PENGUIN REFERENCE BOOKS

THE PENGUIN GUIDE TO COMPACT DISCS & DVDS

Edward Greenfield, until his retirement in 1993, was for forty years on the staff of the *Guardian*, succeeding Neville Cardus as Music Critic in 1975. He still contributes regularly to the record column which he founded in 1954. At the end of 1960 he joined the reviewing panel of *Gramophone*, specializing in operatic and orchestral issues. He is a regular broadcaster on music and records for the BBC, not just on Radios 3 and 4 but also on the BBC World Service, latterly with his weekly programme, *The Greenfield Collection*. In 1958 he published a monograph on the operas of Puccini. More recently he has written studies on the recorded work of Joan Sutherland and André Previn. He has been a regular juror on International Record awards and has appeared with such artists as Dame Elisabeth Schwarzkopf, Dame Joan Sutherland and Sir Georg Solti in public interviews. In October 1993 he was given a *Gramophone* Award for Special Achievement and in June 1994 he received the OBE for services to music and journalism.

Robert Layton studied at Oxford with Edmund Rubbra for composition and with Egon Wellesz for the history of music. He spent two years in Sweden at the universities of Uppsala and Stockholm. He joined the BBC Music Division in 1959 and was responsible for Music Talks, including such programmes as *Interpretations on Record*. He contributed 'A Quarterly Retrospect' to *Gramophone* magazine for thirty-four years and writes for the *BBC Music Magazine*, *International Record Review* and other journals. His books include studies of the Swedish composer Berwald and of the Finnish Sibelius, as well as a monograph on the Dvořák symphonies and concertos for the *BBC Music Guides*, of which he was General Editor for many years. His prizewinning translation of Erik Tawaststjerna's definitive five-volume study of Sibelius was completed in 1998. In 1987 he was awarded the Sibelius Medal and in the following year made a Knight of the Order of the White Rose of Finland for his services to Finnish music. His other books include *Grieg: An Illustrated Life* and he has edited the *Guide to the Symphony* and the *Guide to the Concerto* (OUP). In 2001, at a ceremony to mark the Swedish presidency of the European Union, he was made a Knight of the Royal Order of the Polar Star.

Ivan March is a former professional musician. He studied at Trinity College of Music, London, and at the Royal Manchester College. After service in the Central Band of the RAF, he played the horn professionally for the BBC and travelled with the Carl Rosa and D'Oyly Carte opera companies. He is a well-known lecturer, journalist and personality in the world of recorded music and acts as a consultant to Squires Gate Music Ltd, an international mail order source for classical CDs (www.lprl.demon.co.uk). As a journalist he has contributed to a number of record-reviewing magazines, but now he reviews solely for *Gramophone*.

THE PENGUIN GUIDE TO COMPACT DISCS AND DVDS

2005/6 Edition

IVAN MARCH

EDWARD GREENFIELD AND

ROBERT LAYTON

Edited by Ivan March

Assistant Editor: Paul Czajkowski

PENGUIN BOOKS

PENGUIN BOOKS

Published by the Penguin Group
Penguin Books Ltd, 80 Strand, London WC2R 0RL, England
Penguin Group (USA) Inc., 375 Hudson Street, New York, New York 10014, USA
Penguin Books (Canada), 90 Eglinton Avenue East, Suite 700, Toronto, Ontario,
Canada M4P 2Y3 (a division of Pearson Penguin Canada Inc.)
Penguin Ireland, 25 St Stephen's Green, Dublin 2, Ireland
(a division of Penguin Books Ltd)
Penguin Books (Australia), 250 Camberwell Road, Camberwell, Victoria 3124, Australia
(a division of Pearson Australia Group Pty Ltd)
Penguin Books India Pvt Ltd, 11, Community Centre,
Panchsheel Park, New Delhi – 110 017, India
Penguin Books (NZ), cnr Airborne and Rosedale Roads, Albany,
Auckland 1310, New Zealand (a division of Pearson New Zealand Ltd)
Penguin Books (South Africa) (Pty) Ltd, 24 Sturdee Avenue, Rosebank 2196, South Africa

Penguin Books Ltd, Registered Offices: 80 Strand, London WC2R 0RL, England

www.penguin.com

This edition first published 2005
1

Typeset by Letterpart Ltd, Reigate, Surrey
Printed in Italy by LegoPrint S.p.A.

ISBN-13: 978–0–141–02262–8
ISBN-10: 0–141–02262–0

CONTENTS

THE HISTORY OF THE *PENGUIN GUIDE*

The *Penguin Guide* was the direct descendant of the hardback *Stereo Record Guide*. From its inception, the *Guide*'s editor and publisher, Ivan March, was convinced that the arrival of stereo was the most important step forward in musical technology since the transformation brought about by electric recording in the late 1920s, and that stereo sound was fundamentally more realistic than mono. Not everyone agreed; in particular some hi-fi pundits suggested that 'good mono was better than poor stereo'.

A printed survey was obviously needed to emphasize the superiority of the finest stereo LPs, and with contributors Edward Greenfield and Dennis Stevens offering enthusiastic collaboration, the *Stereo Record Guide* came into being as a hardback, published by the Long Playing Record Library Ltd. The first volume arrived in 1960, and eight more volumes appeared in the following decade. During this period Dennis Stevens moved to the USA and Robert Layton joined the reviewing team.

In the mid-1970s the whole project was taken over by Penguin Books, and the contents of the hardback series were amalgamated and updated in 1975 to become the first *Penguin Stereo Record Guide*, of 1114 pages, covering stereo LPs and a few short-lived quadraphonic issues, and surveying between four and five thousand recordings. The book was so successful that it was immediately reprinted, and it was soon appearing in revised form on an annual basis. In those days the recorded repertoire was comparatively limited, and it was possible to include virtually *all* the stereo recordings available from the major and minor record companies in a single volume.

The arrival of the musicassette initiated the additional *Penguin Cassette Guide*. But it was the appearance of the compact disc in the early 1980s which brought the most successful and widely read of all the early *Guides*. The 1984 publication was called *The Complete Penguin Stereo Record and Cassette Guide*, but it also included reviews of a small number of pioneering CDs, and was sought after by collectors interested in a critical comparison of all three media.

The superiority of the CD as a music carrier was quickly established, and our 1988 revised edition confirmed the new priority, with 'Compact Discs' coming first in the title, and LPs omitted altogether! In 1990 our survey was retitled *The Penguin Guide to Compact Discs*, to which SACDs and DVDs were added in 2003/4.

It is the never-ending improvement in technology which is constantly renewing the recorded repertoire and which continues to place the collecting of recordings of all kinds among the most fascinating and rewarding of musical hobbies.

STEREO, QUADRAPHONY, CD, SACD AND DVD (A HISTORICAL NOTE)

(This technical survey appeared in our first (1975) *Penguin Guide*, but it has been re-edited and updated for this edition.)

When the long-playing record first appeared in 1950, the technology of disc-stereo had already existed for two decades. Its fundamentals had been established in 1931 by A. D. Blumlein, a brilliant engineer who worked for the British Columbia Gramophone Company (later to be amalgamated into EMI). However, besides setting out the basic principles of stereo recording (including microphone and reproducing techniques), Blumlein's early experiments showed (and actual recordings were made) that the coarse-grained shellac used for 78-r.p.m. records was not refined enough to be a satisfactory medium for the system. It is probable too that the economic depression of the time contributed to the postponement of the development of stereo.

With the coming of LP and the use of vinylite as its manufacturing material, Blumlein's obstacles were removed, and by the mid-1950s the Decca company (called London in the USA) under the technical leadership of another brilliant British audio engineer, Arthur Haddy, was already using experimental stereo for commercial recordings. One of the notable early instances was Josef Krips's 1954/5 Vienna *Don Giovanni*, which is still available today.

In America, both Mercury and RCA also began experimenting with stereo in the mid-to-late 1950s, using simple microphone techniques with astoundingly successful results. Orchestral recordings made in the superb acoustics of the Symphony Halls in Chicago and Boston, plus the less glamorous Watford Town Hall in England, combined with the inspirational interpretative skills of Fritz Reiner, Charles Munch, Antal Dorati and others, produced recordings of such naturalness and realism that they remain almost unsurpassed today, especially now that the original three-channel masters can be combined on SACD.

By the dawn of the 1960s, all the major record companies were issuing stereo recordings on a serious basis, and the record-buying public – after first refusing to be overly impressed – began adapting and extending reproducing equipment to handle the new medium. However, the new stereo records needed greater care than their predecessors, and it was soon found that if record wear was not to become a serious problem, a fundamental improvement in pick-up design was needed so that (among other things) the tracking weight at which the pick-up arm moved across the record could be greatly reduced. So began the remorseless progress towards lighter and lighter pick-ups (with improved playing arms to match), until by the time our first *Penguin Guide* was published it was possible to play LPs at tracking pressures of less than one gramme.

As many of our readers will remember, that proved quite unrealistic in an age of atmospheric pollution that produces a situation in which dust adheres gently to the groove surface, and the pick-up, travelling across the disc almost like a feather, is too light to push the dust out of the way, the result being an unnerving series of pops and clicks. It seemed that the reproducing of records had reached a situation where the 'best' modern equipment was so searching in its reproduction of what the record grooves contained that, for the first time in the history of the gramophone, modern LP records were of a lower level of technical refinement than the reproducer on which they might have been played.

However, for those willing to make a sensible compromise in the matter of tracking pressure, it was and is still possible to obtain very satisfactory results from LPs, even if the occasional extraneous interruptions naggingly suggest that the medium is still far from perfect.

At the time of the publication of our initial (1975) *Penguin Guide*, quadraphony was in a rather similar position to that of stereo at the end of the 1950s, but the situation was doubly complicated by the existence of at least two competitive systems, neither of which was compatible with the other. There is no point in going into the claims of the competing technologies for, while the results of both could often be impressive, in the finest instances bringing a genuine further improvement in realism, the concept was stillborn. Some cynics stated that wives rebelled at having to make room for two more loudspeakers in the sitting room! But, whatever the reason, quadraphonic records soon disappeared from the marketplace, and the whole concept of expanding the sound by the use of four sound sources had to wait three more decades, until the arrival of the SACD and DVD.

Meanwhile the musicassette appeared on the scene. It, too, had competition from an alternative system – the eight-track tape cartridge – but it was so obviously superior in its simplicity of format, accessibility and portability (in or out of a car) that it caught the public's imagination. The early classical musicassettes were very low-fi and had a high background tape hiss. But once again Arthur Haddy at Decca stepped into the picture. At the inception of the new medium, he had given his wife a modest portable cassette player and was astonished to find her using it daily, when, as he told us, 'in all the fifty years I have been making records, she never once put a disc record on to the domestic gramophone'.

He immediately set up a production line at a new Decca factory to manufacture quality cassettes, with the surface hiss cut right back by applying the Dolby B noise-reduction system. Other companies followed suit, and when chrome tape replaced iron-oxide stock, the results were often of astonishingly good quality. On top-quality equipment the frequency and dynamic range were usually somewhat inferior to the equivalent LPs, but the sound-balance was often musically very satisfying, and listening was not impaired by those annoying clicks and pops characteristic of the LP. The cassette reigned as a popular second fiddle to the LP for a decade, but a new sound-carrier was already on the horizon that was set to take over from both.

When the digital compact disc arrived in 1983, it was obviously far superior to any previous sound-carrier. Initially expensive to manufacture, it was comparably expensive to buy. But the clarity of the reproduction, the virtually complete absence of extraneous background noise on the new digital recordings, and the potential ease of internal access, often with generous tracking cues, won over most doubting

Thomases or Thomasinas. Music-lovers began to replace their collections with CDs, and the record industry enjoyed a bonanza.

As the pages of our current *Guide* fully demonstrate, the recorded repertoire began to expand, almost without restraint, exploring the musical byways as well as providing a huge choice in the number of interpretations of the standard classics. Moreover, the improvement in transfer technology of older recordings meant that in interpretative terms the CD catalogue was able to reach back into the distant past.

CD manufacturing costs have plummeted, and so have the prices of discs in the shops, led by the always enterprising budget label Naxos. For a period the market has seemed flooded, with more new records appearing than there were potential buyers. But, as we pointed out above, the continuing success of the record industry has always beeen linked to new technology, and just at the right moment the SACD and DVD arrived, together with the return of the concept of quadraphony, and because many homes were investing in Surround Sound for the domestic performance of movies, there is much less resistance than before to the arrival of back speakers, which need not be large or intrusive.

Using the Surround Sound possible with SACD, one can now listen to audio CDs with a vivid sense of being in the auditorium where the recording was made. Certain kinds of music appear to gain more than others, but this may be a purely transitional effect while the aesthetics of four-channel sound are being developed to match the technology. On SACD, in transfers of older recordings, even when using only the normal pair of front speakers, string-tone undoubtedly gains in fullness and naturalness, while in Surround Sound the effect of a brass tutti in a typical nineteenth-century score (or a Renaissance score by Gabrieli or his contemporaries) can be thrilling, while choral music (and especially sixteenth-century choral music) shows a very striking gain in ambient atmosphere and immediacy. DVDs of opera (with surtitles optional) and vintage ballet (with classic choreography preserved) offer a domestic experience and a degree of personal involvement comparable to being at the theatre in the best seat in the house.

EDITOR'S NOTE: THE KEY RECORDINGS

The large number of new or reissued recordings included in our present volume – indicated by the letter (**N**) placed before the catalogue number – demonstrates the continuing and significantly expanded repertoire coverage. We have therefore thought it essential to continue to offer our readers a selection of 'Key' recordings which may be used as a basis for a personal collection or to add to an existing collection.

We have also sometimes included more than one choice, especially where there are attractive alternative couplings of music available, and also where there are highly recommendable versions on both CD and DVD. Of course our recommendations are intended purely for guidance; it is only in the rarest of instances where there are no equally recommendable alternatives, and you are advised to consult the text and make choices according to your own personal inclinations – especially in relation to performances using modern or period instruments. We have included a fair proportion of lower-priced discs, and in some cases a disc has been chosen because of its obvious value for money, where a more expensive alternative might be well worth the extra cost.

Ivan March

FOREWORD

This, our Thirtieth Anniversary Edition, represents something of a watershed in the life of the *Penguin Guide*. Its extraordinarily wide-ranging coverage includes many more CDs than ever before, besides SACDs and the fast-expanding catalogue of DVDs. We are no longer able to encompass all the possible composer listings and reviews in a single volume, and of necessity we have had to concentrate on the cream of the repertoire, which is why our pages include very few discs with an evaluation of only two stars!

Some of the less recommendable recorded versions of major works have been carried forward to our 2006 *Yearbook*, together with music by many interesting minor composers (including, incidentally, William Alwyn, whose centenary falls in 2005, which will bring new recordings, making any present survey premature).

But our Thirtieth Anniversary Edition is rich in new issues and inexpensive reissues, with SACDs often able to bring a marked improvement in sound in older-vintage recordings. No better example of this than Fritz Reiner's marvellous (1960) RCA Chicago recording of Rimsky-Korsakov's *Scheherazade* which, in its enhanced new format, takes its place as a top recommendation for this much-recorded work. A companion anthology of Charles Munch's Boston Berlioz recordings on the same label is hardly less fine, including a fabulous account of the *Royal Hunt and Storm* from *Les Troyens*. The reissued 'Living Stereo' Mercury CDs from the same era are even more alive and vivid, with Dorati's complete recording of Stravinsky's *Firebird* ballet standing out among them.

Telarc, always famous for technical expertise, have produced a CD which is indeed a technological breakthrough in re-creating music-roll performances of Rachmaninov at the piano during the period between 1919 and 1929. Realized by Wayne Stahnke and reproduced digitally on a special Bösendorfer 290SE, the result is astonishing, as if the composer were in the very room, with the most subtle details of rubato and dynamic contrast faithfully captured.

Naxos, too, have been issuing a fascinating series of vintage historical recordings, restored by Ward Marston and Mark Obert-Thorn, which includes the latter's superb retransfer of Karajan's glorious (1953) Kingsway Hall mono recording of Humperdinck's *Hänsel und Gretel* which, remarkably, is finer and sonically more beautiful than EMI's own transfer – and less expensive too.

But the most fascinating of all the Naxos historical reissues is Louis Kaufman's 1947 recording – the first ever – of Vivaldi's *Four Seasons*, with the Concert Hall Chamber Orchestra conducted by Henry Swoboda. Kaufman, a most distinguished violinist, not only pioneered the *Four Seasons* but the whole of *Il Cimento dell'Armonia e dell'inventione*, Op. 8 (with the Winterthur Orchestra under Clemens Dahinden), and the playing is remarkably stylish, in no way dated. The mono sound too (restored by Anthony Casuccio) is remarkably good.

The enterprising Regis label also has us in its debt by reissuing Walter Klien's inspirational and treasurable Vox recordings of Brahms's piano music from the 1960s on five budget-priced discs, and an equally memorable single disc of Sviatoslav Richter playing Chopin in the late 1970s, including fabulous accounts of the four *Scherzi*.

Before leaving the super-budget range, we must mention a cascade of EMI reissues on the HMV label which descended upon us just as we were going to press. We have been able to include only a few; the rest will have to wait for our *Yearbook*. But the role-call of artists is distinguished, they are generous in playing time and offer outstanding value. The snag is they are available only from HMV record shops, or by mail-order at HMV.com; but they are worth looking out for.

SURROUND SOUND

We confess to being initially doubtful as to the advantages of 'surround sound', and so far the range of recordings available in this new compatible technology is limited. It also takes a little time and skill to balance the rear speakers so that, while the ear is subtly aware of the ambient effect, the sound-image itself normally comes from the front. But there have been some surprises. For sheer visceral excitement, the Scherzo of Gergiev's SACD Kirov performance of Tchaikovsky's *Pathétique Symphony* is quite riveting, overwhelmingly realistic, even if some listeners may find the performance itself over-tense. An equally thrilling sense of 'being there' is experienced with an outstanding Capriccio compilation of favourite Handel arias, marvellously sung by Jochen Kowalski, Emma Kirkby, Arleen Augér, Max Emanuel Cencic and others, while the companion Capriccio disc of Weber *Overtures* from the glorious Dresden Staatskapelle under Gustav Kuhn is totally transformed by the vivid immediacy of SACD. Carlos Kleiber's 1977 Bavarian *La Traviata* on DG (with Cotrubas, Domingo and Milnes) is not ideally balanced on CD, but on SACD the party scene in the opening Act is fully three-dimensional, even if the sound itself is not completely refined.

But it is in choral music that SACD comes into its own. Paul McCreesh's vitally alive set of Handel's *Messiah* with the Gabrieli Consort and Players conveys an extraordinarily vivid sense of concert-hall realism in its new SACD transfer. On Coro, The Sixteen, directed by Harry Christophers, sing gloriously Victoria's sublime *Requiem*, the *Officium Defunctorum* of 1605 within the ambience of Saint Silas the Martyr in London, and one has the uncanny feeling of sitting in the church itself.

But it is the Naxos recording, by the Oxford Camerata under Jeremy Summerly, of Tallis's masterly 40-part motet, *Spem in alium*, that heads the choral SACDs issued so far. Tallis wrote the work to be performed by eight choirs of five voices arranged in a circle, and the Oxford singers were arranged in the form of a huge St Chad cross, with two choirs in each quadrant. The result, at the work's climax, is quite overwhelming.

The medium of DVD is proving most exciting of all, and especially in the worlds of ballet (we already have Fonteyn and Nureyev's classic account of *Swan Lake*) and opera. The opera CDs are now flooding out (there are already five versions of *Carmen*!) and there are plenty of outstanding examples to choose from. Among them comes a series recorded in Verona, with consistently fine, traditional productions and starry casts. We hope that this new market may in the future help to prevent the worst idiosyncrasies of self-regarding opera producers who can totally ruin a superb performance with outrageous sets and costumes, and by trying to impose on the production their own subjective interpretative realization, quite foreign to the composer's original intentions. We cannot leave the world of opera without celebrating EMI's outstanding audio recording of *Tristan und Isolde*, conducted by Pappano, with Placido Domingo magnificent in the male title-role. With DVDs now dominating the scene, this may well be one of the last great audio studio recordings of opera; and to make sure it will attract the collector, EMI have included in the CD set an audio DVD of the whole opera, with the screen used just for the surtitles.

INTRODUCTION

As in previous editions, the object of *The Penguin Guide to Compact Discs, DVDs and SACDs* is to give the serious collector a continuing survey of the finest recordings of permanent music on CD, irrespective of price, while also evaluating the quality of the compatible SACDs and video and audio DVDs. As most recordings are issued almost simultaneously on both sides of the Atlantic and use identical international catalogue numbers, this *Guide* should be found to be equally useful in the UK and the USA, as it will in Australia, Canada and New Zealand. The internationalization of repertoire and numbers now applies to almost all CDs issued by the major international companies and also by the smaller ones. Many European labels are imported in their original formats into both Britain and the USA. Those CDs that are available only in England can be easily obtained by overseas collectors via the web address given on page xvii.

We feel that it is a strength of our basic style to let our own conveyed pleasure and admiration (or otherwise) for the merits of an individual recording come over directly to the reader, even if this produces a certain ambivalence in the matter of such a final choice. Where there is disagreement between us (and this rarely happens), readers will find an indication of our different reactions in the text.

We have considered (and rejected) the use of initials against individual reviews, since this is essentially a team project. The occasions for disagreement generally concern matters of aesthetics – in the manner of recording balance for instance, where a contrived effect may trouble some ears more than others, or in the matter of style, where the difference between robustness and refinement of approach appeals differently to listening sensibilities rather than involving a question of artistic integrity. But over the years our views seem to have grown closer together rather than diverging; perhaps we are getting mellower, but we are seldom ready to offer strong disagreement following the enthusiastic reception by one of the team of a controversial recording, providing the results are creatively stimulating.

As playing standards have advanced, our perceptions of the advantages and disadvantages of performances of early music on original (as against modern) instruments seem almost irrelevant. It is the quality of the performance itself which counts, and so expert is the performer's control of period instruments today, while modern-instrument performances have often been so influenced by period-instrument styles, that sometimes one is hardly aware of the difference, especially in orchestral music.

EVALUATION

Most major recordings issued today are of a high technical standard and offer performances of a quality at least as high as is experienced in the concert hall. In adopting a star system for the evaluation of records, we have decided to make use of from one to three stars. Brackets around one or more of the stars indicate some reservations about a recording's rating, and readers are advised to refer to the text. Brackets around all the stars usually indicate a basic qualification: for instance, a mono recording of a performance of artistic interest, where some allowances may have to be made for the sound quality even though the recording has been digitally remastered.

Our evaluation system may be summarized as follows:

***   An outstanding performance and recording in every way

**   A good performance and recording of today's normal high standard

*   A fair or somewhat routine performance, reasonably well performed or recorded.

Our evaluation is normally applied to the record as a whole, unless there are two main works or groups of works and by different composers. In this case, each is dealt with separately in its appropriate place.

ROSETTES

To certain special records we have awarded a Rosette: ❀.

Unlike our general evaluations, in which we have tried to be consistent, a Rosette is a quite arbitrary compliment by a member of the reviewing team to a recorded performance which he finds shows special illumination, magic, a spiritual quality, or even outstanding production values, that places it in a very special class. Occasionally a Rosette has been awarded for an issue that seems to us to offer extraordinary value for money, but that presupposes that the performance or performances are outstanding too. The choice is essentially a personal one (although often it represents a shared view) and in some cases it is applied to an issue where certain reservations must also be mentioned in the text of the review. The Rosette symbol is placed before the usual evaluation and the record number. It is quite small – we do not mean to imply an 'Academy Award' but a personal token of appreciation for something uniquely valuable. We hope that, once the reader has discovered and perhaps acquired a 'rosetted' CD, its special qualities will soon become apparent. There are, of course, more of them now, for our survey has become a distillation of the excellence of CDs issued and reissued over a considerable time-span.

DIGITAL RECORDINGS

Nearly all new compact discs are recorded digitally, but many digitally remastered, reissued analogue recordings are now available, and we think it important to include a clear indication of the difference: all listed CDs are digital *unless* the inclusion of (ADD) in the titling indicates Analogue-to-Digital remastering, while of course the term mono is self-explanatory.

The indication ADD/DDD or DDD/ADD applies to a compilation where recordings come from mixed sources.

LISTINGS AND PRICE RANGES

Our listing of each recording assumes that it is in the premium-price category, unless it indicates otherwise, as follows:

(M) Medium-priced label
(B) Bargain-priced label
(BB) Super-bargain label.

See below for differences in price structures in the UK and the USA.

LAYOUT OF TEXT

We have aimed to make our style as simple as possible. So, immediately after the evaluation and before the catalogue number, the record make is given, sometimes in abbreviated form. In the case of a set of two or more CDs, the number of units involved is given in brackets after the catalogue number.

(N) placed before the catalogue number means that the recording is new to the present volume.

AMERICAN CATALOGUE NUMBERS

The numbers which follow in square brackets are US catalogue numbers if they differ from UK catalogue numbers (and this applies in particular to EMI's 'Great Recordings of the Century', which have a different number on each side of the Atlantic). Some EMI Encore CDs are also differently numbered, so it is always advisable to check. Where a record is available in the USA but *not* the UK, it will appear in square brackets only. But EMI's American label, 'Red Line Classics', is now also available in the UK.

EMI and Virgin have now abandoned the use of alphabetical prefixes, and it is no longer possible to determine the price range from the catalogue listing itself, although budget Encore CDs are clearly marked, as are the two-for-the-price-of-one Gemini, double forte and Virgin reissues.

We have taken care to check catalogue information as far as is possible, but as all the editorial work has been done in England there is always the possibility of error; American readers are therefore invited, when ordering records locally, to take the precaution of giving their dealer the fullest information about the music and recordings they want.

The indications (M), (B) and (BB) immediately before the starring of a disc refer primarily to the British CD, as pricing systems are not always identical on both sides of the Atlantic. When CDs are imported by specialist distributors into the USA this again usually involves a price difference. When mid-priced CDs on the smaller labels are imported they often move up to the premium-price range. American readers are advised to check the current *Schwann* catalogue and to consult their local record store.

ABBREVIATIONS

To save space, we have adopted a number of standard abbreviations in listing record companies, orchestras and performing groups (a list is provided below), and the titles of works are often shortened, especially where they are listed several times. Artists' forenames are usually omitted if they are not absolutely necessary for identification purposes. Also we have not usually listed the contents of operatic highlights and collections.

We have followed common practice in the use of the original language for titles where it seems sensible. In most cases, English is used for orchestral and instrumental music, and the original language for vocal music and opera. There are exceptions, however; for instance, the Johann Strauss discography uses the German language in the interests of consistency.

ORDER OF MUSIC

The order of music under each composer's name broadly follows the following system: orchestral music, including concertos and symphonies; chamber music; solo instrumental music (in some cases with keyboard and organ music separated); vocal and choral music; opera; vocal collections; miscellaneous collections. Within each group our listing follows an alphabetical sequence, and couplings within a single composer's output are *usually* discussed together instead of separately with cross-references. Occasionally (and inevitably because of this alphabetical approach), different recordings of a given work can become separated when a record is listed and discussed under the first work of its alphabetical sequence. The editor feels that alphabetical consistency is essential if the reader is to learn to find his or her way about.

CATALOGUE NUMBERS

Enormous care has gone into the checking of CD catalogue numbers and contents to ensure that all details are correct, but the editor and publishers cannot be held responsible for any mistakes that may have crept in despite all our zealous checking. When ordering CDs, readers are urged to provide their record-dealer with full details of the music and performers, as well as the catalogue number.

DELETIONS

Compact discs regularly succumb to the deletions axe, and many are likely to disappear during the lifetime of this book. Sometimes copies may still be found in specialist shops, and there remains the compensatory fact that most really important and desirable recordings are eventually reissued, often costing less!

Universal Classics have an import service for certain CDs which are not carried in their UK inventory, and these CDs are indicated with the abbreviation (IMS). A small extra charge is made for these discs which may have to be obtained from Germany or Holland.

ACKNOWLEDGEMENTS

Our thanks are owed to our new Penguin copy-editor Emma Littlewood, who came in at the last minute to help with the database corrections, and has proved invaluable; also to Roger Wells, especially for his help during the final assembly of all the back listings and reviews for this book. Paul Czajkowski, as Assistant Editor, helped with the retrieval of earlier reviews (connected with reissues) and contributed a number of specialist reviews, especially in the areas of film music, light music and operetta. He was also responsible for much of the titling – never an easy task. But the most grateful thanks of all go to Alan Livesey, who proofread the book meticulously throughout at great speed, and uncovered many still-existing errors that had occurred earlier in the assembly of the book's reviews.

Grateful thanks also go to all those readers who write to us to point out factual errors and to remind us of important recordings which have escaped our notice.

THE AMERICAN SCENE

CDs are much less expensive in the USA than they are in Great Britain, and because of this (so we are told) many bargain recordings available in England are not brought into the USA by their manufacturers. This applies especially to the Universal group, so that Decca, DG and Philips bargain labels have to be imported by the major US record stores and mail-order outlets. What this means is that while almost any recording mentioned in these pages will be available in the USA, sometimes it will cost more than the buyer might reasonably expect.

Duos and Doubles, where available, remain at two discs for the cost of one premium-priced CD in both countries, and here US collectors have a price advantage. However, many excellent lower-priced discs are not issued in the USA. Where a recording is of extra special interest, American collectors can obtain it readily by mail order from England, through the website address given below. However, it will inevitably cost more than it would domestically.

PRICE DIFFERENCES IN THE UK AND USA

Retail prices are not fixed in either country, and various stores may offer even better deals at times, so our price structure must be taken as a guideline only. This particularly applies to the line drawn between Bargain and Super-bargain CDs (the Helios label is an example). Premium-priced CDs cost on average approximately the same number of dollars in the USA as they do pounds in the UK.

Duos and Doubles are two-for-the-cost-of-one premium-priced discs the world over. Classics for Pleasure and the Virgin Classics 2x1 Doubles are two-for-the-price-of-one mid-priced CDs.

OTHER COMPARABLE PRICES IN THE UK AND USA

Here are comparative details of the other price-ranges (note that sets are multiples of the prices quoted):

Mid-priced series (as indicated by (M) in text)
UK: £10.99; often £9–£10;
USA: Under $13; usually under $12.

Bargain-priced series (as indicated by (B) in text)
UK: £5.50–£7;
USA: Under $7.

Super-bargain budget series (BB)
UK: £5–£6;
USA: $5–$6.

THE AUSTRALIAN SCENE

We have been fortunate in obtaining for review some recordings from the Australian branch of Universal Classics (responsible for the three key labels, Decca, DG and Philips) who have been making a series of local issues of Decca, DG and Philips repertoire of considerable interest, mostly not otherwise available. These are bargain issues in Australia but, because of import costs, are more expensive in the UK and USA. All these Universal Australian CDs can be purchased via the Australian website: www.buywell.com

AN INTERNATIONAL MAIL-ORDER SOURCE FOR RECORDINGS IN THE UK

Readers are urged to support a local dealer if he is prepared and able to give a proper service, and to remember that obtaining many CDs involves expertise and perseverance. However, in recent years many specialist sources have disappeared and for that reason, if any difficulty is experienced in obtaining the CDs you want, we suggest the following mail-order alternative, which offers competitive discounts in the UK but also operates world-wide. Through this service, advice on choice of recordings from the Editor of *The Penguin Guide to Compact Discs, DVDs and SACDs* is always readily available to mail-order customers:

Squires Gate Music Centre Ltd (PG Dept)
Rear 13 St Andrew's Road South,
St Annes on Sea, Lancashire FY8 1SX
United Kingdom
Tel.: (+44) (0)1253 782588; Fax: (+44) (0)1253 782985
website address: www.lprl.demon.co.uk
email address: sales@lprl.demon.co.uk

This organization can supply any recording available in Britain and patiently extends compact disc orders until they finally come to hand. A full guarantee of safe delivery is made on any order undertaken. Please write or fax for further details, or make a trial credit-card order, by fax, email or telephone.

❂ THE ROSETTE SERVICE

Squires Gate also offers a try-before-you-buy weekly loan service (within the UK only) so that customers can try out rosetted recordings at home, plus a hand-picked group of recommended key-repertoire CDs, for a small charge, without any obligation to purchase. A short list of recommended DVDs is also available. If a recording is subsequently purchased, it will be discounted and the trial charge waived. Full details sent on request.

Squires Gate Music Centre also offers a simple bi-monthly or three-monthly mailing, listing a hand-picked selection of current new and reissued CDs, chosen by the Editor of *The Penguin Guide to Compact Discs, DVDs and SACDs*, Ivan March. Customers of Squires Gate Music Centre Ltd, both domestic and overseas, receive the bulletin as available, and it is sent automatically with their purchases.

ABBREVIATIONS

AAM Academy of Ancient Music
Ac. Academy, Academic
Amb. S. Ambrosian Singers
Ara. Arabesque
arr. arranged, arrangement
ASMF Academy of St Martin-in-the-Fields
(B) bargain-price CD
(BB) super-bargain-price CD
Bar. Baroque
Bav. Bavarian
BBC British Broadcasting Corporation
BPO Berlin Philharmonic Orchestra
BRT Belgian Radio & Television (Brussels)
Cal. Calliope
Cap. Capriccio
CBSO City of Birmingham Symphony Orchestra
CfP Classics for Pleasure
Ch. Choir; Chorale; Chorus
Chan. Chandos
CO Chamber Orchestra
COE Chamber Orchestra of Europe
Col. Mus. Ant. Musica Antiqua, Cologne
Coll. Collegium
Coll. Aur. Collegium Aureum
Coll. Voc. Collegium Vocale
Concg. O Royal Concertgebouw Orchestra of Amsterdam
cond. conductor, conducted
Cons. Consort
DG Deutsche Grammophon
DHM Deutsche Harmonia Mundi
Dig. digital recording
E. England, English
E. Bar. Sol. English Baroque Soloists
ECCO European Community Chamber Orchestra
ECO English Chamber Orchestra
ENO English National Opera Company
Ens. Ensemble
ESO English Symphony Orchestra
Fest. Festival
Fr. French
GO Gewandhaus Orchestra
Häns. Hänssler
HM Harmonia Mundi
Hung. Hungaroton
Hyp. Hyperion
IMS Import Music Service (Polygram – UK only)
☛ Key Recording
L. London
LA Los Angeles
LCO London Chamber Orchestra
LCP London Classical Players
LMP London Mozart Players
LOP Lamoureux Orchestra of Paris

LPO London Philharmonic Orchestra
LSO London Symphony Orchestra
(M) mid-price CD
Mer. Meridian
Met. Metropolitan
min. minor
MoC Ministry of Culture
movt movement
(N) New review for this Edition
N. North, Northern
nar. narrated
Nat. National
Nim. Nimbus
NY New York
O Orchestra, Orchestre
OAE Orchestra of the Age of Enlightenment
O-L Oiseau-Lyre
Op. Opera (in performance listings); opus (in music titles)
orch. orchestrated
ORR Orchestre Révolutionnaire et Romantique
ORTF L'Orchestre de la radio et télévision française
Ph. Philips
Phd. Philadelphia
Philh. Philharmonia
PO Philharmonic Orchestra
Qt Quartet
R. Radio
Ref. Références
RLPO Royal Liverpool Philharmonic Orchestra
ROHCG Royal Opera House, Covent Garden
RPO Royal Philharmonic Orchestra
RSNO Royal Scottish National Orchestra
RSO Radio Symphony Orchestra
RTE Radio Television Eireann
S. South
SCO Scottish Chamber Orchestra
Sinf. Sinfonietta
SIS Special Import Service (EMI – UK only)
SNO Scottish National Orchestra
SO Symphony Orchestra
Soc. Society
Sol. Ven. I Solisti Veneti
SRO Suisse Romande Orchestra
Sup. Supraphon
trans. transcription, transcribed
V. Vienna
V/D Video Director
Van. Vanguard
VCM Vienna Concentus Musicus
VPO Vienna Philharmonic Orchestra
VSO Vienna Symphony Orchestra
W. West
WNO Welsh National Opera Company

A HUNDRED OUTSTANDING RECORDINGS

One hundred of the very finest CD and SACD recordings new to, or reissued in, the present volume, personally chosen by the authors.

ADAMS, John

Berceuse élégiac; Shaker Loops; Short Ride in a Fast Machine; (i) *The Wound-Dresser*
(BB) *** Naxos 8.559031. Bournemouth SO, Marin Alsop; (i) with N. Gunn

ARNOLD, Malcolm

Anniversary Overture; Beckus the Dandipratt (Comedy Overture), Op. 5; The Fair Field, Op. 110; A Flourish for Orchestra, Op. 112; A Grand Grand Festival Overture, Op. 57; Peterloo Overture, Op. 97; Robert Kett Overture, Op. 41; The Smoke, Op. 21; A Sussex Overture, Op. 31; Tam o'Shanter Overture, Op. 51
*** Chan. 10293. BBC PO, Gamba

AUBER, Daniel

Overtures: *The Bronze Horse; Fra Diavolo; Masaniello*
❂ (M) *** Mercury **SACD** (ADD) 470 638-2. Detroit SO, Paray (with SUPPÉ: *Overtures: Beautiful Galathea; Boccaccio; Light Cavalry; Morning, Noon and Night in Vienna; Pique Dame; Poet and Peasant*)

BACH, Johann Christian

Overtures: *Adriano in Siria; Alessandro nell'Indie; Amadis des Gaules (including Ballet Music); Artaserse; La calamita de cuori; Carattaco (+ 2 Marches); La Cascina; Cantata a tre voci (Birthday Cantata); Carattaco; Catone in Utica; La clemenza di Scipione (+ 2 Marches); Endimione; Gioas, re di Giuda; La Giulia; Orione; Gli Uccellatori; Lucio Silla; Temistocle; Il tutore e la pupilla; Zanaida. Symphony in D, Op. 18/1*
(M) *** CPO 999 963-2 (2). Hanover Band, Halstead

BACH, Johann Sebastian

Cantatas, Volume 1: 1, 4, 6–7, 11, 23, 28, 30–32, 34, 39–40, 43, 57, 61, 65, 67–8, 72, 76, 82, 85, 87, 92, 103–4, 110, 182, 249
(BB) **(*) Warner (ADD) 2564 61401-2 (10). Giebel, Krebs & soloists, Heinrich Schütz-Ch., Heilbronn, Pforzheimer CO, Werner
Arrangements: Bach–Stokowski: *Chorale Preludes: Ein' feste Burg ist unser Gott; Komm, süsser Tod; Mein Jesu, was vor Seelenweh. Christmas Oratorio: Sinfonia. English Suite 2 in A min., BWV 807: Bourrée. Fugue in G min., BWV 578 (Little Fugue); Orchestral Suite 3 in D, BWV 1068: Air on the G String. Passacaglia and Fugue in C min., BWV 582; Toccata and Fugue in D min., BWV 565; Violin Partitas 1 in B min., BWV 1002: Sarabande; 3 in E, BWV 1006: Preludio*
(M) *** EMI Legend CD/**DVD** (ADD) 5 57758. Symphony O, Stokowski (with **DVD** bonus: DEBUSSY: *Prélude à l'après-midi d'un faune*)

BARBER, Samuel

(i) *Canzonetta for oboe and strings. Capricorn Concerto; Fadograph of a Yestern Scene; Mutations from Bach; Vanessa: Interlude;* (ii) *A Hand of Bridge*
(BB) *** Naxos 8.599135. RSNO, Alsop, with (i) Stéphane Rancourt; (ii) Craigie, Winter, Wall, Williams

BARTÓK, Béla

Dance Suite; Hungarian Pictures; (i) *The Miraculous Mandarin (ballet; complete)*
(BB) *** Naxos 8.557433. Bournemouth SO, Alsop, (i) with Bournemouth SO Ch.

BAX, Arnold

(i–ii) *Winter Legends (for piano & orchestra);* (i) *A Hill Tune; A Mountain Mood;* (i; iii) *Viola Sonata*
(BB) (**(*)) Dutton mono CDBP 9751. (i) Harriet Cohen; (ii) BBC SO, Raybould; (iii) Primrose
Piano Sonatas 1–2; Burlesque; Dream in Exile (Intermezzo); In a Vodka Shop
(BB) **(*) Naxos 8.557439. Ashley Wass

BEETHOVEN, Ludwig van

Piano Concertos (i) *1–4;* (ii) *5 (Emperor). 7 Bagatelles, Op. 33; 6 Bagatelles, Op. 126; 11 Bagatelles, Op. 119; Piano Sonatas: 5 in C min., Op. 10/1; 8 (Pathétique); 17 (Tempest), Op. 31/2; 18, Op. 31/3; 28, Op. 101; 30, Op. 109; 31, Op. 110; 32, Op. 111; 33 Variations on a Waltz by Diabelli, Op. 120*
❂ (B) *** Ph. (ADD) 475 6319 (6). Kovacevich, with (i) BBC SO; (ii) LSO; C. Davis
'The Vienna Horn': *Horn Sonata in F, Op. 17*
(BB) *** Naxos 8.557471. Tomboeck, Inui, Tomboeck, Genia Kuhmeier (with BRAHMS: *Horn Trio, Op. 40;* SCHUBERT: *Auf dem Strom;* SCHUMANN: *Adagio and Allegro in A flat*)
Piano Trios 1 in E flat, Op. 1/1; 2 in G, Op. 1/2; 3 in E flat, WoO38
*** Hyp. CDA 67393. Florestan Trio
String Quartets 8, 10–16; Grosse Fuge
*** Chan. 10191 (8 & 10); Chan. 10269 (11, 14 & Grosse Fuge); Chan. 10292 (12–13); Chan. 10304 (15–16). Borodin Qt (available separately)
String Quartets 11–16; Grosse Fuge
*** Decca 470 849-2 (3). Takács Qt
Piano Sonatas 21–5; 27; 30–32
(M) (***) EMI mono 5 62880-2 (2). Schnabel

BENNETT, Richard Rodney

Film music: (i) *Lady Caroline Lamb (including the Elegy for Viola and Orchestra);* (ii) *Murder on the Orient Express*

(M) *** EMI (ADD) 5 86188-2. Composer, with (i) Mark, New Philh. O; (ii) ROHCG O

BERLIOZ, Hector

(i) *Harold in Italy, Op. 16. Overtures: Béatrice et Bénédict; Benvenuto Cellini; Le carnaval romain, Op. 9; Le Corsaire;* (ii; iii) *La Damnation de Faust;* (iv–v) *L'Enfance du Christ;* (vi) *Les Nuits d'été, Op. 7* (v; vii) *Requiem, Op. 5. Roméo et Juliette, Op. 17* (viii; iii) *1953 mono & (ix; v) 1961 stereo versions); Symphonie fantastique, Op. 14 (1954 & 1962 versions); Les Troyens: Royal Hunt and Storm*
(B) **(*) RCA mono/stereo 82876 60393-2 (10). Boston SO, Munch, with (i) Primrose; (ii) Danco, Poleri, Singher, Gramm, Boatwright; (iii) Harvard Glee Club, Radcliffe Ch. Soc.; (iv) Kopleff, Valletti, Souzay, Tozzi, Olivier; (v) New England Conservatory Ch.; (vi) De los Angeles; (vii) Simoneau; (viii) Roggero, Chabay, Yo-Kwei Sze; (ix) Elias, Valetti, Tozzi
Benvenuto Cellini (original version)
*** Virgin 5 45706-2 (3). Kunde, Ciofi, Di Donato, Lapointe, Naouri, Delaigue, R. France Ch., O Nat. de France, Nelson

BIRTWISTLE, Harrison

(i) *Earth Dances;* (ii) *Theseus Game*
*** DG 477 0702. Ensemble Modern, cond. (i) Boulez; (ii) Brabbins; with Pierre-André Valade

BLISS, Arthur

Clarinet Quintet
(***) Testament mono SBT 1366. Thurston, Griller Qt, or Myers Foggin (with BRAHMS: *Clarinet Quintet; Clarinet Sonata 2*)

BOTTESINI, Giovanni

(i–ii) *Double Bass Cello Concertos 1 in F sharp min.* (orch. Gaydos); *2 in B min.;* (i; iii) *Gran Duo Passione Amorosa* (for two double basses and orchestra, orch. Furtok)
*** CPO 999 665-2. Furtok, with (i) Frankfurt RSO; (ii) Tetzlaff; (iii) Stähle (double bass); Edelmann (cond.)

BOULEZ, Pierre

Figures-Doubles-Prisms; (i) *Pli selon pli;* (ii) *Le Soleil des eaux;* (i–iii) *Le Visage nuptial*
(BB) *** Warner Apex 2564 62083-2 (2). BBC SO, Boulez, with (i) Bryn-Julson; (ii) BBC Singers; (iii) Laurence

BRAHMS, Johannes

Viola Sonatas 1–2; Violin Sonatas 1–3; F. A. E. Sonata
(M) *** Avie AV 2057 (2). Mintz, Golan
Solo Piano: 4 Ballades, Op. 10; 7 Fantasias, Op. 116; 3 Intermezzi, Op. 117; 8 Pieces, Op. 76; 6 Pieces, Op. 118; 4 Pieces, Op. 119; 2 Rhapsodies, Op. 79; Sonata No. 3 in F min., Op. 5; 16 Waltzes, Op. 39; Variations & Fugue on a Theme by Handel, Op. 24; Variations on a Theme by Schumann, Op. 9; 16 Waltzes, Op. 39. (Two Pianos):
(i) *21 Hungarian Dances* (original version); (ii) *16 Waltzes, Op. 39*
(BB) *** Regis/Vox Box CDSX 3612 (5). Walter Klien, with (i) Brendel; (ii) Beatriz Klien

BRIDGE, Frank

String Quartets 2 in G min.; 4; (i) *Phantasy Quartet in F sharp min.* (for piano, violin, viola & cello)
(BB) *** Naxos 8.557283. Maggini Qt, (i) with Roscoe

BRITTEN, Benjamin

String Quartets 1–3; 3 Divertimenti
(M) *** EMI 5 57968-2 (2). Belcea Qt
Death in Venice
*** Chan. 10280 (2). Langridge, Opie, Chance, BBC Singers, City of L. Sinfonia, Hickox

BROWNE, John

O Maria salvatoris; O regina mundi clara; Salve regina I; Stabat iuxta; Stabat mater
*** Gimell CDGIM 036. Tallis Scholars, Phillips

BRUCKNER, Anton

Symphonies 1–9; (i) *Helgoland*
(BB) *** Warner Apex 2564 61891-2 (9). BPO, Barenboim, (i) with Berlin R. Ch., Ernst Senff Ch.

BYRD, William

Consort Songs: *Constant Penelope; Content is rich; He that all earthly pleasures scorns; My mind to me a Kingdom is; My Mistress had a little dog; The noble famous Queen; O Lord, bow down thine heav'nly eyes; O Lord how vain; O that most rare breast; Out of the orient crystal skies; O you that hear this voice; Truth at the first. Pieces for Viols: 2 Fantasias a 6; Galliard a 6; Pavan a 6*
*** HM HMU 907388. Emma Kirkby, Fretwork

CATOIRE, Georgy

Piano Quartet in A min.; Piano Trio in F min.; Elegy in D min. (for violin & piano)
*** Hyp. CDA 67512. Room Music

CHABRIER, Emmanuel

Bourrée fantasque; España (rhapsodie); Joyeuse marche; Suite pastorale; Gwendoline Overture. Le Roi malgré lui: Dance slave; Fête polonaise
(M) *** Mercury **SACD** (ADD) 475 6183. Detroit SO, Paray (with ROUSSEL: *Suite in F*)

CHOPIN, Frédéric

Piano Concertos 1, Op. 11; 2, Op. 21
❂ *** MDG 340 1267-2. Zacharias, Lausanne CO
Ballades 1–4; Scherzi 1–4
(M) *** RCA **SACD** (ADD) 82876 61396-2. Rubinstein
Ballades 1–4; Scherzi 1–4
*** Hyp. CDA 67456. Stephen Hough

CORRETTE, Michel

Laudate Dominum (Psalm 148; based on Spring from Vivaldi's Four Seasons)
(BB) *** Warner Apex (ADD) 2564 60155-2. Alliot-Lugaz, Oudot, Borst, Goldthorpe, Huttenlocher, Lyon Vocal & Instrumental Ens., Cornut or Paillard CO, Paillard (with

MONDONVILLE: *Dominus Regnavit (Psalm 92); Venite Exultemus (Psalm 94))*

DEBUSSY, Claude

Collection: *Images:* (i–ii) *Ibéria;* (iii) *Rondes de printemps; Gigues.* (i; iv) *La Mer;* (i; v) *Nocturnes;* (iv) *Marche écossaise;* (i) *Le Martyre de Saint Sébastien (Fragment symphonique); Petite Suite;* (vi) *Prélude à l'après-midi d'un faune;* (i; vii) *Première Rhapsody for Clarinet and Piano;* (viii) *Première Rhapsody for Saxophone and Orchestra;* (i) *Printemps;* (xi) *Deux Danses;* (i; x) *La Damoiselle élue*
(***) Andante mono AN 2110 (4). (i) Paris CO, Coppola; (ii) Pittsburgh SO, Reiner; (iii) San Francisco SO, Monteux; (iv) NBC SO, Toscanini; (v) Le Grand O des Festivals Debussy, Inghelbrecht; (vi) O des Concerts Straram (Straram, 1930); (vii) Hamelin; (viii) Goodman, NY Philharmonic-Symphony Soc. O, Barbirolli; (xi) Grandjany, Victor String O, Levin; (x) Guyla, Ricquier, Ch. Saint-Gervais

DONIZETTI, Gaetano

Francesca di Foix (complete)
*** Opera Rara ORC 28. Massis, Spagnoli, Larmore, Ford, LPO, Allemandi

DURUFLÉ, Maurice

Organ Music: *Chant Donné (Homage à Jean Gallan); Fugue sur le Thème du Carillon des Heures de la Cathédrale de Soissons, Op. 12; Méditation; Prélude, Adagio et Choral varié sur le thème du 'Veni Creator', Op. 4; Prélude sur l'Introit de l'Épiphanie, Op. 13; Scherzo, Op. 2; Suite, Op. 5*
*** CPO compatible **Surround Sound** SACD 777 042-2. Friedrich Flamme

DVOŘÁK, Antonín

Cello Concerto in B min., Op. 104
*** BBC (ADD) BBCL 4156-2. Du Pré, RLPO, Groves (with IBERT: *Concerto for Cello & Wind Instruments*)
(i) *Piano Concerto;* (ii) *Violin Concerto*
*** Chan. 10309. (i) Hayroudinoff; (ii) Ehnes, BBC PO, Noseda
Piano Trio 4 (Dumky) in E min., Op. 90
*** Warner 2564 61492-2. Beaux Arts Trio (with MENDELSSOHN: *Piano Trio 1* ***)

FAURÉ, Gabriel

Mélodies: (i) *Après un rêve; Arpège; Automne; Au bord de l'eau;* (ii) *C'est l'extase langoureuse; Clair de lune; En sourdine; Green; L'horizon chimérique* (cycle); *Mandoline; Prison; Spleen*
❂ *** Testament mono SBT 1311. Souzay, with (i) Bonneau, (ii) Baldwin (with FALLA: *Canciónes populares españolas;* RAVEL: *Histoires naturelles*)

GABRIELI, Giovanni

'Music for San Rocco': *Canzona 14 a 10; Sonatas 18 a 14; 19 a 15; 20 a 22; 21* (for 3 Violins). Organ Pieces: *Intonazione duodecimo tono; Intonazione del nono tono; Toccata a 4.* Vocal works: *Buccinate in neomenia tuba a 19; Domine Deus meus; In ecclessis a 14; Jubilate Deo a 10; Magnificat a 3* (arr. Keyte); *Misericordia tua Domine a 12; Suscipe clementissime Deus a 12; Timor e tremor a 6*
*** DG **Surround Sound** SACD 477 0862 (2). Gabrieli Consort & Players, Paul McCreesh (with BARTOLOMEO BARBARINO: *Ardens est cor meum; Audi, dulcis amica mea*)

GLAZUNOV, Alexander

Violin Concerto in D
*** Pentatone **Surround Sound** SACD PTC 5186 059. Fischer, Russian Nat. O, Kreizberg (with KHACHATURIAN: *Violin Concerto;* PROKOFIEV: *Violin Concerto 1*)

GLUCK, Christophe

Paride e Elena (complete)
*** DG 477 5415 (2). Koẑena, Gritton, Sampson, Webster, Gabrieli Consort & Players, McCreesh

HANDEL, George Frideric

Messiah (complete)
*** DG **Surround Sound** SACD 477 066-2; CD 453 464-3 (2). Röschmann, Gritton, Fink, Daniels, Neal Davies, Gabrieli Consort & Players, McCreesh
Ode for St Cecilia's Day; Cecilia volgi un sguardo
*** Hyp. CDA 67463. Sampson, Gilchrist, Ch. & King's Consort, King
Partenope (complete)
*** Chan. 0719 (3). Joshua, Summers, Wallace, Zazzo, Streit, Foster-Williams, Early Op. Co., Curnyn
Arias: *Flavio:* (i) *Amor, nel mio penar. Giulio Cesare in Egitto: Va tacito e nascosto. Hercules:* (ii) *Turn thee, youth to joy and love* (with Ch.); (iii) *This manly youth's exalted mind; Mount, mount the steep ascent* (with Ch.). *Messiah:* (iv–v) *He shall feed his flock;* (v) *Rejoice greatly;* (vi) *Why do the nations? . . . Let us break* (with Ch.). *Orlando:* (i) *Fammi combattere. Rinaldo:* (vii) *Or la tromba in suon festante. Rodelinda: Vivi tiranno. Xerxes: Frondi tenere . . . Ombra mai fù.* (viii) *9 German Arias: Süsse Sille, sanfte Quelle.* (ix) *Silente venti* (Motet, with flute & continuo)
❂ *** Capriccio **Surround Sound** SACD 71 024. (i) Axel Köhler; (ii) Hruba-Freiberger; (iii) Augér; (iv) Humphries; (v) Cencic; (vi) Torday, V. Boys' Ch.; (vii) Kowalski; (viii) Monoyios & Berlin Bar. Company; (ix) Kirkby (with various orchestras & conductors)

HAYDN, Josef

The Seasons (Die Jahreszeiten; complete in German)
❂ *** HMC 801829/30 (2). Petersen, Gura, Henschel, RIAS Chamber Ch., Freiburg Bar. O, Jacobs

HOLMBOE, Vagn

Sinfonias 1–4 (Chairos), Op. 73
*** dacapo 8.226017/18. Danish R. Sinf., Koivula

HOLZBAUER, Ignaz

Symphonies: in A, Op. 2/4; E flat, Op. 3/1; D, Op. 3/4; D min.; G (*Il figlio delle selve* Overture)
❂ *** CPO 999 585-2. L'Orfeo Barockorchester, Gaigg

HUMMEL, Johann
(i) *Mass in E flat, Op. 80. Quod in orber, Op. 88; Te Deum*
*** Chan. 0712. Coll. Mus. 90, Hickox, (i) with Gritton, Murray, Gilchrist, Varcoe

LUMBYE, Hans Christian
Amager Polka; Amelie Waltz; Champagne Galop; Columbine Polka Mazurka; Copenhagen Steam Railway Galop; Dream Pictures (Fantasia); The Guard of Amager (ballet): Final Galop. Helga Polka Mazurka; Hesperus Waltz; Lily Polka; Queen Louise's Waltz; Napoli (ballet): Final Galop; Salute to August Bournonville; Salute to our Friends; Sandman Galop Fantastique
(BB) *** Regis RRC 1155. Odense SO, Guth

MAHLER, Gustav
Symphony 8
*** EMI 5 57945-2. Brewer, Isokoski, Banse, Rammert, Henschel, Villars, Wilson-Johnson, Relyea, L. Symphony Ch., CBSO Ch., Youth Ch. & O, Rattle
Symphony 9 in D min.
*** DG 471 624-2. BPO, Abbado

MARTIN, Frank
Mass for double choir; Songs of Ariel (5 pièces tirées de 'La Tempête' de Shakespeare)
*** HM HMC 901834. RIAS Kammerchor, Reuss (with MESSIAEN: *Cinq Rechants; O sacrum convivium*)

MASSENET, Jules
Le Cid (ballet suite)
✪ *** Australian Decca Eloquence (ADD) 476 2742. Israel PO, Martinon (with DVORAK: *Slavonic Dances*; MEYERBEER: *Les Patineurs* – ballet suite, arr. & orch. Lambert)

MILHAUD, Darius
Le Boeuf sur le toit; La Création du monde; (i) L'Homme et son désir. Suite Provençale
(BB) *** Naxos 8.557287. Lille Nat. O, Casadesus, (i) with Makuuchi, Zhao, Vidal, Deletre

MONTEVERDI, Claudio
Il ballo delle ingrate; Il combattiment di Tancredi; Tirsi e Clori; Tempo la cetra
(BB) *** Warner Apex 2564 6181-2. Tragicomedia, Stubbs

MOZART, Wolfgang Amadeus
Piano Concertos 9 (Jeunehomme); 18 in B flat, K.456
✪ *** EMI 5 57803-2. Andsnes, Norwegian Chamber O
Violin Concertos 1–5; Sinfonia concertante, K.364; Concertone, K.190
*** Avie AV 2058 (2). Mintz, Shaham, ECO

MUSSORGSKY, Modest
Night on the Bare Mountain (arr. Rimsky-Korsakov); Pictures at an Exhibition (orch. Ravel)
(M) *** RCA **SACD** (ADD) 82876 61394-2. Chicago SO, Reiner (with TCHAIKOVSKY: *Marche Slave, Marche*

Miniature; BORODIN: *Polovstian March*; KABALEVSKY: *Colas Breugnon Overture*; GLINKA: *Ruslan and Ludmilla Overture*)

OFFENBACH, Jacques
Overtures: Barbe-Bleu; La Belle Hélàne; La Grande Duchesse de Gérolstein; Le Mariage aux Lanternes; Orfée aux Enfers
☉ (***) Australian Decca Eloquence mono 476 2757. LPO, Martinon (with *Overtures*: ADAM: *Si j'étais Roi*; BOIELDIEU: *Le Calife de Bagdad, La Dame Blanche*; HEROLD: *Zampa*)

PALESTRINA, Giovanni Pierluigi di
Ardens est cor meum; Congratulamini mihi omnes; Crucem santam subiit; Crux fidelis; Fratres, ego enim accepi; Dominus Jesus; Haec Dies a 6; Improperium; Magnificat terti toni a 6 (with Plainsong: Et respicientes); Popule meus; Pueri Hebraeorum (with introductory Plainsong: Hosanna filio David); O Domine, Jesu Christe a 6; Stabat Mater a 8; Terra tremuit; Victimae paschali Laudes a 6
*** ASV Gaudeamus CDGAU 333. Cardinall's Musick, Carwood

PROKOFIEV, Serge
(i) *Piano Concertos 1–5; (ii) Violin Concerto 1 in D, Op. 19*
**(*) Testament (ADD) SBT2 1376 (2). Boston SO, Erich Leinsdorf, with (i) John Browning; (ii) Erick Friedmann

PURCELL, Henry
Airs and Duets: Arise my Muse: Hail, gracious Gloriana Hail! Fly Bold Rebellion: Be welcome, then, great sir. Come ye Sons of Art: Sound the Trumpet. The Fairy Queen: Let the fifes and the clarions; Hark the ech'ing air; One charming night. Hail Bright Cecilia: In vain the am'rous flute. If ever I more riches did desire: Here let my life; Ne, O ye Gods. Love's Goddess sure: Many, many such days; Sweetness of nature. Other songs: If Music be the Food of Love; Lord what is mine (Divine Hymn); Lovely Albina's come ashore; Saccharissa's grown old
☉ *** Lyrichord LEMS 8024. Dooley, Crook, Instrumental Ens., Brewer (harpsichord)

RACHMANINOV, Sergei
'A Window in Time': Barcarolle, Op. 10/3; Elégie; Mélodie, Op. 3/3; Etudes-tableaux, Op. 39/4 & 6; Humoresque, Op. 10/6; Polinchinelle; Polka de V. R.; Preludes, Op. 3/2 & 4; Op. 23/5; Lilacs. Transcriptions: Rimsky-Korsakov: Flight of the Bumblebee. Kreisler: Liebesfreud; Liebesleid. Schubert: Wohin?. Bizet: L'arlésienne: Minuet. Mussorgsky; Sorochinsky Fair: Hopak. Trad.: Star-Spangled Banner
☉ *** Telarc CD 80489. Rachmaninov
Piano Concertos 1; 3 in D min., Op. 30
*** Warner 0927 47941-2. Lugansky, CBSO, Oramo
Piano Sonata 2, Op. 36 (rev. 1931); Preludes, Op. 3/2; Op. 23/1–2, 4–5, 10; Op. 32/2, 12; Siren, Op. 21/5; Margaritiki, Op. 38/3; Transcriptions: Scherzo from 'A Midsummer Night's Dream' (Mendelssohn); Flight of the Bumblebee (Rimsky-Korsakov); Lullaby (Tchaikovsky)
☉ *** EMI 5 57943-2. Simon Trpčeski

RAVEL, Maurice
Daphnis et Chloé (complete)
✲ (M) *** RCA **SACD** (ADD) 82876 61388-2. New England Conservatory & Alumni Ch., Boston SO, Munch

Menuet antique; Pavane pour une infante défunte; Le Tombeau de Couperin; (i) *Shéhérazade*
*** DG 471 614-2. Cleveland O, Boulez, (i) with Von Otter (with DEBUSSY: *Danses; Le jet d'eau;* (i) *3 Ballades de François Villon*)

RAWSTHORNE, Alan
Symphonies 1; (i) *2 (A Pastoral Symphony); 3*
(BB) *** Naxos 8.557480. (i) Charlotte Ellett; Bournemouth SO, Lloyd-Jones

RIMSKY-KORSAKOV, Nikolay
Scheherazade (symphonic suite), *Op. 35*
✲ (M) *** RCA (ADD) **SACD** 82876 66377-2. Chicago SO, Reiner (with STRAVINSKY: *Chant du Rossignol*)

ROSSINI, Gioacchino
L'Italiana in Algeri
*** Teldec 0630 17130-2 (2). Larmore, Gimenez, Del Carlo, Corbelli, Grand Theatre Ch., Lausanne CO, Lopez-Cobos

SAINT-SAËNS, Camille
Symphony 3 in C min.
✲ (M) *** RCA **SACD** (ADD) 82876 61387-2. Zamkochian, Boston SO, Munch (with DEBUSSY: *La Mer*; IBERT: *Escales*)

Organ Music: Bénédiction nuptiale, Op. 9; Elévation ou Communion; Fantaisies: in E flat; in D, Op. 101; 2 Improvisations, Op. 150/1 & 7; Prélude & Fugue in E flat, Op. 99/3
✲ *** Capriccio **Surround Sound SACD** 71 046. Joachim Doremüller

SCHOENBERG, Arnold
Gurrelieder
(BB) *** Naxos 8.557518/9. O'Mara, Diener, Lane, Wilson-Johnson, Hill, Haefliger (speaker), Simon Joly Ch., Philh. O, Craft

SCHUBERT, Franz
Piano Sonata 21 in B flat, D.960; (i) *Lieder: Abschied von der Erde; Viola; Der Winterabend*
*** EMI 5 57901-2. Leif Ove Andsnes, (i) with Ian Bostridge

Church Music: Aguste jam coelestium, D.488; 6 Antophonen zu Palmsonntag, D.696; Deutsche Messe, D.872; Graduale in C, D.184; Hymnus an den heiligen Geist, D.964; Kyries: in D min., D.31; B flat, D.45; D min., D.49; F, D.66. Lazarus, D.689; Magnificat in D, D.486; Masses: 1 in F, D.105; 2 in G, D.167; 3 in B flat, D.324; 4 in C, D.452; 5 in A flat, D.678; 6 in E flat, D.950. Offertoriums: (Salve Regina) in F, D.223; (Salve Regina) in A, D.676; (Totus in corde) in C, D.136; (Tres sunt) in A min., D.181; B flat, D.963. Psalms: 23, D.706; 92, D.953. Salve Reginas: in

B flat, D.106, D.379 & D.386; in A, D.676. Stabat Maters: in G min., D.175; F, D.383. Tantum ergos: in C, D.461, D.462, D.739 & D.811; in D, D.750; E flat, D.962
(BB) *** EMI (ADD/DDD) 5 87011-2 (7). Popp, Donath, Rüggerberg, Venuti, Hautermann, Falk, Fassbaender, Greindle-Rosner, Dallapozza, Araiza, Protschka, Tear, Lika, Fischer-Dieskau, Schreier, Capella Bavariae, Bav. R. Ch. & SO, Sawallisch

SCHUMANN, Robert
Symphony 4 in D min., Op. 20
✲ (M) (***) DG mono 474 988-2. BPO, Furtwängler (with HAYDN: *Symphony 88*)

SHOSTAKOVICH, Dmitri
Symphony 5 in D min., Op. 47
*** BBC (ADD) BBCL 4165-2. LSO, Stokowski (with VAUGHAN WILLIAMS: *Symphony 8 in D min.*)

SIBELIUS, Jean
Symphonies 4 in A min., Op. 63; 5 in E flat, Op. 82; Finlandia
(M) (***) EMI Legend mono 557754. Philh. O, Karajan (with bonus **DVD**: BERLIOZ: *Symphonie fantastique: 1st movt only*)
Symphonies 5; 6 in D min., Op. 104
(BB) *** LSO Live LSO 0037. LSO, C. Davis
Songs: Arioso, Op. 3; Den judiska flickans sång (The Jewish Maiden's Song); Belshazars gästabud (Belshazar's Feast); Höstväll (Autumn Evening); Luonnotar; Sancta Maria; Jungfrun på tornet (The Maiden in the Tower); Se'n har jag ej frågat mera (And I Questioned Her No Further); Soluppgång (Sunrise); Våren flyktar hastigt (The Spring is Flying)
*** Warner 8573 8.0243-2. Mattila, CBSO, Oramo (with GRIEG: *Songs*)

SIMPSON, Robert
Symphony 11; Variations on a Theme by Nielsen
*** Hyp. CDA 67500. City of L. Sinfonia, Matthew Taylor

STRAVINSKY, Igor
The Firebird (complete); *Le chant du rossignol; Fireworks; Scherzo à la russe*
✲ *** Mercury **SACD** (ADD) 470 643-2. LSO, Dorati
(i) *Les Noces;* (ii) *Oedipus Rex*
(BB) **(*) Naxos 8.557499. (i) Wells, Bickley, Ewing, International Piano Qt, Tristan Fry Percussion Ens.; (ii) Lane, Cornwell, Wilson-Johnson, Greenan, Fox (speaker); (i–ii) Simon Joly Ch., Philh. O, Craft

SZYMANOWSKI, Karol
King Roger, Op. 46
*** Accord ACD 131-2. Drabowicz, Pasiecznik, Beczala, Tesarowicz, Toczyska, Szymt, 'Alla Polacca' Youth Ch., Polish Nat. Op. O, Kaspszyk

TALLIS, Thomas

Spem in alium (40-part Motet); Salve intemerata (Mass and Motet); I call and cry to thee, O Lord; Discomfort them O Lord; With all our heart
✪ (M) **** Naxos **SACD** 6.110111. Oxford Camerata, Summerly

TANEYEV, Sergei

Piano Quintet, Op. 30; Piano Trio in D min., Op. 22
*** DG 477 5419. Repin, Gringolts, Imai, Harrell, Pletnev

TCHAIKOVSKY, Peter

18 Pieces, Op. 72
✪ *** DG 477 5378. Pletnev (with CHOPIN: *Nocturne, Op. posth.*)

VAUGHAN WILLIAMS, Ralph

Symphony 9 in E min.
(***) Cala mono CACD 0539. O, Stokowski (with RIEGGER: *New Dance*; HOVHANESS: *Symphony 2*; CRESTON: *Toccata, Op. 68* (***))

VERDI, Giuseppe

Aida (complete)
(***) Testament (mono) SBT2 1355 (2). Callas, Baum, Simionato, Walters, Neri, ROHCG O & Ch., Barbirolli

VICTORIA, Tomás Luis de

Officium defunctorum (Requiem), including Taedet animam meam vitae meae; Ave Regina coelorum a 8; Nigra sum; Quam pulchri sunt; Salve Regina; Trahe me post te
*** Coro **Surround Sound SACD** CORSACD 16033. The Sixteen, Christophers

WAGNER, Richard

Tristan und Isolde
✪ *** EMI 5 58006-2 (3). Stemme, Domingo, Fujimura, Pape, Bär, ROHCG Ch. & O, Pappano

WEBER, Carl Maria von

Overtures: Abu Hassan; Der Beherrscher der Geister (Ruler of the Spirits); Euryanthe; Der Freischütz; Jubel; Oberon; Preziosa
*** Capriccio **Surround Sound SACD** 71 045. Dresden State O, Kuhn
Oberon (complete recording in the original English)
✪ *** Ph. 475 6563-2 (2). Davislim, Martinpelto, Kaufmann, Dazeley, Monteverdi Ch., ORR, Gardiner, Allam

WEINGARTNER, Felix

Symphony 1; King Lear (Symphonic Poem)
*** CPO 999 981-2. Basel SO, Letonja

FIFTEEN OUTSTANDING DVDS

Fifteen outstanding DVDs, new to the present volume, personally chosen by the authors.

ARNOLD, Malcolm
'Toward the Unknown Region': Malcolm Arnold – A Story of Survival
*** Isolde Films **DVD** ISO 001. Including performances from Bream, Galway, Lloyd Webber, RTE Nat. SO, Houlihan (V/D: Tony Palmer)

BACH, Johann Sebastian
Christmas Oratorio
*** TDK **DVD** DV-BACHO (2). McFadden, Fink, Genz, Henschel, Monteverdi Ch., E. Bar. Sol., Gardiner

BEETHOVEN, Ludwig van
Violin Concerto in D, Op. 61
*** EMI **DVD** 5 44544-9. Perlman, BPO, Barenboim (Producer: Johannes Müller) (with BRAHMS: *Violin Concerto*)

BERNSTEIN, Leonard
Wonderful Town
✪ *** EuroArts **DVD** 2052299. Criswell, McDonald, Hampson, Barrett, European Voices, Wayne Marshall, BPO, Rattle (Choreography: Candace Allen; V/D: Andreas Morell)

BRITTEN, Benjamin
A Midsummer Night's Dream
*** Warner **DVD** 0630 16911-2. Cotrubas, Bowman, Appelgren, Buchen, Ryland Davies, Duesing, Lott, Bryson, LPO, Haitink (Producer: Peter Hall; TV Director: Dave Heather)

DONIZETTI, Gaetano
Mary Stuart (in English)
*** Warner **DVD** 50467 8028-2. Baker, Plowright, Rendall, Tomlinson, Opie, ENO Ch. & O, Mackerras (V/D: Peter Butler)

HAYDN, Josef
The Creation (*Die Schöpfung*; complete, in German)
*** Capriccio **Surround Sound DVD** 93 507. Cencic, Schmidt, Bauer, Jankowitsch, V. Boys' Ch., Ch. Viennensis, V. Volksoper, SO, Marschik (V/D: Axel Stummer)

MOZART, Wolfgang Amadeus
Le Nozze di Figaro
*** Arthaus **DVD** 101 089. Skram, Cotrubas, Te Kanawa, Luxon, Stade, Rintzler, Condo, Glyndebourne Ch., LPO, Pritchard (V/D: Dave Heather)

PROKOFIEV, Sergei
War and Peace
*** Arthaus **DVD** 100 370-9. Gergalov, Prokina, Volkova, Sonya, Kanunnikova, Alexashkin, Gregoriam, Borodina, Bezukhova, Marusin, Morozov, Kit, Okhotnikov, Gerelo, Kirov Ch. and O, Gergiev (Dir: Graham Vick; V/D: Humphrey Burton)

PUCCINI, Giacomo
Manon Lescaut
*** Warner **DVD** 5050466-7174-2-9. Domingo, Te Kanawa, Allen, ROHCG Ch. & O, Sinopoli (V/D: Humphrey Burton)

RACHMANINOV, Sergei
The Miserly Knight
✪ *** Opus Arte **DVD** OA 0919D. Leiferkus, Berkeley-Steele, Mikhailov, Voynarowsky, Schagidullin, LPO, Jurowski (Producer: Annabel Arden; V/D: James Whitbourn)

ROSSINI, Gioachino
Le Comte Ory (complete)
*** Warner **DVD** 0630 18646-2. Laho, Massis, Montague, Shaulis, Tezier, Robbins, Glyndebourne Ch., LPO, A. Davis (V/D: Brian Large)

STRAUSS, Johann Jr, Strauss, Josef, & Strauss, Eduard
'New Year Concert, 2005': Johann Strauss Jr: Marches: Indigo; Russische. Polkas: An der Jagd; Die Bajadere; Bauern; Ein Herz, ein Sinn; Fate Morgana; Haut-Volée; Klipp-Klapp; Nordseebilder; Pizzicato (with Josef); Vergnügungszug. Waltzes: An der schönen blauen Donau; Geschichten aus dem Wienerwald; 1001 Nacht. Josef Strauss: Polkas: Die Emancipirte; Winterlust. Waltzes: Lustschwärmer. Eduard Strauss: Electrisch Polka (with Suppé: Overture: Die schöne Galathée. Joseph Hellmesberger: Auf Wiener Art)
*** DG **DVD** 073 4020. VPO, Maazel (V/D: Brian Large)

TCHAIKOVSKY, Peter
The Nutcracker, Op. 71 (ballet; complete)
✪ *** BBC Opus Arts **DVD** OA 087 D. Yoshida, Cope, Dowell, Cojocara, Putrov, Royal Ballet, ROHCG O, Svetlanov (Choreography: Lev Ivanov & Peter Wright; Producer: Peter Wright; V/D: Ross MacGibbon)
Swan Lake (ballet; complete)
✪ *** DG **DVD** 073 4044. Fonteyn, Nureyev, V. State Opera Ballet, VSO, Lanchbery (Choreography: Rudolf Nureyev; Dir: Truck Branss)

ABEL, Carl Friedrich (1723–87)

As the first composer to appear in our pages, Abel is certainly worthy of a biographical note. Born, appropriately, at Cöthen, the son of a court musician, he soon became celebrated as a virtuoso on the viola da gamba, and later in life was admired for his improvisational skills on that instrument. He began his career as a member of the Dresden Court Orchestra but, after a period of travel, moved to London in 1758, where his real claim to fame was established as a promoter of subscription concerts in association with Johann Christian Bach. In a way Abel took over from Handel, who died shortly after the first concert in 1759. Bach joined the enterprise five years later, and as partners both composers became friendly and influential with the young Wolfgang Amadeus Mozart when he arrived in London with his father in 1764. The Abel/Bach partnership continued from the mid-1760s until 1781 and encouraged the building of their own concert hall in Hanover Square. In 1782 Abel returned home, where he enjoyed a successful period at the Prussian Court in Potsdam as composer/performer, but in 1785 he returned to London to resume his Hanover Square enterprise until his death. His influence on London music-making at that time was profound. He helped many artists establish their careeers, but above all he was a likeable and generous man, traits that are obvious from his elegant Gainsborough portrait, besides being reflected in the geniality of his music.

Flute Concertos 1–6, Op. 6

(N) *** ASV CDDCA 1178. Beckett, ASMF, Aldwinckle (harpsichord)

These six charming flute concertos date from about 1758/9, around the beginning of Abel's arrival in – and long musical association with – London. They are hardly demanding works but are unfailingly melodic, always elegant and with enough harmonic invention to quash any feeling of blandness. Abel's rhythms often veer towards dance movements in the lively outer movements, while the central adagios have a simple beauty of their own. The minor-keyed Concerto No. 2 is especially enjoyable, and the finales bubble along infectiously. While not using 'authentic instruments', Edward Beckett plays with style, and he is well supported by the ASMF, directed (one presumes) by Robert Aldwinckle from the keyboard, who give the music an admirable lightness and vitality. Good recording.

ADAM, Adolphe (1803–56)

La Filleule des fées (ballet; complete)

*** Marco 8.223734-35 (2). Queensland SO, Mogrelia

This was Adam's third ballet, which was first performed in 1849, and one is struck by the seemingly endless melodic invention and the mastery of orchestration. Adam's wit is irrepressible, while his subtle shifts in metre and harmonic colouring always hold the listener's interest. This makes pleasing home listening, and the recording and performance are both very good.

Giselle (ballet; complete. Choreography: Jean Coralli & Jules Perrot, revised Marius Petipa)

⊕▬ *** TDK DVD DV-BLGIS. Bessmertnova, Vasyuchenko,Vetrov, Bylova, Bolshoi Ballet, directed Grigorovich, Bolshoi Theatre O, Zhuraitis (Producer: Micha Takemori, V/D: Shoukichi Amano)

*** Warner DVD 0630 19397-2. Mezentseva, Zaklinsky, Selyutsky, Terekhova, Kirov Ballet, Leningrad Op. & Ballet Theatre O, Fedotov (Producer: Oleg Vinogradov, V/D: Preben Montell)

These magnificent live performances of Giselle, recorded in 1983 and 1990, preserve a Russian choreographic pattern and dramatic understanding going back to the ballet's first performance there in 1842. The Kirov casting has no weakness. Galina Mezentseva is the epitome of balletic grace in the title-role – and her touching performance at the tragic end of Act I is to be surpassed in Act II, where the opening scene brings more ravishing dancing from Myrtha, Queen of the Wilis (Tatyana Terekhova), and the dazzling corps de ballet. There is intrusive applause here, but it is understandable. Konstantin Zaklinsky as Albrecht and Gennadi Selyutsky as Hilarion are hardly less impressive, and the solo dances and pas de deux in Act II are memorable. The orchestra plays with warmth, finesse and robust vitality under Viktor Fedotov and is richly and vibrantly recorded, with the slight edge on the violins adding to the brilliant effect of the playing. The camera is almost always where you want it to be, with the perspectives imaginatively varied to follow the action. Costumes and scenery are gloriously traditional – the setting for Act III is rightly applauded, and it is only the occasionally over-enthusiastic audience response that is a slight problem.

The Bolshoi DVD recording dates from 1990, with the video direction and audio team from the Japanese Arts Corporation. Although the name of Yuri Grigorovich is given among the choreographic credits, he has primarily acted as stage producer, and the original choreography is retained. Natalia Bessmertnova is superb in the title-role, Yuri Vasyuchenko an imposing and elegantly athletic Albrecht, Yuri Vetrov a lusty Hilarion, and Maria Bylova a wonderfully poised Myrtha. They easily match their Kirov counterparts, and so do the beauty, precision and grace of the corps de ballet, especially in Act II in their extraordinary 'hopping' step. The autumnal Act I set is particularly ravishing in Moscow, but in Act II the Kirov scene, with the moon above, is more romantic; yet the dancing has plenty of tension. In addition, the Kirov manage Giselle's ghostly entry in Act II rather more convincingly than does the Bolshoi version, where she emerges from her grave on an all-too-obvious stage lift. But these are small quibbles; both performances give great pleasure, and the Japanese camera-work is particularly fine and immediate in Moscow; the audio balance also manages to have the applause more muted, even though the orchestral sound is extremely live and vivid. We see the conductor, Algis Zhuraitis, directing his players imperiously at the opening of each Act, but throughout he is also splendidly flexible, turning Adam's melodies with exquisite finesse. So it is very much a case of making an arbitrary choice, for both these sets give enormous pleasure.

Giselle (ballet; complete)

(B) *** Double Decca 452 185-2 (2). ROHCG O, Bonynge

Giselle (older European score)

(BB) *** Naxos 8.550755/6. Slovak RSO, Mogrelia

Giselle (1841) is the first of the great classical ballet scores. Andrew Mogrelia's complete recording uses the normal performing edition. The orchestral playing has grace, elegance and plenty of life: the brass are not ashamed of the melodrama. The recording is resonantly full and warm in ambience, yet well detailed.

Bonynge's performance on Decca restores Adam's original

and is that bit more strongly characterized, while the Decca sound has a slightly sharper and brighter profile. That remains first choice (at Double Decca price) but the Naxos set costs slightly less.

La Jolie Fille de Gand (ballet; complete)
*** Marco 8.223772-73 (2). Queensland SO, Mogrelia

With *La Jolie Fille de Gand*, written in 1842, one year after *Giselle*, Adam was exploring the possibilities of new orchestral colour – cornets and an ophicleide were specified in the overture (not used here), while the finale features an unexpected and dramatic organ entry. There are many such felicities sprinkled throughout this score. If in terms of recording and performance it doesn't quite come up to the level of Bonynge's classic recordings, it is still very good indeed. An essential purchase for all balletomanes or those who simply love sophisticated light music.

OPERA

Le Postillon de Longjumeau (opera; complete)
(BB) **(*) EMI 5 74106-2 (2). Aler, Anderson, Lafont, Le Roux, Ottewaere, Laforge Ch. Ens., Monte Carlo PO, Fulton

Adolphe Adam's opera *Le Postillon de Longjumeau* is best known for the hero's spectacular Act I aria with its stratospheric top notes; however, it contains many other charming moments and is given an excellent complete recording in this EMI set. John Aler, heady in tone throughout his range and with no strain on those top notes, is outstanding as the postillion himself who, soon after singing that aria, leaves his new bride to become an opera singer. As Madeleine the abandoned wife, June Anderson is admirably agile, and she brings a vein of toughness to a heroine who, after inheriting a fortune, seeks revenge on her opera singer husband. Her voice, however, is a trifle raw. The story is preposterous, but there is spike behind the fun, which adds point to the music. Thomas Fulton, conducting the Monte Carlo orchestra, is obviously at home here, giving a lively spring to the many ensembles. The sound has atmosphere and clarity. The only snag is the lack of texts and translations.

ADAMS, John (born 1947)

John Adams: A Portrait. Chamber Symphony; (i) *Gnarly Buttons* (for clarinet & chamber orchestra)
*(**) Arthaus DVD 100 322. (Includes also STEVE REICH: *Eight Lines.* CONLON NANCARROW: *Studies for Player Piano 1 & 7*) Ensemble InterContemporain, Nott; (i) with Trouttet (Producer: Colin Wilson, V/D: Bob Coles)

The '*John Adams Portrait*' is the sort of standard documentary one would expect on a TV arts programme and includes a not very comprehensive summary of his musical output (with brief musical excerpts), concentrating mainly on the operas, especially the violent controversy aroused in America over *The Death of Klinghoffer*. The most interesting comments are from the composer himself, telling of his early rejection of atonal music and the Second Viennese School: 'Webern was the strangest musical experience I have ever encountered in my life.' Adams believes that in the distant future musicians will look back on 'a period in the twentieth century – the era of Schoenberg, Stockhausen and Boulez –

when composers aggressively destroyed the pulse and tonal syntax of music'.

After a year's sabbatical, in 1974 he was exposed to the music of Steve Reich: '*Drumming* was a major event for me.' But he later moved on from Minimalism. He found it provided only 'a limited musical experience . . . its emotional band-width was very small, so I tried to stretch it'. The following concert, which was recorded live in the Paris Théâtre du Châtelet, shows something of his musical progress.

It opens appropriately with Reich's *Eight Lines*, readily demonstrating that Reich helped to create the vocabulary of Minimalism without realizing its musical potential. *Gnarly Buttons* follows, with a virtuoso if lyrically rather cool clarinet soloist (André Trouttet), who nevertheless plays brilliantly and ends the piece hauntingly. Conlon Nancarrow's *Studies*, in their orchestral form, bring a welcome touch of wit, but the Adams *Chamber Symphony* is not easy listening, even though its somewhat doleful, central trombone-led 'Walking Aria' brings lyrical relief from the rumbustiously pungent rhythmic 'jam sessions' of the outer movements. But this is a work which grows in interest with several hearings.

In this kind of repetitive music the visuals don't add a great deal, particularly as the instrumental close-ups do not always reflect the aural detail, and in *Eight Lines* the camera sometimes moves away to look at the chandelier, and the producer splices in some quickened-up night-time traffic imagery! The conductor, Jonathan Nott, is obviously fully in charge, but his self-conscious smiles and wiggling left hand could become irritating with repeated viewing. A fascinating DVD, all the same.

(i) *The Chairman Dances;* (ii; iii) *Chamber Symphony;* (i) *Christian Zeal and Activity; Common Tones in Simple Time;* (iv; v; vi) *Violin Concerto;* (vii; vi) *El Dorado;* (viii; iii; ix) *Eros Piano;* (viii; iii) *Fearful Symmetries;* (i) 2 *Fanfares for Orchestra: Tromba lontana; Short Ride in a Fast Machine;* (ii; iii; x) *Gnarly Buttons;* (ii; iii) *Grand Pianola Music;* (i) *Harmonielehre;* (xi) *Hoodoo Zephyr;* (vii; vi) *Lollapalooza;* (viii; iii) *Shaker Loops;* (vii; vi) *Slonimsky's Earbox.* Instrumental music: (xii) *John's Book of Alleged Dances.* Vocal music: (xiii) *Harmonium;* (xiv; viii; iii) *The Wound Dresser;* (xv; viii; iii) arr. of 5 *Songs* by Charles Ives. Opera: (xvi; vi) *The Death of Klinghoffer: highlights.* (xvii; iii) *I Was Looking at the Ceiling and I Then Saw the Sky;* (xviii) *Nixon in China: excerpts*
(M) *** None. 7559 79453-2 (10). (i) San Francisco SO, De Waart; (ii) L. Sinf.; (iii) composer; (iv) Kremer; (v) LSO; (vi) Nagano; (vii) Hallé O; (viii) O of St Luke's; (ix) with Crossley; (x) with Collins; (xi) composer (synthesizer); (xii) Kronos Qt; (xiii) San Francisco Ch. & SO; (xiv) with Sylvan; (xv) with Upshaw; (xvi) Lyon Opéra Ch. & O; (xvii) instrumental ens.; (xviii) Ch. & O of St Luke's, De Waart

Chamber Symphony; Grand Pianola Music (None. 7559 79219-2)

(i) *Violin Concerto;* (ii) *Shaker Loops* (None. 7559 79360-2)

Fearful Symmetries; (i) *The Wound Dresser* (None. 7559 79218-2)

(i) *Gnarly Buttons.* (ii) *John's Book of Alleged Dances* (None. 7559 79465-2)

This impressive 10-CD box, with many of the performances directed by the composer himself (who is an excellent and persuasive advocate), gives an impressive survey of the achievement of John Adams. As Simon Rattle has aptly commented: 'In almost all of his best pieces, there's a mixture of ecstasy and sadness – the catharsis at the end of *Harmonium*, or the still, sad, personal last Act of *Nixon in China*, or the middle movement of the *Violin Concerto*. It has an immense sadness and depth at the centre of it.'

Many of the discs are available separately and the obvious point of entry is *Grand Pianola Music*, scored for two pianos (John Alley and Shelagh Sutherland) and three female voices, as well as orchestra. The finale, *On the Dominant Divide*, seems custom-made for the Last Night of the Proms, with its 'flag-waving, gaudy tune, rocking back and forth between the pianos, amid ever increasing cascades of B flat major arpeggios'. But you might also begin with the early *Shaker Loops* with its tremolandos and trills, or the *Short Ride in a Fast Machine*.

In the *Violin Concerto* Gidon Kremer's account of the fiendishly demanding solo part is dazzling. The performance is superb, and the dream-like *Chaconne* offers aural and spiritual balm; but with the soloist closely balanced not all listeners will find it easy to last out the bravura battering provided by the 15-minute opening movement. *Shaker Loops*, however, tends to trump previous versions.

Fearful Symmetries, to use the composer's own words, 'is cut from the same cloth as *Grand Pianola Music*, although it is more choreographic in feeling'. In certain ways following on from Ives's *Central Park in the Dark*, 'it resembles one of those Soho nightclubs with a heavy bouncer at the door; it mixes the weight and bravura of a big band with a glittering synthetic sheen of techno pop (samples and synthesizer) and the facility and finesse of a symphony orchestra'. The composer's performance is most exhilarating.

The Wound Dresser is a very moving, elegiac setting (for baritone and orchestra) of Walt Whitman's poem, recalling the author's terrible experiences as a medic during the American Civil War. It is most touchingly sung by Sanford Sylvan and, partly but not entirely because of the music's delicacy of texture, every word is clear.

The clarinet was the composer's own instrument, and his concertante work, *Gnarly Buttons*, is autobiographical and fashioned in three sections, *The Perilous Shore*, *Hoe Down (Mad Cow)* and *Put Your Loving Arms Around Me*, a touchingly 'simple song, quiet and tender upfront'. The work was written for Michael Collins, who gives a haunting performance which the composer describes as ideal. *John's Book of Alleged Dances* is alleged 'because the steps for them have yet to be invented'. The composer's minimalist imagination knows no bounds, and the Kronos players respond with much bravura to his kaleidoscopic ideas.

But much else is new to the catalogue, including the throbbing *Common Tones in Simple Time* ('a pastoral with pulse') and the infernally rhythmic *Lollapalooza*, dedicated to Simon Rattle. The title of the even more explosive *Slonimsky's Earbox*, so obviously Stravinsky-orientated, also celebrates another Russian, the author of a *Thesaurus of Scales and Melodic Patterns*, whose influence Adams also acknowledges. By contrast *Eros Piano* is a ruminative soliloquy, with distinct echoes of Messiaen. *Christian Zeal and Activity*, the earliest work here, has an Ivesian flavour and exists as a framework for an actual revivalist sermon, taken from a radio broadcast.

Perhaps even more remarkable is *Hoodoo Zephyr*, a work for synthesizer, inspired by travel in the deserts of California and Nevada, heard in 'a wash of harmonies that shimmer and oscillate like objects at midday on the broiling floor of a desert sink'. Finally, the orchestration of five famous Ives song-settings should not be forgotten, especially *At the River*, so beautifully sung by Dawn Upshaw.

The set is extensively documented and handsomely packaged, but the lack of track information with each individual disc and the complicated layout of the booklet mean that they are not easy to use together.

Berceuse élégiac; Shaker Loops; Short Ride in a Fast Machine; (i) The Wound Dresser

🔜 (BB) *** Naxos 8.559031. Bournemouth SO, Marin Alsop; (i) with N. Gunn

If you are seeking an introduction to the music of John Adams, you cannot better this splendidly played anthology from Marin Alsop and the Bournemouth Symphony Orchestra, vividly recorded within an ideal acoustic. The whizzing *Short Ride in a Fast Machine* immediately has hit potential but finds its counterpart in the touchingly gentle *Berceuse élégiac*, while the moving lament of the Walt Whitman civil war *Wound Dresser* shows just how naturally Adams writes for the voice. It is finely sung by Nathan Gunn against the simplest orchestral backcloth, with strings dominating. But the highlight of the disc is Adams's early (1978) masterpiece, heard here in a 1983 revision, *Shaker Loops*. Here he draws on the minimalist style of Steve Reich and totally transforms it into a four-movement piece of real lyrical appeal and endless aural fascination. This is now by far its finest performance on disc, with the climax of the third-movement 'Loops and Verses' quite riveting.

(i) Chamber Concerto; Shaker Loops (chamber version). (ii) Phrygian Gates (piano)

*** RCA 09026 68674-2. (i) Ens. Modern, Edwards; (ii) Kretzschmar

Even more than the composer's own version, Sian Edwards's performance of the *Chamber Concerto* creates a dazzling wildness, with the polyphonic tapestries of the outer movements catching both the Stravinskian rhythmic influences in the one and the composer's vernacular jazzy leverage in the other. The string septet version of *Shaker Loops* is just as compelling as the version for string orchestra. Herman Kretzschmar's bravura performance of the piano work *Phrygian Gates* holds the listener's attention throughout its gradual shifts of mood and elliptical metamorphoses. Excellent recording throughout.

(i) El Dorado; (ii) Berceuse élégiaque (arrangement for chamber orchestra of Busoni's Cradle Song of the Man at His Mother's Coffin); The Black Gondola (orchestration of Liszt's La Lugubre Gondola)

*** None. 7559 79359-2. (i) Hallé O, Nagano; (ii) L. Sinf., composer

El Dorado is a diptych of paired orchestral canvases, inspired (in 1991) by two giant paintings. Adams tells us: the first part is 'a musical embodiment of aggressive growth, beginning in a pre-dawn forest and culminating 13 minutes later in a vast crescendo of brutal force'; the second, *Soledades*, is 'a landscape without man, the governing form a grand arch'. *La Lugubre Gondola* is expanded and transformed into a darkly sensuous tone-painting of the gondola gliding through sluggish Venetian waters, carrying a coffin. John Adams is a splendid advocate of his own music, and Nagano's Hallé version of the major work is equally committed and compelling.

Harmonielehre; The Chairman Dances; (i) 2 Fanfares: Tromba lontana; Short Ride in a Fast Machine

🔜 *** EMI 5 55051-2. CBSO, Rattle; (i) with Warren

Harmonielehre is an extraordinary, large-scale (39-minute) work in three parts. *The Chairman Dances* his foxtrot for a full 13 minutes, with unabated energy. The *Two Fanfares* mystically and hauntingly pay their respects to Ives as well as to Copland, while the *Short* (exhilarating) *Ride in a Fast Machine* has an agreeably unstoppable momentum. The performances bring the most persuasive advocacy, and the excellent recording is clear, vivid and spacious.

Naive and Sentimental Music; Mother of Man; Chain to the Rhythm

*** None. 7550 79636-2. LAPO, Salonen

John Adams suggested that *Naive and Sentimental Music* (1998–9) is the most ambitious of his works outside his operas, although at that time *El Niño* had not yet been written. The title serves for the three-part work overall, as well as for its first and longest movement. Its atmosphere is immediately created by the placing of a simple diatonic woodwind melody over strumming chords; but the writing soon moves in new directions, gaining in complexity and passion. The music's peregrinations have infinite variety, and the closing section is very powerful. The second movement is a deeply felt elegy, 'a cradle song of the man at the coffin of his mother', and its melancholy intensity is movingly and gently sustained throughout. In *Chain to the Rhythm* Adams returns to his familiar hypnotic dallying with 'small fragments of rhythmic cells' to form a toccata-like moto perpetuo, finally producing a great surge of energy. A considerable array of percussion is used to enhance the delicacy of texture *en route* to the thundering climax, where the bass drum underlines the coda. Performance and recording are first rate.

Shaker Loops

(M) *** Virgin 5 61851-2. LCO, Warren-Green – GLASS: *Company*, etc.; REICH: *8 Lines*; HEATH: *Frontier* ***

The outstanding performance by Christopher Warren-Green and his London Concert Orchestra is full of imaginative intensity and it received the composer's imprimatur. Outstandingly vivid recording.

CHAMBER & PIANO MUSIC

(i) *Road Movies* (for Violin & Piano); (ii; iii) *Hallelujah Junction* (for 2 pianos). Solo Piano Music (ii) *American Berserk*; *China Gates*; (iii) *Phrygian Gates*

(N) *** None. 7559 79699-2. (i) Josefowicz & Novacek; (ii) Hodges; (iii) Hind

(N) **(*) Black Box BBM 1098 (without *American Berserk*). Russo & Ehnes

These collections represent John Adams in committed minimalist style, whether in his early piano pieces, *Phrygian Gates* and *China Gates* of 1977, or in his much more ambitious piece for two pianos, *Hallelujah Junction*, of 1996. Adams uses the expression 'gates' as a term borrowed from electronic music, acknowledging that *Phrygian Gates* with its kaleidoscopic repetitions is the first piece to use his mature language. *China Gates* uses a similar formula, but with far fewer demands on the pianist, a piece specifically designed for young musicians. *Hallelujah Junction* was inspired by a small truck stop in the High Sierras on the border of California, an isolated place where Adams keeps a cabin. He described it as an '18-minute tableau', and in its variety and colour it represents his minimalist style at its most imaginative. It is only in the three

movements of *Road Movies* that his lyrical vein, so important in his later music, begins to emerge. Written in 1995, it is Adams's only work so far for violin and piano, offering images of the open road, the first a pleasure ride, the second a still picture of isolation, and the third a bumpy ride down a country road.

Apart from including an extra work, the very well-recorded Nonesuch collection is a clear first choice. The performance of *Road Movies* is more vibrant and colloquial in the hands of Leola Josefowicz and John Novacek, with the final 40% *Swing* really taking off. Moreover, both the pianists on the Nonesuch disc have a real feeling for the Adams rhythmic patterns and syncopated percussive accents. In their joint performance of *Hallelujah Junction* they move from the serenity of the centrepiece to an arrestingly jazzy finale, when the full four syllables of the work's title finally materialize to make a powerful and thrilling climax. The composer himself provides indispensable back-up notes about all the music.

The alternative Black Box disc is also impressively played, but the performers, although both vigorous and sympathetic to the music's lyrical passages, miss the last degree of wildness in the more uninhibited moments, even though their virtuosity is in no doubt. In *Hallelujah Junction* James Ehnes moves over from violin to piano.

CHORAL MUSIC

On the Transmigration of Souls

(N) *** None. 7559 79816-2. NY Choral Artists, Brooklyn Youth Ch., P. Smith (trumpet), soloists, NYPO, Maazel

In remembering 9/11, John Adams's moving choral work is the American equivalent of Britten's *War Requiem* in many ways. Yet its means are infinitely more simple and its 25-minute length avoids any hint of inflation or emotional excess. Adams has described the piece as 'a memory space'. Against a shimmering orchestral and choral backcloth is heard a second textural layer of street sounds, muttered phrases from missing persons, their relatives and loved ones, the reading of victims' names by friends and family members. The great 'Why' is created by the quotation of haunting fragments of Ives's *Unanswered Question*, but the choral climax is on the words '*Love*' and '*Light*'. Calm returns, and the final spoken words are 'I see water and buildings' and 'I love you', and the street sounds return the listener to everyday life. The recording laminates the music and sounds with complete success – a remarkable achievement from all concerned.

OPERA

El Niño (complete)

*** Arthaus **DVD** 100 220 (CD version on None. 79634-2 (2)). Hunt Lieberson, Upshaw, White, Theatre of Voices, L. Voices, Berlin Deutsches SO, Nagano (Director: Peter Sellars, V/D: Peter Sellars)

El Niño is essentially a staged oratorio. In this respect it broadly follows on after Bach's *Christmas Oratorio* and Handel's *Messiah* in telling the story of the Annunciation and birth of Christ, the journey to Bethlehem, the visit of the Three Kings, Herod's slaughter of the first-born and the prudent departure of Joseph, Mary and Jesus. The libretto includes Bible texts in the American translation by Richard Lattimore and New Testament Apocrypha, as well as poems by writers from Mexico and Chile, which are sung in Spanish.

The opera staging places the principal singers, chorus and semi-chorus (comprising three counter-tenors) on a plinth below a huge screen on which is projected a two-hour film (made by Peter Sellars and Yreina Cervántez). The narrative is enacted partly in a desert-like location, where we first encounter the passion of Adam and Eve, and later, as the story of Mary, Joseph and Jesus unfolds, in a contemporary American setting. The visit of the Three Wise Men takes place on wasteland near an airport, with jets constantly flying overhead. The massacre ordered by Herod is followed by an angry choral reminder of the slaughter of the Aztecs by Cortès and his troops in Mexico in 1521.

The work opens with typical Adams throbbing chords, and there is a good deal of this minimalist repetition in the score. The role of Mary is shared by mezzo-soprano and soprano; and the long Annunciation aria, set to lyric poetry by Rosario Castellanos (gloriously sung by Lorraine Hunt Lieberson), is an outstanding highlight of the score, as is the same lyricist's soprano/mezzo duet, *Se habla de Gabriel*. Dawn Upshaw, who has more of a narrative role, also sings with great beauty and eloquence.

Much of Willard White's contribution (he takes the part of Joseph) is boldly dramatic recitative, but his performance remains unforgettably powerful. The writing for the three male altos (who together take the part of Gabriel) is imaginatively chorded, and overall the music is consistently inventive, if melodically uneven, and the peaceful closing number for mezzo, baritone, male altos and children's chorus is very touching, even if it does not reach the level of inspiration of the opera's early scenes.

It has to be said that much of the visual imagery (apart from the main events of the story) is confusing, even superfluous, and does not bear repeated viewing; but the three principals all sing with moving eloquence and are always worth watching. So there is a good case for the audio version, which includes full texts, as against the video's surtitles. Whether on CD or DVD, the recording is impressively spacious and clear.

The Death of Klinghoffer (complete; DVD version)

(N) *** Decca **DVD** 074 189-9. Sylvan, Maltman, Howard, Randle, Boutros, Melrose, Marwa, Bickley, Blaze, L. Symphony Ch., LSO, composer (V/D: Penny Woolcock)

John Adams's second opera was entirely reworked for its film/video production. It graphically tells the story of the hijacking of the Italian cruise liner, *Achille Lauro*, by Palestinian terrorists in 1985. The opera had been controversial from its very inception, because in setting the story Adams chose to give equal voices to both sides of the conflict it represents. The two opening choruses are of both exiled Palestinians and exiled Jews; throughout, flashbacks recall the underlying source of the antagonism, showing Palestinian families being violently forced from their homes by the new Jewish settlers in 1948. But the opera still asks the question we all ask: How can a terrorist not only be willing to die but also be able to welcome death and to ignore the human tragedy he is creating? The dramatization of the film narrative is gripping, underpinned by Adams's masterly score. There are many remarkable sequences. Mamoud, the youngest of the hijackers (Kamel Boutros), sings of the night, remembering his harsh youth, and there is an extraordinary scherzando aria for a young Englishwoman, which leads unexpectedly to another young hijacker, Omar (voiced by Susan Bickley), recalling past violence, accompanied by a Wagnerian orchestral

outburst of great power. The orchestral commentary underpins the narrative throughout and creates a powerfully sustained tension, which leads to a great climax at the actual death scene, followed by the poignant '*Gymnopédie*', when the body is thrown overboard and sinks into the ocean. The opera closes with a choral epilogue and the tragic final scene when the Captain (Christopher Maltman) has to tell Marilyn Klinghoffer (Yvonne Howard) of her husband's death, and she recalls their life together.

The performance is in every way outstanding, and even though not all the solo singing is of the highest calibre, the dramatic commitment of the cast, the fine choral singing and superb playing of the LSO are unforgettable when so vividly recorded. The special features include a documentary about the film's conception, including interviews with composer and producer.

The Death of Klinghoffer (complete; CD version)

**(*) None. 7559 79281-2 (2). Nadler, Sylvan, Maddalena, Friedman, Hammons, Felty, E. Op. Ch., Lyon Opéra Ch. & O, Nagano

On CD, Kent Nagano conducts Lyon Opéra forces with the original singers who directly inspired the composer. As Klinghoffer's wife, Marilyn, the mezzo Sheila Nadler rises to the challenge of the closing scene superbly, and the baritone Sanford Sylvan is comparably sensitive as Klinghoffer himself, well matched by James Maddalena as the Captain, an Evangelist-like commentator, and by Thomas Hammons and Janice Felty in multiple roles. The recorded sound is excellent, but the booklet reproduces an unrevised version of the libretto.

I Was Looking at the Ceiling and Then I Saw the Sky

**(*) None. 7559 79473-2. De Haas, Mazzie, McDonald, McElroy, Muenz, Teek, Yang, composer

Inspired by the 1994 California earthquake, using for its title a quotation from one of the survivors, this theatre-piece is an intriguing amalgam of opera and musical. It starts with persistent ostinatos in Adams's early minimalist style, then launches into melodic lines echoing pop and jazz. The dramatic point is lessened on the disc when no linking dialogue is included, but the mixture is undemanding and agreeable, often moving. Even so, it can hardly compare in its impact with Adams's mainstream operas. Conducted by the composer, the performance with a characterful line-up of singers is persuasively idiomatic. Vivid, upfront sound.

Nixon in China (complete)

☛ (M) *** None. 7559 79177-2 (3). Sylvan, Craney, Maddalena, St Luke's Ch. & O, De Waart

It seemed an extraordinary idea to create an opera out of President Richard Nixon's greatest political gamble (which actually paid off): his 1972 visit to China to establish a friendly relationship with the Communist regime and its leader, Chou En-Lai; but those who saw the ENO production will have discovered how grippingly it works in the theatre. Adams's special brand of minimalism works magnetically, and the music itself has a lyrical melodic flow absent from most post-Britten operas. The choral music is especially telling, and Chou's banquet speech/aria is memorable, as is his wife's stirring soliloquy. The singing is generally excellent, as is the recording. A full translation is included.

ADDINSELL, Richard (1904–77)

Warsaw Concerto (orch. & arr. Roy Douglas)
(B) *** Ph. 411 123-2. Dichter, Philh. O, Marriner (with Concert ***)

(M) *** Decca 430 726-2. Ortiz, RPO, Atzmon – GERSHWIN: *Rhapsody* **(*); GOTTSCHALK: *Grand Fantasia* *** (with LISZT: *Hungarian Fantasia*; LITOLFF: *Scherzo* ***)

Richard Addinsell's pastiche miniature concerto, written for the film *Dangerous Moonlight* in 1942, is perfectly crafted; moreover it has a truly memorable main theme. It is beautifully played on Philips, with Marriner revealing the most engaging orchestral detail. The sound is first rate and the Virtuoso reissue has an attractive new livery.

The alternative from Cristina Ortiz is a warmly romantic account, spacious in conception. If the couplings are suitable, this is a rewarding collection, more substantial than Dichter's. The recording is first class.

ADÈS, Thomas (born 1971)

(i; ii; iii) *America (A Prophecy)*. (iii; iv) *Brahms*. (v) *Cardiac Arrest; Les Baricades mystérieuses*. (vi) *The Fayrfax Carol*; (vii) *Fool's Rhymes; January Writ*; (viii) *O Thou, who did with pitfall and with gin; Life Story*; (ix) *The Lover in Winter*
(M) *** EMI 5 57610-2. (i) Bickley; (ii) CBSO Ch.; (iii) CBSO, composer; (iv) Maltman; (v) Composer's Ens., composer; (vi) Poster, Webb, Benjafield; (vii) Bowers Broadbent (organ); (viii) McFadden, Polyphony, Layton; (ix) Blaze

America, for mezzo-soprano, large chorus and orchestra, involves an extraordinary kaleidoscope of original sounds and effects, with Spanish as well as Mayan influences inspiring the musical material. The piece is brilliantly performed and recorded here, with Susan Bickley singing a stylized text drawn from Mayan sources, using a raw, child-like tone. The other works, all much shorter – some (like the four *Lover in Winter* songs for counter-tenor) mere fragments – together make up a colourful survey of Adès and his work, with highly inventive and original choral effects in many of them, superbly presented by Polyphony under its director, Stephen Layton. One very striking example is the setting of lines from *Omar Khayyam* for male voices in 14 parts, using echo effects, *O Thou, who didst with pitfall and with gin*. Comparably memorable are Adès's transcriptions, including *Cardiac Arrest*, involving a jazz number seen through the composer's distorting lens, and *Life Story*, with the singer, Claron McFadden, instructed to sing in the style of Billie Holliday. The Couperin transcription, *Les Baricades mystérieuses*, is improbably dominated by two clarinets, while the final item, *Brahms*, for baritone (Christopher Maltman) and orchestra, is a grand setting of a surreal poem in German by Alfred Brendel. Least radical but still original is the *Fayrfax Carol* that Adès wrote for the King's College Carol Service in 1997. This is an hour of pieces so varied and inventive that it should attract far more than just devotees of new music.

(i–ii) *Asyla, Op. 17*; (i; iii) ... *But All Shall be Well, Op. 10*; (iii–iv) *Chamber Symphony for 15 Players, Op. 2*; (iii–v) *Concerto Conciso for Piano & Chamber Orchestra, Op. 18*; (i; iii) *These Premises are Alarmed, Op. 18*
*** EMI 5 56818-2. (i) CBSO; (ii) cond. Rattle; (iii) cond. composer; (iv) Birmingham Contemporary Music Group; (v) with composer (piano)

Rattle's superbly compelling account of *Asyla* (plural of 'asylum') confirms that this is Adès's major orchestral work so far, one which will surely join the repertoire. The *Chamber Symphony* is extraordinarily intricate in its rhythmic ideas, developing ear-tickling colouristic patterns. The *Concerto Conciso* has the solo piano well integrated into the instrumental group, where rhythms are free and jazzy, but it brings a calm central chaconne before the closing 'Brawl'. *These Premises are Alarmed* is a brief, witty apoplexy, designed as a brilliant orchestral showpiece for the Hallé Orchestra. Balance is restored in ... *But All Shall be Well*, the title coming from *Little Gidding*, the last of T. S. Eliot's *Four Quartets*. Remarkable music, splendidly played and most vividly and atmospherically recorded.

Piano Quintet
(N) *** EMI 5 57664-2. Composer, Arditti Qt – SCHUBERT: *Trout Quintet* ***

The coupling of the Adès *Piano Quintet* with Schubert's *Trout Quintet* suggests a musical irony for, whereas the latter, using all the basic classical forms, is the epitome of musical simplicity, Adès's work, while still cast in a sonata-form structure, presses it to the limits of avant-garde extravagance. The themes are obviously tonal, and indeed one of them is very beguiling, but the complexities of the exposition are hair-raising, with a superimposition of diverse time-signatures, leading to a bizarrely dissonant climax and bringing an equally gargantuan, earth-stopping accelerando. The thorny complexities of the writing are ear-dazzling, yet there is a real underlying lyricism. Not a work for faint-hearts perhaps, but an immensely stimulating attempt to find a contemporary transformation of old forms. The Arditi performance with the composer at the piano was made at The Maltings and has splendid definition and atmosphere.

(i) *Living Toys, Op. 9*; (ii) *Arcadiana, Op. 12*; (iii) *The Origin of the Harp, Op. 13*; (iv) *Sonata da caccia, Op. 11*; (v) Anthem: *Gefriolsae me, Op. 3b*
(B) *** EMI 5 72271-2. (i) L. Sinfonia, Stenz; (ii) Endellion Qt; (iii) Marsh, Robson, Richards, Busbridge, Knight, Boyd, Hopkins, Watkins, Tunnell, Benjafield, cond. composer; (iv) Niesemann, Clark, composer; (v) King's College, Cambridge, Ch., Cleobury; Quinney

Thomas Adès's hushed, deeply devotional anthem, which he wrote in 1990 for King's College Choir, is relatively conventional harmonically, but it is still most original while, conversely, *Living Toys* is a brilliant and colourful sequence of eight movements inspired by the naively heroic ambitions of a Spanish child. *Arcadiana* is Adès's first string quartet, regularly exploiting original timbres and textures and paying tribute, most movingly, to Elgar's *Nimrod*. The *Sonata da caccia* is a trio for baroque oboe, horn and harpsichord, which in its neoclassicism rises well clear of pastiche. The *Origin of the Harp* is an evocation of a symbolic Victorian painting for trios of clarinets, violas and cellos, plus percussion. Excellent performances and recording. Whatever he does, Adès cannot help creating original sounds.

Powder Her Face (opera; complete)
*** EMI 5 56649-2 (2). Gomez, Anderson, Morris, Bryson, Almeida Ens., composer

For his first opera Adès presents what might be described as a cabaret opera. He bases it on the life of the notorious Duchess of Argyll, toast of smart London society in the 1930s, seen in a sequence of flashbacks from the scene in 1990 when, in final penury, she is evicted from her penthouse suite at the Dorchester Hotel. Flashy and superficial, she yet emerges as a pathetic, often ridiculous yet finally touching figure, with Adès's music regularly echoing the popular music of the 1930s but grotesquely distorted. With voices overlapping, words are not always clear but the progress of the plot is never obscured, and the result is both offbeat and attractive. Under the composer's energetic direction, and with the original cast powerfully headed by Jill Gomez as the Duchess, the recording can be warmly recommended, with colourful chamber textures vividly caught.

ADLER, Samuel (born 1932)

Born in Mannheim, Samuel Adler came from a Jewish liturgical and musical background. Fortunately, the family were able to escape from Germany in 1939, moving permanently to the United States, where the young composer was able to study with Walter Piston and Randall Thompson and, later, Copland. He went on to serve as professor of composition at the Eastman School of Music for 20 years, and since 1997 has been a member of the Juilliard composition faculty.

Choral Music: *I Think continually of Thee; It is to God I shall sing; Proclaim God's greatness; L'chah Dodi; Let us rejoice; Mah Tovu; A Prophecy of Peace; Psalms 24, 124 & 146; 2 Psalm Motets; Transfiguration (An Ecumenical Mass); Verses from Isaiah*
(N) *** Gloria Dei Cantores GDCD 038. Soloists, Gloria Dei Cantores, Instrumental Soloists, Synergy Brass Quintet, Patterson or composer

Elisabeth Patterson's excellent choir from Cape Cod, Massachusetts, turns here to the very rewarding music of an American émigré composer with a European Hebrew inheritance (his father was a cantor) and an individual musical style that is universal, rather than selfconsciously American. The Jewish folk element is felt in two of the most attractive items here, but the opening *Prophecy of Peace* displays an invigorating transatlantic freshness that is to reappear regularly throughout the programme. The writing is immediately communicative and, if pieces rarely begin and end in the same key, it is 'because the emotional expression of the texts demands an evolution or metamorphosis'. Adler uses his instrumentalists economically, the full brass with splendour. The Psalm settings are particularly fine and the Hebrew items are colourful, but the highlights are the splendid *Ecumenical Mass* (with its thrilling climactic *Agnus Dei*) and the closing *Verses from Isaiah*, which the composer (who was present throughout the sessions) conducts himself. First-class recording.

AHO, Kalevi (born 1949)

(i) *Violin Concerto; Hiljaisuus (Silence). Symphony 1*
*** BIS CD 396. (i) Gräsbeck; Lahti SO, Vänskä

Aho's *First Symphony* betokens an impressive musical personality at work. *Silence* is an imaginative piece. It is related to (and was conceived as an introduction to) the post-expressionist and more 'radical' and trendy *Violin Concerto*; it is a work of considerable resource and imaginative intensity. Good performances and recording.

Symphonies 2; 7 (Insect Symphony)
*** BIS CD 936. Lahti SO, Vänskä

The *Second Symphony* is a powerfully conceived and cogently argued work in one movement, predominantly fugal in texture, indebted to the world of Shostakovich and Bartók. The *Seventh Symphony* derives its material from an opera, *Insect Life* (based on a play by Karel Čapek). Aho decided to refashion its ideas in symphonic form. Each of the six movements is programmatic, with titles like *Fox-Trot and Tango of the Butterflies*, *The Dung Beetles* and so on. It is more of a symphonic suite than a symphony but is scored imaginatively and with flair. Impeccable performances and extremely fine recording.

(i) *Symphony 11 (for 6 Percussionists & Orchestra). Symphonic Dances (Hommage à Uuno Klami)*
*** BIS CD 1336. Lahti SO, Vänskä, (i) with Kroumata Percussion Ens.

The *Symphonic Dances* derive from a completion Aho made of the ballet *Whirls* by Uuno Klami, whose inspiration, like so much Finnish music, derives from the *Kalevala*, the last act of which the composer left unfinished. It was this project that formed the origin of the *Symphonic Dances*, completed in 2001. Like many of its predecessors, the *Eleventh Symphony* includes an important role for a solo instrument or instruments – in this case a battery of percussion performed expertly by the six members of the Kroumata Ensemble. This is a vital work, which will give pleasure to Aho's growing band of admirers and which is given state-of-the-art recording by the BIS team and some pretty state-of-the-art playing by Osmo Vänskä and his Lahti musicians.

CHAMBER MUSIC

Bassoon Quintet; Quintet for Alto Saxophone, Bassoon, Viola, Cello & Double Bass
*** BIS CD 866. Sinfonia Lahti Chamber Ens.

The *Bassoon Quintet* shows great understanding of the instruments, though it has its longueurs. The *Quintet for Alto Saxophone, Bassoon, Viola, Cello and Double Bass* – an unusual combination but one rich in tonal variety – is the more concentrated of the two and leaves no doubt as to Aho's instrumental resourcefulness and imagination in writing for this ensemble. Virtuoso performances and natural, vivid recording.

Oboe Quintet (for flute, oboe, violin, viola and cello); 7 Inventions & Postlude for Oboe & Cello
*** BIS CD 1036. Sinfonia Lahti Chamber Ens.

The *Quintet for Flute, Oboe, Violin, Viola and Cello* was written in 1977, when Aho was 28, and it is far more concentrated than the overlong *Bassoon Quintet* from the same year. It draws the listener into its world from the first bar. There is a strong feeling for nature, and the melodic invention is fresh, even if interest is not sustained consistently over the piece's 30-minute span. Like the more recent *Inventions and Postlude*, this music is well worth investigating, and both performances and recording are of a high quality.

AKUTAGAWA, Yasushi (1925–89)

Ellora Symphony; Rhapsody for Orchestra; Trinita Sinfonica
(N) (BB) *** Naxos 8.555975. New Zealand SO, Yuasa

A fascinating survey of the music of a Japanese contemporary of Takemitsu whose sound-world could hardly be more different from his better known contemporary's. Where Takemitsu favours subtly luminous textures, Akutagawa is totally extrovert and, above all, melodic, and he goes for spectacularly vivid orchestral panoplies. The 1948 *Trinita Sinfonica* is an immediately engaging three-movement work, Soviet-influenced. The first-movement *Capriccio* opens with a genial bassoon ostinato and then immediately jumps into the brashly witty rhythmic arena of Kabalevsky and lightweight Shostakovich. The beguilingly sensuous central *Ninnerella* has a luscious flavour of film music, and the irrepressible finale has something of the reckless, folksy rhythms of Khachaturian, although the idom is far from Armenian.

The *Ellora Symphony* (1958) opens mysteriously and is closer to the idiom of Takemitsu. It creates a vision of an Indian temple site, celebrating three different religions with erotic carvings and reliefs, all explicitly expressing male and female enjoyment of sexuality as a symbol of prosperity and long life. The work subdivides into 15 brief sections, either slow and feminine or fast and masculine. There is exotic scoring, plus whooping horns and Stravinskian rhythms, well laced with explosions of percussion, all moving to a climax.

Whooping horns also introduce the 1971 *Rapsodia*, which has a more conventional structure, again favouring vibrant allegro ostinatos, with two plaintive central lyrical interludes, very Japanese in pentatonic melodic motivation; and the piece ends with a rumbustious motoric climax and a final roar. All this music is played with enthusiastic gusto and much bravura by the excellent New Zealand orchestra under Yuasa, and they also relish its lyrical colouring. The recording is in the demonstration bracket so, if you enjoy bizarre, tuneful exoticism and lots of orchestral spectacle and noise, this is well worth trying.

ALAIN, Jehan (1911–40)

Organ music

Aria; Chorales; 3 Danses; Danses; Deuxième fantaisie; Intermezzo; Le Jardin suspendu; Litanies; Petite pièce; Préludes; Prélude et fugue; Suite; Variations sur un thème de Jannequin; Variations sur l'hymne Lucis Creator
(BB) *** Naxos 8.553632/3. Lebrun (Cavaillé-Coll organ of the Church of Saint-Antoine des Quinze-Vingts, Paris)

Eric Lebrun is completely attuned to Alain's sound-world and his Cavaillé-Coll organ is ideal. These Naxos performances are thoroughly recommendable and at the price make a real bargain.

Aria; 3 Danses; 2 Danses à Agni Yavishta; Le jardin suspendu; Litanies
☛ **(N)** *** Chan. 10315. Whitehead (organ of Saint Étienne Cathedral, Auxerre, France) – DURUFLE: *Prélude et Fugue,* etc. ***

In the absence of Marie-Claire Alain's outstanding complete recording of Alain's organ music (only Volume 2 is listed in the current Warner catalogue: 8573 85773-2), this splendidly played Chandos recital can serve as an introduction to this highly original composer, alongside the excellent Naxos disc above.

The *Trois Danses*, a masterly triptych, moves from a spectacular opening ritualistic expression of *Joies* to an extended, grief-stricken centrepiece (*Deuils*) suspended over a shimmering oscillation, and the finale suggests an ominously dynamic conflict between life and death. The extraordinary galaxy of sound Alain creates needs the pungency of a French organ, and the instrument at Saint Étienne is surely ideal, both here and in the pair of exotic *Danses à Agni Yavishta* (the Hindu god of fire). The familiar *Litanies* (with its quirky rhythms perhaps not as sharply pointed as usual) and the mystical chaconne of *Le Jardin suspendu* again show the composer's at times almost bizarre palette of colour, as does the surprisingly restless *Aria*, and the Variations on the plainsong, *Lucis Creator,* bring a further pellucid contrast of registration. William Whitehead's outstanding performances are matched by superbly spectacular and wide-ranging Chandos sound.

Sarabande for Organ, String Quintet &Timpani (adapted from *Deuils* by M.-C. Alain)
☛ **(N) (BB)** *** Warner Apex 2564 61912-2. Marie-Claire Alain, Bamberg SO (members), Kantorow – DURUFLE: *3 Dances* etc.; POULENC: *Organ Concerto* ***

Alain conceived his *Trois Danses* (see above) for orchestra, but his premature death prevented him from completing an orchestral score. However, he left an adaptation of the second dance, *Deuils*, scored for a five-part string texture, organ and timpani, calling it *Sarabande*. Marie-Clare Alain has 'restituted and adapted' the sketch for performance. It sounds remarkably different from the organ version, the effect noble and graceful, radiantly translucent and certainly beautiful. The layout is rather like a passacaglia, ending with a recitative-like coda for organ and solo violin. The performance here could hardly be bettered, and this collection as a whole is very rewarding and excellently recorded.

Prière pour nous autres charnels
*** Chan. 9504. Hill, Davies, BBC PO, Y.-P. Tortelier – DUTILLEUX: *Violin Concerto,* etc. ***

Jehan Alain composed this short but beautiful setting of a prayer by Péguy for two soloists and organ; it is a moving piece, modal yet rich in its musical language, and it makes an admirable makeweight to the Dutilleux works.

ALBÉNIZ, Isaac (1860–1909)

Concierto fantástico; Rapsodia española (both for piano & orchestra)
(BB) *** Warner Apex 8573 89223-2. Heisser, Lausanne CO, López-Cobos – FALLA: *Nights in the Gardens of Spain;* TURINA: *Rapsodia sinfónica* ***

Both the *Concierto fantástico* and the *Rapsodia española* (the latter colourfully orchestrated by Georges Ensecu) are given sparkling, idiomatic performances by Jean-François Heisser and the excellent Lausanne Chamber Orchestra under López-Cobos. The *Rapsodia* swaggers along at its close, not unlike Chabrier's *España*. The recording is excellent, and so are the couplings. Thoroughly recommended.

Iberia (suite; orch. Arbós)

*** Chan. 8904. Philh. O, Y.-P. Tortelier – FALLA:
Three-cornered Hat ***

(M) ** Warner Elatus 0927 46720-2. O de Paris, Barenboim –
FALLA: *Nights in the Gardens of Spain* ***

In Arbos's brilliant scoring of Albéniz's piano pieces the
Philharmonia's response brings glowing woodwind colours
and seductive string-phrasing, well projected by the warmly
resonant recording. A clear first choice.

The languorous sophistication of Barenboim's approach is
more in line with the French impressionistic view of Spain
rather than reflecting the brightness and glare of the Spanish
sunshine. The Elatus recording was made at a live performance, and this has not only restricted the range of the sound
but added unwanted bronchial afflictions from the audience.
There is one quite alarming cough in a quiet moment of
Fête-dieu à Seville.

Rapsodia española (arr. Halfter)

(B) *** Decca 448 243-2. De Larrocha, LPO, Frühbeck de
Burgos – RODRIGO: *Concierto de Aranjuez*, etc.; TURINA:
Rapsodia sinfónica ***

(N) *** Australian Decca Eloquence 476 2971. De Larrocha,
LPO, Frühbeck de Burgos – MONTSALVATGE: *Concerto
brève*; SURINACH; *Piano Concerto*; TURINA: *Rapsodia
sinfónica* ***

Alicia de Larrocha's performance is both evocative and dazzling, and she is given splendid support by Frühbeck de
Burgos and brilliant Decca sound. This comes either coupled
with Rodrigo and Turina or as part of an enterprising collection of Spanishry from Australian Decca, including two rare
concertos.

GUITAR MUSIC

Cantos de España: Córdoba, Op. 232/4. Mallorca
(Barcarola), Op. 202; España (6 Hojas de Album), Op. 165.
Iberia (excerpts): *El Puerto; Evocación; El Abaicín; Triana;
Zambra Granadina.* **Suite española:** *Aragón*

**(*) Channel CCS 10397. Peter and Zoltán Katona

The Katona twins are a highly talented duo and they find
plenty of colour and atmosphere in this familiar piano repertoire, very effectively transcribed. The recording too is warm
and pleasing, although the resonance blunts the upper range
just a little. A most attractive recital just the same.

Cantos de España: Córdoba, Op. 232/4; Mallorca
(Barcarola), Op. 202. Suite española: *Cataluña; Granada;
Sevilla; Cádiz, Op. 47/1–4*

🔊 ❂ (B) *** RCA 74321 68016-2. Bream – GRANADOS:
Collection (with MALATS: *Serenata*; PUJOL: *Tango
espagñol; Guajira*) *** ❂

Julian Bream is in superb form in this splendid recital, vividly
recorded in the pleasingly warm acoustic of Wardour Chapel,
near his home in Wiltshire. The playing itself has wonderfully
communicative rhythmic feeling and great subtlety of colour,
and its spontaneity increases the impression that one is
experiencing a 'live' recital. The performance of the haunting
Córdoba, which ends the group, is unforgettable. The super-
bargain reissue includes additionally pieces by Malats and
Pujol.

Suite española, Op. 47 (extended suite, arr. Barrueco)

(M) *** EMI 5 66574-2. Barrueco – TURINA: *Guitar
music* ***

Manuel Barrueco's playing combines warmth with a pleasing
intimacy and a natural, relaxed sense of spontaneity. The
more famous evocations, *Castilla, Granada* and the closing
Sevilla, are subtle in nuance and colour, while the vibrant
Asturias brings a haunting, improvisatory feeling in its calm
middle section. The recording is beautifully judged, not over-
projected.

PIANO MUSIC

L'Automne (Valse); Piano Sonatas 3–5

(N) (B) ** HM Musique d'abord HMA 1957007. Guinovart

As an infant prodigy, Albéniz was already astonishing audiences with his pianistic skill at the age of four. Like the young
Mozart, he made concert tours with his father, but when only
10 he ran away and gave various performances, which he
promoted himself! In his teens he travelled the world, playing
and studying, with Liszt as one of his mentors. Finally in 1883
he returned to Spain, and in Barcelona he married, moving to
Madrid two years later. These three youthful *Sonatas* were
composed during a four-year period which began in 1885.
They appear to be the only survivors out of seven. They were
written along with countless other genre pieces, of which the
charming if perhaps overlong *Autumn Waltz* is one of the
later examples, written in the composer's drawing-room
style. He later dismissed them as 'worthless trifles', but the
Sonatas are more than that. Indeed the *Fifth* (his own favourite) is an engaging little work, with four distinctly individual
movements. Derivative they may be, but this little sonatina
would grace any recital, and the other two are nicely crafted.
The Barcelona pianist Albert Guinovart plays them all with
affection and pleasing freshness, and he is truthfully, if rather
drily, recorded.

**Azulejos; Cantos de España (Preludio (Asturias); Oriental;
Bajo la palmera (Cuba); Córdoba; Seguidillas (Castilla)).
Malagueña; Mallorca (Barcarola); La Vega; Zambra
Granadina; Zaragoza**

(M) *** EMI (ADD) 5 62528-2. De Larrocha

Dating from 1959, this recital is a stimulating example of the
younger Alicia de Larrocha playing with enormous dash and
a glowing palette - the famous *Córdoba* is full of atmospheric
poetry, helped by the warm bass resonance of the recording.

Cantos de España; Suite española

(B) Double Decca ADD/DDD 433 923-2 (2). De Larrocha –
GRANADOS: *Allegro de concierto*, etc. ***

This makes a most rewarding bonus for the coupled Granados collection, and Alicia de Larrocha's playing is imbued
with many subtle changes of colour and has a refreshing
vitality.

Iberia (complete); **Alhambra (Suite)** excerpts: *La vega;
Azulejos; Prelude; Navarra* (both completed Martin Jones).
6 Hojas de Album, Op. 165; Tango; Suite española, Op. 47

(N) (BB) *** Nim. NI 5595/8. Martin Jones – GRANADOS:
Allegro de concierto; Goyescas etc. ***

Iberia (complete); **España (Souvenirs); Navarra** (completed
Bolcom); *La vega; Yvonne en visite!*

🔊 (N) *** Hyp. CDA 67476/7. Hamelin

Iberia (complete); *Suites españolas 1 & 2 (Zaragonza Sevilla)*

(N) **(BB)** **(*)** Naxos 8.554311/2. González

Iberia (complete); *Navarra; Suite española*

❂ *** Decca 417 887-2. De Larrocha

Iberia (complete); *Suite española* (excerpts): *Granada; Cataluña; Sevilla; Cádiz; Aragon; Navarra. Pavana capricho, Op. 12; España (6 Hojas de Album): Tango (only); Recuerdos de viaje: Rumores de la caleta; Puerta de Tierra*

(N) **(M)** *** EMI (ADD) 5 62524-2 (2). De Larrocha

Iberia (complete); *Navarra*

(B) *** Double Decca (ADD) 448 191-2 (2). De Larrocha – GRANADOS: *Goyescas* *** ❂

Marc-André Hamelin has to compete with considerable competition from Alicia de Larrocha, but he emerges with flying colours. He is highly sensitive to the subtle nuances of Albéniz's evocative piano-writing and his gentle, sensuous inflexions are consistently seductive, from the opening *Evocación* of Book I onwards. His pianism is captivating in its delicacy of touch and crisp articulation, but the brilliant playing reflects the bright Spanish sunshine, and throughout he is marvellously recorded. Among modern versions this Hyperion set must now take pride of place alongside de Larrocha, who has special insights of her own to offer.

On her digital Decca version, Alicia de Larrocha brings an altogether beguiling charm and character to these rewarding miniature tone-poems and makes light of their sometimes fiendish technical difficulties. The recording is among the most successful of piano sounds Decca has achieved.

Martin Jones penetrates the ethos of these pieces with a natural feeling for their Spanish atmosphere, and he has sufficient and justified confidence in his own special insights to offer an individual reading with pianism that is brilliantly coloured, rhythmically charismatic and often quite magical in its gentle evocation. Moreover, these performances, even though they were recorded in the studio, have the continued spontaneity of live music-making. The recording is wholly natural, the ambience warm but not too resonant.

The EMI set offers de Larrocha's earliest (1962) stereo recording of Albéniz's great piano suite, *Iberia*. The younger de Larrocha is far tougher, more daring, more fiery and, if anything, even more warmly expressive than she was later. The EMI discs include the haunting *Tango*, deliciously done, the most celebrated of all Albéniz's music; but the sound is not quite as fine as on the Decca sets.

Alicia de Larrocha's second analogue set of *Iberia* was made in 1972, a decade after her earliest stereo version for Hispavox. As in that version, she plays with full-blooded temperament and fire, both here and in *Navarra*. The piano recording is excellent in its realism, and the Double Decca reissue coupled with Granados's *Goyescas* makes a formidable bargain, for – on both artistic and technical merits – *Iberia* loses little ground to her later, digital set, which has rather more subtlety.

Born in Tenerife, Gullermo González plays Albéniz with genuine idiomatic feeling. As the opening *Evocación* of *Iberia* shows, his lyrical style brings a freely romantic rubato, and he produces an exotic brilliance in the bravura pieces. There is no want of sultry Mediterranean atmosphere, and the miniature portraits of Spanish cities which make up the *Suites españolas* are vividly depicted, with the Andalusian and Castilian dance rhythms falling naturally into place. He is very well recorded and the Naxos set has a distinct appeal, even if the playing does not always find quite the degree of spontaneity which illuminates the alternative versions from Hamelin, Alicia de Larrocha and Martin Jones.

Iberia, Book IV: *Málaga; Jerez; Eritaña; 6 Pequeños valses; Serenata árabe; Sonata 3; Suite ancienne 1*

(*) BIS CD 1243. Baselga

The last Book of *Iberia*, which Albéniz premièred in Paris three months before his death, is technically the most demanding of the four. Miguel Baselga studied at the Liège Conservatoire and then with Eduardo del Pueyo, and he is completely at one with the idiom. He has the necessary virtuosity and rhythmic vitality to do justice to this repertoire, though his dynamic range and command of keyboard colour could at times be wider. It may well be, of course, that the balance (which is a little close) and the lively acoustic of the Palacio de Congresos, Zaragoza, contribute to this impression. All the same, there is some very satisfying playing here.

OPERA

Henry Clifford (complete)

(*) Decca 473 937-2 (2). Machado, Marc, Alvarez, Henschel, Martinez, Madrid Ch. & SO, Eusebio

Albéniz's first large-scale opera was premièred in 1895 at the Gran Theatro del Liceo in Barcelona. It was sung in Italian but, like *Merlin*, it was written to an English libretto, and it is in its original form that this Decca recording was made.

The libretto, set during the Wars of the Roses, is dated but ambitious, with even a hint of the supernatural in Act II. However, some of the couplets may induce a smile rather than an aura of menace. For instance, '*Beware of the Witch and her evil eye! … Will she swim or sink? – To the pond and try*'; and Henry's principal aria laments '*Woe is me to love a fairy … Lovely Anna is my Fate!*' If unlikely to take the operatic stage by storm, taken on its own terms the piece nevertheless works well enough on record. The performance overall is more than acceptable, although with one major flaw in that the eponymous hero, sung by Aquiles Machado, is distinctly underpowered, producing some quite disagreeable top notes. His clarion call 'To arms!' sounds desperate rather than heroic, and overall his voice is not particularly ingratiating. Alessandra Marc as his mother, Lady Clifford, is far more commanding and secure, with just the right timbre for the part. Carlo Alvarez's dark baritone is ideally suited to Sir John St John, and Jane Henschel as his wife is in good voice throughout. Ana Maria Martinez is excellent, producing a rich, warm voice for the heroine, Ann. The choruses are especially lively and invigorating. José de Eusebio proves a highly sympathetic conductor, and his excellent Madrid orchestra brings out all the colour of the score and makes the most of the various orchestral dances and entr'actes. Decca's sound is flattering too, warmly atmospheric, well balanced and vivid.

Merlin (complete)

(*) BBC Opus Arte **DVD** OA0888D (2). Wilson-Johnson, Marton, Skelton, Vaness, Odena, Sierra, Madrid Ch. and SO, José de Eusebio

*** Decca 467 096-2 (2). Alvarez, Domingo, Henschel, Martinez, Spanish Nat. Ch., Madrid Comunidad Ch., Madrid SO, Eusebio

This DVD version of Albéniz's Arthurian opera, *Merlin*,

recorded at the staging in Madrid in 2003, makes a valuable supplement to the Decca discs of this rare piece. It may be a flawed opera, seriously impeded by the libretto of the eccentric banker, Francis Burdett Money-Coutts, with its clumsy dramatic structure and doggerel verse, but the score finds Albéniz at his most inspired, and having a video version certainly helps to enhance involvement. As stage director, John Dew sets out the story clearly, helped by stylized sets and costumes, designed respectively by Heinz Balthes and José Manuel Vazquez. They are medieval enough to create the right atmosphere, with a touch of space fiction.

Though the cast is not as starry as that on the discs (which have Plácido Domingo as King Arthur), there is obvious benefit in having English speakers in three of the principal parts: David Wilson-Johnson commanding and noble as Merlin, the American tenor Stuart Skelton as Arthur, powerful rather than subtle, and Carol Vaness, also American, as Nivian, the second of the two main female roles. The big snag in the cast is the singer who might have been counted the star, Eva Marton as the evil Morgan-le-Fay. The unsteadiness of her voice, so extreme that one can hardly tell what pitch she is aiming at, may convey the wickedness of the character, and she acts convincingly, but it is painful on the ear. As her son, Mordred, Angel Odena characterizes well, but he also has bouts of unsteadiness, while Victor Garcia Sierra, taking the role of King Lot of Orkney, is another wobbler.

Happily, the chorus work is first rate and, as in the audio recording, Eusebio draws warmly committed playing from the Madrid Symphony Orchestra. Eusebio also contributes an essay to the booklet about the background to the opera, explaining how the material to complete the score was brought together and rebutting the accusation that the orchestration was by Manuel Ponce. He repeats that rebuttal in the interview (in Spanish) that comes on the second disc, along with interviews (in English) with Eva Marton and David Wilson-Johnson. With so rare an opera it is a pity that the booklet contains no synopsis. Despite the banality of Money-Coutts's verses, what shines out above all is the richness and variety of Albéniz's musical inspiration.

The CD version is very rewarding too, thanks also to a passionate performance under José de Eusebio, spectacularly well recorded. Domingo makes a noble King Arthur, while Carlos Alvarez as Merlin uses his firm, dark baritone with an incisiveness and expressive range worthy of a Wotan.

In the two women's roles, both evil, the American sopranos Jane Henschel as Morgan-le-Fay and Ana Maria Martinez as Nivian, Merlin's treacherous slave, both characterize well, with rich, warm voices. Christopher Maltman is a suitably sinister Mordred, and outstanding among the others is the young tenor, Angel Rodriguez, as Gawain. Chorus and orchestra are outstanding too, intensifying the score's evocative beauty.

ALBINONI, Tomaso (1671–1751)

Adagio in G min. for Organ & Strings (arr. Giazotto)
(M) *** DG (ADD) 449 724-2. BPO, Karajan – RESPIGHI: *Ancient airs*, etc. ***

Karajan's view is stately and measured, and the Berlin Philharmonic strings respond with dignity and sumptuous tone. The anachronism of Giazotto's arrangement is obviously relished.

(i) *12 Concerti a cinque, Op. 5; (ii; iii) 12 Concerti a cinque, Op. 7; (i; ii) 12 Concerti a cinque, Op. 9*
(N) (M) ** Capriccio 67 126/29. (i) Banfalvi; (ii) Lencses; (iii) Bartha; Budapest Strings

This is the only set to include Albinoni's complete *Concerti a cinque*. All these concertos use a three-movement format and are essentially 'Italian Overtures' (fast–slow–fast), although in Op. 5, *Concertos 3, 6* and *9* feature a brief contrasting *Presto* centrepiece in their Adagios. In this first set, the solo violin seems unimportant, although the writing for strings is engagingly inventive. Op. 7 has one or two oboes as soloists, although four are for strings alone; Op. 9 includes three violin concertos, while the rest return to a solo oboe. All are played very pleasingly on modern instruments, with good soloists, and are given warm, full-bodied if not very transparent sound. But in the separate sets listed below, the solo playing has more individuality.

(i) *12 Concerti a cinque, Op. 5; (ii) 12 Concerti a cinque, Op. 7*
(B) **(*) Ph. Duo (ADD) 464 052-2 (2). (i) Carmirelli, I Musici; (ii) Wätzig, Abel, Klinge, Berlin CO, Negri

Philips have recoupled I Musici's Op. 5 with Negri's Op. 7, which meets strong competition. The playing in Berlin combines vitality and polish, but the balance is rather forward: the effect is vivid but the dynamic contrast is reduced. Negri's direction, with its strong, incisive rhythms, also lacks something in flexibility and resilience.

12 Concerti a cinque, Op. 7; 12 Concerti a cinque, Op. 9; Sinfonia for Strings
*** Chan. 0602 (Op. 7/1, 2, 4 & 5; Op. 9/1, 3, 4 & 6; Sinfonia); 0579 (Op. 7/3, 6, 9 & 12; Op. 9/2, 5, 8 & 11); 0610 (Op. 7/7, 8, 10 & 11; Op. 9/7, 10 & 12). Robson, Latham, Coll. Mus. 90, Standage
(BB) *** Naxos 8.553002 (Op. 7/1–3, 6 & 8; Sinfonia); 8.550735 (Op. 7/4, 5, 6, 11 & 12; Op. 9/12); 8.550739 (Op. 9/2, 3, 5, 8, 9 & 11). Camden, Girdwood, Alty, L. Virtuosi, Georgiadis

Anthony Robson plays all eight solo concertos from Opp. 7 and 9 using a period oboe. His tone is most appealing and his phrasing and musicianship are second to none. Simon Standage provides alert accompaniments, also using original instruments, and creates bright, athletic string-timbres. Catherine Latham joins him to complete the Collegium Musicum sets of Opp. 7 and 9, including the works for strings. The artistic results are very lively and refreshing, although the balance is rather close.

The London Virtuosi use modern instruments, but their playing is fresh and refined and the digital recording is natural and beautifully balanced. The calibre of Anthony Camden's solo contribution is readily shown in slow movements, matched by Georgiadis's rapt, sensitive accompaniments. On the first disc Camden's excellent colleague is Julia Girdwood, but for the two other collections Alison Alty takes over, and the partnership seems even more felicitous, with the two instruments blended quite perfectly. Also included is a *Sinfonia* arranged by Camden as a *Sinfonia concertante*. This series can be strongly recommended on all counts.

(i) *Concerti a cinque, Op. 7/2–3, 5–6, 8–9, 11–12; (ii) Adagio in G min.* (arr. Giazotto)
(B) *** DG (ADD) 439 509-2. (i) Holliger, Elhorst, Bern Camerata; (ii) Lucerne Festival Strings, Baumgartner

The playing of Heinz Holliger, Hans Elhorst and the Bern Camerata is refined, persuasive and vital, and the CD could hardly be more truthful or better detailed. The famous *Adagio* (in a perfectly acceptable performance under Baumgartner) has been added to tempt a wider public. Let us hope it does so.

Concerti a cinque, Op. 7/3, 6, 9 & 12; Op. 9/2, 5, 8 & 11

⊶ (BB) *** Regis RRC 1095. Francis, L. Harpsichord Ens.

Those looking for a selection of *Oboe Concertos* from both Op. 7 and Op. 9 will find that Sarah Francis is an immensely stylish and gifted soloist. She is accompanied with warmth and grace, and the recording is first class, transparent yet full and naturally balanced. As a budget-priced Regis reissue this is very attractive indeed.

(i) Concerti a cinque, Op. 9/1–12; (ii) Adagio in G min. (arr. Giazotto)

(B) *** Ph. Duo (ADD) 456 333-2 (2). (i) Ayo, Holliger, Bourgue; (i–ii) Garatti (harpsichord or organ); I Musici

The Philips Duo I Musici alternative of Op. 9 on modern instruments is played with much finesse and style, which comment also applies to the famous *Adagio*. Ayo, Holliger and Bourgue are on top form throughout, and so are the Philips engineers.

Concerti a cinque, Op. 9 (excerpts)

(BB) *** Virgin 2×1 5 61878-2 (2) (9/2, 5, 8, & 11). De Vries, Amsterdam Alma Musica, Van Asperen – TELEMANN: *Oboe Concertos; Sonatas* ***

(BB) *** Warner Apex (ADD) 0927 49020-2 (9/1–3, 5–6,10–11). Pierlot, Toso, Sol. Ven., Scimone

Hans de Vries plays a baroque oboe and produces a most appealing timbre, while his technique is remarkably assured and true. There is one cavil: the solo balance seems a shade too forward. Bob van Asperen's accompaniments are as alert and stylish as the solo playing, and this 2×1 bargain reissue comes in tandem with some equally fine performances of Telemann.

The happily chosen and inexpensive alternative selection comes from Scimone's complete set (deleted) and is equally recommendable, offering a pair each of *Oboe Concertos*, *Double Oboe Concertos* and *Violin Concertos*.

12 Concerti, Op. 10

⊶ (BB) *** Warner Apex 2564 61136-2 (1–6); 2564 61256-2 (7–12). Carmignola, Toso, Sol. Ven., Scimone

Four of the Op. 10 set are violin concertos (Nos. 6, 8, 10 and 12) and three are *concerti grossi* with a small concertino group (Nos. 2, 3 and 4), while the remainder are without soloists and have non-fugal last movements. They radiate simple vitality, a love of life and a youthful exuberance that belies the composer's age. The playing is warm and musical, and the recording is made in an ample acoustic. Some may prefer more sharply etched detail, but the resonant string-timbres are immaculately transferred to CD. They are now even more welcome on the budget Apex label.

Concertos for (solo) Organ in B flat & F (arr. from Op. 2); Flute Sonatas, Op. 4/2 & 6; Op. 6/6 & 7; Oboe Sonata, Op. 6/2; Recorder Sonata, Op. 6/5

*** Mer. CDE 84400. Badinage (with BACH: (Organ) *Fugue in C, BWV 946*, after *Op. 1/12*)

A lightweight but pleasing programme with some particularly deft playing on a slightly watery-sounding baroque flute (a copy of an eighteenth-century instrument) and some very agreeable organ interludes. These are all transcriptions, mostly from violin sonatas. Although it seems likely that Op. 4 is wrongly attributed to Albinoni, the music itself is very agreeable. Good, natural sound.

CHAMBER MUSIC

6 Sonate da chiesa, Op. 4; 12 Trattenimenti armonici per camera, Op. 6

*** Hyp. CDA 66831/2. Locatelli Trio

The set of 'Church' Sonatas, showing the composer at his most lyrically appealing, contrasts with Op. 6. *Trattenimento* indicates 'Entertainment', suggesting a more secular style; and certainly the allegros of Op. 6 are strikingly lively and infectiously dance-like in character. The slow movements are often more formal, though never dull. The performances, using original instruments, are of high quality, well paced, sensitive and fresh, and the recording is well balanced and vivid.

Trio Sonatas, Op. 1/1–12

*** CPO 999 770-2. Parnassi Musici

Albinoni's *Trio Sonatas*, Op. 1, are important not only musically – they make delightful listening – but also historically. For although the four-movement *sonata da chiesa* format (slow–fast–slow–fast) was established by Corelli in the 1680s, it appeared exclusively in Albinoni's Op. 1, with six of these *Trio Sonatas* in the major and six in the minor keys. They are through-composed, i.e. all four movements are based on the same musical material. But Albinoni's variety of invention is inexhaustible, with touchingly expressive slow movements and many individual and often sprightly allegros, although the opening movements of the last two *Sonatas* are especially striking. No. 11 opens with a doleful fugato; No. 12 is built on a ground bass. The period-instrument performances here are first class in every way and they are excellently recorded.

VOCAL MUSIC

12 Cantatas, Op. 4

*** Etcetera KTC 2027 (2). Schlick or Ragin, Selo, Shaw

Albinoni's twelve *Cantatas*, Op. 4, are characteristic pastoral works of their period, lightweight but with plenty of charm; they are written alternately for soprano and alto, with the even-numbered works given to the latter voice. On the whole, the most poignant music is allotted to the soprano voice and the excellent Barbara Schlick responds appealingly, but both soloists rise to the occasion. The continuo too is first class, with Nicolas Selo's beautifully focused and crisply rhythmic cello contribution a particular pleasure. The recording is excellent. Full translations are provided.

ALFVÉN, Hugo (1872–1960)

A Legend of the Skerries, Op. 20; Swedish Rhapsodies 1 (Midsummer Vigil), Op. 19; 2 (Uppsala Rhapsody), Op. 24; 3 (Dala Rhapsody), Op. 47; King Gustav II Adolf, Op. 49: Adagio

*** Chan. 9313. Iceland SO, Sakari

Midsummer Vigil, Alfvén's masterpiece, is quintessential Sweden, and so too is the affecting *Elegy* from the incidental music to Ludwig Nordström's play about *Gustav II Adolf*. Petri Sakari produces musically satisfying results, and this useful anthology can be warmly recommended. The Chandos sound is excellent.

Symphonies: 1 in F min., Op. 7; Revelation Cantata: Andante religioso; Drapa; Uppsala Rhapsody (BIS CD 395). *2 in D, Op. 11; Swedish Rhapsody 1* (BIS CD 385). *3 in E, Op. 23; The Prodigal Son: Suite; Swedish Rhapsody 3* (BIS CD 455. (i) *4 in C min., Op. 39; Legend of the Skerries, Op. 20* (BIS CD 505). *5 in A min., Op. 54; The Mountain King (Suite), Op. 37; King Gustav II Adolf, Op. 49: Adagio* (BIS CD 585)
(N) (M) *** BIS CD 1478/80 (5). Stockholm PO, Järvi; (i) with Högman, Ahnsjö

The five symphonies are all individually available at full price (with fill-ups) or economically in a mid-priced box (five discs for the price of three).

Symphony 1; Andante religioso; Drapa (Ballad for Large Orchestra); Uppsala Rhapsody, Op. 24
*** BIS CD 395. Stockholm PO, Järvi

Symphony 2; Swedish Rhapsody 1 (Midsummer Vigil)
*** BIS CD 385. Stockholm PO, Järvi

Järvi's versions of the *First* and *Second Symphonies* are superior both artistically and technically and leave the listener persuaded as to their merits. The *Uppsala Rhapsody* is based on student songs, but it is pretty thin stuff and the *Andante religioso* is rather let down by its sugary closing pages. *Drapa* opens with some fanfares, full of sequential clichés and with a certain naïve pomp and splendour that verges on bombast. Järvi gives a delightful performance of the popular *Midsummer Vigil*.

Symphony 2; The Prodigal Son (ballet)
(BB) *** Naxos 8.555072. Nat. SO of Ireland, Willén

The *Second Symphony* of 1899 put Alfvén firmly on the map. On Naxos it is coupled with *The Prodigal Son* ballet, which is a delight. Niklas Willén's is an eminently useful and inexpensive alternative to Neeme Järvi's excellent BIS disc.

Symphony 3; Legend of the Skerries, Op. 20; Swedish Rhapsody 3 (Dala Rhapsody), Op. 47
(BB) **(*) Naxos 8.553729. RSNO, Willén

Symphony 3; The Prodigal Son: Suite; Swedish Rhapsody 3 (Dala Rhapsody), Op. 47
*** BIS CD 455. Royal Stockholm PO, Järvi

Neeme Järvi's BIS CD is every bit as fine as its companions and brings the perennially popular suite from *The Prodigal Son*. Excellent playing and recording of real quality.

The sensitive, well-prepared performance by the Scottish players under Niklas Willén also serves the symphony well. Moreover, it comes with equally good accounts of the *Dala Rhapsody* and the *Legend of the Skerries*. The Naxos disc is well worth its modest outlay, although Järvi is to be preferred.

Symphony 4 (From the Outermost Skerries), Op. 39; Festival Overture
(N) (BB) **(*) Naxos 8.557284. Halla, Valdimarsson, Iceland SO, Willén

(i) *Symphony 4. Legend of the Skerries*
*** BIS CD 505. Royal Stockholm PO, Järvi, (i) with Högman, Ahnsjö

The *Fourth* is perhaps Alfvén's most ambitious and in many ways most imaginative symphony, depicting as it does the otherworldly atmosphere of the Stockholm archipelago, one of the best-kept secrets of the Nordic countries in its extent and sheer beauty. There is a romantic programme relating to the emotions of two young lovers, and Alfvén takes a leaf out of Nielsen's book by incorporating two wordless voices into the score in the manner of the *Sinfonia espansiva*. The performance on BIS is sensitive and persuasive; the recording has a natural perspective and admirable detail, and the coupling is apt.

The newer version from Iceland is also well played and is highly competitive, without necessarily being a first choice, unless the Naxos coupling is preferred.

Symphony 5; The Mountain King (Bergakungen): Suite; Gustav II Adolf: Elegy
*** BIS CD 585. Royal Stockholm PO, Järvi

The *Fifth Symphony* draws freely on ideas from the ballet, *The Mountain King*, whose *Suite* completes this CD. *The Mountain King* is an inventive and attractive score; and both works, as well as the touching *Elegy* from the music to *Gustav II Adolf*, could hardly be presented more persuasively. The engineering is absolutely first class.

Choral music: Collection of Part-songs
*** BIS CD 633. Ahnsjö, Alin, Orphei Drängar Ch., Sund

Some of the part-songs Alfvén composed for the Orphei Drängar (Sons of Orpheus) are collected here and are sung to the highest standards of tonal virtuosity. Recommended with enthusiasm even to those who find the symphonies inflated and self-indulgent.

(i) *Revelation Cantata, Op. 31; (ii) Cantata for the 450th Anniversary of Uppsala University, Op. 45*
**(*) Sterling CDS 1058-2. (i) Boman, Zetterström; (ii) Larsson, Zetterström; Malmö Op. Ch. & O, Volmer

Alfvén wrote prolifically for choral forces: there are in all some 60 pieces. The *Revelation Cantata* comes from 1913 for the consecration of the newly erected Church of the Revelation at Saltsjöbaden. It is for two soloists, two choirs, organ, harmonium, celesta, harp and string quartet. More conventional in its scoring, the *Cantata for the 450th Anniversary of Uppsala University* was commissioned in 1927 and is characteristic but not quite top-drawer Alfvén. Both works are certainly worth hearing and get good performances. Charlotta Larsson in the *Uppsala Cantata* is an eloquent artist, and what a fine singer the baritone Fredrik Zetterström is! All the same, at 49 minutes this is short measure for a full-price disc.

ALKAN, Charles-Valentin (1813–88)

Concerti da camera 1 in A min.; 2 in C sharp min., Op. 10/1–2
*** Hyp. CDA 66717. Hamelin, BBC Scottish SO, Brabbins —
HENSELT: *Piano Concerto, etc.* ***

These are early pieces, miniature concertos of no mean interest and individuality. Elegantly played by Marc-André Hamelin and the BBC Scottish Symphony under Martyn Brabbins, they make an excellent foil for the Henselt *F minor Concerto*.

Piano Concerto, Op. 39 (orch. Klindworth); *Concerti da camera 1; 2; 3 in C sharp min.* (reconstructed Hugh Macdonald)

(BB) *** Naxos 8.553702. Feofanov, Razumovsky SO, Stankovsky

Alkan's Op. 39 consists of 12 *Etudes*, of which Nos. 8–10 comprise the *Concerto for Piano*. However, the first movement was orchestrated by the conductor and pianist, Karl Klindworth. Alkan's work is only the core from which the rather long work developed. Feofanov does a heroic job in the Klindworth and shows a sympathy with Alkan that the Slovak-based Razumovsky orchestra and Robert Stankovsky obviously share. Good recording makes this well worth anybody's money.

PIANO MUSIC

Concerto for Solo Piano, Op. 39/8–10

☛ *** M. & A. CD 724. Hamelin

Both John Ogdon and Ronald Smith have recorded the *Concerto*, but the latter's account was not included in the EMI double forte set below, devoted to his Alkan. Marc-André Hamelin's virtuosity is quite simply breathtaking and as masterly as his range of poetic feeling. The 1993 recording is eminently satisfactory and truthful. A remarkable performance, even by this artist's own standards.

Esquisses, Op. 63

(BB) *** Naxos 8.555496. Martin

Alkan's *Esquisses*, 49 little miniatures, are not among his most brilliant virtuoso pieces, but their range of mood and expression is impressively wide. Some, like *Le Staccatissimo* and *Petit prelude à 3*, suggest the world of Couperin and Rameau, while others, such as *Le Premier billet doux*, are miniature mood-pictures. There are occasional foreshadowings of things to come (try the Debussian *Les Soupirs* or *Les Diablotins*), but all these pieces, apart from being expertly crafted, are full of imaginative and original touches. Laurent Martin is an excellent player who understands this music inside out. He made a strong impression when this and other recordings appeared in the early 1990s and is generally well served by the recorded sound.

12 Etudes in the Minor Keys, Op. 39/1–12. Etude, Op. 3/5: Allegro barbaro. Chants: Assez vivement, Op. 38/1; Barcarolle, Op. 65/6. Esquisses: Le staccatissimo; Les Cloches; Les Soupirs; En songe, Op. 63/2, 4, 11 & 48. Les Mois: Gros temps, Op. 74 (Suite 1: 2). Nocturne in B, Op. 22; Preludes: La Chanson de la folle au bord de la mer; Le Temps qui n'est plus; J'étais endormie, mais mon cœur veillait, Op. 31/8, 12–13

*** ASV CDDCS 227 (2). Gibbons

12 Etudes in the Minor Keys, Op. 39; Le Festin d'Esope, Op. 39/12; Scherzo diabolico, Op. 39/3

(BB) *** Naxos 8.555495. Ringeissen

12 Etudes in the Minor Keys: Symphony for Piano, Op. 39/4–7; Alleluia, Op. 25; Salut, cendre du pauvre! Op. 45; Super flumina Babylonis, Op. 52; Souvenirs: 3 Morceaux dans le genre pathétique, Op. 15

*** Hyp. CDA 67218. Hamelin

Alkan's music is almost exclusively for the keyboard, but it rarely finds its way into the modern concert-hall – not surprisingly, given its fiendish, hair-raising difficulties and (to be fair) uneven quality. Jack Gibbons has obviously inherited the mantle of Ronald Smith, to whom his notes pay homage, and he rises to the challenge these pieces present with triumphant virtuosity. Good sound, too.

Bernard Ringeissen gives a very brilliant account of the *Etudes*. The 1990 Naxos recording is very faithful, and at this bargain-basement price the attractions of the set are further enhanced by *Le Festin d'Esope*, also very impressive here.

The *Symphony for Piano* comprises four movements (Nos. 4–7) from the *Douze études*. The *Symphony* and the other pieces on Hyperion must sound effortless, just as a great dancer must seem weightless, and Marc-André Hamelin makes light of their many difficulties. He displays not only a transcendental virtuosity but a great poetic feeling in such pieces as the remarkable *Salut, cendre du pauvre!* Superb playing and very good recording – and noteworthy not only for its dazzling virtuosity but for its refined music-making.

4 Etudes in the Minor Keys, Op. 39; 3 Etudes de bravoure, Op. 16; 3 Grandes Etudes pour les deux mains séparées et réunies, Op. 76; Grande Sonate (Les Quatre Ages), Op. 33; Prélude: La Chanson de la folle au bord de la mer, Op. 31; Sonatine, Op. 61

☛ (B) *** EMI double forte (ADD) 7 75649-2 (2). Smith

Alkan recitals do not last long in the catalogue and readers should not lose the chance of catching up on this compilation of the classic Ronald Smith recordings. All come from the 1970s except for the Op. 16 *Studies* and the *Grandes Etudes*, Op. 76, which this remarkable scholar-pianist made in 1987. We have commented at length on their merits in earlier editions and our admiration has not diminished over the years.

Etudes in the Minor Keys, Op. 39/4–11; Esquisses, Op. 63; Gigue, Op. 24; March, Op. 37/1; Nocturne 1, Op. 22; Petit conte; 3 Petites fantaisies, Op. 41; Préludes, Op. 31/11–13, 15 & 16; Le Tambour bat aux champs, Op. 50/2; Toccatina, Op. 75

(N) (BB) *** EMI Gemini (ADD/DDD) 5 85484-2 (2). Ronald Smith

A further collection from Ronald Smith's impressive and distinguished survey of Alkan's often quite astonishing piano music. Much of the music is almost prophetic, with the Op. 41 *Petites fantaisies* even appearing to presage Prokofiev. Smith plays it all with consummate ease and, as with all his Alkan recordings, his virtuosity is remarkable and his understanding of this repertoire beyond question. The sound remains excellent in this Gemini transfer (Opp. 31, 39 and 41 are analogue, the rest digital).

Grande sonate (Les Quatre Ages); Barcarolle; Le Festin d'Esope; Sonatine, Op. 61

*** Hyp. CDA 66794. Hamelin

Alkan's *Grande sonate* over its four massive movements represents the hero at various ages, with the second, *Quasi-Faust*, the key one. The *Sonatine*, the most approachable of Alkan's major works, is done just as dazzlingly, with the hauntingly poetic *Barcarolle* and the swaggering *Festin d'Esope* as valuable makeweights.

25 Préludes, Op. 31

☛ (M) *** Decca 475 212-2. Mustonen – SHOSTAKOVICH: *24 Preludes* ***

Alkan's (1847) *Préludes* are more poetic than barnstorming. They go through all the major and minor keys, returning to C major in No. 25, and are designed for piano or organ or the pedaler (a piano with pedal-board), the instrument for which the composer had a special affection. Some of the pieces are affecting in their simplicity, and Olli Mustonen (whose début this was on the Decca label) plays them supremely well on the piano. He gives us a very well-filled disc, which won the *Gramophone* Instrumental Award in 1992, for the generous Shostakovich coupling is equally successful. The recording is absolutely first class, though the pedal-stamping in the *Tenth Prélude, Dans le style fugué*, should have been curbed. Strongly recommended, nevertheless.

ALLEGRI, Gregorio (1582–1652)

Miserere

☛— *** Gimell (ADD) CDGIM 339. Tallis Scholars, Phillips –
MUNDY: *Vox patris caelestis*; PALESTRINA: *Missa Papae Marcelli* ***

(M) *** Decca (ADD) 466 373-2. King's College Ch.,
Willcocks – PALESTRINA: *Collection* ***

(B) **(*) CfP 575 5602. St John's College, Cambridge, Ch.,
Guest – LASSUS: *Missa super 'Bell' Amfitrit'alterna'* **(*);
PALESTRINA: *Missa, Veni sponsa Christi* ***

Mozart was so impressed by Allegri's *Miserere* when he heard it in the Sistine Chapel (which originally claimed exclusive rights to its performance) he wrote the music out from memory so that it could be performed elsewhere. On the much-praised Gimell version, the soaring treble solo is taken by a girl, Alison Stamp, and her memorable contribution is enhanced by the recording itself.

The famous 1963 King's performance of Allegri's *Miserere*, with its equally arresting treble solo so beautifully and securely sung by Roy Goodman, is now reissued, impressively remastered in Decca's Legends series – coupled with Palestrina at mid-price.

The 1990 digital recording of this celestial piece from St John's is finely sung, and the three-dimensional balance is very realistic, but the unnamed treble soloist sings less ethereally than his famous predecessors, Alison Stamp and Roy Goodman, with a bold upward leap in the famous repeated phrase.

ALWYN, William (1905–85)

The current centenary of William Alwyn's birth, a composer now remembered mainly for his film music, should bring renewed interest in his other works, with new recordings already announced. We hope to survey his output fully in our 2006 Yearbook.

ANGULO, Eduardo (born 1954)

Guitar Concerto 2 (El Alevín)

*** Guild GMCD 7176. Jiménez, Bournemouth Sinf., Frazor –
RODRIGO: *Concierto de Aranjuez*; VILLA-LOBOS: *Guitar concerto* ***

Angulo's *Concerto* has much in common with its famous Spanish coupling, with the slow movement at first pensive, then full-bloodedly romantic. The finale sparkles with Mexican dance-rhythms, gaudy and gentle by turns. Rafael Jiménez is a highly sensitive and brilliant soloist, and Terence Frazor and the Bournemouth Sinfonietta accompany him with both understanding and gusto. This is a work of considerable popular appeal, and it is recorded very persuasively here.

ANTHEIL, George (1900–59)

Symphonies 1 (Zingareska); 6 (after Delacroix); Archipelago

*** CPO 999 604-2. Frankfurt RSO, Wolff

This CPO coupling of Antheil's first and last symphonies shows the marked contrast between the style of his time in Paris – when he associated with such fellow artists as Joyce, Hemingway, Pound and Picasso – and his later style, influenced by Soviet composers. The gypsy echoes suggested by the title for No. 1, *Zingareska*, are minimal. Far more important are the echoes of early Stravinsky, occasionally mixed with Gershwin, with the finale bringing direct imitations of passages from both *Petrushka* and *The Rite of Spring*. Though it is an attractive, at times brilliant work, the three-movement *Symphony 6* is more consistent, with the central slow movement languorously beautiful in its echoes of Satie's *Gymnopédies*, and with the Soviet-style ostinatos of the outer movements crisply and urgently controlled, helped by brilliant sound, enhanced by sumptuous orchestration. The Rumba, *Archipelago*, dazzlingly scored, makes a delightfully colourful supplement.

*Symphony 3 (American); Capital of the World: Suite.
Hot-Time Dance; McKonkey's Ferry Overture; Tom Sawyer Overture*

(N) *** CPO 777 040-2. Frankfurt RSO, Wolff

Antheil came to prominence in the 1920s as a kind of Dada-esque figure, eager to shock and astonish and be the 'Bad Boy of Music' that he described in his autobiography. Apart from the *Third Symphony* (composed in 1936–9), all the music on this disc is post-war (and the symphony itself was revised in 1946). Hugh Wolff and the Frankfurt Radio Symphony Orchestra give vital accounts of these often colourful, if brashly scored and empty, pieces.

Symphony 4, '1942'

(M) (***) ADD Cala (mono) CACD 0528. NBC SO, Stokowski
– BUTTERWORTH: *Shropshire Lad* **; VAUGHAN WILLIAMS: *Symphony 4* (***)

Symphonies 4; 6; Concert Overture: McConkey's Ferry

(BB) **(*) Naxos 8.559033. Ukraine Nat. SO, Kuchar

There are influences of the composer's East European background in *Symphony 4*, which is probably his best. This music is not deep, but it communicates readily. In February 1944 Stokowski – temporarily replacing Toscanini with the NBC Symphony – conducted a radio performance. Dating from 1942, it relies greatly on march rhythms and persistent ostinatos, often in support of Prokofiev-like melodies; though the radio sound is limited in dynamic as well as frequency range, the clarity and weight are more than enough to convey the power, urgency and dramatic incisiveness of Stokowski's performance, with full and rich string-sound very different from that under Toscanini. With the two English works for coupling, it makes an attractive and revealing disc.

The Naxos issue pairs what are probably Antheil's two most colourful symphonies. They are vividly recorded, with the Ukraine orchestra sounding very idiomatic in Antheil's jazzy syncopations even while they relish the many echoes of Prokofiev and Shostakovich. Though the playing is not as polished as in rival versions, this is well worth considering, with the *Concert Overture, McConkey's Ferry*, dating from the same period, a lively and attractive supplement.

ARENSKY, Anton (1861–1906)

Piano Concerto in F min., Op. 2; Fantasia on Russian Folksongs, Op. 48

*** Hyp. CDA 66624. Coombs, BBC Scottish SO, Maksymiuk – BORTKIEWICZ: *Concerto* ***

Arensky studied with Rimsky-Korsakov but he was closer in feeling to Tchaikovsky, who became his mentor and whose vein of elegiac lyricism he shared. He belongs to the same generation as Liadov, Grechaninov and Taneyev and he taught at the Moscow Conservatoire (1882–95) before becoming Director of the Imperial Chapel at St Petersburg (1895–1901) and then, in the last years of his life, settling on the Gulf of Finland. Arensky's *Piano Concerto in F minor* is an endearing piece, highly Chopinesque in feeling and with some very appealing ideas. Stephen Coombs is an artist of great sensitivity and effortless virtuosity, and he makes out the best possible case for both the *Concerto* and the much shorter *Fantasia on Russian Folksongs*. Good orchestral support and recording.

Violin Concerto in A min., Op. 54

*** Chan. 9528. Trostiansky, I Musici de Montréal, Turovsky – GLAZUNOV: *Concerto ballata*, etc. ***

**(*) Globe GLO 5174. Lubotsky, Estonian Nat. SO, Volmer – RIMSKY-KORSAKOV: *Concert Fantasy*; TCHAIKOVSKY: *Violin Concerto* **(*)

The *Violin Concerto in A minor* is a delightful piece that deserves to be every bit as popular as, say, the Glazunov. On Chandos the concerto is beautifully played by Alexander Trostiansky. He has refinement, musicianship and impeccable taste. He is perhaps balanced rather too reticently, but the case for this concerto is made very persuasively by orchestra and engineers alike.

Mark Lubotsky's fine recording is also one of the best we have had since Aaron Rosand's dazzling Luxembourg Radio account from the early 1970s. Like that, it is coupled with the Rimsky-Korsakov *Concert Fantasy*. Good orchestral playing under Arvo Volmer and naturally balanced sound.

Egyptian Nights, Op. 50

**(*) Marco 8.225028. Moscow SO, Yablonsky

Egyptian Nights was composed in 1900 for Fokine and is based on Pushkin, albeit very loosely. The music cultivates a certain pallid exoticism, with dances for Egyptian girls and, although the invention is not top-drawer, it is often endearing. Arensky was a master of the orchestra; and the ballet, which runs for 50 minutes, is certainly pleasing. Decent playing and recording.

Variations on a Theme of Tchaikovsky, Op. 35a

(B) *** EMI double forte 5 69361 (2). LSO, Barbirolli – RIMSKY-KORSAKOV: *Scheherazade* **; GLAZUNOV: *The Seasons*, etc. ***

These delightful variations, arguably Arensky's best-known work, originally formed the slow movement of the *Second*

String Quartet in A minor, composed in 1894, a year after Tchaikovsky's death, and subsequently arranged for full strings. Sir John Barbirolli's recording, made in the Kingsway Hall in 1965 and first published in harness with the Tchaikovsky *Serenade for Strings*, is warm and spacious. The playing of the LSO under this endearing conductor is suitably affectionate. It comes as part of a quite attractive two-CD Russian music package, let down a little by Svetlanov's rather idiosyncratic *Scheherazade*.

Suites 1 in G min., Op. 7; 2 (Silhouettes), Op. 23; 3 (Variations in C), Op. 33

(BB) **(*) Naxos 8.553768. Moscow SO, Yablonsky

What a good idea to put Arensky's three attractive orchestral *Suites* on a single CD: *Suite 1 in G minor* opens with a Russian theme with variations, and the Russian feel continues in the ensuing three dance numbers, with a bright Scherzo at the centre. *Suite 2 (Silhouettes)*, the best known, is a group of character studies: *The Scholar, The Coquette, The Buffoon*, etc., which all have plentiful invention. *The Dreamer* is especially beautiful, and the work finishes with the spirited portrait of *The Dancer*. *Suite 3* is another set of variations (mainly dance forms), brightly coloured, the *Andante* theme itself beginning in a romantic chorale style and ending as a spirited polonaise. The performances are good and enthusiastic, if not always refined, and, while it all emerges quite vividly, the 1995 sound feels a bit under-recorded, lacking the richness and depth of the finest recordings. It is an enjoyable disc, nevertheless.

Symphony 1 in B min., Op. 4; (i) Fantasia on Themes by I. T. Ryabinin, Op. 48 (for piano & orchestra); Variations on a Theme by Tchaikovsky, Op. 35a; (i; ii) Cantata on the 10th Anniversary of the Coronation, Op. 26; 3 Vocal Quartets with Cello Accompaniment, Op. 57

*** Chan. 10086. Russian State SO, Polyansky; with (i) Tatiana Polyanskaya; (ii) Sharova, Baturkin, Russian State Symphonic Capella

Symphony 2 in A, Op. 22; Intermezzo, Op. 13; Overture: A Dream on the Volga, Op. 16; Suite 3; Nal and Damayanti (opera): Introduction, Op. 47

*** Chan. 10024. BBC PO, Sinaisky

The fluent and inventive *First Symphony* comes from 1883, when Arensky was in his early twenties, and it is a work of not only astonishing promise but very considerable fulfilment. The *Second Symphony* of 1889 is harmonically the more adventurous of the two as well as being tauter: the four movements are rolled into one. These two Chandos issues are of special interest in that they bring some rarities: the *Fantasia on Themes by Ivan Ryabinin* for piano and orchestra and the first recording of the *Cantata on the 10th Anniversary of the Coronation*, as well as giving us the most popular of Arensky's works, the *Variations on a Theme by Tchaikovsky*. None of the above rarities is of much musical substance, though the *Three Vocal Quartets* with cello, which came late in his creative career, could well be the only music ever written for four-part choir and cello! All the performances are very persuasive and very well recorded, and they supersede the Svetlanov recordings in most respects. However, those who acquired the old set should hang on to it for the sake of the charming orchestral suites.

CHAMBER MUSIC

Piano Trio 1 in D min., Op. 32
*** (M) CRD (ADD) 3409. Brown, Nash Ens. –
RIMSKY-KORSAKOV: *Quintet* ***
*** Chan. 8477. Borodin Trio – GLINKA: *Trio* ***

Arensky's *D minor Piano Trio* is delightful. The account by members of the Nash Ensemble is first class in every way, capturing the Slav melancholy of the *Elegia*, while in the delightful *Scherzo* Ian Brown is both delicate and nimble-fingered. The warm, resonant (1982) analogue recording has transferred naturally to CD.

The Borodins, too, give a lively and full-blooded account of the *Trio*. The *Scherzo* comes off well, and the whole does justice to the Borodins' genial playing.

String Quartet 2 in A min., Op. 35
*** Hyp. CDA 66648. Raphael Ens. – TCHAIKOVSKY:
Souvenir de Florence ***

The *A minor Quartet* is unusual in being for only one violin and two cellos. The second movement is a set of variations on Tchaikovsky's *Legend* from the *Children's Songs*, Op. 54. It is marvellously played by members of the Raphael Ensemble, though the recording is a bit close, placing the listener in the front row of the hall.

PIANO MUSIC

Suites for 2 Pianos 1–4
*** Hyp. CDA 66755. Coombs, Munro

All the music here is endearingly fresh. The *Polonaise* which ends the *First Suite* would not disgrace a ballet by Tchaikovsky. *Suite 2*, written four years later, is subtitled *Silhouettes*, and each of its five movements represents a different character. *Suite 3* is a set of nine variations and is the most brilliant and pianistically resourceful of all. *Suite 4* is hardly less beguiling than its companions. Two pianos are difficult to record, and the recording, though too resonant, reproduces them very truthfully. Altogether delightful music and captivating playing.

ARNE, Thomas Augustine (1710–78)

Keyboard Concertos (played as listed): *Harpsichord Concertos: in C; in G min.; Organ Concertos: in B flat; in G; Piano Concertos: in A; in B flat*
*** Hyp. CDA 66509. Nicholson, Parley of Instruments, Holman

The six keyboard concertos of Arne date from different periods in his career and have a wide variety of movement-structures. Holman varies the solo instrument according to the character of each work, with the earliest, *No. 2 in G major*, given on the organ, but the next oldest, *No. 5 in G minor*, played on the harpsichord, when the Scarlattian cross-hands writing is better suited to that instrument. As a sampler, try the delectable *No. 3 in A*, given here on a gentle-toned fortepiano. Exhilarating performances, the instrumental balances perfectly managed, achieving clarity without exaggeration.

Organ Concertos 1–6
**(*) Chan. 8604/5 (2). Bevan Williams, Cantilena, Shepherd

Though Arne's concertos are simpler in style and construction than those of Handel, their invention is consistently fresh. The performances here have admirable style and spirit, and the recording is ideally balanced – the organ seems perfectly chosen for this consistently engaging music. A recommendable set in every respect, except for the playing time (only 86 minutes).

Trio Sonatas 1–7 (complete)
*** Chan. 0666. Coll. Mus. 90 (Standage, Comberti, Coe, Parle)

Arne's seven *Trio Sonatas* (an unusual number for a published set) date from 1757. Unusually in four movements (alternating slow and fast tempi) but framed by two five-movement works, they epitomize the new *galant* manner of the pre-classical period: the part-writing and the discourse amiable, the mildly contrapuntal element in the writing never seeming to predominate in determining the music's style. Where there is a *Gigg* finale there is a flavour of an English country dance, but the slow movements have a comparatively rich expressive character to give the music substance. For instance, the noble opening Siciliana of the five-movement No. 7 is nicely balanced by the closing *Gigg* and fairly brisk Minuet finale. Excellent period-instrument performances, spirited and appropriately genial, truthfully balanced and recorded.

Cymon and Iphigenia; Frolic and Free (cantatas); *Jenny; The Lover's Recantation; The Morning* (cantata); *Sigh no More, Ladies; Thou Soft Flowing Avon; What Tho' His Guilt*
*** Hyp. CDA 66237. Kirkby, Morton, Parley of Instruments, Goodman

The present collection admirably shows the ingenuous simplicity of Arne's vocal writing, very much in the mid-18th-century English pastoral school with its 'Hey down derrys'. Excellent, warm recording, with the voices naturally projected. A most entertaining concert.

STAGE WORKS

Artaxerxes (complete)
*** Hyp. CDA 67051/2. Robson, Bott, Partridge, Spence, Edgar-Wilson, Hyde, Parley of Instruments, Goodman

This sparkling, lively performance impressively explains why Arne's opera was such a success when it was first produced at Covent Garden. The one number that has latterly become popular – thanks largely to Joan Sutherland's brilliant recording – is *The Soldier Tir'd*, but that dazzling climactic number is only one of Mandane's formidable solos, whether expressive or vehement. Catherine Bott gives a masterly performance, with the counter-tenor Christopher Robson also impressive in the castrato title-role, and with Ian Partridge pure-toned and incisive in the role of the villain, Artabanes, even if his sweet tenor hardly conveys evil. With the mezzo-soprano Patricia Spence taking the castrato role of Arbaces, the others are first rate too. On two very well-filled CDs, the set owes much of its success to the inspired direction of Roy Goodman. The reconstruction of the score has been achieved most capably by Peter Holman, who contributes an excellent note.

ARNELL, Richard (born 1917)

Cello Suite; Music for Harp, Op. 72a; Piano Trio, Op. 47; String Quintet, Op. 60; Trio for Flute, Cello & Piano, Op. 168
(M) *** Dutton Epoch CDLX 7122. Locrian Ens. (members)

London-born, Richard Arnell was a student of John Ireland at the Royal College of Music. Visiting New York in 1939, he stayed throughout the war, working as a consultant to the BBC. His music caught the ear of Beecham, and this is how we came to know his ballet suite, *Punch and the Child*.

The five chamber works here represent the full span of his long career, from the powerful *Piano Trio* of 1946, which he himself called 'the most compelling of my chamber works', to the compact two-movement *Trio for Flute, Cello and Piano* of 1991, more quirky in its argument and revealing the composer still full of ideas in his seventies. The *Music for Harp* of 1961 brings another unusual line-up of instruments – a single movement in two halves for harp accompanied by flute, violin and viola. In many ways the tautest of the works here is the four-movement *String Quintet* of 1950, with three relatively brief movements leading to a multi-sectioned *Fantasia*. Justin Pearson is most persuasive in the *Unaccompanied Cello Suite*, which is essentially ruminative but also with a strong baroque underlay, and the Locrian performances throughout are most sympathetic, with the players obviously right inside the music. The recording is excellent. Here is another CD to restore to us yet one more of a generation of British composers which until now have been eclipsed by the avant garde.

ARNOLD, Malcolm (born 1921)

'Toward the Unknown Region': Malcolm Arnold – A Story of Survival
*** Isolde Films **DVD** ISO 001. Includes performances from Bream, Galway, Lloyd Webber, RTE NSO/Houlihan (V/D: Tony Palmer)

Tony Palmer adds to his store of deeply revelatory profiles of composers this moving portrait of Malcolm Arnold at 80. With most of Arnold's own contributions drawn from interviews given earlier in his life, the film follows his career from boyhood in Northampton, through his time as principal trumpet in the LPO – 'it inspired me to compose myself' – and on to his work, writing film music, with the nine symphonies used as cornerstones, plus contributions from such artists as Julian Bream, James Galway and Julian Lloyd Webber, for whom he has written works. It boldly tackles the tragic story of his breakdown and disintegration, largely through drink, and his happy release thanks to the care latterly given to him by his helper and manager, Antony John Day. Day took over when Arnold was given only a year to live, but he has subsequently lived for over 20 years, finally writing his visionary *Ninth Symphony*. The film, originally shown in two parts on Melvyn Bragg's *South Bank Show*, is here given in its full form with over half an hour of important extra material.

(i; ii) *Anniversary Overture, Op. 99; Beckus the Dandipratt Overture, Op. 5;* (iii; ii) *Carnival of the Animals;* (iv; iii; ii) *Concerto for 2 Pianos, 3 Hands (Concerto for Phyllis and Cyril);* (v) *Guitar Concerto, Op. 67;* (vi) *4 Cornish Dances, Op. 91; 8 English Dances, Opp. 27 & 33 (arr. Farr); Fantasy for Brass Band, Op. 114;* (iii; ii) *A Grand, Grand Overture, Op. 57;* (vii) *Larch Trees, Op. 3;* (vi) *Little Suites for Brass Band 1, Op. 80; 2, Op. 93; The Padstow Lifeboat, Op. 94; 4 Scottish Dances, Op. 59 (arr. Farr);* (vii) *Serenade for Small Orchestra, Op. 26*
○— (B) *** RCA (DDD/ADD) 74321 88392-2 (2). (i) BBC Concert O; (ii) Handley; (iii) RPO; (iv) Nettle & Markham; (v) Bream, Melos Ens., composer; (vi) Grimethorpe Colliery Band, Howarth (or composer); (vii) London Musici, Stephenson

This splendid bargain Double gives a useful and generous survey of Arnold works, not forgetting the brass band music which the superb Grimethorpe players under Elgar Howarth recorded with the composer present. Not surprisingly, he gave high praise to Howarth's carefully prepared and winningly spontaneous performances, unerringly paced. Farr's arrangements, too, are extremely effective. The composer himself directs the March, *The Padstow Lifeboat*, with its warning off-key foghorn, based on the pitch of the foghorn at Trevose in Cornwall. The recording is very much in the demonstration bracket.

The short *Anniversary Overture* was written to accompany a Hong Kong fireworks display: it is boisterous and tuneful. Also included is a fizzing performance of Arnold's first orchestral work, *Beckus the Dandipratt*, and the *Double Piano*, originally the '*Concerto for Phyllis and Cyril*'. This was written in 1969 for Phyllis Sellick and Cyril Smith when Cyril lost the use of his left hand and he and his wife continued as a highly successful duo. The piano duo here, Nettle and Markham, are obviously captivated by the piece, which they play with much flair and understanding.

Julian Bream's is a classic account of the *Guitar Concerto*, with the composer directing the accompaniment, and the late-1950s recording has worn its years lightly. The other recordings are all modern. The *Grand, Grand Overture* (with its outrageous special effects) was written for the Hoffnung Festival and comes up remarkably effectively here, with Handley as ever a sympathetic advocate.

Larch Trees dates from as early as 1943, written when Arnold was only 21, and is a nostalgic tone-poem that instantly reveals his natural feeling for evocative instrumentation. It is very sympathetically played, and Mark Stephenson and London Musici are just as convincingly idiomatic in the charming *Serenade*. Altogether excellent value.

Anniversary Overture; Beckus the Dandipratt (Comedy Overture), Op. 5; The Fair Field, Op. 110; A Flourish for Orchestra, Op. 112; A Grand Grand Festival Overture, Op. 57; Peterloo Overture, Op. 97; Robert Kett Overture, Op. 41; The Smoke, Op. 21; A Sussex Overture, Op. 31; Tam O'Shanter Overture, Op. 51
(N) Chan. 10293. BBC PO, Gamba

Sir Malcolm Arnold's genius was particularly well suited to small-scale orchestral works, and every one of these Overtures shows his orchestral personality at its exuberant finest. *Beckus the Dandipratt* came first in 1943, a characterization hailed as a cross between *Till* and *Scapino*, but possibly more of an uninhibited self-portrait. When it appeared on a splendid Decca ffrr 78 disc, it immediately established the composer's reputation, which was to be enhanced a decade later by *Tam O'Shanter*, another flamboyant portrayal, with a spectacular orchestral realization of bagpipes at its witty climax. *A Grand Grand Festival Overture* came a year later – Arnold's contribution to the 1956 Gerard Hoffnung Festival of musical humour. The scoring included four vacuum cleaners and a floor polisher (the participants here faithfully credited in the

CD's documentation). On the night they were despatched by the rifles of a firing squad! But this is far more than an occasional piece, not least because it has a really good tune. The noisily dramatic *Peterloo* also has one. But then so have all the other works here, which, together with their constant inventiveness and brilliant scoring, are all most entertaining. They are marvellously played, with a truly Arnoldinan infectious exhilaration, and the Chandos recording is spectacularly worthy, thrillingly in the demonstration bracket.

Clarinet Concertos 1–2; Divertimento for Flute, Oboe & Clarinet, Op. 37; Fantasy for B flat Clarinet, Op. 87; Sonatina, Op. 29; 3 Shanties for Wind Quintet

*** ASV CDDCA 922. Johnson, Martin, Kelly, Briggs, Cohen, Martineau; ECO, Bolton

With the characterful Emma Johnson as the central figure in all six works, this makes a delightful collection of what is labelled as Arnold's 'Complete Works for Clarinet'. Above all, these performances bring out the fun in Arnold's music, his bluff sense of humour set alongside a vein of warm lyricism matched by few of his contemporaries.

Clarinet Concertos 1, Op. 20; 2, Op. 115; Scherzetto

(BB) *** Hyp. Helios CDH 55060. King, ECO, Wordsworth – BRITTEN: *Clarinet Concerto Movement*; MACONCHY: *Concertinos* ***

Designed in part as a tribute to the great clarinettist, Frederick Thurston, Thea King's collection of short concertante works for clarinet makes an exceptionally attractive disc, beautifully recorded and superbly performed. The *Scherzetto* is a delightfully jaunty piece adapted by Christopher Palmer from Arnold's music for the film *You Know What Sailors Are*. Not only Thea King but the ECO (the orchestra in which she has been a distinguished principal for many years) under Barry Wordsworth bring out the warmth as well as the rhythmic drive.

(i) Guitar Concerto, Op. 67; (ii) 8 English Dances; (iii; iv) Quintet for Brass, Op. 73; (iii; v) Symphony for Brass Instruments, Op. 123

(M) *** Decca mono/stereo 468 803-2. (i) Fernández, ECO, Wordsworth; (ii) LPO, Boult; (iii) Philip Jones Brass Ens.; (iv) Howarth; (v) Snell

Guitar Concerto; Serenade for Guitar & Strings

*** Chan. 9963. Ogden, N. Sinf., Hickox – BERKELEY: *Guitar Concerto*; WALTON: *5 Bagatelles* ***

There are few guitar concertos to match the effectiveness of this jazz-inflected piece, written in 1957 for Julian Bream.

Fernández and the ECO in a fizzing performance, spikily incisive, bring out the jazz overtones. Fernández makes the haunting melody of the first movement's second subject warm and not sentimental, and the full depth of the blues-inspired slow movement is movingly conveyed. Boult's 1954 mono set of the *English Dances* is still the best, and the early mono sound, though lacking in amplitude, is vivid. The 1970s recording for the Philip Jones Brass Ensemble is brilliant and clear, as are the superb performances. The *Symphony* is a longish piece, lasting some 26 minutes. Ultimately, the ideas remain a shade facile, but there are powerful sonorities here. The shorter *Quintet* has bubbling outer movements, with some interesting quirky harmonies, which frame a somewhat more severe central *Chaconne*.

Craig Ogden is a consummate soloist and he is beautifully

recorded. The charming, lyrical *Serenade for Guitar and Strings* which comes as supplement was written by Arnold a couple of years earlier as a trial run for the *Concerto*. An excellent alternative to Julian Bream's recordings, especially if the Berkeley and Walton couplings are preferred.

4 Cornish Dances, Op. 91; 8 English Dances, Set 1, Op. 27; Set 2, Op. 33; 4 Irish Dances, Op. 126; 4 Scottish Dances, Op. 59; 4 Welsh Dances, Op. 138

☛ (BB) *** Naxos 8.553526. Queensland SO, Penny

The advantage this Naxos disc enjoys – to say nothing of its price – is the inclusion of the four *Welsh Dances*, the last to be written and closer in mood to the *Cornish* and *Irish Dances* than to the cheerful ebullience of the masterly *English Dances* of 1950–51. They remain perennial favourites, and Andrew Penny and the Queensland orchestra present them with their colours gleaming. These performances have the composer's imprimatur (he was present at the recording sessions) and can be cordially recommended. The Naxos sound might be thought a shade over-resonant, but it does not lack brilliance.

Film music: The Bridge on the River Kwai (suite for large orchestra); Hobson's Choice (orchestral suite); The Inn of the Sixth Happiness (suite); The Sound Barrier (rhapsody), Op. 38; Whistle Down the Wind (small suite for small orchestra)

*** Chan. 9100. LSO, Hickox

Malcolm Arnold wrote over 100 film scores, and it was the music for *The Bridge on the River Kwai* which (as the composer has acknowledged) put his name before the wider public. All this music is superbly played by Hickox and the LSO (who obviously relish the often virtuoso instrumental scoring), and the recording is as lavish as anyone could wish – very much in the Chandos demonstration bracket.

Film music: David Copperfield; The Roots of Heaven (arr. John Morgan)

*** Marco 8.225167. Moscow SO, Stromberg

The Roots of Heaven (1958), about a white man in central Africa who dedicates himself to preventing the slaughter of elephants, has resonance today. Arnold provides us with a rumbustious five-minute Overture which presents various themes colourfully and imaginatively. The score is imbued with a fair share of exotic local colour: the oboes and percussion in *Fort Lamy* sound suitably jungly.

David Copperfield was written for a much later (1970) TV adaptation of Dickens's famous story. The nostalgia is caught superbly in such numbers as *The Return to Yarmouth*. Dickens's characters are well drawn too, and the *Love for Dora* is heartfelt; indeed the melancholy vein which runs through this score leaves a potent after-effect. Both scores are consistently enjoyable and this is a fine disc in every way, even if the *David Copperfield* suite is even more haunting on Gamba's Chandos collection. The sleeve-notes are remarkably helpful and informative.

Film music: Machines for Brass, Percussion & Strings, Op. 30. Overture: The Roots of Heaven. Arr. & where necessary orch. Philip Lane: (i) Ballad for Piano & Orchestra (from Stolen Face); The Captain's Paradise: Postcard from the Med; David Copperfield (suite); No Love for Johnnie (suite); Trapeze (suite). Arr. Christopher Palmer: The Belles of St Trinian's: Exploits for Orchestra (comedy

suite). *Fantasy on Christmas Carols* from *The Holly and the Ivy*. (ii) *Scherzetto for Clarinet & Orchestra* from *You Know What Sailors Are*

*** Chan. 9851. BBC PO, Gamba, with (i) Dyson; (ii) Bradbury

The suite arranged by Philip Lane from *Trapeze* is a typical example of Arnold's ready flow of invention, including a swinging tune for the horns in the *Prelude*, a delectable blues for saxophone and guitar, an exuberant circus march and a characteristically lugubrious *Elephant Waltz* for a pair of tubas, while the closing sequence features an accordion to set the Parisian scene. The suite from *David Copperfield* opens with a typical melodic sweep, followed by a whimsical *moto perpetuo* representing the Micawbers. This features a solo clarinet, and Christopher Palmer has arranged another witty clarinet scherzetto from an equally capricious theme used in *You Know What Sailors Are*. The concertante ballad for piano and orchestra, arranged by Philip Lane from *Stolen Face*, is rather discursive, but the *Overture* from *The Roots of Heaven* (specially written for the film's New York première) opens with a large-screen flamboyant flourish, followed by more catchy syncopation and a lilting waltz tune. Tender romantic melody comes in *No Love for Johnnie*, while *The Belles of St Trinian's* (the composer's favourite film) brings an audacious sparkle. If *The Holly and the Ivy* offers a rather overfamiliar collection of carols, for the most part not very enterprisingly scored, Arnold's jaunty samba from *The Captain's Paradise*, in which Alec Guinness starred in the bigamous title-role, makes a splendid finale. Rumon Gamba and the excellent BBC Philharmonic provide plenty of infectious zest and a sometimes bitter-sweet lyricism, and the recording is of top Chandos quality. If you enjoy film music, it doesn't come any better than this.

Symphonies 1–9

🔓 (BB) *** Naxos White Box 8.505178 (5). Nat. SO of Ireland, Penny

Andrew Penny's complete set of the Arnold *Symphonies* is a very considerable achievement. The five discs are reviewed separately below, but are here gathered together in one of Naxos's White Boxes with admirable documentation, including a biography of the composer.

Symphonies 1, Op. 22; 2, Op. 40

*** Chan. 9335. LSO, Hickox

(BB) **(*) Naxos 8.553406. Nat. SO of Ireland, Penny

Richard Hickox takes naturally to the Malcolm Arnold idiom and he is particularly impressive in the two slow movements, which are full of atmosphere, vividly coloured and strongly felt. The rumbustious finale of No. 2 brings a splendid release of tension, and the LSO response is powerful and thoroughly committed throughout. The recording is well up to the high standard we expect from this label. A first-rate coupling.

Andrew Penny in his Naxos version matches Hickox closely, but the National Orchestra of Ireland cannot command the richness of sonority of the LSO, and in the poignant *Lento* of the *Second*, with its plangent funeral march, Hickox's more spacious tempo is profoundly moving. Yet the composer was present at these sessions and the slow movement of the *Second Symphony* communicates strongly in the Dublin performance. The Naxos recording is excellent, but the Chandos is very much in the demonstration bracket.

Symphony 3; 4 Scottish Dances, Op. 59

(M) *** Phoenix (ADD) PHD 102. LPO, composer

Arnold made his first recording of the *Third Symphony* at Walthamstow in the late 1950s. In the outer movements the performance has a certain chimerical, spontaneous quality that balances out the deeper feelings beneath the music's surface. The result is uncommonly fresh, even if Hickox's later recording has more gravitas. The early stereo is remarkably spacious and the brass writing is given fine sonority, though the violins are less full-bodied than we would expect today. The reissue on Phoenix includes the original coupling of the *Four Scottish Dances*, which are superbly played (particularly the lovely *Allegretto*), and the current remastering in New York by MacDonald Moore is extremely vivid with a natural perspective and excellent detail.

Symphonies 3, Op. 63; 4, Op. 71

*** Chan. 9290. LSO, Hickox

(BB) *** Naxos 8.553739. Nat. SO of Ireland, Penny

Arnold's *Third Symphony* is notable for the long, expressively austere string-melody in the opening movement and the desolation of its *Lento* slow movement, both played with great expressive intensity under Hickox. The first movement of the *Fourth Symphony* is dominated by one of those entirely winning, Arnoldian lyrical tunes, even though there is jagged dissonance in the central episode. The slow movement brings another long-breathed, almost Mahlerian, melodic flow, and the finale has its bizarre – indeed raucous – moments, including a curious march sequence. Richard Hickox has the work's full measure, and the Chandos recording is superb, full of colour and atmosphere.

Andrew Penny and his Dublin orchestra also give finely played and spontaneous performances that can readily stand alongside the full-price competition, and this Naxos record understandably has the composer's imprimatur. The recording, if not as rich as the Chandos, is of high quality, atmospheric and with the orchestral colours emerging vividly; the special percussion effects in the exuberantly fugal finale of the *Fourth* are also very telling.

Symphony 5, Op. 74; The Belles of St Trinian's (comedy suite); Divertimento 2, Op. 75; Machines (symphonic study); Solitaire: Sarabande & Polka

**(*) Classico CLASSCD 294. Munich PO, Bostock

Symphonies 5; 6, Op. 95

*** Chan. 9385. LSO, Hickox

(BB) *** Naxos 8.552000. Nat. SO of Ireland, Penny

Arnold's *Fifth Symphony* is a consciously elegiac work, written in memory of friends who died young. While the first movement brings moments of valedictory evocation in Hickox's hands, it is also dramatically vibrant, and the *Andante* has a certain restrained warmth of feeling to balance the jocularly brash Scherzo and finale. The disconsolate *Sixth Symphony* is a good deal less comfortable than the *Fifth*, but Hickox handles the powerfully menacing climax of the *Lento* quite superbly, gripping the listener in the music's bleak despair, which then suddenly evaporates with the arrival of the joyous, syncopated brass fanfares of the *rondo* finale. In both symphonies the committed response of the LSO, together with the richly expansive Chandos recording, increases the weight and power of the readings.

Andrew Penny draws fine, concentrated playing from the National Symphony Orchestra of Ireland, with brass and percussion in particular brilliantly caught. As a bargain version this wins the highest recommendation; yet if you go to the Chandos version coupling the same two symphonies, you will get performances that are not just more polished, weightier and even more richly recorded, but are more overtly emotional.

Arnold's *Fifth Symphony* is also idiomatically played in Munich by the excellent resident symphony orchestra, conducted by Douglas Bostock. It is an impressive performance. Bostock is at his finest in three of the four other works included, which are all first recordings. The *Divertimento* is a colourful triptych with a lively *Chaconne* for finale, and there is much uninhibited fun in the early *St Trinian's* film-score, in which the Munich orchestra let their hair down and obviously enjoy themselves. The touching *Sarabande* from *Solitaire* (one of Arnold's most beautiful tunes) and the audacious *Polka* are equally persuasive. Only the symphonic study, *Machines*, gives cause for reservation. The performance is forceful but needs just that bit more bite and propulsion.

Symphonies 7, Op. 113; 8, Op. 124
(BB) *** Naxos 8.552001. Irish Nat. SO, Penny

Andrew Penny and the Irish National Symphony Orchestra round off their fine cycle of the nine Arnold symphonies for Naxos with these two most troubled and challenging works, reflecting the darkest period of the composer's life. Not that these are depressing, for as a creative genius Arnold translates his emotions into symphonic structures at once imaginative and original. The darkness is relieved both by the characteristic colourfulness of Arnold's orchestration (with a battery of percussion prominent in No. 7) and also by the wealth of thematic material, demonstrating the vitality of the composer's imagination through his worst trials.

This Naxos issue comes into direct rivalry with Handley's (currently deleted) Conifer disc of the première recordings of both works. By a fraction Handley's are the more warmly expressive readings of both, with freer rubato, yet Penny and the Irish orchestra gain from the extra clarity of the recording, full and open, bringing out inner detail in often heavy textures, with dramatic contrasts sharply terraced. Particularly at Naxos price, they invite the attention not only of those who already enjoy Arnold's music, but of any collector who enjoys a challenge.

Symphony 9, Op. 128
(BB) *** Naxos 8.553540. Nat. SO of Ireland, Penny

This superb first Naxos recording arrived to confirm the *Ninth Symphony* as a fitting culmination to Arnold's symphonic series. The baldness of the arguments, with two-part writing the general rule, might initially be thought disconcerting. But the music consistently speaks in a true Arnoldian accent, culminating in the long slow finale, almost as long as the other three movements together, registering a mood of tragedy and disillusion. The symphony ends quietly on a major triad, a firm D major chord, a mere sop towards granting release. The other three movements are just as direct, built on instantly memorable material. As to Penny's performance, this is not just concentrated and consistently committed but warmly resonant, with the Dublin strings sounding glorious and the woodwind and brass consistently brilliant. The recording is rich and firmly focused.

CHAMBER MUSIC

Divertimento for Flute, Oboe & Clarinet, Op. 37; Duo for Flute & Viola, Op. 10; Flute Sonata, Op. 121; Oboe Quartet, Op. 61; Quintet for Flute, Violin, Viola, Horn & Piano, Op. 7; 3 Shanties for Wind Quintet, Op. 4
(BB) *** Hyp. Helios CDH 55073. Nash Ens.

Duo for 2 Cellos, Op. 85; Piano Trio, Op. 54; Viola Sonata 1, Op. 17; Violin Sonatas 1, Op. 15; 2, Op. 43; Pieces for Violin & Piano, Op. 54
(BB) *** Hyp. Helios CDH 55071. Nash Ens.

Clarinet Sonatina, Op. 29; Fantasies for Wind, Opp. 86–90; Flute Sonatina, Op. 19; Oboe Sonatina, Op. 28; Recorder Sonatina, Op. 41; Trio for Flute, Bassoon & Piano, Op. 6
(BB) *** Hyp. Helios CDH 55072. Nash Ens.

All the pieces on the first disc show conspicuous resource in the handling of the instruments. The second disc includes two *Violin Sonatas*, which are cool, civilized and intelligent. The *Piano Trio* of 1956 has a powerful sense of direction. The third listing concentrates on the wind music. This is perhaps more for admirers of Arnold's music than for the generality of collectors. The playing is brilliant and sympathetic throughout all three discs and the recording is first rate; good value at bargain price.

String Quartets 1, Op. 23; 2, Op. 118
*** Chan. 9112. McCapra Qt

String Quartets 1–2; Phantasy (Vita abundans) for String Quartet; Quintet for Flute, Violin, Viola, Horn & Bassoon, Op. 7
*** Guild GMCD 7216. Ceruti Ens.

Malcom Arnold's two *String Quartets* were written 26 years apart. The *First*, an early work (and not without influences from Bartók), dates from 1949; the *Second* came in 1974, the year after the *Seventh Symphony*. Both are enigmatic but, like all Arnold's finest music, thoroughly worth coming to terms with, for all their stylistic and musical ambiguities and contradictions. The *Phantasy (Vita abundans)* was written in 1941. In six sections, all drawing on its recurring lyrical opening theme, it teems with 'abundant life', and it is remarkable that it has remained unheard until the arrival of the splendidly alive performance on this Guild CD. The first movement of the engaging *Quintet* (dating from 1944, but revised in 1960) makes a delightful foil and is typical of the jocular, popular Arnold. The performances of all four works by members of the London Ceruti Ensemble are dedicated and full of spirit, and often deeply passionate feeling; and the recording has splendid presence and realism.

The McCapra Quartet are hardly less impressive on Chandos; indeed, theirs were the première recordings of the two *Quartets*. These young players are right inside the music. But they offer only the two *Quartets* and, with a playing time of only 46 minutes, the Chandos disc is completely upstaged by the Guild CD, which plays for over 70!

ARRIAGA, Juan (1806–26)

Symphony in D; Overture: Los esclavos felices
*** Hyp. CDA 66800. SCO, Mackerras – VORISEK: *Symphony in D* ***

(BB) *** Naxos 8.557207. Algarve O, Álvaro Cassuto – (with Concert of music by CARVALHO; MOREIRA; PORTUGAL; SEIXAS **(*))

The *Overture*, which comes before the *Symphony* on Hyperion, is a real charmer, almost Schubertian, but also very much in the style of Rossini, complete with crescendo. The *Symphony* could scarcely be played with more character than it is under Mackerras, and the somewhat resonant but very well-balanced Hyperion recording does not cloud detail. Highly recommended.

The Naxos performances, recorded in Faro, convey the sunny high spirits of the pieces and also bring four other rarities that few readers are likely to know. Good playing and recording.

String Quartets 1 in D min.; 2 in A; 3 in E flat

🎵 *** HM HMI 1987038. Cuerteto Casals

*** MDG 603 0236-2. Voces Qt

(M) **(*) CRD 33123 (2). Chilingirian Qt – WIKMANSON: *String Quartet 2* ***

The three miraculous quartets by the 18-year-old Arriaga still continue to astonish. While we retain a warm affection for the mellow, Schubertian accounts by the Voces Quartet on MDG, these new performances by the youthful Spaniards, recorded in 2003, must now take pride of place. The group was formed in 1997 in Madrid; these young players use modern instruments, yet they show a background understanding of period-instrument practice without creating abrasiveness or linear distortion. Their ensemble is impeccable and their group personality striking, while their playing combines expressive freedom with fine control and matching of timbres. They present the *Andante con variazioni* of the *A major Qartet* with much imagination and a wide range of dynamics; and they are at their finest in the gentle *Andantino* of the *E flat major*, which has a simmering underlying depth of feeling that can suddenly burst passionately to the surface. The work's light-hearted, bouncily rhythmic *Presto Agitato* finale is also splendidly characterized. Excellent, truthfully balanced recording.

The Romanian Voces Quartet is also completely at home in this engaging music and gives warmly refined, polished performances of all three works, full of elegance and spirit. All three slow movements are beautifully played, with just the right degree of gravitas. The spring-like freshness of the first movement of the *Second Quartet* is particularly attractive, and the *Theme and Variations* that follows is most winningly done. The recording is warm and naturally balanced in an attractively warm acoustic.

The Chilingirians play with both conviction and feeling, but they involve a pair of CDs (admittedly with an interesting coupling).

AUBER, Daniel (1782–1871)

Overtures: The Bronze Horse; Fra Diavolo; Masaniello

🎵 ✪ (M) *** Mercury (ADD) SACD 470 638-2. Detroit SO, Paray – SUPPE: *Overtures* ***

Dazzling performances, full of verve and style, which will surely never be surpassed. The present recordings, made in the suitably resonant acoustic of Detroit's Old Orchestra Hall, show Mercury engineering (1959 vintage) at its very finest.

The new SACD transfer, derived from the original three-channnel recording, enhances the recording still more. But the sound is still stunning when the disc is played as a normal CD. Just sample the crisp transients of the opening side drum and the deliciously pointed violins in *Fra Diavolo*, and you'll not be able to stop listening. Why these overtures are never played in concert halls is quite extraordinary: they are elegantly crafted as well as tuneful.

Le Dieu et la Bayadère: Overture & ballet music; L'Enfant prodigue: Overture; Jenny Bell: Overture; La Muette de Portici: Ballet music; Le Premier Jour de bonheur: Overture; La Sirène: Overture; Vendôme en Espagne: Boléro & Air pour le second ballet

**(*) Sterling CDS 1039-2. Gothenburg Op. O, Andersson

Though not all of this music shows Auber at his best, it is all thoroughly entertaining and almost all of it is unknown. Auber had the knack of writing catchy tunes and, with piquant orchestration, splashes of local colour, bacchanales and waltzes, and wit in plenty, one understands how this composer was such a success during the 19th century. The performance and recordings are very good, though they just miss the sheer exhilaration that Paul Paray and his Mercury team brought to this repertoire. This disc will bring much pleasure to those who respond to the repertoire.

OPERA

(i) Le Domino noir (complete); Gustave III ou Le Bal masqué (Overture & ballet music)

✪ *** (M) Decca 476 2173 (2). Jo, Vernet, Ford, Power, Bastin, Olmeda, Cachemaille, L. Voices, ECO, Bonynge

For *Le Domino noir* Auber was inspired to write a sparkling score, full of delightful invention. The opening number directly anticipates the celebrated duet in Delibes's *Lakmé*, and other numbers bring clear anticipations of Gounod's *Faust* and of Verdi's *Il trovatore*, not to mention Gilbert and Sullivan. Three accompanied recitatives, written by Tchaikovsky for a planned performance in St Petersburg, are used very effectively in Act II. Bonynge makes the ideal advocate, moulding melodies, springing rhythms and aerating textures to make the music sparkle from first to last. The playing of the ECO is outstanding. Sumi Jo takes on a role leading her into dazzling coloratura. Bruce Ford as the hero and Patrick Power as his friend, Juliano, sing stylishly in well-contrasted tenor tones, while Isabelle Vernet is excellent as Brigitte. Martine Olmeda and Jules Bastin are both characterful in servant roles. The recording is among Decca's most vivid. On the second disc, after Act III, the fill-up aptly comes from another colourful but more serious opera of Auber, the one that, translated into Italian, prompted Verdi's *Ballo in maschera*.

Fra Diavolo (complete)

(B) **(*) EMI 5 75251-2 (2). Gedda, Mesplé, Dran, Berbié, Corazza, Bastin, Trempont, Laforge Ch. Ens., Monte Carlo PO, Soustrot

Fra Diavolo (complete; in Italian)

**(*) Fonit 3984 27266-2 (2). Serra, Dupuy, Raffanti, Portella, Cambridge University Chamber Ch., Martina Franca Festival O, Zedda

In 1933 *Fra Diavolo* was turned into a film with Laurel and Hardy as the inept pair of bandits, Beppo and Giocomo, but even that failed to bring it back into the general repertory. This lively complete EMI recording presents it as a jolly romp, depending largely on a pastime that is evidently older in France than is generally realized: baiting the English tourist, a Milord and his wife. With Fra Diavolo himself as a kind of swaggering Don Giovanni figure (as the name itself implies, 'Brother Devil'), the twists and turns have a Rossini-like sparkle without quite the same individuality of invention. Ensembles and choruses – well sprung by Soustrot – are generally more important than arias, though Diavolo has his big heroic piece at the opening of Act III, and the second tenor, Lorenzo, has a charming Romance, once a favourite of Richard Tauber's, but here done rather clumsily by Thierry Dran. Gedda in the name part is also strained, but the voice still rings well, and Mady Mesplé is less shrill than usual as the bright, pert Zerline (more overtones of *Don Giovanni*). Other singing too is flawed, but it is the teamwork that brings the fun. The digital recording, basically atmospheric, has just a hint of edge at times on the voices. There is a synopsis but no text and translation.

While the EMI recording offers the French text truncated, as the published score is incomplete, Alberto Zedda in this live festival performance offers the first recording of the Italian version, with all the material preserved and with accompanied recitatives by Auber in place of dialogue. The result is substantially longer and dramatically more convincing. Though the live recording, close and rather dry, brings odd balances and stage noises with occasional rough ensemble, the result is lively and involving, bringing out the winning lyricism of Auber's writing. In the title-role Dano Raffanti characterizes well, using a ringing tenor with flair and only occasional coarseness, relishing the challenge of the big arias. Luciana Serra has a touch of acid at the top of the voice, but this is a bright, agile soprano who brings out the charm in the role of the country-girl, Zerlina. Nelson Portella and Martine Dupuy, clear and firm, are well contrasted as the English Milord and Lady Pamela. An Italian libretto is provided but no translation.

Manon Lescaut (complete)

(B) **(*) EMI 5 75254-2 (2). Mesplé, Orliac, Runge, Bisson,
  Greger, Ch. & O Lyrique of R. France, Marty

Ending like Puccini's setting in 'a desert in Louisiana', Auber's opera, written in the 1850s when he was already 74, bears little relationship to that example of high romanticism. Born 10 years before Rossini, Auber died two years after Berlioz. Here he demonstrates that the liveliness we know from his overtures persisted to the end. Scribe's libretto is a free and often clumsy adaptation of the Prévost novel, but the sequence of arias and ensembles, conventional in their way, restores some of the original poetry. Manon herself is a coloratura soprano (here the small-voiced, agile Mesplé) and Des Grieux a lyric tenor (here the lightweight Jean-Claude Orliac). A recording as lively as this with good sound is very welcome at bargain price, even if no translation is provided, only a synopsis.

La Muette de Portici

(B) *** EMI 5 75257-2 (2). Kraus, Anderson, Aler, Lafont,
  Munier, Jean Laforge Choral Ens., Monte Carlo PO, Fulton

Auber's overture here (usually known as *Masaniello*) was a longtime favourite orchestral work, but the rest of the opera is well worth getting to know. (It was notorious for sparking off a rebellion in Brussels that led to Belgium's separation from the oppressive Dutch.) The opera tells of Masaniello,

hero of the people, defiant against the privileged nobility, a popular theme when Auber wrote the piece in 1829. Wagner praised the opera for both its heroic plot – 'the first really romantic French opera,' he declared – and for Auber's trend towards ridding the opera of set numbers. The writing is not always distinguished, but it is rarely less than entertaining and has several striking melodic ideas, lively ensembles and choruses (some anticipating Gilbert and Sullivan) and a magnificent aria for the hero. In that role, the Spanish tenor Alfredo Kraus sings as stylishly as ever, even if the heroic voice shows signs of age. The other important tenor role, that of Alphonse, the thoughtless Duke's son who seduces and then leaves Masaniello's sister – the mute girl of the title – is sung by the American tenor John Aler. He provides the ideal contrast with Kraus, singing most beautifully. June Anderson in the principal soprano role of Elvira, Alphonse's bride-to-be, sings sweetly. Strongly cast and vigorously conducted by Thomas Fulton, it makes an attractive set, with lively, theatrical sound, even though it lacks a little in richness . No texts are provided, but the set is inexpensive.

AULIN, Tor (1866–1914)

Violin Concerto 3 in C min., Op. 4

(BB) **(*) Naxos 8.554287. Ringborg, Swedish CO, Willén –
  BERWALD: *Violin Concerto;* STENHAMMAR: *2 Sentimental
  Romances* **(*)

Tor Aulin's *Concerto* is a pleasing, well-crafted piece in the Brahms mould, and well worth reviving. A good performance with well-balanced recorded sound in a warm acoustic.

AURIC, Georges (1899–1983)

La Belle et la Bête (complete film score)

(N) (BB) *** Naxos 8.557707. Axios Ch., Moscow SO,
  Adriano

Auric was a major film music composer who scored genres from Ealing comedies to out-and-out horror movies with equal success. (Chan. 9774 is the best all-round recommendation for his film work.) His style was always distinctive and unfailingly inventive. Many consider his score to Cocteau's *La Belle et la Bête* (1945) his finest achievement; indeed its 60 minutes are full of colour and clever invention, with the large orchestra (with chorus) used with great imagination throughout. Unlike many film scores, this one, although a collection of individual numbers, holds together extremely well. One can regard it as a large, Gothic, orchestral tone-poem, often strangely haunting and magical: one easily falls under its spell. Adriano has done his usual impressive work in its reconstruction, presenting it complete and newly recorded for the first time. The Moscow orchestra responds with total commitment and this CD represents a considerable achievement in every way. Originally released in 1996 on Marco Polo, its migration to bargain Naxos means that it is now a must for all film music buffs.

L'Eventail de Jeanne (complete ballet, including music by Delannoy, Ferroud, Ibert, Milhaud, Poulenc, Ravel, Roland-Manuel, Roussel, Florent Schmitt). Les Mariés de la Tour Eiffel (complete ballet, including music by Honegger, Milhaud, Poulenc, Tailleferre)

✪ (N) (M) *** Chan. 10290. Philh. O, Simon

A carefree spirit and captivating wit run through both these composite works; in fact these pieces are full of imagination and fun. Geoffrey Simon and the Philharmonia Orchestra give a very good account of themselves and the Chandos recording is little short of spectacular. This unique recording is even more welcome at mid–price.

Film scores: Suites from: *Caesar and Cleopatra; Dead of Night; Father Brown; Hue and Cry (Overture); The Innocents; It Always Rains on Sunday; The Lavender Hill Mob; Moulin Rouge; Passport to Pimlico; The Titfield Thunderbolt*
*** Chan. 8774. BBC PO, Gamba

It is remarkable that a French composer should have provided the film scores for some of the most famous Ealing comedies, so British in every other respect. But Auric's delicacy of orchestral touch and his feeling for atmosphere (together with his easy melodic gift) made him a perfect choice after his first flamboyant venture with Rank's *Caesar and Cleopatra*. From the witty railway music of *The Titfield Thunderbolt* and the distinct menace of *Dead of Night*, Auric moved easily to the buoyantly spirited *Passport to Pimlico*. But it was *Moulin Rouge* that gave Auric his popular hit, with a charming Parisian waltz song (delicately sung here by Mary Carewe) that was understandably to be a remarkable commercial success. Most of the excerpts are short vignettes but they make enjoyable listening when so well played and recorded.

Film scores: Suite: *Du rififi chez les hommes. Macao, l'enfer du Jeu; Le Salaire de la Peur* (excerpts); *La Symphonie Pastorale:* **Suite, with** *Valse et Tango*
*** Marco 8.225136. Slovak RSO, Adriano

Auric's distinctive language is apparent from the first few seconds on this CD. His style is symphonic, with elements of popular songs (such as the *Valse* and *Tango*, which are heard on a gramophone in *La Symphonie Pastorale*), and all with Gallic flair. *Macao* is largely reconstructed from music that was written for, but not used in, the final edit of the film (including an exotic piece entitled *Chinoiserie*). Auric mixes melodrama and comedy with equal sophistication, and these varied suites stand up remarkably well on their own, which is important as most readers will not have seen the films to which they owe their existence. Auric's imaginative scoring for a large orchestra is always ear-catching: the use of saxophone, high strings and bass drum at the beginning of *Du rififi chez les hommes*, for example, or the eerie *Etude sombre* of *Macao*, which sounds a little like Rachmaninov's *Isle of the Dead*.

Much background work by Adriano was involved in making this recording possible, not least his fascinating and lucid notes. The orchestra plays very well, the sound is atmospheric, and the CD presentation cannot be faulted.

Film scores (suites): *Orphée; Les Parents terribles; Ruy Blas; Thomas L'Imposteur*
*** Marco 8.225066. Slovak RSO, Adriano

Jean Cocteau considered Auric 'his' composer, and the music recorded here was for films that were either directed by Cocteau or for which he was the screenwriter. The elements of fantasy and imagination that marked *Orphée* are reflected in the music: though scored for a large orchestra, it has a classical restraint and is most haunting throughout. Also included is Auric's arrangement of *Eurydice's Lament* from

Gluck's opera – a lovely, piquant bonus. For *Les Parents terribles* Auric dispenses with the strings and uses a large wind band, percussion and piano: a short '*image musicale*' has been assembled for this recording. *Thomas L'Imposteur* starts off in military style and includes a wistful waltz for Clémence and Henriette. For the swashbuckler *Ruy Blas* Auric had to compose straightforward and colourful music, which gave him plenty of scope for his own distinctive brand of orchestration. Adriano has done sterling work in assembling these suites and securing first-class playing from the orchestra, and the recording is good too.

AVISON, Charles (1709–70)

Born in Newcastle-upon-Tyne, Charles Avison has been hailed by the *New Grove Dictionary of Music and Musicians* as 'the most important English Composer of the 18th Century'. He did not stay in the northern provinces but went to London in 1724, where he met the key figure in his musical life, Francesco Geminiani, who had travelled from Italy to England to capitalize on his studies with Corelli. Avison returned to Newcastle a decade later, taking his new musical experience with him; and there, a generation before Abel's comparable London enterprise, he organized a series of subscription concerts, which he continued to direct until the end of his life. As a composer, his most important contribution to English musical life was to write concerti grossi in the Italian style, which Geminiani had taken over from Corelli; but he also composed keyboard music in a style he had absorbed from Rameau. His life was a success story and he died unusually prosperous for an 18th-century musician.

12 Concertos, Op. 6
(N) (BB) *** Naxos 8.557553/54. Avison Ens., Beznosiuk

It is for a very good reason that we know of Avison mainly from his *12 Concerti grossi after Scarlatti* (attractive transcriptions of the latter's keyboard sonatas). Avison's ability to pattern his works on the music of others stood him in good stead throughout his career. While he was a fine musical craftsman, his own creative powers seem to be more limited. He was able to fashion a series of expert concerti grossi in the style he learned from Geminiani, with a deft interplay between the solo *concertino* and the *ripieno*. His concertos are skilfully fashioned, have plenty of vitality and show perceptive use of dynamic contrast; moreover, Avison wrote for the main string group in such a way that it was not too difficult for skilled amateurs to participate in performances. But the music itself, finely wrought as it is, displays no special melodic individuality or any unconventional features. Played as vibrantly and freshly as it is here, on period instruments by this expert ensemble from Avison's own city, and led by the excellent violinist Pavlo Beznosiuk, one cannot help but respond to the vitality of the writing, even if these concertos are not in the same league as the similar works of Corelli or Handel.

Concerti grossi, Op. 9/1, 4, 6–9
(*) Div. Art 2-4108. Georgian Cons.

Charles Avison's set of *Twelve Concertos*, Op. 9, was published in London in 1766. Written in four parts, the composer invites the use of keyboard (notably organ) as a replacement for the violin as the concertino soloist. The music is elegant and easy-going, which is reflected in the pleasingly polished and stylish performances by the Georgian Consort, who play the slightly melancholy slow movements with grace and charm.

Their double-dotting, however, could ideally be a shade crisper, and allegros given more bite (although the finale of No. 8 dances agreeably). The recording is natural and the ambience just right and, with the reservations expressed above, this makes enjoyably relaxed listening.

12 Concerti grossi after Scarlatti
**(*) Alpha 031. Café Zimmermann (3, 5–6, 9, 11 & 12)
**(*) Hyp. CDA 66891/2. Brandenburg Cons., Goodman

The period instrument group Café Zimmermann, with Pablo Valetti expertly leading the concertino, play with great energy and zest, and in slow movements with delicacy of lyrical feeling. These performances are distinctly preferable to those from Roy Goodman and, by not offering a complete set, are placed on a single disc. Even so, the fairly close balance brings a certain 'scratchiness' on tuttis, which is not altogether mitigated by the basically warm ambience. The Alpha CD is beautifully packaged, with excellent documentation, including a chart identifying the Scarlatti sonata movements used by Avison.

Roy Goodman's version has plenty of vitality. Fast movements fizz spiritedly, but the linear style of the slower movements, though not lacking expressive feeling, is altogether less smooth, and these performances are essentially for those who are totally converted to the authentic movement. The recording is excellent.

THE BACH FAMILY,
including Johann Sebastian

Johann Bach (1604–73)

Heinrich Bach (1615–92)

Adam Drese (c.1620–91)

Cyriacus Wilche (?–1667)

Georg Christoph (1642–97)

Johann Christoph (1642–1703)

Johann Michael Bach (1648–94)

Signr Pagh (before 1672)

Johann Ludwig (1677–1731)

Johann Sebastian (1685–1750)

Wilhelm Friedmann (1710–84)

Johann Christoph Friedrich (1732–95)

The Altenbach Archives of J. S. Bach: GEORG CHRISTOPH BACH: *Cantata: Siehe, wie fein und lieblich ist's.* JOHANN BACH: *Motets: Sei nun, wieder zufrieden meine Seele; Unser Leben ist ein Schatten.* JOHANN CHRISTOPH BACH: *Arias: Er ist nun aus; Mit Weinen hebt sich ans. Cantatas: Es erhub sich ein Streit; Herr, wende dich und sei mir gnädig; Meine Freundin, du bist schön. Laments: Ach dass ich Wassers gnug hätt; Wie bist du denn, O Gott in Zorn auf mich entbrannt. Motets: Der Gerechte, ob er gleich zu zeitlich storbt; Herr nun lässest du deinen Diener fahren; Lieber Herr Gott, wecke uns auf; Unsern Herzens Freude hat ein Ende.* JOHANN MICHAEL BACH: *Arias: Ach, wie sehnlich wart ich der Zeit; Auf lasst uns den Herren loben. Cantata: Die Furchte des Herren. Motets: Das Blut Jesu Christi; Herr, wenn ich nur dich habe; Ich weiss, dass mein Erlöser lebt; Nun hab ich überwunden.* JOHANN SEBASTIAN BACH: *Motet: Ich lasse dich nicht, du segnest mich denn.* ADAM DRESE: *Aria: Nun ist alles überwunden.* ANON.: *Aria: Weint nicht um meinen Tod*
☞ ⬤ HM HMC 901783.84 (2). Cantus Cöln, Concerto Palatino, Junghänel

Johann Sebastian Bach was deeply loyal to his extraordinary family, who over the generations produced an unrivalled tribe of composers. Following on after Reinhard Goebel, Konrad Junghänel puts us all in his debt by exploring the 'Altbachisches Archiv' (Archive of the elder Bachs), a group of manuscripts collected by Johann Sebastian himself, which disappeared at the end of the Second World War and was only recently located in the Ukraine and returned to Berlin. All these works obviously meant a great deal to Bach, especially the music of the two composers most generously represented in the collection, notably Johann Christoph and Johann Michael Bach, the eldest sons of Heinrich Bach. Bach was, therefore, their first cousin, once removed. What is remarkable is that this other branch of the family that sprang from Johannes Bach (c.1550–1626) also inherited musically creative genes.

Johann Christoph is clearly the star of the collection: his output was admired by both Johann Sebastian and his son Carl Philip Emanuel. His masterly cantata, *Es erhub sich ein Streit in Himmel*, with its brilliant orchestral and choral opening (with four trumpets), vividly depicts St John's vision of the war of the angels and the fall of the dragon. It was certainly performed in Leipzig, while the wedding cantata, *Meine Freundin, du bist schön*, with its duet-dialogue is a memorably expressive setting of the Song of Solomon. But the lovely Advent motet, *Lieber Herr Gott* (also performed in Leipzig), and the pair of Laments, notably the superbly sung work for solo bass, *Wie bist du denn* (with brilliant writing for solo violin), are hardly less eloquent.

The music of Johann Michael is also distinctive, as is shown by his fluent motets, especially the carol-like *Herr, wenn ich nur dich habe*, with its colourful brass, and the simple strophic solo arias. Johann Bach's main contribution is the touching funeral motet, *Unser Leben ist ein Schatten*, which, alongside a six-part chorus, includes a concealed vocal group in three parts. The composer of the melancholy aria *Weint nicht um meinen Tod* ('Do not weep over my death') is uncertain, but the strophic chorale *Nun ist alles überwunden* has now been ascribed to the Armstedt Kapellmeister, Adam Drese. The closing eight-voice motet, *Ich lasse dich nicht, du segnest mich denn*, was originally attributed to Johann Christoph, but is now established as a work of the young Johann Sebastian, and it ends this fascinating programme on a high plain. Throughout, the singing, whether solo, in dialogue or groups, is of the highest calibre, as is the authentic instrumental contribution, and everything comes over freshly and spontaneously. This is surely the most enterprising and rewarding of the 'Bachiana' collections.

'Bachiana', Volume 1: HEINRICH BACH: *Sonatas 1; 2; 'a cinque' in C & F for 2 Violins, 2 Violas & Continuo.* JOHANN CHRISTOPH BACH: *Aria: Eberliniana pro dormente Camillo for harpsichord.* JOHANN LUDWIG BACH: *Concerto in D for 2 Violins, 2 Oboes & Strings; Orchestral Suite (Overture) in G for 2 Oboes (ad lib.) & Strings.* JOHANN SEBASTIAN BACH: *Concerto in D for 3 Trumpets, Timpani, 2 Oboes, Bassoon & Strings, after BWV 249.* CYRIACUS WILCHE: *Battaglia for 2 Violins, 2 Violas & Continuo.* SIGNR PAGH: *Sonata & Capriccio in G min. for Violin, 2 Violas & Continuo*
*** DG 471 150-2. Col. Mus. Ant., Goebel

'Bachiana', Volume 2 (Double Concertos): C. P. E. BACH: *Double Concerto for Harpsichord & Fortepiano in E flat, Wq.47.* J. C. BACH: *Sinfonia Concertante in A for Violin &*

Cello. JOHANN CHRISTOPH FRIEDRICH BACH: *Double Concerto in E flat for Fortepiano & Viola.* WILHELM FRIEDEMANN BACH: *Flute Concerto*
*** DG 471 579-2. Hill & Soloists, Col. Mus. Ant., Goebel

Reinhard Goebel also offers a wonderfully illuminating pair of discs of pieces by Bach's relatives near and far. On Volume 1 J. S. B. himself is represented by a delightful concerto reconstructed from the *Easter Oratorio*, and the most substantial offerings otherwise are the *Overture (Suite)* and *Concerto* by his near-contemporary – a distant cousin – Johann Ludwig Bach, whose music J. S. B. regularly used as Cantor in Leipzig.

Heinrich Bach and Johann Michael Bach (thought to be the pseudonymous Signr Pagh) are from earlier generations, the grandfather and father respectively of J. S. B.'s first wife and cousin, Maria Barbara, producing music very typical of their period. The piece by Johann Christoph Bach, brother of Johann Michael, is an inventive set of variations for harpsichord, stylistically looking forward, and brilliantly played here by Leon Berben, while Cyriacus Wilche's *Battaglia*, written in 1659 for two violins, two violas and continuo, is the work of the grandfather of Anna Magdalena, Bach's second wife. Reinhard Goebel and his responsive players present the whole collection with a sure feeling for changing idioms and they are brilliantly recorded.

Reinhard Goebel's second collection of 'Bachiana' is primarily devoted to double concertos. Of Bach's sons, by far the most successful were Carl Philipp Emanuel, the Berlin Bach, and Johann Christian, the London Bach, both masters in their own right, who here are represented by superb works, J. C. by a *Sinfonia concertante in A* with violin and cello soloists, and C. P. E. by the fascinating *Concerto for Harpsichord and Fortepiano*, in which with sharp originality the ear-catching tonal contrasts are sharply exploited between the tangy harpsichord and the fluent fortepiano (here brilliantly played by Robert Hill). Reinhard Goebel with his Musica Antiqua of Cologne sets alongside them works by their lesser-known siblings that exceptionally breathe the same exalted air: a *Flute Concerto in D* by Wilhelm Friedemann, the eldest brother, full of breezy invention, and a *Concerto in E flat for Fortepiano and Viola* by Johann Christoph Friedrich, elder brother of J. C. by Bach's second wife, again with tonal contrasts brilliantly exploited. Consistently refreshing performances.

JOHANN CHRISTOPH BACH: Cantatas: *Ach, dass ich Wassers g'nung hätte; Er erhub sich Streit; Die Furcht des Herren; Herr, wende dich und sei mir gnädig; Meine Freundin; Wir bist du denn.* JOHANN MICHAEL BACH: Cantatas: *Ach bleib uns, Herr Jesu Christ; Ach, wie sehnlich wart' ich der Zeit; Auf lasst uns den Herren loben; Es ist ein grosser Gewinn; Liebster Jesu, hör mein Flehen.* GEORG CHRISTOPH BACH: Cantata: *Siehe, wie fein und lieblich.* HEINRICH BACH: *Ich danke dir, Gott*
(M) *** DG Blue 474 552-2 (2). Soloists, Rheinische Kantorei, Col. Mus. Ant., Goebel

Johann Sebastian not only wrote a short family history, he also made a compilation of the family's music (*Altbachisches Archiv*), which he passed on to Carl Philipp Emanuel. These eventually found their way into the archives of the Berlin Singakademie and were published in 1935; the whole collection was destroyed during the war. These two CDs include all the cantatas and vocal concertos by Bach's forefathers that he preserved, with, in addition, a vocal concerto, *Herr, wende*

dich, by Johann Christoph Bach. This survives in an autograph at the Berlin Staatsbibliotek and receives its first publication here in any form.

Johann Michael Bach, who was organist and parish clerk at Gehren for the last two decades of his life and died when Johann Sebastian was nine, is represented by his five delightfully fresh and inventive cantatas. He was obviously familiar with such models as Hassler and Praetorius. All are much shorter even than those of Buxtehude and much less ambitious than *Meine Freundin, du bist schön* by his older brother, Johann Christoph, the greatest of Bach's precursors. This is the most substantial of the works on the first disc, and the five other cantatas of his dominate its companion. Bach praised Johann Christoph as profound, and Carl Philipp Emanuel spoke of him as a 'great and expressive composer'. There are certainly many powerful and haunting passages to be found in *Meine Freundin, du bist schön* and the lament *Ach, dass ich Wassers g'nung hätte*. Only one work by his father, Heinrich Bach, survives, the vocal concerto *Ich danke dir, Gott*, a short piece of some six minutes, which calls to mind the Venetian style of Schütz. The last of the four Bachs represented in the set was his nephew Georg Christoph, a cousin of the brothers Johann Michael and Johann Christoph. His charming wedding cantata, *Siehe, wie fein und lieblich*, records a happy family event.

BACH, Carl Philipp Emanuel (1714–88)
Cello Concertos: in A min., Wq.170; in B flat, Wq.171; in A, Wq.172
🏵 ⊛ *** BIS CD 807. Suzuki, Bach Coll., Japan
(BB) **(*) Naxos 8.553298. Hugh, Bournemouth Sinf., Studt

(i) *Cello Concertos: Wq.170; Wq.171; Wq.172. Hamburg Sinfonias, Wq.183/1-4; Sinfonia in B min., Wq.182/5*
(BB) *** Virgin 2x1 5 61794-2 (2). OAE, Leonhardt; (i) with Bylsma

Hidemi Suzuki creates a dashing flow of energy in the orchestral ritornellos of outer movements, and the Bach Collegium play with great zest and commitment. In slow movements Suzuki's eloquent phrasing, warmth of feeling and breadth of tone are totally compelling, a cello line of heart-stopping intensity. The recording is splendid.

Bylsma's expressive intensity communicates strongly without ever taking the music outside its boundaries of sensibility, and these artists convey their commitment to this music persuasively. The *Hamburg Sinfonias* (for woodwind and strings) are striking works, notable for their refreshing originality. Gustav Leonhardt's account of this second set is the one to have if you want them on period instruments. A splendid bargain recommendation, although the BIS recording of the three *Cello Concertos* by Hidemi Suzuki is special.

Tim Hugh on Naxos is altogether more reticent, but he plays with a persuasive lyrical warmth and Richard Studt's accompaniments are crisp and stylish. The effect is spontaneous, the recording is vividly natural and these modern-instrument performances are alive and enjoyable in their less extrovert way.

(i) *Cello Concerto, Wq. 170;* (ii) *Keyboard Concerto in C, Wq.20. Sinfonias: in G, Wq.173; in E min., Wq.178; in E flat, Wq.179*
*** HM HMC 901711. (i) Bruns; (ii) Alpermann; Berlin Akademie für Alte Musik

C. P. E. Bach's wildly abrupt mood changes and dynamic contrasts are heard at their most intense in the *Sinfonia in E flat*, Wq.179 (1757), which opens the programme here, and there are similar contrasts and surprises in Wq.178. The *G major Sinfonia*, Wq.173, is much earlier, but already shows the same unpredictability, and also has a touchingly simple central *Andante*.

The emotionally charged *Adagio* of the *Harpsichord Concerto* is far more searching, contrasting with the exuberant finale, and no one could complain of a lack of rhythmic energy in the outer movements of the more familiar *A minor Cello Concerto*. In short, with a pair of equally fine soloists and committedly vigorous and alert playing from the orchestra, this extremely generous 79-minute concert provides an ideal introduction to this remarkably original and individual composer. The recording is excellent and the balance places the soloists truthfully in relation to the main string group.

Cello Concerto (2) in B flat, Wq.171

(M) *** Warner Elatus 0927 49839-2. Rostropovich, St Paul CO, Wolff – TARTINI; VIVALDI: *Concertos* ***

The present transcription is played with commanding eloquence and authority not only by Rostropovich but also by the fine Saint Paul orchestra. They produce great warmth along with the transparency of texture to which period-instrument ensembles aspire. The couplings too are well worth having. An excellently focused and fresh recording from 1993, the more welcome at medium price.

Flute Concerto in D

(N) *** CPO 999 888-2. Gurtner, Wiener Akademia, Haselböck – W. F. BACH: *Flute Concerto in D*; F. HOFFMAN: *Flute Concerto in D* ***

You can always rely on C. P. E. Bach to entertain you in his flute concertos, where his lively imagination is always in evidence: he surprises you with modulations and dynamics, never allowing you to be lulled into a *galant* complacency. Superb performances.

Flute Concerto in D min., Wq.22

*** HM HMC 901803. Huntgeburth, Berlin Akademie for Alte Musik, Mai – J. C. BACH: *Harpsichord Concerto*, etc. ***

This highly engaging *Flute Concerto*, written in 1747, is also available in a harpsichord version. But it suits the flute (and indeed the members of the Berlin Akademie) admirably, with its impetuous, brusque outer movements framing an *Andante* that has a melody of great charm. The solo playing from Christoph Huntgeburth is both sensitive and dazzlingly virtuosic, and the recording is excellent.

(i) Flute Concertos: in D min., Wq.22; in A min., Wq.166; in B flat, Wq.167; in A, Wq.168; in G, Wq.169. Sonata for Solo Flute, Wq.132

☞ ✪ (BB) *** Naxos 8.555715/6. Gallois; (i) Toronto Camerata, Mallon

Patrick Gallois is a masterly flautist, and he gives a superb set of performances of these fine concertos written for the court of Frederick the Great and arranged by the composer from works originally featuring the harpsichord as soloist. There is much sparkling vivacity in the allegros, and the expressive range of the slow movements, sometimes quite dark in feeling, is fully captured by both soloist and the excellent Toronto Camerata under Kevin Mallon, who ensures the consistent vitality of the music-making. Gallois uses Bach's

own cadenzas throughout, and he also gives an admirably spontaneous account of the *Solo Sonata* that shows his lovely tone at its most beguiling. With first-rate recording this Naxos set now sweeps the board and supersedes the otherwise excellent recording from Eckart Haupt which omits the *Solo Sonata* (Capriccio 10104-5).

(i) Flute Concertos: in A min., Wq.166; in B flat, Wq.167; in A, Wq.168; in G, Wq.169; (ii–iii) Oboe Concertos: in B flat, Wq.164; in E flat, Wq.165; (ii; iv–v) Solo in G min., for Oboe & Continuo; (v) Solo in G for Harp, Wq.139

(B) **(*) Ph. (ADD) (IMS) Duo 592-2 (2). (i) Nicolet, Netherlands CO, Zinman; (ii) H. Holliger; (iii) ECO, Leppard; (iv) Jucker; (v) U. Holliger

Nicolet uses a modern instrument and plays very well, but the effect with a rather heavy string accompaniment (partly the result of the acoustic) makes less of the music than the rival versions. Heinz Holliger's accounts of the *Oboe Concertos* are masterly. In addition to the excellence of the support from the ECO under Leppard, the Philips engineering is distinguished. The bonuses for oboe and continuo (in this instance harp and cello) and Ursula Holliger's harp *Solo* also add to the attractions of this very generous set.

(i) Flute Concertos, Wq.166 & 168; (ii–iii) Oboe Concerto, Wq.165; (ii; iv) Solo for Oboe & Continuo, Wq.135

(BB) ** Ph. 468 191-2. (i) Nicolet, Netherlands CO, Zinman; (ii) H. Holliger; (iii) ECO, Leppard; (iv) U. Holliger, Jucker

This is drawn from the Philips Duo listed above and has fair appeal, but the Gallois set of the *Flute Concertos* on Naxos stands supreme.

Flute Concertos: Wq.22; Wq.168; Wq.169

*** Hyp. CDA 67226. Brown, Brandenburg Cons., Goodman

Rachel Brown's timbre is small and translucent, but she plays spiritedly and her cleanly articulated roulades are well balanced against Goodman's often aggressively dynamic accompaniments. It is impossible not to respond to such exuberance, and in slow movements the orchestral textures are fined down to support the appealingly gentle flute-line. Excellent recording, resonant but clear.

Complete Solo Harpsichord Concertos

Harpsichord Concertos: 1 in A min.; 2 in E flat; 3 in G, Wq.1–3 (**(*) BIS CD 707); *4 in G ; 7 in A; 12 in F, Wq.4, 7 & 12* (**(*) BIS CD 708); *5 in C min.; 35 in E flat; Sonatinas in D; in G* (*** BIS CD 868); *6 in G min.; 8 in A; 18 in D, Wq.6, 8 & 18* (**(*) BIS CD 767); *9 in G; 13 in D; 17 in D min., Wq.9, 13 & 17* (**(*) BIS CD 768); *11 in D; 14 in E; 19 in A* (**(*) BIS CD 785); *15 in E min.; 25 in B flat; 32 in G min.* (**(*) BIS CD 786); *24 in E min.; 28 in B flat; 29 in A* (**(*) BIS CD 857). Spányi (harpsichord, fortepiano or tangent piano), Concerto Armonico, Szüts

This is an ongoing project in which Miklós Spányi is planning to record all 52 keyboard concertos which Carl Philipp Emanuel wrote between 1733 and 1788, most of which date from the early years of his musical life at the court of Frederick the Great in Berlin, making a direct path to the piano concertos of Mozart.

Spányi has chosen to play the early concertos on a harpsichord with a strong personality. It is very well balanced with a period-instrument string-group (6–2–1–1), which is probably larger than the ensemble the composer would have expected, and the resonance of the recording (made in a Budapest church) also militates against a really intimate effect. But the playing has animation and elegance, and the soloist effectively improvises his own cadenzas at the recording sessions, which increases the sense of spontaneity. Spányi introduces a highly suitable fortepiano (built by Hemel after a 1749 Freiburg) for the *D major Concerto*, Wq.13, which offers contrast of colour and dynamic in the finale, where the string tuttis are so vigorously forthright. All these performances are impressive.

For the later issues in Spányi's ongoing series he turns to the fortepiano (or the slightly more ambitious tangent piano). The *D major Concerto* (H.414), which opens BIS 785, immediately brings an aural surprise in its spectacular and rhythmic use of trumpet and drum parts in the outer movements which here, within a reverberant acoustic, serve to dwarf the fortepiano! On the other hand, the opening ritornello of the *A major* (H.422) recalls Bach's *Brandenburg Concerto No. 6*. H.446 is scored for braying horns as well as strings and is altogether more extrovert. The three-movement concertante *Sonatina in G* again includes flutes, opening with a *Larghetto* and closing with a *Polacca* (with horns). However, the six-movement *Sonatina in D* uses an unusual new format, interchanging *Andante ed arioso* ritornelli for flutes and strings (in which the soloist participates) with delicate solo keyboard fantasias. The finale is vigorous and fully scored. Spányi is inspired to give of his best throughout this collection, especially in the solo fantasias, and the accompaniments are also full of character.

The *A major Concerto* (H.437) has a darkly memorable slow movement; this and the *B flat major* work (H.434) are perhaps better known in alternative versions for cello and flute, yet they are very effective on the fortepiano, even if here the balance is less than ideal, with the rather beefy string-textures given added gruffness of attack by the period instruments.

Keyboard Concertos: in C, Wq.20; in F, Wq.38; Sonatina in D, Wq.102

**(*) BIS CD 1127. Spányi (tangent piano), Concerto Armonico, Szüts

The most fascinating work here is the concertante *Sonatina* of 1763, which is a series of joined-up and attractively diverse movements, alternating *Allegretto* and *Presto* and winningly scored to include flutes and horns. The two *Concertos* both have quite solemn *Adagios*, with the spirits lifted in the finales, although the opening allegro of the *F major* (1763) is also attractively animated. The first movement of the much earlier *C major* work (1746) opens boldly and vigorously in the orchestra and then maintains a contrasting dialogue, with continuing swift interchanges between the rather gruff tuttis and the lighter keyboard writing. Altogether a rewarding collection, very well played and recorded – the tangent piano has a most pleasing and characterful sound.

Keyboard Concerto in D min., Wq.22; Sonatinas: in C & F, Wq.103/4

(N) **(*) BIS CD 1307. Spányi (tangent piano), Concerto Armonico, Szüts

The *D minor Concerto* also exists in a version for flute, which almost certanly came first (see above), but with Bach's comparably restrained rewriting of the solo part it makes an attractive keyboard work, with the strings often playing alongside the soloist. The scoring features boisterous horns in the outer movements, the effect emphasized here by the resonant recording.

The concertante *Keyboard Sonatinas* are of a different genre, composed between 1763 and 1764, and designed to be suitable for amateur as well as professional performance. The C major work is in two movements, with a striking *Arioso* heard twice, as an introduction to each. But it is the *F major* work which is the more memorable. It opens with a solemn movement in the relative minor key, with a solo flute dominating the tutti; then comes a very catchy *Allegro* and finally a moderately fast Minuet, introducing another elegant melody, again using echoing flutes in the accompaniment.

The tangent piano seems highly suitable for these works. It has the attack of the piano (although the strings are struck vertically) and the basic timbre can be varied by stops, which can deaden the sound by slipping strips of leather or cloth against the strings. Alternatively, the *una corda* ensures that only one of the two strings belonging to each note is struck. The result is very pleasing and in this repertoire is often preferable to a drier fortepiano; it is a pity that the resonance of the recording means that the fuller orchestral tuttis are at times very forceful in relation to the smaller keyboard sound.

Harpsichord Concertos: in E, Wq.14; in G, Wq.43

(M) *** CRD (ADD) 3311. Pinnock, E. Concert – J. C. BACH (arr. MOZART): *Harpsichord Concerto* ***

The *E major Harpsichord Concerto* is one of the most ambitious that C. P. E. Bach left us. Trevor Pinnock and his English Concert (using original instruments) give admirable performances, nicely balancing the claims of modern ears and total authenticity. First-rate recording and a fascinating coupling.

Double Concerto for Harpsichord & Fortepiano in E flat, Wq.47

(BB) *** Warner Apex 2564 61137-2. Uittenbosche, Antonietta, Leonhardt Cons. – J. C. BACH: *Sinfonia concertante in F*; W. F. BACH: *Double Concerto for 2 Harpsichords*; J. S. BACH: *Double Harpsichord Concerto 1 in C min. etc.* **(*)

(i) Double Concerto for Harpsichord & Fortepiano in E flat, Wq.47; (ii) Double Concerto, for 2 Harpsichords in F, Wq.46; (i) Sonatina for 2 Harpsichords & Orchestra in D, Wq.109

(BB) *** DHM (ADD) 05472 77410-2. (i) Kelley, Van Immersel (fortepiano or harpsichord); (ii) Curtis, Leonhardt; Coll. Aur., Maier

The spirited and delightful *E flat Concerto for Harpsichord and Fortepiano* comes from Bach's last year. It has a chirpily inviting opening theme and is given a wholly persuasive account by Kelley and van Immersel, with the solo instruments naturally balanced and a warm acoustic assisting a lively, authentic accompaniment. The *Sonatina for 2 Harpsichords and Orchestra* is ambitiously scored for three trumpets, two each of flutes, oboes and horns, bassoon and strings. The first movement (of two) is characteristically quirky and diverse. There are surprises, too, towards the end of the second, which is a Minuet with variations. The *F major Concerto*, scored for strings with the addition of two horns, is still thoroughly representative of this composer, with a memorable *Largo* slow movement. It is also very well played and, at its very economical price, this is a reissue not to be missed.

The Leonhardt performance is also attractive, the fortepiano has a bold, tangible image, and the interplay between the two soloists is felicitous, within a good overall balance.

This comes generously coupled with four other Double Concertos by members of the Bach family, but the Deutsche Harmonia Mundi disc is first choice.

Collection: (i) *Harpsichord Concerto in C min., Wq.43/4 (H.474)*; (ii) *Quartets (Trios) for fortepiano, flute & viola: in A min., D & G, Wq.93/95 (H.537/9)*; (iii) *Flute Sonata (Hamburg) in G, Wq.133 (H.564)*; (ii) *Trio Sonatas: in B min., Wq.76 (H.512)*; *in A, Wq. 146 (H.570)*; *in D (H.585)*. *Keyboard Fantasia in C, Wq.61/6*; *Freye Fantaisie in F sharp min., Wq.67 (H.300)*; *Rondo in C min., Wq.59/4 (H.283)*; *Sonatas: in A min., Wq.49/1 (H.30)*; *in E min., Wq.59/1 (H.281)*; *in G min., Wq.65/17 (H.47)*; *12 Variations in D min. on 'Folie d'Espagne', Wq.118/9 (H.263)*

☞ **(N) (B) ***** DHM/BMG 82876 67374-2 (3). Staier (harpsichord or fortepiano), with (i) Freiburg Bar. O, Hengelbrock; (ii) Les Adieux; (iii) Hazelzet & Hejo Bäss –
J. C. BACH: *Quintets;* J. C. F. BACH: *Quartet ****

A truly outstanding set in every way, with the works all linked by Andreas Staier's outstanding keyboard playing. The *Concerto* is presented with the lightest touch and is splendidly accompanied by the Freiburg group. The *Trio Sonatas* were designated by Bach as quartets, but no bass part survives, and the players of Les Adieux decided against an improvised addition since Bach handles the fortepiano, flute and viola so musically and equally. Certainly the bright, transparent textures of the original instruments here are as delightful as Bach's invention. The little two-movement *Flute Sonata* is also charmingly done The *Trio Sonatas* are no less engaging: they span three decades between them and so give a good idea of the composer's development. All these works are played with admirable style by members of Les Adieux, and are excellently recorded.

But what makes this box so eminently desirable is the disc of solo keyboard music, so full of the composer's quirky rhythmic touches that one often has to smile at his (and Staier's) precociousness, especially so in the *'Freye' Fantaisie* and the *G minor Sonata*. Yet despite the music's unpredictabiliy, each of the sonatas has a delightfully melodic slow movement. Andreas Staier is obviously in his element and relishes each musical twist and turn with remarkable spontaneity. The engaging *Variations* on the theme we know as *La Folia* and the *Sonatas in A minor* and *G minor* are played on the harpsichord and the rest of the programme on a fortepiano. This is the finest collection of the composer's keyboard music in the catalogue.

Oboe Concertos: in B flat, Wq.164; in E flat, Wq.165; (Unaccompanied) Oboe Sonata in A min., Wq.132

(BB) **(*) Naxos 8.550556. Kiss, Ferenc Erkel CO –
MARCELLO: *Concerto **(*)*

József Kiss's playing is sensitive and musical, if without quite the individuality of Holliger (now deleted), but he is very well accompanied and beautifully recorded. The solo *Sonata* is also worth having on disc, although one might have liked more dynamic light and shade here. But with an enjoyable Marcello coupling this is well worth its modest cost.

(i) *Organ Concertos: in G, Wq.34; in E flat, Wq.35. Sinfonia for Strings in C, Wq.182/3. (Solo) Organ Sonatas: in F; A min.; G min.; D, Wq.70/3–6*

(M) *** DHM/BMG 82876 51863-2. Oster; (i) Ens. Parlando, Oster or Adorf

This collection is quite a find. It seems likely that these works

(or most of them) were written for Princess Anna Amalia at the Prussian court; she owned a splendid 22-stop instrument (without pedals). The two *Concertos* are quite different in style. The *G major* of 1754 is written in 'ritornello style' with five orchestral ritornellos alternating with four extended solo episodes. The *E flat major Concerto* (more robustly scored to include horns in the outer movements) has a normal concertante interplay between soloist and orchestra. In between the two concertos comes a *String Sinfonia* in the form of an Italian overture, with a closing *Allegretto*.

The four solo *Sonatas* are fantasia-like, with phrases continually in imitation, using echoing registration, or a chordal sequence, followed by a more florid response. The slow movements are simple and serene, and are registered to bring out the organ colouring, with the *Adagio* of the *G minor*, Wq.70/6, very piquant.

Rainer Oster plays splendidly and uses a highly suitable organ in Saint-Adelphe-in-Albestroff, Moselle, which has a rich palette and fine sonorities. He is able to create a spatial effect with the answering phrases on different stops, which technique the princess must have relished. Don't be put off by the opening tutti of the *G major Concerto* on the first CD, where the period strings are a bit fierce and biting; the quality soon settles down, and it is generally excellent. The orchestra provides characterful accompaniments, while the organ itself sounds first rate.

Berlin Sinfonias: in C; in F, Wq.174/5; in E min.; in E flat, Wq.178/9; in F, Wq.181

*** Cap. 10 103. C. P. E. Bach CO, Haenchen

The playing of Haenchen's excellent C. P. E. Bach group is alert and vigorous, with airy textures and attractively sprung rhythms. Modern instruments are used in the best possible way. Excellent sound.

(i) *Berlin Sinfonias: in C, Wq.174; in D, Wq.176; 6 Hamburg Sinfonias, Wq.182/1–6*; (ii) *Quartets for Flute, Viola, Fortepiano & (optional) Cello: 1 in A min.; 2 in D; 3 in G, Wq.93–5*. (iii) *(Keyboard) Fantasy in C, Wq.59/6*

(B) *** O-L (ADD) (IMS) Double 455 715-2 (2). (i) AAM, Hogwood; (ii) McGegan, Mackintosh, Pleeth, Hogwood; (iii) Hogwood

Christopher Hogwood continually has one responding as to new music, not least in the dark, bare slow movements. The two *Berlin Symphonies* with wind make refreshing listening. The three *Quartets* are all beautifully fashioned, civilized pieces with many of the expressive devices familiar from this composer. Hogwood uses a fortepiano rather than harpsichord and makes a good case for doing so (with documentary support in the notes). The playing overall is absolutely first rate; the recording is most naturally balanced and could hardly be bettered. Moreover the keyboard *Fantasia in C* is a most remarkable work – it is roughly contemporary with Mozart's *C minor Fantasy* and is more than just a bonus. It is splendidly played by Hogwood.

6 Hamburg Sinfonias, Wq.182/1–6

(BB) *** Naxos 8.553285. Capella Istropolitana, Benda

(N) (M) *** DG 476 7109; or DG Blue 477 5000. E. Concert, Pinnock

(BB) ** Warner Apex 2564 60369-2. Franz Liszt CO, Rolla

The six *Hamburg String Sinfonias* are magnificent examples of Bach's later style when, after the years at the Berlin court, he had greater freedom in Hamburg. They are particularly striking in their unexpected twists of imagination, and they contain some of his most inspired and original ideas. Using modern instruments at higher modern pitch, Benda directs light, well-sprung accounts. With more varied textures and tonal contrasts than in most period performances, Benda's have extra light and shade. The darkly chromatic slow movement of No. 3, for example, has a hushed mystery rarely caught. The excellent sound is full and open, as well as immediate. This makes an excellent bargain recommendation.

The performing style of the English Concert concentrates less on abrasive authenticity than on a concern for 18th-century poise and elegance, without losing any degree of validity. This disc in its LP format won the *Gramophone* Early Music Award in 1980, and the excellent recording sounds splendidly fresh and clear in its remastered format. As can be seen above, the disc has been simultaneously reissued in DG's Archiv Blue mid-priced series.

Rolla's are expert performances (especially the *B minor*, Wq.182/5, which receives the liveliest advocacy), but they are a little dry, as are the recordings, which are bright and clinical. The Naxos disc is the one to have.

4 Hamburg Sinfonias, Wq.183/1–4

(BB) **(*) Naxos 8.553289. Salzburg CO, Lee – W. F. BACH: *Sinfonia in F* **(*)

The Naxos Salzburg versions are freshly played, the results spick and span, with polished playing from strings and woodwind alike. Obviously Yoon K. Lee knows about period-performance styles and, though modern instruments are used here, textures are clear and clean. While there is plenty of dramatic contrast, the expressive music seems just a shade cool. But the results are certainly stimulating, and this disc is worth its modest cost.

CHAMBER AND INSTRUMENTAL MUSIC

Duo for 2 Clarinets (Adagio & Allegro), H.636; 6 Sonatas for Pianoforte, Clarinet & Bassoon, H.516–21; Flute Sonatas (for flute and harpsichord): in E, H.506; in C, H.573; Oboe Sonata (for oboe & continuo) in G min., H.549; Pastorale for Oboe, Bassoon & Continuo

(M) *** CPO 999 508-2. Fiati con Tasto, Cologne

This delightfully diverse cross-section of Carl Philipp Emanuel's chamber music for wind instruments could hardly be bettered as a source of exploration. The use of period instruments is expert, and the Flute Sonatas are engagingly perky and given attractively sprightly performances by Karl Kaiser, while Alfredo Bernadini's plaintive oboe timbre is as affecting in the sonatas as it is in the gentle Pastorale (a siciliano), in duet with a doleful bassoon. The felicitous interplay of the six Sonatas for Fortepiano, Clarinet and Bassoon at times anticipates Mozart, and Harald Hoelden's fortepiano contribution here is as nicely judged as his harpsichord playing in the flute sonatas. The recording is very natural and gives a vivid projection to one and all.

Flute Sonatas: Wq.86; in C, Wq.87; in E min., Wq.124; in D, Wq.129; (Solo) Sonata in A min., Wq.132; (i) 12 2- & 3-part kleine Stücke for 2 Flutes, Wq.82

*** ASV CDGAU 161. Hadden, Carolan; Headly; (i) Walker

Flute Sonatas: Wq.124; in G; in A min.; in D, Wq.127–9; in G, Wq.133; in G, Wq.134

*** Cap. 10 101. Haupf, Pank, Thalheim

The *Flute Sonata in A minor* was written in 1747 for Frederick the Great, who, Bach said, 'could not play it'. Nancy Hadden certainly can (using a copy of a Dresden period transverse flute). The 12 *Little Pieces* (1770) alternate trio and duo format and are very jolly and entertaining until the expressively wilting closing *Andante*. Bach favoured the clavichord rather than the harpsichord as appropriate in duo sonatas, and Lucy Carolan proves a fine partner; and the balance is equally well judged in the works with additional viola da gamba.

Six more of the composer's 11 flute sonatas feature on Capriccio in fresh, lively performances, well recorded, ending with one written in Bach's Hamburg period, two years before he died, altogether lighter and more conventionally classical, presenting an interesting perspective on the rest.

11 Flute Sonatas (for flute & continuo), Wq.123–31; 133–4; Sonata for Solo Flute in A min., Wq.132

*** MDG L 3284/5 (2). Hünteler, Bylsma, Ogg

Matthias Claudius said of Carl Philipp Emmanuel, 'I cannot describe his adagio playing better than by comparing it to speech,' and it is in the *A minor Sonata*, Wq.132, that he finds rare expressive artistry. His *G major Sonata*, Wq.133, from his Hamburg years, written for the young blind flautist Friedrich Dulon, shows both wit and virtuosity. The music is rarely predictable, and Bach's mastery and inventiveness are always in evidence. There is nothing watery about the coolly beautiful timbre that Hünteler achieves on his transverse flute, and he proves a masterly exponent of this rewarding repertoire and obviously enjoys an excellent rapport with his continuo partners, Anner Bylsma and Jacques Ogg. The MDG recording is exemplary.

Quartet in D for Flute, Viola, Cello & Fortepiano, Wq.94; Solo Flute Sonata in A min., Wq.132; Sonata in G min. for Viola da gamba & Harpsichord, Wq.88: Larghetto. Trio Sonatas: in C for Flute, Violin & Continuo, Wq.147; in C min. for 2 Violins & Continuo (Sanguineus & Melancholicus), Wq.161

⊶ ✪ *** Channel CCS 11197. Florilegium

A wholly delightful collection. Ashley Solomon's exquisite flute-playing dominates the *D major Quartet*, and the balance with Neal Peres da Costa's delicate fortepiano is quite perfect, registering subtle nuances of dynamic contrast. The *Larghetto* for viola da gamba and harpsichord then makes a melancholy interlude, before Bach's highly imaginative dialogue between Sanguine and Melancholy brings quixotic changes of mood and tempo, even in the central *Adagio*, where Sanguineus eventually wins and makes way for a light-hearted finale. The haunting solo *Flute Sonata* is recorded at a lower pitch to suit the period instrument used; the timbre has an almost alto sonority. Finally comes the diverting *Trio Sonata in C major*, which brings winningly imitative interchanges between flute and violin, particularly exuberant in the finale. The recording balance could hardly be bettered.

Sinfonia a tre voci in D; 12 Variations on 'La Folia', Wq.118/9; Trio Sonatas: in B flat, Wq.158; in C min. (Sanguineus & Melancholicus), Wq.161/1; Viola da gamba Sonata in D, Wq.137

*** Hyp. CDA 66239. Purcell Qt

The *Variations on 'La Folia'* are fresh and inventive, particularly in Robert Woolley's hands, but the remaining pieces are hardly less rewarding. The Purcell Quartet play with sensitivity and seem well attuned to the particularly individual sensibility of this composer. The Hyperion recording is well balanced, faithful and present.

Trio Sonatas *(for flute, violin & continuo), Wq.145–51*
*** CPO 999 496-2 (2). Les Amis de Philippe

The *Trio Sonata in D minor*, Wq.145, shows evidence of being an early work, probably from the early 1730s, as its style has more in common with Johann Sebastian than his son. The *A minor Sonata*, Wq.148 (which opens the first disc), dates from 1735 and shows an advance to a mellower, more richly lyrical character. The other early works are difficult to date as they were revised in 1747, but the three *Berlin Sonatas* (Wq.149–51), which were written in 1745 and 1747, are obviously further advanced in style. The *C major*, Wq.149, opens with a characteristically perky *Allegro di molto*; the *G major*, Wq.150, has a particularly expressive *Adagio*, and Wq.151 in D is strikingly characterful throughout. This is not to say that the earlier works are not personable and appealing, especially in performances as fresh, sensitive and sprightly as by this excellent group of C. P. E.'s 'friends' – Manfredo Zimmermann (transverse flute), Manfredo Kraemer (violin), Ludger Rémy (harpsichord) and Monika Schwamberger (cello). The recording is truthfully balanced in an attractive acoustic.

KEYBOARD MUSIC

Allegretto con variazioni, Wq.118/5; Fantasia & Fugue in C min., Wq.119/7; Sinfonias in G & F, Wq.122/1 & 2; Sonatas in D min. & E, Wq.65/24 & 29
(N) *** BIS CD 1328. Spányi (fortepiano)

Miklós Spányi is curiously unpredictable, but this is one of the very finest collections in his series. He plays the *Allegretto* with its six unpretentious variations with pleasing simplicity, and then gives a bravura account of the *C minor Fantasia* with its rolling chords and the following four-voiced *Fugue*, one of Bach's most impressive works, which at its close echoes the end of the *Fantasia*. Both *Sinfonias* are Bach's own skilful transcriptions of orchestral works and are hence among the most readily attractive of his keyboard pieces, and Spányi plays them straightforwardly and with obvious enjoyment. The *Sonata in D minor*, written in 1749, is unique in being written in five brief movements; however, the first two and last two sections might be regarded as linked. Again Spányi is on excellent form, as he is in the companion *E major Sonata*, which has a normal, three-movement structure. He plays a modern copy of a 1749 Silbermann fortepiano which, very well recorded in a spacious acoustic, has a full sonority that seems just right for this programme. But don't have the volume level too high.

Character pieces: La Borchward; La Pott; La Böhmer; La Complaisante; Les Langueurs tendres; L'Irrésolué; La Journalière; La Capriceuse, Wq.117/17, 18, 26, 28, 30–33; Keyboard Sonatas in E, Wq.62/17; E flat, Wq.65/28
** BIS CD 1087. Spányi (clavichord)

Miklós Spányi is recording all Bach's keyboard sonatas for BIS and previous issues include the *Prussian Sonatas* (BIS 878/9), the early *Sonatinas* and *Sonatas* (BIS 882 and 963), the *'Easy' Sonatas* (BIS 964 and 978), and the works from 1748 to 1749 (BIS 1086). But throughout his survey we have found his curious linear style, with its pauses, somewhat eccentric. That applies also to the present issue, even though both the *Sonatas* here, especially the E flat work, with its bold finale, are well worth having on disc. But what makes this issue worth exploring are the *'Petites pièces de caractère'* written after the style of Couperin, Dandrieu and Rameau. It is a pity Spányi's treatment is not more subtle, but certainly *La Capriceuse*, with its rapid changes of rhythm, sudden interruptions and moments of silence, is strongly portrayed, as indeed is the virtuosic *La Böhmer*, a folk dance with a thumping accompaniment that Spányi obviously relishes. He is well recorded, though the volume control should be restrained in playback.

Petite Pieces: La Gleim; La Bergius; La Prinzett; L'Herrmann; La Buchholz; La Stahl; L'Aly Rupalich, Wq.117/19–21, 23–5 & 27. Sonatas: in A min. & B min., Wq.21/22; in E min., Wq.65/30
(N) *(*) BIS CD 1198. Spányi (clavichord)

Bach's *Petite Pieces* were associated with the composer's friends and acquaintances, and sometimes were obviously intended as portraits. Certainly the most appealing piece here, *La Gleim*, comes over well as a portrayal of a melancholy poet. *La Buchholz* was almost certainly associated with a privy councillor of that name, a patron of literature. But here Spányi's impulsive style negates the elegance of the description, and elsewhere sudden bizarre bursts of *fortissimo* (without explanation in the notes) interfere with the pictorialism. In the *Sonatas* the jerky linear playing remains an irritant and the *A minor* work (for instance) obviously has more potential than is realized here; its Allegretto Siciliano finale, played staccato, loses all its charm. The recording itself is clear and realistic.

Keyboard Sonata in A min. *(Württemberg), Wq.49/1*
(M) **(*) Sony (ADD) SMK 87753. Gould (piano) – J. S. BACH: *Aria variata*, etc.; D. SCARLATTI: *Sonatas* **(*)

The quirky outer movements of this attractive sonata are precisely projected by Glenn Gould's clear, clean articulation, and he finds a contrasting serenity in the slow movement. The recording is dry but truthful.

Keyboard Sonatas: in F sharp min., Wq.52/4; in E min., Wq.59/1; in D, Wq.61/2; in G, Wq.62/19; in G min., Wq.65/17; in C min., Wq.65/31; Andante contenerezza; Rondos: in A, Wq.58/1; in C min., Wq.59/4; in D min., Wq.61/4
☞ ✪ *** DG 459 614-2. Pletnev

Altogether remarkable playing, even by Pletnev's exalted standards. He finds both the wit and depth of this music, and the resource of keyboard colour and refinement of articulation are pretty awesome. And what interesting music it is! He receives very natural recorded sound from the DG team.

Keyboard Sonatas 1–6 *(Damensonaten), Wq.54/1–6*
*** BIS CD 1088. Spányi

The *Six Sonatas 'pour le clavecin à l'usage des Dames'* are from the mid-1760s. Despite their title, which suggests they were written for the composer's less accomplished female students, they require more proficiency than their name implies; although they are mostly light and delicate and require less technical prowess than some of his other keyboard pieces, they also display some degree of complexity and sophistication. And, in these performances, no mean charm. Miklós

Spányi is at his very finest here. He uses a clavichord modelled on an instrument by Christian Gottlob Hubert and is expertly recorded. This is the ninth disc in the survey he is making of the complete C. P. E. Bach sonatas and it is easily the most enjoyable so far.

Keyboard Sonatas: in F & D, Wq.62/9 & 13; in G & G min., Wq.65/26 & 27; Suite in E min., Wq.62/12
**(*) BIS CD 1189. Spányi (clavichord)

Keyboard Sonatas in C, G min. & B flat, Wq.65/16, 17 & 20; Fantasia in E flat, W. deest (H.348)
**(*) BIS CD 1195. Spányi (fortepiano)

The first CD here (BIS 1189) offers four diverse *Sonatas* written in Berlin between 1749 and 1752; they have a *galant* style, although the *E minor* work has more than a little depth. The *Suite* is more strikingly individual and has an attractively expressive *Sarabande* and a lively closing *Gigue*. These works suit the clavichord admirably, and Miklós Spányi uses an appropriate modern copy of a 1785 Dresden instrument, which is recorded most successfully.

The second CD here offers three large-scale *Sonatas* and a *Fantasia*. All three *Sonatas* come from the period 1746–7 and are therefore associated with the new Silbermann fortepiano, which had so captivated Frederick the Great in 1746. Spányi uses a copy of a 1749 Silbermann instrument. The *Sonatas* bear witness to C. P. E. Bach's increasing engagement with the fantasia, for all three have the long, sweeping roulades found in his unmeasured fantasias. Each has some of the rhythmic vagaries that lend them an improvisatory character. As with earlier issues in the series, Spányi plays with scholarly feeling and freshness, although some will not take to his nudging pauses and his *rubato* in slow movements, which sound considered rather than spontaneous. Very truthful recorded sound.

Keyboard Sonatas for Harpsichord: in E min., Wq.62/12; in E min., Wq.65/5; in B flat, Wq.65/20; for Fortepiano: in B flat, Wq.65/44; in C, Wq.65/47; in G, Wq.65/48
**(*) Met. MET CD 1032. Cerasi (harpsichord or fortepiano)

In the *Harpsichord Sonatas* the resonance of the recording does not help Carole Cerasi, but her very free musical line often brings a fussy effect. The opening *Allemande* of the *E minor Sonata*, Wq.62/12, is an obvious example of her very free rubato, and the lively closing *Gigue* too, marvellously articulated as it is, needs a cleaner outline, with the decorations less boldly done.

In the works played on the fortepiano it is the impulsiveness of Cerasi's approach that is daunting, with sudden *forte* accents and forward surges, especially well demonstrated in the finale of the *G major*, Wq.65/48. The preceding *Adagio* is more successful, but even here she seems determined to prove that C. P. E. Bach's music is quixotically temperamental.

Keyboard Sonatas: in B flat, Wq.62/16; in G, Wq.65/22; in E min., Wq.65/30; in A, Wq.65/37; in G, Wq.65/48; in A, Wq.70/1; Rondo in E flat, Wq.61/1
(BB) *** Naxos 8.5536450. Chaplin (piano)

François Chaplin plays these works freshly and confidently on the modern piano rather than on the clavichord (or harpsichord) which the composer would have expected, and he makes no attempt to imitate those instruments. The result demonstrates how forward-looking these sonatas are, especially the appealingly expressive slow movements of the later

works. The closing *Rondo* of 1786 is particularly successful in using the piano's fuller sonority.

ORGAN MUSIC

Organ Sonatas: in F; A min.; D; G min., Wq.70/3–6; Fantasia & Fugue in C min., Wq.119/7; Fugue in D min.; Prelude in D, Wq.70/7; 6 Variations
**(*) Mer. CDE 84313. Gifford (Organ of the Chapel of Hull University)

Carl Philipp Emanuel's organ music is a far cry from the magisterial polyphony of his father's output. The *Prelude* in *D major* opens grandly, but its imitative passage-work is simplicity itself and rather jolly. However, while the four lightweight *Sonatas* make no great technical demands on the performer, they are engaging enough when freshly presented, as here, with a lively, 'orchestral' palette. The *Variations* are in much the same style. The Chapel organ at Hull University has bright, glowing reeds and Gerald Gifford's playing is persuasive.

VOCAL MUSIC

Anbetung dem Erbarmer (Easter Cantata), Wq.243; Auf schicke dich recht feierlich (Christmas Cantata), Wq.249; Heilig, Wq.217; Klopstocks Morgengesang am Schöpfungsfeste, Wq.239
*** Cap. 10 208. Schlick, Lins, Prégardien, Elliott, Varcoe, Schwarz, Rheinische Kantorei, Kleine Konzert, Max

Klopstocks Morgengesang am Schöpfungsfeste ('Klopstock's morning song on the celebration of creation') is a work of many beauties and is well performed by these artists. *Anbetung dem Erbarmer* ('Worship of the merciful') is another late work, full of modulatory surprises. *Auf schicke dich recht feierlich* ('Up, be reconciled') and *Heilig* ('Holy') (1779) are Christmas works. A record of unusual interest, very well performed and naturally recorded.

Die Auferstehung und Himmelfahrt Jesu (The Resurrection and Ascension of Jesus)
*** Hyp. CDA 67364. Schwabe, Christoph Genz, Stephan Genz, Ex Tempore, La Petite Bande, Kuijken
(N) **(*) EuroArts DVD 2054039. Karthäuser, Hardt, Christoph & Stephan Genz, Ex Tempore, La Petite Bande, Kuijken – J. S. BACH: Cantata 11 (Ascension) ***

Carl Philipp Emanuel Bach succeeded his godfather, Telemann, as director of music in Hamburg. There he wrote three superb oratorios, of which this is the last and, as he thought himself, the finest, given a masterly performance here under Sigiswald Kuijken. The 22 sections, most of them brief, present the Resurrection and Ascension of Jesus in a vigorously dramatic way. So the opening recitative is punctuated by violent timpani, and the theme of triumph keeps recurring in a powerful chorus repeated three times, while the baritone soloist echoes that theme in one of his brilliant arias. Striking obbligatos for high baroque trumpet, horn and bassoon colour the arias, most of them brisk, while the work's centrepiece is an ecstatic lyrical duet, a plea for forgiveness, with soprano and tenor lines interweaving in heavenly harmony. All three of the soloists sing with clear, fresh tone, the tenor of Christoph Genz nicely related to the baritone of Stephan Genz, while the choir, Ex Tempore, brings bite and clarity to the dramatic choruses, with each half ending on an elaborate fugue.

Kuijken subsequently re-recorded his interpretation on DVD against the very suitable backcloth of St Nikolai's Church, Leipzig. Two of the soloists are the same, but all four make very fine contributions, with the soprano/tenor duet, *Vater deiner schwachen Kinder*, outstanding. Although the timpanist makes a dramatically visual contribution to the tenor recitative, *Judäa zittert!*, for the most part this is a more lyrical, less dramatic account than the earlier, Hyperion recording, which has greater range and bite. The English translation offered with the EuroArts DVD is pretty feeble, embarrassing at times, but one does not need to use it again after a first hearing. The cameraman explores the church as well as offering every angle of the performers, including a bird's-eye-distance shot; and it can be aurally disconcerting when, after watching the performers directly, the camera moves round to their backs in order to centre on Kuijken while, of course, the sound does not change. When will producers realize that for a complete illusion of a real performance, the camera itself must be more stable. However, this is still musically very enjoyable, and the coupling of Johann Sebastian's *Ascension Cantata* is superbly done.

St Matthew Passion (1785)
(N) ** Capriccio 60 113. Dewald, Jordan, Kupfer, Zelter Ens. der Sing-Akademie zu Berlin, Daus

When C. P. E. Bach finally managed to quit his subservient job in the court of Frederick the Great in Berlin, he inherited the post long held by his godfather, Telemann: director of music for the five principal churches in Hamburg. One of his duties was to write seasonal music, including settings of the Passion story. His approach was severely practical, and this example, his last, dating from 1785 but neglected for over 200 years, demonstrates his story-telling gift rather than any great musical insights. In 53 brief sections lasting a mere 55 minutes, he covers what inspired his father to some of his most sublime flights. C. P. E. borrowed unashamedly, sometimes from his father, and the chorales and recitatives, not too different in style from those of J. S. B., make up the greater part of this setting, with brief turba (crowd) choruses intervening dramatically. There are only three arias, one each for tenor and bass soloists near the beginning and another for the bass near the end, where he develops his own *galant* style. Otherwise the high spots come in several fine choruses, one with chromatic writing worthy of his father. Recorded live, the Zelter Ensemble of the Berlin Singakademie under Joshard Daus give a refreshing performance, rather slow in the chorales but otherwise very well paced, and with three first-rate soloists, the tenor Thomas Dewald and the baritones Daniel Jordan and Jochen Kupfer.

BACH, Johann Christian (1735–82)

Overtures: *Adriano in Siria; Alessandro nell'Indie; Amadis des Gaules* (including *Ballet Music*); *Artaserse; La calamita de cuori; Carattaco* (with 2 *Marches*); *La Cascina; Cantata a tre voci* (*Birthday Cantata*); *Carattaco; Catone in Utica; La clemenza di Scipione* (with 2 *Marches*); *Endimione; Gioas, re di Giuda; La Giulia; Orione; Gli Uccellatori; Lucio Silla; Temistocle; Il tutore e la pupilla; Zanaida. Symphony in D,* Op. 18/1
(N) (M) *** CPO 999 963-2 (2). Hanover Band, Halstead

These opera overtures form an attractive collection from the master of the *galant* style, Johann Christian Bach. Most are in the usual fast–slow–fast pattern, with the fast movements fresh and vigorous, and with the composer's elegant turns of phrase constantly delighting the ear. The extended 25-minute ballet from *Amadis des Gaules* is particularly attractive, with some especially deft writing for the strings and some lively choruses, all finished off with a very catchy *Tambourin*. The Hanover Band under Halstead play with characteristic style, and the CPO recording is excellent.

Amadis des Gaules: Overture & ballet music. **Overtures:** *Endimione; Lucio Silla; Temistocle*
☞ ✧ *** CPO 999 753-2. Hanover Band, Halstead

These four overtures, written for key opera houses in London and Paris and for the Mannheim court, are full of bubbling vitality and striking melodic invention and are sprinkled with attractive orchestral colourings throughout. All the overtures are in the Italian overture form (slow–fast–slow), with central movements of the utmost elegance and grace. The *Amadis des Gaules Overture*, with its crescendi and excited writing, looks to the classical/early romantic period, and one senses a composer embracing all the virtues of a true musical cosmopolitan. The 25-minute ballet music *Amadis* is a delight and includes some vocal items with chorus (curiously not mentioned on the CD leaflet). Performances and recording are both first class, with Halstead providing the right amount of authentic vigour, while allowing the music's charm to come through.

Bassoon Concerto in E flat; Flute Concerto in D; Oboe Concerto 1 in F
*** CPO 999 346-2. Ward, Brown, Robson, Hanover Band, Halstead
Bassoon Concerto in B flat; Flute Concerto in G; Oboe Concerto 2 in F
*** CPO 999 347. Ward, Brown, Robson, Hanover Band, Halstead

These six early concertos had an obvious influence on Mozart's wind concertos, and if you enjoy the Mozart works you will surely enjoy these by J. C. Bach. The *First Oboe Concerto* on the first disc is another version of the *G major* work for flute on the companion CD. The so-described *D major Flute Concerto* is a joining of two separate movements taken from independent manuscripts – and how well they work together! The *Bassoon Concerto in E flat* is an alternative version of the *Sinfonia concertante* in the same key for two violins and cello included below (on CPO 999 348). The *Bassoon Concerto in B flat* is an even more winning piece, with a dignified *Adagio* set against a delectably frivolous finale. The six concertos are played with much felicity by Jeremy Ward, Rachael Brown and Anthony Robson respectively, and Halstead's accompaniments are a model of elegance. The recording is full and natural. Most enjoyable.

5 Berlin Harpsichord Concertos: in B flat; F min.; D min., E & G. Concerto in F min. (attrib.)
*** CPO 999 393-2 & 999 462-2 (available separately). Halstead, Hanover Band

Bach's early Berlin concertos (from the 1750s) in these splendid performances from Anthony Halstead, directing the Hanover Band from the keyboard, are appealingly fluent, full of flair and vitality. Slow movements are deeply expressive and outer movements bustle vigorously. The *F minor* is the best known of the set and it is splendidly played here; however, the *Poco adagio* of the *G major* is in some ways the most searching of all, when the concentration of the hushed *pianissimo* playing is so compelling. The attributed *F minor Concerto* may or may not be by J. C. B. Its outer movements certainly have a fine energetic thrust. The recordings throughout are in the demonstration bracket.

Harpsichord Concertos, Op. 1/1–6

*** CPO 999 299-2. Halstead, Hanover Band

Bach composed three sets of *Clavier Concertos*, each comprising six works. Those wanting a set of Op. 1 on period instruments could hardly better this CPO disc. These are all simple two-movement works, except for No. 4 with its wistful central *Andante* and No. 6, which closes with variations on *God Save the King*. The performances are sprightly and perfectly in scale and the balance quite excellent.

Clavier Concertos, Op. 7/1–6

*** CPO 999 600-2. Halstead, Hanover Band

Clavier Concertos, Op. 13/1–3; Concerto in E flat

*** CPO 999 601-2. Halstead (piano), Hanover Band

Clavier Concertos, Op. 13/4–6; Op. 14 in E flat

*** CPO 999 691-2. Halstead (piano), Hanover Band

Anthony Halstead has recorded Op. 7 in chamber form with just an accompanying string trio. His solo playing is very persuasive and the result is delightfully intimate. *No. 5 in E flat*, the finest of the set, surely anticipates Mozart from the very opening onwards; it has a touchingly expressive slow movement in C minor and a dancing finale; the disc is worth having for this performance alone. With recording of the highest quality, this is one of the most attractive CDs so far in Halstead's Hanover Band series.

Bach's Op. 13 appeared in 1777 and shows him still developing in ideas and orchestration. These are most enjoyable concertos and they are played here with great freshness by Halstead. The *Concerto in E flat* is almost identical with the *Sinfonia concertante* in the same key, but in the present version the soloist has a strongly dominant role.

Op. 14 is more ambitious, although it may have been written earlier. The first movement is characterized by the frequent use of 'Scotch rhythmic snaps' and the finale demands considerable virtuosity from the soloist, readily forthcoming here. Halstead uses a Broadwood pianoforte and accompanies himself brightly and gracefully.

(i) Harpsichord Concerto in B, Op. 13/4; Symphonies: in E flat; G min., Op. 6/6

***** HM HMC 901803. Berlin Akademie for Alte Musik, Mai –
C. P. E. BACH: *Flute Concerto* *****

This collection starts with the *E flat major Symphony* which, as it opens (unexpectedly) with a delicate *Adagio*, may be of questionable authenticity. Here it is introduced very quietly indeed and, although there is a slow crescendo, a diminuendo follows and the listener all but jumps when the *Allegro molto* begins with an explosive *fortissimo*. As usual with the Akademie, the string virtuosity is breathtaking, but *fortissimos* are gruff and accents are strong – although the pizzicato *Allegretto* brings a brief, charming interlude.

The *Keyboard Concerto* that follows is one of Johann Christian's most characterful. It has a bold opening, but the harpsichord enters elegantly, and the contrasts between tutti and the gentle keyboard response are very nicely managed. The *Adagio* brings more pizzicatos and an amiably *galant*

melody, and the finale produces an equally winning set of variations on the Scottish folksong 'The yellow-hair'd laddie'.

Bold, staccato accents underline the vigorous, highly strung opening movement of the *G minor Symphony*, followed by lurching duplets in the similarly tense *Andante*. The finale is played and accented with enormous gusto, and again the orchestra is impressively virtuosic. So, if you like the abrasive style of this period-instrument ensemble, these works show the group at their most virile and exciting, and they are very well recorded. Carl Philipp Emanuel's *Flute Concerto* provides an agreeable light-hearted contrast.

Harpsichord Concerto in D (arr. by Mozart as K.107/1)

(M) * CRD (ADD) 3311. Pinnock, E. Concert – C. P. E.
BACH: *Harpsichord Concertos* *****

It seemed more sensible to list this work here as it tends to get lost in the Mozartian discography. In the early 1770s the teenage Mozart turned three sonatas by J. C. Bach into keyboard concertos, adding accompaniments and ritornellos as well as cadenzas. The first of the group makes an excellent coupling for the two fine C. P. E. Bach concertos.

Sinfonias concertantes: in A for Violin & Cello; in E for 2 Violins, Cello, Flute & Orchestra; in E flat for 2 Clarinets, Bassoon, 2 Horns & Flute. Flute Concerto in D; Andante

*** CPO 999 538-2. Hanover Band, Halstead

Sinfonias concertantes: in B flat for Violin, Cello & Orchestra; in D for 2 Violins & Orchestra; in F for Oboe, Bassoon & Orchestra

*** CPO 999 547-2. Hanover Band, Halstead

Sinfonias concertantes: in C for 2 Violins, Cello & Orchestra; in D for 2 Flutes, 2 Violins & Cello; in E flat for 2 Oboes, 2 Horns, 2 Violins, 2 Violas & Cello

*** CPO 999 628-2. Hanover Band, Halstead

Sinfonias concertantes: in E flat for 2 Violins, Oboe & Orchestra; in E flat & in G for 2 Violins, Cello & Orchestra

**(*) CPO 999 348-2. Hanover Band, Halstead

Johann Christian Bach might well be regarded as the true father of the sinfonia concertante, for (among others, including Karl Stamitz) he wrote over a dozen of them for various solo instruments, and they are of a consistently higher musical quality than those of most of his contemporaries. Even so, these works have rather long (some might feel too long) orchestral ritornellos with which each first movement opens. The solo writing is always effective; the orchestration (with flutes, horns, clarinets) adds to the interest of tuttis and colours slow movements. Finales are usually robust minuets.

The first disc opens with one of Bach's very finest works: in *E major*, with four soloists. The *E flat* work for woodwind has charmingly interwoven solo parts against a busy orchestral backing. The two-movement *A major* work for violin and cello again shows Bach's invention at its most elegantly appealing. With the inclusion of the recently discovered slow movement for the *Flute Concerto in D major* (see above, on CPO 999 346-2), this (first) disc offers the most rewarding collection of the four listed above.

The *B flat Concerto* on the second disc has an ambitious opening *Allegro maestoso* (almost Mozartian), which leads to a *Larghetto* dominated by a melancholy violin cantilena. The piquant oboe solo in the *Andante* of the *E flat* work on the fourth disc is ear-catching; the two works for violins and cello are more uneven.

On CPO 999 628-2 the most attractive movement in the

ambitious but uneven C major work is the finale when the oboes and horns add much to the character of the tuttis; in the D major the interplay of the two solo groups (flutes and string trio) is ear-tickling enough, but the E flat work, with its elaborate scoring for nine instruments (solo oboes, horns and strings) has the most colourful textures of all the sinfonias concertantes here, and the closing Minuet is very diverting. Throughout, the performances have warmth and proper finish and refinement; the balance and recording are excellent and the effect is undoubtedly authentic.

Sinfonia concertante in C for Flute, Oboe, Violin, Cello & Orchestra; Sinfonia in G min., Op. 6/6; Sinfonia for Double Orchestra in E flat, Op. 18/1; Sinfonia in D, Op. 18/4; Overture: Adriano in Siria
**(*) Chan. 0540. AAM, Standage

The *Sinfonia concertante* is perhaps the most conventional piece here, but it has a memorable finale. The *G minor Sinfonia* shows J. C. Bach's imagination at full stretch, lively and intense. Excellent, well-played 'authentic' performances, but the characteristic Chandos resonance prevents the crispest focus.

Sinfonia concertante in F for Oboe, Cello & Orchestra, T.VIII/6
(BB) **(*) Warner Apex 2564 61137-2. Schaeftlein, Bylsma, Leonhardt Cons. – C. P. E. BACH: *Double Concerto for Harpsichord & Fortepiano* ***; W. F. BACH: *Double Concerto for 2 Harpsichords*; J. S. BACH: *Double Harpsichord Concerto 1 in C min.,* etc. **(*)

The *Sinfonia concertante* in F is a pleasing but not distinctive work in two movements, here given a good rather than a distinctive performance. The key work of this collection is Carl Philipp Emanuel's engaging *Concerto for Harpsichord and Fortepiano*.

Complete Sinfonias

6 Sinfonias, Op. 3 (CPO 999 268-2); *6 Sinfonias* (Hummel), *Op. 6* (CPO 999 298-2); *3 Sinfonias* (Markordt), *Op. 8; Sinfonias: in C* (Venier 46) (2 versions) *in F* (manuscript) (CPO 999 383-2); *Sinfonias, Op. 9/1–2* (standard and original versions); *Op. 9/3; Sinfonia in E flat with Clarinets* (CPO 999 487-2); *6 Sinfonias, Op. 18* (CPO 999 752-2)
(M) *** CPO 999 896 (5). Hanover Band, Halstead

J. C. Bach's *sinfonias* shared the same three-part format as the Italian opera overture, and at that time the descriptive titles were interchangeable. Indeed, as we shall discover in Opp. 9 and 18, Bach borrowed overtures from his own operas to include in his published sets. The works were initially intended for his London concerts and the music was usually published concurrently. Although there have been pioneering LP recordings from Marriner of Op. 3, from Zinman of Op. 6, Opp. 8–9 and Op. 18 (on Philips), and a fine set of Op. 18 from Münchinger (on Decca), this is the first complete coverage on period instruments, and very impressive it is. Bach's Op. 3 was premièred in April 1765. They are agreeably spirited works, scored for strings, with oboes and horns in subsidiary roles, offering arguments, both pithy and imaginative, with the vigorous finales particularly enjoyable. They also possess, in the words of Erik Smith, 'an unusual wealth of singing melody', which becomes even more striking in the slow movements of the later *sinfonias*. The very first of the set in D is an outstanding example. Its first movement sounds very like early Mozart, the *Andante* has an easy-going charm

and the infectious finale with its dancing triplets is not a bar too long. This forms the pattern for the works that follow, each of which is still individual. Bach's invention seldom falters, and the *Andante, sempre piano* of No. 4 is particularly engaging.

There is confusion over what constitutes Op. 6 as these symphonies were published in both Paris and Amsterdam (in 1770), and the present set is best identified by the name of the Dutch publisher, Johann Julius Hummel. The works themselves show an advance on Op. 3 in the more prominent use of oboes and horns; first movements, too, are more restlessly energetic, and flutes are introduced in the slow movements of Nos. 2 and 4. The rather striking *Andante* of No. 3 is for strings alone and is in C minor. No. 5, which was very popular in Bach's own time, brings a memorable 'walking' *Andante*, but the finest of the series is No. 6, in the minor key throughout, and an outstanding, forward-looking work in every way. Its remarkable slow movement (again for strings alone) is followed by a very strong finale.

Three of the six symphonies published by the Amsterdam publisher S. Markordt as Bach's 'Op. 8' had already been published by Hummel and are little different from those equivalent versions. The others have a separate identity but are comparatively conventional and are most appealing for their elegant slow movements. No. 3 is attractively vigorous and is more like an opera overture. No. 4 is the most enterprising, with the horns strongly underlining the opening *Allegro molto*, while the closing Minuet brings charm in the Trio and unpredictability in the reprise.

Both versions of the *C major Symphony* were described as *Venier No. 46* by their Parisian publisher. They begin alike, but the second and third movements are enjoyably different, while the Huberty version of Op. 6/1 brings only minor changes, except for the addition of the Minuet and Trio (with an agreeable horn duet) which is almost certainly an interpolation from another composer. However, it seems almost certain that the 'manuscript' *Symphony in F* is authentic. Its restless development certainly anticipates Mozart, and the *Andante*, scored for flute and strings, is delightful, with the lilting finale equally good-natured.

With the Op. 9 *Sinfonias* we enter more familiar territory, and the Hanover Band are in their element, with crisp dynamic allegros while making the most of the sensuous element in slow movements, notably the delectable melody of No. 2. The third of the set is an arrangement of the spirited *Overture Zanaida* with a *galant* central *Andante*, winningly scored, and a brief whirlwind finale. Halstead then gives us the opportunity of hearing the first two symphonies in different versions, first with the familiar economical scoring for strings, oboes and horns, and second in Bach's original scoring, featuring bassoon and clarinets, which colour the music quite differently. The work described as *Symphony in E flat with Clarinets* (but which also includes a bassoon) appears to be the original version of the last of the Op. 9 collection: it is a splendid work with a quite delectable and wholly characteristic *Andante*, and makes full use of the clarinet duetting.

The six ambitious Op. 18 *Sinfonias* represent the peak of Bach's achievement, with the odd-numbered works scored for double orchestra. Here there are two completely separated string groups; the oboes and horns are allotted to the first orchestra, the flutes placed with the second, while the bassoon has divided loyalties.

Of the even-numbered works No. 2 is the *Overture Lucio Silla*, No. 4 draws for its slow movement on an arrangement of the *Andante* from the *Overture Temistocle*, and No. 6 uses music from two other operas from the 1770s, namely *Amadis des Gaules* and *La clemenza di Scipione*, although this work seems likely to have been cobbled together by an arranger rather than by Bach himself. The scoring in the double orchestral works is sophisticated, with much pleasing interplay, the horns and woodwind alternating in the finale of No. 3; the pastoral *Andante* of Op. 18/5 again inimitably joins strings and flutes together. This is the disc to go for if you want a sampler, followed by Op. 9. But the whole set is very rewarding, the playing is both personable and vigorously sparkling, if at times with slightly abrasive strings. The recording is clear and full, perhaps a little dry, but expansive enough in Op. 18, although here the ample tuttis are somewhat less refined.

Sinfonia in G min. Op. 6/6

*** Cap. 10 283. Concerto Köln – C. P. E. BACH: *Harpsichord Concerto*; J. C. F. BACH: *Sinfonias*; W. F. BACH: *Sinfonia*, etc. ***

This remarkable symphony, written in 1770 when Johann Christian was at the height of his fame, is altogether darker than is usual with this most gracious and genial of composers, and the Concerto Köln discover greater dramatic intensity in it than do most ensembles. It is recorded as excellently as it is played.

Sinfonias, Op. 9/1–4; Sinfonia concertante in A for Violin & Cello; Sinfonia concertante in E flat, for 2 Violins, Oboe & Orchestra

(BB) **(*) Naxos 8.553085. Camerata Budapest, Gmür

This disc is of interest, not so much for the symphonies as for the two *Sinfonias concertantes*, which are beautifully played, with stylish and appealing contributions from the soloists, all drawn from the orchestra. The solo writing in the *A major Sinfonia concertante* is quite elaborate, and in the *Andante* of the *E flat* work there is a surprise when the two solo violins introduce Gluck's *Che farò senza Euridice*, which is then taken up by the oboe. The second of the Op. 9 symphonies has a real lollipop *Andante con sordini*, presented over a pizzicato accompaniment. The balance is excellent.

6 Sinfonias (Grand Overtures), Op. 18

(BB) **(*) Naxos 8.553367. Failoni O, Gmür

Hanspeter Gmür and the Failoni Orchestra give warm and graceful accounts of Op. 18. The spirited allegros are slightly cushioned by the resonance, but slow movements are phrased very musically (particularly the lovely, almost Handelian melody of Op. 18/2, which also has a fine oboe solo from László Párkányi). However, Halstead's CPO disc is a clear first choice.

CHAMBER MUSIC

Quintets (for Flute, Oboe, Violin, Viola & Continuo) in G & F, Op. 11/2–3

(N) (B) *** DHM/BMG 82876 67374-2 (3). Staier, Les Adieux – C. P. E. BACH: *Collection*; J. C. F. BACH: *Quartet* ***

These *Quintets* find Johann Christian at his most delightful. The music, delectably scored for unexpected combinations of instruments, is wonderfully fresh and inventive in these spirited performances, which come in a highly recommendable box of chamber and keyboard music mainly by C. P. E. Bach.

6 Symphonies for Wind Sextet (1782)

(N) **(*) Test (ADD) SBT 1345. L. Wind Soloists, Brymer

These six four-movement wind sextets were probably written for Vauxhall and they certainly would make attractive open-air music. The combination of clarinets, horns and bassoons was also that of many mid-eighteenth-century military bands, and three of the six symphonies have a *March* in place of a Minuet, while No. 4 has a closing *Cotillion*. Attractive period music, presented with finesse and polish; but if the writing has plenty of surface charm, there is little real substance – although these players make the most of slightly solemn slow movements. However, for relaxed and undemanding listing, this immaculately transferred CD (of a 1968 Decca recording produced by Erik Smith) can be recommended; performances and recording are of a predictably high standard.

6 Sonatas for the Harpsichord or Pianoforte with an Accompaniment for the Violin or Flute, Op. 16

(BB) **(*) CPO 999 494-2. Salzburger Hofmusik

These attractive, *galant* sonatas (from 1779) are given period performances with plenty of life. They are played alternately on the violin, by Christine Busch, whose timbre is rather thin and edgy, and flute (Karl Kaiser), where the smoothness of sound is nigh perfect. In both cases the balance cannot be faulted and Wolfgang Brunner's contribution (on a most pleasing Viennese fortepiano) is first class throughout. The music itself is lightweight, spontaneously spirited and tuneful. A fair bargain.

KEYBOARD MUSIC

Music for Piano Duet

Sonata for 2 Pianos in G; Sonatas for Piano (4 hands) in C, Op. 15/5–6; in A & in F, Op. 18/5–6

*** CPO 999 848-2. Genova & Dimitrov – W. F. BACH: *Piano Duet Sonatas* ***

Dedicated to the Countess of Abingdon, these are two-movement works of great charm – just sample the delightful tick-tock *Allegretto Rondo* (with variations) of Op. 15/6 which all but anticipates Schubert in its rhythmic felicity and even includes a hint of a drone bass. The writing for two pianos in its companion *G major Sonata* brings an attractive role interchange, well brought out by the (unexaggerated) stereo placement here; while in the works for four hands, which are hardly less inventive and appealing, the players exchange ideas at the same piano. The elegant Minuet which closes the *A major* is quite lyrical, and the *F major* balances an extended classical first movement with an almost Mozartian closing *Rondo*. The performances are first class, bringing out the music's character and touches of wit with attractive geniality and obvious enjoyment. Excellent recording, too.

Solo Keyboard Music

6 Sonatas for Harpsichord or Fortepiano, Op. 5; arr. of Haydn's Symphony 53 (Impériale)

(BB) ** CPO 999 530-2. Hoeren (fortepiano)

The six *Sonatas*, Op. 5, are comparatively simplistic works in two (or, more often, three) movements. Harold Hoeren plays them straightforwardly but does not make them sound distinctive. He is faithfully recorded. The attribution of the arrangement of the Haydn symphony carries a fair degree of doubt; but this disc is inexpensive.

Harpsichord Sonatas: in E & C min., Op. 5/5–6; in C min.; E flat & A, Op. 17/2–3 & 5
(M) ***CRD (ADD) 3453. Black (harpsichord)

Virginia Black plays a modern copy of a Goujon harpsichord, c. 1740, and she is beautifully recorded, the sound clear and robust, with the instrument given a vivid presence (yet not aggressively close) against a warm backgound ambience. Her account of the two-movement *E flat major Sonata*, Op. 17/3, with which she opens her recital, immediately catches the listener's ear, and the *Prestissimo* finale of Op. 17/2, which comes second, is most infectious, the articulation admirably crisp. The *Adagio* of Op. 5/5 is elegant and nicely paced, and again the rhythmically winning finale demands and receives easy virtuosity. A most attractive disc.

Fortepiano Sonatas, Op. 17/1–6
(BB) **(*) CPO 999 788-2. Hoeren

CPO continue their series with Op. 17, which was first published in Paris in 1774 as Op. 12; the London Edition did not arrive until 1779! To complicate matters further, the works themselves were probably written in the 1760s. They are uneven, but contain some attractive individual movements (Brahms had a personal copy of the charming *Andante* of the three-movement *C minor* work, No. 2 of the set, and its finale is equally diverting). Elsewhere there are pre-echoes of Mozart. Harald Hoeren uses an Adlam fortepiano and the performances here are very accomplished and have plenty of character, even if at times the playing is a trifle metrical. Good recording.

VOCAL MUSIC

(i; ii) Laudate pueri Dominum (Vesper psalm); *(i) Salve regina* (antiphon); *(ii) Si nocte tenebrosa* (motet)
*** CPO 999 718-2. (i) Kirkby; (ii) Schäfer; Orfeo Bar. O, Gaigg

Johann Christian's church music was all composed to Latin texts. The lyrical melodic flow has an unmistakable operatic feel to its line and the *Laudate pueri Dominum* is very reminiscent of Mozart in the opera house. The felicitous scoring (especially the use of horns and flutes at the opening of the *Gloria Patri*) is most winning. Both the solo works are very attractive too. Emma Kirkby sings the extended *Salve regina* very beautifully, and she navigates brilliantly the sparkling bravura of the second section, *Ad te clamatus*, before the melting *Ad te suspiramus*. The solo motet, *Si nocte tenebrosa* closes with a supplication to the Virgin. Its wide range of mood is splendidly caught by the pleasing tenor voice of Markus Schäfer. Michi Gaigg's accompaniments are stylish and very well played, and the recording is first class.

BACH, Johann Christoph Friedrich

(1732–95)

Sinfonias: in D min.; E flat, WfV 1/3 & 10
*** Cap. 10 283. Concerto Köln – C. P. E. BACH: *Harpsichord Concerto*; J. C. BACH: *Sinfonia*; W. F. BACH: *Sinfonia*, etc. ***

Both works recorded here are elegantly written and are well worth investigating. The playing of the Concerto Köln is

enthusiastic, sprightly and sensitive, and they are excellently recorded.

Flute Quartet 3 in C, WfV 1/3
(N) (B) *** DHM/BMG 82876 67374-2 (3). Staier, Les Adieux
  – C. P. E. BACH: *Collection*; J. C. BACH: *Quintets* ***

This *Flute Quartet* is untroubled by any depths, but it has a genuine charm that is beautifully communicated by these accomplished players. Excellent recording.

BACH, Johann Michael (1745–1820)

Friedens (Peace) Cantata: Jehova, Vater der Wesen; Advent Cantata: Mache dich auf, werde licht; Christmas Cantata: Das Volk, so im Finstern wandelt; Other Cantatas: Herr, wie sind deine Werke so gross und viel; Wie lieblich sind auf den Bergen die Füss der Boten
*** CPO 999 671-2. Schmithüsen, Crook, Schwarz, Mertens & soloists, Rheinische Kantorei, Kleine Konzert, Max

Johann Michael Bach the younger was of the generation of Johann Sebastian's grandchildren, but a direct relationship to J. S. B. cannot surely be determined. Yet the family genes are strong, for he was a most talented composer and musician. His ambitious *Peace Cantata* was first performed in 1815 and obviously celebrates the end of the Napoleonic wars. It is a remarkable work, with the opening bass recitative evoking the horrors of battle. Then a series of engaging solos and choruses celebrates the spirit of peace and the omnipotence of God. The other four cantatas are equally inventive; each includes a major aria for one of the soloists, often of striking expressive beauty. The music is full of attractive melody and uses the orchestral palette, woodwind and (especially) horns, to provide colourful accompaniments. With a splendid team of soloists, all in fine voice, an excellent chorus and lively orchestral detail this CD is very highly recommended. You cannot fail to enjoy it; even if the sound is a bit over-resonant, the overall balance is good.

BACH, Johann Sebastian (1685–1750)

The Art of Fugue, BWV 1080
**(*) Opus OP30191. Concerto Italiano, Alessandrini
The Art of Fugue; A Musical Offering, BWV 1079
(B) *** Ph. (ADD) Duo 442 556-2 (2). ASMF, Marriner
(B) **(*) Double Decca (ADD) 467 267-2 (2). Stuttgart CO, Münchinger

How to perform *The Art of Fugue* has always presented problems, since Bach's own indications are so sparse. Sir Neville Marriner in the edition he prepared with Andrew Davis has varied the textures most intelligently, giving a fair proportion of the fugues and canons to keyboard instruments, organ as well as harpsichord. Marriner's style of performance is profoundly satisfying, with finely judged tempi, unmannered phrasing and resilient rhythms, and the 1974 recording is admirably refined. Similarly, in the *Musical Offering* Marriner uses his own edition and instrumentation: strings with three solo violins, solo viola and a solo cello; flute, organ and harpsichord. The performance here is of high quality, though some of the playing is a trifle bland. It is excellently recorded and is among the most successful accounts of the work.

Rinaldo Alessandrini's approach to *The Art of Fugue* is to

seek out its underlying expressive and colouristic possibilities. So, after opening with strings, he scores each of the *contrapuncti* for different groups of wind and/or stringed instruments, allotting only the four canons to the harpsichord. The result has distinctive aural appeal, especially as the work proceeds, with *Contrapuncti 12* and *13* engagingly colourful dialogues involving flute, oboe da caccia, violin, viola, bassoon, cello and harpsichord. Alessandrini's solution may not be conventional but the playing (on baroque instruments) is full of life and easy to enjoy. The recording is clear, within a pleasing ambience.

Münchinger's Stuttgart performances also have much to offer. The instrumentation generally allots the fugues to the strings and the canons to the solo woodwind, varied with solo strings. After the incomplete quadruple fugue, Münchinger rounds off the work with the chorale prelude, *Wenn wir in höchsten Nöten sein*, BWV 668a, in principle quite wrong but moving in practice. *The Musical Offering*, although somewhat more relaxed, also brings playing of genuine breadth and eloquence, particularly in the *Trio Sonata* and the performance has many of the fine qualities that distinguished Münchinger's Bach. The recordings were made a decade apart (in the mid-1960s and 1970s) but are of vintage quality, with warmth and excellent presence and detail.

Brandenburg Concertos 1–6, BWV 1046–51

🔘 ✹ *** TDK **DVD** DV-BABBC. Freiburg Bar. O, Von der Göltz

(M) *** Warner Elatus 2564 61773-2 (2). Il Giardino Armonico, Antonini

(B) *** Hyp. Dyad CDD 22001 (2). Brandenburg Consort, Goodman

(M) *** Sony SM2K 89985 (2). Tafelmusik, Lamon

(N) (B) *** CfP 5 86043-2 (2). Hanover Band, Halstead

(BB) *** Virgin 5 61552-2 (2). OAE

*** Telarc CD 80368 (1–3), CD 80354 (4–6) (2). Boston Bar., Pearlman

(N) (BB) **(*) EMI Encore 5 85792-2 (1–4); 5 85795-2 (5–6 & *Orchestral Suite 1, BWV 1066*). ASMF, Marriner

(M) **(*) Astrée ES 9948 (2). Concert des Nations, Capella Reial de Catalunya, Savall

**(*) BIS CD 1151/2 (with additional early version of first movement of No. 5). Bach Coll., Japan, Suzuki

(M) ** Sony (ADD) 515 305-2 (2). Marlboro Festival O, Casals (with rehearsal sequences included)

(i) *Brandenburg Concertos 1–3*; (ii) *Flute Concerto in E min., BWV 1059 & 35* (reconstructed Radeke)

(BB) *** Warner Apex (DDD/ADD) 2564 61363-2. (i) Amsterdam Bar. O, Koopman; (ii) Rampal, Paillard CO, Paillard

Brandenburg Concertos 4–6; (i) Suite 2 in B min.

(BB) *** Warner Apex (DDD/ADD) 2564 61364-2. Amsterdam Bar. O, Koopman, (i) with Rampal

(i) *Brandenburg Concertos 1–6*; (ii) *Flute Concerto in G min., BWV 1056; Double Concerto for Violin & Oboe*

(B) *** Double Decca (ADD) 443 847-2 (2). (i) ECO, Britten; (ii) ASMF, Marriner

Brandenburg Concertos 1–6; (i) Violin Concertos 1–2 in E; (i, ii) Double Violin Concerto in D min., BWV 1041–3

(BB) *** Virgin 2x1 5 61403-2 (2). Scottish Ens., Rees; with (i) Rees; (ii) Murdoch

(i) *Brandenburg Concertos 1–6*; (ii) *Double Violin Concerto*; (ii; iii) *Concerto for Violin & Oboe*

(B) *** Ph. Duo (ADD/DDD) 468 549-2 (2). ASMF; (i) Marriner; (ii) Kremer (violin & cond.); (iii) Holliger

Brandenburg Concertos 1–6; Brandenburg Concerto 5 (early version), *BWV 1050a; Triple Concerto in A min. for Flute, Violin & Harpsichord, BMV 1044*

(M) *** Virgin 5 45255-2 (2). La Stravaganza, Hamburg, Rampe

Brandenburg Concertos 1–3; (i) *Oboe d'amore Concerto in A min., BWV 1055*; (i; ii) *Double Concerto for Oboe & Violin in C min., BWV 1060*

🔘 (M) *** DG Blue 471 720-2. E. Concert, Pinnock; with (i) Reichenburg; (ii) Standage

Brandenburg Concertos 4–6; (i) *Triple Concerto*

🔘 (M) *** DG Blue 464 220-2. E. Concert, Pinnock; (i) with Beznosiuk & Standage

It is remarkable that so early in the DVD era we should have such an outstanding set of period-instrument performances of the *Brandenburgs*, appropriately recorded at Castle Cöthen. For while Bach dedicated and sent them to the Margrave of Brandenburg in 1721, they were composed earlier while Bach was Kappellmeister at the Cöthen court. The castle's Spiegelsaal has been magnificently restored and makes a visually entrancing backcloth for the recordings. The spacious room seems also to have an ideal acoustic for a chamber group.

The Freiburgers play their period instruments with great finesse and warmth. Inner detail is clear, there is no edginess on the strings or linear distortions in the expressively played slow movements. The choice of tempi seems near ideal and Gottfried von der Göltz, who directs proceedings almost impassively but with obvious commitment, plays with an easy virtuosity which is engrossing to watch.

The cameras often cover the players as a group, but also move around among them, and it is fascinating to observe in close-up the pair of horns in No. 1 producing amazing florid passages from simple coils of brass, creating the notes by their controlled embouchures with no valves to press. Similarly, the brilliant soloist in No. 3, Friedemann Immer, uses a primitive early trumpet, with his fingers covering and uncovering holes, rather like a transverse flute. The one effect of balance that is less than ideal (though it often happens in the concert hall) is the harpsichord, which can hardly be heard at all in tuttis, although the solo in the *Fifth Concerto*, played with flexible virtuosity, comes over splendidly. Overall these splendidly alive performances are enormously stimulating and enjoyable. Apart from their very direct musical communication, one learns so much about Bach's contrapuntal writing when the camera directs the eye, without spotlighting, to the performing instruments.

The various competing audio versions of the *Brandenburg Concertos* offer excellence in every price range. The exhilarating set from the Milanese period-instrument group, Il Giardino Armonico, directed by Giovanni Antonini, is among the finest. Tempi seem perfectly judged, buoyantly brisk but never exaggeratedly so. The playing is alive and joyful; slow movements have expressive warmth and serenity. The wind and brass soloists are first rate, the recorder, flute and oboe sounds are equally characterful, and the strings are bright and clean and without edge; the recording is both warm and freshly transparent so that one can hear the harpsichord coming through quite naturally. A splendid achievement.

Pinnock's *Brandenburgs*, from the beginning of the 1980s, continue to hold their place at or near the top of the list, particularly now they are being reissued at mid-price to launch DG Archiv's new 'Blue' label. These performances represent the peak of his achievement as an advocate of authentic performance, with sounds that are clear and refreshing but not too abrasive. Interpretatively he tended to adopt faster speeds in outer movements, relatively slow in *Andantes*, a style that others have since followed, but from first to last there is no routine. Soloists are outstanding, and they are equally persuasive in the concertante works transcribed from better-known originals.

However, Roy Goodman's excellent Hyperion set of the *Brandenburgs* is on a Dyad, with two discs offered for the price of one. The stylish, lively playing is another attractive example of authenticity, lacking something in polish but none in spirit, with the last three concertos especially fresh. Characterization is strong, and slow movements are often appealingly expressive. Tempi of outer movements are very brisk but often bring the lightest rhythmic touch. Very good sound.

Tafelmusik seldom disappoint, and their set of *Brandenburgs* is enjoyably robust and spontaneous, with the horn soloists in No. 1 playing mid-eighteenth-century hand horns with lustily extrovert vigour and bravura, so that one does not mind that intonation is not always exact. Crispian Steele-Perkins, the trumpet soloist in No. 2, plays with remarkable sophistication. Tempi are brisk but never hurried, and slow movements relax warmly as they should, with bulges in phrasing fairly minimal. The recording is excellent and this is now offered at mid-price.

Among period-instrument performances, Anthony Halstead and the Hanover Band are thoroughly recommendable in their own right. The playing is consistently fresh and tempi are admirably chosen to give a feeling of liveliness and a joyful alertness without pressing on too hard, while lyrical lines flow pleasingly throughout and textures are clean and transparent. The recording was made in the Henry Wood Hall and its warm acoustic provides an admirable background ambience.

With the direction shared among four violinists – Monica Huggett, Catherine Mackintosh, Alison Bury and Elizabeth Wallfisch – the Orchestra of the Age of Enlightenment brings all the advantages of light, clear textures and no sense of haste, even when a movement is taken faster than has become traditional.

Martin Pearlman sets attractively lively and spirited tempi in outer movements, yet slow movements are not pressed on but are allowed space to expand. Solo playing is excellent, although Friedemann Immer's trumpet does have a few moments of ungainliness in No. 2. The *Sixth Concerto* is played with one instrument to a part and uses violas da gamba. Not quite a first choice but, with first-class Telarc sound and a feeling that the players are enjoying themselves, this is well worth considering.

Marriner's recording from the mid-1980s was his third and had the advantage of George Malcolm's harpsichord continuo in Nos. 1–3 and 5, while John Constable took his place persuasively in the remainder. The playing brings fine teamwork, superb ensemble and well-judged speeds, never too hectic. However, although the playing is freshly conceived, it also has an urbane quality (though this does not apply to Malcolm's contribution). Yet the vividness of the playing is enhanced by the excellent sound, full in texture

and transparent too, and the *First Orchestral Suite*, included as a bonus, has a comparably easy, stylish quality.

Koopman's account is among the most attractive of those using period instruments, suitable for those who prefer expressive contrasts to be less sharply marked. Like Pinnock, Koopman is not afraid to read *Affettuoso* in the slow movement of No. 5 as genuinely expressive and warm, though without sentimentality. As with Pinnock, the players are one to a part, with excellent British soloists included in the band. In the *Third Concerto*, Koopman effectively interpolates the *Toccata in C*, BWV 916, as a harpsichord link between the two movements. The sound is immediate, but not aggressively so. As a bonus on the first disc, Rampal gives a nimble (1972) performance of what is obviously one of his favourite Bach flute concertos, as he has recorded it more than once. Reconstructed by Winfried Radeke, it is based on a harpsichord concerto fragment, BWV 1059 (originally in D minor), and instrumental material from Bach's *Cantata No. 35*. The second disc is even more generous in including Rampal's participation in the *Second (B minor) Orchestral Suite*.

The La Stravaganza *Brandenburgs* are immensely vigorous and stimulating. Overall, the tempi must be among the fastest on record (disconcertingly so upon first hearing) and the throaty hand-horn playing in the outer movements of No. 1 brings the most extraordinary virtuosity – while the intonation is remarkably accurate. The buoyant outer movements of No. 2 are just as spirited. The strings in No. 3 play with enormous zest, particularly in the finale. Yet throughout, slow movements bring the warmest expressive feeling. No. 5 is offered not only in the 1719 version we know so well but also in an earlier, chamber version, probably written in Carlsbad a year earlier, when Bach had only five players at his disposal. It is refreshingly light-textured. The *Triple Concerto* is played with comparable spirit and finesse. Outstandingly realistic recording.

The Jonathan Rees modern-instrument Scottish *Brandenburgs* are in every way competitive. Directed with much spirit, they are freshly played, with warm, clear recording and excellent internal balance. The tempi seem very apt when the players so convey their enjoyment and the sound has such a pleasing bloom. Rees then becomes the principal soloist in equally warm, buoyant performances of the *Violin Concertos*, with Jane Murdoch matching his stylishness in the *Double Concerto*.

Marriner's 1980 ASMF set of *Brandenburgs* is a leading contender among performances on modern instruments. Above all these performances communicate warmth and enjoyment. In the coupled versions of the two double concertos the violin soloist is Gidon Kremer, who also directs the accompanying ensemble. In the *Double Violin Concerto* he adopts (by electronic means) both solo roles, so these interpretations cannot be accused of any kind of artistic inconsistency – indeed they have the vigour and forward thrust of a determined advocate, in slow as well as fast movements. The result, although stylish, is rather cool, and the same comment might be applied to the *Concerto for Violin and Oboe*, although here Holliger's contribution dominates tellingly, especially in the Adagio. However, these comments do not detract from the appeal of the Marriner *Brandenburgs* which, as a Duo, could still be first choice for those not insisting on the use of period instruments and fast tempi. It is preferable to the Trio alternative including the *Suites* (470 934-2).

Britten made his recordings in the Maltings concert-hall in 1968. The result is a fairly ample sound that in its way goes well with Britten's interpretations. There is some lack of textural delicacy in the slow movements of Nos. 1, 2, 4 and 6; but the bubbling high spirits of the outer movements are hard to resist, and the harpsichordist, Philip Ledger, follows the pattern he had set in live Britten performances, with Britten-inspired extra elaborations a continual delight. As a makeweight for the Double Decca reissue, two more of Marriner's stylish performances of reconstructions of Bach's harpsichord concertos for alternative instruments have been added. First-class (originally Argo) recording, too.

Savall's period-instrument set of the *Brandenburgs* is engagingly fresh. Textures are clear and often translucent, allegros are spirited but never rushed, tempi are well judged (No. 3 is just right), and slow movements are warmly expressive yet in perfect style. There is some breathtaking bravura from the hand horns in No. 1, especially in the closing *Polacca and Trio*, but Friedemann Immer's slightly throttled trumpet sounds in No. 2 are less appealing. At other times, ensemble and intonation are not without flaw, but there is no edginess from the strings, and the spontaneous vitality of this playing carries the day. Not a first choice, but an enjoyable one when the sound is so pleasing.

Suzuki's set of the *Brandenburgs* with his Bach Collegium of Japan proves to be a partial disappointment. Of course there is much fine playing from woodwind soloists and the strings (especially in the finale of No. 3), and Suzuki's own harpsichord contribution, notably in Nos. 4 and 5, is pretty dazzling, with the excellent balance ensuring that he does not dominate the texture too much. Tempi are comparatively relaxed and the overall atmosphere is sunny. But unfortunately the brass players let the side down. The horns are clumsy in the first movement of No. 1, and the trumpet playing of Toshio Shimasda in No. 2, using a specially designed coiled trumpet, sounds strained. He uses lip-pressure instead of valves or 'tone-holes' to 'bend' the upper partials to achieve accurate intonation, and some listeners may find the result slightly uncomfortable; others might relish the extra tension.

Casals was 88 in 1964 when he directed these highly individual performances in the Marlborough Festival in Vermont. By the standards of those days, some of the speeds (especially that for the first movement of No. 2) tended to be fast; now they have fallen into place. Against the fast tempi he gives slow, heavy accounts of the two concertos for strings alone, Nos. 3 and 6. Throughout, his approach to phrasing is unashamedly romantic, with a high degree of warm expressiveness in slow movements (sample the *Adagio* of No. 1). Yet the music-making is full of vitality and affection, and the nimble piano-playing of Rudolf Serkin in the first movement of No. 5 makes a refreshing change from the usual harpsichord. An endearing reminder of a great musician, while the sound is pleasingly full, to suit the warm-hearted nature of the performances.

Brandenburg Concertos 1–6; (i) Violin Concertos 1–2; in D min., BWV 1052; in G min., BWV 1056; (i; ii) Double Violin Concerto; (i; iii) Triple Violin Concerto in D, BWV 1064; (i; iv) Concerto for Violin & Oboe; (i; v) Concerto for Flute, Violin & Harpsichord

(BB) *** Virgin 5 62281-2 (4). OAE, with (i) Wallfisch; (ii) Bury; (iii) Pavlo Beznosiuk, Mackintosh; (iv) oboist unnamed; (v) Lisa Beznosiuk, Nicholson

With the direction of the *Brandenburgs* shared by four violinists – Monica Huggett, Catherine Mackintosh, Alison Bury

and Elizabeth Wallfisch – the Orchestra of the Age of Enlightenment brings all the advantages of light, clear textures and no sense of haste, even when a movement is taken faster than has become traditional. For the *Violin Concertos* Elizabeth Wallfisch takes over as director and principal soloist. Her playing is vigorously stimulating and does not shirk tasteful expressiveness, and her colleagues are equally expert. Their playing has plenty of character, with felicitous, unfussy decoration; the arrangement of the *Triple Harpsichord Concerto* for three violins is particularly convincing. Excellent balance and believable sound make this a highly recommendable budget reissue.

Brandenburg Concertos 1–6; A Musical Offering

(M) *** Virgin (DDD/ADD) 5 61154-2 (2). Linde Cons., Linde

Quite apart from the considerable bonus of the *Musical Offering*, many will prefer the Linde version of the *Brandenburgs*, for the 1981 EMI recording is rather fuller than Pinnock's DG Archiv sound, with the strings very slightly less immediate. In *Brandenburg No. 3* there is a distinct gain in body and warmth, and No. 6 (also for strings alone) again brings a slightly more ample texture, without loss of inner definition. In the *Musical Offering* (recorded a year earlier) Linde is as stylish and accomplished as any of his rivals, and he and his six colleagues offer the preferred version of this work, using original instruments. They are again warmly as well as clearly recorded; indeed the analogue-to-digital transfer is particularly natural, and this set offers remarkable value.

Brandenburg Concertos 3 & 5; Orchestral Suite 3

(B) **(*) DG (IMS) 2-CD 474 287-2 (2). BPO, Karajan –
VIVALDI: *Four Seasons; L'Estro armonico, Op. 3/1, 4, 7, & 10 ***

When Karajan's recordings of the *Brandenburg Concertos* and *Orchestral Suites* first appeared we acknowledged the fine playing but were unenthusiastic about the conductor's interpretations, commenting: 'It is not simply that Karajan uses a large unauthentic orchestra, but that his approach is essentially harmonic rather than contrapuntal – there is little feeling of forward movement.' In his notes (specially written for this reissue, as one of DG's 'Karajan Collection') Richard Osborn, a renowned admirer of the conductor, tells how the *Orchestral Suites*, dating from 1964, received 'unexpected praise from a panel of English musicologists taking part in the BBC's "Interpretations on Record" series. The recordings were heard "blind" and no one was more surprised than the panel to discover that they had been lavishing praise on Berlin Bach.' Certainly the *Third Suite* comes up well enough here. It is more vigorous than we remember – an example (again to quote R.O.) of 'Bach treated in the grand romantic manner.' The opulent string-playing in the famous *Air* may be anachronistic, but it is certainly beautiful, and the current remastering also finds an unexpected freshness of detail in the pair of *Brandenburgs*, which, although tempi are comparatively measured, are neither flaccid nor self-indulgent. In Osborn's assessment they are 'a model of urbane music-making, stylish and acute'.

(i) Brandenburg Concerto 5; Triple Concerto in A min. for Flute, Violin & Keyboard. Italian Concerto

*** Sony SK 87326. Murray Perahia, (i) with Jaime Martin, Kenneth Sillito, Jacob Lindberg, ASMF

Murray Perahia's *Fifth Brandenburg* is among the freshest and most enjoyable we have heard since Serkin and the Busch Chamber Players, which of course it surpasses in recording quality, but also, in many respects, artistically. The excellence of Perahia's Bach is well known, and his peerless pianism is perfectly displayed in the *Concerto in the Italian Style*, where refinement of keyboard colour and feeling for line are much in evidence. Bach playing on the keyboard (piano or harpsichord) does not come better than this.

Complete solo and multiple concertos

(i) *Harpsichord Concertos 1 in D min.; 2 in E; 3 in D; 4 in A; 5 in F min.; 6 in F; 7 in G min., BWV 1052–8;* (ii) *Double Harpsichord Concertos: 1 in C min.; 2 in C; 3 in C min., BWV 1060–2;* (i–iii) *Triple Harpsichord Concertos 1 in D min.; 2 in C, BWV 1063–4;* (i–iv) *Quadruple Harpsichord Concerto in A min., BWV 1065;* (i; v–vi) *Triple Concerto for Flute, Violin & Harpsichord, BWV 1044;* (vi–vii) *Double Concerto for Oboe & Violin in C min., BWV 1060;* (vii) *Oboe d'amore Concerto in A, BWV 1055;* (vi) *Violin Concertos 1 in A min.; 2 in E;* (vi; viii) *Double Violin Concerto in D min., BWV 1041–3*

(B) *** DG (ADD/DDD) 463 725-2 (5). E. Concert, Pinnock, with (i) Pinnock; (ii) Gilbert; (iii) Mortensen; (iv) Kraemer; (v) Beznosiuk; (vi) Standage; (vii) Reichenberg; (viii) Wilcock

Harpsichord Concertos 1–7; Double Harpsichord Concertos 1–3 & in C, BWV 1061a; Triple Harpsichord Concertos 1–2; Quadruple Harpsichord Concerto

⟿ (M) *** DG Trio (ADD/DDD) 471 754-2 (3). Soloists, E. Concert, Pinnock (from above)

Pinnock's performances of the Bach *Harpsichord Concertos* first appeared in 1981 and have dominated the catalogue ever since. In the solo concertos he plays with real panache, his scholarship tempered with excellent musicianship. Pacing is brisk but, to today's ears, used to period performances, the effect is convincing when the playing is so spontaneous, and the analogue sound is bright and clear.

The double, triple and quadruple concertos are digital, and the combination of period instruments and playing of determined vigour certainly makes a bold effect. There is a little more edge on the strings and everything is clearly laid out and forwardly projected. Outer movements emphasize the bravura of Bach's conceptions and, if slow movements could at times be more relaxed, those ears prepared to accept a hint of aggressiveness in the energetic musical flow will find these recordings as stimulating now as when they first appeared.

The transcribed concertos for flute, violin and harpsichord, for oboe and violin, and for oboe d'amore are equally persuasive, both vigorous and warm, with consistently resilient rhythms, while the violin concertos are equally welcome. Rhythms are again crisp and lifted at nicely chosen speeds – not too fast for slow movements – and the solo playing here, led by Simon Standage, is very stylish. Altogether this makes an impressive bargain package in DG's Collectors' Edition, thoroughly recommendable to anyone wanting to obtain all this music economically, in terms of both shelf space and financial outlay.

As can be seen, the solo, double, triple and quadruple concertos are available as a separate Trio at mid-price, properly documented.

Complete harpsichord concertos

Concerto 1; Double Concerto 2; Triple Concerto for Flute, Violin & Harpsichord (*** Chan. 0641); *Concertos 2 & 7; Triple Concerto 2; Quadruple Concerto* (*** Chan. 0611); *Concertos 3 & 5; Double Harpsichord Concerto. Brandenburg Concerto 5 in D* (*** Chan. 0595); *Concertos 4 & 6; Double Concerto 1; Triple Concerto* (*** Chan. 0636). Woolley; Scott; Beckett; Nicholson; Toll; Preston; Mackintosh; Cummings; Purcell Qt

Harpsichord Concertos 1–7; Double Harpsichord Concertos 1–3 & in C; Triple Harpsichord Concertos 1–2; Quadruple Harpsichord Concerto; Triple Concertos for Flute, Violin & Harpsichord; Violin Concertos 1–2; Double Violin Concerto; Italian Concerto

**(*) MDG 309 0680-2 (5). Hollmann, Innig, Lohr, Rémy, Kaiser, Bundies, Röhrig, Musica Alta Ripa

The special feature of the complete set on the Chandos Chaconne label is that the accompaniment is played on period instruments, with one instrument to each part. The warm ambience ensures that the result is not at all thin; indeed the allegros sound striking, firm and full, and of course the balance with the harpsichord or harpsichords is just about ideal. The playing is of high quality, rhythmically fresh and pleasing.

The *Double Concerto in C*, BWV 1061, brings a particularly successful solo interplay in the fugal finale, while in the *Double Concerto in C minor* the interchange of the slow movement is very appealing. The *Quadruple Concerto* works splendidly, with the harpsichords sounding vigorously robust without jangle. The *Fifth Brandenburg Concerto* is an engagingly lithe and sprightly version of what was apparently Bach's very first concerto featuring a solo keyboard instrument. In the *Triple Concerto for Flute, Violin and Harpsichord* the lovely slow movement is exquisitely registered here. Taken as a whole, this set is very successful indeed, with the focus of multiple harpsichords clean and pleasing to the ear. The vitality and finesse of the playing give it claims to be placed alongside the Pinnock and Rousset versions, and in terms of recorded sound it is unsurpassed.

Musica Alta Ripa is another excellent, period-instrument group, and the second of these five discs (which includes the *A minor Violin Concerto* finely played by Usula Bundies) won a Cannes Classical Award. The group favours one instrument to each part in the solo harpsichord concertos, but adds an extra violin to the ripieno in the solo violin concertos, and two extra in the *Double Violin Concerto* and in BWV 1044. The playing of the orchestral group is first class, bright and resilient, with none of the excesses of early period-instrument style. The performances are well paced, and highlights include the *Concerto for Flute, Violin and Harpsichord*, BWV 1044 (and especially the delightfully presented *Adagio ma non tanto e dolce*), and the early version of the *Brandenburg Concerto No. 5.* They also provide a convincing alternative version (for one harpsichord and strings) of the *Alla siciliana* of the *Triple Concerto*, BWV 1063, and include also the solo *Italian Concerto*; but surprisingly the version of BWV 1060 for oboe and violin is omitted. There are two snags to this otherwise lively and enjoyable set. The first is the balance within a fairly reverberant acoustic, with the soloists placed within the chamber orchestral group so that, particularly in the composite keyboard concertos, the harpsichords are almost engulfed by the tuttis. This applies less to the violin concertos, with Anne Röhrig allotted the *E major Concerto* and leading her colleague in BWV 1043, which comes off simply and effectively, if not memorably. The other drawback is the layout over all five discs, which mixes up the genres into composite programmes, whereas most collectors would surely prefer to have, say, the violin concertos grouped together. This makes the separate discs difficult to recommend.

(i) *Harpsichord Concertos 1–8*; (i–ii) *Double Harpsichord Concertos 1–3*; (i; iii) *Triple Harpsichord Concertos 1–2*; *Quadruple Harpsichord Concerto in A min.* Solo pieces: (i) *Fantasia & Fugue in A min., BWV 904; Italian Concerto in F*
(BB) **(*) Virgin 5 61716-2 (4). (i) Van Asperen; (ii) Leonhardt; (iii) Klapprott, Bussi, Lohff; Melante Amsterdam

Harpsichord Concertos 1–7
*** Häns. CD 92.127 (1–3); CD 92.128 (5–7). Levin, Stuttgart Bach Coll., Rilling

Harpsichord Concertos 1–7; (i) *Triple Concerto for Flute, Violin & Harpsichord*
*** HM HMU 907283-84 (2). Egarr, (i) with Brown, Manze; AAM, cond. Manze

Double Harpsichord Concertos 1–3 in C
*** Häns. CD 92.129. Levin, Kahane, Oregon Bach Festival CO, Rilling

Triple Harpsichord Concertos 1–2; Quadruple Harpsichord Concerto; Triple Concerto for Flute, Violin & Harpsichord; Brandenburg Concertos (original version)
*** Häns. CD 92.129. Levin, Videla, Kleiner, Behringer, Gérard, Faust, Stuttgart Bach Coll., Rilling

Double Harpsichord Concertos 1–3; Triple Harpsichord Concertos 1–2; Quadruple Harpsichord Concerto. Fantasia & Fugue, BWV 904; Italian Concerto
(B) **(*) Virgin 2×1 5 62152-2 (2) (from above set with Van Asperen & Soloists, Melante Amsterdam)

Anyone wanting a fine set of the *Harpsichord Concertos* using modern instruments should be well pleased with the performances on Hänssler, which have the additional advantage of the discs being available individually. Herbert Rilling's Bach credentials are impeccable, and the performances combine brisk, sparkling allegros, full of life, with thoughtful slow movements, admirably expressive. Robert Levin, who has already given us a first-class set of the Mozart concertos, plays with style, panache and virtuosity using modern copies of early eighteenth-century instruments by Silbermann and Gräbner which have plenty of projection and personality. They are here admirably balanced with the small but vivid orchestral group in Stuttgart, who show a full understanding of period-instrument practice. The sound is both full-bodied and clear, the acoustic warm and spacious. In the *Double* and *Triple Concertos*, the interplay between the soloists is very effectively projected, with vitality the keynote, and plenty of solo virtuosity. The Oregon Bach Festival Orchestra provide admirable backing. Rilling includes a fine account of the *Triple Concerto*, BWV 1044, plus the early version of the *Fifth Brandenburg* and the original version of BWV 1061a for two unaccompanied harpsichords, and this latter performance is particularly stimulating.

Both Andrew Manze and Bob van Asperen, like the Purcell Quartet on Chandos, favour what is basically a string quartet of period instruments for accompaniment, plus double bass and an added flute and recorders where needed. Even more than in the Chandos set, one has the effect of chamber-music

making. Van Asperen's contribution to the solo concertos is consistently nimble, with an appealing graceful delicacy, and for the most part the accompaniments from the Melante Amsterdam are lightly etched in, although sometimes in slow movements the bass seems a little heavy, and the *Andante* of BWV 1058 could be more imaginative. However, when one turns to the double concertos, where Gustav Leonhardt takes over the leading keyboard role, the effect is more boldly robust, and this applies equally to the triple and quadruple concertos. As can be seen, these composite concertos are also available separately on a Virgin 2×1 bargain Double. The recording balance is excellent throughout.

The performances from Richard Egarr with the Academy of Ancient Music are even more intimate, the authentic harpsichord image quite small. It is a copy of a 1638 Rückers and does not always emerge clearly from the string group, except, of course, in solo passages. But one soon adapts to this very believable balance, and what makes these performances so memorable are the slow movements, which often have a poignant expressive dolour which is very affecting. This is immediately striking in the Adagio of the *First D minor Concerto*, and again in the siciliano of the *C major* and the *Adagio e piano sempre* of the *D major*. The famous Largo of the *F minor* is exquisitely played, and the *dolce* of the slow movement of the *Triple Concerto*, too, is beautifully caught. There is an improvisational quality here in both the solo playing and accompaniments which is very distinctive, even if outer movements have not quite the degree of exuberant brightness that characterizes the Rilling set on modern instruments, which remain equally recommendable in a more extrovert way.

Harpsichord Concertos 1; 2; 5; 6
(M) *(*) Warner Elatus 2564 60329-2. Koopman, Amsterdam. Bar. Ens.

Double Harpsichord Concertos 1–3; (i) Quadruple Harpsichord Concerto in A min.
(N) (M) *(*) Warner Elatus 2564 61775-2. Koopman, Mathot, (i) Mustonen, Marifaldi; Amsterdam Bar. O

Warner are now reissuing Ton Koopman's complete coverage of the *Harpsichord Concertos* from the late 1980s and early 1990s. He is a fine player who has many good Bach recordings to his name. However, the present set is disappointing. The harpsichords are made to sound unpleasantly jangly, with mechanical noise intruding, while the orchestra sounds too heavy, lacking the transparency of period performances, with Koopman often failing to lift rhythms.

Clavier Concertos 1–7
⊙➔ ⊙ *** Sony SK 89245 (1, 2 & 4); SK 89690 (3, 5–7). Perahia, ASMF
(BB) *** Naxos 8.550422 (1–3); 8.550423 (4–7). Chang (piano), Camerata Cassovia, Stankovsky

Murray Perahia's set of the Bach solo keyboard concertos sweeps the board. The performances are totally pianistic, with Perahia's lightness of rhythmic touch in allegros and deliciously crisp ornamentation communicating an exhilarating yet intimate sense of joy. Slow movements are warmly expressive, helped by the elegant fullness of the Academy strings. The many individual touches are never self-aware, but seek to display Bach's music with the freshness of rediscovery, creating a continuing subtlety of colour and feeling. Beautifully balanced recording too. In short, the effect here is to put aside any consideration of period 'authenticity' and instead give this wonderfully life-enhancing music an ageless universality.

Hae-won Chang is a highly sympathetic Bach exponent, playing flexibly yet with strong rhythmic feeling, decorating nimbly and not fussily. Robert Stankovsky directs freshly resilient accompaniments; and both artists understand the need for a subtle gradation of light and shade. The digital recording, made in the House of Arts, Košice, is first class, with the piano balanced not too far forward. A fine super-bargain alternative.

Clavier Concertos (i) 1 in D min., BWV 1052; (ii) 3 in D, BWV 1054; (iii) 4 in A, BWV 1055; (iv) 5 in F min., BWV 1056; (iii) 7 in G min., BWV 1058

(N) **(*) Australian Decca (ADD/DDD) Eloquence 476 2729. (i) Ashkenazy, LSO, Zinman; (ii) Mustonen, Deutsche Kammerphilharmonie; (iii) Schiff, COE; (iv) Larrocha, London Sinf., Zinman

A fascinating disc of Bach's keyboard concertos, all played on the piano, but by different soloists. The standard of performance is generally high, even it is not perhaps always very authentic. Ashkenazy's account of No. 1, for instance, from the mid-1960s makes no concessions to the harpsichord: this is a piano in its own terms, with a wide variety of colour in the first movement and gentle half-tones in the *Adagio*. Zinman accompanies stylishly, especially in the buoyancy of the allegros, and the finale goes well. Olli Mustonen sounds a bit four-square in No. 3, and his German orchestra lacks a certain lightness of touch (the recording is not particularly helpful). András Schiff is excellent with the COE in Nos. 4 & 7, choosing spirited, uncontroversial tempi for the allegros that always add to the joy and sparkle of the music-making. Alicia de Larrocha in No. 5 plays with firm, clear articulation and shapes the slow movement with a cool but moving simplicity, while Zinman's accompaniments throughout are strong and robust.

Clavier Concertos 1; 3; 5–6

(BB) *** Warner Apex 0927 40819-2. Katsaris, Franz Liszt CO, Rolla

Cyprien Katsaris possesses the most remarkable technique and feeling for colour, which are to be heard to excellent advantage in this vividly recorded and well-filled disc. He has an astonishingly vital musical personality and keyboard resource. The playing of the Liszt Chamber Orchestra, surely one of the very finest chamber ensembles in the world, is splendidly supportive. Exciting and imaginative performances all round, and splendid value for money.

Clavier Concertos 1, 5 & 7; in D min. (reconstructed from Cantata 35 by Tureck), BWV 1059

(*) VAI 1192-2 (2). Tureck (piano), Tureck Bach Players – MOZART: *Piano Concerto 24* **(*)**

These are live performances caught on the wing in 1984, and most successfully recorded. Tempi of the allegros are slow (characteristically so for this period of the soloist's career) and the orchestral ensemble is less rhythmically crisp than we would expect today, but Tureck's own solo articulation is characteristically ear-catching. The famous slow movement of the *F minor* (No. 5) is played with a direct simplicity, but the *Andante* of *No. 7 in G minor* brings a long orchestral decrescendo which is overtly romantic yet serves to introduce the soloist very effectively. For all one's reservations, Tureck is always magnetic when playing Bach, and her reconstruction

of the *D minor Concerto* draws on the *Sinfonia* of *Cantata No. 35*, transferring part of the oboe solo to the violin, and using the alto aria, *Geist und Seele wird verwirret*, for the siciliano slow movement.

Double Clavier Concertos 1–2, BWV 1060/61; Triple Clavier Concerto in D min., BWV 1063

(N) *** Warner 2564 61950-2. Güher & Süher Pekinel (pianos), Zurich CO, Griffiths

The Pekinel sisters made their recording début in the 1980s with DG. Their Bach sparkles and delights. These are very vital, crisply articulated and intelligent performances that disarm criticism. The third piano in BWV 1063 is over-dubbed. Howard Griffiths gets very supportive playing from his Zurich players, and the recording is excellently balanced. Recommended with enthusiasm.

Harpsichord Concerto 3; Concerto for Violin & Oboe in C min. Violin Concertos: in D min., BWV 1052; in G min., BWV 1056

*** Virgin 5 45361-2. Ciomei, Biondi, Bernadini, Europe Galante

In the hands of such fine players these four works, all familiar and all reconstructed from other concertos, make a rewarding collection, casting new light on the music, when the performances are so freshly and warmly played (on period instruments) and beautifully recorded. The *Double Concerto for Violin and Oboe* is a highlight, for Alfredo Bernadini's baroque oboe has a most appealing timbre and the balance with the violin is felicitous. Fabio Biondi, playing spiritedly and with easy virtuosity, then makes a good case for the two transcribed *Violin Concertos* (arranged from keyboard concertos), and his expressive line in the two slow movements is also memorable.

(i) Double Harpsichord Concerto 1; (ii) Double Concerto in D min. for Oboe & Violin

(BB) **(*) Warner Apex 2564 61137-2. (i) Leonhardt, Miller, VCM, Harnoncourt; (ii) Schaeftlein, Alice Harnoncourt, Leonhardt Cons. – J. C. BACH: *Sinfonia concertante in F* ****(*)**; C. P. E. BACH: *Double Concerto for Harpsichord & Fortepiano* *******; W. F. BACH: *Double Concerto for 2 Harpsichords* ****(*)**

These are enjoyable performances from two different sources, although the *Andante* of the *Double Harpsichord Concerto* is a little heavy-handed, and in the work for oboe and violin Alice Harnoncourt is balanced rather backwardly, seeming to be placed within the orchestra itself. However, here the *Adagio* is beautifully played and the outer movements have plenty of vitality. The analogue recordings have transferred faithfully to CD. The main interest of this inexpensive reissue is the very winning *Concerto for Harpsichord and Fortepiano* by Carl Philipp Emanuel.

Oboe Concertos: in F (after BWV 49 & 169); in A, BWV 1055; in G min., BWV 1056; (i) Double Concerto in C min. for Oboe & Violin, BWV 1060

(N) (M) *** DHM/BMG 0542 77290-2. Westermann, (i) with Utiger; Camerata Köln

Apart from the *F major Concerto* with its touching central *Siciliana* which derives from cantata movements, the Camerata Köln collection covers much the same ground as the Naxos disc below, although the latter includes an extra work. However, if you prefer the oboe to the oboe d'amore, you will find that Hans-Peter Westermann's timbre on his baroque instrument is quite ravishing and his phrasing equally lovely. In the *Double Concerto* he is partnered by Mary Utiger, who is a fine partner if perhaps just a little recessive. But the Camerata Köln are on top form and the recording is very good indeed.

Oboe d'amore Concertos: in D, BWV 1053; in A, BWV 1055; Oboe Concertos: in G min., BWV 1056; in D min., BWV 1059; Double Concerto in C min. for Oboe & Violin, BWV 1060

(BB) *** Naxos 8.554602. Hommel, Cologne CO, Müller-Brühl

Christian Hommel's outstanding performances of concertos for oboe and oboe d'amore, all of them reconstructions of other works, are lively and sensitive; the recording, with the soloist balanced well in front, is excellent. A most enjoyable disc.

Violin Concertos 1–2, BWV 1041/2; in G min. (from BWV 1056); (i) Double Violin Concerto, BWV 1041

(BB) *** RCA 74321 68002-2. Zukerman, ECO; (i) with Garcia – VIVALDI: *Concertos, RV 187 & 209* ***

(BB) *** EMI Encore (ADD) 5 74720-2. Perlman, ECO, Barenboim; (i) with Zukerman

Zukerman virtually upstages his friend and colleague Perlman in a splendid set of the Bach *Violin Concertos*, with the ECO, but digitally recorded in the early 1990s, producing attractively bright, lithe string-textures, cleaner and more transparent than on the earlier HMV disc. Moreover, he offers equally fine accounts of two top-class Vivaldi concertos as a bonus. The Bach performances have great vitality and Zukerman's solo line in all three slow movements is very beautiful, particularly felt and moving in the *A minor*, using a wide range of dynamic and equally moving in the lovely cantilena of BWV 1056. In the interplay of the *Largo* of the *Double Concerto* José-Luis Garcia matches his style and timbre with that of his colleague very successfully indeed. The solo balance is forward, but the violin timbre is naturally caught and the orchestra well in the picture.

On the Encore disc Zukerman participates only in the *Double Concerto*, where the two famous violinists with their friend and colleague, Barenboim, are inspired to give a very fine account, one in which their artistry is beautifully matched in all its intensity. Perlman is the soloist in the three other works and plays Bach with great naturalness of feeling: his account of the *A minor Concerto* can scarcely be faulted, even if his tempi will not be to all tastes. He is also most impressive in the slow movement of the *E major*. The *G minor* (arranged from the *F minor Harpsichord Concerto* with its sublime Arioso slow movement) is also finely done, and with excellent modern-instrument accompaniments from the ECO this is also a Bach reissue to cherish.

(i) Violin Concertos 1–2; (ii) Double Violin Concerto; (iii) Double Concerto for Violin & Oboe in C min.

⊶ ✿ (M) *** Ph. (ADD) 420 700-2. Grumiaux, with (ii) Krebbers, (iii) Holliger; (i–ii) Les Solistes Romandes, Gerecz; (iii) New Philh. O, de Waart

*** EMI 5 57091-2. Kennedy, BPO; with (ii) Stabrawa; (iii) Mayer

(B) *** Nim. NI 1735(3). Shumsky, Scottish CO; with (ii) Tunnell; (iii) Miller – MOZART: *Concertos 4 & 5*; YSAŸE: *Sonatas* ***

(M) *** Classic fM 75605 57008-2. Hattori, with (ii) Clark, (iii) Williams; SCO, Hattori

(N) (B) ** CFP (ADD) 5 86046-2 (without *BWV 1060*). Bean, Sillito, Virtuosi of England, Davison – HANDEL: *Organ Concertos* **

The maverick Kennedy and the centrally traditional Berlin Philharmonic may make curious partners in Bach, but these are positive, robust readings, marked by fast and fierce speeds in outer movements. Happily, there are none of the idiosyncrasies of Kennedy's version of Vivaldi's *Four Seasons* and, though he discreetly persuades the Berliners to adopt a few ideas from period performance, he is happiest when indulging in warmly expressive slow movements, taken at relatively expansive speeds. His soloist partners – Albrecht Mayer in the work with oboe, Daniel Stabrawa in the sublime *Double Violin Concerto* – make an excellent match.

One has only to sample the simple beauty of Shumsky's playing in the *Andante* of the *A minor Violin Concerto* to be won over to his dedicated Bach style, which is not quite as pure as Grumiaux's but is seductive in its simplicity of line and tonal beauty. John Tunnell makes highly musical exchanges with him in the *Double Violin Concerto*, and Robin Miller is a no less appealing partner in the work for violin and oboe.

The Classic fM disc is also outstanding, offering not just performances which stand high among versions using modern instruments, but full, immediate recording. Joji Hattori, winner of the Menuhin International Competition in 1989, plays with a tone both sweet and pure, flawless in intonation and immaculate in crisply alert passage-work. As director, he draws from the orchestra playing both clear and well sprung, with the clarity enhanced by the recording, and he is well matched by both his duet partners.

Hugh Bean and Kenneth Sillito, both of them distinguished orchestral leaders as well as fine virtuosi, are outstandingly successful as soloists in the *Double Concerto*. This is still one of the most beautiful accounts of the lovely slow movement on record, deeply felt but pure and restrained. The solo concertos are shared, Sillito playing the *A minor* and Hugh Bean the *E major*. If the accompaniments are not always ideally resilient, the performances can be warmly recommended as a bargain issue with an unusual coupling. The 1975 recording still sounds well.

Violin Concertos 1–2; (i) Double Concerto; (ii) Triple Concerto for Flute, Violin & Harpsichord

(B) *** DG (IMS) 463 014-2. Standage, E. Concert, Pinnock; with (i) Wilcock; (ii) Beznosiuk, Pinnock

This collection of violin concertos, played on original instruments, is welcome back into the catalogue. Rhythms are crisp and lifted at nicely chosen speeds – not too fast for slow movements – and the solo playing is very stylish. The *Triple Concerto* is also very successful. The only snag is the edge on violin timbre, which will not please all ears.

(i) Violin Concertos 1–2; (ii) Double Violin Concerto; (iii) Orchestral Suite 4

(B) **(*) DG 449 844-2. (i-ii) D. Oistrakh, RPO, Goossens; (ii) with I. Oistrakh; (iii) Munich Bach O, Richter

David Oistrakh's playing is peerless and can be ranked alongside the Grumiaux versions. In the *Double Concerto* father and son are suitably contrasted in timbre, and the performance of the great slow movement is Elysian. The 1961 recording hardly sounds dated. Richter's account of the *Fourth*

Orchestral Suite is rhythmically unstylish in the matter of double-dotting but is otherwise alert – less heavy than we had remembered.

Violin Concertos (i) *1*; (ii) *2*; (iii) *Double Violin Concerto*; (iv) *Trio Sonata in G, BWV 1038*

(N) (M) ****(*)** Sony (ADD) 518806-2 [SK 92732]. Stern, with
  (i) LSO; (ii) ECO, Schneider; (iii) Perlman, NYPO, Mehta;
  (iv) Rampal, Parnas, Ritter

(i) *Violin Concertos 1–2*; (i; ii) *Double Violin Concerto.*
(Unaccompanied) *Violin Sonata 1*

*** Avie AV 0007. L. St John; (i) New York Bach Ens.; (ii)
  with S. St John

(i–iii) *Violin Concertos 1–2*; (i; ii; iv) *Double Violin Concerto*; (i) (Unaccompanied) *Violin Sonata 2: Andante* (only)

(BB) (*******) Naxos mono 8.110965. (i) Menuhin; (ii) O
  Symphonique de Paris; (iii) cond. Enescu; (iv) with Enescu
  (violin), cond. Monteux

(i–iii) *Violin Concertos 1–2*; (i–ii; iv) *Double Violin Concerto*; (i) *Partita 2: Chaconne*

🏵 (M) (*******) EMI mono 5 67201-2. (i) Menuhin; (ii) O
  Symphonique de Paris; (iii) cond. Enescu; (iv) with Enescu
  (violin), cond. Monteux

Lara St John is a first-rate Bach violinist, her playing lithe and full of communicative intensity. Allegros are exhilaratingly fresh, favouring fleet tempi; indeed, some will feel that the outer movements of the *Double Concerto* are too brisk. Yet they set off the simplicity of approach to the beautiful slow movement in which Scott St John is an admirable partner. With buoyant, polished accompaniments, this collection is very enjoyable indeed, especially as the unaccompanied *G minor Sonata* is equally rewarding, and the recording throughout real and vivid.

Stern's glorious tone and richness of line dominate these solo concertos, although orchestral accompaniments are heavier and tempi slower than we would expect today. Stern directs the *First, A minor, Concerto* himself and plays very beautifully, and the recording, made in the Fairfield Hall in 1966, is warm and very pleasingly balanced. The *E major Concerto* dates from a decade earlier, but the *Double Concerto*, most inspirational of all, came from Stern's 60th birthday concert at the Lincoln Center in the autumn of 1980. Stern nobly concedes the first place to Perlman in this work. Mehta is not perhaps the ideal conductor in this music, but the feeling of a live occasion comes over strikingly and the slow movement is glorious. The applause at the end is well deserved. The *Trio Sonata* is an unexpected bonus and offers some distinguished playing, especially from Rampal, so that one can adjust to the up-front balance. Altogether a most rewarding disc.

Menuhin's 78-r.p.m. recording of the *Double Concerto*, with Georges Enescu his partner (and teacher) and Monteux conducting, is legendary for its rapport and simple expressive beauty. It was recorded in Paris in 1932, the same year that Menuhin recorded the Elgar in London. The two solo concertos – with Enescu on the rostrum – followed in 1933 and 1936. They are hardly less remarkable, with a wonderful purity of line and natural expressive feeling. All these records were made when Menuhin was between sixteen and nineteen years of age and show (as did the Elgar in a quite different way) his unique instinctive musical vision, which came from within rather than from outside influences. The famous *Partita* is

hardly less impressive (see below). In the concertos, the orchestral string-sound is dry, the violins unflattered, but this expert remastering for EMI by Andrew Walter makes the very most of the original 78s and, so moving is the slow movement of the *Double Concerto*, one quite forgets its early provenance. A Bach recording that should be in every collection.

Ward Marston has made impressive transfers of these rightly famous recordings for Naxos, but we marginally prefer the EMI remastering, which is in general smoother and cleaner, if perhaps not always so wide-ranging.

Violin Concerto 2 in E
**(*) Simax PSC 1159. Tellefsen, Oslo Festival Strings,
  Berglund – SHOSTAKOVICH: *Violin Concerto 1* ****(*)**

Arve Tellefsen has never enjoyed the international exposure to which his gifts entitle him, but he is a fine musician who plays with great spirit, and he is well recorded too. Good, stylish playing that should enjoy wide appeal.

(i) *Double Violin Concerto*; (ii) (Unaccompanied) *Cello Suite 1 in C: Bourrée I & II*
(*) EMI **DVD 490449-9. (i) D. Oistrakh, Y. Menuhin, RTF
  CO, Capdevielle; (ii) Rostropovich – MOZART: *Sinfonia concertante*; BRAHMS: *Double Concerto* ****(*)**

The *Double Concerto in D minor* was recorded at the Salle Pleyel in October 1958 with the French Radio Chamber Orchestra under Pierre Capdevielle. The two great soloists first played this together at the 1947 'Prague Spring', and their Paris account affords an admirable opportunity for contrasting the golden tone of the one with the (on this occasion) seraphic playing of the other. Of course the sound calls for some tolerance, but this film is a rarity and is to be treasured. Rostropovich, playing with enormous intensity the *Bourrées* from the *Third Suite for Solo Cello*, recorded in December 1962, is a welcome bonus.

Double Violin Concerto in D min., BWV 1043
(M) ******* RCA (ADD) 09026 63531-2. Heifetz, Friedman,
  London New SO, Sargent – BRAHMS: *Double Concerto*;
  MOZART: *Sinfonia concertante, K.364* *******

It is good to have Heifetz's 1961 stereo recording of the *Double Concerto* as a worthy successor to Menuhin's two versions. Sargent's tempi in the outer movements are brisk but are none the worse for that, and the Elysian dialogue of the slow movement, with Heifetz's pupil Erick Friedman a natural partner, is hardly less inspired and much better recorded.

(i) *Double Violin Concerto. Suite 3: Air* (arr. Wilhelmj).
(Unaccompanied) *Violin Sonata 1: Adagio*
(M) (*******) Biddulph mono LAB 056-7 [id.]. Arnold Rosé, (i)
  with Alma Rosé, O – BEETHOVEN: *String Quartets 4,*
  10 & 14 (*******)

Arnold Rosé's sonata-partner was Bruno Walter and his brother-in-law was Mahler. His daughter, Alma, with whom he is heard in a 1931 recording of the Bach *D minor Double Concerto*, perished in Auschwitz. Interesting though these recordings are, the principal musical rewards in the set come from the three Beethoven quartets with which they are coupled.

A Musical Offering, BWV 1079 (see also above, under *Art of Fugue, Brandenburgs*, and below under Chamber Music)
(BB) ****(*)** Naxos 8.553286. Capella Istropolitana, Benda

Christian Benda uses a small chamber orchestra. Strings

alone, with a minimum of vibrato, play the framing *Ricercars*. The first group of canons add in flute, oboe and bassoon; in the second group, the stringed instruments predominate. A harpsichord joins in the first, and the cor anglais and bassoon dolorously share the last (common) solution of the four offered alternative proposals for solving Bach's so-called 'puzzle canon'. The *Trio Sonata*, at the centre, is given a pleasing performance, expressive and lively, and overall this seems a thoroughly musical interpretation of a work about which any performance is conjectural. The recording is excellent, clear yet with a pleasing bloom, and the result, if a little didactic at times, is undoubtedly fresh.

Orchestral Suites 1–4, BMW 1066–9

𝄽—𝅘 *** Telarc CD 80619. Boston Bar., Pearlman
(M) ***Decca (ADD) 430 379-2. ASMF, Marriner

A spendid new period-instrument recording of the *Orchestral Suites* from the excellent Boston Baroque under Martin Pearlman. All four fit on to a single CD, yet speeds are well judged and lively but not pressed too hard. Pearlman does not present the *Suites* in the usual way but follows the order of composition as suggested by modern scholarship. Thus No. 4 comes first, followed by Nos. 1, 3 and 2. For continued listening this works very well, with the famous *Badinerie* (with stylish flute-playing from Christopher Krueger) making a sprightly end to the programme. Period-instrument playing has come a long way in the last decade, and it is a joy to hear the famous *Air* from the *Third Suite* sounding warmly expressive again instead of vinegary. But what is especially attractive about these performances, apart from their buoyancy, is the internal clarity of the woodwind interplay within a warm acoustic. Altogether these are most enjoyable performances and they are given first-class Telarc recording.

Marriner's 1970 recording of the Bach *Suites* with the ASMF comes on a single CD (77' 48") and the remastering of the fine (originally Argo) recording is fresh and vivid. The playing throughout is expressive, without being romantic, and always buoyant and vigorous. A fine bargain for those not insisting on original instruments; there is nothing remotely unstylish here.

Orchestral Suites 1–4; (i) Double Harpsichord Concertos 1 & 3

(B) *** Double Decca 458 069-2 (2). AAM, Hogwood; (i) with Rousset, Hogwood

Orchestral Suites 1–4; Violin Concerto Movement in D, BWV 1045; Sinfonias from Cantatas 29; 42; 209

(B) *** Hyp. Dyad CDD 22002 (2). Brandenburg Cons., Goodman

Orchestral Suites 1–4; Sinfonias from Cantatas 42 & 174 & Easter Oratorios; (i) Cantata 118: Chorus: Ich liebe den Höchsten von ganzem Gemüte

*** DG 439 780-2. E. Concert, Pinnock; (i) with Ch.

With sound rather warmer and string-tone sweeter, Trevor Pinnock and the English Concert improve on their readings of 16 years earlier. In the dance movements of the *Suite No. 2* Lisa Beznosiuk takes her flute solos faster and more brilliantly than her predecessor, Stephen Preston, but otherwise speeds are generally a fraction broader in all four *Suites*, with allegros more jauntily sprung and phrasing a degree more espressivo. Above all, the great *Air* of *Suite No. 3* sounds far warmer, persuasively phrased on multiple violins instead of on a single, acid-toned instrument. The fill-ups are brief but

make a fascinating bonus, winningly performed.

Hogwood's set of the Bach *Orchestral Suites* illustrates how the Academy of Ancient Music has developed in refinement and purity of sound, modifying earlier abrasiveness without losing period-instrument freshness. That comes out in the famous *Air* from *Suite No. 3* where, with multiple violins and an avoidance of the old squeezed style, the tone is sweet even with little or no vibrato – a movement which in the old Pinnock version on DG Archiv, for example, sounds very sour. Allegros tend to be on the fast side but are well sprung, not breathless. The *Concertos for 2 Harpsichords*, added for the mid-priced reissue, are imaginatively played by Christopher Hogwood and Christophe Rousset. Hogwood aficionados need not hesitate.

Roy Goodman directs brisk and stylish readings of the four Bach *Orchestral Suites*, which are aptly supplemented by four *Sinfonias*, each following a suite in the same key. Though in the *Suites* Goodman in his eagerness occasionally chooses too breathless a tempo for fast movements, the lightness of rhythm and the crispness of ensemble are consistently persuasive, with textures cleanly caught in excellent, full-bodied sound. These are among the finest versions on a long list, with Rachael Brown an exceptionally warm-toned flautist in No. 2. Goodman, like Pinnock, observes all repeats, making the opening overtures longer than usual.

(i) Orchestral Suites 1–4; (ii) 14 Canons from the Goldberg Variations, BWV 1087 (orchestral arrangement)

(M) **(*) Sony (ADD) 517492-2 (2). Marlboro Festival O, with (i) Casals; (ii) Serkin

Everything that Casals touched reveals a profound musical mind, and the *Orchestral Suites* are no exception. This set, made in the mid-1960s, is for musicians, though everyone can learn from it. Devotees of original-instrument performances may not feel at home, but the roll call of the orchestral players is pretty awesome.

Orchestral Suites 2–4

(N) (BB) *** EMI Encore 5860832. ASMF, Marriner

Marriner's 1984 recording (his third) uses an edition prepared by Clifford Bartlett and shows notable differences from his earlier versions. The performance reveals some influence from the authentic movement. On one textual point, the double-dotting in the introduction to the *Third Suite*, he takes a more extreme view than the authentic specialists, turning the three semiquavers at the end of each half-bar into precise demi-semiquavers. In the other introductions, too, there is a return to the clipped, clear manner of his first version – but not to speeds quite so fast. At times the new version may not be quite as precise of ensemble as that Argo/Decca version but, with a slightly more relaxed manner and more spacious recording, it is more genial. As in both previous versions, William Bennett is the brilliant flute soloist in *Suite No. 2*.

Orchestral Suite 3 in D, BWV 1068

(M) **(*) Testament SBT2 1217 (2). BPO, Klemperer –
BEETHOVEN: *Symphony 6*; MOZART: *Symphony 29* **(*)

In May 1964 Otto Klemperer, then aged 79, returned to Berlin to conduct the Berlin Philharmonic in three works that were favourites with him, and he won a rapturous reception. It was over 40 years since his first appearance with the Berlin Philharmonic, and he seemed determined above all to get Karajan's orchestra to produce a distinctive 'Klemperer' sound. The Bach is weightly traditional, with the *Air* expansively romantic.

Collection

(i) *Brandenburg Concerto 5. Orchestral Suite 2; Partita in A min.* (for flute), *BWV 1013; Trio Sonata in G, BWV 1038*

⬥ EMI 5 57111-2. Pahud; Kussmaul; Faust; Schornsheim; (i) Berlin Bar. Sol., Kussmaul

At first sight, this looks like a rather arbitrary collection, but Emmanuel Pahud is a superb artist and the delicacy of his flute playing lights up everything he touches. The solo *Partita* is a model of linear subtlety, and his colleagues play with comparable taste and style in the *Trio Sonata*. The famous *Badinerie* of the *Orchestral Suite No. 2* is exquisitely articulated and the finale of *Brandenburg No. 5* as light as thistledown, while earlier in the same work the harpsichord solo from Christine Schornsheim has similar finesse. The orchestral contribution is wonderfully buoyant and totally free from rhythmic or textural heaviness, the sound itself warm yet completely transparent. In short, this superbly balanced and recorded CD is not to be missed, even if (inevitably) it brings duplication.

CHAMBER MUSIC

The Art of Fugue, BWV 1080

*** Hyp. CDA 67138. Delmé Qt

**(*) DG 474 495-2. Emerson Qt

**(*) ECM 1652. Keller Qt

(N) ** AliaVox Multichannel **SACD** AVSA 9818 A+B (2). Hespèrion XX, Savall

Robert Simpson believed that it is 'essential that the four parts retain their identity throughout', and that 'the quartet is the ideal medium for conveying the beauty of four-part counterpoint with perfect clarity and sensitivity'. As the tessitura lies too low to perform *The Art of Fugue* in D minor, Simpson has transposed the whole sequence into G minor. Incidentally, he includes Tovey's completion of *Contrapunctus XIV*, although the listener can play it without the conjectural ending if preferred. The Delmé Quartet, who have recorded ten of Simpson's own quartets, play with great dedication. Excellent recording. This outclasses other string quartet versions.

The Emerson Quartet move through Bach's fugal masterpiece with great concentration, revealing every detail. They are closely balanced and play immaculately with a fine body of tone, yet with a purposeful briskness that some will find unrelenting, although the cello solo in *Contrapunctus III* has a deep underlying expressive feeling. Then, from the *Canon per Augmentationem* onwards, the players' approach suddenly mellows and becomes quite touching (with vibrato bringing warmth), carrying through to the closing chorale, *Von deinen Thron tret ich Hiermat*, which acts as a reverent epilogue.

The Hungarian Keller Quartet gives the impression of using a fair degree of vibrato, and this brings a more expressive style, so that the cello solo that opens *Contrapunctus III* is almost a lament. There is plenty of variety of both mood and tempo. Nevertheless, keyboard versions delineate the part-writing more pointedly. The recording is full and naturally balanced.

Jordi Savall has felt justified in trying to reinterpret *The Art of Fugue* 'through an ensemble for which the largest repertoire of contrpuntal chamber music of the sixteenth and seventeenth centuries was composed'. A consort of viols is therefore the basis of his performance, to which he has added a further consort of four wind instruments of the period (cornetto, oboe da caccia, sackbut and bassoon). However, while this allows for variety of colour and dynamic intensity, as he intends, and the sounds and textures (especially with the added background ambience possible with SACD) are aurally consistently stimulating, many will find the varying interplay of instrumental blending can distract the ear from the polyphony. The playing is of the highest quality, as is the recording, and the set is beautifully packaged; but this is essentially a performance to sample before committing to a purchase.

(i) *The Art of Fugue: Contrapunctus 1–4; 6; 9; 11; 18;* (ii) Unaccompanied *Cello Suites 1 & 5, BWV 1007 & 1011* (alternating with works by György KURTAG)

(N) (***) EuroArts DVD 2050759. (i) Keller Qt; (ii) Bylsma

The Keller Quartet give outstanding performances of excerpts from the *Art of Fugue*, playing with consistent concentration and intensity. The 'backcloth' in the Bartholomäus-Kirche, Dornheim, with its vertical lines of three plain windows, is also visually satisfying, and the camera follows Bach's contrapuntal exchanges among the players very intelligently. The snag is that the Bach *Contrapuncti* are alternated with very rarefied contemporary works by Kurtág. They too are played with dedicated concentration, and their spare atmosphere is certainly not at odds with the music of Bach. But most listeners will not want to hear them every time and equally will not want to use the controls to move forward. It is a great pity that the excellent Keller group did not choose to record the *Art of Fugue* complete and without interpolations. Anner Bylsma then (uninterrupted) plays the pair of *Cello Suites* very impressively and with striking personal freedom in his phrasing which is entirely convincing. He is naturally recorded and the simple setting is again well chosen.

A Musical Offering, BWV 1079

(B) **(*) HM (ADD) HMA 1951260. Moroney, Cook, See, Holloway, Ter Linden

The introductory *Ricercar* and first group of *Canons* are presented clearly but not pedantically on one or two harpsichords, and the sensitively played *Trio Sonata* follows, given added colour by using flute, violin and continuo. The *Canon perpetua* is then heard on the same combination and, for all the remaining *Canons* except one, Moroney returns to his harpsichord(s). Good recording, truthfully transferred.

(Unaccompanied) *Cello Suites 1–6, BMV 1007–12*

⬤—⬤ ⬥ *** EMI DVD DVA 5 99159 9. Rostropovich

Rostropovich was filmed recording the six Bach *Cello Suites* in 1991 in the Basilique Sainte Madeleine, Vézelay, Yonne, France, a venue he chose for the comparative severity of its interior architecture, which, he felt, created the right backcloth for the music. He introduces the whole project by telling us about his own approach to the interpretation of these masterpieces, with which he has lived all his life, and of his visit to Casals, who played Bach especially for him, creating a rhapsodical dialogue that took his presence into account. Rostropovich then verbally characterizes each onè of the *Suites* before he performs it, moving through sorrow and intensity, brilliance and majesty, and from darkness into the sunlight of the *Sixth, D major* work, which he describes as a

'*Symphony for Solo Cello*'. The analyses he offers on the way are as much connected with emotions and feelings as with the intellect and are easy to follow. Of course, one can choose to hear the music without the commentaries. The performances hardly need recommendation from us: they are totally compelling and are truthfully recorded.

(Unaccompanied) Cello Suites 1–6

☛ ✿ *** EMI 5 55363-2 (2). Rostropovich
(N) (BB) *** EMI Gemini 5 86534-2 (2). Schiff
(B) *** Double Decca 466 253-2 (2). Harrell
(N) (BB) *** Naxos 8.557280/81 (2). Kliegel
(N) (M) ***Avie 0052 (2). Meneses
(N) (BB) *** Virgin 5 62374-2 (4). Kirschbaum – *Violin Partitas & Sonatas* **
(M) *** DG (ADD) 449 711-2 (2). Fournier
(N) (M) *** EMI 5 62878-2 [5 62879] (2). Tortelier
(M) *** Sony SM2K 89754 (2). Ma
(B) *** Ph. (ADD) Duo 442 293-2 (2). Gendron
(N) **(*) DG 477 5228. Jian Wang
(M) (***) EMI mono 5 62611-2 [562617-2] (2). Casals
(BB) **(*) Warner Apex (ADD) 2564 60816-2. Harnoncourt

Rostropovich verbally characterizes each one of the series: 'No. 1, lightness; No. 2, sorrow and intensity; No. 3, brilliance; No. 4, majesty and opacity; No. 5, darkness; and No. 6, sunlight'. True to his word, more than usual he draws distinctions between each, also reflecting the point that the structure of each suite grows in complexity. The results are both moving and strong, with the sound of the cello, as recorded in a warm acoustic, full and powerful, making one hear the music afresh, with *pianissimo* repeats magically achieved.

Heinrich Schiff is straighter but no less concentrated in feeling. Strong and positive, producing a consistent flow of beautiful tone at whatever dynamic level, he here establishes his individual artistry very clearly, his rhythmic pointing a delight. He is treated to an excellent recording, with the cello given fine bloom against a warm but intimate acoustic. This is now an outstanding bargain as a double forte.

Harrell's comparative spareness and restraint contrast strongly with Rostropovich's more extrovert manner, but rarely if ever is the former guilty of understatement. The simple dedication of the playing, combined with cleanness of attack and purity of tone, brings natural, unforced intensity, and in many ways these readings might be compared with Milstein's DG set of the *Unaccompanied Violin Sonatas*. One might disagree occasionally with the tempo, but the overall command is unassailable. The recording quality, forward and real yet aptly intimate in acoustic, suits the performances admirably.

Playing on a Stradivarius cello of 1693, Maria Kliegel gives deeply satisfying performances of these formidable works. With her flawless intonation and well-judged choice of tempi, her intense concentration and direct approach have one enjoying the music without distraction from personal mannerism, with the dark intensity of the *Sarabandes* consistently brought out. Kliegel has made a series of formidable cello recordings for Naxos, and here again she reveals what an inspired artist she can be. Heinrich Schiff offers more individual interpretations, with the dance element strikingly brought out, but Kliegel makes an excellent alternative which many will prefer, beautifully recorded in Budapest.

Antonio Meneses moved from Brazil at the age of 16 to study with Antonio Janigro in Germany, later winning prizes

in Munich and Moscow. He is an experienced chamber-music performer, having collaborated with both the Emerson and Vermeer Quartets, and as a recording artist has worked with Karajan on two occasions. Technically he is a superb player, but the great virtue of his approach to the Bach *Cello Suites* is a deeply musical simplicity. The natural freshness and spontaneity of his playing is disarming; one feels entirely in the presence of Bach and the thoughtful, slightly introvert communing of his performer, rather than sensing any overt virtuosity or emoting. The recording, made in a church in Berkshire, is beautifully judged; and this set is ideal for dipping into on a quiet summer (or winter) evening.

Fournier's richly phrased and warm-toned performances carry an impressive musical conviction. He can be profound and he can lift rhythms infectiously in dance movements, but above all he conveys the feeling that this is music to be enjoyed. This recording has been remastered splendidly and now has even greater presence and realism.

Ralph Kirschbaum's 'authentic' set of the Bach *Cello Suites* is very fine too. He also has the advantage of a very natural recording which displays his full timbre to great advantage. He plays a Domenico Montagnana cello of 1729 and gives it a warmly vivid personality. Articulation in the dance movements is clear; expressive playing is without bulges and does not shirk a degree of vibrato. The performances have intensity, dedication, spontaneity and an intimate thoughtfulness which is genuinely moving. But they are now coupled with Christian Tetzlaff's dazzlingly virtuosic performances of the *Violin Partitas* and *Sonatas* – a stimulating experience, but one which will not be to all tastes.

Recorded in the reverberant acoustic of the Temple Church in London, Paul Tortelier's 1982 performances present clear contrasts with his version of 20 years earlier. They now reappear as one of EMI's 'Great Recordings of the Century'. His approach remains broadly romantic by today's purist standards, but this time the rhythms are steadier, the command greater, with the preludes of each suite strongly characterized to capture the attention even in the chattering passagework. Some will prefer a drier acoustic than this, but the early digital sound is first rate, and the artist's presence is striking.

Yo-Yo Ma's playing has a characteristic rhythmic freedom and favours the widest range of dynamic. The improvisatory effect is seemingly spontaneous and these performances are very compelling indeed, for Ma seems right inside every bar of the music. The first-class recording is very real and natural, with the warm acoustic never blurring the focus. This now appears as a bargain double, a very attractive proposition.

No one artist holds all the secrets in this repertoire, but few succeed in producing such consistent beauty of tone as Maurice Gendron, with the digital remastering firming up an excellent and truthful analogue recording. His phrasing is unfailingly musical, and these readings with their restraint and fine judgement command admiration. At Philips's Duo price, they can be given a warm welcome back to the catalogue.

Born in China, but now living in America, Jian Wang started performing Bach in public at the age of ten. But over the years his connection with the *Cello Suites* has obviously deepened and matured to become intensely personalized. This is communicated throughout these powerfully expressive performances by considerable freedom of phrasing and tempo. The ruminative feeling in the *Prelude* of the *Second Suite* is characteristic of his often introspective approach. His playing of the *Sarabandes*, for instance, is expressively very slow and intense, yet the *Bourrées* in the *Third Suite* and the famous *Gavotte* of the *D major Suite* (No. 6) have the lightest rhythmic touch, and the *Allemande* of the *E flat major* is almost laconic in its geniality. Above all, his is a spontaneous response to Bach, never self-seeking, however wayward, and it carries a resonance that remains with the listener. Wang is beautifully recorded with an appealing tonal warmth in a pleasingly intimate but never dry acoustic.

It was Casals who restored these pieces to the repertory, after long decades of neglect. Some of the playing is far from flawless; passage-work is rushed or articulation uneven, and he is often wayward. But he brought to the *Cello Suites* insights that remain unrivalled, and he brings one closer to the music than most other performers of this extraordinary music. Just sample the *Fourth Suite*, which opens the second disc, to experience the remarkably live and spontaneous character of this Bach-playing. The recordings, dating from 1936 and 1938, have been freshly remastered for this reissue as one of EMI's 'Great Recordings of the Century', and their presence is uncanny.

Nikolaus Harnoncourt's performances, recorded in 1965, remind us that he was a cellist before he became a conductor, and a very good one. They suggest that we are eavesdropping on a solitary musician communing with Bach in private for his own pleasure, rather than projecting the music as at a concert performance. There are moments (for instance, in the *First* and *Fourth Suites*), when the playing could be more positive and rhythmically crisper, yet there are others too when one can feel the cellist's affectionate response to Bach's lyrical phrases. The recording is intimate to match, and this is a fascinating document that should attract all those who admire Harnoncourt's work on the rostrum.

(Unaccompanied) *Cello Suites 1–6;* (i) *Viola da gamba Sonatas 1–2, BWV 1027–8*

(N) (M) **(*) Mercury SACD 470 644–2 (2). Starker, (i) with Sebök

Janos Starker's performances come from 1963 and 1965 and are of great integrity and dedication, without having quite the same electric communication of his earlier, mono recording. The two *Viola da gamba Sonatas* are not ideally balanced and favour György Sebök's piano, though there is no question of his artistry. However, the new SACD transfer of the solo cello works has a remarkable naturalness and realism: Starker might be sitting there beyond the speakers.

(Unaccompanied) *Cello Suites 1, 4 & 5.* (Bonus DVD: *Cello Suite 1 in G, BWV 1007*)

(N) (M) ** EMI Legend DVD/CD 557748. Rostropovich

Rostropovich's 1992 recording of Bach's *Cello Suites* was the first time the great cellist contemplated recording these supreme masterpieces as a complete cycle; the result, in his broadly romantic way, was predictably revelatory, both moving and strong. While one can't help wondering who would want to buy only half the *Cello Suites*, this EMI Legend release does include a superb account of the *First Cello Suite* on DVD, filmed in the Basilique Sainte Madeleine, Vézelay, France, in 1991 (see above).

(Unaccompanied) *Cello Suite 1 in G, BWV 1007*

(M) (***) EMI mono 5 67008-2. Casals – BEETHOVEN: *Cello Sonata 3;* BRAHMS: *Cello Sonata 2* (***)

The *G major Suite* was recorded in 1938, and nobility shines through every bar. Of course this is available with the other suites, but duplication is worthwhile for the sake of its companions.

(Unaccompanied) *Cello Suites 1–6* (transcribed for viola)

(N) (B) *** Ph. Duo 475 6219 (2). Imai (viola)

Nobuko Imai's performance of the *Cello Suites* transcribed for viola is something of a revelation. On the slighter instrument they sound more leonine and less resonant, but they are certainly neither less tonally beautiful nor less compelling. Imai obviously feels the music deeply and she plays with genuine intensity without ever over-emoting. The ruminative *Prelude* of the *Second Suite* has an unforgettable spontaneous expressive feeling and the *Sarabandes* are similarly inspirational, while the dance movements are full of life. Technically, her playing is effortless, and the recording is very real indeed.

(i) *Unaccompanied Cello Suites 1–6.* (ii) *Lute Suites* (arr. for guitar) *1–4, BWV 995–7 & 1006a; Fugue in G min., BWV 1000; Prelude, Fugue & Allegro in E flat, BWV 998; Prelude in C min., BWV 999. Guitar Transcriptions: Arrangements of Cello Suites: 1; 2; 6: Sarabande & Gavotte* (only). *Arrangement of Violin Sonata 3 in C.* **(iii)** *(Unaccompanied) Violin Sonatas 1–3; Partitas 1–3*

(B) **(*) DG 474 641-2 (6). (i) Maisky; (ii) Söllscher (guitar); (iii) Mintz

This compilation in DG's bargain-price Collector's Edition is more of a mixed bag than usual, although all the recordings are digital. Mischa Maisky's performances of the *Cello Suites* are beautifully cultured and played at a high emotional temperature. However, he is rather less inclined to let the music speak for itself than some of his rivals. The *Sarabande* of the *D minor Suite* is a little narcissistic, nor is that of *No. 5 in C minor* free from affectation. There are times in the quicker dance movements when one longs for him to move on – the *Allemande* of No. 6 is taken excessively slowly. However, there is no doubt that he makes an absolutely glorious musical sound and commands an unusually wide range of colour and tone.

By contrast, the distinguished guitarist Göran Söllscher is not in the least self-indulgent in his approach to Bach, and his performances of the *Lute Suites* are thoughtful, highly musical and technically impeccable. There is judicious use of both light and shade; they also have the semi-improvisational quality of a live recital. He uses an eleven-stringed guitar, especially made for Renaissance and Baroque repertoire, which is beautifully recorded here within an agreeably warm acoustic. While the inclusion of his own transcriptions of the works for violin and cello necessitate changes of pitch, there is no reason in principle why they should not work well enough on the guitar. However, although his performances are of the usual high calibre, and he is at his very best in the *Sarabandes*, which are played very freely but not eccentrically, overall the music just fails to lift off in this format.

Shlomo Mintz takes all the technical difficulties of the solo *Violin Sonatas* in his stride, and again he is excellently recorded in a suitable acoustic. His playing has youthful vitality and power, and generally these recorded accounts give much musical satisfaction. But the famous *Chaconne* from the *D minor Partita* finds him wanting. Intonation is generally secure but goes seriously awry in the middle of the *G minor Fugue*. The sound is bold and clear, but this would not be a first choice among recorded versions.

Flute Sonatas 1–6, BWV 1030–35

⊕← (BB) *** ASV Resonance CD RSN 3008. Bennett, Malcolm (harpsichord), M. Evans

Flute Sonatas 1–6; in G min., BWV 1020; A Musical Offering: Sonata in C min.

*** Glossa GCD 920807 (2). Hazelzet, Ogg (harpsichord & fortepiano), Ter Linden (cello)

Flute Sonatas 1–6; in G min.; Partita in A min., BWV 1013

(M) *** CRD (ADD) 3314/5 (2). Preston, Pinnock, Savall

Flute Sonatas 1–6, BWV 1030–35; in G min., BWV 1020; Partita in A min., BWV 1013

(N) (M) *** Artemis Vanguard/Bach Guild (ADD) ATM-CD 1493 (2). Robinson, Cooper; with Eddy (in BWV 1033/35)

Flute Sonatas 1–6; Partita; Trio Sonatas, BWV 1038–9; Suite, BWV 997

(M) **(*) Häns. CD 92.121 (2). Gérard, Azzaloni, Blumenthal, Forchert, Formisano, Kleiner

Flute Sonatas 1–2; 4–6; 1033–5; in G min.

*** RCA 09026 62555-2. Galway, Cunningham, Moll

Flute Sonatas 1, 4 & 6; Trio Sonata in G; Partita, BWV 1013

**(*) MDG 309 0932-2. Kaiser, Musica Alta Ripa

Flute Sonatas 2, 3 & 5; in C min. (from Musical Offering); Trio Sonata, BWV 1038

**(*) MDG 309 0931-2. Kaiser, Musica Alta Ripa

William Bennett uses a modern flute, and in the first three sonatas he and George Malcolm manage without the nicety of using a viola da gamba in the continuo. In *Sonatas Nos. 4–6* the two players are joined by Michael Evans, and the bass is subtly but tangibly reinforced and filled out, though the balance remains just as impressive. The playing, as might be expected of these artists, has superb character: it is strong in personality yet does not lack finesse. Moreover it is strikingly alive and spontaneous and, since the CD transfer brings the most vivid presence without the sound being in the least overblown, this budget reissue can be enthusiastically recommended to all but those who demand the finer points of authenticity above all else. Bennett himself has made the reconstruction of the first movement of BWV 1032.

Two of these *Sonatas*, BWV 1031 and 1033, are unauthenticated, but they still contain attractive music. William Hazelzet plays with a gentle authority and sensitivity and a delicacy of articulation that are altogether most persuasive. He uses two different period instruments, with a subtle difference of colour. Jacques Ogg, his sympathetic partner, uses a modern harpsichord based on models of Couchet, Blanchet and Taskin for the majority of the sonatas, but an attractively bright but shallow fortepiano after Silbermann for BWV 1031, 1035 and 1079 (compare BWV 1021 and 1031, which follow each other on the second disc). Jaap ter Linden adds the cello continuo on BWV 1021 and 1033–5. The balance is expertly judged and, with excellent documentation, this must now take pride of place among period performances of this repertoire.

Using an authentic one-key instrument, Stephen Preston plays with a rare delicacy. Throughout, the continuo playing, led by Trevor Pinnock, is of the highest standard and this is an excellent alternative mid-price choice. This set now comes handsomely repackaged in a box.

The modern-instrument Bach Guild performances from the prize-winning Paula Robinson and Kenneth Cooper are delightful in every way. The recordings date from 1975/6, and the balance between Robinson's nimble flute playing, full of delicacy and charm, and Cooper's unidentified harpsichord is just about ideal, and when Timothy Eddy joins them with a cello continuo in BWV 1033/5 the interplay is equally felicitous. The CD transfer is immaculate, and this set is very enjoyable indeed.

James Galway has now progressed to using period instrumentalists as partners. He is a superb artist and his line in slow movements is exquisite. Vibrato is sparing and the flute timbre is refined, if obviously richer than an 18th-century instrument. The balance in the works with continuo means that Galway tends to dominate the sound-picture aurally as well as musically. But who will grumble when he plays so beautifully, and his companions give excellent support?

Jean-Claude Gérard is a fine player, but it seems curious that all this repertoire should have been recorded (in 1999) with piano instead of harpsichord and using a bassoon continuo. This is all very musical and pleasing enough in its way, but is hardly a first choice.

Karl Kaiser is a thoroughly musical and accomplished soloist, and the members of Musica Alta Ripa all play period instruments very smoothly. Their performances are stylishly pleasing, if at times perhaps a little bland. Twice they use a fortepiano rather than a harpsichord (BWV 1035 and 1039), but to good effect. The set is well balanced and truthfully recorded, but would not be a first choice.

Flute Sonatas 1; 3; 5; 6

(BB) **(*) HM HCX 3957024. See, Moroney (harpsichord), Springfield

Flute Sonatas 1, 4, 5 & 6; (Solo) Partita, BWV 1013

**(*) Channel CCS 15798. Solomon, Charlston

The *American Capital Times* describes the See/Moroney performances as 'wickedly charming'. Janet See's baroque flute has a warm yet watery timbre which is rather appealing, as is her lyrical phrasing, while she is chipper and lively in the allegros. Moroney's support is impeccable, and Mary Springfield adds the viola da gamba part very neatly in the last two works. The balance is excellent and this is certainly refreshing.

Ashley Solomon's solo playing is always flexible and spontaneous in feeling (especially in the solo *Partita*), and Terry Charlston makes up an impressive partnership. They too are well recorded, but the snag here is that the close microphones mean that every time Solomon takes a breath it is all too audible, which could be a problem for some listeners.

Sonatas: (i; ii) 1–3 for Flute & Harpsichord, BWV 1030/32; (i; ii; iii) 4–6 for Flute & Continuo, BWV 1033/5; Partita for Solo Flute, BWV 1013; Sonatas: (iii; ii) for Viola da gamba & Harpsichord, BWV 1027/29; (iv; v) for Violin & Harpsichord, BWV 1014/19; 1019a; (iv; ii; iii) for Violin & Continuo 1021/4; Anh. 153; (iv; v)Suite, BWV 1025; Fugue, BWV 1026 (both for Violin & Harpsichord)

(N) (M) *** DG 476 7117 (5). (i) Hazelzet; (ii) Bouman; (iii) Ter Linden; (iv) Goebel; (v) Hill; Köln Mus. Ant.

Although originally issued as separate sets, these performances were combined in a box to win the 1984 *Gramophone* Early Music Baroque award. Not surprisingly, as the performances are consistently of high quality, Hazelzet's performances of the *Flute Sonatas* are praised above. The *E flat Sonata*, BWV 1031 – at one time thought to be the work of Carl Philipp Emanuel, despite evidence to the contrary in the latter's handwriting – is beautifully played, and the finale of the *E major Sonata*, BWV 1035, is particularly delicate. The

Viola da gamba Sonatas are splendidly played by Jaap Ter Linden and Henk Bouman. The full, cleanly focused gamba timbre is beautifully caught, and the balance with the harpsichord is nigh on perfect. The *Violin Sonatas* are equally fresh and vigorous, also on period instruments, pleasantly abrasive in the violin tone, bringing dance-based movements in particular vividly to life. The *E minor Sonata*, the alternative version of BWV 1019, is welcome too, as is the *Suite in A major*, BWV 1025, which may not be authentic but is probably a composition by Johann Christian Friederich Grieg, but the *G minor Fugue*, BWV 1026, is almost certainly by Johann Sebastian. Highly recommended and very good value, with excellent documentation. The DG Archiv recording is very natural indeed.

Music for lute-harpsichord

Suites 1–2, BWV 996–7; 3 (Prelude, Fugue & Allegro in E flat), BWV 998; Fantasias & Fugues: in B flat, BWV 907; in D, BWV 928; Prelude & Fantasia in C min., BWV 921 & 1121; Prelude in C min., BWV 999
*** Häns. CD 92-109. Hill

The *Suite in E minor*, BWV 996, has the inscription 'Lautenwerck' on its title-page. But the instrument itself is obsolete. We know that it had one, two or three keyboards, used gut strings plucked simultaneously by several jacks and quills, and reputedly possessed an uncannily effective lute stop. So the present instrument, built by Keith Hill in Manchester, Michigan, USA, has had to be reconstructed conjecturally from descriptions of instruments in use in Bach's time. It features only one manual, authentically uses damperless jacks; an ingenious jack-slide, worked by a pedal, replaces the multiple system yet still allows some of the effect of multi-plucking. Robert Hill is a vivid and lively exponent of this experimental instrument; but, perversely, the works which come off best are the *Fantasias and Fugues*, which are less directly associated with the lute. The recording could hardly be better managed, but the resonant, undamped sound means that there is less delicacy of texture than with performances of the three *Suites* on lute or guitar. A fascinating collection none the less.

Lute Suite 1 in G min. BWV 995; Prelude, Fugue & Allegro, BWV 998; Sonata in G min., BWV 1001
(N) **(*) Atma ACD 2238. Stubbs (baroque lute) (available from www.atmaclassique.com)

It is good to hear this music on the lute, although it is not absolutely certain that Bach intended it for that instrument and it is highly effective on the guitar. Stephen Stubbs uses a pair of baroque lutes of either 13 or (in the case of the *G minor Suite*) 14 courses. Judging by the photographs accompanying the documentation, he plays fairly close to the fingerboard, which produces that separateness of plucked sound characteristic of the instrument, and which is especially effective in the two *Fugues*, BWV 998, and the second movement of his transcription of the *First Solo Violin Sonata*, BWV 1001. This is not to suggest that the lute is not able to be ruminatively flexible in the *Sarabande* of BWV 995. The recording is vivid, and altogether this is a stimulating listening experience; however, one does wonder why only three works were included – there would have been room for at least one more *Suite*.

Lute Suites (arranged for guitar) *1–4, BWV 995–7; 1006a*
⊕– ✿ (M) *** Virgin 5 62198-2. Isbin (guitar)
(N) (BB) *** Arte Nova 74321 82492-2. Fernández (guitar)

Lute Suites (arranged for guitar) *1–3; Prelude in C min.; Fugue in G min., BWV 999–1000*
(B) *** Sony (ADD) SBK 62972. Williams (guitar)

Lute Suite 4; Prelude, Fugue & Allegro in E flat, BWV 998. (Unaccompanied) Cello Suite 3: Bourrées 1–2. (i) arr. guitar and organ: Cantata 140: Chorale: Wachet auf!; Fugue à la gigue in G, BWV 877; Italian Concerto: Allegro. Trio Sonata 6 in G, BWV 530; Violin Sonata 4, BWV 1017: Adagio
(B) **(*) Sony ADD/DDD SBK 62973 (2). Williams (guitar); (i) with Hurford (organ)

Surprisingly, Sharon Isbin's reissued Virgin disc (from 1989) is the first single-CD offering all four of the *Lute Suites*, which suit the guitar so well and which here have been edited by Rosalyn Tureck. She gives these performances her imprimatur as 'the product of great talent, impeccable scholarship and extraordinary instrumental techniques'. They also show great sensibility. The opening *Prelude* of the *G minor Suite*, BWV 995 (here played in A minor), has a thoughtful sensitivity that is matched by the beauty of the following *Sarabande*, while the famous *Gavotte en rondeau* of the *E major Suite*, BWV 1006a, has a captivating sparkle and rhythmic lift. In short, this splendid collection even surpasses the classic versions of John Williams in their spontaneity and depth of feeling. The recording is most natural.

Eduardo Fernández now joins Isbin in offering all four *Lute Suites* on a single disc – and very fine they are too. His flexible rubato in the *Sarabandes* has a thoughtful intensity that is very telling, yet he plays the livelier dances with spirit and is particularly appealing in the *Fourth Suite* (a transcription of the *Third Solo Violin Partita*), where there are several favourite moments. His technique has an easy facility, and this is first-class Bach playing in every sense, while the recording cannot be faulted. A most enjoyable disc, and at budget price too.

John Williams shows a natural response to Bach, and his performances of the four *Lute Suites* are among his finest records. The first of these two discs can be recommended unreservedly: the flair of his playing, with its rhythmic vitality and sense of colour, is always telling. The second disc opens with a most winning account of the *Fourth Suite*. The transcriptions of the *Bourrées* from the *Cello Suite* are effective enough; but not all listeners will care for the rest of the programme of rather contrived duets for guitar and organ (an unlikely combination).

(i) Lute Suites 1–2; (ii) Trio Sonatas 1; 5
(M) *** RCA 09026 61603-2. Bream (i) (guitar); (ii) (lute), Malcolm

The two *Lute Suites* are played with great subtlety and mastery on the guitar; the *Trio Sonatas* were originally written for organ; here they are heard on lute and harpsichord and are elegantly played and cleanly recorded within a convincing ambience: the effect is pleasingly transparent and intimate.

Arrangements for Guitar: *Cello Suites: 1, BWV 1007: Prelude & Sarabande. 2, BWV 1008: Minuet. 3, BWV 1009: Sarabande. 4, BWV 1010: Bourrée. 6, BWV 1012: Gavotte. Lute Suites: 1, BWV 996: Allemande; Courante; Sarabande; Bourrée. 2: BWV 997: Sarabande. 3, BWV 995: Sarabande. 5, BWV 1011: Sarabande. Prelude in D, BWV 998; Little Prelude for Lute, BWV 999. Violin Partita 1, BWV 825: Sarabande & Double. Anna Magdalena's Notebook: March; 3 Minuets*
(N) ** Div. Art 24115. Jonathan Richards (guitar)

This collection is described as 'Bach's soothing music for guitar'. It is well played and agreeably recorded, the effect pleasant enough, and is obviously intended as late-evening background music.

Oboe Sonatas: in G min., BWV 1020 & BWV 1030b; in E flat, BWV 1031; in C, BWV 1033. (Organ) *Trio Sonata in C, BWV 529; Well-Tempered Clavier Book II; Prelude & Fugue in C min., BWV 871*
*** Signum SIGCD 034. Hennessy, Parle (harpsichord)

Never mind that these works were not conceived by Bach with the oboe in mind; they sound quite delightful on Gail Hennessy's baroque instrument. Her tone is as pleasing as her playing is stylish; whether in the *Siciliana* of BWV 1031 or the searching *Adagio* of BWV 1033, she provides expressive playing of a high order. She has a fine partner in Nicholas Parle – how beautifully they answer each other in the opening Allegro of BWV 1020, partly because of the excellent balance. The *Trio Sonata*, intended for the organ, works remarkably well in the present arrangement, the finale wonderfully perky and light-hearted.

6 (organ) Trio Sonatas: 1–6, BMV 525–30 (arr. King)
*** Hyp. CDA 666843. King's Consort, King

6 (organ) Trio Sonatas (arr. Gwilt for 2 violins, or violin & viola, cello & harpsichord or organ)
*** BIS CD 1345. L. Baroque, Medlam

Bach's *Organ Sonatas* readily invite transcription, and Robert King makes a good case for presenting them in such arrangements as are offered here, all retaining the original keys. The baroque oboe and oboe d'amore suit Bach's invention especially well and the resulting ranges of colour are very appealing, giving this music a completely new dimension. The playing is joyous and light-hearted and always warm in spirit. First-class recording, too.

London Baroque present the *Trio Sonatas* on strings alone, varying the texture in two cases (BWV 526 and 528) to replace the second violin with a viola, which proves particularly pleasing, with a fuller, warmer texture. Yet the detail of the part-writing emerges clearly. The playing is vivid and full of life, and this makes a fine alternative to the Hyperion version, for the strings here are most attractively recorded.

Viola da gamba Sonatas 1–3, BWV 1027–9
☛ (M) *** Alia Vox AV 9812 (with *Sonata in C, BWV 529*). Savall, Koopman
(M) *** Häns. CD 92.124. Peri (viola da gamba), Behringer (harpsichord)
(M) *** Warner Elatus (ADD) 0927 46717-2. Tortelier (cello), Veyron-Lacroix (harpsichord)
*** DG 415 471–2. Maisky (cello), Argerich (piano)

(i) Viola da gamba Sonatas 1–3. Preludes & Fugues: in D, BWV 850; in G, BWV 860; in G min., BWV 861
*** Signum SIGCD 024. (i) Crum (viola da gamba); Cummings (harpsichord)

(i) Viola da gamba Sonatas 1–3; (ii) Flute Sonatas 1–6
(M) *** Sony SMK 89747. (i) Ma, Cooper (harpsichord); (ii) Rampal, Pinnock, Pidoux

Jordi Savall and Ton Koopman's new set completely supersedes their earlier performance on Virgin. There is a depth of expressive feeling here combined with an intimate rapport between the two players that gives an effect of eavesdropping on live music-making of the highest calibre. The recording is resonant but full, firm and cleanly focused. A clear first choice.

A fine alternative set comes from Alison Crum and Laurence Cummings. Here the harpsichord is very much in the picture, boldly played, with plenty of life and vigour, by Cummings. But Crum's firmly focused gamba is never eclipsed, and the balance overall is better than that on the Hänssler CD. Moreover, Cummings offers sparkling performances of three keyboard *Preludes and Fugues* as a bonus. They are placed to act as interludes between the viola da gamba sonatas. You have only to sample the infectious performance of the *G major Prelude* to find out how attractive they are.

The performances on Hänssler are also warmly sympathetic and alive. Hilde Peri's tone is full – not edgy – and the balance with Michael Behringer's excellently articulated harpsichord-playing is good, the harpsichord a shade backward but still coming through in a warm but not clouding acoustic. A good mid-price alternative.

As the opening *Adagio* of BWV 1027 demonstrates, Tortelier's are warmly expressive, inspirational performances, deeply felt, yet with the allegros spirited and lightly articulated by both artists. The recordings date from 1963, when Tortelier was in his prime. The balance is remarkably successful, and the two instruments are given a natural presence in a pleasing acoustic. The CD transfer is first class, and Tortelier's admirers will not want to be without this fine reissue.

Mischa Maisky is a highly expressive cellist and he opts for the piano – successfully, for Martha Argerich is a Bach player of the first order. A most enjoyable account for collectors who do not care for period instruments.

Yo-Yo Ma plays with great eloquence and natural feeling. His tone is warm and refined and his technical command remains as ever irreproachable. Kenneth Cooper is a splendid partner. However, the colour of the harpsichord does not blend with the cello quite as naturally as with a gamba and there is still a case to be made for the piano as a more appropriate accompaniment. The *Flute Sonatas*, added for this reissue, make a generous bonus. Rampal plays fluently and in good style. The snag is the recording balance, with the flute timbre rich and forward, while the harpsichord (an attractive American instrument, after Hemsch) is relegated to the background. When Roland Pidoux's cello is added to the continuo, the combined sound tends to congeal and detail is opaque.

Violin sonatas

(Unaccompanied) Violin Sonatas 1–3, BWV 1001, 1003 & 1005; Violin Partitas 1–3, BWV 1002, 1004 & 1006
✹ *** EMI 7 49483-2 (2). Perlman
☛ ✹ (N) (M) *** Warner Elatus 2 56461885-2 (2 CDs). Kagan
(M) *** DG (ADD) 457 701-2 (2). Milstein
(M) (***) EMI mono 5 67197-2 (2). Menuhin
*** Testament SBT 2090 (2). Haendel
(B) *** Ph. (ADD) Duo 438 736-2 (2). Grumiaux
(B) *** DG (ADD) Double 453 004-2 (2). Szeryng
(N) *** Pentatone **SACD** PTC 5186 072 (2). Fischer
(B) **(*) EMI (ADD) double forte 5 73644-2 (2). Suk
**(*) Channel CCS 12198 & 14498. Podger
(N) (BB) ** Virgin 5 62374-2 (4). Tetzlaff – *Cello Suites* ***
(N) (BB) **(*) Naxos 8.557563/64. Schröder (baroque violin)

The range of tone in Perlman's playing adds to the power of

these performances, infectiously rhythmic in dance movements but conveying the intensity of live performance in the great slow movements with hushed playing of great refinement. Some may still seek a greater sense of struggle conveyed in order to bring out the full depth of the writing, but the sense of spontaneity, of the player's own enjoyment of the music, makes this set a unique, revelatory experience.

Oleg Kagan made these recordings during live performances in the Concertgebouw in 1989. He died not long afterwards. Fortunately, the CDs are a worthy memento, celebrating his wisdom and supreme musicianship. They have all the magnetism of live music-making and a serenity of spirit that is completely satisfying. As performances they are less reserved and aristocratic than Milstein, not so emotionally extrovert as with Perlman; technically they are almost flawless. The Concertgebouw acoustics add a warm ambience to the beautifully focused violin image and the effect is very real and vivid.

Milstein's set from the mid-1970s remains among the most satisfying of all versions. Every phrase is beautifully shaped, there is a highly developed feeling for line, and these performances have an aristocratic poise and a classical finesse which are very satisfying.

It was the 18-year-old Yehudi Menuhin to whom (between 1934 and 1936) HMV entrusted the very first complete recording of the *Unaccompanied Sonatas* and *Partitas*, and the young musician's remarkable accomplishment more than repaid the company's faith in him. The great *Chaconne* from BWV 1004 is one of most thrilling performances ever put on disc. Elsewhere, the rich, vibrant tone and direct approach (with no swooning or lingering) must have astonished listeners of the time. The microphone is obviously very close, but the secure bowing can take such a scrutiny: the violin image is a little dry, yet is remarkably real and immediate.

Though Ida Haendel's speeds are exceptionally broad, her playing is magnetic, making one welcome her decision to observe all repeats. She takes a full 18 minutes over the great *Chaconne* of the *D minor Partita* but the strong, steady pacing means that the build-up is all the more powerful, with counterpoint clearly defined, helped by vividly immediate recording.

Arthur Grumiaux strikes just the right balance between expressive feeling and purity of style. Some may prefer a rhythmically freer, more charismatic approach, but Grumiaux's readings of all six works are the product of superlative technique and a refined musical intellect.

Henryk Szeryng's tone has never before been caught on record with such leonine fullness and beauty. The technical mastery and polish are quite remarkable, his intonation flawless. These performances are rhythmically free and full of subtle touches.

Julia Fischer was only 21 when she tackled these most challenging of solo violin works but, as she explains in an endearingly frank note, she has loved them since she was nine, has played them daily for many years and performed one of them for Yehudi Menuhin in a masterclass when she was only 11. Broadly traditional in approach, Fischer plays with immaculate purity and clarity, bringing out the separate strands in the *Fugues* of the sonatas, and never forcing her tone. Young as she is, she reveals her individuality in her treatment of the *Sarabandes* in the first two *Partitas*. Where, prompted by the spread chords, some violinists make them monumental, Fischer with her lighter touch makes them thoughtful and contemplative, reflecting the comparable

movements in the *Cello Suites*. Though her tone is refined rather than weighty, she plays the great *Chaconne* of the *D minor Partita* with power and concentration, with big contrasts between sections, again deeply reflective at the start of the major-key section. Her rhythmic pointing is a delight too, her light treatment bringing sparkle to such a movement as the *Gavotte* of the third *Partita*. Her set includes an additional DVD-compatible track, containing an artist interview and session impression.

Josef Suk is a superb artist – but his playing, although technically immaculate, is curiously self-conscious. There seems a tendency to over-inflate the music with broad tempi, and these are not the searching performances one expects in this repertoire.

Rachel Podger uses a period instrument, but her technique and intonation are secure, her tone is full and clean without scratchiness or edge. Only in slow movements is there a minor reservation about the linear style, with moments of minor tonal swelling slightly disturbing the phrasing. There is much to praise in this artist's simplicity of approach, and she is beautifully recorded, but in the last resort this cannot quite compete with the very finest versions.

Sitkovetsky has a beautiful tone and his polished fluency is technically and musically admirable. But everything is too easy-going, there is no sense of grip, of difficulties being surmounted, of a strong forward pulse (Hänssler 92.119).

Christian Tetzlaff's timbre is very appealing and his performance is recorded extremely realistically (by Andrew Keener and Mike Clements). But his reading is most controversial, with extreme tempi, and slow movements are at times almost languorous. The very opening *Adagio* of the *First Sonata* demonstrates his indulgently wayward approach, while the following *Fugue* shows him at his most imaginative. Then the closing *Presto* is very fast indeed and the *Double* of the *First Partita* is faster still, surely too fast. The *A minor Sonata* (No. 2) shows him at his best, and if the closing *Allegro* is again very brisk it has plenty of light and shade. More surprisingly, the famous *Chaconne* of the *D minor Partita* tends rather to slacken in tension as it proceeds. The brilliant playing in the final *Allegro assai* of *Sonata 3* and the quicksilver *Prelude* of the *Third Partita* offer more examples of Tetzlaff's Paganini-like virtuosity, which is easy to enjoy; but this is not a set to recommend except to those who relish bravura in Bach, even if it is over the top.

Jaap Schröder's cycle was made in 1984/5, so it was one of the first in stereo using a baroque violin. The recording (made in a village church) is very bold and close, truthful, but with the dynamic range consequently reduced (particularly striking in the famous *Chaconne* in the *D minor Partita*, which seems to be nearly all on one dynamic level). Schröder's purposeful, direct style brings playing which is secure but at times appears effortful, and the *Sarabande* in the *B minor Partita* seems almost laboured. These performances have undoubted integrity but will not be to all tastes.

Monica Huggett plays her period instrument with skill and accuracy, but she fails to communicate the inner world of this music. She uses considerable nudgings of rubato and momentary pauses, but the result is curiously uninvolving. Although a piece like the fourth-movement *Double* of the *B minor Partita* offers a beautifully articulated stream of notes, which is technically very impressive, the famous *Chaconne* from the *D minor Partita* is made to sound uninvolved and didactic. She is given first-class recording (Virgin 5 62340-2).

(Unaccompanied) *Violin Sonatas 1–3; Violin Partitas 1–3; (i) Violin Sonatas 3–4, BWV 1016–17*

(M) **(*) Ph. (ADD) 464 673-2 (2). Grumiaux; (i) with Sartori (harpsichord)

Grumiaux's set of the solo *Sonatas* and *Partitas* is available economically on a Philips Duo (see above). His musical authority and purity of intonation impress every bit as much as they did in 1960 when they were made, and the sound has striking realism. There is an aristocratic quality to Grumiaux's playing as well as a natural unforced vitality. Here these performances are offered as one of Philips's '50 Great Recordings' at mid-price with two of the *Sonatas for Violin and Harpsichord* thrown in for good measure. But these were Grumiaux's earlier recordings with Egida Giordani Sartori, which, though his own playing is peerless, were less spontaneous in effect than his later set with Jaccottet (see below).

(Unaccompanied) *Violin Sonatas 1–3, Violin Partitas 1–3; Violin Sonata 3, BWV 1016 (2 versions)*

(BB) (***) Naxos mono 8.110918 & 8.110964. Y. Menuhin, with alternatively H. Menuhin or Landowska

Menuhin's early recordings of the solo *Violin Sonatas* and *Partitas* are also available on Naxos. Ward Marston's transfers are expert, but the sound is not quite as smooth as that transferred by the EMI engineers (who had access to the original masters), and there is slightly more background noise. However, the inclusion of Menuhin's two recordings, made in 1938 and 1944 respectively, of the *E major Violin and Harpsichord Sonata* makes a fascinating comparison, the performance with Landowska's harpsichord slower and heavier in style (especially the Adagio) than the fresher version with his sister Hephzibah on the piano.

(Unaccompanied) *Violin Partitas 2 (complete); 3 (Minuets I & II only); Violin Sonatas 1; 3 (complete); (i) English Suite 3 in E: Sarabande; Gavottes I & II*

(M) (***) EMI mono 7 64494-2. Heifetz, (i) with Sándor

Heifetz's Bach was by no means romantic, but his chimerical bowing produces more variety of timbre and subtlety of dynamic shading than would have been likely or possible in Bach's time, while the great *Chaconne* has wonderful detail without losing strength. Such is the spontaneity of effect that the result gives enormous pleasure. The transfer is bright and truthful.

Violin Sonatas (for violin & harpsichord) 1–6, BWV 1014–19

*** Sony S2K 89469 (2). Carmignola, Marcon

*** Naxos 8.554614 (1–4); 8.554783 (5–6 & alternative movements for BWV 1019). Van Dael, Van Asperen

Violin Sonatas 1–6; 1019a; Cantabile from 1019a (2nd version); Sonatas for Violin & Continuo, BWV 1021 & 1023

*** Channel CCS 14798 (2). Podger, Pinnock (with Manson in BWV 1021 & 1023)

Violin Sonatas 1–6; 1019a; Sonatas for Violin & Continuo, BWV 1020–24

⟐ ✿ (B) *** Ph. (ADD) Duo 454 011-2 (2). Grumiaux, Jaccottet, Mermoud (in BWV 1021 & 1023)

Violin Sonatas 1–6; Sonatas for Violin & Continuo, BWV 1021, 1023 & 1024; Fugue in G min., BWV 1026

(M) **(*) Hyp. Dyad CDD 22025 (2). Huggett, Nicholson, Tunnicliffe

Violin Sonatas 1–6; 1019a; Sonatas for Violin & Continuo, BWV 1020–24; Suite, BWV 1025 (arr. Weiss); Fugue in G min., BWV 1026; Harpsichord Sonata in D min., BWV 964 (arr. of BWV 1003); Adagio, BWV 968 (arr. of BWV 1005)

**(*) MDG 309 1073/5-2 (3) (available separately). Musica Alta Ripa

Violin Sonatas 1–6; (i) Sonatas for Violin & Continuo, BWV 1021 & 1023

*** Chan. 0603 (2). Mackintosh, Cole; (i) with Ward Clarke

(BB) **(*) Virgin 5 61650-2 (2) [id]. Holloway, Moroney, Sheppard

Violin Sonatas 1–6, with alternative version of BWV 1019; Sonatas for Violin & Continuo, BWV 1021, 1023 & 1024; Toccata & Fugue in D min., BWV 565 (arr. Manze for solo violin)

**(*) HM HMU 907250.51 (2). Manze, Egarr, Ter Linden

Musica Alta Ripa offer a complete coverage of this repertoire, including arrangements of BWV 1003 and 1005 (originally for solo violin), although three full-priced CDs are involved. The *Suite in D minor*, BWV 1025, is agreeable listening, if of doubtful authenticty: all the movements except the first are transcriptions by Silvius Weiss of a *Lute Suite in A major*. The period-instrument performances here are accomplished, enjoyably musical and well balanced and recorded in a pleasingly resonant acoustic. But they have less individuality than the finest of the performances listed below.

The Bach *Sonatas for Violin and Harpsichord* and for *Violin and Continuo* are marvellously played, with all the beauty of tone and line for which Grumiaux is renowned; they have great vitality, too. His admirable partner is Christiane Jaccottet, and in BWV 1021 and 1023 Philippe Mermoud (cello) joins the continuo. There is endless treasure to be discovered here, particularly when the music-making is so serenely communicative.

A fine new period-instrument version from Naxos goes to the top of the list. It is beautifully played and recorded, and the violinist has a positive relationship with her distinguished keyboard partner. The set gives very great pleasure and satisfaction and includes four alternative movements for BWV 1019.

The Sony set of the six *Violin and Harpsichord Sonatas* from Giuliano Carmignola and Andrea Marcon is outstanding, and could well be a first choice for collectors who do not object to the absence of the *Sonatas for Violin and Continuo* provided by Grumiaux and others. The balance between the two instruments is just about ideal, within an acoustic which adds a nice bloom without obscuring detail. Carmignola plays an eighteenth-century baroque violin whose maker is not known, but which has a sonority to match perfectly the copy of a Mietke harpsichord used by Marcon. The measure here may be short, but the quality is outstandingly high.

Catherine Mackintosh uses a baroque violin, but her timbre is full, her lyrical line flows with an affecting sensitivity. Articulation in allegros is exhilaratingly crisp and clean, and both players express their joy in the music. Maggie Cole's persuasive contribution is well in the picture, and the balance between violin and double-manual harpsichord could hardly be managed more adroitly. In Bach's two *Sonatas for Violin and Continuo* Jennifer Ward Clarke's cello contribution adds to the interest and sonority of the music. Our special allegiance to the Grumiaux performances of the same music on modern instruments remains undiminished, and their

Philips Duo costs half as much as the Chandos set. But these new interpretations are very stimulating.

The performances by Rachel Podger and Trevor Pinnock also carry the highest recommendation, even though the balance places the violin a fraction too near the microphones. This is immediately noticeable in the brightness of timbre of the opening allegro of BWV 1019, which begins the first disc and may trouble some ears. A period violin playing *forte* in its upper range needs no spotlight, and although the balance is excellent in the quieter slow movements, in some of the livelier movements the harpsichord detail is slightly masked by the violin, which is a pity because Trevor Pinnock's contribution is very distinguished. So, too, is the playing of Rachel Podger, always very stylish and warmly phrased. While BWV 1022 and 1024 are omitted, the inclusion of the fine extended *Cantabile* which Bach added to BWV 1019 in 1725 is a distinct asset. Apart from the balance, the recording acoustic is pleasing, but this set should be sampled before purchase.

Andrew Manze is nothing if not individual. Fast movements sparkle vivaciously; slow movements are often played *sotto voce*, creating a withdrawn, almost unearthly sense of repose which is perhaps not quite what Bach intended, but is still very affecting. The balance with the harpsichord or continuo is excellent, yet it is Manze who dominates. For some reason a gamba is also added to the first, *B minor Sonata*, BWV 1014, and it is curiously intrusive. But the highlight of the collection is Manze's breathtaking paraphrase for solo violin of Bach's famous organ *Toccata and Fugue in D minor*, BWV 565. Here Manze's timbre is sweet and full, whereas elsewhere at times it seems unnecessarily meagre, with touches of edginess.

John Holloway too has long experience in the early-music field. His undoubted sensitivity, ability and good taste have won him a wide following, but some will find the actual sound he makes unpleasing: it is vinegary and at times downright ugly. Both Davitt Moroney and Susan Sheppard give excellent support, and the recording cannot be faulted in its clarity and presence.

On the Hyperion Dyad, Monica Huggett often plays exquisitely, as she does in the opening *Dolce* of *No. 2 in A major*. Clearly these marvellous works strike a chord in her sensibility, and she also gives a remarkably spirited display of bravura. One simply has to come to terms with her characteristic timbre, with its thinness (some would say edginess) on top. Yet in the dancing allegros she brings out all the music's joy. The violin is beautifully balanced with Paul Nicholson's sensitive harpsichord backing and, where appropriate, Richard Tunnicliffe's busy cello.

As in his set of the *Solo Violin Sonatas* and *Partitas*, Sitkovetsky plays with great fluency and finish. But his use of vibrato and his indulgently relaxed, lyrical manner are out of style. Robert Hill gives him fine support, but this cannot compete with Grumiaux (Hänssler 92.122).

Violin and Harpsichord Sonatas 1–4, BWV 1014–17
(BB) *** HM Classical Express HCX 395 7084. Blumenstock, Butt (harpsichord)

In what is presumably to become a complete set, the first instalment from Elizabeth Blumenstock and John Butt is very promising indeed. At the opening *Adagio* of the *B minor Sonata*, BWV 1014, John Butt's introduction is pleasingly free and thoughtful, and the violin entry on a gentle crescendo is

just as compelling. Throughout, allegros are engagingly spirited, articulation clean without a hint of didacticism and the interplay between these two artists is constantly stimulating. How delightful is the catchy second movement of the *E major Sonata*, BWV 1016! Elizabeth Blumenstock plays a Strad (and her judicious use of vibrato and her refined style are wholly apt for this repertoire); John Butt uses a modern copy of a 1646 Rückers, enlarged in 1780 by Taskin, and the two players are beautifully balanced and recorded. Most enjoyable – highly recommended.

KEYBOARD MUSIC

The Art of Fugue, BWV 1080; (i) A Musical Offering, BWV 1079. The Well-Tempered Clavier (48 Preludes & Fugues), BWV 846–93
(M) *** HM HMX 2908084/90. Moroney (harpsichord); (i) with Cook, See, Holloway, Ter Linden

If you want all these works played on the harpsichord, and that a modern instrument built in 1980, this Harmonia Mundi mid-priced box is worth considering, for Davitt Moroney has imagination as well as scholarship, and he is eminently well served by the engineers. The *Musical Offering* is also very much dominated by one or two harpsichords, although Moroney is joined by flute and violin in the *Trio Sonata*, and the violin also shares the second of the six regal *Canons*. Again the recording is well balanced and natural. In the *Well-Tempered Clavier* the balance is rather close, the harpsichord image full-bodied and clear. Moroney's considered approach is satisfying in its way. Stylistically, it will suit those who like a thoughtful, unostentatious approach to Bach, yet one that does not lack rhythmic resilience or vitality.

The Art of Fugue (see also string quartet and orchestral versions)
*** Häns. CD 92.134 (2). Hill (harpsichord)
(B) *** HM (ADD) HMX 2901169/70. Moroney (harpsichord)
*** MusicMasters 1612 67173-2. Feltsman (piano)

The Art of Fugue; Partita 2 in C min., BWV 826
(M) **(*) OPS 52-9116/17. Sokolov (piano)

Robert Hill lays out Bach's fugal progression in front of the listener with admirable clarity and concern for the contrapuntal detail, and he varies tempi with excellent judgement to keep the music continually alive. In the *Duet Fugue* he is joined by Michael Behringer. As an appendix he offers four contrapuncti and the *Augmented Canon in Contrary Motion* from Bach's early draft (BWV 1080a). The harpsichord itself has a fine, strong personality and is recorded in a warm acoustic which yet never blurs the interplay of the partwriting.

Davitt Moroney's account commands not only the intellectual side of the work but also the aesthetic, and his musicianship is second to none.

Although he begins gently, Vladimir Feltsman's articulation is at times bold, although it is never hard-edged. He intersperses the *Canons* individually within the body of the work and makes the very most of dynamic contrast. Yet he can be thoughtfully meditative. Feltsman's interpretation is well thought out and thoroughly convincing. He is very well recorded but offers no coupling.

Sokolov's *Art of Fugue* is entirely pianistic. He is neither pedagogic nor didactic, but his linear clarity is admirable. He uses a wide range of dynamic and one can hear the fullest polyphonic detail, yet the music's underlying expressive character emerges readily. The nineteen *Contrapuncti* are played in order, ending – at the beginning of the second disc – with the unfinished No. 19, presented very slowly. He then groups the *Canons* together and closes the work with a deliberate rallentando. The *C minor Partita* makes a lively and characterful encore.

(i) *The Art of Fugue;* (ii) *Applicato in C, BWV 994; Aria & 10 Variations in the Italian Style; Chorale: Joy and Peace, BWV 512; Fantasia in G min., BWV 917; Invention in C, BWV 772 & 772a (1720 & 1723 versions); Italian Concerto; Marches: in D & E flat, BWV Anh. 122 & 127; Musette in D, BWV Anh. 126; 2 Minuets in F, BWV Anh. 115–16; Polonaise in F, BWV Anh. 117a; Prelude & Fugue in A min., BWV 895; Suite in F, BWV 623 (incomplete).* (TELEMANN): *Suite in A, BWV 824 (wrongly attributed to J. S. B.)*
(B) *** Sony (DDD/ADD) SB2K 63231 (2). (i) Rosen; (ii) Tureck (piano)

Charles Rosen's superb account of *The Art of Fugue* is one of the great achievements of Bach keyboard recording. Rosen justifies his choice of a modern piano by his manner of playing, neutralizing any unwanted romantic overtones. The authority of his performance is remarkable and the depth of thought that lies behind the playing creates a satisfying sense of architecture. The 1967 recording is firm and clear, just right for such an exposition, and this performance has total mastery.

Tureck makes a perfect foil for Rosen in offering an essentially lightweight programme, mainly of short keyboard vignettes in which we can hear Bach relaxing and enjoying himself. One of the highlights of the recital is the *Aria in the Italian Style,* followed by ten crisply diverting variations. Tureck's playing not only shows the utmost felicity but also sensitive control of dynamic contrast. The 1981 digital recording is rather forward but not shallow; the *Italian Concerto* dates from 1979 and the sound is more clattery, less well focused. But this set is not to be missed by anyone who enjoys hearing Bach on the piano, and it is a great bargain.

Chromatic Fantasia & Fugue, BWV 903; 4 Duets, BWV 802/5; English Suites 1–6; Fantasia and Fugue in A min., BWV 944; French Suites 1–6; Goldberg Variations, BWV 988; Italian Concerto, BWV 971; 6 Partitatas, BWV 625/30; Partita in B min., BWV 831; (i) *Brandenburg Concertos 1 & 5; Harpsichord Concertos 4 & 5;* (ii) *Triple Concerto for Flute, Violin & Harpsichord, BWV 1044*
(N) (B) **(*) DG 477 013-2 (8). Kirkpatrick, with (i) Lucerne Festival Strings; (ii) Nicolet & Baumgartner

Ralph Kirkpatrick was a key harpsichord soloist on DG's Archiv label in the 1950s and early 1960s. He is a scholarly rather than an intuitive player, yet his thoughts are rarely without interest. Curiously, the *English Suites,* recorded in the famous Munich Herculessaal, are a little dry, probably because of close microphones; the *French Suites,* and the *Fantasy and Fugue in A minor* (something of a tour de force) used the Hamburg studio and are somewhat mellower. The *Goldberg Variations* and *Six Partitas* date from 1958 and were made in stereo in the Jesus-Christus-Kirche. Kirkpatrick is at his best in the *Variations,* providing light and subtle registration. The playing is lively when it should be, controlled and

steady in the slow, stately contrapuntal variations. He certainly conveys the immense feeling of build and momentum that make this work the masterpiece it is.

The *Partitas* show that they can respond to his comparatively inexorable tempi, with his strictness never descending into pedantry, and his modern Neupert harpsichord sounds sonorous and dynamic. He also makes a good deal of the possibilities of the *Chromatic Fantasia and Fugue,* with an impressive increase in tension at the climax of the fugue. However, sometimes his unrelenting rhythmic onward flow and firmness of grip can strike one as too much of a good thing, as in the *Italian Concerto.*

Baumgartner's *Brandenburg* performances are set in the traditional German mould. He is content to go along with the score, contributing relatively little, though his soloists are often excellent; and it is Aurèle Nicolet, the flautist in the *Triple Concerto,* who freshens the music-making and plays delightfully in the *Affetuoso* centrepiece. The *Harpsichord Concertos* again show Kirkpatrick in the very best light, and it is a pity that room was not found for No. 1, also dating from 1958/60. The recordings were models of their time, with fresh, clean performances, beautifully scaled. Here the Lucerne players match the liveliness of Kirkpatrick, who strikes an admirable balance between expressiveness and classical feeling. Fine sound, too.

Chromatic Fantasia & Fugue in D min., BWV 903; 4 Duets, BWV 802–5; Italian Concerto in F; Partita in B min., BWV 831
✿ (M) *** Decca 4761704. Rousset (harpsichord)
(BB) **(*) Warner Apex 8573 89224-2. Ross (harpsichord)

Christophe Rousset's playing combines the selfless authority and scholarly dedication of such artists as Leonhardt and Gilbert with the flair and imagination of younger players, and all the performances here have a taste and musical vitality that reward the listener.

Scott Ross's account of the *Chromatic Fantasia* has less flair than Rousset's. Some may respond to its breadth, which is emphasized by the full-bodied, resonant harpsichord image. These are undoubtedly fine performances, considered and in excellent style, but at times seemingly a little didactic. They are rewarding, but not a first choice in this repertoire, even at budget price.

Chromatic Fantasy and Fugue, BWV 903; English Suite 2 in A min., BWV 807; French Suite 5 in G, BWV 816; Italian Concerto in F, BWV 971; Partita 4 in D, BWV 828; 15 Two-Part Inventions, BWV772/786; The Well-Tempered Clavier, Book 1: Preludes and Fugues 1–2, 5–6, 14 & 17; Book 2: Preludes and Fugues 1, 3, 7, 12 & 24
(N) (B) *** Decca 475 193-2 (2). András Schiff

This compilation of András Schiff's Bach recordings makes an ideal introduction to his way with this composer: the playing has freshness and individuality, and his sparkling ornamentation is always winning. The *Preludes and Fugues* are translated into pianistic terms, rarely if ever imitating the harpsichord, yet one is soon won over. Try the *Gavotte* in the *Fifth Suite* for rhythmic lift or the slow movement of the *Italian Concerto* to experience his sustained line at its most beautiful. Superb recordings, and inexpensive to buy.

Chromatic Fantasia & Fugue; Goldberg Variations; Italian Concerto; Partitas 1–6, BWV 825–8; Little fughettas, BWV 952–3, 961; Little Preludes, BWV 924–8; 930; 933–43; 999;

*Little Preludes with fughettas, BWV 895, 899, 900, 902/902a.
Transcriptions: arr. Busoni: Chaconne in D min. (from
BWV 1004); Preludes & Fugues, BWV 532 & 552; Toccata,
Adagio and Fugue, BWV 564; Toccata & Fugue in D min.,
BWV 565. arr. Hess: Chorale, Jesu, joy of man's desiring*

(N) (BB) *** EMI 5 85878-2 (5). Maria Tipo (piano)

Maria Tipo belongs to the old school. Like the late lamented
Tatiana Nikolayeva, hers is music-making from a different
age, yet it is every bit as living and vibrant as any now before
the public. Her performanec of the *Chromatic Fantasia*, using
a wide dynamic range, is full of flair and virtuosity. The
Italian Concerto has similar panache, with the central
Andante played with exquisite gentleness yet unselfconsciously, to contrast with the robustly vigorous finale. Her
Goldberg Variations is freely romantic in spirit, with a far
from unpleasing variety and subtlety of tonal shading. She
observes first repeats only (even so, the timing runs to 64
minutes) and, generally speaking, is free from excessive idiosyncrasy, with rubati not overdone, though Variations 22
and 26 are an exception. She comes completely into her own
in the six *Partitas*. The part-writing and inner voices all 'tell'
and speak with great sweep and, when required, vigour. She
phrases very musically: her phrasing has breadth and freedom and, what is more, her control of pianistic colour is very
appealing indeed. In its way her set is as good as any in the
catalogue.

The *Little Preludes and Fughettas*, which Bach may well
have written for the use of his 10-year-old son, Wilhelm
Friedmann, are also immensely diverting. The consistently
changing style, tempo and articulation hold the listener
throughout all these miniatures; nothing is mechanical or
remotely metronomic. And, not surprisingly, she is completely at home in the Busoni transcriptions. The opening of
the great *Chaconne* is very commanding indeed: the piece
progresses with unashamed use of romantic light and shade
to build to a powerful climax. In the famous *Toccata and
Fugue in D minor* her flamboyant control of colour is such
that one feels she has heard and been influenced by
Stokowski's orchestral version. The *Toccata, Adagio and Fugue*
has similar panache: the crisp articulation of the *Fugue* is a
joy, and the *Fugue in D major*, BWV 532, is comparably
light-hearted. In complete contrast, her performance of the
famous Myra Hess transcription of *Jesu, joy of man's desiring*
is affectingly gentle. Throughout the set she is beautifully
recorded (in the Salle Wagram, between 1986 and 1991) and
this is an inexpensive reissue to treasure, anticipating the
move back to a freely flexible style of Bach playing on the
piano which has been the hallmark of Angela Hewitt's much
more recent recordings. However, as with the rest of these
French EMI boxes, the notes are sparse and in French only.

*Chromatic Fantasia & Fugue; Goldberg Variations, BWV
988; Italian Concerto; Partita 1 in B flat, BWV 825; Prelude,
Fugue & Allegro, BWV 998; Toccata, Adagio & Fugue, BWV
916*

(BB) *** Virgin 2×1 5 61555-2 (2). Cole (harpsichord)

Maggie Cole plays the *Goldberg Variations* on a copy by
Andrew Warlick of a harpsichord by J. C. Goujon of 1749. She
is recorded with great clarity; as so often, the playback level
needs to be reduced if a truthful and realistic effect is to be
made. Her playing is completely straightforward and she
holds the listener's interest throughout. The remaining items
make up her first solo recital, and very good it is too. She uses
a Rückers harpsichord of 1612 from the Royal Collection,

tuned in unequal temperament. Again her playing is splendidly unfussy, free from interpretative mannerisms and not
bound by rigid rhythms; her virtuosity in the *Chromatic
Fantasia and Fugue* seems effortless and unforced, and there
is an agreeable naturalness about the whole recital. The
recording is thoroughly faithful and the acoustic lively, if
small.

*Chromatic Fantasia & Fugue (Rust version);
Clavier-Büchlein for W. F. Bach: Allemande; Minuets 1 & 3,
BWV 836, 841 & 843. Adagio in G, BWV 968; Fugue in G
min. (after BWV 1000); Partita on the Chorale 'O Gott, du
frommer Gott', BWV 767; Partita in A min. (after BWV 1004,
arr. Mortensen)*

(N) ** Metronome MET CD 1056. Hogwood (clavichord)

This is one of the most truthful available recordings of the
intimate clavichord, reputedly Bach's own favourite keyboard
instrument. Three examples are demonstrated here, for
Christopher Hogwood plays instruments by Hass, Bodechtal
and Schmahl. But his rather laid-back style does not help to
overcome and project the instrument's recessive image, and
the two large-scale *Partitas* lack the breadth and vividness of
organ versions. The pieces from Wilhelm Friedmann's excer-
cise book come off best, but in the 'Rust' version of the
Chromatic Fantasia (which is not very different from the
usual score) Hogwood is unconvincingly wayward, although
the Fugue comes off well. This recital is described as 'The
Secret Bach', and it is not really clear why.

*Chromatic Fantasia & Fugue, BWV 903; (Solo)Concertos:
after Vivaldi, Op. 3/9 & Op.7/8, BWV 972/3; Fantasias &
Fugues in A min. & C min., BWV 904 & 906; Italian
Concerto, BWV 971; Sonata in A min. (after Reincken: Trio
Sonata), BWV 965*

(N) *** HM HMU 907329. Egarr (harpsichord)

Richard Egarr has already given us an outstanding set of the
Bach *Harpsichord Concertos*, and he is no less impressive in
the solo keyboard music. Here he plays a Katzmann harpsichord, modelled on a Ruckert, and it sounds splendidly vivid.
The programme is for the most part familiar; all of it is
played with vigour and sensitivity: the slow movements of
the concertos are pleasingly flexible. As a novelty he includes
a miniature *Suite* derived by the young Bach from the first of
a set of six *Trio Sonatas* by Johann Reincken, published in
1687, and one can readily see how its musical fluency
appealed to him. A most attractive and stimulating recital.

*Concertos (for solo harpsichord): after Vivaldi, 1 in D (after
Op. 3/9), BWV 972; 2 in C (after Op. 7/2), BWV 973; 4 in G
min. (after Op. 4/6), BWV 975; 5 in C (after Op. 3/12), BWV
976; 7 in F (after Op. 3/3), BWV 978; 9 in G (after Op. 4/1),
BWV 980; Italian Concerto*

❀ (M) * Warner Elatus 2564 60362-2. Baumont
(harpsichord)**

We are more used to hearing Bach's transcriptions of Italian
concertos on the organ, but these works were probably
intended for either a harpsichord or even possibly a chamber
organ without pedals. In Olivier Baumont's hands they sound
splendid on the harpsichord, full of vitality and vividly
coloured. Baumont plays a modern French copy of a German
harpsichord 'from the School of Silbermann' of 1735, and it
has a particularly effective range of dynamics. He produces
some impressively dramatic staccato effects in the slow movement of Op. 4/6, but his playing throughout has irresistible

panache. The most famous *Italian Concerto* is used as an encore – and how eloquently Baumont phrases the slow movement. This collection is very enjoyable indeed – a disc to cheer you up on a dull day!

Concertos (arr. for solo piano): *after Vivaldi, Op. 7/2; Op. 4/6, BWV 973 & 975; after Marcello, Op. 1/2, BWV 981, & Oboe Concerto, BWV 974; Italian Concerto, BWV 971; Air de la Pastorale in C min., BWV 590; Andante in B min. after Torelli, BWV 979; Sicilienne from Concerto in D min., after Vivaldi, BWV 596*

(N) **(*) HMC 901871. Tharaud (piano)

Here is yet another novelty: Bach's own transcriptions re-transcribed for the piano, with the result even further removed from the originals. But they are certainly enjoyable when Alexandre Tharaud plays them very persuasively, and he is beautifully recorded. Slow movements are particularly beguiling, especially the individual movement used as encores, which he has arranged himself. But Tharaud's vigorous playing is stimulating too, as the *Italian Concerto* readily demonstrates.

English Suites 1–6, BWV 806–11

☛ *** Hyp. **SACD**: SACDA 67451/2; CD: CDA 67451/2. Hewitt (piano)

*** Sony SK 60276 (1, 3 & 6); SK 60277 (2, 4 & 5). Perahia (piano)

*** Decca 421 640-2 (2). Schiff (piano)

(B) **(*) Sony (ADD) SB2K 62949 (2). Leonhardt (harpsichord)

(M) **(*) Sony (ADD) SM2K 52606 (2). Gould (piano)

With her recordings of the *English Suites* Angela Hewitt caps her outstanding series of Bach's keyboard music on the piano. Of course, they are English only in that they were apparently commissioned by an Englishman; otherwise, like Bach's companion *French Suites*, they offer the usual collection of dance movements, with a mixture of French, German and Italian influences. However, as Hewitt comments in her accompanying notes, the opening *Preludes* (which she relishes) show Bach at his most imaginative and exploratory. But it is in the *Sarabandes* that she finds a depth of feeling and richness of colour that is possible only on the piano, while the exuberant closing *Gigues* (sample that for No. 4) are sparklingly buoyant and spirited. The recording on CD is first class; we see no reason to prefer the SACD.

In Murray Perahia's hands the forward flow is a living thing in itself, and the listener is always made conscious of the richness of the underlying harmony, especially in the *Sarabandes*, which are played very beautifully indeed. The lighter dance movements have a refreshing lightness of articulation, with the decoration made to seem integral. Perahia's mastery is such that, while this is personalized Bach, using a full range of pianistic colour with a disarming naturalness, there is never any suggestion of self-awareness.

András Schiff is straightforward, finely articulated, rhythmically supple and vital. Ornamentation is stylishly and sensibly observed. Everything is very alive, without being in the least over-projected or exaggerated in any way. The Decca recording is altogether natural and present.

On Sony, Leonhardt uses a Skowroneck harpsichord, vividly recorded, and if the volume level is set back a little the effect is very convincing. Leonhardt combines scholarship and artistry. The music flows freshly and expansively, even if

he is not equally inspired in every movement. He is inconsistent in the matter of repeats, sometimes observing them throughout, sometimes not. But this is well worth its modest price.

Glenn Gould has often inspired the adjective wilful, and certainly these reissued performances from the 1970s have much that is eccentric. At the same time, the strength of his musical personality cannot be denied; the music is always alive, phrasing is often strikingly imaginative and textures have appealing inner clarity. On the other hand, there are some bizarre ornamentation and accentuation and the vocalizations are tiresome. The sound is clean and dry, but has more ambient lustre with the present remastering, and the repackaging for the Anniversary Edition is attractive.

English Suites 1–6; French Suites 1–6

(BB) *** Warner Apex (ADD) 0927 40808-2 (1–2); 09027 40814-2 (3–4); 09027 40813-2 (5–6) (available separately). Curtis (harpsichord)

(N) (M) **(*) Sony (ADD) 517 969-2 (4). Gould (piano)

Anyone wanting both the *English* and *French Suites* together at a modest cost, played on a fine period harpsichord, will find Alan Curtis's Teldec set excellent value. By putting them together (with the first *English Suite* followed by the first *French Suite* and so on) the twelve works have fitted neatly on to three discs – each available separately. Curtis uses a harpsichord made by Christian Zell of Hamburg in 1928. The sound is resonant, but pleasingly so, and the full-bodied character of the sound suits Curtis's lively, comparatively robust approach. His playing is both thoughtful and spontaneous. Slow movements go particularly well and there is no feeling of didacticism. Excellent value.

Glenn Gould's piano versions of the *English* and *French Suites* (see above and below) are also available in a single package.

English Suites 1–6; Partitas 1–6

(N) (BB) *** Virgin 5 62379-2 (4). Leonhardt (harpsichord)

Leonhardt's playing here has a flair and vitality that one does not always associate with him, and there is no doubt that he makes the most of the introspective *Sarabande* of the *G minor Suite* (No. 3). He is better served by the engineers than when he last recorded these works for CBS/Sony; his performances, too, are more flexible and relaxed. His set now comes coupled with the six *Partitas*. In terms of sheer sound these are among the most satisfactory versions available, and in terms of style they combine elegance, spontaneity and authority. In many respects this too is musically among the most satisfying of current sets, save for the fact that Leonhardt observes no repeats.

English Suites 2 in A min.; 3 in G min., BWV 807/8

(N) **(*) DG **DVD** 073 4045. Pogorelich (Director: Humphrey Burton) – BEETHOVEN: *Piano Sonata 11* **(*); D. SCARLATTI: *Keyboard Sonatas* ***

Ivo Pogorelich, playing (in the Palazzo Palladiana di Caldogo, Nordera, Italy) comparatively early in his career in 1986, gives cool, pristine accounts of Bach, crisply articulated, with generally brisk tempi in dance movements; some may think the *Gigue* which ends the *Second Suite* is pressed too hard. But his virtuosity undoubtedly dazzles and he is truthfully, if closely, caught by the microphones in an attractive ambience. Pictorially this is very effective; Humphrey Burton and his camera director, Hans Jura, ensure that the camera angles are well judged and the changes of view not too fussy.

French Suites 1–6, BWV 812–17

(N) *** Ambrosie AMB 9942 (2). Rousset (harpsichord)

(N) *** Nim. NI 5744/5. Roberts (piano)

(N) **(*) Zig-Zag Territories ZZT 020401.2 (2). Rannou (harpsichord)

(B) *** DG Double 474 460-2. Gavrilov

(M) **(*) Sony (ADD) SMK 87764. Gould (piano)

French Suites 1–6 (including 3 additional movements); 18 Little Preludes, BWV 924–8; 930; 933–43; 999; Prelude & Fugue in A min., BWV 894; Sonata in D min., BWV 964

☛ *** Hyp. CDA 67121/2. Hewitt (piano)

French Suites 1–6; Italian Concerto; Partita in B min., BWV 831

*** Decca 433 313-2 (2). Schiff (piano)

(i) French Suites 1–6; (ii) English Suite 3; Italian Concerto in F

(B) **(*) EMI double forte 5 69479-2 (2). (i) Gavrilov (piano); (ii) Bunin (piano)

French Suites 1–6; Suites in A min., BWV 818a; in E flat, BWV 819a

(BB) *** Virgin 2×1 5 61653-2 (2). Moroney (harpsichord)

(B) *** Double Decca IMS 466 736-2 (2). Hogwood (with Allemande, BWV 819a)

**(*) BIS CD 1113/4 (with alternative version of the Allemande from the Suite in E flat, BWV 819a). Suzuki (harpsichord)

The comparison between the performances by the extrovert Christophe Rousset (handsomely packaged) and the comparatively laid-back Bernard Roberts is a fascinating one. Rousset chooses a large-scale Ruckers, restored in 1787. He plays the dance movements with real gusto – they are usually faster than with Roberts, who is by no means lacking in impetus, yet the tempi of the Allemandes and Sarabandes are slightly more relaxed in Rousset's hands. That is not to say that Roberts is not wonderfully cool; his slow movements are sensitive and gentle, and you have only to try the famous Gavotte in the Fifth Suite to revel in his spirited elegance. Both are spendidly recorded, so if you like exuberance (and a harpsichord) go for Rousset; if you have already discovered the natural grace and refinement which Roberts brings to Bach on the piano, without any loss of underlying vitality, he is your man.

In many ways the style of Blandine Rannou's reading fits nicely in between Rousset and Roberts. The aural image of her (unnamed) harpsichord image is less spectacular than Rousset's, but is not small-scale either, and she plays the livelier dance movements vigorously, with rhythms strongly pointed. Yet she is thoughtfully restrained in the Sarabandes and her playing in the Allemandes has poise. She opens with a characteristic performance of the Fifth Suite which demonstrates this readily, the Courante and Bourrée are energetic, the Sarabande appealingly ruminative, while the Gavotte and closing Gigue bounce attractively. This set would not perhaps be a first choice, yet it is very enjoyable and well recorded.

Like Hogwood before him, Davitt Moroney plays two further suites, which are almost certainly authentic as they were included in a manuscript copy of the complete set made by Bach's pupil, Heinrich Nikolas Gerber, in 1725. For good measure Moroney also adds a recently discovered second Gavotte belonging to the original version of the Suite No. 4 in

E flat. On artistic grounds too, these performances are very highly recommendable. Ornamentation may be individual, as is the addition of little galanteries, but the expressive content (notably in the Sarabandes) and the flexible spontaneity of his playing continually communicate a sense of 'live' music-making. Pacing is admirable and all repeats are included. He plays a modern harpsichord by John Phillips after Rückers/ Taskin, and the recording gives him a nice presence in a well-judged acoustic. It is a pity that the accompanying notes have been truncated, but in all other respects the present reissue makes a splendid bargain.

Christopher Hogwood uses two harpsichords, a Rückers of 1646, enlarged and modified by Taskin in 1780, and a 1749 instrument, basically the work of Jean-Jacques Goujon and slightly modified by Jacques Joachim Swanen in 1784. They are magnificent creatures and Hogwood coaxes superb sounds from them: his playing is expressive, and the relentless sense of onward momentum that disfigures so many harpsichordists (though not Moroney) is pleasingly absent. These performances have both style and character and can be recommended with some enthusiasm alongside Davitt Moroney; however, the Virgin set has the advantage of a very modest price.

Angela Hewitt's playing is informed by an intelligence and musicianship that are refreshing. Whether in the Preludes, written for Wilhelm Friedemann, or the suites themselves, she displays an imaginative vitality of a high order. The recorded sound is very natural.

Masaaki Suzuki's performances of the French Suites are thoroughly musical and thoughtful and, of course, beautifully played. But his restrained introversion sometimes seems to rob the music of a degree of vitality, although he is lively enough in the Gigues and indeed in the famous Gavotte of Suite No. 5. But these performances are for collectors who like an essentially intimate approach to this repertoire. The recording, as usual with this BIS series, is most natural and pleasing.

Gavrilov conveys the enormous inner vitality of these suites and makes the music vibrant. Such is the conviction he conveys that, while he is playing, one feels there is no other way to play this music and no other instrument to play it on. Very good sound, too. This now comes economically re-priced as a DG Double.

András Schiff gives highly rewarding performances of just Nos. 1–6, his expressive style entirely without personal indulgence, his freedom in slow movements seemingly improvisatory and spontaneous, and his faster dance-movements an unqualified delight. The Partita in B minor is slightly more severe in style than the rest of the programme. As with the rest of his series, the Decca recording is appealingly realistic and an ideal acoustic has been chosen.

Glenn Gould's playing is as idiosyncratic as it is brilliant. Needless to say, as in the English Suites, there are many revealing touches, and there is marvellously clear part-writing and characteristically impressive finger dexterity. There are some odd tempi and a lot of very detached playing that inspires more admiration than conviction. As with the others in Sony's reissued Anniversary Edition, the sound has been improved with the current remastering, although it remains rather dry and close.

Andrei Gavrilov's earlier, 1984 set of the French Suites is full of interesting things, and there is some sophisticated (not to say masterly) pianism. There is an element of the self-conscious here, but there is also much that is felicitous. To fill up the pair of discs, Stanislav Bunin's performances of the

Third English Suite and the *Italian Concerto*, recorded six years later, have been added. His style is bold and direct, less flexible than Gavrilov's approach but totally unselfconscious. Both artists receive excellent recording.

Goldberg Variations, BWV 988

*** Hyp. CDA 67305. Hewitt (piano)

☛— ✪ *** VAI (ADD) VAIA 1029. Tureck (piano)

*** Sony SK 89243. Perahia (piano)

(N) (M) *** Decca 476 7219. Schiff (piano)

(N) (BB) *** BMG Ultimate Classics 82876 64645-2. Dershavina (piano)

*** Häns. CD 92.112 (2). Koroliov (piano)

(B) *** HM HMA 1951240. Gilbert (harpsichord)

(M) *** DG 439 978-2. Kempff (piano)

*** ECM 472 185-2. András Schiff

(M) *** DHM/BMG 82876 60146-2. Leonhardt (harpsichord)

**(*) Opus OP 30-84. Hantaï (harpsichord)

**(*) Delos DE 3279. Víníkour (harpsichord)

(B) ** Warner Elatus 2-CD 2564 60010-2 (2). Barenboim (piano) – BEETHOVEN: *Diabelli Variations* **

(N) (BB) ** Naxos 8.557268. Jandó (piano)

*(**) Sony (ADD) **SACD** SS 37779; CD 517 480-2 [SK 93070]. Gould (1981 recording) (piano)

(M) (**(*)) Sony mono 517 479-2 [SK 90387] (1955 recording) (with *Fugues*, BMV 878 & BMV 883). Gould (piano)

Goldberg Variations; Chromatic Fantasia & Fugue in D min., BWV 903; Italian Concerto

(M) (**(*)) EMI mono CDH5 67200-2. Landowska (harpsichord)

Goldberg Variations; Fughetta in C min., BWV 961; Preludes & Fugues: in A min., BWV 895; D min., BWV 899; E min., BWV 900; F, BWV 901; G, BWV 902

**(*) Mer. CDA 84291. Cload (piano)

Angela Hewitt's performance is totally pianistic, involving the widest range of dynamic contrast, variety of touch and colour. It is imbued with what she calls 'the joyous tone that is characteristic of so much of this work'. She rightly regards the 'black pearl' Variation 25 as 'the greatest of all' and fully reveals its gentle, celestial beauty. After the bold *Quodlibet*, the return of the *Aria* on a magical half-tone reminds one of Tureck – and there can be no higher praise. The Hyperion recording is first class in every way.

Rosalyn Tureck's recording is very special indeed – there is no other record of Bach played on the piano quite as compelling as this, and for I. M. it would be a desert island disc.

Murray Perahia's set is even more personalized than Rosalyn Tureck's VAI version, essentially thoughtful and intimate, often introvert, even ruminative, but with moments of high drama. Some might prefer a more direct, less individualized approach, but Perahia's involvement and dedication are present in every bar of Bach's music, with continual contrasts of pianistic colour and dynamic, yet always with superbly clean articulation (sample Variation 14 – wonderfully crisp and clear). In his personal note Perahia tells us that he regards Variation 24 ('a calming pastoral canon') followed by the famous Variation 25, the 'turning point' of Bach's structure. 'The semitonal intensity of this darkly chromatic piece' is presented as a threnody to imply 'a programmatic description of the Crucifixion'. He then sets off very swiftly in Variation 26, with a sense of release 'like a soul in flight' to suggest a 'programmatic analysis of the Resurrection'. The closing variations are seen as an apotheosis: 'Variation 28

with its very high register and shimmering trills is all transcendence; Variation 29 brings these trills back to earth'; Variation 30 (the *Quodlibet*) brings the climax, and with the restatement of the *Aria*, the 'noble, radiant lines bring the music to rest'. The piano recording is wonderfully true and natural.

It is good to have András Schiff's earlier Decca set back in the catalogue after so long, restored in the Critics' Choice series since it was originally chosen for 'Building a Library' on BBC Radio 3. For those who enjoy Bach on the piano, it can still receive the most enthusiastic advocacy. The part-writing emerges with splendid definition and subtlety. Schiff plays with admirable directness and with a keen sense of enjoyment of the piano's colour and sonority. The Decca recording is excellent in every way, clean and realistic.

We have no knowledge of Ekaterina Dershavina – and apparently nor have BMG, for they don't even put her name on the front of the disc. But she is a first-rate artist and is totally at one with the *Goldberg Variations*, which she plays with disarming freshness and spontaneity. The characterization is keen, the playing both thoughtful and imaginative, deft and sprightly, and the slower variations have genuine depth (sample No. 25). The rapt reprise of the *Aria* is perfectly judged. This compares favourably with the finest versions, irrespective of price, for the recording is natural and beautifully balanced in a most pleasing acoustic. Highly recommended.

Evgeni Koroliov opens the *Aria* rather deliberately, but the performance immediately takes wing and his playing spontaneously gathers excitement as he proceeds. Though there is less variety of dynamic than with Hewitt, his splendidly clear articulation is a joy in itself, and the shaping of each individual variation is compelling. The digital dexterity is remarkable. There is also at times some vocalization, but it is less intrusive than Glenn Gould's. The bold style of the pianism is caught by the clear, forward recording.

Kenneth Gilbert uses a recent copy of a Rückers–Taskin, and it makes a very pleasing sound. His is an aristocratic reading: he avoids excessive display and there is a quiet, cultured quality about his playing that is very persuasive. An essentially introspective account, recorded in a rather less lively acoustic than some others, but he is a thoughtful and thought-provoking player, which makes this an excellent bargain recommendation.

Kempff's version is not for purists, but it has a special magic of its own. Ornaments are ignored altogether in the outlining of the theme, and the instances of anachronisms of style are too numerous to mention. Yet, for all that, the sheer musicianship exhibited by this great artist fascinates and his playing is consistently refreshing. The 1969 recording is very natural.

Since he made his first recording of this work for Decca, András Schiff has clearly rethought his approach to the *Goldberg Variations*, playing with a directness and simplicity and with a consistent crispness of articulation that is at times disarming. Occasionally he presses onwards almost too briskly, but there is no lack of underlying flexibility, and this performance, full of spontaneous zest, is very compelling indeed, even if the earlier, more mellow account is not entirely eclipsed. The recording has splendid clarity and presence.

Gustav Leonhardt recorded the *Goldberg Variations* three times, and this last (1978) version, though the most beautifully recorded, will not necessarily enjoy universal appeal. It is an introverted and searching performance, at times very free rhythmically – and almost mannered. The 'Black Pearl' Variation is a case in point, but the reading is so thoughtful that no one can fail to draw some illumination from it. His instrument is a Dowd copy of a Blanchet and is tuned a semitone flat, as opposed to the Skrowroneck copy of a Dulcken at present-day pitch, which he used in his 1967 record for Teldec. The sound is now altogether mellower and more appealing and, though no repeats are observed, this Deutsche Harmonia Mundi version is fresher and more personal than his earlier Das Alte Werk record.

Wanda Landowska (in 1933) not only rediscovered and reintroduced Bach's complete Goldberg Variations to the European musical public, but soon afterwards made its first recording, and this is it. She plays a large two-manual Pleyel and at times gives it a grand presence, but for the most part her playing is quite restrained, delicate in nuance and often thoughtfully expressive. At other times her virtuosity is very compelling. One must remember that she had to choose her own tempi, for there was no precedent. She is not only convincing but also leads the ear forward most spontaneously. The Italian Concerto is understandably more robust, while the Chromatic Fantasia shows just how fleet her fingers can be. The remastered recording sounds very well indeed, although the problem of slight 'wow' on sustained passages is not solved. But one readily adjusts when the playing is so magnetic.

Pierre Hantaï studied with Gustav Leonhardt, so his credentials are impressive. His account of the Goldberg Variations has received much praise: 'a happy conjunction of heart and mind' suggested the review in Gramophone. The playing is certainly infectiously buoyant and full of life, but his direct manner of presentation and reprise of the Aria is borne out by his response to the 'Black Pearl' 'Adagio, where we feel more expressive flexibility would have been in order. His harpsichord, a Dutch copy of an early eighteenth-century Mietke, is a fine instrument and splendidly recorded.

Jory Vínikour uses an American copy of a 1624 Rückers, which is recorded clearly and cleanly in an attractive acoustic. His playing is alive and has plenty of character; ornamentation is judiciously judged. His inclusion of repeats and choice of tempi mean that this performance, at 85 minutes 39 seconds, runs to a second disc, but the two are offered for the cost of one. There is no doubting the calibre of this playing, but there are a few idiosyncrasies and moments of thoughtful deliberation (Variation 16, for instance) which do not carry the music forward as strongly as with some performances.

Glenn Gould's stereo version of the Goldberg Variations was one of the last records he made. In his earlier record he made no repeats; now he repeats a section of almost half of them and also joins some pairs together (6 with 7 and 9 with 10, for example). Yet, even apart from his vocalizations, he does a number of weird things – fierce staccatos, brutal accents, and so on – that inhibit one from suggesting this as a first recommendation even among piano versions. It is certainly a unique version, and with Gould nothing is either dull or predictable. The recording is, as usual with this artist, inclined to be dry and forward, which aids clarity. This also comes on a Super Audio CD for which a special player is required, but the quality is impressive.

Gould's famous (1955) mono recording enjoyed cult status in its day, and its return will occasion rejoicing among his admirers. He observes no repeats and in terms of sheer keyboard wizardry commands admiration, even if you do not respond to the results. There is too much that is wilful and eccentric for this to be a straightforward recommendation,

but it is a remarkable performance nevertheless.

Additionally available is an elaborately packaged three-disc set including both Gould's mono and stero recordings newly remastered, plus a third disc including the pianist's discussion of his performances with Tim Page. Also included are some studio out-takes from the 1955 recording sessions (SM3K 87703).

Julia Cload observes the repeats in the opening Aria but not elsewhere; she therefore finds room for the 'Little' Preludes and Fugues, which she plays appealingly and fluently. Her account of the Goldberg Variations is strong and thoughtful, not as inspirational as Tureck's; but some may like its directness of manner. The piano is well recorded, but the ear needs to adjust to the 'empty studio' acoustic.

Barenboim's approach is undoubtedly individual, generally thoughtful and fresh, his pianism well adapted to Bach, with (for the most part) well-chosen tempi, a natural pianistic use of light and shade, and a pleasing linear flow. The inclusion of repeats means that the performance stretches over to a second CD, but the break is well placed, coming after the Adagio Variation 25, played very expressively. Then Variation No. 26 seems rather rushed. So this is not a first choice but, if you also want a comparable set of the Diabelli Variations, this might be considered. The recording is excellent.

Jenö Jandó's style is very positive, crisp and direct. He can be very brisk (Variations 6 and 17) sometimes percussive (Variation 14), but he limits his range of dynamics and colour and, despite some good moments, his reading is mostly dry (as indeed is the acoustic).

(i) **Goldberg Variations; Air & Variations in the Italian Style, BWV 989; (ii) Italian Concerto; Prelude & Fugue in A min., BWV 985; Suite in F min., BWV 823. Collection:** Applicato in C, BWV 994; Chorale, BWV 512; Fantasia in G min., BWV 917; Inventions, BWV 772, 772a, 917; March & Polonaise, BWV Anh. 127; Minuets, BWV Anh. 115/6, 122, 126; Musette, BWV Anh 126

(N) (B) **(*) Sony (ADD) 517491-2 (2). Tureck (i) on harpsichord; (ii) on piano

Goldberg Variations; Italian Concerto; Partitas 1–6, & in B min. (French Overture), BWV 825–31

(M) *** DG (ADD/DDD) Trio 474 337-2 (3). Pinnock (harpsichord)

Trevor Pinnock uses four different harpsichords here, including a recently restored copy of a Rückers for the Goldberg Variations, a copy of a Hemsch (tuned to unequal temperament) for the Italian Concerto and the six Partitas, while the French Overture features a copy of a Dulcken. Tempi are generally well judged, rhythms are vital yet free. For the Goldberg Variations Pinnock retains repeats for more than half the variations – which seems a fair compromise, in that variety is maintained yet the performnce can be accommodated on a single disc. The playing is again vital and intelligent, with alert, finely articulated rhythm. In the Partitas he conveys a sense of pleasure that is infectious, and he has great spirit and panache throughout. The recording is eminently truthful and vivid, a bit close in the B minor Partita, which nevertheless still conveys plenty of expressive feeling.

Sony offer Rosalyn Tureck's third recording of the Goldberg Variations, made on a harpsichord in 1978, and, while she still plays all the repeats, perhaps her choice of instrument has led to an interpretation which seems more considered than before, even deliberate at times. The opening Aria is very slow indeed and, although later variations have inreasing vitality, this does not seem as spontaneous as her earlier, piano versions, even though there is much to admire and enjoy. It is the other works which make this set especially attractive. The early (c. 1709) *Aria and Variations* brings an appropriately youthful response, particularly the bravura of Variations 7, 8 and 9. Even more attractive are the shorter works, recorded later (1979 and 1981) and played most beautifully on the piano, especially the lovely *Sarabande* at the centre of the *Suite in F minor*. The group of miniatures, many of which were written to instruct Bach's favourite son, Wilhelm Friede-mann, are delightfully done, especially the opening scalic *Applicato* and some of the brief dance movements and *Inventions*. The recording is truthful throughout, except that in the (boldly played) *Italian Concerto* there is a just a hint of harmonic distortion.

15 2-Part Inventions, BWV 772–86; 15 3-Part Inventions, BWV 787–801

*** BIS CD 1009. Suzuki (harpsichord)

*** Cap. 10 210 (with *6 Little Preludes, BWV 933-8*). Koopman (harpsichord)

(*) Sony (ADD) **SACD SS 6622; CD (M) 517 483-2 [SK 90401]. Gould (piano)

**(*) Decca 411 974-2. Schiff (piano)

15 2-Part Inventions; 15 3-Part Inventions; Ornamented versions: 2-Part Invention 1 in C, BWV 772a; 3-Part Inventions 4–5, 7, 9, 11 & 13, BWV 790–91, 793, 795, 797 & 799

**(*) Astrée E 8603. Verlet (harpsichord)

Masaaki Suzuki plays with perception and skill. These *Inventions* can sound dry, but not in his hands. His response is naturally spontaneous, fresh and alive, never didactic and rigid. Suzuki is one of the finest Bach exponents of our time and he is truthfully recorded.

Ton Koopman scores over rivals in offering the *Six Little Preludes* in addition to the two sets of *Inventions*, and he plays with spontaneity and sparkle.

The *Inventions* are admirably suited to Glenn Gould's clear, didactic style, and they are among his most impressive Bach recordings. As he pairs each of these *Two-* and *Three-Part* works (each in identical keys) listeners are always conscious that they are in the presence of a penetrating musical mind: the clarity of the individual strands is remarkable. The complete set comes in alternative versions: on SACD (which needs a special player) and CD, which is much less expensive. The basic recording is dry, but clear and believable in this remastered form. Side-by-side comparison reveals a slightly fuller sound on CD than SACD, although the difference is minimal. As usual, the ear cannot fail to be exasperated by the vocalizations. One longs for vocal silence.

András Schiff's playing is (for this repertoire) rather gener-ous with rubato and other expressive touches but is elegant in the articulation of the part-writing. Such is his musicianship and pianistic sensitivity, however, that the overall results are likely to persuade most listeners. The recording is excellent.

Blandine Verlet uses a 1624 Rückers which seems quite ideal for this repertoire. She plays with great spirit and the imitation between the parts is admirably clear. Her passage-work is never inflexible and, when the writing is compara-tively expressive, her minor hesitations in the flow prevent any sense of rigidity; this is more striking in the *Three-Part* pieces. Having played through both sets, she then offers a selection with judicious ornamentation, strikingly effective in the very first of the *Two-Part Inventions*.

Italian Concerto; Partitas 1–2, BWV 825–6

(*) Sony (ADD) **SACD SS 6141. Gould (piano)

This SACD certainly offers high-quality reproduction, and the *Partitas* sound strikingly fresh. With the *Italian Concerto*, most notable for Gould's virtuoso (some might say rushed) account of the finale, the sound on the – much less expensive – CD collection below has slightly more fullness, although the difference is marginal. But the measure on the SACD (40') is ungenerous and it is expensive.

Klavierbüchlein for W. F. Bach

**(*) Häns. CD 92.137-2 (2). Payne (harpsichord, clavichord, organ)

Joseph Payne combines organ, harpsichord and clavichord to survey the 63 miniatures which form Bach's *Klavierbüchlein*. Like the companion notebook for Anna Magdalena, it pro-vides fascinating insights into Bach's composing process for, after a series of engaging musical fragments, Bach features early versions of a number of the *Preludes* from the *Well-Tempered Clavier*, of which the shorter version of the famous C major *Prelude*, BWV 846, is notable. These are presented with pleasing simplicity and vitality. Later a series of *Prea-mbulums* and *Fantasias* turn out to be the *Two-* and *Three-Part Inventions*, and here Payne's linear style is a little fussy. But he is generally a fine advocate. The use of three different instruments introduces an appealing variety of colour.

Partitas 1–6, BWV 825–30

*** BIS CD 1313/4 (2). Suzuki (harpsichord)

⊛ (B) ******* Nim. 5673/4. Roberts (piano)

*** None. 7559 79698-2 (1, 3 & 6); 7559 79483-2 (2, 4 & 5). Goode (piano)

*** Häns. CD 92.115 (2). Pinnock (harpsichord)

*** Hyp. CDA 67191/2. Hewitt (piano)

*** Signum SIGD 012. Carolan (harpsichord)

*** Chan. 0618 (2). Woolley (harpsichord)

(N) **(*) Lyrichord LEMS 8038 (2). Troeger (clavichord)

**(*) Decca 411 732-2 (2). Schiff (piano)

(N) (M) **(*) Warner Elatus (ADD) 2564 61778-2 (2). Ross (harpsichord)

Masaaki Suzuki plays a modern Dutch copy of an enlarged two-manual Rückers, which is forwardly recorded and has a strong personality. If you like a bold harpsichord sound, this very realistic BIS disc should provide great satisfaction, for Suzuki's Bach perceptions are fully revealed here and he plays thoughtfully, commandingly and spontaneously.

However, the *Partitas* are heard more often today on the piano, and the splendid set from Bernard Roberts shows why. As the opening *Preambulum* of No. 1 immediately demon-strates, his clear, clean articulation is a constant joy, and the dance movements are delightfully played. Yet the beautiful extended *Allemande* of No. 4 and the later *Sarabande* have a simple expressive depth which is totally disarming. Through-out, Roberts's playing reveals new aspects of these many-faceted works, at times light-hearted but with an underlying profundity that is fully realized here. The Nimbus recording is first class in every way, beautifully focused, with just the right degree of resonance in an ideal acoustic.

Not surprisingly, Richard Goode's Nonesuch set on the piano is equally stylish and appealing. The clean articulation and crisp, well-lifted rhythms (sample the *Gavotta* and *Gigue* of the final *Partita in E minor*) are as arresting as the pianistic use of light and shade, which is not as wide-ranging as with Tureck's approach to Bach and is therefore likely to appeal even to those who usually prefer the harpsichord, for the *Sarabandes* have thoughtful, expressive depth. With piano tone that is clear but never too dry this is very stimulating.

Trevor Pinnock has recorded the six *Partitas* before for DG, but this new set is even finer. He uses a superb American copy of a Hemsch made by David Way in Stonington, Connecticut (with a particularly effective mute stop). As before, he plays these works with a keen sense of enjoyment and projects the music with enormous panache. The harpsichord is superbly recorded and given fine presence in a spaciously resonant acoustic, although the sound may seem a fraction over-resonant to some ears. Nevertheless, playing of this calibre is impossible to resist, and this can be recommended.

Those wanting a set on the piano can also safely turn to Angela Hewitt. Her performances are fluent, deeply musical and, while expressively flexible, less personally wayward than Schiff in the *Sarabandes*, which she still plays very sensitively. The Hyperion recording is first class.

Lucy Carolan's playing, too, is as full of life as it is of imaginative touches. She is both commanding and scholarly, and her ready virtuosity and keen articulation are exhilarating. Yet her touch can also be appealingly delicate. To add variety of colour, she uses a pair of harpsichords, both copies of early instruments. *Partitas* 1, 3 and 6 are played on a copy of a Mietke, and *Partitas* 2, 4 and 5 on a copy of a Goermans–Taskin instrument. Both are excellently recorded.

Robert Woolley's performances are also pleasingly fresh and musical, flowing naturally and spontaneously and with lively rhythmic feeling. He uses a particularly attractive harpsichord, a copy of a Mietke, an instrument of a kind that Bach would have known. It is beautifully recorded within a pleasing open acoustic.

The Boston clavichordist and scholar Richard Troeger makes a good case for playing these works on the clavichord, and Lyrichord have provided him with a truthful recording in an intimate acoustic, reminding the listener not to have the volume level too high. The instrument used is a modern Haas, a Californian copy of a Silbermann. Troeger's playing is direct and thoroughly musical, without idiosyncrasy. He is inclined to be a little didactic, but these are thoughtful performances of some distinction.

Schiff is a most persuasive advocate of Bach on the piano. Though few will cavil at his treatment of fast movements, some may find him a degree wayward in slow movements, though the freshness of his rubato and the sparkle of his ornamentation are always winning. The sound is outstandingly fine.

Scott Ross's set of the *Partitas* dates from 1989. He uses an unidentified but attractive instrument which is recorded with both warmth and clarity. He plays with enjoyable style and panache, and despite one or two minor points (in the *B flat Gigue* not every note speaks evenly and at times greater rhythmic freedom would be welcome) his readings are eminently competitive, reissued on mid-price Elatus.

Partitas 1–6; 6 Little Preludes, BWV 924–930
(M) ** Sony (ADD) SMK 87767 (*Partitas 1–3*); SMK 87768
   (*Partitas 4–6; 6 Preludes*). Gould (piano)

Glenn Gould is as intelligent as he is eccentric. His phrasing and articulation compel admiration, even if he is at times perversely wilful. Many things here prompt one to think again about the music, but the performances are really too individual to qualify for an unreserved recommendation, and

the piano sound, though improved in the new transfer, is still shallow and lacking in timbre.

Partitas 1, 3 & 6
*** Virgin 5 45526-2. Anderszewski (piano)

Piotr Anderszewski orders his choice of *Partitas* very effectively – in reverse order – opening with the enticing *Toccata* of the *E minor*, BWV 830, and ending with the bravura rippling *Gigue* of the *B flat major*, BWV 825. He has the gift of compelling you to listen. This is Bach playing of stature. The pianism is highly articulate and elegant, intelligent and imaginative, and there is a wide range of keyboard colour. This is the sort of playing that disarms criticism. Above all, this comes over as live music-making in the studio, and its spontaneous feeling is totally compelling. Very fine recording too.

7 Toccatas; BWV 910–16
*** Hyp. CDA 67310. Hewitt (piano)
*** Lyr. LEMS 8041. Troeger (clavichord)

Bach's famous journey to Lübeck to meet Buxtehude took place in 1705, and the seven keyboard *Toccatas* were almost certainly written in the following decade, while Bach was under the influence of that master's 'stylus fantasticus'.

Hewitt always holds Bach's disparate motivations convincingly together, as in the *G minor* which, as she comments, can be made to sound uniquely varied and buoyant on the piano, especially the bouncing closing fugue. And how engaging is her sparkling articulation of the first section of the *D major Toccata*, with which she ends her programme. We have no hesitation in declaring this the most stimulating and rewarding CD of these complex and episodic works on any instrument, consistently showing Bach's youthful explorations at their most stimulating. The recording is excellent.

Bach's *Toccatas* are usually played on the harpsichord, organ or piano. But hearing them played so fluently and musically on the more intimate clavichord makes for an enjoyable diversity, and Richard Troeger certainly phrases and articulates with character. The recording engineer has not been tempted to put his microphones too close, and his comment that 'the clavichord is a quiet instrument, but it can fill a room with extraordinary resonance' is borne out here, yet the instrument's essential intimacy is retained.

Toccatas 1–7; Partita 7 in B min. (Overture in the French Style), BWV 831
(M) ** Sony (ADD) SMK 87762 (*Toccatas 1–4*); SMK 87763
   (*Toccatas 5–7 & Partita*). Gould (piano)

Glenn Gould's *Toccatas* were recorded in the mid- to late 1970s. The first disc combines the most fastidious and remarkable pianism with some characteristically impulsive, not to say wilful, touches. Though the playing is of the highest distinction, the piano tone is not, and the wearisome vocalization, on which this artist seems to insist, somewhat dampens one's enthusiasm. On the second disc there is more impressive playing, with the contrapuntal strands being beautifully balanced and clarified, although the recording is still rather wanting in depth and colour.

The Well-Tempered Clavier (48 Preludes & Fugues), BWV 846–93
(N) **(*) EuroArts **DVD** 2050309 (2). Gavrilov (*Book I/1–12*);
   MacGregor (*13–24*); Demidenko (*Book II/1–12*); Hewitt
   (*13–14*)

The idea of filming and recording *The Well-Tempered Clavier* with four different pianists in four different venues is a novel one, and it certainly offers a variety of interpretative manners, none more controversial than Andrei Gavrilov's opening approach, which is both highly individual and wilful, yet obviously deeply considered. He opens Book I by playing the first three *Preludes* and *Fugues* comparatively simply and persuasively (although with a distinctly expressive style). In the *C sharp minor* (No. 4) he becomes more romantically wayward, but reverts to a pointed, Scarlatti articulation in the *Prelude in D major* (No. 5). No. 8 is very slow indeed; *No. 9 in E major* makes a great contrast between the delicacy of the *Prelude* and the forthright *Fugue*, while No. 12 is musingly free and ruminative. Altogether stimulating, but a very personal view.

Joanna MacGregor then creates a complete contrast following her Russian colleague. There is both momentum and character in her playing, which is attractively crisp and clean in the major keys. The minor-key *Preludes* are mellower but they are never romanticized, while the *Fugues* are often bolder. The *B flat major Prelude* is played with great dash, the *Fugue* has engaging imitation; the gentle poignancy of the minor-key *Prelude* which follows is the more striking, and for No. 24 she moves from a thoughtful *Prelude* to a very positive culmination.

Nikolai Demidenko's way is even more bold and direct, his pacing often brisk but never seeming pressed too hard. He can be more relaxed too, as in the *D minor* (No. 6) or the *E* and *F major Preludes*, but the *Fugues* are always purposeful and flowing, and there is never a hint of the romantic dallying which Gavrilov indulges in. Equally, there is no sense of inflexibility or a lack of imagination in the matter of pianistic colour, and certainly there is a sense of a strong personality at work.

Simplicity is Angela Hewitt's hallmark, with well-judged tempi and unexaggerated use of light and shade so that rhythms are precise, the contrapuntal interplay always clear, as in the *A flat major Fugue* (No. 17), while her subtle control of dynamic range and nuance is especially effective in the preceding Prelude. Throughout, the music is allowed to unfold naturally and sometimes quite intimately (the *B flat minor Prelude*). Altogether satisfying: the composer always comes first here.

The visual presentation is far from plain: the producers have endeavoured to seduce the listener's eyes with a background lit in changing colours (often exotic) and the cameras are constantly moving, especially in the angle of approach to the pianist's hands. The palaces at Barcelona and Venice, where MacGregor and Demidenko play, are fully explored (the latter is even photographed from the outside, through a window) and the glory of the interiors at the Wartburg, Eisenach, are realized during Hewitt's final group. The recorded sound is excellent. But only the listener/viewer can decide whether such lavish illustration is really an asset or partially distracting.

The Well-Tempered Clavier (48 Preludes & Fugues), BWV 846–93 (complete)

(M) *** BBC (ADD) BBCL 4109-2 (2) Book I; BBCL 4116-3 (3) Book II. Tureck (piano)

(BB) *** Virgin 5 61711-2 (4). Van Asperen (harpsichord)

⊕─ ⦿ *** Hyp. CDA 67301/2 (Book I); CDA 67303/4 (Book II). Hewitt (piano)

(B) *** Nim. NI 5608/11 (4). Roberts (piano)

*** Decca 414 388-2 (2) (Book I); 417 236-2 (2) (Book II). Schiff (piano)

(M) *** DG (ADD) 463 601-2 (2) (Book I); 463 623-2 (2) (Book II). Kirkpatrick (clavichord)

*** Ongaku 024-113 (2) (Book I); 024-115 (2) (Book II). Schepkin (piano)

*** ECM 835246-2 (2) (Book I); 847936-2 (2) (Book II). Jarrett (piano or harpsichord)

(M) *** DG Blue 474 221-2 (Book 1); 474 546-2 (Book 2). Gilbert (harpsichord)

(BB) (***) Naxos mono 8.110651/2 (Book I); 8.110653/4 (Book II). Fischer (piano)

(M) (***) EMI mono 5 67214-2 (3). Fischer (piano)

(**(*)) DG mono 463 305-2 (4). Tureck (piano)

(N) (M) *(**) Sony (ADD) 517970-2 (4). Gould (piano)

Rosalyn Tureck's legendary Brunswick recordings, offered on LP in the 1950s (and later reissued by DG) pioneered *The Well-Tempered Clavier* as suitable for realization on the piano. At that time she was let down technically by the restricted sound-quality, but her authority shone through. In the autumn of 1975, when she was at her artistic peak, the BBC invited her into the studio to re-record the entire '48' in groups, and the project was completed in November 1976. This time there are no complaints about the realism and naturalness of the recording, and her performance continued to pioneer the use of the widest range of tempi, dynamics and pianistic colour. Yet because of her innate understanding of Bach, the result, for all its remarkable variety of mood, remains essentially pure in a classical sense and immensely satisfying, a miraculous blend of scholarship and personal insight and feeling. She is quoted here as saying: 'In Bach everything is so complex, and yet so simple in the end … the quality of emotion is so remarkably varied. This is what I am aiming for in my playing.' As can be seen, because of Tureck's often measured tempi, Book II extends over three CDs (the third playing for only 40 minutes, but including a 6-minute bonus – a brief conversation between Tureck and Michael Oliver). Throughout, the BBC recording is excellent, and the two Books are available separately.

Collectors wanting a complete modern harpsichord version of the '48' will surely now choose the reissued 1989 Virgin Veritas set from Bob van Asperen. A pupil of Gustav Leonhardt, his account enshrines many of the finest of his master's qualities and outshines most of his rivals on CD. His playing is marked by consistent vitality, elegance and concentration: he plays every note as if he means it and is refreshingly unmetronomic without being too free. He plays a 1728 harpsichord by Christian Zell from the Hamburg Museum, which the engineers capture vividly. The acoustic is less resonant than with Gilbert on DG, which is an advantage, and with its price advantage van Asperen's set is very recommendable indeed.

Angela Hewitt uses all the resources of the modern piano to turn these preludes and fugues into ongoing concert music of great variety and interest. Her range of timbre and dynamic is wide, her articulation can be bold, lightweight or gently searching (as, for instance, in BWV 849). But every bar is imaginatively alive and her thoughtful expressiveness is never self-aware, nor does it obscure the clarity of the part-writing. This is an inspirational set, most naturally recorded.

Bernard Roberts's Nimbus survey is plainer than Angela Hewitt's Hyperion version, which is daringly adventurous in the use of dynamic rise and fall, and in exploring the full range of colour and feeling that is possible with a modern piano. But that is not to suggest that Roberts is unimaginative; indeed, his survey is full of individual touches and insights. Speeds feel undistractingly right throughout and, as in his comparable set of the Beethoven piano sonatas for Nimbus, Roberts refuses to divert attention away from the composer's argument with idiosyncratic gestures. That goes with the deepest concentration, bringing out the full power as well as the beauty, with counterpoint consistently clarified. To confirm the recommendation, the four discs come as a bargain offer, and this is the version, superbly recorded, which for many will be a first choice.

Schiff often takes a very individual view of particular preludes and fugues, but his unexpected readings regularly win one over long before the end. Consistently he translates this music into pianistic terms, and his voyage of discovery through this supreme keyboard collection is the more riveting as the piano is an easier instrument to listen to over long periods. First-rate sound.

It was a bold decision of Ralph Kirkpatrick to pioneer the '48' on the clavichord (in the mid-1960s). Some of the preludes and fugues seem better suited to this instrument. Yet this does not seem a problem for Kirkpatrick, whose expressive powers are never in doubt; nor is his scholarship or musicianship, and he fully realizes the possibilities inherent in the use of his gentler instrument, which is very finely recorded, the sound admirably remastered for this undoubtedly fascinating and rewarding Originals reissue. These are comparatively sober performances in the matter of registration, but there is no doubting Kirkpatrick's grip, or his ability to show a remarkable variety of mood and tone on his more limited instrument.

Sergey Schepkin immediately creates a sharply focused, clear style of articulation, still essentially pianistic but with the extra bite of a 'plucked' keyboard instrument underlying his presentation. He is comparatively chimerical, and attractively so, with tempi in the preludes (though not always the fugues) often faster than with his colleagues. Book II is, if anything, even more stimulating than Book I. American collectors in particular need not hesitate to invest in both volumes. Schepkin's approach is bolder, more vibrant than that of Angela Hewitt, yet the range and variety of the playing is comparable, showing a constantly individual grasp of the essence of Bach's inspiration. The piano is recorded forwardly and truthfully.

Keith Jarrett offers Book I on a modern piano, and we like it very much for its dedication, simplicity and integrity. There is no attempt at any excessive indulgence in keyboard colour, and the recording is very satisfying in its natural sonority. On the face of it, it seems a rather odd idea to revert to the harpsichord for Book II and, if his reasoning does not completely persuade us, his qualities of musicianship do. He is a highly intelligent and musical player whose readings and precise articulation can hold their own against the current competition.

The reissue of Book II completes Kenneth Gilbert's set. This has long been praised by us for readings that are resilient and individual yet totally unmannered. The recording is excellent too, if rather resonant. This can now be recommended as a first choice among harpsichord versions of the '48', alongside Bob van Asperen's set on Virgin – which, however, has a distinct price advantage.

Edwin Fischer's was the first ever '48' to be put on shellac 78s, being recorded in 1933–6. Fischer has often been spoken of as an artist of intellect, but his approach here is neither remote nor cool. Moreover, he produces a beauty of sound and a sense of line that is an unfailing source of musical wisdom and nourishment. Whereas the EMI transfers (7 67214–2) were economically laid out on three mid-priced CDs, each accommodating close on 80 minutes, Naxos has issued each Book on a pair of super-bargain discs, so the saving in cost is less than it might have been. However, these new Naxos transfers are very impressive, the piano-sound surprisingly full and pleasing, distinctly preferable to the EMI CDs. The mastery and subtlety of Fischer's Bach playing needs no re-stating for it has still never been surpassed. An indispensable part of any Bach library.

Rosalyn Tureck's classic mono recording, magnetic and concentrated, was made in New York in the early 1950s. The dry mono sound and limited dynamic range tend to exaggerate the muscularity of the playing, but the tonal contrasts are still brought out strongly, at times echoing in sharp staccato a harpsichord sound. Tureck's Bach is always special; even so, it is disconcerting to find her adopting such idiosyncratically slow speeds for some of the most formidable fugues of Book II. And to reissue such a set at full price seems an extraordinary gesture on DG's part.

Glenn Gould has a large and dedicated following for his Bach recordings, so the fact that we find them eccentric will only be cause for regret to his fans. The very opening *Prelude* of Book I is an instance of his staccato style, and the clarity of his playing is matched by his charisma. There are undoubtedly many imaginative if obdurate touches, and his often curious choice of tempi – sometimes rattlingly fast, sometimes slow and pensive – is wilfully personal, favouring rallentandos at the end of each prelude or fugue. Certainly this is a fascinating set and it has never sounded better: the recording is no longer without bloom, and the ambient effect is more pleasing now, without loss of clarity. But the vocalise also remains, to interfere with one's concentration. For this repertoire on the piano, Tureck or Hewitt are safer recommendations.

The Well-Tempered Clavier, Book I, Preludes & Fugues 1–24, BWV 846–69

⚫ (N) (M) *** RCA (ADD) 82876 62315-2 (2). S. Richter (piano)

*** BIS CD 813/4. Suzuki (harpsichord)

(N) *** Warner 2-CD 2564 61553-2 (2). Barenboim (piano)

*** Häns. 92.116 (2). Levin (harpsichord, clavichord, organ)

(N) *** ECM 476 0482 (2). Feldner (piano)

*** Mer. CDE 84384/5-2. Cload (piano)

**(*) HM Mirare MIR 9930 (2). Hantaï (harpsichord)

Richter's recording of Book I dates from 1970, yet in every way he anticipates the freedom of expression and the pianistic expansion of the music's emotional range which are characteristic of more modern interpretations of Bach's supreme keyboard masterpiece. Richter also uses a wide dynamic range so that, after the simplicity of the C *major Fugue*, the C *minor Prelude* storms in arrestingly, played not unyieldingly but with an accelerando and decelerando just before the arrival of the *Fugue*, which is then presented very strongly and positively. The lightly articulated dexterity of the C *sharp major Prelude* then makes way for a softly reflective account of the C *sharp minor Prelude* with a moving darkness of feeling in the *Fugue* itself, played very slowly. The variety of approach and continual contrast are remarkable, as in the brilliantly played D *major Prelude* (almost a *moto perpetuo*) and its bolder partner, and the D minor diptych, the latter first lilting, then serene. The sheer authority of Richter's playing is consistently commanding, with the spirit of Bach's music faithfully underpinning everything he does. He has clearly thought through the whole span of Book I, creating a stimulating ongoing flow, finally moving from extrovert bravura in the *B flat major Prelude* to a satisfyingly serene conclusion in B minor. The piano is beautifully recorded in a warm acoustic, and this inspired survey, with its many remarkable insights, cannot be recommended too highly.

Suzuki offers only Book I so far, but already he lays claim to being first choice for a harpsichord version of the '48'. His two-manual instrument (by Willem Kroesbergen of Utrecht after an enlarged Rückers) has a fine personality and is splendidly recorded. His pacing is admirably judged, his flexibility never sounds mannered and he brings Bach's great keyboard odyssey fully to life at every turn. A most satisfying achievement.

In a fascinating introductory note with his recording, Daniel Barenboim tells us how he grew up with Bach's keyboard music and when, at the age of twelve, he began studying with Nadia Boulanger, the *Well-Tempered Clavier* was on the music stand of the grand piano. Its content is clearly part of his very being, so this is a very personal interpretation, seeking above all to express the 'powerful bond between the rhythm and harmony'. The playing covers the widest spectrum of feeling, sometimes serene, sometimes dramatic, but always musical, often gently persuasive, and never eccentrically interfering with the line or creating accentuated articulation. This is a thoroughly satisfying musical experience, and if more self-absorbed than with Hewitt or Tureck (see above), Barenboim always communicates directly his own insights about the music.

We know Robert Levin is a fine Bach exponent from his recordings of the harpsichord concertos. The special interest of his set of the '48' is that he alternates between single-manual and double-manual harpsichords, clavichord and organ. His choice of which instrument to use is personal and arbitrary but musically convincing, and certainly throws a fresh slant on this inexhaustible music. He is also very well recorded.

Till Feldner's approach is both direct and free for, as he shows in the minor-key *Preludes* (the *C sharp minor* or *E flat minor*, for instance), he can be thoughtfully reflective, while his tripping staccato for the *D major Prelude* and the clear, positive *Fugue* which follows is appealing in its clarity of focus; and this is found again in the E and F major pairings. Like Hewitt and Barenboim, his playing is completely pianistic, but his style of individuality is less introspective than with Barenboim, if not less personal. Altogether this is thoroughly satisfying, and Feldner is never predictable, offering many individual touches. The recording is excellent.

Julia Cload's new set also promises well, her pianistic style at times comparatively gentle (witness the opening prelude), but her control of dynamic follows Bach's underlying harmonic progressions very subtly. She can be both poetically reserved then suddenly extrovert and sparkling, and always remains faithful to the letter and spirit of this great work.

Born in 1964, Pierre Hantaï has worked with both Gustav Leonhardt and Jordi Savall. He plays the first half of the '48' cleanly and directly, while allowing himself the kind of latitude in the slower movments that one now expects from piano versions. There is a minor degree of nudging linear interference that not all will take to, but this is still very musical playing, and it is enjoyable when the recording is so clearly and pleasingly focused.

The Well-Temperered Clavier, Book 1 (excerpts)

** Ondine ODE 1033-2 (2). Mustonen (piano) –
   SHOSTAKOVICH: *24 Preludes & Fugues, Op. 87* (excerpts)
**

The gifted Finnish pianist Olli Mustonen continues his survey, begun on RCA, interspersing Bach *Preludes and Fugues* with those of Shostakovich, Op. 87. Predictably there is some superb pianism, but the listener's attention tends to gravitate towards the interpreter rather than the composer. His exaggeratedly staccato playing will strike many as attention-seeking rather than musical, wilful rather than just individual. Of course there are good things, but it is all far too self-aware to give consistent satisfaction.

The Well-Tempered Clavier, Book I, excerpts: *Preludes & Fugues 1–3; 5–17; 21–22*
(B) *** DG (ADD) (IMS) 463 020-2. Kempff (piano)

Cool, clear and compelling, Kempff's performances from Book I of the '48' convey pianistic poetry as well as dedication to Bach. A splendid recital, with excellent sound, showing a great artist relaxed and enjoying himself. And so do we.

KEYBOARD RECITAL COLLECTIONS

Rosalyn Tureck recitals

'*Bach and Tureck at Home*' (a birthday offering): (i) *Adagio in G, BWV 968; Aria & 10 Variations in the Italian Style, BWV 989; Capriccio on the Departure of a Beloved Brother, BWV 992; Chromatic Fantasia & Fugue, BWV 903; Fantasia, Adagio & Fugue in D, BWV 912; The Well-Tempered Clavier, Book I: Prelude & Fugue in B flat, BWV 866.* (ii) *English Suite 3 in G min., BWV 808; Italian Concerto; Sonata in D min., BWV 964 (trans. from Unaccompanied Violin Sonata 2 in A min., BWV 1003); Well-Tempered Clavier, Book I: Preludes & Fugues: in C min.; in C, BWV 847–8; Book II: Preludes & Fugues: in C sharp, BWV 872; in G, BWV 884.* (iii) *Goldberg Variations;* (iv) *Partitas 1 in B flat; 2 in C min.; 6 in E min.*

✪ *** VAI (i) VAIA 1041; (ii) VAIA 1051; (iii) VAIA 1029; (iv) VAIA 1040 (available separately). Tureck (piano)

Rosalyn Tureck's Bach playing is legendary, and the performances here show that her keyboard command and fluent sense of Bach style are as remarkable as ever. Tureck uses a wide dynamic and expressive range with consummate artistry, her decoration always adds to the musical effect and she makes us feel that Bach's keyboard music could be played in no other way than this – the hallmark of a great artist.

English Suite 3; 6 Preludes, BWV 933–8; Sonata in D min., BWV 964 (arr. of Unaccompanied Violin Sonata, BWV 1003). Well-Tempered Clavier: Preludes & fugues: BWV 855, 880 & 849

(***) VAI mono VAIA 1085. Tureck (piano)

Recorded (on 78s) at a live event in New York in 1948, this Bach recital shows the young Tureck to be intimately discerning and already completely at home on the piano in Bach's keyboard world. She plays very intimately and the recording is confined, but her thoughtfulness is magnetic throughout and one soon forgets the limited upper range of the sound. Unfortunately, the notes tell the collector little or nothing about the music.

Chromatic Fantasia & Fugue, BWV 903; Italian Concerto; Well-Tempered Clavier, Book I: Preludes & Fugues: BWV 850, 858, 866, 848. Book II: Preludes & Fugues: BWV 871–2, 884–5, 903. Encore: Goldberg Variations: Variation 29
*** VAI (ADD) VAIA 1139. Tureck (harpsichord)

This was recorded live in 1981 at the Metropolitan Museum of Art, New York. The balance is very close but the sharp focus of the instrument suits Tureck's amazingly clean articulation. She opens with five *Preludes and Fugues* from Book II of the *Well-Tempered Clavier*, then, after a dazzling account of the *Chromatic Fantasia* and a reflective fugue, she moves back to give us four *Preludes and Fugues* from Book I which bring the most remarkable bravura articulation; the fugues, however, unfold precisely. Then comes a buoyant *Italian Concerto* with a touchingly thoughtful central *Andante*. The ear soon adjusts to the dry, close, slightly tinkly harpsichord image.

Adagio in G, BWV 968; Aria & 10 Variations in the Italian Style, BWV 989; Capriccio on the Departure of a Beloved Brother, BWV 992; Chromatic Fantasia & Fugue, BWV 903; Partita 2 in C min., BWV 826; Prelude in E flat min., BWV 853; Musette in D (S. Anh. 126)
**(*) VAI VAIA 1131. Tureck (piano)

There is a slight element of disappointment about Tureck's 1995 Russian recital. She does not seem always to relax here as much as usual and, although the *Chromatic Fantasia* is very commanding indeed and the *Partita* is full of characteristic insights, the bold, truthful, but closely observed digital sound seems at times to bring an element of didacticism to her presentation. However, Tureck's full charisma returns in the closing *Prelude* and *Musette*, which are played most movingly. The documentation concentrates on the occasion and says little about the music.

Other keyboard collections

Aria variata alla maniera italiana in A min., BWV 989; Chromatic Fantasia, BWV 903; Concerto in D min. (after Marcello), BWV 974; Fantasies in G min. & C min., BWV 917 & 919; Fantasia & Fugue in C min., BWV 906; Fugues in A & B min. on themes by Albinoni, BWV 950–51
(M) **(*) Sony ADD SMK 87753. Gould (piano) – C. P. E. BACH; D SCARLATTI: *Sonatas* **(*)

Most of this collection was intended for a planned 'Bach Italian Album' that was never completed. Gould was persuaded to record the *Italian Concerto*, even though he disliked it, and also the *Chromatic Fantasia*, though he thought it a 'monstrosity'. Both bring some prodigious virtuosity. Otherwise this is an attractive collection of shorter works, given concentrated performances of characteristic flair. The *Aria variata alla maniera italiana* with its diverse divisions is winningly played, and the *Fantasies* are neatly varied in touch. The spiccato articulation of the outer movements of the *Concerto after Marcello* frame a sensitively expressive middle section, and the pair of fugues on themes by Albinoni are attractively buoyant and clear. The remastered recording is fully acceptable and the couplings add to the attractions of this collection.

Capriccio in E in Honour of Johann Christoph Bach, BWV 993; Capriccio on the Departure of a Beloved Brother, BWV 992; Chromatic Fantasia & Fugue, BWV 903; Fantasia & Fugues: in A min., BWV 944; in C min., BWV 906; Fantasias: in A min., BWV 922; in G min., BWV 917; Fantasia on a Rondeau in C min., BWV 918; Prelude in C
min., BWV 921; Fantasia & Fugue in A min., BWV 944; Fugue in A on a Theme of Albinoni, BWV 950; Prelude & Fugue on a Theme by Albinoni, BWV 923/951
*** BIS CD 1037. Suzuki (harpsichord)

Masaaki Suzuki uses a modern Dutch copy after an enlarged two-manual Rückers harpsichord to spectacular effect. He opens with a dazzlingly bravura account of the *Chromatic Fantasia*, and is equally impressive later in his brilliant articulation of the Albinoni *Prelude* and the engaging *C minor Prelude*, BWV 921 (which is marked *Harpeggiando – Prestissimo*). Yet the fugues are given aptly judged tempi, never rushed. The two *Capricii*, both dedicated to Bach's brothers, are delightfully presented and the illustrative detail of BWV 992 genially realized, while BWV 993 is a lively but light-hearted *Toccata*. The rest of this varied programme is played with comparable flair and all of it is very well recorded. In short, this is a very winning and often exciting collection, and if you are looking for keyboard virtuosity you won't be disappointed here.

Capriccio in E, BWV 993; Capriccio on the Departure of a Beloved Brother, BWV 992; 4 Duets, BWV 802–5; Italian Concerto; Partita in B min., BWV 831
*** Hyp. CDA 67306. Hewitt (piano)

This enticing collection once again confirms Angela Hewitt's reputation for playing Bach on the piano with a distinction comparable to that of Rosalyn Tureck in the five decades before her. Her striking sense of keyboard colour is shown in the 'Departure' *Capriccio*, especially the *Adagissimo*, and, together with an imaginatively wide variety of touch, makes the four *Duets* (so called on account of their two-part counterpoint) unusually diverse, like a suite. The gentle interchanges of No. 3 are particularly captivating. The so-called *Italian Concerto* is subtitled 'Concerto nach Italienischen Gusto', and the vibrant buoyancy of the outer movements readily reflects that feeling, while the central *Andante* is blissful. As for the famous *B minor Partita* (or *French Overture*), the sparklingly rhythmic dance-movements make a perfect setting for the lovely central *Sarabande*. Hewitt is recorded most naturally and provides her own excellent notes.

Chorale Preludes: BWV 639; 659 (both arr. Busoni); Chromatic Fantasia & Fugue, BWV 903; Fantasia & Fugue in A min., BWV 904; Italian Concerto; Fantasia in A min., BWV 922
(M) *** Ph. 442 400-2. Brendel (piano)

Brendel's performances are of the old school, with no attempt to strive after harpsichord effects, and with every piece creating a sound-world of its own. The *Italian Concerto* is particularly imposing, with a finely sustained sense of line and beautifully articulated rhythms. The recording is in every way truthful and present, bringing the grand piano very much into the living-room before one's very eyes. Masterly.

Chromatic Fantasia and Fugue, BWV 903; 4 Duets, BWV 802/5; Italian Concerto; Partita in B min., BWV 831
*** Signum SIGCD 030. Carolan (harpsichord)

Bach keyboard recitals are now proliferating on the piano, so it is good to welcome an outstanding new harpsichord collection from Lucy Carolan that is as fine as any in the catalogue. Her clear, direct style with crisp, unfussy ornamentation brings an account of the *Italian Concerto* which is as buoyant as her *Chromatic Fantasia* is dashing and brilliant, with the following *Fugue* splendidly vital, clean in articulation. The *Four Duets* from the third volume of the *Clavierübung* are usually heard on the organ, but here are made into an attractive miniature keyboard suite, with No. 2 especially winning. The concluding *B minor Partita* (or *French Overture*) makes an impressive conclusion, again full of rhythmic vitality, but with the *Sarabande* eloquently simple. A double-manual harpsichord by Bruce Kennedy after Mietke (*c.* 1702) is used and the recording, made in the warm but not too resonant acoustic St Paul's School, Hammersmith, was balanced by the splendid team of Andrew Keener and Mike Clements, and is nigh perfect in every respect.

Chromatic Fantasia & Fugue, BWV 903; Partitas: 1 in B flat, BWV 825; in B min., BWV 831; Toccata in D min., BWV 913
(B) **(*) DG ADD/DD 463 018-2. Pinnock (harpsichord)

Trevor Pinnock's stylistic sensibility is matched by his technical expertise, and there is no doubt that his explosive burst of bravura at the opening of the *Chromatic Fantasia* is exciting. Sometimes his approach seems too literal, but at others he allows himself more expressive latitude, notably so in the *B minor Partita*. The playing is always rhythmically alive, but the close recording of the harpsichord and the high level combine to create a somewhat unrelenting dynamic level, and the harpsichord timbre is metallic.

English Suite 2 in A min., BWV 807; Partita 2 in C min., BWV 826; Toccata in C min., BWV 911
(M) *** DG (ADD) 463 604-2 (2). Argerich (piano)

Martha Argerich's playing provides a genuinely musical experience: alive, keenly rhythmic, but also wonderfully flexible and rich in colour. There is an intellectual musical vitality here that is refreshing. She is very well recorded indeed, even if the measure (50 minutes) is not especially generous.

French Suite 2 in C min., BWV 813; Italian Concerto; Partita 6 in E min., BWV 830; Toccata in E min., BWV 914
⊕ *** Orfeo C547 011A. Kuschnerova (piano)

Very fine Bach playing here from an artist little known in Britain. Elena Kuschnerova was a pupil of Tatiana Kestner, whose pupils have included Gavrilov and Nikolai Petrov. Since 1992 she has lived in Germany and has, it seems, made records of Prokofiev and Scriabin. Make no mistake, this disc, which derives from a recital given at the Kurhaus, Baden-Baden, in March 2000, is altogether outstanding. Indeed, it is one of the finest Bach recitals on the piano we have had in recent years from a newcomer to the British catalogue. She has a commanding musical presence – the listener is held from beginning to end – and the rhythmic vitality and keenly articulated phrasing betoken a fine musical intelligence. The *C minor French Suite* is wonderfully alive, and both the *E minor Partita* and the *Italian Concerto* are full of spirit and freshness. It was Handel who said that he wrote music 'to make people better', and the present recital leaves the listener feeling exhilarated and purified as only the best Bach playing can. Very good sound.

French Suite 5, BWV 816; Fuga a Tre, BWV 953; Fughetta, BWV 961; Italian Concerto; 3 Minuets, BWV 841–3; 2 Minuets, BWV Anh. 114–15; Partita 1, BWV 825; 6 Preludes, BWV 924–8 & 930; 6 Little Preludes, BWV 939–43 & 999
(B) *** EMI Debut 5 68700-2. Egarr (harpsichord)

Richard Egarr's CD is one of the EMI Debut series and is a welcome reissue. In it the three major solo pieces, the *Partita*

in *B flat*, the *G major French Suite* and the *Italian Concerto*, are interspersed with *Preludes*, *Minuets* and a number of other smaller pieces. Egarr plays a copy of a 1638 Rückers, by Joel Katzman, from which he draws splendid sounds. He is far removed from the rigidity of the sewing-machine school; his playing is unfailingly flexible and musical, and he does not hurry but allows the music to breathe naturally. The recording is pleasing and faithful. An excellent bargain recital.

ORGAN MUSIC

Complete organ music

Helmut Walcha's first mono DG Archiv series (incomplete)

(B) (**(*)) DG mono 474 747-2 (10). Walcha (organs of St-Jacobi-Kirche or St-Peter-und-Paul-Kirche Cappel, Lübeck)

The first three 78-r.p.m. records issued on Deutsche Grammophon's Archiv label in 1947 were of Helmut Walcha playing Bach's six *Schübler Chorales* on the small organ at the St-Jacobi-Kirche in Lübeck. They are included here and are piquantly registered (No. 6, *Kommst du nun*, has a hint of charm – not a quality one usually associates with Walcha's Bach when his playing is so clear, positive and rhythmically clean). He continued with the first and last of the *Trio Sonatas* and the '*Sei gegrüsset*' *Chorale Variations* (which might better have suited a larger organ).

But when in 1950 and 1952 he went on to record the rest of the Bach organ repertoire which he considered authentic, he turned to the Arp Schnitger organ in the Cappel of the St-Peter-und-Paul-Kirche, including the other four *Trio Sonatas* and the *Canonic Variations on 'Vom Himmel Hoch'*. The latter obviously suit the larger instrument, and the *Sonatas*, divided between the two instruments, make a fascinating aural comparison for, even if they are not as spirited as some versions, they are played very beautifully and are never dull.

By then the LP had arrived, with its background quiet, and the DG engineers found that street noise sometimes compromised the recordings made in the St-Jakobi-Kirche (although such problems do not really emerge here). But the suitability of the St-Peter-und-Paul organ is in no doubt, and this is shown by the introductory demonstration of its registrations included with this set. The only snag is that the commentary is in German and no translation is offered, a most curious omission!

Helmut Walcha DG Archiv Stereo Series (incomplete)

The Art of Fugue, BWV 1080 (with *Contrapunctus 18*, completed Walcha); *Allabreve, BWV 589; Chorale Settings: BWV 645–50 (Schübler Chorales), 651–64, 653b, 665–68a, 700, 709, 727, 733, 734, 736; Canonic Variations on 'Vom Himmel hoch', BWV 769; Canzona, BWV 588; Chorale Partita (Sei gegrüsset), BWV 768; Clavier-Übung, Part III (Organ Mass): Prelude & Fugue, BWV 552 & Chorale Settings, BWV 669–89; 4 Duets, BWV 802–5; Fantasias: BWV 562, 572; Fantasias & Fugues, BWV 537, 542; Fugues: BWV 552/2, 578; Fugues on Themes by Legrenzi & Corelli, BWV 574, 579. Orgelbüchlein, BWV 599–644; Pastorale, BWV 590; Passacaglia & Fugue, BWV 582; Preludes &*

Fugues: BWV 531–6, 539, 541, 543–8, 550, 551; Toccatas &
Fugues: BWV 538, 540, 564; Toccata, Adagio & Fugue, BWV
565; Trio Sonatas 1–6, BWV 525–30

(B) **(*) DG (ADD) 463 712–2 (12). Walcha (organs at St
    Laurenskerk, Alkmaar, Netherlands, and
    Saint-Pierre-le-Jeune, Strasburg)

Helmut Walcha's incomplete pioneering stereo series was
recorded between 1959 and 1971. Even if by today's standards
Walcha's Bach style seems very relaxed and sometimes lacking in internal tension, his carefully calculated interpretations
create a genuine sense of organic unity and a deeply musical
sense of line and phrase, which gains from felicitous registration using highly suitable organs, splendidly recorded.

In his distinguished version of The Art of Fugue the registration is admirably varied, yet with the contrasts in register
and timbre heightened by the spatial effect of the stereo. The
Toccatas and Fugues certainly do not lack bravura, and typical
of Walcha's playing at its most monumental is the gigantic
triptych of the Toccata, Adagio and Fugue, a rigorous test of
any organist's technique. It is a work which Walcha comes
through with flying colours, and the Chorale Partita, Sei
gegrüsset, is another expansive piece that comes off very
successfully.

The Preludes and Fugues with their dignified tempi,
although seldom flamboyant, are dedicated performances
which allow every detail to come through, with the E flat
work, BWV 552, especially impressive in its combination of
majesty and clarity. Among the shorter, more colourful pieces
the silvery arpeggios of the Fantasia in G, BWV 572, bring a
fine example of perceptive registration, and in Walcha's hands
the Trio Sonatas are not treated lightly but are used to reflect
the contrapuntal and formal mastery of Bach's middle
period.

Chorale Partita: Sei gegrüsset, BWV 768; Prelude & Fugue in
E flat, BWV 552; 6 Schübler Chorales, BWV 645–50; Toccata
& Fugue in D min., BWV 565; Trio Sonata 1 in E flat, BWV
525

(M) **(*) DG stereo/mono (IMS) 457 704-2. Walcha (St
    Laurenskerk organ, Alkmaar)

DG have, on the whole, chosen well for a programme of
'Originals' to demonstrate Walcha's Bach style. Even if modern ears may find Walcha's approach rather slow and heavy,
the performance of the famous D minor Toccata and Fugue,
although comparatively unflamboyant, is not dull. The Trio
Sonata is engagingly registered, as are the steadily presented
Schübler Chorales. The last four of these are mono, but the ear
hardly registers the difference because of the high quality of
DG's recording.

Peter Hurford Complete Decca Series

Allabreve, BWV 589; Aria, BWV 587; Canonic Variations:
Vom Himmel Hoch, BWV 769; Canzona, BWV 588; Chorale
Partitas: Christ du bist der helle Tag; O Gott, du frommer
Gott; Sei gegrüsset, Jesu gütig, BWV 766–8. Chorale Preludes:
BWV 620a, 730–48, 751–2, 754–5, 757–763, 765, BWV Anh. 55.
Chorale Variations: Ach, was soll ich Sünder machen, BWV
770; Allein Gott in der Höh' sei Ehr, BWV 771.
Clavier-Übung, Part 3: German Organ Mass (Prelude &
Fugue, BWV 552; Choral Preludes, BWV 669–89). Concertos
1–6 (after VIVALDI, ERNST & unnamed composer), BWV
592–7. Fantasias, BWV 562–3, 571–2. Fantasias & Fugues,
BWV 537, 542, 561. Fugues, BWV 574–581, 131a. Kirnberger
Chorale Preludes, BWV 690–713. Kleines harmonisches

Labyrinth, BWV 591. Leipzig Chorale Preludes, BWV 663–8.
Musical Offering: Ricercar, BWV 1079/5. Neumeister
(Arnstadt) Chorale Preludes, BWV 714–15, 742, 957,
1090–1120. Orgelbüchlein: Chorale Preludes 1–46, BWV
599–644. Passacaglia & Fugue, BWV 582; Pastorale, BWV
590; Pedal-exercitium, BWV 598. Preludes, BWV 567–9.
Preludes & Fugues, BWV 531–5; 535a, 536, 539, 541, 543–51; 8
Short Preludes & Fugues, BWV 553–60. Prelude, Trio &
Fugue BWV 545b. Schübler Chorale Preludes, BWV 645–50.
Toccata, Adagio & Fugue, BWV 564. Toccatas and Fugues,
BWV 538, 540, 565–6. Trios, BWV 583–6, 1027a

(B) *** Decca (ADD/DDD) 444 410-2 (17). Hurford (organs
    of Ratzeburg Cathedral, Germany; Church of Our Lady of
    Sorrows, Toronto, Canada; New College Chapel, Oxford;
    Knox Grammar School Chapel, Sydney, Australia; Eton
    College, Windsor; Stiftskirche, Melk, Austria;
    Augustinerkirche, Vienna, Austria; All Souls Unitarian
    Church, Washington, D.C., USA; Domkirche, St Pölten,
    Austria; St Catharine's College Chapel, Cambridge)

With the exception of the 35 Arnstadt Chorale Preludes, as
copied by Neumeister, which were added in 1986, Peter Hurford recorded his unique survey of Bach's organ music for
Decca's Argo label over a period of eight years, 1974–82.
Following the example of Bach himself, who was renowned
for trying out organs, Hurford uses ten different organs,
moving from Ratzeburg in Germany to Toronto in Canada,
back home to New College, Oxford, then to Sydney, Australia,
and so on. Each organ is caught superbly by the recording
engineers, and the registration features a range of baroque
colour that is almost orchestral in its diversity. The digital
recording of the Vienna Bach organ chosen for the Neumeister Chorales is particularly beautiful.

It was Peter Hurford's achievement to influence a complete
change in approach to this repertoire, moving away from an
enduring and essentially pedagogic, German tradition
(shown at its best by organists like Helmut Walcha on DG
Archiv). Vigour and energy are the keynotes of Hurford's
approach to the large-scale works and, without losing their
majesty, he never lets the fugal momentum get bogged down
by the music's weight and scale. We hear Bach's organ writing
with new ears, its human vitality revealed alongside its
extraordinary architecture. The set is supported with very
good notes by Clifford Bartlett which are both scholarly and
readable; full specifications of all the organs used are
included. The recordings are splendidly transferred to CD,
and while newer digital surveys are now appearing, this set of
17 bargain-price CDs remains a cornerstone among available
recordings of this repertoire. Apart from the selection below,
the discs unfortunately are not available separately.

Chorale Preludes, BWV 727, 729–30, 734, 659, 645 & 694;
Fantasias: BWV 562, BWV 572; Fantasias & Fugues: BWV
537 & 542; Passacaglia & Fugue, BWV 582; Preludes &
Fugues, BWV 543, 532 & (St Anne) BWV 552; Toccata, Adagio
& Fugue, BWV 564; Toccatas & Fugues: in D min. (Dorian),
BWV 538; BWV 565

⊶ (B) *** Double Decca (ADD) 443 485-2 (2). Hurford
    (various organs)

A generous 146-minute collection of major Bach organ
works, taken from Peter Hurford's complete survey (see
above), brings two separate recitals, each framed by major
concert pieces, with the beautifully played chorales used in
between the large-scale pieces to add contrast. The current

bright transfers seem to have added an extra sharpness of outline to the sound of some of the big set-pieces, but this is something which will be more noticeable on some reproducers than on others, and the various organs are caught with fine realism and plenty of depth.

Marie-Claire Alain Complete Erato Series

New Series, Volume 1: *Chorales: Ich ruf, zu dir, Herr Jesu Christ, BWV 639; In dulci jubilo, BWV 608; Jesu meine Freude, BWV 610; In dir ist Freude, BWV 610; Concerto in A min. (after Vivaldi), BWV 593; Toccata, Adagio & Fugue in C, BWV 564; Toccatas & Fugues in C, BWV 566; in D min. (Dorian), BWV 538 & BWV 565*
(M) *** Warner Elatus 0927 49834-2. Alain (various organs)

Only Volumes 1, 4–7, 9, 11 and 14 of Marie-Claire Alain's integral survey, made for Erato during the early 1990s, are available separately as we go to print. We discuss them in detail below. However, the complete set is now available again in a box of 14 CDs. Meanwhile, the first of a new Elatus series has arrived, taken from that series, here featuring three different organs all well suited to this repertoire and impressively recorded. Alain opens with a volatile account of the most famous of Bach's *Toccatas and Fugues*, but the other performances are equally compulsive, especially the *Toccata, Adagio and Fugue in C*, and the *Chorales* make a well varied collection. A fine disc.

Volume 1 of the complete coverage was made on the organ of Martinikerk, Groningen, and combines *Leipzig Chorale Preludes* with a pair of *Preludes and Fugues*. However, the results are not entirely satisfactory. The engineers obtain a rich, weighty sound as in the opening *E minor Prelude and Fugue*, but the resonance makes the result rather opaque, which does not enable Alain to clarify detail. The fugue, however, is measured and powerful. This whole programme bears out her comments about tempi, which are essentially relaxed.

The Silbermann organ at Rötha proves ideal for the repertoire in Volume 4, and it stimulates Marie-Claire Alain to some of her most spontaneous performances so far in this variable series. After a robust *Prelude and Fugue in E minor*, BWV 533, Alain is at her most chimerical in the *Christmas Chorale, Nun freut euch, lieben Christen g'mein*, with the registration like tinkling bells, and *In dulci jubilo* is very grand indeed. Alain clearly revels in the elaborate passage on the pedals which opens the *Prelude in C*, BWV 531, and even conveys exuberance, while the fugue is equally alive and vivid. The contrapuntally grand *Herr Gott, dich loben wir* ends the recital massively, and here one feels Alain could have moved the music on a bit.

Alain opens Volume 5 with the early *Prelude and Fugue in C minor* (1703–4) using the Rötha organ's pedals to bravura effect, following with a fairly spontaneous account of the jolly fugue. The first chorale, *Herr Jesu Christ, dich zu uns wend*, BWV 709, is full of gleaming sunshine, while *Erbarm' dich mein O Herre Gott* brings that dedicated feeling of repose which Alain manages so well. The *Partita sopra 'Christ, der du bist der helle Tag'* brings six variations and Alain finds an orchestral range of colour for them, with a gigue movement finally leading to a majestic close.

If the *C major Fugue*, BWV 547, in Volume 6 proceeds on its way somewhat remorselessly, the *Canonic Variations* bring out the very best in Marie-Claire Alain, and the opening presentation, in which the *Christmas Chorale* cantus firmus subtly creeps through the flowing decorative lines is managed very cunningly, while the intricate contrapuntal writing remains clear throughout, and the chorales which follow have plenty of variety in presentation and mood.

Volume 7 offers repertoire which finds Alain at her very finest, for her performances of the *Chorales* clearly identify with their spiritual implications. Splendid recording; this can be strongly recommended.

In Volume 9 the *Très vitement* opening of the *G major Fantasia*, BWV 572, is always appealing, and Alain plays it perkily enough, then returning to her full-bodied style for the *Gravement-lentement*, which she takes very literally. The first of the *Orgelbüchlein* chorales included here, *Nunn komm' der Heiden Heiland*, BWV 599, is also very fully orchestrated, but in *Gottes Sohn ist kommen*, BWV 600, the balance between decoration and chorale is felicitous. The host of ascending and descending angels in BWV 606 is evocatively pictured, but it is in a quietly reflective piece like *Das alte Jahr vergangen ist*, BWV 614, that Alain is at her finest.

The splendid Müller organ used in Volume 11 with its bright, sunny reeds sounds just right for Bach's vivacious Vivaldi transcriptions. The works by Johann Ernst are also most rewarding. Alain's tempi are apt; allegros are not raced, but they are certainly infectious. The *Aria in F* is a Couperin transcription (from *Les Nations*). The two *Preludes and Fugues* are also comparatively lightweight, although still first-class Bach, from the early Weimar period. They are given attractively lively performances. A splendid disc and an ideal sampler to show this artist at her most perceptive.

The famous *Schübler Chorales* are the highlight of Marie-Claire Alain's final volume. They are particularly imaginative and pleasing. Alain takes the famous *Passacaglia in C minor* very spaciously, and here she does not quite generate a high enough degree of tension to carry it at such a slow speed. The *Fugue in G minor* is a little didactic, too – although again very effectively registered. On the other hand, the *Prelude and Fugue in G major* and the *Prelude in G major* are both fine performances.

Kevin Bowyer Nimbus series

Volume 1: *Chorale Preludes, BWV 1099 & 721; Concerto in G (after Prince Johann Ernst), BWV 592; Fantasia & Fugue, BWV 542; Trio Sonata 1, BWV 525*
*** Nim. NI 5280. Bowyer (Marcussen organ of Sct. Hans Kirke, Odense, Denmark)

Volume 2: *Chorale Preludes: BWV 720, 697 & 722, 751 & 729, 738; Fugue (Gigue), BWV 577; Preludes & Fugues, BWV 532 & 541; Trio Sonata 5, BWV 529*
*** Nim. NI 5289

Volume 3: *Chorale Partita: Sei gegrüsset, Jesu gütig, BWV 768; Concerto (after Vivaldi), BWV 596; Preludes & Fugues, BWV 534 & 543*
**(*) Nim. NI 5290

Volume 4: *Fantasia & imitatio, BWV 563; Fugue, BWV 575; 2 Fugues on Themes of Albinoni, BWV 950–51; 8 Short Preludes & Fugues, BWV 553–60; Toccatas, BWV 915 & 916*
● *** Nim. NI 5377

Volume 5: *Aria in F (after Couperin), BWV 587; Concerto (after Vivaldi), BWV 593; Fugue, BWV 576; Prelude & Fugue, BWV 539; Toccata & Fugue, BWV 540*
*** Nim. NI 5400

Volume 6: *Chorale Partita 'Wenn wir in höchsten Nöten sein', BWV Anh. 78; Fantasias super 'Valet will ich dir geben', BWV 735–6; Preludes & Fugues, BWV 533 & 535; Toccata, BWV 566; Toccata, Adagio & Fugue, BWV 564; Trio in G min., BWV 584; Trio Sonata 6, BWV 630*

*** Nim. NI 5423

Volume 7: *Orgelbüchlein: Chorales & Chorale Preludes 1–46, BWV 599–644*

**(*) Nim. NI 5457/8 (2). Bowyer; Fynske Chamber Ch., Joensen

Volume 8: *Chorale Preludes, BWV 653, 709 & 726, 731, 765; (4 Neumeister Chorales): BWV 1098, 1106, 1115–16. Concerto (after Vivaldi); Fantasia & Fugue, BWV 537; Fugue on a Theme by Legrenzi, BWV 574; Preludes & Fugues, BWV 531, 544, 547 & 895 (attrib.); 6 Schübler Chorales, BWV 645–50; Toccata & Fugue (Dorian), BWV 538; Trio Sonata in G, BWV 1039/1027a*

(B) *** Nim. Double NI 5500/1

Volume 9: *Clavier-Übung. Part 3: German Organ Mass: Prelude, BWV 552; Chorale Preludes, BWV 669–89; 4 Duets, BWV 802–5; Fugue (St Anne), BWV 552. Concerto (after Vivaldi), BWV 973; Fugue, BWV 578; Passacaglia & Fugue, BWV 582*

✿ (B) *** Nim. Double NI 5561/2

Volume 10: *Leipzig Chorale Preludes 1–18, BWV 651–68a; 4 Early Chorale Settings, BWV 1104, 1108–4 & 1199; Concerto 3 (after Vivaldi); Fugue, BWV 949*

(B) *** Nim. Double NI 5573/4 (2)

Volume 11: *Canonic Variations on 'Vom Himmel hoch', BWV 769; Chorale Preludes, BWV 690–91, 698, 702, 733, 743, 756; BWV Anh. 55, 60 & 70; 8 Chorale Preludes from the Neumeister Collection (Yale manuscript), BWV 957, 1092, 1096; 1111–13, 1117–18; Fugue on a Theme of Corelli, BWV 579; Preludes & Fugues, BWV 943 & 953; BWV 546; BWV 548; Toccatas, BWV 911, BWV 914; Trios (arr. from BWV 570); BWV 583*

(B) *** Nim. Double NI 5606/7 (2)

Volume 12: *Allabreve, BWV 589; Aria variata, BWV 989; Chorales, BWV 700–701; 710; 1090; Fantasias (Concerto), BWV 571; BWV 572; Fuga chromatisch bearbeitet, BWV Anh. 44; Fugue, BWV 131a; Kleines harmonisches Labyrinthe, BWV 591; Partita on 'Allein Gott in der Höh' sei Ehr', BWV 771; Preludes & Fugues, BWV 545 & 550; Toccata, BWV 918; Trio Sonatas 3–4, BWV 527–8*

(B) **(*) Nim. NI 5647/8 (2)

Volume 13: *Canzona, BWV 588; Chorales, BWV 655c, 694, 696, 699, 703–5, 712, 713/Anh 76; 714, 723, 732, 734, 739, 741, 744, 750, 758, 762/3, 1101, 1105, 1120; Concerto (after Marcello), BWV 974; Partita: O Gott, du frommer Gott, BWV 767; Herr Christ, der einig Gottessohn, BWV Anh. 77; Preludes, BWV 568 & 569; Prelude & Fugues, BWV 551 & 894; Toccatas, BWV 912–13; Trio (after Fasch), BWV 585*

(N) (M) *** Nim. Double NIM 5669/90

Volume 14: *Chorale Partitas: Aus der Tiefe rufe ich, BWV 745; Christ, der du bist der helle Tag, BWV 766; Chorale Preludes, BWV 695, 707, 711, 715–17, 730, 742, 745, 747–9, 754, 757, 1110; 1102; Anh. 171; Concertos: in C (after Ernst), BWV 595; in G min. (after Telemann), BWV 985; in E flat, BWV 597 (attrib.); Fantasia in G min., BWV 917; Fantasia & Fugue, BWV 561; Fugues in C & D, BWV 952 & 580; Preludes*

& Fugues, BWV 533a & 549; Preludes & Fuguettas, BWV 899 & 900; 8 Chorales from the Rudorff Collection; Trios: in D min., BWV 528; in G (after Telemann), BWV 586. 6 Pieces from Anna Magdelena Notebook, BWV Anh. 114–16, 122, 126 & 132

(N) (M) *** Nim. Double NIM 5689/90

Volume 15: *Chorale Preludes, BWV 655b, 660b, 667b, 706, 708, 719, 724, 727, 737, 752, 1085, 1094, 1100, 1103–4; 5 Chorales from Rinck Collection; Concerto in G, BWV 986; Fantasia in C min., BWV 1121; Fantasias: on 'Komm, Heilger Geist', BWV 651a; on a Rondo in C min., BWV 918; Fugues: in A min., BWV 947; in C, BWV Anh. 90; in C min. on a theme by Legrenzi, BWV 574a; in D, BWV 532a; in E min., BWV 956; in G min., BWV Anh. 109; Fuguetta, BWV 961; Partita on 'Ach was soll ich Sünder machen'; Prelude in C, BWV 567; Prelude, Trio & Fugue in B flat, BWV 545a; Sonata in D, BWV 963; Suite in F: Overture, BWV 820. Trio in C min., BWV Anh. 46*

(N) (M) *** Nim. Double NIM 5700/5701

Kevin Bowyer is another of the young-to-middle-aged generation of organists who have recorded a complete coverage of Bach's organ music. But his project is more ambitious than those of any of his competitors in intending, in his own words, 'to set a much wider remit: to offer a survey, an overview of Bach's attribution in the eighteenth and early nineteenth centuries'.

Many of Bach's unfinished works (nearly all of them in manuscripts in Bach's own hand) have been included, plus some completions of fragmentary works by later composers within the limitation of the stated time-period. But in addition, this Nimbus set includes many works, not written by Bach but mistakenly attributed to him, and usually of sufficient musical quality to support the misattribution. Both catagories, in Kevin Bowyer's opinion, include 'delightful, surprising treasures'.

As he has not chosen to record his survey in categorical groups, but in a series of carefully planned recitals, each available separately and enjoyable as an entity, collectors can, if they wish, make an exploration of this rare repertoire at will, in the later volumes, apart from exploring the mainstream works.

The performances have consistent life and integrity and striking spontaneity. The same Danish organ is used throughout, an instrument admirably suited to this repertoire; characteristically, the Nimbus engineers produce a sound-image with plenty of ambience, glowing, colourful pipings and throaty reeds, and plenty of weight when needed, the effect often expansively grand. Each volume is very well documented, and this Nimbus set must be regarded as the most comprehensive Bach organ survey yet published.

Comparing Kevin Bowyer's performances of the *Orgelbüchlein* directly with Christopher Herrick's versions (which in general we find more satisfying) reveals an astonishing difference of sound and characterization. The Danish organ has much more plangent reeds and Bowyer's performances are less warmly mellifluous, more dramatic. Yet those who like a lively presentation will find this set very much to their taste, for Bowyer's tempi are usually brisker than Herrick's. He is recorded very vividly.

Volume 9 centres on Bach's so-called *German Organ Mass*, and this account is unsurpassed on CD. After the powerful introductory *Prelude*, Bach presents each chorale in two contrasting versions, the first elaborate, then a simpler setting without pedals (although occasionally this order is reversed).

Bowyer's imagination is inspired to use all the resources of the splendid organ to emphasize the contrapuntal and stylistic differences and to create the widest variety of mood. Bowyer gives the four deceptively simple *Duets* sparkling registrations to make a foil for the weighty power of the closing *St Anne's Fugue*, which holds the listener from the first bar to the last. Bowyer then continues his recital with a captivating account of Bach's transcription of one of Vivaldi's liveliest violin concertos, and he ends with a superbly eloquent performance of the great *Passacaglia and Fugue in C minor*.

Volumes 13, 14 and 15, which are new to this volume, centre on the *Chorales*, including a group from the so-called Rudorff Collection, and (in Volume 15) five from the Rinck Collection (held at Yale University) which appear to be authentic. In all the *Chorale Preludes* and *Partitas*, however florid or richly registered, Bowyer skilfully ensures that the cantus firmus is clear, so that the listener can easily follow its progress. They are prefaced and interlaced with large and medium-scaled works, all played with characteristic panache. Volume 13 includes a particularly appealing account of Bach's transcription of Marcello's *D minor Concerto*, and there is some brilliant playing too in the *G major Prelude*, BWV 568, which opens the second CD of Volume 13, while Bowyer is at his jaunty best in the *Toccata in D*, BWV 912, which comes later. Here, as elsewhere, Kevin Bowyer is always seeking to use the full palette of colour on his fine organ, and on the second disc of Volume 14 the four chorales based on *Allein Gott in der Höh sei Her* (BWV 711 and 715–17) are splendidly varied; and even the little pieces from Anna Magdalena's Notebook are very entertainingly presented, especially the March and piquant *Musette*. Of the solo *Concertos*, that in E flat, BWV 597, is certainly not, but it is very engaging, and the second recital of Volume 14 closes with a jolly, little-known *Concerto in G minor* derived from Telemann.

Volume 15 opens with a buoyant account of the *Partita on Ach, was soll ich Sünder machen* and then offers a similarly striking performance of the *Fantasia in C minor*. Other highlights here include the extended *Overture in F* and the *Concerto in G*, BWV 986, while all the individual *Fugues* are full of life, the familiar *D major Fugue* being especially winning. Of course, an exhaustive survey such as this includes many works that are not authentic, and in Volume 15 no fewer than 13 such items are included (including the *Fugue* on the composer's own name). There are also variants on other works, of which the *Prelude, Trio and Fugue in B flat* is a lively example; indeed, all these spurious pieces are enjoyable when played with such conviction, for Kevin Bower is never dull.

Volume 16: *18 Anhalt-Cöthen Castle Clock Pieces, BWV Anh. 133–50; Chorales: BWV 653a, 676a, 683a, 691a, 692–3, 695a, 708a, 735a, 753, 759–61, 764, BWV Anh. 57, 73, 200; Concerto in C (after Ernst), BWV 984; 3 Chaconnes, BWV Anh. 82–3; Concerto in D (after Vivaldi), BWV 972; Fantasia in C, BWV 573; Fantasia & Fugue in D min., BWV 549a; Fugues: in B flat, BWV Anh. 45; in C min. on a theme by Legrenzi, BWV 574b; in D min., BWV Anh. 180; in E min., BWV 962; Passacaglia in D min., BWV Anh. 182; Pedalexercitium, BWV 598; Preludes in A, BWV 536a/i; A min., BWV 543a/i; Preludes & Fugues: in B flat, BWV 898; in C, BWV 545a; in E flat, BWV Anh. 177; in G min., BWV 535a (Fragment); Toccata in A, BWV Anh. 178*

(M) *** Nim. Double NIM 5734/35

Volume 16 is a kind of appendix, chosen personally by Kevin

Bowyer, which includes 18 pieces written for the Anhalt-Cöthen Castle grandfather clock, which had a musical mechanism in its upper portion. Traditionally attributed to Johann Sebastian, they were more likely to have been written by one of his sons. Bowyer conveys his enjoyment of these simple but varied miniatures, and he has registered them with much imaginative charm, justifying their inclusion by citing the tradition of mechanical music by Mozart and others being transcribed for the organ.

The programme opens with a spirited account of Bach's familiar transcription of Vivaldi's *Concerto in D* (No. 9 from *L'estro armonico*) in a version not including the pedal, and the first disc concludes with a similar *Concerto* drawing music by Prince Johann Ernst. The rest of the selection includes either music written by others and wrongly attributed to Bach or various alternative versions of authentic works, often with fascinating variants. They are sometimes truncated, as in the case of the *Prelude and Fugue in C*, or incomplete, as with the *Fantasia in C* and the *G minor Prelude and Fugue*, both of which end unexpectedly. Some of the attributions are very attractive, notably the delicately registered *Passacaglia in D minor* (composed by Christian Witte) and the *Fugue in E minor*, an expressive work by Johann Albrechtsberger. The three lightweight *Chaconnes* were probably written by Johann Bernhard, a distant cousin of Johann Sebastian, and the rumbustious *Pedalexercitium*, played here with bravura and relish, might possibly be by C. P. E., as the manuscript is in his handwiting. All in all, a fascinating collection, very well documented.

Volume 17: *The Art of Fugue, BWV 1080; Chorale: 'Wenn wir in höchstein Noten sein', BWV 668a; Capriccio on the Departure of a Beloved Brother, BWV 992; Fantasias in A min., BWV 922; C min., BWV 919; Fantasia & Fugue in A min., BWV 944; Fugues, BWV 945, 948, 954–5, 958; Prelude in G, BWV 902a/1; Preludes and Fughettas, BWV 901–2; Praeludium et Partita del tuono terzo, BWV 833; Ricercare in 3 Voices, BWV 1079/i; Ricercare in 6 voices, BWV 1079/v* (with alternative registration)

(N)(B) *** Nim. Double NIM 5738/40 (3)

Jonathan's Baxendale's extensive and scholarly notes for this final volume make a clear case for the performance of *The Art of Fugue* on the organ or harpsichord 'since the range of the fugues' individual melodic strands would, for the most part, have made them unsuitable for performance on contemporary instruments other than the keyboard'. Moreover, Kevin Bowyer's performance, strong and plainly registered (the *Canons* bringing a brighter interlude), makes the choice of the organ a very convincing one. The other pieces here, used to preface that central masterpiece, are youthful works of some precociousness. The famous *Capriccio* describing a brother's journey is almost certainly a very early work, and Bowyer makes the most of its programmatic character, especially the 'Departure', with its jolly posthorn fugue. The simple *Praeludium et Partita* dates from around 1708: its *Sarabande and Double* here sounds very like a peal of bells, and the *A minor Fantasia* brings a burst of virtuosity to open the second disc. The celebrated chorale, *Wenn wir in höchstein Noten sein*, whether or not (as legend has it) dictated on Bach's deathbed, makes a touchingly gentle coda.

Fantasias & Toccatas, BWV 537–8;540; 542; 564–6; 572. Toccatas BWV 910–16

(N) (M) *** Nim. NI 7077/78. Bowyer (from above complete set)

Preludes & Fugues, BWV 531–6; 539; 541; 543–52
(N) (M) * Nim.** NI 7079/80. Bowyer (from above complete set)

During the lifetime of this book Nimbus are planning to issue a series of mid-priced doubles gathering together groups of major works from Kevin Bowyer's series 'aimed at buyers who were probably frustrated by the recital concept'. If the above are successful, there will be similar packages from the *Chorale Partitas*, (solo) *Concerti* and *Trio Sonatas*.

Christopher Herrick Complete Hyperion Series

Disc 1: *Trio Sonatas 1–6, BWV 525–30.* CDA 66390. Herrick (organ of St Nicholas Church, Bremgarten, Switzerland)

Discs 2–3: *Fantasias: BWV 562, 572, 537, 542; Preludes & Fugues: BWV 536, 543–7, 532, 548, 552, 534 & 541.* CDA 66791/2 (organ of Jesuits' Church, Lucerne)

Disc 4: *Passacaglia in C min., BWV 582; Toccatas & Fugues: in D min. (Dorian), BWV 538; in D min., BWV 565; in F, BWV 540; Toccata, Adagio & Fugue in C, BWV 564.* CDA 66434 (organ of Stadkirche, Zofingen, Switzerland)

Discs 5–6: *Allebreve in D, BWV 589; Canzona in D min., BWV 588; Couperin Aria in F, BWV 587; 4 Duets, BWV 802–5; Fantasias: in A min., BWV 561; in C, BWV 570; Fantasia con imitatione in B min., BWV 563; Fugues, BWV 575–6 & 578; Fugue alla giga, BWV 577; Musical Offering: 3- & 6-part Ricercares in C min., BWV 1079; Pastorale in F, BWV 590; Preludes, BWV 551, 569 & 568; Preludes & Fugues, BWV 533, 535, 539 (Fiddle Fugue), 549a, 550 & 569; Toccata in E, BWV 566; Trios: in D min., BWV 583; in C min. (Fasch), BWV 585; in G (Telemann), BWV 586; in G, BWV 1027a.* CDA 67211/2 (organ of Stadtkirche, Rheinfelden, Switzerland)

Disc 7: *Concertos (for solo organ) 1, BWV 592 (after* ERNST*); 2–3, BWV 593–4 (both after* VIVALDI*); 4, BWV 595 (after* ERNST*); 5, BWV 596 (after* VIVALDI*); Fugue on a Theme of Corelli, BWV 579; Fugue on a Theme of Legrenzi, BWV 574.* CDA 66813 (organ of St Peter and St Paul, Villmergen, Switzerland)

Disc 8: *'Organ Cornucopia': Chorale Preludes, BWV 723, 741, 743, 747, 753–5, 758 (4 verses), 762, 764–5; BWV Anh. 55; Concertos, BWV 571, 597; Fantasia, BWV 575; Fugues, BWV 946, 562, 580; Kleines harmonisches Labyrinthe, BWV 591; Pedal-exercitium, BWV 598; Prelude & Fugue, BWV 531; Prelude, BWV 567; Trio, BWV 584.* CDA 67139 (organ of Pfarrkirche, St Michael, Kaisten, Switzerland)

Disc 9: *Orgelbüchlein: Chorale Preludes 1–46, BWV 599–644.* CDA 66756 (organ of Stadtkirche, Rheinfelden, Switzerland)

Discs 10–11: *19 Kirnberger Chorales, BWV 690–91, 694–713; 18 Leipzig Chorales, BWV 651–68; 6 Schübler Chorales, BWV 645–50.* CDA 67071/2 (organ of Jesuitenkirche, Lucerne, Switzerland)

Discs 12–13: *Clavier-Übung, Part 3: Prelude & Fugue in E flat, BWV 532; Chorale Preludes, BWV 669–89. Chorale Preludes, Fantasias & Fughettas, BWV 672–5; 677, 679, 681, 683, 685, 687, 715–18, 720–22, 724–36, 738–40.* CDA 67213/4 (main and choir organs of Stadtkirche, Zofingen, Switzerland)

Disc 14: *Canonic Variations: Vom Himmel hoch, BWV 769; Chorale Partitas: Christ, der du bist der helle Tag, BWV 766; O Gott, du frommer Gott, BWV 767; Sei gegrüsset, Jesu gütig, BWV 767–8; Ach, was soll ich Sünder machen, BWV 770.* CDA 66455 (organ of St Nicholas Church, Bremgarten, Switzerland)

Disc 15: *36 Neumeister Chorales.* CDA 67215 (organ of the Stadtkirche, Zofingen, Switzerland)

Disc 16: *Attributions: 15 Chorale Preludes, BWV 692–3, 744–6, 748–52, 756–7, 759, 760–61, 763; Chorale Partita, Allein Gott in der Höh' sei Ehr; Fugue in G, BWV 581; 8 Little Preludes & Fugues, BWV 553–60.* CDA 67263 (organ of Pfarrkirche St Michael, Kaisten, Switzerland)

Christopher Herrick, favouring a series of Swiss organs, is very much of the new generation of organists, giving equal precedence to momentum and vitality and colourful registration, alongside a feeling for the musical architecture. This is one of the very finest and most comprehensive of modern surveys of Bach's organ music (including the attributions), offered in a bargain box, excellently documented, with the individual CDs available separately at full price.

Herrick's performances of the *Trio Sonatas* may be comparatively relaxed but the playing has plenty of lift, and he produces colours in slow movements to charm the ear, with the lyrical lines flowing. He has chosen an instrument well suited to this repertoire and he is in full command of its palette, with registration suited to the character of each movement and articulation that is precise without pedantry. The Hyperion recording, too, cannot be faulted, and even the order of works is chosen to make the most of their variety of style.

Volumes 2, 3 and 4 make a very imposing group which centres on some of the most powerfully structured and intellectually cogent of all Bach's major organ works. Herrick offers a presentation which is obviously built on a background of careful preparation, with a spontaneously vivid presentation as emotionally compelling as it is authoritative, with each fugue moving on to a gripping apotheosis. The chosen Swiss instrument seems ideal for the repertoire and it is superbly recorded, giving weight, amplitude and clarity in equal measure.

Volumes 5 and 6 offer a curious mixture entitled 'Miniatures'. Yet not all of these pieces are short (the *Pastorale* – a most attractive performance – is in four movements) and many of the *Preludes and Fugues*, although not extended, are very considerable works and make a strong impression here. The very opening *Allabreve* is commanding, as is the *Toccata in E major* with its weighty pedals. Of course the engaging *Gigue Fugue*, the *Couperin Aria* and the *Telemann Trio* (all delightfully registered) are lightweight and serve well as interludes within the more substantial fare. But the set proves an attractive way of gathering up some of Bach's less obvious masterpieces, and they are all splendidly played and recorded on a fine Swiss organ.

Herrick's *Orgelbüchlein* is in every way recommendable, and these performances can stand among the finest in the catalogue. The Swiss Metzler organ seems just right for these relatively simple yet sometimes florid pieces: it has a wide palette and an equal range of sonorities. The effect is never plangent, yet Herrick readily keeps the cantus firmus in front of the listener without exaggeration. His tempi invariably seem apt and his approach is obviously aware of the word-meaning of each chorale and its expressive implications. The recording is beautiful, smooth yet clear.

Unlike other recitalists, Herrick does not present Part 3 of Bach's *Clavier-Übung*, the so-called 'German Organ Mass', as a complete entity. He has already given us the four *Duets* in the collection of 'Miniatures' above, so here (on the first disc) he frames just the ten large-scale chorale settings with the mighty *E flat St Anne Prelude and Fugue*, using the church's large main organ. Then, on the second CD, he turns to the beautiful single-manual choir organ for the remaining ten lightweight chorales. In principle this works well enough, but it robs the listener of the added stimulation of hearing Bach's simple and elaborate settings of the same chorale side by side. Herrick's performances are well up to standard, but we are inclined to choose Kevin Bowyer's version of Part 3 of the *Clavier-Übung*, which presents the music in the normal published sequence.

The original manuscript for the *Neumeister Chorales* was a comparatively recent discovery, found in a collection at Yale University. The music itself has plenty of variety, for Bach's imagination in this field was inexhaustible, and Herrick is a very persuasive advocate on this fine Swiss organ. The music is admirably paced and always spontaneously alive, while detail remains clear.

Herrick completes his fine series with music long attributed to Bach but almost certainly not written by him. So it is with the *8 Little Preludes & Fugues*, where the basic material is so striking, although scholars feel that the working out is not felicitous enough for J. S. B. Yet the opening of *No. 1* is instantly commanding, the *Fugue* of *No. 2* and the *Prelude* of *No. 4* are attractively jaunty, *No. 6* opens grandly and the *Prelude* of *No. 8* brings a splendid excusion on the pedals which Herrick obviously relishes, followed by an equally appealing *Fugue*. Herrick effectively instersperses these works with the 15 simple chorale settings, where his pacing and registration are so apt that these too are very diverting. Try the utterly different pair of settings of *Vater unser in Himmelreich*, BWV 749 and 750, or the engaging *In dulci jubilo*, BWV 751.

Herrick is perhaps at his finest in the always imaginative registration of the 17 variations which make up the *Chorale Partita, Allein Gott*. As Stephen Westrop comments in the excellent notes which accompany this disc: 'Whoever the composer was, the work employs most of the techniques for varying chorales and displays unbounded energy and invention.' The Swiss Metzler organ Herrick plays has a splendid palette, and is superbly recorded. Bach or not, this is a most rewarding recital, very highly recommended.

Simon Preston DG Series

Disc 1: *Trio Sonatas 1–6, BWV 525–30* (Klais organ, St Katharina, Blankenberg)

Disc 2: *Fantasia & Fugue, BWV 537; Preludes & Fugues, BWV 531, 533–5, 535a, 536, 539, 541; Toccata & Fugue (Dorian), BWV 538* (Marcussen organ, Tonbridge School Chapel)

Disc 3: *Fantasia & Fugue, BWV 542; Pedal-exercitium, BWV 598; Preludes & Fugues, BWV 543–6; Toccata & Fugue, BW 540* (Tonbridge School organ, & Sauer organ, St Peter, Waltrop)

Disc 4: *Fantasias, BWV 562, con imitazione, BWV 563; Preludes & Fugues, BWV 547–51; Toccata, Adagio & Fugue, BWV 564* (Klais organ, St John's, Smith Square, London, & organ of St Peter, Waltrop)

Disc 5: *Fantasias, BWV 570 & 572; Pastorale, BWV 590; Preludes, BWV 568, pro organo pleno, BWV 569; Prelude & Fugue, BWV 532; Toccatas & Fugues, BWV 565–6* (Klais organ, Kreuzbergkirche, & organ of St John's, Smith Square)

Disc 6: *Allabreve, BWV 589; Aria, BWV 587; Canzona, BWV 588; Fugues: on a Theme of Legrenzi, BWV 574; BWV 575, 577–8; on a Theme of Corelli, BWV 579; Passacaglia & Fugue, BWV 582; Trios, BWV 586–7* (organs of St John's, Smith Square, & St Peter, Waltrop)

Disc 7: (Solo) *Concertos 1–5, BWV 592–6* (Marcussen organ, Lübeck Cathedral)

Disc 8: *Orgelbüchlein: Chorale Preludes 1–45, BWV 599–644* (organ of Klosterkirke, Sorø)

Disc 9: *6 Schübler Chorales, BWV 645–50; Leipzig Chorale Preludes 1–18, BWV 651–8* (Metzler organ of Trinity College, Cambridge)

Disc 10: *Leipzig Chorale Preludes 19–36, BWV 659–67; Clavier-übung, Part 3: Organ Mass: Prelude (St Anne), BWV 552; Chorale Preludes, BWV 669–74* (organs of Trinity College, Cambridge, & Nidaros Domkirke, Trondheim)

Disc 11: *Clavier-Übung, Part 3: Organ Mass (cont.): Chorale Preludes, BWV 575–689; 4 Duets, BWV 802–5; Fugue (St Anne), BWV 552* (organ of Nidaros Domkirke, Trondheim)

Disc 12: *Kirnberger Chorales, BWV 690–713; Chorale Preludes, BWV 714–18, 720* (Anderson organ of Frue Kirke, Nyborg, & organ of Klosterkirke, Sorø)

Disc 13: *Chorale Preludes, BWV 721–4, 726–39, 741, 753, 764, BWV Anh. II/55; O Lamm Gottes* (without BWV number) (organ of Klosterkirke, Sorø)

Disc 14: *Chorale Partitas, BWV 766–8, 770; Canonic Variations, BWV 769* (Klais organ of Kreuzbergkirche, Bonn, & organ of Klosterkirke, Sorø)

(B) *** DG 469 420-2 (14). Preston (various organs as listed above)

Simon Preston's survey was recorded over more than a decade from 1987 onwards, beginning with the solo *Concertos*, which set the standard for the entire series. These performances are first class in every way, and the recording of the Lübeck organ admirably clear, yet with an attractively resonant ambience. The *Chorale Partitas* that followed are lucid and beautifully registered, as is the single disc which gathers together all 45 chorales of the *Orgelbüchlein*, persuasively presented. Indeed Preston is at his most individual in this repertoire.

Preston revels in the extrovert brilliance of the early Weimar *Preludes and Fugues* (and indeed also the 'Dorian' *Toccata*) with their elaborately virtuoso use of the pedals, but relishes also the more mature, tightly structured works, which he plays with genuine panache. (Here the organ at St John's, Smith Square, shows its paces, especially in the excitingly played *C minor* and *G major* works, BWV 549 and 550.)

The most ambitious structures, like the *Passacaglia and Fugue in C minor* and the *Toccata, Adagio and Fugue in C minor*, have an impressive sense of purpose and architecture, and the justly celebrated *D minor Toccata and Fugue*, BWV 565, played on the magnificent Sauer organ in Waltrop, has all the necessary panache. It is followed by the ebullient *Fantasia and Fugue in G minor*, an equally outstanding example of Preston's bravura.

Another highlight of the series is the (1993) set of *Trio Sonatas*. The sounds of the Blankenburg organ are sheer delight, with glowing colours in slow movements, while the reeds bring a touch more baroque bite to add character to the allegros, where Preston is always infectiously buoyant. The recording is in the demonstration bracket, but then the sound is state of the art throughout. Part 3 of the *Clavier-Übung*, the so-called 'German Organ Mass', is split over two discs.

Some of the repertoire has been issued on separate recital discs (see below), including a few works not included here, such as the *8 Little Preludes and Fugues*, which are wrongly attributed to Bach. But apart from these omissions the whole series now appears in a DG bargain box, with the various genres sensibly grouped together. The performances are consistently alive and distinguished, and the choice of organs ear-ticklingly perceptive. Good notes, although the analysis of the music itself is general rather than detailed.

Simon Preston DG Series – Earlier Recitals

Canzona, BWV 588; Fantasia con imitazione, BWV 563; Fugue all giga, BWV 577; Preludes & Fugues, BWV 548–50; 8 Short Preludes & Fugues, BWV 553–60; Toccata & Fugue in E, BWV 566

*** DG 449 212-2. Preston

This imposing recital includes music from Bach's Buxtehude-influenced early years, two fine *Preludes and Fugues* from his Leipzig period, very impressively played, and some enjoyable music which was probably not written by Bach at all. The *Gigue Fugue* is irresistible just the same, and the lightweight *Short Preludes and Fugues* are very agreeable listening. No. 8, BWV 560, brings an astonishing burst of virtuosity from Preston in a bravura passage on the pedals. The recording is first class.

Canonic Variations on 'Vom Himmel hoch', BWV 569; Fantasia in G, BWV 572; Pastorale in F, BWV 590; Preludes & Fugue in D, BWV 532; in E flat (St Anne), BWV 552; Toccata & Fugue in D min., BWV 565

⊶ (M) *** DG Entrée 471 734-2. Preston (Klais organ of Kreuzbergerkirche, Bonn)

A fine collection on DG's new mid-priced Entrée label certainly serves as an excellent introduction to Bach's organ music. Recorded in 1988, near the beginning of Simon Preston's ongoing complete survey, it shows this fine player at his freshest and most communicative. The famous *Toccata and Fugue* that opens the programme is not the most sensational account available, but has a sense of fantasy in its vivid baroque palette. There is no lack of virtuosity here, but the opening *Très vitement* of the *G major Fantasia* brings even more brilliant articulation, and this is echoed in the sparkling *D major Fugue*. The four-section *Pastorale*, piquantly registered, makes an engaging interlude before the powerful *St Anne Prelude and Fugue* closes the programme massively. The back-up notes are chatty about Bach, but less informative about the music and say nothing about the organ itself; moreover, the most famous piece here is listed as being in F minor – although the correct key is given on the insert backing slip. One attractive feature is the generous cueing, particularly useful in Preston's colourful set of *Canonic Variations* on the Christmas chorale, *Von Himmel hoch*, where each is separately cued.

Karl Richter DG series

Canzona in D min., BWV 588; Chorale Partitas: 'O Gott du frommer Gott' & 'Sei gegrüsset, Jesu gütig', BWV 767; Chorale Preludes, BWV 645, 650 & 654; Fantasia and Fugue in G min., BWV 542; Passacaglia & Fugue in C min., BWV 582; Preludes & Fugues: in D, BWV 532; in A min., BWV 543; in B min., BWV 544; in C min., BWV 546; in E min., BWV

548; in E flat, BWV 552; Toccatas & Fugues: in D min. (Dorian), BWV 538; BWV 565; in F, BWV 540; Trio Sonatas 1, 2 & 5, BWV 525–6 & 529

(N) (M) **(*) DG (ADD) 477 5337 (3). Richter (organ of Jaegersborg Church, Copenhagen, & Silbermann organ in Freiburg Cathedral)

Karl Richter was best known as a Bach scholar and conductor, and as such he recorded over 70 Bach cantatas as well as all the major oratorios. As the son of a Lutheran pastor, however, he began his career as an organist of renown, being very appropriately appointed to play in Leipzig's Thomaskirche. His technique was immaculate, and he brought to the organ console the same magisterial approach that informed his choral interpretations. These performances are typical of the musician; they are scholarly without being pedantic, relaxed enough to let the music breathe, yet perhaps lacking the final touch of imagination. He chose not to record a complete Bach survey for Deutsche Grammophon but instead hand-picked a selection of the most expressively powerful and epic pieces, although he also included three *Trio Sonatas*, which he registered with easy-going charm, and a handful of *Chorale Preludes*, which he played plainly and simply.

Nearly all these works were recorded in 1964 on a Danish neo-Baroque organ, yet one on which he could still create the most powerful sonorities using its pedals. The *Preludes* to the *Fugues* show him at his most magisterial: the *E flat Prelude* and *Fugue* and the *Fantasia in G minor* are especially memorable in this respect, the pedal opening of the latter caught without a ripple of distortion.

The programme here opens with a truly splendid account of the famous *Toccata and Fugue in D minor*, BWV 565, matching weight with vigour, and excellently paced. For the last three works he chose a historical Silbermann organ – the principal instrument (of four) in Freiburg Cathedral, truly authentic if not always quite in tune with itself. So this three-disc recital ends with the *Dorian Toccata and Fugue*, the *Choral Partita*, '*Sei gegrüsset, Jesu gütig*' and a measured and overwhelmingly powerful account of the magnificent *Passacaglia and Fugue in C*. The recording throughout is of DG's highest quality, but in this last work Richter builds huge climaxes which the engineers capture with a breath-taking range of dynamic. Altogether a worthy set for inclusion in DG's 'Originals'.

Ton Koopman Novalis Series

Disc 1: (i) *Chorale Prelude: Liebster Jesu, wir sind hier, BWV 730/1; Fantasias: in C min., BWV 562; in G, BWV 572; Passacaglia & Fugue in C min., BWV 582; Preludes & Fugues, BWV 532, 543; Toccata, Adagio & Fugue in C, BWV 564; Toccata, BWV 538 (Dorian)*

Disc 2: (ii) *Chorale Preludes, BWV 639, 659; Schübler Chorale: Wachet auf, BWV 645. Fantasia (Prelude) & Fugue in G min., BWV 542; Partita: O Gott, du frommer Gott, BWV 767; Prelude & Fugue (St Anne), BWV 552; Toccata & Fugue in D min., BWV 565*

⊶ (B) *** Regis RRC 2042 (2). Koopman, (i) Dreifaltigkeits organ, Ottobeuren, Christian Müller organ, Leeuwarden, or Garrels organ, Grote Kerk, Maassluis; (ii) Christian Müller organ, Waalse Kerk, Amsterdam

This two-CD set brings together two outstanding recitals drawn from a series for Novalis, using various Dutch organs. Ton Koopman's playing is superb throughout, always using organs admirably suited to Bach's music and all splendidly recorded. The first disc has been put together by Regis to include key items from several individual compilations and to demonstrate three different organs. All three organs are superbly caught by the Novalis engineers.

The second disc brings a complete recital (originally issued on 150 005-2). The Waalse Kerk organ is itself a co-star of this programme, producing magnificent, unclouded sonorities in the spacious tapestry of the *St Anne Prelude and Fugue*, and a wide palette of colour that Koopman uses so effectively in the *Partita* and *Chorale Preludes*. The *Partita* has eight diverse variations but is by no means lightweight. The *Fantasia in G minor* is bold and improvisatory, the fugue swiftly moving and buoyantly paced. The *Chorales* make a contrasting centrepiece, with *Nun komm' der Heiden Heiland*, BWV 659, poignantly serene and the famous *Schübler Chorale*, *Wachet auf*, infectiously jaunty. For the most popular of all Bach's organ pieces Ton Koopman then changes to a more flamboyant style, which he establishes immediately by decorating the opening flourishes so that they become almost a series of trills. The fugue proceeds with exhilarating momentum and ends in a blaze of bravura, a very free reading and a most exciting one that would deserve a standing ovation at a live recital. The recording is in the demonstration bracket, the microphones in the right place for a proper illusion of reality.

Other organ music

The Art of Fugue, BWV 1080

*** BIS CD1034. Fagius (organ of Garnisons Kirke, Copenhagen)

The approach of the Swedish organist Hans Fagius is refreshingly straightforward and unaffected. Here he plays a Danish organ, a reconstruction from 1995 of an instrument made in 1724 by Lambert Daniel Kastens, a pupil of Arp Schnitger. He has the advantage of a first-class recording, as one would expect from this label and the producer-engineer Ingo Petry. This version has a lot going for it, quite apart from the sound, and those who like their Bach plain and unadorned will find it well worth considering.

Concertos (for solo organ) 1–5; 6 in E flat (arr. of concerto by an unnamed composer), BWV 592–7; Trio in C min. (after FASCH), BWV 585; Trio in G (after TELEMANN), BWV 586; Aria in F (from COUPERIN: Les Nations), BWV 587)

(BB) *** Naxos 8.550936. Rübsam (Flenthrop organ of St Mark's Cathedral, Seattle, Washington)

Wolfgang Rübsam's recital for Naxos is strikingly successful. Moreover it is very comprehensive in including the rarely played 'anonymous' concerto transcription, BWV 597. This is a most engaging piece, particularly the jaunty closing section, and it is nicely registered, as are the other individual movements here, by Couperin, Fasch and Telemann. Rübsam's tempi for allegros remain buoyant throughout and the playing is always seemingly spontaneous. The recording is in the demonstration class.

18 Leipzig Chorale Preludes, BWV 651–68; Fantasia in G, BWV 572; Prelude & Fugue in B min., BWV 544; Toccata & Fugue in F, BWV 540; Trio Sonata 4 in E min., BWV 528

(N) (M) *** Priory PRCD 800AB (2). Weir (Gerald Woehl Bach organ of Thomaskirche, Leipzig)

This fine set is a double celebration in offering a first recording of the *18 Chorale Preludes*, which Bach composed in the early 1740s, using the magnificent new organ installed in the

Thomaskirche for the Millennium. Bach's own organ no longer exists – and in any case Bach was not fond of it: he preferred the organ in the Paulinerkirche, and it is appropriate that the case of the new instrument is based on that instrument, and the facade shows Bach's insignia, including his initials. The new Gerald Woehl organ has 61 stops and a magnificent range of colour which Gillian Weir exploits to the full (many of her registrations are captivating; others show the organ's dramatic power), and she is very gentle in the final sublime chorale, *Vol deinem Thron tret ich hiermet*, the first part of which Bach supposedly dictated from his deathbed. She then goes on to play a selection of miscellaneous works to display the organ's full range, from the brilliant filigree of the Arnstadt *Fantasia in G minor* and the charm of the *Trio Sonata* to the full power of BWV 540 and 544. The recording is first class, completely worthy of the occasion, and the documentation excellent.

Orgelbüchlein: Chorale Preludes, 1–46, BWV 599–644

**(*) Häns. CD 92.094. Zerer (organ of Martinkerk, Groningen)

Orgelbüchlein: 19 Chorale Preludes for Advent, Christmas, New Year and the Purification, BWV 599–617; Fantasia in C, BWV 570; Fugue on a Theme of Corelli, BWV 579; Preludes & Fugues, BWV 531 & 534; Prelude in G, BWV 568

(BB) *** Naxos 8.553031. Rübsam (Flenthrop organ of Duke Chapel, Duke University, Durham, USA)

Orgelbüchlein: 27 Chorale Preludes for Passiontide; Easter; Pentecost; and expressing Faith, BWV 618–44; Fantasia in C, BWV 570; Fugue in B min., BWV 579; Preludes & Fugues, BWV 531 & 534; Prelude in G, BWV 568

(BB) *** Naxos 8.553032. Rübsam (Flenthrop organ of Duke Chapel, Duke University, Durham, USA)

Rübsam finds great variety for his presentation of each chorale. The Christmas section is preceded by the flamboyant and joyous *Prelude and Fugue in C*, with its resounding pedals, and the first recital is rounded off with a characteristically spacious account of the imposing *F minor Prelude and Fugue*, BWV 534. The *Easter Chorales* are more robust, while the four *Pentecost Chorales* are touchingly contemplative. There is infinite variety of mood and colour in the last group, opening with a piece symbolizing the ten commandments and showing Bach reflecting on various aspects of the Christian faith. The introduction of the closing *Prelude and Fugue in D minor*, BWV 539, is grave and dignified, but the fugue itself is optimistic and vital, ending the concert satisfyingly. The Duke University Chapel organ is a magnificent instrument, and the recording is superb throughout.

Wolfgang Zerer's set of the *Orgelbüchlein* is of high quality, both in its colouristic range and in its contrasts of mood and tempi. He can be vigorous and flamboyant when required (as in *In dir ist Freude*, BWV 615) but for the most part his presentation is intimate – and effectively so, though he opens up the registration to use the full organ when needed. An enjoyable set, but we are inclined to prefer Rübsam's Naxos set.

6 Trio Sonatas, BWV 525–30 (see also arrangements under Chamber Music, above)

(M) **(*) DG (IMS) 447 277-2. Koopman (organ of Waalse Kerk, Amsterdam)

Ton Koopman's earlier DG set comes from 1982 and is very well recorded on a highly suitable Dutch organ. The opening of the very first sonata promises well, with a buoyant rhythmic lift; the central *Adagio* is nicely coloured and the finale spirited. The *Adagio e dolce* of No. 3 *in D minor* again shows an apt choice of colouring, but the finale (marked *Vivace*) tends to jog along, and the similarly indicated opening movement of No. 6 is also relaxed. Other versions of these works are that bit more spirited but not more glowing, and this is certainly enjoyable.

Organ recitals

Chorales: Nun komm, der Heiden Heiland, BWV 659; Vater unser im Himmereich, BWV 682; Schübler chorale: Wachet auf, BWV 645; Fugue in G min., BWV 578; Passacaglia in C min., BWV 582; Prelude & Fugue in E flat, BWV 552; Toccata & Fugue in D min., BWV 565; Trio Sonata in G, BWV 530
*** Teldec **Audio DVD** 8573 82041-9. Koopman (Christian Müller organ, Grote Kerk, Leeuwarden)

Ton Koopman's ten-volume Teldec coverage has been withdrawn and this seems to be the first volume of an entirely new Das Alte Werke DVD series with the option of surround sound. Even in two-channel stereo the recording has a spectacular spatial dimension and the organ at Leeuwarden is a magnificent instrument. Opening with Bach's most celebrated *Toccata and Fugue*, Koopman adds his usual decorative touches in the introductory flourish, and the following programme could hardly be better planned, with the lively *Fugue in G minor* followed by a rhythmically perky account of the best-known *Schübler Chorale*. The gently solemn *Nun komm, der Heiden Heiland*, darkly coloured, makes a sombre contrast. Then after the large-scale *E flat Prelude and Fugue*, the *Trio Sonata* provides a lighter (if not lightweight) contrast before the massive closing *Passacaglia*. The video content includes a titles menu, the organ specification and pictures of the organ itself.

Allabreve, BWV 589; Chorale Prelude: Ach Gott und Herr, BWV 714; Preludes & Fugues, BWV 532, 553–60; Toccata & Fugue in D min., BWV 565
*** Mer. (ADD) ECD 84081. Sanger (organ of St Catharine's College, Cambridge)

The organ at St Catharine's College, Cambridge, was completely rebuilt in 1978–9. The result is a great success, and its reedy clarity and brightness of timbre are especially suitable for Bach. David Sanger's playing throughout is thoughtful and well structured; registration shows an excellent sense of colour without being flamboyant.

(i) Disc 1: *Chorale Preludes, BWV 622, 680, 721 & 727; Fugues: in B min. on a theme of Corelli, BWV 579; in G (Jig), BWV 577; Passacaglia & Fugue in C min., BWV 582; Pastorale in F, BWV 590; Prelude & Fugue in G, BWV 541; Toccata & Fugue in D min., BWV 565*
(ii) Disc 2: *Aria in F (from* CORELLI: *Trio Sonata), BWV 587; Chorale Preludes, BWV 657, 719, 731, 734–5; Toccata, Adagio & Fugue in C, BWV 64; Trio Sonata 5 in C, BWV 529*
(BB) *** CfP 5 85630-2 (2). Peter Hurford, organs of (i) Martinikerk, Gröningen, Holland; (ii) Ludgerikirche, Norden, Germany

Having left his complete Decca Bach series long behind him, in 1993–9 Peter Hurford set off on this travels again to record familiar Bach repertoire for EMI. He chose two fine Schnitger organs, one in Gröningen, the other in Norden, both recently restored to their former splendour. If the famous *D major Fugue*, BWV 565, is a fraction less flamboyant here than

before, the *Fugue à la Gigue* and *G major Prelude and Fugue* have plenty of character, and the *Toccata, Adagio and Fugue* sounds more sprightly than usual. Characteristically, Hurford brings out a wide range of colour from both instruments, especially in the *Pastorale*, Bach's attractive Vivaldi *Concerto* transcription, and the engaging *Trio Sonata* on the second disc. The chosen *Chorale Preludes* are attractively diverse, sometimes relaxed and thoughtful, at others full of movement: *Nun freut euch*, BWV 734, flows most winningly around the cantus firmus. In the great *C minor Passacaglia and Fugue* that closes the first recital, Hurford demonstrates how magnificently he can hold and build tension when setting off at a measured pace. What a masterpiece this is in his hands! The EMI engineers do him proud with both organs, and it is surprising that this series did not continue.

(i) *Pastorale in F, BWV 590; Passacaglia, BWV 582; 6 Schübler Chorales, BWV 645–50;* (ii) *Toccata, Adagio & Fugue, BWV 564;* (i) *Toccatas & Fugues: BWV 538;* (ii) *BWV 565*
(B) *** DG ADD/DDD 463 016-2. (i) Koopman; (ii) Preston (various organs)

This collection is divided between Simon Preston, on top form in his two contributions, and Ton Koopman, who has the lion's share and uses two different organs. The *Schübler Chorales* are recorded on the organ of the Waalse Kerk, Amsterdam, whose reeds are livelier, underscored by the emphatically rhythmic style of the playing. Excellent contrast is provided by the *Pastorale*, where the registration features the organ's flute stops piquantly. The other performances are well structured and alive, if sometimes rather considered in feeling. Excellent recording throughout.

VOCAL MUSIC

Complete Cantatas: Hänssler Series with Gächinger Kantorei, Bach-Collegium Stuttgart, Helmuth Rilling

Cantatas (i–ii) 1: Wie schön leuchtet uns der Morgerstern; (iii) *2: Ach Gott, vom Himmel;* (ii; iv) *3: Ach Gott, wie manches Herzeleid*
**(*) Häns. (ADD) CD 92.001; with (i) Nielsen, Kraus; (ii) Huttenlocher; (iii) Watts, Baldin, Heldwein; (iv) Augér, Schreckenbach, Harder

Cantatas 4: Christ lag in Todesbanden; 5: Wo soll ich fliehen hin; 6: Bleib bei uns, wenn es will Abend werden
**(*) Häns. (ADD) CD 92.002; with Wiens, Augér, Watkinson, Schreier, Baldin, Kraus, Schöne, Heldwein

Cantatas 7: Christ unser Herr zum Jordan kam; 8: Liebster Gott, wann werd ich sterben; 9: Es ist das Heil uns kommen her
**(*) Häns. (ADD) CD 92.003; with Augér, Sonntag, Watts, Schreckenbach, Kraus, Schöne, Huttenlocher

Cantatas 10: Meine Seel' erhebt den Herren; 12: Weinen, Klagen, Sorgen, Zagen; 13: Meine Seufzer, meine Tränen
**(*) Häns. (ADD) CD 92.004; with Augér, Neubauer, Watts, Watkinson, Baldin, Kraus, Schöne, Heldwein

Cantatas 14: Wär Gott nicht mit uns diese Zeit; 16: Herr Gott, dich loben wir; 17: Wer Dank opfert, der preiset mich; 18: Gleichwie der Regen und Schnee vom Himmel fällt
**(*) Häns. (ADD) CD 92.005; with Laki, Augér, Csapò, Schreckenbach, Schnaut, Baldin, Schreier, Kraus, Huttenlocher, Heldwein, Schöne, Württemberg CO

Cantatas 19: Es erhub sich ein Streit; 20: O Ewigkeit, du Donnerwort
**(*) Häns. (ADD) CD 92.006; with Rondelli, Kessler, Gohl, Kraus, Altmeyer, Nimsgern, Schöne, Frankfurter Kantorei

Cantatas 21: Ich hatte viel Bekümmernis; 20: Jesus nahm zu sich die Zwölfe
**(*) Häns. (ADD) CD 92.007; with Augér, Amini, Watts, Hagerman, Kraus, Robinson, Schöne, Anderson, Indiana University Chamber Singers

Cantatas 23: Du wahrer Gott und Davids Sohn; 24: Ein ungefärbt Gemüte; 25: Es ich nichts Gesundes an meinem Leibe; 26: Ach wie flüchtig, ach wie nightig
*** Häns. (ADD) CD 92.008; with Augér, Watts, Soffel, Baldin, Kraus, Tüller, Heldwein

Cantatas 27: Wer weiss, wie nahe mir mein Ende; 28: Gottlob! Nun geht das Jahr zu Ende; 29: Wir danken dir, Gott
*** Häns. (ADD) CD 92.009; with Wiens, Augér, Watts, Sonntag, Schreckenbach, Graff, Harder, Baldin, Kraus, Tüller, Heldwein, Huttenlocher

Cantatas 30: Freue dich, erlöste Schar; 31: Der Himmel lacht! Die Erde jubilieret
*** Häns. (ADD) CD 92.0010; with Cuccaro, Augér, Georg, Baldin, Kraus, Huttenlocher, Schöne

Cantatas 32: Liebster Jesu, mein Verlangen; 33: Allein zu dir, Herr Jesu Christ; 34: O ewiges Feuer, O Ursprung der Liebe
*** Häns. (ADD) CD 92.0011; with Augér, Watts, Lang, Kraus, Heldwein, Huttenlocher, Schöne

Cantatas 35: Geist und Seele wird verwirret; 36: Schwingt freudig euch empor; 37: Wer da gläubet und getauft wird
*** Häns. (ADD) CD 92.0012; with Augér, Hamari, Schreckenbach, Watkinson, Kraus, Heldwein, Huttenlocher

Cantatas 38: Aus tiefer Not schrei ich zu dir; 39: Brich dem Hungrigen dein Brot; 40: Darzu ist erschienen der Sohn Gottes
*** Häns. (ADD) CD 92.0013; with Augér, Watts, Schreckenbach, Gohl, Harder, Kraus, Huttenlocher, Nimsgern

Cantatas 41: Jesu, nun sei gepreiset; 42: Am Abend aber desselbigen Sabbats
*** Häns. (ADD) CD 92.0014; with Donath, Augér, Hoeffgen, Hamari, Kraus, Huttenlocher, Nimsgern

Cantatas 43: Gott fähret auf mit Jauchzen; 44: Sie werden euch in den Bann tun; 45: Es ist dir gesagt, Mensch, was gut ist
*** Häns. (ADD) CD 92.0015; with Augér, Hamari, Watts, Harder, Baldin, Huttenlocher, Schöne

Cantatas 46: Schauet doch und sehet, ob irgendein Schmerz sei; 47: Wer sich selbst erhöhet, der soll erniedrigt wernen; 48: Ich elender Mensch, wer wird mich erlösen
*** Häns. (ADD) CD 92.0016; with Augér, Watts, Hoeffgen, Kraus, Baldin, Huttenlocher, Schöne

Cantatas 49: Ich geh und suche mit Verlangen; 50: Nun ist das Heil und die Kraft; 51: Jauchzett Gott in allen Landen; 52: Falsche Welt, dir trau ich nicht
*** Häns. (ADD) CD 92.0017; with Augér, Huttenlocher

Cantatas 54: Widerstehe doch der Sünde; 55: Ich armer Mensch, ich Sündenknecht; 56: Ich will den Kreuzstab gerne tragen; 57: Selig ist der Mann
*** Häns. (ADD) CD 92.0018; with Augér, Hamari, Kraus, Fischer-Dieskau, Heldwein

Cantatas 58: Ach Gott, wie manches Herzleid; 59: Wer mich liebet, der wird mein Wort halten; 60: O Ewigkeit, du Donnerwort; 61: Nun komm, der Heiden Heiland
*** Häns. (ADD) CD 92.0019; with Reichelt, Augér, Donath, Watts, Kraus, Schöne, Tüller

Cantatas 62: Nun komm, der Heiden Heiland; 63: Christen, ätzet diesen Tag; 64: Sehet, welch eine Liebes hat uns der Vater erzeiget
**(*) Hans. (ADD) CD 92.020 with Nielsen, Augér, Watts, Hamari, Laurich, Murray, Baldin, Kraus, Huttenlocher, Heldwein, Schöne

Cantatas 65: Sie werden aus Saba alle kommen; 66: Erfreut euch, ihr Herzen; 67: Halt im Gedächtnis Jesum Christ
**(*) Häns. (ADD) CD 92.021 with Schreckenbach, Mitsui, Murray, Kraus, Huttenlocher, Heldwein

Cantatas 68: Also hat Gott die Welt geliebt; 69: Lobe den Herrn, meine Seele; 70: Wachet! betet! betet! wachet!
**(*) Häns. (ADD) CD 92.022 with Augér, Donath, Hamari, Gohl, Kraus, Harder, Huttenlocher, Schöne, Nimsgern

Cantatas 71: Gott ist mein König; 72: Alles nur nach Gottes Willen; 73: Herr, wie du willst, so schicks mit mir; 74: Wer mich liebet, der wird mein Wort halten
**(*) Häns. (ADD) CD 92.023 with Grae, Augér, Schreiber, Donath, Gardow, Schwarz, Schreckenbach, Laurich, Senger, Kraus, Harder, Tuller, Huttenlocher, Schöne

Cantatas 75: Die Elenden sollen essen; 76: Die Himmel erzählen die Ehre Gottes
**(*) Häns. (ADD) CD 92.024; with Reichelt, Augér, Gohl, Hamari, Watts, Kraus, Baldin, Kunz, Nimsgern

Cantatas 77: Du sollst Gott, deinen Herren, lieben; 78: Jesu, der du meine Seele; 79: Gott der Herr ist Sonn, und Schild
**(*) Häns. CD (ADD) 92.025; with Donath, Augér, Hamari, Watkinson, Kraus, Baldin, Schöne, Huttenlocher

Cantatas 80: Ein feste Burg ist unser Gott; 81: Jesus schläft, was soll ich hoffen?; 82: Ich habe genug
**(*) Häns. (ADD) CD 92.026; with Augér, Schreckenbach, Hamari, Harder, Kraus, Huttenlocher, Nimsgern, Württemberg CO

Cantatas 83: Erfreute Zeit im neuen Bunde; 84: Ich bin vergnügt mit meinem Glücke; 85: Ich bin ein Guter Hirt; 86: Wahrlich, wahrlich, ich sage euch
**(*) Häns. (ADD) CD 92.027; with Augér, Watts, Schreckenbach, Kraus, Heldwein, Württemberg CO

Cantatas 87: Bisher habt ich nichts gebeten in meinem Namen; 88: Siehe, ich will viel Fischer aussenden; 89: Was soll ich aus dir machen, Ephraim; 90: Es reisset euch ein schrecklich Ende
**(*) Häns. (ADD) CD 92.028; with Reichelt, Augér, Hamari, Gohl, Watts, Baldin, Kraus, Heldwein, Schöne, Huttenlocher, Nimsgern

Cantatas 91: Gelobet seist du, Jesu Christ; 92: Ich habe in Gottes Herz und Sinn; 93: Wer nur den lieben Gott lässt walten
**(*) Häns. (ADD) CD 92.029; with Donath, Augér, Watts, Schreckenbach, Murray, Hamari, Baldin, Kraus, Huttenlocher, Heldwein, Schöne, Nimsgern, Württemberg CO

Cantatas 94: Was frag, ich nach der Welt; 95: Christus, der ist mein Leben; 96: Herr Christ, der ein'ge Gottessohn
**(*) Häns. (ADD) CD 92.030; with Donath, Augér, Paaske, Höffgen, Baldin, Kraus, Kunz, Heldwein, Schöne, Nimsgern

Cantatas 97: In allen meinen Taten; 98: Was Gott tut, das ist wohlgetan; 99: Was Gott tut, das ist wohlgetan
**(*) Häns. (ADD) CD 92.031; with Donath, Augér, Gardow, Hamari, Watts, Kraus, Harder, Heldwein, Huttenlocher, Bröcheler

Cantatas 100: Was Gott tut, das ist wohlgetan; 101: Nimm von uns, Herr, du treuer Gott; 102: Herr, deine Augen sehen nach, dem Glauben
**(*) Häns. (ADD) CD 92.032; with Augér, Hamari, Watts, Randova, Kraus, Baldin, Equiluz, Huttenlocher, Bröcheler, Schöne

Cantatas 103: Ihr werdet weinen und heulen; 104: Du Hirte Israel, höre; 105: Herr, gehe nicht ins Gericht mit deinem Knecht
**(*) Häns. (ADD) CD 92.033; with Augér, Soffel, Watts, Schreier, Kraus, Heldwein, Schöne

Cantatas 106: Gottes Zeit ist die allerbeste Zeit; 107: Was willst du dich betrüben; 108: Es ist euch gut, dass ich hingehe
**(*) Häns. (ADD) CD 92.034; with Csapo, Augér, Schwarz, Watkinson, Kraus, Baldin, Schreier, Schöne, Bröcheler, Huttenlocher

Cantatas 109: Ich glaube, lieber Herr; 110: Unser Mund sei voll Lachens; 111: Was mein Gott will, das g'scheh allzeit
**(*) Häns. (ADD) CD 92.035; with Graf, Augér, Schreckenbach, Gardow, Watts, Equiluz, Baldin, Harder, Schöne, Huttenlocher

Cantatas 112: Das Herr ist mein getreuer Hirtl; 113: Herr Jesu Christ, du höchstes Gut; 114: Ach, lieben Christen, seid Getrost
**(*) Häns. (ADD) CD 92.036; with Nielsen, Augér, Schnaut, Schreckenbach, Hamari, Baldin, Kraus, Equiluz, Heldwein, Tüller, Schöne

Cantatas 115: Mache dich, mein Geist, bereit; 116: Du Friedefürst, Herr Jesu Christ; 117: Dei Lob' und Ehr dem höchsten Gut
**(*) Häns. (ADD) CD 92.037; with Augér, Watts, Georg, Harder, Kraus, Schöne, Huttelocher, Schmidt

Cantatas 119: Preise Jerusalem, den Herrn; 120, Gott, man lobet dich in der Stille; 121: Christum wir sollen loben schon
**(*) Häns. (ADD) CD 92.038; with Augér, Donath, Murray, Laurich, Soffel, Kraus, Schöne

Cantatas 122: Das neugeborne Kindelein; 123: Liebster Immanuel, Herzog der Frommen; 124: Meinen Jesum lass ich nicht; 125: Mit Fried und Freud ich fahr dahin
**(*) Häns. (ADD) CD 92.039; with Augér, Donath, Watts, Höffgen, Kraus, Balden, Equiluz, Tüller, Huttenlocher, Schöne

Cantatas 126: Erhalt uns, Herr, bei deinem Wort; 127: Herr Jesu Christ, wahr' Mensch und Gott; 128: Auf Christi Himmelfahrt allein; 129: Gelobet sei der Herr, mein Gott
**(*) Häns. (ADD) CD 92.040; with Augér, Watts, Schreckenbach, Kraus, Harder, Balden, Huttenlocher, Schöne

Cantatas 130: Herr Gott, dich loben alle wir; 131: Aus der Tiefen rufe ich, Herr, zu dir; 132: Bereitet die Wege, bereitet die Bahn
**(*) Häns. (ADD) CD 92.041; with Graf, Augér, Schnaut, Watts, Kraus, Equiluz, Schöne

Cantatas 133: Ich freue mich in dir; 134: Ein Herz, das seinen Jesum lebend weiss; 135: Ach Herr, mich armen Sünder
**(*) Häns. (ADD) CD 92.042; with Augér, Soffel, Watts, Baldin, Kraus, Huttenlocher

Cantatas 136: Erforsche mich, Gott, und erfahre mein Herz; 137: Lobe den Herren, den mächtigen König der Ehren; 138: Warum betrübst du dich, mein Herz; 139: Wohl dem, der sich auf seinen Gott
**(*) Häns. (ADD) CD 92.043; with Augér, Nielsen, Watts, Schreckenbach, Bollen, Equiluz, Kraus, Baldin, Tüller, Huttenlocher

Cantatas 140: Wachet auf, ruft uns die Stimme; 143: Lobe den Herrn, meine Seele; 144: Nimm, was dein ist, und gehe him; 145: Ich lebe, mein Herze, zu deinem Ergötzen
**(*) Häns. (ADD) CD 92.044; with Augér, Cszapò, Cuccaro, Watts, Baldin, Kraus, Huttenlocher, Schöne, Schmidt, Frankfurter Kantorei, Württemberg CO

Cantatas 146: Wir müssen durch viel Trübsal; Herz und Mund und Tat und Leben
**(*) Häns. (ADD) CD 92.045; with Augér, Donath, Watts, Hoeffgen, Equiluz, Schöne, Frankfurter Kantorei

Cantatas 148: Bringet dem Herrn Ehre seines Namens; 149: Man singet mit Freuden vom Sieg; 150: Nach dir, Herr, verlanget mich; 151: Süsser Trost, mein Jesus kömmt
**(*) Häns. (ADD) CD 92.046; with Augér, Schreiber, Gamo-Yamamoto, Watts, Georg, Jetter, Laurich, Equiluz, Baldin, Maus, Kraus, Huttenlocher, Kunz, Frankfurter Kantorei

Cantatas 152: Tritt auf die Glaubensbahn; 153: Schau, lieber Gott, wie meine Feind; 154: Mein Liebster Jesus ist verloren; 155: Mein Gott, wie lang, ach lange
**(*) Häns. (ADD) CD 92.047; with Augér, Reichelt, Murray, Lerer, Kraus, Baldin, Melzer, Schöne, Heldwein, Kunz

Cantatas 156: Ich stehe mit einem Fuss im Grabe; 157: Ich lasse dich nicht, du segnest mich denn; 158: Der Friede sei mit dir; 159: Sehet, wir gehn hinauf gen Jerusalem
**(*) Häns. (ADD) CD 92.048; with Laurich, Hamari, Equiluz, Kraus, Baldin, Schöne, Huttenlocher, Figuralchor der Gedächtniskirche

Cantatas 161: Komm, du susse Todesstunde; 162: Ach! ich sehe, itzt, da ich zur Hochzeit gehe; 163: Nur jedem das Seine; 164: Ihr, die ihr euch von Christo nennet
**(*) Häns. (ADD) CD 92.049; with Augér, Wiens, Laurich, Rogers, Watts, Hamari, Kraus, Equiluz, Harder, Schöne, Tüller, Heldwein, Frankfurter Kantorei

Cantatas 165: O heiliges Geist und Wasserbad; 166: Wo gehest du hin; 167: Ihr Menschen, rühmet Gottes Lieb; 168: Tue Rechnung! Donnerwort
**(*) Häns. (ADD) CD 92.050; with Augér, Graf, Burns, Rogers, Watts, Gardow, Gohl, Equiluz, Baldin, Krauss, Altmeyer, Schöne, Tüller, Nimsgern, Frankfurter Kantorei

Cantatas 169: Gott soll allein mein Herze haben; 170: Vergnügte Rühe! beliebt Seelenlust; 171 Gott, wie dein Name, so ist auch dein Ruhm

**(*) Häns. (ADD) CD 92.051; with Augér, Watkinson, Baldin, Heldwein, Württemberg CO

Cantatas 172: Eschallet, ihr Lieder; 173: Erhöltes Fleisch und Blut; 174: Ich liebe den Höchsten von ganzem Gemüte; 175: Er rufet seine Schlafen mit Namen

**(*) Häns. (ADD) CD 92.052; with Cszapò, Beckman, Soffel, Watts, Hamari, Watkinson, Baldin, Kraus, Schreier, Schöne, Tüller, Huttenlocher, Frankfurter Kantorei, Württemberg CO

Cantatas 176: Es ist ein trotzig und verzagt Ding; 177: Ich ruf zu dir, Herr Jesu Christ; 178: Wo Gott der Herr nicht bei uns hält

**(*) Häns. (ADD) CD 92.053; with Nielsen, Augér, Watkinson, Hamari, Schreckenbach, Schreier, Equiluz, Baldin, Heldwein, Schöne

Cantatas 179: Siehe zu dass deine Gottesfurcht nicht Heuchelei sei; 180: Schmücke dich, O liebe Seele; 181: Leichtgesinnte Flattergeister

**(*) Häns. (ADD) CD 92.054; with Augér, Watkinson, Schnaut, Schreckenbach, Equiluz, Kraus, Schöne, Heldwein, Tüller

Cantatas 182: Himmelskönig, sei willkommen; 183: Sie werden euch in den Bann tun; 184: Erwünschtes Freudenlicht

**(*) Häns. (ADD) CD 92.055; with Augér, Soffel, Hamari, Schnaut, Baldin, Schreier, Kraus, Huttenlocher, Heldwein, Tüller

Cantatas 185: Barmherziges Herze der ewigen Liebe; 186: Ärgre dich, O Seele, nicht; 187: Es wartet alles aud dich

**(*) Häns. (ADD) CD 92.056; with Augér, Friesenhausen, Laurich, Watts, Baldin, Equiluz, Huttenlocher, Schöne, Frankfurter Kantorei

Cantatas 188: Ich habe meine Zuversicht; 190: Singet dem Herrn ein neues Lied; 191: Gloria in excelsis Deo; 192: Nun danket alle Gott

**(*) Häns. (ADD) CD 92.057; with Augér, Gamo-Yamamoto, Donath, Hamari, Watts, Baldin, Equiluz, Kraus, Heldwein, Tüller, Württemberg CO

Cantatas 193: Ihr Tore zu Zion; 194: Höchsterwünschtes Freudenfest

**(*) Häns. (ADD) CD 92.058; with Augér, Hamari, Kraus, Watts, Heldwein

Cantatas 195: Dem Gerechten muss das Licht; 196: Der Herr denket an uns; 197: Gott ist unsre Zuversicht

**(*) Häns. (ADD) CD 92.059; with Inhoue-Heller, Soffel, Cuccaro, Graf, Georg, Pfaff, Baldin, Schmidt, Tüller, Huttenlocher, Württemberg CO

Cantatas 198: Lass, Fürstin! lass noch einen Strahl; 199: Mein Herz schwimmt im Blut; 200: Bekennen will ich seinen Namen

**(*) Häns. (ADD) CD 92.060; with Augér, Schreckenbach, Georg, Baldin, Huttenlocher, Württemberg CO

Cantata 201: Geschwinde, ihr wirbelnden Winde (The Contest between Phoebus and Pan)

**(*) Häns. (ADD) CD 98.162; with Rubens, Danz, Odinius, Taylor, Goerne, Henschel

Cantatas 202: Weichet nur, betrübte Schatten; 203: Amore traditore; 204: Ich bin in mir vergnügt

**(*) Häns. (ADD) CD 92.062; with Rubens, Henschel, Behringer

Secular Cantatas

Cantata 205: Der zufriedengestellte Aeolus; Quodlibet, BWV 524

**(*) Häns. CD 92.063; with Rubens, Naff, Danz, Genz, Ullmann, Schmidt

Cantatas 206: Schleicht, spielende Wellen und murmelt Gelinde; 207: Vereinigte Zwietracht der wechselnden Saitern; 207a: Auf, schmetternde Töne der muntern Trompeten

**(*) Häns. CD 92.064; with Schäfer, Petersen, Danz, Olsen, Ullmann, Volle, Häger

Cantatas 207a: Auf, schmetternde Töne der muntern Trompeten; 212 (Peasant Cantata)

**(*) Häns. (ADD) CD 98.163; with Schäfer, Danz, Olsen, Quasthoff, Volle

Cantatas 208: Was mir behagt, ist nur die muntre Jagd (Hunt Cantata); 209: Non sà che sia dolore

**(*) Häns. CD 92.065; with Rubens, Schäfer, Taylor, Quasthoff

Cantatas 208: Was mir behagt, ist nur die muntre Jagd (Hunt); 211: Schweigt stille, plaudert nicht (Coffee)

**(*) Häns. (ADD) CD 98.161; with Rubens, Schäfer, Kirchner, Taylor, Goerne, Quasthoff

Cantatas 210: O holder Tag, erwünschte Zeit (Wedding Cantata); 211: Schweigt stille, plaudert nicht (Coffee Cantata)

**(*) Häns. CD 92.066 with Rubens, Schäfer, Taylor, Quasthoff

Cantatas 212: Mer hahn en neue Oberkeet (Peasant Cantata); 213: Herkules auf dem Schweidewege (Hercules at the Crossroads)

**(*) Häns. CD 92.067; with Schäfer, Rubens, Danz, Ullmann, Quasthoff, Schmidt

Cantatas 214: Tönet, ihr Pauken! Erschallet, Trompeten; 215: Preise dein Glücke, gesegnetes Sachsen

**(*) Häns. CD 92.068; with Rubens, Danz, Ullmann, Schäfer, Schmidt, Henschel

Helmut Rilling has spent a lifetime performing, recording and re-recording Bach. The series has never enjoyed the same exposure as the Leonhardt–Harnoncourt cycle, which was performed on period instruments and included the scores in its LP format, in most cases taken from the *Neue Bach Gesamtausgabe*. Rilling recorded the secular cantatas in the mid- to late 1960s with some fine singers, but Hänssler have replaced these with new accounts recorded in the late 1990s.

For those who generally favour modern as opposed to period instruments and women singers as opposed to boys, this set will be a godsend. There is no question as to the excellence and distinction of many of Rilling's soloists, who feature a number of famous Bach specialists of the last quarter of a century. There are over 20 different sopranos, among then Christine Schäfer, Edith Mathis and the late lamented and much loved Arleen Augér performing at her peak in the period 1979–84. The two dozen mezzos and contraltos include Marga Höffgen, Helen Watts and Doris Soffel. Among the men are Peter Schreier, Dietrich Fischer-Dieskau, Kurt Equiluz, Matthias Goerne, Andreas Schmidt and Jakob Stämpfli, as well as Siegmund Nimsgern and Philippe Huttenlocher.

The choral singing is variable, but it rarely falls below an acceptable standard. Rilling has proved a pragmatist in matters of historical performance practice; he adopts brisk tempos and light accents at times, but allows himself considerable expressive and agogic freedom. It is not easy to make a summary recommendation among the modern-instrument versions, though Rilling's performances are often (but not always) freer than the periodically stiff Karl Richter series that rightly enjoyed such renommé in the 1960s.

Rilling's treatment of recitatives has attracted some criticism, and there are occasions when he too is a little rigid (albeit less so than Richter can be). If one can generalize in these matters, Richter often has the advantage of cleaner recording (much of his DG Archiv series used the Herkulessaal in Munich), and the Stuttgart choral sound is at times rather opaque. However, those who prefer the warmer sound of modern instruments will welcome this Hänssler set, and generally speaking the instrumentalists are of a high quality. Readers who want a complete set should note that the Rilling is comprehensive. The quality of both performances and recordings is variable, but it must be said that Rilling's Hänssler survey is sometimes first rate. All in all, we have derived much satisfaction in either making or renewing our acquaintance with his cycle, which will suit many collectors in search of a scholarly yet intelligently aware approach with a traditional sound. Documentation and transfers are eminently satisfactory but, alas, the series has now reverted to premium price.

Christmas Cantatas 1; 36; 61; 63; 65; 91; 110; 121; 132; 133; 153; 190
(B) *** Häns. CD 94.026 (4). Soloists including Nielsen, Donath, Augér, Watts, Hamari, Kraus, Schreier, Equiluz, Baldin, Huttenlocher, Schöne, Stuttgart Gächinger Kantorei (with Bach Coll. Frankfurter Kantorei, Württemberg CO), Rilling

This four-CD set collects 12 Christmas cantatas from the complete survey of the cantatas by Helmuth Rilling reissued during the Bach celebrations of 2000. The present compilation includes some very fine performances, though collectors who prefer period performances should look elsewhere. This will make a good alternative to the *Christmas Oratorio* as a seasonal present – except, of course, for those who have invested in the complete set that appeared in the Bach year. There are no notes or texts, but these can be downloaded free of charge on the Hänssler website (www.haenssler-classic.de).

Cantatas 21; 38; 51; 56; 76; 79; 80; 82; 93; 106; 137; 140; 149
(B) *** Häns. CD 94.028 (4). Augér, Schreckenbach, Kraus, Heldwein, Harder, Huttenlocher, Hamari, Fischer-Dieskau, Watts, Schöne, Nimsgern, Indiana University Ch. Singers, Stuttgart Bach Coll.; Stüttgart Gächinger Kantorei; Rilling

This second four-CD set collects 13 cantatas on the theme 'Praise and thanks, death and eternity' from the complete Rilling survey. The present recordings were made at various dates between 1975 and 1983. Arleen Augér sings in all but three of the cantatas, and Fischer-Dieskau is the soloist in *Ich will den Kreutzstab gerne tragen* and *Ich habe genug*. Obviously this compilation, and its companion above, will not be of interest to those who have invested in the complete box, which was quite competitively priced in 2000, but those wanting a handful of cantatas may find the selection appealing. It includes such masterpieces as *Gottes Zeit ist die allerbest Zeit* (106) and *Jauchzet Gott* (51), which is the only one to have been recorded digitally. As with the dozen Christmas

cantatas, there are no notes or texts, but they can be downloaded free of charge on the Hänssler website, details of which are given above.

Complete Cantatas: Harnoncourt/Leonhardt Teldec Series

Cantatas 1–14; 16–52; 54–69; 69a; 70–117; 119–40; 143–59; 161–88; 192; 194–9 (complete)
(B) **(*) Teldec (ADD/DDD) 4509 91765-2 (60). Treble soloists from V. Boys' & Regensburg Choirs, Esswood, Equiluz, Van Altena, Van Egmond, Hampson, Nimsgern, Van der Meer, Jacobs, Iconomou, Holl, Immler, King's College, Cambridge, Ch., V. Boys' Ch., Tölz Boys' Ch., Ch. Viennensis, Ghent Coll. Voc., VCM, Harnoncourt; Leonhardt Cons., Leonhardt

Cantatas 1–14; 16–19
(M) *** Teldec (ADD) 4509 91755-2 (6)

Cantatas 20–36
(M) *** Teldec (ADD) 4509 91756-2 (6)

Cantatas 37–52; 54–60
(M) *** Teldec (ADD) 4509 91757-2 (6)

Cantatas 61–9; 69a; 70–78
(M) **(*) Teldec (ADD) 4509 91758-2 (6)

Cantatas 79–99
(M) **(*) Teldec (ADD) 4509 91759-2 (6)

Cantatas 100–117
(M) *** Teldec (ADD) 4509 91760-2 (6)

Cantatas 119–37
(M) **(*) Teldec (ADD) 4509 91761-2 (6)

Cantatas 138–40; 143–59; 161–2
(M) **(*) Teldec (ADD/DDD) 4509 91762-2 (6)

Cantatas 163–82
(M) **(*) Teldec (ADD) 4509 91763-2 (6)

Cantatas 183–8; 192; 194–9
(M) **(*) Teldec (ADD) 4509 91764-2 (6)

This pioneering Teldec project, a recording of most – but not all – of Bach's cantatas, is offered in two alternative choices: as a 60-CD box (with more music on each disc) at bargain price or as a series of ten separate collections, each of six CDs, at mid-price.

The recordings got off to a very good start but, later in the project, various flaws of intonation, and sometimes a feeling that the ensemble would have benefited from more rehearsal, plus occasionally sluggish direction, slightly undermined the overall excellence. However, the authentic character of the performances is in no doubt. Boys replace women not only in the choruses but also as soloists (which brings occasional minor lapses of security), and the size of the forces is confined to what we know Bach himself would have expected. The simplicity of the approach brings its own merits, for the imperfect yet otherworldly quality of some of the treble soloists refreshingly focuses the listener's attention on the music itself. Less appealing is the quality of the violins, which eschew vibrato and, it would sometimes seem, any kind of timbre! Generally speaking, there is a certain want of rhythmic freedom and some expressive caution. Rhythmic accents are underlined with some regularity and the grandeur of Bach's inspiration is at times lost to view. Nevertheless there is much glorious music here which, to do justice to Harnon-court and Leonhardt, usually emerges freshly to give the listener much musical nourishment. The CD transfers are first class. The acoustic is usually not too dry – and not too ecclesiastical either – and the projection is realistic.

Complete Cantatas: Brilliant Series, with Holland Boys' Choir, Netherlands Bach Collegium, Leusink

Volume I: *Cantatas 16; 33; 37; 42; 56; 61; 72; 80; 82; 97; 113; 132; 133; 170*

(BB) ** Brill. 99363 (5); with Holton, Buwalda, Van Der Meel, Schock, Ramselaar

Volume II: *Cantatas 22; 23; 44; 54; 57; 85; 86; 92; 98; 111; 114; 135; 155; 159; 165; 167; 188*

(BB) ** Brill. 99364 (5); with Holton, Buwalda, Van Der Meel, Schock, Ramselaar

Volume III: *Cantatas 17; 35; 87; 90; 99; 106; 117; 123; 153; 161; 168; 172; 173; 182; 199*

(BB) ** Brill. 99367 (5); with Holton, Strijk, Buwalda, Van Der Meel, Schock, Ramselaar

Volume IV: *Cantatas 7; 13; 45; 69; 81; 102; 116; 122; 130; 138; 144; 149; 150; 169; 196*

(BB) ** Brill. 99368 (5); with Holton, Strijk, Buwalda, Van Der Meel, Schock, Ramselaar

Volume V: *Cantatas 6; 26; 27; 46; 55; 94; 96; 107; 115; 139; 156; 163; 164; 178; 179*

(BB) ** Brill. 99370 (5); with Holton, Strijk, Buwalda, Van Der Meel, Schock, Beekman, Ramselaar

Volume VI: *Cantatas 2; 3; 8; 60; 62; 78; 93; 103; 128; 145; 151; 154; 171; 185; 186; 192*

(BB) ** Brill. 99371 (5); with Holton, Strijk, Buwalda, Van Der Meel, Schock, Beekman, Ramselaar

Volume VII: *Cantatas 9; 36; 47; 73; 91; 110; 121; 125; 129; 152; 157; 166; 184; 198*

(BB) ** Brill. 99373 (5); with Holton, Strijk, Buwalda, Van Der Meel, Schock, Ramselaar

Volume VIII: *Cantatas 18 ;30; 40; 49; 79; 84; 88; 89; 100; 108; 136; 140; 176; 187; 194*

(BB) ** Brill. 99374 (5); with Holton, Strijk, Buwalda, Van Der Meel, Schock, Ramselaar

Secular Cantatas: *36c; 201; 202; 203; 204; 205; 206; 207; 208; 209; 210; 211; 212; 213; 214; 215*

(BB) **(*) Brill. 99366 (8). Mathis, Augér, Popp, Watkinson, Hamari, Schreier, Adam, Lorenz, Berlin Soloists and CO, Schreier

On the newly established Brilliant label we have another complete survey of the Bach cantatas that is so economically priced as to make Naxos seem in the luxury price bracket: 15 or 16 cantatas for just under £10 per set, or roughly 60 pence per cantata, is a different proposition from the full-price sets which can be over £5 per cantata. Of course one should not assess this repertoire purely in these terms; once a year or so has passed, it is quality rather than cost that will determine whether you return to these recordings. A substantial number of these performances were recorded in the last four months of 1999; and to accomplish such a venture in so short a time, rather than the many years taken by Karl Richter, Harnoncourt/Leonhardt and Rilling, is in itself no mean feat.

Others were recorded early in 2000, and the secular cantatas, conducted by Peter Schreier and licensed from Edel UK, come from the late 1970s and early 1980s. One does not get far into the set before confirming the suspicion that these accounts are uneven and in some respects a hit-or-miss affair. Although some of the performances sound distinctly under-prepared, there is a great deal of enthusiasm and dedication in Pieter Jan Leusink's enterprise. Some of the performances sound like run-throughs, rather more rough than ready, but others have an eminently acceptable standard of singing and playing; BWV 188, *Ich habe meine Zuversicht*, is remarkably accomplished and features the fine tenor Nico van der Meel. Elsewhere there is some uneven solo singing, uncertain in execution and at times intonation, and certain cantatas do not come off at all well; BWV 198 (*Lass Fürstin, lass noch einen Strahl*) is rather insensitive, and there are more refined and thoughtful accounts of, for example, BWV 112 and 106 (*Gottes Zeit ist die allerbeste Zeit*). However, more of Leusink's performances will give pleasure than not. The Holland Boys are robust and fresh-voiced, and although the instrumental contributions need more polish and rehearsal, there is a straightforward, no-nonsense approach that is welcome. The sound, if again variable, is perfectly acceptable. It is very difficult to give a star rating to these discs. They lack the polish and distinction of the best of the cantata series (by Suzuki, Rilling, Koopman or Gardiner) but are often far from negligible, even when judged by the highest standards, as in BWV 56, *Ich will den Kreuzstab*, which features Bas Ramse-laar's first-rate bass performance. Those who live in univer-sity or cathedral cities with a strong musical tradition will know what to expect and will find these performances con-genial. They are not slick or glamorous, but at this price they valuably fill a gap.

Complete Cantatas: Koopman Series with Amsterdam Baroque Chorus & Orchestra on Challenge Classics

Volume I: *Cantatas 4* (with Appendix: Chorus: *Sie nun wieder zufrieden*); *31; 71; 106* (*Actus tragicus*); *131; 150; 185; 196* (*Wedding Cantata*)

*** Chall. CC 72201 (3). Schlick, Wessel, De Mey, Mertens

Volume II: *Cantatas 12; 18* (with Appendix); *61; 132; 152; 172; 182* (with Appendix); *199; 203: Amore traditore. Quodlibet,* BWV 524

*** Chall. CC 72202 (3). Schlick, Wessel, Prégardien, Mertens

Volume III: *Cantatas 22; 23; 54; 63* (2 versions); *155; 161; 162* (2 versions); *163; 165; 208: Was mir behagt, ist nur die muntre Jagd* (Hunt)

*** Chall. CC 72203 (3). Schlick, Stam, Holton, Bongers, Von Magnus, Scholl, Agnew

Volume IV: *Cantatas 198; 201; 204; 209; 211; 214; 215*

*** Chall. CC 72204 (3). Larsson, Bongers, Grimm, Stam, Von Magnus, De Groot, Agnew, Ovenden, Mertens, Bentvelsen

Volume V: *Cantatas 202; 205; 206; 207a; 212; 213*

*** Chall. CC 72205 (4). Larsson, Rubens, Bongers, Grimm, Von Magnus, Prégardien, Mertens

Previously available on Erato, but now taken over by Chal-lenge Classics, Ton Koopman's cantata cycle looks set to surpass the famous Leonhardt–Harnoncourt set on Teldec (and indeed most of his other competitors). These versions all differ in some important respects, and readers will have to decide for themselves how these various factors weigh in their own balance-sheet. First, Koopman favours an intimate approach to choruses – namely one voice to a part – which seems to rob this repertory of some of its sheer majesty and breadth. Second, unlike Leonhardt–Harnoncourt, Koopman opts for female soloists rather than boys, as would have been the case in Bach's day, and he favours mixed rather than solely male choirs. For many this will be a plus point – and it is good news for fans of Barbara Schlick. Third, and again unlike Leonhardt–Harnoncourt, he goes for slightly higher than normal pitch – a semitone above present-day pitch, which, as Christoph Wolff's notes point out, is what Bach used in Mühlhausen and Weimar, brightening the sonority quite a lot. The singing in virtually all the cantatas is pretty impressive and the instrumental playing is of a high order of accomplishment. Those who set store by security of intonation and excellence of ensemble will probably prefer this survey to the earlier set. Moreover, Koopman offers the collector variants and alternative versions, which will again be an undoubted plus.

Koopman's survey is proceeding on largely chronological lines and Volume III includes the delightful secular cantata 208, *Was mir behagt, ist nur die muntre Jagd*, which includes 'Sheep may safely graze'. All these works come from Bach's Weimar years. For the most part the singing here is of a high order of accomplishment – in particular Andreas Scholl and Elisabeth von Magnus, and the instrumental playing is certainly more finished than is often the case in the Teldec set, though here it is by no means always as fresh or secure as on the Japanese series now under way from BIS. In 54, *Widerstehe doch der Sünde*, Suzuki surpasses Koopman in expressive power, and even when he doesn't the string playing yields in vigour and polish and sonority to the Japanese musicians. Besides offering various appendices, in 63, *Christen, ätzet diesen Tag*, and in 162, *Ach! ich sehe, jetzt, da ich zur Hochzeit gehe*, Koopman gives alternative versions, giving him an undoubted advantage over the opposition.

The fourth volume is given over to secular cantatas of the Leipzig period (1726–34), most not included in the Teldec survey. Foremost among them is the 1727 cantata, *Lass Fürstin, lass noch einen Strahl*, BWV 198, or the 'Funeral Ode' cantata, composed for the funeral ceremonies to mark the death of Christiane Eberhardine, Queen of Poland and Electoral Princess of Saxony. The noble opening chorus is perhaps wanting in breadth (rhythms are often over-accentuated) – memories of Jürgen Jürgens's 1968 version, also with combined Amsterdam and Hamburg forces, are emphatically not erased – and Koopman's soloists are uneven, particularly Lisa Larsson, whose confidence and intonation are occasionally vulnerable (she is better in BWV 209, *Non sà che sia dolore*). Generally speaking, the men are stronger. Koopman is rather breathless in the opening *Sinfonia*. All the same, there are many felicities in the set and some expert and beautifully light wind-playing. The recording is absolutely first class.

The fifth volume completes the survey of the Leipzig secular cantatas up to the so-called *Peasant Cantata, Mer hahn en neue Oberkeet*, BWV 212. There is some distinguished singing from Klaus Mertens and Christoph Prégardien and some highly accomplished and felicitous solo instrumental playing (there are some wonderfully poetic oboe obbligatos). Lisa Larsson seems far more at ease in BWV 202, *Weichet nur, betrübte Schatten*, than she was in the earlier volume, though elsewhere intonation occasionally troubles Elisabeth von Magnus. Generally speaking, this gives more consistent pleasure than earlier releases in the series, and the recordings are excellent.

Volume VI: *Cantatas 50; 59; 69; 69a; 75–6; 104; 179; 186; 190*
(N) **(*) Chall. CC 72206 (3). Ziesak, Von Magnus, Agnew, Mertens, Amsterdam Bar. Ch. & O, Koopman

Volume VII: *Cantatas 24–5; 67; 95; 105; 136; 144; 147–8; 173; 181; 184*
(N) **(*) Chall. CC 72207 (3). Larson, Bartosz, Von Magnus, Türk, Mertens, Amsterdam Bar. Ch. & O, Koopman

Volumes VI and VII inaugurate the long series of sacred cantatas from Bach's Leipzig years. With one exception, the cantatas come from the first annual cycle composed in 1723–4, including (in Volume VII) the well-known *Herz und Mund und Tat und Leben*. The singing of Ruth Ziesak, Paul Agnew and Klaus Mertens is eminently satisfying, and the occasional lapses in intonation which marred some earlier cantatas are absent. The standard of instrumental performances remains high, and the recordings are refreshingly clean and well detailed.

Complete Cantatas, Volume XIII: *Cantatas 1; 33; 38; 62; 92; 93; 96; 122; 133*
*** Chall. CC 72213 (3). York, Gottwald, Agnew, Mertens

Complete Cantatas, Volume XIV: *Cantatas 6; 26; 42; 68; 74; 103; 123; 125; 126; 178; Konzertsatz in D, BWV 1045*
*** Chall. CC 72214 (3). York, Markert, Larsson, Barosz, Gottwald, Dürmüller, Prégardien, Agnew, Gilchrist, Mertens

Complete Cantatas, Volume XV: *Cantatas 3; 28; 85; 87; 108; 110; 128; 146; 168; 175; 176; 183*
*** Chall. CC 72215 (3). York, Piau, Zomer, Rubens, Barosz, Dürmüller, Prégardien, Agnew, Gilchrist, Mertens

Complete Cantatas, Volume XVI: *Cantatas 16; 27; 39; 43; 49; 79; 82; 102; 170*
(N) (M) Chall. CC 72216 (3). Zomer, Piau, Rubens, Bartosz, Markert, Gilchrist, Agnew, Prégardien, Mertens, Amsterdam Bar. O, Koopman

Complete Cantatas, Volume XVII: *Cantatas 13; 17; 19; 32; 35; 56-58; 84; 169*
(N) (M) Chall. CC 72217 (3). Piau, Zomer, Rubens, Bartosz, Stutzmann, Agnew, Dürmüller, Mertens, Amsterdam Bar. Ch. & O, Koopman

Space does not permit the detailed exegesis that this project ideally calls for. With the five volumes listed immediately above, Ton Koopman brings his survey of the Bach cantatas well past its halfway point. Volume 17 contains works from the third annual cycle of cantatas from Leipzig, extending over the period from mid-1725 through to 1727. The high standards which distinguished earlier issues are to be found here, as far as the soloists and instrumentalists are concerned. Some have voiced reservations over Koopman's organ continuo, which is over-embellished, but for the most part these are excellent accounts that can be recommended to followers of the series. Koopman's performances are cultured performances, not quite as full-blooded as the Japanese cycle with Suzuki (see below), but offering some fine singing and scholarly direction. They include exemplary detailed notes from Christoph Wolff and continue to include alternative versions of some movements that Bach used subsequently. Those who have collected earlier issues in this cycle will know their merits, and these newcomers maintain (and at times surpass) the standards of their predecessors, both artistically and in the refined quality of the recorded sound. Some collectors may be deterred by the fact that one must purchase these in batches of three discs with eleven or twelve cantatas per volume, whereas with the BIS each set can be bought singly. Although the latter remains our number one choice, Koopman is highly competitive, and in those parts of the world where Suzuki is not readily available this Challenge coverage is almost every bit as satisfying.

Complete Cantatas: BIS Masaaki Suzuki Series with Japan Bach Collegium

Cantatas 4; 150; 196
*** BIS CD 751; with Kuriso, Tachikawa, Katano, Kooy

Cantatas 5; 80; 115
(N) *** BIS CD 1421; with Rydén, Bertin, Türk, Kooy

Cantatas 7; 20; 94
*** BIS CD 1321; with Nonoshita, Blaze, Kobow, Kooy

Cantatas 8; 33; 113
(N) *** BIS CD 1351; with Nonoshita, Blaze, Türk, Kooy

Cantatas 10; 93; 107; 178
*** BIS CD 1331; with Nonoshita, M. White, Sakurada, Kooy

Cantatas 65; 81; 83; 190
*** BIS CD 1311; with Blaze, Gilchrist, Kooy

Cantatas 78; 99; 114
(N)*** BIS CD 1361; with Nonoshita, Taylor, Sakurada, Kooy

Like Koopman, Suzuki uses a higher pitch (A = 465) with its concomitant brighter sound, and he also favours female voices. This naturally places an additional hurdle before the soprano, Yumiko Kuriso, which she surmounts with conspicuous distinction. In many ways, the results of the pupil outstrip those of the master, for these performances radiate more joy in music-making and give more consistent pleasure than many European ones. The strings are clean, and the sense of inhibition – of excessive awareness of the constraints of period performance that occasionally mar the Harnoncourt–Leonhardt set – is refreshingly absent here. Knowing the problems European languages pose for the Japanese, their German diction is more than acceptable. The continuing evidence below suggests that the remainder of the series (which will also include the other major choral works) is going to be as enjoyable as this first instalment – and as well recorded – and this is obviously going to occupy a key contribution in the Bach discography. If forced to choose from among the cycles currently before the public (Helmut Rilling on Hänssler, the Harnoncourt–Leonhardt set on Teldec and Karl Richter on DG/Archiv), the BIS set would be a very credible first choice.

The above seven discs represent Volumes 21–7 in the Japan Bach Collegium's imposing survey with Masaaki Suzuki. All the cantatas on the first two discs belong to the Leipzig cycle of 1724, the bicentenary of the German hymnbook, and are a treasure house of glorious musical invention. Volume 22 introduces a new departure in Bach's cantata output for, instead of illustrating the gospel appointed for the Sunday in question, each is based on one of the famous Reformation hymns and begins with an imposing introductory movement of magisterial contrapuntal mastery. None is more majestic than the opening of *O Ewigkeit, du Donnerwort*, BWV 20, to which Suzuki and his colleagues bring splendid breadth. All are large-scale works with particularly rich sonorities: trumpet, flute and oboe d'amore respectively adding colour to the usual string and continuo forces. Each new volume in this series from Masaaki Suzuki seems to surpass its predecessor and offer performances of total conviction and consummate artistry. Volume 27, for instance, opens with a magnificent

chorus from the Fifth Cantata, in fact a glorious late work based on the familiar chorale, *Ein feste Burg*, and it could not be done more resplendently, while its two companion cantatas return us to Bach's second year at Leipzig. The BIS recordings are state of the art, and for many they will remain first choice.

Cantatas 12; 54; 162; 182
*** BIS CD 791; with Kuriso, Mera, Sakurada, Kooy

Readers will recognize the opening of 12, *Weinen, Klagen, Sorgen, Zagen*, as a model for the *Crucifixus* of the *B minor Mass*; Suzuki gives it with feeling and gravitas, while his characterization elsewhere – both in 54, *Widerstehe doch der Sünde*, and in 162, *Ach! ich sehe, jetzt, da ich zur Hochzeit gehe* – inspires confidence. No grumbles about the quality of the singing, the instrumental response or the present and pleasing sound, which is in the best traditions of the house.

Cantatas 18; 152; 155; 161; 163
*** BIS CD 841; with Midori Suzuki, Schmithüsen, Mera, Sakurada, Kooy

Cantatas 21 (**with 3 alternative movements**); *31*
*** BIS CD 851; with Frimmer, Türk, Kooy

Cantatas 21; 147
⊕─ *** BIS CD 1031; with Nonoshita, Blaze, Türk, Kooy, Concerto Palatino (BWV 21)

BIS CD 1031 is Volume 12 in Masaaki Suzuki's survey and the fifth devoted to the cantatas that Bach composed in 1723. There are several versions of *Ich hatte viel Bekümmernis* (BWV 21). The so-called Weimar version from 1716, which Bach transposed into D minor for Hamburg in 1720, appeared in Volume 6 of the Suzuki series with some alternative arias. The present version is the revision Bach made in 1723 for Leipzig in which the orchestral texture is enriched. Both cantatas receive performances of great vitality and spirit; the soloists are first rate and the recordings have great presence.

Cantatas 22–3; 75
*** BIS CD 901; with M. Suzuki, Mera, Türk, Kooy

Cantatas 24; 76; 167
*** BIS CD 931; with M. Suzuki, Blaze, Türk, Urano

Cantatas 25; 50; 64; 69a; 77
*** BIS CD 1041; with Nonoshita, Blaze, Sollek-Avella, Türk, Sakurada, Kooy, Concerto Palatino (BWV 25 & 64)

Volume 13 (BIS CD 1041) continues with the cantatas from Bach's first year at Leipzig, 1723. The performances radiate freshness and enthusiasm, and their vitality is matched by a wonderfully present recorded sound.

Cantatas 37; 86; 104; 166
*** BIS CD 1261; with Nonoshita, Blaze, Sakurada, MacLeod

Cantatas 40; 60; 70; 90
*** BIS CD 1111; with Nonoshita, Blaze, Türk, Kooy

Cantatas 44; 59; 173; 184
*** BIS CD 1271. with Nonoshita, Hatano, Türk, Kooy

Cantatas 46; 95; 136; 138
*** BIS CD 991; with M. Suzuki, Wessel, Sakurada, Kooy

Cantatas 48; 89; 109; 148
*** BIS CD 1081; with M. Suzuki, Blaze, Türk, Urano

Cantatas 61; 63; 132; 172
*** BIS CD 881; with Schmithüsen, Mera, Sakurada, Kooy

Cantatas 65, 81, 83, 190
*** BIS CD 1311. with Blaze, Gilchurst, Kooy

Cantatas 66; 67; 134
*** BIS CD 1251; with Blaze, Sakurada, Kooy

Cantatas 71; 106; 131
*** BIS CD 781; with M. Suzuki, Yanagisawa, Mera, Türk, Kooy

BIS CD 781 collects some of the earliest in the canon from Bach's time at Mühlhausen. Some may feel that Suzuki's slow tempo at the opening of 106, the *Actus tragicus* or *Gottes Zeit ist die allerbeste Zeit*, is a little too much of a good thing, but others (like us) may well be convinced by the breadth and space he brings to it. The singing is of a high standard throughout, and Midori Suzuki gives particular pleasure in 71, *Gott ist mein König*, with her freshness and expressiveness – as for that matter do Aki Yanagisawa and Gerd Türk. Freshness is what characterizes the chorus and instrumentalists too, and it communicates a greater intensity of feeling than many rivals. The BIS sound is first class in terms of both clarity and ambience

Cantatas 73; 144; 153; 154; 181
*** BIS CD 1221; with Nonoshita, Blaze, Türk, Kooy

As in the earlier issues, the singers here are uniformly excellent and can give many European soloists and choirs a lesson in diction; their German sounds immaculate. Yoshikazu Mera is a counter-tenor of the highest quality, and the remaining soloists have nothing to fear from comparison with those in the Leonhardt–Harnoncourt set or the Koopman survey on Erato – quite the contrary. Above all, the playing has sensitivity allied to vitality and scholarship blended with imagination. The recordings are very well balanced and finely detailed, very much in the best traditions of BIS. If you find that any of the cantatas listed above fill gaps in your collection, there is no reason to hesitate – and if you are just starting out on a complete collection, this would be a viable first choice.

Cantatas 96; 122; 180
(N) *** BIS CD 1401; with Nonoshita, Kenworthy-Brown, Sakurada, Kooy

The three cantatas here are from 1724 and are linked by their scoring, which in each case includes recorders used to add a variety of special colouring, especially striking in *Das neugeborn Kinderlein* (No. 122). The opening chorus of *Schmücke dich* (No. 180) is fine and, among the soloists, the bass, Peter Kooy, stands out in his arias from this same cantata and also in *Herr Christ, der einge Gottessohn* (No. 96).

Cantatas 105; 179; 186
☛ (M) *** BIS CD 951; with Persson, Blaze, Sakurada, Kooy

Cantatas 119; 194
*** BIS CD 1131; with Hida, Nonoshita, Sollek-Avella, Sakurada, Kupfer, Kooy

BIS CD 951 has the benefit of excellent soloists in Miah Persson, a Swedish soprano of real quality, and the tenor Makoto Sakurada. It seems invidious to single them out, since both the counter-tenor, Robin Blaze, and Peter Kooy are hardly less impressive. *Herr, gehe nicht ins Gericht*, BWV 105, faces formidable competition, but it more than withstands any comparison you might care to make. The balance does not place the soloists too far forward and the sound is as vivid, warm and as clear as you could wish for.

Cantatas (i) 163; (ii) 165; (iii) 185; (iv) 199
*** BIS CD 801; with (i–ii) Yanagisawa; (i–iii) Tachikawa, Sakurada, Schreckenberger; (iii–iv) M. Suzuki

Those who have been collecting this Japanese survey of the Bach cantatas on BIS will know what to expect: secure performances, excellent diction and scholarly yet vital, musically imaginative direction. As each recording appears, the sheer quality of this achievement continues to prove a source of admiration and satisfaction. Masaaki Suzuki is proceeding chronologically and we have in this volume reached the Leipzig cycle of 1724. Although the excellence of rival surveys is not in doubt, this Japanese survey is the strongest and most consistent, and the BIS recordings are altogether exemplary.

Cantatas 210 (Wedding) ; 211 (Coffee)
(N) *** BIS CD 1411; with Sampson, Sakurada, Schreckenberger

While the series of church catatas continues, Suzuki and his team here inaugurate a separate collection of the secular cantatas, including two of the most famous. Carolyn Sampson is the star of both, singing with style and much aplomb in the *Coffee Cantata*, where Stephan Schreckenberger characterizes equally strongly as her father. Perhaps the bold humour of this work suits Suzuki less well than its companion wedding celebration, which is most beautifully sung and is very successful on all counts.

Cantatas: Gardiner DG Archiv Series with Monteverdi Choir and English Baroque Soloists

Cantatas 113; 179; 199
☛ *** Opus Arte **DVD** OA 0816D; with Kožena, Towers, Padmore, Loges

Cantatas for Easter 6; 66
*** DG 463 580-2; with soloists

Cantatas for Ascension Day 11; 37; 43; 128
*** DG 463 583-2; with Argenta, Blaze, Rolfe Johnson, Genz, Varcoe, Hagen

Cantata for Feast of Circumcision: 16; Cantatas for 21st & 23rd Sundays after Trinity 98; 139
*** DG 463 586-2; with Fuge, Ragin, Podger, Schwarz

Cantatas for Whitsun 34; 59; 74; 172
*** DG 463 584-2; with soloists

Cantatas for Advent 36; 61; 62
*** DG 463 588-2; with Argenta, Lang, Rolfe Johnson, Bär

Cantatas for Christmas 63; 64; 121; 133
*** DG 463 589-2; with soloists

Cantatas for 3rd Sunday after Epiphany 72; 73; 111; 156
DG 463 582-2; with soloists

Cantatas for Feast of the Purification of Mary 82; 83; 125; 200
*** DG 463 585-2; with Tyson, Agnew, Harvey

Cantatas for 9th Sunday after Trinity 94; 105; 168
*** DG 463 590-2; with soloists

Cantatas 106; 118; 198
*** DG 463 581-2; with Argenta, Chance, Rolfe Johnson, Varcoe

Cantatas for 11th Sunday after Trinity, 113; 179; 199
*** DG 463 591-2; with soloists

During the 250th anniversary of Bach's death in 2000 John Eliot Gardiner embarked on an ambitious project to perform all the cantatas on the appropriate days of the liturgical year in a variety of English and European venues. Deutsche Grammophon had planned to record the whole series, but the costs involved, the emergence of rival versions at budget price and the magnificent BIS series from Japan prompted them to reconsider the viability of the project.

The DVD offers not just three complete Bach cantatas but an hour-long feature film. The cantatas are very well chosen; the outer ones from 1723 and 1724 respectively are from Bach's Leipzig period, the central one (for solo soprano) dates from 1714 when Bach was in Weimar. Gardiner characteristically relies on fresh young voices, with the Monteverdi Choir typically bright and incisive, matched by the four soloists. The tenor, Mark Padmore, is excellent; the counter-tenor, William Towers, and the young German baritone, Stephan Loges, are consistently firm and clear. But it is the Czech soprano, Magdalena Kožena, who wins first honours with her superb singing in the solo cantata, *Mein Herz schwimmt im Blut*. Aptly, she also appears in the St David's sequence in the feature film, one of the 11 venues visited.

The final outcome was the release of the CDs listed above. Some are live performances and two are reissues: DG 463 581-2 (which includes a memorable account of *Gottes Zeit ist die allerbeste Zeit* from 1990) and the *Advent Cantatas* (DG 463 588-2, from 1992), though it must be noted that both are still offered at premium price, even though the playing time of the former is less than an hour. Come to that, the two newly recorded *Easter Cantatas* (DG 463 580-2) are 48'16" and 16, 98 and 139 (DG 463 586-2) even shorter: 45'30". To be perfectly fair, the *Ascension Day Cantatas* (DG 463 583-2) are better value for money (78'30").

Gardiner's admirers are unlikely to be too concerned about this, as his feeling for style and his sense of drive strike a responsive chord with many music-lovers. His choice of soloists is unerring and the musicianship of the Monteverdi Choir and the English Baroque Soloists always imposing. Rhythmic articulation is light but well defined, and there is great technical finesse and unanimity of ensemble. Some may find him a little too crisp and clean and at times a shade too brisk, even in the poignant funeral cantata, *Lass, Fürstin, lass noch einen Strahl*, BWV 198.

Cantatas 140; 147

⊙━ (M) *** DG Dig. 463 587-2; with Holton, Chance, Rolfe Johnson, Varcoe

These popular Bach cantatas are coupled in highly accomplished performances. The level of instrumental playing is polished, and Ruth Holton, Anthony Rolfe Johnson, Michael Chance and Stephen Varcoe make equally satisfying contributions.

It goes without saying that in the course of these beautifully recorded performances there is much to refresh the spirit alongside much that has spirit rather than a sense of the spiritual. Gardiner is marvellously alive to the texture and is dedicated and enthusiastic, but he can also be unyielding and lacking in breadth and majesty. Despite such reservations and the fact that Suzuki's series with the Bach Collegium of Japan is even more rewarding, Gardiner's performances are undoubtedly of a consistently high calibre. Both the documentation and presentation are of the usual fine Archiv standard. The recordings are immediate and well balanced. A strong recommendation, especially now that it is available at mid-price.

Cantatas: Karl Richter DG Archiv Series with Munich Bach Choir & Orchestra

Cantatas: (i) *4*; (ii) *51*; (i) *56*; (i; iii) *140*; (iv) *147*; (ii) *202*
(B) *** DG Double (ADD) 453 094-2; with (i) Fischer-Dieskau; (ii) Stader; (iii) Mathis, Schreier; (iv) Buckel, Töpper, Van Kesteren, Engen, Ansbach Festival Soloists

Richter's stereo Bach cantata series for DG, which spanned two decades beginning in the late 1950s, is shown at its finest in this well-chosen half-dozen which are all among Bach's finest works in this form. No. 4, *Christ lag in Todesbanden*, is early. Richter seems wholly in sympathy with the music and secures some splendid choral singing and dignified playing from the orchestra. Fischer-Dieskau is featured both here and in the solo cantata, *Ich will den Kreuzstab gerne tragen*. Some might feel that he is at times a little too expressive and over-sophisticated, but he pays characteristic attention to the text. Richter, too, is at times a trifle heavy-handed, but this remains a memorable account. No. 51, *Jauchzet Gott*, demands an abnormally high tessitura from the solo soprano, and Maria Stader is in splendid voice here (a virtuoso performance which is also most moving) and also in the *Wedding Cantata*, *Weichet nur*, which is one of Bach's most immediately appealing works. Here the discipline of the choir is not always impeccable; but these performances truly belong to Stader, and her singing is firm and clear and shows no sense of strain. No. 140, *Wachet auf, ruft uns die Stimme* (which opens the programme), shows Richter's team at their most impressive throughout, with all the soloists on excellent form and the obbligato wind players, Manfred Clement (oboe) and Edgar Shann (cor anglais), making notable contributions, here as elsewhere. The gloriously heartwarming sound from the Munich orchestra is utterly different from what one would expect from a period-instrument performance today. *Herz und Mund und Tat und Leben* is another very successful performance, with both the soprano and contralto arias beautifully sung by Ursula Buckel and the rich-timbred contralto, Hertha Töpper, respectively. The tenor, John van Kesteren, is also impressive. This cantata contains the famous chorale, *Wohl mir, dass ich Jesum habe* (better known as 'Jesu, joy of man's desiring'), and this is presented spaciously and warmly. All in all, this set with its first-class CD transfers can be given the warmest welcome.

Cantatas (for the latter part of the Church year) *5*; *26*; *38*; *55–6*; *60*; *70*; *80*; *96*; *106* (*Actus tragicus*); *115–16*; *130*; *139–40*; *180*
(B) **(*) DG (ADD) 439 394-2 (5); with Mathis, Buckel, Schmidt, Töpper, Schreier, Haefliger, Fischer-Dieskau, Adam, Engen

This Richter box collects cantatas that Bach composed for the last ten Sundays of Trinity, plus three others, a Reformation Festival piece (80), a cantata for St Michael's Day (130) and Bach's funeral cantata, *Gottes Zeit* – the so-called *Actus tragicus*; it is given a first-rate performance, with fine solo singing and committed direction. Most of these cantatas are chorale-based and nearly all emerge with the dignity and majesty one expects from these forces. They were all recorded in the Munich Herkulessaal, for the most part in 1978, and the sound is warm and spacious. Karl Richter's heavy tread seems over the years to have moderated into a more flexible and human gait, though a certain inflexibility and lack of imagination still surface occasionally.

Cantatas (for the middle Sundays after Trinity) *8–9; 17; 27; 33; 45; 51; 78; 100; 102; 105; 137; 148; 178–9; 187; 199*

(B) **(*) DG (ADD) 439 387-2 (6); with Buckel, Mathis, Stader, Hamari, Töpper, Schreier, Haefliger, Van Kesteren, Fischer-Dieskau, Engen

This box offers the cantatas composed for the sixth Sunday after Trinity through to the seventeenth. Again the spacious venue is the Munich Herkulessaal. The chorus is probably larger than it should be, but the results are invariably musical, and Richter shows greater flexibility and imagination than has often been the case. Just occasionally his heavy touch is felt, but so much of this set is first rate that reservations can be all but overruled. The soloists are thoroughly dependable.

Cantatas (for Ascension Day; Whitsun; Trinity) *10–11; 21; 24; 30; 34; 39; 44; 68; 76; 93; 129; 135; 147; 175*

(B) **(*) DG (ADD) 439 380-2 (6); with Mathis, Buckel, Reynolds, Töpper, Schreier, Haefliger, Van Kesteren, Fischer-Dieskau, Moll, Engen

The first performance offered here is the glorious *Ascension Cantata, Lobet Gott in seinen Reichen* (11), which opens and closes joyfully with resplendent trumpets. All four soloists are first rate, and Anna Reynolds is especially memorable in her famous aria, *Ach, bleib doch, mein liebstes Leben*, warmly supported by the strings of the Munich ensemble. Richter's other performances have a breadth and sense of space that are really quite impressive. He makes heavy weather of *Ein ungefärbt Gemüte* (24), but on the whole the dignity of these performances outweighs the occasional pedestrian moments. On the whole a successful box.

Cantatas: Fritz Werner Erato Series

Cantatas, Volume 1: 1, 4, 6–7, 11. 23, 28, 30–32, 34, 39–40, 43, 57, 61, 65, 67–8, 72, 76, 82, 85, 87, 92, 103–4, 110, 182, 249

(N) (BB) **(*) Warner (ADD) 2564 61401-2 (10). Giebel, Krebs and soloists, Heinrich Schütz-Ch., Heilbronn; Pforzheimer CO, Werner

Cantatas, Volume 2: 8, 10, 19, 21, 26, 50–51, 53, 56, 70, 78–80, 85, 90, 98, 102, 104–6, 119, 130–31, 137, 140, 147, 149–50, 160, 180, 200

(N) (BB) **(*) Warner (ADD) 2564 61402-2 (10). Giebel, Krebs, Kelch and soloists, Heinrich Schütz-Ch., Heilbronn; Pforzheimer CO, Werner

Older collectors will recall that from 1957 through to 1973 the Erato label issued a fine Bach cantata series under Fritz Werner that was rather overshadowed at the time by the well-promoted and better-publicized cycle by Karl Richter and his Munich forces on DG's Archiv label. The present sets restore them to circulation in highly competitive and economical packaging. They are divided into four-CD and six-CD boxes, and the presentation material by Nicholas Anderson, who has devised the series, is exemplary in its detail and authority.

Werner's forces are Franco-German and the instrumentalists include such artists as Maurice André, Pierre Perlot and August Wenzinger, all wonderful Bach players, and such soloists as Agnes Giebel, Helmut Krebs, Ingeborg Reichelt and Marga Höffgen among others. *Selig ist der Mann* (57), with Giebel and Barry McDaniel, has been hailed by one authority as the finest account of the cantata on disc. Another highlight is the so-called 'Actus tragicus', *Gottes Zeit ist der allerbeste Zeit*, BWV 106, an affecting performance which is

all the more eloquent for being completely natural. Richter's Munich Bach Choir is perhaps more disciplined and better drilled than Werner's group, but, for all the occasional weaknesses, generally speaking they have greater warmth and spontaneity of feeling. Werner's approach is more humane and, above all, gracious, and it has an unforced expressive eloquence that is to be preferred to the driven and often square phrasing one finds in the generally better-recorded Archiv set.

Cantatas: New Chandos Purcell Quartet Series

Early Cantatas, Volume 1: Cantatas 4; 106; 131; 196

(N) *** Chan. 0715. Kirkby, Chance, Daniels, Harvey, Augmented Purcell Qt

This Chandos disc is the first in a new survey of the Bach cantatas, using period instruments and creating a chamber scale of considerable intimacy. The four cantatas, including the beautiful *Christ lag in Todes Banden* (4) and the celebrated *Gottes Zeit ist die allerbeste Zeit*, were all composed in Mühlhausen in 1707/8, showing the composer in youthfully inspired form. The first-rate soloists join together here to act as the chorus, especially effective in *Aus der Tiefen rufe ich, Herr, zu dir* (131), although it does not quite work in *Gottes Zeit* (106 – the so-called 'Actus tragicus') where the sense of mystery is diminished. No quarrels with the performances at all – they have a great sense of style – or with the excellent recordings, but obviously this is not for those who require a greater amplitude of sonority in this repertoire. Some might feel that the all-but-vibrato-less singing is too pure, and there is inevitably a limited dynamic range, but the result is very refreshing. Whether or not it truthfully reflects the kind of performance Bach would have known, it certainly casts a new light on the music. The acoustic of St Jude on the Hill, Hampstead, adds a gentle glow to the overall sound. Although the Purcell Quartet is listed as the accompanying group, it is augmented by other players, and there are some memorable obbligato contributions – for a pair of seraphic recorders in No. 106, solo oboe in No. 131, and one or two violins in Nos. 4 and 196. An impressive and generous first instalment which augurs well for further issues, although it is a pity that the otherwise excellent documentation does not indicate who is singing in each movement.

Other cantata groupings

Cantatas 2, 20 & 176

*** HMC 901791. Zomer, Danz, Kobow, Kooy, Ghent Coll. Voc., Herreweghe

Two of the soloists (Jan Kobow and Peter Kooy) are common to both this and Masaaki Suzuki's version of *O Ewigkeit, du Donnerwort* with the Japan Bach Collegium. These Ghent performances score in terms of breadth and atmosphere, and the quality of both the singing and the instrumental playing is one of distinction. The refinement of the phrasing gives much pleasure and satisfaction, as does the excellent recorded sound. These are new recordings, and for those not drawn for whatever reason to the various complete sets this will be a good choice. It should belong in any self-respecting Bach cantata collection.

Cantatas . (i) 4; (ii) 56; 82

(M) (**(*)) DG (IMS) mono 449 756-2. (i–ii) Fischer-Dieskau; (i) Frankfurt Hochschule Ch., 1950 Bach Festival O, Lehmann; (ii) Ristenpart CO, Ristenpart

These recordings, reissued as one of DG's 'Originals', come from 1950–51. Fischer-Dieskau's artistry is heard to excellent effect and nowhere better than in *Ich habe genug*, which is sung exquisitely. The choral cantata, *Christ lag in Todesbanden*, receives a dignified and expressive reading. Though the sound is not as vivid or as present as one might expect, it is eminently acceptable. A valuable issue, as a reminder both of an earlier Bach style and of Fischer-Dieskau's consummate artistry.

Cantatas 4; 131

(BB) *** Warner Apex 0927 49574-2. Kendall, Varcoe, Monteverdi Ch., E. Bar. Sol., Gardiner

These performances first appeared within a two-LP format in the early 1980s. This inexpensive reissue includes one of the best loved of all Bach cantatas, *Christ lag in Todesbanden*. At times Gardiner's tempi are characteristically brisk, but there is no question about the vitality of the music-making here, and the recording is truthful and present, without being in the demonstration category.

Cantatas 8; 51; 78; 80; 140; 147

(B) **(*) O-L Double (ADD) 455 706-2 (2). Soloists, Bach Ens., Rifkin

Joshua Rifkin's performances opt for the one-to-a-part principle not only in his instrumental ensemble but also as far as the choruses are concerned. He opts for female sopranos rather than boy trebles but uses adult male altos. Not all will find his solutions congenial, but there is some good singing in this series, and the playing is lively enough. One feels the need for greater weight and a more full-blooded approach at times, but this is outweighed by the sensitivity and intelligence that inform these excellently balanced recordings.

Cantatas 10; 47

(N) **(*) Lyrichord LEMS 8050 (2). Rogers, Le Sage, Minty, Howlett, L. Bach Soc., ECO, Steinitz (with Baroque Sampler)

Lyrichord offers a fascinating reissue from 1965. The recording, originally on the Oryx label, has a fine team of soloists, a full chorus of 20 singers, but a modest-sized chamber orchestra, drawn from the ECO. Indeed, although modern instruments are used, the scale of the performance anticipated the approach of more authentic, later recordings. Paul Steinitz conducts freshly and with plenty of impetus; if, by current standards, the last degree of refinement is missing, this is still very enjoyable. Texts and translations are included, but the listing of the movements of the second cantata, presumably taken from the LP sleeve, returns to re-number the movements 1–5, which does not coincide with the track listings. A sampler disc of excerpts from other Lyrichord issues (even including a brief excerpt from the present disc) is included to tempt collectors to explore the Lyrichord catalogue further.

Cantata 11 (Ascension)

(N) *** EuroArts DVD 2054039. Karthäuser, Hardt, Einhorn, Van de Crabben, La Petite Bande, Kuijken (V/D: Michael Beyer) – C. P. E. BACH: *Die Auferstehung und Himmelfahrt Jesu* **(*)

It was a happy idea to combine a performance of Bach's Ascension Cantata, *Lobett Got* with his son's *Ascension Oratorio*, although the juxtaposition shows that while the latter is a fine work, Johann Sebastian's cantata is a supreme masterpiece. It is splendidly sung here, with excellent soloists and a

first-class period-instrumental group, all working together as a team. The result is very enjoyable indeed, and beautifully recorded.

Cantatas 12; 140. Chorales: *Ertöt uns durch dein' Güte, from BWV 22; In dulci jubilo, BWV 729; Jesu bleibet meine Freude (Jesu, joy of man's desiring), from BWV 147; Kommst du nun, Jesu, BWV 650; Nun danket alle Gott, BWV 386; O Jesuslein süss, BWV 493; Liebster Jesu, wir sind hier, BWV 373; Magnificat in D, BWV 243; Missa brevis in A, BWV 234.* Motets: *Der Geist hilft unserer Schwachheit auf, BWV 226; Lobet den Herrn, alle Heiden, BWV 230; Sanctus in C, BWV 237; Orchestral Suite 3 in D: Air; (Organ) Prelude & Fugue in G, BWV 541*

⊕ *** EMI **Audio DVD** DVC4 92401-9. Gritton, Milne, Chance, Bostridge, George & Soloists, King's College, Cambridge, Ch., AAM, Cleobury (organ)

With the boy trebles soaring up with the trumpets in the King's Chapel acoustic, and with a superb team of starry soloists, Stephen Cleobury's vivid account of the *Magnificat* lies at the centre of an extremely satisfying 153-minute concert of Bach's choral music. It is a shame that this is only an audio rather than a video DVD, but the sound is magnificent, whether heard in normal stereo (side A) or surround sound (side B). The *Magnificat* is framed by a pair of Bach's finest and most famous cantatas, *Weinen, Klagen, Sorgen, Zagen*, which after the sinfonia has a glorious extended choral introduction, and the much less familiar *Missa brevis in A*, which also closes with an exultant *Cum Sancto Spiritu*. Its highlight is the flute-decorated *Qui tollis peccata mundi*, beautifully sung by Rachel Brown. For good measure there are two motets, and the programme is interspersed with chorales, including the famous *Jesu, joy of man's desiring*, while Cleobury also slips in the jubilant but little-known *Sanctus in C*, plus Bach's most famous orchestral *Air* as an interlude. To close the programme he plays the ebullient organ *Prelude and Fugue in G* which is followed by a thrilling postlude – a full-throated account of the familiar *Nun danket alle Gott*. Altogether a Bachian feast!

Cantatas 29: 119; 120

*** HM HMC 901690. York, Danz, Padmore, Kooy, Ghent Coll. Voc., Herreweghe

Unlike the complete survey underway from Suzuki, Philippe Herreweghe is offering a selective approach, linking his cantatas by themes. The three on this CD were composed for the festive openings of the Municipal Councils in 1723, 1730 and 1731. *Gott, man lobet dich in der Stille* contains the first working of the *Et exspecto* of the *B minor Mass*, though the opening mezzo aria is let down by some vulnerable intonation. Herreweghe gets some very cultured playing from his ensemble, and the singing throughout is otherwise very satisfying.

Cantatas 35: Sinfonias (only); (i) 56; 82; 158

*** Decca 466 570-2. (i) Goerne; Salzburg Bach Ch. & Camerata Academica, Norrington

All three cantatas for bass are on the theme of death and the liberation it brings, and they are interspersed on this disc with two spirited instrumental sinfonias. As you would expect from a pupil of Fischer-Dieskau and Schwarzkopf, Goerne's feeling for and projection of words are impeccable and he invests both *Ich habe genug* and *Ich will den Kreuzstab* with great expressive eloquence. Norrington is sometimes given to exaggeration, but for the most part he is supportive. The Decca balance places the voice rather close, perhaps to help the lower end of the register, but the sound is fresh and vivid. Impressive and satisfying accounts of these cantatas.

Cantatas (i) 39, 93 & 107; (ii) 73, 105 & 131; Masses (Missae breves): (iii; iv) in F, A, G min., G, BWV 233–6. Sanctus in D, BWV 238

(BB) *(**) Virgin 5 62252-2 (4). (i; iii) Mellon, Brett; (i; ii) Crook; (i; ii; iii) Kooy; (ii) Schlick, Lesne; (iv) Prégardien; Coll. Voc., Ghent, Ch. & O, Herreweghe

Both discs of cantatas are thoroughly recommendable. Apart from the excellence of the solo singing, one must praise also the fine choral contribution and stylish accompaniments. Herreweghe's pacing cannot be faulted, and the recording has an ideal acoustic so that everything sounds both fresh and warm.

Bach's four short Masses (Missae breves), which come in tandem with the cantatas, are also very well sung with comparably excellent solo contributions. The performances are authentic, spirited and stylish. They are certainly warmly enjoyable. But there is a snag. Unlike the cantatas, they have been recorded in a very resonant ecclesiastical acoustic that, while it provides freedom from period-instrument abrasiveness, takes the edge off the choruses, which often sound muddy, and detracts from the presence of the soloists.

Cantatas for the 1st, 2nd and 3rd days of Christmas, 40; 57; 63; 64; 91; 110; 121; 133; 151

(M) **(*) Teldec (ADD) 0630 17366-2 (3). Soloists, Ghent Coll. Voc., Leonhardt Consort, Leonhardt; VCM, Harnoncourt

A gathering of Bach's cantatas for the Christmas season. The ear has to accept moments of less-than-perfect intonation from the treble soloists of the Vienna Boys' (notably Detlef Bratsch in 91), although on the plus side Peter Jelosits makes a fine contribution to No. 63. Similarly among the original instruments, the horns are sometimes wildly astray in their upper harmonics (as in the introduction for the same cantata, Gelobet seist du, Jesu Christ). The Ghent chorus are not always absolutely reliable either: they are not completely secure in 133; yet they are at their best in 151, a splendid cantata. But overall there is much to enjoy here.

Cantatas. (i) 51 (complete); (ii) 68: Aria: Mein gläubiges Herz (only); 199; (iii) 202 (both complete); (ii) 208: Recitative and Aria: Schafe können sicher weiden (only); (iv) STOLZEL, attrib. BACH: Aria: Bist du bei mir

(M) (***) EMI mono 5 67206-2. Schwarzkopf, (i) Philh. O, Gellhorn; (ii) Dart; (iii) Concg. O, Klemperer; (iv) Moore

EMI have gathered together a superb collection of Schwarzkopf's Bach recordings, made between 1946 (the aria known in English as 'Sheep may safely graze') and 1958 (Cantata 199). What is especially fascinating is the live recording which was taken from a performance of Cantata 202 with Klemperer and the Concertgebouw, even more vehement and characterful at generally faster speeds than in the more controlled studio recording made later the same year, 1957, and now issued on Testament (see below). Bist du bei mir, long attributed to Bach, makes a delightful supplement, with Gerald Moore at the piano. Excellent transfers, though the Netherlands Radio recording with Klemperer is less full, if very atmospheric.

Cantatas 51; 82a; 84; 199; 202 (Wedding Cantata); 209

⊶ (BB) *** Virgin 2x1 5 61644-2 (2). Argenta, Ens. Sonnerie, Huggett

Nancy Argenta recorded these cantatas in the early 1990s. Not only does she give us a radiantly brilliant account of Jauchzet Gott in allen Landen, one that belongs among the best, but also superb versions of both the Wedding Cantata and Non sà che sia dolore. As is well known, Bach was particularly happy with Ich habe genug and scored it for other voices, including soprano, transcribing the oboe obbligato for flute. Argenta's performance is arguably the finest we have in this form and, in all six cantatas included in this package, the Ensemble Sonnerie and Monica Huggett give exemplary support. In every way a distinguished issue and not least in the quality of the recorded sound.

Cantatas 51; 202; 210

*** DG (IMS) 459 621-2. Schäfer, Col. Mus. Ant., Goebel

Christine Schäfer, in this handsomely presented volume, couples two of Bach's wedding cantatas with the familiar Jauchzet Gott in allen Landen. Unusually, this is given in W. F. Bach's arrangement, which adds a second trumpet and timpani to Bach's trumpet, strings and continuo. In all three she is in radiant voice and delights us with her beauty of tone and virtuosity. Reinhard Goebel and his Musica Antiqua Cologne are spirited and vital, though there are times, particularly in the closing Alleluia, when the onward drive is somewhat unremitting. DG have provided one of their most expertly balanced recordings.

Cantatas 54; 169; 170

*** Hyp. CDA 66326. Bowman, King's Consort, King

James Bowman is on impressive form and his admirers need not hesitate here. The present disc is very desirable and the King's Consort under Robert King give excellent support. Good recorded sound.

Cantatas 55; 82a; Sinfonias & Arias from Cantatas 4, 7, 18, 43, 139, 198, 212, & 249

*** Virgin 5 45420-2. Bostridge, Europa Galante, Biondi

Among Bach's copious output there is only one cantata for solo tenor, Ich arme Mensch, ich Sündenknecht, BWV 55. Here Bostridge has attached a transcription of Ich habe genug in its soprano version (BWV 82a). He also performs tenor arias from a number of other cantatas, all of which reveal his fine musical intelligence and beauty of tone. Some may find his diction too carefully projected (he certainly dots his 'i's and crosses his 't's with enormous care) but others will find much to reward them here, not least the superb musicianship of Fabio Biondi and his Europa Galante and the excellent Virgin Classics recording.

Cantatas 56 & 82

(M) *(*) Häns. CD 94.029. Fischer-Dieskau, Bach-Collegium, Stuttgart, Rilling

The performances come from the Hänssler Bach Cantata Edition, which Helmuth Rilling completed in time for the 300th anniversary of Bach's birth. Fischer-Dieskau has recorded Cantatas 56 and 82 several times, but these accounts from the early 1980s give less pleasure than the earlier versions, for they suffer from a certain self-consciousness that sometimes afflicts this great artist. There are no notes (they can be downloaded at www.haenssler-classic.de), and even at its modest price, 44 minutes is short measure.

Cantatas 56; 82; 99; 106 (Actus tragicus); 131; 158

(B) *** Double Decca 458 087-2 (2). Soloists, Bach Ens., Rifkin

Joshua Rifkin's series (where the soloists are one-to-a-part in the chorales) is somewhat uneven, but in the two solo cantatas (56 and 82), Jan Opalach is magnificent and is excellently supported by Rifkin and his group. *Der Friede sei mit dir* (158) is much more of a rarity but is hardly less rewarding. On the companion disc the performance of *Gottes Zeit* (the so-called *Actus tragicus*) has considerable merit. *Aus der Tiefen* (131) is hardly less fine and the singers are all first class. As elsewhere in this series, one feels the need for greater weight, but overall this is a worthwhile reissue.

Cantatas 56; 82; 158

☛ *** DG **Surround Sound SACD** 474 5052. Quasthoff, Berlin Bar. Sol., Kussmaul

Here is one of the most beautiful Bach cantata records in the catalogue. Thomas Quastoff has the warmest bass-baritone voice you could possibly imagine, and his performance of the famous *Ich habe genug* is second to none (even remembering the many famous past recordings). His phrasing is wonderfully musical, and Rainer Kussmaul and his Berlin Baroque Soloists, playing modern instruments with authentic manners, accompany him with comparable warmth and style. The splendid oboe soloist is Albrecht Mayer. The recording is splendid, but if you have four-channel SACD facilities with back speakers, the added realism with a feeling of sitting within the ambience of the Berlin Dahlem Jesus-Christus-Kirche is uncannily real, and it brings an added depth to the voice as well as spaciousness to the accompaniment.

Cantatas 61; 147; Magnificat

(*) TDK **DVD DV-ADCNH. Korondi, Schäfer, Fink, Bostridge, Maltman, Arnold Schoenberg Ch., VCM, Harnoncourt

'Glorious Bach!', as this record is described, is an apt title both for the music and for the performances under Harnoncourt at his most electrifying; but inexcusably sloppy presentation on DVD seriously undermines this issue. This Advent concert of two seasonal cantatas and the *Magnificat*, recorded live at the beautiful baroque Kloster Melk Monastery, comes with only three tracks lasting respectively 16, 32 and 29 minutes. This is the more absurd given that *Cantata 147* contains the best loved of all Bach cantata movements, *Jesu, joy of man's desiring*. Did no one in the TDK team conceive of any purchaser wanting to go straight to that favourite item? This flawed presentation seems perversely designed to turn newcomers off DVD, and is the more frustrating when the performances are so fine. With perceptive camerawork Harnoncourt's face is highlighted at the start of each item, his eyes bulging wide, mouth open and eyebrows raised, a man obsessed, wildly determined to get his singers and players to bring out the drama of the music. The Arnold Schoenberg Choir, some 40-strong for the cantatas, is augmented to 60 or so for the *Magnificat*, singing with fervour throughout. Anna Korondi's creamy tone is nicely contrasted with the fresh, bright tones of the first soprano, Christine Schäfer. Unlike the others, Korondi appears only in the *Magnificat*. In slow movements Harnoncourt keeps a characteristic touch of abrasiveness in his period style, but these are highly enjoyable performances which come like a breath of fresh air.

Cantata 63: Excerpts: 'Bach in Rehearsal'

(N) **(*) Arthaus **DVD** 100 292. Monteverdi Ch., E. Bar. Sol., Gardiner (V/D: Manfred Waffender)

This hour-long DVD offers an illuminating mixture of rehearsal and interview, with Gardiner at his most forthcoming in this recording, made during the preparations in 2000 for his monumental Bach pilgrimage, covering all the cantatas. His message both in his rehearsals (held at the EMI Studios in Abbey Road) and in the interviews is to bring out the fantasy, wit and humour which, he insists, 'flies out of the window' if Bach's music is performed in a heavily Germanic style. Gardiner describes how in early childhood he developed his love of Bach, thanks to the devotion of his parents, giving detailed insight into the cantata being rehearsed, No. 63, *Christen, ätzet diesen Tag*, celebrating the first day of Christmas. The DVD ends with a complete performance of the cantata's magnificent final chorus, and one wonders why Gardiner did not take the opportunity to record and film the whole cantata.

Cantata 82: Ich habe genug

☛ (M) (***) EMI mono 5 62807-2. Hotter, Philh. O, Bernard – BRAHMS: *Lieder ***

One of the greatest cantata performances ever. Glorious singing from Hans Hotter and wonderfully stylish accompanying from Anthony Bernard and the Philarmonia. This 1950 mono recording was never reissued on LP and it sounds vividly present in its current remastering. Moreover, EMI have found some extra Brahms songs to add to the coupling.

Cantatas (i) 82; (i-iii) 159; (ii) 170

✪ (N) *** Australian Decca Eloquence (ADD) 476 2684. ASMF, Marriner; with (i) Shirley-Quirk; (ii) J. Baker; (iii) Tear

Classic accounts of three cantatas, including *Seher, wir geh'n gen Jerusalem* (159), one of Bach's most inspired works. Particularly glorious is the meditation *Es ist vollbracht* ('It is finished'), with its poignant oboe obbligato (played by Rachel Lord). Both Dame Janet Baker and John Shirley-Quirk are in marvellous voice, as they are in Nos. 82 and 170 – hardly less inspired works and performances. Indeed, this collection of cantatas is among the finest in the catalogue and is well worth seeking out. The mid-1960s recordings are of Decca's best vintage quality.

(i) Cantatas 82; 199. (ii) Double Concerto for Oboe & Violin, BWV 1060

*** Priory/Carus 83 302. (i) Kirkby; (ii) Arften, Von der Golz; Freiburg Bar. Ens., Golz

Emma Kirkby's outstandingly fine account of *Ich habe genug* easily ranks alongside the highly praised baritone versions of Hans Hotter and John Shirley-Quirk. This cantata with its lovely transverse flute introduction (beautifully played here by Karl Kaiser) suits Kirkby's sublimely pure soprano voice admirably, and this is claimed to be the first recording of the present E minor version. Kirkby earlier recorded the two principal arias, the lovely *Schlummert ein* as well as *Ich habe genug*, and here her radiant performances are matched by the fresh and stylish playing of the Freiburg Baroque Ensemble with Gottfried von der Golz directing from the violin. What is remarkable about the coupling, *Mein Herz schwimmt im Blut*, is not only the lyrical beauty of the arias, but the way this great baroque soprano invests the recitatives with comparable feeling. Here the obbligato is for oboe, and Katherina

Arften is most sensitive in this role while, as a refreshing interlude, she joins the leader and conductor von der Golz in the engaging *Double Concerto*, BWV 1060. The accompaniments could hardly be bettered, and the recording ambience and balance are just about perfect. A disc that should be in every comprehensive Bach cantata collection.

Cantatas (i) *82; 202 (Wedding);* (ii) *208 (Hunt)*
(B) **(*) Hyp. Dyad CDD 22041 (2). Kirkby; (i) Thomas, Taverner Players, Parrott; (ii) J. Smith, S. Davies, George, Parley of Instruments, Goodman

In the much-recorded BMV 82, *Ich habe genug*, David Thomas gives a good but not inspired account of the solo part, and although the odd intonation blemish is of little importance, memories of Hotter, Souzay, Fischer-Dieskau and others are not banished. Kirkby is much more successful in the *Wedding Cantata* (*Weichet nur*) and as usual delights the listener, though some may feel that the excellent Taverner Players under Parrott could bring greater flair and lightness of touch to this felicitous score. The performance of the *Hunt Cantata*, however, is excellent in every way. The cantata is rich in melodic invention of the highest quality and is well served by excellent soloists (Kirkby again standing out) and first-class instrumental playing. As in the other works, the recording is natural and well balanced. The only snag is the short measure on the second disc (just over 43 minutes), but Kirkby's delightful singing more than compensates.

(i) *Cantata 147;* (ii) *Chorales & Chorale Preludes for Advent & Christmas, BWV 22/601, 36/659, 40/612, 65/603, 104/711, 121/611, 140/645, 151/609, 227/610, 248/700, 294/605, 368/729. 6 Motets, BWV 225/230*
(N) (B) ** EMI Gemini (ADD) 5 86342-2 (2). King's College, Cambridge, Ch., Willcocks; with (i) Ameling, J. Baker, Partridge, Shirley-Quirk, ASMF; (ii) A. Davis or Willcocks (organ)

These are early recordings made by EMI in King's College Chapel, and the choral focus is not particularly clean – most noticeably in the opening chorus of the *Cantata*. This is the work which features the famous chorale, *Jesu, joy of man's desiring*, which comes over freshly; but perhaps the highlight is the dramatic bass aria with trumpets – so well sung by John Shirley-Quirk. The idea of combining sung chorales with the associated organ chorale prelude was pioneered by Willcocks. It is effective enough, but the most impressive performances here are of the six *Motets*, recorded in 1967 and 1970. These represent an older style of Bach performance; however, with their fresh attack and clean rhythms, and with no accompanying instruments (except in *Lobet den Herrn*, which has a continuo), they are undistractingly enjoyable, except for period-performance specialists. The characteristic timbre of the Cambridge trebles is quite well caught, with the stereo spead underlining the antiphonal double-choir effects of *Singet den Herrn*.

Cantatas 158; 203. Arias & Chorales from Cantatas 8; 13; 73; 123; 157; 159
(M) *** EMI 5 67202-2. Fischer-Dieskau, St Hedwig's Cathedral Ch., Schwalbé, Nicolet, Rampal, Koch, Poppen, Picht-Axenfeld, Veyron-Lacroix, BPO, Forster

An outstanding collection, mostly from 1958. For its reissue EMI have added the secular cantata, *Amore traditore*, which dates from 1960, and the excerpts from *Cantata 123*, recorded

a decade later. Fischer-Dieskau, in splendid voice, here sings two complete cantatas plus six individual arias, usually with accompanying chorale. Their range of pitch is wide, of emotion still wider, yet the great baritone proves time and time again that he is absolutely at home in this field. The choir and orchestra under Karl Forster give him excellent support, and the list of obbligato soloists is full of star names, including Aurèle Nicolet and Rampal. The early stereo lends a convincingly spacious realism to what was already a finely balanced ensemble, and the CD transfer is admirable. Full texts and translations are included.

Cantatas 199; 202. Arias from Cantatas 68; 208
*** Testament (ADD) SBT 1178. Schwarzkopf, Philh. O, Dart
– MOZART: *Ch'io mi scordi di te?* (***)

Testament have here gathered together Schwarzkopf recordings made in 1955–8 that for various reasons were never published. What is clear is the superb quality of the singing here, with Sidney Sutcliffe, the principal oboe of the Philharmonia, matching Schwarzkopf's artistry in some of his obbligato solos. It is especially fascinating to compare the two versions (in German) of 'Sheep may safely graze', recorded a year apart in 1957 and 1958 – the second one far more dramatic in the recitative, and generally more freely expressive. The version here of *Cantata 199*, recorded only two days before the one included on the EMI Références issue (67206-2 – see above), is also more romantically expressive at a rather broader speed, a change in the opposite direction. The poised Schwarzkopf predominates, but the vehement Schwarzkopf also repeatedly comes through vividly, directly reflecting the singer's strong, positive character. Excellent transfers.

Cantatas 199; 202; 209
(BB) *** Naxos 8.550431. Wagner, Capella Istropolitana, Brembeck

Mein Herz schwimmt im Blut (BWV 199) comes from Bach's Weimar years, and Friederike Wagner proves both sympathetic and lively; and both *Weichet nur, betrübte Schatten*, popularly known as the '*Wedding Cantata*', and 209, *Non sà che sia dolore*, are given thoroughly enjoyable performances. Not for devotees of authentic-performance practice, but enjoyable for those who prefer a more traditional approach. Decent recording too.

Cantatas 202; 210 (Wedding Cantatas). Cantata 82 (excerpt): Ich habe genug. *Arias (attrib.):* Bist du bei mir *(BWV 508, probably by Gottfried Stölzel);* Gedenke doch, mein Geist *(BWV 509, Anon.)*
☞ *** O-L 455 972-2. Kirkby, AAM, Hogwood

This is among the most delightful of all the records of Bach's solo secular cantatas. Emma Kirkby, in her freshest voice, is ideally cast – as the lovely opening aria, *Weichet nur*, from the more famous of the two *Wedding Cantatas*, immediately shows. Her singing is no less ravishing in *Schlummert ein* from BWV 82, *Schweigt, ihr Flöten* ('Hush, you flutes' – Bach here isn't meaning to be taken seriously) from BWV 210, or the most famous 'Bach aria' which is not written by Bach, *Bist du bei mir*. The accompaniments from Hogwood and his Academy of Ancient Music could not have a lighter touch or more finesse, and the obbligato playing (of which there is a great deal) could not be more sensitive or more fluent. What a long way period-instrument playing has come towards beguiling the ear! The recording is most natural and very well balanced indeed.

Cantata 208 (Hunt Cantata)

**(*) Hyp. CDA 66169. Smith, Kirkby, Davis, George, Parley of Instruments, Goodman

This is a cantata rich in melodic invention of the highest quality. The performance has the benefit of excellent soloists and first-class instrumental playing. However, the measure is short compared with its competitors.

Cantatas 211 (Coffee Cantata); 212 (Peasant Cantata)

*** O-L 417 621-2. Kirkby, Covey-Crump, Thomas, AAM, Hogwood

(N) (B) ** Australian Ph. Eloquence 476 2758. Varady, Baldin, Fischer-Dieskau, ASMF, Marriner

Emma Kirkby is particularly appealing in the *Coffee Cantata* and her father is admirably portrayed by David Thomas. Hogwood opts for single strings, and some may find they sound thin; however, there is a corresponding gain in lightness and intimacy. The recording is altogether first class.

Surprisingly, Julia Varady is the weak link in the Philips performance (reissued on Australian Eloquence); her account of the aria, *Heute noch, liebe Vater*, from the *Coffee Cantata* is curiously wanting in subtlety and delicacy. There are, of course, many good things from Fischer-Dieskau, and Marriner's direction is most enjoyable, but even the good early digital recording is not enough for a strong recommendation.

Major choral works

Christmas Oratorio, BWV 248; Mass in B min., BWV 232; St John Passion, BWV 245; St Matthew Passion, BWV 244

☛ (B) *** DG 469 769-2 (9). Soloists, Monteverdi Ch., E. Bar. Sol., Gardiner

All these performances are among our primary choices for these works, and this bargain box in DG's Collectors' Edition cannot be too highly recommended. The documentation is excellent, although no translations are included.

Christmas Oratorio, BWV 248

*** TDK **DVD** DV-BACHO (2). McFadden, Fink, Genz, Henschel, Monteverdi Ch., E. Bar. S, Gardiner

*** DG 423 232-2 (2). Rolfe Johnson, Argenta, Von Otter, Blochwitz, Bär, Monteverdi Ch., E. Bar. Sol., Gardiner

*** BIS CD 941/2. Frimmer, Mera, Türk, Kooy, Bach Coll., Japan, Suzuki

*** Decca 458 838-2 (2). Bott, Chance, Agnew, King, George, New L. Cons., Pickett

(B) *** EMI (ADD) double forte 5 69503-2 (2). Ameling, Baker, Tear, Fischer-Dieskau, King's College, Cambridge, Ch., ASMF, Ledger

**(*) HM HMC 901630/1 (2). (i) Roschmann, Scholl, Gura, Hager; (ii) Rubens, Kiehr, Fink, Turk, Kooy; Berlin RIAS Chamber Ch., Alte Musik Ac., Jacobs

(BB) **(*) Regis RRC 2004 (2). Russell, Padmore, Wyn-Rogers, George, The Sixteen, Christophers

Recorded live in the beautiful Herdekirche in Weimar, Gardiner conducts an electrifying account of the *Christmas Oratorio*. This was in December 1999, at the beginning of his Bach Pilgrimage year, and he vividly communicates his own exhilaration over the experience in prospect. Characteristically, the performance is brisk and light in fast numbers, yet deeply meditative in the great slow arias, with Bernarda Fink especially moving in her contributions. The high tenor, Stephan Genz, sings with no sense of strain, delivering his recitatives from the pulpit, and the bass, Dietrich Henschel, is

strong and incisive, with Clairon McFadden completing an outstanding quartet of soloists. Choir and orchestra are also in superb form. Each of the discs offers not only three cantatas but also documentaries, one on the Bach Cantata Pilgrimage and the second on Bach in Saxony and Thuringia, with a visit to the St Thomas church in Leipzig where Bach was cantor.

The freshness of the singing and playing in the DG CD set is also a constant pleasure. Far more than usual, one registers the joyfulness of the work, from the trumpets and timpani at the start onwards. Anthony Rolfe Johnson makes a pointful and expressive Evangelist, and also outstanding is Anne Sofie von Otter with her natural gravity and exceptionally beautiful mezzo. Beauty of tone consistently marks the singing of Nancy Argenta, Hans-Peter Blochwitz and Olaf Bär. The sound is full and atmospheric.

As in his recordings of the Bach cantatas, Masaaki Suzuki directs an exceptionally fresh and alert reading of the *Christmas Oratorio*, bringing out the joy of Bach's inspiration, with outstandingly crisp singing from the chorus. Speeds are often fast, but in the beautiful cradle-song, *Schlafe mein Liebster*, relaxed pacing allows full expressiveness, here with Yoshikazu Mera as a characterful male alto soloist. Mera in florid writing does not always avoid the intrusive 'h', but that is one of the few blemishes in the solo singing, with Gerd Türk a fine Evangelist and Peter Kooy a firmly focused bass. Warm, atmospheric sound, though with the choir behind the instruments in the main choruses. This makes a fine alternative to the Gardiner version.

Philip Pickett takes an intimate, relatively small-scale view. Textures are transparent and refinement is the keynote, but this Bach performance also has plenty of vigour, with generally brisk speeds and sprung rhythms. The scale is reflected in the refined singing of Paul Agnew as the Evangelist, but the soprano Catherine Bott and the counter-tenor Michael Chance are the soloists who stand out, not just from the rest but from most rivals in other versions. The tenor Andrew King is crisp and agile in his arias and, though Michael George is not as cleanly focused as he might be, his is a strong, sensitive contribution. Atmospheric recording which sets the limited forces in a helpful acoustic.

With generally brisk tempi (controversially so in Janet Baker's cradle-song, *Schlafe mein Liebster*, in Part 2) Philip Ledger's 1976 King's performance is an intensely refreshing account which grows more winning the more one hears it, helped by four outstanding and stylish soloists. The King's acoustic gives a warm background to the nicely styled performance of choir and orchestra and, although in the CD transfer the choral focus is not absolutely clean, the sound overall is attractively balanced.

René Jacobs, with excellent soloists, offers a fresh, alert reading of the *Christmas Oratorio*, generally well paced but with one idiosyncrasy that for many will be crucial. Though in big choruses Jacobs tends to favour speeds faster than usual, light and crisp, he regularly adopts slow, even ponderous speeds for the chorales, with pauses between lines, reminding one of the old tradition when big choirs were used for this work. He also favours speeds on the slow side for such key numbers as the great cradle-song of Part 2, *Schlafe mein Liebster*, movingly sung by the counter-tenor, Andreas Scholl. The extra time-length involved means that the break between the two CDs comes before the end of Part 3, leaving three numbers to be included on the second disc.

Harry Christophers conducts a crisp and sympathetic reading, very well played and sung, which at speeds generally a little slower than Gardiner's does not quite match that rival in exhilaration and intensity. But it remains an enjoyable performance. He has a first-rate quartet of soloists – where Gardiner has different soloists for the arias from those for the Christmas narrative – with the tenor, Mark Padmore, particularly impressive not just in the arias but as the Evangelist. Good, atmospheric recording, with trumpet and drums dramatically prominent. Now reissued by Regis at bargain price, this is well worth considering.

Easter Oratorio, BWV 249; Cantata 66: Erfreut euch, ihr Herzen
*** HM HMC 901513. Schlick, Wessel, Taylor, Kooy, Coll. Voc., Herreweghe

Easter Oratorio; Magnificat in D, BWV 243
(M) *** Decca (ADD) 466 420-2. Ameling, Watts, Krenn, Krause, V . Ac. Ch., Stuttgart CO, Münchinger

Bach's *Easter Oratorio* derives from a secular cantata, more than once revised. It opens with a joyful *Sinfonia* and an *Adagio* with oboe solo (very well played in the Herreweghe account), followed by a lively chorus ('Come hasten, come running, ye swift feet') with trumpets, but then it depends very much on the soloists, who blend beautifully together in their introductory recitativo before taking their individual roles with distinction – as Mary Magdalene, Peter and John respectively. The chorus and trumpets then return to end the work joyfully. The apt coupling of the *Easter Cantata*, BWV 66, with its lovely closing *Alleluja* completes a disc which is fresh and vivid and will be hard to surpass.

The Decca coupling is one of Münchinger's very best records. The *Easter Oratorio* and *Magnificat* share the same group of soloists – and very impressive they are. Münchinger tends to stress the breadth and spaciousness of both works, and the contribution of the Stuttgart orchestra and the Vienna Academy Choir could hardly be finer, while the vintage Decca recordings have captured the detail with admirable clarity and naturalness.

Epiphany Mass (1740) (includes Cantatas BWV 65 & BWV 180; Missa brevis in F, BWV 233)
*** DG 457 631-2 (2). Monoyios, Davidson, Daniels, Harvey, Gabrieli Cons. & Players, Congregational Choirs of Freiburg & Dresden, McCreesh

Paul McCreesh has assembled here almost three hours of music to represent what might have been heard at Epiphany celebrations in the St Thomas church in Leipzig around 1740, when Bach was in charge. It transforms one's response to the *Missa brevis* in F, for example (in the Lutheran form of *Kyrie* and *Gloria* alone), to hear it like this instead of comparing it unfavourably with the great *B minor Mass*. So too with the cantatas, carols, chorales and organ pieces which make up the varied sequence, all performed superbly.

(i) Magnificat in D; (ii) Violin Concerto 2
*** Sony DVD SVD 45983. BPO, Karajan; with (i) Blegen, Mollinari, Araiza, Holl, Berlin RIAS Chamber Ch.; (ii) Mutter (Director: Humphrey Burton)

There are few better examples on DVD than this of a conductor's magnetism being almost tangible. It is apparent during Anne-Sophie Mutter's fine performance of the *Violin Concerto*, although she is given the limelight; but in the *Magnificat* one can feel the whole orchestra, chorus and soloists responding to the conductor, while Karajan's actual movements are minimal, his face all but impassive. This is gloriously old-fashioned Bach with a large orchestra, and when the camera dwells on the blazing trumpets, one feels almost able to reach out and touch them. It is a thrilling performance, richly and vividly recorded, and one feels right in the middle of it.

Magnificat in D, BWV 243
☛ *** BIS CD 1011. Persson, Nonoshita, Tachikawa, Türk, Urano, Bach Coll., Japan, Suzuki – KUHNAU: *Magnificat;* ZELENKA: *Magnificats in C & D* ***
*** Chan. 0518. Kirkby, Bonner, Chance, Ainsley, Varcoe, Coll. Mus. 90, Hickox – VIVALDI: *Gloria* ***
*** EMI 7 54283-2. Hendricks, Murray, Rigby, Heilmann, Hynninen, ASMF Ch. & O, Marriner – VIVALDI: *Gloria* ***
(BB) *** Warner Apex (ADD) 0927 48681-2. Yakar, J. Smith, Finnilä, Rolfe Johnson, Van Dam, Lausanne Vocal & Instrumental Ens., Corboz – VIVALDI: *Gloria & Kyrie* ***
(BB) *** Naxos 8.554056. Crookes, Whitaker, Trevor, Robinson, Gedge, Oxford Schola Cantorum, N. CO, Ward – VIVALDI: *Gloria* ***

Magnificat in D; Cantata 21
(M) *** Virgin 5 61833-2. De Reyghere, Jacobs, Prégardien, Lika, Netherlands Chamber Ch., La Petite Bande, Kuijken

Magnificat in E flat, BWV 243a; Cantata 10: Meine Seele erhebt den Herren
(N) *** EuroArts DVD 2053419. York, Bartosz, Dürmüller, Mertens, Amsterdam Bar. Ch. & O, Koopman – KUHNAU: *Magnificat*

Magnificat in E flat, BWV 243a
(B) *** Double Decca (ADD) 458 370-2 (2). Palmer, Watts, Tear, Roberts, King's College Ch., ASMF, Ledger – J. C. BACH: *Magnificat;* A. SCARLATTI: *St Cecilia Mass* ***

Koopman chooses the earlier, E flat major version of the *Magnificat*, and it makes a magnificent début on DVD, recorded at St Thomas's Church, Leipzig, where, like its Kuhnau coupling, it was first heard. It differs only marginally from the later version, although the *Esurientes* (for contralto solo) has a delightful obbligato for a pair of recorders – beautifully played here. The performance is thrilling, with its bolder E flat major trumpets and splendidly incisive choral contribution. The soloists too are first class, both individually and as a team. Like Suzuki, Koopman offers the Kuhnau setting and includes also a fine performance of the cantata *Meine Seele erhebt den Herren*, which has associations with the more ambitious work. The camera is used sensibly and follows the music from soloists to chorus to instrumentalists. The usual visual problem, that the sound stays the same whatever the camera angle chosen, remains a little disconcerting, but one adjusts when the performance is so vividly alive and the sound very fine indeed. The cantata too is very successful in all respects

Masaaki Suzuki's account of the better-known D major version of the *Magnificat* with his Japanese forces is quite exhilarating and is the most recommendable now available. He has good soloists, including the Swedish soprano Miah Persson and the German tenor Gerd Türk, as well as some impressive Japanese singers; the instrumental playing is of altogether outstanding quality. Ideal for those who don't now respond either to traditional modern-instrument performances or to authentic period orchestras, for Suzuki's players have the virtues of both: the warmth and vitality of the former and the clarity of the latter.

Both Richard Hickox and Neville Marriner couple the *Magnificat* with the popular D major *Gloria*, RV 589, of Vivaldi, and for collectors seeking this coupling the clear choice is between period and modern instruments. Those who like the former will gravitate towards Hickox, who directs a most musical account and has the benefit of such fine singers as Emma Kirkby, Michael Chance and Stephen Varcoe, and good Chandos recording. Marriner's performance with the Academy is well paced and is executed with precision and fine musical intelligence. No quarrel with the soloists either or with the splendidly warm and present recording. Both can be recommended with confidence.

Splendidly framed by the vigorous opening and closing choruses with their resplendent trumpets, Kuijken's reissued version of the *Magnificat* from 1988 performed by the excellent Netherlanders and La Petite Bande makes a strong mid-priced recommendation. There are some first-class contributions from Greta de Reyghere and Christoph Prégardien, with lovely singing from the soprano and a finely matched oboe obbligato in the aria, *Quia respexit*; there are moments of vulnerable intonation from the oboe, but this is a small blemish. The choral singing is both warmly expressive (especially in *Suscepit Israel*) and as lightly articulated as you could wish. The coupling is one of Bach's most expansive and celebrated Weimar cantatas, *Ich hatte viel Bekümmernis*, which again gives the soprano and tenor plenty of opportunities for *espressivo*, individually and in a duo, after which the trumpets return for the intricate closing chorus of praise. Above all, there is a sense of breadth and majesty fully worthy of Bach. A highly recommendable disc in every way.

Corboz's 1974 recording was the first bargain version that could be strongly recommended. Now it has to compete with the digital Naxos competitor, but stands up well at its Apex price. The professional singers of the Lausanne Choir are generally admirable and the soloists make an excellent team, with the soprano solos from Rachel Yakar and Jennifer Smith particularly beautiful. The music-making is splendidly vigorous and spontaneous, and the CD transfer of the excellent original recording is vividly managed. The Vivaldi couplings are equally recommendable, and Warner have restored the programme notes for this super-bargain reissue.

The fresh and lively Naxos version of the *Magnificat* is now attractively re-coupled with an outstanding version of Vivaldi's *Gloria*, also using modern instruments. None of the soloists from the choir, all of them stylish, is identified on the reissue; our listing of their names is retained from the original issue.

Philip Ledger's account of the E flat version, recorded by Argo in the late 1970s, is also most attractive, highly recommendable if boys' voices are preferred in the chorus, and is excellent value. The soloists are first class. This now comes as a Double Decca, with Alessandro Scarlatti's splendid *St Cecilia Mass* added, also performed with striking vigour and moving expressive feeling.

St Mark Passion (reconstructed Gomme, with recitatives and turbas by Keiser)
**(*) Gaudeamus CDGAX 237 (2). Ovenden, Mirfin, Gomme, Towers, Gilchrist, Thompson, Gonville & Caius College, Cambridge, Ch., Cambridge Bar. Camerata, Webber –
KEISER: *Laudate pueri Domini* **(*)

Markus Passion (1731) (reconstructed Koopman)
(N) *** Chall. **DVD** CCDVD 72141. Prégardien, Kooy, York, Landauer, Agnew, Mertens, Amsterdam Bar. Ch. & O, Koopman

The *St Mark Passion* is lost, and for many years scholars have been conjecturing as to whether its music had found its way into other Bach works. An obvious choice was the *Cantata*, BWV 198, the so-called *Trauerode*, and eventually a setting was cobbled together, based on this cantata plus excerpts from other major sources. The recitatives do not exist either, so these, plus the turba choruses, were purloined from a setting of the *St Mark Passion* by R. Keiser (or N. Bruhns) – it is not clear who actually was its composer.

Ton Koopman has started afresh, abandoning the *Trauerode*, drawing on Bach's music written before Easter 1731 and composing his own recitatives to the text by Christian Friederick Henrici, alias Picander, with the soloists participating in the words of the arias. The result is a triumphant success: a modest work, setting the Passion story with an appealing simplicity, but one which is very convincing in the present splendid performance. Indeed, it is difficult to imagine it being bettered, with superb soloists and Christoph Prégardien as Evangelist telling the story and Peter Kooy as Christ. There are only a limited number of arias but they are finely sung by the starry cast, and the chorus is as dedicated as it is excellent. The performance has all the virtues of a live performance, and the recording and camerawork against the beautiful backcloth of the Chiesa di San Simpliciano, Milan, is well handled. A most rewarding and repeatable experience.

Andor Gomme, editor of the edition used in Cambridge, explains his decision to adapt the recitatives from the *St Mark Passion* of Reinhard Keiser, Bach's senior by a decade, to fill in the narrative sections. The result in no way rivals the two great Bach *Passions* we know, but it offers much fine music normally buried. This performance may not be ideal – with the period instruments of the Cambridge Baroque Camerata often rough – but the Caius Chorus is fresh and alert, as is the solo singing, with Jeremy Ovenden a clear-toned Evangelist, Ruth Gomme the bright, fresh soprano and the countertenor William Towers excellent in the alto arias and such roles as that of Judas. Keiser's ambitious setting of *Psalm 112* provides a welcome makeweight. Warmly atmospheric sound.

(i) *Masses (Missae breves): in F, BWV 233; in G, BWV 236. Trio Sonata in C, transposed to D, BWV 529*
*** Chan. 0653. (i) Argenta, Chance, Padmore, Harvey, instrumental soloists; Purcell Qt

Masses (Missae breves), in A, BWV 234; in G min., BWV 235
*** Chan. 0642. Gritton, Blaze, Padmore, Harvey, Purcell Qt

Masses (Missae breves), BWV 233–6; Magnificat in D, BWV 243
*** Ph. 438 873-2 (2). Bonney, Remmert, Trost, Bär, Berlin RIAS Chamber Ch., C. P. E. Bach CO, Schreier

Masses (Missae breves), BWV 233–4; Kyrie eleison in F, BWV 233a
*** Häns. CD 92.071. Brown, Schäfer, Danz, Taylor, Quasthoff, Schöne, Gächinger Kantorei, Budapest Franz Liszt CO, Bach Coll., Stuttgart, Rilling

Masses (Missae breves): BWV 235–6; Sancti in C; D; G; D, BWV 237–8, 240–41; Christe eleison in G min., BWV 242; Credo in unum Deum, BWV 1081

*** Häns. CD 92.072. Oelze, Ziesak, Danz, Remmert, Prégardien, Quasthoff, Gächinger Kantorei, Bach Coll., Stuttgart, Rilling

There have been various good modern-instrument performances of these so-called short or Lutheran Masses over the years, but the authentic period-instrument performances on Chandos must now take pride of place. Although the soloists provide the one-voice-to-a-part chorus, their voices blend so richly together that one is not conscious of any lack of body or contrast: indeed the effect is glorious, while in the F major work the vigorous trumpeting horns add to the joyfulness of the *Gloria* and *Cum Sancto Spiritu*. The solo singing is splendid, and the overall balance quite excellent. The first disc uses a *Trio Sonata* to act as a kind of extended opening sinfonia, and very effectively too. This is the CD to try first, and you will surely want the other one also.

The Schreier set can be warmly recommended too, for he also includes a fine, fresh account of the *Magnificat*. He has excellent soloists, notably Barbara Bonney and Olaf Bär, and the Philips digital sound is first class. Schreier uses a chamber chorus, and stylistically these modern-instrument performances show that he has absorbed much that is attractive from period-instrument practice, with his lively tempi and fresh orchestral textures. Moreover the ambience is particularly pleasing, bringing atmosphere without clouding detail.

The Masses on the first of the two Hänssler discs were recorded in the early 1990s and the *Kyrie in F*, BWV 233a, in 1999. Similarly, on the second, the recording of the *G minor*, BWV 235, was made in 1992 and the remaining recordings in 1999. These are eminently well recorded (and recommendable) accounts, with fine singing from Christine Oelze and Christoph Prégardien.

Mass in B min., BWV 232

*** DG 415 514-2 (2). Argenta, Dawson, Fairfield, Knibbs, Kwella, Hall, Nichols, Chance, Collin, Stafford, Evans, Milner, Murgatroyd, Lloyd-Morgan, Varcoe, Monteverdi Ch., E. Bar. Sol., Gardiner

*** BBC (ADD) BBCL 4062-2 (2). Hill, J. Baker, Pears, Shirley-Quirk, New Philh. Ch. and O, Giulini

(N) (M) *** Hyp. Dyad CDD 22051 (2). Ritter, Mrasek, Schloderer, Fraas, Rolfe Johnson, George, Tölz Boys' Ch., King's Cons. Ch., King's Cons., King

(N) (BB) *** EMI Gemini 5 86537-2 (2). Donath, Fassbaender, Ahnsjö, Hermann, Holl, Bav. R. Ch. & O, Jochum

(***) BBC mono BBCL 40087-2. Danco, Ferrier, Pears, Boyce, BBC Ch., Boyd Neel O, Enescu

(BB) *** Current Arts 47525-2 (2). Invernizzi, Dawson, Banditelli, Prégardien, Mertens, Swiss R. Ch., Lugano, Sonatori de la Gioiosa Marca, Fasano

(B) *** Virgin 2x1 5 61998-2 (2). Kirkby, Van Evera, Iconomou, Immler, Killan, Covey-Crump, D. Thomas, Soloists from Tölz Boys' Ch., Taverner Cons. & Players, Parrott

(BB) **(*) Naxos 8.550585/6. Wagner, Schäfer-Subrata, Koppelstetter, Schäfer, Elbert, Slovak Philharmonic Ch., Cappella Istropolitana, Brembeck

(B) **(*) Regis RRC 2002 (2). Dubosc, Denley, Bowman, Ainsley, George, The Sixteen & O, Christophers

Mass in B min., (i) (complete); (ii) (excerpts)

(M) (***) EMI mono 5 67207-2 (2). (i) Schwarzkopf, Höffgen, Gedda, Rehfuss, V. Singverein, Philh. O, Karajan; (ii) Schwarzkopf, Ferrier, VSO, Karajan

John Eliot Gardiner gives a magnificent account of the *B minor Mass*, one which attempts to keep within an authentic scale but which also triumphantly encompasses the work's grandeur. Gardiner masterfully conveys the majesty (with bells and censer-swinging evoked) simultaneously with a crisply resilient rhythmic pulse. The choral tone is luminous and powerfully projected. The regular solo numbers are taken by choir members making a cohesive whole. The recording is warmly atmospheric but not cloudy.

In the echoing acoustic of St Paul's Cathedral – remarkably well-tamed by the BBC engineers – Giulini conducts a spacious, dedicated reading. This was a City of London Festival event in 1972, and from first to last one breathes in the atmosphere of a great occasion, thanks not only to the inspired conductor but to a superb quartet of soloists, notably Dame Janet Baker, whose contributions shine out with heart-warming fervour. Peter Pears, then 62, is in fine, clear voice, as is the bass, John Shirley-Quirk, with the soprano, Jenny Hill, fresh and bright. The chorus is not so clearly focused as the soloists, particularly in the meditative numbers, yet in vigorous sections and in the great censer-swinging rhythms of the *Sanctus* the weight and bite of the singing come over thrillingly. Mindful no doubt of the cathedral's reverberant acoustic, Giulini adopts speeds on the broad side even for a traditional, large-scale performance, but soloists and chorus alike sustain them superbly, as do the orchestra, distinguished by such soloists as the horn-player Alan Civil, in the obbligato solo for the *Quoniam*. As an illuminating supplement an interview with Giulini by John Amis is included at the end.

With the distinctive continental tone of the Tölzer Boys, very different from their English counterparts, Robert King's vigorous and alert reading has extra freshness, with 24 boys set brightly against 12 of the King's Consort tenors and basses. The individual finesse of the boy singers is impressively demonstrated in the solos. This is a reading which consistently brings out the joy of Bach's inspiration, not least in the great celestial outbursts of the *Sanctus* and the final *Dona nobis pacem*. Warm, atmospheric recording.

Jochum's memorable, dedicated (1980) performance, marked by resilient rhythms, remains among the most completely satisfying versions even today. The choral singing – by far the most important element in this work – is superb and, though the soloists are variably balanced, they make a fine, clear-voiced team to leave Bach's inspired music resonating in the listener's memory. The digital recording is admirably spacious and clear. Documentation is just about adequate, but with no text.

In the BBC Legends series, the 1951 studio performance is indeed legendary. Suzanne Danco was in her prime, as were Kathleen Ferrier, Peter Pears and Bruce Boyce, Leslie Woodgate's BBC Chorus and, at the helm, the incomparable Georges Enescu. Menuhin pays tribute to his mentor in a moving note. The standards of the orchestral playing fall short of what one might expect in a modern commercial recording (the horn is somewhat tentative in the *Quoniam*) but the singing is glorious and the engineers have worked miracles on the sound which, though two-dimensional, is much better than one might expect. Even if you already have a modern stereo version of the *B minor Mass*, this is an essential supplement.

The Arts label offers a first-rate version at super-bargain price using period instruments. The five soloists are excellent, all with fresh young voices, and with Lynne Dawson radiant in *Laudamus te*. The Lugano Choir of Swiss Radio is outstanding too, with the elaborate counterpoint clean and transparent, thanks also to the recording. Fasano favours fast speeds in period style, giving a joyful lightness to *Et resurrexit*, and making the *Sanctus* happy rather than weighty.

Karajan's 1952 recording was a pioneering set, and the freshness and clarity of the mono sound are astonishing in this excellent EMI transfer. With Schwarzkopf at her most radiant, the quartet of soloists, then still young, stands comparison with any rival since and, though characteristically for the time Karajan adopts a broad speed for the great opening *Kyrie*, the performance is the more remarkable for its period in the briskness and clarity of choruses like the *Gloria*, with the *Sanctus* exhilarating in its combination of freshness and weight, leading to a light, crisp *Osanna*. The five fragmentary excerpts that come as a supplement, recorded at a rehearsal in 1950, are equally valuable, and not only because of Kathleen Ferrier's contribution alongside Schwarzkopf. Karajan's speeds in that 1950 rehearsal are a degree faster than in the studio recording of two years later.

Parrott, hoping to re-create even more closely the conditions Bach would have expected in Leipzig, adds to the soloists a ripieno group of five singers from the Taverner Consort for the choruses. Speeds are generally fast, with rhythms sprung to reflect the inspiration of dance; however, the inner darkness of the *Crucifixus*, for example, is conveyed intensely in its hushed tones, while the *Et resurrexit* promptly erupts with a power to compensate for any lack of traditional weight. Soloists are excellent, with reduction of vibrato still allowing sweetness as well as purity, and the recording, made in St John's, Smith Square, is both realistic and atmospheric.

The Naxos set offers a chamber-scale performance on modern instruments. The orchestral playing is first rate and the soloists are a reliable team, with the contralto, Martina Koppelstetter, outstanding in her two big solos, *Qui tollis* and *Agnus Dei*, the latter taken broadly with fine concentration. In the big extrovert moments like the opening of the *Kyrie* and the *Sanctus*, the chorus are bold and confident; at times elsewhere there is less bite, though one doesn't want to make too much of this; Brembeck's pacing is well judged, and this set is still very recommendable in the budget range.

Harry Christophers, with The Sixteen expanded to 26 singers, gives a fresh, direct period performance, marked by well-chosen speeds and bright choral singing. It wears its period manners easily and the stylistic plainness, less detailed in such matters as appoggiaturas, is certainly refreshing, but it rarely allows the sharply distinctive characterization which marks such versions as Gardiner's on DG. The great *Sanctus* lacks a little in gravity and the slightly distanced recording takes some of the impact from bright, vigorous movements, where trumpets are less forward than usual. The soloists make an excellent team, though Catherine Dubosc's vibrato is obtrusive at times.

Motets: *Singet dem Herrn ein Neues Lied; Der Geist hilft unser Schwachheit auf; Jesu, meine Freude; Fürchte dich nicht, ich bin bei dir; Komm, Jesu, komm!; Lobet den Herrn alle Heiden, BWV 225–30*

(M) *** Teldec 0630 17430-2. Stockholm Bach Ch., VCM, Harnoncourt

(N) *** DHM/BMG 05472 77368-2. Cantus Cöln, Junghänel

**(*) Hyp. CDA 66369. The Sixteen, Christophers

To Bach's motets, which include some of the greatest music he ever wrote for chorus, went the honour of being the first of his vocal music to be issued digitally in 1980. The Teldec recording is very successful indeed, beautifully fresh and clear, the acoustic attractively resonant without clouding detail, and the accompanying instrumental group giving discreet yet telling support. The vigour and joy of the singing come over splendidly. This is one of Harnoncourt's most impressive Bach records, while the Stockholm chorus show stamina as well as sympathy. At mid-price this must now be the prime recommendation for these six works.

There is some fine, expressive singing from the Cantus Cöln under Konrad Junghänel, whose control is flexible and his pacing well judged. They have the obvious colloquial advantage of singing in their own language; the instrumental accompaniment is discreet and supportive, and the recording well balanced and clear within a warm acoustic. But this is not as fine as the Harnoncourt disc.

Harry Christophers and The Sixteen give elegant readings, beautifully tuned and balanced, of the six principal motets, not as strongly characterized as Harnoncourt's but consistently refreshing and satisfying.

St John Passion, BWV 245

☛ *** TDK **DVD** DV-BAJPN. Türk, Midori Suzuki, Blaze, Urano, MacLeod, Bach Coll., Japan, Masaaki Suzuki (includes interview with Masaaki Suzuki)

☛ (BB) *** Naxos 8.557296 (2). Gilchrist, Barnays, Dougan, Littlewood, Bowman, Beale, Baldy, New College, Oxford, Ch., Coll. Novum, Higginbottom

*** DG 419 324-2 (2). Rolfe Johnson, Varcoe, Hauptmann & soloists, Monteverdi Ch., E. Bar. Sol., Gardiner

*** BIS CD 921/22. Schmithüsen, Mera, Türk, Sakurada, Hida, Urano, Kooy, Bach Coll., Japan, Suzuki

(BB) *** Regis RRC 2003 (2). Mark Ainsley, Bott, Agnew, Chance, King's College, Cambridge, Ch., Brandenburg Cons., Cleobury

*** Häns. CD 98.170 (3). Banse, Danz, Schade, Taylor, Goerne, Schmidt, Rilling, Stuttgart Gächinger Kantorei & Bach-Collegium, Rilling

(B) *** Virgin 5 62019-2 (2). Covey-Crump, D. Thomas, Bonner, Van Evera, Trevor, Taverner Cons. & Players, Parrott

Recorded in Suntory Hall, Tokyo, on 28 July 2000 – the day marking the 250th anniversary of Bach's death – this is an outstanding version on DVD of the *St John Passion*, a tribute to the work of Masaaki Suzuki in Japan. In a brief interview which comes as a supplement he comments on the intensive training in period performance he undertook in Holland, and this performance consistently demonstrates the vigour and sensitivity of his approach to Bach. The interpretation remains very similar to Suzuki's earlier CD account on BIS, with fresh, light textures and generally brisk speeds which yet allow for depth of feeling, and the sense of occasion is irresistible. Only Gerd Türk as the Evangelist is presented as a soloist in front of the choir, giving an achingly beautiful performance, with his profound involvement all the more evident when seen as well as heard. Türk also sings the tenor arias, and the other soloists, all first rate, also have double roles, singing in the sixteen-strong choir (4-4-4-4) before stepping forward when needed as soloists: Stephan MacLeod singing Christus as well as the bass arias, Chiyuki Urano singing Pilate and other incidental solos, Robin Blaze a superb alto soloist and the ravishing Midori Suzuki in the two soprano arias. The leaflet offers minimal information and no text, though on DVD one can opt for subtitles in either the original German or the English translation, but not both together.

The Naxos CD version of the *St John Passion*, with the choir of New College, Oxford, at budget price, offers an outstanding period performance which can stand comparison with any in the catalogue. The first distinctive point is that, following Bach's own practice at St Thomas's, only male voices are used, with the soprano arias sung by a boy treble. The choir itself is fresh and bright, singing incisively, with the crowd choruses vividly adding to the drama, helped by the natural balance. Higginbottom's speeds on the fast side follow period practice, except in relatively broad chorales. James Gilchrist is a superb Evangelist, fluent and expressive, and the main quartet of soloists makes a sensitive team, including the confidently firm-toned treble, Joe Littlewood, and the veteran counter-tenor, James Bowman, still in fine voice. The wind instruments of the Collegium Novum have a sharp edge, which brings out the agony implied in the accompaniment to the opening chorus, while the darkness of instrumentation in the great alto aria, *Es ist vollbracht*, adds to the poignancy of Bowman's singing.

Gardiner conducts an exhilarating performance. Speeds are regularly on the fast side but, characteristically, he consistently keeps a spring in the rhythm. Chorales are treated in contrasted ways, which may not please the more severe authenticists; but, as with so much of Gardiner's work, here is a performance using authentic scale and period instruments which speaks in the most vivid way to anyone prepared to listen, not just to the specialist. Soloists – regular contributors to Gardiner's team – are all first rate. Warm and atmospheric, yet clear and detailed recording.

Suzuki directs an urgently refreshing reading of the *St John Passion* on BIS, with fine singing from the chorus giving dramatic impact to the 'turba' choruses. The big choruses at beginning and end are beautifully sung too, though here the voices are set back behind the orchestra and are rather lightweight. Suzuki's feeling for the natural timing of numbers – generally on the fast side in the modern period manner – is impeccable, and the soloists make an excellent team, with Gerd Türk an outstanding Evangelist, light and clear.

Stephen Cleobury conducts a lively, well-paced reading using period instruments, with an excellent team of characterful soloists and with the fresh-toned choir of King's College Choir, including boy-trebles, adding dramatic bite. What specially distinguishes this set is that the alternative numbers which Bach wrote for the revival in 1725 are given in an appendix. John Mark Ainsley is a warmly expressive tenor Evangelist, nicely contrasted with the lighter-toned Paul Agnew, who sings the tenor arias. Among the others, Catherine Bott is warmer and more tenderly expressive than almost any latter-day rival, and the counter-tenor, Michael Chance, sounds in fuller, warmer voice here than in Gardiner's version, a question of recording balance, with the Cleobury performance setting the soloists close so as to counteract the reverberant acoustic of King's College Chapel. Most enjoyable.

The Rilling version on Hänssler uses rather larger forces than in most period versions and, paradoxically, modern instruments are used in period style, using today's higher pitch. Speeds in recitative tend to be broader in a relatively traditional way, but that allows the soloists, notably the superb Evangelist, Michael Schade, to bring out the meaning of the words most vividly, with an electrifying sense of

drama, most important in this work. The other soloists are outstanding too, all of them young singers with firm, characterful voices, and they sound particularly well on record. The third disc comes as a (free) appendix, giving not just the five alternative numbers which Bach wrote for the 1725 revival but also detailed changes in various numbers, setting fragments from the original against the amended versions. These are explained in a spoken commentary between items, so that it is vital for English-speaking listeners to get the English-language version, instead of Hänssler's main German issue, which also has a single-language booklet of notes.

The alternative Hänssler set under Eckhard Weyand offers a crisp and fresh reading, using modern instruments, very well recorded. The manner is plain, the speeds are well chosen, and it is interesting to hear Christine Schäfer at the very beginning of her career, recorded in 1990. Otherwise, at full price hardly a first choice (CD 98.968).

Andrew Parrott's version offers an intimate performance that yet has sharp focus and plenty of power. Though speeds are generally fast and rhythms resilient, he allows himself a broader tempo for the great final chorus and the concluding Chorale, giving them an aptly expressive weight. The Taverner Consort here has only two choristers per part, with soloists included among the singers, while Rogers Covey-Crump as the Evangelist, light and alert, also sings the tenor arias, and David Thomas as Jesus sings the bass arias. The soprano soloists, Tessa Bonner and Emily van Evera, are both bright-toned and boyish, while the alto, Caroline Trevor, has a counter-tenor-like timbre. In compensation for any lack of weight from the scale of forces, the recording balance keeps the voices well forward, both in solo and in choral work. An outstanding recommendation for those who fancy an intimate but powerfully dramatic view.

St John Passion (in English)

⚙ (B) *** Double Decca (ADD) 443 859-2 (2). Pears, Harper, Hodgson, Tear, Howell, Shirley-Quirk, Wandsworth School Boys' Ch., ECO, Britten

Britten characteristically refuses to follow any set tradition, whether baroque, Victorian or whatever, and, with greater extremes of tempo than is common (often strikingly fast), the result makes one listen afresh. The soloists are all excellent, Heather Harper radiant, and the Wandsworth School Boys' Choir reinforces the freshness of the interpretation. A superb bargain.

St Matthew Passion, BWV 244

*** DG 474 200-2 (2). York, Gooding, Ko\u017eena, Bickley, Padmore, Gilchrist, Harvey, Loges, Gabrieli Players, McCreesh

*** DG 427 648-2 (3). Rolfe Johnson, Schmidt, Bonney, Monoyios, Von Otter, Chance, Crook, Bär, Hauptmann, Monteverdi Ch., E. Bar. Sol., Gardiner

*** BIS CD 1000/1002 (3). Türk, Kooy, Argenta, Blaze, Sakurada, Urano, Sollek-Avella, Hagiwara, Odagawa, Bach Coll., Japan, Ch. & O, Suzuki

*** Teldec 8573-81036-2 (3). Fink, Magnus, Röschmann, C. Schäfer, Goerne, Henschel, Prégardien, Schade, M. Schäfer, Widmer, Schoenberg Ch., VCM, Harnoncourt

*** Channel CCS 11397 (3). Türk, Smits, Zomer, Scholl, Mammel, Kooy, St Bavo Cathedral, Haarlem Boys' Ch., Netherlands Bach Society Bar. O and Ch., Van Veldhoven

(M) *** EMI (ADD) 5 67538-2 [67542-2] (3). Pears, Fischer-Dieskau, Schwarzkopf, Ludwig, Gedda, Berry, Hampstead Parish Church Ch., Philh. Ch. & O, Klemperer

(BB) *** Naxos 8.550832/4. Mukk, Gáti, Németh, Verebits, Köves, Cser, Korpás, Kiss, Csenki, Hungarian R. Children's Ch., Hungarian Festival Ch. & State SO, Oberfrank

**(*) HM HMC 901676.78 (3). Bostridge, Selig, Rubens, Scholl, Güra, Henschel, Schola Cantorum Cantate Domino, Ghent Coll. Voc. Ch. & O, Herreweghe

(M) **(*) Ph. Trio 473 263-2 (3). Van der Meel, Sigmundsson, Kiehr, Julsrud, Schubert, Brummelstroete, Bostridge, Spence, Kooy, Van der Kamp, St Bavo Cathedral Boys' Ch., Netherlands Chamber Ch., O of 18th Century, Brüggen

(B) **(*) HMX 2901155.57 (3). Crook, Cold, Schlick, Jacobs, Blochwitz, Kooy, Chapelle Royale Ch., Ghent Coll. Mus., Herreweghe

Though Paul McCreesh uses minimum forces for Bach's masterpiece, with one voice per part, the result has the sharpest dramatic impact, thanks not only to the incisiveness of the performance but to the vivid immediacy of the recorded sound, with words exceptionally clear. The doctrine of reducing forces in Bach's choral works in this way has been exploited in the past by Joshua Rifkin and Andrew Parrott, but this of all Bach's choral works might seem to present insuperable problems, when textures are so complex, with double chorus and descant of trebles involved. The great opening chorus with all those forces sets the pattern. The speed is far faster than usual, with the compound time conveying jollity. Some will miss the darkly meditative mood of more traditional performances, but instead the message of the Passion story is made to bring uplift and rejoicing, with power conveyed not in numbers but through immediacy of impact. Mark Padmore as the Evangelist is fresh and fluent throughout, also taking on the tenor arias with his light, heady tone. Though Peter Harvey, more a baritone than a bass, has his moments of grittiness, as in the bass aria, *Gerne will ich*, with its low tessitura, he makes a suitably grave Jesus in the recitatives. Deborah York as first soprano and Magdalena Kožena as alto, both solo and choral, are excellent with clear, firm voices. The merits of the reduced forces come out very clearly in such a number as the duet with chorus, *So ist mein Jesu*, where the beautiful interweaving of legato lines for soprano and alto are set in sharp contrast with snapping choral comments from the other singers. In the other numbers involving choral comment the contrast of texture between soloist and chorus is also brought out more dramatically than in performances on a bigger scale, and the sharpness of the one-per-part chorus is regularly heightened in detached staccato enunciation. Though the 'turba' choruses of crowd-comment are far fewer in the *St Matthew* than in the *St John Passion*, they too have extra sharpness, and the words of chorales have far more expressive detail than with a full chorus. As the Passion story reaches the Crucifixion, so the mood darkens, not with any change in McCreesh's approach towards traditionally slow, solemn speeds but in the way that Bach's instrumentation affects the emotions conveyed. So the soprano aria, *Aus liebe will mein Heiland sterben*, 'For love my Saviour now is dying', conveys desolation in the instrumental introduction with its bare flute and then has agony intensified through dark-toned oboes da caccia. Those effects come over more sharply with such spare forces, and the alto recitative, *Ach Golgotha*, is similarly darkened with oboes da caccia. As for the supreme alto aria, *Erbarme dich mein Gott*, with its baroque violin obbligato,

Kožena in an intimate atmosphere conveys the ecstatic devotion of resting on God's mercy. In the closing numbers the mood is made to grow lighter, with the reservation that the final chorus with such small forces makes for a downbeat close, hardly weighty enough. One practical result of McCreesh's brisk approach is that this is the first complete version of this expansive masterpiece to come on two CDs instead of three.

Gardiner's version of the *St Matthew Passion*, the culminating issue in his Bach choral series for DG Archiv, brings an intense, dramatic reading which now makes a fine alternative choice, not just for period-performance devotees but for anyone not firmly set against the new authenticity. The result is an invigorating, intense telling of the story, with Gardiner favouring high dynamic contrasts and generally fast speeds, which are still geared to the weighty purpose of the whole work. He and his performers were recorded in what proved an ideal venue, The Maltings at Snape, where the warm acoustic gives body and allows clarity to period textures.

Masaaki Suzuki provides a fresh and beautifully sung reading of the most challenging of all Bach choral works. The light, crisp qualities which have shone out from his previous recordings are present here too, with the bright and resilient, and with a first-rate team of soloists led by the free-toned Gerd Türk as the Evangelist, and with Nancy Argenta outstanding among the others. If the result is a little short on devotional intensity in the culminating sections of this work, that is partly the result of the rather close-up recording, with solo voices and orchestra not always cleanly separated. More seriously, the double choir in the great double-choruses at the beginning and end is more backwardly balanced than elsewhere, set behind the orchestra, so that the dramatic impact is lessened. Nevertheless, this remains a powerful achievement.

When Harnoncourt made his pioneering recording of the *St Matthew Passion* in 1970, he took the doctrinaire view that it should be sung by all-male forces. The result was fresh, if at times abrasive. This new version, recorded in 2000, takes a less extreme view, and the result is lighter, generally faster, yet with a gravity implied that, benefiting from an exceptionally strong and consistent team of soloists, has all necessary weight and intensity. Christoph Prégardien is the mellifluous Evangelist, crisply expressive in his narration, with Matthias Goerne singing not just beautifully but movingly as Jesus. The Arnold Schoenberg Choir has rightly established among the highest reputation among Central European choirs, here singing with power as well as freshness. Harnoncourt's rhythmic control may not be as resilient as some, but his is a consistently imaginative approach, giving concentration and fine detail over the great span of this masterpiece, making this a leading contender among the many rival versions, recorded in clear, open sound.

The Channel Classics version with Jos van Veldhoven was recorded live in 1997 in the same Utrecht venue as Brüggen's (see below). You would never register this from the recording, which is more spacious and is balanced less closely, though van Veldhoven's manner is lighter and more flexible. His team of soloists is also young and fresh, with Gerd Türk a fine Evangelist – as he is for Suzuki in Japan – and with Andreas Scholl singing the alto role beautifully, a real highlight of the set.

While it certainly will not appeal to the authentic lobby, Klemperer's 1962 Philharmonia recording of the *St Matthew Passion* represents one of his greatest achievements on record, an act of devotion of such intensity that points of style and interpretation seem insignificant. The whole cast clearly shared Klemperer's own intense feelings, and one can only sit back and share them too, whatever one's preconceptions.

At bargain price the version from Naxos uses modern, not period, instruments but, following authentic trends, has brisk speeds and well-sprung rhythms. Though the performance takes no less than 35 minutes less than, say, Richter's, in its alertness it never seems rushed, with the Hungarian State Symphony Orchestra and Festival Choir on excellent form, conducted by Géza Oberfrank. A refreshingly lithe and young-sounding Evangelist, József Mukk, leads a team of Hungarian soloists with fresh, clear voices. The obbligato wind-playing is also attractive (if closely balanced) and the recording is spacious and full, and kind to voices.

Herreweghe made his first recording of the *St Matthew Passion* in 1985, a fresh, eager performance with many fine solo contributions. This later version offers more-polished contributions from chorus and orchestra, a degree smaller in scale than before, and again the line-up of mainly young soloists is an impressive one. The set is well worth hearing for the inspired singing of Ian Bostridge as the Evangelist, headily beautiful and finely detailed. Andreas Scholl too is superb in the alto numbers, singing with sensuously beautiful tone, not least in *Erbarme dich*. Werner Güra projects the tenor arias with clear, fresh tone, and the others follow a similar pattern of youthful freshness. It is a fine reading, beautifully paced, but some listeners may well feel that here polish and perfection have not been matched by spiritual intensity. The Harmonia Mundi set comes with an extra CD-ROM disc which helpfully provides a survey of the life of Bach and the background to the Passion, linking it with musical excerpts.

Recorded live in Utrecht in vivid, immediate sound, Frans Brüggen's reading is typically fresh and alert, with speeds generally fast but not invariably so, when Brüggen is consistently thoughtful. With a very light-toned Evangelist (Nico van der Meel) telling the story impressively, this is an intimate reading with the freshness intensified by the singing of the soloists, mostly young. Now reissued as a Trio, this is more enticing at mid-price.

Herreweghe's 1985 recording (recorded on period instruments at lower pitch), now reissued at bargain price, was not altogether superseded by his later version, discussed above. Howard Crook is an excellent, fresh-toned Evangelist, and the other tenor, Hans-Peter Blochwitz, is first rate too. The alto part is taken by the celebrated counter-tenor, René Jacobs, rather hooty in *Erbarme dich*; but Barbara Schlick, with her bright, clear soprano voice, sings radiantly. The instrumental group plays in authentic style, but not abrasively so; Herreweghe's control of rhythm, however, tends to be too heavy. Chorales are often slow and over-accented, and the heavy stressing also mars the big numbers. Nevertheless this is still impressive overall.

(i; ii) *St Matthew Passion* (complete). *Suites.* **(ii)** *2 in B min., BWV 1067;* **(iii)** *3 in D, BWV 1068: Air* (arr. Mahler); **(iv)** *Concerto in D min., for 2 violins & orchestra, BWV 1010*
(***) Naxos mono 8.110880–82. (i) Erb, Vincent, Van Tulder, Durigo, Ravelli, Schey, Amsterdam Toonkunst Ch., Zanglus Boys' Ch.; (ii) Concg. O; (iii) New York Philharmonic SO; (ii; iv) with Zimmerman, Helman; all cond. Mengelberg

Here is the famous Palm Sunday 1939 performance of the *St Matthew Passion*, recorded live by the Netherlands Radio, given in the Concertgebouw. Mengelberg's reading, expansively indulging in slow tempi and rallentandos at every imaginable point, is a monument to a tradition now

departed. He had conducted this same work in Amsterdam every year from 1899 onwards and, whatever the objections to the style of performance that the modern listener may have, the dedication and intensity are irresistible. Chorales are almost unbelievably slow, with rallentandos added, but the devotional quality is clear; and so it is with the singing both of the fine group of soloists and of the choir. Karl Erb was in his sixties when he sang on this recording, and the voice has its thin patches, but he was still unrivalled in Germany as the Evangelist, moving in his narration. Outstanding among the others is the soprano, Jo Vincent, with the alto, Ilona Durigo, firm and strong too, and Louis van Tulder is an attractively light tenor soloist. The recording, made by Dutch Radio using a process that extended the frequency range usual at that time, has come up very vividly in the Naxos transfer. Mengelberg made substantial cuts in the original performance but, unlike the Philips transfer to CD, which cut still further to fit the work on two discs, this one has the original recording complete. That allows Naxos to add all the other Bach recordings made commercially by Mengelberg between 1929 and 1938, notably a Columbia recording of the *B minor Suite* made in the Concertgebouw in 1931 in surprisingly full and vivid sound, using two (unnamed) flute soloists in unison so as to balance the large body of strings. In these other Bach recordings speeds are generally not as expansive as those in the *Passion*, with allegros often well sprung. The instrumentalists include Pier van Egmond and the flautist Hubert Barwahser. It first appeared on four Philips LPs and has been expertly restored by Mark Obert-Thorne on these three CDs. The sleeve speaks of it as being 'abridged' but, apart from a cut after the recitative at 49 to the recitative at 53, and the omission of sections 23, 29, 41, 70 and 75, it is complete. In its way it is glorious in much the same way as was Albert Coates's superb pre-war *B minor Mass*, with its rich string sonority, legato phrasing and great tonal warmth. Obert-Thorne is quite right to claim that at its best the sound approaches the level of 'early 1950s tape', which enables us to hear Mengelberg's forces with an often striking presence.

St Matthew Passion (excerpts)

(N) **(*)** BIS **Surround Sound SACD** 1500 (from above complete recording, with Türk, Kooy, Bach Coll., Japan, Suzuki)

A single-disc selection, however generous, from the *St Matthew Passion* is no more than adequate, but this admirable 81-minute SACD sampler of the fine Suzuki set offers a wonderfully rich and spacious sound-picture. If it does not cure the balance between chorus and orchestra in the opening and closing choruses, it makes the effect very convincing in concert-hall terms.

St Matthew Passion (in English)

(B) **(***)** Dutton mono 2CDAX 2005 (3). Greene, Suddaby, Ferrier, Cummings, Bach Ch., Jacques O, Jacques – PERGOLESI: *Stabat Mater* (**)

In 1947–8 Decca recorded the *St Matthew Passion*, based on the annual performances conducted by Dr Reginald Jacques, and that is what Michael Dutton has here transferred immaculately to CD, with the bonus of the 1946 Decca recording of the Pergolesi *Stabat Mater*, also with Ferrier as soloist. The Bach is very much a performance of its time, with measured speeds and an expressively devotional manner, in the chorales and recitatives as well as in the big choruses. Only the 'turba' choruses commenting on the action are brisk in the way one would now expect. Eric Greene is the noble

Evangelist and the sweet-toned Elsie Suddaby shines out in the soprano arias, but it is Ferrier who instantly on each entry conveys quite a different degree of intensity from the rest, immediately magnetic. Sadly Henry Cummings is too woolly-toned to give much pleasure, but the atmosphere of a performance at that time is vividly caught. Having an English text is well justified, when the words are so clear.

Schemelli's musicalisches Songbook: 57 sacred songs
*** CPO 99407-2 (2). Schlick, Mertens, Van Asperen, Möller

Bach was the principal contributor to the important collection of hymns published in Leipzig in 1736 when he was Kapellmeister there. Some are settings of traditional hymn-tunes, some with improvements by Bach and some are original. This is the biggest selection yet recorded of Bach's work on the *Songbook*, and though this is not a set to play from end to end, it is good to have these dedicated performances from two stylish soloists, very well recorded.

Vocal collections

Arias: *Bist du bei mir; Cantata 202: Weichet nur, betrübte Schatten. Cantata 209: Ricetti gramezza. St Matthew Passion: Blute nur; Ich will dir mein Herze schenken*
**(*) Delos D/CD 3026. Augér, Mostly Mozart O, Schwarz –
  HANDEL: *Arias* **(*)

Arleen Augér's pure, sweet soprano, effortlessly controlled, makes for bright performances of these Bach arias and songs, very recommendable for admirers of this delightful singer, well coupled with Handel arias.

Arias: *Mass in B min.: Agnus Dei; Qui sedes. St John Passion: All is fulfilled. St Matthew Passion: Grief for sin*
(M) (***) Decca mono 433 474-2. Ferrier, LPO, Boult –
  HANDEL: *Arias* (***) ✪

On 7 and 8 October 1952 Kathleen Ferrier made her last and perhaps greatest record in London's Kingsway Hall, coupling four arias each by Bach and Handel. The combined skill of John Culshaw and Kenneth Wilkinson ensured a recording of the utmost fidelity by the standards of that time. Now it re-emerges with extraordinary naturalness and presence.

Orchestral transcriptions and arrangements

Conductors' transcriptions: *Aria: Bist du bei mir?, BWV 508* (Klemperer); *Chorales: Ein feste Burg, BWV 720* (Damrosch) *Herzlich tut mich verlangen, BWV 727* (Leinsdorf); *Ich ruf' zu dir, Herr Jesu Christ, BWV 639* (Gui); *Jesu, Joy of Man's Desiring, from BWV 147* (Ormandy); *Sheep may safely graze, from BWV 208* (Barbirolli); *Fantasia & Fugue in G min., BWV 542* (Mitropoulos); Suite 3, BWV 1068: Air (Sargent); *Suite 6* (arr. from *BWV 848, 992, 827, 811, 867 & 1006*, & orch. Sir Henry Wood); *Toccata & Fugue in D min., BWV 565* (Skrowaczewski)
(N) *** Chan. **SACD** CHSA 5030. BBC SO, Slatkin

What this collection confirms yet again is that Stokowski's orchestral transcriptions, however flamboyant, are almost unique in catching the inate spirit of Bach's music, whereas here only Mitropoulos and Klemperer show a similar total identification. Mitropoulos's spectacular scoring of the *Fantasia and Fugue in G minor* combines panache with individuality. He favours a wide range of dynamic and colour, sometimes intensely dramatic but often gentle in character, using strings and woodwind with finesse; yet the final denouement of the *Fugue* has a real sense of apotheosis.

Klemperer's restrained scoring of the lovely *Bist du bei mir* for strings alone is wonderfully luminous as played here, where Sargent's string version of *Jesu, Joy of Man's Desiring* curiously omits Bach's oboe obbligato, and both this and his semi-luscious treatment of what he calls the *Air on a G String* are somewhat bland. Gui's simple arrangment of the *Chorale Prelude, Ich ruf'zu dir, Herr Jesu Christ* has rather more character: all three pieces are played most sympathetically. The six-movement Suite arranged by Sir Henry Wood is unexpectedly diverse and enjoyable, moving from a Mendelssohnsion treatment of the *C sharp minor Prelude* from the *Well-Tempered Clavier* and a touchingly delicate *Lament* from the *Capriccio on the Departure of his most Beloved Brother* to more robust and heavily scored dance movements.

The programme opens with Skrowaczewski's spectacular alternative transcription of the famous *D minor Toccata and Fugue*, owing much to Stokowski, especially in the use of the horns; although there are extra touches of orchestral detail, the effect is essentially brasher, especially in its use of percussion. Slatkin presents it vigorously and flamboyantly, with a big ritardando at the close of the Fugue emphasizing its gutsy use of the brass; and he is similarly extrovert in Walter Damrosch's full-blooded version of *A Mighty Fortress is our God* which ends the concert spectacularly. Very fine playing throughout from the BBC Symphony Orchestra, and superbly spacious, demonstration-worthy sound from Chandos.

Chaconne from solo *Violin Partita 2, BWV 1004* (orch. Raff); *Chorales: O Mensch, bewein' dein' Sünde gross, BWV 622* (orch. Reger); *Wachet auf, BWV 645* (orch. Bantock); *Fantasia & Fugue in C min., BWV 537* (orch. Elgar); *Fugue à la gigue in G, BWV 377* (orch. Holst); 'Giant Fugue' (Wir glauben all' an einen Gott), BWV 680* (orch. Vaughan Williams & Foster); *Passacaglia & Fugue in C min., BWV 582* (orch. Respighi). *Preludes & Fugues: in C, BWV 545* (orch. Honegger); *in E flat (St Anne), BWV 552* (orch. Schoenberg)
*** Chan. 9835. BBC PO, Slatkin

Flying boldly in the face of period performance, these transcriptions by nine celebrated composers, including Respighi, Elgar, Holst, Vaughan Williams, Schoenberg and Raff, bring out the grandeur of Bach's vision in his organ music. That is greatly helped by the sumptuous Chandos sound and the magnificent playing of the BBC Philharmonic under Leonard Slatkin. The only 19th-century composer here, Raff, tackles not organ music but the great *Chaconne* from the solo *Violin Partita in D minor*, enhancing its epic scale in colourful orchestration. Respighi is weightily dramatic in the *Passacaglia and Fugue in C minor*, and so is Schoenberg in the *St Anne Prelude and Fugue*, while Honegger even uses a saxophone in the *Prelude and Fugue in C*. Most imaginative of all is the *Fantasia and Fugue in G minor*, with Elgar glorying in percussion and harp.

Fantasy & Fugue in C min., BWV537 (arr. ELGAR); *Fugue in G min. (Little Fugue), BWV 579* (arr. STOKOWSKI); *A Musical Offering: Ricercare 2, BWV 1079* (arr. WEBERN); *Prelude & Fugue in E flat (St Anne), BWV 552* (arr. SCHOENBERG); Suite for Organ, Harpsichord & Orchestra (from *Orchestral Suites 2 & 3*, arr. MAHLER); *Toccata & Fugue in D min., BWV 565* (arr. STOKOWSKI)
(N) ** Sony SK 89012. LAPO, Salonen

Salonen's Bach transcriptions CD is certainly well played and recorded, but it lacks the flair of its Chandos rivals (with

Bamert and Slatkin) and the electricity of Stokowski's own recordings. While this CD does offer moments of excitement – the climax of the wonderful Elgar arrangement of the *Fantasy and Fugue in C minor* comes off well – the playing is generally just too strait-laced for these richly upholstered scores, though one enjoys the beauty and refinement of the playing.

Arrangements: Bach–Reger

(i) *Orchestral Suite 2 in B min. for Flute & Strings* (with continuo by Max Reger). *Bach–Reger Suite in G min.* (selected and arr. Reger); *Aria: O Mensch, bewein deine Sünde gross*

*** MDG 321 0940-2. Stuttgart CO, Russell Davies; (i) with Gérard

A fascinating collection. Throughout there is a nineteenth-century amplitude. The *Bach–Reger Suite in G minor*, which is made up of movements from the keyboard *Partitas* and *English Suites*, is scored very like a typical set of Reger variations: the *Courante*, which features oboe, flute and bassoon, may be anachronistic but is very felicitous. The Stuttgart orchestra plays very sympathetically (as does the excellent, nimble flautist) and Dennis Russell Davies seeks a performing style which Reger would have recognized. Excellent recording.

Arrangements: Bach–Stokowski

Chorale Preludes: Ein feste Burg ist unser Gott; Komm, süsser Tod; Mein Jesu, was vor Seelenweh. Christmas Oratorio: Sinfonia. English Suite 2 in A min., BWV 807: Bourrée. Fugue in G min., BWV 578 (Little Fugue); Orchestral Suite 3 in D, BWV 1068: Air on the G String. Passacaglia & Fugue in C min., BWV 582; Toccata & Fugue in D min., BWV 565; Violin Partita 1 in B min., BWV 1002: Sarabande; 3 in E, BWV 1006: Preludio

(N) (M) *** EMI Legend CD/**DVD** (ADD) 5 57758. Symphony O, Stokowski (with DVD Bonus: DEBUSSY: *Prélude à l'après-midi d'un faune*)

A welcome return to circulation of Stokowski's (American Capitol) late-1950s recordings of Bach arrangements which have tended to be overshadowed by his later, more flamboyant Decca Phase Four recordings. The earliest sessions date from 1957, and if the sound, understandably, displays a degree of thinness, it is well balanced, the ambience is remarkably warm, and overall the quality is certainly impressive for its time. Stokowski's richly expressive phrasing engulfs the listener throughout, with the conductor clearly wallowing in the sheer richness of sound he creates in the quiet numbers (which predominate). The *Chorale Preludes* are played with great intensity, while in the spectacular showpieces, such as the *D minor Toccata and Fugue* and the *Passacaglia*, with their generous splashes of romantic colour, plenty of electricity is generated. The bonus DVD records the 1972 film of Debussy's *Prélude à l'après-midi d'un faune*, played at the Royal Festival Hall. It is a joy to watch – deeply felt and magical.

Adagio in C, BWV 564; Chorales: Jesus Christus Gottes Sohn (from Easter Cantata); Komm süsser Tod; Mein Jesu; Sheep may safely graze; Wir glauben all' an einen Gott (Giant Fugue), BWV 680. Fugue in G min. (Little), BWV 578; Passacaglia & Fugue in C min., BWV 582; Suite 3 in D, BWV

1068: Air. Toccata & Fugue in D min., BWV 565; Violin & Harpsichord Sonata 4, BWV 1017: Siciliano; Well-Tempered Clavier, Book 1, Prelude 24

*** Chan. 9259. BBC PO, Bamert

This sumptuously recorded Chandos CD brings together the dozen published Stokowski Bach transcriptions. Bamert's warmly sympathetic readings obviously follow his mentor's way with this music, if without quite managing the naturally spontaneous rubato which was one of Stokowski's special gifts. Nor is the playing as vital and electrifying as the great conductor's own record. But the result is very enjoyable, and the Chandos stereo here is very much in the demonstration bracket.

Harpsichord Concerto in F min., BWV 1056: Arioso (Largo). Chorales: Aus tiefer Noth (De profundis), BWV 1006; Ein feste Burg; Jesu, Joy of Man's Desiring (from Cantata 147); My Soul is Athirst (from St Matthew Passion). Wachet auf, BWV 645; Fantasia & Fugue in G min., BWV 542; Violin Partitas: 1 in B min., BWV 1002: Sarabande. 2 in D min., BWV 1004: Chaconne. 3 in E, BWV 1006: Preludio. Violin Sonata 2, BWV 1003: Andante sostenuto. Well-Tempered Clavier: Fugue in C min., BWV 847; attrib C. P. E. BACH: *Chorale: Aus der Tiefe rufe ich*

(N) *** Chan. 10282. BBC PO, Bamert

Here, more than in his first collection, Matthias Bamert manages the kind of spontaneous, flexible rubato that was Stokowski's personal style and, with superb playing from the augmented BBC Philharmonic and marvellous Chandos recording, the result is spectacular indeed. The chorale preludes, *Aus tiefer Noth* and *Aus der Tiefe rufe ich* (now attributed to C. P. E. Bach), are affectively expressive and deeply felt. Yet, when one turns to the richly opulent scoring of the piece which Stokowski describes as 'Arioso' (the beautiful *Largo* from the *Harpsichord Concerto in F minor*) and the equally lovely *Andante sostenuto* from BWV 1003, the music moves entirely out of Bach's era into Stokowski's own world of ripe romanticism, while *Ein feste Burg* brings flamboyant contrasts of sonorous brass and strings. Of the other transcriptions from the works for unaccompanied violin, the dashing *Preludio in E* from BWV 1006 (thrillingly athletic on full strings) retains some of the character of the original, but with the incredibly flexible Chaconne from BWV 1004 one moves far away from the direct, purposeful momentum of Bach's original. Opening spaciously, with the melodic line constantly ebbing and flowing, it finally reaches an extraordinary, full-bloodedly romantic climax. Yet it is in the *Fantasia and Fugue in G minor* that we are thrilled by the most spectacular Stokowski sound. The piece is recorded here for the first time in the original scoring, which juxtaposes the sonorities of woodwinds (four flutes, three bassoons, double bassoon, three oboes, three clarinets, bass and contrabass clarinets, cor anglais, alto saxophone), brass (six horns, four trumpets, three trombones, tuba), with the fullest possible string sections, and laced with percussion.

Cantata 156: Arioso. Chorales: Ein feste Burg; Komm süsser Tod. Aria: Mein Jesu. Fugue in G min., BWV 578; Orchestral Suite 3, BWV 1068: Air. Passacaglia & Fugue in C min., BWV 582; Toccata & Fugue in D min., BWV 565; Violin Partita 3, BWV 1006: Preludio in E. Violin Sonata 3, BWV 1003: Andante sostenuto. Well-Tempered Clavier: Prelude 8

(M) (**) Cala mono CACD 0527. All-American Youth O, Stokowski

Stokowski formed two different All-American Youth Orchestras in 1940 and 1941, himself auditioning hundreds of players before choosing the excellent final ensemble. With the exception of the *'Little' G minor Fugue*, which belongs to 1940, this was the second group, and these 78-r.p.m. mono recordings were made by Columbia, rather than RCA, in the summer of 1941. They are a bit rough and ready, but Stokowskians will want this version of the famous *Toccata and Fugue* for its exhilarating accelerando (which begins at 4'45"). Much of the programme consists of slow pieces, but the highly expressive style of these young players carries the day, especially in the warmly intense *Ein feste Burg*.

Chorale Prelude: Wir glauben all' an einen Gott ('Giant Fugue'), BWV 680; Easter Cantata, BWV 4: Chorale; Geistliches Lied 51: Mein Jesu, BWV 487; Passacaglia & Fugue in C min., BWV 582; Toccata & Fugue in D min., BWV 565; Well-Tempered Clavier, Book 1: Prelude 8 in E flat min., BWV 853 (all orch. Stokowski)

(M) *** Decca (ADD) 448 946-2. Czech PO, Stokowski (with concert of miscellaneous orchestral transcriptions)

Stokowski's flamboyant arrangements of Bach organ works are presented here with spectacular, closely balanced but truthful Phase Four sound to match. Stokowski, over ninety at the time, challenges his players in expansive tempi, but the results are passionate in concentration. The famous *D minor Toccata and Fugue* is a shade less vital here than in Stokowski's earlier, mono version with the Philadelphia Orchestra, but the stereo sumptuousness is ample compensation. Most remarkable of all is the mighty *Passacaglia and Fugue in C minor*, highly romantic in its decorative detail but moving steadily to an overwhelming climax.

Piano Transcriptions

Chaconne from (unaccompanied) *Violin Partita 2 in D min., BWV 1004* (trans. BUSONI)

(BB) (**(*)) EMI Encore mono 5 75230-2. Michelangeli (piano) – BRAHMS: *Paganini Variations* (**(*)); MOZART: *Piano Concerto 15* (*)

Not surprisingly, Michelangeli plays brilliantly, and if Busoni's influence is increasingly (and excitingly) predominant as the piece proceeds, Bach's structure remains a firm basis for the interpretation. The mono recording is fully acceptable. Michelangeli made few recordings, so this is certainly value for money.

Transcriptions (arr. Busoni): *Chorales: Ich ruf' zu dir, Herr Jesu Christ, BWV 639; Nun freut euch, lieben Christen, BWV 734: Nun komm, der Heiden Heiland, BWV 659; Wachet auf, ruft uns die Stimme, BWV 645*

⊙ *** Sony SK 66511. Perahia – LISZT: *Concert Paraphrases*; MENDELSSOHN: *Songs Without Words* ***

Murray Perahia knows how to make the piano sing as do few of his contemporaries, and how to control pace. His pianism is impeccable in its polish and naturalness of flow, and there is a wonderful bloom about the sound he produces.

Chorales: Ich ruf' zu dir, Herr Jesu Christ; Nun komm der Heiden Heiland; Wachet auf, ruft uns die Stimme. Siciliano in D; Sinfonia in D (all arr. KEMPFF); *Chorales: Alle Menschen müssen sterben; Das alte Jahr vergangen ist; Wenn wir in höchsten Nöten sein* (all arr. HEWITT); *Herzlich tut mich verlangen* (arr. WALTON); *In dulci jubilo* (arr. BERNERS) *Jesu, joy of man's desiring* (arr. MYRA HESS);

Meine Seele erhebt den Herrn (arr. IRELAND); *O Mensch, bewein deine Sünde gross* (arr. HOWELLS); *Sanctify us by Thy goodness* (arr. COHEN); *Die Seele ruht in Jesu Händen* (arr. BAUER); *Sheep may safely graze* (arr. HOWE); *Passacaglia in C min.* (arr. D'ALBERT)

*** Hyp. CDA 67300. Hewitt

Predictably, Angela Hewitt brings the widest range of pianistic style to these often highly individual arrangements by a galaxy of famous names. She finds a natural simplicity in those by Kempff, with *Nun komm der Heiden Heiland* relatively sombre to contrast with the delightful sunlit *Siciliano*. A comparable delicacy of touch is used to evoke Myra Hess herself for her famous version of *Jesu, joy of man's desiring*, while Hewitt's own arrangements are comparably thoughtful. For contrast there is the full-blooded *In dulci jubilo* of Lord Berners, while Eugen d'Albert's version of the great *Passacaglia in C minor* brings a dynamic and colouristic flamboyance within a powerful structure. A most stimulating collection, immensely varied, yet with a thread of underlying profundity throughout. The piano recording could hardly be more natural.

Chorales: Nun komm, der Heiden Heiland; Wachet auf; Ich ruf' zu dir (arr. Kempff); *Sheep may safely graze* (arr. Mary Howe); *Sinfonia in D; Siciliano in G min.; Jesu, joy of man's desiring* (arr. Myra Hess); *Wenn wir in höchsten Nöten sein; Das alte Jahr; Alle Menschen müssen sterben* (arr. Hewitt); *Herzlich tut mich verlangen* (arr. Walton); *Meine Seele erhebt den Herrn* (arr. John Ireland); *O Mensch, bewein dein Sünde gross* (arr. Howells); *Sanctify us by Thy goodness* (arr. Harriet Cohen); *Die Seele ruht in Jesu Händen* (arr. Harold Bauer); *Passacaglia in C min.* (arr. Eugen d'Albert)

**(*) Hyp. CDA 67309. Hewitt (piano)

This collection looks intriguing but is just a little disappointing. Of couse Angela Hewitt's Bach playing is always perceptive, but here there is sometimes a hint of over-characterization. The opening *Sinfonia* is vey bold indeed, as is the *Passacaglia in C minor*, but, as the latter proceeds, in some passages she is almost too gentle. The staccatos at the opening of the *Siciliana* (where the melody itself is played most beautifully) like the accented rhythms in *Wachet auf* seem a shade too precise, though the very clearly focused chorale in *Jesu, joy of man's desiring* works well enough. She is at her very finest when playing very simply, as in Kempff's arrangement of *Ich ruf' zu dir*, Walton's of *Herzlich tut mich verlangen*, and her own of *Alle Menschen müssen sterben*, which ends the programme so serenely.

Partita in B min. (arr. from unaccompanied *Violin Partita 1, BWV 1002*)

(B) *** EMI Debut 5 74017-2. Batiashvili (violin) – BRAHMS: *Violin Sonata 1*; SCHUBERT: *Rondo in B min., D.895* ***

Bach playing of great refinement and beauty of tone by this gifted young player. The Georgian-born Elisabeth Batiashvili studied with Mark Lubotsky and came to international attention when at the age of 16 she won second prize at the Sibelius Competition in Helsinki. She makes her EMI début with this mixed programme. More a calling-card for the artist than a disc for the collector, who will probably want all the Bach *Partitas* or the Brahms *Sonatas*. None the less, this is a most distinguished and satisfying recital that gives pleasure and is well worth the modest outlay.

Toccata & Fugue in D min., BWV 565 (arr. Fox-Lafiche for unaccompanied violin)

*** EMI 5 57384-2. Vengerov – SHCHEDRIN: *Balalaika; Echo Sonata;* YSAŸE: *Solo Violin Sonatas 2, 3, 4 & 6* ***

As well as being a fine, thoughtful artist, Maxim Vengerov is also a showman, as this brilliant live recording of a solo violin recital demonstrates, above all in the arrangement for unaccompanied violin by Fox-Lafiche of Bach's most popular organ piece. In Vengerov's hands it works surprisingly well, backing up the scholarly argument that, stylistically unlike any other Bach organ work (and possibly not by Bach at all), it is better suited to the violin (for which it may have originally been written) than the organ. A welcome makeweight for the four Ysaÿe *Sonatas* and the Shchedrin pieces.

BACH, Wilhelm Friedemann (1710–84)

Adagio & Fugue in D min., F.65; Adagio & Fugue in F min.; (i) Harpsichord Concerto in E min., F.43; Sinfonias in D, F.64; in F, F.67

*** HM HMC 901772. (i) Alpermann; Berlin Akademie für Alte Musik, Mai

This fine Harmonia Mundi disc makes an ideal introduction to the music of Bach's favourite son. It opens with the *Sinfonia in D* with its most engaging woodwind writing, particularly for the flutes in the *Andante*, and closes with the whimsical *Sinfonia in F*, which nevertheless has a gracious *Andante* and ends mellowly with a warm-hearted *Minuet*. The *Concerto* exudes the striking rhythmic life that characterizes this composer's music, but suffers from a recessive balance for the modest-sized chosen harpsichord. However, Raphael Alpermann plays its *Adagio* with appealing delicacy, and survives the rough buffeting of the orchestral tuttis in the finale. Most remarkable of all are the pair of *Adagios and Fugues*, the *F minor* arranged for strings from a keyboard piece by Mozart, who added the spacious introduction. Excellent recording thoughout, apart from the backward balance of the harpsichord.

Flute Concerto in D

(N) *** CPO 999 888-2. Gurtner, Wiener Akademia, Haselböck – L. HOFMANN: *Flute Concerto in D;* C. P. E. BACH: *Flute Concerto in D* ***

A *galant*-style concerto with an especially perky finale, superbly played and recorded on period instruments and part of an attractive programme.

Double Concerto for 2 Harpsichords in D, F.46

(BB) **(*) Warner Apex 2564 61137-2. Uittenbosch, Curtis, VCM, Harnoncourt – J. C. BACH: *Sinfonia concertante in F* **(*); C. P. E. BACH: *Double Concerto for Harpsichord and Fortepiano* ***; J. S. BACH: *Double Harpsichord Concerto 1 in C min., etc.* **(*)

Wilhelm Friedemann's *Double Concerto* is a much less remarkable piece than Carl Philipp Emanuel's *Concerto for Harpsichord and Fortepiano*. It is well enough played here, although tuttis are a bit gruff and rather heavily accented. Nevertheless, this bargain disc is generously full and is well worth its modest cost.

Sinfonia in D, F.64

(BB) **(*) Naxos 8.553289. Salzburg CO, Lee – C. P. E. BACH: *Sinfonias* **(*)

Sinfonia in D, F.64; Adagio & Fugue in D min., F.65

*** Cap. 10 283. Concerto Köln – J. C. F. BACH: *Sinfonia;* C. P. E. BACH: *Harpsichord Concerto;* J. C. BACH: *Sinfonia* ***

Wilhelm Friedemann's three-movement *Sinfonia in D major* was intended for use as an introduction to the Whitsun cantata, *Dies ist der Tag*. The better-known *Adagio and Fugue in D minor* may possibly have originally formed the last two movements of a symphony. It is a very extraordinary and expressive piece. It is played by the Cologne period group with great expressive vitality and is well recorded.

The *Sinfonia* is also given a lively account in Salzburg; modern instruments are used, but textures are clean and fresh and the recording is faithful and well balanced.

6 Sonatas for flute duet, F.54–9

*** MDG 311 984402. Hüteler, Schmidt-Casdorf

These works must be fun to play, especially when the two instruments chirrup together as in the first-movement *Allegro* of No. 2, dance along graciously as in the final *Gigue* of the same work, or chase each other's tails as in the *Presto* finale of No. 4. Slow movements are innocent, yet have a thoughtful melancholy. Overall, the final work in *F minor* is the most individual of the six, but all are different and this simple polyphony stands up to repeated listenings. The performances here are technically immaculate, have a pleasing, spontaneous simplicity and are beautifully recorded.

Fantasias: in C min., F.2; A min., F.23; 12 Polonaises, F.12

(BB) ** CPO 999 501-2. Hoeren (fortepiano)

The extraordinary *Fantasia in C minor* has a darkly dramatic opening, then immediately evokes memories of Johann Sebastian's *Chromatic Fantasia* in its florid brilliance. The *A minor* work is perhaps the best thing on the disc except for the *E minor Polonaise* (No. 10), which is quite touchingly done. The *E flat minor* piece (No. 8) is also thoughtfully presented. Otherwise Hoeren dispatches these works directly and cleanly without trying to make too much of them. Good recording and a very reasonable price.

BACH, Wilhelm Friedrich Ernst (1759–1845)

Wilhelm Friedrich Ernst Bach, the son of Johann Christoph Friedrich Bach (1732–95), was the last direct male descendant of J. S. Bach, and the only professional composer from the generation of Johann Sebastian's grandchildren. Moving to London to visit his uncle (Johann Christian), he adopted the anglicized Christian name of William and determined to stay there and become active as a piano teacher and composer. But when his uncle died suddenly in 1782, he returned home and in 1789 found employment at the Court as music teacher to the family of King Frederick William II.

Music for Piano Duet

Duet for piano (4 hands): in D & G; Sonata for Piano (4 hands) in C

*** CPO 999 848-2. Genova & Dimtrov – J. C. BACH: *Piano Duet Sonatas* ***

Most of his music dates from his last period, including the present duet sonatas, which have previously been wrongly attributed to Johann Christian. Understandably so, for they have much in common with the latter's similar works, with which they are paired on this CD. Indeed the *Rondo* of the *Duet No. 1* has a similar charm to the finale of J. C.'s four-handed *Sonata in C*. But Wilhelm Friedrich Ernst's first-movement style is generally more boldly classical, although he usually relaxes amiably in the *Allegretto* finales. The performances here are first class, as is the recording; this makes a truly fascinating compilation.

BACHE, Edward (1833–58)

Francis Edward Bache (pronounced Baych) was born in Birmingham in 1833, and was founder of the Festival Choral Society. He was first a pupil of Sterndale Bennett and then went to study in Leipzig. But his life was tragically shortened by tuberculosis, and he returned home, where he died at the age of 24.

Duo Brillante (for Violin & Piano); *Piano Trio, Op. 28; Romance* (for Cello & Piano), *Op. 2;* (i) *6 Songs, Op. 18*
(N) (M) **(*)** Dutton CDLX 7145. E. Piano Trio; (i) with Y. Howard

As a violinist Bache played in the Festival Orchestra under Mendelssohn in 1846, and his attractively amiable music was written in that composer's shadow. His *Piano Trio* is characteristic, a most congenial work, traditionally constructed, with pleasingly lyrical themes in the flowing opening movement, while the *Andante espressivo* is an expanded song without words. The pastel-shaded cello *Romanze* (here played simply and eloqently) is engaging, and the *Duo Brillante* is an inventive set of widely contrasted variations on an operatic-styled theme, with the writing steadily increasing in bravura. Both works are elegantly played and given a warmly natural recording. The songs too are Mendelssohnian, and are understandingly sung in the manner of Victorian ballads, although some listeners may find Yvonne Howard's often close vibrato rather intrusive at times.

BAERMANN, Heinrich (1784–1847)

Adagio for Clarinet & Orchestra
*** ASV CDDCA 559. Johnson, ECO, Groves – CRUSELL: *Concerto 2* *** 🔘; ROSSINI: *Introduction, Theme & Variations* ***; WEBER: *Concertino* ***

Heinrich Baermann's rather beautiful *Adagio*, once attributed to Wagner, is offered by a celebrated clarinettist who plays the work warmly and sympathetically.

Clarinet Concertinos: in C min.; E flat; Concertstück in G min.; Sonata in D min.
*** Orfeo Co65011A. Klöcker, Prague CO, Lajèřk

With an unexpected drum-roll beginning the *G minor Concertstück*, which opens this disc, no one could accuse Baermann of not being entertaining in these works. Indeed, these are enjoyably unpretentious concertos, with lively, vivacious writing which fully shows off the prowess of the soloist. Baermann was a celebrated clarinettist in his day and earned the nickname 'The Rubini of the Clarinet' on account of his expressive playing, no doubt put to good use in the lyrical slow movements here, where Bellini-like melodies emerge seductively. With three of these works in a minor key, a certain drama is evident too, but it is Baermann's catchy tunes to which one most readily responds, with the *Polacca* of the *E major Concertino* being especially enjoyable. The *Sonata*

in D minor (also for clarinet and chamber orchestra), uniquely here, begins with an attractive *Adagio*, and is followed by two movements at the composer's perky best. Virtuoso performances from Dieter Klöcker, well supported by the Prague orchestra, and all in good sound, too.

BAIRSTOW, Edward (1874–1946)

Organ Sonata in E flat
*** Priory PRCD 401. Scott (St Paul's Cathedral organ) (with WILLIAM HARRIS: *Sonata 1* ***) – ELGAR: *Sonata 1* ***

Bairstow's *Organ Sonata* was written in 1937 and is Elgarian in feeling; the central Scherzo produces a blaze of orchestral sound unsurpassed by Elgar in either of his works for the instrument. The performance here is admirable and the St Paul's Cathedral organ is just right for it. The third work on the disc, a much more conventional sonata by William Harris (1883–1973), at least has a rather pleasing central *Adagio*.

Anthems and choral settings: Blessed City, Heavenly Salem; Blessed Virgin's Cradle Song; Evening Canticles in D; If the Lord had not helped me; Jesu, grant me this I pray; Jesu, the very thought; Lamentation (from *Jeremiah*); *Let all mortal flesh keep silence; Lord I call upon thee; Lord thou hast been our refuge; Save us, O Lord*
*** Priory PRDC 365. York Minster Ch., Moore; Scott Whiteley

Bairstow is (rightly) best known for his moving and comparatively short anthem, *Let all mortal flesh keep silence*; but, as this collection shows, he wrote much else that gives full rein to his subtle understanding of choral blending and his instinctive response to liturgical texts. The gloriously expansive *Blessed City, Heavenly Salem*, which opens the concert, makes the firmest of Christian statements, and the depth of the composer's religious feeling is expressed touchingly in the poignant *Jesu, the very thought of you*. The performances here are very well prepared and excitingly committed and spontaneous, while the excellent organ accompaniments could hardly be bettered.

BALAKIREV, Mily (1837–1910)

Piano Concertos 1 in F sharp min., Op. 1; 2 in E flat, Op. posth.
*** Hyp. CDA 66640. Binns, E. N. Philh. O, Lloyd-Jones – RIMSKY-KORSAKOV: *Concerto* ***

(i) *Piano Concerto 1; Symphony 2 in D min; Tamara*
*** Chan. 9727. (i) Shelley; BBC PO, Sinaisky

The one-movement *First Piano Concerto* (*Youth*) is modelled on Balakirev's adored Chopin. It is well served by Malcolm Binns's intelligent and sensitive performance, which also has the advantage of fine orchestral support and recording. It also has the only available account of the more characteristic *Second Concerto*. This was left incomplete and was finished after his death by Lyapunov.

Howard Shelley is a powerful soloist in the *Piano Concerto*, relishing the bravura writing, and though the *Second Symphony* cannot compare with the *First* in scale or memorability, Vassily Sinaisky makes a most persuasive case for it in his warm and thrustful performance. He underlines the high dramatic contrasts, drawing playing from the BBC Philharmonic that is incisive and pointed in the Cossack Dance of the *Scherzo* as well as sweetly refined in the lyrical slow movement. *Tamara* is played with similar panache.

Islamey (orch. Lyapunov)

⊙— *** Ph. **SACD** 470 618-2; CD 470 840-2. Kirov O, Gergiev
— BORODIN: *In the Steppes of Central Asia*;
RIMSKY-KORSAKOV: *Scheherazade* ***

Balakirev's virtuoso piano piece as orchestrated by Lyapunov sounds surprisingly like another section of *Scheherazade*, making it an apt and exciting coupling from Gergiev and the Kirov Orchestra, although the resonance clouds detail somewhat, especially on the SACD, where the added hall resonance is the more noticeable.

Symphony 1 in C

⊙— (***) BBC Legends mono BBCL 4084-2. BBC SO,
Beecham — RIMSKY-KORSAKOV: *Le Coq d'or*: Suite;
BORODIN: *Prince Igor: Polovtsian Dances* (***)

Symphony 1; In Bohemia (symphonic poem); *King Lear Overture*
**(*) Chan. 9667. BBC PO, Sinaisky

Symphony 1; Russia; Tamara (symphonic poems)
(BB) *** Regis RRC 1131. USSR State SO, Svetlanov

Symphonies 1–2: Overture on Russian Themes; Russia; Tamara
(B) **(*) Hyp. Dyad CDD 22030 (2). Philh. O, Svetlanov

Balakirev's *First Symphony*, though still neglected, is among the very greatest of Russian symphonies, built on strong, memorable themes, with a ravishingly beautiful slow movement. Yet when Beecham recorded it for EMI in 1955 his usual spark of inspiration was missing in a cautious studio run-through. Here, for a radio broadcast the following year, he conducts the BBC Symphony Orchestra with all the warmth, thrust and sparkle missing from the earlier performance, making this BBC Legends issue very welcome. The recording may be mono, but it is clear and well balanced, as it is in the enjoyable fill-ups: the colourful suite from Rimsky-Korsakov's opera, *Le Coq d'or*, and the *Polovtsian Dances* from Borodin's *Prince Igor*, complete with chorus.

The most recent challenge to Beecham's pre-eminence has come from Chandos, and E. G.'s view is that not since that Philharmonia account has there been a version of this glorious Russian symphony quite so richly expressive, with outstanding playing from the BBC Philharmonic opulently recorded. I. M. and R. L. are less enthusiastic than E. G., but we are all agreed that the two Balakirev rarities make strong and characterful fill-ups.

Svetlanov's earlier (1974) Russian recording of Balakirev's *First Symphony* brings an interpretation that is little different from his later, Hyperion account with the Philharmonia, except that the performance has more grip and tension. The Russian strings give much pleasure, the wonderfully lyrical slow movement is both atmospheric and warmly relaxed, and the Russian clarinettist plays his solo delightfully. The finale has both striking impetus and gleaming Russian woodwind colour. The recording is rich and well detailed. While Beecham reigns supreme in the symphony, this is still a first-rate bargain, for the two melodically attractive symphonic poems are splendidly done, among the finest in the catalogue, and here the 1978 recording is (if anything) even more vividly colourful.

Hyperion have now paired their Svetlanov accounts as a Duo. The performances bring more beautiful playing from the Philharmonia Orchestra: the soaring clarinet solo at the beginning of the slow movement of No. 1 is rapturously done and in the *Second Symphony* the effect is cultured, the sound

pleasingly natural. However, there is some disagreement concerning Svetlanov's grip on the proceedings, and especially so in the first three movements of the *First*, although in the finale the emotional thrust is undeniable. The reading of the *Second* also has a spacious breadth; however, while agreeing that it is tauter than that of the *First*, E. G. suggests that it needs greater concentration. *Tamara* too – almost as extended as a one-movement symphony – needs to be stronger and more purposeful, although *Russia* is more successful.

Piano Sonata in B flat min.
**(*) Kingdom KCLCD 2001. Fergus-Thompson – SCRIABIN: *Sonata 3, etc.* **(*)

The Balakirev is arguably the greatest Russian piano sonata of the pre-1914 era. Gordon Fergus-Thompson is fully equal to its considerable demands and he offers excellent playing, though the recording is reverberant and the piano not always dead in tune. He also includes Balakirev's arrangement of Glinka's *The Lark* as an encore.

BANTOCK, Granville (1868–1946)

Celtic Symphony; Hebridean Symphony; The Sea Reivers; The Witch of Atlas
*** Hyp. CDA 66450. RPO, Handley

Vernon Handley conducts warmly atmospheric performances of four of Bantock's Hebridean inspirations. Most ambitious is the *Hebridean Symphony* of 1913, with nature music echoing Wagner and Delius as well as Sibelius, whose music Bantock introduced into Britain. The two tone-poems are attractive too, but best of all is the *Celtic Symphony*, a late work (written in 1940) which uses strings and six harps. This is in the grand string tradition of Vaughan Williams's *Tallis Fantasia* and Elgar's *Introduction and Allegro*, a beautiful, colourful work that deserves to be far better known. With warm, atmospheric recording to match, Handley draws committed performances from the RPO.

Hebridean Sea Poem 1: Caristiona; Omar Khayyám: Prelude and (i) *Camel Caravan; Orchestral Scene 1: Processional; Song of Songs: Prelude; Thalabala the Destroyer* (symphonic poem)
*** Hyp. CDA 67250. RPO, (i) with Ch.; Handley

Handley and the RPO give performances of great commitment and power, while the splendidly wide-ranging recording is vividly realistic. Not least so in the richly Tchaikovskian *Thalabala the Destroyer*. Bantock had been conducting a number of all-Tchaikovsky concerts, including *Francesca da Rimini*, before writing his tone-poem, and the influences are obvious. But it remains a splendidly successful piece in its own right, full of melodic and orchestral appeal. Elsewhere, and especially in the *Prelude to The Song of Songs* and *Omar Khayyám*, Wagnerian and Straussian influences are equally strong, along with Eastern exoticism, which also comes to the fore in the early *Processional*. But this is not cheap music, and the programme overall is a most rewarding collection that could not be better presented.

Pagan Symphony; Fifine at the Fair; 2 Heroic Ballads
*** Hyp. CDA 66630. RPO, Handley

The *Pagan Symphony* dates from 1928, so it comes mid-way between the *Celtic* and *Hebridean Symphonies*, and the writing brings touches of Elgar as well as German influences. It is tuneful and well crafted. Perhaps it isn't as individual a work as *Fifine at the Fair*, with which Beecham understandably identified; but Handley is equally at home in this colourful tone-poem, and it is good to have it presented in stereo as vivid as this. The two *Ballads* are rather more conventional but still make a considerable impression.

The Pierrot of the Minute: Overture

(M) *** Chan. 6566. Bournemouth Sinf., Del Mar – BRIDGE: *Summer*, etc.; BUTTERWORTH: *Banks of Green Willow* ***

Bantock's overture is concerned with Pierrot's dream in which he falls in love with a Moon Maiden, who tells him their love must die at dawn, but he will not listen. He wakes to realize that his dream of love lasted a mere minute. The writing is often delicate and at times Elgarian, and the piece is well worth investigating. The 1978 recording sounds remarkably fresh.

(i) Sapphic Poem for Cello & Orchestra; (ii) Sappho

*** Hyp. CDA 66899. RPO, Handley, with (i) Lloyd Webber; (ii) Bickley

The passion behind each of these nine songs, introduced by an extended orchestral *Prelude*, is vividly brought out by the RPO under Vernon Handley and sumptuously recorded. The mezzo, Susan Bickley, sings radiantly and with fresh, clear tone, rapt and intense in the final song, *Music of the golden throne*. The concertante piece for cello and small orchestra, written in 1906, makes the perfect coupling – a warmly expressive meditation on the same theme, with Julian Lloyd Webber a dedicated soloist.

Symphony 3 (The Cyprian Goddess); Dante and Beatrice; Helena (Variations on the Theme HFB)

*** Hyp. CDA 66810. RPO, Handley

Vernon Handley again draws from the RPO ripely persuasive performances. *The Cyprian Goddess* echoes Strauss in its sumptuous orchestration and melodic writing, and in its refinement it has something of the elegiac tone of late Strauss. The *Helena Variations*, written in tribute to his wife, echo the freshness and variety of Elgar's newly completed *Enigma*, while *Dante and Beatrice* is a free-ranging programme work which in its warmth and dramatic contrasts recalls Tchaikovsky's *Romeo and Juliet*. Whatever the echoes, in each piece Bantock establishes his own distinctive voice, here more tautly controlled than in his expansive, middle-period works. First-rate sound.

Celtic Songs: At the Rising of the Moon; In the Hollows of Quiet Places; Captain Harry Morgan. Drinking Song: Hafiz to the Sultan Timour. Ghazals of Hafiz: Alá yá! Send the Cup Round; Oh! Glory of Full-mooned Fairness. Jester Songs: In Tyme of Olde; Serenade. Songs from the Chinese Poets: A Dream of Spring; Adrift; Desolation; A Feast of Landerns; The Ghost Road. Songs: The Bluebell Wood; I Go to Prove my Soul; Invocation to the Nile; The Mood Maiden's Song; Ozymandias; Pippa Passes; Song to the Seals; A Woman

(M) *** Dutton CDLX 7121. Rigby, Savidge, Norris

Over his long career Granville Bantock wrote some 400 songs, many of them still unpublished, from which the performers here, guided by Lewis Foreman, writer of the authoritative note, have chosen 22 prime examples. Several items date from the 1890s, when meeting his future wife, Helen, prompted Bantock to write at high speed a great sequence of songs, setting her poems. They include some

inspired by the East, a theme that obsessed Bantock throughout his career, even though musically most of the songs have few oriental fingerprints. Another of his themes was the music of the Highlands, and though as he grew older he would occasionally use pentatonic themes, that was very much the exception. His warm, melodic style, often supported by imaginative piano accompaniment, remained relatively stable over fifty years until his death in 1946. Of the songs here, only the *Song to the Seals* of 1930 has achieved popularity, a hauntingly evocative piece, and the vigorous *Captain Harry Morgan*, celebrating the noted pirate, was a favourite of the bass, Peter Dawson, but all 22 have their striking moments, in clear, well-made music. Though Peter Savidge's baritone does not always focus sweetly, he and Jean Rigby are keenly responsive to the sensitive word-settings, with David Owen Norris a strong, sympathetic partner.

BARBER, Samuel (1910–81)

Adagio for Strings, Op. 11

(N) (M) *** DG 476 7233. LAPO, Bernstein – COPLAND: *Appalachian Spring* ***; GERSHWIN: *Rhapsody in Blue* **(*)

(M) *** DG Entrée 471737-2. LAPO, Bernstein – BERNSTEIN: *Candide: Overture*, etc. *** (with GERSHWIN: *Rhapsody in Blue* **(*))

(N) (M) * EMI 5 57855-2. Munich PO, Celibidache – SHOSTAKOVICH: *Symphonies 1 & 9* **

Bernstein's 1982 reading of the *Adagio* has something of the expansiveness of his interpretation of another slow movement with valedictory associations being given to it, *Nimrod* from Elgar's *Enigma*. In Barber, Bernstein's expressiveness is more restrained and elegiac, but his control of the climax – in what is substantially a live recording – is unerring. Recording somewhat close but full and clear. The original coupling with Copland's *Appalachian Spring* and Gershwin's *Rhapsody in Blue* is now reissued in Universal's 'Critics' Choice' series, but some may prefer the alternative Entrée disc, which offers Bernstein instead of Copland. The Adagio is also available along with Barber's *Violin Concerto* (see below).

Although very well played, in Celibidache's hands Samuel Barber's *Adagio for Strings* is very slow and has insufficient tension to sustain itself.

Adagio for Strings; (i) Cello Concerto, Op. 22. Medea (ballet suite) Op. 23

(BB) *** Naxos 8.559088. (i) Warner; RSNO, Alsop

Barber's *Cello Concerto* of 1945 is more elusive than the *Violin Concertos*, but Wendy Warner concentrates on its sometimes wry lyricism, and she articulates with brilliant point in the gentle scherzando passage of the finale. Marin Alsop is a persuasive partner, relishing the often plangent orchestral backcloth and securing a splendidly committed response from the Scottish players, both here and in the often astringent score for *Medea*. The selection is generous, with the atmospheric central portrayal of Medea herself and her dance of vengeance made the focal point of the score. The famous *Adagio for Strings* then becomes essentially an elegy, but reaches a passionate climax. Fine, vivid recording, though the massed upper strings could have more weight.

Adagio for Strings; (i) *Piano Concerto*; (ii) *Violin Concerto*; (iii) *Four Part Songs*
(M) **(*) ASV PLT 8501. (i) Joselson, LSO, Schenck; (ii) Shapira, Russian PO, Sanderling; (iii) Joyful Company of Singers, Broadbent

Adagio for Strings; (i) *Piano Concerto, Op. 38. Medea's Meditation and Dance of Vengeance, Op. 23a*
*** ASV CDDCA 534. (i) Joselson; LSO, Schenck

Itsai Shapira is Juilliard trained and a warm, lyrical player in the *Violin Concerto*, though he is not as dazzling in the finale as many of his rivals. Stern and, among younger players, Joshua Bell are to be preferred. In the *Piano Concerto* Tedd Joselson is marvellously and dazzlingly brilliant, as well as being highly sensitive and poetic, with an unforced and responsive orchestral contribution from the LSO under Andrew Schenck. The LSO also give a singularly fine account of the *Medea* excerpt (not to be confused with the suite) and a restrained and noble one of the celebrated *Adagio*. The choral pieces make a welcome bonus on the mid-priced alternative.

(i) Adagio for Strings; (i; ii) *Violin Concerto*; (i) *Essays 1–3*; *Medea: Medea's Dance of Vengeance, Op. 23a*; *Overture: School for Scandal, Op. 5*; (iii; iv) *Canzone for Flute & Piano, Op. 38a*; (iv; v) *Cello Sonata, Op. 6*; (iii; v) *Summer Music, Op. 31* (for wind quintet). (iv) (Piano) *Excursions, Op. 20*; *Nocturne (Homage to John Field), Op. 33*; *Souvenirs, Op. 28*
(B) *** EMI Gemini 5 86561-2 (2). (i) St Louis SO, Slatkin; (ii) Oliveira; (iii) Baxtresser; (iv) Margalit; (v) Stepansky; Robinson, Drucker, Le Clair, Myers

A splendid anthology of excellent modern recordings comprising some of Barber's most rewarding music. Slatkin's accounts of the orchestral pieces are superbly played and recorded, and he includes all three of the *Essays*, which is quite rare, as well as the amusing *School for Scandal Overture*. Elmar Oliveira's version of the *Violin Concerto* reacts to the nostalgia of the *Andante* with a vein of bitter-sweet yearning that is most affecting. It is a fine performance overall with a brilliantly played finale. The chamber music is especially valuable, with the performers producing the spontaneous feeling that they have lived with the music before performing it. The *Canzone for Flute and Piano* has an Elysian, soaring melody (slightly French in atmosphere) which Jeanne Baxtresser plays very beautifully. The *Cello Sonata* has a powerful impulse and is given the most eloquent advocacy here, while the *Excursions* have wit and elegance. The shorter pieces are all distinctive and well worth having, and this whole bargain Gemini Double cannot be too highly recommended.

Adagio for Strings; *Essays 1, Op. 12; 2, Op. 17; Music for a Scene from Shelley, Op. 7; Overture: The School for Scandal, Op. 5; Symphony 1, Op. 9*
*** Argo 436 288. Baltimore SO, Zinman

These performances are very alert and vital, particularly that of the *First Symphony*; the recording has superb presence and detail. Apart from the first two *Essays* for orchestra, Zinman's disc includes the more rarely heard *Music for a Scene from Shelley*, sumptuously scored and gloriously atmospheric. This adds greatly to the attractiveness of an already desirable issue, and Zinman and his excellent orchestra play the *Overture* to Sheridan's *The School for Scandal* with equal commitment. Strongly recommended.

(i) Canzonetta for Oboe & Strings. *Capricorn Concerto; Fadograph of a Yestern Scene; Mutations from Bach; Vanessa: Interlude; A Hand of Bridge*
(N) (BB) *** Naxos 8.599135. RSNO, Alsop, with (i) Stéphane Rancourt; (ii) Craigie, Winter, Wall, Williams

The neoclassical *Capricorn Concerto*, which takes its name from the house that Barber and Menotti shared, is a relative rarity, but this excellent budget version does it proud and can more than hold its own against the fine Slatkin account (RCA). The *Canzonetta* was left in short score on Barber's death, but this arrangement with strings is expertly done, and the piece is as moving as the very best of Barber. The *Fadograph of a Yestern Scene* is another rarity, a ruminative and reflective score with a strong vein of melancholy to sustain it. The witty ten-minute opera, *A Hand of Bridge*, which Barber wrote for Menotti's festival at Spoleto, also comes off well. Good recorded sound, too. In short this is a most pleasurable issue and repays repeated hearing.

Cello Concerto, Op. 22
*** Naïve V4961. Gastinel, CBSO, Brown – ELGAR: *Cello Concerto* ***
*** Chan. 8322. Wallfisch, ECO, Simon – SHOSTAKOVICH: *Cello Concerto 1* ***

Like her conductor, Justin Brown, Anne Gastinel is making her début on record, and she couples this fine account of the Barber *Cello Concerto* with a noble and dignified account of the Elgar. Gastinel is a thoughtful and sensitive artist and her recording is among the very finest now available, although the Wendy Warner/Alsop version on Naxos (see above) is also highly recommendable, and for many will have a more suitable coupling. But this new issue does justice to the work's lyricism and freshness and to the gentle melancholy that lies not far beneath the surface at times. Very good sound.

Wallfisch also gives an impressive and eloquent reading, and the elegiac slow movement is especially fine. Wallfisch is forwardly balanced, but otherwise the recording is truthful; the orchestra is vividly detailed.

(i) Cello Concerto; (ii) *Piano Concerto, Op. 38*; (iii) *Violin Concerto, Op. 14*
(N) (BB) *** RCA 82876 65832-2. (i) Isserlis; (ii) Takezawa; (iii) Browning; St Louis SO, Slatkin
(M) **(*) Sony (DDD/ADD) SMK 89751. (i) Ma, Baltimore SO, Zinman; (ii) Browning, Cleveland O, Szell; (iii) Stern, NYPO, Bernstein

This recommendable and generous RCA triptych provides excellent accounts of Barber's three major concertos, the *Piano Concerto* played by John Browning, the pianist for whom the composer originally wrote this formidable half-hour work. He recorded it for CBS not long after the first performance, with George Szell and the vintage Cleveland Orchestra. At rather broader speeds, with the piano balanced more forwardly, this 1990 version is not so high-powered, but in the slow movement it is more sensuous, with figuration magically delicate. The other two concertos were recorded four years later with equal success. Not surprisingly, Stephen Isserlis gives a vigorously committed account of the *Cello Concerto* and he sustains the Andante appealingly. He is very well balanced, as is Kyoko Takezawa in the composer's greatest concertante work for violin, matching a tender lyrical beauty in the first two movements with dazzling virtuosity in the finale. Slatkin's accompaniments are first class, and the St

Louis orchestra responds with both passion and empathy.

It is good to see that Stern's inspired account of the *Violin Concerto* has been additionally recoupled. With his masterly sense of line, Yo-Yo Ma also gives a richly lyrical reading of the *Cello Concerto*. Here the subtleties of the reading are enhanced by having the soloist naturally placed in relation to the well-balanced orchestra. However, the brilliant performance of the *Piano Concerto* by its dedicatee is not helped by the shallowness of the spotlit piano sound, hard in the outer movements with fierce tuttis.

(i) *Cello Concerto; Symphony 2, Op. 19; Medea – Suite, Op. 23*
❋ (**) Pearl mono GEM 0151. (i) Nelsova; New SO, composer

Samuel Barber recorded these three pieces for Decca in 1950. This is their first appearance on CD in very good transfers that have plenty of presence and detail, though the pitch problems that beset the opening bars of the finale of the *Second Symphony* have proved intractable. The ideas of the *Cello Concerto* have a vernal freshness and youthful innocence which still cast a spell and Zara Nelsova's commanding and pioneering account was long the only one available. It is sad that the grievous neglect of the eloquent and powerful *Second Symphony* prompted Barber to succumb to self-doubts and withdraw all but the middle movement. The work is wonderfully lyrical, and the rather Stravinskian *Medea* suite is highly effective and imaginative. The composer could obviously have done with a little more rehearsal with his *ad hoc* orchestra. All the same, there is a special quality and authority about these performances that make them very treasurable.

(i) *Piano Concerto. Medea: Medea's Meditation and Dance of Vengeance. Die Natali; Commando March*
(BB) **(*) Naxos 8.559133. (i) Prutsman; RSNO, Alsop

Stephen Prutsman gives a powerful reading of Barber's formidable *Piano Concerto*, fully in command of the bravura writing of the outer movements and tenderly expressive in the central *Canzone*. As a bargain alternative, this is very welcome, particularly when John Browning's pioneering version with Szell and the Cleveland Orchestra is problematical (see above). With Marin Alsop a most sympathetic Barber interpreter, the *Concerto* is well supplemented by the well-known concert work drawn from the *Medea* ballet, the genial and colourful fantasia on Christmas Carols, *Die Natali*, written at the same period as the concerto in memory of Serge and Natalie Koussevitzky, and the wartime *Commando March*. Well-balanced sound, if with strings on the light side.

(i) *Piano Concerto;* (ii) *Violin Concerto. Souvenirs, Op. 28*
*** Telarc CD 80441. (i) Parker; (ii) McDuffie; Atlanta SO, Levi

Robert McDuffie is a powerful violinist with a formidable technique, if not as individual an artist as many rivals in this warmly romantic *Violin Concerto*. His reading makes an excellent coupling for Jon Kimura Parker's outstanding performance of the *Piano Concerto* and the suite, *Souvenirs*, in its orchestral form. The performance is rather tauter and more purposeful than the fine one which John Browning (the pianist for whom the work was written) recorded for Sony (see above).

Violin Concerto, Op. 14
⊶ (M) *** Decca 476 17235. Bell, Baltimore SO, Zinman – BLOCH: *Baal Shem*; WALTON: *Violin Concerto* ***
*** DG 439 886-2. Shaham, LSO, Previn – KORNGOLD: *Violin Concerto, etc.* *** ❋
*** Sony SK 89029. Hahn, St Paul CO, Wolff – MEYER: *Violin Concerto* ***
(M) *** EMI 5 62600-2. Perlman, Boston SO, Ozawa – BERNSTEIN: *Serenade after Plato's 'Symposium'*; FOSS: *3 American Pieces* ***

(i) *Violin Concerto. Adagio for Strings*
(M) *** Sony 516235-2. (i) Stern; NYPO, Bernstein (with IVES: *The Unanswered Question*; COPLAND: *Fanfare for the Common Man*) – SCHUMAN: *In Praise of Shahn, etc.* ***

Joshua Bell's passionate playing in the Barber, full of tender poetry, is well matched by the excellent orchestra, ripely and brilliantly recorded, with the soloist well forward but not aggressively so. This now takes pride of place. It won the 1998 *Gramophone* Concerto Award and now reappears at mid-price in Universal's Gramophone Award Collection.

Isaac Stern gave the Barber *Violin Concerto* its stereo première in 1964, and his performance, which is consistently inspired, is of superlative quality. It has warmth, freshness and humanity, and the slow movement is glorious. The CBS forward balance for the orchestra is less than ideal, but the recording is otherwise very good and has been impressively remastered. This comes together with Bernstein's 1971 account of the *Adagio*, measured and intense, the version of Copland's *Fanfare for the Common Man* taken from the *Third Symphony*, Ives's masterpiece, *The Unanswered Question*, and the two fine William Schuman works.

Gil Shaham's performance of the Barber also has great virtuosity and is a reading of strong profile, with every moment of dramatic intensity properly characterized. The effect is warm and ripe, with the sound close and immediate, above all bringing out the work's bolder side but not missing the withdrawn, tender lyricism of the heavenly *Andante*. This really *is* good – and worthy to rank alongside the Stern/Bernstein (Sony). Indeed, it is to be preferred to the richly extrovert Perlman account.

Hilary Hahn gives an outstanding performance of the Barber *Concerto*, at once romantic and thoughtful, bringing out heartfelt emotion without overplaying it. This is distinctive, both in using a chamber orchestra, making up in clarity for any loss of weight, and in offering the most unusual coupling, a warmly approachable work specially written for Hahn by the double-bass player and composer, Edgar Meyer. The close balance for the soloist does not allow a genuine *pianissimo*, but otherwise this stands among the finest versions.

For Perlman, also closely balanced, the kernel of the Barber *Concerto* lies in the central slow movement; he plays with a warmth and intensity that even he has rarely matched. Weight, power and virtuoso brilliance then come together in his dazzling account of the finale. His account now comes at mid-price as part of the 'Perlman Edition', retaining its two enterprising couplings.

(i) *Violin Concerto. Music for a Scene from Shelley, Op. 7; Souvenirs* (ballet suite), *Op. 28; Serenade for Strings, Op. 1*
(BB) *** Naxos 8.559044. (i) Buswell; RSNO, Alsop

Marin Alsop with the Royal Scottish National Orchestra backs up the masterly *Violin Concerto* with the witty and delightfully parodic ballet, *Souvenirs*, and two early works, the evocative *Scene from Shelley* and a long-neglected three-movement *Serenade*, which is based on a string quartet written when Barber was nineteen and which anticipates the *Adagio for Strings*. James Buswell is a refined, sensitive soloist, warm without being soupy, if not quite as individual as Isaac Stern in his vintage version with Bernstein.

Essays for Orchestra 1, Op. 12; 2, Op. 17; 3, Op. 47
*** Chan. 9053. Detroit SO, Järvi – IVES: *Symphony 1* ***

In terms of both sonority and approach, Neeme Järvi's account of these appealing works differs from the American competitors. The strings have lightness and subtlety and are highly responsive. The recording is very natural and present, and beautifully balanced.

Essays for Orchestra 2; 3; (i) Toccata Festiva, Op. 36. (ii) Knoxville: Summer of 1915, Op. 24
(BB) *** Naxos 8.559134. RSNO, Alsop, with (i) Trotter; (ii) Gauvin

Marin Alsop continues her outstanding series of Barber recordings for Naxos with an attractive group of works, including one of the most popular of all, the evocative setting of a prose-poem by James Agee, *Knoxville: Summer of 1915*, with the Canadian soprano, Karina Gauvin, as the opulent soloist. The voice is so rich that the diction is not as clear as it might be, but happily the booklet provides the full text. Alsop's reading brings out the contrasts between the different sections more sharply than usual, and similarly in both of the *Essays* (No. 3 a late work, written in 1976) she highlights contrasts to bring out the feeling in both of compressed symphonic structures. The *Toccata Festiva* for organ and orchestra, written for the unveiling of a new organ for the Philadelphia Orchestra, is an exuberant piece that brings the widest expressive range in the organ part and with the orchestra colourful too; surprisingly, this work is a great rarity on disc, here superbly played and recorded.

Symphonies 1, Op. 9; 2, Op. 19; Adagio for Strings; Overture: The School for Scandal
*** Chan. 9684. Detroit SO, Järvi
Symphonies 1; 2; Essay for Orchestra 1; Overture: The School for Scandal
⊶ ✪ (BB) *** Naxos 8.559024. RSNO, Alsop

The two symphonies are played on Naxos with passionate commitment and deep lyrical feeling by the Scottish orchestra. The account of the complete *Second Symphony* will surely confirm the reputation of a wartime work which the composer partly withdrew in despondency after its neglect. The *First Essay for Orchestra* also generates a powerful atmosphere when played with such depth of feeling. With spectacular recording, this exciting collection is very strongly recommended.

The *First Symphony* also comes off well in Neeme Järvi's hands, as does the wartime *Second*. The ubiquitous but none the less moving *Adagio* and the *Overture: The School for Scandal* complete a disc that could well serve as an admirable entry point into Barber's world. The Detroit orchestra turn in polished playing and the recording is rich and vivid, the sound fuller than in the Naxos alternative.

(i) Symphony 1 (in one movement); Essays for Orchestra, 1; 2; (ii) Music for a Scene from Shelley; (i) Night Flight, Op. 19a; (ii; iii) Knoxville (Summer of 1915)
⊶ (BB) *** Regis (ADD) RRC 1139. (i) LSO; (ii) Western Australia SO; Measham; (iii) with McGurk

David Measham proves a splendid advocate of Barber's music, securing passionately committed performances of the *First Symphony* (where at times he brings out its somewhat Waltonian manner) and the powerfully romantic yet mysterious *Music from Shelley*, an inspired early work from 1933, which ought to be better known. The two *Essays for Orchestra* are also very well played, as is the haunting movement, *Night Flight*, all that the composer originally wanted to survive from the *Symphony No. 2*. This was originally a Unicorn collection, to which the two excellent recordings from Western Australia have been addded, notably Molly McGurk's ravishing account of Barber's Coplandesque setting of *Knoxville*, a prose-poem by James Agee. Framed by a lilting, folk-like melody, it is a young girl's nostalgic reminiscence of 'the time of evening when people sit on their porches, rocking gently and talking gently and watching the street'. A rumbustious interlude pictures a streetcar 'raising its iron moan; stopping, belling and starting', and the soloist rises to an ecstatic climax in evoking the 'blue dew' of the night. Finally the child singer is 'taken in, and put to bed'. A miniature masterpiece, the performance (and recording) here could hardly be more warmly evocative. At budget price this reissue cannot be recommended too highly.

CHAMBER MUSIC

String Quartet, Op. 11
(*) DG (IMS) 435 864-2. Emerson Qt – IVES: *Quartets 1–2* *

The Emerson Quartet play with brilliance and technical expertise. The tone is rich, their tonal blend immaculate and their ensemble impeccable; but their expressive eloquence sounds over-rehearsed. All the same, it is in its way stunningly played and eminently well captured by the DG engineers.

Summer Music
*** Crystal (ADD) CD 750. Westwood Wind Quintet – CARLSSON: *Nightwings;* LIGETI: *Bagatelles;* MATHIAS: *Quintet* ***
(BB) **(*) Naxos 8.553851-2. Michael Thompson Wind Quintet – HINDEMITH: *Kleine Kammermusik* **(*); JANACEK: *Mládí* **(*); LARSSON: *Quattro tempi* **

Barber's *Summer Music* is an evocative mood-picture of summer, a gloriously warm and lyrical piece. The Crystal CD offers superbly committed and sensitive playing; a vivid recording.

The Michael Thompson Wind Quintet offer the piece with an enterprising choice of coupling and give an expressive account. The playing is wonderfully accomplished and sensitive, but the close balance does rob it of atmosphere.

PIANO MUSIC

Piano Sonata
(M) *** Phoenix PHCD 105. Browning – CUMMINGS: *24 Preludes* ***

John Browning has long been associated with Barber's music and in 1962 was the soloist in the New York première of his *Piano Concerto*, which was commissioned for him. Here he gives a definitive performance of the *Sonata*, articulating the Scherzo with witty delicacy, readily finding the elusively nostalgic mood of the slow movement and confidently surmounting the technical difficulties of the closing polyphony, with a burst of bravura at the close. He is very well recorded and the coupling is both unexpected and rewarding.

VOCAL MUSIC

Agnus Dei

*** Hyp. CDA 66219. Corydon Singers, Best – BERNSTEIN: *Chichester Psalms;* COPLAND: *In the Beginning*, etc. ***

Barber's *Agnus Dei* is none other than our old friend the *Adagio*, arranged for voices by the composer in 1967. Matthew Best's fine performance moves spaciously and expansively to an impressive climax.

Despite and Still (song-cycle), *Op. 41; 10 Hermit Songs, Op. 29; Mélodies passagères, Op. 27; 3 Songs, Op. 2; 3 Songs, Op. 10; 4 Songs, Op. 13; 2 Songs, Op. 18; 3 Songs, Op. 45; Beggar's Song; Dover Beach; In the Dark Pinewood; Love at the Door; Love's Caution; Night Wanderers; Nuvoletta; Of That So Sweet Imprisonment; Serenades; A Slumber Song of the Madonna; Strings in the Earth and Air; There's Nae Lark*

(M) *** Decca 474 685-2 (2). Studer, Hampson; Browning or Emerson Qt

This distinguished (originally DG) set won the *Gramophone* Solo Vocal Award in 1994 and is in every way recommendable. Barber's style, easily lyrical, sensitively responding to the cadences of English verse, remained remarkably consistent. Cheryl Studer sings beautifully in the *Hermit Songs*, but it is Thomas Hampson who establishes the full flavour of the collection, which includes a sprinkling of vigorous, extrovert songs. He is particularly fine in Barber's best-known song, the extended *Dover Beach*. In that, Hampson is accompanied immaculately by the Emerson Quartet. Otherwise it is John Browning who sharpens the focus and heightens the fantasy in deeply sympathetic accompaniments. Excellent, natural recording, first-class documentation and full texts.

BARGIEL, Woldemar (1828–97)

Octet in C min. for Strings, Op. 15a

(BB) *** Hyp. Helios CDH 55043. Divertimenti – MENDELSSOHN: *Octet* ***

Woldemar Bargiel was Clara Schumann's step-brother and wrote this remarkable *Octet* while a student at the Leipzig Conservatoire. Of course it is not a masterpiece of the same order as the Mendelssohn, with which it is coupled here, but it has natural dignity and real substance. Bargiel has great facility: his invention is of quality and distinction, and his writing shows independence of mind. It would be worth duplicating the Mendelssohn recording for the sake of this compelling music. Divertimenti play it with total commitment and understandable enthusiasm.

BARRIOS, Agustin (1885–1944)

Agustin Barrios was born in southern Paraguay and died in El Salvador. He had no formal musical training and spent his life travelling as an itinerant virtuoso guitarist. For the most

part, the quality of his own music went virtually unrecognized until the 1970s, when the recordings of John Williams revealed the depth of his musicianship, his mastery of his instrument's technique, and a highly individual melodic and harmonic talent.

Las abejas; Aconquija; Aire de Zamba; La catedral; Choro de saudade; Cueca; Julia Florida; Una limosna por el amor de Dios; Maxixa; Mazurka appassionata; Medallon antiguo; Preludios: in C min.; in G min. Un sueño en la floresta; Valses 3–4; Vallancico de Navidad

*** Sony SK 64396. Williams

Aconquija; Aire de Zamba; La catedral; Cueca; Estudio; Una limosna por el amor de Dios; Madrigal (Gavota); Maxixa; Mazurka appassionata; Minuet; Preludio; Un sueño en la floresta; Valse 3; Vallancico de Navidad

(B) *** Sony (ADD) SBK 47669. Williams – PONCE: *Folia de España* ***

The full-price CD duplicates almost all the music on John Williams's first (bargain-priced) recital of music by this fine Paraguayan composer and it has the advantage of the complete background silence of digital recording. The playing is of the highest calibre and has both concentration and charisma. However, the earlier disc offers about 10 minutes' more music, including the Ponce *Variations*, and it remains very attractive in its own right.

Humoresque; Junto a tu corazon – Vals; Mabilita; Madrigal – Gavota; Maxixa; Pepita; Sarita (Mazurka); Suite Andina; Tu y Yo (Gavota romántica); Un sueño en la floresta; Vals, Op. 8/4; Vidalita con variaciones; Vallancico de Navidad

(BB) *** Naxos 8.554558. Goni

The first instalment of Barrios's guitar music from the international prize-winning Greek virtuoso Antigoni Goni plays in a rather more romantic style than John Williams. But Goni's ebb and flow of rubato is a natural response to the line of the music and her playing always sounds spontaneous. She is very well recorded, and the back-up documentation is first class. Incidentally, the attractive four-movement *Suite Andina*, which closes the recital, is an arbitrary grouping of four independent pieces (*Aconquija, Aire de Zamba, Córdoba* and *Cueca*).

Volume 2: Canción de la Hilandera; La catedral; Confesión; Contemplación; Invocación a mi madre; Madrecita; 4 Minuets; Oración (Piegaria); Oración para todos; La Samaritana; El sueño de la muñequita; Variations on a Theme of Tárrega

☛ (N) (BB) *** Naxos 8.555718. Enno Voorhost

For this second volume of their Barrios survey, Naxos have chosen the Dutch guitarist, Enno Voorhost, whose playing is of the highest order. His flexing of rubato and flowing lines are totally spontaneous-sounding, and his beguilingly subtle control of dynamic brings the most disarmingly attractive results. The programme includes the three-movement – not too serious – portrait of *La catedral* (of San José, Montevideo), which is most evocatively done, while the delicately articulated *Confesión* and the fluttering *Canción de la Hilandera* contrast with the romantic *Oración para todos*. Every piece here is melodically enticing and Voorhost is the composer's most seductive exponent. He ends with *Variations on a Theme of Tárrega*, using another very winsome melody, nicely expanded. The recording is very real and properly intimate, and this is an obvious first choice for those wanting to sample the music of this underrated composer.

BARTÓK, Béla (1881–1945)

Mercury Dorati Recordings

(i) *Concerto for Orchestra;* (ii; iii) *Violin Concerto 2;* (iv) *Dance Suite;* (v) *Divertimento for String Orchestra;* (iv) *Mikrokosmos* (arr. Serly): *Bourrée; From the Diary of a Fly.* (v; vi) *The Miraculous Mandarin;* (i) *Music for Strings, Percussion & Celesta;* (iv) *2 Portraits;* (iii) *Second Suite for Orchestra;* (i; vii) *Sonata for Two Pianos & Percussion;* (i) *The Wooden Prince.* (viii) *Bluebeard's Castle*

(N) (M) *** Mercury (ADD) 476 6255 (5). (i) LSO; (ii) Menuhin; (iii) Minneapolis SO; (iv) Philh. Hung.; (v) BBC SO; (vi) BBC Symphony Ch.; (vii) Frid, Ponse; (viii) Szönyi, Skékely; all cond. Dorati

Dorati pioneered the way in recording so much Bartók in the early days of stereo, and this distinguished Mercury box makes a formidable collection. He secures brilliant playing from his various orchestras, especially so with the LSO in the *Concerto for Orchestra.* The work opens evocatively and combines bite with a fiery ardour in the outer movements – the *Elegia* touching, the *Giuoco della coppie* genial and bright-hued – and the finale is exhilarating, with the brass producing a spontaneous burst of excitement near the close. This was recorded in 1964 and shows Mercury's typical skill in the matter of balance, while the 1956 Minneapolis recordings of the *Violin Concerto* and *Second Suite* show just how vivid their earliest stereo recordings were. In the *Violin Concerto* Menuhin demonstrates those special qualities of lyrical feeling and warmth for which he was justly famous – the haunting theme and variations of the central *Andante tranquillo* is especially appealing, and the finale has plenty of impetus and fire. The *Second Orchestral Suite* is a colourful, half-hour-long piece in four movements; the second movement introduces a vibrant fugue and the *Andante* opens with an unusual extended recitative from the bass clarinet. The energetic, folksy finale ends serenely (*molto quieto*). Dorati is a persuasive advocate, and the Mercury recording has no lack of primary colours. The two ballets are both brilliantly played and authentic in spirit: *The Wooden Prince* is given a fresh, dynamically detailed reading, with the reminders of Stravinsky and Bartók's Debussian textures brilliantly caught (1965). *The Miraculous Mandarin,* with its slightly dry yet vivid sound-picture (1965), sounds appropriately chilling, and if it is not quite top choice for this lurid work, the imaginative playing still makes for an impressive account. The *Divertimento,* with which the *Mandarin* was originally coupled, receives a similarly red-blooded, Hungarian performance, even if the finale feels just that bit too steady. The *Music for Strings, Percussion and Celesta* is highly atmospheric, the playing full of tension, with Dorati bringing out all the Hungarian dance inflexions in the finale, while the 1961 sound hardly sounds its age. In the *Dance Suite, Two Portraits* and *Mikrokosmos* items Dorati's fine orchestra of Hungarian émigrés offer distinctive and idiomatic performances, with the late-1950s recordings offering plenty of body without blurring the outlines. The *Sonata for Two Pianos and Percussion* dates from 1960 and is spontaneously compelling. However, in the 1963 recording of *Bluebeard's Castle,* while Dorati secures brilliant playing from the LSO, he finds power rather than mystery in Bartók's unique one-acter. Skékely's portrayal of Bluebeard is taut and intense, using his characterful bass imaginatively. Olga Szönyi is more uneven, strong and incisive but with squally moments. Though rival versions are

more atmospheric than this, Dorati relates this work more clearly to later Bartók. Unfortunately, no libretto is included, but the set overall remains fully recommendable.

Concerto for Orchestra

*** Australian Decca Eloquence (ADD) 467 602-2. Israel PO, Mehta – JANACEK: *Taras Bulba;* KODALY: *Concerto for Orchestra* ***

⊛ (BB) (***) Dutton Lab. mono CDK 1206. Concg. O, Van Beinum – STRAVINSKY: *The Rite of Spring* (***)

(BB) (***) Naxos mono 8.110105. Boston SO, Koussevitzky – MUSSORGSKY: *Pictures at an Exhibition* (**(*))

(M) **(*) Telarc CD 80174. LAPO, Previn – JANACEK: *Sinfonietta* **(*)

It is curious that Mehta's splendid 1976 *Concerto for Orchestra* has had to wait so long for its CD release (though only on Australian Decca). Unlike most Israel Philharmonic recordings, this one was made in Kingsway Hall, London, and the sound is rich and full; and if Mehta's performance lacks the last degree of bite that you find with some others, its combination of brilliance and warm expressiveness is very attractive. The finale has a measure of jollity in it (what Bartók called its ' life-assertion') at a tempo that allows the strings to articulate their rushing semi-quavers clearly. The recording was in the demonstration bracket in its day, with translucent woodwind, firmly focused brass and plenty of sheen on the strings. It is reissued as part of an excellent triptych on the Australian Eloquence label which, unlike the UK series, contains full sleeve-notes.

Eduard van Beinum's recording dates from the early 1950s and it is astonishing how vivid is the work's impact. Bartók's vision springs to life in an extraordinarily fresh way. If you feel a little tired of this piece, listen to van Beinum, for he renews one's enthusiasm for this score as do few others. The sound is quite astonishing in detail and sonority.

The thrilling issue in the Naxos Historical series offers a radio recording of the first performance of the *Concerto for Orchestra* which Koussevitzky gave in Boston on 30 December 1944, four weeks after the New York première. It is a tribute to the virtuoso qualities of the Boston orchestra that the playing is not merely brilliant but has a tension and authority missing from many latter-day performances. Though the sound is limited, with some odd balances and changes of volume, the glowing warmth of the Koussevitzky orchestra, as well as the brilliance, are vividly conveyed, making one easily forget that this is 1944 mono radio sound. The opening of the slow introduction may be more ponderous than we are used to, but that is very much the exception. The textual oddity is that the original five-bar pay-off in the finale is used, where latterly the 24-bar alternative has been universally adopted which is far more effective.

Previn and the Los Angeles Philharmonic give a comfortable, relaxed reading of Bartók's *Concerto.* For Previn, it is above all a work of fun, although there is no lack of excitement in the finale. The Telarc recording captures the full bloom of the orchestra.

(i) *Concerto for Orchestra;* (ii) *Piano Concertos 1–3;* (i; iii) *Violin Concerto 2 in B min.*

(B) *** Ph. (ADD) Duo 438 812-2 (2). (i) Concg. O, Haitink; (ii) Kovacevich, LSO or BBC SO (in 2), C. Davis; (iii) Szeryng

This is as enticing a bargain Bartók collection as you could find. Haitink's 1960 *Concerto for Orchestra* is more subtle, less tense than Solti's mid-priced version, although the element of dramatic contrast is not missing. Szeryng joins Haitink for the *B minor Violin Concerto* with equally satisfying artistic results. Kovacevich's direct, concentrated readings of the three *Piano Concertos* are hardly less persuasive. Sir Colin Davis accompanies sensitively and vigorously. No complaints about the bright, full recording in all four concertos.

(i) *Concerto for Orchestra;* (ii) *Piano Concerto 2;* (iii) *Violin Concerto 2;* (iv; v) *Hungarian Sketches;* (iv; vi) *The Miraculous Mandarin: Suite*

(B) *(**) RCA 2-CD mono/stereo 74321 88690-2 (2). (i) Boston SO, Leinsdorf; (ii) Weissenberg, Phd. O, Ormandy; (iii) Menuhin, Dallas SO, Dorati; (iv) Chicago SO; (v) Reiner; (vi) Martinon

Leinsdorf's *Concerto for Orchestra* is impressively played in Boston, with plenty of colour and warmth in the central movements and some thrilling virtuosity in the finale. The Boston acoustic adds to the warmth of atmosphere, but one wishes that for this compilation RCA had chosen Reiner's Chicago version, which is even finer.

The *Second Piano Concerto* is given a strongly rhythmic performance, not quite so poetic as it might be in the hushed passages of the slow movement, but with red-blooded playing from the Philadelphia Orchestra under Ormandy and atmospheric sound this still makes a vivid impression.

The *Second Violin Concerto* is another matter. This was Menuhin's first recording of a work that obviously inspired him and he never surpassed it. He was at his peak in 1946 and his exquisite solo playing is full of lyrical intensity (especially moving in the slow movement) and technically dazzling. Dorati and the excellent Dallas players give him vibrant, splendidly idiomatic support. The mono recording, with the soloist closely balanced and the orchestral sound two-dimensional, is unflattering, but the ambience of the hall is not entirely lost, and the sheer calibre of the performance triumphs over the technical limitations.

The *Five Hungarian Sketches* are arranged from a set of folk-inspired piano pieces, and in Reiner's hands they show Bartók at his freshest and most original. But this fine (1958) recording is also available more attractively coupled (see below).

Martinon also gives a brilliantly played performance of the so-called *Suite* from *The Miraculous Mandarin* – essentially the ballet minus the final scene. But this conductor's French refinement obviously made it difficult for him to enter fully into the ruthless barbarism of Bartók's conception, and the result is not biting enough to be fully idiomatic. Yet those who find this score normally too brutal may enjoy Martinon's more evocative approach, which is persuasive in a different way when the 1969 recording is so atmospheric.

Concerto for Orchestra; (i) Concerto for 2 Pianos, Orchestra and Percussion. Romanian Folk Dances

(N) **(*) Warner 2564 61947-2. (i) Kärkkäinen, Jumppanan, Erkkilä, Ferchen; Finnish RSO, Oramo

Oramo's account of the *Concerto for Orchestra* has the most vivid colour palette beautifully caught in the recording, but it is not the most excitingly driven version available. However, the main interest here is the *Concerto for Two Pianos with Percussion*, which derives directly from the *Sonata for Two Pianos and Percussion*. Whether you think that this orchestral arrangement robs the piece of its unique textural subtleties or not, here the vivid orchestral contribution is undoubtedly

enjoyable in its own right, and the two soloists and their percussive partners all make a vibrant contribution. The *Romanian Folk Dances* (for strings) make a splendid encore.

Concerto for Orchestra; (i) Viola Concerto

(M) *** Sup. (ADD) SU 3686-2. Czech PO, Ančerl; (i) with Karlovský

This is one of the first of a series of recordings made by Karel Ančerl with the Czech Philharmonic Orchestra in the early 1960s that have been transformed by expert remastering (in this instance by Stanislav Sýkora), so that at last we can hear how good the original recordings were. Certainly that applies to this 1963 recording of the *Concerto for Orchestra*, made in the Rudolfinum Studio, Prague, with the violins bright, clear and biting, and with superb inner detail, yet no lack of ambient lustre on the woodwind. It is not the most ruthless performance on record, as one might have expected from one of the most distinguished Slavonic orchestras; rather it is a highly atmospheric and vigorously understanding one, which demonstrates the virtuosity of both the string section and individual players in the way Bartók intended, culminating in a brilliant and exciting account of the finale. This now projects as one of the finest performances in the catalogue and fully deserves its three-star rating.

The coupling of the *Viola Concerto*, a less coherent work, is not quite on this level. The soloist here does not seem able to make a great deal of the first movement, which is perhaps not altogether his fault – the work has since been re-edited by Bartók's son, Peter. But the violist seems much happier in the *Adagio* and finale, although his playing is without a strong personality. However, the recording is well balanced.

Concerto for Orchestra; Dance Suite; Divertimento; Hungarian Sketches; The Miraculous Mandarin: Suite; Music for Strings, Percussion & Celesta; Romanian Folk Dances

(B) *** Double Decca 470 516-2 (2). Chicago SO, Solti

A self-recommending collection of Solti's digital Bartók recordings. His Chicago performances may not quite have the searing intensity of his classic LSO accounts of the major works here, but the extra warmth of the later readings brings out the lyrical qualities to the music. The *Divertimento* is superbly done too, incisive and full-bodied, and the Hungarian and Romanian dances have all the atmosphere one could wish for. In short, this is excellent value in the Double Decca series and brings typically fine Decca sound.

Concerto for Orchestra; Dance Suite; The Miraculous Mandarin: Suite

(M) *** Decca (ADD) 467 686-2. LSO, Solti

There will be many who prefer Solti's earlier (1965) LSO version of the *Concerto for Orchestra*, for this recording – outstanding in its day – shows its age, though only marginally, in the brightly lit string-tone; in all other respects it is of high quality, with a touch more wit and idiosyncrasy than the later, Chicago version (see above). There is more spontaneity too than in the later, digital account, and one senses Solti's Hungarian upbringing more readily here, for he allows himself certain rubato effects not strictly marked in the score, absorbing the inflexions of Hungarian folksong, very much an influence of Bartók's last-period lyricism. The inclusion of two fill-ups is welcome. The *Dance Suite* may suggest something rather trivial, but Bartók's inspired composition gives us a work that can be enjoyed on many different levels, especially when the performance is so strong and fiery and the recording exemplary. The streak of ruthlessness in Solti's approach that sometimes mars performances of less earthy music is then really given full rein in *The Miraculous Mandarin Suite*, which was recorded with comparable vividness and colour two years earlier, and is benefiting from the Kingsway Hall ambience.

Concerto for Orchestra; Hungarian Sketches; Music for Strings, Percussion & Celesta
(N) (M) *** RCA (ADD) **SACD** 82876 61390-2. Chicago SO, Reiner

Reiner's superlative account of the *Concerto for Orchestra* sounds better than ever in the new compatible-SACD version heard through two speakers. The performances of the *Music for Strings, Percussion and Celesta* and the splendid *Hungarian Sketches* also benefit from the additional presence and sumptuousness of the new transfer. Indispensable, even if you have other accounts of these scores.

Concerto for Orchestra; Kossuth; 3 Village Scenes
(N) (M) *** Ph. 476 7255. Budapest Festival O, Ivan Fischer

The Budapest Festival Orchestra add to their laurels with their outstanding account of the *Concerto for Orchestra*, also offering, as well as the *Village Scenes*, an equally compelling account of the rarely heard symphonic poem, *Kossuth*. Written in 1903, after the young Bartók had heard and admired Strauss's *Ein Heldenleben*, it was inspired by the Hungarian revolutionary hero in the 1848 uprising. Except in the Hungarian rhythms, which the Budapest players inflect so idiomatically, it may give little indication of the mature Bartók, but in its opulence it makes a most satisfying piece, and a modern recording was badly needed. This disc has been reissued by Universal in their 'Critics' Choice' series and quotes the Editor of *Gramophone*, who said of the thrilling orchestral response: 'One senses that the players are being driven to the very limits of their abilities, which only serves to intensify the excitement.' The recording is absolutely first class.

(i) Concerto for Orchestra; (ii) Music for Strings, Percussion & Celesta
(M) *** Praga (ADD) PR 54047. (i) Czech PO, Lehel; (ii) Leningrad PO, Mravinsky

Concerto for Orchestra; Music for Strings, Percussion & Celesta
(M) **(*) DG (ADD) 457 890-2. BPO, Karajan
(M) ** Orfeo (ADD) C551 011B. Bav. RSO, Kubelik

Mravinsky's reading of the *Music for Strings, Percussion and Celesta* is familiar from the days of LP, when it appeared in harness with Honegger's *Symphonie liturgique*, and its sense of mystery and incisive rhythms make for a thoroughly idiomatic reading. But what makes this disc so desirable is György Lehel's magnificent account of the *Concerto for Orchestra*. We remember being carried away by this in its LP incarnation, but renewing its acquaintance on CD, it seems better than ever. It is highly atmospheric, light in texture, full of character and personality, with first-class wind playing: this is very much like hearing the work for the very first time. The recording is very natural, and the performance belongs right up there with the very best. This is recommended with enthusiasm.

Karajan is right in treating Bartók emotionally, but comparison with Solti points the contrast between Berlin romanticism and earthy Hungarian passion. Karajan's moulding of phrases is essentially of the German tradition. The *Music for Strings, Percussion and Celesta* has a well-upholstered timbre, and here Karajan's essentially romantic view combines with the recording to produce a certain urbanity.

Kubelik served as chief conductor of the Bavarian Radio Symphony Orchestra for 18 years, and this account of the *Concerto for Orchestra* was recorded in March 1978 during his tenure; the *Music for Strings, Percussion and Celesta* comes from a guest appearance three years later. There is much to impress here, though neither displaces existing recommendations.

Concerto for Orchestra; 4 Orchestral Pieces, Op. 12
**(*) DG (IMS) 437 826-2. Chicago SO, Boulez

Boulez secures brilliant playing from the Chicago orchestra, but they are able to relax in the central movements, and the finale is very powerfully driven indeed. The *Four Orchestral Pieces* was the nearest that Bartók ever came to writing a symphony, complete with Scherzo and melancholic slow movement.

Piano Concertos 1–3
(M) *** Teldec Elatus 0927 46735-2. Schiff, Budapest Festival O, Fischer
(M) *** DG (ADD) 447 399-2. Anda, Berlin RSO, Fricsay
(BB) **(*) Naxos 8.550771. Jandó, Budapest SO, Ligeti

(i) Piano Concertos 1–2; (ii) 2 Portraits, Op. 5
(M) *** DG (IMS) 457 909-2. (i) Pollini, Chicago SO; (ii) Minz, LSO; Abbado

András Schiff's colourful, winning performances of Bartók's three piano concertos are totally idiomatic, brilliantly and warmly accompanied by the fine Budapest orchestra, bringing out point and sparkle. His depth of meditation in the slow movements matches that which he brings equally to his performances of Bach or Schubert. Now on Elatus, this is a real bargain.

The Géza Anda recordings with Ferenc Fricsay from the beginning of the 1960s are rather special. Both artists show a feeling for the music's inner world and its colouring which is magnetic in the slow movements yet urgent, incisive and red-blooded too. The recording is remarkably atmospheric, yet still tangible in detail.

Jandó is on top form, playing with exciting bravura throughout. The energy of the motoric *First Concerto* is not brutalized, and in the slow movements the resonance of the recording ensures that there is plenty of atmosphere, even if in outer movements the violent brass interjections could be more cleanly focused. Apart from the excess of resonance, the recording is vivid and well balanced.

Pollini's concerto coupling celebrates an exuberant Italian partnership. Rhythms in fast movements are freely and infectiously sprung to bring out the bluff Bartókian high spirits. The vividly recorded Chicago orchestra is in superb form. The ear is then sweetened by Minz's warmth in the *Portraits*. This is an excellent recommendation in its own right, but most collectors will want all three piano concertos.

(i; ii) *Piano Concertos 1–3. Violin Concertos* (iii; iv) *1*; (iii; ii) *2*

🔊— (B) *** Double Decca (ADD/DDD) 473 271-2 (2). (i) Ashkenazy; (ii) LPO; (iii) Chung; (iv) Chicago SO; all cond. Solti

Solti's Bartók recordings are classic accounts and remain top recommendations. If, in the *Violin Concertos*, the soloist is rather forwardly balanced, the hushed intensity of the writing, as well as the biting Hungarian flavour, is caught superbly, thanks to the conductor as well as to the soloist, and there is no sentimental lingering. In the *Piano Concertos*, the partnership between Ashkenazy and Solti works equally well. The *Second* and *Third Concertos* spark off the kind of energy one would expect from a live performance. The *First Concerto* (digital) is even tougher, urgent and biting, and the slow movements in all three work bring a hushed inner concentration, beautifully captured in warmly refined sound. Indeed, the recording throughout, whether analogue or digital, is of vintage Decca quality.

Piano Concerto 3

**(*) EMI 5 56654-2. Argerich, Montreal SO, Dutoit – PROKOFIEV: *Piano Concertos 1 & 3* **(*)

(i) *Piano Concerto 3. Mikrokosmos Vol. 6: 140, 144, 146–9, 151, 153*

(***) Testament mono SBT 1300. Katchen, (i) SRO, Ansermet – PROKOFIEV: *Piano Concerto 3* (***)

Elegant playing from Martha Argerich in the Bartók *Third Concerto* which is new to discography. There is a wonderful, improvisatory feel to much of it, though at times in the slow movement she caresses a phrase in a way that draws attention to her rather than to Bartók. Very distinguished playing, but not a first recommendation. Excellent support from the Montreal orchestra under Dutoit, and good recording.

Katchen's 1953 account of the then relatively new *Third Concerto* was the first LP version issued in Britain, and it superseded György Sandor's première records with Ormandy on 78s. The 1955 edition of *The Record Guide* called his playing 'delicate and imaginative', as indeed it is. Even now, half a century later, its freshness and spontaneity make its reissue welcome, particularly in so excellent a transfer. The excerpts from *Mikrokosmos* are also brilliant (and incidentally first appeared coupled with Ned Rorem's *Second Piano Sonata*).

(i) *Piano Concerto 3*; (ii) *Violin Concerto 2*

(M) *** Sup. SU 3682-2 011. (i) Bernáthová; (ii) Gertler; Czech PO, Ančerl

Bernáthová's is an essentially lyrical reading of the *Third Concerto*, but her skittish, lightly pointed articulation is appealing in the outer movements to make a perfect foil for the mood of the *Adagio religioso* slow movement, which is beautifully played and most affecting. This is well coupled with André Gertler's dedicated performance of the *Violin Concerto*, which also strikes a happy balance between romanticism and technical brilliance. Again the opening is light in style, with nice, snapping rhythms and crisp accentuation, and in the slow movement Gertler treats the music affectingly as a simple song. In the finale he is most successful in bringing out the scherzando humour. Ančerl's accompaniments are characteristically idiomatic in both works, and this is eminently recommendable, with good, atmospheric 1960s recording, naturally transferred to CD.

(i) *Piano Concerto 3*; (ii) *Sonata for Two Pianos & Percussion*

(BB) **(*) EMI Encore (ADD) 5 74991-2. Ogdon, (i) Philh. O, Sargent; (ii) Lucas, Holland, Fry – SHOSTAKOVICH: *Piano Concerto 2* ***

Ogdon gives a fine performance of the *Third Concerto*, although Sargent's accompaniment lacks the last degree of brilliance – the result brings out neither the joy nor the poetry of the work at the fullest intensity. The *Sonata for Two Pianos*, however, receives a stimulating performance from the husband-and-wife team: it is not always as sparkling as it might be (the finale runs down a little) but rarely have two pianists achieved such fine technical and emotional rapport in this music.

(i) *Viola Concerto* (two versions: ed. Péter Bartók & ed. Tibor Serly); *Two Pictures, Op. 10*

(BB) *** Naxos 8.554183. Xiao, Budapest PO, Kovacs – SERLY: *Rhapsody for Viola & Orchestra* ***

Having a première recording of Bartók on Naxos makes an unmissable bargain. His *Viola Concerto* was the uncompleted work which, soon after his death, Tibor Serly put together from sketches. Now Bartók's son Péter, with the scholar Paul Neubauer, has re-edited those sketches. Though the differences are small, this first recording of the revised version, superbly played, proves fascinating, sounding closer to the *Concerto for Orchestra*. With the rich-toned Chinese viola-player Xiao as soloist, that version is here presented alongside Serly's. The warmly atmospheric *Two Pictures* and a viola work by Serly make a good coupling.

(i) *Viola Concerto; Violin Concertos 1–2*; (ii) *Rhapsodies 1–2 for Violin & Orchestra*; (iii) *Duos 28, 31, 33, 36, 41, 42 for 2 Violins. Solo Violin Sonata*

(BB) *** EMI Gemini (ADD) 5 85497-2 (2). Y. Menuhin; (i) New Philh. O, Dorati; (ii) BBC SO, Boulez; (iii) Gotkovsky

Menuhin, with his strongly creative imagination, plays these concertos with characteristic nobility of feeling, and he and Dorati make much of the Hungarian dance-rhythms. There is an appealing, earthy, peasant manner in Menuhin's playing of the *Two Rhapsodies*, which are given an authentic tang, and rather surprisingly this is matched by Boulez's approach, warm, rather than clinical. The great violinist commissioned the *Solo Violin Sonata*, and this is his third recording, made at Abbey Road in 1974/5. The six individually chosen *Duos* make a bonus for what is a very attractive bargain double.

Violin Concertos (i) *1*; (ii) *2*

(BB) *** Naxos 8.554321. Pauk, Polish Nat. RSO (Katowice), Wit

*** Nim. NI 5333. Hetzel, Hungarian State SO, Fischer

György Pauk plays both concertos with exemplary musicianship and is given very good support by the Polish National Radio Orchestra at Katowice. No one investing in this coupling need feel disappointed, and the sound has great warmth and naturalness. Though not a first choice, this offers value for money and gives musical satisfaction.

Gerhart Hetzel also plays both concertos with great feeling and understanding. These are performances of strong but unintrusive personality. Both concertos are very well recorded, with a natural, excellent balance which helps the soloist to just the right extent, and it must rank among the very best now available.

Violin Concerto 2 in B min.
(N) **(M)** **(*) DG 477 5376. Mutter, Boston SO, Ozawa –
DUTILLEUX*Sur le même accord;* STRAVINSKY: *Violin Concerto in D* **(*)
(M) **(*) Orfeo (ADD) C 589021B. Hetzel, VPO, Maazel –
MOZART: *Divertimento 10 in F*, etc. **(*)

Violin Concerto 2; 2 Rhapsodies for Violin & Orchestra
*** DG (IMS) 459 639-2. Shaham, Chicago SO, Boulez

(i) *Violin Concerto 2; Solo Violin Sonata*
(BB) *** Virgin 5 62053-2 (2). Tetzlaff; (i) LPO, Gielen –
JANACEK: *Concerto; Sonata;* WEILL: *Concerto ***
(M) (***) EMI mono 5 74799-2. Menuhin; (i) Philh. O, Furtwängler

Shaham's reading of the *Second Violin Concerto* is full of flair and imagination, taut and intense, while Boulez draws superb playing from the Chicago orchestra. The hushed intensity of Shaham's playing in the slow movement has rarely been matched. The two *Rhapsodies* make an ideal coupling. Full-bodied, well-detailed sound.

Christian Tetzlaff gives a serious and likeable account of the *Violin Concerto* with the LPO. He does not press it into service as a mere vehicle for his own display but, on the contrary, is completely at *its* service. He gets very good support from Gielen and copes well with the formidable difficulties of the *Solo Sonata*. Very good recording and valuable couplings make this well worth considering.

EMI's 'Great Recordings of the Century' series restores the second of Menuhin's four versions of the Bartók *Concerto*, made in the Abbey Road Studios in 1953 with Furtwängler at the helm. It comes not with the pioneering 1947 version of the *Solo Violin Sonata*, which the great violinist had commissioned, but a later, 1957, account. Whichever modern version you might have, this is mandatory listening for anyone who cares about this great music, and it sounds splendid in this new transfer.

DG restore Anne-Sophie Mutter's strongly projected account of the Bartók to circulation, coupling it with a new work by Dutilleux written for her. The recording balance is close and, thrilling though much of the playing is, there is more musical satisfaction to be found in Shaham, Menuhin or Tetzlaff.

Gerhart Hetzel was a pupil and colleague of Wolfgang Schneiderhan, and this present issue pays tribute to his artistry. Hetzel's Bartók *Concerto* has a magisterial quality yet considerable poetic feeling. It has a natural lyricism and musicality as well as the spontaneity of the concert hall rather than the perfection of the studio. In this ORF (Austrian Radio) recording, Hetzel is rather too reticently balanced by comparison with his eminent rivals, and though the Vienna Philharmonic under Maazel give excellent support, the sound does not really match the quality Decca provide for Chung (currently deleted).

Dance Suite; Divertimento; Hungarian Sketches; 2 Pictures
**(*) DG (IMS) 445 825-2. Chicago SO, Boulez

Pierre Boulez and the Chicago orchestra are here rather smoother and less sharply focused than usual. So the *Dance Suite* has its Hungarian flavours muted and in the *Divertimento* the contrasts between solos and tutti are underplayed, though the slow movement and the slower movements among the *Two Pictures* and the five *Hungarian Sketches* are done most poetically.

Dance Suite; Hungarian Pictures; (i) *The Miraculous Mandarin* (ballet; complete)
(N) **(BB)** *** Naxos 8.557433. Bournemouth SO, Alsop, (i) with Bournemouth SO Ch.

Marin Alsop conducts powerful, colourful performances of the controversial and violent ballet, *The Miraculous Mandarin* in its full form, coupled with the *Dance Suite* of 1923, demonstrating in both the orchestra's virtuosity and the conductor's versatility. The recording favours transparency rather than weight, but there is ample bite in the playing, with each contrasted section sharply characterized, and the brass superbly caught. Helpfully, each of the 12 sections is separately banded. The *Dance Suite* in this performance brings together rustic vitality and orchestral refinement, a more genial reading than many, while the *Hungarian Pictures*, with Bartók's own colourful orchestrations of early piano pieces, makes a relaxed tailpiece.

Divertimento for Strings
●–• ✿ *** Chan. 9816. Norwegian CO, Brown – JANACEK: *Idyll*, etc. *** ✿
*** ECM 465 778-2. Camerata Bern, Zehetmair –
SCHOENBERG: *Verklaerte Nacht*; VERESS: *4 Transylvanian Dances ***
*** MDG 321 0180-2. Polish CO, Maksymiuk – BRITTEN: *Variations on a Theme of Frank Bridge ***

Iona Brown gives an arrestingly vibrant account of a piece that can sound dour but here is life-enhancing. The concentration is matched with playing of virtuosity and warmth and demonstration-standard sound of great presence.

While the expertly played account of the *Divertimento* by the admirable Camerata Bern led by Thomas Zehetmair does not displace the Norwegian Chamber Orchestra under Iona Brown, it gives it a good run for its money. Those who are attracted by the coupling, an eloquent reading of *Verklärte Nacht* and the fine *Transylvanian Dances* of Sándor Veress, should consider this as an alternative. The recording is very present and lifelike.

The Polish version under Jerzy Maksymiuk is also among the best. The playing is never less than distinguished and the recording very fine indeed.

Divertimento for Strings; Music for Strings, Percussion & Celesta
(N) *** Linn CKD 234. Scottish CO, Mackerras – KODALY: *Dances of Galánta ***

In his warmth and refinement Sir Charles Mackerras evidently regards Bartók as a composer more expressive than brutal, less sharply contrasted with his friend and colleague, Kodaly, than usual, a point well made by the inclusion of the *Dances of Galánta* as an extra item on the disc. As in that genial and colourful work, the dance element is delightfully brought out in the two fast movements of the *Music for Strings, Percussion and Celesta*, with rhythms wittily pointed and the jazzy syncopations given a lift to bring fun to the finale. There and throughout, Mackerras capitalizes on the advantage of having a smallish band of players so as to achieve a degree of flexibility in rhythm and phrasing such as you get with solo players. In the *Divertimento* that natural, easy flexibility makes for just as much of an idiomatic feeling as in the *Music for Strings, Percussion and Celesta*. Not that there is any lack of weight in any of the performances, with dynamic contrasts dramatically underlined.

(i) *Divertimento for Strings;* (ii) *Music for Strings, Percussion & Celesta;* (iii) *Sonata for 2 Pianos & Percussion*
**(*) Oxford OOCD-CD2 (1/2) (2). (i; ii) Oxford O da Camera, Sacher; (ii; iii) Fry, Holland; (iii) Berman, Lemin

In September 1995, within months of his own ninetieth birthday, the commissionee, Paul Sacher, recorded these live performances with the Oxford Orchestra da Camera, and he here introduces each with his own unique commentary in English. At speeds generally broader than usual, these unique performances may lack the vitality and bite of the finest rivals, but they have a compelling warmth and concentration. The two discs may be obtained from the orchestra direct (2 Axtell Close, Kidlington, Oxford).

Divertimento for Strings; Romanian Folk Dances
(BB) *** Warner Apex 0927 48732-2. St Paul CO, Wolff –
  KODALY: *Dances of Galánta; Dances of Marosszék* **(*)

Hugh Wolff is straight and direct in Bartók, and this approach yields attractive results: the *Romanian Dances* are fresh and very enjoyable, and the *Divertimento* has plenty of energy in the outer movements, yet Wolff allows room for the music to breathe: the slow movement has poise and plenty of atmosphere. These Bartók pieces make an enjoyable and effective contrast to the Kodály items, and they are excellent value.

Hungarian Pictures
(M) *** Chan. 6625 [id.]. Philh. O, Järvi – ENESCU:
  Roumanian Rhapsodies 1–2; WEINER: *Hungarian Folkdance Suite* ***

The *Hungarian Pictures,* drawn from various folk-based pieces and originally written for piano, are lightweight Bartók and vividly entertaining. They are superbly played here and given spectacular sound. They are aptly coupled, not only with Enescu's pair of *Roumanian Rhapsodies* but also with an equally engaging suite by Leó Weiner.

The Miraculous Mandarin (complete ballet), Op. 19
(*) Delos DE 3083. Seattle SO, Schwarz – KODALY: *Háry János,* etc. *
(N) **(*) Australian Decca Eloquence (ADD) 476 2686. VPO, Dohnányi – STRAVINSKY: *Petrushka* **(*)

(i) *The Miraculous Mandarin* (complete); *Hungarian Peasant Songs; Hungarian Sketches; Romanian Folk Dances; Transylvanian Dances*
*** (M) PH. 476 17990. (i) Hung. R. Ch., Budapest Festival O, Fischer

Iván Fischer's account of *The Miraculous Mandarin* is possibly the best ever committed to disc, and certainly the best recorded. The sound is in the demonstration category, with enormous range and depth. It has vivid presence and impact, and the balance is both truthful and refined. The performance has collected golden opinions almost everywhere and has virtuosity, bite and real flair. It won the *Gramophone* Orchestral Award in 1998 and is now reissued at mid-price in Universal's Award Collection: it makes a first-class recommendation for this repertoire.

Gerard Schwarz directs the Seattle orchestra in a powerfully atmospheric account of Bartók's malignant ballet-score, not as idiomatically aggressive as some, but with plenty of grip and excitement at the climax. Aptly and generously coupled with Kodály, this too can be recommended strongly.

Dohnányi's direction of *The Miraculous Mandarin* – which is normally regarded as an unusually barbaric score – is clean, precise and often beautiful. It is far less violent and weighty than usual, and not everyone will respond to what one could almost describe as an unsuspected neoclassical element in the score. That said, the playing of the VPO is very fine, helped by the spacious vintage Decca recording (1977).

The Miraculous Mandarin (Suite), Op. 19
— (N) (BB) *** EMI (ADD) 5 86095-2. Phd. O, Ormandy –
  HINDEMITH: *Concert Music; Symphonic Metamorphoses* ***

Ormandy and the Philadelphia Orchestra had recorded *The Miraculous Mandarin* before, but this 1978 EMI version, recorded at the Old Met., does full justice to the opulence of the Philadelphia strings and the rich sonorities of the cellos and basses. The sheer magnificence of the orchestral sound is a joy in itself, and the effect is dazzling. This reissue is a splendid bargain.

Music for Strings, Percussion & Celesta
(M) **(*) DG (ADD) (IMS) 463 640-2. BPO, Karajan (with
  STRAVINSKY: *Agon* ***)

In DG's latest transfer Karajan's recording (also available coupled with the *Concerto for Orchestra,* see above) offers very beautiful sound, with playing to match. There may not be enough abrasiveness for Bartók, but detail is admirably clear and the overall effect is undoubtedly seductive, as is the equally marvellously played Stravinsky coupling.

2 Portraits, Op. 5
(N) (M) *** Australian Decca Eloquence (ADD) 476 2700.
  VPO, Dohnányi – STRAVINSKY: *The Firebird* **(*)

Dohnányi's Bartók style, rather more mellow than usual, is suited to the *Two Portraits,* the first of which is used also as the first movement of the *First Violin Concerto.* The 1977 recording is warm and spacious.

Rhapsody 1 for Cello & Orchestra
(BB) *** Warner Apex 0927 40600-2. Noras, Finnish RSO,
  Saraste – ELGAR: *Cello Concerto;* DVORAK: *Cello Concerto* **(*)

Bartók scored only the first of his two *Rhapsodies* (originally written for violin and piano) for cello and orchestra, and very effective it is on the responsive bow of Arto Noras. The piece is in two sections, *Lassu* and *Friska,* and the contrasts between the lyrical and fiery elements are managed here with aplomb. Good though not outstanding recording, with the cello dominating the sound-picture.

Rhapsodies for Violin & Orchestra: 1 in G min.; 2 in D min.
(B) *** EMI Red Line CDR5 69806. Chung, CBSO, Rattle –
  DVORAK: *Violin Concerto* ***

Kyung Wha Chung gives commanding, inspired performances, full of fire and imagination.

The Wooden Prince, Op. 13 (complete ballet); Hungarian Pictures
*** Chan. 8895. Philh. O, Järvi

Järvi's red-blooded performance relates *The Wooden Prince* to romantic sources. The drama of the fairy story is told in glowing colours. The opulent playing of the Philharmonia is greatly enhanced by the full, vivid Chandos recording. The suite, *Hungarian Pictures,* provides a colourful if trivial makeweight.

CHAMBER AND INSTRUMENTAL MUSIC

Contrasts for Clarinet, Violin & Piano
*** Delos D/CD 3043. Shifrin, Bae, Lash – MESSIAEN: *Quatuor* ***

(i; ii) *Contrasts for Clarinet, Violin & Piano*; (ii) *2 Rhapsodies; Romanian Folk Dances.* (Solo) *Violin Sonata*
⊶ (BB) *** Hyp. Helios CDH 55149. Osostowicz, with (i) M. Collins; (ii) Tomes

(i) *Contrasts;* (ii) *String Quartet 6 in D;* (iii) *Allegro Barbaro; Dance Suite; Romanian Folk Dances*
(M) **(*) ASV PLT 8502. (i) Stanzeleit, Collins, Fenyö; (ii) Lindsay Qt; (iii) Frankl

(i) *Contrasts. Violin Sonatas 1–2*
(BB) *** Naxos 8.550749. Pauk, Jandó, (i) with Berkes

Hyperion's distinguished coupling of the Bartók *Contrasts* with the *Rhapsodies* and the *Sonata for Solo Violin* now re-emerges on the Helios budget label. All these artists are on excellent form. Krysia Osostowicz is as good as almost any of her rivals in the *Sonata*, and the remainder of the programme is hardly less impressive.

David Shifrin and his colleagues from Chamber Music Northwest also admirably capture the diverse moods of Bartók's triptych, including the mordant wit and vitality of the outer sections and the dark colouring of the centrepiece. They are very well recorded in an agreeable acoustic.

The Naxos collection is very highly recommendable too, particularly when these works are played by such experienced artists as György Pauk and his fellow Hungarian, Jenö Jandó. The refinement and subtlety of Pauk's playing here is very persuasive. In the superb account of *Contrasts*, in which Kálmán Berkes joins them, the balance is better than in the *Sonatas*. Outstanding value.

The Lindsays' performances of the Bartók *String Quartets* were rightly praised on their original release in the early 1980s, and this account of the *Sixth* from that cycle is powerful and expressive, and excellently recorded. Peter Frankl's performances of the piano music have splendid fire and spirit, though the piano tone is not caught flatteringly by the engineers. The *Contrasts* are vibrant, and the sound is exceptionally brilliant, but collectors may find this a bit too closely recorded for comfort.

(i) *44 Duos. Solo Violin Sonata*
(BB) *** Naxos 8.550868. Pauk, (i) with Sawa

György Pauk's impressive recording of the remarkable *Solo Sonata* of 1944 is commanding, and everywhere his pacing seems just right and his playing effortless. In the *44 Duos* Pauk, partnered by the Japanese violinist, Kazuki Sawa, offers expertly judged and splendidly characterful accounts of these pieces. The Naxos recording is very good indeed and enhances the attractions of this super-bargain issue.

(i–ii) *Piano Quintet;* (i; iii) *Andante* (for violin & piano); *Rhapsodies 1 & 2*
(BB) *** Naxos 8.550886-2. (i) Jandó; (ii) Kodály Qt; (iii) Pauk

The *Piano Quintet* dates from 1903–4. A substantial work, it is wholly uncharacteristic. The *Andante* for violin and piano comes from 1902 and is slight but charming. The two *Rhapsodies* come from 1928 and are popular in style. Very good

playing from György Pauk and alert playing from Jandó, whose humming is at times faintly audible. No quarrels with either recording or performances.

Romanian Folk Dances (arr. Székely)
*** Erato 8573-85769-2. Repin, Berezovsky – R. STRAUSS: *Violin Sonata;* STRAVINSKY: *Divertimento* ***

Repin and Berezovsky give an exemplary account of these Székely transcriptions as a makeweight in their outstanding Strauss–Stravinsky recital. There is nothing flashy about this impeccable and relaxed music-making.

Sonata for 2 Pianos & Percussion
*** Chan. 9398. Safri Duo & Slovak Piano Duo – LUTOSLAWSKI: *Paganini Variations* ***; HELWEG: *American Fantasy* **

The Slovak Piano Duo and the Safri Duo, two Danish percussion players, are all dazzlingly alive and vital. All the same, their CD labours under a handicap: it is not good value at full price, lasting about 50 minutes.

(i) *Sonata for 2 Pianos & Percussion. Suite for 2 Pianos, Op. 4b*
(BB) *** Warner Apex 0927 49569-2. Heisser, Pludermacher, with (i) Cipriani, Perotin

Heisser and Pludermacher offer a particularly useful coupling, and it is good to see their eminently vital and intelligent reading of the *Sonata* returning to circulation, particularly as the Argerich–Kovacevich account, arguably the finest, is currently out of circulation. Heisser and Pludermacher and their two percussionists are completely at one and totally idiomatic. The attractions of the disc are considerably enhanced by the coupling, the 1941 two-piano transcription of the *Second Suite for Orchestra* of 1905–7. Decent sound and excellent value.

String Quartets 1–6
⊶ (M) *** DG 476 18331. Tokyo Qt
*** Decca 455 297-2 (2). Takács Qt
*** DG 463 576-2 (2). Hagen Qt
(N) (BB) *** Naxos 8.557543/44. Vermeer Qt
**(*) Simax PSC 1197 (2). Vertavo Qt
*** DG 423 657-2 (2). Emerson Qt
(M) **(*) Auvidis (ADD) V 4809 (3). Végh Qt
(***) Pearl mono GEMS 0147 (2). Juilliard Qt
(B) **(*) EMI double forte 5 75652-2 (2). Alban Berg Qt
(**(*)) ASV CDDCS 301 (3). Lindsay Qt

The DG performances by the Tokyo Quartet bring an almost ideal combination of fire and energy, with detailed point and refinement. The readings are consistently satisfying. Though the polish is high, the sense of commitment and seeming spontaneity are great too. The set now reappears at mid-price in Universal's Award Collection (the Tokyo Quartet won the 1981 *Gramophone* Chamber Music Award).

The Takács Quartet also bring to these masterpieces the requisite virtuosity, tonal sophistication and command of idiom. These are full-blooded accounts of enormous conviction, with that open-air quality which suggests the fragrance of the forests and lakes of Hungary. The recording is excellent, and this Decca set now takes its place near the top of the list.

The Hagen Quartet also have all the requisite fire and virtuosity for these marvellous scores. Apart from their immaculate technical address they bring individual interpretative insights to bear as well. One or two expressive emphases in the *Third Quartet* may disturb some listeners, but on the whole theirs is a set with strong claims to commend it – among which is the vivid recording. Not necessarily a first recommendation, but certainly among the finest in the catalogue.

We are spoilt for choice in this repertoire. The Vermeer are a superbly equipped quartet with first-class ensemble and attack. These are recent recordings and are certainly highly recommendable, though earlier recordings by the Tokyo, Takács and Hagen Quartets are perhaps even more idiomatic. However, the Vermeer recording has a considerable price advantage.

The Vertavo Quartet are a Norwegian group that has been in existence for nearly two decades and has been playing the Bartók *Quartets* for 15 years. They bring a refreshing ardour and commitment and great vitality to the cycle. All the same, their ensemble is not always flawless, and at a time when there are such imposing accounts as the Tokyo or the Takács, for all their spirited dedication they must take second place.

The Emerson Quartet project very powerfully and, in terms of virtuosity, finesse and accuracy, outstrip most of their rivals. If at times their projection and expressive vehemence are a bit too much of a good thing, these are concentrated and brilliant performances that are very well recorded.

The Alban Berg Quartet's are very impressive performances indeed, technically almost in a class of their own. They are very well recorded too, but at times they appear to treat this music as a vehicle for their own supreme virtuosity.

The analogue Végh recordings date from 1972, but the CD transfers are managed splendidly and there is bite without edginess on top. The Végh players sometimes respond with more expressive warmth than some would expect to be applied to Bartók, but this prevents the music from becoming too aggressive and, above all, they produce an effect of seeming spontaneity. But this mid-priced set involves three discs.

Pearl offers new transfers of the famous integral set that American Columbia made in 1950 and Philips issued some years later on its ABL label and which was for long the yardstick by which others were judged. Although all the *Quartets* had been recorded before, this was the first set to be made by the same artists. The Juilliards went on to re-record them in stereo, but there is certainly something special about this pioneering set: a sense of discovery and of awe. It is a core recommendation in the Bartók discography and has been very well transferred.

The Lindsay performances, searching, powerful and expressive, are now reissued together. The digital recording, though first class, occupies three discs which, like the Végh set, places it at a distinct disadvantage.

The DG set by the Hungarian Quartet has considerable authority: the Hungarians were the first to record Nos. 5 and 6, and their leader gave the première of the *Violin Concerto*. But they do not quite convey the full intensity which distinguishes the best rival versions and this seems a curious choice for DG's Legendary 'Originals' (457 740-2).

Violin Sonatas 1–2. (Solo) Violin Sonata
(N) *** Virgin 5 45668-2. Tetzlaff, Andsnes
Violin Sonata 1; Sonatina (trans. André Gertler); Rhapsody 2 for Violin & Piano; Hungarian Folksongs (trans. Tivadar Országh); Hungarian Folk-Tunes (trans. Jozsef Szigeti)
*** ASV CDDCA 883. Stanzeleit, Fenyö

(Solo) Violin Sonata; Violin Sonata 2; Rhapsody 1; Romanian Folk Dances
*** ASV CDDCA 852. Stanzeleit, Fenyö

Christian Tetzlaff and Leif Ove Andsnes offer both the *Violin Sonatas* and the solo work on a single disc and bring a commanding intensity and fine discipline to all three, and their vividly recorded accounts must rank as the finest since the Oistrakh versions with Frida Bauer (No. 1) and Richter (No. 2) in the early 1970s. In the *Solo Sonata* Tetzlaff can withstand the most exalted comparisons.

Susanne Stanzeleit and her partner, Gusztáv Fenyö, are completely inside the idiom. The *Violin Sonata No. 1* and the *Rhapsody No. 2* are every bit as well played and recorded as the *Solo Sonata* and the *Second Sonata* for violin and piano (1922), and the performances are as good as any you can find in the current catalogue. The recording, too, is altogether first rate.

Portrait, Op. 5/1
⊙ (BB) (***) Naxos mono 8.110973. Szigeti, Philh. O, Lambert – BLOCH: *Violin Concerto;* PROKOFIEV: *Violin Concerto 1* (***) ⊙

Szigeti was a stylist and one of the greatest and most individual artists of his day. Not everyone responds to the slightly nasal tone or the nervous vibrato, but there is no questioning the strength of his personality or the quality of his artistry. They are heard to admirable effect in this outstanding account of the first of the Bartók *Portraits*, which he recorded with Constant Lambert on one of his first post-war visits to London. Naxos should reissue the remarkable records he made with Bartók himself in New York.

PIANO MUSIC

Allegro barbaro; 6 Dances in Bulgarian Rhythm; 3 Hungarian Folksongs; 15 Hungarian Peasant Songs; Mikrokosmos (excerpts); 3 Rondos on Slovak Folk Tunes; Sonatina
(BB) **(*) Naxos 8.550451-2. Szokolay

Balázs Szokolay is a highly musical player. His performances are always vitally intelligent and perceptive, and he is acceptably recorded. This is a thoroughly recommendable recital and excellent value, though Szokolay is by no means as well recorded as Kocsis on Philips, nor does he quite have the latter's subtlety or distinction.

Piano Music Vol. 1: *Andante for Piano; 3 Hungarian Folksongs from Csík; 15 Hungarian Peasant Songs, Sz.71; 3 Rondos on Folk Tunes, Sz.84; 7 Sketches, Op. 9b; Sonata, Sz.80; Suite, Op. 14*
(BB) **(*) Naxos 8.554717. Jandó

Piano Music Vol. 2: *Dance Suite; Improvisations, Op. 20; Petite Suite; Romanian Christmas Carols; Romanian Folk Dances 1–6; Slovakian Dance; Sonatina*
(BB) **(*) Naxos 8.554718. Jandó

The benchmark set of the Bartók piano music is the Philips survey by Zoltán Kocsis; of which three of the key CDs are now withdrawn. Jenö Jandó, however, is very well served by the Naxos engineers and gives far more than just serviceable accounts of this repertoire. His playing is thoroughly idiomatic without being really special.

14 Bagatelles, Op. 6; 2 Elegies, Op. 8b; 3 Hungarian Folk tunes; 6 Romanian Folk Tunes; Sonatina
⊙ (M) *** Ph. 476 1657. Kocsis

This was one of the CDs that R. L. chose as being special among the coverage of Bartók's piano music by Zoltán Kocsis, and Universal have now included it in their mid-priced 'Penguin ⊙ Collection'. Not only does it have the advantage of state-of-the-art recording quality, but it also has playing which leads the field in subtlety and imagination.

14 Bagatelles; 3 Hungarian Folk Songs; Out of Doors; 2 Romanian Dances, Op. 8a; Romanian Christmas Carols; Sonatina; Sonata
(M) *** Ph. 464 676-2. Kocsis

This representative collection, chosen as one of Philips's '50 Great Recordings', comes from the Kocsis complete survey, and as it includes the *Sonata* and *Sonatina* and is superbly recorded, it can be highly recommended to those not willing or able to purchase the premium-priced set.

For Children (Books 1–4) complete; Mikrokosmos (Books 1–6) complete
(M) *** Teldec (ADD) 9031 76139-2 (3). Ránki

Dezsö Ránki here shows his musicianship and plays all 85 pieces with the utmost persuasion and with the art that conceals art, for the simplicity of some of these pieces is deceptive; darker currents lurk beneath their surface. He gives us the composer's original edition of 1908–9. Ránki also plays the *Mikrokosmos* with an effortless eloquence and a welcome straightforwardness. He is very clearly (if forwardly) recorded, and he is given a realistic presence.

Mikrokosmos (complete)
**(*) Ph. 462 381-2 (2). Kocsis (with Mocsári in 43–4, 55, 68, 74 & 95; Lukin in 65, 74, 95, 127)
(B) **(*) HM (ADD) HMA 190968/9. Helffer (with Austbö)

Bartók originally intended the piano pieces he began composing in 1926 as a pedagogic exercise with his young son, Péter, in mind and that is exactly the way Kocsis plays the first third of the 153 pieces. Most music-lovers will undoubtedly concentrate on the second half of the work, where the playing really begins to grip the ear, with greater colour and more flexibility of line to bring these brief pieces fully to life. Martá Lukin seems an admirable choice for the four vocal settings, and Karoly Mocsári takes the second part in the pieces for piano duo. The recording is excellent.

Claude Helffer gives an intelligent account of all six books of the *Mikrokosmos*, but his approach at times goes to the other extreme, as he tends to invest detail with rather more expressive emphasis than this most simple of music can bear. However, Harmonia Mundi's cueing is ungenerous (there are only 12 bands to cover the whole series!). If you don't mind that, this is good value in the bargain range.

Out of Doors, Sz 81; Suite, Op. 14
(BB) ** Warner Apex 0927 40911-2. Ranki – STRAVINSKY: Piano Music **(*)

The fine Hungarian pianist Dezsö Ranki is a notable Bartók interpreter. Unfortunately, his accounts of the *Suite* and *Out of Doors*, recorded in 1981, are handicapped by dry recording, which militates against atmosphere. The performances are first class and, were the recording of comparable quality, this would carry a three-star recommendation

OPERA

Bluebeard's Castle (sung in Hungarian)
🎞 *** EMI 5 56162-2. Tomlinson, Von Otter, Elès (nar.), BPO, Haitink
*** DG (IMS) 447 040-2. Norman, Polgár, Chicago SO, Boulez
(M) *** Sony (ADD) SMK 64110. Nimsgern, Troyanos, BBC SO, Boulez
(M) *** Decca (ADD) 466 377-2. Berry, Ludwig, LSO, Kertész
(**(*)) Bluebell mono ABCD 075. Nilsson, Sönnerstedt, Swedish R. O, Fricsay – SCHIERBECK: *The Chinese Flute* (**(*))

(i) *Duke Bluebeard's Castle;* (ii) *Cantata profana*
(M) *** DG stereo/mono (IMS) 457 756-2. (i) Töpper; (i–ii) Fischer-Dieskau; (ii) Krebs, Berlin RIAS Ch., St Hedwig's Cathedral Ch.; (i–ii) Berlin RSO, Fricsay

Never before has Bartók's darkly intense one-acter been given such a beautiful performance on disc, intense and concentrated, as by Bernard Haitink in EMI's live recording of a concert performance with the Berlin Philharmonic. Anne Sofie von Otter conveys new tenderness in Judith, with John Tomlinson magisterially Wagnerian as the implacable Bluebeard, both singing superbly, naturally balanced, not spotlit. Most impressive of all, Haitink builds the performance to a terrifying climax, when Judith is consigned to darkness with her predecessors.

Boulez, in his tautly intense DG version, opts for marginally faster speeds than he did in his earlier, Sony recording, with voices close to add to the involvement. László Polgár is superb as Bluebeard – firm, dark and incisive as well as idiomatic. Jessye Norman is a magisterial Judith. She may not be a believable victim, but this is still a glorious performance, matching the beauty of the Chicago orchestra's playing, weighty and rich on detail.

On Sony, Boulez revealed himself as an impressively warm Bartókian; the soloists are vibrantly committed and the recording is outstandingly vivid, presenting the singers in a slightly contrasted acoustic as though on a separate stage. At the time Boulez had rarely if ever made a finer Bartók record, but his newer, DG version is even finer. A full libretto is provided.

In 1965 Kertész set new standards with his version of *Bluebeard's Castle* with Christa Ludwig and Walter Berry. There is still a strong case for preferring the reading conducted by a Hungarian – especially as the Decca sound reaches demonstration standard in its remastering for Decca's 'Legends' series – but on performance Haitink's later, EMI CD has the balance of advantage.

Fricsay pioneered *Bluebeard's Castle* in stereo in 1958. The snag is that the performance was tactfully cut so that it could fit on to a 12-inch LP. But it certainly stands the test of time. Fischer-Dieskau is a memorable Bluebeard, even if the tone-quality of the voice is perhaps too heroic, not quite sinister enough. Herta Töpper is a superb Judith, even if not always perfectly steady. However, the vivid remastering emphasizes the close balance of the soloists. However, despite this fault and despite the cuts, this remains a fine achievement. For the reissue DG have coupled Fricsay's arresting, indeed inspired, account of the remarkably original *Cantata profana*, recorded seven years earlier, with passionate contributions from both Helmut Krebs and the splendidly incisive chorus. Both recordings were made in the Jesus-Christus-Kirche. Full translations are included.

Bluebell offer a CD taken from a Swedish Radio broadcast from 1953 with Nilsson and Bernhard Sönnerstedt, a wonderful baritone who never sought an international career. Fricsay casts a powerful spell and gets wonderfully eloquent results. There are some cuts which would rule it out of court were it not for the powerfully distilled and extraordinary atmosphere Fricsay evokes, and the superlative quality of both soloists.

BAX, Arnold (1883–1953)

Cathaleen-ni-Hoolihan; (i) *Concertante for 3 Wind Instruments & Orchestra; London Pageant; Tamara Suite* (orch. Parlett)

*** Chan. 9879. BBC PO, Brabbins; (i) with Callow, Bradbury, Goodall

According to the useful notes, the tone-poem *Cathaleen-ni-Hoolihan* began life in 1903 in Bax's student years as the slow movement of a quartet. The score of *Tamara* was inspired by Karsavina, Diaghilev's prima ballerina for whom Bax fell when the Ballets Russes came to London in 1911. He never finished the orchestration, and the present 23-minute suite was compiled by the Bax scholar Graham Parlett. *London Pageant* comes from the Coronation year, 1937. The *Concertante for Cor Anglais, Clarinet, Bassoon and Orchestra* finds Bax at the very end of his creative life as it was being composed for the Henry Wood memorial concert in 1949. The performances are first class, persuasive in every way, and so, too, is the richly sonorous recording.

Christmas Eve; Cortège; Dance of Wild Irravel; Festival Overture; Nympholept; Overture to a Picaresque Comedy; Paean

(M) **(*) Chan. X10158. LPO, Thomson

This collection is perhaps for Bax aficionados rather than the general collector. It includes intriguing novelties, but the compilation is uneven in appeal. The *Overture to a Picaresque Comedy* is first-rate Bax, high-spirited and inventive. *Nympholept* means 'possessed by nymphs' and is another imaginative piece. However, *Christmas Eve* is an early work, coming from the Edwardian era, and is less developed and less interesting, while the *Paean* and *Dance of Wild Irravel* may stretch the allegiance of some listeners. The *Festival Overture* dates from 1909, but was revised in 1918 (and as such is recorded here for the first time). It is certainly spirited, if not distinctive. But all the performances here are sympathetic, and very well played and recorded too.

(i) *Cello Concerto. Cortège; Mediterranean; Northern Ballad 3; Overture to a Picaresque Comedy*

*** Chan. 8494. (i) Wallfisch; LPO, Thomson

The *Cello Concerto* is rhapsodic in feeling and Raphael Wallfisch plays it with marvellous sensitivity and finesse, given splendid support by the LPO under Bryden Thomson. The other pieces are of mixed quality: in the *Overture to a Picaresque Comedy* Thomson sets rather too measured a pace for it to sparkle as it should. The recording maintains the high standards of the Bax Chandos series.

(i) *Cello Concerto;* (ii) *Violin Concerto;* (iii) *Morning Song (Maytime in Sussex)*

(M) *** Chan. X10154. (i) Wallfisch; (ii) Mordkovitch; (iii) Fingerhut; LPO, Thomson

Chandos is re-grouping its vintage Bax recordings at mid-price, and Volume 1 includes two major concertante works plus the short but attractive *Morning Song*, an aubade for piano and chamber orchestra written to celebrate the twenty-first birthday of Princess Margaret, and subsequently made famous by Harriet Cohen. The *Cello Concerto* is discussed above, while Lydia Mordkovitch is equally committed to the *Violin Concerto*. This is full of good, easily remembered tunes, yet there is a plangent, bitter-sweet quality about many of its ideas and an easy, Mediterranean-like warmth that is very appealing. All three soloists are given splendid support by the LPO under Bryden Thomson, and the recording sets and maintains high standards for this Bax series.

(i) *Violin Concerto. Golden Eagle* (incidental music): *Suite; A Legend; Romantic Overture*

*** Chan. 9003. (i) Mordkovitch; LPO, Thomson

The *Violin Concerto*, discussed above, is played by Lydia Mordkovitch with commitment and conviction. The *Romantic Overture* is for chamber orchestra and has a prominent role for the piano. All this music was new to the catalogue, and the concerto deserves to be popular.

(i) *Violin Concerto;* (ii) *Symphony 3*

(M) (***) Dutton mono CDLX 7111. (i) Kersey, BBC SO, Boult; (ii) Hallé O, Barbirolli

Barbirolli's wartime recording of Bax's *Third Symphony*, made in the winter of 1943–4 when he was rebuilding the Hallé Orchestra, has never been surpassed as an interpretation, the first ever recording of a Bax symphony and still one of the finest. EMI did an early CD transfer, but this Dutton version brings astonishingly full and vivid sound, heightening the power of the performance. It is good too to have another powerful performance in the *Violin Concerto*, a work very different in mood from that of the symphonies. Eda Kersey recorded this with Boult and the BBC orchestra in Bedford in 1944, a recording made for the BBC Archive and not for general issue. The result again is astonishingly vivid, with Kersey, sadly short-lived, demonstrating her virtuosic flair and depth of feeling in a reading faster and more urgent in all three movements than the fine modern version from Lydia Mordkovitch on Chandos.

(i) *Concertante for Piano (Left Hand) & Orchestra. In memoriam;* (ii) *The Bard of the Dimbovitza*

*** Chan. 9715. BBC PO, Handley, with (i) Fingerhut; (ii) Rigby

In memoriam is vintage Bax and its main theme was re-used in his score for David Lean's *Oliver Twist*. The *Concertante for Piano (Left Hand)* was written in 1949 for Harriet Cohen, who had injured her right hand the previous year; but after its première under Barbirolli and a Prom performance some weeks later, it languished unheard. Margaret Fingerhut is a most persuasive advocate, and that no doubt helps the positive impression it makes here. *The Bard of the Dimbovitza* offers settings of Romanian peasant songs. Exemplary performances from the BBC Philharmonic under Vernon Handley and state-of-the-art recording.

(i; ii) *Eire: I, Into the Twilight; II, In the Faery Hills; III, Rose-Catha.* (iii; ii) *A Legend;* (i; iv) *On the Sea-Shore* (ed. Parlett); (i; ii) *The Tale the Pine Trees Knew*

(M) *** Chan. X10157. (i) Ulster O, (ii) Thomson; (iii) LPO; (iv) Handley

Volume 4 brings three tone-poems which form an Irish triology. The first two are filled with typical Baxian Celtic twilight, but the last, *Rose-Catha* (meaning 'battle-hymn') presents the composer in vigorous, extrovert mood, making an excellent contrast. Also included is *The Tale the Pine Trees Knew*, one of the better known as well as one of the most evocative of Bax's tone-poems. All are directed with total sympathy by Bryden Thomson. The prelude, *On the Sea-Shore*, makes a colourful and atmospheric companion in the hands of Vernon Handley, played and recorded with similar warmth and brilliance. A fine disc.

Film Music: (i) *Oliver Twist* (complete original score, prepared Graham Parlett). *Malta G.C.*, Part 2: *Gay March; Quiet Interlude; Work and Play; March*
*** Chan. 10126. BBC PO, Gamba; (i) with James

Bax's richly detailed score for David Lean's masterly *Oliver Twist* comes from 1948, during that vintage period in British films when the cream of British composers, including Bliss, Arnold and Walton, were commissioned to provide music of quality that could stand on its own apart from the visual images. Bax's score for *Oliver Twist* is a splendid example, yet it follows the narrative line with the utmost vividness and often with charming detail. In the depiction of Oliver's sleepless night, and again in the amiable depiction of Oliver's happiness at Mr Brownlow's house, Bax writes in effect a concertante piano part, originally written for (and recorded by) Harriet Cohen, but very well played here by Paul James. What is even more impressive is that the writing in the action sequences ('Nancy's hysterical outburst', for instance) never becomes just melodrama but retains its quality.

The writing for *Malta G.C.* is less individual but still attractive. It was the composer's first film score, written in 1942 for a Crown Film Unit propaganda short celebrating the island's valour in the face of fierce and protracted air attacks. Only the music for the first reel is included here, but it features a notable *March* with a genuine *nobilmente* theme in the best Elgarian tradition.

The performances under Rumon Gamba are persuasively sympathetic and spontaneous in their narrative flow and are gloriously recorded – just sample the luscious strings in the opening *Prelude* for *Oliver Twist*. Because of this, the previous coupling of these scores, admirably played by the RPO under Kenneth Alwyn, is to some extent displaced, although the Cloud Nine CD (ACN 7012) while offering only a suite from *Oliver Twist*, includes the full score of *Malta G.C.*, otherwise not available.

The Garden of Fand; The Happy Forest; November Woods; Summer Music
*** Chan. 8307. Ulster O, Thomson

The Celtic twilight in Bax's music is ripely and sympathetically caught in the first three items, while *Summer Music*, dedicated to Sir Thomas Beecham and here given its first ever recording, brings an intriguing kinship with the music of Delius. The Chandos recording is superb.

Golden Eagle; (i) Romantic Overture. Russian Suite; (ii) Saga Fragment (for piano & small orchestra); (iii) 4 Songs: Eternity; Glamour; Lyke-Wake; Slumber Song
(M) ** Chan. X10159. LPO, Thomson, with (i) Nunn; (ii) Fingerhut; (iii) Hill

Bax wrote the incidental music for his brother, Clifford's play, *Golden Eagle* (about Mary, Queen of Scots), which was briefly produced in 1945. Six orchestral numbers survive, of which the closing *Mary Stuart's Prayer* is genuinely touching. The three movements of the *Russian Suite*, all orchestrations of piano pieces, were written as 'symphonic interludes' for Diaghilev's Ballets Russes. As no orchestration of the central *Nocturne* survives, it is here scored by Graham Parlett and is the highlight. The other numbers are more conventional. The *Saga Fragment* (written for Harriet Cohen, but played here with much flair by Margaret Fingerhut) to some extent reflects the contrasts of atmosphere – pungent and wistful – of the *First Symphony*. The *Romantic Overture*, written during a visit to Delius in 1926, also has a concertante piano part, but it is overlong and its more striking idea does not appear until towards the end. The *Four Songs* make strange bedfellows and could not be more individually different. Bax wrote the lyrics of the first two (*Glamour* and *Slumber Song*) in 1910, when he fell ardently and hopelessly in love with a young, sylph-like Ukrainian girl, Natalia Skarginsky. He followed her back to Russia, but was rejected. The musical settings came a decade later, with *Glamour* here orchestrated by Rodney Newton. The third song, *Eternity*, was a setting of Robert Herrick, while *A Lyke-Wake Border Ballad* uses an anonymous sixteenth-century text. Martyn Hill sings them all sensitively, and throughout the collection the playing of the LPO for Bryden Thomson is exemplary in its commitment and refinement. Altogether, Volume 6 of the Chandos series makes an interesting collection, rather than a memorable one.

The Happy Forest; The Garden of Fand; November Woods; Summer Music; Tintagel
(M) *** Chan. X10156. Ulster O, Thomson

After Volume 1, this is perhaps the most attractive so far of these reissued Chandos Bax compilations in including not only *The Garden of Fand* but also Bax's masterly Cornish evocation, *Tintagel*. The Celtic twilight is ripely and sympathetically caught in the first three items, while *Summer Music*, dedicated to Sir Thomas Beecham and here given its first ever recording, brings an intriguing kinship with the music of Delius. The Chandos recording is superb.

(i) Mediterranean. Northern Ballads (ii) 2; (i) 3 (Prelude for a Solemn Occasion). (ii) Spring Fire; Symphonic Scherzo
(M) *** Chan. X10155. (i) LPO, Thomson; (ii) RPO, Handley

Volume 2 gathers together some of Bax's shorter, atmospheric and romantic pieces in highly idiomatic performances, notably those from the RPO under Vernon Handley. *Spring Fire* is an early work, but Bax's command of the orchestra is already richly in evidence. The *Second Northern Ballad* is dark and bleak, strongly tied to the landscape of the rugged northern coasts, while the *Third* is another dark and brooding score. The *Symphonic Scherzo* is of less moment than its companions. Thoroughly lifelike and characteristically well-detailed recording from Chandos.

On the Sea-Shore
*** Chan. 8473. Ulster O, Handley – BRIDGE: *The Sea*; BRITTEN: *Sea Interludes* ***

Bax's Prelude, *On the Sea-Shore*, makes a colourful and atmospheric companion to the masterly Bridge and Britten pieces on the disc, played and recorded with similar warmth and brilliance.

Sinfonietta (Symphonic Phantasy); Overture, Elegy & Rondo
(BB) ** Naxos 8.555109. Slovak PO, Wordsworth

The *Overture, Elegy and Rondo* comes from 1927, a year after the *Second Symphony*, and the *Sinfonietta* from 1932, the year of the *Fifth*. Neither finds Bax at his most inspired, though the *Sinfonietta* has a fine slow movement. The recordings come from 1987 and were previously offered at full price on Marco Polo. As the playing time of the disc is only 45 minutes, its reappearance on Naxos makes it more competitive. Neither piece is available in alternative versions. The performances are not the last word in polish and the recording does not offer distinguished sound, though it is on the whole acceptable.

Spring Fire; Northern Ballad 2; Symphonic Scherzo
*** Chan. 8464. RPO, Handley

Highly idiomatic playing from Vernon Handley and the RPO, and a thoroughly lifelike and characteristically well-detailed recording from Chandos.

Symphonic Variations for Piano & Orchestra; Morning Song (Maytime in Sussex)
*** Chan. 8516. Fingerhut, LPO, Thomson

Margaret Fingerhut reveals the *Symphonic Variations* to be a work of considerable substance with some sinewy, powerful writing in the more combative variations, thoughtful and purposeful elsewhere. This CD is in the demonstration class.

Symphonic Variations; Winter Legends (both for piano & orchestra)
(B) *** Chan. 10209X (2). Fingerhut, LPO, Thomson

It was a sensible idea to pair Bax's two concertante works together as a Chandos bargain Double (two discs for the cost of a single mid-priced record), but why omit the original bonuses of the *Morning Song* and *Saga Fragment*? Margaret Fingerhut's version of the *Symphonic Variations* is discussed above. The *Winter Legends* is reviewed below. The recording is in the demonstration class – a quite outstanding coupling.

Symphonies 1–7
(M) *** Chan. 8906/10. LPO or Ulster O, Thomson

Symphonies 1–7; Rogue's Comedy Overture; Tintagel
☛ ✪ (M) *** Chan. 10122 (5). BBC PO, Handley (set includes free bonus CD of an interview between Vernon Handley and Andrew McGregor)

Vernon Handley has nurtured a life-long ambition to record the seven symphonies of Arnold Bax and, now that Chandos has given him the chance, he has not disappointed us. Generally speaking, this is the most satisfying survey of the cycle we have yet had, and it is difficult to imagine it being superseded. The prodigality of invention in these Bax scores and the luxuriance of their colours and textures are heard to striking effect. Handley holds the scores together very convincingly. His tempi are expertly judged and allow the music to unfold naturally and eloquently. The *Second* (in some ways the most imaginative of them all) comes over impressively (the most satisfying since a memorable broadcast from the BBC Symphony Orchestra under Sir Eugene Goossens in the 1950s), and the *Third* is both tauter yet freer in spirit than any of its rivals, including Barbirolli's wartime pioneering set. Perhaps in the *Fifth* and *Sixth* honours are more evenly divided between Handley and David Lloyd-Jones and the Scottish National Orchestra; both show this music in the best possible light. Listening to Handley's *Seventh*, one is forced to question earlier doubts as to its weakness. The overall impression

it leaves is much stronger than in Raymond Leppard's deleted Lyrita account or Bryden Thomson's earlier Chandos version, and much the same goes for the *Fourth*, even though this is incontrovertibly the weakest of the seven. The orchestral playing is highly responsive and excels in all departments, and the Chandos BBC recording produces sumptuous tonal results (as one expects from any record bearing the names of Mike George and Stephen Rinker). The aural picture is subtle in colourings, less transparent and defined in detail than the recent Naxos versions, but very satisfying, and it all comes at mid-price together with a rarity from the 1930s, the *Rogue's Comedy Overture*, as well as the (rightly) popular *Tintagel*.

The Naxos recordings (see below) are very competitively priced and enable the collector to build up an imposing number of other orchestral pieces. Those who are not total devotees and who want only some of the symphonies (obviously Nos. 2, 3, 5 and 6) will probably gravitate towards Lloyd-Jones's survey (Nos. 5 and 6 are magnificent). But total Baxians will find Handley's set indispensable. In addition to the performances, there is a commentary on the works by the conductor in interview with Andrew McGregor.

Symphony 1; The Garden of Fand; In the Faery Hills
(BB) *** Naxos 8.553525. RSNO, Lloyd-Jones

This first disc in what Naxos also plan to be a Bax series offers warmly idiomatic readings of two early symphonic poems, as well as the *First Symphony*, in recordings less weighty than in the rival Chandos versions but finely detailed. In the two symphonic poems, more specifically inspired by Irish themes, Lloyd-Jones draws equally warm and sympathetic performances from the Scottish orchestra, bringing inner clarity to the heaviest scoring. First-rate sound, though Bryden Thomson on Chandos has even richer recording.

Symphony 3; The Happy Forest (symphonic poem)
(BB) *** Naxos 8.553608. RSNO, Lloyd-Jones

David Lloyd-Jones continues his admirable Bax series with a warmly idiomatic account of the *Third Symphony* of 1929, spacious in the long first movement and the meditative slow movement, defying any diffuseness of argument. The playing of the Scottish orchestra is clear and refined, helped by the transparency of the recording, clarifying often thick textures. From earlier in Bax's career *The Happy Forest*, described as a 'nature poem', provides a refreshing contrast in its youthful energy, tauter, less expansive.

Symphony 5; The Tale the Pine-Trees Knew
☛ (BB) *** Naxos 8.554509. RSNO, Lloyd-Jones

Dedicating his fine symphony of 1932 to Sibelius, Sir Arnold Bax openly echoes the example of that Finnish master, not least in nagging ostinato rhythms. There is also a northern chill in the writing, freshly caught and cleanly recorded in this fine performance from David Lloyd-Jones and the Royal Scottish National Orchestra. Where Bax elsewhere can seem diffuse, with passages rather like improvisations written down, there is a tautness here, again reflecting the example of Sibelius. The music remains very British in flavour, with the triumphant conclusion in a brazen major key affirming that. *The Tale the Pine-Trees Knew* of 1931, another northern inspiration, makes the ideal coupling. An excellent bargain.

Symphony 6; Into the Twilight; Summer Music
☛ ✪ (BB) *** Naxos 8.557144. RSNO, Lloyd-Jones

David Lloyd-Jones's survey of the Bax symphonies goes from

strength to strength, and this account of the magnificent *Sixth* (1933–5) supersedes either of its predecessors (Del Mar on Lyrita and Bryden Thomson on Chandos). His perform-ance has sweep and breadth, and the splendid Naxos record-ing has plenty of range, detail and presence. *Into the Twilight* (1909) is prefaced by a quotation from Yeats and though there are occasional reminders of Rimsky-Korsakov and the Rus-sian school – and also Strauss – its rich, luxuriant textures are fully characteristic of the mature Bax. *Summer Music* (1921, revised 1932) was dedicated to Beecham who had given the first (and, in Bax's lifetime, only) performance of *Into the Twilight*, and it is an affecting piece for a much smaller orchestra than we associate with the composer, though the sonority he produces is characteristically sumptuous. David Lloyd-Jones secures eloquent playing from the Scottish orchestra throughout.

Symphony 7; Tintagel
(BB) **(*) Naxos 8.557145. RSNO, Lloyd-Jones

The *Seventh Symphony* comes from 1939 and was first heard at the New York World Fair that year, conducted by Sir Adrian Boult. It was to be Bax's last symphony and one in which the creative fires seem to burn less intensely than in its two immediate predecessors. David Lloyd-Jones makes out a strong case for it and is as persuasive as (or more persuasive than) his predecessors on record. The late lamented Michael Oliver spoke of its first movement as 'an essay on ambiguity … a complex of unstable components; what appears confi-dently purposeful at one moment becoming tense later on'. Despite its length (it lasts 42 minutes 20 seconds – Handley is even more leisurely at 44 minutes 2 seconds – and is the longest of the seven), the score is still richly stocked. The recording has been called 'uncongenial' and 'unalluring', which strikes us as harsh, though climaxes do not have the transparency of earlier issues in the series nor the strings quite the bloom. David Lloyd-Jones also gives a thoroughly committed account of *Tintagel*.

The Truth about the Russian Dancers (incidental music); From Dusk till Dawn (ballet)
*** Chan. 8863. LPO, Thomson

The *Truth about the Russian Dancers* is vintage Bax, full of characteristic writing decked out in attractive orchestral col-ours. *From Dusk till Dawn* has many evocative ideas with some impressionistic orchestral touches. Not top-drawer Bax, but often delightful, and very well played by the London Philharmonic under Bryden Thomson, and splendidly recorded.

Winter Legends; Saga Fragment
*** Chan. 8484. Fingerhut, LPO, Thomson

The *Winter Legends*, for piano and orchestra, comes from much the same time as the *Third Symphony*, to which at times its world seems spiritually related. The soloist proves an impressive and totally convincing advocate for the score, and it would be difficult to imagine the balance between soloist and orchestra being more realistically judged. The compan-ion piece is a transcription of his one-movement *Piano Quartet* of 1922. A quite outstanding disc.

(i; ii) Winter Legends (for piano and orchestra); (i) A Hill Tune; A Mountain Mood; (i; iii) Viola Sonata
(N) (BB) (**(*)) Dutton mono CDBP 9751. (i) Cohen; (ii) BBC SO, Raybould; (iii) Primrose

Winter Legends is a masterly and imaginative score that enshrines much of the best of Bax. It was originally dedicated to Sibelius, whom he had visited, but Harriet Cohen erased the inscription and put 'written and dedicated to Harriet Cohen' in its place, and Bax had to acquiesce, and instead, some years later, he dedicated his *Fifth Symphony* to the Finnish master! The piano writing places considerable demands on her (she had suffered an accident to her right hand) and, given the small stretch of both hands, this per-formance from a live (1954) BBC studio concert has less authority than the more recent recording by Margaret Finger-hut. However, Clarence Raybould and the BBC Symphony Orchestra give sympathetic support. The two miniatures come from 1942 and the days of 78s, while the *Viola Sonata*, which she recorded with William Primrose, was made in 1937. For Baxians this collection will be of enormous interest, for Cohen is a sensitive advocate, despite her limited pianistic prowess.

CHAMBER AND INSTRUMENTAL MUSIC

Cello Sonata in E flat; Cello Sonatina in D; Legend Sonata in F sharp min.; Folk Tale
** ASV CDDCA 896. Gregor-Smith, Wrigley

The *Cello Sonata* has many characteristic touches and an imaginative slow movement. Bernard Gregor-Smith and Yolande Wrigley are both highly sensitive and responsive players. In the *Sonata* the recording does not give quite enough back-to-front depth and there is a touch of glassiness about the sound. Things are a bit better in the *Folk Tale* (1920), but the recording is sufficiently wanting in bloom to inhibit a three-star recommendation.

Clarinet Sonata
(*) Chan. 8683. Hilton, Swallow – BLISS *Clarinet Quintet*; VAUGHAN WILLIAMS: *6 Studies* *

(i) *Clarinet Sonata*; (ii) *Elegiac Trio* (for flute, viola & harp); (iii) *Harp Quintet*; (iv) *Nonet*; (v) *Oboe Quintet*
☛ *** Hyp. CDA 66807. (i; iv) Collins; (i) Brown (piano); (ii; iv) Davies; (ii–v) Chase; (ii–iv) Kanga; (iii–v) Crayford, Van Kampen; (iii; v) Juda; (iv) Wexler, McTier, Brown (cond.); (iv–v) Hulse

Bax's *Clarinet Sonata* opens most beguilingly, and Janet Hilton's phrasing is quite melting. Moreover the Bliss cou-pling is indispensable.

The Hyperion performances are of exemplary quality. In the chamber-music field Bax wrote with a fantasy and sensi-bility that are no less captivating than in *The Garden of Fand* or *Tintagel*. The members of the Nash Ensemble, including Michael Collins in the *Clarinet Sonata* and Gareth Hulse in the *Oboe Quintet*, seem totally attuned to the idiom, and they play with their usual artistry and dedication. Excellent recording.

Concerto for Flute, Oboe, Harp & String Quartet; In memoriam, for Cor Anglais, Harp & String Quartet; Threnody & Scherzo for Bassoon, Harp & String Sextet; (i) Octet for Horn, Piano & String Sextet; String Quintet
*** Chan. 9602. (i) Fingerhut; ASMF Ch. Ens.

In memoriam is the earliest piece here (it comes from 1917 and originally bore the subtitle, 'An Irish Elegy' – an obvious allusion to the Easter uprising). The *Octet* is arguably the most appealing work in this collection. However, most of this music is captivating; the performances are absolutely first class and the recording in the best traditions of the house.

Elegiac Trio; Fantasy Sonata for Harp & Viola; Harp Quintet; Sonata for Flute & Harp
(BB) *** Naxos 8.554507. Nichols, Ito, Honoré, Pillai, Storey, McGhee

Ideal late-night listening for a balmy summer evening: a collection of Bax chamber music centred around the harp. We have the *Quintet for Harp and Strings* played by an accomplished group called Mobius, who also perform the seductive *Elegiac Trio* for flute, viola and harp, the imaginative *Fantasy Sonata* for viola and harp and the *Sonata for Flute and Harp*. This is all beguiling music (except perhaps for the folksy finale of the *Quintet*), the neglect of which is quite puzzling. There are distinguished alternatives but none are coupled together like this or priced so competitively.

(i) *Harp Quintet;* (ii) *Piano Quartet. String Quartet 1*
*** Chan. 8391. (i) Kanga; (ii) McCabe; English Qt

The *First String Quartet* is music with a strong and immediate appeal. The *Harp Quintet* is more fully characteristic and has some evocative writing to commend it, alongside the *Piano Quartet* with its winning lyricism. These may not be Bax's most important scores, but they are rewarding, and the performances are thoroughly idiomatic and eminently well recorded.

Oboe Quintet
*** Chan. 8392. Francis, English Qt – HOLST: *Air & Variations*, etc.; MOERAN: *Fantasy Quartet*; JACOB: *Quartet ***

Bax's *Oboe Quintet* is a confident, inventive piece. Sarah Francis proves a most responsive soloist, though she is balanced too close; in all other respects the recording is up to Chandos's usual high standards, and the playing of the English Quartet is admirable.

(i) *Piano Quintet in G min. String Quartet 2*
**(*) Chan. 8795. Mistry Qt, (i) with Owen Norris

The *Piano Quintet* is symphonic in scale. The playing of the Mistry Quartet is dedicated and David Owen Norris is the excellent and sensitive pianist. The *Second Quartet* is tauter and more powerful. The performance has plenty of feeling and the recording is excellent.

Rhapsodic Ballad (for solo cello)
*** Chan. 8499. Wallfisch – BRIDGE: *Cello Sonata;* DELIUS: *Cello Sonata;* WALTON: *Passacaglia ***

The *Rhapsodic Ballad* for cello alone is a freely expressive piece, played with authority and dedication by Raphael Wallfisch. The recording has plenty of warmth and range.

String Quartet 3 in F; String Quartet in E: Adagio ma non troppo 'Cathaleen-ni-Hoolihan'; (i) *Lyrical Interlude for String Quintet*
*** (BB) Naxos 8.555953. Maggini Qt, with (i) Jackson

The Maggini Quartet's series of British music recordings for Naxos goes from strength to strength, when the *String Quartet No. 3* of 1936 offers such a revelatory new view of the composer. If in the sequence of seven symphonies that Bax completed between the two world wars the writing often suggests piano improvisation scored for orchestra, this *Quartet* represents Bax at his sharpest, with no meandering. The opening of the first movement sweeps the listener forward in a way that reminds one of Mendelssohn's *Octet*, despite the far more modern idiom. There are many Irish overtones, too, typical of Bax, not least in the finale, which with its sharp rhythms and striking use of pizzicato suggests that he may have been listening to Bartók. The *Lyrical Interlude* is a re-working Bax made in 1922 of the slow movement of his *String Quintet* of 1908. It is a rather beautiful piece, like the *Adagio ma non troppo* from an even earlier quartet that Bax subsequently scored as the tone poem, 'Cathaleen-ni-Hoolihan'. The Magginis are masterly throughout, not just in the four substantial movements of the *Quartet* but in the two evocatively Irish-inspired movements written much earlier.

Viola Sonata in G
(***) Biddulph mono LAB 148. Primrose, Cohen – BLOCH: *Suite;* HINDEMITH: *Sonata* (***)

The legendary William Primrose made this recording of the Bax *Viola Sonata* with Harriet Cohen in the late 1930s, and it serves as a reminder of his sumptuous tone and glorious musicianship.

Violin Sonatas: in G min. in One Movement; 1 in E; Ballad; Legend
*** ASV CDDCA 1127. Gibbs, Mei-Loc Wu

The *G minor Sonata* in one movement is an early piece, dating from 1901 and composed when Bax was still a student at the Royal Academy, and subsequently withdrawn. The *First Sonata* was written in 1910 in the wake of a passionate affair with a Ukrainian girl, but Bax re-wrote the second and third movements during the war, and himself gave its première in 1920 with Paul Kochanski. The *Ballad* and *Legend* are wartime pieces and not otherwise available. Robert Gibbs and Mary Mei-Loc Wu are sympathetic and persuasive Baxians. Excellent sound.

Violin Sonatas 1 in E; 2 in D
*** Chan. 8845. Gruenberg, McCabe

The *Second* is the finer of these two *Sonatas* and is thematically linked with *November Woods*. Rhapsodic and impassioned, this is music full of temperament. Erich Gruenberg is a selfless and musicianly advocate and John McCabe makes an expert partner.

Violin Sonata 2
*** Global Music Network GMN CO113. Little, Roscoe – ELGAR: *Violin Sonata ***

As in the Elgar *Sonata*, with which it is aptly coupled, Tasmin Little gives a powerful, big-scale reading of the four-movement Bax *Sonata No. 2*, relishing the virtuosity of the writing, with Martin Roscoe similarly brilliant. This is a strong, extrovert reading rather than a meditative one, but it leaves you in no doubt as to the strength of this relatively early work, with the second movement a sparkling, fantastic dance and the slow movement a warmly lyrical interlude. An excellent if unusual coupling for Tasmin Little's fine version of the Elgar, very well recorded.

Violin Sonatas 2 in D; 3 (1927); Sonata in F
*** ASV CDDCA 1098. Gibbs, Mei-Loc Wu

Strictly speaking there are four sonatas, but the two numbered sonatas recorded here come from the 1920s. The *Second* was written during the war but revised in 1921, while the two-movement *Third* comes from 1927. The *Sonata in F* comes from the following year and Baxians will recognize it as a kind of prototype of the magical *Nonet* (1930). No Baxian will want to be without it, particularly in these fluent and committed performances.

PIANO MUSIC

Apple-Blossom Time; Burlesque; Ceremonial Dance; Country-Tune; Dream in Exile; From 'Salzburg' Sonata; A Hill Tune; In a Vodka Shop; In the Night; Lullaby; Legend; The Maiden with the Daffodil; Mediterranean; A Mountain Mood; Nereid; O Dame get up and bake your pies (Variations on a North Country Christmas Carol); On a May Evening; Paean; The Princess's Rose-Garden (Nocturne); A Romance; 2 Russian Tone Pictures; Serpent Dance; The Slave Girl; Sleepy-Head; Sonatas 1–4; Toccata; Water Music; What the Minstrel told us; Whirligig; Winter Waters

(M) *** Chan. X10132 (4). Parkin

Eric Parkin proves a sympathetic guide through this repertoire. The *Sonatas* are grievously neglected in the concert hall but are most convincingly presented here. The recording is on the resonant side, but the playing is outstandingly responsive.

Piano Sonatas 1–2; Burlesque; Dream in Exile (Intermezzo); In a Vodka Shop

(N) (BB) **(*) Naxos 8.557439. Wass

Piano Sonatas 3–4; Allegro quasi Andante (Very difficult throughout); Country Tune; O Dame get up and Bake your Pies; Water Music; Winter Tune

(N) (BB) **(*) Naxos 8.557592. Wass

Bax, a brilliant pianist himself, composed naturally at the piano. His early works were much influenced by Russian music, and the one-movement *First Sonata* was actually composed in the Ukraine in 1910. It is here that the influence of Scriabin is perhaps deepest. The *Second Sonata*, also in one movement, is bleak, dark and compelling. The *Third Sonata* of 1926 (Wass's own favourite) is both atmospheric and rhapsodic, the outer movements wild and unpredictable, but with a lyrical slow movement and with an Irish folk influence which reaches a turbulent climax and then subsides into a peaceful postlude. The *Fourth Sonata*, first performed in 1934, although still prolix in many ways the most immediately approachable of the series, with a clear first-movement structure and an engaging secondary theme, an enticing *quasi Andante* marked 'very delicate throughout' and a stormy, toccata-like finale with a distinct underlying romanticism.

Ashley Wass plays all four works with great authority and panache and is equally sympathetic in the shorter pieces, most persuasively bringing out the freely improvisational style. Three of the four pieces on the second disc have real charm, with the evocative *Water Music* (based on a memorable theme from the ballet, *The Truth about Russian Dancers*) and the stormy *Winter Waters* making a powerful contrast. If, even in performances as magnetic as these, the sonatas do come near to outstaying their welcome, anyone attracted to the music of Bax will be delighted by this disc. Excellent recording in Potton Hall, Suffolk, and authoritative notes from Lewis Foreman to guide the listener.

Piano Sonatas 1 in E flat; 2 in G; Legend
*** Continuum CCD 1045. McCabe

Both Bax's *Piano Sonatas* are convincing in John McCabe's hands – in fact, more convincing than the *Legend* – and are excellently recorded. Eric Parkin also proves a sympathetic guide in this repertoire (see above). The recording is on the resonant side, but the playing is outstandingly responsive.

VOCAL MUSIC

Songs: *A Celtic Song Cycle; The Enchanted Fiddle; The Fairies; Far in a Western Brookland; Lullaby; The Market Girl; A Milking Sian; Parting; Roundel; Song in the Twilight; To Eire; When I was one and twenty; When we are lost; The White Peace; Youth*

(N) (M) *** Dutton CDLX 7136. Partridge, Rigby, Dussek

Many of these Bax songs were inspired by his love affairs from his student days onwards, not least his culminating love for the pianist, Harriet Cohen. The opening song, *Youth*, from this sequence is a fine example, and the composer's emotions plus his prowess as a pianist led him to write the most elaborate accompaniments, here brilliantly played by Michael Dussek, making light of the technical difficulties. Ian Partridge with his heady tenor-tone is the ideal interpreter, bringing out word-meaning with fine clarity, and characterizing well in wide-ranging settings of texts ranging from Chaucer to Housman and Bax himself, as well as Yeats and other Irish poets. The mezzo-soprano, Jean Rigby, is similarly persuasive in the *Celtic Song Cycle*, an early work dating from 1904, in a rather simpler, more openly lyrical style.

I sing of a maiden; Mater ora filium; This world's joie
(M) *** EMI 5 65595-2. King's College, Cambridge, Ch.,
    Cleobury – FINZI: *Choral Music;* VAUGHAN WILLIAMS:
    Mass ***

Bax's ambitious setting of a medieval carol, *Mater ora filium*, is one of the most difficult *a cappella* pieces in the choral repertory. Here under Stephen Cleobury the King's College Choir gives it a virtuoso performance, with trebles performing wonders in the taxingly high passages. It is particularly apt, too, when the original inspiration for the piece came from Bax hearing Byrd's *Mass in Five Voices*. The other two Bax pieces, also setting medieval texts, are done most beautifully too, with the unaccompanied voices vividly recorded against the spacious acoustic of King's Chapel. Besides the original Finzi coupling, the reissue includes a splendid analogue performance of Vaughan Williams's beautiful *Mass in G minor*.

BEACH, Amy (1867–1944)

(i) *Piano Concerto in C sharp min., Op. 45;* (ii) *Piano Quintet in F sharp min., Op. 67*
**(*) Ara. Z 6738. Polk; (i) ECO, Goodwin; (ii) Lark Qt

Amy Beach's *Piano Concerto* (1898–9) is an expansive, warmly romantic work written in a post-Lisztian style, with pleasingly lyrical melodies which recall other composers including Grieg and, in the dramatic first movement, Dvořák. The *Concerto* holds the listener's attention throughout, especially in a performance as lyrically sympathetic and sparkling as that by Joanne Polk, persuasively accompanied by Paul Goodwin and the ECO, and very well recorded. It was a pity, though understandable, that the chosen coupling was the ubiquitous *Piano Quintet*. However, this is also presented passionately, with the lovely slow movement movingly done, though the balance here has the string quartet a shade too close and the acoustic lacks depth – those wanting the *Concerto* will certainly not be disappointed at the quality of the performances of either work.

(i) *Piano Concerto, Op. 45. Symphony in E min. (Gaelic)*
☛– (BB) *** Naxos 8.559139. (i) Feinberg; Nashville SO, Schermerhorn

It is Naxos who have had the happy idea of coupling Amy Beach's attractive *Piano Concerto* with the equally diverting *Gaelic Symphony*, which was written in 1894–6 after she had been impressed with the Boston première of Dvořák's *New World Symphony* and determined to build her own symphony by drawing on four traditional Irish tunes of 'simple, rugged and unpretentious beauty'. Yet much of the invention is her own and of high quality to match the concertante work for piano. Alan Feinberg's performance of the latter is in the grand romantic tradition, with splendid digital bravura in the finale, balanced by warm and often passionately lyrical support from the excellent Nashville orchestra. The *Symphony* receives a no less sympathetic and committed reading under Kenneth Schermerhorn. The recording is vivid throughout, not in the very front rank perhaps, but bright and atmospheric. This is surely the disc to start with if you want to discover, inexpensively, the calibre of Beach's music, although Järvi's Chandos disc of the *Symphony* is even finer.

Symphony in E min. (Gaelic)
*** Chan. 8958. Detroit SO, Järvi (with BARBER: *Symphony 1*, etc. ***)

Amy Beach was largely self-taught. Her *Symphony in E minor* operates at a high level of accomplishment and has a winning charm, particularly its delightful and inventive second movement. Once heard, this haunting movement is difficult to exorcize from one's memory. A very persuasive performance by the Detroit orchestra under Neeme Järvi, and good recorded sound.

CHAMBER MUSIC

Pastorale for Wind Quintet, Op. 151; String Quartet (in one movement), *Op. 89; Violin Sonata, Op. 34; 4 Sketches for Piano: Dreaming* (trans. for cello & piano)
⚫ *** Chan. 10162. Ambache

The early *Violin Sonata* of 1897 is characteristically lyrical and very traditional in style, although the *perpetuum mobile* Scherzo brings a distinct personal touch. The slow movement is melodically and harmonically rich, if less individual, but the confident finale establishes the work's distinction, for its secondary theme is memorable. The one-movement *String Quartet*, although begun in 1921 and completed in 1929, was published only after the composer's death. Its character is determined by the three Alaskan folk themes on which it draws. The nostalgic mood created by the simple, poignant chords that dominate the opening *Grave* is dispelled by the central *Più Animato* and *Allegro molto*, but returns hauntingly at the close. The *Pastorale*, which also has a strong personal flavour, was drafted in the same year as the *String Quartet*, but the woodwind scoring was not finalized for another 20 years. It is a charming, gentle, folksy evocation with the balmy atmosphere of a summer afternoon. The arrangement of *Dreaming*, a song without words for cello and piano, gives the cello the gently rhapsodic melodic line, but the piano remains insistent. First-class performances and recording, and worth having for the *String Quartet*, one of Beach's most memorable works.

Piano Quintet in F sharp min., Op. 67
*** ASV CDDCA 932-2. Roscoe, Endellion Qt – CLARKE: *Piano Trio, etc.* ***

(i) *Piano Quintet; Piano Trio in A min., Op. 150;* (ii) *Theme & Variations for Flute & String Quartet*
⚫ *** Chan. 9752. (i) Ambache; (ii) Keen; The Ambache

Amy Beach's glorious 1908 *Piano Quintet* with its passionately lyrical first movement and hauntingly beautiful *Adagio* is already available in a fine performance on ASV, coupled with music by Rebecca Clarke. But the Chandos version from Diana Ambache and her group is even richer, more passionately involving, and the coupling with two other fine chamber works is more apt. The *Theme* for the *Flute Variations* (1916) has a touching nostalgia and, with exquisite flute-playing from Helen Keen, this music comes over as equally deeply felt. The *Piano Trio* is a late work (1939), the opening movement delicate in the manner of Fauré. The catchy finale might almost be a lively dance movement from Dvořák's American period, but the luxuriantly expansive centrepiece is all Beach's own. These are marvellous performances of three very highly rewarding works, superbly recorded.

With Martin Roscoe's characterful playing well matched by the masterly Endellion Quartet, the performance on ASV is magnetic and very well recorded. But the Chandos version is first choice.

Piano Trio in A min., Op. 150; String Quartet in One Movement, Op. 89; Violin Sonata in A min., Op. 34
*** Ara. Z 6747. Polk; Lark Qt

The early *Violin Sonata* (1896), which introduces this highly recommendable collection, opens most beguilingly on the bow of Diane Pascal, its warm lyricism pervading the first movement and the equally melodically fluent *Largo*. A scintillating Scherzo acts as a bridge between them, with its centrepiece looking back lyrically to the opening movement. The finale, if not to be taken too seriously, is more passionate, and in the development neatly produces a three-part fugue.

The elliptical *String Quartet* dates from 1921 and is wholly different in mood, with a haunting Gallic atmosphere, the more surprising as the material includes Alaskan folk themes. The *Piano Trio* draws on older material 'docketed away' in the composer's head (including an early song), its *espressivo* lighter, more romantic in feeling, with the finale dancing along to a catchy, syncopated 'Eskimo' theme. The performances here are first class (Joanne Polk, the pianist, especially worthy of mention) and so is the recording. Most enjoyable and highly recommended.

Piano Trio in A min.; Romance for Violin & Piano. (i) *Songs: 3 Browning Songs; Canzonetta; Chanson d'amore; Ecstasy; Elle et moi; Ich sagte nicht; Je demande à l'oiseau; A Mirage; Nahe des Gelibten; Rendezvous; 3 Shakespeare settings; Stella viatoris; Wir drei*
**(*) BIS CD 1245. Romantic Chamber Group of L.; (i) with Kirkby

The Romantic Chamber Group of London play warmly and certainly romantically, but they are recorded in a resonant acoustic, and both the *Piano Trio* and (especially) the *Romance* create something of the atmosphere of the Palm Court. We are admirers of both the composer and Emma Kirkby, but here she swoons up unabashedly to the climax of the opening song, *Ecstasy*, and *Stella viatoris* is unleashed with comparable ardour. *A Mirage* is more restrained, and the Shakepeare and Browning settings have charm, even if cloying just a little. The French and German settings are attractive in their innocent way, and Kirkby is her sweet-voiced self, and certainly at her best in the sparkle of the closing *Elle et moi*. But she fails to convince us that Amy Beach's songs can find a place in the recital room rather than the salon.

PIANO MUSIC

By the Still Waters; Far Awa'; Gavotte fantastique; A Humming Bird; 3 Morceaux caractéristiques, Op. 28; Out of the Depths; Scherzino: A Peterboro Chipmunk; Scottish Legend; Variations on Balkan Themes, Op. 60; Young Birches
*** Ara. Z 6693. Polk

Ballad, Op. 6; A Cradle Song of the Lonely Mother; The Fair Hills of Eire, O!; A Hermit Thrush at Eve; A Hermit Thrush at Morn; Prelude & Fugue, Op. 81; Les Rêves de Columbine: Suite française, Op. 65; Valse-caprice, Op. 4
*** Ara. Z 6704. Polk

Eskimos, 4 Characteristic Pieces, Op. 64; Fantasia fugata, Op. 87; From Grandmother's Garden, Op. 97; 5 Improvisations, Op. 148; Nocturne, Op. 107; 4 Sketches, Op. 15; Tyrolean Valse-fantaisie, Op. 116. Transcription: R. STRAUSS: *Serenade*
*** Ara. Z 6721. Polk

Arabesque are now exploring Amy Beach's piano music in depth and confirming the consistency of its quality. The *Variations on Balkan Themes* readily demonstrates her ability to sustain a major work. The imaginative pictorial evocations from nature are capped by the beautiful evocation of *Young Birches*, while the nocturnal *Cradle Song of the Lonely Mother* is quite haunting. Beach's ability to assimilate different styles in a single work is never better displayed than in the attractive *Four Sketches*, Op. 15, where at times Schumann, Beethoven, Mendelssohn and Liszt all look over her shoulder; while the disarming simplicity of characterization in *Eskimos* and *From Grandmother's Garden* is quite delightful. Joanne Polk is an understanding and persuasive advocate, capturing the music's special combination of sophistication and innocence with fine spontaneity. She is most truthfully recorded.

SONGS

Ah Love, but a day!; Ariette; Baby; The candy lion; Canzonetta; Come, ah come; Ecstasy; Dearie; Empress of the night; Far awa'; Forgotten; Go not too far; The host; Hush baby dear; Ich sagte nicht; In the twilight; I send my heart up to thee!; I sought the Lord; Je demande à l'oiseau; Juni; May flowers; Nacht; O sweet content; The rainy day; Le Secret; Sheena Van; Sleep little darling; So my love to thee; A thanksgiving fable; Though I take the wings of morning; Der Totenkranz; When far from her; Wir drei; Within my heart; The year's at the spring
(N) (BB) ** Naxos 8.559191. Kelton, Bringerud

Amy Beach was best known in her own lifetime for her piano pieces and songs, of which she wrote over 100. Many are

simple, Victorian-style ballads, but all have accompaniments of quality to give a real backcloth for the singer, as Catherine Bringerud, an excellent accompanist, shows here. Katherine Kelton is at home in the repertoire and, although her vibrato is occasionally too insistent, she responds to the finer examples, such as the Scottish *Dearie, O sweet content, Though I take the wings of morning* and the charming *Candy lion* and *Thanksgiving fable*. Perhaps surprisingly, many of the other, more striking settings are of foreign texts, *Le Secret, Ich sagte nicht and Der Totenkranz* ('The Funeral Wreath'). The recording is well balanced and truthful. Full texts and (where necessary) translations are included.

Evening Hymn, Op. 125/2; Help us O God, Op. 50; Jubilate; Lord of all Being, Op. 146; Nunc Dimittis; Peace I leave with you; Te Deum
*** ASV CDDCA 1125. Harvard University Ch., Somerville; Johnson (organ) – THOMPSON: *Choral Music* ***

Amy Beach's flowing lyrical gift is consistently appealing in these comparatively straightforward but highly eloquent settings. They range from the early serene *Peace I leave with you* and the simple *Nunc Dimittis* – both *a cappella* and from 1891 – and the passionate *Jubilate* with its exuberant organ accompaniment (1905) to the richly harmonized *Evening Hymn* of 1934 and *Lord of all Being* for four-part choir and organ, which has more obvious dissonance, but remains in the musical mainstream. Excellent, committed performances from the Harvard Choir, with the collection made the more attractive by the alternation of items by Randall Thompson.

BEETHOVEN, Ludwig van (1770–1827)

(i) *Piano Concerto 1 in C, Op. 15. Symphony 7 in A, Op. 92; Overture, Coriolan, Op. 62*
*** Arthaus **DVD** 100 148. (i) Perahia; LSO, Solti (V/D: Humphrey Burton)

This is a straight recording directed by Humphrey Burton of a concert at London's Barbican Centre in 1987. The camerawork is discreet and unfussy and the sound impeccably balanced throughout. Nothing distracts the viewer or listener from Beethoven. In spite of some over-emphatic gestures, Solti's accounts of both the *Coriolan Overture* and the *Seventh Symphony* are very fine, and at no point is the LSO sound rough or rhythms overdriven. These are cultured and dedicated performances in every way, and in the concerto Murray Perahia is unfailingly thoughtful, intelligent and imaginative. A memorable concert; and the first-rate recording will give much pleasure.

(i) *Piano Concerto 2 in B flat; (iii) Symphony 9 in D min.*
*** TDK **DVD** DV-EC10A. (i) Pletnev; (ii) Mattila, Urmana, Moser, Schulte, Swedish R. Ch., Eric Ericson Chamber Ch.; BPO, Abbado (Producer: Paul Smaczny, V/D: Bob Coles)

This concert, recorded in the Philharmonie on 1 May 2000, was the tenth conducted by Abbado to mark the centenary of the foundation of the Berlin Philharmonic on 1 May 1882. Pletnev's account of the *B flat Concerto* is immaculate, both artistically and technically, and a model of its kind: expressive eloquence tempered by sureness of musical judgement and taste. In short, it is wonderfully fresh and exhilarating. The *Ninth Symphony*, which Karajan had given on this date in 1963, has a fine line-up of soloists, together with the legendary Eric Ericson Choir and the Swedish Radio Choir, and is a hardly less fine performance, direct and powerful. It comes with a 20-minute documentary, with commentaries and subtitles in English, French, German, Italian, Spanish and Japanese.

Piano Concerto 4 in G, Op. 58

(*) EMI **DVD 492840-9. Rubinstein, LPO, Dorati (with Bonus: CHOPIN: *Polonaise in A flat (Heroic)* – MENDELSSOHN: *Violin Concerto* **; WALTON: *Cello Concerto* ***

Rubinstein made a fine recording of the *G major Concerto* with Josef Krips in New York in the late 1950s – and he recorded three complete cycles in all, playing the *Fourth* most often. The present performance comes from a Royal Festival Hall concert by the LPO under Antal Dorati in December 1967, when the great pianist was already eighty. Although he was more closely identified in the public mind with Chopin, he was a fine Beethoven interpreter, albeit slightly underrated as a Beethovenian by the wider generality of critics (but not, for example, by the composer and scholar Robert Simpson, who spoke with great admiration of Rubinstein's concerto cycle with Krips). Although this performance does not offer the effortless keyboard mastery of Rubinstein's youth and maturity, it is a valuable document and will be treasured by all admirers of this artist.

Piano Concertos (i) 1 in C, Op. 15; (ii) 2 in B flat, Op. 19

🔘 (***) Testament mono SBT 1219. Solomon, Philh. O, (i) Herbert Menges, (ii) Cluytens

Piano Concertos (i) 3 in C min., Op. 37; (ii) 4 in G, Op. 58

🔘 (***) Testament mono SBT 1220. Solomon, Philh. O, (i) Menges, (ii) Cluytens

Piano Concerto 5 (Emperor)

🔘 (***) Testament mono SBT 1221. Solomon, Philh. O, Menges (with MOZART: *Sonatas 11 and 17*)

Olympian performances from Solomon are restored on the Testament label in altogether exemplary sound. The Beethoven concertos with the Philharmonia Orchestra under Herbert Menges and André Cluytens (in Nos. 2 and 4) have been out many times since they were made in the 1950s but have never sounded richer and fresher than they do here. Solomon never interposed his own personality between the composer and listener and his performances celebrate a dedication to musical truth and a timeless purity that place him among the keyboard giants. This is great Beethoven playing.

Piano Concertos 1; 3

(N) (M) *** Telarc CD 80663. Rudolf Serkin, Boston SO, Ozawa

Piano Concertos 2; 4

(N) (M) *** Telarc CD 80064. Rudolf Serkin, Boston SO, Ozawa

Piano Concerto 5 (Emperor)

(N) (M) *** Telarc CD 80665. Rudolf Serkin, Boston SO, Ozawa

Serkin's cycle for Telarc dates from 1981/2, the very beginning of the digital era, yet the sound is excellent: full, warm and natural. It presents a deeply satisfying series of performances. Serkin brings those moments of total magic which are the mark of live performances from a master, here caught in the studio. Technically, the playing of the octogenarian is flawed (there is one amazing slip of finger in the *C major Concerto*);

where in his late Mozart recordings for DG the lack of polish is distracting, here one consistently registers certainty and power. The accompaniments have comparable distinction – Ozawa has never sounded more spontaneous on record.

In the *First Concerto* the conductor opens very gently and then upgrades the tutti with a big, sudden crescendo. The slow movement has Elysian serenity; the finale is joyous. In the *Second*, the natural gravitas of Serkin's playing at the end of the *Adagio* is again lightened by the humour of the playing elsewhere, the inescapable sense of a great musician approaching the music afresh, without a hint of routine. If the *Third* and *Fourth* Concertos lack some of Serkin's youthful fire, and the *Adagio* of the *Third* – taken relatively fast – is a little casual, the concentration is as powerful as ever. The mastery of the soloist's conception is not in doubt, nor is his combination of ruggedness and flights of poetry, not least in the G minor and F minor passages at the beginning of the first-movement development.

In the *G major Concerto*, though strength is the keynote of the outer movements, the compression of the *Andante* again finds Serkin at his most intense, and the detailed poetry is inescapable. With extraordinarily vivid recording, the great pianist is almost as commanding as ever in the *Emperor*, with fire and brilliance in plenty in the outer movements; yet there is also a degree of relaxation, of conscious enjoyment, that increases the degree of communication. The hushed, expressive pianism that provides the lyrical contrast in the first movement is matched by the poised refinement of the *Adagio*; the finale is vigorously joyful and, as throughout the set, Ozawa's accompaniment is first class.

Piano Concertos 1–5

🎼 *** Sony S3K 44575 (3). Perahia, Concg. O, Haitink

*** Ph. 462 781-2 (3). Brendel, VPO, Rattle

(M) *** Teldec 0927 47334-2 (3). Aimard, COE, Harnoncourt

(M) (***) DG mono 474 024-2 (5). Kempff, BPO, Van Kempen – BRAHMS: *Piano Concerto 1*; LISZT: *Piano Concertos 1 & 2*; MOZART: *Piano Concertos 9 & 15*; SCHUMANN: *Piano Concerto* (***)

(i) *Piano Concertos 1–5. 6 Bagatelles, Op. 126; Für Elise*

(B) **(*) Decca (ADD) 443 723-2 (3). Ashkenazy, (i) Chicago SO, Solti

(i) *Piano Concertos 1–5. 7 Bagatelles, Op. 33; 11 Bagatelles, Op. 119; 6 Bagatelles, Op. 126; Fantasia in G min.; 5 Variations on 'Rule Britannia', WoO 79; 7 Variations on 'God Save the King', WoO 78* (i; ii) *Choral Fantasia*

(BB) *** Virgin 5 62242-2 (4). Tan (fortepiano); (i) with LCP, Norrington; (ii) Schütz Ch.

(i) *Piano Concertos 1–5. Piano Sonata 23 (Appassionata), Op. 57*

(M) *** Warner Elatus 2564 60130-2 (1–2); 2564 60433-2 (3–4); 2564 60348-2 (5 & *Piano Sonata 23*). Schiff, Dresden State O, Haitink (available separately)

(i) *Piano Concertos 1–5. 32 Variations in C min., WoO 80*

(N) **(*) Ph. 475 6757. Uchida, (i) Bav. RSO or Concg. O (3 & 4), Sanderling

(i) *Piano Concertos 1–5;* (ii) *Choral Fantasia, Op. 80*

(M) *** EMI (ADD) 7 63360-2 (3). Barenboim, New Philh. O, Klemperer, (ii) with John Alldis Ch.

(B) *** CfP (ADD) 575 7522 (3). Lill, SNO, Gibson

(B) **(*) RCA 82876 55703-2 (3). Ax; (i) RPO, Previn; (ii) NYPO, Mehta

András Schiff with ideal, transparent support from Haitink and the Dresden Staatskapelle offers one of the most refreshing, deeply satisfying Beethoven concerto cycles of recent years. The brightness of Schiff's tone may mean that in hushed passages, such as the solos in the central *Andante* of No. 4, he is reluctant to use a veiled tone, but the singing cantabile of his playing is equally persuasive. He crowns the cycle with a scintillating account of the *Emperor Concerto*, electrifying from first to last, aptly coupled with the most heroic sonata of Beethoven's middle period, the *Appassionata*. Clear, well-balanced sound to match. The discs are available separately.

Perahia, with Haitink a deeply sympathetic partner, gives masterly performances, as close to the heart of this music as any. The sound is full and well balanced. This set has now reverted to full price and is well worth it.

Alfred Brendel offers this new Philips set as his third and last recorded survey of the Beethoven concertos, made in Vienna with Sir Simon Rattle. With each concerto recorded immediately after live performances, the results have an extra spontaneity, usually at speeds marginally faster than in his previous recordings. The dynamic range is greater too, with hushed *pianissimos* more intense, and with Rattle encouraging lightness in his accompaniments. The ambience of the Musikverein casts a warm, natural glow over the proceedings and adds the necessary weight to the *Emperor*. A fine achievement.

Pierre-Laurent Aimard's cycle, recorded live with Harnoncourt and the COE, consistently brings winningly spontaneous, crisply articulated and often poetic playing from a pianist generally associated with twentieth-century music. These are all intensely enjoyable performances, among the very finest to have appeared in recent years, yet, in direct comparison with other pianists like Perahia, who combine poetry with clean articulation and lyrical spontantiety, Aimard is far freer in expression, with rubato much more marked and with Harnoncourt modifying his period-influenced style accordingly, electrifying the inspired players of the Chamber Orchestra of Europe. Excellent sound. The three discs are offered for the price of two.

The combination of Barenboim and Klemperer, recording together in 1967–8, brings endless illumination, with Klemperer's measured weight set against Barenboim's youthful spontaneity, specially compelling in slow movements. The *Choral Fantasia* too is given an inspired performance. The remastered sound is clear and full.

Kempff's earlier Beethoven concerto cycle, here the centrepiece of a collection of his complete 1950s concerto recordings, finds him delightfully carefree, consistently at his most individual (not least in his own cadenzas), turning phrases and pointing ornamentation with rare sparkle and sense of fun. The mono sound is immediate and well detailed. The other concertos in this limited edition include five that he recorded for Decca.

John Lill has never been more impressive on record than in his set of the Beethoven concertos, recorded in 1974–5. In each work he conveys spontaneity and a vein of poetry that in the studio have too often eluded him. Gibson and the Scottish National Orchestra provide strong, direct support, helped by very good analogue recording using the spacious City Hall, Glasgow. Very competitive with other versions at whatever price.

The partnership of Ashkenazy and Solti is fascinating, with Solti's fiery intensity contrasted with Ashkenazy's introspective qualities. Ashkenazy brings a hushed, poetic quality to every slow movement, while Solti's urgency maintains a vivid forward impulse in outer movements. At times, as in the *C minor Concerto*, the music-making may seem too tautly intense, but freshness dominates. On CD the sound is fierce at times, while the piano tone is rather shallow.

Over the years Melvyn Tan has established an enviable reputation on the fortepiano. His playing has a flair and poetic feeling that are rather special, and this partnership with Norrington in the five Beethoven concertos has great spontaneity. The first four bring performances of a natural, unselfconscious expressiveness. Even when Tan's speeds for slow movements are very fast indeed, his ease of expression makes them very persuasive, avoiding breathlessness while simultaneously conveying more gravity than one might expect. Tan's individuality comes over unforcedly to make these readings characterful without unwanted wilfulness. The set is capped by a superb account of the *Emperor* in which Tan displays a poetic fire and brilliance all his own. The reading urgently conveys the feeling of a live performance, and both he and Norrington follow Czerny's brisk (and authoritative) tempo markings. The inspiriting account of the *Choral Fantasia* possesses a mercurial quality and a panache that show this sometimes underrated work in a new and most positive light. Norrington and the chorus and orchestra are no less persuasive, and R. L. gave this coupling a Rosette on its original, full-priced release. Like the rest of the cycle, the recording is splendidly natural, the piano admirably balanced against the period instruments.

The solo recital that follows is no less distinctive. Tan plays on Beethoven's own Broadwood piano. Expert restoration work reveals an instrument which is richly timbred and full-bodied, far more vibrant than any modern copy. Tan plays these pieces with all the spontaneity and flair that he exhibited in the concertos, and in the *G minor Fantasy* conveys an improvisatory quality that is very compelling indeed. He could allow himself more time in some of the *Bagatelles*, but there are no real quibbles here in what is a recital of great interest, offering refreshing insights into the sound-world with which Beethoven himself would have been familiar. The recording has striking realism and presence.

Mitsuko Uchida is obviously at home in the earlier concertos and No. 4 is freely inspirational, both poetic and strongly held together. She finds ample power throughout, with weighty accompaniments from Sanderling and the two orchestras involved. Some may find her spacious approach a little too relaxed at times, but this set is a fine memento of a deeply committed artist, warmly recommended to her many admirers. The early *C minor Variations*, incisively performed, make an apt if rather ungenerous fill-up for the *Emperor*.

Emanuel Ax's boxed set on RCA dates from 1985–6 (although the *Choral Fantasia* was recorded live three years earlier). These are thoughtful, unassertive performances, which in the first two concertos clearly relate the music to Mozart. Previn gives his very musical soloist good support, particularly in the slow movements, which are gentle and touching. Finales are enjoyably brisk and sparkling. The *Third Concerto* is given rather more weight, without ever being forceful: here the finale is more relaxed and measured – pleasingly lyrical in feeling. The *Fourth Concerto* shows these artists at their very best, again warmly lyrical (although the central dialogue could be more dramatic), but the relaxed playing in the *Emperor* makes this a less bitingly compelling version than it can be, with the finale less weighty than usual. Nevertheless this is a most enjoyable set, recorded at Walthamstow (1, 2 & 5) or Abbey Road (3 and 4) with sound that is warmly resonant but clear. The documentation of this bargain reissue is good, and the packaging (as in the rest of RCA's Collections series) is stylishly attractive.

Piano Concertos (i) 1; (ii) 2–4; (i) 5 (Emperor); (iii) Cello Sonata in G min., Op. 5/2. Bagatelle in A min. (Für Elise); Rondo in C, Op. 51/1

(BB) (***) Naxos mono 8.505189 (5). Schnabel, with (i) LSO; (ii) LPO; Sargent; (iii) Piatigorsky – BRAHMS: Piano Concertos 1–2, etc. *(*); SCHUMANN: Kinderszenen (**)

Schnabel recorded the five Piano Concertos between 1932 and 1935, all with Sargent conducting. This early set has a nobility and robustness that makes one realize why audiences of those years identified Schnabel with Beethoven. The playing is in every way typical: in other words, indifferent to surface polish and pianistic elegance, though these are not absent, he is fully aware of the deepest musical currents. Sargent gives him impressive support, even though wind tuning is not always impeccable. These performances are boxed together with his less impressive accounts of the Brahms, but they are also available separately. Decent transfers.

Piano Concertos (i) 1–4; (ii) 5 (Emperor). 7 Bagatelles, Op. 33; 6 Bagatelles, Op. 126; 11 Bagatelles, Op. 119; Piano Sonatas 5 in C min., Op. 10/1; 8 (Pathétique); 17 (Tempest), Op. 31/2; 18, Op. 31/3; 28, Op. 101; 30, Op. 109; 31, Op. 110; 32, Op. 111; 33 Variations on a Waltz by Diabelli, Op. 120

(N) ✪ (B) *** Ph. (ADD) 475 6319 (6). Kovacevich, with (i) BBC SO; (ii) LSO; C. Davis

Steven Kovacevich's Beethoven concerto recordings remain undisputed classics of the catalogue and have been benchmark recordings since their release in the early 1970s. In the first four concertos, with the BBC Symphony Orchestra, Kovacevich and Colin Davis are consistently crisp and fresh, and it is impossible not to respond to their spontaneity, no matter how many times one hears them. In the Emperor, with the LSO, Kovacevich is unsurpassed, and in its time this famous (1973) account set a model for everyone else. The sound remains excellent. This new, economical packaging also conveniently gathers together Kovacevich's Philips piano sonata recordings for the first time. The 1970s recording sounds consistently fresh, full and vivid. Altogether, this box reflects an outstanding achievement.

Piano Concertos 1–4

(B) *** EMI (ADD) double forte 5 69506-2 (2). Gilels, Cleveland O, Szell

(i) Piano Concertos 1–4; (ii) Romances for Violin & Orchestra 1–2, Opp. 40 & 50

(B) *** Ph. (ADD) Duo 442 577-2 (2). (i) Kovacevich, BBC SO, C. Davis; (ii) Grumiaux, Concg. O, Haitink

Gilels is an incomparable Beethoven player, unfailingly illuminating and poetic. Szell, tautly controlled, gives rhythms an exhilarating lift and has tremendous grip, and the playing of the Cleveland Orchestra is beyond reproach. The recordings, made in Severance Hall in 1968, are dry and clear but with ample atmosphere.

The first four Concertos bring characteristically crisp and refreshing readings from Kovacevich and Colin Davis. These are model performances, with Kovacevich conveying a depth and thoughtful intensity that have rarely been matched. The recording, from the early 1970s, is refined and well balanced, and has been admirably transferred to CD. Grumiaux's

Romances date from a decade earlier, but the sound is full and the solo playing is peerless.

Piano Concerto 1 in C, Op. 15

**(*) EMI 5 56974-2. Argerich, Concg. O, Wallberg – MOZART: Piano Concerto 25 **(*)

Argerich, recorded live, offers playing white-hot with the inspiration of the moment, full of sparkle, even if her approach to the slow movement is on the cool side. The radio sound is good, but the coughing of the audience is at times intrusive.

(i) Piano Concerto 1. Piano Sonatas 12 in A flat (Funeral March); 22 in F, Op. 54; 23 (Appassionata)

(B) *** RCA 2-CD (ADD) 74321 84605-2 (2). Richter, (i) with Boston SO, Munch – BRAHMS: Piano Concerto 2 ***

Commanding though Richter's Beethoven C major Concerto is and splendid though it is to have it restored to circulation, it is the Appassionata Sonata (and the Brahms coupling) that makes this so essential an acquisition. Richter's 1961 Appassionata has tremendous electricity, range and majesty. One of the greatest of his Beethoven performances.

(i; iii) Piano Concerto 1; (i; ii; iv) Choral Fantasia, Op. 80; (ii; iv) Meeresstille und glückliche Fahrt, Op. 112

(M) **(*) DG (IMS) 469 549-2. VPO, with (i) Pollini; (ii) V. State Op. Ch.; cond. (iii) Jochum, or (iv) Abbado

In the C major Concerto Pollini is sometimes wilful, but with refreshing clarity of articulation. Brisk rather than poetic, his performance vividly reflects the challenge of an unexpected partnership between pianist and conductor. The recording was taken from live performances but betrays little sign of that. In the big opening solo of the Choral Fantasia, in effect a Beethovenian improvisation written down, Pollini is at his most magnetic, and indeed his performance is compelling throughout. The rare choral work, which acts as filler, also benefits from the spontaneous intensity of feeling conveyed here.

Piano Concertos 1–2

*** Sony SK 42177. Perahia, Concg. O, Haitink
(B) *** Ph. (ADD) 422 968-2. Kovacevich, BBC SO, C. Davis
(M) *** DG (IMS) 445 504-2. Argerich, Philh. O, Sinopoli
*** DG (IMS) 437 545-2. Zimerman, VPO

Piano Concertos (i) 1; (ii) 2. Für Elise

(BB) (***) Naxos mono 8.110638. Schnabel, (i) LSO; (ii) LPO; (i–ii) Sargent

Piano Concertos 1–2; Rondo in B flat, WoO 6

*** Simax PSC 1181. Berezovsky, Swedish CO, Dausgaard

Murray Perahia's coupling of Nos. 1 and 2 brings strong and thoughtful performances which draw a sharp distinction between the two works. No. 2, the earlier, brings a near-Mozartian manner in the first movement; but then, rightly, a deep and measured account of the slow movement takes Beethoven into another world, hushed and intense. The First Concerto finds Perahia taking a fully Beethovenian view from the start. Bernard Haitink proves a lively and sympathetic partner, with the Concertgebouw playing superbly. Warm recording.

Thomas Dausgaard and the Swedish Chamber Orchestra produced an impressively fresh Beethoven cycle based on Jonathan Del Mar's scholarly editions of the symphonies and they have now turned their attention to the piano concertos with Boris Berezovsky as the soloist. Berezovsky was a distinguished Tchaikovsky prize-winner, but he has been rather overshadowed by his countryman Pletnev. His Beethoven has real stature: it has sparkle and zest, and both concertos are paced beautifully and are full of vitality. In terms of their pianism and interpretation they are to be recommended among the best. Very good sound, as one would expect from a record produced by Andrew Keener.

Philips have now restored to the catalogue Stephen Kovacevich's recordings of the Beethoven concertos separately on their Virtuoso label to make a clear first bargain choice for this coupling.

The conjunction of Martha Argerich and Giuseppe Sinopoli in Beethoven produces performances which give off electric sparks, daring and volatile. Argerich is jaunty in allegros, and slow movements are songful, not solemn. Vivid sound in a reverberant acoustic.

Zimerman, completing the cycle he began with Bernstein, directs the Vienna Philharmonic in bright, elegant, often witty performances that bring home the point that these are early works. Bright recording.

Schnabel's performances appeared on LP briefly in the days of the World Record Club and more recently on the Arabesque label. They reigned supreme in the 1930s, when they first appeared, and still make for powerfully compelling listening 70 years on. Mark Obert-Thorn's transfers do justice to the vitality and beauty of sound that Schnabel commanded.

Piano Concertos 1, 2 & 4; 6 Bagatelles, Op. 126

(B) **(*) Double Decca 468 558-2 (2). Ashkenazy, VPO, Mehta

Ashkenazy gives sparkling and relaxed readings of the first two concertos, with Mehta's tactful accompaniments adding to the joyful manner of the first movement of No. 1, where Ashkenazy opts not for Beethoven's biggest cadenza but for the much shorter first option of the three. Each slow movement is thoughtful in an unmannered way, and these are both readings which stay within the brief of early Beethoven. The relaxation and sense of spontaneity which mark this Vienna cycle then bring a performance of the Fourth Concerto that may lack something in heroic drive but which in its relative lightness never loses concentration, bringing a captivating sparkle to the finale. Though this may not be as powerful as Ashkenazy's earlier, Chicago reading with Solti, it is fresher and more natural. The six Bagatelles make an attractive if ungenerous bonus. Good, bright, well-detailed recording, made in the highly suitable ambience of the Sofiensaal.

Piano Concertos 1; 4

*** Ph. 462 782-2. Brendel, VPO, Rattle

In No. 1 Rattle immediately sets the scene with a strong, forward-looking introduction, and Brendel's crisp articulation in the outer movements (and neat touches of wit in the finale) balances the poised, intensely shaped account of the beautiful central Largo. The rare coupling with No. 4 works well, with its highly poetic yet expansive opening, and in the Andante the orchestra weightily contrasts with Brendel's gentle response, which triumphs so touchingly to make way for the joyfully vigorous finale.

Piano Concerto 2

(N) *** Channel Classics SACD CCSSA 19703. Lazic, Klassische Philharmonie Bonn, Beissel – HAYDN: Piano Sonatas 60 & 62 ***

Recorded live in Stuttgart in March 2002, Dejan Lazic's performance of the Beethoven Second Concerto is strongly characterized in its dramatically high contrasts, with muscular playing which yet allows a feather-light touch for the first entry of the piano. The chamber scale is well caught in the recording, and the confidence of this very positive artist is crowned by his choice of cadenza, his own, which with frequent changes of tempo is lively and generally in style, if with some Lisztian touches. Having the two late Haydn sonatas is unusual but illuminating.

Piano Concertos 2–3

(N) *** DG 477 5026. Argerich, Mahler CO, Abbado
*** Ph. 462 783-2. Brendel, VPO, Rattle
(N) (BB) ** EMI Encore 5 86413-2. Barenboim, BPO

There is an element of daring in Martha Argerich's inspired readings of the Second and Third Concertos which, with stylish accompaniment from the Mahler Chamber Orchestra under Abbado, makes it a winning coupling. The clarity and point of her playing in rapid passagework is a delight, with scales that ripple deliciously, so that every idea seems new. This is her first ever recording of No. 3, but she recorded No. 2 in 1985 with Sinopoli and the Philharmonia in a similarly characterful reading, coupled with No. 1. This time her playing has an extra degree of freedom at speeds markedly faster in the first two movements and with agogic hesitations a little more marked. Both have the characterful stamp of a unique artist, and one hopes that both will remain available.

As in the First Concerto, Rattle opens the Second with a strongly rhythmic yet resiliently classical tutti, and Brendel's response shows how close is this musical partnership, both in the reflectively serene Adagio and in the engaging finale. No. 3, with one of Beethoven's most imaginatively developed opening movements, again shows these two artists working in absolute rapport, with the elysian Largo wonderfully sustained in its rapt beauty and the finale lilting joyously. The often subtle use of light and shade continuously illuminates this music-making and the recording balance is most satisfying.

Barenboim's performances on Encore come from his second, digital set of the concertos, recorded in 1985, when he directed the Berlin Philharmonic from the keyboard, not always with total success. The resulting readings lack the character of the earlier cycle, made in collaboration with Klemperer. The orchestral tuttis, too, could be more sharply focused, although this applies more to the C minor than to the B flat Concerto. Having said that, Barenboim's own playing remains impressive, bright and crisply articulated in the Second Concerto and with a fine, spacious account of the Largo of No. 3, not quite matched by the orchestral accompaniment. But in the last resort this is not a distinctive coupling.

Piano Concertos 2; 4

(B) *** Sony (ADD) SBK 48165. Fleisher, Cleveland O, Szell

Leon Fleisher, partnered by George Szell, is both powerful and intense in his spontaneous-sounding performance of No. 2, giving weight to early Beethoven. In No. 4 they are even more searching, with the soloist's refreshingly imaginative playing matched by glorious sounds from the Cleveland Orchestra. The bright, forward recordings have satisfying fullness and body.

Piano Concertos 2; 5 (Emperor)

(N) (B) **(*) RCA 82876 65838-2. Rubinstein, LPO, Barenboim

(*(**)) BBC mono BBCL 4028-2. Hess, BBC SO, Sargent (includes interview with John Amis)

Rubinstein's coupling derives from a complete set of the five concertos, recorded in London's Kingsway Hall in 1975 when the great pianist was 88. In the *Emperor* he plays with spontaneous inspiration in every bar, and the LPO under a relatively young Barenboim accompany with keen understanding. The *B flat Concerto* is not quite so arresting but is still very fine, with a beautifully poised slow movement. On CD the balance is much better than it was on LP, with the soloist still placed forward but with the orchestra vividly in the picture. The piano timbre is truthful and fuller than Rubinstein often received; orchestral wind solos emerge effectively and the strings are laid out convincingly within a reverberant acoustic, but the upper range of the violins is a bit fierce and lacks refinement of focus. A very worthwhile reissue, just the same.

Hess's *Emperor* is the more remarkable for the leonine quality of the performance, a vitally spontaneous reading which exploits the widest expressive range, at once heroic and poetic. The meditative intensity of the slow movement, rapt and refined, leads on to an exuberant account of the finale. No. 2, recorded three years later, also brings a remarkable performance: fresh, poetic and youthfully urgent in the first movement, dedicated in the slow movement, and sparkling and witty in the finale. However, it is important to stress the considerable difference here in recording quality between No. 5 (1957) and No. 2 (1960). It is quite possible that the latter comes from a private off-air tape rather than a BBC mastertape. The sound is more opaque, has *very* limited frequency range and suffers from distortion.

(i) *Piano Concerto 3. Coriolan Overture* (with rehearsal sequence)

(BB) (***) Naxos mono 8.110804. (i) Hess; NBC SO, Toscanini (with WAGNER: *Götterdämmerung: Siegfried's Rhine Journey* (***))

On this live recording of a 1946 broadcast Dame Myra Hess gives a thrilling performance, one of her very finest on disc, with the outer movements crisply articulated and beautifully sprung at high speed and the slow movement warmly expressive, bringing out a rare warmth in Toscanini too. *Coriolan* is high-powered, dry and incisive, and the Wagner makes a welcome fill-up.

(i) *Piano Concerto 3.* (ii) *Piano Sonatas 21 (Waldstein); 24 in F sharp, Op. 78*

(BB) *** Warner Apex 0927 48994-2. (i) Fellner, ASMF, Marriner; (ii) Pommier

Till Fellner is a pianist of keen intelligence and refined musicianship, whose few recordings have made a strong impression. This account of the *C minor Concerto* was made in London in 1994. It deserves to attract a lot of attention and, we hope, will at this competitive price. The sound is first class and the playing of the then 23-year-old is elegant, thoughtful and fresh. The two sonatas, drawn from a set recorded three years earlier by Jean-Bernard Pommier, are not quite in the same league, but the disc is to be recommended.

Piano Concerto 3; Rondo in B flat, WoO 6

(M) *(*) DG (ADD) (IMS) 463 649-2. S. Richter, VSO, Sanderling – MOZART: *Piano Concerto 20* ***

Richter's performance, now reissued as one of DG's 'Originals', is too chilly and detached to be wholly convincing. Like Schnabel, Richter takes the slow movement very slowly

indeed, but unlike Schnabel he provides little warmth and the result is curiously square. The finale is very hard-driven. The *Rondo* is a different matter. Richter's sparkling account is effortlessly brilliant, but not to the exclusion of all else: there is subtlety here and even a touch of humour, but above all complete spontaneity and a sense of enjoyment throughout. The recording has come up well, with clean piano-tone and a fresh overall balance.

Piano Concertos 3 in C min., Op. 37; 4 in G, Op. 58

*** Sony SK 39814. Perahia, Concg. O, Haitink

**(*) DG (IMS) 429 749-2. Zimerman, VPO, Bernstein

(M) **(*) DG (IMS) 471 352-2. Pollini, BPO, Abbado

Piano Concertos 3–4; Rondo in C, Op. 51/1

(BB) (***) Naxos mono 8.110639. Schnabel, LPO, Sargent

Perahia gives readings that are at once intensely poetic and individual but also strong, with pointing and shading of passage-work that consistently convey the magic of the moment caught on the wing, helped by fine, spacious and open recorded sound.

Zimerman finds freshness and poetry in both Nos. 3 and 4, very sympathetically accompanied by Bernstein, who exactly matches his soloist in the thoughtful dialogue of the central *Andante* of No. 4. Bright sound that yet does not allow a full *pianissimo*.

Schnabel re-recorded these concertos after the war with Issay Dobrowen, but this pre-war set, made when he was recording the sonatas for HMV's Beethoven Sonata Society volumes, long dominated the musical scene. Schnabel was about fifty when he embarked on this mammoth enterprise, and the 1933 versions of the *Third* and *Fourth Piano Concertos* with Malcolm Sargent conducting the LPO have long been absent from the catalogues. Their return in these fine transfers is welcome: Schnabel's insights are always special, and although they do not occupy quite the same awesome pinnacle as the sonatas in Schnabel's Beethoven discography, they are still memorable.

DG have chosen the later (1992) recordings of Beethoven's *Third* and *Fourth Piano Concertos*, recorded live, for inclusion in the 'Pollini Edition'. On balance, this newer performance of No. 4 has keener concentration than the earlier, Vienna account with Boehm, while Pollini's playing in the slow movement of No. 3 is more hushed than before. But the balance of advantage does not always favour the later versions, where the piano sound is often shallower and the orchestral recording tends towards harshness in tuttis, lacking bloom.

Piano Concertos (i) *3;* (ii) *5 (Emperor)*

(N) (BB) **(*) Naxos mono 8.110776. Moiseiwitsch, with (i) Philh. O, Sargent; (ii) LPO, Szell

(N) (M) ** Sony 518804-2 [SK 92738]. Serkin, NYPO, Bernstein (Bonus: *Piano Sonata 8: Finale*)

Moiseiwitsch's are performances of stature. The *Emperor* with Szell and the LPO comes from 1938 and long enjoyed classic status. The *Third*, recorded at Abbey Road in December 1950, appeared at the tail end of the 78-r.p.m. era, and we do not recall it appearing on LP. Although it was coolly received at the time, it has had a favourable press in its new incarnation – and rightly so. Moiseiwitsch's playing in the slow movement is poetic and magisterial, and Ward Marston has returned to the original tapes rather than to the shellac dubbings, so the sound is exceptionally good for the period. So, too, is that of the *Emperor*, transferred from Victor pressings, which have much quieter surfaces than the English plum-label 78s. Moiseiwitsch was hailed in the USA as 'a veritable aristocrat of the keyboard' but was underrated here in the 1950s. Perhaps his relegation by EMI to 'plum label' status may account for this in part. This CD leaves no doubts as to his wonderful pianism and his depth of insight.

The remastered CD of the 1964 Serkin/Bernstein account of the *Third Concerto* has improved the sound, which is now relatively spacious. Between them, these two artists give a super-brilliant performance of the first movement, with strong orchestral accents from Bernstein which at times almost brutalize the music. The slow movement is serene and poised, but the aggressive feeling returns in the orchestral tuttis of the finale. Serkin's *Emperor* is characteristically commanding: the reading is strong and nobly sensitive in the great Adagio. The snag is again the rather coarse (1962) recording, which the new transfer can only partly mitigate.

(i) *Piano Concertos 3; 5; Piano Sonata 5 in C min., Op. 10/1; Andante favori in F; Für Elise, WoO 59;* **(ii)** *Choral Fantasia, Op 80*
(B) **(*) Double Decca (DDD/ADD) 468 906-2 (2).
  Ashkenazy, with (i) VPO, Mehta; (ii) Cleveland Ch. & O,
  cond. Ashkenazy

Ashkenazy's digital Beethoven piano concerto cycle of the early 1980s was the first to be issued on CD. (Nos. 1, 2, and 4 are available on Double Decca 468 558-2; see above.) They were generally more relaxed and spontaneous-sounding than the somewhat aggressive Solti Chicago set of the 1970s, though only in the finale of the *Emperor* does the more recent approach bring a slackening of tension that reduces the impact of the reading. The spaciousness of the first movement combined with clarity of texture is most persuasive, and so too is the unusually gentle account of the slow movement. The relaxed approach works well in the *Third Concerto* because, even though it is slower than the earlier recording, it sounds more spontaneous and has fewer distracting agogic hesitations than before. The slow movement is more lyrical, and the finale has much more charm – an excellent performance. Both receive vividly warm recordings, and Mehta accompanies well, though with no particularly memorable insight. Ashkenazy's 1976 account of the Op. 10/1 *Sonata* is both thoughtful and alert, with the freshness of approach silencing any criticism, and the recording is excellent. The vibrantly characterful account of the *Choral Fantasia* was recorded at the time of his later, third set of the Beethoven concertos (1987) when Ashkenazy directed from the keyboard. It makes a compelling bonus.

Piano Concertos 3 in C min.; 5 in E flat (Emperor)
(M) **(*) Sony (ADD) 512867-2. Serkin, NYPO, Bernstein

The remastered CD of the 1964 Serkin/Bernstein account of the *Third Concerto* has improved the sound, which is now relatively spacious. Between them these artists give a super-brilliant performance of the first movement, with strong orchestral accents from Bernstein which at times almost brutalize the music. The slow movement is serene and poised, but the aggressive feeling returns in the orchestral tuttis of the finale, which are similarly fierce, partly the effect of the microphones being so close to the violins. Serkin's *Emperor* is characteristically commanding; the reading is strong and nobly sensitive in the great *Adagio*. The snag is the rather coarse – if extremely vivid – 1962 recording, which the new transfer is unable to mitigate. However, there is no doubt that

this is thrilling music-making, with superb solo playing, and one can adjust to the sound.

(i) *Piano Concerto 3;* **(ii)** *Triple Concerto for Violin, Cello & Piano, Op. 56*
**(*) Simax PSC 1183. (i–ii) Berezovsky; (ii) with Svensson,
  Rondin; (i–ii) Swedish CO, Dausgaard
(BB) (**(*)) Naxos mono 8.110878. (i) Long, Paris
  Conservatoire O; (ii) Odnoposoff, Auber, Morales, VPO;
  Weingartner

More than most Beethoven recordings using a chamber orchestra, this one clearly conveys an intimate scale, with the music in close-up, bringing the sort of impact that early audiences might have expected. Boris Berezovsky in the *Third Concerto* draws on a very wide dynamic range. Despite the relatively small scale, he opts for Beethoven's last and longest cadenza in the first movement. Outer movements are on the fast side, with influences from period-performance practice, yet the slow movements in both concertos are taken at very measured speeds, with Berezovsky allowing himself ample expressive freedom. The finale of the *Piano Concerto* sparkles, thanks to the pianist's exceptionally clean articulation, with passage-work perfectly even. In the *Triple Concerto* the violinist, Urban Svensson, with rather edgy tone as recorded, may not be a perfect match, and Berezovsky rather than the cellist, Mats Rondin, is very much the leader of the team, but the clarity of texture on every level makes for an exceptionally fresh reading.

Marguerite Long's account of the *Third Piano Concerto* was made in June 1939 in the relatively dry acoustic of the Théâtre Pigalle in Paris. The first-movement tempo, as with all Weingartner performances, seems just right, and Long, who is so closely associated with Ravel and Fauré, proves hardly less at home in Beethoven, though she often makes some expressive hesitations at the beginning of phrases, while Weingartner presses on. She comes to grief early in the restatement of the first movement, but hers is a characterful reading of much style and many unashamedly old-fashioned romantic gestures. One soon gets accustomed to the dryish sound over which Mark Obert-Thorne has obviously laboured long – and successfully. Older readers will have made their first acquaintance with the *Triple Concerto* via Weingartner's pioneering (1937) account, a wonderful reading that glows with joy and pleasure and that set a standard which was long unsurpassed.

(i) *Piano Concerto 3;* **(ii)** *Symphony 2*
(N) (M) **(*) DG (ADD) stereo/mono 4749832. (i) S.
  Richter, VPO; (ii) Leningrad PO; Sanderling

Sanderling's 1956 account of the *Second Symphony* was recorded in the Vienna Musikverein on the occasion of the Leningrad orchestra's first post-war European tour, when they astonished their Viennese audience, not only by their expert and idiomatic playing of Beethoven, but also because the orchestra all wore patent-leather shoes! It is indeed a fine, traditional performance, with excellent contributions from the wind soloists as well as the famous string section, and the mono recording is full and well balanced. Richter's 1962 stereo account of the *C minor Piano Concerto* was poorly receieved by us when it first appeared. We found it 'too chilly and detached to be wholly convincing'. But it emerges here, in an excellent transfer, sounding rather warmer than before. Richter (like Schnabel) takes the slow movement very slowly and he is a little square, but again his patrician approach has its impressive side, and the fast, boldly driven finale is less unusual today than it was in the early 1960s.

Piano Concerto 4 in G, Op. 58

(N) ** EMI **DVD** 492840-9. Rubinstein, LPO, Dorati (Bonus: CHOPIN: *Polonaise in A flat (Heroic)* ***) – MENDELSSOHN: *Violin Concerto*, etc. (***); WALTON: *Cello Concerto* (***)

(M) *** Warner Elatus 0927 49617-2. Grimaud, NYPO, Masur – SCHUMANN: *Piano Concerto* ***

*** Sup. SU 3714-2. Moravec, Prague Philh. O, Bělohlávek – FRANCK *Symphonic Variations* ***; RAVEL: *Piano Concerto in G* **(*)

((*))** BBC mono BBCL 4111-2. Hess, LPO, Boult – MOZART: *Piano Concerto 23*, etc. (**(*))

The Rubinstein performance of the *G major Concerto* comes from a TV transmission from the Royal Festival Hall in December 1967. The auditorium was packed so that the sound is a bit dry. Rubinstein is splendidly patrician, though he is not as poetic in fashioning detail as he was in his earlier LP cycle with Krips. The exposition of the first movement is relatively unengaged, though things pick up at the development. Good orchestral playing from the LPO and Dorati, and it is good to see some of the celebrated players of the day, including Richard Adeney. Anthony Craxton directs the viewer's eyes where they need to be and the camerawork is unfussy and economical. The stirring Chopin encore also comes from the Festival Hall, from a recital given a few months later.

Anyone seeking this rare but attractive coupling with the Schumann *Concerto* will find Hélène Grimaud rises to the occasion in both works, and in the Beethoven she has excellent support from Masur, who provides a spacious accompaniment for the first movement, which Grimaud opens with Kempff-like gentleness, and is poetically lyrical throughout. The interchange of the *Andante* is similarly thoughtful, and the vigorous finale brings a joyful, exhilarating conclusion. Warmly resonant recording which adds weight without clouding detail.

This Supraphon CD also offers this unusual coupling, but thanks to the distinctive artistry of the Czech pianist, Ivan Moravec, with his extraordinary clarity of articulation, as well as to the conductor, Jiří Bělohlávek, the result has an attractive consistency, with each work illuminating the others. In the first movement of the Beethoven, Moravec's crisp enunciation of each note in passage-work that can seem routine makes for sparkling results, with the delicate tracery of the piano part in the recapitulation wonderfully clear. With incisive support from Bělohlávek and the Prague Philharmonia, there is no lack of muscular strength either, with Moravec drawing on a wide tonal range, as he does in his deeply meditative reading of the slow movement. In the finale Bělohlávek matches his soloist in drawing from the Prague Philharmonia comparably transparent textures.

Though Dame Myra Hess was among the most celebrated British pianists of her time, she recorded disappointingly little commercially, which makes this coupling of broadcast performances of Beethoven and Mozart specially valuable. In 1961, after a stroke, she decided to retire, and the Beethoven, recorded in September of that year, marked her Prom farewell, while the Mozart *Concerto*, given six weeks later in the Royal Festival Hall, was her very last public performance. You would never know it from the vigour of the playing. Hess

may above all have been noted for the poetry of her performances – the slow movement has a rapt quality and a radiance that compel admiration (and she has great rapport with and support from Sir Adrian and the LPO) – but there is ample evidence here of her power and purposefulness too. This may not be a flawless performance but, even with limited mono sound and a very close balance for the piano, it retains a winning freshness and spontaneity.

Piano Concertos 4; 5 in E flat (Emperor)

(M) *** Sony SMK 89711. Perahia, Concg. O, Haitink

❀ *** Testament SBT 1299. Richter-Haaser, Philh. O, Kertész

(M) *** DG (ADD) 447 402-2. Kempff, BPO, Leitner

❂—☛ ❀ **(M)** *** Decca mono/stereo 467 126-2. Curzon, VPO, Knappertsbusch

(M) *** DG (ADD) 439 483-2. Pollini, VPO, Boehm

(M) *** Ph. 464 681-2. Arrau, Dresden State O, C. Davis

(BB) **(*) Regis (ADD) RRC 1047. Brendel, VSO, Wallberg, or V. Pro Musica SO, Mehta

(BB) **(*) RCA 82876 55267-2. Ax, RPO, Previn

Perahia's accounts are strong and thoughtful, with characteristic touches of poetry. Haitink is a responsive partner – each movement immediately takes wing. These noble performances on Testament, like Hans Richter-Haaser's superb Brahms *B flat Concerto* with Karajan, have not enjoyed much exposure since their appearance on LP in the early 1960s. We recall that the late Robert Simpson, who wrote with special insight and authority on Beethoven, spoke of them with awe and in much the same breath as of Schnabel and Solomon. They stand the test of time well and deserve the strongest recommendation. This is Beethoven playing of the first order, and we hope that Testament will bring other of Richter-Haaser's records back into circulation. The transfer does the original LPs (which we have long cherished) full justice.

In the *Fourth Concerto* Kempff's delicacy of fingerwork and his shading of tone-colour are unsurpassed. Though his version of the *Emperor* is not on an epic scale, Kempff's exceptionally wide range of tone and dynamic gives it power in plenty.

Curzon's refinement and reflective poetry are wonderfully refreshing in both *Concertos*; moreover, he found a perfect partner in Knappertsbusch. The *Fourth Concerto* is an Elysian performance, full of delicate lyrical feeling, the slow movement unsurpassed on record, not even by Kempff. Moreover, the 1954 mono recording, made in the Musikverein, is of outstanding quality, with warm, luminous piano-tone and a clear, transparent orchestral image, not lacking bloom. The *Emperor* is stereo, made in the Sofiensaal three years later. Again it is a refined and thoughtful reading. Curzon's playing in the slow movement is beautifully controlled and it brings out the poetry gently and movingly. The first movement certainly does not lack compulsion, and the finale is the only movement where one feels his approach shifts the viewpoint back almost to Mozart; there is a restraint about the essentially rumbustious movement that some may feel is almost too much of a good thing. Yet the keen intelligence of the playing and the inner concentration working throughout the reading keep it fully alive. The Vienna Philharmonic plays strongly and authoritatively under Knappertsbusch, and the new transfer of the 1957 master has miraculously cleaned up the sound, the orchestral tuttis now full and not edgy and the piano quality very impressive indeed. This makes an ideal coupling for Decca's Legends series. But the Rosette is for the *Andante* of the *G major*, which recalls the notion that

Beethoven had Orpheus's plea for the return of Eurydice in mind. This Decca disc completely replaces Curzon's radio recordings with the Bavarian Radio Symphony Orchestra under Kubelik, made two decades later (Audite 95.459), but his more robust 1971 BBC Festival Hall account of the *Emperor* with Boulez makes a fascinating alternative (see below).

The alternative mid-priced DG coupling offers two of the most strikingly individual performances from Pollini's earlier cycle, excellently transferred. After the poised account of the *Fourth Concerto*, the distinction of Pollini's interpretation of the *Emperor* is never in doubt, with the slow movement elegant and the finale urgent and energetic.

Arrau's 1984 account of the *Emperor* has long been a primary recommendation, standing high among countless other versions. There are technical flaws, and the digital recording, made in Dresden's Lukas Kirche, is rather resonant in the bass. But with Sir Colin Davis and the Dresden State Orchestra as electrifying partners, the voltage is even higher than in his earlier versions of the mid-1960s. Intensely individual, the very opposite of routine, this is from first to last a performance which reflects new searching by a deeply thoughtful musician. It is a thrillingly expansive *Emperor* which will give much satisfaction. The snag is that it is now coupled with No. 4, recorded at the same time, which is altogether less successful. Here Arrau's weighty view brings speeds slower than usual, and for many, despite countless individual touches and excellent orchestral playing, the sluggishness will hamper enjoyment. The bass-heavy recording also adds to the impression of ponderousness. Even so, this disc must be given the strongest recommendation for the superb account of the *Emperor* alone.

It is good that Regis have reissued at budget price Brendel's 1959 Vox performances. Many count these readings the finest of all his Beethoven concerto interpretations, and certainly they have a fresh spontaneity which is very appealing. In No. 4 the orchestral accompaniment is unimaginative: the first-movement tutti for example is rhythmically stodgy. But Brendel's control of phrase and colour is such that his reading rides over this impediment and the contrasts of the slow movement are strongly and poetically made. It is noteworthy that he uses the second of the cadenzas written for the work, one not generally heard. The *Emperor* is a bold and vigorous reading, and here Brendel is well supported by the young Zubin Mehta and the Vienna Pro Musica Symphony Orchestra. The performance is without idiosyncrasy, yet is strong in style and personality, the slow movement raptly serene to contrast with the vitality of the outer movements. In both *Concertos* the piano is well captured and, in spite of the shrill, thin strings (cleanly remastered), the warm resonance brings a fully acceptable overall effect.

This RCA Ax pairing is taken from the complete set above. The *Fourth Concerto* is outstanding in every way; the *Emperor* is thoughtful rather than forceful, the first movement less of a contest than usual, while the flowing speed for the slow movement and the scherzando quality in the finale make for a comparatively lightweight effect, rather thin of piano-tone, powerful though Ax's articulation is.

(i) *Piano Concertos 4; 5 (Emperor). Piano Sonatas 30, Op. 109; 32, Op. 111*
(N) (M) ((*))** RCA mono 74321 987172 (2). Schnabel, (i) with Chicago SO, Stock

At the beginning of the Second World War, Schnabel left Europe for America, where RCA made these recordings in 1942. The *G major Concerto* with Frederick Stock is poetic and is accommodated with the *Emperor* on the first CD, while the Opp. 109 and 111 *Sonatas* occupy the second. The depth and wisdom which we associate with Schnabel's interpretations are much in evidence, and the sound, generally speaking, is an improvement over the earlier 78s. However, his 1932 version of Op. 111 plumbs greater depths and remains unsurpassed by any pianist.

Piano Concerto 4 (arr. for piano & string quintet; reconstructed Küthen); Symphony 2 (arr. for piano trio)
(M) *** DG Blue 474 224-2. Levin (fortepiano), ORR (members)

This most engaging coupling, reissued on the enterprising Archiv Blue Label, was originally issued as part of Robert Levin's complete set of the *Piano Concertos* with Gardiner (now withdrawn). The deft arrangement of the *Second Symphony* was made by Beethoven himself and certainly does not lack strength in piano-trio format. The coupling is more intriguing – an arrangement only recently reconstructed – of the *Fourth Piano Concerto*, with the solo part modified by Beethoven and with the orchestral part neatly transcribed for string quintet. The result is all the more refreshing on period instruments, and this is a disc to snap up before it disappears.

(i) *Piano Concerto 4;* (ii) *Romance 2 in F. Symphony 5*
(M) (**) Sup. mono (i) Páleniček; (ii) D. Oistrakh; Czech PO, Ančerl

Josef Páleníček is a fine artist with engagingly nimble fingers and, though this is a comparatively lightweight performance, it is fresh and enjoyable. Not surprisingly, the *Romance* is beautifully played, but it is Ančerl's *Fifth Symphony* that is most impressive here. The first movement develops powerfully and dramatically, with the Czech players in first-rate form. The slow movement has less impetus but plenty of lyrical warmth, and the finale is the most effective movement of all. Altogether a good, stout performance, with the fine mono recording sounding surprisingly modern in Stanislav Sýkora's impressive remastering.

Piano Concerto 5 in E flat (Emperor), Op. 73
*** Sony SK 42330. Perahia, Concg. O, Haitink
*** DG (IMS) 429 748-2. Zimerman, VPO, Bernstein
(M) *** BBC (ADD) BBCL 4020-2. Curzon, BBC SO, Boulez – MOZART: *Piano Concerto 26* ***
(M) (***) BBC BBCL mono 4074-2. Moiseiwitsch, BBC SO, Sargent – RACHMANINOV: *Piano Concerto 2* (**)

(i) *Piano Concerto 5. Piano Sonatas 8 in C min. (Pathétique); 23 in F min. (Appassionata)*
(B) (**(*)) EMI mono 5 74800-2. Edwin Fischer, (i) Philh. O, Furtwängler

Piano Concerto 5. Piano Sonata 23 (Appassionata)
*** Ph. 468 783-2. Brendel; VPO, Rattle

(i) *Piano Concerto 5. Piano Sonata 30 in E, Op. 109*
☞ ✿ (B) *** Ph. (ADD) 422 482-2. Kovacevich, (i) LSO, C. Davis

(i) *Piano Concerto 5. Overtures: Coriolan, Op. 62; Creatures of Prometheus, Op. 43; Leonora 3*
(M) *** Chan. 6612. (i) Lill; CBSO, Weller

Piano Concerto 5; Grosse Fuge, Op. 133
(B) *** CfP 585 6162. Kovacevich, Australian CO

Piano Concerto 5; (i) *Choral Fantasia, Op. 80*
(M) **(*) EMI 5 67329-2. Barenboim, New Philh. O,
Klemperer, (i) with John Alldis Ch.

Brendel and Rattle combine to present the *Emperor* concerto
as the culmination of their outstanding cycle, weighty and
commanding yet resilient, with a gloriously rich, flowing
Adagio and a finale which is jauntily rhythmic and full of
elation. As throughout this impressive series, the acoustic of
the *Musikverein* is attractively spacious, yet detail is always
clear. The account of the *Appassionata* is comparably distinguished, the obvious product of maturity, with the central
variations especially thoughtful and the finale making a most
satisfying conclusion. Again most realistic sound.

Kovacevich is unsurpassed as an interpreter of this most
magnificent of concertos. His superb account for Philips,
now on Virtuoso, has set a model for everyone and, with its
late sonata coupling, remains the strongest recommendation,
very well transferred.

Kovacevich's later, EMI digital version of the *Emperor*,
sharper and tauter than the earlier, Philips account, now
arrives on Classics for Pleasure. His version with the soloist
directing from the keyboard is recognizably from the same
inspired artist, though speeds are consistently faster and the
manner is sharper and tauter. The piano-sound on the digital
recording is brighter, if not so well balanced. The *Grosse Fuge*
makes an unusual but apt coupling.

Perahia's account of the *Emperor*, strong and thoughtful
yet with characteristic touches of poetry, rounds off an
outstanding cycle of the Beethoven concertos. The approach
is spacious, and with Bernard Haitink and the Concertgebouw Orchestra firm, responsive partners, each movement
immediately takes wing.

Zimerman reserves for the *Emperor* his most powerful
playing and Bernstein sensitively encourages him into
spontaneous-sounding expressiveness, turning phrases with
consistent imagination.

The partnership of the introspective Clifford Curzon and
the incisive Boulez may not seem a promising one, but in this
live performance (recorded in 1971 at the Royal Festival Hall)
the challenge between the two brings electrifying results.
Curzon is at his most taut and incisive, while finding depths
of poetry, and Boulez proves a surprisingly sympathetic
interpreter of Beethoven, matching his soloist in subtle
dynamic shading, while bringing home the work's dramatic
power. Full, forward recording.

On Chandos, John Lill's bold, authoritative Beethoven style
brings breadth and majesty to the opening movement, with
the slow movement serene and the finale vigorously joyful.
Walter Weller's performances of the three overtures are splendidly alive. The CBSO is on top form throughout, and the
full, resonant sound is of the best Chandos vintage. An
outstanding alternative mid-priced choice.

The Barenboim/Klemperer partnership in the *Emperor*
produces a remarkable degree of concentration from pianist
and conductor alike and provides an astonishingly fresh
experience. The performance – with a number of unimportant 'fluffs' unedited – has a striking sense of spontaneity, as
has the magnificent account of the *Choral Fantasia*. The new
transfer of the 1967 Abbey Road recording brings out a hint
of harshness on the massed strings, but the piano is caught
admirably.

Moiseiwitsch's magisterial and noble *Emperor* was
recorded only a month before his death. It is not always
finger-sure in the finale – he was, after all, 73 – but it has a

wisdom and sense of architecture and line that carry all
before it. Sargent and the BBC Symphony give excellent
support, although the recording does not have the clarity and
transparency of a good studio recording of the period. However, connoisseurs of the piano – and of great music-making
– should not neglect this opportunity of collecting it.

Edwin Fischer's 1951 recording of the *Emperor* with Furtwängler and the Philharmonia is one of the great classics of
the gramophone, an *Emperor* both imperious and imperial.
The two *Sonatas* were recorded the following year (also at
Abbey Road) and are equally valuable. However, the current
transfer of the *Concerto* yields a rather opaque, not very
refined orchestral texture, though full-bodied enough, and
the piano timbre too is somewhat bass-heavy.

(i) *Piano Concerto 5. 32 Variations on an Original Theme in
C min., WoO 80; 12 Variations on a Russian Dance from
'Das Waldmädchen' (Wranitzky), WoO 71; 6 Variations on a
Turkish March from 'The Ruins of Athens', Op. 76*
(B) *** EMI (ADD) double forte 5 69509-2 (2). Gilels, (i) with
Cleveland O, Szell – DVORAK: *Symphony 8* **(*)

Of the many versions of the *Emperor Concerto* available, few
are finer than Gilels's, with strength matched by poetry, and
with Szell offering the strongest backing. The *C minor Variations* are superbly done, and the other two sets bring the
strongest characterization too. Bright, full sound.

(i) *Piano Concerto 5;* (ii) *Piano Concerto in E flat, WoO 4*
(arr. & orch. Willy Hess); (iii) *Violin Concerto in D, Op. 61;*
(iv) *Triple Concerto for Violin, Cello & Piano in C, Op. 56*
(B) **(*) Ph. (ADD) Duo 442 580-2 (2). (i) Kovacevich, LSO,
C. Davis; (ii) Grychtolowna, Folkwang CO, Dressel; (iii)
Krebbers, Concg. O, Haitink; (iv) Szeryng, Starker, Arrau,
New Philh. O, Inbal

Kovacevich's superb (1969) account of the *Emperor* is here
part of an attractive Duo compilation which includes also the
early *E flat Piano Concerto* (WoO 4), which the composer
wrote when he was only fourteen, here offered in a spirited
performance in a reconstruction by Willy Hess. Krebbers's
1974 recording of the *Violin Concerto* is outstanding. In his
hands the slow movement has a tender simplicity that is
irresistible. The companion account of the *Triple Concerto*
with Arrau, Szeryng and Starker is less strongly projected,
losing concentration at very unhurried tempi. Yet the set
remains highly recommendable.

(i) *Piano Concerto 5;* (ii) *Triple Concerto for Violin, Cello &
Piano*
(B) *** Sony (ADD) SBK 46549. (i) Fleisher, Cleveland O,
Szell; (ii) Stern, Rose, Istomin, Phd. O, Ormandy

Leon Fleisher, who worked with Szell with special understanding, gives a reading of the *Emperor* impressive for its
dramatic vigour. Stern, Rose and Istomin make an inspired
trio of soloists in the *Triple Concerto*, sadly marred by their
close balance.

(i) *Piano Concerto 5;* (ii) *Cello Sonata in G min., Op. 5/2*
(BB) (***) Naxos mono 8.110640. Schnabel, (i) LSO, Sargent;
(ii) Piatigorsky

Schnabel's *Emperor* was recorded in 1932 (he subsequently
re-made it after the war with the Philharmonia Orchestra and
Alceo Galliera) when he was at the height of his powers and
had London at his feet. It long occupied a dominant position

in the catalogue – and rightly. Schnabel had met Piatigorsky in the 1920s when he was leading the cello section of the Berlin Philharmonic under Furtwängler, and together with Carl Flesch they formed a piano trio in the 1920s. Alas, they made no records, and this 1934 set of the *G minor Cello Sonata* is the sole representation of Schnabel's collaboration with the great cellist. It is very distinguished indeed, although Piatigorsky's post-war set of all five *Sonatas* with Solomon has the greater poise.

(i) *Piano Concertos 1–5*. (ii) *Violin Concerto. Symphonies 1–9; Overtures: Consecration of the House; Egmont; Leonora 3*

(B) **(*) Decca (ADD) 467 892-2 (8). (i) Backhaus; (ii) Szeryng with LSO; otherwise VPO; Schmidt-Isserstedt (with Sutherland, Horne, King, Talvela & V. State Op. Ch. in 9)

Backhaus's authoritative, overtly classical set of the *Piano Concertos* is also available separately (433 891-2), but Schmidt-Isserstedt's vintage cycle of the symphonies, recorded in the Sofiensaal in the mid- to late 1960s, is new to CD. It presents a consistently musical view, not lacking strength, and without distracting idiosyncrasies. All the symphonies are beautifully played – the character of the VPO coming over strongly – and very well recorded. Apart from the *Pastoral*, clean and classically straightforward, but entirely lacking charm, there is no outright disappointment here, and the series culminates in a splendid account of the *Ninth*, one that does not quite scale the heights but which, particularly in the slow movement and the finale (with outstanding soloists), conveys visionary strength. Szeryng's account of the *Violin Concerto* derives from the Philips catalogue and dates from 1965. His is a strongly lyrical performance, withdrawn in the *Larghetto*, yet creating a dreamy, hushed atmosphere in which the gentle beauty of mood is the highlight of the reading, well supported by his partner.

Violin Concerto in D, Op. 61

(N) *** EMI **DVD** 5 44544-9. Perlman, BPO, Barenboim (Producer: Johannes Müller) – BRAHMS: *Violin Concerto* ***

(N) *** EMI **DVD** 490445-9. Grumiaux, O Nat. de l'ORTF, Dorati (Bonuses: BACH: *Violin Partita 2, BWV 1004: Sarabande & Chaconne.* BLOCH: *Nigun (Baal Shem).* PAGANINI: *Caprice, Op. 1/14)* – MENDELSSOHN; *Violin Concerto* (***)

(N) (***) EMI **DVD** 492834-9. Kogan, O Nat. de l'ORTF, Louis de Froment (With recital: BACH: *Violin Partita in D min., BWV 1004: Sarabande.* HANDEL: *Violin Sonata in E, HWV 373* . DEBUSSY: *Beau soir.* SHOSTAKOVICH: *Preludes, Op. 34/10, 15, 16 & 24* (with Andrei Mytnik, piano). BRAHMS: *Hungarian Dance 17.* PAGANINI: *Cantabile.* FALLA: *Suite populaire espagnole* (with Naum Walter, piano). LECLAIR: *Sonata for 2 Violins in C, Op. 3/3* (with Elizaveta Gilels-Kogan, violin) ***)

(M) *** EMI 5 66900-2. Perlman, Philh. O, Giulini

☽ (M) *** DG (ADD) 447 403-2. Schneiderhan, BPO, Jochum – MOZART: *Violin Concerto 5* ***

(N) (M) (***) EMI mono 5 62821-2. Menuhin, Lucerne Festival O, Furtwängler – BRAHMS: *Violin Sonata 3; Hungarian Dances* (**(*))

(M) (***) EMI mono 5 66975-2. Menuhin, Philh. O, Furtwängler – MENDELSSOHN: *Violin Concerto* (***)

(M) (***) EMI mono 5 67583-2 [567584]. Milstein, Pittsburgh SO, Steinberg – BRAHMS: *Violin Concerto* (***) ☽

*** EMI 7 54072-2. Kyung-Wha Chung, Concg. O, Tennstedt – BRUCH: *Violin Concerto 1* ***

(B) *** DG (ADD) (IMS) 453 142-2 (2). Zukerman, Chicago SO, Barenboim – BRAHMS: *Concerto* **(*); MENDELSSOHN; TCHAIKOVSKY: *Concertos* ***

(M) *** RCA (ADD) **SACD** 82876 61391-2. Heifetz, Boston SO, Munch – BRAHMS: *Concerto* ***

(M) *** DG (ADD) (IMS) 463 078-2. Zukerman, Chicago SO, Barenboim – HAYDN: *Sinfonia concertante in B flat* ***

(M) *** RCA (ADD) 09026 68980-2. Heifetz, Boston SO, Munch – MENDELSSOHN: *Violin Concerto* ***

*** Sony SK 60584. Hahn, Baltimore SO, Zinman – BERNSTEIN: *Serenade* ***

(***) BBC (ADD) BBCL 4019-2. Menuhin, Moscow PO, D. Oistrakh – MOZART: *Sinfonia concertante* (***)

(***) Testament mono SBT 1228. Kogan, Paris Conservatoire O, Vandernoot – MOZART: *Violin Concerto 5* (***)

**(*) EMI 7 54574-2. Kennedy, N. German RSO, Tennstedt

(BB) **(*) Virgin 2×1 5 61504-2 (2). Seiler, City of L. Sinfonia, Hickox – HAYDN; MENDELSSOHN: *Concertos* **(*)

(BB) (***) Naxos mono 8.110909. Kreisler, Berlin State Op. O, Blech – MENDELSSOHN: *Violin Concerto* *** (with BACH: *Unaccompanied Violin Sonata 1, BWV 1001: Adagio* (***))

**(*) Sony SK 89505. Bell, Camerata Salzburg, Norrington – MENDELSSOHN: *Violin Concerto* **(*)

(BB) (***) APR Signature mono APR 5506. Huberman, VPO, Szell – LALO: *Symphonie espagnole* (**(*))

(**(*)) Testament mono SBT 1083. Haendel, Philh. O, Kubelik – BRUCH: *Violin Concerto 1* (**(*))

(BB) (***) Naxos mono 8.110946. Szigeti, British SO, Walter – MOZART: *Violin Concerto 4* (***)

(BB) (***) Naxos mono 8.110936. Heifetz, NBC SO, Toscanini – BRAHMS: *Violin Concerto* (***)

(***) Testament mono SBT 1228. Kogan, Paris Conservatoire O, Vandernoot – MOZART: *Violin Concerto 5* (***)

Violin Concerto in D; Romance 1 in G

(M) *** EMI (ADD) 5 62607-2. Y. Menuhin, Menuhin Festival O – TCHAIKOVSKY: *Sérénade mélancolique* ***

(i) *Violin Concerto;* (ii) *Romances 1 in G, Op. 40; 2 in F, Op. 50*

☞━ ☽ (M) *** Warner Elatus 0927 49616-2. Kremer, COE, Harnoncourt

*** DG 471 349-2; **SACD** (compatible) 471 633-2. Mutter, NYPO, Masur

(BB) *** EMI Encore (ADD) 5 74973-2. Y. Menuhin; (i) VPO, Silvestri; (ii) Philh. O, Pritchard

*** EMI 7 49567-2. Perlman, BPO, Barenboim

(***) Testament mono SBT 1109. Menuhin; (i) Lucerne Festival O; (ii) Philh. O, Furtwängler

(BB) *** Naxos 8.550149. Nishizaki, Slovak PO (Bratislava), Jean

Violin Concerto in D; Romance 2 in F

(N) (BB) *** ASV Resonance CDRSN 3032. Shumsky, Philh. O, A. Davis

Whether or not Perlman's 1992 DVD with Barenboim represents his finest recorded performance on record, it is very satisfying, with a particularly beautiful and serene *Larghetto* and a genial, dancing finale. The live recording at the Schauspielhaus, Berlin, is excellent, better balanced than some of his studio recordings, and the camerawork is excellently managed. If you want a recommendable DVD coupling with Brahms, this will give every satisfaction.

Grumiaux came to prominence after the war with a memorable account of the Szymanowski *Fountain of Arethusa* on 78s. He was an artist of princely quality, an aristocrat among violinists, with great purity of spirit and tone. A selfless artist, dedicated to the composer above all and not himself. His Beethoven concerto, made in the Salle Pleyel with the ORTF (French Radio Orchestra) in February 1965, has great naturalness of eloquence – and what a good accompanist Dorati was. The sound is very good, though the quality of the picture is not much more than serviceable. Memorable music-making. The remaining pieces come off equally well, as you would expect from this great artist, and there is a remarkable bonus in the form of a very characterful account of the Saint-Saëns *Introduction et Rondo capriccioso* by Ivrys Gitlis and the young Georges Pludemacher, recorded at the ORTF studios in 1971 which gives much pleasure.

Leonid Kogan was the most natural and supremely classical of artists, whose Beethoven, Brahms and Tchaikovksy concertos were of supreme quality. He was reluctant to allow his concerts to be televised as he found the lighting uncomfortably hot, but this account puts on record one of the great Beethoven concerto performances of the day. Recorded at the ORTF studios in March 1966, Kogan's purity of vision and undemonstrative demeanour are well captured on film. Admirers of this great player should snap this up while it is in circulation. As for the coupled recital: the Handel, Debussy and Dmitri Tsiganov's arrangements of four of Shostakovitch's Op. 34 *Preludes* for piano were recorded on a visit to the BBC studios in 1962 (the Shostakovich are particularly beguiling). The remainder come from the Paris studios of French Radio in 1968. The bonus is a *Sonata for Two Violins* by Leclair, which he recorded with his wife, Elizaveta, the sister of Emil Gilels.

Gidon Kremer's Elatus account with Nikolaus Harnoncourt and the Chamber Orchestra of Europe offers one of his most commanding recordings, both polished and full of flair, with tone ravishingly pure. The controversial point is the cadenza in the first movement, for (like Schneiderhan) he uses a transcription of the big cadenza which Beethoven wrote for his piano arrangement of the work, but with added piano as well as timpani. Kremer also plays violin versions of the other cadenzas and flourishes that punctuate Beethoven's piano version. One of the most refreshing versions of the *Concerto* ever put on disc, backed up by crisp, unsentimental readings of the two *Romances*, and at mid-price too!

Recorded in 1971 but never issued until 2003, Menuhin's version of the Beethoven *Concerto*, with the soloist directing the Menuhin Festival Orchestra from the bow, is on balance the finest he ever made, an inspired reading which brings extra expressive freedom and a sense of urgency beyond his performances with a conductor, however great. The opening tutti instantly establishes the freshness of response from the players closest to him, with transparent textures from a chamber orchestra. In his freedom Menuhin is more impulsive than when another musician is directing the orchestra, allowing himself unmarked accelerandos that sound totally spontaneous. The slow movement has the orchestra very steady in support of the soloist's free flights, with the great third theme dreamily meditative, and the finale brings an affectionate spring to the galloping rhythms, fresh and joyful,

while the silvery beauty of Menuhin's playing above the stave is bewitching throughout. The *Romance* too is light and spontaneous-sounding, and the Tchaikovsky piece makes an attractive filler.

Perlman's outstanding first digital recording of Beethoven's *Violin Concerto* is rightly reissued as one of EMI's 'Great Recordings of the Century' (5 66900-2). This is the finer of his two EMI versions. The element of slight understatement, the refusal to adopt too romantically expressive a style, makes for a compelling strength, perfectly matched by Giulini's thoughtful, direct accompaniment. The beautiful slow movement has a quality of gentle rapture, almost matching Schneiderhan's sense of stillness; and the finale, joyfully and exuberantly fast, is charged with the fullest excitement. The digital recording is satisfyingly full and spacious.

Wolfgang Schneiderhan's stereo version of the *Violin Concerto* is still among the greatest recordings of this work: the serene spiritual beauty of the slow movement has never been surpassed on record. Schneiderhan uses cadenzas transcribed from Beethoven's piano version of the *Concerto*. In DG's 'Legendary Recordings' series, the transfer of the well-balanced 1962 recording is fresh and realistic. The Mozart coupling is apt and generous.

One of the joys of Oscar Shumsky's version of Beethoven's *Violin Concerto* with the Philharmonia is its sense of naturalness and style. His playing is distinguished by a total lack of affectation and by great purity of line, and there seems to be good rapport between soloist and orchestra. The performance is unhurried and refreshingly unaxious to impress: he is agreeably old-fashioned without being overtly romantic (he pulls back for the G minor episode in the first movement, as did Kreisler, whose cadenzas he plays). He has very sympathetic support from the Philharmonia under Andrew Davis. This is one of the very finest versions, quite irrespective of cost, and it includes a comparably sympathetic account of the *F major Romance* to make a marvellous bargain.

Anne-Sophie Mutter's very distinguished performance stands out among recent recordings of Beethoven's great *Concerto*, both for its sheer individuality and for the rapt, lyrical beauty of phrase and tone that often brings one to catch the breath. Until the scintillating lightness of the dancing finale, it is essentially a spacious reading, with the soloist heard against Masur's magnificently authoritative and full-bodied backcloth. The playing is deeply felt in an entirely personal way, often conveyed by moments of magically hushed *pianissimo*, the use of the widest variety of dynamic and great variation of vibrato. If some readers may feel that at times her playing is self-conscious, even wilful, its sincerity of response cannot be gainsaid, and Mutter is obviously determined to think and feel the music through afresh. The two *Romances* are simpler in style: they have never been played more beautifully on disc. The recording is in the demonstration bracket.

It is good that EMI have restored Menuhin's noble, 1949 interpretation of the Beethoven *Concerto* with the Lucerne Festival Orchestra and Furtwängler. It has an authority and intensity that are almost unique in this repertoire. It has been described as 'a great performance: ardent, inward, unhurried'. The Brahms *D minor Sonata* makes an excellent makeweight. Excellent audio refurbishment by Simon Gibson. A self-recommending disc.

Recorded only months before the conductor's death, Menuhin's second EMI version with Furtwängler is another classic which emerges with extraordinary freshness in the latest transfer. Here the bond between the conductor and his younger soloist brought an extra intensity to a natural musical alliance between two inspirational artists, both at their peak. Rarely has the Beethoven *Concerto* been recorded with such sweetness and tenderness, yet with firm underlying strength. With its distinguished coupling, it is a compact disc which defies the years. One hardly registers that it is a mono recording.

A spacious and magisterial account of the Beethoven *Concerto* from Milstein. One of the finest ever recorded, it can rank alongside the greatest of the past and surpass most of the present. It is worthy to be included among EMI's 'Great Recordings of the Century'. The Brahms coupling belongs among the greatest concerto records ever made.

It is good to have Menuhin's first (1960) stereo recording with Silvestri back in the catalogue; it is far preferable to his later versions with Klemperer and Masur. This is a noble performance, very comparable with his mono record with Furtwängler, but of course the sound is greatly improved. Silvestri is surprisingly classical in his outlook and the VPO provide an accompaniment of great character. The *Romances* are simple, straightforward accounts, not quite as memorable as the *Concerto*.

Kyung-Wha Chung's EMI performance, recorded live in the Concertgebouw, is searching and intense. Next to Perlman on another live recording from EMI, Chung is lighter and more mercurial. The element of vulnerability adds to the emotional weight, above all in the wistfully tender slow movement, while the outer movements are full of flair. The recording is full and atmospheric.

Testament offers an alternative Menuhin recording that has been buried for 50 years. Recorded in August 1947, this was his first version of the Beethoven *Concerto* and his first inspired collaboration with Furtwängler. The visionary spaciousness of the reading defied the fashion of the time for a brisk approach (largely promoted by Heifetz and Toscanini). Five years later, Menuhin and Furtwängler made their definitive LP recording, above; but here there is extra poetry and tenderness, particularly in the slow movement; and the CD transfer is first rate.

Those looking for a super-bargain, digital version will find Nishizaki's spontaneous performance a match for many by more famous names. With excellent backing from the Slovak Philharmonic under Kenneth Jean, her playing is individual yet unselfconscious. The *Larghetto* is poised and serene, and the finale buoyant. The two *Romances* are also very well played. The digital recording is excellent, with resonant, spacious orchestral sound.

Zukerman's 1977 recording of the Beethoven *Violin Concerto* comes on a DG Double with three key recordings by Milstein. With Barenboim, Zukerman gives a spacious and concentratedly persuasive account of the first movement. The slow movement is rapt in its simplicity. For anyone wanting these four key concertos, this is an excellent recommendation. It also comes at mid-price, attractively recoupled with a fine performance of the Haydn *B flat Sinfonia concertante*.

Even after half a century, the 1955 Heifetz–Munch account of the Beethoven *Violin Concerto* has lost none of its impact, with the sound astonishingly full and vivid for its date (and with even greater warmth as an SACD in the coupling with Mendelssohn). The supreme mastery of this performance, with speeds generally faster than usual but never sounding rushed, has Heifetz finding time for individuality and imagination in every phrase. For some, the comparative lack of serenity in the first movement (though not in the *Larghetto*) may be a drawback, but the drama of the reading is

unforgettable. Heifetz's unique timbre is marvellously captured, as is Munch's conducting, with its distinctive character, notably its clarity and crispness, and the normal CD transfer of the alternative coupling with Brahms also has a fine sense of realism and presence.

With pure, refined tone, Hilary Hahn gives a dedicated performance, with the poetry of the work never underplayed, but without self-indulgence. The hushed beauty of the central *Larghetto* – taken on the slow side – leads on to a clean-cut, athletic account of the finale. Clear, well-balanced sound.

In 1963 the Moscow Philharmonic Orchestra visited London's Royal Albert Hall, and Menuhin joined them in the Beethoven *Violin Concerto* with no less a figure than David Oistrakh conducting. There is something rather special about this reading with Oistrakh (the slow movement is seraphic) and those who treasure memories of the occasion will welcome its reincarnation in this BBC recording, which is warm and truthful.

Nigel Kennedy's version was recorded live at a single performance in Lübeck, presented complete with encores (movements from the solo Bach *Sonatas* and *Partitas*). Like his interpretation of the Brahms, Kennedy's reading is wilfully slow but always persuasive, even when, after the big Kreisler cadenza in the first movement, he and Tennstedt threaten to come to a dead halt. The cadenza in the finale brings the most controversial point: Kennedy's improvisation which lapses into quarter-tones.

An impressive account from Mayumi Seiler which stands up well against distinguished bargain-priced competition. Hickox is slightly below his finest form and is a bit stiff in the opening of the first movement, but his soloist soars lyrically and is movingly serene in the slow movement, creating an ethereal thread of sound for the secondary theme; she then dances away in the finale. The sound is good, and the couplings include two concertos each by Haydn and Mendelssohn, all offered for the cost of a single medium-priced CD!

Kreisler's technique was unassailable; but his lyrical gifts predominated, his tone was glorious, his phrasing, with its gentle touches of the characteristic *portamenti* of his time, unforgettable. He is at his very peak in this wonderful, poetically rich account of the Beethoven *Concerto*, particularly the ravishing account of the *Larghetto* which causes one to catch the breath at the rapt, Elysian quality of its expressive climax, while the finale releases the tension and is engagingly light-hearted. In Mark Obert-Thorn's splendid transfer the 1926 recording, one of the very first made electrically (in the warm acoustic of the Berlin Singakademie), is astonishingly lifelike, and brings Kreisler's violin vividly into one's presence. Whichever recordings of the Beethoven you already have, this one is a must, with the Bach *Adagio* making a treasurable encore.

Szigeti's searching and magical account of the *Concerto* enjoys legendary status. Its last incarnation was on HMV's plum-label Treasury series during the 1970s, and it is (we believe) new to CD. Made in 1932, when he was at the height of his career, it has the refinement and purity for which he was famous. It belongs among the foremost versions of the *Concerto* on record and is not to be missed in this fine new Naxos transfer.

Joshua Bell's reading has plainly been affected by having a chamber group as partners: the Camerata Salzburg under their period-influenced conductor, Sir Roger Norrington. As for the soloist, his tone seems sparer than in his Decca recordings, clean and bright rather than warmly romantic, aided by the recording quality which is relatively dry, so giving less bloom to the violin tone. It is a powerful performance, but on a smaller scale than usual; but clarity goes with concentration, and a speed rather faster than usual in this long first movement brings an extra tautness and plenty of light and shade. The slow movement is relatively light and delicate, with clean, pure tone from Bell, and the relative intimacy of the reading comes out more clearly than ever in the finale, with crisp timpani. A strong, distinctive reading, well coupled with a similar if more mercurial reading of the Mendelssohn, but hardly a primary recommendation.

Huberman's 1934 performance is another classic version, raptly intense – as in the magical opening to the first-movement coda – but taken at speeds that flow easily, far faster overall than is now the rule. The APR transfer is first rate, with the violin immediate and full of presence.

The partnership of Heifetz and Toscanini in the Beethoven *Violin Concerto* makes for legendary results, uniquely powerful and purposeful, with the purity of the violinist's playing, notably above the stave, making up for any lack of tenderness. Heifetz's example leads Toscanini to a rare gentleness in the slow movement, while the finale is exhilarating in its rhythmic drive. The hard NBC recording is nicely mellowed in the Naxos transfer, if with some audible hiss. An ideal coupling with Heifetz's 1939 version of the Brahms.

Leonid Kogan's mono account of the Beethoven *Concerto* comes from 1957 and, like the Mozart *Concerto* that completes the present CD, was never issued at the time. Kogan re-recorded the work with Constantin Silvestri two years later in stereo so that, although it was passed for release, it was withheld for obvious reasons. Testament have put us in their debt by issuing it now, for it is a reading of the greatest distinction. It has purity and nobility, as does its successor, but there is a slightly freer quality (Tully Potter's sleeve-note calls it 'carefree') and a spirituality too.

Ida Haendel's 1951 recording is an exceptionally powerful one, commanding and concentrated even at spacious speeds. In a transfer of Testament's highest standard, it makes a welcome, if relatively expensive, reissue, in coupling with an outstanding account of the Bruch *Concerto*.

Kyung-Wha Chung's 1979 Decca performance is superseded by her later, full-priced, EMI version with Tennstedt, for the earlier account, measured and thoughtful, lacks compulsion thanks to the prosaic conducting of Kondrashin (460 014-2).

Clarinet Concerto in D (arr. Pletnev from *Violin Concerto, Op. 61*)

*** DG 457 652-2. Collins, Russian Nat. O, Pletnev – MOZART: *Clarinet Concerto* ***

Michael Collins offers a daring transcription for the clarinet of the Beethoven *Violin Concerto*. The warmth of Beethoven's lyricism is brought out more richly in the tone of the clarinet, not just in the slow movement – where Collins feels the advantages are greatest – but in the long first movement too. Apart from the obvious point that no double-stopping is possible on the clarinet, the main difference in the transcription involves a downward octave transposition of the solo line over many sections in all three movements. Pletnev has managed it so deftly that, with passage-work shifted to register comfortably for the clarinet, it consistently sounds natural. The wonder is that Collins makes light of all problems so that one can readily enjoy the music in a new way.

Triple Concerto for Violin, Cello & Piano in C, Op. 56

(M) *** EMI (ADD) 5 66902-2 [5 66954-2]. D. Oistrakh, Rostropovich, S. Richter, BPO, Karajan – BRAHMS: *Double Concerto* ***

(M) *** EMI 5 57773-2. Argerich, Capucon, Maisky, Svizzera-Italiana O, Rabinovitch-Barakovsky – SCHUMANN: *Piano Concerto* ***

(B) *** EMI double forte 5 69331-2 (2). D. Oistrakh, Oborin, Knushevitzky, Philh. O, Sargent – BRAHMS: *Double Concerto*; MOZART: *Violin Concerto 3*; PROKOFIEV: *Violin Concerto 2* ***

(BB) *** DG Entrée 474 569-2. Mutter, Ma, Zeltzer, BPO, Karajan – BRAHMS: *Violin Concerto* ***

(N) (M) **(*) DG ADD 477 5341. Schneiderhan, Fournier, Anda, Berlin RSO, Fricsay – BRAHMS: *Double Concerto* **(*)

(i) Triple Concerto. Piano Concerto in D (arr. from *Violin Concerto*), Op. 61a

(BB) *** Naxos 8.554288. Jandó, (i) with Kang, Kliegel; Nicolaus Esterházy O, Drahos

(i) Triple Concerto; (ii) Piano Concerto 3, Op. 37

(BB) *** EMI Encore (ADD/DDD) 5 74722-2. Zacharias; (i) Hoelscher, Schiff, Leipzig GO, Masur; (ii) Dresden State O, Vonk

(i; ii; iii) Triple Concerto; (ii) 2 Romances for Violin & Orchestra, Opp. 40 & 50; (i; iv) Romance cantabile for Piano, Flute & Bassoon with 2 Oboes & Strings in E min.

**(*) DG (IMS) 453 488-2. (i) Myung-Whun Chung, (ii) Kyung-Wha Chung, (iii) Myung-Wha Chung; (iv) Patrick Gallois, Pascal Gallois; Philh. O, Myung-Whun Chung

(i) Triple Concerto; (ii) Symphony 10: 1st movt (realized & completed Cooper)

(M) *** Chan. 6501. (i) Kalichstein-Laredo-Robinson Trio, ECO, Gibson; (ii) CBSO, Weller

On the EMI analogue recording, a breathtaking line-up, led by David Oistrakh. This is warm, expansive music-making that confirms even more clearly than before the strength of the piece. The new transfer is remarkably vivid and has firmed up the orchestral tuttis most satisfactorily. Now coupled in EMI's 'Great Recordings of the Century' with a similarly commanding account of the Brahms *Double Concerto*, this is an irresistible mid-priced bargain.

This live recording of the *Triple Concerto*, like the Schumann *Piano Concerto* with which it is coupled, was made at the Lugano Festival, reflecting throughout the magnetism of Martha Argerich, inspiring her two younger colleagues. When the piano part (designed for Beethoven's great patron, the Archduke Rudolph) is the least demanding of the three solo roles, it is remarkable how Argerich still emerges as the obvious leader. Not that the cellist Mischa Maisky is any less characterful; but Argerich's powerful presence seems to modify his customary wilfulness, so that even the great cello melody which opens the slow movement is the more moving for its restraint, with the most delicate tonal shading, while the outer movements have a rare vitality.

The soloists in Masur's version of the *Triple Concerto*, led by the cellist Heinrich Schiff, make a characterful but finely integrated trio. Their rhythmic flair prompts Masur in turn to give one of his most sparkling Beethoven performances on record. The long span of the first movement is firmly held together, the brief slow movement has inner intensity without being overweighted, while the finale is ideally clear and light. The sound is both full and detailed. This remains among the very finest of digital versions, and Zacharias's analogue account of the *C minor Concerto* makes an appealingly fresh coupling. With lively support from Hans Vonk, a real bargain.

The vintage EMI recording, now on double forte, features distinguished Russian soloists and dates from the early days of stereo, yet the sound is excellent for its period, the balance one of the most successful this *Concerto* has received even now. Sargent is authoritative, and his soloists make a good team.

The partnership of Dong-Suk Kang, Maria Kliegel and Jenö Jandó may not be familiar, but it is none the less formidable. All three are accomplished soloists and are so good that it seems invidious to single any one of them out. Béla Drahos draws clean-cut, consistently alert playing from the orchestra, more crisply detailed than in most versions. Beethoven's piano version of the *Violin Concerto* makes an apt and exceptionally generous coupling. Jenö Jandó uses his artistry to minimize any ungainliness in the piano-writing, articulating as cleanly and crisply as he does in the *Triple Concerto*.

The DG Entrée version, enjoyably spontaneous, makes a generous coupling for Mutter's fine account of the Brahms *Violin Concerto*.

The 1984 Chandos version of the *Triple Concerto* is exceptionally well recorded. Sharon Robinson, the cellist, takes the lead with pure tone and fine intonation, though both her partners are more forceful artists. A clean-cut, often refreshing view of the work, it is coupled with Weller's strong version of Barry Cooper's completion of the first movement of Beethoven's projected *Tenth Symphony*.

The 1960 recording by Schneiderhan, Anda and Fournier has plenty of atmosphere, but the balance is artificial, with the solo players (clearly separated) well forward and with their contribution dynamically nearly matching that of the orchestra, reducing the natural contrast. Therefore the solo playing has much greater presence than on many rival versions, but Fricsay's vibrant orchestral tuttis still have plenty of impact. The performance has breadth and a genuine grasp of structure, with an eloquent contribution from each of the distinguished soloists. Only in the first movement does one sense a slight want of spontaneity, but there is plenty of personality in this performance. The orchestral sound is generally warm, only really betraying its age in the tuttis.

The Chungs make a characterful trio and give a very fine account of the *Triple Concerto* which conveys a feeling of spontaneous chamber-playing, with the finale taken thrillingly fast, with sparkling results. However, the two *Romances*, beautifully played though they are, and the short, insignificant E minor fragment do not enhance the competitiveness of what is after all a premium-priced disc.

(i) *Triple Concerto;* (ii) *Choral Fantasia*
☞ *** EMI **DVD** 4 91473-9; CD 5 55516-2. BPO, Barenboim, with (i) Perlman, Ma; (ii) Deutsche Staatsoper Ch.

Recorded at concerts on consecutive days in February 1995, with Barenboim directing from the keyboard in both works, this makes an excellent if ungenerous coupling on DVD. These are all spontaneously imaginative artists, never more so than when recorded live. That makes both performances very compelling, with delightful interplay between the soloists in the *Triple Concerto*, led by Yo-Yo Ma on the cello in each emerging theme, producing exquisite *pianissimos* in the slow movement, well caught in the recording. In this work it is notoriously difficult for the engineers to find the perfect balance, and here it helps to have the performers seen as well as heard. Barenboim's piano may be backwardly placed in the sound spectrum but one barely notices it, particularly when the orchestra is satisfyingly full-bodied.

The *Choral Fantasia*, structurally much rougher, depends above all on the solo pianist, and here Barenboim is in his element, not only revelling in the improvisatory quality of the opening solo but also bringing out the fun of the variations on the main theme, a trite melody despite its likeness to the Ode to Joy theme in Beethoven's *Ninth*. The camera follows each solo contribution in turn, with Barenboim injecting manic energy into the csárdás-like variation and swagger into the military march that rounds off the section. The choral contribution comes as an exciting epilogue, very well sung by the singers from the Deutsche Staatsoper, though it is a pity that the DVD provides no subtitles for the text. There is also an alternative CD version.

12 Contredanses, WoO 14; 12 German Dances, WoO 8; 12 Minuets, WoO 7; 11 Mödlinger Dances, WoO 17
(BB) *** Naxos 8.550433. Capella Istropolitana, O. Dohnányi

It is always a delight to catch Beethoven relaxing and showing how warmly he felt towards the Viennese background in which he lived. The excellent Capella Istropolitana group used for the recording is of exactly the right size, and they play the music with light, rhythmic feeling and with plenty of spirit.

Creatures of Prometheus: Overture & Ballet, Op. 43
(N) (BB) *** Hyp. Helios CDH 55196. SCO, Mackerras
(BB) *** Naxos 8.553404. Melbourne SO, Halász

Here, in fresh, vigorous performances, Sir Charles Mackerras and the Scottish Chamber Orchestra bring out not only the drama of the piece but also the colourful qualities which made Beethoven a great composer of light music. The ballet ends with the number which gave him one of his most fruitful themes, used for the finale of the *Eroica Symphony*. Highly recommended, especially at its new Helios price.

The Naxos issue provides an excellent bargain version. The playing is neat and fresh, with rhythms well pointed. Though the string-sound is at times a little cloudy, dramatic passages such as the military trumpets and timpani of the *Allegro con brio* (No. 8) are very well caught, bringing out the panache of the playing. In the big *Adagio* (No. 5) the important cello solo confirms the quality of the Melbourne players.

OVERTURES

Overtures: *The Consecration of the House; Coriolan; The Creatures of Prometheus; Egmont; Fidelio; King Stephen; Leonora 1–3; The Ruins of Athens; Zur Namensfeier*
(N) (M) *** Arte Nova 82876 57831-2 (2). Zurich Tonhalle O, Zinman
(M) *** DG (ADD) (IMS) 427 256-2 (2). BPO, Karajan

It came as a revelation when, five years ago, David Zinman and the Zurich Tonhalle Orchestra – till then not regarded as one of the world's prime recording orchestras – completed a cycle of the Beethoven symphonies which set new standards. More than previous versions using modern instruments, these interpretations took on board the lessons of period performance, even if some of the conductor's elaborations were controversial. Now, in this two-disc set, Zinman applies the same lesson to Beethoven's 11 overtures. The very first, *Prometheus*, sets the pattern with the phenomenal clarity of articulation in an exceptionally fast Allegro, and transparency of texture marks all these performances. As in the symphonies, the drama of Beethoven's writing is underlined in the sharpness of attack and high contrasts of dynamic. Helpfully, the two discs present the sequence of 11 works in an order to make a satisfying programme.

Karajan's set of overtures, recorded in the 1960s, brings impressive performances that have stood the test of time, with a command of structure and detail as well as the virtuosity one expects from the Berlin Philharmonic. The sound is fresh and bright.

(i) **Overtures:** *The Consecration of the House; Coriolan; The Creatures of Prometheus; Egmont; Fidelio; King Stephen; Leonora 1–3; The Ruins of Athens; Zur Namensfeier;* (ii) *12 Contredanses, WoO 14; 12 German Dances, WoO 8; 12 Minuets, WoO 7*

(B) *** Ph. (ADD) Duo 438 706-2 (2). (i) Leipzig GO, Masur; (ii) ASMF, Marriner

Masur's performances of the *Overtures* are more direct than those of Karajan, satisfying in their lack of mannerism. The Philips recording from the early 1970s is of high quality, and the remastering has enhanced its vividness and impact. To complete the second CD, Marriner and the Academy offer a splendid foil with the dance music. Even as a composer of light music, Beethoven was a master.

Overtures: *Coriolan; Creatures of Prometheus; Egmont; Fidelio; Leonora 1–3; Ruins of Athens*

(*) Virgin 5 45364-2. Bremen German Chamber PO, Harding

(N) (M) **(*)** Warner Elatus 2564 61779-2. COE, Harnoncourt

Daniel Harding gives strong, distinctive readings. As the name of the Bremen orchestra suggests, these are performances on a chamber scale. With his chosen players Harding favours extreme speeds, with slow introductions very solemn and measured, leading to hectic allegros which press home the drama of Beethoven's writing. Though all four overtures for *Fidelio* are included, as well as four others, it is a pity that *The Consecration of the House* was not included, if necessary by omitting *The Ruins of Athens*.

Dramatic, taut, exciting and disciplined performances of the Beethoven *Overtures*, very well recorded. The only thing missing is a touch of humanity, so that, for example, the *Creatures of Prometheus Overture* is just that bit too uptight to allow the music to relax and sparkle as it can. However, this is certainly a way to explore Harnoncourt's bracing style in Beethoven.

Overtures: *Coriolan; Leonora 2*

(M) (***) EMI mono 5 65513-2 (3). BPO or VPO, Furtwängler – BRAHMS: *Symphonies 1–4, etc.* (**(*))

These studio recordings of Beethoven overtures, the one from Vienna in 1947, the other from Berlin in 1954, make a fine supplement to Furtwängler's Brahms cycle, with Vienna mellower-sounding than Berlin.

Overture: *Leonora 3, Op. 72a*

*** BBC (ADD) BBCL 4056-2. BBC SO, Kempe – DVORAK: *Symphony 9 (New World)* ❂; PROKOFIEV: *The Love for 3 Oranges: Suite* ***

Like the other two works on Kempe's mixed disc of live Prom performances from August 1975, *Leonora No. 3* brings a performance of tingling intensity. So the emergence of the main allegro theme in a glowing C major leads to violent conflict in the development section, with horns blazing, until the off-stage trumpet has just as powerful an impact as when heard in the opera house. With joy piled on joy the final coda seems to burst over in frenzy.

Romances for Cello and Orchestra 1, Op. 40; 2, Op. 50

**(*) Orfeo C080031A. Müller-Schott, Australian CO, Tognetti – HAYDN: *Cello Concertos 1 & 2* **(*)

Daniel Müller-Schott is a gifted young cellist (in his mid-twenties when this record was made), who has transcribed the two Beethoven *Violin Romances* for his own instrument – and very successfully too! This is playing of some eloquence and finesse, and the two Haydn *Concertos* that comprise the main works can hold their own with the best of the opposition.

Romances for Violin and Orchestra, 1, Op. 40; 2, Op. 50

(M) *** CRD (ADD) CRD 3369. R. Thomas, Bournemouth SO – MENDELSSOHN: *Violin Concerto;* SCHUBERT: *Konzertstück* ***

The purity of Ronald Thomas's intonation (particularly important in the double-stopping at the start of Op. 40) makes for sensitive, clean-cut readings which, along with the Schubert *Konzertstück*, provide enjoyable if unexpected couplings for the Mendelssohn *Concerto*. The recording is first rate.

SYMPHONIES

Symphonies 1–3 (Eroica)

(N) ** EuroArts **DVD** 2050609. SW RSO, Baden-Baden & Freiburg, Gielen

Symphonies 4–6 (Pastoral)

(N) ** EuroArts **DVD** 2050639. SW RSO, Baden-Baden & Freiburg, Gielen

Symphonies 7–9 (Choral)

(N) ** EuroArts **DVD** 2050669. SW RSO, Baden-Baden & Freiburg, Gielen

Michael Gielen's cycle with the South-West Radio Orchestra in Baden-Baden was recorded at public performances between 1997 and 2000. They are unidiosyncratic readings, positive and very well played. Exposition repeats are observed, ensemble is polished and there is both warmth and commitment from the players. Pacing of allegros is usually vigorous – the first movement of the *Eroica* notably so – although the following *Marcia funèbre* lacks intensity and depth. The *Fifth* has plenty of impulse in the outer movements and a warm slow movement, the *Seventh* an exciting finale. But it is the even-numbered symphonies that stay in the memory, notably Nos. 2 and 4, with No. 8 finest of all – a splendid account. They are beautifully played and have genuine spontaneity. However, the brisk tempo of the first movement of the *Pastoral*, elegantly turned as it is, will not appeal to everyone, and although the *Scene by the Brook* is leisurely and affectionate, after a vigorous *Storm* the finale again flows in a very relaxed manner and needs more forward thrust. But the real disappointment is the *Choral Symphony*, which has vigorous choral singing and robust soloists but fails to be in any way memorable. Overall, the sound is well balanced, natural and with the kind of range one would expect from well-balanced broadcast sessions. But the camera is very restless, jumping from player to player at solos; the audience, however, are remarkably unobtrusive, until their applause makes one remember their presence.

Symphonies 1–9; 10 (realized Dr Barry Cooper): 1st movt
(M) *** Chan. 7042 (5). CBSO, Weller (with Barstow, Finnie, Rendall, Tomlinson, CBSO Ch. in 9)

Symphonies 1–9
(M) *** EMI 5 57445-2 (5). VPO, Rattle (with Bonney, Remmert, Streit, Hanson & CBSO Ch. in 9)

(BB) *** Arte Nova 74321 65410-2 (5). Zurich Tonhalle O, Zinman (with Ziesak, Remmert, Davislim, Roth, Swiss Chamber Ch. in 9)

(B) *** CfP 575 7512 (5). RLPO, Mackerras (with Rodgers, D. Jones, Bronder, Terfel, RLPO Ch. in 9)

(N) (B) *** DG (ADD) 474 924-2 (5). VPO, Bernstein (with Jones, Schwarz, Kollo, Moll, V. State Op Ch. in 9)

*** DG 469 000-2 (5). BPO, Abbado (with Mattila, Urmana, Moser, Quasthoff, Swedish R. Ch. in 9)

*** DG 439 900-2 (5). ORR, Gardiner (with Orgonasova, Von Otter, Rolfe Johnson, Cachemaille, Monteverdi Ch. in 9)

(B) *** RCA 74321 20277-2 (5). N. German RSO, Wand (with Wiens, Hartwig, Lewis, Hermann, combined Ch. from Hamburg State Op. and N. German R. in 9)

(M) *** Teldec 0927 49768-2 (5). COE, Harnoncourt (with Margiono, Remmert, Schasching, Holl, Arnold Schoenberg Ch. in 9)

(B) *** DG (ADD) 463 088-2 (5). BPO, Karajan (with Janowitz, Rössl-Majdan, Kmentt, Berry, V. Singverein in 9)

(M) (**(*)) EMI mono 5 67496-2 (5). VPO or Stockholm PO, Furtwängler (with soloists & Ch. in 9)

(i) Symphonies 1–9; Overtures: Consecration of the House; Coriolan; Creatures of Prometheus; Egmont; Fidelio; King Stephen; Leonora 2; The Ruins of Athens; (ii) Missa solemnis
(BB) **(*) Nim NI 1760 (7). Hanover Band, (i) cond. Goodman or Huggett (with Harrhy, Bailey, Murgatroyd, George, Oslo Cathedral Ch. in 9); (ii) Hirsti, Watkinson, Murgatroyd, George, Oslo Cathedral Ch., cond. Kvam

Symphonies 1–9; Overture Coriolan
(BB) *** Warner Apex 2564 60457-2 (5). Sinfonia Varsovia, Y. Menuhin (with Glennon, Schaechter, Janutas, Schollum, Lithuania Kaunas State Ch. in 9)

Symphonies 1–9; Overtures: Coriolan; Egmont; Leonora 3
(B) **(*) Decca (ADD) 430 792-2 (6). Chicago SO, Solti (with Lorengar, Minton, Burrows, Talvela, Chicago Ch. in 9)

Symphonies 1–9; Overtures: Fidelio; Leonora 3
(N) (BB) ** Warner 2564 61890-2 (6). Berlin State O, Barenboim (with Isokoski, Lang, Gambill, Pepe & Berlin Deutsche State Op. Ch. in 9)

Symphonies 1–9; Overtures: Fidelio, Leonore 2, The Creatures of Prometheus, The Ruins of Athens
(M) *** DG mono/stereo 474 018-2 (5). Bav. RSO or BPO, Jochum (with Ebers, Polzinger, Ludwig, Frantz, Bavarian RSO Ch. in 9)

Sir Simon Rattle's Beethoven cycle is not the first to be recorded in concert, but the quality of immediacy and spontaneous expression is something that marks it out more than most of its rivals. The way he encourages the brilliant VPO woodwind and horn soloists to challenge each other in imagination and individuality adds to the impression of joyful discovery. The opening allegro of the *First Symphony* instantly establishes itself as pure Beethoven, music looking forward to the nineteenth century, not back to the eighteenth. So too, even more strikingly, in No. 2, where there is a Beethovenian swagger, which conveys the wit and humour of the writing.

With Rattle's approach reflecting his experience with period performers, textures are clarified and string-tone is thinned down with reduced vibrato, but the string sound still has VPO sweetness. One corollary of the sense of spontaneity is that these are performances with idiosyncrasies. In the heat of the moment Rattle allows himself an element of freedom, and generally his approach is more warmly expressive than that of other performances with modern instruments which, like Harnoncourt's and Zinman's, have taken note of period practice. In the slow movement of No. 2 Rattle moulds the melodies with a warmth that looks forward to the Romantic era.

Whether his idiosyncrasies will seem intrusive is essentially a personal matter, but it helps that these are live performances, not set in stone, with most of the tempo fluctuations natural in their context. It is in the *Eroica* slow movement that Rattle shows his individual interpretative stance most strikingly. Where others, like Harnoncourt and Zinman, regularly follow period practice in adopting flowing speeds for slow movements, Rattle in the *Eroica*, and even more markedly in the great *Adagio* of the *Ninth*, takes note of the Viennese tradition rather than period practice. There is much to be said for that expansive approach in these movements when, with the fast speeds dictated by period practice, the weight of emotion plainly implied is diluted. So the disintegration of the main theme at the end of the Funeral March is almost unbearably moving. In his dialogue with this great orchestra Rattle has plainly sought a midway meeting point.

Overall, Rattle regularly conveys exuberance, not least in the finales, notably in the *Fifth*. In the finale of the *Ninth* Rattle scores palpably with one of the finest quartets of soloists assembled for many years, and the decision to bring over the CBSO chorus is triumphantly justified, with incandescent choral sound. Though Rattle, like Zinman and Abbado, adopts the new Bärenreiter editions of Jonathan del Mar, he does not include the extra repeat of the Scherzo section in the third movement of No. 5 but leaves the structure as we have long known it. The five discs come at mid-price in a lavish presentation package, complete with hardback booklet.

Even more so than Sir Charles Mackerras on Eminence, David Zinman has learnt from the example of period performance and has consistently presented performances of all the symphonies, early and late, which have a transparency not usually achieved with modern instruments, helped by the clear, fresh acoustic of the Zurich hall. There is an important advantage too that this is the first modern-instrument cycle to use the new edition prepared by Jonathan Del Mar, with important modifications in the text. Zinman also allows a degree of ornamentation beyond convention. What matters above all is that not only are the performances electrifying, with the players responding to the challenge of fast speeds in observance of Beethoven's metronome markings, but there is also refinement and tenderness in slow movements, even in the face of fast-flowing tempi. The sound is vivid and beautifully balanced, making this a front-runner among recommendations for cycles using modern instruments.

Sir Charles Mackerras's Beethoven cycle is also among the most recommendable of all at any price, beautifully recorded and interpretatively refreshing, in a refined way steering a satisfying mid-course between traditional and period performance. So the brass have a satisfying braying roundness and the timpani echo period practice, not only in the sharp attack with hard sticks but also in their prominent balance, as in the finale of No. 5. Speeds are on the fast side, but it is a measure of Mackerras's mastery that rhythms are always beautifully sprung without any hint of breathlessness and with consistently refined detail.

Bernstein's late-1970s cycle is dramatic, perceptive, rich in emotion but never sentimental, and it has a natural spontaneous quality that stems in part from his technique of recording. As in other Bernstein/DG recordings of this period, the maestro opted to have live performances recorded and then (with some tidying of detail) edited together. Those who know the thrilling account of the first movement of the *Eroica* in his earlier, New York cycle may be disappointed that the voltage here is lower, but with Bernstein's electricity matched against the traditional warmth of Viennese playing, the results are consistently persuasive. It culminates in a superb account of the *Ninth*, with a fast, tense first movement, a resilient Scherzo, a hushed, expansive reading of the *Adagio* and a dramatic account of the finale. Balances are not always perfect, with microphones placed in order to eliminate audience noise, but the results are generally undistracting, and the CD transfers are very good.

Menuhin's set was originally issued in 1995 (on Carlton) to celebrate his eightieth birthday, and it represents the refreshing response of a great interpretative musician who remained perennially young to the very end of his musical life. It helps that five of the nine symphonies (Nos. 1, 2, 4, 5 and 8) were recorded in the Palais de Musique in Strasbourg, a helpful hall. Though the applause that greets the opening of some of the symphonies is irritating (though it is now edited out on the CD containing *Coriolan* and Nos. 4 and 8), the tensions of live performance regularly bring magical results, as in the dedicated, ecstatic performance of the great *Adagio* of the *Ninth*. Often a disappointment in complete cycles, in Menuhin's hands the *Choral Symphony* brings an impressive conclusion to his series.

In the studio performances, as well as those recorded live, Menuhin uses the chamber scale positively, not only clarifying textures but achieving hushed *pianissimos* of ravishing beauty, as in the *Allegretto* of the *Seventh* or in the broken close of the *Eroica* funeral march. Hairpin dynamics are shaded most subtly throughout, and regularly in slow movements Menuhin's cunning in moulding string melodies, born of his violin mastery, is reflected in the imaginative beauty of line. Only in the *Allegretto* of the *Eighth* does he choose a tempo too slow for rhythms to lift.

Allegros generally tend to be on the brisk side, with lightly sprung rhythms adding to the freshness; some of the very fast speeds, as in the finales of Nos. 5 and 7, seem to reflect not so much latter-day period practice as the early influence of Toscanini. Vigorously rejecting the idea of 'fate knocking on the door' at the opening of the *Fifth* means that in this live performance the effect is deliberately understated and the result, for once, is not very cleanly executed. Such flaws are mimimal next to the shining merits of the set. Exposition repeats are observed, and not everyone will object that Menuhin omits second-half repeats in the Scherzos of Nos. 7 and 9. With recording that puts a fine bloom on the sound without obscuring detail, this is an excellent set for those wanting dedicated performances on a chamber scale, which yet never underplay the strength and power of these masterpieces. The set comes on five individual CDs in jewel cases within a slipcase, and can be ranked alongside those of Rattle, Zinman and Mackerras.

Few conductors change their approach to Beethoven quite as radically as Claudio Abbado has done. The contrasts are astonishing, with overall timings of each work over five minutes shorter this time than before. Moreover, thanks to lighter playing-techniques and the use of smaller string forces, textures are consistently clarified, helped by lighter recorded sound. There is then ample weight in the finale of the *Ninth*, where the chorus and soloists are far better balanced and more cleanly focused than before. Though there is no mention of it, these are live recordings, consistently conveying a dramatic intensity missing in the earlier cycle. Like the conductor, the Berlin players were responding to a challenge.

Eugen Jochum recorded his earlier DG cycle of the nine Beethoven symphonies between 1952 and 1961, the period when mono recording gave way to stereo. It was the first complete Beethoven cycle recorded by DG but has remained in limbo ever since, thanks to the division between mono and stereo, and because Jochum went on to record a stereo cycle with the Concertgebouw orchestra for Philips. In direct comparison, this set of performances is consistently fresher and more spontaneous sounding, even though the interpretative differences are minimal. With two outstanding German orchestras, the Berlin Philharmonic as well as his own Bavarian Radio Orchestra, he inspires even more concentrated playing than with the Dutch orchestra. Extremes of dynamic are superbly caught both in the mono recordings (3, 6, 7 and 9) and in the stereo ones. In the last days of mono the DG engineers achieved astonishing results, full-bodied and with perfect balance, so that the hushed intensity of the *Eroica Funeral March*, for example, is magnetically conveyed. Jochum's characteristic degree of free expressiveness, with the tempo marginally varied to match the needs of each section, rather in the manner of Furtwängler, is achieved so naturally that it is unobtrusive. Even in the *Ninth* the absence of stereo is a minimal drawback, with an outstanding quartet of soloists and a fine choir. Jochum's magnetism is never more impressive than in the finales, which consistently brim with exuberance, giving these studio performances the feeling of live events. With four overtures as fill-ups, the five discs in this limited edition come in a compact box with illuminating notes.

Gardiner's cycle makes a clear first choice for those wanting period versions. These are exhilarating versions which have bite and imagination and a sense of spontaneity. Like others, Gardiner observes Beethoven's own fast metronome markings, but allows himself expansion in the slow movements of the *Eroica* and the *Ninth*. With Jonathan Del Mar a scholarly helper, his amendment of the marking for the Turkish March in the finale of the *Ninth* is twice as brisk as

Norrington's and leads logically into the fugue. The set comes in full, luminous sound, complete on only five discs, with a sixth containing an illustrated talk by Gardiner in three languages.

Wand's digital set with the North German Radio orchestra, recorded between 1985 and 1988, makes another first-class bargain choice, offering performances without idiosyncrasy yet full of character. In the finale of the *Ninth* the combined choruses of North German Radio and Hamburg State Opera, well balanced, sing with fervour, and the closing pages bring a thrilling culmination.

Reflecting his work as a period-performance pioneer, Harnoncourt makes rhythms light and textures clean, with sparing string vibrato. Periodically, as in the first movement of the *Eroica*, he adopts a hectically fast tempo, but that is the exception. Regularly, his choice of speeds is geared to bringing out the refined expressiveness of this brilliant young orchestra. The *Ninth*, recorded almost a year after the rest, makes a fine culmination, though the dry manner in the great *Adagio*, taken at a flowing speed, underplays the emotional depth. Excellent sound. This now comes handsomely repackaged at mid-price with a 120-page booklet.

Of Karajan's four recorded cycles, the 1961–2 set (DG 463 088-2) is the most compelling, combining high polish with a biting sense of urgency and spontaneity. There is one major disappointment, the over-taut reading of the *Pastoral*, which in addition omits a vital repeat in the Scherzo. Otherwise these are incandescent performances, superbly played. On CD the sound is still excellent. On five CDs at bargain price, this offers outstanding value.

Walter Weller's Beethoven cycle for Chandos is among his finest achievements on record. He draws from the City of Birmingham Symphony Orchestra a warm, refined, Viennese quality, to remind you that this conductor started his career as concertmaster of the Vienna Philharmonic. The Chandos sound is full and glowing to match. Now available at medium price, including Barry Cooper's realization of the *Tenth Symphony*.

The pioneering Hanover Band period-instrument performances are well worth considering, when the Nimbus package is so inexpensive. These are all readings which convey the fire and exuberance of live performance; setting them in a reverberant acoustic means that the woodwind sometimes appear disembodied. Monica Huggett directs Nos. 1–2 and 5; Roy Goodman Nos. 3–4 and 6–9. In the latter recordings Goodman draws consistently fresh, individual readings from his team, with rhythms well sprung in exhilarating *allegros*. Consistently the feeling of spontaneity is most winning. The overtures (also shared by the two conductors) are just as characterful, and it is especially good to have the fresh and gripping account of the *Missa solemnis*, conducted by Terje Kvam, chorus-master of the Oslo Cathedral Choir.

Solti's first cycle with his own Chicago orchestra has a firm centrality to it, following the outstandingly successful version of the *Ninth* with which he started the series. The performance of the *Eroica* has comparable qualities, with expansive, steady tempi and a dedicated, hushed account of the slow movement. The CD transfers bring an admirable consistency, with plenty of weight in the bass balancing the bright top register. At bargain price, Solti admirers should not miss this set, particularly as these performances are more satisfying than those in his later, digital series.

By unearthing a live recording of No. 2, made in the Royal Albert Hall in 1948, and borrowing a radio recording of No. 8 made in Stockholm, EMI has put together a complete

Furtwängler cycle – and very impressive it is interpretatively. The sound of those two *ad hoc* recordings may be rough, with heavy background noise, but the performances are electrifying. No. 9 comes in the dedicated performance given at Bayreuth in 1951, but the others are EMI's studio versions, not always as inspired as Furtwängler's live performances but still magnetic and, with well-balanced mono sound, well transferred. Three of the five CDs are now also available separately: *Nos. 1 & 3* (CDH5 67490-2); *Nos. 5 & 7* (CDH5 67492-2); *Nos. 6 & 8* (CDH5 67493-2). The *Choral* is reviewed separately below.

Barenboim, even more than most of today's conductors, has a lifelong devotion to the work of Furtwängler, a point that is regularly reflected in his current readings of the Beethoven symphonies. Speeds tend to be broad in the Furtwängler manner, often very broad, as in the first movements of the *Eroica* and *Ninth*, and he encourages a fair degree of flexibility within movements. This is the orchestra with which he has worked regularly over his years with the Deutsche Oper in Berlin, and they are certainly responsive to his demands. But what undermines most of these performances is a curious lack of tension. In taking a broad, flexible view, the essential factor, as the finest Furtwängler performances demonstrate, is that the expressive freedom must seem to develop spontaneously. In that Barenboim, while still achieving creditable results, tends to fall short. The result is a series of run-throughs rather than genuine performances, not helped by a rounded recording that could with advantage have been brighter. So this set, whether taken as a whole or sampled individually, can be recommended only to Barenboim devotees.

Symphonies 1 in C, Op. 21; 6 in F (Pastoral), Op. 68; 8 in F, Op. 93
*** EuroArts **DVD** DV BPAB 168. BPO, Abbado (V/D: Bob Coles)

Symphonies 2 in D, Op. 36; 5 in C min., Op. 67
*** EuroArts **DVD** DV BPAB 25. BPO, Abbado (V/D: Bob Coles)

These two DVDs offer Abbado's live recordings made in February 2001 in the Santa Cecilia Academy in Rome, exhilarating performances rapturously received by the Italian audience. Interpretatively, they very much follow the pattern set by Abbado in the complete cycle he recorded for DG in Berlin in 1999, using the new edition of Jonathan del Mar, with an extra repeat in the Scherzo of No. 5, for example. Abbado again opts for a performance-style that takes some note of period practice, lighter and more resilient than before, with sharp, clean attack. That particularly applies to slow movements, which flow easily, though Abbado tends to avoid the extreme speeds in fast movements suggested by some of Beethoven's metronome markings. One facility offered in all the symphonies except No.2 is an alternative camera-angle. The first option varies the shots of the conductor with those of different instruments, whereas the second option concentrates the whole time on the conductor. There is a marked discrepancy between the running time of each DVD, with Nos. 1, 6 and 8 lasting almost half an hour longer than Nos. 2 and 5.

Symphony 1
** Sony **DVD** SVD 46363. BPO, Karajan (V/D: Ernst Wild)

Symphonies 2; 3 (Eroica)
** Sony **DVD** SVD 46365. BPO, Karajan (V/D: Ernst Wild)

Symphonies 4; 5
** Sony **DVD** SVD 46366. BPO, Karajan (V/D: Ernst Wild)

Symphonies 6 (Pastoral); 7
** Sony **DVD** SVD 46367. BPO, Karajan (V/D: Ernst Wild)

Karajan's Beethoven has been part of our staple diet since his 1947 account of the *Ninth Symphony*. The sound of the new Sony recordings is first class in every way, though the camera-work tends to be restricted to the same limited number of shots. (Hugo Niebeling's direction in the 1967 *Pastoral* was more imaginative.) All the same, it is good to see as well as hear Karajan and the Berlin Philharmonic. It goes without saying that the orchestral playing is of the highest standard, but at the same time it must be admitted that they do not have the same immediacy and spontaneity of the 1950s and 1960s performances. So this Beethoven set is recommended but without the enthusiasm that Karajan so often inspired.

Symphony 5
🔶 *** EMI **DVD** 492842-9. LPO, Stokowski – SCHUBERT: *Symphony 8 (Unfinished)* *** ⊛ (with LSO: DEBUSSY: *Prélude à l'après midi d'un faune*; WAGNER: *Die Meistersinger: Overture* ***; Bonus: DUKAS: *L'Apprenti Sorcier*; Monteux **)

Stokowski's EMI DVD of Beethoven's *Fifth* is part of one of the very finest of all orchestral concert DVDs and offers an electrifying performance, coupled with a superb Schubert *Unfinished*, with the LPO in peerless form. The camera lets us watch the conductor in close-up a great deal of the time: his almost impassive face, the economy of the flowing hand-movements, a dramatic gesture when needed. In the Beethoven one hand or the other strongly underlines the rhythmic pulse. In the slow movement the glorious tonal richness of the cellos is unforgettable, while the double basses come into their own in the Scherzo (after an unfortunate but momentary slip from the horns). These are both great per-formances, caught on the wing with all the advantages of live music-making, and the wide-ranging recording, made in the attractive ambience of Croydon's Fairfield Halls, is worthy of them, as indeed is the visually appealing colour photography. The expansive Wagner overture and beautifully played Debussy *Prélude*, both featuring the LSO in the London Festival Hall, are fine performances too, but without quite the total memorability of the two main works. As a bonus, the dapper Pierre Monteux directs a lively *L'Apprenti Sorcier*, with a perfectly judged basic tempo, although here the black-and-white photography and compressed sound are a drawback. But this remains an indispensable DVD, both for Stokowski-ans and Beethovenians. One soon becomes totally caught up in the communicated tension of the music-making.

Symphonies. (i) *1*; (ii) *2. Overtures:* (i) *The Creatures of Prometheus*; (iii) *Fidelio*; (ii) *Leonore 2; The Ruins of Athens*
(BB) (***) Naxos mono 8.110854. (i) VPO; (ii) LSO; (iii) LPO, Weingartner

Symphonies. (i) *3 (Eroica)*; (ii) *4*
(BB) (***) Naxos mono 8.110856. (i) VPO; (ii) LPO, Weingartner

(i) *Symphonies 5*; (ii) *Piano Sonata 29 ((Hammerklavier)* arr. Weingartner); (i) *Overture: The Creatures of Prometheus*
(N) (BB) (***) Naxos mono 8.110913. (i) LPO; (ii) RPO, Weingartner

Symphonies. (i) *5*; (ii) *6 (Pastoral)*. (iii) *11 Viennese Dances, WoO 17*
(BB) (***) Naxos mono 8.110861. (i) British SO; (ii) RPO; (iii) LPO, Weingartner

(i) *Symphonies 7; 8. Egmont: Overture*; (ii) *Clärchens Tod; Entr'acte 2*
(BB) **(*) Naxos mono 8.110862. (i) VPO; (ii) LPO, Weingartner

(i) *Symphonies 9 in D min. (Choral)*; (ii) *Overture: Consecration of the House*
(N) (BB) (***) Naxos mono 8.110863. (i) Helletsgruber, Anday, Maikl, Mayr, V. State Op. Ch., VPO; (ii) LPO; Weingartner

Peter Stadlen once memorably referred to Weingartner's 'lean-beef Beethoven'. His accounts of the symphonies are free of the opulence and weight that characterized some of his contemporaries (including the often glorious Furtwän-gler). They have a sinewy classicism, and for many collectors they stood for the voice of Beethoven in much the same way as did Schnabel in the late *Sonatas* or the Busch Quartet in the late *Quartets*. Weingartner was the first conductor to record all the Beethoven symphonies, starting in 1923 in London and ending in 1938 in Vienna with No. 2. The sound is generally more than just acceptable. For many older collec-tors Weingartner's 1936 account was *the Eroica*, speaking with an altogether special authority. It has complete authenticity of feeling, and even younger collectors coming to it without the encumbrance of nostalgia will certainly sense its stature. Mark Obert-Thorn's transfer is not as sensationally good as some of his Schnabel/Beethoven records, and the upper strings in the *Eroica* are not as sweet as they sound in Bryan Crimp's 1975 EMI LP transfer.

Weingartner recorded the *Fifth Symphony* no fewer than four times, and this first version, made in London in 1932 with an *ad hoc* orchestra, is distinguished by sobriety and freedom from any self-regard. His *Pastoral* from 1927 is totally unaffected and sounds strikingly good in this transfer, as do the delightful *Viennese Dances* made with the LPO in 1938.

Weingartner's follow-up 1933 version of the *Fifth Sym-phony* with the LPO was his fourth and most satisfying. But not even Weingartner can make out a totally convincing case for the *Hammerklavier* being transcribed for the orchestra, for all the symphonic dimension of its keyboard writing. An element of struggling against the elements, fighting the very nature of the keyboard medium and storming the heavens, is the essence of the *Hammerklavier*. Once it is orchestrated, this is lost, for the orchestra takes everything comfortably in its stride. For all that, it goes without saying that the thoughts of arguably the greatest Beethoven interpreter of the day about this sonata are well worth hearing at so modest an outlay. Decent transfers.

The *Seventh* and *Eighth* are among the most commanding of Weingartner's Beethoven cycle. The *Seventh* is completely classical in approach, without the (very slightly overdriven) intensity of the contemporaneous Toscanini version, while the *Eighth* has a mercurial quality that is quite special.

(i) *Symphonies 1–9; Overture: Egmont*; (ii) *Missa solemnis, Op. 123*
(B) (***) RCA mono 74321 66656-2 (6 + 1). NBC SO, Toscanini; with (i & ii) Merriman, Robert Shaw Chorale; (i) Farrell, Peerce, Scott; (ii) Marshall, Conley, Hines

There could be no greater contrast than that between those pre-war giants, Weingartner and Furtwängler on the one hand and Toscanini and the NBC Symphony Orchestra on the other. This new refurbishment of the Toscanini Beethoven symphonies and the *Missa solemnis* comes on six CDs together with an additional disc comparing the present transfers with earlier issues. If you were to use an astronomical analogy, you might speak of Toscanini's Beethoven as having the concentration of a white dwarf by the side of Furtwängler's red giant. In any event, those who want these classic and electrifying performances are going to find the sound dramatically improved, warmer and less strident.

Symphonies 1; 2; 3 (Eroica); 8
(B) *** EMI double forte CZS5 73323-2 (2). Concg. O, Sawallisch

Symphonies 4; 5; 6 (Pastoral); 7
(B) *** EMI double forte 5 73326-2 (2). Concg. O, Sawallisch

(i) *Symphony 9 (Choral); (ii) Piano Concerto 5 (Emperor)*
(B) **(*) EMI double forte 5 73329-2 (2). (i) Price, Lipovšek, Seiffert, Rootering, Düsseldorf Städtischer Musikverein, Concg. O; (ii) Egorov, Philh. O; Sawallisch – MOZART: *Piano Concerto 20* **(*)

Much of Sawallisch's Concertgebouw set is greatly admired, but undoubtedly the first of these three double forte reissues is the one to go for. The orchestral playing is of a high standard throughout and Sawallisch has a fine sense of proportion. The *First Symphony* immediately sounds fresh and vibrant; the *Second* and the *Eighth* receive lovely, alert accounts that give much pleasure, and textures are clean and transparent. The *Eroica* receives a performance of some stature and has great breadth and dignity; the orchestral playing is a joy in itself. The mellow acoustic of the Concertgebouw Hall must, however, have encouraged Sawallisch into middle-aged spread for the *Fifth Symphony*, but blazing brass introduces an altogether more electrifying view of the finale. A relaxed view of the *Pastoral* is more sympathetic, but the sound is not ideally clear. Sawallisch's version of the *Choral Symphony* was recorded live, but its sense of occasion is surprisingly muted, with admirably chosen speeds but with playing too relaxed, lacking dramatic tension. Even the finale, with its impressive soloists, is disappointing when the chorus is placed backwardly and the singing lacks sharpness of focus. To fill up the set, Egorov gives a refreshingly direct but still individual account of the *Emperor*.

Symphonies 1–5; 7; (i) 9 (Choral); Missa solemnis
(M) (***) Testament mono/stereo SBT 1284 (1 & 7); SBT 1285 (2 & Overtures: *Coriolan, Egmont, Leonora 3*); SBT 1286 (4 & 5); SBT2 1283 (2) (3 (*Eroica*) & *Missa solemnis*); SBT 1287 (9 (*Choral*)). Gurzenich O, Wand; (i) with Kirschstein, Deroubaix, Schreier, Morbach, Gurzenich Ch.

Though in Britain and elsewhere the mastery of Günter Wand in the central Viennese repertory came to be appreciated only in his later years, these recordings, made between 1955 and 1986 for the Club français du Disque, demonstrate comparable command in Wand's Beethoven interpretations from much earlier in his career. The Gurzenich Orchestra, with which he made the recordings in Cologne, was the one he had trained from 1938 onwards – in effect, the orchestra of the Cologne Opera when performing in concert. The comparisons with Wand's outstanding Beethoven cycle for RCA/BMG, made some twenty-odd years later with the North

West German Radio Orchestra, reveal that the interpretations themselves are remarkably similar. If the ensemble of the Gurzenich Orchestra is not always quite as crisp as that of the Hamburg players – largely a question of rehearsal time, no doubt – there is an extra freshness and spontaneity, helped by the bright forward sound, more sharply focused than on RCA, whether in the earlier mono recordings (*Symphonies 1, 2, 3, 4* and *9*) or the later ones in stereo.

The two-disc package of the *Missa solemnis* and the *Eroica Symphony* is the pick of the series. The *Eroica* is more urgent here than it is in Wand's later recordings, with a dedicated reading of the Funeral March as centrepiece. Finer still is the *Missa solemnis*. Recorded in stereo in 1965, this is a performance that from first to last has a devotional intensity, conveying the impression not of a studio recording but of a great occasion. With high dynamic contrasts Wand is bold, strong and dramatic in the passages where the visionary Beethoven rethought the meaning of the liturgy, weighty in the *Sanctus* and after the hushed dedication of the *Agnus Dei* ever more incandescent in the culmination of the *Dona nobis pacem* with its spine-tingling military incursions. The chorus, despite rather backward placing, sings with admirable freshness, and among the soloists the soprano and tenor (the young Peter Schreier) stand out.

Symphonies 1–2
(BB) *** Arte Nova 74321 63645-2. Zurich Tonhalle O, Zinman
(M) *** Warner Elatus 0927 49003-2. COE, Harnoncourt
**(*) Häns. CD93.084. Stuttgart RSO, Norrington

Symphonies 1–2; Ritterballet, WoO 1
*** Simax PSC 1179. Swedish CO, Dausgaard

Using the Bärenreiter scores newly edited by Jonathan Del Mar, David Zinman conducts electrifying performances of the first two symphonies, with a rather smaller band of strings than in later works. With textures transparent and rhythms crisply sprung at generally fast speeds, the results consistently reflect the influence of period performance. For the *Andantes* in both symphonies there is a hushed dedication.

Harnoncourt's recordings of the first two symphonies are splendidly alive, getting his cycle off to an invigorating start. First-class playing and excellent sound put this coupling high on the list of current mid-priced recommendations.

The Simax coupling is the first volume in what will be a complete survey of Beethoven's orchestral music. These are engagingly fresh performances, stylish and elegant, and with plenty of spontaneous excitement in the outer movements. They combine the vigour of period performance with the richness of a modern orchestra, and if the following discs are as good as this, it will be a cycle of considerable importance. The early but delightful ballet music is a bonus, and the sound is superb.

Recorded live by South West German Radio at the European Music Festival in 2002, Roger Norrington and the Stuttgart Radio Symphony Orchestra performed a complete Beethoven symphony cycle which offers fascinating contrasts with the studio recordings Norrington made earlier for EMI with his period-performance group, the London Classical Players. In Nos. 1 and 2 Norrington's observance of period practice with players using modern instruments results in light, transparent performances at fast speeds. Surprisingly, the *Andante* of No. 1 is even faster than before, so that it sounds more like a Minuet than a slow movement, and the presto Scherzo too is faster. The outer movements of No. 2 are also so fast that the players have problems articulating the notes, but the gain over the EMI performances is that there is greater weight in many of the textures, as in the slow introductions to the first movements of both symphonies, as well as the finale of No. 1.

Symphonies 1 in C; 3 in E flat (Eroica)
*** EMI 5 57564-2. VPO, Rattle
(B) *** CfP 575 9842. RLPO, Mackerras
(BB) *** Warner Apex 2564 60452-2. Sinfonia Varsovia, Y. Menuhin

Symphonies 1; 3 (Eroica); Fidelio: Overture
(BB) (**(*)) Naxos mono 8.110802/3. NBC SO, Toscanini

Recorded live (like the rest of his Vienna cycle), this coupling represents Rattle at his finest. The *First Symphony* brings a powerfully warm and vigorous reading that has the young Beethoven looking forward to the nineteenth century rather than back to tradition, with syncopated cross-rhythms sharply defined and the timpani given prominence. Using Jonathan Del Mar's acclaimed Bärenreiter edition, Rattle takes on board the lessons of period performance without applying them dogmatically. In the *Eroica* his tempo for the first movement is fast but allows an infectious lift to rhythms, while in the Funeral March he gives full emotional weight to the music in his hushed, spacious reading, very different from the fast-flowing period performances that are short on gravity. In the finale, Rattle relishes the inventiveness of the variations, bringing out a playful element, with rhythms delectably sprung.

With Mackerras, the *First* is fresh and alert in a Haydnesque way, while the *Eroica* has ample power, with heightened dynamic contrasts and with the flowing speed for the Funeral March still conveying dedication. First-rate recording.

The one irritant to Menuhin's performances on Apex is the welcoming applause that comes before the music begins and at the close of No. 1, but not before the opening of No. 3. This is intrusive without the visual element. Otherwise these highly musical performances, strong, but on a convincing chamber scale, are among the most satisfying available, with a dedicated reading of the *Eroica* Funeral March. Warm, well-balanced recording.

Though the Naxos transfer is variable – with drying-noises in part of the *Eroica* slow movement and intrusive American radio announcers introducing the performances – Toscanini's 1939 account of the *Eroica* is one of the very greatest ever recorded, incandescent from first to last. The *First Symphony* too has a sparkle missing in later Toscanini.

Symphonies 1; 4; Overture: Egmont
(M) *** DG (ADD) 419 048-2. BPO, Karajan

Karajan's 1977 version of No. 1 is exciting, polished and elegant; in No. 4 the balance is closer, exposing every flicker of tremolando, helped by a recording with fine presence and body.

Symphonies 1; 5
(N) (BB) ** EMI Encore 5 86411-2. Phd. O, Muti

Muti's coupling of Nos. 1 and 5 brings characteristically taut and urgent readings of both symphonies, with early Bethoven treated just as earnestly as if it were from the middle period. The Philadelphia Orchestra in 1985 play with a new brilliance instilled by their conductor; sadly, however, the recording,

made in the Memorial Hall, Fairmount Park, although not without body, is harsh and aggressive in *fortissimos*.

Symphonies 1; 6 (Pastoral)
(M) **(*) Warner Elatus 0927 49833-2. Leningrad PO, Mravinsky
(BB) **(*) Naxos 8.553474. Nicolaus Esterházy Sinfonia, Drahos

Symphonies 1; 6; Overture: Egmont
(B) **(*) Sony (ADD) SBK 46532. Cleveland O, Szell

Recorded live in January 1982, just six years before he died, Mravinsky's performances of the *First* and *Pastoral* are consistently alert and intense, not just in allegros but in the flowing accounts of the slow movements in both symphonies. The *Pastoral* is notable, too, for the aptly rustic quality of the woodwind solos, especially in the first movement (no exposition repeat) and the Scherzo. The sweetness of the Leningrad string-tone also adds greatly to the lyrical beauty of both the slow movement and the finale. Good radio sound, though woodwind solos are balanced too close at times.

Szell's dynamic performance of the *First Symphony* makes up for any absence of charm. In the *Pastoral*, Szell is subtle in his control of phrasing, for all the firmness of his style. However, it is a pity that the close-up sound robs the slow movement of much of its gentleness and delicacy of atmosphere.

In his Beethoven series for Naxos, Drahos offers fresh, spontaneous-sounding performances, beautifully played by a chamber-sized group from Budapest, with recording outstandingly vivid. Plainer and less subtle than the finest versions, these lively, well-sprung performances still make excellent bargains.

Symphony 2 in D, Op. 36
(M) (***) BBC mono BBCL 4099-2. RPO, Beecham – BRAHMS: *Symphony 2* (***)

The *Second Symphony* was the work of Beethoven that Beecham most enjoyed, and he gives an electrifying performance, recorded in the BBC Studio at Maida Vale in December 1956, sadly not in stereo but with clear, well-balanced mono sound. The reading is typical of Beecham, if anything even more magnetic than his EMI studio recording, fiery in the outer movements and warmly persuasive in the *Larghetto* slow movement, affectionately moulded at a steady speed. An excellent coupling for Beecham's incandescent Edinburgh Festival account of the Brahms symphony.

Symphonies 2; 5 in C min., Op. 67
*** EMI 5 57566-2. VPO, Rattle
(B) **(*) Sony (ADD) SBK 47651. Cleveland O, Szell
(BB) **(*) Naxos 8.553476. Nicolaus Esterházy Sinfonia, Drahos

As in No. 1, Rattle registers that the *Second Symphony* is a forward-looking work, the biggest symphony written up to that date. In this live recording the first movement is played with great panache; it is fast and swaggering, while the *Larghetto* slow movement is at once fresh and delicately moulded, and the Scherzo and finale are pointed with wit. The *Fifth Symphony* also benefits from being recorded live, with the first movement at once taut, urgent and weighty, with the slow movement bringing high dramatic contrasts, as do all the movements, not least the dramatic account of the finale. In the Scherzo, unlike David Zinman in his Arte Nova set, which also uses the Del Mar edition, Rattle does not take up the option of having the Scherzo and Trio repeated, before the final mysterious and truncated reprise of the Scherzo. Vivid recording, which allows one to hear the piccolo clearly in the finale of the *Fifth*.

With marvellously clean articulation from the strings in the first movement, Szell's No. 2 has the adrenalin running free; yet here, as in the similarly brilliant account of No. 5, he understands the need to give full scope to the lyrical elements.

Béla Drahos on Naxos conducts clean-cut readings of both works, with the excellent, well-balanced recording capturing the chamber scale very effectively. No. 2 is less dramatic than some. In No. 5, the call of fate at the opening may seem lightweight, but on a chamber scale this is refreshing in its clarity, easily flowing in the middle movements, taut in the outer movements.

Symphonies 2; 6 in F (Pastoral)

(BB) (***) Dutton mono CDBP 9716. Berlin Op. O or LPO; Kleiber

(BB) *** Warner Apex 2564 60453-2. Sinfonia Varsovia, Y. Menuhin

It is too easily forgotten that Erich Kleiber (father of Carlos) was, in the 1920s, a supreme conductor alongside Walter, Toscanini and Klemperer – one whose career temporarily suffered when, during the Hitler period, he went to live in South America. His fine recording of the *Pastoral Symphony*, fresh and alert, was made for Decca in 1948, following up his mould-breaking account of the *Fifth* for that company, one of the earliest LPs. He recorded No. 2 in Berlin much earlier, in 1929; equally strong and magnetic, with full-bodied sound, remarkable for its period. Typically excellent Dutton transfers.

After the opening applause, Menuhin's reading of the *Second Symphony* is weighty and mature-sounding, the first movement lacking a little in bite but not in buoyancy. The *Larghetto* is nobly phrased, the finale vigorous and high-spirited. Alongside the *Choral Symphony*, Menuhin's performance of the *Pastoral Symphony* (which opens without applause) crowns his cycle in its sheer lyrical beauty. The chamber scale and the combination of warmth and lightness of touch bring a joyous momentum. The storm bursts in dramatically, and the heartfelt *Shepherds' Thanksgiving* brings a lyrical apotheosis. Satisfyingly full sound, with a natural brilliance.

Symphonies 2; 7 in A, Op. 92

(M) *** DG (ADD) 419 050-2. BPO, Karajan

(M) (**(*)) BBC mono BBCL 4124-2. Philh. O, Van Beinum

In Karajan's *Second*, the firm lines give the necessary strength. The *Seventh* is tense and exciting, with the conductor emphasizing the work's drama rather than its dance-like qualities.

Eduard van Beinum belonged to the same dedicated school as Weingartner and Sir Adrian Boult, conductors who never sought to impose their own personalities and who were first and foremost servants of the composer. To their number might be added Klemperer, for whom van Beinum was standing in for this 1958 concert. The playing recalls the late lamented Peter Stadlen's description of Weingartner's 'lean beef Beethoven' to mind, for it is completely straight and devoid of idiosyncrasy. Van Beinum's Beethoven received both critical and public acclaim and proved to be his London

swansong, for he died only five months later. Although the *Second* is a good, straightforward account, the *Seventh* is a performance of some stature and an admirable memorial to an underrated master. Well worth investigating, and decent sound.

Symphonies 2; 7; (i; ii) Mass in C, Op. 86; (ii) The Ruins of Athens (incidental music; excerpts), Op. 113

(N) (BB) **(*)EMI Gemini (ADD) 5 86504-2 (2). RPO, Beecham, with (i) Vyvyan, Sinclair, Lewis, Nowakowski; (ii) Beecham Ch. Soc.

In both symphonies Beecham's pacing is highly personal. In the *Second* the extremely expansive speed for the slow movement and his loving manner bring a romantic reading which yet has plenty of Beecham elegance. The *Allegro con brio* of the first movement is extreme in the opposite direction, exhilaratingly fast to challenge the RPO players at their peak; while the last two movements are both taken easily and and wittily. It is a strong, individual performance. Beecham's *Seventh* is comparably brisk; yet, such is his rhythmic control and his ablility to clarify textures – well realized in the vivid recording – the result is exhilarating. Again, in the second movement Beecham reverts to old-fashioned slow manners in what is in effect an *Andante* rather than an *Allegretto*, but his rhythmic sense and care for phrasing still avoid heaviness. The digital transfer of the 1956/7 recording of the *Second Symphony* brings some stridency in the violins, and the analogue hiss is relatively high, but the 1958 sound of the *Seventh* is much more successful, the sound full and well balanced.

On the companion disc, the *C major Mass* is a vintage performance, passionately committed, which makes one appreciate how this strong and dramatic work followed directly on from the late and great Haydn Masses, a commission from Prince Esterhazy. With a first-rate team of soloists and excellent choral singing, Beecham is still a front-runner among modern-instrument performances of this work. The transfer of the 1958 recording is vivid and lively, with clear choral sound. The fill-up of incidental music is equally vibrant, with Beecham roaring through the *Chorus of Dervishes* (finely sung by the Beecham Choral Society), whiskers obviously bristling. Here the fierceness returns in the upper strings, although the chorus is splendidly caught. Yet reservations must be swept aside: these are all memorable performances by a great conductor in his prime, and we must be grateful they were recorded in stereo.

Symphonies 2; 8

(B) *** CfP 575 9852. RLPO, Mackerras

Mackerras rounded off his outstanding Beethoven cycle with performances of these two even-numbered works which bring out the dramatic bite in performances at once refined and full of sharp contrasts, with exhilarating results.

'Eroica': Symphony 3 in E flat, Op. 55: Film Drama

(N)** Opus Arte DVD OA 0908DD. ORR, Gardiner (with Ian Hart, Tim Pigott-Smith, Jack Davenport, Fenella Woolgar, Claire Skinner, Lucy Aikhurst, Leo Bill, Frank Finlay. Director: Simon Cellan Jones)

Eroica is the film, subtitled 'The day that changed music forever', which the won the Prix d'Italia, a graphic re-creation of the occasion when, at the Palace of Prince Lobkowitz in 1804, Beethoven's *Eroica Symphony* was heard for the first time, privately, before a handful of friends. Ian Hart gives a rugged portrait of Beethoven, with Leo Bill as his long-suffering pupil, Ferdinand Ries. The film follows the composer and Ries from his lodgings to the palace, where his arrogance in the face of nobility is clearly established, with Prince Lobkowitz and the Princess (his fervent supporter) ready to accept his own estimate of his greatness. The sceptic in the company is Count Dietrichstein, whose facile comments are no doubt typical of many early listeners to this most revolutionary of symphonies. One has to accept the impossible idea that musicians faced with this extraordinary score could play it immaculately at once without rehearsal or conductor. Granted that, the film not only presents a fine period performance (with Gardiner's ORR for once including no women players) but dramatic presentations of such developments as the rejection of Beethoven's proposal of marriage to Josephine, Countess von Deym, and his hearing from Ries that Napoleon has declared himself Emperor, resulting in his tearing up the title-page of the score.

The main film includes such incidental events as these during the performance, but as a supplement comes an uninterrupted performance of the whole symphony using the same images, with salient passages like the openings of movements illustrated with shots of the manuscript score. Having a complete performance in the main film too involves the film-director, Simon Cellan Jones, devising many shots of the bystanders listening, as well as of the players, but the result is a moving film, made the more so when the aged Haydn appears (Frank Finlay) and pronounces that 'Everything is different from today!' There is an informative booklet with ample documentation.

R.L. comments: However, while Gardiner's performance is outstanding, those who can remember the searching BBC programmes Robert Simpson, Deryck Cooke and Harold Truscott made about Beethoven in the 1950s and 1960s, which added to our knowledge and carried real authority, will find the dramatized feature offered here at best thin and at worst just embarrassing. It is a measure of our dumbed-down times that this is 'Award winning'.

Symphony 3 (Eroica)
(M) **(*) DG (ADD) (IMS) 447 444-2. LAPO, Giulini (with
SCHUMANN: *Manfred Overture* ***)

Symphony 3; Overture: Coriolan
(M) (***) Sony mono SMK 89887. RPO, Beecham

*Symphony 3; Overtures: The Creatures of Prometheus;
Leonora 3*
(M) *** Warner Elatus 2564 60034-2. COE, Harnoncourt

Symphony 3; Overture: Egmont
**(*) DG 439 002-2. BPO, Karajan

Symphony 3 in E flat; Overtures: Leonora 1–2
(M) (***) EMI mono 5 67740-2 [567741]. Philh. O, Klemperer

Symphony 3; Overture: Leonora 3
(**(*)) Testament (mono) SBT 2242 (2). Royal Danish O,
Klemperer – BRAHMS: *Symphony 4;* MOZART: *Symphony
29* (**(*))
(M) **(*) DG (ADD) 419 049-2. BPO, Karajan

Symphony 3; Grosse Fuge
(M) *** EMI (ADD) 5 66793-2. Philh. O, Klemperer

Recorded in April 1957 on Klemperer's last visit to conduct the Royal Danish Orchestra in Copenhagen, the version of the *Eroica* on Testament is even more magnetic than either of his studio recordings with the Philharmonia, fine as they are.

Though the playing in a live account is not quite so polished, the tension is consistently keener, the dramatic points more positive and the overall sense of a great occasion vividly conveyed. The mono sound is not as well balanced as in the studio recordings, but the ear very soon adjusts. The *Third Leonora Overture*, like the Brahms and Mozart symphonies which also come on the first of the two discs in this set, derives from a concert Klemperer conducted in January 1954, and though the slow introduction brings some rough ensemble and the recording is rougher too, not at all kind to the trumpet in the famous off-stage call, the weight and intensity of the performance come over strongly, with the main *Allegro* fiercely dramatic.

The 1954 recording of the *Leonora Overtures Nos. 1* and *2* and the 1955 mono version of the *Eroica* were among the first recordings Klemperer made with the Philharmonia Orchestra, and their success immediately revealed his full strength. This *Eroica* is one of his supreme achievements, with speeds generally more urgent than in his 1961 stereo version (on 5 66793-2, with the *Grosse Fuge* sounding appropriately monolithic). The more spacious later version is keenly concentrated, and the remastered stereo weightily reinforces the work's magnificence. However, many will prefer the even greater incisiveness of the earlier, mono version.

Harnoncourt's *Eroica* brings an extremely fast tempo in the first movement, and his austere view of the great Funeral March is chillingly intense. The result is as individual as it is powerful.

Beecham recorded the *Eroica* only once: in 1951–2, during the period when he was contracted to American Columbia (CBS). Though it is in mono only, the rare combination of qualities – power as well as elegance, warmth without romantic distortion – makes for a magnetic reading. The first movement is marked by extremes of dynamic, while the Funeral March has a natural gravity at a steady, measured pace, with the Scherzo rhythmically bouncy rather than hectic, and the finale thrustful as well as elegant. One specially notes the distinctive sound of Dennis Brain's horn at key moments. The *Coriolan Overture* is comparably powerful and dedicated. Bright, clearly detailed sound.

Karajan's 1977 account (419 049-2) brings fiery intensity, with the Funeral March more concentrated than in his earlier recordings. An exciting performance of *Leonora No. 3* makes a fair bonus. The sound is well defined and clean.

The gain in Karajan's last, digital version of the *Eroica* (439 002-2) lies most of all in the Funeral March, very spacious and intense. The playing lacks something of the knife-edged bite associated with him. The recording is clean and firm, but there is a degree of congestion in big tuttis.

Giulini's refined and individual reading, with its very measured view of the first movement, wins only a qualified recommendation, yet it remains a striking example of a conductor transforming an orchestra.

Symphonies 3; 4
(BB) *** Arte Nova 74321 59214-2. Zurich Tonhalle O,
Zinman
*** DG 471 488-2. BPO, Abbado
*** DG 447 050-2. ORR, Gardiner
**(*) Häns. CD93.085. Stuttgart RSO, Norrington

David Zinman and the Tonhalle Orchestra give outstanding performances of both symphonies. The string and wind articulation in both symphonies is phenomenally crisp and clear so that there is no feeling of excessive haste. In the

Eroica, even with the exposition repeat observed, the first movement lasts barely 15 minutes, and the Funeral March at a flowing speed still conveys darkly tragic intensity, not least at the close. First-rate recording, with ample bloom on the sound.

Abbado's reading of the *Eroica* is at once robust, dramatic and refined, with the lessons of period performance clearly taken on board. Though the tempo for the Funeral March slow movement is flowing rather than measured, with light *pianissimos*, the dedication is intense, building up in this live reading to a deeply affecting coda. The finale is brisk and urgent, yet string textures are transparent, as they are throughout. In No. 4 too, speeds are on the fast side, yet the mystery of the slow introduction is magical, while the Adagio slow movement at a flowing speed is sweet and relaxed in its lyricism, with the power of the outer movements fully conveyed. A splendid, more traditional alternative to Zinman's Tonhalle coupling of the same two symphonies.

Gardiner's briskness means that, like Zinman, he can fit Nos. 3 and 4 on the same disc. The *Eroica*'s first movement is presented purposefully, with full weight and biting intensity. The Funeral March has natural gravity, even at a flowing speed, with high dynamic contrasts. In No. 4, the sublime melody of the slow movement is sweeter than usual with period violins.

Norrington's fast speed for the first movement of the *Eroica* no longer seems surprising, and, compared with his earlier, EMI recording on period instruments, this live performance from Stuttgart brings a more sharply clipped style. Though the opening of the Funeral March is less darkly intense than before, a live occasion brings a growing intensity, until the close is as bleakly tragic as it can be. No. 4 again brings brisk speeds which in the allegro of the first movement sound joyful and carefree but, with violins exposed, the great adagio at a speed faster than before sounds a little perfunctory, though the remaining two movements find Norrington at his most persuasive.

Symphonies 3; 5 in C min., Op. 67
(M) (***) Decca mono 467 125-2. Concg. O, Erich Kleiber

Symphonies 3 (Eroica); 5
(N) (BB) (***) ASV Living Era mono AJC 8551. NBC SO, Toscanini

The superbly remastered reissue in Decca's 'Legends' series joins together two great performances from the early LP era which have never before sounded so impressive on disc. Kleiber's 1950 *Eroica* is wonderfully intense and dramatic, and it includes the repeat of the exposition in the first movement to make the whole structure more staggeringly monumental. If anything, the *Fifth* is even finer. The cumulative excitement of the first movement is achieved without any sense of over-driving, and the slow movement brings a warmly lyrical feeling in the strings to offset the tension elsewhere. The preparation of the finale is unforgettable, and when the great tune sweeps in triumphantly, timpani pounding underneath, it combines dignity and power. Kleiber keeps up the concentration right through to the thrilling coda. The new transfers are wonderfully full and clear, the famous Concertgebouw acoustic faithfully captured, without edginess and stridency.

The second of ASV's new budget series of 'gramophone all-time greats' couples together two of Toscanini's finest and most exciting NBC performances, both from 1939. While the dead acoustics of the infamous Studio 8H are not ameliorated, in these fresh transfers the sound is a good deal more than acceptable, and its vividness is accompanied by only the slightest background noise. The vibrant *Fifth* is famous for its electrifying transition into the finale, with an astonishing range of dynamic for the time. The *Eroica* still grips the listener from the first note to the last and, though the sound is still dry, the transfer is preferable to that offered by Naxos (see above), with the interference in the textural quality of the slow movement minimized and no intrusive radio announcers.

Symphonies 3; 5; 6; 7
(B) *** RCA (ADD) 74321 886 812 (2). Chicago SO, Reiner

Though Fritz Reiner on record has more regularly been associated with exotic repertory, this fine two-disc set establishes what a powerfully dramatic interpreter of Beethoven he was, bitingly direct. In the 1950s he had built the Chicago Symphony into one of the finest orchestras in America, and even the earliest recording here, the *Eroica* from 1954, demonstrates the fullness and brilliance of sound achieved by the RCA engineers in Chicago in the days of experimental stereo. No. 5 dates from the following year, an equally intense performance, while the *Pastoral* comes from 1961, and the *Seventh* from 1959, all of them in sound more vivid than is often found in later Chicago recordings. Following the practice of the time, the exposition repeat is observed only in No. 5. With each of the two discs generously filled, it makes a most attractive package at bargain price.

Symphonies 3; 5; 7
(M) **(*) Decca (ADD) 467 679-2 (2). VPO, Solti

Here is a fascinating encounter with the conducting of the young firebrand Georg Solti, making some of his first records with the VPO in the late 1950s. In the *Eroica* Solti immediately establishes his personality and authority with crisply percussive opening chords and (with the first-movement exposition included) he maintains a high level of tension. The Funeral March is taken simply and slowly, the dynamics well controlled, giving a dedicated rather than an intense account. By contrast the Scherzo is thrillingly fast (with splendid Viennese horn-playing) and the finale romps along to an exciting conclusion.

Alas, the reading of the *Fifth* is much less successful. Solti chooses a very fast tempo for the opening movement, and with such precise, efficient articulation the result cannot help but be physically exciting. But already the feeling is of the playing being too forced, and in the slow movement this comes out in full measure, and the overall effect is one of ponderousness. Solti exaggerates the climaxes, sometimes crudely, and the power of the finale is visceral rather than an expression of incandescent joy. However, the merits of Solti's *Seventh* are substantial: in many ways this is the finest of the three performances. The reading sounds spontaneous and the control of dynamic is particularly impressive throughout, with some fine *pianissimos*, delicate and precise.

Symphonies 3; 8
(B) **(*) Sony (ADD) SBK 46328. Cleveland O, Szell
(BB) **(*) Naxos 8.553475. Nicolaus Esterházy Sinfonia, Drahos
(N) (M) ** RCA 82876 60858-2. NDRSO, Wand

Szell's is a fine performance in the Toscanini tradition, hard-driven and dramatic. The digital remastering is very successful: the sound is firm, full and brilliant. The performance of the *Eighth* is also compelling. The first-movement repeat is taken and the performance is not overdriven.

Drahos's performances on Naxos benefit greatly from superb sound and have the same qualities of freshness and spontaneity that mark the other initial disc in the series, making a good bargain, even if there are more searching readings of the *Eroica*.

Wand's *Eroica* is an honest, direct view, yet full of character. Admirably paced, it is a strong reading, with plenty of underlying lyrical feeling, The orchestral playing is of the highest quality and the horns are very impressive in the Trio of the Scherzo and the joyous finale. The *Eighth* appropriately has a lighter touch, but its vigour and vitality are commanding. Excellent digital recording (from 1985 and 1987 respectively) will make this very recommendable to the conductor's many admirers.

Symphony 4
*** Orfeo (ADD) C 522 991 B. VPO, Boehm – MAHLER: *Lieder eines fahrenden Gesellen*; SCHUMANN: *Symphony 4*
***

Symphonies 4; 5
(M) *** Warner Elatus 2564 60012-2. COE, Harnoncourt

Symphonies 4 in B flat, Op. 60; 5 in C min., Op. 67
(N) **(*) BIS SACD 1416. Minnesota O, Vänskä

Harnoncourt's *Fourth* is a brilliant, vital reading, with high contrasts in the slow movement, bringing soaring lyricism over nagging rhythms. His exuberance does not imply a lack of weight in the *Fifth*. The slow movement is particularly fine, and the finale grows seamlessly out of the Scherzo. The playing has fine bite and lift, and this coupling shows him and the COE at their most compelling.

Boldly, Osmo Vänskä sets out on a projected Beethoven cycle with the Minnesota Orchestra in readings of freshness and dramatic bite. These are performances of extremes, reflecting a youthful approach to the epic task of tackling all nine symphonies. So in the *Fourth Symphony* Vänskä makes the slow introduction dark and intense, leading to an Allegro that is purposeful rather than sparkling, while the slow movement is refined and otherworldly rather than relaxed. The Scherzo brings sharp attack on the offbeat accents, and the finale is full of energy and fire. The *Fifth*, more predictably, is given a performance of similarly high contrasts, with extremes of dynamic from the bitingly intense first movement through to the bold and brassy finale. With full-ranging, well-balanced sound on this compatible SACD, this refreshing disc makes a promising start to the project, though there are many fine alternatives at a fraction of the BIS price.

This Orfeo issue vividly portrays the mastery of Karl Boehm in varied repertoire, electrifying from first to last. His account of No. 4 is bitingly intense in the fast movements, with sharply rhythmic attack, and tender and sweet in the spacious slow movement.

Symphonies 4; 6
☙ ✿ (M) *** Sony (ADD) SMK 64462. Columbia SO, Walter
*** EMI 5 57568-2. VPO, Rattle
(B) *** CfP 575 9862. RLPO, Mackerras

Walter's reading of the *Fourth* is splendid, the finest achievement of his whole cycle. There is intensity and a feeling of natural vigour in every bar. Like his recording of the *Fourth*, the *Pastoral* represents the peak of his Indian summer in the

American recording studios, an affectionate, finely integrated performance from a master, with beautifully balanced sound. This has also been reissued separately on a Super Audio CD (SS 6012) requiring special playback facilities (see below).

In the *Fourth Symphony* Rattle's live recording brings out the dramatic contrast between the mystery of the slow introduction and the exuberance of the main Allegro. As in the rest of his Vienna cycle, he opts for a more moulded, rather more relaxed manner in the lyrical slow movement than other conductors who have taken note of period performance, while the last two movements are full of Beethovenian swagger. The *Pastoral Symphony* makes a fine coupling in a reading that allows a degree of relaxation in each movement, with speeds on the fast side but not too rigid. The *Peasants' Merrymaking* of the Scherzo is liltingly joyful, leading to a dramatic account of the *Storm* and warm relaxation in the finale.

Mackerras adopts consistently fast speeds in both symphonies, except in the slow introduction to No. 4. Crisp, light articulation allows for superb definition from the strings, and Mackerras's subtle rubato ensures that the opening of the *Pastoral* avoids any feeling of rigidity. With hard sticks used by the timpanist, the *Storm* has rarely sounded so thrilling, resolving on an ecstatic, glowing finale.

Symphonies 4; 7
(BB) *** Naxos 8.553477. Nicolaus Esterházy Sinfonia, Drahos

Symphonies 4; 7; King Stephen Overture
(B) *** Sony (ADD) SBK 48158. Cleveland O, Szell

Szell is at his finest in both symphonies. Along with powerful outer movements, tense and spontaneous-sounding, go exceptional accounts of the slow movements in both symphonies, and in No. 7 Szell makes the second movement a genuine *Allegretto*, with keen concentration taking it almost as fast as a period specialist.

The coupling of Nos. 4 and 7 is one of the most successful of the Drahos Naxos series. No. 4 has a joyful vitality, while in No. 7 Drahos keeps a spring in the rhythms without forcing the pace, lifting the finale with bouncing accents, leading to a thrilling coda. An excellent bargain.

Symphonies 4; 8; Coriolan Overture
(BB) *** Warner Apex 2564 60454-2. Sinfonia Varsovia, Y. Menuhin

On the reissued Apex CD the opening applause has been edited, and after the not undramatic *Coriolan Overture* the opening of the *Fourth Symphony* is immediately full of tension, the Allegro joyful and vigorous without being overdriven, and the rapt *Adagio* played most beautifully. There is lyrical feeling underlying the sprightliness of the Scherzo, and the Trio blossoms. The articulate delicacy from wind and strings alike carries into the finale with its vigorous forward impulse. The opening movement of the *Eighth* brings more joyous spirits and a most elegant second subject. This elegance also pervades the *Allegretto*, but here Menuhin's pacing is rather too relaxed and there is a lack of rhythmic uplift. However, all is forgiven when the finale erupts with buoyant energy. Again very fine playing, with the widest dynamic range, adds much to the character of the performances, and the spacious yet clear sound-picture is very satisfying.

Symphony 5 in C min., Op. 67
(N) (BB) (**(*)) Naxos mono 8.110879. BPO, Furtwängler –
WAGNER: *Parsifal: Prelude & Good Friday Music* (***);
FURTWÄNGLER: *Symphonic Concerto: Andante* (**(*))

Symphony 5; (i) Violin Concerto
(N) (M) (***) DG mono 477 5030. BPO, Furtwängler, (i) with
Schneiderhan

Furtwängler's 1937 *Fifth Symphony* (reissued here on Naxos) originally appeared on five 78-r.p.m. HMV discs and was the second of his commercial recordings. (There are 11 recordings in all, some taken from live concerts.) John Ardoin speaks of it as 'a performance of the greatest brilliance and clarity, with incisive attacks, fewer extremes of dynamics and tempo, and despite its fire and fury, more classically controlled than the earlier Polydor or the second EMI version of 1954'. There are all of this conductor's characteristics: impressive weight of tone and utterance, warm and compelling phrasing, even if some of his later readings seem just that shade more personal and involving. These Obert-Thorn transfers were previously available in England on the Biddulph label and are of high quality.

However, Furtwängler's 1947 DG *Fifth Symphony*, recorded live, is gripping from beginning to end, the *Andante* warm and relaxed, and the finale producing a spontaneous burst of adrenalin at the close. The BPO are in fine form and the mono recording is full-bodied; even if the dynamic range is restricted, the contrasts come over in the playing itself. The first-movement exposition repeat is included. Reissued on the 'Dokumente' label (although, disgracefully with such a logo, there *is* no documentaton), this coupling with the *Violin Concerto* should be snapped up before it disappears. Both recordings come from public performances, although the audience noises are really distracting only in Scheiderhan's Elysian account of the *Larghetto* from the *Violin Concerto*. Fortunately, his later, stereo version is unblemished and still available (see above). But this mono account of 1953 is just as inspired, and Furtwängler's contribution makes it equally memorable. Schneiderhan's playing has a wonderful classical lyricism and, apart from the slow movement, one remembers especially the graceful dancing main theme of the finale. Incidentally, he uses quite different cadenzas from his stereo version.

Symphony 5
(N) (M) ** Sony 516237-2 [SK 93012]. Col. SO, Walter (with
rehearsal & overtures: *Coriolan; Egmont* (NYPO))

Symphony 5; (i) Triple Concerto
(BB) (**(*)) Naxos mono 8.110801. NYPO, Toscanini, (i) with
Piastro, Schuster, Dorfman

Symphony 5; (i) Egmont: Overture & Incidental Music,
Op. 84 (complete)
(BB) *** Warner Apex 8573 89078-2. NYPO, Masur; (i) with
McNair, Quadflieg (narr.)

Masur's rugged NYPO account of the *Fifth Symphony* is immensely powerful, compelling from the first bar to the last. The reading is given even greater weight by Masur's observing the repeat both of the Scherzo and of the finale's exposition, which is made doubly successful by the thrust and joyful momentum of the last movement. As if that were not enough, he also provides the finest account of the complete *Egmont* incidental music in the catalogue, opening with a

thrillingly positive account of the *Overture*. The central *Intermezzi* are most sensitively played, and Sylvia McNair is a highly responsive and rich-voiced soloist. Will Quadflieg speaks his melodrama with dignity (separately banded, in German, untranslated in the notes) before the trumpets anticipate the final exultant paean of victory. The full-bodied sound is ideal for both works, with warm string-tone as well as a vivid overall brilliance and projection.

The 1933 account of the *Fifth Symphony* brings a Toscanini performance to treasure, warmer and more refined than his later readings with the NBC Symphony Orchestra, showing a degree of flexibility that was missing later. The *Triple Concerto*, recorded in 1942, brings a tautly controlled performance, with three of Toscanini's favourite players as soloists. They are recorded clearly, but in both works the orchestral sound is very limited, not helped by often-heavy surface noise.

Walter's first movement is taken very fast, yet it lacks the kind of nervous tension which distinguishes Carlos Kleiber's famous version. The middle two movements are contrastingly slow. In the *Andante* (more like an adagio) there is a glowing natural warmth, but the Scherzo at this speed is too gentle. The finale, taken at a spacious, natural pace, is joyous and sympathetic, but again fails to convey the ultimate in tension. The rehearsal excerpts and Overtures hardly make an alternative for another symphony.

Symphonies 5; 6
*** DG 471 489-2. BPO, Abbado
(BB) **(*) Arte Nova 74321 49695-2. Zürich Tonhalle O,
Zinman
**(*) DG 447 062-2. ORR, Gardiner
**(*) DG 439 004-2. BPO, Karajan
** Häns. CD 93.086. Stuttgart RSO, Norrington

Recorded live, Abbado's account of No. 5 is urgently dramatic in the first movement, smoothly refined in the slow movement and by turns strong and mysterious in the Scherzo, with high dynamic contrasts and an extra repeat of the Scherzo section, as prescribed in the Jonathan Del Mar edition, making an ABABA structure as in the *Fourth* and *Seventh Symphonies*. The finale then expands at full power, with the timpani well caught. The *Pastoral* brings the biggest contrast with Abbado's earlier, Vienna recording, when all five movements are faster and lighter than before, bringing out the freshness of inspiration far more effectively. Altogether a superb coupling, hard to beat.

David Zinman conducts the Tonhalle Orchestra in unusually direct and incisive readings. The use of Jonathan Del Mar's Bärenreiter edition in No. 5 brings a full repeat of the Scherzo and Trio before the usual partial and lightweight reprise of the Scherzo, leading into the mysterious link to the finale. If in No. 5 Zinman's approach works extremely well, the *Pastoral* is more problematical. The opening allegro, at a brisk speed, has plenty of energy but not much warmth. The slow movement by contrast is spaciously done, and the *Storm* is biting rather than atmospheric, with the finale plain, strong and intense, rather than warmly persuasive. The sound is fresh and clean, perhaps a little lacking in weight, although this suits the performances.

Gardiner's fast speeds in No. 5, recorded live, bring allegros of manic energy and thrust, pushing the music to the limit. The *Pastoral*, at comparably fast speeds, is crisp and light, with fine shading of phrase and dynamic, not least in the slow movement, though the big violin melody in the finale inevitably lacks the full sweetness of modern strings. Vivid, forward sound, full of presence.

Karajan's digital versions of the *Fifth* and *Sixth* present characteristically strong and incisive readings so that the fast speed for the first movement of the *Pastoral* no longer sounds too tense.

The extra weight of modern instruments in Norrington's later live recording from Stuttgart adds to the impact of the opening Fate motif of the *Fifth*, particularly when he takes it marginally slower than the main allegro, which is even more hectic than in his earlier, EMI version on period instruments. The *Andante* is then markedly faster than before, and less relaxed; but in the finale, as at the start, there is obvious gain in the greater weight of sound and in the dramatic way that the timpani – using hard sticks – rings out. There are gains too in the *Pastoral Symphony*, the least successful of Norrington's earlier cycle. This time the performance is more relaxed, with elegant, unexaggerated phrasing in the *Andante* and freshness and clarity in the *Peasants' Merrymaking*, though the exposed violins in the finale are very sour, with the stilling of vibrato for once disconcertingly extreme.

Symphonies 5; 6; (i) 9 (Choral)

(B) *** DG 2-CD (ADD) 474 260-2 (2). BPO, Karajan; (i) with Tomowa-Sintow, Baltsa, Schreier, Van Dam & V. Singverein

The triptych of Karajan's 1976–7 recordings has been shrewdly chosen for reissue in the 'Karajan Collection' to show the conductor at his very finest, with the clear, digital remastering still allowing ample full-bodied textures. The *Fifth* is magnificent in every way, tough and urgently incisive, with fast tempi bringing weight as well as excitement but no unwanted blatancy, even in the finale. The recording has a satisfyingly wide dynamic range. The *Pastoral* brought a more congenial recording than his earlier, excessively tense 1962 performance with the same orchestra. It is freshly alert, a good dramatic version with polished playing. The *Choral Symphony* remains among the very greatest recordings – see below – and here the remastering is remarkably clean and clear, without loss of weight and amplitude. Incidentally, the disc is additionally cued to mark the entry of the vocalists.

Symphonies 5; 7

●━ ✿ (M) *** DG (ADD) **SACD** 471 630-2; CD 447 400-2. VPO, C. Kleiber

(M) (***) EMI mono/stereo (ADD) 5 67851-2 [576852]. Philh. O, Klemperer

(B) *** CfP 572 849-2. RLPO, Mackerras

(N) (M) (***) DG (ADD) mono/stereo 474 984-2. BPO, Boehm

*** DG (IMS) 449 981-2. Philh. O, Thielemann

(M) **(*) DG Entrée 471 735-2. BPO, Karajan

(BB) **(*) Warner Apex 2564 60455-2. Sinfonia Varsovia, Y. Menuhin

(BB) (**) Naxos mono 8.110926. Berlin State Op. O, Richard Strauss

Symphonies 5; 8; Fidelio: Overture

(M) *** DG (ADD) 419 051-2. BPO, Karajan

In Carlos Kleiber's hands the first movement is electrifying but still has a hushed intensity. The slow movement is tender and delicate, with dynamic contrasts underlined but not exaggerated. In the Scherzo, the horns (like the rest of the VPO) are in superb form; the finale then emerges into pure daylight. In Kleiber's *Seventh*, symphonic argument never yields to the charm of the dance. Incisively dramatic, his approach relies on sharp dynamic contrasts and thrustful rhythms. A controversial point is that Kleiber, like his father, maintains the pizzicato for the strings on the final phrase of the *Allegretto*, a curious effect. The latest digital remastering has again greatly improved the sound, especially on SACD.

Klemperer never surpassed these EMI performances of either symphony, now coupled together as one of EMI's 'Great Recordings of the Century'. Both works have a clarity, immediacy and fidelity of balance that enhance electrifying readings, revealing Klemperer at his best. The *Fifth* is mono only, the *Seventh* stereo.

Sir Charles Mackerras and the Royal Liverpool Philharmonic also give revelatory performances of both the *Fifth* and *Seventh*. Tempi are on the fast side in all four movements but, thanks to rhythmic control, they never sound hectic. The superb recording is both weighty and atmospheric.

Karajan's 1977 version of the *Fifth* (419 051-2) is magnificent in every way, tough and urgently incisive, with fast tempi bringing weight as well as excitement. The coupling is an electrically intense performance of the *Eighth*, plus the *Fidelio Overture*.

Boehm's early recordings of the Beethoven symphonies with the Berlin Philharmonic were upstaged by the orchestra's later partnership with Karajan, and in the analogue-LP era Boehm was celebrated for his later sessions with the VPO, and in particular the *Pastoral Symphony*. This 1953 mono account of the *Fifth Symphony* was his recording début with DG and its excitement and vividness (especially in the finale) belie the idea that his mellow Austrian personality was somehow at odds with the extrovert passion that the work generates. The *Seventh Symphony*, recorded five years later in stereo, is more characteristically weighty, but there is no lack of adrenalin, and the codas of the outer movements bring a thrilling response from the horns. The orchestral playing is not only responsive but superb in ensemble too, with the *Allegretto* of No. 7 particularly beautifully played. The sound in both works reflects the excellent acoustic of the Berlin Jesus-Christus-Kirche and shows just how good DG engineering was in the early years of LP.

Christian Thielemann, opting for broad speeds and resonant textures, reminds one of the weighty Klemperer with this same orchestra – yet with speeds fluctuating in a manner far closer to Furtwängler. The results are magnetic; with outstanding playing from the Philharmonia and vivid digital recording, this is an excellent recommendation for anyone wanting a traditional view with modern sound.

For their entrée into the world of Beethoven symphonies DG have chosen Karajan's digital versions from his last series of recordings, made in the mid-1980s. The *Fifth* is characteristically strong and incisive, recorded in longer takes than previously. In the *Seventh* the bravura is again compelling, and there is no doubt about Karajan's overall command – but much is lost compared with his previous series. The *Allegretto*, taken characteristically fast, is so smooth that the dactylic rhythm at the start is almost unidentifiable. The recording is resonantly full but not as clearly defined in louder climaxes as in the earlier, analogue versions.

After the inevitable opening applause, Menuhin opens the *Fifth* unselfconsciously, if not very sharply, immediately setting a brisk tempo for the allegro, which is played comparatively lightly. The *Andante*, too, begins with a sense of delicate lyricism, and it is in the finale that the performance explodes into joyful illumination. The Allegro certainly dances along in the first movement of the *Seventh*, but here the pacing is relatively steady. The *Allegretto* is deeply eloquent and, as in the *Fifth*, it is the finale that carries the work to its exhilarating yet weighty conclusion. Playing and recording are well up to standard, though the ensemble could be crisper in the first movememt of the *Fifth*.

Richard Strauss, long recognized as a great Mozart interpreter, here demonstrates his mastery in relation to Beethoven. Recorded in the 1920s for what was designed as a Beethoven centenary project, these are above all dynamic, bitingly energetic performances, not always well disciplined but always magnetic. That is so despite the astonishingly fluid tempi, rarely staying quite the same for more than a few bars. In the *Fifth* the sound is limited, but the Naxos transfer is undistracting, never getting in the way of the performance. The *Seventh*, recorded in 1926 just as electrical recording was introduced, comes in drier sound, but the boxiness is something you get used to. Though the second-movement *Allegretto* is rather heavy, the rest is well sprung with a delightfully witty pay-off in the Scherzo. Sadly, the finale brings an enormous cut, designed to fit the movement on to a single 78 side.

Symphony 6 (Pastoral)

◑━ ☀ *** Sony **SACD** (ADD) SS 6012. Columbia SO, Bruno Walter

(M) *** DG (ADD) 447 433-2. VPO, Boehm – SCHUBERT: *Symphony 5* ***

(N) (BB) (***) Naxos mono 8.110877. BBC SO, Toscanini (with MOZART: *Die Zauberflöte: Overture*. ROSSINI: *La Scala di seta: Overture*. WEBER (arr. BERLIOZ): *Invitation to the Dance*. BRAHMS: *Tragic Overture*)

(M) (***) Cala mono CACD 0523. NY City SO, Stokowski – MOZART: *Sinfonia concertante, K.297b* (***)

**(*) Testament SBT2 1217 (2) (with rehearsal). BPO, Klemperer – BACH: *Suite 3 in D*; MOZART: *Symphony 29* **(*)

Symphony 6; Overtures: Coriolan; The Creatures of Prometheus; (i) Egmont: Overture; Incidental Music: Die Trommel gerühret; Freudvoll und leidvoll; Klärchens Tod, Op. 84

(M) *** EMI (ADD) 5 67965-2 [5 67966-2]. Philh. O, Klemperer; (i) with Nilsson

Symphony 6; Overtures: Coriolan; Fidelio; Leonora 2

(M) *** Warner Elatus 0927 49004-2. COE, Harnoncourt

Symphony 6; Overtures: Egmont; Leonora 3

(B) *** Decca 448 986-2. Philh. O, Ashkenazy

Symphony 6; Overture: Leonora 3

(B) **(*) EMI Red Line 5 72551. Phd. O, Muti

Sony's SACD remastering of Bruno Walter's 1958 recording gives the sound an astonishing facelift. The recording is subtly extended in range, notably in the middle and bass, yet there is remarkable added inner detail and a convincing sense of a concert-hall presence. In short, the result has a truly remarkable increase in naturalness and realism, and Walter's wonderfully affectionate performance communicates afresh. Of course, you can get this same performance coupled with the *Fourth Symphony* on an ordinary CD of quality (see above), while you need a special SACD player to reproduce the present issue. But this disc, together with Walter's companion version of Brahms's *Fourth Symphony*, demonstrates that an incompatible SACD has something special to offer.

However, these discs are unnecessarily expensive.

For its reissue as one of EMI's 'Great Recordings of the Century' Klemperer's outstanding account of the *Pastoral* has its previous couplings restored, with the *Coriolan Overture* thrown in for good measure. The extra items act as a prelude to the symphony, with Birgit Nilsson in her prime in the *Egmont* music, effectively cast in the two simple songs, the first made to sound almost Mahlerian. The recordings have been newly remastered by Ian Jones, and the 1957 Kingsway Hall recording of the symphony (transferred at a higher level than previously) now sounds astonishingly vivid, less confined. The *Storm* is very spectacular indeed with its thundering timpani, and the climax of the *Shepherd's Hymn* is thrilling in its power. Yet the warmth and resonant bass line are equally impressive.

Boehm's 1971 version of the *Pastoral* is as fine as any, a beautiful, unforced reading, one of the best-played and (in its day) one of the best-recorded. It still sounds fresh in its current reissue in DG's 'Originals' series with a Schubert coupling.

There is nothing over-tense about Harnoncourt's *Pastoral*, with the brook flowing freely and perhaps bubbling a little over the stream bed. The *Overtures*, recorded live at various venues, after all the symphonies were made, have plenty of character, *Coriolan* powerful in tragic atmosphere, and *Fidelio* and *Leonora No. 2* (with an impressive trumpet solo) not rushed but with plenty of impetus and exciting codas. Excellent sound too.

Ashkenazy's warm performance, thanks to spacious tempi, brings a feeling of lyrical ease and repose, with glowing playing from the Philharmonia and rich Kingsway Hall recording. The two overtures make a good bonus. An excellent bargain.

The famous Toscanini/BBC performance has often been reissued, and the present compilation and transfer can hold its own with the best. A useful reminder that the *Pastoral* with the BBC Symphony Orchestra, with its extra dimension of humanity, more than deserves its classic status.

With the first two movements youthfully urgent, Muti's is an exhilarating performance, fresh and direct. The recording is warm and wide-ranging, though the high violins do not always live up to the 'Philadelphia sound'.

The Cala CD offers Stokowski's first commercial recording of the *Pastoral*, made in Carnegie Hall in 1945. As Edward Johnson points out in his excellent notes, there is 'no want of rustic jollity in the opening movement', but 'Stokowski's *Scene by the Brook* is certainly more *Adagio* than *Andante*'. However, he sustains this leisurely tempo with affectionate ease and gives a radiant account of the finale. The violins sing out freshly and radiantly, and the only real complaint about the sound is the restricted dynamic range. A memorable account just the same.

When in May 1964 Otto Klemperer, aged 79, returned to Berlin to conduct the Berlin Philharmonic after a gap of over 40 years, the climax of the occasion, rapturously received, came with Beethoven's *Pastoral Symphony*. Only a few weeks earlier, Karajan had also conducted the same players in this very symphony, both live and on disc. As the 45-minute rehearsal sequence on the first disc demonstrates, Klemperer was intent on getting the orchestra to produce a distinctive Klemperer sound, making his version fresher, encouraging each soloist to play out individually, undermining the Karajan technique of blending the woodwind into a homogeneous whole. The result is fresh and dedicated, rustic and refined. The rehearsal sequence is spoken in German, but the booklet provides a helpful summary in English.

Symphonies 6; 8 in F, Op. 93
(M) (***) Sony mono SMK 89888. RPO, Beecham

As in his other Beethoven interpretations, Beecham treats the *Pastoral Symphony* as far more than an evocative programme-piece. He tends to prefer steady speeds. The result is wonderfully fresh as well as elegant, while he takes the *Andante* second movement at a slow tempo, finely pointed, allowing himself expressive freedom in the birdsong at the end. The rustic jollity of the Scherzo leads to a fiercely dramatic account of the *Storm* and an exuberant reading of the finale at a fast-flowing tempo. No. 8 is comparably brisk and buoyant in the outer movements, relaxed in the middle movements, with the second-movement *Allegretto* winningly sprung. Transfers of the mono 1951–2 recordings bring commendably clean textures with good inner detail.

Symphonies (i) 6; (ii) 8; (ii; iii) 9 *(Choral)*
(BB) **(*) EMI Gemini (ADD) 5 85490-2 (2). (i) New Philh. O; (ii) LSO; (iii) with Armstrong, Reynolds, Tear, Shirley-Quirk, LSO Ch.; Giulini

Giulini's is essentially a relaxed, lyrical approach to the *Pastoral Symphony* and, with fine playing from the New Philharmonia and full, atmospheric (1968) Abbey Road recording, the result is warm and attractive. The generally slow tempi will not please everyone and, interpretatively at least, the firmer Klemperer approach (also with slow tempi) is more consistently satisfying. Even so, Giulini's version is certainly enjoyable in its leisured progress.

Again in the *Choral Symphony* (recorded four years later, in Kingsway Hall) the tempo of the first movement is unusually slow – like Solti, Giulini insists on precise sextuplets for the opening tremolando, with no mistiness – and he builds the architecture relentlessly, finding his resolution only in the concluding coda. The Scherzo is lithe and powerful, with shattering timpani. The slow movement is warm and Elysian rather than hushed, while the finale, not always quite perfect in ensemble, is dedicatedly intense, helped by fine singing from soloists and chorus alike. The recording is close, immediate and full. The *Eighth Symphony* is less distinguished, but in its lyrical, moulded way remains warmly enjoyable, and the two-disc set is very reasonably priced.

Symphony 7 in A, Op. 92 (see also under *Missa solemnis*, below)
(M) *** BBC BBCL 4076-2. Hallé O, Barbirolli – MOZART: *Symphony 35* ***; WAGNER: *Siegfried Idyll* (***)
*(**) BBC (ADD) BBCL 4005-2. BBC SO, Stokowski – BRITTEN: *Young Person's Guide* **(*); FALLA: *El amor brujo* *** ✪

Barbirolli's live account was recorded by BBC engineers at the Royal Festival Hall in April 1968, with bright, full stereo sound in which the horns bray out superbly. After a weighty account of the slow introduction he then adopts a tempo for the main Allegro which allows plenty of spring in the dotted 6/8 rhythms. The finale too is taken at a tempo which permits fair articulation of the string semiquavers, and characteristically Barbirolli keeps the tempo steadier than most, even through the plain dotted episodes which so often invite a speeding up. Conversely, Barbirolli's speeds for the middle two movements are on the fast side, with an aptly flowing *Allegretto* and a really fast presto for the Scherzo where, following the custom of the time, he omits most of the repeats. With typically warm-hearted accounts of the Mozart

and Wagner items for coupling, this makes a splendid addition to the Barbirolli discography.

Stokowski's reading sounds pretty breathtaking too and has great power and concentration. It is a performance of high contrasts, with the first movement pressed hard and the slow speed for the *Allegretto* made persuasive through subtle phrasing and rhythmic control. Stokowski then mutilates the Scherzo by eliminating the second reprise of the Trio and the third repeat of the Scherzo proper. Nevertheless, this is an exceptional performance. The couplings are outstanding (the Falla in particular is stunning) and the sound very good for its age.

Symphony 7; (i) Egmont (Overture and Incidental Music)
*** Simax PSC 1182. Swedish CO, Dausgaard; (i) with Bonde-Hansen

Recordings of Beethoven symphonies using limited forces have become relatively common but, far more than most, Dausgaard's version of the *Seventh Symphony* and *Egmont* incidental music captures an intimate scale while losing nothing in power and bite. Speeds are on the fast side and textures clear, with the small string section sharply focused and horns braying dramatically. The *Egmont* music begins with an astonishingly brisk account of the *Overture*, minutes shorter than usual; but it works dramatically, with a big pause on 'Egmont's death' and an exhilarating account of the 'Battle Symphony' coda – repeated later at the end of the suite. Henriette Bonde-Hansen is the fresh-toned soprano in the two songs, given a less forward balance than usual for a soloist.

Symphonies 7; 8
*** EMI 5 57570-2. VPO, Rattle
*** DG 471 490-2 BPO, Abbado
(BB) **(*) Arte Nova 74321 56341-2. Zürich Tonhalle O, Zinman
(B) **(*) EMI Red Line 5 69785. Phd. O, Muti
(N) **(*) Häns. CD93.087. Stuttgart RSO, Norrington

Symphonies 7; 8. Overture: The Ruins of Athens
(M) *** Warner Elatus 0927 49620-2. COE, Harnoncourt

Rattle's live recording brings an account of the *Seventh* that is at once warm and weighty, with the dotted dance-rhythms of the main Allegro deliciously pointed, and an element of mystery conveyed in the sudden *pianissimos*. The second-movement *Allegretto* flows easily, marked by sharp *sforzandos* and high dynamic contrasts. The Scherzo, crisply done, has dramatic contrasts too, and the finale is fast – but not so fast as to imperil clarity or rhythmic lift. The *Eighth* brings a joyful performance, conveyed the more clearly in a live recording, with wit in the second-movement *Allegretto* and weight as well as clarity in the outer movements.

Abbado's coupling of Nos. 7 and 8, taken from his complete Berlin cycle, recorded live, brings performances at generally brisk speeds that combine robust power and refinement. The result is more impressive even than his highly praised earlier coupling with the VPO (currently withdrawn). Dynamic contrasts are heightened, and the description 'Little One' of No. 8 is again in no way apt, when the outer movements are so dramatic and the middle two winningly direct, avoiding mere charm while maintaining refinement. Only in the hectic tempo for the finale is there a reservation, when the recording, well balanced in the Philharmonie, obscures the rapid semiquaver articulation. But this remains an outstanding disc.

In the outer movements of Harnoncourt's wonderfully spirited *Seventh* the horns shine out, adding to the joyous release after an *Allegretto* full of under-the-surface tension. No. 8 has drama and resilience too. The overture, opening atmospherically (the horns again impressive, but in a gentler, more lyrical way), soon becomes animated and generates much energy yet with the woodwind retaining the light-hearted spirit.

Zinman's coupling of Nos. 7 and 8 has similar qualities to his earlier, less recommendable coupling of Nos. 5 and 6. That works very well in No. 7, with speeds on the brisk side, which still have rhythmic resilience, notably in the *Allegretto*. In No. 8 Zinman, like Toscanini, takes a rather fierce view of this most compact of the symphonies, with a clipped manner and a fast speed in the first movement and with little or no charm in the middle movements. With clean, crisp ensemble and vivid recording, the power of the piece is reinforced.

The vigour and drive of Muti's account of the *Seventh* are never in doubt – but, surprisingly, the ensemble of the Philadelphia Orchestra is not immaculate. There is spontaneity, but it is paid for by a lack of precision. The *Eighth* is also lively, and it brings greater polish.

As in the rest of Norrington's Stuttgart cycle, the *Seventh* brings a period-style performance on modern instruments, which has both gains and losses compared with his earlier, EMI recording with the London Classical Players. The first movement is even faster than before, but still with a winning rustic spring in the 6/8 rhythms. The *Allegretto* is also faster, more clipped and more metrical, but the fast speeds in the Scherzo and finale are more effective, with the timpani in the finale adding to the impact. In No. 8 the extra weight of modern instruments adds to the impact of the climactic recapitulation in the first movement, but the second-movement *Allegretto* is not just faster but less relaxed than before, and the last two movements also bring a more clipped style.

Symphonies (i) 7; (ii) 9 *(Choral), Op. 125*
(N) (**(*))EMI **DVD** 5 999399. (i) ORTF PO, Ansermet; (ii) Giebel, Hoffgen, Haefliger, Neidlinger, New Philh. Ch. & O, Klemperer

It is fascinating to watch the aged Klemperer fluttering his fingers and inspiring a titanic performance from his New Philharmonia forces. This was in November 1964, barely six months after Walter Legge had attempted to disband the Philharmonia. In this performance at the Royal Albert Hall, the whole ensemble seems determined to demonstrate that even with the adjective 'New' inserted before the name, the results could be just as powerful as before. The Klemperer interpretation is well established, with a first movement of granite strength and a measured, well-sprung Scherzo which, with all the repeats taken, lasts longer than the slow movement. At a flowing speed Klemperer makes that sublime movement easily lyrical rather than portentous, leaving the drama till the choral finale, with four splendid soloists and an incandescent choir. In this black-and-white film the sound is limited but very acceptable. As a bonus item comes Ansermet's reading of the *Seventh* with the ORTF Philharmonic. It reminds us that though Ansermet was always associated with exotic and modern music, he was a stylish Beethovenian, securing crisp and lightly sprung playing from the orchestra in this 'apotheosis of the dance', even though the second-movement *Allegretto* is slower than we would expect today. The sound in this 1967 black-and-white video is brighter than in the Klemperer, but still limited.

Symphony 9 in D min. *(Choral), Op. 125*
(N) **(*) Arthaus **DVD** 100 296. Hruba-Freiberger, Soffel, Wagner, Howell, Leipzig Gewandhaus Ch. & O, Masur (V/D: Rodney Greenberg)

*** EMI 5 57572. Bonney, Remmert, Streit, Hampson, CBSO Ch., VPO, Rattle

(B) *** CfP 575 9882. Rodgers, D. Jones, Bronder, Terfel, RLPO Ch. & O, Mackerras

(BB) *** Arte Nova 74321 65411-2. Ziesak, Remmert, Davislim, Roth, Swiss Chamber Ch., Zurich Tonhalle O, Zinman

*** DG 471 491-2. Mattila, Urmana, Moser, Quasthoff, Swedish R. Ch., Ericson Ch., BPO, Abbado

(N) (M) *** Sony 516 230-2 [SK 93011]. Eaglen, Meier, Heppner, Terfel, Swedish R. Ch., Ericson Chamber Ch., BPO, Abbado *(with Creatures of Prometheus: Finale)*

*** Testament SBT 1177. Nordmo-Løvberg, Ludwig, Kmentt, Hotter, Philh. Ch. & O, Klemperer

(M) *** DG (compatible) **SACD** (ADD) 471 640-2; CD 415 832-2. Tomowa-Sintow, Baltsa, Schreier, Van Dam, V. Singverein, BPO, Karajan

*** DG (ADD) (IMS) 429 861-2. Anderson, Walker, König, Rootering, various Chs., Bav. RSO, Dresden State O, etc., Bernstein

(BB) *** Warner Apex 2564 60456-2. Glennon, Schaechter, Janutas, Schollum, Lithuania Kaunas State Ch., Sinfonia Varsovia, Y. Menuhin

*** DG 447 074-2. Orgonasova, Von Otter, Rolfe Johnson, Cachemaille, Monteverdi Ch., ORR, Gardiner

(M) (***) EMI mono 5 66901-2 [5 66953-2]. Schwarzkopf, Höngen, Hopf, Edelmann, Bayreuth Festival Ch. & O, Furtwängler

(M) *** DG 445 503-2. Norman, Fassbaender, Domingo, Berry, V. State Op. Ch., VPO, Boehm

(M) *** Teldec Elatus 0927 46736-2. Margiono, Remmert, Schasching, Holl, Arnold Schoenberg Ch., COE, Harnoncourt

(BB) *** Naxos 8.553478. Papian, Donose, Fink, Otelli, Nicolaus Esterházy Ch. & O, Drahos

**(*) DG 439 006-2. Perry, Baltsa, Cole, Van Dam, V. Singverein, BPO, Karajan

(**(*)) Testament mono SBT 1332. Giebel, Ludwig, Lewis, Berry, Philh. Ch. & O, Klemperer

(M) **(*) DG (ADD) 463 626-2. (i) Seefried, Forrester, Haefliger, Fischer-Dieskau, St Hedwig's Cathedral Ch., BPO, Fricsay

(M) **(*) Virgin 5 61378-2. Kenny, Walker, Power, Salomaa, Schütz Ch., LCP, Norrington

(N) (M) *(*) DG Entrée 477 500-2. Benacková, Lipovsek, Winberg, Prey, V. State Op. Concert Assoc. Ch., VPO, Abbado

(i) *Symphony 9; Overture: Coriolan*
(M) *** DG (ADD) 447 401-2. (i) Janowitz, Rössl-Majdan, Kmentt, Berry, V. Singverein; BPO, Karajan

(i) *Symphony 9. Overture: Fidelio*
(B) **(*) Sony (ADD) SBK 46533. (i) Addison, Hobson, Lewis, Bell, Cleveland O Ch.; Cleveland O, Szell

(i) *Symphony 9;* (ii) *Choral Fantasia*
(BB) (**(*)) Naxos mono 8.110824. Westminster Ch., NBC SO, Toscanini, with (i) Novotna, Thorborg, Peerce, Moscona; (ii) Dorfman

Rattle's live Beethoven cycle with the Vienna Philharmonic is crowned by an outstanding reading of the *Choral Symphony*. Mystery and power are combined in the first movement, with speeds in the Scherzo not so extreme as to undermine rhythmic point. Where throughout his cycle Rattle has taken clear but undogmatic note of the lessons of period performance, in the slow movement of the *Ninth* he allows himself full expansiveness in a refined and dedicated reading which brings out the contrast between the two variation themes, *Adagio* and *Andante*. Clearly Rattle is unafraid of facing the visionary qualities of this music, so easily minimized by fast speeds. In the finale Rattle benefits from an outstanding quartet of soloists and a warmly robust choir (his own CBSO Chorus). Here more than ever, Rattle gains from the thrust and exhilaration of a live recording, finely balanced.

Mackerras conducts the Royal Liverpool Philharmonic in an inspired account of the *Ninth*, one which has learnt from the lessons of period performance, and, like period specialists, Sir Charles has taken careful note of Beethoven's controversial metronome markings. The recording is outstanding, warm yet transparent and with plenty of body; and the singing in the finale is fine, even if the tenor, Peter Bronder, is on the strenuous side.

David Zinman, too, crowns his Beethoven cycle with a magnificent account of the *Ninth*, using the new Bärenreiter Edition, opting for the fast speeds which have latterly come to be thought authentic, always giving the music the deeper qualities needed and with a sense of hushed dedication in the slow movement, even when taken at a flowing speed. The finale crowns his performance, with the chamber chorus not only fresh and dramatic but deeply dedicated too in the prayerful sections. The soloists are an excellent team of young-sounding singers, and the sound is full and well balanced. On a separate track the last half of the finale is given in an alternative version, with a pause included towards the end, representing Beethoven's first thoughts, later amended.

Already in his live recording of the *Ninth* for Sony (see below), made in 1996, Abbado indicated that his approach to Beethoven was changing, influenced by a study of period practice. Here in his 2000 version, recorded as part of his complete cycle for DG, he takes the process a step further, even faster and more incisive in the first movement, sharper and cleaner in the Scherzo, and even more flowing in the slow movement as well as deeply dedicated. Though in the finale the new account does not quite find the degree of relaxed joy of the 1996 version, the extra incisiveness and fine solo and choral singing, with big dynamic contrasts, make for a very exciting conclusion to a performance which overall is among the very finest available.

Claudio Abbado on Sony directs a recording made at the 1996 Salzburg Easter Festival. Throughout, it captures the electricity of a great occasion. The finale with a superb quartet of soloists and fine Swedish choirs brings the feeling of climax too often missing in recordings of the *Ninth*. Highly recommended; although the bonus of a snippet from the *Creatures of Prometheus* incidental music is hardly generous.

The previously unpublished live recording of Klemperer conducting Beethoven's *Ninth* on Testament is magnetic from beginning to end. The occasion at the Royal Festival Hall in November 1957 was the very first concert of the newly founded Philharmonia Chorus – the culmination of Klemperer's first Beethoven symphony cycle in London. He followed that up immediately by recording the *Ninth* in the studio with exactly the same forces; but in all four movements this live performance has an extra bite and intensity at

marginally faster speeds. In every way it is preferable to the published EMI studio recording, when even the sound is both warmer and kinder to the voices.

Of the three stereo recordings Karajan has made of the *Ninth*, his 1976 account (415 832-2) is the most inspired, above all in the *Adagio*, where he conveys spiritual intensity at a slower tempo than before. In the finale, the concluding eruption has an animal excitement rarely heard from this highly controlled conductor. The soloists make an excellent team. The sound has fine projection and drama. This 1976 Karajan recording, newly remastered, is also available in a two-CD set (see above) together with the *Fifth* and *Sixth Symphonies* and on a single-disc SACD version, which can be played either on a normal CD player or on a SACD/DVD player. However, we cannot feel there is any noticeable advantage here unless the surround sound effect is essential.

Recorded live on the morning of Christmas Day 1989 after the fall of the Berlin Wall, Bernstein's version brings a historic performance that has something special to say, not only because Bernstein substitutes the word '*Freiheit*', 'Freedom', for '*Freude*', 'Joy', in the choral finale. The orchestra, drawn mainly from Germany, also included players of the Kirov Theatre Orchestra in Leningrad, the New York Philharmonic, the Orchestre de Paris and the LSO. The choirs similarly came from East and West Germany, while the soloists represented four countries: America (June Anderson), Britain (Sarah Walker), Germany (Klaus König) and Holland (Jan-Hendrik Rootering). For many, the uniqueness of this version and the emotions it conveys will make it a first choice, despite obvious flaws.

Though the opening applause is distracting and the first movement is less biting than the rest, the *Choral Symphony* here brings a fitting culmination to Menuhin's cycle, thanks also to the fresh, clear singing of the Lithuanian choir and a young, rather lightweight quartet of soloists. Following the Gardiner thesis, the drum-and-fife sequence in the finale of No. 9 is taken very fast, like a French military march. But with a deeply felt slow movement, this must be counted among the very finest of performances on modern instruments at bargain price.

With Gardiner there is no mystery in the tremolos at the start of the *Ninth*, but the movement at its brisk speed builds up inexorably. The slow movement is far faster than usual but still conveys repose. The finale is urgent and dramatic, and the quartet of fresh-voiced soloists is exceptionally strong. An exuberant conclusion confirms this as a clear first choice among period versions.

As bitingly dramatic as Toscanini in the first movement and electrically intense throughout, Szell directs a magnetic account of the *Ninth* which demonstrates the glories of the Cleveland Orchestra. The chorus sings with similar knife-edged ensemble, set behind the orchestra. The performance of the *Fidelio Overture* is electrifying.

It is thrilling to have such a splendid new transfer of Furtwängler's historic recording, made at the reopening of the Festspielhaus in Bayreuth in 1951. The chorus may not be ideally focused in the background, and the audience noises are the more apparent on CD, but the extra clarity and freshness impressively enhance a reading without parallel. The spacious, lovingly moulded account of the slow movement is among Furtwängler's finest achievements on record and, with an excellent quartet of soloists, the finale crowns a performance fully worthy of reissue among EMI's 'Great Recordings of the Century'.

Karl Boehm's reading is spacious and powerful. Overall there is a sense of a great occasion; the concentration is unfailing, reaching its peak in the glorious finale, rugged and strong, with a fine, characterful team of soloists and a freshly incisive chorus of singers from the Vienna State Opera. Strongly recommendable.

Karajan's 1962 version (447 401-2) is less hushed and serene in the slow movement than either of his later versions, but the finale blazes even more intensely, with Janowitz's contribution radiant in its purity. This reflected the electricity of the Berlin sessions, when it rounded off a cycle recorded over two weeks. The *Coriolan* coupling is an added bonus.

For some listeners the fast pace of the slow movement of Harnoncourt's *Ninth* will seem a drawback, but otherwise the performance caps the cycle splendidly, with a very compelling account of the finale.

Béla Drahos with his outstanding chamber orchestra from Budapest gives a refreshingly direct performance of the *Ninth*, typically dramatic, with the *Adagio* following period practice in its flowing speed, sweet and beautifully moulded rather than hushed. With a superb chorus and well-matched soloists, the finale is urgently intense, working to a superb climax. Exceptionally vivid and full sound, well detailed.

The high point of Karajan's digital version of the *Ninth* (439 006-2) is the sublime slow movement, here exceptionally sweet and true, with the lyricism all the more persuasive in a performance recorded in a complete take. The power and dynamism of the first two movements are also striking, but the choral finale is flawed above all by the singing of the soprano, Janet Perry, far too thin of tone and unreliable. The sound of the choir has plenty of body, and definition has been improved in this remastered version.

In December 1939 Toscanini rounded off his Beethoven symphony cycle in New York with these apocalyptic performances of the *Ninth* and the *Choral Fantasia* on Naxos, and the atmosphere of a great occasion comes over vividly. Quite apart from the searing thrust and drama of his approach to both works, it is good to have in the slow movement a keener impression than usual of Toscanini's ability to mould phrases affectionately with hushed intensity. The soloists in the *Ninth* make a superb quartet, with the firm dark bass, Nicola Moscona, particularly impressive. Ania Dorfman's solo playing in the *Choral Fantasia* is marked by a bright tone and diamond-clear articulation. The Naxos transfers, though very limited, have more body than most in this Toscanini series.

Recorded by the BBC in November 1961, Klemperer (on Testament) conducts another searingly powerful performance, well worth preserving, even if in mono only; though with surface noise marring the slow movement, it does not displace the 1957 version, also recorded live in the Royal Festival Hall but in stereo, which also appeared on Testament (SBT 1177). In 1961 Klemperer had just had phenomenal success conducting Beethoven's *Fidelio* at Covent Garden (the opening performance also issued on Testament), and the exhilaration of that achievement is reflected in the *Ninth*, with a ruggedly powerful first movement, a measured but well-sprung Scherzo and a songful slow movement. In all those movements Klemperer is marginally faster than in 1957. Though the finale starts with some untidy ensemble, the electricity of the performance is irresistible, gaining over the 1957 version (and Klemperer's studio version for EMI) in having a finer quartet of soloists.

On DVD comes Kurt Masur, who recorded his video version of Beethoven's *Ninth* in November 1991, when he returned from his post in New York to conduct the orchestra of which he had been music director for so long. It is a strong and biting performance, evidently made warmer by Masur's preference for not using a baton. In the slow movement he draws fine legato from the Leipzig strings, and the choral finale is predictably powerful, even though the chorus is backwardly placed, sounding muffled. Gwynne Howell leads a good but not outstanding quartet of soloists. The camerawork is conventional, but effective enough.

Fricsay's account of the *Ninth* was the first to come out in stereo in the late 1950s. It is undoubtedly a significant performance, well shaped and full of vitality, though tempi are fairly broad, save in the Scherzo. The *Adagio* is particularly beautiful, and only the finale seems lacking in weight. The recording is well balanced (the soloists forward, but the chorus well in the picture) and sounds remarkably good for its age, and though this is not as recommendable as Karajan or Boehm, it is finer than we had remembered it, and a fair choice for inclusion among DG's 'Originals'. The overture is played as an introduction.

Sharp, exhilarating intensity comes over in Norrington's Virgin reading of the *Ninth*, with many of Beethoven's fast metronome markings justified in the results, even the fast-slowing speed for the *Adagio*. A serious snag is the singing of the male soloists, with the baritone, Petteri Salomaa, tremulous, and the plaintive-sounding tenor, Patrick Power, cruelly exposed in the drum-and-fife march passage, taken slowly. Reverberant recording still allows the bite of timpani and valveless horns to cut through the texture.

It was surprising that in his early Beethven cycle, recorded live with the Vienna Philharmonic, Abbado gave such a surprisingly tentative account of the *Ninth* – at least in the first three movements. At generally slow speeds, much of the recording sounds too cautious, as though the conductor is self-consciously looking over his shoulder at great predecessors like Furtwängler. The phrasing often comes to sound self-conscious too. The choral finale works better than the rest, thanks to some good solo and choral singing, but with variable sound – the chorus is ill-focused – this is not competitive and is a disappointing DG choice for an Entrée into the great classics.

Wellington's Victory (Battle Symphony), Op. 91

⊕ (M) *** Mercury (ADD) 434 360-2. Cannon & musket fire directed by Gerard C. Stowe, LSO, Dorati (with separate descriptive commentary by Deems Taylor) – TCHAIKOVSKY: *1812*, etc. *** ⊕

This most famous of all Mercury records was one of the most successful classical LPs of all time, selling some two million copies in the analogue era. Remastered for CD, it sounds even more spectacular than it ever did in its vinyl format, vividly catching Beethoven's musical picture of armies clashing. The presentation, with handsome colour reproductions of appropriate paintings (and excellent documentation), is a model of its kind.

CHAMBER MUSIC

Cello Sonatas 1–5; 7 Variations on 'Bei Männern, welche Liebe fühlen', WoO 46; 12 Variations on 'Ein Mädchen oder Weibchen', Op. 66 (both from Mozart's Die Zauberflöte); 12 Variations on Handel's 'See the conqu'ring hero comes' (from Judas Maccabaeus), WoO45)

⊕➤ (N) *** Ph. 475 379-2 (2). Adrian & Alfred Brendel

This new set of Beethoven's *Cello Sonatas* (and *Variations*) is among the finest ever on disc and is now a clear first choice.

Not only is Adrian Brendel a marvellous artist in his own right, with a clean, pure tone and naturally musical phrasing, but he also inspires his father to spontaneously imaginative playing of the kind that has sometimes eluded him in the recording studio. There are countless details in Alfred Brendel's playing that reveal how thoughtful is his approach to the piano part, which his son matches at every turn. The recording is out of Philips's top drawer, admirably truthful and naturally balanced.

Cello Sonatas 1–2, Op. 5/1–2; (i) 3, Op. 69; 4–5, Op. 102/1–2

☛ (***) EMI **DVD** mono 492848-9. Rostropovich, Richter (Bonus: MENDELSSOHN: *Variations sérieuses* (for piano) (***))

The Rostropovich/Richter DVD was recorded at the Edinburgh Festival in 1964 at a mammoth Usher Hall recital, which, incidentally, began at midnight! Now we can see as well as hear the extraordinary rapport between the two and the intensity of their expressive dialogue. Both artists were in their prime, and Richter never subsequently played these sonatas again. The camerawork is a model of discretion and we are spared the hyperactivity of present-day TV camera technique and allowed to concentrate on the poetic feeling, virtuosity and finesse of this great partnership. The BBC sound balance is actually more natural than the much closer and brighter Philips recording, and there is a splendid bonus in the form of a studio recording of the Mendelssohn *Variations sérieuses*, which Richter made in the late 1950s in Moscow. Here the camerawork is pretty austere (we stay on one angle for long time) but none the worse for that. Although he played the Mendelssohn many times in the 1960s, Richter never recorded it commercially (though there was apparently a pirate LP). In any event, his playing is quite electrifying.

Cello Sonatas 1–2, Op. 5/1–2; 3, Op. 69; 4–5, Op. 102/1–2; 7 Variations on 'Bei Männern'; 12 Variations on 'Ein Mädchen', both from 'Die Zauberflöte', WoO 66

(M) (**(*)) Sony mono 515304-2 (2). Casals, Serkin

These performances come from Prades in 1953, save for the *G minor*, Op. 5, No. 2, and the *Variations*, which were made in Perpignan two years earlier. They are strong, finely shaped accounts that, like the Piatigorsky–Solomon set from the mid-1950s or the Fournier–Schnabel 78s, bring us closer to the spirit of these pieces than most of their successors (Rostropovich and Richter excepted). Serkin is occasionally more aggressive than was Horszowski in their versions; with the latter, one is unaware of the piano's hammers. Some allowances have to be made for the recorded sound, but these transfers are better than any predecessor we have heard.

Cello Sonatas 1–5

(B) *** Ph. (ADD) 464 677-2 (2). Rostropovich, Richter

(***) Testament mono SBT 2158 (2). Piatigorsky, Solomon – BRAHMS: *Sonata 1*; WEBER: *Sonata in A* (***)

Cello Sonatas 1–2, Op. 5/1–2; (i) 3, Op. 69; 4–5, Op. 102/1–2

(BB) (***) Naxos mono 8.1101949/50. Casals, Horszowski or (i) Schulhof (with *Minuet in G*) – BRAHMS: *Cello Sonata 2* (***)

Cello Sonatas 1–2, Op. 5/1–2; Horn Sonata, Op. 15 (arr. cello); 7 Variations on 'Bei Männern'

(BB) *** Naxos 8.555785. Kliegel, Tichman

Cello Sonata in E flat, Op. 64; Cello Sonata 3 in A, Op. 69; Variations on 'Ein Mädchen, Op. 66

(BB) **(*) Naxos 8.555786. Kliegel, Tichman

Cello Sonatas 1–5; 7 Variations on 'Bei Männern'; 12 Variations on 'Ein Mädchen'

(M) **(*) Sony SM2K 89870 (2). Ma, Ax

(i) Cello Sonatas 1–5; (ii) 7 Variations on 'Bei Männern'; 12 Variations on 'Ein Mädchen'; 12 Variations on 'See the conqu'ring hero comes', WoO 45

(B) *** Ph. (ADD) Duo 442 565-2 (2). (i) Rostropovich, Richter; (ii) Gendron, Françaix

(N) (BB) *** EMI Gemini (ADD) 586242-2 (2). Du Pré, Barenboim

(B) *** DG Double (ADD) 453 013-2 (2). Fournier, Kempff

(B) *** EMI (ADD) 5 69422-2 (2). P. Tortelier, Heidsieck

(B) **(*) Hyp. Dyad CDD 22004 (2). Pleeth, Tan (fortepiano)

(i–ii) Cello Sonatas 1–5; (ii–iii) Horn Sonata in F, Op. 17

(B) *** Double Decca ADD/DDD 466 733-2 (2). (i) Harrell; (ii) Ashkenazy; (iii) Tuckwell

Made in the early 1960s, the Philips performances by Mstislav Rostropovich and Sviatoslav Richter, two of the instrumental giants of the day, have withstood the test of time astonishingly well and sound remarkably fresh in this transfer. The performances of the *Variations* by Maurice Gendron and Jean Françaix have an engagingly light touch and are beautifully recorded. The Rostropovich–Richter set has been effectively remastered and has (rightly) been included in the Philips collection of '50 Great Recordings'. But the *Variations* are not included (the two discs together play for 109 minutes), so the Duo alternative is obviously preferable.

The Harrell–Ashkenazy mid-1980s performances are very fine too: they are unfailingly sensitive and alert, well thought out and yet seemingly spontaneous, with superb digital recording. The inclusion in this Double Decca issue of the *Horn Sonata*, equally recommendable (from 1974), makes this particularly attractive for those who regard sound-quality to be of importance.

The set of performances by Jacqueline du Pré with Daniel Barenboim was recorded live for the BBC during the Edinburgh Festival of 1970. The playing may not have the final polish of a studio-made version, but the concentration and intensity of the playing are wonderfully caught.

Fournier and Kempff also recorded their cycle of the sonatas at live festival performances. These fine artists were inspired by the occasion to produce unexaggeratedly expressive playing and to give performances which are marked by their light, clear textures and rippling scale-work, even in the slow introductions, taken relatively fast. In this remastering as a DG Double, the sound is beautifully clear.

The Tortelier set with Eric Heidsieck dates from the early 1970s. The performances are distinguished and make a useful alternative, with a bolder style than that of Fournier and Kempff on DG. The CD transfer is natural and clean.

Casals recorded the *A major Sonata*, Op. 69, with Otto Schulhof in 1930, the *Minuet in G* occupying the last side. He subsequently recorded the *C major*, Op. 102, No. 1, with Mieczyslaw Horszowski and completed the set in Paris not long before the outbreak of war. Their magisterial set of the Brahms comes from 1936 and was long the yardstick by which newcomers were judged – including Casals's subsequent post-war versions.

With the Sony set from Yo-Yo Ma and Emanuel Ax there

are balance problems in the first two (Op. 5) sonatas, with the piano often masking the refined lines drawn by Ma. In the remaining sonatas, Opp. 69 and 102, the balance is much better judged and throughout the sound-quality is well focused and truthful. Ax often produces a big, wide-ranging tone which must have posed problems when related to the more introvert style of the cellist. Ma plays with great sensitivity and imagination, even if there are times when one might think his *pianissimo* a bit overdone. The two sets of Mozartian variations have been added for the reissue, but not the companion Handel set.

The Piatigorsky–Solomon 1954 performances have an aristocratic poise and a patrician elegance that put them in the highest class. The recordings are in mono, and the transfers by Paul Bailey present them in the best possible light.

Though the cello is balanced rather forwardly in relation to the fortepiano, the Hyperion collection makes an attractive issue for anyone wanting period versions. Despite the balance, it is Tan who easily dominates the set and makes the *Allegros* sparkle, notably in the *Variations*.

On her first Naxos disc Maria Kliegel's playing instantly conveys a natural gravity and magnetism. With subtle tonal shading the dedication of the slow sections is sharply contrasted with the exuberance of the *Allegros*, with the American pianist, Nina Tichman, an excellent partner, clear and incisive, springing rhythms infectiously. The variations on the theme from *Die Zauberflöte* are regularly included in sets of the Beethoven cello sonatas, but it is rare to have the *Horn Sonata* given in its cello adaptation. Though not all the horn writing fits the cello well – as at the very start – Kliegel and Tichman give a fresh, compelling performance, like the rest very well recorded.

Maria Kliegel's second Naxos CD continues with an attractively varied recital which can again be confidently recommended. Although the *A major Sonata*, one of the masterpieces of Beethoven's middle period, and the *Zauberflöte* variations (most engagingly presented here) are generously represented on CD, the *E flat Sonata*, Op. 64 is more of a rarity. It is, in fact, a transcription, possibly by Beethoven himself, of the *D major String Trio*, Op. 3, of 1794, and it was published by Artaria the year before its Op. 69 companion. As before, excellent performances and fine recording.

Cello Sonatas 1 in F, Op. 5/1; in E flat, Op. 64 (arr. of String Trio, Op. 3). Variations on Handel's 'See the conqu'ring hero comes', WoO 45
(BB) *** Warner Apex 0927 49595-2. Karttunen, Hakkila (fortepiano)

Cello Sonatas: 2 in F, Op. 17 (trans. of Horn Sonata); 7 Variations on 'Bei Männern'; 12 Variations on 'Ein Mädchen'
(BB) *** Warner Apex 2564 60626-2. Karttunen, Hakkila (fortepiano)

Two discs of Beethoven's works for cello and keyboard, sonatas that were the first of their kind. These Finnish artists play them on instruments of the period, a Benjamin Banks cello from 1770 and a reproduction 1795 Walter fortepiano; and moreover they play them with something of the excitement of first discovery. They have energy, imagination and a fine sense of pace. The recordings, which come from the mid-1990s Finlandia label, also have a lot to recommend them.

Cello Sonata 3 in A, Op. 69
(M) (***) EMI mono 5 67008-2. Casals, Schulhof – BACH: (Unaccompanied) *Cello Suite 1;* BRAHMS: *Cello Sonata 2* (***)

For the *A major Sonata*, way back in 1930, Casals chose Otto Schulhof. He is a thoughtful pianist and their playing is wonderfully natural, unforced and musical. The frail, dry sound soon ceases to worry the experienced ear.

Clarinet Trio in B flat, Op. 11
(M) *** CRD (ADD) 3345. Nash Ens. (with ARCHDUKE RUDOLPH OF AUSTRIA: *Clarinet Trio in B flat* ***)

The Nash Ensemble's account of Beethoven's *Clarinet Trio* has a royal rarity as a coupling. Archduke Rudolph was a son of the Austrian Emperor, but his claim to fame is as a pupil and friend of Beethoven. His *Clarinet Trio* is incomplete: of the closing rondo only a fragment survives, and this performance ends with the slow movement, a set of variations on a theme by yet another prince, Louis Ferdinand of Prussia. The playing is thoroughly persuasive, with some attractive pianism from the excellent Clifford Benson. Much the same goes for the performance of the Beethoven *Trio*, and this is well worth investigating for interest.

Horn Sonata in F, Op. 17
(N) (BB) *** Naxos 8.557471. Tomboeck, Inui – BRAHMS: *Horn Trio;* SCHUBERT: *Auf dem Strom;* SCHUMANN: *Adagio and Allegro in A flat* ***
*** HM HMC 90 9250. Müller, Torbianelli – DANZI; RIES: *Horn Sonatas* ***

The distinctively fruity sound of the Vienna horn is wonderfully caught on the superb Naxos disc with its programme perfectly designed to show off the instrument. Wolfgang Tomboeck, first horn in the Vienna Philharmonic since 1980 and the son of a former principal horn, comes from a family of musicians, and here in all four works he demonstrates what a fine artist he is. His playing is fearless on this notoriously tricky instrument with its seemingly easy bravura, with the most hair-raisingly difficult passages delivered with flair and panache. The Beethoven *Horn Sonata* brings a stylish performance, crisp in attack, yet warm too, with the brief central *Adagio* given the gravity of a funeral march before the sparkling finale. The piano sound is relatively lightweight, which Madoka Inui with her clean articulation turns to advantage in suggesting the sound of a fortepiano.

As Thomas Müller shows here, Beethoven's very classical *Horn Sonata* gains much character from a period instrument with stopped notes. How striking is the opening theme of the first movement (after the bold fanfare) played on the hand horn used here, with the stopped note undisguised at the end of the first phrase. Eduardo Torbianelli's fortepiano, too, makes a naturally supportive partnership. Müller plays with great spirit, and then in the brief *Poco Adagio* he achieves a wan, gentle melancholy, so that the joy of the finale is the more infectious. (Again the ear soon notices the stopped notes.) This is coupled with two other sonatas, and that by Danzi pays its respects to the Beethoven model.

(i) Horn Sonata in F, Op. 17; (ii) Sextet for Horn & Strings, Op. 81b
(B) *** EMI Debut 5 72822-2. (i) Clark, Govier; (ii) Ens. Galant, Montgomery – BRAHMS: *Horn Trio;* MOZART: *Horn Quintet, etc.* ***

Andrew Clark consistently relishes the ripe, fruity, often

tangy tone of the Waldhorn, demonstrating that, although such a piece as the slow movement of the Beethoven sonata brings uncomfortable technical problems, the extra tensions involved can add to the intensity of a performance. There is a flamboyance in the playing which carries the day. Gerald Govier is a persuasive advocate of the fortepiano. On one of EMI's cheapest labels this makes a splendid and stimulating bargain, very well recorded.

Oboe Trio in C, Op. 87; Variations on 'Là ci darem la mano' from Mozart's Don Giovanni

(N) (BB) *(*) Naxos 8.554550. Schachman, Abberger, Spahr –
WRANITZKY: Oboe Trio *(*)

Delightful music, and played with obvious commitment, but the soloists, while not badly out of tune, are nevertheless not quite secure in their intonation, and this is enough to tire the ear after a while. Perhaps it is because they use replicas of period instruments, which might be more difficult to keep in pitch than modern ones. They also sound rather taxed in the fast passages, with the close microphones doing nothing to mask these faults.

Piano Trios 1–9; 10 (Variations on an Original Theme in E flat), Op. 44; 11 (Variations on 'Ich bin der Schneider Kakadu'), Op. 121a; (12) Allegretto in E flat, Hess 48

(B) *** Sony (ADD) SB4K 89979 (4). Stern, Rose, Istomin
(BB) **(*) Naxos 8.550946 (1–2); 8.550947 (3, 8, 10 & 12); 8.550948 (5–6); 8.550949 (7 & 11). Stuttgart Piano Trio

The Stern–Rose–Istomin recordings were made between 1968 and 1970, though the Archduke is earlier and was recorded in Switzerland in 1965. The performances are outstanding: strong, polished and alive. Istomin is always thoughtful and imaginative in slow movements, while Rose, although a less extrovert artist than Stern, holds his own by the warmth and finesse of his lyrical phrasing. One of the highlights of the set is the Archduke, commandingly bold and immediate, with a glorious slow movement; the Ghost Trio also shows these artists at their most communicative. These two performances are available separately (SBK 53514). The recording, improved on CD, is characteristically forward, in the CBS manner of the late 1960s. An excellent bargain.

The Naxos performances have the additional advantage of being available separately. The early Op. 1 set is very successful, played with finesse and with a simplicity of style that is very appealing. The Stuttgart players are good at characterizing variations: Op. 44 is particularly successful and rhythmically most engaging. The first movement of the Ghost Trio is very brisk indeed, and the nervous intensity of the Stuttgart players permeates the performance, although the arrival of the 'Ghost' is eerily effective. The E flat Trio is rather more relaxed and the central movements are played appealingly. The performance of the Archduke is comparatively mellow – not without character, but not really distinctive. The Kakadu Variations come off well, and the Allegretto in B flat, WoO 39, is pleasingly done. Throughout the series the players are not helped by the close microphones in the Clara Wieck Auditorium, but this seems more noticeable in the later works.

Piano Trios 1 in E flat, Op. 1/1; 2 in G, Op. 1/2; 3 in E flat, WoO 38

(N) *** Hyp. CDA 67393. Florestan Trio

Piano Trios 5 (Ghost) in D, Op. 70/1; 6 in E flat, Op. 70/2; Allegretto in B flat, WoO 39

*** Hyp. CDA 67327. Florestan Trio

Piano Trios 7 in B flat (Archduke), Op. 97; 12 (Allegretto in E flat, Hess 48); Variations on 'Ich bin der Schneider Kakadu', Op. 121a

*** Hyp. CDA 67369. Florestan Trio

The Op. 1 performances by the Florestan Trio bring an admirable lightness of touch and inner vitality throughout. The playing of Susan Tomes is particularly felicitous, and the Hyperion recording does it full justice.

The Florestan account of the two Op. 70 trios is outstanding in every way. The playing is quite gripping and masterly, and the sound is very vivid and well balanced. Their commanding, dramatically conceived account of the Archduke is no less superb. Strongly characterized and unfailingly intelligent, this performance, like its companions, can rank among the best to appear for many years, and it is superbly recorded to boot. The fill-up, the Variations on 'Ich bin der Schneider Kakadu', is done with an appealing lightness of touch.

Piano Trios 1–2, Op. 1/1–2

*** MDG 303 1051-2. Trio Parnassus
*** Hyp. CDA 66197. L. Fortepiano Trio

Piano Trios 3, Op. 1/3; 10 (14 Variations in E flat), Op. 44; 11 (Variations on 'Ich bin der Schneider Kakadu'), Op. 121a

*** MDG 303 1052-2. Trio Parnassus

Piano Trios 5 (Ghost); 6, Op. 70/1–2

*** MDG 303 1053-2. Trio Parnassus

Piano Trios 1; 4; Allegretto in B flat, WoO 39

*** Nim NI 5508. Vienna Piano Trio

Piano Trios 2–3, Op. 1/2–3

*** Nim NI 5661. Vienna Piano Trio

The Trio Parnassus use modern instruments, but their spiritedly vibrant style, with bold accents, is every bit a match for their period-instrument competitors. It is balanced by a warm legato from the excellent pianist (Chia Chou) in slow movements, and the finale of Op. 1/2 has exhilarating dynamism. The recording is vividly realistic. The remaining trios, plus the Kakadu and Op. 44 Variations, are hardly less satisfying. Indeed, they can be thought of as the best of the recent versions of these pieces. The playing is unfailingly musical, and the recordings are fresh and vivid.

The London Fortepiano Trio play with considerable virtuosity, particularly in the finales, which are taken at high speed and with fine attack. The use of a fortepiano serves to enhance clarity of texture in this particular repertoire.

The Vienna Piano Trio on Nimbus is a first-class ensemble which gives alert, vital readings that engage the listener's sympathy completely. As with the Dvořák trios from this source, they are well recorded, with a clean, well-focused sound. The performances give pleasure, although competition is stiff in this repertoire; however, in their own right these are superb artistically.

Piano Trios 1–2, Op. 1/1–2; 4, Op. 11

(BB) *** Warner Apex 2564 60364-2. Trio Fontenay

Piano Trios 1; 3; 4

(BB) ** Warner Apex 2564 61366-2. V. Haydn Trio

Piano Trios 2; 5 (Ghost); 6

(N) (BB) ** Warner Apex 2564 61533-2. V. Haydn Trio

Piano Trios 7 (Archduke); 11 (Variations on 'Ich bin der Schneider Kakadu')

(N) (BB) ** Warner Apex 2564 61578-2. V. Haydn Trio

The Fontenay performances offer alert and intelligent playing throughout, with attentive phrasing and bright, well-lit recorded sound. If not quite as distinctive as the Trio Parnassus series, it offers excellent value at Apex price.

The Vienna Haydn Trio is undoubtedly an accomplished ensemble, and for the most part they give good, enjoyable performances, although the slow movement of the *Ghost Trio* is too fast for comfort and occasionally there is a hint of blandness. Not all repeats are observed, yet there would have been plenty of room for them, as playing times are not particularly generous. Although Heinz Medjimorek is a first-class pianist, given the stiff opposition these records must be regarded as an also-ran, even at budget price. The recording is balanced with the piano timbre rather hard and tending to dominate the aural picture at the expense of the strings.

Piano Trio 3 in C min., Op. 1/3; Allegretto in B flat, WoO 39; Variations on 'Ich bin der Schneider Kakadu', Op. 121a

(N) **(*) Simax PSC 1165. Grieg Trio – KAIPAINEN: *Trio III, Op. 29* **

The highly accomplished Grieg Trio's admirable aim is to present the Beethoven trios together with modern works in the medium. Concertgoers may take such exploratory programmes in their stride, but collectors tend not to favour hybrid collections. This group certainly give intelligent and enjoyable accounts of these Beethoven pieces, though they do not observe the first-movement exposition repeat of the *C minor Trio*. Good though he is, their pianist, Vebjørn Anvik, does not quite match Chia Chou of the Trio Parnassus in musical imagination and elegance. So this cannot be a first choice in spite of excellent recording.

Piano Trios 3, Op. 1/3; 7 (Archduke)

(N) *** BIS **SACD** 1172. Kempf Trio

Admirers of Freddy Kempf will welcome the appearance of this Beethoven *Trio* coupling. Kempf himself is eminently thoughtful and at the same time elegant, and his partners, the violinist Pierre Bensaid and the Armenian cellist Alexander Chaushian, are hardly less impressive. The BIS sound is splendidly present and realistic, too. They omit the repeat in the *Scherzo* of the *Archduke*, which excited comment in one periodical, but they are far from alone in this: so do the Beaux Arts in their first recording, Barenboim–Zukerman–Du Pré and many others. In any event, theirs are well-thought-out readings, very musical performances – not perhaps superior to the Florestan among recent rivals, but well worth considering.

Piano Trios 4, Op. 11; 5 (Ghost); 7 (Archduke)

(N) **(*) EMI 5 57506-2. Argerich, Denemark, Drobinsky – MOZART: *Piano Quartet 1* **(*)

Martha Argerich with the Ukrainian clarinettist Marek Denemark and Mark Dobrinsky are recorded at the Lugano Festival in 2002 and give an exuberant account of the piece. Argerich is a delight, fleet-fingered and splendidly alive, and Drobinsky warm-toned and subtly expressive. Denemark gives less pleasure; his tone is thin and reedy, as captured by the recording team. Although it has the atmosphere of a live concert, the performance is not so special that one is likely to return to it very often.

Piano Trios 4, Op. 11; 5 (Ghost); 7 (Archduke)

☛ (M) *** Ph. (ADD) 464 683-2. Beaux Arts Trio

From the Beaux Arts Trio a generous triptych to represent their art among Philips's '50 Great Recordings'. These versions date from 1965 but do not sound their age, and the *Archduke* is a particularly successful transfer, with an attractive bloom on the sound, yet detail is clear. This performance has more spontaneity than their later version and the overall feeling is of lightness and grace. The Scherzo is a delight, and elsewhere there is an attractive pervading lyricism. Some might like a weightier approach, but this is highly rewarding in its own way. The Op. 11 *Trio* is usually heard in its clarinet version. The Beaux Arts players are again on excellent form here and they project the drama and intensity of the *Ghost Trio* to brilliant effect.

Piano Trios 5 (Ghost); 6; 7 (Archduke); 8 in E flat, WoO 38; 10 (Variations in E flat), Op. 44; 12 (Allegretto in E flat), Hess 48

☛ (BB) *** EMI Gemini (DDD/ADD) 5 85496-2 (2). Ashkenazy, Perlman, Harrell

This generous bargain-priced EMI Gemini compilation (which includes both the *Archduke* and *Ghost Trios*) is drawn from the complete set by these artists, which was made over a period of five years between 1979 and 1984. It has long led the field in this repertoire. The playing is unfailingly perceptive and full of those musical insights that make one want to return to the set. The recording is a shade dry but very present and realistic.

Piano Trio 7 in B flat (Archduke), Op. 97

(B) *** EMI double forte (ADD) 5 69367-2 (2). D. Oistrakh, Knushevitzky, Oborin (with KODALY: *3 Hungarian Folksongs*; SUK: *Love Song*; WIENIAWSKI: *Légende*; YSAYE: *Extase* ***) – BRAHMS: *Violin Sonatas 1–2* **(*); SCHUBERT: *Piano Trio 1* ***

On EMI double forte, a well-rounded, thoroughly alive performance by three eminent soloists experienced enough as chamber-music players to allow the necessary blend of personalities. They are rugged and assured in the first movement, brilliant in the last, and only a shade less compelling in the intervening movements. The 1958 recording is smooth and well balanced. The encores come from a concurrent recital disc. Oistrakh is placed rather near the microphones, but his tone is pure and exceptionally rich, with remarkable changes of tone-colour – listen to the little-known but seductive Ysaÿe work and the *Hungarian Folksongs* by Kodály.

Piano Trio 7 (Archduke); 10 (Variations on an Original Theme); 11 (Variations on 'Ich bin der Schneider Kakadu')

(BB) **(*) Virgin 2 x 1 5 62007-2 (2). Castle Trio – SCHUBERT: *Piano Trio 2; Sonatensatz* ***

Those looking for a period-instrument performance of the *Archduke Trio* could well be satisfied with the American Castle Trio. They are generous with repeats, particularly in the Scherzo, playing throughout with vitality, bold accents and plenty of spirit. Indeed at times, in its energy, the music-making has a slightly unsettled quality, and the *Andante cantabile* could ideally be more mellow and relaxed. However, Lambert Ortis's fortepiano (a copy of an 1824 Graf) is not in the least shallow or clattery. Its bright timbre and the sparkling articulation especially suit the two sets of *Variations*, which are presented with great character and charm. The Schubert coupling is even finer.

Piano & Wind Quintet in E flat, Op. 16

(M) *** Sony SMK 42099. Perahia, members of ECO –
MOZART: *Quintet* ***

*** CBC MCVD 1137. Kuerti, Campbell, Mason, Sommerville,
McKay – MOZART; WITT: *Quintets* ***

❂ (***) Testament mono SBT 1091. Gieseking, Philh. Wind
Ens. – MOZART: *Quintet, etc.* (***) ❂

(M) **(*) Warner Elatus 2464 60445-2. Barenboim, Soloists
of Chicago SO – MOZART: *Quintet* **(*)

(N) **(*) CPO 777 010-2. Consortium Classicum – MOZART:
Piano & Wind Quintet; Clarinet Trio **(*)

N) (M) (**) BBC mono BBCL 4164-2. Britten, Leonard &
Dennis Brain, Waters, James – JACOB: *Wind Sextet;*
HINDEMITH: *Horn Sonata;* VINTNER: *Hunter's Moon*

First choice for Beethoven's *Piano and Wind Quintet* lies with
Perahia's CBS version, recorded at The Maltings. The first
movement is given even weight than usual, with a satisfying
culmination. In the *Andante*, Perahia's playing is wonderfully
poetic and serene, and the wind soloists are admirably
responsive. With the recording balanced most realistically,
this issue can be warmly recommended.

A totally winning performance, too, from this group of
leading Canadian wind soloists, appropriately led by the
Viennese-born pianist Anton Kuerti. They play together with
total rapport and their performance has great freshness and
all the spontaneity of live music-making. The finale is particularly infectious. The recording has great vividness and
realism – indeed, it is in the demonstration bracket. This can
be strongly recommended alongside the Sony disc, and it has
the considerable advantage of including additionally the
attractive quintet by Friedrich Witt, who modelled his work
closely on the quintets by Mozart and Beethoven.

Ideal chamber-music-making in this version by Walter
Gieseking and members of the Philharmonia Wind (Dennis
Brain, Sidney Sutcliffe, Bernard Walton and Cecil James).
Recorded in 1955, it has few rivals in tonal blend and perfec-
tion of balance and ensemble. The mono sound comes up
wonderfully fresh in this Testament transfer.

Barenboim here puts down his baton to join players from
the Chicago Symphony Orchestra (Hansjörg Schellenberger,
oboe, Larry Combs, clarinet, Dale Clevenger, horn, and Daniele Damiano, bassoon) who distinguish themselves in the
engaging interplay of the *Andante*. Barenboim too is in good
form – the first movement proceeds jauntily, and the finale is
sprightly but nicely relaxed. This is very enjoyable and well
recorded. Not a first choice, but fair value.

Although there is a touch of heaviness in the first movement, the performance from Consortium Classicum is fluent
and musically communicative, as much as anything because
of the attractive contribution of the pianist, Werner Genuit,
who plays most engagingly in the *Andante* and imbues the
finale with a light touch. Naturally recorded, this disc gains
over most of its competitors by offering an extra work.

The BBC recording is distant and subfusc, although the
internal balance is well integrated. But Dennis Brain's horn
part projects well, and Benjamin Britten takes a sprited lead
throughout: the slow movement is almost Mozartian.

Septet in E flat, Op. 20

(BB) *** Warner Apex 8573 89080-2. Berlin Soloists –
MOZART: *Horn Quintet* ***

(***) Testament mono SBT 1261. V. Octet (members) –
SPOHR: *Nonet* (***)

(B) **(*) DG (ADD) 469 766-2. BPO Octet (members) –
MENDELSSOHN: *Octet* **(*)

**(*) Nim. NI 5461. BPO Octet – HINDEMITH: *Octet* **(*)

Septet, Op. 20; Clarinet Trio, Op. 11

(BB) *** Virgin 2×1 5 61409-2 (2). Nash Ens. (with SCHUBERT:
Octet **)

(i) *Septet, Op. 20;* (ii) *Wind Sextet in E flat, Op. 81b*
❂➡ *** Hyp. CDA 66513. Gaudier Ens.

The young members of the Gaudier Ensemble give an exuberant performance, bringing the *Septet* home as one of the
young Beethoven's most joyfully carefree inspirations. The
rarer *Sextet* for two horns and string quartet makes a generous coupling. Excellent sound, with the wind well forward.

An enchanting version of the evergreen *Septet* from the
Vienna Octet: it oozes Viennese charm but is without any
cloying sentimentality. Its return to the catalogue is very good
news indeed, and it is hoped that other classic accounts from
this source are to resurface soon. The 1956 recording is
astonishingly warm and vivid (a tribute to whoever made this
transfer, as well as to the original Decca engineers). Delightful
coupling, too.

Of the three recordings from Berlin, that by the Soloists on
Apex is a clear first choice. This is a most affectionate
account, beautifully played and warmly recorded in a pleasing acoustic. The players are given a nice presence without
being on top of the listener. The Mozart coupling is attractive
too, and this reissue is most competitively priced.

The Virgin issue brings uneven quality in the coupling.
There is pure magic in these Beethoven performances, and so
the *Clarinet Trio* finds each player, not just the fine clarinettist
Michael Collins, but also the pianist Ian Brown and the cellist
Christopher van Kampen. An apt sense of fun also infects the
Septet, with allegros exhilaratingly fast. Good, atmospheric
sound, but the coupled Schubert *Octet* is not so successful
either technically or musically.

The Berlin Philharmonic Octet on Nimbus also give a
delightful, characterful account of the *Septet* with playing
polished and refined. The only snag is that the recording,
made in the Teldec Studios, Berlin, is rather too closely
balanced. Recommended none the less.

An amiable, refined performance on DG (originally on
Philips) from the excellent Berlin Philharmonic group, with
plenty of life in the outer movements but rather a solemn
view taken of the slow movement. The recording is first class
– many will like its warmth and amplitude – and the new
coupling is more generous than the previous issue of this
performance.

Serenade in D, Op. 25

(N) (B) *** CfP 5 85900-2. London Virtuosi (with BACH: *Flute
Sonata 6, BMV 1035;* TELEMANN: *Trio Sonata in E* ***)

The light and charming combination of flute, violin and viola
inspired the youthful Beethoven to write in an unexpectedly
carefree and undemanding way. The sequence of tuneful,
unpretentious movements reminds one of Mozart's occasional music, and the excellent London Virtuosi, led by James
Galway, find all its charm and natural vivacity. Perhaps the
account of the Bach *Flute Sonata* (with Jane Ryan, viola da
gamba, and David Lumsden, harpsichord) is a little over-
upholstered in its textures, but it is elegantly played, and the
Telemann *Trio Sonata* (in which Archie Camden, oboe, joins
the group) is expressive and sprightly by turns. An excellent

bargain, and the least expensive way of acquiring the Beethoven lollipop.

Serenade in D, Op. 8 (arr. Matiegka)

*** Mer. CDE 84199. Conway, Silverthorne, Garcia – KREUTZER; MOLINO: *Trios* ***

Beethoven's early *Serenade* for string trio was arranged for violin, viola and guitar by the Bohemian composer and guitarist Wenceslaus Matiegka. On Meridian, Gerald Garcia has rearranged it for the present delightful combination, offering the violin part to the flute, and giving the guitar a more taxing contribution. As a companion piece for the rare Kreutzer and Molino items, it makes a charming oddity, very well played and warmly recorded.

STRING QUARTETS

String Quartets 1–16; Grosse Fuge, Op. 133

- (M) *** Valois (ADD) V 4400 (8). Végh Qt
*** Valois (ADD) V 4871 (1 & 5); V 4402 (2–4); V 4403 (6–7); V 4404 (8–9); V 4405 (10 & 12); V 4406 (11 & 15); V 4407 (13 & Grosse Fugue); V 4408 (14 & 16). Végh Qt
(BB) *** ASV Resonance RSB 801 (8). The Lindsays
(B) *** Ph. (ADD) 454 062-2 (10). Italian Qt
(B) *** Cal. ADD CAL 3633.9 (7). Talich Qt
*** EMI 7 54587-2 (4) (1, 3–4, 7, 10, 12–14); 7 54592-2 (4) (2, 5–6, 8–9, 11, 15–16; Grosse Fuge; Cavatina from Op. 130). Alban Berg Qt
(B) *** EMI (ADD/DDD) CZS5 73606-2 (7). Alban Berg Qt
(BB) *** Hyp. Helios CDH 55021/8 (8). New Budapest Qt
(B) **(*) DG 463 143-2 (7). Amadeus Qt
(BB) **(*) Arte Nova 74321 63637-2 (9). Alexander Qt (also available separately)
(N) (B) **(*) Warner 2564 61399-2 (9). Vermeer Qt
(N) (BB) ** RCA 82876 55704-2 (8). Guarneri Qt

For long a first choice, the Végh performances, recorded in the mid-1970s, have rightly been acclaimed for their expressive depth. That intonation is not always immaculate matters little in relation to the wisdom and experience conveyed. There is no cultivation of surface polish, though there is both elegance and finesse. The CD transfers have a far cleaner image than the original LPs. The eight discs are now available together at mid-price.

The great merit in the earlier Lindsay recordings of Beethoven lies in the natural expressiveness of their playing, most strikingly in slow movements, which brings a hushed inner quality too rarely caught on record. The sense of spontaneity necessarily brings the obverse quality: these performances are not as precise as those in the finest rival sets; but there are few Beethoven quartet recordings that so convincingly bring out the humanity of the writing, its power to communicate. They offer superb performances of Op. 59. Their insights are not often rivalled, let alone surpassed, in modern recordings. As to the sound, this set is comparable with most of its competitors and is superior to many; artistically, it can hold its own with the best. The Lindsays also get far closer to the essence of the late quartets than most of their rivals, with the benefit of very well-balanced recording. They regularly find tempi that feel completely right, conveying both the letter and the spirit of the music in rich, strong characterization. These are among the very finest versions to

have been made in recent years and, at budget price, are excellent value.

The Italian performances, superbly stylish, are now offered in a bargain box of unbeatable value. The Végh versions, in some ways even finer, are at mid-price, but on eight discs instead of ten, so the difference in cost is relatively marginal. The latest Philips remastering is most impressive, with the sound much smoother than before and very naturally balanced. In the *Rasumovsky Quartets* in particular, their tempi are perfectly judged and every phrase is sensitively shaped, while the late quartets receive satisfyingly thoughtful and searching interpretations.

The Talich set now returns in a slipcase at bargain price. They have an impressive technical address, not less formidable than any of their rivals. Their performances have the merit of directness and simplicity of utterance; as music-making there is a refreshing naturalness about their approach, which especially suits Op. 18, even if they are sometimes inclined to be a little measured and wanting in urgency. First-movement exposition repeats are observed, except in Nos. 1 and 6. In the middle-period works they win our confidence by the essentially private character of their performances. There is nothing jet-setting here: instead one feels like an eavesdropper on an intimate discourse, with real understanding of what this music is all about. In the late quartets their penetrating accounts can hold their own with the very finest, and the quality of the recorded sound, though not in any way spectacular, is eminently clean and firmly defined, the instruments well placed within a pleasing, not too resonant, analogue ambience.

The Alban Berg's second, digital set, recorded at public concerts, seeks to ensure the greater intensity and spontaneity generated in the presence of an audience. On balance, these performances are freer and more vital than those in the earlier set, but the differences are small. Though the very perfection of ensemble and sheer beauty of sound are not always helpful in this repertoire, these performances are recommended to admirers of this ensemble who are prepared to pay premium price.

The Alban Berg Quartet's earlier performances are characterized by assured and alert playing, a finely blended tone and excellent attack; they generally favour brisk tempi in the first movements, which they dispatch with exemplary polish and accuracy of intonation. Occasionally a tendency to exaggerate dynamic extremes (Op. 59/3, for example) is evident and sounds self-conscious, but by any standards this is superb quartet playing. Other versions have displayed greater depth of feeling in this repertoire – including their own live performance cycle on the same label – but this well-packaged, beautifully recorded set (from 1978–83) at bargain price is well worth considering.

The New Budapest Quartet offer fine performances, always intelligent, with many considerable insights. Throughout the cycle their playing is distinguished by consistent (but not excessive) refinement of sonority, perfect intonation and excellent ensemble and tonal blend. With first-class Hyperion recording, they fully deserve three stars. If the very opening disc of Op. 18/1–2 lacks a little in vitality, this is not a problem elsewhere. They are less searching than the Végh or the Lindsays. At times one feels that they are somehow too clean and occasionally somewhat less than fully characterized. Yet this is always fully committed music-making with plenty of life, and as a super-bargain box (eight CDs for the price of five Helios discs, offered in a slipcase) they are certainly well worth considering: overall; the performances have more depth than those of their Amadeus competitors.

The Amadeus Quartet are at their very best in the Op. 18 *Quartets*, where their mastery and polish are heard to excellent advantage. The smooth and beautifully balanced DG recording from the early 1960s disguises its age. In the middle-period and late quartets, their richly blended tone and refinement of balance are always in evidence and are caught equally well by the DG engineers, but their playing does not always penetrate very far beneath the surface, particularly in the late quartets. There is some superb playing and immaculate ensemble in this cycle, which cannot help but give pleasure, but there are more searching accounts to be found. The set is now offered at bargain price in DG's Collector's Edition and is well documented.

No one investing in the Arte Nova accounts of the Op. 18 *Quartets* listed above will be disappointed. Generally speaking, the Alexander Quartet's approach is selfless and dedicated; the readings are well thought through and distinguished by considerable tonal finesse. In the *E flat*, Op. 127, tempi are intelligently chosen (the scherzando third movement could not be bettered), though there is a certain fierceness in tuttis. The close balance does not rob the slow movement of its sense of mystery, which is a tribute to the tonal finesse these players command. The great *A minor Quartet*, Op. 132 (74321 37312-2), is undeniably impressive. Lovely *pianissimo* playing, both in the opening and in the *Heiliger Dankgesang*, which has keen concentration. One of the best in the set. The *B flat Quartet* and the *Grosse Fuge* (74321 54455-2) come off well. They convey the sense of struggle and possess great lucidity of texture. The *C sharp minor Quartet*, Op. 131 (74321 63675-2), is less successful. In the fugal opening the sense of awe that you find in the greatest performances is missing. Their tempo, too, is just a bit too fast.

The American Vermeer Quartet recorded their Beethoven cycle over almost a decade, from 1983 to 1991. In terms of refinement of tonal blend and unanimity of approach their performances are of a high order; moreover they are artists of keen sensitivity and awareness. They are also the beneficiaries of excellent engineering, and in terms of sound quality there is little here to quarrel with. The image is clear and well focused, albeit forwardly, even if the acoustic is on the dry side. They bring to the Op. 18 set the same qualities of intelligence and musicianship that distinguish the rest of their cycle. Theirs are performances of integrity, free from any expressive idiosyncrasy and very well executed in every respect. However, for all their merits of dedication, they are somewhat lacking in warmth and spontaneity.

While Op. 57 shows their playing at its most concentrated, the performances of the *Harp Quartet* and the *F minor*, Op. 90, are pretty unappealing. It is all very efficient and rather soulless, with aggressive sforzandi. However, the late quartets often show them on top form: their account of Op. 127 is in many ways a very strong one. In Op. 130 they give a perceptive and technically impeccable account of the first movement; but some collectors might find them a shade didactic here – and even more so in the finale, which is also a little too measured. The *Alla tedesca* movement and *Cavatina*, on the other hand, may be a little fast for some tastes; and perhaps there is not enough inwardness of feeling in the *Adagio*, while the middle section of the Scherzo is a bit aggressive and too fast. But Op. 135 is very impressive; tempi seem natural and the slow movement has no lack of depth. Even so, this cycle can hardly be regarded as a first choice.

The Guarneri Quartet was perhaps the most prestigious American ensemble of its day, and it is difficult to flaw their playing. It is impossible not to admire their impeccable technical address, their perfect ensemble and tonal blend. What is missing is the sense of inwardness: these are 'public' performances rather than 'private' music-making, oratory rather than more intimate conversation. It would be wrong to imply that this cycle is shallow, but necessary to point out that there are others who offer greater depths and insights. There is much to admire: well-chosen tempi, abundant finesse and intelligence, as well as the highest accomplishment and virtuosity. The *Grosse Fuge* is pretty stunning. Very good recording and a very competitive price tag, but any recommendation must be qualified.

(i) *String Quartets 1; 9; 11–12; 14–16;* (ii) *Violin Sonata 3 in E flat, Op. 12/3*

⊕ (M) *** EMI mono 5 65308-2 (4). (i) Busch Qt; (ii) Busch, Serkin – SCHUBERT: *String Quartet 8* ***

Listening to the Busch Quartet's pre-war HMV accounts of the quartets, one feels that no group since has ever penetrated deeper into the heart of these scores. In addition to the Beethoven quartets there is a bonus in the form of the *Violin Sonata in E flat*, from Busch and Serkin, playing of warmth and humanity, and a sparkling account of the early *B flat Quartet*, D.112, of Schubert. These are classics of the gramophone and are not to be missed, excellently remastered and transferred.

String Quartets 1–6, Op. 18/1–6; Op. 14/1 (arr. Beethoven); (i) *String Quintet*

*** ASV CDDCA 1111 (1–3); CDDCA 1112 (4–5 & Op. 14); CDDCA 1113 (6 & Quintet). Lindsay Qt; (i) with L. Williams

String Quartets 1–6, Op. 18/1–6

⊕→ *** Decca 470 848-2 (2). Takács Qt

(B) *** EMI 5 62778-2 (2). Alban Berg Qt

(N) (M) *** Sony mono 516024-2. Budapest Qt

(M) **(*) Cal. (ADD) CAL 9633 (1–3); CAL 9634 (4–6). Talich Qt

(B) ** Sony (ADD) SB3K 89975 (3). Juilliard Qt

String Quartets 1 in F; 4 in C min., Op. 18/1 & 4

*** MDG 307 0853-2. Leipzig Qt (with qt movements: SCHUBERT: *in G min., D.173: Allegro con brio*; ROMBERG: *in F, Op. 1/3: Andante*; MOZART: *23 in F, K.590: Allegro* **)

String Quartets 2 in G; 5 in A, Op. 18/2 & 5

*** MDG 307 0855-2. Leipzig Qt

String Quartets 3 in D; 6 in B flat, Op. 18/3 & 6

*** MDG 307 0856-2. Leipzig Qt

The Lindsay Quartet are setting out on a new recorded cycle of the Beethoven string quartets after an interval of almost 20 years. Already in the Op. 18 *Quartets* the trends are clear, all encouraging. Consistently throughout these performances, speeds are a fraction faster than before, in Scherzos often markedly so, with interpretations tauter and more positive, as well as more spontaneous sounding. In the two key *Adagios* which point forward to the visionary qualities of the late quartets – the D minor slow movement of No. 1 in F and the deeply mysterious *Adagio*, *La Malinconia*, at the start of the finale of No. 6 – the speeds, as in the rest, are a fraction more flowing than before, but the hushed intensity is even greater, with no hint of heaviness inappropriate to these early works. It is good to find Beethoven's own transcription for quartet of his little *Piano Sonata*, Op. 14, No. 1, taking its place so naturally among the regular masterpieces, with the finale wittily pointed. The *String Quintet* too is an apt supplement, beautifully done, with Louise Williams as the extra viola.

The Takács Quartet in their ongoing Beethoven cycle maintain the high standards they have achieved in earlier releases. There are so many splendid sets now on the market – some, like the Alban Berg, at highly competitive prices. The Lindsays stretch to a third CD, though they offer the *C major String Quintet* and the arrangement of Op. 14, No. 1; and the deeply musical accounts by the Leipzig Quartet again involve three CDs, but are available separately. Both sets are both well worth considering. However, those collecting the Takács cycle will know the strength and excellence of this ensemble and their command of nuance, sensitive phrasing and musical architecture. Their sound musical intelligence and freshness of approach are always in evidence, and they are given splendid recorded sound.

The Alban Berg's studio recordings of the Beethoven *Quartets* in the late 1970s and early 1980s set high standards. This newer set originates from public concerts in 1989. The performances are not by any means superficial or slick – and admirers of this ensemble need have no hesitation in acquiring them at their new bargain price.

The Leipzig Quartet are not glamorous or glitzy and so have attracted less attention than some of their high-powered colleagues. However, they have immaculate polish and tonal finesse and are immensely musical in their approach. This is humane, old-world music-making, and the performances are unhurried, although they never lack forward movement. The tonal blend and internal balance are impeccable. These readings are full of character, and their apt tempi and total dedication to the score are difficult to fault. They can be recommended alongside the very best and are accorded first-class sound that is as natural and well balanced as the playing.

As the two quartets on the first disc run to less than fifty minutes, MDG fill out the remaining minutes with individual bits and pieces which the assiduous collector may have already acquired. In such a competitive field this will undoubtedly diminish the disc's appeal, given its premium price.

The celebrated set by the Budapest Quartet dates from the early 1950s. Unlike their 1960s remake, the sonority is perfectly focused and the readings have weight, animation and dedication, commanding both the music's architecture and its expressive detail. The performances are captured in mono sound of remarkable fidelity, given the period. The Sony engineers have produced transfers of excellent quality.

The Talich have great directness and simplicity of utterance, even if their accounts are not as inspired as they were later on in the cycle. Most often they find the right tempo and in the first movement of the *A major*, Op. 18/5, have a wonderful freshness and spontaneity. Even if there are moments of prose, there is no lack of poetry elsewhere. Clean, present recording, even if it is a bit on the dry side. Recommended – but not in preference to, say, the Lindsays.

The Juilliard box derives from 'live' performances given at the Library of Congress, Washington, D.C., in 1982, though no information about this is included with this reissue. The sound quality is acceptable but quite dry, and one could well be forgiven for thinking that the venue was a studio. The playing is of a high order of accomplishment, and these are not performances to ignore. But other versions in the lower price range enjoy much superior sound and so this set is mainly recommendable to admirers of these artists.

String Quartet 1 in F, Op. 18/1

(**) BBC mono BBCL 4137-2. Smetana Qt – MOZART: *String Quartet 20* (**(*)); SMETANA: *String Quartet 1* (***)

The Smetana Quartet's performance of Op. 18, No. 1, comes from 1963 when they were at the BBC's Manchester Studios. The sound is in fact better than the Festival Hall Mozart and Smetana performances, made two years later. The slow movement is perhaps a bit fast and almost prosaic, certainly not as searching as such commercial recordings as those of the Végh or the Lindsays. But, generally speaking, the performance still gives a lot of satisfaction. No exposition repeat in the first movement.

String Quartets 1, Op. 18/1; 14, Op. 131

*** Cap. 10510. Petersen Qt

Both in Op. 131 and in the less successful *F major Quartet*, Op. 18, No. 1, the Petersen Quartet prove dedicated and characterful, and this is a satisfying alternative recommendation in digital sound.

String Quartets 3, Op. 18/3; 7, Op. 59/1

*** Channel CCS 6094. Orpheus Qt

The Orpheus Quartet's account of the *First Rasumovsky Quartet* is among the best in recent years. This is very natural playing, well attuned to the period, deeply felt without being over-intense. The recording has clarity and presence.

String Quartets 3, Op. 18/3; 11, Op. 95; 15, Op. 132

(N) (BB) (**(*)) Dutton mono CDBP 8752 (3 & 11); CDBP 9755 (15) (available separately). Griller Qt

When the Griller Quartet recorded Op. 18/3 amd Op. 95 in 1948, there were relatively few other versions, and the position had not greatly improved two years later when Op. 132 followed. The authors of the *The Record Guide* complained in 1955 that 'the shortage of first-rate quartets is alarming' and at the foot of a long list of 78s and LPs they wrote 'there is not one single performance of a Beethoven string quartet that can be recommended'. They were very dismissive of the Griller's Op. 95 ('weak in grasp') and thought there was little to choose between their Op. 132 and the Pascal Quartet's version, which they described as 'inadequate to the depth and power of this music'. The Dutton reissue quotes the famous EMG *Monthly Letter* verdict on Op. 95 which is much more positive. We are glad to have these expert transfers, and not just for reasons of nostalgia but also for the fact that the Grillers, whatever their failings, were thoughtful musicians, able to bring many fresh insights into these scores.

String Quartets 4–5, Op. 18/4–5; 7; 9 (Rasumovsky), Op. 59/1 &3; 11, Op. 95; 13, Op. 130; 15, Op. 132; Grosse Fuge

(BB) **(*) Virgin 5 62258-2 (4). Borodin Qt

Virgin have now combined the Borodin Quartet's recordings in a four-disc budget set. The playing is not superficial – there is plenty of concentration in the slow movements of both Op. 95 and Op. 132, but at the same time the result is not particularly illuminating either. These are the kind of performances that would make a strong impression in the concert hall but that do not resonate in the mind afterwards. Nevertheless, at its modest price this set still offers much to admire and enjoy.

String Quartets 4–5; 13, Op. 130; Grosse Fuge

(BB) **(*) Virgin 2×1 5 61748 (2). Borodin Qt

For finesse and beauty of sound in Beethoven the Borodins are unmatched, even by the Alban Berg. In the early quartets the elegance and warmth of the playing are an undoubted pleasure; yet, eloquent as it is on the surface, the searching quality that Beethoven calls for is passed by. The *Grosse Fuge* demands and receives great attack and gusto, yet the players are even more in their element in the lighter, substituted finale. The sound is very realistic, so at its modest price this set still offers much to enjoy.

String Quartets 4 & 6, Op. 18/4 & 6; 16, Op. 135: Lento assai (only)
(N) (**) EMI Classic Archive mono **DVD** DVB 5996839. Amadeus Qt (Bonus: BRAHMS: *Clarinet Quintet: 3rd movt: Andantino* (with Lancelot); BARTÓK : *Quartet 4: Allegretto Pizzicato;* SCHUBERT: *Quartet 14 (Death and the Maiden): 4th movt* (***)) – MOZART: *String Quintet 3; String Qt 17* (**)

While it is good to see the Amadeus Quartet in concert, this collection is a great disappointment. The performances of the two Op. 18 *Quartets* are very thinly recorded (in 1969) with a fierce aural spotlight on the leader, Norbert Brainin, which makes far from comfortable listening. The brief snippet from Op. 135 is another matter and shows the group at its peak in 1973. So do the other bonuses, the third movement from the Brahms *Clarinet Quintet*, with Jacques Lancelot an eloquently suave soloist, the superbly played Bartók *Pizzicato* and, most impressive all, the fourth movement from Schubert's *Death and the Maiden Quartet*, which brings electrifying ensemble – very like the Emersons, only mellower and more Schubertian.

String Quartets 4; 10 (Harp); 14, Op. 131
(M) (***) Biddulph mono LAB 056-7. Rosé Qt – BACH: *Double Concerto, etc.* (***)

These performances bring us as close as we can possibly get to the kind of strongly characterized playing Brahms and Mahler would have heard. The recordings were made in 1930 and 1932, the *C sharp minor* in 1927, and this accounts for the rather primitive sound.

String Quartets 4, Op. 18/4; 15, Op. 132
*** Cap. 10722. Petersen Qt

The *Heiliger Dankgesang* inspires the Petersen Quartet to playing of great depth, even though at other points they press ahead very slightly. An outstanding recommendation.

String Quartets 7–9 (Rasumovsky), Op. 59/1–3; 10 in E flat (Harp), Op. 74
⌐ *** Decca 470 847-2 (2). Takács Qt

String Quartets 7–9; 10 (Harp); 11, Op. 95
(**(*)) Bridge mono 9099A (2). Budapest Qt

The Takács offer a highly auspicious and successful start to what will be a complete cycle. They omit the *F minor*, Op. 95, and so are able to accommodate the *Rasumovskys* and *Harp* on two CDs instead of the usual three. These are sober and perceptive readings, which make one think anew about this great music. The slow movement of the *E minor*, Op. 59, No. 2, taken more slowly than usual, is searching, and generally they find the right tempi to enable the music to speak effortlessly. Technically impeccable playing, well thought through and scrupulously attentive to detail (with all repeats made), this is a set to rank alongside the very best, and the recording is of Decca's finest quality.

The Budapest Quartet's performances were recorded at concerts given at the Library of Congress during and immediately after the Second World War; only in the *E minor*, Op. 59, No. 2, which was recorded in 1960, do we hear the ensemble in its last years. The *F major Rasumovsky* from 1941 has all the momentum, dramatic contrast and inevitability of growth you find in their later, mono LP version. There is the tremendous grip of the LP version enlivened by the spontaneity of the concert hall. The slow movement of the *E minor* also seems more searching and thoughtful than in the 1950s set, even though its first movement is not as technically immaculate. The recordings from the 1940s are pleasingly full-bodied, and although the acoustic is rather dry there is no lack of colour. The Budapest was always impressive in this repertoire, and the listener soon forgets any sonic limitations or the occasional blemish. A valuable document.

String Quartets 7 in F, Op. 59/1; 10 (Harp), Op. 74
(M) *** Cal. Approche (ADD) CAL 5636. Talich Qt

String Quartets 8, Op. 59/2; 13, Op. 130
(M) *** Cal. Approche (ADD) CAL 5637. Talich Qt

This is an awkward way of reissuing these celebrated Talich performances, as the *Rasumovskys* would have been far better coupled together. However, the performances are another matter. One is immediately gripped by the purity of sound these artists produce and the effortlessness of their phrasing. As a quartet their ensemble and intonation are impeccable, and they possess both depth of feeling and insight. The readings unfold with a totally unforced naturalness; tempi have the feeling of rightness one recognizes in masterly performances, and the dynamic range is wide without being exaggerated. The sound, as usual with their recordings, is just a little bottom-heavy but otherwise very natural, and, like the Végh, they bring a rich humanity to bear on these masterpieces.

String Quartets 7 in F (Rasumovsky); 11, Op. 95
(BB) *** Naxos 8.554181. Kodály Qt

String Quartets 8, Op. 59/2; 10 (Harp), Op. 74
(BB) *** Naxos 8.550562. Kodály Qt

String Quartets 9, Op. 59/3; 12, Op. 127
(BB) *** Naxos 8.550563. Kodály Qt

String Quartet 13, Op. 130; Grosse Fuge
(BB) *** Naxos 8.556593. Kodály Qt

String Quartets 14, Op. 131; 16, Op. 135
(BB) *** Naxos 8.556594. Kodály Qt

String Quartets 15, Op. 132; in F (arr. of Piano sonata, Op. 14/1)
(BB) *** Naxos 8.556592. Kodály Qt

The Kodály have the benefit of very good recorded sound, with a particularly good balance, and the actual playing is very fine, with judiciously chosen tempi and expertly moulded phrasing. Both the *Rasumovsky Quartets* here are very good indeed: thoughtful, decently paced and thoroughly musical accounts, which will give satisfaction. No one getting any of these discs is likely to be disappointed, although they are not a first choice in the bargain range.

String Quartets 8 (Rasumovsky); 10 (Harp)
*** ASV CDDCA 1115. Lindsay Qt

This fifth disc in the new Lindsay series follows the pattern of earlier issues in the extra sharpness of the characterization as well as the extra warmth, compared with the fine performances in their earlier Beethoven cycle for ASV. So in the *Rasumovsky No. 2* the three fast movements are all noticeably faster and sharper than before, fiery in the first and third movements, spiky in the finale, while the sublime *Molto adagio* has an inner hush beyond what was conveyed in the earlier version. The contrast in the *Harp Quartet* is different in that the first two movements are this time lighter in mood, with fun brought out in the first movement with its harp-like pizzicatos, and the *Adagio* treated songfully at a markedly more flowing speed, not as a profound foretaste of the late quartets. In the Scherzo and *Allegretto* variations of the finale bluff Beethovenian qualities are also more clearly brought out. Ensemble is not always as immaculate as it was before, but the vital qualities easily outweigh any reservations. Excellent sound.

String Quartets 8; 10–16; Grosse Fuge

(N) *** Chan. 10191 (*8 & 10*); Chan. 10269 (*11, 14 & Grosse Fuge*); Chan. 10292 (*12–13*); Chan. 10304 (*15–16*). Borodin Qt (available separately)

The Borodin Quartet's Beethoven cycle is collecting excellent reviews, and anyone trying these performances will realize why. It goes without saying that they have magisterial authority: this quartet has been in existence for some 60 years and its original cellist, Valentin Berlinsky, is still with them! They shape each movement with exemplary feeling and there is a pleasing naturalness of phrasing. Some reservations have been expressed about the dynamic range (their *pianissimi* could perhaps be even quieter) but this did not trouble us. They bring us closer to the soul of this music than do many rivals and they are accorded first-rate sound. One small point: those buying Op. 130 will have to invest in the companion disc if they want to end with the *Grosse Fuge*, but this is no great hardship. These accounts can rank along with the finest.

String Quartets 9 in C (Rasumovsky); 10 (Harp)

*** HM HMC 905252. Turner Qt

The Turner Quartet give fine, dedicated performances with well-judged tempi and articulate and vital rhythms. They do not rush things in the finale of Op. 59, No. 3, and find the right tempo for the *Presto* movement of Op. 74, which is so often rushed off its feet. The vibrato-less opening of Op. 74, for all its splendidly transparent textures, may prompt some listeners to long for the warmer, more full-blooded sonority of modern instruments. But both readings are well thought out and distinguished by accomplished and refined musicianship.

String Quartet 10 (Harp), Op. 74

(BB) **(*) Discover DICD 920171. Sharon Qt (with RAVEL: *Quartet* **(*)) – MOZART: *Quartet 1* ***

The Sharon Quartet give a most enjoyable account of the *Harp Quartet*, very well matched, expressive and sensitive in the *Adagio* and perceptive in the closing *Allegretto con variazioni*. The sound is a shade reverberant, but the blend is attractively full.

String Quartets 10 (Harp); 11; 16, Op. 135

**(*) HM HMU 907254. Eroica Qt

These are thought-provoking readings, but at the same time there is some ugly or vulnerable intonation here and there,

most notably in the slow movement of the *F major*, Op. 135, and indeed at the very opening of the *Harp*. All the same, this is an interesting and rewarding disc.

String Quartets 10 (Harp); 11, Op. 95

(N) ** Praga **SACD** PRD/DSD 250 199. Pražák Qt

String Quartet 13, Op. 130 (including alternative finale); Grosse Fuge

(N) ** Praga **SACD** PRD/DSD 250 206. Pražák Qt

The Pražák Quartet produce a good sonority and their playing is both accomplished and perceptive; the *Grosse Fuge* is gutsy and full of vigour. We found their earlier LP recordings not wholly satisfying. Their Op. 130 starts very well, but the rather exaggerated bulges that characterize some of their phrasing will not be to all tastes. The occasional expressive exaggeration will not trouble all listeners, but in this repertoire competition is so abundant and keen that in none of these wonderful works would one turn to the Pražák as a first choice.

String Quartets 11, Op. 95; 12 in E flat, Op. 127

☛— *** ASV CD DCA 1116. Lindsay Qt

String Quartets 11; 12; Grosse Fuge, Op. 133

(B) **(*) Approche Cal (ADD) CAL 5635. Talich Qt

In their sixth disc the Lindsays launch into their biggest challenge yet with the first of the last-period quartets, the Op. 127 *Quartet*. The big contrast in this new version is that the heavenly slow movement flows much more freely than it did before, conveying an even deeper concentration, with subtler shading and sharper contrasts. Also, the more refined recording brings cleaner textures in a reading that is more detailed and sharply characterized throughout. In the Op. 95 *Quartet*, more compact than any, the Lindsay's speeds in all four movements are faster than before, giving an extra bite to the arguments, recognizing this as a halfway house towards the quirky sublimity of the last-period work.

The Talich performances come from the complete set above, recorded in 1977–80. Quartets who play with flawless intonation, precision and attack are, relatively speaking, numerous, but those who play with the degree of *Innigkeit* and concentration that the Talich bring are rare. What marks them out is the essentially private nature of the performances. Along with the Végh or the Lindsays, the Talich bring us Beethoven rather than wonderful quartet playing. On this disc the *Grosse Fuge* prefaces Opp. 95 and 127: the latter is a performance of real stature. The sound is less than state-of-the-art but more than acceptable.

String Quartets 11–16; Grosse Fuge

(N) *** Decca 470 849-2 (3). Tacáks Qt

The Tacáks have collected golden opinions for their Beethoven cycle, and the late quartets in particular have been greeted with much acclaim. It is easy to see why. These performers have steeped themselves in this great music and are unconcerned with interpretative point-making. They have the advantage of working with the new Henle edition by Ernst-Günter-Heinemann and Rainer Cadenbach, and their leader Edward Dusinberre's sleeve-note draws attention to some of the detailed differences. But apart from the letter of the score, it is the spirit they project. The Decca recording, made at St George's, Bristol, is first class and is expertly balanced by Simon Eadon and produced by Andrew Keener. Unlike their rivals, they accommodate the late quartets plus

Op. 95 together on three discs, with two quartets each on the first two CDs, while the final disc includes Opp. 95 and 130 with the alternative finale and the *Grosse Fuge*.

String Quartets 12–16; Grosse Fuge, Op. 133
(M) *** Ph. (ADD) 464 684-2 (3). Italian Qt
(B) **(*) Sony SB3K 89897 (3). Juilliard Qt
(**(*)) Testament mono SBT 3082 (3). Hollywood Qt
(M) **(*) DG Trio 474 341-2 (3). Emerson Qt

String Quartets 12–13; 16; Grosse Fuge, Op. 133
(B) *** Ph. (ADD) Duo 454 711-2 (2). Italian Qt

String Quartets 12, Op. 127; 15, Op. 132
*** MDG 307 0854-2. Leipzig Qt

String Quartets 12; 16, Op. 135
(B) **(*) EMI Encore 5 86415-2. Alban Berg Qt

String Quartet 13, Op. 130; Grosse Fuge, Op. 133
☛ *** ASV CDDCA 1117. Lindsay Qt
(B) **(*) EMI Red Line 5 69792. Alban Berg Qt

String Quartets 14–15
(B) **(*) Ph. (ADD) Duo 454 712-2 (2). Italian Qt
(B) **(*) EMI Red Line 5 69793. Alban Berg Qt

The Lindsays play not just as if they have lived a whole lifetime in the presence of Op. 130 but as if they are discovering it for the first time. The opening movement is perfectly paced – the *Adagio* opening having all the space that it needs – and the *Allegro* unfolding at the *tempo giusto*. Indeed this is a performance that soon has you forgetting the players and concentrating on the score. They speak with a naturalness and understanding that makes for a totally satisfying musical experience. They are splendidly recorded.

Here the Lindsays repeat the *Cavatina*, each time subtly modified, so that the listener can proceed either with that and the *Grosse Fuge* (Tracks 1–6) or with Beethoven's second thoughts (Tracks 1–4, 7 & 8) with the appropriate musical preparation, another performance of the *Cavatina*. The *Grosse Fuge* is given a shattering performance, crisper and more urgent than before, easily lyrical before the regular finale, an ultimate demonstration of the players' responsiveness.

The Leipzig are a first-class ensemble, totally free from expressive exaggeration and surface gloss. Their readings are artistically impeccable and technically immaculate, and MDG gives them first-class sound. Musical through and through, and strongly recommended.

The merits of the Italian Quartet's performances are very considerable and their separate reissue on a pair of Philips Duos is very competitive, even if the second of the two sets seems short measure at only 90 minutes. The remastered sound is very satisfying. But probably the best buy is the three-disc mid-priced set reissued as one of Philips's '50 Great Recordings'.

Sony does not give the date of these Juilliard recordings anywhere in the booklet or on the discs themselves, merely noting both copyright and performance as 2002. It does state that the set consists of previously released material, and presumably this is from the 1980s, since Earl Carlyss is listed as the second violin (nowadays it is Joel Smirnoff). In any event, the performances are far from negligible and the set is economical: Opp. 127 and 131 occupy the first disc, Opp. 132 and 135 the last, and Op. 130 and the *Grosse Fuge* the remaining CD. Vital, intelligent readings, competitively priced and decently enough recorded.

The renowned (1957) Hollywood set of the late Beethoven *Quartets* is one of the classic sets. Technically, the Hollywood players are superior and their virtuosity in the *Grosse Fuge* has to be heard to be believed. But there is no playing to the gallery at any time: this is Beethoven perfectly played without any thought of display. The recordings are mono but have plenty of presence.

Some listeners may find that the sheer polish of the Alban Berg Quartet gets in the way. The recordings do full justice to the magnificently burnished tone that they command and the perfection of blend they so consistently achieve. These performances are drawn from the Alban Berg's second digital cycle of the early 1980s etc.

When the complete Emerson Quartet's recording of the Beethoven cycle of 1994–5 was first issued in 1996, *Gramophone* magazine commented: 'They continually offer new insights into some endlessly enthralling music. Do hear them.' This seems good advice, now they are re-emerging at reduced price, for they have also been praised elsewhere. There are undoubted insights during the course of these performances, and the technical finish of the playing is incredible – amazing, indeed awesome. It goes without saying that there are many incidental beauties too, for the ensemble is immaculate in its precision; its sheer thrust is overwhelming and the DG recording is marvellous. But to our ears the playing concentrates on virtuosity and presentation rather than substance. The group are at their most impressive in the concentration of the last quartets, where their contact with great music is impressive in its unanimity, and this Trio reissue is certainly worth consideration, even if it is by no means a primary choice.

String Quartets 14, Op. 131; 16, Op. 135 (**versions for string orchestra**)
**(*) DG 463 579-2. VPO, Previn – VERDI: *String Quartet* **(*)

André Previn here follows the example of Leonard Bernstein in recording with the Vienna Philharmonic Mitropoulos's understanding arrangement for full strings of this most demanding of quartets. The result is to add weight, while softening the sharpness of inspiration. Unfortunately, the reverberance of the recording softens the focus still further, so that the great set of slow variations of the fourth movement sounds almost Mahlerian in places. None the less, the extra power of the finale brings compensation. With an imaginative coupling in the comparable Verdi arrangement, this certainly makes an illuminating disc.

String Trios 1 in E flat, Op. 3; 2 in G; 3 in D; 4 in C min., Op. 9/1–3; Serenade in D, Op. 8
(B) *** DG Double (ADD) 459 466-2 (2). Italian String Trio

String Trio 1; Serenade in D, Op. 8
*** Hyp. CDA 67253. Leopold String Trio

String Trios 2–4
*** Hyp. CDA 67254. Leopold String Trio

The young Beethoven, in preparation for writing string quartets, composed the three Op. 9 *String Trios* in 1798. They have a winning originality, each well contrasted with the others. The delightful seven-movement *Serenade* was published in 1797. The performances by the prize-winning Leopold Trio are particularly alive and fresh, and the Hyperion recording is remarkably real and vivid.

The Italian performances are immaculately played, full of

vitality and vivid in sound, and choice is a matter of taste: both are equally valid interpretations.

Variations on 'Ich bin der Schneider Kakadu' (for piano trio)

(BB) (***) Naxos mono 8.110188. Thibaud, Casals, Cortot – HAYDN: *Piano Trio in G*; SCHUBERT: *Piano Trio 1* (***)

The celebrated Thibaud–Casals–Cortot Trio was active for barely a decade and made relatively few commercial records. By the standards of the Beaux Arts Trio their repertoire was minuscule, but they were all so active in other fields that they could come together only on rare occasions. This recording was made in 1926 and has been lovingly restored by Ward Marston, even if it undoubtedly shows its age.

VIOLIN SONATAS

Violin Sonatas 1–10 (complete); 'A Life with Beethoven' (documentary by Reiner Moritz)

(N) (M) **(*) DG **DVD** 073 014-2 (2). Mutter, Orkis

Violin Sonatas 5 in F, Op. 24 (Spring); 9 in A, Op. 49 (Kreutzer). 'A Life with Beethoven' (documentary by Reiner Moritz)

** DG **DVD** 073 004-9 (2). Mutter, Orkis

Violin Sonatas 5 (Spring); 9 (Kreutzer)

(*) DG **SACD (compatible) 471 641-2; CD 457 619-2. Mutter, Orkis (from above)

This hour-long documentary follows Anne-Sophie Mutter and Lambert Orkis during their year spent preparing and touring the Beethoven sonata cycle. The performances were recorded at the Théâtre des Champs Elysées in 1999. To follow them over an extended period yields useful insights, though the playing, particularly that of the distinguished violinist, will strike some as being at times just a little self-regarding: there are occasional intrusive expressive exaggerations during these always highly accomplished and intelligent performances. However, the complete set yields considerable rewards and is probably a better investment than the single disc. Good, straightforward camerawork and excellent sound. Subtitles for the English-language documentary are also available in German and French.

The two performances are also available on a very successfully transferred compatible SACD, which readily conveys the sense of 'live' music-making. The variations and finale of the *Kreutzer* are particularly spontaneous sounding.

Violin Sonatas 1–10

🕭― (N) (M) *** DG 476 7256-2 (3). Kremer, Argerich
*** DG 471 495-2 (3). Dumay, Pires
(M) *** Decca 421 453-2 (4); Perlman, Ashkenazy
(B) *** Ph. (ADD) 468 406-2 (4). D. Oistrakh, Oborin
(M) (***) DG mono 463 605-2 (3). Schneiderhan, Kempff
(B) *** Sony DDD/ADD SB3K 89975 (3). Stern, Istomin
(BB) **(*) EMI double forte (ADD) 5 73647-2 (2) (1–6); 5 73650-2 (2) (7–10). Zukerman, Barenboim – TCHAIKOVSKY: *Trio* *(**)
(BB) (***) Naxos mono 8.110969-71 (3). Kreisler, Rupp
(N) (B) (**) Van. Classics mono ATM CD1585 (4). Szigeti, Arrau

Having two such volatile artists as Kremer and Argerich in partnership for the Beethoven *Violin Sonatas* makes for exciting, heart-warming results. Perlman and Ashkenazy may be

more centrally recommendable for being just as communicative and less idiosyncratic, but Kremer and Argerich have one magnetized from first to last by their individuality in performances that consistently sound spontaneous and fresh. Note that all ten sonatas are squeezed on to only three discs at medium price in DG's Critics' Choice series.

The alternative set by Augustin Dumay and Maria João Pires is another of the finest recent surveys. These two artists have a special rapport and play as if they were controlled by one mind. Pires's sense of keyboard colour and pianistic control are to be relished, and the violinist is both thoughtful and individual. He does take some liberties of phrasing, and some may be worried by the odd moment of self-consciousness. But these are intelligently conceived accounts that sound beautiful and are very vividly and naturally recorded. They are elegantly and economically packaged.

Perlman and Ashkenazy's performances offer a blend of classical purity and spontaneous vitality that is hard to resist; moreover, the realism and presence of the recording in its CD format are very striking.

The 1962 versions by David Oistrakh and Lev Oborin are also performances to treasure. There is a relaxed joy in the music-making, an almost effortless lyricism and an infectious sparkle. Some might feel a lack of inner tension, and the recording is rather wider in separation than we favour nowadays, but it is a beautiful sound in every other respect.

The combination of Schneiderhan's refinement and classical sense of poise with Kempff's concentration and clarity makes these 1953 performances highly competitive, even compared with Kempff's later set with Menuhin. Schneiderhan's playing has greater finish and his lyrical line sings sweet and true. One has only to sample the *Spring* or *Kreutzer Sonatas* to discover the calibre of this partnership, spontaneous, dramatic and full of insights, while Kempff's opening of the slow movement of the *C minor Sonata*, Op. 30/2, is unforgettable, and his partner joins him in comparable rapt concentration. The mono recording obviously does not separate violin and piano as clearly as in the stereo set, but the internal balance could hardly be bettered.

The performances by Stern and Istomin have striking rhythmic strengths as well as lyrical appeal: how delightfully the lilting opening theme of *No. 2 in A major* dances along, and how superbly the great *Adagio* of the *C minor*, Op. 30/2, is sustained. This and the very first sonata are analogue and were recorded in 1969; the remainder are digital and date from 1982–3. The *Spring Sonata* is more intense than some versions; the *C minor*, Op. 30/2, has similar electricity, and the *Kreutzer* is splendid. The recording has fine presence, with the close balance suiting the highly projected style of music-making. Excellent value.

Zukerman and Barenboim, friends and colleagues, are both strong and positive artists and they consistently strike imaginative sparks off each other, yet there is a hint too that they may have been conscious of earlier criticism that their collaborations were too idiosyncratic. So these are very much central performances which, although not the most imaginative we have had, are a safe recommendation. At bargain price, in good sound, with an exciting performance of the Tchaikovsky *Piano Trio* as a bonus, this is worth considering.

The Beethoven Sonata Society records, now reissued by Naxos, followed on from Schnabel's cycle of the *Piano Sonatas* and were made in 1935–6. Fritz Kreisler's warm and sensuous vibrato and unique, golden tone come across strongly, even after the passage of almost seventy years, and in some ways they occupy much the same position in the pantheon of great recordings as do the Schnabel. Of course, there are great successors (the Heifetz cycle with Emanuel Bey was underrated in some circles, and the Grumiaux–Haskil, Oistrakh–Oborin cycles offer many insights), but the Kreisler still clamours for a special place. Ward Marston's transfers bring them to life in a vivid fashion and will astonish those who do not know them as well as we do.

The equally famous performances by Szigeti and Arrau were recorded at the Library of Congress in 1944, and the artistry – particularly of Arrau – is formidable. The downside is the sound-quality, which is very dry indeed and does little justice to Szigeti's purity of tone; moreover, applause is cut out very abruptly. The album reproduces the original LP sleeve-notes.

Violin Sonatas 1–3, Op. 12/1–3
(BB) *** Naxos 8.550284. Nishizaki, Jandó

Violin Sonatas 3; 5 (Spring); 9 (Kreutzer)
(BB) (***) Naxos mono 8.110954. Busch, Serkin

Violin Sonatas 4, Op. 23; 10, Op. 96; 12 Variations on Mozart's 'Se vuol ballare', WoO 40
(BB) *** Naxos 8.550285. Nishizaki, Jandó

Violin Sonatas 4; 5 (Spring)
(BB) **(*) EMI double forte (ADD) 5 74293-2 (2). Kagan, S. Richter – MOZART: *Violin Sonatas* **(*)

Naxos offer a winning combination here, in performances wonderfully fresh and alive. Takako Nishizaki's timbre, though not large, is admirably suited to Beethoven and she is in complete rapport with Jandó, who is in excellent form. The *Mozart Variations*, too, are winningly done. The recording is most naturally balanced and the acoustic is spacious without clouding the focus.

The Busch–Serkin accounts of Op. 12, No. 3 and the *Spring Sonata* come from the early 1930s, and the *Kreutzer* was recorded in New York in 1941. These transfers leave no doubt as to the fine musicianship and aristocratic finesse of this playing. Adolf Busch was a Beethovenian of rare quality, and Serkin was at his most responsive and sensitive at this period.

Kagan and Richter offer performances which are very strong on personality, and the results are both distinguished and compelling. There are touches of exaggeration here and there: staccato is very staccato, and the first movement of the *A minor* is fast and nervously intense, but there is no doubting the stature of these readings. The 1976 recording is excellent, and so too is the Mozart coupling.

Violin Sonatas (i) 5 (Spring); (ii) 9 (Kreutzer)
⌀→ (M) *** Decca (ADD) 458 618-2. Perlman, Ashkenazy
(BB) *** Warner Apex 8573 89079-2. Vengerov, (i) Golan; (ii) Markovich
(BB) *** Naxos 8.550283. Nishizaki, Jandó
(B) **(*) EMI Red Line 5 69789. Yehudi & Jeremy Menuhin

Couplings of the *Spring* and *Kreutzer Sonatas* are legion, and the combination of Perlman and Ashkenazy in Decca's 'Legends' series must take pride of place.

Maxim Vengerov recorded the *Kreutzer* first in 1991, the *Spring* a year later. Of his two partners, Alexander Markovich obviously proved the more stimulating, for in the impulsive account of the *Spring Sonata* one feels that Itamar Golan adds comparatively little, although he leads on well enough. But in the *Kreutzer*, and especially in the central variations, Vengerov and Markovich find an affinity. The finale is taken with great

dash and this is undoubtedly infectious when Vengerov's playing is so technically dazzling. The vivid immediacy of the recording – which makes the forwardly placed violin sound larger than life – suits the impetuous manner of the music-making, which is alive in every bar.

If Takako Nishizaki does not produce a large sound, the balance with Jandó is expertly managed, and the result is very natural and real. The performances are delightful in their fresh spontaneity. An excellent bargain.

In 1986 Yehudi Menuhin re-recorded these works, this time with his son. Jeremy plays remarkably well, if not quite matching Hephzibah in the slow movement of the *Kreutzer*. Menuhin's timbre may be less rounded than formerly, and his technique less refined, but the nobility of line is still apparent, and the spontaneity and family chemistry are as potent as ever. The *Kreutzer* finale is joyfully spirited. Excellent recording in a resonant acoustic.

Violin Sonatas (i) 1 in D, Op. 12/1; (ii) 7 in C min., Op. 30/2; (iii) 8 in G, Op. 30/3
*** Concert Recordings WFYI Indianapolis IVCI 1998. (i) Baak, Epperson; (ii) Roussev, Eguchi; (iii) Prunaru, De Silva (website: www.violin.org)

These excellent performances were recorded live by three prize-winners at the 1998 International Violin Competition of Indianapolis, for one of the rules of the semi-final is that each of the soloists shall choose and play a Beethoven violin sonata. All three performances here are polished and full of vitality, amply conveying the urgency of live music-making and in each case demonstrating a true partnership between the two artists. The performance of the *C minor Sonata* is especially fine, but the *G major* is hardly less vivid and gripping. The earlier *D major Sonata* is a little plainer, but has strong classical feeling. A most enjoyable disc, realistically recorded.

Violin Sonatas 6–8, Op. 30/1–3
(BB) *** Naxos 8.550286. Nishizaki, Jandó

All three of the Op. 30 *Sonatas* on one CD represents very good value, particularly with playing of such quality.

Violin Sonatas 8, Op. 30/3; 9, Op. 47; 10, Op. 96
(B) *** Cal. (ADD) CAL 6251. Messiereur, Bogunia

Strong, direct accounts of Beethoven's last three sonatas, of striking spontaneity and recorded with great presence and vividness. This playing, if not always subtle, leaps out of the speakers. This disc is well worth its modest cost.

Violin Sonata 9 in A (Kreutzer), Op. 47
*** EMI 5 56815-2. Perlman, Argerich – FRANCK: *Violin Sonata* ***

Perlman and Argerich, both big musical personalities, strike sparks off each other in this vividly characterful reading of the *Kreutzer*, recorded live. Ensemble is not always immaculate, and audience noises intrude, but this playing could not be more vital, with the first movement fiery and dramatic, the slow movement warmly expressive, and the finale sparkily volatile. The recording, not as immediate as most of Perlman's studio recordings, gives a better idea than usual of his full range of dynamic and tone. Well coupled with a comparable reading of the Franck.

Wind music

Chamber Music for Wind (complete)

(M) **(*) CPO 999 658-2 (4). Consortium Classicum (as below)

Allegro & Minuet for 2 Flutes in G, WoO 26; Duo 1 in C for Clarinet & Bassoon, WoO 27/1; Septet in E flat, Op. 20
**(*) CPO 999 162-2. Consortium Classicum

Duo 2 in F for Clarinet & Bassoon, WoO 27/2; Fidelio: Harmoniemusik: Overture, Arias & Scenes (arr. Sedlak); *Variations on Mozart's 'Là ci darem la mano'*
** CPO 999 437-2. Consortium Classicum

Wind Octet in E flat, Op. 103; Rondino in E flat, WoO 25; Trio for 2 Oboes & Cor Anglais in C, Op. 87
**(*) CPO 999 438-2. Consortium Classicum

Duo 3 in B flat for Clarinet & Bassoon, WoO 27/3; Grenadier March in B flat, WoO 29; Quintet in E flat for Oboe, 3 Horns & Bassoon; Wind Sextet in E flat, Op. 71
**(*) CPO 999 439-2. Consortium Classicum

The Consortium Classicum are a highly musical and eminently stylish group, and anyone wanting all Beethoven's important music for wind ensemble will find the CPO recordings well balanced and pleasing. The *Allegro and Minuet for Two Flutes* and the *Clarinet and Bassoon Duos* are played most winningly and have great charm, while the *Trio for Two Oboes and Cor Anglais*, a little-known but thoroughly rewarding work in the composer's wind output, is most persuasively presented. The *Grenadier March* is an engaging lollipop. However, few will want to repeat the 38-minute selection (*Harmoniemusik*) from *Fidelio* very often and, while Druzěc's wind octet arrangement of the *Septet*, Op. 20, comes off spontaneously here, most collectors will prefer to have the original scoring. The four key works are available together on ASV in rather more characterful performances (see below): their superiority is most apparent in their more imaginative response to slow movements.

(Wind) *Octet in E flat, Op. 103; Quintet in E flat for Oboe, 3 Horns & Bassoon; Rondino in E flat for Wind Octet, WoO 25; Sextet in E flat, Op. 71*
*** ASV CDCOE 807. Wind Soloists of COE

The wind soloists of the Chamber Orchestra of Europe give strong and stylish performances of this collection of Beethoven's wind music, marked by some outstanding solo work, notably from the first oboe, Douglas Boyd. They are recorded in warm but clear sound, with good presence.

PIANO MUSIC

Piano Sonatas 1–32 (complete)
🔾➤ *** Nonesuch 7559 79328-2 (10). Goode
✹ (B) (***) DG mono 447 966-2 (8 + bonus disc). Kempff
(BB) *** EMI (ADD) 5 72912-2 (10). Barenboim
(BB) *** Nim. NI 1774 (11). Roberts
(B) *** DG 463 127-2 (9). Barenboim
✹ (M) (***) EMI mono 7 63765-2 (8). Schnabel

Piano Sonatas 1–32; Bagatelles, Opp. 119 & 125
✹ (B) *** EMI 5 62700-2 (9). Kovacevich

Piano Sonatas 1–32; Diabelli Variations
(M) *** Oehms OCD 229 (10). Perl

Stephen Kovacevich recorded his Beethoven cycle for EMI

between 1992 and 2003 with consistent success, capping the series with an extraordinarily powerful and imaginative account of the *Hammerklavier*. The individual CDs have been highly praised by us. However, some of them have been withdrawn, so the arrival of the complete set at bargain price is doubly welcome. EMI's recording is of consistently high quality, and this cycle must now be counted a first choice, alongside those by Goode, Kempff and (of course) the pioneering Schnabel readings.

It is not just the power of Goode's playing that singles him out, but also the beauty, when he has such subtle control over a formidably wide tonal and dynamic range. Even at its weightiest, the sound is never clangorous. Particularly in the early sonatas, Goode brings out the wit and parody, while slow movements regularly draw sensuously velvety legato. Helped by unusually full and clear recording, with no haze of reverberation, the clarity of his articulation is breathtaking, as in the running semiquavers of the finale of the *Appassionata Sonata*. Above all, Goode has a natural gravity which compels attention. One has to go back to the pre-digital era to find a Beethoven cycle of comparable command and intensity. A first choice for those wanting a modern digital cycle.

Those who have cherished Kempff's later, stereo cycle for its magical spontaneity will find this quality conveyed even more intensely in his mono set, recorded between 1951 and 1956. The interpretations are the more personal, the more individual, at times the more wilful; but for any listener who responds to Kempff's visionary concentration, this is a magical series. No other set of the sonatas so clearly gives the impression of new discovery. Amazingly, the sound has more body and warmth than the stereo set. A ninth disc comes free, celebrating Kempff's achievement in words and music, on the organ in Bach, on the piano in Brahms, Chopin and Beethoven (a masterly pre-war recording of the *Pathétique Sonata*) and accompanying Fischer-Dieskau in four of his own songs.

Barenboim's earlier set of the Beethoven *Sonatas*, recorded for EMI when he was in his late twenties, remains one of his very finest achievements on record. The readings often involve extreme tempi, both fast and slow, but the spontaneous style is unfailingly compelling. At times Barenboim's way is mercurial, with an element of fantasy. But overall this is a keenly thoughtful musician living through Beethoven's great piano cycle with an individuality that puts him in the line of the master pianists. The admirably balanced recordings were made at Abbey Road between 1967 and 1970, and the remastered quality brings a most believably natural piano-image.

Bernard Roberts's cycle – his second for Nimbus – can be warmly recommended, the more so when it too comes at super-bargain price. These are dedicated, undistracting readings which consistently reflect Roberts's mastery as a chamber-music pianist, intent on presenting the composer's arguments as clearly as possible, not drawing attention to himself. Always spontaneous-sounding, Roberts's approach to Beethoven has an element of toughness, whether in the early works or the late, a point that comes out the more clearly when the individual discs mix works of different periods. The mature sonatas are marked by rugged power, with Roberts's virtuosity given full rein, as in the finale of the *Appassionata*. The digital sound is full-bodied, with the piano set in a helpful, quite intimate acoustic.

Spontaneity and electricity, extremes of expression in dynamic, tempo and phrasing, as well as mood, mark Daniel Barenboim's DG cycle, as they did his much earlier one for EMI. Some of the more extreme readings have been modified to fall short of provocation or eccentricity. This time spontaneity is even more evident, though that means he has a tendency at times to rush his fences, particularly in the early sonatas. All three movements of the *Waldstein* are more lyrical this time, and that applies to the late sonatas too, not just in slow movements but equally strikingly in the great fugal movements, where inner parts are brought out more clearly and warmly. The role of such a cycle as this is not to set Barenboim's readings as though in amber, fixed for ever, but to act more nearly as a living document of a performer at a particular point in his career. The sound is full and spacious, more consistent than before. The CD transfers, on one disc fewer than Barenboim's EMI set, are of consistently high quality.

The young Chilean pianist Alfredo Perl responds superbly to the challenge of a complete Beethoven sonata cycle, giving searching accounts of works both early and late, always fresh and spontaneous-sounding, consistently finding depths of concentration in the most demanding of Beethoven's slow movements. Particularly in the early sonatas, his manner is impulsive, often with allegros fast in a Schnabel manner, yet with technical problems masterfully solved and no fudging of detail. Slow movements by contrast are generally spacious, but not so exaggeratedly so that the music loses momentum or a sense of lyrical line. The cycle is splendidly rounded off in accounts of the late sonatas that transcend everything else, not least the *Hammerklavier*, where the slow movement has a sublime purity. The performance of the *Diabelli Variations* is equally commanding and imaginative.

However, although this set was originally issued on Arte Nova at budget price, its reissue at mid-price becomes less competitive when compared with other cycles at bargain price like Kovacevich's or Barenboim's on EMI or Bernard Roberts on Nimbus. The sound is first rate, though inner textures are not always ideally clear, while Perl's use of the pedal is on the generous side, adding to the warmth of the readings. Undoubtedly this Oehms reissue stands alongside the finest surveys of this repertoire, and it is a pity that it is not in a lower price-range. The *Diabelli Variations* (but not the sonatas) are also available separately (OCD 230).

For many music-lovers and record collectors of an older generation, Schnabel was the voice of Beethoven; returning to this pioneering set again, one realizes that his insights were deeper than those of almost anyone who followed him, though his pianism has been surpassed. This is one of the towering classics of the gramophone and, whatever other individual Beethoven sonatas you may have, this is an indispensable reference point.

Piano Sonatas 1–3, Op. 21/1–3
(BB) (***) Naxos mono 8.110693. Schnabel

Piano Sonatas 4, Op.7; 5–6, Op. 10/1–2; 19–20, Op. 49/1–2
(BB) (***) Naxos mono 8.110694. Schnabel

Piano Sonatas 7, Op. 10/3; 8 (Pathétique); 9–10, Op. 14/1–2
(BB) (***) Naxos mono 8.110695. Schnabel

Piano Sonatas 11 in B flat, Op. 22; 12 in A flat, Op. 26; 13 in E flat, Op. 27/1
(BB) (***) Naxos mono 8.110756. Schnabel

Piano Sonatas 14 in C sharp min. (Moonlight; 15 in D (Pastoral; 16 in G, Op. 31/1
(BB) (***) Naxos mono 8.110759. Schnabel

Piano Sonatas 17 in D min. (Tempest; 18 in E flat, Op. 31/3; 21 in C (Waldstein)
(BB) (***) Naxos mono 8.110760. Schnabel

These Beethoven Sonata Society recordings were the classic accounts of the 1930s and the 78-r.p.m. era, and Artur Schnabel brought to this great repertoire a rare depth and vision. There are pianistic inelegances (rushed triplets, etc.), sometimes extreme tempi and a bad-tempered quality that sound totally Beethoven; but the concentration, wisdom and insights (particularly of the late sonatas) remain in a class of their own. There is no question as to the superiority of Mark Obert-Thorn's transfers in comparison with the previous EMI issues: they are more present and vivid, and have much greater body. They also have the advantage of being available singly, so that those who want the greatest performances, such as the *Waldstein*, and the Opp. 110 and 111, can get them without having necessarily to bother with the earlier ones or the very approximate *Hammerklavier*. (This is no match for Solomon's classical and articulate account or his *C major*, Op. 2/3, for example, now on Testament.) But the best are beyond price and they have never sounded better.

Pianistically, these are full of rough edges and do not aspire to sheer pianistic perfection and high polish. However, they come closer to Beethoven than has almost any other musician since, and in these excellent transfers remain an indispensable part of any self-respecting collection.

Piano Sonatas 1, Op. 2/1 ; 3, Op. 2/3; 32, Op. 111
✿ (***) Testament mono SBT 1188. Solomon
Piano Sonatas 7, Op. 10/3; 8 (Pathétique); 13; 14 (Moonlight), Op. 27/1-2
✿ (***) Testament mono SBT 1189. Solomon
Piano Sonatas 17; 18, Op. 31/2–3; 21 (Waldstein); 22, Op. 54
✿ (***) Testament mono SBT 1190. Solomon
Piano Sonatas 23 (Appassionata); 28, Op. 101; 30 & 31, Opp. 109–110
✿ (***) Testament mono SBT 1192. Solomon
Piano Sonatas 26 (Les Adieux); 27, Op. 90; 29 (Hammerklavier)
✿ (***) Testament mono SBT 1191. Solomon

This five-CD set provides a welcome reminder of Solomon's artistry and stature. Alas, it was never completed, as his stroke in 1956 brought his career prematurely to an end. All these discs are available separately, and no one who cares about Beethoven and great piano-playing should lose this opportunity of acquiring them. Solomon was the least assertive of musicians yet the most deeply satisfying, and his interpretations never obscure Beethoven's intentions. His approach has a unique gravity, an Olympian serenity and an unforced naturalness; Bryce Morrison once spoke of the 'outer sobriety yet inner strength and radiance' of his playing. These performances are among the pinnacles of Beethoven playing, and the transfers have never sounded better, surpassing in every respect the earlier, EMI Références issues.

Piano Sonatas 1–3; 5–7; 16–18; 11; 13; 14 (Moonlight); 16; 17 (Tempest); 18–20; 21 (Waldstein); 23 (Appassionata); 25; 26 (Les Adieux)
(N) (BB) *** Virgin 5 62638-2 (5). Tan (fortepiano)

Melvyn Tan began his survey of Beethoven's sonatas using the fortepiano in 1990, continuing in 1991 and 1992; but it was never completed, presumably because of lack of demand, certainly not because of any lack of artistry. Tan has a strong musical personality and in the named middle-period sonatas attacks his instrument with tremendous spirit and flair; every phrase lives, and he is not afraid to present the widest dynamic range. There is consummate artistry and real temperament and fire. Nor is there any want of poetic feeling. In the earlier sonatas he plays with brilliance and sensitivity in equal measure. He uses a copy by Derek Adlam of a Streicher (1814), an instrument for which Beethoven himself expressed a strong preference. The EMI recording is excellent. Even collectors whose taste inclines to the modern piano rather than the fortepiano will surely find both the sounds and musical sense well conveyed here, and perhaps they will be tempted to explore these performances when the cost is so little.

Piano Sonatas 1 in F min.; 2 in A; 3 in C, Op. 2/1–3
*** Sony SK 64397. Perahia
*** Chan. 9212. Lortie
(BB) **(*) Naxos 8.550150. Jandó

As his accounts of the concertos have shown, Murray Perahia is as authoritative and sensitive an interpreter of Beethoven as he is of Mozart. These are commanding accounts of the greatest elegance and freshness. The C major Sonata is arguably the best we have had since the days of Kempff.

Louis Lortie has the benefit of an immediate and truthful recording, greatly enhancing his playing. He brings his usual refined musical intelligence to all three of the Op. 2 Sonatas, giving ample evidence of his instinctive musicianship and artistry.

Jenö Jandó's complete recording of the Beethoven Piano Sonatas is also available in two flimsy slip-cases, each comprising five CDs (8.505002 and 8.505003). This first CD (actually Volume 3) establishes Jandó's credentials as a strong, unidiosyncratic Beethovenian. The piano sound is full and bold.

Piano Sonatas 3 in C, Op. 2/3; 4 in E flat, Op. 7; 27 in E min., Op. 90
☛ (N) (BB) *** Regis (ADD) RRC 1185. S. Richter

A superb disc which, at Regis price, ought to be in every collection, if only for the inspired and very beautful account of the rapt slow movement of Op. 2/3 and the rippling finale of Op. 90, which all but smiles. But all three performances are masterly in their control of structure and intensity, and none sounds either early or immature, just great Beethoven.

Piano Sonatas 3; 29 (Hammerklavier); 6 Bagatelles, Op. 126
(***) BBC (ADD) BBCL 4052-2. S. Richter

Sviatoslav Richter's Beethoven recital of the early C major Sonata, the Hammerklavier and the 6 Bagatelles comes from the Aldeburgh season of 1975 and was unannounced in the Festival brochure. In accordance with Richter's penchant for little-known venues, it was held in Blythburgh Church rather than one of the larger venues. The opening of the Hammerklavier explodes like some galactic force, and the intensity and fire of the performance carries all before it. There is tremendous spontaneity as well as a magnificence about it. Unusually for Richter, he does not repeat the exposition in the first movement of Op. 2, No. 3. Both this piece and the Bagatelles complete a memorable musical occasion, which fortunately escaped oblivion in the BBC Archives. Very acceptable sound.

Piano Sonatas 4 in E flat, Op. 7; 12 in A flat, Op. 26
(M) **(*) BBC mono/stereo BBCL 4064-2. Michelangeli –
    DEBUSSY: Hommage à Rameau **(*); RAVEL: Gaspard de la nuit (***)

The Beethoven sonatas and the Debussy Hommage à Rameau come from a Festival Hall recital that the great pianist gave in 1982. Michelangeli recorded the E flat Sonata for DG, where its 29 minutes were spread over two LP sides. Of the two, this performance sounds the more involving. Michelangeli brings fastidious keyboard articulation and refinement of phrasing to both sonatas here, though he remains curiously aloof.

Piano Sonatas 4; 13 in E flat, Op. 27/1; 19-20, Op. 49/1-2; 22 in F, Op. 54
(BB) **(*) Naxos 8.550167. Jandó

The performances of both the E flat Sonata, Op. 7, and the Sonata quasi una fantasia, Op. 27/1, in which Jandó is totally responsive to Beethoven's wide expressive range, show the excellence of this series, and the three shorter works are also freshly presented.

Piano Sonatas 5–7, Op. 10/1–3; 8 (Pathétique)
(N)**(*) DG 474 810-2. Pollini

Maurizio Pollini continues his magisterial traversal of the Beethoven sonatas, and these marmoreal accounts of the Op. 10 set and the Pathétique offer the superb pianism and intelligence which his admirers rightly treasure. But, as with other recent Beethoven from this artist, they remain for us curiously uninvolving. Excellent sound.

Piano Sonatas 7; 14 (Moonlight); 28, Op. 101
(**(*)) Testament mono SBT 1070. Anda

These recordings come from 1955–8, during the heyday of Géza Anda's years as a Columbia (EMI) artist. The outstanding performance is the otherworldly account of the A major Sonata, Op. 101. All three sonatas are played with a vibrant sense of line, and the recordings are fresh and clean.

Piano Sonatas 7; 23 (Appassionata)
(M) *** Sony SMK 39344. Perahia

Intense, vibrant playing from Perahia in the D major Sonata, with great range of colour and depth of thought, and the Appassionata brings a performance of comparable stature.

Piano Sonatas 8 (Pathétique); 14 (Moonlight); 15 (Pastoral); 17 (Tempest); 21 (Waldstein); 23 (Appassionata); 26 (Les Adieux)
(B) *** Ph. (ADD) Duo 438 730-2. Brendel
(B) *** Double Decca (ADD) 452 952-2 (2). Ashkenazy
(BB) **(*) Decca Eloquence (ADD) 467 487-2 (2). Backhaus

All the performances here are taken from Brendel's analogue cycle for Philips; they are impressive and the recording is consistently excellent. The Tempest, Op. 31/2, is finely conceived and thoroughly compelling, and the central movements of the Pastoral resonate in the memory. Outstanding too is Brendel's account of the Waldstein.

The comparable Decca collection of named sonatas shows Ashkenazy consistently as a penetrating and individual Beethovenian. The Moonlight is poetic and unforced, and he brings concentration together with spontaneity of feeling to the Tempest, with an impressive command of keyboard colour. Taking a broadly lyrical view, the Waldstein is splendidly structured, and the Appassionata is superb. The very good analogue recordings are excellently transferred to CD.

In the early days of LP, Backhaus was Decca's star Beethoven pianist, and he recorded all the piano concertos and sonatas for this label in the Indian summer of a long and distinguished career. Not all ears take readily to his self-consciously authoritative and often brusque manner, yet he found spontaneity in the recording studio, and also an unmistakable Beethovenian spirit. The finest performances here are the *Waldstein* and *Appassionata* (fully three-star). His interpretations had changed little if at all over the years, but had never before been caught on disc so realistically, and this coupling was one of the key Beethoven LPs in the early stereo era. The other works also spring to life here, but his somewhat unyielding manner is less suited to the opening of the *Pastoral Sonata*, although he is at his best in the finale. The surprise is the *Moonlight Sonata*, much more resilient than we had remembered. The recordings (dating from between 1959 and 1964) provide an appropriately bold, full-blooded piano image.

Piano Sonatas 8 (Pathétique); 14 (Moonlight); 17 (Tempest); 23 (Appassionata)
(BB) **(*) Warner Apex (ADD) 8575 89225-2. Pires

Maria-João Pires's recordings date from 1977 and show her already emerging as an individual artist. Her performances are clear and direct, the *Appassionata* strikingly authoritative, the *Tempest* more personalized, and enjoyably so. Fine analogue recording, truthfully transferred. Good value at Apex price.

Piano Sonatas 8 (Pathétique); 14 (Moonlight); 21 (Waldstein); 23 (Appassionata)
(M) *** DG (ADD) 447 404-2. Kempff

Everything Kempff does has his individual stamp; above all, he never fails to convey the deep intensity of a master in communication with Beethoven, as in the magic of his measured reading of the finale of the *Waldstein*. The *Appassionata* is characteristically clear and classically straight. The recording has gained in firmness with the clean sound of the digital remastering.

Piano Sonatas 8 (Pathétique); 14 (Moonlight); 23 (Appassionata)
(N) (M) **(*) EMI CD/DVD (ADD) 557 762. Barenboim (with bonus DVD : BEETHOVEN: Choral Fantasia, with BPO)
(BB) **(*) Naxos 8.550045. Jandó

Barenboim's 1966 performances of the three named sonatas combine impetuosity with a confident control of line. There is a rhapsodic feel to his approach which is very convincing. The *Appassionata*, like the *Pathétique*, is rather wild and rhapsodic in the first movement, and the slow speed for the central variations brings a simple, natural intensity which contrasts well with the lightness and clarity of the finale. The sound is first class. The bonus DVD brings a live (1995) performance of the *Choral Fantasia*; Barenboim (directing from the keyboard) displays much delicacy and charm in the opening sections and builds the work up to a fine climax.

Jandó's clean, direct style and natural spontaneity are particularly admirable in the slow movements of the *Pathétique* and *Appassionata*, warmly lyrical in feeling, yet not a whit sentimental. Only in the coda of the finale of the *Appassionata* does one feel a loss of poise, when the closing *presto* becomes *prestissimo* and the exuberance of the music-making nearly gets out of control.

Piano Sonatas 8 (Pathétique); 14 (Moonlight); 23 (Appassionata); 26 (Les Adieux)
⊕—● ✿ (M) *** RCA (ADD) 09026 63056-2. Rubinstein
(M) *** Ph. 464 680-2. Brendel
(N) (M) **(*) Sony (ADD) 517481-2 [SK 90395]. Serkin

Piano Sonatas 8 (Pathétique); 14 (Moonlight); 23 (Waldstein)
(N) (M) ** Decca (ADD) 476 7218. Radu Lupu

Artur Rubinstein had never recorded the *Moonlight* previously, and he brings to it a combination of freshness and maturity to make it stand out even among many fine recorded versions, with an improvisatory feeling in the opening movement. The *Pathétique* has a youthful urgency in the outer movements, and the impulsive surge of feeling in the *Appassionata* is equally compelling. The recordings, made in the Manhattan Center, New York City, sound firmer and fuller than they did on LP.

Gathered together to be included as one of Philips's '50 Great Recordings', Brendel's performances date from 1994 and are part of his third cycle of the Beethoven sonatas. The gentle, beautifully controlled opening of the *Moonlight* sets the seal on these interpretations, considered and full of wisdom. But Brendel's playing certainly does not lack impulse and spontaneity, as is readily shown by the opening movement of the *Appassionata*. Slow movements are songful yet have depth and character, and Brendel's instinctive feeling for the line of Beethoven's music is never shown more readily than in his wonderfully sympathetic account of *Les Adieux*. The recording, made in The Maltings, is totally real.

Rudolf Serkin's aristocratic approach is immediately apparent at the opening of the *Moonlight Sonata*, and in the allegro he is as incisive and dramatic as ever. As with all master pianists, one finds many points of insight emerging as well as one or two points of personal mannerism. The studio recording dates from December 1962 and the *Les Adieux* Sonata, added for the present reissue, was recorded in Carnegie Hall exactly 15 years later. The present transfers are firmer and more real than in the original LP incarnations, although, surprisingly, the effect is drier in the concert hall than in the studio.

Radu Lupu's more unusual Decca triptych of Beethoven named sonatas, including the *Waldstein* instead of the *Appassionata*, has been out of the catalogue for some years but is now happily restored in the Universal 'Critics' Choice' series, as it was originally chosen on BBC Radio 3 for 'Building a Record Library'. Lupu is an unfailingly sensitive artist and he has the undoubted gift of creating spontaneity in the recording studio. Sometimes his playing can seem mannered, as in his very deliberate approach to the famous slow movement of the *Pathétique Sonata* or at the opening of the *Moonlight*. But his playing carries conviction and the performances of both these works are individual and enjoyable He is less successful in holding the concentration of the *Waldstein* finale, having prepared the opening beautifully, and it is this that lets down an otherwise impressive reissue. The Decca recording is first rate in every way, sonorous and clear, a real piano sound.

Piano sonatas 8 in C min. (Pathétique); 23. (Appassionata); 31 in A flat, Op. 110
✿ (M) *** DG (DDD/ADD) 476 2194. Gilels

If the *Pathétique* does not rank among Emil Gilels's very finest Beethoven performances on record, such are the strengths of his playing that the reading still leaves a profound impression. The account of the *Appassionata* has previously been hailed by us as among the finest ever made, and the 1973 analogue recording is both full and believably present. Op. 110 is given a performance of real stature. Even when Gilels storms the greatest heights in the closing fugue, no *fortissimo* ever sounds percussive or strained. The *Pathétique* and Op. 110 are truthful digital recordings, both made in the Berlin Jesus-Christus-Kirche; the *Pathétique*, made in 1980, has the microphones a bit close, but in No. 31 (dating from five years later) the balance is better judged. An outstanding bargain, all the same. This has now been reissued by Universal as one of the 'Penguin ❂ Collection' at mid-price.

Piano Sonatas 9–10, Op. 14/1–2
(M) (***) BBC mono BBCL 4126-2. Sviatoslav Richter (with CHOPIN: *Etude in F sharp min., Op. 10/4*) – SCHUBERT: *Wanderer Fantasy* (***); SCHUMANN: *Abegg Variations, Op. 1; Faschingsschwank aus Wien* (**)

The two Op. 14 *Sonatas* come from a festival recital in February 1963, two years after Richter's first concert appearances in the West (he had already recorded them commercially for Philips). His very deliberate pace for the *Allegretto* movement of the *E major* lends it a reflective, almost melancholy character, which is unusual, but (as always with this great artist) his readings are the product of much thought. The mono sound is perfectly acceptable.

Piano Sonatas 9–10; 24, Op. 78; 27, Op. 90; 28, Op. 101
(BB) *** Naxos 8.550162. Jandó

Opp. 90 and 101 show this artist at full stretch. These are demanding works and Jandó does not fall short, particularly in the eloquent slow movements. The piano-sound is most believable.

Piano Sonatas 10, Op. 14/2; 19–20, Op. 49/1–2
(M) *** Ph. (ADD) 464 710-2 (2). S. Richter – LISZT: *Piano Concertos 1–2* ***

These three sonatas (sonatinas in all but name) are among those works that most budding amateur pianists have tried to play. Richter presents them with disarming ease and simplicity, and with the utmost eloquence. He is beautifully recorded (in 1963), but this was a curious coupling for his famous versions of the Liszt *Concertos* with Kondrashin, dating from two years earlier, which also had a London venue.

Piano Sonata 11 in B flat, Op. 22
(N) **(*) DG **DVD** 073 4045. Pogorelich (Director: Humphrey Burton) – BACH: *English Suites 2 & 3* **(*); D. SCARLATTI: *Keyboard Sonatas* ***

The second part of Pogorelich's DVD recital (including Beethoven and Scarlatti) moves to the Schloss Eckartsau, near Vienna, a year later in 1987, but the backcloth is equally attractive, and the camerawork follows the previous pattern undistractingly. Pogorelich's Beethoven style is authoritative but slightly detached: the *Adagio*, marked *con molta espressione*, seems a little cool in response. But the later movements loosen up a bit, and there is no doubt that this is a distinctive performance which will more than satisfy the pianist's many admirers.

Piano Sonatas 11–12; 19–20
*** Chan. 9755. Lortie

Performances of vital and unfailing intelligence which make one think afresh about the music itself. What we have heard so far of Louis Lortie's Beethoven odyssey makes one feel that it is worth placing alongside Stephen Kovacevich's sonata cycle on EMI; it is certainly not inferior to it. The Chandos recording is state of the art and wonderfully natural. A most distinguished issue.

Piano Sonatas 11, Op. 22; 29 (Hammerklavier)
(BB) **(*) Naxos 8.550234. Jandó

From its very opening bars, the *Hammerklavier* is commanding; there is rapt concentration in the slow movement, and the closing fugue runs its course with a powerful inevitability. Again, most realistic recording.

Piano Sonatas 12, Op. 26; 16 & 18, Op. 31/1 & 3
(BB) **(*) Naxos 8.550166. Jandó

Volume 7 with its trio of middle-period sonatas can be recommended with few reservations. No. 18 is a considerable success, and there is much to stimulate the listener's interest here. Excellent sound.

Piano Sonatas 12, Op. 26; 13, Op. 27/1; 14 (Moonlight); 19, Op. 49/1; 20, Op. 49/2
*** EMI 5 57131-2. Kovacevich

Stephen Kovacevich's Beethoven always sounds freshly thought out and the first movement of the *A flat Sonata*, Op. 26, is no exception. However well you know it or how often you have heard it, Kovacevich remains an illuminating guide. Yet at no point in the sonata is there any point-making or attention-seeking. The same goes for his poetic and thoughtful account of the *Moonlight* and its beautiful E flat companion, Op. 27, No. 1. Very few pianists command the natural sense of repose that Kovacevich produces in the first movement of the latter, at the point where the main E flat idea gives way to *pianissimo* C major chords. These performances were recorded on the Royal Festival Hall's Steinway in the studios at Lyndhurst Hall and the sound is absolutely first class. A most satisfying and distinguished issue.

Piano Sonatas 14 (Moonlight); 21 (Waldstein); 23 (Appassionata)
(M) *** Virgin 5 61834-2. Pletnev
(N) (M) **(*) RCA (ADD) 82876 62311-2. Horowitz
(N) (M) **(*) Sony (ADD) 518802-2 [SK 92744] Horowitz (with *Sonata 8 Pathétique* excerpts: 1st and 2nd movements only)

Some will find the Pletnev *Moonlight* rather mannered, but he has the capacity to make you listen intently, and he finds the right depths in the slow movement and finale of the *Waldstein*. The account of the *Appassionata* is masterly. The engineering is immaculate. A fine mid-price reissue.

There is some masterly playing here on both discs, and the comparison between the two sets of performances is fascinating. In his 1972 Sony/CBS recording of the *Moonlight Sonata*, Horowitz takes the first movement faster than he did on his earlier 1956 RCA account and the result is undoubtedly less poetic. The other works on the Sony disc are much more succesful, with the finale of the *Waldstein* magically introduced and the *Appassionata* very powerful. This extends to the bonus of the 1963 excerpts from the *Pathétique Sonata*, which are equally impressive. No explanation is given for the omission of the finale. However, the RCA recording of the *Appassionata* was made (in 1959) in Carnegie Hall, and has an electrical spontaneity from the opening bars, and very vivid sound. The RCA 1956 performances of *Waldstein* is also very fine, but like the *Moonlight*, this was recorded (in 1956) at the pianist's home and the sound is dry and close. Even so, of the two discs this is marginally a first choice, unless you want the (very enjoyable) incomplete torso from the *Pathétique Sonata*.

Piano Sonatas 15–18; 30–32

(M) (**) Sony mono SM3K 52642 (3). Gould

'Wilful yet charismatic' is a phrase to which many have recourse whenever Glenn Gould's name is mentioned. There are no doubts as to his pianism or control or the quality of his musicianship; but his late Beethoven, for all its intelligence, is quirky and marred by his vocal contributions. It can be recommended only to his admirers.

Piano Sonatas: 15 (Pastoral); (Kurfürstensonaten) in E flat, F min., D, WoO 47/1–3; in C (incomplete), WoO 51; Sonatinas: in G, F, Anh. 5/1–2

(BB) **(*) Naxos 8.550255. Jandó

Jenö Jandó's playing is fresh, clean and intelligent and, if the two *Sonatinas* are not authentic, they make agreeable listening here. The *Pastoral Sonata* is admirably done.

Piano Sonatas 16–17 (Tempest); 18, Op. 31/1–3

*** Chan. 9842. Lortie

Louis Lortie's ongoing Beethoven sonata cycle is second only to Stephen Kovacevich's magisterial cycle on EMI, and in some instances (thanks to the quality of the Snape recording) it is every bit as fine. Apart from its artistic merits – Lortie rarely puts a finger wrong – it benefits from outstanding natural recording quality. Lortie's playing is tremendously alive and vibrant, and the vivid nature of the sound makes for supremely satisfying listening.

Piano Sonata 17 (Tempest)

◉ (N) (BB) *** EMI (ADD) Gemini 5 86543-2 (2). Sviatoslav Richter – HANDEL: *Suites 9–16* *** ◉

Richter makes the most of possibilities of contrast. He plays the opening extremely slowly and then, when the *Allegro* comes, he takes it unusually fast. Far from being odd, this effect is breathtaking. Excellent Abbey Road sound, and a bargain price.

Piano Sonatas 17 (Tempest); 21 (Waldstein); 26 (Les Adieux)

(BB) **(*) Naxos 8.550054. Jandó

Jenö Jandó offers here three famous named sonatas, and very enjoyable they are in their direct manner.

Piano Sonatas 21–25; 27; 30–32

(N) (M) (***) EMI mono 5 62880-2 (2). Schnabel

Piano Sonatas 22–26

(N) (BB) (***) Naxos mono 8.110761. Schnabel

These classic accounts have rarely been out of the catalogue. Keith Hardwick's 1991 transfers of the eight-CD EMI Références set have been replaced by new ones by Andrew Walter which have considerably more freshness, smoothness and transparency. There are some marvellous things, including a magnificent *Waldstein* and the final Opp. 109–111, which have arguably never been surpassed since they were made in 1932.

Piano Sonatas 22 in F, Op. 54; 23. (Appassionata) (2 versions); 24 in F sharp, Op. 78 (2 versions); 27 in E min., Op. 90

(M) ** DG 474 451-2 (2). Pollini

Pollini recorded all four sonatas in the fine acoustic of the Herkulessaal in the Residenz, Munich, during June 2002, and the sound has impeccable clarity and definition. In addition, we are offered a bonus CD of live performances of Opp. 57 and 78, recorded at the Musikverein in Vienna during the same month. (The little *F sharp major Sonata*, Op. 78, gains in breadth by the observance of both repeats.) However, for all their immaculate pianism there is a want of engagement in all six performances, live or studio, and an unwelcome detachment throughout. Masterly pianism but less masterly as Beethoven.

Piano Sonata 23 (Appassionata); Fantasy in G min., Op. 77

(N) (B) **(*)EMI Debut 5 85894-2. Biss – SCHUMANN: *Davidsbündlertänze* **

Jonathan Biss is a 23-year-old American pianist who has collected golden reviews and numerous awards. This Beethoven–Schumann recital forms part of EMI's invaluable Debut series on which so many young artists have announced their arrival. His accounts of the *G minor Fantasy* and the *Appassionata Sonata* show him in command of superb technical address and a keen dramatic sense. He does not show perhaps the variety of dynamics or subtlety of tonal colouring that would make his undoubtedly compelling playing totally satisfying. The recording captures the timbre and colour of the piano most truthfully.

Piano Sonatas 26 (Les Adieux); 29 (Hammerklavier); Bagatelles, Op. 119

◉━ ✿ *** EMI 5 57520-2. Kovacevich

Stephen Kovacevich opens the *Hammerklavier*, like Schnabel, with an urgent, impatient forward momentum, as if to show Beethoven's ideas straining at the leash and attempting to transcend the constraints of the medium. The slow movement has a depth and imagination that only the greatest interpretations can rival. This is arguably the finest *Hammerklavier* since Gilels and it has the advantage of excellent recorded sound. The *Bagatelles*, Op. 119, and the *Les Adieux Sonata* are worthy companions.

Piano Sonatas 27–28; 29 (Hammerklavier)

(N) (BB) **(*) Regis (ADD) RRC 1205. Brendel
(N) (BB) (***) Naxos 8.110762. Schnabel

Brendel's early Vox/Turnabout recordings make for another enterprising budget reissue on Regis. Brendel's first movement of Op. 101 is disappointingly underplayed, but there is much more *Innigkeit* in the wayward and elusive opening movement of Op. 90, and a smoothly flowing reading of the haunting second movement. The *Hammerklavier* is another matter. The concentration and sense of drama in the first movement are most striking, and only the comparatively unhushed reading of the slow movement – taken on the fast side – mars the interpretation.

Brendel's re-recordings for Philips of the late Beethoven sonatas (see Duo, below) sometimes have not quite the fire and sense of spontaneity that marked his invigorating if variably recorded Turnabout series, and the sound of these Regis transfers is remarkably good. The later Philips *Hammerklavier* is more carefully considered than this earlier version, and it is superbly recorded, so that the great *Adagio* has a genuinely hushed tone and it remains a very distinguished performance. But there is something special too about the earlier Vox version.

The Naxos transfers of Schnabel's recordings are of a very high standard. Comparing Mark Obert-Thorn's transfer of the *E minor Sonata*, Op. 90, with Andrew Walter's is instructive. Walter favours a rather forward sound and a much higher level, while the Naxos is relatively recessed and in some ways does greater justice to the tonal subtlety of Schnabel's playing. The *Hammerklavier*, not included in the EMI set, is perhaps the least technically successful of Schnabel's Sonata Society records, though there are wonderful insights in the slow movement.

Piano Sonatas 27, Op. 90; 28, Op. 101; 29 (Hammerklavier); 30, Op. 109; 31, Op. 110; 32, Op. 111

✿ (B) *** DG Double (ADD) 453 010-2 (2). Kempff

(M) (***) EMI mono 7 64708-2 (2). Solomon

(B) *** Ph. (ADD) Duo 438 374-2 (2). Brendel

Kempff has never been more inspirationally revealing than in these performances of the last six Beethoven sonatas. These are all great performances, and the remastered recordings have been enhanced to an extraordinary degree, to give an uncannily realistic piano-image, helped by the immediacy of Kempff's communication.

Solomon's classic performances present Beethoven pure and unadulterated, with the *Hammerklavier Sonata* one of the greatest recordings of the work ever made. The sound emerges in startling freshness and fullness. Magisterial, thoughtful, lyrical performances that make many later versions sound shallow. But the Testament transfers are even finer (see above).

Brendel's set is among the most distinguished Beethoven playing of the analogue era. The recordings, made in the 1970s, are most realistic and satisfying in the CD transfers. The documentation too is first rate.

Piano Sonata 28 in A, Op. 101; (i) String Quartet 12 in E flat, Op. 127 (trans. Marrion)

(N) **(*) Sony SK 93043. Perahia, (i) with ASMF

Perahia's reading of Op. 101 does not fall short of the highest expectations. Indeed it is one of his most perfect recordings, immaculate in delivery and flawless in musical judgement. He leaves you feeling that there is no other way of playing this work. However, the coupling is more controversial, even though there are precedents. Leonard Bernstein recorded Op. 131 with full string orchestra, and both Weingartner and Klemperer recorded the *Grosse Fuge* in that form. There are gains in the weight of sonority in Paul Marrion's arrangement but a loss of the essential inwardness of the quartet texture. Decent playing, though intonation in the Trio of the Scherzo is problematic on occasion. But Op. 101 is exceptional.

Piano Sonatas 28, Op. 101; 29 (Hammerklavier)

(M) *** DG (ADD) 463 639-2. Gilels

This reissue is an obvious candidate for DG's 'Originals' series. Gilels is at his most inspired in both sonatas, playing with the sort of rapt concentration that makes one forget that these are not live performances. His *Hammerklavier* is a reading of supreme integrity. Olympian, subtle, imperious, one of the finest ever recorded. However, allowances have to be made for the digital recording, which is close and bright and harder than is ideal. The more elusive Op. 101 is also

given a superb reading, with a deeply expressive first movement and *Adagio* before the contrapuntal finale. Here the analogue recording of a decade earlier is first rate and very well transferred.

Piano Sonatas 28–9 (Hammerklavier); 30–32

(B) *** Ph. Duo (ADD) 468 912-2. Arrau

(B) *** Double Decca ADD/DDD 452 176-2 (2). Ashkenazy

(M) **(*) DG 449 740-2 (2). Pollini

Claudio Arrau's famous Beethoven cycle on Philips comes from the 1960s. The *Hammerklavier* is particularly impressive, one of the triumphs of the cycle (Richard Osborne called it 'a torrential performance in full Niagaran spate'). Its middle movement is particularly searching. As always, the Arrau sonority is sumptuous, and the Philips recording still sounds pretty magnificent. Not all this pianist's interpretative decisions will necessarily persuade every listener, but there is nothing here that is not thought-provoking. The booklet reproduces the perceptive notes by the late Philip Radcliffe.

Distinguished performances from Ashkenazy, and an impressive sense of repose in the slow movement of Op. 109, while the account of No. 28 is searching and masterly. This was Ashkenazy's second recording of the *Hammerklavier* and the performance is fresher, more spontaneous than the earlier version, but less monumental. The last two sonatas are played with a depth and spontaneity which put them among the finest available. The analogue recordings date from between 1971 and 1980, and the remastering is very successful. The *Hammerklavier* is a digital recording and has a touch of hardness on top.

Pollini's recordings of the late sonatas, which won the 1977 *Gramophone* critics' award for instrumental music, contain playing of the highest mastery. The remastering for reissue as a DG 'Original' has brought no marked improvement, but the two discs are now packaged like a DG Double and are offered at a special price.

Piano Sonatas 29 (Hammerklavier), Op. 106

(M) **(*) DG (ADD) 474 860-2. Gilels

Emil Gilels's Olympian *Hammerklavier* was certainly worthy of the *Gramophone* magazine's Instrumental Award in 1984. However, this reissue in the 'Awards Collection' is uncoupled, whereas the same performance is also available as a DG 'Original', coupled with Op. 101 and similarly priced (see above).

Piano Sonatas 29 (Hammerklavier) Op. 106; 30 in E, Op. 109; 31 in A flat, Op. 101; 32 in C min., Op. 111; 6 Bagatelles, Op. 126

⊶ ✿ (BB) *** EMI Gemini (ADD) 5 85499-2 (2). Eschenbach

Christoph Eschenbach recorded the *Hammerklavier Sonata* for DG in 1971; it was an impressive account, though it did not survive in the catalogue for very long. He re-recorded it in 1979 for EMI at the Abbey Road Studios with Suvi Raj Grub producing, along with Opp. 109, 110 and 111 and the *Six Bagatelles*, Op. 126. These were not listed in the 1979–82 catalogues (and were not reviewed by *Gramophone* magazine). Nor do they appear to have been issued in the period 1983–99 in Britain. Perhaps they were released on the Continent or there were some contractual problems that stood in their way. Anyway, they are performances of some stature and should be snapped up without delay at this bargain price. The Op. 111 is among the most concentrated, powerfully conceived and sensitive realizations of the score currently before the public, and the *Hammerklavier* is no less magisterial and commanding than its DG predecessor. Listening to Beethoven playing of this quality is a wonderfully satisfying experience and, even if you have the fine accounts of these sonatas by Stephen Kovacevich or any of the other classic versions, do not overlook the present set. These are readings of great musical insight that have the strengths of a master pianist combined with the wisdom of a great musician. The recorded sound is very present and lifelike.

Piano Sonatas 30 in E flat, Op. 109; 31 in A flat, Op. 110; 32 in C min., Op. 111

*** Ph. (IMS) 446 701-2. Brendel

*** MusicMasters 67098-2. Feltsman

(M) *** HM Cal. DDD/ADD CAL 6648. Södergren

(BB) *** Naxos 8.550151. Jandó

(N)(M) **(*) Sony (ADD) 512869-2. Serkin

Brendel's performances are searching and concentrated. They draw one into Beethoven's world immediately, with an eloquence that is all the more potent for being selfless. The recordings, made at the Henry Wood Hall and at The Maltings, Snape, are excellent, real and full of presence.

Vladimir Feltsman demonstrates in the last three sonatas that age is not an essential prerequisite, even with the most searching of Beethoven's works. In the first movement of Op. 109 he is freely rhapsodic to the point of wildness, with the piano made to clatter. In Op. 110 Feltsman's fresh, simple account of the measured paragraphs of the final fugue happily tends to cancel out any disappointment over the bright forcefulness earlier. Op. 111 then comes as a culmination, for here his many qualities focus splendidly, not just in the drama of the compressed first movement but also in the spaciousness of the final *Arietta*.

Inger Södergren's analogue accounts of Opp. 110 and 111 are musically most impressive; she is obviously a pianist of keen musical insights. These performances are fit to keep exalted company, and the recordings are most naturally balanced. A first-class mid-priced recommendation.

The last three sonatas of Beethoven, offered in Naxos's Volume 4, are very imposing indeed in Jandó's hands. There is serenity and gravitas in these readings and a powerful control of structure.

Rudolf Serkin's performances come from different periods: Op. 109 was recorded in New York in 1976, Op. 110 in 1971 and Op. 11 in 1967. There is a commanding rigour and classical feel to his late Beethoven, though he does not always cultivate beauty of tone for its own sake. Whether or not you respond to Serkin, his is playing of stature; some respected critics have ranked his versions of Opp. 109 and 110 among the very finest. It would not be a first choice; indeed, the opening of the finale of Op. 109 sounds distinctly prosaic. Predictably, the sound shows a very considerable improvement over the original LPs.

Piano Sonatas 30–32; Variations on a Theme of Diabelli, Op. 120; 6 Bagatelles, Op. 126; 11 Bagatelles, Op. 119; Ecossaise, WoO 86; Klavierstücken, WoO 61 & 61a; Waltzes, WoO 80

(M) **(*) Naive NC 40001 (2). Heisser

Heisser is a thoughtful pianist whose clear, precise articulation commands admiration and who radiates clarity of thought. There is a strong sense of musical purpose throughout and a refreshing absence of interpretative point-making. If he does not offer the insights of the very finest interpreters

in this very demanding repertoire, his performances are still distinctive, and the sound of the recording is very much in the demonstration bracket.

Miscellaneous piano music

Allegretto in C min., WoO 53; Allegretto, WoO 61; Allegretto quasi andante, WoO 61; Bagatelles, WoO 52 & 56; in B flat, WoO 60; in C; 2 Bagatelles; Für Elise, WoO 59; 12 German Dances, WoO 8; 7 Ländler, WoO 11; 6 Ländler, WoO 15; Minuet in C; 6 Minuets, WoO 10

(BB) **(*) Naxos 8.553795. Jandó

Allegretto in C min., H.69; Bagatelle in C (Lustig-Traurig), WoO 54; Fantasia, Op. 77; 12 German Dances, WoO 13; 7 Contredanses, WoO 14; 6 Ecossaises, WoO 83; Fugue in C, H.64; Minuet in E flat, WoO 82; Polonaise in C, Op. 89; 2 Preludes, Op. 39; Prelude in F min., WoO 55; (Concerto) Rondo in C, WoO 48; (Concerto) Finale in C, H.65

(BB) **(*) Naxos 8.553798. Jandó

It is always a joy to witness Beethoven relaxing. This collection of shorter piano pieces may offer no great music, but they have a freshness and vitality that is an endless delight. Jenö Jandó is at his finest in the two *C minor Allegrettos* and the *C major Rondo*. He opens the second disc with an appropriately impulsive and enjoyable account of the Op. 77 *Fantasia*. Elsewhere his clear, direct manner certainly evokes the spirit of Beethoven. The set of six *Ecossaises* (in essence, contredanses, and little to do with Scotland) are rhythmically very jolly and emerge as an exhilarating offering. The two *Preludes*, Op. 39, modulating through all the major keys in turn, have their fascination too, as has the solo arrangement of the final coda of the *Third Piano Concerto*, which completes the second disc buoyantly. With playing fresh and clear, this is for the most part a delightful supplement to Jandó's cycle of Beethoven sonatas for Naxos.

Allegretto in C min., WoO 53; Andante favori, WoO 57; Für Elise, WoO 59; 6 Variations on an Original Theme, Op. 34

(B) *** Virgin 2x1 5 62233-2 (2). Tan (fortepiano) –

SCHUBERT: *Impromptus*, etc. ***

There are no more persuasive performers on the fortepiano than Melvyn Tan. Here he plays a copy by Richard Adlam of an 1814 instrument by Nanette Streicher, and he brings to these pieces his customary flair and panache. The *F major Variations* come off splendidly: there is plenty of colour and imagination throughout. Despite his rather brisk *Andante favori*, this is a thoroughly enjoyable recital and it is recorded with great realism and presence at The Maltings at Snape.

Andante favori, WoO 57; 2 German Dances, Hess 67; 12 Minuets, WoO 7; Rondo in A, WoO 49; 2 Rondos, Op. 51/1 & 2; Rondo a capriccio in G, Op. 129

(BB) *** Naxos 8.553799. Jandó

With such lightweight items as the two *German Dances* and the *Twelve Minuets* Jandó's fresh, alert manner unobtrusively enhances their charms. That follows the pattern of his earlier Naxos discs of Beethoven's shorter piano pieces. This one also includes equally winning performances of the headlong *Rage over a Lost Penny* and the substantial set of variations, *Andante favori*, that Beethoven originally intended as a middle movement for the *Waldstein Sonata*. Also included are three *Rondos* from early in his career, respectively from 1796, 1798 and 1783, when the composer was only twelve. Excellent sound.

Andante favori, WoO 57; Bagatelles, Opp. 33, 119; WoO 52; C, WoO 56; 6 Minuets, WoO 10; Rondos: 1, 2, Op. 51; WoO 48; WoO 49; 6 Variations on an Original Theme, Op. 34; 9 Variations on a March by Dressler, WoO 63; Variations on a Swiss Song, WoO 64; 24 Variations on Righini's 'Venni Amore', WoO 65; 12 Variations on Haibel's 'Menuet à la Viganò'; 6 Variations on Paisiello's 'Nel cor più non mi sento', WoO 70

*** DG 457 493-2 (2). Pletnev

These performances are extracted from the magisterial DG compilation issued in 1997 to mark the company's own centenary. They are articulated with characteristic mastery and clarity, with no nuance of phrasing or dynamic left unobserved. Pletnev always makes an individual sound and brings his own special insights to bear on this repertoire. The sound is very clean and well focused.

7 Bagatelles, Op. 33; 11 Bagatelles, Op. 119; 6 Bagatelles, Op. 126

(B) *** Ph. 426 976-2. Kovacevich

(BB) **(*) Naxos 8.550474. Jenö Jandó

Bagatelles, Opp. 33; 119; 126; WoO 52 & 56

*** Chan. 9201. John Lill

Beethoven's *Bagatelles*, particularly those from Opp. 119 and 126, have often been described as chips from the master's workbench; but rarely if ever has that description seemed more apt than in these searchingly simple and completely spontaneous readings by Kovacevich.

John Lill characteristically takes a serious view of these miniatures, bringing out their relationship to some of the full masterpieces.

Jandó plays with a crisply rhythmic style, almost at times as if he were thinking of a fortepiano. Then, in the later works, he finds more depth of tone and is thoughtful as well as flamboyant. He is given an excellent, modern, digital recording.

7 Bagatelles, Op. 33; 6 Bagatelles, Op. 126; 6 Variations in F, Op. 34; 15 Variations with Fugue in E flat (Eroica), Op. 35; 32 Variations on an Original Theme in C min., WoO 80

(M) *(**) Sony (ADD) SM2K 52646 (2). Gould (piano)

6 Bagatelles, Op. 126; Polonaise in C, Op. 89; Variations & Fugue on a Theme from 'Prometheus' (Eroica Variations), Op. 35

*** Nim. NIM 5017. Roberts

Bernard Roberts gives a characteristically fresh and forthright reading of the *Eroica Variations*, recorded in exceptionally vivid sound. He may not have quite the flair of Brendel, but the crispness and clarity of his playing are most refreshing. The shorter pieces bring performances even more intense, with the *Bagatelles* – for all their brevity – given last-period intensity.

Glenn Gould's *Bagatelles* and *Variations* are better and less quirky than his Beethoven piano sonatas, which are not competitive. Gould fanatics can invest in them; others who are not converted can be assured that any eccentricity is positive and thought-provoking. Not a first choice but deserving of a place in the catalogue.

Bagatelles, Op 33; in A min. (Für Elise), WoO 59; Fantasia in G min., Op. 77; Minuet in E flat, WoO 82; Rondo in A, WoO 49; 6 Variations on an Original Theme in F, Op. 34; 15 Variations & Fugue on a Theme from Prometheus (Eroica), Op. 35

(N) (BB) (***) Naxos mono 8.110764. Schnabel

These pieces are played by Schabel with a refreshing simplicity: the way he presents the *Original Theme* of Op. 34 is extraordinarily apt, and there is a remarkable amalgam of drama and classicism in the *Eroica Variations* that is totally compelling. Mark Obert-Thorn's transfers of the 1937–8 Abbey Road recordings are as satisfying as ever: the sound is dry but truthful, and Brian Thompson's note is eminently satisfacory.

6 Variations, Op. 34; 6 Variations on 'Nel cor più non mi sento', WoO 70; 15 Variations & Fugue on a Theme from 'Prometheus' (Eroica Variations), Op. 35; 32 Variations, WoO 80

(BB) **(*) Naxos 8.550676. Jandó

6 Variations, Op. 34; 15 Variations & Fugue on a Theme from 'Prometheus' (Eroica Variations), Op. 35; 2 Rondos, Op. 51; Bagatelle: Für Elise, WoO 59

*** Chan. 8616. Lortie

Louis Lortie's readings have both grandeur and authority. This account of the *Eroica Variations* belongs in exalted company and can be recommended alongside such magisterial accounts as that of Gilels.

Jenö Jandó essays the same strong, direct style in his performances of the two major sets of variations as he does in the sonatas. Occasionally his forceful manner in Op. 35 and the *C minor Variations* reaches the point of brusqueness, but no one could deny the strength of his playing. His approach is appropriately lighter in Op. 34 and the very agreeable short set based on the duet by Paisiello. Excellent recording, clear and vivid, to match the other issues in his Naxos series.

33 Variations on a Waltz by Diabelli, Op. 120

⊕↝ *** Virgin 5 454682. Anderszewski

*** Hyp. CDA 66763. Kinderman

*** Ph. (ADD) 426 232-2. Brendel

(B) *** Ph. 422 969-2. Kovacevich

*** DG 459 645-2. Pollini

(N) (M) (**(*)) Sony mono/stereo 5128662. Serkin (with *Bagatelles*, Op.119; *Fantasy*, Op. 71)

(M) ** Warner Elatus 2-CD 2564 60010-2 (2). Barenboim (piano) – BACH: *Goldberg Variations* **

Piotr Anderszewski is the self-critical young Polish pianist who competed at Leeds in 1990 and broke off his performance of the Webern *Variations*, Op. 27, in disappointment at his playing in the semi-finals and withdrew. His Wigmore performance of the *Diabelli* the following year excited rave reviews and this searching and finely recorded account is quite simply the most outstanding, most thoughtful and impressively played version of the *Diabelli Variations* to have appeared for many years.

William Kinderman's version on Hyperion is fresh and well thought out, sparkling with life and character, and it is almost worth buying the present disc for the sake of his illuminating liner-notes. He is very well recorded, too.

On Philips Alfred Brendel, here working in the studio, captures the music's dynamism, the sense of an irresistible force building up this immense structure, section by section. It would be hard to imagine a more dramatic reading, sparked off by the cheeky wit of Brendel's treatment of the Diabelli theme itself. The whirlwind power of the whole performance is irresistible, and the piano-sound is full and immediate.

Stephen Kovacevich also gives one of the most deeply satisfying performances ever recorded. He may at times seem austere, but his concentration is magnetic from first to last, with fearless dynamic contrasts enhanced in the excellent CD transfer. The reading culminates in the most dedicated account of the concluding variations, hushed in meditation and with no hint of self-indulgence. On the cheapest Philips label, it is a bargain that no Beethovenian should miss.

The *Diabelli* is the Everest of variations, along with the *Goldberg*, of course. Maurizio Pollini scales its heights with magisterial aplomb: he is a master pianist whose clarity of articulation and musical intelligence are second to none, and he makes impressive sense of the architecture of this extraordinary work. However, for all his insights and mastery he seems at times cool and aloof: there is a perfection which commands admiration rather than involvement. He rattles off variations 10 and 11 and, although the sublime *Andante* (No. 20) is thoughtful, Schnabel, Horszowski, Brendel and Stephen Kovacevich find infinitely greater depths and a wider range of characterization. The DG recording, made in the Herkulessaal in Munich, has impressive body and presence.

Rudolf Serkin's account of the *Diabelli Variations* was recorded in Marlboro, Vermont, in September 1957; one critic memorably spoke of its 'craggy splendour'. It is indeed a performance of stature, which belonged among the finest of its day. Serkin still holds an honoured place in the *Diabelli* discography. The *Eleven Bagatelles*, Op. 119, and the *G minor Fantasy* were both recorded in New York, in 1966 and 1970 respectively. They are fine performances and enjoy better sound.

Daniel Barenboim first recorded the *Diabelli Variations* in the late 1960s and he is no stranger to their mystery. His later, Elatus account has much to recommend it, and his admirers need not doubt that he is a thoughtful and serious guide in this masterpiece. There are finer versions, but this one comes coupled with a similarly individual set of the *Goldberg Variations*.

VOCAL MUSIC

Adelaide; An die ferne Geliebte, Op. 98; An die Geliebte; An die Hoffnung; Aus Goethes Faust; Klage; Der Liebende; Das Liedchen von der Ruhe; 6 Lieder aus Gellert; Mailied; Neue Liebe, neues Leben; Sehnsucht; Wonne der Wehmut
*** Hyp. CDA 67055. Genz, Vignoles

The German baritone Stephan Genz not only has a voice of warm, velvety beauty, but he already shows a rare depth of understanding. In the very first song here, *An die Hoffnung* ('To Hope') – Beethoven's response to suffering – he sings with rapt concentration, using the widest range of expression, while songs like *Adelaide* bring out his honeyed tone, allied to flawless legato. That contrasts with the youthful energy of the brisk songs and the biting irony of Goethe's *Song of the Flea*, taken very fast. A disc to have one reassessing Beethoven as songwriter, with the mould-breaking cycle, *An die ferne Geliebte*, as a fine climax.

Adelaide; Der Kuss; Resignation; Zärtliche Liebe
(M) *** DG (ADD) 449 747-2. Wunderlich, Giesen –
SCHUBERT: *Lieder*; SCHUMANN: *Dichterliebe* ***

Wunderlich was 35 when he recorded these songs, and the unique bloom of the lovely voice is beautifully caught. Though the accompanist is too metrical at times, the freshness of Wunderlich's singing makes one grieve again over his untimely death.

(i–iv) Cantata on the Death of Emperor Joseph II, WoO 87; (ii–v) Cantata on the Accession of Emperor Leopold II, WoO 88. Meeresstille und glückliche Fahrt, Op. 112; (ii) Opferlied
● *** Hyp. CDA 66880. (i) Watson; (ii) Rigby; (iii) Mark Ainsley; (iv) Van Dam; (v) Howarth; Corydon Singers & O, Best

Arguably Beethoven's first major masterpiece, WoO 87 was one of the few early, unpublished works of which he approved: when he came to write *Fidelio* he used the soaring theme from the first of the cantata's soprano arias for Leonore's sublime moment in the finale, *O Gott! Welch ein Augenblick*. The aria is sung radiantly here by Janice Watson. Relishing the tragic C minor power of the choruses, Matthew Best conducts a superb performance, incisive and deeply moving, with excellent soloists as well as a fine chorus. The second cantata, much shorter, written soon afterwards, brings anticipations of the *Fifth Symphony* and of the choral finale of the *Ninth*, while the two shorter pieces – with Jean Rigby as soloist in the *Opferlied* – make a generous fill-up, equally well performed. The atmospheric recording combines weight and transparency.

Che fa il mio bene? (2 versions); Dimmi, ben mio; Ecco quel fiero istante!; In questa tomba oscura; La partenza; T'intendo, si, mio cor
*** Decca 440 297-2. Bartoli, A. Schiff – HAYDN: *Arianna a Naxos*; MOZART: *Ridente la calma*; SCHUBERT: *Da quel sembiante appresi*, etc. ***

These rare Italian songs come as part of a recital which has an outstanding account of Haydn's *Arianna a Naxos* as its highlight. *La partenza* has a winningly ingenuous simplicity and the *Ariettas* (including two completely contrasting settings of *Che fa il mio bene?*) are also full of charm.

Christ on the Mount of Olives, Op. 85
(BB) *** EMI (ADD) 5 85686-2 [5 85687-2]. Deutekom, Gedda, Sotin, Stadt Bonn Philharmonic Ch., Theaters der Stadt Bonn Ch., Beethovenhalle O, Bonn, Wangenheim
(N) **(*) HM **SACD** 901802. Domingo, Orgonasova, Schmidt, Deutsches RSO, Berlin, Nagano
(B) **(*) HM (ADD) HMA 1955181. Pick-Hieronimi, Anderson, Von Halem, Ch. & O Nat. de Lyon, Baudo

Recorded in 1969/70 in time for the Beethoven bicentenary, the EMI recording of this neglected oratorio had very limited circulation indeed – never appearing in Britain, for example – and here makes its début on CD in an excellent transfer. This is a piece that centres round the figure of Jesus as he meditates on his predestined fate, with the tenor who sings the role of Christ taking on much the greatest burden. Here Nicolai Gedda is superb, radiant of tone and endlessly perceptive in interpreting the text. The Dutch soprano Cristina Deutekom, bright and flexible, is equally positive as the angelic Seraph visiting Christ. If the edge on her voice occasionally brings moments of stridency, she knows how to shade her tone down in duet to match Gedda, as in the big central duet, *So ruhe denn*. The bass soloist, Hans Sotin, is aptly bluff and forthright in the much smaller role of St Peter. Volker Wangenheim draws a warm, sympathetic performance from his Bonn chorus and orchestra, well recorded in the Beethovenhalle in Beethoven's home city.

However, it is good to have a fine modern recording of Beethoven's only oratorio. Domingo as Jesus rarely betrays his age, singing with passion, if not always phrasing with the elegance of Gedda on the older EMI recording. Luba Orgonasova sings beautifully as the Seraph, Andreas Schmidt as Peter is acceptable enough, if less secure than EMI's Hans Sotin. Nagano holds the work together effectively, and the choruses come off especially well, though elsewhere Wangenheim's older EMI account is rather more spontaneous in feeling. The sound is very good – and even better for those with SACD systems. Full texts and translations are included.

Monica Pick-Hieronimi brings powerful Leonore-like qualities to her role as the Seraph. Baudo directs an energetic and lively account which, if lacking the utmost refinement of detail, generates urgency and breadth in the fine closing section.

(i) Egmont: Overture & Incidental Music (complete), Op. 84 (see also Symphony 5); (ii) Leonora Overture 3
(BB) *** Discover DICD 920114. (i) Gauci, Schortemeier, Belgian R. & TV O; (ii) LPO; Rahbari

Alexander Rahbari offers all ten movements of Beethoven's Egmont music. Such rarities as the third and fourth entr'actes and the melodrama, Süsse Schlaf, with Schortemeier as the speaker, may not be important, but they provide an attractive supplement to the well-known items. Both in Egmont and in the Leonora No. 3 Overture (with the LPO) Rahbari conducts crisp, well-sprung, often exciting performances, with Miriam Gauci the warm-toned soprano. Atmospheric recording, pleasantly reverberant.

Mass in C, Op. 86
(BB) *** Belart (ADD) 461 317-2. Palmer, Watts, Tear, Keyte, St John's College, Cambridge, Ch., ASMF, Guest – BRUCKNER: Motets ***

Mass in C, Op. 86; Cantatas: Elegischer Gesang, Op. 118; Meeresstille und glückliche Fahrt, Op. 112
☞ *** Chan. 0703. Evans, Stephen, Padmore, Varcoe, Coll. Mus. 90, Hickox

(i) Mass in C, Op. 86; Meeresstille und glückliche Fahrt (Calm Sea and a Prosperous Voyage), Op. 112
*** DG 435 391-2. Margiono, Robbin, Kendall, Miles, Monteverdi Ch., ORR, Gardiner

Following up the success of his recordings of Haydn and Hummel Masses, Richard Hickox with a choir of modest size (24 singers) brings out the link between Beethoven's Mass in C and those other settings of the Mass also written for the nameday of the Princess Esterházy. Beethoven's Mass was initially a failure, condemned by the Prince as 'totally ridiculous', and latterly it has always suffered from being in the shadow of his massive Missa solemnis of over a decade later. Yet Hickox consistently brings out the way in which, as in that more ambitious work, Beethoven was rethinking the meaning of each phrase of the liturgy and illustrating it with an electric sense of drama. Even more than John Eliot Gardiner on his rival period performance from DG, Hickox brings out the joy of the inspiration, with excellent soloists and a fresh-toned choir, and directs similarly concentrated readings of two brief choral works of 1814, the fine Goethe setting, Meeresstille und glückliche Fahrt, and the simple but deeply felt Elegiac Song (not offered by Gardiner), which come as welcome couplings.

In this long-underrated masterpiece, Gardiner gives just as refreshing a performance as his earlier, prize-winning account of the Missa solemnis. Aptly clear-toned soloists

match the freshness of the Monteverdi Choir. As an imaginatively chosen coupling Gardiner offers the dramatic soprano scena, Ah! perfido, with Charlotte Margiono as soloist, and the brief choral cantata, Meeresstille und glückliche Fahrt.

George Guest's reading is intimate and, with boys' voices in the choir and a smaller band of singers, less dramatic; yet, with splendid recording, the scale works admirably and the result is refreshing. Excellent value at super-bargain price.

Missa solemnis in D, Op. 123
☞ *** DG 435 770-2 (2). Studer, Norman, Domingo, Moll, Leipzig R. Ch., Swedish R. Ch., VPO, Levine
(BB) *** Arte Nova 74321 87074-2. Orgonosova, Larsson, Trost, Selig, Swiss Chamber Ch., Zurich Tonhalle O, Zinman
*** DG 429 779-2. Margiono, Robbin, Kendall, Miles, Monteverdi Ch., E. Bar. Sol., Gardiner
*** HM HMC 901557. Mannion, Remmert, Taylor, Hauptmann, La Chapelle Royale Coll. Voc., O des Champs Elysées, Herreweghe
*** Häns. 93006 (2). Halgrimson, Kallisch, Aler, Miles, N. German R. Ch., South West German R. Vocal Ens. & SO, Norrington
(B) *** DG (ADD) Double 453 016-2 (2). Janowitz, Ludwig, Wunderlich, Berry, V. Singverein, BPO, Karajan – MOZART: Coronation Mass **(*)
(M) **(*) DG 445 543-2 (2). Cuberli, Schmidt, Cole, Van Dam, V. Singverein, BPO, Karajan – MOZART: Mass 16 **(*)
(B) **(*) Warner 9031 74884-2 (2). Mei, Lipovšek, Rolfe Johnson, Holl, Arnold Schoenberg Ch., COE, Harnoncourt
(M) **(*) BBC BBCL 4093-2 (2). Zylis-Gara, Hoffgen, Tear, Arie, New Philh. Ch. & O, Giulini – SCHUBERT: Symphony 4 ***
(BB) *** Naxos 8.557060. Phillips, Redmon, Taylor, Baylon, Van Osdale, Nashville Ch. & SO, Schermerhorn

(i) Missa solemnis in D. Symphony 7 in A, Op. 92
(**(*)) BBC mono BBCL 4016-2 (2). (i) Milanov, Thorborg, Von Pataky, Moscona, BBC Choral Soc.; BBC SO, Toscanini – CHERUBINI: Anacréon Overture ***; MOZART: Symphony 35 (***)

(i) Missa solemnis in D; (ii) Choral Fantasia in C, Op. 80
(M) **(*) EMI (ADD) 5 67546-2 [56747-2] (2). (i) Söderström, Höffgen, Kmentt, Talvela, New Philh. Ch.; (ii) Barenboim, Alldis Ch.; New Philh. O, Klemperer

The 1991 Salzburg Festival honoured its late music director, Herbert von Karajan, in this performance of Beethoven's Missa solemnis, conducted by James Levine. With a starry quartet of soloists, the live recording has an incandescence that conveys the atmosphere of a great occasion, and the DG engineers have obtained rich, weighty sound. For such an intense visionary experience, defying the conventional view of Levine, this is a version not to be missed.

Following up his superb cycle of the Beethoven symphonies, using modern instruments while taking note of period practice, David Zinman with the Tonhalle Orchestra offers an equally exhilarating account of the Missa solemnis on the Arte Nova label at super-bargain price. Again, fast speeds are the rule in a performance which at every point highlights the drama of the liturgy, making the words fresh and clear, helped by bright, immediate singing from the Swiss Chamber Choir, by the sound of it not a small body. Zinman brings out the joy of Et resurrexit as well as of the final Dona nobis *pacem*, made the more intense after Beethoven's dramatic military intrusion has been swept away. Dedication is still part of the equation in this exceptional performance, well recorded.

Gardiner's inspired reading matches even the greatest of traditional performances on record in dramatic weight and spiritual depth, while bringing out the white heat of Beethoven's inspiration with new intensity. Though the performers are fewer in number than in traditional accounts, the Monteverdi Choir sings with bright, luminous tone, and the four soloists are excellent. The recording is vivid too. Even those who normally resist period performance will find this compelling.

Philippe Herreweghe's live recording of the *Missa solemnis* (edited together from two performances) makes a good alternative to Gardiner's prize-winning version on DG Archiv for a period-scale reading. Even at the start, with its odd balance, there is no mistaking that we are on a visionary journey, with an inner quality intensely conveyed. Though the choir is balanced distantly, the sharpness of attack is refreshing, amply justifying a performance on a relatively intimate, period scale. The four young soloists make an excellent team, headed by the sweet, firm, Canadian soprano, Rosa Mannion, previously heard as Dorabella in the Gardiner *Così*.

While the Hänssler version is not a period performance such as one might expect from Norrington, his allegiances are apparent, as in passages where the strings play with little or no vibrato. His speeds, too, reflect a period performer's preference for following Beethoven's own demanding metronome markings. The end of the *Gloria* brings white-hot excitement, as wild syncopations and head-reeling modulations emerge in urgent accelerando. Although this radio recording, made in Stuttgart by the South West German Radio engineers, was not of a live performance, the thrill of it suggests that it was recorded in a straight take. The chorus sing throughout with a winning fervour. The soloists are fresh and cleanly focused, even if the tenor, John Aler, is a little strained under pressure. Alastair Miles repeats his fine reading of the bass part, as already heard in the Gardiner version, while Amanda Halgrimson and Cornelia Kallisch both sing with gloriously firm, full tone. The recording also helps to bring out the highly dramatic contrasts of dynamic that regularly mark this score, again emphasizing the originality of inspiration. One can almost hear Beethoven speaking the words as he revealed their meaning afresh.

On Karajan's earlier (1966) analogue recording, made in the Jesus-Christus-Kirche, both the chorus and, even more strikingly, the superbly matched quartet of soloists convey the intensity and cohesion of Beethoven's deeply personal response to the liturgy, best of all the ill-fated Fritz Wunderlich, singing radiantly. Now on a DG Double, it is attractively coupled with Mozart's *Coronation Mass*.

The glory of Klemperer's set is the superb choral singing of the New Philharmonia Chorus. The soloists are less happily chosen: Waldemar Kmentt seems unpleasantly hard and Elisabeth Söderström does not sound as firm as she can be. This now takes its place among EMI's 'Great Recordings of the Century'.

In his later version for DG, Karajan (445 543-2) conducts a powerful reading, marked by vivid and forward recording for orchestra and soloists, less satisfactory in rather cloudy choral sound. This was one of Karajan's recordings made in conjunction with a video film, which brings both gains and losses. The sense of spontaneity, of a massive structure built dramatically with contrasts underlined, makes for extra

magnetism, but there are flaws of ensemble and flaws of intonation in the singing of Lella Cuberli.

Toscanini's legendary May 1939 account of Beethoven's *Missa solemnis* with a formidable quartet of soloists is a markedly broader, warmer performance than the one from New York once available on RCA; the sound, though limited, is satisfyingly full-bodied. The recordings of Beethoven's *Seventh* and Mozart's *Haffner*, similarly warmer than his New York performances, date from 1935. Though the sound is crumbly at times, the thrill of Toscanini in full flight is vividly conveyed.

Like Levine's performance of a year earlier, Harnoncourt's was recorded live at the Salzburg Festival, but it represents the new, post-Karajan era at that grandest of music festivals. Like Harnoncourt's Beethoven symphony cycle, this performance conveys the dramatic tensions of a live occasion, with finely matched forces performing with freshness and clarity. The rather distanced sound makes the results marginally less involving than either the Levine version or the sparer but inspired Gardiner account.

The BBC radio recording of Giulini in the *Missa solemnis*, made in St Paul's Cathedral in 1968 as part of the City of London Festival, brings a characteristically expansive performance which, in the absence from the catalogue of Giulini's studio recording for EMI, is well worth investigating. Though the sound is far more variable than in the studio performance, with some odd balances, the formidable echo is largely tamed, and the concentration is keener. For coupling on the second CD comes a biting account of Schubert's *Tragic Symphony*, a reading that certainly justifies that nickname.

Kenneth Schermerhorn, best known for his advocacy of twentieth-century music, here demonstrates what power he can bring to Beethoven's supreme choral masterpiece, a work notoriously difficult to interpret. The choral and orchestral sound is full and beefy, reinforcing the thrust of the performance, with the *Credo* at once warm and four-square. Speeds are consistently well chosen, not as fast as those in David Zinman's rival super-bargain issue from Arte Nova, but crisp enough to allow the whole work to be fitted on a single disc. The four soloists are first rate, all with fresh, young-sounding voices, and the enthusiasm of the chorus makes for magnetic singing throughout. The Zinman version on Arte Nova with its clear, transparent sound may provide more new insights, but the Naxos issue is an equally compelling bargain version.

OPERA

Fidelio (complete; DVD versions)

** DG **DVD** 073 052-9. Mattila, Heppner, Struckmann, Lloyd, Pape, Welch-Babidge, Polenzani, Met. Op. Ch. & O, Levine (Dir: Jurgen Flimm, TV Dir: Brian Large)

** Arthaus **DVD** 100074. Beňačková, Protschká, McLaughlin, Archer, Lloyd, Pederson, ROHCG Ch. & O, Dohnányi (Director: Adolf Dresden, V/D: Derek Bailey)

(N) ** TDK **DVD** OPFID. Nylund, Kaufmann, Polgar, Muff, Magnuson, Strehl, Zurich Op. House Ch. and O, Harnoncourt (Dir: Jurgen Flimm, V/D: Felix Breisach)

Updated to the present day with warders in US Army uniform and the prisoners chained in cages, Guantánamo Bay-style, Jurgen Flimm's production of *Fidelio* for the Met., recorded in 2002, is plainly intended to bring home the contemporary associations of Beethoven's opera. As a whole that works effectively, even if the prosaic stage-pictures are not exactly welcoming for video repetition. What is certainly clear is that, with only one flawed member of the cast, and with James Levine at his most intense, tackling a major Beethoven project, the result is an exceptionally powerful reading. Karita Mattila is superb as Leonore, singing with a freedom, beauty and power that cannot be faulted, and though Ben Heppner is in no way a romantic figure he sings with no hint of strain as Florestan. The others sing well too, with Robert Lloyd as Don Fernando made up to look disconcertingly like President George W. Bush. Sadly, the exception is the rough, gritty-toned Pizarro of Falk Struckmann, too often with disagreeable tone singing 'in the cracks' on no recognizable pitch. It takes away some of the impact of the villain of the piece, and the acting in the climactic quartet of Act II, with Struckmann waving a dagger and Leonore finding a revolver only at the last minute, is not as convincing as it might be. But the triumphant finale, as in any great performance of this opera, brings a thrill of excitement and fulfilment.

Very well cast, with Christoph von Dohnányi a dedicated interpreter, the Arthaus DVD of *Fidelio* presents Adolf Dresden's production at Covent Garden in 1991, updated to late Victorian times. The first scene opens in a squalid flat, more appropriate for Berg's *Wozzeck*, with Rocco and Jaquino looking like uniformed officials from some continental railway company. Leonore, the powerful Gabriela Beňačkova, makes little pretence of looking like a man with her long hair in a snood hanging down her back. The squalor persists, with Act II set in the deepest dungeon, reached via a long vertical ladder. None of this helps the drama much, except that Pizarro, presented as an army officer in cocked hat and epaulettes, emerges as a terrifying villain, obsessed with power, determined to have his revenge for earlier slights. The singer is Monte Pederson – tall, handsome and menacing, singing with fine focus and power, an unforgettable portrayal. Beňačkova too sings magnificently, beautifully matched by Marie McLaughlin as Marzelline. There is no weakness in the rest of the cast either, with Josef Protshcká as Florestan singing powerfully and without strain, so that the duet with Leonore, *O namenlose Freude*, is clearer, more precise and less squally than usual. Sadly, the sound of the voices is spoilt by a glassy edginess, and the dry Covent Garden acoustic has been treated to some extra reverberation.

In this production by Jurgen Flimm from the Zurich Opera House, conducted by Harnoncourt and recorded in February 2004, the costumes of Marianna Glittenberg set the piece in the nineteenth century, veering between Napoleonic uniforms for the soldiers and costumes for others from later in the century. That and the sparse sets are generally undistracting, letting one appreciate Harnoncourt's incisive musical direction with a good if not outstanding cast. Finest is the Florestan of Jonas Kaufmann, powerful yet avoiding roughness, while Camilla Nylund as Leonore sings well, but seems on the verge of strain in her big moments, when the video sound hardly lets one appreciate how big or well projected the voice is. Laszlo Polgar is fine as Rocco, but Alfred Muff is a woolly, ill-focused Pizarro. Surprisingly, with Flimm in charge, the acting is often stiff and rudimentary, maybe in reflection of the bare sets.

Fidelio (complete; CD versions)

✿ (***) Testament mono SBT 2 21328 (2). Jurinac, Vickers, Frick, Hotter, Morison, Dobson, ROHCG Ch. & O, Klemperer

☞— ✿ (M) *** EMI (ADD) 5 67364-2 (2) [567361]. Ludwig, Vickers, Frick, Berry, Crass, Philh. Ch. & O, Klemperer (with *Overture: Leonora 3*)

(M) *** DG 474 420-2 (2). Janowitz, Kollo, Jungwirth, Sotin, Popp, Dallapozza, Fischer-Dieskau, V. State Op. Ch., VPO, Bernstein

(BB) *** Naxos 8.660070/71. Nielsen, Winbergh, Moll, Titus, Lienbacher, Pecoraro, Hungarian R. Ch., Nicolaus Esterházy Sinfonia, Halász

(M) *** Teldec 4509 94560-2 (2). Margiono, Seiffert, Bonney, Skovhus, Leiferkus, Polgár, Van der Walt, Arnold Schoenberg Ch., COE, Harnoncourt

(M) *** EMI (ADD) 7 69290-2 (2). Dernesch, Vickers, Kélémen, Ridderbusch, Van Dam, German Op. Ch., BPO, Karajan

(B) *** DG (ADD) Double 453 106-2 (2) (includes *Overture: Leonore 3*). Leonie Rysanek, Haefliger, Fischer-Dieskau, Frick, Seefried, Lenz, Engen, Bav. State Op. Ch. & O, Fricsay

(M) (***) EMI mono 7 64496-2 (2). Flagstad, Patzak, Schoeffler, Greindl, Schwarzkopf, Dermota, V. State Op. Ch., VPO, Furtwängler

**(*) Telarc CD 80439 (2). Beňačková, Rolfe Johnson, Raimondi, Vogel, Kapellman, Mark Ainsley, Edinburgh Festival Ch., SCO, Mackerras

(BB) (*(*)) Naxos mono 8.110054/5. Flagstad, Kipnis, Huehn, Farell, Laufkötter, Met. Op. Ch. & O, Walter

The superb BBC recording of the first Klemperer performance at Covent Garden in February 1961 in many ways even outshines his classic studio recording. Though inevitably in a live performance the ensemble is not always as polished as in the studio version, with stage and audience noises intruding at times, the electricity is of an even higher voltage, so that the drama of the piece comes over the more vividly. This is the opposite of the staid Klemperer, with speeds generally a degree faster than in the studio, and though his decision to include the *Leonore No. 3* overture in the once-traditional place just before the finale is controversial, the performance of it is hair-raisingly exciting, leaving one agog to hear the sublime sequence of the finale. When it comes to the cast, Vickers and Frick are if anything even more magnetic than in the studio recording, and the rest of the cast includes at least one singer who totally outshines her studio counterpart, Elsie Morison, whose enchanting portrait of Marzelline makes her EMI rival seem characterless. The casting of the great Wagnerian, Hans Hotter, as Pizarro brings impressive weight to the role, making this arch-villain far more of a threat than he is with the excellent but relatively lightweight Walter Berry on EMI. John Dobson makes a warmly engaging Jaquino, and Forbes Robinson is a noble Don Fernando; but it is Sena Jurinac singing Leonore for the very first time who sets the seal on the whole performance. She may not have quite the same weight as Ludwig on the studio set, but her projection is superb in singing which combines both brightness and warmth, both noble defiance and womanly compassion. In the excellent Testament transfer the radio sound is astonishingly vivid, with the voices cleanly balanced even when the singers move around on stage.

Klemperer's great set of *Fidelio*, now rightly reissued as one of EMI's 'Great Recordings of the Century', has been freshly remastered by Allan Ramsay. For some reason, the *Overture*, though full-bodied, lacks absolute sharpness of focus; but, once the singers enter, the quality of the splendid (1962) Kingsway Hall recording is very apparent, with the voices beautifully caught in relation to the orchestra, all within a glowing ambience. The result is a triumph to match the unique incandescence and spiritual strength of the performance, superbly cast, which leads to a final scene in which the parallel with the finale of the *Choral Symphony* is underlined. The documentation, including a full translation, is in every way excellent. The *Overture, Leonore No. 3* has been added as a postlude, an outstanding performance excellently transferred.

Bernstein's highly dramatic *Fidelio* brings some splendid singing from a consistently fine cast, with Lucia Popp a delightful Marzelline, Janowitz an outstanding Leonore and Kollo an equally strong Florestan. This now re-emerges as one of DG's 'Originals'.

The new Naxos *Fidelio* from Budapest offers a first-rate modern cast incisively directed by Michael Halász, and very well recorded. Inga Nielsen is an outstanding Leonore, with every note sharply focused, using the widest tonal and dynamic range from bright *fortissimo* to velvety half-tone. Few singers on disc in recent years begin to rival her account of the *Abscheulicher*, ranging from venomous anger to radiant tenderness. Gösta Winbergh makes a formidable Florestan, with Alan Titus a firm, sinister Pizarro and Kurt Moll a splendid Rocco. Only the Don Fernando falls short, with a voice too woolly to focus cleanly. Even making no allowance for price, this version is among the very finest to have arrived in years, gaining in clarity and incisiveness from the relatively small scale.

As you would expect, Nikolaus Harnoncourt, tackling *Fidelio*, reflects the climate of period performance, even though modern instruments are used. The casting matches this approach, with the central role of Leonore given to a singer best known till now for singing Mozart and Bach, Charlotte Margiono. The voice here is warmer than we have known it, so that the *Abscheulicher* has a bite and clarity which make up for not pinning you back in your seat. Barbara Bonney is well contrasted with Margiono. Peter Seiffert sings with unforced clarity as Florestan, and Deon van der Walt is a fresh Jaquino, with Sergei Leiferkus an aptly sinister Pizarro, László Polgár a darkly resonant Rocco and Boje Skovhus a noble Don Pedro. Highlights (70 minutes) are available on Teldec 0630 13800-9.

Comparison between Karajan's strong and heroic reading and Klemperer's version is fascinating. Both have very similar merits, underlining the symphonic character of the work with their weight. Even so, Karajan uses bass and baritone soloists who are lighter than usual, for both the Rocco (Ridderbusch) and the Don Fernando (Van Dam) lack heft in their lower registers. Yet they sing dramatically and intelligently, while the Pizarro of Zoltan Kélémen is made to sound the more biting and powerful. Jon Vickers as Florestan is, if anything, even finer than he was for Klemperer, and Helga Dernesch as Leonore gives a glorious, thrilling performance. The orchestral playing is superb.

The Fricsay set dates from 1957, yet the result is astonishingly modern-sounding, lacking little or nothing in body. As for Fricsay's clear, fresh direction, it matches the excitement and keen tension of a Toscanini performance. Ernst Haefliger is a fine, clear-cut Florestan, lyric in timbre rather than fully heroic, and Frick and Fischer-Dieskau offer strong, intense characterizations, with Pizarro's aria chilling in its villainy. Rysanek's Leonore is also impressive, and her *Abscheulicher* is both dramatic and beautifully shaded. Irmgard Seefried makes an enchanting Marzelline. In this bargain package no libretto translation is included, but there is a well-cued synopsis. The *Leonore No. 3 Overture* is included as a supplement after the opera.

Taken from performances at the Salzburg Festival in 1950, Wilhelm Furtwängler conducts an incomparably starry cast. This is an Austrian Radio recording, previously available only in pirated versions, but here treated to sound which captures the voices on stage with astonishing vividness. The epic scale of Kirsten Flagstad's voice as Leonore sometimes blasts the microphone, but it is a joy to hear such forthright power and security. Elisabeth Schwarzkopf is a delight as Marzelline, vivacious in the dialogue and masterfully sustaining Furtwängler's expansive speed for the Act I quartet. With dialogue included, this is even more compelling than Furtwängler's studio recording.

Like Harnoncourt, Mackerras with modern instruments takes period practice into account. Voices are closer than usual, making the storytelling both more intimate and more intense, most strikingly in the opening scenes. The sudden switch from genial domesticity to the world of the prison and Pizarro comes over with chilling force. That is typical of Mackerras's response to the drama, so that the confrontation quartet of Act II makes one sit up afresh, with Gabriela Beňačková as Leonore bitingly defiant in the face of Pizarro. Beňačková's voice has grown a degree edgier and less predictable at the top, but this is still a warmly expressive as well as a powerful performance. But Anthony Rolfe Johnson as Florestan, responsive though he is, too often brings out an unevenness in the voice, intensified by close-up recording. Siegfried Vogel is a clean-cut Rocco, less elderly than usual, and Ildikó Raimondi is a charming Marzelline, well contrasted with Beňačková.

The second Naxos version offers a historic radio recording of a live performance, given in 1940 at the Metropolitan Opera in New York with Bruno Walter conducting and Kirsten Flagstad as Leonore. For many it will immediately be ruled out by the limited, often crumbly sound, even if the performance under Walter is urgently passionate at high voltage. Flagstad naturally dominates the performance vocally, even more vital than in her Salzburg reading under Furtwängler (EMI). Alexander Kipnis as Rocco and Herbert Janssen as Don Fernando stand out among the rest, with the others in the cast generally disappointing.

Fidelio (complete)

(N) (**(*)) Andante mono AN 3090 (4). V. State Op. Ch. & O, with (i) Neralic, Schöffler, Ralf, Konetzni, Alsen, Seefried, Klein, cond. Boehm; (ii) Poell, Edelmann, Windgassen, Mödl, Frick, Jurinac, Schock, Hendriks, Bierbach, cond. Furtwängler

The Andante set offers a fascinating comparison between a Boehm concert performance of 1944 and a Furtwängler staged performance of 1953. The Boehm version was recorded by the Vienna State Opera company for radio at a time when because of 'total war' the opera house was closed. The studio sound is astonishingly full and clear for its period, letting one appreciate the glorious voice of the young Irmgard Seefried as Marzelline and the characterful, finely focused Pizarro of Paul Schöffler. Herbert Alsen as Rocco is also excellent, a fine singer neglected on disc. Though Hilde Konetzni as Leonore tends to attack notes from below, hers is a powerful performance, while Torsten Ralf as Florestan is strong and well focused. Boehm, rising 50 at the time, gives a well-paced, understanding performance, except that he tends to race through the great Act II Quartet.

Though recorded nine years later, the Furtwängler performance, recorded on stage at the Theater an der Wien, has thinner, more distant sound. The performance took place on

12 October 1953, the day before the EMI sessions for recording the opera with this identical cast. That recording, made in the Musikvereinsaal, may have far fuller sound, but it omits the spoken dialogue, and the voices here are just as impressive as in that long-cherished studio set, notably Martha Mödl, then new to the role of Leonore but already commanding, Sena Jurinac as a creamy-toned Marzelline, Otto Edelmann as a sinister Pizarro, singing with wonderful clarity, and Wolfgang Windgassen as Florestan, heroic and totally unstrained. Gottlob Frick also makes a magnificent Rocco, and Furtwängler is at his most inspired.

Leonore (complete)

*** DG 453 461-2 (2). Martinpelto, Begley, Best, Miles, Oelze, Hawlata, Schade, Monteverdi Ch., ORR, Gardiner
** MDG 337 0826-2 (2). Coburn, M. Baker, Lafont, Martin-Bonnet, Neidhardt-Barbaux, Von Halem, Kobel, Cologne R. Ch., O of Beethovenhalle, Bonn, Soustrot

Gardiner's argument, brilliantly expressed in a note, is that Leonore in 1804 is the more spontaneous and immediate work, while Fidelio of ten years later is retrospective and considered in its response to tyranny and injustice. He goes on to claim that the portraits of both hero and heroine are more poignant in the earlier version, where later they are presented as more self-assured and certain, more universal. Admittedly one misses some dramatic moments, such as the cry of 'Abscheulicher' at the start of the heroine's big aria. One also misses the great fortissimo outburst from the chorus at the start of the final scene, but the Leonore solution is even more evocative, with the chorus getting closer and closer in its signalling of freedom. Hillevi Martinpelto in the title-role on DG conveys youthful ardour as well as power, well contrasted with the sweetly expressive Marzelline of Christiane Oelze. Kim Begley emerges in sharply focused, heroic strength as Florestan, with Michael Schade providing an ideal lyric contrast as Jaquino. Franz Hawlata as Rocco and Alastair Miles as Don Fernando are both first rate, and if Matthew Best as Pizarro comes too close to sing-speech, he is certainly evil-sounding.

Marc Soustrot here offers the première recording of Beethoven's first revision, made for performances in 1806, a year after the original. In practice, this 1806 text, enjoyable in its own right, lacks some of the freshness of 1805, while failing to match the final version of 1814. It does not help that Soustrot is far less dramatic than Gardiner. The performance, well recorded, is reliable rather than inspired, led by Pamela Coburn as a warm-toned Leonore, Mark Baker a lyrical Florestan and Christine Neidhardt-Barbaux a sweetly charming Marzelline, but with Jean-Pierre Lafont a wobbly Pizarro.

BELLINI, Vincenzo (1801–35)

OPERA

Beatrice di Tenda (complete; DVD version)

(N) *(**) TDK DVD DV OPBDT (2). Gruberová, Volle, Kaluza, Hernández, Zurich Op. Ch. & O, Viotti (V/D: Yves Andreé Hubert)

Recorded in December 2001, the TDK DVD version offers an updated production from Zurich Opera House, with modern dress and geometric sets with stairs and handrails as though on an ocean liner. The performance – after Beatrice's delayed entry into the story – revolves round the fine performance of Edita Gruberová in the title-role, bright and agile, if occasionally edgy as recorded. Raul Hernández sings stylishly as the hero, Orombello, and the mezzo, Stefania Kaluza, is strongly cast as Agathe, with Marcello Viotti the purposeful conductor. The opera alone (144 minutes) might have been squeezed on to a single disc, but with a 26-minute interview (in French) with the conductor also included, the set spreads to a second disc.

Beatrice di Tenda (complete; CD version); Arias: Norma: Casta diva. I puritani: Son vergin vezzosa; Oh rendetemi la speme. La sonnambula: Ah, non credea mirarti

(M) *** Decca (ADD) 433 706-2 (3). Sutherland, Pavarotti, Opthof, Veasey, Ward, Amb. Op. Ch., LSO, Bonynge

Beatrice di Tenda, with a story involving a string of unrequited loves, is a splendid vehicle for an exceptional prima donna with a big enough voice and brilliant enough coloratura. Dame Joan Sutherland had made it her own when this recording was made in 1966, a dazzling example of her art with Bonynge, a natural Bellini conductor. The supporting cast could hardly be better, with Pavarotti highly responsive. The recording, of Decca's best vintage, has been transferred to CD with vivid atmosphere and colour. Four famous arias are provided as a filler: one from Sutherland's 1964 Norma, two from her 1963 I puritani and one from the 1962 La sonnambula.

I Capuleti ed i Montecchi (complete)

*** RCA 09026 68899-2 (3). Kasarova, Mei, Vargas, Chiummo, Alberghini, Bav. R. Ch., Munich RO, R. Abbado
*** Teldec 3984 21472-2 (2). Larmore, Hong, Groves, Aceto, Lloyd, SCO, Runnicles
(M) **(*) EMI 7 64846-2 (2). Baltsa, Gruberová, Raffanti, Howell, Tomlinson, ROHCG Ch. & O, Muti
(N) (B) **(*) EMI Gemini (ADD) 5 86055-2 (2). Sills, J. Baker, Gedda, Herincx, Lloyd, John Alldis Ch., New Philh. O, Patanè

Bellini's setting of the Romeo and Juliet story makes a strange opera, enjoyable as long as you can forget any parallel with Shakespeare. The decision to give the role of Romeo to a mezzo-soprano is in itself controversial, but it makes for added interest in that each of the three singers in the major competing sets finds a different slant in the characterization. It is Romeo's music too that provides the focus of interest in an opera in which the material is spread somewhat thinly. Much of the inspiration brings reminders of early Verdi – the exciting opening of the overture, for example – but the whole score is worth the attention of Bellinians.

Taking three discs instead of the usual two, the RCA set offers an important bonus in an alternative version of the Tomb Scene by Nicolai Vaccai, dating from five years before Bellini's version. There are also a couple of alternative versions of arias ornamented by Rossini. Quite apart from that, Roberto Abbado conducts a beautifully sprung, warmly sympathetic reading, less hard-driven than the EMI live recording conducted by Muti. The sound too is warm, full and well balanced, preferable to the EMI. Vocally the principal glory of the set lies in Kasarova's characterful and stylish performance as Romeo, firmer and more consistent than Baltsa's on EMI. Eva Mei makes a sweet and girlish Giulietta, sensitive and true, if lacking some of the deeper insights of Gruberová on EMI. The rest of the cast is first rate, with Ramón Vargas outstanding in the tenor role of Tebaldo (Tybalt).

Donald Runnicles offers a fresh and sympathetic reading of

Bellini's 'Romeo and Juliet' opera with an outstanding cast. The benefit of having the Scottish Chamber Orchestra instead of a full-blown symphony orchestra is that the woodwind and brass have a fairer balance against the strings. Jennifer Larmore is warm, fresh and firm as Romeo, youthfully ardent. Most remarkable of all is the Korean soprano Hei-Kyung Hong as Juliet, at once pure and warm of tone and passionate of expression, equally bringing out the youthfulness of the heroine. As Tebaldo, Paul Groves is clear and stylish, even though the tone is not Italianate, and Robert Lloyd is a commanding Lorenzo. Though the competition is strong, the Teldec set scores both in its casting and in its fullness of sound.

Muti's set was recorded live at Covent Garden in March 1984. With the Royal Opera House a difficult venue for recording, the sound is hard and close. Agnes Baltsa makes a passionately expressive Romeo and Edita Gruberová a Juliet who is not just brilliant in coloratura but also sweet and tender. Muti's conducting is masterly, especially striking at the end of Act I, when the five principals sing a hushed quintet. With excellent contributions from the refined tenor Dano Raffanti (as Tebaldo), Gwynne Howell and John Tomlinson, it is a performance to blow the cobwebs off this once-neglected opera.

In the earlier EMI studio recording, made at Abbey Road in 1975, Janet Baker responds richly to the unfailing lyricism of Bellini's writing. Beverly Sills has her moments of shrillness, but the rest of the singing is very commendable, and the conducting of Giuseppe Patanè is beautifully sprung and the recording is atmospheric. No libretto with translation or synopsis is provided, but the former is available on the EMI Classics Website (www.musicfromemi.com).

Norma (complete; DVD versions)

🅑━ *** Arthaus **DVD** 100 180. Sutherland, Elkins, Stevens, Grant, Opera Australia Ch., Sydney Elizabethan O, Bonynge (V/D: Sandro Sequi)

(*(**) INA **DVD** HCD 4003. Caballé, Veasey, Vickers, Ferrin, Teatro Reggio di Torino, Patanè (Stage Director: Sandro Sequi, V/D: Pierre Jourdan)

Recorded live at the Sydney Opera House in 1978 (not 1991 as the box seems to imply), this Australian Opera production by Sandro Sequi is chiefly valuable for presenting Dame Joan Sutherland in one of her most important roles when she was still at the peak of her powers. Her two audio recordings date from early and late in her career, where this provides an important bridge, with *Casta diva* finding Dame Joan in glorious voice, at once powerful, creamily beautiful and wonderfully secure. With sets by Fiorella Mariani it is a traditional production, springing no surprises, encouraging the diva to relax in the role, never more so than in her big duet with Adalgisa, *Mira o Norma*, ending in a dazzling account of the cabaletta, where Margreta Elkins equally sparkles, and Richard Bonynge draws light, crisply sprung playing from the orchestra. Less satisfying is the singing of Ronald Stevens as Pollione, powerful and heroic, but rather too coarse for Bellinian cantilena. Clifford Grant by contrast could hardly be more cleanly focused as Oroveso. The sound is a little dry, not as full-bodied as in the finest, fully digital recordings, but the sharpness of attack heightens the dramatic thrust of Bonynge's conducting.

Recorded in the open air at the Orange Festival in July 1974, Patanè's DVD offers an exceptionally strong trio of principals. Montserrat Caballé was at her peak at that time, producing a gloriously even flow of legato tone in *Casta diva* and shading dynamics with great sensitivity. Her coloratura, too, is brilliant, as in her cabaletta she defies the high winds in the Festival arena. Her acting is also impressive, with agony movingly conveyed in the scene with her children. Josephine Veasey, equally at her peak in 1974, is rich and firm throughout, offering a perfect foil in the big duet of *Mira o Norma*, even if Patanè presses the cabaletta too hard for comfort. Jon Vickers, perhaps surprisingly for such a heroic tenor, controls his enormous voice with fine precision, projecting superbly, even if his shading of tone is limited. Such casting was ideal for this setting. The others, including Agostino Ferrin as Oroveso, make a first-rate team, but sadly the limited mono recording detracts from the impact of the performance, with voices balanced very close and the orchestra rather thin behind. The staging of Sandro Sequi is conventional and aptly atmospheric. Subtitles are included, but the documentation is paltry, consisting simply of a tribute to Caballé as Norma, with not even a printed list of tracks.

Norma (complete; CD versions)

(M) *** Decca (ADD) 470 413-2 (3). Sutherland, Horne, Alexander, Cross, Minton, Ward, L. Symphony Ch. & O, Bonynge

(M) (***) EMI mono 5 62668-2 (3). Callas, Picchi, Stignani, Vaghi, Rohcg Ch. & O, Gui

(M) (***) EMI mono 5 62638-2 [562642-2] (3). Callas, Stignani, Filippeschi, Rossi-Lemeni, La Scala, Milan, Ch. and O, Serafin

**(*) Decca 414 476-2 (3). Sutherland, Pavarotti, Caballé, Ramey, Welsh Nat. Op. Ch. & O, Bonynge

(M) **(*) EMI (ADD) CMS5 66428-2 (3). Callas, Corelli, Ludwig, Zaccharia, Ch. & O of La Scala, Milan, Serafin

In her first, mid-1960s recording of *Norma*, Sutherland was joined by an Adalgisa in Marilyn Horne whose control of florid singing is just as remarkable as Sutherland's own. The other soloists are very good indeed. A most compelling performance, helped by the conducting of Richard Bonynge; and the Walthamstow recording is vivid but also atmospheric in its CD format. This set has now been reissued at mid-price as part of Decca's 'Compact Opera Collection'. However, there is no printed libretto, only a CD-ROM facility, which carries full text and translation via a computer.

Recorded live at Covent Garden, the 1952 account of *Norma* presents Callas at her very peak. She had already sung the role in a dozen places from 1948 onwards, including La Scala, Milan, but her début at Covent Garden marked a new development, with Ebe Stignani, ideally cast as Adalgisa, a splendid foil. More than her studio recordings of the role, this finds Callas in perfect voice, with none of the flaws that developed later in her career, notably unsteadiness under pressure. Here the tone is unmistakable, with the distinctive timbre well caught in a recording that for most of the time presents the voices vividly, with microphones evidently well placed. Callas's top notes are immaculate, and her coloratura agile, but it is the weight of emotion conveyed that makes this performance unique. Thus, at the start of the duet, *Mira o Norma*, you hear the opening phrase gloriously sung by Stignani in full open tone, with Callas following immediately, shading her tone subtly to add far greater emotional weight. Gui then launches into the brilliant cabaletta at high speed, finding his singers fully equipped to accept the challenge. Interestingly, in the tiny role of Clotilde, companion to Norma, you have Joan Sutherland, then newly recruited to the Covent Garden company: the voice is hardly recognizable, and it might even be that Sutherland the beginner was seeking to match the prima donna next to her as closely as possible. As Pollione, the tenor Mirto Picchi cannot match the women in the cast, but at least he sings with firmer, less strained tone than Mario Filippeschi in Callas's first studio recording of *Norma*, made for EMI in 1954.

In Callas's earlier mono set, the recording is opened out impressively in the new transfer, and the sense of presence gives wonderful intensity to one of the diva's most powerful performances, recorded at the very peak of her powers. Balance of soloists is close but Callas justifies everything, even the cuts. The veteran, Ebe Stignani, as Adalgisa is a characterful partner in the sisters' duets, but Filippeschi is disappointingly thin-toned and strained, and Rossi-Lemeni is gruff. This is now one of EMI's 'Great Recordings of the Century'.

Though Dame Joan Sutherland was 58 when her second *Norma* recording was made, her singing is still impressive, but Pavarotti is in some ways the set's greatest strength, easily expressive as Pollione. Caballé as Adalgisa seems determined to outdo Sutherland in cooing self-indulgently. Full, brilliant, well-balanced recording of the complete score.

By the time Callas came to record her 1960 stereo version, the tendency to hardness and unsteadiness in the voice above the stave, always apparent, had grown serious; but the interpretation was as sharply illuminating as ever, a unique assumption, helped by Christa Ludwig as Adalgisa, while Corelli sings heroically. Serafin as ever is the most persuasive of Bellini conductors. Highlights are available on EMI 5 66662-2.

(i) *Norma* (complete). Excerpts: (ii) *Ite sul colle, o Druidi; Ah! Del Tebro al giogo indegno* (iii) *Merco all'altar di Venere . . . Me protegge!;* (iv) *Sedioze voci . . . Casta diva . . . Ah! bello a me ritorna; Mira, o Norma;* (v) *Sgombra è la sacra selva;* (vi) *Deh! Non voleri vittime*
(N) (BB) (***) Naxos mono 8.110325/7. (i) Callas, Stignani, Filippeschi, Rossi-Lemeni, La Scala, Milan, Ch. & O, Serafin; (ii) Pinza, Met. Op. Ch.; (iii) Merli; (iv) Ponselle; (v) Minghini-Cattaneo; (vi) Cigna, Pasero, Breviario

Mark Obert-Thorn's impressive new transfer has been made from the best portions of two 1950s-era British LP pressings, and he has taken the opportunity to add earlier, historical recordings (made between 1927 and 1937), among which the Pinza and Ponselle items obviously stand out, but the final excerpt (*Deh! Non voleri vittime*) includes some superb singing from Gina Cigna.

Il pirata (complete)
(M) *(**) EMI mono 5 66432-2 (2). Callas, Ego, Ferraro, Peterson, Watson, Sarfaty, American Op. Soc. Ch. & O, Rescigno
(M) ** EMI (ADD) 5 67121-2 (2). Cappuccilli, Caballé, Martí, Raimondi, Rome R. & TV Ch. & O, Gavazzeni

Recorded live at a concert performance in New York in January 1959, the Callas version is flawed, with harsh sound and intrusive audience noises. Though Callas herself shows signs of vocal deterioration, with top notes often raw and uneven, hers is a fire-eating performance, totally distinctive, instantly magnetic from the moment she utters her first word, '*Sorgete*', in Act I. The rest of the cast is indifferent, with Constantine Ego strenuous in the tenor role of Ernesto. The second disc offers an alternative recording of the final scene,

made in Amsterdam six months later, with Rescigno conducting the Concertgebouw Orchestra and with Callas in smoother vocal form, helped by less raw recording.

Gavazzeni's is the first complete recording. Caballé is well suited to the role of the heroine, though by her highest standards there is some carelessness in her singing, with clumsy changes of register. Nor are the conducting and presentation sparkling enough to mask the comparative poverty of Bellini's invention. Caballé's husband, Bernabé Martí, battles valiantly with the difficult part of the pirate. The 1970 recording flatters the voices and has plenty of atmosphere.

I Puritani (complete; DVD version)
(N) * TDK **DVD** DV-OPIP. Gruberová, Bros, Alvarez, Pierotti, Liceu Theatre Ch. & O, Haider (Director: Andrei Serban, V/D Toni Bargallo)

Originally presented by Welsh National Opera, Andrei Serban's production of *I Puritani* with designs by Michael Yeargan involves minimalist sets alongside traditional seventeenth-century costumes apt for this story of the Civil War in England. Though under Friedrich Haider the Orchestra of the Gran Teatre del Liceu in Lisbon can hardly match that of WNO, and chorus-work brings rough ensemble, the pacing of the piece works well. What is disappointing is not only the primitive acting, harking back to a bad old tradition, but the often unstylish singing from an admittedly promising cast. Edita Gruberová as Elvira no longer has such a sweet or fresh soprano as she once had, and her control of coloratura is no longer as certain as it used to be, with scales slithered over. The video regularly views her big moments in close-up which exaggerates her over-acting, as she mouths her words, absurdly so in her efforts to make Elvira's madness convincing. By no stretch of imagination does she emerge as the *vergin vezzosa*, 'charming maiden', described in her brilliant cabaletta, even though she sings that showpiece well enough. As the hero, Arturo, José Bros cuts a handsome, youthful figure, and his sweet-toned tenor is most attractive; but he hangs on to notes even more unstylishly than Gruberová. Among the others, Carlos Alvarez as Riccardo and Simon Orfila as Giorgio sing well enough but, like their colleagues, seem to come from another operatic age. Not a performance worth preserving.

I puritani (complete; CD versions)
*** Decca (ADD) 417 588-2 (3). Sutherland, Pavarotti, Ghiaurov, Luccardi, Caminada, Cappuccilli, ROHCG Ch. & O, Bonynge
(***) EMI mono 5 56275-2 (2). Callas, Di Stefano, Panerai, Rossi-Lemeni, La Scala, Milan, Ch. & O, Serafin
(M) **(*) EMI (ADD) 7 69663-2 (2). Caballé, Kraus, Manuguerra, Hamari, Ferrin, Amb. Op. Ch., Philh. O, Muti

Whereas her earlier set was recorded when Sutherland had adopted a soft-grained style, with consonants largely eliminated, her singing brings fresh, bright singing, rich and agile. Pavarotti emerges as a Bellini stylist, with Ghiaurov and Cappuccilli making up an impressive cast, but with Anita Caminada disappointing as Enrichetta. Vivid, atmospheric recording.

In 1953, when she made this recording, Callas's voice was already hard on top and with some unsteadiness, but her portrayal is uniquely compelling. None of the other soloists is ideal, though most of the singing is acceptable. The mono sound is now opened up and the solo voices project well. Like other EMI/Callas recordings, this has been handsomely redocumented. Highlights are available on 5 66665-2.

When Caballé assumed the role, Riccardo Muti's attention to detail and pointing of rhythm made for refreshing results, and the warm, luminous recording is excellent. But both the principal soloists – here below form – indulge in distracting mannerisms, hardly allowing even a single bar to be presented straight in the big numbers, rarely sounding spontaneous. The big ensemble, *A te, o cara*, at slow speed loses the surge of exhilaration which Sutherland and Pavarotti show so strongly.

La sonnambula (complete)

*** Decca 417 424-2 (2). Sutherland, Pavarotti, D. Jones, Ghiaurov, L. Op. Ch., Nat. PO, Bonynge

(B) *** Naxos 8.660042/3. D'Artegna, Papadjiakou, Orgonasova, Giménez, Dilbèr, De Vries, Micu, Netherlands R. Ch. and CO, Zedda

(M) (***) EMI mono 5 56278-2 (2). Callas, Monti, Cossotto, Zaccaria, Ratti, La Scala, Milan, Ch. and O, Votto

(M) **(*) Decca (ADD) 448 966-2 (2). Sutherland, Monti, Elkins, Stahlman, Corena, Maggio Musicale Fiorentino Ch. & O, Bonynge

Sutherland's singing in her later version is even more affecting and more stylish than before, generally purer and more forthright, if with diction still clouded at times. The challenge of singing opposite Pavarotti adds to the bite of the performance, crisply and resiliently controlled by Bonynge.

The Naxos issue offers the finest version of the opera at any price since Joan Sutherland's. Luba Orgonasova is an expressive and characterful heroine, agile and pointed in her phrasing of coloratura, deeply affecting in the tender legato of *Ah non credea mirarti*, with tone delicately varied. Raul Giménez is equally stylish as Elvino, the rich landowner, using his light Rossinian tenor most sensitively, with Alberto Zedda, scholar as well as conductor, pointing the accompaniment lightly. The other principals are not quite on this level but they make an excellent team. As usual with Naxos opera issues, there is a libretto in Italian but only a detailed summary of the plot in English.

Substantially cut, the Callas version was recorded in mono in 1957, yet it gives a vivid picture of the diva at the peak of her powers. Nicola Monti makes a strong rather than a subtle contribution, but he blends well with Callas in the duets; and Fiorenza Cossotto is a good Teresa. Again, the remastered recording for the Callas Edition shows considerable improvement.

In Sutherland's earlier version, her use of *portamento* is often excessive, but the freshness of the voice is a delight, Bonynge's direction is outstanding, and the casting is first rate too, with Nicola Monti a Bellini tenor. Both Sylvia Stahlman as Lisa and Margreta Elkins as Teresa sing beautifully and with keen accuracy. Even Fernando Corena's rather coarse, *buffo*-style Rodolfo has an attractive vitality. The recording has come up vividly on CD.

BENTZON, Niels Viggo (born 1919)

Feature on René Descartes, Op. 357

(*) BIS (ADD) CD 79. Danish Nat. R. O, Schmidt (with JORGENSON: *To Love Music*; NORBY: *The Rainbow Snake* *)

Krönik om René Descartes ('Feature on René Descartes') comes from 1975. The first movement gives a 'musical version of the Cartesian vortex which refers to a medieval notion of rotating heavenly bodies moving at enormous speed', and the final movement addresses Descartes's celebrated proposition, *Cogito ergo sum*. A well-prepared performance and good recording, but this is not the composer at his best.

Symphonies 3, Op. 46 (1947); 4 (Metamorphoses), Op. 55 (1949)

*** dacapo DCCD 9102. Aarhus SO, Schmidt

Both the symphonies recorded here are teeming with invention: the pastoral opening of the *Third* unleashes a rich flow of ideas, all of memorable quality. The *Fourth* (*Metamorphoses*) is a most imaginative work, visionary music: powerful, concentrated and inventive. Along with the *Sixth* and *Seventh Symphonies* of Holmboe, this is arguably the finest Nordic symphony after Nielsen, and Ole Schmidt and the Aarhus orchestra play it with conviction and passion. The recording is very good indeed, with plenty of detail and a good balance. Two remarkable works.

Symphonies 5 (Ellipser), Op. 61; 7 (De tre versioner), Op. 83

☁ ✸ *** dacapo 8.244111. Aarhus SO, Schmidt

Bentzon's early symphonies offer real vision and their textures glow luminously. Both the *Seventh* and the *Fifth* have a sense of space and individuality (deriving from tonal composers Copland, Nielsen, Hindemith and Stravinsky). It is no exaggeration to call the *Seventh* a masterpiece, an impressive study in thematic metamorphosis. Fine performances and recording.

Cello Sonatas, Opp. 43 & 268; Variations on 'The Volga Boatmen', Op. 354

(N) **(*) dacapo 8.226015. Ullner, Bevan

The *Cello Sonata*, Op. 43, comes from the late 1940s, a vintage period in Bentzon's output, the period of the *Third* and *Fourth Symphonies* and the finest of the piano sonatas. It is a compelling and rewarding score, very well played by these two artists, though some may find the balance unduly favours the pianist. What an inventive, indeed masterly, composer Bentzon was at this period! The later works are both from the 1970s and are perhaps less impressive, though still worth getting to know.

(i) Sextet for Piano and Wind, Op. 278. Wind Quintet 5, Op. 116

*** dacapo 8.224208. Danish Nat. SO Wind Quintet, (i) with N. Bentzon – KOPPEL: *Sextet* ***

The *Fifth Wind Quintet* comes from 1958. This is a thoughtful piece with fresh and original ideas. It is more rewarding than the rather garrulous *Sextet* of 1971, which the composer's son, Nikolaj, plays with the fine Danish Radio Wind players. Among Bentzon's output there are some real masterpieces (the Symphonies 3–7, for example) but the *Sextet* is not in the same class. Nevertheless, this CD is well worth having for the fine *Wind Quintet* and the Koppel piece. Good performances and recording.

Piano Sonatas 3, Op. 44; 5, Op. 77; 9, Op. 104

** dacapo 8.224103. Llambías

Bentzon's *Sonata 3* is an exceptionally fine work, not dissimilar to the sonatas of Tippett or the sole sonata of Robert Simpson, and inferior to neither. Rodolfo Llambías's approach is highly discursive, and he lays bare all of No. 3's many beauties rather too lovingly. All the same, in the absence of any alternatives, these remarkable sonatas demand a hearing. Unfortunately, the acoustic is over-reverberant.

BERG, Alban (1885–1935)

(i; ii) *Chamber Concerto for Piano, Violin & 13 Wind;* (iii) *Violin Concerto (To the Memory of Angel);* (iv) *Lyric Suite: 3 Pieces; 3 Pieces for Orchestra,* Op. 6; (v; vi) *Adagio* from *Chamber Concerto* (arr. for Violin, Clarinet & Piano); (vii) *Lyric Suite for String Quartet;* (vi) *4 Pieces for Clarinet and Piano;* (vii) *String Quartet,* Op. 3; (i) *Piano Sonata,* Op. 1; (viii; iv) *Altenberg Lieder,* Op. 4; (ix) *7 Early Songs* (versions with (x) piano; (iv) orchestra); (xi) *4 Lieder,* Op. 2; (xii) *Lieder: An Leukon; Schlieffe mir die Augen beide* (2 settings); (ix; iv) *Der Wein* (concert aria); (viii; iv) *Lulu: Suite (symphonic pieces).* (xiii) *Lulu* (opera; complete); (xiv) *Wozzeck* (complete). (xv) Transcription of Johann STRAUSS JR: *Waltz: Wein, Weib und Gesang*

(B) *** DG (ADD/DDD) 474 657-2 (8). (i) Barenboim; (ii) Zukerman, Ens. InterContemporain, Boulez; (iii) Mutter, Chicago SO, Levine; (iv) VPO, Abbado; (v) Kremer, (vi) Meyer, Maisenberg; (vii) LaSalle Qt; (viii) Banse; (ix) Von Otter; (x) Forsberg; (xi) Fischer-Dieskau, Reimann; (xii) Marshall, Parsons; (xiii) Stratas, Minton, Schwarz, Mazura, Blankenheim, Riegel, Tear, Paris Op. O, Boulez; (xiv; iv) Grundheber, Behrens, Haugland, Langridge, Zednik; (xv) Boston Symphony Chamber Players

An impressive and inexpensive collection that should satisfy the most demanding Berg enthusiast. Nearly all these recordings are three star and most are still currently available separately and are praised below, including the *Chamber Concerto, Violin Concerto, Three Pieces for Orchestra, Lulu Symphonic Suite,* the *Seven Early Songs* and Boulez's pioneering recording of *Lulu.* Abbado's *Wozzeck,* recorded live, has the inevitable drawback of intrusive stage noises and backwardly balanced singers, but is still very compelling.

Among the other recordings, the LaSalle Quartet provide the most persuasive advocacy in the Op. 3 *String Quartet* and *Lyric Suite* arrangement and are vividly recorded. Sabine Meyer's contribution to the works including clarinet is hardly less impressive, and Barenboim, if not quite a match for Pollini, gives a concentrated account of the *Piano Sonata.*

Juliane Banse sings expressively and lyrically in the *Altenberg Lieder,* atmospherically accompanied by the VPO and Abbado; though some Bergians may prefer tougher, edgier performances, few will resist such a warmly musical response. The contribution of the rich-toned Margaret Marshall and Geoffrey Parsons is hardly less impressive. Fischer-Dieskau with highly sensitive accompaniment from Aribert Reimann is equally communicative in the early Op. 2 *Songs,* and the Boston Chamber Players provide an unexpected bonus in Berg's arrangement of a familiar waltz by Johann Strauss. The documentation is generally very good and includes synopses for the operas but no translations.

Chamber Concerto for Piano, Violin & 13 Wind Instruments, Op. 6

(M) *** DG (ADD) 447 405-2. Barenboim, Zukerman, Ens. InterContemporain, Boulez – STRAVINSKY: *Concerto in E flat,* etc. ***

(i) *Chamber Concerto;* (ii) *Violin Concerto (To the Memory of an Angel)*

(M) *** Warner Elatus 0927 46737-2. Dresden State O, Sinopoli, with (i) Lucchesini; (ii) Watanabe

(i) *Chamber Concerto;* (ii) *3 Pieces for Orchestra;* (iii) *Violin Concerto*

(M) ** Sony (ADD) SMK 68331. (i) Barenboim, Gavrilov; (i–ii) BBC SO; (iii) Zukerman, LSO; (i–iii) Boulez

It would be hard to imagine more romantic readings of Berg's principal orchestral works than those under Giuseppe Sinopoli. The atonal arguments of Berg have never been presented more sinuously, cocooning the ear, helped by sumptuous playing and recording. The violinist, Reiko Watanabe, is totally in sympathy with this approach, using the widest range of expression, tone and dynamic, with the music at the start seeming to emerge out of mists. Romantic readings of the *Violin Concerto* are common enough, but with the pianist, Andrea Lucchesini as a perfectly matched partner for Watanabe, the *Chamber Concerto,* which can seem one of Berg's more cerebral works, is just as seductive.

On DG, Boulez sets brisk tempi in the *Chamber Concerto,* seeking to give the work classical incisiveness; but the strong and expressive personalities of the pianist and violinist tend towards a more romantic view. The result is characterful and convincing, and not at all intimidating. Sadly, Boulez omits the extended repeat in the finale. The recording is attractively atmospheric.

Boulez's personality again strongly dominates the sharply focused Sony performances of the *Chamber Concerto* and Op. 6 *Orchestral Pieces* from 1967. The *Violin Concerto,* with Zukerman as soloist very close indeed, was recorded two decades later, in 1984. His strong, urgent reading matches Boulez's toughness, a robust rather than a subtle or poetic reading, with the elegiac quality missing.

Violin Concerto

*** Warner 2564 60291-2. Hope, BBC SO, Watkins – BRITTEN: *Violin Concerto* ***

(M) *** DG 447 445-2. Perlman, Boston SO, Ozawa (with RAVEL: *Tzigane;* STRAVINSKY: *Concerto* ***)

*** DG 437 093-2. Mutter, Chicago SO, Levine – RIHM: *Gesungene Zeit,* etc. ***

(BB) *** Warner Apex 0927 40812-2. Zehetmair, Philh. O, Holliger – HARTMANN: *Concerto funèbre;* JANACEK: *Concerto* ***

(M) *** Sup. (ADD) SU 3663-2 011. Suk, Czech PO, Ančerl (with BRUCH: *Concerto* **(*); MENDELSSOHN: *Concerto* **(*))

Alban Berg didn't live to hear his *Violin Concerto* performed, and he was therefore unable to correct a number of errors in the copying of the full score. These have now been corrected from primary sources in the critical edition published by Universal in 1996. It was Daniel Hope who, a year before publication, gave the first performance of the corrected version in Manchester; here, in a warm and purposeful performance, he is the soloist in the first recording of it. He sustains spacious speeds with no sense of self-consciousness, intense and concentrated from first to last, subtly varying his vibrato to heighten emotion, notably in the hushed and tender resolution on the Bach chorale theme, *Es ist genug.* The cellist Paul Watkins proves himself a fine conductor, drawing warmly intense playing from the BBC Symphony Orchestra, helped by full, immediate recording with impressively weighty brass. The Britten *Violin Concerto,* written when the young composer was most influenced by Berg, makes an ideal and unique coupling and another outstanding performance.

Perlman's performance is above all commanding. The Boston orchestra accompanies superbly and, though the balance favours the soloist, the recording is excellent. The current transfer shows the Boston acoustic at its most seductive.

Anne-Sophie Mutter begins the *Concerto* with a *pianissimo* of much delicacy. She proceeds to give an intensely passionate reading, both freely expressive and intensely purposeful, with James Levine and the Chicago orchestra matching her in subtle shading. As an imaginative coupling, Mutter offers a concerto written for her by the forty-year-old German composer, Wolfgang Rihm.

On the inexpensive Apex disc Zehetmair plays with great sensitivity and a natural eloquence, and many will prefer this to Mutter on DG. That has tremendous brilliance and panache but Zehetmair's less sensational reading brings one closer to the heart of this poignant music. Moreover, apart from the price advantage, he offers more interesting couplings in the form of the Hartman *Concerto funèbre* and the fragmentary Janáček *Concerto* of 1927–8. The recording, made at The Maltings, Snape, is of exemplary clarity and has great presence, making this triptych a very real bargain.

Suk's sweet, unforced style movingly brings out the work's lyrical side without ever exaggerating the romanticism. A most beautiful performance, with the excellent (1965) recording transferred to CD very firmly and naturally.

(i) *Violin Concerto*; (ii) *Lyric Suite: 3 Pieces*; (iii) *3 Pieces for Orchestra, Op. 6*

(BB) *** Naxos 8.554755. Netherlands RSO, Klas, (i) with Hirsch

(***) Testament mono SBT 1004. (i) Krasner, (i; iii) BBC SO, Webern; (ii) Galimir Qt

This Naxos issue brings together clear, positive versions of three key works by Berg, with the recordings, made in the Hilversum concert hall under the Estonian conductor Eri Klas, presenting each work in close focus. Rebecca Hirsch is an outstanding young violinist who has concentrated on twentieth-century music, and here she combines clean, precise attack with natural tonal warmth. The balance is securely held between weight of emotion and fresh modernity. So it is, too, in the other two works, not just the three-movement orchestral version of the *Lyric Suite*, but Berg's early exercise in Schoenbergian atonality, the *Orchestral Pieces* of 1914–15, where already he demonstrates his genius for the dramatic use of orchestral colour.

The Testament CD is of great interest in bringing back to life a broadcast of the *Violin Concerto* by Louis Krasner (who commissioned it and gave its first performance), laden with a unique intensity of feeling. The sound-quality is poor (it comes from the soloist's own acetates) but the spirit is powerful and vibrant, and the BBC orchestra play superbly. It comes with another 1936 recording, the Galimir Quartet's pioneering Polydor 78s of the *Lyric Suite* – impeccably played but recorded in a horribly dry acoustic.

Lyric Suite

(B) *** None. 7559 79696-2. Upshaw, Kronos Qt

The Nonesuch disc offers a *Lyric Suite* with a difference and so has a special claim on the collector's allegiance. The work was the outcome of Berg's traumatic relationship with Hanna Fuchs-Robettin and originally included a setting of lines from Baudelaire's *Fleurs du mal* in a German translation by Stefan George ('To you, you sole dear one, my cry rises/Out of the deepest abyss in which my heart has fallen'). The American composer and Berg scholar George Perle has reconstructed the original version of the finale and this is its first recording, very eloquently sung by Dawn Upshaw. The

Kronos play with a certain robust intensity and fire (nothing in the least mellifluous here), and they are decently recorded. Since this disc contains only 27 minutes of music, it comes at bargain price.

Lyric Suite: 3 Pieces; 3 Pieces for Orchestra, Op. 6

(M) *** DG (ADD) (IMS) 427 424-2 (3). BPO, Karajan – SCHOENBERG; WEBERN: *Orchestral Pieces* ***

Karajan's purification process gives wonderful clarity to Berg's often complex scores, with expressive confidence bringing out the romantic overtones. For those who resist Berg's style, Karajan's way is most likely to convert, for these are magnificently played and recorded accounts.

Lyric Suite: 3 Pieces; (i) 5 Altenberglieder, Op. 4

☛ (M) *** Warner Elatus 0927 49009-2. Dresden State O, Sinopoli, (i) with Marc

(BB) *** Arte Nova 74321 27768-2. (i) Orsanic; SW German RSO, Gielen – ZEMLINSKY: *Lyric Symphony* ***

The three movements from his *Lyric Suite* make an ideal coupling for the Zemlinsky *Lyric Symphony*, the work which Berg quotes and which prompted his title. They are beautifully played and recorded here, as are the five settings of Altenberg poems, crisp and compact yet full of emotion, here sung superbly with fresh tone and clean attack by the soprano, Vlatka Orsanic. First-rate recording. A pity the documentation does not match the musical excellence.

The Elatus disc is taken from live recordings made at the Saxon State Opera in Dresden in 1997–8, and if anything is even warmer. It offers the very generous coupling of the three-movement orchestral version of the *Lyric Suite* plus the two orchestral works based on Berg's two operas. In those the atmospheric warmth of the playing and conducting is enhanced by the expressive singing of Alessandra Marc, making one wish that these same performers had recorded the complete operas. With late-nineties recording, excellent value.

3 Pieces for Orchestra, Op. 6; 5 Orchestral Songs, Op. 4; (i) Lulu: Symphonic Suite

(M) *** DG (ADD) 449 714-2. (i) M. Price; LSO, Abbado

Abbado makes it clear above all how beautiful Berg's writing is, not just in the *Lulu* excerpts but in the early Op. 4 *Songs* and the Op. 6 *Orchestral Pieces*.

Lyric Suite for String Quartet; String Quartet, Op. 3

*** MDG 307 0996-2. Leipzig Qt (with WEBERN: *3 Pieces* ***)

The *Lyric Suite* is very accessible in its chamber-music format, while the Op. 3 *Quartet* is another of Berg's undoubted masterpieces.

The Leipzig Quartet's performances were coolly received in some quarters but have much warmth and generosity of spirit to commend them. They offer the Webern *3 Pieces* (which take two minutes) as a bonus. (Christine Oelze is the singer in the second.) Recommendable alongside, though not necessarily in preference to, the Alban Berg version.

The Alban Berg Quartet's later (digital) EMI version of the *Lyric Suite* and *Third Quartet* (5 55190-2) is arguably the best ever but now seems short measure at 47 minutes.

Piano Sonata, Op. 1

*** Ph. 468 033-2. Uchida – SCHOENBERG: *Piano Concerto, etc.*; WEBERN: *Variations*

(BB) *** Naxos 8.553870. Hill – SCHOENBERG: *Piano Pieces*, etc.; WEBERN: *Variations* ***
(B) **(*) HM Cal. Approche (ADD) CAL 6203. Södergren (with J. S. BACH: *Keyboard Collection* **(*))

In the Berg *Piano Sonata*, Op. 1, as in the remainder of her programme devoted to the Second Viennese School, Uchida is very persuasive indeed. The main work on the disc, Schoenberg's *Piano Concerto*, receives one of its most successful readings on record.

Peter Hill's account of the Berg *Sonata* on Naxos has more than just its bargain price to commend it. He is a pianist of proven intelligence and sensitivity and is decently recorded. It comes with the Schoenberg piano music, played with no less expertise and authority.

Inger Södergren's performance has real character, but she softens its angst. Those attracted to her enjoyably relaxed Bach coupling may well be converted to enjoying her Berg too. The recording is pleasingly full.

7 Early Songs
*** DG (IMS) 437 515-2. Von Otter, Forsberg – KORNGOLD; STRAUSS: *Lieder* ***
*** Decca 466 720-2. Bonney, Concg. O, Chailly – MAHLER: *Symphony 4* **(*)

In the *Seven Early Songs* of Berg, Anne Sofie von Otter and Bengt Forsberg offer inspired playing and singing, drawing out the intensity of emotion to the full without exaggeration or sentimentality. Along with Strauss and Korngold songs, a fascinating programme, magnetically performed.

Barbara Bonney also sounds spontaneous and warm in the *Seven Early Songs*, which come as a coupling for Mahler's *Fourth Symphony*, and Chailly and the orchestra too sound a degree more involved than in the Mahler.

Lulu (with orchestration of Act III completed by Friedrich Cerha)
(M) *** DG 463 617 (3). Stratas, Minton, Schwarz, Mazura, Blankenheim, Riegel, Tear, Paris Op. O, Boulez
*** Chan. 9540 (3). Haupman, Jaffe, Straka, Juan, Danish Nat. RSO, Schirmer

Boulez's pioneering recording of Berg's *Lulu* in its full three-Act form brings an intensely involving performance, very well cast. Teresa Stratas's bright, clear soprano, well recorded, fits the ruthless heroine perfectly, and Yvonne Minton is most moving as Countess Geschwitz. Firm, clear recording, excellently remastered.

Recorded at a series of live performances, the Chandos version is strongly and purposefully conducted by Ulf Schirmer. Constance Haupman makes Lulu a girlish, vulnerable figure, as well as thrusting and selfish. Her singing is commendably precise, even if under pressure the tone grows shrill. As Dr Schön, Monte Jaffe relies too heavily on unpitched sing-speech, but his is a vividly characterful performance too; and among the others Peter Straka makes a fresh, clear Alwa and Julia Juan a touchingly mature Geschwitz. Boulez's studio version for DG may have a more immediate impact, but this provides an excellent alternative.

Lulu: Symphonic Suite
(BB) *** EMI Encore 5 75879-2. Augér, CBSO, Rattle – SCHOENBERG: *5 Orchestral Pieces*; WEBERN: *6 Orchestral Pieces* ***

Arleen Augér's pure, true soprano in the vocal passages of the *Lulu Suite* is presented as an adjunct to the orchestra, rather than as a salient solo. The sound is of demonstration quality, adding enormously to the attractiveness of a disc that EMI have now reissued in the budget range.

Wozzeck (complete)
(BB) *** Naxos 8.660076-2. Falkman, Dalayman, Qvale, Wahlund, Stregard, Stockholm Royal Op. Ch. & O, Segerstam
(M) *** EMI 5 56865-2 (2). Skovhus, Denoke, Olsen, Merritt, Blinkhof, Sacher, Hamburg State Op. Ch. & State PO, Metzmacher
**(*) Teldec 0630 14108-2 (2). Grundheber, Meier, Baker, Wottrich, Clark, Von Kannen, German Opera, Berlin, Ch. & Children's Ch., Berlin State O, Barenboim
**(*) DG 423 587-2 (2). Grundheber, Behrens, Haugland, Langridge, Zednik, V. State Op. Ch., VPO, Abbado

Segerstam proves a strong, thrusting interpreter, tautly holding the drama together, with the impact heightened by the vividness of the live recording: powerful, immediate and atmospheric, even if the strings are set behind the woodwind, one of the almost inevitable discrepancies in any live recording. There are stage noises too, but the magnetism of the performance and the consistency of the singing with no weak member of the cast quickly make you forget any slight flaws. Though the *Sprechstimme* ('sing-speech') is sometimes free – again not surprisingly – the great merit of all the singers is their musicality, with the Captain and the Doctor less caricatured than usual, and with a firm, central account of the title-role from Carl Johan Falkman. Katarina Dalayman is also superb as Marie, singing with character as well as beauty. A detailed synopsis is provided in the booklet and a complete libretto in German but no translation. An excellent issue which, at the Naxos price, should tempt collectors to experiment with a challenging work that in a performance like this is deeply moving.

Ingo Metzmacher's live recording for EMI was made at the Hamburg State Opera, with Metzmacher drawing powerful, clean-textured playing from his orchestra, firmly establishing this as a high romantic work, whatever its modernist credentials. The casting is strong too, with Bo Skovhus singing with clean focus in the title-role, and with Marie superbly sung by Angela Denoke, sensuous on the one hand, tenderly affecting on the other. Otherwise, the production on a bare stage seems to have encouraged each character to overact, Skovhus included, even while the results are exceptionally vivid, with the sense of a live performance consistently adding to the dramatic impact.

Barenboim's Teldec version of *Wozzeck* was recorded live at the Deutsche Staatsoper in Berlin in 1994. With Grundheber even finer than under Abbado, Barenboim leads a warmly expressive performance. The cast is an outstanding one, with such characterful singers as Graham Clark (Captain) in incidental roles. Less successful is Waltraud Meier as Marie, with an uneven, grainy quality in the voice.

The Abbado version, recorded live in the opera house, is very compelling in its presentation of the drama, given extra thrust through the tensions of live performance. The cast is first rate – but the drawback is that not only do you get intrusive stage noises, but the voices are set behind the orchestra, with the instrumental sound putting a gauze between listener and singers.

Wozzeck (in English)
(M) **(*) Chan. 3094 (2). Shore, Woodrow, Kale, Bayley, Barstow, Rigby, Geoffrey Mitchell Ch., Philh. O, Daniel

Paul Daniel as music director of the English National Opera has proved outstanding in live opera, so it is good to have him following up the success of his English-language recording of Verdi's *Falstaff* with this account of *Wozzeck*, in the 'Opera in English' series, sponsored by the Peter Moores Foundation. The clarity of the words is remarkable in a warm, full-blooded recording which does not underplay the orchestral sound. Coupled with the immediacy, the drama is intensified, even if the sinister element in this story of neurosis is minimized. Andrew Shore, a regular contributor to this series, is strongly cast in the title-role, even if the firm clarity of his singing equally underplays the neurosis. He is strong and positive rather than mad-sounding, at least until the final scenes of Marie's murder and his own suicide. There the atmospheric recording vividly captures the sinister ambience of this disturbing opera. The extremes of expression and dynamic in the scenes with Marie are also very well caught. Dame Josephine Barstow sounds too mature for the role, not quite steady enough, even though dramatically she gives a vivid portrayal, with Jean Rigby a fine foil as Margret. The grotesques among the male characters are all very well portrayed, their characterization the more vivid thanks to the clarity of words.

BERIO, Luciano (1925–2003)

Coro
*** DG (ADD) 471 587-2. Cologne R. Ch. & SO, composer

Coro was written in 1975–6 and revised in 1977, and this recording was made towards the end of 1979. It now reappears, attractively repackaged, and with sung texts and admirable documentation – but still at full price. The work is ambitious, with each of the 40 singers paired with an instrumentalist and with folk verse on basic themes contrasted with poems of Pablo Neruda. The striking line 'Come and see the blood in the streets' keeps recurring to hammer home the composer's political message, though *Coro* makes its impact musically with overtones of the ritualistic elements in Stravinsky's *Les Noces*. Of his generation of leading avant-gardists Berio remains among the most approachable, almost identifiably Italian in his acceptance of melody. The composer here directs a highly committed performance, helped by the impact of forward sound, vividly remastered

Eindrücke; Sinfonia
(BB) *** Warner Apex 8573 89226-2. Pasquier, New Swingle Singers, O Nat. de France, Boulez

In 1969 Berio's *Sinfonia*, written for the New York Philharmonic, made a far wider impact on the music world than is common with an avant-garde composer. Boulez records the complete work for the first time in this fine Erato version. *Eindrücke* is another powerful work, much more compressed, bare and uncompromising in its layering of strings and wind. An outstanding bargain.

(i) *Recital I (for Cathy);* (ii) *Folk-song Suite;* (iii) *3 Songs by Kurt Weill* (arr. Berio)
(M) *** RCA (ADD) 09026 62540-2. Berberian, with (i) L. Sinf.; (ii-iii) Juilliard Ens.; all cond. composer

Recital I is the most elaborate, colourful work that Berio ever wrote for Cathy Berberian. Against fragmentary accompaniment from the instrumental band, the soloist in this semi-dramatic piece thinks back through her repertoire as a

concert-singer from Monteverdi to the present day, a brilliant collage of musical ideas. With Berberian at her most intense, the result is very compelling. Excellent recording. Also included is a sparkling collection of folksongs arranged for Berberian with twinkling ingenuity by Berio. The record concludes with three Kurt Weill songs, arranged by Berio, with Berberian relishing every word.

BERKELEY, Lennox (1903–89)

Guitar Concerto
*** Chan. 9963. Ogden, N. Sinf., Hickox – ARNOLD: *Guitar Concerto;* WALTON: *5 Bagatelles* ***

The Berkeley *Concerto*, one of his last works, begins atmospherically with a duet for two unaccompanied horns, relaxed in its mood, gaining in this performance under Richard Hickox from relatively urgent speeds. It leads via a mysterious slow movement to a finale which starts with a sly quotation from Rodrigo's *Concierto de Aranjuez*. Craig Ogden gives a commanding performance.

The Judgement of Paris (ballet)
(N) (M) *** Dutton CDLX 7149. Royal Ballet Sinfonia, Wordsworth – LAMBERT: *Apparitions;* LANCHBERY: *Tales of Beatrice Potter* ***

We are realizing more and more clearly just what a Diaghilev-like personality Sir Frederick Ashton was in the field of British ballet. Not just as a choreographer (and, as has been rediscovered at Covent Garden recently, his *La Fille mal gardée* is one of the most magical of all lighter ballets) but as an instigator of memorable new ballet scores. Sir Lennox Berkeley's *Judgement of Paris* is perhaps not one of them, but it is genuine ballet music and winningly scored, even if the melodic invention is unmemorable. It is splendidly played by the Royal Ballet Sinfonia under Barry Wordsworth, and the recording is first class in every way.

(i) *Sinfonia concertante, Op. 84; Symphony 3*
*** Chan. 10022. BBC Nat. O of Wales, Hickox, with (i) Daniel – M. BERKELEY: *Oboe Concerto,* etc. ***

In Lennox Berkeley's *Sinfonia concertante* the first two of the five movements are linked by using the same material, while the third and fourth, *Aria* and *Canzonetta,* bring a relaxation before the vigorous finale, with a cadenza in the middle and a thoughtful passage before the strongly rhythmic coda. *Symphony 3,* written in 1968–9, is in a single movement divided into three sections. It represents his late style at its most striking, dark and compressed in the first section, with rapidly contrasting motifs, before a brief, slow, central section leads to a rather more extrovert finale with galloping 6/8 rhythms and a brassy conclusion, all brilliantly caught in the full-ranging Chandos recording.

Symphony 1; Serenade for Strings
*** Chan. 9981. BBC Nat. O of Wales, Hickox – M. BERKELEY: *Horn Concerto; Coronach* ***

The *First Symphony* is one of Lennox Berkeley's most luminous and captivating scores, Gallic in feeling and with a strong sense of momentum and purpose. Completed in 1940, this superbly shaped account is the only recording – and very good it is too. It is a fresh and beautifully written work, prompting a strong, committed performance from the BBC National Orchestra of Wales under Richard Hickox which has been superbly recorded. This symphony deserves to become popular, for its ideas resonate in the mind long afterwards.

The *Serenade for Strings* always sounds fresh, no matter how often you hear it. In four compact movements, it is a delightful piece, carefree until the final *Lento*, where, reflectively, Berkeley touches deeper emotions. In Hickox's hands it comes off splendidly. The BBC National Orchestra of Wales again play with zest and sensitivity, and the recording is extremely vivid and present. Recommended with enthusiasm.

Symphony 4

*** Chan. 10080. BBC Nat. O of Wales, Hickox – MICHAEL BERKELEY: *Cello Concerto; etc.* ***

Lennox Berkeley's *Fourth Symphony* of 1977/8, one of his most ambitious works, is a remarkable piece for a composer in his mid-seventies, starting disconcertingly in darkness but with the slow introduction leading to an energetic first-movement Allegro, followed by a strongly contrasted set of variations and a sharply rhythmic finale, all colourfully orchestrated. Richard Hickox and the BBC National Orchestra of Wales are powerful advocates, brilliantly recorded. The *Symphony* makes a fine coupling for the two major works by the composer's son, Michael.

CHAMBER MUSIC

Concertino, Op. 49; Duo for Cello & Piano, Op. 81/1; Elegy for Violin & Piano, Op. 35/2; Introduction & Allegro for Solo Violin, Op. 24; Oboe Quartet, Op. 70; Petite suite for Oboe & Piano; Sextet, Op. 47; Toccata for Violin & Piano, Op. 33/3
(M) *** Dutton Lab. CDLX 7100. Endymion Ens.

Fine, new recordings of Lennox Berkeley's elegantly fashioned music. It is fastidiously crafted and musically rewarding, unpretentious, urbane and charming. The Endymion Ensemble do it proud, and so does the natural and well-balanced recording.

(i) *Diversions* (for oboe, clarinet, bassoon, horn, piano & string trio), *Op. 61; Oboe Quartet; Sextet* (for clarinet, horn & string quartet), *Op. 47*; (ii) *Piano Duet: Palm Court Waltz, Op. 81/2. Sonatina, Op. 39*
(BB) *** Hyp. Helios CDH 55135. (i) Nash Ens.; (ii) I. Brown; Stott

The Nash Ensemble's eightieth-birthday tribute to Sir Lennox proved opportune, as it was also the year the composer died, so it could act also as a memorial. The ensemble works show the composer at his most effective and refined. *Diversions* is particularly diverting. Both the slow movement and finale are unostentatious essays in counterpoint, yet in addition they manage to be (respectively) lyrically appealing and attractively jaunty. The *Sextet* for clarinet, horn and strings brings an aurally fascinating linear interplay between the wind and string lines. The *Oboe Quartet* is a good deal more than just the usual pastoral excursion. It is dominated and linked by an interval of a third (major or minor) but is far from being a mere intellectual exercise. The slow movement comes last, at first hauntingly sad and mysterious, growing more animated, then returning to the mood of the opening, with each instrument dropping out in turn, leaving the cello alone at the close. The *Palm Court Waltz* for piano duet has a disarming insouciance. If not quite as charming as one might have hoped, it is fun, and it goes well with the elegant *Sonatina*. Of the soloists, the oboist, Gareth Hulse, and the clarinettist,

Michael Collins, deserve special mention; the recording, although a shade resonant in the two piano works, is very good, with woodwind balanced a little forward from the strings.

(i; ii) *Horn Trio, Op. 44*; (ii) *Polka*; (iii) *6 Preludes, Op. 23*; (iv) *3 Greek Songs, Op. 38*; (v; vi) *I Sing of a maiden*; (v; vii) *The Lord is my shepherd*; (iv) *5 Poems of W. H. Auden*; (viii) *4 Poems of St Teresa of Avila, Op. 27*
(M) (***) EMI mono/stereo 5 85138-2. (i) Parikian, Brain; (ii) Smith, Sellick; (iii) Horsley; (iv) Hemsley, Lush; (v) Ch. of King's College, Cambridge; (vi) Willcocks; (vii) Cleobury; (viii) Bowden, Coll. Mus. Londinii, Minchinton

In the *Horn Trio* it is the outstanding horn playing of Dennis Brain that one remembers most, with his bubbling stream of virtuosity offering its own pleasures to the listener. The music itself is expertly written and often very beautiful (the *Lento* especially), all in fine (1954) sound. Colin Horsley is excellent in the short but varied *Six Preludes*, which range from thoughtful and lyrical to showy brilliance, and the 1949 sound is very good. The vocal items are superb: the short but haunting *Three Greek Songs* and imaginative *Five Poems of Auden*, both recorded in 1959, make a welcome return to the catalogue. The *Four Poems of St Teresa of Avila* are regarded by some as the composer's finest work: they are varied and imaginative, with Pamela Bowden's rich contralto providing plenty of contrast and emotion in each of the four movements. The 1958 sound is excellent and, although the soloist is very closely miked, the sound is warm. The programme ends with a jolly *Polka* (with Cyril Smith and Phyllis Sellick) and the only two stereo items (digital): *I sing of a maiden* and *The Lord is my shepherd*, both beautifully atmospheric works with performances to match.

4 Pièces pour la guitare, Op. post.; Sonatina, Op. 1; Theme and Variations, Op. 77
(N) *** Chan. 10261. Craig Ogden – MICHAEL BERKELEY: *Impromptu; Lament, etc.* ***

It was the artistry of Julian Bream that inspired Lennox and Michael Berkeley to compose these works for the guitar. They both find an extraordinarily idiomatic style, so that the *Quatre Pièces*, dedicated to Segovia, sound like anglicized Spanish music, yet they are wholly individual. The invention is consistently ear-catching, as it is in the *Sonatina* (written for Bream), which has a musing slow movement that brings just a faint hint of Rodrigo before the equally appealing and vibrant rondo finale. Finest of all is the *Theme and Variations*, which explores the widest range of guitar figurations and musical divisions, before the haunting closing epilogue, which returns to the mood of the opening. Craig Ogden plays all this music superbly, sustaining great concentration, so that one has a continuing sense of a live performance, borne out by the totally realistic recording. If you enjoy the guitar, this disc is on no account to be missed.

PIANO MUSIC

Concert Study in E flat, Op. 48/2; Improvisation on a Theme of Falla; Paysage, Mazurka, Op. 32/1; 3 Pieces, Op. 2; 6 Preludes, Op. 23; Scherzo, Op. 32/2; Sonata
*** Chan. 10247. Fingerhut (with MICHAEL BERKELEY: *Strange Meeting* ***)

Lennox Berkeley wrote for the piano with exceptional fluency and natural feeling. He was a fine pianist himself and this shows in every bar. Best known are the *Six Preludes, Op. 23*, which were recorded in the days of 78-r.p.m. discs, and though there are alternative accounts of the *Sonata* (one by the late-lamented Christopher Headington) Margaret Fingerhut's vividly recorded account has both eloquence and authority. This is a fine survey of rewarding repertoire, as well played as it is recorded. Piano sound does not come much better than this. As part of the series devoted to both father and son, Michael is represented by an early piece from the early 1970s, *Strange Meeting*, inspired by the poem by Wilfred Owen which his godfather, Benjamin Britten, had used in a decade earlier in his *War Requiem*.

Improvisation on a Theme of Falla, Op. 55/2; Mazurka, Op. 101/2; 3 Mazurkas (Hommage à Chopin), Op. 32; Paysage; 3 Pieces; Polka, Op. 5a; 6 Preludes, Op. 23; 5 Short Pieces, Op. 4; Sonata, Op. 20

**(*) Kingdom KCLCD 2012. Headington (piano)

With the exception of the *Sonata*, all these pieces are miniatures, some of considerable elegance. Christopher Headington is a sympathetic exponent, completely attuned to the idiom. The recording is eminently serviceable and truthful.

6 Preludes, Op. 23

**(*) Paradisum PDS-CD2. Clegg – RAWSTHORNE: *Complete Piano Music* **(*)

John Clegg presents the whole of Rawsthorne's output for the piano. Lennox Berkeley's charming and accomplished miniatures complete a valuable disc: the only snag is the rather claustrophobic acoustic.

(i) *Music for Piano 4 Hands: Sonatina, Op. 39; Theme & Variations, Op. 73; Palm Court Waltz, Op. 81/2. Solo piano music: 6 Preludes, Op. 23; 5 Short Pieces, Op. 4; Sonata, Op. 20*

*** British Music Society BMS 416CD. Terroni, (i) with Beedle

A generous selection of the cultivated and tuneful piano music of Lennox Berkeley: the fine *Sonata* with its sensuously coloured *Adagio*, the often witty *Preludes* and the five charming *Short Pieces*, which often have a whiff of Poulenc, the *Sonatina* with another elegantly individual slow movement, and the more complex *Theme and Variations*. Raphael Terroni is an accomplished and sympathetic exponent, with Norman Beedle an admirable partner in the *Music for Piano Four Hands*. The piano recording is most natural. The CD is available direct from the British Music Society, 7 Tudor Gardens, Upminster, Essex.

OPERA

A Dinner Engagement (complete)

(N) *** Chan. 10219. Williams, Kenny, Rigby, Collins, City of L. Sinfonia, Hickox

In his excellent series for Chandos covering the music of the Berkeleys, father and son, Lennox and Michael, Richard Hickox conducts a performance of Lennox's most popular opera which, with an excellent cast, brings out the light-hearted fun in this comedy of manners. Written to be performed at the 1954 Aldeburgh Festival, it tells of a diplomat and his wife, the Earl and Countess of Dunmow, who, fallen on hard times, have royal guests, the Grand Duchess and her son, Prince Philip, from Monteblanco, where the Earl was ambassador. The comedy lies in the hosts' embarrassment

when, with only the help of a comic char (a stock 1950s figure), their efforts at self-catering go wildly wrong. All comes well in the end, with the Dunmow daughter, Susan, falling in the arms of the Prince. As a comedy it may be dated, but on disc Berkeley's light and lyrical score works well, with excellent singing all round, including Roderick Williams and Yvonne Kenny as the Earl and Countess, Claire Rutter as Susan and Robin Leggate as Philip, with the resonant Anne Collins as a characterful Grand Duchess.

Ruth (complete)

(N) *** Chan. 10301. Rigby, Tucker, Kenny, Rutter, Williams, Joyful Company of Singers, City of L. Sinfonia, Hickox

The story of Ruth and her loyalty to her mother-in-law, Naomi, is among the most touching in the Bible, and Lennox Berkeley, helped by a libretto by Eric Crozier, builds it into a moving opera in three scenes lasting 80 minutes. The mood is lyrical and pastoral, with colourful choruses of reapers and villagers adding movement. After a brief prelude, the opening scene brings a warmly expressive trio, with Ruth and Naomi joined by the other daughter-in-law, Orpah. When Orpah opts to return to the land of Moab, Ruth pledges her loyalty to Naomi in the memorable solo, *Whither thou goest, I will go*, leading on to a duet and an atmospheric chorus to round the scene off. The role of Boaz is taken by a tenor, the farmer who, against the hostility of the villagers, supports the right of Ruth, a Moabite, to glean in his fields with the others. The happy ending comes when Boaz declares his love for Ruth, leading on to the founding of the House of David. Richard Hickox, drawing excellent singing and playing from chorus and orchestra, as well as from the first-rate team of soloists, paces the three scenes most persuasively, bringing out dramatic contrasts in what might have been too gentle a sequence. In the mezzo role of Ruth, Jean Rigby gives a warmly responsive performance, well matched with the soprano, Yvonne Kenny, as Naomi. Though in the Bible story Boaz is an old man, the opera rather counters that, and Mark Tucker gives a fresh, ardent performance, with Roderick Williams forthright as the Head Reaper and Claire Rutter as Orpah. Warm, clear sound.

BERKELEY, Michael (born 1948)

(i) *Cello Concerto. The Garden of Earthly Delights*

*** Chan. 10080. Gerhardt; BBC Nat. O of Wales, Hickox – LENNOX BERKELEY: *Symphony 4* ***

Dating from 1998, *The Garden of Earthly Delights* is a formidable piece for a huge orchestra, including quadruple woodwind and a wide-ranging percussion section, complete with 'lion-roar'. Berkeley uses these forces with a winning exuberance in some of the strongest, most colourful music he has ever written. The piece was inspired by a triptych of Hieronymus Bosch, with the three sections reflecting the three panels depicting, in typically grotesque visions, *The Garden of Eden*, *Carnal Knowledge* and *Hell*. In the first section the atmospheric writing develops powerfully, with a striking horn motif representing the majesty of creation. The *Carnal Knowledge* section contrasts thrusts of energy with recessive string-writing, leading to an energetic dance in the section representing *Hell*. Richard Hickox inspires the BBC National Orchestra of Wales to a brilliant performance, vividly recorded.

The *Cello Concerto*, a less tough piece, dates from 15 years earlier, 1983. Using a relatively small orchestra, it makes the cello soloist very much the centre, with a series of cadenzas, often meditative, punctuated by orchestral passages which emerge almost as interludes rather than the main meat. Well supported by Hickox and the orchestra, Alan Gerhardt's performance is both brilliant and dedicated. This third offering in the Chandos 'Berkeley Edition' is the most powerful yet.

(i–ii) *Clarinet Concerto;* (i) *Flighting;* (iii; ii) *Père du doux repos (Father of Sweet Sleep* from *Speaking Silence)*

*** ASV Single CDDCB 1101. (i) Johnson; (ii) N. Sinfonia, Edwards; (iii) Herford

Michael is the eldest of Lennox Berkeley's three sons. He studied composition with his father and with Richard Rodney Bennett. The *Clarinet Concerto* was written for Emma Johnson. The soloist's concentration leads one magnetically through a thicket of virtuoso writing, often marked by stratospheric shrieks, which she consistently makes compelling, thanks also to the dedicated accompaniment under Sian Edwards. As 'fitting pendants' come two shorter works, a setting of a sonnet by the sixteenth-century French poet, Pontus de Tyard, leading to a solo clarinet piece built on related material.

(i) *Horn Concerto* (for horn and string orchestra); *Coronach* (for strings)

*** Chan. 9981. BBC Nat. O of Wales, Hickox; (i) with Pyatt – L. BERKELEY: *Symphony 1; Serenade* ***

Unlike the works of his father on this CD, the two by Michael are among the darkest and most intense that he has written, giving a sharpness otherwise missing on the disc. *Coronach* is a lament for string orchestra which explores the 'complex emotions of grief; the rage and anger as well as the sadness'. It builds up powerfully in the manner of a funeral dirge, with a quotation from the Scottish ballad, 'The Bonny Earl of Moray'. The *Horn Concerto* in two movements is more powerful still. Written in 1984, it represents a new departure for the composer in its often gritty, uncompromising tone. Yet it makes an immediate emotional impact, with the naggingly energetic first movement giving way to a deeply thoughtful and spacious slow movement. David Pyatt is the superb soloist, magnetically bringing out the logic of each development, with Hickox and the orchestra equally powerful in support. Full, brilliant sound.

(i) *Oboe Concerto; Secret Garden*

☛ *** Chan. 10022. BBC Nat. O of Wales, Hickox with (i) Daniel – L. BERKELEY: *Sinfonia Concertante,* etc. ***

The second Chandos disc of the Berkeley Edition centres round concertante works for oboe by father and son, both written within four years of each other for the inspired, sadly short-lived oboist, Janet Craxton. Next to Lennox Berkeley's *Sinfonia concertante,* a late work, Michael Berkeley's early *Concerto for Oboe and Strings* of 1976–7 seems all the more warmly conservative, with two substantial slow movements framing a relatively brief central Scherzo. One notes the occasional echo of popular music, and the writing for the strings is often sensuous, not least in the finale, entitled *Elegy in memoriam Benjamin Britten,* written within months of the death of Britten, Michael's godfather. The disc is rounded off impressively with the *Secret Garden* of 1997, in which stuttering brass fanfares at the start create what the composer describes as a wall of sound. The long central section with fascinating textures and occasional sensuous moments then aims to reflect the work's title, before the piece is rounded off with the final wall of sound, just as a secret garden is enclosed

by walls. The coda brings a warm echo of the great horn theme in Sibelius's *Fifth Symphony,* reflecting the love of both Berkeleys for that work. As on the companion disc, Richard Hickox and the BBC National Orchestra of Wales give powerfully committed performances, warmly and fully recorded.

Guitar music: *Impromptu; Lament; Sonata in One Movement; Worry Beads*

☛ **(N)** *** Chan. 10261. Craig Ogden – L. BERKELEY: *4 Pièces pour la guitare* etc. ***

Following on after the music of his father, Michael's contribution to this memorable recital is no less magnetic. The haunting *Lament* and the intriguing *Worry Beads* (with a main theme that mirrors a more famous piece by another composer) are followed by a one-movement *Sonata,* improvisatory in feeling, written for Julian Bream; the final encore is an *Impromptu,* a fiftieth birthday present for Bream. Craig Ogden plays all this music with total spontaneity, and is superbly recorded.

Jane Eyre (complete opera)

*** Chan. 9983. Marsh, Wyn, Mills, Bauer-Jones, Slater, Music Theatre Wales Ens., Rafferty

Commissioned to write an opera for the Cheltenham Festival, where the first performance was given in June 2000 and this recording made, Michael Berkeley took on the formidable challenge of adapting Charlotte Brontë's long novel as a compact opera just over 70 minutes long. With a libretto by David Malouf, he has devised a surreal, dream-like sequence that, instead of telling the full story direct, sketches in its outlines with time treated kaleidoscopically, whether in selective moments, flashbacks or offstage voices from the past. Setting the sinister scene, the writing is lyrical in free arioso, with clear tunes emerging. When, for example, Adele, Rochester's ward, refers to the mad scene from *Lucia di Lammermoor,* the main melody from Donizetti's opera is quoted. Michael Rafferty conducts the Music Theatre Wales in a compelling performance, with Natasha Marsh as Jane and Andrew Slater as Rochester singing strongly in the principal roles, and Ffiur Wyn bright and girlish as Adele.

BERLIOZ, Hector (1803–69)

Complete orchestral works

(i) *Grande symphonie funèbre et triomphale, Op. 15;* (i–ii) *Harold in Italy, Op. 16;* (i; iii) *Lélio, Op. 14b; Overtures:* (i) *Béatrice et Bénédict;* (iv) *Benvenuto Cellini;* (i) *Le Carnaval romain, Op. 9; Le Corsaire, Op. 21; Les Francs-juges, Op. 3; Le Roi Lear, Op. 4; Waverley, Op. 1;* (v) *Rêverie et caprice* (for violin & orchestra), *Op. 8;* (vi–vii) *Symphonie fantastique, Op. 14;* (i; vii) *Tristia, Op. 18* (excerpt): *Marche funèbre pour la dernière scène d'Hamlet;* (i) *La Damnation de Faust, Op. 24* (excerpts): *Menuet des follets; Marche hongroise;* (i; viii) *Romeo and Juliet, Op. 17;* (i) *Les Troyens à Carthage, Part II, Prélude, Act III;* (ix) *Les Troyens, Act IV: Royal Hunt and Storm; Marche pour l'entrée de la reine; Ballet Music*

(B) *** Ph. 456 143-2 (6). (i) LSO; (ii) with Imai; (iii) with Carreras, Allen, Constable (piano), Jowitt (clarinet), Scheffel-Stein (harp); (iv) BBC SO; (v) Grumiaux, New Philh. O, De Waart; (vi) Concg. O; (vii) with Alldis Ch.; (viii) with Kern, Shirley-Quirk, Tear, L. Symphony Ch.; (ix) ROHCG O; all (except *Op. 8*) cond. C. Davis

This bargain-priced collection of Sir Colin Davis's Berlioz recordings is self-recommending.

(i) *Grande symphonie funèbre et triomphale;* (ii) *Overtures: Benvenuto Cellini; Le Carnaval romain; Le Corsaire; Les Francs-juges;* (iii) *Les Troyens: Royal Hunt and Storm; Ballet Music; Trojan March;* (iv) *La Mort de Cléopâtre*

(B) *** Erato (ADD/DDD) Double 3984 24229-2 (2). (i) Chorale Populaire de Paris, Musique des Gardiens de la Paix, Dondeyne; (ii) Strasbourg PO, Lombard; (iii-iv) New PO of R. France, Amy, (iv) with Denize

Désiré Dondeyne's 1958 performance of the *Grande symphonie funèbre et triomphale,* spaciously recorded in Notre Dame, is exciting and convincing in a specially French way. The wind and brass group (with a convincing solo trombone) has an authentic tang, with the chorus at the end producing an exhilaratingly robust fervour. The sound has plenty of spectacle and bite. Nadine Denize is equally at home in *La Mort de Cléopâtre,* which combines dramatic flair with a moving closing section. The four key overtures, recorded digitally two decades later, are also very well played, and the programme ends with excerpts from *Les Troyens,* the *Royal Hunt and Storm,* without chorus but still impressive. Excellent recording throughout, but the documentation is totally inadequate, with no texts.

Collection: 'The Berlioz Experience': (i; ii) *Harold in Italy.* (iii; iv) *Rêverie et caprice* (for violin & orchestra). (v) *Symphonie fantastique; Overtures: Benvenuto Cellini; Le Corsaire.* (ii) *Le Carnaval romain.* (iv; vi) *La Damnation de Faust.* (vii) *Mélodies: Adieu Bessy; Amitié, reprends ton empire; La Belle Isabeau; La Belle Voyageuse; Canon libre à la quinte; La Captive; Les Champs; Chanson à boire; Chansonette de M. Léon de Wailly; Le Chant des Bretons; Chant guerrier; Le Chasseur danois; Élégie en prose; Hélène; Je crois en vous; Le Jeune Pâtre breton; Le Matin; La Maure jaloux; Le Montagnard exilé; La Mort d'Ophélie (ballade); Nocturne à deux voix; L'Origine de la harpe; Pleure, pauvre Colette; Prière du matin; Le Roi de Thulé; Sara la baigneuse; Sérénade de Méphistophélès; Le Trébuchet; Zaïde.* (iv; vii) *La Mort de Cléopâtre (scène lyrique).* (iv; viii) *Les Nuits d'été (song-cycle);* (ix) *Requiem (Grande Messe des morts);* (x) *Roméo et Juliette;* (xi) *Te Deum;* (xii) *Tristia.* (xiii) *Les Troyens: Royal Hunt and Storm.* (iv; vi) **Arr. of** DE LISLE: *La Marseillaise*

(B) **(*) DG (DDD/ADD) 474 440-2 (10). (i) Christ; (ii) BPO, Maazel; (iii) Perlman; (iv) O de Paris, Barenboim; (v) O de l'Opéra Bastille, Chung; (iv; vi) with Domingo, Fisher-Dieskau, Minton, Children's Ch., & Ch. de Paris; (vii) Pollet, Von Otter, Aler, Allen; R. Opera Ch., Stockholm (members); Garben (piano) & instrumentalists; (vii) with Norman; (viii) with Te Kanawa; (ix) Pavarotti, Ernst Senff Ch., BPO, Levine; (x) Hamari, Dupouy, Van Dam, New England Conservatory Ch., Boston SO, Ozawa; (xi) Araiza, var. choirs incl. L. Symphony & LPO Ch., European Community Youth O, Abbado; (xii) Cleveland Ch. & O, Boulez; (xiii) Berlin RIAS Chamber Ch. & R. Ch., BPO, Levine

This 10-disc collection, appropriately entitled 'The Berlioz Experience', makes an excellent companion to the Philips set above, and although a good deal of duplication is involved, many of the recordings are of quality and nearly all not otherwise available. Maazel's *Harold in Italy* is undoubtedly

very fine; the structure is held together well, with a vivid sense of forward movement and no lack of poetic feeling. Wolfram Christ is an eloquent and dignified protagonist; there is some imaginative phrasing from soloist and orchestra alike and the performance invariably finds the *tempo giusto*.

Myung-Whun Chung's strongly characterized acccount of the *Symphonie fantastique* is also among the very finest recent recordings, conveying to a rare degree the nervously impulsive inspiration of the young Berlioz. With speeds extreme, the hints of hysteria and overtones of nightmare in Berlioz's programme are freshly brought out, the result volatile rather than symphonically four-square, and the originality of the inspiration seems all the greater. The overtures also reflect this fine conductor's Berlioz credentials.

The set is exceptionally strong on vocal repertoire and (with four outstanding soloists) includes the most comprehensive collection of Berlioz's *mélodies* currently available. Starting magically with the *Nocturne à deux voix,* a little duet for soprano and mezzo with a guitar accompaniment by Göran Söllscher, this two-disc recital of 29 of Berlioz's songs and vocal ensembles includes many rarities previously unrecorded. Despite piano backing from Cord Garben that is sometimes rhythmically too square, this remains very enticing. Among the rarities, such a witty duet for tenor and baritone as *Le Trébuchet* ('The snare') proves a charmer with its bird-like accompaniment, and so does the *boléro, Le Matin,* with castanets as well as piano. Berlioz's last song was written as early as 1850, and it makes one regret that from then on he ignored the genre.

On a separate disc come the scena, *La Mort de Cléopâtre,* superbly sung by Jessye Norman, plus Kiri Te Kanawa in the song-cycle, *Les Nuits d'été.* This makes the most ravishing of Berlioz couplings, with each singer at her very finest. Norman has natural nobility and command as the Egyptian Queen, while Kiri Te Kanawa encompasses the challenge of different moods and register in the song-cycle more completely and affectingly than almost any singer or record in recent years. Barenboim accompanies both performances, and in between comes Perlman's ripely romantic performance of Berlioz's short concertante work for violin and orchestra, the *Rêverie et caprice,* with the soloist bringing out the individuality of the melody and Barenboim's backing giving the work as a whole considerable substance. Barenboim also directs *La Damnation de Faust,* another freely romantic reading and orchestrally most persuasive. But here the variable singing of the choir and controversial casting of the soloists make it less recommendable than it might be. Much will depend on individual responses to Fischer-Dieskau in the role of Mephistopheles, very forceful and detailed but hardly idiomatic, while Domingo is far more cavalier in tackling the role of Faust than he usually is in French music. Moreover, he is not flatteringly recorded, generally too close, and the balance does not help Yvonne Minton either.

Boulez's Cleveland account of *Tristia* is also uneven. The first two sections are warmly atmospheric, with an element of mystery heightened by the distantly placed chorus. But the third section, the weirdly evocative *Funeral March* for the last scene of *Hamlet,* receives a disappointingly plain, detached reading.

Ozawa's 1976 Boston recording of *Roméo et Juliette* is a good deal more successful, if hardly matching Sir Colin Davis or Gardiner, but, with a fine team of soloists, his reading is both warm and dramatic, and his spontaneity helps to unify the work's early fragmentary passages, while the great love scene is convincingly built over the longest span, with a tempo not too expansive. Although the chorus is not sharply focused, the Boston acoustics are pleasing in other ways.

Levine's Berlin Philharmonic account of the *Requiem* is among the most recommendable of modern digital versions, though it cannot match Previn's analogue Walthamstow set; and Abbado's *Te Deum* (also digital) is very impressive. Artistically, too, it is of considerable merit: Abbado brings great tonal refinement and dignity to his reading and the spacious sound helps. Francisco Araiza is altogether first class and has eloquence as well as tonal beauty to commend him. The choirs are responsive, as are the young players Abbado has assembled, and the overall result is most successful. This work comes on the fifth CD, and is capped spectacularly by Berlioz's justly famous choral arrangement of *La Marseillaise*, stirringly led by Domingo.

(i) *Harold in Italy, Op. 16. Symphonie fantastique, Op. 14; La Damnation de Faust: Hungarian March. Roméo et Juliette, Op. 17:* orchestral excerpts: *Roméo seul … Grande fête chez Capulet; Scène d'amour; La Reine Mab (scherzo). Les Troyens:* (ii) *Royal Hunt and Storm*

(B) **(*) Double Decca 455 361-2 (2). Montreal SO, Dutoit; (i) with Zukerman; (ii) with Montreal Ch.

Dutoit's version of *Harold in Italy*, with speeds on the broad side and Zukerman an individual, warmly expressive soloist, is very richly recorded. Again in the *Symphonie fantastique* it is the spectacular, wide-ranging recorded sound that is the first point to note and also the broad speeds. The four extended orchestral excerpts from *Roméo et Juliette* then follow, with Dutoit and his orchestra at their finest, playing warmly as well as brilliantly. The *Royal Hunt and Storm* comes from the complete set of *Les Troyens* and includes the chorus.

(i; ii) *Harold in Italy.* (ii) *Overtures: Le Carnaval romain; Le Corsaire; Les Francs-juges; King Lear; Les Troyens (Overture & March); Waverley;* (iii) *Te Deum, Op. 22*

(M) (***) Sony mono 515300-2 (2). (i) Primrose; (ii) RPO; (iii) Young, LPO Ch., Dulwich College Boys' Ch., D. Vaughan (organ); all cond. Beecham

(i; ii) *Harold in Italy. Overtures:* (ii) *Le Corsaire;* (iii) *King Lear;* (ii) *Les Troyens: Trojan March*

(**(*)) BBC mono BBCL 4065-2. (i) Riddle; (ii) RPO; (iii) BBC SO; Beecham

(i) *Harold in Italy;* (ii) *Tristia (Méditation religieuse; La Mort d'Ophélie; Marche funèbre pour la dernière scène de Hamlet), Op. 18*

*** Ph. 446 676-2. (i) Caussé; (ii) Monteverdi Ch.; ORR, Gardiner

(i) *Harold in Italy. Les Troyens: Ballet Music*

☛ (BB) *** LSO Live LSO 0040. (i) Zimmermann; LSO, C Davis

Recording this Byron-inspired symphony for the third time, Sir Colin Davis demonstrates his supreme mastery as a Berlioz interpreter in a version recorded live, even tauter and more dramatic than his earlier ones made in the studio, with speeds consistently faster, notably in the first movement. Also, the textures are sharper and lighter, partly a question of recording quality, bringing an extra incisiveness. One other benefit of the recording is that the soloist, the magnificent Tabea Zimmermann, is balanced as part of the orchestra instead of being spotlit. The beauty of her tone, with its nut-brown colours down on the C string, is never masked,

but at the other end of the spectrum the balance allows *pianissimos* of unrivalled delicacy. The *Ballet Music*, taken from Davis's prize-winning LSO Live version of *Les Troyens*, makes a warmly atmospheric bonus. The disc comes at super-budget price, complete with authoritative notes by David Cairns, and now becomes a primary recommendation.

Gardiner's pioneering account of *Harold in Italy* on period instruments is searingly dramatic, the more biting in its impact with textures transparent, yet with plenty of weight and high dynamic contrasts. Gérard Caussé here produces spare sounds, making the result quite eerie. The three separate movements of *Tristia* are equally refreshing and dramatic, with sharp dynamic contrasts. Excellent sound.

Beecham's *Harold in Italy* comes from 1951, only a few years after William Primrose had recorded it with Koussevitzky; the *Te Deum* and the *Overtures* come from 1954. Sir Thomas was a masterly interpreter of Berlioz and during that period had few rivals in this repertoire. Fine though it is, his *Harold* does not quite have the incandescent intensity and power of the Koussevitzky, but in the *Te Deum* and the *Overtures* Beecham has an almost unique feeling for this most original of masters, and the RPO play for him with great finesse and subtlety.

The radio recordings of Beecham in full flight are most welcome. The mono radio sound is beefy and immediate, if limited, with fine transfers by Paul Baily. All these items confirm how Beecham in live performances of Berlioz conveyed a red-blooded manic intensity, to match the composer's revolutionary wildness, making almost any rival seem cool. The *Corsaire Overture* has a fierceness and thrust entirely apt to the Byronic subject, culminating in a swaggering climax that verges on the frenetic. *Harold in Italy*, recorded in 1956 with the dynamic range compressed so as to magnify pianissimos, is valuable for having as soloist Beecham's chosen leader of the RPO violas, Frederick Riddle. Here his expressive warmth and responsiveness to Beecham's volatile inspiration make up for intonation problems, highlighted by the close, dry sound. The *Trojan March* makes a swaggering encore, an electrifying performance from the historic opening concert of the Colston Hall in Bristol in 1951.

(i) *Harold in Italy, Op. 16. Overtures: Béatrice et Bénédict; Benvenuto Cellini; Le Carnaval romain, Op. 9; Le Corsaire;* (ii; iii) *La Damnation de Faust;* (iv; v) *L'enfance du Christ;* (vi) *Les Nuits d'été, Op. 7;* (v; vii) *Requiem, Op. 5. Roméo et Juliette, Op. 17:* ((viii; iii) 1953 mono & (ix; v) 1961 stereo versions). *Symphonie fantastique, Op. 14* (1954 & 1962 versions); *Les Troyens: Royal Hunt and Storm*

☛ (N) (B) **(*) RCA mono/stereo 82876 60393-2 (10). Boston SO, Munch; with (i) Primrose; (ii) Danco, Poleri, Singher, Gramm, Boatwright; (iii) Harvard Glee Club, Radcliffe Ch. Soc.; (iv) Kopleff, Valletti, Souzay, Tozzi, Olivier; (v) New England Conservatory Ch.; (vi) De los Angeles; (vii) Simoneau; (viii) Roggero, Chabay, Yo-Kwei Sze; (ix) Elias, Valetti, Tozzi

Charles Munch in his years as principal conductor of the Boston Symphony Orchestra made a series of impressive Berlioz recordings, and here they all sound freshly minted, expertly remastered by Richard Mohr and John Pfeiffer (the second (1960s) version of the *Symphonie fantastique*). Even the earlier (1953) mono set of *Roméo et Juliette* has come up remarkably well. The finest disc of all was of four key overtures, recorded in 1958/9, played with great orchestral virtuosity and élan; included with them was Munch's finest single Berlioz recording: an electrifying account of the *Royal Hunt and Storm* from *Les Troyens*, which out-Beechams Beecham. It was marvellously recorded too, and in the current remastering the vividness, clarity and weight of the storm climax, with the lightning flashing, is riveting in its brilliance, with the lovely, glowing horn-playing in the gentle introduction and postlude equally memorable. Curiously, the 1954 recording of the *Symphonie fantastique* proved a disappointment, not so much in its sound, which is impressive, but in Munch's reading, with its erratic, unspontaneous speed changes, especially in the first movement. The later (1962) reading is very little different. The recording is fuller, but the close balance reduces the dynamic range.

William Primose's earlier mono recording of *Harold in Italy* with Koussevitzky, is praised by us below. The Munch version has the advantage of warmer, more modern recording, although in the loudest passages the stereo does not capture the reverberation of the Boston hall without some loss of focus. However, the first entry of the soloist is magical, and the central movements emerge with much beauty of tone from soloist and orchestra alike. The outer movements are exciting, but the peformance as a whole has not the character and drive of the Bernstein account.

La Damnation de Faust is an undoubted success, even if the reading, vigorous and dramatic, is not always completely idiomatic. Munch's sense of rhythm in vigorous music was not always flexible enough (as in the *Ballet des Sylphes*) and he always preferred a sharp cutting edge – whether in orchestral or in choral sound – to total refinement. David Poleri and the American choruses sing in rather curious French, but none of the shortcomings affects the basic judgement that this is a gripping performance of this unique opera/oratorio. The precision of the orchestra is always impressive, and so generally is the singing, notably that of Suzanne Danco in a dramatic account of Marguerite's music. The CD transfer opens up the (originally mono) 1952 sound remarkably well; the forward sound means that the dynamic range is restricted, but the effect is still atmospheric, and solo voices, orchestra (as in the famous *Hungarian March*) and chorus are all vividly caught.

Once again in *L'Enfance du Christ* the listener is made to realize that Munch's great quality as a Berlioz conductor lies in his consistently sharp sense of drama; his weakness, a failure to realize that Berlioz needs persuasive treatment in his more romantic moments. The *Shepherds' Farewell*, the best-known passage in this magical oratorio, is done in the most extrovert way, and other music too suffers from this absence of feeling for the music's essentially delicate character. But Munch's dramatic flair still tells and, with bright, atmospheric stereo, excellent solo singing (especially from Souzay) and a fine contribution from the chorus, the result is most compelling, possibly more exciting for the uninitiated than a more conventionally evocative performance. *Les Nuits d'été*, from 1955, is a delightful bonus surprise, sung enchantingly by a fresh-toned Victoria de los Angeles, which we have never before discovered.

Munch's recording of the *Requiem* was made as early as 1959 and is an astonishing technical achievement for its time. The four brass groups make a bold effect within the resonant Boston acoustics, and the big climaxes of the *Dies irae* and *Tuba mirum*, though not perfectly focused, are still thrilling. Here Munch's overall direction has an unexpectedly telling lyrical flow; he also brings powerful expressive feeling to the *Lacrymosa*, where the chorus is at its finest. The *Sanctus* – in which Leopold Simoneau, with headily beautiful tone, does

full justice to the tenor solo – is particularly moving. Here the quiet effects of shimmering strings are almost as memorable as the crashing chords of the *Tuba mirum*. Berlioz's trick of orchestration, using low notes on the trombones with a trio of flutes high above, which he features in the *Hostias* and elsewhere, is a strange and ethereal sound in Munch's hands. All in all, this remains a most distinguished set.

Munch also provides what we described at the time (1961) as a 'near-ideal' stereo performance of *Roméo et Juliette* . Predictably his approach is sharp and dramatic as indeed it was in his earlier set, also offered here. In that first version, although the soloists make an impressive team, it is the superb playing of the orchestra that stands out – the gossamer felicity of the *Queen Mab Scherzo* has never been surpassed – even if the violins are made to sound a bit thin and papery elsewhere. The choral contribution is memorable too, as it is in the later recording. This has the advantage of brilliant modern stereo, matched by the virtuosity of excellent soloists and orchestra. But it is Munch's sense of drama that one remembers. The stabbing agony of the frenzied allegro following Juliet's death has a frightening impact, and the jollity of the Capulets' party is taut and brittle. Yet the romanticism of the love music and such tiny numbers as the off-stage chorus for the departing guests show the depth of Munch's sympathy. All in all, this makes a fine tribute to Munch's Boston era, but it is a pity that the vocal works are without texts and translations.

(i) *Harold in Italy, Op. 16;* (ii) *Symphonie fantastique, Op. 14;* (iii) *Overtures: Béatrice et Bénédict; Benvenuto Cellini; Le Carnaval romain; Le Corsaire; Les Francs-juges*
(B) **(*) EMI double forte (ADD) 5 73338-2 (2). (i) McInnes;
(i-ii) O Nat. de France, Bernstein; (iii) LSO, Previn

Bernstein gives a performance of *Harold in Italy* that is both exciting and introspective. With French players, his slightly more relaxed manner than with the NYPO (see above) is in some ways more authentic. Donald McInnes is a violist with a superbly rich and even tone. He responds at all times to the conductor, yet has plenty of individuality. The 1976 recording of this work has an opulent spread and plenty of warmth, but the CD transfer has brought a degree of shrillness to the upper range of the violins, although the solo viola timbre seems unaffected. Bernstein also directs a brilliant and understanding performance of the *Symphonie fantastique*, which captures more than most the wild, volatile quality of Berlioz's inspiration. The overtures provide a rich bonus and are otherwise very well recorded, but it is a pity about the unnatural treble response, which was certainly not on the analogue LPs. Under Previn, the swing-along melody of *Les Francs-juges* swaggers boldly.

Overtures: *Béatrice et Bénédict; Benvenuto Cellini; Le Carnaval romain; Le Corsaire; Les Francs-juges; Le Roi Lear; Waverley*
⊛ ☛ ✿ (N) (M) *** RCA 82876 65839-2. Dresden State O, C. Davis

Overtures: *Béatrice et Bénédict; Le Carnaval romain; Le Corsaire; Rob Roy; Le Roi Lear*
**(*) Chan. 8316. SNO, Gibson

Mercurial, full of vitality and poetic feeling, wonderfully light in articulation, and superbly played and recorded. This RCA disc completely supersedes Sir Colin's recordings on Philips in every way. A glorious issue, outstanding in every way, and now the best Berlioz overtures disc in the catalogue.

Rob Roy is the rarity of the late Sir Alexander Gibson's Berlioz collection. It is if anything even wilder than the other overtures, and with its anticipations of *Harold in Italy* finds Gibson and his SNO at their most dashingly committed. *King Lear*, another rarity, also comes out most dramatically, and though *Béatrice et Bénédict* is not quite so polished, the playing is generally excellent. With first-rate recording, this is attractive enough, but the original dates from 1982, and this should have been reissued at mid-price.

Rêverie et caprice, Op. 8
(M) *** DG (IMS) 445 549-2. Perlman, O de Paris,
  Barenboim – LALO: *Symphonie espagnole;* SAINT-SAENS:
  Concerto 3 ***

Perlman's ripely romantic approach to the *Rêverie* brings out the individuality of the melody and, with a sympathetic accompaniment from Barenboim, the work as a whole is given considerable substance. First-rate digital recording.

Symphonie fantastique, Op. 14
(M) *** Ph. 464 692-2. Concg. O, C. Davis
(M) *** BBC (ADD) BBCL 4018-2. New Philh. O, Stokowski
  (with conversation with Deryck Cooke) – SCRIABIN: *Poème de l'extase* ***
(N) *** BBC BBCL 4163-2. Leningrad PO, Rozhdestvensky –
  TCHAIKOVSKY: *Francesca da Rimini* ***
*** Ph. 434 402-2. ORR, Gardiner
(B) *** EMI Red Line 5 72552. Phd. O, Muti
(M) (***) Dutton Lab. mono CDK 1208. Concg. O, Van
  Beinum (with BEETHOVEN: *Creatures of Prometheus: Overture*
  (LPO)) – SCHUBERT: *Symphony 5* (***)
(M) **(*) Virgin 5 61379-2. LCP, Norrington (with *Les
  Francs-juges*)
(N) (M) ** RCA 82876 60859-2 San Francisco SO, Tilson
  Thomas (with *Lélio: excerpts* with ch.)
(N) ** Telarc **SACD** 60650. Cleveland O, Maazel –
  TCHAIKOVSKY: *Nutcracker Suite* **(*)
(N) (M) (**) DG mono 474 987-2. BPO, Markevitch – BIZET:
  Jeux d'enfants (**)

(i) *Symphonie fantastique;* (ii) *Overture: Le Carnaval romain*
(BB) **(*) Virgin 2x1 5 61513-2. RPO, Menuhin – BIZET;
  CHAUSSON: *Symphonies* **(*)
(M) **(*) DG Entrée 474 165-2. (i) Chicago SO; (ii) BPO,
  Abbado

(i) *Symphonie fantastique; Overture: Le Corsaire;* (ii) *Les
Troyens: March troyenne;* (iii) *Royal Hunt and Storm*
🔊— ✿ (M) *** EMI 5 67971-2 [567972-2]. (i) O Nat. de
  France; (ii) RPO; (iii) with Beecham Ch. Soc., Beecham

*Symphonie fantastique; La Damnation de Faust: Ballet des
sylphes; Menuet des feux follets*
(M) **(*) DG (IMS) 463 080-2. BPO, Karajan

Symphonie fantastique; (i) *Herminie*
** DG 474 209. Mahler CO & Les Musiciens du Louvre,
  Minkowski, (i) with Legay

Symphonie fantastique; (i) *La Mort de Cléopâtre*
**(*) Ph. 475 095-2. VPO, Gergiev, (i) with Borodina

Symphonie fantastique; Roméo et Juliette: Scène d'amour
**(*) Telarc CD 80578. Cincinnati SO, P. Järvi

Beecham's account still enjoys classic status and remains unsurpassed, although it is now nearly fifty years old. While the first two movements show a remarkably spontaneous expressive freedom, the *Waltz* is wonderfully elegant and the *March to the Scaffold* ominously deliberate, the performance overall has a demonic intensity that is immediately compelling and holds the listener on the seat-edge until the work's electrifying close. In this extraordinary new transfer, in which every detail is crystal clear, the strings have an especially rich sheen and the brass a sonority and depth more telling than on any previous incarnation of the 1959 recording. Even the tolling bells of the finale deserve a credit for their remarkable tangibility, while the warm acoustic of the Salle Wagram, Paris, frames a concert-hall balance of remarkable realism.

Gounod wrote that 'with Berlioz, all impressions, all sensations – whether joyful or sad – are expressed in extremes to the point of delirium', and Beecham brought to this score all the fire and temperament, all the magic and affection in his armory. He drew from the French National Radio Orchestra playing of great rhythmic subtlety. This is an indispensable record, made the more so for a tinglingly atmospheric account of the *Royal Hunt and Storm* (with chorus) and the classic account of the *Corsaire Overture*. Ian Jones, the remastering engineer, deserves to share the honours.

Sir Colin Davis's 1974 Concertgebouw recording has dominated the catalogue for two decades. Now reissued at mid-price, it still remains a primary recommendation. The performance has superb life and colour, the slow movement memorably atmospheric and the final two movements very exciting. If the sound does not quite match recent rivals in brilliance and definition, the overall balance is very satisfying and believable.

A really high-voltage performance from Stokowski and the New Philharmonia Orchestra of the *Symphonie fantastique*, recorded in 1968. The great conductor was eighty-six and in astonishing form. Though this would not be a first choice, every bar is stamped with personality. There are characteristic expressive exaggerations, but everything rings true and has conviction. The sound is acceptable, though not all the strands in the texture are ideally balanced. This comes in tandem with an outstanding performance of *Le poème de l'extase* and a conversation between the great conductor and Deryck Cooke.

The high-powered (1971) Prom performance from Rozhdestvensky and the Leningrad Philharmonic demonstrates the orchestra's superlative quality at the time, astonishing British listeners. Though the playing is superbly disciplined, with the strings wonderfully refined, there is an element of wildness in the reading, perfectly suited to the work, encouraged no doubt by the live occasion. Dynamic contrasts are consistently heightened, and the stereo recording, good for its period, brings the drama of that out to the full, even if again inner detail is not always ideally clear. In the fourth-movement *March to the Scaffold* the challenging rapid quaver passage near the start has Rozhdestvensky making no concessions at all to his soloist. The thrill of a great Prom event is vividly caught, not least in the eruption of cheering at the end. The 1960 account of *Francesca da Rimini* makes an equally compelling coupling.

Gardiner with his Orchestre Révolutionnaire et Romantique uses the extra sharpness of focus to add to the dramatic bite. In his electrifying, warmly expressive performance, heightening Berlioz's wild syncopations, he is second to none in conveying the astonishing modernity of music written within three years of Beethoven's death.

Paavo Järvi's impressive version of the *Symphonie fantastique*, generously coupled with the *Love Scene* from *Roméo et Juliette*, celebrated his arrival as the new music director of the

Cincinnati Symphony Orchestra. With vivid Telarc recording, engineered by Jack Renner, the brilliance of Berlioz's orchestration is brought out in finely detailed sound, with textures clarified. The interpretation is fresh and clean-cut, with relatively spacious speeds, yet next to the finest versions there is a lack of spontaneity and dramatic thrust, making it very much a studio account.

Abbado brings the right dreamy atmosphere and feverish intensity to this score, and the playing of the Chicago Symphony Orchestra has all the polish and finesse one could expect. There is much poetic feeling, the slow movement is outstandingly fine and he observes the exposition repeat in the first movement (also in the *March to the Scaffold*). The 1983 DG recording is rich in texture, but the balance is less than ideal. The effect is recessed and, while the background silence of the CD allows the magical pianissimo playing in the slow movement to register effectively, the resonance sometimes clouds the finer points of detail, something that never happens in the remastered Beecham recording.

The balance of fierceness against romantic warmth in Muti's own personality works well in this symphony so that he holds the thread of argument together firmly, without ever underplaying excitement. The sound is among the best that Muti has had in Philadelphia. A strong bargain recommendation.

Eduard van Beinum's *Symphonie fantastique* was the first post-war recording he made, in 1947, on six 78-r.p.m. shellac discs. *The Record Guide*, writing in 1951 and regretting its deletion, called it the 'best of all' at the time – understandably so. Superbly cultured playing from this great orchestra, and the recording is yet another tribute to Decca's post-war engineering.

Menuhin's reading of the *Symphonie fantastique* is full of character and he brings his own humanistic insights, yet the bizarre power of the final two movements is relished. The RPO play very well for him, and the recording is first class, brilliant, but with a satisfyingly full and resonant bass. The overture is enjoyable in a similar way, not just treated as a vehicle for orchestral virtuosity.

Karajan's 1975 performance of the *Symphonie fantastique* brings wonderful playing from the BPO. There is great intensity in the opening movement (without repeat), particularly in the hushed strings, with the orchestra bringing out many subtle nuances of detail. The two final movements are exciting, and the recording is very good. The fill-ups are attractive but not so well recorded. But this is not a top choice.

Norrington does his utmost to observe the composer's metronome markings; but where his Beethoven is consistently fast, some of these speeds are more relaxed than we are used to – as in the *March to the Scaffold* and the *Ronde du sabbat*. His lifting of rhythms prevents the music from dragging, with period instruments giving new transparency; *Les Francs-juges Overture* is disappointingly low-key.

The Telarc SACD is the second of two recordings which Maazel made with the Cleveland Orchestra in 1982, only two years after his coarser CBS/Sony version and much preferable. The Telarc sound is far more refined, and the performance is naturally expressive in a spontaneous-sounding way, without losing the precision of ensemble. It now comes linked to an enjoyable account of Tchaikovsky's *Nutcracker Suite*, with the image somewhat enhanced, although it is not four-channel surround sound; this rather plain account cannot compete with the finest rivals.

Michael Tilson Thomas draws very good playing from his San Francisco forces and is a committed Berliozian, very much at home in the composer's world. Those who have been brought up with a more restrained and classical view of the score may find him a little histrionic at times, although no one could complain of a lack of excitement. Nevertheless, this version cannot be considered a top recommendation. The recording is decent without being state of the art.

Gergiev's reading is above all urgent and weightily dramatic, traditional in not observing the exposition repeat in the first movement and the repeat in the *March to the Scaffold* when arguably such formalities are inappropriate in such a radical work. Not unexpectedly, he also omits the cornets prescribed in the revised score. However, the weight and thrust of Berlioz's dramatic concept come over with thrilling immediacy, and Gergiev draws out the distinctive sound-qualities of the Vienna Philharmonic, recorded in the helpful acoustic of the Musikverein, with ripe horn solos and resonant strings and with waltz rhythms given a Viennese flavour in the second movement, *Le Bal*. The timpani in the fourth movement boom rather too much, but otherwise the sound is full and vivid. The coupling brings Olga Borodina as the powerful soloist in *La Mort de Cléopâtre*, the most adventurous of Berlioz's Prix de Rome entries. It is an early work yet here sounds fully mature and distinctive, with conductor and soloist underlining the high dramatic contrasts.

The *Symphonie fantastique* was the first recording Markevitch made for DG and it comes from November 1954. The presentation is particularly handsome, the original LP sleeve being reproduced along with the recording session report. It appeared in April 1955, at the same time as Karajan's Philharmonia set. Andrew Porter preferred it to the latter and thought it 'full of temperament and fantasy and [recorded] with thrilling realism'. We quote this as a recommendation from a much-respected judge in these matters, while having to report less enthusiastically. Though there is no lack of excitement, some of the interpretative touches seem arbitrary and not really felt, and there is an underlying coolness. This great musician re-recorded it in 1962 with the Lamoureux Orchestra, though again there were unconvincing expressive rubati.

CHORAL WORKS

Le Ballet des ombres, Op. 2; Chanson à boire, Op. 2/5; Chant de chemin de fer, Op. 19/3; Chant guerrier, Op. 2/3; Chante sacré, Op. 2/6 (versions I & II); Le Cinq Mai; Hymne pour la consécration du nouveau tabernacle; Marche funèbre pour la dernière scène d'Hamlet; La Mort d'Orphée; La Mort d'Ophélie; Sara la baigneuse, Op. 11; Scène héroïque (La Révolution grecque); Tantum ergo sacramentum; Tristia, Op. 18; Veni Creator Spiritus

**(*) EMI 5 57499-2 (2). Villazon, Naouri, Riveno, Les Eléments Ch., Capitole Toulouse O, Plasson

Entitled *La Révolution grecque* after the earliest piece in the collection, Michel Plasson's two-disc survey of Berlioz's shorter choral works makes a fascinating study for any lover of Berlioz's music, amplifying the usual portrait we have from his large-scale works. *La Révolution grecque*, written in 1825–33 and described as a *scène héroïque*, harks back to the music of a generation earlier, inspired by the French Revolution, a rousing piece in four sections for two basses, chorus and orchestra. It may be less typical of Berlioz than most of the other works in the collection, but it still brings many moments forecasting the composer's mature style. *Le Cinq Mai*, written to commemorate the death of Napoleon, is equally rare, part of a planned major work to celebrate the defeated Emperor, which Berlioz abandoned. The Op. 2 pieces are taken from a collection of settings of poems by the poet Thomas Moore (in translations by Thomas Gounet), usually given the collective title *Irlande*. Most of the Op. 2 pieces are simple songs, but Plasson has here extracted the choral items, which, like the songs, have piano accompaniment. One of the weirdest pieces here is the ronde nocturne, *Ballet des ombres*, and one of the liveliest the *Chants des chemins de fer*, celebrating the opening of the railway line from Paris to Lille in 1846. The lovely Hugo setting, *Sara la baigneuse*, the three movements labelled *Tristia*, *Méditation religieuse* and *La Mort d'Ophélie* and the *Hamlet Funeral March*, are all relatively well known, here given warmly idiomatic performances. All these works bear the stamp of Berlioz's totally original genius, but curiously two of the later choral works, both settings of Latin for female chorus, *Veni creator spiritus, a cappella*, and *Tantum ergo*, with harmonium accompaniment, are the least typical. Good, warm sound for most items, though the piano in the Op. 2 songs is shallow and clangy.

VOCAL MUSIC

Cantatas: (i) *Herminie*; **(ii)** *La Mort de Cléopâtre*; **(iii)** *La Mort de Sardanapale*; *La Mort d'Orphée*

(BB) **(*) Naxos 8.555810. Ch. Régional Nord, O Nat. de Lille, Régional Nord, Pas-de-Calais, Casadesus; with (i) Lagrange; (ii) Uria-Monzon; (iii) Vallejo

It makes an ideal coupling having on a single disc the four cantatas that the young Berlioz wrote as entries for the Prix de Rome. The work that finally won him the prize in 1829, overcoming conservative opposition, was *La Mort de Sardanapale*, though ironically only a fragment has survived. Ironically too, that fragment is markedly less original than any of the earlier works, even if it is well worth hearing for the hints of Berlioz themes to come. *Herminie*, based on Tasso's *Jerusalem Liberated*, strikingly uses as a central theme the motif that soon after became the *idée fixe* of the *Symphonie fantastique*, while *La Mort de Cléopâtre* even more clearly anticipates the operatic tone of voice that reached its culmination in *Les Troyens*. Even the earliest cantata, *La Mort d'Orphée*, with tenor and a chorus of raging bacchantes, brings a memorable close, though the soloist, Daniel Galvez Vallejo, is coarser than either the excellent soprano, Michele Lagrange, in *Herminie* or the mezzo, Beatrice Uria-Monzon, in *Cléopâtre*, with the Lille orchestra under Jean-Claude Casadesus warm and refined.

(i–ii) *La Damnation de Faust*; *L'Enfance du Christ, Op. 25*; *Herminie*; *Lélio*; *La Mort de Cléopâtre*; *Les Nuits d'été*; *Roméo et Juliette*; *Requiem Mass*; *Te Deum*. **(i) Mélodies:** *La Belle Voyageuse*; *La Captive*; *Le Chasseur danois*; *Le Jeune Pâtre breton*; *Zaïde*

(B) *** Ph. (ADD) 462 252-2 (9). (i) Soloists; (ii) John Alldis Ch., L. Symphony Ch., Amb. S., Wandsworth School Boys' Ch.; LSO, C. Davis

This impressive bargain box of Sir Colin Davis's recordings of the major Berlioz vocal works can be recommended with enthusiasm. Many of them are still available separately and are discussed below. *Roméo et Juliette* has great vitality and atmosphere. *Lélio* is presented without the spoken dialogue, and is convincing within its structural limitations. The *Te*

Deum conveys drama without unwanted excesses of emotion, and the expansive choral climaxes and Nicolas Kynaston's fine organ contribution are impressively contained. Dame Janet Baker sings with passionate intensity in the two dramatic scenes, *Herminie* and *La Mort de Cléopâtre*, but *Les Nuits d'été* is presented with different singers singing different songs, with Sheila Armstrong the finest of the group, especially in the final exhilarating *L'Île inconnue*. In the other songs Josephine Veasey's contribution is also an individual one; but Frank Patterson, the weakest of the soloists, lacks the necessary charm. Nevertheless this is a small blot on what is overall a splendid achievement.

La Damnation de Faust **(complete)**

☞ (BB) *** HM LSO Live LSO 008CD (2). Sabbatini, Shkosa, Pertusi, Wilson-Johnson, L. Symphony Ch., LSO, C. Davis

*** Ph. (ADD) 416 395-2 (2). Veasey, Gedda, Bastin, Amb. S., Wandsworth School Boys' Ch., L. Symphony Ch., LSO, C. Davis

(**(*)) BBC mono BBCL 4006/7 (2). Crespin, Turp, Roux, Shirley-Quirk, L. Symphony Ch., LSO, Monteux

(i) *La Damnation de Faust*; **(ii)** *Harold in Italy*

**(*) DG stereo/mono 463 673-2 (2). (i) Rubio, Verreau, Roux, Mollet, Elisabeth Brasseur Ch., Ch. Enfants RTF, LAP; (ii) Kirchner, BPO; Markevitch

(i) *La Damnation de Faust*; **(ii)** *La Mort de Cléopâtre*

(B) **(*) EMI (ADD) double forte 5 68583-2 (2). Baker; (i) Gedda, Bacquier, Thau, Paris Opera Ch., O de Paris, Prêtre; (ii) LSO, Gibson

Sir Colin Davis's new version at super-bargain price offers a performance and sound which in every way match and even outshine any rival in a strongly competitive field. Recorded at the Barbican in October 2000, it is rivetingly dramatic and yet even more than in his classic 1973 recording for Philips, Davis involves you in the painful quandary obsessing Faust, never letting tension slip for a moment. This time the playing of the LSO is even more refined, with rhythms even more lightly sprung, as in the witty treatment of Mephistopheles's *Flea song*, characterfully sung by Michele Pertusi, weighty yet agile. As Faust, Gabriele Sabbatini is more overtly emotional than any rival, Italianate in his expressiveness helped by his radiant tonal range down to a perfectly controlled head-voice. The Albanian soprano Enkelejda Shkosa is a warm, vibrant Marguerite, with a flicker in the voice giving a hint of the heroine's vulnerability. Not just the LSO but the London Symphony Chorus too are in searing form, and the recording brings out the detail of Berlioz's orchestration with ideal transparency, though the transfer is at rather a low level, needing fair amplification for full impact. The complete text is provided in the booklet, along with Davis Cairns's authoritative notes, if in microscopic print.

Both Nicolai Gedda as Faust and Jules Bastin as Mephistopheles are impressive in Davis's fine 1974 Philips set. The response of the chorus and orchestra is highly intelligent and sensitive, and the recording perspective is outstandingly natural and realistic.

Most valuable in the EMI *Damnation de Faust* is Janet Baker's Marguerite, sung most beautifully. Prêtre is not always perceptive and, though there are many dramatic touches, the set does not outshine Davis. Berlioz's early scena on the death of a famous classical heroine, *La Mort de Cléopâtre*, is most movingly done.

Markevitch's early stereo *Damnation of Faust* last appeared as a bargain Double (without a coupling), but now it is slightly more expensive, reissued at mid-price as one of DG's 'Originals'. But it remains very competitive, even though it has a few small cuts (none serious). The performance is extremely dramatic and compelling, and the recording, which dates from 1955, is in the demonstration class for its period. The orchestral contribution emerges with fine colour, and Markevitch draws the full effect from Berlioz's quirky touches of scoring. As Faust, Richard Verreau, a distinctly Gallic tenor, is especially impressive among the soloists, but Consuelo Rubio is good too, as is Pierre Mollet, with Michel Roux an effective Mephistopheles. The choral contribution is very French, not always too sophisticated, but vibrant and committed, and with plenty of character. In short this is very stimulating and enjoyable when the CD transfer is so successful. The coupling last appeared on another DG Double with Munch's Berlioz's *Requiem*, and the insert notes for the present reissue quote the *Penguin Guide*'s 1994 review as saying: 'This brilliant and exciting mono recording of *Harold in Italy* by Heinz Kirchner, a first-rate soloist with the Berlin Philharmonic, brings a riveting final orgy.' However, re-listening to it immediately after the choral work reveals that the wide-ranging mono recording (which was made four years later in Paris) is less well focused at lower dynamic levels, and does not always flatter the soloist or the orchestral violins in their higher register.

The BBC recording is of a relay from the Royal Festival Hall on 8 March 1962, and it conveys a real sense of occasion. The Monteux performance is a distinguished one with a first-rate cast, and the sound wears its years very lightly.

L'Enfance du Christ, Op. 25

*** Hyp. CDA 66991/2. Rigby, Miles, Finley, Aler, Howell, Corydon Singers & O, Best

(N) (B) **(*) CfP 586 1722 (2). Murray, Thomas Allen, Tear, Wilson-Johnson, Cleobury – HONEGGER: *Cantate de Noël; 4 Motets pour le temps de Noël* ***

(BB) **(*) Naxos 8.553650/1. Viala, Lagrange, Piquemal, Bernardi, Ch. Regional Vittoria de l'Ile de France, Maîtrisse de R. France, Lille Nat. O, J.-C. Casadesus

(i) *L'Enfance du Christ;* (ii) *Méditation religieuse; La Mort d'Ophélie; Sara la baigneuse;* (iii) *La Mort de Cléopâtre*

(B) *** Double Decca (ADD) 443 461-2 (2). (i) Pears, Morison, Cameron, Rouleau, Frost, Fleet, Goldsbrough O; (i–ii) St Anthony Singers; (ii–iii) ECO, (iii) with Pashley; all cond. C. Davis

(i) *L'Enfance du Christ;* (ii) *Roméo et Juliette* (orchestral music only)

(B) *** EMI double forte (ADD) 5 68586-2 (2). (i) De los Angeles, Gedda, Soyer, Blanc, Depraz, Cottret, René Duclos Ch., Paris Conservatoire O, Cluytens; (ii) Chicago SO, Giulini

This atmospheric oratorio for Christmas, so different from almost any other Berlioz work, has been lucky on disc, vividly recorded in beautifully balanced digital sound, immediate yet warm, Matthew Best's version offers a keenly dramatic view. So Alastair Miles conveys pure evil in Herod's monologue at the start and, with words exceptionally clear, Joseph's pleas for shelter are movingly urgent. Jean Rigby is a fresh, young-sounding Mary, with Gerald Finley warm and expressive as Joseph. John Aler is a powerful Reciter and Gwynne Howell a strong, benevolent-sounding Father of the family. This makes

an ideal choice for those who want an intimate view and a superb modern recording.

Sir Colin Davis's 1961 recording of *L'Enfance du Christ* (originally made for L'Oiseau Lyre) is by no means inferior to his later, Philips set. At times the earlier performance was fresher and more urgent, and Peter Pears was a sweeter-toned, more characterful narrator. Elsie Morison and John Cameron are perfectly cast as Mary and Joseph, and Joseph Rouleau makes an impressive contribution as the Ishmaelite Father. This Double Decca reissue in atmospheric sound also offers an invaluable collection of off-beat vocal works, with fine choral singing and a splendid contribution from Anne Pashley.

In Davis's second version, for Philips, the beautifully balanced recording intensifies the colour and atmosphere of the writing, so that the *Nocturnal March* in the first part is wonderfully mysterious. There is a fine complement of soloists, and though Eric Tappy's tone as narrator is not always sweet, his sense of style is immaculate. Others are not always quite so idiomatic, but Janet Baker and Thomas Allen both sing beautifully.

On EMI Gedda may not be as sensitive as Pears in the first Davis version, but de los Angeles is superlative and so is Ernest Blanc as Herod. The orchestra gives sensitive support to the fresh choral singing. The coupling is one of Giulini's best records from the same period (1969). The Chicago orchestra responds with fine discipline and beauty of tone, and also with great conviction in an incandescent performance. Good recording quality, though the focus is not always absolutely clean.

Stephen Cleobury directs a brisk, dramatically taut reading, atmospherically recorded against the reverberant background of King's College Chapel. The freshness is enhanced by the singing of the King's College Choir with its trebles, and the soloists are a characterful team, if not as sweet-toned as some. David Wilson-Johnson is a powerful Herod, though the voice as recorded has a rather rough edge. Ann Murray as Mary sings movingly, but ideally one would look for a firmer tone. Sir Thomas Allen as Joseph is warmer than he was in Sir Colin Davis's Philips version, and Robert Tear is at his most expressive, helped by the acoustic. Cleobury, though occasionally fussy with detail, as in the *Shepherds' Farewell*, has a fine feeling for dramatic timing and tension. This is certain good value with its unexpected new couplings.

On Naxos, Casadesus and the Lille orchestra give a fresh and direct account of Berlioz's sacred trilogy. The tenor, Jean-Luc Viala, makes an excellent narrator and the mezzo, Michèle Lagrange, a touching Mary, and if the others are not so distinguished they form a satisfying team. Casadesus's approach can be well assessed from the flowing speed for the most celebrated number, the *Shepherds' Farewell*. The set includes in its excellent booklet full French text with English translation. Clear, pleasing sound.

Mélodies: *Aubade; La Belle Voyageuse; La Captive; Le Chasseur danois; Le Jeune Pâtre breton; La Mort d'Ophélie; Les Nuits d'été; Zaïde*

(BB) *** Warner Apex 0927 49583-2. Montague, Robbin, Fournier, Crook, Cachemaille, Lyon Op. O, Gardiner

Like Davis before him, John Eliot Gardiner here divides the six keenly atmospheric songs of *Les Nuits d'été* between four singers, in some ways an ideal solution when his choice of singers is inspired and the presiding genius of the conductor makes this a memorable Berlioz bargain disc. In *Les Nuits* d'été Catherine Robbins, with clear echoes of Dame Janet Baker, gives a rich and moving account of *Le Spectre de la rose* (as she does also of the final item from among the miscellaneous orchestral songs, *La Mort d'Ophélie*), and Diana Montague is full and bright in her two songs, coping splendidly with Gardiner's very fast speed for the final *L'Île inconnue*, which brings a delightful pay-off. Pierre Cachemaille gives a thrilling bite to *Sur les lagunes*, and Howard Crook, with his rather thin, reedy tenor, is well suited to *Au cimetière* but is even more striking in the extraordinary *Aubade*, the rarest of the miscellaneous songs, with its accompaniment of two cornets and four horns. The Lyon Opéra Orchestra is helpfully recorded, not in the dry acoustic of the opera house, but atmospherically in a Lyon church. Altogether this Apex reissue is an outstanding bargain.

Mélodies: (i) *La Belle Isabeau; La Belle Voyageuse; La Captive; Le Matin; La Mort d'Ophélie.* (ii) *Les Nuits d'été* (song-cycle); (ii–iii) *Roméo et Juliette: Prologue: Premiers transports (Strophes)*

*** DG 445 823-2. Von Otter, with (i) Royal Stockholm Op. Ch.; Garben; (ii) BPO, Levine; (iii) Berlin RIAS Chamber Ch.

This is a most attractive compilation. The five solo songs here are among the most moving and individual of all, notably the longest, *La Mort d'Ophélie*. In *Les Nuits d'été* von Otter is fresh and radiant, bringing out the dramatic contrasts between the songs, and the poise and weight of *Strophes* from *Roméo* is magical.

Mélodies: 'Chant d'amour': *La Mort d'Ophélie; Zaïde*

*** Decca 452 667-2. Bartoli, Chung – BIZET; DELIBES; RAVEL: *Mélodies* ***

Cecilia Bartoli's collection of French songs is one of the most ravishing of her records yet, and these Berlioz items are among the highlights. Myung-Whun Chung's contribution is both imaginative and supportive.

Messe solennelle; Resurrexit (revised version)

(M) *** Ph. 464 688-2. D. Brown, Viala, Cachemaille, Monteverdi Ch., ORR, Gardiner

This massive work, completed in 1824, is uneven, but the glow of inspiration shines out over any shortcomings. Gardiner conducts with characteristic flair and a sense of drama, bringing brilliant singing from the Monteverdi Choir, though the choral sound is backwardly balanced. A second, modified and slightly expanded version of the violent *Resurrexit* is included as a supplement, a revised version that Berlioz himself acknowledged.

Les Nuits d'été (song-cycle)

◑── (M) *** Decca (ADD) 460 973-2. Crespin, SRO, Ansermet (with recital of French Songs ***) – RAVEL: *Shéhérazade* *** ✪

(***) Testament mono SBT 3203 (3). De los Angeles, Boston SO, Munch – DEBUSSY: *La Demoiselle élue*; MASSENET: *Manon* (***)

(N) (BB) **(*) Naxos 8.557274. Maurus, Nat. O de Lille-Région Nord, Jean-Claude Casadesus – DUKAS: *La Péri*; CHAUSSON: *Poème de l'amour et de la mer* **(*)

(N) (M) ** Telarc CD 80084. Ameling, Atlanta SO, Shaw – FAURÉ: *Pelléas et Mélisande* **

Les Nuits d'été; Mélodies: *La Belle Voyageuse; La Captive; Zaïde*

(BB) *** Virgin 2x1 5 61469-2 (2). J. Baker, City of L. Sinf., Hickox – BRAHMS: *Alto Rhapsody*, etc.; MENDELSSOHN: *Infelice*, etc.; RESPIGHI: *La sensitiva* ***

(i) *Les Nuits d'été*; (ii) *Béatrice et Bénédict: Dieu! Que viens-je d'entendre; Damnation de Faust: D'amour l'ardente flamme*

(B) ** Sony SBK 87797. Von Stade; (i) Boston SO, Ozawa; (ii) LPO, Pritchard – RAVEL: *Shéhérazade* *(*)

With Régine Crespin's richness of tone, and with Ansermet at his finest accompanying brilliantly, this glowing performance is truly legendary – a *tour de force*. Moreover, the Ravel coupling is even more inspired, and the superb new transfers enhance the listener's pleasure further.

This Virgin two-for-one at super-bargain price is a treasure-chest of Janet Baker's later recordings, made in the early 1990s, including her later recording of *Les Nuits d'été* and other orchestral songs (see above).

Victoria de los Angeles's RCA recording of *Les Nuits d'été*, like Debussy's *La Demoiselle élue*, both dating from 1955, makes a splendid, generous bonus to the classic Monteux version of Massenet's *Manon*, recorded in Paris, also in 1955. Though there is more edge on the American recording than on the EMI, making the voice a shade less golden, the charm of the lovely voice is still a delight.

Elly Ameling's version concentrates on pure beauty. Emotionally, the performance is restrained – cautious even – with crisp, calculated, rather reticent playing from the orchestra. The recording, however, is very realistic within a suitably intimate acoustic.

Jean-Claude Casadesus adds to his list of excellent Naxos discs with his talented orchestra based in Lille in this attractive Naxos coupling, atmospherically recorded in rich, clear sound. Elsa Maurus is a high mezzo with a warm, very French timbre and a rapidly flickering vibrato. Sounding very idiomatic, she is well suited to the challenge of *Les Nuits d'été*, with its different songs covering a wide range, while responding to the passion behind Casadesus's conducting. Not a first choice for the song-cycle, perhaps, but an attractive disc just the same.

Frederica Von Stade, always intelligent and naturally musical, sounds less spontaneous than usual in a disappointing version of this most magical of orchestral song-cycles, not helped by Ozawa's cool and uninvolved accompaniment. However, the two operatic scenas show this artist at her finest. *D'amour l'ardente flamme* is particularly fine, and Pritchard's accompaniments are most supportive and beautifully played. Excellent recording.

(i) *Les Nuits d'été*; (ii) *La Mort de Cléopâtre (Scène lyrique)*; (ii; iii) *Les Troyens: Scenes 2 & 4*

✪ (M) *** EMI (ADD) 5 62788-2 [5 62789-2]. J. Baker; (i) New Philh. O, Barbirolli; (ii) LSO, Gibson; (iii) with Greevy, Erwen, Howell, Amb. Op. Ch.

The collaboration of Dame Janet Baker at the peak of her powers and Sir John Barbirolli in what is probably the most beautiful of all orchestral song-cycles produces ravishing results. The half-tones in the middle songs are exquisitely controlled, and the elation of the final song, *L'Île inconnue*, with its vision of an idyllic island, has never been captured more rapturously on record. Berlioz's early scena on the death of a famous classical heroine is also beautifully performed. But even more desirable is Dame Janet's deeply moving rendering of the concluding scenes of Berlioz's epic opera. This makes an essential supplement to the complete recording for any dedicated Berliozian. Baker, helped by a warm and sympathetic accompaniment under Gibson's direction, allows herself a range of tone-colour and a depth of expressiveness not matched by Josephine Veasey, the Dido in the Philips set. Outstanding remastered sound and full translations are included to make this a worthy reissue in EMI's 'Great Artists of the Century' series.

Requiem Mass, Op. 5

☛– (N) *** Telarc **SACD** 60627; CD 806276. Lopardo, Atlanta Ch. & O, Spano

(N) (M) *** RCA **SACD** 82876 66373-2 (2). Simoneau, New England Conservatory Ch., Brass Bands, Boston SO, Munch

(***) BBC mono BBCL 4011-2. Lewis, RPO Ch., RPO, Beecham

(i) Requiem Mass; (ii) Symphonie fantastique

☛– (B) *** EMI double forte (DDD/ADD) 5 69512-2 (2). (i) Tear, LPO Ch., LPO; (ii) LSO; Previn

(i) Requiem Mass; (ii) Te Deum

(M) **(*) Ph. (ADD) 464 689-2 (2). (i) Dowd; (ii) Tagliavini; Wandsworth School Boys' Ch., L. Symphony Ch., LSO, C. Davis

The first big merit of this new Telarc version of the Berlioz *Requiem* is that the recorded sound is of current demonstration quality, spectacular in capturing extremes of dynamic and tonal weight, outshining the previous Telarc version under Robert Shaw. The spectacular sound goes with a reading under the present Atlanta music-director, Robert Spano, which confirms that the chorus and orchestra are still in superb form, with Norman Mackenzie as chorus-master carrying on the tradition so brilliantly established by Shaw. That Spano's speeds are marginally more flowing than in most rival versions means that the whole work has been fitted on a single CD, a palpable advantage. Only in the *Offertorium, Domine Jesu* might Spano's tempo seem a little too fast to convey a fully devotional quality, but the marking is *Moderato*, which clearly justifies Spano's choice of speed. Though both the choral and orchestral sound is thrillingly immediate, with good inner detail, it is amply atmospheric too, conveying the spatial spread of multiple bands of timpani and brass. The excellent tenor soloist in the *Sanctus*, Frank Lopardo, is set at a distance, almost off-stage, a heavenly voice heard from afar.

Munch's Boston version was recorded as early as 1959, yet in some ways it has still not been surpassed, although technically of course the new Telarc version is even more breathtaking. But it was an astonishing technical achievement for its time, and its full glories have not been realized on record until now. The SACD transfer involves three channels (not four), but it sounds very spectacular indeed on two. The four brass groups make a superbly bold effect within the resonant Boston acoustics and the big climaxes of the *Dies irae* and *Tuba mirum* are thrilling. Munch's overall direction has a fine lyrical flow; he brings powerful expressive feeling to the *Lacrymosa*, where the chorus is at its finest. The deep trombone effects come off splendidly in the *Hostias* and the *Sanctus* – where Leopold Simoneau, with headily beautiful tone, does full justice to the tenor solo – is particularly

moving. All in all, this is a most distinguished set, and there is no doubt that this new transfer is in the demonstration bracket, not just for the expansive climaxes, but also for the gentler passages, which have a radiant bloom.

Previn's 1980 Walthamstow recording of Berlioz's great choral work offers spectacular digital sound, with the gradations of pianissimo breathtakingly caught, to make the great outbursts of the *Dies irae* and the *Tuba mirum* the more telling. There is a fine bloom on the voices, while the separation of sound gives a feeling of reality to the massed brass and multiple timpani. Previn's view is direct and incisive, not underlining expressiveness but concentrating on rhythmic qualities. If Previn misses animal excitement, the contrasts of the closing *Agnus Dei* are movingly captured. Robert Tear, balanced close, is a sensitive soloist. The *Symphonie fantastique* in Previn's dramatic, strongly structured reading makes a generous fill-up, also very well recorded.

Though Beecham's live recording, made at the Royal Albert Hall in December 1959, comes in mono only, the BBC sound is warm and full. The weight and intensity of the performance and the sense of a great occasion are caught vividly, not least in the great outburst of brass bands, widely separated, in the *Tuba mirum*. Although the professional choir takes a little time to settle down, the Beecham magic gets to work quickly, to make this one of the most compelling performances on disc. The tenor, Richard Lewis, is in superb form in the *Sanctus*, his voice given a halo of reverberation. A most cherishable historic issue.

For Sir Colin Davis's recording of the *Requiem* Philips went to Westminster Cathedral, and though one can hear individual voices in the choir, thanks to the closeness of the microphones, the large-scale brass sound is formidably caught and the choral fortissimos are glorious, helped by the fresh cutting edge of the Wandsworth School Boys' Choir. The LSO provides finely incisive accompaniment. In the *Te Deum* Davis conveys the massiveness without pomposity, the drama without unwanted excesses of emotion and his massed forces respond superbly. The only disappointment comes in the singing of Tagliavini, reasonably restrained by the standards of most Italian tenors, but not really in style with the others, or, for that matter, Berlioz. The recording is aptly brilliant and atmospheric.

Roméo et Juliette, Op. 17; Les Nuits d'été

(BB) *** HM LSO Live 3CD (2). Barcellona, Tarver, Anastassov, L. Symphony Ch., LSO, C. Davis

(i) Roméo et Juliette; (ii) Overtures: Béatrice et Bénédict; Le Corsaire; Les Francs-juges; Le Roi Lear; Waverley

☛– ⦿ (B) *** Ph. Duo (DDD/ADD) 470 543-2 (2). (i) Borodina, Moser, Miles, Bav. R. Ch., VPO; (ii) LSO; all cond. C. Davis

Sir Colin Davis's first recording of *Roméo et Juliette* is now over 30 years old – although this is hard to believe. It long reigned supreme in the catalogue, but on this bargain Duo Philips have chosen to reissue the later (1993) recording, which is likely to do the same for another thirty! In this Vienna performance, Sir Colin's interpretative approach remains basically unchanged – yet, like vintage wine that has matured, it offers greater depth, colour and body. He has the advantage of fine soloists, and Olga Borodina has the full measure of the Berlioz style. Thomas Moser is no less ardent and idiomatic, and Alastair Miles is a more than acceptable Friar Laurence. Apart from its all-round artistic excellence, this scores over all-comers in sheer quality of sound, which reproduces the whole range of Berlioz's luminous orchestration in all its subtle colourings with remarkable detail and naturalness. The five superbly played and recorded overtures (dating from 1965, except *Béatrice*, which dates from 1977) make this an exceptional bargain on the Philips Duo series, though, sadly, no texts are included.

The LSO Live two-disc issue preserves what by any reckoning was an electrifying event at the Barbican in January 2000. Davis's view of the work has remained fundamentally unchanged, though his speeds at the Barbican are marginally broader until the concluding sections from Juliette's funeral onwards. The live Barbican recording may not match in opulence the 1993 recording with the Vienna Philharmonic, for the Barbican acoustic (as recorded) is drier. Yet the refinement of the sound, with orchestra and chorus set at a slight distance, brings pianissimos of breathtaking delicacy, focused in fine detail. The three young soloists are first rate, characterizing strongly. The Italian Daniela Barcellona controls her vibrant mezzo well in the strophes, and the American tenor, Kenneth Tarver, sings his *Scherzetto* with fluency and sparkle, while the tangily Slavonic timbre of the Bulgarian bass, Orlin Anastassov, stands out well in the Friar Laurence episodes.

Roméo et Juliette (excerpts); *Les Troyens à Carthage: Prelude & Royal Hunt and Storm*

(BB) **(*) Naxos 8.553195. San Diego Ch. and SO, Talmi

Yoav Talmi and the San Diego orchestra offer a far more generous selection from Berlioz's great dramatic symphony than usual, lasting well over an hour. Talmi secures brilliant playing from his orchestra, with admirably crisp ensemble in such show-pieces as the *Queen Mab Scherzo*, and with satisfying warmth in the great Love Scene. It is good too on this very well-filled disc to have the *Prelude* to *Les Troyens* and the *Royal Hunt and Storm* (complete with offstage chorus) as makeweights. The recording is clean and detailed but lacks full weight.

Te Deum, Op. 22

*** Virgin 5 45449-2. Alagna, O de Paris, Nelson; Alain

*** DG 410 696-2. Araiza, L. Symphony Ch., LPO Ch., Woburn Singers, Boys' Ch., European Community Youth O, Abbado

When most of Berlioz's major works have been recorded many times over, it is surprising that the *Te Deum* has been relatively neglected. This latest version under a dedicated Berlioz interpreter, John Nelson, not only has a fuller, more brilliant sound than previous versions, with the complex textures well terraced, it offers two extra instrumental movements that Berlioz suggested should be included for performances celebrating victory, both with military overtones – a Prelude using one of the work's main themes in fugato and a rather corny 'March for the Presentation of the Colours'. It is good too to have Roberto Alagna as an imaginative soloist in the prayer, *Te ergo quaesummus*, and Marie-Claire Alain warmly idiomatic on the organ of the Madeleine, Paris.

The DG recording of the *Te Deum* from Abbado is very impressive. The sound is wide-ranging, with striking dynamic contrasts: Abbado brings great tonal refinement and dignity to this performance, and the spacious sound helps. Francisco Araiza is the fine soloist.

OPERA

Complete operas

(i) *Béatrice et Bénédict*; (ii) *Benvenuto Cellini*; (iii) *Les Troyens, Parts 1 & 2*

(B) *** Ph. (ADD) 456 387-2 (9). (i) Baker, Tear, Watts, Van Allan, Alldis Ch., LSO; (i–ii) Eda-Pierre, Bastin, Lloyd; (ii) Gedda, Massard, Blackwell, Herincx, Cuénod, Berbié, BBC SO; (ii–iii) Soyer, ROHCG Ch.; (iii) Veasey, Vickers, Lindholm, Glossop, Begg, Partridge, Wandsworth School Boys' Ch., ROHCG O; all cond. C. Davis

Sir Colin Davis's recordings of the three Berlioz operas (with *Benvenuto Cellini* made first in 1969, *Béatrice et Bénédict* following in 1972 and the series crowned with *Les Troyens* in 1977) makes another superb bargain package, with consistently fine CD transfers. The one blot on the set is the omission of libretto translations, although the synopses are adequately cued. If Janet Baker and Robert Tear understandably stand out in *Béatrice et Bénédict*, the rest of the cast is also first rate. Similarly, it is Nicolai Gedda in superb form who dominates *Benvenuto Cellini*, but his colleagues do not let him down. Even more than the other two operas, *Les Troyens* was an ambitious team-project, with singers, chorus and orchestra all inspired by Davis and with Josephine Veasey a superb Dido. The Philips engineers rise to the occasion in capturing the opera's spectacle with brilliance, atmosphere and refined detail.

Béatrice et Bénédict (complete)

*** Ph. (ADD) (IMS) 416 955-2 (2). Baker, Tear, Eda-Pierre, Allen, Lloyd, Van Allan, Watts, Alldis Ch., LSO, C. Davis

(B) *** Ph. Duo (ADD) 475 221-2 (2). J. Baker, Tear, Eda-Pierre, T. Allen, Lloyd, Watts, Bastin, Alldis Ch., LSO, C. Davis

*** Erato 2292 45773-2 (2). Graham, Viala, McNair, Robbin, Bacquier, Cachemaille, Le Texier, Lyon Opéra Ch. & O, Nelson

Béatrice et Bénédict presents not just witty and brilliant music for the heroine and hero (on Philips, Janet Baker and Robert Tear at their most pointed) but sensuously beautiful passages too. First-rate solo and choral singing, brilliant playing and sound that is refined and clear in texture, bright and fresh, even if minimal hiss betrays an analogue source. While the original set stays available, it is now also offered inexpensively as a Duo with limited documentation.

The Lyon Opéra version conducted by John Nelson makes an excellent alternative to the vintage Colin Davis recording. In spacious, modern, digital sound it offers substantially more of the French dialogue, well spoken by actors but more dryly recorded than the musical numbers. Susan Graham is a characterful Béatrice, lighter in the big aria than Janet Baker for Davis but aptly younger-sounding. Jean-Luc Viala is a comparably light Bénédict, pointing the fun in his big aria, and Sylvia McNair and Catherine Robbin are superb as Héro and Ursule.

Benvenuto Cellini (original version)

(N) *** Virgin 5 45706-2 (3). Kunde, Ciofi, Di Donato, Lapointe, Naouri, Delaigue, R. France Ch., & O Nat. de France, Nelson

Berlioz's opera *Benvenuto Cellini* has always been a problem work, centred as it is on the casting of a statue. These problems emerged even before the opera was given its first performance in Paris in September 1838, so taxing was Berlioz's writing, with many cuts made. Even then the process of modifying the original had only just begun. In Berlioz's lifetime it was given only 14 times in all, on almost every occasion in a different version, with the most truncated version of all, made for Liszt in Weimar, generally accepted until the 1950s. Then various attempts were made to restore the original Paris version, notably those for Colin Davis when he conducted it in a memorable revival at Covent Garden in 1972, later recorded for Philips. Following the publication of the score in 1996 in the New Berlioz Edition, still more material has emerged, making it possible to re-create Berlioz's original text, even before it was cut for the first Paris performance.

That is what John Nelson has now recorded, after concert performances in Paris. Happily, the Paris Opera had preserved all the material from the beginning, so that it has been possible to un-sew and unglue passages in the score that were cut during the first rehearsals. As the Berlioz scholar, David Cairns, says, this original score 'is Berlioz at his most recklessly inspired', and Nelson's fine performance brings that out, if anything more warmly expressive than Davis's. With one reservation, the cast is first rate, with Laurent Naouri singing characterfully in the equivocal role of Balducci, Treasurer to the Pope, and Patricia Ciofi fresh and pure as his daughter, Teresa, both given important extra material. In the title-role Gregory Kunde has a satisfyingly heroic tenor, but too often finds problems in tackling his top notes cleanly. A fine set, unmissable for anyone interested in the composer.

Les Troyens, Parts I & II (complete)

(*) Arthaus **DVD 100 350 (2). Polaski, Villars, Braun, Martirossian, Lloyd, Levinsky, Le Roi, Vienna State Op. Ch., Slovak PO Ch. (Bratislava), O de Paris, Salzburg PO, Cambreling (V/D: Alexandre Tarta.)

☛ ✿ (BB) *** HM LSO Live 0010CD (4). Heppner, DeYoung, Lang, Mingardo, Mattei, Milling, L. Symphony Ch., LSO, C. Davis

(N) (M) *** Ph. (ADD) 475 6661 (4). Veasey, Vickers, Lindholm, Glossop, Soyer, Partridge, Wandsworth School Boys' Ch. & O, C. Davis

*** Decca 443 693-2 (4). Lakes, Pollet, Voigt, Montreal Ch. & SO, Dutoit

If you need a DVD version of Berlioz's epic opera, this one serves well enough, if with distinct visual reservations. Recorded live at the 2000 Salzburg Festival, this strong, idiomatic version of Berlioz's epic opera comes in the austere production of Herbert Wernicke, who combines the roles of director and designer of sets and costumes. The set throughout is a plain white semicircle framing the stage, with a narrow gap let in at the centre, through which one momentarily sees such essential props as the Trojan horse and Aeneas's ship. Costumes are in a severe black, relieved only by bright red gloves for everyone in the first two Acts, *La Prise de Troie*, and by blue gloves for everyone except the exiled Trojans in the three Carthage Acts. Only royalty is exempt, with a crimson cloak for Priam in the first half and a royal blue one for Dido in the second. Modern military greatcoats are the rule in the first half, with Carthaginian men wearing black lounge suits in the second, while the women have timeless black robes. Happily, this stylization lets you appreciate the music without too much distraction. The great glory of the performance is the singing of Deborah Polaski both as Cassandra in *La Prise de Troie* and as Dido in *Les Troyens à*

Carthage. Rarely on disc has she been quite so commanding, with the voice richly focused and with a subtle contrast made between her vocalization as Cassandra and then, more freely and with less tension until the end, as Dido. John Villars is a powerful Aeneas in both halves, Russell Braun handsome as Choroebus and Robert Lloyd a characterful Narbal, not helped by being costumed as a bespectacled businessman. Sylvain Cambreling draws urgent, idiomatic playing from the Orchestre de Paris, with the choral singing equally powerful, important when the chorus plays such a key role in Wernicke's vision with its stylized movement. The cast list in the booklet omits such essential characters as Anna, Dido's sister (Yvonne Naef), and Iopas (Toby Spence), and others are even omitted from the credits at the end.

Recorded live at performances (and rehearsals) in the Barbican in London, Sir Colin Davis's second recording of this epic opera magnificently crowns his whole career as a Berlioz interpreter on record, generally outshining even his pioneer version of 30 years earlier. The first wonder is that the sound of chorus and orchestra is even fuller, more spacious and certainly brighter and clearer than on the earlier, Philips recording, or even the opulent digital recording given to Charles Dutoit in his Montreal set for Decca. Davis is marginally faster in all five Acts, a degree more thrustful, with the excitement of a live occasion consistently adding extra intensity. The casting too is marginally even finer than before. Petra Lang, a last-minute substitute as Cassandra, is superb: firm, rich and intense, investing every phrase with emotional power, instantly establishing her dominance in the very first scene. Opposite her, Peter Mattei makes a powerful Chorebus. Both in *The Fall of Troy* and *The Trojans at Carthage* Ben Heppner excels himself, not just heroic with his unstrained Heldentenor, but finding a degree of refinement in the love duet of Act III that few rivals can match, let alone on disc. Michelle DeYoung may not be quite so rich and firm a Dido as Josephine Veasey on Davis's earlier set, but the vibrancy of her mezzo is warmly caught by the microphones, and her death monologue is the more moving for the vulnerability she conveys. The rest make an excellent team without any significant shortcoming. Though the set comes on four discs at super-budget price, full libretto and notes are provided, though printed in very small type.

Throughout his earlier, Philips recording Davis compels the listener to concentrate, to achieve the epic logic of Berlioz's masterly setting. Only in the great love scene of *O nuit d'ivresse* would one have welcomed the more expansive hand of a Beecham. Veasey makes a splendid Dido, singing always with fine heroic strength, with Vickers a ringing Aeneas. The Covent Garden Chorus and Orchestra excel themselves in virtuoso singing and playing, and the sound-quality is superbly vivid. However, fine though it is, this set is now superseded by Davis's new LSO Live digital recording.

Dutoit's Decca recording was linked to concert performances of each of the two parts of the opera, recorded in spectacular digital sound. Interpretatively the contrasts between Dutoit and Davis in his first, Philips recording are quickly established. Dutoit is more volatile than Davis, consistently preferring faster speeds – reflecting the metronome markings – bringing not just thrilling allegros but lyrically flowing andantes. However, in his later, LSO set Davis is much closer to Dutoit in his pacing.

On Decca Cassandra's first solo is most persuasively moulded at a flowing speed, with Deborah Voigt far warmer than Berit Lindholm for Davis on Philips. However, both are upstaged by Petra Lang in the newest version. As Dido, the soprano on Decca, Françoise Pollet sings with a rich, even tone, sensuously feminine, even if she lacks the weight of a mezzo, and though Gary Lakes as Dido is less heroic than Jon Vickers, he is more sensitive in the love duet. Dutoit includes the brief Prelude that Berlioz wrote in 1863 for separate performances of the second part of the opera. The other textual addition comes in Act I. After the Andromache scene there is an extra scene, lasting six minutes, which the Berlioz scholar Hugh MacDonald, editor of the Bärenreiter score, has orchestrated from the surviving piano score.

The Trojans: Royal Hunt and Storm

(**(*)) BBC mono BBCL 4113. RPO, Beecham, with BBC Ch.
 – CHABRIER: España; Gwendoline Overture; DEBUSSY: L'Enfant prodigue: Cortège et air de danse; DELIUS: Brigg Fair; MASSENET: La Vierge: Le Dernier sommeil de la vierge; SAINT-SAENS: Le Rouet d'Omphale (with MOZART: Divertimento in D, K.131: excerpts (**(*))

Beecham brought an almost unique gusto and excitement to the Royal Hunt and Storm, heard here with choral interjections, and it is a pity that the BBC recording has not more brilliance and range. Even so, the storm thunder is pretty impressive and the poetic close memorably atmospheric.

Arias and Duets from: Béatrice et Bénédict; Benvenuto Cellini; La Damnation de Faust; L'Enfance du Christ; Lélio; Roméo et Juliette; 8 Scènes de Faust; Les Troyens

*** EMI 5 57433-2. Alagna, Depardieu, ROHOCG, De Billy

This is an inspired collection, bringing together a wide-ranging group of tenor solos from Berlioz's major works. Roberto Alagna is always at his happiest singing in French, and though his voice is less well suited to some of the items, which range from the fully heroic to the tenderly lyrical, the concentration and imagination are most compelling throughout, not least in the Marguerite/Faust duet, Ange adoré, from La Damnation de Faust. The other collaboration is with Gérard Depardieu as speaker in two rare items, Horatio's Ballad from Lélio and Mephistopheles' serenade in its tenor version with guitar from the early Huit Scènes de Faust. Yet Alagna's solo work is central to the success of the disc. He sparkles in such items as the Mab Scherzetto from Roméo et Juliette and Benedict's solo, and is persuasively lyrical in Iopas's solo from Les Troyens in sharp contrast with his power in the solos of Aeneas. As a rousing supplement Algna is the soloist in Berlioz's arrangement of La Marseillaise. For a unique and illuminating Berlioz survey this is both valuable and most enjoyable, with Bertrand de Billy drawing ripely sympathetic playing from the Covent Garden Orchestra.

BERNSTEIN, Leonard (1918–90)

(i) Candide: Overture; (ii) Concerto for Orchestra (Jubilee Games); Divertimento; (iii) Dybbuk (ballet): Suites 1–2. (ii) Facsimile (Choreographic Essay); Fancy Free (ballet); (ii; iv) Halil (Nocturne) for Flute, Strings & Percussion; (ii; v) 3 Meditations from Mass (for cello & orchestra). (ii) A Musical Toast; On the Town: 3 Dance Episodes. On the Waterfront: Symphonic Suite. (vi) Prelude, Fugue & Riffs (for clarinet & jazz ensemble). (ii; vii) Serenade after Plato's Symposium. (ii) Slava; Symphonies Nos. (viii; ii) 1

(Jeremiah); (ix; ii) 2 (Age of Anxiety); (x; xi; ii) 3 (Kaddish: revised version); (x; ii) Chichester Psalms; (xii) Songfest; (i) West Side Story: Symphonic Dances

(B) *** DG (DDD/ADD) 469 829-2 (7). (i) LAPO; (ii) Israel PO; (iii) NYPO; (iv) Rampal; (v) Rostropovich; (vi) Schmidl, VPO (members); (vii) Kremer; (viii) Ludwig; (ix) Foss; (x) V. Jeunesse Ch.; V. Boys' Ch. (xi) Caballé, Wager; (xii) Soloists, Nat. SO

A self-recommending set in DG's Collector's Edition, encompassing virtually all Bernstein's key orchestral and vocal works (but including only the Meditations drawn from the controversial Mass, which he did not re-record for DG). A reminder of the composer's supreme theatical talent comes with the Candide Overture, the excerpts from On the Town and the West Side Story Symphonic Dances. It may be that posterity will decide that his symphonies are too uneven in inspiration to be among the finest to have emerged from the USA in the twentieth century, but no one can doubt the composer's imaginative flair and ready flow of catchy, memorable ideas. Among the other works, the Serenade after Plato's Symposium and the Chichester Psalms are undoubted masterpieces. As can be seen below, Bernstein recorded much of his music earlier with the New York Philharmonic, and those initial accounts have a unique flair and vitality. But if the Israel Philharmonic is not as virtuosic as the NYPO, they respond to the composer committedly and persuasively, and the DG sound is generally fuller and better balanced than the vividly up-front CBS/Sony recordings. There is much to stimulate the listener here, and with good back-up documentation this box is fully worth its modest cost.

Candide: Overture; Fancy Free (ballet); On the Waterfront: symphonic suite; West Side Story: symphonic dances

☞— (M) *** Sony (ADD) SMK 63085. NYPO, composer

(i) Candide: Overture; (ii) On the Town (3 dance episodes); (i) West Side Story: symphonic dances; (iii) America
(M) *** DG Entrée 471 737-2. LAPO, Bernstein – BARBER: Adagio *** (with GERSHWIN: Rhapsody in Blue **(*))

For many, this Sony compilation, issued under the 'Bernstein Century' logo, will be the ideal way of acquiring this orchestral theatre and film music. The fizzing account of the Candide Overture has never been surpassed and the sparkling Fancy Free ballet score is hardly less rhythmically seductive. The symphonic dances from West Side Story confirm Bernstein as a truly great tunesmith; apart from the music's life-enhancing vitality, the closing section is infinitely touching. The recordings, made between 1960 and 1963, have never sounded better: bright and free, with plenty of ambient space.

Bernstein's later, live, Los Angeles account of the sparkling Candide Overture has tremendous flair, his speed a fraction slower than in the earlier, New York studio recording for CBS/Sony. Bernstein's Israeli recordings sound fuller than his earlier versions on Sony, and the Prelude, Fugue and Riffs, also recorded live, is vibrant and rhythmic, with Peter Schmidl a comparatively reticent soloist. The alternative collection offers the same performances but with alternative couplings, including a characteristically intense account of Barber's Adagio. The Rhapsody in Blue is, however, less successful than Bernstein's earlier, CBS/Sony account.

Divertimento for Orchestra; (i) Facsimile (choreographic essay); (ii) Prelude, Fugue & Riffs. West Side Story: symphonic dances (original version)

*** Virgin 5 45295-2. CBSO, Järvi, with (i) Marshall; (ii) Meyer

Järvi and the CBSO clearly enjoy themselves, especially in the elegantly polished and very spirited account of the *Divertimento*. There is some beautiful woodwind-playing in *Facsimile* and, not surprisingly, Wayne Marshall's contribution is glitteringly idiomatic. The same could be said for Sabine Meyer in the very jazzy account of the *Prelude, Fugue and Riffs*, while in the *West Side Story Dances* Järvi relishes the romantic melodies, which are exquisitely played, and finds plenty of rhythmic venom for the *Rumble*.

Serenade after Plato's 'Symposium' (for Solo Violin, String Orchestra, Harp & Percussion)

*** DG 474 500-2. Mutter, LSO, composer – PREVIN: *Violin Concerto* ***

*** Sony SK 60584. Hahn, Baltimore SO, Zinman – BEETHOVEN: *Violin Concerto* ***

(M) *** EMI 5 62600-2. Perlman, Boston SO, Ozawa – BARBER: *Violin Concerto; FOSS: 3 American Pieces* ***

(i) *Serenade after Plato's 'Symposium'*; (ii) *Songfest* (cycle of American poems)

(M) *** DG (ADD) (IMS) 447 957-2. (i) Kremer, Israel PO; (ii) Dale, Elias, Williams, Rosenheim, Reardon, Gramm, Nat. SO of Washington; composer

The *Serenade* ranks among Bernstein's most inspired creations, full of ideas, often thrilling and exciting and equally often moving. Perlman may initially seem almost too confident, missing an element of fantasy. Yet he brings home tellingly how each movement leads thematically out of the preceding one, until the final movement, much the longest, with its references back to the beginning. He also makes it seem a warmer piece, thanks to his range of rich tone-colours, set against the richness of the Boston string-sound.

As in the Beethoven coupling, Hilary Hahn gives an intense, deeply felt performance, crowned by a rapt account of the big *Adagio* fourth section, *Agathon*. Excellent sound.

Though the title suggests a work less weighty than a full concerto, the opposite is true, when Bernstein found his inspiration in Plato's 'Symposium', with the slow movement, *Agathon*, one of his most profound inspirations, beautifully realized by Mutter and Previn.

Symphonies 1 (Jeremiah); 2 (The Age of Anxiety); (i) Chichester Psalms

(M) *** DG (ADD) 457 757-2. Israel PO, composer, (i) with soloists from V. Boys' Ch.

Symphony 2

*** Hyp. CDA 67170. Hamelin, Ulster O, Sitkovetsky – BOLCOM: *Piano Concerto 2* ***

The *Jeremiah Symphony* dates from Bernstein's early twenties and ends with a moving passage from *Lamentations* for the mezzo soloist (on DG, Christa Ludwig). As its title suggests, the *Second Symphony* was inspired by the poem of W. H. Auden, though no words are set to music in this purely orchestral work. The *Chichester Psalms* is one of the most attractive choral works written in the twentieth century: its jazzy passages are immediately appealing, as is the intrinsic beauty of the reflective sequences. These live performances with the Israel Philharmonic are not quite as polished or forceful as those Bernstein recorded earlier in New York, but the warmth of his writing is fully conveyed in these excellent recordings. With a playing time of just under 80 minutes, this DG 'Originals' CD is exceptionally good value.

Any newer version of a major Bernstein work has to stand comparison with Bernstein's own recordings, and even by that test the fine Hyperion account of *The Age of Anxiety* stands up well. As in Bernstein's recording, the piano soloist is presented as a concerto soloist, not only balanced forwardly but encouraged to play characterfully, with expressive warmth. Marc-André Hamelin is outstanding in that role, subtle and with a wider expressive and dynamic range, helped by refined recording and accompaniment. Under Sitkovetsky, the Ulster Orchestra plays brilliantly, giving cogency to the odd, programme-based structure.

(i) Symphony 3 (Kaddish); (ii) Chichester Psalms

(M) *** DG 447 954-2. (i) Caballé, Wager, V. Boys' Ch.; (ii) Soloist from V. Boys' Ch.; (i–ii) Wiener Jeunesse Ch., Israel PO, composer

(M) *** Sony (ADD) SMK 60595. (i) Montealegre, Tourel, Columbus Boychoir; (ii) Bogart; (i–ii) Camerata Singers, NYPO, composer

(M) *** Warner Elatus 0927 46722-2. (i) Mattila, Menuhin; (ii) Mills; French R. Ch. & PO, Sado

The *Third Symphony*, written in memory of John F. Kennedy, also coupled with the *Psalms*, is recorded on DG in its revised version (with a male speaker) which concentrates the original concept of a dialogue between man and God, a challenge from earth to heaven.

The Sony recordings were made in the Manhattan Center in the mid-1960s; the acoustic is agreeably spacious, and many may prefer them to the later, Israeli, DG versions. However, the spoken dialogue in the *Kaddish Symphony* is recited here with melodramatic fervour by Felicia Montealegre (Mrs Bernstein at the time) and this is a serious stumbling block. However, the performance of the *Chichester Psalms* is vividly projected by singers and players alike.

Menuhin, with his thoughtful, measured tones, is the opposite of most narrators in the *Kaddish Symphony*, but the emotion is conveyed just as intensely. Karita Mattila is a radiant soprano soloist and the choir sings brilliantly, but at relatively measured speeds this does not have the dramatic bite of Bernstein's own recordings, though the sound here is fuller and clearer. In the *Chichester Psalms* the choir and orchestra seem more at home in Bernstein's jazzy syncopations, giving a dazzling performance, vividly recorded, with Joseph Mills from the New College, Oxford, choir a fine treble soloist.

VOCAL MUSIC

Chichester Psalms (reduced score)

*** Hyp. CDA 66219. Martelli, Corydon Singers, Masters, Kettel, Trotter; Best – BARBER: *Agnus Dei;* COPLAND: *In the Beginning*, etc. ***

Martin Best uses the composer's reduced orchestration. The treble soloist's chaste contribution is persuasive and the choir scales down its pianissimos to accommodate him. Excellent, atmospheric sound, set in a church acoustic.

Mass (for the death of President Kennedy)

(M) **(*) Sony (ADD) SM2K 63089 (2). Titus (celebrant), Scribner Ch., Berkshire Boys' Ch., Rock Band & O, composer

(N) *(*) HM HMC 901840/41 (2). Hadley, Soloists of the Pacific Mozart Ens., Berlin R. Ch., Staats und Domchor, Berlin, Deutsches SO, Berlin, Nagano

Outrageously eclectic in its borrowings from pop and the avante garde, Bernstein's *Mass*, written for the opening of the Kennedy Center in Washington in 1971, presents an extraordinary example of the composer's creative energy. It still stands as one his most controversial works, very much of its time. Described as a 'theatre-piece', it simultaneously brings a celebration of the Mass, with the five main sections prompting an astonishing range of responses from the composer, including sections he calls 'tropes', with texts of commentary on the liturgy by Stephen Schwarz, questioning and often combative. The composer's own performance remains uniquely persuasive and the Sony (originally CBS) recording is both vividly present and has a convincing ambience.

The newer Harmonia Mundi recording is much less successful. At the centre of the work is the tenor Celebrant, who in the opening section sings a hymn entitled *A Simple Song*, one of the most popular numbers. Sadly, in this performance Jerry Hadley, once a leading interpreter of Bernstein, sings it very unsteadily. Nagano does well in capturing some of the wildness behind Bernstein's scheme, but the Berliners do not begin to match the composer's own chosen participants in the recording he made soon after the first performance. Best are the many choral passages which in their catchy use of jazz rhythms echo the *Chichester Psalms*, including a surprisingly vigorous setting of the *Agnus Dei*. The two longest sections come at the end, a long solo entitled *Things get broken* which verges on the incoherent, and a final chorus which builds up to a splendid climax. This set can be recommended only for those who insist on a modern, digital version.

Songs: *La bonne cuisine* (French and English versions); *I hate music* (cycle); 2 *Love Songs*; *Piccola serenata; Silhouette; So pretty; Mass: A simple song; I go on. Candide: It must be so; Candide's lament. 1600 Pennsylvania Ave: Take care of this house. Peter Pan: My house; Peter Pan; Who am I; Never-Never Land*
*** Etcetera KTC 1037. Alexander, Crone

A delightful collection, consistently bearing witness to Bernstein's flair for a snappy idea as well as his tunefulness. Roberta Alexander's rich, warm voice and winning personality are well supported by Tan Crone at the piano. The recording is lifelike and undistracting.

STAGE WORKS

Candide (final, revised version)
⊕─✲ ✿ (B) *** DG Double 474 472-2 (2). Hadley, Anderson, Green, Ludwig, Gedda, D. Jones, Ollmann, L. Symphony Ch., LSO, composer
(M) *** DG 474 857-2. Hadley, Anderson, Green, Ludwig, Gedda, D. Jones, Ollmann, L Symphony Ch., LSO, composer

(i) *Candide* (final, revised version); (ii) *West Side Story*: complete recording
✿ (M) *** DG 447 958-2 (3). (i) Hadley, Anderson, Green, Ludwig, Gedda, D. Jones, Ollmann, L. Symphony Ch., LSO; (ii) Te Kanawa, Carreras, Troyanos, Horne, Ollmann, Ch. and O; composer

The composer's complete recordings of *Candide* and *West Side Story* have been coupled together on three mid-priced discs for those who have not already acquired one or the other of these inspired scores. *Candide* is a triumph, both in

the studio recording (which Bernstein made immediately after concert performances in London) and in the video recording of the actual concert at the Barbican, bringing out not just the vigour, the wit and the tunefulness of the piece more than ever before, but also an extra emotional intensity. There is no weak link in the cast. Jerry Hadley is touchingly characterful as Candide, and June Anderson as Cunegonde is not only brilliant in coloratura but also warmly dramatic. It was an inspired choice to have Christa Ludwig as the Old Woman, and equally original to choose Adolph Green for the dual roles of Dr Pangloss and Martin. Nicolai Gedda also proves a winner in his series of cameo roles, and the full, incisive singing of the London Symphony Chorus adds to the weight of the performance without inflation.

What is missing in the CD set is the witty narration, prepared by John Wells and spoken by Adolph Green and Kurt Ollmann in the Barbican performance. As included on the video of the live concert (Laser disc DG 072 423-1; VHS DG 072 423-3), those links leaven the entertainment delightfully. Even those with the CDs should investigate the video version, which also includes Bernstein's own moving speeches of introduction before each Act. No doubt this will soon appear on DVD.

Candide also remains available separately, costing approximately the same price.

Bernstein's recording of the complete score of *West Side Story* takes a frankly operatic approach in its casting, but the result is highly successful, for the great vocal melodies are worthy of voices of the highest calibre. Tatiana Troyanos, herself brought up on the West Side, spans the stylistic dichotomy to perfection in a superb portrayal of Anita. The clever production makes the best of both musical worlds, with Bernstein's son and daughter speaking the dialogue most affectingly. Bernstein conducts a superb instrumental group of musicians 'from on and off Broadway', and they are recorded with a bite and immediacy that is captivating. The power of the music is greatly enhanced by the spectacularly wide dynamic range of the recording.

Bernstein's *Candide* won the *Gramophone* magazine's Music Theatre Award in 1992, hence this reissue in the 'Awards Collection'. It is fully documented.

On the Town (complete)
(N) (M) *** DG 476 7145. Von Stade, Daly, McLaughlin, Hampson, Garrison, Ollmann, Ramey, Lear, Cleo Laine, L. Voices, LSO, Tilson Thomas

In the 1992 concert performance of *On the Town* with the LSO (which won the *Gramophone* Music Theatre Award in 1994), it is as though Bernstein himself was performing as well as providing the music. If anything, the full score in the exuberance of youth is even richer in catchy tunes than *Candide*. As in the latter show, the mixing of opera stars with the Broadway tradition works like a charm. Thomas Hampson, rich and resonant, sings Gabey, the leading sailor, in search of Miss Turnstiles, with another fine American baritone, Kurt Ollmann, as Chip and David Garrison giving authentic point to the third sailor, Ozzie. Then in opulent casting, Samuel Ramey sings a series of incidental roles, including the ever-understanding Pitkin, constantly pushed aside by his man-mad girlfriend, Claire. In that role Frederica von Stade establishes herself as the central star, and anyone hesitating should hear the way she leads the ensemble in the climactic nostalgia of *Some other time*. Marie McLaughlin as Ivy, Miss Turnstiles, is slightly less at home, but Tyne Daly as the predatory taxi-driver, Hildy, is winningly larger than life. On CD the numbers are presented dry, as though recorded in the studio, with no linking narrative and no applause. Two of the extra numbers and several encores are omitted to fit the result on a single, well-filled disc. In recompense, an extra number, *The intermission's great*, is included, as are full texts. However, we look forward to the DVD of the video recording, which is even more enjoyable.

Trouble in Tahiti

*** Opus Arte **DVD** OA 0838 D. Novacek, Daymond, Randle, Stafford-Allen, Hegarty, Gibbon, City of London Sinfonia, Daniel (V/D: Tom Cairns)

Directed for video by Tom Cairns, this DVD offers a lively revival of Bernstein's brilliant one-acter of 1952, a work that neatly spans the gap between opera and Broadway musical. In seven scenes introduced by a Prologue it focuses on a couple, Sam and Dinah, whose marriage is under strain in the artificial atmosphere of suburban America in the 1950s, as symbolized by their 'little white house'. From the Prologue onwards their problems are commented on by a vocal trio, often singing in jazzy close harmony. In the staging, period clips heighten the atmosphere of such scenes as the Psychiatrist's Office, where Dinah is having a consultation. Karl Daymond and Stephanie Novacek make an attractive couple, with their monologues and duets set against sharply rhythmic contributions from the vocal trio, helped by idiomatic playing from the City of London Sinfonia under Paul Daniel. Daniel is the principal contributor to a useful introduction, and Humphrey Burton, Bernstein's official biographer, offers a 20-minute personal portrait of the composer as a supplement for the 40-minute opera.

West Side Story: The Making of the Recording

*** DG **DVD** 073 017-9. Te Kanawa, Carreras, Troyanos, Ollmann, Bernstein (V/D: Chris Swann)

With narration from Bernstein himself, this classic feature film about the making of the controversial opera-style recording of *West Side Story* gives a vivid portrait of the composer at work. His unique combination of toughness, warmth, shining charisma and overwhelming genius is vividly conveyed. There is no false modesty in his approach to a work which he had written over 30 years before but never previously conducted. For the first time he had studied it in depth, and was surprised and gratified that it is 'so funky'. He goes on to explain that although it had been tiring listening to play-backs, the experience of recording it 'made me feel very young. It sounds as though I wrote it yesterday.' It is good to see Bernstein's obvious joy as he starts to conduct Kiri Te Kanawa in *I feel pretty*, but his bursts of irritation when someone fails to carry out his instructions are just as telling. The contrasting characters of the four principals come over well, notably the feisty Tatiana Troyanos, and on DVD it is most helpful to have no fewer than 28 chapter points, letting you find any passage quickly. But above all this film is important in giving so illuminating an insight into the character of a great musician and his work. This is of course a supplement to the recording and does not include a complete video performance, only excerpts.

West Side Story (complete)

☛ *** DG **SACD** 471 631-2; CD 457 199-2. Te Kanawa, Carreras, Troyanos, Horne, Ollman, Ch. & O., composer

The composer's own recording of *West Side Story* is now available on one SACD (compatible) or on one CD; the alternative choice combines it with *Candide* at mid-price on three CDs.

Wonderful Town

*** EMI 5 56753-2. Criswell, McDonald, Hampson, Barrett, Gilfry, L. Voices, Birmingham Contemporary Music Group, Rattle

Wonderful Town was one of Leonard Bernstein's earliest successes, but unfairly it has tended to be eclipsed by the later success of *West Side Story*. Here, in a fizzing performance, starrily cast, Rattle rights the balance in a performance at once vigorously idiomatic and also refined in the many lyrical moments. The two characterful sisters finding their feet in the big city are brilliantly played here by Kim Criswell and Audra McDonald, not just charismatic as actresses, but singing superbly. Thomas Hampson as Robert just as commandingly bestrides the conflicting problem of Broadway and the classical tradition, and Brent Barrett in the secondary role of Wreck delightfully brings in the cabaret tradition. Such numbers as 'Ohio', 'A little bit in love', 'Conversation piece' and 'Wrong note rag', rounded off with the big tune of 'It's love', can be appreciated for their full musical quality, with Rattle and his talented Birmingham group relishing the jazzy idiom. Bright, forward sound to match, and a helpful booklet which gives the full text.

BERWALD, Franz (1796–1868)

(i; ii) *Piano Concerto in D*; (i; iii) *Duo in D for Violin & Piano*; (i) *Musical Journal: Tempo di marcia in E flat; Piano Piece 2: Presto feroce. Rondeau-bagatelle in B flat; Theme & Variations in G min.*

** Genesis (ADD) GCD 111. (i) Erikson; (ii) Swedish RSO, Westerberg; (iii) Grünfarb

Greta Erikson's 1971 recording of the *Piano Concerto* is serviceable, very nimble and cleanly articulated, but somewhat wanting in poetry. Josef Grünfarb gives a finely turned account of the *D major Duo*, but this partnership is less persuasive than Marieke Blankestijn and Susan Tomes on Hyperion (CDA 66835).

Violin Concerto in C sharp min., Op. 2

(BB) **(*) Naxos 8.554287. Ringborg, Swedish CO, Willén – AULIN: *Violin Concerto 3*; STENHAMMAR: 2 *Sentimental Romances* **(*)

The Berwald concerto is an early work; its ideas are pleasing and mellifluous, very much in the Spohr tradition. Tobias Ringborg plays well, though he is not as spirited as was Tellefsen (EMI). Good recorded sound. The two Stenhammar pieces are rarities and sound persuasive in his hands. Apart from Christian Bergqvist's record on Musica Sveciae, this newcomer is the only current version of Tor Aulin's well-crafted *C minor Concerto*. A decent performance and good, well-balanced recorded sound.

(i; ii) *Double Concerto for 2 Violins & Orchestra. Drottningen av Golconda: excerpts. Estrella de Soria: Overture & Polonaise. Slaget vid Leipzig (The Battle of Leipzig);* (i) *Theme and Variations for Violin & Orchestra*

(*) Sterling CDS 1061-2. Malmö Op. O, Willén, with (i) Lörstad, (ii) Hagman

Here are some Berwald rarities new to disc. *Slaget vid Leipzig* ('The Battle of Leipzig') comes from 1828, the year after the

Septet, and the *Double Concerto* and the *Theme and Variations* (1816–17) are apprentice works of little originality. *The Battle of Leipzig* is one of Berwald's feeblest efforts, save for the poetic opening paragraphs. The rest is, by Berwald's elevated standards, crude, particularly the end, which quotes *God Save the Queen*, at that time the Swedish National Anthem. The orchestral playing is pretty rough-and-ready – well, rough anyway – and the tonal blend and tuning are poor.

Symphony in A (1820; fragment); Symphonies 1–4; Overtures: Estrella de Soria; The Queen of Golconda
(B) *** Hyp. Dyad CDD 22043 (2). Swedish RSO, Goodman

Symphonies 1–4
(M) *** DG 445 581-2 (2). Gothenburg SO, Järvi

Symphonies 1–2
(N) (B) *** DG Eloquence 477 5031. Gothenburg SO, Neeme Järvi

Roy Goodman's set with the Swedish Radio Symphony Orchestra has the advantage of including the early fragment of the *Symphony in A major* which has been completed – and very well, too – by Duncan Druce, and makes its début on records. Goodman is always alert and intelligent, though he tends to favour brisk tempi. He starts the *Sinfonie singulière* far too quickly and is forced to pull back when the brass enter. There is a certain loss of breadth here, and again in the *Sinfonie sérieuse*. The *Overture* to *The Queen of Golconda* comes off very well. Berwald's orchestration tends to be top-heavy, and the cool acoustic of the Berwald Hall in Stockholm slightly accentuates that. But this set has a distinct price advantage.

Neeme Järvi's set is still highly recommendable; this is music that is wholly in the life-stream of the Gothenburg orchestra. The only reservations one might make concern the brisk opening of the *Sinfonie singulière*, but Goodman is even faster. Järvi's account of the *E flat Symphony* has marginally greater sparkle and lightness of touch. The DG recording is excellent in every way, and the warmer acoustic of the Gothenburg Concert Hall may sway some readers in its favour.

As can be seen, a coupling of Nos. 1 and 2 has been additionally reissued on DG's bargain Eloquence label.

Symphonies 1–4; Overture: Estrella de Soria; Play of the Elves (Elfenspiel); Racing; Reminiscences from the Norwegian Mountains
(B) **(*) EMI double forte (ADD) 5 73335-2 (2). RPO, Björlin

Symphonies 1–4; (i) Konzertstück for Bassoon & Orchestra
🔴➔ *** BIS CD 795/6. (i) Davidsson; Malmö SO, Ehrling

As his earlier recordings of Berwald demonstrate, Sixten Ehrling has a natural feeling for the classic Swedish symphonist. Tempi are all well judged and there is an admirable lightness of touch. There is plenty of breadth in the *Sinfonie sérieuse* and no want of sparkle in the *E flat Symphony*. The *Konzertstück*, composed in 1827 (the year before the *Septet*), is a charming piece, much in its manner. This could well be regarded as a first choice in this repertoire.

The orchestral playing under the late Ulf Björlin is a little deficient in vitality; the recordings were made during a heatwave. Others may be more vital and alert, and Björlin does not succeed in creating the same degree of tension in shaping melodic lines. The *Reminiscences from the Norwegian Mountains* is attractively atmospheric, while *Play of the Elves* is a delightful piece. The *Overture, Estrella de Soria* is full of resourceful and finely drawn ideas. There are no alternatives

at this very reasonable cost, and the EMI engineers have provided excellent recording, clear and quite full-bodied.

Symphonies 1 (Sérieuse); 2 (Capricieuse); Memory of the Norwegian Alps
(N) *** Chan. 10303. Danish Nat. RSO, Dausgaard

Symphonies 3 (Singulière); 4 in E flat; Play of the Elves
*** Chan. 9921. Danish Nat. RSO, Dausgaard

In their day the best all-round version of the two symphonies was by Sixten Ehrling and the LSO on Decca, and the fine DG set by Neeme Järvi and the Gothenburg Orchestra remains very recommendable. But the sheer excellence of the Danish orchestra's playing of these sparkling and original pieces is not in question, nor is the quality of the sound. A strong recommendation. However, first choice for a complete set of the four symphonies rests with Sixten Ehrling on BIS 795/6.

Symphony 1; Overtures: The Queen of Golconda; Estrella de Soria. **Tone-poems:** *Festival of the Bayadères; Play of the Elves; Reminiscences from the Norwegian Mountains*
*** Bluebell (ADD) ABCD 047. Swedish RSO, Ehrling

The *Sinfonie sérieuse* was recorded in 1970 and is arguably the finest account of the work ever recorded (including Ehrling's later, BIS version). It is beautifully played and unerringly paced. The overtures and tone-poems were recorded in 1966. Excellent performances, more vital and imaginative than the RPO versions by the late Ulf Björlin. Very well recorded, too.

CHAMBER MUSIC

Duos: in B flat for Cello & Piano; in D for Violin & Piano; Duo Concertante in A min. for 2 Violins; Concertino in A min. for Violin & Piano: fragment; Fantasy on 2 Swedish Folk Melodies
(BB) *** Naxos 8.554286. Rondin; Lundin; Ringborg, Bergström

The *Duo for Cello and Piano* (1857), played persuasively by Mats Rondin and Bengt-Ake Lundin, alludes to material from the *A minor Quartet*. In both the *Duo* and the *Quartet* the piano is hyperactive, as it tends to be in the roughly contemporaneous *Piano Quintets*. The *Duo Concertante* is quite inventive and well written, although it is nowhere as individual as the *G minor Quartet* (1818). The playing throughout is accomplished, although Lundin dominates in the *Duos* because of the recording balance. The sleeve and cover state incorrectly that the *Duo in D major* is in D minor, but this issue is well worth exploring; in this work Susan Tomes plays with great flair and finesse.

Grand Septet in B flat
(M) *** CRD 3344. Nash Ens. – HUMMEL: *Septet* ***

Berwald's only *Septet* is an imaginative work which deserves a secure place in the repertoire instead of on its periphery. It is very well played by the Nash Ensemble, and is finely recorded.

Grand Septet in B flat; Piano & Wind Quartet in E flat; Piano Trio in F min.
*** Hyp. CDA 66834. Gaudier Ens.

The *Quartet in E flat for Piano and Wind* of 1819 is good but not vintage Berwald, though it could not sound more persuasive in this performance. Delightful performances, on which it would be difficult to improve, and excellent recording too.

Piano Quintet 1 in C min.; Piano Trio 4 in C; Duo in D for Violin & Piano
**(*) Hyp. CDA 66835. Tomes, Gaudier Ens.

The *Piano Quintet* (1853) comes off marvellously. Susan Tomes is both sensitive and expert, and the Gaudier Ensemble are hardly less distinguished. In the *Piano Trio No. 4* and in the less inventive *D major Duo* the balance makes her sound too dominant. True, the *Duo* is for piano and violin – not the other way round – but the violinist, Marieke Blankestijn, an impeccable artist, sounds far too pale and reticent.

Piano Trios 1 in E flat; 2 in F min.; 3 in D min.
(BB) *** Naxos 8.555001. Prunyi, Kiss, Onczay

These three mature piano trios echo the symphonies in their sharp originality, full of surprising twists and turns, often like a more quirky Mendelssohn. The second of the three is the most striking in a troubled F minor, with a broodingly intense first movement. Excellent performances from three Hungarian players, very well recorded.

Piano Trios 4 in C; in C (1845); in C & E flats (fragments)
(BB) *** Naxos 8.555002. Dráfi, Modrian, Kertész

In the second CD the other Hungarian team is first class. The recordings were made respectively in the Italian Institute in Budapest and the Festetič Castle at Keszthely and are bright and well detailed.

String Quartet 1 in G min.
(M) *** CRD (ADD) 3361. Chilingirian Qt – WIKMANSON: *Quartet 2* ***

The *G minor Quartet* is a remarkably assured piece, and the first movement is full of audacious modulations, with themes both characterful and appealing. The Chilingirian players give a well-shaped and sensitive account of it. They are truthfully recorded, and the coupling – another Swedish quartet – enhances the attractions of this issue. Strongly recommended.

String Quartets 1; 2 in A min.; 3 in E flat
*** BIS CD 759. Yggdrasil Qt

First-rate performances by this young Swedish ensemble of their great compatriot's output in this medium. They are both original and rewarding. This gifted ensemble play them very well indeed and are splendidly recorded. Anyone who enjoys the Mendelssohn or Schumann *Quartets* should not delay in investigating this music.

BIBER, Heinrich (1644–1704)

During the lifetime of our *Guide*, and mainly through the medium of recordings, Heinrich Biber has gradually emerged as one of the greatest composers of the latter half of the seventeenth century, perhaps the greatest before Bach. Born in Bohemia, he was a celebrated virtuoso of the violin but, unlike most violinist/composers, his music combined great bravura with genuine expressive depth and musical imagination of the highest order. His instrumental works are capped by the extraordinary *Rosary Sonatas*, but in his later years as Court Musician and Kapelmeister at Salzburg he was to compose some equally extraordinary and original vocal music.

(i) *Ballettae a 4 Violettas, 1–7; Battaglia in D; Peasants' Churchgoing Sonata in B flat a 6; Sonata Sancti Polycarpi a 9 (for 8 trumpets & bass); Sonatas 1–2 a 8 for 2 Clarini, 6 violae; 3–4 a 5 Violae; Sonata a 7 for 6 Trumpets, Taburin & Organ; (ii) Requiem in F min.; (iii) In festo trium regium, muttetum Natale (Epiphany Cantata) à 6; Laetatus sum à 7*
(N) (BB) *** Warner Apex 2564 61031-2. (i) V. Concentus Musicus, Harnoncourt; (ii; iii) with Equiluz, Von Egmond, Villesech, Soloists of Vienna Boy's Ch.; Ch. Viennensis; (ii) cond. Gillesberger

This is a good, varied and inexpensive introduction to Biber's music. The *Battle* sequence itself has some hair-raising instrumental effects, including barbaric pizzicati representing the cannon. The picture of 'the dissolute company' brings a half-minute of well-organized instrumental cacophony. In the *March* there is a bizarre drum-and-fife imitation by violin and double-bass. The *Polycarp Sonata*, using eight trumpets, makes a thrilling sound. The piece closes with a *Lament of the Wounded Musketeers*. The *Sonatas* for strings and clarini (and notably the *Peasants' Churchgoing*) show lyrical effects as well as dramatic ones. The performances have great character – Nikolaus Harnoncourt was always good at explosive accents – and are very well recorded. The *Requiem* has since been recorded with even greater success. The present version tends to lack some consistency of musical purpose, but still has fine moments. The two *Cantatas* contain music that is both beautiful and striking and are well sung, and the sound is excellent.

Battaglia; (Lute) Passacaglia in C min.; Partita VII for 2 Viole d'amore & Continuo; Violin Sonata (Solo representativa) with Continuo
**(*) Teldec 3984 21464-2. Il Giardino Armonico (with ZELENKA: *Fanfare; anon.: Tune for the Woodlark*; ONOFRI: *Ricercare for Viola da gamba & Lute*) – LOCKE: *The Tempest* **(*)

The most impressive work here is the *Partita for Two Viole d'amore and Continuo*, a powerful piece concluding with a very fine *Arietta variata* which is in essence a chaconne. It is very well played indeed. So too is the *Solo Violin Sonata representativa*, a much lighter piece whose main interest is an ingenious series of bird and animal imitations: nightingale, cuckoo, cock and hen, and even a miaowing cat. If the lute *Passacaglia* is rather pale, the familiar *Battle* sequence is just the opposite and suits the generally rather aggressive period-instrument style, which also affects the coupled music by Matthew Locke. Rather bitty, anyway.

Battaglia à 10; (i) Requiem à 15 in A
*** Alia Vox AV 9825. (i) Soloists; La Capella Reial de Catalunya, Concert de Nations, Savall

Jordi Savall's *Battaglia* opens with a dance-like vigour and has more musical light and shade. The closing *Lament* is gently touching. The *Requiem* is recorded – like the *Missa Bruxellensis* below – in Salzburg Cathedral, which was its original setting. It opens with a most imposing *Marcia funèbre*, a fully scored instrumental version of the *Sanctus*, which accompanied the solemn processional entry into the cathedral before the *Mass* received its (probable) first performance in 1687. This immediately demonstrates the wide reverberation of the cathedral acoustic, which Savall accommodates in a spacious performance that moves forward strongly – in every way a superbly eloquent account with splendid soloists. The elaborate and sumptuous documentation even includes a reproduction of the cathedral interior showing where the various vocal *soli in concerto*, the antiphonal brass and the string group were placed for the recording. The overall balance is amazingly successful, the separation is natural, but all is bathed in the richly resonant cathedral ambience. This is a magnificent disc in every way and almost certainly first choice for the *Requiem*, although other fine versions are mentioned below.

(12 Sonatae) Fidicinium sacro-profanum; Balletti lamentabili; (i) Passacaglia for Solo Violin; (ii-iii) Laetatus sum; (iii) Nisi Dominus; (ii) Serenada (der Nachtwächer)

*** Chan. 0605 (2). (i) Mackintosh; (ii) Harvey; (iii)
   Wistreich; Augmented Purcell Qt

The *Fidicinium sacro-profanum* (1682) are characteristically inventive works, varying between three and eight linked sections of considerable variety (rhythmic as well as melodic) and interest, very much the precursor of the concerto grosso. They are presented here with great freshness and give consistent pleasure. To add contrast, the Purcell Quartet intersperse them with other key works: the solo *Nisi Dominus* (Richard Wistreich in excellent form) and the dramatic duet setting of *Laetatus sum*, which is equally stimulating. Later, Peter Harvey returns as the Nightwatchman, singing against a winning pizzicato accompaniment. The famous *Battle* evocation is as impressive here as in any competing version. The second disc opens with the *Balletti lamentabili*, in which a haunting *Sonata* and a delicate closing *Lamenti* frame an *Allemande*, *Sarabande*, *Gavotte* and *Gigue*, all of which, for all their dance rhythms, maintain a mood of gentle melancholy. The programme ends with Biber's masterly *Passacaglia for Solo Violin*, which undoubtedly anticipates Bach's unaccompanied violin music. It is played superbly by Catherine Mackintosh. A splendid set, among the Purcell Quartet's finest achievements. The recording is very real indeed.

Harmonia artificiosa-ariosa (7 Partitas), 1–3 & 5 for 2 Scordatura Violins & Continuo; 4 for Scordatura Violin, Viola di braccio & Continuo; 6 for 2 Violins & Continuo; 7 for 2 Violas d'amore & Continuo (complete)

*** Astrée E 8572. Rare Fruits Council
(M) *** Chan. 0575/6. Purcell Qt, with Wallfisch

These complete recordings of Biber's masterly *Harmonia artificiosa-ariosa* show us the amazing range of these seven partitas (or suites) which were published posthumously in 1712. In many ways the two sets of performances are alike, and they certainly share the spontaneity and scholarship of the very best period-instrument performances. Tempi are usually similar, although the Purcell Quartet tend to bring a slightly more spacious *espressivo* to slower movements. Their extra weight (with use of organ continuo) is especially telling in the passacaglias. The curiously named Rare Fruits Council also play with great energy and virtuosity and, again, effectively use an organ to add colour and weight to the texture. They are balanced rather forwardly, which reduces the dynamic range somewhat, but some of the solo passages have striking delicacy, and the chaconne-like variations of the closing *Seventh Partita* are very powerfully integrated. In short, you cannot go wrong with either of these recordings. We have listed the Rare Fruits Council first, as Auvidis manage to squeeze all seven partitas on to a single CD. Chandos have been forced to use a pair, playing for 43 minutes and 47

minutes respectively. But the cost has been reduced accordingly to upper-mid-price.

Harmonia artificiosa-ariosa: Partitas III & V. Rosenkranz Sonata 10; Passacaglia 16 for Solo Violin; Sonata VI; Sonata representativa (for violin & continuo)

*** BIS CD 608. Lindal, Ens. Saga

Biber's melancholy *Passacaglia* for solo violin is totally memorable. But the hit of the programme is the *Sonata representativa* with its bird evocations – they are more than just imitations – including the nightingale, thrush, cuckoo (a most striking approach) and cockerel. Maria Lindal is a splendid soloist and the style of the playing here is vibrantly authentic: the ear quickly adjusts to the plangent (but in no way anaemic) timbres which suit this repertoire admirably.

Mensa sonora (Instrumental Taffel-Music) (Parts 1–6); (i) Sonatina violino representativa

(N) (M) **(*) DG 477 5001. Mus. Ant. Köln, Goebel, (i) solo
   violin

Completed in 1680, the six chamber sonatas which make up Biber's *Mensa sonora* were subtitled 'Instrumental table-music with fresh-sounding violins'. Each has the usual mixture of baroque movements, including Allamanda, Courante, Sarabanda and Gigue, and sometimes a Balletto or Ciacona. They are lightweight but inventive and are readily appealing, and the performances are spirited. However, the snag is the buzzy abrasiveness of the closely observed string timbre which will not be to all tastes. If in the sonatas Biber anticipates Telemann, in the remarkable programatic *Sonatina violino representativa* he also foreshadows Vivaldi. He titillates his audience with extraordinary miniature portraits, including the nightingale and cuckoo, a squawking frog, a cock and hen, quail, and not least a miaowing cat. Reinhard Goebel plays with splendid panache, and here the astringent solo timbre serves to add to the cartoon-like characterizations.

Mystery (Rosenkranz) Violin Sonatas (complete)

(N) *** HM HMU 907321.22 (2). Manze, Egarr (with
   McGillivray in Sonata XII)
⊕━ ✹ (BB) *** Virgin 5 62062-2 (2). Holloway, Moroney,
   Tragicomedia
(N) *** ASV Gaudeamus CDGAU 350 (1–9); CDGAU 351
   (10–16). Huggett, Sonnerie
(B) **(*) Signum SIGCD 021 (2). Reiter, Concordia

Mystery (Rosenkranz) Violin Sonatas (complete; with (i) readings from the Rosemary Psalters)

**(*) Avie AV 0038 (2). Pavlo Beznosiuk, Roblo, Chateauneuf,
   Tunnicliffe; (i) Timothy West (reader)

Biber's emergence as one of the great composers of the seventeenth century is more than ever borne out by his set of *Mystery* (or *Rosary*) *Sonatas* for violin and continuo, which is surely his instrumental masterpiece, and which tells the Christian story in instrumental terms. There are 15 Sonatas divided into three groups: *The Five Joyful Mysteries* (The Annunciation; Visitation; Nativity; Presentation of the Infant Jesus; and the Twelve-year-old Jesus in the Temple); *The Five Sorrowful Mysteries* (Christ on the Mount of Olives; the Scourging at the Pillar; Crowning with Thorns; Carrying of the Cross; and the Crucifixion) and *The Five Glorious Mysteries* (The Resurrection; Asension; Descent of the Holy Ghost; Assumption of the Virgin; and Coronation of the Virgin). The work ends with an expressively powerful extended slow

Passacaglia which becomes steadily more complex.

Each of the *Sonatas* has an introductory *Prelude* followed by variations and dance movements. The programmatic element, where it appears, is usually limited to the opening section, as in the very first *Sonata*, where the soloist represents the Annunciation with a flourishing bravura passage, or in the touching *Lamento* which opens No. VI, or the powerful hammering of the nails in Sonata No. X (The Crucifixion). That effect is accentuated by the use of scordatura, where the solo violin's strings are retuned, affecting the instrument's sonority. The solo writing is immensely demanding and John Holloway's strong instrumental personality is very telling. David Moroney (chamber organ or harpsichord) and Tragicomedia provide an imaginative continuo, using viola da gamba, lute, harp and a regal for the Crowning with Thorns. The recording gives a most vivid presence to the soloist.

Needless to say, Andrew Manze's playing is of the highest quality. He is a master of this repertoire, and his timbre is strikingly full, his lyrical phrasing highly responsive, his use of scordatura has plenty of edge, and his supreme virtuosity is ever apparent, without exaggeration. In the extensive notes he suggests that to over-dramatize the work's programmatic details (i.e. the hammering of nails) is not what the composer intended, that Biber's descriptive intention is at a 'deeper symbolic level'. He also opts for a comparatively simple backcloth for the solo violin. He could not have chosen a more distinguished accompanist than Richard Egarr, who provides a chamber organ continuo in nine of the sonatas, and uses a harpsichord in the remaining three. Alison McGillivray (cello) joins them in Sonata XII (*The Ascension*) to lead the way up to heaven and add to the sonority. The effect here is less dramatic than in the Virgin set, much plainer than in the Gaudeamus, but even more emotionally telling in its relatively austere presentation. This is especially striking in the sequence covered by Sonatas VI–IX, while *The Crucifixion and Death of Jesus* (Sonata X) forms the emotional climax of the performance of Part I, and his restrained and dedicated account of the final *Passacaglia* makes a very moving apotheosis at the close of Part II. The recording is finely balanced, and this set is made the more attractive not only by its lavish packaging and the separate cueing of individual movements throughout, but also by an appendix, including Andrew Manze's spoken explanation of what scordatura means, with plenty of examples.

Monica Huggett is also very persuasive in these wonderful sonatas and, besides vigorous bravura and characteristic sensitivity, she brings a sense of fantasy to her solo playing which is particularly appealing. Moreover, the sounds made by Sonnerie are aurally captivating, with Mathew Hall's organ continuo adding a rich background of colour to underpin the rest of the continuo. This is attractively varied from sonata to sonata, including theorbo, harp, viola da gamba, harpsichord, guitar, achlute and lirone in various combinations. The recording balance is close, but the overall effect is most vivid within a pleasing acoustic. One drawback, however, is that there are only 12 separating bands, one for each sonata, with no cues for individual movements. However, this is makes a genuine alternative to the Harmonia Mundi set.

The Concordia version on Signum is rather more intimate and less flamboyant, although Walter Reiter is obviously deeply involved in the music, and this too is a fine performance. Although the Virgin set has a great price advantage, Andrew Manze's performance must take pride of place.

The Avie performace is equally fine, if not even finer, and is beautifully recorded in an ideal acoustic. However, it is introduced by and interwoven with a spoken narration by Timothy West of the entire Christian story and, while the narrative is presented with pleasing simplicity and is separately cued, one would not imagine that listeners would want to repeat it at every performance (except, perhaps, as an act of devotion). One can, of course, programme the player to play the music only (the booklet identifies all the musical cues), but that means setting up the CD player especially, and not every listener will want to take the trouble to do this. We hope therefore that Avie will consider a separate issue of the music alone, which could well be a first choice.

12 Sonatae tam Aris, quam Aulis servientes

*** Astrée E 8630. Rare Fruits Council, Karemer

*** Chan. 0591. Bennett, Laird, McGillivray, Cronin, Purcell Qt

(N) **(*) Chall. CC 72129. Amsterdam Combattimento Consort, De Vriend

(BB) ** Hyp. Helios CDH 55041. Parley of Instruments, Goodman, Holman

Biber's *Sonatae tam Aris, quam Aulis servientes* are among his most immediately attractive works, their direct appeal comparable with the Bach *Brandenburgs*. They combine appealing expressive elements and great rhythmic vitality. The robustly extrovert new recording from the Rare Fruits Council is full of character, vividly colourful and alive. In about half the *Sonatas* (Nos. 1, 4, 7, 10 and 12) the authentic string group of seven players plus continuo is joined by one or two trumpets, and here the effect is quite spectacular. The works for strings alone, however, are splendidly full-bodied and colourful (helped by the liberal use of organ in the continuo). The energy and expressive vigour of the music-making here bubbles over. Highly recommended.

The Chandos complete set from the augmented Purcell Quartet is also excellent in every way, full of life and imaginative detail. The sound is first class, but the Rare Fruits Council remains first choice.

The Amsterdam account too is both lively and authentic, with some very good trumpet playing. Although the character is of a chamber performance, with contrasts not as dramatic as in the Astrée version, the rhythmic jollity is still persuasive, and the recording, made in the Hilversum Radio studio, is well balanced and vivid.

Indeed, by their side the much more intimate performances from the Parley of Instruments, sympathetically played though they are, sound rather pale. This Helios reissue is inexpensive, but the Auvidis Astrée disc is well worth the extra money.

Unam Ceylum: Violin Sonatas 3, 4, 6, 7; in A & in E (unpublished)

(N) *** ECM 472 084-2. Holloway, Assenbaum, Mortensen

John Holloway has already proved himself another master of this repertoire with his dramatic account of the *Rosary Sonatas*. His bold, extrovert approach and ready bravura are especially suited to these works of 1681 which, he tells us, 'are a complete compendium of Biber's then playing technique' (on a shorter fingerboard than today's instruments) including of course (in *Sonatas 4* and *6*) scordatura. Biber is presented here as the Paganini of his time. The writing, always entertaining, is both dazzling and tuneful and includes, besides the occasional *Gigue* and *Gavotte*, plenty of examples of his inventive writing in variation, passacaglia and chaconne styles. John Holloway presents the sonatas with great panache and obvious pleaure in their technical intricacies, while the continuo is admirably realized by Aloysia Assenbaum (organ) and Lars Mortensen (harpsichord). The recording is truthful – forwardly balanced in a warm acoustic.

8 Violin Sonatas (for violin & continuo) (1681); **Sonata pastorella; Sonata representativa in A** (for solo violin); **Passacaglia for Solo Violin; Passacaglia for Lute**
*** HM HMX 2907344/45 (2). Romanesca (Manze, North, Toll)

These phenomenally difficult *Sonatas*, with their high tessitura and bizarre effects, can be played only by a violinist of remarkable technical gifts. Such is Andrew Manze. He conveys to the full the tension that always springs from strong performances of technically demanding music, yet at the same time he retains an essentially expressive style, also featuring the improvisatory feeling in the writing, to say nothing of its sublimely volatile unpredictability. The recording has a fine, spacious acoustic, and only those who find the abrasiveness of authentic fiddling aurally difficult should stay away from this highly stimulating pair of discs.

Violin Sonatas 2, 3, 5, 7 (1681); **Passacaglia for Solo Violin;** (i) **Nisi Dominus for Violin, Bass Voice & Continuo**
*** Gaudeamus CDGAU 203. Huggett, Sonnerie; (i) with Guthrie

Monica Huggett's period-instrument timbre and style of attack are no less gutsy and vibrant than those of Andrew Manze, with plenty of vibrant edge on the phrasing. But this is superbly alive playing and the unaccompanied solo flourishes of the *Second Sonata in D minor* surely anticipate Bach, as the unaccompanied *Passacaglia* reminds one initially of his famous *Chaconne*. But it comprises 65 repetitions of the ground – G, F, E flat, D – and some might feel that – for all Monica Huggett's skill – it outlasts its welcome; others may find it hypnotic. The Psalm setting, so resonantly, dramatically and touchingly sung by Thomas Guthrie, recalls Monteverdi. Here the violin figurations are clearly as important as the vocal line, and the continuo, using organ as well as theorbo, gives fine support. Excellent, vividly forward recording.

Violin Sonatas (with continuo, 1681), **3–4; 6–8; 81 in A; 84 in E** (unpublished)
*** ECM 472 084-2. Holloway, Assenbaum, Mortensen

Composed two years before the *Mystery Sonatas*, this 1681 set of *Sonatas* with continuo (chamber organ or harpsichord) is, to quote John Holloway, 'a complete compendium' of the composer's dazzling playing technique. 'All the possibilities for double-stopping and three- and four-note chord playing are there, including contrapuntal writing in two and three voices.' Two sonatas (Nos. 4 and 6) use scordatura re-tuning of the strings (which Holloway plays on a different violin), but the most striking aspect of these works is their variety of invention, plus a most appealing lyricism which balances the great bravura of the extended flourishes. There are fine Passacaglias in both *Sonata No. 6* and the unpublished *E major Sonata*, the latter being preceded by a dazzling fantasia-like introduction. Holloway's performances have great flair. He creates a beautiful timbre on his Hoog copy of a 1649 Amati violin, and he obviously revels in the music's ready fund of melody. The continuo backing is very supportive and ideally balanced and recorded. This is not just a historical

curiosity: it provides a most stimulating and enjoyable listening experience.

VOCAL MUSIC

Missa Alleluia
(BB) **(*) DHM 05472 77856-2. Soloists, Gradus ad Parnassum, Junghänel – SCHMELZER: *Sonata and Vespers* **(*)

The *Missa Alleluia* of 1698 anticipates the spectacle of the *Missa Bruxellensis*, demanding eight soloists and a double chorus, plus two cornets, six trumpets, three trombones, timpani and continuo. Konrad Junghänel uses Schmelzer's *Sonata per chiesa* for Brass, Strings and Organ as a sonorous opening prelude and intersperses the Propers appropriate for church dedication (which are beautifully sung). With excellent soloists, it is an impressive performance, spaciously recorded, although the wide reverberation takes some of the brightness from the sound. However, this reissue is very recommendable at its modest cost.

Mass in B flat a 6; Requiem in F min.
(N) *** DG 474 7172. Hemington, Holton, Auchinloss, Grant, Pott, Gabrieli Consort & Players, McCreesh (with MUFFAT: *Ciacona*; SCHMELZER: *Sonatas II & XIII*; MEGERLE: *Peccator et consolator a 2*; ANON.: *Praeludium; Praeludium legatura*; LASSUS: *Ave verum corpus a 6; Media vita in morte sumus a 6*)

Paul McCreesh offers a chance to enjoy and compare the relatively small-scale *Mass for Six Voices and Continuo* with the more familiar and more spectacular *F minor Requiem* which was probably written for performance in Salzburg Cathedral and which is here performed with a string ensemble and the chorus reinforced with trombones in the generous acoustic of Tonbridge School Chapel in Kent. Biber's *Mass* setting is here introduced by a *Ciacona* by Muffat and interspersed with other contemporary music to form a quasi-litigical sequence in which the *Ave verum* and (closing) *Media vita* of Lassus stand out for their serene beauty. Characteristically McCreesh directs the proceedings with great vitality: the *Gloria* and *Credo* of the *Mass*, sung with resplendent vigour, really move along, and the *Requiem* too is never left to languish. The choral singing is splendid, and the Gabrieli Consort and brass players add a fine backing sonority. One of the highlights of the recording is the *Offertory* in the *Mass*, a setting of *Peccator et consolator* for two soprano voices, beautifully sung by Susan Hemmington and Ruth Holton, in which the second voice is placed distantly to achieve an echo effect. If you acquire this superbly recorded disc, this is the excerpt you will be playing to your friends as an unforgettable sampler.

Missa Bruxellensis
⊕⌐ ✺ *** Ala Vox AV 9808. Soloists, La Capella Reial de Catalunya, Concert des Nations, Savall

This gloriously festive *Missa Bruxellensis* – a late (perhaps final) work, dating from 1700 – is scored for two eight-voice choirs, groups of wind, strings, trumpets, horns and trombones, and a bass continuo of organs and bassoons. The disposition of the soloists, choristers and instruments in the stalls, around the transept and in the cathedral choir was designed to add to the sense of spectacle, and the music is fully worthy of its ambitious layout. Its imaginative diversity, with continual contrasts between tutti and soli of great expressive power, shows the composer working at full stretch. The *Kyrie* opens in great splendour with the two antiphonal choirs and festive trumpets (*cornets à bouquin*). The closing *Agnus Dei* has the soloists singing radiantly but with piercing dissonance from Biber's extraordinary sustained suspensions, with the full forces then entering for the closing *Amen*. The performance here, superlatively recorded in the echoing – but never blurring – acoustics of Salzburg Cathedral, re-creates the work's première and is truly inspired. This marvellous disc cannot be recommended too highly.

Missa Salisburgensis

*** DG **SACD** 471 632-2; CD 457 611-2. Gabrieli Cons. & Players, Col. Mus. Ant., McCreesh; Goebel

**(*) Erato 3984 25506-2. Soloists, Amsterdam Bar. Ch. & O, Koopman

Paul McCreesh in partnership with Reinhard Goebel turns to one of the grandest of all ecclesiastical events, when in Salzburg Cathedral in 1682 they celebrated the 1,100th anniversary of Salzburg as a centre of Christianity. Though the score survived, there is no specific mention of the composer – all was created for the glory of God alone – but shrewd detective work, described in the note, clearly points to Heinrich von Biber, who was soon to be appointed Kapellmeister to the archbishop. The blaze of sound on the disc is magnificent, with widely spaced antiphonal groups, choirs and instrumentalists, thrillingly capturing massive contrasts of sound, especially in the surround-sound SACD format.

Koopman's version of Biber's spectacular score has the obvious merit of being recorded in its original venue, Salzburg Cathedral. But the long reverberation period tends to blur the choral clarity, and it also affects the brilliance of the trumpets. Koopman's spacious approach must also have been dictated by the problems of resonance and, fine though his account is, it cannot match the superb DG version.

Requiem à 15 in A (see also under *Battaglia à 10*)

(M) *** DHM/BMG 82876 60149-2. Alamanjo, Van der Sluis, Elwes, Padmore, Huijts, Van der Kamp, Netherlands Bach Festival Ch. & O, Leonhardt – STEFFANI: *Stabat Mater* ***

Leonhardt's account of Biber's *A major Requiem* is very fine indeed. There is no lack of aural spectacle, but the acoustic of Pieterskerk, Utrecht, is ideally free from excessive resonance so that the results are particularly fresh, with remarkably clear detail, yet there is the right warmth of ambience and bloom on the excellent soloists, choir and orchestra alike. The performance has plenty of vitality and, for those interested in having a beautiful setting of the *Stabat Mater* by Biber's contemporary, Agostino Steffani, this is an excellent mid-priced recommendation.

Requiem in F min.; In festo trium regium muttetum Natale (Epiphany cantata); Laetatus sum à 7 (cantata)

(BB) **(*) DHM 05472 77842-2. Piau, Van der Sluis, Lettinga, Elwes, Van der Kamp, Netherlands Bach Fest. Bar. O, Leonhardt – VALS: *Missa Scala Aretina* **(*)

Requiem in F min.; Offertories: Huc Poenitentes; Lux perpetua; Ne cedite mentes; Quo abiit dilectus

**(*) Ambroisie AMB 9936. Arsys Bourgogne, Cao

If you want just the *F minor Requiem*, Leonhardt's performance is a fine one and he has good soloists. He is committed

and his reading has genuine spontaneity and fervour; moreover he is richly recorded.

The Arsys Choir of Burundy give a fine, dedicated performance of the *F minor Requiem*, beautifully recorded; the end effect is warm if very slightly bland. The great interest of this disc lies in the first recording of the four beautiful offertories, again very well sung, although the excellent soloists from the choir are not individually distinctive. *Quo abiit dilectus* stands alone in its restrained accompaniment for viols, but the closing *Lux perpetua* for double choir and brass is the most sonorously spectacular.

BINCHOIS, Gilles (*c.* 1400–60)

Agnus Dei; Kyrie; Sanctus. Domitor Hectoris; Nove cantum melodie

(N) *** Hyp. CDA 67474. Binchois Consort, Kirkman – DUFAY (attrib.): *Mass for St Anthony Abbot* ***

Gilles Binchois, the close contemporary of Dufay, matched him in mastery, even though he wrote far less within a shorter career. These five superb examples of his work demonstrate the range and variety of his choral writing, making an excellent and illuminating coupling for the fine *Mass for St Anthony Abbot* attributed to Dufay. If *Domitor Hectoris* represents a smooth style of polyphony, with the three voices forming various duo combinations, the other motet, written in 1431 to celebrate the baptism of the new heir to the duchy of Burgundy, *Novum cantum melodie*, is wonderfully elaborate and celebratory, a magnificent piece. The three *Mass* movements, compact as they are, bring refreshing variety of expression in a lyrical style. The Binchois Consort under Andrew Kirkman give dedicated performances, very well recorded, and the disc benefits from scholarly notes by Philip Weller, helpful not just for the specialist but for the newcomer.

BIRTWISTLE, Harrison (born 1934)

Carmen Arcadiae mechanicae perpetuum; Secret Theatre; Silbury Air

*** Etcetera KTC 1052. L. Sinf., Howarth

Silbury Air is one of Birtwistle's 'musical landscapes', bringing ever-changing views and perspectives on the musical material and an increasing drawing-out of melody. With melody discarded, *Carmen Arcadiae mechanicae perpetuum* (*The Perpetual Song of Mechanical Arcady*) superimposes different musical mechanisms to bring a rhythmic kaleidoscope of textures and patterns. The title of *Secret Theatre* is taken from a poem by Robert Graves which refers to 'an unforeseen and fiery entertainment', and there is no doubting the distinctive originality of the writing, utterly typical of the composer. Howarth and the Sinfonietta could hardly be more convincing advocates, recorded in vivid, immediate sound.

(i) Earth Dances; (ii) Endless Parade (for trumpet, vibraphone & strings); (iii) 5 Distances for 5 Instruments; (iv) Panic; (iii) Secret Theatre; Tragoedia; (iii; vi) 3 Settings of Celan for Soprano & 5 Instruments

(M) *** Decca 468 804-2 (2). (i) Cleveland O, Dohnányi; (ii) Hardenberger, BBC PO, Howarth; (iii) Ens. InterContemporain, Boulez; (iv) Harle, BBC SO, A. Davis; (vi) with Whittlesey

There is no more individual or intractable voice in British music today than Harrison Birtwistle. Pierre Boulez, who directs the majority of the items here, has been his champion for many years, and he delivers performances sharply focused and powerfully intense. It was *Tragoedia* which in 1965 alerted us to a formidable new voice in British music, conveying deep, dark emotions behind a brutal façade. It is not a tragedy in the conventional sense but a ritual in eight compact, tensely argued sections. *Secret Theatre* over a span of nearly half an hour presents another ritual, contrasting timbres and moods, dance and song, with the brutality tempered by overt lyricism. The close of the piece is hauntingly poetic, one of Birtwistle's most telling moments.

The five players in *Five Distances* are widely separated (an instruction not well conveyed in the otherwise excellent (originally DG) recording) and this shorter piece is comparably intense. The Celan settings are a poignant and eloquent tribute to a Romanian-Jewish poet who suffered severely in the Second World War. The soloist, Christine Whittlesey, manages its angular vocal lines with richly beautiful tone throughout.

Earth Dances is yet another slow-moving ritual, brilliantly written for the orchestra, here superbly played in Cleveland, while the piece for trumpet and orchestra moves the solo instrument through a kaleidoscopic processional of constantly changing aural images of great imaginative diversity. Its language is yet again far from easily assimilable, but both performances and the Philips recording are outstandingly fine. The most famous item here is *Panic*, performed at the Last Night of the Proms in September 1995, its seemingly interminable progress caused near panic among the audience, many of whom found it chaotic and completely incomprehensible. So does I. M. Neither he nor R. L. finds Birtwistle's music particularly rewarding: the enthusiasm expressed above belongs to E. G.

(i) *Earth Dances;* (ii) *Theseus Game*
(N) *** DG 477 0702. Ensemble Modern, cond. (i) Boulez; (ii) Brabbins; with Pierre-André Valade

Earth Dances, written in 1985/6, is one of Birtwistle's most powerful works, a half-hour span for full orchestra which, with six 'strata' combining and recombining, piled on one another, builds up inexorably. Brassy and with bold use of percussion, it has been fairly described a 'Rite of Spring for the 1980s', and here comes in a superb live recording under Pierre Boulez, a formidable rival for the pioneering Decca version from the Cleveland Orchestra under Dohnányi. The apt coupling is *Theseus Game*, recorded live at the first performance in 2003 at the Ruhr Triennale. This is another massive work of over half an hour, this time for two chamber ensembles working independently under two conductors. The classical image inspiring a ritual typical of the composer is that of the thread given to Theseus by Ariadne, which is here represented by a thread of melody carried on by a sequence of soloists, who emerge from each ensemble to perform centrestage. Inevitably, without visual help, a recording cannot match the dramatic effect of an event actually witnessed, but the power of the writing, often abrasive, comes over splendidly, and this can be warmly recommended to admirers of this unique and uncompromising composer. Sadly, only two tracks are provided, with no indication of different sections.

(i) *Gawain's Journey; The Triumph of Time;* (ii) *Ritual Fragment*
(N) *** NMC Do 88. (i) Philh. O; (ii) London Sinf.; Howarth

These superb recordings of *Gawain's Journey* and *The Triumph of Time* were originally issued on the Collins label. NMC here enterprisingly restores them to the catalogue with the bonus of *Ritual Fragment*, the piece which the composer wrote in 1989 as a memorial tribute to Michael Vyner, artistic director of the London Sinfonietta from 1972 until his death. Here Birtwistle gives important solos to ten players, starting with the trumpet and ending with the flute.

The Triumph of Time, inspired by the Brueghel engraving, presents the idea of Time as a remorseless destroyer. Typically of the mature Birtwistle, it is a grindingly slow and relentless processional, with Elgar Howarth bringing out the biting power of the piece, just as Pierre Boulez did in the original recording. It relates to the massive opera, *The Mask of Orpheus*; even more directly, *Gawain's Journey* recycles various sections of Birtwistle's next major opera, *Gawain*. The orchestral interlude from the beginning of Act II forms a centrepiece, framed by material from different sections, including the very opening and the close, making a weighty as well as a violent piece. Under Elgar Howarth the Philharmonia plays both pieces brilliantly, stunningly recorded.

Tragoedia
(N) (M) *** EMI (ADD) 586187-2 (2). Melos Ens., Foster –
   MAXWELL DAVIES: *Leopardi Fragments; Revelation and Fall*, etc. ***

Recorded in 1967, *Tragoedia* instantly established the Birtwistle sound, with its abrasive writing for woodwind. It is a work, less than 20 minutes long, which in its concentration makes clear that this is a major piece, one that provides a foretaste of Birtwistle's striking first opera, *Punch and Judy*. It also provides an early example of Birtwistle's devotion to ritual in his music, with sections balanced against each other after the example of Greek tragedy – hence the title. With the early works by his close contemporary, Peter Maxwell Davies, for coupling, this first CD transfer of the original recording could not be more welcome, superbly played and recorded.

VOCAL MUSIC

(i; iii) *Melencolia I;* (ii; iii) *Meridian;* (iii) *Ritual Fragment*
*** NMC CD 009. (i) Pay; (ii) King, Thompson, Van Kampen; L. Sinf. Voices; (iii) L. Sinf. (members); Knussen

The NMC Birtwistle disc has the London Sinfonietta under Oliver Knussen in three works revealing the composer at his most uncompromising. *Ritual Fragment* was inspired by the death of Michael Vyner, the dynamic and influential artistic director of London Sinfonietta. Just as dark and even more obsessive are the two longer works on the disc, *Melencolia I* and *Meridian*, the latter the grimmest of love-songs.

An Interrupted Endless Melody; Duets for Storab; Entr'actes & Fragments; 9 Settings of Niedecker; The Woman & the Hare
*** Black Box BBM 1046. McFadden, Watson, Nash Ens., Brabbins

Entitled 'The Woman and the Hare' after the most ambitious work on this disc, a setting of a text specially written by David Harsent, this collection of Birtwistle chamber works spans his whole career, from *The Entr'actes* and *Sappho Fragments* of 1962–4, his uncompromising style already established along with his love of a ritualistic structure, to the Harsent setting of 1999. Harsent was the librettist for Birtwistle's opera,

Gawain, but when his verses proved too long for the composer's purpose, he set the salient lines for soprano and interwove them with recitations of the rest, to striking effect. In response to the verses, the music evokes the wildness of nature and of man himself in a sequence of fragments that characteristically still holds firmly together, thanks also to the performers here, including the soprano Claron McFadden and the reciter, Julia Watson. The Niedecker settings were developed from what began as a tribute to Elliott Carter on his ninetieth birthday, again built on brief evocative images, while the *Duets for Storab* (1983) take their inspiration from a legendary Neolithic king and comprise duets for two unaccompanied flutes with echoes of Stravinsky. *An Interrupted Endless Melody* was written in 1991–4 in memory of the oboist, Janet Craxton, with a single melody varied by strongly contrasted accompaniments on the piano. A fascinating collection, vividly recorded.

Pulse Shadows

*** Teldec 3984 268672-2. McFadden, Arditti Qt, Nash Ens., De Leeuw

This sequence of laments, inspired by the cryptic verses of the poet, Paul Celan, is one of the most moving of Birtwistle's later works. In it he interleaves two works that had a separate genesis – his nine settings of Celan and the nine pieces for string quartet – making a two-tier sequence of over an hour which, among much else, enshrines the composer's response to the Holocaust. In this version the English translations of Paul Hamburger are used for all the poems except one, *Todtnauberg*, which is recited in English while the song is sung in German. Whatever the influences, Birtwistle's writing is totally distinctive, not just in his response to the strangely allusive poems of Celan, but in his equally cryptic writing for string quartet in the intervening pieces. The eighteen sections, most of them brief, far from seeming fragmentary, hang together in a kaleidoscope of sharp inspiration, superbly realized here by all the performers, not least the soprano, Claron McFadden, totally unfazed by the cragginess of the writing and helped by the vividly immediate sound.

Secret Theatre; Ritual Fragment; (i) Nenia: The Death of Orpheus

(B) *** CPO 999 360-2. (i) Hardy; Musikfabrik NRW, Kalitzke

It is fascinating to compare this German reading of Birtwistle's impressive *Secret Theatre* with Boulez's on DG. The playing of Musikfabrik may not seem so powerful, partly because of a less forward recording, but the concentration builds up with comparable intensity, and the final climax is, if anything, even more uninhibited. *Nenia: The Death of Orpheus*, the earliest work here, is an elegiac piece in which the soloist's vocalizing is punctuated by percussive singspeech, an early example of the composer's obsession with the Orpheus legend which culminated in the large-scale opera, *The Mask of Orpheus*. *Ritual Fragment*, dating from 1990, is not just dark and intense but at times angry, demonstrating that, for all the brutality of expression, Birtwistle's emotions are fundamental.

OPERA

The Mask of Orpheus (complete)

(M) *** NMC D 050 (3). Garrison, Bronder, Rigby, Owens, Opie, Ebrahim, BBC Singers & O, A. Davis

Birtwistle's *The Mask of Orpheus* is one of the most challenging operas ever written. The telling and retelling of the Orpheus legend, with one version superimposed on another and with the music reflecting that, makes it hard to take in for the listener who is unprepared. Even so, one cannot miss the magnetic intensity of Birtwistle's score. Act I is broadly based on the death of Eurydice, poisoned by a snake; Act II follows Orpheus in his progress through the Underworld over 17 arches; and Act III, with its structure echoing the movement of the tide on a beach, rounds off the epic scheme, ending in Orpheus's death at the hands of the Dionysiac women, and the final fading of the myth.

With Andrew Davis controlling his massed forces masterfully, helped by Martyn Brabbins as assistant conductor, the intense originality of a score dotted with havens of sheer beauty is never in doubt. Central to its success is the thrilling performance of the American tenor, Jon Garrison, as Orpheus the man, well supported by Peter Bronder as Orpheus the myth. Jean Rigby and Anne-Marie Owens, less prominent in the story, similarly take on the divided and superimposed role of the heroine, Eurydice woman and myth. The recorded sound is superb, vivid in conveying the different musical layers, electronic as well as instrumental and vocal. The documentation is very full. It is good that NMC have issued this important set as 'three discs for the price of two'.

Punch and Judy (opera; complete)

*** Etcetera KTC 2014 (2). Roberts, DeGaetani, Bryn-Julson, Langridge, Wilson-Johnson, Tomlinson, L. Sinf., Atherton

Punch and Judy is a brutal, ritualistic piece. It may not make easy listening, but nor is it easy to forget: behind the aggressiveness, Birtwistle's writing has a way of touching an emotional chord, just as Stravinsky's so often does. Stephen Roberts is outstanding as Punch, and among the others there is not a single weak link. David Atherton, conductor from the first performances, excels himself. The clear, vivid recording, originally made by Decca for their enterprising LP Headline series, has been licensed by Etcetera.

BIZET, Georges (1838–75)

L'Arlésienne (complete incidental music; ed. Riffauld)

*** EMI 7 47460-2. Orféon Donostiarra, Toulouse, Capitole O, Plasson

The score of the complete incidental music that Michel Plasson and his excellent French forces have recorded is based on the 1872 autograph, and the singing of the Orféon Donostiarra is as excellent as the orchestral playing. The less familiar music is every bit as captivating as the suites, so that the performance has great charm, and the EMI recording is very good indeed. Strongly recommended.

L'Arlésienne: Suite 1; Suite 2: Farandole (only)

*** Sony (ADD) **SACD** SS 89414. Cleveland O, Szell – GRIEG: *Peer Gynt Suite 1;* MUSSORGSKY: *Pictures; Khovanshchina: Prelude* ***

Szell's 1966 recording was highly praised by us in its LP format for its beautifully refined playing and warmth from the Cleveland Orchestra under Szell. The remastering for SACD has added body to the sound while retaining the vividness, and the couplings are equally successful.

L'Arlésienne: Suites 1–2; Jeux d'enfants
*** Decca Australia Eloquence (ADD) 460 505-2. Cleveland O, Maazel – FRANCK: *Symphony ***

L'Arlésienne: Suites 1–2; Patrie Overture, Op. 19; Symphony in C
(**(*)) Testament mono SBT 1235. Fr. Nat. R. O, Cluytens

(i) *L'Arlésienne: Suites 1–2; (ii) Symphony in C*
(M) *** EMI (ADD) 5 67231-2 [567259]. (i) RPO; (ii) Fr. Nat. R. O; Beecham
(B) **(*) EMI Red Line CDR5 69881. ASMF, Marriner

L'Arlésienne: Suites 1–2; Carmen: Suite 1
(M) *** DG (ADD) (IMS) 423 472-2. LSO, Abbado

L'Arlésienne: Suites 1–2; Carmen: Suites 1–2
☛ (M) *** Decca 466 421-2. Montreal SO, Dutoit

L'Arlésienne Suites 1–2; Carmen: Extended Suite; Jeux d'enfants
(N) (M) ** DG Entrée 471 736-2. O de la Bastille, Chung

L'Arlésienne: Suites 1 & 2; Carmen: Suites 1 & 2; Ouverture: Patrie (Ouverture dramatique); Scènes bohémiennes; Symphony in C
(B) **(*) Double Decca 475 190-2 (2). Montreal SO, Dutoit

L'Arlésienne: Suites Nos. 1 & 2; Carmen Symphony (arr. Serebrier)
** BIS CD 1305. Barcelona SO and Nat. O of Catalonia, Serebrier

With playing that is both elegant and vivid, and with superb, demonstration-worthy sound, Dutoit's polished yet affectionate coupling of the *L'Arlésienne* and *Carmen* suites makes a clear first choice.

Beecham's famous Bizet coupling now rightly reappears as one of EMI's 'Great Recordings of the Century'. His magical touch is especially illuminating in the two *L'Arlésienne* suites, and the early (1956) stereo gives the RPO woodwind striking luminosity yet plenty of body. The *Symphony* too sounds freshly minted. Although the playing here has slightly less finesse, its zest is in no doubt, especially in the finale, and the oboe soloist in the slow movement distinguishes himself.

Among other analogue couplings of the *L'Arlésienne* and *Carmen* suites, Abbado's 1981 DG recording also stands out. The orchestral playing is characteristically refined, the wind solos cultured and eloquent, especially in *L'Arlésienne*, where the pacing of the music is nicely judged.

Maazel chooses fast tempi in the *L'Arlésienne* suites, though not so fast that it sounds rushed, while the *Jeux d'enfants* is a delight, with some really delicate pianissimo playing from the Cleveland Orchestra. Unfortunately the coupling is not so outstanding (though still acceptable). Although Beecham and Dutoit are in a class of their own in *L'Arlésienne*, this Australian disc will surely appeal to audiophiles.

In French music there is a lot to be said for the special Gallic sonority the national Radio Orchestra produces. André Cluytens's 1953 account of the *Symphony in C* with this orchestra was the first on LP. It is an eminently stylish account and has a refreshingly unaffected quality about it. The finale is completely unforced, with great lightness of touch and clarity of articulation. The same goes for the *L'Arlésienne* suites, also from 1953. Very good mono sound and a worthwhile addition to the Bizet discography.

Marriner's EMI account of Bizet's *Symphony*, which is generous with repeats in the outer movements, does not quite

re-create the sparkling lightness of touch of his earlier Argo (Decca) version. In the first movement there is plenty of energy, but not the same sense of complete spontaneity. But it is still very enjoyable, and the two *L'Arlésienne* suites are beautifully played, the *Adagietto* given a gossamer delicacy. The Abbey Road recording is first class.

From Dutoit an enjoyable and comprehensive collection of Bizet's most popular orchestral works, and some rarer items. In the *Carmen* and *L'Arlésienne Suites*, the playing is elegant and vivid, with superb, demonstration-worthy sound. This *Montreal Collection* is a top recommendation in its original, single-disc format. However, the second CD, recorded later, which includes the *Symphony*, *Scènes bohémiennes* and the overtures, is not quite so successful. The playing is of good quality, animated and spirited, but the music-making does not possess the charm and sparkle which the best performances (Beecham and Martinon, for example) bring to this repertoire. This music-making is still enjoyable, nevertheless, especially as Decca provide such good sound throughout; but it is a pity that the first CD was not reissued independently.

Myung-Whun Chung's 1991 collection is a disappointment. The playing of the Bastille orchestra is polished but in no way distinctive, and the players are not helped by being set back in a very resonant acoustic which clouds detail and almost blunts Bizet's vivid scoring.

Unlike Sir Thomas Beecham, the conductor and composer José Serebrier has apparently long been dissatisfied with the conventional orchestral suites drawn from Bizet's *Carmen*, not just on points of orchestration but on the random order of the movements selected. Somewhat self-consciously, his alternative has been to devise a sequence of orchestral movements that broadly follow the development of the plot – though, finding the final death scene inappropriate for orchestral transcription, he has used Carmen's 'Gypsy Dance' instead, from the opening of Act II. So, to take one example, following the opening *Prélude*, we have a movement called 'The Cavalry', the mustering scene without the chorus of children.

Carmen: Suite 1; Suite 2 (excerpts)
(BB) *** Regis 1137. LSO, Frühbeck de Burgos (with collection: 'Grand Opera Choruses' L. Symphony Ch.; LSO, Hickox ***)

Frühbeck de Burgos offers the six favourite items and has the advantage of budget price and full, modern, digital recording, made in Watford Town Hall. The LSO playing is bright-eyed and polished, and this remains good value for those attracted to the coupling, an outstanding collection of operatic choruses (and not just from *Carmen*).

Jeux d'enfants (Children's games), Op. 22
(*) BBC (ADD) BBCL 4039-2. Philh. O, Boult – RAVEL: *Daphnis et Chloé: Suite 2*; SCHUBERT: *Symphony 8 (Unfinished)*; SIBELIUS: *Symphony 7 *(*)
(N) (M) (**) DG mono 474 987-2. LOP, Markevitch – BERLIOZ: *Symphonie fantastique ***

Was Sir Adrian stepping in for Giulini on this occasion (a Prom from 1964), for *Jeux d'enfants*, the *Unfinished Symphony* and Ravel's *Daphnis* were very much Giulini repertoire? In any event the Bizet is performed with the elegance, sparkle and tenderness one associates with the younger, Italian maestro. Marvellous playing from the Philharmonia and a good BBC recording which lacks only the last degree of range and sparkle.

An attractive, neatly performed account of Bizet's enchanting score too from Markevitch, recorded in 1957, by which time he had taken over as chief conductor of the Lamoureux Orchestra. All the same, others have brought greater charm to these pieces.

La Jolie Fille de Perth: Suite

(*) Testament SBT 1238 Fr. Nat. R. O, Cluytens – RAVEL: *Daphnis et Chloé Suites*, etc.; ROUSSEL: *Le Festin de l'araignée* *

Unfussy, straightforward and fresh, even if the last ounce of polish is missing. But this CD is a must for the coupling, Cluytens's inspired and atmospheric account of Roussel's *Le Festin de l'araignée*.

Symphony in C

(M) *** Häns. CD 93013. Stuttgart SW RSO, Prêtre – RAVEL: *Daphnis et Chloé: Suite 2; La Valse* ***

(BB) **(*) Virgin 2×1 5 61513-2 (2). SCO, Saraste – BERLIOZ: *Symphonie fantastique*, etc.; CHAUSSON: *Symphony* **(*)

(M) ** Sony (ADD) SMK 61830. NYPO, Bernstein – OFFENBACH: *Gaîté parisienne*, etc. ** (with SUPPE: *Beautiful Galathea: Overture* ***)

Prêtre's tempo for the opening movement (exposition repeat included) is just right, with a nice rhythmic lift, and the *Adagio* brings a memorable oboe solo. The unnamed principal has an almost vocal vibrato, and he phrases exquisitely. In the very brisk *moto perpetuo* finale the strings articulate with tremendous bustling precision, yet the second theme is able to relax and lilt seductively. The Liederhalle, Stuttgart, has a most attractive acoustic and the recording, although digital, has an almost analogue ambient warmth. If you want the couplings this disc is highly recommendable.

Saraste gives a distinctly purposeful account of the first movement, rhythmically strong and bold; the *Adagio*, with a rich-timbred oboe solo, blossoms romantically in the strings, and the *Scherzo* has striking impetus to lead to a high-spirited finale. The effect of the recording is full and the Scottish performance is enjoyable in its own way. Good value if you want all three works.

Bernstein's 1963 performance brings much to enjoy. The finale, in particular, has tremendous brilliance, which is most infectious, and the slow movement is affectionately done. On the downside, the first movement lacks the charm it ideally needs and the recording sounds a bit glassy, though it is better than it was on LP.

PIANO MUSIC

Jeux d'enfants, Op. 22

(N) (BB) **(*) EMI Gemini 5 86510-2 (2). Collard, Béroff – DEBUSSY & RAVEL: *Music for piano, 4 hands & 2 pianos*; DUKAS: *L'Apprenti Sorcier* **(*)

Jeux d'enfants is a collection of 12 engaging piano miniatures, of which Bizet scored just five for his familiar orchestral suite. While he adroitly picked the highlights, many of the other pieces are delightful too, and this – so far as we can trace – is their only appearance on CD. Jean-Philippe Collard and Michel Béroff play them appealingly, with items like *Les Chevaux de bois* and *Les Quatre Coins* standing out. The digital recording, made in the Paris Salle Wagram in 1994, is not flattering, but very acceptable when the repertoire is so rare.

Chants du Rhin; Nocturne

(B) **(*) RCA 2-CD 74321 88678-2 (2). Luisada – CHOPIN: *Piano Concerto 1; Recital* **(*)

Bizet's piano music is much neglected in the concert hall, although Glenn Gould has championed it on records. Bizet's set of 'songs without words', *Chants du Rhin*, has great charm, although perhaps not all of it is realized here. The Tunisian-born Jean-Marc Luisada is a fluent and often sensitive artist, but he is perhaps a touch heavy-handed in these slight vignettes. He is much more at home in the Chopinesque *Nocturne*, which he presents quite persuasively. Good recording.

VOCAL

'Chant d'amour': Mélodies: Adieux de l'hôtesse arabe; Chant d'amour; La Coccinelle; Ouvre ton cœur; Tarantelle

*** Decca 452 667-2. Bartoli, Chung – BERLIOZ; DELIBES; RAVEL: *Mélodies* ***

These delightful Bizet songs come as part of an outstanding recital of French repertoire, readily demonstrating the versatility of Cecilia Bartoli, who is so sympathetically accompanied by Myung-Whun Chung. Both voice and piano are recorded beautifully. The collection is considered more fully in our Recitals section, below.

Te Deum

(N) **(*) Australian Decca Eloquence 476 2947. Greenberg, Winbergh, Lausanne Pro Arte Ch., Swiss R. Ch., SRO, Lopez-Cobos – POULENC: *Gloria; Stabat Mater* ***

Bizet's *Te Deum* of 1858 is a product of his youth and was written while he was still at Rome; indeed, it was composed for the Rodrigues Prize which was open only to the winners of the Prix de Rome, and it did not win. It is very much a student work, with little of the effortless mastery that distinguishes the even earlier *Symphony*, and there is much that is derivative. There are some entertaining moments in the course of its 25 minutes, along with some obviously manufactured ideas, not all of which are effective. However, with such a good performance and recording, there is enough of interest here to make it worth considering.

OPERA

Carmen (complete; DVD versions)

(N) *** DG **DVD** 073 4032. Bumbry, Vickers, Freni, Diaz, V. State Op. Ch., VPO, Karajan (Dir. & V/D: Karajan)

*** Columbia Tristar **DVD** CDR 10530. Migenes, Domingo, Raimondi, Esham, Fr. Nat. RSO and Ch., Maazel (V/D: Franco Rossi)

(*) DG **DVD 073 000-9. Baltsa, Carreras, Ramey, Mitchell, Met. Op. Ch. & O, Levine (V/D: Brian Large)

(N) **(*) TDK **DVD** DV-OPCAR. Domashenko, Dashuk, Pastorello, Josipovic, Berti, Aceto, Verona Arena Ch. & O, Lombard (V/D: George Blume)

*(*) Opus Arte **DVD** OA 0867 D (2). Von Otter, Haddock, Naouri, Milne, Glyndebourne Ch., LPO, Jordan

Based on a lavish Salzburg Festival production, directed (like the video production) by Karajan himself, his film of *Carmen* was made in 1967 with the starriest of casts. Though the sound recording was made in the Sofiensaal in Vienna, the filming was done in Munich, using an expansion of Teo Otto's impressive stage sets. That involved the singers miming to their own voices, so that when the film regularly uses revealing close-ups of the soloists, the discrepancies between lips and voice become obvious. That is one of the few flaws in an exceptionally powerful production. Grace Bumbry as Carmen is at her most seductive, sensuous in both voice and looks, establishing herself as sultry and provocative even before she starts singing in Act I. Jon Vickers is equally powerful as Don José, defiant of authority from the very beginning, and though his tenor is of heroic scale, he shades it down beautifully for such an aria as the *Flower Song*, using a perfectly controlled head-voice at the end in genuinely hushed singing. Mirella Freni is an enchanting Micaëla, girlish and fun-loving, with Justino Diaz a powerful and handsome Escamillo completing a quartet of principals not just characterful but vocally firm and clear. The rest of the cast cannot be faulted either, and Karajan conducts with a combination of bite and warmth to match and even outshine his two regular CD versions. Recitatives are preferred to spoken dialogue, and the full ballet is included.

Filmed on location in the most atmospheric of sites, few operatic films add so vividly to the music as this version of *Carmen*, directed by Franco Rossi. It starts with a striking visual coup: the credits are shown with merely the murmur of a bullring crowd in the background, while a matador is seen playing with a bull. He finally brings his sword down for the kill, and it is at that moment that Bizet's opening *Prélude* thunders out.

The film is set to a recording specially made in the studio, and issued on CD by Erato. An excellent performance, under Lorin Maazel, on DVD it projects as sharply dramatic, with Plácido Domingo at his finest and Julia Migenes the most vibrantly characterful of Carmens. Ruggero Raimondi makes a noble Escamillo, and though Faith Esham's voice is not ideally sweet as Micaëla, it is a tender, sensitive performance. The sound is first rate, and having the singers miming to the music is not too distracting. The DVD is markedly sharper in focus than the equivalent VHS. Unfortunately no booklet is provided, just a leaflet with only sketchy details given, even of the cast.

DG's DVD version of *Carmen* offers a grandly traditional production from the Met. in New York. It is starrily cast, with James Levine bringing out all the brilliance of the score, almost to a fault, when the sound is bright to the point of edginess. This 1988 production, directed for the stage by Paul Mills and imaginatively directed for television by Brian Large, has the most lavish, solidly realistic sets and costumes by John Bury, so grand that at each curtain-rise the stage picture prompts loud applause. Happily, at the time the four principals, all noted for taking their respective roles, were at their peak. Agnes Baltsa, who earlier sang Carmen for Karajan, is as ever a tough, defiant heroine, sultry, with rarely a smile on her face, initially sneering at the attentions of the glamorous Escamillo of Samuel Ramey. Her mezzo is firm and dark if hardly beautiful, with none of the vocal unevenness that developed later. Similarly, José Carreras as Don José is in superb voice, singing with a honeyed range of tone before his voice was affected by leukaemia. The *Flower Song* is exquisitely shaded with a perfectly controlled head-voice for the *pianissimo* high note at the end. Samuel Ramey, more noble than flamboyant or dangerous, makes a powerful Escamillo, and Leona Mitchell with her warm soprano is an appealing Micaëla. Though Levine's fast speeds occasionally trip up the very large chorus, they sing brilliantly, even though stage movement is on the primitive side. Though this cannot match Rosi's film of Migenes and Domingo in imagination, it

makes a fine recommendation for a live performance filmed in the opera house.

It says much for latter-day standards of opera in the Verona Arena that not only is Franco Zeffirelli the director of the colourful TDK DVD production, but the briskly idiomatic performance under Alain Lombard features two outstanding young singers in the two principal women's roles. As Carmen herself, Marina Domashenko is both glamorous and an electrifying actress, flashing her teeth menacingly from the start, and she has a rich, superbly focused mezzo which she uses with flair. As Micaëla, Maya Dashuk, girlish and pretty, has a bright, clear soprano which projects perfectly and, though Marco Berti as Don José is unashamedly Italianate in his singing of Bizet, his is a strong, well-controlled performance. With some grit in the voice, Raymond Aceto is less successful as Escamillo, but he still gives an acceptable performance. The chorus sings incisively, and the elaborate staging in front of panoramic background scenery involves dozens of extras, some riding horses. The sound of the orchestra is rather dry, but the voices come over vividly, evidently helped by clever microphone placing. An extravagant entertainment, as Zeffirelli no doubt intended.

The DVD of the 2002 Glyndebourne production is disappointing, when the miscasting of Anne Sofie von Otter as Carmen is all the more apparent in filmed close-up. She sings wonderfully, but it is impossible to take this imperious heroine seriously when, endlessly pouting and rolling her eyes, she is simply arch and knowing, never voluptuous. Marcus Haddock also sings well as Don José, but he too lacks the right looks, though Laurent Naouri is an imposing Escamillo and Lisa Milne a deeply affecting Micaëla. At least on DVD you see the brilliant young conductor Philippe Jordan at work in the *Prélude* and *Entr'actes*, wielding his baton like a toreador with his sword.

Carmen (complete; CD versions)

⊕•🔴 *** EMI 5 57434-2 (3). Gheorghiu, Alagna, Hampson, Mula, Les Elements Ch., Toulouse Capitole O, Plasson

*** DG 410 088-2 (3). Baltsa, Carreras, Van Dam, Ricciarelli, Barbaux, Paris Op. Ch., Schoenberg Boys' Ch., BPO, Karajan

(M) **(*) EMI 5 67357-2 [567353] (3). De los Angeles, Gedda, Micheau, Blanc, French R. Ch. & O, Beecham

(B) *** DG Trio 471 750-2 (3). Horne, McCracken, Krause, Maliponte, Manhattan Op. Ch., Met. Op. O, Bernstein

(M) *** RCA 74321 39495-2 (3). L. Price, Corelli, Merrill, Freni, Linval, V. State Op. Ch., VPO, Karajan

**(*) Decca 414 489-2 (2). Troyanos, Domingo, Van Dam, Te Kanawa, Alldis Ch., LPO, Solti

(N) (M) **(*) DG (ADD) 477 5342 (2). Berganza, Domingo, Cotrubas, Milnes, Amb. S., LSO, Abbado

** EMI 5 56281-2 (2). Callas, Gedda, Guiot, Massard, Duclos Ch., Children's Ch., Paris Nat. Op. O, Prêtre

(BB) (**) Naxos mono 8.110238/9 (2). Michel, Jobin, Dens, Angelici, Opéra Comique Ch. & O, Cluytens

It is only the first of the delights of EMI's richly enjoyable set of *Carmen* with Angela Gheorghiu that it is restored as a grand opera, returning to the traditional version, with spoken dialogue replaced by the recitatives that Ernest Guiraud provided at the suggestion of the composer just before he died. Here we have another soprano version, and Angela Gheorghiu excels herself, immediately taking her place among the greats. This is a Carmen at once threatening and seductive, using a glorious range of tone, with a hearty chest register and the subtlest control of vibrato to give moments of heightened emotion extra intensity. So in the Quintet, leading up to Carmen's confession, '*Je suis amoureuse*', her vibrancy is suddenly transformed into rich, glowing tone on that confession, a moment of rapture. This is a performance full of just such imaginative detail, and it includes as a fascinating supplement the first version of what became the *Habañera* in Act I.

Gheorghiu is well matched by Roberto Alagna as Don José, always at his happiest singing French and, most moving as the beaten victim in Act IV. Thomas Hampson is a heroic, swaggering Escamillo and Inva Mula a touching Micaëla, idiomatically French, with Michel Plasson drawing crisp and incisive playing from his Toulouse team, bringing lightness to ensembles, often at speeds faster than usual.

Otherwise Karajan's DG set of *Carmen* makes a first choice among modern versions. In Carreras he has a Don José who is lyrical and generally sweet-toned. José van Dam is incisive and virile, the public hero-figure; which leaves Agnes Baltsa as a vividly compelling Carmen, tough and vibrant, yet with tenderness under the surface.

Beecham's speeds are not always conventional but they always *sound* right. And, unlike so many strong-willed conductors in opera, Beecham allows his singers room to breathe and to expand their characterizations. De los Angeles's portrayal of Carmen is absolutely bewitching, and when in the Quintet scene she says *Je suis amoureuse* one believes her absolutely. Naturally the other singers are not nearly as dominant as this, but they make admirable foils; Nicolai Gedda is pleasantly light-voiced as ever, Janine Micheau is a sweet Micaëla, and Ernest Blanc makes an attractive Escamillo. The glowing stereo recording was made in the Salle Wagram, Paris, at widely separated sessions between 1958 and 1959, but in Allan Ramsay's excellent new transfer this hardly shows at all. The hall acoustic makes the chorus sound very resonant but gives an attractive theatrical atmosphere to the solo voices, caught naturally and without edginess, and well balanced in relation to the orchestra. At its new mid-price, this famous set reasserts its position near the top of the list of recommendations and makes a worthy addition to EMI's 'Great Recordings of the Century'. Beecham adds his own special touch to the orchestral interludes. The documentation cannot be faulted, including session photographs and a full translation.

Bernstein's 1973 *Carmen* was recorded at the New York Metropolitan Opera. Some of his slow tempi are very controversial, but what really matters is the authentic tingle of dramatic tension which permeates the whole entertainment. Marilyn Horne – occasionally coarse in expression – gives a fully satisfying reading of the heroine's role, a vivid characterization. The rest of the cast similarly works to Bernstein's consistent overall plan. It is very well transferred and comes as a Trio offered with only a cued synopsis.

Karajan's RCA version, made in Vienna in 1964, owes much to Leontyne Price's seductive, smoky-toned Carmen. Corelli has moments of coarseness but his is still a heroic performance. Robert Merrill sings with gloriously firm tone, while Mirella Freni is enchanting as Micaëla. With recording full of atmosphere, and attractively repackaged at mid-price, this is a very strong contender.

Solti's Decca performance is remarkable for its new illumination of characters. Tatiana Troyanos is one of the subtlest Carmens on record. Escamillo too is more readily

sympathetic, not just the flashy matador who steals the hero's girl, whereas Don José is revealed as weak rather than just a victim. Troyanos's singing is delicately seductive too, with no hint of vulgarity, while the others make up a consistent singing cast. Though the CD transfer brings out the generally excellent balances of the originally analogue recording, it exaggerates the bass, although the voices retain their fine realism and bloom.

Superbly disciplined, Abbado's 1977 performance nails its colours to the mast at the very start in a breathtakingly fast account of the opening prelude. Through the four Acts there are other examples of idiosyncratic tempi, but the whole entertainment hangs together with keen compulsion, reflecting the fact that these same performers, Sherrill Milnes as Escamillo excepted, took part in the Edinburgh Festival production directly associated with this recording project. Conductor and orchestra can take a large share of the credit for the performance's success, for though the singing is never less than enjoyable, it is on the whole less characterful than on some rival sets. Teresa Berganza is a seductive if somewhat unsmiling Carmen – not without sensuality – producing consistently beautiful tone, but lacking some of the flair which makes for a three-dimnsional portrait. If Ileana Cotrubas as Micaëla is not always as sweetly steady as she can be, Milnes makes a heroic matador. The spoken dialogue is excellently produced, and the sound is vivid and immediate, with the CDs hardly betraying the fact that the sessions took place in different studios (in London as well as Edinburgh). All in all, this deserves its place among DG's 'Originals', and a full text and translation is included.

The Naxos historical issue brings an excellent CD transfer of one of the very first versions of *Carmen* to appear on LP and one of the first to use the *opéra comique* version with dialogue, fluently spoken by the francophone cast. The singing is fresh and clean rather than inspired, with Solange Michel as Carmen firm and direct but never sensuous, and with Raoul Jobin a forthright ringing Don José with few subtleties, Michel Dens a reliable rather than a characterful Escamillo and Marthe Angelici a bright Micaëla. The big disappointment is the conducting of André Cluytens, too often metrical at fast speeds, not letting the music breathe, perfunctory even.

Maria Callas was ideally suited to the role of Carmen, but her complete recording is disappointing. One principal trouble is that the performance, apart from her, lacks a taut dramatic rein, with slack ensemble from singers and orchestra alike. The moment the heroine enters, the tension rises; but by Callas's standards this is a performance rough-hewn, strong and characterful but lacking the full imaginative detail of her finest work. The set has been remastered and a new booklet prepared for this latest reissue.

Carmen (highlights)

(M) *** Decca (ADD) 458 204-2 (from above complete set, with Troyanos; cond. Solti)

(M) *** DG (ADD) 457 901-2 (from above complete set, with Horne; cond. Bernstein)

(M) *** EMI 5 57502-2 (from above complete set, with Gheorghiu; cond. Plasson)

(B) **(*) DG (ADD) 439 496-2 (from complete set, with Berganza, Domingo, Cotrubas, Milnes, Amb. S., LSO, Abbado)

(M) ** EMI (ADD) 5 66663-2 (from above complete set, with Callas; cond. Prêtre)

(BB) ** EMI Encore CDE5 74955-2 (from complete recording with Bumbry, Vickers, Freni, Paskalis, Paris Opéra Ch. & O, Frühbeck de Burgos)

We have been enthusiastic about Angela Gheorghiu's Carmen, and she is well matched by Alagna and Hampson, and with Inva Mula an appealingly vulnerable Micaëla (see above). The highlights are generous (70 minutes 31 seconds) and well selected, reflecting all four acts, with an excellent cued synopsis.

The reissued mid-price set of highlights from Solti's sharply characterful set is generous (75 minutes) and handsomely repackaged in a slipcase. A full translation is included, and the remastered recording sounds both brilliant, full-bodied and atmospheric, though still somewhat over-weighted in the bass.

The DG Galleria disc can also be recommended, offering 70 minutes of well-chosen excerpts from the Bernstein set recorded at the Met., the only snag being that the synopsis is not linked to the 14 different cues. Luckily, however, *Carmen* is not a difficult opera to follow!

The bargain highlights selection on DG Classikon offers a fairly generous sampler of the Berganza–Domingo–Abbado set, with some 69 minutes of well-chosen excerpts, including all the hits. The documentation relates the music to the narrative in a brief but succinct synopsis.

The Callas set of highlights returns to the original (1964) selection, offering 61 minutes of key items relevant to the narrative; so Callas sings in only about half the excerpts.

Frühbeck de Burgos's account of 1970 was the first to use the original (1875) version of Bizet's score, without the cuts that were made after experience in the theatre, and with spoken dialogue instead of the recitatives, which Guiraud composed after Bizet's early death. The EMI Encore disc offers a comprehensive selection (76 minutes) from a set with a less-than-compelling Carmen in Grace Bumbry, who sings with firm tone but too rarely with musical or dramatic individuality. Vickers makes a strong Don José and Paskalis a rich-toned Escamillo, so with the opera well paced this makes a more than acceptable and well-recorded sampler, even if the synopsis is very sparse.

Carmen (in English)
(M) **(*) Chan. 3091 (2). Bardon, Gavin, Magee, Plazas, Geoffrey Mitchell Ch., Philh. O, Parry

For the first time the Chandos version offers this most popular opera in English in a modern recording. The problem is that English words tend to make these characters sound too proper, not earthy enough; but once that discrepancy is recognized, there is much to enjoy in this lively, generally well-cast performance. Patricia Bardon, who has sung Carmen for Scottish Opera, is a warm-toned heroine, whose drawback for recording is that the voice tends to spread under pressure at the top, but this is a strong and convincing portrayal, and Julian Gavin makes an outstanding Don José with his ringing tenor, never for a moment under strain, even in the *Flower Song*, with a baritonal quality adding weight in dramatic moments. Mary Plazas is a charming, innocent-sounding Micaëla, and though Gary Magee's baritone is hardly dark enough for Escamillo, it is a pleasing, forthright portrayal, and the others make an excellent team, not least in the lightly sprung, tripping account of the *Quintet*. The choral contributions of the Geoffrey Mitchell Choir are excellent, and David Parry generally paces the piece well, with excellent playing from the Philharmonia, even if at times

one would welcome more rhythmic spring. The full-bodied, well-balanced Chandos recording lets one appreciate not only the brilliance of Bizet's orchestration but the beauty too, as in Micaëla's Act III aria. Using a new edition of the *opéra comique* version by Richard Langham-Smith, which wisely adopts most of Bizet's own cuts made during the original rehearsals, David Parry has himself provided the translation, with spoken dialogue nicely compact.

Carmen (highlights; in English)
(B) **(*) CfP (ADD) 585 0082. Johnson, D. Smith, Herincx, Robson, Hynter, Sadler's Wells Opera Ch. & O, C. Davis

This was one of the most successful Sadler's Wells discs of the 1960s, thanks both to the forceful conducting of Colin Davis and to the rich-voiced, reliable singing of Patricia Johnson as Carmen. Not that Johnson is merely reliable and no more; time and again her phrasing is most imaginative and memorable. It is good that the microphones catch her voice so well, and Donald Smith, the Don José, provides a wonderfully attractive, ringing tone. The selection is brief (51 minutes) but well made, and the ensemble work has the authentic enthusiasm of a live performance, helped by the vivid sound.

Les Pêcheurs de perles (complete)
(M) (***) EMI mono 5 65266-2 (2). Angelici, Legay, Dens, Noguera, Théâtre Nat. de l'Opéra-Comique Ch. & O, Cluytens

Unavailable since the early days of LP, this superb EMI/Cluytens set of 1954 offers the finest, most warmly expressive performance on disc of this delectable opera. Ironically, its nearest rival is the Philips set of the previous year under Jean Fournet, also in mono (currently unavailable), both of them outshining later, stereo sets. Cluytens is an even more sensitive conductor than his Philips rival, less four-square, getting the music to flow flexibly; and his cast, idiomatically French, has no weak link. Martha Angelici as the heroine, Leila, is both sweet and bright, with no Gallic shrillness, and Henry Legay has a degree of heroic timbre in the rounded, lyric quality of his tenor, while Michel Dens, as in other French opera recordings of the period, proves a firm, characterful baritone. With excellent choral and orchestral work, one gets the impression of a stage experience translated to the studio. The mono transfer is a little dull on orchestral sound, but it captures voices vividly.

BLISS, Arthur (1891–1975)

Adam Zero (ballet; complete); A Colour Symphony
☛ (BB) *** Naxos 8.553460. N. Philh. O, Lloyd-Jones

Full of striking ideas and effects to illustrate four heraldic colours, the *Colour Symphony* here receives a refined and idiomatic reading, marked by superb wind-playing. More valuable still is the first complete recording of the ballet, *Adam Zero*, in which the process of creating a ballet is presented as an allegory for the ongoing life-cycle. Lloyd-Jones directs a dramatically paced performance, amply confirming this as one of Bliss's most inventive, strongly co-ordinated scores, shamefully neglected. Full, well-balanced sound.

Checkmate (ballet); Prologue; 5 Dances
(BB) *** Hyp. Helios CDH 55099. E. N. Philh. O, Lloyd-Jones
– LAMBERT: *Horoscope* *** ❂; WALTON: *Façade* ***

David Lloyd-Jones is a highly sympathetic advocate of Bliss's ballet suite, and he includes also the *Prologue*. The Hyperion recording, while warm enough to convey the score's lyricism, has plenty of bite in the *Red Knight's Mazurka*. This is most enjoyable, but it is the superb couplings that make this triptych both distinctive and now very desirable at Helios price.

(i) *Checkmate: Suite; Hymn to Apollo;* (ii) *Music for Strings;* (iii) *Clarinet Quintet;* (ii, iv) *Lie strewn the white flocks*
(B) *** Chan. 2-for-1 241-1 (2). (i) Ulster O, Handley; (ii) N. Sinfonia, Hickox; (iii) Hilton, Lindsay Qt; (iv) D. Jones, N. Sinfonia Ch.

The *Music for Strings* is surely the key work here, and Hickox directs it spontaneously and with deeply expressive feeling. Vernon Handley conducts with complete authority and evident enthusiasm both the *Checkmate Suite* and the less familiar *Hymn to Apollo*. In the masterly *Clarinet Quintet* (see below) Janet Hilton and the Lindsays are totally persuasive, and the recording is most naturally balanced. The *Pastoral, Lie strewn the white flocks*, is another of the composer's most memorable works and is brought vividly to life by the passionate singing of the Northern Sinfonia Chorus. Della Jones sings the *Pigeon song* touchingly, and the recording is in the demonstration bracket. On the whole, this is to be preferred to the Hyperion version (see below).

Checkmate (ballet): 5 Dances
(M) *** Chan. 6576. West Australian SO, Schönzeler – RUBBRA: *Symphony 5* ***; TIPPETT: *Little Music* **(*)

The five dances from *Checkmate* on the Chandos issue are well played under Hans-Hubert Schönzeler and, with its valuable Rubbra coupling, this is welcome back in the catalogue at mid-price.

(i) *Cello Concerto. A Colour Symphony;* (ii) *The Enchantress* (scena for contralto and orchestra)
(N) (M) *** Chan. 10221X. (i) Wallfisch; (ii) Finnie; Ulster O, Handley

Raphael Wallfisch is a powerful soloist in the *Cello Concerto*. This is a reading which brings out the red-blooded warmth of the writing, with the soloist strongly supported by the Ulster Orchestra under Handley. They are equally persuasive accompanying Linda Finnie in the extended scena which Bliss wrote for Kathleen Ferrier nearly 20 years earlier. There, Bliss was inspired by the individual artistry of a great musician – even though, as he himself said, he found it hard to reconcile the goodness of Ferrier with the character of Simaetha, the central figure in the passage of Theocritus which he chose to set. For this reissue Chandos have added Vernon Handley's authoritative and enthusiastic account of the *Colour Symphony* and throughout the recording is warm and atmospheric throughout.

Piano Concerto
⚙ (***) British Music Society mono BMS 101 CDH. Mewton-Wood, Utrecht SO, Goehr – STRAVINSKY: *Concerto for Piano & Wind* (***); SHOSTAKOVICH: *Piano Concerto 1* (***)
(M) **(*) Divine Art (ADD) 2-4206. Barnard, Philh. O, Sargent

Bliss's *Piano Concerto* (1939) is a powerful work in the nineteenth-century Romantic tradition, and at the time it was hoped it could prove to be a British 'Emperor' concerto.

The snag is that its themes, although often lyrically attractive, are not strong or memorable enough in themselves. Bliss was so impressed with Noel Mewton-Wood's playing of his *Concerto* that he wrote a sonata especially for him. The *Concerto* was recorded in 1952, and it is a truly prodigious performance, full of flair and with a vein of easy lyricism that invests the slow movement with magical, poetic feeling. There is a real burst of bravura in the first-movement cadenza, and the finale has the kind of impulsive virtuosity that one associates with Horowitz. Alec Robertson, reviewing the original LP in *Gramophone*, said, 'Mewton-Wood gives the performance of his life ... and is evidently at one with the conductor ... and the orchestra sound as if they are enjoying themselves'. Most remarkable of all is the exciting spontaneity of the playing, which sounds for all the world like a live performance. The concert hall recording of the orchestra is two-dimensional and lacks body, but the piano is well caught, and one adjusts when Brian Crimp's remastering is clear and clean and the playing so thrillingly compulsive.

Trevor Barnard's excellent performance with Sargent and the Philharmonia is commanding, and there is much to enjoy. The recording of the piano is excellent but rather forward, while the orchestra is recessed and not ideally transparent, as is obvious in the opening tutti. Nevertheless, a thoroughly worthwhile CD reissue.

Discourse for Orchestra; Miracle in the Gorbals (complete ballet); Things to Come (complete film score, reconstructed Christopher Palmer)
(BB) **(*) Naxos 8.553698. Queensland SO, Lyndon-Gee

The Naxos issue is most valuable for offering not only a première recording of the *Discourse for Orchestra*, but the complete ballet-score of *Miracle in the Gorbals*, colourful and vigorous in illustrating the sordid but moving tale of murder and salvation in the slums of Glasgow. The 18 brief sections are strongly contrasted in mood and atmosphere and are here given a warmly committed performance by the Queensland orchestra, as is the *Discourse*, even though the strings are challenged by the violin writing. The five movements from *Things to Come* are also welcome in Christopher Palmer's reconstruction of the original opulent scoring, though it is astonishing to find the famous *March* omitted. Good, warm sound.

Film music: Caesar and Cleopatra: Suite (ed. & arr. Easterbrook and Binney); Royal Palaces Suite; Things to Come: Concert Suite (reconstructed Lane); War in the Air: theme; March: Welcome the Queen
⊶ ⚙ *** Chan. 9896. BBC PO, Gamba

It seems extraordinary that Bliss's great pioneering film-score for *Things to Come*, some 45 minutes of music, became lost in its original form. Bliss had collaborated closely with H. G. Wells on the project, but in the final cut of the movie the recorded score no longer matched the action. Lionel Salter was called in at the last moment to edit Bliss's score and Muir Mathieson to record it. Various records and arrangements were made but, fortunately for posterity, Sir Henry Wood had kept the test pressings of his (1935) 78s of the original score, and eight of the ten sides were discovered in the late 1990s in the Archive Library of the Royal Academy of Music. Now, thanks to Philip Lane, we can at last hear this inspired, wonderfully orchestrated score as Bliss conceived it, with the closing *Epilogue* so full of Elgarian nobilmente spirit.

Caesar and Cleopatra had a chequered career as a film, with almost everything going wrong in production, and Bliss's score was never used. Fortunately it exists in a faded working manuscript, and again shows him in inspirational form. *War in the Air*, with its Waltonesque opening fanfare, was a splendid title and closing-credits piece of considerable panache, written for the BBC, who produced this 15-episode documentary in 1954, as an answer to the famous American NBC series, *Victory at Sea*.

The *Royal Palaces Suite* was written twelve years later for a BBC TV documentary broadcast on Christmas Day 1966, with a narration by Sir Kenneth Clark. It displays plenty of regality and also shows the composer at his most diverting and tuneful in the charming Waltz for *The Ballroom in Buckingham Palace*. This admirable programme opens with Bliss's best march in the Elgarian tradition, written for a Pathé newsreel, and altogether this splendid CD confirms Bliss as a composer of resource, who could write good tunes to order – at least in the early part of his career.

CHAMBER MUSIC

Conversations; Madam Noy; (i–ii) *Rhapsody;* (ii) *Rout. The Women of Yueh; Oboe Quintet*

*** Hyp. CDA 66137. Nash Ens., with (i) Rolfe Johnson; (ii) Gale

The predominant influence in *Rout*, for soprano and chamber orchestra, and in the *Rhapsody*, with its two wordless vocal parts, is Ravel. The *Oboe Quintet* is a work of considerable quality. The music assembled here represents Bliss at his very best. A lovely disc which can be warmly recommended, and eminently well engineered, too.

Clarinet Quintet

*** Redcliffe RR 010. Cox, Redcliffe Ens. – RAWSTHORNE: *Clarinet Quartet*; ROUTH: *Clarinet Quintet* ***

(N) (***) Testament mono SBT1366. Thurston, Griller Qt – BRAHMS: *Clarinet Quintet; Clarinet Sonata 2* ***

*** Chan. 8683. Hilton, Lindsay Qt – BAX: *Sonata*; VAUGHAN WILLIAMS: *Studies* ***

(i) *Clarinet Quintet. String Quartet 2*

(N) ☛ (BB) *** Naxos 8.557394. Maggini Qt, (i) with Campbell

The *Clarinet Quintet* of 1932 is arguably Bliss's masterpiece, and David Campbell and the Maggini Quartet give an authoritative and searching account, even finer than Nicholas Cox's alternative Bristol version. Bliss dedicated his *Second Quartet* of 1950 to the Grillers, and in terms of intensity and imagination the Maggini come pretty close to them. These are totally dedicated performances, concentrated in feeling and expertly finished, which should do much to restore these pieces to their rightful place in the repertoire. A valuable and in every way distinguished release, and an essential issue for admirers of the composer.

The *Quintet* is also played very beautifully by Nicholas Cox and members of the Redcliffe Ensemble, who readily catch the flowing lyricism of the opening movement and the intense valedictory feeling of the *Adagietto*, in which the composer remembers his younger brother, Kennard, who was killed at the Somme in 1916. The recording too, in the glowing acoustic of St George's, Brandon Hill, Bristol, is quite ideal. Moreoever the Rawsthorne coupling may be perceived by some collectors as being more appropriate than the Bliss *Quartet*.

Frederick Thurston recorded the *Quintet* for Decca with the Griller Quartet in 1935, only four years after its composition. Its restoration to the catalogue after some 70 years is something of an event, for three generations of music lovers will not have heard it. It is altogether superb in every respect, and these impeccable transfers from the four 78s bring it vividly to life. Thurston was a legendary player in his day and listening to his understated eloquence in this consummate performance of Bliss's masterpiece is living testimony to his artistry.

Janet Hilton and the Lindsays also have the measure of the *Clarinet Quintet*'s autumnal melancholy; the recording is natural and well focused. But this needs a mid-price reissue.

(i; ii) *Oboe Quintet;* (ii; iii) *Piano Quartet;* (iv) *Viola Sonata*

☛ (BB) *** Naxos 8.555931. (i) Daniel; (ii) Maggini Qt; (iii) Donohoe; (iv) Outram, Rolton

It is surprising that Bliss's *Piano Quartet* is not better known. An early (1915) folk-tune-inspired work it may be, yet it is brim full of attractive melody and, in the hands of Peter Donohoe and the Maggini Quartet, is quite captivating. The later (1927) *Oboe Quintet*, written for and premièred by Leon Goossens, is more intimately atmospheric, mainly pastoral in feeling, but with a vigorous *Vivace* finale which quotes from *Connell's Jig*. Nicholas Daniel is a nimble, elegant soloist and catches the work's light-hearted mood to perfection. Like so many other English works for viola, Bliss's *Sonata* was written for Lionel Tertis. It is highly demanding for both participants, both in the rhapsodic expressive lyricism of the *Andante* and in the *Furiant* Scherzo; but the main challenge for the violist comes in the passionate closing section, where the violist is taken up to the instrument's stratospheric heights. Martin Outram, with Julian Rolton a fine partner, rises to the occasion in a highly persuasive account of another work that deserves a more frequent hearing. Excellent recording throughout, and good documentation.

Piano Quartet in A min.; Bliss; The Rout Trot; Triptych (for piano). (i) *Angels of the Mind* (for voice & piano); *4 Songs* (for voice, violin & piano)

*** ASV CDDCA 1128. De Pledge, Chamber Domaine, (i) with Meyerhoff

This accomplished ensemble bring us some Bliss rarities, including the first recording of the early *Piano Quartet in A minor* (1915) and the *Triptych* for piano (1971). The former, written when he was in his early twenties, is well crafted, though the debt to Vaughan Williams and English folksong is still to be discharged. The jazzy *Bliss* and *The Rout Trot* are well done, as is the *Triptych*, which is muscular and well held together. There are moments when one's thoughts turn to John Ireland, though the writing is still very characteristic. *Angels of the Mind* is another late piece of some quality, which Helen Meyerhoff sings with great musical intelligence though less vocal beauty. The recording is dryish and more air is needed round the aural image.

String Quartets 1 in B flat; 2 in F min.

*** Hyp. CDA 66178. Delmé Qt

These performances by the Delmé Quartet are not only thoroughly committed but enormously persuasive, and they can be recommended even to readers not normally sympathetic to this composer.

Piano Sonata

** Div. Art 2-5011. Barnard – BUSONI: *24 Preludes* **

Piano Sonata; Pieces: Bliss (One-Step); Miniature Scherzo; Rout Trot; Study; Suite; Triptych. arr. of BACH: *Das alte Jahr vergangen ist* ('The old year has ended')
*** Chan. 8979. Fowke

The biggest work on the Chandos disc is the *Sonata*. Its neo-romantic rhetoric is less convincing than some of the earlier pieces Bliss composed, in particular the *Suite* (1925). There are some other lighter pieces, like the *The Rout Trot* and *Bliss* (*One-Step*), written in the 1920s when his inspiration was at its freshest. Good performances and excellent recording, made in The Maltings, Snape.

Trevor Barnard played the *Sonata* to Bliss in the late 1950s and the composer made some annotations and corrections in the printed score that are incorporated here. But collectors should note that the Divine Art recording is distinctly monochrome and lacklustre. The Chandos disc is the one to go for.

VOCAL MUSIC

Song-cycles: 2 American Poems (Millay); *7 American Poems; Ballads of the Four Seasons* (Li-Po); *A Knot of Riddles; 2 Nursery Rhymes* (Cornford); *3 Romantic Songs* (Walter de la Mare); *4 Songs. The Tempest* (incidental music). Other songs: *Angels of the mind; At the window; A child's prayer; Auvergnat; Elegiac sonnet; Fair is my love; The fallow deer at the lonely house; The hammers; In praise of his Daphnis; Rich or poor; Simples; 'Tis time I think by Wenlock town; Three jolly gentlemen; The tramps; When I was one-and-twenty*
*** Hyp. CDA 67188/9. McGreevy, Spence, Herford, Sturrock, Nash Ens., Brabbins

The very variety of this splendid collection of Bliss's songs will come as a surprise to many, for the composer refused to be limited by the usual constraints of the English tradition, let alone to be influenced by the folk tradition. The collection spans the full extent of his composing career, from a boyhood song like the Housman setting, *'Tis time, I think, by Wenlock town*, through to two of his last works, *A Knot of Riddles* (for baritone and 11 instruments) and *Angels of the Mind*, another song-cycle for soprano and piano setting poems by Kathleen Raine, a work he wrote not on commission but simply for his own enjoyment. Geraldine McGreevy is the outstanding soloist in that and the other soprano items, and the others also respond sensitively to Bliss's distinctive word-setting, often helped by sharply rhythmic accompaniments. It is striking how often Bliss liked to have more than a piano in accompaniment, not just in *A Knot of Riddles* but in such an isolated song as his *Elegiac sonnet* for tenor, string quartet and piano to words by Cecil Day Lewis, written for the memorial concert commemorating the pianist, Noel Mewton-Wood. Kathleen Sturrock is the excellent pianist in most of the songs, with members of the Nash Ensemble ever stylish in the rest. First-rate recording. A most valuable, comprehensive essay, 'An introduction to Arthur Bliss as Songwriter' by Giles Easterbrook, is included in the booklet.

Lie strewn the white flocks
*** Hyp. CDA 66175. Minty, Pierce, Holst Singers & O., Davan Wetton – BRITTEN: *Gloriana: Choral Dances;* HOLST: *Choral Hymns from Rig Veda* ***

Bliss's *Pastoral* is given a winning performance by the Holst Singers and Orchestra, with the choral sections (the greater part of the work) aptly modest in scale but powerful in impact. With glowing sound and very attractive works for coupling, this is an outstanding issue.

BLOCH, Ernest (1880–1959)

(i) *America (Epic Rhapsody)*; (ii) *Concerto Grosso 1 for Strings & Piano*
*** Delos DE 3135. Seattle SO, Schwarz; (i) with Seattle Ch.; Michaelian

Bloch's *America* overflows with an endearingly naïve and sentimental patriotism. Its three sections, lasting in total some 39 minutes, describe the struggles and hardships and the hours of joy and sorrow of the emerging of the American nation, leading to a finale which declares, in the words of Walt Whitman: 'As he sees the farthest he has the most faith.' The work climaxes with a heartfelt anthem of praise which, the composer recounted, came to him on the steamer on his arrival in New York harbour in August 1916. It makes a superbly grandiloquent end to an endearingly contrived patchwork-quilt of ideas from both the Old and New Worlds, ranging from *Half a pound of tuppenny rice* to *Swanee River*.

The performance could hardly be better, the playing (and singing) more enthusiastic and more spectacularly recorded, and the documentation includes not only the words and melody of the anthem but a layout of the musical narrative, detailing the source of the melodies and quoting from Whitman's prose. The *Concerto Grosso* with its piano obbligato (one of the composer's finest shorter works) makes a refreshing postlude, again splendidly played and recorded.

Baal Shem
(M) *** Decca 476 17235. Bell, Baltimore SO, Zinman –
BARBER: *Violin Concerto*; WALTON: *Violin Concerto* ***
(B) *** EMI Début 5 73501-2. Shapira, ECO, Hazlewood –
BRUCH: *Violin Concerto 1* **; BUNCH: *Fantasy* **;
SARASATE: *Zigeunerweisen* **(*)

Bloch's own (1939) orchestrations of his three popular Hasidic pieces for violin and piano, *Baal Shem*, offers a fine, unusual makeweight for Bell's prize-winning disc of the Barber and Walton concertos; it won the 1998 *Gramophone* Concerto Award and now re-appears at mid-price in Universal's *Gramophone* Award Collection.

The EMI account of *Baal Shem* forms part of a début recital by the 24-year-old Israeli violinist, Ittai Shapira, designed to show off his artistry. A gifted player, who is perhaps more at home in this triptych than he is in the Bruch. A very fine performance and very well recorded too.

Violin Concerto in A min.
✿ (BB) (***) Naxos mono 8.110973. Szigeti, Paris Conservatoire O, Munch – BARTOK: *Portrait*; PROKOFIEV: *Violin Concerto 1* (***) ✿

(i) *Violin Concerto. Baal Shem*
*** ASV CDDCA 785. (i) Guttman; RPO, Serebrier (with SEREBRIER: *Momento; Poema* **)

(i) *Violin Concerto; Hebrew Suite for Violin & Orchestra*; (ii) *Schelomo (Hebrew Rhapsody)*
(M) ** Sup. SU 3169-2 011. (i) Bress, Prague SO, Rohan; (ii) Navarra, Czech PO, Ančerl

Szigeti's pioneering record of the Bloch *Concerto* has long been a classic of the gramophone. So authoritative is it and so revered by violinists that Menuhin waited for almost thirty years before venturing on his recording with Kletzki. Since then there have been few successors, and while Szigeti's 1938 records were transferred to LP in the USA (on Vox Turnabout) this is – unaccountably – its first appearance on CD. A wonderfully serene yet intense performance from both Szigeti and Munch that penetrates to the core of Bloch's masterpiece. Szigeti's nervous vibrato is heard to perfect effect here, as it is in the first of the Bartók *Portraits*, and the classic première recording of the Prokofiev *D major Concerto* with Sir Thomas Beecham and the LPO.

The performance from Michael Guttman has both fire and colour, and no attempt is made to rein in the freely rhapsodic flow of the piece. It also has well-balanced, modern, digital recording.

Hyman Bress's recording is a thoughtful, ruminative account, well worth hearing and totally unforced. At the time of writing the *Hebrew Suite* is not otherwise available in its orchestral form. André Navarra's 1964 account of *Schelomo* is more high-voltage. Not a first choice, but those investing in these performances will find that there is musical satisfaction to be had here.

Schelomo (Hebraic Rhapsody) for cello & orchestra

*** Virgin 5 45664-2. Truls Mørk, Fr. R. PO, Paavo Järvi – BRUCH: *Kol Nidrei*; SCHUMANN: *Cello Concerto* ***

(BB) *** Virgin 2x1 5 61490-2. Isserlis, LSO, Hickox – ELGAR: *Cello Concerto*; KABALEVSKY: *Cello Concerto 2*; R. STRAUSS: *Don Quixote*; TCHAIKOVSKY: *Andante cantabile*, etc. ***

(M) *** DG 457 761-2. Fournier, BPO, Wallenstein – BRUCH: *Kol Nidrei*; LALO: *Cello Concerto*; SAINT-SAENS: *Cello Concerto 1* ***

(M) **(*) Sup. (ADD) SU 3667-2. Navarra, Czech PO, Ančerl – SCHUMANN: *Cello Concerto* **(*); RESPIGHI: *Adagio con variazioni* ***

Truls Mørk gives a superb account of Bloch's *Schelomo*, concentrated and powerful. The solo rhapsodizings suit his freely expressive style perfectly, and Paavo Järvi draws from the French Radio Philharmonic a performance of wonderful weight and clarity. So the two big orchestral climaxes have the most satisfying thrust, resolving the soloist's musings. The clarity of the sound heightens the magnetic impact of the playing of both soloist and orchestra. Interestingly coupled with two other concertante works for cello.

The dark intensity of Isserlis's solo playing and the sharp, dramatic focus of Hickox in the big, climactic orchestral tuttis are magnetic, preventing Bloch's youthful outpouring on Solomon and the Song of Songs from sounding self-indulgent. Warm, refined recording. This now comes as part of a highly recommendable and very generous bargain Virgin Double which includes key cello works by five different composers, all in first-class performances.

Fournier is a bit too closely balanced in this fervent performance, but the sound is very beautiful and he is excellently supported by the Berlin Philharmonic under Wallenstein. Apart from the balancing of the cello, the 1967 recording is excellent.

André Navarra is a fine cellist and, although he is less commanding than Fournier, his too is a warmly eloquent account, and he is well supported by Ančerl. The remastering has made the solo cello very real and vivid, but the inner orchestral focus is not quite so sharp. Yet the sound remains natural, and for those wanting the couplings this disc is worth considering.

Voice in the Wilderness

**(*) Australian Decca Eloquence 466 907-2. Starker, Israel PO, Mehta – BERLIOZ: *Harold in Italy* **(*)

Voice in the Wilderness is a rather diffuse piece which at times sounds for all the world like the soundtrack of a Hollywood biblical epic, while at others its textures are so vivid and imaginative that such thoughts are promptly banished. Starker's is a finely played account, vividly recorded. Mehta seems just a bit lacking in intensity, but there is little current competition on CD, so this is well worth considering if the coupling is attractive.

3 Nocturnes for Piano Trio

*** Simax PSC 1147. Grieg Trio – MARTIN: *Piano Trio on Irish Folktunes*; SHOSTAKOVICH: *Piano Trios* ***

The first *Nocturne* (*Andante*) finds Bloch in Hebraic-Debussy mode, while the second (*Andante quieto*) is more overtly romantic and less interesting, though the Grieg Trio play it with much feeling, as they do the final *Tempestuoso*. The couplings further enhance the value of this issue, arguably the best the Grieg Trio have given us.

String Quartets 1–4

✪ (***) Decca mono 475 6071 (2). Griller Qt

It hard to believe that these performance of Bloch's *String Quartets* (No. 5 had not been written at the time of these recordings) have had to wait so long to appear (although the *Second* was released on Dutton – see below); but it makes their return all the more welcome, especially as these works have been neglected in general. The Griller Quartet were closely associated with Bloch and became his friends and favourite interpreters, with the composer supervising these recordings, made in 1954. Tully Potter's sleeve-note informs us that, after the 1946 première of the *Second Quartet*, Bloch told the Quartet, 'It is a composer's dream come true to hear his work played as you have played it', and he dedicated his *Third Quartet* to them. These are clearly great performances, with any slight faults of intonation made irrelevant in the thrust of the music-making. The *First Quartet* (1916) lasts almost an hour, yet in this magnetic performance it doesn't feel a moment too long; Bloch's wonderfully rich, haunting harmonies are played by the Grillers with spine-tingling concentration, often producing sounds of otherworldly beauty, casting a powerful spell indeed. Tully Potter counts it among *the* great string quartet recordings, with the *Second* not far behind.

The material in the *Second Quartet* (1945) is strong and memorable, and it is worked into tautly constructed arguments, never heard more convincingly than in this pioneering performance. The *Third Quartet* (1952) is more terse than the previous two, with robust, gritty outer movements (the finale has an especially infectious rhythmic bite), separated by an *Adagio* of great beauty. The *Fourth Quartet* (1953) is more reflective in character than the *Third*, opening most atmospherically, and, although it is not without strenuous passages, it is the quieter writing that makes the most effect. All in all, a worthy, enterprising (and unexpected) release on Decca's 'Original Masters' series, and the transfers of the relatively dry but atmospheric (1954) sound are excellent.

String Quartet 2 (1945); Night (1925).

(BB) (***) Dutton mono CDBP 9713. Griller Qt – DVORAK: *Quartet 12 (American)*; MOZART: *Adagio & Fugue* ***

It is sad that the string quartets of Ernest Bloch have become so neglected. In No. 2 the material, strong and memorable, is worked into tautly constructed arguments, never more convincingly than with the Griller Quartet in their heyday just after the war. It was then the leading British quartet of the time, perfectly matched, and helped here by early Decca *ffrr* recording, superbly transferred by Dutton. The Dvořák and Mozart items are equally recommendable.

Violin Sonatas 1–2 (Poème mystique); Abodah; Melody; Nuit exotique
*** Hyp. CDA 67439. Hagai Shaham, Arnon Erez

Violin Sonatas 1; 2 (Poème mystique); Abodah (Yom Kippur Melody); Melody; Suite hébraïque
(BB) *** Naxos 8.554460. Kremer, Over

The Bloch *Violin Sonatas* come from the 1920s and in recent years have rather fallen out of favour. This fine Israeli duo bring appropriate fervour and mystical feeling to this repertoire, and they are vividly recorded in Hyperion's high standard. This is now a first recommendation in this repertoire.

In Miriam Kremer and Simon Over the sonatas also have sympathetic advocates: both artists play with exemplary taste and sensitivity, and Simon Over produces a wonderful range of colour. So, for that matter, does Kremer, who has great refinement of tone. Good recordings, with plenty of space round the aural image.

Suite in A min. for Viola & Piano
(***) Biddulph mono LAB 148. Primrose, Kitzinger – BAX; HINDEMITH: *Sonatas* (***)

Primrose and his excellent partner make the strongest case for this piece and, considering its provenance, the sound is amazingly good.

Enfantines, 5 Sketches in Sepia; In the Night; Nirvana; Piano Sonata; Visions and Prophecies
*** Chan. 9887. Fingerhut

Bloch composed relatively little for the piano: the majority of the smaller pieces on the disc, *Enfantines, Five Sketches in Sepia, In the Night* and *Nirvana*, come from the period 1921–3. The *Piano Sonata* was written in the mid-1930s at the time he was working on *Voice in the Wilderness* for cello and orchestra, which is very much in the spirit of his *Hebrew Rhapsody, Schelomo*. Bloch's muse is essentially rhapsodic and improvisatory and his piano writing cries out for the colours of the orchestra. Much of the writing is amorphous and wanting in direction, but it is difficult to imagine it better played than it is here by Margaret Fingerhut or more naturally recorded.

Sacred Service
(N) (M) ** Chan. 10288X. Berkman, Zemel Ch., L. Chorale & Concord Singers, LSO, Simon

Bloch's *Sacred Service* has long been neglected by the gramophone since the composer's own pioneering recording and Leonard Bernstein's version made in the 1960s. So the reappearance of this 1978 version must be welcomed, particularly in such vivid sound. The singing is perhaps wanting in ardour and intensity, and there could be greater attention to dynamic nuances. However, it would be unfair to dwell on the shortcomings of this performance in the light of so much that is good, not least of which is the orchestral playing. The recording is spacious and well focused.

BLOW, John (1649–1708)

(i) *Ode on the Death of Mr Henry Purcell. Fugue in G min.; Grounds: in C min.; in D min.; Sonata in A; Suite in G*
**(*) Virgin 5 45342-2. (i) Lesne, Dugardin; La Canzona – PURCELL: *Songs & Duets* **(*)

Ode on the Death of Mr Henry Purcell: Mark how the lark and linnet sing. Ah, heav'n! What is't I hear?
*** Hyp. CDA 66253. Bowman, Chance, King's Consort, King – PURCELL: *Collection* ***

The *Ode on the Death of Mr Henry Purcell* is a most welcome addition to the catalogue. There are some striking chromaticisms and dissonances and some inventive and noble music. Robert King's spontaneous style is infectious, with the orchestral comments engagingly animated. Both performances are highly rewarding, and in the last resort couplings will dictate choice.

Gérard Lesne and his fellow counter-tenor give a stylish performance, reflecting that of the younger master, but it is good to identify the character of Blow himself more clearly in the instrumental pieces of his which punctuate the series of Purcell songs and duets. The recorder players of La Canzona are on the abrasive side, not helped by the close recordings, but this makes an attractive and illuminating disc.

Venus and Adonis
(B) *** HM HMX 2901684. Joshua, Finley, Blaze, Clare College Chapel Ch., OAE, Jacobs

(i) *Venus and Adonis*; (ii) *Organ Voluntaries in D min.; A min.; G (2 versions)*
(M) *** Decca 473 713-2. (i) Bott, George, Crabtree, Gooding, King, Grant, Robson, Agnew, Westminster Abbey School Choristers, New L. Cons., Pickett; (ii) Leonhardt

Venus and Adonis has been well served on record, but Pickett's version has a pair of trump cards to play: Catherine Bott's imaginative, enticing Venus and Michael George's strongly characterized Adonis. The result is that this simple drama springs to life with unexpected vividness. The supporting cast is excellent, and so is the (1992) recording, and we are made to realize that this is a far finer and deeper work than hitherto suspected. Now offered at mid-price, with four short but attractive organ voluntaries added as a bonus, and with texts included, this is an excellent reissue in Decca's British Music Collection.

René Jacobs conducts a lively performance of *Venus and Adonis*, bringing out the dramatic bite of a piece that inevitably suffers by comparison with Purcell's *Dido and Aeneas*. Speeds are on the brisk side, never rushed, and Rosemary Joshua makes a delightful Venus, bright and sweet, singing with ravishing tone in her big solo towards the end. Gerald Finley, clear and firm, makes a splendid Adonis, and it is good to have a counter-tenor, not a soprano, in the role of Cupid, the excellent Robin Blaze. Fresh, incisive singing from the Clare College Chapel Choir, and clear, atmospheric sound. A bargain.

BOCCHERINI, Luigi (1743–1805)

Luigi Boccherini, long underestimated, was born in Tuscany and came from a cultivated family. His father was a professional double bass player and Luigi was already a proficient cellist by the age of thirteen, which explains his fondness for concertos for this instrument. He was soon a much-travelled virtuoso, and it was in Paris in 1767 that he had his first chamber works published. He went on to Spain the following year, where the Spanish Infanta became his patroness and, after subsequently being granted a small pension by the king, he established a base in Madrid. So the Spanish influence on much of his music is not surprising.

COMPLETE CELLO CONCERTOS

Cello Concertos 1 in E flat, G.474; 2 in A, G.475; 3 in D, G.476; 5 in D, G.478

(BB) *** Naxos 8.553572. Hugh, SCO, Halstead

Cello Concertos 4 in C, G.477; 6 in D, G.479; 7 in G, G.480; 8 in C, G.481

(BB) *** Naxos 8.553571. Hugh, SCO, Halstead

Cello Concertos 3 in D, G.476; 7 in G, G.480; 9 in B flat, G.482. (i) Aria accademica in B flat, G.557

**(*) Astrée E 8517. Coin, Limoges Bar. Ens., Coin; (i) with Almajano

Cello Concertos 4 in C, G.477; 6 in D, G.479; 7 in G, G.480; 8 in C, G.481

☞ (BB) *** Warner Apex (ADD) 0927 49805-2. Bylsma, Concerto Amsterdam, Schröder

Cello Concertos 7 in G (G.480); 10 in D (G.483); Sinfonias: in D min. (La casa del diavolo), Op. 12/4; in B flat, Op. 21/5 (G. 497)

✪ (M) *** DHM 82876 60150-2. Bylsma, Tafelmusik, Lamon

Cello Concertos 9 in B flat, G.482; 10 in D, G.483; 11 in C; 12 in E flat

(N) (BB) *** Naxos 8.557589. Wallfisch, N. CO, Ward

Naxos has now begun an impressive new series covering Boccherini's twelve cello concertos. (Our listing uses the Gérard catalogue, so the collector must be careful to identify the contents of each CD by the Gérard numbers.) They are beautifully performed on modern instruments but with concern for period practice, and superbly recorded. There is dedicated playing not just from the soloist but also from the excellent Scottish Chamber Orchestra under Anthony Halstead. Tim Hugh offers substantial cadenzas not only in the first movements of each work but also in slow movements and finales too. The formula in all these works is similar, even though each has its individual delights, with strong, four-square first movements, slow movements that sound rather Handelian, and galloping finales. Throughout, Hugh and Halstead make a stimulating partnership and all these works spring appealingly to life.

For Volume 3, Naxos have turned to Raphael Wallfisch and the Northern Chamber Orchestra under Nicolas Ward, with predictably stimulating results. Indeed, this is one of the finest single discs of Boccherini cello concertos in the catalogue; it includes a first-class account of No. 9 with its noble original *Andante grazioso*. Yet No. 10 proves an equally fine work, on an altogether grander scale, with rich scoring for horns and oboes in the tutti, and alternating with the cello in the *Andante lentarello* in the style of a sinfonia concertante. The horns make an immediately striking contribution to the rumbustious finale. No. 11 by contrast is more economically scored, and its *Largo cantabile* features the unaccompanied cello with orchestral ritornelli as a prelude and postlude. No. 12 is a recent discovery and is a fine, mature work, with an

eloquent slow movement of considerable depth and a popular *Rondo* finale almost like Haydn. The performances are peerless and the recording excellent in every way (like the documentation).

Anner Bylsma on Apex is a fine player, well suited to this repertoire, while Schröder's accompaniments are most stylish and full of vitality. The 1965 recording is first class and the immaculate CD transfer makes the very most of the sound.

Bylsma (a superb cellist) was at his peak in the *G major Concerto*, and the slow movement is played with ravishing delicacy, followed by an infectious finale. Its companion has a darker *Andante lentarello* as its centrepiece, phrased with comparable eloquence, and a jolly, horn-led closing *Allegro e con moto*, in which Bylsma's dashing virtuosity is hair-raising. He is lucky to have Jeanne Lamon's Tafelmusik as his accompanying group, one of the most elegant and polished of all period-instrument ensembles. They come into their own in the pair of symphonies, playing with a Mozartian grace and zest; the dancing violins in the *vivace* finale of the *B flat major Symphony* matched by the fierce vigour of the 'furies' in the devilish finale of the D minor work. The recording is absolutely first class.

Christophe Coin directs his excellent Limoges period-instrument group from the cello, and they accompany most stylishly. With his small-toned baroque cello, his playing is subtle and fastidiously elegant, its expressive feeling never worn on the sleeve. He is the exact opposite of Rostropovich, and those who enjoy intimacy in these works will find this much to their taste.

Cello Concerto 9 in B flat, G.482

☞ (N) *** DG 474 236-2. Jian Wang, Camerata Salzburg (with COUPERIN: *Pièces en concert* (arr. Bazelaire); FRESCOBALDI: *Toccata* (arr. Toister) – MONN: *Cello Concerto* ***

The Chinese cellist Jian Wang gives as eloquent an account as any in the catalogue and enjoys wonderful support from the Camerata Salzburg. He makes the most of this charming and affecting score, for so long known in Friedrich Grützmacher's curious arrangement in which he added a slow movement from a different concerto, together with his arrangement of a Boccherini sonata. Jian Wang was a star pupil in Shanghai, and then studied at Yale with Aldo Parisot. He commands great beauty of tone and expressive subtlety and obviously enjoys a good rapport with the Salzburg players. The *Pièces en Concert*, Bazelaire's arrangement of movements from the *Concerts Royaux* of Couperin, were frequently heard just after the war but are rarities now; Jian Wang plays them with great finesse, as he does the remarkable Frescobaldi piece. A rewarding programme.

(i) *Cello Concerto 9 in B flat* (original version, revised Gendron); (ii–iii) *Flute Concerto in D, Op. 27* (attrib.; now thought to be by Franz Pokorny); (iv) *Symphonies 3 in C; 5 in B flat, Op. 12/3 & 5*; (v) *Guitar Quintets 4 in D (Fandango); 9 in C (La Ritirata di Madrid)*; (vi) *String Quartet in D, Op. 6/1*; (iii) *String Quintet in E, Op. 13/5: Minuet* (only)

(B) *** Ph. Duo 438 377-2 (2). (i) Gendron, LOP, Casals; (ii) Gazzelloni; (iii) I Musici; (iv) New Philh. O, Leppard; (v) Pepe Romero, ASMF Chamber Ens.; (vi) Italian Qt

This most attractive anthology is well documented, and the famous *Minuet* could hardly be presented more winningly, the one digital recording here. It is also good that Gendron's version of the *Cello Concerto* is included, for he pioneered the return of the original version (without Grützmacher's reworking), and he plays it admirably. The *Flute Concerto* is a *galant* piece, elegantly played by Gazzelloni, and one can see why it was mistakenly attributed. Both *Symphonies* are full of vitality in these excellent performances under Raymond Leppard and are very well recorded. The Italian Quartet's performance of the *D major Quartet* is notable for its freshness and refinement. The charming *Guitar Quintets* are unfailingly warm and sensitive, and they are well recorded too, although there is a touch of thinness on top.

Cello Concerto in B flat (arr. Grützmacher)
(M) *** EMI (ADD) 5 66896-2 [5 66948-2]. Du Pré, ECO,
  Barenboim – HAYDN: *Concertos 1–2* ***
(BB) *** Naxos 8.550059. Kanta, Capella Istropolitana,
  Breiner – HAYDN: *Cello Concertos 1–2* ***

Working for the first time in the recording studio with her husband, Daniel Barenboim, Jacqueline du Pré was inspired to some really heart-warming playing, broadly romantic in style – but then that is what Grützmacher plainly asks for. Du Pré's admirers will surely feel that this is an apt choice for reissue as one of EMI's 'Great Recordings of the Century', and the disc now offers two Haydn cello concertos instead of one.

Ludovít Kanta's playing is distinguished by imaginative and musicianly phrasing and a warm tone. The Slovak players under Peter Breiner give a good account of themselves, and this can hold its own against versions costing twice or three times as much.

Complete symphonies

28 Symphonies (complete)
(M) *** CPO 999 401 (8). Deutsche Kammerakademie,
  Neuss, Goritzki

In this first complete survey of the Boccherini symphonies, Johannes Goritzki's achievement is remarkable. Himself a cellist, he shows a natural feeling for Boccherini's special combination of *galant* and classical styles, revealing the music's strengths rather than its weaknesses, The playing – on modern instruments – of the German Chamber Academy Orchestra of Neuss is alert, polished and warm-hearted, besides showing a nice feeling for Boccherini's delicate *Andantinos*, which are never sentimentalized. The recording is excellently balanced and has plenty of life and bloom. All the discs are now available separately at budget price.

Volume 1: *Sinfonia in D, G.490; Sinfonia concertante in C for 2 Violins & Cello, Op. 7, G.491; Sinfonia with Solo Guitar in C, Op. 10/3, G.523*
*** CPO 999 084-2

Volume 2: *Symphonies: in D; in E flat; in C, Op. 12/1–3, G.503-5*
*** CPO 999 172-2

Volume 3: *Symphonies: in D min.; in B flat; in A, Op. 12/4–6, G.506–8*
*** CPO 999 173-2

Volume 4: *Symphonies: in B flat; in E flat; in C; in D; in B flat, Op. 21/1–5, G.493–7*
*** CPO 999 174-2

Volume 5: *Symphonies: in A, Op. 21/6, G.498; in D; in E flat; in A, Op. 35/1–3, G.509–11*
*** CPO 999 175-2

Volume 6: *Symphonies: in F; in E flat; in B flat, Op. 35/4–6, G.512–14; in C, Op. 37/1, G.515*
*** CPO 999 176-2

Volume 7: *Symphonies: in D min.; in A, Op. 37/3–4, G.517–18; in C min., Op. 41, G.519*
*** CPO 999 177-2

Volume 8: *Symphonies: in D, Op. 42, G.520; in D, Op. 45, G.522; in D, G.500*
*** CPO 999 178-2

The early *Sinfonia in D, G.490*, originated as an (Italian) overture to a cantata, *La confederazione del Sabini con Roma*. Dating from 1765, it has a most engaging, dancing finale, while the charming central *Andante grazioso* was also featured in the *Cello Concerto, G.478*. The *Sinfonia concertante, G.491*, first heard in Paris in 1768, is a wholly different matter – an ambitious work of considerable character and immediate appeal. The *Sinfonia* with obbligato solo guitar is an arrangement of G.491, made some years later for the Marquis de Benevent, an amateur guitarist.

The Op. 12 *Symphonies* of 1771 mark Boccherini's full entry into his own *galant* symphonic world, even if at times he is still thinking in terms of concertante writing, especially in Op. 12/3. Allegros are full of vigour, yet that melancholy element which is part of his musical personality is always apparent.

Boccherini composed his Op. 21 set of 1775 during a congenial period in his life when he was living in Aranjuez, and this is reflected in their generally lighthearted manner; the flutes frequently colour the scoring appealingly, as in the opening movement of the first of the set. The slow movements are usually dainty *Andantinos*, and the composer favours *dolce* and *con grazia* flavourings. Finales are usually vigorous, with bouncing energy; alternatively, those of the second and third of the set are gracious Minuets.

The last of the set is in A and is richly scored, with aurally striking use of the highly crooked horns.

The Op. 35 group of 1782 marks a further step forward in maturity. They are all still three-movement works, but the scoring is more expansive, yet the ideas in the allegros are as invigorating as ever.

The energetic first symphony of the Op. 37 set (one of the composer's most fertile works) is in four movements, setting the pattern for the rest of the series. Its first movement returns to Boccherini's concertante style, with pairs of oboes, bassoons, flutes and a solo violin, and the spirited monothematic finale brings a panoply of colour, with chirping trills adding to the gaiety.

By the time he wrote his Op. 37 symphonies in 1786–7 Boccherini was established as the director of the Duchess of Osuna's court orchestra in Madrid. These mature four-movement works are obviously Haydn-influenced, but the lively invention and rich scoring remain Boccherini's own. The horns shine through in the *A major* finale which, with its single striking theme, is reminiscent of the finale of Haydn's *Symphony No. 88*. Moreover, the outer movements of the powerful C minor work, Op. 41 (1788), have much in common with Haydn's *Sturm und Drang*, with a lovely *Pastorale* to give peaceful contrast. This key work is one of the composer's most imaginative symphonies.

Boccherini's last two symphonies, Opp. 42 and 45, were written in 1789 and 1792 respectively, while the composer was in the employ of the King of Prussia. They are both first-class works, clearly following the pattern Haydn had established; but, as ever with Boccherini, they remain highly individual in colour. After this, G.500 is unduly simplistic and unadventurous, and it is more likely to be spurious than an early work wrongly catalogued. However, Goritzki makes the very most of its brief *Presto* finale, avoiding any sense of anticlimax.

Other recordings

Symphonies: in A, Op. 15/6, G.508; in E flat, Op. 35/5, G.513; in C min., Op. 41, G.519; in D, Op. 42, G.520
(B) **(*) HM Musique d'abord HMA 1951597. Berlin Akademie für Alte Musik

Four characteristic Boccherini *Symphonies*, given bold and energetic performances by the Berlin Akademie. In the A major work of 1771 Boccherini writes engagingly for the flutes, but the high horns here dominate the *fortissimos*. The string playing in the *Larghetto* is pleasing and, after the Minuet, the work ends with another (*Grave*) slow movement. *No. 19 in E flat* (1782) is a three-movement work with a Minuet finale that hardly sounds like a Minuet at all. Nos. 26 and 27 were written in 1788 and 1789 respectively and are obviously more mature. The *C minor* has a winning *Pastorale* slow movement, sympathetically presented here, and the cascading finale demands and receives considerable virtuosity from the violins, But the *D major* is the finest of the four with a memorable Minuet (with violin obbligato) and a charming, Laendler-like trio, followed by a vigorous finale full of contrasts. The playing throughout lacks neither polish nor strength, but tuttis are gruff, with powerful accents, and at times one wishes the orchestra could relax more and convey a greater sense of elegance, as Tafelmusik do.

Symphonies: in D; in E flat; in A; in F; in E flat; in B flat, Op. 35/1–6
**(*) Hyp. CDA 66903. L. Festival O, Pople

Symphonies: in C; in D min.; in A, Op. 37/1, 3 & 4, G.515, 517–18; in D, Op. 42, G.520
**(*) Hyp. CDA 66904. L. Festival O, Pople

In the mid-1990s, Hyperion embarked on a Boccherini series with Ross Pople directing lively, characterful and polished performances with his excellent chamber orchestra. As can be seen above, these are attractive and mature works. The Hyperion sound is pleasingly fresh and open, and this is a most enjoyable pair of discs, but not necessarily preferable to the CPO series.

CHAMBER MUSIC

Cello Quintet, Op. 37/7
*** Australian Decca Eloquence (ADD) 421 637-2. ASMF –
MENDELSSOHN: *Octet* ***

The *Quintet* is an inspired piece and makes this disc worth getting for its own sake, though the coupled performance of Mendelssohn's *Octet* is a particularly fine one. The 1968 recording remains rich and full, and this Australian Eloquence CD has full sleeve-notes.

Cello Sonatas: in C min., G.2 (first version); in A, G.4 (first version); in G, G.5; in C, G.17; in F min.
(BB) *** Naxos 8.554324. C. & S. Benda

Boccherini could hardly be boring if he tried, and these cello sonatas (of which he wrote thirty-four!) are full of attractive invention. They could hardly be more persuasively played. The *A major Sonata* which opens the disc is particularly enticing, warmly melodic and with fizzing display passages which Christian Benda handles with easy virtuosity against the simple fortepiano backing. The finale is marked *Affetuoso*, which sums up this team's approach throughout. The jolly opening movement of the *G major* is an *Allegro militaire*, while the *moto perpetuo* finale of the *C major* is as busy as a bumble-bee. The *F minor Sonata* was discovered as recently as 1987 and has a lovely *Cantabile siciliano* for its slow movement which is quite haunting in the hands of these players. In short this is a first-class disc, very naturally recorded.

Cello Sonatas: in D min., G.2b; in A, G.4; in G, G.5; in A, G.13; in G, G.15; in C min., G.18
**(*) HM Praga PRD 250 147. Kaňka, Tůma, Hejný

These Prague recordings feature a full continuo, and the result is like a cello duet accompanied by a (dwarfed) backwardly balanced harpsichord. The playing is eloquent and spirited, but the effect is muddled and much less enjoyable than the splendid Naxos versions.

Flute Quintets (for flute, violin, viola, 2 cellos), Op. 17/1–6, G.419–24)
(BB) *** Naxos 8.553719. Magnin, Janáček Qt

The Op. 17 *Quintets* are comparatively familiar and certainly rewarding, and they are very well played and recorded here. This Naxos disc is excellent value.

Flute Quintets, Op. 55/1–6, G.431-6 (for flute & string quartet)
(M) *** CPO 999 382-2. Faust, Auryn Qt

These six *Flute* (or oboe) *Quintets* are late works, dating from 1797, and show the composer at his most felicitous and charming. No. 6 is the only work in the minor key and it ends delicately. Michael Faust is a first-rate flautist and his performances here are vivacious and elegant, and recorded with a vivid presence.

Guitar Quintets 1–7, G.445–51; 9 (La ritirata di Madrid), G.453
(B) *** Ph. Duo (ADD) 438 769-2 (2). P. Romero, ASMF Chamber Ens. (members)

Boccherini wrote or arranged 12 guitar quintets, but only the present eight have survived, plus another version of *No. 4 in D* (*Fandango*), G.448. Although some of the music is bland, it is nearly all agreeably tuneful in an unostentatious way, and there are some highly imaginative touches, with attractive hints of melancholy and underlying passion. These performances by Pepe Romero (often willing to take a relatively minor role) and members of the ASMF Chamber Ensemble are wholly admirable, and Philips are especially good at balancing textures of this kind in the most natural way, the guitar able to be assertive when required without overbalancing the ensemble.

Guitar Quintets 4 in D (Fandango), G.448; 5 in D, G.449; 6 in G, G.450
(BB) *** HM HCX 3957026. Savino, Artaria Qt

It is good to have performances on period instruments which create such a natural balance between the strings and the guitar. Although textures are less ample, they can also be attractively delicate, and there is no lack of warmth in the lovely *Pastorale* which forms the second movement of the most famous work (No. 4), with its *Fandango* finale. Here there is a spirited contribution from Peter Mund with his castanets. The other *D major Quartet*, G.449, has a charming opening movement and a diverting closing Theme and Variations, based on the same theme. Performances are stylishly intimate with recording to match. Most recommendable.

Guitar Quintets Nos. (i) 4 in D (Fandango), G.448; 7 in E min., G.451; 9 in C (La ritirata di Madrid), G.453

⊶ (B) *** DG (ADD) 449 852-2. Yepes, Melos Qt; (i) with Tena

In the DG bargain compilation from 1971 the playing is expert and, in the boisterous *Fandango* finale of No. 4, Lucero Tena also makes a glittering contribution with his castanets. *La ritirata di Madrid* is used as the finale of the C major work. This picturesque evocation is created with a set of 12 brief variations set in a long slow crescendo, followed by a similarly graduated decrescendo, a kind of Spanish patrol, with the 'night watch' disappearing into the distance at the end.

Guitar Quintets Nos. (i) 4 in D (Fandango), G.448; 9 in C (La riterata di Madrid), G.453. String Quartet in G min., Op. 24/6 (G.194)

**(*) Virgin 5 45606-2. (i) Pinardi, Europa Galante, Biondi

The Virgin coupling of the *Fandango* and *Riterata di Madrid* Quintets is the most dramatic on record, with Mauro Occhinieri's castanets as spectacular in the one as the histrionic *crescendo* and *decrescendo* in the other, with the music finally fading away completely into the distance. The playing itself is immensely vigorous, but it is the lack of charm (an important feature in Boccherini's music), entirely absent in the *Adagio* of the G minor String Quartet. The recording is vividly projected and it is easy to respond to the visceral power of this playing, but this is not the whole story. The Yepes–Melos DG pairing of the two main works may be picturesque rather than theatrically overwhelming, but its elegance is more in keeping with the composer's intentions (DG 449 852-2).

Guitar Quintet 9: La ritirata di Madrid ('Procession of the Night Watch in Madrid'): orchestral version

(M) *** DG (ADD) 457 914-2. BPO, Karajan – ROSSINI: String Sonatas **(*)

This colourful and original work, which sets out to evoke music heard in Madrid at night, responds wonderfully to the full Karajan treatment. The playing is glorious, with sound to match, but it is also available, with better couplings, on one of DG's 'Originals' (449 724-2) as a bonus for Respighi's *Pines* and *Fountains of Rome*.

Piano Quintets, Op. 56/1–2 & 5, G.407–8 & G.411; Op. 57/2–3 & 6, G.414–15 & G.418

(M) *** Astrée E3001 (2). Cohen, Mosaïques Qt

There are 12 piano quintets, and Patrick Cohen and the Mosaïques Quartet are obviously embarking – so far with great success – on a complete set. There is drama and grace and warmth of feeling, balanced by elegance, in this music; and the playing here also emphasizes its vitality. Slow movements are particularly eloquent, and the use of period instruments in no way inhibits the expressive range of the music.

Piano Quintets: in E flat; in A min.; in E min.; in C, Op. 56/3 & 6, Op. 57/3 & 6, G.410, G.412, G.415, G.418

⊶ (B) *** DHM (ADD) 05472 77448-2. Les Adieux

This is a particularly attractive group of Boccherini works, and it is made the more so by its reissue on the bargain Baroque Esprit label. The lovely *E minor* and the *A minor* both have those hints of beguiling, almost sultry melancholy that makes this composer's musical language so distinctive. This accomplished period-instrument group turn in performances of great finesse and charm, though the recording balance places the listener very much in the front row of the salon.

String Quartets, Op. 32/1–6

(B) *** Warner Elatus (ADD) 2564 60028-2 (2). Esterházy Qt

String Quartets, Op. 32/1–2; String Quartet in A, Op. 39

(BB) *** Naxos 8.555042. Borciani Qt

String Quartets, Op. 32/3–6

(BB) *** Naxos 8.555043. Borciani Qt

The Esterházy Quartet set dates from 1780, about the same period as Haydn's Op. 33. They may ultimately lack the depth and vision of Haydn and Mozart, but to listen to this pioneering Elatus recording is to be amazed that music of this quality has been so long neglected. The Esterházy Quartet are led by Jaap Schröder and theirs is thoroughly rewarding music-making. The Quartet was beautifully recorded in Haarlem, Holland, in 1976 and the new CD transfer of these two *Das alte Werk* discs is outstandingly natural. The documentation is sparse, and the overall playing time of the pair of CDs is only 89 minutes, but they are all enjoyable and the set now comes in the lowest price range.

The Quartetto Borciani offer an equally accomplished alternative on moden instruments, which have plenty of character and vitality and are always sensitive to Boccherini's gentle touches of expressive melancholy. But they have an advantage over the Teldec set in including Boccherini's later *A major Quartet*, Op. 39 (1787), which has a particularly touching *Grave* third movement, most affectingly played here. The Naxos recording is vivid and truthful and there are excellent notes, whereas the Teldec set is very sparsely documented.

String Quartets: in C; in G min.; in A, Op. 32/4–6

(BB) *** CPO 999 202-2. Nomos Qt

These are three most attractive works, of Boccherini's best quality. All three slow movements are expressively potent; the *Andantino lentarello* of the *A major* is particularly searching, and the following Minuet is hardly less striking. The Nomos is a first-class group, using modern instruments but in such a way as to provide textures which are fully blended and sweet while avoiding nineteenth-century opulence. The recording is excellent.

String Quartet in E flat, Op. 58/2

(M) *** HM Cal. (ADD) CAL 5698. Talich Qt – HAYDN: Quartet 74; MENDELSSOHN: Quartet 2; MICA: Quartet 6 ***

The Talich are on top form and are recorded very naturally, so that this well-planned collection amounts to more than the sum of its parts.

String Quintets: in A, Op. 10/1; in D min., Op. 18/5; in A (Della disgrazia), Op. 28/2 ; in A, Op. 29/4; in A, Op. 40/4; in F, Op. 41/2

(***) Testament mono SBT 1245. Quintetto Boccherini

String Quintets: in F, Op. 11/3; in C min. (Di Nina), Op. 18/1; in D min., Op. 25/1; in C min., Op. 29/2

(***) Testament mono SBT 1244. Quintetto Boccherini

String Quintets: in E, Op. 11/5; in D (L'Uccelliera), Op. 11/6; in G, Op. 25/3; in E flat, Op 31/1: Grave in D (Fandango), Op. 40/2

(***) Testament mono SBT 1243. Quintetto Boccherini

For so long dismissed as 'la femme d'Haydn', Boccherini has been underrated and taken for granted. Yet at his finest and most eloquent – and many of these quintets are just that – they show how inventive and poignant he can be. Under the elegant surface, there is a melancholy that is often affecting and, though his music does not show the range and depth of his greatest contemporaries, his art can be deeply rewarding. These mono recordings were all made in the mid-1950s by one of the finest ensembles of the day; they produce a finely balanced sound of great refinement and tonal beauty. This is most civilized music-making and much to be cherished. Each disc is available separately and few collectors having sampled one will be able to resist its companions. Very little allowance need be made for the 1950s recording, and the transfers are eminently truthful and present.

String Quintets, Op. 11/4–6

⊕↝ (BB) *** DHM 05472 77851-2. Smithsonian Chamber Players

Boccherini's Op. 11 dates from 1771. No. 5 of the set in A major contains *the* famous Minuet and it is presented elegantly here. But the extraordinary Trio of the Minuet of Op. 11/4 fragmented over a drone bass is almost as memorable, and the first movement of Op. 11/6 called *L'uccelliero* ('The Aviary') brings a series of exotic bird calls, plus shepherds' pipes in the slow movement. So this stylishly played collection scores three out of three for novelty. The recording is faithful if perhaps a little close.

String Quintets Op. 11/5; Op. 25/1, 4 & 6

*** Virgin 5 45421-2. Europa Galante

Boccherini's quintets are an unfailing delight and their sunny, gentle aspect at times masks a touching melancholy. Europe Galante play with great sympathy and style and round things off with the famous minuet. A most attractive issue.

String Quintets: in E , Op. 13/5, G.275; in G min., Op. 37/13, G.348; in F min., Op. 37/19, G.351

*** Hyp. CDA 67287 Vanbrugh Qt, with Lester

It is particularly refreshing in the Vanbrugh performance to hear Boccherini's famous *Minuet* in context with the work's other three movements; their approach pays obvious tribute to period practice in the choice of tempo, far faster than one usually associates with this well-known 'lollipop', light and crisp. The other movements are comparably striking, starting with a leisurely first movement marked *amoroso*, and ending with a relaxed Rondo finale, marked *sotto voce*, with much pointed dialogue between the instruments.

Both the other quintets here were composed in 1789, 18 years after the *E major*, and regularly rely on the characteristic Boccherini device of quickly switching between major and minor keys. In the *G minor* Boccherini again uses the marking *amoroso* in the Larghetto slow movement, before leading in the finale to a movement which has something of the flavour of Haydn in *Sturm und Drang* mood, not a rondo but a compact sonata-form structure. Vividly recorded and with

fine performances, both polished and refreshing, with Richard Lester a perfect partner for the prize-winning Vanbrugh Quartet, this is an outstanding disc in every way.

String Quintets: in C, Op. 28/4, (G 310); in C, Op. 42/2 (G 349); (Quintettino) in B min., Op. 42/3 (G 350); in D, Op. 43/2 (G 353)

*** Hyp. CDA 67383. Vanbrugh Qt, with Lester

The prize-winning Vanbrugh Quartet, with Richard Lester now a seasoned member of the ensemble, continue their exploration of the Boccherini *String Quintets*, using a second cello. The earliest in C major, Op. 28/4, dates from 1779. It opens amiably and is characteristic of the composer's bonhomie, mixed with touches of melancholy, noticeable in the minor-key Trio of the Minuet and the tranquil *Grave*, then offset by the bouncing closing Rondeau. Its companion work in the same key, written a decade later, opens nostalgically, but its congenial Minuet has a catchiness that is similar to the composer's most famous movement in this form, yet again with a minor-key centrepiece. The spirited *Allegro assai* is then followed by a galant finale.

The two-movement *Quintettino* (again from 1789) makes a direct contrast between wistful espressivo and vigorous – but not entirely convincing – jollity. The *D major Quintet*, written a year later, opens positively and follows with graceful Minuet, which leads to a touchingly simple *Andante*; all melancholy is then banished by the good-natured finale. Throughout the four works Boccherini's invention nevers fails him, and these excellent players relish all the felicities of his writing. Excellent recording.

String Quintets, Op. 39/1–3, G.337–9; String Quartet, Op. 64/2, G.249

*** MDG 603 1040-2. Frankfurt Ens. Concertante

The three *Quintets* of Op. 39, dating from 1787, are scored for a double bass in the place of second cello, which adds considerably to the body of the sound. In any case, it is always good to hear Boccherini with the added warmth of modern instruments, as the lovely Pastorale, second movement of the first *Quintet*, readily shows. The Adagio of the second, which opens over a pizzicato accompaniment, is also most engaging, and its busy finale has a gentle close. Then the ever-innovative Boccherini subdivides the brief central movement of the third work into four contrasted sections, while the perky closing Rondeau has a central Minuet. The *String Quartet*, Op. 64/2, of 1804 was Boccherini's last composition, and he completed the first movement only. But it has characteristic charm and would make a good encore, although here it forms a central interlude. First-class performances throughout, polished and committed, and fine recording make this collection very recommendable.

String Sextets, Op. 23/1, 2 & 5

(B) **(*) HM Musique d'abord HMA 1951478. Ens. 415, Banchini

Boccherini's special vein of melancholy, which yet never suggests gloom and indeed refreshes the spirit, is heard at its most appealing in these works, notably the *Andantino* of *No. 2 in B flat major* and the *Grave*, which opens the D major (No. 5). He is never a conventional composer, and even the minuets are unpredictable (one has several trios). In short, these are very appealing works and they are played with refined polish and feeling by this sensitive ensemble, who use original instruments with much finesse. However, it must be said that the overall texture produced here is somewhat meagre, and at times one feels the need for the fuller, more robust sound of modern instruments.

Violin Sonatas, Op. 5/1–6, G.25–30
** Glossa GCD 920306. Ogg, Moreno

Boccherini's Op. 5 originated as a set of sonatas for violin and fortepiano. He then promptly made an arrangement of the keyboard part for harpsichord, and it was published in Paris in 1769. There are notable differences between this and the original version for fortepiano, but the present performers have chosen the published version in preference to the composer's manuscript, for reasons that are not altogether convincing. Indeed, their performances here fail to convince, for Jacques Ogg does not create a very sonorous timbre and the recording is not too flattering either, letting the rather clattery harpsichord, which often has the major role, dominate rather more than necessary.

(i) Stabat Mater, G.532 (First Version); Concert Arias: Ah, no! son io che parlo; Care luci. Symphonies: in D min. (La Casa del Diavolo), Op. 12/4 (G.506); in C, Op. 23/3 (G.523); in A, Op. 37/4 (G.518)
☛ (N) (BB) *** Warner Apex 2564 61689-2 (2). (i) Gasdia; Sol. Ven., Scimone

Boccherini wrote comparatively little vocal music but his *Stabat Mater*, in its original version an extended solo setting for soprano, here gloriously sung by Cecilia Gasdia, must be counted among his most inspired works. The beautiful sequence of movements towards the close – *Eja mater fons amoris . . . Tui nati vulnerati . . . Virgo virginum praeclara*, sung most affectingly here – contains some exquisite music, and in the despairing closing *Quando corpus moretur*, Gasdia is very moving indeed. The music has a Mozartian purity of line, and the two concert arias which follow also take Mozart as their model. They are brilliantly sung: Claudio Scimone provides highly sensitive support. Then on the second disc (with his I Solisti Veneti) offers vital and expressive accounts of three *Symphonies*, including not only *La Casa del Diavolo*, but a most appealing concertante work in C major. This was the composer's last symphony to be published (in 1798) and has prominent obbligato parts for oboe, violin and guitar, which are most sympathetically played here and are especially effective in the gentle *Grave* slow movement. The digital sound is bright and immediate, but there is plenty of ambient warmth.

KEYBOARD MUSIC

6 Duet Sonatas for 2 Harpsichords (from String Quartets, G.195/200); Fandango (from String Quintet in D, G. 341)
(B) ** HM HMA 1951233. Christie and Rousset (harpsichords)

These are transcriptions for two harpsichords of string quartets – or rather *quartettinos* (they are in two movements, hence the diminutive) – composed by Boccherini in 1778. They sound less idiomatic in this instrumental form than the *Fandango*, an arrangement of a movement from the *Quintettino*, Op. 40/2, written ten years later. Boccherini himself transcribed it for guitar and quartet. It certainly works more successfully in the keyboard medium than the other quartets. The playing here by a distinguished partnership is lively but

closely balanced and is recorded at a high level so that the overall effect is somewhat unremitting.

VOCAL MUSIC

(i) Stabat Mater (first version); (ii) String Quintet in C min., Op. 31/4, G.328
(M) **(*) HM HMC 901378. (i) Mellon, Ens. 415, Banchini; (ii) Banchini, Gatti, Moreno, Dieltiens, Brugge

Stabat Mater (1800 version)
☛ *** Hyp. CDA 67108. Gritton, Fox, Bickley, Agnew, Harvey, King's Consort, King – D'ASTORGA: Stabat Mater ***

Boccherini originally wrote his *Stabat Mater* in 1781 for solo soprano and strings. But, stimulated by the ongoing success of Pergolesi's famous 1736 setting of the same text, he revised the work in 1800 for two sopranos and a tenor, increasing its dramatic range and power.

The pure-voiced Agnès Mellon makes a gently touching case for the earlier version and she is expressively and authentically supported by the refined playing of Chiara Banchini and her four colleagues of Ensemble 415, who also give a sensitive account of the *String Quintet* which acts as filler. If the effect of the vocal work with period-instrument accompaniment is comparatively restrained, many will enjoy the gently luminous sense of spirituality which pervades this Harmonia Mundi version. The recording is very natural.

Boccherini's ambitious revision is masterly in increasing the range and expressive power of the work. With first-class soloists, Robert King's performance is as moving as it is gripping in the more dramatic moments. Notable are the lovely soprano duets, so beautifully sung by Susan Gritton and Sarah Fox, contrasting with the dramatic trios with tenor, and the closing *Quando corpus morietur* (another trio) is exquisitely managed. The apt coupling, a fine setting of the same text, written nearly a century earlier by an almost unknown Spanish composer, increases the value of this disc.

BOËLLMANN, Léon (1862–97)
Cello Sonata in A min., Op. 40; 2 Pieces for Cello & Piano, Op. 31
*** Hyp. CDA 66888. Lidström, Forsberg – GODARD: Cello Sonata in D min., etc. ***

Boëllmann is best known for his organ music and in particular the *Suite gothique*, whose final Toccata is a familiar *cheval de bataille*. The A minor Sonata reveals him to be a cultured and imaginative musician. Mats Lidström and Bengt Forsberg play with such passion and conviction that they almost persuade one that this piece is worthy to rank alongside the Brahms *Sonatas*. The recording is very acceptable, if rather close. Strongly recommended.

BÖHM, Georg (1661–1733)
Keyboard Suites 1–11; Prelude, Fugue & Postlude in G min.
(N) *** Glossa GCD 921801 (2). Meyerson

Georg Böhm was one of the leading Baroque masters of the organ and harpsichord. When the young J. S. Bach went to Lüneburg in 1700, he spoke of Böhm as the greatest keyboard virtuoso he had ever met. And Carl Philipp Emanuel reported that he had loved and studied this master with reverence and transcribed in his own hand *Menuet fait par Mons. Böhm* in Anna Magdalena Bach's Notebook. Böhm's suites followed the formal conventions of the period with stylized dance movements, and were in all likelihood conceived in the years before 1700, during his period in Hamburg. They are of high quality and keen musical interest and are splendidly played by Mitzi Meyerson on a modern instrument by Keith Hill, tuned to mean-tone temperament. Also of much interest is the *Prelude, Fugue and Postlude in G minor*, which came to light in 1837 and which Schumann described as *eine gespenstige Kaprice* ('an eerie Caprice'). Very good sound too.

BOÏELDIEU, François (1775–1834)

Harp Concerto in 3 Tempi in C
☜— ✿ (M) *** Decca 425 723-2. Robles, ASMF, Brown – DITTERSDORF; HANDEL: *Harp Concertos*, etc. *** ✿

Boïeldieu's *Harp Concerto* has been recorded before but never more attractively. The (originally Argo) recording is still in the demonstration class and very sweet on the ear. To make the reissue even more attractive, three beguiling sets of *Variations* have been added, including music by Handel and Beethoven and a *Theme, Variations and Rondo Pastorale* attributed to Mozart.

La Dame blanche (complete)
(M) *** EMI 5 56355-2 (2). Blake, Verzier, Naouri, Fouchécourt, Deletré, Massis, Delunsch, Brunet, Dehont, Vajou, R. France Ch., Paris Ens. O, Minkowski

Completed in 1826, this lighthearted adaptation of Walter Scott's novel sparkles from first to last, helped by the inspired direction of Marc Minkowski with an excellent team of soloists who all sing with a natural feeling for the idiom. This is a piece which with its many lively ensembles points directly forward to Donizetti's *Daughter of the Regiment* and even to Offenbach's two gendarmes from *Geneviève de Brabant*. Here the cast has no weak link, with the outstanding Rossinian tenor Rockwell Blake matched by the others, not least Annik Massis as Anna and Mireille Delunsch as Jenny. For some non-French speakers there may be rather too much dialogue, but that can easily be worked around on CD. Warm, well-balanced sound.

BOITO, Arrigo (1842–1918)

Mefistofele (complete)
(N) (M) *** Decca 475 6666 (2). Ghiaurov, Pavarotti, Freni, Caballé, L. Op. Ch., Trinity Boys' Ch., Nat. PO, Fabritiis
(M) **(*) Decca (ADD) 440 054-2. Siepi, Del Monaco, Tebaldi, Cavalli, St Cecilia Ac., Rome, Ch. & O, Serafin
(M) *(*) Sony SM2K 90478 (2). Domingo, Marton, Ramey, Hungarian State Op. Ch. & O, Patanè

Boito's *Mefistofele* is a strange and episodic work to come from the hands of the master-librettist of Verdi's *Otello* and *Falstaff*, but it has many fine moments. The early digital recording gives the brass and percussion plenty of weight – most importantly in the heavenly prologue. With the principal soloists all at their best – Pavarotti most seductive in *Dai campi, dai pratti*, Freni finely imaginative on detail, Caballé consistently sweet and mellifluous as Elena, Ghiaurov

strongly characterful, if showing some signs of strain – this is a most recommendable set, though Fabritiis in his last recording lacks a little in energy, and the chorus is placed rather distantly. Texts and translation are included in its new Classic Opera release.

On the 1958 Decca Rome set, Serafin, the most persuasive Italian conductor of his day, draws glorious sounds from his performers, even from Mario del Monaco, who is here almost sensitive. Tebaldi is a rich-toned Margherita – almost too rich-toned for so frail a heroine – and Siepi makes an excellent Mefistofele. The Decca engineers came up trumps: the stereo remains remarkably spacious, particularly in the Prologue.

Patanè's is a stiff, rather perfunctory reading of this vivid opera about heaven and hell, not helped by a studio acoustic which, with the chorus cleanly and unatmospherically placed, makes it sound more like an oratorio than an opera. Plácido Domingo sings well, but there is little bloom on the voice and, noble and commanding as Samuel Ramey's performance is, he does not sound sinister. The biggest snag is the singing of Eva Marton, far too heavyweight and unsteady a soprano for Margherita, and hardly better suited to the role of Elena (Helen of Troy) which she doubles – another drawback to the set. Moreover the documentation is unacceptably sparse, with neither libretto nor cued synopsis. First choice for this opera still rests with the vintage Decca recording conducted by Fabritiis, with Pavarotti most seductive and Caballé a fine Elena.

BOLCOM, William (born 1938)

Piano Concerto
*** Hyp. CDA 67170. Hamelin, Ulster O, Sitkovetsky – BERNSTEIN: *Symphony 2* ***

William Bolcom is above all a communicator, never afraid of drawing on popular music of every kind, and translating his sources. So this colourful piano concerto, written in 1976 as an offbeat celebration of the US Bicentennial, ranges wide in its moods, with the first movement bringing a jewelled sequence of ideas, both bright and dark, and with the slow movement a gentle dialogue between piano and orchestra. The most striking and provocative movement is the finale, in which Bolcom, Ives-like, hilariously offers a whirling potpourri of American popular themes, from *Yankee Doodle* by way of Sousa and others to ragtime and jazz, punctuated by a sort of Last Post on a cornet, using a hymn-tune. It is great fun, but intentionally with sinister overtones, and Hamelin and his accompanists respond superbly. An unusual and attractive fill-up for the Bernstein.

Songs of Innocence and of Experience
(N) (BB) *** Naxos 8.559216/18 (3). Brewer, Brueggergosman, Davidson, Hohenfeld, Pelton, Morris, Simpson, Young, Gord, Graham, University of Michigan School of Music SO, University Musical Soc., Slatkin

When still in his teens William Bolcom was bowled over by Blake's *Songs of Innocence and Experience*, and promptly composed two of the settings which 20 years later resulted in this work of epic length. Using a daringly wide range of styles, including echoes of country music, folk-tunes, Broadway songs, spirituals and jazz, he has built this complex and attractively varied anthology of settings. The two and a quarter hours of music involve a series of musical arches in nine clear movements, each with a related theme. Not only does the piece run to impressive length, it requires vast vocal and instrumental forces, some 450 performers in this recording, made with musicians from Bolcom's home University of Michigan. With soloists ranging from the dramatic soprano, Christine Brewer, to the folk/blues singer, Peter 'Madcat' Ruth, the performance under Leonard Slatkin is most compelling. Backing the wide-ranging roster of soloists, the amateur choruses achieve remarkably good ensemble in often tricky writing. The work ends with a setting of the poem, *A Divine Image*, prompting Bolcom not to a grand finale but to an attractively jazzy, Bernstein-style number for blues-singer and choruses, with guitar prominent. The booklet gives not only Bolcom's own informative note but full texts of the songs. Full, atmospheric sound.

BORODIN, Alexander (1833–87)

'The World of Borodin': (i) *In the Steppes of Central Asia; Prince Igor*: (ii) *Overture*; (ii–iii) *Polovtsian Dances*; (iv) *Symphony 2 in B min.*; (v) *String Quartet 2: Nocturne*; (vi) *Scherzo in A flat*; (vii–viii) *Far from the shores of your native land*; (vii, ix) *Prince Igor: Galitzky's Aria*

☛ (M) *** Decca (ADD) 444 389-2. (i) SRO, Ansermet; (ii) LSO, Solti; (iii) with L. Symphony Ch.; (iv) LSO, Martinon; (v) Borodin Qt; (vi) Ashkenazy; (vii) N. Ghiaurov; (viii) Z. Ghiaurov; (ix) L. Symphony Ch., LSO, Downes

'Essential Borodin': Symphonies . (i) *1 in E flat*; (ii) *2 in B min.*; (iii) *3 in A min.*; *In the Steppes of Central Asia*; (iv) *String Quartet 2 in B min.*; (v–vi) *Song: Far from the shores of your native land. Prince Igor*: (vii) *Overture*; (vii–viii) *Polovtsian Dances*; (v; viii–ix) *Galitzky's Aria; Konchak's Aria*

(B) *** Double Decca (ADD) 455 632-2 (2). (i) RPO, Ashkenazy; (ii) LSO, Martinon; (iii) SRO, Ansermet; (iv) Borodin Qt; (v) N. Ghiaurov; (vi) Z. Ghiaurov; (vii) LSO, Solti; (viii) L. Symphony Ch.; (ix) LSO, Downes

The 'World of Borodin' is an extraordinarily successful disc. There can be few if any other collections of this kind that sum up a composer's achievement so succinctly or that make such a rewarding and enjoyable 76-minute concert. Solti's *Prince Igor Overture* is outstanding. The *Nocturne* follows the *Overture* so effectively that one might have thought it the composer's own plan. Ansermet's *In the Steppes of Central Asia* is warm and atmospheric. After Nicolai Ghiaurov has reminded us of the melancholy side of the Russian spirit, we come finally to Martinon's unsurpassed 1960 LSO performance of the *B minor Symphony*: the sound has remarkable presence and sparkle.

Decca have now happily expanded the programme to fit on to a Double, and in doing so they represent the composer even more comprehensively for very little extra outlay. Ashkenazy's reading of the *First Symphony* is less high-powered than Martinon's superb account of No. 2, but its many delights come over richly, thanks not only to the quality of the RPO playing but also to the warm (1992) digital recording. Ansermet's touch in the unfinished *Third* is most attractive, with some delightful moments from the SRO woodwind. What makes this extended programme especially attractive is the inclusion of the whole of the *Second String Quartet*, rather than just the slow movement. The performance by the eponymous Borodin Quartet is masterly in every respect. In *Prince Igor* Ghiaurov now adds a second role by

singing Konchak's aria from Act II in addition to Galitzky's aria from Act I.

In the Steppes of Central Asia

*** Ph. SACD 470 618-2; CD 470 840-2. Kirov O, Gergiev – BALAKIREV: *Islamey*; RIMSKY–KORSAKOV: *Scheherazade* ***

Borodin's evocative tone-poem in a concentrated performance provides a well-judged contrast with the main work, *Scheherazade*, in Gergiev's exciting reading. The recording's rich atmosphere is undoubtedly enhanced on the surround-sound SACD stereo version.

In the Steppes of Central Asia; (i) *Nocturne* (from *String Quartet 2*) arr. for violin & orchestra by Rimsky-Korsakov; *Petite suite* (orch. Glazunov); (ii; iii) *Requiem* (orch. Stokowski, arr. Simon); *Prince Igor: Overture*; (iii) *Chorus of Polovtsian Maidens; Dance of Polovtsian Maidens; Polovtsian March; Polovtsian Dances*

(M) **(*) Cala CACD 1029. Philh. O, Simon, with (i) Chase; (ii) Boughton; (iii) BBC SO Ch.

In the Steppes of Central Asia; Prince Igor: Polovtsian Dances

(BB) **(*) EMI Encore (ADD) 5 74763-2. Phil O, Cluytens – RIMSKY-KORSAKOV: *Capriccio espagnol*, etc.; MUSSORGSKY: *Night on the Bare Mountain* **(*)

An interesting and valuable anthology on Cala. Borodin's five-minute piano piece called *Requiem* is played in Stokowski's flamboyantly expansive orchestration, to which Geoffrey Simon has very effectively added solo tenor and male chorus. The piece is ingeniously based on 'Chopsticks' but has an exaggerated dynamic range. *In the Steppes of Central Asia* would have been more effective with greater dynamic contrast, a warmly languorous performance. In the March and the famous *Polovtsian Dances*, the singing of the BBC Chorus is of a high standard, though Geoffrey Simon's direction is lively rather than electrifying, both here and in the Overture. Rimsky-Korsakov's concertante arrangement of the famous *Nocturne* for violin and orchestra – in spite of Stephanie Chase's pleasing advocacy – gives the piece the character of a salon encore, charming but insouciant. The *Petite suite*, a set of six piano miniatures orchestrated by Glazunov, comes off very engagingly.

From Cluytens come a beautifully controlled performance of *In the Steppes of Central Asia* and a lively *Polovtsian Dances*, both enjoyable. The 1958 recording sounds astonishingly well, with only a touch of thinness betraying its age. Part of an attractive bargain CD of Russian show-pieces.

Symphonies 1–3

(N) (M) **(*) RCA 82876 62321-2. Nat. PO, Tjeknavorian

Symphonies 1–3; In the Steppes of Central Asia; Nocturne (orch. Nicolai Tcherepnin); *Petite suite; Prince Igor: Overture*; (i) *Polovtsian Dances*

*** DG (IMS) 435 757-2 (2). Gothenburg SO, Järvi; (i) with Gothenburg Ch.

For those wanting all three symphonies, the Järvi DG set remains recommendable. The alternative versions by Serebrier (ASV CDDCA 706) and Gunzenhauser (Naxos 8.550238) each have the advantage of being offered on a single CD but are undistinctive.

Järvi's *First* has plenty of individuality and colour; the slow movement is radiant, the Scherzo beautifully sprung and the finale made to anticipate the *Prince Igor Overture* in its bright, rhythmic pointing. The *Second* is a strong, spacious reading; however, alongside Martinon (see below), the first movement is somewhat lacking in bite and thrust. The *Third Symphony* (completed by Glazunov), comes off vividly, although it is not as strong a work as the other two. The other pieces are played equally well by the excellent Gothenburg orchestra, notably the *Petite suite*, although there are some reservations about Tcherepnin's very exotic orchestration of the famous *Nocturne* from the *D major String Quartet*, and perhaps Järvi doesn't pull out all the stops in his undoubtedly vivid account of the *Polovtsian Dances*. Yet the Swedish choral singing, if not uninhibited, is vital enough and even includes a brief solo interpolation representing the Khan. The digital recording throughout is from DG's top drawer.

Tjeknavorian's performances, while lacking the last ounce of character, are polished and full of colour, and the orchestral response is on the whole lively. The RCA recordings are certainly vivid and well balanced with wide range and a warm ambience. However to have all three symphonies in modern recordings on a single disc is very attractive.

Symphony 1 in E flat

(BB) **(*) Warner Apex 0927 40597-2. Norwegian R. O, Rasilainen – TCHAIKOVSKY: *Symphony 2* ***

A very enjoyable and recommendable account of this delightful symphony from the Norwegian Radio Orchestra and their Finnish conductor is spirited, and is well enough played and recorded if you want the coupling. It certainly gives pleasure.

Symphony 2 in B min.

(***) Testament mono SBT 1048. Philh. O, Kletzki – TCHAIKOVSKY: *Manfred Symphony* (***)

(M) *(*) Ph. (ADD) 464 735-2. Concg. O, Kondrashin (with RIMSKY-KORSAKOV: *Scheherazade* ***)

(BB) *(*) Belair BAM 9724. New Russian O, Poltevsky – RIMSKY-KORSAKOV: *Tsar Saltan: Suite* ***

Kletzki draws superb playing from the Philharmonia at a vintage period in the mid-1950s. The ravishing account of the slow movement has Dennis Brain at his peak in the big horn solo, backed by Bernard Walton on the clarinet and Sidney Sutcliffe on the oboe producing whispered pianissimos that caress the ear. The first movement is brisk and dramatic, while in the Scherzo the tonguing of the woodwind makes for phenomenal precision. As for the transfer, after a dull opening the bite and immediacy of the brass and woodwind are so vivid they give an illusion of stereo.

Kondrashin's rather brisk live account of the *Second Symphony* has the advantage of fine orchestral playing, though it is let down by some intrusive audience noise and a lapse of intonation in the slow movement. Kondrashin's outstanding *Scheherazade* is a different matter, but fortunately it is also available alternatively coupled with other works by Rimsky-Korsakov.

At super-bargain price on the Belair label comes Poltevsky's version with an excellent orchestra drawn from a range of Moscow orchestras. Impossibly heavy at the start, with fluctuation of tempo in the first movement, and the other three movements are taken broadly too. A disc worth hearing for an electrifying account of the *Tsar Saltan Suite*.

Symphonies (i; ii) 2 in B min.; (iii) 3 in A min.; (i; iv; v) Prince Igor: Overture; Polovtsian Dances

(BB) *** Decca Eloquence (ADD) 467 482-2. (i) LSO; (ii) Martinon; (iii) SRO, Ansermet; (iv) Solti; (v) L. Symphony Ch.

Martinon's electrifying account of the *B minor Symphony* remains unsurpassed. Notable for its fast tempo for the famous opening theme, the strong rhythmic thrust suits the music admirably; the Scherzo is vibrant, the slow movement, with a beautifully played horn solo, is most satisfying, and the finale is a blaze of colour. The early 1960s sound is astonishingly vivid. Solti's *Prince Igor Overture* both unexpectedly romantic and very exciting: there is no finer version in the catalogue. The same can be said of the *Polovtsian Dances*, with splendid choral singing, even if the chorus takes a little longer to warm up than in the famous Beecham version. Both items date from 1966 and have vintage Decca sound.

If the playing of the Suisse Romande Orchestra is not a match for the LSO, Ansermet brings out all the colour in his alive and spontaneous account of the *Third Symphony*, with some delightful moments from the SRO woodwind. Any slight reservations are swept aside, however, when the rest of the programme is so stimulating, and this makes a splendid bargain on the Eloquence label.

Sextet (2 movements)

** Mer. CDE 84211. Arienski Ens. – ARENSKY: *Quartet* ***; TCHAIKOVSKY: *Souvenir de Florence* **

Borodin composed his *Sextet* on a visit to Heidelberg in 1860 but, unfortunately, only two of its movements survive. The Arienski Ensemble play with enthusiasm and conviction and are decently recorded.

String Quartets 1 in A; 2 in D

*** Chan. (ADD) 9965. Borodin Qt

Borodin's *First Quartet* had occupied him over a long period, the best part of the 1870s, while the *Second* was composed in the course of a few summer weeks in 1881 when he was in the country at Zhitovo. It is one of the most lyrical quartets in the repertoire, and its familiarity prompts some music-lovers to underrate its consummate mastery of form. The Borodins made this classic recording in 1979, and it remains the yardstick by which all others are judged.

String Quartets 1 in A; 2 in D; (i) String Sextet in D min.

*** ASV CD DCA 1143. The Lindsays, (i) with Williams, R. Wallfisch

The Lindsays add to their repertory of warm, intense recordings this splendid coupling of Borodin's two *String Quartets* alongside a rarity from early in the composer's career, the *String Sextet*, composed in Heidelberg in 1860, of which only two movements survive. It is a most attractive makeweight in which Borodin was plainly seeking to emulate Mendelssohn's masterly *String Octet* with writing similarly light and exuberant. The *Second Quartet*, with its haunting second-movement *Notturno*, has long been a favourite work, but the *First Quartet*, more ambitious in scale, brings similar finesse and melodic warmth. The Lindsays, very well recorded, give glowing, ripely expressive and finely balanced performances that confidently bring out the light and shade of the writing of both scores, as well as a more convincing reading of the *Sextet* than any other we have heard.

The eponymous Borodin Quartet has a special claim on this repertoire and is now to be found on the Chandos mid-price Historic label. But this sumptuously recorded new ASV triptych has splendid eloquence and will probably be a first choice for those readers who are looking for an up-to-date recording.

String Quartet 2 in D

(M) *** Classic fM 75605 57027-2. Chilingirian Qt –
DVORAK: *Quartet in F*; SHOSTAKOVICH: *Quartet 8* ***

(***) Testament mono SBT 1061. Hollywood Qt –
GLAZUNOV: *5 Novelettes*; TCHAIKOVSKY: *String Quartet 1*
(***)

(M) **(*) HM Cal. (ADD) CAL 5202. Talich Qt –
TCHAIKOVSKY: *Quartet 1* ***

(M) **(*) Decca (ADD) 425 541-2. Borodin Qt –
SHOSTAKOVICH; TCHAIKOVSKY: *Quartets* **(*)

(**(*)) BBC mono BBCL 4063-2. Borodin Qt – RAVEL:
Quartet (**(*)); SHOSTAKOVICH: *Quartet 8* (**(*))

(M) **(*) Telarc CD 80178. Cleveland Qt – SMETANA:
Quartet 1 **(*)

On the Classic fM label the Chilingirian Quartet offer powerful, incisive performances of an apt and generous coupling. With Levon Chilingirian an exceptionally alert leader, rhythms in the Borodin are consistently well sprung, with no sentimentality, in a warmly expressive account of the celebrated slow movement.

Although later recordings may match the Hollywood version, it is still a performance with persuasive freshness and ardour. The sound has been improved, and the addition of the Glazunov, which is new to the catalogue, enhances the disc's value. The playing time runs to one second short of 80 minutes.

The Talich performance is characteristically refined and beautifully played, although the performance lacks something in Slavonic voluptuousness. The digital recording, however, is first class, full and naturally balanced. Moreover, the Tchaikovsky coupling is outstanding in every way.

The Borodins' version of the *Second Quartet* on Decca is very fine, though the forward recording, rich-textured, approaches fierceness in the present CD transfer, and most will prefer a softer-grained effect.

The Borodins made their professional début in 1946, though it was not until 1955 that they assumed their present name. Such was their refinement of sonority, wonderful blend and superb unanimity of ensemble that they soon acquired a legendary reputation. The BBC performance and its companions come from 1962, when the Edinburgh Festival concentrated on Russian music and artists and the Borodin Quartet made their first appearance in Britain. After Edinburgh they recorded the Shostakovich and Borodin *Quartets* at the Decca studios (425 541–2). This mono performance is not quite its equal, although it has great immediacy and flair; in any event, it is still well worth having and sounds very good for its age.

The Cleveland Quartet give a brilliantly prepared and vital account on their four Stradivariuses but, as is the case with the Smetana coupling, their performances are stronger on polish than they are on spontaneity. Not a first choice, though it is impossible not to admire their expertise or gainsay the excellence of the Telarc recording.

Prince Igor (complete; DVD versions)

*** Ph. **DVD** 074 173-9 (2). Putilin, Gorchakova, Akimov,
Aleksashkin, Vaneev, Borodina, Kirov Ballet Ch. & O,
Gergiev (Producer: Paul Smaczny, V/D: Arno Cronvall)

*** Ph. **DVD** 075 099-9 (6). As above – GLINKA: *Ruslan and
Ludmilla*; MUSSORGSKY: *Boris Godunov*

The Kirov production was mounted six years after the CD recording below, in 1998, with a different but equally strong cast. Both Galina Gorchakova and Olga Borodina sing the same roles (Yaroslavna and Konchakova respectively) but the Khan Konchak is Vladimir Vaneev while the performance is dedicated to the memory of the Khan in the earlier set, the incomparable Bulat Minjelkiev; most of the other male roles are differently (but no less superbly) cast. The notes replicate the scholarly account in the CD set of what this edition restores. It includes passages discovered among Borodin's papers that were rejected by Rimsky-Korsakov in his superb edition, and they have been specially orchestrated for this new production by Yuri Faliek. (Rimsky-Korsakov's style and orchestration are very close to Borodin's – and the completion and scoring of Act III was an altogether phenomenal feat on Glazunov's part.) Of Borodin's 20 years of autograph material for the opera, less than a third was included in the published score, and all of that was edited by Rimsky. Some 1,680 bars were the work of Glazunov, who also orchestrated 157 of the 710 pages of full score. Rimsky scored another 368, and only 185 pages remained of Borodin's own scoring. The Gergiev production reverts to a structural outline of 1883, which proposed alternating the Russian and Polovtsian acts. This is not the place to discuss the re-ordering of the material of the opera, but its artistic interest and success are not in question.

The Royal Opera House production from the early 1990s conducted by Haitink was available on video and two Laser-Discs (Decca 071 421-1) and it is well worth seeing for the Igor of Sergei Leiferkus, the Galitsky of Nikola Ghiuselev and Burchuladze's Khan Konchak. However, for obvious reasons it is completely superseded by this superb Philips version. The sets and costumes are sumptuous and the choreography for the *Polovtsian Dances* is that of Fokhine which Diaghilev presented in Paris. The Kirov set is now also included in an attractive package with two other classic productions (presumably at an attractive discount) to mark Valery Gergiev's 25th anniversary at the opera house; those who do not have these performances should take advantage of this. All three are outstanding.

Prince Igor (complete; CD versions)

*** Ph. 442 537-2 (3). Kit, Gorchakova, Ognovienko,
Minjelkiev, Borodina, Grigorian, Kirov Ch. & O, St
Petersburg, Gergiev

(M) **(*) EMI (ADD) 5 66814-2 (2). Chekerliiski, Christoff,
Todorov, Sofia Nat. Theatre Op. Ch. & O, Semkow

Gergiev's electrifying account of Borodin's epic opera reflects not only his own magnetic qualities as a conductor but also the way he has welded his principal singers as well as the chorus and orchestra into a powerful team. Acts I and II are given in reverse order from the usual, with the substantial Prologue here followed by the first Polovtsian scene and its spectacular dances. Only then do you get the scene at Prince Galitsky's court, leading up to Yaroslavna's great lament, here sung superbly by Galina Gorchakova. Otherwise Gergiev generally follows the well-established edition, but he has included material omitted from Borodin's copious sketches, notably an extended monologue of lament for Igor himself as a prisoner of Khan Konchak in Act III: 'Why did I not fall on the field of battle?' That alone puts this ahead of the fine rival

Sony recording from Tchakarov with Bulgarian forces (currently deleted on Philips), and Gergiev is even more sharply dramatic, generally adopting faster speeds. On the solo casting, honours are much more even. The two principal women, not just Gorchakova but Olga Borodina too as Konchak's daughter, Konchakovna, are both magnificent, even finer than their Bulgarian rivals, but neither principal bass Vladimir Ognovienko as Galitsky nor Bulat Minjelkiev as Konchak can match the vocal richness or character of the Bulgarians, Ghiuselev and Ghiaurov, both older-sounding but still compelling. Gegam Grigorian in the tenor role of Igor's son gives a lusty performance, while Mikhail Kit as Igor himself, though often gritty and even fluttery of tone, sings thoughtfully and intelligently, making him a fair match for his Bulgarian rival.

In the colourful EMI recording, Act III is omitted entirely, on the grounds that it was almost completely the work of Rimsky-Korsakov and Glazunov. Boris Christoff as both Galitzky and Konchak easily outshines all rivals. Jerzy Semkow with his Sofia Opera forces is most sympathetic, but the other soloists are almost all disappointing, with the women sourtoned and the men often strained and unsteady. The sound is limited but agreeably atmospheric.

Prince Igor: Overture & Polovtsian Dances
⊕— (M) *** EMI 5 66983-2 [p5 66998-2]. Beecham Choral Soc., RPO, Beecham – RIMSKY-KORSAKOV: *Scheherazade* ***
(BB) *** Virgin 2×1 5 61751-2 (2). RLPO Ch. & O, Mackerras – MUSSORGSKY: *Pictures*, etc. **; RIMSKY-KORSAKOV: *Scheherazade* **(*); TCHAIKOVSKY: *The Tempest* ***

Prince Igor: Polovtsian Dances
(N) (M) **(*) Mercury SACD (ADD) 475 6194. LSO, Dorati – RIMSKY-KORSAKOV: *Capriccio espagnol*, etc. ***
(***) BBC mono BBCL 4084-2 RPO & Ch., Beecham – BALAKIREV: *Symphony 1*; RIMSKY-KORSAKOV: *Le Coq d'or: Suite* ***
(BB) (***) Dutton mono CDBP 9712. LPO, Fitelberg – RIMSKY-KORSAKOV: *Scheherazade; Skazka* ***

Beecham's 1957 performance of the *Polovtsian Dances* – now reissued as one of EMI's 'Great Recordings of the Century' – sweeps the board, even though it omits the percussion-led opening *Dance of the Polovtsian Maidens*. Beecham draws an almost Russian fervour from his choristers. The recorded sound is little short of astonishing in its fullness, vividness and clarity.

Though the live broadcast performance is less polished than Beecham's studio version, and it comes in mono instead of stereo, it is the full version with chorus, making a powerful fill-up to the superb account of the Balakirev symphony.

A splendid account of the *Prince Igor Overture* from Mackerras. The *Polovtsian Dances* proceed with comparable brilliance and fervour, with the Royal Liverpool Philharmonic Choir producing an expansive lyrical tone and joining in the frenzy of the closing section with infectious zest. Excellent recording too, vivid and full; if only the Mussorgsky and Rimsky-Korsakov couplings had produced comparable electricity, this super-bargain double would have been a world-beater. As it is, it is good value.

Dorati's Mercury recording is not among the most refined from this source, but no one could say that it lacks vividness in this new SACD transfer; the performance has plenty of boisterous vitality and the climax is exhilarating.

The Polish conductor Gregor Fitelberg recorded the *Polovtsian Dances* for Decca in 1946, a fresh, colourful reading enhanced by early Decca *ffrr* recording at its most impressive, very well transferred by Dutton. It makes an attractive fill-up for the Rimsky-Korsakov items from Ansermet and Constant Lambert.

BORTKIEWICZ, Sergei (1877–1952)

Piano Concerto 1 in B flat min., Op. 16
*** Hyp. CDA 66624. Coombs, BBC Scottish SO, Maksymiuk – ARENSKY: *Piano Concerto* ***

Sergei Bortkiewicz's concerto is conservative in idiom, a conventional, romantic, virtuoso offering without much individual flavour. Stephen Coombs takes its considerable difficulties in his stride and plays the work as if it was great music – and at times he almost persuades one that it is. He receives excellent support from the BBC Scottish Orchestra under Jerzy Maksymiuk, and good recording quality.

BOUGHTON, Rutland (1878–1960)

(i) *Oboe Concerto 1 in C; Symphony 3 in B min.*
(BB) *** Hyp. Helios CDH 55019. (i) Francis; RPO, Handley

Rutland Boughton's *Third Symphony* is expertly fashioned, often imaginative and, save in the rumbustious Scherzo (where the closing pages are clumsily scored), hardly puts a foot wrong. The *Oboe Concerto* is hardly less rewarding. The recording of the *Symphony* approaches the demonstration bracket and the performances are totally committed, even if the strings of the RPO are not quite on top form. A bargain well worth seeking out.

(i) *Oboe Quartet 1; 3 Songs without Words (for Oboe Quartet). String Quartets: in A (On Greek Folk Songs); in F (From the Welsh Hills)*
(BB) *** Hyp. Helios CDH 55174. (i) Francis; Rasumovsky Qt

Nearly all this music is inspired by the countryside, and indeed the folk-styled melodies in the delightful *A major 'Greek' Quartet*, might well have had a British source, rather than a Greek derivation. The second movement of the *F major Quartet* hauntingly evokes the *Landscape from the* (Welsh) *Hilltops*. The *Oboe Quartet* has two perky movements and a third, more reflective *Andante con variazione*. Sarah Francis, who has already given us a fine account of Boughton's *First Oboe Concerto* (see above), is equally persuasive both here and in the three equally winning *Songs without Words*, opening with an *Andante delicato* and closing sensuously with a *Barcarolle* marked *Andante languido*. The Rasumovsky Quartet gives sympathetic support throughout and, with good, clear recording, this inexpensive disc has much to offer.

Pastoral
(BB) *** Hyp. Helios CDH 55008. Francis, Rasumovsky Qt – HARTY: *3 Pieces*; HOWELLS: *Sonata*; RUBBRA: *Sonata* ***

Boughton's enchanting *Pastoral* for oboe and string quartet makes a delightful pendant to this fine collection of English music for oboe and piano. It has a disarmingly attractive, folksy pastoral melody which haunts the memory. The performance could hardly be more persuasive.

Bethlehem (choral drama)

*** Hyp. CDA 66690. Field, Bryan, Bryson, R. Evans, Bowen, Peacock, Opie, MacDougall, Van Allan, Seaton, Campbell, I. Boughton, Matheson-Bruce, Holst Singers, New L. Children's Ch., City of L. Sinf., Melville

Boughton's score, lyrical and undemanding, with carols punctuating the scenes as chorales punctuate the Bach *Passions*, is an aptly fresh and innocent setting of an edited version of the Coventry Nativity Play. The role of the villainous Herod unexpectedly is consigned to a tenor. Alan G. Melville conducts a warm, fluent performance that is generally well sung, though for the central role of the Virgin Mary it would have been better to have had a sweeter voice than Helen Field's. Alan Opie and the two other wise men are outstanding, and the three shepherds characterize well in their pastoral cavortings. The score has been discreetly cut to fit the two Acts on to a single CD with little loss. First-rate, well-balanced sound.

The Immortal Hour (opera; complete)

(B) *** Hyp. Dyad CDD 22040 (2). Kennedy, Dawson, Wilson-Johnson, Davies, George Mitchell Ch., ECO, Melville

Analysed closely, much of *The Immortal Hour* may seem like Vaughan Williams and water; but this fine performance, conducted by a lifelong Boughton devotee, brings out the hypnotic quality which had 1920s music-lovers attending performances many times over, entranced by its lyrical evocation of Celtic twilight. The simple tunefulness goes with a fine feeling for atmosphere. The excellent cast of young singers includes Anne Dawson as the heroine, Princess Etain, and Maldwyn Davies headily beautiful in the main tenor rendering of the *Faery song*. Warm, reverberant recording, enhanced in its CD format, and this delightful opera is not to be missed at its new Dyad price.

BOULANGER, Lili (1893–1918)

(i) *Clairières dans le ciel* (song-cycle); (ii) Choral Music: *Hymne au soleil; Les Sirènes; Pour les funérailles d'un soldat; Renouveau; Soir sur la plaine*

(N) (BB) **(*) Hyp. Helios CDH 55153. (i) Hill, Ball; (ii) New L. Chamber Ch., Wood

Christopher Palmer, who supplies the excellent extended notes for this coupling of a major song-cycle and five short choral works with soloists, suggests that *Clairières dans le ciel* ('Clearing in the Heavens') is the most important of Lili Boulanger's secular works. A setting of a series of 13 verses (out of 24) by Francis Jammes, it draws a picture of a tall, beautiful and certainly mysterious young girl who entrances the poet, haunts his consciousness, then vanishes. The music is fragrantly sensuous in a particularly French way, the introduction balmy and exotic, the passionate epilogue summing up the unrequited lover's final words: 'I have nothing left to sustain me.' Martyn Hill fully captures the work's essence and for the most part sings beautifully, though his bursts of intensity bring an intrusive vibrato. Andrew Ball's accompaniment, rippling and ardent, is delightfully supportive. The short choral works each have a soloist, *Renouveau* and *Soir sur la plaine* have three each. The piano accompaniments are but a substitute for the original orchestral scores, but they serve well enough when the choral writing is so exquisitely

sumptuous in the blending of female voices, richly impressionistic. The most striking piece, however, is essentially male in character: a dark evocation of a soldier's funeral, a de Musset setting using a solo baritone, powerfully ritualistic. The New London Chamber Choir admirably catch the lavish impressionistic colouring of this highly original writing and sing with fervour, and Andrew Ball again rises to the occasion, although not all the accompaniments are very pianistic. Excellent recording and full texts and translations make this a bargain.

Faust et Hélène; Psaume 24; Psaume 130: Du fond de l'abîme; D'un matin de printemps; D'un soir triste

*** Chan. 9745. Dawson, Murray, Bottone, MacKenzie, Howard, CBSO Ch., BBC PO, Y.-P. Tortelier

Faust et Hélène has astonishing beauty and a natural eloquence. Like *Psaume 24*, *Du fond de l'abîme* and the other music on the disc, it offers testimony to an altogether remarkable talent. There is a distinguished team of soloists (Lynne Dawson and Bonaventura Bottone in the cantata and Ann Murray in one of the Psalms) and first-rate contributions from the Birmingham chorus and the BBC Philharmonic under Yan-Pascal Tortelier.

Psaume 24; Psaume 130: Du fond de l'abîme; Pie Jesu

❀ **(*) BBC (ADD) BBCL 4026-2. Price, Greevy, Partridge, Carol Case, BBC Ch., BBC SO, N. Boulanger – FAURE: *Requiem* **(*) ❀

Lili Boulanger died in her mid-twenties, but not before committing some remarkable music to paper, including the *Pie Jesu*, dedicated to her sister Nadia. The latter certainly conveys her fervour and belief in these remarkable scores, and *Du fond de l'abîme* is a work of astonishing originality and imagination. Recorded at a live concert in the Fairfield Halls, Croydon, the BBC engineers provide more than acceptable sound, and the balance is skilfully done. A rather special musical document.

BOULEZ, Pierre (born 1925)

Eclat-Multiples; Rituel: In memoriam Bruno Maderna

(M) *** Sony (ADD) SMK 45839. BBC SO, Ens. InterContemporain, composer

Eclat-Multiples appeared first in 1964 simply as *Eclat*, a brilliant showpiece, an exuberant mosaic of sounds; but then, in 1970, it started developing from there in the pendant piece, *Multiples*. *Rituel* is the most moving music that Boulez has ever written, inspired by the premature death of his friend and colleague, Bruno Maderna. This record, very well played and recorded, provides both a challenge and a reward.

(i) . . . explosante-fixe . . . ; (ii) Notations; (iii) Structures pour deux pianos, Livre II

(N) *** DG 477 5385. (i) Ens. InterContemporain, composer, with Cherrier, Ophèle, Valade; (ii; iii) Aimard; (iii) Boffard

With works written between 1945 and 1993, this disc offers an illuminatingly broad view of Boulez as composer. Earliest is the set of 12 brief piano pieces, *Notations*, which he wrote in 1945, demonstrating his application of serialism to the widest range of parameters. Jean-Pierre Aimard proves magnetic in holding the often fragmentary writing firmly together, building the varied sequence powerfully. Book 2 of Boulez's *Structures for Two Pianos* dates from the period 1956–61, but where in Book 1 he kept strictly to serial techniques, in this second work for two pianos he felt tempted to exploit the special effects that the medium itself offered, echoing electronic effects at times. Aimard with Florent Boffard again proves magnetic, but it is with the main work on the disc, . . . *explosante-fixe* . . ., 37 minutes long, that Boulez as composer emerges at full stretch in the colour and energy of his writing for chamber orchestra with electronic effects. Three concertante flutes take centre stage, with Sophie Cherrier on the midi-flute leading the other two. After the piano works the impact is all the more telling, with Boulez drawing incisive playing from the members of the Ensemble InterContemporain, very well recorded.

Figures-Doubles-Prisms; (i) Pli selton pli; (ii) Le Soleil des eaux; (i; ii; iii) Le Visage nuptial

(N) (BB) *** Warner Apex 2564 62083-2 (2). BBC SO, Boulez, with (i) Bryn-Julson; (ii) BBC Singers; (iii) Laurence

Issued to celebrate Boulez's 80th birthday, this compilation of some of his finest recordings from the 1980s is very welcome at super-budget price, covering a wide range of his vocal music. *Pli selon pli*, his fascinating setting of words by Mallarmé, has long been accepted as a modern classic with its exotic instrumental writing, often surprisingly delicate. Phyllis Bryn-Julson is the superb soloist, and in duet with the contralto, Elizabeth Laurence, she is just as persuasive in the more sumptuous sounds of *Le Visage nuptial*, a cantata setting of a deeply complex poem by Renée Char, with the two interweaving soloists supplemented by the BBC Singers. The BBC Singers then take centre stage for another setting of Char, *Le Soleil des eaux*, giving a virtuoso performance in the vigorous choral writing. As a coda comes the orchestral work, *Figures-Doubles-Prismes*, by turns darkly intense and powerfully abrasive. The seeming wildness of inspiration is superbly controlled in this performance under the composer, as it is in all the works. First-rate digital sound all through.

CHAMBER MUSIC

Dérive (for flute, clarinet, violin, cello, vibraphone & piano); (i) Dialogue de l'ombre double; (ii) Flute Sonatine; Mémoriale (... explosante-fixe ... originel) for Flute & 8 Instruments; (iii) Piano Sonata; (iv) Cummings ist der Dichter

(BB) *** Warner Apex 0927 49987-2. (i) Daimins; (ii) Cherrier; (iii) Aimard; (iv) BBC Singers; Ens. InterContemporain, composer

Here is an inexpensive way of exploring a wide range of Boulez's chamber and instrumental music in expert performances that are directed by the composer and very well recorded. No one could suggest that the recklessly spiky progress of the *Sonatine for Flute* (a most assured performance) and the *Piano Sonata* are anything but intractable. But the *Dialogue de l'ombre double* (another superbly played work for clarinet in electronic duet with itself) is both imaginative and aurally fascinating, while *Dérive* and *Mémoriale* (which are not too long) are similarly exotically ear-tickling, if with no formal logic. Most strikingly original of all is the longest piece here, the weirdly atmospheric choral work, *Cummings ist der Dichter*, which is a setting of a poem attempting to link birdsong with space. The vocal melismas are taken up and shared with the instrumental ensemble, and the result is nothing if not extraordinary.

(i) Dialogue; (ii) Répons

(*) DG 457 605-2. (i) Damiens; (ii) Soloists, Ens. InterContemporain, composer

Boulez chose the title *Répons* in reflection of the interplay of solo and ensemble voices in Gregorian chant; but even an unprepared listener can appreciate the sensuous element in this work for six contrasted soloists, an instrumental ensemble of 24 players, and computerized sound developed from that of the soloists. Though a two-channel stereo recording cannot convey the full impact, this is a powerful performance that gives a fair impression of the live event. *Dialogue* applies similar techniques to a solitary clarinet, with more limited but tonally revealing results.

Domaines

(B) ** HM HMA 195930. Ens. Portal, Musique Vivante, Masson

Domaines was first performed in 1968 as a work for solo clarinet, but two years later Boulez rewrote the score to include a responding concertante ensemble of 20 additional instrumentalists including percussion, divided into five groups arranged in a circle. The solo clarinet moves among them throughout the performance, yet remains a fulcrum, and in the first half of the work the soloist determines the order in which these shall be played and dominates the proceedings. In the second *Mirror* half, the conductor of the ensemble makes the choice and the soloists reflect the instrumental tuttis which are now more elaborate. Clearly any performance has a strong visual element which an audio recording cannot capture, but the stereo here readily conveys the mobility of the soloist. Although this is a bargain reissue, the playing time is only just over half an hour, which many will say is quite long enough!

Pli selon pli

*** DG 471 344-2. Schäfer, Ens. InterContemporain, composer

First composed in 1957 but repeatedly revised since, *Pli selon pli* is a key work in Boulez's development, a portrait of the poet Mallarmé, setting his texts to craggy vocal lines that blossom in such a performance as this, with Christine Schäfer singing radiantly. Boulez has recorded this piece, well over an hour long, twice before, but this definitive version is the first to take account of his last revision in 1989. With vivid sound the composer brings out the contrast between the complex textures of the outer movements and the chamber-like precision of the three central settings of Mallarmé or 'Improvisations' as he calls them. The recording was made after a series of live performances, so that the talented players of Ensemble InterContemporain convey rapt concentration in obedience to the composer-conductor's precise demands, magnetic from first to last.

Piano Sonatas 1–3

(BB) *** Naxos 8.553353. Biret

The Boulez sonatas are well served by the gramophone – particularly No. 2, which Pollini has recorded for DG. Those with an interest in this repertoire will be well rewarded by Idil Biret on Naxos; she is more than equal to their technical demands and is given good sound.

Piano Sonata 2

(M) (***) DG (ADD) (IMS) 471 359-2. Pollini – DEBUSSY: 12 Etudes **

'It is the performer's absolute responsibility', Pollini has said, 'to put new music into their programmes … the only interesting works are those composed in an uncompromisingly modern musical language,' as Beethoven's was in his time. Boulez's *Second Sonata* certainly meets that criterion. Pollini also felt that the hugely destructive energy of the piece also calls up comparisons with late Beethoven, and in particular the *Hammerklavier Sonata*, which is perhaps a little unfortunate. The composer's stated intention was to 'destroy what was first-movement sonata form, to dissolve slow-movement form by means of the trope, to dissolve repetitive scherzo-form by means of variation form, and in the fourth movement to destroy fugal and canonic form'. Indeed in the finale the pianist at one point has an instruction to 'pulverize the sound'. So, if you like musical disintegration, this is the piece for you, and in the accompanying note Paul Griffiths (the author of a book on Boulez) analyses its content and defines its progress with considerable skill. Pollini truly believes in this sonata, readily demonstrated by the forceful driving momentum of his playing throughout. Its inclusion in the 'Pollini Edition' was therefore inevitable, even though many listeners will not take readily to it, fine though the playing is.

BOWEN, York (1884–1961)

York Bowen belongs to the same generation as Bax and, like him, was a formidably gifted pianist. By 1912 he had written three piano concertos and two symphonies, prompting Saint-Saëns no less to hail him as 'the most remarkable of the young British composers'. Sorabji wrote that he was 'in the great tradition to which, for all their idiosyncratic differences, men such as Ravel, Rachmaninov and Medtner belong' and rated him as the greatest of English keyboard composers of his day.

Viola Concerto in C min., Op. 25
*** Hyp. CDA 67546. Power, BBC Scottish SO, Brabbins – FORSYTH: *Viola Concerto in G min.* ***

York Bowen's *Viola Concerto*, dating from 1908, was one of the first works inspired by the leading viola-player, Lionel Tertis, who by his example over the years transformed the viola repertory. Bowen was himself a viola-player as well as a pianist and he exploits the instrument masterfully, launching powerfully in the first subject of the opening *Allegro assai*. That restless theme is quickly set against a warmly relaxed second subject. The central *Andante cantabile* brings a rich, song-like melody, exploiting the viola's lower register, leading to a jaunty finale, witty in its use of woodwind, which combines elements of scherzo and finale. Well coupled with another rarity, the *Viola Concerto* of Bowen's contemporary, Cecil Forsyth, the disc makes a valuable addition to the growing list of Bowen's works on disc, superbly played by Lawrence Power, with Martyn Brabbins and the BBC Scottish Orchestra as ever warmly understanding accompanists, very well recorded, with the viola well forward.

Cello Sonata; Suite for Violin & Piano; Violin Sonata in E min.
(M) *** Dutton CDLX 7120. Endymion Ens.

Anyone who enjoys English music of the early twentieth century should investigate this collection of three formidably powerful chamber works, representing the music of York Bowen over the full span of his long career. His *Violin Suite* of 1909, premièred by the dedicatee, Fritz Kreisler, was one of the works that established Bowen before the First World War at the forefront of young British composers. The post-war musical world then turned against him, and though he continued to write prolifically, such works as the *Cello Sonata* of 1921 and the *Violin Sonata* of 1945 were largely ignored as being unfashionably out of date. What these keenly intense performances consistently demonstrate is the cogency of York Bowen's writing, with strongly argued structures built on striking thematic material. So the *Violin Suite* in four movements is framed by strongly rhythmic movements in sonata form, with a flowing *Barcarolle* for slow movement and a *Humoresque* Scherzo that Kreisler himself might have written as one of his encore pieces. The later works bring no lessening of passion behind the writing. Whatever the lack of appreciation, the composer never seems to have become disillusioned, maybe even foreseeing that a later era might come round to appreciating such strongly committed music. With Krysia Osostowicz the outstanding violinist and Jane Salmon the fine cellist, these very well-recorded performances could not be better designed to bring that about.

Horn Quintet; Piano Trio; Rhapsody Trio
(M) *** Dutton CDLX 7115. Endymion Ens.

Three more superb chamber-works, dating respectively from 1927, 1926 and 1945, bear out the quality of Bowen's writing, a composer never afraid to write a good tune, offering well-made works that never seem routine, particularly in outstanding performances like these. The *Horn Quintet* is a glorious piece, with Stephen Stirling magnificent in the central horn part, and if the main motif of the first movement reminds one of Vaughan Williams's *Fifth Symphony*, York Bowen was writing almost 20 years earlier. One looks forward to hearing much more.

String Quartets 2 in D min., Op. 41; 3 in G, Op. 46b; (i) Phantasy-Quintet for Bass Clarinet & String Quartet, Op. 93
*** British Music Society BMS 426CD. Archaeus Qt, (i) with Timothy Lines

Here is yet another record of York Bowen's chamber music to confirm that he is more of a major figure in British music than has hitherto been thought. The two *String Quartets* are remarkably similar in atmosphere and layout and were probably written at about the same time, around the end of the First World War. The *Second Quartet in D minor*, with its hauntingly melodic first movement, was published in 1922 as the recipient of a Carnegie Trust Award and soon forgotten. The *Poco lento* is unforgettably nostalgic and the busily folksy finale of contrasting brilliance, offset by more appealing lyricism.

The *Third Quartet* opens with another lovely melodic contour reminding one a little of Dvořák, with the slow movement following in the same mood of intimate melancholy. The finale matches the pattern of the last movement of No. 2, opening with pizzicati and leading to a dashing main theme and a warmly lyrical counterpart.

The bass clarinet does not dominate the *Phantasy-Quintet*, but adds a beguiling touch of darkness to its texture, interwoven with solo interludes. The work is continuous, opening and closing in gentle reverie, but with quixotic tempo changes in its middle sections. Highly sympathetic performances and excellent recording ensure this CD receives a strong recommendation.

*Viola Sonatas 1 in F; 2 in C min.; Phantasy for Viola &
Piano, Op. 54*

(M) *** Dutton CDLX 7126. Boyd, Forsberg

With James Boyd the rich-toned soloist, this collection of
Bowen's music for viola and piano is equally welcome. The
two sonatas are both early works, written in 1905 when
Bowen was just completing his studies at the Royal Academy
of Music. He was directly inspired by the mastery of the viola
virtuoso, Lionel Tertis, a tireless advocate of the viola's claims
as a solo instrument, for whom Bowen wrote all these works,
often accompanying him at the piano. In the unashamedly
lyrical style that brought him such early success as a composer, this is warmly approachable music built on sharply
memorable thematic material, with vigorous outer movements in both sonatas framing a Dvořákian cantabile slow
movement in No. 1, and a dark minor-key *Grave* in No. 2. The
Phantasy, adopting the fluid, Elizabethan-influenced form in
linked sections prescribed for the Cobbett Prize, is more
individual, starting with a haunting slow meditation on
unaccompanied viola, with the main allegro in a galloping
6/8 time. The Swedish accompanist, Bengt Forsberg, proves as
understanding an accompanist as he is in the song repertory.

PIANO MUSIC

*Ballade 2, Op. 87; Berceuse, Op. 83; Moto perpetuo from
Op. 39; Preludes, Op. 102, 1 in C; 2 in C min.; 6 in D min.; 7
in E flat; 8 in E flat min.; 10 in E min.; 15 in G; 16 in G min.;
18 in G sharp min.; 19 in A; 20 in A min.; 21 in B flat; 22 in B
flat min.; Romances 1, Op. 35/1; 2, Op. 45; Sonata 5 in F min.,
Op. 72; Toccata, Op. 155*

⊕– ✿ *** Hyp. CDA 66838. Hough

Few recent discs of piano music are as magical as this:
magnetic performances that come as a revelation, demonstrating that this long-neglected composer was a master of
keyboard writing. Hough, always compelling on disc, not
only technically brilliant but spontaneously expressive, consistently conveys his love for Bowen's music, starting with 13
of the 24 *Preludes*. He puts them in his own very effective
order, bringing out the contrasted qualities of jewelled miniatures, reflecting Rachmaninov on the one hand, Ireland and
Bax on the other, but with a flavour of their own. The most
powerful, most ambitious work is the *Sonata No. 5*, with two
weighty, wide-ranging movements separated by an *Andante*
interlude. Vivid piano-sound and illuminating notes by Francis Pott and Hough himself.

*24 Preludes, Op. 102; Sonata 6 in B flat min., Op. 160;
Reverie, Op. 86*

(N) *** Chan. 10277. Celis

The *B flat minor Sonata*, Op. 102, was York Bowen's last
composition, composed just before he died in 1961, and he
never wrote anything finer. It is a magnificent work,
Brahmsian in its volcanic first movement (which also has a
memorable second-subject group). But the tranquil pastoral
Intermezzo is very much his own and very English, followed
by a brilliant Toccata finale which rounds off the piece
buoyantly. But it is the 24 *Preludes*, in all major and minor
keys, written just before the Second World War, which demonstrate the full range of Bowen's piano writing. Stephen
Hough has already recorded a selection, but the Dutch pianist, Joop Celis, gives us the lot and shows us just how
fascinating and rewarding they are. There are touches of

Rachmaninov, Scriabin and Debussy, and they stem from the
spiritual world of Brahms – yet, like in the *Sonata*, there is
something unmistakably English about them. To listen right
throught the sequence is to discover the composer's full
personality, and the final *Prelude in B minor*, marked *serioso e
tragico*, surely sums up the whole admirably, followed by the
Rêverie which makes a touching but by no means inconsequential encore. Fine, realistic recording makes this a most
desirable issue.

BOYCE, William (1711–79)

Apart from Handel, the London-born William Boyce was the
most important English composer of the eighteenth century.
Trained as a chorister at St Paul's Cathedral, he took up a
career as an organist, later both composing for the Chapel
Royal and conducting at the Three Choirs Festival. He also
wrote music for the theatre and for Vauxhall Gardens. He
became Master of the King's Music in 1755. But his main
musical association remained with the annual festivals at St
Paul's, where he was buried under the dome.

Overtures 1–12; Concerti grossi: in B flat; B min. & E min.

(B) *** Chan. Double 6665 (2). Cantilena, Shepherd

Though these works do not have quite the consistent originality which makes the Boyce *Symphonies* so refreshing, the
energy of the writing – splendidly conveyed in these performances – is recognizably the same, with fugal passages that turn
in unexpected directions. Cantilena's performances readily
convey the freshness of Boyce's inspiration, and this is one of
the most recommendable of all their recordings, the more
attractive for being reissued as a bargain Double. They are
oddly balanced but the sound is both atmospheric and vivid
and provides a refreshing musical experience.

Symphonies 1–8, Op. 2

(M) *** Decca 473 081-2. AAM, Hogwood

*** DG 419 631-2. E. Concert, Pinnock

(M) *** CRD 3356. Bournemouth Sinf., Thomas

(N) (B) ** CfP 5 86047-2. Menuhin Festival O, Y. Menuhin

Christopher Hogwood and the Academy of Ancient Music
turn in performances that are every bit as lively and well
played as Trevor Pinnock's rival set with the English Concert,
and perhaps more sensitively shaped. By comparison, Pinnock sounds just a bit bright and business-like, making the
Hogwood top choice among the period-instrument versions,
especially at its new mid-price in Decca's 'British Collection'.
Excellent recording.

Pinnock's disc of the Boyce *Symphonies* wears its scholarship very easily and in so doing brings not only lively, resilient
playing but fresh revelation in the treatment of the *vivace*
movements. Nicely scaled recording, bright but atmospheric.

Thomas's tempi are often brisk, and are certainly swifter-
paced than Pinnock's 'new look'. But even against such strong
competition as this, the buoyant playing of the Bournemouth
Sinfonietta still gives much pleasure by its sheer vitality.
Bright, clear sound and a price advantage.

The eight symphonies recorded here are wonderfully
inventive and entertaining with the orchestration nicely varied. The influence of Handel is apparent, and these Handelian associations are especially relished by Menuhin, whose
gracious phrasing and elegant manner are supported by
excellent orchestral playing that brings out the warmth. The
recording from 1971/2 still sounds well if a little dated, and

this bargain disc is still worth considering even if later period-instrument performances are more revelatory.

12 Trio Sonatas (1747)
**(*) Chan. 0648 (2). Coll. Mus. 90, Standage

12 Trio Sonatas (1747); Sonatas 13–15 (unpublished)
*** Hyp. CDA 67151/2. Parley of Instruments or Parley B. O, Holman

Boyce gave the English trio sonata a new lease of life at a time when the format was in danger of falling into neglect, and they are consistently inventive and a good example of baroque 'easy listening'. Not only that, but they seem to get more and more attractive, and the second disc is more enjoyable than the first. As an appendix, Peter Holman has discovered three extra sonatas (here numbered 13–15) which survive in a manuscript in the Cambridge Fitzwilliam Museum. There is evidence to suggest that these sonatas were sometimes played in orchestral form, so the Hyperion recording alternates orchestral and chamber performance, with Nos. 1, 3, 5, 7–9, 11 and 13 heard on a full string group. These period performances are vigorously alert and stylish, with slow movements refined yet warmly relished, especially those that remind the listener a little of Handel. Excellent recording without edginess.

Simon Standage and Collegium Musicum 90 offer one instrument to a part throughout. The performances are fresh and alive, the recording clean and clear. However, the competing set from Peter Holman, with the Parley instrumental groups on Hyperion, is in almost every way preferable.

Anthems: *By the waters of Babylon; I have surely built thee an house; The Lord is King, be the people never so impatient; O give thanks; O praise the Lord; O where shall wisdom be found?; Turn thee unto me; Wherewithal shall a young man?; Organ Voluntaries 1, 4 & 7*
(M) *** CRD 3483. New College, Oxford, Ch., Higginbottom, Cooper

These five verse anthems and three others in a rather more ambitious ternary format are all of high quality, broadly following a Purcellian tradition. The beautiful *By the waters of Babylon* is perhaps the finest of the latter, but the verse anthem, *I have surely built thee an house*, is also very commanding, as is the opening *O where shall wisdom be found?*. Three organ voluntaries are included to add variety and, with such strong, well-integrated performances and excellent recording in a highly suitable acoustic, this can be truly recommended.

Ode for St Cecilia's Day
♦── *** Gaudeamus CDGAU 200. Burrowes, Purefoy, Watts, Edgar-Wilson, George, New College, Oxford, Ch., Hanover Band, Lea-Cox

Boyce's *Ode for St Cecilia's Day* uses a text by his friend John Lockman, celebrating Apollo and the Muses as well as St Cecilia, patron saint of music. It is only at the very end that the saint herself appears in the last aria, sung in this performance by a boy chorister, the fresh-voiced Patrick Burrowes. This has similar vigour to *The Secular Masque*, recorded earlier by Graham Lea-Cox with the same choir and orchestra, with comparably lively results in the choruses, if with less distinguished singing from the soloists. Good, atmospheric sound.

The Secular Masque. Overtures: *Birthday Ode for George III* (1768); *King's Ode for the New Year* (1772); *Ode for St Cecilia's Day*
*** Gaudeamus CDGAU 176. Howarth, Kuhlmann, Daniels, Robinson, Varcoe, Thomas, New College, Oxford, Ch., Hanover Band, Lea-Cox

The Secular Masque represents Boyce at his freshest and most unbuttoned. So 'Diana's song' – which Boyce published separately – with elaborate horn parts, brims with rustic jollity and is sung radiantly here by Judith Howarth. 'Mars's song', *Sound the trumpet, beat the drum*, also has Boyce responding with engaging directness, vigorous and colourful. Each of the overtures here, including the one for the *Secular Masque*, follows a similar form in two, three or four brief movements. Graham Lea-Cox draws lively performances from the Hanover Band, the choir and his excellent team of soloists. Warm, full sound.

Solomon (serenata)
*** Hyp. CDA 66378. Mills, Crook, Parley of Instruments, Goodman

William Boyce's *Solomon* is a totally secular piece, a dialogue between She and He, with the verses freely based on the *Song of Solomon*. As this stylish and alert period performance using young, fresh-voiced soloists makes clear, it has some delightful inspirations, less influenced by Italian models than by popular English song. First-rate sound.

BRAHMS, Johannes (1833–97)

(i) *Academic Festival Overture;* (ii) *Hungarian Dances, 1–21;* (i) *Serenades 1 in D, Op. 11; 2 in A, Op. 16; Tragic Overture*
(N) (B) **(*) DG (ADD/DDD) 477 5424 (2). (i) BPO; (ii) VPO; Abbado

The *Serenade No. 1*, recorded in 1981, is very beautifully played, imaginative and sensitive, with the digital recording sounding better than it did on LP. The Berlin Philharmonic also play superbly in the *Second Serenade*, and the 1967 analogue recording has also come up well, though neither shows DG quite at its finest. In the *Hungarian Dances*, Abbado has great sparkle and lightness. The VPO is hardly less impressive than the BPO; the two overtures go well too, and the set is certainly recommendable if the programme appeals.

Piano Concertos. 1 in D min., Op. 15; 2 in B flat, Op. 83
(BB) *** Virgin 2×1 5 61412-2. Hough, BBC SO, A. Davis
** DG 457 837-2 (2). Pollini, BPO, Abbado

(i) *Piano Concertos 1–2; Academic Festival Overture, Op. 80; Tragic Overture, Op. 81*
(B) **(*) Sony (ADD) SB2K 89905 (2). (i) Serkin; Cleveland O, Szell

(i) *Piano Concertos 1–2;* (ii) *Academic Festival Overture; Tragic Overture; Variations on a Theme of Haydn, Op. 56a*
(B) *** EMI double forte (ADD) 5 72649-2 (2). (i) Barenboim, Philh. O; (ii) VPO; Barbirolli
(B) **(*) Ph. (ADD) Duo 438 320-2 (2). (i) Arrau; Concg. O, Haitink

(i) *Piano Concertos 1–2. Tragic Overture; Variations on a Theme of Haydn*
(B) **(*) DG (ADD) Double 453 067 (2). (i) Pollini; VPO; Boehm (1) or Abbado (2)

(i–iii) *Piano Concertos 1*; (i; iii; iv) *2*; (i; v) *Variations & Fugue on a Theme of Handel, Op. 24* (orch. Rubbra); *Variations on a Theme of Haydn*

(B) **(*) Double Decca 470 519-2 (2). (i) Ashkenazy; (ii) Concg. O; (iii) Haitink; (iv) VPO; (v) Cleveland O

(i) *Piano Concertos 1–2. Variations & Fugue on a Theme of Handel; Waltzes, Op. 39*

(M) *** Sony Heritage (ADD) MH2K 63225 (2). Fleisher; (i) Cleveland O, Szell

(i) *Piano Concertos 1–2. Fantasias, Op. 116*

(M) *** DG (ADD) 447 446-2 (2). Gilels, (i) BPO, Jochum

Piano Concertos (i) 1; (ii) *2. Intermezzos in A min., Op. 116/2 & E flat, Op. 117/1; Rhapsody in G min., Op. 79/2*

(BB) (*(*)) Naxos mono 8.505189 (5). Schnabel, with (i) LPO, Szell; (ii) BBC SO, Boult – BEETHOVEN: *Piano Concertos* (***); SCHUMANN: *Kinderszenen* (**)

(i) *Piano Concertos 1–2*; (ii) *2 Lieder, Op. 91; 5 Lieder, Op. 105*

(N) (B) *** EMI double forte 5 75655-2 (2). (i) Kovacevich, LPO, Sawallisch; (ii) Murray, Imai

The Gilels performances can still hold their own against virtually all the competition, but the two concertos are also available separately (see below). However, the present set is offered at a reduced price and the remastered recording is quite outstanding.

Barenboim's performance of the *First Piano Concerto* with Barbirolli is among the most inspired ever committed to disc. The playing is heroic and marvellously spacious. In the *Second Concerto* the first two movements remain grandly heroic and the slow movement has something of the awed intensity you find in the middle movement of the *First*, while the finale erupts gracefully into rib-tickling humour. This is a performance to love in its glowing spontaneity. Of the fill-ups, the *Academic Festival Overture* could do with more sparkle, while the *Tragic Overture* and *Haydn Variations* show the conductor at his finest. The late-1960s recordings have transferred splendidly to CD.

Stephen Hough gives keenly distinctive and deeply thoughtful readings of both Brahms concertos, so that with refined recording the transparency of textures may be disconcerting to those who insist on a fat Brahms sound. He adopts the widest range of tone and dynamic, with the recording beautifully capturing the hushed pianissimos in both works, not least in both slow movements. Both recordings were made in 1989.

Leon Fleisher's two concerto recordings are both masterly examples of joint inspiration, bringing out the point that these are in many ways symphonies with piano, when Szell's direction is so powerful and incisive as well as warmly expressive. Not that Fleisher in any way lacks individuality, for the crisp confidence of his virtuosity has a sureness in its musical and emotional thrust that carries one magnetically on. The sound is among the best offered by CBS/Sony at that period, with the piano balanced forwardly but not aggressively so. Generously, this Heritage issue also includes solo recordings by Fleisher of the *Handel Variations* and *Waltzes*, similarly crisp and concentrated, though the 1956 mono sound here is rather clattery.

Serkin's 1968 account of the *First, D minor Concerto*, his third on LP, brought tremendous command and grandeur, and the support from Szell and the Cleveland Orchestra has

great power. In the *Second, B flat major Concerto*, Serkin achieves an ideal balance between straightforwardness and expressiveness, while the slow movement has a genuine 'inner' intensity, with some wonderfully expressive playing by the Cleveland principal cellist. The CBS/Sony recordings have been considerably improved in the current remastering, but in No. 1 the piano tone is not as full as one would ideally like and the balance still lacks a natural perspective. However, in No. 2 the piano tone has more body and the orchestral sound is also fuller. The two overtures are brilliantly played, the *Academic Festival Overture* being particularly ebullient.

Noble and dedicated, Stephen Kovacevich's EMI account of the Brahms *D minor Concerto* is a performance of stature which belongs in the most exalted company; indeed, it must now take precedence. Moreover it is accorded fine digital sound which has all the warmth and spaciousness one could ask for, together with splendid presence and detail. There is a welcome fill-up in the form of the two Op. 91 *Songs* with viola, admirably presented by Ann Murray and Nobuko Imai, plus the five *Lieder*, Op. 105.

However, after his noble and dedicated account of the *First Piano Concerto* with Wolfgang Sawallisch and the LPO, Stephen Kovacevich's version of its successor brings admiration tinged with disappointment. It does not match this partnership's *First* and does not take wing in quite the same way.

Arrau's Philips readings undoubtedly have vision and power, and the *D minor Concerto* is majestic and eloquent. There is some characteristic agogic distortion that will not convince all listeners and, by the side of Gilels, Arrau seems idiosyncratic. In the *Second Concerto* his playing has a splendid combination of aristocratic finesse and warmth of feeling, and in both concertos Haitink and the Royal Concertgebouw Orchestra give excellent support.

Ashkenazy gives a commanding and magisterial account of the solo part of the *First Concerto* that is full of poetic imagination. The *Second Concerto*, with the VPO, is not as successful. It is spacious in conception and thoughtful in detail, but curiously lacking in impulse, with cautious speeds, and it is overtly expressive in the lyrical episodes of the second movement. The slow movement is very beautiful and the finale offers the proper contrast; but in the last resort, in spite of the excellent recording, this is slightly disappointing. For the fill-ups, Ashkenazy adopts the role of conductor: the *Haydn Variations* receives an excellent performance in very plush Cleveland sound – sound that also brings out all the vibrant colour in Rubbra's extravagant orchestration of the *Variations and Fugue on a Theme by Handel* – a substantial bonus – which is similarly well played and is highly enjoyable. A mixed bag then, but worth considering by Ashkenazy admirers.

Although Pollini and the Vienna Philharmonic under Karl Boehm are given finely detailed recording in the *First Piano Concerto*, other versions (notably Gilels) provide greater wisdom and humanity. Not that Pollini is wanting in keyboard command, but he is a little short on tenderness and poetry. All too often here he seems to have switched on the automatic pilot and, although the *B flat Concerto* under Abbado is much fresher and offers some masterly pianism, there are warmer and more spontaneous accounts to be had.

DG have also paired together Pollini's two Brahms concertos, recorded live with Abbado in 1997–8. No. 1 is handicapped by a balance that places the piano very forward in relation to the orchestra. The *Second Concerto* is much more acceptable in this respect: indeed the sound is very satisfactory. The performance too is of some distinction, but this set is poor value at premium price.

Both Schnabel's Brahms discs come in the box alongside the Beethoven and are also available separately (8.110664/5). He recorded the *D minor Concerto* with Szell in 1938, but it does not show him at his best: rhythms are unstable, and there is a sense of struggle. The first movement is rather pedestrian and heavy-going. The *B flat Concerto* was recorded in 1935 with the then newly formed BBC Symphony Orchestra under Sir Adrian Boult and occupied classic status then. Although it has a sense of space and wisdom, there are all too many splashes and moments of insecurity for it to give universal satisfaction. Sir Adrian is supportive, but Schnabel is best remembered by his late Beethoven sonatas. Very good transfers, though the sound is distinctly dated.

(i) *Piano Concerto 1. Piano Quartet 1* (orch. Schoenberg)

⊕━ *** EuroArts **DVD** 2053659 (i) Barenboim; BPO, Rattle (Director: Bob Coles, Producer: Paul Smaczny)

The Barenboim/Rattle DVD of the *First Concerto*, coupled with Schoenberg's orchestration of the *First Piano Quartet*, (curiously scored minus a piano) is visually and sonically one of the most successful of all the available orchestral concert DVDs, and the *Concerto* is an overwhelming musical experience. The opening visual images as the camera zooms in on the huge open-air auditorium of the Odeon of Herodes Atticus, at the foot of the Acropolis, packed with a large audience, are spectacular enough. But when Sir Simon Rattle passionately launches into the opening of the *Concerto* and one perceives the Berlin Philharmonic Orchestra seated on a relatively small covered stage and playing marvellously, one cannot believe what one is hearing. The sound is magnificent – full, rich, resonant and vivid in its detail, as if the recording were made in a normal concert hall with perfect acoustics. When Barenboim enters, the balance, both sonically and artisically, is just as outstanding. It is a superb performance, with free-running adrenalin, to match Barenboim's much earlier studio partnership with Barbirolli: the first movement comparably heroic, the movingly sustained *Adagio* full of tension which is released in the gloriously vivacious finale. Moreover, the camerawork is marvellously edited – the visuals of Barenboim are strikingly well chosen, and the orchestral coverage is equally prescient – we always seem to be watching the important instruments for every section of the score, with long shots equally artistically judged. Indeed, it is remarkably like being present at the concert itself. The choice of Schoenberg's orchestration of the *Piano Quartet* for the second half of the concert was a curious one, yet that too is played with great conviction. But this disc is an essential purchase for the *Concerto* alone.

Piano Concerto 1 in D min., Op. 15

(N) (M) **(*) RCA (ADD) Compatible **SACD** 8276 66378-2. Rubinstein, Chicago SO, Reiner

*** Ph. 420 071-2. Brendel, BPO, Abbado

(M) *** Decca (ADD) 466 376-2. Curzon, LSO, Szell – FRANCK: *Symphonic Variations;* LITOLFF: *Scherzo* ***

(M) *** Warner Elatus 0927 46768-2. Grimaud, Berlin State O, Sanderling – STRAUSS: *Burleske* ***

(M) (***) DG mono 474 024-2 (5). Kempff, Dresden State O, Konwitschny – BEETHOVEN: *Concertos 1–5;* MOZART: *Concertos 9 & 15;* LISZT: *Concertos 1–2;* SCHUMANN: *Concerto in A min.* (***)

(i) *Piano Concerto 1. Variations & Fugue on a Theme of Handel, Op. 24*

(***) Testament mono SBT 1041. (i) Solomon; Philh. O, Kubelik

(N) (M) **(*) Sony (ADD) 512875-2. R. Serkin, Cleveland O, Szell

(i) *Piano Concerto 1;* (ii) *4 Ballades, Op. 10*

** Australian Decca (ADD) 466 724-2. (i) Rubinstein, Israel PO, Mehta; (ii) Katchen

Rubinstein's account of the *D minor Concerto* was one of the very first stereo recordings made by RCA, in Chicago Symphony Hall in April 1954, and, thanks to the sympathetic hall acoustics, it must have delighted its producers, Richard Mohr and John Pfeiffer. The originally two-track recording is here remastered for SACD, but it also sounds impressive on a normal CD player. This is a poetic and essentially lyrical reading, impulsive and intent on avoiding Brahmsian stodginess, for Reiner's control of the orchestra, volatile and imaginative, has a spacious strength. This deserves a warm welcome back to the catalogue, but the playing time is only 46 minutes, and the previous reissue also included Rubinstein's performances of two of Brahms's major piano pieces.

Brendel produces a consistently beautiful sound and balances the combative and lyrical elements of the work with well-nigh perfect judgement.

Clifford Curzon's 1962 recording, produced by John Culshaw in Kingsway Hall, returns to the catalogue, superbly remastered. The fierceness of attack in the upper strings, especially in the powerful opening tutti, sounds naturally focused on CD, adding a leonine power to Szell's orchestral contribution, and the piano tone is admirably natural.

As the very opening reveals, Serkin's partnership with Szell generates the same kind of adrenalin and ardour as the Decca version with Curzon and the LSO. The slow movement has fine lyrical feeling, and the overall reading has a fine grip and is undoubtedly compelling. Although it does not match the Decca sound, the 1968 recording has been opened up for this reissue. The *Handel Variations*, recorded a decade later and also commandingly played (although not absolutely immaculate technically), is rather closely balanced in the American manner of the time.

Hélène Grimaud is an impressive Brahms interpreter and totally attuned to his world, while Kurt Sanderling, whose Brahms symphony cycle with the Dresden Orchestra from the early 1970s remains among the best, is equally persuasive here. Grimaud's is a performance to reckon with and the recording has splendour and presence. No one buying this, particularly at so modest a price, is likely to be disappointed on any count.

Solomon's magisterial account with Rafael Kubelik and the Philharmonia Orchestra has a majestic grandeur and blends the dramatic power of youth with the wisdom of old age. Of course the 1952 recording does not possess the range or bloom of subsequent versions, but the transfer succeeds in making it sound astonishingly present. Of his celebrated 1942 set of the Brahms *Handel Variations* one is tempted to say the same.

Kempff's characteristic magnetism, expressed in his masterly control of lyrical legato and clarity of texture, makes for a reading of this massive concerto that is totally distinctive. It may lack the weight of some – though there is no lack of power in the big climax of the slow movement – but it is totally compelling, as are the other concerto recordings from the 1950s in this limited edition box.

Rubinstein admirers will be happy to learn that his 1975 Decca recording of Brahms's *First Concerto* has made it on to CD. With more than a sprinkling of wrong notes, this can never be a general recommendation, but the character and drive of the man in his late eighties emerge vividly. To hear such a performance in the concert hall one would readily pay far more, though here the piano is balanced too forwardly. Katchen's characterfully played and recorded *Ballades* make a useful coupling. This CD is nothing if not a collector's item.

Piano Concerto 2 in B flat, Op. 83

*** Ph. 432 975-2. Brendel, BPO, Abbado

*** Naïve V4944. Guy, LPO, Berglund

(M) (***) BBC mono BBCL 4125-2. Arrau, SCO, Gibson –
SCHUBERT: *3 Klavierstücke* (***)

(**(*)) Testament mono SBT 1170. Fischer, BPO, Furtwängler
– FURTWANGLER: *Symphonic Concerto: Adagio* (**)

(M) **(*) DG (ADD) 474 838-2. Anda, PO, Karajan – GRIEG:
Piano Concerto **

(N) (BB) (**(*)) Santuary Living Era mono AJC 8550.
Rubinstein, LSO, Coates – TCHAIKOVSKY: *Piano Concerto 1* (**(*))

(BB) (**) Naxos mono 8.110671. Horowitz, NBC SO,
Toscanini – TCHAIKOVSKY: *Piano Concerto 1* (***) ✪

(i) *Piano Concerto 2;* (ii) *Cello Sonata in D* (arr. of *Violin Sonata in G, Op. 78*)

**(*) Sony SK 63229. Ax; with (i) Boston SO, Haitink; (ii) Ma

(i) *Piano Concerto 2. Intermezzi: in B flat min., Op. 117/2; in C, Op. 119/3; Rhapsody in G min., Op. 79/2*

(***) Testament mono SBT 1042. Solomon, (i) Philh. O,
Dobrowen

(i) *Piano Concerto 2. Piano Sonata 1, Op. 1/2*

☞ (N) (B) *** RCA 82876 60860-2. S. Richter, (i) Chicago
SO, Leinsdorf

Richter's Brahms B flat is one of the very finest performances of this great work. There is nothing self-conscious or studied here; the music is allowed to unfold naturally and with warmth and eloquence. This belongs alongside the greatest. This two-CD package also includes Richter's classic version of the early *C major Sonata*, Op. 1, an outstanding performance in every way, and both 1960 recordings sound very good indeed.

Brendel is massive and concentrated and has greater depth than in his earlier account with Haitink. It is a worthy successor to their *D minor*, though in terms of humanity and wisdom it does not displace the celebrated Gilels–Jochum version (now available coupled with No. 1).

The young French pianist François-Frédéric Guy caused quite a stir with his Prokofiev at London's Wigmore Hall a year or two ago, and we hailed his recording of the *Sixth* and *Eighth Sonatas* in extravagant terms in our main volume as being worthy of ranking alongside the likes of Richter, Pollini and Pletnev. This account of the Brahms *B flat Concerto* is hardly less commanding. It comes from a concert given at the Royal Festival Hall on 30 May 2003 – and it is quite simply a straight performance rather than a compilation drawn from two or more performances. It can hold its own against the finest – and, having the electricity of a live occasion, is in some ways to be preferred to many rivals. Berglund is a supportive and sympathetic accompanist and audience noises are unobtrusive. The Festival Hall acoustic does not flatter the upper strings but, that apart, readers should find this a most rewarding issue.

The magisterial and autumnal *Second Piano Concerto in B flat* from Emanuel Ax and the Boston Symphony under Bernard Haitink on Sony has tremendous breadth. It strikes the right balance between the rhapsodic and the symphonic, the seemingly improvisatory solo writing and the sinewy orchestral texture. Ax is a perceptive and thoughtful artist whose beautiful pianism impresses, as does the eloquent orchestral playing. The fill-up, an arrangement by an unknown hand of the *G major Sonata* transposed to D major for cello, is played with refinement but is hardly an urgent addition to the catalogue.

Arrau could be a masterly interpreter of the Brahms concertos, often performing both at the same concert. He recorded the *Second* twice during the 1960s and '70s, once with Giulini and again with Haitink. This concert performance was given in Glasgow in 1963 and shows him in splendid form: there is a breadth, warmth and luminosity of tone that are peculiar to Arrau at his finest, and an intenstity he brought to everything he did in the concert hall. The mono sound is very faithful and, although the performance does not necessarily add substantially to what we know from his commercial recordings, it is still a worthwhile addition to his concert discography.

The commanding Solomon version of the *B flat Concerto* with Issay Dobrowen and the Philharmonia Orchestra comes from 1947. There is a leonine nobility about this performance and an immediacy, spontaneity and dramatic fire that sweep all before it. Like his *D minor Concerto*, this is a classic account which no admirer of this artist (or of Brahms, for that matter) should pass over. The piano is not always perfect (the C above the stave is out of tune in one passage) but the pianist is! One soon forgets the sonic limitations and is swept along by the performance.

The 1968 partnership of Géza Anda and the BPO provides much fine playing from soloist and orchestra alike. The performance opens slowly and is rhapsodically free; it has plenty of impulse and, if Anda is wayward at times, he is always commanding. There is poetry here and undoubted power. The slow movement is often richly eloquent and the finale has a persuasive, lyrical charm. There is much to enjoy, not least in the glorious orchestral response, even if this is not a primary recommendation. The recording is appropriately bold and full, and the balance good, no doubt improved in this new 'Originals' transfer.

The partnership of Edwin Fischer and Wilhelm Furtwängler produced inspired music-making, both in the 1943 wartime German radio recording of the Brahms concerto and in the slow movement from the conductor's own ambitious concerto, recorded in 1939. The sound in the Brahms is limited, but the piano is bright and clear, and the performance has such energy and warmth, rapt in the slow movement, that one readily forgives any flaws and intrusive audience noises.

Rubinstein's performance with the LSO conducted by Albert Coates was his very first concerto recording for HMV, made in 1929 in London's Queen's Hall, under less than ideal conditions. Yet the result was remarkably successful, especially in terms of balance. Coates's relatively brisk tempi (except in the *Andante*) and Rubinstein's chimerical response bring a comparatively lightweight reading compared with some versions, but Rubinstein's patrician manner and glitteringly luminous articulation is a pleasure in itself. The transfer is undistractingly clear and clean and, as the Tchaikovsky *Concerto* is of comparable historical interest, this augurs well for Santuary Classics' new budget series of 'all-time gramophone greats'.

This Horowitz–Toscanini version of the Brahms *B flat Concerto* dates from around the same time as their famous coupled recording of the Tchaikovsky *B flat minor Concerto*. Both were made in Carnegie Hall, but Toscanini generates little Brahmsian expansiveness (and Horowitz matches his lean textures with bare pedalling). For all its energy and bravura we are not drawn into the tension of the performance as we are in the Tchaikovsky, and only in the finale does Horowitz's scintillating fingerwork restore the *grazioso* feeling. Mark Obert-Thorn's admirably vivid transfer cannot be faulted.

Violin Concerto in D, Op. 77 (see also under *Symphonies 3–4*)

☛— (N) *** EMI DVD 5 44544-9. Perlman, BPO, Barenboim (Producer: Ursula Klein, V/D: Klaus Lindemann) – BEETHOVEN: *Violin Concerto* ***

(N) (B) *** Decca 475 6703 (2). Bell, Cleveland O, Dohnányi – SCHUMANN; TCHAIKOVSKY; WIENIAWSKI: *Violin Concertos* ***

✪ (M) (***) EMI mono 5 67583-2 [567584]. Milstein, Pittsburgh SO, Steinberg – BEETHOVEN: *Violin Concerto* (***)

(M) *** RCA (ADD) 09026 61742-2. Heifetz, Chicago SO, Reiner – BEETHOVEN: *Violin Concerto* ***

(BB) *** DG Entrée 474 569-2. Mutter, BPO, Karajan – BEETHOVEN: *Triple Concerto* ***

(M) *** DG 445 515-2. Mutter, BPO, Karajan – MENDELSSOHN: *Violin Concerto* ***

*** Sony SK 89649. Hahn, ASMF, Marriner – STRAVINSKY: *Violin Concerto* ***

(BB) (***) Dutton mono CDBP 9710. Neveu, Philh. O, Dobrowen – RAVEL: *Tzigane;* SUK: *4 Pieces* (***)

(M) (***) EMI mono 7 61011-2. Neveu, Philh. O, Dobrowen – SIBELIUS: *Violin Concerto* (***)

*** Chan. 8974. Udagawa, LSO, Mackerras – BRUCH: *Concerto 1* ***

(BB) (***) Naxos mono 8.110936. Heifetz, Boston SO, Koussevitzky – BEETHOVEN: *Violin Concerto* (***)

(***) Testament mono SBT 1037. Martzy, Philh. O, Kletzki – MENDELSSOHN: *Violin Concerto* (***)

(***) Testament mono SBT 1038. Haendel, LSO, Celibidache – TCHAIKOVSKY: *Violin Concerto* (***)

(M) *** EMI (ADD) 5 66977-2 [5 66992-2]. Perlman, Chicago SO, Giulini

(N) (M) *** EMI Legend CD/DVD (ADD) 557764. Perlman, Chicago SO, Giulini (with bonus DVD: BEETHOVEN: *Violin Concerto in D, Op. 61:* 1st movt only)

(N) **(*) Warner 2564 61561-2. Rachlin, Bav. RSO, Jansons – MOZART: *Violin Concerto 3* **(*)

(BB) **(*) EMI Encore (ADD) 5 74724-2. D. Oistrakh, Fr. Nat. RSO, Klemperer – MOZART: *Sinfonia concertante* **

**(*) EMI 7 54187-2. Kennedy, LPO, Tennstedt

(B) **(*) DG (ADD) Double (IMS) 453 142-2 (2). Milstein, VPO, Jochum – BEETHOVEN; MENDELSSOHN; TCHAIKOVSKY: *Violin Concertos* ***

(B) **(*) Cedille Double CD 9000068 (2). Barton, Chicago SO, Kalmar – JOACHIM: *Violin Concerto 2* **(*)

(BB) **Warner Apex 0927 4959-2. Zehetmair, Cleveland O, Dohnányi – SCHUMANN: *Fantasy* ***

(*) DG 457 075-2. Mutter, NYPO, Masur (with SCHUMANN: *Fantasy, Op. 131* *)

(M) **(*) Warner Elatus 2564 60806-2. Vengerov, Chicago SO, Barenboim – DVORAK: *Concerto* ***

(BB) ** EMI Encore 5 85455-2. F. P. Zimmermann, BPO, Sawallisch – MOZART: *Violin Concerto 3* ***

(i) *Violin Concerto;* (ii) *Hungarian Dances 1, 2, 7 & 9; Sonatensatz in C min. (Scherzo)*

(M) *** EMI 5 62598-2. Perlman; (i) BPO, Barenboim; (ii) Ashkenazy (piano)

(i) *Violin Concerto;* (ii) *Violin Sonata 3 in D min., Op. 108*

(M) **(*) EMI stereo/mono 5 67973-2 [5 67974-2]. D. Oistrakh; (i) Cleveland O, Szell; (ii) Yampolsky

Perlman's DVD, recorded live in 1992 at the Berlin Schauspielhaus with the Berlin Philharmonic under Barenboim, is in every way satisfying but is especially notable for the raptly beautful performance of the *Adagio*, with the cameraman not missing the movement's famous introductory oboe solo, played very tenderly. It is in every way memorable, and is followed by a sparkling account of the finale. Barenboim is a splendid partner, and the Berlin Philharmonic are on top form; the balance is unusually good for a Perlman recording, though he certainly dominates the performance. The sound itself is excellent, and the producer has directed the changing camera angles very perceptively, not missing out the conductor. If you want a DVD of the coupling with Beethoven, this will give every satisfaction.

Joshua Bell's commanding performance of the Brahms *Violin Concerto* is full of flair, demonstrating not only his love of bravura display, but also his ready gift for turning a phrase individually in a way that catches the ear, always sounding spontaneous. Full, atmospheric recording and no less outstanding couplings put this among the very finest versions. This now comes as part of a bargain-priced two-CD set which, if you want the couplings, is very recommendable indeed.

The EMI mono Milstein–Steinberg recording originally appeared on Capitol in Britain and was long treasured. Returning to it after many years, its stature impresses more than ever before. It is quite simply glorious: a performance of surpassing beauty, its virtuosity effortless, and with a tremendous breadth, warmth and eloquence. There is, above all, a nobility here that shines through. Milstein re-recorded it in the 1980s in Vienna with Jochum – very well, too – but this remains in a class of its own.

Like the Beethoven with which it is coupled, the CD transfer of Heifetz's dazzling performance makes vivid and fresh what on LP was originally a rather harsh Chicago recording, more aggressive than the Boston sound in the Beethoven. With the CD, the excellent qualities of RCA's Chicago balance for Reiner come out in full, giving a fine, three-dimensional focus.

Mutter's early partnership with Karajan proved naturally spontaneous, and her 1981 account of the Brahms *Concerto* has stood the test of time, to make an excellent choice for DG's Entrée label.

In many ways her playing combines a natural feeling with the flair and individuality of Perlman. Needless to say, Karajan's accompaniment is strong in personality and the Berlin Philharmonic play beautifully; the performance represents a genuine musical partnership between youthful inspiration and eager experience. Both alternative couplings are hardly less attractive.

Perlman's 1992 'live' recording remains highly recommendable, finding him at his most commanding, powerful and full of nonchalant flair, and conveying an extra warmth of commitment, with no sense that the performance has been achieved too easily. Now, reissued as part of the 'Perlman Edition', it has an apt and delightful collection of encores (recorded a decade earlier, with Ashkenazy an admirable partner). The Joachim arrangements of the four *Hungarian Dances* bring the most carefree playing, but the *Scherzo* is hardly less brilliant.

Hilary Hahn's very first entry establishes her total command, coupled with a purity and precision which make for a magnetic reading from first to last, sensitively matched by the full and incisive playing of the Academy under Sir Neville Marriner. The close balance means that Hahn is much less hushed in the slow movement, but then her urgent reading of the finale is given extra impact.

Ginette Neveu's is a magnificent performance, urgently electric, remarkable not just for sweetness of tone and her pinpoint intonation but also for the precision and clarity of even the most formidable passages of double stopping. The EMI transfer from the original 78s brings satisfyingly full-bodied sound, surprisingly good on detail. Not surprisingly, the Dutton transfer is even more realistic and full-blooded than the EMI version. That is coupled with her magnetic account of the Sibelius concerto, whereas Dutton chooses music by Ravel, Suk and others.

Hideko Udagawa gives a powerful, persuasively spontaneous-sounding reading. Her biting attack on the most taxing passages is often thrilling, even if her violin-sound is not always the sweetest. Mackerras draws comparably powerful playing from the LSO. Warm, full and well-balanced recording.

Recorded in 1939 with Koussevitzky and the Boston orchestra as powerful partners, Heifetz's first recording of the Brahms concerto is typically strong and purposeful, with the structure firmly held together. Speeds in all three movements are faster than we are now used to, but never seem rushed or perfunctory. The patrician purity of Heifetz's playing brings concentration to the slow movement, while the finale is incisive and dramatic, with double-stopping crisply in time. The Naxos transfer is relatively mellow, masking the roughness in the mono sound. An ideal coupling with the Heifetz/Toscanini Beethoven.

Johanna Martzy's is an exceptionally warm and persuasive account of the Brahms, marked by a very wide range of dynamic and tone. Few versions of whatever period can match the hushed tenderness of Martzy in the coda of the first movement, and so it is too in the slow movement, while the finale is played with Hungarian point and flair. Kletzki proves an ideal accompanist. The Testament reissue, superbly transferred, at last does justice to a long-underappreciated artist.

Ida Haendel, too, gives a powerful, full-toned reading of the Brahms. Recorded in mono in 1953, it comes up very freshly and intensely in this superb CD transfer from Testament, and the clarity and bite of the playing, as well as its strength and nobility, are splendidly caught, confirming the mastery of a great violinist too little heard on disc.

EMI have chosen Perlman's distinguished earlier account of 1976 for reissue in their 'Great Recordings of the Century' series. He is finely supported by Giulini and the Chicago Symphony Orchestra and gives a reading of a darker hue than is customary, with a thoughtful, searching slow movement, rather than the autumnal rhapsody which it so often becomes. The spacious recording is warm and full-bodied. It places the soloist rather too forward, but admirers of Perlman looking for an alternative performance need not hesitate.

Perlman's 1976 account with Guilini and the Chicago Symphony Orchestra also comes on a Legend reissue with a DVD bonus of the first movement of the Beethoven *Violin Concerto*, filmed in Berlin in 1992, with the Berlin Philharmonic Orchestra under Barenboim.

David Oistrakh's 1969 recording of the *Violin Concerto* with Szell must certainly be numbered among the finest versions. The performance is full of controlled feeling and disciplined vitality, with a particularly memorable account of the slow movement. Playing of this order is certainly worthy of EMI's 'Great Recordings of the Century', even if the remastered sound of the orchestral violins sounds a bit thin on top in tuttis. The performance of the *D minor Violin Sonata* is also a fine one, and again it is Oistrakh's warm lyricism in the slow movement that stands out. Yampolsky is a fine partner if somewhat backwardly balanced, and here the 1955 mono recording does show its age. One wonders why EMI did not choose Oistrakh's later 'live' recording with Richter.

However, the conjunction of two such positive artists as Oistrakh and Klemperer makes for a reading characterful to the point of idiosyncrasy, monumental and strong rather than sweetly lyrical. Oistrakh sounds superbly poised and confident; in the finale, if the tempo is a shade deliberate, the total effect is one of clear gain. The 1961 recording seems smoother than in its most recent incarnation.

If lightness and refinement mark out Julian Rachlin's reading, it is not in any way a small-scale account, but rather that the moments of reflection are even more individual than those of outward-going bravura. With Mariss Jansons drawing comparably refined playing from the Bavarian Radio Orchestra, it is a compelling reading, very well recorded. Lithuanian-born, but trained in Vienna, Rachlin's tone is finely focused rather than fat with vibrato, so that the slow movement is as elegant as it is romantic, while the finale is athletic and incisive, helped by the clarity of the recording of the orchestra.

Kennedy's version of the Brahms is by a fair margin the slowest ever put on disc, but his devotion to the work gives an intensity to sustain all the eccentricities. Tennstedt draws concentrated playing from the LPO, the whole richly recorded.

For all the beauty and brilliance of the playing, this DG account is not quite the flawless Milstein reading of the Brahms that he had previously put on record for EMI. Jochum secures playing of great warmth and distinction from the Vienna Philharmonic, and the hint of unease in the soloist is only relative. Those who want to hear Milstein in fine (1974) analogue sound can be safely directed here, for there are no such reservations about the other three performances on this DG Double.

On the Cedille label the Brahms *Violin Concerto* comes in an apt coupling in a two-for-the-price-of-one package with the Joachim *Violin Concerto*. Though it starts unpromisingly with a stodgy account of the opening tutti, the performance is instantly transformed by the entry of the soloist, Rachel Barton. She proves a magnetically imaginative artist who makes every phrase sound fresh and spontaneous, with free rubato totally natural. Technically too she shows complete mastery, using at the end of the movement her own formidably demanding and expansive cadenza. The disc then includes as a bonus track the usual Joachim cadenza leading again into the reflective coda. The slow movement, like the first, has a lacklustre opening tutti, before the soloist transforms the atmosphere, and the finale is fresh and bright, thanks to Barton. Though the Brahms masterpiece completely outshines the Joachim concerto of 17 years earlier, it is illuminating to have them side by side.

Zehetmair's is a warm and thoroughly musical account: his timbre is sweet, and both he and Dohnányi, who accompanies sympathetically, offer a natural response to Brahmsian lyricism. The Cleveland Orchestra's playing is beyond criticism and the (originally Teldec) sound balance is impressively natural. But other versions of the concerto have a stronger profile, and this performance fails to resonate in the memory.

In her New York recording, Anne-Sophie Mutter cannot quite match the mastery of her early version with Karajan. Her tone, as recorded, is less evenly beautiful, and live performance brings idiosyncrasies and the occasional flaw. It remains an enjoyable, warm-hearted version, recommendable for the unusual Schumann coupling.

We have mixed feeling about Vengerov's Brahms *Violin Concerto* (originally coupled with the *Third Violin Sonata*). For E. G., Vengerov plays not just for display, but with far deeper insights, the inspiration of the moment captured at white heat. Using the widest dynamic and tonal range, this is a performance of extremes, just as felicitous in bravura as in lyrical purity. R.L., while not denying that Vengerov's technique is dazzling and admitting that he produces a wonderful sound, finds the performance open to the charge of being a bit too gleaming and slick. But it is certainly an account to magnetize the listener.

Zimmermann's recording is taken from live performances given in the Philharmonie in Berlin, but only in the finale does this add to the lift and imagination of the reading. Until then his clean, direct approach seems a little too well-mannered for such a bravura work, beautiful as the playing is. Well recorded and coupled with an inspired, quicksilver performance of Mozart, this is fair value but hardly makes a strong contender. First choice rests with Joshua Bell (on Decca 475 6703).

Violin Concerto (with cadenzas by Busoni, Joachim, Singer, Hermann, Auer, Ysaÿe, Ondricek, Kneisel, Marteau, Kreisler, Tovey, Kubelik, Busch, Heifetz, Milstein, Ricci)
*** Biddulph LAW 002. Ricci, Sinfonia of London, Del Mar

The veteran Ruggiero Ricci not only gives a strong, assured performance of the concerto, he adds no fewer than 16 cadenzas as well, any of which can be programmed into the main performance on CD. Though Ricci is no longer as fiery or incisive as he once was, his is an attractive performance of the concerto, well recorded.

(i) *Violin Concerto*; (ii) *Double Concerto for Violin, Cello & Orchestra, in A min., Op. 102*
(M) *** RCA (ADD) 82876 59410-2. Heifetz, with (i) Chicago SO, Reiner; (ii) Piatigorsky, RCA Victor SO, Wallenstein
(B) **(*) Sony (ADD) SBK 46335. Stern, (i) with Rose; Phd. O, Ormandy

An excellent and logical coupling of these two vintage accounts for RCA's new 'Classic Library' series. The speeds in all the movements of the *Violin Concerto* may be on the fast side, but Heifetz's ease and detailed imagination make them more than just dazzling, while the central *Andante*, at a flowing speed, is delectably songful. Wallenstein, accompanying the *Double Concerto*, may not quite be in the same league of brilliance as that of Reiner in the *Violin Concerto*, but he nevertheless provides a sympathetic back-cloth for the 1960

Heifetz–Piatigorsky partnership. Even if this account does not quite match Heifetz's earlier version with Feuermann, it is still a strong, warm-hearted performance with a strikingly brilliant finale. The sound for both these recordings has been vastly improved in recent incarnations, and this CD certainly retains its classic status.

Stern's glorious (1959) account of the *Violin Concerto* with Ormandy is now given a coupling that is both generous and suitable, the mid-1960s' collaboration with Leonard Rose in the *Double Concerto*. The two soloists unfailingly match each other's playing, with Ormandy always an understanding accompanist. The only drawback is the characteristically forward balance of the soloists.

(i) *Violin Concerto* ; (i; ii) *Double Concerto for Violin, Cello & Orchestra. Symphonies 1–4; Academic Festival Overture, Op. 80; Tragic Overture, Op. 81; Variations on a Theme by Haydn, Op. 56a*
(N) (B) ** DG 474 930-2 (5). VPO, Bernstein, with (i) Kremer; (ii) Maisky

In the *Violin Concerto* with Bernstein, Kremer is powerful in attack and has strikingly clean articulation (the first movement is tauter than in his earlier, Karajan version) but he replaces the Joachim cadenza with a longer one by Reger, which will diminish its appeal for many collectors. The second movement is hardly a true *Adagio*, and Bernstein is much broader than the soloist, who tries to move things on. The finale is very fast indeed – the *ma non troppo vivace* marking being ignored. Even through Bernstein gets sumptuous results from the VPO, Kremer is too self-admiring and idiosyncratic to carry a firm recommendation. The same comments also apply to the *Double Concerto*, where Kremer's playing is often posturing and narcissistic. Even Mischa Maisky – a similarly superb player – is affected, with some extreme dynamic extremes coming across as self-conscious. The first two movements lack any real momentum and, though one enjoys the superb playing of the VPO (and excellent DG recording), this is another of Bernstein's least impressive concerto recordings, although both are taken from live performances.

However he is back on characteristic form in the early-1980s set of the *Symphonies*. They were edited together from live performances and – with the exception of the *Third Symphony*, which at slow speeds loses impulse – they represent a warmly spontaneous response to much-loved music. Unfortunately, as a Brahmsian, Bernstein is a Jekyll and Hyde figure. Though the thrust and urgency of the playing is rarely in doubt, he often dallies self-indulgently, as in the drawn-out account of the main theme in the finale of the *First Symphony* or the extreme *allargando* on the chorale motif at the end, or the Elgarian moulding in the slow movement of the *Fourth*. Like any Bernstein live performance, these readings are fascinating to listen to once, but less recommendable for constant listening. The digital recordings sound better in their CD incarnation, even if the balance and clarity are not always ideal.

Double Concerto for Violin, Cello & Orchestra in A min., Op. 102
(*) EMI **DVD 490449-9. (i) D. Oistrakh, Rostropovich, Moscow PO, Kondrashin – BACH: *Double Violin Concerto*, etc.; MOZART: *Sinfonia concertante* **(*)
☛ (M) *** EMI (ADD) 5 66902-2 [5 66954-2]. D. Oistrakh, Rostropovich, Cleveland O, Szell – BEETHOVEN: *Triple Concerto* ***

(B) *** EMI double forte (ADD) 5 69331-2 (2). D. Oistrakh,
Fournier, Philh. O, Galliera – BEETHOVEN: *Triple
Concerto;* MOZART: *Violin Concerto 3;* PROKOFIEV: *Violin
Concerto 2* ***

(BB) *** EMI Encore 5 75865-2. Menuhin, Tortelier, LPO,
Berglund – DVORAK: *Cello Concerto* **(*)

(BB) (***) Naxos mono 8.110940. Heifetz, Feuermann, Phd.
O, Ormandy – BRUCH: *Scottish Fantasy;* GLAZUNOV:
Violin Concerto (***)

(N) (M) **(*) DG (ADD) 477 5341. Schneiderhan, Starker,
Berlin RSO, Fricsay – BEETHOVEN: *Triple Concerto* **(*)

(M) *** RCA (ADD) 09026 63531-2. Heifetz, Piatigorsky, RCA
Victor SO, Wallenstein – J. S. BACH: *Double Violin
Concerto in D min.;* MOZART: *Sinfonia concertante* ***

(BB) *** Naxos 8.550938. Kaler, Kliegel, Nat. SO of Ireland,
Constantine – SCHUMANN: *Cello Concerto* ***

(BB) (***) Naxos mono 8.110930. Thibaud, Casals, Barcelona
O, Cortot – DVORAK: *Cello Concerto* (***)

**(*) Testament SBT 1337. Ferras, Tortelier, Philh. O, Kletzki
– TCHAIKOVSKY: *Violin Concerto* **(*)

David Oistrakh and Rostropovich were recorded during the
Moscow Philharmonic's visit to London in October 1965. It is
a highly charged account which shows both artists at their
most emotionally intense yet profoundly disciplined. As
usual at this period, the camerawork, expertly produced by
the young Brian Large, is very restrained, with a limited
number of angles and the minimum of visual distraction. Of
course the sound is less transparent and present than the
commercial records of the period, but this DVD does convey
the sense of occasion and musical excitement.

This 1969 EMI recording of the *Double Concerto* has claims
to be regarded as one of the finest of all versions. If it places
David Oistrakh and Rostropovich too far forward, few will
grumble when the playing is so ripely, compellingly
Brahmsian and the solo timbres so richly projected. The
Andante is glorious. Szell's powerful tutti and warmly sympathetic backing keeping the Cleveland Orchestra well in the
picture. Coupled with an equally arresting version of
Beethoven's *Triple Concerto*, this is fully worthy of its reissue
as one of EMI's 'Great Recordings of the Century'.

David Oistrakh's first stereo account with Fournier dates
from 1959, but the recording was balanced by Walter Legge
and the sound is remarkably satisfying. The performance is
distinguished, strong and lyrical – the slow movement particularly fine – and, with Galliera and the Philharmonia
providing excellent support, this version, coupled with three
other outstanding concerto recordings, makes an ideal choice
for bargain-hunters.

The version by Menuhin and Tortelier presents two outstandingly warm and individual soloists against the background of strong, steadily paced accompaniment. The
soloists are placed well forward, but the result is genial as well
as big and positive. The challenge between two volatile,
inspirational artists brings out the best in both of them, with
the slow movement sweet and relaxed and the finale slower
than usual, but nicely lilting and crisply pointed. Excellent,
full, 1984 recording, debatable (like the Dvořák coupling)
only on the question of the forwardness of the soloists. In
every other respect a genuine bargain.

Recorded in December 1939 in very good sound for the
period, the Philadelphia account of the Brahms *Double Concerto* finds Heifetz perfectly matched with Emanuel Feuermann, as near a cellist counterpart to the violin wizard as
could ever be found. This is the most powerful performance

ever put on disc, passionate as well as purposeful, if lacking a
little in tenderness. The incisiveness of the playing in the
most taxing bravura passages makes for exciting results.
Generously coupled with Heifetz's pioneering account of the
Glazunov concerto and his 1947 version of the *Scottish Fantasy*, the Naxos issue brings a first-rate transfer.

Although Wallenstein is not as fine an accompanist as
Ormandy, he provides a sympathetic backcloth for the 1960
Heifetz–Piatigorsky partnership which, even if it does not
quite match Heifetz's earlier version with Feuermann, is still a
strong, warm-hearted account with a strikingly brilliant
finale. The 1960 recording, although a bit close, has been
improved out of all recognition compared to the harsh
quality of the LP, and there is certainly no lack of warmth
here.

We have always enjoyed the Schneiderhan/Starker/Fricsay
account of the Brahms *Double Concerto* since it came out in
1961. The soloists are placed rather too forwardly (which
reduces the dynamic contrast with the orchestra) but the
effect is better on CD than it ever it was on LP, and there is
plenty of warmth and atmosphere. Fricsay shapes the work
splendidly and there is plenty of impetus.

The Brahms and Schumann concertos make an excellent
and apt coupling, here presented on the Naxos super-budget
label in warmly spontaneous-sounding recordings, very well
recorded. Ilya Kaler is as clean in attack and intonation as is
Maria Kliegel, who earlier impressed with her Naxos coupling
of the Dvořák and Elgar *Cello Concertos*.

Collectors who grew up in the 1930s and 1940s will probably have got to know the *Double Concerto* in the Thibaud–
Casals version with the Barcelona Orchestra conducted by
Cortot. It is a performance of incandescent intensity and
humanity, which reigned supreme until the Heifetz–
Feuermann set came along. This new transfer is probably as
good as any we are likely to get. The 1929 original was
scrawny and strident, and Mark Obert-Thorn has succeeded
in taming it more successfully than did Dutton – almost the
latter's only failure!

The performance of the *Double Concerto* by Christian
Ferras, Paul Tortelier and the Philharmonia Orchestra under
Paul Kletzki was recorded at the Kingsway Hall in 1962,
though it was reissued in a box devoted to Tortelier first in
the days of LP and then on CD, it has not been released on
one disc. The two French artists have a good rapport and
deliver a finely integrated account of the work, and Kletzki
gives admirable support. Those who believe that recording
has rarely been more natural or truthful than it was in the
first few years of stereo will take further solace in the spacious
and pleasing sound, excellently remastered by Paul Baily.

(i) *Double Concerto for Violin, Cello and Orchestra.
Symphony 1, Op. 98*

(M) *** Warner Elatus 0927 49615-2. (i) Perlman, Ma;
Chicago SO, Barenboim

From Elatus an unexpected but outstandingly successful
re-coupling. In the *Double Concerto*, Perlman, in collaboration with Yo-Yo Ma, is volatile, more flexible than when his
partners were Rostropovich and Haitink on EMI (7 49486-2).
Although in the outer movements the speeds are noticeably
faster than before, Perlman and Ma are both freer, broadening more markedly in moments of repose, while the finale
dances with extra lightness. A great performance, well
recorded. Moreover, Barenboim's Chicago performance of
the *First Symphony* was the finest from his cycle of the late

1990s. It is grippingly compulsive. He takes the *Andante* more slowly than marked, but with a richly ardent response from the Chicago strings, the result is eloquently convincing, with much refined orchestral detail. After an excitingly ebullient Scherzo, the finale sets off with a powerful thrust that carries through to the final bar, though Barenboim's flexible style prevents any feeling of rigidity. Throughout, the sound is suitably full-bodied, within the aptly resonant acoustics of Chicago's Orchestral Hall.

(i) *Double Concerto. Symphony 2, Op 73*
(N) (BB) *** LSO Live LSO 0043. (i) Nikolitch, Hugh; LSO, Haitink

Gordon Nikolitch and Tim Hugh, the soloists in Haitink's live LSO version of the *Double Concerto*, recorded at the Barbican in 2003, are both leaders of their respective sections in the LSO, co-ordinating superbly in a powerful performance, taut and thrusting in the first movement, warm and flowing in the central *Andante*, and clean and incisive in the finale. The weight and warmth of the sound help to make this the finest of Haitink's Brahms series, with an equally persuasive account of the *D major Symphony*. At the very start, the ripeness of the horn, played by the section-leader, David Pyatt, sets the pattern for a performance at once warm and powerful. There is no exposition repeat in the first movement, but that adds to the tautness and concentration, relaxing in an exceptionally charming account of the third movement, before a strong and steady reading of the finale, exciting yet with no headlong rush at the end.

Hungarian Dances 1–21 (complete)
☛ ❂ (BB) *** Naxos 8.550110; (1–2; 4–21). Budapest SO, Bogár
(M) **(*) Chan. 7072. LSO, Järvi
**(*) Ph. (IMS) 462 589-2. Budapest Festival O, I. Fischer

The Budapest Symphony Orchestra recording of the Brahms *Hungarian Dances* is sheer delight from beginning to end. The playing has warmth and sparkle, and the natural way in which the music unfolds brings a refreshing feeling of rhythmic freedom. Bogár's rubato is wholly spontaneous. The recording is warm and full yet transparent, with just the right brilliance on top. This is an outright winner among the available versions.

The Chandos recording is characteristically sumptuous and Järvi is warmly affectionate, attractively coaxing the rubato of a dance like No. 7 in F major. There is plenty of spirit and flexibility elsewhere, and this set is certainly warmly enjoyable. Yet both Weller and (especially) Bogár are even more spontaneously Hungarian in spirit.

Ivan Fischer's performances are warmly enjoyable and obviously have an authentic Hungarian underlay, including players of the 'gypsy violin' and cimbalom. But it is the gentler numbers (Nos. 3 and 4, for instance) which come off best, and even here, for all the elegance of the playing, at times the rubato sounds just a trifle calculated. The recording is full and natural, but this does not alter our allegiance to the splendid Naxos set.

Hungarian Dances 1, 3, 5–6, 17–20
(M) *** DG (ADD) (IMS) 447 434-2. BPO, Karajan – DVORAK: *Scherzo capriccioso*, etc. **(*)

Karajan's performances have great panache and brilliance and the brightly lit (1959) recording is given added fullness in the

current remastering, and the superlative orchestral playing is by turns warmly affectionate and dazzling.

Serenades 1 in D, Op. 11; 2 in A, Op. 16 (see also above)
(B) *** Sony SBK 89899. LSO, Tilson Thomas
❂ *** Australian Decca Eloquence [ADD] 466 672-2. LSO, Kertész
(BB) **(*) Warner Apex 2564 61138-2. (i) Royal Stockholm O, A. Davis; (ii) Ens. O de Paris, Jordan

Serenades 1–2; (i) Liebeslieder Waltzes, Op. 52 & 65
(M) **(*) Orfeo C008 102A (2). VSO, Bertini; (i) with Sieghart, V. Singverein

Michael Tilson Thomas's digital recordings of the two *Serenades* tend to sweep the board, irrespective of price. His account of the glorious D major work has a sunny geniality and a youthful radiance that are most persuasive, and the A major is equally fresh. He gets admirable results from the LSO, and these readings have both vitality and sensitivity. The Sony recordings are natural and well detailed.

It is a great pity that Kertész's classic performances are available only as an import, which means that although they are on a bargain label in Australia, they cost much more here. But these readings remain as fresh as ever. Recorded in the mid-1960s, they have an unforced spontaneity, as well as robust vigour when called for. The recording in its new transfer is full and vivid, and this remains very highly recommendable on all counts.

Andrew Davis and the Stockholm orchestra give a spirited account of Brahms's masterly early *D major Serenade*. Davis's direction is as sympathetic as the players' response, and the 1998 recording is very good, even if the texture could be more transparent. For the budget reissue it has been joined to Armin Jordan's more mellow performance of the companion A major work, which is a shade less vital, but has a warmly played slow movement, and an engaging closing Rondo. Again the sound, with a nice bloom on the woodwind, is pleasingly full, if not sharply detailed. Excellent value at Apex price.

Gary Bertini's account of the opening movement of the *D major Serenade*, with its rollicking horns, has a boisterous quality which is engaging, and throughout both works he draws much fine playing from the Vienna Symphony Orchestra; the woodwind provide appealing colour. Bertini maintains a good momentum for the *Adagio* slow movements, which is sensible enough, but he captures the relaxed atmosphere better in Op. 16 than in Op. 11. The resonant recording sounds rich-textured at lower dynamic levels, but in *fortissimos* the opulence also brings a touch of heaviness. However, there is much agreeable warmth here and the reissue throws in a second CD with an equally agreeable performance of the seductive *Liebeslieder Waltzes*, liltingly sung by the Vienna Singverein, although Ingrid Sieghart is not a soloist to banish memories of more famous names.

(i) Serenades 1–2; Academic Festival Overture; (ii) Tragic Overture; (i) Variations on a Theme of Haydn; (i, iii) Alto Rhapsody, Op. 53
(B) **(*) EMI double forte (ADD) 5 68655-2 (2). (i) LPO; (ii) LSO; (iii) with J. Baker, Alldis Ch.; all cond. Boult

Sir Adrian Boult's warmly lyrical approach to the two *Serenades* is less ebullient and sparkling than that of Andrew Davis or Bertini, yet he gives pleasure in a different way. Boult's way with these delightful scores is engaging enough to blunt any criticism, when the late-1970s Abbey Road recording is suitably full. What makes this inexpensive double forte reissue even more attractive is the inclusion of Janet Baker's devoted account of the *Alto Rhapsody*, the performance essentially meditative. The *Academic Festival Overture* opens the programme in a rather more extrovert fashion, and the *Variations* are also vividly presented and strongly characterized, the sound here rather more lively. The eloquent *Tragic Overture* also shows Boult as a true Brahmsian. In playing time (just under two hours), however, this is rather less generous than some double fortes.

Serenade 1 in D, Op. 11

*** Finlandia 3984-25327-2. Royal Stockholm PO, A. Davis –
 STENHAMMAR: *Serenade for orchestra* *** ●

Andrew Davis and the Stockholm orchestra give a spirited account of Brahms's early masterpiece. Davis's direction is as sympathetic as the players' response. The recording is very good, even if the texture could be more transparent. However, Stenhammar's glorious *Serenade* is a logical and useful coupling, and this performance is very special.

SYMPHONIES

Symphonies 1–4

☞ (B) *** DG (ADD) Double 453 097-2 (2). BPO, Karajan

(N)(B) (**(*)) Sony 2-CD mono 517187-2 (2) NYPO, Walter

(B) **(*) RCA 74321 89103-2 (2); or 74321 89102-2 (1 & 3); 74321 89101-2 (2 & 4). N. German RSO, Wand

(M) **(*) DG 429 644-2 (3). BPO, Karajan

(B) **(*) DG 2-CD (DDD/ADD) 474 263-2 (2). BPO, Karajan

Symphonies 1–4; Academic Festival Overture; Tragic Overture; Variations on a Theme of Haydn

(BB) **(*) Warner 2564 61892-2 (4). Chicago SO, Barenboim

Symphonies 1–4; Academic Festival Overture; Tragic Overture; Variations on a Theme of Haydn; (i) Alto Rhapsody

(M) *** EMI (ADD) 5 62742-2 [5 627602] (3). Philh. O, Klemperer; (i) with Ludwig, Philh. Ch.

Symphonies 1–4; Academic Festival Overture; Tragic Overture; Variations on a Theme of Haydn; (i) Alto Rhapsody; Fragment from Goethe's Harz Journey in Winter; (ii) Gesang der Parzen (Song of the Fates); Nänie; Schicksalslied

*** DG 435 683-2 (4). BPO, Abbado; (i) with Lipovšek, Senff Ch.; (ii) Berlin R. Ch.

Symphonies 1–4; Hungarian Dances 1, 3 & 10; Variations on a Theme of Haydn

(M) (**(*)) EMI mono 5 65513-2 (3). BPO or VPO, Furtwängler – BEETHOVEN: *Overtures* (***)

Symphonies 1–4; Tragic Overture; Variations on a Theme by Haydn

(***) Testament mono SBT 3167 (3). Philh. O, Toscanini

(BB) *** RCA Navigator (ADD) 74321 30367-2 (3). Dresden State O, K. Sanderling

*** Telarc CD-80450 (4). SCO, Mackerras

(***) Testament mono/stereo SBT 3054 (3). BPO, Kempe

Abbado's remains the most successful of the modern, digital cycles and still makes a clear first choice, with playing at once polished and intense, glowingly recorded. The set gains from

having a generous collection of imaginatively chosen couplings: the rare, brief, choral works, as well as the usual supplements in the *Overtures* and *Variations*.

Anyone wanting Karajan's readings of the four Brahms symphonies should be well satisfied with the DG Double, which offers his recordings made in the late 1970s. The current remastering makes the most of the analogue sound. The playing of the Berlin Philharmonic remains uniquely cultivated: the ensemble is finely polished yet can produce tremendous bravura at times, and there is no lack of warmth. Karajan's interpretations, with lyrical and dramatic elements finely balanced, changed little over the years. A very real bargain, hard to beat.

Klemperer's monumental set – now reissued as one of EMI's 'Great Recordings of the Century' – remains highly desirable. The sound was effectively refurbished (in 1999) for the separate issues of the symphonies, and the commanding strength of these readings continues to recommend them. In that respect No. 1 is unsurpassed; Nos. 2 and 3 may be a trifle austere for some tastes, but their emotional power is in no doubt, and in No. 2 the balance between the lyrical and histrionic elements is held in perfect balance. The combination of gravity and drama in No. 4 makes a continuing impact on almost all listeners (although R. L. confesses that its comparative severity means he has never really enjoyed this *Fourth*). The *Tragic Overture* is done with equal strength, and the *Alto Rhapsody* also shows the conductor at his most masterful and, with Christa Ludwig on fine form, it is a beautifully expressive performance. The *Haydn Variations* is chosen to open the first disc, as it was one of his first (mono) recordings made with the Philharmonia, made in 1954; yet the orchestra immediately responds to him, and he enters fully into the spirit of the *Academic Festival Overture*.

Otherwise Kurt Sanderling's 1971–2 Dresden recordings make an excellent choice. They have a warmth and humanity that stand out from the general run of Brahms cycles, with the Dresden orchestra responding to Sanderling's direction with playing of an unaffected and natural eloquence, so that the performances can stand comparison with any in the catalogue at any price. Their return to circulation is cause for celebration.

Günter Wand's Brahms set is also highly recommendable for providing spontaneously compelling readings of all four works, very well played. RCA have carefully remastered the 1982–3 recordings (as far as is possible with digital masters) and the sound-balance seems fuller, with the tendency to shrillness on violin tone now less problematic; certainly the effect gives the playing plenty of bite. Wand's is a consistently direct view of Brahms, yet the reading of each symphony has its own individuality. No. 1 has striking impetus throughout, and the *Second* (the finest of the four) is a characteristically glowing but steady reading, with the recording adding fullness and bloom. In the *Third* the forward thrust returns excitingly in the outer movements, yet overall Wand's wise way with Brahms, strong and evenly paced, works beautifully. The reading of No. 4 initially seems understated, but the remastering with its rather more expansive sound adds to the weight and strength of what is a generally satisfying conclusion of a fine cycle. Wand's admirers need not hesitate. The two discs are available separately.

The concerts on Testament preserve the two legendary occasions in the autumn of 1952 when, in a Brahms cycle at the Royal Festival Hall, Toscanini conducted the Philharmonia Orchestra on his one visit to London after the war. It is fascinating to compare these readings of the Brahms symphonies with those which Toscanini recorded in the same twelve months with the NBC Symphony Orchestra in New York. Where the New York performances, resonant and superbly drilled, have a hardness and rigidity, with dynamic contrasts ironed out, the Philharmonia ones consistently bring a moulding of phrase and subtlety of rubato which bear out the regular Toscanini instruction to 'Sing!'. And, in contrast with most Toscanini recordings, the hushed playing is magical. Though mono recordings made in the Royal Festival Hall are inevitably limited in range, the clarity and definition of the EMI recording quickly make one forget such limitations and the intrusive coughing. There are a couple of blips to note, which in context hardly matter. The chorale on trombones just after the great horn theme in the introduction to the finale of No. 1 brings a series of split notes, and the finale of No. 4 is disturbed by firecrackers, let off by pranksters. Toscanini was completely unfazed. A set to restore Toscanini's unique reputation as a conductor without equal, when too many of his commercial discs give only a limited view of his mastery.

For their reissue in the 'Karajan Collection', DG have chosen the later digital versions of Nos. 1–3 but wisely reverted to the 1978 analogue version of No. 4, which in many ways sounds finest of all. In his 1987 version of the *First Symphony* Karajan draws a typically powerful and dramatic performance, beautifully played, which sounds warm and spontaneous. The sound is full and weighty to match, but the recording is thick and generalized in tuttis. It is comfortable enough overall, but could be better defined. The *Second Symphony* suffers less than the first from the thick, undifferential digital recording, when textures in this later work tend to be lighter. It is a magnificent reading, in some ways warmer and more glowing than his previous versions, with consistently fine playing from the Berlin Philharmonic, who approach with striking freshness a symphony they must have played countless times. However, Karajan's last recording of the *Third Symphony* brings a relatively perfunctory performance, seemingly more so when at a fastish tempo, the first movement (as with Nos. 1 and 2) has no exposition repeat. The sound is full although tuttis are not ideally clear, and there is a hint of shrillness. The analogue performance of No. 4 readily compensates. The performance is richer and more imaginative than the later digital version, satisfyingly spacious, yet the *Passacaglia* has splendid grip and so does the slow movement. The recording is full, firm and wide ranging. But for a complete Karajan set of the four symphonies the DG Double mentioned above is more satisfying overall.

Bruno Walter's earlier mono LP set of the Brahms *Symphonies* was recorded in 1951 and 1952 with the NYPO in Carnegie Hall. These are all outstanding performances, the interpretations not so markedly different from the later stereo set made with the Columbia Symphony Orchestra in the conductor's 'Indian summer' of 1959/60, although the *First Symphony* here is more consistent in its spirited vitality. On the other hand, the later set has an even more persuasive, glowing warmth, helped by the breadth of the stereo set. The current transfer of the mono discs was made in France and is not entirely flattering to the upper range of the strings (particularly in the odd-numbered symphonies), although the recordings do not lack body. A valuable reissue nevertheless.

Like Furtwängler, Kempe is freely expressive, but his freedom is very different, with far less extreme changes of tempo. Speeds and timings are often very similar, but results are strikingly different. First and foremost, Kempe has his finger on the natural flow and pulse of these symphonies in a way that calls to mind only the most exalted comparisons. The

Second and the *Fourth* are both mono, and the sound is less transparent and fresh – but, ironically, they are at least as vivid and are rather better focused. The *Tragic Overture* is one of the best ever committed to disc. Excellent transfers.

Mackerras uses forces of the same size as Brahms would have had at his disposal in Meiningen. The smaller numbers remove some of the thick-textured, overweight quality that the strings can produce in Brahms, while retaining their warmth and richness. The strings are often thinned out to single part at times, and the effect is – strangely enough – enriching. The set includes the very first version of the slow movement of the *First Symphony* as it was originally performed at Karlsruhe and Cambridge. There are fascinating differences both in the order of the material and, at times, in the harmony. The playing is exemplary and has no lack of warmth, and the same must be said of the recording. Well worth getting.

As with his Beethoven set, Barenboim dons his Furtwänglerian mantle for his Chicago accounts of the first two Brahms symphonies which, though very well played, suffer from his wilful waywardness and eccentric structural control. His inspirational flexibility works well in the *Third Symphony*, which does not lose its ongoing purpose and brings beautiful orchestral playing in the central movements. No. 4 is the finest of all, a highly concentrated interpretation that moves forward powerfully; even though the tempo for the *Andante* is slow, it is presented ardently and is capped by a gripping performance of the closing *Passacaglia*. We hope this may be issued separately, like No. 3 (see below).

Furtwängler's EMI compilation brings together the live recording of the *First Symphony* that he made with the Vienna Philharmonic in 1952 and live recordings of the remaining three symphonies made with the Berlin Philharmonic in 1948 and 1952, presumably taken from radio sources. The performance of the *First* is perhaps the best and it has the best sound, which otherwise is disappointingly thin, lacking in body and with some harshness; but the electricity of Furtwängler in Brahms is vividly captured.

Eschenbach's set could compete only if the Houston performances were truly outstanding, which they are not. They are beautifully played and very well balanced and recorded. But Eschenbach, highly musical Brahmsian as he is, has not yet entirely mastered the art of bringing a performance fully to life in the recording studio. Easily the finest performance is of the *Fourth Symphony*, where the tension is consistently maintained and Eschenbach's steady lyrical flow, often impassioned, reminds one of Karl Boehm. One of the highlights of the set is the moving account of the *Alto Rhapsody*. Dunja Vejzovic is in glorious voice and the choral entry is a moment of serene magic, with the Houston chorus beautifully balanced with the solo voice. But as a general recommendation, this Virgin set is a non-starter (5 62081-2).

Symphonies 1–2
(N) (M) (**(*)) RCA mono 82876 62322-2. NBC SO, Toscanini

Toscanini's NBC Brahms from 1951/2 is high-powered but full of lyricism and an Italian warmth. The *First Symphony* starts very fast and intensely, but the *Second*, although not exactly relaxed, is not too hard-driven to lose the music's lyrical chacater, and its energy is characteristically compelling. The Carnegie Hall resonance brings both ambience and body to counteract the harshness on high violins, and although the fierceness suits No. 1 rather than No. 2, in the latter the impetus of the recapitulation in the finale thrillingly holds the listener in its grip.

Symphonies 1–3; Academic Festival Overture; Tragic Overture

❀ (B) *** EMI double forte (ADD) 5 69515-2 (2). LPO, Jochum

Jochum's EMI stereo versions of the Brahms symphonies were made in the Kingsway Hall in 1976; the analogue recordings, produced by Christopher Bishop, are outstandingly full and vivid. These remastered discs indeed sound better than almost any of their mid- or bargain-priced competitors. The LPO playing is excellent, the spontaneity of its performances carrying the listener along on a wave of inspiration, and this also applies to the exuberant *Academic Festival Overture* and the hardly less vibrant *Tragic Overture*. The high drama of the *First Symphony* immediately shows Jochum at his most persuasive. Equally, No. 2 is a warmly lyrical reading, expansive in the first movement, fast and exciting in the finale. The inner movements are beautifully played. The *Third Symphony* represents the peak of Jochum's cycle, and this is among the most rewarding versions of this work, irrespective of price. He conveys the full weight and warmth of the work with generally spacious speeds, finely moulded.

Symphony 1 in C min., Op. 68

(M) *** DG (ADD) 447 408-2. BPO, Karajan – SCHUMANN: *Symphony 1* ***

*** Simax PSC 1206. Oslo PO, Jansons – JOACHIM: *Hamlet Overture* ***

(BB) **(*) Dresden Staatskapelle Live VKJK 0414. Dresden State O, Haitink – WEBER: *Oberon Overture* **(*)

(BB) (***) Dutton Lab. mono CDBP 9705. Hollywood Bowl SO, Stokowski – FALLA: *El amor brujo* (**(*))

Symphony 1; Academic Festival Overture; Tragic Overture

(N) (BB) *** Naxos 8.557428. LPO, Alsop

Symphony 1; Tragic Overture

(N) (BB) **(*)LSO Live LSO 0045. LSO, Haitink

Symphony 1; Tragic Overture; (i) Alto Rhapsody

☞ ❀ (M) *** EMI (ADD) 5 67029-2. Philh. O, Klemperer, (i) with Ludwig, Philh. Ch.

Symphony 1; Variations on a Theme of Haydn

(M) **(*) DG Entrée 474 166-2. VPO, Giulini

(BB) ** Naxos 8.550278. Belgian R. PO, Brussels, Rahbari

(i) Symphony 1; Variations on a Theme of Haydn; (ii) Hungarian Dances 17–21

(B) **(*) Sony (ADD) SBK 46534. (i) Cleveland O, Szell; (ii) Phd. O, Ormandy

Symphony 1; Variations on a Theme of Haydn

(N) (BB) ** EMI Encore 5 86092-2. LPO, Sawallisch

Symphony 1; (i) Gesang der Parzen (Song of the Fates)

*** DG 431 790-2. BPO, Abbado, (i) with Berlin R. Ch.

Klemperer's 1956–7 Kingsway Hall recording remains among the greatest performances this symphony has ever received on disc. This is Klemperer at his very finest, and his reading remains unique for its authority and power, supported by consistently superb Philharmonia playing. The sound is both clear and full-bodied. The *Alto Rhapsody* also shows Klemperer at his most masterful and Ludwig on fine form: it is a beautifully expressive performance.

After a spacious introduction, Abbado launches into a warm, dramatic reading, rhythmically well sprung and finely shaded, with the full power of the great dramatic climaxes brought out in the finale, from the rapt pianissimo of the opening onwards. The *Gesang der Parzen* makes an unusual and warmly attractive coupling, very well sung. A clear first choice among modern recordings.

Karajan's 1964 recording of Brahms's *First Symphony* (the conductor's third version of five – DG 447 408-2) seems by general consensus to be regarded as his finest. The control of tension in the first movement is masterly, the orchestral playing is of superlative quality and the result is very powerful, with the finale a fitting culmination. The remastering has restored the original, full, well-balanced, analogue sound, with plenty of weight in the bass. The coupling with Schumann's *First Symphony* makes this a very desirable record indeed.

Marin Alsop conducts the LPO in a strong, thrusting performance of the *First Symphony*, very well recorded and persuasively paced. After the power of the first movement Alsop brings out the tenderness of the following *Andante* and the lyrical freedom of the third movement, before unleashing more power in the finale. Only her slowing for the two big statements of the great march theme fails to sound entirely convincing. The two overtures are just as taut and fresh. An excellent start to a projected Brahms cycle.

Following up his other Brahms symphony recordings for Simax, Jansons in a live recording directs a spacious reading of the *First* which brings out its lyricism as well as its weight of argument. He is helped by a spacious acoustic in a venue, the Oslo Concert Hall, once counted difficult and dry. The refinement as well as the power and intensity of the playing cannot be faulted. Warmly recommended for those who have collected Jansons's earlier Brahms discs, as well as those curious about the rare and atmospheric Joachim overture.

Szell's account of No. 1 is one of the most impressive of his set. His bold, direct thrust gives the outer movements plenty of power and impetus, and the inner movements bring relaxation and a fair degree of warmth.

Haitink, with the LSO, conducts a forthright, rugged account of the *First Symphony*. Recorded live, it brings no exposition repeat in the first movement but remains powerfully convincing, weighty even in the slow movement and incisive throughout. The slightly dry acoustic of the Barbican makes the recording less atmospheric than it might be, but the sound is undistracting, as it is in the *Tragic Overture*.

It was unfortunate timing that the Dresden Staatskapelle's own-label live recording with Haitink should appear immediately after the LSO Live version with him. The sound is warmer and more refined, with a pleasant bloom on the strings and glorious ripe horn-playing. But the first movement, marginally broader than the LSO version, is less taut; and generally the results are heavier, making the disc marginally less recommendable. More refinement in the Weber *Overture*.

Opening powerfully with thundering timpani in the manner of Klemperer, though with generally more relaxed tempi, Alexander Rahbari on Naxos gives a strong, direct reading, spacious yet with plenty of impetus. A fair choice for those with limited budgets, even if there are many finer versions of all four symphonies.

Stokowski's characteristic ebb and flow of rubato is individual yet warmly felt, following the Brahmsian contours persuasively and giving the performance a constant expressive power. His rich lower strings combine with mellow wind and resonant brass, while the violins soar. The urgent, crisply articulated rhythms in the first movement give the reading a consistently strong momentum, and in the slow movement the violins play with extrovert lyrical passion. Similarly, in the finale, after the noble horn fanfare, the strings articulate their famous tune with gutsy bow contact. There is an involving sense of 'live' music-making here, and as usual the sophisticated Dutton transfer makes the very most of the original master.

Like the other performances in Giulini's cycle with the VPO from the early 1990s, No. 1 brings speeds far slower than usual, almost eccentrically so in the *Allegro* of the first movement. Yet such is the weight and tension of the reading that the result is compelling, with the sound of the Vienna Philharmonic gloriously full and rich. The *Variations* are similarly expansive and compelling, a welcome coupling. Even so, one wonders about DG's decision to choose Giulini's idiosyncratic approach as an ideal entrée for novice collectors into Brahms's symphonic world, for all the intensity of the playing.

Sawallisch's lyrical approach makes for a warm, persuasive reading, lacking dramatic bite in outer movements, not helped by rather edgy LPO violins, but with the slow movement raptly simple. The couplings are generous and the reissue inexpensive, but this is not really competitive.

Symphonies 1; 3
(BB) **(*) RCA 74321 68009-2. N. German RSO, Wand

In the opening movement of the *First Symphony* Wand brings fierce intensity to the slow introduction by choosing an unusually fast speed, then leading naturally by modular pacing into the main allegro. The extra unity is clear. There is comparable dramatic intensity in the finale, though the choice of tempo for the main marching melody, far slower than the rest, brings uncomfortable changes of gear. Yet with a sense of spontaneity matching that of a live perfomance, the reading remains convincing. The *Third Symphony*, steadily paced, strong and easy, with the exposition repeat observed, again demonstrates Wand's singularity, here bringing out the work's autumnal moods and ending with a sober view of the finale. The sound in both works is inclined to be edgy on top, which affects the violins and in the *Third Symphony* underlines the reedy twang of the Hamburg woodwind, especially in the slow movement, while the solo horn is none too secure in his solo in the third movement.

Symphony 2 in D, Op. 73
(N) **(*) Ph. **DVD** 070 161-9. VPO, Carlos Kleiber (Director: Horant Hohlfeld) – MOZART: *Symphony 36 in C (Linz)* **(*)

(M) *** Cala CACD 0531. Nat. PO, Stokowski – MENDELSSOHN: *Symphony 4* ***

(N) (M) (**(*)) DG mono 474 989-2. BPO, Boehm – REGER: *Variations on a Theme by Mozart* **(*)

(M) (***) BBC mono BBCL 4099-2. RPO, Beecham – BEETHOVEN: *Symphony 2* (***)

(***) Testament mono SBT 1015. BBC SO, Toscanini – MENDELSSOHN: *Midsummer Night's Dream:* excerpt; ROSSINI: *Semiramide: Overture* (***)

Symphony 2; (i) Alto Rhapsody
*** DG 427 643-2. (i) Lipovšek, Senff Ch.; BPO, Abbado

Carlos Kleiber's DVD account comes from a live concert in the Musikverein, recorded in 1991. He looks surprisingly young, and obviously enjoys directing the VPO in front of the cameras. We see quite a lot of him, and although his hand movements are minimal the Vienna Philharmonic play superbly for him; their Brahmsian response is warmly idiomatic. The highlight of the performance is the *Adagio*, which is affectionately detailed and has many memorable moments, matched by the the beautifully delicate oboe solo in the *Allegretto grazioso*, on which the camera dwells lovingly. The horns shine through a texture which is not as warm as would be ideal and which is light in the bass. One assumes this was because the acoustic of the famous hall has been robbed of some of its natural ambience by the presence of the audience. Nevertheless this is a distinctive and enjoyable performance, with penty of impetus in the finale (the horns come through splendidly in the galloping second subject).

Among modern CD versions Abbado's still stands as an easy first choice, particularly when, with Marjana Lipovšek a radiant soloist, it also contains a gravely beautiful account of the *Alto Rhapsody*. Abbado's approach to Brahms is generally direct, but his control of rhythm and phrase makes the performance instantly compelling.

Stokowski's recording of the *D major Symphony* was one of the last he made, in London in 1978. It is a performance of warmth and power and, for all his free rubato, the effect is totally spontaneous, with the symphonic structure unimpaired, first-movement exposition repeat included. The concert-hall acoustic adds richness and breadth to the sound and the reading itself grips the listener throughout; after the reprise of the second subject of the finale, the brass ring out to make a thrilling conclusion. The CD transfer is first class and, with its equally impressive Mendelssohn coupling, this is one of Stokowski's very finest later recordings.

There is a naturalness and dignity about the 1956 Boehm performance which is very satisfying. It is a broadly conceived reading, leisurely and spacious, with fine playing from the Berlin Philharmonic and excellent recording. There is a substantial and satisfying coupling which further enhances the value of this reissue.

The radio recording of Brahms's *Second Symphony*, always a favourite work with Beecham, comes from an Edinburgh Festival performance given in August 1956 which has become legendary. Though the dry Usher Hall acoustic and the bronchial audience prevent it from matching in sound Beecham's stereo recording for EMI (currently withdrawn), the incandescence of the performance makes it magnetic, at once warm and impulsive in the first movement, richly expressive in the second and elegant in the third, leading to the fieriest, most biting account of the finale, with a marked *stringendo* in the coda and wild cheering from the audience before the last chord has ended. The excitement of the event is vividly caught despite the limited sound.

Toscanini's account with the BBC Symphony Orchestra on Testament, recorded in 1938, will come as a revelation to those who view the legendary Italian as a hard-driving, demonic maestro. Tempi are relaxed, the first movement is unhurried and the mood is sunny and smiling. There is none of the hard-driven momentum and over-drilled intensity that marked his final, NBC version. The sound calls for tolerance, but the playing is worth it.

Symphonies 2–3
*** Simax PSC 1204. Oslo PO, Jansons

☞ (M) *** Sony (ADD) SMK 64471. Columbia SO, Walter

(M) *** EMI (ADD) 5 67030-2.. Philh. O, Klemperer

(B) *** DG (ADD) 429 153-2. BPO, Karajan

(B) *** Sony (ADD) SBK 47652. Cleveland O, Szell

Jansons draws incandescent playing from his Oslo Philharmonic in outstanding versions of both symphonies. The refinement of the playing and the subtlety of Jansons's dynamic shading go with an approach which is at once direct and refreshing, with generally steady speeds yet warmly expressive on detail. Whereas in No. 3 Jansons observes the exposition repeat in the first movement, in No. 2 he omits it, a justifiable decision when it is very much a question of proportion. These now stand among the very finest versions of both symphonies, a formidable addition to the Simax catalogue, recorded in full, well-detailed sound.

The Bruno Walter coupling of the *Second* and *Third Symphonies* is very recommendable indeed. Walter's performance of the *Second* is wonderfully sympathetic, with an inevitability and a rightness which makes it very hard to concentrate on the interpretation as such, so cogent is the musical argument. Walter's pacing of the *Third Symphony* is admirable, and the vigour and sense of joy which imbue the opening of the first movement (exposition repeat included) dominate throughout, with the second subject eased in with wonderful naturalness.

Klemperer's account of No. 2 is also a great performance, the product of a strong and vital intelligence. Alongside Walter he may seem a trifle severe and uncompromising, but he was at his peak in his Brahms cycle and he underlines the power of the symphony without diminishing its eloquence in any way. Again in No. 3 there is a severity about his approach which may at first seem unappealing but which comes to underline the strength of the architecture. The remastered recording, made concurrently and in the same venue as No. 1, is very impressive.

Karajan's 1964 reading of the *Second* is among the sunniest and most lyrical accounts, and its sound is competitive even now. The companion performance of the *Third* is marginally less compelling but is still very fine. He takes the opening expansively and omits the exposition repeat. But clearly he sees the work as a whole: the third movement is also slow and perhaps slightly indulgent, but the closing pages of the finale have a memorable autumnal serenity. A bargain.

The Cleveland Severance recordings have been improved immeasurably. The orchestral virtuosity still remains and at times Szell's care for detail does become predominant, but the underlying ardour and warmth are in no doubt, especially in the *Adagio*, while the *Allegretto grazioso* has an appealing simplicity. The *Third* is a magnificent performance. Overall, this is a reading to set alongside that of Bruno Walter, even if (as in the *Second Symphony*), the exposition repeat is omitted.

Symphony 3 in F, Op. 90
*** BBC (ADD) BBCL4058-2. BBC N. SO, Monteux (with ROSSINI: *L'Italiana in Algeri Overture* **(*)) – SCHUMANN: *Symphony 4* ***

(***) Testament mono SBT 1173. Philh. O, Cantelli – MENDELSSOHN: *Symphony 4* (***)

Symphony 3; Serenade 2 in A, Op. 16
(N) (BB) ** LSO Live LSO 0056. LSO, Haitink

Symphony 3; Tragic Overture; (i) Song of Destiny (Schicksalslied)
*** DG 429 765-2. BPO, Abbado; (i) with Senff Ch.

Symphony 3; Variations on a Theme of Haydn
*** Erato 4509 95193-2. Chicago SO, Barenboim

Abbado directs a glowing, affectionate performance of *Symphony 3*, adopting generally spacious speeds and finely moulded phrasing but never sounding self-conscious, thanks to the natural tension which gives the illusion of live, spontaneous music-making. The rich, well-balanced, clean-textured recording underlines the big dramatic contrasts. This now heads the list of modern, digital recordings of this symphony.

Monteux's musical schooling was in Mozart, Beethoven and Brahms, and they were his first love. This bears fruit in a performance that is beautifully played, admirably shaped and full of vigour.

Barenboim's volatile approach works well in the *Third Symphony* and, although there must be some minor reservations about his freely spacious treatment of both central movements, they are beautifully played and warmly lyrical. The first movement (exposition repeat very much part of the interpretation) has plenty of power and a glowing lyrical feeling. The finale has exciting thrust and the valedictory ending is managed most sensitively. The *Variations*, too, are full of imaginative touches.

Cantelli's 1955 version of Brahms's *Third*, justly famous in the mono LP era, is among the warmest, most glowing accounts ever put on disc, with Dennis Brain's glorious horn-playing, ripely recorded, crowning the whole incandescent performance. Sadly, in mono, it has been available only rarely in the years since 1955, making this superbly transferred reissue very welcome, particularly when the coupling is an equally unforgettable, previously unissued version of the Mendelssohn.

Haitink introduces the *Symphony* with a delightful, care-free account of the *Serenade*, capturing the youthful exhilaration of this early inspiration. With no violins in the orchestra, the LSO's fine wind soloists have a field day in their lightly sprung playing. The *Symphony* is less successful, not helped by a recording that is less helpful than others in this LSO series, with the limitations of the Barbican acoustic apparent than usual, so that the violins sound thin at times. The middle two movements are on the slow side, but finely shaped, while the finale brings the tautest playing, sharply dramatic.

Symphonies 3–4
(M) *** DG (ADD) 437 645-2. BPO, Karajan
(M) **(*) Warner Elatus 0927 49835-2. BPO, Harnoncourt

In his 1978 recording Karajan gives superb grandeur to the opening of the *Third Symphony* but then characteristically refuses to observe the exposition repeat. Comparing this reading with Karajan's earlier (1964) version (coupled with No. 2), one finds him more direct and strikingly more dynamic and compelling. In the *Fourth Symphony* Karajan refuses to overstate the first movement, starting with deceptive reticence. His easy, lyrical style, less moulded in this 1978 reading than in his 1964 account, is fresh and unaffected and highly persuasive. The Scherzo, fierce and strong, leads to a clean, weighty account of the finale.

Recorded live in the Berlin Philharmonie in April 1997, Harnoncourt's performances of Nos. 3 and 4 are marked by a clarity and precision that are typical of a conductor who built his reputation on period performance. In the fascinating interview that comes in place of a conventional note, he emphasizes his view that Brahms was a craftsman who, like sculptors in a medieval cathedral, made sure that every detail was right even where no one would ever see the result. Harnoncourt's approach to both works reflects that, with fine detail meticulously highlighted, at times to the detriment of forward movement, as in the second and third movements of No. 3 and the slow movement of No. 4, where evenly stressed rhythms detract from carefully moulded phrasing. Vigorous allegros work far better, with the finales of both symphonies and the Scherzo of No. 4 fiery and dramatic. Good, firm sound, occasionally not ideally transparent.

Symphony 4 in E min., Op. 98

(N) **(*) DG DVD 073 4017. Bav. State O, Carlos Kleiber (Producer Harald Gerick) (with BEETHOVEN: *Overture Coriolan* ***) – MOZART: *Symphony 33* **(*)

☛— *** Sony **SACD** (ADD) SS 6113. Columbia SO, Walter

(N) (B) *** DG (ADD/DDD) 477 5324 (2). VPO, Carlos Kleiber – SCHUBERT: *Symphony 8 (Unfinished)* **(*); WAGNER: *Tristan und Isolde: Act III excerpts* ***

*** Simax PSC 1205. Oslo PO, Jansons – JOACHIM: *Overture: Heinrich IV* ***

**(*) BBC (ADD) BBCL 4003-2. BBC SO, Kempe – SCHUBERT: *Symphony 5* **(*)

**(*) Testament (ADD) SBT 1278. RPO, Kempe

(N) (BB) **(*) LSO Live LSO 0057. LSO, Haitink

(N) (M) **(*)EMI (ADD) 5 62882-2 [5 62883-2] (2). Chicago SO, Giulini (with *Tragic Overture; Variations on a Theme of Haydn*: Philh. O; also '*Giulini at 90*': Broadcast Profile)

(**(*)) Testament mono SBT 2242 (2). Royal Danish O, Klemperer – BEETHOVEN: *Symphony 3*, etc.; MOZART: *Symphony 29* (**(*))

Symphony 4; Academic Festival Overture

(M) *** EMI (ADD) 5 67031-2. Philh. O, Klemperer (with SCHUMANN: *Overtures: Genoveva; Manfred* **)

Symphony 4; Tragic Overture

(M) *** DG (IMS) 445 508-2. VPO, Bernstein

Symphony 4; Variations on a Theme of Haydn; (i) Nänie

*** DG (IMS) 435 349-2. BPO, Abbado, (i) with Berlin R. Ch.

Carlos Kleiber's DVD version is a performance of some distinction, even if the interpretation does not match his earlier, VPO account. It is a pleasure to watch this unexpectedly genial-looking conductor caressing the detail of this great symphony and receiving such a warm response from the Bavarian players, especially the strings, who play so beautifully and relaxedly in the slow movement. In Munich 1996, while Kleiber did not exert quite the overall grip which made his VPO CD version so memorable a decade earlier, the closing *Passagaglia* still makes an impressive and satisfying finale, and here it is a pleasure to watch the camera move round the orchestra during Brahms's variations, and especially the moment when the solo flute has the stage to himself. The concert opens with a superbly dramatic account of Beethoven's *Coriolan Overture*; if the symphony had sustained this degree of tension, it would have been a world-beater. The Herkulessaal is a visually pleasing venue – although we watch the conductor quite a lot of the time – and its acoustics provide a warmer Brahms sound than the Vienna Musikverein in the *Second Symphony* (see above).

This SACD transfer of Bruno Walter's inspired 1959 account of Brahms's *Fourth Symphony* is (like his companion disc of Beethoven's *Pastoral Symphony*) a true revelation of the astonishing enhancement that Sony's (non-compatible) SACD remastering can bring. The recording expands in range, warmth and body of tone in the strings, inner detail is more tangible, yet above all one receives a true concert-hall effect. The conductor's refusal to linger by a wayside painted

in glowing colours has a cumulative effect, with the glorious slow movement ripely intense in the strings, balanced by a vivacious exhilarating Scherzo (splendid brass) before the great *Passacaglia* finale is built up and sustained by Walter's underlying impetus. The result is thrillingly 'live' from the first bar to the last. A remarkable achievement, but this disc is very expensive.

Abbado rounds off his outstanding series with an incandescent performance of the *Fourth*, marked by strong, dramatic contrasts and finely moulded phrasing. The coupling is exceptionally generous, not just the *Haydn Variations* but the rare choral piece to words by Schiller, *Nänie*.

Carlos Kleiber's famous CD version is a performance of real stature and much strength, with the attention to detail one would expect from this great conductor. A gripping and compelling performance, at the opposite end of the scale from Walter's coaxingly lyrical approach. DG have successfully remastered the 1981 sound, which now has more than sufficient weight in the bass and more bloom than before. The violins under pressure still sound somewhat shrill at *fortissimo*, but this adds to the edge of the performance, and there is room for the strings to expand in the *Andante*. The finale has tremendous thrust. With its generous new couplings, this carries the strongest recommendation at mid-price.

Klemperer's granite strength and his feeling for Brahmsian lyricism make his EMI version one of the most satisfying ever recorded. The finale may lack something in sheer excitement, but the gravity of Klemperer's tone of voice, natural and unforced in this movement as in the others, makes for compelling results. Among the fill-ups the *Academic Festival Overture* is made to sound grand rather than high-spirited, but the Schumann couplings are muscularly massive and Germanic, rather than incandescent. Excellent transfers.

Jansons with the Oslo Philharmonic directs a performance which underlines the contrasts between the first two movements, predominantly lyrical and reflective, and the last two, with their sharper impact. As in the rest of Jansons's Brahms series, the playing is polished and refined, the more magnetic for being recorded live. The recording beautifully captures the delicacy of the *pianissimo* playing of the strings, while offering ample warmth and power in the last two movements. The Joachim overture, *Heinrich IV*, finer than the earlier *Hamlet Overture*, makes an apt if not very generous bonus, when it was so admired by Brahms.

Bernstein's 1981 Vienna version of Brahms's *Fourth*, recorded live, is exhilaratingly dramatic in fast music, while the slow movement brings richly resonant playing from the Vienna strings, not least in the great cello melody at bar 41, which with its moulded rubato comes to sound surprisingly like Elgar. This is easily the finest of Bernstein's Vienna cycle and, with generally good sound, is well worth considering.

Kempe's later account with the BBC Symphony Orchestra comes from 1974 and (according to the label information) the Festival Hall. Such is the warmth and openness of the acoustic that the Albert Hall would seem the more likely venue. It is a beautifully natural account, relaxed and yet held together well, and totally free from eccentricity. Kempe gets excellent playing from the BBC Symphony Orchestra, and the CD captures all the atmosphere of a live occasion.

Rudolf Kempe's earlier account of the *Fourth Symphony* with the RPO comes from 1960 and sounds remarkably well. It enjoyed considerable *renommé* during the 1960s and was preferred at the time by many collectors to the famous Klemperer version with the Philharmonia and the Karajan

Berlin account. Kempe's is a masterly reading, which well deserves its new lease of life and even forty years on, still ranks among the best, if not holding a place at the very top of the current list.

As in the *First Symphony*, Haitink's reading with the LSO of No. 4 is notable for its rugged symphonic strength, with unexaggerated speeds and a forthright directness of approach. In a live performance, recorded in June 2004 at the Barbican, these qualities build up impressively. Even though the Scherzo is powerful rather than jovial, the finale crowns the reading, with the contrasted sequence of *Passacaglia* variations held tautly together. Recording clear, if on the dry side. Unlike Haitink's LSO versions of the first three symphonies, this one has no coupling, making it less competitive, even in this price-range.

It goes without saying that the Chicago orchestra played with magnificent discipline and tonal refinement for Giulini in 1969, and they were well served by the HMV engineers. As a whole, however, the performance of the *Fourth Symphony* is not as commanding as one night have expected, though there are eloquent moments. The slow movement is most beautifully done, but elsewhere, both in the first movement and in the *Passacaglia*, Giulini does not resist the temptation to underline interpretative points. The challenge of variation form seems to suit him better than the symphony. One of his great qualities is to come fresh to well-worn classics, and this performance with the Philharmonia of the *Haydn Variations* and that of the *Tragic Overture* are a complete success. The CD transfers are excellent. The reissue in EMI's 'Great Recordings of the Century' series includes a second disc with a 77-minute profile of the conductor, his life and career, supervised by Steven Robinson for WFMT Radio Network.

Though the Copenhagen audience in January 1954 is disagreeably bronchial, and the ensemble is rough by the standards that Klemperer came to achieve with the Philharmonia for EMI, the electricity of his Testament reading of Brahms's *Fourth* is most compelling, warmer and more spontaneously expressive than one might expect from this rugged conductor. Though in the *Passacaglia* of the finale the solo playing is not always refined, the power of the piece is inescapable, making one understand the glowing memories of players in the orchestra as quoted in the Testament note.

(i) *Symphony 4;* (ii) *German Requiem, Op. 45;* (iii) *Schicksalslied, Op. 54*
(B) **(*) EMI double forte (ADD/DDD) 5 69518-2 (2). (i) LPO, Jochum; (ii) Norman, Hynninen; (ii–iii) BBC Symphony Ch., LPO Ch., Tennstedt

In the *Fourth Symphony*, Jochum's very opening phrase establishes the reading as warmly affectionate, and he combines a high degree of expressive flexibility with a rapt concentration which holds the symphonic structure strongly together. It demonstrates Jochum's passionate feeling for Brahms, with its spirit of soaring lyricism and – in the finale especially – a strong, even irresistible forward momentum. Although the performance has its idiosyncrasies of tempo, it is highly compelling in every bar, and it is a great pity that the appeal of this inexpensive reissue is somewhat diluted by the performance of the coupling, which may not be to all tastes.

In the *Requiem* Tennstedt brings speeds slower than on any rival version. His dedication generally sustains them well. What does sound monumental rather than moving is Jessye Norman's solo, *Ihr habt nun Traurigkeit*, though the golden tone is glorious. The *Schicksalslied* is also given a spacious,

strong performance, with the London Philharmonic Choir singing dedicatedly, and the 1984–5 digital recording spacious to match.

(i) *Variations on a Theme of Haydn;* (ii) *Variations & Fugue on a Theme by Handel, Op. 24* (arr. Rubbra)
*** Australian Decca Eloquence (ADD/DDD) 467 608-2. (i) VPO, Kertész; (ii) Cleveland O, Ashkenazy – DVORAK: *Symphonic Variations* ***

Rubbra's orchestration of the *Handel Variations* is hugely enjoyable, with a vivid orchestral palette which becomes ever more imaginative as it goes along. Beginning in a very neo-Baroque manner, with Clarke's *Trumpet Voluntary* springing to mind, all 25 variations are a delight. Ashkenazy's performance is superb and the digital recording excellent. The more familiar *Haydn Variations* is warmly recorded and receives a strongly affecting performance under István Kertész, perhaps more so with the knowledge that the conductor drowned just before the final sessions ended. The orchestra completed the recording without him, and it was released as a tribute to this much-admired musician.

CHAMBER MUSIC

Cello Sonata 1 in E min., Op. 38
(***) Testament mono SBT 2158. Piatigorsky, Rubinstein – BEETHOVEN: *Cello Sonatas;* WEBER: *Sonata in A* (***)

Piatigorsky's patrician account of the *E minor Sonata* with Artur Rubinstein was recorded in Paris in the summer of 1936. It has been out of the catalogue for nearly half a century, and Testament has put matters right with this exemplary transfer.

Cello Sonatas 1 in E min., Op. 38; 2 in F, Op. 99
⊶ *** DG 410 510-2. Rostropovich, Serkin
(N) (B) *** Double Decca 475 6210 (2). Harrell, Ashkenazy – MENDELSSOHN: *Cello Sonatas, etc.* ***
*** Channel CCS 5483. Wispelwey, Komen
*** Hyp. CDA 66159. Isserlis, Evans
(M) (**(*)) EMI mono 5 57293-2. Du Pré, Barenboim – BRUCH: *Kol Nidrei* **(*)
(N) (B) *(*) EMI Gemini (ADD) 5 82633 (2). Du Pré, Barenboim – CHOPIN; FRANCK: *Sonatas* **
(N) (M) ** EMI Legend CD/**DVD** (ADD) 557 750. Du Pré, Barenboim (bonus DVD: excerpts from BEETHOVEN: *Cello Sonata 3, Op. 69; Piano Trio (Ghost);* ELGAR: *Cello Concerto*) – BRUCH: *Kol nidrei* *(**)
(M) **(*) RCA 82876 59415-2. Ma, Ax

Cello Sonatas 1-2; Songs without Words: Feldeinsamkeit; Die Mainacht; Minnelied; Mondenschein; Nachtwandler; Sommerabend; Der Tod, das ist die kühle Nacht
**(*) DG (IMS) 459 677-2. Maisky, Gililov

The partnership of the wild, inspirational Russian cellist and the veteran Brahmsian, Serkin, on DG is a challenging one. It proves an outstanding success, with inspiration mutually enhanced, whether in the lyricism of Op. 38 or the heroic energy of Op. 99. Good if close recording.

Harrell and Ashkenazy also give almost ideal performances of the two Brahms *Cello Sonatas*, strong and passionate as well as poetic. They are naturally recorded and balanced, but in their LP incarnation we complained that in the resonant acoustic the imagery lacked sharpness of focus. On CD, this fault is greatly lessened – indeed, the cello sounds vividly clear – and this Double Decca is warmly recommended.

The Dutch partnership, Pieter Wispelwey and Paul Komen, offers something rather different. The cellist plays a nineteenth-century Bohemian cello and the pianist a Viennese period-instrument: thus theirs is the only version of the sonatas to approximate to the sound Brahms himself might have heard. There is nothing anaemic or academic about their playing, and no sense of scholarly inhibition. These are full-blooded performances, vivid in feeling and passionate, at no time wanting in eloquence.

Using gut strings, Isserlis produces an exceptionally warm tone, here nicely balanced in the recording against the strong and sensitive playing of his regular piano partner. In every way these perceptive and well-detailed readings stand in competition with the finest.

What is fascinating is to find how different the unpublished version by Du Pré and Barenboim of the *Second Sonata* is from the studio recording which they made in that same period, soon after they had married in 1967. The first movement, at 6'41", is over two minutes shorter than in the studio recording, increasing the passionate urgency of the reading, although the repose in the central development section then becomes if anything more intense. Du Pré's characteristic wildness means that intonation occasionally strays, and detail is less cleanly delivered than in the studio performance. No other movement in either sonata offers quite such a marked contrast, though in each the extra bite of spontaneity adds to the magnetism. Though the mono sound – presumably from the film sound-track – is cramped, with the piano rather shallow and clattery, no devotee of this inspired partnership is likely to be disappointed.

On RCA, Ma produces tone of great beauty and refinement, and Ax plays with great sensitivity, though there are times when he is in danger of overpowering his partner. As in the later, Sony performances, by Ma and Ax (SK 48191) the balance favours the piano, for Ax sometimes produces too thick a sound in climaxes and Ma is, as always, sensitive and smaller in tone. Theirs is an essentially romantic view, and some might find the *E minor Sonata* rather too wayward. They are certainly more measured in their tempi than almost any of their rivals. The claims of these readings reside in their refined lyricism rather than their muscularity, and these artists have splendid rapport. The RCA recording is very truthful. The coupled transcription of the *G major Violin Sonata*, whether or not made by the composer, as is claimed here, is more controversial. Starker plays it boldly, but the cello line generally lies low, and is less well projected than the piano part. However, the couplings are worthwhile and generous (although the Rachmaninov *Sonata* also has balance problems), and this reissue is certainly worth its asking-price.

The stereo recordings of the two Brahms *Cello Sonatas* that Du Pré and Barenboim made in 1968 are flawed by Jacqueline du Pré's undeniable stylistic self-indulgence; even if these players tackle the second and more taxing of the sonatas with the sense of heroic size that the music demands, the result is not entirely convincing. This is on the whole the more successful of the two performances. The Abbey Road recording is well balanced and realistic, but this is not recommended for those who find themselves resisting the Du Pré–Barenboim brand of romantic expressiveness, and the coupling now comes in the Legend series with a DVD of Beethoven and Elgar excerpts, interspersed with an interview with Du Pré, which makes a fascinating (if piecemeal) bonus.

These 1968 Du Pré/Barenboim performances are also available on an inexpensive Gemini two-CD set, coupled with Chopin and Franck.

(i) *Cello Sonatas 1–2;* (ii) *Violin Sonatas 1–3; F.A.E. Sonata: Scherzo*
(B) **(*) Virgin 2×1 5 61415-2 (2). (i) Rose; (ii) Laredo; (i–ii) Pommier

Rose achieves a fine partnership with Pommier, with whom he is ideally balanced, and though the recording is a trifle too close it is very truthful. Not surprisingly, these are strong, searching performances, especially the passionate *F major Sonata*. The *Violin Sonatas* used the same venue the previous year, but here Laredo is not flattered by the close microphones, and this makes his ardent Brahmsian response seem a bit fierce at times. Once that is said, these too are impressively committed performances.

Cello Sonata 2 in F, Op. 99
(M) (***) EMI mono 5 67008-2. Casals, Horszowski – BACH: (Unaccompanied) *Cello Suite 1 in G;* BEETHOVEN: *Cello Sonata 3* (***)

(i) *Cello Sonata 2;* (ii) *Clarinet Quintet in B min., Op. 115;* (iii) *Horn Trio in E flat, Op. 40;* (iv) *Piano Trio 1 in B, Op. 8;* (v) *Violin Sonata 3 in D min., Op. 108*
(B) *** Double Decca (ADD) 452 341-2 (2). (i; iv) Starker; (i; iv–v) Katchen; (ii) Brymer, Allegri Qt; (iii) Tuckwell, Perlman, Ashkenazy; (iv–v) Suk

The recordings of the *Piano Trio* and the *Cello Sonata* represent the results of Julius Katchen's last recording sessions before his untimely death. They were held at The Maltings, and the results have much warmth. The *Cello Sonata* is given a strong and characterful performance, while Jack Brymer gives a masterly and finely poised account of the *Clarinet Quintet* which in terms of polish and finesse can hold its own with the very best. The highlight of this set is the superbly passionate performance of Brahms's marvellous *Horn Trio* from Tuckwell, Perlman and Ashkenazy. By contrast, Josef Suk's personal blend of romanticism and the classical tradition in the *Violin Sonata* is warmly attractive but small in scale.

The celebrated (1936) Paris recording of the Brahms *F major Sonata*, Op. 99, with Casals and Horszowski has had numerous incarnations, most recently on EMI Références, but its splendours do not fade. It remains one of the most moving accounts of this leonine score on disc.

Clarinet Quintet in B min., Op. 115
*** DG 459 641-2. Shifrin, Emerson Qt – MOZART: *Clarinet Quintet* ***
(BB) *** Warner Apex 0927 44350-2. Leister, Berlin Soloists – MOZART: *Clarinet Quintet* ***
(N) (**(*)) Testament mono SBT 1282. Alfred Boskovsky, Vienna Octet (members) – MOZART: *Clarinet Quintet* **(*)

(i) *Clarinet Quintet;* (ii) *Clarinet Sonata 2*
(M) *** Chan. 6522. Hilton, (i) Lindsay Qt; (ii) Frankl

(i) *Clarinet Quintet in B min.;* (ii) *Clarinet Sonata 2 in E flat, Op. 120/2*
(N) (***) Testament mono SBT 1366. Thurston, (i) Griller Qt; (ii) Myers Foggin – BLISS: *Clarinet Quintet* (***)

(i) *Clarinet Quintet*; (ii) *Clarinet Trio in A min.*

⊖→ *** Hyp. CDA 66107. King, (i) Gabrieli Qt; (ii) Georgian, Benson (piano)

(BB) **(*) Naxos 8.550391. Balogh, (i) Danubius Qt; (ii) Jandó, Onczay

*** MDG 307 079-2. (i) Leister; Leipzig Qt

(i) *Clarinet Quintet*; (ii) *String Quintet 2 in G, Op. 111*

(B) *** HM HMA 1951349. (i) Portal; (ii) Caussé; Melos Qt

David Shifrin's newest recording of the Brahms *Quintet* is outstandingly fine. He establishes a natural partnership with the Emersons; the outer movements, while warmly lyrical, are much more characterful and positive than in his earlier version. Yet the *Adagio* achieves a gentle, ruminative, almost improvisational quality. The recording is admirably balanced and the equally recommendable Mozart coupling has an appealing simplicity.

Thea King and the Gabrieli Quartet give a radiantly beautiful performance of the *Clarinet Quintet*, as fine as any put on record, expressive and spontaneous-sounding, with natural ebb and flow of tension as in a live performance. The recording of the strings is on the bright side, very vivid and real.

On Apex, Karl Leister's easy-going lyricism does not mean that there is not a firm overall grip on the proceedings, yet in the Elysian slow movement he seems to be tenderly and thoughtfully improvising, and his relaxed warmth is captivating. The mellow *grazioso* of the Minuet is then followed by a *con moto* finale which retains the overall mood yet lightens and becomes more passionate as the variations develop. His supporting Berlin Soloists match his playing serenely and they are well balanced and beautifully recorded. A lovely performance, well matched by the Mozart coupling – and this CD is very inexpensive.

His later performance with the Leipzig Quartet is second to none. The quartet and its distinguished soloist produce impressive results in what is surely Brahms's most serene utterance, and the *A minor Quartet* also receives an authoritative and musical performance. For those wanting this particular coupling, this disc can certainly be recommended.

Janet Hilton's essentially mellow performance of the *Clarinet Quintet*, with the Lindsay Quartet playing with pleasing warmth and refinement, has a distinct individuality. Her lilting syncopations in the third movement are delightful. Hilton's partnership with Peter Frankl in the *E flat Clarinet Sonata* is rather less idiosyncratic and individual; nevertheless, this performance offers considerable artistic rewards.

The warm resonance of the recording gives an almost orchestral richness of timbre to the Melos group, joined by Gérard Caussé, yet they open the *Adagio* of Op. 111 (which comes first on the disc) with an exquisite delicacy of texture and feeling. The sound in the *Clarinet Quintet* is equally beguiling and Michel Portal matches the strings with his gently luscious tone in the *Clarinet Quintet*, with the beautiful slow movement dreamily ruminative and the theme-and-variations finale hardly less delightful. This coupling is highly recommendable in all respects.

József Balogh is a highly sensitive player with a lovely tone. He is well supported by the Danubius Quartet, and their account of the *Clarinet Quintet* is a rewarding one, with warmth and atmosphere, rising to considerable heights of intensity in the *Adagio*. The *Clarinet Trio* is an enjoyably fresh account, though not quite so memorable, except in the *Andantino grazioso*, which is delightfully done; with excellent

recording, this is still a worthwhile disc, and inexpensive to boot.

Alfred Boskovsky's early Decca performance of the *Clarinet Quintet*, famous in its day, is very beautiful indeed, relaxed in an old-fashioned way and with a lovely Viennese warmth. The 1953 mono sound is vivid and truthful, if a bit close.

Frederick Thurston and the Grillers recorded the Brahms in the wartime Decca studios in 1941, but Thurston never passed it for release. Sidney Griller treasured his set of the four 78s and always hoped that they would reach the public domain. His copies were used in this important transfer. One point of interest concerns the very opening, which is a shade quicker than we are used to (Mühlfeld, its dedicatee, was responsible for passing down the slower tempo – which had Brahms's blessing – to Charles Draper and Reginald Kell). Though they were admirers of Draper, Thurston and the Grillers never followed the tradition. Theirs is an immaculate performance (there were no re-takes at all) and its appearance greatly enriches the catalogue. Very informative notes by Tully Potter.

(i) *Clarinet Quintet*; (ii) *Clarinet Sonatas 1–2*; (iii) *String Quintet 2*

(B) **(*) Delos Double DE 3706. (i-ii) Shifrin; (i; iii) Chamber Music Northwest; (ii) Rosenberger (with SCHUMANN: *Fantasiestücke, Op. 73* **(*))

David Shifrin's earlier (1988) account of the *Clarinet Quintet* has a glowing delicacy of feeling and is played with lovely tone and much warmth from the supporting Northwest string group. However, the mellow atmosphere persists throughout and, although the performance is very easy to enjoy, there is too little difference of character between the four movements. One would have liked more bite and character from the strings, especially in the finale. This applies equally to the *G major Quintet*, where it is the lyrical warmth of the *Adagio* that remains in the memory. The two *Clarinet Sonatas* are songful and have great warmth, and again Shifrin's richly lyrical phrasing gives much pleasure. He has fine support from Carol Rosenberger. These performances, less volatile than those of Ralph Manno and Alfredo Perl on Arte Nova (see below), are very satisfying in a quite different way, for Shifrin's tone is consistently beautiful. So are the three Schumann *Fantasy Pieces*, especially the wistful opening number, which might well be another movement by Brahms.

(i; ii) *Clarinet Quintet*; (ii–iv) *Clarinet Trio*; (i; iv) *Piano Quintet, Op. 34*; (i) *String Quartets 1–3*; (i; v) *String Quintets, 1–2*; (i; v; vi) *String Sextets 1–2*

(BB) ** DG (ADD) 474 358-2 (5). (i) Amadeus Qt; (ii) Leister; (iii) Donderer; (iv) Eschenbach; (v) Aronowitz; (vi) Pleeth

Among the best things in this Amadeus Brahms collection are the *String Quartets*, where the group's rich tone, effortless technique and subtle internal rhythms combine to make these performances of stature. They are warm and unaffected readings, but the snag is that the late-1950s sound has come up rather stridently in this transfer, especially above the stave. Eschenbach gives a powerful – sometimes over-projected – account of his part in the *Piano Quintet*, yet this is undoubtedly a moving performance with plenty of vitality, and the Amadeus players remain well in the picture. With the *Quintets* and *Sextets* the playing is as polished as one would expect, and the 1960s sound remains warm and full; but there are times when a certain mannered blandness creeps in, which detracts from the music's freshness. It may strike some ears that these performances are too suave and lacking in depth, though, of course, the players display fine tonal blending and excellent ensemble. Leister is a good soloist in the clarinet works (he was the principal clarinet of the Berlin Philharmonic), though his readings could be a little more imaginative at times. The Amadeus give lush support, some might say a bit overheated in their contribution to the Quintet, and this version will not convince all listeners. The performance of the Clarinet Trio is more consistently successful. But overall, the attractions of this bargain box are limited by one's awareness that there have been so many even finer versions of all these works released over the past three decades.

(i) Clarinet Quintet; (ii) Piano Quintet. String Quintets 1–2

☛ (B) *** Ph. (ADD) Duo 446 172-2 (2). (i) Stähr; (ii) Haas; BPO Octet (members)

The Berlin performance of the Clarinet Quintet is both beautiful and faithful to Brahms's instructions. The delicacy with which the 'Hungarian' middle section of the great Adagio is interpreted gives some idea of the insight of these players. It is an autumnal reading, never forced, and is recorded with comparable refinement. The two String Quintets are also admirably served by these same players (with Dietrich Gerhard, viola, replacing the clarinettist, Herbert Stähr). The performances combine freshness and polish, warmth with well-integrated detail. For the Piano Quintet Werner Haas joins the group and they give a strongly motivated, spontaneous account of this splendid work that is in every way satisfying. The piano is balanced most convincingly. The recordings come from the early 1970s and the sound is remarkably full and warm, the richness of texture suiting the String Quintets especially well. This is among the finest bargains in the Philips Duo list.

Clarinet Sonatas 1 in F min.; 2 in E flat, Op. 120/1–2

☛ *** Chan. 8563. De Peyer, Prior

(BB) *** Naxos 8.553121. Berkes, Jandó

(M) *** Oehms OCD 232. Manno, Perl

Superb performances from Gervase de Peyer and Gwenneth Prior, commanding, aristocratic, warm and full of subtleties of colour and detail. The recording too is outstandingly realistic.

No one buying the Naxos CD coupling the two late Clarinet Sonatas is likely to have any regrets. They are beautifully played and freshly recorded by this distinguished Hungarian duo, and they would be recommendable even in a higher price-bracket.

Ralph Manno has a succulent tone, highly suitable for Brahms. He establishes a strong partnership with Alfredo Perl, and these volatile performances are full of imaginative light and shade. In the F minor, the slow movement is freely ruminative, the E flat major opens most persuasively and is equally strong on contrast. There is some most winning playing in the Andante and the brief finale is full of energy. The well-balanced recording is most realistic and vivid.

Clarinet Sonatas 1–2; (i) Clarinet Trio

*** Nim. NI 5600. Leister, Bognár; (i) with Boettcher

The Nimbus recording gives the artists rather less space round the aural image than we would like. All the same, Karl Leister and his two distinguished colleagues play with expressive eloquence and artistry. These performances have warmth and spontaneity.

(i) Clarinet Sonatas 1–2; (ii) String Quartets 1–3

(B) *** Ph. (ADD) Duo 456 320-2 (2). (i) Pieterson, H. Menuhin; (ii) Italian Qt

The Clarinet Sonatas are very well played by George Pieterson and Hephzibah Menuhin. The autumnal twilight of the lovely Andante un poco adagio of the F minor is appealingly caught, and the following Allegretto grazioso flows engagingly. The E flat Sonata is more direct, less coaxing but strongly characterized, with plenty of light and shade. Vivid recording from 1980 adds to the feeling of boldness. The three String Quartets are marvellously played by the Quartetto Italiano. As always with the Philips remastering of analogue recordings (here from 1967, 1970 and 1971 respectively), the CD transfers are admirably truthful in timbre and balance.

Clarinet Trio in A min., Op. 114

*** RCA 09026 63504-2. Collins, Isserlis, Hough – FRUHLING: Clarinet Trio; SCHUMANN: Märchenerzählungen, etc. ***

It would be hard to imagine a finer performance of the Brahms Clarinet Trio than on the RCA disc. All three of these fine young musicians are natural recording artists, never failing to sound spontaneously expressive, always conveying the feeling of live music-making, so that their interchanges are magnetic. It makes an imaginative coupling having the Brahms masterpiece alongside the long-buried but delightful Frühling Trio and the arrangements of Schumann items from the same forces.

(i) Clarinet Trio, Op. 114; (ii) Horn Trio, Op. 40

(N) (BB) *** Warner Apex 2564 61792-2. (i) Portal; Lodeon; (i; ii) Dalberto; (ii) Del Vescovo, Amoyal

A persuasively warm performance of the Clarinet Trio from Michel Portal, whose tone is rich and succulent, Frédéric Lodeon and Michel Dalberto, recorded in a suitably resonant, Brahmsian acoustic. It is joined to an equally fine – if not even finer – account of the Horn Trio from the full-timbred Pierre Del Vescovo, a first-class horn player, and the ever sensitive Pierre Amoyal. Here the pianist makes an even stronger contribution: the Adagio mesto is very beautifully and delicately done, and both the Scherzo and the irrepressible Rondo finale are infectiously spirited. The recording, again in a warm acoustic, is even more vivid and clear. A first-class bargain, if you want both works.

(i) Clarinet Trio; (ii) Horn Trio. Piano Trios 1–3

☛ *** Hyp. CDA 67251/2. Florestan Trio, with (i) Hosford; (ii) Stirling

(i) Clarinet Trio; (ii) Horn Trio; (iii) Piano Trios 1–4

(B) *** Ph. (ADD) Duo 438 365-2 (2). (i) Pieterson; (ii) Orval, Grumiaux, Sebök; (i; iii) Beaux Arts Trio

The Florestan set is among the finest since the Beaux Arts' comparable grouping, in terms of both performance and recording. There is a freshness and spontaneity that rekindles one's own enthusiasm for this music, and such is its dedication that one is left marvelling at the richness and quality of Brahms's inventive resource. The same must be said of the Horn Trio and the late A minor Clarinet Trio. The recorded sound is very natural and lifelike and brings the players into your living room.

George Pieterson is a first-rate artist and his account of the Clarinet Trio with members of the Beaux Arts group offers masterly playing from all three participants. The balance in the *Horn Trio* is perhaps the most successful on record. The fine horn player, Francis Orval, achieves this without any loss of personality in his playing. As for the *Piano Trios*, the performances are splendid, with strongly paced, dramatic allegros, consistently alert and thoughtful, and with sensitive playing in slow movements. The sound is first class and the resonance of Bernard Greenhouse's cello is warmly caught without any clouding of focus. The CD transfer has brightened the top a little, but not excessively.

Horn Trio in E flat, Op. 40 (see also above)

👤 (B) *** EMI Debut 5 72822-2. Clark, Martin, Govier –
BEETHOVEN: *Horn Sonata*, etc; MOZART: *Horn Quintet*,
etc. ***

(N) (BB) *** Naxos 8.557471. W. Tomboeck, Inui, J.
Tomboeck – BEETHOVEN: *Horn Sonata*; SCHUBERT: *Auf dem Strom*; SCHUMANN: *Adagio and Allegro in A flat* ***
*** Chan. 9964. Danish Horn Trio – LIGETI: *Horn Trio* ***

Andrew Clark's performance using a period Waldhorn is most stimulating. There is a flamboyance in the playing which makes such a movement as the finale of the Brahms *Trio* thrilling, and Clark's virtuosity is well matched by his partners, also using period instruments. On one of EMI's cheapest labels it makes a splendid bargain. Warm, full sound.

Wolfgang Tomboeck, first horn in the Vienna Philharmonic since 1980 and the son of a former principal horn, comes from a family of musicians, and here in all four works he demonstrates what a fine artist he is, producing the ripest tones on the Vienna horn. The galloping rhythms of the second and fourth movements of the Brahms have an infectious brilliance and swagger. With Tomboeck's son, Johannes, playing the violin, they have a lift and energy to make some rival versions seem cool, while the *Andante* first movement is warm and relaxed, freely expressive in a very Viennese way. It would be hard to imagine a more persuasive demonstration of the instrument than this.

The Danish Horn Trio are a warmly persuasive Brahmsian team led by Jakob Keiding, a very fine horn player. The opening seems just a little deliberate, but the *allegro* surges away spontaneously, and throughout, the music's romantic ripeness is fully captured, with the Scherzo both lively and bold, its Trio richly lyrical. But the kernel of the reading is the deeply expressive *Adagio mesto*. The atmosphere here is far more than *mesto* ('sorrowful'), combining the elements of a berceuse and a lament. Then the sunshine blazes forth in the ebullient finale, the horn gallumphing off with glorious vigour, and at the close Keiding caps the whole performance with that exuberant top E flat. The recording is immensely vivid if a bit over-resonant but not every collector will want the Ligeti coupling, enterprising though it is.

(i) Horn Trio in E flat; (ii) Piano Quintet in F min., Op. 34

(M) *** CRD 3489. Nash Ens. (members); (i) Lloyd; (ii) Brown

The CRD reissue of the *F minor Piano Quintet* and the *Horn Trio*, played by the Nash Ensemble is very competitive. The playing is refreshingly unforced, with the *Quintet* underpinned firmly by the incisive playing of the pianist, Ian Brown. In the *Horn Trio* Frank Lloyd produces an exceptionally rich tone and helps the group to give a raptly beautiful account of the *Adagio*; the galloping finale is then performed with joyful panache. Tempos are well chosen and there is great naturalness of phrasing. These players convey the sense

of music-making in the home rather than the concert hall, and they have lively, faithfully recorded sound in their favour.

Hungarian Dances 1–2, 4 & 7

*** EMI 7 54753-2. Chang, Feldman – TCHAIKOVSKY: *Violin Concerto* ***

It may be an ungenerous coupling for the Tchaikovsky *Concerto*, but Chang's performances of four of the Brahms *Hungarian Dances* – recorded with Jonathan Feldman in New York – are delectable.

(i) Piano Quartets 1–3; Piano Trio in A, Op. posth

(B) *** Ph. (ADD) Duo 454 017-2 (2). Beaux Arts Trio, (i) with Trampler

The Beaux Arts set of *Piano Quartets* is self-recommending at Duo price, with the *A major Piano Trio* thrown in as a bonus. Thoughtful, sensitive playing in slow movements, lively tempi in allegros, characteristic musicianship plus spontaneity combine to make these recordings highly recommendable throughout, alongside the Stern Sony set, which is in a higher price-bracket.

(i) Piano Quartets 1–3; Piano Quintet; String Quartet 2

(***) Testament mono SBT 3063 (3). (i) Aller; Hollywood Qt – SCHUMANN: *Piano Quintet* (***)

The Hollywood Quartet's versions of the Brahms *Piano Quartets* have hardly been surpassed, and the *A minor Quartet* has tremendous grip and an ardent lyricism. They seem to be more or less ideal performances. Due to the microphone placement there is a strident quality in the upper register in the *A minor Quartet*, but it can easily be tamed. There was nothing in the least strident about their tone in the flesh. Performances of this integrity do not come often.

(i) Piano Quartet 1. 4 Ballades, Op. 10

(M) **(*) DG (ADD) 447 407-2. Gilels, (i) with Amadeus Qt

Gilels is in impressive form, and most listeners will respond to the withdrawn delicacy of the Scherzo and the gypsy fire of the finale. The slow movement is perhaps somewhat wanting in ardour, and the Amadeus do not sound as committed or as fresh as their keyboard partner. The DG recording is well balanced and sounds very natural in its new transfer. Moreover, in the *Ballades* Gilels offers artistry of an order that silences criticism.

Piano Quartet 1 in G min. (orch. Schoenberg); Variations & Fugue on a Theme by Handel, Op. 24 (orch. Rubbra)

*** Chan. 8825. LSO, Järvi

The current craze for Schoenberg's transcription of the Brahms *Piano Quartet in G minor* is puzzling. However, Neeme Järvi's new version with the LSO is as good as any. It is performed with some enthusiasm and is well recorded.

Piano Quintet in F min., Op. 34

👤 *** BBC (ADD) BBCL 4009-2 (2). Curzon, Amadeus Qt – SCHUBERT: *Trout Quintet* ***

(N) (M) *** MDG 307 1218-2. Staier (early piano), Leipzig Qt

(N) **(*) Mer. CDE 84459. Denk, Concertante (members) – DVORAK: *Piano Quintet* ***

(M) **(*) DG (ADD) 474 839-2. Pollini, Italian Qt

(BB) *** Naxos 8.550406. Jandó, Kodály Qt – SCHUMANN: *Piano Quintet* ***

Clifford Curzon is captured at his most spontaneously expressive in his live performance with the Amadeus Quartet, recorded at the Royal Festival Hall in 1974. Similarly the Amadeus Quartet are at their most compelling. Ensemble may not be quite as polished as in a studio performance, but the warmth and power are ample compensation, and the bonus disc of Schubert's *Trout Quintet* makes a very attractive package.

The MDG disc offers a performance short on playing time but long on excellence. The Leipzig Quartet has an almost unrivalled reputation in the Viennese classical repertoire, and Andreas Staier is unfailingly illuminating and sensitive. He plays a 1901 Steinway which is much lighter in colour and body than the modern concert grand. All too often this work seems to inhabit a war zone, with the quartet struggling to make themselves heard above the combative pianist. This version demands to be heard and, though there is no fill-up, it is competitively positioned at mid-price and deserves a strong recommendation. Natural recorded sound.

The Meridian disc provides a surprisingly rare coupling of *Piano Quintets* by Brahms and Dvořák by Concertante, a group of musicians from the Juilliard School. The excellent pianist Jeremy Denk and the violinist Xiaio-Dong Wang are common to both; the other artists change for each of the two performances, which are in consequence somewhat different in character. The Brahms is a strong reading, yet intimate too, with fine detail and a genuinely spontaneous feeling, the recording well balanced, although not in the very top bracket. But if you want the coupling, this is certainly enjoyable, if not a first choice, and the Dvořák *Quintet* is even finer.

There is some electrifying and commanding playing from Maurizio Pollini, and the Italian Quartet is in eloquent form. The balance, however, is in the pianist's favour, though the effect in this new 'Originals' transfer seems a touch improved over the original (1980) LP release. There are some minor agogic exaggerations but none that should put off admirers of the pianist. However, the playing time of under 44 minutes for this disc undoubtedly will, even if one is hardly short-changed on quality.

The fine Naxos account has a great deal going for it, even though it does not include the first-movement exposition repeat. The playing is boldly spontaneous and has plenty of fire and expressive feeling. The opening of the finale also has mystery; overall, with full-bodied recording and plenty of presence, this makes a strong impression. It is certainly a bargain.

Piano Trios 1 in B, Op. 8; 2 in C, Op. 87; 3 in C min., Op. 101; 4 in A, Op. posth.
(N) (BB) *** Warner Apex 2564 61259-2 *(1 & 2)*; 2564 61690-2 *(3 & 4)*. Trio Fontenay

Powerful, spontaneous playing with a real Brahmsian spirit, given excellent, modern recording, puts these admirable performances by the Trio Fontenay (originally on Ultima, but now at budget price) at the top of the list.

Piano Trios 1–2
(N) *** Quartz QTZ 2011. Gould Piano Trio
(M) *** Decca (ADD) (IMS) 421 152-2. Katchen, Suk, Starker
*** DG (IMS) 447 055-2. Pires, Dumay, Wang

(i) Piano Trios 1–3; (ii) Cello Sonata 2 in F; (iii) F.A.E. Sonata: Scherzo
(B) *** Double Decca (ADD) 448 092-2 (2). Katchen, with (i–ii) Starker; (i; iii) Suk

No, the Gould Trio does not feature the famous American pianist of that name, but introduces an excellent new ensemble, founded by the violinist, Lucy Gould, the current leader of the Academy of St Martin-in-the-Fields. She had shrewdly picked Benjamin Frith as her pianist, and it is he and the cellist, Alice Neary (winner of the Pierre Fournier award), who immediately win the listener over at the gloriously noble introduction of the *B major Trio* which is opened by Frith. He is equally impressive in the rapt account of the *Adagio*. But this is a performance as full of passion as it is of warmth and poetry, and he comes into his own with brilliant playing in the Scherzo as he does in the Scherzo and finale of the companion work, played with comparable commitment and a strongly spontaneous impetus. The recording is excellent, as well detailed as it is full-bodied.

The Katchen/Suk/Starker performances of the first two *Piano Trios* are warm, strong and characterful, while the tough *C minor Trio* and the epic, thrustful *Cello Sonata* bring a comparably spontaneous response. If the sound of the CD transfers is a little limited in the upper range, the ear is grateful that no artificial brightening has been applied, for it provides a real Brahmsian amplitude which is very satisfying. Highly recommended in either format.

Augustin Dumay and Maria João Pires are joined by the young Chinese cellist, Jian Wang. His contribution is certainly eloquent here and the performances overall have authority and finesse. Though the recording is not absolutely ideal in every respect, it does have a pleasing warmth and amplitude. The performance has personality and earns three stars.

String Quartets 1 in C min.; 2 in A min., Op. 51/1–2; 3 in B flat, Op. 67 (see also under Clarinet Sonatas)
➡ (B) *** Teldec (ADD) 4509 95503-2 (2). Alban Berg Qt (with DVORAK: *String Quartet 13 ***)
*** EMI 7 54829-2 (2). Alban Berg Qt
**(*) Claves 50-9404/5 (2). Quartet Sine Nomine

String Quartets 1–3; (i) Piano Quintet in F min., Op. 34
(M) *** Hyp. Dyad CDD 22018 (2). (i) Lane; New Budapest Qt

String Quartets 1–2
*** Chan. 8562. Gabrieli Qt
(BB) *** Naxos 8.554271. Ludwig Qt
**(*) Simax PSC1156. Vertavo Qt

String Quartets 1, Op. 51/1; 3, Op. 67
(BB) **(*) Warner Apex 0927 49985-2. Borodin Qt

String Quartets 2–3
(N) (M) (**) Decca mono Heritage 475 6155. Végh Qt

The analogue Teldec Alban Berg performances were made in the mid-1970s when the quartet was on peak form, highly polished yet completely fresh in their musical responses. This set is strongly recommended and can stand alongside the best in the catalogue, even if the Dvořák coupling is not quite as fine as the Brahms.

The New Budapest Quartet bring warmth and spontaneity to all three scores, responding to their dramatic fervour and lyrical flow in equal measure. Their intonation is altogether impeccable and they are scrupulously attentive to Brahms's dynamic markings, with pleasing results in terms of clarity and transparency. They also offer an excellently shaped and musicianly account of the *F minor Piano Quintet*, with responsive playing from Piers Lane, and they are among the best and most naturally recorded to have appeared in recent years.

On EMI, the performances have all the finesse and attack one expects from the Alban Berg Quartet, along with impeccable technical address. The *A minor* has just the right kind of dramatic intensity and the range of colour and dynamics they produce in all three works is impressive. The EMI engineers produced well-detailed, truthful sound. These are all performances of quality and can be recommended even to those who find this ensemble at times a little too glossy.

The Sine Nomine Quartet are splendidly recorded in a helpful acoustic and the effect here is just like a series of live performances. The playing, though well integrated, responsive and with plenty of Brahmsian spirit, has not the degree of sophistication and finesse the Alban Berg Quartet displays, but it does have consistent vitality and spontaneity; the *Third, B flat major Quartet* is particularly alive: it leaps out of the speakers towards the listener, and again the closing variations are a highlight of the performance.

Richly recorded in an agreeably expansive ambience, the Gabrielis give warm, eloquent performances of both the Op. 51 *Quartets*, deeply felt and full-textured without being heavy; the *Romanze* of Op. 51, No. 1, is delightfully songful. There are both tenderness and subtlety here, and the sound is first class.

The Naxos issue is an eminently satisfactory bargain. Indeed, it provides more musical pleasure than one might find from more celebrated ensembles, and the recording has good presence and is well balanced.

On Apex there is marvellously sophisticated playing from the Borodins, with wonderful tonal blending, absolute security of intonation and immaculate ensemble. The first movement of No. 1 sets off with considerable impetus, but the thoughtfulness of the performance establishes itself within a few bars, and the inner movements of this quartet have much grace and delicacy of feeling. In No. 3 the subtle treatment of the variations that make up the last movement is a high point of the record. The digital recording is firm and truthful, if a shade close and bright, but the main reservation here is that these performances, although they offer much to admire and enjoy, lack the kind of spontaneity that really grips the listener; moreover many listeners might prefer their Brahms to sound more robust.

The Vertavo are a young Norwegian quartet. There is evident feeling in these well-prepared performances, though a trace of self-consciousness can be discerned in the wide dynamic range they cultivate. When they play softly, they certainly let you know it. All the same, these are thoroughly recommendable accounts even if they do not displace first recommendations.

Expressive and characterful accounts of Brahms's *String Quartets* 2 and 3 from the Végh Quartet, dating from 1955. The reflective passages have affection and there is no lack of momentum (first-movement repeats are omitted). The sound is bright and forward, but the upper violin register is not especially ingratiating, becoming a little wearing after a while.

String Quartet 1, Op. 51/1 ; (i) String Sextet 2 in G, Op. 36

(N) *** MDG 307 1261-2. Leipzig Qt, (i) with Rohde, Peter Bruns

This Leipzig Quartet survey of Brahms goes from strength to strength. The playing is wonderfully civilized and musicianly, and completely free of superficial gloss. The sound that MDG give them is as faithful a recording as we have come to expect from this source.

String Quintets 1 in F, Op. 88; 2 in G, Op. 111

☛ *** Hyp. CDA 66804. Raphael Ens.

(N) *** MDG 307 1251-2. Leipzig Qt, Rohde

*** DG (IMS) 453 420-2. Hagen Qt, Caussé

With the *First Quintet* opening seductively, these are fine, vital performances of both works from the Raphael Ensemble. Indeed, these performances are on the same level of distinction as their accounts of the *String Sextets* and, like that companion Hyperion disc, the recording is very present indeed, which to some ears may seem a minor drawback.

The Leipzig Quartet and the violist Hartmut Rohde give warm and musicianly accounts of these masterpieces. This is music-making in the old style, selfless and totally dedicated. Our first choice in these *Quintets* has been members of the Rafael Ensemble on Hyperion, but this splendidly recorded version makes an excellent alternative.

The Hagen Quartet and Gérard Caussé also give highly enjoyable accounts of the two *Quintets*, and the DG engineers give them good recorded sound. No need to say more than that it can also rank alongside the Raphael Ensemble on Hyperion.

String Quintet 2 in G, Op. 111

*** Naim CD 010. Augmented Allegri Qt – BRUCH: *String Quintet* ***

*** Nim. NI 5488. Brandis Qt, with Dean – BRUCKNER: *String Quintet* ***

The second of the two string quintets makes the ideal coupling for the long-buried Bruch *Quintet*, which was also the product of old age. Very well played and recorded by the Allegri.

The Brandis version of the *G major Quintet* offers good value in being coupled with Bruckner's *F major Quintet*. The Brandis are a fine quartet and they give a warm and sympathetic account of this lovely work; the Nimbus recording is natural and lifelike.

String Sextet 1 in B flat, Op. 18

(***) Biddulph mono LAB 093. Pro Arte Qt, with Hobday, Pini – SCHUBERT: *String Quintet in C* (***)

String Sextets 1 in B flat, Op. 18; 2 in G, Op. 36

☛ *** Hyp. CDA 66276. Raphael Ens.

*** Chan. 9151. ASMF Chamber Ens.

*** Signum SIGCD 013. Hausmusik, London

(M) *** EMI (ADD) 5 74957-2. Y. Menuhin, Masters, Aronowitz, Wallfisch, Gendron, Simpson

The *Sextets* are among Brahms's most immediately appealing chamber works. The Raphael Ensemble are fully responsive to all their subtleties as well as to their vitality and warmth. In short, these are superb performances; the recording is very vivid and immediate, although some ears might find it a shade too present.

The Chandos alternative is also highly recommendable, with both *Sextets* again accommodated on one CD without sacrificing the exposition repeats, so that at almost 78 minutes the Academy of St Martin-in-the-Fields offer excellent value for money. Moreover, these well-prepared and musical performances are perceptive and intelligent, and they receive finely detailed and present recording.

Hausmusik are dedicated to the performance of nineteenth-century music on the instruments of the time. The instrumental timbre is lighter and more transparent, but there is no lack of warmth. The sonority is less well upholstered and rich than in modern versions, but tempi are well chosen and the playing is unfailingly sensitive and musical. It is a more than welcome addition to the catalogue, but for most collectors it will be a supplement rather than an alternative to the existing recommendations.

Menuhin's group of star players integrate well together and transmit their enjoyment of these warmly lyrical works. The performances are relaxed and agreeably affectionate, with the *G major* work particularly beguiling. Perhaps both opening movements could have more grip but there is spontaneity here, and the mid-1960s recording has retained its original warmth and now has greater freshness and better definition, without edginess. The humanity of the playing comes over fully.

The impeccable technical address of the Pro Arte Quartet shows on the Pro Arte reissue here, and their warmth and finesse make their Brahms as satisfying as any account recorded since. Needless to say, some allowance has to be made for the 1935 recording, eminently well transferred though it is.

Viola Sonatas 1–2; F.A.E. Sonata: Scherzo
**(*) Chan. 8550. Imai, Vignoles – SCHUMANN: *Märchenbilder* **(*)

Viola Sonatas 1–2; (i) 2 Songs with Viola, Op. 91
*** RCA 09026 63293-2. Bashmet, Muntian

The *Viola Sonatas* are played superbly by Yuri Bashmet, whose sumptuous tone and refined musicianship, along with the expert support of Mikhail Muntian, are persuasive. Finely poised and well-proportioned accounts, among the finest around.

Nobuko Imai is an almost peerless violist and it is difficult to flaw her accounts of the two Op. 120 *Sonatas* with Roger Vignoles. The reverberant acoustic does not show the piano to good advantage but, apart from that, this is an impressive issue.

Viola Sonatas 1–2; Violin Sonatas 1–3; F.A.E. Sonata: Scherzo
(N) (M) *** Avie AV 2057 (2). Mintz, Golan
(B) *** DG Double (ADD) 453 121-2 (2). Zukerman, Barenboim

The Zukerman–Barenboim performances of the *Viola Sonatas* may be a little sweet for some tastes, but they are easy to enjoy, with the expressiveness never sounding contrived, always buoyant. In the *Violin Sonatas*, they produce songful, spontaneous-sounding performances that catch the inspiration of the moment. The sound itself is very natural, with good presence. The lively *Scherzo in C minor* from the *F.A.E. Sonata* is thrown in for good measure.

Following in the footsteps of Zukerman and Barenboim, Shlomo Mintz and Itamar Golan give highly spontaneous performances of all five sonatas, with Mintz obviously equally at home on violin and viola, but creating a different sound-world for each instrument. At times there is a richly ruminative quality in the *Violin Sonatas* which is very special, and slow movements are most beautifully played, by violinist and pianist alike. These performances have a natural Brahmsian warmth that is second to none. The *F.A.E. Scherzo* makes a vibrant postlude and, throughout, the recording is of the highest quality.

Violin Sonata 1 in G., Op. 78
(M) *** EMI Debut 5 74017-2. Batiashvili, Chernyavska – BACH: *Partita 1*; SCHUBERT: *Rondo in B min.* ***

The Georgian-born Elisabeth Batiashvili makes her EMI début with a mixed programme. The disc is a calling-card for the artist rather than the collector who will probably want all

three Brahms sonatas. Taken purely on its merits, however, this is a lovely performance, suitably relaxed and lyrical. Ms Batiashvili is sensitively partnered by Milana Chernyavska and the balance on the recording is expertly judged.

Violin Sonatas 1–2
(B) **(*) EMI (ADD) double forte 5 69367-2 (2). I. Oistrakh, Ginzburg – BEETHOVEN: *Archduke Trio;* SCHUBERT: *Piano Trio 1* ***

Violin Sonatas 1 in G, Op. 78; 2 in A, Op. 100; 3 in D min., Op. 108
☞ (BB) *** Hyp. Helios CDH 55087. Osostowicz, Tomes
(M) *** EMI 5 66893-2 [5 66945-2]. Perlman, Ashkenazy
*** DG (IMS) 435 800-2. Dumay, Pires
(M) *** Decca (ADD) 466 393-2. Suk, Katchen
(***) Testament mono SBT 1024. De Vito, Fischer; Aprea (in 2)

Violin Sonatas 1–3; F.A.E. Sonata: Scherzo
(M) **(*) DG (ADD) (IMS) 463 653-2 (2). Schneiderhan, Seeman

Violin Sonata 2 in A
*** Orfeo (ADD) C489981B. D. Oistrakh, S. Richter – PROKOFIEV: *Sonata 1* ***

Krysia Osostowicz and Susan Tomes give performances of such natural musicality that criticism is almost disarmed. They phrase with great spontaneity yet with apparently effortless care and artistry, and the interplay between the two partners is instinctive. The Hyperion engineers manage the sound and balance with their customary skill, and theirs is certainly to be preferred to some of the more glamorous rivals now on the market. At its new bargain Helios price this goes straight to the top of the recommended list.

Perlman and Ashkenazy bring out the trouble-free happiness of these lyrical inspirations, fully involved yet avoiding underlying tensions. In their sureness and flawless confidence at generally spacious speeds, these are performances which carry you along, cocooned in rich sound. But not all will agree that this is a suitable candidate for EMI's 'Great Recordings of the Century'.

Augustin Dumay and Maria João Pires on DG are certainly among the most interesting of the other CD couplings. They bring temperament and finesse to all three sonatas and, though there are one or two interpretative touches that may not enjoy universal appeal, these are unlikely to inhibit pleasure. These are artists of strong personality; certainly those with a special admiration for this partnership need not hesitate.

The Suk/Katchen partnership was recorded in the Kingsway Hall in 1967. Suk's personal blend of romanticism and the classical tradition is warmly attractive but small in scale. These are intimate performances, but none the worse for that, and they are refreshingly enjoyable, particularly as the sound and balance are excellent.

Gioconda De Vito's accounts of the *G major* and *D minor Sonatas* with Edwin Fischer from 1954 show warmth and finesse in equal measure, and her playing conveys a sense of expressive freedom. Fischer's playing is characteristically magisterial; and the *A major Sonata*, which she recorded with her usual partner, Tito Aprea, is hardly less beautiful. This is all rather special playing, and few allowances need be made for the excellent mono recording.

Schneiderhan and Seeman, for all their classical expertise, give the impression in the first and third sonatas of an unromantic, almost cool approach which hardly agrees with

Brahms in his pastoral *G major* mood, or his fiery *D minor* mood. However, No. 2 shows the team in a much more favourable light. The *A major*, a sunny and radiant work, here benefits from a warm approach, stressed by the violinist's rounded tone and the pianist's glowing left-hand playing, especially of the arpeggio passages. They are also in good form for the delightful and less often heard *Scherzo* from a sonata based on the motto 'F.A.E.' (*frei aber einsam* – free but lonely), whose other movements were written by Schumann and Dietrich.

Igor Oistrakh finds a rich tone and a fine lyrical line for two essentially lyrical works, and he is accompanied sympathetically by Anton Ginzburg. The recording of both instruments is beautiful, but the piano is backwardly balanced in a resonant acoustic and the violin is well forward. This is not disastrous, but it may irritate those who rightly consider that these are works for violin *and* piano.

The Orfeo disc is rather special. It records the Oistrakh–Richter partnership at the very top of its form in a live concert at the 1972 Salzburg Festival. The playing silences criticism and the recording from ORF (Austrian Radio) is perfectly serviceable.

Violin Sonatas (i) *2*; (ii) *3*
(M) *** Warner Elatus 2564 60661-2. Vengerov, (i)
   Markovich; (ii) Barenboim – ELGAR: *Violin Sonata* ***

Vengerov's partnership with Alexander Markovich works admirably. They both catch the *amabile* of the first movement of the *A major Sonata*, and the Brahmsian mellowness is sustained both in the *Andante tranquillo* and in the easy grace of the *Allegretto grazioso* finale. Yet there is an underlying vitality, and Vengerov rises to the climaxes. The account of the *D minor Sonata* is also very fine, with Vengerov bringing out the mystery of this minor-key work, and with Barenboim at the piano also freely spontaneous. Excellent recording and, while it is a pity that the *First Sonata* could not have been added for this reissue, the coupled performance of the Elgar is passionately convincing.

(i) *Violin Sonata 3, Op. 108;* (ii) *Hungarian Dances 1, 4, 6–7 & 17* (arr. Joachim)
(N) (M) (**(*)) EMI mono 562821-2. Y. Menuhin, with (i) H.
   Menuhin; (ii) M. Gazelle – BEETHOVEN: *Violin Concerto*
   (***)

The Brahms *D minor Sonata* makes an excellent bonus for Menuhin's outstanding 1949 account of the Beethoven *Violin Concerto*, if not of quite the same calibre. It was recorded in the Studio Albert, Paris, in 1936 when Yehudi was 20 and Hephzibah 16, and the five *Hungarian Dances* recorded with that fine pianist Marcelle Gazelle also come from the same year.

PIANO MUSIC

Piano music for four hands

(i) *21 Hungarian Dances* (original version); (ii) *16 Waltzes, Op. 39.* Solo Piano: *4 Ballades, Op. 10; 7 Fantasias, Op. 116; 3 Intermezzi, Op. 117; 8 Pieces, Op.76; 6 Pieces, Op. 118; 4 Pieces, Op. 119; 2 Rhapsodies, Op. 79; Sonata 3 in F min., Op. 5; 16 Waltzes, Op. 39; Variations & Fugue on a Theme by Handel, Op. 24; Variations on a Theme by Schumann, Op. 9; 16 Waltzes., Op. 39*
⊕ ✿ (N) (BB) *** Regis CDSX 3612 (5). Walter Klien, with
   (i) Brendel; (ii) Beatriz Klien

We first discussed this splendid anthology of Brahms piano music in the early 1960s in our *Guide to Bargain Classics*. It was a marvellous bargain then, and it still is; indeed, it is cherishable. As a Brahms pianist, Walter Klien is in the front rank and his recordings can be discussed in the same breath as those of Katchen and Kempff, although his style is nearer to that of the latter than the former. He has a natural sensitivity to Brahms's melodic line and in the shorter *Pieces* and *Intermezzi* his gentle touch and subtle control of nuance and colour is magical; always his pianistic textures are fresh and lacking in turgidity. The performance of the *F minor Sonata* has all the spontaneous buoyancy of youth, and this alone is worthy of the Rosette. Moreover, Klien shows he is as able to bring out the classical power of the *Handel Variations* as he is willing to evoke the romanticism of the Schumann set. For this reissue, Alfred Brendel joins Klien for equally fine performances of the piano-duo version of the *16 Waltzes*, and the original version for piano, four hands, of the *Hungarian Dances*, and it is unlikely that we shall have a jollier performance of the latter. Fortunately, the Vox engineers excelled themselves, for the the piano-tone is fully convincing and often very beautiful. We must be grateful to Regis for making these fine discs available again.

German Requiem, Op. 45 (arr. for piano, 4 hands)
(BB) ** Naxos 8.554115. Matthies, Köhn

Brahms's piano-duet arrangement of his great choral work succeeds better than might be expected. Though the whole project may seem odd, what does come out of this warmly expressive performance is the spring-like lyricism of Brahms's writing. On the other hand, having piano tone alone does emphasize the fact that the work is predominantly slow. A curiosity, well recorded.

Hungarian Dances 1–21; 18 Liebeslieder Waltzes, Op. 52a
(BB) *** Naxos 8.553140. Matthies, Köhn

The Naxos edition of Brahms piano duets brings lively and winning performances. It makes a generous and very attractive coupling to have all 21 *Hungarian Dances* in their original form, coupled with the piano-duet version of the first and more popular set of *Liebeslieder Waltzes*. Crisp, clean ensemble, matched by well-focused sound.

Piano Quartet 2 (arr. for one piano, four hands); *5 Waltzes, Op. 9* (arr. for 2 pianos)
(N) (BB) *** Naxos 8.554821. Matthies, Köhn

The *Second Piano Quartet* also works well in its piano-duet format and is played here robustly but with plenty of light and shade, dynamic and emotional. The five *Waltzes* make a vivacious encore, ending with a beguiling account of the most famous, in A flat.

Serenades 1 in D, Op. 11; 2 in A, Op. 16
(BB) *** Naxos 8.553726. Matthies, Köhn

Brahms's two *Serenades*, among his earliest orchestral works – the *Second* without violins – have an open innocence which translates well to the plainer medium of piano duet in Brahms's own arrangements. The duo of Matthies and Köhn, very well recorded, brings out an extra freshness and clarity. An attractive addition to their Naxos series.

Sonata for 2 Pianos in F min., Op. 34b; Variations on a Theme of Haydn, Op. 56b
(BB) *** Naxos 8.553654. Matthies, Köhn

This third volume in Naxos's series brings fresh and alert performances of two of the most important works, each of them better known in alternative forms. What the German duo demonstrates is that the two-piano format brings formidable advantages in bite and attack, as well as some disadvantages. Speeds are sensibly chosen for the sonata, as they are in Brahms's own piano-duet version of the *Haydn Variations*, again clarified. Bright, clear sound to match.

Solo piano music

4 Ballades, Op. 10; 7 Fantasias, Op. 116; Hungarian Dances 1–10; (i) 11–21; 3 Intermezzi, Op. 117; 8 Piano Pieces, Op. 76; 6 Piano Pieces, Op. 118; 4 Piano Pieces, Op. 119; Piano Sonatas 1 in C, Op. 01; 2 in F sharp min., Op. 2; 3 in F min., Op. 5; 2 Rhapsodies, Op. 79; Variations on a Hungarian Song, Op. 21/2; Variations on a Theme by Paganini, Op. 35; Variations & Fugue on a Theme by Handel, Op. 24; Variations on a Theme by Schumann, Op. 9; Variations on an Original Theme, Op. 21/1; Waltzes, Op. 39

(B) *** Decca (ADD) stereo/mono 455 247-2 (6). Katchen, (i) with J.-P. Marty

Katchen's magisterial survey of Brahms's keyboard music was made for Decca between 1962 and 1965, save for the last three *Ballades*, which come from the 1950s and are in mono. Although we would rank the Gilels *Ballades* and some of the Kempff recordings of the later pieces as special (not to mention Solomon's mono account of the *F minor Sonata* (on Testament) and, indeed, some of the other recordings of this work listed separately below), those wanting a comprehensive survey need look no further. Katchen is an eminently faithful and sound interpreter who brings refined musicianship and a natural authority to this repertoire; he is given the benefit of Decca recording which was excellent for its period, and remains so. The six CDs are offered at a very low price and, although they are not available separately, they still make a tremendous bargain. In addition to the three *Ballades*, the following are mono recordings: the *Schumann Variations*, Nos. 1, 5 and 7 of the *Fantasias* and Nos. 11–21 of the *Hungarian Dances.*

4 Ballades, Op. 10

(M) *** DG (ADD/DDD) (IMS) 457 762-2. Michelangeli – SCHUBERT: *Piano Sonata in A min.* **; BEETHOVEN: *Piano Sonata 4* *

Michelangeli produces a wonderfully blended tone and fine, mellow sonority. The *Ballades* are given a performance of the greatest distinction, without the slightly aloof quality that sometimes disturbs his readings; and the 1981 digital recording is excellent. The couplings, alas, are not in the same league.

4 Ballades, Op. 10; Intermezzo, Op. 117/2; 6 Piano Pieces, Op. 118; Piano Sonata 3, Op. 5; 2 Rhapsodies, Op. 79; Variations & Fugue on a Theme by Handel, Op. 24; Variations on a Theme by Paganini, Op. 35

(B) **(*) Double Decca (ADD) 452 338-2 (2). Katchen

Julius Katchen's style in Brahms is distinctive. In general the bigger, tougher pieces come off better than, for example, the gentle *Intermezzo*. But such pieces as the two *Rhapsodies* are splendidly done, and so are the *Ballades*. The *Sonata* receives a commanding performance.

7 Fantasias, Op. 116

*** Ottavio OTRC 39027. Cooper – SCHUMANN: *Abegg variations*, etc. ***

(M) **(*) DG 445 562-2. Kissin – LISZT: *Concert Paraphrases of Schubert Lieder*, etc. ***; SCHUBERT: *Wanderer Fantasia* **(*)

Imogen Cooper's stirring account of the *Capriccio* which opens the set captures the listener immediately, and the variety of colour and mood gives enormous pleasure throughout. The gentle *Intermezzi* are most beautiful, for the recording does this memorable playing full justice. The listening experience here is as if one was present at a live recital.

The Kissin recording comes from 1991 and finds the young virtuoso in masterful form. There is perhaps more to these extraordinary pieces than he uncovers but his pianism is glorious, and he is beautifully recorded too.

7 Fantasias, Op. 116; 3 Intermezzi, Op. 117; 8 Pieces, Op. 76; 6 Pieces, Op. 118; 4 Pieces, Op. 119

(B) *** EMI double forte (ADD) 5 69521-2 (2). Alexeev – SCHUMANN: *Etudes symphoniques* ***

Fantasias, Op. 116; 3 Intermezzi, Op. 117; 6 Pieces, Op. 118; 4 Pieces, Op. 119

(M) **(*) DG (ADD) 437 249-2. Kempff

(N) (M) **(*) Erato Elatus 2564 60805-2. Grimaud

Dmitri Alexeev's playing has authority and he produces an ideally weighted sonority, with the correct blend of colour. He brings the right kind of tenderness and insight to the quieter pieces. His mastery of rubato is consummate and these performances generally hold their own against any now before the public. With its excellent Schumann coupling this is very highly recommendable.

Kempff's style in Brahms is characteristically individual: poetry emphasized rather than brilliance, subtle timbres rather than virtuosity. It follows that Kempff shines in the gentle fancies of Brahms's last period, with his magic utterly beguiling in the *Intermezzi in A minor, E major* and *E minor* from Op. 116, and especially in the lovely *E flat major Andante* of Op. 117.

Hélène Grimaud's survey of late Brahms comes from the 1990s. She is admirably attuned to the Brahmsian sensibility, which speaks naturally and thoughtfully in her hands. Good though she is, the inwardness of this intensely private music is even better conveyed in many other discs, including the relatively recent recital from Lars Vogt on EMI (see below).

(i) Fantasias, Op. 116; Intermezzi, Op. 117; (ii) Pieces, Op. 76; (i) Pieces, Opp. 118/119; (ii) Rhapsodies 1 in B min.; 2 in G min., Op. 79/1–2; (i) Variations & Fugue on a Theme by Handel, Op. 24; (iii) Variations on a Theme by Paganini, Op. 35

(B) *(**) Ph. Duo (ADD/DDD) 442 589-2 (2). (i) Kovacevich; (ii) Varsi; (iii) Harasiewicz

The performances by Stephen Kovacevich can receive the strongest recommendation. He finds the fullest range of emotional contrast in the Op. 116 *Fantasias* but is at his finest in the Op. 117 *Intermezzi* and the four *Klavierstücke*, Op. 119, and it seems perverse that Philips then turned to recordings by Dinorah Varsi of the two *Rhapsodies* and eight *Klavierstücke*, Op. 76, when Kovacevich has also recorded them. However, these are already available, coupled with the two *Piano Concertos*, on another Duo. Varsi's playing is at times very impulsive. Adam Harasiewicz, however, plays the

Paganini Variations with some flair and towards the end produces some exciting bravura. Generally the recordings are very good; Kovacevich's Op. 116 and Op. 118 are digital.

7 Fantasias, Op. 116; 8 Pieces, Op. 76; 2 Rhapsodies, Op. 79
(BB) **(*) Naxos 8.550353. Biret

Idil Biret readily captures the graceful intimacy of the *A flat* and *B flat Intermezzi*. Of the two *Rhapsodies*, the second is particularly fine, boldly spontaneous, its dark colouring caught well. The *Fantasias*, Op. 116, bring some beautifully reflective playing, notably in the three *Intermezzi* grouped together (in E major and E minor), while the framing *G minor* and *D minor Capriccios* are passionately felt, the latter ending the recital strongly. This is all impressively characterized Brahms playing, and the recording does not lack sonority.

3 Intermezzi, Op. 117; 6 Pieces, Op. 118; 4 Pieces, Op. 119; 2 Rhapsodies, Op. 79
*** Decca (ADD) 417 599-2. Lupu
(B) **(*) HM Cal. (ADD) CAL 6679. Södergren

Radu Lupu's late Brahms is quite outstanding in every way. There is great intensity and inwardness when these qualities are required, and a keyboard mastery that is second to none. This is undoubtedly one of the most rewarding Brahms recitals currently before the public.

Inger Södergren's Brahms is imaginative and poetic: her performances of the three *Intermezzi* are enticingly intimate, while there is a commanding volatility and passion in the *Rhapsodies*. She brings out all the colour of the Op. 118 *Pieces* and captures their variety of mood and atmosphere.

3 Intermezzi, Op. 117; 6 Pieces, Op. 118; 4 Pieces Op. 119
𝄐 *** EMI 5 57543-2. Vogt

Issued simultaneously with his Brahms duo discs from the Heimbach Chamber Music Festival, Lars Vogt's disc of the three last sets of piano pieces offers a different slant on his Brahms interpretations in a conventional studio recording. There are profound things in these extraordinarily forward-looking late Brahms pieces, and Vogt is a Brahmsian of real quality who is completely inside this repertoire. His speeds, far from being fast, as they tend to be in his live performances, are on the broad side, but his natural warmth and ability to convey the sense of spontaneous invention make these very much a welcome supplement to the festival performances. The EMI disc offers natural, lifelike and wide-ranging recorded sound that does justice to a thoughtful and highly musical artist.

Piano Sonatas 1 in C, Op. 1; 2 in F sharp min., Op. 2
*** Decca (IMS) 436 457-2. S. Richter

Recorded in Mantua in February 1987, these performances show Sviatoslav Richter at his most commanding. He makes the most heavily chordal piano writing sound totally pianistic and there is exquisite shading of tone and flawless legato. Both slow movements are coloured most subtly and the opening of the finale of the *F sharp minor Sonata* has a wonderful improvisatory feeling. The playing throughout has the spontaneity of live music-making and the Decca engineers have secured most realistic sound.

Piano Sonata 3; 4 Ballades, Op. 10
𝄐 *** Hyp. CDA 67237. Hough
(M) *** Warner Elatus 0927 49562-2. Barenboim

(BB) **(*) Naxos 8.550352. Biret

Piano Sonata 3, Op. 5; Capriccio in B min., Op. 76/2; Hungarian Dances 1 in G min.; 2 in D min.; 3 in F; 6 in D flat; 7 in A; Intermezzo in A min. Op. 76/7
** RCA 82876 52737-2. Kissin

Piano Sonata 3; 7 Fantasias, Op. 116; 4 Pieces, Op. 119
(N) **(*) HM HMU 907339. Nakamatsu

Piano Sonata 3; 3 Intermezzi, Op. 117; 2 Rhapsodies, Op. 79
(M) **(*) Sony SMK 89802. Ax

Piano Sonata 3 in F min., Op. 5; 16 Waltzes, Op. 39
*** Ondine ODE 1044-2. Siirala

The *F minor Sonata* and the *Ballades*, Op. 10, are virtually contemporary, separated by less than a year. They are a young man's music – the composer only just having entered his twenties. Stephen Hough gives us a finely conceived, naturally paced and beautifully controlled account of both pieces. The intellect and emotions, the 'classical' Brahms and youthful romanticism are well balanced. The recorded sound is very good and lifelike.

The young Finnish pianist Antti Siirala has collected innumerable prizes (the Beethoven Competition in Vienna, 1997, London, 2000, Dublin and Leeds in 2003) and is still only in his mid-twenties. His Brahms *F minor Sonata* announces the arrival of a serious artist whose musical armoury, while it has no want of bravura and virtuosity, is profoundly well equipped to deal with the artistic challenges posed by this great work. Siirala's recording is to be ranked along with the very best, and he is hardly less impressive in the Op. 39 *Waltzes*. First-class piano recording.

Barenboim's *Sonata* and *Ballades* are distinguished by an effortless technical command and excellent musical characterization and insight. Although he is not necessarily a first choice, this generally well-recorded account is certainly most impressive. Good value too.

As a pupil of Kempff, Idil Biret has a fine understanding of this repertoire, although her approach is more muscular than Kempff's. Thus the first of the four *Ballades* opens with enticing lyrical feeling but has the most powerfully dramatic climax, to match the feeling of the Scottish ballad, *Edward*, on which it is based. The fourth *Ballade* is gravely beautiful and shows her at her finest. The *Sonata* opens commandingly and its lyrical side is well balanced. These performances are full of character. Good recording, made in the Heidelberg studio.

Emanuel Ax gives an appropriately massive performance of the *F minor Sonata*, but the fortissimo he produces is never ugly and his pianissimo tone is always most refined and of great beauty. The slow movement in particular is played with great tenderness and poetic feeling. There is plenty of space round the aural image and the sound is a joy in itself. Although he is an artist of the highest intelligence, Ax is at times prone to moments of expressive exaggeration and phrases are sometimes self-consciously moulded, almost cosseted, as if he did not quite trust the music to speak for itself.

Masterly and magisterial playing in the *F minor Sonata*, but there is a studied, self-conscious quality about Yevgeni Kissin's playing that is a little disturbing. There is little spontaneity of feeling and not everyone will respond. It is undoubtedly very impressive in its way, but in the sonata readers will be better served by Stephen Hough.

Jon Nakamatsu was Gold Medal winner in 1997 at the Tenth Van Cliburn International Piano Competition and he is a talent to be reckoned with. He clearly has a natural feeling for Brahms, yet his account of the *F minor Sonata* is not entirely convincing. The very opening lacks the sense of sudden unleashed youthful energy, the rhythm of the Scherzo is a little mannered in its accentuation, and the finale too has a lack of consistent impetus, But the *Andante* is played very beautifully, and in Opp. 116 and 119 it is the reflective pieces that are memorable, although the closing *Rhapsodie* of Op. 119 is a vigorous *Allegro resoluto*. The recording is excellent.

Variations & Fugue on a Theme of Handel, Op. 24

(N) (M) *** Warner Elatus 2564 61762-2. Schiff (piano) – HANDEL: *Keyboard Suite in B flat (HWV 434)*; REGER: *Variations & Fugue on a Theme of Bach* ***

Schiff's splendid performance is made the more attractive by being preceded by the Handel *Suite* from which Brahms draws his theme. The Reger *Variations* are also given a first-class, highly imaginative performance of wide dynamic contrasts, lyricism alternating with strength. The (excellent) recording comes from a live recital at the Concertebouw in 1994.

Variations on a Theme by Paganini, Op. 35

(BB) *** Discover DICD 920423. Brancart – LISZT: *Paganini Etudes* ***

(BB) (**(*)) EMI Encore mono 5 75230-2. Michelangeli – BACH/BUSONI: *Partita 2: Chaconne* (**(*)); MOZART: *Piano Concerto 15* (*)

Evelyne Brancart has superb technique, fine musicianship and sensitivity; the recording is rather bright and forward but yields pleasing results. An enjoyable recital – though, even at super-bargain price, rather short measure at 47' 40".

Michelangeli's prodigious virtuosity here (in 1950) is dazzling, with not a note out of place, and Paganini's own legendary bravura looms over Brahms's variations, although there is no lack of light and shade. The piano recording is shallow on top, but acceptable.

Variations on a Theme of Schumann (trans. for 2 hands by Theodor Kirchner)

** Athene ATHCD 23. Boyde – SCHUMANN: *Impromptus; Variations* **

Brahms published his variations on the so-called Schumann *Geister Variations* for piano duet as Op. 23, and his friend, the composer Theodor Kirchner, transcribed it for solo piano. It comes as the make-weight for an intelligently planned Schumann recital by the German pianist Andreas Boyde. The playing is very convincing but the recording somewhat too close and shallow.

ORGAN MUSIC

11 Chorale Preludes, Op. 122; Chorale Prelude & Fugue on 'O Traurigkeit, O Herzeleid'; Fugue in A flat min. (original and published versions); Preludes & Fugues: in A min.; G min.

*** Nim. NI 5262. Bowyer (organ of Odense Cathedral)

11 Chorale Preludes, Op. 122; Chorale Prelude & Fugue on 'O Traurigkeit, O Herzeleid'; Fugue in A flat min.; Preludes & Fugues: in A min.; G min.

*** CRD 3404. Danby (organ)

Kevin Bowyer has the advantage of the splendid Danish organ in Odense Cathedral, which combines a full tone and a warmly coloured palette with a clear profile. Like Nicholas

Danby, Bowyer is obviously at home both in the early *Preludes and Fugues*, in which he produces considerable bravura (helped by the fresh, bright sound of the organ), and in the very late set of *Chorale Preludes*. He then closes the recital with Brahms's original manuscript forms of the two earliest pieces (which we have already heard in their published formats), the *Chorale Prelude and Fugue on 'O Traurigkeit'* and the unpolished *A flat minor Fugue*. The disc is very well documented.

Nicholas Danby, playing the organ of the Church of the Immaculate Conception in London, gives restrained, clean-cut readings which yet have a strong profile. Choice between these two discs might well depend on preference for the type of organ used. The effect on CRD is rather more incisive but has firmness and weight of tone and certainly does not lack amplitude.

VOCAL MUSIC

Alto Rhapsody, Op. 53

(N) (BB) (***) Regis mono RRC 1146. Ferrier, LPO Ch. & O, Krauss – MAHLER: *Das Lied von der Erde* (**)

(i) *Alto Rhapsody*; **(ii)** *Botschaft; Sapphische Ode*; **(ii; iii)** *2 Songs with Viola, Op. 91*; **(iv)** *Vier ernste Gesänge*

(N) (BB) (*(*)) Naxos mono 8.111009. Ferrier, LPO Ch. & O, Krauss – (ii) Spurr; (iii) Gilbert; (iv) Newmark – SCHUMANN: *Frauenliebe und Leben* (**(*))

The *Alto Rhapsody* was one of Kathlen Ferrier's own favourites among her records, and well it might have been, for the spacious phrases of Brahms's setting of Goethe suited the glorious tonal beauty of her voice to perfection, and the closing section with chorus is particularly moving. The Regis transfer is admirable, bringing out all the vocal warmth and radiance; the Naxos sound is undoubtedly clearer and brighter, but this has been achieved by Mark Obert-Thorn controversially re-pitching the recordings at A = 440 Hertz instead of 428 Hertz of the original Decca masters. Those wanting Mahler's *Das Lied* as a coupling will find the Regis sound again satisfactory, but here Decca's own transfer is even finer, and in any case the Naxos collection is more tempting. Botschaft and the *Sapphische Ode* are most touching, with Phyllis Spurr accompanying sensitively. John Newmark is a less imaginative participant, and Max Gilbert's viola timbre is meagre as recorded; but in the *Four Serious Songs* the dark intensity of Ferrier's singing is unforgettable, and again the transfers are excellent and equally truthful to the vocal timbre and piano. No translations are included on either disc.

LIEDER

Lieder: *Ach, wende diesen Blick; Die Mainacht; Heimweh; Mädchenlied; Meine Liebe ist grün; O kühler Wald; Ständchen; Unbewegte laue Luft; Von ewiger Liebe; Wie rafft' ich mich auf; Wiegenlied*; **(i)** *2 Songs with Viola (Gestilte Sehnsucht & Geistliches Wiegenlied), Op. 91*; *3 Volkslieder: Dort in den Weiden; Sonntag; Vergebliches Ständchen. 8 Zigeunerlieder, Op. 103/1-7 & 11*

*** DG (IMS) 429 727-2. Von Otter, Forsberg, (i) with Sparf

Anne Sofie von Otter gives these Brahms Lieder the natural freshness of folksong which so often they resemble. She phrases unerringly, holding and changing tension and mood as in a live recital, and her accompanist is strongly supportive. In the Op. 91 settings they are joined by Nils-Erik Sparf, who plays with admirable taste.

Lieder: *Agnes; Alte Liebe; Dein blaues Auge hält so still; Dort in den Weiden; 2 Songs, Op. 91; Gold überwiegt die Liebe; Immer leiser wird mein Schlummer; Der Jäger; Klage I-II; Die Liebende schreibt; Liebesklage des Mädchens; Liebestreu; Des Liebsten Schwur; Das Mädchen, Op. 85/3; Mädchenfluch, Op. 95/1; Mädchenlied. Op. 107/5; Das Mädchen spricht; 5 Ophelia Lieder; Regenlied; 6 Romanzen und Lieder, Op. 84; Salome; Sapphische Ode; Spanisches Lied; Der Schmied; Therese; Todessehnen; Die Trauernde; Vom Strande; Von waldbekränzter Höhe; Vorschneller Schwur; Wie melodien zieht; 8 Zigeunerlieder, Op. 103*

⊶ (B) *** DG (ADD) Double 459 469-2 (2). Norman, Barenboim

This double CD concentrates on Brahms's 'women's songs'. Jessye Norman's tone is full and golden. Her imagination even matches that of Fischer-Dieskau, and no praise could be higher. Her voice is ideally suited to many of these songs, and if occasionally there is a hint of an over-studied quality this is of little consequence, considering the overall achievement. Barenboim's accompaniments are superb, contributing much to the success of this recital. The recording is excellent and this is a real bargain.

Lieder: *An die Nachtigall; Bottschaft; Dein blaues Auge hält so still; Feldeinsamkeit; Der Gang zum Liebchen; Geheimnis; Im Waldeseinsamkeit; Komm bald; Die Kränze; Die Mainacht; Meine Liebe ist grün; Minnelied; Nachtigall; O wüsst ich doch den Weg zurück; Sah dem edlen Bildnis; Salamander; Die Schale der Vergessenheit; Serenade; Sonntag; Ständchen; Von ewiger Liebe; Von waldbekränzter Höhe; Wie bist du, Meine Königin; Wiegenlied; Wir Wandelten*

(BB) *** Virgin 2×1 5 61418-2 (2). Allen, Parsons – WOLF: *Lieder* ***

Thomas Allen gives fresh, virile performances of a particularly attractive collection of Brahms songs. There is less underlining of words than Fischer-Dieskau or Bär give us but still a keen and detailed feeling for meaning as well as mood. There are many such felicities here, with Geoffrey Parsons an ever-sympathetic accompanist and with sound more cleanly focused than in earlier Lieder issues from this source. Now coupled with an equally desirable recital of Wolf songs, with the two CDs offered for the cost of one mid-priced disc, this is a set not to be missed by any lover of German Lieder, even though no translations are provided.

(i) *Alto Rhapsody. Academic Festival Overture*

(M) *** EMI (ADD) 5 62791-2. J. Baker, Alldis Ch., LPO, Boult – SCHUBERT: *Symphony 9* ***

Dame Janet Baker's devoted (1970) recording of the *Alto Rhapsody* with Boult was originally coupled with the *Second Symphony*. Now it comes equally attractively paired with Schubert. The Brahms remains meditative, even though the tempo is unlingering and the manner totally unindulgent. The warm Abbey Road recording is transferred very successfully to CD.

Alto Rhapsody; 4 Songs, Op. 17

⊶ (BB) *** Virgin 2×1 5 61469-2 (2). J. Baker, L. Symphony Ch., City of L. Sinf., Hickox – BERLIOZ: *Les Nuits d'été*, etc.; MENDELSSOHN: *Infelice*, etc.; RESPIGHI: *La Sensitiva* ***

Though the Virgin recording of the *Alto Rhapsody* was made after Janet Baker's retirement from the concert platform, the voice is in glorious condition, superbly controlled. This is a more openly expressive and spacious reading than her earlier, EMI one with Boult, matching her performances in the two Mendelssohn items. The four early Brahms songs, Opus 17, for women's chorus with two horns and harp accompaniment, are delightfully done.

(i) *Alto Rhapsody;* (ii) *German Requiem, Op. 45;* (iii) *Song of Destiny (Schicksalslied), Op. 54;* (iv) *Geistliches Lied, Op. 30;* (v) *Vier ernste Gesänge (4 Serious Songs), Op. 121;* (vi) *2 Songs with Viola, Op. 91*

(B) **(*) Double Decca (ADD/DDD) 452 344-2 (2). (i; vi) Watts; (i) SRO, Ansermet; (ii) Te Kanawa, Weikl, Chicago Ch. & SO, Solti; (iii) Amb. Ch., New Philh. O, Abbado; (iv) King's College, Cambridge, Ch., Cleobury; (v) Holl, A. Schiff; (vi) Parsons, Aronowitz

Solti favours very expansive tempi, smooth lines and refined textures in the *Requiem*. There is much that is beautiful, even if the result overall is not as involving as it might be. Kiri Te Kanawa sings radiantly, but Bernd Weikl with his rather gritty baritone is not ideal. Fine recording, glowing and clear. Helen Watts gives a sensitive account of the *Alto Rhapsody*, while the *Song of Destiny* brings a refined contribution from the Ambrosian Chorus with Abbado directing strongly. Helen Watts, too, is in good form in her sensitive performances of the two songs with viola as well as piano accompaniment. Cecil Aronowitz plays his obbligato with great finesse, and the combination of voice, viola and piano is particularly effective in *Gestillte Sehnsucht*. The contributions of Robert Holl, accompanied by András Schiff, are slightly marred by the slow tempi chosen but are well sung, with due note taken of the texts.

Lieder: *Auf dem Kirchhofe; Botschaft; Feldeinsamkeit; Minnelied III; Heimweh II (O wüsst ich doch den Weg zurück); Sapphische Ode; Sonntag; Ständchen; Verrat; Wie bist du, Meine Königin; Wie melodien zieht es mir. Wir wandelten; Vier ernste Gesange, Op. 121*

⊶ ✿(M) (***) EMI mono 5 62807-2. Hotter, Moore – BACH: *Cantata 82: Ich habe genug* (***) ✿

Glorious singing from Hans Hotter, wonderfully accompanied by Gerald Moore. A splendid transfer of the 1950 recordings – an indispensable coupling, with two extra songs included that were not on the old Références CD.

Ave Maria, Op. 12; Nänie, Op. 82; Schicksalslied, Op. 54; (i) *Triumphlied, Op. 55*

*** Chan. 10165. Danish Nat. Ch. & SO, Albrecht; (i) with Skovhus

It is fascinating to find Brahms banging the patriotic drum in his *Triumphlied*, written to celebrate the Prussian victory over the French in 1870 and the establishment of the German empire. Sadly, though the writing is masterly, this three-movement cantata has been neglected over the years, partly for political reasons (though the text is hardly jingoistic, being taken from the Book of Revelations) and partly for the great difficulty for the singers of a piece for eight-part chorus. Albrecht's performance with the Danish National Choir and Orchestra may be less polished than Sinopoli's DG version, but it is markedly warmer and more idiomatic, well coupled with a devotional reading of *Schicksalslied, Song of Destiny* (with a Hölderlin text) and the valedictory *Nänie*. The rare setting of *Ave Maria* for women's voices, an early work, makes a charming supplement.

Lieder: *Dein blaues Auge hält; Dort in den Weiden; Immer leiser wird mein Schlummer; Klage I & II; Liebestreu; Des Liebsten Schwur; Das Mädchen; Das Mädchen spricht; Regenlied; Romanzen und Lieder, Op. 84; Salome; Sapphische Ode, Op. 94/4; Der Schmied; (i) 2 Songs with viola, Op. 91; Therese; Vom Strande; Wie Melodien zieht es; Zigeunerlieder, Op. 103*
(M) *** DG 474 856-2. Norman, Barenboim; (i) with Christ

Winner of the *Gramophone* Solo Vocal Award in 1983, this delightful and strongly contrasted selection from DG's Lieder Box in the Brahms Edition shows Jessye Norman at her finest. For the CD equivalent of an earlier digital LP, the two *Songs with Viola* have been added to make a highlight of the new recital. The task of recording a complete set of women's songs seems in this instance to have added to the warmth and sense of spontaneity of both singer and pianist in the studio, while Wolfram Christ makes a distinguished contribution to Op. 91. The heroic scale of *Der Schmied* is superb, as is the open simplicity of *Zigeunerlieder*, while the gentler songs find the gloriously ample voice exquisitely scaled down. The recording is wonderfully vivid, giving the artists a tangible presence. An outstanding reissue.

Deutsche Volkslieder (42 **German folksong settings**)
(B) *** EMI Gemini (ADD) 5 85502-2 (2). Schwarzkopf, Fischer-Dieskau, Moore

In Brahms's simple folk-settings no singers in the world can match Schwarzkopf and Fischer-Dieskau in their musical imagination and depth of understanding. Gerald Moore as ever is the ideal accompanist, and the recording quality is natural and vivid, with some enchanting conversation pieces between the soloists. However, no translations are included and no attempt is made to explain the meaning of each song.

German Requiem, Op. 45
⊟~ *** TDK **DVD** DV-MUSIK. Bonney, Terfel, Swedish R. Ch., Eric Ericson Chamber Ch., BPO, Abbado (V/D: Coles)
⊟~ ✿ *** Ph. 432 140-2. Margiono, Gilfry, Monteverdi Ch., ORR, Gardiner
(BB) *** Warner Apex 8573 89081-2. M. Price, Ramey, Amb. S., RPO, Previn
(BB) *** HM LSO Live LSO 0005CD. Blackwell, Wilson-Johnson, L. Symphony Ch., LSO, Previn
(M) *** EMI 5 66903-2 [5 66955-2]. Schwarzkopf, Fischer-Dieskau, Philh. Ch. & O, Klemperer
(M) **(*) DG (ADD) 463 661-2. Janowitz, Waechter, Vienna Singverein, BPO, Karajan
(M) (***) EMI mono 7 64705-2. Grümmer, Fischer-Dieskau, St Hedwig's Cathedral Ch., BPO, Kempe
(M) (***) EMI mono 5 62811-2 [5 62812-2]. Schwarzkopf, Hotter, V. Singverein, BPO, Karajan
(B) **(*) Sony (ADD) SBK 89308. Cotrubas, Prey, New Phil. Ch. & O, Maazel

(N) (B) ** RCA 82876 60861-2. Battle, Hagegård, Chicago Ch. & SO, Levine

(i) *German Requiem;* (ii) *Alto Rhapsody; Song of Destiny (Schicksalslied), Op. 54; Academic Festival Overture; Tragic Overture; Variations on a Theme by Haydn*
(B) **(*) Ph. (ADD) (IMS) Duo 438 760-2 (2). (i) Lipp, Crass; (ii) Heynis; V. Singverein; VSO, Sawallisch

(i) *German Requiem; Burial Song, Op. 13*
(M) *** Virgin 5 61605-2. (i) L. Dawson, Bär; L. Schütz Ch., LCP, Norrington

Abbado's DVD of the *Requiem* with Barbara Bonney and Bryn Terfel as soloists and the Swedish Radio and Eric Ericson choirs, together with the Berlin Philharmonic itself, was recorded at the Vienna Musikverein in April 1997. It is in every way highly impressive, and there is a moving directness of utterance. We are also spared any attempts at visual gimmickry. This is Brahms pure and simple, with sympathetic and intelligent direction from Bob Coles and the camera completely at the service of the music. Strongly recommended.

Gardiner's 'revolutionary' account of the *German Requiem* brings a range of choral sound even more thrilling than in the concert hall. With period instruments and following Viennese practice of the time, speeds tend to be faster than usual, though the speed for the big fugue is surprisingly relaxed. Charlotte Margiono makes an ethereal soprano soloist, while Rodney Gilfry, despite a rapid vibrato, is aptly fresh and young-sounding. One could not ask for a more complete renovation of a masterpiece that is often made to sound stodgy and square.

It is the seeming simplicity of Previn's dedicated approach in his earlier, Apex recording, with radiant singing from the chorus and measured speeds held steadily, that so movingly conveys an innocence in the often square writing, both in the powerful opening choruses and in the simple, songful *Wie lieblich*. The great fugatos are then powerfully presented. Both soloists are outstanding, Margaret Price golden-toned, Samuel Ramey incisively dark. The recording, of high quality, is warmly set against a helpful church acoustic with the chorus slightly distanced.

This second recording from André Previn, on LSO Live, is a powerful, dedicated reading which emphasizes the drama of the piece in high contrasts. The impact of the chorus is all the greater when the recording gives the impression of a relatively compact group – more a question of the Barbican acoustic rather than actual size. In its freshness it defies any idea of this as a turgid piece, as once condemned by Bernard Shaw. Though speeds are on the fast side – with the overall timing some ten minutes shorter than in most rival versions – the flow makes the music all the more magnetic, removing any hint of sentimentality. Good, clear soloists and first-rate sound.

Norrington, using period forces, comes into direct rivalry with Gardiner in his Philips version, recorded 18 months earlier. At speeds even faster and taking a plainer view, but drawing equally fine singing from his choir, Norrington lacks some of Gardiner's dramatic flair, but Lynne Dawson sings with ravishing sweetness in her central solo and Olaf Bär brings a Lieder-like intensity to the baritone solos, even if he lacks a degree of darkness. Unlike Gardiner and most other rivals, Norrington offers a brief coupling, the dark *Burial Song* with wind accompaniment.

Klemperer's reading has been effectively remastered for

reissue as one of EMI's 'Great Recordings of the Century'. Measured and monumental, the performance defies preconceived doubts. The speeds are consistently slow – too slow in the *vivace* of the sixth movement, where Death has little sting – but, with dynamic contrasts underlined, the result is uniquely powerful. The solo singing is superb and the Philharmonia Chorus were at the peak of their form. The new CD transfer is excellent.

Karajan's beautifully refined performance of Brahms's big choral work emerges more vividly in its new 'Originals' transfer, and one enjoys its many beauties, not least Gundula Janowitz's fresh approach to the music. Other versions may convey more immediate power, but although it is not a prime recommendation, this recording will not disappoint Karajan's admirers.

Rudolf Kempe's mono recording of 1955 is incandescent, glowing with warmth, a characteristic example of his dedicated intensity and, though the mono recording is limited on orchestral sound, the voices are caught vividly and atmospherically, with the choir the more involving for being forwardly balanced. There is vintage singing too from Fischer-Dieskau, and Elisabeth Grümmer sounds sweetly radiant, superbly sustaining Kempe's exceptionally slow speed for *Ihr habt nun Traurigkeit*.

Recorded in October 1947 and issued on ten short-playing 78rpm discs, Karajan's mono version of the *German Requiem* was – surprisingly – the first ever complete recording of this work, and it is fully worthy of inclusion among EMI's 'Great Artists of the Century' series. It was also something of a breakthrough in Karajan's early career. It is in part a tribute to his unique collaboration with Walter Legge, not only that this is a performance – which has been rarely matched since on record, incandescent and intense – but that even now the sound has such vivid presence. There is inevitably some surface noise, but nothing too distracting, and the brightness and fullness of the sound are astonishing. The chorus is in superb, incisive form, and the two soloists are both at their peak, the young Schwarzkopf fresh-toned and Hotter far firmer than he later became.

Maazel directs a strong, unaffected performance, most impressive in the great choral climaxes, notably so in *Denn alles Fleisch*. There is a fair sense of spontaneous music-making here, and the warm (1976) recording is apt for the music. The soloists are both in good voice, though Cotrubas's beautiful tone has a hint of unsteadiness, no doubt exaggerated by the recording. Fair value, as Sony provide texts and translations.

In the *German Requiem* Sawallisch may not penetrate the spiritual depths as deeply as a conductor like Kempe, but the music flows naturally. It is a deeply satisfying version, with an account of the final movements both dramatic and ethereal. Franz Crass's dark bass colouring make his solos tonally distinctive, but the singing of Wilma Lipp in *Ihr habt nun Traurigkeit* is a blot, wobbly and plaintive-sounding. However, what makes this inexpensive set worth considering, even against the competition, is Aafje Heynis's lovely singing in the *Alto Rhapsody*. It is even more dedicated and 'inner' than Kathleen Ferrier's, and the tonal shading is most beautiful. The emotionally more turbulent *Song of Destiny* is also a considerable success. Not all collectors will need the overtures, but they are well enough played and recorded, although the early date (1959) of the *Variations* shows in the violin timbre.

Levine's 1973 version starts with two assets: the celebrated Chicago Symphony Chorus is probably the finest in America,

and in addition the two soloists both prove excellent, Kathleen Battle pure and sweetly vulnerable-sounding, Hagegård clear-cut and firm. Nor does Levine race the music: the outer movements of the seven may seem faster than usual, so that the first is hardly meditative, but there is no sense of haste. More serious is Levine's choice of an exceptionally slow speed for the second movement, *Denn alles Fleisch*, sounding rhythmically stodgy if undeniably powerful in impact. Levine may not be the most illuminating conductor in this work, and the recording is not ideal – with inner textures growing cloudy in tuttis – but overall the performance gives considerable pleasure.

German Requiem, Op. 45 (sung in English)

*** Telarc CD 80501. Chandler, Gunn, Mormon Tabernacle Ch., Utah SO, Jessop

(BB) (**) Naxos mono 8.110839. Chiesa, Janssen, Westminster Ch., NBC SO, Toscanini

Craig Jessop directs a dedicated reading of a new translation by Robert Shaw which for English-speaking listeners will communicate warmly, not least thanks to the extra immediacy of the words. The choir, which too often has been recorded mushily, here emerges far fresher than before, and the two soloists are both first rate. Janice Chandler has a warm, creamy soprano, and Nathan Gunn has a youthfully clear baritone which he uses with finesse and passion. Full, warm sound, not always ideally transparent; but this remains a fully worthy tribute to Shaw.

In January 1943, at the height of the Second World War, Toscanini conducted his performance of the Brahms *Requiem* in New York, understandably choosing an English text rather than German. As one would expect, it is high-powered, starting with a refreshing, urgent account of the opening Beatitude setting, *Blessed are they*. After that the next movement, *Behold, all flesh is as the grass*, is very broad indeed, prevented from sounding sluggish only by Toscanini's high-voltage intensity, which equally sustains the other movements. Herbert Janssen as the baritone soloist, dramatic and clean-cut, provides Lieder-like detail. Viviane della Chiesa is the fresh, creamy-toned soprano in the fourth movement, and the Westminster Choir adds to the drama, even though backwardly balanced. Limited mono sound, less harsh than many commercial NBC recordings of the period.

(i) Vier ernste Gesang (4 Serious Songs), Op. 121; (ii) 2 Songs with viola, Op. 91

(BB) (***) Regis mono RRC 1153. Ferrier, (i; ii) Spurr, Gilbert – MAHLER: *Kindertotenlieder* etc. (***) ❁

This vintage Kathleen Ferrier record brings together a group of the great contralto's early Decca Brahms recordings from 1949–50, showing the richness of the voice and her natural expressive involvement. These recordings are also available elsewhere, notably in Decca's various Ferrier groupings, but these Regis transfers are appealingly smooth and natural, and the recording is inexpensive.

Vier ernste Gesänge, Op. 121; Lieder: Auf dem Kirchhofe; Botschaft; Feldeinsamkeit; Im Waldeseinsamkeit; Minnelied III; Mondenschein; O wüsst ich doch den Weg zurück; Sapphische Ode; Sommerabend; Ständchen

❁━ ❁ (M) (***) EMI (ADD) 7 63198-2. Hotter, Moore – BACH: *Cantata 82: Ich habe genug* (***) ❁

Glorious singing from Hans Hotter, wonderfully accompanied by Gerald Moore. An excellent transfer.

3 Gesänge, Op. 42; (i) *4 Gesänge, Op. 17; 5 Gesänge, Op. 104;*
(ii) *6 Quartette, Op. 112; Zigeunerlieder, Op. 109*
❻ *** Chan. 9806. Danish Nat. R. Ch., Parkman; with (i)
Yeats, McClelland, Lind; (ii) Forsberg

Brahms's shorter choral works are still too little known by
many collectors, who are almost over-familiar with his
orchestral and chamber music, so we have given this Chandos
disc a Rosette, not only in response to the splendid performances it contains, but also in the hope of enticing readers to
explore. The Danish National Radio Choir have already
brought us a fine collection of motets, including the *Marienlieder* (see below). Here they turn their attention to some of
the lovely unaccompanied *Gesänge*, and include also as a
highlight of the concert the luscious settings of Op. 17, which
have delectable harp accompaniments and obbligatos for one
or two horns. *Sehnsucht*, the first of the six piano-
accompanied *Quartets* which follow, has one of the composer's most seductive melodies, and the robust set of
Zigeunerlieder which close the recital, sung with great vigour,
show the composer at his most infectiously boisterous.

Liebeslieder Waltzes, Op. 52
*** BBC (ADD) BBCB 8001-2. Harper, J. Baker, Pears,
Hemsley, Britten & Arrau (piano duet) – ROSSINI: *Soirées
musicales;* TCHAIKOVSKY: *4 Duets* ***

Britten was allergic to the music of Brahms, but you would
never know that from this magical performance of the *Liebeslieder Waltzes*. As an inspired accompanist he is joined by
Claudio Arrau in a perfect partnership. The soloists make an
outstanding and characterful team, whoopsing away
throughout, with Janet Baker striking a deeper note in the
poignant seventh waltz. Full, clear, radio sound.

*Liebeslieder Waltzes, Op. 52; New Liebeslieder Waltzes,
Op. 65; 3 Quartets, Op. 64*
*** DG (IMS) 423 133-2. Mathis, Fassbaender, Schreier,
Fischer-Dieskau; Engel & Sawallisch (pianos)

On DG one of the most successful recordings yet of the two
seductive but surprisingly difficult sets of *Liebeslieder Waltzes*.
The CD has fine realism and presence.

(i–ii) *Liebeslieder Waltzes, Op. 52* (2 performances); (iii)
Waltzes, Op. 39; Waltzes for Piano Duet, Op. 39, (iv) *2,
6 & 15;* (v) *1, 2, 5, 6, 10, 14 & 15*
(M) (***) EMI mono 5 66425-2. (i) Seefried, Höngen,
Meyer-Welfing, Hotter; (i, iv) Wührer; Von Nordberg; (ii)
De Polignac, Kedroff, Cuénod, Conrad; (ii, v) Lipatti,
Boulanger; (iii) Backhaus

This historic tribute to Brahms in waltz-time makes a fascinating study, with two early recordings of the first *Liebeslieder
Waltzes* – one very Viennese, one very French – set in contrast
and the Opus 39 *Waltzes* offered in a variety of performances,
with the popular *Waltz in A flat*, as well as two others,
appearing in no fewer than three versions each, from Backhaus solo, from Wührer and Von Nordberg in Vienna and
from Lipatti and Boulanger in Paris, all very different and
equally winning. The vocal teams in the *Liebeslieder Waltzes*
are strikingly different too, with the Viennese much slower
and more inclined to linger, with voices beautifully blended,
where the Parisian performances are brisk and incisive, with
voices (not least Hugues Cuénod's high tenor) clearly separated, despite the limited mono recording of 1937. Good,
smooth transfers.

Motets

Sacred motets: *Ach, arme Welt, du trügest mich, Op. 110; Es
ist das Heil uns kommen her, Op. 29; O Heiland reiss die
Himmel auf, Op. 74*
**(*) Paraclete Press GDCG 107. Dei Cantores, Patterson –
MENDELSSOHN: *Motets* **(*)

Brahms's *Es ist das Heil* owes a debt to Bach in its four-part
chorale followed by a five-part fugue, where the part-writing
could be more sharply delineated. But the other two works
have a simple eloquence which is well caught by these persuasively committed performances, beautifully recorded.

*Ave Maria, Op. 12; 3 Fest- und Gedenksprüche, Op. 109;
Geistliches Lied, Op. 30; 2 Motets, Op. 29; 2 Motets, Op. 74; 3
Motets, Op. 110; Psalm 13, Op. 27*
(BB) *** Naxos 8.553877. St Bride's Ch., R. Jones; Morley
(organ)

Throughout his composing career, from his Hamburg days
onwards, Brahms was devoted to writing choral music, both
religious and secular, superbly crafted. In their first recording,
Robert Jones and the choir of St Bride's, Fleet Street, give
fresh, clear performances. They are beautifully scaled to give
the illusion of church performance, helped by warm, atmospheric recording.

*3 Fest- und Gedenksprüche, Op. 109; Marienlieder, Op. 22; 2
Motets, Op. 29; 2 Motets, Op. 74; 3 Motets, Op. 110*
*** Chan. 9671. Danish Nat. R. Ch., Parkman

The programme from the Danish Radio Choir is made
especially attractive by the inclusion of the seven *Marienlieder*, which include some of Brahms's simplest and most
beautiful lyrical inspirations. They are gloriously sung by this
justly famous Danish choir, who are on splendid form
throughout the disc and are beautifully recorded.

*3 Fest- und Gedenksprüche, Op. 109; Missa canonica, Op.
posth.; 2 Motets, Op. 29; 2 Motets, Op. 74; 3 Motets, Op. 110*
*** HM HMC 901591. Berlin RIAS Chamber Ch., Creed

This collection of Brahms's *a cappella* choral music includes
the rare fragments (*Sanctus, Benedictus* and *Agnus Dei*, all set
in German, from the *Missa canonica*. There is a distinctive
advantage in having German-born singers in this repertoire,
and the performances by the RIAS Chamber Choir directed
by Marcus Creed could hardly be more eloquent, especially
the four beautiful *Festal & Commemorative Sentences*,
Op. 109. The recording is first class.

(i) *Rinaldo, Op. 50;* (ii) *Alto Rhapsody. Gesang der Parzen,
Op. 89*
(N) *** Chan. 10215. (i) Stig Andersen; (ii) Larsson; Danish
Nat. Ch. & SO, Albrecht

Brahms's cantata, *Rinaldo*, like operas by Handel and Gluck
among others, tells of the crusader Rinaldo, ensnared by the
enchantress Armida. His fellow-knights finally rescue him,
persuading him to return to the cause. Brahms's setting for
tenor soloist, male chorus and orchestra, with a text by
Goethe, moves from the ecstasy inspired by Armida to his
final mood of resolution, backed up in a stirring final chorus,
written long after the rest. It is hardly a dramatic sequence
but it is a moving one, here superbly realized by Danish
forces under Gerd Albrecht. It is very well coupled with two
other Goethe settings by Brahms, the radiant *Alto Rhapsody*,
with Anna Larsson the rich-toned soloist, and the greatest

and darkest of his shorter choral works, *Gesang der Parzen*, 'Song of the Fates'.

Die schöne Magelone (song-cycle)
(N) **(*) Orfeo C050 041A. Jarnot, with Borkh (narrator), März
**(*) Orfeo C490 981B. Fischer-Dieskau, S. Richter

The song-cycle, *Die schone Magelone*, in 15 settings of poems by Ludwig Tieck, illustrates the high-romantic story of the beautiful Magelone, wooed by the knight, Count Peter of Provence. The songs, rather than providing a narrative, merely reflect on the fairy-tale story behind them, with the baritone soloist impersonating not only Peter himself but several incidental characters. On Orfeo, the baritone, Konrad Jarnot, London-trained and latterly a pupil of Dietrich Fischer-Dieskau, with the pianist Carl-Heinz März gives a glowing performance, masterly in his control of legato phrasing, shading his voice down to honeyed *pianissimos*, as in the song he himself regards as the key to the whole cycle, expressing Peter's agony on the disappearance of Magelone. Jarnot has the advantage even over his teacher, Fischer-Dieskau, a noted interpreter of this work, that his baritone is so fresh and youthful. To hold the sequence of songs together more firmly, Jarnot has persuaded the veteran soprano, Inge Borkh, to provide a spoken narration between the songs, explaining the story. Frustratingly for those who are not German-speakers, texts and translations are given only for the songs themselves, not for the narration, with the story not even given in synopsis in the booklet.

Dietrich Fischer-Dieskau has done more than any other singer to bring this once-neglected song-cycle back into the repertory, a love-story from the age of chivalry. This Orfeo version offers a live Salzburg Festival recording, made in July 1970, and though audience noises occasionally intrude, the thrust and impulse of the reading are irresistible. As a bonus come his three encores of other Brahms songs. No texts are given nor even translations of titles.

BREIMER, Peter (20th century)
Songs and Dances of the Silk Road
(BB) *** Naxos SACD 611082; CD 8.557348. Nishizaki, New Zealand SO, Judd – CHEN GANG: *Butterfly Lovers' Concerto* ***

The *Songs and Dances of the Silk Road* by the Slovak composer, Peter Breimer, are an obvious coupling for the more famous *Butterfly Lovers' Concerto*, also based on traditional Chinese melodies. There are nine movements, all titles. The first, *A Beloved Rose*, is very seductive, and Nishizaki plays it delightfully; the second, *Half Moon Climbs*, is rather like a film theme. The others are all colourfully inventive, and one of the most attractive is the fifth movement, *Sa li Hong ba*, which opens with a romantic horn solo but is turned into a charming and jaunty dance, led by the soloist. The sixth, *Lan hua hua*, brings a melancholy flute solo, much in the style of *Butterfly Lovers*, and that is no coincidence, as the original folksong tells a similar story of a young girl forced to marry against her wishes. The boldly rhythmic No. 8 is less oriental, including bongo drums, and the final dance begins with a rhythm that would not be out of place in the music of Spain. The performances are excellent, with Nishizaki on top form. James Judd and the New Zealand Symphony Orchestra enjoy their oriental excursion and play spiritedly: their principal flute shows a natural feeling for the sinuous Chinese melodies, and the recording is first class.

BRIDGE, Frank (1879–1941)
Berceuse; Canzonetta; Rosemary; Suite for Strings; There is a willow grows aslant a brook; Serenade; The Two Hunchbacks: Intermezzi. Threads: Andante and Waltz
(BB) *** BMG/RCA 74321 98708-2 (2). Britten Sinf., Cleobury
– DELIUS: *Violin Sonatas 1–3, etc.* *** ✪

This delightful collection – originally issued on Conifer – has much in common with similar compilations of the lighter miniatures of Elgar. The beautiful *Suite for Strings* and the inspired Butterworth-like *There is a willow grows aslant a brook* are masterpieces, but the vignettes are charming, notably the *Intermezzi* from incidental music for a children's play, *The Two Hunchbacks*, and the gentle *Andante* and winning little *Waltz* from another play called *Threads*. The playing is warmly sympathetic and polished, and beautifully recorded. The new coupling is unexpected but welcome.

String Quartets 1 (Bologna); 3
(N) (BB) *** Naxos 8.557133. Maggini Qt
String Quartets 2 in G min.; 4; (i) Phantasy Quartet in F sharp min. (for piano, violin, viola & cello)
(N) (BB) *** Naxos 8.557283. Maggini Qt, (i) with Roscoe

String Quartet 4
*** Redcliffe RR 020. Bochmann Qt (with PURCELL: *Chacony in G min.*, ed. Britten ***) – Alan BUSH: *Suite of Six* **

This brilliantly follows up the success of the Magginis' earlier Naxos disc of the Bridge *Quartets 1* and *3*, completing an outstanding cycle, arguably the finest British contribution to quartet literature. The *Quartet No. 2*, written in 1914–15, represents the composer in his transitional phase from early lyrical style to late experimental, a powerful piece in three movements, with the darkly intense slow introduction to the quirky finale taking the place of a full slow movement. It won the Cobbett Prize in 1915, when the rules allowed not just phantasy quartets in contrasted sections but works in sonata form. The *Quartet No. 4* of 1937 was written for Elizabeth Sprague Coolidge – also the benefactor of Bartók – and follows No. 3 in exploiting a dissonant chromatic idiom while adopting more conventional structures. The long first movement is in sonata form, featuring wild passages with such markings as *agitato* and *frenetico*, while the central minuet is surprisingly sinister in its 'wrong-note' neo-classicism. The finale is an energetic rondo with a slow introduction. The *Phantasy Quartet*, with Martin Roscoe joining three of the quartet members, is a fine example of the Cobbett formula, in seven sections lasting only 12 minutes, another striking piece in Bridge's early style. Passionate performances and vivid recording.

The alternative version of the *Fourth Quartet* on Redcliffe is rather upstaged by this new Naxos version, fine though it is, and very well recorded. But the coupled Alan Bush *Suite* is less enticing, and the Purcell *Chacony*, in Britten's rich-textured arrangement, although it makes an attractive encore and is presented with expressive warmth and dignity, is only partial compensation. The recording is of high quality throughout.

Cherry Ripe; Enter Spring (rhapsody); *Lament; The Sea* (suite); *Summer* (tone-poem)

☙ (M) *** EMI (ADD) 5 66855-2. RLPO, Groves

Writing in the early years of the last century, the composer confidently produced a magnificent seascape in the wake of Debussy, *The Sea*, but *Summer* was free of conventional pastoral moods, while in the last and greatest of Bridge's tone-poems, *Enter Spring*, he was responding to still wider musical horizons. Groves's warm advocacy adds to the impressiveness. First-rate recording, most successfully remastered.

(i) *Enter Spring*; (ii) *The Sea*

(M) *** BBC mono/stereo BBCB 8007-2. (i) New Phil. O; (ii) ECO, Britten – HOLST: *Fugal Concerto*, etc. BRITTEN: *The Building of the House: Overture* ***

Benjamin Britten as Frank Bridge's devoted pupil conveys a warmth and depth of understanding which transform two of Bridge's finest, most ambitious orchestral works, both evocative and intensely imaginative, giving them a focus that other interpreters do not always find. The radio recordings have been very well transferred.

The Sea (suite)

*** Chan. 8473. Ulster O, Handley – BAX: *On the Sea-Shore*; BRITTEN: *Sea Interludes* ***

The Sea receives a brilliant and deeply sympathetic performance from Handley and the Ulster Orchestra, recorded with a fullness and vividness to make this a demonstration disc.

Suite for String Orchestra

*** Chan. 8390. ECO, Garforth – IRELAND: *Downland Suite*, etc. ***

*** Nim. NI 5068. E. String O, Boughton – BUTTERWORTH: *Banks of Green Willow*, etc.; PARRY: *Lady Radnor's Suite* ***

Suite for String Orchestra; Summer; There is a willow grows aslant a brook

(M) *** Chan. 6566. Bournemouth Sinf., Del Mar – BANTOCK: *Pierrot of the Minute*; BUTTERWORTH: *Banks of Green Willow* ***

Summer is beautifully played by the Bournemouth Sinfonietta under Norman Del Mar. The same images of nature permeate the miniature tone-poem, *There is a willow grows aslant a brook*, an inspired piece, very sensitively managed. The *Suite for Strings Orchestra* is equally individual. Its third movement, a *Nocturne*, is lovely. The CD transfer is excellent and one can relish its fine definition and presence.

The ECO also play well for David Garforth in the *Suite for Strings Orchestra*. This performance is extremely committed; it is certainly recorded excellently, with great clarity and presence.

The Nimbus collection is more generous and is certainly well chosen. Here Bridge's *Suite* again receives a lively and responsive performance, from William Boughton and his excellent Birmingham-based orchestra, treated to ample, sumptuously atmospheric recording, more resonant than its competitors.

CHAMBER MUSIC

Cello Sonata

*** Chan. 8499. Raphael & Peter Wallfisch – BAX: *Rhapsodic Ballad*; DELIUS: *Sonata*; WALTON: *Passacaglia* ***

Bridge wrote his *Cello Sonata* during the First World War. It is a distinctive world that Bridge evokes in the *Cello Sonata* and one to which Raphael Wallfisch and his father, Peter, are completely attuned, and they are beautifully recorded.

Cello Sonata; Berceuse; Cradle Song; Elegie; Meditation; Melodie; Scherzo; Serenade; Spring Song

*** Simax PSC 1160. Birkeland, Anvik – BRITTEN: *Cello Sonata* ***

The Norwegian partnership of Øystein Birkeland and Vebjørn Anvik is totally inside the Bridge idiom and they give fluent and impressive accounts not only of the *Sonata* but also of the companion pieces. Sympathetic performances and excellent recorded sound.

3 Idylls for String Quartet

*** Hyp. CDA 66718. Coull Qt – ELGAR: *Quartet* **(*); WALTON: *Quartet* ***

As this superb, purposeful performance by the Coull Quartet shows, the *Three Idylls*, each marked by sharp changes of mood as a phantasie-form, make up a satisfying whole, a quartet in all but name. They provide a superb bonus to a fine performance of the Elgar and an outstanding one of the Walton *Quartet*. Excellent sound.

(i) *Phantasie Quartet. Phantasie Trio in C min.; Piano Trio 2*

☙ (BB) *** Hyp. Helios CDH 55063. Dartington Trio, (i) with Patrick Ireland

The playing of the *Phantasie Trio* by the Dartington Trio is of exceptional eloquence and sensitivity. They are no less persuasive in the *Phantasie Quartet*. Their account of the visionary post-war *Piano Trio No. 2* of 1929 is completely inside this score. The Hyperion recording is altogether superb, in the demonstration bracket, perfectly natural and beautifully proportioned, and this is even more attractive on the bargain Helios label.

String Quartets 1 in E min.; 4 (1937)

** Mer. CDE 84369. Bridge Qt

The Bridge Quartet give committed and dedicated accounts of the *First Quartet* of 1906 and the much darker, searching *Quartet* Bridge completed four years before his death. The overall sound is lustreless and uninviting, and to be honest the playing could have a little more finish. However, we are not spoilt for choice in this interesting repertoire.

String Quartets 2 in G min.; 3

*** Mer. CDE 843111. Bridge Qt

Bridge's *Second Quartet*, written in 1915, immediately captures the listener's attention and brings together a sequence of movements thematically linked, each of which has a wide range of moods and tempi, fantasy-style. The *Third Quartet*, written a decade later, shows affinities with the Second Viennese School, yet, after the intensity of the argument and a haunting central *Andante*, the work has a valedictory close. The two quartets are superbly played by this eponymous group, who are right inside the music. The recording is first class.

String Sextet

*** Chan. 9472. ASMF Chamber Ens. – GOOSSENS:
Concertino, etc. ***

Frank Bridge's *Sextet* is a substantial piece that fills in the
picture of the development of the composer before the First
World War. The Academy of St Martin-in-the-Fields Chamber Ensemble plays with great eloquence.

PIANO MUSIC

*Arabesque; Capriccios 1–2; Dedication; Fairy Tale Suite;
Gargoyle; Hidden Fires; In Autumn; 3 Miniatures; Pastorals,
Sets 1–2; Sea Idyll; 3 Improvisations for the Left Hand;
Winter Pastoral*
*** Continuum CCD 1016. Jacobs

*Berceuse; Canzonetta; 4 Characteristic Pieces; Dramatic
Fantasia; Etude Rhapsodic; Lament; Pensées fugitives; 3
Pieces; 4 Pieces; 3 Poems; Scherzettino*
*** Continuum CCD 1018. Jacobs

*Piano Sonata; Graziella; The Hour-glass; 3 Lyrics; Miniature
Pastorals, Set 3; Miniature Suite* (ed. Hindmarsh); *3
Sketches.* arr. of BACH: *Chorale: Komm, süsser Tod, BWV
478*
*** Continuum CCD 1019. Jacobs

Peter Jacobs provides a complete survey of the piano music of
Frank Bridge, and it proves an invaluable enterprise. The
recorded sound is very good indeed: clean, well defined and
present, and the acoustic lively. Calum MacDonald's excellent
notes tracking Bridge's development over these years are
worth a mention too.

VOCAL MUSIC

Songs: Disc 1: *Adoration; Blow, blow, thou winter wind;
Come to me in my dreams; Cradle Song; Dawn and evening;
A dead violet; The Devon maid; A dirge; E'en as a lovely
flower; Fair daffodils; Far, far from each other; Go not,
happy day; If I could choose; Lean close thy cheek; Music,
when soft voices die; My pent-up tears oppress my brain;
Night lies on the silent highways; The primrose; So perverse;
Tears, idle tears; The violets blue; When most I wink;
Where'er my bitter tear drops fall; Where is it that our soul
doth go?*
Disc 2: *All things that we clasp; Day after day; Dear, when I
look into thine eyes; Dweller in my deathless dreams;
Goldenhair; Into her keeping; Isobel; Journey's end; The last
invocation; Love is a rose; Love went a-riding; Mantle of the
blue; O that it were so!; Speak to me my love; So early in the
morning, O; Strew no more red roses; Thy hand in mine; 'Tis
but a week; What shall I your true love tell?; When you are
old and gray; Where she lies asleep*
*** Hyp. CDA 67181/2(2). Watson, Winter, MacDougall,
Finley, Chase; Vignoles

Bridge's song output was extensive and of quality. The first
disc covers the songs from 1901 through to 1908, ending with
the *Three Songs with Viola* with Louise Winter and Roger
Chase; and the second carries them through to the Tagore
settings and Humbert Wolfe *Journey's End* of 1925. By this
time Bridge's musical language had undergone a complete
change. Not that the early songs are ever mere Edwardian
ballads, but one would be hard put to guess that they were by

the same composer as *Dweller in my deathless dreams*. All four
singers give thoroughly committed performances, and it
would be invidious to single any one of them out for special
praise. Roger Vignoles is superb throughout and Hyperion's
recording is expertly balanced. Special mention, too, for the
informative and judicious presentation.

BRITTEN, Benjamin (1913–76)

*An American Overture; Ballad of Heroes; The Building of
the House; Canadian Carnival;* (i) *Diversions for Piano (left
hand) & Orchestra. Occasional Overture; Praise we great
men; Scottish Ballad; Sinfonia da Requiem; Suite on English
Folk Tunes: A time there was; Young Apollo;* (ii) *4 Chansons
françaises*
(B) *** EMI double forte 5 73983-2 (2). (i) Donohoe; (ii)
Gomez; CBSO Ch., CBSO, Rattle

A valuable compilation from the various recordings of Britten's music, most of it rare, which Rattle has made over the
years. It is good to have the *Diversions for Piano (left-hand) &
Orchestra,* with Peter Donohoe as soloist – amazingly this was
the first version in stereo – and the most cherishable item of
all is the radiant performance given by Jill Gomez of the four
Chansons françaises, the remarkable and tenderly affecting
settings of Hugo and Verlaine composed by the 15-year-old
Britten. This fine collection is now all the more desirable at its
new bargain price.

*An American Overture, Op. 27; Canadian Carnival; Sinfonia
da Requiem; Suite on English Folk Tunes (A time there was)
Op. 90; Young Person's Guide to the Orchestra*
(M) *** EMI 5 55394-2. CBSO, Rattle

A generous single-disc anthology taken from the above compilation, which is equally recommendable.

An American Overture; (i) *King Arthur Suite* (arr.
Hindmarsh); (i–ii) *The World of the Spirit* (cantata)
*** Chan. 9487. BBC PO, Hickox, with (i) Britten Singers; (ii)
Gordon, Rigby, Mitchell, Reed

The two main works here both derive from music written for
radio productions, an epic dramatization of the *King Arthur*
story by D. G. Bridson in 1937 and the religious cantata, *The
World of the Spirit,* in 1938, using a sequence of texts prepared
by R. Ellis Roberts. Though the mature Britten style is identifiable only occasionally, the invention and imagination are
characteristic from first to last. The fanfares which open the
King Arthur music have the flavour of the film music of the
period, but with a clear, Britten-like slant. The religious
cantata, *The World of the Spirit,* follows the pattern of *The
Company of Heaven* of the previous year, but the wide range
of texts prompts Britten to use an astonishing range of
techniques. The result is a fascinating mosaic of contrasting
elements, culminating at the end of the second of the three
parts in an open imitation of Walton's *Belshazzar's Feast.* Full
texts are given. *An American Overture* makes a good
companion-piece to the radio-inspired works. First-rate singing from soloists and choir alike in the cantata, helped by full
and rich recording.

*An American Overture; Sinfonia da Requiem, Op. 20; Peter
Grimes: 4 Sea Interludes & Passacaglia, Op. 33*
(BB) **(*) Naxos 8.553107. New Zealand SO, Fredman

Myer Fredman conducts warm and purposeful performances

of this group of orchestral works from early in Britten's career. Dramatic and atmospheric points are well made with the help of a warm hall acoustic and full-ranging recording. Recommendable at super-budget price.

The Building of the House: Overture, Op. 79

(M) *** BBC mono/stereo BBCB 8007-2. ECO, composer – BRIDGE: *The Sea*, etc.; HOLST: *Fugal Concerto*, etc. ***

(M) *** BBC BBCL 4140-2. New Philh. Ch. and O, Giulini – SCHUBERT: *Symphony 9*; WEBER: *Der Freischütz: Overture* ***

Written for the opening of the Maltings Concert Hall in June 1967, *The Building of the House Overture* comes in a performance Britten conducted only two days after the première. The excitement of the occasion is carried over, even though the choral entry is initially off-pitch. A historic supplement to Britten's revealing interpretations of Bridge and Holst, well transferred from a radio recording.

When Giulini made this live recording at the Royal Festival in January 1968, Britten's overture, written for the opening of the Snape Maltings, was barely six months old. It is a dramatic rather than a polished reading, with the New Philharmonia Chorus brought in to sing the passages from Psalm 127 that distinguish this energetic but relatively lightweight piece. An unexpected and valuable addition to Giulini's discography on this disc, issued to celebrate the conductor's ninetieth birthday.

Clarinet Concerto Movement (orch. Matthews)

(BB) *** Hyp. Helios CDH 55060. King, ECO, Wordsworth – ARNOLD: *Clarinet Concertos 1–2*; *Scherzetto*; MACONCHY: *Concertinos* ***

Benny Goodman commissioned the young Benjamin Britten to write a concerto for him. Sadly, just before Britten returned to England, Goodman suggested a delay, and the composer never even sorted out the sketches. Colin Matthews, who worked closely with Britten during his last three years, has here fathomed what Britten intended and has orchestrated the result to make a highly attractive short piece, alternately energetic and poetic, with material adroitly interchanged and percussion used most imaginatively. Thea King, as in the rest of the disc, plays the piece most persuasively, making one deeply regret that it was never completed.

Piano Concerto in D, Op. 13

(M) **(*) Chan. (ADD) 6580. Lin, Melbourne SO, Hopkins – COPLAND: *Concerto* **(*)

(M) **(*) Hyp. CDA 66293. Servadei, LPO, Giunta – KHACHATURIAN: *Piano Concerto* **(*)

(i) *Piano Concerto;* (ii) *Violin Concerto, Op. 15*

(M) *** Decca (ADD) 473 715-2. (i) Richter; (ii) Lubotsky; ECO, composer

(i; ii) *Piano Concerto;* (ii) *Johnson Over Jordan: Suite;* (iii) *Overture: Paul Bunyan* (arr. Colin Matthews)

⊶ (N) (BB) *** Naxos 8.557197. (i) MacGregor; (ii) ECO; (iii) LSO; Bedford

Richter is almost incomparable in interpreting the *Piano Concerto*, not only the thoughtful, introspective moments but also the Liszt-like bravura passages. With its highly original sonorities the *Violin Concerto* makes a splendid vehicle for another Soviet artist of the time, Mark Lubotsky. Recorded in The Maltings, the playing of the ECO under the composer's direction matches the inspiration of the soloists.

Joanna MacGregor's powerful performance of Britten's *Piano Concerto* has a formidable advantage over rival versions when it includes as a supplement the slow movement from the original (1938) version of the *Concerto*, which Britten replaced with the impressive *Impromptu* when he revised the work in 1945. Though this movement, labelled *Recitative and Aria*, is too long for its material, it is good to hear the composer's first thoughts. Steuart Bedford is the ever-sympathetic conductor in this and the other two works. Earlier issued on Collins with a different coupling, this Naxos reissue of the *Concerto* offers two rarities instead, the overture for the early opera, *Paul Bunyan*, with orchestration amplified by Colin Matthews, and the incidental music which Britten wrote in 1939 for J. B. Priestley's *Johnson over Jordan*, one of his 'time' plays. Written at high speed, the score is strong and colourful but often sounds strangely unlike Britten, often more like Shostakovich. Even so, it is most enjoyable and includes one gem in the delightful dance-band parody, *The Spider and the Fly*.

Gillian Lin cannot match Richter in detailed imagination but, from her sharp attack on the opening motif onwards, she gives a strong and satisfying reading, well accompanied by Hopkins and the Melbourne orchestra.

With good, well-balanced, digital recording, Annette Servadei gives a strong, dedicated, muscular performance. She is particularly impressive in the hushed and sustained passacaglia, entitled *Impromptu*, which provided Walton with the theme of his *Variations on an Impromptu of Britten*.

Violin Concerto in D min., Op. 15

⊶ *** Warner 2564 60291-2. Hope, BBC SO, Watkins – BERG: *Violin Concerto* ***

*** Chan. 9910. Mordkovitch, BBC SO, Hickox – VEALE: *Violin Concerto* ***

*** Classico CLASSCD 233. Azizjan, Copenhagen PO, Vänskä – WALTON: *Violin Concerto* **(*)

(i) *Violin Concerto, Op. 15;* (ii) *Symphony for Cello & Orchestra, Op. 68*

(BB) *** Naxos 8.553882. (i) Hirsch; (ii) Hugh; BBC Scottish SO, Yuasa

As in the Berg *Concerto*, with which his account of the Britten is coupled, Daniel Hope sustains broad speeds in the spacious outer movements, conveying passionate intensity without expressive exaggeration. The slow passacaglia of the finale is particularly moving, from Hope's ethereal first entry to the inner meditation of the closing pages, while fast music finds him playing with sharp clarity of articulation. The cellist Paul Watkins demonstrates his formidable powers as a conductor, drawing comparably warm, sympathetic playing from the BBC Symphony Orchestra, fully and brilliantly recorded.

Lydia Mordkovitch gives an outstandingly thoughtful and intense reading. The hushed opening, which can seem just sweet and easy, here conveys mystery and expectation thanks to Mordkovitch, and the tautness and purposefulness of her bravura playing then keep the wayward structure together, helped by warmly responsive playing from the BBC Symphony under Hickox. The opulent Chandos recording, finely detailed, bringing out the richness of Mordkovitch's tone and the high dramatic contrasts of the orchestra, adds greatly to the impact.

Like the Naxos coupling of Walton's *Violin* and *Cello Concertos*, this Britten pairing is an outstanding disc in every way, not just a fine bargain. As in the Walton, Tim Hugh gives a superb reading of Britten's *Cello Symphony*, strong and purposeful, making light of the formidable technical demands and the gritty double-stopping, with lyrical moments standing out. Rebecca Hirsch gives a spacious reading of the *Violin Concerto*, her tone clear and fresh rather than warmly romantic. The scherzando writing of the middle movement is full of fun, and the elegiac close of the finale is made poignant by understatement. Full, clear recording, with timpani specially vivid.

Sergej Azizjan adopts a manner at once lighter in the quicksilver bravura passages and more intimate and poetic in lyrical writing, ending with a deeply felt account of the closing pages, one of Britten's deepest inspirations up to that time. Though some will still prefer the bigger-boned approach of Ida Haendel, such a fine and illuminating performance as Azizjan's is equally welcome, as is the coupling.

(i) *Double Concerto in B min. for Violin, Viola & Orchestra. 2 Portraits for Strings; Sinfonietta* (version for small orchestra); (ii) *Young Apollo* (for piano, string quartet & strings), Op. 16
(M) *** Warner Elatus 0927 46718-2. (i) Kremer, Bashmet;
  (ii) Lugansky; Hallé O, Nagano

Of the many works which Britten left in his bottom drawer to be discovered only after his death, none is more rewarding than this striking three-movement *Double Concerto for Violin and Viola*. What he left was the short score with indications of orchestration, which Colin Matthews had little difficulty in completing. Though the chromatic writing in the *Double Concerto* betrays something of the same influence, it is stylistically less radical than the *Sinfonietta*, warmer and more recognizably the work of Britten, with its distinctive melodies and orchestration both spare and striking. It receives a magnetic reading here from the two high-powered Russian soloists, with Kent Nagano and the Hallé Orchestra. The *Sinfonietta* comes in a version that Britten made in America, for small orchestra rather than solo instruments, and the *Two Portraits*, written when Britten was 16, offers a vigorous, purposeful picture of a friend and a reflective, melancholy one of himself, with the viola solo beautifully played by Bashmet. A revelatory disc.

(i) *Lachrymae, Op. 48a. Movement for Wind Sextet;* (ii) *Night Mail* (end sequence). *Sinfonietta; The Sword in the Stone* (concert suite for wind & percussion); (iii) *Phaedra, Op. 93*
*** Hyp. CDA 66845. (i) Chase; (ii) Hawthorne; (iii) Rigby;
  Nash Ens., Friend

Lachrymae, for viola with string accompaniment, is played here with the beauty intensified, thanks to the firm, true playing of Roger Chase. Both the *Sinfonietta* and the *Wind Sextet* movement of 1930 are astonishingly accomplished for a teenage composer, reflecting the mature Britten style only occasionally. The concert suite for wind and percussion was drawn from music for a radio production of T. H. White's ironic Arthurian piece, *The Sword in the Stone*, and brings some delightful Wagner parodies. It is also good to have the final sequence from Britten's music for the GPO film documentary, *Night Mail*, with Auden's rattling verse spoken by Nigel Hawthorne. In the dramatic scena, *Phaedra*, Jean Rigby sings beautifully but lacks the biting intensity of Janet Baker. Excellent playing from the Nash Ensemble, and first-rate recording.

(i; ii) *Lachrymae;* (i) *Prelude & Fugue, Op. 29; Simple Symphony; Variations on a Theme of Frank Bridge;* (ii) *Elegy for Solo Viola*
☛ ✿ (B) *** Virgin 2x1 5 62179-2. (i) Norwegian CO,
  Brown; (ii) Tomter – GRIEG: *At the Cradle*, etc; NIELSEN:
  At the Bier; Little Suite ***

Iona Brown gives performances of the *Simple Symphony* and the *Frank Bridge Variations* to match the composer's own. The *Simple Symphony* fizzes with youthful energy, yet Brown brings an unusually wide and expressive range to the poignant *Sentimental Sarabande* which elevates Britten's writing far beyond any suggestion of juvenilia. The *Frank Bridge Variations* have never sounded more emotionally powerful on record and in the *Lachrymae* Lars Anders Tomter is an outstanding soloist, not least in the touching full presentation of Dowland's tune in the haunting coda. He follows the *Lachrymae* with an ardent account of the solo *Elegy*. The recording is of demonstration quality. This now comes as part of an outstanding Virgin Double.

Lachrymae; Prelude & Fugue for 18-part String Orchestra; Simple Symphony; A time there was . . . (suite on English folk tunes), Op. 90; Variations on a Theme of Frank Bridge; Young Person's Guide to the Orchestra. (i) Song-cycles: *Les Illuminations, Op. 18; Nocturne, Op. 60;* (ii) *Serenade for Tenor, Horn & Strings, Op. 31. Gloriana: Courtly Dances. Peter Grimes: 4 Sea Interludes*
(B) **(*) Nim. NI 1751 (3). E. String O or ESO, Boughton;
  with (i) Hadley; (ii) Halstead

This inexpensive bargain box will seem to many collectors an admirable way of collecting Britten's key orchestral works plus the three major song-cycles. In the latter, Jerry Hadley is a dramatic and involving soloist; his is not far short of an operatic approach, with the crystal-clear projection of words and histrionic power of his singing compensating for some lack of subtlety in word-colouring. *Les Illuminations* (in easily colloquial French) is strikingly fresh and spontaneous, and in the *Nocturne*, which opens magnetically and evocatively, the orchestral playing is full of tension. Anthony Halstead's horn contribution in the *Serenade* is hardly less impressive. William Boughton shows himself a fine Britten advocate throughout, and the works both for strings and for full orchestra are most sympathetically played and certainly do not lack vitality. The recording (for the most part made in the Great Hall of Birmingham University) is outstandingly rich and resonant in a characteristic Nimbus way, while the powerful evocation of the *Peter Grimes Sea Interludes* is enhanced by the acoustic of Birmingham's Symphony Hall – one of the first recordings to be made there. Excellent value.

(i) *Lachrymae, Op. 48a. Simple Symphony, Op. 4; Suite on English Folk Tunes, Op. 90;* (ii) *Temporal Variations* (orch. C. Matthews); (iii) *A Charm of Lullabies, Op. 41* (orch. C. Matthews)
(N) (BB) *** Naxos 8.557205. N. Sinf., Bedford, with (i)
  Dukes; (ii) Daniel; (iii) Wyn-Rogers

This fine disc emanates from the old Collins Classics Britten edition and is to be welcomed back to circulation with enthusiasm. Steuart Bedford brings the keenest intelligence and intuitive feeling to everything here. The anthology spans the whole of Britten's career. The *Temporal Variations* of 1936, originally for oboe and piano, are effectively scored for strings by Colin Matthews – as, for that matter is his orchestration of *A Charm of Lullabies* of 11 years later. The elegiac, valedictory *Suite on English Folk Tunes* is touching and affecting, and Bedford's is the finest reading of it in the current catalogue. All the soloists are impeccable and the disc fills an important gap in the Britten discography with real distinction, to say nothing of economy.

(i; ii) *Lachrymae;* **(i)** *Simple Symphony; Variations on a Theme of Frank Bridge; Young Apollo, Op. 16.* **(iii)** *Death in Venice: Suite* (arr. Bedford); **(iv)** *Peter Grimes: 4 Sea Interludes & Passacaglia*

(B) *** Chan. 2-for-1 241-2 (2). (i) Montreal I Musici, Turovsky; (ii) Golani; (iii) ECO, Bedford; (iv) Ulster O, Handley

Young Apollo is particularly successful here, with vivid recording capturing the unusual textures with piano and string quartet as well as strings. Rivka Golani is a resonant soloist in *Lachrymae*, and the *Variations* and *Simple Symphony* have similar heft, helped by the rich, upfront recording. Representing Britten's operas, Steuart Bedford's *Death in Venice Suite* is well worth having, and Handley's *Peter Grimes* excerpts are second only to Previn's splendid EMI recording, helped by richly atmospheric digital sound of demonstration quality. This is one of the most recommendable of Chandos's new two-for-one Doubles.

(i) *Matinées musicales; Soirées musicales;* **(ii; iv)** *Young Person's Guide to the Orchestra;* **(iii; iv)** *Peter Grimes: 4 Sea Interludes & Passacaglia*

(M) *** Decca (ADD) 425 659-2. (i) Nat. PO, Bonynge; (ii) LSO; (iii) ROHCG O; (iv) composer

Bonynge's sparkling versions of the *Matinées* and *Soirées musicales* are here reissued, coupled with Britten's accounts of the *Young Person's Guide to the Orchestra* and the *Sea Interludes and Passacaglia.*

Occasional Overture; Prelude & Fugue for 18-Part String Orchestra; Variations on a Theme of Frank Bridge; Young Person's Guide to the Orchestra.

(N) **(BB)** *** Naxos 8.557200. LSO or ECO, Bedford

The *Occasional Overture* was written for the opening of the BBC Third Programme in 1946. It is a rumbustious piece that might almost have been written by Malcolm Arnold rather than Britten. The other works are more familiar and often recorded, but all three performances here under Steuart Beford are of the highest calibre, with superb playing from the strings of the ECO in the *Frank Bridge Variations* and *Prelude and Fugue*, and the LSO on top form in the other two works. Excellent recording too. Orginally issued by Collins, this is a genuine Naxos bargain.

Prelude & Fugue for 18 Solo Strings, Op. 29; Simple Symphony Op. 4; Variations on a Theme of Frank Bridge, Op. 10

(N) **(B)** *** ASV Resonance CD RSN 3042. N. Sinf., Hickox

This ASV reissue is notable for an outstandingly fine account of the *Frank Bridge Variations* which stands up well alongside the composer's own version. Hickox's reading encompasses the widest range of emotion and style, from the genial, exuberant bravura of the *Moto perpetuo* to the powerful intensity of the *Funeral March* and the hauntingly atmospheric, ethereal passage before the final bars. The earlier parodies have a wittily light touch; throughout, the string

playing is commitedly responsive, combining polish with eloquence, the rich sonorities resonating powerfully in the glowing ambience of All Saints Quayside Church, Newcastle. The reverberation also recalls Britten's own famous account of the *Simple Symphony*, made in The Maltings. Even if Hickox does not quite match the composer's rhythmic bounce in the *Playful Pizzicato*, he finds a strain of nobilmente in the *Sentimental Sarabande*. The *Prelude and Fugue* is comparably eloquent, although here the playing is marginally less assured. The 1987 recording is excellent.

The Prince of the Pagodas (complete)

❂ *** Virgin 7 59578-2 (2). L. Sinf., Knussen

The multicoloured instrumentation – much influenced by Britten's visit to Bali – is caught with glorious richness in Oliver Knussen's really complete version. Most importantly, he opens out more than 40 cuts, most of them small, which Britten sanctioned to fit his own Decca recording on to four LP sides. The performance is outstanding and so is the sound.

Simple Symphony, Op. 4.

(N) **(BB)** *** Warner Apex 2564 61437-2. RPO, Warren-Green – BUTTERWORTH: *Banks of Green Willow;* ELGAR: *String Serenade;* HOLST: *St Paul's Suite;* VAUGHAN WILLIAMS: *Fantasia on a Theme of Tallis* ***

A truly outstanding super-bargain anthology. Christopher Warren-Green is an underrated conductor of English music and here he is at his most spontaneously successful. The outer movements of the *Simple Symphony* sparkle with vivacity, the *Playful Pizzicato* bounces with joy and the *Sentimental Sarabande* has never been more touchingly expressive. Excellent sound.

(i) *Simple Symphony;* **(ii)** *The Young Person's Guide to the Orchestra (Variations & Fugue on a Theme of Purcell); Peter Grimes: 4 Sea Interludes*

(B) *** EMI Red Line 5 72564. (i) ASMF; (ii) Minnesota O; Marriner

(i) *Simple Symphony;* **(ii)** *Variations on a Theme of Frank Bridge;* **(iii)** *Young Person's Guide to the Orchestra; Peter Grimes: 4 Sea Interludes*

**(*) Australian Decca Eloquence mono/stereo 467 237-2. (i) ECO, composer; (ii) ASMF, Marriner; (iii) Concg. O, van Beinum

The composer's incomparable performance of the *Simple Symphony*, and Marriner's vivid account of the *Frank Bridge Variations*, are both classic versions. The stereo recordings are quite superb. Rarely have the *Four Sea Interludes* been recorded with such bite and dramatic flair as here under van Beinum. Though the *Young Person's Guide* has some wildness in the playing, the excitement of the performance makes it memorable, and the mono sound is basically full and warm.

Marriner's Minnesota accounts of the *Young Person's Guide* and the *Peter Grimes Interludes* are very well played and, if his direct approach is a little stiff, the digital sound is first rate, clean and clear, yet warmly atmospheric. The youthful *Simple Symphony* is delightfully spirited and fresh.

(i) *Simple Symphony;* **(ii)** *Les Illuminations, Op. 18; Nocturne, Op. 60;* **(iii)** *Rosa Mystica*

(M) **(*) ASV PLT 8503. (i) N. Sinfonia, Hickox; (ii) Rolfe Johnson, LMP, Glover; (iii) Eton College Chapel Ch., Allwood

Any new recording of *Les Illuminations* and the *Nocturne* is bound to be compared with the classic Decca Pears/Britten version, and this ASV recording lacks the intensity and sheer personality, not to mention the clearly detailed projection, of that classic account. However, the more atmospheric (though not blurred sound) of the ASV recording brings out other aspects of the score and the performance has its own insights. Readers who do not respond to Peter Pears will find refreshment here, with the opening of the *Nocturne*, for example, very haunting. Anthony Rolfe Johnson's approach is warmly lyrical, and he colours the vocal line with subtle detail, without any distracting idiosyncrasy, while Jane Glover's relaxed direction coaxes some lovely playing from the LMP. The sound is warm and well balanced. Hickox's version of the *Simple Symphony*, though not as electrifying as the composer's own, is beautifully played and among the best of the digital versions, and the short *Rosa Mystica* makes an unusual bonus. Texts are not included.

Sinfonia da Requiem Op. 20

(BB) *** EMI Encore 5 75868-2. CBSO, Rattle – HOLST: *The Planets* **(*)

Rattle's passionate view of the *Sinfonia da Requiem* is unashamedly extrovert, yet it finds subtle detail too. The EMI recording is admirably vivid and clear. It now comes unexpectedly coupled with *The Planets* on EMI's budget Encore label.

(i) Sinfonia da Requiem; (ii) Symphony for Cello & Orchestra, Op. 68; (iii) Cantata misericordium, Op. 69

(M) *** Decca (ADD) 425 100-2. (i) New Philh. O; (ii) Rostropovich, ECO; (iii) Pears, Fischer-Dieskau, L. Symphony Ch., LSO; composer

All the performances on the Decca CD are definitive, and Rostropovich's account of the *Cello Symphony* in particular is commanding. The CD transfers are managed admirably.

Sinfonia da Requiem; The Young Person's Guide to the Orchestra, Op. 34; Peter Grimes: 4 Sea Interludes & Passacaglia, Op. 33

(M) **(*) Virgin 5 61835-2. RLPO, Pešek

Though Libor Pešek fails to convey the full ominous weight of the first movement of the *Sinfonia da Requiem*, he then directs a dazzling account of the central *Dies Irae* Scherzo, taken breathtakingly fast, and finds an intense repose in the calm of the final *Requiem aeternam*. The *Sea Interludes* sound relatively unatmospheric, but the *Young Person's Guide* is very well detailed. The recording is comfortably reverberant.

Sinfonia da Requiem, Op. 20; Gloriana: Symphonic Suite, Op. 52a; Peter Grimes: 4 Sea Interludes & Passacaglia

(N) (BB) *** Naxos 8.557196. LSO, Bedford

In his Britten series (originally for Collins), Steuart Bedford conducts strong, idiomatic performances of these works, helped by exceptionally vivid recording. The atmosphere of the *Peter Grimes Interludes* is caught superbly, and the *Sinfonia da Requiem*, treated expansively, culminates in a radiant acount of the final *Requiem aeternam*. Recommended all the more, now that it reappears on the Naxos budget label.

Sinfonia da Requiem, Op. 20; Peter Grimes: 4 Sea Interludes & Passacaglia

☓ ✪ (M) *** EMI 5 62615-2 [5 62616-2]. LSO, Previn – HOLST: *Egdon Heath*, etc. ***

(B) *** EMI double forte (ADD) 5 72658-2 (2). LSO, Previn – SHOSTAKOVICH: *Symphonies 4 & 5* **(*)

Previn gives a passionately intense reading of the *Sinfonia da Requiem*, the most ambitious of Britten's early orchestral works, written after the death of his parents. It is warmer than the composer's own, less sharply incisive but presenting a valid alternative. So too in the *Four Sea Interludes*, with Previn springing the bouncing rhythms of the second interlude – the picture of *Sunday Morning in the Borough* – even more infectiously than the composer himself. These superb performances are presented in expansive 1970s recordings of demonstration quality. With its new Holst coupling, this is one of Previn's finest CDs, fully worthy of inclusion among EMI's 'Great Recordings of the Century'. It is a pity that the Shostakovich coupling on the alternative double forte issue is only partly recommendable: the *Fourth Symphony* is very successful but the *Fifth* fails to take off.

Sinfonietta, Op. 1

*** BIS CD 540. Tapiola Sinf., Vänskä – *Nocturne*, etc. ***

The *Sinfonietta* is busier in its textures than mature Britten; it is here presented with rare strength and warmth to make it totally convincing. It is very well recorded and comes with an attractive collection of vocal music.

Symphony for Cello & Orchestra, Op. 68

*** Virgin 5 45356-2. Mørk, CBSO, Rattle – ELGAR: *Cello Concerto* ***

(*) Russian Disc RDCD 11108. Rostropovich, Moscow PO, composer – SAUGUET: *Mélodie concertante* *

(i) Symphony for Cello & Orchestra, Op. 68. Death in Venice: suite, Op. 88 (arr. Bedford)

(M) *** Chan. 10274X. (i) Wallfisch; ECO, Bedford

This is the second recording Truls Mørk has made of the *Cello Symphony*. He is completely attuned to the Britten sensibility, playing with ardour and vision. Rattle gets a superb response from the Birmingham players and the sound is state-of-the-art, with particularly impressive depth and naturalness of perspective. The best account of the piece to have appeared for some years, and highly recommended.

Sounding less improvisatory than Rostropovich, Wallfisch and Bedford are more purposeful, and the weight and range of the brilliant and full Chandos recording quality add to the impact, with Bedford's direction even more spacious than the composer's. Steuart Bedford's encapsulation of Britten's last opera into this rich and colourful suite makes a splendid coupling.

The special interest of the Russian Disc issue is that it includes a recording of the very first performance of the *Cello Symphony* on 12 March 1964, given by its dedicatee and 'onlie begetter', with Britten himself conducting. It is not as well recorded as the version Rostropovich and Britten made for Decca not long afterwards, but there is great intensity and concentration here.

A time there was (suite on English folk tunes); Johnson over Jordan (suite, arr. P. Hindmarsh); Young Person's Guide to the Orchestra; Peter Grimes: 4 Sea Interludes

*** Chan. 9221. Bournemouth SO, Hickox

A time there was is the suite which Britten wrote at the very end of his life, characteristically original and with a new, elusive vein. The *Johnson over Jordan Suite* is drawn from the incidental music which Britten wrote in 1939 for an experimental play of J. B. Priestley, in which music and mime played an integral part. If the style is uncharacteristic of the later Britten, the colour and vitality are most winning, played here with verve.

Variations on a Theme of Frank Bridge, Op. 10

*** MDG 321 0180-2. Polish CO, Maksymiuk – BARTOK: *Divertimento* ***

Among recent accounts of Britten's youthful masterpiece, this Polish version under Jerzy Maksymiuk is among the best. Each variation is expertly shaped and well characterized, and the piece is held together very well by Maksymiuk. Rather short measure at 52 minutes, but nevertheless an issue of quality.

Variations & Fugue on a Theme by Frank Bridge; Young Person's Guide to the Orchestra; Peter Grimes: 4 Sea Interludes & Passacaglia

●━ (BB) *** Warner Apex 8573 89082-2. BBC SO, A. Davis

In his admirable British music series, Andrew Davis gives full weight as well as brilliance to these masterpieces from early in Britten's career, making a particularly attractive triptych. The *Frank Bridge Variations*, set here against the more popular Purcell set, gain particularly from large-scale treatment, with each variation strongly characterized. Excellent recording. This is one of the outstanding bargains among the Warner Classics super-bargain Apex series.

Young Person's Guide to the Orchestra (Variations & Fugue on a Theme of Purcell), Op. 34

(N) (B) *** CfP 586 1752. LPO, Sian Edwards (with DEBUSSY: *Children's Corner: 3 Pieces*: ECO Wind Ens.) – PROKOFIEV: *Peter and the Wolf* **(*); RAVEL: *Ma Mère l'Oye* ***

(*) BBC (ADD) BBCL 4005-2. BBC SO, Stokowski – BEETHOVEN: *Symphony 7* *(**); FALLA: *El amor brujo* * ✪

(M) **(*) Virgin 5 61782-2. RLPO, Pešek – PROKOFIEV: *Peter and the Wolf* (***); SAINT-SAENS: *Carnival of the Animals* (chamber version) ***

The underrated Sian Edwards, always impressive in the recording studio, does not press the earlier variations too hard, revelling in the colour of her wind soloists, yet the violins enter zestfully and the violas make a touching contrast. The brass bring fine bite and sonority, and the fugue has plenty of vitality, with the climax spectacularly expansive in the resonant acoustics of Watford Town Hall. The three pieces from *Children's Corner*, skilfully scored for wind by Graham Sheen, make a pleasing bonus, with the *Golliwog's Cake-Walk* easily the most effective.

Stokowski's 1962 Prom performance with the BBC Symphony Orchestra is quite spectacular. The whole occasion was highly charged and the quality of the orchestral response pretty breathtaking. Even if the opening is very relaxed, almost lethargic, this is a reading of outstanding personality and intensity, the sound very good for its age.

Libor Pešek and the Royal Liverpool Philharmonic Orchestra give a detailed and brilliantly played account of Britten's *Young Person's Guide to the Orchestra*. Tension is comparatively relaxed, but the closing fugue is lively and boldly etched.

Young Person's Guide to the Orchestra (with narration)

(BB) *** Naxos 8.554170. Everage, Melbourne SO, Lanchbery – POULENC: *The Story of Babar* *** ✪; PROKOFIEV: *Peter and the Wolf* ***

(M) **(*) Decca Phase Four 444 104-2. Connery, RPO, Dorati – PROKOFIEV: *Peter and the Wolf*, etc. **(*)

Using her own enthusiastically expanded version of the original commentary, Dame Edna Everage is sure to draw any young possum into the world of the orchestra. Her exuberance offsets any twee moments, and the Melbourne orchestra illustrate vivid instrumental descriptions with splendidly alive and colourful playing. The Naxos recording is excellent and, with its highly enjoyable couplings, this inexpensive triptych is warmly recommendable.

Sean Connery's voice is very familiar and his easy style is attractive. His narration should go down well with young people, even if some of the points are made heavily. The orchestral playing is first rate and the vivid, forwardly balanced recording – with a Decca Phase Four source – is effective enough. The performance has plenty of colour and vitality.

CHAMBER MUSIC

Cello Sonata in C, Op. 65

*** Simax PSC 1160. Birkeland, Anvik – BRIDGE: *Cello Sonata*, etc. ***

(i) *Cello Sonata in C;* (Unaccompanied) *Cello Suites 1, Op. 72; 2, Op. 80*

●━ (M) *** Decca (ADD) 421 859-2. Rostropovich; (i) with composer

The *Cello Sonata* was written specially for Rostropovich. The idiom itself is unexpected, sometimes recalling Soviet models, as in the spiky *March*, perhaps in tribute to the dedicatee. Although technically it demands fantastic feats from the cellist, it is hardly a display piece. It is an excellent work to wrestle with on a record, particularly when the performance is never likely to be outshone. The recording is superb in every way. It is here aptly coupled with two of the *Suites for Unaccompanied Cello*.

On Simax these Norwegian artists give as sympathetic and idiomatic account of the Britten *Sonata* as any now in the catalogue. Britten and Rostropovich command a special authority, but those wanting an alternative with up-to-date recorded sound need not hesitate.

Cello Suites (Suites for Unaccompanied Cello) 1, Op. 72; 2, Op. 80; 3, Op. 87

*** Virgin 5 45399-2. Mørk

*** BIS CD 446. Torleif Thedéen

The Norwegian cellist Truls Mørk gives richly eloquent accounts of all three suites. He produces a magnificent sound and has a flawless technique. There is an impressive sense of space, a refusal to impress us or be rushed, and a depth of insight that is quite special. Even if you have the pioneering Rostropovich set or one of its successors, you will find something new here.

Torleif Thedéen has magnificent tonal warmth and eloquence, and he proves a masterly advocate of these *Suites*, which sound thoroughly convincing in his hands, if not quite as powerful as Rostropovich in the concertos and sonatas.

Cello Suite 3

(M) *** Virgin 5 61849-2. Isserlis – TAVENER: *The Protecting Veil* ***

Steven Isserlis brings out the spiritual element in a work

which draws on traditional Russian themes, including Orthodox Church music, and such a performance relates well to the Tavener work with which it is coupled.

(i) Gemini Variations (for violin, flute & piano duet), Op. 73; (ii) 2 Insect Pieces (for oboe & piano); (iii) Russian Festival (for brass); (iv; v) A Birthday Hansel, Op. 92; (iv; vi–viii) Cantata academica, Op. 62; (iv; vii; ix; x) Cantata misericordium, Op. 69; (iv; xi; xii) Canticle II (Abraham and Isaac); (xiii; x) Children's Crusade, Op. 82; (iv; xii) 6 Hölderlin Fragments, Op. 61; (xiv) Poet's Echo
- (M) *** Decca ADD 468 811-2 (2). (i) Gábor & Zoltán Jeney;
  - (ii) Holliger, Schiff; (iii) Philip Jones Brass, Iveson; (iv) Pears, (v) Ellis; (vi) Vyvyan, Watts, Brannigan, (vii) L. Symphony Ch., LSO, (viii) Malcolm; (ix) Fischer-Dieskau; (x) cond. Burgess; (xi) Procter; (xii) composer (piano); (xiii) Soloists, Wandsworth School Boys' Ch.; (xiv) Vishnevskaya, Rostropovich

This collection is called 'Rarities' and ranges from the *Insect Pieces* for oboe and piano of 1935 and the sonorous *Russian Funeral* of 1936 to *A Birthday Hansel* (a Burns setting celebrating the seventy-fifth birthday of the Queen Mother), completed the year before the composer's death. The 1957 recording of *Abraham and Isaac*, with an eloquent contribution from Norma Procter, is new to the catalogue. The *Gemini Variations* were commissioned by the Hungarian Jeney twins, who perform the piece here. Britten's ingenuity in switching the two young performers between one instrument and another (violin, flute and piano) is never interrupted and the final cadence brings a real coup, when all four instruments are somehow sounded together.

More than anything the *Cantata academica*, written for Basle University, is an expression of joy and optimism, while in the *Cantata misericordium* (telling the story of the Good Samaritan) the composer's theme is the resolution of stress in peace and tranquillity which come from within. At its close the beautiful *Dormi nunc* ('Sleep now') in a gentle 9/8 rhythm makes a blissful resolution.

The *Children's Crusade* is darker, a setting of a Brecht poem which in the most direct way, with vivid percussion effects, tells of children lost in Poland in 1939. *The Poet's Echo*, Britten's setting of Pushkin in the original Russian, was written for Vishnevskaya. Her voice, with its Slavonic unevenness, is not the most suited in controlling the subtle line of such delicate songs, but with the help of her husband the performance is warm and highly atmospheric. The six *Hölderlin Fragments*, with Peter Pears responding eloquently, reflect a highly individual response to the German language and the sensitive word-painting of Hölderlin. (Surprisingly for Decca, no translations are included for either of these cycles.)

(i; ii) Lachrymae; (ii; iii; iv) Canticle 3: Still falls the rain, Op. 55; (iii; v) Our Hunting Fathers; (ii; iii) Who are these children?, Op. 84
- (M) (**(*)) BBC mono/stereo BBCB 8014-2. (i) Major; (ii) composer (piano); (iii) Pears; (iv) Brain; (v) LSO, composer

Our Hunting Fathers created something of a scandal when it was first performed, at the Norwich Festival in 1936, thanks to its anti-blood-sports theme, prompted by W. H. Auden. The composer in his interpretation here, biting and urgent to the point of violence in climaxes, reflects what he must have felt in writing the work. Pears is in superb voice too, focused

sharply in this rather dry mono BBC studio recording of 1961. In *Lachrymae*, the playing of Britten at the piano magnetizes the ear almost as in an improvisation, with the viola player Margaret Major characteristically warm in a beautifully sustained reading.

Who are these children? may initially seem a relatively lightweight piece, but it only serves to intensify, by contrast, the darkness of the four more substantial war-inspired songs, with both Britten and Pears at their finest. It is good, too, to have this 1956 Aldeburgh Festival account of the *Canticle No. 3* with Dennis Brain as horn soloist, warm even in face of a dry acoustic. The big snag is the absence of texts – particularly serious in the case of the little-known Soutar poems.

6 Metamorphoses after Ovid, Op. 49; Phantasy Quartet, Op. 2; 2 Insect Pieces; Temporal Variations
- **(*) MDG MDG 3010925-2. Schmalfuss, with Mannheim Qt (members) or Watanabe

(i) 6 Metamorphoses after Ovid; (i; ii) Phantasy Quartet (for oboe, violin, viola & cello), Op. 2; (i; iii) 2 Insect Pieces; Temporal Variations; (iii) Holiday Diary, Op. 5; Night Piece; 5 Waltzes
- (BB) *** Hyp. Helios CDH 55154. (i) Francis; (ii) Delmé Qt (members); (iii) Dussek

(i) 6 Metamorphoses after Ovid; (ii) 2 Insect Pieces; (iii) Suite for Harp, Op. 83
- *** Mer. (ADD) CDE 84119. (i–ii) Watkins; (ii) Ledger; (iii) Ellis – Tit for Tat, etc. ***

Sarah Francis has long had a special association with Britten's oboe music, studying the *Ovid* pieces with the composer himself. She gives strong and distinctive characterizations not only to those six unaccompanied pieces but also to the early *Phantasy Quartet* and to the pieces for oboe and piano as well. Michael Dussek proves a magnetic interpreter of the solo piano music, bringing out the sparkle of the boyhood waltzes (or 'Walztes' as Britten originally called them) and the *Holiday Diary*. He then finds intense poetry and magic in the *Night Piece*, written for the first Leeds Piano Competition, with deliberately awkward keyboard layout.

Sarah Watkins gives biting and intense performances of the unaccompanied *Metamorphoses*, as well as the two early *Insect Pieces* with Philip Ledger. The sound is full and immediate, set convincingly in a small but helpful hall. It was for Osian Ellis that Britten wrote the *Harp Suite*, and Ellis remains the ideal performer.

Gernot Schmalfuss plays expertly and is excellently supported by the pianist Mamiko Watanabe and members of the Mannheim Quartet. Excellent recording, too, though it is not very realistically marketed – 46′ 47″ seconds' playing time is rather short measure for a premium-price disc.

String Quartets: in F (1928); in D (1931); 2, Op. 36
- *** Chan. 9664. Sorrel Qt

String Quartets 1 in D, Op. 25; 2 in C, Op. 36; 3 Divertimenti
- (BB) *** Naxos 8.553883. Maggini Qt

String Quartet 3, Op. 94; Quartettino (1930); Alla marcia (1933); Simple Symphony
- (BB) *** Naxos 8.554360. Maggini Qt

String Quartets 1–3; 3 Divertimenti
- (M) *** EMI 5 57968-2 (2). Belcea Qt

String Quartet 1 in D, Op. 25

(M) *** CRD 3351. Alberni Qt – SHOSTAKOVICH: *Piano Quintet* ** (*)

String Quartet 1 in D, Op. 25; 3 Divertimenti, Op. 36

☛ ✿ *** Challenge CC 72106. Brodsky Qt –
TCHAIKOVSKY: *String Quartet 1* *** ✿ (Available from www.challengeclassics.com)

String Quartets 2 in C, Op. 36; 3, Op. 94

☛ *** Challenge CC 72099. Brodsky Qt

(M) *** CRD 3395. Alberni Qt

(i) *String Quartets 2–3*; (ii) *Sinfonietta, Op. 1*

(M) *** Decca (ADD) 475 051-2. (i) Amadeus Qt. (ii) V. Octet (members)

String Quartet 3, Op. 94

*** ASV CDDCA 608. Lindsay Qt – TIPPETT: *Quartet 4* ***

It is a revelation to find Britten at fourteen strongly influenced by Beethoven. This première recording by the Sorrel Quartet of the *F major* work of 1928, his first written under the tutelage of Frank Bridge, is strong and confident, with hints of later Britten. The *D major Quartet* of 1931 was revised by the composer himself not long before he died, tonally equivocal, with hints of Bergian influence. Warmly performed, they make a fine coupling for the magnificent *Second Quartet*, here made to start waywardly, leading to a passionate, concentrated reading, helped by wide-ranging sound.

In a compact two-disc package, the Belcea Quartet offer outstanding performances of all Britten's works for string quartet published in the composer's lifetime: the three numbered *Quartets* plus the brightly inventive *Divertimenti* of 1936, assembled from pieces written earlier. With the help of warm, full recorded sound, these are performances which from first to last bring out the originality of the timbres which Britten created in all the numbered *Quartets*, from the ethereal sounds at the start of the *Quartet No. 1* onwards. As a string player himself, his approach to matching and contrasting the four instruments was remarkably adventurous. It is a point which the Belcea fully appreciate, giving warmly idiomatic performances, regularly with a sense of fantasy. In the *Quartet No. 2* the Belcea players give a performance of high contrasts, finding mystery in the *pianissimos* of the long final *Chacony*, set against powerful climaxes. Mystery is an important element too in the rarefied writing of the *Quartet No. 3*, Britten's last major work. EMI earlier issued an excellent set by the Endellion Quartet of all the quartet music written by Britten, including the early works published posthumously. Yet in their chosen works, the key ones, the Belcea versions are even finer, unlikely to be surpassed. They are certainly well recorded by the John Fraser–Arne Akselberg team in the sympathetic acoustic of Potton Hall, Suffolk.

The spontaneity of the playing of the Brodsky Quartet immediately grips the listener, with the gleamingly luminous opening of the *D major Quartet* bringing a raptly concentrated pianissimo, and this degree of intensity pervades the whole performance. The crisply impetuous, sardonic Scherzo and the deep feeling of the *Andante calmo* contrast with the bustle of the finale, its fugato and broad lyrical melody jostling with each other for our attention. The *Three Divertimenti* of 1936 are equally vividly characterized, the flimsy central *Waltz* delectably slight and transparent and

full of charm. The recording could hardly be more real and present.

The Maggini give clean, direct performances of the first two numbered quartets, not as intense as some but fresh and thoughtful, well coupled with the three colourful *Divertimenti* of 1936. Clean, slightly distanced sound. This makes a formidable bargain as its competitors all involve more than one disc.

The Maggini's second CD is even finer than their first. They give a strongly characterized reading of Op. 94. The *Poco adagio* of the *Quartettino* is particularly searching, while the account of the *Simple Symphony* (which opens the programme) is as sprightly and sparkling as you could wish. First-class recording. The almost Mahlerian *Alla marcia* is the musical source of the penultimate movement of the song-cycle, *Les Illuminations*, written six years later. This pair of Naxos discs all but trumps the opposition.

The Brodsky Quartet follow up their outstanding account of Britten's *First Quartet* with an equally dedicated and passionate account of the *Second*, with its forceful *Chaconne*, written in 1945 to commemorate the 250th anniversary of Purcell's death. That movement is contrasted with the Brodskys' approach to the brooding *Passacaglia* of the *Third Quartet*, a spare, seemingly wayward, but valedictory work, with great depth of feeling, written at the very end of the composer's life. Both these performances embody the seemingly spontaneous response that illuminated their account of No. 1, and the recording, made at the Snape Maltings, is fully worthy of the playing.

Comparison with the Alberni performances (which are less smoothly integrated) shows the latter's sharp appreciation of the seemingly fragmentary pattern of argument of No. 3; the Alberni, too, have good ensemble and intonation. Moreover this is playing from the heart, vividly recorded and strongly characterized. However, first choice lies with the Belcea and Brodsky performances, while the Naxos discs offer a splendid bargain alternative and are more generous too.

The *Third Quartet* was written for the Amadeus, who play it convincingly, finding an underlying depth of feeling which comes to the surface in its brooding *Passacaglia*. The *Second* ends with a forceful *Chaconne*. The contrasts of style are developed well here, in performances which in their day were considered definitive. The *Sinfonietta* was written when Britten was in his teens, its style pointing towards central Europe, so the 1965 Viennese chamber performance seems thoroughly appropriate.

The Lindsay performance also brings one of the most expansive and deeply expressive readings on record. The ASV recording is vivid, with fine presence; but extraneous sounds are intrusive at times: heavy breathing, snapping of strings on finger-board, etc.

Suite for Violin & Piano, Op. 6

(B) *** EMI Début 5 72825-2. Zambrzycki-Payne, Presland –
GRIEG: *Violin Sonata 3*; SZYMANOWSKI: *Violin Sonata, Op. 9* ***

Unlike some Début releases which concentrate on pieces that serve more purpose as a visiting card for the artist than as a useful addition to the catalogue, this makes good sense on both scores. The Britten is a rarity, and though there is a rival account this has tremendous personality and life. What an imaginative and characterful piece it is! Rafal Zambrzycki-Payne's partner, Carole Presland, is a superb player too. The Abbey Road recording is expertly balanced and sounds very natural. A most desirable disc.

VOCAL MUSIC

Advance Democracy; (i) *A Boy Was Born, Op. 3; 5 Flower Songs, Op. 47; Sacred and Profane, Op. 91*
*** Chan. 9701. Finzi Singers; (i) Lichfield Cathedral Choristers, Spicer

Advance Democracy, with its adventurous choral writing, sets the seal on a wide-ranging group of works representing Britten: both early (the nativity cantata, *A Boy Was Born,* written at the age of 19) and late (*Sacred and Profane,* dating from 1975, the year before Britten died, which poignantly sets death-obsessed medieval lyrics). The five *Flower Songs,* written in 1949, demonstrate Britten's gift for writing occasional music, pointful and elegant. Under Paul Spicer the Finzi Singers give virtuoso performances, vividly caught in the warm and atmospheric Chandos recording.

A.M.D.G.; Chorale after an Old French Carol; 5 Flower Songs; Hymn to the Virgin; Sacred and Profane, Op. 91; Gloriana: Choral Dances
*** Hyp. CDA 67140. Polyphony, Layton

Under Stephen Layton the brilliant group, Polyphony, give superb performances of a wide range of Britten's unaccompanied choral music, from the *Hymn to the Virgin,* written in 1930 when the teenage composer was confined to the school sickbay, to *Sacred and Profane,* one of his last works, settings of medieval texts both religious and secular. Originally written for solo voices, they present a formidable challenge for a choir, taken up masterfully by Polyphony. They combine refinement and strength equally in the other, widely varied works, from the delicate *Flower Songs* to the often lusty dances from the Elizabethan opera, *Gloriana,* incisively done. *A.M.D.G.* is a work not performed until long after Britten's death, sensitive settings of poems by Gerard Manley Hopkins, written in 1939 when Britten was in the United States, and remaining unperformed, when Britten and Pears stayed on in America for three years. Finely balanced sound to match the refined beauty of the performances.

Antiphon; Festival Te Deum; Hymn to St Cecilia; A Hymn of St Columba; Hymn to St Peter; Hymn to the Virgin; Jubilate Deo; Missa brevis; Rejoice in the Lamb; Te Deum in C. (Organ) Prelude & Fugue on a Theme of Vittoria
⊶ (BB) *** Naxos 8.554791. St John's College Ch., Robinson

This collection of 11 choral works may omit the much-recorded *Ceremony of Carols* but as a result it gives a wider view of Britten's achievement in this area, with Barry Holden's excellent notes relating each work to the composer's career and personal associations. The biting attack of these young singers is enhanced by refined recording which thrillingly brings out the wide dynamic contrasts. The *Prelude and Fugue* for organ with its elaborate counterpoint is also brilliantly done. The booklet includes full texts.

A Boy Was Born, Op. 3; A Ceremony of Carols, Op. 28; Rejoice in the Lamb, Op. 30
**(*) Australian Decca Eloquence 467 612-2. Masters, Barley, King's College, Cambridge, Ch., Cleobury

Stephen Cleobury's refined, beautifully controlled readings from 1990, originally on Argo, now reappear on Australian Decca's Eloquence label. This was always an excellent grouping of these three early Britten works, all with the sound of boy trebles as a source of inspiration. These performances, set

against a reverberant acoustic, may lack the bite and earthiness of the readings Britten himself is known to have preferred, but they have plenty of energy and can still be recommended as they possess a character of their own.

A Boy Was Born; Christ's Nativity; Hymn to the Virgin; Jubilate in C; Shepherd's Carol; Te Deum in C
*** Hyp. CDA 66285. Gritton, Wyn-Rogers, Holst Singers, St Paul's Cathedral Choristers, Layton; Goode (organ)

Here is a disc to illustrate Britten's special fascination with the Christmas story, including *Christ's Nativity*. The writing has many bold and original touches typical of the mature composer, not least in the opening cries of *Awake!* Steven Layton conducts a finely controlled performance, full of sharp dynamic and rhythmic contrasts. Despite speeds slower than usual, the performance of the cantata *A Boy Was Born,* of 1934, has similar merits, with the *Jubilate* and *Te Deum* made the more vigorous by the organ accompaniment of David Goode. Atmospheric, spacious choral sound.

A Boy Was Born; Festival Te Deum, Op. 32; Rejoice in the Lamb, Op. 30; A Wedding Anthem, Op. 46
*** Hyp. CDA 66126. Corydon Singers, Westminster Cathedral Ch., Best; Trotter (organ)

All the works included here are sharply inspired. The refinement and tonal range of the choirs could hardly be more impressive, and the recording is refined and atmospheric to match.

Canticles 1–5
*** Hyp. CDA 66498. Rolfe Johnson, Chance, Opie, Vignoles, Williams, Thompson – PURCELL, arr. BRITTEN: *An Evening Hymn*, etc. ***

Canticles 1, My beloved is mine, Op. 40; 2, Abraham and Isaac, Op. 51; 3, Still falls the rain, Op. 55; 4, Journey of the Magi, Op. 86; 5, Death of St Narcissus, Op. 89. A Birthday Hansel. arr. of PURCELL: *Sweeter than roses*
(M) *** Decca (ADD) 425 716-2. Pears, Hahessy, Bowman, Shirley-Quirk, Tuckwell, Ellis, composer

Canticles 1–5; Folksongs, arr. Britten: *The ash grove; The plough boy; The foggy, foggy dew; Greensleeves; O Waly Waly; The Salley Gardens; There's none to soothe*
*** Virgin 5 45525-2. Bostridge, Daniels, Maltman, Drake, with Brown, Brewer

The Decca CD brings together on a single record all five of the miniature cantatas to which Britten gave the title 'Canticle', plus the *Birthday Hansel,* written in honour of the seventy-fifth birthday of Queen Elizabeth the Queen Mother, and a Purcell song-arrangement. A beautiful collection as well as a historical document, with recording that still sounds well.

Ian Bostridge's heady tenor is ideally suited to the inflexions of Britten's music, and he gives colourful, vigorously dramatic readings of pieces that can seem wayward, helped by inspired accompaniment from Julius Drake. The longest of the five, No. 2, setting the story of Abraham and Isaac in the words of the Chester Miracle Play, brings the most striking performance, with Bostridge joined by the countertenor, David Daniels, each characteristically distinctive, yet well matched. The settings of Edith Sitwell and of T. S. Eliot (with Christopher Maltman as baritone) are also made the more dramatic with high dynamic contrasts, and the *Fifth Canticle,* with harp accompaniment, brings ear-tweaking textures. The seven folksong arrangements, including the most popular ones, are shared among the three singers. Excellent recording.

The Hyperion versions make an excellent alternative. Rolfe Johnson's tenor is sweeter even than Pears's, most of all in the fifth of the *Canticles*, *The Death of St Narcissus*, written with harp accompaniment at the very end of Britten's life. Like the fourth, *The Journey of the Magi*, it sets a T. S. Eliot poem. The three Purcell realizations are shared among the soloists, one apiece, all representing Purcell at his most beautiful and intense.

(i) *Canticles 1–3.* Folksong arrangements: *The ash grove; La belle est au jardin d'amour; The bonny Earl o' Moray; The brisk young widow; Ca' the yowes; Come you not from Newcastle?; The foggy, foggy dew; The Lincolnshire poacher; Little Sir William; The minstrel boy; O can ye sew cushions?; Oliver Cromwell; O Waly, Waly; The plough boy; Quand j'étais chez mon père; Le roi s'en va-t'en chasse; The Salley Gardens; Sweet Polly Oliver; The trees they grow so high.* Song-cycles: *On this Island, Op. 11; 7 Sonnets of Michelangelo, Op. 22; Winter Words, Op. 52*

(M) *** EMI (ADD) 5 73995-2 (2). Tear, Ledger; (i) with Bowman; Tuckwell

Tear, trained in the Aldeburgh tradition, gives renderings that are both individual and authentic, but his performances cannot quite match those on Decca (see above). However, they are still very sensitive, and the mid-1970s stereo is even more atmospheric than on the earlier disc. The use of a counter-tenor (Bowman) for the second voice in *Abraham and Isaac* allows the eerie setting of God's words (the two soloists in octaves) to be more smoothly matched to produce an aptly disembodied effect.

Tear is at his freshest and most communicative in the three cycles and the folksong arrangements. It was a generous idea to include not only the intensely atmospheric Hardy settings of *Winter Words* and the deeply expressive Michelangelo settings but also the rarer settings of Auden (*On this island*), which date from the beginning of Britten's career. These last may be less felicitous than the later songs, but they are still strikingly individual. In the folksongs, close as Tear's interpretations are to those of Peter Pears, he has a sparkle of his own, helped by the resilient accompaniment of Philip Ledger. In any case, some of these songs are unavailable in Pears versions, and the EMI collection is a delight on its own account. *Oliver Cromwell* (which ends the first of the two discs) is among the most delectable of pay-off songs ever written. Excellent recording throughout.

Canticle 1; Folksong arrangements: Down by the Salley Gardens; Little Sir William; The trees they grow so high; O Waly Waly; 7 Sonnets of Michelangelo, Op. 22; Winter Words, Op. 52

(BB) *** Hyp. CDH 55067. Rolfe Johnson, Johnson

In this 1985 recording, now reissued at bargain price, the *Michelangelo Sonnets* have a freshness and exuberance apt for that earliest of the song-cycles with piano, and the folksongs are deliciously pointed, notably *Little Sir William*. Even more valuable are the first of the *Canticles*, setting an equivocal poem by the Jacobean Francis Quarles, as well as the Hardy song-cycle, *Winter Words*, which contains some of the most striking and atmospheric of all Britten's songs, exactly evoking the world of Hardy. Graham Johnson proves an ideal accompanist. Refined, well-balanced sound.

(i) *A Ceremony of Carols;* (ii) *A Boy Was Born; Jesus, as Thou art our Saviour; Shepherd's Carol*

(M) *** ASV CDWHL 2097. Christ Church Cathedral Ch., Grier; with (i) Kelly; (ii) Bicket (with collection: 'Carols from Christ Church' ***)

A first-class account of Britten's *Ceremony of Carols*, attractively vigorous, full of rhythmic energy. There is an earthy quality which reflects the composer's own rejection of over-refined choirboy tone, yet the two treble solos are both delicate and radiantly assured. The dialogue *Shepherd's Carol* is also sung most effectively. The reissue is combined with a dozen carols by various composers, mainly English, making for an enticing Christmas CD.

(i) *A Ceremony of Carols.* (ii) *Deus in adjutorium meum; Hymn of St Columba; Hymn to the Virgin; Jubilate Deo in E flat; Missa brevis, Op. 63*

*** Hyp. CDA 66220. Westminster Cathedral Ch., Hill; (i) with S. Williams; (ii) J. O'Donnell (organ)

Particularly impressive here is the boys' singing in the *Ceremony of Carols*, where the ensemble is superb, the solo work amazingly mature and the range of tonal colouring a delight. Along with the other, rarer pieces, this is an outstanding collection, beautifully and atmospherically recorded.

(i) *A Ceremony of Carols; Festival Te Deum; Hymn to St Cecilia;* (ii) *Jubilate Deo;* (i) *Missa brevis in D;* (ii) *Rejoice in the Lamb* (Festival Cantata); *Te Deum in C*

(M) *** EMI (ADD) 5 62796-2. Soloists, King's College, Cambridge, Ch., (i) Willcocks; (ii) Ledger

A worthy inclusion in EMI's 'Great Artists of the Century' series. The King's trebles may have less edge in the *Ceremony of Carols* than their Cambridge rivals at St John's College, and the *Missa brevis* can certainly benefit from a throatier sound, but the results here are dramatic as well as beautiful. Philip Ledger's 1974 version of the cantata *Rejoice in the Lamb* has timpani and percussion added to the original organ part. Here the biting climaxes are sung with passionate incisiveness, while James Bowman is in his element in the delightful passage which tells you that 'the mouse is a creature of great personal valour'. The *Te Deum* setting and *Jubilate* make an extra bonus and are no less well sung and recorded.

(i; ii) *A Ceremony of Carols;* (i; iii) *Friday Afternoons, Op. 7; Francie; King Herod and the cock; The oxen;* (i) *Sweet was the song;* (iv) *Song: The birds;* (iv; v; iii) *3 2-part Settings of Walter de la Mare: The Ride-by-nights; The Rainbow; The Ship of Rio. A Wealden Trio*

(BB) *** Naxos 8.553183. (i) New L. Children's Ch., Corp; (ii) Kanga; (iii) Wells; (iv) Hopper; (v) Attree; Kenyon

Ronald Corp directs bright, refreshing performances of a delightful collection of Britten choral pieces written for children's voices. The New London Children's Choir is relatively large and is recorded against a lively hall acoustic, but there is no lack of impact, and the tenderness of expression as well as the liveliness is consistently refreshing. Though the *Processional* is recorded statically, losing in atmosphere, the *Ceremony of Carols* brings ensemble remarkably crisp for a biggish choir, and these performances justify the decision to have full ensemble treatment for all of the *Friday Afternoons* sequence. A splendid bargain.

(i) *A Ceremony of Carols; Hymn to St Cecilia; Hymn to St Peter; Hymn to the Virgin; Te Deum in C*

(BB) *** ASV Resonance CD RSN 3007. Christ Church Cathedral Ch., Grier; (i) with Kelly

On ASV Christ Church Cathedral Choir gives attractively vigorous performances, full of the right sort of rhythmic energy for these strongly characterful choral works. There is an earthy quality that reflects the composer's own rejection of over-refined choirboy tone, but the *Hymn to St Cecilia* with its setting of a brilliant Auden poem is a degree too rough, and it loses some impact when the choir is rather backwardly balanced.

(i) *A Ceremony of Carols;* (ii) *St Nicholas*

(M) *** EMI (ADD) 5 65112-2. King's College Ch., Willcocks; with (i) Ellis; (ii) Tear, Russell, Cambridge Girls' Ch.

The King's trebles may have less edge than their rivals at St John's College but, felicitously partnered by Osian Ellis, their performance of Britten's most famous choral work is both beautiful and full of character. In *St Nicholas*, though the balance of the solo voices – the Saint as a boy and a man respectively – is rather too close, the performance is vivid and dramatic, with particularly fine contributions from the trebles of the choir, belying the old idea that their style was too pure to be adapted to rugged modern works. A delightful coupling.

(i) *4 Chansons françaises; Les Illuminations;* (ii) *Serenade for Tenor, Horn & Strings*

(M) **(*) Chan. 10192X. (i) Lott; (ii) Rolfe Johnson, Thompson; RSNO, Thomson

Felicity Lott gives a strong and sensitive performance of the four *French Songs*, as she does of the other early French cycle on the disc, *Les Illuminations*, bringing out the tough and biting element rather than the sensuousness. Anthony Rolfe Johnson, soloist in the *Serenade*, gives a finely controlled performance, but Michael Thompson is not as evocative in the horn solo as his most distinguished predecessors. Bryden Thomson draws crisp, responsive playing from the SNO, and this is the more attractive at mid-price.

(i) *4 Chansons françaises;* (ii) *Our Hunting Fathers;* (i) *Serenade for Tenor, Horn and Strings*

(N) (BB) *** Naxos 8.557206. (i) Lott; Bryn-Julson; ECO, Bedford

In the anti-blood-sports cantata, *Our Hunting Fathers*, Phyllis Bryn-Julson is refreshingly fluent and agile, and if in the even earlier cycle, *4 Chansons françaises*, Felicity Lott could be warmer, the characterful, heady-toned Philip Langridge is superb in the *Serenade* (horn soloist Frank Lloyd). Bright, forward sound, originally engineered by Mike Hatch for the Collins label.

Curlew River (1st parable for church performance)

(M) *** Decca (ADD) 421 858-2. Pears, Shirley-Quirk, Blackburn, soloists, Instrumental Ens., composer and Tunnard

In Britten's own version, which has its own special character, Harold Blackburn plays the Abbot of the monastery who introduces the drama, while John Shirley-Quirk plays the ferryman who takes people over the Curlew River and Peter Pears sings the part of the madwoman who, distracted,

searches fruitlessly for her abducted child. The recording is outstanding even by Decca standards.

Folk Song Arrangements (complete): Volume I: *British Isles; Folk Songs* (published poshumously); Volume 2: *France;* Volume 3: *British Isles* (unpublished); *Pray Goody* (published poshumously); Volume 4; *Moore's Irish Melodies;* Volume 5: *British Isles;* Volume 6: *England;* (i) *German Folk Song* (published posthumously); (i) *Unidentified Setting*

(N) (BB) *** Naxos 8.557220/21. Lott, Langridge, Johnson (piano); Bonell (guitar); Van Kampen (cello)

(i; ii) *8 Folk Song Arrangements for High Voice and Harp;* Choral Folk Songs: (iii) *The Holly and the Ivy;* (i; iv) *King Herod and the Cock; The Twelve Apostles.* (unpublished): *The Bitter Withy* . (i; v) *14 Folksong with Orchestra* (5 French & 9 English)

(N) (BB) *** Naxos 8.557222. (i) Langridge, (ii) Ellis; (iii) Feaviour, J. Harris, Kirk, Joly, BBC Singers; (iv) Wenhaston Boys' Ch., Barnet; Norris (piano); (v) T. Allen, N. Sinfonia, Bedford

This three-disc collection was originally published by Collins as a boxed set, closely following Hyperion's two-disc set. In this Naxos reissue, the first two CDs are together in a single jewel-case, and the third comes separately. The important extras are 10 unpublished settings, as well as 14 orchestral arrangements. With Philip Langridge, Felicity Lott and Thomas Allen more positively characterful than their opposite numbers on Hyperion, and with Graham Johnson grippingly imaginative at the piano, one appreciates far more here that Britten's folksongs were not simple settings but original art songs. Among the extra 10, *I wonder as I wander* (unaccompanied, except for an interstanza commentary on the piano) is specially moving, a song that Peter Pears often performed with Britten but which was never included in the regular collection. Tantalizingly, no one has yet identified the words for one tenderly beautiful song, superbly performed here on the cello by Christopher van Kampen.

Folksong Arrangements: *The ash grove; At the mid hour of night; Avenging and bright; La Belle est au jardin d'amour; Bird scarer's song; Bonny at morn* (2 versions); *The bonny Earl o' Moray; The brisk young widow; Ca' the yowes; Come you not from Newcastle?; David of the white rock; Dear harp of my country!; Early one morning; Eho! Eho!; The false knight along the road; Fileuse; The foggy, foggy dew; How sweet the answer; Il est quelqu'un sur terre; I was lonely and forlorn; I will give my love an apple; The last rose of summer; Lemady; The Lincolnshire poacher; Little Sir William; Lord! I married me a wife!; Master Kilby; The miller of Dee; The minstrel boy; La Noël passée; O can ye sew cushions?; O the sight entrancing; Oft in the stilly night; Oliver Cromwell; O Waly, Waly; The plough boy; Quand j'étais chez mon père; Rich and rare; Le roi s'en va-t'en chasse; Sail on, sail on; Sailor-boy; The Salley Gardens; Sally in our alley; She's like the swallow; The shooting of his dear; The soldier and the sailor; Sweet Polly Oliver; There's none to soothe; The trees they grow so high; Voici printemps*

(B) *** Hyp. Dyad CDD 22042 (2). Anderson, Nathan, MacDougall; Martineau, Lewis, Ogden

Now reissued as a Dyad Double, this is a delightfully varied set, conveniently bringing together the seven volumes of folksong settings, five with piano accompaniment, and one each with guitar and harp. Jamie MacDougall, youthfully fresh and clear, has the majority of the songs, and though he may not be as characterful as Peter Pears, for whom they were written, his directness and clear diction are just as winning, undaunted as he is by singing not just in French but in Welsh for two of the songs in the volume with harp. Lorna Anderson, also fresh and clear, provides contrast in six of the seven volumes, with the second soprano, Regina Nathan, warmer in tone, singing all nine of the Irish songs in the final volume. Much of the success of the collection, certainly its variety, is owed to Malcolm Martineau, who relishes the sharp originality of Britten's piano-writing, making one regret that he wrote so few solo piano pieces. Bryn Lewis on the harp and Craig Ogden on the guitar are equally idiomatic. First-rate sound. Full texts are given in the notes.

Folksong arrangements: *The ash grove; Avenging and bright; La Belle est au jardin d'amour; The bonny Earl o' Moray; The brisk young widow; Ca' the yowes; Come you not from Newcastle?; Early one morning; The foggy, foggy dew; How sweet the answer; The last rose of summer; The Lincolnshire poacher; The miller of Dee; The minstrel boy; Oft in the stilly night; O Waly, Waly; The plough boy; Le roi s'en va-t'en chasse; Sally in our alley; Sweet Polly Oliver; Tom Bowling*

(M) *** Decca 476 1976-2. Pears, Britten

It is good to have the definitive Pears–Britten collaboration in the folksong arrangements. Excellent, faithful recording, well transferred to CD.

(i) *The Golden Vanity;* (ii) *Noye's Fludde*

⊕— (M) *** Decca (ADD) 436 397-2. (i) Wandsworth School Boys' Ch., Burgess, composer (piano); (ii) Brannigan, Rex, Anthony, East Suffolk Children's Ch. & O, E. Op. Group O, Del Mar

The Wandsworth boys are completely at home in *The Golden Vanity* and sing with pleasing freshness. The coupling was recorded during the 1961 Aldeburgh Festival, and not only the professional choristers but the children too have the time of their lives to the greater glory of God. All the effects have been captured miraculously here, most strikingly the entry into the Ark, while a bugle band blares out fanfares, with the stereo readily catching the sense of occasion and particularly the sound of *Eternal Father* rising above the storm at the climax of *Noye's Fludde*.

6 Hölderlin-Fragmente; Um Mitternacht; Who are these children?

(N) *** Hyp. CDA 67459. Padmore, Vignoles – FINZI: *A Young Man's Exhortation;* TIPPETT: *Boyhood's End ****

Mark Padmore, brilliantly accompanied by Roger Vignoles, here couples four cycles, all undeservedly neglected, on the theme of youth and friendship. In the ease of his fine control of the two Britten works, he even outshines the example of Peter Pears, for whom they were all written. On this showing, Padmore bids fair to rival Ian Bostridge among young tenors. Written in 1969, late in his career, Britten's cycle, *Who are these children?*, sets 12 brief poems by William Soutar, most of them in the Scots dialect, while the *Six Hölderlin Fragments* bring Britten's only essay in setting German verse, supplemented here by his setting of Goethe's *Um Mitternacht*, discovered only after his death.

The Holy Sonnets of John Donne, Op. 35; Harmonia sacra (realizations of Pelham Humfrey): *Hymn to God the Father; Lord I have sinned* (realization of William Croft): *A Hymn on Divine Musick. The Way to the Tomb* (incidental music for Ronald Duncan's masque): *Evening; Morning; Night.* W. H. Auden settings: *Fish in the unruffled lakes; Night covers up the rigid land; To lie flat on the back with the knees flexed.* Songs: *Birthday song for Erwin; Cradle song for Eleanor; If thou wilt ease thine heart; Not even summer yet; The Red Cockatoo; Um Mitternacht; When you're feeling like expressing your affection; Wild with passion*

⊕ *** Hyp. CDA 66823. Bostridge, Johnson

In the Donne *Sonnet* cycle, written when the composer returned in deep shock after playing at the death camp of Belsen at the end of the war, Bostridge makes one concentrate afresh on Britten's powerful response to Donne's grittily uncompromising poems. His voice may be lighter than that of Pears, but in its lyrical beauty it can encompass a wider range of tone and dynamic. So in the opening sonnet one registers the anger of the words even more bitingly than with Pears, thanks also to the inspired accompaniment of Graham Johnson. The disc also offers inspired performances of 18 of the Britten songs which earlier fell by the wayside: the four Auden settings, which include a provocatively sexual one, a dreamily atmospheric setting of *Fish in the unruffled lakes* and a jolly cabaret song. The evocative title given to this CD collection, *The Red Cockatoo*, refers to the shortest song of all, a striking setting of Arthur Waley.

The Holy Sonnets of John Donne, Op. 35; 7 Sonnets of Michelangelo, Op. 22; Winter Words, Op. 52; The Children and Sir Nameless; If it's ever Spring again

(BB) *** Naxos 8.557201. Langridge, Bedford

On these reissued 1995/6 recordings, originally available on the Collins label, Philip Langridge gives intense and dramatic performances of the three most important Britten song-cycles with piano, originally written with Peter Pears in mind. With Steuart Bedford, Britten's long-term collaborator, as accompanist, this reading of the Donne sonnet-cycle is marked by high contrasts of dynamic and tone, so that one hears echoes of Peter Grimes's music. In the other two cycles Langridge is just as expressive but is generally lighter in manner, certainly more than Pears in his recordings. Valuably, Langridge adds two more Hardy settings, originally intended for *Winter Words* but that neither fit the main pattern nor quite match the rest in imagination.

(i) *Les Illuminations* (song-cycle), *Op. 18;* (ii) *Nocturne;* (iii) *Serenade for Tenor, Horn & Strings, Op. 31*

⊕— (M) *** Decca (ADD) 436 395-2. Pears; (i) ECO; (ii) wind soloists; (ii–iii) LSO strings, composer; (iii) with Tuckwell

(B) *** CfP 575 5632. Mark Ainsley, with (i) Britten Sinf. wind soloists; (ii) Pyatt; Britten Sinf. Strings; Cleobury

(BB) ** Naxos 8.553834. A. Thompson, M. Thompson, Bournemouth Sinf., Lloyd-Jones

With dedicated accompaniments under the composer's direction, these classic Pears versions of *Les Illuminations* and the *Serenade* (with its horn obbligato superbly played by Barry Tuckwell) make a perfect coupling, with the *Nocturne* from 1960 making an ideal addition on CD. Pears, as always, is the ideal interpreter, the composer a most efficient conductor, and the fiendishly difficult obbligato parts are played superbly. The recording is brilliant and clear, with just the right degree of atmosphere, although the transfer of *Les Illuminations* is brighter than the other two works.

The ideal triptych of Britten's three great orchestral song-cycles finds John Mark Ainsley echoing the example of the inspirer, Peter Pears, in the shading and moulding of each phrase, above all in the *Serenade*, where the brilliant horn-playing of David Pyatt provides an extra reason for recommending the CfP disc. Mark Ainsley's range of expression is wide, and under pressure the voice grows a little rough, as in the final Shakespeare setting of the *Nocturne*. But that is contrasted with an exceptionally beautiful use of the head-voice, with total freedom in the upper register, as in the *Lyke-Wake Dirge* from the *Serenade*. Warm, immediate recording.

This same coupling is welcome at super-bargain price, and David Lloyd-Jones draws vivid and responsive playing from the Bournemouth Sinfonietta, with Michael Thompson an outstanding horn soloist. Adrian Thompson is a sensitive and characterful singer who understands the idiom, unafraid of high tessitura, but the microphone brings out the heavy vibrato in the voice, often as a disagreeable wobble.

Nocturne, Op. 60

(M) **(*) BBC (ADD) BBCB 8013-2. Pears, ECO, Britten –
SHOSTAKOVICH: *Symphony 14* **(*)

Nocturne; Now sleeps the crimson petal; Serenade, Op. 31
(both for tenor, horn & strings)
*** BIS CD 540. Prégardien, Lanzky-Otto, Tapiola Sinf.,
Vänskä – *Sinfonietta* ***

This vivid live broadcast performance contrasts well with Britten and Pears's studio recording for Decca (see above). Peter Pears here sounds warmer and sweeter, balanced a little backwardly and so set against a helpful ambience. The obbligato instrumentalists in each song, by contrast, are more closely balanced than in the Decca recording, adding to the impact of such a song as the Wordsworth with its terrifying timpani solo, superbly played by James Blades. Not just Blades but all the soloists here from the ECO are even more attuned to Britten's idiom than their LSO counterparts on Decca. Sadly, no texts are included.

Osmo Vänskä brings together not only the two best-loved orchestral song-cycles but also the supplementary Tennyson setting intended for the *Serenade* and the elusive work, the *Sinfonietta*, which Britten honoured as his Opus 1. Christophe Prégardien has an ideally light and sweet tenor which, even in the high tessitura of the *Lyke-Wake Dirge* from the *Serenade*, shows no strain whatever. Though one detects that he is not English, that is a tribute to his articulation, and he is totally in tune with the idiom. Excellent, spacious sound, if with the tenor soloist slightly backward.

(i) Noye's Fludde, Op. 59. A Ceremony of Carols, Op. 28

*** Somm SOMMCD 212. (i) Wyn-Rogers, Luxon,
Wilson-Johnson; Finchley Children's Music Group, Wilks

Noye's Fludde is here delightfully fresh and energetic, capturing the atmosphere of a live performance very well, with its processions of birds and animals and the off-stage Voice of God. With Benjamin Luxon providing a sonorous Voice of God, David Wilson-Johnson a characterful Noye and Catherine Wyn-Rogers a fruity Mrs Noye, all the other roles are performed sharply and incisively by members of the

group. *A Ceremony of Carols*, given with comparable freshness and confidence, makes an ideal coupling, also well recorded.

On This Island; Folksong arrangement: The Salley Gardens

(M) *** BBC (ADD) BBCB 8015-2. Pears, composer –
SCHUBERT: *7 songs*; WOLF: *7 Mörike Lieder* *** (with
ARNE: *Come away death; Under the greenwood tree*;
QUILTER: *O mistress mine*; TIPPETT: *Come unto these
yellow sands*; WARLOCK: *Take, O take those lips away* ***)

Britten's early song-cycle, set to poems by his friend W. H. Auden, is especially valuable, as he did not otherwise record it, and typically it brings a bitingly dramatic reading. Inspired performances of the Lieder by Schubert and Wolf, as well as the sharply contrasted Shakespeare settings by a wide range of British composers.

Our Hunting Fathers, Op. 8

(N) (BB) *** LPO LPO 0002. Harper, LPO, Haitink – ELGAR:
Enigma Variations, etc. ***

Bernard Haitink's first contribution to the LPO's own-label discs is outstandingly fine. The cantata, *Our Hunting Fathers*, is a curious work. The young Britten wrote it in 1936 to words by W. H. Auden for the Norwich Triennial Festival, knowing that this attack on fox-hunting would be counted provocative. The music itself is darkly original and difficult to interpret, not least for the singer, whether soprano or tenor. Not only does Haitink conduct a high-voltage performance, Heather Harper in this live (1979) recording, made during the Proms at the Royal Albert Hall, is at her peak, commandingly impressive even in the tricky song, *Rats Away*. Well coupled with noble accounts of the two Elgar works.

(i) Our Hunting Fathers, Op. 8; (ii) Serenade for Tenor, Horn & Strings, Op. 31; (i) Folksong arrangements: Oliver Cromwell; O Waly, Waly

**(*) EMI 5 56871-2. Bostridge, with (i) Britten Sinf., Harding;
(ii) Neunecker, Bamberg SO, Metzmacher

Ian Bostridge's radiantly lyrical tenor is ideally suited to the works which Britten wrote for Peter Pears, providing new insights in the *Serenade*; and the early song-cycle on an anti-blood-sports theme, *Our Hunting Fathers*, makes a welcome alternative. Bostridge gives a most illuminating account of the solos, bringing out the bite of the texts prepared by W. H. Auden, and Daniel Harding's direction is beautifully textured at spacious speeds – but next to the venom of Britten's own urgent performance it seems a degree too relaxed.

Purcell realizations: Orpheus Britannicus: The knotting song; 7 Songs (1947); 6 Songs (1948); O Solitude; 5 Songs (1960); Celemene; 6 Duets (1961). Harmonia sacra: The Blessed Virgin's expostulation; The Queen's Epicedium; Saul and the Witch of Endor; 3 Divine Hymns (1947); 2 Divine Hymns & Alleluia (1960). Miscellaneous songs (1971): Dulcibella; When Myra sings

*** Hyp. CDA 67061/2 (2). Lott, Gritton, S. Walker, Bowman,
Mark Ainsley, Bostridge, Rolfe Johnson, Jackson,
Keenlyside; Johnson

As a result of giving recitals with Peter Pears during and after the war, Britten was encouraged to make a series of realizations using the figured basses Purcell provided in his big collections, *Orpheus Britannicus* and *Harmonia sacra*. The accompaniments for piano may defy latter-day ideas of authenticity, but Britten imaginatively follows the harmonic indications given, to produce entirely distinctive results, introducing a lyricism rare in keyboard continuo. With an outstanding team of soloists and with Graham Johnson as the inspired pianist, this collection stands as a monument to the devotion of one English master to another. The first disc, drawn from the *Orpheus Britannicus* collection, includes songs like *Fairest isle*, better known in the context of *King Arthur* or other entertainments. The second, from *Harmonia sacra*, has darker, weightier and more extended items, notably the magnificent scena, *Saul and the Witch of Endor*, involving three singers and with side-slipping chromatics as daring as any Purcell ever imagined. The tenor Ian Bostridge displays high mastery and Simon Keenlyside sings magnificently in the dark, bass items like *Job's curse* and the late *Let the dreadful engines*. Excellent, well-balanced sound.

(i) *The Rescue of Penelope*; (ii) *Phaedra*
(M) *** Warner Elatus 0927 49010-2. (i) Hagley, Wyn-Rogers, Mark Ainsley, Dazeley, Baker (narrator); (ii) Hunt; Hallé O, Nagano

Soon after his return from America at the height of the war, Britten wrote the incidental music for a radio play by Edward Sackville-West on the Homeric subject of Odysseus' return to Penelope. Drawn from the complete score, with barely any amendments of the original and compressed into a 36-minute cantata with the help of Colin Matthews, Britten's last amanuensis, the result is extraordinarily powerful, with emotions intensified. The most important role is that of the narrator, here masterfully taken by Dame Jane Baker to bring the story vividly to life despite the stylized classical language – 'Odysseus, Lord of sea-girt Ithaca' or 'His fair white-armed Penelope', for example. The commentaries, beautifully sung, regularly add to the atmospheric beauty of the piece. In its richness of idiom this may not be distinctly Britten-ish, with unexpected echoes of Walton's film music and even of Wagner, but it is endlessly inventive in a very Britten-like way, not just illustrative but strong and purposeful, a valuable addition to the Britten *oeuvre*. Lorraine Hunt's performance of *Phaedra*, Britten's last vocal work, characteristically spare, may not quite match that of the dedicatee, Dame Janet, in conveying the heroine's agony, but the portrait of a deranged woman is chillingly powerful, with singing comparably beautiful and intense.

Saint Nicolas, Op. 42
(N) (M) (***) Decca Heritage mono 475 6156. Pears, Hemmings, Girls' Ch. of Sir John Leman School, Boys' Ch. of Ipswich School Preparatory Dept, Aldeburgh Festival Ch. & O, composer

St Nicholas; Hymn to St Cecilia
*** Hyp. CDA 66333. Rolfe Johnson, Corydon Singers, St George's Chapel, Windsor, Ch., Girls of Warwick University Chamber Ch., Ch. of Christ Church, Southgate, Sevenoaks School, Tonbridge School, Penshurst Ch. Soc., Occasional Ch., Edwards, Alley, Scott, ECO, Best

With rare exceptions, Britten's first recordings of his own works have a freshness and vigour unsurpassed since. *Saint Nicolas* was recorded in 1955 and possesses both those qualities, as well as atmosphere in abundance, all sounding uncannily vivid in this Decca Heritage transfer. Britten's performance captures the element of vulnerability superbly, with the children's contributions especially touching. While

the use of the original cover is a big plus point, the minuscule facsimile of the LP notes is not.

For the first time in a recording, the congregational hymns are included in Matthew Best's fresh and atmospheric account of *St Nicholas*, adding greatly to the emotional impact of the whole cantata. Though the chorus is slightly distanced, the contrasts of timbre are caught well, with the waltz-setting of *The birth of Nicholas* and its bath-tub sequence delightfully sung by boy-trebles alone. The *Hymn to St Cecilia* is also beautifully sung, with gentle pointing of the jazzy syncopations in crisp, agile ensemble and with sweet matching among the voices.

(i) *Serenade for Tenor, Horn & Strings, Op. 31*; (ii) Arr. of folksongs: *Avenging and bright; The bonny Earl o' Moray; The last rose of summer; Sally in our alley*
(M) (**(*)) Decca mono 468 801-2. Pears, with (i) Brain, Boyd Neel String O, composer; (ii) composer (piano) –
WALTON: *Façade* ***

This early (1944) account of the *Serenade*, with Pears in freshest voice and Dennis Brain's superb horn playing, has never been surpassed. The transfer from 78s is admirably faithful, complete with surface rustle, and one soon forgets the dry acoustic and early provenance of the recording. Yet surely the clicks could have been removed! Four folksongs recorded in stereo have been added for this reissue.

Songs & Proverbs of William Blake, Op. 74; Tit for Tat; 3 Early Songs: Beware that I'd ne'er been married; Epitaph; The clerk. Folksong arrangements: Bonny at morn; I was lonely; Lemady; Lord! I married me a wife!; O Waly, Waly; The Salley Gardens; She's like the swallow; Sweet Polly Oliver
**(*) Chan. 8514. Luxon, Williamson

Benjamin Luxon's lusty baritone gives an abrasive edge, whether to early songs, folksong settings or the Blake cycle. Only rarely does he become too emphatic. Excellent, sensitive accompaniment and first-rate recording.

(i; iii) *Spring Symphony Op. 44*; (ii) *5 Flower Songs* (for chorus); (ii–iv) *Hymn to St Cecilia*; (v) *War Requiem*
(M) **(*) DG 459 509-2 (3). (i) Hagley, Robbin, Mark Ainsley, Choristers of Salisbury Cathedral; (ii) Monteverdi Ch.; (iii) Philh. O; (iv) with Preston-Dunlop, Ross, Vickers, Mitchell, Savage; (v) Orgonasova, Johnson, Tölz Boys' Ch., N. German R. Ch. & SO; Gardiner

(i) *Spring Symphony, Op. 44; Peter Grimes: 4 Sea Interludes*
(M) *** EMI (ADD) 7 64736-2. (i) Armstrong, J. Baker, Tear, St Clement Dane's School Boys' Ch., L. Symphony Ch.; LSO, Previn

(i) *Spring Symphony*; (ii) *Welcome Ode, Op. 95*; (iii) *Psalm 150, Op. 67*
**(*) Chan. 8855. (i) Gale, Hodgson, Hill, Southend Boys' Ch., LSO; (ii) City of London Schools' Ch., LSO; (iii) City of London Schools' Ch. and O; Hickox

Previn makes this above all a work of exultation, a genuine celebration of spring; but here, more than in Britten's recording, the kernel of what the work has to say comes out in the longest of the solo settings, using Auden's poem, *Out on the lawn I lie in bed*. With Janet Baker as soloist it rises above the lazily atmospheric mood of the opening to evoke the threat of war and darkness. The *Four Sea Interludes*, which make a generous bonus, are presented in their concert form, with tailored endings.

With more variable soloists – the tenor Martyn Hill outstandingly fine, the soprano Elizabeth Gale often too edgy – Hickox's version of the *Spring Symphony* does not quite match the composer's own in gutsy urgency. But this CD brings the advantage of a first recording of Britten's last completed work, the *Welcome Ode*. The third work, equally apt, is the boisterous setting of *Psalm 150*.

DG now offer Gardiner's account of the *Spring Symphony* and *War Requiem* in a mid-priced package. In the former he clarifies the textures at speeds generally flowing more briskly than usual, but the result is less wild and rustic-sounding in the bluff final chorus. Both here and in the two bonuses the Monteverdi Choir sing with astonishing virtuosity, with the syncopated rhythms of the *Hymn to St Cecilia* superbly projected and the *Flower Songs* just as fresh. By contrast, the live recording of *War Requiem* is undermined by dim, inconsistent sound, with soloists and chorus from the North German Radio often ill-focused. The reading is thoughtful rather than dramatic, although not without intensity and power.

(i) *Tit for Tat;* (ii) Folksong arrangements: *Bird scarer's song; Bonny at morn; David of the White Rock; Lemady; Lord! I married me a wife!; She's like the swallow*
*** Mer. CDE 84119. Shirley-Quirk; (i) Ledger; (ii) Ellis – *6 Metamorphoses* etc. ***

John Shirley-Quirk is unrivalled in the sharp yet subtle way he brings out the irony in these boyhood settings of De la Mare poems. It is also good to have him singing the six late folk-settings with harp accompaniment, here played by Osian Ellis, for whom they were originally written.

War Requiem, Op. 66
*** Decca 414 (ADD) 383-2. Vishnevskaya, Pears, Fischer-Dieskau, Bach Ch., L. Symphony Ch., Highgate School Ch., Melos Ens., LSO, composer
☛ *** BBC (ADD) BBCL 4046-2. Woytowicz, Pears, Wilbrink, Wandsworth School Boys' Ch., Melos Ens., New Philh. Ch. O, Giulini
*** EMI 7 47034-8. Söderström, Tear, Allen, trebles of Christ Church Cathedral Oxford Ch., CBSO Ch., CBSO, Rattle
(BB) ** Naxos 8.553558/9. Russell, Randle, Volle, Scottish Festival Ch., St Mary's Episcopal Cathedral, Edinburgh, Ch., BBC Scottish SO, Brabbins (with Boddice)
** Teldec 0630 17115-2 (2). Vaness, Hadley, Hampson, American Boychoir, Westminster Symphonic Ch., NY PO, Masur

(i) *War Requiem;* (ii) *Ballad of Heroes, Op. 14; Sinfonia da Requiem, Op. 20*
*** Chan. **SACD** CH5A 5007 (2); CD: Chan. 8983/4. (i) Harper, Langridge, Shirley-Quirk; (ii) Hill; St Paul's Cathedral Choristers, L. Symphony Ch., LSO & CO, Hickox

Richard Hickox's Chandos version rivals even the composer's own definitive account in its passion and perception. Hickox thrusts home the big dramatic moments with unrivalled force, helped by the weight of the Chandos sound. The boys' chorus from St Paul's Cathedral is exceptionally fresh. Heather Harper is as golden-toned as she was at the very first Coventry performance, fearless in attack. Philip Langridge has never sung more sensitively on disc, and both he and John Shirley-Quirk bring many subtleties to their interpretations. Adding to the attractiveness of the set come two substantial choral works, also in outstanding performances. The recording is now also available on Compatible SACD with multi-channel surround sound.

Britten's own 1963 recording of the *War Requiem* comes near to the ideal. Though Vishnevskaya is abrasive in the soprano solos, she sings with incomparable emotional intensity. The recording has been carefully and lovingly remastered and it now also includes a rehearsal sequence. The vivid realism of the sound-balance now comes over the more strikingly, with uncannily precise placing and balancing of the many different voices and instruments, and John Culshaw's contribution as producer is the more apparent. A remarkable achievement.

Recorded live by the BBC in 1969, this thrilling account of the *War Requiem* finds Giulini as the principal conductor bringing the sort of biting, even wild intensity and deep dedication to Britten's score that marked his readings of the Verdi *Requiem*. The spacious Albert Hall acoustic enhances the electric atmosphere, while Britten himself conducts the Melos Ensemble just as dramatically in the Wilfred Owen settings. Peter Pears as tenor soloist is matched by the fresh, clear Dutch baritone, Hans Wilbrink, while Stefania Woytowicz is the bright, incisive soprano, alongside the New Philharmonia Chorus at its most brilliant. A bargain squeezed on to a single disc at rather more than mid-price.

With Elisabeth Söderström a more warmly expressive soloist than the oracular Vishnevskaya, the human emotions behind the Latin text come out strongly on EMI. If Robert Tear does not always match the subtlety of Pears on the original recording, Thomas Allen sounds more idiomatic than Fischer-Dieskau. Rattle's approach is warm, dedicated and dramatic, with fine choral singing (not least from the Christ Church Cathedral trebles). The various layers of sound are well managed on the digital recording, if not quite with the definition of the finest rivals.

The glory of the Naxos version, on two bargain discs, is the sound, with spatial contrasts captured thrillingly and atmospherically, and the boys' choir in particular beautifully caught, clear but at a distance. The choral singing generally is excellent, vivid and immediate in the big climaxes of such sections as *Dies irae*. Under Martyn Brabbins for the full orchestral sections, and under Nigel Boddice for the chamber orchestra settings of the Wilfred Owen poems, the BBC Scottish Symphony Orchestra plays with fine point and precision, underlining the drama of the piece. The weakness is the solo singing, with Thomas Randle sounding strained and Michael Volle unidiomatic, and with Lynda Russell's fruity soprano too often edgy and uneven.

It is always revealing to have non-British performances of British music, and Kurt Masur directs a thoughtful, dedicated reading of the *War Requiem* with three first-rate American soloists. The virtuoso chamber group accompanying the Owen poems is made up of excellent players from the New York Philharmonic, and the choirs cannot be faulted, with the off-stage boys precisely placed. That said, this does not have the dramatic intensity of the finest versions, and the soloists are not helped by a relatively dry acoustic. With no fill-up it makes an expensive purchase compared with the fine Hickox Chandos set.

OPERA

(i) *Albert Herring;* (ii) *Billy Budd;* (iii) *Owen Wingrave;* (iv) *Peter Grimes*
☛ **(N) (B)** *** Decca 475 6020 (8). (i; iv) Pears; (i; iii) ECO; (ii) Glossop, Amb. Op. Ch., LSO; (iii) Luxon; (iv) ROHCG Ch. & O; all cond. composer

An indispensable set, an obvious basis for any collection, large or small, offering the composer's definitive performances, admirably recorded between 1959 and 1971, and since unsurpassed. The documentation is sparse but adequate, including cued synopses.

Albert Herring (complete)

*** Chan. 10036 (2). Gilchrist, Stephen, Williams, Bullock, Burgess, Opie, Tear, City of L. Sinfonia, Hickox

(BB) *** Naxos 8.660107/08 (2). Gillett, Taylor, Finley, Barstow, Palmer, Savidge, Kale, N. Sinfonia, Bedford

**(*) Decca (ADD) 421 849-2 (2). Pears, Fisher, Noble, Brannigan, Cantelo, ECO, Ward, composer

Richard Hickox more than any rival brings out the fun of Britten's comic chamber opera, lifting rhythms in an infectious way. The result is warm and welcoming, helped by a full, rich Chandos recording. In the title-role of the hapless Albert, James Gilchrist is outstanding, with a tenor light enough to sound wimpish in the first half of the opera, and then to convey the anger of the character in the monologue that marks his change of heart at the end of Act II, 'Heaven helps those who help themselves'. The threnody that follows, when the whole company assumes that Albert is dead, is all the more telling with Hickox, when he conveys a quasi-religious, devotional quality to Britten's heavily ironic writing. Pamela Helen Stephen as Nancy and Roderick Williams as Sid, the two lovers, are also the more convincing for having relatively light voices, and the line-up of village characters, all of them larger than life, is taken by an excellent team, even if Susan Bullock as Lady Billows sounds rather young for such a battleaxe of a woman.

On Naxos, on what was originally a Collins recording, Steuart Bedford offers a performance that brings out the fun of the piece even more infectiously than Britten himself. It constantly gives the illusion of stage comedy rather than a studio recording. Bedford has long made a speciality of conducting this opera in the theatre, a very English piece that, amazingly, has been among the most widely appreciated Britten operas throughout the world. It helps that Christopher Gillett in the title-role has a clear, youthful-sounding tenor, whereas Pears, recording in his mid-fifties, seventeen years after the first performance, inevitably sounds old as the gawky hero, no matter how inspired his acting. As Lady Billows, Josephine Barstow, with rasp in the voice, is every bit as formidable as Sylvia Fisher was before, and Felicity Palmer is wonderfully characterful as her prim housekeeper, Florence Pike. The other village worthies are also strongly cast, while the lower orders in this class-conscious comedy are earthier and lustier than their predecessors, with the love duet of Syd (Gerald Finley) and Nancy (Ann Taylor) tenderly touched in. What seals the set's success is the way that in the ensembles – whether the fast chattering ones or the great threnody when they think that Albert is dead – Bedford secures such crispness, wittily lifting rhythms, making the music swagger. At the Naxos reissue price this is a phenomenal bargain and, like full-price sets, this one includes a full libretto.

Britten's own 1964 recording of the comic opera, *Albert Herring*, remains a delight. Peter Pears's portrait of the innocent Albert was caught only just before he grew too old for the role, but it is full of unique touches. Sylvia Fisher is a magnificent Lady Billows, and it is good to have such a wide range of British singers of the 1960s presented so characterfully. The recording, made in Jubilee Hall, remains astonishingly vivid.

Billy Budd (original four-act version; DVD version)

*** Arthaus **DVD** 100278. Allen, Langridge, Van Allan, Howlett, ENO Ch. & O, Atherton (Dir: Albery; V/D: Gavin)

Billy Budd (CD versions of original score)

*** Erato 3984 21631-2 (2). Hampson, Rolfe Johnson, Halfvarson, Manchester Boys' Ch., Hallé Ch. & O, Nagano

(**) VAIA mono 1034-3 (3). Pears, Uppman, Dalberg, Alan, G. Evans, Langdon, ROHCG Ch. & O, composer

Billy Budd (revised version; complete)

*** Chan. 9826 (3 for 2). Keenlyside, Langridge, Tomlinson, Opie, Bayley, Best, L. Symphony Ch., LSO, Hickox

*** Decca (ADD) 417 428-2 (3). Glossop, Pears, Langdon, Shirley-Quirk, Wandsworth School Boys' Ch., Amb. Op. Ch., LSO, composer (with *Holy Sonnets of John Donne; Songs & Proverbs of William Blake* ***)

Tim Albery's production of *Billy Budd* with Thomas Allen powerful in the title-role was one of the classic English National Opera presentations of the 1980s. This 1988 video version, made originally for BBC Television, with an introduction by Michael Berkeley, vividly captures the intense atmosphere. It is helped by the bare, stylized sets of Tom Cairns and Antony McDonald and by David Cunningham's clever lighting; they have one imagining the scenes with a chilling intensity that a more realistic approach could hardly match. The performance under David Atherton is outstanding, with Philip Langridge as Captain Vere, disguised as E. M. Forster in the solo prologue and epilogue sequences, bringing out the character's scholarly side, interpreting the role in a strikingly different way from Peter Pears, for whom it was written, but just as magnetically. Thomas Allen may in 1988 have seemed rather old for the role of the innocent Billy, but the power not just of his singing but of his acting too, with the voice clear and fresh, makes his performance deeply moving. Just as striking is the venomous figure of Claggart, superbly taken here with terrifying intensity by Richard Van Allan in one of his finest recorded performances. Barrie Gavin's direction for video adds to the power of the performance with imaginative camerawork. The DVD is provided with plentiful index-points.

Hickox's brilliant Chandos version of *Billy Budd*, with the finest cast of principals yet assembled, uses the revised two-Act score. In Philip Langridge the role of Vere has found its most thoughtful interpreter yet, so that from the start his self-searching is the key element in the whole work. Comparably magnetic is John Tomlinson's Claggart, the personification of evil, chillingly malevolent in every inflexion, oily in the face of authority. Equally, Simon Keenlyside as Billy gains over all rivals in the fresh, youthful incisiveness of the voice, movingly shaded down to a rapt half-tone for the lyrical monologue sung by Billy about to die. Helped by sound of spectacular quality, Hickox at marginally broader speeds conveys more mystery in reflective moments than even Britten himself did. His expansiveness means that the set spills over on to a third disc but, with three discs for the price of two, that brings no disadvantage.

On Erato we have a complete recording of Britten's original, four-Act version of his opera, *Billy Budd*, above all urgent and intense, more dramatic, less reflective than Britten's own recording for Decca of the revised, two-Act version. Not only that, Thomas Hampson brings to the title-role an extra beauty alongside heroic power. It includes the important assembly scene on the deck of HMS *Indomitable* – removed in the revision – when the crew greet Captain Starry Vere, establishing his character. It also provides a thrilling fortissimo close to the original Act I, superbly achieved in Kent Nagano's powerful performance with the Hallé Orchestra and Choir. Set against the velvet-toned Hampson, Anthony Rolfe Johnson as Vere has some grit in his voice, creating a believable character at once rugged and introspective. Eric Halfvarson as the evil Claggart is not as sinister as some of his predecessors but, apart from some roughness in the upper register, it is a forceful, incisive performance, matching the urgency of Nagano's approach. Among the others, Gidon Saks is superb as the Sailing Master, Mr Flint; Martyn Hill is most characterful as the whining Red Whiskers, and the veteran, Richard Van Allan, is ideally cast as old Dansker, with Andrew Burden clear-toned as the victimized Novice. Coming on two discs instead of three, this has a clear price advantage over existing sets.

On Decca, Britten himself has an outstanding cast, with Glossop a bluff, heroic Billy and Langdon a sharply dark-toned Claggart, making these symbol-figures believable. Magnificent sound, and the many richly imaginative strokes – atmospheric as well as dramatic – are superbly managed. The extravagant layout on three CDs begins with the *John Donne Holy Sonnets* (sung by Pears) and the *Songs & Proverbs of William Blake* (sung by Fischer-Dieskau), with the Prologue and Act I of the opera beginning thereafter. They are equally ideal performances.

Though the sound is very scrubby, disconcertingly so at the very start, the historic recording of the very first performance of the opera in December 1951 is valuable for the fresh, youthful-sounding performance of Theodor Uppman in the title-role, as well as Peter Pears as Captain Vere, clearer and more flexible than in his studio recording of 16 years later. There is no libretto. It is interesting that, though the orchestra sounds dim and limp at the start, Britten as conductor whips up searing tension through the opera.

Death in Venice (complete; DVD version)
** Arthaus **DVD** 100 172. Tear, Opie, Chance, Glyndebourne Ch., L. Sinf., Jenkins (S/D: Stephen Lawless, Martha Clarke. Producer: Dennis Marks)

Death in Venice (complete; CD versions)
(N) *** Chan. 10280 (2). Langridge, Opie, Chance, BBC Singers, City of L. Sinf., Hickox
*** Decca (ADD) 425 669-2 (2). Pears, Shirley-Quirk, Bowman, Bowen, Leeming, E. Op. Group Ch., ECO, Bedford

This Glyndebourne production of Britten's last opera offers a stark, even brutal view of a piece which originally, thanks both to Britten's score and to John Piper's sets, highlighted the beauty of Venice. With Lawless and Clarke, using bare sets by Tobias Hoheise, predominantly black, blotting out the beauty of the city on water, the result seen in close-up is claustrophobic. Robert Tear's vividly detailed, totally compelling portrayal of Aschenbach is masterly, and his characterization may prompt many to consider the set, even though the voice itself is wanting in bloom, and very different from the moving but more relaxed approach of Peter Pears, for whom the role was written. Similarly Alan Opie in the multiple baritone roles of characters dogging Aschenbach's path is far more sinister than John Shirley-Quirk, plainly representing evil, and even the boy Tadzio is finally made to leer at Aschenbach, suggesting that he is after all the messenger of evil too, something quite different from Britten's original concept. In the counter-tenor role of Apollo, Michael Chance

is also ideally cast, the opponent of evil and death, finally worsted.

But the production is another matter: the action is confined within a distinctly cramped, small arena and there is no feeling of space or sense of atmosphere. This shoe-box dimension of the sets really lets the opera down badly. Nor is the recording as ample as one could wish, and the piano sound is pretty uningratiating. Thus, vision adds little if anything to the musical experience and even detracts from it. Subtitles are provided in French, German and Spanish but there is no original English text, which at times would have been helpful. The Decca and Chandos CDs offer a far more satisfying experience in every way.

Richard Hickox's superb account of *Death in Venice*, the composer's last opera, matches and in many ways even outshines the fine model of the original recording conducted by Steuart Bedford (instead of the ailing Britten himself), with Peter Pears in the central role. Philip Langridge proves an inspired interpreter of the role of Ashenbach, more passionate than Pears, conveying the character's self-torture from the start as he faces writer's block, injecting energy when he confesses to himself that 'the boy Tadzio shall inspire me'; and in his death scene he is even more poignant. Even so, he fails to convey quite the same agony of self-realization as Pears at the end of Act I on the whispered line *I love you!* Equally, Alan Opie makes a more robust figure than John Shirley-Quirk in the seven contrasted portraits of the tormenting figures who beset Aschenbach on his fatal trip to Venice, varying them vividly. The counter-tenor Michael Chance sings even more eerily as the Voice of Apollo, helped by distancing by the engineers, while the recording throughout is even more open and vividly atmospheric than the original Decca, fine as that is. Add to that Hickox's powerful, finely timed pacing of a work which is largely meditative, and the result is totally magnetic.

Peter Pears's searching performance in the central role of Aschenbach is set against the darkly sardonic singing of John Shirley-Quirk in a sequence of roles as the Dionysiac figure who draws Aschenbach to his destruction and, though Steuart Bedford's assured conducting lacks some of the punch that Britten would have brought, the whole presentation makes this a set to establish the work outside the opera house.

Gloriana (complete)
*** Decca 440 213-2 (2). Barstow, Langridge, D. Jones, Summers, Welsh Nat. Op. Ch. & O, Mackerras

Without effacing memories of earlier interpreters, Josephine Barstow gives a splendid performance as the Virgin Queen, tough and incisive, with the slight unevenness in the voice adding to the abrasiveness. Only in the final scene when, after the execution of Essex, the queen muses to herself in fragments of spoken monologue, does her reading lack weight, but, just before that, the final confrontation between Elizabeth and Essex brings a thrilling climax, when Elizabeth attacks her lover not for infidelity but for treason. Philip Langridge's portrait of Essex is just as striking, consistently bringing out the character's arrogant bravado. The rest of the cast is equally starry, with Alan Opie as the queen's principal adviser, Sir Robert Cecil, balefully dark rather than sinister, with the warm-toned Della Jones as Essex's wife and the abrasive Yvonne Kenny as his sister, Lady Penelope Rich, equally well cast. Sir Charles Mackerras directs his Welsh National Opera forces in a performance that brings out the full splendour of this rich score. The Decca recording is comparably splendid.

Gloriana: Choral Dances

*** Hyp. CDA 66175. Hill, Owen, Holst Singers & O, Davan Wetton – BLISS: *Lie strewn the white flocks;* HOLST: *Choral Hymns from the Rig Veda* ***

The composer's own choral suite, made up of unaccompanied choral dances linked by passages for solo tenor and harp, makes an excellent coupling for the equally attractive Bliss and Holst items. Excellent, atmospheric recording.

A Midsummer Night's Dream (DVD version)

(N) *** Warner **DVD** 0630 16911-2. Cotrubas, Bowman, Appelgren, Buchen, Ryland Davies, Duesing, Lott, Bryson, LPO, Haitink (Producer: Peter Hall; TV Director: Dave Heather)

Recorded at Glyndebourne in 1981, the Warner DVD offers a magical production of Britten's fairy opera based on Shakespeare. The atmospheric sets of John Bury brilliantly exploit the limited space of the Glyndebourne stage in the old theatre, with forest trees manipulated by wood spirits amid mists, with moonlight adding to the mystery, and with fantastic costumes for the fairy characters. Peter Hall, as ever at Glyndebourne, is an inspired director, capturing the unique mixture of fantasy, comedy and downright farce with the surest hand, and with Bernard Haitink adding to the fun in his conducting, when in the final play scene with the Rude Mechanicals he brings out the parodies of Berg (in the music for Wall), Verdi (for Bottom) and Donizetti (for Flute). The cast is a vintage one, with James Bowman as Oberon and Ileana Cotrubas as Tytania unsurpassed, and with Felicity Lott, Ryland Davies and Dale Duesing outstanding among the lovers. Curt Appelgren is rightly dominant among the Rude Mechanicals as Bottom, both imposing and funny, with Patrick Power comic in his embarrassment as Flute. A fine memorial to traditional stage values in opera.

A Midsummer Night's Dream (complete; CD version)

*** Decca (ADD) 425 663-2 (2). Deller, Harwood, Harper, Veasey, Watts, Shirley-Quirk, Brannigan, Downside and Emanuel School Ch., LSO, composer

Britten again proves himself an ideal interpreter of his own music and draws virtuoso playing from the LSO. Peter Pears has shifted to the straight role of Lysander. The mechanicals are admirably led by Owen Brannigan as Bottom; and among the lovers Josephine Veasey (Hermia) is outstanding. Deller, with his magical male alto singing, is the eerily effective Oberon.

Owen Wingrave; The Hidden Heart

*** Arthaus **DVD** 100 372. Finley, Hellekant, Hill, Savidge, Barstow, Dawson, Gale, Marlton, Westminster Cathedral Ch., Deutches SO, Berlin, Nagano (DVD Dir: Margaret Williams)

After its first presentation on television, *Owen Wingrave* has been staged regularly, but it works best on the small screen, as this television production, originally made for Channel 4 in Britain, demonstrates. It presents the piece evocatively and convincingly in a setting updated to 1958, with khaki battledress for the soldiers. Surprisingly, it makes Owen's dilemma more convincing than the original over his pacifism and refusal to complete his military studies, with Gerald Finley singing and acting superbly. The unsympathetic fiancée, Kate, also seems a more complex character than before, well taken

by Charlotte Hellekant, and the gallery of disagreeable family-members is strongly cast too, notably Martyn Hill as the old, unforgiving Sir Philip Wingrave and Josephine Barstow as Miss Wingrave. Peter Savidge sings well in the role of the tutor, Spencer Coyle, the lone voice of sanity, with Anne Dawson as Mrs Coyle and Hilton Marlton as the wimpish Lechmere. Set mainly in the Wingrave country house, the result is nicely evocative, with the misty ghost scenes sufficiently creepy. With the orchestral score evidently recorded separately by the Deutsches Symphony Orchestra of Berlin under Kent Nagano, the musical results are still well co-ordinated.

What makes this issue especially valuable is that it also contains as an extra the moving film, *The Hidden Heart*, made for Channel 4 by Teresa Griffiths. Subtitled 'A Love Story in Three Pieces', this hour-long film gives a striking portrait of Benjamin Britten from the 1930s onwards, centring on his lifelong love for the tenor, Peter Pears. The discussion of Britten's homosexuality is treated intelligently and sympathetically, with the film's three sections built round three key works, *Peter Grimes* of 1945, the *War Requiem* of 1962 and *Death in Venice* of 1973, his last opera, which, as John Evans of BBC Radio 3 suggests, was the most autobiographical of his works. It consistently comes out that Britten and Pears were in many ways deeply conventional figures, 'like two pre-school masters' as the counter-tenor James Bowman says, with Britten even described as 'straight-laced'. Many of Britten's closest friends and associates give their views, and the film is well illustrated with period clips, not least of Peter Pears singing.

Paul Bunyan (complete)

⊕ **(M)** *** EMI 5 85139-2 (2). Lawless (spoken part), Dressen, Comeaux, Nelson, Soloists, Ch. & O of Plymouth Music Series, Minnesota, Brunelle

*** Chan. 9781 (2). Gritton, Streit, Robinson, Egerton, Broadbent, White, Coleman-Wright, Graham, Royal Opera Ch. & O, Hickox

Aptly, this first recording of Britten's choral operetta comes from the state, Minnesota, where the story is set. When the principal character is a giant who can appear only as a disembodied voice, the piece works rather better on record or radio than on stage. Musically, Britten's conscious assumption of popular American mannerisms does not prevent his invention from showing characteristic originality. Well cast and recorded in clean, vivid sound, with Philip Brunelle a vigorous conductor, this excellent first recording deserves all the prizes it won in its original issue on Virgin Classics.

The much-admired Covent Garden production of *Paul Bunyan* was recorded live at the Sadler's Wells Theatre in 1999. Though there are intrusive stage noises, the Chandos sound vividly captures the dramatic atmosphere of this ballad opera with its witty libretto by W. H. Auden, so full is it of colourful, distinctive invention. Hickox directs a warmly idiomatic reading which gains over the only previous version in featuring such fine singers as Susan Gritton as Tiny and Kurt Streit as Johnny Inkslinger. The Chandos sound is more open and atmospheric than the studio recording for Virgin, which yet in many ways gains from the closeness of the voices.

Peter Grimes (DVD versions)

☛ *** Arthaus **DVD** 100 382. Langridge, Cairns, Opie, Howard, Orton, ENO Ch. & O, Atherton (V/D: Barrie Gavin)

(N) *** Warner **DVD** 0630 16913-2. Vickers, Harper, Bailey, ROHCG Ch. & O, C. Davis (Dir: Elijah Moshinsky; V/D: John Vernon)

Peter Grimes (CD versions)

*** Chan. 9447/8 (2). Langridge, J. Watson, Opie, Connell, Harrison, Opera London, L. Symphony Ch., City of L. Sinf., Hickox

☯ ✿ (M) *** Decca (ADD) 467 682-2 (2). Pears, C. Watson, Pease, J. Watson, Nilsson, Brannigan, Evans, Ch. and O of ROHCG, composer

*** EMI 7 54832-2 (2). Rolfe Johnson, Lott, Allen, Ch. & O of ROHCG, Haitink

(B) *** Ph. (ADD) Duo 462 847-2 (2). Vickers, Harper, Summers, Bainbridge, Cahill, Robinson, Allen, ROHCG Ch. & O, C. Davis

Tim Albery's darkly intense production of *Peter Grimes* for ENO, updated to the interwar period, makes a powerful impression on DVD, thanks not just to the outstanding performance and production but also to Barrie Gavin's television presentation. Instead of filming a live performance, it uses the dark, stylized designs of Hildegard Bechtler as the background for a studio performance on the wide Coliseum stage, with close up shots restoring the claustrophobic atmosphere that such a large venue tends to undermine. One does not see David Atherton and the orchestra; instead, seascapes are shown during the important orchestral interludes. This is a production in which the chorus is a protagonist, and that, too, is vividly brought home in Gavin's presentation. As for the principals, their singing, vivid and characterful from first to last, can hardly be faulted, with Philip Langridge even more moving as Grimes than on CD, thanks to his deeply involved acting, with his big solos, notably the one in his hut in Act II and the final mad monologue, bringing the most powerful climaxes. Janice Cairns makes a touching Ellen, clear and firm throughout, with just a touch of the stiffness of a schoolmistress adding to the effectiveness of her acting. Alan Opie is an ideal Balstrode, even more than usual emerging as a central figure in the action, and the individual characters from the Borough are all vividly drawn, notably the Mrs Sedley of Susan Orton and the Auntie of Ann Howard. The women's quartet in Act II is radiantly sung, and the option on DVD of having English subtitles even with an opera in English adds powerfully to the impact of the piece.

Though the composer himself disapproved, Jon Vickers's radical portrayal of the role of Grimes in this unforgettably powerful Covent Garden production by Elijah Moshinsky was generally acclaimed as both musically inspired and powerfully convincing. With justice he portrayed this Suffolk fisherman as rough and rugged, darkly resentful of his treatment by the citizens of the Borough, at once violent and brooding. With Vickers such a solo as *What harbour shelters peace* brings a sudden transformation from an agonized mood into one of fleeting hope, and Vickers rises superbly to the challenge of the final monologue, with paranoia tipped over into madness. Heather Harper is equally moving as Ellen Orford, unsurpassed in the role, with Norman Bailey powerful as Balstrode. The other characters are also colourfully portrayed, with fine singing all round. Colin Davis, as on his Philips audio recording, proves an inspired interpreter, taut in control as well as warmly expressive, drawing vividly atmospheric playing from the orchestra to supplement the brilliantly effective sets, minimal but wonderfully evocative in their dark picture of the Borough. Irritatingly, no cast list is given on the box, only at the very end of the film.

The rhythmic spring which Hickox gives this colourful score harks back to the composer's classic set, and Chandos backs him up with an exceptionally rich recording, with bloom on the voices and full, immediate orchestral sound. The casting of Philip Langridge in the title-role is central to the set's success. As on stage, he is unrivalled at conveying the character's mounting hysteria, and the result is chilling. Janice Watson makes a most touching Ellen Orford, younger and less maternal than her rivals, but all the more tender, with the golden tones of the voice well caught. The others make a superb team, with Alan Opie an outstanding Balstrode and John Connell commanding as lawyer Swallow at the start.

The Decca recording of *Peter Grimes* was one of the first great achievements of the stereo era. Few opera recordings can claim to be so definitive, with Peter Pears, for whom it was written, in the name-part, Owen Brannigan (another member of the original team) and a first-rate cast. Britten conducts superbly and secures splendidly incisive playing, with the whole orchestra on its toes throughout. The recording, superbly atmospheric, has so many felicities that it would be hard to enumerate them, and the Decca engineers have done wonders in making up aurally for the lack of visual effects. Reissued on the 'Legends' series at mid-price, this costs far less than it did but lacks text or libretto.

On EMI, Anthony Rolfe Johnson brings out the inward intensity of Grimes, singing most beautifully, hardly troubled by the high tessitura. Felicity Lott makes a tenderly sympathetic Ellen Orford, and Sarah Walker is unforgettable as Mrs Sedley, the laudanum-taking gossip. Thomas Allen is a wise and powerful Balstrode, making the Act III duet with Ellen an emotional resolution. The Covent Garden Chorus and Orchestra benefit from the extra range and vividness of EMI's digital recording and this adds to the impact.

Sir Colin Davis takes a fundamentally darker, tougher view of *Peter Grimes* than the composer himself. Jon Vickers's powerful, heroic interpretation sheds keen new light on what arguably remains the greatest of Britten's operas. Heather Harper as Ellen Orford is most moving, and there are fine contributions from Jonathan Summers as Captain Balstrode and Thomas Allen as Ned Keene. The recording is full and vivid, with fine balancing. Now reissued as a Duo, this is a genuine bargain.

Peter Grimes: 4 Sea Interludes & Passacaglia

*** Chan. 8473. Ulster O, Handley – BAX: *On the Sea-shore*; BRIDGE: *The Sea* ***

(N) (B) * DG 474 936-2 (3). Boston SO, Bernstein – ELGAR: *Enigma Variations* *(*); SIBELIUS: *Symphonies 1–2, 5 & 7* (*)

Handley draws brilliant, responsive playing from the Ulster Orchestra in readings that fully capture the atmospheric beauty of the writing, helped by vivid recording of demonstration quality.

Although the Boston Symphony Orchestra create beautiful sounds, Bernstein's performance is devoid of real adrenalin: even the storm fails to generate excitement, with the slow tempi veering towards eccentricity, to put it mildly; this, like the rest of the collection, is far from Bernstein at his best.

The Rape of Lucretia (complete)

*** Chan. 9254/5. Rigby, Robson, Pierard, Maxwell, Miles, Rozario, Gunson, City of L. Sinf., Hickox

(i) *The Rape of Lucretia* (complete); (ii) *Phaedra, Op. 93*
*** Decca (ADD) 425 666-2 (2). (i) Pears, Harper,
Shirley-Quirk, J. Baker, Luxon, ECO, composer; (ii) J. Baker,
ECO, Bedford

In combining on CD *The Rape of Lucretia* with *Phaedra*, Decca celebrates two outstanding performances by Dame Janet Baker, recorded at the peak of her career. Among other distinguished vocal contributions to the opera Peter Pears and Heather Harper stand out, while Benjamin Luxon makes the selfish Tarquinius into a living character. The seductive beauty of the writing – Britten then at his early peak – is caught splendidly, the melodies and tone-colours as ravishing as any he ever conceived.

Though the soloists in the Britten recording – notably Janet Baker in the title-role – are more sharply characterful and well contrasted, the alternative views presented on Chandos are comparably convincing. Jean Rigby as Lucretia may lack the warmth and weight of Baker, but she gains from having a younger-sounding voice. Equally, the timbre of Nigel Robson as the Male Chorus, rather darker than Peter Pears's, adds to the dramatic bite of his characterization, virile in attack. Catherine Pierard as the Female Chorus has a more sensuous voice, making it a more involved commentary. Quite apart from its unique authority, Britten's Decca set (also at full price) comes with a valuable fill-up in *Phaedra*, the work he wrote for Janet Baker; but the Chandos rival gives an equally strong, in some ways more dramatic, view of a masterly opera.

The Turn of the Screw (DVD version)
(*) Arthaus **DVD 100 198. Field, Davies, Greager, Obata,
Stuttgart RSO, Bedford (Dir: Michael Hampe. V/D: Claus
Viller)

The Turn of the Screw (CD versions)
*** Virgin 5 45521-2 (2). Bostridge, Rodgers, Henschel,
Tierney, Leang, Wise, Mahler CO, Harding
(BB) *** Naxos 8.660109/10. Langridge, Lott, Pay, Hulse,
Cannan, Secunde, Aldeburgh Festival Ens., Bedford
(M) (***) Decca mono 425 672-2 (2). Pears, Vyvyan,
Hemmings, Dyer, Cross, Mandikian, E. Op. Group O,
composer

The hero of this Arthaus DVD production is Steuart Bedford, who gets vibrant singing and playing from all concerned. Helen Field is a thoroughly convincing Governess and the cast is in every respect excellent, even if Machita Obata looks a little too mature for Flora. A good production, very atmospheric, and with generally unobtrusive video direction.

Vividly recorded in atmospheric sound at the Snape Maltings, Britten's own concert-hall, with the chamber orchestra regularly adding to the dramatic impact, notably in the writing for timpani, Harding's CD version on Virgin of this most tautly constructed of Britten's operas brings many qualities to distinguish it from previous recordings. The headily fluent performance of Ian Bostridge in the Peter Pears roles of the Prologue and Peter Quint is specially memorable. Bostridge is lighter with his exceptionally free upper register, creepy though not as darkly sinister as Peter Pears or other predecessors. As the Prologue makes clear, Bostridge and Harding bring a freely volatile, at times improvisatory quality to the music with plenty of light and shade, again helped by the wide-ranging digital recording. Joan Rodgers is very well cast as the Governess, spontaneously expressive, vividly conveying her growing fears without seeming as neurotic as some rivals. It is good too to have not just the role of Miles

sung by a boy treble but the role of Flora sung by a girl of the appropriate age rather than by an adult. That adds to the horror of innocence corrupted, while Jane Henschel as Mrs Grose and Vivien Tierney as Miss Jessel are first rate, clear and firm, characterizing well.

Steuart Bedford's vividly recorded, warmly atmospheric version of *The Turn of the Screw* (originally issued on the Collins label) could not be more welcome in this super-bargain Naxos reissue. Bedford, who took over from Britten himself when the composer could no longer conduct his own recordings, here presents a similarly idiomatic performance with a comparable sharpness and magnetism that, thanks to the spacious recording, brings out the eerie atmosphere of the piece, the quality which originally attracted the young Britten to Henry James's ghost story. The recording also allows one to appreciate the sharp originality of the instrumentation in what by any standards is the tautest of Britten's operas. The singers too have been chosen to follow the pattern set by the original performers. Langridge here, like Pears before him, takes the double role of narrator and Peter Quint, echoing Pears's inflexions, but putting his own stamp on the characterization. Felicity Lott is both powerful and vulnerable as the Governess, rising superbly to the big climaxes which, thanks to the recording quality, have a chilling impact, not least at the very end. Sam Pay is a fresh-voiced Miles, less knowing than David Hemmings in the Britten set, with Eileen Hulse bright and girlish as Flora. Nadine Secunde is a strong Miss Jessel, and Phyllis Cannan matches up to the strength of her predecessor, Joan Cross. An outstanding set, with the Aldeburgh Festival Ensemble including such fine artists as Jennifer Stinton on the flute, Nicholas Daniel on the oboe, Richard Watkins on the horn and the Brindisi String Quartet.

Though the recording is in mono only, the very dryness and the sharpness of focus give an extra intensity to the composer's own incomparable reading of his most compressed opera. Peter Pears as Peter Quint is matched superbly by Jennifer Vyvyan as the Governess and by Joan Cross as the housekeeper, Mrs Grose. It is also fascinating to hear David Hemmings as a boy treble, already a confident actor. Excellent CD transfer.

Collection

'*The World of Britten*': (i–ii) *Simple Symphony*; (iii; ii) *Young Person's Guide to the Orchestra*; (iv–v) Folksong arrangements: *Early one morning; The Plough Boy*; (vi) *Hymn to the Virgin*; (iv; vii; iii; ii) *Serenade for Tenor, Horn & Strings: Nocturne.* Excerpts from: *Ceremony of Carols; Noye's Fludde; Spring Symphony; Billy Budd; Peter Grimes*
🠒 (M) *** (ADD) Decca 436 990-2. (i) ECO; (ii) cond.
composer; (iii) LSO; (iv) Pears; (v) composer (piano); (vi)
St John's College Ch., Guest; (vii) Tuckwell; & various
artists

The Britten sampler is well worth having for the composer's own vibrant account of the *Variations on a Theme of Purcell* and the *Simple Symphony*, where the *Playful Pizzicato* emerges with wonderful rhythmic spring and resonance (in the warm Maltings acoustics). The Pears contributions are very enjoyable too, notably the haunting *Nocturne* from the *Serenade*, with Barry Tuckwell in splendid form. Excellent sound throughout, although the tuttis in the *Young Person's Guide to the Orchestra* could with advantage have had a more expansive sonority.

BROWNE, John (c. 1490)

O Maria salvatoris; O regina mundi clara; Salve regina I;
Stabat iuxta; Stabat mater

(N) *** Gimell CDGIM 036. Tallis Scholars, Phillips

We know very little about John Browne except that he was
ahead of his time, both in the richness of sonorities he
created and in the remarkable length of his melodic lines. The
beauty is self-evident in these superb performances from the
Tallis Scholars, recorded in the sumptuous acoustic of the
Church of St Peter and St Paul, Salle, Norfolk. All this music
is to be found in the earlier folios of the Eton Choirbook,
dating from about 1490 to 1500, alongside more pieces that
are lost. The richness of the soaring treble texture is immediately striking in the opening *Salve regina*, but the radiant
antiphon *O Maria salvatoris*, is even more remarkable. This is
the longest work and the climactic piece in this programme,
written in the most lavish eight-part polyphony. It was so
celebrated in its day that it was given pride of place as the
opening item in the Choirbook. It is an extraordinary piece,
in its time a work almost as unprecedented as Tallis's 40-part
motet, *Spem in alium*, although its means are more modest.

BRUCH, Max (1838–1920)

Double Concerto in E min., for Clarinet, Viola & Orchestra,
Op. 88

(B) *** Hyp. Dyad CDD 22017 (2). King, Imai, LSO, Francis
(with Concert ***)

*** Sup. SU 3554-2. Peterkova, Besa, Prague Philh.,
Bělohlávek – MENDELSSOHN: 2 *Concert Pieces*; ROSSINI:
Introduction, Theme and Variations, etc. ***

Bruch's *Double Concerto* is a delightful work with genuinely
memorable inspiration in its first two lyrical movements and
with a roistering finale making a fine contrast. Clarinet and
viola are blended beautifully, with melting phrasing from
Thea King. The recording is excellent. This is part of an
excellent two-disc set, including other attractive concertante
works by Mendelssohn, Crusell, Spohr and other, less familar
names.

With the viola-player, Alexander Besa, as an inspired partner, the Czech clarinettist, Ludmila Peterkova, includes the
Double Concerto in a delightfully off-beat collection of
neglected clarinet music, warmly accompanied by Jiri
Bělohlávek and the Prague Philharmonia. She is an artist who
is not only warmly expressive, but sparkles in everything she
plays.

(i) *Double Concerto in E min. for Clarinet, Viola &*
Orchestra; (ii) *Romance for Violin & Orchestra;* (i) *8 Pieces*
for Clarinet, Viola & Piano

⊶ (BB) *** Warner Apex 8593 89229-2. Caussé, (i; iii)
Meyer, (i; ii) Lyon Op. O, Nagano; (iii) Duchable

The performance of the *Double Concerto* from Paul Meyer
and Gérard Caussé is affectionately mellow, yet does not miss
the lilt of the lively finale. Caussé's timbre is so warm and full
that here the balance between wind and stringed soloists is
more equal than on Hyperion. Caussé then goes on to give a
richly romantic account of the *Romance*, another work with
an endearing melodic flow. The *Eight Pieces* are much rarer,
another late work (from 1910). They are full of charm, their
romanticism pastel-shaded, but they are by no means insubstantial (No. 3 extends to nearly eight minutes). These highly

sympathetic performances are beautifully recorded, and this
Apex reissue makes a fine bargain.

Double Piano Concerto in A flat min., Op. 88a

*** Chan. 9711. Güher and Süther Pekinel, Philh. O, Marriner
– MENDELSSOHN: *Double Concerto*; MOZART: *Double*
Concerto ***

The Max Bruch *Double Concerto* is well worth hearing in a
performance as strong, sympathetic and well recorded as the
one on Chandos. With some attractive themes it makes a
welcome rarity, whatever its limitations.

Violin Concertos: 1 in G min.; 2 in D min., Op. 44; 3 in D
min., Op. 58; Serenade for Violin & Orchestra, Op 75;
Scottish Fantasy, Op. 46

(B) *** Ph. (ADD) Duo 462 167-2 (2). Accardo, Leipzig GO,
Masur

This Philips Duo gathers together Bruch's three *Violin Con-*
certos, plus two other major concertante works. Although no
other piece quite matches the famous *G minor Concerto* in
inventive concentration, the delightful *Scottish Fantasy*, with
its profusion of good tunes, comes near to doing so, and the
first movement of the *Second Concerto* has two soaringly
lyrical themes. The *Third Concerto* brings another striking
lyrical idea in the first movement and has an endearing
Adagio and a jolly finale. The engagingly insubstantial *Ser-*
enade was originally intended to be a fourth violin concerto.
Throughout the set Accardo's playing is so persuasive in its
restrained passion that even the less inspired moments bring
pleasure. With the soloist balanced rather close, the orchestral
recording is full and spacious.

Violin Concerto 1 in G min., Op. 26

*** Sony SK 87740. Midori, BPO, Jansons – MENDELSSOHN:
Concerto ***

*** EMI 7 54072-2. Chung, LPO, Tennstedt – BEETHOVEN:
Concerto ***

(M) *** EMI (ADD) 5 66906-2 [5 66958-2]. Menuhin, Philh.
O, Susskind – MENDELSSOHN: *Concerto* ***

(N) (M) *** EMI Legend (ADD) 557766. Menuhin, Philh. O,
Susskind (with bonus **DVD**: MOZART: *Violin Concerto 3*) –
MENDELSSOHN: *Violin Concerto* ***

(M) *** DG (IMS) 449 091-2. Mintz, Chicago SO, Abbado –
DVORAK: *Concerto* ***

(M) *** DG 463 641-2. Mutter, BPO, Karajan –
MENDELSSOHN: *Concerto* ***

(N) (BB) *** Regis RRC 1152. Jaime Laredo, SCO –
MENDELSSOHN: *Concerto* ***

(**(*)) Testament mono SBT 1083. Haendel, Philh. O,
Kubelik – BEETHOVEN: *Concerto* (**(*))

*** Chan. 8974. Udagawa, LSO, Mackerras – BRAHMS:
Concerto ***

*** EMI 7 49663-2. Kennedy, ECO, Tate – MENDELSSOHN:
Concerto; SCHUBERT: Rondo ***

(BB) (***) Naxos mono 8.110977. Milstein,
Philharmonic-Symphony O, New York, Barbirolli –
MENDELSSOHN; TCHAIKOVSKY: *Violin Concertos* (***)

(M) **(*) Sup. (ADD) SU 3663-2 011. Suk, Czech PO, Ančerl
– BERG: *Concerto*; MENDELSSOHN: *Concerto* ***

(B) **(*) Sony SBK 48274. Zukerman, LAPO, Mehta – LALO:
Symphonie espagnole; VIEUXTEMPS: *Concerto 5* **(*)

**(*) EMI 5 56906-2. Znaider, LPO, Foster – NIELSEN:
Concerto **(*)

(*) Australian Decca Eloquence (ADD) 461 369-2. Ricci, LSO, Gamba – MENDELSSOHN: *Concerto* **(*); SAINT-SAENS: *Havanaise*, etc. *

(N) (B) **(*) Decca 475 6700. Bell, ASMF, Marriner – MENDELSSOHN; MOZART: *Violin Concertos* **(*)

(M) ** DG (ADD) 463 651-2. Morini, Berlin R.O, Fricsay – DVORAK: *Concerto* ***; GLAZUNOV: *Concerto* **

(B) ** EMI Début 5 73501-2. Shapira, ECO, Hazlewood – BLOCH: *Baal Shem* ***; BUNCH: *Fantasy* **; SARASATE: *Zigeunerweisen* **(*)

(BB) (**) Naxos mono 8.110902. Menuhin, LSO, Ronald – ELGAR: *Concerto* (***)

It is a tribute to Midori that she can tackle this traditional, much-duplicated coupling with such individuality, particularly when in live recordings her inspired partners are the Berlin Philharmonic under Mariss Jansons. Her first entry in the Bruch is musingly reflective, with the recording heightening contrasts between soloist and orchestra, even though the violin is placed relatively close. The panache of her performance of the first movement is followed by a rapt account of the second. The finale again benefits from bold orchestral playing, with high contrasts setting off the sparkle of the soloist. Here we have a disc that – in the face of formidable competition – remains a clear winner.

Compared with her earlier, Decca recording (see below), Kyung Wha Chung's expressive rubato in her EMI version is more marked, with her freedom vividly conveying magic such as you find in her live performances, and the finale is again impulsive in its bravura. An exceptionally attractive version.

Menuhin's performance with Susskind, now reissued as one of EMI's 'Great Recordings of the Century', has long held an honoured place in the catalogue. The performance has a fine spontaneity, the work's improvisatory quality very much part of the interpretation, and there is no doubting the poetry Menuhin finds in the slow movement or the sparkle in the finale. The bright, forward sound of the 1960 recording has transferred vividly and naturally to CD.

Menuhin's recording is now issued additionally in EMI's Legend series, with a bonus DVD of Mozart's *Third Concerto*. It was filmed with the Orchestre de chambre de l'ORTF in Paris in 1967 and makes an interesting and generous but not exceptional encore.

Shlomo Mintz's compelling playing makes the listener hang on to every phrase. The vibrato is wide, but his approach is so distinctive and interesting that few listeners will resist. The Chicago Symphony Orchestra plays with great brilliance and enthusiasm, and Abbado's direction is most sympathetic. The vivid recording has transferred splendidly to CD.

In Anne-Sophie Mutter's hands the concerto has an air of chaste sweetness, shedding much of its ripe, sensuous quality, but retaining its romantic feeling. There is a delicacy and tenderness here which is very appealing and, although the tuttis have plenty of fire, Karajan sensuously scales down his accompaniment in the lyrical passages to match his soloist. The digital recording provides a natural balance and a vivid orchestral texture.

Long recommended by us as a first-class budget version, Jaime Laredo with consistently fresh and sweet tone gives a delightfully direct reading, never for a moment self-indulgent. His is a beautifully reflective account of the slow movement. He directs from the bow and the orchestral

ensemble is particularly iprssive. With excellent dgital recording from the mid-1980s, this is a genuine bargain.

Ida Haendel's magnificent (1948) reading of the Bruch, rather like her accounts of the Brahms and Tchaikovsky, reissued earlier by Testament, combines power and great warmth, with the first movement strong and purposeful, the second passionate in its lyricism, and the third brilliant and sparkling. An excellent transfer, but it is a pity that this is offered at full price.

Full of temperament, Hideko Udagawa gives a persuasively passionate performance of the Bruch, very well recorded, and, with strong, colourful playing from the orchestra, the hushed opening of the slow movement is caught beautifully.

Kennedy's totally unsentimental view may not have quite the individual poetry of the very finest versions, but it is coupled with an outstanding account of the Mendelssohn and the rare Schubert *Rondo*.

Milstein recorded the Bruch Concerto three times; this, his first, made in New York in 1942, sounds amazingly spontaneous and rich-toned. At this time American Columbia were beginning to record on to 33⅓rpm lacquer master discs, after which the approved takes were dubbed on to wax 78rpm discs. Although the resultant 78s were not as impressive as direct-to-wax discs, when they were transferred to LP in the early 1950s there was a much wider frequency range as well as quieter surfaces. The recordings sound as well as 1950s early tape masters. Many critics see the present account as Milstein's finest version of the Bruch: it is certainly exhilarating and wonderfully fresh.

Suk's account may not be as imaginative or individual as some; but his sweet timbre, rich in the slow movement without over-emoting, is combined with a naturally sympathetic feeling for the music's melodic line. The very simplicity of his approach brings its own rewards and while the finale, taken rather slowly, is perhaps a little lacking in lift-off, the performance overall, like the paired Mendelssohn, is endearing. Ančerl accompanies warmly and the 1963 Supraphon recording has been remastered most effectively: it remains pleasingly reverberant but is now better defined. Moreover the new Berg bonus is outstanding.

Zukerman's reissued Sony triptych shows him at his finest, and it is a pity that the close-up balance brings inevitable reservations. His Bruch is a passionately extrovert performance, tempered by genuine tenderness in the slow movement. The brilliantly lit recording with its larger-than-life effect is overwhelming.

Joshua Bell chose the Bruch for his Decca début recording in 1985. He demonstrates a flawless technique and plays with plenty of warmth and poetry, if missing something of the withdrawn, 'inner' quality of the slow movement. He is not heped by a very forward balance which places him in a spotlight at the expense of the orchestra, although Marriner's fine accompaniment is not enirely masked. The effect is to boost the romantic boldness of his playing, and many will respond to such powerful projection. This is certainly enjoyable, but the uneven partnership between soloist and orchestra is a drawback.This has now been issued as a Decca Double, including *Violin Concertos* of Mozart as well as the original Mendelssohn coupling.

Ricci has an outstanding technique and very characteristic tone which, alongside Perlman's rich sound, for example, sounds more febrile. But the performance here has fine intensity and there is a natural warmth which brings out the music's temperament without indulging it. The 1958 recording only hints at its age in the tuttis, but is amazingly full and vivid, and this performance – especially with Gamba's full-blooded conducting, remains individual and enjoyable.

Nikolaj Znaider comes from Denmark and his Bruch *Concerto* is very fine indeed, well thought out and fervent. He has very good support from Lawrence Foster and the LPO but there is a slight self-awareness that prevents it going to the top of the list.

Erica Morini's account with Fricsay dates from the late 1950s, but it still sounds remarkably fresh, and the tender performance of the famous slow movement is quite memorable. However, on LP this version last appeared on DG's bargain label, which is where it belongs. The current reissue is most notable for Martzy's coupled account of the Dvořák *Concerto*.

Wonderfully talented though Ittai Shapira is, this account of the *G minor Concerto* does not sweep all before it. He needs a little more sense of abandon, though Charles Hazlewood's rather steady, almost sedate tempi do not help.

The young Yehudi Menuhin's first recording dates from 1931 (the year before the coupled Elgar concerto). The transfer, made by Mark Obert-Thorn from pre-war RCA Victor pressings, is not very flattering to Menuhin's tone in the outer movements, which is thin and edgy, and the orchestra sounds very rough in the main tutti of the first movement. However, the slow movement shows Menuhin's true eloquence both in his richness of timbre and in his beauty of line.

Violin Concerto 1 in G min., Op. 26; Scottish Fantasy, Op. 46

🔑 (M) *** Decca (ADD) 460 976-2. Chung, RPO, Kempe – MENDELSSOHN *Concerto* ***

(M) *** RCA (ADD) 09026 61745-2. Heifetz, New SO of L., Sargent – VIEUXTEMPS: *Concerto 5* ***

The magic of Kyung Wha Chung, always a spontaneously inspired violinist, comes over beguilingly. Chung goes straight to the heart of the famous *G minor Concerto*, finding mystery and fantasy as well as more extrovert qualities. Just as strikingly in the *Scottish Fantasy* she transcends the episodic nature of the writing to give the music a genuine depth and concentration, above all in the lovely slow movement. Kempe and the RPO accompany sympathetically, well caught in a glowing recording.

Heifetz plays with supreme assurance, and the slow movement shows this fine artist in masterly form. Heifetz's panache and the subtlety of his bowing and colour bring a wonderful freshness to Bruch's charming Scottish whimsy. Sargent accompanies sympathetically, and though the soloist is balanced much too closely, there is never any doubt that Heifetz can produce a true *pianissimo*.

Violin Concertos 1; 3 in D min., Op. 58

*** Warner 0927 45664-2. Hanslip, LSO, Brabbins – SARASATE: *Navarra* ***

Still in her early teens, Chloë Hanslip here builds formidably on the success of her début disc of violin showpieces, tackling not only the popular *G minor Violin Concerto* of Bruch but the far more demanding *Third Concerto*, almost twice as long. For Hanslip the bigger the challenge, the greater her success. Warm and confident as she is in No. 1, she tends to underline phrasing rather heavily, where in the expansive No. 3 she is fresher, more imaginative and more individual. With clean attack, flawless intonation and crisp double-dotting, she gives a winningly spontaneous-sounding reading, revelling in the beauty of the violin writing and its range of expression, while Martyn Brabbins draws incisive playing from the LSO. The Sarasate showpiece – in which Hanslip is joined in duet by Mikhail Ovrutsky – with its jaunty Spanish dance rhythms makes a delightful supplement.

Violin Concerto 2 in D min., Op. 44

*** Delos DE 3156. Hu, Seattle SO, Schwarz – GOLDMARK: *Concerto* ***

Violin Concerto 2; Scottish Fantasy, Op. 46

(M) *** EMI (ADD) 5 62589-2. Perlman, New Philh. O, Lopez-Cobos

**(*) EMI 7 49071-2. Perlman, Israel PO, Mehta

(i) ***Violin Concerto 2. Symphony 3 in E, Op. 51***

*** Chan. 9738. (i) Mordkovitch; LSO, Hickox

In such warmly expressive, spaciously conceived readings as these, the coupling of symphony and concerto on Chandos offers a welcome, very well recorded alternative to the general run of Bruch issues. In the *Third Symphony* Hickox takes an affectionate view of the work. Speeds are broad in the first three movements, markedly so in the *Adagio*, with the chorale theme spacious and dedicated, and the surging theme which opens the finale has a hint of English folksong. In the *Second Violin Concerto*, Lydia Mordkovitch gives a raptly intense reading, making the long, slow first movement (in sonata form) into a deeply reflective meditation, punctuated by virtuoso flurries, readily justifying her spacious speeds.

Nai-Yan Hu is ideally balanced and well accompanied by Schwarz and the Seattle orchestra. Hu's soaring lyrical lines underline the music's warmth and consistent melodic inspiration. Though Perlman strikes a high profile in his EMI version, the sympathetic warmth of this Hu/Schwarz partnership and the concert-hall fullness of the Delos recording is preferable.

EMI have chosen Perlman's more intimately reflective 1976 New Philharmonia coupling for reissue in the 'Perlman Edition'. His superlative playing invests the first movement of the *Second Violin Concerto* with such warmth that it compares favourably with the more famous, G minor work. In his hands, both the main themes are given a soaring memorability and the coda is exquisitely managed. If the rest of the work has a lower level of inspiration, it is still richly enjoyable, and Perlman's account of the *Scottish Fantasia* is wholly delectable, showing the same degree of stylish lyricism and eloquence of phrasing. The EMI analogue recording is fully worthy of the performances and is well transferred to CD.

In his later, Israel recording, Perlman may be less intimately reflective in both works than he was when he recorded this coupling with the New Philharmonia, but in the fast movements there are ample compensations in the sharp concentration from first to last.

(i) ***Violin Concerto 3 in D min., Op. 58. Symphony 1 in E flat, Op. 28***

*** Chan. 9784. (i) Mordkovitch; LSO, Hickox

The *Third Violin Concerto* is laid out spaciously; yet Bruch characteristically allows himself plenty of lyrical lingering, which inspires Lydia Mordkovitch to playing of rapt intensity down to magical *pianissimos*. The slow movement is most typical of Bruch, again with Mordkovitch responding warmly to this hushed meditation, before the vigorous *moto perpetuo* finale. The *Symphony No. 1*, written soon after the popular *Violin Concerto in G minor*, is also based on striking material. As in the earlier disc, Hickox is a warmly expressive but never self-indulgent interpreter, and the Chandos recording is full and atmospheric.

(i) Double Concerto for Violin & Viola, Op. 88.; Kol Nidrei, Op. 47; Romance for Viola & Orchestra, Op. 85

*** RCA 09026 63292-2. Bashmet, LSO, Järvi; (i) with Tretyakov – WALTON: *Viola Concerto* ***

Bruch's fund of melodic invention, usually a youthful gift, stayed with him well into his seventies, as the *Double Concerto* and the *Romance* winningly demonstrate. The latter work for viola and orchestra of 1912 harks straight back to the slow movement of the *G minor Violin Concerto*. It is a radiant piece and draws a heartfelt performance from Bashmet, as does the well-known *Kol Nidrei*, made the more poignant with viola taking the place of cello. The *Double Concerto* brings extra sensuousness, thanks also to the pure-toned playing of Viktor Tretyakov, a perfect foil for the resonant Bashmet.

Kol Nidrei, Op. 47

*** Virgin 5 45664-2. Truls Mørk, French RPO, Paavo Jarvi – BLOCH: *Schelomo*; SCHUMANN: *Cello Concerto* ***

*** EMI 5 56126-2. Chang, LSO, Rostropovich – FAURE: *Elégie* ***; SAINT-SAENS: *Cello Concerto 1* ***; TCHAIKOVSKY: *Rococo Variations* *** ✪

(M) *** DG (ADD) 457 761-2. Fournier, LOP, Martinon – BLOCH: *Schelomo*; LALO: *Cello Concerto*; SAINT-SAENS: *Cello Concerto 1* ***

(N) (M) **(*) Mercury **SACD** 475 6608. Starker, LSO, Dorati – DVORAK: *Concerto*; TCHAIKOVSKY: *Rococo Variations* **(*)

(**(*)) EMI mono 5 57293-2. Du Pré, Israel PO, Barenboim – BRAHMS: *Cello Sonatas 1–2* (**(*))

(N) (M) *(**) EMI CD/**DVD** Legend mono 557 750. Du Pré, Israel PO, Barenboim – BRAHMS: *Cello Sonatas* (**(*))

Like Bloch's *Schelomo*, Bruch's *Kol Nidrei* is a Jewish rhapsody, even though the composer was not Jewish himself. It suits Mørk's freely expressive style just as well as the Bloch, resulting in a deeply concentrated reading, with *pianissimo* playing magically refined.

The phenomenally gifted 13-year-old Korean-born cellist, Han-Na Chang, catches the intense atmosphere of Bruch's Hebrew melody with a natural sensitivity, spontaneous in her dynamic contrasts; and indeed the extraordinary poise and assurance of this playing, matched by her ability to touch the listener, reminds one of the young Yehudi Menuhin. Her mentor accompanies her with great sympathy and the Abbey Road recording is beautifully balanced.

If Fournier's performance lacks the last degree of romantic urgency, it makes up for it in the beauty and style of the solo playing, and he is well supported by Martinon's Lamoureux Orchestra.

Starker's Mercury recording is utterly transformed by the new SACD transfer, wonderfully warm and glowing. The performance may lack romantic urgency but it has a relaxed, ruminative quality which is very endearing. Dorati accompanies most persuasively, providing a highly sympathetic orchestral backcloth.

Du Pré's account of Bruch's *Kol Nidrei*, like the Brahms sonatas discovered by Christopher Nupen in his film archive, was recorded in 1968 when the Israel Philharmonic was visiting London. It also sweeps one along in its spontaneous warmth, deeply dedicated in the prayerful first half and passionate at the climax. A most welcome bonus to the store of Jacqueline Du Pré's recordings.

Du Pré's account of Bruch's *Kol Nidrei* also comes on a Legend reissue, including some bonus excerpts on a companion DVD – see under the Brahms coupling.

Scottish Fantasy (for violin & orchestra), Op. 46

⊶ (N) (B) *** Decca (ADD) 476 7288-2 (2). D. Oistrakh, LSO, Horenstein – MOZART: *Sinfonia concertante*, etc. **(*); HINDEMITH: *Violin Concerto* ***

(B) *** CfP 575 8022. Little, RSNO, Handley – LALO: *Symphonie espagnole* ***

(BB) (***) Naxos mono 8.110940. Heifetz, LPO, Barbirolli – BRAHMS: *Double Concerto*; GLAZUNOV: *Violin Concerto* ***

The extrovert 1962 Oistrakh/Horenstein performance of the *Scottish Fantasia* owes nearly as much to the conductor as to the soloist. The expansive dignity of the opening of the brass shows immediately how fine the orchestral contribution is going to be, and Oistrakh's playing throughout is ravishing, enhancing the stature of the work immeasurably. The slow movement is especially memorable and, with superb 1962 sound, this is one of the top choices for this work, now in Universal's Critics' Choice series.

It is an excellent idea to couple Bruch's evocation of Scotland with Lalo's of Spain, both works in unconventional, five-movement, concertante form. Tasmin Little takes a ripe, robust and passionate view of both works, projecting them strongly, as she would in the concert hall. In this she is greatly helped by the fine, polished playing of the Scottish orchestra under Vernon Handley, a most sympathetic partner. The recording is superb, with brass in particular vividly caught. Little plays the Guerriero finale absolutely complete.

Bruch's *Scottish Fantasy* was always a favourite work with Heifetz, and although his pioneering 1947 version cannot quite match his stereo remake with Sargent and the LSO in thoughtful intensity, the passion and brilliance of the playing are most compelling, with the songful *Adagio* section even more moving in its simpler, more flowing manner, hushed and dedicated. Generously coupled with the powerful Brahms performance and the exuberant account of the Glazunov, another first recording. Good Naxos transfers, if with audible surface hiss and not quite as sophisticated as the EMI remastering.

(i) Scottish Fantasy, Op. 46. Serenade, Op. 75

(N) (BB) **(*) Naxos 8.557395. (i) Fedotov; Russian PO, Yablonsky

It is good to have one of Bruch's rarer concertante pieces for violin coupled with the colourful *Scottish Fantasy*. In warm, thrustful performances Maxim Fedotov may be a little short on the subtler qualities of mystery and tenderness, but the bravura of his playing, helped by full-blooded accompaniment from Dmitry Yablonsky and the Russian Philharmonic, makes the results compelling enough. The *Serenade*, Op. 75, dating from 1900, 20 years after the *Fantasy*, belies its lightweight title in its breadth and weight over four substantial movements. Not surprisingly, Bruch originally had the idea of putting this among his numbered concertos.

Symphonies 1 in E flat, Op. 28; 2 in F min., Op. 36; 3 in E, Op. 51

(B) *** EMI double forte 5 75157-2 (2). Gürzenich O or Cologne PO, Conlon – SCHREKER: *Prelude to a Grand Opera* ***

In James Conlon's convincing performances, both orchestras (it is not clear which plays which work) emphasize the music's Brahmsian and Schumannesque derivations. A good case is made for the *Third Symphony* here, with the romantic opening richly done, the slow-movement variations warmly effective, and the Scherzo (which the composer regarded as the finest movement in each of these works) is made to sound original in its scoring. Only the finale lets the piece down. The orchestral playing is committed throughout, even if at times greater drive is needed from the conductor. However, reservations are put to one side when the reissue is not only inexpensive but includes a red-blooded account of Schreker's vividly colourful *Prelude to a Grand Opera*.

String Quintet in A min., Op. posth.
*** Naim CD 010. Augmented Allegri Qt – BRAHMS: *String Quintet 2* ***

Bruch's *A minor Quintet* was one of two he wrote for sheer joy at the age of eighty. It is an unashamed throwback in idiom to Beethoven and Brahms, but the freshness of ideas and argument is most winning. Like the Brahms *G major Quintet*, with which it is ideally coupled, it is very well performed and vividly recorded.

VOCAL MUSIC

Moses (oratorio; complete)
*** Orfeo C 438 982 H. Volle, Gambill, Whitehouse, Bamberg Ch. & SO, Flor

Bruch's oratorio celebrating the story of Moses – as the composer said, from where Handel's *Israel in Egypt* leaves off – regularly recalls Mendelssohn's *Elijah*. The fresh, bright opening chorus leads on to a series of strong and colourful choruses. The story is then filled in with solos from the three characters: Moses a baritone, Aaron a tenor and The Angel of the Lord a soprano. The result may not be as vividly dramatic as *Elijah*, but in a warm and purposeful performance under a conductor with strong Mendelssohnian sympathies it makes its mark, thanks also to striking melodic material. Bright, clear, well-balanced sound.

BRUCKNER, Anton (1824–96)

Symphonies 0; 1–9; Symphony 4: Volksfest finale (1878)
(BB) *** Naxos 8.501101 (11). RSNO, or Nat. SO of Ireland, Tintner

Symphonies 0; 1–9
(B) **(*) Decca (DDD/ADD) 448 910-2 (10). Chicago SO, Solti

Symphonies 1–9 (complete)
(M) *** DG (ADD) 429 648-2 (9). BPO, Karajan
(B) *** EMI (ADD) 5 73905-2 (9). Dresden State O, Jochum
(B) *** DG (ADD) 469 810-2 (9). BPO or Bav. RSO, Jochum
(M) **(*) RCA (ADD) 09026 63930-2 (8). Cologne RSO, Wand (also available separately: 1 (09026 63931-2); 2 (09026 63932-2); 3 (09026 63933-2); 4 (09026 63934-2); 5 (09026 63935-2); 7 (09026 63937-2); 8–9 (09026 63938-2 (2))
(N) (B) ** RCA 87876 60395-2 (9). Leipzig GO, Masur

Symphonies 1–9; (i) Helgoland
(N) (BB) *** Warner 2564 61891-2 (9). BPO, Barenboim, (i) with Berlin R. Ch., Ernst Senff Ch.

Recorded between 1990 and 1997, Daniel Barenboim's cycle of the Bruckner *Symphonies* is among his finest achievements with the Berlin Philharmonic. These are powerful, concentrated performances, with tension and impact heightened by the fact that all but two of them, Nos. 4 and 7, were recorded live in concert. They also gain in competition with direct rivals – certainly in the super-bargain category – by enjoying spectacular sound, with Barenboim's preference for extreme dynamics fully and thrillingly caught, even though the extremes may be too great for easy domestic listening for some. The studio recording of No. 4 is the only one in which tension and ensemble slacken a little, but that is only a marginal flaw. The cycle rises to a climax with Barenboim's masterly readings of the last two symphonies. No. 8 in the full Haas edition is dedicated in all four movements, with the hushed expanse of the slow movement leading thrillingly into the incisive, brassy attack of the finale. No. 9 is equally dedicated, with Barenboim bringing out the adventurousness of the writing, with fragments coalescing into towering climaxes, ending on a noble account of the finale so satisfying that one has no regrets that Bruckner failed to complete a finale. The symphonic chorus for male voices and orchestra, *Helgoland*, makes a valuable supplement as a fill-up for No. 1, the last work that the composer completed, while writing No. 9. The nine discs come in a convenient compact box with full notes in a booklet.

The reappearance of Karajan's magnificent cycle, long a yardstick by which others were measured – and at mid-price – must be warmly welcomed. We have sung the praises of these recordings loud and long, and in their new format they are outstanding value.

Jochum's DG cycle was recorded between 1958 (No. 5) and 1967 (No. 2), all but four (Nos. 2, 3, 5 and 6) with the Berlin Philharmonic. It enjoys the advantage of accommodating one symphony per disc. No apology need be made for either the performances or the quality of the recorded sound, which wears its years lightly. One of the finest is the 1957 *Fifth*, in which Jochum brought a unique sense of mystery and atmosphere to Bruckner, and it more than compensates for the occasional freedom he permitted himself. He communicates a lofty inspiration to his players, and many of these readings can more than hold their own with later rivals. The set now comes economically packaged and priced and well documented in DG's Collector's Edition and can be thoroughly recommended.

Eugen Jochum's second Bruckner cycle was recorded in Dresden with the magnificent Staatskapelle between 1975 and 1980 in the last days of analogue recording. There is little difference in his approach here when compared to his earlier, DG set: he always favoured the Nowak editions, but the Dresden set has the richer, more opulent sound. Jochum had wisdom and nobility as well as a sense of vision, and his lifelong feeling for Bruckner's music and his grasp of its architecture shine through in every bar. At a bargain price, this is very competitive indeed.

There are few more persuasive Bruckner conductors than Georg Tintner, and his symphonic cycle on Naxos is uniquely complete in including not only *Die Nullte* and the 'Study Symphony', but also the 'Volksfest' Finale of No. 4. The performances are very well played by the Royal Scottish National Orchestra, the readings dedicated and intense, often inspired, and the recordings are full, atmospheric and clear. The Naxos White Box includes admirably extensive documentation, and this set must receive the strongest recommendation, quite irrespective of its modest cost.

Solti had previously recorded the *Eighth* with the VPO for John Culshaw in the Sofiensaal as early as 1966. With the Chicago Symphony Orchestra he recorded the whole cycle between 1979 (No. 6) and 1995 (No. 5). The two early symphonies are very impressive, but the *Third* is the one failure, relatively crude and coarse. Otherwise, the *Seventh*, with refined playing, lacks tension in the outer movements, but the series culminates in an inspired account of the *Eighth* and the *Ninth*, similarly spacious, with the music given full time to breathe. Other performances may be more deeply meditative, but the power of Solti and the brilliance of the playing and the digital recording are formidable.

Günter Wand's final survey of the Bruckner symphonies (1974–81) with the Cologne Radio Symphony Orchestra shows him as a dedicated Brucknerian who rarely falters in his majestic progress. His accounts of Nos. 5 and 6 do not match Jochum, but elsewhere (in Nos. 2 and 8 particularly) he is sometimes to be preferred. In No. 1 he uses the 1891 version of the score with its richer tonal palette and the planners were wise to choose the 1979 recording of the *Eighth*, rather than Wand's more recent and less convincing account with the North German Radio Symphony Orchestra. The *Ninth* then makes a dignified and spacious close to the series. As a whole the cycle has much to recommend it and at times he and the fine Cologne orchestra achieve real inspiration. The studio recordings are all analogue and the current remastering brings much-improved sound compared with the older LPs. The symphonies are additionally all available separately at mid-price, and alongside the complete set RCA have issued a brand-new digital recording of the *Fourth Symphony* (the reading even more spacious than the earlier account), coupled with Schubert's *Fifth Symphony* (74321 93041–2). Both are 'live' performances, made not long before the conductor died. They are of high calibre, the Schubert particularly warm, gracious and vital, beautifully recorded. Additionally this two-disc set includes an interview, 'Serving Music with Devotion', illustrated with excerpts from *Symphonies Nos. 4, 5, 6* and 9. Being spoken in German, this is perhaps of less interest to English-speaking collectors, although a translation is included in the accompanying booklet.

Recorded between 1974 and 1978, Masur's set comes from much the same period as Jochum's later, EMI cycle and some (though by no means all) of the symphonies appeared on CD during the late 1970s. Masur chooses the *Linz* version of No. 1, the 1889 version of No. 3 and the original versions of the remainder. Generally speaking, it is what one might call a sound rather than an inspired cycle. He is a dedicated Brucknerian and the Leipzig Gewandhaus Orchestra is a responsive body, but for those who (rightly) attach importance to continuity its reissue on nine CDs has brought a break between discs after the third movement of No. 8.

Symphony oo in F min.; Overture in G min.

(M) *** Oehms OC 208. Saarbrücken RSO, Skrowaczewski

Unlike most cycles of the Bruckner symphonies, Skrowaczewski's with the Saarbücken Orchestra includes this first attempt at writing a symphony, completed in 1863 when the composer was already in his late thirties. It is a fine performance, very well recorded, making an outstanding bargain. The inspiration is fresh and open with many echoes of Mendelssohn and Schumann, but already there are Bruckner fingerprints, notably in the hushed and tender slow movement and the Scherzo with its rugged contrasts. The *Overture*

in D minor from the same period makes an ideal fill-up with its mysterious slow introduction leading to a light, Mendelssohnian Allegro. Now reissued on the Oehms label, this series is at mid rather than budget price.

Symphony oo in F min. (Study Symphony); String Quintet: Adagio (arr. for strings)

*** Ondine ODE 920-2. German SO, Berlin, Ashkenazy

Symphony oo in F min. (Study Symphony); Symphony 4: Volkfest Finale (1878)

(BB) *** Naxos 8. 554432. RSNO, Tintner

It is good that Tintner in his superb Bruckner cycle for Naxos here fills in what might easily have been two gaps. The composer was 39 when he completed this *F minor Symphony*, but the progressions and effects point forward to what we now recognize as fully Brucknerian, with sharp contrasts and sudden changes of direction in the argument. With excellent playing and recording – as in the rest of the series – Tintner could not be more persuasive; as a welcome bonus he adds the very rare second version of the finale of the *Fourth Symphony*, which Bruckner entitled *Volksfest*, 'Festival of the People'. Strikingly different, particularly at the start, from the 1880 version of that movement, which is generally performed, it is well worth hearing in a fine performance like this, even if it hardly displaces the usual version.

Ashkenazy conducts his Berlin orchestra in a strong and purposeful reading. His speeds are consistently fast, his manner direct but still expressive, so that he brings out the inner intensity of the fine slow movement. The lovely *Adagio* of the *String Quintet* in string orchestra format brings just as dedicated a performance, an excellent bonus. Full, warm sound. However, the Naxos version has a considerable price advantage.

Symphonies o in D min. (Die Nullte); 8 in C min. (1887 Nowak edition)

☞ (BB) *** Naxos 8.554215/6. Nat. SO of Ireland, Tintner

In a moving note George Tintner passionately argues the case for Bruckner's original (1887) version of No. 8, fresh and spontaneous. Most conductors opt for the 1889–90 revision, edited by either Haas or Nowak. The differences are major and there is much that will take you completely by surprise. The result is an intense, keenly concentrated reading, with total dedication in the playing, which rises to supreme heights in the long *Adagio* slow movement, where the refined *pianissimo* playing of the Irish orchestra is magically caught by the Naxos engineers. Even for those with rival versions, this makes a very necessary recommendation, particularly when the two-disc package brings so generous and revealing a coupling as the *D minor Symphony (Die Nullte)* in a very good performance. Tintner powerfully brings out the Brucknerian qualities in embryo, and again he is served very well by the Irish orchestra, even if the weight of big tuttis is less than in some others of this series.

Symphony 1 in C min.

(M) *** Oehms OC 210. Saarbrücken RSO, Skrowaczewski

Skrowaczewski draws dedicated, tautly sprung playing from the Saarbrücken orchestra in what remains a problematic work. At speeds on the fast side, this is a fresh and urgent reading, which yet brings out the hushed intensity of the spacious second movement *Adagio*. Beautifully recorded in a helpful acoustic, it is a match for any version at whatever price.

Symphonies 1 in C min. (1866 version, revised Carragan); 3 in D min.: Adagio (1876)
(BB) *** Naxos 8.554430. RSNO, Tintner

As with other symphonies in his mould-breaking Bruckner series for Naxos, Georg Tintner opts for the earliest version of the *Symphony No. 1*. The principal differences here are in the finale, which brings angular writing and orchestration that is more radical than in the revisions. Tintner in his dedicated performance, with refined playing from the Scottish orchestra, amply justifies his choice, powerfully bringing out the bald originality of the writing. The generous makeweight also offers a rare text, a version of the slow movement of *Symphony No. 3* unearthed by the Bruckner editor, Leopold Nowak, which was composed in 1876, between the original one of 1873 and the shortened one of 1877. Again the intensity and refinement of the performance sustain the expansiveness compellingly. Clear, atmospheric sound, at once transparent and weighty in climaxes.

Symphonies (i) 1 in C min. (Linz version); 9 in D min.; (ii) Te Deum
☛ (B) *** Ph. Duo (ADD/DDD) 473 886-2. (i) Concg. O; (ii) Mattila, Mentzer, Cole, Holl, Bav. R. Ch., VPO; Haitink

This is one of the finest of the reissues from Haitink's analogue Concertgebouw series. The orchestra produces an opulent, deeply Brucknerian sound in the wind department as well as in the strings, and both performances have real stature, with a tremendous grip in the *Ninth* and a vision that penetrates its sense of tragedy and dramatic power as do few others. Even if Haitink misses some of Jochum's mystery and Walter's gentler poetry, his mighty reading still shows the dramatic force of the work. The *Te Deum* is also finely done and makes an added inducement to invest in this coupling.

Symphony 2 in C min. (original, 1872 score)
☛ (BB) *** Naxos 8.554006. Nat. SO of Ireland, Tintner

In his Bruckner series for Naxos, Georg Tintner here firmly favours the composer's first thoughts, arguing that later revisions are not improvements. He therefore opts for the edition of the original (1872) score, presenting the work at its most expansive and with the big two movements in reverse order from usual. The Scherzo has an extra repeat, but more important is the expansion of both the slow movement and the finale, here presented in concentrated performances that feel not a moment too long. The coda of the *Andante* brings a horn solo at the very end (substituted by Herbeck in 1876), challenging to the player, which is more strikingly beautiful than the clarinet solo with which Bruckner replaced it. Excellent, refined playing from the Irish orchestra and full, rich sound, with the brass gloriously caught.

Symphonies 2 in C min. (1877 version); 4 in E flat (Romantic)
(B) **(*) EMI (ADD) 5 74837-2 (2). Dresden State O, Jochum

Jochum's Bruckner has a special magnetism, though some will have reservations on points of style with his free variation of tempo within a movement, especially his accelerandi in the big crescendi, evident in both these symphonies, recorded in 1975 (No. 2) and 1980 (No. 4); this is a characteristic that occurs throughout his cycle (available in a bargain box). However, Jochum's natural affinity of temperament with the Austrian master gives these massive structures a compelling, unforced concentration that brings out their

architectural grandeur. At budget price, this is well worth considering if the coupling is desired.

Symphony 3 in D min. (original, 1873 version)
(BB) *** Naxos 8.553454. RSNO, Tintner
(BB) **(*) Warner Apex 2564 60005-2. Frankfurt RSO, Inbal

With characteristic boldness, Georg Tintner opts here to record the very rare first version, far more expansive than the final, revised version normally heard. The score was lost for almost a century and was finally published only in 1977. Tintner holds the vast structure together masterfully, even though his speeds in the three expanded movements are daringly slow. The first movement alone lasts over half an hour, yet the concentration of the performance, with dynamic contrasts heightened, never falters for a moment, with playing from the Scottish orchestra both powerful and refined. The slow movement too is rapt and dedicated, with *pianissimos* of breathtaking delicacy. The Scherzo is then fast and fierce, before the spacious account of the finale. Tintner in every way justifies his daring and revelatory choice of text.

It was Eliahu Inbal who pioneered the original version of this symphony, and the playing of the Frankfurt Radio Orchestra shows a keen feeling for atmosphere and refined dynamic contrasts. The recording, too, is very acceptable, but Tintner's Naxos version remains a preferable and more imaginatively atmospheric performance.

Symphony 3 in D min. (1877 version)
(*) Arthaus **DVD 100 320. Bav. RSO, Solti – STRAVINSKY: *Symphony in 3 Movements* *(*)
(M) *** Oehms OC 212. Saarbrücken RSO, Skrowaczewski
(M) **(*) Warner Elatus 2564 60533-2. BPO, Barenboim
(M) (**) BBC mono BBCL 4161-2. Hallé O, Barbirolli –
　　WAGNER: *Tannhäuser Overture & Venusberg Music* (**)

Symphony 3 in D min. (1877 version with 1876 Adagio)
*** Hyp. CDA 67200. BBC Scottish SO, Vänskä

Recorded for television by Bavarian Radio in 1993, this Arthaus DVD offers straightforward video presentations of Solti conducting the Bavarian Radio Orchestra in two sharply contrasted works, with the Bruckner rather curiously coupled with the Stravinsky *Symphony*. Solti is a dramatic Brucknerian rather than a warmly expressive one. The sound as well as the interpretation is bright and incisive, with the orchestral balance on DVD rather light on bass. Dynamic contrasts are extreme, bringing out the monumental quality of the outer movements, with the third-movement Scherzo fiercely rhythmic. It is a characteristic Solti reading which will please his admirers. However, the Stravinsky coupling is much more controversial.

Skrowaczewski offers a mid-priced version of the *Third*, which in both performance and recording rivals any more expensive version. Unlike Tintner he opts for the usual text, following Bruckner's final reworking in his third version of the work. As in Skrowaczewski's other Bruckner recordings now being reissued on the Oehms label, the playing of the Saarbrücken orchestra is strong and intense, with opulent sound to match. So the slow movement is sweet and warm in its lyrical flow, and the finale glows with resplendent brass.

The key point about Vänskä's version, given a brilliant and refined performance by the BBC Scottish Symphony, is that he uses a long-buried text for the *Adagio* slow movement. It was discovered only when the orchestral parts for the 1877 performance of the revision completed that year were found to have extensive corrections and pastings-over. Once these were removed, another complete version of the *Adagio* was revealed, more expansive, with more quotations from Wagner included. The liner-notes clarify these points, making an excellent case for preferring this text. Vänskä effectively heightens the Wagnerian qualities of the score, while drawing a ripe, Brucknerian sound from his players, helped by full, atmospheric recording.

Barenboim uses the 1877 version of the score, gets impressive results and draws opulent sound from the Berlin Philharmonic, and the recorded sound does them justice. This has considerable passion and musical conviction, and the performance and recording would not disgrace any collector's library. However, it does not have the the same blend of natural eloquence and architectural strength as the Haitink digital Vienna version, nor is it quite as beautifully recorded. That comes with an equally outstanding version of the *Eighth Symphony* on a Philips Duo (see below).

On the BBC Legends label, it is good to have so persuasive an example of Barbirolli in Bruckner, with generally steady speeds and warmly expressive phrasing. The bite and dramatic tension of a live performance are well caught. However, the mono recording, made in the Free Trade Hall in Manchester in 1964, is rather boxy and limited in range, with not enough body in the strings.

Symphonies 3 in D min.; 7 in E
(B) *** EMI double forte (ADD) 5 68652-2 (2). Dresden State O, Jochum

Eugen Jochum gives these massive structures an easy, warm, unforced concentration that brings out their lyricism as well as their architectural grandeur. He uses the Nowak edition; with his understanding of Bruckner developing towards a more direct and monumental approach, the authority is never in doubt, and this is matched by splendid playing from the Dresden orchestra.

Symphonies 3 in D min. (1877 version); 8 in C min.
☛ (BB) *** Ph. Duo 470 534-2 (2). VPO, Haitink

Haitink's was one of the first digital recordings of the 1877 version of the *Third Symphony,* which Bruckner embarked on after Hermann Levi had rejected the *Eighth Symphony,* making a number of cuts suggested by the Schalk brothers. This version is favoured by many Bruckner scholars. Questions of editions apart, this is a performance of enormous breadth and majesty, and Philips give it a recording to match. The playing of the VPO is glorious throughout, and even collectors who have alternative versions should consider this magnificent issue. No less enticing is the recording of the *Eighth Symphony,* with the same formidable combination of conductor and orchestra, and outstanding engineering (by the doyen of Philips engineers, Volker Strauss), and the results are outstanding. The performance is remarkable for its breadth and nobility, and Haitink has the full measure of its majesty and grandeur. Not only does it possess great dramatic sweep, its slow movement has greater depth than his earlier reading. The VPO play with great fervour and warmth, and the recorded sound is sumptuous. If it doesn't quite match Karajan's magisterial DG accounts, it is still among the most satisfying versions available. In short, these two symphonies make an outstanding bargain on the Philips Duo label.

Symphony 4 in E flat (original, 1874 version)
(BB) **(*) Warner Apex 2564 61371-2. Frankfurt RSO, Inbal

(N) (BB) (*) Arte Nova 82876 60488-2. Linz Bruckner O, Russell Davies

Like the *Third,* there are three versions of the *Romantic Symphony,* and no one had recorded the original version before Inbal. The Scherzo here is a completely different and more fiery movement, and the opening of the finale is also totally different. Inbal's performance is good, with a genuine feeling for the Bruckner idiom, paying scrupulous attention to dynamic refinements. The recording is well detailed, though the climaxes almost (but not quite) reach congestion. A fascinating issue, and especially attractive at budget price.

Eliahu Inbal's pioneering account in 1983 of the first version of the *Fourth Symphony* is unchallenged by Dennis Russell Davies and his Linz players; the orchestra is no match for the Frankfurt orchestra and there is an unwelcome detachment about the conductor's approach. Good sound, but not recommended.

Symphony 4 in E flat (Romantic)
☛ *** RCA 09026 68839-2. BPO, Wand
(M) *** DG (IMS) 449 718-2. BPO, Jochum (with SIBELIUS: *Night Ride and Sunrise, Op. 55,* with Bav. RSO (***))
(M) *** DG (ADD) Entrée 477 500-2. BPO, Karajan
(BB) *** Naxos 8.554128. RSNO, Tintner
(M) *** Decca (ADD) 466 374-2. VPO, Boehm
*** Testament (ADD) SBT 1298. LSO, Kertész
(M) *** Oehms OC 213. Saarbrücken RSO, Skrowaczewski
(M) **(*) EMI (ADD) 5 62315-2 [5 62816-2]. Philh. O, Klemperer – WAGNER: *Siegfried Idyll* ***
(B) **(*) EMI Red Line 5 69795. BPO, Muti

Symphony 4 in E flat; Overture in G min.
(***) Testament mono/stereo SBT 1050. Philh. O, Von Matačič

Günter Wand's Berlin version of the *Fourth Symphony* crowns his achievement as one of our greatest Bruckner conductors. The recording derives from a concert at the Philharmonie in Berlin and conveys a sense of occasion so often missing in the studio. Wand knows what this music is about and has the command of its architecture and space. One feels immediately comfortable under his guidance, dedicated and purposeful, with consistently warm textures from the Berlin Philharmonic. Speeds are judged perfectly; rubato is more extreme than in most studio readings, but the massive structure is held together lucidly in total concentration. Keenly dramatic, capped by towering climaxes, it offers full, rich sound, if with *pianissimos* not quite as hushed as they might be. This is much more successful than Wand's earlier recordings with the NDR Cologne Orchestra and must rank alongside the finest now in the catalogue; for collectors wanting a premium-priced version, this will probably be first choice.

Jochum's way with Bruckner is unique. So gentle is his hand that the opening of each movement or even the beginning of each theme emerges into the consciousness rather than starting normally. The purist may object that, in order to do this, the conductor reduces the speed far below what is marked, but Jochum is for the listener who wants above all to love Bruckner. The recording has been enhanced in this reissue in DG's 'Originals' series, and a fascinating mono recording of Sibelius's *Night Ride and Sunrise* has been added. Jochum was not thought of as a Sibelian, but this performance is most impressive.

Karajan's opening (on his DG version) has more beauty

and a greater feeling of mystery than almost anyone else on CD. As in his earlier, EMI record, Karajan brings a keen sense of forward movement to this music as well as showing a firm grip on its architecture. His slow movement is magnificent. The current remastering of the 1975 analogue recording, made in the Philharmonie, is very impressive. The sound may lack the transparency and detail of the very finest of his records, but it is full and firmly focused.

There are not many versions as fine as Georg Tintner's on Naxos, at whatever price. With extreme *pianissimos* magically caught, full of mystery, this is an exceptionally spacious reading, deeply reflective and poetic, which brings out the Schubertian qualities in Bruckner, sweet and songful as well as dramatic. The playing of the Royal Scottish National Orchestra is as refined as the recording, with subtly terraced dynamics beautifully clear.

There are many who admire Boehm's Bruckner, and he certainly controls the lyrical flow of the fourth symphony convincingly, helped by first-rate playing from the VPO, and vintage Decca sound from 1973, with the advantage of the spacious acoustics of the Sofiensaal. The balance provides splendid detail and a firm sonority. Boehm's sobriety was also his strength; in every bar he gives the impression that he knows exactly where he is going and, choosing the Nowak edition, he shapes the structure compellingly.

Skrowaczewski's reading of Bruckner's most popular symphony is characteristically strong and refined, with extreme dynamic contrasts heightened by the excellent recording, so that the crescendo at the start of the finale is exceptionally powerful. Only in the third movement Scherzo does he adopt a tempo at all out of the ordinary, challenging the horns in daringly fast hunting calls, which yet are finely disciplined.

Klemperer's 1965 performance with the Philharmonia is for those primarily seeking architectural strength. The reading is magisterial and the finale has impressive weight and strength. Alongside Jochum's flexible approach, Klemperer's view seems severe, even marmoreal. But there is no question as to its power or the vividness of the remastered EMI recording. It now comes with the bonus of the *Siegfried Idyll*, giving a playing time of 79 minutes.

Although a Kertész/LSO performance was briefly available on BBC Radio Classics, this Decca account has been out of circulation since its original appearance in the 1960s. It is a performance of some distinction, as fresh as the famous Dvořák cycle that Kertész recorded in the late 1960s and without the slightest trace of affectation. It has a Schubertian directness and keen dramatic sense to commend it. Very fine playing from the LSO and impressive sound. Not a first choice but an impressive reissue nonetheless.

With warm, slightly distanced sound, the sensuous beauty of the Berlin Philharmonic string section has rarely been caught so beautifully. Muti as a Brucknerian has a fine feeling for climax, building over the longest span, and his flexible phrase-shaping of Brucknerian melody, very different from traditional rugged treatment, reflects a vocal style of expressiveness. With that extra warmth and high dramatic contrasts, Muti takes Bruckner further south than usual.

Lovro von Matačič's Philharmonia account of the *Fourth Symphony* dates from 1954 and used the Franz Schalk/Karl Loewe edition of 1889, with cuts in the Scherzo and finale. This fine Testament transfer pays tribute to the acute ears of the Walter Legge/Douglas Larter recording team, with the sound beautifully blended. When it was issued in the USA, the *Overture in G minor* was added two years later, and this was also recorded in stereo. The performance has both

lucidity and majesty, with Dennis Brain's horn-playing outstanding.

Symphonies 4 in E flat (Romantic); 5 in B flat
(B) **(*) Sony SB2K 87742 (2). Phd. O, Ormandy

Eugene Ormandy has never been closely associated with Bruckner on record, yet his reading of the *Fourth Symphony* from 1967 (using the Nowak edition) has a warmth and power and a natural expressiveness that are most persuasive. Very well played in opulent Philadelphia string-tone and with glorious horns in the hunting motif of the Scherzo, this could be well worth considering. There is some edge on high violins in the transfer, but the recording has a concert-hall acoustic and plenty of body. However, the coupling is unfortunate and unnecessary, as each symphony is complete on a single CD and the *Fifth* has less atmosphere and mystery. Here the recording is comparatively two-dimensional, with the brass brash in tuttis. The Philadelphia strings are eloquent but are much less flatteringly caught.

Symphonies 4 in E flat (Romantic); 9 in D min.
☞ ✪ (M) *** Sony (ADD) 515302-2 (2). Columbia SO, Walter

Bruno Walter's recordings of Bruckner's *Fourth* and *Ninth Symphonies* represented the peak of his Indian summer of recordings for CBS in 1959 and 1960; and both sound splendid in this current paired reissue, with glorious strings and richly sonorous brass. Although not quite as impressive as the *Ninth*, the *Fourth* is still a memorable account. Walter makes his orchestra of Californian musicians sound remarkably European in style and timbre, and the superbly played 'hunting' Scherzo is wonderfully vivid. The reading is characteristically spacious. His special feeling for Bruckner meant that he could relax over long musical paragraphs and retain his control of the structure, while the playing has fine atmosphere and no want of mystery.

The *Ninth* is finer still. Walter's mellow, persuasive reading leads one on through the leisurely paragraphs so that the logic and coherence seem obvious where other performances can sound aimless. Perhaps the Scherzo is not vigorous enough to provide the fullest contrast – though the sound here has ample bite – yet it exactly fits the overall conception. The final slow movement has a nobility that makes one glad that Bruckner never completed the intended finale. After this, anything would have been an anticlimax.

Symphony 5 in B flat
☞ ✪ *** DG 476 7097-2. Dresden State O, Sinopoli
*** RCA 09026 68503-2. BPO, Wand
*** BBC (ADD) BBCL 4033-2. BBC SO, Horenstein
(BB) *** EMI Encore 5 75862-2. LPO, Welser-Möst
(N) **(*) Australian Decca Eloquence (ADD) 476 2746. VPO, Maazel
(N) (M) ** RCA SACD 82876 60749 (2) (with rehearsals). VPO, Harnoncourt

Sinopoli's disc appeared in the very month of his untimely death, a wonderful memorial, characterful and strong in a positive, even wilful way distinctively his. The Dresden Staatskapelle responds with playing of incandescent intensity, totally allied with the conductor in silencing any stylistic reservations. This is a reading of high dramatic contrasts, with the towering climaxes of the outer movements both rugged and refined, purposeful and warm, with the variegated structure of the finale tautly held together. This is a live recording, and the inspiration of the moment comes over at full force. The energy of the *Scherzo* and the passion of the slow movement complete the picture of an exceptionally high-powered reading, recorded in glowing sound, now part of the Penguin Rosette collection.

In his later version Günter Wand forsakes the Cologne and Hamburg orchestras (with which he made his earlier recordings) in favour of the Berlin Philharmonic. The present disc was put together from three concert performances given in January 1996. Wand, an experienced and selfless interpreter, gives a noble reading, magnificently played.

Horenstein's magisterial account of the *Fifth Symphony* with the BBC Symphony Orchestra has the advantage of relatively rich and vivid sound and comes from a 1971 Prom. It is an eloquent and compelling performance of a symphony which Horenstein (to the best of our knowledge) never recorded commercially.

Welser-Möst's 1993 performance has worn well and makes a very competitive version at bargain price. It is well thought out and concentrated in feeling, and if not a first choice is still recommendable. The recording made in the Konserthaus, Vienna, before an attentive audience, is both wide ranging and well balanced.

Although Maazel's 1973 account of the *Fifth Symphony* lacks a certain spiritual dimension which the finest versions possess, it has a great deal to commend it. It is beautifully played and recorded, with plenty of detail and body. Moreover, Maazel's control of tempo changes is masterly, combining flexibility with firmness of grip. If not a top choice, it is still worth considering.

The first disc of Harnoncourt's RCA double offers the complete performance of the symphony and the second (not in SACD) gives us 75 minutes of rehearsals. Scrupulously prepared and well thought out, the performance is very well recorded, with an exceptionally wide dynamic range. The brass of the Vienna Philharmonic resound brightly rather than sonorously, and the texture has detail and transparency. Harnoncourt's *Adagio* is on the brisk side and some of the phrasing in the Scherzo is heavy-handed with unnecessarily overemphatic accents. Thought-provoking rather than wholly satisfying; recommended to Harnoncourt's band of admirers rather than to the generality of collectors.

Symphonies 5 in B flat (1878 edition); *6 in A* (original version)
(B) **(*) EMI double forte 5 72661-2 (2). Dresden State O, Jochum

Jochum's DG account of the *Fifth Symphony* (with the Bavarian Radio Orchestra) was one of the earliest and one of the finest of his first cycle, and DG should consider issuing it as one of their 'Originals'. However, the Dresden version also has a very impressive slow movement, and the *Sixth* is similarly compelling. The CD transfers are admirably spacious and the Dresden strings have plenty of depth. But the brass is rather too brightly lit and, especially in the climaxes of the *Sixth Symphony*, the effect is brash.

Symphony 6 in A
(BB) *** LSO Live LSO 0022. LSO, C. Davis
(M) *** EMI (ADD) 5 62621-2 [5 62622-2]. New Philh. O, Klemperer (with Overtures: GLUCK: *Iphigénie en Aulide*; HUMPERDINCK: *Hänsel und Gretel* **)
(M) *** EMI (ADD) 5 67037-2. New Philh. O, Klemperer − WAGNER: *Wesendonk Lieder* **

(N) *** Australian Decca Eloquence (ADD) 476 2745. VPO, Stein − WEBER: *Overtures* ***
(M) **(*) Oehms OC 215. Saarbrücken RSO, Skrowaczewski

Sir Colin Davis's live recording of the *Sixth*, made in February 2002, is above all warm and purposeful. The high contrasts of the outer movements are superbly caught, with weighty resonant string-tone bringing incandescent climaxes. The weight of strings adds to the slow-paced moment of the expansive slow movement too, inexorably building up over long paragraphs, with the second subject treated *con amore*. The conductor's concentration finally brings sharp coherence to the wayward structure of the finale, with the engineers confirming their mastery over the Barbican acoustic in full-bodied sound.

Klemperer's 1964 version has been reissued as one of EMI's 'Great Recordings of the Century'. It remains a characteristically strong and direct reading. It is disarmingly simple rather than overly expressive in the slow movement (faster than usual) but is always concentrated and strong, and the finale is held together particularly well. Splendid playing from the New Philharmonia Orchestra, and the Kingsway Hall recording is clear and bright, but even more full-bodied in the present remastering. The two overtures are earlier (1960) and feature the Philharmonia: *Hänsel und Gretel* is richly atmospheric, but the Gluck is heavy-going, and some collectors may prefer the alternative Wagner coupling in the 'Klemperer Legacy' series.

Horst Stein's is a nobly wrought account of the *Sixth Symphony* with the Vienna Philharmonic. The slow movement has genuine eloquence and gravity, and the performance of the other three is refreshingly free of eccentricity, striking the right degree of breadth and dignity. Stein brings both imagination and feeling to this score, and he is excellently recorded in vintage (1973) Decca sound.

Stanislaw Skrowaczewski has proved himself an impressive Bruckner interpreter. This Arte Nova recording, made in the Saarbrücken Congress Hall in 1997, is very serviceable indeed and Skrowaczewski guides his forces with unerring purpose and nobility. Tempi are well judged throughout and phrases shaped with refinement. The string-tone needs perhaps to be weightier, but this is a very good performance, recommendable alongside Tintner on Naxos, whose account has slightly less gravitas but still has its own appealing individuality.

Symphony 6 in A; (i) *Te Deum*
(N) (**(*)) Testament mono SBT 1354. BBC SO, Klemperer, (i) with Harper, J. Baker, R. Lewis, M. Nowakowski, BBC Symphony Ch.

Those who heard the 1961 Third Programme broadcast have long treasured memories of Klemperer's dedicated performance of the *Sixth Symphony*. Although he recorded the symphony commercially three years later with the New Philharmonia, he never committed the *Te Deum* to disc. The BBC account is glorious, perfectly paced and wonderfully sung by the fine team of soloists, including the then youthful Janet Baker and the BBC Chorus making a last appearance under their legendary chorus-master, Leslie Woodgate, who retired shortly afterwards. The *Symphony* was a rarity at this time and much of the 18 hours of rehearsal must have been spent on familiarizing the orchestra with it. The downside in this set is the cramped acoustic of Studio 1, Maida Vale; the commercial set was made at Abbey Road and the orchestral playing is undoubtedly finer. Brucknerians will want this for an outstanding *Te Deum* and will still find much to interest them in the *Sixth*.

Symphonies 6 in A; 7 in E
(B) ** Ph. Duo (ADD) 473 301-2 (2). Concg. O, Haitink

These are eminently acceptable performances – and inexpensive, too. But this market is now fiercely competitive, and there are other more recommendable versions, not least by Haitink himself. The *Sixth* dates from the early 1970s, and Haitink's grasp of the Brucknerian architecture and his direct approach has many merits, including breadth and a certain atmosphere, though the opening could be played a little slower. The *Seventh* was recorded in 1966 and, once again, his directness and understanding ensures a sound performance, but his later, more expansive recording for Philips (1979) has far greater sensitivity to atmosphere. The sound remains full and warm in both.

Symphony 7 in E (original version)
(BB) ** Warner Apex 0927 40817-2. Frankfurt RSO, Inbal

For excellence of orchestral playing and vividness of recording, Inbal's *Seventh* is well up to the standard of his Bruckner series, using the original scores; but the performance itself, although not lacking an overall structural grip, is without the full flow of adrenalin that can make this symphony so compulsive. The great climax of the slow movement is much less telling without the famous contribution from the cymbals.

Symphony 7 in E
⊙━ *** Teldec 3984 24488-2. VPO, Harnoncourt
(M) *** BBC (ADD) BBCL 4123-2. Philh. O, Giulini – FALLA: *Three-Cornered Hat* (excerpts); MUSSORGSKY: *Khovanshchina: Prelude* ***
(BB) *** Naxos 8.554269. RSNO, Tintner
(N) (M) *** RCA 82876 62323-2. BPO, Wand
(M) (***) Dutton Lab. mono CDK 1205. Concg. O, Van Beinum (with TCHAIKOVSKY: *Waltz from Serenade for Strings* (***))
**(*) Häns. CD 93.027. SW German RSO, Stuttgart, Sanderling

Harnoncourt's outstanding performance of the *Seventh* was recorded live in the Sofiensaal and is one of his very finest records. The sound is magnificent: the Viennese strings have a radiant sheen and the brass is gloriously sonorous. The performance could hardly be more compelling. In the slow movement the cymbal crash at the climax is omitted, but even this does not spoil its impact, and in the beautiful coda Harnoncourt draws out the resemblance in the valedictory overlapping horn parts to Wagner's *Das Rheingold*. The *Scherzo* is extremely vivid, yet what is so striking about the reading overall is its appealing lyrical feeling, with its moments of gentle restraint. This has to compete with Tintner, but it is very highly recommendable in its own right. Harnoncourt admirers need not hesitate.

Giulini's account of the *Seventh Symphony* with the Philharmonia Orchestra comes from the BBC's 1982 Prom season, a performance totally dedicated from beginning to end. Those who were there have not forgotten its breadth and nobility, nor the spirituality of its slow movement. This was the period when the Philharmonia was at its peak, and it is fascinating to compare this live recording with the studio version that Giulini made for DG with the Vienna Philharmonic later in the 1980s. The Philharmonia playing is just as

refined as that of the Viennese, not least the strings, while the live interpretation has an extra intensity and concentration, with speeds consistently faster and more flexible, so that climaxes are all the more thrilling. This ranks among the finest non-studio accounts of this great work, and the sound achieved by the BBC engineers, though not state of the art by the standards of 2004, is very fine indeed, natural in perspective and finely balanced. The Falla fill-up comes from an earlier Prom season (1963) and the *Khovanshchina Prelude* from an Edinburgh Festival concert at the Usher Hall. Strongly recommended.

Like his other Bruckner recordings for Naxos, Tintner's account of No. 7 brings a performance both subtle and refined, concentrated from first to last, often at spacious speeds. The glow of Brucknerian sound is caught beautifully, with the full nobility of the slow movement brought out. The *Scherzo* is not as rugged as it can be but, with sprung rhythms, the dance element is infectious. An outstanding bargain to rival any version.

The RCA reissue offers Günter Wand's third recording of the *Seventh Symphony*; the earlier performances were with the Cologne Radio or NDR orchestras. It has the benefit of the Berlin Philharmonic and excellent recorded sound. As always with Wand, everything is phrased beautifully, and there is a fine balance between beauty of incident and the grandeur of the whole. It is thoroughly recommendable and the conductor's admirers need not hesitate, but overall it would not be a first choice.

Eduard van Beinum's reading, one of the finest ever put on record, brings a wonderfully persuasive response from the Concertgebouw Orchestra, not only rich in sonority but refined and often surprisingly transparent in texture, so that the effect of Bruckner's scoring is lighter than usual, especially in the lilting *Scherzo*. The great *Adagio* has superb concentration. Given another of Dutton's miraculous transfers, the 1947 Decca recording sounds both spacious and full-bodied. The Tchaikovsky *Waltz* which acts as encore is sheer delight.

Sanderling's is a spacious, powerfully expressive reading and he gets fine playing and rich string-tone from the Stuttgart orchestra. The advantage of a live performance is that, with the musicians fully committed, he feels able to relax instead of pressing on, and this brings moments when the tension ebbs somewhat, while in the slow movement the climax falls short of being overwhelming. The recording is good but not nearly as fine as Harnoncourt's.

Symphony 8 in C min. (1887 Nowak version)
(N) (BB) * Arte Nova 82876 62856-2 Bruckner O, Linz, Russell Davies

Like the Naxos version under Georg Tintner (coupled with *Die Nullte*), also at super-bargain price, Dennis Russell Davies's version uses the rarely performed first version of the *Eighth* in the Nowak Edition. This live recording offers a strong and idiomatic reading, but one that lacks the rapt dedication, the visionary quality of Tintner, with playing less refined. It is partly that Tintner builds climaxes with finer control of crescendo, with monumental results at broader tempi. The Naxos discs also offer an important fill-up, the *Symphony No. o*, where on Arte Nova there is no extra item.

Symphony 8 in C min. (ed. Haas)
⊙━ ✹ (M) *** DG 476 1654. VPO, Karajan
*** DG 459 678-2. VPO, Boulez
*** RCA 74321 82866-2 (2). BPO, Wand

(M) *** DG (ADD) 463 081-2. VPO, Boehm

(M) **(*) Chan. 7080 (2). LPO, Järvi – REGER: *Variations & Fugue on a Theme of Beethoven* ***

**(*) BBC (ADD) BBCL 4067-2. Hallé O, Barbirolli

(N) **(*) BBC (ADD) BBCL 4159-2 (2). Philh. O, Guilini – DVORAK: *Symphony 8 in G* (**(*); ROSSINI: *Semiramide Overture* ***

Karajan's last version of the *Eighth Symphony* is with the Vienna Philharmonic Orchestra and is the most impressive of them all. The sheer beauty of sound and opulence of texture is awe-inspiring but never draws attention to itself: this is a performance in which beauty and truth go hand in hand. The recording is superior to either of its predecessors in terms of naturalness of detail and depth of perspective. Understandably, Universal have picked it for reissue in their mid-priced 'Penguin ❂ Collection'.

With taut control Pierre Boulez directs a tough, intense reading of this most expansive of the Bruckner symphonies, one which is also warmly expressive in the great Bruckner melodies, helped by glowing playing from the Vienna Philharmonic. The terracing of the textures, as well as their clarification, typical of Boulez, is beautifully caught by the fine DG recording and the great slow movement proceeds magnetically, in Boulez's hands a powerful symphonic structure rather than a visionary statement. The finale – using the more expansive text of the Haas Edition – is then rugged and bitingly dramatic, with Boulez's use of rubato warmly idiomatic.

Recorded live in the Berlin Philharmonie in January 2001, Wand's reading of the massive *Eighth Symphony* in the Haas Edition brings a deeply dedicated performance, weightier and more expansive than his 1979 version with the Cologne Radio Symphony Orchestra. With full-bodied sound, the power of his interpretation comes over at full force, even if the lack of a true pianissimo means that the slow movement is less poignant than before, warm and open-hearted rather than mysterious, yet superbly controlled over the massive span of the *Adagio*. The tensions of a live event also add to the impact of the performance, with the *Scherzo* and the finale both conveying a degree of wildness in their thrusting power. A valuable alternative to the earlier version.

Though he never recorded a complete Bruckner symphony cycle, Karl Boehm was a Brucknerian to rival the greatest, as is movingly demonstrated in this superb reading of the longest and most challenging of the symphonies, the *Eighth*. Recorded in 1976, this is a performance that in the most natural way combines ruggedness and refinement. With the Vienna Philharmonic incandescent, the dynamic contrasts are sharply extreme. Boehm characteristically prefers steady speeds, so that the pulse of the expansive slow movement, for example, moves with unerring momentum as in a live performance, hushed in its intensity. Boehm also holds the diffuse structure of the finale tautly together in a manner that is natural and unforced yet powerful. Excellent, well-balanced sound, recorded in the Musikvereinsaal.

Neeme Järvi's reading with the LPO is warmly spontaneous from first to last, helped by opulent Chandos sound in this 1986 recording. The thrust of argument is conveyed persuasively throughout, as in a live performance, thanks to Järvi's easy control of rubato, with weighty brass set against silky string-tone. The Scherzo is warm, with no hint of menace, and the slow movement cocoons one in a sensuous bath of sound, before the weighty finale, even if the result is not always quite as detailed as in the finest versions. At

mid-price with the rare Reger fill-up it is still a good recommendation.

Barbirolli's Hallé version comes from a live Royal Festival Hall broadcast of 1970. The recording is well balanced, but limited in range and dynamic and the brass tuttis could ideally be more expansive. But its Festival Hall brightness is fully acceptable when the performance is so concentrated. Barbirolli's reading of the slow movement is deeply felt and warmly passionate in his characteristic manner, and the Hallé players respond eloquently both here and in the beautifully shaped and thrilling finale. The applause at the close is well deserved.

The Giulini BBC Legends recording comes from a 1983 concert at London's Royal Festival Hall and is a spacious, deeply felt and unhurried account which at 86 minutes bestrides two discs. The acoustic is well managed by the BBC engineers though it is less than ideally opulent. The coupling offers a Dvořák symphony, recorded at a much earlier stage in his association with the Philharmonia.

Symphonies (i) *8 in C min.;* (ii) *9 in D min.*
*** BBC (ADD) BBCL 4017-2 (2). (i) LSO; (ii) BBC SO; Horenstein
(B) *** EMI double forte (ADD) 5 73827-2 (2). Dresden State O, Jochum

These BBC recordings of performances at the Royal Albert Hall in 1970 reveal the genius of Jascha Horenstein more tellingly than almost any of his studio recordings. Though he draws out the warm expressiveness in Bruckner's lyrical writing, moulding phrases, he takes a rugged view of the overall structure, not least in his rapt account of the great *Adagio* in *Symphony No. 8*. Fine as the LSO is in that symphony with its brighter string-tone, the performance of the *Ninth* with the BBC Symphony brings even finer playing, strong and purposeful. Warm, atmospheric, rich sound.

With the benefit of wide-ranging, full-blooded recording, Jochum's Dresden version of the *Eighth* is a performance of incandescent warmth. His flexible, spontaneous-sounding style in Bruckner is here consistently persuasive from the mysterious opening of the first movement onwards. As in his earlier vesion for DG, Jochum opts for the Nowak edition. The quality is vivid for much of the time, but the climaxes are not without a touch of harshness and a hint of congestion. The Dresden account of the *Ninth* is another splendid example of Jochum's art, with the strings made to sound weighty and sonorous by the Dresden acoustic. Jochum is again at his most convincing here, giving an impression of spontaneity such as you would expect in the concert hall.

Symphony 9 in D min.
❂ (N) (M) *** Sony 518812-2 [SK 92737]. Cologne SO, Walter (with *Te Deum*: Yeend, Lipton, Lloyd, Harrell, Westminster Ch., NYPO, Walter)
(M) *** DG (IMS) 429 904-2. BPO, Karajan
(BB) *** Naxos 8.554268. RSNO, Tintner
(M) *** Teldec Elatus 0927 46746-2. BPO, Barenboim
(N) (M) (***) DG mono 474 990-2. Bav. RSO, Jochum
*** DG (IMS) 427 345-2. VPO, Giulini
(BB) **(*) LSO Live LSO 0023. LSO, C. Davis

Bruno Walter's 1959 account of Bruckner's *Ninth Symphony* represents the peak of his achievement during his Indian summer in the CBS recording studios just before he died. His mellow, persuasive reading leads one on through the leisurely paragraphs so that the logic and coherence seem obvious where other performances can sound aimless. Some may not find the *Scherzo* vigorous enough to provide the fullest contrast, but the final slow movement has a nobility which suggests that after this, anything would have been an anticlimax.

For the reissue Sony have added Walter's fine (1959) Carnegie Hall mono recording of the *Te Deum*, a characteristically spacious account with a well-matched team of soloists and an excellent contribution from the Westminster Choir. The transfer of the very good mono recording is well managed.

The DG Galleria reissue of Karajan's 1966 recording offers a glorious performance of Bruckner's last and uncompleted symphony, characteristically moulded and displaying a simple, direct nobility that is sometimes missing in this work. Even in a competitive field, this disc stands out at mid-price, to rank alongside Bruno Walter's noble 1959 version.

Like others in his Bruckner series, Georg Tintner's Naxos recording of the *Ninth Symphony* is a match in every way for the finest rival versions, whatever the price. The refinement of *pianissimos* brings out the full mystery of the massive outer movements, while the delicate fantasy of the *Scherzo* is brilliantly touched on at high speed, with a touch of wildness. The final *Adagio* builds up in exultation: this may not have been planned as the finale, but here it becomes the most deeply satisfying conclusion. The playing of the Royal Scottish National Orchestra is superb, with recording at once transparent and refined, as well as weighty.

Daniel Barenboim's Berlin account has depth and strength, with the advantage of superb orchestral playing, and the recorded sound has splendid body and transparency. One of the strongest of newer recommendations.

Giulini's *Ninth* is also a great performance, the product of deep thought. There is the keenest feeling for texture and beauty of contour, and he distils a powerful sense of mystery from the first and third movements. The DG recording is spacious and transparent.

Recorded in 1954 in the Herkulessaal, Munich, Jochum's was the earliest LP version of the *Ninth Symphony*, save only for the Horenstein account on Vox. It enjoyed classic status in its day and remained in the catalogue until the early 1960s. There is a spirituality and authenticity of feeling about Jochum's Bruckner, and the revival of this fine performance deserves a place in any comprehensive Bruckner collection. It is little short of amazing how well the DG mono recording has come up. It is very handsomely presented too, reproducing the original sleeve and session details.

Sir Colin Davis's account with the LSO comes from a concert recorded at the Barbican Hall in February 2002. He takes a very leisurely view of the first movement, one of the very slowest on record, and takes 66 minutes over the whole work. Some will find this too much of a good thing. The LSO give intensive and responsive playing in all departments. Not a first choice in what is an intensely competitive field but one that Brucknerians ought to hear. Decent sound.

CHAMBER MUSIC

String Quintet in F
*** Nim. NI 5488 Brandis Qt, with Dean – BRAHMS: *String Quintet 2* ***

(N) *** Australian Decca Eloquence (ADD) 476 2455. VPO Quintet, with H. Weiss – SCHMIDT: *Piano Quintet* ***

String Quintet in F; Intermezzo for String Quintet
(*) Hyp. CDA 66704. Raphael Ens. – R. STRAUSS: *Capriccio: Sextet* *

(M) **(*) CRD 3456. Alberni Qt

Bruckner's beautiful *Quintet* dates from 1878, immediately after the revision of the *Third* and *Fourth Symphonies*. It is music of substance and depth, and this superb account by the Vienna Philharmonic Quintet remains an excellent way of getting to know this fine work. The rich (1974) Decca/ Sofiensaal sound – full and sweet – retains its qualities on CD.

The Brandis version of the *Quintet* offers a splendid coupling in Brahms's *G major Quintet*, Op. 111, and their playing stands up well alongside the current competition. They are well recorded and have a natural feeling for the space and pacing of this piece. For those attracted by the coupling, this could well be a first choice.

The Raphael Ensemble, coupling their performance with the *Intermezzo in D minor* and the opening *Sextet* from Strauss's *Capriccio*, are ardently full-blooded in an eloquent account and have the benefit of rich recorded sound.

The Alberni version comes from the early 1980s without any additional fill-up. It is well played without affectation and, taken in isolation, is most satisfying. Hardly a first choice though.

VOCAL MUSIC

Masses (i) *1 in D min.; 2 in E min.;* (ii) *3 in F min.*
✪(M) *** DG (ADD) 447 409-2 (2). (i) Mathis, Schiml, Ochman, Ridderbusch; (ii) Stader, Hellman, Haefliger, Borg; Bav. R. Ch. & O, Jochum

Bruckner composed his three *Masses* between 1864 and 1868, although all three works were revised two decades later. Each contains magnificent music. Eugen Jochum is surely an ideal interpreter, finding their mystery as well as their eloquence, breadth and humanity. The *Kyrie* of the *E minor* swelling out gloriously from its gentle opening is breathtaking, while the fervour of the passionate *F minor* work is extraordinarily compelling, with the intensity and drive of an inspirational live performance. Throughout all three works, the scale and drama of Bruckner's inspiration are fully conveyed, and in these newest transfers the warmly atmospheric analogue recordings from the early 1970s are given remarkable vividness and presence.

Masses 1–3; Aequalis 1 & 2; Motets: Afferentur regi virgines; Ave Maria; Christus factus est; Ecce sacerdos magnus; Inveni David; Locus iste; Os justi; Pange lingua; Tota pulchra es, Maria; Vexilla regis; Virga Jesse; Libera me; Psalm 150; Te Deum
*** Hyp. CDS 4407 (3). Soloists, Corydon Singers and O; ECO Wind Ens., Best; T. Trotter (organ)

It makes good sense to assemble all of the Bruckner choral music that the Corydon Singers and Matthew Best have recorded during the last few years in one three-CD set. They are very fine indeed and make a splendid modern alternative to Jochum; when eloquent and natural, Best's direction is imaginative and he achieves a wide tonal range.

Mass 2 in E min.; Mass in C
*** Chan. 9863. Kuznetsova, Golub, Russian State Symphonic Cappella, Russian State SO, Polyansky

There is something seraphic about the *E minor Mass*. It may not have the grandeur and majesty of the later symphonies, but there is a simplicity of invention and an elevation of feeling that are affecting, particularly when it is recorded so beautifully and performed with the eloquence of Polyansky and his Russian forces on Chandos. The early *C major Mass* is a most welcome coupling.

Masses (i) 2 in E min.; (ii) 3 in F min.; (iii) 5 Motets: Ave Maria; Christus factus est; Locus iste; Os justi; Virga Jesse; (iii; iv) Te Deum
(BB) ** EMI Gemini (ADD) 5 85508-2. (i) John Alldis Ch., ECO; (ii) Harper, Reynolds, Tear, Rintzler; (iii) New Philh. Ch., (iv) Pashley, Finnilä, Tear, Garrard; (ii; iv) New Philh. O; Barenboim

Barenboim's approach to the *E minor Mass* and the *Te Deum* is one of dramatic extremes, with meditative passages exceptionally slow and fast passages unusually urgent, the contrasts emphasized by the flamboyant EMI sound with its wide dynamic range. But there is no lack of dynamism and the *Te Deum* is a vivid, boisterous performance, relying not so much on massive choral effects (the recording was done with a comparatively small choir in a smallish church) as on rhythmic energy. The *F minor Mass* is by no means dull or without character but, even more here, one feels that Barenboim does not quite capture the right atmosphere. The motets are well sung; but this is not a first choice for this repertoire.

(i) Mass 3 in F min. (original version). Motets: Ave Maria; Locus iste; Virga Jesse Floruit
(N) (B) **(*) DG Eloquence 477 5032. Stader, Hellman, Haefliger, Borg; (i) Bav. R. Ch. & SO, Jochum

This was Jochum's first stereo recording of the *F minor Mass*, using the original score and dating from 1963. Not unexpectedly, Jochum achieves fine singing and playing from his Bavarian forces, and he has a good team of soloists whose soprano and tenor are outstanding. The *Motets*, too, are finely sung, but the later recordings are even finer.

Missa solemnis in B flat min.; Psalms 112, 150
(BB) *** Virgin 2×1 5 61501-2 (2). Oelze, Schubert, Dürmüller, Hagen, Bamberg Ch. & SO, Rickenbacher – MOZART: Requiem ***

Bruckner's *Missa solemnis* is a comparatively early work (1854), written a decade before the *D major Mass*. It is given a strong, fresh performance here, with a good solo team, although the soprano, Christiane Oelze, sounds a bit hard at times. The two Psalm settings are 30 years apart, with *Psalm 150* (1892) obviously the more mature: both are sung eloquently. The chorus, as in the Mozart coupling, are set back in a spacious acoustic. Altogether this makes a thoroughly worthwhile bargain Double, unexpectedly pairing early Bruckner with late Mozart.

Motets: Afferentur regi; Ave Maria; Christus factus est; Ecce sacerdos; Iam lucis orto sidere; Inveni David; Libera me; Locus iste; Os justi; Pange lingua; Salvum fac populum tuum; Tantum ergo; Tota pulchra es; Vexilla regis; Virga Jesse
(BB) *** Naxos 8.550956. St Bride's Church Ch., Jones

(i) Motets: Afferentur regi; Ave Maria; Christus factus est; Ecce sacerdos; Locus iste; Os justi; Pange lingua; Tota pulchra es; Vexilla regis; Virga Jesse. (ii) Psalm 150; Te Deum
(M) *** DG (ADD) 457 743-2 (2). (i) Bav. R. Ch.; (ii) Stader, Wagner, Haefliger, Lagger, German Op. Ch., Berlin, BPO; Jochum

Motets: Afferentur regi; Ecce sacerdos; Inveni David; Os justi; Pange lingua
(BB) *** Belart (ADD) 461 317-2. St John's College, Cambridge, Ch., ASMF, Guest – BEETHOVEN: *Mass in C* ***

This Naxos disc is the first commercial recording of the St Bride's Church Choir, and very impressive it is, for with crisp, clear ensemble and fresh tone from boyish-sounding sopranos they give warmly sympathetic performances of these fine Bruckner motets, an excellent selection covering most of the best known. The recording is full and vivid, set against a helpful church acoustic which does not obscure detail.

On DG, the ten motets are sung superbly and are among Jochum's most distinguished recordings. With excellent soloists, the performances of the two larger-scale works here have fine eloquence and admirable breadth and humanity and no lack of drama and, with some fine singing from Maria Stader and Ernst Haefliger, as well as superbly loving orchestral support from the Berliners, this has a special eloquence. The original recordings tended to be distanced; in making the sound more present and clear the remastering is undoubtedly fresher and brighter.

The St John's performances are of the highest quality and the recording is marvellously spacious. They come in the lowest price-range, coupled with a fine account of Beethoven's *C major Mass*.

Requiem in D min.; Psalms 112 & 114
**(*) Hyp. CDA 66245. Rodgers, Denley, M. Davies, George, Corydon Singers, ECO, Best; T. Trotter (organ)

Matthew Best here tackles the very early setting of the *Requiem* which Bruckner wrote at the age of 25. The quality of the writing in the Psalm settings also varies; but with fine, strong performances from singers and players alike, including an excellent team of soloists, this is well worth investigating by Brucknerians. First-rate recording.

Te Deum
●► (B) *** Warner Apex 8573 89128-2. Spreckelsen, Ankerson, Adalbert Kraus, Moll, Bielefeld Musikverein Ch., Philh. Hung., Stephani – VERDI: *Te Deum* ***
(B) **(*) DG Double (ADD) 453 091-2 (2). Tomowa-Sintow, Baltsa, Schreier, Van Dam, V. Singverein, VPO, Karajan – VERDI: *Requiem Mass* **(*)

An outstanding account of Bruckner's 1884 setting of the *Te Deum* from Martin Stephani, vibrantly direct and gripping, with an excellent team of soloists and very fine choral singing over a wide range of dynamic. Stephani is fully sympathetic to the composer's deeply felt religious feeling. The well-balanced recording provides a warm acoustic while giving the chorus bite and amplitude. Text and translation are included. A bargain.

Karajan's analogue account of the *Te Deum* is spacious and strong, bringing out the score's breadth and drama. This is very satisfying and, if the Verdi coupling is acceptable, is self-recommending.

BRUMEL, Antoine (c. 1460–c. 1520)

Missa: Et ecce terrae motus; Sequentia: Dies irae, Dies illa
●► ✿ (M) *** Sony SMK 89613. Huelgas Ens., Van Nevel

Missa: Et ecce terrae motus; Lamentations; Magnificat secondi toni
*** Gimell CDGIM 026. Tallis Scholars, Philips

Brumel succeeded Josquin as *maestro di cappella* at Ferrara. Lassus himself prepared and took part in a performance of the 12-part Mass, *Et ecce terrae motus*, in Munich in the 1570s, and this is the only copy of the work that survives. It is not just the contrapuntal ingenuity of Brumel's music that impresses but the sheer beauty of sound with which we are presented. Brumel was not only one of the first to write a polyphonic *Requiem* but the very first to make a polyphonic setting of the sequence *Dies irae, Dies illa*. This is a more severe work than the glorious 12-part Mass which occupies the bulk of this CD, and it is written in a more medieval tonal language. The performances by the Huelgas Ensemble under their founder–director, Paul van Nevel, are fervent and eloquent and vividly bring this music back to life. This recording, made in the ample acoustic of the Irish Chapel in Liège, is resplendent.

The Tallis Scholars are hardly less impressive than the Huelgas Ensemble. In some respects their disc is complementary in that they opt for a different solution to the *Agnus Dei*, which is incomplete in the Munich manuscript. Van Nevel favours a Danish source that Philips and his editor reject on the grounds that it uses six voices and voices of different range. The texture in their performance has greater transparency and clarity than the richer, darker sonority of the Van Nevel. Both can be recommended. However, the reissued Sony version now has a distinct price advantage and readers who have not already acquired it (or the Hyperion alternative) should lose no time in securing a copy, before Sony delete it again!

BRUSA, Elisabetta (born 1954)

Adagio; Favole; Firelights; Requiescat; Suite grotesque; Wedding Song
(BB) **(*) Naxos 8.555267. Nat. SO of Ukraine, Mastrangelo

Elisabetta Brusa was born in Milan and studied at the Conservatoire, before moving on to participate at Dartington and Tanglewood. Of the two Naxos discs of her orchestral music, this is the more enticing. The glittering Scherzo, *Firelights*, is characteristic of her orchestral skill, but the expressive eloquence of the following 16-minute Adagio would not be out of place in almost any late twentieth-century symphony, and the engagingly rhapsodic *Wedding Song* ('an ode to the inner and outward joy of love and marriage') that follows is memorable in a lustrously romantic way,

The yearning *Requiescat* for large orchestra ('a freely structured musical prayer in a single movement') is dedicated to the composer's mentor, Hans Keller, and ends with a soaring solo soprano voice adding to the passionate celebration of the coda. The *Suite grotesque* might be regarded as a sinfonietta, with its slightly weird opening Scherzo, a darkly atmospheric slow movement, and a vigorous finale that gathers together the themes of the preceding movements 'in quadruple counterpoint', to reach a very positive apotheosis.

In the *Fables* Brusa uses the same orchestral identifications as did Prokofiev in *Peter and the Wolf*, so the listener has no trouble in identifying the characters. Most imaginative are Hans Andersen's *The Real Nightingale and the Mechanical*

One, and the innocently poignant portrait of *The Ugly Duckling*. Most picaresque is La Fontaine's *The Ant and the Grasshopper* (a saxophone), but *The Philosophical Fly* (Aesop) meets his end spectacularly, and Perrault's *Puss in Boots* is given a jolly royal march, with a winningly jaunty main theme. First-class performances and a splendidly vivid recording, with the only real reservation being the unflattering sound of the Ukrainian upper strings.

Fanfare; Florestan (orchestral portrait); Nittemero Symphony; Messidor (fantasy); La Triade (symphonic poem)
(BB) **(*) Naxos 8.555266. Nat. SO of Ukraine, Mastrangelo

Messidor is the most immediately attractive work here, an orchestral fantasy inspired by 'A Midsummer Night's Dream'. It reminds one of early Delius, though dissonance clouds the coda. *Florestan* (1997) evokes Schumann's imaginary character. It opens ardently and melodramatically with strings and horns, but it is the atmospherically lyrical music that is more memorable.

'Rain pours down incessantly' in *La Triade* (1994), an orchestral 'curtain of water', its scenario drawn both by an Aesop fable (with a fox and snake the central characters) and by Leonardo da Vinci's description of 'The Deluge'. The *Nittemero* ('Night and Day') *Symphony* (1985–8) is scored for 14 players, and again the ear is immediately struck by the composer's vivid orchestral world. The three-movement work is cyclic, depicting the 24 hours, from midday to midday. The work ends very confidently, as does the Adams-like minimalist *Fanfare*, which brings a positive end to the programme.

The performances here are bold and committed and generally well recorded, except that the Ukrainian violins sound thin in their upper range. But this is a promising début, and worth sampling at Naxos price.

BRYARS, Gavin (born 1943)

(i) *Cello Concerto*; (ii) *Les Fiancailles*; (iii) *The Green Ray* (for saxophone & orchestra); (ii) *The North Shore*; (iv) *One Last Bar, then Joe can sing* (for percussion ensemble); (ii) *The Sinking Titanic*; (ii; v) *Adnan Songbook*; (vi) *Jesus's Blood Never Failed Me Yet* (2 versions)
*** Ph. 473 296-2 (2). (i) Lloyd Webber, ECO, Judd; (ii) Gavin Bryars Ens.; (iii) Harle, Bournemouth Sinf., Bolton; (iv) Nexus; (v) Anderson, Smith; (vi) Waits

This two-disc compilation celebrating the sixtieth birthday of Gavin Bryars, one of the most approachable of contemporary British composers, brings together an attractive and wide-ranging cross-section of his works. Each disc begins with one of the two most ambitious works, concertante pieces with the original soloists: Julian Lloyd Webber in the *Cello Concerto* and the saxophonist John Harle in *The Green Ray*, which was inspired by a novel of Jules Verne and evokes the west of Scotland. The *North Shore*, for viola (Bill Hawkes) and chamber group, was similarly inspired by a place, the cliffs by St Hilda's Abbey near Whitby, Yorkshire, with another Jules Verne reference. Predominantly lyrical and reflective, at times skirting the edge of Minimalism, these and the other works are at once approachable and challenging, with Bryars's most popular piece, *Jesus's Blood Never Failed Me Yet*, inspired by the singing of a tramp, here given in two compact versions, designed for a record 'single' instead of an LP or CD. Excellent performances from a wide variety of sources in America as well as Britain.

BUNCH, Kenji (born 1973)

Fantasy for Violin & Orchestra
(B) ** EMI Début 5 73501-2. Shapira, ECO, Hazlewood –
   BLOCH: *Baal Shem* ***; BRUCH: *Violin Concerto 1* **;
   SARASATE: *Zigeunerweisen* **(*)

This piece forms part of a début recital. It was written for this gifted player, who is described by the composer as playing a Joachim-like role in its gestation. It would be unkind to press the parallel with Brahms further, for this is a very thin, amorphous piece – quite sub-Bloch.

BURGON, Geoffrey (born 1941)

At the round earth's imagined corners; But have been found again; Laudate Dominum; Magnificat; Nunc dimittis; A Prayer to the Trinity; Short Mass; This World; 2 Hymns to Mary
**(*) Hyp. CDA 66123. Chichester Cathedral Ch., Thurlow

Burgon's famous *Nunc dimittis* is well matched here with the *Magnificat* which he later wrote to complement it and a series of his shorter choral pieces, all of them revealing his flair for immediate, direct communication, and well performed. First-rate recording.

(i) *The Calm; Merciless Beauty; (ii) A Vision*
*** ASV CDDCA 1059. (i) Bowman; (ii) Jenkins; (i) City of London Sinfonia, (ii) ASMF, (i; ii) composer

In *Merciless Beauty* the alto voice blends so closely with the orchestra that James Bowman seems an integral part of the texture, within semi-voluptuous scoring. All these seven songs are about love, but the most striking is the title-number (a setting of Chaucer) while the closing *Campionesque for Anna* matches the opening *Western wind* in its languorously exotic line. The tenor cycle, *A Vision*, offers settings of John Clare (1793–1864) and pictures the countryside as seen through the eyes of a sensitive farmworker-poet. These songs are generally more restrained and reflectively touching. An interlude, *Voices from the Calm* (originally a ballet score), offers instrumental writing, with the counter-tenor voice again laminated in, and is no less evocative in feeling. The closing *Voices from the Calm*, a dream couplet by Walt Whitman (which also inspired the ballet), returns to voices – overlapping vocal lines. All the performances are warmly sensitive and beautifully recorded in an ideally warm ambience.

BUSH, Alan (1900–95)

(i) *Violin Concerto, Op. 32; (ii) Dialectic for String Quartet; (iii) 6 Short Pieces for Piano, Op. 99*
☞━ *** Claudio (ADD) CB 5151-2. (i) Parikian, BBC SO, Del Mar; (ii) Medici Qt; (ii) composer

Alan Bush – a pupil of John Ireland and Professor of Composition at the Royal Academy of Music for half a century – was one of the major figures of British music in the 1920s to 1940s, and in his earlier works he developed a promising 'thematic' variation of serialism, which retained a tonal base. He joined the British Communist Party in 1935 and remained a blinkered devotee of the Soviet political mirage throughout his life, even moderating his slightly thorny early lyricism into a more easily communicative style in 1948, loyally following the Soviet directive. Sadly, when he was in his nineties (as

John Amis relates in his excellent notes for the Meridian CD) he was 'not even aware of the crumbling of the Soviet Union', for 'his memory of the last fifty years had disappeared'. In Britain his politics alienated many in positions of power, and his works in consequence went unheard. He observed somewhat wryly: 'Well, I suppose you might say I asked for it.'

The excellent recordings on the Claudio disc date from the early 1980s and are of high quality. The vividly attractive and comparatively mellow *Violin Concerto* of 1948 marked Bush's change to a more easy-going, rhapsodic style, here balancing the structure of the piece after its pulsing rhythmic opening and before the closely related dance-like finale. The writing has an attractive element of neoclassicism and altogether this is a concentrated work that readily communicates, especially in a solo performance as persuasively assured and sympathetic as that given by Manoug Parikian, admirably accompanied by the BBC orchestra under Del Mar.

The *Dialectic* is the composer's masterpiece and it is marvellously played. Tersely argued but brimming over with passionate lyricism, it reaches a fugal climax of thrusting intensity, even recalling Beethoven's *Grosse Fuge*. The immediately attractive late *Piano Pieces* are also appealingly characterful as presented here by the composer.

Symphonies 1 in C, Op. 21; 2 (Nottingham), Op. 33
(N) ** Classico CLASSCD 484. Royal N. College of Music SO, Bostock

Of the first two Alan Bush symphonies, No. 1 is overtly political. Although written during the troubled early war years, the work's uneasy, fretting character is more concerned with the 'class conflicts' of British society, as observed through the eyes of a dedicated Communist Party member. The first movement is based on a tone row but the music never loses its tonal basis. It evolves into a 'Dance of Death' to which 'capitalist policy has brought the peoples of the world'. Ironically, its traits can be more readily linked with the consequences of the Stalinist regime. The slow movement broods in despair, producing a passionately protesting climax and an impotently furious coda. The finale is more cheerful, supposedly representing communist dynamism, but also apparently associated with Marshal Tito, 'Defender of Peace'.

The *Second (Nottingham) Symphony* (1949) is altogether mellower. Bush responded to the Zhdanov doctrine of 1948 and decided to compose music with more direct, popular appeal. But the result is more of a suite than a symphony, and the first movement is almost like a film scene in its ingenuous portrayal of *Sherwood Forest*, complete with hunting-calls and galloping horses, and the slow movement (*Clifton Grove*) suggests the idyllic scene of the flowing River Trent. The Scherzo (*Castle Rock*) is animated and includes both a passacaglia and a fugue, yet fails to charm the ear, with its violent climax remembering a popular political uprising against the Duke of Newcastle in 1931 (over the Reform Bill). *Goose Fair*, the finale, is essentially more genial, and is brightly scored. It ends not very convincingly, with celebratory bells. Both these splendidly played peformances by the excellent Royal Northern College of Music Symphony Orchestra under Douglas Bostock are as persuasive as they could be. The recording, too, is excellent. But this is not music one is compelled to return to.

Cello Sonata, Op. 120; 3 Contrapuntal Studies for Violin and Viola, Op. 13; Phantasy for Violin and Piano, Op. 3; Piano Quartet, Op. 5
(M) *** Dutton CDLX 7130. London Piano Qt

Listed below is an attractive programme of Bush's chamber

music on Meridian, and this new collection from Dutton is, if anything, even more enjoyable. The *Cello Sonata* was written in 1989, sixty years after the other works here, and it shows the mature composer at his finest. Its bold *Allegro energico* immediately establishes the music's strength of purpose, and the expressive *Larghetto molto espressivo*, with its modal harmonic flavour, is memorable in such a sympathetic performance as this by David Kennedy and Philip Fowke. The *Piano Quartet* (1924, revised 1929) is also highly inventive and full of character, its harmonic language individual but never becoming aggressive: its warm underlying lyricism ensures the music's ready communication throughout.

The equally appealing *Phantasy for Violin and Piano* (1923) is similarly lavish in its melodic flow and it brings matching rhythmic freedom, while the three *Contrapuntal Studies* are as aurally enticing as they are skilfully contrived. (They probably date from 1929, the year of Bush's most stimulating chamber work, the *Dialectic* for string quartet.)

All these performances from members of the London Piano Quartet are deeply felt and show how well these four fine artists identify completely with the composer. The recording too, is very lifelike, to make this a most rewarding collection.

(i; ii) *Concert Piece for Cello & Piano, Op. 17;* (i–iii) *3 Concert Studies for Piano Trio, Op. 31;* (i; ii) *2 Easy Pieces for Cello & Piano;* (ii; iii) *2 Melodies, Op. 47;* *Sonatina, Op. 88* (both for viola & piano); (i; ii) *Summer Valley for Cello & Piano*

*** Mer. CDE 84458. (i) Spooner; (ii) C. Summerhayes; (iii) A. Summerhayes

The instrumental programme on Meridian is stimulating and includes the other key work in the composer's output, the riveting *Concert Piece* for cello and piano of 1936, written prophetically as war clouds were gathering in Europe. The music's harmony is bleakly astringent, yet there is a touchingly poignant central cantilena, before the malevolent closing section with its march rhythms builds to an uncompromisingly hostile climax. The balm of the *Viola Sonatina* with its pastoral feeling and the lovely, very English evocation of a *Summer Valley* (both ravishingly played here) offer genuine solace.

The three artists on Meridian play very sympathetically indeed and with fine ensemble. There is all the expressive power needed in Op. 17, while the central *Nocturne* of the Op. 31 *Concert Studies* for piano trio is haunting in its evocative feeling, and the closing *Alla Bulgaria* is enjoyably spirited. The two charming *Easy Pieces* for cello, and the pair for viola (both with piano) show Bush's disarming melodic gift. Let John Amis have the final word. He tells us: 'Bush was a delightful man' who 'wrote music for head and heart, and many times managed to combine the two elements … these [works] are all masterly and endearing.'

(i) *Lyric Interlude, Op. 26;* *Meditation on a German Song* (The Trooper's Pledge), *Op. 22;* *Le quatorze juillet: esquisse, Op. 38;* *Preludes & Fugues 1–2, Op. 108;* *Serenade and Duet, Op. 111;* *Song and Dance, Op. 117a.* *3 Râga Melodies for Unaccompanied Violin, Op. 59*

(N) *** Mer. CDE 844481. Alan Summerhayes; (i) Catherine Summerhayes

Alan Bush's splendid four-movement *Lyric Interlude* (1944) shows the composer at his most appealingly melodic. Its intensity of feeling derives from the tragic death of one of his daughters in a road accident. The *Andantino* is full of tender

warmth; the Scherzo is engagingly light-hearted, a portrait perhaps, and the passionately lyrical finale is full of life rather than a threnody. The *Meditation on a German Song* of 1848 perhaps expresses the composer's feelings about death even more tellingly. It introduces a beautiful and very disconsolate German melody, taken from a song, which tells of a conscripted horse-soldier's pledge as he rides 'for freedom's sake' to almost certain death. The central section suggests the 'bitter dregs' of battle, and the work ends elegiacally.

Le quatorze juillet, both jaunty and reflective, is a very French tribute to the wartime Résistance. The *Three Râga Melodies* (1961), for solo violin, although written in classic Râga styles, still have a surprisingly Western feeling. Apart from the concentration of the writing, there is little Bachian influence in the two late *Preludes and Fugues* (1986) and the connecting rhapsodic 'Interlude' emphasizes the lyricism of the composer's style. With the *Serenade and Duet*, Op. 111, and the delightful miniatures of Op. 117a Bush finally moves into a distinctly English modal style and an appealing personal simplicity of uuterance. Altogether this is a first-class survey. Adam Summerhayes proves a committed, accomplished and understanding advocate, admirably partnered by Catherine, and the Meridian balance and recording cannot be faulted.

Suite of Six (for String Quartet), Op. 81

*** Redcliffe RR 020. Bochmann Qt (with PURCELL: *Chacony in G min.*, ed. Britten ***) – BRIDGE: *String Quartet 4* ***

Dating from 1975, Alan Bush's *Suite of Six* is his final work for string quartet. It is most imaginatively structured and splendidly inventive. An *Introduction* and *Postlude* frame the six central movments, displaying and recalling the six different modes in which they are written. Four are in dance format: a resourceful, imitative *Pavane* with the instruments in pairs, followed by a spirited *Reel*, a snappy *Moto perpetuo* jig and a bold but more lyrical *Sword Dance*. The two slow movements provide serene central interludes, the first an engaging folk-styled Aeolian *Andante*, the second a lovely *Air*. The writing consistently shows the composer at his finest. The Bochmann Quartet give a subtly detailed and expressive performance of high quality, and they are beautifully recorded. The coupled Frank Bridge *Quartet* is a harder nut to crack, but Purcell's *Chacony* makes a heart-warming encore.

Prison Cycle (with Rawsthorne)

(*) Campion Cameo 2001. Wells, Swallow – RAWSTHORNE: *Songs* **(*); MCCABE: *Folk Songs* *

Alan Bush contributed three of the five songs that make up the sombre *Prison Cycle*, set to poems by the German socialist poet Ernst Toller, the first and last of which picture him endlessly pacing up and down in his restricted space, and the second in which he dwells on the increasing familiarity and friendliness of all the everyday objects that surround him in his otherwise bare cell. Alison Wells's sympathetic performances are discussed under the Rawsthorne coupling.

BUSH, Geoffrey (born 1920)

Farewell, Earth's Bliss; 4 Hesperides Songs; A Menagerie; (i) *A Summer Serenade*

*** Chan. 8864. Varcoe, Thompson, Westminster Singers, City of L. Sinfonia, Hickox, (i) with Parkin

The delightful *Summer Serenade* of seven song-settings has long been Bush's most frequently performed work, and this first recording glowingly brings out the sharp contrasts of mood within and between the songs, with instrumentation just as felicitous as the choral writing. It is well coupled with a solo song-cycle of comparable length, *Farewell, Earth's Bliss*, with Stephen Varcoe the baritone soloist; four songs from Herrick's *Hesperides*, also for baritone and strings; and three for unaccompanied voices, including an insistently menacing setting of Blake's *Tyger*. The tenor Adrian Thompson, not ideally pure-toned, contributes to only two of the *Serenade* songs; otherwise these are near-ideal performances in warm, open sound.

BUSNOIS, Antoine (c. 1430–92)

Antoine Busnois was an adventurous and controversial cleric by any standards, and a well-travelled musician. In the 1460s, while serving as chaplain at Tours Cathdral, he was involved in violence against a priest, for which he was excommunicated, but subsequently he was pardoned by Pope Pius II. He later relocated to Poitiers, where he established a more peaceful reputation as poet and musician. He moved on to join the Duke of Burgundy's Court Chapel, and was present at the Duke's major battles, fought during the decade from 1467 to 1475. He ended his ecclesiastical career at Bruges. Manuscripts and prints of his music have been found in a number of countries, including Italy and England, demonstrating how well he was esteemed during his lifeime.

Chansons: Amours nous traitte honnestement/Je m'en voy; A une damme j'ay fait veu; Est-il merchy de quoy on puet finer?; Ja que li ne s'i attende; Missa O Crux lignum;
Chanson-Motet: Resjois-toy, terre de France; Motets: Gaude caelestis Domina; Incomprehensibilia/Praeter rerum ordinem
(N) *** HM HMU 907333. Orlando Consort

The present collection displays the scope of Busnois's musical personality, for the chansons and the patriotic chanson-motet are strikingly colloquial and very different from the ecclesiastical music, something well understood by the four members of the Orlando Consort. The Hymn, *Conditor alme siderum* ('Kindly creator of the Stars') is surprisingly memorable, the performance notable for its rhythmic accents. The lines of the *Missa O Crux lignum* flow more smoothly, and the cantus firmus remains admirably clear throughout when, performed by just four voices, the part-writing is so clear. The disc is beautifully packaged, and full texts and translations are included.

Missa l'homme armé; Motets: Anima mea liquefacta est; Gaude celestis
*** Hyp. CDA 67319. Binchois Consort, Kirkman (with PULLOIS: *Flos de spina*) – DOMARTO: *Missa Spiritus almus* ***

The disappointment for the non-specialist listener in Busnois's Mass setting using *L'homme armé* is that the composer's long, pliable, melismatic lines disguise the nature of the original chanson, so that it becomes submerged in the flowing textures. It is a fine work nevertheless, reaching its climax at the powerful *Sanctus*. But the plangent motet, *Anima mea liquefacta est*, is even more striking with its darker sonorities and use of low voices. *Gaude celestis* also has a low bass line, but the upper voices dominate celestially. The ravishingly rich-voiced *Flos de spina* by Ockeghem's contemporary and colleague, Jean Pullois, makes a splendid postlude.

BUSONI, Ferruccio (1866–1924)

Berceuse élégiaque, Op. 42; (i) *Concertino for Clarinet & Small Orchestra. Geharnischte Suite; 2 Studies for Doktor Faust, Op. 51; Tanz Walzer*
*** Chan. 9920. (i) Bradbury; BBC PO, Järvi

The *Geharnischte Suite* is the rarity here. It was written in 1895 during Busoni's time in Helsinki and dedicated to members of his circle there – Sibelius (whose cause he championed in Germany), Armas and Eero Järnefelt, and the writer Adolf Paul. It was revised in 1903, and although not top-drawer Busoni, it is still rewarding and inventive. Neeme Järvi and the BBC Philharmonic produce sumptuous performances of the moving, dream-like *Berceuse élégiaque*, written on the death of the composer's mother, and the inspired *Sarabande* and *Cortège*, the *Studies for Doktor Faust*. The *Tanz Walzer* also found their way into *Doktor Faust*, where they were used to depict festivities at the Court of Parma. The BBC Philharmonic play with evident commitment, and John Bradbury is the elegant and sensitive soloist in the *Concertino for Clarinet and Small Orchestra*. The sound is first class and in the best traditions of the house.

Berceuse élégiaque; 2 Studies for Doktor Faust; Turandot Suite, Op. 41
(BB) **(*) Naxos 8.555373. Hong Kong PO, Wong

Popularity seems to rest as much on chance as on merit, for it is difficult to understand why the *Turandot Suite* has never become a popular repertory piece. Sir Malcolm Sargent conducted it with the BBC Symphony Orchestra in the late 1950s and early 1960s, but it remains virtually unplayed these days, and only in recent years has it been recorded (by Muti in 1994). Given its bargain price, it should now reach a wider audience. It has all the qualities of melodic appeal (its fifth movement quotes *Greensleeves*), resourceful invention and brilliant orchestral colour that should ensure its popularity. The two *Studies*, the *Sarabande* and *Cortège*, written in preparation for his opera, *Doktor Faust*, remain the composer's masterpiece, highly searching and imaginative music that can claim to be profound, as, indeed, can the *Berceuse élégiaque*. Both performances and recording are very good, and this disc serves as an admirable and inexpensive introduction to a fascinating and underrated master, although on the assumption that Neeme Järvi goes on to record the *Turandot Suite* in his Busoni series, readers may want to hold their hand before acquiring this.

Piano Concerto, Op. 39
☛ *** Hyp. CDA 67143. Hamelin, CBSO Ch., CBSO, Elder
(M) *** Telarc CD 80207. Ohlsson, Cleveland O & Ch., Dohnányi
(M) (*(**)) Somm mono BEECHAM 15. Mewton-Wood, BBC Ch., BBC SO, Beecham

Busoni's *Piano Concerto* is arguably the most formidable in his repertory, but in such an inspired reading as Hamelin's it emerges as a genuine Everest of a work. The challenge it presents has already sparked off an impressive list of recordings, but Hamelin's is the finest yet. Even before the piano enters, the opening tutti, four minutes long, establishes the rapt, glowing intensity of the performance, thanks to Mark Elder's dedicated conducting of the Birmingham orchestra, with radiant recording to match. Above all, Hamelin and Elder bring out the warmer, more colourful qualities behind the five massive movements, the dedication of the long *Pezzo serioso* beautifully sustained.

It is good to have a recommendable mid-priced alternative in first-rate digital sound. With extra prominence given to the solo instrument, Garrick Ohlsson's bravura display is very exciting, and the pianist's own pleasure in virtuosity enhances his electricity and flair. However, in the choral finale the CBSO Chorus on Hyperion has more impact than the Cleveland Orchestra Chorus, creating a more impressive culmination.

Beecham's recording with Noel Mewton-Wood derives from two live performances, broadcast on successive days from the BBC's Maida Vale No. l Studio on 3 and 4 January 1948. As it is a BBC recording (presumably made on acetate discs) it is surprising that the sound is so resonant, and the quality of the tuttis is often coarse and sometimes confused – as the very opening demonstrates. Mewton-Wood was only seventeen at the time, yet he plays with tremendous dash and fire and with prodigious virtuosity, especially in the *Pezzo giocoso* second movement and the *All'italiana Tarantella.* Beecham conducts with vigour, often rumbustiously and always with great flair, and of course he creates a magical woodwind palette in the gentler passages. The BBC Symphony Orchestra rises to the occasion, although the playing is not always polished, and the singing of the BBC Male Voice Choir is not as sophistcated as we would expect today. Nevertheless, Beecham is Beecham, and he had an astonishingly brilliant young soloist, so the performance is well worth preserving on CD.

(i) *Indianische Fantasie, Op. 44. Lustspiel Overture, Op. 38; Gesang vom Regen der Geister; Die Brautwahl: Suite*
(N) *** Chan. 10302. (i) Goerner; BBC PO, Järvi

Starting attractively with the sparkling *Lustspiel Overture* – amazingly the product of a single night's work – this instalment in Neeme Järvi's Busoni series offers a good cross-section of this elusive composer's work. Even if there is a feeling that Busoni, as a far-sighted musical thinker, should have written even more imaginative music, there is much to enjoy here, not least in the two works built on 'Indian' themes, the music of Native Americans, not from the subcontinent. The *Indian Fantasy* is a substantial piece, in effect a piano concerto in a single movement of eight contrasted sections, and Nelson Goerner copes brilliantly with the virtuoso writing that Busoni designed for himself. On a much smaller scale *Gesang vom Regen der Geister*, 'Song of the Spirit Dance', involves equally colourful use of similar ideas, for strings, wind and timpani. *Die Brautwahl*, 'Bridal Choice', was Busoni's first opera, based on a story by E. T. A. Hoffmann, and in this suite he puts together an atmospheric sequence of segments from it, with instruments taking over vocal lines in vivid orchestration, with an element of grotesquerie. Brilliant playing under Järvi and vivid recording.

Violin Sonatas 1 in E min., Op. 29; 2 in E min., Op. 36a
*** Chan. 8868. Mordkovitch, Postnikova

Violin Sonatas 1–2; in C (1876), BN52
(N) *** Finlandia 2564 61078-2. Lev, Raekallio

The two Busoni *Sonatas* are rewarding pieces, already recorded by Lydia Mordkovitch and Victoria Postnikova, but these new Finlandia performances are coupled with an early sonata, written when Busoni was ten. Lara Lev and her Finnish partner should succeed in convincing any doubters

as to the stature of the *Second Sonata*, a one-movement work dating from 1898. This playing is utterly compelling and has an authenticity of feeling and dedication that is completely persuasive, and these fine players serve it to perfection. Very natural recorded sound.

Lydia Mordkovitch and Victoria Postnikova are also impressive advocates of the *First Sonata* and give a sympathetic reaing of the *Second*, especially its beautiful *Andante* section leading to a set of variations. The recording is excellent, but first choice rests with their Finlandia competitors, who also offer more music.

SOLO PIANO MUSIC

Indianisches Tagebuch (4 Studies); Sonatinas 1–6; Toccata
(M) *** CPO 999 702-2. Pontinen

Busoni composed his six *Sonatinas* over a decade between 1910 and 1920. His choice of title is deceptive, for they are by no means simply structured works and their textures are characteristically prolix. (One often feels with this composer that there are too many notes!) The most famous is No. 6 (*Super Carmen*), which is rather like a Lisztian concert paraphrase, only more sophisticated in its seductive interweaving of themes from Bizet's opera. Pontinen plays with matching subtlety and he is equally sensitive to the essentially serene atmosphere of No. 4, subtitled *In die Nativitas Christi MCMXVII*. No. 5 is a free reworking of the *Fantasy and Fugue in D minor*, once attributed to Bach, but since discovered to be unauthentic.

The four studies which make up the *Indian Diary* are based on Native American folk themes. All this music is technically very demanding, and the closing Toccata prodigiously so, but Roland Pontinen not only responds warmly to Busoni's lyrical writing, but meets all the many challenges with easy virtuosity and flair. He is excellently recorded.

An die Jugend: Giga bolero e variazione. Elegies: All'Italia; Berceuse; Turandots Frauengemach. Exeunt omnes; Fantasia nach J. S. Bach; Indianisches Tagebuch (Red Indian Diary), Book I; Sonatinas 2; 6 (Kammerfantasie on 'Carmen'); Toccata. Transcription of BACH: *Prelude & Fugue in D, BWV 532*
*** Chan. 9394. Tozer

This collection is thoroughly worthwhile. The Chandos disc assembles nearly 80 minutes of Busoni's piano music and makes an admirable and well-chosen introduction to it. Most pieces come off very well indeed, and often brilliantly, from the *Exeunt omnes* and the *Elegien* to the *Indianisches Tagebuch* and the attractive *Turandots Frauengemach*. This is an excellent CD, very well recorded and thoroughly recommendable.

4 Elegies; Sonatina seconda; Toccata; arr. of BACH: Toccata & Fugue in D min., BWV 565; Chorales: Ich ruf' zu dir, Wachet auf
☛ *** MDG 312 0436-2. Tanski

Claudius Tanski proves a most persuasive Busoni interpreter, having the questing mind and sensitivity this repertoire calls for, not to mention the abundant technical prowess. He plays four of the *Elegies*, Nos. 3–6. Both in Busoni's visionary pieces and in the transcriptions of the Bach, he is more than equal to the technical and imaginative challenges this music presents. Artistically this is three-star playing and, though the recording is not in the demonstration bracket, it is superior to Trevor Barnard (see below).

Fantasia contrappuntistica; Fantasia after J. S. Bach; Toccata
**(*) Altarus (ADD) AIR-2-9074. Ogdon

Ronald Stevenson calls Busoni's remarkable *Fantasia contrappuntistica* a masterpiece and, listening to John Ogdon's performance, one is tempted to agree. The *Fantasia after J. S. Bach* was written a year earlier and is among Busoni's most concentrated and powerful piano works. The balance places Ogdon rather far back and, as the acoustic is somewhat reverberant, the piano sounds a little clangy.

24 Preludes, Op. 37
** Div. Art 2-5011. Barnard – BLISS: *Piano Sonata* **

Trevor Barnard offers an intelligently planned disc, since neither the Bliss *Piano Sonata* nor the Busoni *Preludes* are otherwise available. However, the recording is a bit monochrome and shallow; the playing itself, though serviceable and conscientious, falls short of distinction.

OPERA

(i) Arlecchino (complete); (ii) Turandot (complete)
*** Virgin 7 59313-2 (2). (i) Richter, Mohr, Holzmair, Huttenlocher, Dahlberg, Mentzer; (ii) Gessendorf, Selig, Dahlberg, Schäfer, Kraus, Holzmair, Struckmann, Sima, Rodde; Lyon Op. Ch. & O, Nagano

Arlecchino ('Harlequin') is a sparkling comedy that builds on *commedia dell'arte* conventions with a point rarely matched in opera, though for the non-German-speaking listener a snag of the piece is that the title-role is a speaking part, a deterrent to frequent repetition. Even so, it would be hard to imagine a finer performance than this, with the conductor's finesse matched by a brilliant German cast with no weak link.

Busoni's *Turandot* evokes a fantasy fairy-tale atmosphere in a piece that is light in texture, with motivation aptly quirky rather than realistic. The surreal atmosphere is enhanced when the improbable theme for the evocative interlude before Act II is not Chinese but English – *Greensleeves*. Again Nagano's conducting gives a thrusting intensity to a piece that might seem wayward, and the casting is comparably brilliant, with Mechthild Gessendorf masterly as Turandot and Stefan Dahlberg heady-toned as Kalaf. The recording is vividly atmospheric, with plenty of presence.

Doktor Faust (complete)
**(*) Erato 3984 25501-2 (3). Henschel, Begley, Hollop, Jenis, Kerl, Fischer-Dieskau, Lyon Op. Ch. & O, Nagano
(M) **(*) DG (ADD) 427 413-2 (3). Fischer-Dieskau, Kohn, Cochran, Hillebrecht, Bav. Op. Ch. & R. O, Leitner

Kent Nagano and his Lyon Opéra forces fill an important gap in the catalogue with this first really complete recording of Busoni's masterpiece, using the score as completed after Busoni's death by his pupil, Philipp Jarnach. The set seeks to get the best of both worlds by also offering the extended realization of the closing scenes prepared by Anthony Beaumont with the help of newly discovered extra sketches. Fischer-Dieskau here recites the opening and closing superscriptions, normally omitted in stage productions. Dietrich Henschel may not be as searching or weighty an interpreter as Fischer-Dieskau, but the clarity and incisiveness of his singing are most impressive, leading to a noble account of the death scene, one of the passages expanded in the Beaumont version. He is well contrasted with the powerful Mephistopheles of Kim Begley, a tenor role that is Wagnerian in its demands. The rest of the cast is first rate, with voices well forward; but the impact of the performance is slightly blunted by the backward balance of the orchestra, distanced in a more spacious acoustic.

Unfortunately, the DG recording is full of small cuts; however, with superb, fiercely intense conducting from Leitner, it fully conveys the work's wayward mastery, the magnetic quality which establishes it as Busoni's supreme masterpiece, even though it was finished by another hand. The cast is dominated by Fischer-Dieskau, here in 1969 at his very finest; and the only weak link among the others is Hildegard Hillebrecht as the Duchess of Parma.

BUTTERWORTH, Arthur (born 1923)

Summer Music, Op. 77
(M) *** ASV CD WHL 2132. Salvage, Royal Ballet Sinfonia, Sutherland (with Collection of Bassoon Concertos and Concertinos ***)

Although a concertante piece, led by the soliloquizing bassoon, Arthur Butterworth's unforgettably atmospheric triptych is more like a three-part symphonic poem, organically whole in the way of Sibelius, yet reflecting not Nordic scenery but the North Yorkshire moors, which, as the composer tells us, 'despite the exhilaration of sun and wind on the high hills in summertime' (tellingly evoked in the finale), 'there ever seems to be a faint indefinable air of lonely melancholy brooding'. This is imaginatively caught by the soloist here; and Butterworth's subtly vivid use of orchestral colour increases the music's evocation and intensity, reaching a peak in the central *Nocturne*, moving slowly forwards, with its tolling bells and underlying persistent timpani. The performance is altogether first class and so is the recording. It comes within an attractive collection of more lightweight bassoon concertos and the disc is well worth investigating.

Symphony 1, Op. 15
*** Classico CLASSCD 274. Munich SO, Bostock –
GIPPS: *Symphony 2* ***

How is it possible for a symphony of this quality to be so neglected by the British musical establishment? It is powerful, imaginative and atmospheric. Arthur Butterworth comes from Manchester and played in the Hallé and Scottish National Orchestras. His *First Symphony* is a large-scale, 40-minute work which Sir John Barbirolli premièred in 1957. Sibelian in outlook (but none the worse for that) and with an innate feeling for the landscape of northern England and Scotland, it is powerfully argued and arresting – the product of a resourceful musical mind. It resonates in the memory, and Douglas Bostock and the Munich orchestra capture both its sombre mood and its stormy climaxes; the composer had the desolate Cape Wrath in mind in the last movement, where the music's whirlwind energy is splendidly conveyed. The recording is excellent, spacious and full-bodied.

MUSIC FOR BRASS

3 Impressions for Brass, Op. 36; Passacaglia on a Theme of Brahms, Op. 87; Sinfonia concertante, Op. 111; arr. for brass of BRAHMS: *Variations on a Theme of Handel, Op. 24*
*** Doyen DOYCD 130. Black Dyke Band, Childs

With the moorlands of northern England for his inspiration, Arthur Butterworth's *Three Impressions for Brass* draws a parallel with Malcolm Arnold's nostalgic *Cornish Dances*, although moving northeast to reflect the nineteenth-century industrial heritage of Northumberland. The triptych includes haunting evocations of a busy working coal mine, an old deserted farmhouse on which the colliery has encroached, and it closes with a vigorous portrayal of coal trains traversing George Stephenson's Royal Border Railway Bridge at Berwick-upon-Tweed.

A direct association with Brahms then brings a brilliant *Passacaglia* on (an inverted version of) the main theme of the final movement of that composer's *Fourth Symphony*, itself a *Passacaglia*, with Brahms's original chorale emerging thrillingly to dominate the climax.

The confidently structured *Sinfonia concertante*, with tenor horn and (brass) baritone as soloists, moves from a pastoral first movement (with distinct echoes of Vaughan Williams's *Fifth Symphony*) through a brilliant *Scherzo*, and a slow movement called *Night Music*, where there are darker, even sinister, undercurrents, and on to an excitingly ebullient closing *Rondo*.

For the final item the band offers Butterworth's brilliant transcription for brass of Brahms's *Variations and Fugue on a Theme of Handel, Op. 24*. Although the scoring is brilliantly imaginative and resourceful, the arrangement cannot efface memories of the piano original. Nor would one want to return to it very often. The playing of the Black Dyke Band is pretty marvellous throughout, and in the notes the composer expresses his own praise for the conductor of what he calls 'these magnficent and stunning performances'. The recording is excellent.

BUTTERWORTH, George

(1885–1916)

The Banks of Green Willow

⊶ (N) (BB) *** Warner Apex 2564 61437-2. RPO, Warren-Green – BRITTEN: *Simple Symphony;* ELGAR: *String Serenade;* HOLST: *St Paul's Suite;* VAUGHAN WILLIAMS: *Fantasia on a Theme of Tallis* ***
*** Chan. Compatible **SACD** CHSA 5001; CD CHAN 9902. LSO, Hickox – VAUGHAN WILLIAMS: *London Symphony (Original Version)* ***
(M) *** Chan. (ADD) 6566. Bournemouth Sinf., Del Mar – BANTOCK: *The Pierrot of the Minute: overture;* BRIDGE: *Summer,* etc. ***

The Banks of Green Willow; 2 English Idylls; A Shropshire Lad (rhapsody)

*** Nim. NI 5068. E. String O, Boughton – BRIDGE: *Suite;* PARRY: *Lady Radnor's Suite* ***

The RPO, woodwind and strings alike, play most beautifully in Christopher Warren-Green's idyllic performance which brings out the music's pastoral colouring as well as its rapture. The recording is first class, and the couplings are equally recommendable.

Butterworth's idyll makes a warmly atmospheric coupling for Vaughan Williams, and it is available additionally in multi-channel sound, where it sounds even more richly atmospheric. These Chandos SACDs will reproduce on a normal CD player.

Boughton secures from his Birmingham-based orchestra warm and refined playing in well-paced readings. In an ample acoustic, woodwind is placed rather behind the strings.

On Chandos, Del Mar gives a glowingly persuasive performance of *The Banks of Green Willow,* which comes as part of another highly interesting programme of English music devoted also to Butterworth's somewhat older contemporaries, Bantock and Frank Bridge. The digital transfer of a 1979 analogue recording has the benefit of even greater clarity without loss of atmosphere.

(i) *The Banks of Green Willow; 2 English Idylls; A Shropshire Lad* (rhapsody); (ii) *A Shropshire Lad* (cycle of 6 songs); *Bredon Hill* and other songs: *O fair enough are sky and plain; When the lad for longing sighs; On the idle side of summer; With rue my heart is laden*
(M) *** Decca (ADD) 468 802-2. (i) ASMF, Marriner; (ii) Luxon, Willinson

In his orchestral pieces and songs (almost all of which are included here) George Butterworth's music created an idealized picture of a rural England before the First World War, in which the composer was killed by a sniper's bullet. The orchestral rhapsody, *A Shropshire Lad,* with its yearning lyricism, represents the English folksong school at its most captivatingly atmospheric, and the other three works are in a similarly appealing pastoral vein, and again have moments of passionate feeling. Marriner's performances with the Academy have stood the test of time. They are very beautiful and utterly evocative. The recording, vivid and wide-ranging, dates from 1976 and the CD remastering shows just how good it is.

Benjamin Luxon's performances of the songs, in partnership with David Willinson, are equally persuasive. Unlike the orchestral works they do not draw on actual folk-tunes. Luxon's approach, dramatic as well as sympathetic, reveals these settings as not quite the unassuming miniatures they may sometimes seem. But while he can project his tone and words with great power, his delicate half-tones are equally impressive, and he underlines the aptness of music to words often set by British composers, but never more understandingly than here. Again well-balanced, vivid recording from the mid-1970s.

A Shropshire Lad (rhapsody)

(M) (**) Cala mono CACD 0528. NBC SO, Stokowski – ANTHEIL: *Symphony 4;* VAUGHAN WILLIAMS: *Symphony 4* (***)

Stokowski in this evocative Butterworth tone-poem draws ravishing, sensuous sounds from the NBC Orchestra, notably the strings, unrecognizable as Toscanini's players. Sadly, the 1944 radio recording, cleanly focused and well transferred, is marred by some 'wow' on the tape.

Love Blows as the Wind (3 songs)

(M) *** EMI (ADD) 7 64731-2. Tear, CBSO, Handley – ELGAR; VAUGHAN WILLIAMS: *Songs* ***

These three charming songs (*In the year that's come and gone, Life in her creaking shoes, Coming up from Richmond*), to words by W. E. Henley, provide an excellent makeweight for a mixed bag of orchestral songs based on the first recording of Vaughan Williams's *On Wenlock Edge* in its orchestral form. The sound is clear, yet enjoyably warm and atmospheric.

BUXTEHUDE, Dietrich (c. 1637–1707)

In the last two decades, Dietrich Buxtehude, alongside Biber, has emerged as one of the greatest composers of the latter half of the seventeenth century, mainly through the influence of the gramophone. Bach's famous prolonged visit was obviously based on a great deal more than Buxtehude's fame as an organist. Buxtehude's own father was himself a fine organist and held a position in Helsingborg (then part of Denmark, now in Sweden) where his son was probably born. Dietrich soon revealed his own skills on the instrument and, after taking over from his father, later moved to St Mary's Church, Lübeck, which was to be his musical centre for over three decades. He was a famed perfomer, not only on the organ but also on the violin and lute. As a composer he wrote music of very high quality in all fields, including chamber and instrumental works, and a great many vocal works of all kinds, including secular and sacred cantatas, plus a remarkable organ literature that clearly had much influence on the young Johann Sebastian.

CHAMBER MUSIC

(i) *Fried- und Freudenreiche Hinfart, BuxWV 76: Contrapunctus/Evolutio I–II; Klag-Lied; Trio Sonatas, Op. 1/1, 2 & 6, BuxWV 252–3 & 257; Op. 2/3, BuxWV 257; in C & D BWV 266–7; (ii) (Keyboard) Ciaccona, BuxWV 160; Passacaglia, BuxWV 161*

(M) *** DHM/BMG 82876 60151-2. Capriccio Stravagante, Sempé; (ii) Weiss and Sempé (harpsichords)

Here is another useful and characteristic period-instrument selection of Buxtehude's *Trio Sonatas* for those not wanting the complete series. They are very persuasively played by this excellent period-instrument group and include the *D major Sonata*, BuxWV 267, the composer's sole surviving piece of its kind for two bass instruments, here viola da gamba and cello, which enjoy a fascinating interplay. The closing *G major Sonata*, Op. 1/2, is also one of the most attractively inventive of these fertile works. The solemn *Klag-Lied* with the associated *Contrapuncti* (1674) was composed on the death of the composer's father. Of the two keyboard duos, the *Ciaconna* is marginally the more interesting and vital, although the *D minor Passacaglia* may have served as a model for the C minor work of Bach.

6 String Sonatas (without Opus numbers): in C min. D, BuxWV 266–7; in F, BuxWV 269; in G; in A min.; in B flat, BuxWV 271–3

*** da capo 8.224005. Holloway, Weiss, Ter Linden, Rasmussen, Mortensen

*** da capo 8.224121 (as above, in a box with complete da capo catalogue)

These unpublished works come from an (undated) collection held in Uppsala, Sweden. They are scored for a more varied ensemble than the Op. 1 and Op. 2 *Sonatas* and their other principal difference is that they contain considerably more solos than in the published collections. They are certainly no less inventive. Both the *G major*, BuxWV 271 (which opens the disc), and the *B flat major*, BuxWV 273 (which is a

considerably expanded version of Op. 1/4), are particularly attractive; the former, with a series of violin solos and a sprightly closing fugato, shows the composer at his most varied and light-hearted. BuxWV 266 (which closes the disc) is the most concentrated and complex of all. The same thematic material is re-used and varied throughout the work. There is a central, freely ruminative ('fantastic') violin solo, and the *Sonata* culminates with a brief, sustained slow finale. The writer of the excellent accompanying notes, Nils Jensen, suggests that this (appropriately) C major work deserves the epithet of Buxtehude's 'Jupiter Sonata'. Performances throughout are excellent in every way and the recording well up to standard. As can be seen above, this CD comes either in a normal jewel-case or also (subject to availability) in a box with a complete da capo catalogue.

7 Trio Sonatas, Op. 1, BuxWV 252–8

⊕– (N) (BB) *** Naxos 8.557248. Holloway, Mortensen, Ter Linden

*** HM HMC 901746. Kraemer, Quintama, Roberts, Börner

*** Hyp. CDA 67236. Wallfisch, Tunnicliffe, Nicholson

7 Trio Sonatas, Op. 2, BuxWV 259–65

*** da capo 8.224004. Holloway, Mortensen, Ter Linden

Trio Sonatas: in G; B flat & D min., Op. 1/2, 4 & 6 (BuxWV 253, 255 & 257); in D & G min., Op. 2/2–3, (BuxWV 260–61)

*** ASV (ADD) CDGAU 110. Trio Sonnerie

Buxtehude was nearly sixty when he published his *Sonatas*, Op. 1 and Op. 2. Each contains seven works and together they ambitiously explore all the major and minor keys, beginning with F major and omitting only F minor and B flat minor. What is immediately striking about both Op. 1 and Op. 2 is not just the variety of invention, but the way Buxtehude heightens the contrasting vitality of his allegros by introducing them with *Lentos* or *Adagios* of considerable expressive intensity. On the whole, the sonatas of Opus 2 are less quirky and seem more mature than those of Op. 1 and are very well balanced in their expressive and vigorous content. With John Holloway a very stylish leader, the performances on Naxos are expert, fresh and alive, using period instruments brightly without edginess or unattractive linear squeezing. The group is very well balanced and the recording immediate and real.

Of the other sets of Op. 1, the Hyperion recording is rather more intimate than the Harmonia Mundi version. Much depends on the lead violin in these works, and Manfredo Kraemer's virtuosity and strong instrumental personality are reminiscent of Andrew Manze, although of course Elizabeth Wallfisch who leads the Hyperion group certainly does not lack a strong profile and she and her colleagues make an impressive team. But Kraemer is especially appealing both in the lyrical writing, and in his witty pointing of the rhythmic snaps which are a feature of the splendid *Ciaconna Vivace* which opens the *Fourth Sonata*. The volatility of tempo is a splendid example of Buxtehude's 'stylus fantasticus' which so impressed Bach and which is particularly well handled by Kraemer and his colleagues. In short, both these sets of performances are first class, but to us the Harmonia Mundi disc is marginally the more appealing, and it is very well recorded.

In their well-chosen selection, the Trio Sonnerie show enthusiasm and expertise, and their virtuosity is agreeably effortless and unostentatious.

KEYBOARD MUSIC

Complete harpsichord music

Volume 1: *Aria in A min., BuxWV 249; Canzona in C, BuxWV 166; Canzonetta in A min., BuxWV 225; Chorale Variations: Wie schöne leuchtet der Morgernstern, BuxWV 223; Fugue in B flat, BuxWV 176; Partita: Auf meinen lieben Gott, BuxWV 179; Suites: in C, BuxWV 226; in D, BuxWV 233; Toccata in G, BuxWV 165*
*** da capo 8.224116. Mortensen

Volume 2: *Aria: More Palatino in C, BuxWV 247; 2 Canzonettas in G, BuxWV 171-2; Chorale: Nun lob, meine Seele, den Herren, BuxWV 215; Courante zimble in A min., BuxWV 245; Fugue in C, BuxWV 174; Suites: in E min., BuxWV 235; in G min., BuxWV 242*
*** da capo 8.224117. Mortensen

Volume 3: *Aria: La Capricciosa in G, BuxWV 250; Canzonetta in D min., BuxWV 168; Prelude in G, BuxWV 162; Suites: in F, BuxWV 238; in A, BuxWV 243*
*** da capo 8.224118. Mortensen

Buxtehude's keyboard and organ music is not clearly defined: much of it could be played on organ, harpsichord or clavichord, although the works requiring the pedal were obviously intended primarily for the organ. In his excellent survey Lars Ulrik Mortensen has carefully chosen the works most suitable for the harpsichord, including chorales and other sets of variations (notably the *Arias*) which were Buxtehude's strongest suit and in which he displays consistent ingenuity and musical skill, always holding the listener's interest. The selected fugues are all jauntily appealing. Mortensen uses a copy of a Rückers harpsichord made by Thomas Mandrop-Poulsen, an excellent instrument on which he produces a remarkable range of colour (it includes also a muted effect). His performances are of the highest order, spontaneous and flexible, and exciting in their sheer dexterity.

Volume 3 brings what is undoubtedly Buxtehude's keyboard masterpiece, *La Capricciosa*, a virtuoso showpiece nearly 30 minutes in length, consisting of 32 variations on an *Aria in G minor*. The composer's kaleidoscopic invention knows no bounds, and this work clearly anticipates Bach's *Goldberg Variations*. It is less profound but is continually diverting, and it requires both imagination and brilliance from its performer. Superbly played here, it makes this third collection the obvious point for the collector to enter Buxtehude's very rewarding keyboard world.

Aria with 2 Variations in A min., BuxWV 249; La Capricciosa (32 Variations on the Bergamasca), BuxWV 250; Chorale Partita: Auf meinen lieben Gott, BuxWV 179; Praeludia in G & G min., BuxWV 162 & 163; Suite in G min., BuxWV 241; Toccata in G, BuxWV 165
☞ (BB) *** Naxos 8.557413. Wilson

An outstanding recital to show the full range and scope of Buxtehude's keyboard writing. The key work here is *La Capricciosa*, a set of 32 greatly diverse variations on a German folk melody, which Glen Wilson suggests is Buxtehude's equivalent of Bach's *Goldberg* set, with which it has some striking parallels. (It even, in variation 27, includes a parody of a bad harpsichordist!) The two *Praeludia* are written in the very free style known as *stylus phantasticus*. The *Suite in G minor* is particularly attractive, while the *Chorale Partita* is in a hybrid format, using the same four dance movements to characterize the variants of the chorale theme. Wilson plays

with great flair, and in addition provides excellent back-up documentation. He uses a modern copy of a 1626 Ruckers, which is vividly if somewhat resonantly recorded; this means that one needs to set not too high a volume in the opening virtuoso *G major Toccata*.

ORGAN MUSIC

Complete Organ Music, Volume 1: *Ciaconas, BuxWV 159–60; Chorales: BuxWV 182; 189–90; 197–200; 202; 208–9; 211; 217; 317; Passacaglia in D min., BuxWV 161; Praeludia, BWV 137; 148–9*
(N) **(*) MVD dacapo 8.226002. Bryndorf (organ of St Mary's Church, Elsinore)

Complete Organ Music, Volume 2: *Chorales, BuxWV 178; 180; 206; 214–15; 220–24; Praeludia, BuxWV 136; 142; 151–3*
(N) **(*) MVD dacapo 8.226008. Bryndorf (organ of St Mary's Church, Elsinore)

Bine Bryndorf's new survey of Buxtehude's organ music has the distinction of being recorded on the organ at the church where the composer himself played. However, the instrument he knew has undergone much renovation since his time, being converted and re-converted in 1662–3 and 1854, while the modern instrument was built by Frobenius & Sons in 1960, if using the original casework. It sounds very good indeed; the pedals are particularly characterful and the overall sonority is rich in colour. Bryndorf's registration is eminently well chosen, and she is not dull; but there is a certain sobriety here too, and at times one wishes for a little more flair. However, the *Praeludia* show her at her best and fully in touch with the composer's *stylus phantasicus* – well demonstrated in BuxWV 137, which ends Volume 1, and in BuxWV 152 and 142, which frame the second recital.

Canzona in E min., BuxWV 169; Canzonetta in G, BuxWV 171; Ciacona in E min., BuxWV 160; Chorales: Ach Herr, mich armen Sünder, BuxWV 178; In dulci jubilo, BuxWV 197; Komm, Heiliger Geist, Herre Gott, BuxWV 199; Vater unser im Himmelreich, BuxWV 219; Magnificat primi toni, BuxWV 203; Preludes: in C, BuxWV 137; in D, BuxWV 139
**(*) Chan. 0514. Kee (organ of St Laurent Church, Alkmaar)
– SWEELINCK: *Collection* ***

Piet Kee's performance of the opening *Magnificat primi toni* is magnificent. The closing *Ciacona in E minor* is impressive too, while the *Canzonetta in G* is deliciously registered, with piping flute colouring. One's reservations concern the presentation of the chorales, which, Kee suggests, 'require poetic expression'. Perhaps they do, but they also need to be moved on rather faster. The Chandos recording is superb.

Ciacona in E min., BuxWV 160; Chorale Fantasia: Wie schön leuchtet der Morgernstern, BuxWV 223. Chorale Preludes: In dulci jubilo, BuxWV 197; Komm, Heiliger Geist, Herre Gott, BuxWV 199; Nun bitten wir den Heiligen Geist, BuxWV 208; Nun lob, mein Seel, den Herren, BuxWV 212; Von Gott will ich nicht lassen, BuxWV 221. Chorale Variations: Vater unser im Himmelreich, BuxWV 207; Mit Fried und Freund ich fahr dahin, BuxWV 76; Fugue in C, BuxWV 174. Preludes: in A min., BuxWV 153; in C, BuxWV 137; Toccata in G, BuxWV 164
(BB) ** Naxos 8.555775. Brown (Brombaugh organ of Central Lutheran Church, Eugene, Oregon)

Julia Brown is an accomplished and musical player and the

splendid organ in Oregon seems admirably suited to this repertoire. Her registration cannot be faulted in its use of colour, and she opens and closes very impressively with the *C major* and *A minor Preludes*, with full use of the pedals. Her account of the celebrated *Ciacona in E minor* is also very effective. The *Chorales* are played thoughtfully, with fractional pauses in the line, and at times one could welcome a stronger forward pulse in the other works, even though every detail is clear. The 'Gigue' *Fugue in C* is quite lively but could ideally be more rhythmically buoyant. The recording is first class and so is the documentation.

Chorales: *Auf meinen lieben Gott, BuxWV 179; Gott der Vater wohn uns bei, BuxWV 190; Nimm uns, Herr du treuer Gott, BuxVW 207; Nun komm der Heiden Heiland, BuxWV 211; Puer natus in Bethlehem, BuxWV 217; Von Gott will ich nicht lassen* (2 settings), *BuxWV 220/221*

*** Chan. 0539. Kee (organ of Roskilde Cathedral, Denmark) (with BRUHNS: *Preludes* ***)

The restored baroque organ at Roskilde Cathedral has a palette to tempt the most jaded listener and, although Piet Kee still persists in playing these chorales and their variants rather slowly, his piquant registration is very effective, so that they serve as attractively serene interludes between the remarkably flamboyant *Preludes* by Buxtehude's precociously inspired pupil, Nicolaus Bruhns, whose genius was sadly cut short when he predeceased his mentor, at the early age of 32. The recording is of demonstration quality.

VOCAL MUSIC

Choral works: (i) *Alles, was ihr tut, BuxWV4; Fürwahr, er trug unsere Krankheit, BuxWV 31; Der Herr ist mit mir, BuxWV15; Das neugeborne Kinderlein, BuxWV 13.* Attrib Buxtehude: *Magnificat anima me, BuxWV 38*

**(*) da capo 8.224160. (i) Reuter; Copenhagen Royal Chapel Ch., Dufay Collective, Munk

Though not quite as memorable as its companion volume below, this collection of Buxtehude's choral music has considerable attractions. The opening *Das neugeborne Kinderlein*, celebrating the baby Jesus, dances along with much pastoral charm, and *Der Herr ist mit mir* ('The Lord is with Me'), is similarly light-hearted. Both are pleasingly and freshly sung by this competent if perhaps not really distinguished Danish choir. But in *Fürwahr, er trug unsere Krankheit*, although the solo bass, Johan Reuter, sings expressively, the treble soloists are less secure. In *Alles, was ihr tut* the opening section is repeated at the close to frame a work which includes choruses that often anticipate Handel. The main aria is sung (homophonically) in four parts by the chorus, and the bass is only given the arioso which introduces the second chorus. The closing choral *Magnificat* is almost certainly spurious, but its simplicity of style is certainly appealing, although the upper voices here are again not too stable. Even so, with good recording, pleasingly balanced in a warm acoustic, this collection has much to recommend it. As with the first volume, full texts and translations are included.

Cantatas: *Befiehl dem Engel, BuxWV 10; Fürwahr, er trug unsere Krankheit, BuxWV 31; Gott hilf mir, BuxWV 34; Herzlich lieb hab ich Dich, O Herr, BuxWV 41; Ich suchte des Nachts, BuxWV 50; Nun danket alles Gott, BuxWV 79*

*** HM HMC 901629. Cantus Köln, Junghänel

This eminent German group give extremely stylish and cultured accounts of these lovely pieces, and no one wanting a representative anthology of Buxtehude cantatas is likely to be unpersuaded by this splendid recording.

Sacred Cantatas: *Cantata Domino, BuxWV 12; Herr, wenn ich nur dich hab, BuxWV 38; Ich habe Lust abzuscheiden, BuxWV 47; Ich halte es dafür, BuxWV 48; Jesu meine Freude, BuxWV 60; Salve, Jesu, Patris gnate unigenite, BuxWV 94; Jesu dulcis memoria, BuxWV 56; Mein Herz ist bereit, BuxWV 73.* (**Organ**) *Fugue in C, BuxWV 174*

☞ *** Chan. 0691. LeBlanc, Kirkby, Harvey, Purcell Qt; Woolley

A wholly admirable collection in which Emma Kirkby, although given prime billing, takes second place to the similarly light-timbred Canadian soprano, Suzie LeBlanc. Their voices match admirably in the many delightful passages of imitative part-writing that Buxtehude writes so deftly, never more so than in the lovely *Jesu dulcis memoria* and *Salve Jesu*. The closing sections of each work are almost like miniature choruses, notably so in *Ich habe Lust abzuscheiden*, which was written for two sopranos and bass (the excellent Peter Harvey), and the similarly scored *Jesu meine Freude*, perhaps the most striking work here, which even has a *Gute Nacht*, 'farewell to life', in its penultimate verse. Harvey also has his own confidently affirmative solo cantata, *Mein Herz ist bereit*, and Suzie LeBlanc enjoys both a memorable duet canata with the bass, *Ich halte es dafür* and a brief solo cantata, *Herr, wenn ich nur dich hab*. The Purcell Quartet accompany beautifully, and are usually given an introductory sonata to open the proceedings. As an interlude Robert Woolley plays the *C major 'Gigue' Fugue*, which provided the inspiration for Bach's *G major Fugue*, BWV 577. The recording is warm and intimate, and this collection cannot be too highly recommended.

Sacred Cantatas and Arias: *Fried und freudenreich Hinfahrt; Organ Contrapuncti I–III; Klag-Lied, BuxWV 76. Gen Himmel zu dem Vater main, BuxWV 98; Herr, wenn ich nur dich hab, BuxWV 38; O dulcis Jesu, BuxWV83; O fröliche Stunden, BuxWV95; Schaff in mir, Gott, BuxWV95; Sicut Moses exaltavit serpentem, BuxWV97; Singet dem Herrn, BuxWV98; Was mich auf dieser Welt betrübt, BuxWV105*

*** da capo 8.224062. Kirkby, Holloway, Kraemer, Ter Linden, Mortensen

Buxtehude wrote his *Fried und freudenreich Hinfahrt* at the time of his father's death in 1674. The three *Contrapuncti* (used here effectively as interludes) were probably intended to manifest the learning of the deceased, but the *Klag-Lied* is a poignant strophic song of mourning, sung here with infinite tenderness. Yet the programme opens with the delightfully jubilant aria, *O fröliche Stunden* ('Oh Happy Hours'), which is then followed by the beautiful sacred concerto (or cantata), *O dulcis Jesu*, in which Kirkby alternates expressive richness with a more florid, arioso style. *Was mich auf dieser Welt betrübt* is another simple aria of great charm. But the most ambitious work here is *Singet dem Herrn* (a setting of the first four verses of Psalm 98) in which the soprano voice duets delightfully with a solo violin, while the closing *Herr, wenn ich nur dich hab* is in the form of a chaconne. With Emma Kirkby in freshest voice, this is a wholly enjoyable disc. Throughout, her radiant and nimble singing is matched by the refinement and warmth of the accompaniments, mostly featuring two violins (John Holloway and Manfredo Kraemer in perfect accord). But the contribution of organist Lars Mortensen, who also doubles on harpsichord, is hardly less musical and pleasing. Full texts and translations are included.

Membra Jesu nostri, BuxWV 75

♀→ (M) *** DG (IMS) 447 298-2. Monteverdi Ch., E. Bar. Sol., Gardiner – SCHUTZ: *O bone Jesu* ***
*** BIS CD 871. Hida, Midori Suzuki, Yanagisawa, Anazawa, Mera, Sakurada, Ogasawara, Bach Coll., Japan, Masaaki Suzuki
(BB) *** Naxos 8.553787. Trogu, Invernizzi, Balconi, Cecchetti, Carnovich, R. Svizzera (Lugano) Ch., Sonatori de la Gioiosa Marca, Treviso, Accademia Strumentale Italiana, Verona, Fasolis (with ROSENMULLER: *Sinfonia XI* ***)

Membra Jesu nostri; Heut triumphieret Gottes Sohn, BuxWV 43

(B) **(*) HM HMA 1951333. Concerto Vocale & Instrumental Ens., Jacobs

The *Membra Jesu nostri* is a cycle of seven cantatas, each addressed to different parts of the body of the crucified Christ, all of a simple, dignified, expressive power that make a strong impression. John Eliot Gardiner's is the most searching and devotional; the Concerto Vocale, though beautifully sung, is less atmospheric both as a performance and as a recording. The Harmonia Mundi is more forwardly balanced; the Gardiner has more space and the sense of one of Buxtehude's own *Abendmusik*. Compare the sixth of the cantatas, *Ad cor*, and the more reverential approach and feeling of the Gardiner version tells. But both issues can be recommended; the impressive *Heut triumphieret Gottes Sohn* comes with the Harmonia Mundi disc and a Schütz *Geistliches Konzert*, *O bone Jesu*, related in spirit, comes on the Archiv recording, which is now offered at mid-price.

On BIS, Suzuki's Japanese ensemble bring a remarkably authentic feeling for period to this lovely work (Masaaki Susuki worked with Ton Koopman for many years) and, although the recording is made in a rather reverberant acoustic environment, this does not seriously diminish the pleasure this set gives. However, unlike both its competitors, it is without a coupling.

The performance from the Swiss-Italian Radio and ensembles from Verona and Treviso under Diego Fasolis is marginally less polished and accomplished vocally, but it has feeling and depth. They are most expertly balanced and the sound is excellent in every way. Those wanting a bargain need not hesitate.

Sacred Cantatas: In te, Domine, speravi, BuxWV 53; Jesu meine Freude, BuxWV 59; Jubilate Dominum, BuxWV 64; Sicut Moses, BuxWV 97; Was frag'ich nach der Welt, BuxWV 104; Wenn ich, Herr Jesu, habe dich, BuxWV 107; Wir schmeckt es so lieblich und wohl, BuxWV 108

(N) (BB) *** Naxos 8.557041. Hill, White, Graindlay, Artia Ens., Mallon

Buxtehude's sacred cantatas are in no way laden with heavy religious symbolism but are remarkable fresh. The opening *Was frag'ich nach der Welt* ('What is the world to me') has a pastoral character, and the following *Jesu meine Freude* is full of joy. *Wenn ich, Herr Jesu, habe dich*, which follows the measured string *Passacaglia*, is more sombrely expressive in feeling, but *Jubilate Domino* (a solo cantata, nimbly sung here by the counter-tenor, Matthew White) demands considerable virtuosity. The concerted *Wie schmeckt es so lieblich und wohl*

('How lovely and good the saviour') is full of light-hearted praise. The performances here are pleasingly intimate, well sung (Katherine Hill, the soprano soloist in *Sicut Moses*, particularly fresh) and truthfully recorded. Full texts and translations are included, plus excellent documentation.

BYRD, William (1543–1623)

The Byrd Complete Edition, Volume I: (i) Alma redemptoris mater a 4; Audivi vocem de caelo a 5; Christe qui lux es a 5; Christe redemptor omnium a 4; De lamentorum Jerimiae prophetae a 5; Domine quis habitat a 9; Ne perduas cum impiis a 5; Omni tempore benedic Deum a 5; Peccavi super numerum a 5; Vide Dominum quoniam tribulor a 5. Propers for the Lady Mass in Advent a 5 (Rorate caeli; Tollite portas/Ave Maria; Ecce virgo). Consort pieces: (i) Christe qui es lux a 4; Miserere a 4; Sanctus a 3; Sermone blando a 4

*** Gaudeamus CDGAU 170. Cardinall's Musick, Carwood; (i) Friedeswide Consort

Cardinall's Musick are putting us in their debt by providing (in new editions by David Skinner) a complete recorded survey of the vocal music of William Byrd. Although not all of his music is of equal quality, the overall standard is very high, and most of it was published during the composer's lifetime, though not the superb *Peccavi super numerum*, which closes the recital. Volume I commences the series with a programme of the early manuscript works, which are used to frame the three Gradualia for the Lady Mass in Advent. At a centre point in each group of motets, a recorder consort provides two contrasting instrumental pieces. Most of this music is virtually unknown: it is all sung with great conviction, richly blended and convincingly paced. The recording was made in the Fitzalan Chapel at Arundel Castle, which provides an ideal acoustic, resonant yet never blurring detail.

The Byrd Complete Edition, Volume II: Ad Dominum, cum tribularer a 8i Alleluya – Confitemi Domino a 3; Alleluya – Laudate pueri Dominum a 3; Ave regina caelorum a 5; Decantabat populus a 5; Deus in adjutorium a 6; Hodie Christus natus est a 4/6; O admirabile commertium a 4/7; O magnum mysterium a 4/8-9; O salutaris hostia a 6. 5 Propers for the Nativity a 4 (1607). BYRD/SHEPPARD/MUNDY: In exitu Israel a 4

*** Gaudeamus CDGAU 178. Cardinall's Musick, Carwood

Volume 2 is, if anything, even more stimulating than Volume 1, including as it does *O salutaris hostia* with its extraordinarily plangent harmonic clashes – the most musically daring work in the composer's whole output. The Propers for Christmas and the three associated Gradualia provide the central core of the recital. But the exultant *Decantabat populus* and the two closing motets – the noble and melancholy *Deus in adjutorium* (here reconstructed) and the heartfelt and passionate *Ad Dominum cum tribularer* – are among the composer's finest, most individual and most passionate works.

The Byrd Complete Edition, Volume III: Early Latin church music: Benigne fac Domine; Christus qui lux est; Circumspice Jerusalem; Domine ante te omne desiderium; Domine Deus omnipotens; Petrus beatus; Reges Tharsis et insulae; Sacris solemnis; Super flumina Babylonis; Te lucis; 4 Propers for Epiphany

*** Gaudeamus CDGAU 179. Cardinall's Musick, Carwood (with Philippe DE MONTE: *Quomodo cantabimus* ***)

In Volume 3, Cardinall's Musick turn to rare music, mainly pieces which Byrd left unpublished. The four Propers for Epiphany come from an incomplete set of Gradualia, published in 1607, yet this music shows Byrd at his most imaginative. Most moving of all is the culminating item, an eight-part setting of four verses from Psalm 136, reflecting the trials of a recusant Catholic in Elizabeth I's England, with the poignant message (in Latin), 'How shall we sing the Lord's song in a strange land?' Performances throughout are beautifully shaped, yet with great underlying intensity.

The Byrd Complete Edition, Volume IV: *Cantiones sacrae, Book I* (1575): complete
*** Gaudeamus CDGAU 197. Cardinall's Musick, Carwood

Byrd published the first of his three collections of *Cantiones sacrae* in conjunction with his teacher and mentor, Thomas Tallis, contributing 17 motets to this initial collection. Although these ASV performances encounter considerable competition in the present catalogue, this is, at present, the only recommendable CD (74 minutes) offering the entire contents of Book I, and the performances are beautifully blended, while Andrew Carwood's tempi move the music on at what seems a natural pacing. The recording is well up to the fine standard of this series.

The Byrd Complete Edition, Volume V: (i) *Masses for 3, 4 & 5 Voices;* (ii) *Organ Fantasia in C & D min.; Voluntary a 3*
✪ *** Gaudeamus CDGAU 206. (i) Cardinall's Musick, Carwood; (ii) Russill

Byrd's three great Masses were written for recusant private performance in English country houses. Perhaps the most beautiful is the *Mass for 3 Voices*, which comes second here and is performed with great eloquence. The three organ voluntaries which act as introductions and interludes are taken from *My Ladye Nevell's Booke* and are admirably played on an appropriate (modern) chest organ by Patrick Russill. It is difficult to conceive of finer or more moving performances or more natural sound, and the clarity of detail is remarkable.

The Byrd Complete Edition, Volume VI: *Music for Holy Week and Easter* (1605 & 1607): (i) *Adoramus te; Angelus Domini; Christus resurgens; Haec dies; Holy Saturday Vespers; Mane vobiscum; Mass Propers for Easter Day; Passion Domini nostri Jesu Christi secundum Johannem; Plorans plorabit; Post dies octo*
*** Gaudeamus CDGAU 214. Cardinall's Musick, Carwood, (i) with Russill (organ)

Shortly after publishing his three Masses Byrd began his comprehensive anthology of Gradualia (Mass Propers for the Church Year). The First Book was published in 1605, the Second Book in 1607; all the music in this collection comes from these two books. The penitential opening lament, *Plorans plorabit* ('My eyes shall weep sore') is one of his finest, very moving in its expressive polyphony.

Yet a warning has to be given that roughly half the disc consists, not of polyphony, but of chanting by solo voices. With complete text and translation it becomes hypnotic, but hardly an experience to be repeated often. The rest of the programme, however, is richly appealing, especially the *Holy Saturday Vespers* which in their 'Alleluias' anticipate the joyous and imaginative *Mass Propers for Easter Day* (the word *Alleluia* is not spoken in Lent).

The Byrd Complete Edition, Volume VII: *Cantiones sacrae* (1589) 1–8: *Deficit in dolore; Domine praestolamur; O Domine adjuva me; Tristitia anxietes; Memento Domine; Vide Domine afflictionem; Deus venerunt gentes; Domine tu jurasti; Propers for Lady Mass from Christmas to the Purification* (1605)
*** Gaudeamus CDGAU 224. Cardinall's Musick, Carwood

By the time Byrd came to publish what he described as his own first Book of his *Cantiones sacrae* in 1589, the position of practising Catholics in Protestant England had become extremely vulnerable and dangerous. Byrd was undoubtedly associated with the Jesuits, yet, a favourite of the queen, he was allowed to write his music unharmed, and in his *Cantiones sacrae* expresses the anguish of his fellow Catholics.

These beautiful motets are used to frame Byrd's first volume of Gradualia, settings of Proper texts for the whole church year. The performances from Andrew Carwood and his fine group are as movingly committed and expressive as ever, and are beautifully recorded. The editor, David Skinner, as usual provides the excellent notes.

The Byrd Complete Edition Volume VIII: *Cantiones Sacrae* (1589) 8–15: *Vigilate; Inresurrectione tua; Aspice Domine de sede; Ne irascaris Domine; O quam gloriosam; Tribulationes civitatum; Domine secundum multitudinem; Laetentur coeli. Propers for the Feast of the Purification*
*** Gaudeamus CDGAU 309. Cardinall's Musick, Carwood

Volume VIII concludes the 1589 *Cantiones Sacrae*, written to be sung at domestic devotions against the background of the increasing Catholic oppression. The message of the texts is cryptic: *Vigilate* ('Keep watch, for you know not when the Lord of the House will come'), which surely has an underlying message to the faithful that deliverance might be at hand. A brief interlude of joy is provided by *O quam gloriosam*, and if the darkness of mood returns in the profound melancholy of *Tribulationes civitatum*, for the final piece, *Laetentur coeli*, the gloom at last lifts with the opening 'Let the Heavens rejoice', and the closing words affirm 'He shall take pity on his afflicted people'.

As with Volume VII, these deeply expressive motets are used to frame Byrd's often inspired Gradualia, in this instance the *Propers for the Feast of the Purification*, which make a welcome change to a more positive mood. The performances and recordings are well up to the high standard of this remarkable series, as are David Skinner's excellent notes.

OTHER RECORDINGS

Music for Consorts and Virginals: *Browning; The Carman's whistle; A fancie; Fantasia a 6; French Corantos; The Irish March; My Lord of Oxenford's Maske; Pavan; Pavan a 5; Pavan: Belle qui tiens ma vie; Pavan: Mille Regretz; 2 Pavans & Galliards; Pavan & Galliard a 6; Pavan & Galliard: Kinbourough Good; Praeludium & Ground; The Queen's Alman*
*** Astrée E 8611. Capriccio Stravagante, Sempé

Skip Sempé and his colleagues play every note with that authenticity of feeling which is so often missing from period performance. Sempé has poetic feeling, an astonishing keyboard flair and rare artistry. *Browning* has the alternative title of *The leaves be green* and consists of divisions on a popular song, while the *Fantasia a 6* which closes the concert is a masterly compression of ideas into a fluid structure as powerful as Purcell's famous *Chaconne*. The sound of his Skowroneck harpsichord is vividly reproduced. One of the best CDs of its kind to have appeared in recent years, and a splendid introduction to the composer.

Music for viols: *Browning; 2 Fantasias a 3 in C; Fantasias a 4 in D & G; Prelude & Voluntary;* (i) *Prelude (Pavana, Gagliarda Ph. Tregian); Ut re mi fa sol la (for harpsichord);* (ii–iii) *Delight is dead;* (ii) *Farewell false love;* (iii) *My mistress had a little dog; Rejoice unto the Lord;* (ii–iii) *Who made thee, Hob, forsake the plough?* (ii) *Ye sacred muses*
*** Lyrichord LEMS 8015. (i) Bagger; (ii) Crout; (iii) Lipnik; NY Cons. of Viols

The New York Consort of Viols play with an attractive blend of timbre, and everything they play is thoroughly alive. The harpsichordist, Louis Bagger, plays with great bravura when *Ut re mi fa sol la* becomes more and more florid as it proceeds. The two vocal soloists work well together, especially in the rustic dialogue song, *Who made thee, Hob, forsake the plough?* Tamara Crout sings with great charm in her solo numbers: with the lightest touch in the charming song about the 'murdered' pet dog, and very expressively in *Rejoice unto the Lord* and the touching *Ye sacred muses*. In every way this is a most rewarding programme, excellently balanced and recorded.

Consort, keyboard music, anthems and songs: *Fantasia for 4 viols; Fantasia 2 for 6 viols; Fantasia 3 for 6 viols; Galliard; Have mercy upon me, O God; In nomine 2 for 4 viols; In Nomine 5 for 5 viols; Pavane;* (i) (Keyboard) *John, come kiss me now; Pavan in A min.; Qui passe (for my Ladye Nevell);* (Vocal) (ii) *Christ rising again; Fair Britain Isle; In angel's weed; Rejoice unto the Lord; Susanna fair; Triumph with pleasant melody*
☯– (BB) *** Naxos 8.550604. Rose Consort, Red Byrd; (i) Roberts (harpsichord or virginals); (ii) Bonner

Here is a useful and inexpensive cross-section of Byrd's secular output that gives a good idea not only of its artistic riches but of its sheer variety. Both the ensembles recorded here, the Rose Consort of viols and Red Byrd, are in good form, and Timothy Roberts and Tessa Bonner are sensitive and expert exponents of this repertoire. The recorded sound is eminently clean and well balanced, and there is plenty of space round the aural image, which greatly enhances the undoubted attractions of a pleasant anthology.

Complete keyboard music
(M) *** Hyp. CDA 665551/7. Moroney (harpsichords, muselar virginal, organ, chamber organ, clavichord)

Keyboard music: *The Battell: Marche; The Trumpets; The Bells; The Carman's Whistle; Christe qui lux; Fantasia; Galliard; Galliard for the Victorie; Galliard to Johnson's Delighte; Go from my window; A Grounde; Miserere I & II; Have with yow to Walsingham; My Ladye Nevell's Grownde; O quam gloriosum est regnum; 7th Pavan; A Pavion; Praeludium to the Fancie; Ut, re, mi, fa, sol, la*
*** Hyp. CDA 66558. Moroney (harpsichords, muselar virginal, organ, chamber organ, clavichord)

Davitt Moroney's impressively comprehensive *Gramophone* award-winning undertaking includes also the organ music played on the highly suitable Ahrend organ of L'Eglise-Musée des Augustins, Toulouse. To add maximum variety, he also uses a number of keyboard instruments based on north European seventeenth-century models, including a clavichord by

the estimable Thomas Goff, a chamber organ by Martin Goetz and Domenic Gwynn, and harpsichords by Hubert Bédard and Reinhard von Nagel. The most fascinating of these instruments is the so-called muselar virginal (by John Philips of Berkeley after a 1650 Couchet), which has a remarkably rich timbre. Moroney tells us that, for all its fullness of sound, the instrument fell out of favour because of a drawback: its very characteristic 'amplified' mechanical clicks, especially in rapid left-hand scales. However, this instrument is heard at its finest and most spectacular (on Disc 7) in Byrd's description of *The Battel*, with its introductory *Marche* and a *Galliard for the Victorie*. Quite as fascinating aurally are the five items with which Moroney closes his programme. Four different versions of the *Praeludium to the Fancie* from Book 12 are given, each heard on a different instrument, and he concludes with the *Fantasia* from Book 13, one of the composer's most complex and original pieces, presented with considerable flair. Throughout, the playing is committed, authoritative and nicely embellished, if at times a shade didactic. The recording is most realistic, though it is important not to set the volume level too high. The accompanying notes are as thorough as they are scholarly and comprehensive. The set is offered at a special price: seven discs for the cost of five.

A well-chosen 78-minute programme from Davitt Moroney's distinguished survey, including favourite items like the hypnotic portrayal of *The Bells*, the jolly *Carman's Whistle* (on chamber organ), and *The Trumpets* from *The Battell*, to demonstrate the extraordinary sound of the muselar virginal (here sounding something like a highly amplified jew's harp!), but given a less bizarre image in the following *Galliard for the Victorie*. In complete contrast the pair of delicate *Misereres* are played on a small clavichord, so you will have to be careful with the volume control. As with the complete set, the documentation is first class.

My Ladye Nevells Booke (42 Keyboard pieces) (1591)
✹ (M) *** Decca 476 1530 (3). Hogwood (virginals, harpsichord or chamber organ)

This collection of Byrd's keyboard music was compiled by John Baldwin of Windsor, 'a gentleman of the Chapel Royal', and must be reckoned the finest collection of keyboard music in Europe of the sixteenth century. Christopher Hogwood rings the changes by using a variety of instruments, a virginals, two harpsichords (one Flemish and the other Italian) and a fine chamber organ, all of which he plays with sympathy and vitality. Hogwood's scholarly gifts are shown in the fine notes that accompany the set, but, more important, his masterly keyboard technique and artistic sensitivity are sustained throughout the three CDs (originally four LPs), excellently recorded in the early 1980s. A most enterprising choice for Universal's 'Penguin ✹ Collection', originally issued by L'Oiseau-Lyre, and now appearing on compact disc for the first time.

VOCAL MUSIC

Anthems: *Praise our Lord, all ye Gentiles; Sing joyfully; Turn our captivity.* **Motets:** *Attolite portas; Ave verum corpus; Christus resurgens; Emendemus in melius; Gaudeamus omnes; Justorum animae; Laudibus in sanctis Dominum; Non vos relinquam; O magnum mysterium; O quam suavis; Plorans plorabit; Siderum rector; Solve iubente Deo; Veni, Sancte Spiritus; Visita quaesumus Domine*
(M) *** Coll. CSCD 507. Cambridge Singers, Rutter

John Rutter brings a composer's understanding to these readings, which have a simple, direct eloquence, the music's serene spirituality movingly caught; and the atmospheric recording is very faithful, even if detail could be sharper. The programme is divided into four groups: Anthems; then Motets: of penitence and prayer; of praise and rejoicing; and for the Church year.

Cantiones sacrae, Book 1: Aspice Domine; Domine secundum multitudinem; Domine tu iurasti; In resurrectione tua; Ne irascaris Domine; O quam gloriosum; Tristitia et anxiestas; Vide Domine afflictionem; Vigilate

(M) **(*) CRD 3420. New College, Oxford, Ch., Higginbottom

Cantiones sacrae, Book 2: Circumdederunt me; Cunctis diebus; Domine, non sum dignus; Domine, salva nos; Fac sum servo tuo; Exsurge, Domine; Haec dicit Dominus; Haec dies; Laudibus in sanctis Dominum; Miserere mei, Deus; Tribulatio proxima est

(M) **(*) CRD 3439. New College, Oxford, Ch., Higginbottom

Although all three Books of *Cantiones sacrae* were written to be sung in Latin, some of the more successful were translated and sung in English. Their musical range is wide. Though the New College Choir under its choirmaster, Edward Higginbottom, does not sing with the variety of expression or dynamic which marks its finest Oxbridge rivals, it is impossible not to respond to the freshness of its music-making. The robust, throaty style suggests a Latin feeling in its forthright vigour, and the directness of approach in these magnificent *Cantiones sacrae* is most attractive, helped by recording which is vividly projected, yet at once richly atmospheric.

Cantiones sacrae: Laetentur coeli; Tristitia et anxietas

*** Proud Sound PROUCD 1149. King's College Ch., London, Trendell – TAVERNER: *Missa Corona Spinea; Audivi vocem de coelo* ***

The exuberant *Laetentur coeli*, the Advent motet that concludes Byrd's 1589 collection of *Cantiones sacrae*, and the magnificent *Tristitia et anxietas* from the same collection make a fine supplement to the fresh-voiced performance of Taverner's wide-ranging *Missa Corona Spinea*. Warmly atmospheric recording.

Gradualia (1607): Masses for 5 Voices: In tempore Pascchali & In Assumptione Beata Mariae Virginis: Propers; Antiphons (for 4 voices): Ave Regina coelorum; Salve Regina. Motet: Regina coeli

(N) (B) *** HM Classical Express HCX 3955182. Chanticleer

Byrd published this music rather bravely in 1607 for clandestine use by Catholics in Protestant England. Propers for actual private performances of the Masses for Easter and the Assumption are included, alongside a pair of beautiful Marian Antiphons, and the lovely motet, *Regina coeli*. The music has a uniquely intimate spirtual serenity and is very beautifully sung here, and equally beautifully recorded.

The Great Service (with anthems)

*** Gimell CDGIM 011. Tallis Scholars, Phillips

Peter Phillips and the Tallis Scholars give a lucid and sensitively shaped account of Byrd's *Great Service*. Theirs is a more intimate performance than one might expect to encounter in one of the great English cathedrals; they are fewer in number

and thus achieve greater clarity of texture. The recording is quite excellent: it is made in a church acoustic (the Church of St John, Hackney) and captures detail perfectly. It includes three other anthems.

Lamentations: Tenebrae for Good Friday. Mass for 4 Voices

(N) (M) *** CRD 3499. Clerks of New College Oxford, Ch., Higginbottom – TALLIS: *Lamentations I & II* etc. ***

Only one set of *Lamentations* by Byrd survives: the first lesson at Tenebrae on Good Friday. Deeply felt, radiant in its simplicity, Byrd's setting of Jeremiah's lament on the destruction of Jerusalem undoubtedly had a double significance for its composer, a devout Catholic, deploring the reformation of the English church. The *Mass in four parts*, written for private performance, has a similar combination of simplicity and deep feeling. The closing *Agnus Dei* is particularly intense, with the closing words '*dona nobis pacem*' ('grant us peace') given a gentle, musical emphasis. The Clerks of New College, Oxford, 16 in number, give admirably scaled performances, richly recorded in an ideal acoustic.

Masses for 3, 4 and 5 Voices; Ave verum corpus; Diffusa est gratia; Magnificat (Great Service); Nunc dimmitis; Prevent us, O Lord; Tristitia et anxuetas; Vigilate

*** Gimell **DVD** GIMDP 901. Tallis Scholars, Phillips

Tudor and Renaissance music is not well represented in the DVD catalogue (understandably so, perhaps) but this, a model of its kind, may encourage others to explore early music. Some of these performances (the *Missa à 3*, and many of the remaining items) are recorded in Tewkesbury Abbey and beautifully filmed by candlelight, while the two remaining Masses were (appropriately enough, given the period) filmed in the Chapel of Merton College, Oxford. As one expects from the Tallis Scholars, these are expert performances, impeccable in intonation and tonal blend. In addition, there is a feature on Byrd. Time was when the BBC would have turned to a leading authority on the music of the period to present such a programme, but this 70-minute feature is fronted by the ubiquitous Charles Hazlewood. Although he is unfailingly pleased with himself, many viewers respond positively to him and the feature is undoubtedly informative.

Mass for 3 voices; Mass for 4 voices

⊕ ✸ (N) (M) *** Decca 4767090 King's College Cambridge Ch., Willcocks

Mass for 3 voices; Mass for 4 voices; Mass for 5 voices

(B) **(*) HM (ADD) HMA 190211. Deller Cons.

Masses for 3, 4 & 5 voices; Ave verum corpus

*** Gimell CDGIM 345. Tallis Scholars, Phillips

Masses for 3, 4 & 5 voices; Ave verum corpus; Magnificat; Nunc dimittis

⊕ (B) *** Double Decca 452 170-2 (2). King's College, Cambridge, Ch., Willcocks – TAVERNER: *Western Wynde Mass* ***

Although later versions of the *Mass for 5 voices* have produced singing that is more dramatic and more ardent, the King's Choir versions of the *Masses for 3 and 4 voices*, dating from 1963, remain classics and the original issue has now joined Universal's Penguin Rosette collection. On Double Decca the 1959 recordings of the *Ave verum*, *Magnificat* and *Nunc dimittis* have been added, representing a more reticent, less forceful style than some might expect. But the singing is still affectingly beautiful and the sound comparably spacious, and the coupled Taverner programme shows the choir on top form.

Peter Phillips is a master of this repertoire; undoubtedly these performances have more variety and great eloquence so that, when the drama is varied with a gentler mood, the contrast is the more striking. The sound made by the Tallis Scholars in Merton College Chapel is most beautiful, both warm and fresh.

Whether or not it is historically correct for Byrd's Masses to be sung by solo voices, the great merit of the French Harmonia Mundi performances is their clarity, exposing the miracle of Byrd's polyphony, even though the tonal matching is not always flawless. The 1968 recording is clean and truthful, although it lacks something in ecclesiastical atmosphere.

Mass for 4 voices; Mass for 5 voices; Infelix ego
(BB) *** Naxos 8.550574. Oxford Camerata, Summerly

This coupling from the Oxford Camerata represents one of Naxos's most enticing bargains. The full-throated singing has spontaneous ardour but no lack of repose in the music's more serene moments. Summerly offers the motet, *Infelix ego*, as a bonus. These readings are distinctive in a different way from those by the Tallis Scholars. The recording is outstandingly vivid.

Masses for 4 & 5 voices with the Propers for the Feast of Saints Peter and Paul (Gradualia 1607) and All Saints (Gradualia 1605). Motets: Ad Dominum cum tribularer; Diliges Dominum; Hodie Simon Petrus; Quodcunque ligaveris; Quomodo cantabimus?; Tu es Pastor ovium
(B) *** Virgin 2 x 1 5 62013-2 (2). The Sixteen, Christophers
    (with DE MONTE: Super flumina Babylonis)

The Byrd *Masses* for three, four and five voices can be (and are) accommodated on a single CD, but the advantage of this bargain Virgin double is that the two *Masses* included here are placed in a wider musical context: the *Mass for Four Voices* is contrasted with some of the richer six-part motets from the 1607 Gradualia, including *Quomodo cantabimus?* Similarly the *Mass for Five Voices* is joined with the Propers for the Feast of All Saints, which come from the Gradualia of 1605 and includes the eight-part motet *Ad Dominum cum tribularer*, notable for its rich-textured, poignant false relations. Suitably appended is Philippe de Monte's *Super flumina Babylonis*, which the composer had sent to Byrd in 1583 and to which the *Quomodo cantabimus?* is a response. The singing is very impressive, the recording excellently focused and the acoustic appropriately spacious.

Motets in paired settings: Ave verum corpus (Philips); Haec dies (Palestrina); Lustorum animae (Lassus); Miserere mei, Deus (G. Gabrieli); O quam gloriosum; Senex puerem portabet (Victoria); Tu es Petrus (Palestrina). Hodie beata virgo Maria
⚫ (N) (B) *** CfP 5 86048-2. King's College, Cambridge, Ch., Willcocks (with SWEELINCK & PALESTRINA: *Hodie Christus natus est*. VICTORIA: *O magnum mysterium*. GIBBONS & WEELKES: *Hosanna to the son of David*. WILKES: *Gloria in excelsis Deo*. ECCARD: *When to the temple Mary went*)

These were the first recordings made by the EMI team (Ronald Kinloch Anderson, Christopher Bishop and Neville Boyling) when in 1964 they took over the recording of the King's College Choir from Argo. Considering the acoustic problems inherent in the reverberation of the chapel, they immediately achieved remarkable results, as this excellent CD

transfer readily shows. The focus is mistier than we would expect today, but it is ideal for the repertoire. Two LPs were recorded at the time and and nearly all the contents of both are included here (76 minutes), making this disc an amazing bargain.

The first collection ('Byrd and his contemporaries') was an imaginatively devised programme in which settings of Latin texts by Byrd are directly contrasted with settings of the same words by some of his greatest contemporaries. Often the mood of the setttings is similar (as in the lovely paired settings of *Ave verum corpus* and *Miserere mei, Deus*, but at other times there is greater contrast, as with *Tu es Petrus*. But – as was Sir David Willcocks' intention – the juxtaposition makes one listen to the individual qualities of these polyphonic masters the more keenly and register their individuality.

The second collection (originally entitled 'Christmas to Candlemas') follows on naturally from the first and brings a juxtaposition of settings by Sweelinck and Palestrina: *Hodie Christus natuts est* (fascinatingly different), Gibbons and Weelkes: *Hosanna to the son of David* (with more in common). One of the most memorable is Byrd's own contribution, the celestial *Hodie beata virgo*. No texts and translations are included, but there is a good note by Andrew Parker.

Psalmes, Sonets and Songs of Sadness (1588): excerpts: All as at sea; Care for thy soul; Come to me grief; If women could be fair; In fields abroad; Lullaby; The match that's made; O God give ear; O Lord how long?; O that most rare breast; Susanna fair; What a pleasure to have great princes
(M) *** Decca (ADD) 475 049-2. Cons. of Musicke, Rooley

Byrd's *Psalmes, Sonets and Songs of Sadness* of 1588 enjoyed such popularity in their time that they were reprinted twice in their first year of publication. They are more than just a collection of madrigals, as the title suggests, and are given exemplary performances here. Anthony Rooley's fine vocal group is led by Emma Kirkby, and they give many of them as consort pieces, some with the full number of repeated stanzas, which the artists discreetly embellish. This is a first-class reissue, excellently recorded and an invaluable addition to Decca's 'British Music Collection'.

SONGS

Consort Songs: An aged Dame; Ah silly Soul; All as at sea; Come to me, grief, for ever; Constant Penelope; How vain the toils; Lullaby: My sweet little Baby; O dear life, when may it be; O God that guides the cheerful Sun; O that most rare breast; Rejoice unto the Lord; Who likes to love; Ye sacred Muses
🎵 *** Hyp. CDA 67397. Blaze, Concordia

In his preface to *Psalmes, Sonets and Songs of Sadness* (1588) Byrd suggested that his stimulus was 'to perswade everyone to learne how to sing – it is the onely way to know where Nature hath bestowed the benefit of a good voice: which guift is so rare, as there is not one among a thousand that hath it'. Well certainly Robin Blaze 'hath it'; indeed the natural beauty of his vocal colouring stands out among contemporary countertenors as being ideal for illuminating these lovely, expressive songs of sadness, like *O dear life, when may it be* (with lute accompaniment) and the two Funeral Consort Songs for Sir Philip Sydney, *Come to me, grief, for ever*, and *O that most rare breast*, and the song of pietie, *How vain the toils that mortal man do take*. Of course there are lighter songs here too, including the jaunty *Who likes to love* (again with lute), while the opening *Rejoice unto the Lord* is full of confidence. But the gem of the collection is also one of the earliest and most extended. *My sweet little Baby* dates from that collection of 1588, and is an entirely delightful Christmas lullaby, which was much and rightly praised by the Earl of Worcester for its immediately communicated beauty. With highly pleasing accompaniments, beautifully balanced, and ravishing singing throughout, this is a record to treasure and draw upon, though not to play all at once.

Consort Songs: *Ah, silly soul; Ambitious Love; Come, Pretty Babe; Constant Penelope; Fair Britain Isle (An Elegy for Henry, Prince of Wales); If Women could be Fair* (with ANON: *Fie Fie my Faith*). Pieces for viols: *Browning my Dear (on the Leaves be Green); In nomine a 4 in D min.*
*** Globe GLO 5159. Cordier, Royal Consort – GIBBONS: *Fantasias; In nomines* ***

Although there is a pervading atmosphere of dolour, these fine Byrd songs, interspersed with *Fantasias* and *In Nomines* of Orlando Gibbons, make a highly rewarding programme when this Dutch gamba group play with such warmth, sensibility and refinement. Moreover, the counter-tenor David Cordier, has just the right delicacy of timbre for these Elizabethan songs, which he sings with spirit and deep expressive feeling (especially Byrd's poignant elegy for the Prince of Wales and the touching *Ah, silly soul*). First-class recording.

Consort Songs: *Constant Penelope; Content is rich; He that all earthly pleasures scorns; My mind to me a Kingdom is; My Mistress has a little dog; The noble famous Queen; O Lord, bow down thine heav'nly eyes; O Lord how vain; O that most rare breast; Out of the orient crystal skies; O you that hear this voice; Truth at the first.* Pieces for Viols: *2 Fantasias a 6; Galliard a 6; Pavan a 6*
(N) *** HM HMU 907388. Emma Kirkby, Fretwork

Emma Kirkby's voice is as fresh as ever, a little brighter and clearer perhaps, but extraordinarily true, and her singing is full of charm. Here she is authentically accompanied by a consort of six viols, who also provide interludes. In songs as varied as *O Lord how vain, My mistress has a little dog, The noble famous Queen* and *O that most rare breast* (not belonging to a lady, but an elegy for Sir Philip Sidney) she is equally eloquent in different ways. Unless you do not respond to the viol's sonority, this collection, nicely varied and generous (75 minutes), is self-recommending and very well recorded.

Fair Britain Isle; In fields abroad; Lullaby; My Mistress had a little dog; O Lord how vain; Rejoice unto the Lord; Susanna fair; Though Amaryllis dance in green; Though I be Brown; La Verginella; Ye sacred muses; Fantasia a 4; In nomine 1–2 a 4
*** Simax PSC 1191. McGreevy, Partridge, Phantasm

Geraldine McGreevy dominates this attractive recital, opening with the lovely *La Verginella*, and very touching in the surprisingly melancholy *Fair Britain Isle* and the poignant *Lullaby*, though perking up for *Susanna fair* and *Though Amaryllis dance in green*. Ian Partridge is in good voice too, although his contribution is perhaps less striking. These are all songs in which the vocal line is part of the polyphonic texture of the viol accompaniment, which Phantasm handle admirably, as they do their three, solo consort pieces. Excellent recording with no edginess on the string timbres.

CAGE, John (1912–92)

Concerto for Prepared Piano & Chamber Orchestra (1950/51); The Seasons (ballet); Seventy-Four (for orchestra), Versions I & II; Suites for Toy Piano (original and orchestral version, scored by Lou Harrison)
*** ECM 465 140-2. (i) Tang (prepared piano; toy piano); American Composers' Orchestra, Russell Davies

Seventy-Four, hypnotic in atmosphere, is nevertheless remarkably static. *The Seasons* is, in the composer's own words, 'an attempt to express the traditional Indian view as quiescence (winter), creation (spring), preservation (summer), and destruction (fall)'. It is not easy to follow, but certainly has plenty of movement, and its textures are exotic. The simplistic *Suite for Toy Piano* has also been ingeniously scored by Lou Harrison and most listeners will respond to the vividly contrasting sonorities of this instrumental version, which has instant appeal. The performances here are dedicated and of the highest calibre, and the recording excellent.

CALDARA, Antonio (c. 1670–1736)

Sonata da camera in E min., Op. 1/5; Trio Sonata in D, Op. 2/3; (i) Cantatas: *D'improviso amore felice; Medea in Corinto; Soffri mio caro Alcino; Vicino a un rivoletto*
(B) **(*) Virgin 2x1 5 61588-2 (2). (i) Lesne, Il Seminario Musicale – STRADELLA: *Motets* **(*)

Gérard Lesne is in his element in these fine cantatas. The most immediately striking is *Medea in Corinto*, based on the legend of the betrayal of Medea by Jason of the Golden Fleece fame. But the finest and most extended is the memorable *Vicino a un rivoletto*, where the voice shares a long, echoing interchange with a solo violin (splendidly played here) followed by a gravely noble arioso with cello obbligato. The two *Sonatas* are used as interludes, but they are fine works in their own right – the melancholy *Adagio* of the four-movement *Trio Sonata*, Op. 1/5, is particularly affecting. These performances could hardly be more authentic or more communicative, and they are naturally balanced and recorded. The one great snag is the absence of either translations or adequate notes about the music.

Christmas Cantata (Vaticini di Pace); Sinfonias 5 & 6
(B) *** Naxos 8.553772. Haines, Dayiantis-Straub, Lane, Arnot, Aradia Baroque Ens., Mallon

Caldara, an Italian contemporary of Bach and Handel, wrote this rare and delightful cantata for the Christmas celebrations in Rome in 1712. Preceded by an overture, it is a free-running sequence of 14 arias for the allegorical characters of Peace, Human Heart and Divine Love, with Justice initially representing Old Testament values. Peace, in the longest and most beautiful of the arias, a siciliano, then woos Justice to mercy through a vision of the Infant Christ. This Canadian performance is fresh and lively, with four excellent soloists (notably Mary-Enid Haines as Peace) and a good period-instrument ensemble. A rarity made doubly enticing at Naxos super-bargain price.

Crucifixus
(B) *** Double Decca (ADD) 443 868-2 (2). Palmer, Langridge, Esswood, Keyte, St John's College, Cambridge, Ch., Philomusica, Guest – BONONCINI: *Stabat Mater* ***; PERGOLESI: *Magnificat in C; Stabat Mater* **(*);

D. SCARLATTI: *Stabat Mater;* A. SCARLATTI: *Domine, refugium factus es nobis; O magnum mysterium;* LOTTI: *Crucifixus* ***

The *Crucifixus* is an elaborate 16-part setting of great eloquence, texturally rich and concentrated into a few seconds short of five minutes. It follows on naturally after Bononcini's beautiful *Stabat Mater*.

Maddalena ai piedi di Cristo (oratorio; complete)
*** HM HMC 905221/22. Kiehr, Dominguez, Fink, Scholl, Messthaler, Türk, Schola Cantorum Basiliensis O, Jacobs

This oratorio about Mary Magdalene at the feet of Christ, an early work dating from around 1700, inspired Caldara to an astonishing sequence of *da capo* arias, most of them brief, but with several longer ones given to Maddalena herself, notably the heartfelt *Pompo inutile*, inspiring Maria Cristina Kiehr to warm, golden tone, or the agonized *In lagrime stemprato*, depicting falling tears. In contrasting characterization, her sister Marta has such jolly numbers as *Vattene, corri, vola*, with Rosa Dominguez bright and agile. The role of Christ is given to a tenor, but neither of his two arias is reflective, and the biggest proportion of arias go to the counterpart characters of Earthly Love (a mezzo, Bernarda Fink) and Heavenly Love (a counter-tenor, Andreas Scholl), both of them singing superbly, subtly contrasted in tone. René Jacobs draws fresh and alert playing from the Schola Basiliensis Orchestra, with the instruments, including varied continuo, set in a warm acoustic slightly behind the singers.

Trio Sonatas: in G min., A & F Op. 2/4, 6 & 8; Ciacona, Op. 2/12; (i) *Cantatas: L'anniverario amoroso; La Fama; Vincino a un rivoletto* (for alto, violin & cello)
**(*) ASV Gaudeamus CDGAU 347. Four Nations Ens., Appel; (i) with Lane

The expert American original-instrument group, the Four Nations, provide an attractively interwoven concert of Caldara's vocal and instrumental music, and their full-voiced mezzo soloist (who sounds more like an alto) contributes stylishly and ardently. The group are at their finest in the splendid instrumental *Chaconne* and the beautiful closing cantata, *Vincino a un rivoletto* ('By a stream'), where there are obbligati for both solo violin and cello. The closing (virtual) duet for voice and cello, *Aimé sento il mio core* ('Alas my heart swoons with pain'), beautifully balanced, makes a moving finale. In the *Trio Sonatas* the transparency of string texture is characteristic of period-instrument style, and if Jennifer Lane is less subtle than Gérard Lesne in this repertoire, she communicates readily and with much feeling.

CAMPRA, André (1660–1744)

Campra was born in Aix-en-Provence, but after training and serving in the cathedral there he moved on to St Etienne in Toulouse, where he stayed for 11 years, then to Paris to became maître de chapelle at Notre Dame Cathedral. If it was to be in the world of opera that his prime reputation was to flourish, his cantatas and motets were also justly popular.

Cantatas: *Arion; La Dispute de l'Amour et de l'Hymen; Enée et Didon; Les Femmes*
(B) *** HM HMA 1951238. Feldman, Visse, Gardeil, Les Arts Florissants, Christie

Jill Feldman is at her most spirited and eloquent in the dramatic narrative of *Arion*, and Dominique Visse's tangy

alto is equally telling in the altercation of the conflicting interests of Marriage and Love which need to be resolved harmoniously. *Les Femmes* is sung with both feeling and sparkle by Jean-François Gardeil. The most ambitious of the four works is a brilliant duet celebrating the nuptials of Aeneas and Dido. With sensitive and strongly paced accompaniments from William Christie and Les Arts Florissants, it is difficult to imagine that these works could be re-created more tellingly, helped by the presence and atmosphere of the excellent recording.

Grands Motets: *De profundis; Exaudiat te Dominus; Notus in Judae Deus*. Requiem: *Introit*
(N) *** Virgin 5 45619-2. Soloists, Les Arts Florissants Ch. & O, Christie

This is a wholly delightful disc, with Christie, his soloists, chorus and instrumentalists at their very finest. These are wonderfully engaging works, spirited and expressive by turns. The outgoing quality of the music bubbles to the surface: sample the opening of *Exaudiat te Dominus*, a setting of Psalm 19, with its blazing trumpets and exuberant solo and choral singing. Or try the Recitative, *A custodia* from *De profundis* with its engaging writing for woodwind; both are worthy of Handel, even though their syle is French. The programme closes with a lovely setting, serene and exultant, of *Requiem aeternam*, the Introit from Campra's *Mass of the Dead*, richly sung by the chorus, with a solo interlude and polyphonic decoration, both vocal and instrumental. This is an obvious place to start if you want to explore Campra's music.

Petits Motets: *Florete prata; Insere Domine; Quemadmodum desiderat cervus; Salve Regina*
(N) **(*) Virgin 5 45720-2. Agnew, Les Arts Florissants, Christie – François COUPERIN: *Petits Motets* **(*)

Here are four of Campra's petits motets for solo voice, three deeply expressive in their melancholy – although they are interspersed with others, slightly more varied, by Couperin. *Florete prata* ends the programme joyously. They are very well presented by Christie and his group, with Paul Agnew the responsive and highly individual soloist. But this is a specialized collection, perhaps not for the general collector.

Requiem Mass
**(*) HM (ADD) HMC 901251. Baudry, Zanetti, Benet, Elwes, Varcoe, Chapelle Royale Ch. & O, Herreweghe

This *Requiem* is a lovely work, with luminous textures and often beguiling harmonies, and its neglect is difficult to understand. Herreweghe's performance, with refined solo and choral singing, is pleasing and sympathetic if comparatively cool. The recording is refined, to match the performance.

CANTELOUBE, Marie-Joseph (1879–1957)

Dans le montagne (for Violin & Piano)
(N) *** Hyp. CDA 67427. Graffin, Devoyon – BREVILLE: *Violin Sonata 1* ***

It is good to have an instrumental work from Canteloube, albeit an early one, written in 1904–5, submitted to his teacher and mentor, D'Indy, then (much revised) finally published in 1906. It is a work of great charm. Canteloube loved the mountains and lived among them in his early years. The first two movements, *En plein vent* and the evocative and poetic *Le soir*, are melodically endearing. Canteloube marked the second, *Lent. Très calme*, and commented 'this is a gentle hilltop breeze, not a mountain squall'. The third, *Jour de fête*, opens and closes with a quaint, donkey-like ostinato and then sparkles exotically; the finale, *Dans le bois au printemps*, opens impressionistically and then introduces Canteloube's famous melody from the Auvergne, looking back at the mountains. Altogether this is as delightful and ingenuous as the more famous songs, and it is most persuasively performed here, and excellently recorded.

Songs of the Auvergne: Series 1–5 (complete)

(B) *** Double Decca 444 995-2 (2). Te Kanawa, ECO, Tate –
VILLA-LOBOS: *Bachianas brasileiras 5* ***

*** Decca **DVD**/CD 475 6145 (as above)

*** Erato 0630 17577-2 (2). Upshaw, Lyon Op. O, Nagano –
EMMANUEL: *Chansons bourguignonnes* ***

Dawn Upshaw sings with tenderness and character in a style less sensuous than that of Kiri Te Kanawa (notably so in the fresh, open account of the famous *Baïlèro*, where she uses greater variety of dynamic, with an echo effect). Her line in the lyrical numbers is often very beautiful, while in the quirkier items her manner is nearer to the more folksy idiom of Natania Davrath. She is persuasively accompanied by Kent Nagano and the Lyon Opera Orchestra, with their distinctly French colouring. What makes this Erato set particularly enticing is the inclusion of a half-dozen rather similar and no less charming arrangements of Burgundian songs by Maurice Emmanuel. Full translations are provided, if in minuscule print.

In Dame Kiri Te Kanawa's recital the warmly atmospheric Decca recording brings an often languorous opulence to the music-making. In such an atmosphere the quick songs lose a little in bite, and *Baïlèro*, the most famous, is taken extremely slowly. With the sound so sumptuous, this hardly registers and the result remains compelling, thanks in large measure to sympathetic accompaniment from the ECO under Jeffrey Tate. There is also a paired CD/DVD combined with a DVD filmed in the Auvergne countryside (Deccca 475 6145). However, the photography is pleasing but unmemorable.

Chants d'Auvergne (excerpts): *L'Antouèno; Baïléro; 2 Bourrées; 3 Bourrées; Brezairola; La délaïssádo; Jou l'pount d'o Mirabel; La-haut, sur le rocher; Lou boussu; Lou coucut; Lou diziou bé; Malurous qu'o uno fenno; Oï ayaï; Passo pel prat; La pastoura als camps; Pastourelle; Quand z'eyrou petitoune; Uno jionto postouro*

(N) (BB) *** Naxos 8.557491. Gens, O Nat. de Lille,
Jean-Claude Casadesus

Véronique Gens, one of the finest French singers of her generation, is generally associated with baroque music, but here with her fresh, finely projected voice she gives performances of this generous selection of the *Chants d'Auvergne* that bring out the folk qualities far more than usual. Where these songs have often been recorded by singers with sensuous, velvety voices, like Victoria de los Angeles or Kiri Te Kanawa, Gens gives them an authentic French timbre, whether in the melismatic phrases of *Baïléro*, always a favourite item, or the vigour of the two sets of *Bourrées*. Jean-Claude Casadesus conducts the excellent Lille orchestra in similarly idiomatic performances, atmospherically recorded. Full texts and translations make this a genuine bargain.

Chants d'Auvergne: L'Antouèno; Baïlèro; 3 Bourrées; Brezairola; Chut, chut; La Délaïssádo; Lo Fïolairé; Là-haut, sur le rocher; Hè! beyla-z-y dáu fél; Lo Calhé; Lou Boussu; Lou coucut; Malurous qu'o uno fenno; Obal, din lo combuè; Oï ayaï; Passo pel prat; La pastrouletta è lo chibaliè; La Pastoura als camps; Pastourelle; Tè, l'co tè; Uno jionto

(M) *** EMI (ADD) 5 66978-2 [5669932]. De Los Angeles, LAP, Jacquillat

The warmth and sweetness of Victoria De Los Angeles's tone when her own pioneering recordings were made (1973 and 1975) match the allure of Canteloube's settings, bringing them into the concert hall. In the lighter numbers, the *Bourrées* for instance, the singing combines sparkle with a natural feeling for the folk idiom, and there is the most engaging vocal colour in *Hè! beyla-z-y dáu fél* and *Tè, l'co tè*; elsewhere De Los Angeles can be ravishing with her fine-spun vocal timbre, as in *La Delissádo* or the gentle *Lou Boussu*, while *Lou coucut* speaks for itself. The accompaniments are highly sympathetic (fine wind solos at the opening of *Lo Calhé*) and the atmospheric recording is attractive too, though at times not ideally clear in focusing orchestral detail (*L'Antouèno* has rather washy strings). But these are quibbles; this is a most enjoyable disc and well worthy of remembering as one of EMI's 'Great Recordings of the Century'.

Chants d'Auvergne: L'Antouèno; Baïlèro; 3 Bourrées; Lou Boussu; Brezairola; Lou coucut; Chut, chut; La Délaïssádo; Lo Fïolairé; Jou l'pount d'o Mirabel; Malurous qu'o uno fenno; Passo pel prat; Pastourelle; Postouro, sé tu m'aymo; Tè, l'co, tè

☛ ✿ (B) *** CfP 575 1382. Gomez, RLPO, Handley –
FAURÉ: *Masques et bergamasques; Pavane* ***

Jill Gomez's selection of these increasingly popular songs, attractively presented on a bargain-price label, makes for a memorably characterful record which, as well as bringing out the sensuous beauty of Canteloube's arrangements, reminds us, in the echoes of rustic band music, of their genuine folk base. An ideal purchase for the collector who wants just a selection. The inclusion of the charming Fauré works makes this reissue more attractive than ever.

Chants d'Auvergne: Baïlèro; 2 Bourrées; 3 Bourrées; Brezairola; La Délaïssádo; Lo Fïolairé; La pastoura als camps; Lou Boussu; Lou coucut; Malurous; Pastourelle; Postouro sé tu m'aymo; Qu'o uno fenno. Chants des Pays Basques: Chori erresiñoula; Chorietan buruzage; Egun batean; Lurraren pian; Nik badut matteñobat

*** Auvidis V 4811. Bayo, Tenerife SO, Perez

María Bayo is a most engaging artist and has just the temperament to sing her selection of favourites idiomatically (*Lo Fiolairé* is deliciously done), and yet in *Baïlèro* and *La Délaïssádo* her line and timbre are ravishing. Víctor Pablo Perez directs the accompaniments with sultry Mediterranean warmth and real character. The solo wind playing (oboe and clarinet) is particularly diverting. What makes this collection especially attractive is the bonus of five *Chants de Pays Basques*, not included by Natania Davrath. The orchestrations are slightly more conventional than for the Auvergne songs, but the use of horns in the jaunty *Egun batean* is most winning and this and *Nik badut matteñobat* are among the highlights. The recording is first class and gives orchestra and voice a most attractive bloom. Full translations are included.

Chants d'Auvergne: Baïlèro; 3 Bourrées; Brezairola; Lou Boussu; Lou coucut; Chut, chut; La Délaïssádo; Lo Fïolairé; Uno jionto postouro; Jou l'pount d'o Mirabel; Malurous qu'o uno fenno; Oï ayaï; Pastourelle; La pastrouletta; Postouro, sé tu m'aymo; Tè, l'co, tè

(B) *** Virgin Classics 2×1 5 61742-2. Augér, ECO, Tortelier – RAVEL: *Alborada; Shéhérazade*, etc. **(*)

Arleen Augér's lovely soprano is ravishing in the haunting, lyrical songs like the ever-popular *Baïlèro*. In the playful items she conveys plenty of fun, and in the more boisterous numbers the recording has vivid presence. Augér returns to sing Ravel's exotic song cycle *Shéhérazade* as part of a new coupling, which includes four of that composer's key orchestral works.

CAPLET, André (1878–1925)

Epiphany (Fresco for Cello & Orchestra after an Ethiopian Legend)

(B) *** EMI Début 5 73503-2. Phillips, Bav. Chamber PO, Plasson – FAURE: *Elégie;* LALO: *Cello Concerto* ***

'Fresco' is a perfect description of this impressionistically etched evocation which depicts the arrival in Bethlehem of Caspar, the black member of the three kings, the bringer of gold to 'honour the King of the World'. Caplet creates a fascinating opening texture of woodwind colour, which the cello first embroiders, then rhapsodically dominates. There is a long central cadenza placed against a steady drumbeat, then the work ends with an exotic dance when the king's young black retainers join in the celebration. Caplet's sound imagery is oriental and yet French (just as Ravel's can be), but the work demands, and receives here, enormous bravura from the cello soloist. The clear recording and the skill of the conductor ensure that, without loss of allure, every detail is in focus.

CARDOSO, Frei Manuel (c. 1566–1650)

Lamentatio; Magnificat secundi toni

(BB) *** Naxos 8.553310. Ars Nova, Bo Holten – LOBO: *Motets;* MAGALHAES: *Missa O Soberana luz*, etc. *** (with Concert of Portuguese polyphony ***)

Cardoso's serene, flowing polyphony with its forward-looking use of augmented chords is heard at its most striking in the *Magnificat*, while his *Lamentatio* for six voices is touchingly beautiful. Remarkably eloquent singing from this fine Danish choir and good recording in a suitably ecclesiastical acoustic. The rest of the programme is hardly less stimulating.

Requiem (Missa pro defunctis)

(BB) *** Naxos 8.550682. Oxford Schola Cantorum, Summerly – LOBO: *Missa pro defunctis* ***

Requiem; Magnificat; Motets: Mulier quae erat; Non mortui; Nos autem gloriari; Sitivit anima mea

⊕ ☛ ✿ *** Gimell (ADD) CD GIM 021. Tallis Scholars, Phillips

Cardoso's *Requiem* opens in striking and original fashion. The polyphony unfolds in long-breathed phrases of unusual length and eloquence, and both the motets, *Mulier quae erat* ('A woman, a sinner in that city') and the short *Nos autem gloriari* ('Yet should we glory'), are rich in texture and have

great expressive resplendence. Cardoso's use of the augmented chord at the opening of the *Requiem* gives his music some of its distinctive stamp. The Tallis Scholars sing with characteristic purity of tone and intonation, and they are splendidly recorded. A glorious issue.

In Summerly's Naxos account, Cardoso's *Missa pro defunctis* is not as dramatic in its contrasts as the coupled setting of Duarte Lôbo. As with the Lôbo coupling, a solo treble makes a brief but effective introduction for each movement, a device which works very touchingly. The performance by Oxford Schola Cantorun is beautifully paced and the calibre of the singing itself is very impressive indeed, as is the Naxos recording.

CARISSIMI, Giacomo (1605–74)

Representing the generation following Monteverdi, Giacomo Carissimi wrote a vast amount of vocal music, notably for the oratorios of Italy. He built a formidable reputation as a teacher as well, with Marc-Antoine Charpentier among his pupils. The range and magnificence of his music is only just beginning to be discovered.

Cantatas: Ahi, non torna; Piangete, ohimè piangete; Si dia bando, alla sperenza; Siam tre miseri piangente; Va dimanda al mio pensiero. Motets: Benedictus Deus et Pater; Exulta gaude, filia Sion; O dulcissimum Mariae nomen; Omnes gentes gaudate cum victore; Surrexit pastor bonus (with keyboard interludes by FRESCOBALDI; KAPSBERGER; ROSSI)

(N) **(*) Signum SIGCD 0040. Concerto delle Donne

All but three of the cantatas and motets here are settings for two or (mainly) three soprano voices, the remainder are solo works. There is plenty of musical variety; Carissimi's invention is unflagging and the contrapuntal interplay of the three voices is appealing when all three soloists have fine, rich voices which match well together and there are no wobblers. Each of the three soloists, Donna Dream, Gill Ross and Elin Thomas, has a solo work, but Donna Dean, the leader of the team, is allotted the most striking, *Piangete, ohimè, piangete,* with its melancholy semitone droops (which gives its name to the collection), while the duet cantata which follows, *Si dia bando,* is delightfully fresh, as if its hopeless message about the contradictions and unreliability of love are not be be taken too seriously. The instrumental accompaniments are stylishly managed and vocal works are interwoven by keyboard interludes, intimately played by Alastair Ross. Even so, this is not a disc to be taken at a single sitting. Full texts and translations are included.

Historia di Abraham et Isaac; Historia di Ezechias (Oratorios). Mass for 8 Voices; Motets: O vulnera doloris; Salve, salve, puella

(N) (M) *** Erato 2564 60590-2. Soloists, Lisbon Gulbenkian Foundation Ch. & O, Corboz

Although originally published in the early 1970s, these recordings have not found their way into the British catalogue before now. The *History of Hezekiah* is a memorably concise oratorio with superb choral writing, splendidly sung here. Resourcefully, Carissimi sets King Hezekiah's plea for divine mercy in the minor key, while God's music is always in the major. The narrator's role is given to two sopranos and then to the final chorus. The story of Abraham's willingness to sacrifice his son at God's command makes for another compressed but dramatic setting. Here the role of narrator (Historicus) is, perhaps less effectively, given to a tenor voice, though again taken over by the chorus at the close to glorify God. The kernel of the work is the dialogue between Isaac and Abraham, at first apprehensive, but later expressing joy at the happy reprise. The three *Mass* movements (which may not be authentic) offer rich polyphony, with the serene *Kyrie* contrasted with the vigorous settings of the *Gloria* and *Credo*. The dramatic dialogue of *Tolle sponsa* (for soprano, bass and chorus) is then followed by a pair of solo male cantatas of which *Salve, salve puella* is floridly very demanding of the tenor soloist. This is a very stimulating collection, well sung and recorded, but it is let down by the absence of documentation. Only the Latin texts of the two oratorios are provided, with no cueing or translations.

The Story of Jephtha; The Story of Jonah; Dai piu riposti abissi

(N) (BB) *** Naxos 8.557390. Consortium Carissimi, Zanon

(i) *Jephte;* (ii) *Jonas;* (iii) *Judicium Salomonis (The Judgement of Solomon)* (oratorios)

*** Mer. CDE 84132. Coxwell, Hemington Jones, Harvey, Ainsley, Gabrieli Cons. 8 Players, McCreesh

Both the Historia di Jephte and the *Historia Jonae* involve free treatment of texts from the Old Testament. In 16 sections lasting a mere 21 minutes, *The Story of Jephtha* has interlacing solos, some for characters in the story, others involving narration (Historicus) in free arioso. Punctuating this crisp telling of the story come four choruses in six parts, and a duet for two sopranos. They add to the attractive variety of the piece in madrigal-like numbers, ending with the longest and most impressive. *The Story of Jonah* follows a similar pattern, with the dialogue between Jonah and the Sailors playing an important part, and ending with a fine eight-part chorus for the people of Nineveh, *We have sinned Lord*. Described as a Serenade, the third work is equally mellifluous, involving more chordal writing. It is here given with the top lines taken by two tenors instead of two sopranos. The brilliant singers of Consortium Carissimi – with the director, Vittorio Zanon, only indicated in small print at the end of the long list of artists – give magnetic performances, beautifully recorded. In this outstanding bargain issue full texts are given, very necessary for complete enjoyment, and this CD supersedes its Meridian competitor.

No opening sinfonia survives for *Jephte*, and Paul McCreesh chooses to preface this oratorio with a Frescobaldi *Toccata*, which works well. *Jephte* is affectingly presented, and the McCreesh performance brings overt expressive feeling, despite some vocal insecurities at the very top. Overall these are well-prepared and intelligent accounts. The continuo part is imaginatively realized, with some pleasing sonorities (organ, double harp, chitarrone, etc.) and, despite some undoubted minor shortcomings, these are most convincing accounts of all three works, if on a fairly intimate scale However, the back-up documentation is inadequate.

De Tempore interfecto Sisar; Dialogo del Gigante Golia; Diluvium Universale (Dialogo del Noe); Regina Hester (Oratorios)

(N) *** CPO 999 983-2. Mauch, Backes, Carmignani, Jochens, Van der Kempe, Musica Fiesta., La Capella Ducalle, Wilson

This enterprising disc gathers together four contrasted oratorios, hitherto thought to have been lost. Most striking among

them are *The Dialogue of the Giant Goliath*, and the *Dialogue of Noah*. In the former, Harry van de Kempe, from his very opening aria, is lugubriously sinister as the deep-voiced Goliath, and Constanze Backes a contrastingly fresh-voiced David. Van der Kempe then transforms himself into a warmly sympathetic Noah, to plead with an unrelenting God (Wilfried Jochens), and it is the choral interplay which represents the rushing winds and the downpour of rain. The variety of the music which follows, with solos from the other singers interspersed with orchestral ritornelli (strings and brass) and lively choruses crying out against the cruelty of God, is all vividly histrionic, until finally the future covenant is established and a peaceful future promised. The singing here is fresh, the ornamentation impressive and the vigorous rhythmic articulation has plenty of vigour, while the expressive music is most sympathetically sung. The recording is very good and full translations are included; the only snag is that individual arias and ensembles are not cued and, apart from the main roles, it is very difficult to determine who is singing what!

CARLSSON, Mark (born 1952)

Nightwings

*** Crystal CD 750. Westwood Wind Quintet – BARBER: *Summer Music;* LIGETI: *Bagatelles;* MATHIAS: *Quintet* ***

In *Nightwings* the flute assumes the persona of a dreamer, the taped music may be perceived as a dream-world, and the other four instruments appear as characters in a dream. On this evidence, however, the conception is in some respects more interesting than the piece itself. Excellent playing and recording.

CARTER, Elliott (born 1908)

(i; ii) *Oboe Concerto;* (iii) *Esprit rude;* (ii) *Penthode* (for 5 groups of instruments); (iv; ii) *A Mirror on Which to Dwell*
(BB) *** Warner Apex 8573 89227-2. (i) Holliger; (ii) Ens. InterContemporain; (iii) Cherrier, Troutet; (iv) Bryl-Julson, Boulez

A recording of a concert given for the composer in Paris to celebrate his eightieth birthday. The *Oboe Concerto* was written for Heinz Holliger, who gives a superb performance of a work which is underlyingly lyrical and appealing. *Esprit rude* ('rough breathing') is an even less predictable duet for flute and clarinet, and the atmospheric *Penthode* ('concerned with the experiences of connectedness and isolation') written for five groups of four players, is no more easy to unravel.

In the song-cycle, setting poems of Elizabeth Bishop, one cannot but admire the expertise of Phyllis Bryn-Julson, accurately leaping from note to note against often bizarre accompaniments, and producing a remarkably expressive line of real tonal beauty. The recording is admirable, clear and well balanced. A classic and indispensable reissue.

Concerto for Orchestra

(M) *** Sony (ADD) SMK 60203. NYPO, Bernstein – IVES: *Central Park in the Dark*, etc. ***

It is apt that on the Bernstein CD, Elliott Carter's key avant-garde orchestral work from 1969 should follow on after Ives, for its writing seems naturally to derive from that earlier master in its complexity. However, the argument here is much more thorny, the texture densely interwoven and prismatic; its energy is unquestioned, but its linear fragmentation is daunting. Certainly it could hardly be played with more expertise or display more conviction; and the close (1970) recording-balance ensures that every detail is well defined.

(i) *Piano Concerto. Holiday Overture; Symphony 1*
(BB) **(*) Naxos 8.559151. Nashville SO, Schermerhorn; (i) with Wait

The three works on the disc in Naxos's enterprising American Classics series make plain the strong contrast between early Carter works, very much in the American open-air tradition developed by Copland and Roy Harris, and the much thornier, more challenging music he came to write from the 1960s onwards. Both the *Holiday Overture* (1945) and the *Symphony No. 1* (1942) are fresh and open in his earlier manner. The *Holiday Overture* is a lively piece and well worth having on disc. The *Symphony* is rewarding, close in idiom to Copland and Piston. Its material is interesting and the feeling for form strong. The disc is worth having for this alone, particularly in this strong, understanding and well-recorded performance, culminating in a sparkling account of the finale. Between those works and the *Piano Concerto* of 1965 (written for the 85th birthday of Stravinsky) Carter concentrated mainly on chamber works, developing the uncompromising personal idiom that has won him universal critical acclaim.

The *Piano Concerto* is pretty rebarbative, highly intricate rhythmically, its ideas firmly embedded in barbed wire and its spikey charms eminently resistible. In short, it is deeply unappealing, even given the virtuosity of the remarkable soloist and the supportive playing of the Nashville orchestra. Other respected musicians feel differently and, at this modest price, collectors can afford to try it for themselves. The pianist, Mark Wait, copes well with the daunting technical problems of the piano writing, well supported by the Nashville orchestra, renowned for its adventurous recordings of modern music. First-rate sound, if with the piano balanced rather too forwardly.

(i) *Piano Concerto; Variations for Orchestra*
*** New World (ADD) NW 347. (i) Ursula Oppens; Cincinnati SO, Gielen

The *Concerto* is a densely argued piece, complex in its structure, with a concertino of seven instruments, surrounding the piano, who act as 'a well-meaning but impotent intermediary'.

Michael Gielen directs strong, purposeful readings, very well played, of this taxing music, clarifying the thornily complex arguments with Ursula Oppens a powerful soloist.

The *Variations* is an inventive and fascinating work, splendidly played by the Cincinnati forces. The recording was made at concert performances and is excellent.

CARULLI, Ferdinando (1770–1841)

Guitar Concerto in A
(M) **(*) DG (IMS) (ADD) 439 984-2. Behrend, I Musici – GIULIANI: *Concerto in A* ***; VIVALDI: *Guitar Concertos* **(*)

The Italian virtuoso Ferdinando Carulli made his reputation in Paris, where this innocent post-Mozartian one-movement piece was written. It is elegantly played by Behrend and I

Musici and immaculately recorded. A touch more vitality would have been welcome, but this is enjoyable enough.

CASELLA, Alfredo (1883–1947)

La Giara (Symphonic Suite), Op. 41 bis; Paganiniana (Divertimento for Orchestra), Op. 65; Serenata for Chamber Orchestra, Op. 46 bis
(BB) *** Naxos 8.553706. Italian Swiss RSO, Benda

The performance of *Paganiniana* by the Italian Swiss Radio under Christian Benda is as bright-eyed, polished and sympathetic as its competitor, below. Both the *Serenata*, which is precociously good-humoured (it opens with a droll bassoon solo) and touchingly nostalgic by turns, and the ballet, *La Giara*, are unashamedly eclectic. But Casella has a ready fund of good tunes and they are delectably scored. The ballet also includes a melancholy vocal interlude, *The Story of the Girl Seized by Pirates*, sensitively sung by Marco Beasley, affecting but not in the least sentimental. The recording is first class, vividly atmospheric. This collection is well worth having, but don't play all three works at once.

Paganiniana, Op. 65
(***) Testament mono SBT 1017. St Cecilia, Rome, O, Cantelli (with DUKAS: *L'Apprenti sorcier*; FALLA: *Three-cornered Hat*; RAVEL: *Daphnis et Chloé: Suite 2* (***))

Paganiniana is a delightful, effervescent score. Cantelli's pioneering record dates from 1949 and comes up sounding very well in a marvellously transferred Testament issue which also offers his 1955–6 Philharmonia recording of the *Daphnis* suite and his 1954 *Three-cornered Hat*. Elegant playing.

PIANO MUSIC

A la manière de ... Op. 17/1 & 2 serie; Barcarola; Berceuse triste; 2 Canzoni popolari italiane; Cocktail's Dance; 2 Contrasts; Inezie, Op. 32; Notturnino; Nove pezzi, Op. 24; Pavane; 2 Ricercari sul nome B.A.C.H; Ricercare sul nome Guido M. Gatti; Sarabande; Sei studi, Op. 70; Sinfonia, Arioso e Toccata; Sonatina, Op. 28; Studio sulle terze maggiori; Toccata; Undici pezzi infantili, Op. 35; Variations sur une Chaconne
(M) *** Warner (ADD) 0927 47043-2 (3). Lye de Barberiis

Of the three major Italian composers of the Ottocento – Malipiero, Pizzetti and Casella – the last named was the most active in the cause of contemporary music as a pianist, conductor, teacher and organizer. He studied in Paris with Fauré and rubbed shoulders with the likes of Stravinsky, Ravel and Enescu. Casella was a leading exponent of neo-classicism and a driving force behind the ISCM (International Society for Contemporary Music) and as a pianist he recorded the Bloch *First Piano Quintet* and Roy Harris's *Piano Trio*. He was easily the most influential figure in Italian music between the two world wars, but his own output, which is extensive and of quality, has fallen into neglect. Apart from *Paganiniana*, which has been recorded by Ormandy, Muti and Kondrashin, his *Violin Concerto* was championed by André Gertler on Supraphon and there is a 1936 broadcast, albeit incomplete, of the *Triple Concerto* conducted by Koussevitzky, no less. This three-CD set collects his piano music, and the idiomatic quality of the writing leaves no doubt as to his natural feeling for the keyboard. The idiom is eclectic and the mature style often brittle and dryish, yet his is a cultured, well-stocked musical imagination and the writing is unfailingly inventive, even if it is not a good idea to play too much of it at once. Not great music, perhaps, but eminently intelligent and rewarding – and well played here. Readers who do not want everything can choose the excellent Naxos recital by Luca Ballerini listed below.

11 Children's Pieces, Op. 35; 2 Ricercari on the Name B.A.C.H, Op. 52; 9 Pieces, Op. 24; 6 Studies, Op. 70
(BB) *** Naxos 8.554009. Ballerini

What an interesting composer Casella is and how strange that he is so neglected! Like Strauss, his role in the fascist era has attracted the opprobrium of various armchair heroes, usually American academics, who have never faced such realities, but Egon Wellesz, a scholar-composer of proven anti-Nazi credentials, never wavered in his admiration of him. The *Nine Pieces*, Op. 24, are all exploratory in idiom, reflecting the worlds of Stravinsky, Busoni and Ravel. The third, *In modo elegiaco*, even foreshadows the harmonic world of Frank Martin. The *Children's Pieces* of 1920, dedicated to Castelnuovo-Tedesco, are imaginative and full of resource and charm, the last being reminiscent of the circus music of Stravinsky's second *Little Suite*. The *Ricercari on the Name B.A.C.H*, Op. 52, were written for Gieseking in 1932 and are as exploratory in idiom as the charming wartime *Etudes*, Op. 70. Very convincing performances, as intelligent as befits this music, and very well recorded too.

CASTELNUOVO-TEDESCO, Mario (1895–1968)

Guitar Concerto 1 in D, Op. 99
(M) *** Sony (ADD) SMK 89753. Williams, ECO, Groves –
   RODRIGO: *Concierto de Aranjuez, etc.*; VILLA-LOBOS: *Concerto* ***
(BB) *** Naxos 8.550729. Kraft, N. CO, Ward – RODRIGO; VILLA-LOBOS: *Concertos* ***

John Williams's more recent version of Castelnuovo-Tedesco's engaging concerto with Groves is more vividly recorded than his earlier account with Ormandy and the Philadelphia Orchestra, but that was fresher and had more pace. He is placed too far forward here, so that it is not always possible to locate him in relation to his colleagues. But if the sound is unreal as far as perspective goes, it is by no means unpleasing. These artists make the most of the slow movement's poetry and the performance has no lack of charm. The generous couplings and distinguished performances (about which there are few reservations) make this new compilation highly recommendable.
On Naxos another first-class version of this slight but attractive concerto, which is well suited by the relatively intimate scale of the performance. The recording is well balanced and vivid, and the soloist, Norbert Kraft, has plenty of personality; and the accompaniment is fresh and polished. Typically excellent Naxos value.

Cello Sonata, Op. 50; Notturna sull'acqua, Op. 82a ; Scherzino, Op. 82b; I Nottambu i (Variazione fantastiche), Op. 47; Paraphrase on Rossini's 'Largo al factotum'; Toccata, Op. 83; Valse on the Name of Gregor Piatigorsky
*** Biddulph LAW 024. Green, Moyer

Castelnuovo-Tedesco's *Cello Sonata* is a splendid work, opening with a striking main theme (marked *Arioso e sereno*) followed by a highly inventive *Aria with Variations* to act as slow movement and finale combined. The two nocturnal pieces are full of Mediterranean atmosphere. Serenity and passion are interchanged and whirling Spanish dance-rhythms follow, but the perfumes of the night return to end the work gently. The two witty encores sparkle, with Tchaikovsky's *Sleeping Beauty Waltz* making a surprise entry in the Piatigorsky tribute. Nancy Green is in full sympathy with this repertoire and she plays very persuasively indeed, with excellent support from her partner, Frederick Moyer.

SOLO GUITAR MUSIC

Aranci in fiore, Op. 87a; Capriccio, Op. 195/18; Escarramán, Op. 177/1-5; La guarda cuydadosa, Op. 177/6; 3 Preludi mediterranei, Op. 176; Variations à travers les siècles, Op. 71; Variations plaisantes sur un petit air populaire, Op. 95; Tarantella, Op. 87b
(BB) **(*) Naxos 8.554831. Micheli

This is the début CD of the young Italian, Lorenzo Micheli, who won first prize in the 1999 Guitar Foundation of America Competition. To his credit he refrains from duplicating the familiar Villa-Lobos or Sor repertoire and concentrates on rarities by his countryman, Castelnuovo-Tedesco. The music is slender in substance but appealing. Artistically this is first rate, as Micheli plays with assurance and elegance, but he is balanced very closely.

CASTILLON, Alexis de (1838–73)

Piano Quartet in G min., Op. 7
(N) (BB) *** Virgin 2x1 4 82061-2 (2). Kandinsky Qt –
   CHAUSSON; LEKEU; SAINT-SAENS: *Piano Quartets* ***

Like Chausson and Lekeu, with whom he shares this two-CD set, Alexis de Castillon was a pupil of César Franck. He graduated from Saint-Cyr and combined a military career with composition. His Op. 7 Piano Quartet of 1869 is an engaging piece, much indebted to Schumann. The performance, like the others in this coupling, comes from the early 1990s and is expert and well recorded. This is a valuable and rewarding issue.

CATALANI, Alfredo (1854–93)

A Sera; Serenatella; String Quartet in A
*** ASV CDDCA 909. Puccini Qt – PUCCINI: *Crisantemi; Fugues; Quartet etc.* ***

The elegant *Serenatella* and the romantically melancholy *A Sera*, were arranged by the composer from piano originals, and Catalani understandably thought well enough of the latter to use it for the prelude to Act III of his most famous opera, *La Wally*. The *String Quartet in A* is less consistent, but its scale is impressive, with the extended slow movement providing a moving expressive climax, confidently handled. A delightful disc, warmly played and atmospherically recorded.

La Wally (opera; complete)
(B) *** Double Decca (ADD) 460 744-2 (2). Tebaldi, Del Monaco, Diaz, Cappuccilli, Marimpietri, Turin Lyric Ch., Monte Carlo Op. O, Fausto Cleva

The title-role of *La Wally* prompts Renata Tebaldi to give one of her most tenderly affecting performances on record, a glorious example of her singing late in her career. Mario del Monaco begins coarsely, but the heroic power and intensity of his singing are formidable, and it is good to have the young Cappuccilli in the baritone role of Gellner. The sound in this late-1960s recording is superbly focused and vividly real. Reissued as a Double, this is now one of Decca's prime operatic bargain sets. The new-style synopsis should prove attractive to newcomers to the opera.

CATOIRE, Georgy (1861–1926)

Despite his French-sounding surname, Georgy Catoire was Russian, born in Moscow in April 1861, an exact contemporary of Arensky and four years older than Glazunov. At 14 he started studying the piano in Berlin with Karl Klindworth, the friend and champion of Wagner who prepared the piano scores of the Wagner operas. The young Catoire became a dedicated Wagnerian, which led him – after he had developed his talent for composing – to look to German romanticism rather than to Russian nationalism for his inspiration. But he later studied with Rimsky-Korsakov and Liadov in St Petersburg, before returning to settle in Moscow. He received encouragement from both Tchaikovsky and Taneyev, and in 1916 he was appointed professor of composition at the Moscow Conservatory, a post he held until his death in 1926. Yet he was of French descent, and something of his Gallic origins shines through his music.

Piano Quartet in A min.; Piano Trio in F min.; Elegy in D min. (for violin & piano)
(N) *** Hyp. CDA 67512. Room Music

Room Music, the talented group led by the pianist Stephen Coombs, here act as persuasive advocates in passionate and brilliant performances of two of Catoire's major chamber works. The *Piano Trio*, dating from 1900, is remarkable both for its well-planned structure and for the virtuosity of the piano writing, particularly in the dashing finale. Although the influence of Franck and his circle can be felt, some of the thematic material has a hint of a Russian flavour, as do the main themes of the *Piano Quartet*, written in 1916. In this later work the additional influence of Scriabin becomes clear, but again the structural control of this Russian Wagnerian plays an important part. The song-like *Elegy for Violin and Piano* makes an attractive supplement to the major works. Coombs provides excellent notes (both from his pen and his fingers), and the other performers are equally committed and persuasive. The recording is in the finest Hyperion tradition, the sound very lifelike and well balanced. This is highly civilized and rewarding music, well worth investigating.

Piano music: Caprice, Op. 3; Chants de crépuscule (4 Morceaux), Op. 24; Intermezzo, Op. 6/5; 3 Morceaux, Op. 2; 5 Morceaux, Op. 10; 4 Morceaux, Op. 12; Poème, Op. 34/2; Prélude, Op. 6/2; 4 Préludes, Op. 17; Prélude, Op. 34/3; Scherzo, Op. 6/3; Valse, Op. 36; Vision (Etude), Op. 8
*** Hyp. CDA 67090. Hamelin

Georgy Catoire's music has been all but forgotten, which makes this dazzling collection of his piano music especially welcome, prompting Marc-André Hamelin to astonishing feats of virtuosity, combined with poetry. Catoire left a big collection of piano miniatures, of which this collection of 28 is an attractive sample. They are played in order of opus

number, giving an idea of Catoire's development from echoing Chopin, Liszt and Tchaikovsky to adventuring more towards the world of Wagner and of the French Impressionists. If there is a Russian he echoes, it is Scriabin, and it is the fluency of his writing for the keyboard rather than memorability of material that strikes home, with Hamelin an ideal interpreter. Yet for all these influences, in many ways he is his own man, and his music, particularly the *Morceaux*, is often very seductive. Hamelin also shows how he can tickle the ear with a scherzando lightness, as in the two engaging pieces from Op. 6. This is not a recital to play continuously but, drawn on, it will give much refreshment and pleasure. Hamelin is given an outstandingly natural recording, bright, yet with full sonority and colouring.

CAVALLI, Francesco (1602–76)

Francesco Cavalli was born Francesco Caletti in the Venetian city of Creme, where he became a choirboy in the cathedral. When the Venetian govenor, Federico Cavalli, offered his patronage, he also offered his name, and the young musician subsequently became chorister, organist and finally *maestro de capella* at St Mark's, Venice. His main claim to fame is as an operatic composer, of which he wrote more than 30. But no doubt in due course we shall discover more of his sacred and instrumental music.

Messa Concertata; 4 Canzonas; Motets: O bone Jesu; O quam suavis et decora
(N) (BB) *** Hyp. Helios CDH 55293. Hyde, Carwood, Seicento, Parley of Instruments, Holman

Much of Cavalli's church music was published in his *Musica Sacre* of 1656. It begins with a concerted setting of the *Messa Concertata*, and that is what Peter Holman has recorded here He follows the custom at St Mark's at the time of interspersing the five movements of the Ordinary with offertory and communion motets and ensemble sonatas, sonorously but modestly scored. The Mass uses two four-part choirs of voices, with two violins, three trombones and continuo, reflecting Monteverdi's *Magnificat* setting of 1641, which tends to confirm that Cavalli was the latter's pupil. His own music, with its jolly three-bar dactylic rhythms and rich chording for voices and brass, is extrovert and vigorous, although the soprano Philippa Hyde's contribution to the two motets shows the depth of his touching lyrical writing. Cavalli is no carbon copy of his mentor but a fine composer in his own right. The performance, with excellently blended voices and instruments, is most appealing and is very well recorded. Full texts and translations are included.

OPERA

La Calisto (complete version; freely arranged by Raymond Leppard)
☉ (M) *** Decca 476 2176 (2). Cotrubas, Trama, J. Baker, Bowman, Gottlieb, Cuénod, Hughes, Glyndebourne Festival Op. Ch., LPO, Leppard

No more perfect Glyndebourne entertainment has been devised than this freely adapted version of an opera written for Venice in the 1650s but never heard since. It exactly relates that permissive society of the seventeenth century to our own. It is the more delectable because of the brilliant part given to the goddess, Diana, taken by Dame Janet Baker. In

Leppard's version she has the dual task of portraying first the chaste goddess herself, then in the same costume switching immediately to the randy Jupiter disguised as Diana, quite a different character. The opera is splendidly cast. Parts for such singers as James Bowman draw out their finest qualities, and the result is magic. No one should miss Dame Janet's heartbreakingly intense singing of her tender aria *Amara servitù*, while a subsidiary character, Linfea, a bad-tempered, lecherous, ageing nymph, is portrayed hilariously by Hugues Cuénod. The opera has transferred admirably to a pair of CDs, with each of the two acts offered without a break; the recording, made at Glyndebourne, is gloriously rich and atmospheric, with the Prologue in a different, more ethereal acoustic than the rest of the opera. This has now been reissued by Universal as one of the 'Penguin ● Collection' – at mid-price and with full documentation included.

La Calisto (complete)

(B) **(*) HM HMX 2901515.7 (3). Bayo, Lippi, Keenlyside, Pushee, Mantovani, Concerto Vocale, Jacobs

Jacobs directs a lively account, recorded in vivid, immediate sound, helped by some characterful, generally well-sung solo performances. In the title-role Maria Bayo is sweet and fresh, and Alessandra Mantovani as Diana sings warmly, though with some unsteadiness. The disappointment is that when Jove is disguised as Diana, the part is sung by the weighty baritone, Marcello Lippi, taking the role of Jove, in a piping falsetto. Graham Pushee, a reliable but hooty counter-tenor, takes the role of Endimione, and the comic role of the nymph, Linfea, is taken by a male singer, Gilles Ragon, capable but nowhere near as characterful as Hugues Cuénod at Glyndebourne. The vigour and variety of Cavalli's inspiration are brought out well by Jacobs and his team. The set now comes at bargain price, handsomely packaged with full libretto and translation.

Arias and Duets from: *Calisto; Didone; Egisto; Giasone; Ormindo*

(N) (BB) **(*) Naxos 8.557748. Banditelli, Frisandi, Abbandanza, Doro, Cecchetti, Mediterraneo Concento, Vartolo

Here is a well-planned and ideally documented aural window opening on to five of Cavalli's key operas, very well sung by a fine cast who are obviously at home in this repertoire. If there are no stellar names in the cast list, there was no star system in Cavalli's time, and the vocal acting here is at one with the melodramatic (and sometimes sexually explicit) story-lines. While the music itself often has distinct reminders of Monteverdi, Cavalli was still his own man, and the lovely lyrical theme of the final duet of Act III of *Didone* is almost Handelian, while the farewell scene between Erisbe and Ormindo is dramatically most affecting. The operas are full of laments (Dido's is sensitively sung, if not as memorable as Purcell's famous setting), but Hypsipille's grieving from Act III of *Giasone* shows Cavalli at his best, dramatically volatile and very touching. Equally, Cavalli readily captures the sensuous atmosphere of the highly immoral interchanges in *Calisto*, while Endymion's Act II aria is quite luscious. All in all, while this is a piecemeal selection, there is a great deal to enjoy, and it does give the listener a sense of the range of Cavalli's operatic writing. The accompaniments are most stylishly managed, and the conductor, Sergio Vartolo, is also to be praised for his sensitive accompaniments at the harpsichord.

CHABRIER, Emmanuel (1841–94)

Bourrée fantasque; España (rhapsody); *Joyeuse marche; Suite pastorale; Gwendoline: Overture. Le Roi malgré lui: Danse slave; Fête polonaise*

*** Mercury (ADD) **SACD** 475 6183. Detroit SO, Paray – ROUSSEL: *Suite* **(*)

Mercury are bringing out some of their most admired recordings on SACD and the new format should go some way to further enhance the already spectacular results afforded by the 'Living Presence' technology. This finely played and idiomatically conducted Mercury collection of Chabrier's best orchestral pieces does not disappoint. Paray's whimsically relaxed and sparkling account of *España* gives great pleasure and his rubato in the *Fête polonaise* is equally winning. The *Suite pastorale* is a wholly delightful account, given playing that is at once warm and polished, neat and perfectly in scale, with the orchestra beautifully balanced. The *Joyeuse Marche* was recorded in Detroit's Old Orchestral Hall a year before the rest of the programme. The slightly dry acoustic suits the music, the quality now enhanced on SACD, with its original three channels now remastered most tellingly. The Roussel coupling makes an excellent and imaginative bonus.

España; Fête polonaise; Gwendoline overture; Habanera; Joyeuse marche; (i) *Larghetto for Horn & Orchestra; Prélude pastorale; Suite pastorale*

*(**) DG (IMS) 447 751-2. (i) Janezic; VPO, Gardiner

España; Gwendoline Overture

(**(*)) BBC mono BBCL 4113. RPO, Beecham (with spoken introduction) – BERLIOZ: *The Trojans: Royal Hunt and Storm;* DEBUSSY: *L'Enfant prodigue: Cortège et air de danse;* DELIUS: *Brigg Fair;* MASSENET: *La Vierge: Le Dernier Sommeil de la vierge;* SAINT-SAENS: *Le Rouet d'Omphale* (with MOZART: *Divertimento in D, K.131: excerpts*) (**(*))

España; Habanera; Joyeuse marche; Lamento; Prélude pastorale; Suite pastorale; Le Roi malgré lui: Danse slave; Fête polonaise

(BB) **(*) Naxos 8.554248. Monte-Carlo PO, Niquet

España; Suite pastorale

*** Chan. 8852. Ulster O, Y. P. Tortelier – DUKAS: *L'Apprenti sorcier; La Péri* **(*)

Beecham's BBC recording of *España* comes from a 1956 live broadcast concert of 'Lollipops', and enjoyable though it is, it does not quite match his earlier studio recording with the LPO, partly because the sound has less range and sparkle. However, it does have a spoken introduction from the conductor, and the *Gwendoline Overture*, recorded a year earlier, does not lack either charm or gusto. The excerpts from the Mozart *Divertimento* were part of the main concert and bring some predictably fine string and horn playing.

A very well-recorded programme on Naxos, played with considerable idiomatic flair if without always the very last degree of finesse (*Sous-bois*, for instance, could be more delicate in the bass). But the rumbustious pieces have plenty of sparkle and *España* does not lack gusto. Enjoyable, and good value for money.

Yan Pascal Tortelier and the excellent Ulster Orchestra give an altogether first-rate account of Chabrier's delightful *Suite pastorale*, distinguished by an appealing charm and lightness of touch. There is a spirited account of *España*, too.

Gardiner's DG collection is disappointing. The *fortissimos* bring coarseness into the music-making and readily become tiring to listen to. Easily the most attractive and refined playing comes in the charming *Suite pastorale*, with the rustling leaves in *Sous-bois* delicately caught. The performances certainly do not lack vigour but are hardly subtle in rhythmic feeling. Clearly the VPO are not at home in this repertoire and, for all the brilliance of Gardiner's approach, *España* becomes heavy going, with its over-enthusiastic bass drum, while the orchestra is not very seductive either in nudging the rhythms of the *Habanera*.

PIANO MUSIC

Aubade; Ballabile; Caprice; Feuillet d'album; Impromptu; Pièces pittoresques; Ronde champêtre; (i) 3 Valses romantiques
(BB) *** Regis RRC 1133. Stott; (i) with Burley

For those wanting a representative single-CD selection, Kathryn Stott provides the ideal answer. She plays this long-neglected but rewarding repertoire with intelligence, wit and elegance. Perhaps the very last ounce of charm is missing, but there is enough of it to provide delight. She is, moreover, recorded with great presence and fidelity; the piano sound is very alive, natural and fresh.

VOCAL MUSIC

Mélodies (complete): Adieux à Suzon; Ah! petit démon; Ballade des gros dindons; Chanson pour Jeanne; Chants d'oiseaux; Les Cigales; Couplets de Mariette; Credo d'amour; Duo de l'ouvreuse de l'Opéra Comique et de l'employé du Bon Marché; L'Enfant; España (arr. Emile Louis); *L'Ile heureuse; L'Invitation au voyage; Ivresses!; Lied* (De Banville); *Lied* (Mendès); *Le Pas d'armes du roi Jean; Pastorale des cochons roses; Ronde gauloise; Le Sentier sombre; Sérénade; Sérénade de Ruy Blas; Sommation irrespectueuse; Tes yeux bleus; Toutes les fleurs; Villanelle des petits canards*

Folksong arrangements: Les plus jolies du pays de France: Bèrgere et chasseur; La Bien-aimée; Le Désereur; Entrez, la belle, en vigne; Les Filles de trente ans; Le Flambeau éteint; La Fleur dorée; Les Garçons de Bordeaux; Joli dragon; Marion s'en va-t-a l'ou; Les Métamorphoses; La Mie du voleur; La Morte de la brune; Nique nac no muse!; Que les amants ont de la peine!; Sur le bord de l'île; Ode à la musique
*** Hyp. CDA 67133/4. Lott, Burden, Varcoe, Spence, Johnson, McGreevy, Polyphony, Layton

These two generously filled discs, appropriately sub-titled 'Musique adorable!' offer a wide-ranging selection of Chabrier's songs, as well as the *Ode à la musique* (sung by Geraldine McGreevy with the choral group, Polyphony), and a curious duo for a programme-seller at the Opéra Comique and an assistant at the Bon Marché department store. That jokey piece, with each section ending in a Swiss yodelling song, demonstrates the humorous side of Chabrier, and his lighter manner also comes out in the vocal arrangement of his popular Spanish rhapsody, *España*, made under his supervision by Emile Louis with patter-like words by Eugène Adenis, a fun piece. Yet many of these songs are deeply expressive, even some of those which date from 1862 when he was only

21. They include a setting of Victor Hugo, *Sommation irrespectueuse*, which darkly hints at madness, and a setting of Baudelaire's *L'Invitation au voyage*, which has always been eclipsed by the supreme setting of that poem by his friend, Duparc, but which is intensely original, with sustained notes on a bassoon producing distinctive tone-colours (finely played by Ursula Leveaux). The song which opens the second disc, *Tes yeux bleus*, is also most evocative, hinting at Wagner's *Traume*, while that second disc also includes 16 regional folksong settings, bright and characterful. As always in his song recordings for Hyperion, Graham Johnson greatly adds to one's enjoyment, not only with his ever-sensitive playing but in his comprehensive, scholarly notes. Felicity Lott, Geraldine McGreevy, William Burden and Toby Spence are all in fine voice, singing stylishly.

OPERA

Briseis (complete)
✿ *** Hyp. CDA 66803. Rodgers, Padmore, Keenlyside, Harries, George, BBC Scottish SO, Jean-Yves Ossonce

Starting with a ripely seductive sailors' chorus, few operas are as sensuous as *Briseis*. On disc it matters little that this is a torso. The writing is not just sensuous but urgent, a warm bath of sound that is also exhilarating. Casting is near ideal, with Joan Rodgers in the title-role rich and distinctive, and with Mark Padmore as the sailor, Hylas, equally warm, producing heady, clear tenor tone. Symbolizing the forces of Christian good, Simon Keenlyside as the Catechist and Kathryn Harries as the mother of Briseis, cured through faith, both sing with character and apt resonance. Full, atmospheric sound.

Gwendoline (complete)
*(**) ED 13059 (2). Kohutková, Henry, Garino, Brno Philharmonic Ch., Slovak PO, Penin

Like the unfinished *Briseis*, recorded by Hyperion, *Gwendoline* is a high romantic opera written in the shadow of Wagner, with many sensuous sequences, not just the love-duets but such evocative choral passages as the *Epithalamium*. The final love-death brings more echoes of the final trio of Gounod's *Faust* than it does of Wagner, with the idiom identifiable French throughout. This live recording offers a performance flawed vocally but with Jean-Paul Penin drawing playing that is both sensitive and passionate from the Slovak Philharmonic. In the title-role Adriana Kohutková sings sympathetically but with bright tone that leads to shrillness on top. Didier Henry's grainy baritone grows rough under pressure, hardly heroic-sounding, and Gérard Garino's fine, clear tenor sounds far too youthful for the aged Armel. Nevertheless, a very enjoyable first recording, with first-rate sound.

L'Etoile (complete)
✿ *** EMI 7 47889-8 (2). Alliot-Lugaz, Gautier, Bacquier, Raphanel, Damonte, Le Roux, David, Lyon Opéra Ch. and O, Gardiner

This fizzing operetta is a winner: the subtlety and refinement of Chabrier's score go well beyond the usual realm of operetta, and Gardiner directs a performance that from first to last makes the piece sparkle bewitchingly. Colette Alliot-Lugaz and Gabriel Bacquier are first rate, and numbers such as the drunken duet between King and Astrologer are hilarious. Outstandingly good recording, with excellent access.

CHADWICK, George (1854–1931)

Aphrodite; Angel of Death; Overtures: Euterpe; Melpomene; Thalia

(BB) *** Naxos 8.559117. Nashville SO, Schermerhorn

Although an American composer, George Chadwick still relates to the world of Brahms and Dvořák, if with an attractive transatlantic flavour in the manner of the *New World Symphony*. But these tone-poems and (symphonic) overtures, though substantial and colourful works, are not on that level, and although they have engaging invention, they do not always fully sustain their length. The three overtures are each named after one of the muses. *Thalia* (the muse of comedy) highlights Chadwick's particular skill at writing wittily and lightheartedly; the more substantial *Melpomene* (the muse of tragedy) was one of the composer's most often performed works during his lifetime, its opening almost *Tristanesque*, while *Euterpe* (the muse of music), is enjoyably colourful.

The *Angel of Death*, one of Chadwick's last orchestral ventures, has a Straussian flavour, and rather melodramatically depicts a dying sculptor's attempt to finish his masterpiece before succumbing to death. It is a flamboyant score with its ominous low brass chorales, and the drum roll signifying the artist's death is followed by sweeping strings and harp. But the longest work here is the tone-poem *Aphrodite*, which lasts just under 30 minutes. With its depictions of 'Moonlight on the Sea', 'Storms', 'Lovers', 'Children Playing' and 'The Approach of a Great Army', it suggests the sights the statue of the goddess might witness overlooking the sea. The Nashville orchestra seems thoroughly inside the music and the recording is very good, if not in the demonstration league.

Overtures: Melpomene; Rip van Winkle. Tam O'Shanter (symphonic ballad)

*** Chan. 9439. Detroit SO, Järvi – RANDALL THOMPSON: *Symphony 2* **

The *Rip van Winkle* overture, new to the catalogue, is an early work that is well laid out for the orchestra, as for that matter are the other two pieces. *Melpomene* has been compared by some commentators to the symphonic poems of Franck or Dukas. *Tam O'Shanter* (1915) is brilliantly scored and enormously vital and rumbustious. Good playing from the Detroit orchestra under Neeme Järvi and natural, life-like recording.

Serenade for Strings

*** Albany TROY 033-2. V. American Music Ens., Earle – GILBERT: *Suite* ***

This very well-crafted piece by the so-called 'Boston classicist' gives much pleasure. It is quite beautifully played by this excellent Viennese group, drawn from younger members of the Vienna Symphony Orchestra. The sound too is first rate, a successful example of a 'live recording' bringing no loss in realism and a gain in spontaneity.

Symphonies 2 in B flat; 3 in F

*** Chan. 9685. Detroit SO, Järvi

Chadwick's *Second Symphony* dates from the early 1880s, though its delightful *Scherzo* was premièred two years ahead of the rest of the work. When this was first heard it had to be encored, which is hardly surprising. It has an engaging,

cheeky quality (one contemporary review in the Boston *Transcript* wrote that 'it positively winks at you') and Järvi makes the very most of it. The *Third Symphony* is hardly less fresh and appealing. It breathes much the same air as Brahms, Dvořák and Svendsen; it is very compelling in so persuasive a performance as is given here by Järvi and his Detroit orchestra. The *Largo* is beautifully shaped and the *Scherzo* delightfully light and piquant. Absolutely first-class recording too.

CHAMINADE, Cécile (1857–1944)

Music for violin & piano: *Capriccio, Op. 18; Rondeau, Op. 97; Sérénade espagnole; Valse carnavalesque, Op. 73;* Music for 2 pianos: *Dance payenne; Pas des cymbales;* Songs: *Alleluia; Auprès de ma mie; L'amour captif; L'anneau d'argent; Attente (Au pays de Provence); Bonne humeur; Chanson triste; Ecrin; Espoir; L'été je voudrais; La lune paresseuse; Malgré nous; Ma première lettre; Menuet; Mignonne; Mots d'amour; Nice-la-berre; Rond d'amour; Si j'étais jardinier; Sombrero; Te souviens-tu?; Viens! mon bien-aimé!; Villanelle; Voisinage*

(N) *** DG 476 7110. Forsberg, Sparf, Von Otter, Jablonski

Those who associate the Victorians' favourite composer Cécile Chaminade with slight, genteel piano pieces will be surprised to find a far greater variety in this winning collection of her songs, as well as pieces for violin and piano and for two pianos. The sparkle and energy of many of them chimes perfectly with the artistry of Anne Sofie von Otter, here at her most vivacious. One may look in vain for any kind of profundity, with the poems chosen by the composer rarely rising above the banal, but the vocal lines are easily elegant and often colourful, and the piano accompaniments unusual and demanding. The picture is completed by equally winning performances of the six instrumental pieces. This CD won the *Gramophone* Vocal Award in 2002 and now appears at mid-price with full documentation, including texts and translations.

CHARPENTIER, Gustave (1860–1956)

Louise (complete)

(B) (***) Naxos mono 8.110102/4. Moore, Jobin, Pinza, Doe, Met. Op. Ch. & O, Beecham

This completely gives the lie to any idea that Grace Moore was primarily a film star rather than a genuine prima donna. Helped by Sir Thomas Beecham at his most warmly understanding, obviously enjoying his wartime stint at the Met. in New York (1943), she gives an enchanting performance as Charpentier's heroine. The voice is not just brilliant and flexible, with trills and ornaments flawlessly executed, but warm too, bringing out the tenderness of the writing. Her French is totally idiomatic, with the Canadian, Raoul Jobin, a stylish hero and Ezio Pinza gloriously resonant as the heroine's father. Clearer, fuller, if limited mono sound than in most radio recordings from this source.

Louise (gramophone version conceived and realized by the composer)

(M) (***) Nim. mono NI 7829. Vallin, Thill, Pernet, Lecouvreur, Gaudel, Ch. Raugel & O, Eugène Bigot

These substantial excerpts from *Louise* were recorded in 1935 under the 75-year-old composer's supervision; they feature two ideally cast French singers as the two principals, Ninon Vallin enchanting in the title-role and the tenor, Georges Thill, heady-toned as the hero, Julien. The original eight 78-r.p.m. records are fitted neatly on to a single CD, and – in the selection of items, made by the composer himself – just the delights and none of the longueurs of this nostalgically atmospheric opera are included. The voices are caught superbly in the Nimbus transfers, but with an early electrical recording like this the orchestral sound becomes muddled. Yet even Nimbus has rarely presented voices as vividly as here.

CHARPENTIER, Marc-Antoine
(1643–1704)

Les Antiennes 'O' de l'Avent, H.36–43, with *Noëls pour les instruments, H.534; Canticum in navitatem Domini nostri Jésus Christ, H.416; Pastorale sur la naissance de Notre Seigneur Jesus Christ, H.482* (HMX 2908141). *Canticum in nativitatem Domini nostri Jésus Christ, H.414; Pastorale sur la naissance de notre Seigneur Jésus Christ, H.483* (HMX 2908140). *Litanies de la Vierge, H.83; Missa Assumpta est Maria, H.11; Te Deum, H.146* (HMX 2908144). *Méditations pour le Carême; Le Reniement de St Pierre* (HMX 2908143). *Les Arts Florissants* (opéra et idylle en musique). (HMX 2908142)

(B) *** HM (ADD) HMX 2908140/44 (5). Les Arts Florissants, Christie

These two pioneering collections from William Christie and his Arts Florissants of the music of Charpentier, made over two decades, are complementary, the Harmonia Mundi compilation being recorded between 1981 and 1989 and the Warner Classics box between 1995 and 2001. Charpentier wrote numerous works in celebration of Christmas, and he set the words of the *Canticum in nativitatem Domini* four times, only one of which (H.416) is included in both compilations.

The solemn '*O*' *Antiphons* on the first disc listed here are so called because of their opening invocation: *O salutaris hostia, O Sapientia*, etc. Charpentier explained in his manuscript that custom demanded that *Noëls* were performed between them when they were sung on the days preceding the Nativity. Charpentier places the emphasis on these opening invocations in his settings, often with striking results, and the pastoral interludes form a refreshing contrast. The musical delights are considerable. The coupled setting of *In nativitate Domini* (also available, below, in a later performance on Warner Classics, coupled with the *Midnight Mass*) was composed for Marie de Lorraine, Duchesse de Guise, whose ensemble Charpentier directed until her death in 1688. The term 'Canticum' was used for both a motet and an oratorio, and this work has much of the character of an oratorio, and it affirms the composer's debt to his master, Carissimi. The invention throughout all this music has great appeal and variety, and the same high standards of performance and recording that are found here prevail throughout the box.

The *Canticum in nativitatem Domini*, H.414, also has invention of great appeal and variety and the coupled Pastorale is another most rewarding piece: its grace and charm continue to win one over to this eminently resourceful composer and his so fertile imagination.

Christie's performance of the *Te Deum* is almost certainly the finest in the catalogue. It is introduced not only by the famous fanfare *Prélude* but, before that, by Philidor's *Marche des timbales*. The disc also includes the much less familiar but no less beautiful *Missa Assumpta est Maria* and the more restrained *Litanies de la Vierge*. Framed by a *Kyrie* and closing *Agnus Dei*, the seven movements each radiantly describe one of the Virgin's mystical attributes, followed by an intercessionary prayer. This is a deeply devotional work for eight singers, two viols and continuo, and the composer himself participated in its first performance.

The *Méditations pour le Carême* are a sequence of three-voice motets for Lent with continuo accompaniment (organ, theorbo and bass viol) that may not have quite the same imaginative or expressive resource as their coupling, but they are full of nobility and interest. *Le Reniement de St Pierre*, however, is one of Charpentier's most inspired and expressive works, and its text draws on the account in all four Gospels of St Peter's denial of Christ. The performance and recording maintain the high standards of this series.

With *Les Arts Florissants* (from which Christie's ensemble takes its name) we move into the world of miniature opera. This is a short entertainment in five scenes; the libretto tells of a conflict between the Arts, who flourish under the rule of Peace, and the forces of War, personified by Discord and the Furies. This and the little Interlude that completes the music include some very invigorating and fresh ideas, performed very pleasingly indeed. The five CDs come in a box, each in an elegantly illustrated cardboard inner, and there is an excellent booklet, including full texts and translations.

Concert for viols in 4 Parts, H.545; Il faut rire et chanter: Dispute de bergers, H.484; La Pierre Philosophale, H.501. Airs: Ah! laissez-moi rêver; Ah! qu'ils sont courts les beaux jours; Ah! qu'on est malheureux d'avoir eu des désirs; Auprès du feu l'on fait l'amour; Ayant bu du vin claire; Charmantes fleurs, naissez; En vain rivaux assidus; Fenchon, la gentille Fenchon; Non, non, je ne l'aime plus; Quoi! Je ne verrai plus; Quoi! rien ne peut vous arrêter?; Rentrez, trop indiscrets soupirs; Tristes déserts, sombre retraite. Chaconne: Sans frayeur dans ce bois (3984 25485-2) (with Daneman, Petibon, Eikenes, Agnew, Sinclair, Piolino, Le Monnier, Ewing). *Canticum in nativitatem Domini, H.416; Messe de Minuit pour Noël, H.9; 4 Noëls sur les instruments* (8573 85820-2) (with soloists). (i) *Amor vince ogni cosa* (pastoraletta); (ii) *Les Plaisirs de Versailles*; (iii) *3 Airs on Stanzas from 'Le Cid'* (0630 14774-2) (with (i) Petibon, Lallouette; (i; ii) Daneman, Piolino; (ii) Károlyi, Duardin, Gardeil; (i; iii) Agnew). *La Descente d'Orphée aux Enfers* (chamber opera; complete). (0630 11913-2) (with Agnew, Daneman, Zanetti, Petibon, Károlyi, Gardeil)

(B) *** Warner 2564 61758-2 (4). Les Arts Florissants, Christie

The first disc in the later, Warner Classics box, described as 'Divertissements and Airs et Concert', shows something of the range of Charpentier's instrumental and secular vocal writing. The programme is framed by a dramatic setting, the first, *La Pierre Philosophale* (1681) is a so-called machine-play, written for the Comédie Française, in which the music took second place to the spectacular stage effects. In this instance the production failed, and all we are left with is eight minutes of charmingly scored music. Its choruses of Four Elements glorify the victory of love, while the central arias are sung by a gnomide celebrating her forthcoming wedding, and a Marquis (disguised as a sylph) who seeks her hand, though wishing she were taller. The union of such opposites is appropriately acclaimed by a duet of Fire and Water, and the Marquis is then astonished at the metamorphosis of his bride into a voluptuous, full-sized beauty!

The centrepiece of the programme is a collection of *chansonettes* and *airs sérieux*, of which the dolorous *Rentrez, trop indiscrets soupirs* ('Return, sighs'), *Quoi!, je ne verrai plus* ('Never more shall I see him') and the poignant *Ah! Qu'on est malheureuse* (despairing of a lost love) are contrasted with the delicately engaging *Ah! qu'ils sont courts* (about the short life of a springtime flower) and the following tender duet, '*Charmantes fleurs*' (with recorder obbligato). These are then followed by the more successful amours experienced after a glass or two of wine, *Ayant bu du vin claire*. The songs are made the more appealing for being interspersed with attractive movements from Charpentier's *Concert pour quatre parties de violes* which he wrote especially for the Marquise de Guise in 1680/81, as she preferred viols to modern violins.

The programme ends with *Il faut rire et chanter: Dispute de Bergers*, a miniature pastoral chamber-opera. The arguments are about the winter weather, which is then banished and spring celebrated. After a lament about the suffering of mortals, the shepherds join forces to dispel the melancholy. The message is: pastoral life is bearable, music and laughter (a little overdone here, perhaps) are life's best medicine. The performance is splendidly sung and played, and the recording is full of atmosphere. The documentation is admirable but sadly omits to tell who is singing the solo airs.

Christie's apt coupling of the beautiful *Canticum in nativitatem Domini*, H.416, and its interpolated instrumental *Noëls*, with the *Messe de Minuit pour Noël*, seems made in heaven. He has recorded the *Canticum* before, for Harmonia Mundi, with the freshest results (see above), but the new performance is just as warmly persuasive, and the *Midnight Mass*, using 11 different carol melodies, is even more memorable. In the *Kyrie* the use of *Joseph est bien marié*, given first to violins then to flutes, is an enchanting instance, and the whole work is a marvellous example of simple means used to maximum musical effect. The performance is unlikely to be surpassed.

Amor vince ogni cosa is a charming pastoral conversation-piece (with shepherds' chorus) about unrequited love. *Les plaisirs de Versailles* is a 'mini-opera' in which the characters are Music, Conversation, Le Jeu, Comus and Un Plaisir. They engage in a vociferous dialogue which is in turns lyrical, dramatic and bizarrely humorous, arguing at length about which is the most essential of the King's pleasures, with Comus mediating and suggesting fine wines, pastries and sweetmeats. Finally the protagonists are reconciled and the piece ends with a happy chorus. The three ardent airs from Corneille's *Le Cid* make a passionate central interlude. Throughout, the solo singing is delightful and full of lively and charming characterization, while Charpentier's orchestration is equally diverting when Christie provides such sparkling accompaniments.

La descente d'Orphée aux enfers is another dramatic entertainment on an intimate scale, lasting just under an hour, which Charpentier wrote for a private function at Mlle de Guise's mansion, around 1686. It is sad that, through lack of opportunity, Charpentier was given little chance to develop as a composer for the theatre as opposed to the church. The piece starts with lightweight, sparkling movements in dance rhythms, but then dramatically changes tone with the death of Euridice, a moment superbly interpreted by Sophie Daneman. The following lament for Orphée is just the first of his

moving and expressive solos, each of them brief but intense, beautifully sung by Paul Agnew. They culminate in a sequence when he seeks to charm Pluton in the Underworld, finally succeeding. Their impact is the greater by being regularly set against light, rhythmic numbers. The work ends with the lamenting of Pluton's subjects at losing Orphée and his musical magic. The pattern is far more compact than in the great settings of this favourite classical subject by Monteverdi and Gluck on either side; but with Christie drawing superb singing and playing from his well-chosen team, it is good to have such a rarity revived, probably given only once at the time and no more. The four discs come in their original jewel cases in a sleeve, and throughout there is excellent documentation, plus full texts and translations.

(i) *Ballet intermèdes d'Andromède. Le Ballet de Polieucte*
**(*) Gaudeamus CDGAU 303. (i) Elliott, Gilchrist, Guthrie, Underwood, New Chamber Op., Band of Instruments, Cooper

Charpentier wrote nearly three-quarters of an hour of incidental music for the 1682 revival of Pierre Corneille's *Andromède*, which is all included here. The play was notable for its special effects, including spectacular aerial flights, which the music accompanies rather tamely. Indeed, the writing for the soloists, although agreeable enough and well sung, is often somewhat pale. It is the intermezzi that contain the most striking ideas.

Le Ballet de Polieucte featured in another play of Corneille (for which Charpentier drew on precomposed music) is more memorable. It consists of an Overture (originally composed for Molière's *Le Dépit amoureux*) and a dozen brief but graceful dance movements, including a jolly *Marche de triomph*. The performances here are elegant and polished and well recorded, but a little more vitality would not have come amiss. The documentation cannot be faulted.

Ballet music: *La Descente d'Orphée aux Enfers; Médée; Les Plaisirs de Versailles*
*** Erato 3984 26129-2. Les Arts Florissants, Christie – RAMEAU: *Les Fêtes d'Hébe; Hippolyte et Aricie ***

This recording celebrated the twenty-fifth anniversary of William Christie and Les Arts Florissants by combining colourful, lightweight ballet sequences from major dramatic works by Charpentier with more extended ballets of Rameau. These shorter selections are characteristically colourful and are played with great vivacity and colour.

Motets: *Alma redemptoris; Amicus meus; Ave regina; Dialogus inter Magdalenam et Jesum; Egredimini filiae Sion; Elevations; O pretiosum; O vere, o bone; Magdalena lugens; Motet du saint sacrement; O vos omnes; Pour le Passion de notre Seigneur* (2 settings); *Salve regina; Solva vivebat in antris Magdalena lugens*
*** HM (ADD) HMA 1951149. Concerto Vocale

Half of the motets on this record are for solo voice and the others are duets. Among the best and most moving things here are *O vos omnes* and *Amicus meus*, which are beautifully done. Another motet to note is *Magdalena lugens*, in which Mary Magdalene laments Christ's death at the foot of the Cross. Expressive singing from Judith Nelson and René Jacobs, and excellent continuo support. Worth a strong recommendation.

Ave Maris stella, H.63; Domine salvum sine organo in C, H. 290; Messe pour le Port-Royal, H.5; Motet: Flores o Gallia, H.342; Magnificat pour le Port-Royale, H.81; O salutaris hostia, H.261; Psaume Laudate Dominum, H.182; Veni creator pour un dessus sel au catechisme, H.69

*** Astrée E 8598. Les Demoiselles de Saint-Cyr, Mandrin

In the mid-1680s, Charpentier composed several works 'for Port Royal'. There were two convents: one in the Chevreuse valley, south of Versailles, which was situated on a low-lying, marshy site; and the second, to which many of the nuns repaired, in the Faubourg Saint-Jacques in Paris, for which most of this repertoire was written. The music is scored for female voices only and is generally austere in style. The main work, after which the record is titled, is the *Messe pour le Port-Royal* for three soloists, chorus and organ. This is supplemented by various other pieces, psalm settings and the fine *Magnificat*, also written for the convent. This is reposeful music, predominantly meditative in character, and very persuasively performed by Les Demoiselles de Saint-Cyr under Emmanuel Mandrin, with Michel Chapuis providing the solo organ interludes. A rewarding issue.

Caecilia, virgo et martyr; Filius prodigus (oratorios); *Magnificat*

⊕━ (B) *** HM HMA 195066. Grenat, Benet, Laplenie, Reinhard, Studer, Les Arts Florissants, Christie

The music's stature and nobility are fully conveyed here. The *Magnificat* is a short piece for three voices and has an almost Purcellian flavour. One thing that will immediately strike the listener is the delicacy and finesse of the scoring. All this music is beautifully recorded; the present issues can be recommended with enthusiasm, especially at Musique d'Abord price.

Canticum in nativitatem Domini, H.393; In nativitatem Domini canticum, H.314; In nativitatem Domini canticum: Chanson, H.416; In nativitatem Domini Nostri Jesus Christi, H.414; 9 Noëls

⊕━ (BB) *** Naxos 8.554514. Aradia Ens., Mallon

In this Christmas disc with a difference, the talented Canadian group, the Aradia Ensemble, warmly recorded, present the nine charming sets of simple variations Charpentier wrote on French Christmas carols, or *Noëls*. Standing out from the rest is the minor-key *Ou nous dites Marie*, with chromatic writing like Purcell's. These instrumental pieces are set alongside a sequence of lively vocal motets on a Christmas theme, culminating in a miniature Nativity oratorio.

Canticum in nativitatem Domini, H.416; Dialogus inter angelos et pastores Judeae in nativitatem Domine, H.420; Noël: Un flambeau, Janette, Isabelle (3 versions), *H.460*

⊕━ (BB) *** Naxos 8.557036. Smith Bessette, Stelmacovitch, Nortman, Streetman, Aradia Ens., Mallon

Here is a natural and equally beguiling follow-up to the Aradia Ensemble's first Naxos collection of Christmas music, including *Noëls*. The two cantatas both use the same text from St Luke, telling of the angel's dialogue with the shepherds. Each then creates a nocturnal atmosphere, followed by the shepherds' joyful 'awakening', devotion and exultation. The innocence of the pastoral scene is richly conveyed in Charpentier's simple but inspired settings. The three versions of the *Nöel* (the first for soloists and organ, the second for

choir, the third instrumental) act as prelude, intermezzo and postlude in the most effective way, so that the concert makes a perfect whole. Singing, playing and recording are of high quality and so is the documentation.

Canticum in nativitatem Domini nostri Jesus Christi, H.416; Pastorale sur la naissance de notre Seigneur Jésus Christ, H.482

*** HM (ADD) HMC 905130. Les Arts Florissants Vocal & Instrumental Ens., Christie

The cantata, a finely balanced edifice in two complementary halves, is separated by an instrumental section, an eloquent evocation of the night. The little pastorale was written in the tradition of the *ballet de cour* or divertissement. This is enchanting music, elegantly played and excellently recorded.

Canticum pro pace, H.392; Josué, H.404; Mors Saülis et Jonathae, H.403; Praelium Michaelis Archangeli factum in coelo cum dracone, H.410; Quam dilecta tabernacula tua, H.167; Troisième Leçons de ténèbres du mercredi, du jeudi et du vendredi Saint, H.135/7

(N) (BB) **(*) Warner Apex 2564 61745-2 (2). Schlick, Wessel, Prégardien, Mertens, Rooy, Zijlstra, Visse, Van Berne, Amsterdam Bar. O, Koopman

The present collection centres on music which Charpentier wrote for double choir after his return from Italy (see below); although in the *Trois Leçons* the six-part grouping is not used until the closing '*Jerusalem*'. These are late settings, maintaining a beautifully serene melancholy, spiced by dissonances 'at the heart of the dark and sad key of C minor'. Curiously, Charpentier often wrote for double choir in a warlike ambience, and the *Canticum pro pacem* (1674–6), which opens with a Prelude suggesting 'the clamour of war', probably celebrated the successful outcome of one of Louis XIV's battles with the Dutch. *Josué* and *Mors Saülis et Jonathae* are motet/oratorios based on Old Testament stories, and the latter is very theatrical, almost operatic, opening with an even more dramatic orchestral *Rumor bellicus* ('Noise of War'). The chorus (often in very lively fashion) both narrates the story and takes part in the action, making a lively contrast to the dialogues between Saul, David, and the Soldier who kills the lamenting Saul at his own request. There is a memorably expressive aria for the Witch, and the closing section with David's *Air* and a choral lament is very touching. The performances here, with a first-class group of soloists who join together for the choruses, are in every way excellent, with the experienced directing hand of Ton Koopman and members of his Amsterdam Baroque Orchestra ensuring that standards of ensemble are the highest, and the recording is of equal excellence. The one snag is that, while full texts and translations are included, there is only a single cue for each work, which makes finding one's way very difficult. *Mors Saülis et Jonathae*, for instance, is in two parts, playing together for 35 minutes, and there is not even a separate track for Part II.

Canticum Zachariae: Benedictus, H.345; Mass, H.1; Te Deum, H.147

(BB) *** Naxos 8.553175. Le Concert Spirituel, Niquet

The *Canticum Zachariae* dates from 1687, and its lovely six-part *Benedictus* shows Charpentier in characteristically fluent lyrical and contrapuntal form. The four-part *Mass* – the first of the composer's eleven settings – which opens simply, extends to six voices in the *Sanctus*, with the spirited *Hosanna* extended to double choir. But it is the short *Agnus*

Dei, serenely beautiful, that haunts the memory.

The *Te Deum* was the composer's last setting, written not too long before his death. If without the instrumental spectacle of his most famous setting, it is supremely confident in its variety of style, superbly written, ending exultantly. The performances here are splendid, not inflated, but in every way satisfying. The recording is excellent and there is full documentation.

La Couronne de fleurs (Pastorale); *Caprice, H.542; 2 Menuets, H.541; Préludes: in A min.; in F min., H.528; Prélude, Menuet & Passepied in G min., H.520; Suite in D min., H.545; Symphonie in G, H.529. Airs: Oiseaux de ces bocages; Profitez du printemps; Dialogue d'Angélique et Médor, H.506; Tout renaît, tout fleurit, H.468; 3 Trios: Beaux petits yeux d'écariate, H.448; Compère Grégoire, H.470; Fanchan, la gentille Fanchon, H.454*

(N) *** Ambroisie AMB 9954. Berthon, Gabail, Getchell, Novelli, Dumora, Amarillis, Gaillard

Charpentier's pastoral, *La Couronne de fleurs*, derives in part from *Le Malade imaginaire*, the first work in which he collaborated with Molière in 1673, intended for the entertainment of the King. It is very lightweight Charpentier, but charmingly scored, and the performance is very French and highly idiomatic, with Cassandre Berthon shining in the joint roles as the goddess Flora and Hyacinthe, while Valérie Gabail is equally pleasing as the sheperdess Roselie. As the piece only runs to just under 30 minutes, the excellent period-instrument group, Amarillis, have framed it with an introductory *Suite* (originally for viols, but here played by flutes, oboes and violins), and followed it with a programme of airs and short instrumental pieces, closing with a *Symphonie* in the form of a chaconne. Again, everything is expertly sung and played, but the effect is rather piecemeal. Yet one's spirits perk up at the three vocal *Trios parodiques* (humorous drinking songs), which are most engagingly spirited and deliciously vulgar, quite unlike the Charpentier we know in church. Excellent recording and documentation, and lavish presentation, but this will not appeal to all Charpentierian tastes.

Elévation; In obitum augustissimae nec son piissimae gallorum Reginae lamentum; Luctus de morte augustissimae Mariae Theresiae Galliae

(N) (BB) *** Warner Apex 2564 61743-2. Degelin, Verdoodt, Smolders, Crook, Vandersteene, Widmer, Namur Chamber Ch., Musica Polyphonica, Devos

All three works here lament the death of the queen, Marie Thérèse. Clearly the event moved Charpentier deeply, and each reflects the paradox of the Christian faith in contrasting grief with joy and hope in the life hereafter. Here Devos's performances could hardly be bettered, bringing out all the music's drama, joy, and depth of feeling. The recordings, both made in spacious acoustics, are also first class and this Apex reissue is highly recommended. Such a collection can only further enhance the growing recognition of Charpentier's stature.

9 Leçons de ténèbres, H.120–125; H.136–137

(N) (BB) ** Warner Apex 2546 61742-2 (2). Widmer, Verschaeve, Crook, Caals, De Meulenaere, Ruhl, Musica Polyphonica, Devos

The first six *Leçons de ténèbres* for solo voices included here (H.120–125) come from Volume XXII and were probably written in 1680 for the Abbaye-aux-Bois; the remainder are for three voices and, though not unrelated to the earlier ones, are later still. Neither set duplicates the repertoire already covered by the Harmonia Mundi and Virgin issues above; but the performances here, although sensitive and lyrically eloquent, lack something in vitality. In that respect the solo works are rather more positive than those for three voices. The stylish instrumental accompaniments using original instruments are suitably pastel-shaded, and the recording is excellent; but one feels that a rather stronger characterization would have made these performances even more appealing.

Leçons de ténèbres for Maundy Thursday

(B) *** HM (ADD) HMC 901005. Jacobs, Nelson, Wieland Kuijken, Verkinderen, Christie, Concerto Vocale, Jacobs

The first of the *Leçons de ténèbres* sung on Maundy Thursday concerns the *Lamentations of Jeremiah*, and Charpentier's melismatic setting is sung with great eloquence by René Jacobs. Yet one must remember that this music was written for nuns (the names of the sisters who sang them are known) and Charpentier observed that the leading soprano should possess a '*voix touchante*' rather than a '*voix brillante*'. So it is here, in the second and third lessons, with Judith Nelson's *dolce* leading the small female group, accompanied (as the composer suggested) by a continuo of bass viol, organ and theorbo. They are beautifully recorded and this reissue is a real bargain.

Mass for 4 Choirs & Orchestra

(N) (BB) **(*) Warner Apex 2564 61745-2. Mellon, Poulenard, Brett, Aubin, Elwes, Laplenie, Cantoe, Gardell, Regional Ch. of N. Pas-de-Calais, Jean Bridier & Françoise Herr Vocal Ensembles, Gabrieli Ch., Grande Ecurie et la Chambre du Roy, Malgoire (with BOYVIN: *Organ Pieces* ***)

Charpentier wrote his *Mass for Four Choirs* when he returned to Paris in the early 1670s after spending three years in Italy, where he would certainly have encountered such multichorus antiphonal works. Though these were not part of the French tradition, he adapted them to the style of the French organ mass, interspersing organ interludes between the Propers. For the present live performance, Jean-Claude Malgoire has used – to great effect – organ pieces by Jacques Boivin (1646–1707) whose characterful music is exactly contemporary with that of Charpentier. The choral writing is essentially homophonic, often serene and always beautiful, with the soloists singing together, often in more lively part-writing as a further contrasting group. The *Christe* features two quartets of soloists, the *Gloria* is opened delicately and luminously by four solo voices and is followed by a rich choral sequence in 16 parts, and the *Et Resurrexit* is a more complex, contrapuntal sequence for the soloists. The performance here is of high quality, but the 1990 recording, made in the Abbaye of Saint-Michel en Thiérache, although providing a richly atmospheric ambience does not give clear separation between the various choral groups. Nevertheless, this is a thoroughly worthwhile disc, with Latin text included.

Messe de minuit pour Noël (Midnight Mass for Christmas Eve); Dixit Dominus; Te Deum

(BB) *** Naxos 8.557229. Aradia Ens., Mallon

Kevin Mallon and his excellent Canadian group, the Aradia Ensemble, give bright, clear readings of two of the most popular of Charpentier's choral works. This period performance of the *Prélude* for the *Te Deum* is very different from the one that used to introduce Eurovision programmes; it is altogether lighter and more joyful, with an exuberant display of timpani at the start and with bright trumpet flourishes throughout. In the *Christmas Mass* Mallon equally brings out the joy of the writing, giving more prominence than usual to the carols that punctuate the *Kyrie*, and springing rhythms infectiously in writing that in many sections offers a thoughtfully original setting of the liturgy. The *Dixit Dominus*, with its unexpectedly gentle minor-key introduction, makes an attractive extra item. Clear, well-balanced sound.

(i) *Messe de minuit pour Noël (Midnight Mass for Christmas Eve)*; (ii) *Te Deum*

(B) *** EMI Encore 5 74726-2 (ADD). (i) Cantelo, Gelmar, Partridge, Bowman, Keyte, King's College Ch., ECO, Willcocks; (ii) Lott, Harrhy, Brett, Partridge, Roberts, King's College Ch., ASMF, Ledger

There is a kinship between Charpentier's lovely *Christmas Mass* and Czech settings of the Mass that incorporate folk material, even the *Kyrie* having a jolly quality about it. The King's performance is warm and musical, but there isn't much Gallic flavour. The recording comes from the late 1960s and certainly now has more bite than it did; but reservations remain about the basic style of the singing. The coupling is the best known of the *Te Deum* settings, and this time the King's performance has a vitality and boldness to match the music and catches also its douceur and freshness. A splendid bargain on EMI's new super-bargain label.

Messe en la mémoire d'un Prince (Messe pour les trépassés, H.2; Motet pour les trépassés, H.311; Miserere des Jésuits, H.193/193a) (with ROBERDAY: *Fugue et caprice sur le même sujet*)

*** Virgin VC5 45394-2. Pelon, Bertin, Mammel, Sarragosse, Namur Chamber Ch., Ens. La Fenice, Tubéry

The *Messe pour les trépassés* and the associated Motet were commssioned in the mid-1670s from young Charpentier as funeral music for members of the Guise family, of whom the deeply religious Marie (her married name was de Lorraine) was the musical driving force. Charpentier set only the Ordinary of the Mass, with the plainsong of the *Pie Jesu* forming a melancholy melodic core. The *Motet*, with its heartfelt refrain *Miseremini mei* is interpolated after the *Kyrie*.

Later the composer returned to the motet and reworked and extended it for the Jesuits. It is set to one of the seven Penetential Psalms, and he developed it into an extended work of great poignancy for six-part chorus, flutes and strings, but with passages for one, two and three solo voices. Much of the music is very positive in feeling with the final chorus, *Tunc acceptabis* ('Thou shalt be pleased with the sacrifices of righteousness') joyfully animated and reaching a splendid polyphonic resolution.

A great deal of research and preparation went into this project by the French musicologist Jean Lionnet, and the recording is posthumously dedicated to him. Most importantly, he filled out the instrumental parts in the middle range to double the voices according to practice in Charpentier's time, including the use of the serpent. The CD opens with tolling bells, then Louis Couperin's organ voluntary *Carillons de Paris*, acts as a prelude to the Mass, while the Roberday *Fugue* forms an interlude before the *Miserere des Jésuits*. The performances could hardly be more dedicated – finely sung and played – with the recording admirably atmospheric and clear.

Miserere, H.219; Motets: Pour la seconde fois que le Saint Sacrament vient au même reposoir, H.372; Pour le Saint Sacrement au reposoir, H.346; Motet pour une longue offrande, H.434
*** HM HMA 195 1185. Mellon, Poulenard, Ledroit, Kendall, Kooy, La Chapelle Royale, Herreweghe

Charpentier's *Motet pour une longue offrande* is one of his most splendid and eloquent works. The *Miserere* was written for the Jesuit Church on Rue Saint-Antoine, whose ceremonies were particularly sumptuous. All four works on the disc are powerfully expressive and beautifully performed. The recording, made in collaboration with Radio France, is most expertly balanced.

Les Quatre Saisons (Quatuor anni tempestates). Psalms of David 41: Quemadmodum desiderat cervus; 75: Notus in Judaea Deus; 126: Nisi Dominus

(B) **(*) Opus OP 10004. Rimi, Delétré, Parlement de Musique, in Gester

Charpentier's *Four Seasons* is a group of four motets for two voices, drawing its inspiration from the 'Song of Songs', but it is a comparably routine inspiration. In the celebration of *Spring*, the two soprano voices here (the second unnamed) are not ideally matched and their vibratos clash. But in *Summer* and *Autumn*, their dialogue interchanges are much more pleasing, and in *Winter* the bravura scales (suggesting the gales, perhaps) come off quite effectively. With the Psalm settings the vocal writing is of an altogether different order and the three singers respond to Charpentier's stimulating variety of colour and mood. *Nisi Dominus* brings some lovely solo work from Noémi Rimi and the vocal blending is often impressive. After a charming 'piping' instrumental introduction, the bass opens Psalm 75 rather gruffly, but the agreeable vigour of this opening makes way for a very touching centrepiece, before the buoyant close. The style of Le Parlement de Musique is robust rather than refined and, while the recording is vivid, the focus is not always quite clean. But this inexpensive disc is still worth trying. Full texts and translations are provided.

OPERA AND THEATRE MUSIC

Actéon (complete)

(B) *** HM HMA 1951095. Visse, Mellon, Laurens, Feldman, Paut, Les Arts Florissants Vocal & Instrumental Ens., Christie

Actéon is particularly well portrayed by Dominique Visse; his transformation in the fourth tableau and his feelings of horror are almost as effective as anything in nineteenth-century opera! The other singers are first rate, in particular the Diane of Agnès Mellon. Alert playing and an altogether natural recording, as well as excellent presentation, make this a most desirable issue and a real bargain.

David et Jonathas (complete)

(B) **(*) HM (ADD) HMA 190 1289/90. Lesne, Zanetti, Gardeil, Visse, Les Arts Florissants, Christie

Christie's version of *David et Jonathas* may not always be especially dramatic, but it has a notably sure sense of authentic Baroque style and scale, as well as fine choral singing. However, only one of Christie's soloists is really outstanding: the characterfully distinctive counter-tenor, Dominique

Visse, who gives a vivid, highly theatrical performance. Those who relish authenticity above all else will clearly take to this version, very well recorded.

Médée (complete)

⊛ *** Erato 4509 96558-2 (3). Hunt, Padmore, Delétré, Zanetti, Salzmann, Les Arts Florissants, Christie

In his second recording of this rare opera, again with his group, Les Arts Florissants, Christie was glad to be able to open out the small cuts that were made before so as to fit the LP format. The success of his new interpretation is readily borne out in the finished performance, which easily surpasses the previous one in its extra brightness and vigour, with consistently crisper and more alert ensembles, often at brisker speeds, with the drama more clearly established. The casting is first rate, with Lorraine Hunt outstanding in the tragic title-role. Her soprano has satisfying weight and richness, as well as the purity and precision needed in such classical opera; and Mark Padmore's clear, high tenor copes superbly with the role of Jason, with no strain and with cleanly enunciated diction and sharp concern for word-meaning. The others follow Christie's pattern of choosing cleanly focused voices, even if the tone is occasionally gritty.

CHAUSSON, Ernest (1855–99)

Poème for Violin & Orchestra

(M) *** Decca (ADD) 460 006-2. Chung, RPO, Dutoit – DEBUSSY; FRANCK: Violin Sonatas *** ◉

(M) *** EMI 5 62599-2. Perlman, O de Paris, Martinon (with MASSENET: Thaïs: Méditation: Abbey Road Ens., Foster) – RAVEL: Tzigane; SAINT-SAENS: Introduction and Rondo capriccioso etc. ***

(M) **(*) RCA (ADD) 09026 61753-2. Heifetz, RCA Victor SO, Solomon – LALO: Symphonie espagnole (**(*)); SAINT-SAENS: Havanaise, etc.; SARASATE: Zigeunerweisen (***)

(BB) **(*) CfP 585 6192. Kennedy, LPO, Kamu – TCHAIKOVSKY: Violin Concerto **(*)

Chung's performance is deeply emotional, if not as opulent as Perlman's; but, with committed accompaniment from the RPO and excellent (1977) recording, this makes an apt bonus for superb performances of the Debussy and Franck Violin Sonatas.

Perlman's 1975 account of Chausson's beautiful Poème, with the Orchestre de Paris under Martinon, is a classic account by which all newcomers are measured. What a glorious and inspired piece it is when played with such feeling! It now returns to the catalogue at mid-price in the 'Perlman Edition' as part of a particularly distinguished anthology that includes a brilliant account of Ravel's Tzigane and the eternally fresh Saint-Saëns pieces so beloved of virtuosi – and of the public too, when played like this. The digital transfer exchanges some of the opulence of the original for a gain in presence (not that Perlman isn't near enough already), but it still sounds full. A luscious account of the Thaïs Méditation, recorded digitally two decades later, has now been added.

Heifetz too is recorded very closely, as if in the glare of a spotlight, and the performance is robbed of much of its subtlety. Even so, the playing itself is quite remarkable.

Nigel Kennedy's version of the Poème, unusually expansive and sensuous, with ripe and powerful build-up of climaxes, comes as a welcome, if not very generous, coupling for his warmly romantic reading of the Tchaikovsky Concerto, recorded in similarly rich, full sound.

(i) Poème for Violin & Orchestra; (ii) Poème de l'amour et de la mer

*** Chan. 8952. (i) Y. P. Tortelier; (ii) Finnie; Ulster O, Tortelier – FAURE: Pavane, etc. ***

No quarrels with Yan Pascal Tortelier's playing in the Poème, which he directs from the bow. There is consistent beauty of timbre and, what is more important, refinement of feeling. In the Poème de l'amour et de la mer Linda Finnie can hold her own with the very best; her feeling for the idiom is completely natural and her voice is beautifully coloured; among newer recordings this has very strong claims. Indeed in rapport between singer and orchestra none is better.

Symphony in B flat, Op. 20

(B) *** Virgin 2x1 5 61513-2 (2). Fr. RPO, Janowski – BERLIOZ: Symphonie fantastique; Le Carnaval romain; BIZET: Symphony ***

Symphony in B flat; Soir de fête, Op. 32; La Tempête, Op. 18; Viviane, Op. 5

❽➡ *** Chan. 9650. BBC PO, Y. P. Tortelier

Symphony in B flat; Soir de fête; La Tempête: 2 Scenes

**(*) Chan. 8369. Radio-Télévision Belge SO, Serebrier

Symphony in B flat, Op. 20; Viviane (Symphonic Poem)

(BB) **(*) Warner Apex 0927 49518-2. Basle SO, Jordan

Yan Pascal Tortelier and the BBC Philharmonic give thoroughly idiomatic and well-played accounts of all these Chausson pieces. They more than hold their own against any of the competitors and, given the excellence of the sound, may well be a first choice for collectors wanting an up-to-date recording of the Symphony.

Serebrier's account is also logically coupled with other Chausson pieces, Soir de fête plus two scenes from the incidental music for The Tempest. Serebrier's account of the Symphony has real conviction and receives good recording, but on balance Tortelier is preferable.

Armin Jordan and the Basle orchestra give a well-shaped account of the Symphony and are thoroughly atmospheric in the Wagnerian slow movement. The orchestral playing is responsive, and the recording has an agreeable warmth, with plenty of space around the sound. Jordan is a fine (and much underrated) conductor with an obvious sympathy for this work, and he is thoroughly convincing both here and in the symphonic poem. An excellent bargain, though not to be preferred to the Serebrier and Tortelier on Chandos.

Janowski's highly idiomatic reading is the finest of the performances on this inexpensive Virgin Double. It is very well played, and the performance has a strong impetus, particularly in the passionate finale, with the Franckian undertones well brought out throughout the work. The recording is obviously modern and is very good, if not absolutely top drawer. If you want the couplings, this is well worth considering.

CHAMBER MUSIC

Andante & Allegro (for clarinet and piano); Piano Trio in G min., Op. 3; Pièce for Cello & Piano, Op. 39; Poème Op. 25 (arr. for violin, string quartet & piano)

*** Hyp. CDA 67028. Neidlich, Devoyon, Hoffman, Graffin; Chilingirian Qt

The *Poème* appears here in a newly discovered arrangement by the composer. There is a complete naturalness and conviction about this performance in which Graffin is a wonderfully persuasive soloist. The remaining pieces, including the early *Piano Trio*, come off well and can hold their own against any rival. The rich acoustic environment enhances the appeal of these dedicated performances.

Concert in D for Violin, Piano & String Quartet, Op. 21

(*) Essex CDS 6044. Accardo, Canino, Levin, Batjer, Hoffman, Wiley – SAINT-SAENS: *Violin Sonata 1* ***
(N) (B) ** Decca 2-CD 475 6709. Thibaudet, Bell, Takács Qt – DEBUSSY; FAURÉ; FRANCK: *Violin Sonatas* **; RAVEL: *Piano Trio* ****

Salvatore Accardo and Bruno Canino and their four colleagues convey a sense of effortless music-making and of pleasure in making music in domestic surroundings. Accardo is particularly songful in the third movement, light and delicate elsewhere. It is a thoroughly enjoyable account, recorded in a warm acoustic.

Decca's team compromises Yves Thibaudet, Joshua Bell and the Takács Quartet, and they give a good account of themselves. Bell is perhaps a little too forceful and thrustful in tone in the main theme of the first movement, and they are rather on the fast side in the finale and wanting in breadth. These artists do not convey much period feeling or atmosphere, and are less inside Chausson's sensibility than are their Essex competitors. The recording is bright and well focused.

Piano Quartet in A, Op. 30

(N) (BB) *** Virgin 2x1 4 82061-2 (2). Kandinsky Qt – CASTILLON; LEKEU; SAINT-SAENS: *Piano Quartets* ***

The Chausson *Piano Quartet* comes from 1896, three years before the composer was killed in a cycling accident. It is an enormously civilized piece which reinforces the oft-quoted claim that Chausson is the connecting link between Franck and Debussy. There are parallels between it and the Debussy *G minor Quartet* of 1893. If you enjoy the Fauré *Piano Quartets*, this is your kind of music. It is the centrepiece of this rewarding two-CD compilation, and the performance from the early 1990s is most alive and satisfying.

Poème (for violin and piano) Op. 25

(N) *** New Note Quartz QTZ 2002. Liebeck, Apekisheva – PROKOFIEV; SAINT-SAENS; YSAŸE: *Violin Sonatas* ***

Katya Apekisheva's piano introduction prepares the way for Jack Liebeck's entry very seductively and his playing is full of passionate feeling. There may be more subtle accounts of Chausson's *Poème* on record, but none more deeply felt or ardent. The balance places the violin vividly forward, but with this degree of pasionate advocacy one is swept away, and the close of the piece is exquisitely gentle. The rest of this enterprising début programme is not less stimulating.

String Quartet in C min., Op. 35 (completed d'Indy)

*** Hyp. CDA 67097. Chilingirian Q. – D'INDY: *String Quartet 1* ***
(BB) *** Naxos 8.553645. Quatuor Ludwig – FRANCK: *Piano Quintet* ***

Prompted by César Franck in 1889, French composers produced a series of fine string quartets, of which only Debussy's and Ravel's remain in the regular repertory. This superb disc from the Chilingirians, sensitively played and beautifully recorded, is a revelation. Chausson's work, completed by

Vincent d'Indy after the composer's tragic death, has echoes of his teacher, Franck, touched in with point and elegance.

The Quatuor Ludwig also play it with conviction and aplomb. The recording is excellent, and this is also highly recommendable if you want the coupling.

VOCAL MUSIC

Mélodies: *Cantique à l'épouse; Le charme; Le colibri; Nanny; Les Papillons; Sérénade italienne; Le temps des lilas*
(N) (M) (***) Decca (mono) 475 041-2. Souzay, Bonneau – FAURÉ: *Mélodies* ***

The inclusion of these rare Chausson songs in this Decca reissue is particularly welcome. They were recorded in 1955 when Souzay was at his vocal peak, and Jacqueline Bonneau proved the ideal accompanist. John Culshaw produced the original sessions, and voice and piano are most naturally balanced. The Fauré songs offered as coupling, if less rare, are hardly less valuable, and this reissue deservedly won the *Gramophone* Historical Vocal Award in 1991. Full texts and translations are included.

(i) *Chanson perpétuelle, Op. 37;* **(ii)** *Poème de l'amour et de la mer, Op. 19;* **(iii) Mélodies:** *Le Charme; Le Colibri; La Dernière Feuille; Sérénade italienne; Les Papillons*
(BB) *** Warner Apex 0927 48992-2. Norman; (i) Monte Carlo Qt; (ii) Monte Carlo PO, Jordan; (i; iii) Dalberto

Although Jessye Norman's account of the glorious *Poème de l'amour et de la mer* does not wholly eclipse memories of Dame Janet Baker's version, it is still very recommendable in its own right. The orchestral texture is splendidly opulent and atmospheric, and Jessye Norman makes an impressive sound throughout. Sometimes her voice seems a bit too big for these pieces – and the closer than ideal balance does not help here – but her artistry is never for the moment in doubt. Even if the playing time (45') is comparatively short, this is a real bargain at Apex price.

3 Chansons de Shakespeare; 3 Lieder de Camille Mauclair; 2 Poèmes de Verlaine; Mélodies: L'albatross; L'âme de bois; Amour d'antan; Apaisement; L'aveu; Cantique à l'épouse; La caravanne; Chanson; Chanson perpétuelle; Le charme; La cigale; Le colibri; Dans la forêt; La dernière feuille; Hébé; Marins dévots à la vierge Marie; Les morts; Nanny; Nocturne; Nos souvenirs; Nous, nous aimerons; La nuit; Les papillons; La pluie; Printemps triste; Le rideau de ma voisine; Le reveil; Sérénade; Sérénade italienne; Serres chaudes; Le temps des lilas
*** Hyp. CDA 67321/2. Lott, Murray, Trakas, Greevy, Johnson; Chilingirian Qt

These two superb, revelatory discs contain all the regularly published songs of Chausson, plus five songs drawn from manuscript sources. Beautifully performed, they come with the same kind of scholarly notes that Johnson provides for his Schubert and Schumann series, plotting the composer's development from his student years to his untimely death in a cycle accident. What consistently comes out far more than in Chausson's instrumental music is his gift of tunefulness, fresh and memorable. Not that they are lacking in refinement in any way, and the piano accompaniments, particularly in the early songs, from the sparkling first item, *Les papillons*, are models of refinement and imagination, consistently inspiring Johnson as accompanist.

The singers, too, are all fine artists. Ann Murray is charming throughout in the great majority of the songs for female voice, with Dame Felicity Lott confined to five intense Maeterlinck settings, written in 1896, four years before Chausson's death, when he and Debussy were encouraging each other's enthusiasm for that poet. The third principal singer, the American, Chris Pedro Trakas, is a great discovery, with his heady light tenor and unfailingly sensitive response to the French words. The last songs, setting Verlaine and Shakespeare, lead finally to a delicate setting of Albert Jounet, and as an apt conclusion a ravishing song with string quartet accompaniment to words by Charles Cros, a poet also credited in France with inventing the gramophone. Vignettes of each poet as well as the commentary add to the delights of the set.

Poème de l'amour et de la mer, Op. 19
(N) *** Warner 2564 61938-2. Graham, BBC SO, Yan Pascal Tortelier – DEBUSSY: *Poèmes de Charles Baudelaire*; RAVEL: *Shéhérazade* ***

(N) (BB) **(*) Naxos 8.557274. Maurus, Nat. O de Lille Région Nord, Jean-Claude Casadesus – DUKAS: *La péri*; BERLIOZ: *Les Nuits d'été* **(*)

Susan Graham is in her element in Chausson's lovely song cycle, phrasing with a natural sensuous charm and producing an unstrained beauty of line. She is very sensitively accompanied and beautifully recorded. But the great interest of this triptych is the Debussy coupling, re-orchestrated by John Adams.

Le roi Arthus (complete)
(N) *** Telarc CD-80645 (3). Schroeder, Bullock, O'Neill, Le Roux, Okulitch, McIntyre, Apollo Voices, BBC SO, Botstein

Recorded in association with BBC Radio 3, the Telarc version of *Le roi Arthus*, Chausson's opera based on the Arthurian legend, brings out the sensuality of this piece which is much influenced by Wagner. Chausson aimed to transcend that influence, and with sumptuous sound and a passionate approach to the score Leon Botstein clearly demonstrates that this is not just a Wagnerian imitation but a work that brings out Chausson's distinctive voice. In its ripe melodic writing it is moving in a way that reminds one that Puccini too was much influenced by Wagner. The dreamy beauty of the first big love duet between Queen Guinevere (in French Genièvre) and Lancelot brings the clearest echoes of the Act II love duet from *Tristan und Isolde*, and the love-triangle, with Arthur himself the rejected husband, directly reflects the situation in Tristan.

In the absence from the catalogue of the pioneering Erato version with Armin Jordan conducting French Radio forces, this new set is particularly welcome, even if the cast, good though it is, cannot quite match the outstanding quality of the earlier one. In the title-role Andrew Schroeder sings with noble authority but cannot match Gino Quilico on Erato in vocal warmth. Susan Bullock as Genièvre sounds bright and girlish but grows edgy under pressure, while Simon O'Neill as Lancelot has clear, open tone but cannot equal Gosta Winbergh in range of expression. Even so, they are most convincing, as are François Le Roux as Merlin and Daniel Okulitch as the malicious Mordred. Fine playing and choral singing, with consistently richer ensembles and more powerful climaxes than on Erato.

CHERUBINI, Luigi (1760–1842)

Overtures: Les Abencérages, ou L'Etendard de Grenade; Anacréon, ou L'amour fugitif; Eliza, ou Le voyage aux glaciers du Mont St-Bernard; Faniska; L'hôtellerie Portugaise; Les deux journées, ou Le Porteur d'eau; Medée; Concert Overture

☞ **(B)** *** EMI double forte 5 75160-2 (2). ASMF, Marriner
  – WOLF-FERRARI: *Overtures and Intermezzi* ***

Although Marriner's performance of *Anacréon* does not have the sheer incandescent energy of Toscanini, its close is brilliantly done. All these overtures, which are brimming with attractive invention, are played with characteristic finese and warmth by the Academy of St Martin-in-the-Fields. *L'hôtellerie Portugaise* has much dexterity and charm, and the combination of drama, energy and elegance in *Les deux journées* and *Faniska* is most winning. Here, and even more in the witty touches in *Les Abencérages*, there are hints of Rossini, but Cherubini's style is that bit weightier and the very fine *Concert Overture*, with its grave opening, is both dramatic and full of grace. Incidentally, it is more substantial than the incorrect playing time given on the leaflet would suggest. An outstanding disc, very naturally recorded at Abbey Road in 1991, again reminding us why Beethoven admired Cherubini.

Anacréon Overture
(***) BBC BBCL mono 4016-2 (2) BBC SO, Toscanini –
  BEETHOVEN: *Missa solemnis; Symphony 7* **(*);
  MOZART: *Symphony 35 (Haffner)* ***

Cherubini's fine *Anacréon Overture* enjoyed considerably more exposure in the 1930s and 1940s. (At the time of writing there is no modern recording at all!) Toscanini's account comes from 1935 and finds the BBC Symphony Orchestra at its most responsive and alert. For a 1930s broadcast the sound, though not the highest of fi, is really very good indeed.

String Quartets 1–6
(M) *** CPO 999 949-2 (3). Hausmusik
*** CPO 999 463-2 (Nos. 1 & 6); 999 464-2 (Nos. 2 & 5); 999 465-2 (Nos. 3 & 4) (available separately). Hausmusik

String Quartets 1 in E flat; 2 in C
☞ *** BIS CD 1003. David Qt

String Quartets 3 in D min.; 4 in E
*** BIS CD 1004. David Qt

Cherubini's quartets are of very high quality and it is good to have outstanding new recordings of them. Listening to them makes one realize the justice of Beethoven's admiration for the composer, for Cherubini's melodic inspiration is often distinguished and instinctive, there is always a fine musical intelligence at work and polished craftsmanship is always in evidence.

The first four works bring an exhilarating response from this excellent BIS group, who are superb individual players yet perfectly integrated tonally. They are thoroughly at home in Cherubini's sound-world. In short these modern-instrument performances could hardly be bettered, and the recording, as one expects from this label, is in every way first class.

The performances by Hausmusik on period instruments are also of the very highest quality. Although textures are less ample, inner detail is wonderfully clear, there is no lack of warmth and the playing itself is highly eloquent. As it so happens, the *Fifth Quartet in F*, which they alone offer, is one of their finest performances. The opening of No. 6 is similarly perceptive and, throughout, finales are full of zest and energy. In short, except for those allergic to period instruments, this set leads the field, and the recording is strikingly vivid and present. The six quartets are also available together in a mid-priced box.

(i) Coronation Mass in A for King Charles X; March religieuse; (ii) Solemn Mass in G for the Coronation of Louis XVII; (iii) Requiem in C min.

(N) (B) *** EMI Rouge et Noir 5 85258-2 (2). (i) Philh. Ch. & O; (ii) LPO Ch. & O; (iii) Amb. S., Philh. O; Muti

The *G major Mass* was finished in 1819, but meanwhile Louis XVIII had postponed his coronation a number of times, and in the end it never took place, so Cherubini's music remained unperformed and the full score was prepared for publication only recently. As is so often the case with Cherubini, the musical inspiration is not only dignified but noble – and, on occasion, inspired. Muti seems persuaded of its distinction and performs the work with dedication and conviction.

The *Coronation Mass for Charles X* dates from 1825 and there are signs in the *Gloria* that Cherubini was influenced by both Beethoven's *Fidelio* and the *Ninth Symphony*, and in the *Incarnatus* and *Crucifixus* by the *Missa solemnis*. But Cherubini's church music has a character of its own, beautifully crafted, with moments of real memorability, such as the closing bars of the *Kyrie*. Muti presents the music with an intensity to hide any limitations, and both chorus and orchestra respond superbly. He secures the widest dynamic refinements and the digital sound is bold and full, with ceremonial trumpets braying magnificently. There is an instrumental appendix in the form of a *Marche religieuse*, a very fine piece. The *C minor Requiem* was praised extravagantly by Berlioz with the claim that 'no other production of this great master can bear any comparison with it for abundance of ideas, fullness of form and sustained sublimity of style'. Muti's fine account is discussed below, but the present Rouge et Noir set is the most economical way of approaching this repertoire.

Mass in F (Di Chimay)

*** EMI 5 57589-2. Ziesak, Lippert, Abdrazakov, Bav. R. Ch. & SO, Muti

Riccardo Muti, most persuasive interpreter of Cherubini, follows up his earlier recordings of that neglected composer's choral music with a lively account of the *Mass in F*, which in 1809 broke a creative block then afflicting the composer. In his enthusiasm Cherubini wrote what was then his most ambitious work. It is a massive 75-minute structure that in its inventiveness brings out the drama of the liturgy just as Haydn's last Masses had in the immediately preceding years. Muti's live recording is not always perfectly polished, but in thrust and concentration the performance is most compelling, with the hushed account of the *Crucifixus* bringing rapt choral singing. Characterful soloists too, with the soprano Ruth Ziesak singing radiantly.

Mass 2 in D min.

♦━ ❁ *** Häns. CD 98.325. Coburn, Kallisch, Thompson, Will, Stuttgart Gächinger Kantorei & Bach Collegium, Rilling

Cherubini began composing his *D minor Mass* in 1811, but

added a newly composed *Sanctus* in 1822. Thus it was contemporary with Beethoven's *Missa solemnis*, and it has much of that work's lyrical gravitas and depth. This outstanding Hänssler recording by the Gächinger Kantorei and Stuttgart Bach Collegium is fully worthy of this glorious work. The choral and orchestral contribution is particularly fine. Cherubini makes great demands on his soloists, both individually and in concert, and the singers here rise eloquently to the occasion. They often favour a noticeable vibrato style, yet the close matching and blending of their voices means that this is not a problem. Introduced by some lovely woodwind playing, the ensemble, which opens the *Et incarnatus est* led by the solo female voices, is radiantly beautiful; then the trumpets regally announce the *Et resurrexit* and the choral response is thrilling. Similarly the rapturous closing *Agnus Dei*, which Rilling paces admirably, leads on the genially life-assertive, and finally exultant *Donna nobis pacem*. This is one of Rilling's very finest records and the demonstration-worthy recording, made in 1992 in the Stadhalle Leonberg, could not be more satisfyingly balanced.

Requiem in C min.

(N) (BB) *** EMI Gemini 5 86239-2 (2). Ambrosian Ch., Philh. O, Muti – verdi: *Requiem* ***

The *C minor Requiem*, the best known, was called by Berlioz 'the greatest of the greatest of his [Cherubini's] works'. Muti directs a tough, incisive reading, underlining the drama. The digital recording is excellent.

CHOPIN, Frédéric (1810–49)

Complete Chopin Editions

DG Complete Chopin Edition

(B) **(*) DG (DDD/ADD) 463 047-2 (17)

To commemorate the 150th Anniversary of Chopin's death in 1999, DG assembled for the first time the complete works of Chopin - even making several new recordings to fill in the gaps. There are many outstanding Chopin recordings here notably from Argerich, Pollini and Zimerman, but almost all of these are available separately. However there are several where DG might have made a better choice, the *Waltzes* and *Mazurkas*, for instance. At a bargain price and with a lavishly illustrated booklet, this is still good value, especially for those beginning a Chopin collection. The full list of individual issues can be found in our previous editions and, subject to continued availability, will be given a detailed review in our 2006/7 Yearbook but most collectors will want to make their own choices from the various available CDs in the following pages.

Idil Biret Complete Chopin Edition

The Turkish pianist, Idil Birit, has all the credentials for recording Chopin. Among others she studied with both Cortot and Wilhelm Kempff. She has a prodigious technique and undoubtedly overall her Chopin survey for Naxos is an impressive achievement. Like Argerich, she is inclined to impetuosity, especially in the *Ballades* (Naxos 8. 550508) and more appropriately in the *Polonaises* (8.550361), while the *Nocturnes* are beautifully played (8.550356/7). The three *Sonatas*, fitted comfortably onto a single CD, are one of her finest achievements (8.550363), but if you want a single disc to show her at her most prodigious and glittering, try the collection of little-known novelties called *Rondos and Variations* (8.550367). We shall include a complete coverage of these CDs in our 2006/7 Yearbook.

Concertos and concertante music

Andante spianato et Grande polonaise, Op. 22

(***) BBC mono 4031-2. Richter, LSO, Kondrashin – LISZT: *Piano Concertos 1–2*, etc. (***)

Both in the *Andante* and the *Polonaise*, Richter is at his most magical, not just brilliant but intensely poetic too, the more moving in a live performance. The playing has great delicacy and bravura. The BBC's mono recording balances him much closer than the orchestra and at times his pedalling is audible.

(i) *Piano Concertos 1–2. Ballades 1–4; Barcarolle; Fantasia in F min.; Impromptus 1–4 (Fantaisie-impromptu); Nocturnes 1–21; Preludes 1–28; Scherzos 1–4; Waltzes 1–19.*
(B) **(*) Ph. (ADD) 468 391-2 (7). Arrau; (i) with LPO, Inbal

Arrau's survey was recorded over a decade in the 1970s. The two piano concertos came first and set the seal on his approach: immaculately aristocratic, but with personal touches of rubato which will not convince everybody. His expressive hesitations do not always grow naturally out of what has gone before. The LPO under Inbal give loyal support, but the piano is forwardly balanced to dominate the proceedings.

The *Préludes* followed in 1974, with each and every one bearing the imprint of a strong personality to which not all listeners respond. Yet these performances appear to spring from a strong inner conviction. The *Ballades*, too, are particularly impressive and, as always with the Philips recordings of this artist, there is unfailing beauty of tone. Among the *Impromptus* the *Fantaisie-impromptu*, with its nobly contoured central melody, is a highlight: the piano timbre is richly coloured and full in the bass. Some of the rubato Arrau adopts in the *Nocturnes* may again strike some listeners as a shade too personal, but his artistry is unique and he is eminently well served by the engineers.

Piano Concertos (i) *1 in E min.*; (ii) *2 in F min.*

●━ ✿ (N) *** MDG 340 1267-2 Zacharias, Lausanne CO
(M) *** RCA (ADD) **SACD** 82876 67902-2. Rubinstein, London New SO, Skrowaczewski, or Symphony of the Air Wallenstein
**(*) Sony SK 44922. Perahia, Israel PO, Mehta
*** EMI 5 56798-2. Argerich, Montreal SO, Dutoit
(BB) *** Regis RRC 1096. Tirimo, Philh. O, Glushchenko
(BB) *** Naxos 8.550123. Székely, Budapest SO, Németh
(M) **(*) EMI ADD 5 67232-2 [567261]. François, Monte-Carlo Op. O, Frémaux
** DG 459 684-2. Zimerman, Polish Festival O

An inspired new coupling of the two Chopin *Concertos* goes straight to the top of the list. Zacharias directs the Lausanne Chamber Orchestra from the keyboard, but the result is in no way small-scale. Indeed, the opening tuttis of both first movements have never been more commandingly full of life and grace, and in each case the second subject is introduced most poetically, to be delectably echoed at the piano entry. Zacharias finds new insights in both works and notably in the development section of the *F minor Concerto*. Both slow movements are magical: the recitative-like section in the *Larghetto* of No. 2 is wonderfully spontaneous-sounding. Throughout, the passagework is gleamingly full of interest

and the finales sparkle, without putting virtuosity before musical values. The sound is well up to MDG standards, a resonantly full-bodied orchestral picture, with the piano foward but recorded with absolute naturalness. A disc to treasure.

Rubinstein's performances are more than welcome back in remastered form, for there is much that is unforgettably magical in the performances. His shaping of the main theme of the *E minor Concerto* is memorable and in the *Larghetto* his control of colour and rubato are inimitable. Again in the *F minor Concerto*, although the Carngie Hall acoustic proved less than ideal, Rubinstein's contribution is an object lesson in the delicate playing of Chopin's poetic moments; his rubato is so natural that the music sounds as if it were extemporized. As with all the reissues of Rubinstein's early recordings, the piano timbre is much warmer than it sounded on the original LPs, and although the orchestral quality is more variable, the new SACD transfer makes the very most of the sound.

Perahia's effortless brilliance and refinement of touch recall artists like Hofmann and Lipatti. Mehta provides a highly sensitive accompaniment once the soloist enters but is curiously offhand and matter-of-fact (indeed almost brutal) in the orchestral ritornelli. The sound is dryish and far from ideal. The three stars are for Perahia's playing, not the sound!

In Martha Argerich's newest EMI coupling her pianism remains as mercurial and her virtuosity as incandescent as ever; indeed, she has rarely sounded as captivating or characterful. Charles Dutoit gets good playing from the Montreal orchestra. Admirers of Argerich (and, we might add, of Chopin) need not hesitate.

Martino Tirimo's readings often bring exquisite delicacy and they are totally without barnstorming, yet there is spontaneity in every bar, and both slow movements bring playing where one has an impression of musing reverie. In outer movements passage-work is scintillatingly alive, and finales have a beguiling rhythmic lift. There is strong orchestral support from Glushchenko and the Philharmonia players in the sparkling dance rhythms. Excellent (originally Conifer) recording, too.

István Székely is particularly impressive in the *E minor Concerto*, but in both works he finds atmosphere and poetry in slow movements and an engaging dance spirit for the finales, with rhythms given plenty of character. Németh accompanies sympathetically; the orchestral contribution here is quite refined. The recording is resonantly full, not absolutely clear on detail; but the piano image is bold and realistic. A splendid bargain in every sense of the word.

If François's rather grand first entry in the *E minor* is slightly mannered, there is much fine playing here, and the solo contribution in the finales of both concertos often scintillates. Frémaux's accompaniments of outer movements are strong in vitality and certainly supportive in the beautiful *Larghettos*, where again much of the solo playing is persuasive. The remastering of the late–1960s recordings gives both the forwardly placed soloist and the orchestra a vivid presence.

DG marked the 150th anniversary of the composer's death with a newly recorded pairing of the two concertos from Krystian Zimerman. Alas, any sense of momentum or naturalness is submerged by uncharacteristically disruptive rubato. Both concertos are the same – full of intrusive touches and pulled out of shape. Far better to have his earlier set with Giulini and the Los Angeles orchestra: elegant, aristocratic and sparkling. But you cannot: Zimerman has asked that it should be withdrawn as he prefers the Polish disc which he directs himself.

Piano Concerto 1 in E min., Op. 11

(M) *** DG (ADD) 449 719-2 Argerich, LSO, Abbado – LISZT: *Concerto 1* ***

(BB) **(*) Naxos 8.550292. Székely, Budapest SO, Németh – LISZT: *Concerto 1* **(*)

(i) *Piano Concerto 1. Ballade 1; Nocturnes 4 & 5, Op. 15/1–2; 7, Op. 27/1; Polonaise 6, Op. 53*

🟐➼ (M) *** EMI (ADD) 5 67548-2 [567549]. Pollini, (i) Philh. O, Kletzki

(i) *Piano Concerto 1. Berceuse; Fantaisie in F min., Op. 49; Fantaisie-impromptu*

*** DG (IMS) 457 585-2. Pires, (i) COE, Krivine

Pollini's classic recording still remains among the best available of the *E minor Concerto*. This is playing of such total spontaneity, poetic feeling and refined judgement that criticism is silenced. The digital remastering has been generally successful. The additional items come from Pollini's first EMI solo recital, and the playing is equally distinguished, the recording truthful.

Maria João Pires's concerns centre on the more inward-looking side of Chopin rather than its incandescence or brilliance, but this is a performance of substance and she is given eminently responsive support from the Chamber Orchestra of Europe and Emmanuel Krivine. The solo pieces are thoughtful, sensitive accounts and there are no quarrels with the DG recording.

With persuasive support from Abbado, Martha Argerich provides some lovely playing, especially in the slow movement. Perhaps in the passage-work she is rather too intense, but this is far preferable to the rambling style we are sometimes offered. This version is now reissued in two different formats. The first comes as one of DG's 'Originals' in a coupling with an equally individual and charismatic account of Liszt's *First Concerto*; for the bargain Classikon alternative a miscellaneous programme of encores has been added, showing well the impulsive qualities of her solo playing.

István Székely's account is also available with the *F minor Concerto* (see above), but those preferring a Liszt coupling should find this alternative equally satisfactory.

(i) *Piano Concerto 1; Etudes: in G flat, Op. 10/5; in E min., Op. 25/5*

(B) (*(*)) EMI mono 5 74802-2. Lipatti, (i) with Zurich Tonhalle O, Ackermann – GRIEG: *Piano Concerto* (***)

Lipatti's is a lovely performance but, despite the recent remastering at Abbey Road by Simon Gibson, its sonic limitations (which also apply to the pair of *Etudes*) will prove something of an obstacle to all but his most fervent admirers.

(i) *Piano Concerto 1; (ii) Romanze only. Berceuse; Chant polonaise (arr. Liszt); Etudes: in E, Op. 10/1; in G flat, Op 10/5 (2 versions); Mazurkas: in B flat min., Op. 24/4; in C sharp min., Op. 63/3 (3 versions); in G, Op. 67/1; Waltzes: in C sharp min., Op. 64/1; in E min., Op. posth.*

(***) Biddulph mono LHW 040. Rosenthal; with (i) Berlin State Op. O, Weissmann; (ii) NBC SO, Black

Listening to this painstaking transfer by Ward Marston, it is easy to understand why Moriz Rosenthal was held in such veneration. His poetic feeling and extraordinary delicacy of touch come across in the smaller pieces. In the *E minor*

Concerto his playing is of enormous elegance and refinement of tone, which can be discerned even in this primitive 1930 recording. The recordings all date from 1929–31 when this artist was in his late sixties to early seventies, save for the slow movement of the *Concerto*, which survives in a live broadcast marking the pianist's seventy-fifth birthday. Some allowances must be made for the frail sound, but the playing has unfailing beauty and finesse.

(i) *Piano Concerto 1 (piano & string quintet version). Recital: Ballade 3; Etude in C sharp min. (Revolutionary), Op. 10/12; Fantaisie in F min.; Mazurkas, Op. 17/3–4; Op. 24/2; Nocturnes: in D flat, Op. 27/2; in B, Op. 62/1; Préludes, Op. 28/7, 17 & 22; Scherzo 2 in B min.; Waltz in E flat (Grande valse brillante), Op. 18*

(B) **(*) RCA 2-CD 74321 88678-2 (2). Luisada; (i) Augmented Talich Qt – BIZET: *Chants du Rhin; Nocturne* **(*)

Chopin himself performed this arrangement of the *E minor Piano Concerto* in Paris in 1832 when a full orchestra was not available. But Jean-Marc Luisada's decision to record it seems curious. Certainly, the restricted scoring highlights the piano (especially at its initial entry in the first movement), but elsewhere there is a loss of colour, for Chopin's orchestration is often very effective. It is in the slow movement when the refined and tenderly romantic contribution of the Talich Quartet (augmented with a double bass played by Benjamin Berlioz) adds much to the interpretation, and pianistically it is a first-class performance throughout, with a sparkling finale. The solo recital further demonstrates the wide range of Luisada's Chopin sympathies. He is often boldly individual, and his playing is full of temperament and fire, yet there is no lack of poetry and the two *Nocturnes* are beautifully done. Excellent recording throughout and an unexpected coupling.

Piano Concerto 2 in F min., Op. 21

(BB) (***) Naxos mono 8.110612. Cortot, O, Barbirolli – SCHUMANN: *Concerto* (***)

(i) *Piano Concerto 2; Ballades 1–4; Barcarolle, Op. 60; Berceuse (2 versions); Chants polonais (trans. Liszt); Etudes, Op. 10/1–12 (2 versions); Op. 25/1–12 (2 versions); Nouvelles études; Impromptus: Nocturnes Op. 9/2; 15/1–2; 27/1; 55/1–2; 24 Preludes; Prelude in C sharp min., Op. 45; Piano Sonatas 2; 3; Waltzes 1–14*

(M) (***) EMI mono 7 67359-2 (6). Cortot, (i) with O, Barbirolli

Cortot, who recorded so much Chopin between the wars and for so many embodied the spirit of Chopin at that period, never committed the *E minor Concerto* to disc. The *Second*, recorded in 1935 at the Abbey Road Studios, sounds wonderfully fresh and is as individual as one would expect from this great artist. Mark Obert-Thorn gets a very good sound from the shellac originals.

Cortot's spontaneity, poetic feeling and keyboard refinement are also heard to prodigal effect on the six EMI CDs. Several alternative versions (for example, both sets of the Opp. 10 and 25 *Etudes* from 1934 and 1942 are included) offer food for thought. But in any event this is playing of a quite special quality: aristocratic yet full of fire and spontaneity. The transfers are strikingly good and bring Cortot very much before one's eyes.

(i) *Piano Concerto 2. Ballade 1; Barcarolle, Op. 60; Berceuse; Fantaisie-impromptu; Mazurkas: in B flat, Op. 7/1; in D,*

Op. 33/2; in A min., Op. 68/2; Nocturnes: in E flat, Op. 9/2; in G min., Op. 37/1; Polonaises: 3 in A (Military), Op. 40/1; 6 in A flat, Op. 53; Scherzo 2 in B flat min., Op. 31; Sonata 2 in B flat min. (Funeral March). Waltzes: in A flat, Op. 34/1; in D flat (Minute), Op. 64/1; in E min., Op. posth.

(B) *** RCA (ADD) Twofer 74321 34175-2 (2) Rubinstein, (i) Symphony of the Air, Wallenstein

Including as it does complete performances of the *F minor Piano Concerto* and an unsurpassed *Funeral March Sonata*, this RCA Twofer must be counted a top choice among all the bargain collections of Chopin's piano music. Rubinstein's playing was in a class of its own. The orchestral tuttis in the *Concerto* are dry and studio-ish, but the piano timbre and colouring are unimpaired, especially in the delicate filigree of the slow movement. Otherwise the sound is always good, and often very good.

Les Sylphides (ballet; orch. Douglas)

&—- ● (B) *** DG (ADD) 429 163-2. BPO, Karajan – DELIBES: *Coppélia*: suite; OFFENBACH: *Gaîté parisienne*: excerpts ***

Karajan conjures consistently beautiful playing from the Berlin Philharmonic Orchestra, and he evokes a delicacy of texture which delights the ear throughout. The sound is full and atmospheric, and this is one of Karajan's very finest recordings. At bargain price it is unbeatable, coupled on CD not only with *Coppélia* (although the suite is not complete) but also with Offenbach's *Gaîté parisienne*.

CHAMBER MUSIC

Cello Sonata in G min., Op. 65; Grand duo concertante in E on Themes from Meyerbeer's 'Robert le Diable'; Nocturne in C sharp min., Op. posth. (arr. Piatigorsky); *Etudes: in E min., Op. 25/7; D min., Op. 10/6* (arr. Glazunov; ed. Feuermann); *Waltz in A min., Op. 34/3* (arr. Ginsburg)

(BB) *** Naxos 8.553159. Kliegel, Glemser

Fresh and ardent performances of the *Sonata* and the remaining two pieces that comprise Chopin's complete output for cello and piano. The Naxos collection also throws in some cello arrangements for good measure. These gifted and accomplished young artists are very well recorded indeed and, at the price, this is a bargain.

Cello Sonata in G min., Op. 65

(B) *** EMI 5 74333-2 (2). Tortelier, Ciccolini – FAURE; MENDELSSOHN; RACHMANINOV: *Cello Sonatas* ***

(M) *** Somm SOMMCD 026. Walton, Owen – RACHMANINOV: *Cello Sonata* ***

(N) (B) **(*) EMI Gemini (ADD) 5 82633 (2). Du Pré, Barenboim – BRAHMS: *Sonatas 1 & 2* *(*); FRANCK: *Sonata* ***

**(*) BIS CD 1076. Thedéen, Pöntinen – SCHUMANN: *Adagio & Allegro, etc.* **(*)

Tortelier's recordings of the Chopin and Rachmaninov *Sonatas*, which were made in the 1960s in the Salle Wagram, come up sounding fresh. They occupied a commanding position in the catalogue during the early 1970s and, rightly so! The same goes for the Fauré, which Tortelier recorded with Eric Heidsieck as a fine partner. Although he is accompanied less well in the two Mendelssohn *Sonatas* (recorded in 1978), this reissue is still highly competitive at the price.

A fine new coupling of the Chopin and Rachmaninov *Sonatas* from an excellent new duo on Somm, both individually prize-winners, but who play very sympathetically together, their spontaneous style both passionate and refined. The slow movement of the Chopin is presented with winning simplicity. The recording balance is very good, the sound natural, although at higher dynamic levels one would have liked rather more separation.

Torleif Thedéen and Roland Pöntinen give an eloquent and convincing account of the *Cello Sonata*, with a particularly beautiful slow movement, even if they are not helped by a reverberant acoustic, though the overall sound is not unpleasing. Most readers will probably want to stick with Tortelier, but this partnership is well worth considering.

The easy lyrical romanticism of the Chopin *Sonata* is beautifully caught by Jacqueline du Pré and Daniel Barenboim. There is an autumnal quality in the writing which they present most persuasively. Though the cellist phrases with her usual spontaneous-sounding imagination, this was one of her more reticent records, perhaps aptly so. Finely balanced recording.

Piano Trio in G min., Op. 8

(BB) *** Warner Apex 0927 40822-2. Trio Fontenay – SMETANA: *Piano Trio* **

The Trio Fontenay give a vividly characterized and well-projected account of the *Piano Trio*, written when Chopin was eighteen and not exactly one of his greatest works. It is well worth hearing all the same when the cost of the disc is so reasonable. Good, clear recording.

Waltzes, arranged for cello & piano, Vol. I: Etude in E min., Op. 25/7; Grande valse brillante in D, Op. 18; Mazurkas: in G min., Op. 67/2; in C, Op. 67/3; in A min., Op. 67/4 & Op. 68/2; in B flat (op. posth.); Nocturne in C sharp min. (op. posth.); Polonaise brillante in C, Op. 3; Preludes 2 in A min., Op. 28; 3 in G; 4 in E min., Op. 28; 6 in B min., Op. 28; 7 in A, Op. 28; Scherzo (from Cello & Piano Sonata, Op. 65); Valse brillante in A, Op. 34/1 & A min., Op. 34/2; Valse in A, Op. 42

**(*) Channel Classics CCS 16298. Wispelwey, Lazic

This is an oddity. Pieter Wispelwey has followed up the example of the nineteenth-century Russian cellist and composer, Carl Davidov, in transcribing Chopin piano pieces for cello and piano. The opening one, the popular *D major Waltz*, Opus 18, arranged by Davidov, is unpromising, with the cello not bright enough to sustain the melody well. Wispelwey's own transcriptions in partnership with his pianist, Dejan Lazic, of *Mazurkas*, *Preludes* and other Chopin pieces, are much more effective, and they find both players in sparkling form, though the closeness of the sound is unhelpful. Other transcriptions by Glazunov and Piatigorsky are also included, as well as the *Scherzo* from Chopin's *Cello Sonata* and an early *Polonaise in C*, which Chopin himself wrote for cello and piano. Recommended above all for cellists.

PIANO MUSIC

Vladimir Ashkenazy Chopin Edition

Albumblatt in E; Allegro de concert in A, Op. 46; Barcarolle; Berceuse; Boléro in A min., Op. 19; 2 Bourrées; Cantabile in B flat; Fugue in A min.; Galop marquis; Hexameron: Variation in E min.; Largo in E flat; 3 Nouvelles études; Rondo in E flat, Op. 16; Souvenir de Paganini; Tarantelle in

A flat, Op. 43; Variations brillantes in B flat, Op. 12; Wiosna (Spring) from Op. 74/2. Ballades 1–4; Scherzi 1–4. 12 Etudes, Op. 10; 12 Etudes, Op. 25. Impromptus 1–3; 4 (Fantaisie-impromptu). 24 Preludes, Op. 28; Preludes: in C sharp min., Op. 45; in A flat. Mazurkas 1–29; 30–68 (including 2 versions of Op. 68/4). Nocturnes 1–12; 13–21. Polonaises 1–6; 7, Polonaise-fantaisie; 8–16. Sonatas 1–3; Contredanse in G flat; 3 Ecossaises; Marche funèbre in C min., Op. 72/2; Rondos: in C min., Op. 1; à la Mazur in F, Op. 5; in C, Op. 73; Variations on a German National Air; Variations in D (for piano duet – with Vovka Ashkenazy). Sonatas; Fantaisie in F min. Waltzes 1–19
(B) *** Decca (ADD/DDD) 443 738-2 (13)

Ashkenazy made his Chopin recordings for Decca over a decade from 1974 to 1984, using seven different locations, yet the recorded sound is remarkably consistent, always natural in colour and balance and with a good presence, whether from an analogue or a digital source. Consistently persuasive, these readings combine poetry with flair and (as in the Ballades) often bring a highly communicated warmth. The bravura brings genuine panache, whether in the large-scale, virtuoso pieces like the Scherzi or in the chimerical approach to a miniature like the Souvenir de Paganini. At bargain price this set makes an unbeatable investment.

(i) Andante spianato & Grande Polonaise brillante; (ii) Polonaises 1–7; (iii) 3 Polonaises, Op. 71; 6 Polonaises, Op. posth.; Album Leaf in E; 2 Bourrées; Cantabile in B flat; Fugue in A min.; Galop marquis in A flat; Largo in E flat
(N) (M) *** DG (DDD/ADD) 2-CD 477 5430 (2). (i) Argerich; (ii) Pollini; (iii) Ugorski

This is a straight reissue of Volume 5 from DG's Chopin Edition. Pollini offers magisterial playing, in some ways more commanding than Rubinstein (and better recorded) though not more memorable. Argerich's Andante spianato (1974) is everything it should be: wonderfully relaxed to start with and extrovertly sparkling in the Grande polonaise. Ugorski fills in the gaps with some of Chopin's early works: interesting to hear, sometimes entertaining, but containing only glimpses of the greatness that was to emerge. Excellent value.

Andante spianato & Grande Polonaise brillante, Op. 22; Polonaises 4–6; Polonaise-Fantaisie, Op. 61
(N) (M) ** Van. SACD AM-SC 1589. Brendel

Although not possessing a natural affinity for the music of Chopin – the least effective piece here is the Andante spianato – nothing Brendel does in unstimulating, and these Schumanesque performances certainly have their interest. This is strong, intelligent playing, the rubato sensitive and the character of each piece well realized. They were very well recorded in 1968, and the natural piano-timbre with a full, resonant bass has been expertly transferred to SACD.

Ballades 1–4; Allegro de concert, Op. 45; Introduction & Variations on 'Je vends des scapulaires', Op. 12
(M) *** CRD (ADD) CRD 3360. Milne

Ballades 1–4; Barcarolle; Berceuse; Fantaisie in F min.; Scherzo 3 in C sharp min., Op. 39
(N) **(*) Tavros 8253466528. Primakov (available from www.tavrosrecords.com)

Ballades 1–4; Barcarolle; Berceuse; Scherzo 4
**(*) RCA 09026 63259. Kissin

Ballades 1–4; Barcarolle; Fantaisie in F min.
*** DG (IMS) 423 090-2. Zimerman

Ballades 1–4; Etudes: in E; C sharp min., Op. 10/3-4; Mazurkas: in F min., Op. 7/4; in A min., Op. 17/4; in D, Op. 33/2; Nocturne in F, Op. 15/1; Waltzes: in E flat (Grande valse brillante), Op. 18; in A flat, Op. 42
🔊 ⬤ *** Sony SK 64399. Perahia

Ballades 1–4; Fantasia in F min.; Prelude Op. 45
**(*) DG 459 683-2. Pollini

Ballades 1–4; Nocturnes 1–21 (complete)
(B) *** Double Decca (ADD) 452 579-2 (2). Ashkenazy

Ballades 1–4; Nocturnes 1–20; Scherzi 1–4; Waltzes 1–17
(B) **(*) DG Trio (ADD) 469 350-2 (3). Vásáry

Ballades 1–4; Scherzi 1–4
(N) (M) *** RCA SACD (ADD) 82876 61396-2. Rubinstein
(N) *** Hyp. CDA 67456. Hough

Ballades 1–4; Scherzi 1–4; Prelude, Op. 45
(M) *** Decca (ADD) 466 499-2. Ashkenazy

Ballades 1–4; Sonata 3 in B min., Op. 58
(N) (BB) ** Hyp. Helios CDH 55182. Demidenko

One has to go back to Hofmann, recorded in 1937, to find a more searching or poetic account of the G minor Ballade than Murray Perahia's. His Waltzes prompt one's thoughts to turn to the classic post-war Lipatti set, but comparison does not find Perahia less poetic. Moreover, the Sony engineers do him justice. In every respect a masterly recital which readers should not miss.

Krystian Zimerman's impressive set of the Ballades and the other two works on this disc are also touched by distinction throughout and have spontaneity as well as tremendous concentration to commend them, and the modern digital recording is of fine DG quality.

However, Rubinstein's readings are unique and the digital remastering has been highly successful. The performances of the Ballades are a miracle of creative imagination, with Rubinstein at his most inspired. The Scherzi, which gain most of all from the improved sound (they were originally very dry), are both powerful and charismatic, and the recording is further enhanced on SACD.

Among present-day pianists, Stephen Hough has not only the keyboard virtuosity but also the vision and poetic insight this music calls for. His playing serves as a reminder of just what an original master Chopin was and how vital was his genius. One of the best modern versions of either sets of pieces.

Ashkenazy's readings of the Ballades are thoughtful and essentially unflashy; the rubato arises naturally from his personal approach to the music. The intimacy of the recording allows him to share this with the listener. The recording is admirably natural and satisfying. The Nocturnes were recorded over a decade, from 1975 to 1984. The playing is splendidly imaginative and atmospheric. As always, Ashkenazy is completely attuned to Chopin's unique sound-world, and the CD transfers are impeccable.

Those wanting the alternative coupling with the Scherzi will find the reissue in Decca's 'Legends' series equally attractive. In the Scherzi the playing is chimerically dazzling, and the isolated Op. 45 C sharp minor Prelude, a pianistic tone-poem in its own right, makes an ideal interlude before the B minor Scherzo bursts in on the listener. Very good recording, particularly impressive in the *Scherzi*, which have a fine depth of sonority.

Hamish Milne gives thoughtful and individual performances of the *Ballades*. They may initially sound understated, but in their freshness and concentration they prove poetic and compelling. Similarly he plays the two rarities with total conviction, suggesting that the *Allegro de concert* at least (originally a sketch for a third piano concerto) is most unjustly neglected. The recorded sound is first rate.

Kissin's *Four Ballades* were recorded in the Sudwestfunk Studios in Freiburg and, although the sound is natural enough, climaxes tend to be muddy in the reverberant acoustic. The *G minor Ballade* is curiously wayward and wanting in momentum. Of course, there are many beautiful things – particularly the *Barcarolle* – but at other times Kissin is intrusive and not content to leave Chopin to speak for himself.

Vassily Primakov was born in Russia but made his New York début in 2004, playing Rachmaninov's formidable *Third Concerto* to considerable acclaim; and this is a remarkable first CD recital. He is an artist of immense talent and remarkable technical accomplishment. But, like many Slavonic pianists, his very free and often mannered style brings a personalized degree of rubato that, even if it sounds spontaneous, is stretching the limits of interpretative licence too far – as in the *Fantaisie*, which comes first in his programme. He is undoubtedly a natural Chopin pianist and, for all their wilfulness, these beautifully played performances have magnetic poetic feeling. The *Berceuse* is exquisite, and the four *Ballades* have a flowing romantic ardour, balanced with moments of great delicacy, that is very appealing. But the *C sharp minor Scherzo* needs more structural cohesion, and he would do well to study Sviatoslav Richter's recording of this piece to learn how poetic freedom and a planned overall view can hold the piece together. The other remarkable feature of this CD is the vivid presence of the recording, which in a curious way is more real than real. One almost seems to have one's head inside the keyboard (!), with the bass resonating richly. It is a curious effect but, although the piano timbre itself is full and true, the overall impression is not quite natural. But hi-fi enthusiasts will surely be using this as a larger-than-life demonstration disc.

Pollini's CD is so modestly filled that, however impressive the playing, it strikes us as poor value. Only 48 minutes of music at full price is a lot to ask – even if it is Pollini. The performances are commanding, masterly and well recorded.

Vásáry's *Ballades* are imaginatively played here and the readings are individual in their combination of poetry and bravura, with the *G minor* outstanding in its romantic sweep. The *Nocturnes*, too, demonstrate a flexibility in delicately moulding a Chopin phrase to find the kernel of poetry, even if the relaxation in the melodic line sometimes seems just a shade calculated. But it is the *Scherzi* that show the pianist at his best, played boldly and brilliantly and with much resilience. The *Waltzes* offer clean, stylish phrasing and crisp articulation, but sometimes lack charm, perhaps partly because here the piano timbre is drier. The recordings were made in the mid-1960s and are of good if slightly variable quality.

Nikolai Demidenko plays with plenty of bravura, but he is too wilful in the *Ballades* to be totally convincing. He opens each poetically, if a little self-consciously, and then he storms away passionately and not entirely convincingly. The *Sonata* is much more successful, with some very dextrous virtuosity in the Scherzo and finale, while the Largo is thoughtfully expressive. The recording is vivid but a little hard in *fortissimos*.

Barcarolle; Berceuse; Fantaisie in F min.; Impromptus 1–3
*** Sony MK 39708. Perahia

Perahia is a Chopin interpreter of the highest order. There is an impressive range of colour and an imposing sense of order. This is highly poetic playing and an indispensable acquisition for any Chopin collection. The CBS recording does him justice.

Barcarolle; Berceuse; Scherzi 1–4
**(*) DG (IMS) 431 623-2. Pollini

Berceuse; Fantaisie in F min.; Scherzi 1–4
*** Chan. 9018. Shelley

Howard Shelley offers much the same programme as Maurizio Pollini on DG. He has the advantage of a more sympathetic recording. But there is a greater freshness and tenderness about his approach and, though he is obviously totally inside this music, he manages to convey the feeling that he is discovering it for the first time.

There is no want of intellectual power or command of keyboard colour in Maurizio Pollini's accounts of the Chopin *Scherzi*. This is eminently magisterial playing, with powerfully etched contours and hard surfaces that inspires more admiration than pleasure.

Berceuse; 12 Etudes, Op. 25; Sonata 2
(M) *** DG (IMS) (ADD/DDD) 471 357-2. Pollini

A programme of reissues, specifically designed for the 'Pollini Edition'. Pollini plays the *Berceuse* coolly and elegantly, and with beautiful precision. The *Sonata* is very commanding: the slow movement is particularly fine, and the *Etudes* are masterly. But who would want Op. 25 without Op. 10?

Etudes, Op. 10/1–12; Op. 25/1–12; 3 Nouvelles études
✿ *** Erato 8573-80228-2 (2). Lugansky
(BB) *** Warner Apex 8573 89083-2. Berezovsky
*** Chan. 8482. Lortie

Etudes, Op. 10/1–12; Op. 25/1–12; Impromptus 1–3; Fantaisie-impromptu
☞ ✿ (M) *** Sony 518807-2. Perahia
*** DG (ADD) 413 794-2. Pollini
(*) BIS **SACD 1390. Kempf

Etudes, Op. 10/1–12; Op. 25/1–12; Ballades 1 & 3
(B) *** EMI Encore 5 86417-2. Gavrilov

Etudes, Op. 10/1–12; Op. 25/1–12; Fantaisie in F min., Op. 49; Sonatas 1–3
(N) (BB) *** Double Decca (ADD) 466 250-2 (2). Ashkenazy

Murray Perahia's expressive range, along with his variety of keyboard colour and musical imagination, are of exceptional quality. His virtuosity is totally self-effacing, so that the listener's engagement with Chopin's world is complete. There is not the slightest trace of self-awareness, only a total dedication to the musical vision on the page. The value of the set is further enhanced by the outstanding quality of the recorded sound. For the reissue the *Impromptus* have been added as a bonus.

Nikolai Lugansky produces a beautiful sound at every dynamic and is unconcerned with showmanship or high-voltage display. He is a real artist with consummate delicacy of fingerwork and fluidity of phrasing. We much admired his Vanguard recording of the Rachmaninov *Fourth Concerto*, and this set of the Chopin *Etudes* is every bit as fine. It is a musician's Chopin and for the serious music lover rather than the piano fancier. A most distinguished and valuable recording.

Ashkenazy recorded his Chopin survey as far as possible in chronological order. The sets of *Etudes* from 1975 offer playing of total mastery and can be recommended alongside Pollini and, more recently, Louis Lortie on Chandos (offering the finest recorded sound of all). The *C minor Sonata* (No. 1) is an early work (1827) and not deeply characteristic. Ashkenazy's account (1976) enjoys classic status alongside the more recent version of Andsnes. His 1980 performance of the *Funeral March Sonata* (No. 2) is no less dazzling than his earlier live recording of 1972 and in some respects surpasses it. It has wonderful panache. The *B minor Sonata*, recorded a year later, is also memorable and involving. An authoritative account of the *F minor Fantasy* provides an excellent makeweight in very realistic sound.

Marvellous playing, too, from the 23-year-old Boris Berezovsky in 1991. He had been placed fourth at Leeds in 1987 and first at Moscow in 1990, and this was his first major recording for Teldec. Just try the dazzling Op. 10/2 or the gentle poetry of the famous *E major Etude* which follows, while the three final *Studies* of Op. 25 show his wide range of dynamic, natural sensitivity, and compelling power. Then the closing *Nouvelles études* are coaxed disarmingly. In short this is a thrilling disc, and would be highly recommendable even if it cost far more. The recording brings a touch of hardness at fortissimo level, but is certainly truthful in all respects and readily reflects Berezovsky's warm colouring of the lyrical writing.

Louis Lortie's set of the 24 *Etudes* can also hold its own with the best. His playing has a strong poetic feeling and an effortless virtuosity. He is beautifully recorded at The Maltings, Snape (the acoustics of which occasionally cloud the texture).

Pollini's record also comes from 1975 and sounds splendidly fresh in its digitally remastered form. These are vividly characterized accounts, masterly and with the sound eminently present, although not as full in sonority as the more recent versions.

With the two sets of Chopin *Etudes* Freddy Kempf comes up against the stiffest competition and in many of them holds his own with the very finest. Overall, however, this is not a set to prefer to those of Perahia, Berezovsky and Pollini. Kempf's playing does not lack fire or poetic sensibility, though not all his interpretative points seem to arise naturally from his music-making but rather seem artificially transplanted (as in Op. 10, No. 11). Yet this survey should be heard, for Kempf has undoubted flair and brilliance to commend him. However, his instrument sounds a shade too bright and glassy.

Andrei Gavrilov's performances of the *Etudes* bring an exuberant virtuosity that is impossible to resist. Even if some of the tempi are breathtakingly fast, the sustained legato and his poetic feeling are indisputable. The impulsive bravura is often engulfing, so that one feels the need to take a breath on the soloist's behalf after the furious account of the *Revolutionary Study*; but this is prodigious playing, given a bold, forward recording to match. The *Ballades* are also impulsive but full of romantic feeling too.

(i) *Etudes, Opp. 10 & 25* ; (ii) *Préludes, Op. 28* ; (iii) *Sonata 2 in B flat min., Op. 35*
(M) **(*) BBC Opus Arte **DVD** OA 08893D. (i) Perl; (ii) Kempf; (iii) Hewitt

It is good to have some outstanding new Chopin performances on DVD. The *Études* and *Preludes* originally opened broadcasting each night on BBC Four during 2004 and always left one wanting more. Alfredo Perl is recorded in Hopetoun House, Edinburgh, and Freddy Kempf at the Château de Neuville, Gambais, both providing a handsome backcloth for what on the whole are enjoyable performances. Unlike her companions here, who both use a Steinway, Angela Hewitt, recorded at the Wimbledon Theatre, plays a Fazioli, about which the accompanying leaflet is silent and there is no mention of this maker in *Grove*. In fact, the DVD is pretty well silent about everything: no notes, merely a bald statement of the number and key of the pieces, and their timings. A few words about the artists would have made sense. Played in sequence, the pauses between the *Préludes* and the *Études* are far too long – particularly in the *Préludes*. Perl emotes somewhat, but his playing is first rate, and the camerawork is sensitive and varied. Kempf is even better served by the camera and is more photogenic; he is splendidly alive in Op. 25/4 but a trifle self-conscious in Op. 25/1 and effortful in Op. 10/2. These *Studies* are by no means as special as some of his BIS recordings have been, but, that said, he is always an interesting player. Angela Hewitt is as wonderful a Chopin interpreter as she is a Bach player and she gives a vividly characterized performance of the *Sonata*. Some will find the camerawork in the Wimbledon Theatre obtrusive; one minute she is observed from the gallery, the next we are at her feet; and then the camera will roam restlessly. However, it cannot detract from her fine playing. At its modest price (less than a CD) however, this is highly recommendable and will give pleasure.

Etudes, Op. 10/4, 10 & 11; Op. 25/5, 11 & 12; Nocturnes in E, Op. 62/2 & E min., Op. 72/1
(N) (M) *(*) Praga (ADD) PR 54056. Richter – SCRIABIN: *Piano Sonatas 2 & 5* ***

Richter's *Études* were recorded by Czech Radio in 1988, but the microphone is uncomfortably close and the result unpleasing. But the two *Nocturnes* are earlier, made in 1972, and are much better; they come with some pretty dazzling and unmissable Scriabin.

Etudes, Op. 25/1–12; 24 Preludes, Op.25; Sonata 2 in B flat min., Op. 35 (Funeral March)
*** Opus 111 OP 30-289 (2). Sokolov

These performances are extracted from a ten-volume set produced for the Chopin celebrations in 1999 (and discussed above). Grigory Sokolov's electrifying playing of the *Etudes*, Op. 25, and of the *Second Piano Sonata* is something of a must: he is a virtuoso whose technique is matched by real insight. When Olejniczak Sokolov 'sits down in front of an 1831 Pleyel piano', the sleeve tells us, 'Chopin's strength, tenderness, and virtuosity re-emerge as never before.'

Fantasy in F min., Op. 49; Piano Sonata 3, Op. 38
(N) (M) ***EMI (ADD) 5 62884-2 [5 62885-2]. Arrau (with MENDELSSOHN: *Andante and Rondo capriccioso*; WEBER: *Konzertstücke* ***)

Arrau was on his finest form in 1960 when he recorded the *B minor Sonata* and the forthright reading of the *Fantasy in F minor*. In the Sonata he evokes a dreamy quality in the quieter music – the *Largo* is especially beautiful – yet he can find plenty of vigour for stronger writing. This is a very fine performance indeed and he is very seductive in the delightful fairy world of Mendelssohn's *Andante and Rondo capriccioso*, an excellent mono recording from 1951 which sounds almost as real as the beautifully recorded Chopin items. This is fully worthy of inclusion among EMI's 'Great Recordings of the Century'.

Mazurkas 1–59, Op. 6/1–4; Op. 7/1–5; Op. 17/1–4; Op. 24/1–4; Op. 30/1–4; Op. 33/1–4; Op. 41/1–4; Op. 50/1–3; Op. 56/1–3; Op. 59/1–3; Op. 63/1–3; Op. 67/1–4; Op. 68/1–4 & Op. 68/4 (revised version); 60–68, Op. posth.
(B) *** Double Decca DDD/ADD 448 086-2 (2). Ashkenazy
(BB) **(*) EMI Gemini (ADD) 5 86767-2 (2). Smith

Mazurkas 1–51
(M) *** RCA (ADD) 09026 63050-2 (2). Rubinstein

As can be seen, Ashkenazy's survey of Chopin's *Mazurkas* is the most comprehensive available. They are finely articulated, aristocratic accounts and he includes all the posthumously published *Mazurkas*. The Decca recordings (often digital) are more modern and more natural than that afforded to Rubinstein.

Rubinstein could never play in a dull way to save his life, and in his hands these 51 pieces are endlessly fascinating, though on occasion in such unpretentious music one would welcome a completely straight approach. As with the *Ballades* and *Scherzi*, the digital remastering has brought a much more pleasing piano-timbre.

That Ronald Smith's technique is of a high order is evidenced by his numerous Alkan recordings. If there are times, as one listens to his finely drawn account of the Chopin *Mazurkas*, when one would welcome greater poetic intensity or characterization, these moments are few by comparison with the pleasure this comprehensive and well-recorded set gives, particularly at so reasonable a cost.

Nocturnes 1–19
(see also under *Ballades*)
☛ (M) *** RCA (ADD) 09026 63049-2(2) Rubinstein

Nocturnes 1–21
*** DG 447 096-2 (2). Pires
(BB) *** Arte Nova 74321 82185-2 (2). Castro
(B) *** DG 453 022-2 (2). Barenboim
**(*) Hyp. CDA 66341/2. Rév

Nocturnes 1–21; Barcarolle; Fantaisie-impromptu
(BB) **(*) Regis RRC 2034 (2). Stott

Nocturnes 1–21; Barcarolle; Fantaisie in F min.
(M) *** Ph. (ADD) 464 694-2 (2). Arrau

Nocturnes 1–21; Impromptus 1–3, 4 (Fantaisie-impromptu)
(N) *** Hyp. CDA 67371/2. Hewitt
(B) **(*) Ph. (ADD) Duo 456 336-2. Arrau

Nocturnes 1–21; Mazurkas 13 in A min., Op. 17/4; 32 in C sharp min., Op. 50/3; 35 in C min., Op. 56/3; Waltzes 3 in A min.; 8 in A flat, Op. 64/3; 9 in A flat; 10 in B min., Op. 69/1–2; 13 in D flat, Op. 70/3
(B) **(*) EMI double forte (ADD) 5 73830-2 (2). Weissenberg

Rubinstein in Chopin is a magician in matters of colour; his unerring sense of nuance and the seeming inevitability of his rubato demonstrate a very special musical imagination in this repertoire. The recordings were the best he received in his Chopin series for RCA, and this mid-priced reissue is most handsomely repackaged.

Angela Hewitt is so established in the public consciousness as an eminent Bach interpreter that the idea of her playing anything else seems as unlikely as it was with Rosalyn Tureck. Hewitt gave us some impressively idiomatic Ravel last year, and this Chopin is no less authentic in feeling and magisterial in accomplishment. A very satisfying collection and beautifully recorded too.

However, Pires gives performances of great character, her playing often bold as well as meltingly romantic and brings the right poetic feel to this music. Hers is the art that conceals art, and that serves the composer to perfection. She uses the widest dynamic range and is recorded with a brilliant presence as well as a basically warm sonority.

Ricardo Castro offers a series of performances to compete with almost any in the catalogue. The degree of concentration and thoughtful simplicity of approach is consistent throughout both discs, his nuancing and rubato managed with convincing spontaneity. The recording, made in two quite different venues, is of high quality, clear and natural.

Barenboim recorded the *Nocturnes* in 1981 and he was very beautifully recorded. Phrasing is beautifully moulded, seemingly spontaneous, thoughtful and poetic, and becoming really impetuous only in the music's more passionate moments.

Arrau's approach creates tonal warmth coupled with inner tensions of the kind one expects in Beethoven and this is a very compelling cycle, full of poetry, the rubato showing an individual but very communicable sensibility. Although Arrau's Chopin is seldom mercurial, it is never inflexible, and it has its own special insights. The *Fantaisie-impromptu* with its finely contoured central melody is a highlight. As always, the Philips piano recording is of the highest standard. Arrau's set also comes as one of Philips's '50 Great Recordings', coupled with the *Barcarolle* and *Fantaisie in F minor*, which are among his finest Chopin recordings.

As is immediately apparent in the *Fantaisie-impromptu* which acts as an introduction to her survey, Kathryn Stott's Chopin is very romantic, seldom understated and uses the widest dynamic range. Yet at times she touches the listener by her very calmness. Rubato is convincingly managed and overall her playing has a strong profile. She is most realistically recorded.

Lívia Rév is an artist of refined musicianship and impeccable taste, selfless and unconcerned with display or self-projection. Indeed, there are times when she comes too close to understatement. But these are still lovely performances and the recording has great warmth.

Alexis Weissenberg is a thoughtful, serious artist and a natural Chopin player with highly poetic feeling for rubato. But at times he gets impulsively carried away, and occasionally some of the elusive nocturnal quality is lost. The *Mazurkas* too are very volatile, but here the strong rhythmic pointing is more appropriate, and the *Waltzes* sparkle more delicately. Overall one would not want to make too much of Weissenberg's passionate outbursts, for much of his playing is memorably gentle and affecting, helped by a natural piano-sound, which has fine colour and sonority.

Nocturnes 1–21; 24 Preludes, Op. 28; Preludes 25–26
(N) (BB) **(*) EMI Gemini (ADD) 5 86507-2 (2). Ohlsson

While still barely out of his teens, Garrick Ohlsson won the 1970 Chopin Contest, and subsequently, to make his début on disc, recorded the *Polonaises*, then the *Preludes* (in 1974), and between 1977 and 1979 the *Nocturnes*, all at Abbey Road. He has a positive style and technique very much of the modern

American school, but with it he is thoughtful and often engagingly poetic. He is always at the service of the composer and is seldom wilful. Just at times his touch can be heavy (sample the *G sharp minor Prelude*, Op. 28/12), then equally he can display the lightest touch as in the following *F sharp major* piece. The penultimate *Prelude in C sharp minor*, Op. 45, is particularly beautiful; then he throws off the brief, posthumous *A flat* work to make a neat conclusion.

He is at his very best in the *Nocturnes*, played with pleasing flexibility and control of colour, the rubato spontaneous and nicely judged (sample Op. 15/2). Just occasionally he is carried away, as in the central section of Op. 9/3. He is well recorded, with the sound in the *Nocturnes* often very good indeed. This set is to be welcomed back to the catalogue after so long an absence, and is well worth its modest cost.

Nocturnes 1–19; Scherzi 1–4
(BB) (**(*)) Naxos mono 8.110659/60. Rubinstein

The Naxos transfers are of Rubinstein's London recordings made at Abbey Road in 1932 (the *Scherzi*) and 1937 (the *Nocturnes*). They are transferred from 78-r.p.m. originals (in excellent condition) by Stuart Rosenthal, with some background noise still present at times. One also feels that in the *Nocturnes* a little more space could have been allowed between each piece. But although the sound is less impressive, not as wide-ranging as EMI's own transfers, this is fair value at the Naxos price.

Nocturnes in E flat, Op. 9/2; F, F sharp & G min., Op. 15/1–3; C sharp min., Op. 27/1; B, Op. 32/1; G, G min., Op. 37/1–2; C min., F sharp min., Op. 48/1–2; F min., Op. 55; E, Op. 62/2; E min., Op. 72/1 (posth.)
(M) *** DG Entrée 471 743-2. Barenboim

This well-chosen collection of thirteen *Nocturnes* drawn from Barenboim's 1980 complete survey is eminently recommendable. But Ricardo Castro offers all nineteen on Arte Nova – see above – for the same cost, and his admirably recorded performances are every bit as enticing as these.

Polonaises 1–16, Op. 26/1–2; Op. 40/1–2; Op. 44; Op. 53; Polonaise-fantaisie, Op. 61; Op. 71/1–3; Op. posth./1–6. Albumblatt; Allegro de concert, Op. 46; Barcarolle; Berceuse; 2 Bourrées; 3 Nouvelles études; Fugue in A min.; Galop marquis; Tarantelle in A flat; Wiosna (arr. from Op. 74/2)
(B) *** Double Decca ADD/DDD 452 167-2 (2). Ashkenazy

Polonaises 1–7; Andante spianato et Grande polonaise brillante
●— (M) *** RCA (ADD) 09026 63048-2. Rubinstein
(N) *** SACD 471 648-2; (M) CD 457 711-2. Pollini

Ashkenazy's performances of the *Polonaises* are of the highest calibre and the recording is of Decca's best. The second CD contains some items that are quite short (the piano transcription of Chopin's song *Wiosna* lasts for barely a minute, but it is very fetching). But there are substantial works too: the *Barcarolle* and *Berceuse*, the latter meltingly done, and the *Allegro de concert* and *Nouvelles études* also show Ashkenazy at his finest. At Double Decca price this pair of CDs is self-recommending.

Master pianist that he was, Rubinstein seems actually to be rethinking and re-creating each piece, even the hackneyed *Military* and *A flat* works, at the very moment of performance in this recording, made in Carnegie Hall. His easy majesty and natural sense of spontaneous phrasing give this

collection a special place in the catalogue, and the *Andante spianato and Grande polonaise* obviously inspire him.

Pollini's set offers playing of outstanding mastery as well as subtle poetry, and the DG engineers have made a satisfactory job of the new transfer, although the hardness on top remains something to which the ear must adjust. Nevertheless this is magisterial playing, in some ways more commanding than Rubinstein (and rather more tangibly recorded), though not more memorable.

24 Preludes, Op. 28; Preludes 25–26; Scherzi 1–4; Waltzes 1–19
(B) *** Double Decca (ADD) 460 991-2 (2). Ashkenazy

24 Preludes, Op. 28; Prelude in C sharp min., Op. 45. Andante spianato et Grande polonaise, Op. 22; Polonaise-fantaisie in A flat, Op. 61
●— *** Chan. 9597. Lortie

24 Preludes, Op. 28; Etudes, Op. 10/4–6; Op. 25/1–2; 6 & 12
(BB) **(*) Warner Apex 2564 60158-2. Lympany

24 Preludes, Op. 28; Scherzi 1–4
*** Naim NAIMCD 028. Gimse

24 Preludes, Op. 28; Sonata 2; Polonaise in A flat, Op. 53
** RCA 09026 63535-2. Kissin

Louis Lortie's expertly recorded account of the *Preludes* is among the best we have had in recent years. He has poetic feeling, character and finesse in equal measure. Not all his interpretative decisions will convince everyone, but on the whole this is enjoyable and distinguished Chopin playing.

Ashkenazy's 1979 set of the *Preludes* combines drama and power with finesse and much poetic delicacy when called for. The *Waltzes* were recorded over the best part of a decade. There is an impressive feeling for line throughout, an ability to make each waltz seem spontaneous and yet as carefully wrought as a tone-poem. The *Scherzi* have characteristic panache, the playing imbued with imaginative insights and spontaneity. Again excellent recording.

Håvard Gimse is a cultured player whose talent is primarily lyrical. He is at his best in the self-communing, poetic side of these wonderful pieces but there is no want of fire, though perhaps more could be made of the dramatic and dynamic contrasts in the *B minor Scherzo*. The Sofienberg Church in Oslo offers an excellent acoustic and the recording is pleasingly natural.

Dame Moura Lympany plays the whole set as an ongoing sequence and then adds a baker's half-dozen hand-selected *Etudes* for good measure in which her pedalling covers the not always quite precise articulation (in Op. 25/12, for instance). The piano recording is truthful, warm rather than brilliant.

Kissin's recital offers some masterly, indeed dazzling pianism, but we miss the fresh, spontaneous quality that has distinguished most of his earlier recitals. He makes pretty heavy weather of the *E minor Prelude* (No. 9) though the close RCA balance probably makes him sound heavier than he is.

Preludes, Op. 28, 1–11; 14–16; 20 & 23
(M) ** Nim. NI 8810. Busoni (piano) – BACH: *Chaconne*; LISZT: *Etudes d'exécution transcendante*, etc. ***

Busoni's Duo-Art piano-roll recordings (from 1923) project his Chopin manner truthfully, and he proves no stylist in this music. Indeed much of his playing, if strong in character, is heavy going. *No. 20 in C minor* opens very stolidly indeed, but the closing *F major* (No. 23), recorded four years after the rest of the sequence, brings a much lighter touch. Excellent sound.

Scherzi 1–4; Ballade 3 in A flat; Berceuse in D flat; 3
Ecossaises; Prelude in C sharp min., Op. 45
(N) (BB) ** Warner Apex (ADD) 2564 61261-2. Freire

Nelson Freire's performances are accomplished and idiomatic, and they are well recorded. While enjoyably thought out and not lacking virtuosity or expressive feeling, the *Scherzi* are less imaginative than with Richter, less volatile than in Demidenko's hands. The *Ecossaises* are charming trifles; but the most memorable performance here is the *Berceuse*, which most beautifully played. The analogue recording has transferred realistically to CD.

Scherzi 1–4; Introduction & Variations on a German Air;
Variations on 'Là ci darem la mano', Op. 2
(N) (BB) **(*) Hyp. Helios CDH 55181. Demidenko

Nikolai Demidenko plays with magisterial keyboard authority and command of colour. There are narcissistic and idiosyncratic touches to which not all listeners will respond; all the same, there is still much that will (and does) give pleasure.

This Regis coupling derives from two separate Richter recitals of 1977 and 1979, originally published by Olympia. There is some marvellous playing in the *Préludes*. It is an odd but substantial assortment: Nos. 4 through 10 in the published sequence, then 13, 19, 11, 2, 23 and 21. These obviously derive from a public concert, as there is applause at the end. He is distinctly ruminative and wayward at times, but always poetically so. As for the *Scherzi*, they are inspired: there are no more imaginatively spontaneous performances in the catalogue. Chopin's markings are either *Presto* or *Presto con fuoco* and, while there is bravura in plenty, there is also an extraordinarily rich, expressive lyricism in the central sections. Everywhere there are fresh insights that seize the listener by the ear, none more frisson-creating than the centrepiece of the *Third Scherzo*, when simple chords are answered by a magical filigree in the right hand. This is Chopin playing of a truly remarkable calibre, and fortunately the remastering by Paul Arden-Taylor is of a high order: the piano quality is very real, full and immediate.

Piano Sonatas 1 in C min., Op. 4; 2 in B flat min. (Funeral
March), Op. 35; 3 in B min., Op. 58
(M) * Decca (ADD) 448 123-2. Ashkenazy**

Piano Sonatas 1–3; Etudes: Op. 10/6; Op. 25/3–4, 10–11;
Mazurkas, Op. 17/1-4
⊶ (BB) * Virgin 2x1 5 61618-2 (2). Andsnes**

Leif Ove Andsnes has the advantage of state-of-the-art piano-sound and his recital comes in a slim, two-for-the-price-of-one CD pack. Andsnes proves as idiomatic an interpreter of Chopin as he has done of Grieg. He also makes out a very good case for the early *C minor Sonata*, Op. 4, which is less well represented on disc and which he plays with real conviction and flair. The other pieces generally come off well and collectors can invest in this set with complete confidence.

Ashkenazy's accounts enjoy classic status, and they are certainly well recorded, with very vivid sound. They are also available as part of a Double Decca combined with the *Etudes* and *Fantasy in F minor* – see above.

Piano Sonata 2 in B flat min., Op. 35
(M) * DG 463 678-2. Pogorelich – PROKOFIEV: *Sonata 6*;**
RAVEL: *Gaspard* *** ◐**
(***) Testament mono SBT 1089. Gilels – MOZART: *Sonata*
17; SHOSTAKOVICH: *Preludes & Fugues 1, 5 & 24* (***)

It was obvious from this 1981 debut recording that the Yugoslav pianist, Ivo Pogorelich, possesses an outsize personality and a keen awareness of colour. He is a commanding artist of undoubted charisma, and his playing has temperament and fire in abundance. There are many wilful touches here and some agogic mannerisms that will not have universal appeal. All the same, these are performances to be reckoned with, and he went on a year later to record the outstanding Prokofiev and Ravel couplings. Here the balance is close and probably does not do full justice to the quality of his pianissimo tone, which nevertheless sounds remarkable. This reissue is an obvious candidate for DG's 'Originals'.

Gilels's account of the *B flat minor Sonata* was recorded in New York and first appeared in 1984. The passage of time has not dimmed its classic status or its poetic intensity and, although some allowances have to be made for the recorded sound, they are few.

Piano Sonata 2; Barcarolle; Nocturnes: 5 in F sharp, Op. 15/2;
13 in C min., Op. 48/1; 15 in E, Op. 62/2; 20 in C sharp min.,
Op. posth.; Scherzo 2
(M) **(*) Virgin 5 61836-2. Pletnev

Pletnev is a master pianist: in his hands the finale of the *Sonata* has a wizardry comparable only with Horowitz and Rachmaninov. However, this is not a self-effacing performance and the expressive posturing will disappoint his growing circle of admirers. Of course, there are marvellous things here too – the *C minor Nocturne* is one – but on the whole this is masterly pianism first and Chopin second.

Piano Sonatas 2 in B flat min. (Funeral March); 3
***** DG (ADD) 415 346-2. Pollini**

Piano Sonatas 2 (Funeral March); 3; Barcarolle; Berceuse;
Fantaisie in F min.
(M) * RCA (ADD) 09026 63046-2. Rubinstein**

Rubinstein's readings of the two finest *Sonatas* are unsurpassed, with a poetic impulse that springs directly from the music and a control of rubato to bring many moments of magic. The sound is also improved, and the addition of the *Barcarolle* and *Berceuse* make this mid-priced reissue all the more desirable.

Pollini's performances are commanding; his mastery of mood and structure gives these much-played *Sonatas* added stature. The slow movement of Op. 35 has both drama and atmosphere, so that the contrast of the magical central section is all the more telling. Both works are played with distinction, but the balance is just a shade close.

Piano Sonata 3; Barcarolle; Impromptus 1–3;
Fantaisie-impromptu
***** Chan. 9175. Shelley**

Piano Sonata 3 in B min., Op. 58; Etude, Op. 10/3
(N) *(*) RCA 82876 64561-2. Luisada – LISZT: *Sonata* *(*);
SCRIABIN: *Sonata 9* *

Piano Sonata 3; Mazurkas: in A min., Op. 17/4; in B flat
min., Op. 24/4; in D flat, Op. 30/3; in D, Op. 33/2; in G; in C
sharp min., Op. 50/ 1 & 3; in C, Op. 56/2; in F sharp min.,
Op. 59/3; in B; in F min.; in C sharp min., Op. 63/1-3; in F
min., Op. 68/4
***** RCA 09026 62542-2. Kissin**

Piano Sonata 3; Polonaise 6 in A flat, Op. 53
(B) **(*) EMI Début 5 73500-2. Slobodyanik – SCHUMANN:
Kinderszenen, etc. **

Piano Sonata 3; Prelude in C sharp min., Op. 45; Scherzo 4 in E, Op. 54

(***) BBC mono/stereo BBCL 4138-2. Perlemuter

Evgeny Kissin plays not only with an effortless mastery but with a naturalness and freshness that silence criticism. His sense of poetry and his idiomatic rubato are combined with impressive technical address and impeccable taste.

An outstanding Chopin recital from Howard Shelley, whose interpretative powers continue to grow in stature. His playing has poetic feeling and ardent but well-controlled temperament. Very good sound.

Alex Slobodyanik is now in his mid-twenties and on the brink of a promising career. His account of the *B minor Sonata* is sensitive and intelligent and, along with the Schumann couplings, serves as an admirable visiting-card for this young artist. At the same time, it does not have quite the strong personality of some of his CD rivals.

Considering his standing in the musical world, Vlado Perlumeter made relatively few commercial recordings. The *Sonata* comes from a 1964 recital and is mono, while the *E major Scherzo* and the *Prelude* (both stereo) are from the early 1970s, when Perlumeter was already in his late sixties. There is some wonderfully perceptive music-making here and the musical importance of this disc is enhanced by exceptionally good notes by Jeremy Siepmann. Strongly recommended.

Jean-Marc Luisada made a good impression in the Warsaw Competition, way back in 1985, and is a far from insensitive player. But these highly mannered Chopin interpretations are not really satisfactory: they are disfigured by disruptive *rubati* and other interpretative distortions, and convey little sense of authority.

Waltzes 1–14; Impromptus 1–3, 4 (Fantaisie-impromptu); Boléro, Op. 19

(M) *** RCA (ADD) 09026 63047-2. Rubinstein

Waltzes 1–14; Impromptus 1–4 (Fantaisie-impromptu)

(M) *** RCA (ADD) 82876 59422-2. Rubinstein

Waltzes 1–14; Barcarolle; Mazurka in C sharp min., Op. 50/3; Nocturne in D flat, Op. 27/2

⊶ ✪ (M) (***) EMI mono 5 66904-2 [66956]. Lipatti

Waltzes 1–19; Impromptus 1–4 (Fantaisie-impromptu)

(BB) * EMI Encore (ADD) 5 74975-2. Cziffra

Rubinstein's performances of the *Waltzes* have a chiselled perfection, suggesting the metaphor of finely cut and polished diamonds, and his clear and relaxed accounts of the *Impromptus* make most other interpretations sound forced by comparison. The digital remastering has softened the edges of the sound-image, and there is an illusion of added warmth.

Dinu Lipatti's classic performances were recorded by Walter Legge in the rather dry acoustic of a Swiss Radio studio at Geneva in the last year of Lipatti's short life, and with each CD reincarnation they seem to have grown in wisdom and subtlety. The reputation of these meticulous performances is fully deserved, and they are rightly reissued as part of EMI's 'Great Recordings of the Century' series.

Georges Cziffra's performances date from the 1970s, and although his technique is not in question, there is a feeling of skating on the surface of the music. The effect is exacerbated by the thin, almost brittle quality of the recording, which was poor by 1970s standards, never mind today. With Rubinstein and Lipatti around, this is a non-starter and does scant justice to the artist.

RECITAL COLLECTIONS

Allegro de Concert in A, Op. 46; Berceuse in D flat, Op. 57; Boléro in A min., Op. 19; 6 Polonaises, Op. posth.; Tarantella in A flat, Op. 43

(N) (BB) *** Hyp. Helios CDH 55183. Demidenko

Most of these pieces are early works: the *Polonaises in G minor* and *B flat major* (with which he frames the recital) date from 1817, that in *G sharp minor* from 1822, the *G flat major* from 1829 and the *Boléro* from 1833, while the *Allegro de Concert* and *Tarantella* were composed at the beginning of the 1840s. The two masterpieces, the *Berceuse* and *Polonaise-Fantasy* (both superbly played) date from 1843–4 and 1846; so here Nikolai Demidenko demonstrates Chopin's progress from youthful precociousness to genius. Yet he plays the earliest pieces with such winning affection and idiomatic feeling that, much more than with Ugorski, above, these charming miniatures are all pointing towards the future. He is excellently recorded.

Andante spinanato & Grande polonaise brillante in E flat, Op. 22; Fantaisie in F min., Op. 49; Piano Sonata 3 in B min., Op. 58; Polonaise Fantaisie in A flat, Op. 61

(N) (BB) **(*) Warner Apex 2564 61691-2. Pommier

Jean-Bernard Pommier's playing is as natural and fresh as the recorded sound; the venue for his recital was Fontfroide Abbey in Provence, with its specially installed studio. Pommier's approach is completely free from self-consciousness and he allows the flow of the music to unfold by itself. There is much to admire in his control of the polyphonic subtleties in the first movement of the *Sonata*, but it is possible to imagine a more varied tonal palette flow both here and in the Scherzo. Yet readers investing in this modestly priced reissue will find more to reward than to disappoint, and the sound is very good indeed.

Andante spianato et Grande Polonaise brillante, Op. 22; Ballades 1–4; Fantaisie-impromptu; Polonaise-fantaisie, Op. 61

** BIS CD 1160. Kempf

Freddy Kempf plays with great virtuosity, but there are some attention-seeking touches that make the listener more aware of the gifted pianist than of the great composer. They are sufficient to diminish the appeal of this eminently well-recorded issue.

Andante spianato et Grande Polonaise brillante; Fantaisie-impromptu; 3 Mazurkas, Op. 59; Nocturne in E flat, Op. 9/2; Piano Sonata 3

*** EMI 5 57702-2. Lim

The then nineteen-year-old Korean pianist, Dong-Hyek Lim made a strong impression in his debut recital of Chopin, Ravel and Schubert. This appeared in 2003, issued in the 'Martha Argerich Presents' series. He has distinguished himself at the Moscow Competition and in Paris, and was still only nineteen when he recorded this all-Chopin recital at the Abbey Road Studios, thus reaffirming his musical credentials. His range of colour and command of dynamic nuance are masterly and he has a strong and individual musical personality. Apart from his effortless technical fluency, he brings a rich poetic imagination to this music and, in the *Sonata*, no mean command of structure. This is the finest Chopin CD to have appeared for a long time (even in a year that has seen Piotr Anderszewski's fine recital on Virgin, reviewed below) and signals the arrival of an outstanding and exciting pianistic talent. EMI give him an excellent and very natural recording.

Ballade 1 in G min.; Etudes: in E; in C sharp min., in G flat (Black Key); in C min. (Revolutionary), Op. 10/3–5 & 12; in A flat; in E min., Op. 25/1 & 5; Mazurkas: in F min., Op. 7/3; in D flat, Op. 30/3; in E min., Op. 41/2; in F sharp min., Op. 59/3; Nocturne in F min., Op. 55/1; Polonaises: in A flat (Heroic); Prélude in B min. (Raindrop), Op. 28/6; in A (Military); Scherzo 1 in B min., Op. 20; Waltzes: in A min., Op. 34/2; C sharp min., Op. 64/2

(N) (M) (**) Sony 518801-2. Horowitz

It is almost as if there were two pianists playing here, although each has a dazzling technique. But the opening 'Heroic' Polonaise sounds incredibly hard, with the microphones far, far too close, and the following Mazurka is no less brittle and shallow, very like a fortepiano. Then, in the Waltz in C minor, the sound is transformed and is soft-grained and poetic, like the playing. The following Polonaise is again much too sharp-edged, and the Etude in E major is again pleasing, and so on. There are performances here which reveal Horowitz as a unique master of the keyboard – but, alas, he had to wait until he could record for Deutsche Grammophon in Europe before he received sound worthy of his wonderful playing.

Ballades: 1 & 3 ; Barcarolle; Etudes: in E; in G flat (Black Keys); in C min. (Revolutionary), Op. 10/3, 5 & 12; in A min. (Winter Wind), Op. 25/11; Fantaisie-impromptu; Mazurkas: in B flat, Op. 7/1; in D, Op. 33/1; Nocturnes: in E flat, Op. 9/2; in F sharp min., Op. 15/2; in B, Op. 32/1; in F min., Op. 55/1; Polonaises: in A (Military), Op. 40/1; in A flat, Op. 53; Preludes: in D flat (Raindrop), Op. 28/15; in C sharp min., Op. 45; Scherzos 1 & 3; Waltzes: in E flat (Grande valse brillante), Op. 18; in A min., Op. 34/2; in D flat (Minute); in C sharp min., Op. 64/1-2; in A flat, Op. 69/1; in B min., Op. 69/2; in G flat, Op. 70/1

(B) *** Double Decca DDD/(ADD) 444 830-2 (2). Ashkenazy

Most music-lovers would count themselves lucky to attend a recital offering the above programme with a total playing time of 130 minutes. The first CD, which is all-digital, opens commandingly with the Grande valse brillante and closes with the Polonaise in A flat; the second (an analogue collection, but of excellent technical quality) begins with the A flat Ballade and ends with the Scherzo in C sharp minor. Overall the recordings date from between 1972 and 1984.

Ballades 1 & 4; Barcarolle; Etudes: Op. 10/5; Op. 25/7; Nocturnes: Op. 9/2–3; Op. 15/1; Op. 27/1; Polonaise-fantaisie; Waltz in A flat, Op. 16/1

(BB) *** RCA stereo/mono 74321 68008-2. Horowitz

Although the Andante spianato and Grande Polonaise is omitted, this super-bargain reissue is a rather more extended recital than its mid-priced predecessor, but again all these performances derive from live recitals. The Nocturnes (in E flat major, Op. 23/2, and C sharp minor Etude, Op. 25/7) are in excellent mono from 1957, with the rest coming from between 1979 and 1982. The performances are fabulous; to the end of his career Horowitz's technique was transcendental and his insights remarkable. There is much excitement, but even more that is unforgettably poetic, and not a bar that is predictable. With the sound so realistic, his presence is very tangible. Not to be missed.

Ballade 1; Mazurkas: 19 in B min., 20 in D flat, Op. 30/2–3; 22 in G sharp min., 25 in B min., Op. 33/1 & 4; 34 in C, Op. 56/2; 43 in G min., 45 in A min., Op. 67/2 & 4; 46 in C; 47 in A min., 49 in F min., Op. 68/1–2 & 4; Prelude 25 in C sharp min., Op. 45; Scherzo 2

**(*) DG (ADD) (IMS) 413 449-2. Michelangeli

Although this recital somehow does not quite add up as a whole, the performances are highly distinguished. Michelangeli's individuality comes out especially in the Ballade and is again felt in the Mazurkas, which show a wide range of mood and dynamic. The Scherzo is extremely brilliant, yet without any suggestion of superficiality. The piano tone is real and lifelike.

Ballades 3–4; Mazurkas 1–3, Op. 59/1–3; Op. 63; in F min., Op. 68/4; Polonaises 5 in F sharp min., Op. 44; 6 in A flat

*** Virgin 5 45620-2. Anderszewski

Piotr Anderszewski's Chopin recital has had almost as rapturous a press as his Bach – and with good reason. Along with Dong-Hyek Lim's recital discussed above, it has the right blend of sensibility and poetic feeling with classical finesse. Anderszewski is obviously an artist of quality, whose Chopin has a sense of real flair and vision as well as splendid control.

Ballade 3; Barcarolle; Berceuse; Etudes 13 in A flat; 21 in G flat, Op. 25/1 & 9; Fantaisie in F min.; Impromptu 1 in A flat; Mazurka 13 in A min., Op. 17/4; Nocturnes 5 in F sharp min., Op. 15/2; 20 in C sharp min., Op. posth.; Preludes: in A flat & C min., Op. 28/17 & 20; Scherzo 2 in B flat min., Op. 31; Waltzes 5 in A flat, Op. 42; 14 in E min. (op. posth.)

(BB) *** Naxos 8.555799. Idil Biret

Idil Biret's impetuosity and brilliance both combine to make the E minor Waltz which opens this recital arresting in its bravura, but she plays with both character and poetry in the Barcarolle and the two Ballades, while the Berceuse has a touching simplicity worthy of a young pupil of Wilhelm Kempff ('Uncle Kempff' as she called him). Indeed, overall this admirably planned recital demonstrates what a natural feeling Biret has for Chopin. Her complete survey is greatly prized in France and the mixture here of Etudes, Preludes and Mazurkas shows her control of colour and rubato in different ways, while the dashing account of the Scherzo in B flat demonstrates both her easy virtuosity and her willingness to slip back readily into gentle lyricism. The recording is excellent, with a real sense of presence.

Ballade 4; Barcarolle; Berceuse; Mazurkas in A min., A flat & F sharp min., Op. 59/1–3. Nocturnes in B & E, Op. 62/1–2. Polonaise 7 (Polonaise-fantaisie), Op. 61; Waltzes in D flat (Minute), C sharp min. & A flat, Op. 64/1–3

**(*) Decca SACD (Compatible) 470 608-2. Ashkenazy

Vladimir Ashkenazy's recital is new, recorded in Finland in 1999. The sound is first class, Decca's finest – whether played back as a CD or SACD, with or without surround sound. The programme is well planned and beautifully played, with the Barcarolle, Berceuse and Nocturnes as highlights. But there was a natural spontaneity in Ashkenazy's earlier Chopin records that is less consistently achieved here.

Ballade 4; Berceuse; Etudes: Opp. 10/3, 8 & 9; 25/1-3; Fantaisie in F min.; Mazurka in A min., Op. 68/2; Nocturne: in E flat, Op. 9/2; D flat, Op. 27/2; Polonaise in A, Op. 40/1; A flat, Op. 53; Waltzes: in A flat, Op. 42; E min., Op. posth.

(**(*)) Testament mono SBT 1030. Solomon

This anthology affords ample proof of Solomon's power to distil magic in pretty well whatever composer he touched. Most of these 78-r.p.m. recordings were made between 1942 and 1946; the *F minor Fantaisie* is pre-war (1932), a wonderfully searching account, and the sheer delicacy and poetry of the playing shine through the often frail recorded sound. Good transfers.

Barcarolle; Berceuse; Mazurkas: 13 in A min., Op. 17/4; 23 in D, Op. 33/2; 33 in B, Op. 56/1; Nocturnes: 1 in B flat min., Op. 9/1; 8 in D flat, Op.27/2; 10 in A flat, Op. 32/2; 12 in G, Op. 37/2; 17 in B, Op. 62/1; Polonaises: 3 in A, Op. 40/1; 6 in A flat; Scherzo 2; Waltz: in C sharp min., Op. 64/2
(M) (**(*)) EMI mono 5 67007-2. Rubinstein

The present selection, carefully arranged to make a satisfactory ongoing recital, dates from between 1928 (the charismatic account of the *Barcarolle*, which sounds unbelievably good) and 1939 (the B flat Mazurka, Op. 56/1). Certainly the younger Rubinstein (he was in his forties) has a wonderfully chimerical touch, especially in some of the *Nocturnes* and indeed the *Berceuse*, which he paces fairly briskly. In the *Mazurkas* his rubato is as uniquely personal as it is convincing. The transfers are a shade dry, and at times a little lacking in sonority, but pretty faithful otherwise.

Berceuse, Op. 57; Boléro, Op. 19; Mazurkas, Op. 24/1–4 & Op. 26/4; Nocturne in C sharp min.; Polonaises: in A flat; B flat ; G min.; Rondo in C min., Op. 1; Sonata, Op. 4: 3rd movt. Souvenir de Paganini; Variations brillantes, Op. 12; Waltzes, Op. 64/2–3
(N) (M) ** Divine Art 24116. Katin (Collard & Collard Square Piano)

The interest here lies in the piano rather than in the performer, a restored Collard & Collard square piano of around 1836. Although there is no suggestion that Chopin used it, it approximates to the period in which most of the music here was written. Certainly Peter Katin, who is a highly experienced Chopin player, produces an attractive singing tone in the *Berceuse* and *Nocturne*, and he demonstrates the glitter of the upper range in Paganini's *Variations* on the 'Carnival of Venice' and the *Variations brillantes* with which he opens the recital. So far as we can judge (with no means of comparison), the 1996 recording, previously available on the Athene label, is admirably truthful.

Berceuse; Impromptus 1–4 (Fantaisie-impromptu); Sonata 3
(M) (**(*)) Decca mono 475 6157. Magalov

Dating from 1954, this Heritage reissue reintroduces Nikita Magalov to the catalogue. This is intelligent and sensitive Chopin playing: the *Berceuse* is one of the finest performances of this elusive piece on record. The four *Impromptus* are played as a set and make very satisfying listening when heard together. The *Sonata* is also very successful, if not quite on the level of Rubinstein or Pollini. The mono recording has warmth as well as clarity.

Etudes: Op. 10/1–12 (Kilenyi); 3 & 5 (Paderewski & Brailowsky); 5 (Busoni); 7 (Planté); Etudes: Op. 25/1 (Darré); 2 (Planté & Brailowsky); 3 (Sofronitsky); 4 (Kilenyi); 5 (Cortot & Busoni); 6 (Darré); 7 (Koczalski); 8–10 (Cortot); 11 (Brailowsky); 12 (Emil von Sauer). Mazurkas: 7, 20–21, 26, 32, 38, 40–41 (Horowitz); 17, 25–6, 31, 44 & 47 (Friedman); 3–4, 10, 22, 27, 39–40, 45–6 & 48 (Sofronitsky); 9, 14, 24, 35 & 44 (Kapell); 19, 43, 49 & 52

(Maryla Jonas). *Nocturnes: 2, 7 & 15 (Rubinstein); 2 & 5 (Paderewski); 4, 12–13 (Sofronitsky); 4 & 7 (Cortot); 5 (Busoni); 8 (Lipatti); 17 (Koczalski); 19–20 (Maryla Jonas). Polonaises 1–7 (Rubinstein); 3 (Paderewski); 6 (Friedman & Sofronitsky); 9, Op. 71/2 (Maryla Jonas)*
(N) (***) Naïve Andante mono AN 1190 (4)

A cornucopia of great musical riches; a collection of quite exceptional documentary value, four CDs housed in an excellently annotated and sumptuously produced 104-page hard-covered book. There are almost too many rarities to detail: Edward Kilenyi (1884–1968), not to be confused with his son of the same name, was a pupil of Mascagni and the teacher of Gershwin. His 1937 records of the Op. 10 *Etudes* made in Paris are contrasted on the first CD with Brailowsky (1928), Busoni (1922) and Francis Planté (1839–1934), a pupil of Marmontel and a protégé of Liszt, who made seven Chopin records in 1928 when he was nearly 90. He was renowned for his 'floating tone'. Raoul Koczalski (1884–1948) is of particular interest as he studied with Chopin's pupil, Karol Mikuli, and so represents an authentic link with the composer. The Cortot, Horowitz, Lipatti and Rubinstein records are well known, but the William Kapell (1951) and Sofronitsky performances (1949) are not. A set which will reward and fascinate for countless hours and prove enriching for both the less knowledgeable and the connoisseur. Good transfers. A companion set (Andante AN 1189) of the *Preludes* with Friedman, Casadesus, Cortot, Horowitz and others (the 'others' include Rachmaninov) has not been submitted for review but sounds pretty self-recommending.

Etudes: in G flat, Op. 10/5; in G sharp min.; in C sharp min., Op. 25/6–7; 3 Ecossaises, Op. posth. 72/3; Fantasy in F min.; Impromptu in A flat, Op. 29; Sonata 3; Waltzes: in A flat; A min., Op. 34/1–2; in E min., Op. posth.
*** DG 453 456-2. Pletnev

Opening with the great *F minor Fantasy* and closing with the *B Minor Sonata*, both superbly done, Pletnev's well-planned recital has all the hallmarks of a live recital, plus the technical advantage of studio recording. Such is his command of tonal colour elsewhere that one is scarcely aware of the piano's hammers even in fortissimo passages. But interpretatively things are less straightforward and he is often wilful. His rubato in the *B minor Sonata* is at times intrusive. The *G flat* and *G sharp minor Etudes* are dazzling, as is the famous *E minor Waltz* (written when the composer was twenty); and the *Ecossaises*, which are even earlier, are deliciously frothy. Yet the *C sharp minor Etude* takes the listener into a wholly different world and is very touching, as is the slow movement of the *Sonata*. For all one's reservations about the personal element, this is very distinguished playing indeed.

Fantaisie in F min.; Nocturnes: in C sharp min.; in D flat, Op. 27/1–2; in A flat, Op. 32/2 ; Polonaise in F sharp min., Op. 44; Scherzo 2; Waltzes: in A flat; in A min., Op. 34/1–2; in A flat, Op. 42
🎧 ⊕ *** RCA 09026 60445-2. Kissin

Evgeny Kissin's Chopin anthology comes from a Carnegie Hall recital given early in 1993 when he was still only twenty-one. His virtuosity and brilliance are always harnessed to musical ends and there is total dedication to Chopin and no indulgence. Chopin playing of real quality and well recorded, though the sound is a bit thick in the bass.

Fugue in A min., Op. posth.; Lento con gran espressione in C sharp min., Op. posth.; Nocturnes: in E flat, Op. 9/2; in C min., Op. posth.; Polonaise in B flat min., Op. posth.; Waltzes: in A min., Op. 34/2; in A min.; in E min.; in F sharp min., Op. posth.

(*) Etcetera KTC 1231. Antoni – FIELD: *Largo; Nocturnes,* etc. ***

The primary purpose of this CD is to make a direct comparison with similar works, written even earlier, by John Field, who invented the *nocturne* in the year Chopin was born. Some of the similarities between the two young composers have already been documented (notably Field's *E flat major Romance* and Chopin's famous *Nocturne* in the same key from Opus 9). But other musical links are equally fascinating. Helge Antoni plays simply and poetically, and this serves to point up his comparisons. He is naturally recorded in a pleasing acoustic.

VOCAL MUSIC

Songs: *The bridegroom; Drinking song; Faded and vanished; Reverie (Dumka); Handsome lad; Hymn from the tomb; Lithuanian song; The maiden's wish; Melodia (Elegy; Lamento); The messenger; My darling; Out of my sight; The ring; Sad river; Spring; There where she loves; The two corpses; The warrior; Witchcraft.* Songs arr. Pauline Viardot from Chopin *Mazurkas: Berceuse* (from Op. 33/3); *Faible cœur* (from Op. 7/3); *La Danse* (from Op. 50/1); *La Fête* (from Op. 6/4); *Plainte d'amour* (from Op. 6/1)

*** Hyp. CDA 67125. Kryger, Spencer

Chopin wrote these songs for relaxation, just to please himself, never publishing them, and that may explain why the Polish flavour is so strong. He was reflecting his own early background, and the results are charming. *Mazurka* rhythms abound, as in the haunting *Handsome lad*, with the collection rounded off in the one song which goes deeper, *Melodia*, the heartfelt lament of an exile. The five arrangements of Chopin *Mazurkas* made for her own use by the leading singer, Pauline Viardot, are comparably charming, making the ideal fill-up. Urszula Kryger, with her vibrant Slavonic tone well controlled, makes the most sympathetic interpreter, sensitively accompanied by Charles Spencer.

CILEA, Francesco (1866–1950)

Adriana Lecouvreur (DVD version)

*(*) TDK **DVD** 10 5009-9 DV-OPADL. Dessi, Borodina, Larin, Giuseppini, Guelfi, La Scala Ch. & O, Brignoli (Stage and TV Dir. Puggelli)

Adriana Lecouvreur (CD version)

*** Decca (IMS) 425 815-2 (2). Sutherland, Bergonzi, Nucci, d'Artegna, Ciurca, Welsh Nat. Op. Ch. & O, Bonynge

This DVD from TDK brings a rare opportunity to see Cilea's warmly colourful opera about a celebrated French actress and her love rival, with the Princesse de Bouillon, based on a play by Eugène Scribe. The plot may be contrived, with a preposterous pay-off when Adriana is poisoned by a bunch of violets sent by her rival, but it offers a good range of character roles for the principals. It is presented here in Lemberto Puggelli's lavish production for La Scala, Milan, first seen in 1989, and here revived in January 2000. The ingenious sets of Paolo Bregni give you views from behind the scenery, with Adriana seen on stage from behind in Act I, and with the

garden of the Prince's palace in Acts II and III. The traditional production sets the scene accurately in 1730, with handsome costumes by Luisa Spinatellli, though in Act I the heroine's elaborate gown with blue and gold spangles has a silly little hat to match. The big problem in this performance, warmly conducted by Roberto Rizzi Brignoli, is that Olga Borodina as the Princess is a far more compelling singer and actress, far richer and firmer, than Daniela Dessi as Adriana, taking the role of the greatest actress of her day. Her spoken monologue from Racine's *Phèdre*, flung out as an insult to the Princess, is limply done, and Dessi's singing, often edgy under pressure, conveys generalized emotions, even in the two big arias, *Io son l'umile ancella* in Act I and *Poveri fiori* in Act IV. Cilea's use of the big tune from that first aria is most effective. It does not help that Sergei Larin as the beloved, Maurizio, makes an unromantic figure, even though he sings well. The character roles of the Prince (Giorgio Giuseppini) and Michonnet (Carlo Guelfi) are both strongly taken. The voices are well caught, but the orchestra is relatively thin.

On CD Sutherland's performance in the role of a great tragic actress could not be warmer-hearted. She impresses with her richness and opulence in the biggest test, the aria *Io son l'umile ancella*, an actress's credo, and her formidable performance is warmly backed up by the other principals, and equally by Richard Bonynge's conducting, not just warmly expressive amid the wealth of rich tunes, but light and sparkling where needed, easily idiomatic.

CLARKE, Rebecca (1886–1979)

(i) *Piano Trio;* (ii) *Viola Sonata*

⊶ ✿ *** ASV CDDCA 932. Roscoe, with (i) Watkinson, Waterman; (ii) Jackson – BEACH: *Piano Quintet* ***

Born and educated in Britain, Rebecca Clarke was a frequent visitor to the United States and lived there permanently from the Second World War onwards. She played the viola herself, and the bitingly romantic *Sonata*, superbly written for the instrument, is here given a warm and purposeful performance. The *Piano Trio* of two years later (1921) is, if anything, even more striking, with clean-cut, thrusting themes bringing echoes of Bartók and Bloch which never submerge Clarke's individual voice. The performances by Martin Roscoe with members of the Endellion Quartet are masterly, with full-bodied, well-balanced recording.

Complete Choral Music

Ave Maria; Away, delights; Come, O come; Daybreak; He that dwelleth in a secret place; Hymn to Pan; A lover's dirge; Music when soft voices die; My spirit like a charmed bark; Nacht für Nacht; Now fie on love; Philomela; Shelley's hellas chorus; Sleep; Spirits; Take, O take those lips away; There is no rose; Weep you no more; When cats run home

*** ASV CDDCA 1136. Gonville and Caius College Choir, Webber

There has been a welcome revival of interest in the music of Rebecca Clarke, who died in 1979 at the age of 93. The first woman pupil of Stanford at the Royal College of Music, she was also one of the leading viola-players of her time, and her prize-winning *Viola Sonata* is now firmly re-established in the regular repertory. Her songs too have been widely revived, but this collection of her choral music, very well sung and recorded, breaks new ground. These nineteen items were written between 1906, when she was still a student, and 1943, when she had just settled in New York, where she stayed for the rest of her life. Although her writing for voices is not as adventurous stylistically as her instrumental music, each piece is unfailingly imaginative, starting with refined echoes of her teacher, Stanford, and later reflecting both the English church tradition and the Elizabethan madrigal.

CLEMENS NON PAPA, Jacob

(c. 1510/15–c. 1555/6)

Jacob Clement or Clemens non Papa was jokingly known as Clement-not-the-Pope, so as to distinguish him from either Pope Clement VII or the Flemish poet, Jacobus Papa. However, we know very little about him. It seems likely that he was in Bruges from 1544–5, and he certainly spent most of his life in the Low Countries. However, he was very prolific and much respected in his time (over a dozen of his Masses have survived, over 200 motets and many chansons).

Missa and Motet: *Ecce quam bonum.* Motets: *Accesserunt ad Jesum; Carole, magna est; Job tonso capite; Pascha nostrum; Veni electa mea*

(N) *** Signum SIGCD 045. Brabant Ens., Rice

This admirable Signum disc serves alongside the fine Gimell CD to provide a magnetic introduction to the music of Clemens non Papa, a sixteenth-century composer of great individuality and distinction, whose music is so little known. Based on the composer's own motet, the *Mass Ecce quam bonum* is in five parts, extended to six from the *Sanctus* onwards, and is an essentially joyful celebration of the unity of the church, and God's benediction on those who lead a peaceful life. The soaring opening phrase is instantly recognizable throughout each of the movements, although it is given a neat variant in the *Osanna.* The motets interspersed between the Propers of the Mass add melodic and textural variety and vary from the Easter Anthem, *Pascha nostrum,* a sensuous excerpt from the Song of Songs (*Veni electa mea*) and even a warning mention of the predicament of Job. Glorious singing throughout and outstandingly fine recording in the chapel of Merton College, Oxford, where the impressive conductor of the Brabant Ensemble is based; and it is he who provides the notes. Full texts and translations are provided.

Missa Pastores quidnam vidistis; Motets: *Pastores quidnam vidistis; Ego flos campi; Pater peccavi; Tribulationes civitatum*

✿ *** Gimell CDGIM 013. Tallis Scholars, Phillips

The beauty of line and richness of texture in the masterly *Missa Pastores quidnam vidistis* are unforgettable in this superb performance by the Tallis Scholars. The programme opens with the parody motet associated with the Mass, which has a glorious eloquence. Of the other motets, *Pater peccavi,* solemnly rich-textured, is especially memorable; but the whole programme is designed to reveal to modern ears another name hitherto known only to scholars. The recording is uncannily real and superbly balanced. It was made in the ideal acoustics of the Church of St Peter and St Paul, Salle, Norfolk.

CLEMENTI, Muzio (1752–1832)

Symphonies: 1; in B flat & D, Op. 18/1-2

*** Chan. 9234. LMP, Bamert

Symphonies 1-4

*** Erato (ADD) 4509 92191-2 (2). Philh. O, Scimone

Six of Clementi's 20 symphonies survive. The four numbered works are all scored for much larger forces than the Op. 18 set and even include trombones. Their musical content explains Clementi's high reputation in his lifetime as a composer for the orchestra, not just the piano. If the *Great National Symphony* is the most immediately striking, with *God save the King* ingeniously worked into the third movement, the other works are all boldly individual. The *Fourth* is a remarkably powerful symphonic statement which brings some striking modulations, and there is some unexpected chromatic writing. Moreover Clementi's use of the orchestra is often very imaginative, though his indebtedness to the Haydn of the *London Symphonies* is very striking.

Bamert's performances are on a chamber scale and are refreshingly alive and polished. They are given top-class Chandos sound. If you want just one CD of Clementi symphonies, this is the one to have, and indeed the music here is rather engaging.

The performances by Claudio Scimone and the Philharmonia Orchestra are strong and sympathetic, and the recording (made in London's Henry Wood Hall in 1978) is full, resonant and natural, bringing weight as well as freshness. They deserve a warm recommendation even though they have now reverted to premium price.

PIANO MUSIC

Capriccio in B flat; Fantasia with Variations on 'Au clair de la lune', Op. 48; Preludio 1 alla Haydn in C; Preludio 1 alla Mozart (both from Op. 19); Sonatas: in F min., Op. 13/6; in F, Op. 33/11; in G min., Op. 34/11

⌕ (M) *** Warner Elatus 2564 60676-2. Staier (fortepiano)

The reissue of Andreas Staier's splendid recital on Elatus gives it a fair claim to being the most desirable introduction to the music of Clementi in the catalogue. The anticipation of Beethoven appears in nearly all this music, even in the *Preludio alla Haydn,* although the companion *Prelude* is undoubtedly closer to Mozart, as is the *Capriccio.* The *Sonatas* are all considerable works, and Staier's flexibility of style brings out their individuality strongly.

Piano Sonatas in A, Op. 2/4; G min., Op. 8/1; B flat, Op. 8/3; F min., Op. 13/6; G, WO14

⌕ (BB) *** Naxos 8.555808. Alexander-Max (piano)

Playing on an attractively mellow-toned, untwangy fortepiano, the American pianist, Susan Alexander-Max, gives magnetic performances of five sparkling and original early sonatas by Clementi, on what one hopes is the start of a series from Naxos. Some eighteen years older than Beethoven, Clementi – Italian-born but based from boyhood in England – wrote these sonatas for his own use on his European tours as a leading virtuoso, one of those whom the Emperor Joseph II pitted in contest against Mozart. Even the earliest sonata, in G major, written when Clementi was only sixteen and hitherto unpublished, develops striking material, and the two minor-key sonatas in particular point forward to Beethoven and beyond, exploiting the keyboard in adventurous ways with a wide dynamic range and bold harmonies.

Piano Sonatas in G min., Op. 7/3; in F min., Op. 13/6; in B flat, Op. 24/2; in F sharp min.; in D; Op. 25/5-6

**(*) D & J Athene ATH CD 4. Katin

Peter Katin plays a square piano which has subsequently been restored. So the sounds he creates are as authentic as one could find. The work which comes off best in his recital is the *G minor Sonata*, Op. 7/3, which sounds so effective on the fortepiano. The slow movement of the *F sharp minor*, Op. 25/5, sounds very direct, seeking no romantic overtones; generally, Peter Katin's approach is plainspun to suit the somewhat dry sonority of his instrument. He is very realistically recorded.

Piano Sonatas: in F min., Op. 13/6; in B flat, Op. 24/2; in F sharp min., Op. 25/5; in G, Op. 37/1
*** Accent ACC 67911D. Van Immerseel (fortepiano)

Very fleet and brilliant performances from Jos van Immerseel. The slow movements of these *Sonatas* have considerable expressive depth, and the outer ones are full of a brilliance that is well served by this eminently skilful and excellent artist.

Piano Sonatas: in B flat, Op. 24/2; in G; in F sharp min., Op. 25/2 & 5; in D, Op. 37/2; 6 Progressive Sonatinas, Op. 36
(BB) *** Naxos 8.550452. Szokolay

Balázs Szokolay's Naxos anthology is very successful and his playing inspires enthusiasm. Decent recording; excellent value.

Piano sonatas: in D, Op. 25/6; in A, Op. 33/1; in A, Op. 50/1; in G min. (Didone abbandonata), Op. 50/3
(M) *** CRD 3500. Roscoe

Martin Roscoe makes a very persuasive case for playing these sonatas on a modern instrument. He is particularly searching in the *Adagio sostenuto* of the late *A major Sonata*, Op. 50/1, and how impressively he pedals in the dolorous *Introduzione (Largo patetico e sostenuto)* of the *G minor Sonata (Didone abbandonata)*, then presenting the *Adagio dolente* most touchingly and finding plenty of drama in the agitated finale. Yet the gallant early D major work is joyfully spirited and full of charm. The recording is very natural, well up to the high standard we expect from this label.

Piano Sonatas in G; B min.; D, Op. 40/1–3
(BB) *** Naxos 8.553500. De Maria

Pietro de Maria's account of the three sonatas of Op. 40 is impeccable not only in terms of virtuosity but in musicianship and artistry. His playing is meticulous, beautifully articulated, his command of dynamics and naturalness of phrasing admirable. He is accorded first-class sound, fresh and present, as one might expect from the acoustic of St George's, Brandon Hill, Bristol. Very good value for money.

CLÉRAMBAULT, Louis-Nicolas
(1676–1749)
Sonata 1 (Anonima) in G; Simphonie à 5 in G min.; (i) Harpsichord Suite 2 in C min.; (ii) Cantatas: Orphée; Léandre et Héro
(BB) **(*) Naxos 8.553744. Les Solistes du Concert Spirituel; (i) Rannou; (ii) with Piau

Nicolas Clérambault's sonatas followed the Corellian model, but the invention of No. 1 is indeed very anonymous. and does not show him at his best. The three-minute *Simphonie*, however, turns out to be an engaging single-movement *Chaconne*. The *Harpsichord Suite* follows the French style of Couperin, but Blandine Rannou fails to make the most of it

by choosing consistently slow tempi, until the closing *Gigue*, which sparkles. However, as can be seen below, it was his cantatas which made Clérambault's reputation, and two of the finest are included here, beautifully sung by Sandrine Piau. Both include 'strong and tender airs', which are exquisite duets with a solo flute. The accompaniments by Les Solistes du Concert Spirituel are admirably alive and stylish and this Naxos disc is well worth getting for the cantatas alone.

Cantatas: Apollon et Doris; L'Isle de Délos; Léandre et Héro; Pirame et Tisbé
(M) *** Opus OP 10006. Poulenard, Ragon, Ens. Amalia

Both *Léandre et Héro* and *Pirame et Tisbé* come from 1713; they are redolent of tragedy and exhibit a sensibility of great refinement. *L'Isle de Délos* comes from 1716 and evokes the pleasures of the island, while *Apollon et Doris* (1720) serves to reaffirm the feeling that as a master of the secular chamber cantata he was second to none. Affecting performances from Isabelle Poulenard and Gilles Ragon, well supported throughout by the Ensemble Amalia. The recording is first rate.

Le Triomphe d'Iris (pastorale)
(BB) *** Naxos 8.554455. Méchaly, Geoffroy-Dechaume, Goubioud, Bona, Duthoit, Novelli, Lombard, Le Concert Spirituel, Niquet

Clérambault also produced lively court entertainments like this delightful Pastorale; and the present work presents a story of two pairs of shepherd and shepherdess lovers, Daphnis and Sylvie, and Tircis and Philis, brought together at the end by the goddess, Iris, representing Love. What matters most is the vitality of Clérambault's writing in a sequence of brief arias, choruses and dances, underlined in the rhythmic bite of this performance from the period instruments of Le Concert Spirituel. The refined, very French team of singers is well drilled and agile, untroubled by brisk speeds. Clear, refined recording to match.

COATES, Eric (1886–1957)
(i) *By the Sleepy Lagoon; (ii) Calling all Workers: March; (iii) Cinderella (Phantasy); From Meadow to Mayfair: Suite; London Suite; London again Suite; (i) The Merrymakers Overture; (iii) Music everywhere: March; (iii; iv) Saxo-Rhapsody; (i) The Three Bears (phantasy); (ii) The Three Elizabeths: Suite; (i) The Three Men: Man from the Sea (only); (iii) Wood Nymphs (valsette)*
☛ (B) *** CfP (ADD) 762 5572 (2). (i) LSO, Mackerras; (ii) CBSO, Kilbey; (iii) RLPO, Groves; (iv) with Brymer

It is good to welcome back this key collection of the music of Eric Coates, 'the man who writes tunes', much loved by orchestral players as he also writes so gratefully for their instruments, being an ex-orchestral player himself. On the whole, Groves, who has the lion's share of the repertoire here, proves a persuasive advocate, although occasionally his approach is slightly bland. Jack Brymer is the excellent soloist in the *Saxo-Rhapsody*; and the other piece with a diluted jazz element, *Cinderella*, also goes with a swing. However, not surprisingly, the performances from Sir Charles Mackerras and the LSO are even more lively, and there are also several really outstanding ones from the CBSO under Reginald Kilbey. He proves the ideal Coates conductor, with a real flair for catching the sparkle of the composer's leaping allegro figurations, notably in the first movement of *The Three Elizabeths*, where also his shaping of the central, slow movement – one of the composer's finest inspirations, dedicated to the late Queen Mother – has an affectionate grace. The marches are splendidly alive and vigorous. With good transfers this is the best Coates compilation currently available.

Ballad; By the Sleepy Lagoon; London Suite; The Three Bears (phantasy); *The 3 Elizabeths* (suite)
(M) *** ASV CDWHL 2053. East of E. O, Nabarro

Malcolm Nabarro has the full measure of Coates's leaping allegros and he plays the famous marches with crisp buoyancy. *The Three Bears* sparkles humorously, as it should; only in *By the Sleepy Lagoon* does one really miss a richer, more languorous string-texture. Excellent, bright recording, and the price is right.

Cinderella (Phantasy); *Dam Busters March; Joyous Youth* (Suite); *London Suite; Miniature Suite; The Selfish Giant* (Phantasy); *The Three Bears* (Phantasy)
🎵➔ ⊕ *** Chan. 9869. BBC PO, Gamba

This is easily the best Eric Coates collection ever. It is a joy to hear his imaginatively coloured orchestration on a full-sized orchestra with an ample string-group splendidly served by these superb performances and Chandos's demonstration-worthy recordings. The finest of the three *Phantasies* is *The Three Bears*, with its opening rhythmic phrase, 'Who's been sleeping in my bed?' and its later, utterly beguiling waltz theme. *Cinderella* boasts another richly romantic example, and two more, both deliciously lightweight, close the *Joyous Youth Suite* and the *Miniature Suite*, which shows the composer at his most elegant and graceful. More robust is the *London Suite*, with its vigorous, pacy evocation of the old Covent Garden Market, followed by a romantic portrayal of *Westminster*, complete with chimes. The *Knightsbridge March* finale was famous as a signature tune for the BBC. The programme ends appropriately with *The Dam Busters*. All orchestral musicians love playing Coates's music and this is conveyed by the orchestra throughout this wonderfully enjoyable CD.

Cinderella (Phantasy); *Footlights* (Concert Waltz); *London Again Suite; The Selfish Giant* (Phantasy); *Summer Days Suite; Three Men Suite; TV March*
(N) *** Avie AV 2070. RLPO, Wilson

The Liverpool Phil. have not recorded Eric Coates since the days of Sir Charles Groves, but they have not lost their touch, and under the excellent John Wilson they play this attractively tuneful music with verve and affection. How well Coates builds the introduction to the *Footlights Waltz* before the beguiling tune arrives, and how effectively Wilson and his players respond! Alongside the waltz, the engaging *Three Men Suite* (as distinct from the catchy finale) and the charmingly scored lightweight *Summer Days* are new to the CD catalogue and they are most winningly played and recorded here.

COINCY, Gaultier de (c. 1177–1236)

Gaultier de Coincy, born in Coincy-l'Abbaye, eventually became Abbot of St Médard in Soissons. His literary works, the narrative *Miracles de Nostre-Dame*, survive in more than eighty manuscripts, of which twenty-two also contain groups

of chansons with music, the haunting melodies not necessarily composed by de Coincy, but collected by him.

Miracles de Nostre-Dame: *Amours; Chançonetes; Conductus; Royne Celestre; Ma Viele*
(N) *** HM HMU 903317. Harp Consort, Laurence-King

This is a very well-planned collection, dividing Gaultier's music into five groupings. Most of the pieces are short, but they are surprisingly tuneful. Of the three love songs the intoductory *Cui donrai* is almost romantic, and the concerted dance-song *Hui matin a l'ajournee* has a rich but simple harmonization. The chansonettes (instrumental as well as vocal) are brief but melodically catchy. The Harp Consort is a great deal more than that, and throughout this very entertaining programme, besides the many vocal pieces, there are contributions from medieval harp, psaltery, cornetto, shawm (an unforgettable sound), vielle, chamber organ, and even a solo (*Pour Dieu*) for bagpipes. Playing and singing has lots of character and the recording is splendidly vivid. Whether early medieval music could have been as polished as the performances are here, one still feels drawn back in time.

Miracles de Nostre-Dame: *Chants des Anges: Amours, qui bien ses enchanter; Entendez tuit ensemble; Hui enfantez; Hui matin a l'ajournee; Ma vièle; Mere Dieu, Virge senee; S'amour dont sui espris; Talenz m'est pris orendroit*
🎵➔ ⊕ *** Decca 460 794-2. New L. Consort, Pickett

Gaultier de Coincy's poems (splendidly translated by Professor J. H. Marshall) are mostly in ecstatic praise of the Virgin Mary (but with allusions to earthly love and desire), while *Hui matin*, which evokes the break of a spring day and the discovery of a 'little flower of lovely hue', opens with a perky recorder solo. *Ma vièle* is translated as 'My fiddle would fain play a fine tune' and opens instrumentally. *Amours, qui bien ses enchanter, Talenz m'est pris orendroit* and the closing *Entendez tuit ensemble* are swinging dance songs, sung in consort, but Pickett often alternates choral unisons with solo voices. *Hui enfantez* (celebrating the Christchild) is more solemn, but the repeated chant is no less appealing. Although the basic atmosphere is medieval, the lyrical flow of the music's lines is often surprisingly modern, and the soprano voices here of Joanne Lunn, Heddvid Aberg and Faye Newton are sweetly celestial, balanced by the male group. The engaging accompaniments, while obviously conjectural, are convincing and delightfully scored, with Pickett himself leading the ensemble on recorder. This is infectiously individual music, beautifully sung and played, which could become popular in the way of Hildegard von Bingen, given sufficient exposure.

COLERIDGE-TAYLOR, Samuel (1875–1912)

4 Characteristic Waltzes, Op. 22; Gipsy Suite, Op. 20; Hiawatha Overture, Op. 30; Othello Suite, Op. 79; Petite Suite de concert, Op. 77; Romance of the Prairie Lilies, Op. 39
*** Marco 8.223516. Dublin RTE Concert O, Leaper

Coleridge-Taylor wrote much delightful orchestral music, the most famous being the charming *Petite Suite de concert*. The composer's feeling for the genre is also apparent in the *Four Characteristic Waltzes*. Each is nicely coloured: there is a nostalgic *Valse bohémienne*, a countrified *Valse rustique* (the oboe so easily conjuring up the countryside), a stately *Valse de la reine*, and a lively *Valse mauresque*. The *Gipsy Suite* is a piquantly coloured four-movement work of considerable appeal, while the *Othello Suite*, beginning with a lively dance, has an engaging *Willow Song* and ends with a stirring *Military March*. Performances and recording are excellent, and this is altogether a winning if essentially lightweight collection, perhaps more for aficionados than for the general collector.

Violin Concerto in G min., Op. 80

*** Hyp. CDA 67420. Marwood, BBC Scottish SO, Brabbins –
  SOMERVELL: *Violin Concerto in G* ***
**(*) Avie AV 0044. Graffin, Johannesburg PO, Hankinson –
  DVORAK: *Violin Concerto* **(*)

When in 1910 Samuel Coleridge-Taylor went to the United States to conduct his cantata, *Hiawatha*, he was introduced to the great American violinist, Maud Powell. He promised to write a concerto for her, but his first attempt, using spirituals as thematic material, failed to satisfy him or her. His second attempt – with some themes again echoing spirituals – was performed in America in 1912, though the composer was by then too ill to attend, and he died three months later. It is a warmly lyrical work in keeping with his other music, here passionately performed by the excellent French violinist, Philippe Graffin, whose Hyperion recordings of the Saint-Saëns *Violin Concertos* are such a success. Sadly, his virtuosity is not matched by the playing of the Johannesburg Philharmonic, which may be enthusiastic and is forwardly recorded, but which is rough in ensemble.

Fortunately, the newer Hyperion version has no such drawback, for the playing of the BBC Scottish Orchestra is polished, although perhaps it could do with greater fervour. It is good to hear such a fine, committed performance as this: Anthony Marwood is an accomplished advocate and a convincing exponent of this worthwhile score. Very good sound from the Andrew Keener–Simon Eadon team. It is well coupled with a first recording of the impressive *Violin Concerto* of Sir Arthur Somervell.

African Dances, Op. 58; Hiawatha Sketches, Op. 16; Petite suite de concert, Op. 77; Violin Sonata, Op. 28

(M) *** Dutton Epoch CDLX 7127. Juritz, Dussek

One of Stanford's favourite composition students, the young Coleridge-Taylor was encouraged by his mentor to write very traditionally. After the huge success of *Hiawatha* (from which, alas, he received no royalties), he took every opportunity to earn money from light music of the kind displayed here, suitable for the palm court and spa or pier orchestras. His most successful and characteristic piece was the *Petite suite de concert*, sprightly and with a flimsy charm. The other suites here are typical, groups of tuneful, deftly characterized vignettes. He had a genuine lyrical melodic gift, as is shown by the delightful *Andantino* from the *African Dances* and the central movement of the *Hiawatha Sketches*. This predated the famous choral work by a year, but had no thematic connection. The *Violin Sonata* was written immediately before his masterpiece, *Hiawatha's Wedding Feast*, and was taken up by Albert Sammons. As the very opening shows, it is permeated with attractive folksy themes: the first has a rhythmic snap that surely shows the influence of Dvořák, but it is a long work, its material is slight, the *Larghetto* has a flavour of the salon, and the *con fuoco* finale if dashing, is over-extended until the rather touching close. The performances here are excellent as is the recording, but are unable to persuade one that this amiable music is likely to survive in the concert hall.

Scenes from The Song of Hiawatha (complete); (i) Symphonic Variations on an African Air, Op. 63

(M) *** Decca 473 431-2 (2). Field, Davies, Terfel, Welsh Nat.
  Op. Ch. & O, Alwyn; (i) RLPO, Llewellyn

(i-iii) Hiawatha's Wedding Feast. (ii;iv) Petite Suite de Concert, Op. 77 (v) La Bamboula (Rhapsodic Dance)

☛ (N) (B) *** CfP 587 0242. (i) Richard Lewis & Royal
  Choral Soc. (ii) Philh. O; (iii) Sargent; (iv) Weldon; (v)
  Bournemouth SO, Alwyn

Hiawatha's *Wedding Feast*, the first part of Coleridge-Taylor's choral triology based on Longfellow's epic poem, is still regularly performed by choral societies in the north of England. The reasons for the neglect of parts two and three, The *Death of Minnehaha* and *Hiawatha's departure* are made only too clear by Alwyn's complete recording: there is a distinct falling off in the composer's inspiration, so attractively tuneful in *Part One*. Alwyn's performance is freshly spontaneous, with excellent soloists (including an early appearance on CD by Bryn Terfel as Hiawatha), though the Welsh Opera Choir do not seem at home in the idiom. For its reissue Decca have provided the *Symphonic Variations on an African Air*, a colourfully attractive work of some twenty minutes.

However this is upstaged by HMV's budget reissue of Sargent's splendid 1961 Abbey Road recording of just *Hiawatha's Wedding Feast*, with the Royal Choral Society. Everything about this is a success, including of course Richard Lewis's stylish performance of *Onaway! Awake, Beloved!*. We happen to know that Arthur Haddy, the Chief Recording Engineer of Decca, admired the recording in its LP format, and that is was an accolade indeed!. The CD transfer is not sharply focused, but the sound remains warmly atmospheric. The *Petite Suite de Concert* is the composer's best-known orchestral work a salon pastich of great charm. The seond movement, 'Demande et response' with its delicate string melody was a favourite in long-gone Palm Court days. George Weldon's polished Philharmonia performance is wholly sympathetic and not in the least sentimental, and it is given first class sound. *La Bamboula*, which the composer wrote for his third visit to the USA in 1910, is a 'series of evolutions' on a West Indian dance also used by Gottschalk, and it makes an attractive encore.

COLLINS, Antony (1893–1963)

Elegy in Memory of Edward Elgar

(N) (M) *** Dutton CDLX 7148. BBC Concert O, Lloyd Jones
  – ELGAR: *Piano Concerto, etc.* ***

Written during the Second World War while Collins, a composer as well as a conductor, was in California, this *Elegy* has a nostalgic flavour, based on a motif from the sketches for the slow movement of Elgar's *Symphony No. 3*. It makes a welcome rarity, together with the other pieces supplementing the première recording of the *Piano Concerto*. The outer sections are sombrely Elgarian, with a biting Sibelian climax in the middle. First-rate performance and sound. Collins wrote a great deal of music, including another, more light-hearted, morsel called *Vanity Fair* (part of his film score of that name). We need to explore his output further.

CONUS (KONIUS, or KONYUS), Julius (1869–1942)

Violin Concerto in E min.
*** DG (IMS) 471 428-2. Garrett, Russian Nat. O, Pletnev – TCHAIKOVSKY: *Violin Concerto* ***
**(*) Chan. 9622. L. Edwin Csüry, I Musici de Montréal, Turovsky – DAVIDOV: *Cello Concerto 2 in A min.;* GLAZUNOV: *Piano Concerto 2* **(*)

Here Conus's musical ideas are long marinaded in Tchaikovsky and Rachmaninov. The *Violin Concerto* (1898) is the only work of his to maintain a foothold on the repertory. Its tunes are pleasing at the time but no one would pretend that it is a masterpiece. Nevertheless, it has been recorded by Heifetz and Perlman no less. David Garrett is the young virtuoso whose account of the Paganini *Caprices* (with accompaniments by Schumann) excited much attention when it appeared some time ago, and this seventeen-year-old soloist plays it with great conviction and sweetness of tone, and he is splendidly partnered by Pletnev and the Russian National Orchestra. Perlman (and Heifetz) remain peerless in this kind of repertoire, but Garrett is impressive too and well worth hearing.

Csüry is a most musical player and he plays this *Concerto* very sympathetically, even if he is no match for Perlman. Turovsky's Montreal band give him admirable support.

COOKE, Arnold (born 1906)

Clarinet Concerto
(BB) *** Hyp. Helios CDH 55069. King, Northwest CO of Seattle, Francis – JACOB: *Mini-Concerto*; RAWSTHORNE: *Concerto* ***

Arnold Cooke's music contains an element of Hindemithian formalism, carefully crafted, but the slow movement of this *Concerto* soars well beyond. Thea King makes a passionate advocate, brilliantly accompanied by the Seattle orchestra in excellent (1982) analogue sound, faithfully transferred. This triptych is the more attractive at bargain price.

Clarinet Quintet
(BB) *** Hyp. Helios CDH 55105. King, Britten Qt – HOLBROOKE: *Eilean Shona;* HOWELLS: *Rhapsodic Quintet;* FRANKEL; MACONCHY: *Clarinet Quintets* ***

How could we have come to miss a collection as rewarding and generous as this, recorded in 1990 and centring on the outstanding clarinet playing of Thea King in partnership with the Britten Quartet? No matter. Here it is reissued at budget price and not to be missed.

Like his *Clarinet Concerto*, Arnold Cooke's *Quintet* has a slightly sinewy lyrical flow in the manner of Hindemith, but, though the composer does not always seek to 'charm', Thea King's playing is so seductive in the *Andante* that the listener is aurally cajoled. The first movement is characteristically unpredictable in line and flow, but the performance here finds its slightly wan melodic appeal and the perky finale is most winning. Excellent recording.

COPLAND, Aaron (1900–90)

Appalachian Spring (complete recording of full score); *Billy the Kid* (ballet suite); *Rodeo: 4 Dance Episodes*
🔁 ✹ (M) *** RCA 82876 65840-2. San Francisco SO, Tilson Thomas

It was Eugene Ormandy who in 1954 persuaded Copland to score the complete *Appalachian Spring* – hitherto available only in its original chamber version – for full orchestra. It is still not in print, existing only in manuscript, but Michael Tilson Thomas's superb recording confirms Ormandy's view that the work would expand magnificently. In the ballet the variations on *Simple Gifts* which form the climax are presented in, and interrupted by, an additional episode in which a revivalist appears and warns the central couple in the story of what Copland called 'the strange and terrible aspects of human fate'.

The complete ballet here runs to 36 minutes, and in this magnificently played and very moving performance is revealed as a twentieth-century masterpiece to rank alongside the three key Stravinsky ballets, including *The Rite of Spring*. The opening is wonderfully serene, and Tilson Thomas finds infinite detail and colour throughout, while creating a richly evocative tapestry of great beauty, helped by a recording of extraordinary breadth. The performances of the two cowboy ballets are similarly imaginative and compelling, giving the impression of coming to the music for the first time. This is not to be missed, even if you already have other versions of this vivid music.

Appalachian Spring (ballet suite: original chamber version); *Billy the Kid* (ballet suite); *Fanfare for the Common Man; Music for the Theatre*
(M) **(*) Classic fm 75605 570362. Eos O, Sheffer

The Eos *Appalachian Spring* is more striking for its rhythmic zest and vivid woodwind detail than for the richer sweep of string-tone which comes with a full orchestral version like Tilson Thomas above. The same approach gives the sharpest focus to the popular rhythmic elements of *Music for the Theatre* and the *Billy the Kid* ballet suite, where the gentle nostalgia of *Prairie Night* and *Billy's Death* are caught more by the small string-group. The *Celebration Dance* is very wittily pointed, while the final view of *The Open Prairie* certainly does not lack evocative power; but again some might prefer a more lavish patina of orchestral tone.

'Celebration' Vol. 1: (i) *Appalachian Spring* (ballet: complete original chamber version; with rehearsal sequence); (ii) *Billy the Kid* (ballet): Suite. *Danzón Cubano; Down a Country Lane;* (iii) *El salón México;* (ii) *Fanfare for the Common Man; Quiet City; Rodeo* (4 dance episodes). (iv) *Nonet for Strings*
(M) *** Sony (ADD) SM2K 89323 (2). (i) Columbia Chamber Ens.; (ii) LSO; (iii) New Philh. O; (iv) Columbia String Ens.; all cond. composer

This is the first of two mid-priced Doubles celebrating the centenary of Copland's birth. The *Nonet for Strings* (recorded in 1962), which has not appeared on CD before, is a powerful triptych with two 'Slow and solemn' sections framing a rhythmic centrepiece. The recording is good if a bit close. The other novelty, *Down a Country Lane*, began life as film music. The original version of *Appalachian Spring* brings an alert, refreshing account, although only 13 instruments are used. A rehearsal sequence is included, with the composer's directions to his players as pertinent as they are clear.

Appalachian Spring (ballet) Suite

(M) *** DG 476 7233-2. LAPO, Bernstein – BARBER: *Adagio for Strings* ***; GERSHWIN: *Rhapsody in Blue* **(*)

Bernstein's DG version of *Appalachian Spring* was recorded at a live performance, and the conductor communicates his love for the score in a strong yet richly lyrical reading and the compulsion of the music-making is obvious. The recording is close but not lacking in atmosphere, and it sounds extremely vivid, reissued in DG's Critics' Choice series.

(i) *Appalachian Spring; Billy the Kid* (complete ballet); (ii) *Dance Symphony;* (iii) *Danzón Cubano; El salón México;* (ii) *Fanfare for the Common Man; The Red Pony* (suite); (i) *Rodeo* (complete ballet)

(B) *** EMI Double forte 5 73653-2 (2). (i) St Louis SO, Slatkin; (ii) Mexico City PO, Bátiz; (iii) Dallas SO, Mata

Slatkin's was the first complete recording of *Billy the Kid*. The complete ballet *Rodeo* consists essentially of the usual four colourful movements, though here a piano interlude is included. Both are given terrific performances under Slatkin, and the sound is superb. Bátiz's orchestra doesn't have the technical excellence of Slatkin's, but he is a lively and persuasive interpreter of Copland. The *Dance Symphony* is well done, though the ensemble is not as precise as it could be. *The Red Pony* suite – a colourful and nostalgic score for Lewis Milestone's film – is among the most endearing lighter scores Copland wrote and is very enjoyable. Mata's Dallas performance of *Danzón Cubano* and *El salón México* are as good as any – brilliant performances in demonstration sound. In every sense this set is a splendid bargain.

(i) *Appalachian Spring* (ballet) *Suite; Billy the Kid: Suite;* (ii) *Clarinet Concerto;* (i) *Danzón Cubano; Fanfare for the Common Man; John Henry; Letter from Home;* (i; iv) *Lincoln Portrait;* (iii) *Music for Movies;* (i) *Our Town; An Outdoor Overture; Quiet City; Rodeo (4 Dance Episodes);* (iii) *El salón México;* (i) *Symphony 3;* (v) *Las agachadas*

(M) *** Sony (ADD) SM3K 46559 (3). (i) LSO; (ii) Goodman, Columbia Symphony Strings; (iii) New Philh. O; (iv) with H. Fonda; (v) New England Conservatory Ch.; composer

Sony here offer a comprehensive anthology of the major orchestral works, ballet suites and film scores dating from Copland's vintage period, 1936–48. The composer directs with unrivalled insight throughout. The remastering for CD is done most skilfully, retaining the ambience of the originals, while achieving more refined detail.

Appalachian Spring (ballet) Suite; Billy the Kid: Suite; Fanfare for the Common Man; Rodeo (4 Dance Episodes)

(B) **(*) Naxos 8.550282. Slovak RSO (Bratislava), Gunzenhauser

(i) *Appalachian Spring* (ballet) *Suite;* (ii) *Billy the Kid* (suite); *Rodeo (4 Dance Episodes)*

(B) *** RCA Navigator (ADD) 74321 21297-2. (i) Boston SO, composer; (ii) Morton Gould and his O

(N) **(*) Telarc SACD 60648. Atlanta SO, Lane – HINDEMITH: *Symphonic Metamorphoses on Themes of Weber* **(*)

(N) (M) **(*) Telarc CD 80078. Atlanta SO, Lane

The Bratislava orchestra play with such spontaneous enjoyment in *Rodeo* and *Billy the Kid* that one cannot help but respond. Gunzenhauser, a fine conductor of Czech music, is equally at home in Copland's folksy, cowboy idiom and all this music has plenty of colour and atmosphere. If some of the detail in *Appalachian Spring* is less sharply etched than with Bernstein, the closing pages are tenderly responsive. The recording is admirably colourful and vivid, with a fine hall ambience, and the spectacle of the *Fanfare for the Common Man* is worth anybody's money. A bargain.

Copland's first recording of *Appalachian Spring*, recorded in Boston in 1959, has an appealing breadth and warmth of humanity, helped by the Symphony Hall resonance: the Shaker climax is wonderfully expansive. Morton Gould conducts the other two ballets with enormous zest and vitality, and 'his' orchestra play as if their very lives depended on it. The early (1957) stereo is a little dated but remains arrestingly spectacular, and the quieter, more evocative writing is haunting, distilling a special combination of tender warmth and underlying tension. The *Corral Nocturne* and wistful *Saturday Night Waltz* in *Rodeo* are especially fine, and here Gould also includes the *Honky-Tonky Interlude* on an appropriate piano. The closing *Hoe-Down* is refreshingly folksy and has great rhythmic energy.

In its day (1982) Louis Lane's performances on Telarc were given recording of demonstration quality, naturally balanced, although the bass drum and tam-tam at the opening of the *Fanfare* are forwardly placed to enhance the feeling of spectacle. Lane's account of *Appalachian Spring*, without missing the score's lyrical qualities, has an attractive feeling of the ballet theatre about it. *Rodeo* is not as bitingly dramatic as with Bernstein, but it is folksy and enjoyable. The recording is very slightly enhanced on the SACD, and this includes the – not particularly appropriate – Hindemith coupling. The CD version, with little loss of fidelity, is at mid-price. But both are upstaged by the Tilson Thomas RCA collection.

(i) *Appalachian Spring* (ballet) *Suite;* (ii) *Ceremonial Fanfare;* (iii) *Dance Symphony; El salón México;* (i) *Fanfare for the Common Man;* (i; iv) *Lincoln Portrait;* (v) *Music for Movies;* (vi) *Quiet City;* (iii) *Rodeo: 4 Dance Episodes;* (vii) *Old American Songs* (excerpts): *Simple gifts; Ching-a-ring-chaw; Long time ago; I bought me a cat; At the river*

(B) *** Double Decca ADD/DDD 448 261-2 (2). (i) LAPO, Mehta; (ii) Philip Jones Brass Ens.; (iii) Detroit SO, Dorati; (iv) Peck; (v) L. Sinf., Howarth; (vi) ASMF, Marriner; (vii) Horne, ECO, C. Davis

Mehta's performance of *Appalachian Spring* is one of the most distinguished of several fine recordings he made for Decca in the late 1970s, which also included the spectacular *Fanfare for the Common Man* and the *Lincoln Portrait*, with Gregory Peck a comparatively laid-back narrator who speaks Lincoln's prose with dignity and restraint. Dorati's performances of the *Dance Symphony*, *El salón México* and *Rodeo* were digitally recorded in 1981. They are notable for their bright, extrovert brilliance, having evidently been chosen for their immediate, cheerful qualities, and the only reservation is that, somewhat surprisingly, Dorati's treatment of jazzy syncopations is rather literal. But as sound this is very impressive, and the performances have much vitality. The evocative opening picture of the *New England Countryside* occupies the same musical world as *Appalachian Spring*. Again, fine playing from the London Sinfonietta under Elgar

Howarth, and vivid recording. Marriner's account of *Quiet City* is second to none, but the highlight of the second CD is Marilyn Horne's delightful performances of five *Old American Songs*. Excellent value.

Appalachian Spring (ballet): Suite; (i) *Clarinet Concerto. 3 Latin-American Sketches; Quiet City*

(BB) **(*) Naxos 8.559069. Nashville CO, Gambill, with (i) Arden

This useful Naxos collection at budget price of key works by Aaron Copland gets off to a promising start with the three jolly *Latin-American Sketches*, bright and alert with a refined string section of chamber size. The *Clarinet Concerto*, originally written for Benny Goodman, brings in the first movement tender pianissimo playing from the soloist, Laura Arden, principal of the Atlanta Symphony Orchestra. That leads via a freely spontaneous account of the central cadenza to a clean, sharp reading of the jazzy finale. The orchestral suite from the ballet, *Appalachian Spring*, with chamber forces including limited strings set in a warm yet intimate acoustic, effectively reflects the fact that the original ballet, substantially longer, involved solo strings. The evocative tone-poem, *Quiet City*, with a deeply expressive cor anglais solo from Paula Engerer, next to the fruity trumpet of Scott Moore, may lack something in concentration, but it makes a welcome supplement. Annoyingly, there are no separating tracks between the different sections of either the Concerto or the Ballet Suite.

Appalachian Spring (ballet) *Suite*; (i) *Piano Concerto. Symphonic Ode*

**(*) Delos DE 3154. (i) Hollander; Seattle SO, Schwarz

The glowing acoustics of the Seattle Opera House smooth some of the abrasiveness away from Lorin Hollander's impressive account of Copland's *Piano Concerto* and also filter out some of the glitter from the jazzy piano-writing. Similarly, *Appalachian Spring* loses some of the bite in the dance rhythms, although the glowing woodwind detail and the richly expansive closing variations on *A Gift to be Simple* are more than compensation. The exultantly monumental close of the pungently flamboyant *Symphonic Ode* is given similar weight and breadth. The Seattle orchestra plays splendidly throughout and Schwarz is a master of all this repertoire.

'The World of Copland': (i) *Appalachian Spring* (ballet): Suite ; (ii) *Danzón Cubano*; (iii) *Fanfare for the Common Man*; (iii; iv) *Lincoln Portrait*; (v) *Quiet City*; (vi) *El salón México* (trans. for piano by L. Bernstein); (vii) *5 Songs from 'Old American Songs'* (excerpts)

(N) (B) *** Decca ADD/DDD 473 146. (i) Detroit SO, Dorati; (ii) Baltimore SO, Zinman; (iii) LAPO, Mehta; (iv) Peck; (v) ASMF, Marriner; (vi) Jablonski; (vii) Horne, ECO, C. Davis

An excellent single-disc anthology, making a fine introduction to Copland's music. Mehta's vivid *Fanfare for the Common Man* gets the collection off to an arresting start; the same conductor is on good form, too, for the *Lincoln Portrait*, with Gregory Peck as the relatively laid-back narrator. Dorati has the full measure of Copland's masterly *Appalachian Spring* suite, creating a haunting evocation at the opening and a feeling of serene acceptance at the close, while the witty portrayal of *The Revivalist and his Flock* is characterized with sparklingly precise rhythms and splendid string and woodwind detail. The sound is arresting in its range and vividness

and confirms the excellence of the acoustic of Detroit's Old Orchestral Hall. Zinman is not quite so impressive in the *Danzón Cubano*, which generates a lower voltage, but it is very well played and recorded. The piano version of *El salón México* is unexpected but enjoyable (it was Copland who suggested to Bernstein that the transcription be made). *Quiet City* is very beautifully played by Marriner's Academy with outstanding cor anglais and trumpet soloists, and Marilyn Horne's performances of five *Old American Songs* are winningly idiomatic: the rhythmic sparkle of 'Ching-a-ring-chaw' and the charm of 'I bought me a cat' contrasting with the moving simplicity of the closing 'At the River'.

Billy the Kid (excerpts); *Down a Country Lane*; (i) *Old American Songs* (Sets 1–2); (ii) *8 Poems of Emily Dickinson*

(N) (BB) *** Warner Apex 2564 62089-2. St Paul Chamber O, Wolff, with (i) Hampson; (ii) Upshaw

Hugo Wolff and his fine St Paul Chamber Orchestra are completely at home here, and it is good to have the composer's own scoring of *Down a Country Lane* (originally a piano piece). It is a pity that only three excerpts were included from *Billy the Kid* (there is plenty of room for the whole ballet). However, the highlights are the two superbly sung song-cycles. In the *Old American Songs*, Thomas Hampson is in a special class, and he includes both sets. So is Dawn Upshaw's eloquent set of the *Emily Dickinson Poems*, now easily the finest version on record.

Billy the Kid (Ballet Suite); *Rodeo: 4 Dance Episodes*

(N) (BB) **(*) Resonance CDRSN 3042 Bournemouth SO – GERSHWIN: *Porgy and Bess Symphonic Picture* **(*)

When these Bournemouth performances on Resonance were first issued in 1993, the disc was chosen for BBC Radio 3's 'Building a Record Library'. We too have praised the performance of *Rodeo*, and certainly both the ballet scores are vividly alive and John Farrer moulds the romantic string-tunes very persuasively. The recording too is excellent. But finer versions have appeared since, and unless the Gershwin coupling is especially wanted, this is not a primary recommendation.

Clarinet Concerto

*** Chan. 8618. Hilton, SNO, Bamert – NIELSEN: *Concerto*; LUTOSLAWSKI: *Dance Preludes* ***

(i) *Clarinet Concerto. Music for the Theatre; Music for Movies*; (ii) *Quiet City*

**(*) Music Masters 7005-2. (i) Blount; O of St Luke's, Russell Davies; (ii) with Gekker, Taylor

Janet Hilton's performance is soft-grained and has a light touch, yet she finds plenty of sparkle for the finale and her rhythmic felicity is infectious. She is at her very finest, however, in the gloriously serene opening, where her tender, poetic line is ravishing.

William Blount is a rich-toned soloist, with spacious, long-drawn phrasing in the opening movement which some might find too languid, contrasting with the brilliant central cadenza and roisterously jazzy finale. The vibrant *Music for the Theatre* with its brash *Prologue* and *Dance* and ironic *Burlesque* nicely offsets the mellower New England evocations of *Music for Movies*, although here *Sunday Traffic* makes another lively contrast and the *Threshing Machines* are very busy too. *Quiet City* is beautifully evoked. This is a reissue of a 1988 CD, but the vivid projection and warmth of the sound suggest more modern provenance.

(i) *Clarinet Concerto*; (ii) *Rodeo: 4 Dance Episodes*; (iii; iv) *Piano Quartet*; (iii–v) *Sextet for Clarinet, Piano and String Quartet*

☮– (M) *** ASV Platinum PLT 8504. (i) Hosford, COE, Fischer; (ii) Bournemouth SO, Farrer; (iii) Vanbrugh Qt (iv) Roscoe; (v) Collins

A fine account of Copland's delightful *Clarinet Concerto* from Richard Hosford, who plays beautifully as well as with character. The *Sextet*, a tersely argued work with sharply etched colours, and the more challenging *Piano Quartet* receive fine, committed performances by the Vanbrugh Quartet (and the excellent soloists), who bring out plenty of detail and colour in these scores, be it in the vibrant contrasts of the *Sextet* or the haunting beauty of the first movement of the *Piano Quartet*. The recording is ideal, vivid and warm. The well-known *Rodeo* excerpts are brightly done, though the acoustic is a little dry.

(i; ii) *Piano Concerto*; (iii) *Dance Symphony*; (ii) *Music for the Theatre*; (iii) *2 Pieces for String Orchestra*; *Short Symphony (Symphony 2)*; *Statements*; *Symphonic Ode*; (iv; ii) *Symphony for Organ & Orchestra*

(M) *** Sony (ADD) SM2K 47232 (2). (i) Composer (piano); (ii) NYPO, Bernstein; (iii) LSO, composer; (iv) with E. Power Biggs

This second Sony Copland collection covers early orchestral and concertante music written between 1922 and 1935 and is, if anything, more valuable than the first box. The 1923 *Rondino*, the second of his *Two Pieces for String Orchestra*, is the earliest work here. The *Lento* is a totally memorable piece. The *Symphony for Organ and Orchestra* is a powerful and strikingly innovative work, dating from 1924. It is given an extremely idiomatic and responsive performance by E. Power Biggs, and Bernstein balances the overall sounds with great skill. The pungently flamboyant *Symphonic Ode*, commissioned by the Boston Symphony, helped the orchestra to celebrate its fiftieth anniversary. All these performances have a definitive authority combined with total spontaneity of response from the participants, which makes them compelling listening, and the recordings – dating from between 1964 and 1967 – are very well engineered, extremely vivid in the excellent CD transfers.

Piano Concerto

(M) **(*) Chan. 6580. Lin, Melbourne SO, John Hopkins – BRITTEN: *Piano Concerto* **(*)

Gillian Lin is undoubtedly successful in the Copland *Concerto*, bringing out the jazz element in this syncopated music. The 1978 stereo recording is well balanced and realistically transferred to CD.

Symphony 3; Quiet City

☮– *** DG 419 170-2. NYPO, Bernstein

With Bernstein conducting Copland's *Third Symphony*, you appreciate more than with rival interpreters that this is one of the great symphonic statements of American music. The electricity of the DG performance is irresistible. The recording is full-bodied and bright, but its brashness is apt for the performance. The hushed tranquillity of *Quiet City*, another of Copland's finest scores, is superbly caught by Bernstein in the valuable fill-up.

CHAMBER MUSIC

'Celebration' Vol. 2: (i; ii) *Duo for Flute & Piano*; (i; iii) *Piano Quartet*; (i; iii; iv) *Sextet for Clarinet, Piano & String Quartet*; (i; v) *Vitebsk (Study on a Jewish Theme for Piano Trio)*; (vi) *Billy the Kid* (excerpts, arr. for piano, Lukas Foss). (Vocal) (vii; i) *Old American Songs, Sets I-II* (viii; i) *12 Poems of Emily Dickinson*; (with (ix) *Lincoln Portrait*)

(M) **(*) Sony SM2K 89326 (ADD) stereo/mono (2). (i) composer; (ii) Shaffer; (iii) Juilliard Qt (members); (iv) Wright; (v) Carlyss, Adam; (vi) Levant; (viii) Lipton; (ix) Sandburg, NYPO, Kostelanetz

Copland wrote very little chamber music, obviously preferring to express himself on a fuller orchestral canvas. The early *Vitebsk* (1928) opens with a spiky two-note rhythmic violin figure, but the music's underlying lyricism soon comes to the fore. The performance has both intensity and impetus, but one could wish that the microphones were not so very close. The *Sextet* is the composer's 1936 arrangement of the *Short Symphony* of three years earlier, its concentration and terse argument the more sharply etched by the sparse instrumentation. The performance could not be more spontaneously committed and the close balance, if far from ideal, is not destructive.

In the masterly and challenging *Piano Quartet* (1950) Copland so thoroughly absorbed twelve-note technique into his own harmonic and rhythmic vocabulary that, from the haunting opening *Adagio serio* onwards, one could hardly guess this is a serial work. The *Duo for Flute & Piano* (1971) is very listener-friendly, melting and poetic on Elaine Shaffer's lips and, in the finale, witty and Gallically diverting; and Oscar Levant's performance of the piano arrangements of *The Open Prairie*, *Street in a Frontier Town* and *Celebration Day* from *Billy the Kid* are attractively fresh and idiomatic.

Martha Lipton's pioneering mono LP of the *Emily Dickinson Poems* has an appealing directness, feeling for the words. The voice is very well caught by the microphones. Similarly William Warfield sings the *Old American Songs* with great freshness, and his mono set with the composer is vividly projected. It was André Kostelanetz who commissioned the *Lincoln Portrait*, which explains the inclusion of his 1958 recording. He conducts it dramatically and committedly. Carl Sandburg was Lincoln's biographer and his narration is attractively unpontificating and warmly casual. The orchestral recording is brilliant but lacks a really rich amplitude.

PIANO MUSIC

Piano Fantasy

*** Mode 93. Laimon – IVES: *Piano Sonata 3* ***

Copland began writing his 32-minute *Fantasy* in 1951, intending it to be a piano concerto to be premièred by William Kapell. But the proposed soloist died and the original commission fell through, and by 1955 it had become a solo work, finally receiving its première in 1957. Here Sara Laimon certainly seems to be right inside this initially intractable work, following the composer's continually changing directives as written on the score with apparent spontaneity, right through to the reflective closing pages. She is very well recorded, so if you are musically adventurous you might try this example of Copland's music, which could not be further removed from *Billy the Kid*! (The disc can be obtained from Mode, PO Box 1262, New York 10009 or www.mode.com.)

Piano Fantasy; Passacaglia; Piano Sonata; Piano Variations
(N) (M) ✱✱✱ Divine Art 25016. Clarke

Piano Fantasy; Piano Sonata; Piano Variations
(N) (BB) ✱✱(✱) Naxos 8.559184. Pasternack

Raymond Clarke now provides what is the most satisfying single disc of Copland's piano music. He opens with the early *Passacaglia*, composed in (1921–2) while the composer was in Paris and dedicated to Nadia Boulanger. It is a self-consciously serious work, easy to follow, and in Clarke's hands attractively diverse. The 'craggy' *Piano Variations* of 1930 follow on naturally after it (even the keys are related). Clarke then proves completely at home in the *Sonata*. His opening is arresting and the first movement develops thoughtfully and naturally, the main theme quite haunting. The jazzy syncopations that arrive later are handled with aplomb; the Scherzo is played with sparkling bravura, so that the serene lyricism of the finale is the more moving. The *Fantasy* is handled with equal understanding, especially in its changes of mood and tempo, and altogether this collection leads the field. The recording is outstandingly vivid and realistic, with a full sonority in the bass. A most satisfying and rewarding collection.

It is easy to be put off by the first few notes of the *Piano Fantasy* on the Naxos disc, for Benjamin Pasternack opens very percussively, emphasized by the bright recording. But the performance soon finds its own level, although it is more impetuous and volatile, indeed faster than with Raymond Clarke (29 minutes overall, instead of 33). Copland described it as 'a spontaneous and unpremeditated sequence of events', and it certainly is that here. The *Sonata* too is strongly characterized, especially the jazz-inspired central movement, and the work closes meditatively. The *Variations* make an enjoyably diverse final item. The sound, once one adjusts to its vivid presence, is fully acceptable, and this disc should suit bargain-hunters.

Piano Sonata
(N) ✱✱✱ Hyp. CDA 67469. Hamelin – IVES: *Piano Sonata 2 (Concord)* ✱✱✱

Marc-André Hamelin, first-prize winner at the 1985 Carnegie Hall International America Music competition, was an ideal choice for this apt coupling of Copland and Ives (even if reputedly Copland did not admire Ives's piano writing). In Hamelin's hands Copland's complex first movement unravels spontaneously to demonstrate both uncompromising power and underlying lyricism, and the bravura fleetness of his jazzy articulation of the catchily syncopated Scherzo is matched by the thoughtful threnody of the halcyon close to the finale. He is superbly recorded.

Piano Sonata; 4 Piano Blues; Scherzo humoristique: The Cat and the Mouse
✱✱✱ Nim. NI 5585. Anderson – GERSHWIN: *3 Preludes; Arrangements of Songs; An American in Paris* ✱✱✱

Mark Anderson also gives an outstanding account of the *Piano Sonata*, making it seem emotionally warmer and texturally and harmonically less spare than usual. His reading will surely make new friends for the work; it is 'freely expressive' (as the first movement is marked by the composer) and with the restless rhythmic mood of the central *Vivace* spontaneously caught, with even a brief jazz inflexion. The closing *Andante sostenuto* is tapered down movingly and leaves the listener aware that this is a remarkably individual and original work. The *Four Piano Blues* are in Copland's easily

accessible style and are also very well characterized, while the witty portrait of *Le Chat et la souris* makes a brilliant encore for what is a live recital in Nimbus's own concert hall.

VOCAL MUSIC

(i) *In the Beginning. Help us, O Lord; Have mercy on us, O my Lord; Sing ye praises to our King*
✱✱✱ Hyp. CDA 66219. (i) Denley; Corydon Singers, Best – BARBER: *Agnus Dei;* BERNSTEIN: *Chichester Psalms* ✱✱✱

In the Beginning is a large-scale, 15-minute motet for unaccompanied chorus and soprano solo, written in 1947, and the long span of the work is well structured with the help of the soprano soloist, here the fresh-toned Catherine Denley. The chorus is just as clear and alert in its singing, not only in the big motet but also in the three delightful little pieces which come as an appendix. Vivid recording, full of presence.

(i) *In the Beginning. 5 Old American Songs; Motets: Have mercy on us; Help us, O Lord; Sing ye the Praises to our King; Thou, O Jehova*
(N) ✱✱✱ Gloriae Dei Cantores GDCD 029. (i) Bybee; Gloriae Dei Cantores, Patterson – VIRGIL THOMSON: *Hymns; Mass* etc. ✱✱✱

An outstanding account of *In the Beginning* with warmly expressive singing from this splendid choir, based in Cape Cod, Massachusetts. The mezzo, Luretta Bybee, is an eloquent, full-voiced soloist, though her vibrato is somewhat intrusive. Five favourite *American Songs* follow, with *Simple gifts*, *The Boatmen's Dance* and the infectiously rousing *Ching-a-Ring-Chaw* standing out. Then come four equally diverse miniature motets, ending with the joyful *Sing ye the praises*, which show the choir at their very finest. Excellent recording, and an even more imaginative Virgil Thomson programme as coupling, make this a very desirable issue indeed.

'Celebration' Vol. 3: **(i; ii)** *In the Beginning;* **(ii; iii)** *Lark;* **(iv)** *Old American Songs, Sets I–II;* **(v)** *12 Poems of Emily Dickinson;* **(vi)** *The Tender Land* (opera: abridged version)
(M) ✱✱(✱) Sony (ADD) SM2K 89329 (2). (i) Miller, (ii) New England Conservatory Ch., composer; (iii) with Hale; (iv) Warfield, Columbia SO, composer; (v) Addison, composer (piano); (vi) Clements, Turner, Treigle, Cassily, Fredericks, Choral Arts Soc., NYPO, composer

By the time he came to re-record the orchestral settings of the *Old American Songs* in 1962 William Warfield had made them completely his own and he sings them with great warmth and affection. Needless to say, Copland's direction of the orchestra is a delight from start to finish. In the settings of Emily Dickinson, he accompanies at the piano with even more relish than he did previously for Martha Lipton, and Adele Addison's creamy voice adds to the listener's pleasure and this performance is more seductive than the earlier version, if perhaps characterized less strongly.

The two choral works, *In the Beginning* more ambitious in scale than *Lark*, both have strong soloists, but in neither case is the singing of the New England Conservatory Chorus ideally vibrant and biting, although, with the composer directing, the performances are still compelling, and they are well enough recorded.

The abridged recording of *The Tender Land* is another matter, for Copland proves a first-class opera conductor. The excerpts are atmospherically and vividly recorded and there is no weak link in the cast. *The promise of living*, which closes Act I, is thrillingly sung.

Old American Songs: Sets 1 & 2 (original versions)
** Chan. 8960. White, McNaught (with collection: *American Spirituals; Folk-songs from Barbados and Jamaica* ***)

Characteristically Willard White's opulent bass comes with a pronounced vibrato which on disc tends to get exaggerated. Yet with its helpful acoustic the Chandos recording captures the richness of his voice most attractively, very characterfully black in its evocations.

(i; ii) Old American Songs (Sets I & II); 12 Poems of Emily Dickinson. (ii) 4 Piano Blues
*** Black Box BBM 1074. (i) Chilcott; (ii) Burnside

The tragically early death of the soprano Susan Chilcott has sadly robbed us of an outstanding singer, characterful and imaginative. When her voice, clear and fresh, was ideally suited to recording, it is doubly sad that she made far too few recordings. This superb collection of Copland songs, bringing together 25 of his most approachable pieces, plus the *Four Piano Blues*, comes from Iain Burnside's series, 'Voices', for BBC Radio 3, beautifully recorded as well as masterfully performed. Though the *Old American Songs* with their open-air, folk-based inspiration are more readily suited to a man's voice, Chilcott is strong and magnetic in each one, and she equally relishes the touching simplicity of the *Emily Dickinson Poems*, with Burnside the ideal accompanist, crisp and pointed in the songs as well as in his solo pieces.

CORELLI, Arcangelo (1653–1713)

Concerti grossi, Op. 6/1–12
☛ (B) *** Hyp. Dyad CDD 22011 (2). Brandenburg Consort, Goodman

(M) *** DG 474 907-2. E. Concert, Pinnock

(BB) *** Naxos 8.550402/3. Capella Istropolitana, Krechek

(BB) **(*) HM HCX 3957014/5. Philh. Bar. O, McGegan

(B) **(*) Double Decca (ADD) 443 862-2. ASMF, Marriner

Concerti grossi, Op. 6/1–6
*** HM Opus OP 30-147. Europa Galante, Biondi

Concerti grossi, Op. 6/7-12
*** HM Opus OP 30-155. Europa Galante, Biondi

Corelli's glorious set of *Concerti grossi*, Op. 6, is now very well represented in the catalogue in all price-ranges. For those who prefer period performances there is plenty of choice. Roy Goodman and the Brandenburg Consort use 17 string players plus harpsichord continuo, archlute and organ; however, there is a sense of style and a freshness of approach in the Goodman version that is very persuasive. The recorded sound is first class.

But the newest set, from the appropriately named Europa Galante, is as fine as any. The chamber-sized ripieno of period instruments (2,2,2,1,1) offers crisp detail yet no feeling of any lack of sonority, and the elegant playing is alert and vital yet smiles pleasingly: these musicians are obviously enjoying the music, and so do we. The soloists are excellent, as is the recording.

This DG performance of Corelli's masterly set of concertos won the Gramophone Early Music Baroque Award in 1989.

Pinnock and his English Concert bring not only an enthusiasm for this music but a sense of grandeur. They are entirely inside its sensibility, and the playing of the concertino group (Simon Standage, Micaela Comberti and Jaap ter Linden) is wonderfully fresh-eyed and alert, yet full of colour. This is most welcome in its new mid-price format.

For those preferring the richer textures of modern instruments, the Naxos set by the Capella Istropolitana under Jaroslav Krechek represents very good value indeed. The players are drawn from the Slovak Philharmonic and have great vitality and, when necessary, virtuosity to commend them. The digital recording is clean and well lit, but not over-bright, and makes their version strongly competitive.

McGegan's 1990 complete set makes a good recommendation for those wanting a super-bargain set of the concertos on period instruments. The performances, intimately small-scaled as they are, combine a spirited vivacity with expressive feeling, and although slow movements are moved on more briskly than with Pinnock (who still leads the authentic field) the balance of tempi is generally convincing. One might like rather more textural warmth, but the transparency is appealing and the continuo comes through as it should, and overall the balance is very good.

The reissued ASMF version uses a performing edition by Christopher Hogwood and has been prepared with evident thought and care. Yet compared to the issues mentioned above, there is at times a hint of blandness.

Oboe Concerto (arr. Barbirolli)
(B) *** Dutton Lab./Barbirolli Soc. CDSJB 1016. Rothwell, Hallé O, Barbirolli HAYDN; MARCELLO: *Oboe Concertos* *** (with Recital: C. P. E. BACH; LOEILLET; TELEMANN: *Sonatas*, etc. **

Barbirolli's *Concerto* is cunningly arranged from a *Trio Sonata* and in its present form it makes one of the most enchanting works in the oboe repertoire. The performance here is treasurable and the clear, natural recording projects the music admirably.

CHAMBER MUSIC

Sonate da chiesa, Op. 1/1–12; Op. 3/1–12; Sonate da camera (Trio Sonatas), Op. 2/1–12; Op. 4/1–12
*** Chan. 0692 (4). Purcell Qt

The admirable Purcell Quartet (joined by Catherine Weiss in Op. 4), with a continuo from Jakob Lindberg, theorbo and archlute, plus Robert Woolley (organ in Opp. 1 and 3 and harpsichord in Opp. 2 and 4) surveys all Corelli's Sonatas of Opp. 1–4. Their playing is vibrant and stylish, and expressive in slow movements, and in that respect, although allegros are admirably spirited, makes somewhat less of the lighter character of the *Sonate da chiesa*, than Medlam and the London Baroque, although the difference is hardly consequential. The Chandos recording is first rate, and this complete set is highly recommendable. But the Harmonia Mundi versions (described in more detail below) are much less expensive and have their own very considerable merits.

Sonate da chiesa, Op. 1/1–12; Op. 3/1–12
(B) *** HM HMA 1951344/5. L. Bar., Medlam

Corelli's two dozen *Church Sonatas* Op. 1 (1681) and Op. 3 (1689) are different from the chamber sonatas in that the continuo is for organ (most winningly presented here), while the structure opens with a slow *Grave* or *Largo*, followed by three more movements, usually (but not invariably) fast-slow-fast. The sparkling final sonata of Op. 12, after the opening *Grave*, has four fast movements in a row. Throughout these works each movement is brief, but the contrapuntal writing is ever felicitous and the music brims over with appealing invention. These period performances from Charles Medlam and his excellent London Baroque group could not be fresher or more appealing, and they are beautifully recorded.

Sonate da camera (Trio Sonatas), Op. 2/1–12; Op. 4/1–12
(B) *** HM HMA 1901342/3. L. Bar., Medlam

Corelli was incapable of writing trivially, and of the earlier *Chamber Sonatas* of Op. 2, the *Second* and *Sixth* both have extended slow opening *Allemandes* while the remarkable *No. 4 in E minor* has a very touching central *Adagio* in addition to its solemn opening *Prelude*. The final work of Op. 2 is a single-movement *Ciacona* which deserves to be better known. London Baroque under Charles Medlam catch the varying moods of these rewarding works to perfection, and they are beautifully recorded.

Trio Sonatas, Op. 1/9; Op. 2/4 & 12 (Ciacona); Op. 3/12; Op. 4/3; Op. 5/3, 11 & 12 (La Folia)
*** Hyp. CDA 66226. Purcell Qt

The Hyperion disc is one of six designed to illustrate the widespread use in the eighteenth century of the famous *La Folia* theme. It includes a varied collection of *sonate da chiesa* and *sonate da camera*. Excellent performances from all concerned, and recording to match.

Violin Sonatas, Op. 5/1–12
✿ *** HM HMU 907 298.99 (2). Manze, Egarr
(B) *** Virgin 2 × 1 5 62236-2 (2). Huggett, Meyerson (harpsichord or organ), Cunningham, North

Corelli's twelve *Violin Sonatas*, Op. 5, were published in 1700. Nos. 1–5 are in five-movement *sonata la chiesa* form, Nos. 7–11 are *sonate da camera*, usually in four movements, although Nos. 10 and 11 each includes a brief additional section. Corelli's invention is inexhaustible and the set closes with perhaps the most celebrated set of variations on the traditional *La Follia* theme. Andrew Manze is in his element here. Dazzling playing on a baroque instrument, with slow movements touchingly lyrical, full of subtle detail, and plenty of gusto and character in allegros, yet with unwanted acerbities banished. Richard Egarr is a true partner, and there are countless felicities. The balance is natural, with the violin obviously dominating, yet the harpsichord comes through.

Corelli's writing is basically for two instruments, but Hugget and Meyerson incorporate a variety of continuo group combinations, adding colour with the use of organ as well as harpsichord, cello, archlute, theorbo and guitar. The performances here are as authentic as they are imaginative and stylish, and the recording balance is admirable.

12 Violin Sonatas, Op. 5; Sonata in A, Op. 5/9 (elaborated Geminiani)
*** Hyp. CDA 66381/2. Locatelli Trio

Corelli's *Violin Sonatas*, Opus 5, were enormously popular and influential in their day and were even used by his contempories as vehicles for improvised or written elaboration and ornamentation. The Hyperion set includes Geminiani's elaborated version of No. 9, using a manuscript in the latter's own handwriting. Needless to say, the originals stand up perfectly well without such accretions. They are in essence suites of usually five (sometimes four) movements and the later works incorporate dance forms – *Corrente, Sarabanda, Giga*, etc. No. 12 is a set of variations on the famous *La Folia*. These period performances by the Locatelli Trio are eminently alive and stylish. *Allegros* sparkle, decoration seems entirely apt and *Adagios* have a sympathetic expressive line, and there is imaginative use of dynamic contrast. The recording balance cannot be faulted.

6 Violin Sonatas, Op. 5
(N) (BB) **(*) Naxos 8.557165. Van Dael, Van Asperen (organ or harpsichord)

The period performances on Naxos are of quality, choosing to omit the cello of the basso continuo. Lucy van Dael is a fine violinist and Bob van Asperen's keyboard credentials are impeccable. The snag lies in the balance. He plays the first three sonatas on an organ which looms too large in the sound picture in relation to the violin, and Nos. 4–6 on an apparently small harpsichord which is backwardly balanced and is rather dwarfed by its partner.

Trio Sonatas, Op. 5/1, 3, 6, 11 & 12 (La Folia)
*** Accent ACC 48433D. S. & W. Kuijken, Kohnen

When authenticity of spirit goes hand in hand with fine musical feeling and accomplishment, the results can be impressive, as they undoubtedly are here, drawing one into the sensibility of the period. This is a thoroughly recommendable selection which deserves to reach a wider audience than early-music specialists; the recording is natural and the musicianship refined and totally at the service of Corelli.

CORIGLIANO, John (born 1938)

Symphony 2; (i) The Red Violin: Suite from the film
(N) *** Chan. **SACD** CHSA 5035. I Musici de Montréal, Yuli Turovsky, (i) with Eleonora Turovsky & Ch.

Symphony 2 for String Orchestra; The Mannheim Rocket
*** ODE 1039-2. Helsinki PO, Storgårds

John Corigliano's *Second Symphony*, commisioned by the Boston Symphony Orchestra, draws on his 1996 *String Quartet*, but the adaptation involved rewriting three of the five movements. The opening *Prelude* combines synchronous threads of sound which oscillate hauntingly, leading to a climax and a serene chordal apotheosis. The Scherzo is slashingly aggressive, but the middle section is gentle, bearing a lyrical passacaglia. The *Nocturne* opens ethereally and creates a richly sustained string tapestry to picture a serene Moroccan night, interrupted by a pattern of muezzin calls from the city's many mosques. Then comes a complex *Fugue*, which the composer describes as 'anti-contrapuntal'. He uses a single theme in separate voices moving at different tempi; the work closes with a *Postlude* in valedictory mood, with a high solo violin 'meant to impact a feeling of farewell'. The synchronous sound threads of the *Prelude* return, and the symphony ends as it began, fading into silence. It is a remarkably imaginative piece, not nearly as difficult to follow as it sounds.

The Mannheim Rocket is a phantasmagorical orchestral picture of Baron von Munchausen's Wedding Cake Rocket taking off, but it is also a pun on a musical term made famous by the Mannheim orchestra in the eighteenth century to describe a rising musical sequence that speeded up and grew louder as it went higher. Corigliano quotes the stately opening of a Stamitz *Sinfonia* to lift his rocket clear, but in the end it crashes to the ground, and the piece returns to its Mannheim device for its coda. The performances here are first class and so is the spectacular recording. This is all real music and well worth trying.

The alternative Chandos version is also very well played and recorded under the composer's supervision. Those with SACD facilities will find the sound very impressive indeed. The suite drawn from the composer's music for the François Giraud film, *The Red Violin*, is in 11 brief sections, in effect a violin concerto, with the solo violin emerging ever more prominently in writing both brilliant and lyrical, with a gypsy cadenza towards the end. The *Suite* is rounded off with a beautiful development of the main theme, representing the heroine Anna, not just on the violin and the orchestra but briefly with a wordless chorus (unidentified on the disc). Whether you choose this coupling or *The Mannheim Rocket* of Ode, the symphony itself is well worth having.

CORNYSH, William (c. 1468–1523)

Adieu, adieu my heartes lust; Adieu, courage; Ah Robin; Ave Maria, mater Dei; Gaude, virgo, mater Christi; Magnificat; Salve regina; Stabat Mater; Woefully arrayed

☛ ✿ *** Gimell CDGIM 014. Tallis Scholars, Phillips

Cornysh's music is quite unlike much other polyphony of the time and is florid, wild, complex and, at times, grave. The Tallis Scholars give a magnificent, totally committed account of these glorious pieces – as usual their attack, ensemble and true intonation and blend are remarkable. Excellent recording.

Ave Maria, mater Dei; Gaude, virgo, mater Christi (motets); *Magnificat; Salve regina*

*** Gaudeamus CDGAU 164. Cardinall's Musick, Carwood – TURGES: *Magnificat;* PRENTES: *Magnificat* ***

In his survey of early Tudor polyphony, Andrew Carwood, with his keenly responsive group, Cardinall's Musick, here presents all four of Cornysh's surviving liturgical works, including a fine *Magnificat* and a radiant *Salve regina*, alongside even more elaborate *Magnificats* by two composers far less well-known but just as inspired. Complex and beautiful, the *Magnificat* of Turges is the most expansive of all, while Prentes's *Magnificat*, closely following Cornysh's, even outshines that model in both scale and sublimity.

CORRETTE, Michel (1709–95)

6 Organ Concertos, Op. 26

(B) *** HM (ADD) HMA 195 5148. Saorgin (organ of L'Eglise de l'Escarène, Nice), Bar. Ens., Bezzina

These lively and amiable *Concertos* are here given admirably spirited and buoyant performances, splendidly recorded using period instruments. The orchestral detail is well observed, and René Saorgin plays vividly on an attractive organ. Michel Corrette's invention has genuine spontaneity, and this makes an enjoyable collection to dip into, though not to play all at one go.

Sonatas: for Bassoon & Continuo: in F & G (Les Délices de la solitude), Op. 20/1 & 5; for Flute & Continuo: in E min.; D

min., Op. 13/2 & 4; for Harpsichord & Flute in E min., Op. 15/4; for Oboe & Continuo in D min. (L'Ecole d'Orphée). Suite for Recorder & Continuo in C min. (from Les Pièces, Op. 5). (Harpsichord): Les Amusements du Parnasse: La Furstemberg & Variations; Le Sabotier hollandois & Variations; Premier livre de pièces de clavecin: Suite in D (complete); Suite 3 (Les Etoiles): Rondeau, Op. 12 (both from Op. 12)

*** Mer. CDE 84325. Carroll, Rowland, Civil

The rather agreeable *Oboe Sonata* comes from *L'Ecole d'Orphée*, a violin tutor, and the Op. 5 *Pièces*, from which the *Suite for Recorder and Continuo* is taken, were primarily designated for the musette (an aristocratic set of bagpipes). However, the composer suggested a whole range of alternatives. The versatile and expert Paul Carroll has mastered all the baroque instruments featured in these works and plays each of them with spirit and character. But it is perhaps his harpsichord music for which Corrette is best remembered – and justly so. The *D major Suite* is strikingly inventive. David Rowland plays them on excellent modern copies of two different period instruments, and he is beautifully recorded. The instrumental works, too, are naturally balanced. An entertaining 73 minutes – but not necessarily to be taken all at once.

Laudate Dominum (Psalm 148)

(N) (BB) *** Warner Apex (ADD) 2564 60155-2. Alliot-Lugaz, Oudot, Lyon Vocal & Instrumental Ens., Cornut – MONDONVILLE: *Dominus Regnavit* etc. **(*)

We have a little gem here: Corrette's *Laudate Dominum*, based on the *Spring* movement of Vivaldi's *Four Seasons*, is an indication of how popular the *Four Seasons* remained in the years after his death, before it disappeared into obscurity. Corrette's work dates from 1768, and Vivaldi's music is treated to some especially felicitous writing (the *Adagio* is hauntingly beautiful). As the sleeve-note writer says, the work is full of Italianate freshness, with plenty of virtuosic passages for flute, violins and voice. It is quite captivating and for most collectors will be a real find. Excellent performance and good (1975) sound.

COUPERIN, Armand-Louis (1725–1789)

Pièces de clavecin excerpts: L'Affligée; Allemande; L'Arlequine ou la Adam; La Blanchet; La de Boisgelou; La du Breüil; La Chéron; Courante la de Croissy; L'Enjouée; La Foucquet; Gavottes 1 & 2; La Grégoire; L'Intrépide; Menuets 1 & 2; La Seimillante ou la Joly; Les Tendres Sentimens; La Turpin; La Victoire

(BB) **(*) CPO 999 312-2. Hoeren (harpsichord)

Armand-Louis Couperin was distantly related to both François and Louis. His *Pièces de clavecin* were published in 1751 in two books, and here we are offered a good selection of 19 pieces. Some, such as the *Allemande* and *La Grégoire*, show a debt to Rameau but others, such as *L'Affligée* and *La Chéron*, are more forward-looking. Harald Hoeren, a pupil of Kenneth Gilbert and Gustav Leonhardt, plays an instrument by Klaus Ahrend based on Flemish models of the 1750s. He is a persuasive artist, though he is not helped by the rather close recording-balance. Satisfactory results can be obtained by a low-level setting of the volume control.

Pièces de clavecin: L'Affligée; La du Breüil; Les Tendres Sentimens

**(*) BIS CD 982. Hirosawa (harpsichord) – François COUPERIN; Louis COUPERIN: *Pièces de clavecin* **(*)

Another thunderous harpsichord so closely balanced that immediate action is called for to reduce the level setting. No quarrels however with Asami Hirosawa's playing, which has great expressive feeling. Her account of *L'Affligée* has greater poignancy than Harald Hoeren's, and if the volume is turned down a satisfactory result can be secured.

COUPERIN, François (1668–1733)

Les Apothéoses: L'Apothéose composé à la mémoire immortelle de l'incomparable M. de Lully; La Parnasse ou l'Apothéose de Corelli

(M) *** Astrée ES 9947. Hespèrion XX, Savall

Couperin's two great linked instrumental works, both called *Apothéoses*, between them ardently espouse the virtues of the conflicting French and Italian influences on early eighteenth-century music. The composers Lully and Corelli are thus united in the Elysian fields, with the French and Italian muses playing each other's music. It is a delightful concept. Each work has a sequence of stylized classical vignettes. *L'Apothéose de Lully* is programmatic and evokes Apollo and Mercury; *L'Apothéose de Corelli* is an eloquent Trio sonata, but also with titled movements, grave, expressive and lively by turns. The performances by Savall and Hespèrion XX have splendid life, grace and refinement of feeling. The gossamer delicacy of *Plainte des mêmes* in the former is matched by the exquisite playing in the fourth section, *Corelli ... s'endorf ...* in the latter. Each movement is introduced briefly in French by Bernard Hervé (who never outstays his welcome), and the documentation includes translations. This rewarding music could hardly be more attractively presented, and the recording is excellent.

Concerts royaux 1 in G; 2 in D; 3 in A; 4 in E min.

☛ *** Alia Vox **Multi-channel SACD** AVSA 9840. Le Concert des Nations, Savall

*** ASV CDGAU 101. Trio Sonnerie

The *Concerts royaux* can be performed in a variety of forms. On the ASV Gaudeamus disc, the Trio Sonnerie give them in the most economical fashion (violin, viola da gamba and harpsichord) and the contribution of all three musicians is unfailingly imaginative. Excellent recording.

However, the Trio Sonnerie are upstaged by Jordi Savall (bass viol and director) whose period-instrument ensemble, Les Concert des Nations, includes flute, oboe, violin, bassoon and continuo. They play this music delightfully, with warmth and spirit, and the recording has an ideal ambience and fine presence. On four-channel SACD, the illusion of sitting in the concert hall is very real.

Les Goûts Réunis: Le DoDo ou l'amour au berceau; Sonades: La Sultanne; La Superbe. Suites for Viola da Gamba & Harpsichord: 1 in E min.; 2 in A

(N) (M) *** DHM/BMG 05472 93545-2. Bernfeld, Capriccio Stravagante, Sempé

The manuscripts for Couperin's *Pièces de violes* were published in 1728, then were lost for two centuries, being rediscovered in 1919. The *Sonades* include violins (here performed on two superb period instruments from the Metropolitan Museum of Modern Art in New York); they are written in the contemporary Corellian *sonata da chiesa* form, with alternation of brief quick and slow movements, but using French language terms to describe each. The *First Suite for Viola da Gamba* is more ambitious, including the expected layout of Prélude, Allemande, Courante, Sarabande and so on, finishing with a spirited Passacaille; the *Second* is in four movements, with the noble and dignified third named 'Pompe funèbre', perhaps in memory of Marais, who had died the year the *Pièces* were published. *Le Dodo* or 'the sleep or love in the cradle' is curious little gamba novelty whose evocation is obscure. The performances are authentic and full of life – but be warned, the viola da gamba has a much more raspy personality than the cello, and the violin timbre here is also abrasive. The recording is excellent, but the notes are sparse.

KEYBOARD MUSIC

Harpsichord Suites, Book 1: Ordre 1; Concerts royaux 1-2

(BB) *** Naxos 8.550961. Cummings (harpsichord)

Harpsichord Suites, Book 2: Ordres 6 & 8; Book 3: Ordre 18

☛ *** Hyp. CDA 67440. Hewitt (piano)

Harpsichord Suites, Book 3: Ordre 13

**(*) BIS CD 982. Hirosawa (harpsichord) – Armand-Louis COUPERIN; Louis COUPERIN: *Pièces de clavecin* **(*)

Laurence Cummings plays a modern instrument by Michael Johnson modelled on a Taskin, and he produces pleasing and musical results. Both artistically and in terms of recorded sound, this is a valuable addition to the catalogue.

Asami Hirosawa couples the marvellous *Treizième ordre* with two of Louis Couperin's *Suites* and three pieces by Armand-Louis. She is thoroughly inside the French style and shows a natural feeling for its rhythmic flexibility. A very close microphone-balance produces pretty deafening results, but a drastic reduction of volume makes for more satisfactory listening.

Having had a great success with Bach's keyboard music, Angela Hewitt now turns to Couperin, and the present disc is the first of three in which she has chosen music that she feels is best suited to the piano. In her admirable accompanying notes she comments on the composer's extensive and explicit ornaments: 'Leaving them out is not an option! It is all related to gesture: ornamentation is there for an expressive purpose, to emphasize one note, to make you wait for another. It is all part of the melodic line.' Certainly, in her hand the ornamentation is both crisply decorative and flexible and always inherent in the music's forward flow.

All these pieces have descriptive titles, some ambiguous (like *Les Baricades mystérieuses*, in which she subtly responds to the adjective), but often picaresque, and the range of colour and dynamic possible on the piano certainly increases their evocative effect. The crisply-articulated opening, *Les Moissonneurs* ('The Reapers'), is both rustic and jolly and if the melodic line of *Les Langeurs tendres* is indulged somewhat, that is surely forgivable, when *Le gazouïllement* ('The warbling') chirps engagingly and *Le Commère* chatters with a Scarlattian lightness of touch. Later *Soeur Monique* and *L'attendrissante* are portrayed tenderly and gently, to be contrasted with the engagingly lively *Le Turbulent* and the quaintly nimble *Le Tic-toc-choc*. In short, this playing is endlessly diverting and the piano is most naturally recorded.

Harpsichord Suites, Book 4, Ordres 21, 24–27
*** Hyp. CDA 67480. Hewitt (piano)

Angela Hewitt's selection from Book 4 (with the Ordres not played consecutively) is even more enticing than her first collection from Books 2 and 3 (CDA 67440 – see our main volume).

All the pieces have intriguing titles and not all of them are obviously reflected in the mood of the music, though *La Mistérieuse* is certainly atmospheric and *La Muse Victorieuse* is full of self-confidence. Among the most enigmatic are *Les Ombres errantes* ('Wandering souls'), the rondeau *L'Epineuse* ('The Thorny One'), which in the event is most engaging, and the poised and friendly representation of the composer's own name, which may or may not be intended as a self-portrait. *L'Amphibie* is certainly ambitious, a memorable passacaglia minus a ground bass, while *La Petite Pince-sans rire* ('The Straight-faced Wag') is agreeably ironic. The four pieces from the 17th *Ordre* (all in the key of B minor) are kept until last and make a splendidly satisfying closing set. The allemande *L'Esquise* is aptly named, but *Les Pavots* ('The Poppies') and *Les Chinoises* (not at all Chinese) are charming fancies, and the closing *Saillie* ('Leap') serves to end the *Ordre* positively and with satisfying finality. Splendid alive and sensitive performances, really fine recording and excellent documentation.

VOCAL MUSIC

Petits Motets: *Audite omnes et expavescite; Quid retribuam tibi Domine; Respice in me; Salve Regina; Usquequo,Domine*
(N) **(*) Virgin 5 45720-2. Agnew, Les Arts Florissants, Christie – CAMPRA: *Petits Motets* **(*)

Couperin's small-scale solo motets have only recently been rediscovered. Their vocal style mixes melancholy, expressive writing and drama. The *Salve Regina* is the most ambitious example here, although *Quid retribuam tibi Dominum* is also eloquently poignant. They are finely sung here by Paul Agnew, and William Christie and his group provide authentic accompaniments. But this is a specialist compilation, rather than one for the small collection.

Laudate pueri Dominum; Motet à Sainte Suzanne; 4 Versets d'un Motet composé de l'ordre du Roy (1703); 7 Versets d'un Motet composé de l'ordre du Roy (1704); 7 Versets d'un Motet composé de l'ordre du Roy (1705); Verset du motet de l'année dernière: Qui dat nivem
🔊 (N) (BB) *** Virgin 2x1 5 62419-2 (2). Piau, Pelon, Fouchécourt, Corréas, Les Talens Lyriques, Rousset – Henri DU MONT: *Motets* ***

Any collector who has not previously discovered the riches of Couperin's *Petits motets* should immediately dive in here, for the style of the music in this generous compilation is extraordinarily wide-ranging and rewarding. There is much vocal treasure in the brilliantly florid versets, with their no less complex instrumental obbligati. Although the overall standard of solo singing and instrumental playing is high, Sandrine Piau is the star of the occasion. She takes the place of her agile and apparently ethereal-voiced predecessor, Marguerite-Louise, Couperin's cousin, for whom the music was written, and is the leading soloist in the first of the psalm versets (1702) 'composed by order of the King'. Here in the exquisite 'Adolescent sum ego' she is in duet with the hardly less impressive Caroline Pelon and a pair of celestial flutes. The

flutes return to accompany her in the equally demanding single verset, *Qui dat nivem*, but she also contributes to the other versets and the closing *Laudate pueri Dominum* (the earliest of Couperin's motets written for the Chapel Royal).

But perhaps the finest work of all here is the joyful *Motet à Sainte Suzanne*, written much later and showing the composer's mature style at its most persuasive. With first-class recording this is an outstanding disc in every way, and it is linked inexpensively to a rewarding collection of music by Couperin's much lesser-known predecessor, Henry du Mont.

Leçons de ténèbres pour le Mercredi Saint
(B) *** HM (ADD) HMA 195 210. Deller, Todd, Perulli, Chapuis
(N) ** Australian Decca Eloquence 476 2454. Les Talens Lyriques, Rousset

Leçons de ténèbres pour le Mercredi Saint, 1–3; 4 versets du motet
*** Erato 0630 17067-2. Daneman, Petibon, Les Arts Florissants, Christie

Sophie Daneman, Patricia Petibon and Les Arts Florissants must probably rank as the best. The first two *Leçons* are divided between the two sopranos, who join together for the last. As the *Trois leçons de ténèbres* take less than 40 minutes, the *Quatre versets du motet* (eight minutes) make an ungenerous fill-up. However, these are exquisite performances and are beautifully recorded.

Deller's version is not authentic, since this music, written for a convent, did not envisage performances by male voices. In every other respect, however, his account has a wonderful authenticity of feeling and a blend of scholarship and artistry that gives it a special claim on the attention of collectors.

One might have thought that the Australian Decca performances would have been ideal, with two excellent soloists and the accompaniments directed by Christophe Rousset. Sandrine Piau and Véronique Gras take turns in the first two *Leçons* and match their voices convincingly in the third and, later, in the *Magnificat* and motets. Yet the result is disappointingly cool and chaste and curiously unmoving. The most effective piece here is the fervent closing Easter motet, *Victoria! Christo resurgenti*, where the *Alléluias* have real emotional resonance.

COUPERIN, Louis (*c.* 1626–61)

Pièces de clavecin: Galliarde in G; 5 Pièces in D; 6 Pièces in C; Preludes in F, A, G & F sharp min.; Preludes (Toccades) in A min. & D min.; Tombeau de M. Blancrocher
(BB) *** Naxos 8.555936. Wilson

Louis Couperin wrote far less than his celebrated nephew, but his small output is of great quality. Glen Wilson's notes speak of Couperin achieving in a few bars 'a synthesis between boldness and balance, between grace and grandeur, emotional depth and economy of means'. And indeed there is a greater eloquence and more feeling in many of these miniatures than in much of the comparable output of François. These are intimate and often inward-looking pieces, and Glen Wilson, who has recently published a reconstruction of Couperin's lost *Préludes non mesurés*, brings us totally inside their world. He plays a copy of a 1628 instrument by Rückers the Younger and is expertly recorded. This fine disc leaves one wondering whether it is not Louis who deserves to be called 'le-grand'.

Harpsichord suites: in A min.; in C; in D; in F (including *Le Tombeau de M. de Blancrocher*)

(BB) *** Naxos 8.550922. Cummings (harpsichord)

Pièces de clavecin: Suites in A min. & C

**(*) BIS CD 982. Hirosawa (harpsichord) – Armand-Louis COUPERIN; François COUPERIN: *Pièces de clavecin* **(*)

Laurence Cummings plays a modern copy of a Rückers, which is very well recorded by Naxos. His selection is generous and he arranges his own groupings. His decoration is convincing and he plays with much spontaneity and flair. The CD offers some 75 minutes of music and is one of Naxos's best bargains.

Asami Hirosawa couples two of Louis Couperin's suites with pieces by Armand-Louis, and the *Treizième ordre* by Couperin-le-grand. She is an impressive advocate, admirably flexible in such pieces as the *Prélude à l'imitation de M. Froberger*. We occasionally felt the need for greater variety of colour, though in this respect she is not helped by a very close microphone-balance.

COUPERIN, Marc Roger Normand

(1663–1734)

Livre de tablature de clavecin (*c.* 1695): complete

*** Hyp. CDA 67164. Moroney (harpsichord)

Marc Roger Normand's book contains 57 pieces – many attributed to other composers, including Chambonnières, Le Bègue and Lully. His choice is unerringly perceptive. Virtually all these miniatures are very personable, especially those by Paul de la Pierre and members of his family. Normand was a first cousin of François Couperin and was clearly a first-rate musician. Apart from his own works he includes an extended set of variants (27 couplets) on the famous *Folies d'Espagnes*. Moroney is a persuasive advocate. He plays with style and spontaneity and consistently entertains the listener. He uses a splendid Italian virginal dating from the seventeenth century, which is beautifully recorded, and this collection can be very highly recommended.

CRESTON, Paul (1906–85)

Symphonies 1, Op. 20; 2, Op. 35; 3 (Three Mysteries), Op. 48

☞ (BB) *** Naxos 8.559034. Ukraine Nat. SO, Kuchar

Paul Creston was among the most approachable of American symphonists. The *First* is exuberantly colourful and strongly rhythmic, with clean-cut themes. The titles of the four compact movements – *With Majesty, With Humour, With Serenity* and *With Gaiety* – reflect the openness of the emotions. No. 2 is much darker, with each of its two substantial movements moving from darkness towards a lightened mood. No. 3 outlines the life of Christ with a peaceful opening, almost pastoral, representing the Nativity and leading to a joyful allegro. The second movement, representing the Crucifixion, is a heartfelt lament, avoiding bitterness and anger, before the Resurrection finale, where Creston is at his most specifically American, almost Copland-like, with jagged syncopations leading to a triumphant close. The Ukraine orchestra, very well rehearsed, plays with warmth and an idiomatic flair surprising from a non-American band, and it is very well recorded.

Symphony 2, Op. 35

*** Chan. 9390. Detroit SO, Järvi – IVES: *Symphony 2* ***

Järvi's well-recorded and excellently performed Chandos version of No. 2 can be recommended if the Ives coupling is desired.

Symphony 3 (Three Mysteries), Op. 48; Invocation & Dance; Out of the Cradle; Partita for Flute, Violin & Strings

*** Delos DEL 3114. Seattle SO, Schwarz

Gerard Schwarz gives a fervent and committed account of No. 3, drawing excellent playing from his Seattle orchestra. The exhilarating *Invocation and Dance*, the *Partita* (which is somewhat more austere) and the less successful *Out of the Cradle* benefit not only from Schwarz's committed advocacy but also from superb engineering. The sound is in the demonstration class.

Symphony 5, Op. 64; Invocation and Dance, Op. 58; Out of the Cradle, Op. 5; Partita, Op. 12; Toccata, Op. 68

(BB) *** Naxos 8.559153. Seattle SO, Schwarz

Collectors who have his *Second Symphony* will know just how inventive Paul Creston can be and how expertly he writes for the orchestra. The *Toccata* from 1957 has much of the same vitality and rhythmic flair as the symphony, and the wild clarinet solos we recall in the *Second Symphony* resurface here, calling to mind the *Danse générale* from *Daphnis et Chloé*. The *Fifth Symphony* (1956) is a three-movement work, exuberant and full of spirit, and as expertly fashioned as most of Creston's music. *Out of the Cradle* and the *Partita* are early and of lesser interest. Creston was grievously neglected in the 1960s and '70s when tonal composers were considered 'uninteresting' and the likes of Barber patronizingly dismissed. Creston may not be as gifted as the latter, but readers who respond to Barber and Copland will find themselves at home in Creston's world. Splendid performances and recording.

String Quartet, Op. 8

(***) Testament mono SBT 1053. Hollywood Qt – DEBUSSY: *Danse sacrée*, etc.; RAVEL: *Introduction & Allegro*; TURINA: *La oración del torero*; VILLA-LOBOS: *Quartet 6* (***)

The *String Quartet*, Op. 8, is a pleasing, well-fashioned piece, slightly Gallic in feeling. The *Adagio* unfolds with eloquence. It could not be better served than it is by the Hollywood Quartet, recorded in 1953: the playing is stunning, and the recording, too, is very good for its period, even if the acoustic is on the dry side.

CRUSELL, Bernhard (1775–1838)

Concertino for Bassoon & Orchestra in B flat; Introduction et air suédois for Clarinet & Orchestra, Op. 12; Sinfonia concertante for Clarinet, Horn, Bassoon & Orchestra, Op. 3

*** BIS CD 495. Hara, Korsimaa-Hursti, Lanski-Otto, Tapiola Sinf., Vänskä

The most substantial piece here is the *Sinfonia concertante for Clarinet, Horn, Bassoon and Orchestra*. The finale is a set of variations on a chorus from Cherubini's opera, *Les Deux Journées*. The much later *Concertino for Bassoon and Orchestra* is an altogether delightful piece, which quotes at one point from Boïeldieu. It is played with appropriate freshness and virtuosity by László Hara. The *Introduction et air suédois for Clarinet and Orchestra* is nicely done by Anna-Maija Korsimaa-Hursti. The Tapiola Sinfonietta, the orchestra of Esspoo, play with enthusiasm and spirit for Osmo

Vänskä, and the BIS recording has lightness, presence and body.

Clarinet Concertos 1 in E flat, Op. 1; 2 in F min., Op. 5; 3 in E flat, Op. 11

🔑 ❁ *** ASV CDDCA 784. Johnson, RPO/ECO, Herbig; Groves; or Schwarz

*** Ondine ODE 965-2. Kriiku, Finnish RSO, Oramo

(B) *** Virgin 2x1 5 61585-2 (2). Pay, OAE – WEBER: *Clarinet Concertos* ***

(N) (BB) *** Hyp. Helios CDH 55203. King, LSO, Francis

Crusell, born in Finland but working in Stockholm for most of his career, was himself a clarinettist and these delightful concertos demonstrate his complete understanding of the instrument. There are echoes of Mozart, Weber and Rossini in the music, with a hint of Beethoven. No one brings out the fun in the writing quite as infectiously as Emma Johnson, and this generous recoupling (74 minutes), bringing all three Concertos together, is a delight. With well-structured first movements, sensuous slow movements and exuberant finales, Johnson establishes her disc as a first choice above all others.

Kari Kriiku gives dazzling performances, even more daring than his rivals on disc, regularly choosing speeds that stretch virtuosity to the limit, particularly in the finales. By choosing exceptionally fast speeds in Nos. 1 and 2 Kriiku brings out an extra scherzando quality, sharp and spiky, with crisply dotted rhythms. Partly as a result of the immediacy of the recording, Kriiku's pianissimos are not as extreme as they might be, yet in flair and panache he is second to none, superbly supported by the purposeful playing of the Finnish National Radio Orchestra under Sakari Oramo.

Pay uses a reproduction of a nine-key clarinet as made around 1810 by Heinrich Grenser; Crusell himself is known to have used a ten-key Grenser clarinet. The slight edginess of the sound goes well with Pay's preference for fastish – often very fast – speeds which yet never get in the way of his imaginative rhythmic pointing. The results in outer movements are exhilarating. They sparkle with wit, while slow movements have a flowing songfulness that is comparably persuasive. The Virgin recording, made at Abbey Road studio, is clear, well balanced and atmospheric.

Thea King with her beautiful, liquid tone also makes an outstanding soloist. Her approach is often more serious, especially in the *Second Concerto*, where she brings out the Beethovenian character of the first movement, while the *Andante pastorale* slow movement is played with the widest range of tone-colour. Throughout, she is well accompanied by Alun Francis; and the resonant Hyperion recording, with the soloist balanced forward, emphasizes the feeling of added gravitas, making this a fine budget recommendation.

Clarinet Concerto 1 in E flat, Op. 1

*** ASV CDDCA 763. Johnson, RPO, Herbig – KOZELUCH; KROMMER: *Concertos* ***

Even though many collectors may prefer the CD containing all three of the Crusell concertos, Emma Johnson's version of the *First Clarinet Concerto* makes a highly attractive compilation with lesser-known but enticing works by Kozeluch and Krommer.

Clarinet Concerto 2 in F min., Op. 5

❁ *** ASV CDDCA 559. Johnson, ECO, Groves – BAERMANN: *Adagio;* ROSSINI: *Introduction, Theme & Variations;* WEBER: *Concertino* ***

Crusell's *Second Clarinet Concerto* made Emma Johnson a star, and in return she put Crusell's engagingly lightweight piece firmly on the map. Her delectably spontaneous performance is now caught on the wing and this recording sounds very like a live occasion.

Introduction & Variations on a Swedish Air (for clarinet and orchestra), *Op. 12*

(B) *** Hyp. Dyad CDD 22017 (2). King, LSO, Francis (with *Concert* – see below ***)

The Weberian Crusell *Variations* show Thea King's bravura at its most sparkling. It is far from being an empty piece; its twists and turns are consistently inventive. This is part of an excellent two-disc set including other attractive concertante works by Max Bruch, Mendelssohn, Spohr and other less familiar names.

Clarinet Quartets 1 in E flat, Op. 2; 2 in C min., Op. 4; 3 in D, Op. 7

(BB) *** Hyp. Helios CDH 55031. King, Allegri Qt (members)

These are captivatingly sunny works, given superb performances, vivacious and warmly sympathetic; Thea King's tone is positively luscious and the sound is generally excellent. The CD transfer is highly successful and its migration to the bargain-price Helios label makes it even more attractive.

Divertimento in C, Op. 9

(BB) **(*) Hyp. Helios CDH 55015. Francis, Allegri Qt – KREUTZER: *Grand Quintet;* REICHA: *Quintet* **(*)

Crusell's *Divertimento* has charm and grace, and the performance here is nicely played and recorded; it is now offered at bargain price.

CUMMINGS, Richard (born 1928)

24 Preludes

(M) *** Phoenix PHCD 105. Browning – BARBER: *Piano Sonata* ***

Richard Cummings, born in Shanghai and raised in Manila, was schooled on the American West Coast and studied music at the San Francisco Conservatory. His mentors included Bloch, Schoenberg and Sessions, although their influence was obviously not profound! He is primarily a composer of music for the theatre, but as a fine pianist shows a natural facility for the instrument. He wrote the *24 Preludes* between 1966 and 1969 especially for John Browning, who plays them with aplomb and obvious enjoyment. These are not in essence a theme and variations, although each one seems to grow naturally from its predecessor. The idiom is readily accessible, eclectic, but none the worse for that. The invention explores a wide variety of musical styles and is unfailingly diverting, when played so stylishly and sympathetically. The recording is excellent.

DALLAPICCOLA, Luigi (1904–75)

Frammenti Sinfonici dal Balletto Marsia; 2 Pezzi; Piccola Musica Notturna; (i) *Tartiniana. Variazioni per Orchestra*

(N) *** Chan. 10258. BBC PO, Noseda, (i) with Ehnes

Dallapiccola, a composer of fastidious sensibility, is seldom encountered in the concert hall these days and his representation in the catalogue is not generous. The Chandos programme makes an excellent introduction to his output: a good starting point is the sensitive and evocative nocturnal landscape depicted in *Piccola Musica Notturna* of 1954, a haunting piece written for Herman Scherchen. After that, try the fragments from the ballet, *Marsia* (1942–3) which is full of inventive resource and even has some of the lushness of Respighi, though not the harmonic vocabulary. The ghostly *Sarabande* of the *Due Pezzi* almost reminds one of the spirit of Busoni's *Sarabande* from *Doktor Faust*, and the *Variations for Orchestra* show Dallapiccola's delicacy of colouring at its finest. James Ehnes is an excellent soloist in the more traditional *Tartiniana*, modelled on Casella's *Paganiniana* or Respighi's reworkings of Rossini and Boccherini. Very truthful sound from the Manchester partnership of Mike George and Stephen Rinker, and good sleeve-notes, too, from Calum MacDonald. A rewarding issue which deserves the widest currency.

2 Studies for Violin & Piano

(**) VAI mono VAIA 1124. Ricci, Tureck – DIAMOND: *Piano Sonata* (***); SCHUMANN: *Piano Concerto* (*(**))

Dallapiccola's *Two Studies*, written in 1947, consist of a wan *Sarabande* and an aggressive *Fanfare and Fugue*. This was their New York première in 1952. Ricci plays them impeccably, in partnership with Rosalyn Tureck, though the recording balance places the violin unacceptably and unflatteringly close.

VOCAL MUSIC

(i) *Canti di Prigionia*; (i; ii) *2 Cori di Michelangelo Buonarroti il Giovane*; (iii) *5 Fragmenti di Saffi*; *2 Liriche di Ancreonte*; *6 Carmina Alcani*; (ii) *Tempus destruendi – Tempus aedificandi*

(BB) *** Warner Apex 8593 89230-2. (i) New L. Chamber Ch., (ii) Jansen, Gwynn; (iii) Moffat; Ens. InterContemporain, Zender

This excellently sung and atmospherically recorded collection offers a fine survey of Dallapicola's highly individual vocal writing, from the comparatively direct madrigal style of the early *Michelangelo Cori* (1933), to the unpredictable choral lines and sustained dissonances – gentle and passionate – of *Tempus destruendi – Tempus aedificandi*, written nearly 40 years later. The evocatively ear-tweaking *Preghiera* of the *Canti di Prigionia* (1938–41) for chorus, with pianos, harps and percussion, moves inexorably towards its first and subsequent climaxes, while the second movement (*Invocazione di Boezio*) surprises by introducing the *Dies irae*, no doubt influenced by the composer's reaction at the time of composition to Mussolini's announcement of Italy's adoption of fascism.

But it is in the three central song-cycles of the early 1940s, with their colourful and often dextrous accompaniments, where Dallapiccola shows himself as both an original and an expressive communicator. Even if the melodic lines twist about impulsively, and not always logically, the effect is aurally magnetic when they are so confidently and sympathetically sung and accompanied. The one snag is that, while texts are provided, there are no translations.

DANZI, Franz (1763–1826)

Bassoon Concertos 1–2 in F; 3 in C; 4 in G min.

(BB) *** Naxos 8.554273. Holder, New Brandenburg Philharmonie, Pasquet

Danzi was himself a cellist and wrote a fine concerto for his own instrument; but he also, perhaps not surprisingly, had a natural affinity for the bassoon, and all four of these tuneful concertos readily exploit the instrument's potential for gentle melancholy and humour. Albrecht Holder (who prepared the *C major* work for publication) is a splendidly stylish soloist with a most appealing timbre, and his cadenzas are nicely judged. He is most sympathetically accompanied by Nicolás Pasquet and his excellent Brandenburg chamber orchestra. The Naxos recording balances the soloist forwardly, but the orchestra is well in the picture and the warm resonance is flattering. A first-class CD in every way which will be hard to surpass.

(i; ii) Concertante for Flute & Clarinet in B; Op. 41; (i) Flute Concerto 2 in D min., Op. 31; (ii) Fantasia on Mozart's 'La ci darem la mano' for Clarinet & Orchestra

*** RCA 09026 61976-2. (i) Galway; (ii) Meyer; Württemberg CO, Faerber

Danzi wrote four flute concertos which suggest a style midway between eighteenth-century classicism and the more romantic manner of Weber. The dramatic minor-key opening of No 2, included here, is remarkably like Mozart's *D minor Piano Concerto*, but James Galway's entry immediately lightens the mood; he also plays the charming *Larghetto* very persuasively, and the finale trips along delightfully. His partnership with Sabine Meyer affords equal felicity in the *Concertante*, with the two soloists carolling together most engagingly. They have plenty of good tunes to share, and in Danzi's *Fantasia* Meyer clearly enjoys all the bravura roulades with which Mozart's famous theme is decorated, after its delectably gentle entry. The accompaniments by Faerber with his Württemberg Chamber Orchestra are stylishly supportive and the recording is both full and well balanced.

Horn Concerto in E.

(BB) *** Teldec (ADD) 0630 12324-2. Baumann, Concerto Amsterdam, Schröder – HAYDN; ROSETTI: *Concertos* ***

Danzi's *Horn Concerto* is straightforward but attractive. The Romance is Weberian, smoothly contoured and pleasing in line, but the pertly amiable closing Rondo is the most winning of the three movements and demands and receives some very nimble tongueing from Baumann, who gives a most sympathetic performance overall. The 1969 recording has been pleasingly remastered.

Bassoon Quartets 1 in C; 2 in D min.; 3 in B flat

(M) *** CRD CRD 3503. Thompson, Coull Qt

These three charming *Quartets* have a *galant* innocence and a gentle, lyrical feeling. Danzi seeks primarily to capture the bassoon's doleful, lyrical character; its lighter side is not dismissed but he never becomes too jocular. In short, these are slight but appealing works, and they are presented here with affectionate warmth and spirit, and they are beautifully recorded.

Horn Sonata in F, Op. 17

*** HM HMC 90 5250. Müller, Torbianelli – BEETHOVEN; RIES: *Horn Sonatas* ***

Danzi obviously knew Beethoven's *Horn Sonata*, and his work opens with an almost identical arpeggio flourish. When the principal theme arrives it is also obviously following the Beethoven model, if more romantically. The pleasing *Larghetto* is a proper slow movement instead of just an interlude, and in the finale the *galant* Bohemian elegance of the writing and the greater virtuousity required of the soloist make the music very much Danzi's own. This is an excellent performance, with Thomas Müller playing expertly on a hand horn, and Eduardo Torbianelli a fine partner. The recording balance is well managed; and Müller's plump timbre is caught most naturally.

(i) *Piano Quintet in F, Op. 53. Wind Quintets, Op. 67/1–3*
*** BIS CD 539. (i) Derwinger; BPO Wind Qt

Danzi was one of the first composers to cultivate the wind quintet; these diverting pieces, played with much distinction and recorded with great clarity and presence, offer unexpected pleasure. The *Piano Quintet* is insubstantial, but rather delightful all the same.

Wind Quintets, Op. 56/1–3; Wind Sextet in E flat
(BB) *** Naxos 8.553076. (i) Michael Thompson Wind Quintet

(i) *Wind Quintets, Op. 67/1–3;* (ii) *Horn Sonata 1 in E flat, Op. 28*
(BB) *** Naxos 8.553570. (i) Michael Thompson Wind Quintet; (ii) Thompson; Fowke

(i) *Wind Quintets, Op. 68/1–4;* (ii) *Horn Sonata 2 in E min., Op. 44*
(BB) *** Naxos 8.554694. (i) Michael Thompson Wind Quintet; (ii) Thompson; Fowke

Danzi's three sets of ever-engaging *Wind Quintets* were published in 1821 and 1823–4 respectively. For these elegant recordings the horn soloist, Michael Thompson, has gathered around him a superbly balanced group of London's leading wind players, Jonathan Snowden (flute), Derek Wickens (oboe), Robert Hill (clarinet) and John Price, a bassoonist with a particularly appealing musical presence. They combine to give polished and beautifully blended performances of this charmingly conversational music, for which Danzi had such a ready penchant. Their melodic invention is innocent but is as appealing as it is seemingly inexhaustible.

The first disc also includes Danzi's *First Horn Sonata* of 1804, probably modelled on Beethoven's similar work of three years earlier, although the style is more romantic in its writing for the horn. Thompson and Philip Fowke are admirable partners. The *Second Horn Sonata* of 1813 is even more lyrically *galant* (the piano part especially so), particularly in the theme and variations finale.

The *Wind Sextet*, which is the bonus on the second CD, is in the tradition of wind *Harmoniemusik*, which reached its zenith with Mozart's later serenades. Danzi's work is not quite on that level, but is fluently appealing, with a spirited finale which has much in common with Mozart's *Gran partita* for thirteen wind instruments. Again, excellent sound.

Wind Quintets, Op. 56/1–2; Op. 68/1–2
(M) *** Sup. 11 1264-2. Academia Wind Quintet

Czech players seem to have a special feeling for the Bohemian light-heartedness of Danzi's writing for wind instruments. The Academia Wind Quintet from the Prague Conservatory offer here a pair of hand-picked quintets from Opp. 56 and 68 and play them with a rippling facility and endearing insouciance. They are beautifully recorded.

DAQUIN, Louis-Claude (1694–1772)

Nouveau Livre de Noëls 1–12
*** Hyp. CDA 66816. Herrick (organ of Church of St Rémy de Dieppe)

Louis-Claude Daquin was a keyboard prodigy, and at the age of six he is reported to have played for the king, who correctly predicted his later fame. Daquin became organist at Notre Dame in 1735. He is best known for his *Noëls*, which are often used as piquant organ encore pieces. The composer's title page suggests that they could also be played on harpsichord or violins and woodwind; but they were obviously meant primarily for the organ and were intended for performance at Christmas Mass – acting as seasonal voluntaries, usually heard just before midnight.

Each uses a popular melody, to which a cumulative bravura variation style is applied, with the decoration and variants steadily gaining in pace and brilliance. Above all, performances were required to be buoyant and spirited, as indeed they are here, and Christopher Herrick, who registers a colourfully varied palette, obviously enjoys himself throughout. The Dieppe organ seems an ideal choice (sample Nos. 4, 6 or 10) and it is beautifully recorded. Not a disc to play all at once, but very engaging to dip into.

DARNTON, Christian (1905–81)

Piano Concertino in C
(N) (BB) *** Naxos 8.557290. Donohoe, Northern Sinfonia –
ROWLEY; GERHARDT; FERGUSON: *Piano Concertos* ***

Warmly lyrical, with a touch of Stravinskian neo-classicism and a dash of Shostakovich, and ending with a bravura display in the finale, Christian Darnton's *Concertino* for piano and strings makes a valuable addition to this imaginative collection of four British concertos, superbly performed by Peter Donohoe directing the Northern Sinfonia from the keyboard.

D'ASTORGA, Emanuele (c. 1680–1757)

Stabat Mater
❂ (M) *** DHM/BMG 82876 60145-2. Monoyios, Mammel, Happel, Balthazar-Neumann Ch., Freiburg Bar. O, Hengelbrock – DURANTE: *Magnificat in B flat*;
PERGOLESI: *Confitebor tibi Domine* *** ❂
*** Hyp. CDA 67108. Gritton, Bickley, Agnew, Harvey, King's Consort Ch., King's Consort, King – BOCCHERINI: *Stabat Mater* ***

Baron Emanuele d'Astorga came from the Spanish nobility and was a self-taught composer; he settled for a while in Italy, travelled to London and Lisbon, but eventually returned to his homeland. He led an adventurous life, which was pictured in both a romantic novel and an opera in which the deranged hero is sustained by hearing his own *Stabat Mater*. D'Astorga's setting was justly renowned in its time for its intensity of lyrical feeling and its broad flow of lyrical melody, notably in the solos and duets. Yet, unusually, it ends exultantly, celebrating Christ's 'victory' over the cross, with a lively if unadventurous extended final chorus. The German performance here is in every way persuasive, beautifully sung and played, and directed with much spirit by Hengelbrock.

The recording is first class, and texts and translation are included.

Emanuele d'Astorga's *Stabat Mater* predates Boccherini's – with which it is coupled on Hyperion – by nearly a century and, unlike that work (and the Pergolesi setting on which it is based), is written like a miniature oratorio with soloists and chorus. The chorus opens and closes the work – the opening with touching melancholy, but the closing *Christe quam sit hinc exire* much more upbeat. In between, the various solos and duets are expressively quite intense, and overall this is a remarkably accomplished and rewarding piece, especially when sung as eloquently as it is here, with excellent soloists and a fine choral contribution, all very well recorded.

DAVIES, Sir Henry Walford (1869–1941)

Everyman (Oratorio; complete)
(N) (M) *** Dutton CDLX 7141. Putnins, Staples, Ferrari, Johnston, London Oriana Ch., Kensington SO, Drummond

Sir Henry Walford Davies, largely forgotten now except for the haunting piece, *Solemn Melody*, was one of the most popular musical figures in Britain in the interwar period. That was largely through his radio broadcasts on music, genial and informal in a way that was rare at the time. He was even chosen in 1934 to succeed Elgar as Master of the King's Music, and earlier had a distinguished career as a choirmaster. That is reflected in this fine oratorio, *Everyman*. Written in 1904, it follows the progress of Everyman from earth to heaven, a theme which echoes Elgar's *Dream of Gerontius* of four years earlier in a more homespun way. The impact of this performance is greatly enhanced by the clarity of the words, both from the four excellent soloists and from the vigorous chorus. It is true that Davies makes Death, a tenor-role, into rather too amiable a figure, and the melodic material could be more striking, but this is a powerful piece that richly deserves revival, here well directed by David Drummond in full, brilliant sound.

DAVYDOV, Karl (1838–89)

Cello Concerto 2 in A min., Op. 14
**(*) Chan. 9622. Ziumbrovsky, I Musici de Montréal, Turovsky – CONUS: *Violin Concerto*; GLAZUNOV: *Piano Concerto 2* **(*)

Davydov (or Davïdov) was one of the greatest cellists of his day – Tchaikovsky described him as 'the king of cellists'. His *A minor Concerto* is rather bland, almost Mendelssohnian, but it is an excellent visiting card for the soloist, Alexander Ziumbrovsky, who plays with a fine and natural musicianship.

DEBUSSY, Claude (1862–1918)

Concertante and Orchestral Music (almost complete)
(B) *** Chan. X10144 (4). Queffélec, Masters, Bell, King, McChrystal, Ulster O, Y. P. Tortelier

Chandos have now assembled Debussy's orchestral music (previously coupled with Ravel) in a bargain box in recordings which generally reflect the state of the art. There are excellent soloists in the concertante works. The subtlety and atmosphere of *La Boîte à joujoux* are captured splendidly, and

the concertante works are equally sensitive. Not all the performances are a first choice, but the shorter works come off particularly well.

(i; ii) *Berceuse héroïque*; (iii) *La Boîte à joujoux* (ballet); *Children's Corner* (both orch. Caplet); (i; iv) *Danse (Tarantelle styrienne)*; (i; v; vi) *Danses sacrée et profane for Harp and Strings*; (vii) *Fantaisie for Piano and Orchestra*; (iii) *Images; Jeux*; (i; v) *Khamma* (orch. Koechlin); (i; vi) *Marche écossaise*; (iii) *Le Martyre de Saint Sébastien* (fragments symphoniques); *La Mer; Nocturnes*; (viii) *Petite suite* (orch. Büsser); (iii) *La Plus que lente* (orch. composer); *Prélude à l'après-midi d'un faune*; (ix) *Prélude: La Cathédrale engloutie* (orch. Stokowski); (viii; x) *Première Rapsodie for Clarinet and Orchestra*; (iii) *Printemps* (orch. Büsser); (viii) *Suite bergamasque: Clair de lune* (orch. Caplet)
(B) **(*) Decca 475 313-2 (4). (i) Concg. O; (ii) Van Beinum; (iii) Montreal SO, Dutoit; (iv) Chailly; (v) Vera Badings; (vi) Haitink; (vii) Kars, LSO, Gibson; (viii) SRO, Ansermet; (ix) New Philh. O, Stokowski; (x) Gugholz

This Decca compilation is based on the outstanding series of recordings of the major works, made in the late 1980s and early 1990s by Dutoit in Montreal, notable both for colourfully expansive recording, richly atmospheric, and the conductor's highly sympathetic approach, vital and flexible yet strong. For the *Berceuse* and the *Danses sacrée et profane* Concertgebouw recordings from the Philips catalogue have been chosen, conducted with great finesse by Eduard van Beinum and Haitink respectively, and for the *Fantaisie for Piano and Orchestra* the soloist is Jean-Randolph Kars, a very persuasive Debussian, given excellent support by Gibson. Ansermet contributes too, and if his *Petite suite* is not as polished as its Chandos competitor, it is certainly vivid. We return to the Concertgebouw Orchestra, this time conducted by Chailly, for the rare *Khamma*, and Stokowski's astonishing orchestration of *La Cathédrale engloutie* makes for an unexpected bonus. Excellent value, although Tortelier's similar but not identical Chandos compilation is more consistent in the quality of the orchestral playing and recording.

(i) *Berceuse héroïque*; (ii; iii) *Danses sacrée et profane* (for harp and strings); (ii) *Images; Jeux; Marche écossaise; La Mer*; (ii; iv) *Nocturnes*; (ii) *Prélude à l'après-midi d'un faune*; (ii; v) *Première rapsodie for Clarinet & Orchestra*
🔾 ✿ (B) *** Ph. Duo (ADD) 438 742-2 (2). Concg. O, (i) Van Beinum; (ii) Haitink; with (iii) Badings; (iv) Women's Ch. of Coll. Mus.; (v) Pieterson

This Duo ranks as probably the finest Debussy collection in the CD catalogue. Although the programme as a whole is directed by Haitink, it is good that his distinguished predecessor, Eduard van Beinum, is remembered by the opening *Berceuse héroïque*, played with great delicacy and a real sense of mystery, with the early (1957) stereo highly effective. For the *Danses sacrée et profane* Haitink takes over, with elegant playing from the harpist, Vera Badings, who is excellently balanced. Haitink's reading of *Images* is second to none and is beautifully played by the wonderful Dutch orchestra; this applies equally to *Jeux*, while in the *Nocturnes* the choral balance is judged perfectly, and few versions are quite as beguiling and seductive as Haitink's. His *La Mer* is comparable with Karajan's 1964 recording. The hazily sensuous *Prélude à l'après-midi d'un faune* and the undervalued *Clarinet Rhapsody* are also played atmospherically, although the former is more overtly languorous in Karajan's hands. Again, the Philips recording is truthful and natural, with beautiful perspectives and realistic colour, a marvellously refined sound.

Berceuse héroïque; Images; Jeux; Marche écossaise; La Mer; Musiques pour le Roi Lear; Nocturnes; Prélude à l'après-midi d'un faune; Printemps

(B) *** EMI double forte (ADD) 5 72667-2 (2). Fr. R. & TV Ch. & O, Martinon

Martinon's is a very good *Images*, beautifully played, with the orchestral detail vivid and glowing. *Jeux* is also very fine, with the sound attractively spacious. *La Mer* enjoys the idiomatic advantage of fine French orchestral playing, even if it does not quite match Karajan or Haitink. The *Musiques pour le Roi Lear* is a real rarity; the colourful *Fanfare* remains impressive, and *Le Sommeil de Lear* is highly evocative. The *Nocturnes* are beautifully played, as indeed is *Printemps*, with Martinon penetrating its charm. At bargain price these are competitive recommendations, and the current transfers are warmly atmospheric; even if the upper end of the range is rather brightly lit, there is plenty of depth in the sound.

La Boîte à joujoux; Children's Corner (orch. Caplet)

(***) Testament mono SBT 1236 French Nat. R.O, Cluytens – RAVEL: *Le Tombeau; Valses Nobles* (**)

Like *Le Martyre de Saint Sébastien* and the ballet *Khamma*, *La Boîte à joujoux* was one of those scores that the composer left for others to orchestrate. Caplet's scoring was made in 1923, some five years after Debussy's death. The ballet, effortless and charming in its inventive flow, tells of a triangular love affair among marionettes who live in a large toy box. Cluytens conveys its charm very expertly and gets good playing from his French Radio forces – and a mono recording of outstanding quality for the period which still impresses today. Both pieces are very enjoyable indeed.

La Boîte à joujoux; Children's Corner (orch. Caplet); Danse (orch. Ravel); (i) Danses sacrée et profane. (ii) Fantaisie for Piano & Orchestra; La plus que lente; Khamma; Petite suite (orch. Büsser); (iii) Première rapsodie for Clarinet & Orchestra. (iv) Rapsodie for Saxophone

(B) *** EMI double forte (ADD) 5 72673-2 (2). Fr. R. & TV O, Martinon; with (i) Jamet; (ii) Ciccolini; (iii) Dangain; (iv) Londe

Children's Corner and *La Boîte à joujoux* contain much to enchant the ear, as does the tuneful *Petite suite*. The rarity here is *Khamma*. This and the two *Rapsodies* are underrated and, although there are alternative versions of all these pieces, none is more economically priced. The performances are sympathetic and authoritative, and the recordings have been remastered successfully. The sound is full and spacious, with an attractive ambient glow.

Danse (Tarantelle styrienne); Sarabande (orch. Ravel)

(BB) *** Virgin 2 × CD 5 62050-2 (2). Lausanne CO, Zedda – MILHAUD: *La création du monde*; PROKOFIEV: *Symphony 1 (Classical)* ***; SHOSTAKOVICH: *Chamber Symphony; Symphony 14* **

(N) **(*) Australian Decca Eloquence 476 2452. Concg. O, Chailly – RAVEL: *Boléro*; MUSSORGSKY: *Pictures at an Exhibition* **(*)

Zedda's performances with the Lausanne Chamber Orchestra are neat and polished, full of character and well recorded.

The Milhaud and Prokofiev couplings are excellent too, the Shostakovich more controversial.

Ravel's orchestrations of two Debussy piano pieces, the *Sarabande* from the suite *Pour le piano*, and *Danse*, an arrangement of the early *Tarantelle styrienne*, make delightful and comparatively rare items in Chailly's disc demonstrating Ravel's genius as an orchestrator. *Danse* really outshines the original in fantasy, but in the *Sarabande* it is harder for a full orchestra to play with the subtlety of rubato that this stylized music seems to demand. Ripely brilliant recording.

Danse; Images: Ibéria. Marche écossaise; La Mer; Nocturnes: Nuages; Fêtes (only); (i) La Damoiselle élue

(B) (***) Naxos mono 8.110811-2. NBC SO, Toscanini, (i) with Novotna, Glaz, Schola Cantorum Women's Ch.

These are incandescent, sharply focused performances, quite unlike any others and offering the longest of the irascible rehearsals which are a fascinating feature of the series. It is specially valuable to have the three rare works – the *Marche écossaise* of 1908; the *Danse*, an early piano piece orchestrated by Ravel; and the early lyric poem, *La Damoiselle élue* – with clean-cut soloists.

Danse sacrée et danse profane (for harp and string orchestra)

(***) Testament mono SBT 1053. Mason Stockton, Concert Arts Strings, Slatkin – CRESTON: *Quartet*; RAVEL: *Introduction & Allegro*; TURINA: *La oración del torero*; VILLA-LOBOS: *Quartet 6* (***)

Felix Slatkin and his Hollywood colleagues give as atmospheric an account of the *Danse sacrée et danse profane* as any on record, and Anne Mason Stockton is the excellent harpist. The mono recording dates from 1951 but is uncommonly good. This comes as part of a remarkably fine anthology of Hollywood Quartet recordings.

(i) Danses sacrées et profanes; Images; Jeux; La Mer; Prélude à l'après-midi d'un faune; (ii) Nocturnes; Printemps; (iii) Première rapsodie for Clarinet & Orchestra

(M) **(*) Sony (ADD) SM2K 68327 (2). New Philh. O or (i) Cleveland O; Boulez; with (i) Chalifoux; (ii) Alldis Ch.; (iii) De Peyer

Jeux, a work of seminal importance in Boulez's development, is here given very persuasively. The *Images* are carefully shaped and balanced and, like the coolly distinctive *Danses sacrées et profanes*, were recorded in Cleveland and gain from the ambience of Severance Hall, even if the balance is close. *La Mer* and the *Prélude à l'après-midi d'un faune* (which certainly does not lack passionate feeling) are a good deal better than some accounts, but *La Mer* cannot compare with the Karajan version from the same era. Needless to say, Gervase de Peyer gives a distinguished account of the lovely *Clarinet Rhapsody*, and the contribution of the John Alldis Choir to *Sirènes*, the third of the *Nocturnes*, is poised, even if the effect overall is cool rather than ethereal. But those who respond to Boulez's clarity of vision in this repertoire will find that the Sony engineers have made a marvellous job of these transfers to CD, maximizing the ambient effect and retaining the sharply defined detail.

Danses sacrées et profanes; Images; Jeux; Prélude à l'après-midi d'un faune

(M) *** Sup. (ADD) SU 3478-2 011. Czech PO, Baudo (with Patras)

Recorded in the attractive acoustics of the Dvořák Hall of the Rudolfinum, Prague, these were among the finest recordings Supraphon made during the analogue LP era. *Jeux* is clothed in richly glowing colours, with ravishingly seductive string-textures, while Baudo displays a subtle feeling for the music's ebb and flow. He also lets the famous *Prélude* unfold with a natural progress and the central climax of the piece flowers quite spontaneously. At the very opening of *Images* the piquant oboe solo is ear-catching. *Les Parfums de la nuit* waft languorously in the evening breeze, and the opening of *Le Matin d'un jour de fête* is hauntingly evocative before the orchestra blazes into life. This, like the *Danses sacrées*, was recorded a decade later with comparable success.

(i) *Danses sacrée et profane*; (ii) *3 Ballades de François Villon*; *Le Jet d'eau*

(N) *** DG 471 614-2. Cleveland O, Boulez, with (i) Wellbaum; (ii) Hagley – RAVEL: *Menuet antique, etc.* ***

An evocative account of the *Danse sacrée et danse profane*, ideal listening to cool you on a summer evening, perfectly done by Lisa Wellbaum and the Cleveland Orchestra. Alison Hagley, the *Mélisande* in Boulez's Welsh National Opera DVD of *Pelléas*, gives highly appealing accounts of the Baudelaire setting, *Le jet d'eau* and the *Trois Ballades de François Villon*. Altogether a lovely recital.

6 *Epigraphes antiques* (orch. Ansermet); *Jeux*

(***) Testament mono SBT 1324. SRO, Ansermet (with SAINT-SAENS: *Danse macabre*) – DUKAS: *L'Apprenti Sorcier*, etc. **(*)

Ansermet's *Jeux* and *Six Epigraphes antiques* were only the second recording of the pieces to appear. Although the Suisse Romande Orchestra's wind intonation is not impeccable, it is better than on some issues from the early days of stereo. *Jeux* first appeared in 1953 and the *Six Epigraphes antiques* the following year. Ansermet's scoring is most felicitous. The performances have great atmosphere and real style; and it is good to have the Ansermet account of his own transcription, whose tempi are so perfectly judged and textures so perfectly balanced, back in circulation. Very decent sound. A most winning reissue, well worth investigating.

6 *Epigraphes antiques* (orch. Ansermet); *Estampes: Pagodes* (orch. André Caplet); *Printemps* (suite symphonique; original (1887) choral version, reconstructed Emil de Cou); *Prélude: La puerta del vino* (orch. Henri Büsser); *Suite bergamasque* (orch. Gustave Cloez & André Caplet)

**(*) Ara. Z 6734. San Francisco Ballet O, De Cou; (i) with soloists and Ch.

A fascinating disc, and most fascinating of all is the original choral version of *Printemps*, which sounds positively voluptuous in this superbly rich recording. Emil de Cou has gone back to the full original manuscript and provided his own highly convincing re-scoring. The result will intrigue all Debussians and its seductive impact will surely thrill all listeners. The orchestrated piano pieces are also very successful. In the *Suite bergamasque*, *Clair de lune* sounds lovely on strings, and both the *Minuet* and *Passepied* are effective in orchestral dress. In his fastidiously scored *Epigraphes antiques* de Cou goes for atmospheric evocation and certainly No. 2 (*Pour le tombeau sans nom*), with its instant reminder of *Images*, is very beguiling; and the whole set is made to sound lustrous in its impressionistic colouring. The San Francisco Ballet Orchestra plays very well indeed, and the spacious

acoustic provides an impressively full and naturally balanced sound-picture.

Fantaisie for Piano & Orchestra

(BB) *** Warner Apex (ADD). 8573 89232-2. Queffélec, Monte Carlo Op. O, Jordan – RAVEL: *Piano Concertos* ***

The Warner Apex disc offers an inexpensive coupling of the major works for piano and orchestra by both Debussy and Ravel, and in Anne Queffélec's hands the *Fantaisie* makes a very pleasing impression indeed and is very well recorded.

(i) *Images: Ibéria*; (ii) *Jeux; La Mer; Prélude à l'après-midi d'un faune*

(B) *** CfP 586 1672. (i) LSO, Previn; (ii) LPO, Baudo

Images: Ibéria. La Mer

☛ ✹ (B) *** RCA 2-CD 74321 88692-2 (2). Chicago SO, Reiner – MUSSORGSKY: *Pictures* **(*); RAVEL: *Alborada*, etc. ✹ ***

Images: Ibéria. La Mer*; (i) *Nocturnes. Prélude à l'après-midi d'un faune

(N) (M) *** RCA SACD 82876 6674-2. Boston SO, Munch – RAVEL: *Boléro*, etc.

(M) *** Ph. (ADD) 464 697-2. Concg. O, Haitink; (i) with female Ch.

***Images; Jeux; Le Roi Lear* (incidental music)**

(BB) *** EMI Encore 5 75218-2. CBSO, Rattle

Images; La Mer*; (i) *Nocturnes

(***) Australian Decca Eloquence mono/stereo 464 636-2. Concg. O, Van Beinum, with (i) Women's voices of the Coll. Mus.

Images; La Mer; Nocturnes: Nuages; Fêtes* (only); *Prélude à l'après-midi d'un faune

(M) *** RCA (ADD) 82876 59416-2. Boston SO, Munch

***Images*; (i) *Nocturnes. Le Martyre de Saint Sébastien:* (symphonic fragments); *La Mer; Prélude à l'après-midi d'un faune; Printemps* (orch. Büsser)**

(B) *** Double Decca 460 217-2 (2). Montreal SO, Dutoit, (i) with chorus

Haitink's magical performances and recordings (from the mid- to late-1970s), extracted from Haitink's Duo above, have stood the test of time and remain unsurpassed. Indeed, the allure of the orchestral sound as remastered here is quite unforgettable. An admirable choice for Philips's set of '50 Great Recordings'.

Previn's account of *Images* was the first EMI digital record to appear, as early as 1979, and understandably it was also included in the first release of EMI compact discs. Detail emerges clearly, yet there is no highlighting and no interference in the natural perspective. Every colour and sonority, however subtle, registers so vividly in the sound-picture that this factor outweighs any slight reservations one might have about the performances. There is much felicitous wind-playing and no lack of atmosphere in *Gigues*. Baudo's recordings of the other three works come from a decade later and can still be ranked among the very best. The sound is beautifully balanced and natural, and the performances have even more character than Previn's *Images*. Baudo's lovely account of the *Prélude* is as atmospheric as any in the catalogue and more beautifully shaped than many. In the faster sections, *Jeux* is at times brisker than with Haitink, and it well conveys the playfulness of the tennis match, with the sound wonderfully refined and transparent. This Classics for Pleasure reissue is a very real bargain.

At last RCA have paired together Reiner's *Ibéria* and *La Mer*, recorded in the late 1950s, coupled with Ravel and Mussorgsky – though, curiously, Ozawa's (excellent) *Pictures* has been chosen rather than Reiner's version. *Ibéria* is immaculate in execution and magical in atmosphere, a marvellously evocative performance recorded in a natural concert-hall balance. *La Mer* has, if anything, even greater warmth and fullness in the current remastering, while the *pianissimo* opening has enormous evocative feeling and *Jeux de vagues* a haunting sense of colour. The closing *Dialogue du vent et de la mer* generates great excitement. Of course the marvellous acoustic of the Chicago Hall contributes to the appeal of this superbly played account, as it does to the couplings.

In *Images* Rattle is memorably atmospheric, while in *Jeux* he is just a touch more expansive than most rivals and also more evocative, although he does not depart from the basic metronome markings. Haitink probably remains a first choice in this score, for he has atmosphere and a tauter grip on the music's flow. The *King Lear* excerpts sound splendid. First-rate recording, very vivid but beautifully balanced. At Encore price this is a truly remarkable bargain.

Munch's vintage accounts of Debussy were transformed on CD, with the Boston acoustic now casting a wonderfully warm aura over the orchestra, the sound gloriously expansive and translucent. There is marvellous Boston playing here, especially from the violins. Munch's inclination to go over the top may not appeal to all listeners, but the results are compelling and the orchestral bravura is thrilling. The *Prélude à l'après-midi d'un faune* makes a ravishing interlude, expanding to a rapturous climax.

As can be seen, *Ibéria* has ben reissued separately in SACD format, coupled with Ravel's *Boléro*, *Rapsodie espagnole* and *La valse*, with the sound even more glamorous, but losing something in the upper range.

In *Images* and the *Nocturnes* Dutoit is freer than some with rubato, as well as in his warm, expressive moulding of phrase. His sharp pointing of rhythm, as in the Spanish dances of *Ibéria* or the processional march in *Fêtes*, is also highly characteristic of his approach to French music. By contrast, the remaining works are strong rather than evocative, although few versions of *L'après-midi* match this one in the seductive beauty of Timothy Hutchins's flute-playing. For those who like these impressionistic masterpieces to be presented in full colour, with a vivid feeling for atmosphere, this is an ideal choice.

Van Beinum's performances here have genuine atmosphere and beauty: nothing overstated, yet much nuance and detail captured. The *Images* are mono recordings from the 1950s but sound remarkably full and sophisticated, while the rest of the stereo recordings, from the late 1950s, sound only just a bit dated under pressure, though they always remain warm. Well worth investigating at its bargain price.

Images: (i; ii) *Ibéria*; (iii) *Rondes de printemps; Gigues.* (i; iv) *La Mer*; (i; v) *Nocturnes*; (iv) *Marche écossaise*; (i) *Le Martyre de Saint Sébastien (Fragments symphoniques); Petite Suite*; (vi) *Prélude à l'après-midi d'un faune*; (i; vii) *Première Rhapsody for Clarinet & Piano*; (viii) *Première Rhapsody for Saxophone & Orchestra*; (i) *Printemps*; (xi) *Deux Danses.* (i; x) *La Damoiselle élue*
(N) (***) Andante mono AN 2110 (4). (i) Paris Conservatoire O, Coppola; (ii) Pittsburgh SO, Reiner; (iii) San Francisco

SO, Monteux; (iv) NBC SO, Toscanini; (v) Le Grand Orchestre des Festivals Debussy, Inghelbrecht; (vi) Orchestre des Concerts Straram, Straram, 1930; (vii) Hamelin; (viii) Goodman, NY Philharmonic-Symphony Society O, Barbirolli; (xi) Grandjany, Victor String O, Levin; (x) Guyla, Ricquier, Chorale Saint-Gervais

This handsomely produced four-CD set offers a cornucopia of great Debussy recordings in the confines of an 80-page, sturdily bound book in English, French and German. Collectors of the older generation will find here the 1938 HMV 78s of the *Nocturnes* from Piero Coppola and the Paris Conservatoire Orchestra that they grew up with, alongside the even more rare set under Inghelbrecht from 1934, Walter Straram's 1930 *Prélude à l'après-midi d'un faune* and Coppola's wonderfully idiomatic and unhurried *La Damoiselle élue* (1934). The second CD offers three accounts of *La Mer*, two famous, one not: from Coppola (1932), superbly natural; Roger Désormière and the Czech Philharmonic (1950) as well as Toscanini's electrifying NBC account from the same year. (It might have been even more valuable if the Koussevitzky *La Mer* had been chosen, as the Toscanini has been widely and frequently available.) On the third CD it is good to have the *Petite Suite* conducted by Henri Büsser, to whom Debussy entrusted its orchestration, along with Coppola's excellent account, both from the early 1930s, together with his atmospheric *Martyre de Saint-Sébastien* and *Clarinet Rhapsody* with Gaston Hamelin, the latter contrasted with Benny Goodman's 1940 performance with Barbirolli. The last CD contrasts the *Ibéria* of Coppola, with its highly evocative *Les parfums de la nuit*, with Reiner's 1941 account with the Pittsburgh orchestra which we do not recall ever having been transferred before. Some of the Coppola records were included in a six-CD set devoted to the orchestra, discussed some years back (Vogue VG 665001) and now difficult to track down; but in any event these are better transfers. Some of these recordings were made only a decade or so after Debussy's death and bring us nearer than any other to a performance tradition that he would have recognized in his lifetime. This is real treasure trove.

Jeux; La Mer; Nocturnes: Nuages, Fêtes (only)
(***) Testament mono SBT 1108. St Cecilia Ac., Rome, O, De Sabata – RESPIGHI: *Fountains of Rome* (***)

Victor de Sabata's 1947 account with his Rome orchestra of *Jeux* brings great character and atmosphere to this wonderful score. Although the two purely orchestral *Nocturnes* first appeared on record in 1948, de Sabata's account of *La Mer* did not; it makes its first appearance now, but it is still music-making of quality that deserves a place in any Debussy collection.

Le Martyre de Saint-Sébastien: La Cour des lys; Danse extatique
*** Arthaus DVD 100 314. Rotterdam Philh. O, Gergiev (V/D: Bob van den Burg) – PROKOFIEV: *Scythian Suite*; STRAVINSKY: *Piano Concerto* etc. ***

This DVD shows something of the breadth of Gergiev's musical sympathies (and, in the rehearsal sequences, his charm, which persuades his players to give of their best). He has a geniuine feeling for Debussy and we can imagine him directing a distinguished *Pelléas*.

Le Martyre de Saint Sébastien (symphonic fragments);
Prélude à l'après-midi d'un faune

☛ *** MDG Audio DVD 9371099-5; CD 337 1099-2.
Orchester der Beethovenhalle, Bonn, Soustrot – RAVEL:
Ma Mère l'Oye; La Valse ***

Soustrot gives highly atmospheric, slightly understated but
not under-characterized accounts of these scores, with no
exaggerated nuances, only unforced music-making. The
recorded sound is beautifully balanced too, with the details
emerging with both clarity and subtlety. Altogether a most
distinguished coupling. It sounds particularly real in its
Audio DVD format – this is one of the finest Debussy
recordings in the catalogue.

*Le Martyre de Saint-Sébastien: 2 Fanfares & Symphonic
fragments;* (i) *Nocturnes; Printemps (Symphonic Suite)*

☛ ✪ (M) *** DG 476 1653. O de Paris; (i) & Ch.,
Barenboim

This is one of Barenboim's very finest records and it has been
out of the catalogue since the early 1990s. We welcome it back
as part of Universal's 'Penguin ✪ Collection'. Its 72 minutes
include not only the early *Printemps* and the *Symphonic
fragments* from *Le Martyre de Saint-Sébastien* but also his
splendid set of *Nocturnes*. The latter performance, though
highly individual in its control of tempo, has great fervour:
Sirènes develops a feeling of soaring ecstasy, and the closing
pages with chorus are rapturously beautiful. Comparably, in
Le Martyre Barenboim succeeds in distilling an intense, rapt
quality and brings to life its evocative atmosphere in a way
that has not been matched since Cantelli's mono HMV
recording. If Barenboim does not expound the score with
quite the same delicacy of feeling as Cantelli secured, he still
refrains from any expressive indulgence and allows the music
to speak for itself. He is no less persuasive in *Printemps*
(which had to be re-orchestrated by Henri Büsser – following
the composer's instructions – when the original was lost in a
fire). This receives a performance as good as any in the
catalogue. Barenboim succeeds in balancing intensity with
atmospheric feeling, and the result is very persuasive. The
1977–8 recordings, made in either Notre Dame du Liban or
the Paris Mutualité, are spacious, rich in texture and well
balanced, with good definition and range, and the CD transfer has refined detail without reducing the allure.

La Mer

(M) *** DG (ADD) 447 426-2. BPO, Karajan –
MUSSORGSKY: *Pictures;* RAVEL: *Boléro* ***

(N) (M) *** RCA SACD (ADD) 82876 61387-2. Boston SO,
Munch – IBERT: *Escales* ***; SAINT-SAENS: *Symphony 3
in C min.* *** ✪

*** Naïve V 4946. O. Nat. de France, Svetlanov – SCRIABIN:
Poème de l'extase ***

(N) **(*) DG 477 5082 (2). Lucerne Festival O, Abbado –
MAHLER: *Symphony 2* **(*)

La Mer; Nocturnes

✪ (M) *** EMI 5 62746-2 [5 627592]. Philh. Ch. & O, Giulini
– RAVEL: *Alborada; Daphnis et Chloé: Suite 2* *** ✪

La Mer; (i) *Nocturnes. Prélude à l'après-midi d'un faune;
Printemps*

(BB) *** Regis RRC 1177. LSO; (i) L. Symphony Ch.; Frühbeck
de Burgos (without *Printemps*)

(BB) **(*) EMI Encore 5 74727-2. Capitole Toulouse O,
Plasson; (i) with female Ch.

La Mer; Nocturnes: Nuages; Fêtes (only); *Le Martyre de
Saint Sébastien* (symphonic fragments); *Prélude à
l'après-midi d'un faune*

(***) Testament mono SBT 1011. Philh. O, Cantelli

La Mer; Prélude à l'après-midi d'un faune

☛ (M) *** DG (ADD) 427 250-2. BPO, Karajan – RAVEL:
Boléro, etc. ***

After more than three decades Karajan's 1964 account of *La
Mer* is still very much in a class of its own. It enshrines the
spirit of the work as effectively as it observes the letter, and
the superb playing of the Berlin orchestra, for all its virtuosity
and sound, is totally self-effacing. It is now available, coupled
with Karajan's outstanding (1966) record of Mussorgsky's
Pictures at an Exhibition and a gripping account of Ravel's
Boléro, but we prefer the original coupling of the *Prélude à
l'après-midi d'un faune* and Ravel's *Daphnis et Chloé,* which
are equally unforgettable.

Giulini's early stereo recordings of Debussy (from 1962)
remain very distinguished indeed. It would be difficult to
fault his reading of *La Mer,* and the *Nocturnes* are played with
great delicacy of feeling and refinement of detail. *Nuages* and
Sirènes are perhaps a little too dreamy, but they are magically atmospheric, with a fine contribution from the Philharmonia Chorus, which gives the final movement great allure.
Both works here are beautifully recorded; indeed, the Kingsway Hall sound is of demonstration quality for its time, and
the first-rate CD transfer combines ambience and bloom
with inner clarity. The Ravel coupling is equally fine, and this
CD is fully worthy of its inclusion among EMI's 'Great
Recordings of the Century', ranking alongside Karajan's celebrated DG recordings of *La Mer* and *Daphnis,* with marginally even finer sound.

Munch's account of *La Mer* dates from 1956, yet this new
transfer makes it sound better then ever, incredibly vivid for
its period (or any period, for that matter). Even though the
sound is close-miked, the Boston acoustic provided plenty of
atmosphere to match the performance's undoubted excitement. Outstanding couplings and expanded sound on offer
to those with SACD systems.

Michael Plasson and the Orchestre Capitole de Toulouse
offer value for money on EMI's super-budget label Encore, in
that the traditional coupling of *La Mer, Nocturnes* and the
Prélude is supplemented by a lovely performance of
Printemps, very refined and beautifully recorded. The very
well characterized and equally finely played *La Mer* can hold
its own with the best. The two orchestral *Nocturnes* have
plenty of atmosphere, but *Sirènes* is let down by uncertain
intonation and poor tone from the female voices of the
Chœur de Toulouse Midi-Pyrénées. The reverberance of
Halle-aux-Grains poses some problems, but they are more
completely overcome here than in many earlier recordings.

Cantelli's account of the four symphonic fragments from
Le Martyre de Saint Sébastien is one of the most beautiful
performances he ever committed to vinyl; the textures are
impeccably balanced and phrases flawlessly shaped. Its
atmosphere is as concentrated as that of the legendary first
recording under Coppola. *La Mer* and the *Prélude à l'après-
midi d'un faune* are hardly less perfect, and the transfers are
excellent.

Although strong in Mediterranean atmosphere, Frühbeck
de Burgos's account of *La Mer* has an underlying grip, so he
can concentrate on evocation at the opening and continue to
lead the ear on spontaneously. Overall there is plenty of
excitement and much subtlety of detail, both here and in the

Nocturnes, where textures again have the sensuousness of southern climes, and no lack of glitter. The *Prélude à l'après-midi d'un faune* brings lovely, delicate flute-playing from Paul Edmund-Davies and a richly moulded string climax. If these are not conventional readings, they are full of impulse and are superbly recorded.

The Naïve CD provides an impressive memento of Svetlanov's last visit to France in January 2001, a year before his death. *La Mer* was recorded on 25 January at the Théâtre des Champs-Elysées, and *Le Poème de l'extase* three days later in Nantes. Although he is primarily associated with Russian repertoire, Svetlanov obviously has an intuitive feeling for Debussy's masterpiece, and he established excellent rapport with these fine players. A very atmospheric account, which is finely paced and superbly played. There would have been room on this 54-minute disc for another piece from these concerts, but doubtless reasons of either time or quality militated against its inclusion. This is a performance of stature, as is that of the Scriabin. An excellent note by Marc Vignal and very good sound.

Abbado's version, recorded live at the Lucerne Festival in 2003, has undoubted impetus and is very well played. But this is an essentially refined ocean view, the *Jeux des vagues* have little sense of underlying stresses, and the *Dialogue du vent et de la mer*, although it obviously excited the audience, stops short of being *tumultueux*.

Prélude à l'après-midi d'un faune; La Cathédrale engloutie (orch. Stokowski)

(M) (**(*)) Cala mono CACD 0526. NBC SO, Stokowski –
  GOULD: *2 Marches for Orchestra;* HOLST: *The Planets* (***)

The *Prélude à l'après-midi d'un faune* derives from an NBC broadcast dating from March 1943. Apart from a couple of blemishes (the opening has a fair amount of swish), the sound is acceptable, but the performance is more than that: it is individual and compelling, with the faun's reverie celebrated with some particularly lush string-playing. The same comments apply to Stokowski's superb account of his transcription of *La Cathédrale engloutie*, dating from a February 1944 broadcast but sounding rather shrill. There are some technical faults: a sudden brief drop in level quite early on, some pitch fluctuation, etc., but the magnetism of the performance is never in doubt. Two attractive fill-ups for an individual account of *The Planets*.

Première rapsodie (for clarinet and orchestra)

*** EMI 5 56832-2. Meyer, BPO, Abbado – MOZART: *Clarinet Concerto;* TAKEMITSU: *Fantasma/Cantos* ***

This evocative Debussy work reveals to the utmost Sabine Meyer's special gift for using the clarinet seductively. Not only is this a beautiful performance, it is a dramatic one too, with high contrasts underlined, helped by immaculate playing from the Berlin Philharmonic under Abbado. An unusual but magical coupling for the Mozart masterpiece.

(i) Première rapsodie (for clarinet and orchestra); (ii; iii) Danses sacrée et profane; (iii; iv) Sonata for Flute, Viola and Harp; (v) String Quartet; (vi) 2 Arabesques. (vii) Suite bergamasque: Clair de lune

(M) **(*) ASV PLT 8505. (i) Johnson, ECO, Tortelier; (ii) Prometheus Ens.; (iii) Thomas (harp); (iv) Blake, Inoue; (v) Lindsay Qt; (vi) Fergus-Thompson; (v) Cherkassky

Debussy's lovely *First Rhapsody* for clarinet and orchestra (he

never wrote a second) also brings out the most persuasive qualities in Emma Johnson's artistry. The range of expression, with extreme contrasts of tone and dynamics, makes this an exceptionally sensuous performance, yearningly poetic and well recorded. The Lindsays play with their usual aplomb and panache in the *String Quartet*. There are splendid things here, notably the youthful fire of the opening movement and the finely etched finale. They do not always match the *douceur* and *tendresse* that the Quartetto Italiano, the Hagen and the Melos find, but they are always stimulating. The Prometheus Ensemble provide an attractive performance of the *Danses sacrée et profane*, and the *Sonata for Flute, Viola and Harp* is sensitively done too by Richard Blake and his partners. Gordon Fergus-Thomson's *Deux Arabesques* are engagingly played, but Cherkassky's account of *Clair de lune* isn't as magical as it might be.

COLLECTIONS

2 Arabesques (arr. MOUTON); Bruyères (arr. GRAINGER); La Cathédrale engloutie (arr. STOKOWSKI); Children's Corner (arr. CAPLET); Danse (Tarantelle styrienne, arr. RAVEL); L'Isle Joyeuse (arr. MOLINARI); La Mer

(M) **(*) Cala CACD 1024. PO, Simon

Geoffrey Simon's warm, urgent reading of *La Mer* is coupled here to various orchestrations of Debussy's piano music. Debussy himself approved of Caplet's sensitive orchestration of *Children's Corner* ('so gorgeously apparelled', he said), with its reference to *Tristan* in the final *Golliwog's Cakewalk* underlined by the orchestration. The recording is good, if a bit cavernous, and doesn't capture the bass drum in the delectable *Tarantelle styrienne* in the way that Ansermet's old Decca recording did. But it is all enjoyable, and is offered at mid-price.

Clair de lune (arr. CAPLET); The Girl with the Flaxen Hair (arr. GLEICHMANN); Night in Granada (arr. STOKOWSKI); Nocturnes; Pagodas (arr. GRAINGER); Petite suite (arr. BUSSER); Première rapsodie

(M) **(*) Cala CACD 1025. Philh. O, Simon

The second Geoffrey Simon Debussy CD, like the first, includes several rarities, plus an excellent account of the *Nocturnes*. Grainger's arrangement of *Pagodas* is especially charming, with its elaborate percussion section simulating Balinese gamelan, and Büsser's famous arrangement of the *Petite suite* is always a delight. As with the companion CD, the sound is a bit cavernous, clouding some of the textures at times.

CHAMBER MUSIC

Cello Sonata in D min.

(M) *** Decca (ADD) 460 974-2. Rostropovich, Britten –
  SCHUBERT: *Arpeggione Sonata* **(*); SCHUMANN: *5 Stücke in Volkston* ***

(BB) *** Warner Apex 0927 40599-2. Noras, Rigutto –
  FRANCK; FAURE: *Cello Sonatas* ***

**(*) ASV CDDCA 796. Gregor-Smith, Wrigley – BRIDGE;
  DOHNANYI: *Sonatas* **(*)

(i) Cello Sonata; (ii) Violin Sonata

(*) Chan. 8458. (i) Turovsky; (ii) Dubinsky; Edlina – RAVEL: *Piano Trio* *

Cello Sonata; Petite pièce for Clarinet & Piano; Première rapsodie for Clarinet & Piano; Sonata for Flute, Viola & Harp; Violin Sonata; Syrinx for Solo Flute

*** Chan. 8385. Athena Ens.

Like Debussy's other late chamber works, the *Cello Sonata* is a concentrated piece, quirkily original. The classic version by Rostropovich and Britten has a clarity and point which suit the music perfectly. The recording is first class and, if the couplings are suitable, this holds its place as first choice. It is fully worthy of reissue in Decca's latest 'Legends' series.

From Arto Noras and Bruno Rigutto comes as fine a performance of the *Cello Sonata* as any in the catalogue (excepting Rostropovich and Britten). Noras was recorded in 1995, and the sound is good. At the price it is a real bargain.

The most ethereal of the pieces from the Athena Ensemble on Chandos is the *Sonata for Flute, Viola & Harp*, whose other-worldly quality is beautifully conveyed here. In the case of the other sonatas, there are strong competitors but, as a collection, this is certainly recommendable.

Bernard Gregor-Smith and Yolande Wrigley play with great refinement and authority, as well as much sensitivity. They are perhaps too closely balanced but this does not prevent their record being highly desirable.

Yuli Turovsky gives a well-delineated, powerful account with Luba Edlina. In the *Violin Sonata*, Rostislav Dubinsky and Edlina (his wife) are in excellent form, though this is red-blooded Slavonic Debussy rather than the more ethereal, subtle playing of a Grumiaux.

(i) Danses sacrée et profane; (ii) Cello Sonata; (iii) Sonata for Flute, Viola & Harp; (iv) String Quartet; (v) Syrinx; (vi) Violin Sonata

(B) **(*) Cal. DDD/ADD CAL 3822.4 (3). (i; iii) Pierre; (i) La Follia Ens.; (ii) Pernoo; (ii; vi) Rigollet; (iii) Xuereb; (iii; v) Beaumadier; (iv; vi) Roussin – RAVEL: *Chamber Music, etc.* **

The *String Quartet in G minor* was recorded in 1972 – and very good it is, too. The three sonatas are digital and recent and, like the *Danses sacrée et profane* and *Syrinx*, come from 1997. They are very well played, though none would necessarily be a first choice. A more than serviceable recommendation all the same.

Le Petit Nègre; Petite pièce; Première rapsodie; Rapsodie for Cor Anglais; Rapsodie for Saxophone; Sonata for Flute, Viola & Harp; Syrinx

(M) *** Cala CACD 1017 (2). Bennett, Daniel, Campbell, Gough, Watkins, Haram, Tapping, Jones – SAINT-SAENS: *Chamber Music* ***

The *Rapsodie for Cor Anglais*, with which this Cala Duo opens, is more familiar in its form for alto saxophone; it was originally to have been called *Rapsodie mauresque*. Nicholas Daniel plays it with great sensitivity. It is also heard in its alternative form, splendidly played by Simon Haram. The performance of the *Sonata for Flute, Viola & Harp* is also highly sensitive.

Piano Trio in G (1880)

*** Hyp. CDA 67114. Florestan Trio – FAURE; RAVEL: *Piano Trios* ***

(*) Ara. Z 6643. Golub Kaplan Carr Trio – FAURE: *Piano Trio* *; SAINT-SAENS: *Piano Trio* **(*)

(BB) **(*) Naxos 8.550934. Joachim Trio – RAVEL: *Piano Trio*; SCHMITT: *Piano Trio: Très lent* **(*)

Debussy's *Piano Trio*, a product of his teenage years, may reveal few signs of his mature style but it makes a very apt and delightful coupling for the Ravel and Fauré works. With personnel led by the pianist Susan Tomes, the Florestans follow up the success of their prize-winning Schumann disc for Hyperion in a strong and urgent reading, at once highly polished and flexibly expressive. Vivid sound.

The Golub–Kaplan–Carr Trio also give a very good account of this slender piece, and they are decently recorded.

The Joachim Trio play with consistent sensitivity and finesse. This is a thoroughly musical account and beautifully recorded; but it would not necessarily be a first choice, though the attractive price-tag (and the agreeable Schmitt bonus) makes it competitive.

String Quartet in G min., Op. 10

⊕ ⊚ (M) *** DG 463 082-2. Melos Qt – RAVEL: *String Quartet* *** ⊚

*** DG (IMS) 437 836-2. Hagen Qt – RAVEL; WEBERN: *Quartets* ***

(M) *** Ph. 464 699-2. Italian Qt – RAVEL: *Quartet* ***

(B) *** CfP 568 1472. Chilingirian Qt – RAVEL: *Quartet* ***

(B) *** EMI Début 5 74020-2. Belcea Qt – DUTILLEUX: *Ainsi la nuit;* RAVEL: *String Quartet* ***

(M) **(*) Chan. (ADD) 9980. Borodin Qt – RAVEL: *String Quartet* **(*)

(B) **(*) Calliope (ADD) CAL 5893. Talich Qt – RAVEL: *String Quartet etc.* ***

**(*) ASV CDDCA 930. Lindsay Qt – RAVEL: *String Quartet* **(*); STRAVINSKY: *3 Pieces* **(*)

(BB) **(*) Naxos 8.550249. Kodály Qt – RAVEL: *Quartet, etc.* ***

(M) **(*) EMI 5 67550-2 [5 67551-2]. Alban Berg Qt – RAVEL: *String Quartet* **(*); STRAVINSKY: *Concertino; Double Canon; 3 Pieces* ***

The outstanding Melos recording was made in 1979 and is in every way a great performance. The playing of the Melos Quartet is distinguished by perfect intonation and ensemble, scrupulous accuracy in the observance of dynamic markings, a natural sense of flow and great tonal beauty. It would be difficult to imagine a finer account of the Debussy than this, and the sound in its latest Galleria format remains very impressive.

The Hagen Quartet on DG produce the greatest refinement of sound without beautifying the score; they also enjoy the benefit of superb engineering. Indeed, if pressed, this might well be a first choice among recent issues.

It need hardly be said that the playing of the Quartetto Italiano is outstanding. Perfectly judged ensemble, weight and tone still make this a most satisfying choice and, even if it is rather short measure, the Philips recording engineers have produced a vivid and truthful sound-picture. However, it has now been promoted from bargain to mid-price.

At bargain price, the Chilingirian coupling is in every way competitive. They give a thoroughly committed account with well-judged tempi and very musical phrasing. The Scherzo is vital and spirited, and there is no want of poetry in the slow movement. The recording has plenty of body and presence and has the benefit of a warm acoustic: the sound is fuller than on the version by the Italian Quartet.

The Belcea Quartet pay scrupulous attention to dynamics and make fine judgements regarding tempos and can hold their own with the best. They have enviable tonal finesse, and their phrasing is sensitive and internal balance excellent. A brightly lit recording, although there is a touch of glare.

The Borodin Quartet's Chandos version comes from the late 1960s and is not to be confused with their later Virgin CD. The playing is very committed and polished and the recorded sound is eminently satisfactory, but this is not a first choice.

The Talich Quartet recorded their Debussy–Ravel coupling in 1984, the Debussy in the studio and the Ravel at a public concert. It goes without saying that they are distinguished by refinement, perfect ensemble and warmth, and by well-judged tempi and playing that is completely free from idiosyncratic or egocentric touches. The recording is not in the first flight but is more than serviceable.

The Lindsays play with their usual aplomb and panache. There are splendid things here, notably the youthful fire of the opening movement and the finely etched finale. They do not always match the *douceur* and *tendresse* which the Quartetto Italiano and the Hagen find, but they are always stimulating. Fine recording.

As we know from their Haydn recordings, the Kodály Quartet are an excellent ensemble, and they too give a thoroughly enjoyable account. There are moments here (in the slow movement, for example) when the Kodály are touched by distinction. This music-making has the feel of a live performance; these players also have the benefit of a generous fill-up and very good recorded sound. Excellent value.

Technically the Alban Berg are in a class of their own, yet, strangely enough, one finishes listening to this with greater admiration than involvement. Not that they are in any way outside Debussy's world; rather the performance beautifies the work and has comparatively little spontaneous feeling. It is superbly recorded but is not a first choice, unless the outstanding Stravinsky coupling is wanted.

Syrinx; Bilitis (arr. Lenski). (i) *La plus que lente*

*** EMI 5 56982-2. Pahud; (i) Kovacevich – PROKOFIEV: *Flute Sonata*; RAVEL: *Chansons madécasses* ***

Syrinx has rarely sounded more erotic or other-worldly. The *Bilitis* is a transcription by Karl Lenski of the *Six épigraphes antiques* for piano duet (1914). Emmanuel Pahud, first flute of the Berlin Philharmonic, is sensitive both to every nuance and dynamic subtlety and to the spirit of this highly effective transcription. Stephen Kovacevich gives a beautifully characterized account of Debussy's satire of a salon waltz, *La plus que lente*, as good as any and better than most.

Violin Sonata

⊙— ❀ (M) *** Decca (ADD) 460 006-2. Chung, Lupu – FRANCK: *Violin Sonata* *** ❀; CHAUSSON: *Poème* ***

(N) (M) *** DG 477 5448 (2). Mintz, Bronfman (with **Recital of Encores** by ALBÉNIZ; COUPERIN; GLAZUNOV; GRANADOS; KREISLER; WEBER; WIENIAWSKI) – FAURÉ; FRANCK; RAVEL: *Violin Sonatas* ***

*** DG (IMS) 445 880-2. Dumay, Pires – FRANCK: *Violin Sonata*; RAVEL: *Berceuse*, etc. ***

(B) *** CfP 575 80422. Little, Lane – POULENC: *Violin Sonata*; RAVEL: *Violin Sonata*, etc.***

(N) (B) ** Decca 2-CD 475 6709. Bell, Thibaudet – CHAUSSON: *Concert for Piano, Violin & String Quartet*; DEBUSSY; FAURÉ; FRANCK: *Violin Sonatas* **; RAVEL: *Piano Trio* ***

Kyung Wha Chung plays with marvellous character and penetration, and her partnership with Radu Lupu could hardly be more fruitful. Nothing is pushed to extremes and everything is in perfect perspective. The recording sounds admirably real.

Shlomo Mintz gives a performance that is difficult to fault and which gives much pleasure. This can be recommended alongside – though not in preference to – Chung and Lupu. However, Mintz and Bronfman have the additional advantage of offering fine accounts of the Fauré and Ravel *Sonatas* and a magnificent one of the Franck, with an attractive collection of encores thrown in for good measure.

Augustin Dumay and Maria João Pires give as idiomatic and sensitive an account of the Debussy *Sonata* as one could wish for, and those wanting their particular coupling with Franck and Ravel need not really hesitate.

Tasmin Little and Piers Lane also give a highly dedicated performance which tautly holds together the often fragmentary argument, making the result sound spontaneous in its total concentration. Excellent sound and a first-rate coupling.

Joshua Bell and Jean-Yves Thibaudet play the *Sonata* with no want of ardour and much accomplishment, but they are not fully attuned to its spirit. Dynamic markings are carefully observed, but this performances makes more of the work's outward virtuosity than of its searching, intimate quality. The rather up-front recording balance does not help either artist, and competition is very keen here.

Violin Sonata; Nocturne et Scherzo; Beau soir; La fille aux cheveux de lin; Minstrels; Il pleure dans mon coeur

(N) *** Avie AV 2059. Graffin, Désert – ENESCU: *Impressions d'enfance*; RAVEL: *Sonata*; *Tzigane* ***

The performance of the *Violin Sonata* from Philippe Graffin and Claire Désert is delightfully chimerical, sensitively small-scaled. But this very musical partnership offers also the early *Nocturne et Scherzo* which Debussy originally conceived for violin and piano and performed himself (in 1882), but which he later re-wote for cello and piano. Graffin has re-transcribed the violin part, leaving the piano part untouched, and it works very well. The other transcriptions are by Arthur Hartmann, except *Minstrels*, which Debussy himself arranged in 1914. The recording througout has an attractive intimacy, and the couplings are all well worth having, especially the Enesco, which is essentially a ten-movement children's suite.

PIANO MUSIC

Music for Piano Duet and Two Pianos

Danses sacrée et profane; En blanc et noir; Lindaraja; Nocturnes (trans. RAVEL); Prélude à l'après-midi d'un faune

(BB) *** Hyp. Helios CDH 55014. Coombs, Scott

Stephen Coombs and Christopher Scott made an outstanding début with this fine recording, which leads the field in this repertoire. Very highly recommended.

6 épigraphes antiques; Marche écossaise sur un thème populaire; Petite suite (all for piano, 4 hands). En blanc et noir. Lindajara; 2 Nocturnes: Nuages; Fêtes (trans. Ravel). Prélude à l'après-midi d'un faune (arr. composer) (all for 2 pianos)

(N) (BB) ** EMI Gemini (ADD/DDD) 5 86510-2 (2). Collard, Béroff – RAVEL: *Music for 2 pianos*; BIZET: *Jeux d'enfants*; DUKAS: *L'apprenti sorcier* **(*)

This is a most important, indeed unique, set, including all the four-handed and two-piano works of Debussy and Ravel. It is let down by indifferent recording, made in the Paris Salle Wagram in the early 1980s, with the microphones too close, hardening the piano-timbre. But the playing of Jean-Philippe Collard and Michel Béroff is generally distinguished, notably so in *En blanc et noir*, one of the most inspired of Debussy's works, and the aurally fascinating *Six épigraphes antiques*. *Lindajara* is also most impressive but suffers from the shallow piano-timbre, while the engaging *Petite suite* lacks charm. Ravel's transcription of the (digitally recorded) pair of *Nocturnes*, however, is a distinct success, and the composer's arrangement of the *Prélude à l'après-midi d'un faune* comes off surprisingly well, although one misses the sensuous strings in the central climax. For all the reservations about the sound, this generous set, with its enterprising couplings (153 minutes of music overall) is well worth having.

(i) *En blanc et noir; 6 Epigraphes antiques; Lindaraja; Marche écossaise; Petite suite.* (Solo piano): *Ballade slave; Berceuse héroïque; Danse (Tarantelle styrienne); Danse bohémienne; D'un cahier d'esquisses; 12 Etudes; Hommage à Haydn; Masques; Nocturne; Le Petit Nègre; La plus que lente; Rêverie; Suite bergamasque; Valse romantique*
(B) *** Ph. Duo (ADD) (IMS) 438 721-2 (2). Haas, (i) with Lee

2 Arabesques; Children's Corner; Estampes; Images, Books 1-2; L'Isle joyeuse; Mazurka; Pour le piano; Préludes, Books 1-2
(B) **(*) Ph. Duo (ADD) 438 718-2 (2). Haas

The playing of Werner Haas is rarely routine. Book 2 of the *Préludes* and many of the pieces from Book 1 are very well worth having; the *Images* are pretty good too, and many of the shorter pieces in the second listed volume are neatly and sensitively characterized. What makes its companion pair of CDs indispensable is the splendid collection of Debussy's music for piano duet (four hands or two pianos), recorded a decade later, in which Haas is joined by Noël Lee. The *Petite suite* is delightfully fresh, and *En blanc et noir* and the *Six épigraphes antiques* are very distinguished indeed. The (early 1960s) piano recording throughout is well up to Philips's high standard.

Solo piano music

2 Arabesques; Ballade; Berceuse héroïque; Children's Corner; Danse; Danse bohémienne; D'un cahier d'esquisses; Estampes; 12 Etudes; Hommage à Haydn; Images 1-2; L'Isle joyeuse; Masques; Mazurka; Nocturne; Le Petit Nègre; La plus que lente; Pour le piano; Préludes, Books 1-2; Rêverie; Suite bergamasque; Valse romantique. (i) *Fantaisie for piano & orchestra*
(M) (***) EMI mono 5 65855-2 (4). Gieseking; (i) with Hessischen R. O, Schröder

Gieseking's Debussy enjoyed legendary status in the 1930s and 1940s, and EMI are to be congratulated for not only restoring to circulation the famous recordings he then made but also even adding to them. The two sets of *Préludes* date from 1953 and 1954, as indeed do most of the recordings collected here. The earliest is *Children's Corner* from 1951, which is also the date of the Frankfurt recording of the *Fantaisie*. The latter calls for some (albeit not great) tolerance, but the remaining performances sound better than ever. Gieseking's artistry is too well known to need further exegesis or advocacy. A marvellous set which all pianists should investigate.

2 Arabesques; Ballade; Danse bohémienne; Danse (Tarantelle styrienne); Images (1894); Nocturne; Pour le piano; Rêverie; Suite bergamasque; Valse romantique
(BB) **(*) Regis RRC 1121. Tirimo

This is a useful and inexpensive collection and Tirimo's playing is distinguished: there is never any doubt as to his Debussian credentials. He plays only the two outer movements of the 1894 *Images*, arguing quite reasonably that the differences between the two versions of the *Sarabande* are only slight. The acoustic of Rosslyn Hill Chapel, Hampstead, is pleasing and allows the sound to expand; but the balance is close and the microphone even picks up the pedal mechanism (try the opening of the *Danse* on track 8). This will worry some listeners more than others, and otherwise this is a fine disc.

2 Arabesques; Berceuse héroïque; D'un cahier d'esquisses; Hommage à Haydn; Images, Books I & II; L'Isle joyeuse; Page d'album; Rêverie
⊶ ✿ (M) *** Decca 475 210-2. Kocsis

Winner of the *Gramophone* 1990 Instrumental Award, Zoltán Kocsis's Debussy recital, originally issued by Philips, is in every way outstanding. The recording of the piano is still among the most realistic we have heard and artistically this collection is even more distinguished in terms of pianistic finesse, sensitivity and tonal refinement than his earlier, 1983 collection (Philips 412 118-2, now withdrawn).

2 Arabesques; Children's Corner; Estampes; Etudes, Books 1-2; Images, Books 1-2; Le Petit Nègre; La plus que lente; Pour le piano; Préludes, Books 1-2
(BB) *(**) EMI 5 74122-2 (3). Béroff

On the original LPs Michel Béroff's accounts of the *Préludes* and *Estampes* had a compelling sense of atmosphere and a wonderful sensitivity and tonal finesse. However, these transfers have brought the aural image forward and succeed in robbing the performances of much of their magic. Some tinkering with the controls will help, and there is still pleasure to be derived from Béroff's artistry, but justice has not been done to the sonority that this fine Debussian produces.

2 Arabesques; Children's Corner; Estampes; Images, Books 1-2; L'Isle joyeuse; Pour le piano; Préludes, Book 1; Rêverie; Suite bergamasque
(B) *** Double Decca (ADD) 443 021-2 (2). Rogé

Pascal Rogé's playing is distinguished by a keen musical intelligence and sympathy, as well as by a subtle command of keyboard colour, and this Double Decca set must receive the warmest welcome. *Children's Corner* is played with neat elegance and the characterization has both charm and perception, while the *Suite bergamasque*, *Pour le piano* and *Images* are no less distinguished. In *Estampes* there are occasional moments when the listener senses the need for more dramatic projection, but Rogé brings genuine poetic feeling to the first book of the *Préludes*. The CD transfers are clear and firm.

2 Arabesques; Children's Corner; Estampes; L'Isle joyeuse; Le Petit Nègre; La plus que lente; Rêverie; Suite bergamasque: Clair de lune
*** Chan. 9912. Tabe

Among newer recordings of Debussy piano music Kyoko Tabe's recital is eminently successful. She has a good feeling for atmosphere and a keen musical intelligence. The playing time runs to 65 minutes, so there would have been room for the whole of the *Suite bergamasque*. All the same, this is a fine issue on every count.

2 Arabesques; Children's Corner; Images, Books I & II; Etudes, Book II; Estampes; L'Isle joyeuse; Masques; La plus que lente; Pour le piano; Préludes, Books I & II; Rêverie; Suite bergamasque

(N) (B) ** EMI 5 859902-2 (4). Samson François – RAVEL: *Piano Music* **

There is some spirited playing from Samson François, and the piano is well enough recorded (between 1968 and 1970), but François, although much admired by his compatriots, is not consistently sensitive, not does he observe the dynamic nuances so important in this repertoire. Robust rather than refined, and no match for Rogé.

2 Arabesques; Danse bohémienne; D'un cahier d'esquisses; Estampes; Images oubliées; L'Isle joyeuse; Morceau de concours; Nocturne; Pour le piano; Préludes, Books 1-2 (complete); Masques; Rêverie

*** Decca 452 022-2 (2). Thibaudet

Beautifully recorded, Jean-Yves Thibaudet's wide range of tone and dynamic is used with great imagination, and his playing often suggests an improvisatory quality. The music's subtlety of colour, with half-lights as well as sudden blazes of light (as in the stunning *Feux d'artifice*), is fully understood by this fine artist, and there is no question as to the spontaneity of his playing. The *Préludes* are among the finest on record.

Ballade; Berceuse héroïque; Children's Corner; Danse (Tarantelle styrienne); Elégie; Etudes, Books 1 & 2; Etude retrouvée (reconstructed Roy Howatt); Hommage à Haydn; Images 1–2; Mazurka; Page d'album; Le Petit Nègre; La plus que lente; Suite bergamasque; Valse romantique

*** Decca 460 247-2 (2). Thibaudet

This completes Jean-Yves Thibaudet's survey of Debussy's solo piano music, and Debussy-playing doesn't come any better than this. As before, these performances are full of evocative atmosphere (especially the *Images*), and ever imaginative in their infinite variety of colour and dynamic. But most impressive are the *Etudes*, unsurpassed on record in their strong characterization, flair and virtuosity – not even by Mitsuko Uchida's famous Philips set – and, with Decca's recording so real and immediate, they project with vivid spontaneity as at a live recital. These two CDs make a clear first choice among modern digital recordings of this totally absorbing repertoire.

Children's Corner Suite

(BB) **(*) Naxos 8.550885. Biret – SCHUMANN: *Kinderszenen;* TCHAIKOVSKY: *Album for the Young* ****

Idil Biret takes the opening movement very briskly and impetuously, but the performance then settles down and is sensitive and well characterized, especially the closing *Golliwog's Cakewalk*. Good recording and recommendable couplings too.

Children's Corner Suite; Danse (Tarantelle styrienne); 3 Estampes; Images: Poissons d'or; Reflets dans l'eau. Mazurka; Pour le piano: Toccata. Préludes, Book I: La cathédrale engloutie; La fille aux cheveux de lin; Minstrels. Suite bergamasque; Valse romantique

(N) (BB) * Naxos 8.555800. Thiollier

There is nothing special here; indeed the the playing is less than first rate and, with so many alternative collections available, readers are advised to look elsewhere.

Children's Corner; D'un cahier d'esquisses; Hommage à Joseph Haydn; Morceau de concours; Le Petit Nègre; La Plus que lente; Préludes, Book 1

*** BIS CD 1205. Ogawa

Children's Corner; Estampes; Homage à Joseph Haydn; Images, Books 1–2; Masques; Le Petit Nègre; La Plus que lente; Préludes, Books 1–2

(B) *(*) Naïve 2-CD (ADD) V 1001 (2). Lee

Noël Lee's Debussy comes from 1971 and was well thought of in its day, even though the recorded sound is a little wanting in transparency and bloom. The two books of *Préludes* and *La Plus que lente* are accommodated on one CD and the rest on its companion. Noël Lee is completely inside this repertory and his playing is often distinguished, but the recorded sound is no match for its finest analogue competitors, Thibaudet or the BIS recording listed above. Moreover, the notes are to be found only on www.naiveclassique.com, which will not suit collectors who prefer them to be more readily available with the disc.

Children's Corner; Images, Books 1–2; Préludes, Books 1–2

**(*) DG (ADD) 449 438-2 (2). Michelangeli

'Immaculate' is one of the words that spring to mind when one hears Michelangeli's Debussy. There is no doubt that his performances of *Children's Corner* and the two sets of *Images* are very distinguished. The *Préludes* undoubtedly bring piano playing which is pretty flawless. At the same time, it is very cool and detached and, although Book 2 excited enormous enthusiasm in some quarters, both Books here will strike many as somewhat glacial and curiously unatmospheric. Moreover the set is uncompetitively priced.

Children's Corner; Estampes; L'Isle joyeuse; Images I & II; La Plus que lente; Suite bergamasque

(M) (***) EMI mono 5 62798-2. Gieseking

A self-recommending disc, drawing on Walter Gieseking's four-disc survey listed above. The mono recordings are of excellent quality.

Estampes; Images, Books 1–2, Images oubliées; L'Isle joyeuse; Masques pour piano

*** BIS CD 1105. Ogawa

These first two volumes of Noriko Ogawa's Debussy survey bode well. She has an unerring feeling for the Debussy sound world and the delicacy and refinement of touch to do it full justice. This Japanese pianist is the equal of Thibaudet, and her elegance and finesse are matched by a magnificent sense of atmosphere. The BIS recording is in the very first flight.

Estampes: Soirée dans Grenade; Jardins sous la pluie. Images: Reflets dans l'eau; Hommage à Rameau; Poissons d'or. Masques; La plus que lente; Préludes: La Fille aux cheveux de lin; La Cathédrale engloutie; Minstrels; La Terrasse des audiences du clair de lune; Ondine

(B) *** RCA 2CD (ADD) stereo/mono 74321 846062.
Rubinstein – FAURE: *Nocturne 3*; FRANCK: *Symphonic Variations; Prélude, choral et fugue*; RAVEL: *Valses nobles et sentimentales; Le tombeau de Couperin*: excerpts; *Miroirs*; SAINT-SAENS: *Piano Concerto 2* (with CHABRIER: *Pièces pittoresques: Scherzo-valse*) ****

The source of these Debussy pieces is not clear, but most were recorded in the 1960s. The excerpts from *Estampes* and *Reflets dans l'eau* are listed as mono (1945) but still sound real and immediate. The performances are poised and refined and have great atmosphere, showing Rubinstein as a natural Debussian. *Jardins sous la pluie* and *Reflets dans l'eau* bring an easy virtuosity, always at the service of the composer. The remastering is most impressive.

Etudes, Books 1–2
⊕– ✿ (M) *** Ph. 464 698-2. Uchida
(M) ** DG 471 359-2. Pollini – BOULEZ: *Piano Sonata 2* (***)

Etudes, Books 1–2; Estampes; L'Isle joyeuse
(BB) *** Regis RRC 1091. Tirimo

12 Etudes; Images, Books 1–2
*** Warner 8573 83940-2. Aimard

Mitsuko Uchida's remarkable account of the *Etudes* on Philips is not only one of the best Debussy piano records in the catalogue and arguably her finest recording, but also one of the best ever recordings of the instrument. It is even more attractive at mid-price and is certainly worthy of inclusion among Philips's selection of '50 Great Recordings'.

Debussy playing of some stature from Pierre-Laurent Aimard, though his playing does not project the mists and atmosphere of this music so much as its extraordinary colour, inner vitality and originality. The *Images* are vibrant and as good as any in the catalogue, and the musical and technical challenges of the *Etudes* are surmounted with magisterial aplomb. This holds its own even alongside the wonderful Uchida set. Crystalline, clean recording that is in the demonstration category.

Martino Tirimo offers not only the *Etudes*, played with imagination and much subtlety of colour, but he also includes a set of *Estampes* and *L'Isle joyeuse*, neither quite as impressive, but still worth having. He is very well recorded and this Regis reissue is very competitive in the cheapest price-range.

In terms of atmosphere and poetic feeling, Pollini is no match for Uchida or indeed for Pierre-Laurent Aimard. He offers impressive and distinguished pianism, but there is little sense of magic, no doubt the fault of the rather close and analytical recording balance. In climaxes there is a certain hardness.

Hommage à Rameau
(M) **(*) BBC mono BBCL 4064-2. Michelangeli –
BEETHOVEN: *Sonatas 4 & 12* **(*); RAVEL: *Gaspard de la nuit* (***)

The Debussy *Hommage à Rameau* is beautifully delivered and controlled. It comes with an almost miraculous account of Ravel's *Gaspard*, which alone is worth the price of the disc. The notes by William Robson, Michelangeli's BBC producer, serve to bring the whole occasion vividly to life.

Images I & II; Préludes, Book I (from above set)
(N) (M) **(*) DG (ADD) 477 5345. Michelangeli

As can be seen, both sets of *Images* and Book I of the *Préludes* (discussed above) have been reissued separately as one of DG's 'Originals'.

Préludes, Books 1–2 (complete)
⊕– ✿ (M) *** EMI mono 5 67233-2 [5 67262-2]. Gieseking

(N) *** Onyx 4004. Rogé
*** DG 435 773-2 (2). Zimerman
(BB) *** Regis RRC 1111. Tirimo

Gieseking's classic set of both Books of the Debussy *Préludes* takes its rightful place as one of EMI's 'Great Recordings of the Century' and now has proper documentation. The current remastering again confirms the natural realism of the 1953–4 Abbey Road recording, with Book 1 produced by Geraint Jones and Book 2 by Walter Legge, although there is a touch of hardness on *forte* passages.

When Pascal Rogé embarked on his Debussy recordings for Decca in the 1970s, he did not include the Second Book of *Préludes*. He is among the finest exponents of this inexhaustible and fascinating repertoire now before the public, and his expertly recorded performances are totally gripping.

There is no want of atmosphere or poetic feeling in Krystian Zimerman's account of the *Préludes*. This is a very distinguished performance indeed, though some may find the level of intensity too much to live with. Yet his playing is imaginative and concentrated. The DG recording is sensitively balanced, but there is more than a hint of hardness in climaxes.

No grumbles about value for money or quality from Martino Tirimo on Regis. His playing is very fine indeed and can withstand comparison with most of his rivals – and, apart from the sensitivity of his playing, the recording is most realistic and natural. This could well be a first choice for those wanting a modern digital recording offering the complete set on one disc.

Préludes, Book 1
(**) TDK **DVD** DV-DOCEQY. Barenboim. (Film by Paul Smaczny)

This is not a straight performance of the First Book of the *Préludes* by Daniel Barenboim, but a film in which they feature, sometimes with a narrative overlay. Readers may well find, as we did, that it breaks the spell to find *Nuages* or the *Sonata for flute, viola and harp* cropping up in the background during the commentary, and various quotations being offered between the individual *Préludes*. Generally, the film is atmospheric and the photography both striking and tasteful. A great deal of care has been lavished on it, and though there are one or two tiresome conceits (the beautiful young lady who swans around in the first two pieces and traipses down alleyways in *La Sérénade interrompue*, and the puzzling chess game in one of the others), there is more to admire than to cavil at. Barenboim's playing is sensitive enough – without exactly eclipsing memories of the finest Debussians – and his commentary on the whole is thoughtful, as one would expect. (Perhaps his producer should have saved him from one embarrassment when he speaks of Debussy as a 'loner', then confesses that he doesn't know whether this is true of his private life! There is plenty of literature, from Lockspeiser onwards, which he might have consulted.) But this is a pedantic small point: he plays decently, the photography and the settings are sumptuous and the occasional irritant is outweighed by the visual and musical pleasures on offer. But frankly we feel that this is not the way to present performances on DVD: they should be kept separate from any commentary.

Préludes, Book 1; Images oubliées (1894)
(M) **(*) Channel CCS 4892. Van Immerseel

The special interest of Jos van Immerseel's recording of the first Book of *Préludes* lies in his instrument, an Erard of 1897, of the kind which Debussy would have known and played. The sonority is gentle and veiled and curiously seductive except in *forte* passages; the timbre, particularly in the upper register of the instrument, is monochrome and dry, and this tells in a piece such as *La Sérénade interrompue*. There is a real turn-of-the-century feel to the shadowy sound-world of *Des pas sur la neige* and the first of the *Images oubliées*. An interesting appendix for a Debussy discography, but essentially this is an issue for specialist collections.

VOCAL MUSIC

Early Songs: Poèmes de Théodore de Banville: *Aimons-nous; Fête galante; Il dort encore; Le Lilas; Nuit d'étoiles; Pierrot; Rêverie; Les Roses; Sérénade; Souhait; Zéphyr.* **Poèmes de Paul Bourget:** *Les Cloches; Musique; Paysage sentimental; Romance d'Ariel; Romances 1 & 2; Regret; Voici que le printemps.* **Poème de Gautier:** *Coquetterie posthume.* **Poème de Mallarmé:** *Apparition.* **Poèmes de Verlaine:** *Clair de lune; En sourdine; Fantoches; Mandoline; Pantomime*
*** Deux-Elles DXL 1052. Keith, Lepper

Gillian Keith, winner of the Kathleen Ferrier Award in 2000, with her fresh, bright soprano proves a sensitive interpreter of these early Debussy songs. It is not easy for a singer to soften the impact of such a voice, and Keith with her fine control of dynamic does wonders in shading her tone in songs which demand subtlety above all. There is a sensuous element even in Debussy's earliest songs, and this generous selection gets one marvelling at the range and finesse of the composer even in his teens. Keith is sensitively accompanied by a young colleague, also trained at the Royal Academy of Music, Simon Lepper. First-rate sound.

Mélodies: *L'Ame évaporée; Auprès de cette grotte sombre; Beau soir; Chevaux de bois; Les Cloches; Crois mon conseil; L'Echelonnement des haies; Fêtes galantes 1 (En sourdine; Fantoches; Clair de lune); Fêtes galantes 2 (Les Ingénus; Le Faune; Colloque); Green; Je tremble en voyant ton visage; Le Jet d'eau; Mandoline; La Mer; Pour ce que plaisance est morte; Le Son du cor; De soir; Le Temps a laissié son manteau*
(M) *** DG (ADD) 463 664-2. Souzay, Baldwin

This is one of the great Debussy song-recitals of the age. Recorded in 1961, it opened the eyes of many music-lovers of the time to the mastery of these inspired songs. Quite apart from the beauty of his voice itself, it is the sheer intelligence and consummate artistry that Gérard Souzay brings to bear that silences criticism. He is admirably partnered by Dalton Baldwin. Excellent recorded sound.

Mélodies: *La Belle au bois dormant; Beau soir; 3 Chansons de Bilitis; Fêtes galantes 1; Fleur des blés; Noël des enfants qui n'ont plus de maison; Nuit d'étoiles*
*** Virgin 5 45360-2. Gens, Vignoles – FAURÉ; POULENC: *Mélodies ***

Véronique Gens gives an impressive and imaginative account of these songs, allowing Debussy's subtle art to register without any expressive exaggeration. She certainly makes a beautiful sound and has the benefit of Roger Vignoles's intelligent support, and excellent and natural recording.

3 Ballades de François Villon
(N) (***) Testament mono SBT 1312. Souzay, Bonneau – DUPARC: *Chanson triste; Elégie,* etc.; CHAUSSON: *Songs;* RAVEL: *Don Quichotte à Dulcineé* (***)

The *Villon Ballades* are heard in their orchestral form (*Le Promenoir des deux amants* and *La Grotte* in the orchestration by Louis Beydts) although, as in the Ravel *Don Quichotte,* the balance is not ideal. Souzay is very close to the microphone and masks some of the orchestral detail. But this is superb singing by a master of this repertoire, and Jacqueline Bonneau is an ideal partner.

3 Ballades de François Villon; 3 Chansons de France; Fêtes galantes (2nd series); Noël des enfants qui n'ont plus de maison; 3 Poèmes de Stéphane Mallarmé; Le Promenoir des deux amants
(M) **(*) Naïve V 4803. Kruysen, Lee

Bernard Kruysen was perhaps the most distinguished Dutch baritone of his day. The present recital comprises the contents of one 1971 LP which, at just under 40 minutes, is distinctly poor value even at mid-price. Artistically these are strong performances, aristocratic in demeanour and well characterized. Kruysen is sensitively and perceptively accompanied by Noël Lee, and well recorded too.

3 Ballades de François Villon; Fêtes galantes (2nd series); Fleur des blés; Mandoline; 3 Mélodies; Nuit d'étoiles; 5 Poèmes de Baudelaire; Voici que le printemps
*** Hyp. CDA 67357. Maltman, Martineau

Christopher Maltman proves himself equal to the challenges of Debussy, Verlaine and Baudelaire, and in no small measure the success of his recital resides in the superb support of Malcolm Martineau. Maltman's feeling for line and his sense of style are impressive, and the Hyperion recording team produce excellent and naturally balanced sound. This is a most successful and enjoyable recital.

3 Chansons de Charles d'Orléans
*** Ph. 438 149-2. Monteverdi Ch., ORR, Gardiner – FAURÉ: *Requiem;* RAVEL; SAINT-SAENS: *Choral Works ***

With Gardiner and his period forces bringing out the medieval flavour of these charming choral settings, this adds to a generous and unusual coupling for Gardiner's expressive reading of the Fauré *Requiem.*

La Damoiselle élue
(***) Testament mono SBT 3203 (3). De los Angeles, Boston SO, Munch – BERLIOZ; *Les Nuits d'été;* MASSENET: *Manon ***

The combination of Munch's purposeful understanding of this wayward work, together with the charm of Victoria de los Angeles, make this an exceptional performance, even though in limited (1955) mono sound. As in the Berlioz song-cycle, the RCA recording may not capture the full golden beauty of the singer's voice, but these two works make a valuable bonus for the classic Monteux version of Massenet's *Manon.*

L'Enfant prodigue (scène lyrique): Cortège et Air de danse
(M) (**(*)) mono BBCL 4113. RPO, Beecham (with spoken introduction) – BERLIOZ: *The Trojans: Royal Hunt and Storm;* CHABRIER: *España; Gwendoline Overture;* DELIUS: *Brigg Fair;* MASSENET: *La Vierge: Le dernier sommeil de la vierge;* SAINT-SAENS: *Le rouet d'Omphale* (with MOZART: *Divertimento in D, K.131:* excerpts) (**(*))

This famous Beecham encore, played with characteristic charm and finesse, comes from a live broadcast concert of 1956. The recording is acceptable but not of the BBC's finest standard.

4 Poèmes de Charles Baudelaire (orch. John Adams)
(N) *** Warner 2564 61938-2. Graham, BBC SO, Yan Pascal Tortelier – CHAUSSON: *Poème de l'amour et de la mer*; RAVEL: *Shéhérazade* ***

It was surely an extraordinary venture of John Adams to orchestrate four of these songs; he omits *La mort des amants*. The result is to give the words an entirely new atmosphere, a richer background patina, and in *Recueillement* he even brings in horns, apparently to suggest a Wagnerian ethos. Certainly Susan Graham responds to this new backcloth, so different from a piano, and she sings tenderly and often very beautifully indeed. A fascinating and daring experiment, well brought off by conductor and singer alike.

OPERA

Pelléas et Mélisande (DVD versions)
*** DG **DVD** 073 030-9. Hagley, Archer, Maxwell, Cox, Walker, Welsh Nat. Op. Ch. & O, Boulez (V/D Peter Stein)
** Arthaus **DVD** 100 100. Le Roux, Alliot-Lugaz, Van Dam, Soyer, Taillon, Golfier, Schirrer, Lyon Op. Ch. & O, Gardiner. (S/D: Pierre Strosser. V/D: Jean-François Jung)

Boulez's account of *Pelléas* with the Welsh National Opera was much acclaimed at the time, and, judging from the 1992 DVD recording, rightly so. Boulez produces much greater atmosphere than he did in the celebrated CBS version. On DVD the first four acts are accommodated on the first disc, Act V on the second. The soloists are impressive; Alison Hagley's Mélisande especially is both good to look at and to listen to. Her vocal and stage characterization are excellent, and she conveys an appealing sense of innocence. Neill Archer's Pelléas is no less intelligently projected, and Kenneth Cox's Arkel is splendidly sung and finely acted. Peter Stein's production is effective, simple and beautifully lit. During the orchestral interludes, which Debussy composed to cover scene changes in the first production, we are shown the full score but at no time either the orchestra or Boulez. Yet this is infinitely more satisfying than the alternative Lyons production with its perverse setting.

On DVD the Lyon cast is strong: François Le Roux's Pelléas, familiar from Abbado's DG recording, has innocence and vulnerability, and the Mélisande of Colette Alliot-Lugaz is subtly drawn, more so than in her Decca recording with Dutoit. José van Dam, who also recorded the role with both Abbado and Karajan, conveys Golaud's torment of spirit to perfection, and it is difficult to fault any of the remaining characters.

Special interest lies in Gardiner's musical direction: he corrects various textual errors and removes the interludes Debussy wrote to cover scene changes in the original production, producing an altogether tauter dramatic experience. Gardiner also lays out the orchestra in the way Debussy had originally directed, with a distinct gain in transparency.

The stage director shows no comparable respect for the original: the action is placed indoors in the large room of a château at the turn of the nineteenth century at the time when Debussy was composing the opera: so there are no tower, no sea-shore, no forest, no grotto, no sense of the sunless castle and no mystery.

A rather run-down Golaud is seen in a dressing-gown, turning over the past in his mind, and we lose the fountain, the impact of light when the lovers emerge from the vault – and so on. In any profession other than opera production this would be condemned as vandalism, although it is not quite as dire and impertinent as the 1997 Glyndebourne production which pictured Mélisande perched in a chandelier! This performance comes from 1987.

Pelléas et Mélisande (CD versions)
☛ *** DG 435 344-2 (2). Ewing, Le Roux, Van Dam, Courtis, Ludwig, Pace, Mazzola, Vienna Konzertvereinung, VPO, Abbado
(M) *** Naïve Radio FranceV4923 (3) Von Otter, Holzmair, Naouri, Schaer, Vernhes, Couderc, R. France Ch. & Nat. O, Haitink
(M) *** EMI 5 67168-2. Stilwell, Von Stade, Van Dam, Raimondi, Ch. of German Op., Berlin, BPO, Karajan
(B) *** Naxos 8.660047-9 (3). Delusch, Theruel, Arapian, Bacquier, Jessoud, Ch. Regional Nord/Pas de Calais, O Nat. de Lille, J.-C. Casadesus
(M) **(*) Sony (ADD) SM3K 47265 (3). Shirley, Söderström, McIntyre, Ward, Minton, ROHCG Ch. & O, Boulez
(M) (***) EMI mono 7 61038-2 (3). Joachim, Jansen, Etcheverry, Paris CO, Désormière (with *Mélodies*)
(***) Testament mono SBT 3051 (3). Jansen, de los Angeles, Souzay, Froumenty, Collard, French Nat. R. O, Cluytens
(M) **(*) Decca (ADD) 473 351-2 (2). Maurane, Spoorenberg, London, Hoeckmann, Veasey, Geneva Grand Theatre Ch., SRO, Ansermet

Claudio Abbado's outstanding version broadly resolves the problem of a first CD recommendation in this opera, which has always been lucky on record. If among modern versions the choice has been hard to make between Karajan's sumptuously romantic account, almost Wagnerian, and Dutoit's clean-cut, direct one, Abbado satisfyingly presents a performance more sharply focused than the one and more freely flexible than the other, altogether more urgently dramatic. The casting is excellent, with no weak link.

Haitink even in the opening prelude establishes the dedication of his reading, spacious, capturing an intensity that unmistakably evokes a great live event. Though speeds are often on the slow side, the thrust of the drama is presented with an extraordinary vividness, largely a question of Haitink's control of tempo, so that climactic moments are thrust home with often chilling impact. Never is there the feeling that this is a static work. Though neither of the two principals is a native French-speaker, their performances are totally idiomatic, with Holzmair a fresh, lyrical Pelléas, believably ardent in his obsession with Mélisande, and with von Otter also characterizing superbly, tender and subtle, not just an innocent. The Golaud of Laurent Naouri is the more moving when with his youngish baritone he is such a believable lover, not merely a predator. The others too are first rate, with firmness and clarity the keynote, with the soprano of Florence Couderc fresh and bright if obviously feminine in this young boy's role. The three discs avoid the need to break in the middle of Act III, and come in a three-for-the-price-of-two offer, but the CD index points are limited to the beginnings of scenes, not even separating the preludes and interludes, so that the third disc, containing just Act V, has only a single index point.

EMI have restored the rich and passionate Karajan set to

the catalogue, still at full price. It is a performance that sets Debussy's masterpiece as a natural successor to Wagner's *Tristan*, with the orchestral tapestry at the centre and the singers providing a verbal obbligato; but Karajan's concentration carries one in total involvement through a story that can seem inconsequential. Frederica von Stade is a tenderly affecting heroine and Richard Stilwell a youthful and upstanding hero, set against the dark, incisive Golaud of Van Dam. The playing of the Berlin Philharmonic is both polished and deeply committed.

Though the spaciousness of Casadesus's sensitive and poetic reading means that the Naxos set stretches to three discs rather than two, the result is most compelling, with fresh, young voices helping to make the drama more involving. Mireille Delusch is a bright and girlish Mélisande, well matched against the high baritone of Gérard Theruel as a boyish Pelléas. The others are first rate too, including the veteran, Gabriel Bacquier, aptly sounding old as Arkel. The voices are to the fore in the recording, with every word made clear, and the orchestra, with a modest band of strings, adds to the chamber-scale intimacy. The libretto comes in French only, but with good notes and a synopsis in English. An outstanding bargain nevertheless.

Boulez's sharply dramatic view of Debussy's atmospheric score on Sony is a performance which will probably not please the dedicated Francophile – for one thing there is not a single French-born singer in the cast – but it rescues Debussy from the languid half-tone approach which for too long has been accepted as authentic. Boulez is supported by a strong cast; the singing is not always very idiomatic but it has the musical and dramatic momentum that stems from sustained experience on the stage. In almost every way this has the tension of a live performance.

In Roger Désormière's wartime recording, Etcheverry is arguably the most strongly characterized Golaud committed to disc, and neither Joachim's Mélisande nor Jansen's Pelléas has been readily surpassed. A *Pelléas* without atmosphere is no *Pelléas*, and this classic reading puts you under its spell immediately. A further inducement for collectors is a generous selection of Debussy songs from Maggie Teyte and the celebrated recording of *Mes longs cheveux* by the original Mélisande, Mary Garden, accompanied on the piano by Debussy himself in 1904. A very special set.

The Cluytens (1956) recording is a welcome return to the catalogue. Victoria de los Angeles as Mélisande is often affecting and always sings the role exquisitely, and readers will obviously want the set for her. Souzay's Golaud is also magnificent vocally. André Cluytens gets superior playing from the Orchestre National de la Radiodiffusion Française and casts a strong spell, even if he does not always distil as powerful an atmosphere. The transfer is altogether exemplary, a model of its kind, and the well-focused mono sound gives unalloyed pleasure.

It is good to have Ansermet's 1964 recording return to currency in Decca's mid-priced 'Compact Opera Collection'. The presentation is attractive and now includes an excellent cued synopsis, as well as making the complete libretto with translation available on the Internet. The analogue stereo recording remains in the demonstration bracket; but Ansermet is curiously literal, and rarely does the undoubted beauty of the sound bring with it that evocative frisson that the composer surely intended. It is largely a question of tension, and Ansermet's direction tends to be in a low key. Camille Maurane's Pelléas is excellent and Erna Spoorenberg has a simple charm without ever seeming quite at home in the

part. George London's Golaud is coarse and ill-defined, but that is perhaps right with so unpleasant a character. Even so, the performance still carries the Ansermet charisma, and his admirers will not want to be without this reissue.

Rodrigue et Chimène (opera; completed Langham Smith; orch. Denisov)

*** Erato 4509 98508-2 (2). Brown, Dale, Jossoud, Van Dam, Bastin, Le Texier, Lyon Op. Ch. & O, Nagano

In the years immediately before he started work on his masterpiece, *Pelléas et Mélisande*, Debussy all but completed this opera to a much more conventional libretto, telling the story of El Cid. Richard Langham Smith reconstructed the rest, and Edison Denisov did the inspired orchestration, adding music from other sections to fill in a few gaps. The best comes first, with radiant singing from Laurence Dale, ideal as Rodrigue, and the fresh and expressive soprano, Donna Brown, as Chimène. Atmospheric off-stage choruses are distinctive too, but little of Act III gives much clue as to the identity of the composer, enjoyable though it is. Kent Nagano's superb recording brings vividly atmospheric sound. José van Dam sings strongly and clearly as the heroine's father, Don Diègue, with the veteran, Jules Bastin, in splendid voice as Don Gomez.

DELAGE, Maurice (1879–1961)

4 Poèmes hindous

*** Testament mono SBT 1135. Micheau, Fr. R. O, Cluytens – STRAVINSKY: *Le Rossignol* *** ❂

The *Quatre Poèmes hindous* make an ideal coupling for *Le Rossignol*. These four songs are very much in the received post-Debussian tradition and are exquisitely sung by Janine Micheau. While the mono sound is less transparent than is ideal, the recording is expertly transferred and gives great pleasure.

DELALANDE, Michel-Richard (1657–1726)

Premier Caprice ou Caprice de Villers-Cotterêts

(M) **(*) Erato (ADD/DDD) 2564 60578-2. Ch. Caillard, Jean-François Paillard O, Paillard – LULLY: *Armide; Isis* (extracts) **(*)

Michel-Richard Delalande was closely associated with the courts of Louis XIV (he taught his daughters and was made Master of the King's chamber music in 1685) and Louis XV (he was director of the Royal Chapel in 1714–23), holding in total seven court posts during his lifetime. Delalande extracted music from his elaborate court ballets into suites or symphonies (sometimes called Caprices), which were performed every 15 days during the supper of Louis XIV and Louis XV. This *First Caprice* is named after the *Château de Villers-Cotterêts*, residence of the king's brother, presumably written for some occasion connected with him. This (digital) recording is eminently enjoyable, though Paillard's style, using modern instruments, does seem a little heavy at times, if not enough to seriously mar enjoyment. The music is tuneful and thoroughly entertaining, a nice mixture of lively drums and trumpet numbers with more gently melancholy ones – there is particularly attractive writing for the woodwind (the bassoons and oboes in the *Augmentation, premier air neuf* are delightful). It makes an original bonus for the Lully suites.

La grande pièce royale (Fantasy or Caprice) for oboe, strings & continuo); Te Deum; Motets: Panis Angelicus; Venite, adoremus; Venite, exultemus

⊕— * Hyp. CDA 67325. Sampson, Clifton-Griffith, Gilchrist, Agnew, Gunthorpe, Mustard, Ex Cathedra, Skidmore

Entitled '*Music for the Sun King*', this is an anthology which readily demonstrates the wide range and quality of Delalande's music which is clearly the equal of that by his more celebrated colleague, Marc-Antoine Charpentier. Indeed, this magnificent *Te Deum* setting, with its trumpets and drums at the opening and returning equally regally at the closing *In te Domine speravi*, is every bit as compelling as Charpentier's more famous setting, with Carolyn Sampson singing radiantly in the lovely *Tu ad liberandum*, and with the other soloists here hardly less impressive.

Venite, exultemus is another optimistic work of praise, more modestly scored, but in the *Venite, adoremus*, for three soloists and chorus, he introduces a deeply expressive central section ('Let us weep before the Lord'), accompanied by two celestial flutes, and the penultimate *Hodie si vocen ejust*, which has an elaborate violin obbligato, as usual closes with a joyful chorus.

Panis Angelicus, again simply and tenderly sung by Carolyn Sampson, interweaves the vocal line with a solo flute. But what makes this collection particularly desirable is the inclusion of the rare intrumental fantasy, *La grande pièce royale*, scored for oboes, strings and continuo (here a bassoon). Its six movements (*Doucement, Gracieusement, Gaiement*, etc.) all derive from a gravely noble theme fully worthy of a monarch. It is beautifully played here, and the vocal works, too, are superbly done within a spacious acoustic that emphasizes their grandness, but which seems just as effective in the gentler music.

Grand Motets: Audite coeli quae loquor; Beati quorum remissae sunt; Quam dilecta

*** Virgin 5 45531-2. Haller, Guillon, Crook, Lamy, Buet, Les Pages & Les Chantres de Versailles, La Grand Ecurie et La Chambre du Roy, Schneebeli

With his grand motet, *Beati quorum*, the young Delalande was chosen by Louis XIV at a 'musical tournament' in April 1683 to take charge (alongside three other musicians) of the Royal Chapel 'Pages'. It is a spectacular work for soloists, chorus and orchestra with many individual touches, not least the apparent refusal, '*Non, non*', in the passage *Verumtamen in diluvio aquarum multarum* ('Surely in the floods of great waters'). *Audite coeli* is even more imaginative, using a wide variety of almost operatic effects to illustrate Moses' dramatic warning, 'Give ear, O ye heavens, and I will speak.' The darkly powerful bass solo, *Vidit Dominus*, with its increasingly restless accompaniment (admirably sung by Alain Buet) leads to a frenzied double-chorus, *Foris vestabit*, but again the motet ends in genial rejoicing. *Quam dilecta* is a richly expressive but less spectacular work, with lovely, mellifluous scoring, telling of the joyfully tender response of the soul 'at the foot of the tabernacle'. The performances here are in every way authentic, expressive and stirring, with splendid contributions from soloists, chorus and instrumentalists, and the recording is first class.

Cantate Domino; De profundis; Regina coeli

*** Gaudeamus CDGAU 141. Ex Cathedra Chamber Ch. & Bar. O, Skidmore

Jeffrey Skidmore with his fine, Birmingham-based choir and orchestra presents vividly characterized performances of three of Delalande's '*grands motets*', written to be performed simultaneously with the daily celebration of Mass at Louis XIV's court. *De profundis* is a magnificent piece, as are the two lighter, joyful motets. As the title indicates, *Regina coeli* has a Marian text, while *Cantate Domino* represents the peak of Delalande's long career. With their sequences of brief, sharply contrasted movements, these motets, in performances as lively and sensitive as these, can be warmly recommended to many more than baroque specialists. Warm, full sound.

Motets: Confitebor tibi Domine; De profundis; (i) Miserere

(BB) *** Warner Apex 0927 49983-2. (i) Fisher; soloists, New College, Oxford, Ch., King's Consort, Higginbottom

This is an excellent and inexpensive introduction to three of Delalande's most inspired motets. *Confitebor tibi Domine* (Psalm 110) is essentially a song of praise, but it has many gentle and touching expressive moments for soloists and chorus alike. It closes with an exultant, contrapuntally brilliant choral *Gloria Patri. De profundis clamavi* (Psalm 129), with its valedictory opening, also has great expressive variety, with fine writing both for soloists and for small vocal ensemble, and delightful scoring. It too closes radiantly in a spirit of optimism. *Miserere* (Psalm 50) is set for solo soprano (here the glorious-voiced Gillian Fisher), with alternate verses sung in celestial plainchant by the female chorus (originally the nuns). Edward Higginbottom, who conducts the other two works admirably, here plays the chamber organ accompaniment and the effect is very moving indeed. The recording is resonantly atmospheric, using spatial dimensions tellingly and, with excellent documentation and full translations included, this budget anthology cannot be recommended too highly.

Confitebor tibi Domine; Super flumina Babilonis; Te Deum

(B) *** HM HMA 1951351. Gens, Piau, Steyer, Fouchécourt, Piolino, Corréas, Les Arts Florissants, Christie

Confitebor tibi Domine (1699) and *Super flumina Babilonis* (1687) have much expressive writing, and the performances under William Christie are light and airy but not wanting in expressive feeling. The more familiar *Te Deum* is given as good a performance as any that has appeared in recent years. The sound is airy and spacious, and the performances combine lightness and breadth.

DELIBES, Léo (1836–91)

Coppélia (ballet; complete. Choreography: Ninette de Valois)

⊕— ✲ * BBC DVD 1024. Benjamin, Acosta, Heydon, Royal Ballet, ROHCG O, Moldoveaunu (Production: Ninette de Valois/Anthony Dowell. V/D: Bob Lockyer)

Coppélia (ballet; complete. Choreography Maguy Marin)

(N) Arthaus DVD 100 337. Françoise Joullie, Josu Zabala, Nerses Boyadjian, Maria Brown, Lyon Nat. Op. Ballet, Lyon Nat. Op. O, Nagano (Produced & Directed Thomas Grimm)

With this production the Royal Ballet celebrated its return to Covent Garden after the Opera House's two-year closure. Ninette de Valois's choreography and production and Osbert Lancaster's colourful sets of *Coppélia* made a return after 20 years. It was televised in February 2000 and, were you to compare a VTR of that broadcast with the present DVD, you would appreciate the greater sense of presence, cleaner focus and altogether firmer image that the new medium offers. In fact the colour is quite spectacular.

Leanne Benjamin's Swanhilda has much charm and the Cuban, Carlos Acosta, brings the appropriate ardour, grace and virtuosity to the role of Franz, while Luke Heydon's Dr Coppélius is exemplary. There is first-class dancing from the Corps and lively, well-paced orchestral playing under Nicolae Moldoveanu. Moreover, the sound is well defined and musically balanced.

Deborah Bull introduces the ballet, and the DVD includes a short feature about the Royal Ballet on the move after the closure of the Royal Opera House and another on the work of Osbert Lancaster. An altogether delightful set which will give much pleasure.

The choreographer of this Lyon production of *Coppélia*, Maguy Marin, transposes Delibes's delightful ballet into a modern, run-down urban environment, abandoning ballet dresses for modern clothes. As the orchestra plays the prelude we see Coppélius walk across the square outside hs modern appartment and – picking up his mail on the way – go to his living room and carry a sexy-looking blonde Coppélia on to the balcony. Below, in the square, Swanhilda appears, eating an apple, then Franz arrives on his bicycle, looks up and is attracted to Coppélia, and forthwith abandons Swanhilda, joining a strident gang of young people to which he apparently belongs. All this occurs with 'dancing' of little grace, as Delibes's magical score runs its course. As the booklet suggests: 'From this point onwards the dances seem to have little to do with the plot of the classical ballet.' Various cinematic devices are employed. The problem of the *Dance of the Automatons* is managed by Coppélia using a film projector; later she becomes a multi-imaged creaure, and so on. It all beggars belief that a major company would want to mount something so far divorced from the composer's intentions as this. The only good things about this DVD are the splended playing of Lyon National Opera Orchestra, elegantly and vibrantly conducted by Kent Nagano, and the excellent sound. You could, of course, play the recording without the visuals, and then it would be enjoyable.

Complete ballets: (i) *Coppélia;* **(ii)** *Sylvia;* **(iii)** *La Source*
(B) *** Decca (ADD/DDD) 460 418-2 (4). (i) Nat. PO; (ii) New Phil. O; (iii) ROHCG O; Bonynge

Bonynge's digital *Coppélia* recording sparkles from start to finish. There is tremendous energy in the many vigorous numbers and the contribution of the woodwind is a continual delight. Not as consistently inspired as *Coppélia*, *Sylvia* is more serious and symphonic in approach but there are many exciting set-pieces, much piquant colouring and a haunting *leitmotif* which runs throughout. The New Philharmonia play with tremendous energy and style, and the 1972 recording is as brilliant as you could wish. *La Source* was the composer's first ballet, though he wrote only Acts II and III. Its elegantly lightweight style alerted the world to his talent for writing for the dance theatre, with his felicitous use of the orchestral palette readily discernible – clearly showing this as a forerunner for *Coppélia* and *Sylvia*. The complete ballet is

given here, with Acts I and IV written by Minkus, whose contribution is rather more melancholy than Delibes's but is well written and enjoyable. The ROHCG Orchestra plays with great style and the digital recording is warm and detailed – well up to the house standard. At bargain price, this set is exceptional value.

Coppélia **(ballet): complete**
(B) *** Double Decca (ADD) 444 836-2. SRO, Bonynge –
MASSENET: *Le Carillon* ***

Coppélia **(ballet; complete);** *La Source: Suites 2 & 3;*
Intermezzo: Pas de fleurs
(BB) *** Naxos 8.553356/7. Slovak RSO (Bratislava), Mogrelia

On the Double Decca reissue of his earlier (1969) analogue set, Bonynge secures a high degree of polish from the Suisse Romande Orchestra, with sparkling string- and wind-textures, and with sonority and bite from the brass. The Decca recording sounds freshly minted and, with its generous Massenet bonus, little-known music of great charm, this set remains competitive.

The Bratislava orchestra plays with characteristic finesse and grace and with glowing lyrical feeling. There is both drama and vitality in this *Coppélia*. The recording is warm and spacious, with the orchestra set slightly back. Other versions may have more surface brilliance, but most lovers of ballet music will enjoy the naturalness of perspective and the attractively smooth string-quality. *La Source* comes off equally well. The *Pas de fleurs grande valse* is a real lollipop and in the two suites the music (selected rather arbitrarily) has plenty of colour and rhythmic life.

Coppélia **(ballet; highlights)**
☛ (BB) *** Warner Apex 2564 60365-2. Lyon Opéra O, Nagano

A very generous and comprehensive selection from Delibes's delightful score for *Coppélia*, which Tchaikovsky admired so much. Every bar of the music-making is of the highest quality, and the recording with its nicely judged acoustic is as attractive as the playing. Self-recommending, unless you want the complete score, which costs twice as much.

Coppélia: extended excerpts; Sylvia: extended excerpts
(B) *** EMI (ADD) 5 69659-2 (2). Paris Op. O, Mari

Jean-Baptiste Mari uses ballet tempi throughout, yet there is never any loss of momentum, and the long-breathed string-phrasing and felicitous wind solos are a continual source of delight. Mari's natural sympathy and warmth make the very most of the less memorable parts of the score for *Sylvia* (and they are only slightly less memorable). Seventy-five minutes are offered from each ballet. The sound is fresh.

Coppélia **(ballet): suite**
(B) *** DG (ADD) 429 163-2. BPO, Karajan – CHOPIN: *Les Sylphides* *** ◉; OFFENBACH: *Gaîté parisienne:* excerpts ***

Karajan secures some wonderfully elegant playing from the Berlin Philharmonic Orchestra and his lightness of touch is generally sure. The *Csárdás*, however, is played very slowly and heavily, and its curiously studied tempo may spoil the performance for some. The recording is very impressive; but it is a pity that in assembling the CD the suite had to be truncated (with only 71 minutes' playing time, at least one more number could have been included). As it is, the *Scène et valse de la poupée, Ballade de l'épi* and the *Thème slav varié*, all present on the original analogue LP, are omitted here.

Coppélia; Sylvia (excerpts)

(BB) **(*) EMI Encore (ADD) 5 75221-2. New Philh. O, Mackerras – MESSAGER: *Les Deux Pigeons* (excerpts); GOUNOD: *Faust: Ballet Music* **(*)

With only three numbers from *Coppélia* and four from *Sylvia* included – admittedly among the most popular movements – this CD captures only a few of the highlights from Delibes's scintillating ballets, but these late-1960s recordings are lively and enjoyable, only a touch dated in sound, and they form part of an enjoyable and inexpensive programme of French ballet music.

Coppélia: suite; Kassya: Trepak; Le Roi s'amuse: suite; La Source: suite; Sylvia: suite

(BB) **(*) Naxos 8.550080. Slovak RSO (Bratislava), Lenárd

An attractive hour of Delibes, with five key items from *Coppélia*, including the *Music for the Automatons* and *Waltz*, four from *Sylvia*, not forgetting the *Pizzicato*, and four from *La Source*. Perhaps most enjoyable of all are the six pastiche ancient 'airs de danse', provided for a ballroom scene in Victor Hugo's play, *Le Roi s'amuse*. They are played most gracefully, and the excerpts from the major ballets are spirited and nicely turned. Vivid sound.

Sylvia (ballet): complete

(BB) *** Naxos 8.553338/9. Razumovsky Sinfonia, Mogrelia – SAINT-SAENS: *Henry VIII Ballet Music* ***

Mogrelia's performance of *Sylvia* is above all spacious, bringing out the music's pastel-shaded lyricism yet finding plenty of weight for the more vigorous music depicting the hunters. The *Divertissement* of Act III (which includes some of the best numbers, including the famous *Pizzicato*) is vividly done. However, in the performance as a whole, glowing sentience takes precedence over vitality, and some might find the atmosphere a little sleepy at times. Excellent, naturally balanced recording.

VOCAL MUSIC

Les Filles de Cadiz

*** Decca 452 667-2. Bartoli, Myung-Whun Chung (with VIARDOT: *Les Filles de Cadiz; Hai Luli!; Havanaise* ***) – BIZET; BERLIOZ; RAVEL: *Mélodies* ***

Cecilia Bartoli could hardly be more seductive or more Carmen-like than she is here in Delibes's most famous song, *Les Filles de Cadiz*; here, within a delectable recital of French songs, it is placed alongside the setting of the same poem made by the great prima donna, Pauline Viardot, giving a refreshingly different view. The other Viardot items too are highly engaging in this memorable collection of French mélodies.

OPERA

Lakmé (complete)

*** EMI 5 56569-2 (2). Dessay, Kunde, Van Dam, Haldan, Toulouse Capitole Ch. & O, Plasson

(B) *** Double Decca 460 741-2 (2). Sutherland, Berbié, Vanzo, Bacquier, Monte Carlo Op. Ch. & O, Bonynge

The glory of the EMI set is the fresh, girlish portrayal of the heroine by Natalie Dessay, starrily seductive with her silvery, girlish tone, first heard ravishingly from afar. Technically, she is superb too, and the *Bell Song* becomes a narrative, not just a coloratura display piece. As Gerald, Gregory Kunde has an appealingly light and heady tenor, sounding totally idiomatic. José van Dam as the vengeful Nilakantha is not as menacing as some, but he sings with satisfying firmness. Delphine Haldan's fruity mezzo contrasts rather than blends with Dessay's soprano in the popular *Flower duet*, but with Plasson warmly expressive, generally taking an expansive view, the sensuousness of the score is well brought out, helped by the atmospheric Toulouse recording, though not as sharply focused as the vintage Decca recording, with Bonynge more bitingly dramatic.

The performance on Decca seizes its opportunities with both hands. Sutherland swallows her consonants, but the beauty of her singing, with its ravishing ease and purity up to the highest register, is what matters; and she has opposite her one of the most pleasing and intelligent of French tenors, Alain Vanzo. Excellent contributions from the others too, spirited conducting and brilliant, atmospheric recording. The reissue as a Double Decca makes a splendid bargain and the new-style synopsis will prove especially helpful for newcomers to this opera.

Lakmé (highlights)

(N) (M) (**(*)) Decca Heritage mono 475 6158. Robin, Disney, De Luca, Borthayre, Opéra Comique Ch. & O, Sébastian

These highlights date from 1952, and the voices – very much in front of the orchestra – are warmly and vividly caught (John Culshaw was the producer). Mado Robin's highly individual timbre is certainly affecting, and her amazing vocal agility and freak high notes are used to predictably impressive effect in the *Bell Song*. The rest of the cast, if not outstanding, are all characterful and, with the French forces, it all sounds authentic.The highly attractive original LP cover is reproduced for this reissue.

DELIUS, Frederick (1862–1934)

(i) *Air and Dance; La Calinda (Koanga); Hassan: Intermezzo and Serenade;* (ii) *In a Summer Garden; Paris;* (iii) *Sea Drift;* (iv) *A Song of the High Hills;* (ii) *A Song of Summer; Summer Night; A Village Romeo and Juliet: The Walk to the Paradise Garden;* (v) *Cello Sonata*

(M) **(*) Decca mono/stereo 470 375-2. (i) ASMF, Marriner; (ii) LSO, Collins; (iii) Shirley-Quirk, L. Symphony Ch., RPO, Hickox; (iv) Evans, Hoare, Welsh Nat. Op. Ch. & O, Mackerras; (v) Lloyd Webber, Forsberg

Some notable Delius performances here, the earliest contribution coming from Anthony Collins. Dating from 1953, the mono recorded sound retains its ambient warmth and the glow of sound that made these accounts famous in their day and which is so essential for Delius. *Paris* is full of spontaneous passionate evocation, and Collins's mastery in this repertoire is confirmed in the rest of his items. In his 1980 account of *Sea Drift*, rather than lingering, Hickox is urgent in his expressiveness, but there is plenty of evocative atmosphere, too. John Shirley-Quirk sings with characteristic sensitivity, and the chorus – trained by Hickox – is outstanding; the remastering is excellent. Marriner's 1977 items have always been admired: they are lovely performances, warm, tender and eloquent. They are superbly played and recorded in a flattering acoustic, the sound not in the least bit dated.

Air & Dance; Florida Suite; North Country Sketches; On Hearing the First Cuckoo in Spring
(M) *** Chan. 6628. LPO or Ulster O, Handley

Vernon Handley's splendid Ulster coupling of the comparatively rare *Florida Suite* (written in America) and the *North Country Sketches* (which evokes the seasons on the Yorkshire moors) has always been a staple of the CD catalogue. In the latter work a Debussian influence is revealed and Handley's refined (yet warm) approach to the early (1887) *Florida Suite* clearly links it with later masterpieces, with the famous *La Calinda* delightfully presented. The recording is superbly balanced within the very suitable acoustics of the Ulster Hall, and it is hardly less impressive in the two bonuses from the LPO, which are equally beautifully played. The *Air and Dance* dates from 1915 and was dedicated to the National Institute for the Blind. A highly recommendable reissue.

Air and Dance; On Hearing the First Cuckoo in Spring; Summer Evening; Summer Night on the River
(M) ** Chan. 10174X. LPO, Handley – VAUGHAN WILLIAMS: *Serenade to Music; The Wasps Overture* **

Handley as an interpreter of Delius generally takes a more direct, less gently lingering view than is common, but here that refusal to sentimentalize – which can miss the more sweetly evocative qualities of the music – goes with the most subtle nuances in performance, fresh as well as beautiful and atmospheric. *Summer Evening* is little more than a salon piece, but is no less attractive for that. The tonal richness of the LPO playing is superbly caught in the outstanding Chandos recording, but this collection plays for only 46 minutes overall, which is ungenerous these days.

American Rhapsody (Appalachia); Norwegian Suite (Folkeraadet: The Council of the People); Paa Vidderne (On the Heights); Spring Morning
** Marco Polo 8.220452. Slovak PO, Bratislava, Hopkins

Paa Vidderne, the most substantial piece here, is rather melodramatic but has a distinct melodic interest. *Spring Morning* is shorter and similarly picaresque, but the *Folkeraadet Suite* displays a sure orchestral touch and is most attractive in its diversity of invention. The *American Rhapsody* is a concise version of *Appalachia* without the chorus, given here in its original (1896) format. John Hopkins brings a strong sympathy and understanding to this repertoire and secures a committed and flexible response from his Czech players in music which must have been wholly unknown to them.

2 Aquarelles (arr. Fenby); Brigg Fair; Dance Rhapsodies 1-2 (ed. Beecham); Florida Suite; In a Summer Garden; North Country Sketches; On Hearing the First Cuckoo in Spring; Summer Night on the River (both edited Beecham); The Walk to the Paradise Garden
(B) **(*) Double Decca 460 290-2 (2). Welsh Nat. Op. O, Mackerras

Mackerras is just as warmly sympathetic in these Delius orchestral pieces as in his complete opera recording, *A Village Romeo and Juliet*. The contrast between the two performances of the interlude, *The Walk to the Paradise Garden*, reflects the contrast between the orchestras, the Welsh more direct and passionate. The *Dance Rhapsodies*, music which is far from

rhapsodic, here receive fresh, taut performances. In the shorter works Mackerras is warmly sympathetic, with the woodwind playing particularly excellent. But the recording, made in the Brangwyn Hall, Swansea, is less spacious, less sensuous than the Austrian-made one of the opera, lacking Delian mystery. The massed strings in particular have too much brightness; one requires more lambent textures in this music.

(i) 2 Aquarelles; Dance Rhapsodies 1 & 2; Florida Suite; Irmelin Prelude (ed. Beecham); North Country Sketches; Over the Hills and Far Away; (ii) Romance; (iii) Appalachia
(M) **(*) Decca 473 716-2 (2). (i) Welsh Nat. Op. O, Mackerras; (ii) Webber, Fosberg; (iii) Washington, Welsh Nat. Op. Ch.

A further shuffling of Mackerras's Delius recordings, mainly in order to include *Appalachia*. His stimulating accounts of the *Aquarelles*, *Dance Rhapsodies* and *North Country Sketches* are included above, while the other works are equally persuasively done. The Brangwyn Hall recordings are again a little bright – this repertoire ideally calls for more lambent textures, the effect being rather too strident in the climaxes. Julian Lloyd Webber gives a sensitive account of the short *Romance*. In *Appalachia*, a refreshing and direct reading, the wide dynamic range means that the *fortissimos* are almost overwhelming, though some will respond to the vividness of the music-making. These performances are, in general, less subtle than Beecham's, less lovingly affectionate than Barbirolli's, but are still enjoyable.

2 Aquarelles (arr. Fenby); Fennimore and Gerda: Intermezzo. Hassan: Intermezzo & Serenade (all arr. Beecham); Irmelin: Prelude. Late Swallows (arr. Fenby); On Hearing the First Cuckoo in Spring; A Song Before Sunrise; Summer Night on the River
(M) *** Chan. 6502. Bournemouth Sinf., Del Mar

This 49-minute concert creates a mood of serene, atmospheric evocation – into which Eric Fenby's arrangement of *Late Swallows* from the *String Quartet* fits admirably – and the beauty of the 1977 analogue recording has been transferred very well to CD, with all its warmth and bloom retained.

2 Aquarelles; Fennimore and Gerda: Intermezzo. On Hearing the First Cuckoo in Spring; Summer Night on the River
(M) *** DG (ADD) 439 529-2. ECO, Barenboim – VAUGHAN WILLIAMS: *Lark Ascending*, etc.; WALTON: *Henry V* ***

Barenboim's luxuriant performances have voluptuous sensuousness, and their warm, sleepy atmosphere should seduce many normally resistant to Delius's pastoralism. The couplings are no less enticing.

Brigg Fair
(M) (**(*)) BBC mono BBCL 4113. RPO, Beecham – BERLIOZ: *The Trojans: Royal Hunt and Storm*; CHABRIER: *España; Gwendoline Overture*; DEBUSSY: *L'Enfant prodigue: Cortège et Air de danse*; MASSENET: *La Vierge: Le dernier sommeil de la vierge*; SAINT-SAENS: *Le rouet d'Omphale* (with MOZART: *Divertimento in D, K.131*: excerpts (**(*))

Beecham's BBC recording of *Brigg Fair* comes from a live broadcast concert of 1956. The playing of Gerald Jackson (flute), Terence MacDonagh (oboe), Jack Brymer (clarinet) and Gwydion Brooke (bassoon) ensures its evocative delicacy, but the recording itself leaves something to be desired, and the EMI stereo version is preferable.

(i) *Brigg Fair; La Calinda* (arr. Fenby); *In a Summer Garden; Fennimore and Gerda: Intermezzo. Hassan: Intermezzo* and (iii) *Serenade* (arr. Beecham); (ii) *Irmelin: Prelude;* (i) *Late Swallows* (arr. Fenby); *On Hearing the First Cuckoo in Spring; A Song before Sunrise;* (ii) *A Song of Summer;* (i) *Summer Night on the River;* (ii) *A Village Romeo and Juliet: Walk to the Paradise Garden* (arr. Beecham); (i; iv) *Appalachia* (with brief rehearsal sequence)

(M) *** EMI (ADD) 5 65119-2 (2). (i) Hallé O; (ii) LSO; (iii) with Tear; (iv) Jenkins, Amb. S; all cond. Barbirolli

Sir John shows an admirable feeling for the sense of light Delius conjures up and for the luxuriance of texture his music possesses. The gentle evocation of *La Calinda* contrasts with the surge of passionate Italianate romanticism at the climax of the *Walk to the Paradise Garden*. Barbirolli's style is evanescent in repose and more romantic than the Beecham versions but, with lovely playing from both the Hallé and the LSO, the first-rate analogue sound from the mid- to late 1960s adds to the listener's pleasure. *Appalachia* is given an admirably atmospheric reading that conveys the work's exotic and vivid colouring.

(i; ii) *Brigg Fair*; (iii; i; iv) *Piano Concerto*; (v; vi) *Violin Concerto*; (vi) *On Hearing the First Cuckoo in Spring*; (vii) 2 *Pieces for Cello and Piano: Caprice; Elegy*

(M) **(*) Decca mono/stereo (ADD/DDD) 470 190-2. (i) LSO; (ii) Collins; (iii) Kars; (iv) Gibson; (v) Little; (vi) Welsh Nat. Op. O, Mackerras; (vii) Lloyd Webber, Forsberg

Anthony Collins's mono 1953 account of *Brigg Fair* is a classic one, its ardour totally English in feeling. The sound is superb for its time, although its coupling with much later stereo and digital recordings might not suit all listeners. That said, there are no poor performances here: Tasmin Little, often shading her tone down to hushed pianissimos in the *Violin Concerto*, is ravishing, with the close of the work bringing a moment of total repose, while Mackerras draws strong, sympathetic playing from the orchestra of the WNO, as he does in *On Hearing the First Cuckoo in Spring*, although here the forwardness and clarity of the recording tends to make the results less evocative than they might be. Jean-Rudolph Kars proves a superb and eloquent advocate of the rare *Piano Concerto* in this persuasive (1969) reading. Gibson provides admirable support, and the recording demonstrates an excellent balance between soloist and orchestra. With the *Two Pieces for Cello and Orchestra* making a pleasing bonus, this is certainly a worthwhile collection.

Brigg Fair; Dance Rhapsody 2; Fennimore and Gerda: Intermezzo* (arr. Fenby); *Florida Suite: Daybreak - Dance (La calinda)* (revised & edited Beecham). *Irmelin: Prelude; On Hearing the First Cuckoo in Spring; Sleigh Ride; Song before Sunrise; Summer Evening* (arr. Beecham); *Summer Night on the River

🔑 ❁ (M) *** EMI 5 67552 [5 67553-2]. RPO, Beecham

The further remastering of Beecham's stereo Delius recordings, made at Abbey Road at the end of the 1950s, continues to demonstrate a technological miracle. The result brings these unsurpassed performances into our own time with an uncanny sense of realism and presence. The delicacy of the gentler wind and string textures is something to marvel at, as is the orchestral playing itself. Beecham's fine-spun magic, his ability to lift a phrase is apparent from the very opening of *Brigg Fair*, which shows Delius at his most inspired and Beecham's orchestra at their most incandescent. The shorter pieces (especially the ravishing *Intermezzo* from *Fennimore and Gerda*) bring superb wind solos, while Beecham often conjures a lazy sentient warmth from the strings – as in *On Hearing the First Cuckoo in Spring*, but more especially in *Summer Night on the River*, which no other conductor has matched since. The *Sleigh Ride* shows Beecham twinkling and sparkling, and he is no less persuasive in the excerpt from the *Florida Suite*. But why is this not complete? The admirable documentation is by Lyndon Jenkins. Sheer magic, and fully worthy to be included in EMI's 'Great Recordings of the Century'.

Brigg Fair; Dance Rhapsody 2; On Hearing the First Cuckoo in Spring; In a Summer Garden

(B) *** Sony (ADD) SBK 62645. Phd. O, Ormandy – VAUGHAN WILLIAMS: *Fantasias*, etc. ***

Ormandy and his great orchestra, on peak form in the early 1960s, give warm, stirring and highly romantic performances of these four masterpieces. Ormandy and his engineers do not seek the fragility, the evanescence of Delius's visions; for that one can turn to Beecham. But this music responds well to a riper approach and there is no danger here of Delius sounding faded. The sound is remarkably full and expansive, far more convincing than the original LP. With its equally involving coupling, this is a true bargain.

(i) *Brigg Fair; Eventyr; In a Summer Garden;* (ii) *A Song before Sunrise;* (i) *A Song of Summer;* (ii) *Summer Night on the River; A Village Romeo and Juliet: Walk to the Paradise Garden*

(B) *** CfP (DDD/ADD) 575 3152. (i) LPO; (ii) Hallé O; Handley

Vernon Handley's beautifully played Hallé performances were recorded in 1981, and the digital sound is of EMI's best quality, matching clarity of definition with ambient lustre and rich colouring. This very generous reissue adds three hardly less fine LPO performances recorded in the Henry Wood Hall three years earlier, where the analogue quality is very nearly as good. Handley's approach to *The Walk to the Paradise Garden* is strongly emotional, closer to Barbirolli than to Beecham. Incidentally, the variations which make up *Brigg Fair* – one of the disc's highlights – are grouped in six separate bands, a very useful feature, unique on CD.

Brigg Fair; In a Summer Garden; On Hearing the First Cuckoo in Spring; Paris (The Song of a Great City); Summer Night on the River; A Village Romeo and Juliet: Walk to the Paradise Garden

(BB) *** Warner Apex 8573 89084-2. BBC SO, A. Davis

A superb disc. Beecham may be very special in these lovely scores but it is good to have state-of-the-art modern recordings, admirably spacious and atmospheric and with an excitingly wide dynamic range. The closing section of *Brigg Fair*, with Davis's slow sustained march tempo leading to an impulsive accelerando and a great surge of passion, is thrilling, and shows, like the similarly volatile account of *Paris*, how deeply Andrew Davis responds to this music. But he can be languorous too (a legacy from Barbirolli perhaps), as at the beginning of the *Walk to the Paradise Garden*; later the BBC strings sing out with full-blooded fervour at the climax, superbly caught by the engineers, and Davis tapers down the coda very beautifully indeed. *On Hearing the First Cuckoo in Spring* and the *Summer Night on the River* both bring a feeling of hazy rapture, with lovely woodwind detail. In short this is post-Beecham Delius with a new approach from a conductor who feels this music in his very being.

(i) *Caprice & Elegy;* (ii-iii) *Piano Concerto;* (iv-v) *Violin Concerto;* (vi; iii) *Hassan: Intermezzo & Serenade; Koanga: La Calinda;* (v) *On Hearing the First Cuckoo in Spring;* (vii) *Legend for Violin & Piano*

(***) Testament mono SBT 1014. (i) Harrison, CO, Fenby; (ii) Moiseiwitsch, Philh. O; (iii) Lambert; (iv) Sammons; (v) Liverpool PO, Sargent; (vi) Hallé O; (vii) Holst, Moore

The greatest treasure is the first ever recording of the *Violin Concerto*, made in 1944 and featuring the original soloist, Albert Sammons, arguably the most eloquent and moving account of the work ever committed to disc. Moiseiwitsch's recording of the *Piano Concerto*, also the first ever, is hardly less powerful, making a very good case for this warm but less cogent piece. The other items range from the 1930 recording of the *Caprice and Elegy* by Beatrice Harrison, the dedicatee, with suspect intonation and plentiful portamento, to Sargent's 1947 recording of the *First Cuckoo*, very warm and free in its rubato. Constant Lambert is also a first-rate interpreter of Delius, as the *Hassan* and *Koanga* excerpts show. This transfer has higher surface-hiss than later issues on this label, but the disc must be strongly recommended.

Cello Concerto
*** EMI 5 55529-2. du Pré, RPO, Sargent (with Recital) ***

The EMI disc offers what was du Pré's first concerto recording, and the recital is a transfer of the material mainly from her very first EMI sessions in 1962 which gave such clear promise of glories to come. Most recommendable, although readers will note that it remains at full price.

(i) *Cello Concerto;* (ii) *Double Concerto for Violin & Cello. Paris (The Song of a Great City)*
*** CfP 575 8032. (i; ii) Wallfisch; (ii) Little; RLPO, Mackerras

This superb recording of the *Double Concerto*, with soloists who easily outshine their predecessors on record (however distinguished), confirms the strength of a piece which establishes its own logic, with each theme developing naturally out of the preceeding one. Rafael Wallfisch is just as persuasive in the *Cello Concerto*, and Mackerras proves an understanding interpreter of the composer in the big tone-poem, *Paris, The Song of a Great City*. The recording is comparably full and atmospheric.

Piano Concerto in C min.
(B) *** CfP 575 9832. Lane, RLPO, Handley – FINZI: *Eclogue;* VAUGHAN WILLIAMS: *Piano Concerto* ***
(BB) (***) Naxos mono 8.110689. Moiseiwitsch, PO, Lambert (with solo pieces by DEBUSSY; GODOWSKY; GRANADOS; IBERT; POULENC; PROKOFIEV; RAVEL; STRAVINSKY (***))

Piers Lane gives a masterly performance of the Delius *Piano Concerto*, weighty without pomposity, which effectively counters ideas of being 'sub-Grieg', early though it is. Lane's measured, concentrated reading of the slow movement is particularly compelling.

Benno Moiseiwitsch was a keen advocate of the *Piano Concerto* Delius wrote at the beginning of the 1900s and pressed its claims on the likes of Rachmaninov and Medtner who didn't know it. No one has played it with greater

eloquence and sensitivity (though Jean-Rudolphe Kars, recently reissued on Decca (see above), came close). It is not the greatest Delius but has wonderful moments, which Moiseiwitsch plays with great sensitivity and imagination. Lambert shows that it was not only Beecham and Barbirolli who could conduct Delius, as those who remember his *On Hearing the First Cuckoo* will already know. The rest of the disc is made up of mostly well-known pieces: Debussy's *Jardin sous la pluie* and Ravel's *Jeux d'eau* will delight not only those who grew up when these 78s were in currency but also younger collectors, who have not yet encountered them.

Violin Concerto
(BB) (**(*)) Naxos mono 8.110951. Sammons, Liverpool PO, Sargent – ELGAR: *Violin Concerto*. (**(*))
(M) **(*) EMI (ADD) 7 64725-2. Menuhin, RPO, M. Davies – ELGAR: *Violin Concerto* ***

Albert Sammons's première account of the Delius *Violin Concerto*, recorded in 1944, is by general consent still unsurpassed even by the likes of Ralph Holmes and Tasmin Little, except in terms of recording quality. The World Record LP transfer by A. C. Griffith (coupled with Moiseiwitsch's 1946 account of the *Piano Concerto*) was very fine, but those who have been surviving on that may now turn with confidence to the Naxos transfer.

Menuhin's account, well accompanied and recorded in 1976, does not show the polish of his playing in earlier years, and the timbre is not always ideally sweet; but he gives a heartfelt performance, and the semi-improvisatory freedom and radiant beauty of the writing above the stave are caught superbly. The Abbey Road recording is truthful, warmly atmospheric and well balanced.

Dance Rhapsodies 1-2; In a Summer Garden; North Country Sketches; A Village Romeo and Juliet: Walk to the Paradise Garden
**(*) Chan. 9355. Bournemouth SO, Hickox

Hickox is a sensitive and flexible Delian and the Bournemouth orchestra play passionately for him, especially in the *Walk to the Paradise Garden*. The *Dance Rhapsodies* are not held together quite as persuasively as by Mackerras. *In a Summer Garden* is both ardent and luxuriant in its shimmering summer heat-haze, while the wintry landscape of the *North Country Sketches* brings almost crystalline iciness from the violins. But the recording, made in the Winter Gardens, Bournemouth, although basically full and spacious, brings a somewhat two-dimensional effect in catching the fervent sweep of violin-tone, as if the microphones were a little too close.

Eventyr (Once upon a Time); Sleigh Ride; (i) *Song of the High Hills;* (ii) *5 Songs from the Norwegian* (orch. Holten)
*** Danacord DACOCD 592. Aarhus SO, Holten; with (i) Høyer Hansen, Kjøller, Aarhus University Ch., Aarhus Chamber Ch.; (ii) Bonde-Hansen

Bo Holten and the excellent Aarhus Symphony Orchestra follow up their earlier Danacord disc of Delius's Danish inspirations with this collection of works inspired by Norway, a country to which Delius was specially attracted. *Sleigh Ride*, a piano piece buried for many years which finally surfaced in the composer's orchestration in 1946, is a jolly little piece, not at all Delian in style, and by rights it should have been a popular hit from the start. The *Five Songs from the Norwegian* are charming, the more seductive in Bo Holten's sensitive orchestrations, with Henriette Bonde-Hansen the delightfully fresh, pure-toned soprano. *Eventyr*, inspired by the folk-tales of Christen Asbjornsen, was written much later, but the most ambitious Delius work inspired by Norway is *The Song of the High Hills*. Over its 25-minute span it offers some of the most hauntingly atmospheric music that Delius ever wrote, notably in the passages for wordless choir. Holten conducts a beautiful, refined performance, which keeps the music moving, never letting it meander, building to powerful climaxes and thrillingly recorded with a fine feeling for atmosphere.

Fennimore and Gerda: Intermezzo; Irmelin: Prelude; Koanga: La Calinda (arr. Fenby); *On Hearing the First Cuckoo in Spring; Sleigh Ride*

(B) *** CfP (ADD) 575 3162. LPO, Handley – VAUGHAN
  WILLIAMS: *Lark Ascending; Wasps Suite*, etc. ***

These five favourite Delius items belong to the same 1977 Henry Wood Hall sessions as the LPO items included in the companion Handley collection above. The playing is equally sensitive and the warm, spacious analogue recording is most attractively transferred. The Vaughan Williams items are hardly less attractive.

Florida Suite; Idylle de printemps; Over the Hills and Far Away; La Quadroone; Scherzo; (i) *Koanga: Closing Scene*

(BB) *** Naxos 8.553535. E. N. Philh. O, Lloyd-Jones; (i) with
  Glanville, Lees, Evans, Francis, Peerce, Thomas

Several of the works here are new to disc, including the *Idylle de printemps*, fresh and charming, leading to an ecstatic climax. *La Quadroone* and *Scherzo* were originally planned as movements in a suite. Lloyd-Jones has clearly learnt from Beecham's example in his glowing and intense readings of the other three works, with the orchestra's woodwind soloists excelling themselves in delicate pointing, not least in the haunting *La Calinda*, included in the *Florida Suite*. *Over the Hills and Far Away*, raptly done, is richly evocative too, and the epilogue to the opera, *Koanga*, rounds off a generously filled disc with music both sensuous and passionate, featuring six female vocal soloists from Opera North, three sopranos and three mezzos.

Florida Suite; Over the Hills and Far Away; (i) *Songs of Sunset*

⊶ (M) *** EMI (ADD) 5 75788-2. RPO, Beecham

Delius's *Florida Suite*, with its haunting reminiscences of the composer's stay at the family orange plantation in the late 1880s, was first performed in Leipzig in 1887. It was then forgotten until Beecham unearthed it fifty years later. It is a delightful score, with the first movement featuring the famous *La Calinda*, which subsequently became a favourite lollipop. The whole work is given a magical performance here, and Beecham's ability to lift a phrase is also apparent at the evocative opening of *Over the Hills and Far Away*, which dates from almost a decade later. The *Songs of Sunset*, composed between 1906 and 1908, was also left to Beecham to première in 1911. Here the choral focus is soft-grained, but the words are surprisingly audible, and the backward balance of the soloists is made to sound natural against the richly atmospheric orchestral textures. With excellent transfers of fine recordings made at Abbey Road in 1956 and 1957, this makes an essential supplement to the stereo orchestral collection from the same period listed above (EMI 5 67752).

On the Mountains (symphonic poem); (i) *Paa vidderne* (melodrama); (ii) *7 Songs from the Norwegian*

*** Classico CLASSCD 364. RLPO, Bostock; (i) Hall; (ii) Lund
  (with GRIEG: *Norwegian Bridal Procession*, orch. Delius ***)

'Vidde' is unique to Norwegian and means the desolate heather and rock of the high mountains rather than just plain mountain. So both Delius's *Paa vidderne* and the slightly earlier tone-poem are best translated as *On the Heights*. Douglas Bostock uses Lionel Carley's fine English translation from the Ibsen original. There is a lot of Grieg here, but much that only Delius could have written, often highly imaginative and rather haunting. However, the medium is not really satisfactory and Peter Hall has to assert himself over the full orchestra, and in climaxes the result is not pleasing. All the same the piece is always interesting and often moving. The *Songs from the Norwegian* are also given in English. Bostock is a first-rate conductor and gets vitally fresh and responsive playing from the Liverpool Philharmonic. There is plenty of air round the aural image, and the recording-balance is judged most musically.

Over the Hills and Far Away; Paris (The Song of a Great City); (i) *Sea Drift*

(M) (*(**)) Sony mono SMK 89430. RPO, Beecham; (i) with
  Boyce & BBC Ch.

Beecham's interpretations of Delius are uniquely compelling: the early tone-poem, *Over the Hills and Far Away*, comes over with great atmosphere and both *Paris* and *Sea Drift*, with Bruce Boyce as soloist, are special, so it is sad that Sony's standards of transfer have deteriorated since these mono recordings of the early 1950s first appeared on CD. An extra top-emphasis goes with more muddled inner textures, so that even in *Paris* – the most successful of the transfers here – the percussion sounds shallow and unnatural. When Beecham never managed to record *Sea Drift* in stereo sound, it is specially sad that the chorus sounds ill-focused and rather crumbly in a work that cries out for evocative atmosphere. With all the reservations over transfers, the performances remain irreplaceable.

(i) *2 Pieces for Strings;* (ii) *7 Danish Songs; Irmelin Suite*

** Dinemic DCCD 019. (i) Philh. O; (ii) Farley, Rhein PO;
  Serebrier

Delians will welcome this issue, which brings rare repertoire: the Danish songs have not been recorded before. However, the value of these performances is diminished by the recording, which is far too reverberant and by no means well focused.

CHAMBER MUSIC

Cello Sonata

*** Chan. 8499. R. and P. Wallfisch – BAX: *Rhapsodic Ballad;*
  BRIDGE: *Cello Sonata;* WALTON: *Passacaglia* ***

In the Chandos version of the *Cello Sonata* the performers give as strong and sympathetic an account as is to be found. They are also excellently recorded.

String Quartet

*** ASV CDDCA 526. Brodsky Qt – ELGAR: *Quartet* ***

In this music, the ebb and flow of tension and a natural feeling for persuasive but unexaggerated rubato is vital; with fine ensemble but seeming spontaneity, the Brodsky players consistently produce that. First-rate recording.

Violin Sonatas 1–3; in B, op. posth

•—◦ ✿ (BB) *** BMG/RCA 74321 98708-2 (2). Little, Lane –
BRIDGE: *Orchestral Music* ***

This is the first disc to bring together all four of Delius's
Violin Sonatas, here magnetically performed, with Tasmin
Little's deeply felt playing superbly matched by Piers Lane;
these are works that find Delius at his most meltingly lyrical.
The rarity is the earliest and longest, written in 1892 but not
published until 1977, less distinctive than the three numbered
works, but already very characteristic. The others are tauter
and more compact than one expects of Delius, culminating
in the haunting masterpiece that, when blind and paralysed,
he dictated to his amanuensis, Eric Fenby. The Bridge coupling is no less recommendable and this Twofer is a very real
bargain.

Violin Sonata 2

(**(*)) Testament mono SBT 1319. Rostal, Horsley – ELGAR:
Violin Sonata in E min.; WALTON: *Violin Sonata* (**(*))

The myth that only a British-born musician can give idiomatic readings of British music, whether of Elgar, Delius or
Walton, is exploded in these recordings by Max Rostal who,
fleeing from the Nazis in 1934, became a key musical figure in
Britain. All three sonatas, differently coupled, were among the
first issues on the Argo label, founded by Harley Usill in the
early days of LP, setting a pattern of imaginative enterprise all
too rare at that period. The Delius, more than the other two,
suffers from the dryness of the mono recording and the close
balance of the violin. Yet the artistry and natural understanding of the performers still make it a compelling reading of an
elusive sonata, with Colin Horsley, Rostal's regular pianist,
the most sympathetic partner.

PIANO DUET

Dance Rhapsodies 1 & 2; In a Summer Garden; North Country Sketches; On Hearing the First Cuckoo in Spring; A Song before Sunrise; Summer Night on the River (arranged for piano, four hands, by Peter Warlock)

*** BIS CD 1347. Ogawa, Stott

When subtly evocative instrumental colouring lies at the
heart of Delius's magic, it might seem an odd exercise recording these piano-duet arrangements by Delius's young friend,
Peter Warlock. Some were made when Warlock was still in his
teens – at a time before Delius's music was recorded for the
primitive gramophone. The artistry of the two brilliant pianists Noriko Ogawa and Kathryn Stott, who have formed a
most sensitive duo partnership, completely justifies the
project, even if the first item on the disc, *On Hearing the First
Cuckoo in Spring*, is the least effective in transcription. When
finally the distant call of the cuckoo is revealed, that magic
moment on the piano conveys none of the overtones you get
from a clarinet played *pianissimo*. By contrast, the companion
piece, *Summer Night on the River*, acquires an attractive
freshness transferred to the piano, as does *In a Summer
Garden* with its flickering imitations of birdsong. Generally
the more rhythmic the writing the more effective it is in
piano transcription, as in the 6/8 of *A Song before Sunrise*.
When it comes to the *North Country Sketches*, which Warlock
transcribed somewhat later in 1921, these arrangements
sound like original piano music, just as Ravel's own piano
versions are valid in their own right as keyboard music. The

subtle shading of the first piece, *Autumn*, is magically conveyed, and so are the dance rhythms of the last two pieces,
Mazurka and *The March of Spring*, as, more predictably, are
the dance themes on which the two *Dance Rhapsodies* are
built.

VOCAL MUSIC

(i) Appalachia; Sea Drift; (ii) A Song before Sunrise; Koanga: La Calinda

*** Australian Decca Eloquence (ADD) 467 601-2. (i)
Shirley-Quirk, L. Symphony Ch., RPO, Hickox; (ii) ASMF,
Marriner

Hickox's 1977 LP of *Appalachia* and *Sea Drift* is an early
example of this conductor's natural affinity with Delius.
These are fresh and dedicated performances, urgent in their
expressiveness rather than lingering. John Shirley-Quirk sings
with characteristic sensitivity, and the chorus is outstanding.
The trusty Marriner items are always good to hear, and the
sound throughout this generous CD is superb. Texts are
included in this Australian Eloquence release, as are excellent
notes by Christopher Palmer.

(i) Appalachia: Chorus (arr. B. Suchoff) Songs: An den Sonnenschein; Ave Maria; Durch den Wald; Frühlingsabruch; Her ute skai gildet saa; Little birdie; On Craig Ddu. Two Songs to be Sung of a Summer Night on the Water: 1, without words; 2, with tenor solo; Sonnenscheinlied; The splendour falls on castle walls; The streamlet's slumber song. Hassan, Act I: Chorus; Act II: Chorus of beggars and dancing girls; Irmelin, Act I (arr. E. Lubin): (i) Chorus. A Village Romeo and Juliet: Wanderer's Song (male voices); Wedding music

(M) *** Somm SOMMCD 210. Douse, Ball, Elysian Singers
of London, Greenhall, with (i) Nolan

Though you would hardly recognize the early part-songs of
1887 as the work of Delius, their Englishness is attractive,
making a delightful prelude to an evocative sequence freshly
performed. In chronological order, it follows the composer's
development through his early operas, with appropriate
sequences turned into separate numbers – those from *A
Village Romeo and Juliet* and *Appalachia* involving accompaniments by organ and piano respectively. The climax comes
with the two haunting *Songs to be Sung of a Summer Night on
the Water*. The *Hassan* items too are vintage Delius, before the
final Tennyson setting rather pales in face of Britten's far
more vivid setting in the *Serenade*. Warm, atmospheric
sound.

(i) An Arabesk. A Mass of Life: Prelude. (ii) Songs of Sunset, Parts 1-7; (iii) Part B. Songs: (iv) I-Brasil; Le ciel est pardessus le toit; Cradle Song; Irmelin Rose; Klein Venevil; The Nightingale; Twilight Fancies; The Violet; Whither

(M) (***) Somm mono BEECHAM 8. (i, ii) Henderson, L.
Select Ch.; (ii) Haley; (iii) Evans, Llewellyn, BBC Ch. (iv)
Labbette; LPO or RPO, Beecham (or (iv) Beecham, piano)

Drawn from discs in Beecham's own private collection,
mostly unissued till now, this collection includes several
treasures, notably the live recording of the *Songs of Sunset*,
made at the 1934 Leeds Festival. Far more than any rival,
Beecham conveys a virile thrust and energy in the writing,
partly by opting for faster speeds. Both in this, with its seven
linked sections, and in the single span of *An Arabesk*, a setting

of Jens Peter Jacobsen in Philip Heseltine's translation, the line of the argument is clarified. Roy Henderson is the clean-cut, sensitive baritone soloist in both, sounding very English, with Olga Haley a fresh, bright mezzo soloist in the *Songs of Sunset*. The test pressings sadly lack the final section, but a substitute is provided for that section, taken from a 1946 recording with Nancy Evans and Redvers Llewellyn which Beecham initially rejected. The ends of 78-r.p.m. sides tend to have a noisy surface, but there is ample body in the sound.

Dora Labbette is the enchanting soprano soloist in all the separate songs, bright and silvery, attacking even the most exposed high notes with astonishing purity and with magical *pianissimos*. Four of the ten come in the beautiful orchestral versions, with the rest accompanied at the piano by Beecham himself. He may have been only a good amateur pianist, but his natural magnetism still shines out.

An Arabesk; 2 Danish Songs; 5 Danish Songs (orch. Bo Holten); 7 Danish Songs (1897); Fennimore and Gerda: Intermezzo. Lebenstanz; Sakuntala
*** Danacord DACOCD 536. Bonde-Hansen, Reuter, Danish Nat. Op. Ch., Aarhus Chamber Ch. and SO, Holten

Tending to favour speeds a shade faster than usual, Bo Holten brings out the emotional thrust of such a piece as *An Arabesk*, rather as Beecham used to. The *Seven Danish Songs* of 1897 come in Delius's own sensuous orchestrations, with the self-quotations in the ballad-like *Irmelin Rose* the more telling in orchestral form, while *Summer Nights* is magically transformed in its atmospheric evocation of a sunset.

Delius also orchestrated two separate Danish songs, *The Violet* and *Summer Landscape*, as well as *Sakuntala*, which has prompted Holten to orchestrate five other Danish songs, so as to form another orchestral cycle. These, too, are more beautiful than with piano. Singing in the original Danish, the two soloists have fresh, young voices, clear and precise. The choral singing in *An Arabesk* is also excellent.

Life's Dance, inspired by a play of Helge Rode, is a rarity, originally conceived in 1899, with the depiction of death at the end peaceful, not at all tragic. The Aarhus orchestra responds warmly to Holten's idiomatic direction, with refined playing closely balanced in a helpful acoustic.

(i–iii) Idyll (Once I Passed Through a Populous City); (i–iv) Requiem; (i; v) A Song Before Sunrise; (i; iv; v) Songs of Farewell
(M) **(*) EMI (ADD) 5 75293-2. (i) RPO; (ii) M. Davies; (iii) with Harper, Shirley-Quirk; (iv) Royal Choral Soc.; (v) Sargent

Delius's *Requiem* is far sparer than most of the composer's other works of the period, and much of it is rewarding. This was its recording première. The *Idyll* is much earlier, or at least its material is, and the music, though uneven in inspiration, is often extremely impressive. These excellent pioneering Meredith Davies performances date from 1968 and still sound excellent, if lacking a little richness by modern standards. The *Songs of Farewell*, dedicated to Eric Fenby, are among the most ambitious works the composer attempted to write after he had become blind and paralysed. Sir Malcolm Sargent conducted the first performance in March 1932, and this, his 1964 account, is committed and warm-hearted in the best tradition of Delius recording. *A Song Before Sunrise* provides a haunting and atmospheric makeweight. The recordings are excellent for their period.

(i) A Mass of Life (sung in German); (ii) Requiem
*** Chan. 9515 (2). (i) Rodgers, Rigby, Robson; (ii) Evans; (i-ii) Coleman-Wright; Waynflete Singers, Bournemouth Ch. & SO, Hickox

Hickox gives a glowing account of this ambitious setting of a German text drawn from Nietzsche's *Also sprach Zarathustra*. He is helped by excellent singing and playing from his Bournemouth forces, and by fine solo singing, notably from the soprano, Joan Rodgers. The full and atmospheric Chandos recording confirms the primacy of this version even over the excellent previous recordings. The *Requiem*, half an hour long, makes the ideal coupling, emerging as a fine example of Delius's later work, not as distinctive in its material as the *Mass*, but with an element of bleakness tempering the lushness of the choral writing. Here too – with Rebecca Evans this time as soprano soloist – Hickox conducts a most persuasive performance, ripely recorded.

4 Old English Lyrics. Songs: I-Brasil; Indian love song; Love's philosophy; The nightingale; The nightingale has a lyre of gold; Secret love; Sweet Venevil; Twilight fancies
**(*) Chan. 8539. Luxon, Willison – ELGAR: Songs **(*)

This group of Delius songs draws most persuasive performances from Luxon and Willison, sadly marred by the rough tone which has latterly afflicted this fine baritone. Excellent, well-balanced recording.

(i) Sea Drift; Songs of Farewell; (i; ii) Songs of Sunset
☍ *** Chan. 9214. (i) Terfel; (ii) Burgess; Bournemouth Symphony Ch., Waynflete Singers, Southern Voices, Bournemouth SO, Hickox

In this second recording of Delius's masterpiece Hickox finds even more magic, again taking a spacious view – which keeps the flow of the music going magnetically. Bryn Terfel adds to the glory of the performance, the finest since Beecham, as he does in the *Songs of Sunset*, with Sally Burgess the other characterful soloist. The *Songs of Farewell*, helped by incandescent choral singing, complete an ideal triptych, presented in full and rich Chandos sound.

(i) The Song of the High Hills. Hassan: Intermezzo & Serenade. Irmelin: Prelude. (ii) Koanga: Final Scene. (ii; iii) A Village Romeo and Juliet
(N) (BB) (***) Naxos mono 8.110982-3 (2). RPO, Beecham, with (i) Hart, Jones, Luton Ch. Soc.; (ii) RPO Ch.; (iii) Dyer, Soames, Dowling, Sharp, Ritchie, Bond

In 1946 Beecham made an important first recording of Delius, *The Song of the High Hills*. Written in 1911, it is one of his most ambitious choral works, very evocative in its use of wordless chorus to represent man in nature, while expressing the composer's 'joy and exhilaration one feels in the Mountains'. That is a spirit which Beecham captures perfectly, again never letting the music meander.

A Village Romeo and Juliet was recorded two years later. Central to this Swiss slant on the famous love story (based on a novella of Gottfried Keller) is the sequence of duets between the lovers, Sali and Vreli, making the casting of those roles crucial in any recording. René Soames was a tenor with a very English sound; to say the least, he does not sound sufficiently ardent, and his dry, thin tone is somewhat uningratiating, making his portrayal of Sali seem a little stiff, though musically the clarity and precision are impressive. Lorely Dyer as Vreli is fresh and bright, but she has a small voice and her intonation at the beginning of scene 4 is vulnerable. However, the Naxos transfer captures the voice better than the 1992 EMI transfer of this historic Beecham recording, with less emphasis on her rapid vibrato. It is also good to hear such vintage singers of the period as Dennis Dowling and Frederick Sharp as the respective fathers of the hero and heroine, with an excellent line-up of soloists in the many incidental roles. What stands out most of all in this performance, as it does in all the items on the disc, is the thrust and vigour of Beecham's approach to Delius. If Delius's music has often seemed to meander, it is rarely so with a Beecham interpretation. The extra items are very welcome too, notably the surgingly warm final scene from his earlier opera, *Koanga*, again with chorus.

OPERA

Fennimore and Gerda (complete)

*** Chan. 9589. Stene, Howarth, Tucker, Coleman-Wright, Danish Nat. R. Ch. & SO, Hickox

Fennimore and Gerda, the sixth and last of Delius's operas, may suffer from a lopsided libretto but it has some of his most inspired vocal music. Fennimore, the first heroine, dominates the first nine of the eleven scenes, with Gerda, the second heroine, introduced only at the end to provide an idyllic conclusion. Using the original German, Hickox's reading is aptly sensuous – far warmer than the only previous recording on EMI, conducted by Meredith Davies (5 66314-2) – with fresh-voiced principals headed by Randi Stene as Fennimore, Judith Howarth as Gerda and Peter Coleman-Wright and Mark Tucker as rivals in this very Scandinavian love-tangle.

(i) Koanga (opera; complete); (ii) Song of the High Hills

(M) *** EMI (ADD) 5 85142-2 (2). (i) Holmes, Lindsay, Herincx, Erwen, Allister, Estes, Alldis Ch., LSO; (ii) RLPO & Ch.; Groves

With big Verdian ensembles and Puccinian ariosos (the style is still unmistakably Delian) *Koanga* is a big, red-blooded opera, which makes a striking impact on record. Koanga is a proud African prince brought as a slave to a Mississippi plantation. He falls in love with a mulatto girl who is then abducted. Told in flashback, this simple story gives Delius the chance to write a marvellous sequence of evocative passages, not least the Negro choruses. The recording uses a revised libretto, much more effective than the original. When it first appeared in 1974, Groves's powerful reading plus excellent singing from the whole cast suggested that this was a work that could readily have been taken into regular repertory in the opera house. But that was not to be, which makes this reissue uniquely valuable. The splendid analogue recording has transferred most vividly and atmospherically to CD, and the set is well documented. *The Song of the High Hills*, with its wordless chorus, was recorded in the same year, and is perceptively interpreted, but here Groves is inclined to understatement.

A Village Romeo and Juliet (complete)

☛ (M) *** EMI (ADD) 5 75785-2 (2). Luxon, Mangin, Harwood, Tear, John Alldis Ch., RPO, M. Davies (includes illustrated talk by Eric Fenby)

Meredith Davies's great quality is his inspired pacing of a score that can easily stagnate, when central to this Swiss slant on the 'Romeo and Juliet' story (based on a novella of Gottfried Keller) is a sustained sequence of duets between the lovers, Sali and Vreli, as their calf-love blossoms into something deeper. Just as much as echoing the Romeo and Juliet story, the plot is a variant of the Tristan and Isolde legend, leading to the final love-death as the lovers, in ecstatic suicide-pact, drift down the river in their sinking barge. Davies ensures that the music never meanders. He sets the love-duets in dramatic contrast to the vigorous writing, above all in the lively fair scene. The plot is made to unfold with a feeling of inevitability, and the overall freshness is enhanced by the use of Tom Hammond's radically revised text for the libretto in place of the grotesquely stilted original, written by Delius himself. Davies is, if anything, even more passionate than Beecham in his 1946 recording, as at the climax of the great orchestral set-piece, *The Walk to the Paradise Garden*.

Elizabeth Harwood and Robert Tear are both excellent as Vreli and Sali, winningly characterful and clearly focused, with the role of Sali as a boy in the opening scene taken by a bright treble, Corin Manley, against the fresh soprano of Wendy Eathorne for Vreli as a child. Benjamin Luxon and Noel Mangin can hardly be bettered as the warring fathers, dark and incisive, while John Shirley-Quirk in the equivocal role of the Dark Fiddler – representing the spirit not of evil but of raw nature – is firm and forthright with an apt hint of the sinister. As transferred, the 1971 recording still has plenty of body, with the evocative offstage effects beautifully handled. The only serious snag in having the opera in this compact format at mid-price is that there is no libretto. Instead, Eric Fenby provides a very detailed synopsis and (as a supplement on the second disc) the recorded talk by Fenby on Delius and his career, with a fascinating reconstruction of how the blind and paralysed composer used to dictate his final inspirations to Fenby, a terrifying exercise.

(i) A Village Romeo and Juliet (complete); (ii) Songs of Sunset

(M) (***) Somm BEECHAM 12-2. (i) Soames, Hambleton, F. Smith, Sharp, Clinton, Terry, Davies; (ii) Haley, Henderson; BBC Theatre Ch., RPO, L. Select Ch.; LPO, Beecham

Beecham's radio recording of Delius's opera, *A Village Romeo and Juliet*, was made for the BBC Third Programme only a week before he went to the EMI studio to record the opera with substantially the same cast. The wonder is how different it is interpretatively. The timing alone provides an indication of the contrast, with the studio recording some eleven minutes shorter than the radio recording in an opera lasting under two hours. Surprisingly, the more expansive radio recording is the one which sounds more passionate at almost every point, with the spontaneity of the live performance far outweighing any advantages of precision and balance in the studio version. Though the studio recording is better balanced, it is the radio version which, despite flaws, is the more atmospheric, with more air round the voices.

René Soames, a fine, sensitive tenor, sings with fresh, cleanly focused tone as the hero in both recordings, yet the radio version again wins out as the more lively. Other singers who appear in both include Gordon Clinton in the sinister role of the Dark Fiddler, and Frederick Sharp as Marti, father of the heroine, Vreli, both strong and clear in a very English way. Fabian Smith, who sings the role of Sali's father, is even firmer than his quarrelling rival, Sharp, and every bit as impressive as the excellent Denis Dowling on the EMI version. More surprising still, Vera Terry as the heroine, Vreli, on the radio recording outshines her EMI rival, Lorely Dyer, who has a distracting flutter in the voice, though at the top Terry's soprano grows shrill. The only pity is that at mid-price Somm have been unable to provide a libretto, and the indexing is limited to just one track per scene.

The revised version of Beecham's 1934 Leeds Festival performance of the *Songs of Sunset* makes a welcome bonus on the second disc, an astonishingly vivid and atmospheric live performance of these sensuous settings of poems by Ernest Dowson, with Olga Haley and Roy Henderson the excellent soloists.

DIAMOND, David (1915–2005)

(i) *Violin Concerto 2; The Enormous Room; Symphony 1*
⊶ (BB) *** Naxos 8.559157. (i) Seattle SO, Schwarz, (i) with Talvi

What a good composer David Diamond is – and how good it is to have the present repertoire reissued on Naxos. Like Barber, Piston and Roy Harris, Diamond was pushed aside in the late 1950s when the march of serialism and post-serialism seemed unstoppable, and Boulez and his followers dismissed such music as irrelevant. However, this generation is returning with a vengeance and Diamond has enjoyed considerable exposure in the last decade or so. The *First Symphony* was composed after the outbreak of war had forced Diamond to abandon his studies with Nadia Boulanger in Paris and return to America. Mitropoulos conducted its première in 1941 and the piece is undoubtedly an auspicious beginning to his impressive symphonic portfolio. The lyrical *Second Violin Concerto* (1947) is a bit Stravinskian with a dash of Walton. It is finely played by the Finnish-born Ilkka Talvi; and the fantasia, *The Enormous Room* (1948), takes its inspiration from the e. e. cummings description of his incarceration in a French detention camp in 1918. The poet described his eighty-by-forty-foot room at La Ferté Macé (shared with many others) as 'filled with a new and beautiful darkness, the darkness of snow outside, falling and falling with the silent gesture which has touched the soundless country of my mind as a child touches a toy it loves'. Diamond's score is rhapsodic in feeling, with orchestral textures of great luxuriance; it is both imaginative and atmospheric, and throughout he is well served by Gerard Schwarz, the Seattle orchestra and the Delos team who originally recorded it. Indeed, the recording is outstanding.

(i) *Concert Piece for Flute & Harp. Concert Piece for Orchestra.* (i) *Elegy in Memory of Ravel. Rounds for String Orchestra; Symphony 11: Adagio*
⊶ *** Delos DE 3189. Seattle SO, Schwarz, (i) with Glorian Duo

The *Rounds for String Orchestra* (1944) is a masterpiece and ought to be part of the international repertoire. It conjures up the vastness of the American continent but suggests also the presence of humanity, while the vigorous closing movement encapsulates barn-dance energy. The *Concert Piece for Orchestra* is also snappily rhythmic, more jagged, with a cool, elegiac counterpart and a sudden resolution. The *Elegy for Ravel* is unexpectedly troubled and dissonant, but the delicately evoked *Concert Piece for Flute and Harp* is far closer to

Ravel's world. The eloquent *Adagio* from the *Eleventh Symphony* has been described as Brucknerian. All this music is played superbly by the fine Seattle orchestra, and the disc is worth considering for the *Rounds* alone.

(i) *Kaddish for Cello & Orchestra. Psalm; Symphony 3*
(N)(BB) *** Naxos 8.559155 (i) Starker; Seattle SO, Schwarz

The *Third Symphony* is a four-movement work of no mean power. This and the *Psalm* show Diamond as a real man of the orchestra, and the Seattle orchestra proves an eloquent advocate. *Kaddish* is a more recent piece and is played here by its dedicatee, János Starker. A highly recommendable Naxos reissue.

Symphonies 2 & 4
(BB) *** Naxos 8.559154. Seattle SO, Schwartz

In spite of attracting attention after the Second World War, David Diamond's music (with a few exceptions) was grievously neglected in the 1960s and '70s. The *Fourth Symphony* is very diatonic, tonal, impeccably crafted and sophisticated, qualities that were not highly praised at the time. The *Second Symphony* is a large-scale work, lasting nearly three-quarters of an hour, written in 1942–3 at the height of the war, and it has great sweep and power. There is a lot of Roy Harris in the opening measures, and the music unfolds with a similar sense of inevitability and purpose. Overall, his music is less what one might in the vernacular call 'macho'. There are also reminders both of Shostakovich and of the Copland of *Appalachian Spring*. It is beautifully crafted and envinces a continuity of musical thought that defines the real symphonist. These excellent performances were originally recorded by and released on Delos, along with the *Concerto for Small Orchestra*, with the New York Chamber Orchestra, which has, sadly, been removed for its Naxos incarnation. However, at bargain price, with such dedicated and expert playing, all set in a spacious and well-balanced, ventilated acoustic (though some may find it too reverberant), it still represents good value at the asking price.

Symphony 8; Suite 1 from the Ballet, Tom; (i) *This Sacred Ground*
(BB) *** Naxos 8.559156. Seattle SO, Schwarz; (i) with Parce, Seattle Girls' Ch. & NorthWest boychoir

The *First Suite from the Ballet, Tom* inhabits much the same musical world as Aaron Copland. The *Eighth Symphony* makes use of serial technique but will still present few problems to those familiar with Diamond's earlier music, for it remains lyrical and thought-provoking. It culminates in a double fugue of considerable ingenuity. *This Sacred Ground* is a short setting for soloist, choirs and orchestra of the Gettysburg Address, and it may not travel so well. Committed performances and excellent, natural, recorded sound.

Piano Sonata
(***) VAI mono VAIA 1124. Tureck – DALLAPICCOLA: 2 *Studies for Violin & Piano* (***); SCHUMANN: *Piano Concerto* (*(**))

David Diamond wrote his *Sonata* especially for Rosalyn Tureck, bearing in mind her special experience in contrapuntal playing which was to prove very telling in the double fugue of the powerful finale. But her light, clear articulation gives a splendid sparkle to the Scherzo, which comes as the centrepiece of the highly expressive *Adagio*. This is the work's world première performance, in front of an audience in New

York's Town Hall, and it has great intensity and power. The recording is very close and is hard in *fortissimo*, but acceptable. Miss Tureck especially requested that her CD should be included in our *Guide*, and understandably so. Perhaps she will now be invited to re-record the work.

DIEPENBROCK, Alphons (1862–1921)

Elektra Suite; (i) *Hymn for Violin & Orchestra. Marsyas Suite; Overture: The Birds*
*** Chan. 8821. (i) Verhey; Hague Residentie O, Vonk

The *Birds Overture*, written for a student production of Aristophanes, is rather delightful if very Straussian, with some vaguely Impressionistic touches. The *Marsyas Music* (1910) is expertly and delicately scored with touches of Strauss, Reger and Debussy. Good performances from the Residentie Orchestra under Hans Vonk, and eminently truthful recording quality. Recommended.

(i) *Hymne an die Nacht;* (ii) *Hymne;* (i) *Die Nacht;* (iii) *Im grossen Schweigen*
*** Chan. 8878. (i) Finnie; (ii) Homberger; (iii) Holl; Hague Residentie O, Vonk

This second volume brings four symphonic songs, all of great beauty and with an almost Straussian melancholy. There are touches of Reger and Debussy as well as Strauss, and all four pieces are expertly and delicately scored. Good performances from all three soloists and the Residentie Orchestra under Hans Vonk, and very good recording indeed.

D'INDIA, Sigismondo (c. 1582–c. 1630)

Amico, hai vinto; Diana (Questo dardo, quest' arco); Misera me (Lamento d'Olympia); Piangono al pianger mio; Sfere fermate; Torna il sereno zefiro
*** Hyp. CDA 66106. Kirkby, Rooley (chitarone) –
MONTEVERDI: *Lamento d'Olympia*, etc. ***

Sigismondo d'India's setting of the *Lamento d'Olympia* makes a striking contrast to Monteverdi's and is hardly less fine. This is an affecting and beautiful piece and so are its companions, particularly when they are sung as superbly and accompanied as sensitively as they are here. A very worthwhile CD début.

Il primo libro de madrigali (1606): *Interdette speranz'e van desio. Ottavo libro de madrigali: Il pastor fido,* Act IV, Scene 9: *Se tu, Silvio crudel, mi saetti* (five madrigal cycle)
●—◖ (M) *** Virgin 5 61165-2. Chiaroscuro, L. Bar., Rogers
– MONTEVERDI: *Madrigals* *** ◉

It is in the cycle from his Eighth Book of Madrigals, *Se tu, Silvio crudel, mi saetti,* that one experiences not only the composer's lyrical originality to the full but also his affinity with the operatic writing of his greater contemporary, Monteverdi. The vocal dialogue, which alternates solo and ensemble singing, is touching and dramatic by turns, and requires effortless vocal virtuosity. The quality of the performances is superlative, refined without a hint of preciosity, and always alive, while the accompaniments on the oboe and harpsichord are delicately balanced. An outstanding collection in every way.

DITTERSDORF, Carl Ditters von (1739–99)

Double-Bass Concertos 1 in D; 2 in D (Krebs 171/2)
*** Hyp. CDA 67179. Nwanoku, Swedish CO, Goodwin –
VANHAL: *Double-Bass Concerto in D* ***

The double-bass can make a cumbersome concerto soloist, but Chi-Chi Nwanoku, regular member of distinguished ensembles ever since her student days, makes light of any problems in these concertos. She is amazingly agile and incisive in allegros, well tuned and expressive in lyrical slow movements. Jan Vaňhal and Carl Ditters von Dittersdorf, exact contemporaries, were both inspired to write these works by the playing of the eighteenth-century virtuoso, Johann Matthias Sperger, himself the composer of 17 double-bass concertos. The Vaňhal is charming enough, but the two Dittersdorf works are more distinctive, making up an ideal coupling, very well recorded.

Harp Concerto in A (arr. Pilley)
❋ (M) *** Decca (ADD) 425 723-2. Robles, ASMF, Brown –
BOIELDIEU; HANDEL: *Harp Concertos*, etc. *** ❋

Dittersdorf's *Harp Concerto* is a transcription of an unfinished keyboard concerto with additional wind parts. It is an elegant piece, thematically not quite as memorable as the Boieldieu coupling, but captivating when played with such style.

6 Symphonies after Ovid's Metamorphoses
**(*) Chan. 8564/5 (2). Cantilena, Shepherd

All the *Ovid Symphonies* have a programmatic inspiration and relate episodes from the *Metamorphoses* of Ovid, such as *The Fall of Phaeton*, which are vividly portrayed. *The Rescue of Andromeda by Perseus* is a particularly effective work (it has an inspired *Adagio*) and the slow movement of the *D major, The Petrification of Phineus and his Friends,* is a delight. *The Transformation of the Lycian Peasants into Frogs* could hardly be more graphic and is full of wit. This is inventive and charming music that will give much pleasure, and it is generally well served by Cantilena under Adrian Shepherd. There is also a set on Naxos (8.553368/9) acceptably performed by the Failoni Symphony Orchestra under Hanspeter Gmür, but the Chandos versions have much more character and are worth the extra cost.

Symphonies in A min. (Il delirio delli compositori, ossia Il gusto d'oggidi) (Grave a2); in A (Sinfonia nazionale nel gusto di cinque nazioni) (Grave A10); in D (Il Combattimento delle passioni umani) (Grav D16)
(BB) *** Naxos 8.553975. Failoni O, Grodd

Of these three symphonies, descriptive of human moods rather than programmatic, the *A minor,* concerned with the delirium of the composer, is obviously not meant to be taken too seriously. The D major *Battle of the Human Passions* of 1771, with its seven movements, is more of a suite than a symphony. Opening with a portentous 'Halleluja' *maestoso* ('*Pride*'), it includes a '*Mad*' (but not very mad) *Minuet* for strings alone, and depicts a tender humility, contentment, a very positive constancy and a touching melancholia. The finale is the epitome of vivacity, yet with mercurial mood-changes.

The *Sinfonia of Five Nations* – Germany, Italy (unflatteringly crude), France, England and (surprisingly) Turkey –

dates from around 1766 and is really another suite, given its variety by rhythm as much as by melody. Excellent performances throughout – Uwe Grodd is a persuasive exponent – and good recording; but, apart from the ingenious *A minor Symphony*, musically this is far less rewarding than the companion triptych of untitled symphonies below.

Symphonies: in D min. (Grave d1); F (Grave F7); G min. (Grave g1)
(BB) *** Naxos 8.553974. Failoni O, Grodd

The three works collected here show Dittersdorf at his most inventive, learning and absorbing influences from both Haydn and Mozart. The *F major Symphony* is the earliest here, probably dating from the early 1760s, and a very personable little work it is. The *G minor Symphony*, which comes from the close of the same decade, is altogether more turbulent. It must have been highly regarded in its day, for the manuscript survives in a number of copies and is listed in three major publishers' catalogues of the time. The *D minor Symphony* dates from the mid- to late 1770s and its warmly lyrical opening *Adagio* immediately coaxes the ear with just a hint of Beethoven's *Pastoral Symphony*, although its mood is darker. The performances here are first class in every way, the playing polished, responsive and vigorous, and the recording is excellent. This is an easy first choice among the available discs of Dittersdorf symphonies.

DODGSON, Stephen (born 1924)

(i) *Flute Concerto* (for flute and strings); (ii) *Duo Concertant for Violin, Guitar & Strings*; (iii) *Last of the Leaves* (cantata for bass, clarinet and strings)
*** Biddulph LAW 015. (i) Stallman; (ii) Kantorow, Gifford; (iii) George, Bradbury; N. Sinfonia, Zollman

Dodgson wrote his *Flute Concerto* for the American flautist, Robert Stallman, who is the fine soloist on this disc. The *Duo Concertant* also receives a persuasive performance. With its hints of an English Stravinsky, this is another work that is at once thoughtful and charming. *Last of the Leaves* is a cantata for bass soloist accompanied by clarinet and strings, more consistently autumnal and elegiac. Framing the work are settings of poems by Austin Dobson and Harold Monro, with the necessary contrast provided by the best-known poem, G. K. Chesterton's *The Donkey*. Though Michael George's noble bass voice is not caught as sweetly as it might be, it is a tenderly moving performance, with John Bradbury equally expressive, and with the Belgian conductor, Ronald Zollman, as in the other works, a sympathetic accompanist.

(i) *Guitar Concerto* (for guitar and chamber orchestra). *Partita 1 for Solo Guitar*
(B) **(*) Sony (ADD) SBK 61716. Williams; (i) with ECO, Groves – RODRIGO: *Concierto de Aranjuez*, etc. **(*)

John Williams proves an eloquent and authoritative exponent, and the *Concerto* could hardly hope for a more persuasive performance. Much the same goes for the *Partita*, and these make original and worthwhile couplings for the ubiquitous Rodrigo works. The recording is good but not exceptional.

Piano Sonatas 1; 3 (Variations on a Rhythm); 6
*** Claudio CC 4941-2. Roberts

Piano Sonatas 2; 4; 5
*** Claudio CC 4431-2. Roberts

Those who know Stephen Dodgson's guitar music may initially be disconcerted that the style here is grittier, more demanding and quirky at times, as in the multiple movements of the *Sonata No. 4*. In that work the note-writer, Professor Wilfrid Mellers, highlights an 'Alice in Wonderland' quality – apt from a composer distantly related to the Dodgson who was author of that fantasy, Lewis Carroll.

That comes on CC 4431-2, but the companion CD, CC 4941-2, gives a wider insight into the composer's development, from the *Sonata No. 1* of 1959, in which English echoes can still be detected, to the more freely expansive writing of the *Sonata No. 6* of 1994, inspired by Bernard Roberts's performances on the first disc. Most ingenious in its complex organization is the *Sonata No. 3* of 1983, subtitled *Variations on a Rhythm*, with Dodgson at his most original. Excellent, well-balanced sound.

DOHNÁNYI, Ernst von (1877–1960)

(i) *Harp Concertino, Op. 45*; (ii) *Piano Concerto 2 in B min., Op. 42*; (iii) *Violin Concerto 2 in C min., Op. 43*
(N) *** Chan. 19245. (i) Lantaff; (ii) Shelley; (iii) Ehnes; BBC PO, Bamert

The latest issue in the ongoing Chandos series brings the *Second Piano Concerto*, played with great panache by Howard Shelley, and the soloists in the other works are hardly less fine; the *Harp Concertino* is a most engaging work in Lantaff's hands. Chandos and the BBC team at Manchester provide excellently balanced sound.

Piano Concertos 1 in E min., Op. 5; 2 in B min., Op. 42
*** Hyp. CDA 66684. Roscoe, BBC Scottish SO, Glushchenko

These concertos are well wrought, with a melodic warmth that fails to be indelible, but they provide bravura for the soloist and contrast for the orchestra. The present performances are surely unlikely to be surpassed for their commitment, and the playing is finished as well as ardent; the recording, too, is excellent.

Piano Concerto 1 in E min., Op.5; Ruralia Hungarica
*** Chan. 9649. Shelley, BBC PO, Bamert

Howard Shelley, the brilliant soloist in Bamert's version of the *Variations on a Nursery Tune* (CHAN. 9733), is here the powerful, warmly expressive soloist in a work which first brought Dohnányi success when still a student, the *First Piano Concerto*. With Bamert a dedicated interpreter of this composer, as he is in the rest of his excellent Chandos series, Shelley magnetically sustains the massive length of the outer movements, relishing the Lisztian fluency of the improvisatory writing and bringing a natural gravity to the chorale theme of the Bruckner-like central Andante. As an attractive coupling Bamert conducts the five movements of the orchestral version of *Ruralia Hungarica*, just one of the five folk-based works to which he gave this title. This makes a recommendable alternative to the rival Hyperion version of the *Concerto*, which has the *Second Concerto* for coupling. Full, vivid recording, not always ideally clear on detail.

Konzertstück for Cello & Orchestra, Op. 12
*** Chan. 8662. Wallfisch, LSO, Mackerras – DVORAK: *Cello Concerto* ***

Dohnányi's *Konzertstück* has many rich, warm ideas, not least a theme in the slow movement all too close to *Pale hands I loved beside the Shalimar*, and none the worse for that.

Wallfisch's performance, as in the Dvořák, is strong, warm and committed, and the Chandos sound is first rate.

Serenade in C, Op. 10
*** Hyp. CDA 67429. Leopold String Trio – MARTINU; SCHOENBERG: *Trios* ***

This delightful *Trio* with its overtones of Brahms and Dvořák always gives pleasure. Its famous première recording with Heifetz, Primrose and Feuermann has never been equalled or surpassed, but this superb account by the Leopold Trio will do very nicely. They play with great conviction and convey much pleasure in their music-making.

Symphony 1; American Rhapsody, Op. 47
*** Chan. 9647. BBC PO, Bamert

Dohnányi's *First Symphony* is something of a find. It is not just accomplished; the scoring shows real flair. A large-scale piece, some 55 minutes in duration, it reveals a strong sense of form. Matthias Bamert directs both works impressively and has the advantage of the BBC Philharmonic and excellent engineering from the BBC/Chandos team. You will find this most rewarding music.

Symphony 2, Op. 40; Symphonic Minutes, Op. 36
*** Chan. 9455. BBC PO, Bamert

Dohnányi's *Symphonic Minutes* are richly inventive and have enormous charm. The *Second Symphony* is a generally well-argued and finely crafted piece and is well worth getting to know, even if (at nearly 50 minutes) it rather outstays its welcome. The playing of the BBC Philharmonic under Matthias Bamert is vital and sensitive, and the Chandos recording is in the best traditions of the house.

Variations on a Nursery Tune, Op. 25
(B) *** Double Decca (ADD) 458 361-2 (2). Katchen, LPO, Boult – LISZT: *Piano Concertos 1-2*, etc. ***

Variations on a Nursery Tune, Op. 25; Suite in F sharp min., Op. 19; The Veil of Pierrette: Suite, Op. 18
☛ *** Chan. 9733. Shelley, BBC PO, Bamert

For all their popularity, Dohnányi's variations on 'Twinkle, twinkle, little star', with their witty parodies, have been meanly treated on disc. The brilliant version with Howard Shelley the sparkling soloist is especially welcome when it offers two other examples of Dohnányi the charmer. The *Wedding Waltz* from the mimed entertainment, *The Veil of Pierrette*, was once well known, dashingly Viennese, as are the other three movements, previously unrecorded, including a *Merry Funeral March* which parodies Mahler. The *Suite* too is engagingly colourful. Brilliant performances, sumptuously recorded.

Katchen's 1959 remake of the *Nursery Variations* has the advantage of Decca's finest vintage stereo. The performance is both perceptive and spontaneous, as full of wit as it is of lilt and flair, and the recording is very beautifully balanced – indeed, in the demonstration bracket for its period.

(i) Piano Quintet 1 in C min., Op. 1. String Quartet 2 in D flat, Op. 15
**(*) Chan. 8718. (i) Manz; Gabrieli Qt

Piano Quintets 1; 2 in E flat min., Op. 26; Serenade in C, Op. 10
*** Hyp. CDA 66786. Schubert Ens. of London

(i-ii) Piano Quintets 1-2; (i) Suite in the Old Style, Op. 24
*** ASV CDDCA 915. (i) Roscoe; (ii) Vanbrugh Qt

Dohnányi wrote the first of his two *Piano Quintets* when still in his teens; it is ripely Brahmsian, built strongly on memorable themes. The *Second Quintet*, dating from 20 years later, just after the *Nursery Variations*, is sharper and more compact, with Hungarian flavours more pronounced, if never Bartókian. The *Suite in the Old Style*, for piano alone, is an amiable example of pre-Stravinsky neo-classicism, again beautifully written for the instrument. The Vanbrugh Quartet is well matched by Martin Roscoe in keen, alert performances, warmly recorded.

The Schubert Ensemble give us in addition the *Serenade for String Trio*. A clear three-star recommendation for the Hyperion disc and their excellent pianist, William Howard.

Wolfgang Manz's performance of Dohnányi's *First Piano Quintet* lacks something in fantasy and lightness of touch. But the bigger-boned, somewhat Brahmsian effect of this performance is certainly compelling, if less strong on charm. The *Second String Quartet* is a strong piece, splendidly played by the Gabrielis, and beautifully recorded.

Serenade for String Trio
(B) *** Virgin 2×1 5 61904-2 (2). Domus – MARTINU: *Piano Quartet 1*, etc.; DVORAK: *Bagatelles*; KODALY: *Intermezzo*; SUK: *Piano Quartet* ***

The Dohnányi *Serenade for String Trio* comes from 1902 and was first recorded in an unforgettable performance by Heifetz, Primrose and Feuerman. The three players from the Domus team meet its demands with admirably alert and sensitive playing and can more than hold their own against recent rival accounts. This performance comes as part of a rewarding and inexpensive programme from Domus which has an eminently natural recorded sound.

Serenade for String Trio; Sextet
☛ ✹ (BB) *** Naxos 8.557153. Spectrum Concerts Berlin, Dodge

The two chamber works here, representing the full span of Dohnányi's composing career, from the early *Serenade* to the *Sextet* of 1935, are among the composer's most winning music, making up a superb disc, brilliantly played and recorded. The *Serenade for String Trio* is Dohnányi's most popular chamber work, with four of its five movements crisply compact and undemanding, but with a Variation movement, *Andante con moto*, fourth in the sequence, which on a more ambitious scale delves deeper, a point movingly brought out here in playing of hushed intensity. The *Sextet* is even more distinctive, with a strong first movement prominently featuring the horn, and a slow movement which builds up powerfully, before the two lighter movements which follow. The delicately pointed Scherzo leads to an exuberant finale, with jagged cross-rhythms, comic false entries and deliciously surreal waltz-references. It is played here breathtakingly fast, with the waltz parodies wittily highlighted, and the fun of the final 'wrong-key' cadence nicely pointed under the direction of the cellist, Frank Sumner Dodge. Brilliant, full-bodied sound to match.

Sextet in C for Piano, Clarinet, Horn, Violin, Viola & Cello, Op. 37
*** ASV CDDCA 943. Endymion Ens. – FIBICH: *Piano Quintet* ***

The Endymions play with great feeling and panache; they are

splendidly recorded and can be strongly recommended if the couplet is wanted.

String Quartets 2 in D flat, Op. 15; 3 in A min., Op. 33
*** ASV CDDCA 985. Lyric Qt – KODALY: *Intermezzo for String Trio* ***

These two quartets are separated by two decades. Dohnányi's emerging personality is already much in evidence. The *Third Quartet* is a finely crafted and richly inventive score, conservative in idiom. The Lyric Quartet play with commitment and conviction that more than outweigh the odd moment of inelegance.

Violin Sonata in C sharp min., Op. 21; Andante rubato (Ruralia Hungarica)
**(*) Biddulph LAW 015. Shumsky, Lipkin – WEINER: *Violin Sonatas 1 & 2* **(*)

Oscar Shumsky and Seymour Lipkin were recorded in New York in 1993 and they make an excellent case for this neglected but fine sonata. Shumsky's playing is not quite as polished or masterly as it was in the early 1980s, but it is still supremely musical. A worthwhile addition to the catalogue.

PIANO MUSIC

6 Concert Etudes, Op. 28; Pastorale; Ruralia Hungarica, Op. 32a; Variations on a Hungarian Folk Song, Op. 29
☛━ ✪ (BB) *** Naxos 8.553332. Pawlik

The *Six Concert Etudes*, Op. 28, of 1916 are among the most technically demanding pieces in the repertoire. Markus Pawlik was still in his twenties when he recorded these pieces, and his playing is remarkable for its dazzling virtuosity, sensitivity, finesse and good taste. His dexterity and wonderful clarity of articulation in the *D flat Etude* are exceptional. His is a formidable talent, and we hope to hear much more of him. Decent recorded sound. Recommended with all enthusiasm.

DOMARTO, Petrus de (c. 1450)

Missa Spiritus almus
*** Hyp. CDA 67319. Binchois Consort, Kirkman (with PULLOIS: *Flos de spina*) – BUSNOIS: *Missa l'homme armé; Motets* ***

The *Missa Spiritus almus* of Petrus de Domarto is strikingly more richly lyrical than the coupled work of Busnois, even though the two Masses were composed little more than a decade apart. Petrus's flowing, serene textures are apt for the 'nourishing spirit' of the title. Little is known of the composer except that he spent part of his career in Antwerp alongside Ockeghem. But this is a memorable work, and the performance and recording are of high quality.

DONIZETTI, Gaetano (1797–1848)

Il barcaiolo; Cor Anglais Concerto in G; Oboe Sonata in F; (Piano) Waltz in C
*** Mer. (ADD) CDE 84147. Polmear, Ambache O, Ambache (with PASCULLI: *Concerto on Themes from 'La Favorita'; Fantasia on 'Poliuto'*; LISZT: *Réminscences de Lucia di Lammermoor*)

The *Sonata in F* is an agreeable piece with a fluent *Andante* and a catchy finale; and the vignette, *Il barcaiolo*, is even more engaging. The *Cor Anglais Concerto* centres on a set of variations that are not unlike the fantasias on themes from his operas by Pasculli. However, these demand the utmost bravura from the soloist. Diana Ambache proves a sympathetic partner and gives a suitably flamboyant account of Liszt's famous *Lucia* paraphrase.

(i) Clarinet Concertino in B flat; (ii) Cor Anglais Concertino in G; (iii) Flute Concertino in C min.; (iv) Oboe Concertino in F; (v) Double Concertino in D min. for Violin & Cello; (vi) Sinfonia a soli instrumenti di fiato in G min. Sinfonia in D min. per la Morte di Capuzzi
☛━ ✪ (N) (BB) *** Naxos 8.557492. (i) B. Kovács; (ii) Girgás; (iii) I. Kovács; (iv) J. Kiss; (v) A. Kiss, J. Kiss Domonkos; (vi) Soloists, Budapest Camerata, L. Kovács

We already know the *Concertino for Cor Anglais*, which is played here with a delectable timbre and a nice feeling for light and shade. The *Clarinet Concertino* brings a touch of melancholy to its opening cantilena, yet the finale chortles. The *Flute Concertino* also opens with an eloquent aria, but the closing rondo is irrepressibly light-hearted, with an infectiously carefree, Rossinian wit. The *Oboe Concertino* has a vigorous hunting finale, played here with bouncing zest. The *Double Concertino*, in three movements, is the most ambitious work. In short, all these concertos are most winning, as elegant as they are inventive, and all the expert soloists (several of whom seem to be interrelated) smilingly convey the music's Italian sunshine. The concertos are framed by two contrasting *Sinfonias*. Both are played very persuasively, and throughout the collection László Kovács and his Budapest chamber orchestra provide supportive and stylish accompaniments. The recording could hardly be bettered, and the result is a collection which will give great and repeated pleasure. Now at Naxos price it is a great bargain.

Sinfonias in A; D min. (both arr. Benedek); D (arr. Angerer)
**(*) Marco Polo 8.223577. Failoni CO, Oberfrank

These works are well played and flatteringly recorded; a touch more wit and sparkle would not have come amiss, but the music is well worth having.

CHAMBER MUSIC

Introduzione for Strings; String Quartets 10 in G min.; 11 & 12 in C
(M) *** CPO 999 279-2. Revolutionary Drawing Room

This excellent CPO series reveals Donizetti to be a considerable contributor to the string quartet medium, offering works that in their craftsmanship and quality of invention can stand comparison with all but the very finest of Haydn. These three and the following four, Nos. 13–16, all date from around 1821, when the composer was in his early twenties. They are very much Haydn-influenced (in the best sense). These players are completely at home on their period instruments: their execution is fresh, vital and expressive, without any linear eccentricities.

String Quartet 13 in A
(M) *** CRD 3366. Alberni Qt – PUCCINI: *Crisantemi*; VERDI: *Quartet* ***

This is an endearing work with a Scherzo echoing that in Beethoven's *Eroica* and with many twists of argument that are attractively unpredictable. It is given a strong, committed performance and is well recorded.

String Quartets 13 in A; 14 in D; 15 in F
(M) **(*) CPO 999 280-2. Revolutionary Drawing Room

No. 14 in D is programmatic, and we hear the storm gathering immediately at the opening: its full force is soon sweeping through the music. The hushed *Adagio* sadly contemplates the havoc left behind, but the genial Minuet suggests that life goes on, with repairs carried out in the Trio, while the hammering workmen sing to themselves. The *F major* opens thoughtfully, but the genial spirit of the first movement again recalls Haydn, and that master's humanity is also reflected in the *Andante*. All these quartets are played with spirit, warmth and finesse, and the recording is vivid, though this disc is not quite as smooth as CPO 999 279, revealing a degree of edge on the timbre of the lead violin.

String Quartets 16 in B min.; 17 in D; 18 in E min.
(M) *** CPO 999 282-2. Revolutionary Drawing Room

No. 16 is the last of the 1821 quartets; the jolly, energetic triplets of its first movement are clearly forward-looking, almost Schubertian. The *Largo* is thoughtfully serene, even sombre. No. 17 was written four years later and is noticeably more warmly romantic. Finest of the whole series is the mature *E minor Quartet* of a decade later, splendidly assured in its light-hearted first movement, which the composer used as a basis for his *Linda di Chamonix Overture*. It is splendidly played; indeed, the performances throughout this CD are among the finest in the series, and the recording is first class, too – that edge on the leader's tone (noticed above) has disappeared, and the balance is excellent.

OPERA

Anna Bolena (complete)
(M) (**(*)) EMI mono 5 66471-2 (2). Callas, Simionato, Rossi-Lemeni, G. Raimondi, Carturan, La Scala, Milan, Ch. & O, Gavazzeni

The Callas recording was made live at La Scala in 1957, with the great diva at her most searingly magnetic. This is a performance which, despite the occasional sour note, has one marvelling at the imaginative phrasing and subtlety of dynamic shading, with top notes firm and clear, if characteristically edgy. Gavazzeni proves a most sympathetic conductor and, though the rest of the cast is no match for Callas, there is characterful if rather inflexible singing from Simionato as Giovanna and a fresh, clear contribution from Gianni Raimondi in the relatively small tenor role of Percy, here made the smaller by cuts. Nicola Rossi-Lemeni as Henry VIII is positive but gritty of tone in a less than convincing characterization. The radio sound is dry and limited and with occasional interference, but for Callas fans this is well worth hearing.

L'assedio di Calais (complete)
*** Opera Rara (ADD) OR 9 (2). Du Plessis, D Jones, Focile, Serbo, Nilon, Platt, Glanville, Smythe, Treleaven, Harrhy, Bailey, Mitchell Ch., Philh. O, Parry

The Opera Rara set is one of the most invigorating of all the complete opera recordings made over the years by that enterprising organization. With Della Jones and Christian du Plessis in the cast, as well as a newcomer, Nuccia Focile, as Queen Eleanor, David Parry conducts the Philharmonia in a fresh, well-sprung performance which gives a satisfying thrust to the big ensembles. The one which ends Act II, including a magnificent sextet and a patriotic prayer for the chorus, brings the opera's emotional high point. When, in Act III, Edward III's big aria turns into a sort of jolly waltz song, the music seems less apt.

Don Pasquale (DVD version)
(N) **(*) TDK **DVD** DV-OPDP. Mei, Siragusa, Corbelli, De Candia, Gatti, Ch. & O of Teatro Lirico-Cagliari, Korsten (Producer: Andreina de Porto)

Don Pasquale (complete) (CD versions)
⊝➛ *** RCA 09026 61924-2 (2). Bruson, Mei, Allen, Lopardo, Bav. R. Ch., Munich R. O, R. Abbado

*** EMI 7 47068-2 (2). Bruscantini, Freni, Nucci, Winbergh, Amb. Op. Ch., Philh. O, Muti

Recorded at the Teatro Lirico in Cagliari in Feburary 2002, the TDK DVD demonstrates the traditional qualities of productions in provincial Italian opera houses. Traditional costumes and sets consistently help to enhance the comedy in this lively production by Andreina de Porto. The comedy revolves round the sure-fire *buffo* performances of the veteran, Alessandro Corbelli, in the title-role (only half-singing, but acting superbly) and Roberto de Candia as Dr Malatesta, just as confident and singing the part full out. Eva Mei is an equally assured Norina, not as fresh-sounding as she once was, but still a strong performer, and with Antonino Siragusa as Ernesto rightly presenting him as something of an opportunistic layabout rather than a conventional hero. After a fierce start, Gerard Korsten proves a warm and purposeful conductor, pacing the comedy well.

Roberto Abbado's Munich set for RCA is on balance the finest modern version of Donizetti's sparkling comedy. Not only does Abbado spring rhythms cleanly and lightly, they are made the more infectious by the clarity of focus. The cast has no weak link. Renato Bruson may accentuate Pasquale's comic lines with little explosions of underlining but that helps to distinguish him sharply as a *buffo* character from his opposite number, Malatesta, here sung with rare style and beauty by Thomas Allen, as well as with a nicely timed feeling for the comedy. Frank Lopardo as Ernesto shades his clear tenor most sensitively, singing his *Serenade* with far more refinement than most latter-day rivals. Eva Mei sings the role of Norina with an apt brightness and precision (including an excellent trill), even if others have presented a more characterful heroine.

Muti's is a delectably idiomatic-sounding reading, one which consistently captures the fun of the piece. Freni is a natural in the role of Norina, both sweet and bright-eyed in characterization, excellent in coloratura. The *buffo* baritones, the veteran Bruscantini as Pasquale and the darker-toned Leo Nucci as Dr Malatesta, steer a nice course between vocal comedy and purely musical values. Muti is helped by the beautifully poised and shaded singing of Gösta Winbergh, honey-toned and stylish as Ernesto. Responsive and polished playing from the Philharmonia, and excellent studio sound.

Don Pasquale (complete; in English)
(M) *** Chan. 3011 (2). Shore, Dawson, Banks, Howard, Mitchell Ch., LPO, Parry

David Parry and a lively team of soloists, using Parry's own translation, deliver a well-paced, jolly and amiable performance. The interplay of characters is caught well and the celebrated patter duet between Don Pasquale and Dr Malatesta, wonderfully articulated, brings none of the traditional comic wheezing at the end – on the whole, an advantage. Andrew Shore and Jason Howard are good *buffo* singers, characterful if a little gruff, with Howard's Malatesta rather younger-sounding than usual, a believable brother of Norina. Lynne Dawson is fresh, sweet and agile as the heroine, and Barry Banks is a clear and unstrained Ernesto. Full sound, atmospheric enough to give warmth to the voices without obscuring words. If your preference is for opera in English, you can't go wrong with this.

L'elisir d'amore (DVD version)
🎥 *** Decca **DVD** 074-103-9. Gheorghiu, Alagna, Scaltriti, Alaimo, Lyon Op. Ch. & O, Pido

L'elisir d'amore (CD versions)
🎥 *** Decca 455 691-2 (2). Gheorghiu, Alagna, Scaltriti, Alaimo, Lyon Op. Ch. & O, Pido

(M) *** Erato 4509 98483-2 (2). Devia, Alagna, Spagnoli, Praticò, Tallis Chamber Ch., ECO, Viotti

*** Decca (ADD) 414 461-2 (2). Sutherland, Pavarotti, Cossa, Malas, Amb. S., ECO, Bonynge

(B) **(*) Double Decca (ADD) 443 542-2 (2). Gueden, Di Stefano, Corena, Capecchi, Mandelli, Maggio Musicale Fiorentino Ch. & O, Molinari-Pradelli

(BB) (***) Naxos mono (ADD) 8.110125/26 (2). Sayao, Tagliavini, Valdengo, Baccaloni, Lenchner, Met. Op. Ch. & O, Antonicelli (with excerpts from LEONCAVALLO: *Pagliacci*; PUCCINI: *La Bohème* (**))

(M) **(*) EMI (ADD) 5 65658-2 (2). Carteri, Alva, Panerai, Taddei, La Scala, Milan, Ch. & O, Serafin

Updated to the 1920s with jolly sets in primary colours, Frank Dunlop's production for Lyon Opéra on Decca makes an attractive DVD, very well produced by Brian Large, involving the same cast as on the excellent Decca CD recording, also made in 1996. As Alagna explains in the 52-minute feature film on the making of the recording, which comes as a valuable supplement, he tries in his characterization of the innocent Nemorino to bring out the youthful rather than the comic element, with results a degree weightier than usual. Angela Gheorghiu as Adina emerges in Act I brandishing a riding-crop, more than a match for Belcore, let alone Nemorino, and singing enchantingly. As Belcore Roberto Scaltriti is young and virile, with Dulcamara equally impressive, arriving in a vintage Rolls-Royce drawing a streamlined caravan. Under Evelino Pido the comedy of the piece fizzes winningly, with something of a circus atmosphere created by the staging.

Angela Gheorghiu and Roberto Alagna equally help to make the new Decca CD version of Donizetti's sparkling comedy a winner. Alagna's voice is recorded closer than in his earlier, Erato version, a portrait of the innocent Nemorino on the hefty side, with a newly unearthed variant of the great aria, *Una furtiva lagrima*, which proves no advantage, neither tender nor subtle. Otherwise the set is excellent all round, with Gheorghiu an enchanting Adina, tenderly poignant in her final solo.

The mid-priced Erato set is a light, generally brisk account of the score, and it provides an ideal modern alternative to Richard Bonynge's version. Mariella Devia cannot match Sutherland for beauty of tone in the warmly lyrical solos but she sparkles more, bringing out what a minx of a heroine this is. Roberto Alagna's tenor timbre was then lighter, if not quite so firm, and, like Devia, he brings out the lightness of the

writing delectably. His performance culminates in a winningly hushed and inner account of the soaring aria, *Una furtiva lagrima*. Rounding off an excellent cast, Pietro Spagnoli is a fresh, virile Belcore, and Bruno Praticò a clear, characterful Dr Dulcamara, an excellent *buffo* baritone, making the very most of a voice on the light side. The sound is first rate. Highlights are available on an Apex disc (2564 61496-2) which makes a good sampler.

Joan Sutherland makes Adina a more substantial figure than usual, full-throatedly serious at times, at others jolly like the rumbustious Marie; in the key role of Nemorino, Luciano Pavarotti proves ideal, vividly portraying the wounded innocent. Spiro Malas is a superb Dulcamara, while Dominic Cossa is a younger-sounding Belcore, more of a genuine lover than usual. Bonynge points the skipping rhythms delectably and the recording is sparkling to match, with striking presence.

With Hilde Gueden at her most seductive, the very early (1955) Decca stereo recording offers a delightful, spontaneous-sounding performance. Not just Gueden but the other soloists too are strikingly characterful, with Giuseppe di Stefano at his most headily sweet-toned, singing with youthful ardour, Fernando Corena a strong and vehement Dulcamara and Renato Capecchi well contrasted as Sergeant Belcore, though not quite so firm of tone, but both splendidly comic. Even without a libretto it makes a good bargain, with two CDs offered for the price of one.

One great benefit from the Naxos Historical series has been to expand our knowledge of the Brazilian soprano Bidu Sayao, who for many years was such a favourite at the Met. in New York, but who was hardly known in Europe, making far too few commercial recordings. As a total charmer among lyric sopranos she is perfectly cast here as Adina, giving a sparkling portrayal opposite the young, golden-toned Tagliavini as Nemorino. Like all Italian tenors of his generation, he has his unstylish habits, but echoing Gigli he gives a winningly delicate account of *Una furtiva lagrima*, as well as entering into the fun of the piece. Giuseppe Valdengo could hardly be stronger as a firm, powerful Belcore, and the veteran, Salvatore Baccaloni, in traditional *buffo* bass style milks every comic point as the quack, Dulcamara, with Antonicelli timing the comedy to a nicety. Clear, if limited, mono sound. As a supplement come two delightful live recordings of Sayao: Nedda's communing with the birds in *Pagliacci* and the *Bohème* duet, *O soave fanciulla*, with Giuseppe di Stefano.

The La Scala set had a fine cast in its day (1959). Alva is a pleasantly light-voiced and engaging Nemorino. Carteri's Adina ideally should be more of a minx than this, but the part is nicely sung all the same. Panerai as Belcore once again shows what a fine and musical artist he is, and Taddei is magnificent, stealing the show as any Dulcamara can and should. The drawback is Serafin's direction. The La Scala chorus is lively enough, and it is not that the orchestral playing is slipshod, but they provide less sparkle than they should.

The Elixir of Love (complete; in English)
(M) **(*) Chan. 3027 (2). Banks, Plazas, Holland, Shore, Williams, Mitchell Ch., Philh. O, Parry

This lively account in English under David Parry brings out the high spirits of the piece, even if inevitably there are resulting echoes of Gilbert and Sullivan. Central to the performance's success is the vivacious Adina of Mary Plazas, sparkling and sweet-toned, guaranteed to ensnare any man around. Barry Banks gives a forthright performance as the innocent hero, Nemorino, even if the tone is not really Italianate enough for this music, whatever the language. Ashley Holland as Sergeant Belcore and Andrew Shore as Dr Dulcamara are lively and characterful, agile in rapid patter, even if their voices could be more sharply focused.

Elvida (complete)

(N) *** Opera Rara ORC 29. Massis, Spagnoli, Larmore, Ford, LPO, Allemandi

Written in 1826, when Donizetti was still in his twenties, *Elvida* is his only serious one-Act opera. It was commissioned for a royal gala performance at San Carlo in Naples with an exceptionally starry cast, including Luigi Lablache and Giovanni Rubini. The one-Act format was dictated by the royal timetable, and it results in a delightfully compact *dramma per musica*, involving the conflict of Castilian and Moorish forces in Spain. Elvida, from Castile, is held captive in Granada by the Moorish leader, Amur, whose son, Zeidar (a trouser role beautifully sung by the mezzo, Jennifer Larmore) falls in love with her. After various complications, she is finally rescued by the Castilian prince, Alfonso, who himself claims her hand. With a cast of principals identical to those in Opera Rara's recording of *François di Foix*, the performance is similarly strong and lively under the direction of Antonello Allemandi. Annick Massis is again outstandng in the title-role. Though the invention is not quite as striking as that in *François di Foix*, there are many delightful passages, such as the galloping 6/8 stretta which rounds off the Act I duet of Elvida and Zeidar.

Emilia di Liverpool (complete). L'eremitaggio di Liwerpool (complete)

*** Opera Rara (ADD) OR 8 (3). Kenny, Bruscantini, Merritt, Dolton, Mitchell Ch., Philh. O, Parry

The very name, *Emilia di Liverpool*, makes it hard to take this early opera of Donizetti seriously. In this set, sponsored by the Peter Moores Foundation, we have not only the original version of 1824 but also the complete reworking of four years later, which was given the revised title noted above. Such a veteran as Sesto Bruscantini makes an enormous difference in the *buffo* role of Don Romualdo in *Emilia*, a character who speaks in Neapolitan dialect. His fizzing duet with Federico (the principal tenor role, sung superbly by Chris Merritt) sets the pattern for much vigorous invention. With fresh, direct conducting from David Parry, this is a highly enjoyable set for all who respond to this composer.

La favorita (complete)

(M) **(*) Decca (ADD) 430 038-2 (3). Cossotto, Pavarotti, Bacquier, Ghiaurov, Cotrubas, Teatro Comunale Bologna Ch. & O, Bonynge

La Favorita may not have as many memorable tunes as the finest Donizetti operas, but red-blooded drama provides ample compensation. Fernando is strongly and imaginatively sung here by Pavarotti. The mezzo role of the heroine is taken by Fiorenza Cossotto, formidably powerful if not quite at her finest, while Ileana Cotrubas is comparably imaginative as her confidante, Ines, but not quite at her peak. Bacquier and Ghiaurov make up a team which should have been even better but which will still give much satisfaction. Bright recording.

La Fille du régiment (DVD version)

(*) TDK **DVD DV-OPLFDR. Devia, Kelly, Podles, Pratico, La Scala Ch. & O, Renzetti. (Dir. Crivelli, TV Dir. Protasoni)

La Fille du régiment (CD version)

☛— *** Decca (ADD) 414 520-2 (2). Sutherland, Pavarotti, Sinclair, Malas, Coates, ROHCG Ch. & O, Bonynge

Recorded live at La Scala, Milan, in June 1996, the DVD of *La Fille du régiment* is taken from a film for Italian television (RAI) with pretty sets and costumes by Franco Zeffirelli using flat, bright colours echoing those in an eighteenth-century print. The performance centres round the characterful Marie of Mariella Devia, a diminutive figure, bossy in a military way, who, defying her size, sings with a loud, penetrating voice, agile up to the highest register but not very steady in the middle. She generally sings well, though she guys her singing-lesson solo in Act II with grotesquely raucous tone. Opposite her, the Tonio of Paul Austin Kelly is a handsome roly-poly figure, sporting a great cushion of fuzzy hair. What matters is that he has a clear, firm, lyrical tenor, with a formidably unstrained top register, so that he copes superbly with the notorious arietta, *Pour mon âme*, in the finale of Act I with its clutch of high Cs. Eva Podles is magnificent in the character role of the Marquise de Berkenfield, commanding both in her singing and in her acting, completely dominating the compliant Sulpice of Bruno Pratico in Act II. The ensembles both with and without the chorus are brilliantly done, though the reunion trio, *Tous les trois réunis*, is taken absurdly fast. Otherwise the conducting of Donato Renzetti is warm and idiomatic. Note that nowadays even La Scala prefers the French text of this opera to the Italian version of Donizetti's score.

It was with the Decca cast that *La Fille du régiment* was revived at Covent Garden, and Sutherland immediately showed how naturally she takes to the role of Marie, a *vivandière* in the army of Napoleon. She is in turn brilliantly comic and pathetically affecting, and Pavarotti makes an engaging hero. Monica Sinclair is a formidable Countess in a fizzing performance of a delightful Donizetti romp that can confidently be recommended both for comedy and for fine singing. Recorded in Kingsway Hall, the CD sound has wonderful presence and clarity of focus.

(i) Gabriella di Vergy (1838 version); (ii) Scenes from 1826 version

**(*) Opera Rara ORC 3 (2). (i) Andrew, du Plessis, Arthur, Tomlinson, J. Davies, Winfield; (ii) Harrhy, Jones; RPO, Francis

Dating from 1979 and transferred well to CD, this Opera Rara set of *Gabriella di Vergy* (not to be confused with *Gemma di Vergy*) presents the rediscovered score, written in the composer's hand, of a piece which Donizetti himself never heard. It was unearthed by Don White and Patric Schmid and makes one wonder how this inventive score with its many sparkling cabalettas and superb Act II finale could have been neglected for so long. The cast is a capable one, with Alun Francis, as ever, a sympathetic conductor; it is interesting to hear John Tomlinson early in his career, slightly miscast. It is fascinating to have as appendix three excerpts from the original, 1826 score, with Della Jones taking the role of the hero, Raoul, later rewritten for tenor.

François di Foix (complete)

(N) *** Opera Rara ORC 28. Massis, Spagnoli, Larmore, Ford, Antoniozzi, LPO, Allemandi

Patric Schmid of Opera Rara has the rare gift of lighting on rarities among early nineteenth-century operas that have been unfairly forgotten. Here he has produced a splendid account of one of Donizetti's one-Act operas, 75 minutes long, *François di Foix*, described as a *melodramma giocoso*. This story of the Countess mistreated by her husband, before he meets his comeuppance, may be far-fetched, but it inspired Donizetti to write a sparkling sequence of numbers which never outstay their welcome, with one bright idea leading on to another, including a chorus which anticipates one in *L'elisir d'amore*. The piece ends, after many duets and ensembles, in a big tournament scene. This first recording, well paced by the conductor, Antonello Allemandi, is also notable for bringing forward an outstanding young coloratura soprano, Annick Massis, who takes the title-role, wonderfully bright and agile, rising up to the challenge of her big numbers. Jennifer Larmore sings warmly as the Page, with the bass, Alfonso Antoniozzi, aptly gritty as the malicious Count, the tenor, Bruce Ford, lyrical as the attendant Duke, and Pietro Spagnoli magisterial as the King.

Lucia di Lammermoor (complete)

O→ *** Decca (ADD) 410 193-2 (2). Sutherland, Pavarotti, Milnes, Ghiaurov, Davies, Tourangeau, ROHCG Ch. & O, Bonynge

(B) *** Double Decca (ADD) 460 747-2 (2). Sutherland, Cioni, Merrill, Siepi, St Cecilia Ac., Rome, Ch. & O, Pritchard

*** DG 435 309-2 (2). Studer, Domingo, Pons, Ramey, Amb. Op. Ch., LSO, Marin

(N) (BB) (***) EMI mono 5 86197-2 (2). As below, with Callas, Di Stefano, Gobbi, cond. Serafin

O→ (M) (***) EMI mono 5 62747-2 [5 62764-2] (2). Callas, Di Stefano, Gobbi, Arie, Ch. & O of Maggio Musicale Fiorentino, Serafin

(M) **(*) Westminster 471 250-2 (2). Sills, Bergonzi, Cappuccilli, Diaz, Amb. Op. Ch., LSO, Schippers

**(*) EMI 5 56284-2 (2). Callas, Tagliavini, Cappuccilli, Ladysz, Philh. Ch. & O, Serafin

(i) Lucia di Lammermoor (complete); (ii) Highlights (from Historical Recordings)

(N) (BB) *** Naxos mono 8.110131/2. (i) Callas, Di Stefano, Gobbi, Arie, Ch. & O of Maggio Musicale Fiorentino, Serafin; (ii) Merrill, Pinza, Vellicci (1952); Galli-Curci, Schipa (1928); Barrientos, Hackett, Stracciari, Mardones, Meader, Noé, Pinza (1920); Dal Monte (1926); Gigli (1925); McCormack (1910)

Though some of the girlish freshness of voice which marked the 1961 recording had disappeared by the 1971 set, Sutherland's detailed understanding was intensified. Power is there as well as delicacy, and the rest of the cast is first rate. Pavarotti, through much of the opera not as sensitive as he can be, proves magnificent in his final scene. The sound-quality is superb on CD. In this set, unlike the earlier one, the text is absolutely complete.

The 1961 Sutherland version of *Lucia* is a bargain in Double Decca format. Though consonants were being smoothed over, the voice is obviously that of a young singer, and dramatically the performance was close to Sutherland's famous stage appearances of that time, full of fresh innocence. Her coloratura virtuosity remains breathtaking, and the cast is a strong one, with Pritchard a most understanding conductor. The reissue has Decca's new-style synopsis, with a 'listening guide' for newcomers to the opera.

On DG, Cheryl Studer makes an affecting heroine, singing both brilliantly and richly, and Plácido Domingo rebuts any idea that his tenor is too cumbersome for Donizetti. This is the finest version yet in digital sound, with the young Romanian, Ion Marin, drawing fresh, urgent playing from the LSO. The rest of the cast is outstandingly strong too, with Juan Pons as Lucia's brother, Enrico, and Samuel Ramey as the teacher and confidant, Raimondo, Bide-the-Bent.

Callas's earlier, mono set dates from 1953. The diva is vocally better controlled than in her later, stereo set (indeed some of the coloratura is excitingly brilliant in its own right), and there are memorable if not always perfectly stylish contributions from Di Stefano and Gobbi. As in the later set, the text has the usual stage cuts, but the remastered sound is impresssive. This was an obvious choice for EMI's 'Great Recordings of the Century' (5 62747-2), and it has been newly remastered for the reissue. However, EMI have brought out an alternative budget version (5 86197-2) to compete with Naxos; it comes without libretto but with an acceptable booklet with a cued synopsis. Naxos (who also include a cued synopsis) offer not only the complete opera but seven fascinating historical recordings. Among the historical recordings, the Galli-Curci/Toto Schipa duet and Totti Dal Monte's pristine Mad Scene stand out, and it is always a pleaure to hear Gigli's golden tenor. The famous Sextet was recorded primitively in New York in 1920, and is for aficionados of acoustic recordings only! The Naxos transfer of the complete opera by Mark Obert-Thorn 'is made from the best portion of five LP copies, and the slightly flat pitch of the EMI CD version has been corrected'. Comparison with the budget EMI transfer reveals a somewhat smoother upper focus on Naxos, both on voices and on orchestra, which we are inclined to prefer, although some might think that Callas is given slightly more presence on EMI.

The giving personality of Beverly Sills has never been so warmly conveyed on record as in the formidable performance originally issued on LP by EMI (it was recorded at Abbey Road), now a 1970 Westminster set. Sills's Mad Scene in particular is deeply moving. The initial 'takes' were recorded at the very end of a taxing six hours of sessions in which, like the heroine, Sills was literally at the end of her tether. That tension has been retained in the finished recording and, with glass harmonica adding an authentic – if hideously out-of-tune – dimension to the score, Sills devotees need not hesitate. Her coloratura is as effortless as ever, and though the decorations to the cabaletta of the First Act aria are uncomfortably elaborate, the technical assurance is never in doubt. But, as in the opera house, the voice has an uneven register towards the top of the stave, and when it comes to the sheer beauty of tone she cannot compare with Sutherland. However, her supporting cast is first rate and so is the vigorous direction of Thomas Schippers. The recording balance is not always consistent, but the sound is full and faithful.

The Callas stereo version was recorded in Kingsway Hall in 1959, with her edgy top notes cleanly caught. Her flashing-eyed interpretation of the role of Lucia remains unique, though the voice has its unsteady moments. One instance is at the end of the Act I duet with Edgardo, where Callas on the final phrase moves sharpwards and Tagliavini – here past his best – flatwards. Serafin's conducting is ideal, though the score, as in Callas's other recordings, still has the cuts which used to be conventional in the theatre. An hour of highlights from this set is available on EMI 5 66664-2.

Lucrezia Borgia (complete)

(M) *** Decca (ADD) 421 497-2 (2). Sutherland, Aragall, Horne, Wixell, London Op. Voices, Nat. PO, Bonynge

Sutherland is in her element here. Aragall sings stylishly too, and although Wixell's timbre is hardly Italianate he is a commanding Alfonso. Marilyn Horne in the breeches role of Orsini is impressive in the brilliant *Brindisi* of the last Act, but earlier she has moments of unsteadiness. The recording is characteristically full and brilliant.

Maria Padilla (complete)

**(*) Opera Rara (ADD) ORC 6 (3). McDonall, Jones, Clark, Du Plessis, Earle, Caley, Kennedy, Davies, Mitchell Ch., LSO, Francis

Maria Padilla even matches *Lucia di Lammermoor* in places, with the heroine ill-used by the prince she loves, Pedro the Cruel. When the obligatory mad scene is given not to the heroine but to her father, even a tenor such as Graham Clark – future star in Bayreuth – can hardly compensate, however red-blooded the writing and strong the singing. In the title-role Lois McDonall is brightly agile, if at times a little raw. Alun Francis directs the LSO in a fresh, well-disciplined performance and, as ever with Opera Rara sets, the notes and commentary contained in the libretto are both readable and scholarly.

Maria Stuarda (complete)

(M) *** Decca (ADD) 425 410-2 (2). Sutherland, Tourangeau, Pavarotti, Ch. & O of Teatro Comunale, Bologna, Bonynge

In the Decca set of Donizetti's tellingly dramatic opera on the conflict of Elizabeth I and Mary Queen of Scots, the contrast between the full soprano Maria and the dark mezzo Elisabetta is underlined by some transpositions, with Tourangeau emerging as a powerful villainess in this slanted version of the story. Pavarotti turns Leicester into a passionate Italian lover, not at all an Elizabethan gentleman. As for Sutherland, she is at her most fully dramatic too, and the great moment when she flings the insult *Vil bastarda!* at her cousin brings a superb snarl; Richard Bonynge directs an urgent account of an unfailingly enjoyable opera. Unusually for Decca, the score is slightly cut. The recording is characteristically bright and full.

Mary Stuart (in English)

(N) *** Warner DVD 50467 8028-2. Baker, Plowright, Rendall, Tomlinson, Opie, ENO Ch. & O, Mackerras (V/D: Peter Butler)

(M) *** Chan. 3017 (2). Baker, Plowright, Rendall, Tomlinson, Opie, ENO Ch. & O, Mackerras (V/D: Peter Butler)

Dame Janet Baker chose this opera for her farewell to the operatic stage in London in 1982, understandably when the role of the tragic queen was one of her most powerful assumptions. Her deeply moving performance, with her voice ringing gloriously, is well known from the audio version, but this video greatly intensifies the experience. John Copley's inspired production, with evocative sets and costumes by Desmond Heeley, makes the perfect background for her brilliant acting. The joyful mood of her first aria is powerfully transformed into anger as she confronts Queen Elizabeth. That leads to resigned dedication as she sings her prayer in the last scene. Rosalind Plowright in her prime makes an excellent, statuesque foil to Elizabeth, and the other principals are first rate too – the young John Tomlinson as Talbot, David Rendall a ringing tenor as Leicester and Alan Opie characterful as Cecil. Sir Charles Mackerras as conductor strongly underlines the drama of the piece.

Poliuto (complete)

(M) (***) EMI mono 5 65448-2 (2). Callas, Corelli, Bastianini, Zaccaria, La Scala Ch. and O, Votto

In 1960 Maria Callas returned to La Scala, having missed the two previous seasons, and had a triumph. This live recording, made at the time, demonstrates the scale of that triumph, with Callas's musical imagination and intensity of communication at their very peak. Corelli gives a heroic performance, noticeably subtler and more sensitive in scenes opposite Callas than when he is on his own. Callas herself consistently shows why this role inspired her, both in her natural gravity and poised intensity in slow music and in her biting brilliance in coloratura, marred slightly by the characteristic edge on the voice. Bastianini and Zaccaria complete the top Scala team of principals and, though the chorus is often rough, Votto heightens the dramatic impact in his conducting. Variable and limited mono sound, now effectively remastered.

Roberto Devereux (complete)

**(*) Opera Rara ORC24 (2). Miricioiu, Bros, Ganassi, Frontali, ROHCG Ch. & O, Benini

Where both *Maria Stuarda* and *Anna Bolena* have achieved consistent success both on disc and in the opera house, this other Tudor opera of Donizetti has been seriously neglected. The orchestral prelude is striking enough, with the slow introduction based, anachronistically, on a mournful account of *God Save the Queen*. The plot is then set entirely after Robert, Earl of Essex, has returned from Ireland to face the charge of treason, with Sara, Duchess of Nottingham, and her husband, the Duke, providing the subplot. The Queen's inner conflict between her love for Essex and what she knows to be her duty to remove a traitor, is nicely set against her realization that Sara is her rival in love. That leads to the most moving final scene when, after Essex has sung his final defiant aria on the way to the block (part of it improbably in waltz time), Elizabeth, just too late, receives the ring she had given him as a token of her love. The cannon signalling his execution roars out just as she decides to reprieve him, leaving her distraught.

Central to the success of this new set is the singing of the Romanian, Nelly Miricioiu, as Elizabeth, a fine, characterful soprano who has been unjustly neglected on disc. With a voice far warmer than Sills', yet just as flexible in coloratura, she gives a most moving account of the key role of the Queen, and she is well matched by the fresh, young tenor, Jose Bros, as Essex, who, instead of belting his words out like his predecessor on disc, shades his tone with a delicacy all too rare with tenors today in this repertory. The contrast of youth and maturity is equally effective in the casting of the clear-toned Sonia Ganassi as Sara, while Maurizio Benini draws warmly dramatic, idiomatic singing and playing from the Covent Garden chorus and orchestra. The only snag of this live performance is that the audience is so enthusiastic that wild applause punctuates the performance all too often. As usual with Opera Rara, the booklet is a model of scholarship, with profiles and portraits of great singers of the past who have sung the principal roles, though curiously nothing about the present cast except their photos.

Rosmonda d'Inghilterra: highlights

*** Opera Rara ORR 214. Fleming, Ford, Miricioiu, Miles, Montague, Philh. O, Parry

It was in 1994, just before her spectacular rise to international superstar status, that Renée Fleming contributed to Opera Rara's splendid recording of this long-neglected Rossini opera. Shrewdly that company here offers 76 minutes from the opera, covering substantially all the vocal high spots involving the heroine. The result is a formidable demonstration of Fleming's art, with her sumptuous voice then at its freshest. With starry casting for the other characters too, the quality of her contribution, far from being dimmed, is enhanced still further, with Nelly Miricioiu and Diana Montague nicely contrasted, and with Bruce Ford and Alastair Miles ideally cast. Strong, purposeful direction from David Parry and full, vivid sound. Unlike most Opera Rara issues, this one does not provide texts, only a summary of plot for each item.

Ugo, conte di Parigi (complete)

*** Opera Rara (ADD) (3). D. Jones, Harrhy, J. Price, Kenny, Arthur, du Plessis, Mitchell Ch., New Philh. O, Francis

The 1977 recording of *Ugo, conte di Parigi* was the result of formidable detective work, revealing in this early opera of 1832 a strong plot and some fine numbers, including excellent duets. Matching such singers as Janet Price and Yvonne Kenny, Maurice Arthur sings stylishly in the title-role with a clear-cut tenor that records well. Della Jones and Christian du Plessis, regular stalwarts of Opera Rara sets, complete a stylish cast. Reissued on CD, thanks to the Peter Moores Foundation, it offers a fresh and intelligent performance under Alun Francis, and the scholarly, readable notes and commentary, as well as libretto and translation, are models of their kind.

Collection: 'Donizetti Divas': excerpts from: (i) *Alfredo il Grande*; (ii) *L'assedio di Calais*; (iii) *Chiara e Serafina*; (iv) *Dom Sébastien de Portugal*; (v) *Emilia di Liverpool*; (vi) *Gabriella di Vergy*; (vii) *Maria De Rudenz*; (viii) *Maria Padilla*; (ix) *Rosmonda d'Inghilterra*; (x) *Ugo, Conte di Parigi*; (xi) *Zoraisa di Granata*

*** Opera Rara (ADD) ORR 213. (i; iii) D. Jones; (ii) Focile, du Plessis; (iii; v) Kenny; (iii) Davies; (iv) Elkins; (vi) Andrew; (vii; ix) Miricioiu; (vii) MacFarland, Ford; (viii) McDonall; (ix) Fleming; (x) Price, Harrhy; (xi) Cullagh, Montague; with variations orchestras & conductors

Recorded with various singers and orchestras between 1977 and 1990, this collection of Donizetti rarities brilliantly exploits the sparkling style of Della Jones as exponent of Donizetti. The various items have been compiled from earlier recordings from Opera Rara, complete operas as well as the earlier volumes of the '100 Years of Italian Opera' series, yet in sound and above all in vocal quality the results are splendidly consistent. Anyone looking to explore the neglected side of Donizetti's vast output without venturing into complete operas will find this most illuminating.

Arias from: (i; ii) *Belisario*; (ii; iii) *Gemma di Vergy*; (i) *Parisina d'Este. Torquato Tasso*

(N) (M) *** RCA (ADD) 82876 62309-2 (2). Caballé, Amb. Op. Ch., LSO, Cillario, with (i) Elkins; (ii) McDonnell; (iii) Fyson, Mauro – ROSSINI; VERDI: *Arias* ***

Three famous LP recital 'rarities' discs are generously brought together here for the first time. Caballé's conviction as well as her technical assurance makes for highly dramatic results in these still rare Donizetti scenas. The placing of the voice in the *Belisario* item is superbly assured, as is the control of tone, with never a hint of forcing, even in the most exposed *fortissimo*. The cabaletta from *Torquato Tasso* goes equally impressively, helped by Cillario's sympathetic conducting; and there is much elsewhere to enjoy, for these late-1960s recordings display some of Caballé's finest qualities. The recording is full and

vivid, though there is some minor distortion when the voice presses hard. Texts and translations included.

Arias: *L'Elisir d'amore: Prendi, prendi per me sei libero. La figlia del reggimento: Convien partir. Lucrezia Borgia: Tranquillo ei posa! ... Come'è bello!*

** EMI (ADD) 5 66464-2. Callas, Paris Conservatoire O, Rescigno – ROSSINI: *Arias* **(*)

Reissued as part of EMI's Callas Edition, and very well recorded in 1963–4, this is a good example of the latter-day Callas, not always sweet-toned, and at times demonstrating less than the usual fire. If the singing rarely shows her at her most imaginative, and if there are fewer phrases that stick in the memory by their sheer individuality, that is not Donizetti's fault. Yet there is still much to admire, and the remastering flatters the voice by providing a warmly atmospheric orchestral backing. Excellent documentation: full translations are provided.

DOWLAND, John (1563–1626)

The Collected Works (complete)

(B) *** O-L (ADD) 452 563-2 (12). Kirkby, Simpson, York Skinner, Hill, D. Thomas, Consort of Musicke, Rooley

This set, recorded over half a decade in the late 1970s, is a remarkable achievement. The discs originally appeared separately, but are now available only in a bargain box, well documented and with full texts provided. The contents of the *First Booke of Songes* of 1597 were recorded in the order in which they are published, varying the accompaniment between viols, lute with bass viol, voices and viols, and even voices alone.

The *Second Booke* contains many of Dowland's best-known songs, such as *Fine knacks for ladies*, *I saw my lady weep* and *Flow my tears*. Incidentally, the last two are performed on lute and two voices, the bass line being sung by David Thomas; this is quite authentic, though many listeners will retain an affection for its solo treatment. The solo songs are given with great restraint and good musical judgement, while the consort pieces receive expressive treatment. Emma Kirkby is at her freshest and most appealing in *Come, ye heavy states of night* and *Clear or cloudy*.

In the *Third Booke* David Thomas gives an excellent account of himself in *What poor astronomers they are*, and Emma Kirkby's voice is again a delight. Apart from a certain reluctance to characterize, this disc also commands admiration.

A Pilgrimes Solace (1612), Dowland's *Fourth Booke of Songs*, appeared when he was fifty, and here it spreads over more than a single CD. In a collection pervaded by melancholy, variety has been achieved here by using contrasts of texture: some of the songs are performed in consort, others are given to different singers. The second of the two CDs also includes some interesting 'transcriptions', but they are less 'transcriptions for the keyboard of Dowland', rather pieces composed 'after' Dowland.

Volumes 6 and 7 offer a superb collection of motets and sacred songs, an invaluable counterpart to the better-known secular works, instrumental and vocal. The recording is first rate. The *Lachrimae* are most beautiful pieces and are played with splendid taste. The instrumental music which closes Volume 7 is an anthology of arrangements of Dowland's music, presented not as second-best (as we today think of arrangements) but as a genuine illumination, a heightening of the original inspiration. Particularly attractive are the items for two or more lutes.

Volumes 8, 9, 10 and 11 concentrate on Dowland's huge output of lute music. Though Dowland is best known for his melancholy – *semper dolens*, etc. – he has far greater range than the popular imagination would give him credit for. Of particular note are some of the *Fantasias* from Jakob Lindberg (who uses a bandora as well as a lute); their chromatic boldness and fantasy place them among the greatest music for this instrument. Both Christopher Wilson and Anthony Bailes play very freely and expressively.

The second half of Volume 11 and the first part of Volume 12 concentrate on the consort music. Three of the *Pavans* and *Galliards* come from Thomas Simpson's *Opusculum* (1610) and two of the *Pavans* are direct recompositions of Dowland's *Lachrimae*. Marvellous playing comes in the pieces from Simpson's *Taffel-consort* (1621).

The final volume concludes with 'A *Musicall Banquet*' (1610) which Robert Dowland, the great lutenist's son, compiled and published but which he did not compose. The composers range from his celebrated father to lesser-known masters such as Holborne and Tessier, or more familiar ones such as Caccini. Not all the performances are equally satisfying, but overall this box cannot be recommended too highly, though essentially it is meant to be dipped into rather than taken a whole CD at a time. The CD transfers are of the very highest quality.

First Booke of Songes (1597): *Unquiet thoughts; Whoever thinks or hopes; My thoughts are wing'd with hope; If my complaints; Can she excuse my wrongs; Now, O now I must needs part; Dear, if you change; Burst forth my tears; Go crystal tears; Think'st thou then by thy feigning; Come away, come sweet love; Rest awhile; Sleep wayward thoughts; All ye whom Love or Fortune; Wilt thou unkind thus leave me; Would my conceit; Come again, sweet love doth now invite; His golden locks; Awake, sweet love; Come, heavy sleep; Away with these self-loving lads*

☛ (M) *** Decca (ADD) 475 048-2. Cons. of Musicke, Rooley

This collection, first issued in 1976, was the first of a continuing series which was to embrace Dowland's entire output. Here Rooley and the excellent Consorte of Musicke have recorded all the contents of the *First Booke of Songes* in the order in which they are published, varying the accompaniment between viols, lute and bass viol, but also offering voices and viols, and even voices alone. There is hardly any need to stress the beauties of the music itself, which is eminently well served by this stylish ensemble, and beautifully recorded.

CONSORT MUSIC

Instrumental Pieces: *Captain Digorie Piper his Galiard; Earl of Essex Galiard; Fantasie for Lute; Frog Galiard; Lord Strangs March; M. Bucton's Galiard; Mistresse Nichols Almand; M. Thomas Collier, his Galiard with 2 Trebles; Pavan: La mia Barbara.* **Songs:** *Awake, sweet love; Come again, sweet love doth now invite; Come away, come sweet love; Fine knacks for ladies; Flow my tears; From silent night; Go nighly cares; If my complaints could passions move; In darkness let mee dwell; Lasso mia vita; Sorrow, sorrow stay; Time stands still*

(N) **(*) Virgin 5 45288-2. Virelai

An agreeably intimate programme of songs, including many

of the best known, pleasingly sung by Catherine King, accompanied by various groupings of viol, or viols, lute, and tenor flute. The instrumental pieces are similarly variously scored. *Lord Strang's March, Fine knacks for ladies,* and *Mistress Nichols Almand,* for instance, are played by the piquant combination of tenor flute, bass viol and cittern, and *The Frog Galliard* is sonorously allotted to bass flute and bass lute. An enjoyable collection, well recorded – but, because of Dowland's pervading melancholy, the ear craves more variety of mood, so this is a concert to be dipped into rather than heard right through.

Consort music: *Captain Digorie Piper, his pavan and galliard; Fortune my foe; Lachrimae; Lady Hunsdon's almain; Lord Souche's galliard; Mistress Winter's jump; The shoemaker's wife (a toy); Sir George Whitehead's almain; Sir Henry Guildford's almain; Sir Henry Umpton's funeral; Sir John Smith's almain; Sir Thomas Collier's galliard; Suzanna*

*** Hyp. CDA 66010. Extempore String Ens.

The Extempore Ensemble's technique of improvising and elaborating in Elizabethan consort music is aptly exploited here in an attractively varied selection of pieces by Dowland; on record, as in concert, the result sounds the more spontaneous. Excellent recording.

Consort music, lute solos and songs: *Captain Digorie Piper his galliard; The King of Denmark's galliard; M. Buctons galliard; The Earle of Essex galliard; M. George Whitehead his galliard; M. Giles Hobies galliard; M. Henry Noel his galliard; M. Nicholas Gryffith his galliard; Mistress Nichols almand; Mr John Langton's pavan; M. Thomas Collier his galliard; Semper Dowland semper dolens; Sir Henry Umpton's funerall; Sir John Such his galliard.* **Lute:** *A Fancy; Farewell (In nomine).* **Lute and bass viol:** *Dowlands adieu for Master Oliver Cromwell.* **Songs:** *All ye who love or fortune; Burst forth my tears; Can she excuse my wrongs; Lasso vita mia; A shepherd in a shade; Stay sweet awhile*

☛ (BB) *** Naxos 8.553326. Rose Consort of Viols, with Heringman and King

Catherine King's fresh voice and simplicity of line are all her own and she is very touching in the melancholy songs. The Rose Consort, lively enough in the galliards, also show their sensitivity to Dowland's doleful moods, notably in the famous *Semper Dowland semper dolens,* but also in the lament for Oliver Cromwell, (not the famous Oliver Cromwell), played sombrely on bass viol and lute. The two lute solos, very well played by Jacob Heringman, offer further contrast, and the whole programme is recorded most naturally.

Lachrimae, or Seaven Teares

*** BIS CD 315. Dowland Consort, Lindberg

Jakob Lindberg and his consort of viols give a highly persuasive account of Dowland's masterpiece. The texture is always clean and the lute clearly present.

Lachrimae: 7 Passionate pavans. **Consort settings:** *Captain Piper his galliard; The Earl of Essex galliard; The King of Denmarks galliard; M. Bucton his galliard; M. George Whitehead his almand. M. Giles Hoby his galliard; M. Henry Noell his galliard; M. John Langtons pavane; M. Nicholas Gryffith his galliard; M. Thomas Collier his galliard with two trebles; Mrs Nichols Almand; Semper Dowland, semper dolens; Sir Henry Umptons funerall; Sir John Souch his galliard*

☛ *** Virgin 5 45005-2. Fretwork, with Wilson

This is a reissue of Fretwork's 1989 recording of excerpts from the *Lachrimae*, for which the 'passionate' pavans serve as introduction. Structurally they form a variation sequence, linked by a falling fourth at the opening of the first *Lachrimae antiquae* and by other common motifs of melodic line and harmony, an innovative procedure at the time. They are distinguished also by their pervading melancholy but are followed by a newly recorded collection of Dowland's own galliards, so one can choose to move over to more cheerful music at any time. All the performances are of undoubted merit and are well recorded.

(i) *Lachrimae: 7 Passionate Pavans. Captain Piper his Galliard; The Earl of Essex Galiard; M. Buctons Galiard; M. George Whitehead his Almand; M. Giles Hobies Galiard; M. Henry Noel his Galiard; Mr John Langtons Pavan; King of Denmark's Galiard; M. Nicholas Gryffith his Galiard; Mistress Nichols Alman; Semper Dowland, semper dolens; Sir John Souch his Galiard.* Songs: (ii) *Come heavy sleepe; Flow my teares; Go crystall teares; I saw my lady weepe; Sorrow Stay*

(N) **(*) HM HMU 907275. (i) The King's Noyse, Douglass; (ii) Hargis, O'Dette (lute)

The King's Noyse also give a very affecting performance of the *Lachrimae*, plus a generous programme of other pieces for viols. In a similarly dolorous mood, Ellen Hargis contributes just five lute songs, which she sings touchingly and beautifully, and they are expertly accompanied by Paul O'Dette. They are interspersed with the instrumental music, and one could have wished that the balance was more even betweem vocal and instrumental items. However, the recording is most natural and full texts are included.

LUTE MUSIC

Complete Lute Works played by Paul O'Dette
*** Volume 1 (HM HMU 907160); Volume 2 (HM HMU 907161); Volume 3 (HM HMU 907162); Volume 4 (HM HMU 907163); Volume 5 (HMU HMU 907164) (available separately)

Dowland wrote about 100 lute solos, using every musical form familiar at the time. Where either divisions (variations) or ornaments are obviously missing, Paul O'Dette has supplied his own – and very convincing they are. The music on this first disc is particularly rich in ideas. *Orlando sleepeth* is a hauntingly delicate miniature and it is played, like *Mrs Winters jumpp* and *Go from my window*, on the orpharion, a wire-strung instrument very like the lute but with a softer focus in sound because 'the fingers must be easily drawn over the strings, and not sharply gripped or stroked, as the lute is'. O'Dette is an acknowledged master of this repertoire: his playing, which can be robust or with the most subtle nuance, is characterized by a natural and unexaggerated expressive feeling. Dowland's use of other composers' music is very prevalent in Volume 2, and several of the works are not certainly his, but they are of such a quality that the attribution is just. Dowland was never satisfied with his music; he was always revising and rethinking earlier works. The exotic *King of Denmark's galliard*, the opening item on Volume 3, was originally called the 'Battle galliard' because of its bugle-calls, so engagingly portrayed on the lute. *Queen Elizabeth's* not dissimilar *galliard* was originally written for someone else. Generally the third volume of this excellent series has

more extrovert music, but there are still interludes of melancholy. The closing *Semper Dowland semper dolens* (extended to seven minutes) speaks for itself. For his fourth volume, Paul O'Dette uses two different lutes as appropriate, an 8-course and a 10-course, both after Hans Frei. For the most part this is a low-key programme, very much in the '*semper dolens*' mood. Of course there are highlights, like the famous *Fantasia*, P 71, and the mood perks up for the galliard written for the Earl of Essex, while the galliard after Daniel Bachelar is also very striking and the penultimate piece, *La mia Barbara*, is very charmingly presented. But overall this is not one of the more memorable of the O'Dette collections. Volume 5 includes a fascinating mixture of genuine Dowland and music written by other composers very much in the Dowland manner. *Une jeune fillette* (with its extended divisions) is probably by Bachelar. The sombrely memorable *Sir Henry Umpton's Funerall* is certainly by Dowland but was originally conceived as a consort piece, as was *Hasellwood's Galliard*. Three items are probably by Dowland's son, Robert, including the rather fine *Pavin and Gaillard for Sir Thomas Monson* and the very characterful *Almande*, which appears to be derived from a piece by Robert Johnson. Dowland's own splendid closing *Fantasie* comes from a late manuscript, but in a profusely ornamented version, which suggests that it is not completely authentic. Dowland was known not to favour excessive ornamentation, which he called 'blind divisions'. Yet it makes a lively ending to a fine concert which is full of good things.

Music for lute or (i) orpharion: (i) *Can she excuse me; A Dream. Fancies, P 6 & P 73; Fantasie, P 1a; Farewell; Frog galliard; Lachrimae, P 15; Lady Hunsdon's puffe; Melancholy galliard; Mignarda; The most high and mightie Christianus, the fourth King of Denmark, his galliard; Mr Knights galliard; Mrs Brigide Fleetwood's pavan alias Solus sine sola; Mrs Vaux Jig; (i) Mrs Winters jump; My Lord Willoughby's welcome home; (i) Orlando sleepeth; Resolution; The Right Honourable The Lord Viscount Lisle, his galliard; Semper Dowland semper dolens; The Shoemaker's wife; Sir John Smith his almain; Tarleton's riserrection; Walsingham*
☞ *** BIS CD 824. Lindberg (lute or (i) orpharion)

Those not collecting Paul O'Dette's complete series will find this BIS CD offers a cross-section of many of the finest of Dowland's lute pieces. The programme is generous (75 minutes) and Jacob Lindberg is no less at home in this repertoire than his colleague on Harmonia Mundi. He is particularly successful in the lively (battle) galliard written for the King of Denmark, which is full of personality, as is the gentle piece called *Resolution*. The orpharion is used to atmospheric effect in the four works for which it was intended. *Semper Dowland, semper dolens* is presented most eloquently, as is the remarkable *Farewell*; and the divisions on *Walsingham* are played with a nice flow and an unexaggerated bravura. The recording is first class.

VOCAL MUSIC

A Musicall Banquet (Collection, 1610)
*** Decca 466 917-2. Scholl, Karamazov, Märkl, Coin

As can be seen above, *A Musicall Banquet* (although compiled by his son) is included in the final volume of the collected works of John Dowland, and while several of the finest songs are attributed to him, most of them are by others, including two engaging chansons by Pierre Guédron, and Caccini's very beautiful *Amarilli mia bella* (ravishingly presented by Andreas Scholl) and the equally touching *Dovro dunque morire?* Bachelar's *To plead my faith* is hardly less memorable and another highlight is Guillaume Tessier's delicate *In a grove most rich of shade*, while the anonymous *Sta notte mi sognana* brings some delectably nimble decoration. Indeed this repertoire is perfectly designed for Scholl's lovely voice and subtle musicianship, and the continuo accompaniment is never intrusive. The recording is most naturally balanced, but with the pervading melancholy atmosphere it might have been a good idea to have used more than one voice to add variety of timbre.

Lute songs, Book I (1597): *Awake sweet love; All ye whom love or fortune hath betraid; Can she excuse my wrongs with vertues cloak?; Come again: sweet love doth now invite; Deare, if you change, ile never chuse again; Goe crystal teares; If my complaints could passions move; Sleep wayward thoughts.* **Book II (1600):** *Come ye heavie states of night; Fine knacks for ladies; Flow my teares fall from your springs; If fluds of teares could cleanse my follies past; I saw my lady weepe; Shall I sue, shall I seek for grace?; Stay sorow stay; Tymes eldest sonne, old age the heire of ease … Then sit thee down and say thy 'Nunc dimittis' … When others sings 'Venite exultemus'*
*** Metronome METCD 1010. Agnew, Wilson

Lute songs, Book III (1603): *Behold a wonder here; Flow not so fast ye fountaines; I must complaine, yet do enjoy; Lend your eares to my sorrow good people; Say love if ever thou didst finde; Time stands still; Weepe you no more sad fountaines; What if I never speed; When Phoebus first did Daphne love.* **A Musicall Banquet (1610):** *In darkness let me dwell; Lady if you so spight me.* **A Pilgrim's Solace (1612):** *If that a sinners sighes be angels foode; Love those beames that breede Shall I strive with wordes to move; Stay time while thy flying; Thou mightie God … When Davids life by Saul … When the poore criple*
*** Metronome METCD 1011. Agnew, Wilson

Paul Agnew's tenor voice has a certain darkness of colouring in the middle range that seems just right for the dolour of such songs as *Come ye heavie states of night* and *Flow not so fast ye fountaines*, or the despondent *If that a sinners sighes be angels foode* (a lovely performance), yet he can lighten it attractively for lively numbers like *What if I never speede* or *Fine knacks for ladies*. On the first disc, *Come again: sweet love doth now invite* has a passionate forward flow that is almost operatic. In the tripartite *Tymes eldest sonne* Dowland separates the three stanzas with excerpts from the actual liturgy, while *Thou mightie God* maintains its lamenting mood consistently throughout its three semi-narrative sections. Christopher Wilson's intimate accompaniments could not be more gently supportive, and the recording balance is admirable within a pleasingly atmospheric acoustic. Each disc is handsomely presented with a beautifully printed booklet containing full texts and illustrations, all within a slipcase.

Four-part lute songs, Book I: *Awake with these self-loving lads; If my complaints could passions move; Now! oh now I needs must part; Think'st thou then by thy feigning.* **Book II:** *Fine knacks for ladies.* **Book III:** *Me, me and none but me; Say love, if ever thou didst find; What if I never speed?; When Phoebus first did Daphne love.* **Book IV:** *In this trembling shadow; Stay, sweet awhile; Tell me true love; Wherever sin sore wounding.* **Solo:** *Tell me true love*
**(*) Lyrichord LEMS 8031. Saltire Singers, Dupré

The Saltire Singers are a superb vocal group from the early 1960s. Patricia Clark and Edgar Fleet were both performers with Deller's Consort, and Desmond Dupré was Deller's lutenist. The vocal blend here is ravishing. Seldom have individual singers matched their voices more richly in this repertoire, with Patricia Clark leading with a sweet, soaring soprano, her gentle touch of vibrato ideal for Dowland's melodic lines. The choice of songs too is admirable, offering some of Dowland's very finest inspirations. The extended *Tell me true love* brings opportunities for lovely solo contributions from each member of the team; but most touching of all is the melancholy *Wherever sin sore wounding*, which shows Dowland at his most profound. The recording of the voices could hardly be bettered, except that at times they tend to overwhelm the lute. The only other small caveat is the relatively short measure (44 minutes), but the quality of the singing more than compensates. Full texts are provided.

Lute Songs: *All ye whom love; Awake sweet love; Behold a wonder here; Can she excuse my wrongs?; Dear, if you change; Die not before thy day; The Earl of Derby's, his galliard; Farewell too fair; The lowest trees; Me, me and none but me; Mister Dowland's midnight; Mistress Winter's jump; Mourn! mourn!; Now cease, my wandering eyes; Semper Dowland, semper dolens; Shall I strive; Sorrow stay!; Stay Time; Thou mighty God; Woeful heart*
(N) (BB) **(*) Virgin 2x1 5 64210-2 (2). Kirkby, Rooley

Emma Kirkby seldom disappoints, and she sings these songs with simple beauty, often touching. But her white, pure timbre does not always find quite enough variety of colour and intensity in Dowland's more poignant expressions of dolour. Anthony Rooley accompanies very supportively on either his lute or a 7-course orpharion. What makes this inexpensive double especially attractive is the coupled selection of songs by Robert Jones, which suit Kirkby's voice very persuasively. Excellent balance and truthful recording.

Ayres and Lute-lessons: *All ye whom love; Away with these self-loving lads; Come again sweet love; Come heavy sleep; Go Christal teares; If my complaints; My thoughts are winged; Rest awhile;* **(Lute):** *Semper Dowland, semper dolens.* *A shepherd in a shade; Stay sweet awhile; Tell me, true love; What if I never speede; When Phoebus first did Daphne love; Wilt thou unkind.* **(Lute)** *Prelude & Galliard*
(B) **(*) HM (ADD) HMA 1901076. Deller Consort, M. Deller; Spencer

Dowland's 'ayres' were designed for a consort of singers as well as for solo singer and lute, and it is good to hear them in this form. Two of the Lute Lessons are excellently played by Robert Spencer. The performances for the most part give consistent pleasure. The sound is excellent.

Can she excuse my wrongs?; Come again! Sweet love doth now invite; Come, heavy sleep; Fine knacks for ladies; Flow my tears; His golden locks; If my complaints could passions move; In darkness let me dwell; I saw my lady weep; Lady, if you so spite me; Me, me and none but me; Now, O now I needs must part; Say love if ever thou did'st find; Sorrow stay; Stay awhile thy flying; Think'st thou then by feigning?; Time stands still; When Phoebus first did Daphne love; Wilt thou unkind thus reave me?. Lute solos: *Fortune my foe; Melancholy galliard.* (With *Galliards* by Mary, Queen of Scots. Attrib. FRANCIS CUTTING: *Greensleeves (Divisions).* ANON.: *Bonny Sweet Robin; Callino; Kemp's Jig.*)
(BB) *** Naxos 8.553381. Rickards, Linell (lute)

Steven Rickards has a light, precise counter-tenor voice which he uses very imaginatively in this sequence of 19 madrigals, including many of Dowland's finest. So a lively number like *Fine knacks for ladies* has a crispness and spring to bring out its lightness; even more impressively Rickards, with tone rock-steady and little or no hooting, superbly sustains the long legato lines of such great madrigals as *Flow my tears, I saw my lady weep* and *Come, heavy sleep*. There are also well-chosen lute solos from Dorothy Linell, supplementing her excellent accompaniments. The recording, made in New York, is clear and well balanced. Full texts and good notes are provided.

Can she excuse my wrongs?; Come again! Sweet love doth now invite; Far from triumphing court; Flow so fast, ye fountain; In darkness let me dwell; I saw my lady weep; Lady, if you so spite me; Thou almighty God; Shall I sue?; Weep you no more, sad fountains. Lute solos: *Lachrimae antiquae pavane; Semper Dowland, sempre dolens*
*** Lyrichord (ADD) LEMS 8011. Oberlin, Iadone (lute)

One can hardly believe that this recital was recorded in 1958, so fresh and vivid is the sound. Russell Oberlin's very special counter-tenor timbre is beautifully caught. *I saw my lady weep* is most moving, while *Flow my tears* soars; but most touching of all is the closing *In darkness let me dwell*. Joseph Iadone contributes two of Dowland's most famous instrumental pieces. The only drawback to this disc is the comparatively short playing-time of 48 minutes.

Can she excuse my wrongs?; Come again, sweet love; Come heavy sleep; Flow not so fast, ye fountains; From silent night; Go nightly cares; In darkness let me dwell; I saw my lady weep; Shall I sue?. Consort pieces: *Captain Digory Piper's pavane and galliard; The First galliard.* Lute lessons: *Melancholy galliard; Mistess White's nothing; Mistress Winter's jump; My Lady Hunsdon's puff.* Lute duets: *My Lord Chamberlain's galliard; My Lord Willoughby's welcome home.* Lute lessons: *Orlando sleepeth; Sir John Smith's almain; Tarlton's resurrection*
(M) *** HM (ADD) HMX 290244/45 (2). Deller, Consort of Six, Spencer

Alfred Deller's collection is admirably planned and beautifully recorded. He is in excellent voice, while variety is provided by interweaving his solos with lute pieces and music for Elizabethan consort of six instruments (two viols, flute, lute, cittern and bandora). The recording is naturally balanced and nothing in the recital outstays its welcome.

'Earth, water, air and fire': Lute songs: *Come again, sweet love doth now invite; Shall I strive; Sleep, wayward thoughts; Woeful heart; Would my conceits.* Pilgrims Solace: *Toss not my soul; From silent night; Go nightly cares; Sorrow stay; In darkness let me dwell; Though mighty God*
⊙━ *** Gaudeamus CDGAU 187. Consort of Musicke, Rooley (with LOCKE: *Break, distracted heart*; MORLEY: *Deep lamenting; Leave now mine eyes*; TOMKINS: *O let me live for true love; Weep no more*; WEELKES: *Cease sorrows now*; DE SERMISY: *Las, je m'y plains* ***)

The note accompanying this stimulating concert suggests that the four elements were 'everywhere in English lyrics' during Dowland's time, 'celebrating England as a veritable Arcadia'. Fresh response to word-meaning is the keynote, not just in Dowland but in items by his friends, Tomkins, Morley and Weelkes and, notably, Matthew Locke's melodramatic *Break,*

distracted heart, sung by 'Two despairing men and two despairing women', ending with a spoken dialogue between the two principal characters, before they do away with themselves! The closing sequence, in complete contrast, brings the most intense illumination of all: Dowland's five devotional songs, *The Pilgrimes Solace*, crowned by an extended motet, *Thou Mighty God*, visionary and uplifting.

DREYSCHOCK, Alexander (1818–69)

Piano Concerto in D min., Op. 137
*** Hyp. CDA 67086. Lane, BBC Scottish SO, Willén –
  KULLAK: *Piano Concerto in C min.* ***

This is one of the very finest of Hyperion's 'Romantic Piano Concerto' series. Piers Lane rises to the occasion with glittering dexterity and fine romantic flair, while the orchestra provides enthusiastic support, introducing the endearing main theme of the *Andante* with affectionate warmth. As in the coupled Kullak *Concerto*, there are echoes of Liszt and Chopin in the passage-work, and the strong finale combines Weberian brilliance with Mendelssohnian sentiment in the charming secondary theme. The splendidly balanced recording presents the polished dialogue between solo piano and the often flamboyant orchestra in an ideal perspective.

DU FAY, Guillaume (c. 1400–1474)

Secular Music (complete)
(B) *** O-L 452 557-2 (5). Penrose, Covey-Crump, Elwes, Elliott, Hillier, George, Medieval Ens. of L., P. and T. Davies

What will surprise those who dip into these discs is the range, beauty and accessibility of this music. There is nothing really specialized about this art beyond the conventions within which the sensibility works. The documentation is thorough and the performances have great commitment and sympathy to commend them. The actual sound-quality is of the first order, and readers who investigate the contents of this box will be rewarded with much delight. The discs are not available separately, but we are glad to see that the box is available on both sides of the Atlantic.

Sacred Music from the Bologna Manuscript. Q15: *Agnus Dei; Credo & Gloria; Gloria Spiritus et alme; Inclita stella maris; Kyrie Fons bonitatis; O beata Sebastiane; O gemma lux, et speculum; O sancte Sebastiane; Sanctus et Benedictus; Supremum est mortalibus bonum; Vasilissa, ergo gaudes*
*** Signum SIGCD 023. Clerks' Group, Wickham

Edward Wickham and his excellent Clerks' Group here explore the Bologna Manuscript, Q15, which is one of the great surviving collections of fifteenth century music. Their selection aims to show the changes in Du Fay's style. The early *Vasilissa, ergo gaude* of 1420, with its very simple, bare polyphony and passing moments of dissonance, is written in the isorhythmic style of the previous century in which the rhythms of the second half of the motet exactly repeat those of the first half. On the other hand the later *O beata Sebastiane* is written in a freer manner, its melisma more lyrical. The paired *Gloria* and *Credo* are also agreeably flowing, and *Supremum est mortalibus bonum* has an even more striking melodic line. But all this music is characteristically stimulating, for Du Fay has a strong musical personality. The Clerks' Group always seem completely at home in this repertoire and

Wickham's pacing is always convincing. A fine and beautifully recorded collection.

Chansons: *Adieu ces bons vins de Lannoys; Belle, que vous ay je mesfait; Bon jour, bon mois; Ce jour de l'an; Donnes l'assault à la fortress; Helas mon dueil; J'ay mis mon cuer; Mon cher amy; Par droit je puis bien complaindre; Pas le regard de vos beaux yeux; Pour l'amour de ma doulce amye; Puisque vous estez campieur; Quel fronte signorille La doce vita; Resvelliés vous et faites chiere lye; Resvelons nous; Se la face au pale; Vergene Bella*

(BB) ** Naxos 8.553458. Landauer, Unicorn Ens., Posch

This Naxos anthology offers some 17 items, which are freely interpreted, taking the text as a guideline rather than a rigid musical framework, and they are given with some panache. There is an improvisatory freedom that would doubtless delight in the concert hall but is perhaps less satisfying on repetition. Well recorded, but ultimately not as rewarding as the performances in the more authoritative Oiseau-Lyre set.

Missa Ecce ancilla Domine (with **Propers:** *Dei angelis Dei officium*)

(B) **(*) Virgin 2x1 5 61818-2 (2). Ens. Gilles Binchois, Vellard
   (with *Le Banquet du Voeu (The Feast of the Pheasant)* 1454)

Du Fay's magnificently rich and resourceful *Missa Ecce ancilla Domine* dates from the early 1460s, with the composer using two different plainchants as the cantus firmus, suggesting that he did not expect his Mass to be linked to any particular feast-day. Appropriate propers have been chosen for this eloquent performance, although it is not certain that they were composed by Du Fay himself. The coupling, however, is a curious choice, for it has little to do with Du Fay. 'The Feast of the Pheasant' was associated with the Crusades where, amid great courtly extravagance, the nobles assembled to pledge their vows. The range of entertainments included a wide range of 'table music', instrumental and vocal, which was performed between the courses of the feast, and the tapestry of unidentified works here attempts to simulate that occasion. One wonders if this is music many collectors would wish to return to, even though the performances have plenty of vitality.

Missa L'homme armé; Motet: *Supremum est mortalibus bonum*

☛— (BB) *** Naxos 8.553087. Oxford Camerata, Summerly

Jeremy Summerly and his Oxford Camerata give a powerfully expressive and wholly convincing account of Du Fay's masterly cyclic Mass using a Burgundian chanson as its basis. We hear this sung first in its original format as an introduction, and its message, 'The armed man should be feared', makes a dramatically appropriate contrast with the motet, *Supremum est mortalibus*, which is a peace song. The latter was written some 30 years earlier, yet it shows just as readily the remarkable inventiveness and eloquence of this fifteenth-century French composer. The Mass movements are interspersed with plainchant in the same Dorian mode. With vivid yet atmospheric recording this can be given the strongest recommendation.

Missa Santi Anthoni de Padua. Motet: *O proles Hispaniae / O sidus Hispaniae*

*** Hyp. CDA 66854. Binchois Cons., Kirkman

Mass for Saint Anthony Abbot (attrib.)

(N) *** Hyp. CDA 67474. Binchois Consort, Kirkman –
BINCHOIS: *Agnus Dei; Kyrie; Sanctus*, etc. ***

Through clever detective work this fine ten-movement plenary Mass (with four sections of the Ordinary – *Introit, Gradual, Alleluia* and *Offertory* – added to the Proper) is now attributed with fair confidence to the great Guillaume Du Fay, the towering figure in the music of his time. The background to this is brilliantly explained in scholarly notes by Philip Weller, adding to the enjoyment of a superb performance by the Binchois Consort. As he says, this is music which brings 'flashes of brilliance and moments of grandeur', making this recording very welcome, whatever its source. Sensitive singing from the six singers of the Binchois Consort under Andrew Kirkman, and a splendid coupling in the five items by Du Fay's contemporary, Gilles Binchois, all very well recorded.

The Binchois Consort is a small, intimate, all-male group and the Hyperion ambience is comparatively dry and the inner detail emerges with great clarity. The Binchois Consort also performs a motet with two texts associated with St Anthony. The recording is first class and the disc is highly recommendable.

Motets: *Apostolo glorioso; Balsamis et munda cera; Ecclesie militantis; Fulgens iubar ecclesiae Dei; Magnanime gentes laudes; Moribus et genere; Nuper rosarum flores; O gemma lux; O Sancte Sebastiane; Rite majorem Jacobus; Salve flos Tusce gentis; Supremum est mortalibus; Vasilissa ergo gaude; Virgo, virga virens*

*** HM HMC 901700. Huelhas Ens., Van Nevel

Du Fay was especially renowned in his time for his rhythmic motets, all 13 of which are included here. The polyphonic character of these works is dependent on a constantly repeated rhythmic formula or period (of no determined length). But, as always with this composer, the expressive character of the music still predominates, and its underlying structural complexity is seldom obvious to the listener – nor should it be. The music soars and there is no better example than the celestial polyphony of *Ecclesie militantis* with its complex final pages, or the more sombre motet which gives the disc its title, *O gemma lux*. The exultant *Rite majorem Jacobus* ends with a bold stroke of dissonance in its final cadence, but the flowing *Virgo, virga virens* which closes the concert creates a lovely expressive serenity. The voices are underpinned by instruments, usually sonorous sackbuts, which support the implied harmony without weighing down the polyphony. The performances here are most eloquent, very well paced, and beautifully recorded in a very suitable abbey acoustic.

DU MONT, Henry (1610–1684)

Allemande à 3; Pavane à 3; Saraband à 3; Symphonie à 3 (for 2 violins & continuo); *Allemande en tablature; Allemande grave; Allemande sur les anches* (all for organ); *Pavane pour clavecin.* Dialogue motets: *Dialogue angelis et peccatoris; Dialogus de Anima; In lectulo meo; In te Domine; Litanies à la Vierge*

(BB) *** Virgin 2x1 5 62419-2 (2). Les Talens Lyriques,
   Rousset – F. COUPERIN: *Motets* ***

Henry de Thier was born near Liège and probably adopted the title Du Mont, the French translation of his Walloon name, to help his advancement when he settled in Paris just before 1640. It was a shrewd move, for he was to become Master of Music in the King's Chapel, a shared post, but one in which he prospered.

Rousset, in his diverse collection with Les Talens Lyriques, introduces some of the chamber and instrumental music, in which a noble expressive gravity predominates, although there are engaging dance-like interludes. He has chosen (quite authentically) to use mean-tone temperament, a tuning system based on thirds, which lends a distinctive colour to the organ music. And, in the interests of an ideal balance, his singers and instrumentalists are sited in the organ loft!

The harpsichord *Pavane* with which Rousset closes the concert himself is one of its highlights, and the other is the echo motet, *In lectulo meo*, in which Sandrine Piau shines radiantly in a duet with herself. The five-voice *Litanies à la Vierge* (with continuo) is another serenely beautiful work. But the most important and striking of these dialogue motets is the ambitious *Dialogus de Anima* – almost an oratorio – for five singers, in which God, a sinner and an angel converse, with the piece ending with a splendid five-part chorus. This is most vividly performed, and recorded, and with full texts and translations this Virgin bargain Double, while perhaps of specialist appeal, can be recommended highly, the more so as the Couperin coupling is equally stimulating.

Symphonies: in D; G.* Motets: *Benedic anima mea; Domine quid multiplicati sunt; Magnificat; Nisi Dominus; O panis angelorum; Pulsate tympane

(M) *** Virgin 5 61675-2. Les Pages et Chantres de la Chapelle, Musica Aeterna Ens., Schneebeli

The collection of Du Mont's *grands motets*, composed for the Chapel Royal, shows the composer at his most inspired. They are in an exultant post-Renaissance style, using soloists, solo ensembles, small chorus and large five-part chorus in combination. Grandest of all is the superb *Magnificat* featuring a double choir (large and small) and solo group to make a kind of three-dimensional intercourse. The sense of spectacle here reminds the listener of Gabrieli, even if Du Mont's instrumental scoring is much more modest.

The performances rise to the occasion, and if there is a momentary slight lapse of intonation among the soloists, it is not of great moment when overall these singers and instrumentalists are fully worthy of this exuberant music. The recording is first class and the only snag is that texts and translations are omitted.

DUKAS, Paul (1865–1935)

L'apprenti sorcier (The Sorcerer's Apprentice)

(key) *** DG 419 617-2. BPO, Levine – SAINT-SAENS: *Symphony 3* ***

(M) **(*) Chan. 6503. SNO, Gibson – ROSSINI (arr. Respighi): *La Boutique fantasque*; SAINT-SAENS: *Danse macabre* **(*)

(***) Testament mono SBT1017. Philh O, Cantelli – CASELLA: *Paganiniana*; FALLA: *Three-Cornered Hat*; RAVEL: *Daphnis et Chloé: Suite 2* (***)

Levine chooses a fast basic tempo, though not as fast as Toscanini (who managed only two 78 sides), but achieves a deft, light and rhythmic touch to make this a real orchestra Scherzo. Yet the climax is thrilling, helped by superb playing from the Berlin Philharmonic. The CD has an amplitude and sparkle which are especially telling.

Cantelli's 1954 mono account still remains one of the very best performances ever recorded, and it is splendidly transferred.

Gibson secures excellent playing from the SNO, if without the sheer panache of some of his competitors. The recording (made in City Hall, Glasgow, in 1972) is less overtly brilliant than Levine's but has plenty of atmosphere. The Chandos disc, however, is ungenerous in playing time (37 minutes).

***L'Apprenti sorcier (The Sorcerer's Apprentice)* (with spoken introduction)**

(BB) **(*) Naxos 8.554463. Morris (nar.), Slovak RSO, Jean – RAVEL: *Ma Mère l'Oye* ***; SAINT-SAENS: *Carnival of the Animals* **(*)

In this Naxos triptych clearly aimed at young children, Johnny Morris provides a concise and effective narrative introduction. The performance is alive and well paced; it takes a while to generate the fullest tension, but any child should respond to this imagery. The recording is excellent, spacious and vivid.

L'Apprenti Sorcier; La Péri

*** Chan. 8852. Ulster O, Y.-P. Tortelier – CHABRIER: *España*, etc. ***

**(*) Testament SBT 1324. Paris Conservatoire O, Ansermet (with SAINT-SAENS: *Danse macabre*) – DEBUSSY: *Jeux; 6 Epigraphes antiques*, etc. (***)

Symphony in C; Polyeucte: Overture

*** Chan. 9225. BBC PO, Y.-P. Tortelier

L'Apprenti sorcier; La Péri: Poème dansé* (with *Fanfare*); *Symphony in C

*** RCA 09026 68802-2. O. Nat de France, Slatkin

(BB) *** Warner Apex 0927 48725-2. (i) Nouvel PO; (ii) SRO; Jordan

L'Apprenti sorcier; La Péri* (with *Fanfare*); *Polyeucte: Overture

(M) *** Sup. (ADD) SU 3479-2 011. Czech PO, Almeida

Dukas's *La Péri* was written for Diaghilev in 1912. Yan Pascal Tortelier gives a very good performance, with plenty of atmosphere and feeling, and *L'Apprenti sorcier* is equally successful.

Very fine playing from the Orchestre National under Leonard Slatkin and a very well-shaped account of Dukas's fine *Symphony* plus a highly persuasive and atmospheric account of *La Péri*. Extremely well recorded too. This can be warmly recommended alongside Yan Pascal Tortelier on Chandos; the different choice of couplings will no doubt be a decisive factor, but there is not a great deal to choose between them if it is just the *Symphony* you are after.

The super-bargain Apex disc offers a reissue of what were the first accounts of the Dukas *Symphony* and *La Péri* to reach CD, and the 1985 recording sounds splendid in this new transfer, especially in *La Péri*, which is spectacular, atmospheric and clear. Jordan's reading of the *Symphony* has both vitality and musical conviction, and he is equally sensitive to the richly languorous evocation of *La Péri*, while building a thrilling climax. *L'apprenti sorcier* has been added for the present reissue, and very good it is too. The 1992 sound is again spacious and vivid, and the admirably paced performance is among the best in the catalogue. An outstanding bargain: indeed this would be recommendable if it cost far more. However, it does not displace the Tortelier account of the *Symphony* on Chandos as a first recommendation.

Almeida's Dukas collection, made in 1973 is hardly less successful, although he rightly sought to give the strings added brilliance for the passionate climax of *La Péri*. Almeida's performance is sensuous and gripping, and the orchestral playing has both intensity and allure. *Polyeucte*, an early work with Wagnerian echoes, is also extremely successful, especially the closing *Andante tranquillo*. But what makes this Supraphon disc very competitive is the sparkling *L'Apprenti sorcier*, the main theme winningly jaunty and ideally paced, and reaching a brilliant climax, with superb roistering horns and the whole orchestra on its toes.

Ansermet's first mono recording of *La Péri* comes from 1954. His re-make, with the prefatory *Fanfare* added, dates from 1959 and was one of the demonstration LPs of the day. This earlier account with the Paris Conservatoire Orchestra, which was originally coupled with Rachmaninov's *Isle of the Dead*, omits the *Fanfare*. The sound, even in this transfer of the experimental stereo master (made alongside the mono but never released at the time), is obviously more detailed. If the 1959 account is undoubtedly superior sonically, the earlier version is a reading of great breadth and style. *L'Apprenti Sorcier* is also very successful, and there is an added bonus of Saint-Saëns's *Danse macabre*. Well worth investigating.

La péri (with Fanfare)

(N) (BB) **(*)** Naxos 8.557274. Nat. O de Lille-Région Nord, Jean-Claude Casadesus – BERLIOZ: *Nuits d'été*; CHAUSSON: *Poème* **(*)**

Jean-Claude Casadesus with his fine Lille orchestra conducts a warmly atmospheric reading of Dukas's 'poem for orchestra', introduced (as it should be) by the fanfare written as a brief prelude. The recording is both warm and clear, with the brass beautifully caught. Not perhaps a first choice, but an excellent supplement to the two vocal pieces.

Piano Duet

L'apprenti sorcier (arr. for 2 pianos)

(N) (BB) **(*)** EMI Gemini (ADD/DDD) 5 86510-2 (2). Collard, Béroff – DEBUSSY & RAVEL: *Music for piano, 4 hands & 2 pianos*; BIZET: *Jeux d'enfants* **(*)**

The composer's own piano-duet transcription of his most famous work is surprisingly successful, particularly the opening and closing pages; but Collard and Béroff are spirited throughout and the digital recording is fully acceptable.

Piano Sonata in E flat min.; La Plainte, au loin, du faune; Prélude élégiaque; Variations, Interlude and Finale on a Theme of Rameau

(N) **(*)** Simax PSC 1177. Aspaas

(BB) **(*)** Warner Apex 0927 48996-2. Hubeau

The *Piano Sonata* comes from the turn of the century, four years after *The Sorcerer's Apprentice*, and is a substantial piece, some 45 minutes in duration, permeated with the aura of Franck and d'Indy. Debussy said that 'it breathes a kind of mystic emotion', and is grand in scale and ambition. Dukas was studying the late Beethoven sonatas at the time, and there are allusions to both the *Hammerklavier* and Op. 111 here. The *Rameau Variations*, obviously modelled on the Brahms *Handel Variations*, followed only two years later. On Simax the recorded sound is very satisfactory, though some may be

troubled by the over-reverberant acoustic and a certain bass-heaviness. When the ear adjusts, Aspaas's thoughtful and musicianly performances will give pleasure, although Hubeau costs less and is still worth considering.

Jean Hubeau may not always show the greatest subtlety of keyboard colour and dynamic, but he has the advantage of having studied with Dukas himself, so these performances, recorded in French Radio studios in 1987 when Hubreau was seventy, have a certain authority and documentary value.

DUNSTABLE, John (d. 1453)

Missa Rex seculorum. Motets: *Albanus roseo rutilat - Quoque ferundus eras - Albanus domini Laudus; Ave maris stella; Descendi in ortum meum; Gloria in canon; Preco preheminence - Precursor premittur - textless - Inter natos mulierum; Salve regina mater mire; Specialis Virgo; Speciosa facta es; Sub tuam protectionem; Veni sancte spiritus - Veni creator spiritus*

*** Metronome METCD 1009. Orlando Cons.

The Orlando Consort present their generous, 74-minute survey with an impressive combination of direct, impassioned feeling and style. If the splendid *Missa Rex seculorum* is of doubtful attribution, every piece here, motets and antiphons alike, is clearly by a major composer with a highly individual voice. The recording is excellent in every way and this CD, which won the *Gramophone*'s Early Music Award in 1996, offers the collector an admirable and highly rewarding entry into this composer's sound-world.

Motets: *Agnus Dei; Alma redemptoris Mater; Credo super; Da gaudiorum premia; Gaude virgo salutata; Preco preheminenciae; Quam pulcra es; Salve regina misericordiae; Salve sceme sanctitatis; Veni creator; Veni sancte spiritus*

*** Virgin 5 61342-2. Hilliard Ens., Hillier

These motets give a very good idea of Dunstable's range, and they are sung with impeccable style. The Hilliard Ensemble has perfectly blended tone and impeccable intonation, and their musicianship is of the highest order. Some collectors may find the unrelieved absence of vibrato a little tiring on the ear when taken in large doses; but most readers will find this a small price to pay for music-making of such excellence, so well recorded.

DUPARC, Henri (1848–1933)

Mélodies (complete): *Au pays où se fait la guerre; Chanson triste; Elégie; Extase; La fuite* (duet)*; Le galop; L'Invitation au voyage; Lamento; Le Manoir de Rosamonde; Phidylé; Romance de Mignon; Sérénade; Sérénade florentine; Soupir; Testament; La vague et la cloche; La vie antérieure*

*** Hyp. CDA 66323. Walker, Allen, Vignoles

The Hyperion issue is as near an ideal modern Duparc record as could be. Here are not only the 13 recognized songs but also four early works – three songs and a duet – which have been rescued from the composer's own unwarranted suppression. Roger Vignoles is the ever-sensitive accompanist, and the recording captures voices and piano beautifully, bringing out the tang and occasional rasp of Sarah Walker's mezzo and the glorious tonal range of Thomas Allen's baritone.

Mélodies: *Chanson triste; Elégie; Extase; L'Invitation au voyage; Lamento; Le Manoir de Rosemonde; Phidylé; Sérénade florentine; Soupir; Testament; La Vague et la cloche; La Vie antérieure*

(N) (***) Testament mono SBT 1312. Souzay, Bonneau –
RAVEL: *Don Quichotte à Dulcineé*; DEBUSSY: *3 Ballades* ***; CHAUSSON: *Mélodies* (***)

Souzay's recordings of 12 of Duparc's 16 songs, made with Jacqueline Bonneau for Decca, comes from 1953 and is superior, both vocally and interpretatively, to his 1970 set for HMV. The voice has a wonderful freshness and bloom, and the monaural sound is also remarkably good – and not just for its period. The balance is well judged and every syllable registers. Some of the songs have never been surpassed, even by Bernac or Panzera. These are very special performances and exquisitely accompanied.

Mélodies: *Chanson triste; Elégie; Extase; L'Invitation au voyage; Lamento; Le Manoir de Rosemonde; Phidylé; Soupir*

(N) *** Nim. (ADD) NI 5736/7 (2). Cuénod, Parsons –
FAURÉ: *Mélodies* ***

Older readers will recall that Hugues Cuénod took part in Nadia Boulanger's famous (1937) records of Monteverdi madrigals and, even in the 1980s, sang the role of the Astrologer in Rimsky-Korsakov's *Le Coq d'or* at Covent Garden. He was born in 1902 and, as we go to press, is 103! He was already 70 when he made these recordings, though this hardly shows: the voice is light and steady, and his sense of style impeccable. Both the accompanists (the documentation does not indicate who accompanies what) are highly sensitive and match the refined intelligence that this great artist brings to this repertoire.

DUPRÉ, Marcel (1886–1971)

ORGAN MUSIC

6 Antiennes pour le Temps de Noël, Op. 48; 79 Chorales, Op. 28, 21–23, 36–41 & 66; Symphony 2, Op. 26; Vision, Op. 44; Zephyrs

(BB) ** Naxos 8.554542. Baker (organ)

The trouble (if it is a fault) with Marcel Dupré's music is that every piece of substance sounds like a masterly improvisation. Not that this need worry the listener until a long piece such as the *Deuxième Symphonie*, in which a certain want of concentration becomes manifest. George Baker is a committed interpreter but, in spite of the competitive price-tag and decent recording, he must yield to Ben van Oosten's impressive cycle on MDG on artistic grounds. However this Naxos disc is part of a 12-CD series covering Dupré's complete organ works which we hope to cover fully in our 2006/7 Yearbook.

79 Chorales, Op. 28, 4, 8, 13, 20, 44, 49–51, 67 & 77; Elévation, Op. 2; 15 Pieces, Op. 18; Psalm XVIII, Op. 47

*** MDG 316 0955-2. Van Oosten (organ)

MDG are in the process of recording Marcel Dupré's complete organ music and this is the fifth volume. The longest piece here is the Op. 18 *Versets sur les Vêpres de la Vierge*, recorded (like the remainder of his programme) on the Cavaillé-Coll organ at Saint-Ouen, Rouen. This set comes from 1918, and each of its short movements is inspired by the plainchant proper for the sections of the Vespers. Dupré

performed them to great acclaim at his London début in 1920, when they were interspersed with liturgical chant, sung by 600 singers assembled by the Gregorian Association. They were originally improvisations, which greatly moved Claude Hoodman Johnson, a founder of Rolls-Royce, who had heard Dupré play them at Notre-Dame and asked him to notate them. They are short, musically unrelated pieces without any trace of 'display', which the Dutch organist Ben van Oosten has recorded at Saint-Ouen, Rouen, where Dupré himself was at one time active. They include some highly expressive and deeply felt music. Van Oosten is organist of the Grote Kirk in Amsterdam, a considerable scholar and author of the standard work on Widor. Admirers of Dupré cannot do much better than explore this and the other records in the series, and the MDG recording is of a high standard.

6 Chorales, Op. 28; 2 Chorales, Op. 59; 24 Inventions, Op. 50; 4 Modal Fugues, Op. 63

(BB) *** Naxos 8.553862. Biery

The 24 *Inventions*, Op. 50, which are divided to begin and end this CD, are, like Bach's *Well-Tempered Clavier*, composed in all the major and minor keys. They are distinguished by fastidious craftsmanship and considerable imagination, as are the 6 *Chorales*, Op. 28 (1930). The *Chorales*, Op. 59, and the *Four Modal Fugues* come from the 1960s. James Biery is an excellent advocate and the recording, made on the Casavant organ of the Cathedral of Saints Peter and Paul, in Providence, Rhode Island, is splendidly lifelike and has great clarity and definition. A rewarding issue.

Chorale & Fugue, Op. 57; 3 Esquisses, Op. 41; Preludes & Fugues: in B; G min., Op. 7/1 & 3; Le Tombeau de Titelouse: Te lucis ante terminum; Placare Christe servulis, Op. 38/6 & 16; Variations sur un vieux Noël, Op. 20

*** Hyp. CDA 66205. Scott (St Paul's Cathedral organ)

An outstandingly successful recital, more spontaneous and convincing than many of the composer's own recordings in the past. Dupré's music is revealed as reliably inventive and with an atmosphere and palette all its own. John Scott is a splendid advocate and the St Paul's Cathedral organ is unexpectedly successful in this repertoire.

Cortège et Litanie, Op. 19/2; Evocation, Op. 37: Allegro deciso. Prelude and Fugue in F min., Op. 7/2; Symphony 2 in C sharp min., Op. 26; Symphonie-Passion, Op. 23

*** Hyp. CDA 67047. Scott

John Scott's recording on the organ of St Paul's Cathedral is one of the most impressive Dupré CDs of recent times and a worthy companion to CDA 66205. The *Symphonie-Passion* sounds splendidly opulent and his account of the *Second Symphony* is pretty stunning. There is always an improvisatory, rhapsodic feel to Dupré's music, but these are concentrated and powerfully atmospheric accounts which use the acoustic to maximum effect.

DURANTE, Francesco (1684–1755)

Magnificat in B flat

↦ ✷ (M) *** DHM/BMG 82876 60145-2. Landauer, Oswald, Abele, Balthazar-Neumann Ch., Freiburg Bar. O, Hengelbrock – D'ASTORGA: *Stabat Mater*; PERGOLESI: *Confitebor tibi Domine* *** ✷

Francesco Durante's briefly succinct setting of the *Magnificat* has been described as 'one of the loveliest works of its kind' and 'the ideal of a musical work of praise'. Durante was apparently by nature taciturn, introverted, and shabby in appearance. Yet he was Pergolesi's teacher and here he shows himself a consummate master of the styles and influences of his time. Moreover, his musical inspiration is in no doubt: the opening and closing choruses are exultantly life-enhancing; the *Et misericordia*, beautifully sung by Bernhard Landauer, is lyrically memorable, as is the tenor/bass duet, *Suscepit Israel*, which is equally touching. Indeed, the performance is first class in every way, with fine contributions from soloists, chorus and orchestra alike, with Thomas Hengelbrock directing the music vividly and sympathetically.

DUREY, Louis (1888–1979)

Mélodies and song-cycles: *Le bestiaire; Chansons basques; Epigrammes de Théocrite; Hommage à Erik Satie; Images à Crusoé; Inscriptions sur un oranger; 2 Lieder romantiques; 3 Poèmes de Pétrone*

*** Hyp. CDA 67257. Le Roux, Johnson

Louis Durey is the forgotten member of 'Les Six', the group of young French composers nominated in 1920 for their adventurousness. All the songs in this illuminating collection date from 1918 and 1919, the brief period leading up to the arrival of 'Les Six', with the composer's own commentary on each group of songs included as well as the texts. An exception is the opening item, *Hommage à Erik Satie*, a song found among Satie's papers on his death, with its stylistic mixture of Poulenc, Stravinsky and Satie himself. The rest reveal a subtly evocative response to French texts and a characterful use of the piano, often angular in the three Basque songs to words by Cocteau and in the 26 songs setting *Le bestiaire* of Apollinaire.

Most of the 48 songs in the seven collections are very brief, pointful fragments merely, but the sequence, sensitively devised by Johnson, leads up to Durey's masterpiece, *Images à Crusoé*, which, to texts by Saint-John Perse, tackles a deeper theme – the alienation of Crusoe from the world when he returned from his desert island. Though, under pressure, Le Roux's baritone has its moments of strain, these are all wonderfully idiomatic performances from singer and pianist alike, ideally recorded and presented.

DURUFLÉ, Maurice (1902–86)

(i) *3 Dances for Orchestra*; (ii) *Prélude et Fugue sur le nom d'Alain, Op. 7*

(N) (BB) *** Warner Apex 2564 61912-2. (i) Bamberg SO, Kantorow; (ii) Marie-Claire Alain – ALAIN: *Sarabande for Organ, String Quintet and Timpani*; POULENC: *Organ Concerto* ***

Duruflé's *Three Dances for Orchestra* are a revelation. The composer studied under Paul Dukas and shows an extraordinary flair for orchestration, creating sounds that are vividly colourful, translucent and richly exotic. The *Dances* are full of attractive ideas and the central *Danse lente* is lustrously sensuous; the exciting finale, opening with Dukas's bassoon, increases in vigour and then produces a hauntingly melancholy theme on the saxophone, before the bassoon returns with the spirit of the dance. After a brilliant climax, the busy, motoric rhythms fade away into silence. The performance

here sparkles irresistibly and the recording is brilliant, sumptuous and wide-ranging. Needless to say, Marie-Claire Alain's account of the composer's best-known organ work is in every way distinguished, as are the coupled works by Jehan Alain and Poulenc. A disc not to be missed.

ORGAN MUSIC

Chant Donné (Homage à Jean Gallan); Fugue sur le thème du Carillon des Heures de la Cathédral de Soissons, Op. 12; Méditation; Prélude, Adagio et Choral varié sur le thème du 'Veni Creator', Op. 4; Prélude sur l'Introit de l'Épiphanie, Op. 13; Scherzo, Op. 2; Suite, Op. 5

☞ (N) *** CPO compatible Surround Sound SACD 777 042-2. Flamme (Mülheisein organ, Stiftskirche, Bad Gandersheim)

**(*) Delos D/CD 3047. Wilson (Schudi organ of St Thomas Aquinas, Dallas, Texas)

The producer of the Delos record, which includes all the music Duruflé wrote for the organ, consulted the composer before choosing the present organ, and the performances of Duruflé's often powerful and always engagingly inventive music are of the highest quality. The account of the closing *Toccata* of the *Suite*, Op. 5, has breathtaking bravura, and if here (as elsewhere) detail is not sharply registered, the spontaneity and power of the playing are compulsive.

However, this Delos disc is now completely upstaged by the superb new CPO SACD, in surround sound. If a suitable player is available, linked to back speakers, one has the extraordinary feeling of sitting in the Stiftskirche, where the recording was made. Not only is the climax of the Op. 5 *Toccata* overwhelming but in the gentler music the pedals still make their presence felt, even on a normal CD playback. Flamme plays a magnificent new organ, installed in 2000, for which the *manufacturer d'orgue*, Mülheisein, was awarded the *Meilleurs Ouvriers de France* prize. It is entirely suitable for this repertoire, and as its sonorities reach the whole church, because of its 'ground-tone intonation', it is especially effective in a recording which captures a four-dimensional sound-picture. Friedhelm Flamme's playing is highly sensitive, and he can articulate with great delicacy when needed, as in the *Scherzo* and the *Prélude*, Op. 4, while he creates a fine climax for the *Carillon des Heures*. The two extra works on the CPO CD are not specifically organ pieces, the simple *Chant Donné* (just over a minute long) was part of an anthology of tributes to Duruflé's composition teacher from his students; the *Méditation* of 1964 is a gentle piece in Rondo form whose theme Duruflé used again in the *Agnus Dei* of the *Missa Cum jubilo*. Very highly recommended.

Danse lente, Op. 6/2; Prélude et Fugue sur le nom d'Alain, Op. 7

☞ (N) *** Chan. 10315. Whitehead (organ of Saint Étienne Cathdral, Auxerre, France) – ALAIN: *Aria; Danses*, etc. ***

The well-known *Prélude et Fugue* weaves the name, Alain, into both sections and even quotes from the composer's *Litanies* at the conclusion of the *Prélude*. The transcribed *Danse lente* is the middle movement of Duruflé's orchestral *Trois Danses*, and almost turns the organ into an orchestra in its own right. Its moods change from the mysterious to the whimsical and, after climaxing, the dance themes mysteriously disappear. In this spendidly played recital, both pieces are interwoven with an highly stimulating programme of music by Alain on an organ ideal for this repertory.

Organ Music: *Fugue sur le carillon des heures de la Cathédrale de Soissons, Op. 12; Méditation, Op. posth.; Prélude, adagio et choral varié sur le 'Veni Creator', Op. 4; Prélude et fugue sur le nom d'Alain, Op. 7; Prélude sur l'introit de l'Epiphanie; Scherzo, Op. 2; Suite, Op. 5*
*** BIS CD 1304. Fagius

Duruflé's music is closely identified with the Cavaillé-Coll sonority; but John Scott, who recorded his work on the organ of St Paul's Cathedral more than a decade ago, showed how impressively its character could be conveyed on other instruments. Hans Fagius uses the four-manual 89-stop 1928 Frobenius organ of Aarhus Cathedral in Denmark for his recital, and a particularly fine instrument it is. Apart from his good musicianship and taste, Fagius has the additional advantage of authority, since he also studied with the composer. Fagius's liner-notes are also exemplary and he has the additional advantage of superbly realistic BIS recording.

Requiem, Op. 9
(M) *** Warner Elatus 0927 49001-2. Larmore, Hampson, Amb. S., Philh. O, Legrand – FAURE: *Requiem* ***
(B) *** Sony (ADD) SBK 67182. Te Kanawa, Nimsgern, Amb. S., Desborough School Ch., New Philh. O, A. Davis – FAURE: *Requiem* ***
(B) *** Decca Eclipse 448 711-2. Palmer, Shirley-Quirk, Boys of Westminster Cathedral Ch., L. Symphony Ch., LSO, Hickox – FAURE: *Pavane*; POULENC: *Gloria* ***
**(*) York Ambisonic YORK CD177. White, Martin, Canterbury Cathedral Ch., Flood – FAURE: *Requiem* **(*)
Requiem, Op. 9; Messe Cum jubilo, Op. 11; 4 Motets sur les thèmes grégoriens, Op. 10; Notre père, Op. 14 (both for a cappella choir)
*** EMI 5 56878-2. Von Otter, Hampson, Alain; Orfeon Donostiarra, O de Capitole Toulouse, Plasson
*** Nim. NI 5599. Turpin, Clements, Morton (treble); Farrington, St John's College Cambridge Ch., Robinson

(i; ii; v) *Requiem, Op. 9;* (iii; iv; v) *Messe cum Jubilo, Op. 11;* (iii) *4 Motets on Gregorian Themes, Op. 10;* (v) (Organ) *Prélude et fugue sur le nom d'Alain, Op. 7*
☛ (BB) *** Warner Apex 2564 61139-2. (i) Bouvier, Depraz, Philippe Caillard Ch., LAP; (ii) Stéphane Caillat Ch.; (iii) Soyer; (iv) O Nat. de l'ORTFM; all cond. composer; (v) Duruflé-Chevalier (organ)

Requiem, Op. 9 (3rd version); 4 Motets, Op. 10
*** Hyp. CDA 66191. Murray, Allen, Corydon Singers, ECO, Best; Trotter (organ)

(i–iii) *Requiem. Op. 9;* (ii) *4 Motets, Op. 10;* (iii) (Organ) *Prélude et fugue sur le nom d'Alain*
(B) *** Double Decca (ADD) 436 486-2(2). (i) King, Keyte; (ii) St John's College, Cambridge, Ch.; (iii) Cleobury (organ); Guest – FAURE: *Requiem*, etc.; POULENC: *Messe*, etc. ***

Duruflé wrote his *Requiem* in 1947, overtly basing its layout and even the cut of its themes on the Fauré masterpiece. Michel Legrand uses the full orchestral version and makes the most of the passionate orchestral eruptions in the *Sanctus* and *Libera me*. He strikes a perfect balance between these sudden outbursts of agitation and the work's mysticism and warmth. The Ambrosian Choir sing ardently yet find a treble-like purity for the *Agnus Dei* and *In Paradisum*, while Jennifer

Larmore gives the *Pie Jesu* more plangent feeling than its counterpart in the Fauré *Requiem*. The recording, made in Watford Town Hall, is spacious and most realistically balanced. A clear first choice and now in the medium price-range.

However, on Sony, Andrew Davis directs a warm and atmospheric reading of Duruflé's beautiful setting with the Desborough School Choir, and this makes an excellent bargain alternative. He too uses the full orchestral version with its richer colourings. Kiri Te Kanawa sings radiantly in the *Pie Jesu*, and the darkness of Siegmund Nimsgern's voice is well caught. In such a performance Duruflé establishes his claims for individuality, even in the face of Fauré's setting. The recording is nicely atmospheric.

This Apex budget reissue is particularly valuable as it replaces a previous Ultima set and centres on the now familiar *Requiem*, given a spontaneously dedicated performance under the direction of the composer that blossoms into great ardour at emotional peaks. The less familiar but no less beautiful *Messe cum Jubilo* receives a comparatively inspirational account, its gentler passages sustained with rapt concentration, with beautiful playing from the French Radio Orchestra. The soloists in both works rise to the occasion, and the choral singing combines passionate feeling with subtle colouring: the Chorale Stéphane Caillat are at their finest in the four brief *a cappella* motets, which are no less memorable. The composer proves a splendid exponent of his own works, as does his daughter playing the *Prélude et Fugue* on the organ of Soissons Cathedral. The spaciously atmospheric recordings were made between 1959 (the *Requiem*) and 1971. Not to be missed.

Using the chamber-accompanied version, with strings, harp and trumpet – a halfway house between the full orchestral score and plain organ accompaniment – Best conducts a deeply expressive and sensitive performance. With two superb soloists and an outstandingly refined chorus, it makes an excellent recommendation, well coupled with the motets, done with similar freshness, clarity and feeling for tonal contrast. The recording is attractively atmospheric yet quite clearly focused.

Hickox tempers the richness of the orchestral version by using boys' voices in the choir. He relishes the extra drama of orchestral accompaniment with biting brass at the few moments of high climax. Felicity Palmer and John Shirley-Quirk sing with deep feeling and fine imagination, if not always with ideally pure tone. The recording has a pleasantly ecclesiastical ambience, which adds to the ethereal purity of the trebles, and the stereo spread is wide.

The (originally Argo) St John's version also uses boy trebles instead of women singers, even in the solo of the *Pie Jesu* – exactly parallel to Fauré's setting of those words, which was indeed first sung by a treble. The alternative organ accompaniment is used here, not as warmly colourful as the orchestral version, but very beautiful nevertheless. The 1974 recording is vividly atmospheric. To this have been added the *Four Motets*, on plainsong themes, which are also finely sung. The organ piece, another sensitive example of Duruflé's withdrawn genius, makes a further bonus, especially when one realizes that this generous pair of CDs includes also the *Mass* and *Salve Regina* of Poulenc.

The later St John's performance under Christopher Robinson also uses the highly effective organ-accompanied score. With a superb contribution from Ian Farrington, this works admirably, especially in the *Libera me*, but it has to be admitted that an orchestra makes a spectacular contribution to the *Gloria* (and elsewhere) and again later adds much colour to the lovely *Messe cum Jubilo*.

Plasson's performance was recorded in the spaciously resonant acoustic of Toulouse's Notre Dame La Daurade and, as is immediately obvious in the opening *Kyrie*, the chorus is backwardly placed, floating in a misty atmosphere; although at climaxes the vocal sound expands thrillingly, at other times Plasson's comparatively relaxed pacing means that the music-making has less tension. The warmer voice of Thomas Hampson has a special appeal; on the other hand, while Anne Sophie von Otter sings beautifully and eloquently, her vibrato brings a hint of the opera-house at the climax of the *Pie Jesu*.

In the Canterbury Cathedral version, helped by exceptionally vivid Ambisonic recording as well as David Flood's direction, the dramatic bite of the Duruflé *Requiem* is brought out in high dynamic contrasts, where often the devotional element comes over to the exclusion of any dramatic bite. So in the third movement, *Domine Jesu Christe*, the *fortissimo* choral attack is thrilling in the references to the punishments of hell. The sharpness of focus for the choir and accompanying instruments (but not, alas, the baritone soloist, Ian White) goes with a relatively intimate scale, with the brightness of the 18 trebles beautifully caught. More than usual, one registers the differences between this and the Fauré coupling. The version with organ accompaniment is used, which means that one misses the trumpet trimmings of the orchestral version, and Flood opts to have the melody of the *Pie Jesu* sung not by a soloist but by the trebles of the choir.

DUŠEK, Franz Xaver (1731–99)

Keyboard Sonatas: in D, Op. 31/2 (C133); in B flat, G & C min., Op. 35/1–3 (C 149–51); Elégie harmonique, Op. 61 (C211); Fantasia & Fugue in F min., Op. 55 (C199); Sonata (Le retour à Paris), Op. 64 (C221)
(N) (B) ******* DHM/BMG 82876 67377-2 (2). Staier (fortepiano)

The four *Sonatas* on Andreas Staier's first CD come from Dušek's London years in the 1790s, when he was befriended by Haydn and John Broadwood the piano-maker, for whose five-and-a-half-octave grand the three sonatas of Op. 36 (1797) were written. Staier's exhilarating recital is recorded on a Broadwood of 1806, restored by Christopher Clarke, who describes it as 'loud, sonorous, dramatic, and a little vulgar'. It has all the weight to cope with the dramatic flair which Staier brings to these highly interesting and occasionally prophetic sonatas. At one point the *B flat Sonata* anticipates Schubert, and the *C minor* has often been compared with Beethoven's *Pathétique*. The recital opens with the flamboyantly improvisational *Fantasia* and simpler *Fugue*, dedicated to the composer's friend, J. B. Cramer, publisher and piano manufacturer. Dušek fled London (in 1799) to avoid his creditors (among them Lorenzo da Ponte), abandoning his young wife and settling in Hamburg.

The *Elégie harmonique* paid tribute to his friend and patron, Prince Louis Ferdinand of Prussia, who was killed at the Battle of Saalfeld in 1806. It opens with an improvisatory introduction which quotes one of Haydn's *Seven Last Words*. The piece is in two movements, with the closing *Tempo vivace e con fuoco* providing a strong contrast, suggesting that the prince was a man of vigour and feeling.

The *A flat Sonata* marks Dušek's final return to Paris in 1807 (he had been a favourite of Marie Antoinette and left in 1789, so avoiding her fate) and is a bold and forward-looking work with its touchingly expressive *Molto adagio*, quirky

Minuet/Scherzo and boisterously rhythmic finale. Once again the playing throughout has great impetus and all the panache needed to bring these remarkable works back to life on the same Broadwood fortepiano that was used for the first disc. Overall, these are compelling performances of music that has much individuality and fantasy.

DUTILLEUX, Henri (born 1916)

Cello Concerto (Tout un monde lointain)
⊶ ******* EMI (ADD) 5 67867-2 [567868]. Rostropovich, O de Paris, Baudo – LUTOSLAWSKI: *Cello Concerto* *******

(i; ii) *Cello Concerto;* (ii; iii) *Violin Concerto (L'Arbre des songes);* (i) *3 Strophes sur le nom de Sacher* (for unaccompanied cello)
**(*) Virgin 5 45502-2. (i) Mørk; (ii) R. France PO, Chung; (iii) Capuçon

(i) *Cello Concerto (Tout un monde lointain);* (ii) *Métaboles;* (iii) *The Shadows of Time*
(N) (BB) ******* Warner Elatus 0927 49830-2. (i) Noras, Finnish RSO, Saraste; (ii) O Nat. de France, Rostropovich; (iii) Boston SO, Ozawa

(i) *Cello Concerto; Métaboles; Mystères de l'instant*
*** Chan. 9565.(i) Pergamenschikov; BBC PO, Y.-P. Tortelier

The Erato disc offers a first-rate introduction to the French master. The *Cello Concerto* is intense in feeling and rich in those glowing timbres and luminous textures which he is so successful in creating. The Finnish cellist, Arto Noras, is a committed and authoritative soloist and is given excellent support from Saraste and the Finnish Radio Orchestra. Both performances and recordings of the *Métaboles* and *The Shadows of Time* have been recommended in earlier editions of the *Guide* and make an excellent coupling.

Rostropovich plays the *Cello Concerto* with enormous virtuosity and feeling; the Orchestre de Paris under Serge Baudo gives splendid support, while the 1975 recording is immensely vivid, with Rostropovich looming larger than life but given great presence. This has now rightly been reissued as one of EMI's 'Great Recordings of the Century'.

Boris Pergamenschikov rises to the challenge and, although Rostropovich's remains an almost mandatory recommendation, thanks to the composer's authority, the excellence of the orchestral playing under Yan Pascal Tortelier and the Chandos recording earn it a three-star grading. The *Métaboles* and the *Mystères de l'instant* are played expertly and persuasively.

Truls Mørk is also an impressive exponent of *Tout un monde lointain*, though the solo cello is rather too forwardly placed. The recording, made in the Salle Olivier Messiaen at Radio France, is impressively detailed even if the balance is slightly synthetic. Renaud Capuçon is recorded in the Salle Pleyel and the splendid recording reveals plenty of orchestral detail: Myung-Whun Chung holds everything together in magisterial fashion. The Virgin disc also has the solo piece, played with great authority and fine characterization by Truls Mørk.

(i) *Cello Concerto (Tout un monde lointain). Symphony No. 1; Timbres, Espace, Mouvement (La Nuit Etoilée)*
(N) (BB) ****(*)** Arte Nova 74321 92413-2. Queyras, O. Nat. Bordeaux Aquitaine, Graf, (i) with Queyras

A fine performance of the *Cello Concerto*, too, from Jean-Guihen Queyras. The acoustic of the Salle Franklin, Bordeaux, is very resonant, but the balance in all three works is most musically judged and the sound is most vivid and present; this can certainly be recommended and is well worth acquiring, even at the risk of duplication. Those just wanting the two symphonies coupled together at mid-price have the Barenboim set (see below), but these bargain issues from Bordeaux, while separating them, are better value, particularly as they bring much more than adequate performances. The Bordeaux orchestra is almost the equal of the Toulouse Capitole, it is well disciplined and has an excellent wind section.

(i) (*Violin Concerto*) *L'Arbre des songes*; (ii) *La Geôle*; 2 Sonnets de Jean Cassou; Mystère de l'instant
(N) (BB) *** Arte Nova 82876 63825-2. O Nat. Bordeaux Aquitaine, Graf, with (i) Charlier; (ii) Le Roux

In *L'Arbre des songes* Charlier has commanding authority and unforced eloquence, shaping every phrase and balancing each texture to perfection, and this newcomer with the Orchestre National Bordeaux Aquitaine is very recommendable. New to the catalogue is *La Geôle*, composed in 1944 during the war to a text by Jean Cassou, two of whose sonnets he set ten years later. Good sound and excellent value.

(i) *Violin Concerto (L'Arbre des songes)*. *Timbres, espaces, mouvement*; (ii) 2 Sonnets de Jean Cassou
*** Chan. 9504. (i) Charlier; (ii) Hill, N. Davies; BBC PO, Y. P. Tortelier – ALAIN: *Prière* ***

In terms of artistry and musicianship Charlier yields nothing to his rivals, and Yan Pascal Tortelier gives us the *Timbres, espaces, mouvement* (*La nuit étoilée*) from 1979 as a makeweight. The *Deux sonnets de Jean Cassou* come in Dutilleux's own orchestral transcription, in which Martyn Hill and Neal Davies are effective soloists.

Métaboles
(BB) *** Warner Apex (ADD) 0926 48686-2. O Nat. de l'ORTF, Munch – HONEGGER: *Symphony 4* ***

Métaboles was commissioned in 1964 by the Cleveland Orchestra and only three years later taken into the studio by Charles Munch, one of Dutilleux's most notable champions. In its day (1967) it was a state-of-the-art recording, and though there are many more recent accounts, it still sounds vivid and exhilarating. Munch's account of the Honegger symphony is also outstanding.

Métaboles; The Shadows of Time; Symphony 2 (Le Double)
(N) (BB) **(*) Arte Nova 74321 80786-2. O Nat. Bordeaux Aquitaine, Graf

The Bordeaux orchestra play with finesse and sensitivity throughout this disc and those above, though in the two symphonies (which are separated on Arte Nova) they do not supersede the performances by the BBC Philharmonic under Yan Pascal Tortelier on Chandos. However, given the price and the excellence of the recorded sound, they make a perfectly valid alternative recommendation, and the other orchestral works are impressive too.

Sur le même accord
(N) (M) *** DG 477 5376. Mutter, O Nat. de France, Masur – BARTOK: *Violin Concerto 2*; STRAVINSKY: *Violin Concerto in D* ***

Dutilleux's *Sur le même accord* is a short work (under nine minutes) and was commissioned for Mutter by Paul Sacher when she was 16; she was in her thirties when the score finally arrived. This performance was recorded at its Paris première in 2003, and very fine it is too. *Sur le même accord* is 'on the same chord' and the music is derived from the six plucked notes heard at the beginning. Like all Dutilleux's music, it is highly imaginative and atmospheric, and makes a welcome addition to his growing discography.

Symphonies 1–2
🔗 ✹ *** Chan. 9194. BBC PO, Y.-P. Tortelier
(M) ** Warner Elatus 2564 60334-2. O de Paris, Barenboim

Marvellously resourceful and inventive scores, which are given vivid and persuasive performances by Yan Pascal Tortelier and the BBC Philharmonic Orchestra. The engineers give us a splendidly detailed and refined portrayal of these complex textures – the sound is really state-of-the-art.

The exhilarating *First Symphony* is not as well served by Barenboim and the Orchestre de Paris as it is on the alternative Chandos coupling . In Paris the Scherzo is scrambled and the opening notes of the *Passacaglia* are clipped. Equally the *Second Symphony* is well enough played with an eminently serviceable recording. But the Munch version (below) is far superior.

Symphony 2; Métaboles
(M) *** Erato 2564 60572-2. O Nat. de l'ORTF, Munch – HONEGGER: *Symphony 4* ***

Symphony 2; Métaboles; Timbres, espace, mouvement
**(*) Finlandia 3984 25324-2. Toronto SO, Saraste

Munch's account of the *Second Symphony*, which he commissioned for the seventy-fifth birthday of the Boston Symphony Orchestra, is in a special category. He was its first interpreter and his performance is not only uniquely authoritative, it is also powerfully evocative. *Métaboles* was commissioned in 1964 by the Cleveland Orchestra, and only three years later was taken into the studio by Munch. In its day the recording was state-of-the-art, and if today it is not quite as fine as Chandos provide for Yan Pascal Tortelier (who also offers No. 1 on Chan. 9194), it still sounds vivid and exhilarating. Munch's account of the Honegger coupling is also outstanding.

Jukka-Pekka Saraste and the Toronto Symphony Orchestra's performances are eminently serviceable and, having been made in the presence of Dutilleux himself, must, we assume, carry his imprimatur. But the recording does not have quite the transparency or body of the Harmonia Mundi disc.

Ainsi la nuit (String Quartet)
(B) *** EMI Début 5 74020-2. Belcea Qt – DEBUSSY, RAVEL: *String Quartets* ***

The Belcea accounts of the Debussy and Ravel quartets are pretty impeccable, and their Dutilleux is hardly less sensitive. One's first impression of *Ainsi la nuit* is of fragmentation and delicate wisps of texture, but gradually its power and logic emerge. The Belcea players are extraordinarily sensitive to its dynamic range and produce a performance of great finesse. At budget price and with good sound, this enjoys a strong competitive advantage.

DVOŘÁK, Antonín (1841–1904)

'Deo Gratias': A documentary on the life of Dvořák (written and directed by Martin Suchanek)

(N) *** Supraphon **DVD** SU 7007-9 (includes performances of the composer's music by various Czech artists)

Dvořák's own final comment on his life was *'Deo Gratias'*, 'Thanks be to God'. That makes an apt title for this admirably direct and informative documentary surveying the composer's career. The story is told without fuss, with plenty of relevant illustrations, whether of the characters involved or the places referred to, tricked out with historic film material. It is fascinating to find that Dvořák's reports from his first music school were unflattering, with the exception that he was 'strong on counterpoint'; that in London he would get up at 6 a.m. to wander round the city; and that the salary he received in New York as Director of the Conservatoire was 30 times higher than what he was getting at home.

The biography is illustrated with a sequence of performances, filmed live, single movements rather than complete works. The selection is fair enough, with Vaclav Neumann warmer in his conducting than he has often been in his studio recordings. Those items – the finale of the *New World Symphony* and the first movement of the *Cello Concerto* with Gustav Rivinius as soloist – are vintage recordings, but the brilliantly played finale of the *Piano Concerto* dates from only three years ago, from the same performance (with Martin Kasik as soloist and with Jiri Kout conducting) that Supraphon has also issued complete on CD.

Warner 100th Anniversary Edition: (i) *American Suite in A, Op. 98b;* (ii) *Carnival Overture;* (iii) *Czech Suite;* (iv) *The Golden Spinning Wheel;* (ii) *In Nature's Realm, Op. 91;* (i) *Legends, Op. 59a;* (ii) *Othello, Op. 93;* (iv) *The Noon Witch, Op. 108; The Water Goblin, Op. 107; The Wild Dove, Op. 110; Symphonies: 7; 8; 9 (New World)*

(N) (B) *** Warner 2564 61530-2 (5). (i) Rochester PO, Zinman; (ii) NYPO, Masur; (iii) Lausanne CO, Jordan; (iv) Concg. O, Harnoncourt

The collection here is not altogether predictable, with the *American* and *Czech Suites* especially welcome. With Harnoncourt conducting the last three symphonies (including a first-class account of the *New World*) and the four key symphonic poems, this is certainly excellent value, and the standard of recording is high.

(i) *American Suite, Op. 98b;* (ii) *Czech Suite, Op. 39; Nocturne for Strings in B, Op. 40; Polka for Prague Students in B flat, Op. 53a; Polonaise in E flat; Prague Waltzes;* (i) *Slavonic Dances 1–16, Op. 46/1–8, Op. 72/1–8;* (ii) *Slavonic Rhapsody 3, Op. 45*

(B) *** Double Decca DDD/ADD 460 293-2 (2). (i) RPO; (ii) Detroit SO; Dorati

Dvořák's *American Suite* has clear influences from the New World. It is slight but charming music. Dorati has its measure and the RPO are very responsive. The Kingsway Hall recording balance suits the scoring rather well, but the *Slavonic Dances,* recorded at the same time (1983), are not so sweet here in the upper range of the strings, although otherwise the sound is full and pleasing. Dorati's performances have characteristic brio, the RPO response is warmly lyrical when necessary and the woodwind playing gives much pleasure. The *Czech Suite* can sometimes outstay its welcome, but

certainly not here. The other items too have the brightness and freshness that mark out the *Slavonic Dances,* especially the *Polka* and *Polonaise* with their attractive rhythmic spring. The most charming piece of all is the set of *Waltzes,* written for balls in Prague – Viennese music with a Czech accent – while the lovely *Nocturne* with its subtle drone bass makes a winning interlude. The *Slavonic Rhapsody,* with its opening suggesting a troubadour and his harp, makes a vivacious end to what the documentation rightly describes as 'two-and-a-half hours of Dvořák's most tuneful orchestral music'.

American Suite; 7 Interludes for Small Orchestra; (i) *Mazurka for Violin & Orchestra. Nocturne in B; Polka in B flat; Polonaise in E flat; 5 Prague Waltzes;* (ii) *Rondo for Cello & Orchestra; Silent Woods for Cello & Orchestra*

(N) (BB) *** Naxos 8.557352. (i) Trostianski; (ii) Yablonsky; Russia PO, Yablonsky

This is a tidying-up compilation, offering just short of 80 minutes of lesser-known Dvořák, although *Silent Woods* and the *Nocturne* are not entirely unfamiliar. The highlight is the *American Suite,* written originally for piano and orchestrated a year later (in 1894, before the composer returned home from America). It is delectably scored and, although lightweight, has great charm. The *Seven Interludes* were written much earlier, in 1867: they are agreeable enough, but very slight. The *Mazurka* (1879) for violin and orchestra, has something of the flavour of the *Slavonic Dances.* The dance movements are jolly and infectious, the *Polonaise* suitably boisterous. The performances here are all of good quality, as is the recording, and with good documentation the disc earns its three stars for enterprise as well as enjoyment.

Carnival Overture; Czech Suite; The Golden Spinning-Wheel; A Hero's Song; Husitska; In Nature's Realm; My Home; The Noon-Day Witch; Othello; Symphonic Variations; Water Goblin; Wood Dove

(N) (BB) ** Brilliant Classics 92297 (3). Janáček PO, Kuchar

The performances by the Janáček Philharmonic of Dvořák's *Symphonic Poems* and *Overtures,* recorded in Slovenia over a period of only eight days, may not be as refined as some, but under their American conductor, Theodore Kuchar, they are all colourful, strongly characterized and idiomatic. The playing is not always helped by the recording, up-front to the point of coarseness, so that heavy tuttis often become congested, as in the opening of the *Carnival Overture* or the climax of *The Water Goblin,* with detail obscured, and the exposed violins are not as sweet as they might be. Yet this is a highly enjoyable collection which has one admiring more than ever the composer's happy inventiveness, and it is temptingly inexpensive.

Cello Concerto in B min., Op. 104

⊶ ✿ (M) *** DG (ADD) 447 413-2. Rostropovich, BPO, Karajan – TCHAIKOVSKY: *Rococo Variations* *** ✿

(N) *** BBC (ADD) BBCL 4156-2. Du Pré, RLPO, Groves – IBERT: *Cello and Wind Concerto* ***

*** Teldec 8573-85340-2. Du Pré, Swedish RSO, Celibidache – SAINT-SAENS: *Cello Concerto 1* ***

*** Chan. 8662. Wallfisch, LSO, Mackerras – DOHNANYI: *Konzertstück* ***

(N) (M) *** RCA **SACD** 82876 66375-2. Piatigorsky, Boston SO, Munch – WALTON: *Concerto*

(BB) **(*) EMI Encore (ADD) 5 75865-2. Tortelier, LSO, Previn – BRAHMS: *Double Concerto* **(*)

(BB) (***) Naxos mono 8.110930. Casals, Czech PO, Szell –
BRAHMS: *Double Concerto* (***)

(M) (***) EMI mono 5 62952-2 [5 62953-2]. Casals, Czech PO,
Szell – ELGAR: *Concerto* (**(*)); BRUCH: *Kol Nidrei* (***)

**(*) EMI (ADD) 5 55527-2. Du Pré, Chicago SO, Barenboim
– ELGAR: *Concerto* ***

**(*) Virgin 5 61838-2. Mørk, Oslo PO, Jansons –
TCHAIKOVSKY: *Variations on a Rococo Theme* **(*)

(N) (M) **(*) Mercury SACD 475 6608. Starker, LSO, Dorati
– BRUCH: *Kol Nidrei;* TCHAIKOVSKY: *Rococo Variations*
**(*)

(M) **(*) EMI (ADD) 5 62803-2 [5 62805-2]. Du Pré, Chicago
SO, Barenboim – SCHUMANN: *Cello Concerto* **(*)

(B) **(*) Warner Apex 0927 40600-2. Noras, Finnish RSO,
Oramo – BARTOK: *Rhapsody 1;* ELGAR: *Cello Concerto* ***

(i) *Cello Concerto;* (ii) *Rondo in G min.;* (iii) *Silent Woods*
**(*) Channel CCS 8695. Wispelwey; (i) Netherlands PO,
Renes; (ii-iii) Giacometti (piano or harmonium) (with
ARENSKY: *Chant triste;* DAVIDOV: *Am Springbrunnen, Op. 20/2;*
TCHAIKOVSKY: *Andante cantabile, from Op. 11* **(*))

Cello Concerto; Silent Woods
**(*) Guild GMCD 7253. Kreger, Philh. O, Yu – HERBERT:
Cello Concerto **(*)

The intensity of lyrical feeling and the spontaneity of the
partnership between Karajan and Rostropovich ensures the
position of their DG disc at the top of the list of recommendations for this peer among nineteenth-century cello concertos. The orchestral playing is glorious. Moreover, the
analogue recording, made in the Jesus-Christus-Kirche in
September 1969, is as near perfect as any made in that vintage
analogue era, and the CD transfer has freshened the original.

On the BBC Legends label comes a live broadcast recording, made in July 1969 at the Proms, which thrillingly captures Jacqueline du Pré's astonishing range of expression and
tone-colour in this masterpiece, with Charles Groves warmly
supportive. There are some magical things and a liberal use of
portamento. This may have fallen out of fashion now, but it
would have been perfectly natural in Dvořák's day, as it was in
Elgar's. Of course some may feel that she wears her heart just
a bit too visibly on her sleeve, but hers is a big-hearted
reading, full of passion and sensitivity. By comparison, the
studio version is effortful, with du Pré's highly individual
expressive pointing too heavily underlined, whereas in this
Prom performance her natural freedom sounds totally spontaneous and persuasive, bringing out a poignancy in the work
to tug at the heart. The lightweight Ibert *Concerto*, recorded
in 1962, with the cello the first among many soloists, makes a
welcome coupling, a work that du Pré never otherwise
recorded.

Jacqueline du Pré's Swedish Radio recording brings excellent sound, even better than on her EMI studio recording
made in Chicago two years later. Her reading here is even
more warmly spontaneous than the later one. Evidently, du
Pré did not just tolerate the typical exaggerations of a Celibidache reading, but responded positively to them.

Rafael Wallfisch's is also an outstanding version, strong and
warmly sympathetic, masterfully played. The excitement as
well as the warmth of the piece comes over as in a live
performance, and Wallfisch's tone remains rich and firm in
even the most taxing passages. The orchestral playing, the
quality of sound and the delightful, generous and unusual

coupling all make it a recommendation which must be given
the strongest advocacy.

Piatigorsky's superb (1960) recording is praised below in its
normal CD coupling with the *Eighth Symphony*. But in the
new SACD transfer, the orchestral sound is transformed,
richer and fuller in colour, worthy of the composer's vivid
scoring. Of course the balance of the cello remains too
forward, but in all other respects the recording is greatly
improved, and the coupling with Walton is most welcome.

Tortelier's recording with Previn has a satisfying centrality,
not as passionately romantic as Rostropovich on DG, but
with the tenderness as well as the power of the work held in
perfect equilibrium. What is less perfect is the balance of the
recording, favouring the cellist a little too much, though the
richness and body of the 1977 EMI sound is impressive, with
the strongly rhythmic playing of the LSO well caught. A
bargain.

Casals plays with astonishing fire and the performance
seems to spring to life in a way that eludes many modern
artists; the rather dry acoustic of the Deutsches Haus, Prague,
and the limitations of the 1937 recording are of little consequence. This perfomance is one of the classics of the gramophone. The Naxos coupling restores to circulation the
intensely felt Brahms *Double Concerto* with Thibaud and
Casals. There is not a great deal to choose between Mark
Obert-Thorn's transfer of the Dvořák and the EMI version –
both have been done with great care – though if pressed to a
choice, we would prefer the slightly more detailed Naxos.

Jacqueline du Pré's celebrated early recording with Barenboim conveys the spontaneous passion that marked her
playing in public, and it is a performance that captures very
vividly the urgent interpretative flair of both husband and
wife, conductor and soloist. Though the exaggeratedly forward balance of the cello remains very noticeble, in the new
transfer the sound has filled out nicely and is clearly detailed.
The recoupling is also sensible.

The Dutch cellist, Pieter Wispelwey, here gives a more
intimate reading than most on disc, with rather more *portamento* than usual, bringing out autumnal tone-colours, as he
does in the shorter pieces which come as fill-up. The performance may be less bitingly dramatic than most, but the
concentration and expressive warmth make it extremely
compelling. Three of the shorter pieces – in all of which
Wispelwey uses gut strings – have harmonium accompaniment. That is most effective in the Tchaikovsky and the
Arensky (which sounds as though it is about to turn into
Tchaikovsky's song, *None but the lonely heart*), but then
sounds muddled in Dvořák's *Silent Woods.* Happily the *Rondo*
comes with piano accompaniment, as does the Davidov.
Excellent sound.

A fine lyrical performance from an impressive young Norwegian soloist. Truls Mørk has not the largest instrumental
personality, but Jansons provides a refined orchestral introduction to set the scene for the arrival of his young soloist,
who phrases both with ardour and with gently hushed tenderness when playing on a half-tone. The elegiac episode
recalling earlier ideas just before the close of the finale is
touchingly done. An enjoyable performance, given vivid,
modern sound, but one which pales beside the glorious
romanticism of the Rostropovich–Karajan partnership.

Starker and Dorati, Hungarians both, bring a partnership
of contrasts to the Dvořák *Concerto.* The exciting orchestral
introduction immediately establishes the electricity of
Dorati's contribution, but Starker is less extrovert. He plays
with consistent eloquence and much beauty of phrase; and

now, for the first time, the new SACD transfer shows the full warmth of his tone, and he is very naturally balanced. The result is endearingly warm-hearted, if not the most intense account on record.

James Kreger, a pupil of Leonard Rose, won the Piatigorsky Award in his time at Juilliard when he was only 18 years old. He first came to wider notice at the Moscow Tchaikovsky Competition in 1974 and has an impressive *curriculum vitae*. His dedication and artistry come across in this fine Guild version of the *Cello Concerto*, whose slow movement is most eloquent. He is rather too forwardly balanced in comparison with the orchestra and draws out the central section of the first movement rather too much, but this is still a rewarding performance, and the addition of the rarely recorded *Silent Woods* is another plus point.

The excellent Finnish cellist Arto Noras gives a sensitive reading of the Dvořák *Concerto*, responsively accompanied by Oramo. He is rather too backwardly balanced, but better this than a spotlight, and the orchestra is vividly and warmly caught. There is no lack of vigour, but most impressive are the tender moments, not least the *Epilogue*, raptly done. With fine couplings this is a real bargain.

(i) *Cello Concerto;* (ii) *Symphony 8 in G, Op. 88*
(M) **(*) Sony SMK 89871. BPO; (i) with Ma, cond. Maazel; (ii) cond. Giulini
(M) **(*) RCA (ADD) 82876 55302-2. Boston SO, Munch, (i) with Piatigorsky

The partnership of the passionately extrovert Lorin Maazel and the more withdrawn artistry of Yo-Yo Ma is unexpectedly successful when the recording is so vivid and atmospheric and the orchestral playing superb. Ma's rapt concentration and refined control of colour bring at times an elegaic dimension to the performance, and Maazel accompanies with understanding and great sensitivity, fining down the orchestral textures so that he never masks his often gentle soloist, yet provides an exuberant contrast in orchestral fortissimos. Giulini's account of the *G major Symphony* is warm-hearted and has those touches of refinement which distinguish this conductor's interpretations. The Berlin Philharmonic, too, play most beautifully throughout. But the performance is studio bound and, although not without intensity, refuses completely to take off. Furthermore, Giulini makes comparatively little of the lilting lyrical melody which is the glorious centrepiece of the *Allegretto grazioso*.

Piatigorsky's classic 1960 account of the *Cello Concerto* emerges again on RCA's Red Seal label – remastered and sounding better than ever – though that cannot alter a balance, which places the cello too close, not always flattering to the soloist. The tuttis are somewhat two-dimensional, though the sound is now fully acceptable. There is no lack of orchestral colour and the acoustic of Symphony Hall is well conveyed behind the music-making. The performance is the very opposite of routine, with Piatigorsky and Munch in complete rapport, producing a totally spontaneous melodic flow. Although there are moments when intonation is less than immaculate, the inspiration of the performance carries the day. The *Symphony* was recorded a year later but sounds better than in earlier transfers. Munch's reading is strongly characterized and, though he occasionally presses hard, the thrust comes from a natural ardour. Some might feel the finale a bit over-driven, but there is plenty of feeling in the slow movement and few would fail to respond to the passionate blossoming in the strings of the inspired lyrical theme

that forms the centrepiece of the third-movement *Allegretto*. In short, a fresh, individual account and a desirable coupling.

(i) *Cello Concerto;* (ii) *Symphony 9 (New World)*
☛– (BB) *** Warner Apex (ADD) 0927 49919-2. (i) Hoelscher, Hamburg PO, Keilberth; (ii) NW German Philharmonie, Lindenberg
(BB) (***) Naxos mono 8.110901. (i) Feuermann; Berlin State Op. O, cond. J. Taube, (ii) E. Kleiber
(M) **(*) DG Entrée 474 167-2. (i) Fournier, BPO, Szell; (ii) Dresden State O, Levine

This Apex reissue is a real rediscovery. When Ludwig Hoelscher recorded Dvořák's *Cello Concerto* in 1958, he was Germany's leading solo cellist, an artist of the very front rank, with a really big, resonant tone and a big, heroic sense of style to go with it. This performance ranks with the very finest on record, including the famous Rostropovich–Karajan account. With Hoelscher one has a sense of real striving, and that is just how it should be. The passion of the slow movement is conveyed wonderfully, and the orchestral playing is excellent here: witness the famous horn trio. The finale has no less ardour and excitement. The recording, full and warm and vivid, is astonishingly good. If the balance favours the soloist unduly, the tone he gives us is so glorious that one finds it hard to carp over such a matter. Lindenberg's account of the *New World Symphony* is not quite on this level, but it is a direct, persuasively simple reading, again with a beautifully played slow movement. Only the rather easy-going trio in the Scherzo lets the interpretation down a little, but it is agreeably elegant, and the finale makes amends. Again, good sound (from 1969). This is a bargain disc to seek out, even if duplication is involved.

Emanuel Feuermann's pioneering account of the *Cello Concerto* was made in 1928–9. Feuermann, a passionate soloist, at times seems intent on showing just how fast he can play, with phenomenally clean articulation but with the occasional flaw of intonation. Well transferred by Mark Obert-Thorn from pre-EMI Parlophone pressings, the sound is limited but clear. Erich Kleiber's 1929 recording of the *New World Symphony* equally brings an electrifying performance, fast and furious in allegros and tenderly expressive in the slow movement. The surface noise is sometimes obtrusive but hardly detracts from the impact of an at times inspirational reading.

Fournier's richly distinguished stereo account of the *Cello Concerto*, with Szell an admirable partner, is coupled on Entrée with a good but not distinctive *New World Symphony* from Levine. Its main interest lies in the conductor's rare partnership with the great Dresden Staatskapelle, who certainly play gloriously in the first two movements. But the Scherzo lacks Bohemian rhythmic jauntiness, and the finale is exciting without carrying all before it. Moreover the timpani sound oppressively close in the introduction, and there is no exposition repeat. Nevertheless, the sheer quality of the orchestral playing carries the day.

Warner 100th Anniversary Edition: (i) *Cello Concerto;* (ii) *Piano Concerto;* (iii) *Violin Concerto;* (iv) *Romance in F min., Op. 11;* (v) *Silent Woods, Op. 68/5;* (vi) *Serenade for Strings, Op. 22;* (vi) *Serenade for Wind, Op. 44;* (vii) *Slavonic Dances 1–16, Opp. 46 & 72;* (viii) *Slavonic Rhapsody 3;* (ix) *Requiem Mass;* (x) *Rusalka: 2 Arias*
(N) (B) ** Warner 2564 61528-2 (6). (i) Rostropovich, Boston SO, Ozawa; (ii) Aimard, Concg. O, Harnoncourt; (iii) Vengerov, NYPO; (iv) Zehetmair, Philh. O, Inbal; (v) Noras,

Kuopio SO, Lehtinen; (vi) St Paul CO, Wolff; (vii) COE, Harnoncourt; (viii) Czech PO, Neumann; (ix) Zylis-Gara, Toczyska, Dvorsky, Mróz, R. France Ch. & New PO, Jordan; (x) Urbanova, Prague SO, Lenárd

This is a more mixed offering than its companions: Rostropovich's account of the *Cello Concerto*, for instance, is disappointing, as is Jordan's of the *Requiem*. But the accounts of the *Piano* and *Violin Concertos* are much more recommendable and Harnoncourt's *Slavonic Dances* are very exciting.

Piano Concerto in G min., Op. 33

(M) *** EMI (ADD) 5 66895-2 [5 66947-2]. Richter, Bav. State O, C. Kleiber – SCHUBERT: *Wanderer Fantasia* ***

(i) *Piano Concerto*; (ii) *Violin Concerto*

(N) *** Chan. 10309. (i) Hayroudinoff; (ii) Ehnes, BBC PO, Noseda

Having Dvořák's *Piano* and *Violin Concertos* on a single disc makes an apt and generous coupling. The Canadian violinist, James Ehnes, gives a strong, incisive performance of the *Violin Concerto*, with speeds on the fast side in the first two movements and with the furiant finale bitingly fresh. His rapid vibrato gives a distinctive timbre to his playing, making the slow movement less warmly romantic than it often is, and the recording, generally well balanced, is yet less full and warm than in the *Piano Concerto*. That receives a superb performance from the Russian, Rustem Hayroudinoff, one which stands the closest comparison with the classic version by Sviatoslav Richter. Even more than Richter, Hayroudinoff brings out the joyful, carefree quality of Dvořák's inspiration, bringing home what a wonderful fund of good melodies it contains. The clarity of his articulation in the often tricky passagework is phenomenal. Helped by full, rich sound which yet allows fine detail, Noseda and the BBC Philharmonic match the subtlety and point of the soloist's playing, establishing this as an outstanding modern version.

Richter plays the solo part in its original form (and not the more pianistically 'effective' revision by Wilém Kurz which is published in the Complete Edition), and his judgement is triumphantly vindicated. This is the most persuasive and masterly account of the work ever committed to disc; its ideas emerge with an engaging freshness and warmth, while the greater simplicity of Dvořák's own keyboard writing proves in Richter's hands to be more telling and profound. Carlos Kleiber secures excellent results from the Bavarian orchestra, and the 1977 recording has clarity and good definition to recommend it.

(i) *Piano Concerto, Op. 33. The Water Goblin (symphonic poem), Op. 107*

(BB) *** Naxos 8.550896. (i) Jandó; Polish Nat. RSO, Wit

An infectiously fresh and warmly lyrical account from Jandó and the highly supportive Polish National Radio Orchestra under Antoni Wit. Jandó conveys his own pleasure, and Wit's accompaniment glows with colour; he then offers a splendidly vibrant and colourful portrayal of *The Water Goblin*, one of the composer's most vividly melodramatic symphonic poems. The recording is spacious and realistically balanced. The violins are a shade overbright but otherwise the sound is excellent. Very enjoyable and well worth its modest cost.

(i) *Piano Concerto*; (ii) *Piano Quintets, Op. 5, & Op. 81*

(B) *** RCA 2-CD 74321 88683-2 (2). Firkušný, with (i) Czech PO, Neumann; (ii) Ridge Qt – JANACEK: *Concertino; Concerto* ***

Rudolf Firkušný has played the Dvořák *Piano Concerto* in both the original version and that by Vilém Kurz, as well as this Czech version on RCA, a *mélange* of the two. The recording conveys its sunny geniality to good effect and, although the great pianist was 79 when this record was made, the playing still sounds both youthful and aristocratic. The performance of the famous Opus 81 *Piano Quintet* is equally memorable, wonderfully warm and spontaneous. These players are right inside the music and Firkušný's contribution is full of special insights. What is more remarkable is how the performers also invest the early, immature *Piano Quintet* (from 1872, but revised in 1887) with such vivacity in the outer movements and warmth of lyrical feeling in the *Andante*. Here Firkušný is at his finest and his playing excites a similar response from his colleagues to make the work almost sound a forgotten masterpiece and certainly one that should be heard more often. This bargain Double cannot be recommended too highly, and its claims are enhanced by the Janáček coupling.

Violin Concerto in A min., Op. 53

(M) *** Warner Elatus 2564 60806-2. Vengerov, NYPO, Masur – BRAHMS: *Violin Concerto* **(*)

(B) *** CfP 575 8062. Little, RLPO, Handley – SIBELIUS: *Concerto 1* ***

(M) *** Virgin 5 61910-2. Tetzlaff, Czech PO, Pešek – LALO: *Symphonie espagnole* ***

(M) *** DG (IMS) 449 091-2. Mintz, BPO, Levine – BRUCH: *Concerto 1* ***

(M) *** DG (IMS) (ADD) 463 651-2. Martzy, Berlin RSO, Fricsay – BRUCH: *Concerto 1*; GLAZUNOV: *Concerto* **

(BB) (***) Naxos mono 8.110975. Milstein, Minneapolis SO, Dorati – MOZART: *Adagio in E* etc.; GLAZUNOV: *Violin Concerto*. (***)

(*) Sup. SU 3709-2 031. Sporcl, Czech PO, Ashkenazy – TCHAIKOVSKY: *Violin Concerto* *

**(*) Avie AV 0044. Graffin, Johannesburg PO, Hankinson – COLERIDGE-TAYLOR: *Violin Concerto* **(*)

Violin Concerto; Masurek

*** Ph. (IMS) 464 531-2. Suwanai, Budapest Festival O, I. Fischer – SARASATE: *Carmen Fantasy*, etc. ***

Violin Concerto; Romance in F min., Op. 11

(B) *** EMI Red Line 5 69806. Chung, Phd. O, Muti – BARTOK: *Rhapsodies* ***

(BB) *** Naxos 8.550758. Kaler, Polish Nat. RSO (Katowice), Kolchinsky – GLAZUNOV: *Concerto* ***

(M) *** Sup. (ADD) SU 1928-2 011. Suk, Czech PO, Ančerl – SUK: *Fantasy* ***

(BB) **(*) Warner Apex 0927 49517-2. Zehetmair, Philh. O, Inbal – SCHUMANN: *Violin Concerto* ***

(i) *Violin Concerto; Romance in F min., Op. 11*; (ii) *Sonatina in G, Op. 100; 4 Romantic Pieces, Op. 75*

(M) **(*) EMI 5 62595-2. Perlman, (i) LPO, Barenboim; (ii) Sanders

Maxim Vengerov performs not only with the effortless brilliance and dazzling technical command that one expects but with poetic feeling, freshness and spontaneity. Here virtuosity is at the service of artistry. He receives splendid support from Kurt Masur and the New York Philharmonic (they are recorded at a concert performance) and the balance between the soloist and orchestra is judged expertly. However, there are some reservations about the Brahms coupling.

Tasmin Little brings to this concerto an open freshness and

sweetness, very apt for this composer, that are extremely winning. The firm richness of her sound, totally secure on intonation up to the topmost register, goes with an unflustered ease of manner, and the recording brings little or no spotlighting of the soloist; she establishes her place firmly with full-ranging, well-balanced sound that co-ordinates the soloist along with the orchestra.

Akiko Suwanai is daring, urgent and volatile, adopting the widest range of dynamic and tone down to whispered *pianissimos* that convey a mood of deep meditation, as in the opening of the slow movement. The finale, taken faster than usual, is above all exciting, if with rhythms rather less sprung than in more relaxed readings. Slavonic flavours have rarely been brought out so vividly in this boldly rhapsodic concerto. The colourful *Masurek* (or mazurka) makes an apt link between the Sarasate showpieces and the concerto. Full, brilliant sound, with the violin marginally spot-lit.

Tetzlaff's performance, distinguished by quicksilver lightness in the passage-work, is both full of fantasy and marked by keen concentration and a sense of spontaneity. With the violin balanced naturally, not spot-lit, the slow movement has a hushed intensity at the opening, which gives extra poignancy to Tetzlaff's tender, totally unsentimental phrasing. In romantic freedom of expression characteristically, Pešek makes orchestral textures clear, bringing out extra detail even in the heaviest tuttis, despite reverberant recording. Very recommendable.

There is dazzling playing from Shlomo Mintz, whose virtuosity is effortless and his intonation astonishingly true. There is good rapport between soloist and conductor, and the performance has the sense of joy and relaxation that this radiant score needs. The digital sound is warm and natural in its upper range.

Suk's earlier performance is back in the catalogue at mid-price, effectively remastered, recoupled with the Suk *Fantasy*. Its lyrical eloquence is endearing, the work is played in the simplest possible way, and Ančerl accompanies glowingly. Readers will note that, since its last appearance, the *Romance* has been restored, an equally delightful performance. This is one of Suk's very finest records.

Kyung Wha Chung gives a heartfelt reading of a work that can sound wayward. The partnership with Muti and the Philadelphia Orchestra is a happy one, with the sound warmer and more open than it has usually been in the orchestra's recording venue. She finds similar concentration in the *Romance*.

The Perlman and Barenboim partnership is at its peak in the both the *Concerto* and the delectable *Romance*, and this coupling remains very competitive, the more so in that this reissue in the 'Perlman Edition' is at mid-price, and now offers the double bonus of the enchanting *Sonatina* plus the hardly less attractive set of *Four Romantic Pieces*. Both are beautifully played and well recorded, save for the imbalance between the celebrated violinist and the more recessed pianist.

Martzy possesses a virtuoso technique dominated by the mind of a fine musician, so that the listener feels an agreeable sense of security and pleasure even in the most fiery passages. The several luscious and lyrical tunes emerge with the bloom of youthful innocence upon them, and their kinship with folk-song adds constantly to their all-pervading charm. Fricsay's accompaniment is masterly, and if he is not ideally served by the recording acoustic, his insistence on clarity of texture compensates for this small disadvantage.

The performance of the Russian violinist, Ilya Kaler, has great romantic warmth and natural Slavonic feeling, and he is given excellent support by Kolchinsky and the Polish orchestra. The very resonant acoustics of the recording, made in the Concert Hall of Polish Radio, give the soloist a somewhat larger-than-life image against a widely resonant orchestral backcloth. But the effect is easy to enjoy when the playing is so ardent; moreover these artists offer (besides the Glazunov) the *Romance in F minor*, and that is also beautifully played.

Zehetmair plays the concerto with brilliance and precision. He is satisfyingly clean in attack and is very sympathetic in the lovely *Romance*. He is well accompanied by Inbal and the (originally Teldec) recording is natural and well balanced. Even so, this is a performance in the central Viennese tradition, with the Czech flavours played down and with little feeling for the Czech idiom, even in the Slavonic dance of the finale. But the Schumann coupling is first class, and altogether this is a welcome bargain reissue.

Milstein's account of the Dvořák *Concerto* with Steinberg and the Pittsburgh orchestra enjoyed great and justified celebrity in the early 1960s and reappeared in the six-CD box EMI issued some years ago devoted to his art. This version sounds pretty exhilarating too, and Dorati gets very supportive playing from the Minneapolis orchestra.

Pavel Sporcl is a charismatic violinist, with natural flair and imagination as well as formidable virtuoso technique. It helps that both performances on this Supraphon disc were recorded live, in the Rudolfinum in Prague, with the electricity of each occasion vividly conveyed. At the end of the Dvořák there is a wild yell of enthusiasm before the applause, suggesting that Sporcl's flamboyant appearance as well as his musical gifts have attracted a youthful following. The Czech audience was obviously roused by hearing so warmly idiomatic a reading of a work that can easily seem wayward. Though in the slow movement Sporcl does not quite match his finest rivals in inner intensity, the finale is delightful, with the Slavonic dance-rhythms lightly sprung.

As in the Coleridge-Taylor *Concerto* with which it is aptly coupled, Philippe Graffin is a warmly committed soloist in the Dvořák, but with flawed orchestral playing, vigorous but rough in ensemble, this version is hardly a strong competitor, except for those wanting the rare work with which it is coupled.

(i) *Violin Concerto*; (ii) *Piano Quintet, Op. 81*

*** EMI 557521-2. Chang, with (i) LSO, C. Davis; (ii) Kerr, Christ, Faust, Andsnes

It makes a very attractive and unusual disc to have the brilliant young violinist, Sarah Chang, coupling her warm and powerful account of the Dvořák *Violin Concerto* not with another concerto but with one of the composer's most popular chamber works. As in her fine coupling of the Dvořák *String Sextet*, coupled with Tchaikovsky's *Souvenir de Florence*, she shows what a warmly sympathetic chamber-player she is, with the pianist Leif-Ove Andsnes sharing the leadership of the group in equally inspired playing in the *Piano Quintet*. As though making music for fun, they are freely spontaneous-sounding in their expressiveness, with the *Dumka* slow movement seemingly improvisatory, and the Scherzo very light, taken at a challengingly fast tempo. The performance of the *Concerto*, with Sir Colin Davis a powerful and understanding Dvořákian, similarly draws freely expressive playing from Chang in a performance which treats the unconventional structure of the first movement as rhapsodic without letting tensions slip. The sense of fantasy is irresist-ible, with Chang using extremes of dynamic, there and in the slow movement, and with the Slavonic dance of the finale given a winning spring. The recording, made at the Watford Colosseum, enhances the feeling of a big-scale performance, with full-bodied sound set in a lively acoustic.

(i) Violin Concerto; (ii) Piano Trio in F min., Op. 65
(N) *** HM HMC 901833. Faust, with (i) Prague Philh., Bělohlávek; (ii) Queyras, Melnikov

The Harmonia Mundi coupling of the composer's solitary Violin Concerto with one of his chamber works is unexpect-edly attractive. Isabelle Faust's account of the former is most distinctive in its biting vitality. In all three movements speeds are on the fast side, and the playing of the Prague Philharmo-nia under Bělohlávek adds to the bite, bringing out the authentic Czech flavour of dance-based rhythms. Faust and her Czech collaborators are magnetic throughout, never let-ting the tension slip, with drama rather than reflectiveness the keynote in all three movements. In the F minor Trio, Faust, in a partnership of equals, leads a most persuasive performance, marked by warmth and spontaneity. With vivid recording, made in the Rudolfinum in Prague, this is one of the most distinctive of all the many versions of the Concerto.

Czech Suite; A Hero's Song, Op. 111; Festival March, Op. 54; Hussite Overture, Op. 67
(BB) **(*) Naxos 8.553005. Polish Nat. RSO (Katowice), Wit

Antoni Wit is most impressive in A Hero's Song. There is an outburst of patriotic hyperbole towards the close (with thun-dering trombones), but Wit generates excitement without letting things get out of hand. The performance of the Czech Suite is warm and relaxed, nicely rustic in feeling, but again is affected by the resonance.

Czech Suite; Notturno for Strings, Op. 40; Serenade for Strings, Op. 22
*** Ara. Z 6697. Padova CO, Golub

David Golub takes a more relaxed view than usual of the opening movement of the adorable Czech Suite (no harm in that), and he presents the quicker movements with an unforced charm that is captivating. The Padua Chamber Orchestra respond to his sensitive direction with evident sympathy in the Serenade, though he tries to make a little too much of the contrasting idea of the first movement. Gener-ally very well-judged tempi. Enjoyable and musical playing, enhanced by a natural recording.

Overtures: Carnival; Hussite; In Nature's Realm; My Home; Othello. Symphonic Poems: The Golden Spinning Wheel; The Nooonday Witch; The Wood Dove; Symphonic Variations, Op. 78; Slavonic Dances 1–16, Op. 46/1–8; Op. 72/1–8
→ (B) *** DG Trio ADD 469 366-2 (3). Bav. RSO, Kubelik

This is among the finest of the Universal Trios (three discs for the price of two mid-priced CDs, with excellent documenta-tion) so far issued. Kubelik has a special feeling for Dvořák, and these performances are among his finest on record and they are superbly played, with the Slavonic Dances displaying both virtuosity and panache. He is also splendidly dashing in Carnival; and the other two overtures, Opp. 91 and 93 – all three linked by a recurring main theme – which Dvořák wrote immediately after his first visit to America in 1892, are comparably successful and full of colouristic subtlety.

The patriotic Hussite Overture is superbly passionate, while the opening of The Golden Spinning Wheel is gentle and elfin-like. There is some bewitching playing from the wood-wind throughout this performance, matched by tender strings and a noble restraint from the trombones. In both The Water Goblin and The Noonday Witch the dramatic urgency is most compelling, with stabbing rhythms in the former, and the lyrical sections of the score played with much poignancy. The Wood Dove is more difficult to bring off, but here, as in its companions, there is magic and lustre in the orchestral textures and the atmospheric tension is striking. The Sym-phonic Variations open warmly and graciously, and Kubelik is obviously determined to minimize the Brahmsian associa-tions. The recordings, made in the Munich Hercules-Saal between 1973 and 1977, are freshly transferred to CD and generally sound very good indeed.

Overtures: Carnival; In Nature's Realm; Othello; Scherzo capriccioso
**(*) Chan. 8453. Ulster O, Handley

Overtures: Carnival; In Nature's Realm; Othello; Scherzo capriccioso; Symphonic Variations
**(*) ASV CDDCA 794. RPO, Farrer

Overture: The Cunning Peasant
(M) (**) Sup. mono SU 1914 011. Czech PO, Sejna – SKROUP: The Tinker Overture; SMETANA: Festive Symphony, etc. (***)

Overture: My Home. Symphonic Poems: The Golden Spinning Wheel; A Hero's Song, Op. 111; The Noonday Witch; The Water Goblin; The Wood Dove, Op. 110
(B) **(*) Chan. 2-for-1 241-3 (2). RSNO, Järvi

Many will be attracted to Neeme Järvi's collection by the modern, digital sound, warmly atmospheric in typical Chan-dos style, not always clean on detail but firmly focused. These recordings were all fill-ups for Järvi's integral set of the symphonies. The real rarity here is A Hero's Song, Dvořák's very last orchestral work. Järvi's strongly committed, red-blooded performance minimizes any weaknesses. My Home is given an exuberant performance, bringing out the lilt of the dance rhythms, and Järvi is a dramatic advocate of The Water Goblin. He also brings out the storytelling vividly in The Noonday Witch, while the most memorable of all the sym-phonic poems, The Golden Spinning Wheel, has plenty of drama and atmosphere, helped by the fine bloom of the recording. The only snag here is the relative short measure.

Handley's excellent performances put the four works in perspective. Superbly recorded, this now seems short measure at premium price.

John Farrer scores over Handley by including also the Symphonic Variations, here given a performance of great freshness. The three linked overtures have comparable warmth and delicacy of colouring. There is plenty of drama too, and the only slight disappointment is that Carnival, while vigorous enough and with a richly hued central section, could have been even more exuberant. The Scherzo capric-cioso is brightly vivacious.

The Cunning Peasant is not one of Dvořák's greatest over-tures, though Karel Sejna makes the most positive case for it in his mono recording. Acceptable sound and a useful fill-up to Smetana's exhilarating Festive Symphony.

The Golden Spinning Wheel; The Noonday Witch; The Water Goblin; The Wild Dove

☛ ✿ (M) *** Teldec 2-CD 2564 60221-2 (2). Concg. O, Harnoncourt

Harnoncourt's collection of Dvořák's four most vivid symphonic poems is one of his finest pairs of records and one of Teldec's most realistic recordings. The performances offer superlative playing from the Concertgebouw Orchestra, and Harnoncourt's direction is inspired, lyrical and dramatic by turns, ever relishing Dvořák's glowing scoring for woodwinds and, in the famous *Spinning Wheel*, the horns and, towards the close, a gloriously sonorous passage for the trombones. These are all quite long works and their colourful descriptive narrative means that they need holding firmly together. Harnoncourt does that, yet keeps the narrative flow moving along with an exciting momentum. The end of *The Water Goblin* is superbly melodramatic and *The Golden Spinning Wheel* is unsurpassed on record, even by Beecham. The recording and ambience are so believable that one feels one has the famous Dutch concert hall just beyond the speakers.

The Golden Spinning Wheel, Op. 109; The Noonday Witch, Op. 108; The Wood Dove, Op. 110

(BB) *** Naxos 8.550598. Polish Nat. RSO (Katowice), Gunzenhauser

The Polish orchestra seem thoroughly at home in Dvořák's sound-world and Gunzenhauser gives warm, vivid performances and is especially evocative in the masterly *Golden Spinning Wheel*. There is shapely string phrasing and a fine, sonorous contribution from the brass. The concert hall of Polish Radio in Katowice has expansive acoustics – just right for the composer's colourful effects.

Legends, Op. 59; Miniatures, Op. 75a; Notturno in B, Op. 40; Prague Waltzes

☛ ✿ (M) ***Ph. 476 2179. Budapest Festival O, Fischer

The *Legends* are endearing, captivating, gloriously inventive pieces, the charm and character of which are conveyed wonderfully by Iván Fischer and the Budapest Festival Orchestra and recorded as sumptuously as their outstanding Bartók discs. All of these pieces, including the poignant *Notturno* and the delightful *Prague Waltzes*, are performed with great feeling and style and convey Fischer's affection for them. The *Legends* have been well served in the past, and Fischer's version is every bit as idiomatic and better recorded. Now reissued in Universal's 'Penguin ✿ Collection' at mid-price, this recording remains a top recommendation.

Scherzo capriccioso, Op. 66; Slavonic Dances, Opp. 46/1, 3 & 7; 72/2 & 8

(M) **(*) DG (IMS) (ADD) 447 434-2. BPO, Karajan – BRAHMS: *8 Hungarian Dances* ***

Virtuoso performances from Karajan which remain stylish because of the superbly polished ensemble. The *Scherzo capriccioso* is exhilarating, but the lilt of the lyrical secondary tune does seem a trifle calculated. However, coupled with eight of the Brahms *Hungarian Dances*, this reissue certainly shows the Karajan/BPO combination in dazzling form.

Serenade for Strings in E, Op. 22

(M) **(*) Decca (ADD) 470 262-2. ASMF, Marriner – GRIEG: *Holberg Suite*; TCHAIKOVSKY: *Serenade* ***

(BB) **(*) Naxos 8.550419. Capella Istropolitana, Krček – SUK: *Serenade* ***

Serenade for Strings in E; Serenade for Wind in D min.

☛ *** ASV CDCOE 801. COE, Schneider

*** Ph. (IMS) (ADD) 400 020-2. ASMF, Marriner

Serenade for Strings; Serenade for Wind; Miniatures, Op. 74a

(BB) *** Discover DICD 920135. Virtuosi di Praga, Vlček

The young players of the Chamber Orchestra of Europe give winningly warm and fresh performances of Dvořák's *Serenades*, vividly caught in the ASV recording.

Marriner's Philips performances are direct without loss of warmth, with speeds ideally chosen, refined yet spontaneous-sounding; in the *Wind Serenade* the Academy produce beautifully sprung rhythms, and the recording has a fine sense of immediacy.

Marriner's 1970 Decca (originally Argo) account of the *Serenade* is very richly textured, almost velvety, which some may find a bit too indulgent for the innocent simplicity of the music. But after a slightly mannered start, it is hard not to respond to such beguiling and engaging playing. The sound remains rich and full in this 'Legends' transfer, and both couplings are first class.

The wind players of the Virtuosi di Praga give a bright, idiomatic performance of Opus 44, using characteristically reedy tones. The *String Serenade* is done with equal understanding, though the recording catches an edge on high violins. The rare *Miniatures* for string trio provides an attractive makeweight. An excellent bargain in full, bright sound.

Fine playing from the Capella Istropolitana on Naxos, and flexible direction from Jaroslav Krček. His pacing is not quite as sure as in the delightful Suk coupling, and the *Adagio* could flow with a stronger current, but this is still an enjoyable and well-recorded performance.

Christopher Warren-Green's rather languorous approach to the work for strings verges dangerously upon the sentimental and, despite glowing sound and fine playing from the Philharmonia strings and wind alike, neither *Serenade* is as effectively characterized as the competition.

Serenade for Wind in D min., Op. 44

☛ (N) *** Arthaus **DVD** 100 725. Members of BPO Wind (V/D: Klaus Lindemann) (with BEETHOVEN: *Octet in E flat, Op. 103* ***)

(M) *** CRD (ADD) CRD 3410. Nash Ens. – KROMMER: *Octet-Partitas* ***

(BB) *** Naxos 8.554173. Oslo PO Wind Soloists – ENESCU: *Dixtuor*; JANACEK: *Mládi* ***

(**(*)) Testament mono SBT 1180. L. Bar. Ens., Haas – MOZART: *Serenades 11 & 12* (**(*))

The blending of the Berlin Philharmonic Wind is richly urbane, but this does not mean their performance of Dvořák's delightful *Serenade* is in any way lacking in vitality and spirit; indeed, the *Allegro molto* finale is irresistibly zestful, bubbling over with bravura. The Beethoven *Wind Octet* is rightly treated in a more robust fashion, presented with the freshness of a masterpiece, and there is wonderful geniality in the *Menuetto* (taken at a fair lick) and much infectious virtuosity (especially from the horns) in the *Presto* finale. The ensemble is recorded within the Jaspissaal of the Neue Kammern (new chambers) of the summer palace of Frederick the Great in Potsdam-Sanssouci, which is a visual delight and has a superb acoustic for a wind ensemble: the sound is in every way first class. The camera follows individual players and the whole ensemble in alternation and is usually just where you would want it to be.

The Nash Ensemble can hold their own with the competition in the *D minor Serenade*, and their special claim tends to be the coupling, a Krommer rarity that is well worth hearing. The CRD version of the Dvořák is very well recorded and the playing is very fine indeed, robust yet sensitive to colour, and admirably spirited.

The Oslo wind soloists on Naxos give us a genuine bargain. Here is a performance of real quality that can stand alongside the finest on offer. Crisp rhythms predominate, and a good sense of line and tonal finesse. These artists recorded this repertoire on the Victoria label in the early 1990s under a conductor. These are different and better accounts in every way. No need to hesitate.

Karl Haas's preference for fast speeds and metrical rhythms is well illustrated in this reading of Dvořák's *Wind Serenade*, in which the opening march has more of a military flavour than usual. As a generous supplement to Mozart's two great serenades for wind octet, this makes an ideal coupling of three of the greatest of all wind works, performed by an ensemble that included some of the finest British players of the post-war period, including Dennis Brain, Frederick Thurston and Terence Macdonagh. Vivid, immediate sound, well transferred.

Slavonic Dances 1–16, Op. 46/1–8; Op. 72/1–8

🔑 *** Teldec 8573 81038-2. COE, Harnoncourt

*** Ph. **SACD** (compatible) 470 601-2; CD 464 601-2. Budapest Festival O, I. Fischer

(M) *** DG (ADD) 457 712-2. Bav. RSO, Kubelik

❁ (M) *** Sony **SACD** SS7208; SBK 48161. Cleveland O, Szell

(BB) **(*) Warner Apex (ADD) 0927 48999-2. Czech PO, Neumann

(M) **(*) Chan. 6641. RSNO, Järvi

Harnoncourt's excitingly uninhibited new set of the *Slavonic Dances*, with the Chamber Orchestra of Europe, combines great exuberance and virtuosity with vivid colouring. Harnoncourt's direction has tremendous zest and vitality. The *Dumka* character of Op. 46/2 is spectacularly caught, moving from a relaxed lyrical charm and warmly flexible phrasing to spontaneously hot-blooded bursts of energy, with the trombones electrifyingly unleashed. The delicacy of the string and woodwind playing in No. 6 of the first set is particularly beguiling, as is the seductive rubato at the opening of Op. 72/2. But even here the relaxation of the shapely phrasing is underpinned by an inherent vitality, with the last two chords given a firm finality.

Not surprisingly the playing of the Budapest Festival Orchestra under Iván Fischer is attractively idiomatic and the Philips recording is first class in every way, richer and more natural than the Teldec sound for Harnoncourt. It sounds even finer on SACD. If by the side of Harnoncourt the performances seem comparatively easy-going, they are certainly not without moments of brilliance, even if they lack the sheer zest which makes the COE playing so compelling. But those who find Harnoncourt too rashly uninhibited will find this a mellower but satisfying alternative set, beautifully played and even more idiomatic in feeling. The recording is also available in surround sound compatible CD.

Kubelik's set, now issued as one of DG's 'Originals', offers polished, sparkling orchestral playing. The sound has greater refinement and a rather wider range of dynamic than the competing Sony disc and for that reason many will choose it in preference to Szell, for Kubelik has a very special feeling for Dvořák, and the playing of the Bavarian orchestra brings a thrilling virtuosity and a special panache of its own.

In Szell's exuberant, elegant and marvellously played set of the *Slavonic Dances* the balance is close (which means pianissimos fail to register) but the charisma of the playing is unforgettable and, for all the racy exuberance, one senses a predominant feeling of affection and elegance. The warm acoustics of Severance Hall ensure the consistency of the orchestral sound. This is also available on one of Sony's new Super Audio CDs, which require a special CD player. The sound is enhanced, with a much greater warmth in the middle and bass, and a pleasing ambience.

Neumann's (originally Teldec) set dates from 1972. He was to re-record the *Slavonic Dances* later for Decca with the same orchestra in Phase 4, but the earlier set is preferable. The Czech Philharmonic bring a special idiomatic quality to these dances, which are vivaciously played with convincingly flexible rubato, and the recording is characteristic of Telefunken's bright-eyed analogue presentation. Not a first choice, but excellent value at Apex price.

Järvi undoubtedly has the measure of this repertoire and he secures brilliant and responsive playing from the RSNO. The recording, made in the SNO Centre, Glasgow, has the orchestra set back in an acoustic of believable depth, but the upper strings are brightly lit and the fortissimos bring some loss of body and a degree of hardness on top, so that after a while the ear tends to tire.

Slavonic Dances 1–8 & 15, Op. 46/1–8; Op. 72/7

(**N**) (B) *** Australian Decca Eloquence (ADD) 476 2742. LSO, Martinon – MASSENET: *Le Cid*; MEYERBEER: *Les Patineurs* *** ❁

An exuberantly vivacious collection of the *Slavonic Dances*, with Martinon adding a touch of Gallic wit to make these performances unique in every way. Full, warm sound from 1959, making this a fine bonus to the outstanding Massenet/ Meyerbeer coupling.

(i) ***Slavonic Dances 1, 3 & 8, Op. 46/1, 3 & 8; 9 & 10, Op. 72/1–2;*** (ii) ***Slavonic Rhapsody 3, Op. 45/3***

(**N**) (B) *** Decca (ADD) 476 2453. (i) Israel PO, Kertész; (ii) Detroit SO, Dorati – ENESCU: *Romanian Rhapsody I*; SMETANA: *Má Vlast: Vltava*, etc. ***

As in the Smetana items, Kertész generates playing that is irresistible in its idiomatic vivacity. The furiants go like the wind, but Kertész maintains the underlying lyricism of the music. The 1962 recording is warm and exceptionally vivid, and this coupling was rightly regarded as a classic in its day. The recording quality is obviously more refined in Dorati's *Slavonic Rhapsody* from 1979, and there is much to enjoy in this highly sympathetic and colourful performance which makes a fine bonus.

Slavonic Dances 1, 3, 8-10

(M) **(*) Decca (ADD) 467 122-2. VPO, Reiner – BRAHMS: *Hungarian Dances*. STRAUSS: *Death and Transfiguration; Till Eulenspiegel* **(*)

Reiner's way with Dvořák is indulgent but has plenty of sparkle, and the VPO are clearly enjoying themselves; any reservations about the conductor's idiosyncrasies are minor when the playing is so vivacious. Good (1960) recording and splendid Strauss couplings make this disc worth considering.

(i) 3 Slavonic Rhapsodies, Op. 45; (ii) Rhapsody in A min., Op. 14

(BB) *** Naxos 8.550610. Slovak PO, (i) Košler; (ii) Pešek

Dvořák's three *Slavonic Rhapsodies* of 1878 are much more like symphonic poems without a programme and, while overflowing with characteristic ideas and colourful scoring, they are also loosely constructed and melodramatic. But it is the earlier *Rhapsody in A minor* that is the most ambitious work here. Libor Pešek's performance is splendid, with a vigorous response from the orchestra, who even bring off the bombastic, patriotic coda. This is every bit as enjoyable as the Op. 45 *Rhapsodies*, although it is not as sophisticated as No. 3. This Naxos collection would be recommendable even if it cost far more.

Slavonic Rhapsody 1, Op. 45

(BB) *** Warner Apex (ADD) 0927 48752-2. Czech PO, Neumann – FUCIK: *The Bear with the Sore Head*, etc. ***

This excellent version of Dvořák's charming *Slavonic Rhapsody No. 1* makes an intelligent fill-up for a stimulating programme of music by one of the composer's pupils, Julius Fučik.

Suite in A, Op. 98b

(M) (***) Sup. mono SU 1924-2 001. Czech PO, Sejna – MARTINU: *Concerto for Double String Orchestra*, etc. (***)

A lovely performance of the beautiful *A major Suite*, recorded in mono in 1956; but the real attraction on this disc is the Martinů pieces – especially the *Third Symphony* – which are very special.

Symphonic Variations

*** Australian Decca Eloquence (ADD) 467 608-2. LSO, Kertész – BRAHMS: *Haydn Variations* ***

Kertész's account of the underrated *Symphonic Variations* is outstanding, with the conductor bringing out all the Brahmsian overtones as well as the Czech composer's freshness of spirit. The 1970s recording remains vivid and full, and with two excellent couplings this is certainly a desirable CD.

SYMPHONIES

Symphonies 1–9

(M) *** Chan. 9991 (6). SNO, Järvi

(N) (B) *** Sup. SU 3802-2 (6). Prague RSO, Vladimir Valek

Symphonies 1–9; American Suite; Carnival Overture; Czech Suite; Overtures: My Home; Othello; In Nature's Realm; Scherzo capriccioso; The Wild Dove

(BB) **(*) Virgin 5 61853-2 (8). RLPO, or Czech PO, Pešek

Symphonies 1–9; Overtures: Carnival; In Nature's Realm; My Home. Scherzo capriccioso

❂ (B) *** Decca (ADD) 430 046-2 (6). LSO, Kertész

Symphonies 1–9; Overture: Carnival. Scherzo capriccioso; The Wood Dove

(B) **(*) DG 463 158-2 (6). BPO, Kubelik

Now reissued at mid-price, Järvi's Chandos set makes a clear first choice for those wanting first-class digital recordings of these symphonies, the sound full and naturally balanced. There are no fillers, as with Kertész on Decca (and there would have been room for some on the first, second and sixth CDs), but each symphony can now be heard without a break,

and Järvi is a consistently persuasive Dvořákian.

In the bargain range, the Supraphon box is very welcome when, with refined, finely detailed recording, it makes a formidable rival to the long-established Kertész, LSO set on Decca. Valek's preference is for brisk speeds which yet allow ample lift to Czech dance-rhythms. Even with swift pacing in opening allegros, Valek at once keeps the tempo steady while allowing a more expressive style in the lyrical themes than Kertész tended to do. Helped by clean, well-balanced recording, this goes with admirably clear textures, even in the heaviest tuttis. Slow movements too are affectionately played, even with more flowing speeds than Kertész's, with delectable pointing of detail. Throughout all these performances, there is a natural, idiomatic feeling of players tackling works they already know well, even in the rarer early symphonies. The only seriously questionable tempo is in the first movement of No. 6, which is on the slow side, but there an initial heaviness quickly evaporates when the playing is so crisp and well sprung. Nos. 5 and 7 gain in many ways from having been recorded live in the Rudolfinum in Prague, but there is no lack of tension in any of these performances, whether recorded live or in the studio.

For those not wanting to go to the expense of the digital Chandos/Järvi set, István Kertész's bargain box is first choice among the remaining collections of Dvořák symphonies. The CD transfers are of Decca's best quality, full-bodied and vivid, with a fine ambient effect. It was Kertész who first revealed the full potential of the early symphonies, and his readings gave us fresh insights into these often inspired works. To fit the symphonies and orchestral works onto six CDs, some mid-work breaks have proved unavoidable; but the set remains a magnificent memorial to a conductor who died sadly young.

Kubelik's set from the late 1960s and early 1970s has much to recommend it, first and foremost being the glorious playing of the Berlin Philharmonic and the natural idiomatic warmth Kubelik brings to his music-making. He seems less convinced by the earlier symphonies, and in No. 3 there is an element of routine, something which does not happen with Kertész on Decca. In spite of some idiosyncratic touches, however, Kubelik achieves glowing performances of Nos. 6–9, and especially No. 7; in No. 8 he is also more compelling than his Decca competitor. The remastered DG sound is impressively wide-ranging and is especially fine in the last (and greatest) three symphonies. Many will also be glad to have his memorable account of *The Wood Dove*.

Symphony 1; A Hero's Song, Op. 111

*** Chan. 8597. SNO, Järvi

Symphony 1; Legends, Op. 59/1-5

(BB) *** Naxos 8.550266. Slovak PO or Slovak RSO, Gunzenhauser

The first of Dvořák's nine symphonies is on the long-winded side. Yet whatever its structural weaknesses, it is full of colourful and memorable ideas, often characteristic of the mature composer. Järvi directs a warm, often impetuous performance, with rhythms invigoratingly sprung in the fast movements and with the slow movement more persuasive than in previous recordings. The recording is warmly atmospheric in typical Chandos style.

Though on a super-bargain label, the competing Bratislava version rivals Järvi's Chandos disc both as a performance and in sound. The ensemble of the Slovak Philharmonic is rather crisper, and the recording, full and atmospheric, has detail less obscured by reverberation. The first five of Dvořák's ten *Legends* make a generous coupling: colourful miniatures, colourfully played.

Symphony 2 in B flat, Op. 4; Legends, Op. 59/6–10
(BB) *** Naxos 8.550267. Slovak PO or Slovak RSO, Gunzenhauser

Symphony 2; Slavonic Rhapsody 3 in A flat, Op. 45
**(*) Chan. 8589. SNO, Järvi

With speeds more expansive than those of Neeme Järvi, his Chandos rival, Gunzenhauser gives a taut, beautifully textured account, very well played and recorded, clearly preferable in every way, even making no allowance for price. The completion of the set of *Legends* makes a generous coupling (73 minutes).

Järvi's performance, characteristically warm and urgent, is let down by the reverberant Chandos sound, here missing the necessary sharpness of focus, so that the tangy Czech flavour of the music loses some of its bite. The *Slavonic Rhapsody* is done with delicious point and humour, with the sound back to Chandos's normal high standard.

Symphony 3 in E flat, Op. 10; Carnival Overture, Op. 92; Symphonic Variations, Op. 78
*** Chan. 8575. SNO, Järvi

Järvi's is a highly persuasive reading, not ideally sharp of rhythm in the first movement but totally sympathetic. The recording is well up to the standards of the house, and the fill-ups are particularly generous.

Symphonies 3; 6 in D, Op. 60
(BB) *** Naxos 8.550268. Slovak PO, Gunzenhauser

These exhilarating performances of the *Third* and *Sixth Symphonies* are well up to the standard of earlier records in this splendid Naxos series. Gunzenhauser's pacing is admirably judged through both works, and rhythms are always lifted. Excellent, vivid recording in the warm acoustics of the Bratislava Concert Hall.

Symphony 4 in D min., Op. 13; (i) Biblical Songs, Op. 99
*** Chan. 8608. SNO, Järvi, (i) with Rayner Cook

Järvi's affectionate reading of this early work brings out the Czech flavours in Dvořák's inspiration and makes light of the continuing Wagner influences, notably the echoes of *Tannhäuser* in the slow movement. This is a performance to win converts to an often underrated work. The recording is well up to the Chandos standard.

Symphonies 4–6; Overtures: Carnival; In Nature's Realm. Scherzo Capriccioso
☞ (B) *** Double Decca (ADD) 473 798-2. LSO, Kertész

Kertész gives a good dramatic account of the *Fourth Symphony*, accepting the Wagner crib in the slow movement and making the most of the Scherzo with its attractive lolloping theme, which unfortunately gives way to a blatant march trio with far too many cymbal crashes in it. No. 5, with its pastoral atmosphere and further echoes of Wagner, is particularly successful and full of vitality. No. 6 clearly reflects the influence of Brahms, particularly of the *Second Symphony*. Not only the shape of the themes but the actual layout of the first movement has strong affinities with the Brahmsian model, but Kertész's performance effectively underlines the individuality of the writing as well. Outstanding versions of the

dashing *Carnival Overture*, an equally sparkling *Scherzo capriccioso* and the colourful *In Nature's Realm* make admirable bonuses.

Symphonies 4; 8 in G, Op. 33
(BB) **(*) Naxos 8.550269. Slovak PO, Gunzenhauser

Gunzenhauser's *Fourth* is very convincing. In his hands the fine lyrical theme of the first movement certainly blossoms, and the relative lack of weight in the orchestral textures brings distinct benefit in the Scherzo. The slow movement, too, is lyrical without too much Wagnerian emphasis. The naturally sympathetic orchestral playing helps to make the *Eighth* a refreshing experience, even though the first two movements are rather relaxed and without the impetus of the finest versions. The digital sound is excellent, vivid and full, with a natural concert-hall ambience.

Symphony 5 in F, Op. 76; Othello Overture; Scherzo capriccioso
☞ ❀ (BB) *** EMI Encore 5 85702-2. Oslo PO, Jansons

Jansons directs a radiant performance of this delectable symphony, and the EMI engineers put a fine bloom on the Oslo sound. With its splendid encores, equally exuberant in performance, this 1989 reissue remains one of the finest Dvořák CDs in the catalogue and is now in addition incredibly inexpensive.

Symphony 5 in F, Op. 76; The Water Goblin, Op. 107
*** Chan. 8552. SNO, Järvi

Järvi is most effective in moulding the structure, subtly varying tempo between sections to smooth over the often abrupt links. His persuasiveness in the slow movement, relaxed but never sentimental, brings radiant playing from the SNO, and Czech dance-rhythms are sprung most infectiously, leading to an exhilarating close to the whole work, simulating the excitement of a live performance.

Symphonies 5; 7 in D min., Op. 70
(BB) *** Naxos 8.550270. Slovak PO, Gunzenhauser

Gunzenhauser's coupling is recommendable even without the price advantage. The beguiling opening of the *Fifth*, with its engaging Slovak wind solos, has plenty of atmosphere, and the reading generates a natural lyrical impulse. The *Seventh*, spontaneous throughout, brings an eloquent *Poco adagio*, a lilting Scherzo and a finale that combines an expansive secondary theme with plenty of excitement and impetus.

Symphonies 5; 7–8; 9 (New World)
(BB) *** Decca Eloquence (ADD) 467 472-2 (2). LSO, Kertész

The four most popular (and, of course, most recorded) symphonies are offered on a budget two-disc Eloquence set (which also means limited documentation). Kertész's performances are again direct and dramatic and are very well played. Curiously, the *Fifth*, with its beautiful slow movement and glorious bouncing Scherzo, involves duplication, for it is also included on the Double Decca above. The voltage is lower in Kertész's *Seventh*, yet there is no lack of warmth, and the *Eighth* is particularly successful, freshly spontaneous throughout. The *New World* capped his cycle impressively, still one of the finest performances on disc, with a most exciting first movement (exposition repeat included) and a *Largo* bringing playing of hushed intensity to make one hear the music with new ears. The remastered recordings from the 1960s still sound very well indeed.

Symphony 6 in D, Op. 60.
(N) (BB) **(*) LSO Live LSO 0059. LSO, C. Davis
(M) **(*) Orfeo C 55201B. Bav. RSO, Kubelik – JANACEK: *Sinfonietta* **(*)

Symphony 6 in D, Op. 60; The Wood Dove, Op. 110
*** Chan. 9170. Czech PO, Bělohlávek

Bělohlávek conducts a glowing performance of No. 6, rich in Brahmsian and Czech pastoral overtones, helped by satisfyingly full and immediate Chandos sound. This easily takes precedence over the Järvi version (CHAN 8350). His reading of the late symphonic poem is comparably warm and idiomatic in a relaxed way.

The LSO Live disc of No. 6 makes a welcome supplement to Davis's accounts of the last three symphonies on the same label. Recorded at the Barbican in 2004, It is an admirable and infectiously spirited performance. Sir Colin Davis and his fine players are wonderfully idiomatic and offer a performance of exceptional clarity of detail. At the very start the syncopated thrumming on horns and violas has every note sharply defined, where most recordings make it an indistinctly defined sound. The clarity is mainly due to Davis's cleanly focused reading, but is also a question of the Barbican acoustic, here sounding rather drier than on some other LSO Live discs; it is rather closely balanced and does not leave the orchestral textures quite enough space to open out. For the Scherzo, Davis adopts a fastish tempo, and the snapping rhythms come out with extra sharpness, leading to a light, delicate account of the Trio section. In the finale he brings out the warmly Brahmsian qualities. Not a first choice perhaps, but a stimulating one.

Kubelik's broadcast account from 1971 is eminently satisfactory, straightforward and idiomatic, though not superior to his Berlin version. But readers who would welcome this particular coupling need not really hesitate. It is musically satisfying and well recorded.

Symphonies 6; 8 in G, Op. 88
*** DG 469 046-2. VPO, Chung

The first movement of No. 6 surpasses in breadth and power (and in the natural way in which it unfolds) almost anything between the *C major (Great)* of Schubert and the *Second* of Brahms, the shadows of both of which are clearly visible. It is luminous and innocent, as is the *Eighth*, another glowing and life-enhancing score, generously coupled here. Both symphonies are served supremely well by Chung and the Vienna orchestra and the DG engineers. It is certainly the best we have had since the famous Decca set from Kertész (with the Breugel covers!).

Symphony 7 in D min., Op. 70
(BB) *** LSO 0014. LSO, C. Davis

Sir Colin Davis's live recording of the *Seventh* with the LSO was made at the Barbican in March 2001, a powerful reading, a shade freer and more warmly expressive than his earlier (1975) version for Philips with the Concertgebouw Orchestra (see below). Though each movement is a degree broader than before, over a minute longer in each of the first two movements, that does not bring either a slackening of tension this time nor an inflation. Rather the opposite when, with more immediate sound, the power and expressive range are intensified, culminating in a towering account of the finale which, unlike many, here emerges as a fully satisfying conclusion, after the masterly originality of the earlier movements.

(i) *Symphony 7 in D min., Op. 70;* (ii) *Carnival Overture, Op. 92;* (i; iii) *Romance in F min., for Violin & Orchestra, Op. 11*
(N) (BB) ** Warner Apex 2564 61427-2. (i) Philh. O, Inbal; (ii) LPO, Conlon; (iii) Zehetmair

Inbal's *Seventh* is a nicely relaxed, idiomatic reading, the Scherzo gently lilting and the finale gathering force at the end; it was regarded as one of the finest of his cycle. However, in this strongly competitive field, there are other, more distinctive and characterful versions and, despite the enjoyable couplings, this version is only fair value.

Symphony 7 in D min., Op. 70; Nocturne for Strings, Op. 40; The Water Goblin, Op. 107
*** Chan. 9391. Czech PO, Bělohlávek

Bělohlávek knows better than his direct rivals how to draw out idiomatic warmth from the Czech Philharmonic, and he is helped by satisfyingly full and glowing Chandos sound. Fresh, well paced and intelligently shaped, this is a thoroughly recommendable reading, paired with an excellent account of *The Water Goblin* and the eloquent, poignant *Nocturne for Strings*. In this spacious reading of the *Nocturne* the Czech strings produce ravishing sounds, and *The Water Goblin* is similarly relaxed and warm rather than sharply dramatic.

Symphonies 7; 8 in G, Op. 88
(M) *** DG (IMS) (ADD) 457 902-2. BPO, Kubelik
(B) **(*) Sony (ADD) SBK 67174. Philh. O, A. Davis

Kubelik's glowing approach to the *Seventh Symphony* is essentially expressive, but his romanticism never obscures the overall structural plan and there is no lack of vitality and sparkle. The acccount of the *Eighth* is a shade straighter; it is discussed below in its alternative coupling with the *New World Symphony*.

Andrew Davis's comparatively lightweight account of the *Seventh* has an attractive lyrical freshness; the *Eighth* is much more compulsive and dramatically spontaneous, making the most of the music's dynamic contrasts, with high drama in the climaxes of the *Adagio*, which also has plenty of expressive feeling, and a sense of vibrant energy throughout the outer movements. The finale is thrilling (although there is some raucous tone from the brass) and there is no doubt about the individuality of the reading as a whole.

Symphonies 7–9; Overture Carnival
(B) **(*) Sony (ADD) 517 495-2 (2). Cleveland O, Szell (with SMETANA: *Bartered Bride Overture; String Quartet 1 (From my Life)*: orchestral version, arr. Szell)

Symphonies (i) 7; (ii) 8; 9 (New World); Overture: Carnival; Scherzo capriccioso
(B) **(*) EMI double forte (ADD) 5 68628-2 (2). (i) LPO; (ii) Philh. O; Giulini

(i) *Symphonies 7–9;* (ii) *Romance in F min., Op. 11.* (i) *Symphonic Variations*
(B) *** CfP 2-CD 575 7612 (2). (i) LPO, Mackerras; (ii) Gonley, ECO)

Symphonies (i) 7–8; (ii) 9 (New World); (i) Symphonic Variations, Op. 78
(B) *** Ph. (ADD) Duo 438 347-2 (2). (i) LSO; (ii) Concg. O; C. Davis

At bargain price Mackerras's tryptich offers performances of all three symphonies which are among the finest ever, with first-rate digital recording throughout. With Mackerras, tragedy is not uppermost in the *D minor Seventh Symphony*, but rather Dvořákian openness. After a hushed, mysterious opening, it is the lilting joy of the inspiration which makes the performance so winning. No. 8 easily matches its companion in effervescence. The colour and atmosphere of the piece are brought out vividly and with a lightness of touch that makes most rivals seem heavy-handed. Mackerras takes a warmly expansive view of the *New World*, remarkable for a hushed and intense account of the slow movement and superb playing from the LPO. In the *Symphonic Variations*, too, his relaxed treatment is consistently winning. Stephanie Gonley, the leader of the ECO (who take over for this one item), is a sensitive and characterful soloist in the haunting *Romance in F minor*, originally coupled with the *Legends* and added for this generous and highly recommendable reissue.

Szell's performances of the last three symphonies come from the late 1950s. The recordings have a characteristically forward balance; although brightly lit, the sound is full-bodied in its current transfer, with the Severance Hall ambience well caught. Throughout, the playing combines polish with vitality; hardly ever does one feel that the characteristic Szell discipline interferes with the music's spontaneity. No. 7 has a strong forward impulse. It may be lacking in geniality but it has plenty of character: the slow movement has a strong foward impulse and there is no lack of sparkle elsewhere. No. 8 is superbly played, the pick of the bunch, and no one should be disappointed with the *New World* with taut outer movements, a responsive yet refined *Largo* and an attractive rhythmic lilt in the Scherzo. The *Carnival Overture* (from 1963) is predictably super-brilliant, as is Smetana's *Bartered Bride Overture*. The surprise bonus is Szell's fully scored orchestral transcription of Smetana's *First String Quartet*, which is made to sound more like a symphony. It is played spontaneously and with much zest and brings a passionately felt slow movement. The 1949 mono recording is a bit fierce in *fortissimo* but has supporting weight and warmth. The result is memorable.

Giulini is at his finest in both the *Seventh* and the *New World*. In the *D minor Symphony* he and the LPO players really make the music sing, and the Dvořákian sunshine keeps breaking out. The glowing (1976) recording encourages rounded textures and rounded phrases. No. 8 (like the *New World*), recorded with the Philharmonia 14 years earlier, brings a similar mellow approach, but the result is comparatively disappointing. Giulini's speeds are on the slow side, especially in the *Adagio* and rather bland *Allegretto*, while the finale opens in a somewhat subdued fashion. Frankly this does not altogether come off. The *New World* is a different matter, refreshingly direct. The remastering gives the sound plenty of warmth and projection.

Sir Colin Davis's Philips performances of Nos. 7 and 8, with their bracing rhythmic flow and natural feeling for Dvořákian lyricism, are appealingly direct yet have plenty of life and urgency. In the *New World*, however, the very directness has its drawbacks. The cor anglais solo in the slow movement brings an appealing simplicity. The reading is completely free from egotistical eccentricity and, with beautiful orchestral playing throughout, this is enjoyable in its way. The set is made the more attractive by the inclusion of the *Symphonic Variations* – one of Dvořák's finest works, much underrated by the public – and here Davis's performance has striking freshness. The remastering of all the recordings is very successful.

Symphonies 7; 9 (New World)
(B) *(**) RCA Double 74321 68013-2 (2). Chicago SO, Levine

Levine's virile account of the *Seventh Symphony* is hampered by a sound-balance that makes tuttis seem aggressive (particularly the slow movement climax) and the upper strings thin and febrile. The reading itself is direct and well played but lacks charm: the sparkle of the Scherzo is there, but Levine's inflexion of the main idea is less than ideal. The *New World Symphony* is similarly problematic. The reading is lively and exciting, with some excellent playing, but in spite of a fresh transfer the digital recording is rough, again with an edge on the violins and internal congestion in tuttis.

Symphony 8 in G, Op. 88
(N) (**(*)) BBC (ADD) BBCL 4159-2 (2). Philh. O, Giulini – BRUCKNER: *Symphony 8* **(*); ROSSINI: *Semiramide Overture* ***
(N) (***) BBC mono BBCL 4154-2. RPO, Beecham – SIBELIUS: *Symphony 2* (***)
(BB) *(*) Warner Apex 0929 48732-2. NYPO, Masur – JANACEK: *Sinfonietta* **(*)

Symphony 8 in G; The Golden Spinning Wheel
**(*) Chan. 9048. Czech PO, Bělohlávek

(i) Symphony 8; Nocturne for Strings; (ii) Overtures: Carnival; In Nature's Realm
(M) *** Chan. 7123. (i) LPO; (ii) Ulster O; Handley

Symphony 8; Slavonic Dances 3, Op. 46/3; 10, Op. 72/2
(B) *** EMI double forte (ADD) 5 69509-2 (2). Cleveland O, Szell – BEETHOVEN: *Piano Concerto 5*, etc. ***

Symphony 8; The Wood Dove, Op. 110
*** Chan. 8666. SNO, Järvi

Järvi's highly sympathetic account of the *Eighth* underlines the expressive lyricism of the piece, the rhapsodic freedom of invention rather than any symphonic tautness, with the SNO players reacting to his free rubato and affectionate moulding of phrase with collective spontaneity. The warm Chandos sound has plenty of bloom, with detail kept clear, and is very well balanced.

Handley's admirable (1983) recording has an ongoing freshness, and its affectionate touches – as in the way Handley lilts the glorious string-melody at the centre of the Scherzo – are subtle, not egocentric. Indeed, with first-class playing from the LPO, the life and spontaneity of the performance are most winning. The *Nocturne* makes a most agreeable encore and is also beautifully played. The Ulster Orchestra takes over in the two overtures, both most attractively done. The recording contributes, of course: it is of Chandos's usual high standard.

Szell's reading of the *Eighth Symphony* is strong and committed, consistent from first to last, and marvellously played. With full-bodied (1970) sound, it remains both distinctive and very enjoyable. The pair of *Slavonic Dances* are mellower than the earlier, complete set on Sony but are still a fine example of Cleveland orchestral bravura. The transfers are first class – this is a richer sound than on many records from this source.

Bělohlávek directs the Czech Philharmonic in a warmly idiomatic reading of No. 8. He is helped by a satisfyingly beefy recording with plenty of bloom that yet focuses the players more sharply than most recordings with this orchestra. Though basic speeds are on the fast side, Bělohlávek is never reticent over giving full expansiveness to linking passages, so adding to the warmth. The longest and richest of

Dvořák's late symphonic poems is given similarly idiomatic treatment – but in a version with cuts, a considerable drawback.

Giulini's concert performance comes from a 1963 Prom. The warm acoustic of the Albert Hall adds to this spontaneous and inspiriting reading. Rossini's *Semiramide Overture* comes from later in the same year and makes a sparkling *bonne-bouche*. This is a very enjoyable account, although the recording does not quite match the finest studio versions.

Beecham's account comes from an RPO concert of 1959. He had a strong feeling for Dvořák, and the playing here is both lively and cultured, not quite as electrifying as the Sibelius with which it was originally coupled in the 1960s but nonetheless pretty memorable. A fine momento of Beecham and his orchestra in this repertoire. The transfer does not reproduce the earlier HMV ALP issue but is a new one from the original tapes.

Masur's 1993 account of the *Eighth Symphony* is very well played and recorded, but it lacks real vitality and character. An element of blandness creeps in from time to time, and the slow movement fails to get to the heart of the score, despite some beautiful playing. The finale, too, lacks adrenalin.

Symphonies 8 in G; 9 (New World)
⊶ *** Ph. **SACD** 470 617-2; 464 640-2. Budapest Festival O, I. Fischer
*** Sony (ADD) **SACD** SS 89413. Cleveland O, Szell
(M) *** DG (ADD) 447 412-2. BPO, Kubelik
(N) (BB) *(**) EMI Encore 5 86419-2. Phd. O, Sawallisch

A superb new coupling of Dvořák's two greatest symphonies goes straight to the top of the list. Needless to say, Iván Fischer includes the exposition repeat of the *New World*, and both performances are uncommonly imaginative and marvellously played. Fischer's readings combine freshness with refinement and thoughtfulness with passion, and he has a splendid ear for detail. One notes in particularly the magical *pianissimo* at the reprise of the main theme of the finale of the *G major Symphony* on the strings, with the following passage touchingly nostalgic, to match a similar delicacy of feeling at the gentle close of the *Largo* of the *New World*. This is ravishingly played, with a meltingly simple cor anglais solo. Yet the brass can blaze brilliantly when required and the Budapest trombones have a splendidly exuberant rasp. The recording is of Philips's very finest and also available in surround sound on compatible CD.

Szell's Cleveland recordings were made in 1959 when the Cleveland Orchestra was at its very peak. But they have never sounded as richly expansive on record as they do now. The Sony SACD remastering has not been able to alter the relatively close-up sound-balance, but the dynamic range is widened, the brilliance retained without edge, and (especially in No. 8) the middle and bass fills out appreciably within the attractive Severance Hall acoustic. Szell obviously loved the *G major Symphony* in particular, for he recorded it three times, and this is by far the finest of the three. He opens the first movement comparatively gently, but with an affectionate, expressive warmth, and he observes the exposition repeat. The slow movement is glorious: passionate, but also lyrically relaxed, not least in the closing pages, with the orchestral detail always glowing. The Scherzo is again relaxed, but in the Trio the violins take over the lovely melody from the oboe to sweep up exultantly, and with an unashamed portamento, to the climax. The trumpets announce the finale regally and the first tutti is exuberant, with rollicking horns. But again it is

the warm lyricism of the variations that is so telling, until the thrilling coda.

Szell's *New World Symphony* is vividly dramatic, combining vitality, marvellous orchestral discipline and expressive resilience. The *Largo* offers warmth and refinement and a sense of repose, the Scherzo has splendid rhythmic bite, and the finale constant exhilaration. Altogether a superb coupling.

Rafael Kubelik's performances of the last Dvořák symphonies are also among the finest ever recorded. They are superbly played, and the recordings sound admirably fresh, full yet well detailed, the ambience attractive. Kubelik's account of the *Eighth* is without personal idiosyncrasy, except for a minor indulgence for the phrasing of the glowingly lyrical string-theme in the trio of the Scherzo. The orchestral balance in the *G major Symphony* is particularly well judged. Kubelik's marvellously fresh *New World*, recorded in the Jesus-Christus-Kirche, also remains among the top recommendations, providing one does not mind the omission of the first movement's exposition repeat.

Sawallisch, on an EMI budget Encore disc, conducts as honeyed an account of the *New World* as you will find in a long list of versions. With playing from the Philadelphia Orchestra that is outstandingly refined and beautiful, this should by rights be among the most desirable of all versions – but sadly, as with Muti's Philadelphia recordings of this period, made in the intractable Memorial Hall in Fairmount Park in the late 1980s, the sound is disappointing. Sawallisch draws sweeter and more rounded tone from the players than Muti generally did, but the textures grow thick and opaque in any loud tutti. The slow movement in particular is frustrating when the lightly scored passages ravish the ear, only to give way to boomy, ill-focused pizzicati in the contrasting central section. In the *Eighth*, recorded a year later, it is disappointing to find that the playing is not so easily spontaneous-sounding. Once again Sawallisch gives a thoughtful, sympathetic reading, but the glow of enjoyment is less obvious. Additionally, the sound still presents the violins with an edge in loud tuttis which is very un-Philadelphian.

Symphony 9 in E min. (From the New World), Op. 95
*** Sony **DVD** SVD 48421. VPO, Karajan
**(*) DG 439 009-2. VPO, Karajan – SMETANA: *Vltava* **(*)
*** BBC (ADD) BBCL 4056-2. BBC SO, Kempe – BEETHOVEN: *Overture: Leonore 3.* PROKOFIEV: *The Love for Three Oranges: Suite ***
(M) *** DG 463 650-2. BPO, Fricsay – LISZT: *Les Préludes;* SMETANA: *Má Vlast: Vltava ***
(N) (B) *** RCO Live RCO 0400-2. Concg. O, Jansons
**(*) Pentatone SACD PTC 5186 019. Netherlands PO, Kreizberg – TCHAIKOVSKY: *Romeo and Juliet (Fantasy Overture)* **(*)
(M) (***) Teldec mono 8573 83025-2. Concg. O, Mengelberg – FRANCK: *Symphony in D min.* (***)
(BB) ** EMI Encore (ADD) 5 74961-2. New Philh. O, Muti – TCHAIKOVSKY: *Romeo and Juliet* **(*)
(M) ** Virgin 5 61837-2. Houston SO, Eschenbach (with TCHAIKOVSKY: *Francesca da Rimini* **)

Symphony 9; Overture Carnival
(N) (M) ***RCA **SACD** 82876 66376-2. Chicago SO, Reiner – SMETANA: *Bartered Bride Overture;* WEINBERGER: *Schwanda Polka & Fugue*

Symphony 9. Overtures: *Carnival; In Nature's Realm; Othello*

☛— (M) *** Ondine Double ODE 962-2 (2). Czech PO, Ashkenazy

Symphony 9 *(New World); Overture: Othello*
**(*) DG (IMS) 457 651-2. BPO, Abbado

Symphony 9; (ii) *Czech Suite; Prague Waltzes*
(B) *** Decca 448 245-2. (i) VPO, Kondrashin; (ii) Detroit SO, Dorati

Symphony 9; Overture: *My Home, Op. 62*
*** Chan. 8510. SNO, Järvi

(i) *Symphony 9;* **(ii)** *Serenade for Strings*
(B) **(*) Sony SBK 46331. (i) LSO, Ormandy; (ii) Munich PO, Kempe

Symphony 9; Slavonic Dances 1, 3 & 7, Op. 46/1, 3 & 7; 10 & 15, Op. 72/2 & 7
(M) *** DG (ADD) 435 590-2. BPO, Karajan

Symphony 9; Slavonic Dances 6, 8, & 10, Op. 46/6 & 8, Op. 72/2.
(BB) **(*) Warner Apex 8573 89085-2. NYPO, Masur

Symphony 9 *(New World); The Water Goblin, Op. 107*
*** Teldec 3984 25254-2. Cong. O, Harnoncourt

Karajan recorded this symphony four times with the Berlin Philharmonic (for Polydor in 1940, for Columbia, EMI, in 1958, for DG in 1964 and for EMI/HMV in 1977). This present account comes from February 1985 and is also available on a DG CD (439 009-2) (see below). At the time we thought the playing of the Vienna Philharmonic not quite as refined as the previous, Berlin version. Seeing as well as hearing this performance on DVD gives one pause. Does seeing the players and their conductor affect the listener's judgement? Whether or not it equals earlier versions, it is certainly a very fine account, its beauty of sonority is quite affecting, and the remaining movements are strikingly fresh. The sound has an impressively wide dynamic range and the visual direction keeps the eye's attention where it would be in the concert hall. At 43' 30" it is perhaps short measure, but artistically it is very satisfying and well worth the money.

Ashkenazy's Ondine recording is not only an outstanding new recommendation, but it also makes an excellent coupling, offering Dvořák's trilogy of overtures, originally conceived as a group under the title of 'Nature, Life and Love', together with his most popular symphony in a two-for-the-price-of-one package. The performances from this great Czech orchestra are excellent, conveying wonderfully the warmth and thrust of a live experience, with musicians playing their hearts out. Incidentally, Ashkenazy follows the instruction from Dvořák to ignore the first-movement exposition repeat. Textures are not ideally transparent, largely a question of the immediate recorded sound, warm rather than clear.

Recorded live, Harnoncourt's first movement, with its bold, clipped rhythms and a nice relaxation for the lyrical second group, generates plenty of excitement, with exposition repeat made part of the structure. The *Largo* by contrast is gentle, with the cor anglais solo very delicate, almost like an oboe, and with some superb *pianissimo* string-playing to follow. The Scherzo lilts as it should, and the finale is well thought out so that it moves forward strongly, yet it can look back to the composer's reprise of earlier themes with touching nostalgia. This CD is made the more attractive by the superbly atmospheric and magnetic account of *The Water Goblin*, one of Dvořák's most colourful symphonic poems.

Kempe's *New World Symphony* brings another memorable performance, dedicated, with *pianissimos* of breathtaking delicacy. In a rapt account of the slow movement, taken at a flowing speed, the opening cor anglais solo has a folk-like innocence. The other three movements have a similar Slavonic flavour, each involving dramatic extremes of dynamic, vividly caught by the BBC engineers and superbly transferred. This is a quite exceptional account, most illuminating and compelling to have appeared for some years. And while they make a curious mixture for a single disc, each of the three contrasted works on this CD have a rare intensity, coming from the two Prom concerts that Kempe conducted in August 1975 on the eve of his taking over as Chief Conductor of the BBC Symphony Orchestra in succession to Pierre Boulez.

Kondrashin's Vienna performance of the *New World Symphony* was one of Decca's first demonstration CDs. Recorded in the Sofiensaal, every detail of Dvořák's orchestration is revealed within a highly convincing perspective. Other performances may exhibit a higher level of tension but there is a natural spontaneity here. The cor anglais solo in the *Largo* is easy and songful, and the finale is especially satisfying, with the wide dynamic range adding drama and the refinement and transparency of the texture noticeably effective as the composer recalls ideas from earlier movements. The budget-priced Eclipse CD is enhanced by Dorati's bright, fresh Detroit versions of the *Czech Suite* and the even rarer *Prague Waltzes* (Viennese music with a Czech accent).

Reiner's 1957 *New World* is an essentially lyrical performance without idiosyncratic disturbances. There is no first-movement exposition repeat, but how naturally the second subject is ushered in, and how well the music flows, both here and in the *Largo*, with consistently lovely playing, specially in the rapt closing section. The Scherzo sparkles and its lilting rustic interlude is especially beguiling, while there is plenty of excitement in the finale. As with all these RCA SACD reissues, one notices the added warmth of the sound and firm but resonant bass. What makes this disc the more attractive are the fill-ups, and not just the brilliant *Carnival Overture*, which bursts with energetic orchestral bravura and yet has a ravishing Slavonic feeling in the middle section.

The *New World Symphony* issued without a coupling offers very short measure for a new CD, but this first issue on the Royal Concertgebouw's own label marked the occasion of Mariss Jansons taking over as music director, and the quality of the performance is obvious compensation, reflecting the players' response to their new leader. The slow introduction instantly conveys warmth and tension, reflecting a live occasion. Set against the helpful, open acoustic of the Concertgebouw, the results are magical, particularly in the slow movement, where the orchestra's unrivalled string section is inspired to playing of breath-taking refinement.

Fricsay's reading is unashamedly romantic and is a favourite of I.M.'s. He makes a considerable and affectionate *ritardando* at the entry of the first movement's secondary theme, but with superb playing from the Berlin Philharmonic his unashamed use of rubato and *accelerando* is managed so spontaneously that it becomes part of the structure. The great *Largo* opens gently and luminously, and is imbued throughout with tender warmth. The sparkling dance rhythms of the Scherzo are full of verve, and the finale is similarly exhilarating, with its central nostalgic interlude hardly less telling. The first-movement exposition repeat is omitted, and this remains a splendid example of Fricsay's vibrantly personal style. The recording has been vividly remastered.

Karajan's 1964 DG analogue recording has a powerful lyrical feeling and an exciting build-up of power in the outer movements. The *Largo* is played most beautifully, and Karajan lets the orchestra speak for itself, which it does, gloriously. The rustic qualities of the Scherzo are brought out affectionately, and altogether this is very rewarding. The recording is full, bright and open. This is now reissued, sounding as good as ever, coupled with five favourite *Slavonic Dances*, given virtuoso performances.

Järvi's opening introduction establishes the spaciousness of his view, with lyrical, persuasive phrasing and a very slow speed, leading into an allegro which starts relaxedly but then develops in big, dramatic contrasts. The expansiveness is underlined when the exposition repeat is observed. The *Largo* too is exceptionally spacious, with the cor anglais player taxed to the limit but effectively supported over ravishingly beautiful string-playing. The Scherzo is lilting rather than fierce, and the finale is bold and swaggering.

Abbado's opening *Othello Overture* is superbly done. In the *New World*, the Berlin Philharmonic often play gloriously, but excitement is more sporadic – welling up at the end of the first movement, and emerging throughout a sparkling account of the Scherzo. But, although beautifully played, the *Largo* is very relaxed, and the forward sweep one needs in the finale is elusive.

Kurt Masur's recording was taken from a live concert given in the Avery Fisher Hall in October 1991, and the Teldec engineers have made light of the hall's notoriously unhelpful acoustic. Though the sound is on the dry side, it not only has a fair bloom but conveys an extremely wide dynamic range. The slow movement is particularly fine, with *pianissimos* that have you catching your breath, and with Masur's very straight, simple phrasing conveying a tender intensity. Moreover, there is a precision of ensemble to rival that of a studio performance. Masur's very direct manner in the fast movements brings strong, dramatic results, but with very forward sound and the percussion standing out (the timpani almost deafening at times) the results are on the aggressive side. This is not among the warmer readings of this much-recorded work, yet with an attractive coupling of three *Slavonic Dances*, winningly done, it makes a worthwhile addition to the catalogue at its very modest cost.

The Netherlands Philharmonic (not to be confused with the Radio Orchestra) was founded as recently as 1986, a merger of the Amsterdam Philharmonic, the Utrecht Symphony and the Netherlands Chamber Orchestra. It boasts a complement of 130 players and claims to be the largest orchestral organization in the country. Jakov Kreizberg has just taken over as chief conductor, prompting the Dutch company Pentatone to make a series of recordings, including this coupling of two favourite works, not otherwise available together on a single disc. The performance of the *New World* is strong and incisive. Kreizberg takes a fresh, direct view. He eases the tempo for the haunting little flute melody of the third subject in the first movement, but that is as near to an idiosyncratic approach as he gets, and in the slow movement he chooses a very spacious, steady pacing, with extremes of dynamic very well caught by the recording and with the strings admirably refined. Crisp ensemble and articulation mark the Scherzo and finale. Those without the facility of Surround Sound will find the recording coming over at a slightly lower level than usual.

Mengelberg took up his appointment at the Amsterdam Concertgebouw in 1895, only two years after Dvořák had finished his *Symphony, From the New World*. Mengelberg gave its Amsterdam première in 1896. He conducted it with an enormous lyrical intensity, and gets such eloquent playing in these wartime performances that criticism is almost silenced. Both performances here are strongly narrative, so that they totally compel attention throughout, and the expressive self-indulgence of which his detractors complain does not unduly disturb. Such is the dramatic fire and ardour of this playing that most listeners will take his mannerisms in their stride. Mind you, he pulls the contrasting idea of the Scherzo horribly out of shape, and the end of the first movement is rather steeply faded, perhaps to avoid some blemish, but the sound has striking presence and sonority.

Under Ormandy, the playing of the LSO has life and spontaneity, and the rhythmic freshness of the Scherzo (achieved by unforced precision) is matched by the lyrical beauty of the *Largo* and the breadth and vigour of the finale. Perhaps the reading has not the individuality of the finest versions, but the sound is full and firm in the bass to support the upper range's brilliance. For coupling, we are offered an essentially mellow account of the *String Serenade*, directed by Kempe with affectionate warmth.

Muti's 1976 *New World* is a sweet and amiable performance, unsensationally attractive but hardly memorable. The recording is quite rich and smooth but makes the great cor anglais melody of the slow movement sound a little bland. The price is low but the competition is ferocious. However the Tchaikovsky coupling is very fine.

CHAMBER AND INSTRUMENTAL MUSIC

Warner 100th Anniversary Edition: (i) *Cypresses, B.152;* (ii) *Piano Quartet 2, Op. 87; Piano Quintet in A, Op. 81;* (iii) *Piano Trios 1–4 (Dumky); String Quartets:* (iv) *9 in D min., Op. 34; 10 in E flat, Op. 54;* (v) *12 (American), Op. 96;* (vi) *13 in G, Op. 106;* (v) *String Quintet in E, Op. 97;* (vii) *String Sextet in A, Op. 48*

(N) (B) ****(*)** Warner 2564 61527-2 (6). (i) New Helsinki Qt;
(ii) Schiff, Panocha Qt; (iii) Trio Fontenay; (iv) American Qt; (v) Keller Qt; (vi) Alban Berg Qt; (vii) Boston Symphony Chamber Players

A pretty good cross-section of performances here, and this box will undoubtedly give satisfaction. Certainly Schiff and the Panocha Quartet, the Trio Fontanay and the American and Alban Berg Quartets will give pleasure, and these are all among the composer's finest chamber works.

Piano Quartets 1 in D, Op. 23; 2 in E flat, Op. 87

🌎 ✪ ******* Hyp. CDA 66287. Domus

(N) ******* Australian Ph. Eloquence (ADD) 470 6622. Beaux Arts Trio, Trampler

The Dvořák *Piano Quartets* are glorious pieces, and the playing of Domus is little short of inspired. This is real chamber-music playing: intimate, unforced and distinguished by both vitality and sensitivity. Domus are recorded in an ideal acoustic and in perfect perspective; they sound wonderfully alive and warm.

The playing of the Beaux Arts Trio is as fresh and spontaneous as the music itself, and the early 1970s recording still sounds remarkably well – warm and beautifully balanced.

Piano Quartet 2 in E flat, Op. 87; Piano Quintet, Op. 81
(M) **(*) Warner Elatus 2564 60336-2. Schiff, Panocha Qt

Both the *Piano Quintet* and the *E flat Quartet*, Op. 87, enjoy distinguished representation on CD, but in only one instance are they coupled together (by Menaham Pressler and the Emerson Quartet on DG 439 868-2 – see our main volume). And so András Schiff and the Panocha Quartet offer a welcome alternative, particularly at so competitive a price. The performances are musical and very well recorded and, though neither is a first choice if price is no object, they are both very enjoyable.

(i) *Piano Quartet 2*; (ii) *Romantic Pieces, Op. 78; Violin Sonatina in G, Op. 100*
*** Sony SK 62597. (i) Ax, Laredo, Stern, Ma; (ii) Stern, McDonald

A starry line-up here for the *E flat Piano Quartet* with Emanuel Ax, Jaime Laredo, Yo-Yo Ma and Isaac Stern, who also plays the *G major Sonatina* and the *Romantic Pieces* with the pianist Robert McDonald. The *E flat Piano Quartet* was sketched immediately after the famous *A major Piano Quintet* and, though not quite its equal, is full of character and appealing melodic inspiration. The *Violin Sonatina* and the *Romantic Pieces* are rather light in comparison, though such is their charm that few will complain.

Piano Quintets: in A, Opp. 5 & 81 (see also under *Piano Concerto*)
**(*) Praga PRD 250 175. Klánsky, Pražák Qt

The early Opus 5 *Piano Quintet* was composed during the summer of 1872, but it remained in manuscript until 1887 when Dvořák revised and shortened it. In three movements, with a fine lyrical *Andante*, the sparkling finale takes the place of the *Scherzo*. Ivan Klánsky and the Pražák Quartet play it zestfully and freshly, but they do not uncover all its secrets, nor do they realize the full richness of its melodic lyricism as do Firkušný and the Ridge Quartet (see above). The same comments apply to the familiar and masterly Opus 81 *Quintet*, also in A major. The performance here is alive and sensitive, and the first movement is pressed forward with great zest and passion (the modern, digital recording is a shade fierce) where just a little more resilience and relaxation would have paid greater dividends. Fine playing then, but the Firkušný performances are the ones to have, and the RCA Double offers much more music for the same cost.

(i) *Piano Quintet in A, Op. 81. String Quartets 5, Op. 9: Romance; 10 in E flat, Op. 51; 12 in F (American), Op. 96; 13 in G, Op. 106; 14 in A flat, Op. 105; String Quintet in E flat, Op. 97; 5 Bagatelles for 2 Violins, Cello & Harmonium, Op. 47; Cypresses; 2 Waltzes (for string quartet); Terzetto (for 2 violins & viola in C), Op. 74*
(M) *** ASV CDDCS 446 (4). The Lindsays, with (i) P. Frankl

A splendid compilation, gathering together many of Dvořák's key chamber works and including not only the *American Quartet* but also the lovely *Quintet*, which has similar transatlantic connections. Incidentally and importantly, they include the repeat in the first movement of this work, with its lead-back. The less well-known *E flat major Quartet* has a slow movement marked *Dumka (Elegia)*: its mood is at first wistful then more energetic, but there is a nostalgic *Romanza* to follow before the dancing finale. The twelve *Cypresses* are arrangements of songs but are so winningly melodic that the words are not missed. The two *Waltzes* are also charmingly

folksy, characterful and strongly contrasted. The *Bagatelles* feature a by no means backward harmonium, the effect engagingly piquant. None of this music is uninspired and most of it shows the composer at his finest. The performances are characteristically warm and vital, and the recording is first class, clearly focused but with a pervading bloom.

Piano Quintet in A, Op. 81
*** ASV CDDCA 889. Frankl, Lindsay Qt – MARTINU: *Piano Quintet 2* ***
(N) *** Mer. CDE 84459. Denk, Concertante (members) – BRAHMS: *Piano Quintet* **(*)

Piano Quintet in A; Piano Quartet 2 in E flat, Op. 87
**(*) DG (IMS) 439 868-2. Pressler, Emerson Qt (augmented)

Piano Quintet in A; Piano Trio 4 (Dumky), Op. 90
(BB) *** Virgin 2x1 5 61516-2 (2). Nash Ens. – SAINT-SAENS: *Carnival of the Animals*, etc. ***

(i) *Piano Quintet in A; String Quartet 12 in F (American), Op. 96*
*** Testament (ADD) SBT 1074. (i) Stepán; Smetana Qt – JANACEK: *String Quartet 1* ***

(i) *Piano Quintet in A. String Quintet 2 in G, Op. 77*
*** Hyp. CDA 66796. Gaudier Ens., (i) with Tomes

This ASV account of Dvořák's glorious *Piano Quintet* by the Lindsays with Peter Frankl can readily stand comparison with the famous early Decca account with Clifford Curzon. Apart from Peter Frankl's fine contribution, one especially responds to Bernard Gregor-Smith's rich cello-line. Because of the resonance, the recording is full and warm, and if there is just a hint of thinness on the violin timbre the balance with the piano is particularly well managed.

With Susan Tomes the inspired pianist, the Gaudier Ensemble give a sparkling performance of the *Piano Quintet*, full of mercurial contrasts that seem entirely apt and with rhythms superbly sprung. The *G major String Quintet* is lighter than most rival versions, with speeds on the brisk side and with Marieke Blankestijn's violin pure rather than rich in tone. Very well recorded, this makes an excellent recommendation if you fancy the coupling. In neither work are the exposition repeats observed.

Concertante is a group of musicians from the Juilliard School; they offer the rare coupling of the *Piano Quintets* of Brahms amd Dvořák. This latter is a particularly fine performance, full of passionate spontaneity in the opening movement and with a balancing warmth throughout. Here the lead violin is Colin Jacobson, while Xiao-Dong Wang (who leads in the Brahms) is on the second desk; and this may acount for the even greater impetus, although the well-balanced pianist, Jeremy Denk, also makes a first-class contribution. The closing pages are most beautifully managed. The recording is very good without being in the demonstration bracket; but if you want the coupling, the disc can certainly be recommended.

It is surprising that the coupling of the *A major Piano Quintet* and the *Dumky Trio* has not been chosen more often. The Nash Ensemble offer warmly enjoyable performances of both, with genuine intimacy of feeling and no lack of vitality. They are eminently well recorded and give considerable satisfaction. The Saint-Saëns couplings are delightful, and this inexpensive Virgin Double is splendid value for money.

In terms of tonal finesse and bloom, the Smetana Quartet had few peers, and their ensemble is perfect. Moreover the quality of the mid-1960s recorded sound is as good as many being produced today. The *Piano Quintet*, in which they are joined by Pavel Stepán, is glorious, even if the acoustic is slightly drier than is ideal. No quarrels with the *F major Quartet* either. The sound is analogue and has great warmth.

Menahem Pressler joins the Emerson Quartet in powerful, intense accounts of these two magnificent works. The *Lento* of the *Second Piano Quartet* is given with a rapt, hushed concentration to put it among the very finest of Dvořák's inspirations. The performance of the *Quintet* is comparably positive in its characterization, but the DG New York recording gives an unpleasant edge to high violins, making the full ensemble abrasive.

(i) *Piano Quintet in A. String Quintets 1-3, Opp. 1, 77 & 97; String Sextet in A, Op. 46*
(B) *** Ph. (ADD) Duo 462 284-2 (2). (i) Kovacevich; BPO Octet (members)

This is the first time all these works have been gathered together on CD, and they make up a very enticing Duo. The Opus 1 *String Quintet in A minor* was written in 1861 when the composer was twenty; the *G major String Quintet* is a much later work, and there is plenty to be found in its beautiful *Poco andante* and the vital finale. The masterly and endearingly characteristic Opus 97 *Quintet* (1893) dates from the composer's American years. The Berlin Philharmonic soloists play most eloquently; these performances are both musical and polished. They are splendidly matched in the *Piano Quintet* by Stephen Kovacevich, who at times is perhaps a little over-reticent but whose clarity of articulation is a marvel. The recordings, from 1968 and 1972, occasionally show their age just a little in the upper range of the string-timbre in *fortissimos*. But there is a pleasing ambient fullness and the sound is generally well balanced.

Piano Trios 1 in B flat, Op. 21; 2 in G min., Op. 26; 3 in F min., Op. 65; 4 in E min. (Dumky), Op. 90
(N) (B) *** Chan. 2x1 241-24 (2). Borodin Trio
*** Ara. Z 6726-2 (2). Golub, Kaplan, Carr.
(M) **(*) Sup. (ADD) SU 3545-2 (2). Suk Trio
(B) **(*) Ph. (ADD) Duo 454 259-2 (2). Beaux Arts Trio

Piano Trios 1 in B flat, Op. 21; 3 in F min., Op. 65
(N) *** MDG 342 1262-2. V. Piano Trio

Piano Trios 2 in G min. Op. 26; 4 (Dumky), Op. 90
(N) *** MDG 342 1261-2. V. Piano Trio

The Borodin performances, recorded live at various venues between 1983 and 1985, have all been issued previously, and the *Dumky* remains as a separate issue, coupled with Smetana (see below). However, collectors wanting the complete set will find these are all finely shaped performances. There is characteristic ardour and fire; such imperfections as there are arise from the natural spontaneity of live music-making. The recording varies a little from venue to venue but gives a very real illusion of presence. Although we have a special regard for the newest MDG set from the Vienna Piano Trio, this Chandos bargain reissue remains strongly recommendable in Chandos's two-for-the-price-of-one series.

The talented young players of the Vienna Piano Trio bring out to the full the dramatic contrasts of Dvořák's writing. They are not just sharp in attack but rapt and intense in bringing out the mystery of the slow movement, *Adagio molto e mesto* of the B flat Trio, with the folk-rhythms of the feather-light Scherzo deliciously pointed. The performance of the *F minor Trio* has similar contrasts of light and shade, with the Brahmsian weight of the piano-writing powerfully brought out and with the expressive range of the violin and cello similarly wide in performances that consistently give the illusion of a live experience. On the second disc, the ear immediately registers the wide range of dynamic of the playing of the first movement of the *G minor Trio*, and the Scherzo is again delectably pointed and the finale equally infectious. The constant changes of mood and tempo in the *Dumky* are handled with chimerically spontaneous Slavonic feeling, and the playing is superb.

David Golub, Mark Kaplan and Colin Carr make an ideally balanced group; Golub produces a wide range of keyboard colour and combines subtlety with a vital yet flexible rhythmic grip. Kaplan plays with great artistry, and we can't remember hearing cello-playing of greater eloquence in these trios than we get from Colin Carr. Splendidly characterized playing and totally idiomatic in style. Throughout there is feeling and freshness, yet nothing is overstated. The recording places one fairly near the artists, but there is room for the music to expand in climaxes and the overall effect has plenty of presence. An altogether delightful set which gives great pleasure.

One has only to listen to these glorious Dvořák performances from the Suk Trio to hear their complete rapport with the composer and their warmth for the music surfacing again and again. Notably in the often inspired pianism of Jan Panenka, and Josef Suk's delicate lyricism; but the cellist, Josef Churchro, is also a most responsive player. Throughout the set their readings have the benefit of great concentration and intellectual grip. They hold the architecture of each movement together most impressively, yet can relax in an instant. They are perhaps finest of all in the *Dumky*, with its constant changes of mood, and ebb and flow of tempi. The original recordings, dating from 1977–8 were of high quality, but while the analogue warmth and ambient glow are fully retained in the CD transfer, and the piano sounds especially fresh, the recording shows its age in the violin timbre, which is a little thin in the higher register, and this may trouble some ears. But these performances remain unsurpassed.

The Beaux Arts' earlier versions of the *Piano Trios* come from the end of the 1960s. The *F minor* is played with great eloquence and vitality. And what sparkling virtuosity there is in the Scherzo of the *G minor*, Op. 26. The splendours of the *Dumky* are well realized in an account of great spontaneity and freshness. The recording is naturally balanced and splendidly vivid; only a degree of thinness on the violin-timbre gives any grounds for reservation. At Duo price this is excellent value.

Piano Trios 1–2
(BB) *** Naxos 8.55439. Joachim Trio

Piano Trios 1; 4 (Dumky)
*** Nim. NI 5472. V. Piano Trio

The Vienna Piano Trio show admirable musicianship and sensitivity in the *B flat Trio* and in the famous *Dumky Trio*, and they are very well recorded too.

Fresh, vital playing from this excellent Naxos group. Very good recording too, and though not to be preferred to the Beaux Arts, this is eminently recommendable and worth the money.

Piano Trio 3 in F min., Op. 65
*** Chan. 8320. Borodin Trio

Piano Trios 3–4 (Dumky)
*** Hyp. CDA 66895. Florestan Trio
(M) **(*) Ph. (ADD) (IMS) 426 095-2. Beaux Arts Trio

Piano Trio 4 in E min. (Dumky), Op. 90
*** Chan. 8445. Borodin Trio – SMETANA: *Piano Trio* ***
(N) *** Warner 2564 61492-2. Beaux Arts Trio –
MENDELSSOHN: *Piano Trio 1* ***

The Hyperion disc offers musicianly and refined performances that will give much pleasure, and the recording, too, is excellent.

The Beaux Arts made their début on LP some 36 years ago with their performance of the *Dumky Trio* (alone on one full-priced LP) and, although some of the personnel has changed, the youthfulness and grace of the playing has not. Menahem Pressler is every bit as sensitive and fleet of finger as he was in the mid-1950s. The new Warner recording is of course more realistic and wide-ranging. It is splendidly balanced and makes a very happy tribute to this wonderful ensemble.

The Beaux Arts' 1969 Philips performances of Op. 65 and the *Dumky* still sound fresh and sparkling, though the recording on CD is a little dry in the violin-timbre; the *F minor*, arguably the finer and certainly the more concentrated of the two, is played with great eloquence and vitality.

The playing of the Borodin Trio in the *F minor Trio* has great warmth and fire; such imperfections as there are arise from the natural spontaneity of a live performance, however this now seems short measure. But in the *Dumky Trio* it is the spontaneous flexibility of approach to the constant mood-changing that makes the splendid Borodin performance so involving, as well as the glorious playing from each of the team. The recording is naturally balanced and the illusion of a live occasion is striking.

4 Romantic Pieces, Op. 75; Slavonic Dance, Op. 46/2 (original version); Violin Sonatina in G, Op. 100.
(N) (M) *** Sup. SU 3772. Suk, Holec – SMETANA: *From the Homeland;* SUK: *Ballade; 4 Pieces* ***

4 Romantic Pieces, Op. 75; Violin Sonatina in G, Op. 100; Humoresque (for solo piano)
(N) *** Analekta FL2 3191. Ehnes, Laurel – JANACEK: *Violin Sonata 1;* SMETANA: *From the Homeland* ***

Idiomatic and beautifully turned performances, as one would expect from the composer's grandson and his accomplished partner. The *Sonatina* is an utterly delightful work, particularly the slow movement, which is played exquisitely. It is good, too, to hear the *E minor Slavonic Dance* in its original form, before Dvořák scored it for orchestra. The 1971 recording is excellent and the faithful CD transfer quite transforms the original LP sound.

On Analekta, the collection of violin and piano music by the three greatest Czech composers inspires not just the brilliant Canadian violinist, Ehnes, but his piano-partner, Eduard Laurel, to performances which with rare understanding bring out the special, most winning qualities of each work. In Dvořák's *Four Romantic Pieces*, Ehnes and Laurel convey a sense of spontaneity, the immediacy of the moment, which yet goes with purposeful control. The gravity of the final *Larghetto*, twice as long as any of the other three movements, is magnetically caught, while the *Sonatina*, product of Dvořák's American years, brings a delectably sprung performance. The finale, with its syncopations and melodic shapes typical of the 'American' Dvořák, sounds like a cross

between a Slavonic dance and a Hoe-down. As a charming coda, Ehnes, switching to the piano, offers a reading, albeit a little wayward, of Dvořák's ever-popular *Humoresque*.

String Quartets 1–14; Cypresses, B.152; Fragments in A min.; F, B.120; 2 Waltzes, Op. 54, B.105
(B) *** DG (ADD) 463 165-2 (9). Prague Qt

Dvořák's *Quartets* span the whole of his creative life. The glories of the mature *Quartets* are well known, though it is only the so-called *American* which has achieved real popularity. The beauty of the present set, made in 1973–7, is that it offers more *Quartets* (not otherwise available) plus two *Quartet Movements*, in *A minor* (1873) and *F major* (1881), plus two *Waltzes* and *Cypresses* for good measure, all in eminently respectable performances and decent recordings. The present transfers are managed most satisfactorily, with a nice balance between warmth and presence. At bargain price, neatly packaged and with good documentation, this is self-recommending.

String Quartets 5 in F min., Op. 9; 7 in A min., Op. 16
(BB) *** Naxos 8.553377. Vlach Qt

String Quartets 8 in E., Op. 80; 11 in C, Op. 61
(BB) *** Naxos 8.553372. Vlach Qt

String Quartet 9 in D min., Op. 34; Terzetto in C (for 2 violins and viola), Op. 74
(BB) *** Naxos 8.553373. Vlach Qt

String Quartets 10 in E flat, Op. 51; 14 in A flat, Op. 105
☛ (BB) *** Naxos 8.553374. Vlach Qt

String quartets 12 in F (American), Op. 96; 13, in G, Op. 106
☛ (BB) *** Naxos 8.553371. Vlach Qt

Although there is stiffer competition now that DG have reissued the Prague Quartet set of the Dvořák canon at budget price, the Vlach is as good a way of exploring this repertoire as any. Their tonal matching seals their claims to be an outstanding international group, and there is nothing 'bargain basement' about the performances except their price. The playing is cultured and has warmth and vitality, and there can be no grumbles so far as the quality of the recorded sound is concerned; it is natural, well focused and warm. The dark intensity on a whispered *pianissimo* which marks the hushed opening of Op. 105, one of Dvořák's masterpieces, leads on to performances of exceptional strength and refinement, and throughout the series the vigorous movements bring exhilaratingly sprung rhythms and slow movements that are deeply expressive. So far this has been one of Naxos's success stories, and we are inclined to think the series strongly competitive.

They prove equally successful, both artistically and as recorded sound. At the price there is no need to hesitate with this series: the Vlach are as fresh and persuasive as any of their rivals on premium-priced labels.

String Quartet 7 in A min., Op. 16; Cypresses
**(*) Chan. 8826. Chilingirian Qt

String Quartets 8 in E, Op. 80; 9 in D min., Op. 34
**(*) Chan. 8755. Chilingirian Qt

String Quartets 10 in E flat; 11 in C, Op. 61
**(*) Chan. 8837. Chilingirian Qt

Chandos provide very fine recorded sound for the Chilingirians, who play with sensitivity in all five *Quartets*. These are straightforward, well-paced readings that are eminently serviceable. Some collectors may perhaps feel that they fall short of the very highest distinction, but they are unfailingly musicianly and vital.

String Quartets 8 in E flat, Op. 80; 9 in D min., Op. 34
*** Praga HMCD 90. Kocian Qt

Outstanding performaces from the Kocian Quartet, naturally idiomatic and full of vitality. Both slow movements are played most beautifully, the *Adagio* of the *D minor* is very tender, and both Scherzos have a real Slavonic rhythmic feel. The outer movements of the *E flat major* are particularly appealing. The recording is real and present, perhaps a shade close (there is a hint of shrillness on the violins) but well balanced. This is much more characterful and authentic than the coupling of the same two works by the Chilingirians on Chandos.

String Quartets 9 in D min., Op. 34; 10 in E flat, Op. 51
(BB) *** Warner Apex 7559 79671-2. American String Qt

Although the Dvořák *Quartets* are well served on CD, their representation at bargain price is limited to the fine Naxos series by the Vlach Quartet, which includes these two works, differently coupled. The *D minor*, Op. 34, has one of Dvořák's most deeply expressive and affecting slow movements. These 1985 performances are very sensitive and imaginative, and the recorded sound is perfectly serviceable. Strongly recommended alongside the Vlach versions.

String Quartets 9, Op. 34; 14 in A flat, Op. 105
(M) *** Somm SOMMCD 231. Delmé Qt

With this issue the Delmé Quartet celebrate their fortieth birthday (they were founded in 1962). They are a refreshingly musical ensemble, unglamorous and free from gloss, and though there are some infelicities, both quartets are very well served. The sublime slow movement of Op. 34 is eloquently played, and the recording, made in Leiston Abbey, is eminently truthful and well balanced.

String Quartet 12 in F (American), Op. 96
(B) *** Calliope CAL 6262. Annesci Qt – GLAZUNOV: Quartet 3 ***
*** EMI 7 54215-2. Alban Berg Qt – SMETANA: Quartet ***
(M) *** Classic fM 75605 57027-2. Chilingirian Qt – BORODIN: Quartet 2; SHOSTAKOVICH: Quartet 8 ***
(BB) (***) Dutton mono CDBP 9713. Griller Qt – BLOCH: Quartet 2; Night; MOZART: Adagio & Fugue (***)
(***) Testament mono SBT 1072. Hollywood Qt – KODÁLY; SMETANA: Quartets (***)
(M) **(*) DG (IMS) (ADD) 437 251-2. Amadeus Qt – SMETANA: String Quartet 1 **(*)
(M) **(*) Virgin 2x1 5 62437-2 (2). Endellion Qt – SMETANA: String Quartet 1 – MARTINU: Double Concerto etc. ***

String Quartet 12 (American); Cypresses
*** DG (IMS) 419 601-2. Hagen Qt – KODÁLY: Quartet 2 ***

The Hagen Quartet make an uncommonly beautiful sound, and their account of this masterly score is very persuasive indeed. Their playing is superbly polished, musical and satisfying, and they play the enchanting *Cypresses*, which Dvořák transcribed from the eponymous song-cycle, with great tenderness. The recording is altogether superb, very present and full-bodied.

A warmly refined account from the rich-timbred Annesci Quartet, with the second subject of the first movement shaped most affectionately. This is essentially a mellow performance (helped by richly atmospheric recording), but there is no lack of underlying impulse, and there is plenty of dash in the sparkling finale. The Glazunov coupling is equally recommendable.

The Alban Berg have their finger on the vital current that carries its musical argument forward. Phrasing is shaped dextrously and the polish and elegance of their playing are never in danger of diminishing the spontaneous-seeming character of this music.

On Classic fM, the Chilingirian Quartet give powerful, incisive performances, though they are recorded a bit too forward. Levon Chilingirian's violin-tone is given a slight edge by the full, immediate recording. In the Dvořák the big contrasts of mood and atmosphere are brought out, with the slow movement yearningly beautiful and the fast movements given an infectious spring.

When this brilliant version of Dvořák's *American Quartet* was recorded in 1948, the Grillers were at their peak, unassailably the leading such group in Britain. Perfectly matched, they bring out the exhilaration of the fast music, notably in a dazzling account of the finale and the yearning beauty of the slow movement. This was a fine early example of Decca's prowess in using its ffrr process, and Dutton in the CD transfer secures astonishingly vivid results. Well coupled with the masterly but neglected Bloch *Quartet* and the Mozart masterpiece.

The Hollywood Quartet is pretty well self-recommending, and their account of the *F major Quartet* is everything one would expect: impeccable in terms of execution, ensemble and taste. This was a quartet which brought real artistry to everything they played.

Admirers of the Amadeus will certainly want their 1977 coupling of Dvořák and Smetana, recorded in Finland. This is a strongly conceived performance, full of ardour. The Scherzo and exhilarating finale show their brilliance of ensemble at its most appealing and infectious. The sound is vivid, full and immediate.

The Endellion Quartet give a generally excellent account. Mind you, one is pulled up with a start at the second theme of the first movement which the leader, Andrew Watkinson, pulls out of shape. However, these players are robust in style, their music-making has conviction they are eminently well recorded, and the couplings are as generous as they are unexpected.

String Quartets 12 (American); 13 in G, Op. 106
*** ASV CDDCA 797. Lindsay Qt

In the *American Quartet* the Lindsays' account is certainly among the very best in terms of both performance and recording. The *G major* is also played very well, with much the same dedication and sensitivity. An outstanding coupling.

String Quartets 12 (American); 14 in A flat, Op. 105
**(*) Chan. 8919. Chilingirian Qt

These Chilingirian performances are well up to the standard of their fine series, even if their version of the *American Quartet* would not be a first choice. The recording is first class, and those needing this coupling will not be disappointed.

String Quartet 12 (American); (i) String Quintet in E flat, Op. 97
(BB) *** Warner Apex 0927 44355-2. Keller Qt, with (i) Deeva

Dvořák wrote the second of his string quintets (the one with the extra viola) in the same period as the popular Op. 96

Quartet, similarly using thematic material with American inflexions, so that the two works make an apt and attractive coupling. The Keller Quartet give outstanding readings of both works, crisp and fanciful, with light, clear textures and speeds generally on the fast side. The tenderness of the lyricism is beautifully caught in consistently imaginative phrasing, and the Erato recording is beautifully balanced. A real bargain.

String Quartet 13 in G, Op. 106; Quartet Movement in F, B.120; 2 Waltzes, Op. 54
**(*) Chan. 8874. Chilingirian Qt

The playing of the Chilingirians has momentum and vitality and, though there are moments when they could make more of dynamic nuance, these are sympathetic and well-recorded performances. They include the *Quartet Movement in F major* that Dvořák had originally intended for the piece, as well as two of the *Waltzes* he arranged from the Op. 54 piano pieces.

String Quartet 14; Terzetto in C, Op. 74
*** Testament SBT 1075. Smetana Qt – JANACEK: *String Quartet 2* ***

The Smetanas observe the traditional cut in the finale of Op. 105, from 11 bars before fig. 11 until 4 bars after fig. 12. This is a wonderful performance. Moreover it comes with the *Terzetto in C* for two violins and viola, a rarity in the concert hall, played freshly and elegantly, and with their outstanding account of Janáček's *Intimate Letters*, which is new to the British catalogues.

String Quintets in A min., Op. 1; E flat, Op. 97
⊘→ (BB) *** Naxos 8.553376. Vlach Qt, with L. Kyselac

An intelligent coupling by the Vlach of the earliest *Quintet* coupled with one of the most masterly of all his chamber works, the *E flat*, Op. 97. No need to worry about this performance or recording, for both are excellent and, although there are numerous alternatives of quality, none is priced so competitively.

String Quintets: (i) in G, Op. 77; (ii) in E flat, Op. 97
*** Bayer BR 100 184CD. Stamitz Qt, with (i) Hudec; (ii) Talich

String Quintets: in G, Op. 77; in E flat, Op. 97. Intermezzo in B, Op. 40
*** Chan. 9046. Chilingirian Qt, with D. McTier

String Quintets in G, Op. 77; E flat, Op. 97; Nocturne in B, Op. 40
*** Sony SK 89605. L'Archibudelli

The Dutch-based group, L'Archibudelli, more than holds its own against the competition and offers also the beautiful *Notturno*, which originally formed part of the *G major Quintet*, Op. 18, before Dvořák revised it as Op. 77. The Op. 97 *E flat Quintet*, composed in America, is a strong work, rather eclipsed by the famous Op. 96 *American Quartet*, and is distinguished by a particularly eloquent slow movement.

Otherwise, honours are pretty evenly divided between the Stamitz Quartet and the Chilingirians in the *Quintets*. The Stamitz Quartet is perhaps balanced more forwardly but is recorded pleasantly, and the Chilingirian set on Chandos has more air round the sound but without any loss of focus. Both performances have the warmth and humanity that Dvořák exudes, but the Chilingirians undoubtedly score in including the beautiful *B major Intermezzo* that the composer had

originally intended for the *G major Quintet* and which he subsequently expanded into an independent work for full strings, the *Nocturne*, Op. 40. This tips the balance in their favour.

String Quintet in E flat, Op. 97; String Sextet in A, Op. 48
*** Hyp. CDA 66308. Raphael Ens.

The *E flat major Quintet*, Op. 97, is one of the masterpieces of Dvořák's American years, and it is most persuasively given by the Raphael Ensemble, as is the coupled *Sextet*. It is also very well recorded, though we are placed fairly forward in the aural picture.

String Sextet in A, Op. 48
(*) Sup. **DVD SU 7004-2. Augmented Smetana Qt – SMETANA: *String Quartets 1–2 (plus documentary on the Smetana Quartet)* **(*)

The *Sextet* makes an admirable fill-up for the two Smetana *Quartets* and is given without intrusive camerawork. Musically very satisfying, though the documentary in which the members of the quartet look back over their career is curiously stiff.

String Sextet in A, Op. 48
(BB) *** Warner Apex 7559 79679-2. Boston Symphony Chamber Players – SMETANA: *Piano Trio* ***
*(**) EMI 5 57243-2. Chang, Hartog, W. Christ, T. Christ, Faust, Maninger – TCHAIKOVSKY: *Souvenir de Florence* *(**)

This 1983 performance finds Joseph Silverstein leading some eminent colleagues from the Boston Symphony and giving as sensitive an account of Dvořák's endearing *Sextet* as any now before the public. Decent if rather forward recording.

Sarah Chang's warm individual artistry is superbly matched by players drawn from the Berlin Philharmonic, past and present. These are players who not only respond to each other's artistry, but do so with the most polished ensemble and a rare clarity of inner texture, not easy with a sextet. The subtlety as well as the energy of Dvořák's *Sextet* is consistently brought out, using the widest dynamic range. Sadly, the sound is top-heavy with little bass, the cello registering fully only in the work's gentler moments. On some reproducers the adjective 'scrawny' might describe the string tuttis.

Violin Sonatina in G, Op. 100 (see also under Violin Concerto – Perlman)
*** Praga PRD 250 153. Remés, Kayahara – JANACEK; MARTINU; SMETANA: *Violin Sonatas* ***

Considering its disarmingly melodic freshness, it is astonishing that Dvořák's *Violin Sonatina* is so rarely heard and recorded. Although it is full of charm, its four movements are by no means diminutive in character, and the composer probably chose the title to emphasize its unpretentiousness. This splendidly sensitive account from Václav Remés, admirably partnered by Sachiko Kayahara, is sheer delight from beginning to end and has an authentic Czech lilt, yet is full of character. The recording is very good indeed, and so are the couplings.

Piano duet
Slavonic Dances 1–16, Op. 46/1–8; Op. 72/1–8
(BB) *** Naxos 8.553138. Matthies, Köhn

The brilliant piano duo of Silke-Thora Matthies and Christian Köhn are most persuasive performers, radiating their own enjoyment, bringing out inner parts, giving transparency to even the thickest textures, subtly shading their tone and, above all, consistently springing rhythms infectiously, with an idiomatic feeling for Czech dance music. The forwardly balanced recording brings out the brightness of the piano while letting warmth of tone come forward in such gentler dances as *No. 3 in D*. An excellent bargain.

7 Organ Preludes & Fugues

(*) BIS CD 1101. Ericsson – GLAZUNOV: *Preludes & Fugues*, etc.; SIBELIUS: *Intrada*, etc. *

These pieces – five preludes, a fughetta and two fugues – are graduation exercises that Dvořák wrote on leaving the Prague Organ School. They are played very well here and show the fluency and technical proficiency you would expect from any gifted student, but no sign of individuality.

VOCAL AND CHORAL MUSIC

Cypresses ((i) **Instrumental and (ii) Vocal Versions**), *B11 & B152*

(N) *** Somm SOMMCD 236. (i) Delmé Qt; (ii) Robinson, Johnson

The charming sequence of 12 pieces for string quartet that Dvořák entitled *Cypresses* has been recorded fairly often, but the set of 18 songs on which they are based has been seriously neglected. Here, as an ideal and generous coupling, comes a disc setting the two cycles side by side, with illuminating results. The vocal versions, written in 1865, marked Dvořák's first essays in song-writing, but he left them unpublished. It was not until much later, in 1887, that he transcribed 12 of them for string quartet. Both sets in their reflection on youthful love provide a touching portrait of the composer. Predictably, the quartet versions are subtler in their presentation of folk-based ideas. Though the present recording of the song versions sets the singer at a slight distance, with occasional roughness at the top disturbing the general sweetness of tenor-tone, Timothy Robinson's performances are warmly sympathetic, helped by ever-responsive accompaniment from Graham Johnson. The Delmé Quartet plays the instrumental versions with exceptionally sweet matching, generally opting for relatively broad speeds and warmly expressive phrasing. The disc also offers excellent detailed notes and full texts and translations.

Biblical Songs, Op. 99; Gipsy Melodies, Op. 55; In Folk Tone, Op. 73; Love Songs, Op. 83.

*** Sup. SU 3437-2. Peckova, Gage

Dagmar Peckova's is an ideal voice for this repertory, unmistakably Slavonic in timbre, yet firm and pure as well as rich. She retains a freshness that is specially apt for the songs inviting a girlish manner, including the most famous of this composer's songs, the fourth of the seven *Gipsy Songs*, *Songs My Mother Taught Me*, sounding fresh and new. Earliest in inspiration are the eight *Love Songs*, charming pieces which already reveal an unquenchable lyrical gift. Next chronologically are the *Gipsy Songs* of 1880, bold and colourful, which are here nicely contrasted by Peckova and Gage with the four simpler, less exotic songs, *In Folk Tone*, of six years later. Last and longest is the cycle of ten *Biblical Songs*, setting texts from the Psalms. More usually they are sung by male singers, gaining from weight and gravity, but here with the mezzo, Peckova, they prove just as moving and intense. Full texts are given, but translations in German and French as well as

English come on separate pages, making it far more difficult to follow songs line by line. Clear, well-balanced sound.

(i) Requiem, Op. 89; (ii) 6 Biblical Songs from Op. 99

⊶ ✿ (B) *** DG Double (ADD) 453 073-2 (2). (i) Stader, Wagner, Haefliger, Borg, Czech PO & Ch., Ančerl; (ii) Fischer-Dieskau, Demus

This superb DG set from 1959 brings an inspired performance of Dvořák's *Requiem* which here emerges with fiery intensity, helped by a recording made in an appropriately spacious acoustic that gives an illusion of an electrifying live performance, without flaw. The passionate singing of the chorus is unforgettable and the German soloists not only make fine individual contributions but blend together superbly in ensembles. DG have added Fischer-Dieskau's 1960 recordings of six excerpts from Op. 99. He is at his superb best in these lovely songs. (The numbers included are: *Rings an den Herrn*; *Gott, erhöre meine inniges Flahen*; *Gott ist mein Hirte*; *An den Wassern zu Babylon*; *Wende dich zu mir*; and *Singet ein neues Lied*.) Jörg Demus accompanies sensitively, and the recording-balance is most convincing.

(i) Requiem, Op. 89; (ii) Mass in D, Op. 86

(B) *** Double Decca (ADD) 448 089-2 (2). (i) Lorengar, Komlóssy, Isofalvy, Krause, Amb. S., LSO, Kertész; (ii) Ritchie, Giles, Byers, Morton, Christ Church Cathedral Ch., Oxford, Cleobury (organ), Preston

Kertész conducts with a total commitment to the score and he secures from singers and orchestra an alert and sensitive response. The recording, which has the advantage of the Kingsway Hall ambience, has a lifelike balance, and for this Double Decca reissue the work has been sensibly recoupled with Simon Preston's beautifully shaped Christ Church account of the *Mass in D*, recorded six years later. In both works the CD remastering shows how good were the original recordings.

Saint Ludmila (oratorio), Op. 74

*** Orfeo C 513992H (2). Aghová, Breedt, Beczala, Vele, Prague Chamber Ch., WDR Cologne Ch. & SO, Albrecht

Saint Ludmila is a winningly vigorous, dramatic work, reflecting the composer we know from the symphonies in its rhythmic strength and lyrical warmth. It is a piece full of white-hot inspiration, punctuated with lively choruses and arias, often feeling operatic. As is to be expected, since it comes from the same period as the *Seventh Symphony*, there are many glorious pages. The final section leads to a triumphant choral finale which in places echoes that of Beethoven's *Ninth*. This Orfeo issue offers a strong, colourful performance which points the drama well, using four first-rate Czech-speaking soloists and with the Cologne choir augmented by the Prague Chamber Choir. The result is both polished and idiomatic, helped by warm, full sound, even though the chorus is set behind the orchestra.

The Spectre's Bride (cantata)

*** Delos DE 3296. Krovytska, Aler, Kusnjer, Westminster Symphony Ch., New Jersey SO, Macal

The Spectre's Bride, Dvořák's most vigorous dramatic cantata, in its freshness offers a strong contrast with his devotional choral works, which have few Czech echoes. Based on a Czech legend, the melodramatic story of a maiden seduced by the ghost of her long-missing lover may seem corny, reflecting

Victorian taste, but Macal – Czech-born but now an American citizen – sweeps any cobwebs away in an idiomatic performance that is both incisive and warmly expressive. The choral singing is first rate, and among the soloists Oksana Krovytska stands out with her bright pure soprano as the all-too-innocent maiden, rising to the challenge of her *Prayer to the Virgin* with its foretaste of Rusalka's *Invocation to the Moon*. Surprisingly, the weak link here is the most celebrated soloist, John Aler, his tenor not always well focused. The original Czech text is used. Though the booklet gives only the stilted English translation, this new issue scores over Czech rivals in the quality of its sound.

Stabat mater; Psalm 149, Op. 79

(BB) **(*) Naxos 8.555301/2 (2). Brewer, Simpson, Aler, Gao, Washington Ch. & O, Shafer

(i) *Stabat Mater;* (ii) *Legends 1–10, Op. 59*

(B) *** DG Double (ADD) 453 025-2 (2). (i) Mathis, Reynolds, Ochman, Shirley-Quirk, Bav. R. Ch. & SO; (ii) ECO; Kubelik

The *Stabat Mater* blazed the trail for Dvořák's cause during his lifetime. Kubelik is consistently responsive and this is a work which benefits from his imaginative approach. The recording, made in the Munich Herkulessaal, is of very good quality. The ten Legends are beautifully played by the ECO. This music ought to be better known, with its colourful scoring and folksy inspiration of a high order. Again very good recording.

Robert Shafer conducts his chorus and the Washington Orchestra in a fresh, well-disciplined reading. The chorus is rather backwardly placed, but Shafer's clean-cut directness helps to avoid any feeling of sentimentality. Outstanding among the soloists is Christine Brewer, and John Aler, though not as sweet-toned as usual, sings very sensitively too. The mezzo, Marietta Simpson, is tremulous as recorded, and Ding Gao is clear and reliable in the bass solos.

OPERA

Dimitrij

(N) *** Sup. SU 3793-2 (3). Vodička, Drobková, Hajóssyová, Aghová, Mikuláš, Kusnjer, Prague Philharmonic Ch., Prague R. Ch., Czech PO, Albrecht

This first complete recording of Dvořák's ambitious historical opera was made in 1989, an opera memorable for carrying on the story of Boris Godunov after the Tsar died. Four of the principal characters are the same as in Mussorgsky's masterpiece: the Polish Princess Marina, Boris's daughter Xenia, and Prince Shuisky, as well as Dimitrij himself. The big difference is that Dimitrij here genuinely believes in his right to claim the throne as the son of Ivan the Terrible, where in *Boris* he is an unashamed pretender. It puts a completely different slant on his character, a noble figure tragically brought down as a sham. This is a fine recording, idiomatically conducted by Gerd Albrecht, with the choirs from Prague making the most of the many ensembles, not least the double-choruses representing the conflicting Polish and Russian forces. As has regularly been pointed out, Dvořák was less influenced in these by the rugged example of Mussorgsky than by the grand operas written for Paris by Meyerbeer.

Though it can hardly compare with *Boris Godunov*, the confrontation between Dimitrij and his rejected wife,

Marina, in Act III is certainly powerful, as is the final, hesitant admission of Marfa in Act IV that Dimitrij is not her son. In the title-role Leo Vodička is a strong, very Slavonic-sounding tenor, singing sensitively if at times with strain. Sweetest on the ear among the women is Livia Aghová as Xenia, pure, fresh and precise in attack. As Marina, Magdalena Hajóssyová is bright and fresh, if with an occasional edge on the voice; and the contralto, Drahomira Drobková, is a warm, rich-toned Marfa. Good sound, with the singers' diction admirably clear.

The Jacobin

(M) *** Orfeo C641 043F (3). Bronikowski, Lehotsky, Aghová, Stephinger, Holland, Danková, Mikuláš, Lorenz, Georg, Cologne Children's Ch., Prague Chamber Ch., Cologne R, Symphony Ch. & O, Albrecht

(*) Fone **SACD 024 2 SACD (2). Pivovarov, Werba, Grato, Monogarova, Lehotsky, Panova, Elliot, Wexford Op. Ch., Nat. PO of Belarus, Voloschuk

*** Sup. (ADD) 11 2190-2 (2). Zítek, Sounová, Přibyl, Machotková, Blachut, Průša, Tuček, Berman, Katilena Children's Ch., Kuhn Ch., Brno State PO, Pinkas

This opera is a strange but attractive mixture. The main plot involves the hero, Bohuš, son of Count Vilém, being falsely accused of being a revolutionary Jacobin. But Dvořák – having made him a baritone, not a tenor – centres his emotions on the sub-plot involving village life and the love between the gamekeeper, Jiří, and Terinka. Terinka's father, the village musician-schoolmaster, Benda, is the focus of delectable rehearsal scenes with the schoolchildren and villagers. Gerd Albrecht, the conductor who has recorded so many of Dvořák's major works, is warmly understanding of the Czech folk idiom, and he points rhythms delectably; set in an open acoustic, using large forces both in the orchestra and in the multiple choruses, the Orfeo version achieves a fine balance between high drama and rustic colour. One is forced to take the mortal threat to Bohuš from the evil Adolf very seriously.

Michael Lehotsky, a tenor, sweetly Slavic in timbre, takes the role of Jiří, as he does on the Wexford set from Fone, and again he gives an animated performance. Opposite him is the soprano, Lívia Aghová, as Terinka, again both Slavic in timbre and sweet-toned, charmingly provocative. Though Andrea Danková, as Bohuš's wife Julie, is more variable and with a more pronounced vibrato and a tendency to shrillness under pressure on top, the apt weight of the voice establishes the character well, making the necessary contrast with Terinka. As Bohuš the baritone, Marcin Bronikowski, lyrical in his early scenes, rises splendidly to the challenge of the final scene when he appeals to his father, convincing him of his innocence, so bringing the happy ending. In the key role of Benda the character tenor, Eberhard Francesco Lorenz, paints a colourful portrait of the schoolmaster without caricaturing him, and the fine bass, Christoph Stephinger, sings nobly as the Count, with Peter Mikuláš strongly cast as the Count's Burgrave. As Adolf, Mark Holland sounds gritty at times, but that is only apt for so villainous a character, and he sings with fine projection in his big moments. The important choruses – with big ensembles ending each Act – are superbly sung too. This is a piece that by rights should have become a far closer rival to *The Bartered Bride* than it has. Though the set takes three discs instead of two for rival versions, that brings the advantage of having each Act complete on a single disc.

It is good to welcome a recording made live at the ever-enterprising Wexford Festival in Ireland. This warmly enjoyable set was recorded at three performances in the tiny Festival Theatre there in 2001, with excellent results. The orchestra as well as many in the cast were drawn from the National Opera of Belarus, Slav performers naturally in tune with this delightful folk-based opera by a Slavonic composer.

The Wexford performance under the lively direction of Alexander Voloschuk, with no weak link in the cast, captures the folk atmosphere very attractively, with stage effects more vivid than they might have been in the studio and with few disturbing stage noises. As Jiří, Michal Lehotsky has an agreeable, if very Slavonic, tenor, with Mariana Panova bright and clear as Terinka and Alasdair Elliot catching the right idiom in the gift role of her father. The relative dryness of the theatre acoustic in Wexford adds to the clarity without taking bloom away from the voices, with choruses of children as well as adults well caught. The rival Supraphon version under Jiří Pinkas, recorded in Brno in 1977, offers a performance on an altogether bigger scale, but the intimacy of the Wexford production is just as compelling and the performance just as lively. The snag of the Fone set is that, unlike the Supraphon set, it contains no libretto but only a sketchy synopsis, hardly adequate with such an offbeat story.

Jiří Pinkas draws lively and idiomatic performances from a first-rate cast, including such stalwarts as Vilem Přibyl as the hero (a little old-sounding but stylish) and the veteran tenor Beno Blachut giving a charming portrait of the heroine's father. Václav Zítek sings the heroic part of the Jacobin himself with incisive strength and Daniela Sounová is bright and clear as the heroine. The analogue sound is clear and firmly focused. A full libretto/translation is included.

The Jacobin: highlights
**(*) Sup. (ADD) 11 2250-2 (from above complete recording, cond. Pinkas)

The highlights disc is at medium price and, with 62 minutes' playing time, makes a good sampler. However, there is no libretto included, not even a synopsis, which is unhelpful in an unfamiliar work of this kind.

Kate and the Devil (complete)
**(*) Sup. (ADD) 11 1800-2 (2). Barová, Ježil, Novák, Sulcová, Suryová, Horáček, Brno Janáček Op. Ch. & O, Pinkas

This is a charming comic fantasy about the girl who literally makes life hell for the devil who abducts her. It inspired a score that might almost be counted an operatic equivalent of his *Slavonic Dances*, full of sharply rhythmic ideas, colourfully orchestrated. The role of Kate is very well taken by Anna Barová, firm and full-toned, with Jirka sung attractively by Miloš Ježil, though his Slavonic tones are strained on top. The snag is the ill-focused singing of Richard Novák as the Devil, characterful enough but wobbly. Jiří Pinkas persuasively brings out the fun and colour of the score, drawing excellent singing from the chorus; and the 1979 recording has plenty of space, agreeably warm and atmospheric. The libretto is well produced and clear, but it assumes that the set is on three CDs instead of two, with Acts II and III together on the second.

Rusalka (DVD versions)
(N) *** Sup. **DVD** SU 7008-9. Subrtová, Zidek, Miková, Mixová, Haken, Ovčačiková, Prague Nat. Ch. & O, Chalabala (V/D: Bohumil Zoul)

(**) TDK **DVD** DV-OPRUS (2). Fleming, Diadkova, Larin, Hawlata, Urbanová, Sénéchal, Deshayes, Paris Nat. Op. Ch. & O, Conlon (Director: Robert Carsen; V/D: Francois Roussillon)

Rusalka (CD versions)
⊙— *** Decca 460 568-2 (3). Fleming, Heppner, Hawlata, Zajick, Urbanová, Kusnjer, Kloubová, Kühn Mixed Ch., Czech PO, Mackerras

*** Sup. 10 3641-2 (3). Beňačková-Cápová, Novák, Soukupová, Ochman, Drobková, Prague Ch. & Czech PO, Neumann

What the film director, Bohumil Zoul has done in the Supraphon DVD is to use the 1961 Supraphon audio recording as the soundtrack for an imaginative re-creation of the story, using actors chosen for their looks. So Rusalka, sung freshly and brightly by Milada Subrtová, is played by a very pretty young girl, Katerina Machackova, and the Prince, sung by the legendary Ivo Zidek, has film-star good looks in the person of Miroslav Nohinek. The Foreign Princess, formidably sung by Alena Miková, is portrayed by the handsomely implacable Marie Malkova, while the Turnspit, sung by a girl, Ivana Mixová, is played by a young boy (Michal Mikes). Among the principals, only the old Watersprite is sung and played by the same artist, Eduard Haken.

The opening scene between Rusalka and the Watersprite makes clear their supernatural character by using superimposed images, making their green complexions and bodies transparent. The superimposed images continue until the Prince arrives on his horse, and we see the transformation of Rusalka into a human being, so losing her fussy green complexion and acquiring a blouse and skirt. Though the camerawork tends to be fussy, the result is certainly evocative. One trouble, which increases towards the end of the film, is the coordination of words and lips, and the 1961 audio recording, clear and full on voices, tends to have rather thin orchestral sound. That said, this is a most traditional presentation following the composer's vision, with a first-rate performance allied to an idealized setting of the story. Like the Solti DVD of Tchaikovsky's *Eugene Onegin*, it certainly points the way to the future. Who knows, one day we may have a really realistic DVD *Ring*, perhaps filmed by Stephen Spielberg!

This live video recording of *Rusalka*, made in 2002 for French television, offers a DVD of Robert Carsen's Paris Opera production. Like some other DVDs, it permanantly exposes the pitfalls of so many modern opera productions that ignore the intentions of the composer and wilfully place the producer's sometimes bizarre conceits before the needs of the music, distorting the presentation of the principal characters. Here a fine performance is all but ruined by such tasteless visual arrogance.

As in her audio recording for Decca, Renée Fleming confirms her special love for the piece, helped by a supporting cast that could hardly be starrier, with James Conlon a warmly Dvořákian conductor. Fleming is in glorious voice, with the recording balance tending to favour singers rather than the orchestra. Yet there are striking differences in her reading here on stage compared with her studio recording. On stage her expression is far freer, which to a degree brings added warmth but which also makes for singing stylistically far less pure, with sliding between notes and under-the-note attack. When so much is so moving, and Fleming's acting matches her unfailingly heart-felt singing, it may be a minor problem, but on musical grounds the audio version is preferable.

Sergei Larin as the Prince is similarly positive, with his clear Slavonic tenor only occasionally roughening under strain. In Carlsen's modern-dress production, with costumes by Michael Levine, he cuts an even less romantic figure than he might, not helped by his outfits of winter overcoat and trilby, and baggy lounge suit. Larissa Diadkova makes a characterful figure of the witch, Jezibaba, even when in Act III she appears in what initially looks like a padded pulpit, but then in a surreal way turns out to be a vertically upended bed! Franz Hawlata, a fine bass, sings with richness and power as the Water Spirit, an imposing figure even in a lounge suit and wire-framed spectacles. Power and projection also mark the singing of Eva Urbanová as the Prince's seducer, the Foreign Princess, and it is good to have the veteran Michel Sénéchal taking the character role of the Gamekeeper, though both he and the excellent Karine Deshayes as the Kitchen Boy are not helped by the morning dress of tail coat and striped trousers given to all the palace servants. This Paris production with its unflattering modern costumes and prosaic sets – sometimes a bare box, more often a gigantic hotel bedroom – has little magic, despite some clever lighting devised by the director himself. The format is relatively extravagant on two DVDs, with a collection of trailers for other discs from TDK as the only substantial extra. Not recommended. The Decca CD set is in every way a more satisfying musical experience.

This offers not only ripely atmospheric sound but what in almost every way is the ideal cast, with the Czech Philharmonic incandescent under Sir Charles Mackerras. Renée Fleming gives a heartfelt, sharply detailed performance, with the voice consistently beautiful over the widest range. Ben Heppner too, with his powerful tenor at once lyrical and heroic, is ideally cast as the Prince. Franz Hawlata as the Watergnome, Rusalka's father, and Dolora Zajick as the witch, Ježibaba, are both outstanding too, with even the smaller roles cast from strength, using leading singers from the Prague Opera. In his inspired conducting Mackerras does not resist the obvious Wagnerian overtones, yet Czech flavours are never underplayed in the many colourful dance rhythms.

Dvořák's fairy-tale opera is also given a magical performance by Neumann and his Czech forces, helped by full, brilliant and atmospheric recording. The title-role is superbly taken by Gabriela Beňačková-Cápová, and the famous *Invocation to the moon* is enchanting. Vera Soukupová as the Witch is just as characterfully Slavonic in a lower register, though not so even; while Wieslaw Ochman sings with fine, clean, heroic tone as the Prince, his timbre made distinctive by tight vibrato. Richard Novák brings out some of the Alberich-like overtones as the Watersprite, though the voice is not always steady. The banding could be more generous, but a full translation is included. However, the Decca set makes a clear first choice.

Rusalka (abridged CD version)

(N) ** Orfeo (ADD) C638 0421 (2). Beňačková, Dvorsky, Randová, Nesterenko, V. State Op. Ch. & O, Neumann

This live recording from Austrian Radio was made at the first night of the belated Viennese production on 10 April 1987, 85 years after its planned Viennese première, vividly capturing the atmosphere of a great and moving occasion. The casting of the five principal roles could hardly be starrier, an unrivalled Slavonic quartet, with three Czech singers joined by the Russian bass, Evgeni Nesterenko, as the Watergnome. Neatly, the resonant Eva Randová doubles in the roles of the witch, Jezibaba, and the Foreign Princess. To add to the authenticity, Vaclav Neumann conducts far more warmly than in many of his studio recordings. The stereo recording is full and vivid, marred only occasionally by stage and other noises. The snag is that the performance comes in a cut version, taking away some half hour of music, largely a question of the elimination of the Hunter and the Turnspit from the story. In compensation, the cuts bring the advantage that the opera can be readily fitted on to two CDs instead of three. Gabriela Beňačková as Rusalka is even warmer in tone and often weightier than Renée Fleming in the excellent Decca version, just as fearless in tackling the exposed top notes. Peter Dvorsky at the peak of his form is light and lyrical as the Prince, while Randová is impressive in both her roles, weighty and characterful.

Rusalka: highlights

*** Decca 466 356-2 (from above complete recording, with Fleming, Heppner; cond. Mackerras)
(M) **(*) Sup. 11 2252-2 (from above complete recording; cond. Neumann)

The splendid Decca recording of *Rusalka* runs to three CDs and there will be those collectors who will be satisfied with just highlights; and here the heroine's famous *Invocation to the moon* opens a well-chosen 74-minute selection. Texts and translations are included.

The Supraphon disc offers an hour of music. But the current mid-priced reissue has neither libretto nor synopsis, merely a list of the excerpts.

The Stubborn Lovers (complete)

*** Sup. SU 3765-2. Janál, Březina, Sýlkorová, Kloubová, Beláček, Prague Philharmonic Ch. & Philh., Bělohlávek

This sparkling one-act comic opera with an amiably nonsensical plot is guaranteed to delight all lovers of Dvořák's music. In a sequence of 16 brief scenes it gives an amusing picture of village life, mainly in brisk ensembles. A few years before Dvořák wrote it in the autumn of 1874, Smetana's *The Bartered Bride* was given its first performance, and Dvořák follows that iconic example in tone of voice. Yet in keeping with his progressive outlook, this is a piece which links numbers together. This splendid account of an opera otherwise unrecorded, very well sung and played, with Jiří Bělohlávek a most persuasive conductor, makes its mark tellingly, with one winning tune after another from the Overture onwards.

The reluctant lovers of the title are Toník and Lenka, whose parents (Vávra, father of Toník, and Ríhová, mother of Lenka) demand that they marry. Naturally, the young ones want to choose for themselves, but the godfather of both of them, Reřicha, understands the youngsters better than their parents. He succeeds in making them jealous, demonstrating that they are actually in love with each other, by suggesting that their parents are themselves scandalously intent on marrying across the generations, Vávra with designs on Lenka, Ríhová with Toník. This involves a sequence of farcical overhearings and misunderstandings that, needless to say, are sorted out in the end with little or no pain.

Rather like Alfonso in *Così fan tutte*, Reřicha is the manipulator, contributing to almost every number, a role strongly taken here by the bass, Gustáv Beláček, coping splendidly with solos rather like patter-songs. The mellifluous light tenor Jaroslav Březina is splendid as Toník, characterizing well and making his change of heart convincing, as Zdena Kloubová does as Lenka when, seeing Toník as the choice of her mother, she wonders why tears have come into her eyes. The respective parents, Vávra and Ríhová, are well taken too, though they have less opportunity to establish positive characters. A welcome rarity.

Wanda (complete)

**(*) Orfeo C149003F (3). Romanko, Tchistjakova, Straka, Daniluk, Kusnjer, Breedt, Prague Chamber Ch., WDR Ch., & SO Cologne, Albrecht

In five Acts, *Wanda* dates from 1876, the year after Dvořák composed his eternally fresh *Fifth Symphony*, and much of that freshness is carried over to the opera, with orchestration light and transparent. Sadly, he was not a natural opera-composer and, for all the delights of the music, this Polish subject involving Princess (later Queen) Wanda and two rivals for her love, the Cracow knight Slavoj and the German Prince Roderick, is hardly gripping dramatically.

Yet on disc it is well worth investigating, and Gerd Albrecht, using a revised and expanded edition of a score thought to be lost in the Second World War, conducts a strong, purposeful performance, with fine teamwork in the ensembles. The principal male soloists, Peter Straka as Slavoj and Ivan Kusnjer as Roderick, are both first rate, but the warm, idiomatic singing of the principal women, Olga Romanko in the title-role and Irina Tchistjakova as her sister, Božena, is marred by the unevenness of their very Slavonic voices. Excellent singing from the joint Czech and German choirs, and full, well-balanced radio recording.

DYSON, George (1883–1964)

Sir George Dyson's career was based on his love for, and his wish to continue, the great tradition of English church music. 'If a man would live again the musical history of a thousand years,' he wrote, 'let him sit in the choir of a cathedral and listen.' It was a limited view but a deeply sincere one, and his recorded output demonstrates his own ability to perpetuate his musical in heritance.

(i) Violin Concerto. Children's Suite (after Walter De La Mare)

⊶ ✿ *** Chan. 9369. (i) Mordkovitch; City of L. Sinfonia, Hickox

Dyson's *Violin Concerto* is a richly inspired, warmly lyrical work, and the third-movement *Andante* for violin and muted strings, divided into variations, brings a rare hushed beauty, superbly achieved in this dedicated performance. Lydia Mordkovitch gives a reading that is both passionate and deeply expressive. The *Children's Suite* reflects qualities similar to those in the *Concerto*, not least a tendency to switch into waltz-time and a masterly ability to create rich and transparent orchestral textures, beautifully caught in the opulent Chandos recording. Two rarities to treasure.

(i) Concierto leggiero (for piano & strings); Concerto da camera; Concerto da chiesa (both for string orchestra)

*** Chan. 9076. (i) Parkin; City of L. Sinfonia, Hickox

This splendid Chandos CD brings not only an engagingly light-textured concertante item for piano but also two powerful and eloquent works in the great tradition of English string music. The writing shows both a strongly burning creative flame as well as new influences from outside. The performances here are wonderfully fresh and committed and the string recording has plenty of bite and full sonority, while the balance with the piano is quite admirable. Highly recommended.

Symphony in G; At the Tabard Inn: Overture. Concerto da chiesa for Strings

(N) (BB) *** Naxos 8.557720. Bournemouth SO, Lloyd-Jones

(i) *Symphony in G;* (ii) *At the Tabard Inn: Overture;* (ii; iii) *In Honour of the City*

(N) (M) **(*) Chan. 10308X. (i) City of L. Sinfonia; (ii) LSO; (iii) L. Symphony Ch.; Hickox

First heard in 1937, Dyson's *Symphony in G* is the most ambitious of his orchestral works. Welcomed at its first performance, it subsequently fell into neglect, when it followed such a striking sequence of symphonies written by British composers in the 1930s: Vaughan Williams, Walton, Bax, Moeran and others. In the first two movements Dyson's determination to strike a contemporary pose in that Sibelian era seems to inhibit his melodic gift, with thematic material fragmentary, and the charming second-movement *Andante* is slight. But in the third-movement variations – taking the place of a Scherzo – and most of all in the colourful finale, his inhibitions depart in writing that is warm, free and colourful, using ideas from *The Canterbury Pilgrims*, with majestic scoring for the brass. Helped by clear, well-balanced recording, David Lloyd-Jones conducts a brilliant performance which clarifies often heavy textures. In the *Concerto da chiesa* for strings of 1949, each of the three movements develops a medieval hymn melody, with *Veni Emmanuel* inspiring a darkly dedicated slow first movement, among Dyson's finest inspirations. That melody returns, transformed, at the end of the finale which is based on the vigorous psalm-tune, *Laetatus sum*. With solo strings atmospherically set against the full string band, this is a neglected masterpiece. *At the Tabard Inn* was originally designed as an overture for his choral work, *The Canterbury Pilgrims*, and completes a first-rate disc, superbly played.

By its side, the more expensive Hickox version, although very well played, seems less convincing, especially the first movement, which tends to flag a little. The Chandos disc also includes two fill-ups, originally issued with *The Canterbury Pilgrims*, *At the Tabard Inn* and the choral *In Honour of the City*, both excellently performed; they are discussed below. But the Naxos CD is first choice for the symphony.

CHAMBER MUSIC

(i) *Cello Sonata;* (ii) *3 Lyrics for Violin & Piano; 3 Violin Pieces. Bach's Birthday; Epigrams for Piano; My Birthday; Prelude & Ballet for Piano; Primrose Mount; Twilight; 3 War Pieces*

(M) *** Dutton CDLX 7137. Owen Norris, with (i) Spooner; (ii) Juritz

From a working-class background Dyson won music scholarships to become the leading champion of public school music in the 1920s and subsequently Director of the Royal College of Music. On disc his major works have been well treated, but in this charming collection, master-minded by the pianist, David Owen Norris, quite a different side is revealed, most strikingly in the piano pieces that make up the greater part of the programme. With Owen Norris an ideal interpreter, pointing rhythm and phrase seductively, the wit of the ten tiny *Epigrams* at the start has one appreciating Dyson's lightness of touch. Just as witty are the four pieces entitled *Bach's Birthday*, with counterpoint that strays into atonality, intended as a joke for his friend the pianist and scholar Harold Samuel. *Three War Pieces*, unpublished until now, were written when Dyson was in service in the trenches in the First World War, while other groups of pieces like *Twilight* and *My Birthday* from the 1920s were designed for amateurs to play, as are the two sets of violin pieces.

3 Rhapsodies (for string quartet)
(BB) *** Hyp. Helios CDH 55045. Divertimenti – HOWELLS: *In Gloucestershire (String Quartet 3)* ***

Although its spirit is lighter, more capricious, the first of Dyson's *Rhapsodies* follows on quite naturally after the gentle close of Howells's haunting portrayal of the Gloucestershire countryside. The second, a dark elegy, makes a haunting contrast, but the third is again essentially light-hearted in its lyrical grace. Surprisingly, the work was inspired by Dante and written after a Mediterranean holiday. Its changing moods are caught most sensitively by this excellent group, and the Hyperion recording is of high quality.

VOCAL MUSIC

Benedicite; Evening Service in D; Hail Universal Lord; Live forever, glorious Lord; Te Deum; Valour; (i) (Organ) Prelude; Postlude; Psalm-tune Prelude (I was Glad); Voluntary of Praise
(BB) *** Regis RRC 1161. St Catherine's College, Cambridge, Ch., Owen Rees; (i) Rees (organ) (with HOWELLS: *Dyson's Delight*)

An excellent bargain anthology of Dyson's music. His writing here may not always be strikingly individual, but every so often its invention soars. There are some well-made organ pieces here too (plus an admiring contribution from Herbert Howells, based on two themes from Dyson's *Canterbury Pilgrims*), but it is the vocal music that is the more memorable. It is all sung with striking freshness by choristers who seem to have its inflexions in their very being. Excellent recording in a spacious acoustic, though the words come over well. Even so, there is an excellent leaflet with this reissue (of an originally Unicorn disc), setting them out and giving much useful information about the composer and his music, a model of its kind.

3 Choral Hymns; (Organ) Fantasia & Ground Bass; Hierusalem; Psalm 150; 3 Songs of Praise
*** Hyp. CDA 66150. Hill, St Michael's Singers, Trotter, RPO, Rennert

Where the organ piece unashamedly builds on an academic model, *Hierusalem* reveals the inner man more surprisingly, a richly sensuous setting of a medieval poem inspired by the thought of the Holy City, building to a jubilant climax. It is a splendid work and is backed here by the six hymns and the Psalm setting, all of them heart-warming products of the Anglican tradition. Performances are outstanding, with Jonathan Rennert drawing radiant singing and playing from his team, richly and atmospherically recorded.

(i–ii) The Canterbury Pilgrims. Overture at the Tabard Inn; (i) In Honour of the City
*** Chan. 9531 (2). (i) Kenny, Tear, Roberts; (ii) London Symphony Ch.; LSO, Hickox

Chandos provide us with the long-awaited recording of Dyson's best-known work, preceded by the Overture based on its themes. Here the soloists all have major contributions to make, for Dyson's characterization of the individual pilgrims is strong; but the glory of the piece is the choruses, which are splendidly sung here. *In Honour of the City*, Dyson's setting of William Dunbar, appeared in 1928, nine years before Walton's version of the same text; Dyson, however, unlike Walton, uses a modern version of the text, as he does in *The Canterbury Tales*, and to fine, direct effect. The splendid Chandos recording is fully worthy of the vibrant music-making here.

Quo Vadis
*** Chan. 10061 (2). Barker, Rigby, Langridge, Williams, Royal Welsh College of Music & Drama Chamber Ch., BBC Nat. Ch. & O of Wales, Hickox

Quo Vadis can be related to such works of the same period as Howells's *Hymnus Paradisi*, Finzi's *Intimations of Immortality*, Vaughan Williams's *Sancta civitas* and *Dona nobis pacem*, representing 'agnostics at prayer', as Lewis Foreman says in his note. More than the others, Dyson draws on the widest array of sources, rearranging texts from such poets as Campion, Vaughan, Herrick, Shelley, Newman and Bridges in an elaborate kaleidoscope of words, mixing different sources together in all but one of the nine substantial movements, even rearranging individual lines from Wordsworth's *Intimations of Immortality*. Far from sounding disjointed or bitty, each section is given a seamless quality, with ecstatic choral climaxes designed to exploit the all-embracing acoustics of a great cathedral. The warm but well-defined Chandos recording helps to heighten the impact of the incandescent singing of the Welsh choristers, semi-chorus as well as full choir, inspired by the dedicated direction of Richard Hickox. Each of the four soloists – here a strong, firm and characterful quartet – in turn takes a leading role in the nicely balanced sequence of movements. They also sing as a quartet in the movements ending each half. Dyson's idiom may not be strikingly original but, with its lyrical warmth and fine control of texture, and with emotions often heightened by striking key-changes, the result will delight all devotees of the British choral tradition.

ECCLES, John (c. 1668–1775)

Semele (opera; complete)
(N) *** Forum FRC 9203. Mangrum, Taylor, Ferrill, Philips, Roberson, Grau, Clements, Valsson, Florida State University Op. O, Rooley

In 1707, some 36 years before Handel wrote his *Semele*, John Eccles used the same drama of William Congreve as the basis of his last opera, collaborating closely with the celebrated dramatist. At the time, Eccles was regarded very much as Purcell's successor, the country's principal composer of dramatic music, but he and Congreve both saw the way that Italian opera was pushing out English opera, and Eccles's *Semele* was never performed. This première recording of the work comes through the enterprise of the Opera Department of Florida State University and thanks to the enthusiasm of Anthony Rooley, who likens the collaboration of Eccles and Congreve to that of Gilbert and Sullivan. Each brief number, solo, duet or ensemble, is fluently linked by recitative very similar in style to that of Purcell, and takes you crisply on with nothing outstaying its welcome, even if little can compare with Handel in memorability. With jolly numbers in compound time predominating, the emotional range is much more limited than with Handel, but the writing is certainly inventive, as in the 'soft symphony' which opens Act III on gentle pizzicatos from the strings.

With a cast of young singers, some of them with voices not fully formed, Rooley directs a most enjoyable performance, cleanly recorded, with voices well forward. Standing out is the characterful Juno of Brenda Grau, well contrasted with the sweet, fluent Semele of Leslie Mangrum. The orchestra too reflects excellent teaching by the University's Early Music Department, limited to solo strings, baroque oboe and continuo.

EDWARDS, Ross (born 1943)

Piano Concerto

**(*) Australian ABC Eloquence 426 483-2. Henning, Queensland SO, Fredman – WILLIAMSON: *Double Piano Concerto*; SCULTHORPE: *Piano Concerto* **(*)

An enterprising disc of Australian piano concertos. Ross Edwards's example is no masterpiece, but it has a certain enjoyable vitality. The slow movement, using pentatonic scales, gives it a Japanese flavour, and the finale is tuneful and fun. The performance is good, though the recording is only average.

EGK, Werner (1901–83)

The Temptation of St Anthony (cantata)

(M) *** DG (IMS) (ADD) 449 097-2. J. Baker, Koeckert Qt, Bav. RSO (strings), composer – ORFF: *Catulli Carmina* ***

Egk's *Temptation of St Anthony* shows him at his best: it is in effect a song-cycle, and Janet Baker, who was in particularly good voice at this period of her career (the mid-1960s), sings it with great beauty. The recording, too, is good, and this can be recommended as a sampler for those who want to investigate Egk's music for themselves.

ELGAR, Edward (1857–1934)

(i–ii) *Adieu; Beau Brummel: Minuet*; (i; iii) *3 Bavarian Dances, Op. 27; Caractacus, Op. 35: Woodland Interlude. Chanson de matin; Chanson de nuit, Op. 15/1–2; Contrasts, Op. 10/3; Dream Children, Op. 43*; (iv) *Enigma Variations, Op. 36*; (i; iii) *Falstaff, Op. 68: 2 Interludes*. (iv) *Pomp and Circumstance Marches 1–5, Op. 39*; (i; iii) *Salut d'amour; Sérénade lyrique*; (i; iii; v) *Soliloquy for Oboe* (orch. Gordon Jacob); (i–ii) *Sospiri, Op. 70; The Spanish Lady: Burlesco. The Starlight Express: Waltz. Sursum corda, Op. 11*

(B) *** Chan. 2-for-1 241-4 (2). (i) Bournemouth Sinf.; (ii) Hurst; (iii) Del Mar; (iv) RSNO, Gibson; (v) with Goossens

Sir Alexander Gibson's reading of *Enigma* has stood the test of time and remains very satisfying, warm and spontaneous in feeling, with a memorable climax in *Nimrod*. The 1978 recording, made in Glasgow's City Hall, remains outstanding. The *Pomp and Circumstance Marches*, too, have fine *nobilmente* and swagger. The rest of the programme is a collection of miniatures directed by either George Hurst or Norman Del Mar, both understanding Elgarians. Elgar wrote the *Soliloquy* for Leon Goossens, who plays it with his long-recognizable tone-colour and feeling for phrase. Most of the other pieces in Norman Del Mar's programme are well known, but they come up with new warmth and commitment here, and the 1976 recording, made in the Guildhall, Southampton, has an appealing ambient warmth and naturalness. George Hurst

recorded his Elgar rarities a year earlier in Christchurch Priory, and again the recording has plenty of body, but there is more thinness in the sound of the violins in these items than with Del Mar.

'*A Portrait of Elgar*': *3 Bavarian Dances, Op. 27; Carissima; Chanson de matin; Chanson de nuit, Op. 15/1–2; Cockaigne Overture, Op. 40; Dream Children, Op. 43; Enigma Variations, Op. 36; Froissart Overture, Op. 19; Gavotte (Contrasts), Op. 10/3; Introduction & Allegro for Strings, Op. 47; May Song; Mazurka, Op. 10/1; Nursery Suite; Pomp and Circumstance Marches 1–5, Op. 39; Rosemary (That's for remembrance); Sérénade lyrique; Serenade for Strings, Op. 20; Salut d'amour, Op. 12; Spanish Lady (suite); The Wand of Youth Suite 2, Op. 1b*

(B) **(*) Nim. NI 1769 (4). E. SO or E. String O, Boughton

This very inexpensive four-disc set is made up of four separate Elgar collections, and Disc 3 duplicates the *Chanson de matin* and *Chanson de nuit*, already included on Disc 2. However, the latter collection (including the *Nursery Suite* plus *Dream Children* and most of the miniatures) is particularly attractive, for William Boughton's performances are graceful and sympathetic and have plenty of character. The *Introduction and Allegro* has a ripely overwhelming climax, but the fugal argument is not lost. The *Enigma Variations* have many pleasingly delicate touches of colour, with the brass and organ making a fine effect in the finale. There is an easy swagger about the *Pomp and Circumstance Marches*. The warmly reverberant acoustic of the Great Hall of Birmingham University gives the performances of these larger-scale works a spaciousness that is entirely apt. What is more questionable is the scale conveyed by the recording (in the same acoustic) for the other, lighter and more intimate pieces. The manner is sparkling, the playing refined and well detailed, with rhythms nicely sprung, but the large scale implied tends to inflate the music, particularly in the *Wand of Youth* excerpts.

(i) *3 Bavarian Dances*; (ii) *Caractacus: Triumphal March; Woodland Interlude*; (i) *Carissima; 3 Characteristic Pieces, Op. 10; Elegy; The Kingdom: Prelude. May Song; Minuet, Op. 21; Nursery Suite; Rosemary; Severn Suite, Op. 87; Wand of Youth Suites 1–2*; (iii) *5 Piano Improvisations*

(N) (M) (***) EMI mono 5 85153-2 (2). (i) LSO, LPO, BBC SO or New SO, composer; (ii) LSO, Collingwood; (iii) composer (piano)

A feast of essentially lightweight Elgar, with nearly all the music conducted by the composer and drawn from EMI's deepest archives. The sparkling vigour of Elgar's own performances is of course well known; one only has to play such items as the lively *Mazurka* from *Three Characteristic Pieces* to be instantly drawn into Elgar's world (or, for that matter, the deliciously pointed *Gavotte* from the same triptych). These two CDs are full of delight, not least in the *Five Piano Improvisation*, where we have Elgar himself as pianist. If they hardly represent the very best of his music, they are beautifully crafted and often very touching.

3 Bavarian Dances, Op. 27; Caractacus, Op. 35: Triumphal March. The Light of Life, Op. 29: Meditation. Polonia, Op. 76. Wand of Youth Suites 1–2, Op. 1a–b

(B) *** EMI (ADD) 5 75295-2. LPO, Boult

Sir Adrian's outstanding performances of the *Wand of Youth Suites* catch both the innocence and the intimacy of the music, very much reflecting Elgar's personal world. The fragile charm of the delicate scoring is well realized and there is plenty of schoolboy gusto for the rollicking *Wild Bear* (only playfully wild, of course). The orchestral playing is first rate and conveys to the listener the conductor's obvious affection for this music. The 1968 recording is of vintage EMI quality and has adapted splendidly to CD remastering, with little loss of ambient warmth. The *Bavarian Dances* are also genuinely inspired, and the climax of *The Marksman* brings a real frisson. *Polonia* was written as a gesture to help Polish refugees at the beginning of the First World War and shows the composer's flair for flag-waving orchestral sounds.

'*The Lighter Elgar*': (i) *Beau Brummel: Minuet;* (ii) *Carissima;* (i) *Chanson de matin, Op. 15/2;* (ii) *3 Characteristic Pieces, Op. 10: Mazurka; Sérénade mauresque; Contrasts: The Gavottes AD 1700 & 1900.* (i) *Dream Children, Op. 43;* (ii) *May Song; Mina; Minuet, Op. 21; Rosemary (That's for remembrance);* (ii–iii) *Romance for Bassoon & Orchestra, Op. 62;* (i) *Salut d'amour, Op. 12;* (ii) *Sevillana, Op. 7; Sérénade lyrique;* (i; iv) *The Starlight Express, Op. 78:* Organ grinder's songs: *My old tunes; To the children.* (i) *The Wand of Youth Suite 1:* excerpt: *Sun Dance*

🔑 ❁ (M) *** EMI (ADD) 5 65593-2. (i) RPO, Collingwood; (ii) N. Sinfonia, Marriner; with (iii) Chapman; (iv) Harvey

This beautifully recorded CD combines almost all the contents of two LPs. In the first, Frederick Harvey joins the orchestra for two organ grinder's songs from the incidental music for *The Starlight Express*, and they have seldom been sung more winningly on record. It is these items one remembers most, but the second collection under Sir Neville Marriner is hardly less successful. All the music is pleasingly delightful in its tender moods and restrained scoring, favouring flute, bassoon and the clarinet in middle or lower register. Very much worth having is the rhapsodic *Romance for Bassoon and Orchestra* with Michael Chapman the elegant soloist. The Northern Sinfonia play with style and affection. Throughout, EMI have provided that warm, glowing sound that is their special province in recording Elgar's music.

Caractacus: March. Coronation March; Empire March; Grania and Diarmid: Funeral March. March of the Moghul Emperors. Polonia; Pomp and Circumstance Marches 1–5, Op. 39

(N) (BB) *** Naxos 8.557273. New Zealand SO, Judd

James Judd here follows up the excellent Naxos disc of the two *Wand of Youth Suites* and the *Nursery Suite* with a splendid collection of Elgar marches. The five *Pomp and Circumstance Marches* in brisk, well-sprung readings are flanked by four rather longer pieces – three more extended marches plus, as a final item, *Polonia*, Elgar's First World War tribute to Poland, with its sequence of Polish martial themes made to sound very British. The clarity and crisp ensemble of the *Pomp and Circumstance* pieces (as well as speeds on the brisk side) give them a winning freshness, with the brass particularly impressive. The *Coronation March* of 1911, written for the coronation of George V, has symphonic dimensions, with Judd drawing the disparate elements strongly together, while the solemn *Funeral March* from Elgar's incidental music to a play by W. B. Yeats and George Moore, *Grania and Diarmid*, is here enhanced when it includes not just the march itself but the substantial introduction, usually labelled 'Incidental Music'. The *Empire March*, written for the opening of the Wembley Exhibition of 1924, and *Polonia* are relative rarities on disc, both persuasively done, while the *March of the Moghul Emperors*, with its exotic percussion, is a welcome rarity too. The *Triumphal March* from *Caractacus* has the brassiest opening of any of the marches, and Judd makes it swagger infectiously. Warm, clear, well-balanced recording.

***Caractacus, Op. 35: Woodland Interlude. Crown of India Suite, Op. 66; Grania & Diarmid, Op. 42: Funeral March. The Light of Life, Op. 29: Meditation. Nursery Suite; Severn Suite, Op. 87* (orchestral version)**

(B) **(*) EMI (ADD) 5 75294-2. RLPO, Groves

It is good to have these performances by Sir Charles Groves restored to the catalogue. They were recorded in 1969 and 1970, while he was principal conductor of the Royal Liverpool Philharmonic Orchestra. This is all music that he understands warmly, and the results give much pleasure. One does not have to be an imperialist to enjoy any of the occasional pieces, and it is interesting to find the patriotic music coming up fresher than the little interlude from *The Light of Life*, beautiful though that is. Both the *Nursery Suite* (written for Princesses Elizabeth and Margaret Rose) and the orchestral version of the *Severn Suite* (written for a brass band contest) come from Elgar's very last period, when his inspiration came in flashes rather than as a sustained searchlight. The completely neglected *Funeral March* was written in 1901 for a play by W. B. Yeats and George Moore; it is a splendid piece. The CD transfer retains the bloom of the original recordings.

Chanson de matin; Cockaigne Overture; Enigma Variations* (including original version of ending)*; Serenade for Strings

(M) *** Hallé CD HLL 7501. Hallé O, Elder

Recorded live in Bridgewater Hall, Manchester, in October 2002, this version of the *Enigma Variations* under Mark Elder on the Hallé's own label is very strongly characterized, with playing delicate and refined on the one hand and powerfully incisive on the other; the oboe in R.B.T. is jauntily pointed, and W.M.B. brings powerful contrasts over its brief span, while *Nimrod*, taken at a steady, measured speed, builds up with exceptional power, with the organ adding to the weight of the finale. As a bonus the disc offers the shorter, original version of the finale, as used in the ballet *Enigma Variations.* The clarity of texture is ideal, not just in *Enigma* but also in the other items: the *Serenade for Strings* with a spacious and refined central *Larghetto*, *Cockaigne* (also with organ) and *Chanson de matin*, which is light and delicate.

Civic Fanfare;* (i) *Piano Concerto: Slow movement. Crown of India: March; Hail Immemorial Ind. Empire March. Polonia; The Spanish Lady: suite; Une voix dans le désert; The wind at dawn

**(*) Classico CLASSCD 334. (i) Fingerhut; Ostergard, Hall, Munich SO, Bostock

The two items here from the *Crown of India* are the only two to have survived beyond the regular suite. The *March* is not as characterful as the well-known *March of the Mogul Emperors*, and the extended song, *Hail Immemorial Ind*, is no better than the corny opening words suggest, but this music is typically Elgarian, and so is the *Empire March* of 1924, written for the Wembley Exhibition.

The song, *The wind at dawn*, like the *Crown of India* items a first recording, is the earliest music here, setting a poem by Elgar's future wife, similar in mood to *Sea Pictures*, with the mezzo-soprano, Mette Christina Ostergard, a clear, girlish soloist. The words (by the Belgian poet, Emil Cammaerts), are an embarrassment in the wartime piece, *A voice in the desert*, which, starting with melodramatic funeral drumbeats, involves both a speaker and a mezzo soloist in uneasy harness. *Polonia*, involving orchestra alone, has its moments of banality too, but works far better, even though the performance could be stronger.

The Spanish Lady Suite here with the five brief movements – March, Morning Minuet, Fitzdottel, Fantastico and Bolero – rather more striking than those in the well-known suite edited by Percy Young. The slow movement of the *Piano Concerto* was also edited by Dr Young, but even with a sympathetic performance from Margaret Fingerhut, that is a disappointing trifle, more of a salon piece than a genuine concerto movement. The strings of the Munich Symphony are not always as well nourished as they might be, but Douglas Bostock is always persuasive with his Elgarian rubato. Lewis Foreman's scholarly notes greatly add to one's enjoyment.

(i) *Cockaigne Overture;* (ii) *Cello Concerto in E min.;* (iii) *Violin Concerto;* (i) *Enigma Variations, Op. 36;* (iv) *Pomp and Circumstance Marches 1-5, Op. 39*

(B) *** Sony (ADD) SB2K 63247 (2). (i) Phd. O, Ormandy;
(ii) Du Pré, Phd. O, Barenboim; (iii) Zukerman, LPO,
Barenboim; (iv) Philh. O, A. Davis

Jacqueline du Pré's outstanding second recording of the Elgar *Cello Concerto* is discussed below, as is Zukerman's ardent account of the *Violin Concerto*, recorded six years later, also with Barenboim. Andrew Davis brings plenty of imaginative flair to the five *Pomp and Circumstance Marches* and is sumptuously recorded. Ormandy's view of *Enigma* is characteristically forthright, lacking some Elgarian nuance – although *Nimrod* is finely shaped – but, with the help of glorious Philadelphia string-playing, urgently convincing just the same. Ormandy paints his picture of Edwardian London with even broader strokes of the brush in vivid primary colours and the Philadelphia players rise to his exultant direction. Again the expansively resonant sound adds to the sense of spectacle.

Cockaigne Overture, Op. 40; Enigma Variations, Op. 36; Introduction & Allegro for Strings; Serenade for Strings, Op. 20

⊶ ✪ (BB) *** Warner Apex 09027 413712-2. BBC SO, A. Davis

Andrew Davis's collection of favourite Elgar works is electrifying. The very opening of *Cockaigne* has rarely been so light and sprightly, and it leads on to the most powerful characterization of each contrasted section. The two string works are richly and sensitively done. Similarly, the big tonal contrasts in *Enigma* are brought out dramatically, notably in Davis's rapt and spacious reading of *Nimrod*, helped by the spectacular Teldec recording. This is surely a worthy successor to Barbirolli in this repertoire and is an outstanding disc in every way. At its new Apex price it is one of the great Elgarian bargains.

Cockaigne Overture; Enigma Variations; Serenade for Strings, Op. 20.

(N) (M) **(*) Telarc CD 80192. Baltimore SO, Zinman

David Zinman is a persuasive Elgarian, though his readings are affectionate rather than dramatically robust, and the cockney spirit of *Cockaigne* seems a little undercharacterized

alongside Beecham. However, the fine Baltimore string playing is idiomatically warm and expansive: the opening of *Enigma* has a gentle, touching lyricism, *Nimrod* is almost elegiac, while the great cello variation (B.G.N.) is gloriously rich. The Telarc recording is magnificent, with superbly resonant brass: the Guards ride by in *Cockaigne* grandiloquently, and the close of both the *Overture* and the *Variations* are sonically thrilling (bass drum and organ come through splendidly). The *Serenade* is beautifully played, the *Larghetto* touchingly nostalgic, and again the sound is first class.

Cockaigne Overture; Falstaff; Introduction and Allegro for Strings; Serenade for Strings

(B) *** CfP (ADD/DDD) 575 3072. LPO, Handley

Vernon Handley directs a superb performance of *Falstaff*, and the achievement is all the more remarkable because his tempi are unusually spacious (generally following the composer's markings). The playing of the LPO is warmly expressive and strongly rhythmic. *Cockaigne* is also given a performance that is expansive yet never hangs fire. The *Introduction and Allegro* and *Serenade* are digital and date from 1983. They were made in Watford Town Hall, but the balance is closer, the string outline more brightly lit. The *Introduction and Allegro* is passionate, yet with lyrical contrasts tenderly made; the *Serenade* brings a somewhat indulgent treatment of the *Larghetto*, and here comparison with Boult is not in Handley's favour. Nevertheless this reissue is a real bargain.

Cockaigne Overture; Froissart Overture, Op. 19; In the South (Alassio), Op. 50; Overture in D min. (arr. from HANDEL: Chandos Anthem 2)

(M) **(*) Chan. 8309. SNO, Gibson

Sir Alexander Gibson's Chandos collection dates from 1983, but it shows him at his best. The Scottish orchestra make a vividly cohesive sound and they are given a brilliant digital recording with a firm bass, though the strings are just a little lacking in richness of timbre. The picture of London is full of bustle and pageantry, with bold brass and flashing percussion, and Gibson's directness serves *Froissart* and the Handel arrangement equally well. *In the South*, too, does not lack impetus, if not matching the famous (deleted) Silvestri version, and the overall effect is extremely vivid and tangible, even though there are finer individual versions of these works available and the present collection has a playing time of only 54 minutes.

(i) *Cockaigne Overture;* (ii) *Froissart Overture, Op. 19; Pomp and Circumstance Marches, Op. 39,* (i) *1 in D;* (ii) *2 in A min.; 3 in C min.;* (i) *4 in G;* (ii) *5 in C*

(M) *** EMI (ADD) 5 66323-2. (i) Philh. O; (ii) New Philh. O;
Barbirolli

It is good to have *Cockaigne*, Barbirolli's ripe yet wonderfully vital portrait of Edwardian London, back in the catalogue – one of the finest of all his Elgar records. *Froissart* is very compelling too (though the CD transfer is slightly less flattering here), and Barbirolli makes a fine suite of the five *Pomp and Circumstance Marches*. The lesser-known Nos. 2 and 5 are particularly gripping, with plenty of contrast in No. 4 to offset the swagger elsewhere. Here the sound is as expansive as you could wish.

Cockaigne Overture; Introduction & Allegro for Strings, Op. 47; Serenade for Strings, Op. 20

(M) (***) EMI mono 5 66543-2 (2). Hallé O, Barbirolli – VAUGHAN WILLIAMS: *Oboe Concerto*, etc. (***)

Barbirolli later recorded all three of these works in stereo, but these mono versions from the early post-war period have an immediacy and positive strength rarely matched. Transfers are vivid and clear, with fine detail, only rarely thin or edgy. With the important Vaughan Williams recordings, an outstanding double-disc issue.

Cello Concerto in E min., Op. 85

⊶ ✿ (N) (M) * EMI (ADD) 5 62886-2 [5 62887-2]. Du Pré, LSO, Barbirolli (with *Cockaigne Overture*)– *Sea Pictures* *** ✿

*** EMI (ADD) 5 55527-2. Du Pré, LSO, Barbirolli – DVORAK: *Cello Concerto* **(*)

(M) *** Sony SMK 89712. Ma, LSO, Previn – WALTON: *Cello Concerto* ***

*** Virgin 5 45356-2. Mørk, CBSO, Rattle – BRITTEN: *Cello Symphony* ***

(M) (***) Revelation mono RV 10100. Rostropovich, Moscow PO, Rakhlin – BRITTEN: *Cello Symphony* (***)

*** BIS CD 486. Thedéen, Malmö SO, Markiz – SCHUMANN: *Concerto* ***

*** Naïve V 4961. Gastinel, CBSO, Brown – BARBER: *Cello Concerto* ***

(BB) *** Warner Apex 0927 40600-2. Noras, Finnish RSO, Saraste – BARTOK: *Rhapsody 1* ***; DVORAK: *Cello Concerto* **(*)

(N)(M) (**(*)) EMI mono 5 62592-2 [5 62953-2]. Casals, BBC SO, Boult – DVORAK: *Concerto* (***) (with BRUCH: *Kol Nidrei* (***))

(i) *Cello Concerto;* (ii) *Enigma Variations*

*** Australian Decca 450 021-2. (i) Harrell, Cleveland O, Maazel; (ii) LAPO, Mehta

(i) *Cello Concerto. Enigma Variations; Pomp and Circumstances Marches, Op. 39, 1 & 4*

(M) **(*) DG 474 561-2. Philh. O, Sinopoli, (i) with Maisky

(i) *Cello Concerto. Falstaff;* (ii) *Romance for Bassoon.* (iii) *Smoking Cantata*

(M) *** Hallé CD HLL 7505 (i) Schiff; (ii) Salvage; (iii) Shore; Hallé O, Elder

(i) *Cello Concerto. Falstaff, Op. 68.* BACH arr. Elgar: *Fantasia and Fugue in C min., BWV 537;* HANDEL arr. Elgar: *Overture in D min.*

(N) (M) *** EMI (ADD) 5 85152-2. LPO, Boult, (i) with Tortelier

Jacqueline du Pré was essentially a spontaneous artist. Her style is freely rhapsodic, but the result produced a very special kind of meditative feeling; in the very beautiful slow movement, brief and concentrated, her inner intensity conveys a depth of espressivo rarely achieved by any cellist on record. Brilliant virtuoso playing too in the Scherzo and finale. CD brings a subtle extra definition to heighten the excellent qualities of the 1965 recording, with the solo instrument firmly placed. Alongside the original pairing with Janet Baker's *Sea Pictures* comes Barbirolli's superb account of *Cockaigne*, and the disc is now offered at mid-price.

EMI have now given an alternative coupling with the Dvořák *Concerto*, and this much-loved recording is given extra warmth and clarity in the new transfer. However, we retain our allegiance to the original pairing, which has been revamped as one of EMI's 'Great Recordings of the Century'.

In its rapt concentration Yo-Yo Ma's recording with Previn is second only to du Pré. The first movement is lighter, a shade more urgent than the du Pré/Barbirolli version, and in the Scherzo he finds more fun, just as he finds extra sparkle in the main theme of the finale. The key movement with Ma, as with du Pré, is the Adagio, echoed later in the raptness of the slow epilogue, poised in its intensity. Warm, fully detailed recording, finely balanced, with understanding conducting from Previn. At mid-price a splendid bargain.

It is quite a coup for Mark Elder in this third Elgar issue on the Hallé's own label to have so masterly a cellist as Heinrich Schiff in the *Cello Concerto*. This is one of the very finest versions ever, in many ways even more impressive than Schiff's earlier version, which was recorded not with a British orchestra but with the Dresden Staatskapelle under Sir Neville Marriner. The new version has even more intensity, with the first movement played with patrician nobility, very Elgarian, yet without inflation. The Scherzo is dazzlingly played, and in the other two movements the reading is markedly different from Schiff's earlier version, with a more flowing speed in the slow movement, less heavy, more songful and just as deeply felt, and a breathtakingly fast account of the main allegro in the finale, crisply articulated and very exciting. *Falstaff* brings a thrustful account that carries one magnetically over the many contrasted sections, giving the illusion of a live performance; and the *Romance for Bassoon* makes an attractive supplement, with Graham Salvage, the orchestra's principal bassoon, as soloist, bringing out the glowing lyricism. As a tiny extra squib comes the first ever performance and recording of one of Elgar's 'japes', a protest for baritone and orchestra against a ban on smoking in the hall, imposed in his home by the composer's host and close friend, Edward Speyer. Only nine bars long, it lasts less than a minute, a Wagnerian flourish to demonstrate Elgar's tongue-in-cheek humour, with Andrew Shore the robust soloist.

Truls Mørk has the requisite blend of fervour and dignity, yet there is a freshness and directness here which is affecting. Rattle and the Birmingham orchestra give excellent support, and the recording has excellent internal balance and naturalness of perspective.

Lynn Harrell's deeply felt reading balances a gentle nostalgia with extrovert brilliance. The slow movement is tenderly spacious, the Scherzo bursts with exuberance and, after a passionate opening, the finale is memorable for the poignantly expressive reprise of the melody from the slow movement. The recording of the orchestra is brightly lit, but attractively so, and the cello image is rich and full. In the *Enigma Variations*, Mehta proves a strong and sensitive Elgarian, and this is a highly enjoyable performance which has long been admired. The vintage Decca recording, with the organ entering spectacularly in the finale, is outstanding in its CD transfer.

Paul Tortelier gives a noble and retrained account of the *Cello Concerto*, with Boult providing tactful support, producing an eminently satisfying overall performance. Boult treats *Falstaff* essentially as a symphonic structure. It follows therefore that some of the mystery is missing, some of the delicate sense of atmosphere that impregnates the interludes, for example, is under-characterized. But the crispness of the playing and Boult's unfailing alertness amply compensate for that. The present re-shuffling of Boult's Elgar recordings opens unexpectedly with the brilliant arrangement of Handel's *Overture in D minor*, as well as the hardly less impressive transcription of Bach's *Fantasia and Fugue in C minor*, both unfailingly enjoyable and available on CD for the first time. Warm, 1970s sound.

The mid-priced mono Revelation disc offers an early account from Rostropovich. In the main arguments of each movement he uses the widest dynamic range, conveying a raptly reflective intensity, full of poignancy, to match even du Pré. Rakhlin proves a most sensitive Elgarian and has great feeling for the reticence and longing that this music conveys. The cello is far too forwardly balanced, making the orchestra sound dim by comparison, but the warmth of the reading is powerfully conveyed.

Anne Gastinel does not wear her heart on her sleeve but gives an account in which a certain reticence and dignity enhance the all-pervasive melancholy of this glorious score. The performance was recorded in Birmingham in September 2003 and, although it may not be free from blemish, it is a thoughtful and sensitive reading of genuine memorability. Her Barber *Concerto*, with which this is coupled, is among the very finest committed to disc.

The Finnish cellist Arto Noras, like his Swedish colleague Torleif Thedéen (on BIS 486), seems completely attuned to the Elgar sensibility and gives a moving account of this marvellous work, balancing vigour with a reticent serenity. He is very well accompanied, and this bargain triptych is highly recommendable. Thedéen has a nobility and reticence that are strongly appealing and Noras is hardly less impressive. Neither will disappoint; both enrich and do justice to the Elgar discography.

Mischa Maisky is highly persuasive in the *Cello Concerto* and, with Sinopoli a willing partner, gives a warmly nostalgic, if perhaps not absolutely distinctive performance, essentially valedictory in feeling. The slow movement is deeply felt, but not in an extrovert way, and the soloist's dedication is mirrored in the finale. The mood of the *Concerto* is carried over into the *Enigma Variations*, where the lyrical variations are expressively relaxed and *Nimrod* has a simple, direct nobility. Sinopoli avoids the usual speeding up at the end of the finale, the thrust of that and other vigorous climaxes is pressed home passionately. The rich recording adds to the character of the readings, with the Philharmonia playing superbly. With two marches added for this release (not quite so well recorded), this CD is an undoubted bargain.

Casals recorded the Elgar *Cello Concerto* in London in 1946, and the fervour of his playing caused some raised eyebrows. A powerful account, not least for Sir Adrian's contribution, even though its eloquence would have been even more telling were the emotion recollected in greater tranquillity. A landmark of the gramophone all the same, and the strongly characterized Max Bruch *Kol Nidrei* makes a fine encore.

(i; ii) *Cello Concerto.* (iii; iv) *Violin Concerto;* (ii) *Cockaigne Overture; In the South (Alassio); Enigma Variations; Froissart Overture;* (iii; iv) *Salut d'amour;* (ii) *Serenade for Strings; Symphonies 1–2*
(B) RCA **(*) 82876 60389-2 (4). (i) Starker; (ii) LPO; (iii) Zukerman; (iv) St Louis SO; all cond. Slatkin

János Starker was in his seventies when he recorded the *Cello Concerto* with Leonard Slatkin, and the performance reflects both his understanding and the intellectual strength that has always marked his playing. In Elgar, his tough, slightly wiry tone goes with a relatively objective approach, with flowing speeds generally kept steady; and Slatkin, as in many of his other Elgar recordings, shows his natural feeling for the idiom. Sadly, in spite of Slatkin's sympathetic direction, Pinchas Zukerman's account of the *Violin Concerto* is far less involved than his earlier, Sony version. He tends to lack the sheer energy and, to make matters worse, the recording, being set at a distance, lacks body. In the *First Symphony* Slatkin's credentials as an Elgarian of understanding are very much on display. With bracing tempi, in the manner of Elgar's own performances, Slatkin brings the right sort of surging qualities to the first movement that ideally it needs, helped by brilliant playing from the LPO. The slow movement too is very impressive, though not quite achieving the rapt intensity of the greatest accounts, but noble all the same; the finale is superbly paced and completely satisfying. The account of the *Second Symphony* is equally splendid, timed beautifully to deliver authentic frissons, and it also has extra power in the finale by the addition of pedal notes on the organ, just before the epilogue – as Elgar once suggested to Sir Adrian Boult. Previously, only Vernon Handley had included them on his equally understanding version on CfP, though Slatkin's version is much more expansive than his. After such stirring accounts of the symphonies, it is sad to report that his reading of *Enigma* fails to catch fire, with the theme and *Nimrod* done very sluggishly indeed. *Froissart* is on the stiff side, but better, and *Cockaigne* goes reasonably well, but not much more than that. He is, however, back on form for both the *In the South Overture*, a fast, bracing performance, often exciting and superbly recorded, and a persuasive reading of the *Serenade for Strings*. A mixed bag, but worth considering.

(i) *Cello Concerto;* (ii) *Violin Concerto*
(N) (BB) **(*) Virgin 2x1 5 62425-2 (2) (i) Isserlis, LSO, Hickox; (ii) Sitkovetsky, RPO, Menuhin – *Sea Pictures* **(*)
(B) (***) Avid mono AMSC 587. (i) Casals, BBC SO, Boult; (ii) Sammons, New Queen's Hall O, Wood

The most distinctive point about Steven Isserlis's version of Elgar's *Cello Concerto* on Virgin is his treatment of the slow movement, not so much elegiac as songful. Using a mere thread of tone, with vibrato unstressed, the simplicity of line and the unforced beauty are brought out. The very placing of the solo instrument goes with that, rather more distant than is usual, with the refinement of Elgar's orchestration beautifully caught by both conductor and engineers.

Dmitri Sitkovetsky's sensitive reading of the *Violin Concerto* has been seriously underrated, making it now a fine coupling in this two-disc bargain compilation with the *Cello Concerto* and *Sea Pictures* in well-established versions. Even before the soloist enters, Menuhin's conducting of the RPO, evidently remembered from working with the composer himself, clearly establishes the performance's credentials, thrustful yet warmly expressive, with Elgarian rubato finely controlled. Sitkovetsky himself proves equally persuasive, when his pure, finely focused tone never grows soupy, and his wide dynamic range is matched by the refinement of the orchestral playing. His mercurial reading of the main theme in the finale leads to a deeply meditative account of the accompanied cadenza, rounded off excitingly in the final coda. First-rate recording, made in Abbey Road in 1990, and better balanced than the *Cello Concerto*.

In some ways Albert Sammons's 1929 recording of the *Violin Concerto* has never been surpassed, although of course Menuhin's with the composer himself is also very special. The first Avid CD transfer of these recordings was singularly unsuccessful. But the second, current version is infinitely superior. The sound in both works is now excellent, the *Cello Concerto* full and with the soloist firmly focused, the *Violin Concerto* even more remarkable in its warmth and natural clarity, with the solo violin caught vividly and cleanly. Sammons's high level of concentration and the atmospheric magnetism generated in the unsurpassed account of the finale come over very directly to complete a remarkably compelling listening experience.

(i) *Cello Concerto in E min., Op. 85*; (ii; iii; v) *Violin Concerto in B min., Op. 61*; (iii; v) *Cockaigne Overture, Op. 40*; (iv; v) *Enigma Variations, Op. 36*

(M) **(*) Decca (ADD/DDD) 473 085-2 (2). (i) Lloyd Webber, RPO, Y. Menuhin; (ii) Chung; (iii) LPO; (iv) Chicago SO; (v) Solti

Lloyd Webber's account of the *Cello Concerto* (originally Philips) is the more satisfying for its fidelity to the score and the absence of exaggeration. The speeds – as in the flowing *Moderato* in the first movement – are never extreme, always well judged. Kyung-Wha Chung's 1977 account of the *Violin Concerto* also maintains its position as one of the finest available. It is an intense and deeply committed reading which rises to great heights in the heart-felt account of the slow movement – made the more affecting by its vein of melancholy – and the wide-ranging performance of the finale. The first movement itself brings much beautiful playing too, but there are one or two tiny flaws of intonation, and here Solti's accompaniment does not have quite so firm a grasp, though the performance will undoubtedly be refreshing to any Elgarian.

Solti is back on top form in an exciting and sharply dramatic account of the *Cockaigne Overture* in vintage (1976) Decca sound, though the 1974 *Enigma Variations* become a dazzling showpiece. But if the charm of the work is given short measure, the structure emerges even more strongly. The main disappointment is *Nimrod*, where, from a basic tempo faster than usual, Solti allows himself to get faster and faster still, in a style that misses the feeling of *nobilmente*.

(i) *Piano Concerto* (realized Walker). *Adieu* (orch. Geehl); *Suite of Four Songs* (transcribed for orchestra, Haydn Wood); (ii) Choral Music: *The Immortal Legions; So Many True Princesses* (orch Payne); *Spanish Serenade*

(N) (M) *** Dutton CDLX 7148. (i) Owen Norris; (ii) BBC Singers; BBC Concert O, Lloyd-Jones – COLLINS: *Elegy in Memory of Elgar* ***

Like the *Symphony No. 3*, the Elgar *Piano Concerto*, 40 minutes long, has been realized from the composer's sketches, written between 1913 and his death. Robert Walker has ingeniously put together a host of fragments (explained in detail in a note by the pianist, David Owen Norris), but the result fails to hang together in the way the *Symphony No. 3* does in Anthony Payne's realization, partly because the material is not as striking and has been drawn from a wider range of sources. Nevertheless, Walker has done an excellent job so that, with Owen Norris displaying formidable concentration and virtuosity and David Lloyd-Jones drawing warmly idiomatic playing from the BBC Concert Orchestra, the result is always enjoyable. The long first movement is more sectional than the rest, with the central *Poco Andante* – the only movement that Elgar came near to completing – a light interlude, and the finale a dashing Sonata Rondo with a march-like main theme.

The other items make a charming supplement, not just the *Suite* compiled by Haydn Wood and *Adieu*, a late piano piece orchestrated by Henry Geehl, but the three choral items. Anthony Payne provides the orchestration for *So Many True Princesses*, to words by Masefield, originally written with military band accompaniment. *The Immortal Legions*, another late work, is drawn from *The Pageant of Empire* with words by Alfred Noyes. The Anthony Collins piece, based on a motif in the sketches for the *Third Symphony*, is another enjoyable rarity for Elgarians. First-rate sound.

Violin Concerto in B min., Op. 61

☛ *** EMI 5 56413-2 Kennedy, CBSO, Rattle – VAUGHAN WILLIAMS: *The Lark Ascending* ***

(B) *** CfP 575 1392. Kennedy, LPO, Handley

(BB) (***) Naxos mono 8.110902. Menuhin, LSO, composer – BRUCH: *Concerto 1* (**)

(BB) (**(*)) Naxos mono 8.110951. Sammons, Liverpool PO, Sargent – DELIUS: *Violin Concerto* (**(*))

(BB) (***) Naxos mono 8.110939. Heifetz, LSO, Sargent – WALTON: *Violin Concerto* (***)

(***) Beulah mono 1PD 10. Campoli, LPO, Boult – MENDELSSOHN: *Violin Concerto* (***)

(N) ** DG 474 504-2. Hahn, LSO, C. Davis (with VAUGHAN WILLIAMS: *The Lark Ascending* **)

(i) *Violin Concerto in B min. Cockaigne Overture, Op. 40*

(BB) *** Naxos 8.550489. (i) Kang; Polish Nat. RSO (Katowice), Leaper

With this impressive remake of the Elgar *Violin Concerto*, Kennedy launched masterfully into his new career, refreshed after years of self-imposed exile from the regular concert platform. He made this new recording in Birmingham immediately after giving his first live concerto performance in years, and the reading has extra thrust and passion compared with his earlier recording of this epic work. The outer movements are faster and more freely expressive than before, the slow movement more expansive, with *pianissimos* of magical intensity, qualities equally impressive in the evocative Vaughan Williams piece.

For many ears, Nigel Kennedy's earlier (1984) recording of the *Violin Concerto* has an even greater freshness than his later recording in Birmingham with Rattle. It is certainly commanding, and with Vernon Handley as guide it is centrally Elgarian in its warm expressiveness, but its steady pacing also brings out more than usual the clear parallels with the Beethoven and Brahms concertos. This is particularly striking in the first movement and, both here and in his urgent account of the allegros in the finale, Kennedy shows that he has learnt more than any recorded rival from the example of the concerto's first great interpreter, Albert Sammons. Yet the influence of Yehudi Menuhin is also apparent, not least in the sweetness and repose of the slow movement and in the deep meditation of the accompanied cadenza which comes as epilogue. The recording, produced by Andrew Keener, with the soloist balanced more naturally than usual, not spotlit, is outstandingly faithful and atmospheric. The CfP reissue makes a remarkable bargain.

Mark Obert-Thorn's transfer of the classic first Menuhin recording with the composer is taken from what he describes as pre-war RCA Victor 'Z' shellac pressings, and the result is surprisingly successful, the soloist truthfully caught with a minimum of background noise, and the orchestral strings given plenty of body. The coupled Max Bruch, recorded the previous year, is less successful.

It is difficult to imagine the concerto being better played than it is in this inspired 1928 recording by Albert Sammons, who had recorded it in abridged form in the days of acoustic recording. Even the classic Menuhin–Elgar version, made four years later, wonderful though it is, is in some ways outclassed. The HMV Treasury LP transfer by A. C. Griffith was very fine, but collectors may now turn with confidence to the Naxos transfers.

Dong-Suk Kang, immaculate in his intonation, plays the Elgar with fire and urgency. This is very different from most latter-day performances, with markedly faster speeds; yet those speeds relate more closely than usual to the metronome markings in the score, and they never get in the way of Kang's ability to feel Elgarian rubato naturally, guided by the warmly understanding conducting of Adrian Leaper. Irrespective of price, this is a keenly competitive version, with excellent, wide-ranging, digital sound, if with rather too forward a balance for the soloist.

Jascha Heifetz's unique reading of the Elgar is well transferred on Naxos in mellower sound than on previous RCA transfers. The ease of his virtuosity leads to dazzling bravura at speeds faster than usual, bringing a rare volatile quality in music that can easily seem a struggle. Yet that ease goes with a passionate warmth in Elgar's great lyrical moments, with wide vibrato perfectly controlled, and with high harmonics ethereally pure. The great second-subject melody is the more tenderly poignant for flowing easily. Heifetz treats the slow movement as a lyrical interlude, before the brilliant display of the finale leads to a deeply reflective account of the unaccompanied cadenza. Any idea of Heifetz as a chilly interpreter is firmly rebutted. Good (1949) mono sound.

Campoli gives a deeply felt but highly individual account of Elgar's great concerto. One can judge one's reaction to this performance by the control of vibrato on the opening phrase of his first entry. This is an essentially romantic approach, full of warmth; but Campoli applies himself here with dedication to a work he obviously loves, and the result – with Boult securely and compellingly at the helm – is most rewarding. The 1954 Kingsway Hall recording has been impeccably transferred from the *ffrr* master tape by Tony Hawkins at the Decca studios. With its outstanding Mendelssohn coupling this is a fully worthy memento of a strikingly fine soloist.

Hilary Hahn, in taking on the challenge of the Elgar *Violin Concerto*, plays everything flawlessly, but remains curiously detached. Though she phrases with sympathy, the emotion of the piece fails to come across and, with Sir Colin Davis taking a weighty view of the score, the LSO seems relatively detached too. For once the magic of the accompanied cadenza summing up the work seems to disappear. *The Lark Ascending* is again well played, but without any special insights.

(i) *Violin Concerto in B min., Op. 61;* (ii) *Enigma Variations, Op. 36*
(M) (***) EMI mono 5 66979-2 [566994]. (i) Menuhin, LSO; (ii) Royal Albert Hall O; composer

The 1932 Menuhin/Elgar recording of the *Violin Concerto* emerges on this newly remastered EMI CD with a fine sense of presence and plenty of body to the sound. As for the performance, its classic status is amply confirmed; in many ways no one has ever matched – let alone surpassed – the sixteen-year-old Menuhin in this work, even if the first part of the finale lacks something in fire. Elgar's own 1926 recording of *Enigma* is too well known for much further comment. But his accelerando surge just before he broadens the climax

of *Nimrod* and the hustle and bustle of *G.R.S.* emphasize the spontaneous individuality of the reading. Although allowances have to be made for the sound, which is somewhat recessed at lower dynamic levels, the engineers have done wonders with the current remastering, and this coupling is surely worthy to take its place among EMI's 'Great Recordings of the Century'.

(i; ii) *Violin Concerto in B min.;* (iii; iv) *Piano Quintet in A min.;* (v) *String Quartet in E min.;* (i; vi) *Violin Sonata in E min;* (iii) **(Piano):** *Concert Allegro; Serenade*
(B) **(*) CfP 585 9082 (2). (i) Bean; (ii) RLPO, Groves; (iii) Ogdon; (iv) Allegri Qt; (v) Music Group of L.; (vi) Parkhouse

Hugh Bean recorded the *Violin Concerto* in 1972 in the wake of Menuhin's re-recording and, if his performance does not quite match that, it is still a very fine one and – as the splendid opening tutti immediately shows – it is strongly and authoritatively conducted by Sir Charles Groves. There is no question about Bean's technical assurance or his natural identification with the work and, although his performance is more relaxed, less tense than Menuhin's, it has a warmth and simplicity that are disarming, with the first movement's second subject beautifully played, and the serene beauty of the slow movement well caught, followed by a successful finale with some very fine moments, especially in the closing pages. The EMI recording catches Bean's tonal beauty and gives plenty of body to the orchestra. Not quite a first choice then, but well worth having when the rest of this collection is so desirable, including the *Piano Quintet*, the most ambitious of Elgar's three major chamber works. Its slow movement is among the composer's greatest, and every bar is distinctive and memorable. John Ogdon and the Allegri Quartet give a strong performance, which misses some of the deeper, warmer emotions but which still gives considerable satisfaction. The *String Quartet* is well done too, but not so understandingly as the later account by the Britten Quartet on a budget Regis CD (RRC 1015 – see below). The *Violin Sonata* has both an autumnal quality and a Brahmsian flavour, and it responds to ripe treatment such as Hugh Bean and David Parkhouse provide. The *Concert Allegro* for piano is a valuable oddity, rescued by John Ogdon (the music was long thought to be lost) and splendidly played, while the *Serenade* brings some charming ideas, even if it reveals Elgar's obvious limitations when writing for the keyboard. All these works are well recorded, and this CfP set is more than worth the modest price asked for it.

Dream Children; Elegy; In Moonlight; Nursery Suite; (i) *Romance for Bassoon and Orchestra, Op. 62. Serenade for Strings; Sospiri*
**(*) HM HMU 907258. ECO, Goodwin; (i) with Price

A warmly nostalgic collection, beautifully played and recorded, if not quite as idiomatic in feeling as the performances by Boult and Handley . The *Serenade* and the boisterous items in the *Nursery Suite* bring contrast to what is all essentially gentle music. A programme for a late summer evening which would be even more attractive at a lower price.

Dream Children, Op. 43; Nursery Suite; Wand of Youth Suites 1 & 2, Op. 1a and 1b
(BB) *** Naxos 8.557166. New Zealand SO, Judd

It makes an ideal coupling on Naxos to have the two *Wand of Youth Suites*, using themes Elgar had written in boyhood for a family play, alongside his other two works inspired by childhood, *Dream Children* of 1902 and the *Nursery Suite* of 1930, dedicated to the then Duke and Duchess of York and the Princesses Elizabeth (now the Queen) and Margaret Rose. The freshness of inspiration is a delight, superbly brought out in these fine performances from New Zealand, recorded in Wellington in full, well-balanced sound, with James Judd always an idiomatic Elgarian. The *Wand of Youth Suites* in particular range wonderfully wide in mood and invention, culminating in the most brilliant movement of all, *The Wild Bears*, an orchestral showpiece here given a spectacular performance.

Enigma Variations: 'A Hidden Portrait' (**with complete performance**)

(**N**) *** BBC Opus Arte **DVD** OA 0917D. nar. A. Davis; BBC SO, A. Davis (V/D: Diana Hill)

Sir Andrew Davis's fine performance of the *Enigma Variations*, with *Nimrod* hushed, slow and steady, was recorded in the atmospheric surroundings of Worcester Cathedral, where Elgar said everyone should hear his music. Davis introduces a highly enjoyable documentary about the work and 'the friends pictured within'. In the documentary he suggests that each variation, as well as reflecting the character of a particular friend, reveals much about Elgar himself, 'like an actor playing many roles'. He sets the work clearly against the composer's career, 'the masterpiece that catapulted him to fame in 1899', and each section is illustrated with archive material and in-period reconstructions, happily with no dialogue, only Davis's narration. He concentrates on describing and analysing nine of the 14 variations, his favourites, with plentiful orchestral clips of the music and illustrations played on the piano. Though the visual illustrations are fussy and irrelevant at times, the actual performance has no unwanted intrusions, just a sepia photo of the subject as each variation begins.

Enigma Variations (Variations on an Original Theme), Op. 36

(**M**) *** Decca (ADD) 452 303-2. LSO, Monteux – HOLST: *Planets* ***

(**BB**) *** DG (ADD) 439 446-2. LSO, Jochum – HOLST: *Planets* ***

**(*) Cala (ADD) CACD 0524. Czech PO, Stokowski (with BRAHMS: *Symphony 1 in C min., Op. 68* **(*))

(**M**) *** EMI 5 67748-2 [567749]. LSO, Boult – HOLST: *Planets* ***

(**M**) **(*) BBC (ADD) BBCM 5002-2. BBC SO, Sargent – HOLST: *Planets* **(*)

(**N**) (**M**) *(*) DG 474 936-2 (3). BBC SO, Bernstein – BRITTEN: *4 Sea Interludes* *; SIBELIUS: *Symphonies 1–2, 5 & 7* (*)

Monteux's *Enigma* remains among the freshest versions ever put on disc, and the music is obviously deeply felt. The reading is famous for the real *pianissimo* which Monteux secures at the beginning of *Nimrod*, the tension electric, and the superb climax is more effective in consequence. Differences from traditional tempi elsewhere are marginal and add to one's enjoyment. The vintage Kingsway Hall stereo was outstanding in its day and it is almost impossible to believe that this dates from 1958; with its stunning Holst coupling, this is one of the very finest (and most generous – 78 minutes) reissues in Decca's 'Classic Sound' series.

Like others (including Elgar himself) Jochum sets a very slow *Adagio* at the start of *Nimrod*, slower than the metronome marking in the score; unlike others, he maintains that

measured tempo and, with the subtlest gradations, builds an even bigger, nobler climax than you find in *accelerando* readings. It is like a Bruckner slow movement in microcosm, around which the other variations revolve, all of them delicately detailed, with a natural feeling for Elgarian rubato. The playing of the LSO matches the strength and refinement of the performance.

Stokowski adroitly guides the players of the Czech Philharmonic through Elgar's masterpiece, illuminating every bar with his special affection, and the result is gloriously rich in spontaneous feeling, casting an entirely new slant on a work that one felt one knew very well indeed. Stokowski's insights are special to himself. The coupling is a splendid version of Brahms's *First Symphony*, recorded live with the LSO at the Royal Festival Hall in 1972.

Boult's *Enigma* comes from the beginning of the 1970s, but the recording has lost some of its amplitude in its transfer to CD: the effect is fresh, but the violins sound thinner. The reading shows this conductor's long experience of the work, with each variation growing naturally and seamlessly out of the music that has gone before. Yet the livelier variations bring exciting orchestral bravura and there is an underlying intensity of feeling that carries the performance forward.

With the BBC engineers capturing the atmospheric thrill of a Prom performance in the Royal Albert Hall, Sir Malcolm Sargent's 1966 account may be a degree less polished, but its thrust and urgency are irresistible, building up superbly to the final variations in which the BBC brass and the obbligato organ convey an extra frisson, even if the sound is pretty opaque and there are too many extraneous noises. But, with an equally warm and expressive account of *The Planets* as the generous coupling, in many ways this makes a more persuasive case for the conductor than the older EMI pairing of Sargent's studio recordings of the same works.

Bernstein's is quite the most perverse reading of *Enigma* ever recorded (1982), and few listeners will respond to its outrageous self-indulgence, not least in *Nimrod*, which is dragged out to interminable length. Though wilful, Bernstein is always passionate and, with good playing and recording, this account may possibly attract those who want a fresh view of the work; but there surely can't be too many collectors who will want the Sibelius symphonies in this boxed set – or, at least, play them more than once.

Enigma Variations; Coronation March, Op. 65; In the South (Alassio), Op. 50

(**BB**) *** Naxos 8.553564. Bournemouth SO, Hurst

George Hurst with the Bournemouth orchestra inspires richly expressive playing, full of subtle rubato which consistently sounds natural and idiomatic, never self-conscious. Like Elgar himself, he tends to press ahead rather than linger, as in the great climactic variation in *Enigma*, *Nimrod*, as well as in the finale and in the overture, *In the South*. The *Coronation March* also inspires an opulent, red-blooded performance, and the recording thoughout is rich and sumptuous.

Enigma Variations; Elegy for Strings (2 versions); *Introduction & Allegro for Strings* (2 versions); *Symphony 1 in A flat, Op. 55*

(**B**) (***) Dutton Double mono/stereo CDSJB 1017 (2). Hallé O, Barbirolli

Barbirolli recorded both the *Enigma Variations* and the beautiful *Elegy* (for which he had a special affection) three times, and the *Introduction and Allegro* six times! Here we are offered the third (1947 – mono) and fifth (1956 – stereo) versions of the latter. In the earlier, mono account the recapitulation of the big striding theme in the middle strings already has superb thrust and warmth. The *Enigma* recording is the first (in mono), also from 1947, and it sounds very well in the present transfer, though the later and very exciting Pye stereo version, and the 1962 HMV version (see below) are finer both on performance and sonic grounds. Which is not to say that this strikingly fresh, earlier version is not worth having. But what makes the present collection special is the inclusion of the first (1956), originally Pye, stereo account of the *First Symphony*. The Hallé plays at a good sparkling allegro, and the music surges along. In the slow movement too there is greater warmth, with really affectionate playing in the three glorious main themes – the last one reserved for the very end of the movement. The remaining movements have comparable intensity, and in this new Dutton transfer the sound, though not as ripe as the later, EMI version, is much more than acceptable.

Enigma Variations; Falstaff; Grania and Diarmid: Incidental Music & Funeral March

*** EMI 5 55001-2. CBSO, Rattle

In *Enigma*, Rattle and the CBSO are both powerful and refined, overwhelming at the close, and they offer a generous and ideal coupling. *Falstaff* is given new transparency in a spacious reading, deeply moving in the hush of the final death scene, with the *Grania and Diarmid* excerpts as a valuable makeweight.

Enigma Variations; Froissart Overture, Op. 19; (i) Grania and Diarmid (incidental music), Op. 42. The Sanguine Fan (ballet; complete), Op. 81

(N) (M) **(*) Chan. 6692. LPO, Thomson; (i) with Miller

Bryden Thomson conducts a broad, characterful reading of *Enigma*, warmly expressive but never mannered, leading the ear on persuasively in a purposefully structured whole. *Froissart* goes well too, without being truly memorable, and he finds all the charm of *The Sanguine Fan* ballet, characterizing it well without inflating it; while the unexpected mixture of Elgar and Celtic twilight in the *Grania and Diarmid* incidental music brings a simlarly agreeable response, notably in the fine, measured *Funeral March*. The little Yeats song, *There are seven that pulled the thread*, is warmly sung by Jenny Miller, though the microphone exaggerates her generous vibrato.

Enigma Variations; In the South (Alassio), Op. 50; Serenade for Strings

(M) *** Virgin 5 62200-2. RPO, Litton

When Andrew Litton made these recordings in 1987, he had little experience of Elgarian repertoire, yet he showed a natural flair for the idiom. His performance of *Enigma* may not be traditional in every detail – *Nimrod* is intense and strong rather than elegiac – but each variation is vividly characterized, without eccentricity. *In the South* and the *Serenade* also confirm Litton's innate feeling for Elgarian rubato, phrasing and rhythm, the qualities which are implied rather than specified in the score. This reissue, warmly and atmospherically recorded in EMI's St John's Wood studio, can certainly be recommended in its own right to anyone who fancies the coupling.

Enigma Variations; Introduction and Allegro for Strings

(N) (B) *** LPO LPO 0002. LPO, Haitink – BRITTEN: *Our Hunting Fathers* ***

Bernard Haitink's live recordings of the *Enigma Variations* and the *Introduction and Allegro*, dating respectively from 1986 at the Royal Albert Hall and 1984 at the Royal Festival Hall, make an excellent coupling for his outstanding Prom performance of the rare Britten cantata. Characteristically, his speeds are on the broad side but never involve a loss of tension, with nobility the keynote, not least in the radiant account of *Nimrod*. Well recorded, the LPO strings, with David Nolan as leader, are in first-rate form.

Enigma Variations; Introduction and Allegro for Strings, Op. 47; In the South (Alassio) Overture, Op. 50; Sospiri, Op. 70

**(*) DG 463 265-2. VPO, Gardiner

On the evidence of this disc John Eliot Gardiner is not an instinctive Elgarian. His reading of *Enigma* is very personal in its moulding of line, and while the VPO provide virtuosity and finely etched detail, they fail to get to the heart of the music, especially in *Nimrod*, which is spacious and serene rather than heart-tugging. The *Introduction and Allegro* is again brilliantly played, but the great striding tune in the middle strings, which Barbirolli shapes so passionately, is here without real depth of expressive feeling and the final climax, too, falls short. But *In the South* is a different matter. It bursts vividly into life with a Straussian surge of ardour; the Roman Juggernaut sequence is almost overwhelming, with a balancing tenderness on the touching central section. The closing section carries all before it. The Vienna Philharmonic strings also bring a Mahlerian warmth to *Sospiri*, which is very affecting. But *Enigma* is a disappointment – in spite of first-class recording.

(i) Enigma Variations; (ii) Pomp and Circumstance Marches 1-5, Op. 39

(M) *** (ADD) DG 429 713-2. RPO, Del Mar
(M) *** EMI (ADD) 7 64015-2. (i) LSO; (ii) LPO; Boult

In the *Enigma Variations* Del Mar comes closer than any other conductor to the responsive rubato style of Elgar himself, using fluctuations to point the emotional message of the work with wonderful power and spontaneity. The RPO plays superbly, both here and in the *Pomp and Circumstance Marches*, given Proms-style flair and urgency – although some might feel that the fast speeds miss some of the *nobilmente*. The reverberant sound here adds something of an aggressive edge to the music-making.

Boult's *Enigma* (also available coupled with Holst's *Planets* – see above) is self-recommending. His approach to the *Pomp and Circumstance Marches* is brisk and direct, with an almost no-nonsense manner in places. There is not a hint of vulgarity and the freshness is most attractive, though it is a pity he omits the repeats in the Dvořák-like No. 2. The brightened sound brings a degree of abrasiveness to the brass.

(i) Enigma Variations; Pomp and Circumstance Marches 1 & 4; Salut d'amour, Op. 12; (ii) Serenade for Strings in E min., Op. 20

(BB) *** Naxos 8.554161. (i) Czecho-Slovak RSO; (ii) Capella Istropolitana; Leaper

Though Leaper's slow account of the 'Enigma' theme makes an unpromising start, his reading of the *Variations* is most beautiful, with ripely resonant string-playing and with warmly expressive rubato in *Nimrod* suggesting that the Slovak players had been won over to Elgar by Leaper's advocacy. Most refined of all is the Capella Istropolitana's account of the *Serenade*, with the slow movement specially beautiful, finely shaded. An excellent compilation of Elgar's most popular orchestral pieces, brilliantly recorded.

Enigma Variations; Serenade for Strings, Op. 20
(B) **(*) CfP 574 8802. LPO, Handley – VAUGHAN
  WILLIAMS: *The Lark Ascending*, etc. ***

Vernon Handley's generously full CfP disc is given brilliant, wide-ranging (1983) digital sound. The readings are in the Boult tradition and very well played. But Handley's strong personal identification with the music brings a consciously moulded style that tends to rob the *Enigma Variations* of its forward impulse. The Elgarian ebb and flow of tension and dynamics is continually underlined by a highly expressive manner and, although he uncovers much imaginative detail, there is a consequent loss of spontaneity. The performance of the *Serenade* is more direct, although the *Larghetto* again has a more personal idiosyncrasy.

Falstaff, Op. 68; Elegy, Op. 58; The Sanguine Fan (ballet), Op. 81
(BB) *** Naxos 8.553879. N. Philh., Lloyd-Jones

Rich, full Naxos sound with high dynamic contrasts adds satisfying weight to David Lloyd-Jones's taut and dramatic account of Elgar's elaborate Shakespearean portrait. Speeds are often on the fast side, but idiomatically so, with a natural feeling for Elgarian rubato and sprung rhythms. Both in *Falstaff* and in *The Sanguine Fan*, Lloyd-Jones draws fragmented structures warmly and persuasively together so that the late ballet-score emerges strongly, not just a trivial, occasional piece. The beautiful *Elegy* is most tenderly done, modest in length but no miniature. An outstanding bargain, competing with all premium-price rivals.

Introduction & Allegro for Strings
*** Ara. Z 6723. San Francisco Ballet O, Lark Qt, Jean-Louis
  Le Roux – HANDEL: *Concerto grosso in B flat, Op. 6/7*;
  SCHOENBERG: *Concerto for String Quartet & Orchestra
  after Handel's Concerto grosso, Op. 6/7*; SPOHR: *Concerto
  for String Quartet & Orchestra* ***

A passionately committed performance from the excellent San Francisco string-players, with a warmly tender contribution from the solo group. They are not entirely idiomatic – they do not quite let rip in the striding unison string-tune in the way that British players would – but their slower tempo remains convincing when the underlying fervour is in no doubt. The final climax is superb. Splendidly vivid recording.

(i–ii) *Introduction & Allegro for Strings*; (i) *Serenade for Strings*; (iii) *Elegy, Op. 58; Sospiri, Op. 70*
☞ ✹ (M) *** EMI 5 67240-2 [567264]. (i) Sinfonia of L.; (ii)
  Allegri Qt; (iii) New Philh. O; Barbirolli – VAUGHAN
  WILLIAMS: *Greensleeves & Tallis Fantasias* *** ✹

Barbirolli's famous record of English string music (the *Elegy* and *Sospiri* were added later) might be considered the finest of all his records, and it remained in the catalogue at full price for over three-and-a-half decades. Now not only does it cost less, it rightly takes its place as one of EMI's 'Great Recordings of the Century', with the current remastering of

an originally magnificent recording losing nothing, combining bite and excellent inner definition with the fullest sonority.

King Arthur: Suite; (i) *The Starlight Express* (suite), *Op. 78*
(M) **(*) Chan. 6582. (i) Glover, Lawrenson; Bournemouth
  Sinf., Hurst

The *King Arthur Suite* is full of surging, enjoyable ideas and makes an interesting novelty on record. *The Starlight Express Suite* is taken from music Elgar wrote for a children's play, with a song or two included. Though the singers here are not ideal interpreters, the enthusiasm of Hurst and the Sinfonietta is conveyed well, particularly in the *King Arthur Suite*. The recording is atmospheric if rather over-reverberant, but the added firmness of the CD and its refinement of detail almost make this an extra asset in providing a most agreeable ambience for Elgar's music.

Nursery Suite; Wand of Youth Suites 1 and 2, Opp. 1a & b
☞ *** Chan. 8318. Ulster O, Thomson

The playing in Ulster is attractively spirited; in the gentle pieces (the *Sun Dance, Fairy Pipers* and *Slumber Dance*) in the *First Wand of Youth Suite*, which show the composer at his most magically evocative, the music-making engagingly combines refinement and warmth. The *Nursery Suite* is strikingly well characterized, and with first-class digital sound this is highly recommendable.

Serenade for Strings in E min., Op. 20
☞ (N) (BB) Warner Apex 2564 61437-2. RPO, Warren-Green
  – BRITTEN: *Simple Symphony*; BUTTERWORTH: *Banks of
  Green Willow*; HOLST: *St Paul's Suite*; VAUGHAN
  WILLIAMS: *Fantasia on a Theme of Tallis* ***

With the RPO players ever responsive, Warren-Green's latest RPO performance – part of an outstanding anthology of English music – is even finer than his earlier, deleted Virgin account in bringing out the grace of Elgar's string writing and the tender feeling of the *Larghetto*.

Symphonies 1–2; Overtures: Cockaigne; In the South
(B) *** Double Decca (ADD) 443 856-2 (2). LPO, Solti

Symphonies 1–2; Pomp and Circumstance March 5
(B) **(*) EMI (ADD) double forte 5 69761-2 (2). Philh. O,
  Haitink

Solti's accounts of the two Elgar *Symphonies* must be counted among his most successful recordings and certainly remain among the top choices for this repertoire several decades later. Before he recorded the *First* he made a searching study of Elgar's own 78-r.p.m. recording, and the modifications of detailed markings implicit in that account are reproduced here, not with a sense of calculation but with very much the same rich, committed qualities that mark out Elgar's performance. Solti seems freed from emotional inhibitions, with every climax superbly thrust home and the hushed intensity of the glorious slow movement captured magnificently on CD. The *Second* receives an equally incandescent reading, once again closely modelled on Elgar's own surprisingly clipped and urgent performance, but benefiting from virtuoso playing and, as with the *First*, vintage Decca sound. Fast tempi bring searing concentration and an account of the finale that for once presents a true climax. Whilst no one can grumble at the couplings on the mid-priced set – Britten's full-blooded and distinctive account of the *Introduction and*

Allegro and Marriner's *Serenade for Strings* (perhaps a little stiff in manner) – the Double Decca original LPO couplings of the *Cockaigne* and *In the South* overtures were more logical, even if *In the South*, recorded in 1979, is over tense.

With consistently slow tempi, Haitink's is a spacious reading of No. 1. The result is hardly idiomatic but, with superb playing from the Philharmonia under Haitink's concentrated direction, it is profound and moving, elegiacally glowing with genuine Elgarian warmth. The *Second Symphony* is more controversial, and here the CD transfer remains just a little disappointing, with the sound of the strings not as expansively opulent as expected. The opening movement in particular is very volatile, and throughout there are many wayward touches that fail to convince entirely on repeated hearing. Elgarians will miss some of the usual spring in the 12/8 compound time of the first movement. But for many the performance will be a revelation in its strength and depth of feeling.

Symphony 1 in A flat, Op. 55
(BB) *** LSO Live LSO 0017. LSO, C. Davis

Symphony 1; Chanson de matin; Chanson de nuit; Serenade for Strings, Op. 20
(M) *** EMI (ADD) 7 64013-2. LPO, Boult

Symphony 1; Imperial March, Op. 32
(BB) *** Naxos 8.550634. BBC PO, Hurst

Symphony 1; In the South, Op. 50
(***) Testament mono SBT 1229. LPO, Boult

(i) Symphony 1; In the South Overture; (ii) Canto popolare: In Moonlight
(M) *** Hallé CD HLL 7500. (i) Hallé O, Elder; (ii) Rice, Elder

Symphony 1 in A flat; Introduction and Allegro for Strings, Op. 47
⊶ ✪*** BBC (ADD) BBCL 4106-2. Hallé O, Barbirolli

Symphony 1; Pomp and Circumstance Marches 1–5
(B) *** CfP (ADD/DDD) 575 3052. LPO, Handley

On 24 July 1970 Sir John Barbirolli conducted (and recorded) an inspired Hallé performance of Elgar's *First Symphony* in St Nicholas's Chapel as his major contribution to the King's Lynn Festival. Four days later he suffered a fatal heart attack. There could be no finer memorial.

Fascinatingly, the interpretation, rather than following on from the conductor's later, 1962 Philharmonia reading, looks back to his first 1956 Pye recording with his own orchestra. Both performances play for a little over 52 minutes, and the timings of each movement and the flexible inner relationships of tempos are remarkably close throughout. But this final version has not only great depth of feeling but also the frisson of live music-making: it matches and even surpasses that first venture in its surging forward momentum, and the acoustic of the chapel provides a wonderfully warm glow and the richest amplitude for the Hallé brass and strings, without blunting the *fortissimos*. Most memorable of all is the sheer richness of the opening of the *Adagio*, sustained throughout with Barbirolli's characteristic warmth of feeling, while the impassioned Hallé string playing is as rich in tone as it is heartfelt.

Barbirolli recorded the *Introduction and Allegro* six times between 1927 and 1962. Two versions are included on the Dutton Double listed above under the coupled *Enigma Variations*. Both have that characteristic richness and thrust when the big striding theme in the middle strings is reprised

(something matched by no other conductor) and it happens again here, with a mellow body to the recording to increase the amplitude. Everyone has their favourite version among the six, but no Elgarian will be disappointed with the present account, which still has the Hallé strings sitting on the edge of their seats, responding to the ardour of 'Glorious John'.

Vernon Handley directs a beautifully paced reading which can be counted in every way outstanding. The LPO has performed this symphony many times before but never with more poise and refinement than here. It is in the slow movement above all that Handley scores; his account is spacious and movingly expressive. The coupled *Marches* are exhilaratingly brilliant and if Nos. 2 and (especially) 3 strike some ears as too vigorously paced, comparison with the composer's own tempi reveals an authentic precedent. Certainly the popular *First* and *Fourth* have an attractive, gutsy grandiloquence. With very good sound, well transferred to CD, this is highly recommendable indeed.

It was the Hallé Orchestra under Hans Richter which first played Elgar's *First Symphony* in 1907, and Mark Elder triumphantly follows up the example of his predecessors, notably Sir John Barbirolli, with an outstanding performance, recorded for the Hallé's own label in September 2001. Elder's pacing is ideal, building the symphonic structure unerringly, with the slow movement bringing playing of exceptional refinement and beauty, with breathtaking *pianissimos*, and with the finale, taken fast, leading to a movingly triumphant return of the motto theme. *In the South* brings an equally compelling performance, again with textures remarkably clear, making the piece as colourful a representation of Italy as anything by Respighi, full of bold contrasts. As a bonus, a first recording is included of the haunting *Canto popolare* from the overture in a vocal version, *In Moonlight*, with the mezzo, Christine Rice, as soloist and Mark Elder at the piano.

Reflecting the emotions of a live event, Colin Davis's use of rubato and expressive hesitations on Warner Apex is greater than it might have been in a studio performance, notably in the tender account of the slow movement, but the concentration of the playing is so intense that the results are magnetic, not self-conscious. The performance builds up to a thrilling account of the finale, which prompts wild applause. Excellent sound. A first-rate recommendation at super-bargain price, even if the reissue of Vernon Handley's CfP version offers not only a generous coupling as well but a performance a degree more idiomatic still.

On the bargain Naxos label comes a warmly sympathetic version of the *Symphony No. 1* from the BBC Philharmonic under George Hurst. Masterly with Elgarian rubato, he refreshingly chooses speeds faster than have become the norm, closer to those of Elgar himself. No one will be disappointed with Hurst's powerful reading, well coupled with the *Imperial March*.

The first wonder of the superb transfer of Boult's 1949 version of Elgar's *First Symphony* from Testament is the astonishing quality of the sound: mono only but full-bodied and finely detailed to give a keen sense of presence, with a surprisingly wide dynamic range. As to interpretation, this mono version, beautifully paced, has far more thrust and tension than the later one, notably in the finale. Also, the heavenly *Adagio* has an extra meditative intensity in the way that Boult presents each of the great lyrical themes, pure and poignant in their beauty. Nobility is the keynote of the whole interpretation. Boult's recording of the overture, *In the South*, made in 1955, brings out his thrustful side even more strikingly, with urgent speeds giving way in the lovely *Canto popolare* section to a honeyed beauty, with George Alexander the superb viola soloist. Sadly, the 1955 sound is shallower than that of six years earlier for the *Symphony*.

In his later, stereo version Boult clearly presents the *First Symphony* as a counterpart to the *Second*, with hints of reflective nostalgia amid the triumph. His EMI disc contains a radiantly beautiful performance, with no extreme tempi, richly spaced in the first movement, invigorating in the syncopated march rhythms of the Scherzo, and similarly bouncing in the Brahmsian rhythms of the finale.

Symphony 2 in E flat, Op. 63
(BB) *** LSO Live LSO 0018. LSO, C. Davis
(BB) *** Naxos 8.550635. BBC PO, Downes

Symphony 2; The Crown of India (suite), Op. 66
(M) *** Chan. (ADD) 6523. RSNO, Gibson

Symphony 2; In the South (Alassio)
(BB) *** Warner Apex 0927 49586-2. BBC SO, A. Davis

Symphony 2; Introduction and Allegro for Strings
(N) (M) *** Hallé CDHL 7507. Hallé O, Elder

Symphony 2; (i) Sea Pictures
☛ (B) *** CfP (DDD/ADD) 575 3062. LPO, Handley; (i) with Greevy

Handley's remains the most satisfying modern version of a work which has latterly been much recorded. What Handley conveys superbly is the sense of Elgarian ebb and flow, building climaxes like a master and drawing excellent, spontaneous-sounding playing from an orchestra which, more than any other, has specialized in performing this symphony. The sound is warmly atmospheric and, at the peak of the finale, vividly conveys the added organ part in the bass (which Elgar himself suggested 'if available'): a tummy-wobbling effect. As a generous coupling Bernadette Greevy – in glorious voice – gives the performance of her recording career in *Sea Pictures*. Handley's sympathetic accompaniments are no less memorable, with the LPO players finding a wonderful rapport with the voice. In the last song Handley uses a telling ad lib. organ part to underline the climaxes of each final stanza.

Mark Elder follows up his brilliantly successful earlier Elgar recordings on the Hallé Orchestra's own label with this glowing account of the *Second Symphony*. With speeds on the broad side in the first two movements, he draws muscular playing from the orchestra, taut and compelling, with the brass particularly impressive. Elder's control in the gradual building of climaxes is splendidly demonstrated in the Funeral March slow movement, helped by full, clear sound, recorded in the BBC's Manchester studios. The finale, rather brisker than usual, rounds off a deeply satisfying performance. As a pendant, Elder reads the Shelley poem, *Song*, from which Elgar's superscription is taken, 'Rarely, rarely comest thou, Spirit of Delight'. The *Introduction and Allegro*, recorded in the helpful acoustic of Bridgewater Hall, brings a performance of big, dramatic contrasts, with the Hallé strings ideally refined. These performance have lucidity and warmth and an admirable feeling for detail and pace. There is a feeling of authenticity in both; the sound is present and vivid. Though there are excellent rival versions, like Handley (on CfP, even cheaper than this mid-price issue), the bonus item is certainly welcome, and this version of the *Symphony* deserves recommendation alongside the best.

Recorded live in the autumn of 2001 as part of his Elgar series, Sir Colin Davis's LSO account of No. 2 follows a similar pattern to No. 1 in a spacious, refined reading that readily sustains speeds broader than usual, notably in the development section of the first movement and in the whole of the slow movement. Particularly for a live recording, the dynamic range is remarkable with whispered *pianissimos* of breathtaking gentleness, set against ripe *fortissimos* with glorious brass sounds. Though in the finale Davis adopts a fast speed, his account of the lovely epilogue with its hushed reference back to the opening theme of the whole work is exceptionally spacious and tender, making a haunting close. But, as with No. 1, Handley remains the primary recommendation.

Andrew Davis's *Second* is the finer of his two performances of the two symphonies. It is an impetuous performance, strong and passionate. The slow movement has great eloquence, matched by the impetus of the finale, and it is coupled with a similarly exciting *In the South*. With first-class recording, this is eminently recommendable at budget price and well worth having as an alternative to Handley and Boult.

Downes uses an expansive speed in the first movement to give the writing its full emotional thrust, and the hushed tension of the slow movements leads up to towering climaxes, well controlled. The Scherzo is brilliant, delicate and witty, and the finale with its sequential writing is perfectly paced. The valedictory feeling at the close is very moving. Indeed, the only reservation is that the sound, though warm and refined, is a degree too distanced, so that the noble opening of the work does not have its full impact.

Gibson's recording shows his partnership with the RSNO at its peak, and this performance captures all the opulent nostalgia of Elgar's masterly score. The reading of the first movement is more relaxed in its grip than Handley's, but its spaciousness is appealing and, both here and in the beautifully sustained *Larghetto*, the richly resonant acoustics of Glasgow City Hall bring out the full panoply of Elgarian sound. The finale has splendid *nobilmente*. In the *Crown of India* suite Gibson is consistently imaginative in his attention to detail, and the playing of the Scottish orchestra is again warmly responsive.

Symphony 3 (from the composer's sketches, realized by Anthony Payne)
☛ (BB) *** Naxos 8.554719. Bournemouth SO, Daniel
(BB) *** LSO Live LSO 0019. LSO, C. Davis

Symphony 3 (completed from sketches, elaborated by Payne)
*** NMC NMCD 053. BBC SO, A. Davis

Symphony 3: sketches and commentary by Payne
(B) *** NMC NMCD 052. Gibbs, Norris, BBC SO, A. Davis

The original NMC recording of Anthony Payne's realization of Elgar's fragmentary sketches became a bestseller. Andrew Davis gave an inspired performance and the playing of the BBC Symphony Orchestra is thoroughly committed. The symphony is very well recorded. Anthony Payne's illustrated talk on the sketches gives precise details of his thinking and procedures. He discusses the exact state in which Elgar left the sketches, many of which were in full score, and what problems any conjectural completion would encounter, confirming that, whatever extra inspiration Elgar himself would have added to a finished score, this remains a wonderful bonus to our knowledge of the composer. The majority of the sketches were written out for violin and keyboard, and (on NMCD 052) Robert Gibbs plays the very instrument on which Elgar himself ran through the fragments with Reed. This bargain-price CD makes a splendid supplement to the recording of the complete work. But the performance by the Bournemouth orchestra under Paul Daniel matches the earlier one from Andrew Davis. If on NMC the BBC Symphony sounds richer and more sumptuous, relating the work to earlier Elgar, the leaner sound of the Bournemouth orchestra brings out the originality even more, with textures clear and transparent. The passages such as the opening exposition section, which Elgar completed himself, again make it clear that he was pointing forward, developing his style. Daniel is particularly successful too in drawing the threads together in the finale, the movement which was the most problematic for Payne. The slow epilogue is even more moving here than in the earlier performance, ending in mystery on a question mark. First-rate sound.

The Colin Davis LSO version, recorded live, comes into direct rivalry with Paul Daniel's superb Naxos disc with the Bournemouth Symphony, offering a performance just as powerful and concentrated, marked by refined string-playing, with *pianissimos* magically caught, even if the weight of tuttis is not quite as great as in the more forwardly balanced Naxos recording. Davis's reading of the finale is particularly fine with its clear pointing of sections, leading up to Payne's imaginative treatment of the close, and indeed this can be recommended alongside Daniel's account.

The Wand of Youth Suites 1 and 2; Organ Sonata in G (orch. Gordon Jacob)

(B) *** CfP 575 9792. RLPO, Handley

Handley's *Wand of Youth Suites* date from 1988 but have not been reviewed by us before. He is a true Elgarian and catches all the impetuous energy of the *Sun Dance*, the intimate magic of the *Fairy Pipers* and *Moths and Butterflies*, the warm serenity of the *Slumber Scene* and the contrasts of *Fairies and Giants* and the *Tame* and roisterous *Wild Bears*. The Liverpool orchestra plays with delicacy and vigour, warmth and finesse. It is welcome to have as an unexpected fill-up Handley's splendid account of the magnificent *Organ Sonata*, vividly orchestrated by Gordon Jacob to create what might almost be counted Elgar's 'Symphony No. o'. The recording, from the partnership of Andrew Keener and Mike Hatch, is in every way first class.

MUSIC FOR BRASS

Severn Suite, Op. 87

(N) (BB) **(*) Hyp. CDH 55070. L. Brass Virtuosi, Honeyball
– IRELAND: *Downland Suite*, etc.; VAUGHAN WILLIAMS: *Prelude on 3 Welsh Hymns* **(*)

Elgar was was commissioned to write his *Severn Suite* for the 1930 Crystal Palace Brass Band Festival. It was scored by Henry Geehl, who apparently also had quite a hand in its construction (he complained that the composer's sketches were inadequate). Elgar later orchestrated it, but the original is very effective indeed, with the characteristic flourish of the opening *Prelude* (the theme of which returns at the work's close) contrasting with the sombre *Elegy* – all highly telling on brass alone. This is an excellent performace, though it could perhaps have had more swagger at the end, and ideally one would have liked a full-sized brass band, instead of this more modest-sized group of players, fine as they are. Excellent recording.

CHAMBER AND INSTRUMENTAL MUSIC

(i) *Piano Quintet in A min., Op. 84. String Quartet in E min., Op. 83* (see also under *Violin Concerto*)

*** Chan. 9894. Sorrel Qt, (i) with Brown

(BB) *** Naxos 8.553737. Maggini Qt, (i) with Donohoe

(BB) *** Discover DICD 920485. Aura Ens., (i) with Fink

Piano Quintet; Violin Sonata in E min., Op. 82

*** Hyp. CDA 66645. Nash Ens. (members)

The Sorrel Quartet, perfectly matched by Ian Brown in the *Piano Quintet*, give exceptionally searching readings of these two late chamber works of Elgar. These are dedicated performances which understandingly bring out the contrast between the expansive *Quintet*, bold in its rhetoric, and the more intimate *Quartet*, with its terse, economical structure. The breadth of expression, using the widest dynamic range down to the most delicate *pianissimos*, intensifies the impact of each performance, magnetic and concentrated as if recorded live.

The Naxos and Discover versions appeared simultaneously, both at super-bargain price, both very recommendable. The Naxos issue with the young British Maggini Quartet, joined by Peter Donohoe, offers stylish, nicely pointed, slightly understated readings. Yet it is the Aura Ensemble of Switzerland which, perhaps surprisingly, offers even more red-blooded, urgently expressive readings, helped by rich, forward sound.

With the violinist, Marcia Crayford, and the pianist, Ian Brown, both as the duo in the *Sonata* and as the key players in the *Quintet*, the performances on Hyperion are more volatile than usual; but it is the slow movements above all that mark these performances as exceptional. The central *Adagio* of the *Quintet*, far slower than usual, then brings the most dedicated playing of all, making this not just a lyrical outpouring but an inner meditation. Warm, immediate recording.

String Quartet in E min., Op. 83

*** Regis RRC 1015. Britten Qt – WALTON: *Quartet* ***

*** ASV CDDCA 526. Brodsky Qt – DELIUS: *Quartet* ***

(*) Hyp. CDA 66718. Coull Qt – BRIDGE: 3 *Idylls*; WALTON: *Quartet* *

There is a poignancy in this late work which the beautifully matched members of the Britten Quartet capture to perfection. Not only do they bring out the emotional intensity; they play with a refinement and sharpness of focus that give superb point to the outer movements. With more *portamento* than one would normally expect today, the result is totally in style. Warmly expressive as the Gabrieli Quartet are in the Chandos coupling of the same works, the Brittens are even more searching.

The young players of the Brodsky Quartet take a weightier view than usual of the central, interlude-like slow movement, but they amply justify it. The power of the outer movements, too, gives the lie to the idea of this as a lesser piece than Elgar's other chamber works. First-rate recording.

Though in the Elgar the Coulls sound almost too comfortable, less successful at conveying the volatile mood-changes, their relaxed warmth is still very persuasive; and the Walton performance, with the melancholy of the slow movement intensified, is very fine. Excellent sound.

Violin Sonata in E min., Op. 82

*** Globe Musical Network GMN CO113. Little, Roscoe –
BAX: *Violin Sonata 2* ***

*** Nim. NI 5666. Hope, Mulligan – FINZI: *Elegy;* WALTON:
Violin Sonata ***

(M) *** Warner Elatus 2564 60661-2. Vengerov, Chachamov
– BRAHMS: *Violin Sonatas 2–3* ***

(N) (BB) (***) Naxos mono 8.110957. Sammons, Murdoch
(with SCHUBERT: *Rosamunde: Entr'acte.* DVORAK:
Humoresque, Op. 101/7. MASSENET: *Thaïs: Méditation.*
NACHEZ: *Passacaglia on a Theme of Sammartini.* SAMMONS:
Bourrée. TRAD.: *Londonderry Air*) – MOZART: *Sinfonia
Concertante in E flat*

(**(*) Testament mono SBT 1319. Rostal, Horsley – DELIUS;
WALTON: *Violin Sonatas* (**(*))

*Violin Sonata; Canto popolare; La Capricieuse, Op. 17;
Chanson de matin, Op. 15/2; Chanson de nuit, Op. 15/1; Mot
d'amour, Op. 13/1; Offertoire, Op. 11* (arr. Schneider); *Salut
d'amour, Op. 12; Sospiri, Op. 70; Sursum corda, Op. 11*
✿ *** Chan. 9624. Mordkovitch, Milford

*Violin Sonata; Canto popolare; Chanson de matin; Chanson
de nuit; Mot d'amour; Salut d'amour; Sospiri; 6 Easy pieces
in the first position*
*** Chan. 8380. Kennedy, Pettinger

Lydia Mordkovitch here transforms the elusive Elgar *Violin
Sonata*. In rapt and concentrated playing she gives it new
mystery, with the subtlest pointing and shading down to
whispered *pianissimos*. The shorter works include not only
popular pieces like *Salut d'amour, Chanson de matin* and
Sospiri, but rarities like a version of *Sursum corda* never
previously recorded and a little salon piece of 1893 which
Elgar inexplicably published under the pseudonym, Gustav
Francke.

Tasmin Little gives a warmly romantic, freely expressive
reading of the *Sonata*, presenting it as a big-scale virtuoso
work, where so often it has been underplayed. She allows
herself fair freedom over tempo, so that the second subject is
exceptionally broad, yet convincingly so, when (as ever) she
conveys spontaneity in every phrase. Equally, the fantasy of
the slow movement is brought out, even while she prefers a
rich rather than an intimate tonal palette. Her volatility in the
finale leads up to a magnificent conclusion. Very well
recorded, with the Bax *Sonata No. 2* an excellent coupling,
dating as it does from exactly the same period as the Elgar.

On Nimbus the Elgar *Sonata* brings a performance of high
contrasts both in dynamic range – with Daniel Hope using
daringly extreme *pianissimos* – and in flexibility of tempo. So
in the first movement the opening at an urgent speed gives
way to a very broad reading of the second subject, hushed
and introspective. Hope then treats the enigmatic slow movement as more than an interlude, bringing out gravity through
his dark violin-tone. In the finale, too, Hope conveys an
improvisational quality, again using the widest dynamic
range, finely matched by Simon Mulligan – like Hope, a
Menuhin protégé. Warm, atmospheric recording, less reverberant than many from this source.

At the start of the *Sonata*, Kennedy, also on Chandos,
establishes a concerto-like scale, which he then reinforces in a
fiery, volatile reading of the first movement, rich and biting in
its bravura. The elusive slow movement, *Romance*, is sharply
rhythmic in its weird Spanishry, while in the finale Kennedy
colours the tone seductively. As a coupling, Kennedy too has a
delightful collection of shorter pieces, not just *Salut d'amour*

and *Chanson de matin* but other rare chips from the master's
bench, although here he is less subtle than Mordkovitch.
Kennedy is matched beautifully throughout the recital by his
understanding piano partner, Peter Pettinger, and the recording is excellent.

Originally linked with the Dvořák *Violin Concerto* and now
recoupled with Brahms, Vengerov's performance is at once
passionate and large scale. He also brings out the thoughtful
poetry of the piece, with a vein of fantasy in the elusive slow
movement.

Albert Sammons was the greatest English violinist of his
day; he possessed a wonderful breadth of phrasing and sense
of line. His interpretation of the Elgar was rather eclipsed in
the 1930s and '40s by the youthful Menuhin conducted by
Elgar himself, but it remains *hors de concours* and, among
many Elgarians, reigns supreme. So should this wonderfully
idiomatic and richly expressive yet restrained account of the
Sonata.

Max Rostal, a refugee from Hitler's Germany, became an
inspired interpreter of English music, as all three of the *Violin
Sonatas* on this fine Testament disc demonstrate. In the Elgar,
Rostal is totally idiomatic, with a powerful, thrusting reading
of the first movement and an account of the slow movement
that, as with Vengerov, brings out the element of free fantasy.
He then plays the finale with a naturally expressive flexibility,
which relates the movement more than usual to the accompanied cadenza in the Elgar *Violin Concerto*. The mono
recording is on the dry side, but Rostal's refined tone defies
the lack of bloom, with Colin Horsley a most responsive
partner.

Music for wind

*Adagio cantabile (Mrs Winslow's Soothing Syrup); Andante
con variazione (Evesham Andante); 5 Intermezzos; Harmony
Music 1*
(M) *** Chan. (ADD) 6553. Athena Ens.

4 Dances; Harmony Music 2–4; 6 Promenades
(M) *** Chan. (ADD) 6554. Athena Ens.

As a budding musician, playing not only the violin but also
the bassoon, Elgar wrote a quantity of brief, lightweight
pieces in a traditional style for himself and four other wind-
players to perform. He called it 'Shed Music'; though there
are few real signs of the Elgar style to come, the energy and
inventiveness are very winning, particularly when (as here)
the pieces – often with comic names – are treated to bright
and lively performances. Excellent recording, with the CD
transfers sounding as fresh as new paint.

PIANO MUSIC

Solo piano music

*Adieu; Carissima; Chantant; Concert Allegro; Dream
Children; Griffinesque; In Smyrna; May Song; Minuet;
Pastorale; Presto; Rosemary; Serenade; Skizze; Sonatina*
**(*) Chan. 8438. Pettinger

*Adieu; Concert Allegro, Op. 46; Dream Children, Op. 43;
Enigma Variations, Op. 36* (arr. Elgar); *Griffinesque; In
Smyrna; Presto; Salut d'amour; Serenade; Skizze; Sonatina*
*** ASV CDDCA 1065. Garzón

The Chandos record includes nearly all of Elgar's piano
music. This has not established itself in the piano repertoire
but, as Peter Pettinger shows, there are interesting things in

this byway of English music (such as the *Skizze* and *In Smyrna*). We get both the 1889 version of the *Sonatina* and its much later revision. Committed playing from this accomplished artist, and a pleasing recording too, with fine presence on CD.

The main work on ASV is Elgar's own transcription of the *Enigma Variations*, which preceded the orchestral version by three months. It is marvellously played here but was, of course, made before the days when one could get to know the piece through the gramophone. However, if you are going to have this in its keyboard form, it could hardly be better played. The Spanish pianist María Garzón has sensitivity and fervour, and she plays it and the other Elgar pieces, such as the *Concert Allegro*, the *Sonatina* and *In Smyrna* (which Elgar composed after a Mediterranean cruise as a guest of the Royal Navy), as if she had been born and bred in Worcester rather than Madrid.

ORGAN MUSIC

Organ Sonata 1 in G, Op. 28

*** Priory PRDC 401. Scott (organ of St Paul's Cathedral)
(with HARRIS: *Sonata* ***) – BAIRSTOW: *Organ Sonata* ***

Elgar's *Organ Sonata* is a ripely expansive piece, a richly inspired work, more of a symphony than a sonata. John Scott gives an excitingly spontaneous performance and the St Paul's Cathedral organ seems an ideal choice, although some of the *pianissimo* passages become rather recessed. The recording has plenty of spectacle and the widest dynamic range.

VOCAL AND CHORAL MUSIC

Angelus; Ave Maria; Ave maris stella; Ave verum corpus; Ecce sacardos magnus; Fear not, O land; Give unto the Lord; Great is the Lord; I sing the birth; Lo! Christ the Lord is born; O hearken thou; O salutaris hostia 1–3

(BB) *** Hyp. Helios CDH 55147. Worcester Cathedral Ch., Hunt; A. Partington (organ)

In this group of 14 sacred choral works, Dr Donald Hunt, choirmaster of Worcester Cathedral, here provides a refreshing supplement to his fine collection of Elgar part-songs (Hyperion CDA 66271/2 – see below). Though in the grand setting of Psalm 48, *Great is the Lord*, one misses the impact of a big choir, the refinement of Dr Hunt's singers, their freshness and bloom as recorded against a helpful acoustic are ample compensation, particularly when the feeling for Elgarian phrasing and rubato is unerring. The coronation anthem *O Hearken thou* would also benefit from larger-scale treatment, convincing as this refined performance is; but most of these 14 items are more intimate, and the Worcester performances are near ideal, with clean ensemble, fine blending and taut rhythmic control. Vividly atmospheric recording, which still allows for full detail to emerge.

Ave Maria; Ave Maris stella; Ave verum corpus; Benedictus. Op. 34/2; Give unto the Lord (Psalm 29), Op. 74; Go Song of mine, Op. 57; Great is the Lord (Psalm 48), Op. 67; The Light of Life, Op. 29: Seek Him that maketh the seven stars; Light

of the World. O hearken Thou, Op. 64; O salutaris hostia; Te Deum laudamus, Op. 34/1; The Apostles: The Spirit of the Lord is upon me

●━ (BB) *** Naxos 8.557288. St John's Cambridge, College Ch., Robinson; J. Vaughan (organ)

This is the last of the series of ten highly successful CDs made by the St John's College Choir under Christopher Robinson, before he retired in 2002. Elgar's shorter Latin settings, *Ave verum corpus*, *Ave Maria*, *Ave Maris stella*, *O hearken Thou* and *O salutaris hostia*, are all quite lovely. The more ambitious *Te Deum* and *Benedictus* was written for the Hereford Three Choirs Festival of 1897 and, like the Psalm setting *Great is the Lord* (first heard at Westminster Abbey in 1912), shows Elgar at full stretch. It is also good to have the serene *Prologue* to *The Apostles* (1903), *The Spirit of the Lord* and, finally, the two memorable excerpts from Elgar's first oratorio, *The Light of Life*, notably the stirring *Light of the world*, which is the exultant closing chorus. Splendid singing throughout and excellent recording make this a collection to treasure.

The Apostles, Op. 49

*** Chan. 8875/6. Hargan, Hodgson, Rendall, Roberts, Terfel, Lloyd, L. Symphony Ch., LSO, Hickox
(M) *** EMI (ADD) 7 64206-2 (2). Armstrong, Watts, Tear, Luxon, Grant, Carol Case, Downe House School Ch., LPO Ch., LPO, Boult (with *Light of Life: Meditation*)

Where Boult's reading has four-square nobility, Hickox is far more flexible in his expressiveness, drawing singing from his chorus that far outshines that on the earlier reading. Most of his soloists are preferable too, for example Stephen Roberts as a light-toned Jesus and Robert Lloyd characterful as Judas. Only the tenor, David Rendall, falls short, with vibrato exaggerated by the microphone. The recording, made in St Jude's, Hampstead, is among Chandos's finest, both warm and incandescent, with plenty of detail.

Boult's performance gives the closing scene great power and a wonderful sense of apotheosis, with the spacious sound-balance rising to the occasion. Generally fine singing – notably from Sheila Armstrong and Helen Watts – and a 1973/4 Kingsway Hall recording as rich and faithful as anyone could wish for. The powerfully lyrical *Meditation* from *The Light of Life* makes a suitable postlude without producing an anticlimax, again showing Boult at his most inspirational.

(i) The Black Knight (symphony for chorus and orchestra); Part-songs: Fly singing bird; The snow; Spanish serenade. (ii) Scenes from the Saga of King Olaf, Op. 30

(M) **(*) EMI 5 65104-2 (2). (i) RLPO Ch. & O, Groves; (ii) Cahill, Langridge, Rayner Cook, LPO Ch., LPO, Handley

The Black Knight, Op. 3; Scenes from the Bavarian Highlands, Op. 27

◉ *** Chan. 9436. L. Symphony Ch., LSO, Hickox

The cantata *The Black Knight* is based on a similar story to that of Mahler's early cantata, *Das klagende Lied*, but Elgar's inspiration is more open and less tortured, with the orchestration already showing the mastery which was to bloom in *Enigma*. Hickox, helped by exceptionally rich and full recording, with vivid presence, consistently brings out the dramatic tensions of the piece as well as the refinement and beauty of the poetic sequences, to make the previous recording under Sir Charles Groves sound too easy-going, enjoyable though it is. The part-songs inspired by the composer's visit to Bavaria then add even more exhilaration, with the vigour and joy of the outer movements – better known in Elgar's orchestral versions – brought out winningly, and with the London Symphony Chorus at its freshest and most incisive. A disc to win new admirers for two seriously neglected works.

Charles Groves conducts a fresh performance of *The Black Knight*, and the happiness and confidence of the writing are what come over, even though Elgarians must inevitably miss the deeper, darker and more melancholy overtones. The emotional thrust in Handley's reading confirms *King Olaf* as the very finest of the big works Elgar wrote before the *Enigma Variations* in 1899. Though strained at times by the high writing, Philip Langridge makes a fine, intelligent Olaf, Teresa Cahill sings with ravishing silver purity and Brian Rayner Cook brings out words with fine clarity; but it is the incandescent singing of the London Philharmonic Chorus that sets the seal on this superb set, ripely recorded.

(i) *Caractacus* (complete). *Coronation March; Imperial March; Enigma Variations*
(M) *** EMI 7 63807-2 (2). (i) Armstrong, Tear, Glossop, Rayner Cook, King, Stuart, RLPO Ch.; RLPO, Groves

(i) *Caractacus, Op. 35. Severn Suite* (full orchestral version)
*** Chan. 9156/7. (i) Howarth, Wilson-Johnson, Davies, Roberts, Miles, L. Symphony Ch.; LSO, Hickox

Caractacus, based on the story of the ancient British hero pardoned by the Emperor Claudius, dropped out of the regular repertory long ago, forgotten except for the rousing *Triumphal March* and some notorious lines about the nations 'standing to hymn the praise of Britains like brothers hand in hand'. In fact, only a tiny proportion of the piece is at all jingoistic, and such passages as the duet between Caractacus's daughter and her lover are as tenderly beautiful as anything Elgar wrote before *Enigma*. Groves offers a very fine performance with consistently excellent soloists and fine choral singing which with ripe recording brings out all the Elgarian atmosphere (even if it does not manage the clearest projection of the words). But it partly explains the neglect. The dramatic interest is limited, and the melodies are generally not as memorable as they might be. Yet *Caractacus* gives a rich insight into Elgar's early career, showing him as a composer still limited but delightfully approachable.

Elgar's *Caractacus* draws from Hickox and his splendid LSO forces a fresh, sympathetic reading, generally very well sung, with David Wilson-Johnson in the title-role, recorded in opulent Chandos sound. Much the most memorable item is the well-known *Imperial March*, introducing the final scene in Rome, made the more exciting with chorus. The only reservation is that the earlier, EMI recording conducted by Sir Charles Groves was crisper in ensemble and even better sung, with even more seductive pointing of rhythm. For coupling, Hickox has the full orchestral arrangement of Elgar's very last work, originally for brass band, the *Severn Suite*.

(i) *Coronation Ode, Op. 44. The Spirit of England, Op. 80*
(M) *** Chan. 6574. Cahill, SNO Ch. and O, Gibson; (i) with Collins, Rolfe Johnson, Howell

Gibson's performances combine fire and panache, and the recorded sound has an ideal Elgarian expansiveness, the choral tone rich and well focused, the orchestral brass given plenty of weight, and the overall perspective highly convincing. He is helped by excellent soloists, with Anne Collins movingly eloquent in her dignified restraint when she introduces the famous words of *Land of hope and glory* in the finale; and the choral entry which follows is truly glorious in

its power and amplitude. *The Spirit of England*, a wartime cantata to words of Laurence Binyon, is in some ways even finer, with the final setting of *For the fallen* rising well above the level of his occasional music.

(i) *Coronation Ode;* (ii) *The Spirit of England, Op. 80; Oh hearken thou (Offertory), Op. 64;* (i) *National Anthem* (arr. Elgar)
(M) *** EMI (ADD/DDD) 5 85148-2. (i; ii) Lott; (i) Hodgson, Morton, Roberts, Cambridge University Music Socety, King's College, Cambridge, Ch., New Philh. O, Band of Royal Military School of Music, Ledger; (ii) L. Symphony Ch., N. Sinf., Hickox – PARRY: *I was glad* ***

Ledger is superb in capturing the necessary swagger and panache of the *Coronation Ode*. The 1977 analogue recording, of demonstration quality, is one of the finest made in King's College Chapel – and with extra brass it presents a glorious experience. Excellent singing and playing, though the male soloists do not quite match their female colleagues. A decade later, Hickox conducted a rousing performance of *The Spirit of England*, magnificently defying the dangers of the composer's wartime bombast, adding also a short but telling setting of Psalm 29, composed as the Offertory in the coronation service of King George V in 1911. The London Symphony Chorus is in radiant form, and Felicity Lott is a strong soloist in both major works. First-rate Abbey Road digital sound. The disc opens with Elgar's grandiloquent version of the National Anthem, which includes a last-verse reference to *Pomp and Circumstance No. 1*.

The Dream of Gerontius, Op. 38
(B) *** EMI (ADD) 5 73579-2 (2). Baker, Lewis, Borg, Hallé & Sheffield Philharmonic Ch., Amb. S., Hallé O, Barbirolli
*** Chan. 8641/2. Palmer, A. Davies, Howell, L. Symphony Ch. & LSO, Hickox – PARRY: *Anthems* ***
(B) **(*) CfP 2-CD 575 7642 (2). Rolfe Johnson, Wyn-Rogers, George, Huddersfield Ch. Soc., RLPO Ch. & O, Handley – WALTON: *Belshazzar's Feast* **

(i) *The Dream of Gerontius;* (ii) *Cello Concerto*
(***) Testament mono SBT 2025 (2). (i) Nash, Ripley, Noble, Walker, Huddersfield Ch. Soc., Liverpool PO; (ii) P. Tortelier, BBC SO; Sargent

(i) *The Dream of Gerontius;* (ii) *The Music Makers, Op. 69*
🏵 ⊕ (M) *** EMI (ADD) 5 66540-2 (2). (i) Gedda, Watts, Lloyd, Alldis Ch., LPO Ch., New Philh. O; (ii) Baker, LPO Ch., LPO; Boult

Boult's total dedication is matched by his powerful sense of drama. Indeed, it is difficult to conceive of a more powerful conclusion to Part I when Robert Lloyd (a magnificent Priest and Angel of Agony) and the chorus send Gerontius's soul on its way. The spiritual feeling is intense throughout, but the human qualities of the narrative are also fully realized. Nicolai Gedda in the role of Gerontius brings a new dimension to this characterization. He is perfectly matched by Helen Watts as the Angel. It is a fascinating vocal partnership and is matched by the commanding manner which Robert Lloyd finds for both his roles. The orchestral playing is always responsive, and often, like the choral singing, very beautiful, while the dramatic passages bring splendid incisiveness and bold assurance from the singers. The 1976 Kingsway Hall recording has been remastered quite stunningly: the sound has great presence as well as ideal ambient warmth and atmosphere. It is technically, as well as musically, a truly great recording. The performance and recording of *The Music Makers*, made at Abbey Road a decade earlier, is also very successful. If only the whole piece lived up to the uninhibited choral setting of the *Nimrod* variation from *Enigma*, it would be another Elgar masterpiece. Nevertheless, Boult's dedication, matched by Janet Baker's masterly eloquence, holds the listener throughout, and the current transfer has brought a new vividness to the choral contribution.

Barbirolli's red-blooded reading of *Gerontius* is the most heart-warmingly dramatic ever recorded; here it is offered, in a first-rate CD transfer, in coupling with Janet Baker's rapt and heartfelt account of *Sea Pictures*. No one on record can match her in this version of *Gerontius* for the fervent intensity and glorious tonal range of her singing as the Angel, one of her supreme recorded performances; and the clarity of CD intensifies the experience. In terms of pure dedication the emotional thrust of Barbirolli's reading conveys the deepest spiritual intensity. The recording may have its hints of distortion, but the sound is overwhelming. Richard Lewis gives one of his finest recorded performances, searching and intense, and, though Kim Borg is unidiomatic in the bass role, his bass tones are rich in timbre, even if his projection lacks the dramatic edge of Robert Lloyd on the reissued Boult set.

Sir Malcolm Sargent in 1945 paced the score perfectly, drawing incandescent singing from the Huddersfield Choral Society. The soloists too, superbly led by Heddle Nash as Gerontius, have a freshness and clarity rarely matched, with Nash's ringing tenor consistently clean in attack. Though Gladys Ripley's fine contralto is caught with a hint of rapid flutter, she matches the others in forthright clarity, with Dennis Noble as the Priest and Norman Walker as the Angel of the Agony both strong and direct. The mono recording captures detail excellently; even if inevitably the dynamic range is limited and the chorus lacks something in body, such a climax as *Praise to the Holiest* has thrilling bite. The first and finest of Paul Tortelier's three recordings of the Elgar *Cello Concerto* makes an ideal coupling, emotionally intense within a disciplined frame.

Hickox's version outshines almost all rivals in the range and quality of its sound. Quite apart from the fullness and fidelity of the recording, Hickox's performance is deeply understanding, not always ideally powerful in the big climaxes but paced most sympathetically, with a natural understanding of Elgarian rubato. The soloists make a characterful team. Arthur Davies is a strong and fresh-toned Gerontius; Gwynne Howell in the bass roles is powerful if not always ideally steady; and Felicity Palmer, though untraditionally bright of tone with her characterful vibrato, is strong and illuminating. Though on balance Boult's soloists are even finer, Hickox's reading in its expressive warmth conveys much love for this score, and the last pages with their finely sustained closing *Amen* are genuinely moving.

(i) *The Kingdom, Op. 51;* (ii) *Coronation Ode, Op. 34*
(M) *** EMI (ADD) 7 64209-2. (i) M. Price, Minton, Young, Shirley-Quirk, LPO Ch., LPO, Boult; (ii) Lott, Hodgson, Morton, Cambridge University Music Soc., King's College, Cambridge, Ch., New Philh. O, Band of Royal Military School of Music, Kneller Hall, Ledger

The Kingdom; Sursum corda; Sospiri
*** Chan. 8788/9. Marshall, Palmer, A. Davies, Wilson-Johnson, L. Symphony Ch., LSO, Hickox

Boult was devoted to *The Kingdom*, identifying with its comparative reticence, and his dedication emerges clearly throughout a glorious performance. The melody which Elgar wrote to represent the Holy Spirit is one of the noblest that even he created, and the soprano aria, *The sun goeth down* (beautifully sung by Margaret Price), leads to a deeply affecting climax. The other soloists also sing splendidly, and the only reservation concerns the chorus, which is not quite as disciplined as it might be and sounds a little too backward for some of the massive effects which cap the power of the work. The coupling of the *Coronation Ode* is handy and certainly welcome, rather than particularly appropriate. Both works are generously cued.

Hickox proves a warmly understanding Elgarian and his manner is more ripely idiomatic. His soloists make a characterful quartet. Margaret Marshall is the sweet, tender soprano, rising superbly to a passionate climax in her big solo, *The sun goeth down*, and Felicity Palmer is a strong and positive – if not ideally warm-toned – Mary Magdalene. David Wilson-Johnson points the words of St Peter most dramatically, and Arthur Davies is the radiant tenor. The fill-ups are not generous: the intense little string adagio, *Sospiri*, and the early *Sursum corda*.

The Light of Life (Lux Christi), Op. 29
*** Chan. 9208. Howarth, Finnie, A. Davies, Shirley-Quirk, L. Symphony Ch., LSO, Hickox

Notably more than Sir Charles Groves in the earlier, EMI recording, Hickox conveys the warmth of inspiration of *The Light of Life* in glowing sound, with the chorus incandescent. The solo singing is richly characterful, even if the microphone catches an unevenness in the singing of the mezzo, Linda Finnie, and of John Shirley-Quirk; nevertheless he sings nobly as Jesus in the climactic 'Good Shepherd' solo. Arthur Davies, as the blind man, and the soprano, Judith Howarth, are both excellent, singing with clear, fresh tone.

The Music Makers; Sea Pictures, Op. 37
*** Chan. 9022. Finnie, LPO Ch., LPO, Thomson
(M) **(*) EMI 5 65126-2. Palmer, L. Symphony Ch., LSO, Hickox

On Chandos the song-cycle and the cantata make a good coupling, with a contralto soloist as the key figure in each work. Bryden Thomson directs warmly expressive, spontaneous-sounding performances of both works, easily flexible in an idiomatic way, and this now makes a first choice among modern recordings.

Hickox's coupling of *Sea Pictures* and the big cantata, *The Music Makers*, brings strong, powerful performances, very individual in the song-cycle thanks to the urgent, tough and indeed characterful singing of Felicity Palmer. Hickox gives a convincing, red-blooded reading of the cantata, atmospherically recorded and with the voices well caught, but with reverberation masking some of the orchestral detail.

3 Partsongs, Op. 18; 4 Partsongs, Op. 53; 2 Partsongs, Op. 71; 2 Partsongs, Op. 73; 5 Partsongs from the Greek anthology, Op. 45; Death on the hills; Evening scene; Go, song of mine; How calmly the evening; The Prince of Sleep; Weary wind of the West
*** Chan. 9269. Finzi Singers, Spicer

Elgar's partsongs span virtually the whole of his creative career, and the 22 examples on the Finzi Singers' disc range from one of the most famous, *My love dwelt in a northern land*, of 1889 to settings of Russian poems (in English translation) written during the First World War. The Finzi Singers under Paul Spicer give finely tuned, crisp and intense readings of all the pieces. The Hyperion two-disc collection (see below) also includes Elgar's ecclesiastical motets, but for the secular partsongs the Chandos performances are even finer.

4 Partsongs, Op. 53; 5 Partsongs from the Greek anthology, Op. 45. Choral songs: *Christmas greeting; Death on the hills; Evening scene; The fountain; Fly, singing bird; Goodmorrow; Go, song of mine; The herald; How calmly the evening; Love's tempest; My love dwelt; The Prince of sleep; Rapid stream; Reveille; Serenade; The shower; Snow; Spanish serenade; They are at rest; The wanderer; Weary wind of the West; When swallows fly; Woodland stream; Zut! zut! zut!*
*** Hyp. CDA 66271/2. Worcester Cathedral Ch.; Donald Hunt Singers, Hunt; Swallow, Ballard; Thurlby

The finest item on the Hyperion CD is the last, in which both choirs join, the eight-part setting of *Cavalcanti* in translation by Rossetti, *Go, song of mine.* It is also fascinating to find Elgar in 1922, with all his major works completed, writing three charming songs for boys' voices to words by Charles Mackay, as refreshing as anything in the whole collection. Atmospherically recorded – the secular singers rather more cleanly than the cathedral choir – it is a delightful collection for anyone fascinated by Elgar outside the big works.

Songs: *After; Arabian Serenade; Is she not passing fair; Like to the damask rose; Oh, soft was the song; Pleading; Poet's life; Queen Mary's song; Rondel; Shepherd's song; Song of autumn; Song of flight; Through the long days; Twilight; Was it some golden star?*
**(*) Chan. 8539. Luxon, Willison – DELIUS: *Songs* **(*)

Benjamin Luxon seemingly cannot avoid the roughness of production that has marred some of his later recordings, but he gives charming freshness to this delightful selection. Brilliant and sensitive accompaniment, and a very fine recording-balance.

Scenes from the Bavarian Highlands, Op. 27; Ecce sacerdos magnus; O salutaris Hostia (3 settings); *Tantum ergo; The Light of Life: Doubt not thy Father's care; Light of the World*
(M) **(*) Chan. 6601. Worcester Cathedral Ch., Robinson; Wibaut; Bramma

It is good to have a fine, mid-priced performance of the original, piano-accompanied version of the charmingly tuneful *Bavarian Scenes.* Even without the orchestra, the music lifts up with remarkable freshness when the singing in Worcester is appropriately committed and spontaneous. The three versions of *O salutaris Hostia* are also worth having, and the strong performances of *Tantum ergo* and *Ecce sacerdos magnus* add to the interest of this reissue.

Songs: *Pleading; 3 Songs (Was it some golden star?; Oh, soft was the song; Twilight), Op. 59; 2 Songs (The torch; The river), Op. 60*
(M) *** EMI (ADD) 7 64731-2. Tear, CBSO, Handley – BUTTERWORTH: *Songs;* VAUGHAN WILLIAMS: *On Wenlock Edge, etc.* ***

At his most creative period in the early years of the century, Elgar planned another song-cycle to follow *Sea Pictures,* but he completed only three of the songs, his Op. 59. The other songs here are even more individual, a fine coupling for Vaughan Williams and Butterworth. Incisive and characterful, yet expressively sympathetic performances from Robert

Tear. The recording, well focused, is appropriately warm and atmospheric.

Sea Pictures (song-cycle), *Op. 37*
⊶ ❋ (N) (M) *** EMI (ADD) 5 62886-2. Baker, LSO, Barbirolli – *Cello Concerto* (with *Cockaigne Overture*) *** ❋
(N) (BB) **(*)Virgin 2x1 5 62425-2 (2). Palmer, LSO, Hickox – *Cello & Violin Concertos* **(*)
** ABC Classics (ADD) 461 922-2. Elkins, Queensland SO, Albert – SHIELD: *Rosina;* WILLIAMSON: *The Growing Castle* ***

Like du Pré, Baker is an artist who has the power to convey on record the vividness of a live performance. With the help of Barbirolli she makes the cycle far more convincing than it usually seems, with often trite words clothed in music that seems to transform them. On CD, the voice is caught with extra bloom, and the beauty of Elgar's orchestration is enhanced by the subtle added definition. This unique coupling has now been reissued at mid-price as one of EMI's 'Great Recordings of the Century'.

Felicity Palmer's performance with Hickox is individual and strong, thanks to her urgent and indeed characterful singing, more powerful than with Janet Baker, if less endearing.

Albert's warm-hearted, atmospheric and beautiful account of the *Sea Pictures* makes an unexpected fill-up to Shield's sparkling rustic opera, *Rosina.* Margreta Elkins's voice is well captured in the 1983 recording. Though the orchestra lacks richness, it is perfectly acceptable. Texts are included, along with very full documentation.

The Starlight Express (incidental music), *Op. 78*
(B) *** CfP (ADD) 585 9072. Masterson, Hammond-Stroud, LPO, Handley

It has been left to latterday Elgarians to revive a 1916 score (incidental music for a children's play) that was not a success in its day but that reveals the composer at his most charming. On CD in this dedicated reconstruction (without the spoken dialogue) one is conscious of the element of repetition. But the ear is constantly beguiled and the key sequences suggest that this procedure would have won the composer's approval. Much of the orchestral music has that nostalgically luminous quality that Elgarians will instantly recognize. Both soloists are excellent, and the LPO plays with warmth and sympathy. The 1976 recording is excellent and it matters little that, in order to fit the piece complete on to a single CD, some minor cuts have had to be made.

ELLER, Heino (1887–1970)

Dawn (tone-poem); (i) *Elegia for Harp & Strings; 5 Pieces for Strings*
*** Chan. 8525. (i) Pierce; SNO, Järvi – RAID: *Symphony 1* ***

Dawn is frankly romantic – with touches of Grieg and early Sibelius as well as the Russian nationalists – and the *Five Pieces for Strings* have a wistful, Grieg-like charm. The *Elegia for Harp and Strings* of 1931 strikes a deeper vein of feeling and has nobility and eloquence, tempered by quiet restraint; there is a beautiful dialogue involving solo viola and harp which is quite haunting. Excellent performances and recording. Strongly recommended.

EMMANUEL, Maurice (1862–1938)

6 Chansons bourguignonnes du Pays de Beaune
*** Erato 0630 17577-2 (2). Upshaw, Lyon Op. O, Nagano –
CANTELOUBE: *Songs of the Auvergne: Series 1–5* ***

Maurice Emmanuel's attractive orchestral arrangements
enhance these Burgundian songs from the Beaune region, in
very much the same way as Canteloube's *Chants d'Auvergne*.
The six included here are nicely contrasted, and they are
delightfully sung and most idiomatically accompanied. *Le
Pommier d'Août* and *Noël* are particularly engaging, but most
memorable of all is the haunting closing *Farewell to the
shepherdess*.

ENESCU, Georges (1881–1955)

The Romanian composer, Georges Enescu, was an immensely
gifted child prodigy, already a precocious violinist at the age
of seven and by 13 entering the Paris Conservatoire, where he
studied composition under Massenet and, later, Fauré. But, as
his career developed, his creative achievements were long
overshadowed by his role as violinist, teacher (to the youthful
Yehudi Menuhin, among others) and conductor. He was long
famous only for his *First Romanian Rhapsody*, and this, and
even the visionary *Third Violin Sonata*, give little inkling of
his true stature, although his opera, *Oedipe*, certainly does,
and now that it has been recorded – see below – justice is at
last being done.

Romanian Rhapsody 1
*** Mercury (ADD) **SACD** 475 6185. LSO, Dorati – LISZT:
Hungarian Rhapsodies 1–6 **(*)
(N) (B) *** Decca (ADD) 476 2453. Detroit SO, Dorati –
SMETANA: *Má Vlast: Vltava. The Bartered Bride: Overture;
Polka; Furiant* ***; DVORAK: *Slavonic Dances*, etc. ***

Dorati finds both flair and exhilaration in this enticing piece,
especially in the closing pages, and the Mercury sound from
the early 1960s is of a vintage standard. The coupling with the
Liszt *Hungarian Rhapsodies* is entirely appropriate. The new
SACD format further enhances the already spectacular results
afforded by the 'Living Presence' technology. It is very
impressive indeed.

Another very well-played and -recorded account of Enescu's chimerical *First Rhapsody*, also under Dorati, with the
Detroit orchestra clearly enjoying its Eastern gypsy influences
and building up plenty of excitement. It makes a fine bonus
to Kertész's classic Dvořák and Smetana coupling, but the
Mercury version in its new SACD format is finer still, with
the recording very near the demonstration bracket.

Romanian Rhapsodies 1–2, Op. 11/1–2.
(M) *** Chan. 6625. RSNO, Järvi – BARTOK: *Hungarian
Pictures*; WEINER: *Hungarian Folkdance Suite* ***

Järvi has a warmly idiomatic feeling for these amiable,
peasant-inspired rhapsodies, moulding phrases and linking
passages with spontaneity, drawing committed playing, with
plenty of subtle touches from the Royal Scottish National
Orchestra, ripely recorded. Although the first of the two
rhapsodies is much the more popular, and justly so, the
second is also lively and colourful. They are now aptly
coupled with comparably entertaining and colourful folk-
inspired music by Bartók and Weiner.

Romanian Rhapsodies 1–2; (i) Symphonie concertante for
Cello & Orchestra, Op. 8. Suites for Orchestra: 1 & 2 in C,
Opp. 9 & 20; 3 (Villageoise) Op. 27; (ii) Poème roumaine,
Op. 1
(N) (BB) **(*) Warner Apex 2564 62032-2 (2). Monte Carlo
PO, Foster, with (i) Maggio-Ormezowski; (ii) Male Ch. of
Colonne O, & Ens. Audita Nova

An inexpensive and worthwhile introduction to Enescu for
those wanting to explore beyond the *Romanian Rhapsodies*.
The *Symphonie concertante* is an attractively written piece,
again using national dances. The cello soloist is excellent. The
first two of the *Three Suites for Orchestra* are well crafted
without being in the very first rank, yet they are expertly laid
out for the orchestra and have a charm and appeal that ought
to ensure them a wider following. The *Third (Village) Suite*
brings a series of pastoral scenes and more national dances to
conclude. The *Poème roumaine* has lyrical appeal and uses an
evocative wordless male chorus with bells at the opening, and
later a solo violin; it features the Romanian national anthem
as its finale. All this is well enough served by the Monte Carlo
orchestra under Lawrence Foster and is given the benefit of
natural, spacious recording.

Symphonies (i) 1 in E flat, Op. 13; 2 in A, Op. 17; (ii; iii) 3 in
C, Op. 21; (ii; iii; iv) Vox Maris (Symphonic Poem), Op. 31
(N) (B) *** EMI 5 86604-2 (2). (i) Monte Carlo PO, (ii) O
Nat. de Lyon; Lawrence Foster; with (iii) Les Eléments
Chamber Ch.; (iv) Brenciu; Sydney

The *First* and *Second Symphonies* predate the First World
War; No. 1 (1905) and 2 (1912–14) inherit the mantle of
Strauss, Franck, Dukas – and even Brahms – and are scored
with great flair. They have never been played with such vigour
and conviction as here, nor as well recorded. Lawrence Foster,
who has recorded a good deal of Enescu, directs the Monte
Carlo orchestra with tremendous fire and an infectious
enthusiasm, and the players respond as if their lives depended
on it. The even more opulent *Third Symphony* (1918) is more
intractable; its expansive first movement is not easy to hold
together; but Foster is clearly back on top form in the
second-movement march/scherzo, and sustains the fullest
tension in the ecstatic finale with its wordless chorus (helped
by the passionate singing of the Les Eléments Choir).

Vox Maris (a score discovered only after the composer's
death, although probably written in the 1920s) takes the
unearthly evocation a stage further, using offstage soprano
and tenor soloists and chorus, and even drawing on a motif
borrowed from *Oedipe*. Based on a Breton poem by René
Willy in French translation, it is essentially a seascape with
shipwreck, and is powerfully evocative, if over-inflated. Alas,
no text and translation are included here; otherwise performance and recording show Lawrence Foster again at his finest,
with another impressive choral contribution, although the
wobbly soprano soloist is not an asset.

(i) Symphony 3. Romanian Rhapsody 1
** Chan. 9633. (i) Leeds Festival Ch.; BBC PO,
Rozhdestvensky

The *Third Symphony* dates from the middle of the First
World War and is a long, loosely constructed piece, scored for
large forces including six horns, organ, piano, two harps and
wordless chorus. Rozhdestvensky conducts with much sympathy, though he could perhaps have adopted a brisker tempo
for the first movement. The performance lacks the last ounce

of urgency, and the same goes for the popular *Romanian Rhapsody No. 1*. Good Chandos sound.

CHAMBER MUSIC

Dixtuor, Op. 14

(BB) *** Naxos 8.554173. Oslo PO Wind soloists – DVORAK: *Wind Serenade*; JANACEK: *Mládi* ***

The *Dixtuor* or *Decet* is one of Enescu's most glorious scores: its sophisticated counterpoint and idyllic charm are most appealing. The plaintive slow movement is haunting. The Oslo wind soloists are artists of quality whose reading challenges the finest at any price. Crisp rhythms, a good sense of line and tonal finesse. These artists recorded this piece on the Victoria label in the early 1990s, but these are different and better accounts in every way.

Impressions d'enfance (for Violin & Piano), Op. 28

(N) *** Avie AV 2059. Graffin, Désert – DEBUSSY: *Violin Sonata; Nocturne et Scherzo*, etc.; RAVEL: *Sonata; Tzigane* ***

Written in 1940, during a period when Enescu had returned home to Romania, *Impressions d'enfance* is a series of charming nostalgic glimpses of the composer's childhood, beautifully evoked in the performance here. Opening with the sound of a fiddler on the street, there follow brief portraits, first a melacholy old beggar, then a stream trickling at the bottom of a garden, a bird in its cage and a cuckoo clock, a cricket; then, more atmospherically, moonlight and the wind in the chimney; and, finally sunrise, with night-time banished in a rhapsodic finale in which one feels the composer returning forcefully to the present.

Piano Quartet 2 in D min., Op. 30; Piano Quintet, Op. 29

(BB) **(*) Naxos 8.557159. Solomon Ens.

The *Piano Quintet* had a long period of gesation and was not completed until 1940 and not performed until the mid-1960s, a decade after the composer's death. The *Piano Quartet No. 2* (1943–4) is dedicated to Fauré, with whom Enescu studied in the 1890s. Indeed, it has something of the subtlety and finesse of late Fauré and, like the *Quintet*, is a work of real substance which rewards the serious listener. This music does not try to impress with effect or originality but by its continuity of thought and finely paced musical development. With every new record we hear, Enescu emerges as a composer with something important to say. The Solomon Ensemble play well but the balance is not ideal: there is not enough air round the sound and the first violin is placed too reticently, hence the reservation. Strongly recommended all the same, particularly at its competitive price.

String Quartets 1 in E flat; 2 in G, Op. 22/1–2

(BB) *** Naxos 8.554721. Ad Libitum Qt

The Enescu quartets share the same opus number but are separated by over three decades; the *First* comes from the end of the First World War and the *Second* from the 1950s, towards the end of the composer's life. Few works by this extraordinary musician are without their rewards, and although neither quartet rises to the same imaginative heights as *Oedipe* or the *Dixtuor* they are full of good things. They are well played by this fine Romanian team and priced at the right level. The adventurous collector will not baulk at

a fiver for repertoire that he or she does not know and will find the outlay worthwhile.

Violin Sonatas 2, Op. 6; 3, Op. 25; Torso

(BB) *** Hyp. Helios CDH 55103. A. Oprean, J. Oprean

Enescu's *Second Violin Sonata* is an early work, written in 1899 when he was seventeen and still studying in Paris with Fauré. The *Third* (1926), together with the opera, *Oedipe*, is his masterpiece and shows an altogether different personality; the difference in stylistic development could hardly be more striking. Adelina Oprean is thoroughly inside the idiom, as befits a Romanian, and she deals with its subtle rubati and quarter-tones to the manner born. She exhibits excellent musical taste but her partner (and brother) is somewhat less scrupulous in his observance of dynamic nuance. The additional *Torso* is a sonata movement from 1911, which was published only in the 1980s.

PIANO MUSIC

Suites 1–3

(N) *** Avie AV0013. Borac

Enescu wrote for the piano with flair. He was a great violinist and conductor, and a formidable pianist. Cortot once asked him, 'Why is it that you, a violinist, have a better piano technique than I do?' The *First Suite*, Op. 3 (*In the Olden Style*), comes from 1897, the *Second*, Op. 10, from the early years of the last century, and the *Third*, Op. 18 (*Pièces impromptues*), was written between 1913 and 1916. A warm welcome to the present collection of the three *Suites* by the Romanian Luiza Borac, who won the 1991 Enescu International Prize, along with two dozen other awards and prizes. She proves a dedicated and authoritative interpreter of this interesting and rewarding music. The recording is present and bright, though at times a little bottom-heavy.

Oedipe (opera): complete

*** EMI 7 54011-2 (2). Van Dam, Hendricks, Fassbaender, Lipovšek, Bacquier, Gedda, Hauptmann, Quilico, Aler, Vanaud, Albert, Taillon, Orfeon Donostiarra, Monte Carlo PO, Foster

This is an almost ideal recording of a rare, long-neglected masterpiece, with a breathtaking cast of stars backing up a supremely fine performance by José van Dam in the central role of Oedipus. The idiom is tough and adventurous, as well as warmly exotic, with vivid choral effects, a revelation to anyone who knows Enescu only from his *Romanian Rhapsody*. The only reservation is that the pace tends to be on the slow side, but the incandescence of the playing of the Monte Carlo Philharmonic under Lawrence Foster and the richness of the singing and recorded sound amply compensate for that, making this a musical feast.

ENGLUND, Einar (1916–99)

Einar Englund first made a name in the days of LP with his incidental music to Max Frisch's play *The Great Wall of China*. Afterwards he emerged from relative neglect to really generous exposure. All seven symphonies have been recorded, together with a fair number of his concertos and other pieces. Writing in the early 1970s in *Twentieth Century Composers*, R.L. spoke of him as possessing 'perhaps the most spontaneous and natural gift' of his generation and was impressed by his 'Prokofievian exuberance and skill'. Englund was born in Gotland, the large Swedish island in the Baltic, but settled in Helsinki, where he studied and, after a spell in Tanglewood with Copland, later taught. The idiom owes much to Shostakovich, but his invention is fresh and lively. He was a highly accomplished pianist and wrote for the instrument with great naturalness and flair.

Piano Concertos 1 & 2; Epinika
*** Ondine 1015-2. Matti Eaekallio, Tampere PO, Eri Klas

Symphonies 1 (War) (1946); 2 ('Blackbird') (1948)
**(*) Ondine ODE 751-2. Estonian SO, Lilje

Einar Englund's *First Symphony* is, in his own words, 'an expression of euphoric joy'. He has a spontaneous and natural gift, and his musical language is closer to Shostakovich than to anyone else. The *Second Symphony* presumably acquired its nickname from the apparent evocation of bird-song at the very opening. Good performances and very acceptable (though not outstanding) recorded sound.

The *First Piano Concerto* comes from 1955 and is fluent and likeable. There is plenty of Prokofiev and Shostakovich and there are times when we are fleetingly reminded of Rawsthorne or Britten. In the *Second Concerto*, written nearly twenty years later, the debt to Shostakovich remains strong, and it is musically less interesting and satisfying than No. 1. *Epinika*, written for the first post-war Olympic Games, is a lively and skilfully wrought *pièce d'occasion*. Good performances and recordings, but there is a more than serviceable account of the *First Concerto* on Naxos, coupled with the *Second* and *Fourth Symphonies* (8.553758).

Symphonies 2 (Blackbird); 4 (Nostalgic); (i) Piano Concerto 1
(BB) *** Naxos 8.553758. Turku PO, Panula, (i) with Sivelöv

The *Second Symphony* (1948) is full of imaginative things, though, like the *Fourth*, its debt to Shostakovich is heavy. In the *First Piano Concerto* (1955), with its touches of Prokofiev and strongly Gallic overtones, Niklas Sivelöv proves a most musical and accomplished soloist. Rather good performances and recording make this an admirable introduction to this gifted composer.

Symphonies 4 (Nostalgic); 5 (Fennica); The Great Wall of China (suite)
*** Ondine ODE 9612. Tampere PO, Eri Klas

The Great Wall of China is the incidental music for the play by Max Frisch. It sounds fresh and there is no lack of parody and pastiche, with touches of jazz. The *Fourth Symphony* was composed following the death of Shostakovich, from whose works it quotes. The *Fifth Symphony* recalls Englund's service in the Second World War with the spirit of tranquil recollection, unlike the *First*, which was written in the immediate wake of those terrible years. There are powerful things here, although the debt to Shostakovich undoubtedly hangs too heavily.

(i) Symphony 6 (Aphorisms); (ii) Cello Concerto
*** Ondine ODE 951-2 [id.]. Tampere PO, Klas; with (ii) Gustafsson, (i) Tampere Philh. Ch.

The *Cello Concerto* (1954) precedes the *First Piano Concerto* and is highly imaginative. Shostakovich is still a presence in Englund's musical make-up, but his music is nevertheless quite haunting and his writing both inventive and resourceful; there is always something happening and the music unfolds naturally. The *Sixth Symphony* (1986) is a choral

setting of Heraclitus, again inventive and direct in utterance. Jan-Erik Gustafsson is the eloquent soloist in the *Cello Concerto* and the orchestral support under Eri Klas is first class. The recording has much greater body and richness of detail than the Naxos disc listed above.

(i) Piano Quintet. String Quartet
(N) *** BIS CD 1197. Sinfonia Lahti Chamber Ens., (i) with Peter Lönnqvist

This disc couples the eminently eclectic *Piano Quintet*, written in his mid-twenties, with the mature *String Quartet* of 1985. Englund himself spoke of the earlier work as 'a mixture of Franck, Reger, Brahms and Ravel but the cocktail is of course Englund'. Englund's teacher alerted Sibelius's attention to the piece and he spoke warmly of it, though he thought the composer had 'squeezed too much musical activity into the work'. It is fresh, inventive and inspiriting. The *Quartet* is a powerful and concentrated piece, with less immediate appeal than the *Quintet*, but nonetheless a welcome addition to Englund's representation in the catalogue.

FALLA, Manuel de (1876–1946)

(i) Harpsichord Concerto; (ii; iii) El amor brujo; (ii; iv; v); Nights in the Gardens of Spain; (vi) The Three-Cornered Hat: Miller's Dance; Final Dance. (vii) La vida breve: Interlude & Dance 1
**(*) Australian Ph. (ADD) 468 313-2. (i) Puyana, O, Mackerras; (ii) Markevitch; (iii) Spanish RTV SO; (iv) Lamoureux O; (v) Haskil; (vi) Paris Nat. Op. O, Benzi; (vii) Minneapolis SO, Dorati

Markevitch provides real atmosphere at the beginning of *El amor brujo* and the orchestra is lively and committed. Clara Haskil's admirers will be glad to have her dazzling and sultry account of the *Nights in the Gardens of Spain*, and Mackerras's direction of the *Harpsichord Concerto* is idiomatic and Puyana is a fine soloist – the rather dry acoustic suiting the music admirably. Benzi's excerpts from *The Three-Cornered Hat* with the Paris Opéra Orchestra have a typically French twang in the brass department, and Dorati's *La vida breve* excerpt is vividly played and recorded in the Mercury manner. The 1960s sound throughout is generally good if not as rich and vivid as the rival Decca recordings of the same period.

(i; ii) Harpsichord Concerto; (iii; iv; v) El amor brujo; (iv, vi, vii) Nights in the Gardens of Spain; (viii) The Three-Cornered Hat; (ix) La vida breve: Interlude and Dance; (x) Homenaje 'Le tombeau de Claude Debussy'; (vii) 4 Spanish Pieces; (xi) 7 Canciones populares españolas; (ii; xii) Psyché
●-- ✿ (B) *** Double Decca (ADD/DDD) 466 128-2 (2). (i) Constable; (ii) L. Sinf., Rattle; (iii) New Philh. O; (iv) Frühbeck de Burgos; (v) Mistral; (vi) LPO; (vii) De Larrocha; (viii) Montreal SO, Dutoit; (ix) SRO, Ansermet; (x) Fernández; (xi) Horne, Katz; (xii) with Jennifer Smith

A myriad of performances have been perceptively gathered together for this 'Essential Falla' compilation, which is surely rightly named. Dutoit's 1984 complete version of *The Three-Cornered Hat* is wonderfully atmospheric as well as brilliantly played – one of the first Decca digital demonstration recordings, and still a top recommendation. Recorded in 1966, Frühbeck de Burgos's *El amor brujo* enjoys exceptionally vivid sound, yet with plenty of light and shade: the superbly graduated crescendo after the opening is immediately compelling, and the control of atmosphere in the quieter passages is masterly, while Nati Mistral has the vibrant, open-throated production of a real flamenco singer.

Alicia de Larrocha's later digital version of *Nights in the Gardens of Spain* is unsurpassed among modern recordings: it has rich, lustrous sound and refined detail. The piano image is well forward, and this allows the listener to relish the freshness and brilliance of the soloist's articulation in the work's later sections. The playing has undoubted poetry and in the first movement there is a thoughtful, improvisatory quality which captures the evocative feeling of the shimmering Andalusian night. Her playing of the *Four Spanish Pieces* glitters.

The other shorter works are equally worthwhile. Ansermet's *Interlude and Dance* from *La vida breve*, with its melodramatic opening and lively dance section, is always enjoyable, and Marilyn Horne's *Spanish Folksongs* are vibrantly idiomatic. John Constable's crisply vivid account of the delightful *Harpsichord Concerto* (with Rattle) and the haunting rarity, *Psyché*, for voice – Jennifer Smith a fine soloist – and orchestra complete an extraordinarily generous survey. This Double Decca is the finest and most comprehensive Falla collection in the catalogue.

El amor brujo (Love, the Magician; ballet) (original version, complete with dialogue); (i) (Piano) *Serenata; Serenata andaluza. 7 Canciones populares españolas*
*** Nuova Era 6809. Senn, Carme Ens., Izquierdo; (i) Bodini

By including the dialogue, spoken over music, the Nuova Era issue provides the complete original conception of *El amor brujo*, rather like a one-Act zarzuela, with chamber scoring. Martha Senn is perfectly cast in the role of the gypsy heroine. She sings flamboyantly and often ravishingly, both here and in the delectable *Canciones populares* and the other two songs offered as coupling, and she is accompanied very sympathetically. Luis Izquierdo directs the main work atmospherically and finds plenty of gusto for the piece we know as the *Ritual Fire Dance*; and the recording is suitably atmospheric and vivid.

El amor brujo (complete)
✹ *** BBC (ADD) BBCL 4005-2. Lane, BBC SO, Stokowski –
  BEETHOVEN: *Symphony 7* *(**); BRITTEN: *Young Person's Guide to the Orchestra* **(*)
(B) (**(*)) Dutton Lab. mono CDBP 9705. Merriman, Hollywood Bowl SO, Stokowski – BRAHMS: *Symphony 1* (***)
(M) **(*) BBC (ADD) BBCB 8012-2. Reynolds, ECO, Britten (with TCHAIKOVSKY: *Francesca da Rimini; Romeo and Juliet* **)

(i) *El amor brujo* (complete); (ii) *Nights in the Gardens of Spain*
(M) *** Decca 430 703-2. (i) Tourangeau, Montreal SO, Dutoit; (ii) De Larrocha, LPO, Frühbeck de Burgos –
  RODRIGO: *Concierto* *** ✹

Stokowski's BBC account of Falla's *El amor brujo* was given at a Prom in 1964 and has all the electricity of a live occasion. This is an outstanding and thrilling performance. In almost every movement Stokowski opts for fast speeds, with the players of the BBC Symphony Orchestra challenged to the limit, as in the *Ritual Fire Dance*, which is electrifying. Consistently Stokowski finds colour and atmosphere, and his soloist, Gloria Lane, with her fruity mezzo tone-colours, sounds comparably idiomatic. In short, this is the most gripping and hypnotic performance on or off record, and the recording quality is very good indeed.

With recording in the demonstration class, Dutoit's performance has characteristic flexibility over phrasing and rhythm and is hauntingly atmospheric. The sound in the coupled *Nights in the Gardens of Spain* is equally superb, rich and lustrous and with vivid detail. Alicia de Larrocha's lambent feeling for the work's poetic evocation is matched by her brilliance in the nocturnal dance-rhythms.

Stokowski's magnetism is just as apparent in his 1956 recording of *El amor brujo* with the Hollywood Bowl Orchestra. In this Dutton transfer the mono recording is amazingly sharp and vivid, and the vibrant soloist, Nan Merriman, is very much with us. The Spanish rhythms and colours are seductively caught, with plenty of bite in the famous *Ritual Fire Dance*. But in this instance Stokowski upstages himself, for the later, BBC recording is even more electrifying.

Britten conducts a warmly evocative reading of the Falla ballet. Not only does he bring out the atmospheric beauty of the writing, he characteristically points rhythms in a seductively idiomatic way, as in his treatment of the haunting *Pantomime*. Anna Reynolds may not sound very Spanish, but she too is warmly responsive and characterful. However, the Tchaikovsky coupling ultimately lacks the kind of strong adrenalin flow so essential in this repertoire.

(i) *El amor brujo* (complete); (ii) *Nights in the Gardens of Spain. The Three-Cornered Hat: Dance of the Neighbours; Dance of the Miller; Finale (Jota)*
(B) *** Sony (ADD) SBK 89291. (i) Phd. O, (ii) Stokowski; (iii) with Verrett; (iv) Ormandy (v) with Entremont
(BB) **(*) RCA Navigator (ADD) 74321 24215-2. (i) Mistral; (ii) Achucarro; LSO, Mata

(i) *El amor brujo* (complete); (ii) *Nights in the Gardens of Spain. La vida breve: Interlude and Dance*
(M) *** Chan. 10232X. (i) Walker; (ii) Fingerhut; LSO, Simon

The brightly lit Chandos recording emphasizes the vigour of Geoffry Simon's very vital account of *El amor brujo*, and Sarah Walker's powerful vocal contribution is another asset, her vibrantly earthy singing highly involving. The Simon/Fingerhut version of *Nights in the Gardens of Spain* also makes a strongly contrasted alternative to Alicia de Larrocha's much-praised reading, and the effect is more dramatic, with the soloist responding chimerically to the changes of mood. The *Interlude and Dance* from *La vida breve* make a very attractive encore.

Stokowski's charismatic stereo Philadelphia recording of *El amor brujo* is fierce and sumptuous by turns. The orchestra play with passionate conviction, and Shirley Verrett ranges between rich vibrato and raucous flamenco-like tone. The *Nights in the Gardens of Spain* receives a flamboyantly expressive performance from Entremont and Ormandy – both artists forming a true partnership, with a well-judged balance between glitter and a delicate blending of textures. The dances from the *Three-Cornered Hat* are strongly characterized too, though the violins sound a bit glassy here.

Eduardo Mata has an uninhibited vocal soloist in Nati Mistral and her singing is more earthy than many of her competitors. *Nights in the Gardens of Spain* brings a highly sympathetic contribution from Joaquín Achucarro, and the performance is both evocative and exciting. The dances from *The Three-Cornered Hat* are more rhythmically subtle than usual, although here the LSO violin-timbre sounds thinner. A good super-bargain triptych, nevertheless.

(i) *El amor brujo (Love, the Magician)*; (ii) *The Three-Cornered Hat* (ballets; both complete)

(M) *** EMI (ADD) 5 67587-2 (2) [567590-2]. de los Angeles, Philh. O, (i) Giulini; (ii) Frühbeck de Burgos – *La vida breve* ***

(B) *** DG (ADD) 457 878-2. Berganza, (i) LSO, Navarro; (ii) Boston SO, Ozawa

(i) *El amor brujo (Love, the Magician)*; (ii) *The Three-Cornered Hat* (ballet). *La vida breve: Interlude and Dance*

(M) *** Decca (IMS) (ADD) 466 991-2. SRO, Ansermet, with (i) de Gabarain; (ii) Berganza

(N) (BB) **(*) Naxos 8.557800. Asturias SO, Valdés, with (i) Nafé; (ii) Martos

Listening to Ansermet's early 1960s version of *The Three-Cornered Hat*, you understand why his recordings are cherished by audiophiles: the sound is glitteringly brilliant and full. The performance has lots of character and shows the conductor and his orchestra on top form. *El amor brujo* is not quite so brilliant as a recording, or as a performance, but it is still very good, with plenty of nice touches here and there. It is always a pleasure to hear the *Interlude and Dance* from *La vida breve*: the *Dance* of which – a most catchy tune – is especially vivid here. A very colourful and worthy addition to Decca's 'Legends' label.

A beautifully civilized and atmospheric account of *El amor brujo* from Giulini, warmly and atmospherically recorded. Thoroughly enjoyable, even if the performance is not as vivid and red-blooded as Frühbeck de Burgos's *Three-Cornered Hat*, where the *'Olés'* were recorded separately and dubbed on, but which has greater high spirits. Victoria de los Angeles does not sound quite earthy enough, but she sings splendidly throughout and the CD transfers are excellent. This is now recoupled with *La vida breve* as one of EMI's 'Great Recordings of the Century'.

Teresa Berganza links the comparable DG pairing. Both the recordings date from the late 1970s, and at that time Ozawa's Boston sound is vividly alive, even more so on CD, and has a wide dynamic range yet an admirable presence without distorting perspectives. *El amor brujo*, recorded in London's Henry Wood Hall, brings a slightly more recessed effect and the score's magical moments of evocation are beautifully done, while Berganza's contribution is vibrantly idiomatic, and the responsive LSO playing (wind and strings alike) is comparably seductive in the *Pantomime* sequence.

Though Maximiano Valdes and the Asturias Symphony Orchestra have a natural feeling for the Spanish idiom, the performances of both ballets are lusty rather than refined, not helped by a slight distancing of violins in the recording. In *El amor brujo*, with Alicia Nafé as mezzo soloist, the roughness of ensemble goes with a rhythmic heaviness even in the *Ritual Fire Dance*. The *Three-Cornered Hat* again brings rough ensemble, and the mezzo, Maria José Martos, has her raw moments, but the performance has far more vigour and bite to bring out the folk qualities in Falla's writing.

(i; ii) *Nights in the Gardens of Spain*; (iii) *El amor brujo: Ritual Fire Dance; The Magic Circle*

** Arthaus **DVD** 100 034. (i) Barenboim (piano); Chicago SO; (ii) Domingo; (iii) cond. Barenboim – SIBELIUS: *Violin Concerto*. **(*) (Producer: Bernd Hellthaler; V/D: Bob Coles)

Nights in the Gardens of Spain

(BB) *** Warner Apex 8573 89223-2. Heisser, Lausanne CO, López-Cobos – ALBENIZ: *Concierto fantástico*, etc.; TURINA: *Rapsodia sinfónica* ***

The Arthaus DVD offers a 1997 recording made while the Chicago orchestra was in Germany. On the face of it this should have strong claims on the collector, a master-pianist as soloist and a great Spanish singer-now-conductor on the podium. Yet despite the latter, the performance is curiously wanting in mystery and atmosphere, and one remains untransported to the magical Sierra de Córdoba. Barenboim plays with customary aplomb and the video direction is expert and unobtrusive. The encores, the *Ritual Fire Dance* and *The Magic Circle* from *El amor brujo*, come off well under Barenboim's baton.

The performance by Jean-François Heisser (with López-Cobos a highly idiomatic partner) is first class in every way, combining warm evocation, brilliant colouring and excitement. The playing could hardly be more grippingly spontaneous, and the modern (1996) digital sound is vividly real. The couplings are equally attractive and this comes in the lowest price range.

The Three-Cornered Hat (ballet; complete)

*** Chan. 8904. Gomez, Philh. O, Tortelier – ALBENIZ: *Iberia* ***

Yan Pascal Tortelier is hardly less seductive than Dutoit in handling Falla's beguiling dance-rhythms, bringing out the score's humour as well as its colour. The fine Chandos recording is full and vivid, if rather reverberant, and Jill Gomez's contribution floats within the resonance; but the acoustic warmth adds to the woodwind bloom, and the strings are beguilingly rich. The closing *Jota* is joyfully vigorous.

The Three-Cornered Hat (ballet): *3 Dances*

(***) Testament mono SBT1017. Philh. O, Cantelli – CASELLA: *Paganiniana*; DUKAS: *L'Apprenti sorcier*; RAVEL: *Daphnis et Chloé: Suite 2* (***)

It is good that Cantelli's excellent (1954) performances of these vivid dances are back in such fine transfers. Elegant, polished accounts, given very good mono sound.

The Three-Cornered Hat (ballet): *Miller's Dance, Danse finale*

*** BBC (ADD) BBCL 4123-2. Philh. O, Giulini – BRUCKNER: *Symphony 7*; MUSSORGSKY: *Khovanshchina: Prelude* ***

The Falla dances, recorded live, make a lively contrast to Giulini's dedicated reading of Bruckner's *Seventh Symphony*, the main work on the disc.

GUITAR MUSIC

7 Spanish Popular Songs (Suite populare españolas; arr. for guitar)

(B) *** EMI Red Line CDR5 69850. Barrueco – GRANADOS: *Danzas españolas* ***

Barrueco is a magician among the new school of guitarists, and his delicate nuances of colouring in these song transcriptions are matched by his seemingly spontaneous rhythmic freedom. Excellent recording too.

VOCAL MUSIC

Seite canciones populares españolas (7 Spanish Popular Songs)

(N) (***) Testament mono SBT 1311. Souzay, Bonneau –
FAURE: *Mélodies* *** ❂; RAVEL: *Histoires naturelles* (***)

The late Gérard Souzay is wonderfully captured here in this 1951 set, made only six years after his Paris début and finding the youthful bloom of his voice at its peak. Highly characterized performances, and expertly accompanied by Jacqueline Bonneau. No need to make any allowances for the age of the Decca recording in Paul Bailey's scrupulous remastering.

PIANO MUSIC

Fantasía bética; 4 Piezas españolas

(B) *** Double Decca (ADD) 433 926-2 (2). De Larrocha –
ALBENIZ: *Iberia; Navarra*, etc. ***

These welcome and attractive couplings for Albéniz's *Iberia* are given exemplary performances and most realistic recording.

OPERA

La vida breve (complete)

(M) *** EMI (ADD) 5 67587-2 (2) [567590-2](2). De los
Angeles, Higueras, Rivadeneyra, Cossutta, Moreno, Orféon Donostiarra Ch., Nat. O of Spain, Frühbeck de Burgos – *El amor brujo; Three-Cornered Hat* ***

La vida breve is a kind of Spanish *Cavalleria rusticana* without the melodrama. Unquestionably the opera's story is thin, the heroine expiring of a broken heart when her lover deserts her for another; but if the music for the final scene is weakened by a fundamental lack of drama in the plot, Frühbeck de Burgos makes the most of the poignancy of the closing moments. Victoria de los Angeles deepened her interpretation over the years and her imaginative colouring of the words gives a unique authority and evocation to her performance. The flamenco singer in Act II (Gabriel Moreno) also matches the realism of the idiom with an authentic 'folk' style. The other members of the cast are good without being memorable; but when this is primarily a vehicle for de los Angeles and the orchestral interludes are managed so colloquially, this is readily recommendable. The recording remains atmospheric but has increased vividness and presence. It is now offered, coupled with Falla's two celebrated ballet scores, as one of EMI's 'Great Recordings of the Century'.

FARRENC, Louise (1804–75)

Louise Farrenc, not a familiar name, was an important force in French music during her lifetime, not only in her quest to revive earlier keyboard music, but also by paving the way for France's musical renaissance of the 1870s. She was the sister of the laureate sculptor, Auguste Dumont, and wife of Aristide Farrenc, flautist and music publisher, whom she significantly helped in his work in publishing *Le trésor des pianistes*, an important anthology of harpsichord and piano music spanning some three hundred years.

Symphony 2 in D, Op. 35; Overtures: 1 in E min., Op. 23; 2 in E flat, Op. 24

(N) **(*) CPO 999 820-2. NDR Radiophilharmonie, Goritzki

The *Second Symphony* was premièred in 1846 and very much follows the early German classical models (especially Beethoven), with the spirit of Mendelssohn and Schumann felt from time to time. It is eminently tuneful and attractively scored, and the references to Bach's *The Art of Fugue* in the finale add an unusual twist. It is worth a hearing, as are the two *Overtures* (1834), which bring plenty of Romantic drama. While these are not forgotten masterpieces, Farrenc's invention is never less than appealing. This collection makes a good case for these pieces. The recording is basically warm and well balanced, though the details can become a little blurred in the louder, fast passages. However, with under 50 minutes offered, this is might have been more enticing on a cheaper label.

FASCH, Johann (1688–1758)

Bassoon Concertos: in C; D min. Concerto in A (for Violin Obbligato) in A. Double Oboe Concertos: in G; in E flat; in C min. Overture in G

*** CPO 777 015-2. Azzolini, Skuplik, La Stravaganza, Köln

A delightful collection from the German composer Johann Fasch. These lively and inventive works are thoroughly entertaining, the composer bridging the gap between the baroque and classical eras, clearly pushing forward new ideas, with some often bold writing, most notably in the woodwind department. The orchestra clearly relishes the music and revels in the brilliance of the writing. The double concertos are especially enjoyable and there is little here that falls below a high standard. One takes pleasure in the bold array of colour and sound that the soloists produce – often rich and earthy – for its own sake. The accompaniments are superb and the recording is sharply vivid.

Trumpet Concerto in D

(B) *** Sony **SACD** SS 57497. Marsalis, ECO, Leppard –
HAYDN; HUMMEL; LEOPOLD MOZART: *Concertos* ***

Fasch's *Trumpet Concerto* is notable for its fine *Largo* slow-movement cantilena. It is brilliantly played by Wynton Marsalis and is here reissued on non-compatible SACD with obvious couplings. The sound is very impressive, but these famous concertos are available elsewhere, more generously coupled and less expensively priced.

(i) *Trumpet Concerto. Symphonies for Strings in G and A*

(BB) ** Warner Apex 0927 49980-2. (i) André, Paillard CO,
Paillard – PACHELBEL: *Canon; Suites* **

Fasch's *Trumpet Concerto* is very well played here by Maurice André. The two *Symphonies* are also agreeable little works, touchingly expressive and lively by turns, and the performances are warm and polished, if perhaps not distinctive.

FAURÉ, Gabriel (1845–1924)

(i; ii) *Après un rêve; Elégie* (both for cello and orchestra);
(iii) *Masques et bergamasques;* (ii; iv) *Pavane;* (ii; v) *Pelléas et Mélisande: Suite;* Harp: (vi) *Une châtelaine en sa tour;* Piano: (vii) *Dolly;* (viii) *Barcarolle 2; Nocturne 4;* (ix) *Cantique de Jean Racine;* Mélodies: (x) *Les Berceaux; Le Secret; Soir; L'Horizon chimérique* (cycle). (xi) *Requiem*

(B) **(*) DG Panorama (ADD) 469 268-2 (2). (i) Erskin; (ii)
Boston SO, Ozawa; (iii) Orpheus CO; (iv) Tanglewood Festival Ch.; (v) Hunt; (vi) Zabaleta; (vii) Alfons & Aloys

Kontarsky; (viii) Rogé; (ix) King's College Ch., Cambridge, Cleobury; (x) Souzay, Baldwin; (xi) Battle, Schmidt, Philh. Ch. & O, Giulini

Although some of the performances here are inclined to excessive reticence, overall this well-planned collection makes a good introduction to Fauré's special sensibility. In the orchestral items *Pelléas et Mélisande* includes the rarely heard *Chanson de Mélisande* sung simply and sweetly by Lorraine Hunt. However, neither she nor the eminently musical cello soloist (Jules Erskin) in the two concertante pieces displays a strong individuality. *Masques et bergamasques* springs to life in the hands of the Orpheus Chamber Orchestra and is played vigorously and warmly. Similarly, the Kontarskys give a vividly sympathetic account of *Dolly*, and Pascal Rogé plays the two piano pieces beautifully. Nicanor Zabaleta too is very beguiling in his own arrangement of *Une châtelaine en sa tour*, and Souzay is in his element in the mélodies. However, though the King's performance of the *Cantique* cannot be faulted, Giulini returns to a comparatively withdrawn mood for the *Requiem*. His care for detail in textures and his unexaggerated expressive style keep the result hushed and prayerful rather than sugary. Kathleen Battle sings glowingly in the *Pie Jesu*, sounding sumptuous but not really in style. Throughout the programme the warmly atmospheric recording is a considerable plus point, and this is certainly value for money, even if no texts are included.

Ballade for Piano & Orchestra, Op. 19

⊙ (BB) (***) Dutton mono CDBP 9714. K. Long, Nat. SO, Boyd Neel – LEIGH: *Concertino;* MOZART: *Piano Concertos 15 & 24* (***)

*** Chan. 8773. Lortie, LSO, Frühbeck de Burgos – RAVEL: *Piano Concertos* **(*)

(BB) **(*) Naxos 8.550754. Thiollier, Nat. SO of Ireland, De Almeida – FRANCK: *Symphonic Variations;* D'INDY: *Symphonie sur un air montagnard français* **(*)

Recorded in 1944, Kathleen Long's classic recording of Fauré's *Ballade* remains among the most inspired ever, at once subtle and immediate in its communication, a perfect demonstration of Long's refined artistry. A fine supplement to the equally subtle readings of Mozart *Concertos* and the hauntingly effective Leigh *Concertino*. A magical (and very generous) CD, very well recorded and transferred.

Louis Lortie is a thoughtful artist and his playing has both sensitivity and strength. This is as penetrating and well recorded an account of Fauré's lovely piece as any now available; however, the coupling is not one of the preferred versions of the Ravel concertos.

Naxos offer an intelligently planned triptych. François-Joël Thiollier shows some imagination and sensitivity in Fauré's lovely *Ballade*, which is not represented as generously on CD as it should be. The orchestral playing is perfectly acceptable, without being in any way out of the ordinary; likewise the recording. All the same, it is worth the money.

Ballade for Piano & Orchestra, Op. 19; Berceuse for Violin & Orchestra, Op. 16; Caligula, Op. 52; Les Djinns (orchestral version), Op. 12; Elégie for Cello & Orchestra, Op. 24; Fantaisie for Piano & Orchestra, Op. 111; Masques et bergamasques, Op. 112; Pelléas et Mélisande, Op. 80; Pénélope: Prélude; Shylock, Op. 57

⊙➔ (B) *** EMI double forte 5 74840-2 (2). Collard, Y. P. & P. Tortelier, Von Stade, Gedda, Bourbon Vocal Ens., Toulouse Capitole O, Plasson

This set of Fauré's orchestral music contains much that is very rewarding indeed. It includes the delightful *Masques et bergamasques* and the *Pelléas et Mélisande* and *Shylock* music, as well as such rarities as *Les Djinns* and *Caligula*. Plasson gets an alert and spirited response, and the recordings are very good. He shows a genuine feeling for the Fauréan sensibility, and the fine-spun lyricism of the Nocturne from *Shylock* is nicely conveyed. Jean-Philippe Collard gives a really distinguished account of both the early *Ballade* and the seldom heard *Fantasie*, Op. 111. Although the vocal items no longer have texts and translations, as on the original issues, the set is now offered at bargain price. Altogether this is a lovely collection in every way, offering many delights, and it cannot be too warmly recommended.

(i) Ballade for Piano & Orchestra, Op. 19. Dolly Suite; (ii) Elégie for Cello & Orchestra; (iii) Fantaisie for Flute & Orchestra (orch. I. Aubert). Masques et bergamasques; Pavane (orch. H. Rabaud); Pénélope: Prelude

*** Chan. 9416. (i) Stott; (ii) Dixon; (iii) Davis; BBC PO, Tortelier

Beautifully played and richly recorded, with Yan Pascal Tortelier a most understanding interpreter, this neatly brings together the most popular orchestral pieces of Fauré, miniatures which often convey surprising weight of feeling as well as charm, as for example the celebrated *Elégie*, here tenderly played by Peter Dixon. Kathryn Stott brings out not only the poetry in the *Ballade for Piano and Orchestra*, but also the scherzando sparkle of the virtuoso passages. Just as convincing are the *Fantaisie for Flute* (soloist Richard Davis) and the ever-popular *Dolly Suite*, both arranged by other hands. The four brief movements of *Masques et bergamasques* are charmingly done and Tortelier's account of the *Overture to Masques et bergamasques* is second to none. Indeed, he has the measure of all the music on this disc, be it the poignancy of the *Pénélope Prelude* or the delicacy of the *Dolly Suite*.

(i) Berceuse, Op. 116. Dolly Suite, Op. 56; Masques et bergamasques, Op. 112; Pelléas et Mélisande (suite), Op. 80; (ii) Shylock (suite), Op. 57

(BB) *** Naxos 8.553360. Dublin RTE Sinf., Georgiadis, with (i) Healy; (ii) Russell

John Georgiadis with his rhythmic flair not only brings out the colour and vigour of the fast movements but, as a fine violinist himself, persuades his Irish players to draw out the expressive warmth of such numbers as *Tendresse* in the *Dolly Suite*. *Masques et bergamasques*, the *Dolly Suite* and the incidental music to *Pelléas et Mélisande* are all among Fauré's best-loved works, and it is good too to have the rarer music for the Shakespeare-based play, *Shylock*, complete with two vocal movements sweetly sung by Lynda Russell. Michael Healy is the expressive violin soloist in the lovely *Berceuse*. Warm, atmospheric recording, transferred at rather a low level.

Elégie in C min. (for cello and orchestra), Op. 24

*** EMI 5 56126-2. Chang, LSO, Rostropovich – BRUCH: *Kol Nidrei* ***; SAINT-SAENS: *Cello Concerto 1* ***; TCHAIKOVSKY: *Rococo Variations* *** ⊙

(B) *** EMI Début 5 73503-2. Phillips, Bav. Chamber PO, Plasson – CAPLET: *Epiphany;* LALO: *Cello Concerto* ***

Han-Na Chang is a naturally inspirational artist, and on her sensitive bow the lovely and sometimes elusive *Elégie* is made to sound like a vocal aria, the shaping and use of light and shade unerring, with a dedicated accompaniment from her mentor, Rostropovich. The recorded sound is very beautiful.

From the impressive Xavier Phillips, a poetically songful and only marginally recessive performance, with orchestra and soloist at one in their response to Fauré's emotional and dynamic contrasts.

Fantaisie for Piano & Orchestra, Op. 111

(N) *** Australian Decca Eloquence (ADD) 476 235-2. De Larrocha, LPO, De Burgos – FRANCK: *Symphonic Variations*; RAVEL: *Piano Concertos in G & for the Left Hand ***

The Fauré *Fantaisie* is a late work, but an aristocratic one of great distinction, beautifully played and recorded in this 1972 performance. The couplings are recommendable too: altogether this is an impressive anthology.

Masques et bergamasques; Pavane

(B) *** CfP (ADD) 575 1382. LPO, Handley – CANTELOUBE: *Chants d'Auvergne *** ⦿

These performances under Vernon Handley are very enjoyable, fresh and sympathetic, with excellent recording to add bloom to the fine playing. A fine bonus for the outstanding Canteloube coupling.

Pavane, Op. 60

(B) *** Decca 448 711-2. ASMF, Marriner – DURUFLE: *Requiem; POULENC: Gloria ***

Marriner's warmly elegant account of the famous *Pavane* is used effectively on this Decca disc as an interlude between Duruflé's *Requiem* and Poulenc's *Gloria*, both fine performances.

Pelléas et Mélisande Suite, Op. 80; (i) Pavane, Op. 50

*** Chan. 8952. (i) Renaissance Singers; Ulster O, Tortelier – CHAUSSON: *Poème*, etc. ***

(N) (M) ** Telarc CD 80084 (without PAVANE). Atlanta SO, Shaw – BERLIOZ: *Nuits d'été **

These finely finished and atmospheric Chandos performances come in harness with a fine account from the soloist-conductor of Chausson's *Poème* and a perceptive and idiomatic performance of the *Poème de la mer et de l'amour*. Very good orchestral playing and exemplary recording.

Beautifully recorded in clear, natural sound, Robert Shaw and the Atlanta orchestra give a refined, beautifully shaped performance of the four movemnts of Fauré's tenderly atmospheric suite, but it makes an odd and ungenerous coupling for the similarly reticent account of the Berlioz song-cycle.

CHAMBER MUSIC

(i) *Allegretto Moderato for 2 Cellos;* (ii) *Andante. Elégie, Op. 24; Papillon, Op. 77; Romance, Op. 69; Sérénade, Op. 98; Sicilienne, Op. 78; Sonatas 1 in D min., Op. 109; 2 in G min., Op. 117*

**(*) RCA 09026 68049-2. Isserlis, Devoyon; with (i) Waterman; (ii) Greer

Steven Isserlis understands the essential reticence and refinement of Fauré's art. Perhaps he is at times a shade too reticent in the music and could allow himself to produce a more ardent and songful tone. The balance, which slightly favours his partner, contributes to this impression. Pascal Devoyon is

a no less perceptive and sensitive artist. A welcome, then, for the artistry of these performances, but tinged with slight disappointment at the less than ideal balance.

Cello Sonata 1 in D min., Op. 109

(BB) *** Warner Apex 0927 40599-2. Noras, Rigutto – DEBUSSY, FRANCK: *Cello Sonatas ***

Cello Sonatas 1 in D min., Op. 109; 2 in G min., Op. 117

(B) *** EMI (ADD) 5 74333-2 (2). Tortelier, Heidsieck – CHOPIN; MENDELSSOHN; RACHMANINOV: *Cello Sonatas ***

Cello Sonatas 1–2; Après un rêve (trans. Casals); Elégie, Op. 24; Papillon, Op. 77; Romance, Op. 69; Sérénade, Op. 98; Sicilienne, Op. 78

*** Opus 111 OP 30-242. Bruns, Ishay

Cello Sonatas 1–2; Elégie; Sicilienne

(M) *** CRD (ADD) CRD 3316. Igloi, Benson

Moving performances from the late Thomas Igloi and Clifford Benson that do full justice to these elusive and rewarding Fauré sonatas, and the recording is clear, if not one of CRD's finest in terms of ambient effect.

Noble performances too from both Tortelier and Heidsieck, who play with fervour and eloquence within the restrained expressive limits of the music. The fine EMI recording brings both instruments into the living room most vividly.

Peter Bruns plays the Tonino cello that Casals once owned and Roglit Ishay plays an Erard. This has a more brittle timbre than the modern piano but Fauré himself much liked its lighter action. Those who want the sonatas in the sonorities the composer himself might have heard should investigate this. These two artists both play with appropriate eloquence and the miniatures come off well.

An eloquent performance too on Warner Apex of the wonderful *D minor Sonata* by this aristocratic Finnish cellist, who plays with subtlety and finesse. If the couplings appeal, this makes an excellent bargain.

(i) Cello Sonatas 1–2; (ii) Andante in B flat, Op. 75; Berceuse, Op. 16; Elégie; (iii) Fantaisie, Op. 79; Morceau de concours; (ii) Morceau de lecture; (i) Papillon, Op. 77; (i-ii) Piano Trio in D min., Op. 120; (ii) Romance, Op. 28; (i) Serenade in B min., Op. 98; Sicilienne, Op. 78; (ii) Violin Sonatas 1 in A, Op. 15; 2 in E min., Op. 108

(B) *** EMI (ADD) 5 85279-2 (2). Collard; with (i) Lodéon; (ii) Dumay; (iii) Debost

Piano Quartets (i; ii) 1 in C min., Op. 15; (i; iii) 2 in G min., Op. 45; Piano Quintets 1 in C min., Op. 89; 2 in C min., Op. 115; (iii) String Quartet in E min., Op. 121

(B) **(*) EMI (ADD) 5 85282-2 (2). (i) Collard; (ii) Dumay, Pasquier, Lodéon; (iii) Parrenin Qt

Dumay and Collard bring different and equally valuable insights, and the performances of the *Piano Quartets* are masterly. In addition, there are authoritative and idiomatic readings of the two *Piano Quintets*, the enigmatic and otherworldly *Quartet* and, on the first set above, the *Piano Trio*, the two *Cello Sonatas* (what a fine player Lodéon is!), plus all the smaller pieces. True there are excellent accounts of the *Violin Sonatas* elsewhere, from Grumiaux/Crossley and Amoyal/Rogé, and the *Cello Sonatas* are well served by both Igloi and Isserlis (see above); but many of the smaller pieces are more elusive, and they are presented here with a generally admirable standard of performance and recording. This is enormously civilized music whose rewards grow with each hearing; however, one has to accept that, because the Paris Salle Wagram was employed for the recordings (made between 1975 and 1978), close microphones have been used to counteract the hall's resonance. The remastering has both increased the sense of presence and brought a certain dryness to the ambient effect, although the string timbres are fresh.

Piano Quartets 1 in C min., Op. 15; 2 in G min., Op. 45

☞ ✿ *** Hyp. CDA 66166. Domus

(M) *** Sony 518805-2 [SK 92745]. Ax, Stern, Laredo, Ma
  (Bonus: MASSENET: *Thaïs: Méditation:* Ma, Stott)

Domus have the requisite lightness of touch and subtlety, and just the right sense of scale and grasp of tempi. Their nimble and sensitive pianist, Susan Tomes, can hold her own in the most exalted company. The recording is excellent, too, though the balance is a little close, but the sound is not airless.

The mid-priced reissue of Sony's starry version of the two *Piano Quartets* with Emanuel Ax, Isaac Stern, Jaime Laredo and Yo-Yo Ma offers a serious challenge to the Domus account on Hyperion. The performances are of high quality and anyone could rest happy with them. But Domus convey the more idiomatic feel; theirs is domestic music-making at the highest level of accomplishment and it conveys an altogether special freshness and spontaneity. Ma throws in a transcription for cello of Massenet's *Méditation* as an appealing encore.

Piano Quartets 1 in C min., Op. 15; 2 in G min., Op. 45;
Piano Quintets 1 in D min., Op. 89; 2 in C min., Op. 115

(B) *** Double Decca 475 187-2 (2). Rogé, Ysaÿe Qt

It goes without saying that Pascal Rogé and the Ysaÿe Quartet give performances of great finesse and sensitivity. On the first CD they are more successful in the *Quintet 1* than in the early *Quartet 1*, where they must yield to Domus (Hyperion), who find greater delight and high spirits in the Scherzo. The recording here is very good, though there is an occasional moment when the reverberant acoustic affects the focus. The *Second Quintet* and *Quartet* were recorded in a different location a year later – though, curiously, the aural image is still not quite perfect: Rogé is just that bit too much to the fore, and the quartet is not set in an ideal focus. That said, the playing of all concerned is excellent, alive and subtle, with expert and sensitive contributions from the distinguished pianist. The musical values of these performances sweep aside any of the slight reservations concerning the sound, especially as this set is offered so inexpensively.

Piano Quintets 1–2

☞ ✿ *** Hyp. CDA 66766. Domus, with Marwood

*** Claves CD 50-8603. Quintetto Fauré di Roma

The playing of Domus in these two masterpieces is as light, delicate and full of insight as one would expect. They make one fall for this music all over again. The second is among the masterpieces of Fauré's Indian summer as he approached his eighties. As this concentrated performance suggests, its autumnal lyricism brings likenesses to late Elgar, with the pianist, Susan Tomes, at her most sparkling in the mercurial Scherzo. Excellent sound.

The Quintetto Fauré di Roma also have the measure of Fauré's subtle phrasing and his wonderfully plastic melodic

lines, and their performances are hard to fault. The recording, made in a Swiss church, is warm and splendidly realistic. This music, once you get inside it, has a hypnotic effect and puts you completely under its spell.

(i) *Piano Quintet 2;* (ii) *Violin Sonata 1 in A, Op. 13;* (iii) *Dolly Suite* (for piano duet), *Op. 56*

(M) **(*) CRD CRD 3505. (i) Nash Ens.; (ii) Crayford, Brown;
  (iii) Brown, Tomes

The balance in the *Second Piano Quintet* is less than ideal, the piano being rather too dominant, and in this respect the Domus version on Hyperion is to be preferred. A very fine account from Marcia Crayford and Ian Brown of the *A major Violin Sonata*, sensitive yet vital. Some may feel that they are brought too close to the artists, but the balance between the two instruments is musically judged. The *Dolly Suite* is beautifully done, and Ian Brown and Susan Tomes convey its charm and innocence in exemplary fashion. Overall the sound on this disc is a bit too bright, but the playing is full of conviction and artistically this must carry a strong recommendation.

Piano Trio in D min., Op. 120

*** Ara. Z 6643. Golub/Kaplan/Carr Trio – DEBUSSY: *Piano Trio* ***; SAINT-SAENS: *Piano Trio* **(*)

*** Hyp. CDA 67114. Florestan Trio – DEBUSSY; RAVEL: *Piano Trios* ***

Piano Trio; (i) *La Bonne Chanson, Op. 61*

(M) *** CRD (ADD) CRD 3389. Nash Ens., (i) with Walker

David Golub, Mark Kaplan and Colin Carr give as understanding and idiomatic a performance of the sublime Fauré *Trio* as is to be found. They convey its understatement and subtlety of nuance to perfection, and the interplay among them is a model of the finest chamber-music-making. The recording is very good indeed, with plenty of warmth.

The Florestans offer a very apt coupling of three sharply contrasted French works. Fauré is represented in mellow old age, Debussy as a teenager and Ravel in high maturity. With personnel drawn from the piano quartet group Domus, led by the pianist Susan Tomes, they give an exceptionally strong, unapologetic reading, at once highly polished and flexibly expressive, revealing what power Fauré retained to the end of his life. Vivid sound.

The members of the Nash Ensemble also give a dedicated performance of the late, rarefied *Piano Trio*, capturing both the elegance and the restrained concentration. They are hardly less persuasive in the song-cycle, where the characterful warmth and vibrancy of Sarah Walker's voice, not to mention her positive artistry, come out strongly in this beautiful reading of Fauré's early settings of Verlaine, music both tender and ardent. The atmospheric recording is well up to CRD's high standard in chamber music.

(i; ii) *Piano Trio, Op. 120; Après un rêve* (arr. for piano trio by Eguchi); (i) *Violin Sonata 1 in A, Op. 11; Andante, Op. 25. Berceuse, Op. 28; Masques et bergamasques: Clair de lune, Op. 46/2* (arr. Périlhou); *Pelléas et Mélisande: La Fileuse* (arr. Auer); *Sicilienne. Morceau lecture a vue; Romance, Op. 28; Serenade Toscane* (arr. Ronchini)

*** Van. ATM-CD 1239. Shaham; with (i) Eguchi, (ii) Brinton Smith

Gil Shaham, among the most inspired violinists of his generation, here offers what he describes as a 'Fauré Album'. Two major works, the *First Violin Sonata*, ardently lyrical, and the

Piano Trio, one of the finest of the late chamber works, are complemented by eight shorter pieces, including some favourites. *Après un rêve* comes in an arrangement for piano trio, and other songs arranged for violin and piano include *Clair de lune* and *Serenade Toscane*. There are also two numbers from Fauré's incidental music for Maeterlinck's *Pelléas et Mélisande*, not just the popular *Sicilienne* but a spectacular arrangement of *La Fileuse* by the teacher and virtuoso, Leopold Auer, in which the muted violin imitates a spinning-wheel. Shaham plays with a phenomenal range of tone and dynamic, consistently caressing the ear. In the two major works too his free expressiveness brings a winning sense of spontaneity, well matched by the pianist, Akira Eguchi.

String Quartet in E min., Op. 121

☛ ✪ (BB) *** Naxos 8.554722. Ad Libitum Qt – RAVEL: *Quartet ***

The Ad Libitum Quartet are from Romania, all the members having been students of the Georges Enescu Academy in Iasi, and they came to wider notice when they won first prize at the Evian Competition in 1997. Their ensemble and intonation are perfect, their tone is silken and they give a wonderfully expressive and beautifully characterized account of Fauré's elusive late *String Quartet* – one of the best we have ever heard and one of the best in the catalogue. It is recorded in the Moldava Philharmonic Hall in Iasi and is very natural and lifelike.

Violin Sonata 1 in A, Op. 13

(N) (B) ** Decca 2-CD 475 6709. Bell, Thibaudet – CHAUSSON: *Concert for Piano, Violin & String Quartet*; DEBUSSY; FRANCK: *Violin Sonatas **; RAVEL: *Piano Trio ***

While Joshua Bell and Jean-Yves Thibaudet have the measure of Fauré's ardour, his reticence and subtlety register less successfully. The recording is far from airless, but there could be more space round the aural image.

(i) *Violin Sonata 1 in A, Op. 13. 6 Nocturnes: 1–2, 6–7, 12–13*

(N) *(*) RCA 82876 62312-2. Luisada, (i) with Korcia

Jean-Marc Luisada's six *Nocturnes* are mannered, if not seriously so, but they are pretty prosaic. They were recorded in Metz six years ago in a rather unglamorous and dry acoustic. The *A major Sonata* was recorded in the more ample acoustic of The Maltings, Snape, in 2001; but again the playing of Laurent Korcia is not particularly persuasive and the balance does not flatter his tone.

Violin Sonatas 1 in A, Op. 13; 2 in E min., Op. 108

(BB) *** Hyp. Helios CDH 55030. Osostowicz, Tomes

(N) (M) *** DG 477 5448 (2). Mintz, Bronfman (with Recital of Encores by ALBENIZ; COUPERIN; GLAZUNOV; GRANADOS; KREISLER; WEBER; WIENIAWSKI) – DEBUSSY; FRANCK; RAVEL: *Violin Sonatas ***

(M) *** Ph. 426 384-2. Grumiaux, Crossley – FRANCK: *Sonata **(*)

Violin Sonatas 1–2; Andante, Op. 75; Berceuse, Op. 16; Morceau de concours – Romance, Op. 28

☛ ✪ (M) *** Decca 476 2180. Amoyal, Rogé

Violin Sonatas 1–2; Andante in B flat, Op. 75; Berceuse, Op. 16; Romance in B flat, Op. 28

(BB) *** Naxos 8.550906. Kang, Devoyon

Readers wanting a modern recording of the two Fauré *Violin Sonatas* need look no further. Pierre Amoyal and Pascal Rogé play them as to the manner born. As one would expect, they are totally inside the idiom and convey its subtlety and refinement with freshness and mastery. There are admirable alternatives from Grumiaux and Crossley at mid-price and from Krysia Osostowicz and Susan Tomes, but Amoyal and Rogé more than hold their own against them and throw new light on the three slight miniatures that they offer as a bonus. Impeccable recording, too. A lovely disc, now available at mid-price in Universal's 'Penguin ✪ Collection'.

Dong-Suk Kang, splendidly partnered by Pascal Devoyon, gives us performances which are very fine indeed. Without disturbing our allegiance to other, earlier issues, this is a welcome newcomer – and very good value for money.

Krysia Osostowicz and Susan Tomes bring an appealingly natural, unforced quality to their playing and they are completely persuasive, particularly in the elusive *Second Sonata*. The acoustic is a shade resonant but, such is the eloquence of these artists, the ear quickly adjusts. At Helios price, this is highly recommendable.

Splendid playing, too, from Shlomo Mintz, who is also rather swamped by the pianist, Yefim Bronfman, though his virtuosity and sensitivity are not in question. nor is the lyrical intensity of Mintz's playing. It is the resonant acoustic of the Deutschlandfunk Sendesaal which takes some getting used to

These *Sonatas* are also beautifully played and recorded on the Philips reissue. Moreover the two artists sound as if they are in one's living-room; the acoustic is warm, lively and well balanced. An excellent mid-priced recommendation.

PIANO MUSIC

Solo piano

Ballade in F sharp, Op. 19; Barcarolles 1–13; (i) Dolly Suite, Op. 56. Impromptus 1–5; Impromptu, Op. 86; Mazurka in B flat, Op. 32; 13 Nocturnes; Pièces brèves 1–8, Op. 84; 9 Préludes, Op. 103; Romances sans paroles 1–3; (i) Souvenirs de Bayreuth. Theme & Variations in C sharp min., Op. 73; Valses-caprices 1–4

☛ ✪ *** Hyp. CDA 66911/4 (4). Stott, (i) with Roscoe

(B) *** CRD (ADD) 5006 (5). Crossley (without *Dolly Suite; Souvenirs de Bayreuth*)

Both the *Thirteen Barcarolles*, written between 1880 and 1921, and the *Thirteen Nocturnes*, from an even wider period between 1875 and 1921, give a most illuminating view of Fauré's career, gentle and unsensational like the music itself, but with the subtlest of developments towards a sparer, more rarefied style. That comes out all the more tellingly when, as here, they are given in succession and are played with such poetry and spontaneous-sounding freshness. Kathryn Stott earlier recorded for Conifer a generous selection of Fauré piano music, but, quite apart from the warmer, clearer and more immediate sound on the Hyperion issue, allowing for velvet tone-colours, the later performances are more winningly relaxed, ranging wider in expression. Each of the four discs contains well over 70 minutes of music, logically presented, with the *Nocturnes* spread between the third and fourth discs, framing the lighter pieces, including such duets as the witty Wagner quadrille, *Souvenirs de Bayreuth*, and the ever-fresh *Dolly Suite*, both with Stott ideally partnered by Martin Roscoe. A masterly set.

Paul Crossley's recordings come from the 1980s. He shows

an instinctive feeling for Fauré's elusive, expressive language and subtle artistry. We pay tribute to the individual discs below and welcome their appearance in collected form. The recorded sound is a little variable but never less than good, though Kathryn Stott scores with extremely fine Hyperion recording. Another drawback to the CRD set is that five CDs are involved, and the piano duet items are not included. Stott must remain a first recommendation. Those who do not want to buy the complete oeuvre but are looking for a very well-recorded anthology of Fauré's piano music should investigate Kun-Woo Paik's Decca CD.

Ballade in F sharp, Op. 19; Barcarolle 1, Op. 26; Impromptu 2, Op. 31; Improvisation (8 Pièces brèves), Op. 84/5; Nocturnes 1; 3, Op. 33/1 & 3; 6, Op. 63; 11, Op. 104/1; 13, Op. 119; Préludes, Op. 103, 2 & 7; Romance sans paroles, Op. 17/3
*** Decca 470 246-2. Paik

The Korean-born, Paris-based Kun-Woo Paik continues to impress in French music. This Fauré recital is the finest single-disc anthology of this great composer's music to have appeared for some time. Paik is completely attuned to the outwardly gentle but powerful and subtle vein of feeling that Fauré exhibits and is completely inside his sensibility. Even if Fauré is well represented in your library, you should add this excellently recorded recital, which would make a fine introduction for those new to this repertoire.

Ballade in F sharp, Op. 19; Mazurka in B flat, Op. 32; 3 Songs Without Words, Op. 17; Valses-caprices 1–4
(M) *** CRD (ADD) 3426. Crossley

Paul Crossley is especially good in the quirky *Valses-caprices*, fully equal to their many subtleties and chimerical changes of mood. He is extremely well recorded too.

Ballade in F sharp, Op. 19; Nocturnes 1–13 (complete); 9 Préludes, Op. 103; Theme & Variations in C sharp min., Op. 73
(B) **(*) EMI (ADD) 5 85174-2 (2). Collard

Barcarolles 1–13; (i) Dolly Suite. Impromptus 1–5; Mazurka, Op. 32; Pièces brèves 1–8, Op. 84; Romances sans paroles 1–3; (i) Souvenir de Bayreuth. Valses-caprices 1–4
(B) **(*) EMI (ADD) 5 85261-2 (2). Collard, (i) with Rigutto

This is glorious music which ranges from the gently reflective to the profoundly searching. The *Nocturnes* offer a glimpse of Fauré's art at its most inward and subtle. The *Préludes* are comparably intimate, and this is all music to which Jean-Philippe Collard is wholly attuned. His account of the *Theme and Variations* is no less masterly, combining the utmost tonal refinement and sensitivity with striking keyboard authority. Collard has the qualities of reticence yet ardour, subtlety and poetic feeling to penetrate Fauré's intimate world, but the only regret is that full justice is not done to it by the French engineers.

Barcarolles 1–13 (complete); Theme and Variations in C sharp min., Op. 73
(***) Testament mono SBT 1215. Thyssens-Valentin

Nocturnes 1–13 (complete)
(***) Testament mono SBT 1262. Thyssens-Valentin

Impromptus 1–5; Impromptu, Op. 86; 8 Pièces brèves; Valses-caprices 1–4
(***) Testament mono SBT 1263. Thyssens-Valentin

These three Testament CDs, superbly transferred from Ducretet-Thomson discs in mono, offer Fauré interpretations that have rarely been matched for their poetry and natural spontaneity of expression, coupled with a flawless technique. These discs, recorded respectively in 1955, 1956 and 1959, consistently have one marvelling at the fluidity of Thyssens-Valentin's playing, which yet is combined with sparkling control, in a way that few rival versions can begin to match. It almost feels as though she herself is actually creating this music as she plays. Any lover of Fauré's subtly nuanced piano music should immediately investigate these magnetic, revelatory performances. For each disc the pianist's daughter, Jeannine Lançien, provides a fascinating account of her mother's idiosyncratic career, and Bryce Morrison, a lifelong devotee, adds a critical assessment.

Barcarolles 1–13 (complete)
(M) *** CRD (ADD) CRD 3422. Crossley

Paul Crossley has a highly sensitive response to the subtleties of this repertoire and is fully equal to its shifting moods. The CRD version was made in the somewhat reverberant acoustic of Rosslyn Hill Chapel, and is more vivid than the 1974 EMI recording of Collard.

Barcarolles 1, 5 & 6; Nocturnes 1, 8 & 13; Romance sans paroles 1–3; Valse-caprice 1; Theme and Variations
(BB) *** Regis (ADD/DDD) RRC 1187. Crossley

This makes an admirable 75-minute recital, taken from Paul Crossley's five-disc coverage for CRD. The engaging *Theme and Variations* is especially welcome. Crossley never forces the music, yet his purity of style is never chaste and his concentration and sense of scale demonstrate his full understanding of this repertoire. The recorded sound is consistently good, though reflecting slightly different recording balances between 1983 and 1987. A bargain.

Barcarolles 1, Op. 26; 6, Op. 70; Impromptus 2, Op. 31; 3, Op. 34; Nocturnes 1, 3, Op. 33/1 & 3; 4, Op. 36; 6, Op. 63; 13, Op. 119; 8 Pièces brèves, Op. 84; Romance sans paroles 3, Op. 17/3
*** Hyp. CDA 67074. Stott

An admirably chosen collection, arranged in the form of a recital, taken from Kathryn Stott's complete survey. The opening *Romance Without Words* is inviting and the *A minor Barcarolle* and *E flat major* and *minor Nocturnes* are particularly winning, as are the charming eight miniatures of Op. 84. A pity the *C sharp minor Theme and Variations* was not included, but what is (69 minutes) is well worth having when played and recorded so persuasively.

Impromptus 1–5; 9 Préludes, Op. 103; Theme & Variations in C sharp min., Op. 73
(M) *** CRD (ADD) CRD 3423. Crossley

The *Theme and Variations in C sharp minor* is one of Fauré's most immediately attractive works. Paul Crossley plays it with splendid sensitivity and panache. The recorded sound, too, is extremely well judged.

Nocturnes (complete); Pièces brèves, Op. 84
(M) **(*) CRD (ADD) CRD 3406/7. Crossley

Here the recording is rather closely balanced, albeit in an ample acoustic, but the result tends to emphasize a percussive element that one does not normally encounter in this artist's playing. There is much understanding and finesse, however, and the *Pièces brèves* are a valuable fill-up.

VOCAL MUSIC

Mélodies: (i) *Après un rêve; Arpège; Automne; Au bord de l'eau;* (ii) *C'est l'extase langoureuse; Clair de lune; En sourdine; Green; L'horizon chimérique* (cycle); *Mandoline; Prison; Spleen*

⊕ **(N)** (***) Testament mono SBT 1311. Souzay, (i) Bonneau or (ii) Baldwin – FALLA: *Canciónes populares españolas*; RAVEL: *Histoires naturelles* ***

Writing in 1955, the authors of *The Record Guide* spoke of Souzay surpassing his earlier achievements, and they hailed these Fauré songs on Decca LXT 2543 (from which this Testament issue in part derives) as 'one of the most satisfactory LP song recitals yet issued'. Half a century later it has lost none of its ability to enchant and remains one of the most eloquent of all Souzay's song records.

Mélodies: *Après un rêve; Aurore; Automne; La bonne Chanson; Au bord de l'eau; Clair de lune; L'horizon chimérique; Lydia; 5 Mélodies 'de Venise'; Mirages; Nell; Le parfum impérissable; Le plus doux; Les présents; Prison; Les roses d'Ispahan; Soir; Spleen*

(N) *** Nim. (ADD) NI 5736/7 (2). Cuénod, Isepp – DUPARC: *Mélodies: Chanson triste, etc.* ***

Hugues Cuénod took part in Nadia Boulanger's famous 1937 records of Monteverdi madrigals and even in the 1980s sang the role of the Astrologer in Rimsky-Korsakov's *Le Coq d'or* at Covent Garden. He was born in 1902 and as we go to press, is 103! Cuénod was already 70 when he made these well-balanced recordings, though this hardly shows: the voice is light and steady and his sense of style impeccable. Both the accompanists (the documentation does not indicate who accompanies what) are highly sensitive and match the refined intelligence this great artist brings to this repertoire.

Mélodies: *Après un rêve; Arpège; Au bord de l'eau; C'est l'extase; Claire de lune; En sourdine; Green; L'horizon chimérique* (cycle); *Mandoline; Prison; Spleen; Tristesse*

(N) (M) (***) Decca mono 475 041-2. Souzay, Bonneau – FAURÉ: *Mélodies* (with CANTELOUBE: *Brezairola; Malurous qu'o uno fenno.* BOËSSERT: *Me veux tu mourir*; BATAILLE: *Ma bergère non légère*; TRAD: *Tambourin; Cahez, beaux yeux*)

Winner of the *Gramophone* Historical Vocal Award in 1991, this treasurable collection is drawn from recordings made in the 1950s, including some of those on the Testament recital above. The partnership of Gérard Souzay and Jacqueline Bonneau was almost unique in the field of French mélodie, and this disc, like its companion, is very special indeed. The Canteloube items make a refreshing bonus. The arrangements of folksongs are also welcome.

Mélodies: *Après un rêve; Au bord de l'eau; Aurore; Clair de lune; Dans les ruines d'une abbaye; En sourdine; Fleur; Green; Ici-bas; Mai; Mandoline; Nell; Nocturne; Notre amour; Le Papillon et la fleur; Le Pays des rêves; Les Présents; Prison; Les Roses d'Ispahan; Le Secret; Soir*

(BB) *** Virgin 2×1 5 61433-2. Yakar, Lavoix (with BIZET: *Pastorale; Rose d'amour; Sonnet*; CHABRIER: *Chanson pour Jeanne; L'Ile heureuse; Lied* ***) – HAHN: *Mélodies* ***

Rachel Yakar with her warm, very French-sounding timbre is an ideal interpreter of French mélodie, bringing out the subtleties of word-meaning, though it is a pity that in this super-bargain double-disc issue no texts are provided, only a cursory survey of the genre. The selection of 22 songs could hardly be more attractive, with settings of individual poets grouped together, so that early and late settings of Verlaine can be compared and contrasted. Excellent (1991) recording from Radio France. Coupled with an equally imaginative collection of Hahn songs, plus extra cherishable items from Bizet and Chabrier, it is a delightful issue.

Mélodies: *Après un rêve; Au bord de l'eau; Les Berceaux; Clair de lune; Lydia; Mandoline; Le Papillon et la fleur; Sylvie*

*** Virgin 5 45360-2. Gens, Vignoles – DEBUSSY; POULENC: *Mélodies* ***

Véronique Gens is a highly accomplished artist and certainly makes a beautiful sound. She allows Fauré's art to speak for itself, although there are times when you feel stronger characterization would not come amiss. She is sensitively accompanied by Roger Vignoles and recorded with great naturalness.

La Chanson d'Eve, Op. 95; Mélodies: Après un rêve; Aubade; Barcarolle; Les Berceaux; Chanson du pêcheur; En prière; En sourdine; Green; Hymne; Des jardins de la nuit; Mandoline; Le Papillon et la fleur; Les Présents; Rêve d'amour; Les Roses d'Ispahan; Le Secret; Spleen; Toujours!

⊕ *** Hyp. CDA 66320. Baker, Parsons

Dame Janet Baker gives magical performances of a generous collection of 28 songs, representing Fauré throughout his long composing career, including many of his most winning songs. Geoffrey Parsons is at his most compellingly sympathetic, matching every mood. Many will be surprised at Fauré's variety of expression over this extended span of songs.

Requiem, Op. 48

(M) *** Teldec 0927 49001-2. Bonney, Hampson, Amb. S., Philh. O, Legrand – DURUFLE: *Requiem* ***

(B) *** Sony (ADD) SBK 67182. Popp, Nimsgern, Amb. S., New Philh. O, A. Davis – DURUFLE: *Requiem* ***

(M) *** EMI (ADD) 5 66894-2 [5 66946-2]. De los Angeles, Fischer-Dieskau, Brasseur Ch., Paris Conservatoire O, Cluytens

⊕ **(*) BBC (ADD) BBCL 4026-2. Price, Carol Case, BBC Ch., BBC SO, Boulanger – BOULANGER: *Psaumes 24 & 130; Pie Jesu* **(*) ⊕

(*) HM HMC 901771. Zomer, Genz, La Chapelle Royale, Coll. Voc. Ghent, O des Champs-Elysées, Herreweghe – FRANCK: *Symphony* *

**(*) York Ambisonic YORK CD177. Rawlins, White, Martin, Canterbury Cathedral Ch. & O, Flood – DURUFLE: *Requiem* **(*)

(i) *Requiem.* (ii; iii) *Après un rêve, Op. 7/1*; (ii) *Dolly (Suite), Op. 56*; (ii; iii) *Elégie, Op. 24*; (ii; iv) *Pavane, Op. 50*

(BB) **(*) DG Entrée 474 562-2. (i) Battle, Schmidt, Philh. Ch. & O, Giulini; (ii) Boston SO, Ozawa; (iii) Eskin; (iv) Tanglewood Festival Ch.

Requiem; Pavane, Op. 50

(M) *** EMI (ADD) 7 64634-2. Armstrong, Fischer-Dieskau, Edinburgh Festival Ch., O de Paris, Barenboim – BACH: *Magnificat* **

*** Ph. 446 084-2. (i) McNair, Allen; ASMF Ch. & O, Marriner (with KOECHLIN: *Choral sur le nom de Fauré*; SCHMITT: *In memoriam 2: Scherzo sur le nom de Gabriel Fauré*; RAVEL: *Pavane pour une infante défunte* ***)

(i) *Requiem, Op. 48*; (ii) *Pavane*; (iii) *Pelléas et Mélisande: Suite, Op. 80*

*** Decca 421 440-2. (i) Te Kanawa, Milnes; (i–ii) Montreal Philharmonic Ch.; (i–iii) Montreal SO, Dutoit

(M) **(*) Ph. (ADD) 464 701-2. (i) Ameling, Kruysen, Chorzempa; (i–ii) Netherlands R. Ch., Fournet; (iii) Gomez, cond. Zinman; (i–iii) Rotterdam PO

Requiem (1893 version); *Ave Maria, Op. 67/2; Ave verum corpus, Op. 65/1; Cantique de Jean Racine, Op. 11; Maria, Mater gratiae, Op. 47/2; Messe basse; Tantum ergo, Op. 65/2*

☛– *** Coll. (ADD) COLCD 109. Ashton, Varcoe, Cambridge Singers, L. Sinfonia (members), Rutter

Requiem (1893 version); *Ave verum corpus; Cantique de Jean Racine; Messe basse; Tantum ergo*

*** Hyp. CDA 66292. Seers, Poulenard, George, Corydon Singers, ECO, Best

(i) *Requiem*; (ii) *Cantique de Jean Racine*; (ii; iii) *Messe basse*

(BB) *** Naxos 8.550765. Beckley, Gedge, Schola Cantorum of Oxford, Oxford Camerata, Summerly (with DE SEVERAC: *Tantum ergo*; VIERNE: *Andantino*; with Carey, organ ***)

(B) *** Double Decca (ADD) 436 486-2 (2). (i) Bond, Luxon; (ii) Cleobury; (iii) Brunt; (i–iii) St John's College, Cambridge, Ch., Guest (i) with ASMF – DURUFLE: *Requiem*; POULENC: *Mass*, etc. ***)

Requiem; Cantique de Jean Racine; La Naissance de Vénus, Op. 29

*** Australian ABC Classics 472 045-2. Macliver, Tahu Rhodes, Cantillation, Sinf. Australis, Walker

(i; ii; iv) *Requiem*; (ii; iii) *Les Djinns, Op. 12*; (ii) *Madrigal, Op. 35*

*** Ph. 438 149-2. (i) Bott, Cachemaille; (ii) Monteverdi Ch., Salisbury Cathedral Boy Choristers; (iii) Vatin; (iv) ORR, Gardiner – DEBUSSY: *3 Chansons de Charles d'Orléans*; RAVEL: *3 Chansons*; SAINT-SAENS: *3 songs* ***

(i) *Requiem*; (ii) *Messe basse*

(B) **(*) CfP 512 8112. (i) Augér, Luxon; (ii) Smy, King's College, Cambridge, Ch., Ledger

Requiem (1893 version); *Messe des pêcheurs de Villerville*

(M) **(*) HM HMC 801292. Mellon, Kooy, Audoli, Petits Chanteurs de Saint-Louis, Paris Chapelle Royale Ch., Musique Oblique Ens., Herreweghe

John Rutter's inspired reconstruction of Fauré's original 1893 score, using only lower strings and no woodwind, opened our ears to the extra freshness of the composer's first thoughts. Rutter's fine, bright recording includes the *Messe basse* and four motets, of which the *Ave Maria* setting and *Ave verum corpus* are particularly memorable. The recording is first rate but places the choir and instruments relatively close.

Michel Legrand uses the full orchestral version of 1900 in

the most dramatic way possible, yet the delicacy of the *In paradisum* reflects an equally sympathetic response to the gentler, mystical side of the music. Barbara Bonney's *Pie Jesu* with its simplicity and innocence is very touching. Thomas Hampson makes an eloquent contribution to the *Libera me*, and after the climax the flowing choral line shows the subtle range of colour and dynamic commanded by the Ambrosian Singers (as well as the orchestra). With superb, spacious recording this performance is very compelling indeed, and it is coupled with an equally fine account of the Duruflé work which was inspired by Fauré's masterpiece.

The directness and clarity of Andrew Davis's reading on Sony go with a concentrated, dedicated manner, the fresh vigour of the choral singing achieves an admirable balance between ecstasy and restraint in this most elusive of *Requiem* settings, culminating in a wonderfully measured and intense account of the final *In paradisum*. Lucia Popp is both rich and pure, and Siegmund Nimsgern (if less memorable) is refined in tone and detailed in his pointing. The recording, made in a church, matches the intimate manner and, with its equally fine Duruflé coupling, this is a very highly recommendable bargain version.

John Eliot Gardiner, like Rutter but with period forces, also chooses the version of the *Requiem* with the original instrumentation. The darkness matches Gardiner's view of the work, which he makes more dramatic than it often is. The mellow recording takes away some of the bite but, with excellent soloists – Catherine Bott radiantly beautiful in the *Pie Jesu*, Gilles Cachemaille vividly bringing out word-meaning – it makes an excellent choice. *Les Djinns* is specially welcome, with piano accompaniment on a gentle-toned Erard of 1874; and all the other pieces, including Fauré's enchanting *Madrigal*, are in various ways inspired by early French part-songs, with the medieval overtones brought out in the Debussy and with the humour of the Ravel nicely underlined.

Matthew Best's performance with the Corydon Singers also uses the Rutter edition but presents a choral and orchestral sound that is more refined, set against a helpful church acoustic. *In paradisum* is ethereally beautiful. Best's soloists are even finer than Rutter's, and he too provides a generous fill-up in the *Messe basse* and other motets, though two fewer than Rutter.

Barenboim's 1975 recording has been splendidly remastered. The sound is firmer and better focused without loss of atmosphere. The Edinburgh Festival Chorus are freshly responsive so that, although their tone is beefier than in some versions, the effect is never heavy and the performance is given a strong dimension of drama. Sheila Armstrong's *Pie Jesu* is even more successful here than with de los Angeles. Fischer-Dieskau is not quite as mellifluous as in his earlier account with Cluytens, but he brings a greater sense of drama. A first-rate version, including a sensitive account of the *Pavane*.

The de los Angeles/Fischer-Dieskau version, made under the late André Cluytens in the early 1960s, has great expressive eloquence and the choir, if not as fine as Rutter's or Gardiner's (to name but two), has a certain idiomatic advantage. It has always been a highly recommendable version with dedicated contributions from both soloists, and the full, warmly atmospheric recording sounds very beautiful. However, it has no coupling.

Nadia Boulanger's account, recorded at Croydon's Fairfield Hall with the BBC Chorus and Symphony Orchestra, has dignity and gravity. Tempi throughout are on the slow side but seem absolutely right. The *Introitus* has what John War-rack's excellent notes call 'an almost tragic severity'. There may be better sung and played accounts of the *Requiem*, but this has a keenly devotional feeling throughout and a special radiance that is moving. A rather special musical document.

The Naxos version makes an excellent bargain choice for the *Requiem* in its original orchestration. The fresh, forward choral tone goes with a direct, unmannered interpretation from Jeremy Summerly, with soloists comparably fresh-toned and English-sounding. The recording brings out the colour-ings of the orchestra in sharp detail, with the organ and brass vividly caught. The performance of the *Messe basse* is compa-rably direct, made to sound a little square at times, but the *Cantique de Jean Racine* is most winningly done. The little meditative organ piece by Vierne and the unaccompanied motet by de Severac are pleasing makeweights.

The Australian artists on ABC give a translucent, sensuous performance, and their well-blended sound and fine balance are enhanced by the singing of Cantillation, which is is a relatively small choir. Teddy Tahu Rhodes is a bass-baritone with a slightly grainy finish to his voice, but an uncommon agility, while Sara Macliver's lovely *Pie Jesu* is effortless and pure. The performance of the *Cantique de Jean Racine* is very fine too. However, the special interest of this release is the inclusion of *La Naissance de Vénus*, in essence a single-scene mythological opera, intended for the concert hall. Fauré con-sidered it one of his best compositions. Again Tahu Rhodes, in the role of the deity Jupiter, shows considerable agility, this time in a high baritone register. This is the only available recording of this work, except for an EMI version which used a piano reduction. Here we can enjoy the orchestral passages, depicting the miraculous transformation of the sea, for the first time. A worthwhile addition to the catalogue. Full texts and translations are included, with excellent documentation.

Philippe Herreweghe, in his earlier recording using the original score (HMC 801292), unlike Rutter and Best, tends to adopt speeds that are a degree slower than those marked. His soloists are more sophisticated than their British rivals, ton-ally very beautiful but not quite so fresh in expression. The recording has chorus and orchestra relatively close, but there is a pleasant ambience round the sound.

Not surprisingly, the acoustics of St Eustache, Montreal, are highly suitable for recording the regular full orchestral score of Fauré's *Requiem*, and the Decca sound is superb. Dutoit's is an essentially weighty reading, matched by the style of his fine soloists, yet the performance has both fresh-ness and warmth and does not lack transparency. There are attractive bonuses.

The St John's account has a magic that works from the opening bars onwards. Jonathon Bond and Benjamin Luxon are highly sympathetic soloists and the 1975 (originally Argo) recording is every bit as impressive as its digital competitors, while the smaller scale of this version is probably nearer to Fauré's original conception. The Double Decca reissue offers exceptionally generous couplings, not only the Duruflé *Req-uiem* but other fine music by both Duruflé and Poulenc, but for those collectors who want just the pair of *Requiems* the single disc is fair value.

Marriner in his 1993 recording for Philips also returns to the fuller re-orchestration. But where many larger forces encourage expansive speeds, Marriner's pacing is ideal, and the clean choral attack is matched by superb singing from Sylvia McNair and Thomas Allen. Though other versions convey even more magic, Marriner can be warmly recom-mended, particularly for those who fancy the instrumental pieces offered as coupling, including charming rarities by Koechlin and Schmitt.

Some thirteen years after making his recording of the Fauré *Requiem*, using the original version of the score, Her-reweghe has followed it up with the full-orchestra version of 1901, again using period instruments and style. Once again, so many of the speeds, notably in the opening *Introit* and *Kyrie*, are very slow. The *Introit* (setting *Requiem aeternam*) is also repeated later as an introduction to the *Libera me*. With fine singing from soloists and choir, this is a distinctive account, fresh and refined, not a primary choice perhaps, but filling an obvious gap and offering a generous, apt and unique cou-pling in a period-instrument performance of the Franck *Symphony*.

Fournet's account of the *Requiem* is very dramatic, and while the singing of the Netherlands Radio Chorus rises to climaxes powerfully, in some other respects the performance is rather cool. The recording tends to make both soloists (who sing well enough) sound rather too close, and it does not flatter Kruysen. However, the major coupling, David Zinman's highly refined and beautifully played account of the *Pelléas et Mélisande* suite, is in every way outstanding. There is a pervasive tenderness and delicacy. The (1979) recording is in the demonstration bracket here, and for that matter the 1975 recording of the *Requiem* has also come up pretty well in this remastering. Full texts and translations are included, but this is hardly, as Philips suggest, a 'Great Recording'.

In the later (1982) digital King's College recording, Ledger presents the *Requiem* on a small scale, with considerable restraint. This is less beautiful a performance than the earlier one, which was made with the same choir by Sir David Willcocks. On the Classics for Pleasure reissue the compara-tively brief *Messe basse*, also sweetly melodic, makes an apt but ungenerous coupling.

The York Ambisonic engineers project the Canterbury Cathedral Choir and Orchestra, as well as the powerful organ, with an impressive weight and immediacy, with the perform-ances unaffected by cloudy reverberation despite being recorded in the Cathedral. John Rutter's edition is used. The baritone soloist is very much part of the choir, hardly at all separated from his colleagues and not well focused. One big advantage is that the intimacy of scale comes over clearly, while the sharpness of focus for the choir and accompanying instruments also brings out the differences between the two works, where mistier sound tends to twin them very closely. Thanks to David Flood's direction as well as to the recording, the drama is underlined in high dynamic contrasts. The treble soloist, Joseph Rawlins, is bright and fresh in the *Pie Jesu*.

Giulini with large-scale Philharmonia forces adopts con-sistently slow speeds and a very reverential manner in the *Requiem*. That view usually makes the work too sentimental, but Giulini's care for detail in textures and his unexaggerated expressive style keep the result hushed and prayerful rather than sugary, with warm, atmospheric recording to match. Kathleen Battle sings with glowing warmth in the *Pie Jesu*, sounding sumptuous but not really in style. The music-making springs to life in the delectable opening movement of *Dolly*, and Ozawa's performance has the deftest touch throughout; indeed, this was the most attractive recorded account (it dates from 1986) since Beecham's and, like the rest of the Ozawa items, it is very pleasingly recorded within a warm concert-hall ambience. A mixed but worthwhile bar-gain.

FAYRFAX, Robert (1464–1521)

Missa Albanus; Missa O bone Ihesu (with Elevation Motet: Anima Christi ... Resurrexio Christi); Missa O quam glorifica; Missa Regali ex progenie; Missa Tecum principium
(M) *** Gaudeamus CDGAX 353 (3). Cardinall's Musick, Carwood

This fine mid-priced set gathers together all Fayrfax's known Masses, plus a bonus in the newly discovered and magnificent *O bone Ihesu* and an incomplete four-part setting of *Anima Christi* (an 'elevation motet' sung during the elevation of the host). The surviving text begins with '*Resurrexio*' and David Skinner, whose editions are used throughout, tells us in the notes that there is no doubt about the connection of this motet with the Mass. The performances and recordings are of outstanding quality, and anyone who has not yet sampled this glorious music could do no better than start here.

FERGUSON, Howard (1908–99)

A wonderfully gifted musician, Howard Ferguson gave up composing at a relatively early stage in his career, feeling that he had nothing more to say and that his language was out of step with the way contemporary music was moving.

Piano Concerto (for piano and strings)
(N) (BB) *** Naxos 8.557290. Donohoe, Northern Sinfonia –
    DARNTON; GERHARD; ROWLEY: *Piano Concertos* ***

Howard Ferguson wrote sparingly but with the most acute discrimination. This *Concerto for Piano and Strings*, written in 1951, is conceived in structure on neo-classical lines, with an opening orchestral tutti, but it follows the warmly attractive idiom that is typical of the composer, very British, with brilliant writing for the soloist, not least in the finale with its jazzy syncopations, slightly Waltonian, leading to a climax in waltz time. The central *Theme and Variations* comes nearer to the pastoral tradition, building up powerfully. Peter Donohoe, directing the Northern Sinfonia from the keyboard, is the most persuasive interpreter. Well-balanced sound. An excellent, varied and imaginative coupling.

Overture for an Occasion, Op. 16; Partita, Op. 5a; (i) *2 Ballads, Op. 1;* (ii) *The Dream of the Rood, Op. 19*
*** Chan. 9082. (i) Rayner Cook; (ii) Dawson, L. Symphony Ch.; LSO, Hickox

This collection includes a striking setting of the *Lyke-Wake dirge*, written in 1928 long before Britten. The *Partita* of 1935–6 is surprisingly dark until the last movement, with a weirdly enigmatic second movement and a lamenting slow movement. The *Overture for an Occasion*, written for the Queen's coronation, has the warmth and colour of comparable Walton works, and further echoes of Walton flavour the *Dream of the Rood*, a setting of an Anglo-Saxon poem with a radiant soprano solo introducing a sequence of richly atmospheric choruses. Hickox proves an ideal advocate, drawing incandescent singing and playing from his performers, with rich and clear Chandos sound to match.

(i) *Octet;* (ii; iii) *Violin Sonata 2, Op. 10;* (iii) *5 Bagatelles*
*** Hyp. CDA 66192. (i) Nash Ens.; (ii) Chilingirian; (iii) Benson – FINZI: *Elegy* ***

Ferguson's *Octet* is written for the same instruments as Schubert's masterpiece, a delightful counterpart. Those seeking a first-class modern version will find that the Nash Ensemble fill the bill admirably. The other works on the Hyperion disc display the same gift of easy, warm communication, including the darker *Violin Sonata* and Finzi's haunting *Elegy for Violin & Piano.*

(i) *Violin Sonatas 1, Op. 2; 2, Op. 10;* (ii) *4 Short Pieces;* (iii) *3 Sketches, Op. 14;* (iv) *Discovery* (song-cycle), *Op. 13;* (v) *5 Irish Folksongs, Op. 17;* (vi) *Love and reason;* (iv) *3 Mediaeval Carols, Op. 3*
*** Chan. 9316-2. (i) Mordkovitch; (ii) Hilton; (iii) Butt; (iv) Mark Ainsley; (v) Burgess; (vi) Schneider-Waterberg; all with Benson

This generous collection of Ferguson's chamber music, beautifully performed, provides a fine counterpart to Hickox's orchestral and choral disc. It is framed by the two *Violin Sonatas* (1931 and 1946), both powerful works, with Lydia Mordkovitch a rich and persuasive interpreter. Clifford Benson is the linchpin among the performers, contributing to all the works here. The *Four Short Pieces* for clarinet and the *Three Sketches* for flute are delightful miniatures, as is the counter-tenor song, *Love and reason,* and the *Carols* and the *Discovery* cycle for tenor. Best of all is the colourful cycle of Irish folksongs for mezzo, vividly performed by Sally Burgess. Excellent, well-balanced sound.

(i) *Partita for 2 Pianos, Op. 56. Piano Sonata in F min., Op. 8*
*** Hyp. CDA 66130. Shelley, (i) Macnamara

Ferguson's *Sonata* is a dark, formidable piece in three substantial movements, here given a powerful and intense performance, a work which, for all its echoes of Rachmaninov, is quite individual. The *Partita* is also a large-scale work, full of good ideas, in which Howard Shelley is joined for this two-piano version by his wife, Hilary Macnamara. Excellent, committed performances and first-rate recording, vividly transferred to CD.

5 Bagatelles; Sonata in F min.
(N) (M) *** Somm SOMMCD 038. Bebbington – GURNEY: *Nocturnes* ***

Ferguson's muscular *Piano Sonata* (1938–40), written in memory of his teacher, Harold Samuel, is a work of deep, controlled, yet passionate intensity. Its language is frankly romantic and splendidly laid out for the piano, at times even reminding the listener of Brahms, Rachmaninov or, nearer home, Bliss – and none the worse for that! But it is still the product of an individual sensibility, powerfully argued and finely structured. Mark Bebbington gives convincing performances, though the recording is decent rather than distinguished.

FERNSTRÖM, John (1897–1961)

Wind Quintet, Op. 59
*** Phono Suecia PSCD 708. Amadé Wind Quintet –
    KALLSTENIUS: *Clarinet Quintet, Op. 17;* KOCH: *Piano Quintet* ***

Although John Fernström was a prolific composer, much of his energy and time was consumed by work with orchestras and choirs in southern Sweden. However, the *Wind Quintet* is well fashioned and civilized. The playing of the Amadé Quintet has plenty of finesse and elegance and scores over its Oslo rival on Naxos.

FERRABOSCO, Alfonso I (1543–88)

FERRABOSCO, Alfonso II (1578–1628)

A. F. sr: *Almain a 5; Di sei bassi a 6; Dovehouse Pavan a 5; Fantasies 3, 6, 14 & 16; Fuerunt mihi lachrimae a 4; In nomine 1–2; Solo e pensoso a 5; Uy re mi a 3*

A. F. jr: *3 Almains in C a 5; Fantasia a 4 (1); Fantasies 2 & 8 a 6; Hexachord Fantasies 1–2; In nomine 2 a 6; In nomine through all parts a 6; Pavan in C a 5; Susanne un jour a 5*

(N) *** CPO 999 859-2. Rose Consort of Violins

This disc reveals the music of a fascinating father-then-son musical relationship with the Court of Queen Elizabeth I. Alfonso Ferrabosco senior arrived in England at the beginning of the 1560s and served the Queen as lutenist and composer for a decade and a half, before returning to Turin in 1578, leaving his son behind as the Queen's ward. She tried hard without success to get his father back and so the younger Alfonso later took over. Both were fine composers, but their music is strikingly different: the father's has greater depth of melancholy, whereas the son's writing is more extrovert but no less skilful. But the father's works are the more memorable. The Rose Consort are persuasive performers and are very well recorded.

FIBICH, Zdeněk (1850–1900)

Symphonies 1 in F, Op. 17; 2 in E flat, Op. 38; 3 in E min., Op. 53

(B) *** Chan. Double 9682 (2). Detroit SO, Järvi

There is a strong Bohemian feel to these works and if, like so much of Fibich's music, the *First Symphony*, which opens so invitingly, is a little square, such is the excellence of Neeme Järvi's performance that it does not feel so. It is the best account so far on record. The performances of the *Second* and *Third* come into competition with a Supraphon issue from the Brno Orchestra under Jiří Walddans and Bělohlávek (11 0657-2) respectively. But on Chandos, opulent sound adds to the rustic charm of much of the writing, as well as heightening the warmth and drama of the playing. Moreover the Chandos recording scores in terms of fidelity and space, and the Detroit orchestra respond with enthusiasm to these scores. Overall this set is well worth exploring and far preferable to the Naxos alternative.

Piano Quartet in E min., Op. 11; Quintet for Violin, Clarinet, Horn, Cello & Piano, Op. 42

*** MDG 304 0775-2. Villa Musica Ens.

The *E minor Piano Quartet* is an early piece, which enjoyed the approval of Hanslick, while its companion comes from 1893. The ideas though pleasing are a little square; they do not have the fresh, outdoor quality of Fibich's great compatriots. This is well-wrought music and is beautifully played by these accomplished artists and excellently recorded.

Piano Quintet, Op. 42

*** ASV CDDCA 943. Endymion Ens. – DOHNANYI: *Sextet* ***

Fibich's *Piano Quintet* is a relatively late piece; it comes from the last decade of his life and has much lively invention and no mean charm. The Endymions give a first-rate account of it and are excellently recorded.

Moods, Impressions and Reminiscences, Opp. 41, 44, 47 & 57

*** Chan. 9381-2. Howard

William Howard is sensitive to the varying moods of these pieces, and he is convincingly recorded.

Sarka (complete)

*** Orfeo C 541 002H (2). Urbanová, Lotric, Kirilova, Jenis, Vienna Concert Ch., Vienna RSO, Cambreling

**(*) Sup. (ADD) SU 0036-2 612 (2). Depoltavá, Pribyl, Randová, Zítek, Brno Janáček Op. Ch., Brno State PO, Stych

Completed in 1897, only three years before the composer's death, Fibich's *Sarka*, based on the Czech legend of the predatory Sarka and her fellow Amazons. Fibich was aiming directly at writing a Wagnerian opera, especially in his echoes of *Tristan und Isolde* in the love duet for Sarka and Ctirad, the knight with whom she falls in love against her will. As in so many grand romantic operas the weakness lies in melodic material that only fitfully sticks in the memory. Yet on disc this is a piece well worth hearing. On Orfeo Sylvain Cambreling conducts a strong and purposeful performance in a good, well-balanced radio recording. Both the principals, Eva Urbanová as Sarka and Janez Lotric as Ctirad, are outstanding, with their characterful Slavonic voices that yet focus beautifully, and the others make a strong team.

The Supraphon version dates from 1978, with warmly atmospheric analogue sound. Its great strength is the idiomatic conducting of Jan Stych, even though Eva Depoltavá in the title-role is less characterful than Urbanová on Orfeo. Vilem Pribyl is a first-rate Ctirad, but the most outstanding singing comes from Eva Randová as the leader of the Amazons, Vlasta, rich and distinctive.

FIELD, John (1782–1837)

Piano Concertos 1 in E flat; 2 in A flat

*** Chan. 9368. O'Rourke, LMP, Bamert

Míceál O'Rourke embarks on a complete cycle of the Field concertos. The music of the present pair of concertos is uneven, but the Scottish slow movement of No. 1 features the folk tune *Within a mile of Edinburgh town* rather winningly. No. 2 brings a characteristic Field rondo with an engaging principal theme which becomes catchier as it is given more rhythmic treatment. The soloist is very persuasive, and he receives admirable support from Bamert and the London Mozart Players. First-class, naturally balanced recording.

Piano Concertos 1 in E flat; 3 in E flat

☛ (BB) *** Naxos 8.553770. Frith, Northern Sinfonia, Haslam

Benjamin Frith has the bargain field to himself. His playing is characteristically sensitive and fresh, and he is well supported by the Northern Sinfonia and David Haslam. Very good, warm recording, in a decent acoustic.

Piano Concertos 2 in A flat; 3 in E flat

(M) **(*) Warner Elatus 0927 49610-2. Staier, Concerto Köln, Stern

The performances on Elatus are certainly authentic, with Staier's nimble, twinkling (some would say tinkly) roulades contrasting with the robust orchestral tuttis. But, as with the music of Chopin, it is difficult to prefer the sound here to that of the modern piano, except perhaps in the innocent *Rondo* which closes No. 2, which is delightfully pointed by Staier's crisp keyboard articulation. However this disc is now in the medium price range.

Piano Concertos 3 in E flat; 5 in C (*L'Incendie par l'orage*)
*** Chan. 9495. O'Rourke, LMP, Bamert

Míceál O'Rourke is well up to form in the *Third Concerto*. The coupling (No. 5) is notable mainly for its histrionic storm effects in the middle of the first movement, which climax with a bold stroke on the tam-tam. After this, the weather breaks and we are ready for the songful *Andante*, before the comparatively robust and spirited finale which brings delicacy as well as brilliance of articulation from the soloist. Excellent support throughout from Bamert, and first-class recording.

Piano Concertos 4 in E flat; 6 in C
*** Chan. 9442. O'Rourke, LMP, Bamert

O'Rourke continues his Chandos series with highly persuasive accounts of Nos. 4 and 6, with both works providing delightful slow movements. The *C major Concerto* is the more interesting of the two, giving the soloist some scintillating passage-work in the first movement and a lolloping *Rondo* finale. Excellent, sympathetic accompaniments and first-rate recording.

Piano Concertos 5 (*L'Incendie par l'orage*); 6 in C
☻ (BB) *** Naxos 8.554221. Frith, Northern Sinfonia, Haslam

These two concertos are exhilaratingly performed by Benjamin Frith with the Northern Sinfonia, with Frith's sparklingly clear articulation in rapid scales and figuration magnetizing the attention in music that can easily seem just trivial. The title of the *Fifth Concerto*, *L'Incendie par l'orage* ('Fire from Lightning'), reflects a dramatic storm passage in the long and ambitious first movement, while the lovely slow movement of the *Sixth Concerto* is a nocturne in all but name, with the outer movements full of bright ideas.

(i) Piano Concerto 7 in C. Divertissements 1–2; Nocturne 16 in F; Rondeau in A flat. (ii) Quintetto
*** Chan. 9534. O'Rourke; (i) LMP, Bamert; (ii) Juritz, Godson, Bradley, Desbruslais

Although the finale of Field's *Seventh Piano Concerto* is characteristically chirpy, some of the passage-work is a shade garrulous (not the fault of the soloist, who is well on form). However, the opening movement has a beautiful central *Lento* section which the composer later extracted and published as one of the Nocturnes. What makes this disc treasurable is the series of lollipops which follow – the two *Divertissements*, *Rondeau* and *Nocturne*, every one of which has a really good tune. The serene single-movement *Piano Quintet* is also delicately charming. Performances and recordings are well up to the high standard of this excellent Chandos series.

Air du bon roi Henri IV; 2 Album Leaves in C min.; Andante inédit in E flat; Fantaisie sur un air russe, 'In the Garden'; Fantaisie sur l'air de Martini; Irish Dance: Go to the Devil; Marche triomphale; Nocturne in B flat; Nouvelle fantaisie in

G; *Polonaise en rondeau; Rondeau d'écossais; Rondo in A flat; Sehnsuchtswalzer; Variations in D min. on a Russian Song, 'My dear bosom friend'; Variations in B flat on a Russian Air, Kamarinskaya*
*** Chan. 9315. O'Rourke

Míceál O'Rourke presents this (nearly 80-minute) recital with intelligence and taste. Most of this repertory is not otherwise available, and much of it has the quiet charm one expects from this delightful composer. O'Rourke proves a dedicated interpreter of real artistry. Recorded at The Maltings, Snape, he is admirably served by the Chandos team.

Nocturnes 1–16
**(*) Athene ATH CD 1. Leach (fortepiano)

Joanna Leach uses three 'square' fortepianos, by Stodart and Broadwood (both from the 1820s) and a D'Almain from a decade later. The latter instrument most closely approaches the quality of a modern piano, though the Broadwood is not far behind. Leach coaxes poetic sounds from these comparatively recalcitrant instruments and plays this repertoire very sensitively. However, it cannot be denied that for most ears this music (with its remarkable anticipations of Chopin) sounds even better on a modern concert grand.

Nocturnes 1–9; Piano Sonatas 1 in E flat; 2 in A, Op. 1/1–2
☻ (BB) *** Naxos 8.550761. Frith

Nocturnes 10–17; 18 (Midi); Piano Sonata 3 in C min., Op. 1/3
☻ (BB) *** Naxos 8.550762. Frith

Benjamin Frith's playing is delectably coaxing, and he makes these *Nocturnes* so often seem exquisitely like Chopin, yet still catches their naïve innocence, especially in the *A flat major* work. He hops, skips and jumps delightfully in the Irish *Rondo* finale of the *First Sonata* and is hardly less beguiling in the rather more imposing opening movement of the *Second*.

The second CD includes the famous *Nocturne 18* whose original title was *Midi* (or '*Twelve O'clock Rondo*'). The *Third Sonata* occupies the mid-way point in the recital. Its first movement is just a little hectoring (Beethovenian *con fuoco* was not Field's natural element) but the closing *Rondo* simulates another popular air for its basis. As before, the recording is very natural.

Largo in C min.; Nocturnes in B flat; C min.; E min.; Prelude in C min.; Romance in E flat; Waltzes: in A; E (Sehnsucht)
*** Etcetera KTC 1231. Antoni – CHOPIN: *Recital* **(*)

Under the title 'Crossfire' this fascinatingly devised recital readily demonstrates links and influences between the music of John Field (who invented the Nocturne) and Chopin, his young Polish successor. Helge Antoni is a notably sensitive advocate of Field's music, and his simple style readily draws parallels with alternated pieces by Chopin. Field's *Nocturne in C minor* of 1812 is presented alongside Chopin's work in the same key, written 25 years later, and there are similar influences to be found in the *Waltzes*. A recital that is both stimulating and musically enjoyable too, as it is naturally recorded.

Piano Sonatas: 1 in E flat; 2 in A; 3 in C min., Op. 1/1–3; 4 in B
**(*) Chan. 8787. O'Rourke

Míceál O'Rourke plays these two-movement *Sonatas* written by his countryman with some flair. He is particularly good in the famous *Rondo* finale of the *First Sonata*, which he plays with real Irish whimsy and sparkling touch. The *Allegretto scherzando* of No. 3 also has hit potential.

FILS, Anton (1733–60)

Symphonies in A; C; D; E flat; G min.
*** CPO 999 778-2. Orfeo Bar. O, Gaigg

Here is another composer emerging from eighteenth-century obscurity (this time from Bavaria), and with the opening of the *Symphony in C*, with its dramatic *crescendi*, it comes as no surprise to find that he was very much part of the Mannheim music scene. Interestingly, unlike many composers from this period, Fils's music came into fashion just after his death. Perhaps its freshness, with pleasing folk-music elements, especially in some snappy rhythmic patterns, made it stand out. The minuets in general have a charmingly rustic dance quality, and the *Prestissimo* finale of the *A major Symphony* interrupts its headlong rush with a very characteristic sequence, complete with bass-drone. The finale of the *D major Symphony* displays the composer's ability to build up tension steadily, starting off with unison strings, and includes a particularly striking pedal point (on violas) lasting some 26 bars. The poignant oboe solo in the minuet of the *C major Symphony* is another highly attractive episode. Indeed all these symphonies are melodically appealing and lively, and the *G minor Symphony* is particularly exhilarating. The Orfeo Barockorchester plays excellently under Michi Gaigg: the string ensemble is elegantly pointed, and the often piquant woodwind writing is delightfully brought out. The recording is both warm and vivid.

FINE, Irving (1914–62)

(i) *Serious Song: Lament for String Orchestra;* (ii) *Symphony;* (i) *Toccata Concertante*
(M) *** Phoenix PHCD 106. Boston SO, (i) Leinsdorf; (ii) composer

Born in Boston, Irving Fine studied composition at Harvard with Walter Piston and later Nadia Boulanger. Although his main career was academic, his music was admired by Copland for its 'quality, sincerity and vitality', and Copland placed him in the 'Stravinsky School' of American composers. That composer's strong influence is certainly felt in the three-movement *Symphony*, a passionately argued work achieving consistent tension, with the closing *Ode* finally summing up the musical material. The *Lament* for strings is powerfully lyrical and comparably intense, while the equally approach-able and catchy *Toccata Concertante* is full of rhythmic energy, its syncopations only rarely flirting with the world of popular American music. It ends very powerfully, and these two contrasted pieces would work well together to represent this fine composer at a concert. The performances are vital and very well played indeed. The recording, too, is excellent. Worth exploring.

FINZI, Gerald (1901–56)

Cello Concerto
*** Chan. 9949. Wallfisch, RLPO, Handley – LEIGHTON: *Cello Concerto* ***

(i) *Cello Concerto;* (ii) *Eclogue for Piano and Strings; Grand Fantasia & Toccata*
(BB) *** Naxos 8.555766. (i) Hugh; (ii) Donohoe; N. Sinfonia, Griffiths

The *Cello Concerto* is arguably Finzi's greatest work, not just ambitious but deeply moving, written under the stress of knowing he was terminally ill. Marking the centenary of Finzi's birth, Chandos here reissues Raphael Wallfisch's richly romantic reading, still at full price but with a rather more generous coupling than on Naxos, the tautly argued *Cello Concerto* of Kenneth Leighton. Wallfisch finds all the dark eloquence of Finzi's central movement, and the performance overall has splendid impetus, with Handley providing the most sympathetic backing. The Chandos recording has a very natural balance.

The Naxos version, with Tim Hugh a most sensitive soloist, has the advantage not only of bargain price but of a very apt coupling in two of Finzi's concertante works with piano, originally designed for a concerto. Peter Donohoe is the powerful soloist, not always as tender as he might be, but still very sympathetic. A good bargain alternative choice.

Clarinet Concerto, Op. 31
(BB) *** Hyp. Helios CDH 55101. King, Philh. O, Francis – STANFORD: *Clarinet Concerto* ***

(i) *Clarinet Concerto, Op. 31; 5 Bagatelles for Clarinet & Strings* (arr. Ashmore), *Op. 23a; Love's Labour's Lost: 3 Soliloquies, Op. 28.* (ii) *Introit in F for Solo Violin & Small Orchestra, Op. 6; Romance in E flat for String Orchestra, Op. 11; A Severn Rhapsody, Op. 3*
(BB) *** Naxos 8.553566. (i) Plane; (ii) Hatfield; N. Sinfonia, Griffiths

(i) *Clarinet Concerto;* (ii) *Eclogue for Piano & Strings; Love's Labour's Lost: Suite; Prelude for String Orchestra; Romance for Strings*
(M) *** Nim. NI 5665. (i) Hacker; (ii) Jones; E. String O, Boughton

(i; ii) *Clarinet Concerto;* (iii) *Eclogue;* (iv) *Forlana* (arr. Ashmore); (v) *Magnificat;* (ii) *New Year Music: Nocturne. Romance* (for strings); (vi) *Earth and Air and Rain;* (vii) *In terra pax;* (viii) *Let us garlands bring;* (ix) *Dies natalis;* (x) *Amen* (from *The Full, Final Sacrifice*)
(B) *** Decca 476 2163 (2). (i) A. Marriner; (ii) ASMF, N. Marriner; (iii) Lane, ECO, Daniel; (iv) Johnson, RPO, Reynolds; (v) City of L. Sinf., Hickox; (vi) Luxon, Willison; (vii) Crabtree, Sweeney, Waynflete Singers, Winchester Cathedral Ch., Bournemouth SO, Hill; (viii) Terfel, Martineau; (ix) Langridge, LSO, Hickox; (x) New College, Oxford, Ch., Higginbottom

(i) *Clarinet Concerto;* (ii) *Introit for Violin & Orchestra*
(M) *** BBC (ADD) BBCM 5015-2. (i) Hilton, BBC N. SO, Thomson; (ii) Jarvis, LPO, Boult – LEIGH: *Harpsichord Concertino* *** (with Concert: 'English Music' ***)

(i) *Clarinet Concerto. Romance for Strings, Op. 11;* (ii) *Dies natalis, Op. 8;* (iii) *Let us garlands bring, Op. 18*
**(*) CBC SMCD 5204. (i) Campbell; (ii) V. Anderson; (iii) Braun; Manitoba CO, Streatfeild

(i) *Clarinet Concerto, Op. 31;* (ii) *5 Bagatelles for Clarinet & Piano*
*** ASV CDDCA 787. Johnson; (i) RPO, Groves; (ii) Martineau – STANFORD: *Clarinet Concerto, etc.* ***

Andrew Marriner's account of the *Clarinet Concerto* (originally Philips) is a particularly sensitive one: Marriner *père* is an admirable partner and secures some ravishingly gentle playing from the ASMF in the *Adagio*, and the finale lilts engagingly. The lyrical *Nocturne* flows in the finest pastoral tradition. Piers Lane's excellent version of the *Eclogue*, in fine Decca sound, will give much pleasure, as will Richard Hickox's performance of *Dies Natalis*. The Christmas work, *In terra pax*, is equally free. The boldly set *Magnificat* of 1951 receives a strongly convincing performance. It is a pity that there was room only for the brief *Amen* from *Lo, the Full, Final Sacrifice*, but the full work is available on EMI (see below). In *Earth and Air and Rain*, Finzi's distinctive setting of Hardy, there is sometimes a flavour of Vaughan Williams, and in *When I set out for Lyonnesse* a distinct reminder of Stanford's *Songs of the Sea* emerges. Excellent accompaniments from David Willison – his gentle postlude for the finale song, *Proud songsters*, ends the cycle movingly. The five Shakespearean settings, *Let us garlands bring*, are just as memorable in their contrasted ways.

Emma Johnson is even more warmly expressive in the concerto than Thea King on her Helios disc, and with Sir Charles Groves and the RPO ideally sympathetic accompanists. Finzi's sinuous melodies for the solo instrument are made to sound as though the soloist is improvising them, and with extreme daring she uses the widest possible dynamic, ranging down to a whispered *pianissimo* that might be inaudible in a concert-hall

Thea King also gives a definitive performance, strong and clean-cut. Her characterful timbre, using little or no vibrato, is highly telling against a resonant orchestral backcloth. Alun Francis is a most sympathetic accompanist. With Stanford's even rarer concerto this makes a most attractive bargain reissue, and the sound is excellent.

Finzi's *Concerto* is also played most nimbly by Janet Hilton, admirably supported by Bryden Thomson, especially in the lovely *Adagio*, which is memorably intense. The *Introit for Violin and Orchestra*, which brings another memorable theme, is a meditative, thoughtful piece, very well played by Gerald Jarvis and the LPO under Sir Adrian Boult in 1969. This is part of a 77-minute concert of English music, including the delicious *Harpsichord Concertino* of Walter Leigh.

Robert Plane's highly responsive performance of the concerto also uses a wide range of dynamic, and movingly brings out the work's sense of improvisatory lyricism. Not to be outdone, the Naxos collection offers the *Three Soliloquies*, plus an orchestration of the five lovely *Bagatelles*, which is even more evocative than the original version with piano. The *Introit for Violin and Orchestra* is most sensitively played by Lesley Hatfield. The *Romance* is hardly less engaging, while *Severn Rhapsody* shows its composer spinning his pastoral evocation in the manner of Butterworth. All this music is most persuasively presented by the Northern Sinfonia under Howard Griffiths and the Naxos recording has plenty of warmth and atmosphere.

Alan Hacker's reading of the *Concerto* is also improvisatory in style and freely flexible in tempi, with the slow movement at once introspective and rhapsodic. The concert suite of incidental music for Shakespeare's *Love's Labour's Lost* is amiably atmospheric and pleasing in invention and in the colour of its scoring. The two string-pieces are by no means slight and are played most expressively; the *Romance* is particularly eloquent in William Boughton's hands. For the reissue a sensitive account of the *Eclogue* has been added.

The warmly expressive playing of the strings of the Manitoba orchestra under Simon Streatfeild immediately strikes the ear at the opening of this alternative Finzi collection from Canada, and they play the lovely *Romance* very beautifully. It was enterprising to offer a version of *Dies natalis* (written for 'high voice') with a soprano soloist, but although Valdine Anderson sings freshly and sensitively, her close vibrato will not seduce all ears, and she is no match for Ian Bostridge. However, Russell Braun is much more persuasive in the baritone cycle of Shakespearean songs, *Let us garlands bring*, and James Campbell is equally impressive in the *Clarinet Concerto*, playing very gently in the ravishing *Adagio* and with appealing whimsy in the catchy finale. Excellent recording too.

(i) *Concerto for Violin & Small Orchestra. Prelude, Op. 25; Romance, Op. 11* (both for strings); (ii) *In Years Defaced* (song-cycle, orchestrated by Finzi, Alexander, Roberts, Matthews, Payne and Weir)
*** Chan. 9888. (i) Little; (ii) Mark Ainsley; City of L. Sinfonia, Hickox

The *Concerto for Violin and Small Orchestra* was the first orchestral work of Finzi's to be performed, but was then neglected for over 70 years, until these outstanding performers took it up for this recording. Drawing on Finzi's distinctive brand of pastoral writing, the outer movements are strong and vigorous, the central slow movement ethereally reflective. The warmly expressive *Prelude for Strings* was salvaged from a *Chamber Symphony* that was never completed, while the *Romance* is the most ravishing piece of all, with rich string-writing echoing both Elgar and Vaughan Williams in its emotional surge. Ideal performances, richly recorded.

Taking their cue from Finzi's own setting of *When I set out for Lyonnesse*, the five other composers involved, all Finzi admirers, offer sensitive settings of a sequence of poems (four by Hardy) which together form a satisfying cycle, designed to celebrate the composer's centenary in 2001. All very much in style, they heighten the emotional thrust of each of these beautiful songs, all among Finzi's finest, and are sympathetically sung by John Mark Ainsley. Colin Matthews brings out the mystery of Flecker's evocative poem, *To a Poet a Thousand Years Hence*, while Anthony Payne (the understanding 'realizer' of Elgar's *Third Symphony*) provides a brilliant conclusion, more radical than the rest, with the compound-time setting of Hardy's *Proud Songsters*, quite different from Britten's setting of the same poem in *Winter Words*.

Eclogue for Piano & String Orchestra
(B) *** CfP 575 9832. Lane, RLPO, Handley – DELIUS: *Piano Concerto*; VAUGHAN WILLIAMS: *Piano Concerto* ***

This is the central movement of an uncompleted piano concerto which the composer decided could stand on its own. It was Howard Ferguson who edited the final manuscript and set the title. The mood is tranquil yet haunting, and Piers Lane gives it a tenderly sympathetic reading.

Grand Fantasia & Toccata (for piano and orchestra), Op. 38; (ii) Intimations of Immortality, Op. 29
(M) *** EMI 7 64720-2. (i) Fowke; (ii) Langridge, RLPO Ch.; RLPO, Hickox

Finzi's setting of Wordsworth, with its rich, lyrical cantilena, brings constant reminders of the Elgar of *Gerontius*, while the writing remains essentially within the pastoral tradition of

English song-setting. The performance here is wholly committed, with the fervour of the chorus echoing the dedication of the soloist. The choral recording is both spacious and brilliant. The coupling, a Bachian *Grand Fantasia*, is followed by a genial *Toccata*, fugal in style. The piece is played compellingly by Philip Fowke, and Hickox is a fine partner. Again vividly realistic sound. Highly recommended.

(i) *Romance for Strings, Op. 11;* (ii) *Dies natalis, Op. 8;* (iii) *Earth and Air and Rain, Op. 16;* (ii) *For St Cecilia;* (iv) *Lo, the Full, Final Sacrifice, Op. 26: Amen* (only); (v) *Magnificat, Op. 36;* (vi) *In terra pax, Op. 39;* (vi) *Let us garlands bring, Op. 18*

(M) *** Decca (ADD) 468 807-2 (2). (i) ASMF, Marriner; (ii) Langridge, L. Symphony Ch., LSO, Hickox; (iii) Luxon, Willinson; (iv) New College, Oxford, Ch., Higginbottom; (v) Hickox Singers, City of L. Sinfonia, Hickox; (vi) Sweeney, Winchester Cathedral Ch., Bournemouth SO, Hill; (vii) Terfel, Martineau

Marriner's account of the eloquent if brief *Romance for Strings* is second to none, and Hickox's performance of *Dies natalis* brings a notably sensitive and passionate soloist in Philip Langridge, who also contributes impressively to the cantata commissioned for the St Cecilia's Day celebration in 1947 (with a text by Edmund Blunden). Its opening is full of pageantry in the Elgarian tradition, although the mood softens in the second section. *In terra pax* is another Christmas work, opening atmospherically with the baritone's musing evocation of the pastoral nativity scene. It is admirably sung by Donald Sweeney. Then comes a burst of choral splendour at the appearance of the Angel of the Lord, and after her gentle declaration of the birth of Christ comes an even more resplendent depiction of the 'multitude of the heavenly host', magnificently sung and recorded, and the music returns to the thoughtful recessed mood of the opening. The boldly set *Magnificat* of 1951 was an American commission and all three of these performances are strongly convincing. But why include only the brief *Amen* from *Lo, the Full, Final Sacrifice?*

In *Earth and Air and Rain*, Benjamin Luxon demonstrates the versatility of Finzi's word settings. The five Shakespearean settings, *Let us garlands bring*, are beautifully sung by Bryn Terfel. All in all this is a thoroughly worthwhile compilation, given excellent recording throughout.

Elegy for Violin & Piano

*** Nim. NI 5666. Hope, Mulligan – ELGAR: *Violin Sonata;* WALTON: *Violin Sonata* ***

*** Hyp. CDA 66192. Chilingirian, Benson – FERGUSON: *Octet,* etc. ***

The Finzi *Elegy* is a very apt makeweight for the Elgar and Walton sonatas, the only surviving movement from a projected violin sonata written in a hectic period for Finzi at the beginning of the Second World War.

Finzi's moving little *Elegy* also makes an apt fill-up for the record of chamber music by his friend, Howard Ferguson.

VOCAL MUSIC

Song-cycles: *Before and After Summer, Op. 16; I said to Love, Op. 19b; Let Us Garlands Bring, Op. 18*

(N) (BB) *** Naxos 8.557644. Williams, Burnside

Thomas Hardy was the poet who inspired Finzi more than any other, and here Roderick Williams frames his beautifully

crafted recital with two of the cycles or 'sets', as Finzi preferred to call them. *Before and after Summer* consists of 10 Hardy songs which Finzi assembled in 1949, notably the dark, powerful setting of *Channel Firing* which comes as a centrepiece. Finzi may underplay the ruggedness of Hardy, the poet's earthy qualities, but his feeling for words is always most sensitive. *I said to Love* is a collection of five settings assembled after the composer's death by his widow and son, three dating from the 1930s when he was at his most creative, and two, far darker, dating from his last months before he died in 1956. *Let Us Garlands Bring,* better known, consists of five Shakespeare settings, dedicated to Vaughan Williams, which bring refreshing new illumination to texts set many times before, with *Come away Death* and *Fear no more the Heat of the Sun* among the finest of all Finzi songs. Firm, even tone from Roderick Williams and beautifully clear diction, with immaculate playing from Iain Burnside.

Dies natalis (see also above, under *Clarinet Concerto* and *Romance for Strings*)

(M) *** EMI 5 65588-2. W. Brown, ECO, Finzi – HOLST: *Choral Fantasia; Psalm 86;* VAUGHAN WILLIAMS: *5 Mystical Songs,* etc. ***

Dies natalis is one of Finzi's most sensitive and deeply felt works, using meditative texts by the seventeenth-century writer, Thomas Traherne, on the theme of Christ's nativity. Finzi's setting is very well sung here by Wilfred Brown, although Ian Bostridge (see above) is even finer. The remastered recording sounds wonderfully fresh and is naturally balanced within a glowing acoustic.

Dies natalis; Intimations of immortality

**(*) Hyp. CDA 66876. Mark Ainsley, Corydon Singers & O, Best

Matthew Best, with John Mark Ainsley as soloist in both works, uses a relatively small orchestra. This is a more intimate reading of the latter work than on the earlier, EMI recording from Richard Hickox, yet it conveys an almost comparable concentration. Mark Ainsley has a sweet if small voice, very apt for both works, even if under pressure there is some unevenness. The chorus sings with feeling, though the recording is not as vividly immediate as the analogue EMI recording.

God is Gone Up; Lo, the Full, Final Sacrifice; Magnificat

(M) *** EMI 5 65595-2. King's College, Cambridge, Ch., Cleobury; Farnes – BAX: *Choral Music;* VAUGHAN WILLIAMS: *Mass* ***

Both the extended anthem, *Lo, the Full, Final Sacrifice,* setting Richard Crashaw's version of an Aquinas hymn, and the *Magnificat* were commissioned works, the one for St Matthew's, Northampton, the other for Massachusetts; in their rich climaxes they bring out a dramatic side in Finzi along with his gentle beauty, splendidly conveyed by the King's choir. The recording, made in the Chapel, is so nicely balanced that part-writing is clear even against the ample acoustic.

God is gone up; Magnificat; Let us now praise famous men; Lo, the full final sacrifice; My Lovely One; Thou didst delight my eyes; Welcome, Sweet and Sacred Feast; 7 Unaccompanied Part-Songs, Op. 17.

(BB) *** Naxos 8.555792. St John's College, Cambridge, Ch., Robinson

Gerald Finzi, from a prosperous Jewish family, but very much the English gentleman, wrote a handful of anthems and motets for the Anglican Church, here freshly and warmly sung by the choir of St John's College, Cambridge, under their choirmaster, Christopher Robinson. Best known is the strong and vigorous motet, *God is gone up*, with a triumphant shout, setting a text by the seventeenth-century poet, Edward Taylor; and most of the other settings use verse by the mystic poets of that period, much loved by Finzi. Crowning the collection is the extended setting of Richard Crashaw's poem, *Lo, the full final sacrifice*, ending on an ecstatic 'Amen' with scrunching harmonies. Unlike most offerings in this excellent St John's series from Naxos, this one includes secular items, unaccompanied part-songs, beautifully wrought, setting poems by Robert Bridges.

Oh Fair to See; Till Earth Outwears; A Young Man's Exhortation

(N) *** Linn CKD 253. Gilchrist, Tillbrook

James Gilchrist's fine disc of Finzi, with Anna Tillbrook the most sensitive accompanist, makes the perfect complement to the Naxos issue of Finzi songs, with very few duplications. Again Hardy is the poet whom Finzi chooses for most of the songs, with *Till Earth Outwears* and the two parts of *A Young Man's Exhortation* devoted exclusively to him, and with a Hardy setting opening the compilation cycle, *Oh Fair to See*. That group of seven songs concludes movingly with a setting of Robert Bridges, *Since we loved*, the last song Finzi wrote before his untimely death in 1956, addressed to his wife. Gilchrist with his clear tenor tone brings out the reflective beauty of Finzi's response to words, and brings vitality to the relatively few vigorous songs. Well-balanced sound.

A Young Man's Exhortation

(N) *** Hyp. CDA 67459. Padmore, Vignoles – TIPPETT: *Boyhood's End*; BRITTEN: *7 Hölderlin-Fragmente; Um Mitternacht*, etc. ***

Finzi's delightful cycle, dating from 1933, offers 10 more settings of Hardy poems, which are among the most warmly lyrical songs he ever wrote, with the poet's often earthy verse matched by the composer's English pastoral idiom. Mark Padmore is an ideal interpreter, warmly accompanied by Roger Vignoles, who provides a perceptive commentary in the notes. Well coupled with other cycles on the theme of youth and friendship.

FIOCCO, Joseph-Hector (1703–41)

Missa Solemnis in D; (i) Motets: Ave Maria; Homo Quidam

(BB) *** Naxos 8.557120. Coppé, Nirouët, Elsacker, Crabben, Mechelen, Snellings, Cappella Brugensis, Coll. Instrumentale Brugense, Peire, (i) with Reyghere

Joseph-Hector Fiocco was the eighth child of the Venetian composer, Pietro Antonio Fiocco. He moved to Brussels in 1682 and had 14 children in all, by two wives! He was briefly 'Sangmeester' at Antwerp Cathedral in succession to Willem de Fesch and he then returned to Brussels as master at the Collegiate Church of St Michael and St Gudule. His output is mainly vocal and instrumental sacred music, motets, Masses, *leçons de ténèbres* and the like, though there are some instrumental pieces, which were published in 1730 as his Op. 1. Both the *Missa Solemnis* and the two motets have been prepared from autograph copies in the Brussels Conservatoire by the conductor, Patrick Peire, who provides scholarly notes. In this refreshing music Vivaldi and the Italian style mingle with the influences of Lully, Couperin, Charpentier and Campra. The recordings, made in Ghent, are clean and well focused and the acoustic is warm.

FIORILLO, Federigo (1755–after 1823)

Violin Concerto 1 in F

(BB) *** Hyp. Helios CDH 55062. Oprean, European Community CO, Faerber – VIOTTI: *Violin Concerto 13* ***

Fiorillo's *Concerto* is charmingly romantic. Adelina Oprean's playing can only be described as quicksilver: her lightness of bow and firm, clean focus of timbre are most appealing. She is given a warm, polished accompaniment, and the recording is eminently truthful and well balanced.

FLOTOW, Friedrich (1812–83)

Martha (opera; complete)

(M) *** RCA 74321 32231-2 (2). Popp, Soffel, Jerusalem, Nimsgern, Ridderbusch, Bav. R. Ch. and O, Wallberg

Martha is a charming opera, and the cast of this 1978 recording (originating with Eurodisc) is as near perfect as could be imagined. Lucia Popp is a splendid Lady Harriet, the voice rich and full yet riding the ensembles with jewelled accuracy. Doris Soffel is no less characterful as Nancy, and Siegfried Jerusalem is in his element as the hero, Lionel, singing ardently throughout. Siegmund Nimsgern is an excellent Lord Tristan, and Karl Ridderbusch matches his genial gusto. Wallberg's direction is marvellously spirited and the opera gathers pace as it proceeds. The Bavarian Radio Chorus sings with joyous precision and the orchestral playing sparkles. The first-class recording has been vividly transferred, though there is a touch of edge on the voices of Lady Harriet and Nancy. The libretto promised on the back of the box is in German only, but the story of this opera is very easy to follow.

FLOYD, Carlisle (born 1926)

Susannah (opera; complete)

*** Virgin 5 45039-2 (2). Studer, Ramey, Hadley, Lyon Op. Ch. & O, Nagano

This is an updating of the story of Susannah and the Elders in the Apocrypha, which readily adapts to the background of a traditional community in the Appalachian mountains. The idiom is tuneful and unashamedly tonal, influenced by American folk-music. Most effective are the two big solos for the heroine, one in each of the compact Acts, both gloriously sung by Cheryl Studer, who as a native American sounds easily in character, taking to the idiom naturally. Samuel Ramey is similarly at home in this music, singing strongly with his richest tone, even if one can hardly believe in him as a vile hypocrite. With Jerry Hadley ideally cast as the tenor hero, Sam, Susannah's brother, who finally murders the predatory Blitch, the rest of the cast is first rate. The chorus and orchestra of the Lyon Opéra are also inspired by their American conductor to give heartfelt, idiomatic performances. Excellent sound, as in previous Lyon Opéra recordings with Nagano.

FOERSTER, Josef Bohuslav (1859–1951)

Symphony 4 in C min. (Easter), Op. 54; Springtime and Desire, Op. 93

(M) *** Sup. (ADD/DDD) 111 822-2. Prague SO, Smetáček

This beautiful if overlong symphony is both dignified and noble; its Scherzo is infectiously memorable and could be as popular as any of the *Slavonic Dances* if only it were known, and there is a sweep to the first movement that is most impressive. The finale is the least successful of the four movements, and here attention flags. All the same, the symphony wears well. To this analogue recording Supraphon add a 1985 account, digitally recorded, of his *Springtime and Desire*, a symphonic poem with a strong emphasis on the symphonic, and this, like the symphony, is a most welcome addition to the catalogue. Good performances, decent recording.

FORQUERAY, Antoine (1671–1745)

Pieces for 3 Viols in D min.; Suite for 3 Viols in D

*** Virgin 5 45358-2. Hantaï, Uemura, Verzier, Hantaï – MARAIS: *Pièces à violes* ***

It is not absolutely sure that these works are by Forqueray, but they share the austere style we recognize in that composer's writing for viol consort. Whoever composed this six-movement *Suite*, it is music of considerable expressive depth, especially the eloquent *Sarabandes*, and it ends with a lively extended *Chaconne*. The performances here are sympathetically expert and very well recorded.

Pièces de viole (1747): Divertissements 1–4

(N)**(*) Signum SIGCD 008. Charivari Agréable Simfonie

Pièces de viole, Volume I: Suites 1–2

(N) **(*) Astrée Naïve ES 9977. Savall, Coin, Koopman

Jordi Savall is a gamba player with a strong, bold instrumental personality. He undoubtedly has something in common with Antoine Forqueray himself, who was often held in awe by his contemporaries. Forqueray's virtuosity even intimidated people and, like Paganini, he was compared with the Devil. Savall's darkness of tone gives his performances a comparably special character: the result is powerfully expressive but totally lacking in charm. He has admirable support from the second gamba player, Christophe Coin, and from Ton Koopman, but the results will not appeal to all listeners.

The alternative collection on Signum is remarkably different in tone. The programme concentrates almost entirely on Forqueray's character pieces for viols, and includes a high proportion of pieces named after contemporary musicians. Charivari Agréable are well named: they are altogether more friendly in performance, responding to Forqueray's markings *très tendrement* and *gracieusement* and even bringing an element of charm. The piece named after Leclair, *très vivement et détaché*, is delightfully gay and spirited, but there is plenty of variety elsewhere, and the performances here are alive, sympathetic and seemingly authentic.

(i) Pièces de viole; (ii) Pièces de clavecin

(M) *** DHM/BMG 82876 60165-2. (i) Bernfield; (ii) Sempé

Antoine Forqueray was a younger contemporary of Marin Marais and enjoyed a reputation as one of the greatest gamba players of his day, though he responded more favourably to the Italian music of his time (Corelli and Vivaldi) than did Marais. This record contrasts some of his character pieces with the harpsichord transcriptions made by his son, Jean-Baptiste (1699–1782), and published in 1747, two years after his death. The latter was also a formidable player; indeed it has been suggested that the father's denunciation of him to the Paris Police for 'gambling, womanising and theft', when he was beginning to establish himself in the 1720s, was in part motivated by jealousy of his enormous talent! The transcriptions are, as such things should be, re-creations and remarkably free rhythmically. Nor is there a hint of rigidity in Skip Sempé's performances; they have all the expressive freedom and poetic feeling that the music calls for. The music has an intimacy and character that is beguiling, and Jay Bernfeld's playing has a comparable instinctive artistry. Both players are well served by the engineers who do not attempt to make either instrument larger than life. This is one of the most rewarding reissues in the current Deutsche Harmonia Mundi mid-priced series.

Pièces de clavecin; Harpsichord Suites 1–5

**(*) MDG 605 1101-2 (2). Meyerson

The present suites were edited in 1747 by his son, Jean-Baptiste (1699–1782). They exist in two forms: for solo viola de gamba with a second gamba as continuo and for solo harpsichord. Forqueray père's prowess as a gamba player was so impressive that he was engaged by the royal household as tutor to Louis XIV himself. His music is of much originality and considerable beauty and is given with great character by both players. Unusually, as MDG has high standards in these matters, the excellent Mitzi Meyerson is closely balanced and the aural image is too upfront so that the ear tires. A pity, as the playing is very fine.

Harpsichord Suites 1 in D min.; 3 in D; 5 in C min.

(BB) *** Naxos 8.553407. Beauséjour (harpsichord)

These suites are transcriptions of music for the viol of uncertain provenance, and they were long thought to be by Forqueray's son, Jean-Baptiste. Whatever the case may be, the music itself is of quality and originality, and it is well served by the Canadian harpsichordist, Luc Beauséjour, as recorded at the Church of St Alphonse-de-Rodriguez in Quebec. He plays with great flair and zest, and the sound is first class.

Harpsichord Suites 1: La Laborde; 2 in G; 3: La Moranglis ou la Plissay; 4 in G min.; 5 in C min.; La Rameau; La Guignon; La Léon

(BB) *** Naxos 8.553717. Beauséjour (harpsichord)

This second CD completes the Naxos coverage of Forqueray's five transcribed *Harpsichord Suites* and includes movements for which there was no room on the first CD (which has a playing time of 76 minutes). Of the three missing excerpts from the *Fifth Suite*, *La Guignon* is notably spirited, and the closing sarabande, *La Léon* (marked *tendrement*), touchingly sombre. The performances and recording continue the high standard of the first disc.

Harpsichord Suites 3 in D; 5 in C min.

(BB) *** Virgin 2x1 5 61872-2 (2). Meyerson (harpsichord) – RAMEAU: *Pièces de clavecin en concerts* ***

Mitzi Meyerson duplicates the *D major Suite* offered on Naxos, but includes also the equally ambitious *C minor* work which, like its companion, has titled movements, with the majestic introduction dedicated to Rameau (whose *Pièces de* clavecin en concerts act as an attractive coupling for this inexpensive Double CD set). She plays a 1974 Rubio after a 1769 Taskin, its rich sonority well conveyed in the warm acoustic of Forde Abbey, Chard, Somerset, especially in the dramatically forceful closing portrait of *Jupiter*.

FÖRSTER, Christoph (1693–1745)

Horn Concerto in E flat

*** Ara. Z 6750. Rose, St Luke's Chamber Ens. – HAYDN; L. MOZART; TELEMANN: *Horn Concertos* ***

Christoph Förster was a contemporary of Bach and this, the earliest of the four concertos in this outstanding collection, is no less demanding of the soloist's virtuosity. The eloquent minor-key theme of the *Adagio* is genuinely touching, and its distinctly baroque cantilena is well understood by soloist and orchestra alike. The dancing finale has an almost Vivaldian tinge and demands great virtuosity, which is readily forthcoming here. Stewart Rose is a splendid player, secure in technique, his style buoyant and expressive by turns, and the orchestra of which he is principal provides him with warmly stylish accompaniments. The recording is first class.

FORSYTH, Cecil (1870–1941)

Best-known for his book on orchestration, the standard work for many years, Cecil Forsyth was also a fine composer, especially early in his career, when he wrote two successful comic operas. He emigrated to the United States in 1914, where he remained until his death in 1941, concentrating on his work in a publishing firm.

Viola Concerto in G min.

(N) *** Hyp. CDA 67546. Powers, BBC Scottish SO, Brabbins – BOWEN: *Viola Concerto* ***

Forsyth's *Viola Concerto*, a confident work built on clear, well-defined themes, was written in 1903, not for Lionel Tertis but for another leading viola-player of the time, Emile Ferir, who gave the first performance at a Promenade concert under Sir Henry Wood. The memorable opening has the viola musing, unaccompanied, in an introduction punctuated by sharp *sforzando* chords from the orchestra. That leads to a main *Allegro* built on a dashing theme marked by triplets. The central *Andante* brings a yearningly tender main melody in elegiac mood. As a viola-player himself, Forsyth writes confidently for the instrument, notably introducing striking double-stopped passages, particularly in the finale, in which a sharply rhythmic, march-like theme is contrasted with a ballad-like second subject. Superbly played and recorded, with Lawrence Powers a masterly soloist, it makes a valuable rarity and an ideal coupling for the York Bowen concerto from the same period.

FOSS, Lukas (born 1922)

3 American Pieces

(M) *** EMI 5 62600-2. Perlman, Boston SO, Ozawa – BARBER: *Violin Concerto*; BERNSTEIN: *Serenade after Plato's 'Symposium'* ***

As the title suggests, Foss's *Three American Pieces* have a strong element of Copland-like folksiness, married to sweet, easy lyricism and with some Stravinskian echoes. Skilfully orchestrated for a small orchestra with prominent piano, all three of the pieces, not just the final *Allegro*, *Composer's Holiday*, but also the first two, *Early Song* and *Dedication*, have a way of gravitating into hoe-down rhythms, often with a surprising suddenness. They make a fine bonus for the two key works of Barber and Bernstein, and it is good that this uniquely valuable triptych is now offered at mid-price.

Fantasy Rondo; For Lenny; Grotesque Dance; Four 2-Part Inventions; Passacaglia; Prelude in D; Scherzo ricercato; Solo

(N) (BB) *** Naxos 8.559179. Scott Dunn

An impressing pianist, Lukas Foss was also a prolific composer, and the *Inventions* and *Grotesque Dance* were written when he was 16. This disc collects all his piano music from his teens through to *Solo* (1981) and *For Lenny* (1987). They are inventive and at times delightful pieces. Anyone who feels at home in the musical worlds of Barber and Copland will find this highly congenial. It would be good to have his rather Stravinskian but highly stimulating *Second Piano Concerto* back in circulation. Highly recommended.

FOULDS, John (1880–1939)

String Quartets 9 (Quartetto intimo), Op. 89; 10 (Quartetto geniale), Op. 97; Aquarelles, Op. 32

⊕ *** Pearl SHECD 9564. Endellion Qt

The *Quartetto intimo*, written in 1931, is a powerful five-movement work in a distinctive idiom more advanced than that of Foulds's British contemporaries, with echoes of Scriabin and Bartók. Also on the disc is the one surviving movement of his tenth and last quartet, a dedicated, hymn-like piece, as well as three slighter pieces which are earlier. Passionate performances and excellent recording, which is enhanced by the CD transfer. A uniquely valuable issue.

PIANO MUSIC

April, England; Egoistic; English Tune with Burden, Op. 89; Essays in the Modes, Op. 78; Music-Pictures Groups VI (Gaelic Melodies), Op. 81; VII (Landscapes), Op. 13; Variations & Improvisations on an Original Theme, Op. 4

*** BIS CD 933. Stott

Kathryn Stott proves brilliant and persuasive in this repertoire. She also has the advantage of quite exceptionally truthful and vivid recording quality. The *Essays in the Modes* (1928), which opens the disc, is interesting stuff; one is reminded of *Petrushka* in the first and of Busoni elsewhere. Stott characterizes these pieces and everything here with strong personality. Try *Prismic*, the last of the *Essays*, and the intelligence and wit of her playing will make a striking impression. Foulds wrote for the piano throughout his life, and if his music from the 1920s is obviously the more rewarding, even the youthful *Variations and Improvisations on an Original Theme* shows a pleasing fluency. Not great music but, played like this, one is almost persuaded that it is.

FRANÇAIX, Jean (1912–97)

(i) Piano Concertino; Les Bosquets de Cythère; Les Malheurs de Sophie

☛ *** Hyp. CDA 67384. (i) Cassard; Ulster O, Fischer

We still have a very special affection for the Mercury performance of the *Piano Concertino* by the composer's daughter, Claude Françaix, and we hope Universal will find a way to reissue this on SACD in the UK. Meanwhile, this new account by Philippe Cassard on Hyperion is to be warmly welcomed. The first movement *Presto* is exhilaratingly brisk, yet Cassard's articulation is immaculate, and the other three movements are full of the delicacy and charm for which the work is celebrated, especially the whimsical finale.

Les Bosquets de Cythère might have been a ballet but is in essence a suite of waltzes. The island of Cythère was traditionally the birthplace of Aphrodite and it is celebrated as the home of intoxicating sensual pleasure. This is hinted at daintily in several of the gentler movements, such as the sadly fragile portrait of *Aminte délaissée*, *Le Consolateur facétieux*, and *Subtile tendresse*, with its echoes of Ravel. Yet the rumbustious *Introduction à la vie joyeuse* has something of the spirited *galanterie* of Milhaud.

Les Malheurs de Sophie depicts the misadventures of the ill-behaved three-year-old heroine and her cousin, Paul, who is two years older. Although the ballet opens boisterously, there are many exquisite touches to show the composer's affection for his heroine, including the idyllic *Andante tranquillo* that opens the Second Tableau and the charming *Allegretto* that opens the Third, while the *Pas de deux of Sophie and Paul* is ingenuously light-hearted. Like the other works here, the score is played with great affection and elegant attention to detail by the Ulster Orchestra under Thierry Fischer, and the Hyperion recording is in the demonstration class.

Ouverture anacréonique; Pavane pour un génie vivant; Scuola de ballo; Sérénade; Symphony 3 in G
*** Hyp. CDA 67323. Ulster O, Fischer

Françaix did not number his symphonies, but this amiable G major work is his *Third* (1953), composed light-heartedly in memory of Papa Haydn. What a happy work this is! The *Sérénade*, written 20 years earlier, is even more jocular, opening with fake-rhythmic abrasiveness before a melancholy bassoon introduces the *Andantino*. But high spirits return in the chirping *Poco Allegretto* and dashingly ribald finale.

A touching calm then dominates the rather lower lovely opening of the *Ouverture anacréonique* (1978): the composer tells us he is trying to portray an imaginary world without conflict. But the music soon livens up vivaciously and reaches a confident, jazzy climax. The exquisite *Pavane pour un génie vivant*, a homage to Ravel, is the most recent composition here (1987) and evokes that composer's world idyllically. The programme then ends winningly with a pastiche *Scuola de ballo*, based on the music of Boccherini. It is in a direct line with Stravinsky's *Pulcinella* (although less corrosive) and Tomasini's *Good Humoured Ladies*, but wittier. The whole programme is played with warmth, polish and vitality in equal measure, the recording is first class and this is very highly recommended. We hope that the enormously sympathetic Thierry Fischer will continue his exploration of Françaix's orchestral output.

À huit (Octet); Clarinet Quintet; Divertissement for Bassoon & String Quintet; (i) L'Heure du berger
🎵 *** Hyp. CDA 67036. Gaudier Ens., (i) with Tomes

À huit (Octet); Clarinet Quintet; Divertissement for Bassoon & String Quintet
**(*) MDG MDGL 3300. Charis Ens.

À huit, written for the Vienna Octet in 1972 and dedicated to the memory of Schubert, is a delight. The *Clarinet Quintet* is a relatively late work (1977) but full of the beguiling charm that distinguishes so much of Françaix's invention. Despite its wartime provenance, the *Divertissement for Bassoon and String Quintet* manages to smile, while *L'Heure du berger*, background music for a brasserie, comes off equally well. Highly polished and characterful playing from all concerned in Hyperion and excellent recording.

Highly accomplished playing, too, from the Charis Ensemble and eminently acceptable recording. But the Gaudier Ensemble offer the same repertoire as well as an elegant performance of *L'Heure du berger*. Though the Charis are very good, the Gaudier have the competitive edge over them.

Les Demoiselles de la nuit; Le Roi nu (ballets; complete)
(N) *** Hyp. CDA 67489. Ulster O, Thierry Fischer

These two ballets perfectly illustrate the imaginative skill of Jean Françaix, a composer who consistently kept his creative aim within set limits and was ever ready to charm the ear. *Le Roi nu*, written for Serge Lifar and his company in 1935, is based on Hans Andersen's story, 'The Emperor's New Clothes', and after an imposing fanfare launches into brilliant, illustrative music, light and varied. The 11th of the 12 brief sections culminates in the voice of a child saying the famous pay-off line, '*Mais le roi est nu*', 'But the King is naked', sparking off a surprisingly jolly final section, *Panic*. *Les Demoiselles de la nuit* of 1948 is much darker, a surreal story based on a scenario of Jean Anouilh, described as 'a cat ballet in one Act'. The action is set among a seedy community of cats, with Agathe, the coquettish white kitten, the centre of attention – a role originally danced by the young Margot Fonteyn. She falls in love with a human, a violinist, but quickly reverts to type when she kills a caged bird, then runs off with the other cats. The violinist chases them but falls to his death. Agathe returns to his body 'in animal devotion and human love'. Starting with a wonderfully evocative *Nocturne* (repeated later), the predominantly melancholy tone is dotted with lighter passages typical of Françaix, always keenly illustrative. Thierry Fischer conducts the Ulster Orchestra in compellingly idiomatic performances, vividly recorded.

Wind Quintets 1 & 2; (i) L'Heure du berger
*** MDG 603 0557-2. Kammervereinigung Berlin; (i) with Zichner

These Berliners put over Françaix's delightful *Wind Quintets* with great charm and delicacy. These are performances that radiate freshness and fun and, apart from the virtuosity of the performances, the naturalness of the recording and the balance are a continuing source of delight. *L'Heure du berger* is a piano and wind sextet, but this is as good in its different way. Delicious playing and enchantingly light-hearted music.

CHAMBER MUSIC

8 Bagatelles for Piano Quintet; Divertissement for Piano Trio; Dixtuor for Wind Quintet and String Quintet; Nonette after the Quintet, K.452, of Mozart; String Quartet; (i) Theme & Variations for Clarinet & Piano; (ii) Violin Sonatine
*** Disques Concord Erol ER 96004 (2). L'Octuor de France (members), composer (piano); with (i) Sajot; (ii) Naganuma

The Octuor de France under the direction of the composer, who also participates vividly on the piano, provide here an admirably representative collection of Françaix's chamber music written over five decades. The *String Quartet* (1934), like the well-known *Piano Concertino*, is small-scale but delightfully so, apparently slight, and certainly amiable, but with a touching *Andante* and a sparkling pizzicato *Scherzo*, full of syncopations, followed by a simpler *moto perpetuo* finale with a tranquil coda, with something of the luminosity of Ravel.

The early *Divertissement* was written like a concerto grosso a year later, but here, in the 1974 revision, a piano replaces the orchestral ripieno and the result is delightfully insouciant. The bustling finale is very French in its uninhibited animation, yet the *Andante* again has a gentle inner feeling, which is to return touchingly in the last movement before the closing whirlwind.

The violin *Sonatine* (1934) has a will-o'-the-wisp precocity, yet once more there is an underlying lyrical tractability. A set of variations as its centrepiece produces a kaleidoscope of unpredictable moods and much dashing bravura from both participants. Similarly, the *Clarinet Variations* bring a series of brief, spirited vignettes, full of charm, with the witty *Tempo di Valzer* particularly catchy.

Turning now to the pair of late works, we find the subdivided first movement of the *Dixtuor* (1987) opening with a seductively lazy *Larghetto tranquillo*, then moving into a similarly easy-going *Allegro*. The lightweight Scherzo chortles in 3/8 time and almost becomes a waltz, and the finale combines pastoral and folksy elements. The *Eight Bagatelles* of 1980 are in the composer's kaleidoscopic vignette style, and include two rather spare but expressive solo movements for viola and cello, before the penultimate poignant graduated crescendo in which all the participants gradually join, with the composer's skittish mood reappearing in the finale.

The *Nonette* is a fairly straightforward transcription of Mozart's *Piano and Wind Quintet*, K.452, for four wind instruments and string quintet, including a double bass. Françaix takes some liberties with the original, but the Mozartian spirit remains predominant, and there is plenty of charm. All the performances here are of the highest order, and the recording too is first class. But this is a set to be dipped into rather than taken in a single draught.

FRANCK, César (1822–90)

(i) *Le Chasseur maudit*; (ii) *Les Eolides*; (i) *Psyché*; *Rédemption*; (i; iii) *Nocturne*
(N) (B) *** Australian DG Eloquence (ADD) 476 2800. (i) O de Paris, Barenboim; (ii) SRO, Ansermet; (iii) Ludwig

What a good idea to gather together Barenboim's 1976 Franck recordings, yet not include the obvious *Symphony* (which was not one of his recording successes) instead of the rarer works here. *Rédemption* is given a splendidly convincing performance, with glorious brass antiphonies. *Le Chasseur maudit* opens with a most evocative Sunday morning ambience, and the devilish chase which follows, with its arresting horn calls, is vividly exciting. The orchestral sections of *Psyché* are richly done, showing real *tendresse*, and the relatively simple and brief *Nocturne*, beautifully sung by Christa Ludwig, makes a

beguiling bonus. The 1967 sound for Ansermet's *Les Eolides* is even more vivid, a work that suits him well, with much expressive feeling in the ebb and flow of the string writing of this haunting piece.

Symphonic Variations for Piano & Orchestra

🞉 ⬤ (B) *** Decca (ADD) 433 628-2. Curzon, LPO, Boult –
GRIEG: *Concerto* ***; SCHUMANN: *Concerto* **(*)
(M) *** Decca (ADD) 466 376-2. Curzon, LPO, Boult –
BRAHMS: *Piano Concerto 1*; LITOLFF: *Scherzo* ***
*** Sup. SU 3714-2. Moravec, Prague Philh. O, Bělohlávek –
BEETHOVEN: *Piano Concerto 4* ***; RAVEL: *Piano Concerto in G* **(*)
(BB) **(*) Naxos 8.550754. Thiollier, Nat. SO of Ireland, De Almeida – FAURE: *Ballade*; D'INDY: *Symphonie sur un chant montagnard français* **(*)

Clifford Curzon's 1959 recording of the Franck *Variations* has stood the test of time; even after four decades there is no finer version. It is an engagingly fresh reading, as notable for its impulse and rhythmic felicity as for its poetry. The vintage Decca recording is naturally balanced and has been transferred to CD without loss of bloom. The Grieg *Concerto* coupling is hardly less desirable, and there is also an alternative coupling with Brahms and Litolff, reissued in Decca's 'Legends' series.

François-Joël Thiollier shows imagination, and the orchestral playing is perfectly acceptable without being in any way distinguished. All the same, many will find it tempting at this price.

As in his transparent account of the Beethoven *G major Concerto*, Moravec's ability to convey expressive warmth without exaggeration comes out in the Franck *Symphonic Variations*, with the improvisatory writing for the soloist sounding totally natural and spontaneous in free rubato. The faster variations bring bright, clear textures, not just in the piano part but also in the orchestral writing, with Bělohlávek drawing the most responsive playing from the orchestra he founded.

(i) *Symphonic Variations for Piano & Orchestra* with *Prélude, choral et fugue*

(B) *** RCA 2CD (ADD) 74321 846062 (2). Rubinstein, (i) Symphony of the Air, Wallenstein – CHABRIER: *Pièces pittoresques: Scherzo-valese*; DEBUSSY: *Estampes*, etc.; FAURE: *Nocturne 3*; RAVEL: *Valses nobles et sentimentales*, etc.; SAINT-SAENS: *Concerto 2* ***
(N) (B) *** Australian Decca Eloquence (ADD) 476 235-2. De Larrocha, LPO, Frühbeck de Burgos – FAURE: *Fantasie* ***; RAVEL: *Piano Concertos in G and for the Left Hand* ***

Rubinstein's fine, 1958 recording of the *Symphonic Variations* (the first in stereo) has refinement and charm, yet his bravura tightens the structure while his warmth and freedom prevent it from seeming hard or in any way aggressive. The 1968 recording has a warm atmosphere. The present RCA Double also includes his persuasive piano version of the *Prélude, choral et fugue*.

The Spanish interpreters, Alicia de Larrocha and Frühbeck de Burgos, provide a reading that (perhaps surprisingly) brings out the French delicacy of the *Variations* more than usual. It is most enjoyable, very well recorded (1972), and makes a very welcome return to circulation in this very recommendable anthology.

(i) *Symphonic Variations for Piano & Orchestra;* (ii)
Symphony in D min.; Les Eolides; (iii) *Violin Sonata in A;*
(iv) (Piano) *Prélude, choral et fugue;* (v) (Organ) *Cantabile
in B; Choral 2; Pièce héroïque in B min.;* (vi) *Panis angelicus*
(B) **(*) Ph. (ADD) Duo 442 296-2 (2). (i) Bucquet, Monte
   Carlo Op. O, Capolongo; (ii) Concg. O, Otterloo; (iii)
   Grumiaux, Hajdu; (iv) del Pueyo; (v) Cocherau (organ of
   Notre-Dame de Paris); (vi) Carreras

Although the performances are variable, this Philips Duo set is
certainly worth its asking price. Its highlights are Otterloo's
splendid (1964) account of the *Symphony* (plus *Les Eolides*)
and the Grumiaux/Hajdu performance of the *Violin Sonata*
(see below). Otterloo's reading of the *Symphony* has tremendous thrust and its romantic urgency is impossible to resist
when the orchestral playing is so assured. *Les Eolides* is a
welcome bonus. Marie-Françoise Bucquet gives a perfectly
satisfactory account of the *Symphonic Variations*, and Carreras
sings his heart out in *Panis angelicus*. But del Pueyo's piano
contribution is a routine one and Cocherau's organ pieces are
also unmemorable, not helped by wheezily unflattering sound.

Symphony in D min.

☙ ✿ (M) *** RCA (ADD) **SACD** 82876 67897-2. Chicago
   SO, Monteux – STRAVINSKY: *Petrushka* ***
(M) *** DG (IMS) (ADD) 449 720-2. Berlin RSO, Maazel –
   MENDELSSOHN: *Symphony 5* ***
*** HM HMC 901771. O des Champs-Elysées, Herreweghe –
   FAURE: *Requiem* **(*)
(M) (***) Teldec mono 8573 83025-2. Concg. O, Mengelberg
   – DVORAK: *Symphony 9 (From the New World)* (***)
** Australian Decca Eloquence (ADD) 460 505-2. Cleveland
   O, Maazel – BIZET: *L'Arlésienne: Suites 1-2; Jeux
   d'enfants* ***

(i) *Symphony in D min.; Le Chasseur maudit;* (ii)
Symphonic Variations for Piano & Orchestra
(N) (B) **(*) RCA 82876 65833-2. (i) Boston SO, Munch; (ii)
   Pennario, Boston Pops O, Fiedler

Symphony in D min.; Le Chasseur maudit
(B) **(*) EMI Red Line 5 73235-2. Phd. O, Muti

Symphony in D min.; Les Eolides
(BB) **(*) Warner Apex 0927 41372-2. NYPO, Masur

Symphony in D min.; Les Eolides; (i) Symphonic Variations
for Piano & Orchestra
*** Chan. 9875. (i) Lortie; BBC PO, Tortelier

Symphony in D min.; Psyché: Four Orchestral Extracts
*** Avie AV 003. Strasburg PO, Latham-König

Monteux exerts a unique grip on this highly charged Romantic
symphony, and his control of the continuous ebb and flow of
tempo and tension is masterly, so that any weaknesses of
structure in the outer movements are disguised. The splendid
playing of the Chicago orchestra is ever responsive to the
changes of mood, and the most recent remastering for SACD
brings a further improvement; indeed, now the quality reflects
the acoustics of Chicago's Orchestra Hall in the same way as
the Reiner recordings, with textures full-bodied and glowing,
without loss of detail. The newest coupling is Monteux's
uniquely authoritative 1962 Boston recording of *Petrushka*.

With brilliantly full Chandos recording enhancing Tortelier's warm, urgent reading of the *Symphony*, this Chandos
CD makes an outstanding recommendation for Franck's two
most popular orchestral works, an ideal coupling not as

common as one might expect. The evocative tone-poem, *Les
Eolides*, inspired by a poem of Leconte de Lisle, light and
fanciful in its luminously scored evocation of the breezes of
heaven, makes an attractive bonus. In the *Symphony*, with
speeds far faster than usual, making the overall timing over
five minutes less than with such rivals as Chailly and Karajan,
Tortelier totally avoids the heaviness and sentimentality that
can afflict this work. In the central *Allegretto*, after his urgent
account of the first movement, Tortelier adopts a conventional tempo, with fine gradations of dynamic and a slightly
raw-sounding cor anglais adding to the freshness. In the
finale Tortelier is more distinctive than anywhere, with his
fast speed for the *Allegro non troppo* challenging the players of
the BBC Philharmonic to produce exciting rather than genial
results. Louis Lortie is the excellent soloist in the *Symphonic
Variations*, spontaneously poetic in the slow sections, sparkling and light in the scherzando finale.

Munch's 1957 performance of the *Symphony in D minor*
was always among the finest ever recorded. It is held together
very tautly. But it suffered – as it still does – from the internal
balance of the orchestra, which lets the trumpets (with a
nasal edge to their tone) coarsen the texture of the loud
moments. Otherwise the warm Boston acoustics are heard to
good effect, although in the slow movement the harp is very
forward. The finale begins with tremendous élan, and the
quotations from previous movements are not allowed to halt
the onward flow of the music. *Le Chasseur maudit*, with its
eight horns (recorded five years later), is still one of the most
exciting performances of this rarity on disc and here sounds
spectacular: the horn calls come over arrestingly. The *Symphonic Variations* are brilliantly played by Leonard Pennario,
and if Fiedler's support is strong rather than subtle this is still
very enjoyable. A thoroughly worthwhile reissue.

Jan Latham-König's account of the Franck *Symphony* is the
finest to have appeared for some years. It is superbly played by
the Strasbourg orchestra, but the interpretation is by no means
conventional. Latham-König daringly uses constantly varying
tempi and the widest dynamic range. His reading is wayward
but full of warmth, and he keeps a splendid grip on the structure; the passionate outburst of excitement as the secondary
theme swings into the listener's presence is visceral. The *Allegretto* makes a gentle, serene interlude; but the forward sweep
of the finale is again interrupted as earlier themes are recalled,
and the very close proves a most satisfying culmination. He
then offers Franck's second orchestral version of *Psyché* (omitting the chorus), which is essentially a tone-poem in four
sections. The radiant opening (*Le Sommeil de Psyché*), rapturously phrased on the clarinet, is followed by the most lustrous
string-playing, which languorously captures the music's sensuous evocation. After the 'awakening breezes' of what acts as a
Scherzo, the thrilling climax of the third section, *Le Jardin
d'Eros*, is later to be ardently capped by the strings in a mood of
'ravishing luxuriance and ecstatic fulfilment', to quote Julian
Haylock's sleeve-note. The recording is spaciously spectacular
– very much in the demonstration bracket.

Maazel's DG account is beautifully shaped, both in its
overall structure and in incidental details. He adopts a fairly
brisk tempo in the slow movement, which, surprisingly
enough, greatly enhances its poetry and dignity; his finale is
also splendidly vital. The work gains enormously from strong
control and deliberate understatement, as well as from the
refinement of tone and phrasing which mark this recording, for
there is no lack of excitement. The recording, admirably well
blended and balanced, is enhanced in this new CD transfer
for DG's 'Originals'.

Offered as an unusual but apt coupling for the Fauré *Requiem*, Herreweghe's reading of the Franck *Symphony* – written during the same period – is quite different in style. Generally urgent speeds add to the freshness and clarity brought by period instruments – the only version so far to use them – with sentimentality completely avoided. Clear, warm sound to match.

Masur creates a sound-world with the New York Philharmonic which is totally different from that achieved by his predecessor, Zubin Mehta. The performances of both *Les Eolides* and the *Symphony* are very fine, sensitively shaped and with the architecture held together well. All the same, Masur's account of the *Symphony* does not generate quite the same excitement and blazing conviction that Monteux brought to it, and it does not displace existing recommendations. Moreover, even at bargain price, it offers rather less than top value with a playing time of only 48 minutes.

Muti's is a strongly committed but unsentimental reading. The cor anglais solo in the *Allegretto* is most beautiful and the finale is particularly refreshing in its directness. *Le Chasseur maudit* is strongly presented, and the 1983 recording, robust and vivid, is certainly improved in its CD format, generally well integrated and among EMI's better Philadelphia records made in the 1980s, but there is a degree of glare on the otherwise brilliant digital recording.

Maazel's Decca account is exciting and brilliantly played and recorded, but a lack of lyrical tenderness robs the work of some of its more appealing qualities. The rich melody of the second subject finds Maazel introducing tenutos, which in so clipped and precise a performance seem obtrusive. Maazel's earlier account with the Berlin Radio Orchestra on DG is in almost every way preferable.

When Mengelberg took up his appointment at the Amsterdam Concertgebouw in 1895, both the Franck *Symphony* and the *New World* were new music, and although the Franck had been composed in 1888 it was not published until the mid-1890s, when it soon appeared at a Concertgebouw concert. Mengelberg conducted it with an enormous lyrical ardour and gets such responsive playing from his wartime orchestra that criticism is almost silenced. Bryan Crimp's transfer reveals a sound that is extraordinarily vivid and rich for its period. Of course, the same agogic mannerisms that are so characteristic of this conductor are in evidence, but we have to say that such is the dramatic fire and fervour of this playing that most listeners will surely be willing to take them in their stride.

CHAMBER MUSIC

Cello Sonata in A (trans. of *Violin Sonata*)

(BB) *** Warner Apex 0927 40599-2. Noras, Rigutto –
   DEBUSSY; FAURE: *Cello Sonatas* ***
(N) (B) *** EMI Gemini (ADD) 5 82633 (2). Du Pré,
   Barenboim – BRAHMS: *Sonatas 1 & 2* *(*); CHOPIN:
   Sonata **(*)
**(*) CRD (ADD) CRD 3391. Cohen, Vignoles (with DVORAK:
   Rondo) – GRIEG: *Cello Sonata* **(*)

Franck's *Violin Sonata* in its original form emerges as a strikingly brilliant work. Inevitably when translated to the cello it is mellower, less extrovert, but its originality of structure, based on strikingly memorable material, is underlined all the more.

Arto Noras's performance is as good as any, particularly at this competitive price. He is an elegant player of much finesse, and both the Debussy and Fauré sonatas come off well.

Du Pré and Barenboim also give a fine, mature, deeply

expressive reading of a richly satisfying work, beautifully recorded. However, their couplings are uneven in appeal.

Robert Cohen gives a firm and strong rendering of the Franck *Sonata* in its cello version, splendidly incisive and dashing in the second-movement *Allegro*, but the recording is more limited than one expects from CRD, a little shallow. The addition of the Dvořák *G minor Rondo*, Op. 94, makes a pleasing bonus.

Flute Sonata in A (trans. of *Violin Sonata*)

(M) *** RCA (ADD) 09026 61615-2. Galway, Argerich –
   PROKOFIEV; REINECKE: *Flute Sonatas* ***
(N) *** EMI 557 813-2. Pahud, Le Sage – STRAUSS: *Flute
   Sonata* ***; WIDOR: *Suite, Op. 34* ***

Although the prospect of hearing the Franck *Violin Sonata* arranged for flute may strike you as unappealing, it is surprising how well this music responds to James Galway's transcription and his sweet-toned virtuosity. Argerich is in absolutely superb form here, and the recording, if just a trifle close, is truthful, pleasingly fresh and well defined. An outstanding reissue.

Pahud also gives a commanding performance, using a wide tonal and dynamic range (partly a question of recording balance), and Eric Le Sage's positive qualities come out impressively. That transcription is well matched by the comparable transcription of the Strauss *Violin Sonata*, supplemented by the delightful four movements of the Widor *Suite* – the composer's most popular work outside the organ repertory – making a winning disc, although choice here will probably depend on couplings.

Piano Quintet in F min.

(BB) *** Naxos 8.553645. Levinas, Quatuor Ludwig –
   CHAUSSON: *Quartet in C min.* ***
(***) Testament mono SBT 1077. Aller, Hollywood Qt –
   SHOSTAKOVICH: *Piano Quintet* (***)

Michaël Levinas and the Quatuor Ludwig give a very impressive account of 'the king of piano quintets' (the phrase is Tournemire's). This is a very competitive account which is well worth its modest asking price. Levinas is a sensitive player, and those who are attracted by the enterprising Chausson coupling should consider the present disc. Both the playing and the recorded sound are of a high standard.

Edward Sackville-West and Desmond Shawe-Taylor, the authors of *The Record Guide*, spoke of the Aller/Hollywood version five decades ago as a 'clean-limbed performance ... the players' attack is extraordinarily vivid and the instrumental balance beautifully maintained'. Even if there is no mistaking the (1953) mono sound as being of its time, the performance has such eloquence and power that the music leaps out of the speakers with a vibrant intensity.

Viola Sonata in A (transcription of *Violin Sonata*)

*** Chan. 8873. Imai, Vignoles – VIEUXTEMPS: *Viola
   Sonata*, etc. ***
*** Simax PSC 1126. Tomter, Gimse – VIEUXTEMPS: *Viola
   Sonata*, etc. ***

An all-Belgian coupling from these two violists, Imai and Tomter. The Franck loses a certain amount of its flamboyance and passion, and gains in a kind of measured dignity. Both performances listed above are exemplary if you want it in this form. There is absolutely nothing to choose between them; both are commanding performances and have an impressive eloquence.

Violin Sonata in A

☛━🗝 ✿ (M) *** Decca (ADD) 460 006-2. Chung, Lupu –
DEBUSSY: *Violin Sonata* *** ✿; CHAUSSON: *Poème* ***

(N) (M) *** DG 477 5448 (2). Mintz, Bronfman (with *Recital
of Encores* by ALBÉNIZ; COUPERIN; GLAZUNOV;
GRANADOS; KREISLER; WEBER; WIENIAWSKI) –
DEBUSSY; FRANCK; RAVEL: *Violin Sonatas* ***

(N) *** EMI 557679-2. Chang, Vogt – SAINT-SAENS: *Violin
Sonata No. 1;* RAVEL: *Violin Sonata* ***

*** EMI 5 56815-2. Perlman, Argerich – BEETHOVEN: *Violin
Sonata 9 in A (Kreutzer)* ***

*** DG (IMS) 445 880-2. Dumay, Pires – DEBUSSY: *Violin
Sonata in G min.;* RAVEL: *Berceuse,* etc. ***

(M) *** DG (IMS) (ADD) 431 469-2. Danczowska, Zimerman
– SZYMANOWSKI: *Mythes,* etc. *** ✿

**(*) EMI 5 57505-2 [5 57497-2]. Capucon, Gurning –
RACHMANINOV: *Cello Sonata* **(*)

(M) **(*) Ph. (ADD) 426 384-2. Grumiaux, Sebök – FAURE:
Sonatas ***

(N) (B) ** Decca 2-CD 475 6709. Bell, Thibaudet –
CHAUSSON: *Concert for Piano, Violin & String Quartet;*
DEBUSSY; FAURE: *Violin Sonatas* **; RAVEL: *Piano Trio*
***

Kyung Wha Chung and Radu Lupu give a glorious account,
full of natural and not over-projected eloquence, and most
beautifully recorded. The slow movement has marvellous
repose and the other movements have a natural exuberance
and sense of line that carry the listener with them. The 1977
recording is enhanced on CD and, with an apt Chausson
coupling, this reissue remains very desirable indeed.

On DG, Shlomo Mintz and Yefim Bronfman give a
superbly confident account of the *Sonata*. It is impeccably
played, with wonderfully true intonation from the violinist
and highly accomplished support from the pianist. They are
splendidly recorded, and the couplings are very recommendable too.

Sarah Chang and Lars Vogt also make a winning partnership and give a commanding account of the *Sonata*. Vogt
proves particularly impressive in the challenging piano part.
This is probably one of the best versions to have appeared for
some time, and if the coupling appeals (and it should)
readers need not hesitate. Good recorded sound too.

As in the Beethoven *Kreutzer Sonata*, Perlman and Argerich challenge each other to thrilling effect in this live EMI
recording, made in Saratoga in 1999. Here, in a less formally
structured sonata, their spontaneous interplay makes for an
apt feeling of rhapsodic improvisation. The very opening
finds Argerich deeply reflective, before Perlman launches into
the *Allegro* at a far faster tempo. Some may resist the expressive freedom, whether in phrasing, rubato or in fluctuations
of speed, but the magnetism will for most be irresistible, even
when the playing is not immaculate, as in the second-
movement *Allegro*. As in the Beethoven coupling, audience
noises are intrusive at times.

The distinguished partnership of Augustin Dumay and
Maria João Pires offers as assured and powerful an interpretation of Franck's indestructible *Sonata* as any now in the
catalogue. They have a firm grip on line and combine both
intellectual conviction and tenderness of feeling. The DG
recording is more than acceptable, and readers wanting this
particular coupling need not hold back.

Kaja Danczowska's account of the Franck is distinguished
by a natural sense of line and great sweetness of tone, and she
is partnered superbly by Krystian Zimerman. Indeed, in

terms of dramatic fire and strength of line, this version can
hold its own alongside the finest, and it is perhaps marginally
better balanced than the Kyung Wha Chung and Radu Lupu
recording.

Renaud Capucon and Alexandre Gurning give a big-scale,
warmly expressive reading of the Franck *Violin Sonata*. If not
perhaps a first choice, it is magnetically made the more
dramatic by being recorded live. Well coupled with the Rachmaninov *Cello Sonata*, played by Capucon's brother, Gautier.

Grumiaux's account, if less fresh than Chung's, has nobility
and warmth to commend it. He is slightly let down by his
partner, who is not as imaginative as Lupu in the more poetic
moments, including the hushed opening bars.

Joshua Bell and Jean-Yves Thibaudet bring no want of
passion and an impressive technical address to the *Sonata*.
Theirs is an outgoing performance that would fire enthusiasm
in the heat of the concert hall. But while it would be quite
unjust to call them shallow, it must be said that their insights
are not as penetrating as those of some of their distinguished
rivals, and the acoustic in which they are recorded is less than
ideal, for there is too little ambience to help them.

ORGAN MUSIC

Andantino in E (arr. Vierne); *Cantabile; Chorals 2–3; Pièce
héroïque; Prélude, fugue et variation, Op. 18*

*** Chan. 8891. Kee (Cavaillé-Coll organ of Basilica de Santa
Maria del Coro, San Sebastian)

The Dutch composer-organist Piet Kee omits the *Choral 1*, for
which room could surely have been found, as the playing-
time is only 61 minutes 43 seconds; but, apart from this, there
can be few grumbles about his record. His interpretations
strike an excellent balance between expressive freedom and
scholarly rectitude.

*3 Chorals (in E; B min.; A min.); 3 Pièces (Fantaisie in A;
Cantabile; Pièce héroïque); 6 Pièces (Fantaisie 1 in C, Op. 16;
Grande pièce symphonique, Op. 17; Prélude, fugue et
variation, Op. 18; Pastorale, Op. 19; Prière, Op. 20; Final,
Op. 21)*

☛━🗝 ✿ (N) (BB) *** Warner Apex 2564 61428-2 (2). Alain
(Cavaillé-Coll organ of Saint-Etienne, Caen)

*3 Chorals (in E; B min.; A min.); 3 Pièces (Fantaisie in A;
Cantabile; Pièce héroïque); 6 Pièces (Fantaisie 1 in C; Grande
pièce symphonique; Prélude, fuge et variation; Pastorale;
Prière; Final) Opp. 16–21*

(N) (B) *** Cal. (ADD) CAL 5920/21. Isoir (Cavaillé-Coll
organ of Luçon Cathedral)

(N) (BB) *** Regis RRC 2054 (2). Bate

The two Apex CDs include all of Franck's most important
works for organ: the *Six pièces*, written between 1860 and
1862, the *Trois pièces* of 1878 and the *Trois chorals* of 1890, the
last year of the composer's life. Marie Claire Alain recorded
all these works on LP for Erato on a Cavaillé-Coll organ at
Lyons. Now she has returned to them, using an even finer
instrument at Caen. The Cavaillé-Coll organs are as closely
related to Franck's music as, say, Peter Pears's voice was to
Britten's. These new performances are even finer than the
earlier ones, full of spontaneous feeling, and the registration
brings some glorious sounds, notably in the Op. 16 *Fantaisie*,
the *Third Choral*, where the detail is quite remarkably clear,
and the exultant closing *Final*. The sympathy which this
player brings to this music and the authority of the results

give this survey a special claim on the allegiance of collectors, and the digital recording is superb, very much in the demonstration bracket.

André Isoir's performances are also recorded on a Cavaillé-Coll organ (in 1975), and very impressively too. His performances, with their improvisatory character, are just as authentic as Marie Claire Alain's and his recording justly won a Grand Prix du Disque. The *Grande pièce symphonique* is especially successful, the *Chorals* are appropriately cool, and the *Pièce héroïque* is also strikingly spontaneous. However, the digitally recorded Warner Apex set remains first choice on grounds of both excellence and economy.

Jennifer Bate plays the Danion-Gonzalez organ at Beauvais Cathedral and is given the benefit of an excellent digital recording. The spacious acoustic contributes an excellent ambience to the aural image, and Bate's brilliance is always put at the service of the composer. The *Pièce héroïque* seems rather well suited to the massive sounds which the Beauvais organ can command and all the music chosen here – the content of three CDs, previously available on the Unicorn label – shows the instrument to good advantage. The only small criticism is that Bate rushes the opening of the *A minor Choral*, some of whose detail does not register in this acoustic at the speed. However, this is a splendid bargain issue by any standards.

Choral 2

*** Chan. 9785. Tracey (organ of Liverpool Cathedral), BBC PO, Tortelier – GUILMANT: *Symphony 2 for Organ & Orchestra*; WIDOR: *Symphony 3 for Organ & Orchestra* ***

Franck's *Second Choral* is an expansive *Passacaglia* which reaches a great climax and then gently fades away in the valedictory closing bars. Although the Liverpool organ is not entirely right for it (one needs better definition), Ian Tracey's performance can hardly be faulted, and the result is nothing if not spectacular, enough to make a suitable encore for the two concertante works.

PIANO MUSIC

Choral 3; Danse lente; Grand caprice; Les Plaintes d'une poupée; Prélude, aria et final; Prélude, choral et fugue

*** Hyp. CDA 66918. Hough

Stephen Hough's impressive *Prélude, choral et fugue* is worthy to rank alongside Murray Perahia's account (currently withdrawn), and no praise could be higher. In addition to the piano music, Hough gives us his own transcription of the *Third* of the organ *Chorals*, which in his hands sounds as if it had been written for the piano, so splendidly is it played. A most distinguished record in every way.

Eglogue (Hirtengedicht), Op. 3; Les Plaintes d'une poupée; Prélude, aria et final; Prélude, choral et fugue; Premier grand caprice, Op. 5

(BB) *** Naxos 8.554484. Wass

Ashley Wass hails from Lincolnshire and came to international attention as first-prize winner of the 1997 World Piano Competition. Both the *Eglogue*, meditative with a massive central climax, and the *Grande caprice*, a flamboyant showpiece, were written when Franck was in his early twenties. What Wass brings out in those and the major items is the technical brilliance of the keyboard writing. He uses a ravishing range of tone, lightening the *Prélude, aria et final* with a flowing speed in the *Prélude* and a mysterious opening for the

Final. The two lyrical miniatures are charmingly done, but most impressive is the finest of Franck's piano works, the *Prélude* and *Choral*, leading to a powerful, clean-cut account of the *Fugue*, which makes one want to hear Wass in Bach. Heavy *fortissimos* tend to clang – partly the eager pianist's fault – but otherwise the sound is full and vivid.

VOCAL MUSIC

Psyché (symphonic fragments)

(***) Testament mono SBT1128. René Duclos Ch., Paris Conservatoire O, Cluytens – RAVEL: *Daphnis et Chloé* ***

It is logical that André Cluytens's sensitive account of *Daphnis* should be coupled with Franck's most sumptuous and imaginative score. Both are inspired by classical mythology. The 1954 recording is mono but the transfer is of high quality and no collector will fail to respond.

FRANKEL, Benjamin (1906–73)

(i) Viola Concerto, Op. 45; (ii) Violin Concerto (In Memory of the Six Million), Op. 24; (iii) Serenade Concertante for Piano Trio & Orchestra, Op. 37

(M) *** CPO CPO 999 422-2. (i) Dean; (ii) Hoelscher; (iii) Smith, Lale, Emmerson; Queensland SO, Albert

The *Violin Concerto* comes from 1951 when the holocaust was still a vivid and horrific memory. Its emotional core is the expressive and eloquent slow movement. Yet apart from its elegiac centre, the overwhelming impression the work leaves is powerful and positive, a testament to the strength of the human spirit. The *Viola Concerto* is much later and is hardly less memorable. Frankel's lyricism and his musical ingenuity are always in evidence. The composer describes the *Serenata concertante*, which is for piano trio and orchestra, as 'a street scene' in which passing traffic, a distant jazz band, lovers dancing and much else besides can be heard. It wears its serial organization lightly. Both Ulf Hoelscher and Brett Dean are impressive soloists in the two concertos and the Queensland orchestra respond with supportive playing. The recording engineers serve these fine players faithfully and produce an impressive and wide-ranging sound. Strongly recommended.

Film music from: The Curse of the Werewolf; Footsteps in the Fog; The Importance of Being Earnest; The Night of the Iguana; Trottie True; The Years Between

(BB) **(*) CPO 999 809-2. Queensland SO, Albert

Perhaps the most enjoyable music here is the lively opening and closing theme to the 1952 film of *The Importance of Being Earnest*, which instantly raises a smile. The slow section in the middle is not quite as memorable, and that reflects the main reservation of this disc: much of the music is rather slow, if often brooding, and there are few really striking melodies. Even so, the short *Pastoral* from *The Curse of the Werewolf* is (believe it or not) quite memorable, while *Trottie True* features frothy music in the best light-music tradition. There are imaginative orchestral effects in the sombre score to *The Night of the Iguana*, which includes the wistful *Hanna and Shannon Theme*. That said, the performances and recording are very sympathetic, and the documentation is generous. But this CD will appeal mainly to admirers of film music rather than to those who appreciate the orchestral repertoire and powerfully conceived symphonies for which this composer is best known.

Symphonies 1–8; Overtures; Mephistoteles Serenade and Dance

(B) *** CPO 999 661-24. Queensland SO, Albert

Symphonies 1, Op. 33; 5, Op. 46; May Day Overture, Op. 22

*** CPO 999 240-2. Queensland SO, Albert

Benjamin Frankel is a master of the orchestra, and the *First Symhony* (1959) leaves no doubt that he was also a master symphonist. The music develops organically; Frankel has something of the strength of Sibelius combined with a Mahlerian anguish, and his serialism, like that of Frank Martin, never undermines tonal principles. The *Fifth Symphony*, too, is a well-argued and impressive score. The Queensland orchestra play with dedication, and the performances of both symphonies and the inventive *May Day Overture* are very well recorded too. However, this has now been withdrawn as a separate issue.

Symphonies 4, Op. 44; 6, Op. 49; Mephistopheles' Serenade and Dance, Op. 25

*** CPO 999 242-2. Queensland SO, Albert

The *Fourth Symphony* is arguably one of the very finest of Frankel's works. It has a more restrained palette than its predecessors, yet its invention is both powerful and distinctive. The Scherzo has a memorable delicacy and the elegiac finale has great eloquence. The *Sixth* is dark and powerfully argued and gets very persuasive advocacy from the Queensland orchestra under Werner Andreas Albert, and very fine recording. However, this is no longer available as a separate issue.

Symphonies 7, Op. 50; 8, Op. 53; A Shakespearean Overture, Op. 29; Overture to a Ceremony, Op. 51

*** CPO 999 243-2. Queensland SO, Albert

This issue completes the cycle of Benjamin Frankel's symphonies. The *Seventh* was commissioned by the Peter Stuyvesant Foundation for the LSO, who gave its première under André Previn in 1970. A thoughtful and searching piece, it was underrated at the time and we now have the opportunity of getting to know it for ourselves. The opening of the *Eighth* (1971) is vintage Frankel and the work as a whole has a sense of logic and purpose that marks his best music. All the same, those starting to investigate the cycle should not begin here; the *First* and *Fourth* are better entry points into Frankel's world. The resourceful and imaginative *Shakespearean Overture* was first given at the Edinburgh Festival by the National Youth Orchestra of Great Britain under Walter Susskind, and it is a welcome addition to the Frankel discography. As can be seen all eight symphonies are now available in a box.

Bagatelles for 11 Instruments (Cinque pezzi notturni), Op. 35; Clarinet Quintet, Op. 28; Clarinet Trio, Op. 10; Pezzi pianissimi, Op. 41 (for clarinet, cello & piano); Early Morning Music

(BB) *** CPO 999 384-2. Dean, Australian String Qt (members); Queensland Symphony Chamber Players

The *Clarinet Quintet* is beautifully crafted and is expertly played by these Australian artists. The *Clarinet Trio* was composed in 1940, but Frankel's musical language and fluent invention are already in place. The short but disturbing *Pezzi pianissimi* are thoughtful, gentle pieces which resonate in the memory afterwards, as do the *Bagatelles for Eleven Instruments* of 1959. This work is serial but not 'atonal' – much in the same way as Frank Martin's is. Excellent playing and recording make this another most desirable introduction to a much-neglected and underrated composer whose work is at last gaining ground.

Clarinet Quintet, Op. 28

(BB) *** Hyp. Helios CDH 55105. Thea King, Britten Qt – COOKE: *Clarinet Quintet;* HOLBROOKE: *Eilean Shona;* HOWELLS: *Rhapsodic Quintet;* MACONCHY: *Clarinet Quintet* ***

Frankel's *Clarinet Quintet* (1956) was a BBC commission for the Cheltenham Festival. It is perhaps the least harmonically tractable work in Thea King's Helios anthology, but it communicates strongly in a performance as strong as this, especially the quirky central Scherzo, while the elegiac finale, written in memory of the distinguished clarinettist, Frederick Thurston, is utterly haunting.

FRESCOBALDI, Girolamo
(1583–1643)

KEYBOARD MUSIC

Primo libro di toccate (1616): excerpts. Il Secondo libro di toccata, canzoni, Versi d'hinni; Magnificat; Gagliarde, corrente: excerpts. Partite sopra l'aria della romanesca (1624); Aria di balletto (1637)

(BB) *** Virgin 2×1 5 61869-2 (2). Ross (harpsichord) – BACH: *Goldberg Variations* **(*)

Scott Ross here surveys the keyboard music of a composer whose music demands a free, improvisatory style of performance, of which Ross is obviously a master. Indeed, he presents this repertoire in a most appealing way, opening with four (very free) *Toccatas* from Book I. The excerpts from the Second Book are framed by two highly inventive sets of variations; the second is a rather engaging *Aria di balletto*, not unlike Handel's variations known as *The Harmonious Blacksmith*. Ross's easy bravura is particularly attractive here, and his Jean-Louis Val harpsichord is very vividly recorded. This now comes inexpensively coupled to Ross's lively set of Bach's *Goldberg Variations*.

Primo libro di Toccate (1616): excerpts: Capriccio del Soggetto scritto sopra l'Aria di Roggiero; Corrente quatro; Partita II sopra l'Aria di Monicha; Toccata prima. Secondo libro di Toccate: excerpts: Aria detto Balletto; Aria detta la Frescobalda; Toccata prima; Toccata decima; Toccata undecima

**(*) Audivis E 8654. Verlet

Frescobaldi's art is intensely personal and his highly expressive idiom makes him a particularly rewarding figure. Blandine Verlet offers four pieces from the *First Book of Toccatas* (1615) and five from the *Second* (1627), both republished and revised in 1637. The music is full of surprises and colour, and Verlet has a good feel for this repertoire. She uses an early instrument which may be Flemish and close to a Rückers; or it may possibly be a French copy of a Flemish instrument. The recording, which dates from the 1970s, places the instrument very far forward and it should be replayed at a low level setting.

VOCAL MUSIC

Fiori musicali: Messa della Madonna (Missa cum jubilo & Vesper)

(N) (M) *** DHM/BMG 05472 77345-2. Canticum, Erkens; Ghielmi (organ)

Frescobaldi published his *Fiori musicali* while in Venice in 1635, including the present Mass setting, which is one of three. It is written in the alternatim style, with the organ playing in alternation with the vocal text, the latter set by Frescobaldi in the simplest way, with its roots in plainsong. Here the organ pieces vary between toccatas, ricercares, canzonas and capriccios, and it is the *Capriccio sopra la Girolmeta* that closes the Mass after the Marian antiphon, *Ave Regina*. The performance here by Canticum (a vocal octet) directed by Christoph Erkens is of high quality, with the serenely melismatic vocal lines balancing beautifully with Lorenzo Ghielmi's organ voluntaries; the recording, made in the church of San Maurizio, in the primary Milan Monastery, is admirable.

Il primo libro de' madrigale a 5 (1608)
*** Opus 111 OP 30-133. Concerto Italiano, Alessandrini

Frescobaldi, born in Ferrara, was 25 when his first book of madrigals was published in 1608. They are songs about lovers, longing, admiring, often not daring to speak directly, about parting and loss, and always about passions unrequited. They produced a glorious stream of lyrical invention and a skill in construction remarkable in a composer at the outset of his career. Rinaldo Alessandrini and the Concerto Italiano have been winning golden opinions in this repertoire, and these delightful performances bear out their reputation for fine tuning and blending, and a richly expressive line. They not only give pleasure but should at last put this composer's name firmly in front of the public.

FRICKER, Peter Racine (1920–90)

Symphony 2, Op. 14
(M) (***) EMI mono 5 75789-2. RLPO, Pritchard – SIMPSON: *Symphony 1* (***); ROBIN ORR: *Symphony in One Movement* ***

Peter Racine Fricker (the Racine indicates that he claimed descent from the great French dramatist) studied with R. O. Morris and, after the war, with Mátyás Seiber. He made his breakthrough into the LP catalogue with this symphony which the Liverpool Philharmonic Orchestra commissioned for the 1951 Festival of Britain. Stronger in its sense of flow and logic than in endearing thematic ideas, it is a powerfully concentrated and well-argued work which enjoyed some success in the 1950s. In 1964 Fricker became Professor of Composition at the University of California at Santa Barbara, and he spent the remainder of his life there. As a result, his later works, including three more symphonies, his impressive cantata, *The Vision of Judgment*, and other choral works have received relatively little exposure in Britain, and his major works are unrepresented on CD. The transfer of the *Second Symphony* to CD together with the *First* of his contemporary, Robert Simpson, both written in 1951, is to be welcomed with enthusiasm, and the sound is remarkably fresh and well detailed.

FROBERGER, Johann (1616–67)

Froberger was a particularly interesting composer who, like so many of his contemporaries including his friend Schütz, was sent to study in Italy. He studied with Frescobaldi, becoming court organist in Vienna under Ferdinand III, and composed exclusively for the keyboard. He drew inspiration from the French style and visited both Paris and

London. His music is contemplative and often inward-looking

Keyboard Works, Volume 1: *Allemande, FbWV 635; Capriccio, FbWV 519; Fuga, FbWV 307; Partitas, FbWV 618a; 639–641 644–6; 652; Toccata 2nd Toni, FbWV 130*
(N) *** MDG 341 1186-2. Rampe (harpsichord, clavichord or organ)

Keyboard Works, Volume 2: *Allemande, FbWV 650; Capriccio, FbWV 503a; Partitas, FbWV 606a (Mayerin); 638, 642–3, 648 (Dolorosa); 649–51; Sarabande, FbWV 640; Toccata Quinti toni, FbWV 116a*
(N) *** MDG 341 1195-2. Rampe (harpsichord, clavichord or organ)

Strasburg Manuscript: 14 Harpsichord Suites
(N) *** CPO 999 750-2 (2). Rémy (harpsichord)

Froberger's *Partitas* or *Suites* for harpsichord, apart from their musical interest, are important historically in that in their make-up the composer pioneered the layout of the so-called 'French suite' to include the regular group of dance movements that Bach inherited – Allemande, Gigue, Courante, Sarabande and Gigue. Here those latter two movements regularly exchange places; sometimes Froberger chooses an expressive finale, at others a lively one. The Strasburg manuscript, copied by Michael Bulyowsky, a pupil and admirer of the composer, was recently discovered in the Dresden State Library. The music is very attractive indeed, as are the CPO performances, which are thoughtful, expressive and full of lively spontaneity. Rémy uses a modern copy of a Franco-Flemish instrument, which is beautifully recorded. This CPO set makes an admirable introduction to Froberger's keyboard suites and will give much satisfaction.

On MDG, Siegberg Rampe offers a wider selection of what is suggested are 'the unknown works', using for the most part a French copy of a Couchet harpsichord of 1679, and, for a few pieces in each volume, either a modern copy of a late-seventeenth-century clavichord or a suitable organ, which adds to the variety of his presentation. His keyboard style is more robust that Rémy's, certainly it is full of life, and he is very well recorded. But on the whole we find Rémy's performances more satisfying, although there is not a great deal in it.

Lamentation faite sur la mort très douloureuse de Sa Majesté Impériale, Ferdinand le troisième, An. 1657, FbWV 633; 4 Partitas: Auff Die Mayerin, FbWV 606; Lamento sopra la dolorosa pedita della Real Maestà di Ferdinando IV, FbWV 612; Méditation sur ma mort future, FbWV 629; Plainte faite à Londres pour passer la mélancolie, FbWV 630; Tombeau sur la mort de Monsieur Blancheroche, FbWV 632; 3 Toccatas (Book 2), *FbWV 101–3; 3 Toccatas* (Book 4), *FbWV 107–8; 112*
(N) (BB) *** Naxos 8.557472/73. Vartolo (harpsichord)

Lamentation sur la mort de Ferdinand III in F; Partitas (Suites) XVIII in G min.; XIX in C min.; XX in D; XXX in A min.; Toccatas II in D min.; IX in C; XIV in G; XVIII in F; Tombeau sur la Mort de M. Blancheroche in C min.
🎵 (B) *** HM HMA 1951372. Rousset (harpsichord)

Those wanting just a selection of this repertoire can turn either to Rousset on Harmonia Mundi or to Sergio Vartolo on Naxos, who also provides excellent and informative notes. He uses an Italian harpsichord for the *Toccatas* and a French instrument for the *Partitas*, *Lament* and the *Tombeau sur la mort de Monsieur Blancheroche*. Incidentally, the *Partita Auff Die Mayerin*, FbWV 606, included by both Vartolo and Rampe, is a piquant set of variations on a popular German song of the time. Vartolo plays with authority and flair, and conveys the spirit as well as the letter of this fascinating composer. The recording is very lifelike, though it needs to be played at a lower setting than normal.

Froberger composed almost solely for the keyboard; he published three major collections of his works: in 1646 and 1656 and, towards the end of that decade, a further undated Book of Capricci and Ricercari. The influence of his teacher, Frescobaldi, is apparent in the freedom of the writing: the *Toccatas* are often unpredictable, a factor that Christophe Rousset clearly relishes in his playing. He uses a restored (1652) Couchet double-manual harpsichord which suits all these works admirably in his hands. Its pitch (A392) brings a comparatively bright sonority which is very effective in the *Gigues*; but some listeners might like a more sonorous effect in the *Allemandes*. Yet Rousset's playing is both searching and imaginative, and he creates an expressive emphasis in the meditative *D major Suite* by taking the *Sarabande* quite slowly. In the *Lamentation for Ferdinand III* and *Tombeau for M. Blancheroche* (a famous lutenist and Froberger's great friend) he reveals considerable expressive poignancy, and the descending scale at the end of the latter piece probably pictures M. Blancheroche's fall down a flight of stairs (in 1652), before dying in the composer's arms. A fine and inexpensive introduction to the music of this remarkable French master.

FRÜHLING, Carl (1868–1937)

Clarinet Trio, Op. 114

*** RCA 09026 63504-2. Collins, Isserlis, Hough – BRAHMS: *Clarinet Trio*; SCHUMANN: *Märchenerzählungen*; *Träumerei* ***

It was the cellist Steven Isserlis who unearthed this warmly seductive trio for clarinet, cello and piano. Frühling was a composer writing against fashion in a frankly Brahmsian idiom which yet has strong purpose and individuality, built on memorable themes. The Schumann suite is a fine make-weight, with Isserlis tackling the viola part on the cello. Michael Collins and Stephen Hough, equally magnetic as recording artists, are ideal partners.

FRYE, Walter (died 1475)

Missa Flos Regalis; Song: Alas, alas

*** Signum SIGCD 015. Clerks' Group, Wickham (with ANON.: *Kyrie: Deus creator* from *Sarum Chant Pryncesse of Youthe*. BEDYNGHAM: *Myn hertis lust; Fortune alas; Mi very joy; So ys emprentid* ***) – PLUMMER: *Missa Sine nomine* ***

This enterprising and very rewarding Signum collection is entitled '*Brussels 5557*', as all the music is taken from a manuscript catalogued under that number, held in the Brussels Bibliothèque Royale. The presence of English music in an anthology which includes works by Du Fay confirms its importance, and indeed the *Missa Flos Regalis* is a remarkably individual setting. Frye's melismatic style is all his own, with the serene *Sanctus* followed by an even more beautiful *Agnus Dei*. We are then offered a group of memorable secular songs, including three by another virtually unknown composer,

John Bedyngham, which are equally individual, especially the delightful *So ys emprentid*, although Frye's *Alas, alas* is perhaps finest of all. The performances, as one anticipates from this splendid group, are dedicated and impressively secure. The recording too could hardly be bettered, nicely set back in a warm ambience.

Tut a par moy

*** Gaudeamus CDGAU 302. Clerks' Group, Wickham – JOSQUIN DESPREZ: *Motets; Missa Faisant regretz* ***

We still know very little about the hugely influential English composer, Walter Frye. Yet it is fascinating to discover that this touching three-part rondeau, *Tut a par moy* ('Everything comes to me alone: in order not to see me as sad as I could possibly be'), reached the ears of Josquin. He used a four-note motif from the song on which to base his *Missa faisant regretz*. But the rondeau is memorable in its own right and is beautifully sung here.

FURTWÄNGLER, Wilhelm
(1886–1954)

Symphonic Concerto: Adagio

(**) Testament mono SBT 1170. Fischer, BPO, Furtwängler – BRAHMS: *Piano Concerto 2* (**(*))

(N) (BB) (**) Naxos mono 8.110879. Fischer, BPO, Furtwängler – BEETHOVEN: *Symphony 5*; WAGNER: *Parsifal: Preludes* (***)

Edwin Fischer's sympathetic account of the *Adagio solenne* from the B minor *Symphonic Concerto* is available on both Naxos and Testament. While Mark Obert-Thorn's Naxos transfer is not as full-blooded as Paul Baily's, it is eminently serviceable if the couplings are preferred. The *Adagio* is a noble piece, with an autumnal feel to it. It may not be great music, but with its echoes of Bruckner leading to passionate climaxes it makes agreeable listening in the 1939 studio recording, even with limited sound.

GABRIELI, Andrea (1510–86)

(i) *Ricercar a 4 del primo tuono; Ricercar a 4 del sesto tuono; Ricercar a 4 del duodecimo tuono; Ricercar per sonar a 8.* (ii) (Organ) *Canzon alla Francese: Petit Jacquet; Intonazione del sesto tuono; Madrigal: Ancor che co'l partire; Ricercar del settimo tuono.* (i; ii; iii) *Missa Pater peccavi; Motets: (i; iii) De profondis clamavi; (iv; i) O sacrum convivium*

*** Hyp. CDA 67167. (i) His Majestys Sackbutts & Cornets; Roberts (organ); (iii) His Majestys Consort of Voices, Roberts, (iv) with Pickard

It is good to have first-class performances of some of Andrea Gabrieli's *Ricercari* on record, even if they are less spectacular and, indeed, less varied than those of his nephew, Giovanni. The Mass setting (based on Andrea's own motet, *Pater peccavi in coelum*) settles for very simple counterpoint but springs to life in the *Sanctus*.

The solo motet, *O sacrum convivium*, is simply and beautifully sung by Anna Sarah Pickard, whose vocal line is integrated within the 'accompaniment' by four sackbuts. The organ interludes are played by the group's director, Timothy Roberts, and the concert closes with the eight-part *Ricercar per sonar*, which is rather impressive. Excellent recording in a well-judged acoustic.

Madrigals: *Amami, vita mia, ch'io t'amo anchora; Ancor che col partire; Asia felice hor ben posso chiamarmi; Caro dolce ben mio, perche fuggire; Chi'nde darà la bose al solfizar; Del gran Tuonante la sorella e moglie; Felici d'Adria e dilettose rive; Hor ch'a noi torna la stagion novella; Io mi sento morire; I'vo piangendo i miei passati tempi; Lasso, Amor mi trasporta ov'io non voglio; Laura soave, vita di mia vita; Mentr'io vi miro, vorrei pur sapere; Mirami, vita mia, miram'un poco; O beltà rara, o santi modi adorni; O passi sparsi, o pensier e pronti; Sassi, palae, sabbion, del Adrian lio; Sento, sent'un rumor ch'al ciel estolle; Voi non volete, donna.* **Instrumental Pieces:** *Amami, vita mia, ch'io t'amo anchora; Dunque il comun poter; Fuor fuori a sì bel canto*

(N) *** Chan. 0697. I Fagiolini, Hollingworth (with GIOVANNI GABRIELI: Madrigals: *Sacri di Giove augei sacre Fenici* (2 versions). Instrumental Pieces: *Canzon I: La Spiritata)*

Andrea Gabrieli has been somewhat overshadowed by his nephew Giovanni, yet his music has an expressive character and colour very much its own. These little-known madrigal settings show a ready musical response to the Renaissance poetic vision of love which, although embroidered with elegant words, is quite explicit in its expressions of earthly desire. *O beltà rara* and *Laura soave* pay a pasionate tribute to the beauty of, and a hoped-for amorous reaction from, women, while *Amami, vita mia, Caro dolce ben mio* and *Voi non volete, donna* are touchingly plaintive responses to unrequieted and unresponsive love. The lovely Petrarch setting, *Lasso, Amor mi transporta ov'io non voglio*, makes it plain that love carries the lover 'where I do not wish to go', while in the intense dialogue between Cloris and Adonis, *Io mi sento morire*, ecstatic 'death' does not quite mean what it says!

Gabrieli was nothing if not versatile, and his touching tribute on the death of Willaert contrasts with *Asia felice*, depicting a celebration of the Turkish defeat at the Battle of Lepanto (with cornett, three trombones, organ and percussion). This, like the later, popular dialect numbers, receive I Fagiolini's lively and enthusiastic treatment, making the most of their earthy colour in their use of cornetts and sackbuts, while the love songs could hardly be sung with greater longing. Excellent recording, and full texts and translations are included in this very valuable addition to Renaissance repertoire.

Madrigali e canzoni: *Angel del terzo ciel; Cantiam di Dio, Cantiamo; Canzona a 4; Come havrò pace in terra; Caro dolce ben mio; A le guacie i rose; Gratie che'l mio Signor; I'vo piangendo i miei passati tempi; Mentre la greggia errando; Mentr'io vi miro; Quanti, sepolti giù nel foco eterno; Hor che nel suo bel seno; O Dea; Piangi pur, Musa; Ricercare a 4; Rimanti, Amor; O soave al mio cor dolce catena; Sento, sent' un rumor; Tirsi, che fai cosi dolente a l'ombra; Tirsi morir volea; Vaghi augeletti; La verginella è simile alla rosa; Vostro fui e sarò mentre ch'io viva*

**(*) CPO 999 642-2. Weser-Renaissance Bremen, Cordes

Andrea Gabrieli composed prolifically in most genres and this collection of madrigals, performed here by singers and instrumentalists of the Weser-Renaissance, brings together pieces from several different publications. Where the singers and instrumentalists are together, there is a tendency for nuances of word-colouring and dynamics to be ironed out. Although there are moments of dubious intonation, performances are generally dedicated, and the recording is clean and well focused. A useful addition to the catalogue.

Benedictus Dominus Deus a 8; Gloria in excelsis Deo a 16; Magnificat a 12; O crux splendidior a 8; Ricercar del duodecimo tuono a 4

(N) *** CfP (ADD) 586 0492. Amb. S., String & Brass Ens., Stevens – GIOVANNI GABRIELI: *Angeles ad pastoris ait;* etc. ***

When these recordings were first issued in 1967, the transfer to LP could not convey the full amplitude of the original recording. With the coming of CD these technical problems have vanished, and the added spaciousness is very apparent. There are some splendidly grandiloquent gestures here and the massive sonorities of the *Gloria in excelsis Deo*, with voice and brass textures interweaving, move towards their climax without strain. The textures in *O crux splendidior* are lighter and the *Ricercar* for brass is particularly successful. The singing is impressive throughout and the brass playing has the proper richness of sonority. A pioneering collection that is still highly recommendable.

Psalmi Davidi 6; 31; 37; 50; 101; 129; 143. Antiphon: Ne remimiscaris Domini

(N) (M) **(*) CPO 999 863-2. Capella Ducale Venetia, Picotti

Andrea Gabrieli's setting of the *Seven Penitential Psalms* of David, which was published in 1583, show a deeper, more expressive side of a composer who is nearly always twinned with his nephew, Giovanni, with his spectacular brass writing. The title-page suggests that the *Psalmi Davidi* were 'suitable, whether for every type of instrument or to be modulated with the voice', which is open-ended. However, Picotti has settled for darker brass sonorities, which are blended in with the homophonic choral sound in a resonant acoustic. The singing is warmly mellifluous and the sombre character of the music is preserved throughout, one might have liked more variety of dynamic range and (at times) more vigour, but the beauty of the simple vocal lines is well sustained and the third part of the last Psalm (142), 'Show me the path that I should follow', brings real intensity to this final plea. The opening and closing chanted Antiphon, *Lord do not look to my guilt*, also underlines the penitent atmosphere of Gabrieli's intentions. The recording is warmly atmospheric rather than clear.

GABRIELI, Giovanni (1554–1612)

'Music for San Rocco': Canzona 14 a 10; Sonatas 18 a 14; 19 a 15; 20 a 22; 21 **(for 3 Violins).** **Organ pieces:** *Intonazione duodecimo tonol; Intonazione del nono tono; Toccata a 4.* **Vocal works:** *Buccinate in neomenia tuba a 19; Domine Deus meus; In eccelessis a 14; Jubilate Deo a 10; Magnificat a 3* (arr. Keyte); *Misericordia tua Domine a 12; Suscipe clementissime Deus a 12; Timor e tremor a 6*

(N) *** DG Surround Sound **SACD** 477 0862 (2). Gabrieli Consort & Players, McCreesh (with Bartolomeo – BARBARINO: *Ardens est cor meum; Audi, dulcis amica mea)*

This is easily the most spectacular recording of Giovanni Gabrieli's music currently available and, played through four speakers, it does give – in the living room! – some idea of what breadth of vocal and instrumental sonorities he achieved in St Mark's, Venice, during the feast days at the end of the sixteenth century. The present recordings, however, were made in the equally spacious acoustics of the Scuola Grande di San Rocco, not far away. The concert, which is entirely conjectural, is inspired by a Saturday festival held at San Rocco on 6 August 1608, about which a contemporary told us, 'I would willingly goe an hundred miles a foote at any time to heare the like . . . I was for the time even rapt up with Saint Paul into the third heaven'.

Canzoni da sonare: I (La spiritata) a 4; I a 5 (1615); I toni a 10 (1597); II a 4 (1606); III a 6 (1615); VII a 7 (1615); XII toni a 10 (1597; 2 versions); XXIV a 8 (1608); XXVII a 8 (1608); Ricercar sopra 'Re fa me don' a 4

🎵 (BB) *** Virgin 2×1 5 62028-2 (2). Hespèrion XX, Savall (with A. GABRIELI: *Canzon sopra 'Qui la dira'*; GUAMI: *Canzon: 'La accorta' a 4*; *Canzon sopra 'La battaglia' a 4*; *Canzon 'La cromatica' a 4*; *Canzon 'La guamina'*; *Canzon XXIV a 8*; *Canzon XXV a 8*) – SCHEIN: *Banchetto musicale*; SCHEIDT: *Ludi Musici* ***

A fine selection of Giovanni Gabrieli's *Canzonas*, together with half a dozen more by his contemporary Giuseppe Guami, which are in much the same style. Also included is a *Canzon sopra 'Qui la dira'* by Giovanni's uncle, Andrea (with whom he studied), based on a song. This is played on the harpsichord and makes an attractive interlude. But Jordi Savall varies the scoring throughout, so that some works are for strings (including the solemn *Ricercar*), others include brass to splendid effect. Guami's '*La Accorta*' is melancholy, and his '*Battaglia*' is disappointingly low key, but many of the others are very jolly, notably Giovanni's dancing *Canzon VII a 7* and Guami's *Canzon XXV a 8*. This and Giovanni's florid closing *Canzon XII toni* in ten parts demand great bravura from all concerned. The performances are splendid, and so is the recording. This is one of the finest collections of Renaissance music in the catalogue.

Canzoni e Sonate per concertar con l'organo: Canzoni (1615) V & VI a 7; VIII, X & XII a 8; XIV a 10; XVI a 12. Sacrae Symphoniae (1597): Canzon septimi toni a 8 (2 versions); primi toni a 10; noni toni a 8; duodecimi toni a 8 & a 10; in echo duodecimi toni a 10 accomodata per concertar con l'organo; Ricercare del primo rono; Sonata octavi toni a 12

(N) **(*) HM 901688. Concerto Platino, Dicket or Toet; Jansen & Tamminga (organs)

The church of San Petronio, Bologna, has a pair of recently restored organs which have similarities to those at St Mark's, Venice, so they are highly suitable for recording this music antiphonally. It is splendidly played and the church acoustic is suitably spacious to give a sonorous effect. However, though the comparatively familiar '*Echo*' *Sonata* stands out and the *Ricercare* also makes a contrast, and though the *Canzoni* of 1597 and *Sonate* of 1615 are alternated in the progamme, there is not enough variety here for extended listening: the ear familiar with Gabrieli craves some vocal music. Performances are first class.

Music for Brass, Vol. 1: *Canzon a 12 in double echo; Canzon septimi toni a 8 2; Canzon septimi e octavi toni a 12; Canzon noni toni a 8; Canzon noni toni a 12; Canzoni duodecimi toni a 10, 1 & 3; Canzoni VII; VIII; IX; XI; XIII; XIV; XVII; XXVIII; Sonata pian' e forte alla quarta bassa a 8*

(BB) *** Naxos 8.553609. LSO Brass, Crees

Starting with the *Canzon XVII* of 1615 in 12 parts, involving three choirs of instruments, Eric Crees and his brilliant players from the brass section of the LSO demonstrate at once what variety of tone they can produce, with the finest shading of timbre and texture. In the great *Sonata pian' e forte*

of 1597 in eight parts and the even more striking *Double Echo Canzon in 12 Parts*, the playing is remarkable as much for its restraint and point as for its dramatic impact. Beautiful sound, both clear and atmospheric, not aggressive.

Music for Brass, Vol. 2: *Canzon La Spirita à 4; Canzon à 12; Canzon II; Canzon III; Canzon V; Canzon VI; Canzon XII; Canzon XVI à 12; Canzon primi toni à 8; Canzon seconda à 4; Canzon serza à 4; Sonata XVIII; Sonata XIX; Sonata octavi toni à 12*

(BB) *** Naxos 8.553873. LSO Brass, Crees

Music for Brass, Vol. 3: *Canzon IV; Canzon X; Canzon XV; Canzon primi toni à 10: Canzon in echo duodecimi toni à 10; Canzon duodecimi toni à 10 2; Canzon prima; Canzon quarta à 4; Canzon quarti toni à 15; Canzon septimi toni à 8 1; Sonata XX; Sonata XXI (with organ)*

(BB) *** Naxos 8.554129. LSO Brass, Crees

The *Canzon in echo duodecimi toni à 10* in Volume 3 is obviously the most spectacular piece, but the paired *Sonatas XX* and *XXI* (with organ) thrillingly combine rich sonorities with complex decoration, and in Volume 2 there are several very striking pieces, notably *La Spiritata* and *Canzon XVI à 12*, which closes the disc.

Sonata pian'e forte

(***) BBC BBCL mono 4059-2. LSO, Stokowski – LISZT: *Mephisto Waltz 1*; NIELSEN: *Symphony 6*; TIPPETT: *Concerto for Double String Orchestra* ***

The *Sonata pian'e forte* was a repertory piece in the 1940s and '50s, before the period-instrument movement got under way, and Stokowski evokes a rich individual sonority from his fine players.

Angelus ad pastores ait; Buccante in neomenia tuba; Canzon septimi toni a 8; Hodie Christus natus est; Hodie completi sunt; O Domine Jesu Christe; O magnum mysterium; Omnes gentes, plaudite manibus

(B) **(*) EMI double forte (ADD) 5 68631-2 (2). Cambridge University Musical Soc., Bach Ch., King's College Ch., Wilbraham Brass Soloists, Willcocks (with SCHEIDT: *In dulci jubilo* ***) – SCHUTZ: *Psalm 150* **(*); MONTEVERDI: *Vespers* *(*)

Originally recorded in King's College Chapel, using quadraphonic sound, the CD transfer brings stereo which is notable for the opulent richness of brass and choral textures rather than inner clarity, yet is resonantly resplendent. There is an impressively wide dynamic range, as is shown by the serene motet, *O Domine Jesu Christe*. Added to the Gabrieli works is Scheidt's setting in eight parts of the famous *In dulci jubilo*, which is particularly successful. It is a pity that the principal Monteverdi coupling is not more recommendable.

(i) *Angelus ad pastoris ait a 12; Buccante in neomenia tuba; Canzon septimi toni a 8; Hodie Christus natus est a 10; Hodie completi sunt a 8; O Domine Jesu Christe a 8; O magnum mysterium a 8; Omnes gentes plaudite manibus a 16;* (ii) *Buccante in neomenia tuba a 19; Canzon septimi toni; In eccelessis a 14; Timor et tremor*

(N) *** CfP (ADD) 586 0492. (i) King's College, Cambridge, Ch., Cambridge University Musical Soc., Bach Ch., Wilbraham Brass Soloists, Willcocks; (ii) Amb. S., String & Brass Ens., Stevens – ANDREA GABRIELI: *Benedictus Dominus Deus*, etc. ***

This generous Classics for Pleasure reissue combines the

above impressive performances, directed by Sir David Willcocks in 1973, with a pioneering stereo programme from 1966, recorded at Abbey Road. The latter collection, directed by Denis Stevens, pioneered these multi-voiced works; if the massive sonorities of *Buccinate in neomenia*, with its 19-part ensemble divided into four separate choirs, sounds a little too close, the sound is otherwise very impressive. The lighter vocal texture of *Timor et tremor* is very successful, and *In eccelessis*, with its attractive answering between higher and lower voices, is more expansive. The King's recordings have much more space, and performances and recordings are of the quality we would expect from this source. A fine disc, and a bargain too.

'A Venetian Christmas'
*** DG 471 333-2. Gabrieli Consort and Players, McCreesh (with DE RORE: *Missa praeter rerum serie*)

Paul McCreesh adds to his evocative series re-creating great religious occasions with what might have been heard at Christmas in St Mark's in Venice around the year 1600. Punctuated by chant, a variety of pieces by Giovanni Gabrieli for choir, for organ and for brass ensemble sets the central liturgy in context. Gabrieli characteristically exploits the wide-ranging antiphonal effects inspired by St Mark's, with the first motet, *Audite principes*, involving no fewer than 16 parts divided into three separate groups, each led by a solo voice. Most striking is the setting of the Mass chosen, dating from half a century earlier, a so-called parody Mass by Cipriano de Rore in seven parts (one more than the complex motet by Josquin Des Prez on which it is based), a magnificent example of polyphony, superbly performed here.

GADE, Niels (1817–90)

Andante & Allegro (arr. Rachlevsky); *Novelettes, Opp. 53 & 58*
*** Claves CD 50-9607. Kremlin CO, Rachlevsky

This is eminently civilized writing, inventive and intelligent, full of charm, and the performances by the Kremlin Chamber Orchestra under Misha Rachlevsky are beyond praise. It is a joy to hear such natural and beautifully shaped phrasing, and the recording is pleasingly natural and warm.

(i) *Capriccio in A min. for Violin and Orchestra* (orch. Reinecke). *Overtures: Echoes of Ossian, Op. 1; Hamlet, Op. 37; Mariotta*
**(*) Danacord DACOCD 510. (i) Astrand; Danish PO, South Jutland, Brown – AXEL GADE: *Violin Concerto 2* **(*)

Niels Gade exerted enormous influence on Danish musical life: in addition to his eight symphonies, he was an influential teacher. This disc includes his well-known Op. 1, the *Overture, Echoes of Ossian* (1840), as well as two other overtures and a *Capriccio* for violin and orchestra, new to disc. As always, the mantle of Mendelssohn weighs heavily on Gade's muse. Good performances and decent recording.

Novelettes: in F, Op. 53; in E, Op. 58
*** CPO 999 516-2. German Chamber Ac. Neuss, Goritzki – HAMERIK: *Symphony 6* ***

These miniatures for strings, like most of Gade's music, are full of charm, and are excellently played by the Deutsche Kammerakademie with their splendid cellist-conductor Johannes Goritzki. They have great lightness of touch and vital rhythmic articulation. First-rate sound.

Symphony 1 in C min. (On Sjølund's Fair Plains), Op. 5; Overture, Echoes of Ossian, Op. 1; Hamlet Overture, Op. 37
🔊━ *** Chan. 9422. Danish Nat. RSO, Kitaenko

This performance of the engaging, folksong-inspired *First Symphony* has an unaffected quality and an unforced eloquence that give much delight. The two shorter works, *Hamlet* and the *Echoes of Ossian Overture*, are also very well played. The recording, made in the fine concert hall of Danish Radio, is absolutely first rate, natural in perspective, with plenty of presence and detail.

Symphonies 1; (i) 5 in D min., Op. 25
**(*) Chan. 10026. Danish Nat. RSO, Hogwood with (i) Brautigam

Christopher Hogwood brings great freshness to the *First Symphony*, and were the *Fifth* as successful, it would be arguably the finest of what has proved a highly impressive cycle. *On Sjølund's Fair Plains*, so called because of the folksong it quotes, offers what is perhaps the most convincing reading here. In addition to its freshness, it has breadth and feeling. So, too, does the delightful *Fifth Symphony* for piano and orchestra, but Ronald Brautigam uses an Erard fortepiano of 1837, which will strike those who know the recordings under Neeme Järvi and Michael Schønwandt as papery in timbre and clattery, even though the playing has great elegance. Although Hogwood reduces the size of the string body, the sound is not quite as clean as the BIS, Chandos and dacapo sets.

Symphonies 1 in C min.; 8 in B min., Op. 47
*** BIS CD 339. Stockholm Sinf., Järvi

Thirty years separate the *First Symphony* from Gade's *Eighth* and last symphony, like the *First* much indebted to Mendelssohn. Despite this debt, there is still a sense of real mastery and a command of pace. The Stockholm Sinfonietta and Neeme Järvi give very fresh and lively performances, and the recording is natural and truthful.

Symphonies 2 in E, Op. 10; 7 in F, Op. 45
**(*) BIS CD 355. Stockholm Sinf., Järvi

Symphonies 2 in E, Op. 10; 8 in B min., Op. 47; Allegretto, un poco lento; Overture: In the Highlands, Op. 7
*** Chan. 8962. Danish Nat. RSO, Hogwood

Schumann thought No. 2 'reminiscent of Denmark's beautiful beechwoods'. The debt to Mendelssohn is still enormous here, but it is very likeable, more spontaneous than the *Seventh*, though this work has a delightful Scherzo. Splendid playing from the Stockholm Sinfonietta under Järvi, and good recording too.

The *Eighth Symphony* (1871) is very civilized. Hogwood also gives us the *Allegretto, un poco lento*, the original slow movement of the *Eighth Symphony* (which Gade subsequently discarded) and an early overture, *In the Highlands*, with which Gade followed up the success of his *Ossian Overture*. Well-shaped, solid performances and recommendable, although Neeme Järvi and the Stockholm Sinfonietta have the lighter touch and have greater transparency of sound.

Symphonies 3 in A min., Op. 15; 4 in B flat, Op. 20
*** BIS CD 338. Stockholm Sinf., Järvi

Gade's *Third* has great freshness and a seemingly effortless flow of ideas and pace, and a fine sense of musical proportion. No. 4 was more generally admired in Gade's lifetime, but its companion here is the more winning. It is beautifully played and recorded.

Symphonies 3 in A min., Op. 15; (i) 5 in D min., Op. 25
**(*) dacapo DCCD 9004. (i) Malling; Coll. Mus., Copenhagen, Schønwandt

Michael Schønwandt's performances of these two Gade symphonies are most musical, and are distinguished by sensitive phrasing and a fine feeling for line. In the *Fifth Symphony*, the piano is less closely observed than it is in the BIS recording. Amalie Malling is the more reticent player, too, and plays with taste and grace. However, the 1988 recording though perfectly acceptable, is not as good or as fresh sounding as its BIS rival, which on balance is to be preferred.

Symphonies 3; 6; Overture, Echoes from Ossian, Op. 1
*** Chan. 9795. Danish Nat. RSO, Hogwood

The symphonies of the nineteenth-century Danish composer, Niels Wilhelm Gade, may bring many echoes of his mentor, Mendelssohn, but No. 3 is undoubtedly one of the most attractive. Written in 1846–7 when he was still working in Leipzig, it has an invigorating bite to it, starting as it does with a vigorous *Presto* movement in a dark A minor. It seems that this striking movement was only a second thought. Quite apart from its excellence as a performance, this newcomer is of special interest in that it includes its first version, which Gade subsequently discarded. More expansive, with a slow introduction, that abandoned movement is less integrated and less symphonic in feeling than the definitive version.

The *Sixth*, composed nearly ten years later, does not have the same lightness and vibrant spirit, yet it conveys little sense of tragedy, even though it was written in the immediate wake of Gade's wife's death in childbirth. The first movement proceeds as if on automatic pilot and the first group remains untouched by distinction. Things look up later on: the slow movement has a lot of charm and the Scherzo a certain sparkle.The warmth and weight of Hogwood's readings of both symphonies, brilliantly recorded, give him a certain advantage over rivals on disc, with some distinguished wind-playing from the Danish orchestra, and if the recordings are not as beautifully transparent as Järvi's on BIS (differently coupled) they are still very good. In addition to the rejected movement of No. 3, there is a further bonus in the form of the endearing and evocative *Concert Overture, Echoes from Ossian*, Gade's most popular orchestral work, a valuable makeweight.

Symphonies 4; 7; Concert Overture 3, Op. 14
**(*) Chan. 9957. Danish Nat. RSO, Hogwood

In No. 4, best known of his eight symphonies, as in most of his works, Gade charmingly echoes Mendelssohn. The *Seventh Symphony* has great geniality and charm, and is winningly played on this disc. The only reservation concerns the sound which, though naturally balanced and with plenty of presence, places the listener far too close to the orchestra. Neeme Järvi's recordings of both symphonies with the Stockholm Sinfonietta (on BIS) have the greater tonal finesse and transparency of texture, and sound much fresher. The *Concert Overture No. 3* is an appealing piece, a first recording and well worth having, and the disc can certainly be recommended for the spirited playing of the Danish orchestra and the elegance of Hogwood's direction.

Symphonies (i) 5 in D min., Op. 25; 6 in G min., Op. 32
*** BIS CD 356. Stockholm Sinf., Järvi, (i) with Pöntinen

The *Fifth Symphony* is a delightfully sunny piece which lifts one's spirits; its melodies are instantly memorable, and there is a lively concertante part for the piano, splendidly played by the young Roland Pöntinen. The *Sixth Symphony* is rather more thickly scored and more academic. The recording is very good and, given the charm of the *Fifth Symphony* and the persuasiveness of the performance, this coupling must be warmly recommended.

CHAMBER MUSIC

Allegro in A min., for String Quartet; (i) Andante & Allegro molto in F min., for String Quintet. String Quartet in F (Wilkommen und Abschied); (ii) Octet in F, Op. 17
**(*) BIS CD 545. Kontra Qt, with (i–ii) Nygaard; (ii) Egendal, Madsen, Ranmo

All this music is youthful, and has charm and freshness of invention. Gade's work has a spontaneity – particularly the *F minor Quintet* – which is quite captivating. This is a useful supplement to the Kontra's recording of the three later *Quartets* discussed below, and in many ways it is to be preferred. The excellent performances are well recorded, but there is a slightly strident edge in tutti passages which inhibits a full three-star recommendation.

Octet, Op. 17; Sextet, Op. 44
*** MDG 308 1102-2. Berlin Philharmonic String Octet

As always with Gade, the craftsmanship is impeccable and the musical architecture is finely balanced, but the musical ideas in both works are heavily indebted to Mendelssohn. It is all very mellifluous, even if neither piece ever approaches Mendelssohn in quality of inspiration or distinction of mind. The playing of the Berlin ensemble is thoroughly dedicated and enthusiastic, and although the recording places us fairly far forward in the recital room there is plenty of air around the sound. Both are available in alternative recordings, but neither is superior to the present issue.

String Quartets 1 in F min.; 2 in E min.; 3 in D, Op. 63
*** BIS CD 516. Kontra Qt

These are pleasing works of great facility and are worth hearing, particularly in such good performances and recordings as we are given here. If they show too strong a gravitational pull from Mendelssohn, in terms of invention and craftsmanship they give a certain pleasure.

VOCAL MUSIC

(i) Efterklange af Ossian (Echoes of Ossian), Op. 1; (ii) Elverskud (The Elf-King's Daughter), Op. 30; (iii) 5 Partsongs, Op. 13
*** Chan. 9075. (ii) Johansson, Gjevang, Elming, Danish Nat. R. Ch.; (iii) Danish Nat. R. Chamber Ch., Parkman; (i; ii) Danish Nat. RSO, Kitaienko

(i) Elverskud; Op. 30; (ii) Forårs-fantasi (Spring Fantasy), Op. 23
*** dacapo 8.224051. (i) Elmark, Paëvatalu; (i; ii) Dolberg; (ii) Dahl, Henning-Jensen, Byriel, Westenholz; (i) Tivoli Concert Ch.; Tivoli SO, Schønwandt

Gade's *Elverskud*, variously translated as *The Elf-King's Daughter*, *The Erl-King's Daughter*, *The Fairy Spell* or *The Elf-Shot*, is a work of great appeal and the opening of the second half – an evocation of the moonlit world of the fairy hill – is little short of inspired. Michael Schønwandt's account has a good deal to recommend it. In some ways this Marco Polo disc scores over its Chandos rival: the solo singers are generally more satisfying and the conductor keeps a firmer grip on proceedings without any loss of poetic feeling or atmosphere. It also has the advantage of the more adventurous coupling, the *Forårs-fantasi* (*Spring Fantasy*), another of Gade's most delightful inspirations, radiant in its happiness and full of sun.

On Chandos, *Elverskud* comes with Gade's very first opus, the delightful *Ossian Overture*. A further bonus is the set of *Five Partsongs*, Op. 13, beautifully sung by the Danish Radio Chamber Choir; the fourth, *Autumn song*, is particularly memorable and haunting. *Elverskud* again gives unfailing pleasure, particularly in such a persuasive performance and excellent recording.

Korsfarerne (The Crusaders), Op. 50

**(*) BIS CD 465. Rorholm, Westi, Cold, Canzone Ch., Da Camera, Kor 72, Music Students' Chamber Ch., Aarhus SO, Rasmussen

Gade's *Korsfarerne* is in three sections, *In the Desert*, *Armida* and *Towards Jerusalem*, and lasts the best part of an hour. The Danish forces assembled here do it proud, as do the BIS recording team, but the debt to Mendelssohn, say in the *Chorus of the Spirits of Darkness* which opens the second section, overwhelms any feeling of originality.

GALUPPI, Baldassare (1706–85)

Piano Sonatas, Volumes 1–3

**(N) (M) **(*) Divine Art 2-5006 (8 *Sonatas*); 2-5007 (9 *Sonatas*); 2-25015 (8 *Sonatas*). Seivewright (piano)

Galuppi's keyboard music was brought to the notice of record collectors by a *C major Sonata* included by Michelangeli in a Decca mono LP recital, and he turned it into a little pearl. Galuppi was also celebrated by Browning, but alas the 'Toccata' his poem describes does not actually exist. However, some 90 sonatas do, and they are all being recorded by Peter Seivewright, using a modern piano but with only modest pedalling in slow movements and crisp, clean articulation in *Allegros*. He is a sensitive artist and obviously enjoys this repertoire, and he communicates this enjoyment to us.

These works appear to be the epitome of simplicity, but in fact they are usually through-composed, so that movements are built, often quite imaginatively and always resourcefully, out of the same basic material. Certain movements stand out, for instance the bouncing *Presto* second movement of the three-movement *Sonata in C minor* on the first disc, which is surprisingly like the second movement of the *Sonata in G minor* which then reuses the same idea for an *Allegretto grazioso* finale. The sonata which follows (in E major) brings an engaging set of Variations for its second movement (of two), and the final sonata of the first volume opens with a delightful *Andante, e con espressione*, the longest movement on the whole disc.

The second volume opens with a winning two-movement *Sonata in C*, and the works which follow are inventively varied, but in much the same style. When we continue into the third volume, we realize that Galuppi is not seeking to break any formal barriers or make harmonic explorations, but applies his ideas within straightforward musical frameworks. Yet the three-movement *C major Sonata* included here

is really very fetching in its simplicity, and the *G major* and *B flat major Sonatas* are also most appealing.

The one unforgivable aspect of this series is the lack of proper documentation, how the sonatas relate to each other in a time framework. We are told merely that they were probably middle-period works and nothing more – except the key of each sonata.

Motets: Arripe alpestri ad vallem; (i) Confitebor tibi, Domine

☛ ❂ (BB) *** Virgin 2x1 5 62413-2 (2). Lesne, (i) with Gens, Harvey; Il Seminario Musicale – VIVALDI: *Salve regina* etc. ***

These two very beautiful motets show Galuppi at his most inspired, and they are performed superbly by Gérard Lesne, who is joined by Véronique Gens and Peter Harvey in *Confitebor tibi* (praising God for His munificence), which brings a skill in its overlapping part-writing worthy of Mozart. The accompaniments from Il Seminario Musicale are refreshingly sensitive, alive and polished, while the recording has a natural presence.

OPERA

La Diavolessa (complete)

**(N) **(*) CPO 999 947-2 (2). Dilcheva, Vieweg, Allen, Maldonado, Pahn, Lautten Compagney Berlin, Katschner

Baldassare Galuppi was one of the most popular and successful eighteenth-century Venetian composers of his day and about his operas Charles Burney wrote, 'Many of the refinements in modern melody, and effects in dramatic music, seem to originate in the genius of Galuppi', and indeed, in this recording of *La Diavolessa*, there is much to enjoy, not least in the second-Act finale, where a seance is evoked with some divertingly mock-mysterious writing. The plot of lovers thwarted by lack of money – and their endeavours to obtain it – bringing mistaken identity, Machiavellian tactics and the like, but all ending happily, is the stuff of *opera buffa*. The cast is competent if not outstanding: Kremena Dilcheva as Dorina (an alto) is not as consistently secure as she might be, and she lacks the sparkle the role should ideally have, with her low- and high-lying tessitura coming off best. Bettina Pahn is very good as the Countess, and all the men are lively and characterful. Wolfgang Katschner's direction throughout the many tuneful arias, duets and ensembles is generally lively and, with CPO's recording full and theatrical, this is worth exploring. Texts and translations are included.

Il mondo alla roversa (opera; complete)

*** Chan. 0676 (2). Italian Swiss R. Ch., I Barochisti, Fasolis

Galuppi, working in collaboration with the playwright Carlo Goldoni, might be counted the father of comic opera in Italy, finding much greater success with his comic works than with his formal operas. First seen in Venice in 1750, this delightful piece, *Il mondo alla roversa* ('The Topsy-Turvy World'), subtitled *Le donne che commandano* ('Women in Command'), helps to explain why, with its brisk sequence of short solo numbers and ensembles, punctuated by brief recitatives. The idea of an island where a council of women has taken over control from the men is lightly treated, and predictably the non-feminist age leads to their final overthrow and their capitulation in love. The Italian studios of Swiss Radio have lately produced a number of impressive recordings of early music, and this fresh, lively account is no exception.

GAUBERT, Philippe (1879–1941)

Complete Flute Music, Vol. 1: *3 Aquarelles* (for flute, cello & piano); *Divertissement grec* (for 2 flutes & harp); *Madrigal* (for flute & piano); *Médailles antiques* (for flute, violin & piano); *Pièce romantique* (for flute, cello & piano); *Tarentelle* (for flute, oboe & piano); *Suite. Soir païen* (for voice, flute & piano)

(N) (BB) *** Naxos 8.557305. Fenwick Smith, Pinkas, Pearce Zoon, Pilot, Ferrillo, Lowe, Jayne West

Complete Flute Music, Vol. 2: *Flute Sonatas 1–3; Sonatine Quasi Fantasia*

(N) (BB) *** Naxos 8.557306. Fenwick Smith, Pinkas

Flute Sonatas 1–3; Madrigal; Orientale; 3 Aquarelles; Pièce romantique (both for flute, cello & piano)

**(*) Deux-Elles DXL 923. Thomas, Shaw, Scott

Philippe Gaubert was a virtuoso flautist and composed extensively for the instrument. This anthology shows his refinement of craftsmanship and freshness of inspiration. Not great music but full of Gallic charm, which is well conveyed in these accomplished performances by Kathryn Thomas and Richard Shaw, who are joined in the *3 Aquarelles* and the *Pièce romantique* by the cellist Phoebe Scott. Decently recorded, even if the acoustic is over-reverberant.

Volume I of the Naxos set is devoted to Gaubert's shorter pieces, many of which feature extra solo instruments which give the music added colour and, in works like the *Divertissement grec*, a certain piquancy. There is much attractive writing here, often with a touch of the exotic colouring (the *Berceuse orientale* from the *Suite*, and the *Soir païen*, for voice, flute and piano, are obvious examples). The second volume features the more substantial *Flute Sonatas*. The *Third* of the three is the most dramatic, with an especially virtuosic finale. Fenwick Smith is superb in the repertoire and is well supported by Sally Pinkas's sympathetic partnership. The extra soloists on volume one are all very good too, and the Naxos sound is both full and atmospheric. These bargain CDs are recommended alongside, though not in preference to, the excellent Chandos set below, which, of course, costs a great deal more.

Music for Flute and Piano: *Sonatas 1–3; Sonatine. Ballade; Berceuse; 2 Esquisses; Fantaisie; Nocturne et allegro scherzando; Romance; Sicilienne; Suite; Sur l'eau*

*** Chan. 8981/2. Milan, Brown

Gaubert had a genuine lyrical gift and his music has an elegance and allure that will captivate. He is eminently well served by Susan Milan and Ian Brown, and they are well balanced by the Chandos engineers. Truthful sound; civilized and refreshing music, not to be taken all at one draught but full of delight.

GEMINIANI, Francesco (1687–1762)

Concerti grossi, Op. 2/1–6; Op. 3/1–4

☞ (BB) *** Naxos 8.553019. Capella Istropolitana, Krěcek

This is part of an ongoing Naxos project to record all Geminiani's *Concerti grossi* using modern instruments but in a style which clearly reflects the freshness and vitality of period-instrument practice. The Capella Istropolitana offer excellent accounts of the whole of Op. 2 and the first four concertos of Op. 3, all invigoratingly enjoyable and very well recorded.

Concerti grossi, Op. 3/5–6; Op. 7/1–6

☞ (BB) *** Naxos 8.553020. Capella Istropolitana, Krěcek

This CD continues the Naxos series of Geminiani's *Concerti grossi*, concluding Op. 3 and including the whole of Op. 7. However, the extra parts (in Nos. 3, 4 and 5 for flutes, and 6 for bassoon) are not used here as they are in Iona Brown's outstanding set with the ASMF (see below), which remains a primary recommendation for Op. 7. Nevertheless the performances by the Capella Istropolitana match those on their first disc in freshness and vitality, and they are very well recorded. Bargain-hunters need not hesitate.

12 Concerti grossi, Op. 5 (after Corelli's *Violin Sonatas, Op. 5*)

(N) **(*) Zig-Zag Territories ZZT 040301 (2). Soloists, Ens. 415, Banchini

(i) 12 Concerti grossi, Op. 5 (after Corelli); (ii; iii) Cello Sonata in D min., Op. 5/2; Ornamented arrangement of Corelli's Sonata in A for Violin & Cello

*** HM HMU 907261/62 (2). (i) AAM, Manze; (ii) Watkin; (iii) McGillivray

The period-instrument performance by the players of the Academy of Ancient Music are led from the bow by Andrew Manze. He is a superb soloist, but so are his colleagues, and the transparency of the sound and refinement of textures in no way preclude warmth. *Allegros* are full of vigour (and bravura) while the exquisite delicacy of the solo contribution to slow movements makes the strongest possible case for authenticity in this music. If you want to sample the vigour and dynamic contrasts of this music-making, try the final work of the set with its winning variations on *La folia*. As a bonus, two further arrangements are offered, equally persuasive in performance. The recording is excellent and this makes a clear first choice for Op. 5, unless you are unable to enjoy period performance-manners – which here are totally without eccentricity.

Banchini's performances are also lively; sometimes very lively indeed, and slow movements are expressively played in the authentic style. But the effect has much less subtlety of detail and refinement in the matter of light and shade. The Zig-Zag recording is very good, but Andrew Manze's set is the one to go for.

Concerti grossi: in D min. (La folia, from CORELLI: *Sonata in D min., Op. 5/12); in G min., Op. 7/2; Trio Sonatas 3 in F (from Op. 1/9); 5 in A min. (from Op. 1/11); 6 in D min. (from Op. 1/12); Violin Sonatas: in E min., Op. 1/3; in A, Op. 4/12*

*** Hyp. CDA 66264. Purcell Band & Qt

This record comes from Hyperion's 'La folia' series, though the only piece here using that celebrated theme is the arrangement Geminiani made of Corelli's D minor Sonata. Apart from the G minor Concerto, Op. 7, No. 2, the remainder of the disc is given over to chamber works. The Purcell Quartet play with dedication and spirit and convey their own enthusiasm for this admirably inventive music to the listener.

Pièces de clavecin (London 1743)

(N) ** Glossa GCD 921504. Bonizzoni (harpsichord)

Geminiani's *Pièces de clavecin*, published during one of his visits to London, of which 13 movements are included here, were transcribed from his *Violin Sonatas*, mostly Opus 4, but also including items from Opp. 1 and 2. The arrangements work well enough, and if they are not especially distinctive in Fabio Bonizzoni's performances, he is not helped by the resonant acoustic of the Castello Sforzesco in Milan, which tends to cloud the sound of the Pascal Taskin harpsichord in louder passages.

GERHARD, Roberto (1896–1970)

(i) *Harpsichord Concerto. Symphony (Homenaje a Pedrell)*
*** Chan. 9693. (i) Tozer; BBC SO, Bamert

Gerhard's unnumbered *Symphony* of 1941, written in homage to his teacher, Felipe Pedrell, is a far more approachable, less radical piece than his later works. Based on themes from an opera by Pedrell, it is openly tonal, with a Dvořák-like first movement, a warmly elegiac central slow movement and a jolly finale, with Spanish flavours increasingly emerging. The *Harpsichord Concerto*, written for Thurston Dart, is altogether grittier, revealing Gerhard's increasing confidence in handling serial argument. Excellent performances and full-ranging sound.

Piano Concerto (for Piano & Strings)
(N) (BB) *** Naxos 8.557290. Donohoe, Northern
  Sinfonia – DARNTON: ROWLEY; FERGUSON: *Piano
  Concertos* ***

Roberto Gerhard's *Concerto for Piano and Strings*, very different in style as it is from its companions on this Naxos disc, makes a valuable and refreshing addition to Peter Donohoe's imaginative collection of four British piano concertos. After fleeing from his native Catalonia after the Spanish Civil War, Gerhard settled in Cambridge and became a stimulating influence on British music. This was the first work in which he fully adopted Schoenbergian serial techniques, yet in its energy and inventiveness it is far from daunting, with each movement reflecting Spanish music. The first movement has the label, *Tiento*, in effect 'Toccata', with scurrying piano-writing in whirlwind neoclassical rhythms, and the central *Adagio*, much the longest movement, labelled *Diferencias*, brings a set of variations, a dark lament for his homeland, with guitar-like repetitions for the piano. The finale, *Folia*, is a fantasy piece using a ground bass. A brilliant performance from Peter Donohoe, directing the Northern Sinfonia from the keyboard.

(i) *Piano Concerto. Epithalamion; Symphony 3 (Collages)*
*** Chan. 9556. BBC SO, Bamert, (i) with Tozer

The key work here is the *Third Symphony* of 1960, which brings out Gerhard's fascination with electronic sounds, set in contrast with a large orchestra, hence the subtitle, *Collages*. The visual inspiration here was seeing a sunrise from a high-flying aircraft, with the physical element vital in Gerhard's ever-inventive, thornily complex writing. That is vividly captured in Bamert's powerful performance, which easily outshines those on earlier recordings. The *Piano Concerto* of 1951 is also complex in its thought, but is readily approachable, and the *Epithalamion*, written for the wedding of friends, using a very large orchestra, represents the composer at his wildest. This recording reveals a very full, rich sound.

Concerto for Orchestra; Symphony 2 (original version)
☮ *** Chan. 9694. BBC SO, Bamert

Gerhard's *Concerto for Orchestra* provides an excellent introduction to this fascinating composer. Like the *Fourth Symphony*, it reflects a mood of controlled wildness, with the composer's exuberant enjoyment of exotic sound exploited to the full. It receives a warm, incisive performance from Bamert and the BBC orchestra, who are comparably persuasive in the grittier arguments of the *Second Symphony*. This is the first recording, which goes back to his original score of 1959. It is a powerful work, in two long movements, each subdivided in two, with the pent-up energy of the first giving way to the stillness and concentration of the second. Outstandingly rich and full recording.

(i) *Violin Concerto. Symphony 1*
*** Chan. 9599. BBC SO, Bamert, (i) with Charlier

It was the belated first performance in 1955 of the *Symphony No. 1* that sparked off the surge of creativity which marked Gerhard's last years. The work's rejection of athematicism makes it initially less approachable than the coupled *Violin Concerto*, but it is a brilliant and rewarding piece. It is a work which richly repays repeated listening, and here under Bamert receives a powerful performance. The *Violin Concerto* is more immediately inviting, a neo-Romantic and haunting score with a strong sense of atmosphere: its slow movement has a sultry languor that recalls the Mediterranean. It is also a bravura work and the piece includes Spanish references, very like those in the opera *The Duenna*, written soon afterwards. Olivier Charlier is a brilliant advocate, not least in the dazzling finale. Rich, full-bodied sound. A fascinating and highly recommendable issue.

Symphony 4 (New York); Pandora Suite
*** Chan. 9651. BBC SO, Bamert

Roberto Gerhard's *Fourth Symphony* can be seen as the culminating achievement of his extraordinary last period. Throwing caution aside, he here indulges in his exuberant love of wild and exotic orchestral sounds. This half-hour, single-movement span is at once uninhibited yet tautly conceived, with complex and highly original textures that emerge with pin-point clarity in this superb recording conducted by Matthias Bamert. The *Pandora Suite* from 1942, written for the Kurt Jooss ballet in colourful tonal writing, reveals Gerhard at his most approachable.

(i) *Concert for 8; Gemini; Leo; Libra.* (ii) *3 Impromptus*
*** Largo LARGO 5134. (i) Nieuw Ens., Spanjaard; (ii) Snijders

'I have a certain weakness for astrology in general and for horoscopes in particular,' wrote Gerhard in 1968, having just completed the third of his three astrological pieces for chamber ensemble. It is specially valuable to have all three on a single disc. With contrasted instrumental groups in each, this is Gerhard at his most personal: taut and abrasive, thornily inventive. The strongest and boldest of the three, as well as the longest, is *Leo*, his last completed work, a celebration of the star sign of his wife, Poldi. That association makes the close, written in the face of serious illness, specially poignant. The *Concert for 8* – with an accordion among the instruments – is an apt extra, as are the three little piano *Impromptus*. Clean-cut performances and recording.

The Duenna (opera; complete)
*** Chan. 9520 (2). Van Allan, Clark, Glanville, Powell, Archer, Taylor, Roberts, Wade, Opera N. Ch., E. N. Philh. O, Ros Marbá

Sheridan's play, *The Duenna*, was originally presented with music by Thomas Linley. But Gerhard resolved to turn it into an opera, and here the characteristic hints of atonality simply add extra spice to the Spanish flavours, with sensuously colourful instrumentation and lively dance-rhythms to produce a superbly crafted, consistently inspired work, even if there is rather too much reliance on speech over music to fill gaps in the story. As the heroine, Donna Luisa, Susannah Glanville sings charmingly, rising to the challenge of her big monologue in Act II, one of the most tenderly lyrical passages in the whole opera. Richard Van Allan makes an aptly gruff and characterful Don Jerome, the heavy father, and Neill Archer is an ardent hero. In the title-role of the Duenna, Claire Powell is firm and fruity, delightful in her duet with Don Isaac, the rich Jew who is tricked into marrying her. The recording, made in the Royal Concert Hall, Nottingham, is vivid and immediate, with fine presence, letting words be heard with commendable clarity even over the richest orchestral background.

GERSHWIN, George (1898–1937)

An American in Paris; Catfish Row (Suite); (i) Concerto in F. Cuban Overture; Lullaby; Mexican Dance; (i) Rhapsody in Blue (original, 1924 version). (ii) Second Rhapsody; (i) Variations on 'I got Rhythm'. Walking the Dog; (Piano Solo) (i) Rialto Ripples; (ii) O Land of mine, America

(N) (M) **(*) Telarc 2-CD 80445. Cincinnati Pops O, Kunzel; with (i) Tritt; (ii) Goodyear; (iii) Central State University Ch., Caldwell

An American in Paris; Cuban Overture; Lullaby; (i) Variations on 'I got Rhythm'; Rialto Ripples (from above); (ii) Piano Prelude 2; (iii) Porgy & Bess: Summertime

(N) (M) ** Telarc CD 80542. Cincinnati Pops O, Kunzel; with (i) Tritt; (ii) O'Conor; (iii) Blackwell

The Telarc two-disc anthology, originally assembled for the Gershwin Centenary in 1998, is pretty comprehensive and includes the 1924 Whiteman scoring of the *Rhapsody*, with William Tritt lively enough, yet without the breathless momentum of the famous piano-roll account with the composer. The performance is also notable in including some 44 bars of music which Gershwin later cut out (not necessarily to disadvantage). The *Concerto* has a nostalgically memorable slow movement, but the outer movements are somewhat lacking in sheer verve. However, Stewart Goodyear makes a surprising success of the *Second Rhapsody* and both the *Rialto Ripples* rag and the engaging '*I got Rhythm*' *Variations* are played with stylish flair by his colleague. The other main items are also available differently coupled, and nearly all the shorter pieces are worth having. The *Lullaby* is hauntingly seductive on the Cincinnati strings; *Walking the Dog*, a clarinet solo, is played with neat insouciance by Richard Hawley, but the *Mexican Dance* is a conventional genre piece. The sentimental choral work which ends the concert, although sung ardently, needs more Sousa-like pep than it receives here; the recording, too, is not up to the usual Telarc standard.

The single disc, surprisingly, omits the *Rhapsody* but includes the *Piano Prelude No. 2*, simply and appealingly played by John O'Conor, and *Summertime* from *Porgy and Bess*, very well sung by Harolyn Blackwell with chorus, a curious substitution, but very welcome.

An American in Paris; Piano Concerto in F; Cuban Overture; 'I Got Rhythm': Variations for Piano & Orchestra; Porgy and Bess: Symphonic Suite (arr. Robert Russell Bennett); Rhapsody in Blue; 2nd Rhapsody for Orchestra with Piano; Songs: Girl Crazy; Strike up the Band (both orch. Don Ross)

(B) *** Virgin 2×1 5 62056-2 (2). Marshall, Aalborg Symphony

With this dazzling Gershwin programme Wayne Marshall both acts as soloist and directs the orchestra. *An American in Paris* and the *Cuban Overture* are full of character, with superbly idiomatic orchestral playing; and the orchestral soloists shine individually in Robert Russell Bennett's brilliant orchestration of the music from *Porgy and Bess*, while the strings are gorgeously seductive in both tone and inflexion. This is consistently exhilarating.

The performance of the *Rhapsody in Blue* in some ways outshines even Bernstein's famous New York account in its audacious, glittering brilliance, although Bernstein still has a special place in the catalogue. But Marshall manages spontaneously to coalesce both the 'symphonic' and the jazz character of the piece, with the accent on the latter (where with Bernstein the balance is more even). Here the players of the Aalborg Symphony produce a hell-for-leather 'pizazz' in the fast brass tuttis, contrasting with a rapturous bluesy account of the the big tune. The '*I Got Rhythm*' *Variations* are played with comparable bravura and panache, full of affection and witty touches.

Marshall opens the *Concerto* much faster than usual, and this too is a peppy, transatlantic reading but one that relaxes wonderfully for the heart-touching trumpet blues theme of the slow movement, splendidly played here. The *Second Rhapsody* is almost as dazzling as the first, with the closing pages winningly brought off. *Girl Crazy* and *Strike up the Band* are lively pot-pourris, presumably following the outline of the original theatre overtures. The recording is first class, full of ambient atmosphere, while the violins have just the right degree of brightness and tonal body to add sumptuousness and bite where needed. In every way this set leads the field.

(i) An American in Paris; Cuban Overture; (ii) Porgy and Bess: Symphonic Portrait; (i; iii) Rhapsody in Blue

(B) **(*) Decca Eloquence (ADD/DDD) 467 410-2. (i) Cleveland O, Maazel; (ii) Detroit SO, Dorati; (iii) with Davis

Ivan Davis is both a brilliant and sophisticated soloist in the *Rhapsody*; the boisterous account of *Cuban Overture* is immensely spirited, and *An American in Paris* is given an upbeat reading, well held together. There are more sumptuous versions but, with superb Cleveland playing, these performances are easy to enjoy. Dorati's digital recording of Robert Russell Bennett's famous *Porgy and Bess* arrangement is quite superb, both as a recording and as a performance. The opening is evocatively nostalgic, and each one of these wonderful tunes is phrased with a warmly affectionate feeling for its character, yet never vulgarized. A good bargain – though, as usual in the UK Eloquence series, notes are not provided.

(i) An American in Paris; (ii) Concerto in F; (iii) Rhapsody in Blue (original, 1924 score)

(N) (M) ** RCA 82876 60862-2. (i) San Francisco SO, Tilson Thomas, (ii) with Ohlsson; (iii) Tilson Thomas (piano), New World Symphony

Michael Tilson Thomas's account of the *Rhapsody in Blue*

with the New World Symphony is an attempt to re-create his earlier performance of the score on Sony using Gershwin's piano-roll and the original reduced orchestration (see below). But it is only partially successful, and both here and in Garrick Ohlsson's reading of the *Concerto in F* the solo playing brings some indulgent rhythmic touches which do not wear well on repetition, although the *Concerto's* slow movement is very beautifully played. *An American in Paris* goes well enough, but there are more convincing Gershwin collections than this.

An American in Paris; Piano Concerto in F; Rhapsody in Blue

(M) *** EMI 5 66891-[566943]. Previn (piano & cond.), LSO

The digital remastering of Previn's EMI set, made at the beginning of the 1970s, has brought a striking enhancement of the recording itself; there is now much more sparkle. The performance of the *Concerto* was always an outstanding one by any standards, but now in the *Rhapsody* one senses many affinities with the famous Bernstein account. *An American in Paris* is exuberantly volatile, and the entry of the great blues tune on the trumpet has a memorable rhythmic lift.

An American in Paris; (i) Piano Concerto in F. Cuban Overture; (i) Rhapsody in Blue; Variations on 'I got Rhythm'

(N) (M) *** RCA **SACD** 82876 61393-2. (i) Wild; Boston Pops O, Fiedler

The RCA SACD, with just short of 80 minutes' playing time, offers the contents of two 'Living Stereo' LPs, recorded in 1959 and 1961 respectively, now with enhanced sound. Besides the usual triptych, Fiedler's *Cuban Overture* is added, which has great élan, and Earl Wild includes a bouncy account of the '*I got Rhythm*' *Variations*, given plenty of rhythmic panache and a nice touch of wit. Indeed (while not stretching the boundaries beyond the limit, like the Ozawa/Marcus Roberts DVD), these are essentially jazzy performances. Wild's playing is full of energy and brio, and he inspires Arthur Fiedler to a similar infectious response.The outer movements of the *Concerto* are comparably volatile and the blues feeling of the slow movement is strong. In *An American in Paris* Fiedler adds to the exuberance by bringing in the bevy of motor horns indicated in the original score (though Paris is without them these days). The slightly brash recording sounds newly minted, much clearer in focus than before, without loss of the Boston amplitude.

(i) An American in Paris; (i; ii) Concerto in F; Rhapsody in Blue (both arr. Roberts). *(i) Strike up the Band* (Selection). *(ii) I got Rhythm.* ROBERTS: *Cole after Midnight.* LINCKE: *Berliner Luft*

(N) *(**) EuroArts **DVD** 2053098. (i) BPO, Ozawa; (ii) Marcus Roberts Trio

Described as 'A Gershwin Night', this live open-air concert in the spectacular Berlin stadium, the Waldbühne – holding an audience of thousands – is rather a mixture of Gershwin and jazz improvisations, which will not appeal to all listeners. The opening performance of *An American in Paris* is magnificent. Ozawa knows just how this masterpiece should be shaped, and the Berlin Philharmonic players (after a period with Rattle at the helm) inflect the rhythms with élan: their playing is remarkably idiomatic, gorgeous in sonority and thrilling in its impetus. The recorded sound is superb and there is no lack of ambient resonance).

However, in the concertante works the orchestra (who

again play resplendently) is joined by not just Marcus Roberts (a fine jazz pianist) but also by his rhythm group. They are virtuoso players, but in the *Rhapsody* and *Concerto* they add extended improvisations in the place of cadenzas and, in the finale of the *Concerto* especially, these brilliant rhythmic interludes are too much of a good thing. Similarly, the simple melody of *I got Rhythm* is extended – quite wittily in its way – to over six minutes. *Strike up the Band* is a selection; the memorable tune of that name forms the climax but is underused. The concert ends with an uproarious account of the Berliners' equivalent of the finale of the Last Night of the Proms, and the audience let their hair down in Lincke's *Berliner Luft*, enthusiastically adding the prescribed repeated three whistles to the refrain.

An American in Paris; (i) Rhapsody in Blue

🔊 💿 (M) *** Sony (ADD) **SACD** SS 89033; CD 516234-2; [SK 90393]. NYPO, Bernstein, (i) Bernstein (piano) – GROFÉ: *Grand Canyon Suite* ***

(N) ** Telarc **SACD** 60646. Cincinnati SO, Kunzel, (i) with Eugene List – TCHAIKOVSKY: *Capriccio Italien; 1812, etc.* **(*)

Bernstein's 1958–9 coupling set the standard by which all subsequent pairings of *An American in Paris* and *Rhapsody in Blue* came to be judged. It still sounds astonishingly well as a recording. Bernstein's approach is inspirational, exceptionally flexible but completely spontaneous. The performance of *An American in Paris* is vividly characterized, brash and episodic; an unashamedly American view, with the great blues tune marvellously timed and phrased as only a great American orchestra can do it. This coupling is also available on one of Sony's Super Audio CDs, which needs special playback equipment but which offers richer and more expansive sound, approaching demonstration standard.

Eugene List is as always an impressive soloist in Gershwin, and the Telarc performance using the full symphonic scoring is recorded very sumptuously indeed. The rich sound is ideal for those who like to wallow in the melodic richness of *An American in Paris*. The blues tune certainly sounds expansive and there is no real lack of vitality, although in both works there seems an over-prominence of the bass drum (a characteristic of Telarc CDs). Originally issued on their own, these Gershwin performances now come with an even more spectacular Tchaikovsky triptych.

(i–ii) An American in Paris; (ii–iii) Rhapsody in Blue; (ii; iv) Overtures: Funny Face; Girl Crazy; Let 'em eat Cake; Of thee I sing; Oh Kay!; Strike up the Band; (ii; v) Promenade (Walking the Dog); (ii; v; vi) Fascinatin' Rhythm

🔊 (N) (B) *** Sony 516241-2 [SK 93080]. (i) NYPO; (ii) Tilson Thomas; (iii) composer (from 1925 piano roll), Columbia Jazz Band; (iv) Buffalo PO; (v) LAPO; (vi) Sarah Vaughan

Alongside Bernstein's great vintage recording of the *Rhapsody* in its orchestration for full symphony orchestra comes this remarkable re-creation of the composer's own performance, taken from a 1925 piano roll, using Ferdé Grofé's initial scoring for Paul Whiteman. Gershwin's own recording was made possible by the dedication of Tom Shepard and the record's producer, Andrew Kadzin, who meticulously covered every hole on the composer's piano roll which did not refer to the piano part. A group of eminent musicians was then gathered in the studio to play Grofé's scoring, which featured mostly wind, a variety of saxophones, clarinet and brass, plus eight violins. Gershwin's solo performance was recorded from the pianola, and the tape was then used by Michael Tilson Thomas and his 'Columbia Jazz Band', who skilfully fitted the accompaniment around it. The spontaneity of the finished performance is quite riveting. Gershwin's virtuosity is remarkable, his tempi often disconcertingly fast, and there is much bravura from the accompanying group (the first big tutti for the band makes one really sit up). But when one adjusts there is no doubt that the music-making has an irresistible flavour of the 1920s, although when the big tune arrives it is introduced richly and spaciously. This is an account that makes one rethink a piece that is usually heard less quirkily in its equally valid symphonic dress.

Fortunately the main coupling is a very fine account of *An American in Paris* with the NYPO on top form, while the excellent Buffalo Philharmonic are equally on their toes and enjoying themselves in sparkling performances of the six overtures. These pot-pourris demand both vivacity and affectionate detail – which they receive here in good measure. The two bonuses are also splendidly done, with Sarah Vaughan's *Fascinatin' Rhythm* a great closing encore.

Broadway and Film Music: *A Damsel in Distress* (suite, arr. McGlinn.); *Stiff Upper Lip: Funhouse Sequence.* **Overtures:** *Girl Crazy; Of Thee I Sing; Oh, Kay!; Primrose; Tip-Toes*
(B) **(*) EMI double forte 5 68589-2 (2). New Princess
    Theatre O, McGlinn – KERN: *Overtures* **; PORTER:
    Overtures & Film Music ***

This inexpensive two-disc double forte set makes a pretty good collection for those who enjoy authentic re-creations of Broadway music composed by three of its greatest names. John McGlinn has recorded his selections using the original scores. The extended dance-sequence, *Stiff Upper Lip*, comes from a 1937 movie and has some good tunes. So has *Oh Kay!* (half a dozen) while *Girl Crazy* offers the irresistible *I got rhythm*. Elsewhere the famous melodies are more thinly spread, but the marvellous playing of the New York pick-up orchestra (gorgeous saxes and brass) has splendid pep. The lively, close-miked sound gives an authentic theatre-pit brashness, with very bright violins, although the background ambience is warm enough.

Catfish Row (suite from *Porgy and Bess*)
*** Telarc CD 80086. Tritt, Cincinnati Pops O, Kunzel –
    GROFE: *Grand Canyon Suite* ***

Catfish Row was arranged by the composer after the initial failure of his opera. It includes a brief piano solo, played with fine style by William Tritt in the highly sympathetic Telarc performance, which is very well recorded.

Piano Concerto in F
(N) (B) *** DG 2-CD 477 5439 (2). Szidon, LPO, Downes –
    IVES: *Piano Sonatas;* MACDOWELL: *Piano Concerto 2;*
    VILLA-LOBOS: *Piano Music* ***

Robert Szidon on DG treats the *Concerto* as he would any other romantic concerto and, with the rhythm superbly lithe and tonal colouring enchantingly subtle in its range, the result gives new stature to the music. The jazz idiom is seen (as it regularly and naturally is, for example, in the Ravel *Concertos*) as an essential, but not overwhelmingly dominant element – a refreshing alternative to the totally jazz-dominated performance on Ozawa's DVD. Downes and the LPO match the soloist in understanding and virtuosity, while the recording is of demonstration standard for its time

(1970). This comes within a stimulating two-CD collection of 'Piano music from the Americas'.

Piano Concerto in F; Rhapsody in Blue
(N) (M) (**) Decca Heritage mono 475 6159. Katchen,
    Mantovani and his O

Mantovani was an unexpected choice for Katchen in this repertoire, but the results are surprisingly successful (Mantovani was a fine musician and always had excellent players). Katchen displays all his characteristic energy and there is no lack of bravura. The mono (1955) sound is quite dry, but vivid, and the use of the original cover on this Decca Heritage release is highly evocative. However, the playing time of under 45 minutes is ungenerous.

Piano Concerto in F; Rhapsody in Blue; 2nd Rhapsody for Piano & Orchestra; Variations on 'I got rhythm'
(M) *** Classic fM 76505 57012-2. Boriskin, Eos O, Sheffer

Michael Boriskin is a native New Yorker, and he and Jonathan Sheffer immediately establish a partnership which brings an idiomatic and freshly individual approach to these two concertante masterpieces which uniquely span the jazz world and the ethos of the concert hall. The keenly sophisticated and inventive 'I got rhythm' *Variations* are no less glittering and are wonderfully infectious. The orchestral detail throughout is a joy (especially illuminating in the less inspired *Second Rhapsody*), while in the concerto the big climaxes open out to engulf the listener expansively and ardently. Boriskin's brilliant pianism is wittily skittish in the most infectious way, both in the *Rhapsody* and in the delectably played central section of the concerto's slow movement, which Neil Balm has opened so languorously with his trumpet. The finale brings dazzling yet totally unforced bravura. The recording is first rate.

Porgy and Bess Symphonic Picture (arr. Robert Russell Bennett)
(N) (BB) **(*) Resonance CDRSN 3042. Bournemouth SO,
    Farrer – COPLAND: *Billy the Kid; Rodeo* **(*)

John Farrer presents the famous Robert Russell Bennett *Symphonic Picture* with some panache, and the Bournemouth players respond with spirited flair, the brass especially. However, the orchestral sound could ideally be more sumptuous. Dorati's famous Detroit version is not upstaged – see above.

Rhapsody in Blue (see also above, under *An American in Paris*)
(M) **(*) DG 476 7233. Bernstein (piano & cond.), LAPO –
    BARBER: *Adagio for Strings;* COPLAND: *Appalachian Spring* ***

In his last recording of this work for DG, Bernstein rather goes over the top with his jazzing of the solos in Gershwin. Such rhythmic freedom was clearly the result of a live rather than a studio performance. This does not match Bernstein's inspired (1959) analogue coupling for CBS.

Arrangements of Songs: *Embraceable you; Fascinatin' rhythm; A foggy day; Funny Face; He loves and she loves; I got rhythm; Liza; Love is here to stay; The man I love; Nice work if you can get it; Oh, Lady be good; Summertime; 'S wonderful; They all laughed; They can't take that away from me*
(BB) *** EMI Encore (ADD) 5 85081-2. Y. Menuhin &
    Stéphane Grappelli

This is an attractive bargain re-assembly of the Gershwin numbers taken from the vintage Menuhin–Grappelli series of studio collaborations, recorded during the 1970s and early 1980s, in which two distinguished musicians from different musical backgrounds struck sparks off each other to most entertaining effect. The songs are all famous and the treatments highly felicitous. The sound has excellent presence.

PIANO MUSIC

Impromptu in 2 Keys; 3 Preludes; Three-quarter Blues; Ballet (from *Primrose*); *Jazzbo Brown* (from *Porgy and Bess*); *Merry Andrew* (from *Rosalie*); *Overtures: Girl Crazy; Lady be Good. Promenade* (from *Shall we Dance*); *2 Waltzes in C* (from *Pardon My English*). **Song arrangements:** *Clap yo' hands; Do do do; Do it again; Fascinatin' rhythm; I got rhythm; I'll build a stairway to paradise; Liza; The man I love; My one and only; Nobody but you; Oh, lady be good; Somebody loves me; Strike up the band; Swanee; Sweet and low down; 'Swonderful; That certain feeling; Who cares?*
(BB) *** Hyp. CDH 55006. Brownridge

Angela Brownridge offers Gershwin's meagre output of solo concert pieces for piano, opening with a Joplinesque early rag, *Rialto Ripples*, Gershwin's first instrumental number from 1916. She plays the *Three Preludes* very well indeed, and also includes piano interludes from various shows, like the pair of *Waltzes in C* which the composer and Kay Swift played as a piano duet in *Pardon My English*.

There are also two pot-pourri *Overtures* which are very spirited and then – by offering just chorus and verse – she finds room for 18 of Gershwin's finest song-arrangements, her playing scintillating and romantic by turns, yet always stylish. The recording is excellent. A bargain.

3 Preludes; An American in Paris (arr. Daly); *Songs* (arr. Gershwin): *Fascinatin' rhythm; I got rhythm; I'll build a stairway to paradise; The man I love; Oh, lady be good; Liza; Somebody loves me; Sweet and low down; 'Swonderful; Who cares?*
(*) Nim. NI 5585. Anderson – COPLAND: *Piano Sonata*, etc. *

Recorded at a live recital in Nimbus's own concert hall, this is an enjoyable enough collection of Gershwin favourites. Mark Anderson plays very well, if without those subtle rhythmic inflexions that mark most American performances and especially Gershwin's own piano-roll recordings. But why transcribe *An American in Paris*? It sounds so much better in its full orchestral costume.

Piano Rolls

'The Piano Rolls' Vol. 1: (i) *An American in Paris;* (ii) *Idle dreams; Kicking the clouds away; Novelette in fourths; On my mind the whole night long; Rhapsody in Blue; Scandal walk; So am I; Swanee; Sweet and lowdown; That certain feeling; When you want 'em you can't get 'em, when you've got 'em you don't want 'em*
*** None. 7559 79287-2. (i) Milne and Leith; (ii) composer

This series, recorded by the composer between 1916 and 1926 using the Welte-Mignon and Duo-Art piano-roll systems, was reproduced through a 1911 pianola (operated by Artis Wodehouse) and then recorded in digital stereo – with the utmost realism. The result is as if Gershwin himself was playing in the studio. The four-handed arrangement of *An*

American in Paris is a marvellous 'orchestral' performance and matches the composer in its flamboyance and breadth of style. *Rhapsody in Blue* is the composer's special arrangement. The sound is first class and admirably present.

'*The Authentic George Gershwin*' (piano arrangements of songs)

Volumes 1–3 (complete)
(M) **(*) ASV CDWLS 328 (3). Jack Gibbons

Jack Gibbons has transcribed Gershwin's own piano transcriptions from the records and piano rolls made by the composer himself, and in certain cases from recorded radio programmes and film sound-tracks. His playing is brightly idiomatic, fresh and spontaneous, and has received much praise for its closeness to the composer's own keyboard style. The modern digital recording adds to the appeal of this set. But the arrangements of the orchestral works and the solo piano versions of the *Rhapsody in Blue*, the *Second Rhapsody* and the '*I got rhythm*' *Variations* (drawn from the composer's four-handed versions) often sound rather prolix and are much less effective and enjoyable than the songs, although played with the same sense of style. There are also more impressive versions on disc of the three *Piano Preludes*. In many ways Volume 4 is the most attractive of the Jack Gibbons anthologies so far. Opening with the original version of the *Girl Crazy Overture*, he concentrates on numbers from two shows, *A Damsel in Distress* (which includes a pair of fascinatingly different versions of *The jolly tar and the milkmaid*) and *Shall We Dance*. Both are full of striking numbers, and he ends with the ever-engaging *Love walked in* from *The Goldwyn Follies*. His easy, undemanding style is as idiomatically engaging as ever, and the recording is well up to standard. The full listings will appear in our 2006/7 Yearbook.

VOCAL MUSIC

'*Kiri Sings Gershwin*': *Boy wanted; But not for me; By Strauss; Embraceable you; I got rhythm; Love is here to stay; Love walked in; Meadow serenade; The man I love; Nice work if you can get it; Somebody loves me; Someone to watch over me; Soon; Things are looking up. Porgy and Bess: Summertime*
**(*) EMI 7 47454-2. Te Kanawa, New Theatre O, McGlinn (with chorus)

In Dame Kiri's gorgeously sung *Summertime* from *Porgy and Bess*, the distanced heavenly chorus creates the purest kitsch. But most of the numbers are done in an upbeat style. Dame Kiri is at her most relaxed and ideally there should be more variety of pacing: *The man I love* is thrown away at the chosen tempo. But for the most part the ear is seduced; however, the pop microphone techniques bring excessive sibilants on CD.

OPERA AND MUSICALS

Girl Crazy (musical)
(M) *** None. 7559-79250-2. Blazer, Luft, Carroll, Korbich, O, Mauceri

Girl Crazy, despite its hit numbers – *Embraceable you, I got rhythm* and *Bidin' my time* – has always been counted a failure; but this lively recording, with an ensemble of distinguished New York musicians conducted by John Mauceri, gives the lie to that. The story of love and misunderstanding is largely irrelevant, but the score has point and imagination from beginning to end, all the brighter here for having had the sugar-coating which Hollywood introduced in the much-mangled film version of 1943 removed. The casting is excellent. Judy Blazer takes the Ginger Rogers role of Kate, the post-girl, while Judy Garland's less well-known daughter, Lorna Luft, is delightful in the Ethel Merman part of the gambler's wife hired to sing in the saloon. David Carroll is the New Yorker hero, and Frank Gorshin takes the comic role of the cab driver, Gieber Goldfarb. The only serious reservation is that the recording is dry and brassy, aggressively so – but that could be counted typical of the period too. Undoubtedly a bargain at mid-price.

Lady Be Good (musical)

*** None. 7559 79308-2. Teeter, Morrison, Alexander, Pizzarelli, Blier, Musto, Ch. & O, Stern

This charming score, dating from 1924 (just after *Rhapsody in Blue*), emerges as one of the composer's freshest. Such numbers as the title-song, as well as *Fascinatin' rhythm* and the witty *Half of it, dearie, blues*, are set against such duets as *Hang on to me* and *So am I*, directly reflecting the 1920s world that Sandy Wilson parodied so affectionately in *The Boy Friend*. *Lady Be Good* was the piece originally written for the brother-and-sister team of Fred and Adele Astaire, and the casting of the principals on the disc is first rate. These are not concert-singers but ones whose clearly projected voices are ideally suited to the repertory, including Lara Teeter and Ann Morrison in the Astaires' roles and Michael Maguire as the young millionaire whom the heroine finally marries. The score has been restored by Tommy Krasker, and an orchestra of first-rate sessions musicians is conducted by Eric Stern.

Oh Kay!

*** None. 7559 79361-2. Upshaw, Ollman, Arkin, Cassidy, Westenberg, Larsen, Ch. & O of St Luke's, Stern

The last in this splendid Nonesuch series of Gershwin musicals is in many ways the finest of all. With the music (including hits like *Someone to watch over me*, *Clap yo' hands*, *Do do do* and the very catchy *Fidgety feet*) fitting neatly on to one CD, this is a fizzing entertainment. Dawn Upshaw is a highly enticing Kay, and she gets vivid support from Kurt Ollman as Jimmy, Adam Arkin as Shorty McGee and Patrick Cassidy as Larry. The cast could hardly be more naturally at home in Gershwin's sparkling score. Eric Stern directs with great flair and the recording is admirably vivid. Not to be missed.

Porgy and Bess (opera; complete)

⊶ ✱ *** EMI **DVD** 4 92496-9. White, Haymon, Blackwell, Hubbard, Baker, Clarey, Evans, Glydebourne Ch., LPO, Rattle

⊶ ✱ *** EMI 5 56220-2 (3). Details as above

After the huge success of the Glyndebourne production of *Porgy and Bess*, EMI took the whole cast to the Shepperton Studios, where it was produced for video by Trevor Nunn and Yves Baignere, using the giant stage to move the actions around freely as in a film. The result is stunningly successful, bringing the story to life with extraordinary vividness. This is one of the most creative of all such productions so far, fully worthy of Gershwin's masterly score.

On CD, Simon Rattle conducts the same cast and orchestra as in the opera house, and the EMI engineers have done wonders in establishing more clearly than ever the status of *Porgy* as grand opera. By comparison, Lorin Maazel's Decca

CD version sounds a degree too literal, and John DeMain's RCA set is less subtle. More than their rivals, Rattle and the LPO capture Gershwin's rhythmic exuberance with the degree of freedom essential if jazz-based inspirations are to sound idiomatic. The chorus is the finest and most responsive of any on the three sets, and the bass line-up is the strongest. Willard White is superbly matched by the magnificent Jake of Bruce Hubbard and by the dark and resonant Crown of Gregg Baker. As Sportin' Life, Damon Evans gets nearer than any of his rivals to the original scat-song inspiration without ever short-changing on musical values. Cynthia Haymon as Bess is movingly convincing in conveying equivocal emotions, Harolyn Blackwell as Clara sensuously relishes Rattle's slow speed for *Summertime* and Cynthia Clarey is an intense and characterful Serena. EMI's digital sound is exceptionally full and spacious.

Porgy and Bess (highlights)

*** EMI 7 54325-2 (from above recording, with White, Haymon; cond. Rattle)

Rattle's highlights disc is generous (74 minutes) and most comprehensive. However, not all the tailoring is clean: *Summertime* ends rather abruptly and there is at least one fade.

Porgy and Bess: excerpts (i) 1935, 1940; & (ii) 1942 original cast recordings; (iii) 1935 RCA recordings; (iv) *Lullaby: Summertime; Livin's easy; A woman is a sometime thing; Takes a long pull to get there; It ain't necessarily so.* (v) Arr. Heifetz: *Summertime; A woman is a sometime thing; My man's gone now; It ain't necessarily so; Bess, you is my woman now; There's a boat dat's leavin' soon for New York (Tempo di blues).* (vi) *Symphonic Picture* (arr. R. R. Bennett)

(BB) (**(*) Naxos mono 8.110 219-2 (2). (i) Brown, Duncan, Robeson, Eva Jessye Ch., O, Smallens; (i; ii) Long; (ii) Dowdy, Matthews, O, Reisman; (iii) Jepson, Tibbett, O, Smallens; (iv) Robeson, O, Greenwood; (v) Heifetz, Bay; (vi) LAPO, Wallenstein

These two discs in the Naxos historic series vividly bring together the earliest recordings of numbers from Gershwin's great opera. The first of the two discs contains the recordings made for American Decca by the original casts, both from the pioneering 1935 production (not recorded till 1940, the first 'original cast album') and from the West Coast revival of 1941, recorded the following year. All the principal numbers are included, though not always with the original singers taking their old roles. Todd Duncan and Anne Brown are the principals, firm, clear and characterful, with Edward Matthews another fine contributor. Avon Long and Helen Dowdy are the principals in the 1942 recordings; excellent too, though by then even the principal numbers are jazzed up with blaring brass commentary. Curiously, the very first original-cast recording, made in 1935 by Edward Matthews, was of two numbers in strict tempo 'for dancing'. That was the year when two principal singers from the Met., Lawrence Tibbett and Helen Jepson, recorded for RCA a collection of nine excerpts, the principal items on the second disc, all of them magnificent. Also included are four items recorded by Paul Robeson in London in 1938: uniquely resonant, with the soprano aria, *Summertime*, transposed for bass. Heifetz's arrangements of six numbers, recorded for American Decca in 1945, are also magnetic. The Robert Russell Bennett *Symphonic Portrait* also comes in a première recording, rough in sound but a reasonable filler. Voices, and Heifetz's violin, come over well in the rest of the transfers, though orchestral sound is thin.

Strike Up the Band (musical)

**(*) None. 7559 79273-2 (2). Barrett, Luker, Chastain, Graae, Fowler, Goff, Lambert, Lyons, Sandish, Rocco, Ch. & O, Mauceri

Strike Up the Band was the nearest that George and Ira Gershwin ever came to imitating Gilbert and Sullivan, although its two hit numbers, *The man I love* and *Strike up the band*, are entirely characteristic. For all its vigour, the performance lacks something of the exuberance which marks the recordings of musicals conducted by John McGlinn for EMI. It may be correct to observe the dotted rhythms of *The man I love* as precisely as this performance does, but something is lost in the flow of the music, and to latter-day ears the result is less haunting than the customary reading. The singers are first rate, but they would have been helped by having at least one of their number with a more charismatic personality. The second disc includes an appendix containing seven numbers used in the abortive 1930 revival.

GESUALDO, Carlo (c. 1561–1613)

Ave, dulcissima Maria; Ave, regina coelorum; Maria mater gratiae; Precibus et meritus beatae Mariae (motets). Tenebrae responsories for Holy Saturday

⊶ *** Gimell CDGIM 015. Tallis Scholars, Phillips

Ave, Dulcissima Maria; Peccantem mei quotidie; Tribularer si nescirem; Tribulationem et delorem (motets). Tenebrae, responsories for Holy Saturday

(N) (B) *** HM Musique d'abord HMA 1951320. Ens. Vocal Européen, Herreweghe (with GORLI: *Requiem*)

The astonishing dissonances and chromaticisms may not be as extreme here as in some of Gesualdo's secular music but, as elaborate as madrigals, they still have a sharp, refreshing impact on the modern ear which recognizes music leaping the centuries. The performances are superb, finely finished and beautifully blended, with women's voices made to sound boyish, singing with freshness and bite to bring home the total originality of the writing with its awkward leaps and intervals. Beautifully recorded, this is another of the Tallis Scholars' ear-catching discs, powerful as well as polished.

Herreweghe's performances with his European group of singers are also very fine, not as volatile as those by the Tallis Scholars, but serenely intense and moving. Apart from *Ave dulcissima Maria*, which he shares with Phillips, he chooses three different motets, all suitably penitential. Moreover, he offers a bonus of an extraordinary, even bizarre *Requiem* by Sandro Gorli (born in Como in 1948). The composer has provided his own text, and the music's modern dissonances, although even more flagrantly pungent, are curiously in the spirit of medieval writing; and the work ends in a desperately wild call of 'Father, why hast thou forsaken me?'

Leçons de ténèbres: Responsories for Maundy Thursday

⊶ *** Signum SIGCD 048. King's Singers

(B) *** HM (ADD) HMA 190220. Deller Cons., Deller

Gesualdo's *Responses for Holy Week* of 1611, with their surprising chromatic dissonances, are among the most remarkable and original of all *Tenèbre* settings. We already have a fine performance of them from Alfred Deller's Consort on Harmonia Mundi, but this new, ground-breaking account from the

King's Singers is even more expressively powerful. Immediately, as *In Monte Oliveti* opens, the King's Singers demonstrate a very flexible approach to tempo and dynamic that is to characterize their whole performance. The impeccable intonation and tonal matching also give a special richness to the chordal writing; and its moments of dissonance and the drama of *Amicus meus osculi* ('the betrayal with a kiss') and *Judas mercantor pessimus* are very tangible. The performance closes simply with the chant, *Christus factus est*, and this is treated as a brief recessional. A superbly sung performance, expressively poignant but dramatic too, which brings a new dimension to this remarkable music. The recording is outstanding.

The Deller Consort here bring much the same approach as distinguishes their handling of the madrigal literature. The colouring of the words is a high priority, yet it never oversteps the bounds of good taste. The consort blends remarkably well and intonation is excellent. Temptingly inexpensive.

Leçons de ténèbres: Responsories for Good Friday (1611)

(N) **(*) Sony SK 62977. Taverner Consort, Parrott

Parrott's collection is beautifully sung and recorded, if not quite achieving the degree of passionate flexibility which is a feature of the Signum performances. But Parrott consistently includes all the antiphon chants which precede each of the responsories, which is absolutely authentic. But some of them are quite long, and (for non-ecclesiastical performance) perhaps this is too much of a good thing.

GIBBONS, Orlando (1583–1625)

Consorts for Viols: *Fantasias a 2, 1–6; Fantasias a 6, 1–6; Go from my window; Galliard; Pavan;* (i) **Songs:** *Ah dear heart; The Silver Swan; What is our life?*

*** Metronome MET CD 1039. Concordia, (i) with Elliott

Consorts for Viols: *Fantasies a 3, 1–4; Fantasies a 6, 1–5; In Nomines a 5, 1–2.* **Keyboard Pieces arranged for Viols:** *Fantasia; Galliard; Go from my Window; Pavan; Pavan Lord Salisbury; Peascod Times.* **Vocal works arranged for Viols:** *Hosanna to the son of David; O Lord, in thy wrath. The Silver Swan*

⊶ *** Avie AV 0032. Phantasm

The *Fantasies* for viol consort by Orlando Gibbons are among the most sublime works in the string repertory, leading on to the *Fantasias* of Purcell, even breathing the same air as the late Beethoven *Quartets*. Sadly, on disc they have too often been treated to performances that slice your ears off in period abrasiveness; happily, the group, Phantasm, is different, at once authoritative and beautifully matched. The complexity of the *Fantasies in six parts*, presented here as a cohesive group, is astonishing both in rhythm and in counterpoint, and the two six-part *In Nomines*, more austere, have a similar intensity. Four *Fantasies in three parts* demonstrate Gibbons's contrapuntal mastery just as clearly. Quoting the composer, Phantasm supplement this music written specifically for viols with transcriptions of such keyboard pieces as the superb *Lord Salisbury Pavan*, as well as three of Gibbons's greatest vocal pieces, the anthems *O Lord, in thy wrath* and *Hosanna to the Son of David*, as well as the lovely madrigal, *The Silver Swan*. Well-balanced sound, though with a limited dynamic range.

The performances from Concordia are similarly warm, tonally full and without abrasiveness, with sensitive use of light and shade, and they can be recommended alongside (but not in preference to) those by Phantasm. However, the advantage of the Metronome collection is that it includes three delightful songs, beautifully sung by Rachel Elliott.

Consort Music: *Fantasias a 4: 1–2 in C. In Nomines: a 4 in D min.; a 5: 1 in C; 2 in G min.* (i) *Ye Sacred Muses (Elegy on the Death of Thomas Tallis)*
*** Globe GLO 5159. Royal Consort, (i) with Cordier – BYRD: *Consort Songs* ***

These *Fantasias* and *In Nomines* are played with warmth and refinement, and with subtle variations of dynamic light and shade. As we have commented on the Byrd couplings, a consistent atmosphere of dolour pervades. But that lies within the music itself, and David Cordier's sensitive account of Gibbons's posthumous tribute to Tallis, *Ye Sacred Muses*, is most touchingly sung.

Consort music: (i) *Fantazia 1 for 2 Treble Viols; Fantazias 3 & 5 a 6; Fantazia 1 for Great Double Bass (for Organ & 3 Viols); Galliard a 3; Galliard a 6; Go not from my window a 6; In nomine a 4; Pavane a 6.* **Keyboard pieces:** (ii) *Almain in F; The fairest nymph (mask); Lincoln's Inn mask; The Lord of Salisbury his pavane and galliard. Organ Preludium in G.* **Vocal:** (i; iii) *Behold thou hast made my days; Glorious and powerful God (both for 5 voices & 5 viols).* **Solo voice & viols:** (i; iv) *Dainty fine bird; Fair is the rose; I feign not friendship where I hate; I see ambition never pleased; I tremble not at noise of war; I weigh not fortune's frown; The silver swan*
☛ (BB) *** Naxos 8.550603. (i) Rose Consort of Viols; (ii) Roberts; with (iii) Red Byrd; (iv) Bonner

This makes the perfect supplement to the excellent Naxos issue of Gibbons's church music (see below), with 22 items that cover a wide range of songs as well as instrumental music. The players of the Rose Consort, with agreeably tangy string-tone, contribute most of the instrumental pieces, culminating in two magnificent *Fantazias* in six parts: No. 3 with ear-catching harmonic clashes, No. 5 with side-slipping chromatic writing, pointing forward to later centuries.

Timothy Roberts is the soloist in keyboard music on harpsichord, virginals and organ, while the soprano, Tessa Bonner, is the bright-toned soloist in a sequence of songs with consort accompaniment. Also standing out are two fine anthems, one written for the funeral of a Dean of Windsor, with Red Byrd accompanied by the consort, five voices and five instruments.

Harpsichord Pieces: *2 Almaynes; Fancy; 3 Fantasias; French Air, Almayne & Coranto; 3 Galliards; 4 Pavins; 3 Preludiums; The Kings Jewell; Whoope doe me no harm good man*
(N) ** Globe 5168. Egarr (Muselar virginal or harpsichord)

Gibbons's keyboard music is slight, well crafted and pleasing, if not as memorable as his consort music. Richard Egarr (not surprisingly) has its full measure, whether on virginal or harpsichord. He is attractively recorded.

Anthems and verse anthems: *Almighty and everlasting God; Hosanna to the Son of David; Lift up your heads; O Thou the central orb; See, see the word is incarnate; This is the record of John.* **Canticles:** *Short service: Magnificat & Nunc dimittis. 2nd Service: Magnificat & Nunc dimittis.* **Hymns & Songs of the church:** *Come kiss me with those lips of thine;*

Now shall the praises of the Lord be sung; A song of joy unto the Lord. **Organ Fantasia:** *Fantasia for Double Organ; Voluntary*
*** Gaudeamus CDGAU 123. King's College Ch., L. Early Music Group, Ledger; Butt

This invaluable anthology was the first serious survey of Gibbons's music to appear on CD. It contains many of his greatest pieces. Not only are the performances touched with distinction, the recording too is in the highest flight and the analogue sound has been transferred to CD with complete naturalness. Strongly recommended.

Anthems: *Almighty and everlasting God; Hosanna to the son of David; O clap your hands; O God, the King of glory; O Lord, in thy wrath; O Lord of Lords; Lift up your heads; Out of the deep; See, see, the word is incarnate; 2nd Service: Magnificat; Nunc dimittis. Short Service: Nunc dimittis. (Organ) Fantazia of 4 parts; Preludes in D min.; G*
☛ (BB) *** Naxos 8.553130. Oxford Camerata, Summerly; Cummings

Using his small professional choir, 12 singers at most, and often fewer, Jeremy Summerly directs fresh, finely focused readings of an outstanding collection of Gibbons's anthems. This may not have so much of the ecclesiastical aura of a traditional cathedral performance with boys' voices, but it amply makes up in clarity and incisiveness for any lack of weight and warmth. That is particularly so in the six magnificent unaccompanied full anthems which are included, where the astonishing harmonic clashes and progressions in the counterpoint come out with wonderful impact, generally with just a single voice per part.

In addition there are three fine verse anthems, drawing on the full complement of singers, with organ accompaniment, plus Gibbons's two evening services, the short one much simpler than the second one. Three organ pieces are also included, though Laurence Cummings's account of the extended *Fantazia* in four parts is not as varied as it might be. Fine, clear, atmospheric sound.

Anthems and verse anthems: *Behold, thou hast made my days; Blessed are they that fear the Lord; Glorious and powerful God; Great King of Gods; Hosanna to the son of David; If ye be risen again with Christ; O clap your hands; O God, the King of glory; O Lord in thy wrath rebuke me not; Sing unto the Lord; This is the record of John; Thou God of wisdom; 2nd Evening Service: Magnificat; Nunc dimittis. Organ Fantasia in A min (MB XX/12)*
*** Hyp. CDA 67116. Blaze, Varcoe, Winchester Cathedral Ch., Hill; Farr or Baldock

Orlando Gibbons's *Hosanna to the son of David* is among the very finest anthems of the period, a glory of English music, and aptly that is the opening item for this excellent collection of Gibbons's church music, very well performed and recorded. Robin Blaze is an outstandingly sweet-toned counter-tenor soloist, well matched by Stephen Varcoe in the verse anthems. The only pity is that the collection concentrates on verse anthems, nine of them plus the *Second Evening Service*, as against only three full anthems with their excitingly elaborate counterpoint. The *Fantasia in A minor* for organ makes an apt supplement.

Anthems and Church Anthems: *Blessed are all they; Hosanna to the Son of David; I am the Resurrection; Lord we beseech thee; O clap your hands; O Lord how do my woes* *increase; O Lord, I lift my heart to thee; O Lord, in thy wrath; Praise the Lord, O my Soul; Preces and Psalm 145; See, see the world is incarnate; Sing unto the Lord.* Hymns and Songs *1, 3–5, 9, 13, 18, 20, 22, 24, 31, 47, 67*

(N) (B) ** Calliope (ADD) CAL 4611. Clerkes of Oxenford

These recordings were highly praised when first issued in 1976, and they are certainly sung with feeling by a richly blended choir. However, the transfer to CD has not been entirely successful: the sound is full but rather opaque, and the disc is upstaged by more recent issues.

Madrigals and Motets (1612): *Ah dear heart; Dainty fine bird; Fair is the rose; Fair ladies that to love; Farewell all joys; How art thou thralled; I feign not friendship; I see ambition never pleased; I tremble not at the noise of war; I weigh not fortune's frown; Lais now old; 'Mongst thousands good; Nay let me weep; Ne'er let the sun; Now each flowery bank of May; O that the learned poets; The silver swan; Trust not too much fair youth; What is our life?; Yet if that age*

(N) (B) *** Decca 2-CD 476 7227 (2). Consort of Musicke, Rooley – MORLEY; WILBYE: *Madrigals ****

Gibbons left only one book of madrigalian pieces, and the Consort of Musicke here present it complete. The vocal group includes well-known names and is led by the young Emma Kirkby, who opens this 1975 programme with a delightfully fresh, young-voiced solo performance of *The silver swan*. She is accompanied by a quartet of viols, and half the pieces here are sung *and* played with viols, and sensitive attention is paid to phrasing and colour. Performances are eminently thoughtful though diction is not always first class; but it would be curmudgeonly to dwell on minor criticisms in so enjoyable an enterprise, for the set is expertly recorded and beautifully produced. It is not only a welcome addition to Gibbons's representation on record, but is equally valuable for the coupled repertoire by Morley and Wilbye. This set is now reissued as one of Universal's 'Critics' Choice' series, with full texts included.

GILBERT, Antony (born 1934)

(i) *On Beholding a Rainbow;* (ii) *Certain Lights Reflecting;* (iii) *Into the Gyre; Unrise*

(N) *** NMCD 105. (i) Marwood, Royal N. Coll. Mus. SO, Walker; (ii) Bickley, BBC SO, A. Davis; (iii) Royal N. Coll. Mus. Wind Ens., Rundell

Issued to celebrate the 70th birthday of Antony Gilbert, noted composition teacher in Manchester, these four works admirably illustrate not only his unfailing craftsmanship, with not a note wasted, but his warmth and imagination. That is specially true of the most ambitious of the works, *On Beholding a Rainbow*, a full-scale violin concerto, with Anthony Marwood the excellent soloist, in which a formidable Passacaglia, set out in a broad sonata form, is followed by an elegiac slow movement, more easily lyrical than most of Gilbert's music, and a dashing moto perpetuo finale in variation form. *Certain Lights Reflecting*, written in Sydney in 1988, is a sequence of four contrasted orchestral songs, setting words by the Australian poet, Sarah Day, full of colour and superbly sung by Susan Bickley. The two shorter works, *Into the Gyre* and *Unrise* for wind band draw out the brilliance of the Wind Ensemble of the Royal Northern College of Music, where Gilbert has taught since 1973.

GILBERT, Henry (1868–1928)

Suite for Chamber Orchestra

*** Albany TROY 033-2. V. American Music Ens., Earle – CHADWICK: *Serenade for Strings ****

Henry Gilbert belonged to a time when almost all musical influences came from Europe and the American public did not value the output of its indigenous composers. This *Suite*, which is harmonically innocuous but has an agreeable nostalgic languor, has something in common with Delius's *Florida Suite*, although Gilbert's invention is less indelible. An excellent performance here from members of the Vienna American Ensemble, who are completely at home in the music, as well they might be. The recording is excellent.

GILLES, Jean (1668–1705)

Messe des Mortes (Requiem Mass)

⊶ (BB) *** Warner Apex 2564 61260-2. Azema, Nirouër, Hite, Mason, Aix-le-Provence Festival Ch., Sagittarius Vocal Ens., Provençaux Ens. de Tambours, Boston Camerata, Cohen

(M) *** DG (ADD) 471722-2. Rodde, Nirouët, Hill, U. Studer, Kooy, Ghent Coll. Voc., Col. Mus. Ant., Herreweghe (with CORRETTE: *Carillon des morts ****)

Messe des Morts (Requiem Mass); Motet: *Diligem te Domine*

(BB) *** HM HMC 901341. Mellon, Gens, Crook, Lamy, Philips, Kooy, Chapelle Royale Ch. & O, Herreweghe

Gilles's *Requiem*, which for many years was a favourite work in France, was rejected by the two families who originally commissioned it, so Gilles decreed that it should be used for his own funeral. So great was the regional pride in eighteenth-century Provence that the work was often heard alongside the *Requiem* of Campra, with alternating movements from each!

The music is preceded by an introductory drum processional, gradually approaching, here provided by the Provençal Ensemble of Tambours, and they end the work with an equally atmospheric recessional. (A solo tambour also heads the *Communion*.) This was obviously intended to simulate the local custom of giving the open coffin a *tour de ville* before burial. In the interests of complete authenticity, the present performance also interpolates the liturgical chants in their appropriate places in the Mass, solemnly and resonantly sung by members of the Sagittarius Ensemble.

Gilles carries over the introductory march rhythm into the extended *Introit* which, like the splendid *Sanctus* and touchingly beautiful *Agnus Dei*, gives the soloists much that is rewardingly florid and expressively beautiful to sing. The solo team here rises to the occasion, each individually first class and working eloquently together. The chorus writing too is imaginative and demanding, and the Provençal choir is excellent, crisply directed by Joël Cohen, while the period-instrument accompaniment could hardly be more stylishly involved in the proceedings. Most attractive of all is to have this authentic performance so well recorded in Aix-en-Provence Cathedral, where the composer began his musical career as a choirboy and subsequently learned his craft as a composer. Altogether, this Apex reissue cannot be recommended too highly.

Gilles's rhythmic and harmonic vigour (with plentiful false relations to add tang) is well caught in this alternative DG performance on original instruments, and the singers find the music's expressive style admirably. The *Carillon* was included by Michel Corrette in his own edition of the Gilles *Requiem*, printed in 1764, and is appropriately included here as a postlude.

Herreweghe, too, gives a stylish performance of the *Requiem*, including the introductory march with drums but not the Corrette *Carillon*. He has fine soloists and an excellent chorus, and the *Post Communion* is particularly moving. Moreover he includes the grand motet, *Diligem te* ('I will love Thee, Lord, my strength'), for double choir, using his soloists also as the *petit choeur* in contrast with the *grand choeur*. *Commata est, et contranuit terra* ('When the earth shook and trembled') brings a vigorous chorus, with soloists, rather than any special effects, but the following *Inclinavit coelos, et descendit* ('He bowed the heavens also, and came down') makes a serene contrast, before the happy closing chorus. In short this is another fine work by this little-known composer, and it is very well performed and recorded here.

GILLIS, Don (1912–78)

The Alamo; (i) The Man Who Invented Music; Portrait of a Frontier Town; Saga of a Prairie School; Symphony 5½ (for Fun)
(N) (M) (***) Dutton mono CDLK 4163. New SO, composer, (i) with Kilty (nar.)

Don Gillis had a long and active career in America from the 1930s to the 1970s. He was a trombone player and later joined a jazz band; he became a composer and arranger and, eventually, programme director and producer for NCB, New York, 1944–54, working with Toscanini. His *Symphony No. 5½* is undoubtedly his best-known piece, enjoying quite a vogue in the 1950s. It is indeed a fun work, brightly and wittily scored. *The Alamo* is a 1947 tone-poem depicting the dramatic events associated with the famous fort in San Antonio, Texas. The folk-like atmosphere of the opening and closing sections is nostalgically caught here, contrasting with the later melodrama. The *Saga of a Prairie School* is overtly sentimental, but it similarly shows the composer's skill at evocative scene-painting, with the reflective 'prayful' scenes set against more vigorous writing where one marvels at the brilliance of the orchestral playing under the composer, especially the brass. The *Portrait of a Frontier Town* is a bright and breezy portrayal of Fort Worth, Texas, including everything you would expect to find, from square-dancing to 'Prairie Sunsets', scenes of *Night Life* as well as (less believably) a portrait of *The Chamber of Commerce*! *The Man Who Invented Music* was devised for radio and was first broadcast (conducted by Dorati) in 1949. The story (by the composer) is about a grandfather who in order to get his grandchild, Wendy, to go to sleep, spins a tale about how he invented music, and acts as a kind of young person's guide to the orchestra. It is a charming period piece. The performances on this CD can be thought of as definitive, and the (originally Decca) sound is remakably bright and vivid, with Dutton's remastering technique heard at its finest.

GINASTERA, Alberto (1916–83)

Harp Concerto, Op. 25
*** Chan. 9094. Masters, City of L. Sinfonia, Hickox – GLIERE: *Concertos* ***

Ginastera's 1956 *Harp Concerto*, full of vivid colours and snappy, incisive rhythms, also has a highly atmospheric slow movement. All its kaleidoscopic moods are keenly projected by Rachel Masters in this refreshing and invigorating performance. Alert playing, too, from the City of London Sinfonia under Richard Hickox. Strongly recommended, as are the two Glière concertos with which it is coupled.

(i) Harp Concerto, Op. 25; (ii) Piano Concerto 1. Estancia (ballet suite), Op. 89
*** ASV CDDCA 654. (i) Allen; (ii) Tarrago; Mexico City PO, Bátiz

The *Harp Concerto* is brought fully to life here by Nancy Allen and the Mexican orchestra. *Estancia* is a comparably vivid piece of Coplandesque machismo, its character also very successfully realized. The *First Piano Concerto* is mildly serial but far from unattractive – and very brilliantly (and sensitively) played by Oscar Tarrago. An excellent introduction to this composer.

Estancia (ballet): Dances, Op. 8a. Glosses sobre temes de Pau Casals, Op. 48; Obertura para el Fausto criollo, Op. 9; Pampeana 3 (Symphonic Pastoral), Op. 24
(N) *** Chan. 10152. Berlin SO, Castagna

Ginastera (no relation of Fredastaira) was the leading composer produced in the Argentine in the last century, and this disc collects some of his most popular and colourful scores. Best known are *Estancia* and the *Overture for a Creole Faust*. The *Pampeana No. 3* is a particularly strong and imaginative work and alone worth the cost of the disc, which will serve as an admirable visiting card for this unjustly neglected composer whose music is eminently approachable and stimulating. Excellent recorded sound.

(i) Cello Sonata, Op. 49. Danzas argentinas, Op. 2; Estancia, Op. 8; (i) Pampeana 2, Op. 21 (rhapsody for cello and piano). Pequeña danza; Piano Sonata 1, Op. 22; 5 Canciones populares argentinas; (i) Triste (arr. Fournier)
*** ASV CDDCA 865. Portugheis, (i) with Natola-Ginastera

The four-movement *Cello Sonata*, ardently rhapsodic, chimerical and full of atmosphere, is dedicated to Ginastera's wife, who is the soloist here, while *Pampeana* is a rhapsody which has an Argentinian flavour without using folk melodies. The *Piano Sonata No. 1* (1952) is a powerful, integrated piece with a desolate *Adagio* and a brilliant, rhythmically chimerical folk-dance finale. Alberto Portugheis is thoroughly at home in this repertoire and plays compellingly throughout. He is well recorded.

Canciones, Op. 3: Milonga. Malambo, Op. 7; 3 Piezas, Op. 6; Piezas infantiles; Rondo sobre temas infantiles argentinos, Op. 19; Sonatas 1, Op. 53; 3, Op. 58; Toccata
*** ASV CDDCA 880. Portugheis

The pieces for children are most welcoming and are delightfully varied and intimate: the *Milonga* is seductive in a Latin-American way, as are the *Three Pieces*, Op. 6. The *Sonatas* are harder nuts to crack: the first has a formidable opening movement and a ferocious closing toccata, and the *Toccata*, written for the organ and played with great bravura here, is also a piece to make one sit up. Alberto Portugheis is a first-rate artist, and his natural sympathies for the music's idiom are apparent throughout. He is very well recorded.

GIORDANO, Umberto (1867–1948)

Andrea Chénier (DVD version)
*** Warner NVC Arts **DVD** 5050466-8357-2-7.
   Tomowa-Sintow, Domingo, Zancanaro, ROHCG Ch. & O,
   Rudel (V/D: Humphrey Burton)

Dating from 1985, the DVD of Michael Hampe's production offers a traditional staging that vividly captures the atmosphere of Giordano's melodramatic presentation of Revolutionary France. Under the experienced conducting of Julius Rudel, the three principal characters are powerfully drawn, all three at the peak of their powers. Plácido Domingo cuts a flamboyant figure as Chénier, with the widest range of tone and expression in his key monologues. Though Anna Tomowa-Sintow's creamy soprano grows a little rough under pressure, she makes a tenderly sympathetic Maddalena; but it is Giorgio Zancanaro as Gérard who emerges as the most powerful figure, singing gloriously and bringing out the more human side of this revolutionary leader, convincingly making the transition from the defiant flunky he is in Act I. Other roles are well taken, too. No booklet is provided and no synopsis, with no indication on the box who is singing which roles.

Andrea Chénier (CD versions)
☞— (M) *** RCA (ADD) 74321 39499-2 (2). Domingo,
   Scotto, Milnes, Alldis Ch., Nat. PO, Levine
**(*) Decca (IMS) 410 117-2 (2). Pavarotti, Caballé, Nucci,
   Kuhlmann, Welsh Nat. Op. Ch., Nat. PO, Chailly
(M) **(*) EMI (ADD) 5 65287-2 (2). Corelli, Stella, Sereni,
   Rome Op. Ch. & O, Santini

Andrea Chénier with its defiant poet hero provides a splendid role for Domingo at his most heroic, and the former servant, later revolutionary leader, Gérard, is a character well appreciated by Milnes. Scotto gives one of her most eloquent and beautiful performances, and Levine has rarely displayed his powers as an urgent and dramatic opera conductor more potently on record, with the bright recording intensifying the dramatic thrust of playing and singing.

Pavarotti may motor through the role of the poet-hero, singing with his usual fine diction; nevertheless, the redblooded melodrama of the piece comes over powerfully, thanks to Chailly's sympathetic conducting, incisive but never exaggerated. Caballé, like Pavarotti, is not strong on characterization but produces beautiful sounds, while Leo Nucci makes a superbly dark-toned Gérard. Though this cannot replace the Levine set, it is a colourful substitute with its demonstration sound.

The glory of the 1964 EMI version is the Chénier of Franco Corelli, one of his most satisfying performances on record, with heroic tone gloriously exploited. The other singing is less distinguished. Though Antonietta Stella was never sweeter of voice than here, she hardly matches such rivals as Scotto or Caballé. The 1960s recording is vivid, with plenty of atmosphere, and has been transferred to CD most naturally, but the RCA set in the same price range, with Domingo and Scotto, remains a clear first choice.

Fedora (complete; DVD version)
(N) **(*) DG **DVD** 073 2329. Freni, Arteta, Domingo, Croft,
   Hartman, Met. Op. Ch. & O, R. Abbado (V/D: Brian Large)

Fedora (complete; CD version)
(M) ** Sony (ADD) SM2K 91138 (2). Marton, Carreras,
   Kincses, Hungarian R. & TV Ch. & O, Patanè

Like Puccini's *Tosca*, Giordano's *Fedora* was based on a play by Victorien Sardou, designed as a vehicle for Sarah Bernhardt. Though it gives many opportunities for the soprano heroine to shine, the irony is that by far the most memorable number, very brief, is the declaration of love by the hero, Loris, *Amor ti vieta*. This video, taken from a live performance in 1997, offers a typically lavish production by Beppe de Tomasi from the Met. in New York with a cast as starry as could be assembled anywhere. Mirella Freni in 1997 was vocally past her best but the voice is still very beautiful, and maturity is an apt quality for a singer characterizing the beautiful widow, Fedora. Plácido Domingo makes a handsome Loris, relishing his big moment in *Amor ti vieta*. In the subsidiary roles Ainhoa Arteta as Countess Olga and Dwayne Croft as the diplomat, De Siriex, both sing with clear, firm tone, while Roberto Abbado paces the work well. The big snag is that the enthusiasm of the Met. audience involves prolonged applause at Freni's entrance and after the big moments of both Freni and Domingo. Brian Large's sensitive video direction homes in on the principals effectively but fails to display the grandeur of Ferruccio Villagrossi's sets fully enough.

On Sony, Eva Marton is aptly cast as Fedora, the Romanov princess, but in a work that should sound sumptuous it is not a help that the voices are placed forwardly, with the orchestra distanced well behind. The balance exaggerates the vibrato in Marton's voice, but it is a strong, sympathetic performance; Carreras, too, responds warmly to the lyricism of the role of the hero, Loris, giving a satisfyingly forthright account of the key aria, *Amor ti vieta*. The rest of the cast is unremarkable, and Patanè's direction lacks bite, again partly a question of orchestral balance. The other snag is inadequate documentation, offering neither libretto nor a cued synopsis. The superior, older Decca set with Olivero and Del Monaco is currently withdrawn, but should return to the catalogue shortly.

GIPPS, Ruth (born 1921)

Symphony 2, Op. 30
*** Classico CLASSCD 274. Munich SO, Bostock –
   BUTTERWORTH: *Symphony 1* ***

Ruth Gipps studied with Vaughan Williams and during the war years played the oboe in the City of Birmingham Symphony Orchestra. She became a tireless champion of neglected repertoire and an excellent teacher. Her *Second Symphony* comes from 1945 and, though indebted to Vaughan Williams, is well argued and inventive. It is decently played and recorded.

GIULIANI, Mauro (1781–1829)

(i; ii) *Guitar Concertos 1 in A, Op. 30; 2 in A, Op. 36; 3 in F, Op. 70; Introduction, Theme with Variations & Polonaise (for Guitar & Orchestra), Op. 65.* (i) *Grande ouverture, Op. 61; Gran sonata eroica in A; La Melanchonia; Variations on 'I bin a Kohlbauern Bub', Op. 49; Variations on a Theme by Handel, Op. 107;* (i; iii) *Variazioni concertati, Op. 130*
(B) *** Ph. Duo (ADD) 454 262-2 (2). (i) Pepe Romero, (ii)
   with ASMF, Marriner; (iii) with Celedonio Romero

Pepe Romero is a first-rate player, and his relaxed musicmaking and easy bravura bring an attractive, smiling quality.

But what makes these concertos so distinctive are the splendid accompaniments provided by the Academy of St Martin-in-the-Fields under Marriner, and throughout there are many delightful touches from the orchestra. The *F major Concerto* begins with an engaging little march theme whose dotted contour reminds one of Hummel, and the amiable *Siciliano* that forms the slow movement is matched by an unforceful closing Polonaise. Hummel again comes rhythmically to mind in the first movement of the *Second Concerto*, which is for strings alone. The *Introduction, Theme with Variations and Polonaise* is like a mini-concerto and is given a performance of vitality and charm. The Op. 49 *Variations* are agreeable but slight, but the *Sonata eroica* hardly merits its grand sobriquet. The *Variations concertanti* for two guitars, in which Pepe is joined by Celedonio, is played with affection and ready virtuosity. The mid-1960s recording is warm and refined throughout, very easy on the ear.

Guitar Concerto in A, Op. 30

(M) *** DG (IMS) (ADD) 439 984-2. Behrend, I Musici –
   CARULLI: *Concerto in A* ***; VIVALDI: *Guitar Concertos* **(*)
(B) **(*) Decca (ADD) 448 709-2. Fernández, ECO, Malcolm
   – PAGANINI: *Sonata*; VIVALDI: *Concertos* **(*)

Giuliani's *A major Concerto* is presented by Siegfried Behrend with much elegance and finesse and is immaculately recorded. Its catchy main theme is endearing; though the music overall is slight, it is nicely crafted.

A rather low-key, essentially chamber performance from the highly musical Eduardo Fernández, who refuses to show off. He is accompanied elegantly by Malcolm and the ECO and is most naturally recorded.

Duo concertante for Violin & Guitar, Op. 25

(BB) *** H M HCX 3957116. Huggett, Savino – PAGANINI: *Grand Sonata*, etc. ***

Monica Huggett adopts her most silky timbre and plays most winningly in Giuliani's ingenuous but extended *Duo* (37 minutes). Richard Savino has less to do but does it expertly. The *Theme and Variations* second movement also has considerable charm. The recording is ideally balanced and most realistic.

Variations on a Theme by Handel, Op. 107

(B) *** Sony (ADD) SBK 62425. Williams (guitar) –
   PAGANINI: *Caprice 24*, etc.; D. SCARLATTI: *Sonatas*;
   VILLA-LOBOS: *5 Preludes* ***

The *Variations* are on Handel's famous *Harmonious Blacksmith* theme. Their construction is guileless but agreeable, and they are expertly played and well recorded. This is only a small part of a well-planned and exceptionally generous collection devoted mainly to Paganini and Domenico Scarlatti.

GLASS, Philip (born 1937)

(i) Cello Concerto; (ii) Concerto Fantasy for 2 Timpanists and Orchestra

(N) *** Dunvagen Music (ASCAP) 0014. (i) Julian Lloyd
   Webber; (ii) Glennie, Haas; RLPO, Schwarz

Glass's *Cello Concerto* opens darkly and atmospherically, with a combined cadenza and characteristic ostinato featuring the soloist, to introduce a rolling semi-minimalist sequence that dominates the music; but the work's warmly lyrical strain is immediately apparent, and Glass's writing is genuinely melodic, hauntingly so, especially in the central movement, which brings what the soloist describes as 'an almost trance-like serenity'. The finale again combines powerfully nagging minimalist motivation with an expansive further outpouring of lyrical energy. A remarkable work, marvellously played.

The *Concerto Fantasy* is in four movements, all dominated by thundering timpani, with the third a cadenza duet for the two soloists. It is very noisy and invigorating. You will either find it thrilling or sonically overwhelming. Both performances here are surely definitive.

(i; ii) Concerto for Saxophone Quartet & Orchestra; (ii) Symphony 2; (iii) Orphée, Act II, scene III: Interlude

*** None. 7559 79496-2. (i) Rascher Saxophone Qt; (ii)
   Stuttgart CO; (iii) V. RSO; composer

Philip Glass's *Symphony No. 2*, in three substantial movements, represents his music at its most mellifluous, his second-generation brand of minimalism. Written in 1993, it uses polytonality as a basic element, to a degree taking the place of contrasts traditional in symphonic form. The first movement, longest of the three, is lush and lyrical, with melodies turning back on themselves, while the central slow movement jogs along similarly with minimalist 'till-ready' rhythms. The finale is bolder and brassier, with a piano bringing echoes of *Petrushka*. The *Interlude* from *Orphée* is vintage Glass, while the more compact *Saxophone Quartet Concerto* brings the liveliest music, with jazzy syncopations in the second movement and Spanish-American flavours in the finale varying Glass's persistent *moderato* writing. Excellent performances and well-balanced recording.

Violin Concerto

*** Telarc CD 80494. McDuffie, Houston SO, Eschenbach –
   ADAMS: *Violin Concerto* ***

(i) Violin Concerto. Company; Akhnaten: Prelude & Dance

(BB) **(*) Naxos 8.554568. (i) Anthony; Ulster O., Yuasa

Glass's *Violin Concerto*, with its hypnotic minimalist exploration of simple basic material, is one of his best and most approachable works. The repeated four-note downward scale on which the soloist weaves his serene soliloquy in the slow movement is particularly haunting, the effect very like a chaconne, which links it readily to the coupled Adams concerto. On Telarc McDuffie gives a first-class performance and is very well recorded indeed.

Adele Anthony is a talented violinist from Tasmania, who here gives a sweetly expressive reading, despite a rather plodding account of the very opening. In the central movement she finds a rare tenderness, as well as on the high harmonics at the end of the whole work. The concerto makes an excellent centrepiece for a complete disc of Glass's music, with Yuasa and the Ulster Orchestra equally persuasive in the four brief movements of *Company* and the two orchestral passages from the opera, *Akhnaten*.

Company; Façades

(M) *** Virgin 5 61851-2. LCO, Warren-Green – ADAMS:
   Shaker Loops ***; REICH: *8 Lines* ***; HEATH:
   Frontier ***

Company consists of four brief but sharply contrasted movements for strings; *Façades* offers a haunting cantilena for soprano saxophone, suspended over atmospherically undulating strings. The performances are full of intensity and are expertly played, and the recording is excellent.

Symphonies 1 & 4
(N) (BB) *** Naxos 8.559202. Bournemouth SO, Alsop

Marin Alsop's accounts of these two symphonies by Philip Glass make a powerful contribution to the Naxos American Classics series, magnetically performed and brilliantly recorded. No. 2, much the longer work in three substantial movements, dates from 1994 and, though this is unreconstructed minimalism with unrelenting kaleidoscopic repetitions, Glass's skill in controlling shifting textures and rhythms makes the result compelling, with the full orchestra colourfully used, and the occasional scalic motif taking the place of full melodies. No. 3, first heard in 1995, is little more than half the length, a piece for 19 strings and optional percussion, with the gentle opening movement serving as prelude to the second and third movements, the one fast, the other a measured chaconne. The fourth movement is brief and brilliant, drawing threads together.

String Quartets 2 (Company); 3 (Mishima); 4 (Buczak); 5
*** None. 7559 79356-2. Kronos Qt

Happily, the quartets here are presented in reverse order, for the last of the four, No. 5, dating from 1991, presents Glass at his most warmly expressive and intense. Textures are luminous, shimmering in their repetitions rather than thrusting them home relentlessly. The Kronos Quartet, for whom the work was written, give a heartfelt performance, as they do of the *Quartet No. 4* (1990), written in memory of Brian Buczak, who died of AIDS. The valedictory mood is intensified by a lyrical and poignantly beautiful middle movement, leading to a noble finale. The *Quartet No. 2* (1983) consists of four brief movements originally written to accompany the staged soliloquy of a dying man, entitled *Company*. Again it is valedictory in tone but is far less tender. The *Quartet No. 3* (1985) is repetitive in the characteristic Glass manner, this time with six brief movements. Though Nos. 4 and 5 most clearly reveal the hand of a master, the earlier works also represent Glass at his most approachable, the more so when they are treated to magnetic performances by the Kronos Quartet, superbly recorded.

ORGAN MUSIC

(i) Dances 2 & 4; (ii) Duets & Canons (suite); Satyagraha (opera), Act III: Finale
*** Nim. NI 5664. (i) Broadbent; (ii) Bowyer (Marcusson organ in St Augustin's Chapel, Tonbridge School, Kent)

Sometimes one wonders with the music of Philip Glass whether the composer always means to be taken seriously, or if he is sometimes pulling our musical legs. The two *Dance* movements were written in the early 1970s. *Dance 2* represents the most basic form of minimalism, offering a hypnotically relentless ostinato for nearly 25 minutes, with very minor changes of the harmonic implications in the pedals. *Dance 4* is more musically eventful. Below the toccata-like sequence there is a galumphing figure in the bass and frequent if repetitious harmonic movement. A good deal more happens during this piece, although one feels that the composer, rather than creating forward movement, is going round in circles. The shorter (seven-minute) *Satyagraha* finale is sandwiched in between the two *Dances*, more lyrical in feeling, but hardly more motivated. All three pieces are played with devoted determination by Christopher Bowers-Broadbent, who never puts a foot or finger wrong.

Kevin Bowyer takes over for the *Duets and Canons* (1996) creating a thoughtful, improvisatory feeling. All ten are brief and have liturgical titles, which the composer tells us are based on the plainsong of the Third Mass of the Nativity. They are rhythmically free (often quirkily so) and the changes in mood are provided primarily by the changes in registration (and modest variations in tempo). The *Sanctus*, for instance, is surprisingly dark and sombre, *Viderunt omnes* celestial, but the closing *Agnus Dei and Benedictus* finally leave the listener in mid-air. The recording of the fine Marcusson organ at Tonbridge cannot be faulted.

OPERA

La Belle et la bête (opera based on the film of Jean Cocteau; complete)
*** None. 7559 79347. Felty, Purnhagen, Kuether, Martinez, Neill, Zhou, Philip Glass Ens., Riesman

What Glass has done here is to provide a new musical accompaniment to a showing of Cocteau's 90-minute film, *La Belle et la bête*, dispensing with Auric's original film-music and synchronizing the singing-parts with the speech of the actors in the film. In the opening scenes the music is far lighter and more conventionally beautiful than most Glass, but then the poignancy of the story is more and more reflected in the score, both tender and mellifluous. The hypnotic quality of Glass's repetitions helps to enhance the magical atmosphere, while the use of the original French film-script prompts Glass to be more warmly melodic than usual. Glass's justification lies in the intensity of the score overall, with Janice Felty and Gregory Purnhagen both clearly focused in the central roles, though Purnhagen's baritone suggests from the start a heroic, not a bestial, figure. Vividly atmospheric sound.

Einstein on the Beach (complete)
*** None. 7559 79323-2 (3). Soloists, Philip Glass Ens., Riesman

Glass himself explains the need for a new recording of this bizarre and relentless opera – as the surreal title implies, more dream than drama. Where the earlier recording had an abrasive edge, this new one is more refined, melding the different elements, electronic alongside acoustic, more subtly and persuasively than before. Even so, the first train episode, over 20 minutes long, remains mind-blowing in its relentlessness. The impact is heightened by the vividness of the recording, with spoken voices in particular given such presence that they startle you as if someone had burst into your room. The vision remains an odd one, but with a formidable group of vocalists and instrumentalists brilliantly directed, often from the keyboard, by Michael Riesman, the new recording certainly justifies itself.

Satyagraha (DVD version)
*** Arthaus **DVD** 100 136. Goeke, Harster, Danniker, Nielsen, Greiwe, Württemburg State Theatre O, Russell Davis

Philip Glass's second opera, *Satyagraha*, is a curiosity, an opera with virtually no plot, using a text in Sanskrit. This video, recorded live at the Würrtemburg State Theatre in Stuttgart in 1983, offers a staging by Hugo Kach which is comparably bizarre. There is no music for several minutes at the start, with various fetish figures walking about, though that seems to have little relevance to the main theme of the opera, a tribute to Mahatma Gandhi as peace-maker. Glass seeks to use Gandhi's involvement in South Africa in the years between 1893 and 1914 as a comment on latter-day political and religious problems. Glass and Constance de Jong based the libretto on the ancient Indian didactic poem, *Bhagavadgita*, 'Song of the Blessed One', much quoted by Gandhi. The title *Satyagraha* means 'dedication to the truth', and each of the three long Acts, almost an hour each, has a superscription paying tribute to other leaders, Tolstoy, the poet Rabindranath Tagore, and Martin Luther King. Reflecting Glass's minimalist score, the dream-like staging involves little movement, though Glass's detailed inventiveness induces a hypnotic effect, clearly related to oriental meditation. Dennis Russell Davis with an excellent cast, led by three singers sharing the role of Gandhi, conducts a persuasive performance.

GLAZUNOV, Alexander (1865–1936)

A la mémoire de Gogol, Op. 86; A la mémoire d'un héros, Op. 8; (i) Chant du ménestrel for Cello & Orchestra, Op. 71; Concerto ballata for Cello & Orchestra, Op. 108; 2 Pieces for Cello & Orchestra, Op. 20
(BB) *** Naxos 8.553932. Moscow SO, Golovschin, (i) with Rudin

The *Concerto ballata* is a late work, written for Casals and dating from 1931. The *Chant du ménestrel* is much earlier and comes from 1900, between the *Sixth* and *Seventh Symphonies*. It has an easy charm that delights the ear. *A la mémoire de Gogol* is a dignified, well-shaped piece which belies (as does the *Concerto ballata*) Glazunov's reputation for scoring too thickly. We admired Alexander Rudin's recording of the Kabalevsky *Cello Concertos*, and his playing here is no less eloquent. The Moscow orchestra plays well for Igor Golovschin and the sound has pleasing warmth and clarity.

Carnaval Overture, Op. 45; Concert Waltzes 1–2, Opp. 47 & 51; Spring, Op. 34; Salomé (incidental music), Op. 90: Introduction; Dance
(BB) **(*) Naxos 8.553838. Moscow SO, Golovschin

This collection of shorter pieces by Glazunov makes up a delightful disc, bringing out the composer's amiable side. There are some attractive ideas in *Spring* (*Vesna*), a charming work, refined and transparent in its orchestration, playing on birdsong and building to a sensuous climax. The more familiar *Concert Waltzes* contain some of Glazunov's most winning tunes, the one Tchaikovskian in flavour, the other Viennese. The novelty most likely to excite curiosity here is Glazunov's music for Oscar Wilde's *Salomé*, with Salome's dance leading to a Polovtsian climax. It is surprisingly conventional and tame, and Salome sheds her veils in a most unerotic fashion. But this cannot be blamed on the conductor, and generally these are warm, idiomatic performances, richly recorded.

Le Chant du destin, Op. 84; 2 Préludes, Op. 85; Suite caractéristique in D, Op. 9
(BB) **(*) Naxos 8.553857. Moscow SO, Golovschin

Le Chant du destin, written in 1907, is dominated by a sombre two-phrase theme which curiously reminds one of Gershwin's song, 'Swonderful, only the mood and colouring are utterly different. The music, which is presented eloquently, still has its longueurs. The eight-movement *Suite caractéristique*, from two decades earlier, is vintage Glazunov, an orchestral transcription of piano pieces. The two *Preludes*

date from 1906 and 1908 respectively. One remembers, in a sombre and valedictory mood, Vladimir Stassov (famous for naming Balakirev and his contemporary group of Russian composers 'the mighty handful'); the second (much more extended) opens surprisingly like Tchaikovsky's *Francesca da Rimini* and this curious leitmotif dominates the early part of the piece. It is well played, as indeed is the *Suite*. The recording is very good, too. At Naxos price this is worth considering.

Chant du ménestrel (for Cello & Orchestra), Op. 71
*** Chan. 8579. Wallfisch, LPO, Thomson – KABALEVSKY; KHACHATURIAN: *Cello Concertos* ***

Glazunov's *Chant du ménestrel* shows the nostalgic appeal of 'things long ago and far away'. It is a short but appealing piece and is very well played by Wallfisch and becomes a welcome makeweight on the Chandos CD.

(i) Concerto ballata for Cello & Orchestra, Op. 108; (ii) Piano Concerto 1, Op. 92
*** Chan. 9528. (i) Dyachkov; (ii) Pirzadeh; I Musici de Montréal, Turovsky – ARENSKY: *Violin Concerto* ***

The highly romantic *First Piano Concerto* is already well served by Stephen Coombs (see below). The *Concerto ballata* is also available on Naxos, but Yegor Dyachkov is a fine soloist, and the young Iranian-born Canadian pianist, Maneli Pirzadeh, proves a most poetic and brilliant exponent of the *Piano Concerto*. All in all, this makes a highly recommendable coupling.

Piano Concertos 1 in F min., Op. 92; 2 in B flat
**(*) Hyp. CDA 66877. Coombs, BBC Scottish SO, Brabbins – GOEDICKE: *Concertstück* **(*)
(BB) ** Naxos 8.553928. Yablonskaya, Moscow SO, Yablonsky

These two piano concertos are ripely lyrical, like a mixture of Brahms and Rachmaninov, but the inspiration is anything but tired or faded. As in his survey of Glazunov's piano music for the same label, Stephen Coombs is a persuasive advocate, and he always leaves one with the feeling that this music means more than it does. The BBC Scottish Symphony Orchestra under Martyn Brabbins give sympathetic support, and the only serious reservation one might make concerns the over-resonant recording acoustic.

Very good performances of both these genial pieces by this partnership on Naxos but they do not by any means supplant the Hyperion alternative with Stephen Coombs, who is the more subtle pianist. We would continue to recommend his recording in spite of the price advantage of this newcomer.

Piano Concerto 2 in B flat, Op. 100
**(*) Chan. 9622. Herskowitz, I Musici de Montréal, Turovsky – DAVIDOV: *Cello Concerto 2* **(*); CONUS: *Violin Concerto* **(*)

Matthew Herskowitz is not quite as persuasive an artist as, say, Stephen Coombs on Hyperion. However, the merit of this record is to explore Russian concertos of the second rank which deserve a place in your library.

Violin Concerto in A min., Op. 82
☛ ✪ *** RCA 74321 87454-2. Znaider, Bav. RSO, Jansons – PROKOFIEV: *Violin Concerto 2*; TCHAIKOVSKY: *Méditation* *** ✪
(N) *** Pentatone SACD PTC 5186 059. Fischer, Russian Nat. O., Kreizberg – KHACHATURIAN: *Violin Concerto* ***; PROKOFIEV: *Violin Concerto 1* ***

(M) *** Warner Elatus 0927 49567-2. Vengerov, BPO, Abbado – PROKOFIEV: *Concertos 1–2* ***

*** DG 457 064-2. Shaham, Russian Nat. O, Pletnev – KABALEVSKY: *Concerto;* TCHAIKOVSKY: *Souvenir d'un lieu cher,* etc. ***

(M) *** Erato 0927 49014-2. Mutter, Nat. SO, Rostropovich – PROKOFIEV: *Violin Concerto 1;* SHCHEDRIN: *Stihira* ***

(M) (***) EMI mono 7 64030-2. Heifetz, LPO, Barbirolli – SIBELIUS: *Violin Concerto* (**); TCHAIKOVSKY: *Violin Concerto* (***)

(BB) (***) Naxos mono 8.110940. Heifetz, LPO, Barbirolli – BRAHMS: *Double Concerto;* BRUCH: *Scottish Fantasy* (***)

(M) *** EMI 5 62593-2. Perlman, Israel PO, Mehta – SHOSTAKOVICH: *Violin Concerto 1,* etc. ***

(N) (M) *** RCA (ADD) 82876 66372-2. Heifetz, RCA Victor SO, Hendl – PROKOFIEV: *Violin Concerto 2;* SIBELIUS: *Concerto* ***

(BB) (***) Naxos mono 8.110975. Milstein, RCA Victor SO, Golschmann – DVORAK: *Violin Concerto;* MOZART: *Adagio in E,* etc. (***)

(BB) *** Naxos 8.550758. Kaler, Polish Nat. RSO (Katowice), Kolchinsky – DVORAK: *Concerto,* etc. ***

(M) ** DG (IMS) (ADD) 463 651-2. Morini, Berlin R.O, Fricsay – BRUCH: *Violin Concerto 1* **; DVORAK: *Violin Concerto* ***

Nikolaj Znaider's Glazunov reveals an artist who not only has commanding technical address but eloquence and taste. His approach is fresh and so he makes one fall for this glorious work all over again. He is given splendid support by Mariss Jansons and the excellent Orchester des Bayerischen Rundfunks. A special mention should be given to the recording engineer, Wolfgang Karreth, who gets the ideal balance between soloist and orchestra and a very natural and lifelike sound.

The unique coupling of three Russian violin concertos on Pentatone could hardly be more recommendable, with warmly compelling performances from the brilliant young German virtuoso, superbly recorded in full, bright, clear sound, given added sonority in SACD. In the Glazunov *Concerto* it is the clarity and subtlety of Julia Fischer's playing that marks her reading out, in rivalry with even the finest. She finds yearning tenderness in the slow middle section of this one-movement work and gives an easy swing to the bouncy rhythms of the final section.

Originally coupled with Tchaikovsky, Vengerov's version is now paired, even more attractively, with his outstanding Prokofiev performances. His account of the Glazunov is hardly less exceptional, for again he gives a familiar concerto extra dimensions, turning it from a display piece into a work of far wider-ranging emotions, when he contrasts and shades the tone-colours so magically, keeping the richest tone in reserve for the third theme. Predictably, his dashing final section is breathtaking in its brilliance.

Gil Shaham gives a pretty dazzling account of the *Concerto* with Mikhail Pletnev and the Russian National Orchestra, which can well hold its own with the current opposition. The coupling is unusual and readers attracted by it need not hesitate. Good, ample sound.

Anne-Sophie Mutter is here more volatile and more freely expressive than she has usually been on disc, sounding totally spontaneous, and that is particularly impressive in the Glazunov. The recording, made in the Kennedy Center, Washington, is more airy and spacious than many from this venue.

The command and panache of Perlman are irresistible in this showpiece concerto, and the whole performance, recorded live, erupts into a glorious account of the galloping final section in playing to match that of the supreme master in this work, Heifetz. The acoustic of the Mann Auditorium in Tel Aviv is not an easy one for the engineers, and tuttis are rather rough, but this is more atmospheric than most from this source.

In the winter of 1934 Heifetz came to London to record the Glazunov, a work previously unrecorded. The exuberance of his playing, well matched by Barbirolli's sympathetic accompaniment, makes it a uniquely compelling version, freely improvisational, with a dedicated account of the *Andante sostenuto* and an exuberant one of the swaggering finale. The Naxos transfer is well balanced, if not quite as sophisticated as the previous, EMI remastering, with surface hiss occasionally intrusive. A generous coupling just the same and a splendid alternative.

For those who accept slightly dated 1963 stereo sound, Heifetz is again incomparable, his later account among the strongest and most passionate in the catalogue, and the RCA Orchestra under Hendl gives fine support. The remastered recording sounds really good in its new SACD format.

Milstein brings a special authority to the Glazunov *Violin Concerto,* as he played it under the composer's baton in 1915, many times during his youth, and at his American début concert in 1928 with the Philadelphia Orchestra under Stokowski. He recorded it, with Beecham conducting, in 1934 and again in 1951 with the RCA Victor Symphony Orchestra and Steinberg. No one plays it with greater virtuosity, aristocratic finesse or tonal beauty, and we would decline to choose one from among the five recordings he made. All of them show this enchanting work as the masterpiece it is and they both exhilarate and move the listener.

The Russian violinist Ilya Kaler gives a rapturously lyrical performance, and Camilla Kolchinsky's accompaniment is equally warm and supportive. The resonant acoustic of the Concert Hall of Polish Radio gives a big, spacious orchestral sound, but Kaler's tone is full to match, and the violin playing can certainly accommodate the scrutiny of the fairly close microphones.

Erica Morini's sweetly lyrical account is eminently acceptable, even if it is no challenge to the finest versions. Whether it is worthy of a place among DG's 'Originals' is another matter. However, Morini's is in every respect a pleasing and well-recorded performance (it was made in the late 1950s).

(i) *Violin Concerto. The Seasons* (ballet), *Op. 67*
*** Chan. 8596. (i) Shumsky; SNO, Järvi

Neeme Järvi obtains good results from the Scottish National Orchestra in *The Seasons,* though tempi tend to be brisk. The Chandos acoustic is reverberant and the balance recessed. In the *Violin Concerto,* Oscar Shumsky is perhaps wanting the purity and effortless virtuosity of Heifetz, but the disc as a whole still carries a three-star recommendation.

From the Middle Ages, Op. 79; Scènes de ballet, Op. 52
*** Chan. 8804. SNO, Järvi (with LIADOV: *A Musical Snuffbox* ***)

From the Middle Ages (suite), *Op. 79; The Sea, Op. 28; Spring, Op. 34; Stenka Razin, Op. 13*
(M) *** Chan. 7049. SNO, Järvi

Järvi makes out an excellent case for these charming Glazunov suites. Although this music is obviously inferior to Tchaikovsky, Järvi has the knack of making you think it is better than it is, and the Chandos recording is up to the best standards of the house. The first disc also includes a fine account of Liadov's delightful *A Musical Snuffbox*.

The tone-poem *Spring* was written two years after *The Sea* and is infinitely more imaginative; in fact it is as fresh and delightful as its companion is cliché-ridden. At one point Glazunov even looks forward to *The Seasons*. *Stenka Razin* makes a colourful enough opening item for this alternative collection.

Raymonda (ballet; complete)

(N) *** Arthaus **DVD** 100 719. Bessmertnova, Vasyuchenko, Taranda, Nobrova, Bolshoi Ballet, directed Grigorovich; Bolshoi Theatre O, Zhuraitis (V/D: Shuji Fujii)

Glazunov's *Raymonda* (his first major theatrical score, premièred in 1898) is a traditional romantic ballet with a simple story and a happy ending; and this admirable DVD is especially valuable for preserving a lavish (1989) Bolshoi production which draws on the original choreography (*Raymonda* was the last ballet in which Petipa participated). At the opening, the heroine is celebrating her birthday with all her friends and her fiancé, the knight Jean de Brienne, in affectionate attendance. But the two lovers must part, for Jean must go off to fight in the Hungarian war and Raymonda is left disconsolate.

That night the apparition of a mysterious White Lady appears and takes Raymonda to a magic garden where (in her dream) her lover is restored to her; suddenly he is whisked away and in his place a fierce Arab Sheik appears, determined to make Raymonda his own. In Act II Abderakhman actually arrives, pursues his suit even more determinedly and proposes passionately; as evidence of his resources, his entourage provide an exotic divertissement (which includes Spanish as well as oriental dances, and a Bacchanale). He plans an abduction, but fortunately at the key moment Jean de Brienne returns triumphant, with the Hungarian king at his side, to claim his bride to be.

A battle ensues, but the situation is saved by the king, who suggests a duel between the two suitors for the hand of Raymonda. However, the White Lady's influence intervenes, and Jean (also costumed in white) prevails, and Abderakhman falls, dying, still professing his great love – the one moment of real dramatic pathos in a rather tame storyline. So the original planned wedding can go ahead, and the celebrations bring a further extended divertissement in which Hungarian dances predominate, although the Hungarian idiom is rather diluted in Glazunov's music. But he provides a thoroughly professional score with a good deal of pretty and charmingly scored music, none better than *Valse fantastique* with variations at the end of Act I. Much of the rest is amiably melodic and full of romantic writing for the strings, without the piquant memorability of *The Seasons*. The hero and heroine (who dance a musically engaging *pas de deux*) are standard ballet characters, and much of the choreography is traditional; but Natalya Bessmertnova is a charmingly graceful heroine, and she is well partnered by her elegant Knight (Yuri Vasyuchenko). Yet it is the Sheik – sinisterly portrayed by Gedminas Taranda – who steals the show. He makes a spectacular entry, with a thrilling repeated sideways leap, and with flashing eyes establishes a formidable characterization throughout. Undoubtedly this is the Bolshoi at their peak, and the orchestral playing under Algis Zhuraitis is first class, as is the recording. The camerawork cannot be faulted, although the Bolshoi stage is huge, and some of the long shots are inevitably rather distantly focused. The audience applause is at times an irritant, especially the constant demands for repeated bows from the principals after key dance numbers. But this remains an indispensable set for ballet lovers.

Raymonda (complete ballet)

(BB) **(*) Naxos 8.553503/4. Moscow SO, Anissimov

This Naxos version is played elegantly and affectionately, and the Moscow upper strings are full and warm as recorded. It does not lack life. But in seeking atmosphere, the playing creates a less than vibrant effect, although this is partly caused by Alexander Anissimov's tendency to luxuriant tempi.

Raymonda (ballet), *Op. 57:* extended excerpts from Acts I & II

**(*) Chan. 8447. SNO, Järvi

Järvi chooses some 56 minutes of music from the first two Acts, omitting entirely the Slavic/Hungarian Wedding *Divertissement* of the closing Act, and this contributes to the slight feeling of lassitude. But with rich Chandos recording this is a record for any balletomane to wallow in.

The Seasons (ballet; complete), *Op. 67*

⊙— (B) *** Double Decca 455 349-2 (2). RPO, Ashkenazy – PROKOFIEV: *Cinderella* ***
(M) **(*) Decca 460 315-2. SRO, Ansermet – KHACHATURIAN: *Gayaneh*; *Spartacus*: excerpts ***
(BB) **(*) Naxos 8.550079. Czech RSO (Bratislava), Lenárd – TCHAIKOVSKY: *Sleeping Beauty Suite* **
(N) (***) Dutton mono CDBP 9754. SO, composer – PROKOFIEV: *Romeo and Juliet: Suite 2* (***)

The Seasons (ballet; complete), *Op. 67*; Concert Waltzes 1 in D, Op. 47; 2 in F, Op. 51

(B) *** EMI double forte (ADD) 5 69361-2 (2). Philh. O, Svetlanov – ARENSKY: *Variations on a Theme of Tchaikovsky* ***; RIMSKY-KORSAKOV: *Scheherazade* **

The Seasons (ballet; complete); *Scènes de ballet, Op. 52*

*** Telarc CD 80347. Minnesota O, De Waart

Ashkenazy's account of Glazunov's delightful ballet is the finest it has ever received. The RPO playing is dainty and elegant, refined and sumptuous, yet the strings respond vigorously to the thrusting vitality of the Autumnal *Bacchanale*. The Decca engineers, working in Watford Town Hall, provide digital sound of great allure and warmth, very much in the demonstration bracket. As can be seen this recording is available on a Double Decca, coupled with Prokofiev's *Cinderella* ballet.

But if you want *The Seasons* separately on a single CD, you will be hard put to better the Minnesota performance, elegant, polished, warm and alive, and given Telarc's top-drawer sound. The famous thrusting tune of *Autumn* is only marginally less athletic than with Ashkenazy. The *Scènes de ballet* make an ideal coupling, not quite as melodically distinctive but still very enjoyable and cosily tuneful, although the second-movement *Marionettes* matches Delibes at his most piquant.

Svetlanov's account is played most beautifully. His approach is engagingly affectionate; he caresses the lyrical melodies persuasively so that, if the big tune of the *Bacchanale* has slightly less thrust than usual, it fits readily into the overall conception. The glowing Abbey Road recording is excellent and vividly remastered. It comes in harness with a very Russian *Scheherazade*, which he recorded with the LSO but about which we have some reservations (see below), and Barbirolli's highly persuasive version of the endearing Arensky *Variations* for strings.

Ansermet's recording dates from 1966 and is of vintage Decca quality. The performance takes a little while to warm up, but perhaps that is not inappropriate in the opening *Winter* sequence, where the conductor's meticulous ear for detail is a plus point, for the wind playing throughout is engagingly pointed. At the opening of *Summer* one might wish for a richer, more sumptuous sound from the Suisse Romande violins, but the zestful opening of *Autumn* is firm to the point of fierceness.

Ondrej Lenárd gives a pleasing bargain account of Glazunov's delightful score, finding plenty of delicacy, while the entry of Glazunov's most famous tune at the opening of the *Autumn Bacchanale* is very virile indeed. The sound is atmospheric, yet with plenty of fullness.

Recorded for the Columbia label in 1929, the composer's own reading of *The Seasons* brings a vigorous and colourful performance, with surprisingly good ensemble from what was evidently a pick-up orchestra, even if wind solos are often more raw-toned than they would be from a modern orchestra. The impact of the performance, not least in the exuberant *Bacchanale* for *Autumn* with lifted rhythms, is greatly heightened by the vivid and full-bodied transfer by Michael Dutton. The value of having the composer's own view of his most popular orchestral work is heightened by the excellent coupling of Prokofiev conducting music from his *Romeo and Juliet* ballet.

Stenka Razin (symphonic poem), Op. 13
*** Chan. 8479. SNO, Järvi – RIMSKY-KORSAKOV: *Scheherazade* ***

Stenka Razin has its moments of vulgarity – how otherwise with the *Song of the Volga Boatmen* a recurrent theme? – but it makes a generous makeweight for Järvi's fine version of *Scheherazade*. The recording is splendid.

Symphonies 1 in E, Op 5; 5 in B flat, Op. 55
(N) **(*) Orfeo C 093101A. Bav. RSO, Neeme Järvi

Symphony 2 in F sharp min., Op. 16; Concert Waltz 1
(N) **(*) Orfeo C 148101A. Bamberg SO, Neeme Järvi

Symphony 3 in D, Op. 33; Concert Waltz 2
(N) *** Orfeo C 157101A. Bamberg SO, Neeme Järvi

Symphonies 4 in E flat, Op. 48; 7 in F, Op. 77
(N) **(*) Orfeo C 148201A. Bamberg SO, Neeme Järvi

Symphony 6 in C min., Op. 58; Poème lyrique, Op. 12
(N) *** Orfeo C 157201A. Bamberg SO, Neeme Järvi

Symphony 8 in E flat, Op. 83; Overture solennelle, Op. 73; Wedding Procession
(N) **(*) Orfeo C 157201A. Bav. RSO, Neeme Järvi

Now that Orfeo CDs are distributed by Chandos, Neeme Järvi's cycle of the Glazunov *Symphonies* has been restored to the catalogue. Alas, they are all still at full price, but they are also all available separately, and they include some attractive bonuses. The *Third* and *Sixth Symphonies* are among the finest of the set, full of vigour and benefiting from the polish of the Bambergers' playing. But all these performances are cultivated. No. 1 is highly sympathetic in Järvi's hands, cogent and engagingly fresh. No. 2 is comfortable, both in music and in sound, but is undoubtedly enjoyable; and Järvi brings out

the full charm of No. 4. No. 5 (like No. 8 played by the Bavarian Radio Orchestra) may lack something in glitter, but the balance is full and pleasing. Above all, Järvi avoids bombast which can too easily take over in these works, which are nothing if not civilized.

Symphonies 1 in E, Op. 5; 6 in C min., Op. 58
*** BIS CD 1368. BBC Nat. O of Wales, Otaka

Symphony 1; (i) Violin Concerto, Op. 82
*** Chan. 9751. Russian State SO, Polyansky, (i) with Krasko

What a remarkable and delightful work the Glazunov *First Symphony* is – not only on account of the composer's youth (he was a mere sixteen at the time) but also because of the quality and fertility of its invention and its expert craftsmanship! Polyansky's pacing keeps the music alive throughout, and the finale, delightfully scored and in effect a set of variations on a simple theme, is one of the most successful closing movements for any of the composer's symphonies. Polyansky manages the tempi changes in an engagingly spontaneous way and the Chandos sound, full and with glowing wind colouring, is flattering. Julia Krasko plays the *Violin Concerto* warm-heartedly and with confidence and ready bravura, and she receives fine support from the Russian orchestra. The Chandos sound is well up to standard.

Otaka gives a first-class account of the *First*, every bit as fine as Polyansky, although perhaps the Chandos recording is marginally more vivid. But Otaka's *Sixth* is superb, one of the very finest performances and recordings of any Glazunov symphony on disc, with enchantingly affectionate detail. The music moves forward naturally and spontaneously, and there is delightful wind-colouring and the most elegant string-playing, especially in the central *Theme and Variations* and *Intermezzo*; yet the finale is a great success too. Highly recommended.

Symphony 2; From Darkness to Light, Op. 53; Mazurka in G
*** BIS CD 1308. BBC Nat. O of Wales, Otaka

Symphony 2 in F sharp min., Op. 16. (i) Coronation Cantata, Op. 56
*** Chan. 9709. Russian State SO, Polyansky, (i) with Lutiv-Ternovskaya, Kuznetsova, Grivnov, Stepanovich, Russian State Symphonic Capella

Glazunov's *Symphony No. 2* is full of very Russian themes that echo Borodin's *Prince Igor*, which Glazunov himself helped to complete after the composer's death. Though Polyansky's performance loses some concentration in the finale, it is warmly expressive and colourful, helped by rich, full recording. What makes the disc especially attractive is the substantial fill-up, the première recording of the *Coronation Cantata* which Glazunov wrote to celebrate the coronation of the last Tsar, Nicolas II. Framed by forthright choruses, the opening one in a swinging triple time, the middle five movements feature the four soloists in turn, culminating in an exhilarating movement, *Heaven and earth*, enriched with sensuously beautiful orchestration. A winning rarity, very well performed, with a strong team of soloists, all attractively Slavonic in timbre, even if the soprano grows edgy under pressure.

Tadaaki Otaka provides a very convincing account of the *Second Symphony*, mastering its rhetoric and revelling in its profusion of attractive, very Russian themes. He opens arrestingly and maintains the concentration of the playing to the end even more successfully than Polyansky on the competing Chandos recording of this same work. However, Polyansky's coupling is the *Coronation Cantata*, a rare and very attractive piece which is given an excellent performance. The *Mazurka* on the BIS CD is rhythmically buoyant; perhaps its material is overstretched, but there is variety of mood which Otaka manipulates very convincingly. *From Darkness to Light* is an unsettled piece, as enigmatic as its title. It produces a rather striking lyrical theme, but the intervening episodes, with heavy brass and cymbals, are less convincing. However, it is very well played indeed, and the recording throughout is excellent, full-bodied and spacious with a resonant concert-hall acoustic. For the *Second Symphony* this is now probably a first choice.

Symphony 3 in D, Op. 33; Ballade in F, Op. 78
*** BIS CD 1358. BBC Nat. O of Wales, Otaka

Symphony 3 in D, Op. 33; Concert Waltzes 1–2
**(*) Chan. 9658. Russian State SO, Polyansky

(i) *Symphony 3;* (ii) *Serenades 1 in A, Op. 7; 2 in F, Op. 11;* (i) *Stenka Razin, Op. 13*
**(*) ASV CDDCA 903. (i) LSO; (ii) RPO; Butt

Not for nothing did David Brown call Glazunov 'the Mendelssohn of Russian music'. His precocious talent is well known: he was still in his early twenties when he started work on the *Third Symphony*, which was dedicated to Tchaikovsky, who took a great interest in the score. The Tristanesque passages in the slow movement show a Wagnerian influence, though it is still the Borodin inheritance that strikes one most forcibly, and if the ideas are not perhaps as characterful as in the *Fifth Symphony*, they are still touched with distinction. Tadaaki Otaka gives a splendidly vital and sensitive account, full of warmth and passion, and this is now a clear first choice among available recordings. The *F major Ballade* of 1902, with its Rimsky-like middle section, makes an attractive makeweight, and the notes by Marina Lobanova are admirable. The recording has a natural perspective and depth.

Polyansky freely varies the music's forward impetus but keeps the tension fairly high, helped by a passionate response from his string section. The finale opens with a conventional Russian folk-dance theme, but is too extended for its material, in spite of the excellent, committed playing and plenty of momentum. The two *Concert Waltzes*, however, are most winning and they are played with affection and finesse. One cannot fault the performance of the *Symphony* either, but, apart from the Scherzo, Polyansky does not convince us that it shows the composer at his most imaginative. The Chandos recording is excellent if resonant.

Yondani Butt's performance of the *Symphony* is a good one and very well played. One would have liked a greater sense of soaring (over the throbbing wind chords) at the opening, but the response of the LSO catches the colour and melancholy of the slow movement, and the Scherzo (easily the best movement) has sparkle. But it is the two charming early *Serenades* that catch the ear, seductively played by the RPO.

Symphonies 4 in E flat, Op. 48; 5 in B flat, Op. 55
*** Chan. 9739. Russian State SO, Polyansky
*** ASV CDDCA 1051. Philh. O, Butt

The *Fourth Symphony* dates from the year of Tchaikovsky's death (1893) and is a charming and well-composed work, held together structurally by a theme which Glazunov uses in all three movements. The *Fifth*, written two years later, is more imposing, but not so very different really, although the first movement is more vigorous. Throughout both works the Philharmonia playing under Butt is persuasively warm and

sympathetic, helped by the spacious, well-balanced recording.

However, the Chandos competitor has the advantage of a fine Russian orchestra which immediately establish a richly Slavonic atmosphere of melancholy for the languorous opening theme of No. 4. The Chandos recording is glowingly warm in capturing string and woodwind timbres alike, yet the Scherzos of both symphonies sparkle translucently. The resonance means that the finales have less bite than with the ASV recording and, while they are played with robust, Russian-dance vigour, Butt is exceptionally spirited in the finale of No. 5. It is a case of swings and roundabouts, for the ASV recording is clearer, if not more lustrous.

Symphonies 4 in E flat, Op. 48; 8 in E flat, Op. 83
(N) BIS **(*) CD 1378. BBC Nat. O of Wales, Otaka

Otaka makes the most of the melancholy opening of the *Fourth Symphony*, which is very delicately and affectionately done. The central brilliant *Scherzo* has similar delicacy, with elegant woodwind playing, and the following *Andante* is most beautifully done. Not that these performances are lacking in energy, and both symphonies are well laid out, with no attention to detail skimped. The opening of the finale of No. 4 sounds more noble than usual, with the ebb and flow of the movement well judged. Refined rather than brilliant sound to match the performances. But in the last resort this disc would not offer a first choice for either work.

Symphony 5 in B flat; The Seasons (ballet; complete)
⊶ (N) *** Warner 2564 61434-2. RSNO, Serebrier

Jose Serebrier with the Royal Scottish National Orchestra here couples two of Glazunov's most warmly attractive works. The one-Act ballet *The Seasons* is the most popular of his orchestral works, deservedly so. The *Fifth Symphony*, dating from five years earlier, 1895, opens with a bouncing *Allegro* in triple-time, here given an exhilarating performance. That is followed by a Scherzo which echoes Mendelssohn's fairy music, a lyrical slow movement, lovingly done, and an energetic finale full of vigorous syncopations. With outstanding recorded sound giving clarity and weight, the refinement and power of the performance are superbly caught.

Symphonies 5 in B flat, Op. 55; 7 in F, Op. 77
(N) **(*) BIS CD 1388. BBC Nat. O of Wales, Otaka

Otaka brings clear thinking and refined playing to the *Fifth Symphony*, but Serebrier brings more energy and spirit to his Warner version (though nothing compares in excitement to Fedoseyev's old HMV/Melodia account, where the finale is electrifying). In the *Seventh*, refinement and beauty of playing are paramount, and much of the woodwind detail is very attractive indeed. With Otaka's unrushed tempi, the rhythms are nicely pointed, and one can appreciate all the details in busy movements, such as the lovely, rustic-sounding Scherzo. Only in the finale does one occasionally feel a more extrovert approach would bring a benefit, though there is nothing here to mar one's enjoyment, especially when the strings are so beautifully phrased. Refined, well-balanced sound to match.

Symphonies 5; 8 in E flat, Op. 83
⊶ (BB) *** Naxos 8.553660. Moscow SO, Anissimov

These are both delightful symphonies, even if the *Eighth* is rather thickly scored. However, Alexander Anissimov does his best to make the textures as clear and well ventilated as possible, and pays great attention to details of dynamics and balance. Try the Scherzo of the *Fifth Symphony* and you will find much lightness of touch and a greater transparency than is often encountered in records of these works. His is a far more persuasive account of the *Eighth* than Svetlanov's LP version from the 1980s. Strongly recommended, especially at such a modest cost.

Symphony 6 in C min., Op. 58; Characteristic Suite in D, Op. 9
(N) *** Chan. 10238. Russian State SO, Polyansky

(i) *Symphony 6 in C min., Op. 58; Raymonda (ballet), Op. 57a: Suite;* (ii) *Triumphal March, Op. 40*
**(*) ASV CDDCA 904. (i) LSO; (ii) RPO; Butt

Symphony 6; The Forest (tone-poem), Op. 19
(BB) **(*) Naxos 8.554293. Moscow SO, Anissimov

Valéry Polyansky's current Glazunov symphony cycle is proving very satisfying, with thoroughly idiomatic and sound interpretations, and the present coupling is no exception. Polyansky's reading of the *Sixth Symphony* has plenty of impetus and excellent detail, and the *Characteristic Suite* is well worth having on disc. Very good playing from the Russian State Symphony Orchestra and excellent Chandos recording make this another desirable addition to the catalogue.

Yondani Butt is helped by the open sound of the ASV recording and the fine wind and brass contributions from the LSO; the brass chorale at the end of the *Variations* is effectively sonorous. However, this performance is now outclassed by Otaka on BIS. The selection from *Raymonda* concentrates on the first two Acts and offers only a brief *Entr'acte* from Act III; most of the music in fact comes from Act I, some 21 minutes out of a selection lasting just over half an hour. The playing is both graceful and lively, and the recording has plenty of amplitude and warmth.

Anissimov also handles the symphony admirably and, with the Moscow players responding persuasively, the performance is a great success. However, *The Forest* is an overextended pantheistic tone-poem with an ingenuous programme. The performance is sympathetic, the recording very good, but Anissimov fails to persuade us that this piece is not too long for its material. Yet the work is rarely if ever performed, and the fine account of the symphony is worth its modest Naxos price.

Symphony 8, Op. 83; Poème lyrique, Op. 65; (i) *Commemorative Cantata, Op. 65*
⊕ *** Chan. 9961. Russian State SO, Polyansky; (i) with Kuznetsova, Grivnov, Russian State Symphonic Capella

Polyansky's performance of the *Eighth Symphony* is thoroughly persuasive throughout, especially in the finale, which is both exciting and satisfyingly cumulative. The *Poème lyrique*, too, is given a rapturous account, with Polyansky revelling in the Russianness of the melodic line. But what makes this disc especially compelling is the lovely cantata commemorating the centenary of the birth of Pushkin. It is full of richly lyrical invention, and the performance is in every way outstanding. Soloists, chorus and orchestra combine to give a passionately dedicated performance of what is surely one of the composer's finest choral works. The recording is well up to Chandos's excellent standard.

CHAMBER MUSIC

5 Novelettes, Op. 15
(***) Testament mono SBT1061. Hollywod Qt – BORODIN: *String Quartet 2;* TCHAIKOVSKY: *String Quartet 1* (***)

The Hollywood Quartet bring a freshness and ardour to these charming compositions that are most persuasive.

String Quartet 3 in G (Slavonic)
(B) *** Cal. CAL 6262. Annesci Qt – DVORAK: *String Quartet 12 (American)* ***

Glazunov's *Slavonic Quartet* is so named because of its finale (*'Une fête slave'*), which the Annesci players despatch with attractive geniality, neatly catching the dance rhythms. They are equally fetching in the *Alla Mazurka*, with its underlying drone, while the first two movements are full of lyrical warmth. A first-rate coupling for the Dvořák performance is no less endearing.

String Quartets 2 in F, Op. 10; 4 in A min., Op. 64; Elegy, Op. 105
(N) *** MDG 603 1237-2. Utrecht Qt
String Quartets: 3 in G (Slave), Op. 26; 5 in D min., Op. 70
*** MDG 603 1236-2. Utrecht Qt

Both *Quartets* on MDG 603 1237-2 are youthful, as is the *Quatuor slave* on the previously issued second disc. The *F major* comes from 1881, when the composer was 16 and had already written the *First Symphony*; the *A minor* dates from only two years later and the *Quatuor slave* was composed in two parts, in 1886 and 1888. The 'Slavonic' influences in the Mazurka third movement and the *Fête slave* finale bring Russian dance influences at their most civilized, while the slow movement of the *A minor Quartet* is particularly beautiful. What elegantly written music this is! For those starting to collect these works, the Utrecht versions can be thoroughly recommended. They are warmly and pleasingly recorded.

String Quintet in A, Op. 39
*** Chan. 9878. ASMF Chamber Ens. – TCHAIKOVSKY: *Souvenir de Florence* ***

Glazunov's *String Quintet* (with second cello) is a work of characteristic warmth and lyricism. The performance is thoroughly committed and persuasive, and very well recorded too. There is no alternative version in the catalogue – but, even if there were, this would be hard to beat.

Complete piano music

Piano Sonata 1 in B flat min., Op. 74; Grande valse de concert, Op. 41; 3 Miniatures, Op. 42; Petite valse, Op. 36; Suite on the Name 'Sacha'; Valse de salon, Op. 43; Waltzes on the Theme 'Sabela', Op. 23
*** Hyp. CDA 66833. Coombs

Easy Sonata; 3 Etudes, Op. 31; Miniature in C; 3 Morceaux, Op. 49; Nocturne, Op. 37; 2 Pieces, Op. 22; 2 Poèmes-improvisations; Sonatina; Theme & Variations, Op. 72
*** Hyp. CDA 66844. Coombs

Marking the start of a new Russian series, each of these two discs contains a major work, the *Piano Sonata No. 1* on the first and the *Theme and Variations*, Op. 72, on the second. For the rest, you have a dazzling series of salon and genre pieces, full of the easy charm and winning tunefulness that mark Glazunov's ballet, *The Seasons*. Stephen Coombs proves a most persuasive advocate, consistently conveying sheer joy in keyboard virtuosity to a degree rare in British pianists. Coombs plays with a natural warmth and a spontaneous feeling for line which give magic to pieces which otherwise might seem trivial. As well as the engaging *Variations*, simple in outline but elaborate and colourful in texture, the second disc offers what might be counted Glazunov's most assured piano work, the set of three *Etudes*, Op. 31.

(i) *Piano Sonata 2 in E min., Op. 75; Barcarolle sur les touches noires; Idyll, Op. 103; 2 Impromptus, Op. 54; In modo religioso, Op. 38; Prelude & 2 Mazurkas, Op. 25; Song of the Volga Boatmen, Op. 97* (arr. Siloti); (ii) *Triumphal March, Op. 40*

*** Hyp. CDA 66866. (i) Coombs; (ii) Holst Singers, Layton

The most substantial work here is the *Second Sonata* of 1901, which is better played than by any of its rivals we have heard. The most unusual piece is the transcription of a Wagnerian *Triumphal March*, written for the Chicago Exposition, which eventually introduces *Hail Columbus*, sung in Russian! Not all the music on this generously filled CD is of equal merit but most of it is rewarding, and the recording serves the music well.

4 Preludes & Fugues, Op. 101; Prelude & Fugue in D min., Op. 62; in E min. (1926)

*** Hyp. CDA 66855. Coombs

The *D minor Prelude and Fugue* is not just a powerful essay in Bachian counterpoint, but a dramatic and compelling piece. The set of four, Op. 101, are not only intellectually rewarding but they are also artistically most satisfying and inventive pieces. The *E minor* from 1926 opens dramatically and is another impressive piece. The recording is eminently satisfactory, without any excessive reverberance.

ORGAN MUSIC

Fantasy, Op. 110; Preludes & Fugues: in D, Op. 93; in D min., Op. 98

*** BIS CD 1101. Ericsson – DVORAK: *Preludes & Fugues* **(*); SIBELIUS: *Intrada*, etc. ***

These pieces leave no doubt as to Glazunov's contrapuntal mastery. The *Prelude and Fugue in D* was composed in the immediate wake of the *Eighth Symphony*, and the *D minor* (which also exists in a version for piano), with its powerfully wrought fugue, will surprise those who think of Glazunov as a dyed-in-the-wool conservative. The *Fantasy* was written for Marcel Dupré in 1934–5, towards the end of Glazunov's career, and is well worth getting to know. Hans Ola Ericsson produces some splendid effects from the powerful new Gerald Woehl organ at St Petrus Canisius, Friedrichshafen. The recording is in the demonstration class and has tremendous presence and range.

VOCAL MUSIC

Tsar Iudesyskiy (King of the Jews)

*** Chan. 9467. Russian State Symphony Ch. & SO, Rozhdestvensky

Tsar Iudesyskiy (King of the Jews); Salome* (incidental music): *Introduction and Salome's dance

*** Chan. 9824. (i) Russian State Symphonic Capella; Russian State SO, Polyansky

Glazunov's incidental music to Konstantin Romanov's *Tsar Iudesyskiy* (*King of the Jews*) offers considerable artistic rewards. There is an unaffected simplicity that is quite touching, and the naturalness of the musical inspiration outweighs any of its longueurs or miscalculations. Rozhdestvensky shapes each phrase with feeling and imagination, and he gets good results from his chorus and orchestra. Moreover, the quality of the recorded sound is first rate in every respect, with well-balanced choral and orchestral forces and a lifelike perspective. There are informative and helpful notes by David Nice.

Astonishingly Chandos have followed up Rozhdestvensky's CD with another, using similar forces conducted by Valéry Polyansky. His version is hardly less compelling, although perhaps Rozhdestvensky is that bit more dramatic at the opening, and in portraying the Levite's trumpets (actually horns). But Polyansky's account is richly atmospheric and his singers are splendid. There is little in it, although some may be swayed by the more recent CD's inclusion of the music that Glazunov wrote in 1908 for a production of Oscar Wilde's *Salome*. It is agreeably sinuous and sumptuous, but the music for the famous *Dance* (for which Fokine provided choreography) is anything but erotic.

GLIÈRE, Reinhold (1875–1956)

(i) *Concerto for Coloratura Soprano, Op. 82;* (ii) *Harp Concerto, Op. 74*

*** Chan. 9094. (i) Hulse; (ii) Masters; City of L. Sinfonia, Hickox – GINASTERA: *Harp Concerto* ***

This digital recording of Glière's lush concertos is highly competitive in both works. The recording is suitably rich and opulent, yet every detail is audibly in place. Eileen Hulse is an impressive soloist with excellent control, well-focused tone and a good sense of line, and she is excellently supported by the City of London Sinfonia and Richard Hickox. Nor need Rachel Masters fear comparison with her predecessor, Osian Ellis; so, given such excellent sound, this is all highly self-indulgent and sybaritic.

Symphony 2 in C min., Op. 25; Zaporozhy Cossacks, Op. 64

**(*) Chan. 9071. BBC PO, Downes

Not even the advocacy of Sir Edward Downes with his magnificent Manchester orchestra can conceal the banality of some of the writing in this early symphony – it cannot compare with Glière's later and grander *Symphony No. 3*. *Zaporozhy Cossacks* is less ambitious but also contains banalities. Excellent performances and outstanding recording.

Symphony 3 in B min. (Ilya Mourometz), Op. 42

☛ *** Telarc CD 80609. LSO, Botstein

*** Chan. 9041. BBC PO, Downes

(i) *Symphony 3 (Ilya Mourometz);* (ii) *Cello Concerto, Op. 87.*

(BB) **(*) Regis RRC 2068 (2). (i) RPO, Faberman; (ii) Sudzilovsky, Russian Cinematographic O, Skripta

Fine as its Chandos competitor is, this new Telarc recording of Glière's *Ilya Mourometz Symphony* is even more impressive. Botstein uses the uncut original score of 1911, and even though both outer movements run to over 22 minutes, their length is well sustained. What Botstein also does is to bring out the underlying Russian folksong inspiration of the writing. The spaciously spectacular recording is well up to the high standard we expect from this label.

Downes and the BBC Philharmonic in magnificent form give an urgently passionate performance of this colourful programme piece. Downes, taut and intense, relates the writing very much to the world of Glière's close contemporary, Rachmaninov. The recording, made in the concert hall of New Broadcasting House, Manchester, is one of Chandos's finest, combining clarity and sumptuousness. But the new Telarc recording is even finer.

Faberman made the first complete digital recording of Glière's epic symphony in 1978 (originally for Unicorn). His conducting cannot be described as volatile, and he is never led into introducing urgent stringendos to add to the passion of a climax; but his very patience, helped by excellent recording, makes for very compelling results. If, at the start of the main *Allegro* of the first movement, cellos and basses have limited resonance, that is clearly a reflection of how the players actually sounded in the hall, and though the long finale is is marginally less clean in its textures, the sound from first to last has a natural balance and warmth. This is not a first choice, but it is inexpensive and includes also the bonus of the *Cello Concerto*, an agreeable piece (with an extended slow movement) but not distinctive. The solo cellist, Sergei Sudzilovsky, has a small tone and the effect is at times rather wan. But he is well balanced with the orchestra and the lack of vividness must be partly attributed to the recording, which is rather lacking in impact.

Octet, Op. 5; Sextet, Op. 11
*** MDG 308 1196-2. Berlin Philharmonic String Octet

Although he is best known for the huge *Ilya Mourometz Symphony* and his ballet *The Red Poppy*, Glière's chamber-music output was also extensive. His music is firmly rooted in the great post-nationalist Russian style, and as a teacher he exerted a great influence on Miaskovsky, Khachaturian, Lev Knipper and the eleven-year-old Prokofiev. His *Octet* comes from 1900, when the composer was in his mid-twenties, and the *Sextet*, his third essay in the medium, was composed five years later. Both works show a mastery not only of the genre (Glière was a fine violinist) but the impeccable craftsmanship that one would expect from a pupil of Taneyev, while the melodic ideas are both beautifully fashioned and finely paced. Everything unfolds as you feel it should, there is a keen sense of forward movement and nothing outstays its welcome. The spiritual world is that of Borodin and Glazunov, even if the thematic ideas do not have the former's distinction. The Berlin Philharmonic String Octet play with enthusiasm and persuasiveness, and the MDG sound is very lifelike. An appealing and welcome issue.

GLINKA, Mikhail (1804–57)

Capriccio brillante on the Jota aragonesa (Spanish Overture 1); Kamarinskaya; Souvenir of a Summer Night in Madrid (Spanish Overture 2); Valse-fantaisie; A Life for the Tsar: Overture & Suite (Polonaise; Krakowiak; Waltz; Mazurka; Epilogue)
*** ASV CDDCA 1075. Armenian PO, Tjeknavorian

Capriccio brillante on the Jota aragonesa (Spanish Overture 1); Kamarinskaya; Overture in D; Ruslan and Ludmilla:

Overture & Suite; Souvenir of a Summer Night in Madrid (Spanish Overture 2); Symphony on Two Russian Themes; Valse-Fantaisie
*** Chan. 9861. BBC PO, Sinaisky

The key work on ASV here is *Kamarinskaya*, a kaleidoscopic fantasy on two Russian folksongs. Tchaikovsky said it contained 'the whole of Russian music, just as the acorn holds within itself the oak tree'. The two Spanish overtures created another genre, the orchestral 'picture postcard', which Russian composers brought home from their travels abroad. Glinka's two pieces have a glitter and atmospheric appeal all of their own, especially the *Capriccio brillante*, featuring a 'jota aragonesa' also used by Liszt. But the seductive scoring of *Summer Night in Madrid* was in some ways even more influential. The *Valse-fantaisie* is a charmer, but the overture and suite from *A Life for the Tsar* are more conventional. The whole programme is played here with a natural vitality and a delightful feeling for its Russianness under a conductor who is a composer himself. The bright recording, full-bodied and glowing, is one of the finest we have received from ASV.

Sinaisky duplicates the main items in Tjeknavorian's programme, but includes also the seductive *Symphony on Two Russian Themes*: not great music, but alluring in its orchestral palette and its anticipations of Borodin. Many will also prefer the fizzingly brilliant *Overture, March* and *Dances* (effectively a charming ballet suite) from *Ruslan and Ludmilla* to the excepts from *A Life for the Tsar*. Moreover, not only is the playing of the BBC Philharmonic under Sinaisky both warmly responsive and sparkling, but the state-of-the-art Chandos recording (brass, woodwind and strings alike) is even finer than the ASV alternative. Highly recommended.

Polka 1 (orch. Balakirev); Spanish Overtures 1 (Jota aragonesa); 2 (Summer Night in Madrid); Waltz Fantasia; Ivan Susanin (A Life for the Tsar): Overture. Prince Kholmsky: Overture and Entr'actes to Acts II–IV; Ruslan and Ludmilla: Overture; Chernamor's March
(BB) *** Regis (ADD/DDD) RRC 1142. USSR SO & Bolshoi Theatre O, Svetlanov

These Russian recordings have been selected from a two-disc Melodiya set that last appeared on BMG/RCA. The performances embrace a considerable time-span (1963–84). The playing of the USSR Symphony Orchestra, which provides the majority of the items, is nothing if not expert and idiomatic, and the remastered recordings, though variable in quality, are generally very good indeed.

CHAMBER MUSIC

Grand Sextet in E flat
(BB) *** Hyp. Helios CDH 55173. Capricorn –
RIMSKY-KORSAKOV: *Quintet for Piano & Wind* ***

Glinka's *Sextet* is rather engaging, particularly when played with such aplomb as it is here. The contribution of the pianist, Julian Jacobson, is brilliantly nimble and felicitous. The balance places the piano rather backwardly, but the CD provides good detail and presence.

Trio pathétique in D min.
*** Chan. 8477. Borodin Trio – ARENSKY: *Piano Trio* ***

Glinka's *Trio* is prefaced by a superscription: *'Je n'ai connu l'amour que par les peines qu'il cause'* ('I have known love only through the misery it causes'). It is no masterpiece – but the

Borodins almost persuade one that it is. The Chandos recording is vivid and has excellent presence.

OPERA

Ruslan and Ludmilla (complete)

☐— * Ph. **DVD** 075 096-9 (2). Ognovienko, Netrebko, Diadkova, Bezzubenkov, Gorchakova, Kirov Op. Ch. & O, Gergiev – (Producer: Wilson; V/D: Hulscher) (Bonuses: **Gergiev**: 'Introducing Ruslan' and 'Catching up with Music' – biographical tour)

*** Ph. **DVD** 075 099-9 (6). As above – BORODIN: Prince Igor; MUSSORGSKY: Boris Godunov

Gergiev in his Kirov recording, done live on stage, launches into this classic Russian opera with a hair-raisingly fast and brilliant account of the overture, and then characteristically brings out the subtlety of much of the writing, as well as the colour. The voices come over well, with Vladimir Ognovienko characterful as Ruslan, bringing out word-meaning, most impressively in his big Act II aria. Anna Netrebko is fresh and bright as Ludmilla, as well as agile, not as shrill as many Russian sopranos, but it is Galina Gorchakova as Gorislava who takes first honours; she is rich and firm, as is Larissa Diadkova in the travesti role of Ratmir, especially impressive in the delightful duet with Finn (Konstantin Pluzhnikov). There is much refinement and sensitivity from all concerned and a vivid sense of that fairy-tale quality that makes its charm pretty irresistible. The layout is on two sharply defined and colourful DVDs with Acts I–III on the first and Acts IV and V on the second disc. In addition there are two bonuses, the first an introduction to the opera of some 18 minutes and a 50-minute feature about Gergiev. The staging is colourful, if at times a bit static, and the whole production will give much pleasure. Good essays in English, French and German, from different authorities (and subtitles in Italian, Spanish and Mandarin). Ruslan is a great work, and this version will delight all who invest in it. The discs are also included in the excellent Philips set, 'The Glory of Russian Opera'.

GLUCK, Christoph (1714–87)

Don Juan (ballet; complete)

(N) *** Australian Decca Eloquence (ADD) 476 2440. ASMF, Marriner – HANDEL: Ariodante; Il Pastor Fido (suites) ***
(BB) *** Warner Apex 8573 89233-2-2. E. Bar. Sol., Gardiner

Gluck's Don Juan is a wonderful score, revolutionary in its day, and it comes across to modern ears as a tuneful work full of striking ideas, with plenty of charm and drama. The pizzicato Andante in Act I is one of many incidental delights on the way, and the finale is suitably dramatic. Marriner's classic 1967 recording has great lightness of touch, beautiful playing and vintage Decca sound. If Gardiner's (Erato) version brought out more of the work's drama, there is nothing in the least bland about Marriner's direction and, with its very enjoyable coupling, this makes a welcome return to circulation.

Originally part of the Gardiner Collection, the alternative Gardiner version has much to recommend it at Apex price. The 1981 recording is full and modern. The performance too has a clean and dramatic profile.

OPERA

Alceste (Vienna version 1767; complete)

(B) *** Naxos 8.660066/68 (3). Ringholz, Lavender, Degerfeldt, Treichl, Martinsson, Drottningholm Theatre Ch. & O., Ostman

This is the first recording of the Vienna version of Alceste, rather simpler and more direct in manner than the far better-known French version of 1776. Here, Alceste's powerful aria Divinités du Styx becomes Ombre, larve, less imposing, and the intimate scale of the Drottningholm presentation reflects that, with a cast of young singers remarkable for their freshness rather than for their power.

The self-sacrificing heroine is more girlish, more vulnerable, as portrayed by the American Teresa Ringholz, who is clear and true in every register, if a little lacking in variety. Her sweetness and purity are matched by the young Swedish soprano Miriam Treichl, in the role of Ismene, Alceste's confidante – a most promising singer, even if it is at times confusing to have such similar singers juxtaposed. The clear-toned British tenor Justin Lavender sings stylishly in the relatively small role of Admeto, husband of Alceste, with Jonas Degerfeldt, aptly lighter and more youthful, as his confidant, Evandro.

After a dull start the chorus warms up well in Act II, with the period orchestra a little edgy but always alert under Ostman's direction. At the Naxos price one can hardly complain that the opera is laid out rather extravagantly on three discs, when in any case that brings the advantage of one disc per Act. Well-balanced sound, with voices well to the fore. Full libretto, synopsis and translation are provided.

Armide (complete)

*** DG 459 616-2. Delunsch, Workman, Podles, Naouri, Ch. & Musiciens du Louvre, Minkowski

Armide, the fifth of Gluck's 'reform' operas, written for Paris in 1777, is both passionate and dramatic in telling the story of the sorceress, Armide, and her unwilling love for the knight Renaud. It leads to a sensuous love duet in Act V before Renaud finally rejects her love. Using a libretto set by Lully almost a century earlier, Gluck develops a compellingly flexible structure, with arias, duets and recitatives merging in quick succession. Minkowski's treatment could not be more dramatic, persuasively leading one on at speeds on the brisk side. The cast is strong, powerfully led by Mireille Delunsch in the title-role, singing with rich, firm tone, and with Charles Workman fresh and clean-cut as the tenor hero, Renaud. In the brief but important role of La Haine, Ewa Podles sings with commanding intensity, and the minor roles are also well taken. The live recording gives weight and bite to the substantial instrumental band.

Iphigénie en Aulide (complete)

(M) *** Erato 2292 45003-2 (2). Van Dam, Von Otter, Dawson, Aler, Monteverdi Ch., Lyon Op. O, Gardiner

Gardiner here reconstructs the score as presented in the first revival of 1775; the recording conveys the tensions of a live performance without the distractions of intrusive stage noise. The darkness of the piece is established at the very start, with men's voices eliminated, and a moving portrait built up of Agamemnon, here sung superbly by José van Dam. In the title-role Lynne Dawson builds up a touching portrait of the heroine. Her sweet, pure singing is well contrasted with the positive strength of Anne Sofie von Otter as Clytemnestra, and John Aler brings clear, heroic attack to the tenor role of Achilles. The performance is crowned by the superb ensemble-singing of the Monteverdi Choir in the many choruses. A highlights disc is also available on Apex (2564 61507-2).

Iphigénie en Aulide (complete, in German; arr. Wagner)

(M) **(*) RCA (ADD) 74321 32236-2 (2). Moffo, Fischer-Dieskau, Schmidt, Spiess, Stewart, Augér, Bav. R. Ch., Munich R. O, Eichhorn

Wagner's arrangement used here is, by the standards of modern purism, a total travesty and the use of German instead of French only reinforces the stylistic conflict. But with an urgently dramatic performance, with a formidable list of soloists, excellent choral singing and fine playing, this is enjoyable entertainment in its own right, with its enriched orchestration and harmony, its cuts and additions and its amended plot. Wagnerians at least need not hesitate. Good stage atmosphere in the recording. The German libretto comes without a translation.

Iphigénie en Tauride (DVD version)

(N) ** Arthaus **DVD** 100 376. Galstian, Gilfry, Van der Walt, Scharinger, Jankova, Soranno, Zurich Op. Ch. & O, Christie (V/D: Thomas Grimm)

Iphigénie en Tauride (complete; CD versions)

☛ ✿ (M) *** Ph. 476 171-2 (2). Montague, Aler, Allen, Argenta, Massis, Monteverdi Ch., Lyons Op. O, Gardiner

*** DG 471 133-2 (2). Delunsch, Keenlyside, Beuron, Naouri, Louvre Ch. & O, Minkowski

*** Telarc CD 80546 (2). Goerke, Gilfry, Cole, Salters, Baker, West, Boston Baroque, Pearlman

On DVD, with an impressive cast, William Christie conducts the Zurich Opera House Orchestra in a performance with period overtones, bringing out the drama of this 'reform' opera. But he is not helped by the updated production by Bernhard Fleischer, with Thoas (incongruously wearing a silver crown) and the male chorus in tailcoats. The chorus also makes feeble movements during the ballet sequence. All told, the modern dress adds nothing, making the story less involving, particularly when Thoas is dispatched with a large carving-knife. Not only is Juliette Galstian a fine Iphigénie, bright, clear and wonderfully agile, the roles of the two friends, Pylade and Oreste, are strongly taken, respectively by Deon van der Walt and Rodney Gilfry. As a bonus, the disc also contains an hour-long film about Gluck, including interviews with William Christie and John Eliot Gardiner among others. But most collectors will get far more satisfaction from the CD audio versions.

Indeed, Gardiner's electrifying reading of Iphigénie en Tauride is a revelation. Though his Lyon orchestra does not use period instruments, its clarity and resilience and, where necessary, grace and delicacy are admirable. Diana Montague in the name-part sings with admirable bite and freshness and Thomas Allen is an outstanding Oreste, characterizing strongly but singing with classical precision. John Aler is a similarly strong and stylish singer, taking the tenor role of Pylade. The recording is bright and full. This is now part of Universal's 'Penguin Rosette Collection'.

Marc Minkowski launches into his characterful, highly distinctive reading in a performance of the overture with characteristically extreme speeds in both directions. Where Pearlman's Telarc version consistently takes a safe course,

Minkowski's regularly offers a more personal, more challenging view, giving new insights into the music. It also sounds more idiomatic, thanks to having a cast almost entirely made up of French speakers, who enunciate their words clearly to heighten the meaning. That is especially true of Mireille Delunsch in the title-role, golden-toned and deeply affecting in her great aria, O malheureuse Iphigénie! Simon Keenlyside as Oreste is hardly less idiomatic and characterful, with his sharply focused baritone. Yann Beuron as Pylade and Laurent Naouri as Thoas complete an outstanding team. Balance of merits between Minkowski and Pearlman could not be closer, and there is also the outstanding Gardiner version which, despite using modern instruments, combines many of the merits of both.

With an excellent cast, led by Christine Goerke radiantly pure-toned in the title-role, Martin Pearlman directs his Boston forces in a fresh, direct reading of the last of Gluck's 'reform' operas, which unaffectedly brings out the dramatic bite as well as the beauty. Pearlman's choice of speeds is never extreme, always natural, and, besides Goerke, Rodney Gilfry as Oreste and Vinson Cole as Pylade with clean, heady tenor tone are both excellent. An excellent, safe choice for anyone wanting this masterpiece in a period performance.

Orfeo ed Euridice (DVD versions)

(N) **(*) Warner **DVD** 5050467-3921-2-0. Baker, Speiser, Gale, Glyndebourne Festival Ch., LPO, Leppard (V/D: Rodney Greenberg)

(N) **(*) Arthaus **DVD** 100 417. Kowalski, Webster, Budd, ROHCG O and Ch., Haenchen

Orfeo ed Euridice (complete; CD versions)

☛ (M) *** Ph. 470 424-2 (2). Ragin, McNair, Sieden, Monteverdi Ch., E. Bar. Sol., Gardiner

(M) *** EMI C5 56885-2 (2). Hendricks, Von Otter, Fournier, Monteverdi Ch., Lyon Opéra O, Gardiner

(M) *** Erato 2292 45864-2 (2). J. Baker, Speiser, Gale, Glyndebourne Ch., LPO, Leppard

*** Teldec 4509 98418-2 (2). Larmore, Upshaw, Hagley, San Francisco Op. Ch. & O, Runnicles

(BB) *** Naxos 8.660064. Biel, Boog, Avemo, Drottningholm Theatre Ch. & O, Ostman

Peter Hall's classic Glyndebourne production of Orfeo, here recorded in 1982, is valuable above all for marking one of Dame Janet Baker's last operatic appearances. It is good to be reminded how powerful the result is when her passionately intense singing is matched by her equally involved and compelling acting. To see her cradling the dead Euridice in her arms as she sings Che faro is deeply moving. Raymond Leppard draws biting attack and warm expressiveness from the LPO, though the impact of the musical clarity is slightly muted by the rather soft focus of the camerawork. Leppard has opted for a version of the score broadly based on the composite Berlioz edition, but using the Italian rather than the French text, including at the end Gluck's sequence of ballet numbers as a grand finale, here imaginatively staged. John Bury's sets are stylized and evocative, with the final scene involving a central pathway in exaggerated perspective into the distance, brilliantly effective for the final scene between Orfeo and Euridice. As Euridice, Elisabeth Speiser sings powerfully but has an edge on her voice, less noticeable on video than on the Erato CD. As Amor, Elizabeth Gale sings brightly, seemingly unhampered by being suspended at a height, pantomime-wise, throughout the opera. The Glyndebourne Chorus sings with superb attack.

The Arthaus DVD brings a live recording, made at Covent Garden in 1991, of Harry Kupfer's much-praised production. Central to its success is the brilliant and moving performance of the title-role by the counter-tenor Jochen Kowalski, singing flawlessly. Though Kupfer updates the action to the present day, with Orpheus wearing leather jacket and jeans and carrying a guitar rather than a lyre, he justifies that by making the result so involving. The bizarre production never undermines the musical impact, which is heightened by the period-style practices that Harmut Haenchen persuades the Covent Garden Orchestra to adopt. Haenchen opts for the original, Vienna version of the score, sharp, direct and concise, even though that omits some of the favourite numbers which Gluck added after the original Vienna presentation. Euridice is sung very sweetly by Gillian Webster, with her white dress cloaked in black for the journey back to Hades. The character of Amor is imaginatively presented, with a boy treble, Jeremy Budd, singing very freshly from the side of the stage, while a very young child plays on stage around the meditating Orpheus. Comparably, the chorus is set on the left, singing from choir-stalls. Bright, forward sound.

On CD Gardiner's newest set for Philips could not be more sharply contrasted with the earlier recording he made for EMI in 1989. Then he was persuaded at the Lyon Opéra to record the Berlioz edition, in French. But all along Gardiner has much preferred the tautness of the original, Vienna version in Italian, which here on Philips he presents with a bite and sense of drama both totally in period and deeply expressive. The element of sensuousness, not least in the beautiful singing of the counter-tenor, Derek Lee Ragin, in the title-role, complements the Elysian beauty Gardiner finds in such passages as the introduction to *Che puro ciel*. Sylvia McNair as Euridice and Cyndia Sieden as Amor complete Gardiner's outstanding solo team. One's only regret is that the set does not provide as a supplement such numbers written for Paris as *The Dance of the Blessed Spirits*.

EMI have reissued Gardiner's earlier recording of the Berlioz edition of Gluck's opera, sung in French. It is now at mid-price and many will be glad to have this set, which aimed at combining the best of both the Vienna and Paris versions, although he omits the celebratory ballet at the end of the opera. Anne Sofie von Otter is a superb Orphée, dramatically most convincing. The masculine forthrightness of her singing matches the urgency of Gardiner's direction; and both Barbara Hendricks as Euridice and Brigitte Fournier as Amour are also excellent. The chorus is Gardiner's own Monteverdi Choir, superbly clean and stylish, and the recording is full and well balanced. However, his newest set, for Philips, is even finer (even though once again he does not include the ballet sequence).

The Erato version of *Orfeo ed Euridice*, directly based on the Glyndebourne production in which Dame Janet Baker made her very last stage appearance in opera, was recorded in 1982. Leppard presents the score with freshness and power, indeed with toughness. Nowhere is that clearer than in the great scene leading up to the aria, *Che farò*, where Baker commandingly conveys the genuine bitterness and anger of Orpheus at Eurydice's death. Elisabeth Speiser as Eurydice and Elizabeth Gale as Amor are both disappointing but, as in the theatre, the result is a complete and moving experience centring round a great performance from Dame Janet. The complete ballet-postlude is included, delightful celebration music. The recording has been enhanced in the CD transfer, bright and vivid without edginess, and there is an excellent (74-minute) budget CD

of highlights including the Ballet Music on Apex (2564 61497-2).

Donald Runnicles also conducts a performance based on the 1869 Berlioz edition, generally adopting speeds a degree broader than those preferred by Gardiner in his EMI set, and with a smoother style. Jennifer Larmore makes a strong and positive Orphée, brilliant in the aria which in this edition ends Act I, rich and warm in rather broad treatment of the big aria, *J'ai perdu mon Eurydice*. Next to von Otter for Gardiner she sounds very feminine, and not quite as flexible. Dawn Upshaw is a charming Eurydice, and Alison Hagley a sweet-toned Amour, though she is balanced very backwardly, as is the chorus at times in what is otherwise a good recording. Unlike Gardiner, but like Leppard on Erato, Runnicles includes ballet music at the end.

Using the original Italian text of the first Vienna version of 1762, Ostman's Naxos version offers a refreshingly robust account using period forces, recorded live in the beautiful Drottningholm Theatre near Stockholm. Without any of the extra items that Gluck composed for Paris, the result fits neatly on a single CD, which, unlike most bargain opera issues, includes a complete libretto and translation. The performance has its uneven moments, but all three soloists have fresh, clear voices, with the warm mezzo, Ann-Christine Biel, sustaining the title-role well, even if she is not specially characterful. Clear, undistracting sound. Not a first choice, but well worth having.

Orphée et Eurydice (1774, Paris version)

(N) (BB) *** Naxos 8.660185/86 (2). Fouchécourt, Dubose, Le Blanc, Lafayette Ch. & O, Brown

(N) ** DG 474 9932 (2). Croft, Delunsch, Harousseau, Delgado-Boge, Louvre Ch. & O, Minkowski

Like Minkowski's DG Archiv set, Ryan Brown's, recorded at the University of Maryland in 2002, uses the 1774 Paris version of the score, with a tenor in the title-role. Lightness is the keynote of the whole performance, with rhythms crisp, textures sparklingly clear, and speeds which never fall into heaviness or sentimentality, flowing easily. Not only that, Brown has the great advantage of having in the title-role one of the finest tenors in the French eighteenth-century tradition, Jean-Paul Fouchécourt. Not only is his tone headily beautiful throughout, his upper register is consistently sweet and free, with elaborate divisions negotiated stylishly and without strain, as in the brilliant Arietta which ends Act I. At a flowing speed *J'ai perdu mon Eurydice* is tender and moving, though sadly Naxos hide that salient number at the very end of a long track. Having too few tracks is one of the very few flaws in an outstandingly stylish set, with Catherine Dubosc as Euridice and Suzie Le Blanc as Amour, both sweet-toned but nicely contrasted, as with Fouchécourt benefiting from being native French-speakers. Though the 1774 text is complete, Brown omits the ballet music at the end, pointing out in his excellent note that Gluck drew it largely from other sources after the initial performances. Clear, fresh sound.

Recorded live at the Théâtre de Poissy in Paris, Marc Minkowski's account of the Paris version of Gluck's setting of the Orpheus legend brings extreme speeds in both directions, fast and slow, characteristically for this conductor. What makes the result far less compelling than usual with him is the heavy-handedness of the reading, lacking elegance, with instrumental textures not as clear as they might be and with rhythms unlifted. The soloists are good, but the tenor, Richard Croft, in the title-role seems to have been chosen for his weight of voice, no doubt apt for a big theatre, for his performance too, dramatic as it is, seems heavy-handed, with the high tessitura bringing obvious strain. Even the most famous aria, *J'ai perdu mon Eurydice*, is heavy and sluggish. Though a few cuts are made, Minkowski includes the ballet music which Gluck added at the end. A disappointment, when the French version of the piece has too often been neglected on disc.

Orphée et Eurydice (composite Berlioz Edition of 1859)
(N) * Farro **DVD** D108045. Kasarova, Joshua, York, Bav. State Op. Ch. & O, Bolton

On DVD, using the composite Berlioz Edition of 1859, Ivor Bolton – usually associated with period performance – conducts a large-scale reading of the opera, with wind and heavy brass bringing out the adventurousness of Gluck's harmonies. The language is French, even though neither the principals nor the large chorus are native French-speakers. Their artistry carries them through, with Vesselina Kasarova a powerful and characterful Orpheus and Rosemary Joshua as Eurydice combining tenderness and clear projection. In this updated Bavarian State Opera production, directed by Nigel Lowery, Amor, sung by Deborah York, slightly hooty, is not helped by appearing as a red-nosed clown. Equally, having a mezzo Orpheus in black slacks and wearing a gold cross is unhelpful in clarifying the story, whatever the symbolic overtones the producer may have intended. Other oddities include the device of having the chorus impersonating an orchestra on stage during the instrumental numbers and a bizarre ballet at the end, with dancers pretending to be puppets re-enacting the story in a massive set like a television screen. Though the booklet has helpful articles, there is no list of chapters except on the disc itself, making it more awkward to use. Bright, forward sound.

Paride e Elena (complete)
☛ (N) *** DG 477 5415 (2). Koz̆ená, Gritton, Sampson, Webster, Gabrieli Consort & Players, McCreesh

First heard in 1770, *Paride e Elena* was the third of the 'Reform' operas that Gluck wrote with Calzabigi in Vienna but, unlike *Orfeo* and *Alceste*, it was never adapted later for Paris. Instead, Gluck borrowed some of its numbers for later operas, but the original remains a masterpiece, as Paul McCreesh amply demonstrates in his starrily cast version with the Gabrieli Consort and Players. The plot is simple, with Paris the most ardent of lovers in pursuit of the initially reluctant Helen. In the castrato role of Paris, Magdalena Koz̆ená sings ravishingly, not least in the glorious finale of Act II, with comments not just from Helen (the excellent, characterful Susan Gritton) but from Cupid, here called Amore. Carolyn Sampson sings that role very sweetly, and Gillian Webster is well cast too as Pallas Athene, the goddess predicting doom at the end. This ideal set includes two versions of the final scene, the revised and shortened version as well as the published one. Beautifully balanced sound.

Italian arias from: *Antigone; La clemenza di Tito; La corona; Ezio; Il parnaso confuso; La Semiramide riconasciuta*
*** Decca **SACD** 470611-2; CD 467 248-2. Bartoli, Berlin Akademie für alte Musik, Forck

In this fine collection of eight formidable arias from Gluck's Italian operas, all to libretti by Metastasio and written early in his career before his 'reform' operas, Cecilia Bartoli reinforces her claims as a *prima donna* who delights in making new

discoveries, bringing her magnetism and vitality to bear on music that would otherwise be forgotten. Her vocal range, spanning far more than the mezzo register, as well as her range of expression, is astonishing. Bravura items like the opening aria from *La clemenza di Tito* are thrown off with flawless technique and obvious enjoyment, sharply contrasted with tender arias which draw out her expressive depth. Fascinatingly, one of the three items from *La clemenza* is an early version of one of the heroine's big arias from *Iphigénie en Tauride*. This formidable display of singing is splendidly supported by crisp, alert playing from the Berlin orchestra of period instruments. Clear, full recording. Decca presents the disc attractively in fascsimile-style book form, and this also comes in surround sound compatible CD form.

Arias from *La clemenza di Tito; Paride e Elena*
*** DG 471 334-2. Koz̆ená, Prague Philh., Swierczewski – MOZART; MYSLIVECEK: *Arias* ***

An outstanding stylist in whatever she sings, Magdalena Koz̆ená is seemingly untroubled by any of the formidable technical problems in this fine collection of arias, producing glorious tone from beginning to end. Well coupled with familiar Mozart and rare Mysliveček, this fine Gluck group includes a fascinating aria from his version of *Clemenza di Tito*. Under Swierczewski the Prague Philharmonia equal the Czech Philharmonic in the refinement of their playing.

Arias from: *Iphigénie en Tauride; Orphée et Eurydice; Paride e Elena*
*** Erato 8573 85768-2. Graham, OAE, Bicket – MOZART: *Arias* ***

Masterly as is Susan Graham's singing of Mozart, in a wide range of arias, her Gluck performances are if anything even more revelatory, making one of the outstanding recital discs of recent years. These are all characters that she has portrayed on stage, and the characterization and ease with French words could not be more compelling, particularly in the three contrasted *Iphigénie* arias. The voice is creamily beautiful, and though the best known of these items, Orpheus's *J'ai perdu mon Eurydice*, is on the slow side, Graham sustains her line flawlessly. Polished playing and well-balanced sound.

Arias: *Orfeo ed Euridice: Che farò; Che puro ciel. Telemaco: Se per entro*
*** Virgin 5 45365-2. Daniels, OAE, Bicket – MOZART; HANDEL: *Arias* ***

Even in a generation that has produced an extraordinary crop of fine counter-tenors, the American David Daniels stands out for the clear beauty and imagination of his singing. The best-known items here – the two principal solos from Gluck's *Orfeo* – are done with a tender expressiveness that matches any performance by a mezzo, with Daniels's natural timbre, at once pure and warm, completely avoiding counter-tenor hoot. Not only that, his placing of the voice is flawless, with the florid singing equally impressive in its brilliance and precision.

GODOWSKY, Leopold (1870–1938)

Piano Sonata in E min.; Passacaglia
*** Hyp. CDA 67300. Hamelin

Marc-André Hamelin has here had the idea of coupling for the first time Godowsky's two biggest piano works. First performed by the composer in 1911, his *E minor Sonata* is a massive, 47-minute piece in five movements. It is framed by the two longest movements, both predominantly slow and intense, ending darkly with a sombre funeral march. It is a work which Hamelin, a Godowsky devotee, relates to such similarly massive masterpieces as Bach's *Goldberg Variations* and Beethoven's *Diabelli Variations*. That is a serious overestimate of a work which in places outstays its welcome. However, Hamelin's intense commitment makes the most persuasive case for it, with brilliant pianistic effects never used for mere display. The *Passacaglia*, well under half the length, is far tauter, offering an impressive set of 44 variations plus cadenza and fugue on the theme which opens Schubert's *Unfinished Symphony*. Again Hamelin, brilliant technician that he is, refuses to treat this closely argued piece as mere display. Fine sound, atmospheric and full of presence.

53 Studies, Based on the Etudes of Chopin, Op. 10 & Op. 25 (complete)
⊛ *** Hyp. CDA 67411/2. Hamelin

Ian Hobson offers a selection of these legendary pieces on the Arabesque label and Carlo Grante has done them all in masterly fashion on Altarus, but Marc-André Hamelin supersedes them both. Godowsky's celebrated studies are of unbelievable difficulty, and arouse both excitement and admiration and, in some places, horror that some of their contortions should have been attempted at all. Godowsky's *tour de force* is realized with supreme virtuosity and – more to the point – artistry by Hamelin. It is quite stunning, an extraordinary achievement even by Hamelin's own standards. No one with an interest in the piano should pass this by.

GOEDICKE, Alexander (1877–1957)

Concertstück in D (for piano and orchestra), Op. 11
**(*) Hyp. CDA 66877. Coombs, BBC Scottish SO, Brabbins
– GLAZUNOV: *Piano Concertos 1 & 2* **(*)

Alexander Goedicke's *Concertstück* is far from negligible, both in its melodic invention and in its musical structure. Stephen Coombs is a brilliant and sympathetic interpreter of this music and the BBC Scottish Symphony Orchestra under Martyn Brabbins give every support. The recording is too reverberant – and this perhaps inhibits a full three-star recommendation.

GOEHR, Alexander (born 1932)

Violin Concerto
(N) *** EMI 5 86189-2. Parikian, RPO, Del Mar –
HAMILTON: *Violin Concerto; Sinfonia* ***

The *Violin Concerto* comes from 1962 and was dedicated to Manoug Parikian, who premièred the piece that same year. It is serial without being anonymous 'mittel-Europa' in style, and there is obviously a sophisticated imagination at work. Expertly laid out for the orchestra and splendidly recorded at the Abbey Road Studio No. 1. Not a piece for those who want 'easy listening' but a rewarding score for the more exploratory and thoughtful listener.

GOLDMARK, Karl (1830–1915)

Violin Concerto in A min., Op. 28
☛ ⊛ *** Delos DE 3156. Hu, Seattle SO, Schwarz –
BRUCH: *Violin Concerto 2* ***
(BB) *** Naxos 8.553579. Tsu, Razumovsky Sinfonia, Yu Long
– KORNGOLD: *Violin Concerto* ***

The Taiwanese soloist Nai-Yuan Hu (pronounced Nigh-Yen Who) makes an outstanding début on CD with a coupling of two underrated concertos which on his responsively lyrical bow are made to sound like undiscovered masterpieces. The Goldmark is a tuneful and warm-hearted concerto that needs just this kind of songful, inspirational approach: Hu shapes the melodies so that they ravishingly take wing and soar. Moreover, Schwarz and the Seattle orchestra share a real partnership with their soloist and provide a full, detailed backcloth in a natural concert-hall framework.

Vera Tsu is another outstanding soloist. Her tone is rich, bringing out to the full the ripe romanticism of the Goldmark *Concerto*. Her attack is fearless in the many bravura passages, so that the dance rhythms of the dance-finale have a rare sparkle, and her hushed playing in the central slow movement at a very broad speed movingly demonstrates her inner concentration, helped by the equally beautiful, finely varied playing of the Razumovsky Sinfonia of Bratislava. Rich, full, open sound.

Rustic Wedding Symphony, Op. 26
☛ (M) *** Sony SMK 87780. RPO, Beecham – HANDEL:
Faithful Shepherd Suite (***)

Rustic Wedding Symphony, Op. 26; Overtures: In Italy, Op. 49; In the Spring, Op. 36
(BB) **(*) Naxos 8.550745. Nat. SO of Ireland, Gunzenhauser

Rustic Wedding Symphony, Op. 26; Sakuntala Overture, Op. 13
*** ASV CDDCA 791. RPO, Butt

No recorded performance of Goldmark's engaging *Rustic Wedding Symphony* has ever matched Beecham's. He made the work his very own and, as Neville Cardus is quoted as saying about a live performance in the notes with this reissue: 'The loveliness of his phrasing of Goldmark's delicately sentimental melodies in the "Garden" movement and the warm yet gentle tone of the RPO were such that I shall try never to forget their ingratiating appeal. The symphony sounded a miniature masterpiece, the first-movement variations flowed beautifully and abundantly.' So it is here, with the horns, led by Dennis Brain, at the work's opening quite irresistible, and the galumphing Bohemian dance finale wonderfully jolly. Fortunately the 1952 Abbey Road mono recording is fully worthy: warm, full and vivid. Not to be missed.

Yondani Butt and the RPO clearly enjoy themselves. The recording has brightly lit violins, but plenty of bloom on the woodwind, and the only miscalculation of balance concerns the trombone entry in the first movement, which is too blatant and too loud. Otherwise this is in every way enjoyable. The *Overture Sakuntala* opens impressively but does not quite sustain its 18 minutes. Butt presents it with persuasive vigour and lyrical feeling, and does not shirk the melodrama.

Gunzenhauser gives a fresh, bright-eyed account. He takes both the opening movement and the *Andante* (*In the Garden*) appreciably faster than does Butt, and he loses something in poise and spacious eloquence in consequence. But the overall performance is spontaneous and enjoyable. It is well recorded and, although the violins sound thin, that is almost certainly not the fault of the engineers. Of the two jaunty overtures, *In Italy* is especially vivacious and sparkling.

Symphony 2 in E, Op. 35; In Italy Overture, Op. 49; Prometheus Bound, Op. 38
*** ASV CDDCA 934. Philh. O, Butt

Goldmark's *Second Symphony* is a highly confident piece with a strong opening movement, an ambivalent but appealing *Andante*, a vivaciously delicate Scherzo, which is Mendelssohn undiluted, and a characteristically folksy, dance-like finale. Yondani Butt has the work's full measure. The Lisztian *Prometheus Bound* on the other hand is overlong and melodramatic, and the main *Allegro* is routine in its working out. Yet it has some winning lyrical ideas and Butt does his very best for it. The *Italian Overture* is genuinely vivacious, though not especially Italianate: it has a rather beautiful nocturnal sequence as a central episode. The ASV recording is in every way excellent.

String Quartet in B flat, Op. 8; (i) String Quintet in A min., Op. 9
**(*) ASV CDDCA 1071. Fourth Dimension String Qt, (i) with Smith

Goldmark's *String Quartet in B flat* is a fluent, beautifully fashioned piece, very much in the Schumann and Mendelssohn tradition, though one is in no doubt that the musical argument is guided by a sense of purpose. The *String Quintet* is an even stronger piece, sure in its feeling for musical movement and with some good ideas. The Fourth Dimension String Quartet makes its début, with David Smith as the second cello in the quintet. Decent performances, though the tonal blend leaves something to be desired, and one would welcome greater richness of timbre.

GOMBERT, Nicolas (c.1495–c.1560)
Magnificats I–IV (with plainchant Antiphons)
*** Gimell CDGIM 037. Tallis Scholars, Phillips

Magnificats V–VIII (with plainchant Antiphons)
*** Gimell CDGIM 038. Tallis Scholars, Phillips

The eight *Magnificat* settings of Nicolas Gombert (his last major works) are among the most glorious music of the Flemish Renaissance, and this superbly sung set of performances from the Tallis Scholars will surely confirm this neglected composer's position as a major figure of his era. The flowing lines of his joyous polyphony bring tightly knit harmonic implications, with plenty of passing dissonance to spice the part-writing, but also rich sonorities. All the *Magnificats* set the even-numbered verses in polyphony, while the odd-numbered ones are in thematically linked chant, which brings appealing contrasts of texture. Appropriate antiphons have been chosen, and are sung twice, used effectively to frame each *Magnificat*. Outstanding recording, as is usual from this series. Try the first disc and you will surely want to move on to the second.

GOOSSENS, Eugene (1893–1962)
Concertino for Double String Orchestra, Op. 47; Fantasy for 9 Wind Instruments, Op. 36; Symphony 2, Op. 62
*** ABC 8.770013. Sydney SO, Handley

The *Second Symphony* is an important work – and something

of a discovery: its material is strong and the imaginative landscape it inhabits quite individual. There is a dark, Nordic feeling about the opening and a fertility of invention in the Scherzo that recalls Prokofiev. The *Concertino* is more effective for full strings than in its chamber form (see below), and the *Fantasy for Wind Instruments* (1924) has a touch of Stravinsky and Les Six. Expert playing from the ABC Sydney Orchestra of which Goossens was conductor in the 1950s, and well-prepared and meticulously shaped readings from Vernon Handley. Recommended with enthusiasm.

Concertino for String Octet, Op. 47; Phantasy Sextet, Op. 37
*** Chan. 9472. ASMF Chamber Ens. – BRIDGE: *String Sextet* ***

The *Concertino for String Octet*, Op. 47, was subsequently scored for double string orchestra (see above). It has brightness and vitality, and is expertly laid out for the instruments, as is the 1923 *Phantasy Sextet*, Op. 37, commissioned by Elisabeth Sprague Coolidge. Intelligent and inventive music, well played by the Academy of St Martin-in-the-Field and eminently well recorded by the ever-enterprising Chandos.

GÓRECKI, Henryk (born 1933)
(i) Harpsichord Concerto; (ii) Little Requiem for a Polka (Kleines Requiem für eine Polka); (iii) Good Night (In Memoriam Michael Vyner) for soprano, alto flute, 3 tam-tams and piano
*** None. 7559 79362-2. L. Sinf.; (i) Zinman; (ii) Chojnacka, cond. Stenz; (iii) Upshaw, Bell, Constable, Hockings

The *Little Requiem* (1993) opens with a single quiet bell-stroke; a piano (John Constable) then engages in a tranquil dialogue with the violins, to be rudely interrupted by a burst of bell-ringing; the energetic, marcato *Allegro impetuoso* follows. The piece ends with a raptly sustained elegiac *Adagio*, still dominated by the quietly assertive tolling bells. The two-movement *Harpsichord Concerto*, written a decade earlier, combines soloist and strings in a vibrant, jangly ménage. *Good Night* is nocturnally serene. The soprano voice enters only in the third movement, with a cantilena to Shakespeare's words from *Hamlet*: 'Good night ... and flights of angels sing thee to thy rest!' Both here and in the *Little Requiem* the very atmospheric recording brings an added dimension to the communication from performers who are obviously totally committed to the composer's cause.

Symphony 3 (Symphony of Sorrowful Songs), Op. 36
*** None. 7559 79282-2. Upshaw, L. Sinf., Zinman
*** Australian ABC Classics 472 040-2. Kenny, Adelaide SO, Yuasa

Symphony 3 (Symphony of Sorrowful Songs), Op. 36; 3 Pieces in the Olden Style
☞ (BB) *** Naxos 8.550822. Kilanowicz, Polish Nat. RSO, Wit

Scored for strings and piano with soprano solo in each of the three movements, all predominantly slow, Górecki's *Symphony No. 3* sets three laments taking the theme of motherhood. The first movement, nearly half an hour long, resolves on the central setting of a fifteenth-century text from a monastic collection. The second movement incongruously brings a switch to a sensuously beautiful idiom, with the soprano solo soaring radiantly. The third movement is the setting of a folksong with a two-chord ostinato as accompaniment, concluding in a passage of total peace. The Sinfonietta's fine performance, beautifully recorded, is crowned by the radiant singing of Dawn Upshaw.

Zofia Kilanowicz on Naxos has also obviously become immersed in the word-settings. In the work's closing section, with its hint of a gentle but remorseless tolling bell, Wit achieves a mood of simple serenity, even forgiveness. The *Three Pieces in Olden Style* make a fine postlude, the second with its dance figurations, the third with its fierce tremolando violins, like shafts of bright light, suddenly resolving to a very positive ending. All in all, this seems in many ways a 'best buy'.

Despite its several predecessors, this Australian recording of Górecki's *Third Symphony* finds new things to say. Where others tend to blend the differences between the movements, Yvonne Kenny treats the work almost like an opera, comprising three very distinct dramatic soliloquies: the sorrowful *Stabat mater* figure of the first movement contrasting with the terrified imprisoned girl of the second, and the shattered, bereft mother of the last. Kenny is never given to melodrama, but her expressive warmth and intensity bind her portrayal together, and the result makes this symphony less abstract and, in a way, more powerful. Kenny's eloquent singing and her sense of drama are well supported by the Adelaide Symphony Orchestra. The CD is very well documented and full texts and translations are included. However, there is no coupling, whereas the fine Naxos version includes also the *Three Pieces in the Olden Style*.

VOCAL MUSIC

(i) *Good Night* (*Requiem* for soprano, alto flute, 3 tam-tams and piano), *Op. 63*; (ii) *Little Requiem for a Polka* (for piano & 13 instruments), *Op. 64*; *3 Pieces in Old Style for Strings*
*** Telarc CD 80417. I Flamminghi, Werther; with (i)
   Szmytra; Edmund-Davis; Righarts; (ii) Gleizes

Górecki's *Requiem* was written for and dedicated to Michael Vyner, the conductor who did much to establish the composer's music in the West. He died in 1989, only a year after directing an important introductory London concert, and Górecki immediately set about writing this simple valedictory piece for solo soprano, darkly resonant alto flute and, in the epilogue, three tam-tams (gongs of indefinite pitch), played very gently indeed. The quotation in the title is from Shakespeare's *Hamlet* – 'Good night … flights of angels sing thee to thy rest' – and the work's prevailing elegiac quietness has much in common with the *Little Requiem*, written three years later. The *Three Pieces in Old Style* make a perfect foil and are beautifully played by this excellent group under Roldof Werther. Needless to say, the Telarc recording is in the demonstration bracket, although it has a very wide dynamic range, so that one has to be careful in not setting the volume level too high when the music opens on a sustained *pianissimo*.

(i) *Miserere, Op. 44*; *Amen, Op. 35*; *Euntes ibant et flebant, Op. 32*; (ii) *Wuslo moja (My Vistula, Grey Vistula), Op. 46*; *Szeroka woda (Broad Waters): Choral Suite of Folksongs, Op. 39* (Oh, our River Narew; Oh, when in Powistle; Oh, Johnny, Johnny; She picked wild roses; Broad waters)
*** None. 7559 79348-2. (i) Chicago Symphony Ch. & Lyric
   Op. Ch., Nelson; (ii) Lyra Chamber Ch., Ding

Górecki's powerful *Miserere* was prompted by the political upheaval in Poland in 1981. Górecki set a text of only five words: *Domine Deus noster, Miserere nobis*; although the work's span is ambitious, it is sustained by profound intensity of feeling. The combined Chicago choirs maintain the sombrely atmospheric opening *pianissimo* with impressive concentration, and the dynamic climax of the piece, when the combined choirs sing in ten parts, is very compelling. The following *Euntes ibant et flebant* (for unaccompanied chorus) is simpler, more serene. The five folksong settings are also essentially expressive (even *Oh, Johnny, Johnny* is marked *Molto lento – dolce cantabile*) and all are harmonically rich. They are beautifully sung by the smaller group. The recording, made in the Church of St Mary of the Angels in Chicago, is admirable.

GOSSEC, François-Joseph (1734–1829)

Symphonies: in E flat; in D (Pastorella), Op. 5/2–3; in E flat; in F, Op. 12/5–6; in D (1776)
*** Chan. 9661. L. M. P., Bamert

François-Joseph Gossec, composer of a remarkably forward-looking *Requiem*, also wrote some three dozen symphonies, the first dating from the 1750s and his last from 1809. His style is often close to Haydn – witness the delightful chirping second subject of the first movement of the *F major*, Op. 12/6 (published in 1769), the tenderly lyrical slow movement using muted strings, and the jovial finale. The two symphonies from Op. 5 date from seven years earlier and here the scoring, which includes clarinets, brings a Mozartian elegance, besides a *galant* charm in the *Romanza* second movement. The stately *Adagio* of the so-called *Pastorella*, however, looks backwards in its classical poise. In some ways most striking of all is the later three-movement D major work, with its striding opening theme, boldly Haydnesque, gentle central lament and cheerful finale. Its full scoring, which includes trumpets, shows a fine feeling for orchestral colour. But these are all highly enjoyable and rewarding works, especially when played with such spirit and finesse, and so beautifully recorded.

Requiem (Missa pro defunctis)
☛ (BB) *** Warner Apex 8573 89234-2. Degelin, De
   Reyghere, Crook, Widmer, Maastricht Conservatory Ch.,
   Musica Polyphonica, Devos

Symphony (a più stromenti) in E flat, Op. 5/2; Symphonies: in E flat; in F, Op. 8/2; in G, Op. 12/2; Suite de danses (orch. Calmei); Gavotte in D
**(*) ASV CDA 1124. O. de Bretagne, Sanderling

Requiem (Missa pro defunctis); (i) Symphony à 17
(BB) *** Naxos 8.554750-51 (2). Invernizzi, Arruabarrena,
   Crook, Darbellay, Gruppo Vocale Cantemus, Svizzera R.
   Ch., Svizzera Italiana O, Hauschild, or (i) Fasolis

The Belgian composer François-Joseph Gossec was a bold innovator, some of his writing even foreshadowing Berlioz. The opening of this 80-minute *Requiem* of 1760, with its ominous timpani and string-writing, is quite commanding, and the ensuing movements have a period mixture of baroque and classical writing, some interesting harmonic progressions and certainly some beautiful writing. It is in passages such as the *Mors stupebit et natura*, with its tremolo strings punctuated by the timpani, that one realizes how forward-looking this composer was. The performance on

Naxos, using modern instruments, is enjoyable, and generally well sung and played, though it's possible to imagine that Minkowski, for example, would make it more exciting. The sound is good – the San Lorenzo Cathedral doesn't produce an acoustic that is too wallowy. The 27-minute *Symphony* makes an enjoyable bonus, and this set is well worth investigating at the price, with full texts and translations included, along with informative sleeve-notes.

The alternative version from Devos uses period instruments and has the advantage of being on a single CD. It too is very enjoyable and has plenty of commitment and gusto. The soloists (with Howard Crook common to both versions) are good without being outstanding, but the chorus is impressive, with fine, authentic-sounding brass support at the *Mors stupebit*. The recording too is excellent, so if you are not worried about the symphony and don't mind the absence of text and translation, this could be a best buy.

Of the symphonies recorded on ASV, the *G major* has a delightfully graceful centrepiece and an especially vivacious finale. The *F major*, with its haunting minor-key introduction, then launches into another lively allegro. The *Symphony a più stromenti* has both melody and rhythmic drive, often taking unexpected turns, showing the experimental side of the composer which emerged more fully in his later works. And it is easy to see why Gossec's *Gavotte in D* was so popular in its day: it is a charming lollipop which raises a smile and remains in the mind. The *Suite de danses* offers more modern dress. It was orchestrated in 1964 and makes agreeable listening, never more so than in another *Gavotte* with a minor-key middle section. The Breton orchestra, while not in the first rank, play with enthusiasm and some flair, and they are warmly recorded.

GOULD, Morton (1913–96)

Fall River Legend (ballet; complete)
*** Albany TROY 035. Peters, Nat. PO, Rosenstock (with recorded conversation between Agnes de Mille and Morton Gould)

This complete recording of *Fall River Legend* opens dramatically with the Speaker for the Jury reading out the Indictment at the trial, and then the ballet tells the story of Lizzie Borden in flashback. Gould's music has a good deal in common with the folksy writing in Copland's *Appalachian Spring*, and it is given a splendidly atmospheric performance and recording by the New York orchestra under Rosenstock. There is also a 26-minute discussion on the creation of the ballet between Agnes de Mille and the composer.

2 Marches for Orchestra
(M) (***) Cala mono CACD 0526. NBC SO, Stokowski – DEBUSSY: *Prélude à l'après-midi d'un faune*, etc. (**(*)); HOLST: *Planets* (***)

These two stirring wartime marches were 'written in tribute to two of our gallant allies': the first is Chinese in character (complete with marching effects), the second colourfully employs two Red Army songs. An enjoyable end to a fascinating Stokowski disc; and the sound, emanating from an NBC broadcast from March 1943, is fully acceptable.

Symphony 3
(*) Albany **SACD TROY 515. Albany SO, Miller – HARRIS: *Symphony 2* **(*)

Although such pieces as the *Fall River Legend* and the *Latin-American Symphonette* have been recorded more than once, Morton Gould's symphonies are little heard, even in America. He proves to be a symphonist of quality, though his musical personality is too indebted to Stravinsky, Copland, Roy Harris and William Schuman for a distinctive and individual voice to be discerned. But there is an engaging vigour and a keen feeling for the cut-and-thrust of the musical argument. Decent, well-characterized playing, though the strings could perhaps have greater richness of sonority.

GOUNOD, Charles (1818–93)

Faust: Ballet music
(BB) **(*) EMI Encore (ADD) 5 75221-2. New Philh. O, Mackerras – DELIBES: *Coppélia; Sylvia* (excerpts); MESSAGER: *Les Deux Pigeons* (excerpts) **(*)

This lively and nicely pointed reading of the *Faust* ballet music from Mackerras, very well played indeed, forms part of an attractive collection of French music. The 1969 recording is a little thin by modern standards but is certainly vivid enough.

Symphonies 1 in D; 2 in E flat
☛ *** ASV CDDCA 981. O of St John's, Smith Square, Lubbock

The beautifully sprung and subtly phrased performances from John Lubbock and the Orchestra of St John's bring out the charm of these delightful symphonies. Lubbock's care for detail and the refreshingly polished playing is matched by a pervading warmth. We hope ASV will decide to reissue the Gounod pairing on the Quicksilva label, when it would again be fully competitive.

Petite symphonie in B flat (for 9 wind instruments)
(M) *** Chan. (ADD) 6543. Athena Ens. – IBERT: *3 Pièces brèves*; POULENC: *Sextet* ***

An astonishingly fresh and youthful work, the *Petite symphonie* in fact has impeccable craftsmanship and is witty and civilized. It makes ideal listening at the end of the day, and its charm is irresistible in a performance as full of *joie de vivre* as that provided by the Athena group, who are particularly light-hearted in the finale.

Mélodies and songs: *L'Absent; The arrow and the song; Au rossignol; Ave Maria; Boléro; Ma belle amie est morte; La Biondina* (song-cycle); *Ce que je suis sans toi; Chanson de printemps; Clos ta paupière; Envoi de fleurs; The fountain mingles with the river; If thou art sleeping, maiden; Ilala; A lay of the early spring; Loin du pays; Maid of Athens; Mignon; My true love hath my heart; Oh happy home! o blessed flower!; Où voulez-vous aller?; La Pâquerette; Prière; Rêverie; Sérénade; Le Soir; Le Temps des roses; Trust her not!; Venise; The worker*
*** Hyp. CDA 66801/2. Lott, Murray, Rolfe Johnson, Johnson

Graham Johnson here devises an enchanting programme of 41 songs presenting the full span of Gounod's achievement not just in French *mélodie* (on the first of the two discs) but also in songs Gounod wrote during his extended stay in England. The soloists here are at their very finest. So on the first disc, after charming performances of the opening items from Felicity Lott, Ann Murray enters magically, totally transforming the hackneyed lines of *Ave Maria*, before tackling the most joyous of Gounod songs, the barcarolle-like *Sérénade*. Anthony Rolfe Johnson is comparably perceptive in *Biondina*, bringing out the Neapolitan-song overtones, as well as in six of the English settings. As in the Schubert series, Johnson's notes are a model of scholarship, both informed and fascinating.

Messe Chorale

(BB) *** Warner Apex 8573 89235-2. Lausanne Vocal Ens., Corboz; Alain (organ) – SAINT-SAENS: *Mass* **(*)

Gounod's *Messe Chorale*, an early work, could not be more different from his *Messe solennelle de Sainte-Cécile*. Drawing on the eighteenth-century tradition of French organ Mass, it intersperses choral sections with organ interludes, all based on the chosen Gregorian theme which acts as a leitmotif, reaching an expressive peak in the *Hosanna in excelsis* of the *Sanctus*. The *Benedictus* then leads via a brief fugue and a grand organ coda into the richly harmonized and finally serene *Agnus Dei*. Gounod's setting has an endearing simplicity, and it is beautifully sung and recorded here under Michel Corboz, with Marie-Claire Alain making a splendid foil for the choir on the magnificent organ of Lausanne Cathedral.

Messe solennelle de Sainte-Cécile

*** EMI 7 47094-2. Hendricks, Dale, Lafont, Ch. and Nouvel O Philharmonique of R. France, Prêtre

Gounod's *Messe solennelle*, with its blatant march setting of the *Credo* and sugar-sweet choral writing, may not be for sensitive souls, but Prêtre here directs an almost ideal performance, vividly recorded, with glowing singing from the choir as well as the three soloists.

Faust (complete)

⊕ ✿ *** Teldec 4509 90872-2 (3). Hadley, Gasdia, Ramey, Mentzer, Agache, Fassbaender, Welsh Nat. Op. Ch. & O, Rizzi

*** EMI 5 56224-2 (3). Leech, Studer, Van Dam, Hampson, Ch. & O of Capitole de Toulouse, Plasson

(M) **(*) EMI (ADD) 5 67967-2 (3) [5 67975-2]. De los Angeles, Gedda, Blanc, Christoff, Paris Nat. Op. Ch. & O, Cluytens

(N) (BB) (***) Naxos mono 8.111083/85 (3). Bjoerling, Kirsten, Siepi, Met. Op. Ch. and O, Cleva. (Appendix: Bjoerling: SCHUBERT: *Ständchen*. SIBELIUS: *Var det en dröm?*; *Svarta rosor*; *Säv, saäv, susa.* HERBERT: *Princess Pat: Neapolitan Love Song.* Excerpts from: PUCCINI: *La Bohème* (with Anna-Lisa Bjoerling); GOUNOD: *Roméo et Juliette*; DONIZETTI: *L'elisir d'amore*; MASCAGNI: *Cavalleria rusticana*; WAGNER: *Lohengrin*)

Rizzi, with an outstanding cast and vividly clear recording, makes the whole score seem totally fresh and new. Jerry Hadley as Faust has lyrical freshness rather than heroic power, brought out in his headily beautiful performance of *Salut! demeure* and, like Rizzi's conducting, his singing has more light and shade in it than that of rivals. The tenderness as well as the bright agility of Cecilia Gasdia's singing as Marguerite brings comparable variety of expression, with the *Roi de Thulé* song deliberately drained of colour to contrast with the brilliance of the *Jewel Song* which follows. Her performance culminates in an angelic contribution to the final duet, with Rizzi's slow speed encouraging refinement, leading up to a shattering moment of judgement and a fine apotheosis. Alexander Agache as Valentin may be less characterful than Hampson on the EMI Toulouse set, but his voice

is caught more richly; but it is the commandingly demonic performance of Samuel Ramey as Mephistopheles that sets the seal on the whole set, far more sinister than José van Dam on EMI. Like that EMI set, the Teldec offers a valuable appendix, not just the full ballet music but numbers cut from the definitive score – a drinking song for Faust and a charming aria for Siebel. EMI's supplementary items, four, all different, are more generous but musically less interesting.

On EMI, Plasson comes near to providing another recommendable *Faust*, even if José van Dam's gloriously dark, finely focused bass-baritone does not have the heft of a full-blooded bass voice such as is associated with the role of Mephistopheles. Cheryl Studer conveys the girlishness of Marguerite, using the widest range of dynamic and colour. If Richard Leech's voice might in principle seem too lightweight for the role of Faust, the lyrical flow and absence of strain make his singing consistently enjoyable. As Valentin, Thomas Hampson is strongly cast, with his firm, heroic baritone. The sound has a good sense of presence, set in a pleasantly reverberant acoustic which does not obscure necessary detail. In addition to supplementary numbers, the appendix offers the complete ballet music.

In the reissued Cluytens set, the seductiveness of Victoria de los Angeles's singing is a dream and it is a pity that the recording hardens the natural timbre slightly. Christoff is magnificently Mephistophelian. Gedda, though showing some signs of strain, sings intelligently, and among the other soloists Ernest Blanc has a pleasing, firm voice, which he uses to make Valentin into a sympathetic character. Cluytens's approach is competent but somewhat workaday. The set has been attractively repackaged and remastered and the libretto has strikingly clear print, to make a good mid-priced choice for this popular opera. This now comes effectively remastered as one of EMI's 'Great Recordings of the Century'.

Taken from a Metropolitan Opera broadcast in 1950, the Naxos historical set offers a vividly dramatic performance under Fausto Cleva featuring three of the star singers of the time in a theatre sometimes dubbed the *Faustspielhaus*. Jussi Bjoerling as Faust is in ringing voice, full-bloodedly caught at full throttle, firm and clear. Cesare Siepi, a pillar of the Met., sings magnificently as Mephistopheles, happier in French than most Italian singers, while Dorothy Kirsten makes a clear, firm Marguerite, fresh and forthright rather than charming. The voices come over superbly, and one quickly adjusts to the limited orchestral sound. Exceptionally, the ballet music is included in Act IV, and as a supplement on the third disc there are arias and songs from Schubert and Wagner to Sibelius and Victor Herbert, recorded by Bjoerling in American and Swedish broadcasts.

Faust (abridged version)

(B) (**(*)) Naxos mono 8.110016/7. Jepson, Crooks, Pinza, Warren, Olheim, NY Met. Op. Ch. & O, Pelletier

Naxos offers a performance broadcast from the Boston Opera House in April 1940. Richard Crooks's ringing tenor sounds more Italianate than French, but he makes an ardent Faust, and Ezio Pinza gives a vividly dynamic and characterful portrait of Mephistopheles, singing superbly and offering what must be the fastest account of the *Calf of Gold* aria on disc. Leonard Warren even in 1940 did not sound youthful enough for Valentin, with vibrato already obtrusive, and though Helen Jepson as Marguerite is a little shrill at times under pressure, it is a winning performance. Wilfred Pelletier proves an inspired conductor. Pacing the music very well, he draws excellent ensemble from the whole company, even if the radio recording has the orchestra presented rather dimly, well behind the singers. Applause and stage noises tend to be obtrusive, with the performance preceded and punctuated by an announcer summarizing the plot.

Faust: highlights
(M) *** CfP (ADD) 764 8042 (from above complete set, with de los Angeles, Gedda; cond. Cluytens)

In the EMI (75-minute) set of excerpts, the singing gives much pleasure, particularly that of de los Angeles and Christ-off, and the choral contribution is spirited. Excellent value and an ideal way of sampling a performance which has many virtues.

Faust (complete; in English)
(M) *** Chan. 3014 (3). Clarke, Plazas, Miles, Magee, Montague, Walker, Geoffrey Mitchell Ch., Philh. O, Parry

Faust, in a good English translation by Christopher Cowell, works brilliantly. The dramatic intensity is consistently heightened by David Parry's lively conducting, with the music paced to bring out the full impact of the big climaxes, and with freshness and sparkle given to such familiar numbers as the Soldiers' Chorus. The chorus is electrifying, and the cast of principals is first rate. Paul Charles Clarke sings strongly in the title-role (if not always sweetly), well experienced from appearing in the Welsh National Opera production. Alastair Miles, who also sang with WNO, is outstanding in every way as Mephistopheles, dark, firm and incisive, if not always sinister. Mary Plazas brings out the girlish innocence in Marguerite, sweet and pure, making light of the vocal challenges, above all giving joy to the Jewel Song. With singers as characterful as Diana Montague and Sarah Walker in smaller roles, this is the finest issue yet in the excellent 'Opera in English' series promoted by the Peter Moores Foundation. The third disc includes the complete ballet music as a supplement.

Roméo et Juliette (complete)
*** EMI 5 56123-2 (3). Alagna, Gheorghiu, Vallejo, Van Dam, Keenlyside, Capitole de Toulouse Ch. & O, Plasson

With Gheorghiu and Alagna inspired as the lovers, the EMI Toulouse set offers the finest performance on disc yet, in almost every way. Gheorghiu does not just sing sweetly, without strain, the subtlety of her expression and her ability to rise to the demands of tragedy set her apart, and Alagna – who made such an impact in this role at Covent Garden early in his career – is youthfully ardent and unstrained. The rest of the cast is generally excellent too, with José van Dam as Frère Laurent and Simon Keenlyside as Mercutio both outstanding, though Marie-Ange Todorovitch, bright and agile as Stephano, is rather shrill. Given absolutely complete with the Act IV ballet music (not a dramatic gain) the set takes three discs instead of two, but is well worth it. Warm, atmospheric sound.

Roméo et Juliette (abridged)
** Arthaus DVD 100 706. Gheorghiu, Alagna, Kriz, Hendrych, Kuhn's Ch., Czech Phil. CO, Guadagno (TV Dir: Barbara Willis Sweete; Producer: Christopher Hunt)

The DVD of Gounod's Shakespearean opera, cut down to 70 minutes for the purposes of television, should not be confused with the EMI CDs, though the two principals equally demonstrate that this is a favourite opera of theirs in warmly expressive singing and sympathetic acting. The film was shot at the atmospheric Gothic castle of Zvikov in the Czech Republic, beautifully set beside a lake. The singers were recorded in the helpful acoustic of the Rudolfinum in Prague, and for the film Gheorghiu and Alagna mime their parts, while the other roles are mimed by Czech actors. The drastic cutting – much played down in the notes – means that each of the five Acts is reduced to 12 minutes or less, with Act III shortened simply to the finale. Rightly, the duetting between the two lovers takes up the greater part of the film, and there the exotic setting enhances the impact of the performance, with Anton Guadagno the sympathetic conductor.

GRAINGER, Percy (1882–1961)

Blithe Bells; Colonial Song; English Dance; Duke of Marlborough's Fanfare; Fisher's Boarding House; Green Bushes; Harvest Hymn; In a Nutshell (Suite); Shepherd's Hey; There Were Three Friends; Walking Tune (symphonic wind band version); We Were Dreamers
*** Chan. 9493. BBC PO, Hickox

Hickox is masterly here, with rhythms always resilient, both in bringing out the freshness of well-known numbers like Shepherd's Hey and in presenting the originality and charm of such little-known numbers as Walking Tune. The BBC Philharmonic is in superb form, warmly and atmospherically recorded. By far the longest item is the suite, In a Nutshell, which includes pieces like the Arrival Platform Humlet, well known on their own, and which has as its core a powerful and elaborate piece, Pastoral, which with its disturbing undertow belies its title.

Blithe Bells (Free Ramble on a Theme by Bach: Sheep may safely graze); Country Gardens; Green Bushes (Passacaglia); Handel in the Strand; Mock Morris; Molly on the Shore; My Robin is to the Greenwood Gone; Shepherd's Hey; Spoon River; Walking Tune; Youthful Rapture
☞ (M) *** Chan. 6542. Bournemouth Sinf., Montgomery

For those wanting only a single Grainger orchestral collection, this could be first choice. Among the expressive pieces, the arrangement of My Robin is to the Greenwood Gone is highly attractive, but the cello solo in Youthful Rapture is perhaps less effective. Favourites such as Country Gardens, Shepherd's Hey, Molly on the Shore and Handel in the Strand all sound as fresh as new paint. The 1978 recording, made in Christchurch Priory, has retained all its ambient character in its CD transfer.

(i) *Country Gardens*; (ii) *Green Bushes*; (i) *Handel in the Strand*; (iii) *Harvest Hymn*; (iv) *The Warriors*; (ii) *Irish Tune from County Derry*; (i) *The Immovable 'Do'*; (ii) *Molly on the Shore*; (v) *Shepherd's Hey*; (vi) *Let's Dance Gay in Green Meadow* (for 2 pianos); (vii) *In Dahomey*; (viii) *Tribute to Foster*; Songs: (x) *Brigg Fair*; (xi) *The Sprig of Thyme Died for Love*
(M) *** Decca (ADD/DDD) 470 126-2. (i) Eastman-Rochester Pops O, Fennell; (ii) ECO, Bedford; (iii) ASMF, Marriner; (iv) Philh. O, Gardiner; (v) ECO, Britten; (vi) Britten, Tunnard; (vii) Feinberg; (viii) Kazimierczuk, Higgins, Podger, Savage, Monteverdi Ch., E. Country O, Gardiner; (x) Pears, Linden Singers; (xi) Von Otter, Forsberg

By raiding the Mercury, Philips and DG as well as the Decca archives, Universal has assembled on Decca an excellent

Grainger collection which fully justifies its 'World Of' heading. The Mercury recordings are famously bright and vivid, while the well-known Bedford and Britten items are beautifully recorded and superbly played. There is a good mix of Grainger's imaginative orchestrations interspersed with piano and vocal items, including Pears's famous *Brigg Fair* and Anne Sofie von Otter's haunting *The Sprig of Thyme*. The disc closes with one of Grainger's most flamboyant works, the extravagantly scored music to *The Warriors*. It was written between 1913 and 1916 for a ballet which never materialized, hence the work's subtitle: '*Music for an Imaginary Ballet*'. The *Tribute to Foster* comes from a particularly attractive collection of folksong arrangements selected and directed by John Eliot Gardiner and is an unexpected highlight.

Irish Tune from County Derry; Lincolnshire Posy (suite); *Molly on the Shore; Shepherd's Hey*

(M) *** ASV (ADD) CDWHL 2067. L. Wind O, Wick –
  MILHAUD; POULENC: *Suite française* ***

First-class playing and vivid recording, with the additional attraction of delightful couplings, make this very highly recommendable.

The Warriors (music for an imaginary ballet)

*** DG **SACD** 471 634-2; CD 445 860-2. Philh. O, Gardiner –
  HOLST: *The Planets* ***

Colourful and vigorous, *The Warriors* throbs with energy, at one point – in a gentler interlude – involving an offstage orchestra in Ivesian superimpositions. The result is hugely enjoyable in such a fine performance as Gardiner's. It makes an unexpected and valuable coupling for his brilliant account of the favourite Holst work. Dazzling sound.

(i) *Ye Banks and Braes o' Bonnie Doon;* (ii) *Colonial Song; Country Gardens;* (i) *The Gum-Suckers' March; Faeroe Island Dance; Hill Song 2;* (ii) *Irish Tune from County Derry;* (i) *The Lads of Wamphray March;* (ii) *Lincolnshire Posy;* (i) *The Merry King; Molly on the Shore;* (ii) *Shepherd's Hey*

*** Chan. 9549. Royal N. College of Music Wind O, with (i) Rundell, (ii) Reynish

Even more than most issues in the Chandos Grainger series, this is a fun disc, with the brilliant young players of the Royal Northern College relishing the jaunty rhythms. Many of the pieces are well known in Grainger's alternative arrangements, but this version of Grainger's most popular piece, *Country Gardens*, is not just an arrangement of the piano version but, as he explained himself, 'a new piece in every way'. The *Faeroe Island Dance* in this late band version of 1954 has a pivoting ostinato for horns that echoes the opening of Vaughan Williams's *Fifth Symphony*, before launching into the dance proper with echoes of *The Rite of Spring*.

PIANO MUSIC

Country Gardens; In a Nutshell (suite): *Gay but Wistful; The Gum-Suckers' March. Jutish Medley; March-Jog (Maguire's Kick); Molly on the Shore; One More Day My John; Ramble on the Last Love-Duet from Strauss's 'Der Rosenkavalier'; Sheep and Goat Walkin' to the Pasture; Shepherd's Hey; Spoon River; Sussex Mummers' Christmas Carol; Turkey in the Straw; The Warriors.* STANFORD: *Irish Dances* arr.
GRAINGER: *Leprechaun's Dance; A Reel*

*** Nim. NI 8809. Grainger (from Duo-Art piano rolls)

We have always been admirers of the Duo-Art player-piano recording system, and here Grainger's personality leaps out from between the speakers, yet the original rolls were cut between 1915 and 1929! It is good to have such a winningly vigorous *Country Gardens* and such a characterful *Shepherd's Hey*, while *Sheep and Goat Walkin' to the Pasture* has rhythmical character of the kind that makes one smile. *Gay But Wistful* is neither – nonchalant, rather – but endearing. The lyrical numbers like the touching *Sussex Mummers' Christmas Carol*, *One More Day My John* and the lilting Zanzibar boat-song have a winningly relaxed flair, and Grainger makes his arrangement of the Richard Strauss love-duet from *Der Rosenkavalier* sound intimately luscious and deliciously idiomatic. The recording is first class.

Complete: '*Dished up for Piano*', Volumes 1–5

(B) *** Nim. NI 1767 (5). Jones

Martin Jones's splendid Nimbus survey of Grainger's piano music is no longer available on separate CDs, but they do now come together in a slip-case at bargain price. The playing is refreshingly alive and spontaneous. Volume 1 is particularly attractive, and that is the place to start, for there is not a dull item here. There is plenty of dash in the folksong arrangements, and charm too, and they display a much greater range than one might have expected. The transcriptions are fascinating. The fourth and fifth volumes are the most enjoyable of all. Grainger's arrangements in Volume 4 are often very free, but Jones plays them with such spontaneity that they are freshly enjoyable in their own right. The opening *Four Irish Dances* of Stanford are attractively spiced. His 'concert version' of Bach's most famous *Toccata and Fugue* in based on the arrangements by Tausig and (mainly) Busoni: Jones excitingly gives the full bravura treatment. But there are gentle, original pieces too, and the *Eastern Intermezzo* features peals of bells. *Tiger-Tiger* is simplicity itself, as is *At Twilight*, but this piece then ends with a bluesy 'added sixth' chord.

Volume 5 offers the original works for up to six hands, and the opening *Children's March*, in which Jones is joined on one piano by Richard McMahon, could not be more rumbustiously attractive. In *Ye Banks and Braes* (prolix but effective) and the lilting *Zanzibar Boat-Song* three players share a single piano. But in the intricate *Passacaglia on Green Bushes* (a *tour de force* which steadily increases in pace and excitement), Philip Martin joins the other two to make up the six hands, on three pianos, and this is the complex scoring of both the 'rambling' *English Dance*, which is very diverting, and the closing *Warriors* ballet (which is complete). All the playing here is splendidly secure technically, and the performances not only have panache but also readily convey the enjoyment of the participants. The pianos are recorded reverberantly in the Nimbus manner – but it rather suits this repertoire, and the image is absolutely truthful. A full listing will be included in the 2006/7 Yearbook.

Colonial Song; Country Gardens; Handel in the Strand; Harvest Hymn; The Hunter in his Career; In a Nutshell (Suite): *Gum-Suckers' March. In Dahomey (Cakewalk Smasher); Irish Tune from County Derry; Jutish Medley; A March-Jig; The Merry King; Mock Morris; Molly on the Shore; Ramble on the Last Love-Duet from Richard Strauss's 'Der Rosenkavalier'; A Reel; Scotch Strathspey & Reel; Shepherd's Hey; Spoon River; Walking Tune*

**(*) Hyp. CDA 66884. Hamelin

Marc-André Hamelin's articulation is phenomenally crisp,

and the recording is excellent, but he misses the charm of some of these pieces when he is often too metrical, pushing ahead a shade too fast in such pieces as *Country Gardens* or *Shepherd's Hey*, so that rhythms fail to spring infectiously as they should. Yet the choice of items is generous and apt.

VOCAL MUSIC

Choral Music (unaccompanied): *Agincourt song; At twilight; Australian up-country song; Early one morning; The gypsy's wedding day; Irish tune from County Derry; Jungle-Book verses; Love at first sight; My dark-haired maiden; My love's in Germanie; Mary Thomson; Near Woodstock Town; O mistress mine; Recessional; Six dukes went a-fishin'; Soldier soldier; Ye banks and braes*
*** Chan. 9987. ASMF Ch., Hickox

Beautifully sung by the St Martin's Academy Chorus, it is the favourite folk-songs, like *My dark-haired maiden, Ye banks and braes, Early one morning* and the *Londonderry air* which resound in the memory. Yet there are attractive novelties too, with Grainger's version of the *Agincourt song*, the four diverse *Jungle-Book verses* and *Love at first sight* receiving their first recording. The latter was written by Grainger's wife Ella, though harmonized and arranged for soprano solo and mixed chorus by her husband; she questions in a moment of happiness whether such love can really last after the seductive initial impulse. The result is charming. Excellent, warmly atmospheric recording does not muffle the words, although full texts are included, and excellent documentation by Barry Ould.

Anchor song (setting of Rudyard Kipling); *Thou gracious power* (setting of Oliver Wendell Holmes); Arrangements of folksongs: *Afterword; Air from County Derry; Brigg Fair; Early one morning; Handel in the Strand; I'm seventeen come Sunday; The lonely desert-man sees the tents of the Happy Tribes; Marching tune; Molly on the shore; 2 Sea shanties; Shallow Brown; Six dukes went a-fishing; There was a pig went out to dig; Ye banks and braes o' bonnie Doon*
*** Chan. 9499. Padmore, Varcoe, Joyful Company of Singers, City of L. Sinf., Hickox; Thwaites

In the darkly intense *Shallow Brown* Hickox has a clear advantage in opting for an excellent baritone soloist (Stephen Varcoe), with an equally fine choral ensemble. In Hickox's version of the *County Derry* (the 'Londonderry air') he has chosen an extended, elaborate setting. *Ye banks and braes* is another item given in a version previously unrecorded, with a whistled descant. Among the pieces completely new to disc are the *Marching tune* and *Early one morning*. Also most striking is the brief, keenly original choral piece, *The lonely desert-man sees the tents of the Happy Tribes*, here given a dedicated performance, with the tenor intoning a theme from Grainger's orchestral piece, *The Warriors*, and the distant chorus chattering a chant borrowed from his *Tribute to Foster*.

(i) *Bell Piece. Blithe Bells;* (ii) *Children's March; Hill Songs I & II; The Immovable 'Do'. Irish Tune from County Derry; Marching Song of Democracy; The Power of Rome and the Christian Heart*
*** Chan. 9630. Royal N. College of Music Wind O, Reynish or Rundell; with (i) Gilchrist; (ii) vocal group from band

Where in their first collection (above) the splendid players of the Royal Northern College of Music Wind Orchestra clearly so enjoy Grainger's rhythmic buoyancy, here they equally relish his feeling for wind colour, as in the engaging *Hill Songs*, and rich sonorities, as in the powerful and remarkable *The Power of Rome and the Christian Heart*, and equally so in this characteristically imaginative arrangement of the *Londonderry Air* for band and pipe organ. *Bell Piece* (a 'ramble' on Dowland's melancholy air, *Now, O Now I Needs Must Part*) begins with a tenor solo with piano, before the wind players gently steal in. In the *Children's March* members of the band are invited twice to sing a vocalise when they are not playing. Altogether a fascinating and greatly enjoyable programme, strikingly well directed by Timothy Reynish and Clark Rundell.

The Crew of the Long Serpent; Danish Folk Song Suite; Kleine Variationen-Form; Stalt Vesselil (Proud Vesselil); To a Nordic Princess; (i) (Vocal) *Dalvisa; Father and Daughter (Fadit og Dóttir); The merry wedding; The rival brothers; Song of Värmland; Under un Bro (Bridge)*
*** Chan. 8721. Danish Nat. RSO, Hickox; (i) with Stephen, Reuter, Danish Nat. R. Ch.

From his earliest years Grainger was drawn to Scandinavian and Icelandic literature. This stimulating and rewarding collection centres on music directly influenced by his immersion in those cultures, all little known, except perhaps the *Danish Folk Song Suite*, with its highly exotic orchestration, winningly presented here. Among the other orchestral items the rollicking *Crew of the Long Serpent*, the colourful *Variations*, and the much more extended and lusciously scored *Tribute to a Nordic Princess* stand out. In the complex opening choral piece, *Father and Daughter*, a traditional Danish folk dance is mixed up with a theme of Grainger's own. The jolly, concerted *Merry wedding* is sung in English: it draws on a folk poem for its text, but is musically original. *Dalvisa* is a delightful vocalise, using the same melody Alfvén featured as the centrepiece in his *Midsummer Rhapsody*. Splendid performances and top-class Chandos sound.

Bold William Taylor; Colonial song; The Bridegroom Grat; Died for love; Free music; Harvest hymn; Hubby and Wifey; The Land O' the Leal; Lisbon; Lord Maxwell's goodnight; Lord Peter's Stable-Boy; Molly on the Shore; The Nightingale; The old woman at the christening; The only son; The power of love; The shoemaker from Jerusalem; The twa corbies; The two sisters; Walking tune; Willow willow; Ye Banks and Braes O' Bonnie Doon
**(*) Chan. 9819. D. Jones, Hill, Varcoe, ASMF Chamber Ens.

The present volume of the Chandos Grainger series is devoted to pieces (with or without vocal contributions) accompanied by various chamber ensembles. Grainger's scoring is as vividly captivating as ever, and never more so than in his arrangements of *Lisbon* and *Walking tune* (both for wind quintet), or in accompanying the delightful melody of *The shoemaker of Jerusalem* (with flute, trumpet, strings and piano (four hands)). In the solo songs some might feel that Della Jones is a bit precocious in her sharp word-enunciation (as in *The old woman at the christening*), but her gusto is endearing. Stephen Varcoe adopts a much simpler style most effectively in *Bold William Taylor*, and Martyn Hill spins the line of *Lord Maxwell's goodnight* and *The twa corbies* very touchingly, accompanied by a rich string patina. *Free music* is set for a normal string quartet and opens with eerie glissandi, and the quartet returns, cello-led, to end the recital with a rapturous account of *Molly on the Shore*. Excellent recording, as usual from this source.

The Bride's Tragedy (for chorus & orchestra); *Brigg Fair* (for tenor & chorus); *Danny Deever* (for baritone, chorus & orchestra); *Father and daughter* (*A Faeroe Island dancing ballad;* for 5 solo narrators, double chorus & 3 instrumental groups); *I'm seventeen come Sunday* (for chorus, brass & percussion); *Irish tune from County Derry* (*Londonderry air;* for wordless chorus); *The Lost lady found; Love verses from The Song of Solomon* (for tenor & chamber orchestra); *The merry wedding* (*Bridal dances;* for 9 soloists, chorus, brass, percussion, strings & organ); *My dark-haired maiden* (*Mi nighean dhu;* for mixed voices); *Scotch strathspey and reel – inlaid with several Irish and Scotch tunes and a sea shanty* (orchestral version); *Shallow Brown* (for solo voice or unison chorus, with an orchestra of 13 or more instruments); *The Three Ravens* (for baritone solo, mixed chorus & 5 clarinets); *Tribute to Foster* (for vocal quintet, male chorus & instrumental ensemble)

🔊 (M) *** Decca 475 213-2. Soloists, Monteverdi Ch., English Country Gardiner O, Gardiner

It would be difficult to imagine a more exhilarating disc of Grainger's music than this (originally Philips) collection of 'Songs and Dancing Ballads', which won the *Gramophone*'s Choral Award in 1996. John Eliot Gardiner met the eccentric composer as a child and has become devoted to his music. The variety is astonishing, even among the folksong settings, which often use melodies transcribed from original sources by Grainger himslf. Gardiner singles out the hypnotically measured sea-shanty *Shallow Brown* as the most 'searingly original' of Grainger's works and the most haunting. The performance here backs that up, with furious tremolandos from guitars and banjos, which Grainger called 'wogglings'. The richest, most exotic piece is the setting of *Love verses from The Song of Solomon*, while the longest and most elaborate items bring astonishingly original effects for both voices and orchestra, the richly evocative *Tribute to Foster* and the setting of a mock Scottish ballad by Swinburne, *The Bride's Tragedy*, which Grainger described as a pained 'grumble-shout'. All 14 items, many of them first-ever recordings, bring typically quirky inspirations, superbly interpreted. Even if the choir's attempts at various dialects, from Mummerset onwards, may not be to everyone's taste, the virtuosity of the singing is breathtaking. The bitter element in some of the numbers provides a clue to the inspiration that fired Grainger, as in the grim setting of Kipling's *Danny Deever*, with its refrain, 'Oh they're hanging Danny Deever in the morning'. Echoing Mahler in its subject, it is far more angry. Superb sound, though (because of the complexity of textures) words are often inaudible. Full text and really outstanding notes – a model of what documentation should be.

Duke of Marlborough Fanfare; Green Bushes (Passacaglia); Irish Tune from County Derry; Lisbon; Molly on the Shore; My Robin is to the Greenwood Gone; Shepherd's Hey; Piano Duet; Let's Dance Gay in Green Meadow. Vocal and Choral: *Bold William Taylor; Brigg Fair; I'm Seventeen Come Sunday; Lord Maxwell's goodnight; The Lost Lady Found; The Pretty Maid Milkin' Her Cow; Scotch Strathspey and Reel; Shallow Brown; Shenandoah; The Sprig of Thyme; There Was a Pig Went Out to Dig; Willow Willow*

*** Australian Decca Eloquence (ADD) 467 234-2. Pears, Shirley-Quirk, Amb. S. or Linden Singers, Wandsworth Boys' Ch., Britten or Bedford

This collection is one of the best single-disc anthologies of Grainger's music. The bulk of the collection derives from Britten's 1969 LP, and the sound in this transfer is extraordinarily full and vivid: indeed, the clarity of *There Was a Pig Went Out to Dig* has uncanny presence. It is altogether a delightful anthology, beautifully played and sung throughout. If Grainger's talent was smaller than his more fervent advocates would have us believe, his imagination in the art of arranging folksong was prodigious. The *Willow Song* is a touching and indeed haunting piece and shows the quality of Grainger's harmonic resource. The *Duke of Marlborough Fanfare* is strikingly original, and so is *Shallow Brown*. Vocal and instrumental items are felicitously interwoven, and Decca's Australian team are to be congratulated in making this CD available.

Songs of the North (*4 Scottish settings*); *6 settings of Rudyard Kipling; The secret of the sea; Sailor's shanty.* Traditional folksong settings: *Bold William Taylor; British waterside; Creepin' Jane; Hard-hearted Barb'ra; The lost lady found; The pretty maid milking her cow; Shallow Brown; Six dukes went afishin'; Willow willow*

**(*) Chan. 9503. Varcoe, Thwaites

Stephen Varcoe is obviously at home in these folksongs. Most of them are set fairly simply, as in the lovely opening of *Willow willow*, or the bold, jiggy narrative of *The lost lady found*, while *The pretty maid milking her cow* is very touching. These are essentially concert performances. However, Varcoe's vernacular account of Kipling's *Soldier soldier come from the wars* is especially successful, and *Hard-hearted Barb'ra* is delightfully done, as is Grainger's own setting of Longfellow's *The secret of the sea*. *Shallow Brown*, which ends the programme, is very dramatic indeed, although some might feel that Varcoe goes over the top here, helped by Penelope Thwaites's strong accompaniment; indeed, she makes an admirable contribution throughout this well-recorded recital.

GRANADOS, Enrique (1867–1916)

(i) *Dante* (symphonic poem); *Goyescas: Intermezzo;* (ii) *La maja y el ruiseñor. 5 Piezas sobre cantos populares españolas* (arr. Ferrer)

*** ASV CDDCA 1110. Gran Canaria PO, Leaper; with (i) Herrera; (ii) Lucey

Dante is unexpectedly confident in its use of the orchestral palette. The first section opens in sombre despair to evoke Dante's journey with Virgil into the 'black malignant air' of the Inferno, while in the second we meet Paolo and Francesca, their love already anticipated in a sadly yearning theme in Part One. Granados evokes his narrative using luscious post-Wagnerian chromaticism and even introduces voluptuous hints of Scriabin and early Schoenberg. *Francesca's Story* is a straightforward setting of Canto V of Dante's poem, and here there are even hints of Puccini's *Madame Butterfly*. The vocal line is affectingly sung by Nancy Herrera, her fully coloured mezzo darkening the lower notes entreatingly. Adrian Leaper and the excellent Gran Canaria Orchestra play this remarkable score with languorous intensity. The enchanting highlight of *Goyescas, La maja y el ruiseñor* is simply and beautifully sung by Frances Lucey, and the opera's *Intermezzo* follows vibrantly. Anselm Ferrer's orchestration of five of the *Piezas sobre cantos populares* skilfully re-creates the music orchestrally – sultry and sparkling by turns. They are most winningly and flexibly presented, to make an entertaining centrepiece in a first-class collection, atmospherically and vividly recorded.

12 *Danzas españolas* (orch. Ferrer)

☛⊸ (BB) *** Naxos 8.555956. Barcelona SO & Catalonia Nat. O, Brotons

This overtly nationalistic music, using original tunes, has encouraged various composers to orchestrate them, of which this set by Rafael Ferrer is colourful and effective. The flutes and oscillating strings in No. 2 have a haunting atmosphere, and the delicacy of writing in the central sections of No. 5, flanked with its strong, brooding theme, is imaginative also. If, in its orchestral format, this is hardly the most subtle music, it is all colourful and enjoyable. The recording is vivid and bright, matching the performance, and this inexpensive CD is worth its modest price.

12 *Danzas españolas; Escenas poeticas, Book I* (arr. for guitar and orchestra)

(BB) *** Naxos 8.553037. Kraft, Razumovsky Sinf., Breiner

These are attractive transcriptions for guitar and orchestra of Granados's piano pieces. The Canadian guitarist Norbert Kraft is a brilliant and effective player. If you want to try Granados in this orchestral garb rather than in its original, keyboard form, you can invest in this with confidence.

(i) *Piano Quintet in G min.* Piano music: *A la Cubana, Op. 36; Aparición; Cartas de amor - Valses intimos, Op. 44; Danza caracteristica; Escenas poéticas* (2nd series)

(M) *** CRD (ADD) CRD 3335. Rajna; (i) with Alberni Qt

The *Piano Quintet* is a compact work, neat and unpretentious, in three attractive movements, including a charming lyrical *Allegretto* and a vigorous finale where the piano is most prominent. Among the solo items, the evocative pieces in the *Escenas poéticas II* are the most valuable, but even the more conventional colour-pieces that make up the rest of the disc are worth hearing in such perceptive readings. The CRD analogue recording is very good indeed and so are the CD transfers.

GUITAR MUSIC

Cuentos de la juventud, Op. 1: Dedicatoria. Danzas españolas 4 & 5, Op. 37/4-5; Tonadillas al estilo antiguo: La maja de Goya. Valses poéticos

☛⊸ ⊙ (BB) *** RCA 74321 68016-2. Bream (guitar) –
ALBENIZ: *Collection* (with pieces by MALATS and PUJOL)
*** ⊙

Like the Albéniz items with which these Granados pieces are coupled, these performances show Julian Bream at his most inspirational. The illusion of the guitar being in the room is especially electrifying in the middle section of the famous *Spanish Dance No. 5*, when Bream achieves the most subtle *pianissimo*. Heard against the background silence, the effect is quite magical. But all the playing here is wonderfully spontaneous. This is one of the most impressive guitar recitals ever recorded, and for this super-bargain reissue RCA have generously added the *Tres piezas españolas* of Rodrigo, recorded a year later and no less distinguished.

12 *Danzas españolas* (trans. for guitar)

(B) *** EMI Red Line CDR5 69850. Barrueco – FALLA: *Spanish Popular Songs* ***

As in the Falla coupling, this is masterly playing, warmly coloured, subtly nuanced and naturally idiomatic in its rhythms, so that one might think that these piano pieces had been orginally intended for the guitar.

PIANO MUSIC

Piano Music (complete)

(BB) *** Nim. NI 1734 (6). M. Jones

Allegro de concierto; Escenas románticas; Goyescas (complete); *Goyescas: Intermezzo. Goyesca (El pelele); Oriental, canción, variada, intermedio y final; Rapsodia aragonesa; Valse de concert; Reverie* (Improvisation; transcribed from a Duo Art piano roll)

(BB) *** Nim. NI 5595/8 (4). M. Jones – ALBENIZ: *Iberia, etc.* ***

The Nimbus six-disc set is described as 'the complete published works for the piano', but you will look in vain in the contents list for the *Goyescas*: as they are listed (on the second CD) as *Los majos enamorados*, Parts I and II. The *Libro de horas* come between the two Books (which works well enough), with *El pelele* played quite separately. No reason is given for this in the sparse notes, the one drawback to the set which is otherwise highly recommendable at its modest price. A full listing will be included in the 2006/7 Yearbook. As can be seen, there is an equally recommendable shorter collection (which includes the *Goyescas* and also the Duo Art piano-roll transcription of the composer playing an improvisation).

A la antigua; Bourrée; Bocetos: colección de obras fáciles; Cartas de amor: Valses intimos; Esquise . . .! Vals tzigane; 7 Estudios; 6 Estudios expresivos en forma de piezas fáciles; La góndola: Escena poètica L'himne dels morts; Minuetto; Valses sentimentales

(BB) *** Naxos 8.557141. Riva

A la cubana; Aparición; Apariciones: Valses románticos. Cuentos de la juventud; Escenas infantiles; 'Miel de la Alcarrie': Jota. Rapsodia aragonesa; Valses opéticos

(BB) ** Naxos 8.554629. Riva

A la pradera; Arabesca; Azulejos; Canción árabe; Canción morisca; Escenas poéticas; Fantasia – Cheherezada; Moresque; Oriental Theme with Variations, Intermezzo & Finale; Valse de Concert

(BB) ** Naxos 8.555325. Riva

Allegro appassionato; Allegro de concierto; Barcarola; Capricho español; Danza lenta; Escenas románticas; Libro de horas; Paisaje; Preludio in D

(BB) ** Naxos 8.554 628. Riva

Danza característica; El jardi d'Elisenda; Jácara; 3 Impromptus; Pastoral; Parramda-Murcia; Países soñados: Palacio encantado en el mar. Piezas sobre cantos populares españols; Sardana; Serenata

(BB) ** Naxos 8.555323. Riva

Granados's piano music is extensive and of quality, and Naxos's survey with the American pianist Douglas Riva provides an inexpensive introduction to this repertoire. As well as his accomplishments as a pianist, he is a scholar and assistant editor of the 18-volume edition of the complete piano music. His playing has earned the praises of Spanish critics as well as the imprimatur of Xavier Montsalvatge. He is a sympathetic interpreter rather than a distinguished one, and after a while the ear longs for greater subtlety and finesse. There is all too little variety of colour. He is rather closely recorded, but the sound is generally pleasing.

A la pradera; Barcarola, Op. 45; Bocetos; Cuentos de la juventud, Op. 1; Mazurka, Op. 2; Moresque y Arabe; Sardana; Los soldados de cartón
(M) *** CRD (ADD) 3336. Rajna

Allegro de concierto; Capricho español, Op. 39; Carezza vals, Op. 38; 2 Impromptus; Oriental; Rapsodia aragonesa; Valses poéticos
(M) *** CRD (ADD) 3323. Rajna

Danzas españolas, Op. 37
(M) *** CRD (ADD) 3321. Rajna

Escenas románticas; 6 Piezas sobre cantos populares españols; Danza lenta
(M) *** CRD (ADD) 3322. Rajna

6 Estudios espresivos; Estudio, Op. posth.; Impromptu, Op. 39; 3 Marches militaires; Paisaje, Op. 35; Pequeña suite (In the garden of Elisenda)
(M) *** CRD (ADD) 3337. Rajna

Goyescas; Escenas poéticas (1st series); Libro de horas
(M) *** CRD (ADD) 3301. Rajna

Thomas Rajna plays with great sympathy and flair. Apart from the *Danzas españolas*, some of the finest music is to be found in the *Escenas románticas* and in the other pieces on CRD 3322 and 3323. The later volumes, however, excellently played and recorded, are well worth considering, and not merely for the sake of completeness. The eight pieces on CRD 3336, opening with the beguilingly innocent *Moresqe y Arabe*, are delightful, pleasingly contrasted in style and played with great character and spontaneity. The *Six Estudios* serve to point the formative influences in Granados's style – Schumann and, to a lesser extent, Fauré – while the other pieces, including the *Marches militaires* (in which Rajna superimposes the second piano part) are unfailingly pleasing. His account of *Goyescas* must yield to Alicia de Larrocha, but his interpretations are clear and persuasive and the music's greatness does not elude him. The fill-ups, more immediately charming, less ambitious, are valuable, too. A distinguished set, welcome in the CD catalogue at mid-price.

Allegro de concierto; Danza lenta; 12 Danzas españolas; El pele; Goyescas (complete); Valses poéticos
(B) *** RCA 2-CD 74321 84610-2 (2). de Larrocha (with: MONTSALVATGE: *Dinagación; Sonatine pour Yvette ***)
(N) (M) *** RCA 82876 60863-2. *Goyescas & Las Danzas españolas* only. De Larrocha

Alicia de Larrocha has recorded much of this repertoire before, both for Spanish Hispavox and later, perhaps definitively, for Decca (see below). Her view of these pieces has not changed substantially since, although her responses in the earlier recordings are sometimes marginally fresher. However, her newest, RCA set of the *Danzas españolas* is every bit as perceptive and sparkling, and her Spanish temperament remains naturally attuned to this music. The spontaneity of feeling is still there too, and the *Valses poéticos* are especially charming. The RCA recording is natural, fully coloured and with fine sonority; it is very present and vivid: the listener is closer to the instrument than with Decca, where there is a shade more space round the instrument. The set of *Goyescas* and six *Danzas españolas* are also available on a single mid-priced CD. However, the RCA Double is not only generous, it offers two delightful encores by Montsalvatge. Although Spanish by birth and training, his piano miniatures, harmonically ambivalent, are very much after the French style of Satie and Poulenc. *Divagación* was dedicated to Alicia de Larrocha, and the delectably frivolous *Sonatine* was written in 1962 as a tenth-birthday present for his granddaughter, appropriately quoting '*Twinkle, twinkle, little star*' in the finale.

Allegro de concierto; 12 Danzas españolas; El pelele
(B) *** Double Decca ADD/DDD 433 923-2 (2). De Larrocha – ALBENIZ: *Cantos de España; Suite española ***

Alicia de Larrocha has an aristocratic poise to which it is difficult not to respond, and she plays with great flair and temperament in the *Danzas españolas*. *El pelele* is an appendix to the *Goyescas* collection and is brilliantly played, as is the *Allegro de concierto* (which is digitally recorded).

Goyescas (complete)
⊕—ꞷ ✿ (B) *** Double Decca 448 191-2 (2). De Larrocha – ALBENIZ: *Iberia, etc. ***

Goyescas: Los majos enamorados, Parts I–II
(N) (B) *** Nim. 2-CD NI 7718/9. Martin Jones – ALBENIZ: *Iberia ***

Goyescas (complete); Escenas románticas; El pelele; 6 Piezas sobre cantos populares españoles; Valses poéticos
(M) *** EMI (ADD) 5 62581-2. De Larrocha

Alicia de Larrocha brings special insights and sympathy to the *Goyescas* (given top-drawer Decca sound in 1977); her playing has the crisp articulation and rhythmic vitality that these pieces call for, while she is hauntingly evocative in *Quejas ó la maja y el ruiseñor*. The overall impression could hardly be more idiomatic in flavour or more realistic as a recording. This Double Decca coupling with Albéniz's *Iberia* is very distinguished.

Alicia de Larrocha's EMI set of *Goyescas* derives from the Spanish Hispavox catalogue and was made in 1963, a decade before her first Decca set. The performance is more impulsive, at times more intensely expressive, if less subtle in feeling than the later version, and the recording, if not as fine as the Decca, is eminently realistic. The closing *Zapateado* of the *Cantos populares españoles* has a fire and sparkle characteristic of her playing at this stage of her career.

As in the coupled *Iberia* of Albéniz, Martin Jones's instinctive sympathy with the Spanish idiom brings a remarkable freshness to the music of Granados, and the recording is very real and natural.

Goyescas (complete); El pelele
**(*) Chan. 9412. Parkin

Eric Parkin is obviously comfortable in the balmy Spanish climate and his performance of *Quejas ó la maja y el Ruiseñor* is as seductive as any. His approach to the gentler music is thoughtfully intimate, yet the brilliantly played *El pelele* brings plenty of extrovert sparkle. However, in the two more extended pieces of *Goyescas*, *Los requiebros* ('Flatteries') and especially *El amore y la muerte*, Alicia de Larrocha's combination of impulsiveness with ruminative evocation is that bit more temperamentally spontaneous. The Chandos recording cannot be faulted, but this is not a first choice.

GRAUN, Carl Heinrich (1704–59)

GRAUN, Johann Gottlieb (1703–71)

C. H. GRAUN: (i) *Harpsichord Concerto in C min.*; (ii) *Oboe d'amore Concerto (Trio Sonata) in D*; (iii) J. G. GRAUN: *Flute Sonata in C*; (ii; iii) *Flute and Oboe Sonatas in D & G*
*** MDG 601 0505-2. (i) Doling; (ii) Schmaulfuss; (iii) Lieberknecht, Sophia Soloists, Tabokov

Carl Heinrich and Johann Gottlieb Graun were the 'Tweedle-dee and Tweedledum' of the court of Frederick the Great of Prussia. Having first worked separately, the two brothers joined forces in 1735. Carl Heinrich, appointed Court Kapell-meister and opera composer, was the senior figure (for whom Frederick built the Unter den Linden Opera House), while Johann Gottlieb became concertmaster in the court orchestra. As this engaging collection shows, both were accomplished composers, although they wrote in very different styles. Johann Gottlieb balanced the inherited baroque manner with the new classicism, while Carl Heinrich favoured *cantabile* lines and *galant* geniality. Even so, the identity of their musical manuscripts became mixed up, for many of their works were simply assigned to 'Graun', with no further identification. All but one of the works here seem to belong to Carl Heinrich – and very attractive they are, the more so as the continuo line is assigned to an excellent bassoonist (Helman Jung). The equally pleasing *Harpsichord Concerto* (with strings) must be attributed to Johann Gottlieb: it is very much an inherited Vivaldi model, though by no means a slavish copy. The engaging *Concerto* (*Trio Sonata*) for oboe d'amore has certain characteristics of both musicians; but it may not be by either of them, as this instrument was supposedly not available at the Prussian court at that time. All the performances here are first class, as is the recording, so we leave curious collectors to decide for themselves the identity of the last-named piece.

Cleopatra e Cesare (opera; complete)
(B) *** HM HMX 2901561.3 (3). Williams, Vermillion, Dawson, Gambill, RIAS Chamber Ch., Concerto Köln, Jacobs

Cleopatra e Cesare is certainly by Carl Heinrich, and very enjoyable it is in a performance as outstanding as this. The work was used in 1742 to inaugurate Frederick the Great's newly built Unter den Linden Opera House in Berlin. It is based on a libretto by Giovanni Botarelli, centring on the passion between the two main characters, and it ends happily, with even Pompey (who has murdered Cleopatra's brother, Ptolemy) forgiven, and the chorus singing rather unrealistically: '*Long life and joy to the loving wife with the august monarch on the throne.*' Graun may not match in imagination his contemporaries in Berlin such as C. P. E. Bach, but his music – arias, ensembles and the two choruses which open and close the opera – is consistently refreshing and full of vitality. Much of Graun's melodic writing (Cornelia's lovely Act I aria, *Son risoluto, mi si spezza*, for instance) is all but worthy of Handel. All the principals here sing most stylishly with clean, agile attack, not least Janet Williams whose cabaletta, *Tre le procelle assorto* ('In the midst of the tempest'),

brings some hair-raising, beautifully focused coloratura, while she is sweetly affecting in her big Act III aria. Lentolo (Jeffrey Francs) has another virtuoso aria (*Non so se io clebba*) which he despatches with thrilling aplomb. Lynne Dawson sings most beautifully as Cornelia, widow of Pompey (the only character who is left unhappy at the end of the story); and Iris Vermillion with her firm, strong mezzo makes a most characterful Caesar. Under René Jacobs, a sensitive director, there is no weak link in the rest of the cast either, and the excellent sound-balance conveys an apt scale for the music. The performance fizzes along and is consistently entertaining, as a full text and translation are provided.

GRAY, Steve (born 1947)

Guitar Concerto (for guitar & small orchestra)
✿ *** Sony SK 68337. Williams, LSO, Daniel – HARVEY: *Concerto antico* *** ✿

The kernel of Steve Gray's *Guitar Concerto* (1987), written for its performer here, John Williams, is the long, expressively atmospheric slow movement, which reaches a bold, expansive climax. The effect is haunting, but the jocular finale also brings loudly vociferous, even vulgar, orchestral outbursts – reflecting the composer's jazz-orientated background – and these probably come off better at a concert than on disc. However, the work ends with music of the utmost delicacy. The performance here is surely definitive and the recording first class.

GRECHANINOV, Alexander (1864–1956)

(i) *Cello Concerto, Op. 8. Symphony 4, Op. 102*; (ii) *Missa festiva, Op. 154.*
*** Chan. 9559. Russian State SO, Polyansky, with (i) Ivashkin; (ii) Russian State Symphonic Cappella, with Golub (organ)

The *Cello Concerto* is an early work, rather pale and conventional, but the *Fourth Symphony* is intensely Russian and its idiom more reminiscent of the 1880s than the 1920s. It is no masterpiece but if you feel at home in the world of Glière and Glazunov, it is worth investigating. Decent performances.

Symphony 1 in B min., Op. 6; (i) *Snowflakes, Op. 47*; *Missa Sancti Spiritus, Op. 169*
*** Chan. 9397. (i) Russian State Symphonic Cappella; Russian State SO, Polyansky

The *First Symphony* is well-schooled music and, like so much Russian music of the period, its craftsmanship is not in question. *Snowflakes* is a middle-period work, written before Grechaninov moved to America after the Revolution; and it has charm. The *Missa Sancti Spiritus* comes from the other end of Grechaninov's long career, when he was living in America. Good performances and excellent recording.

Symphony 3, Op. 100; (i) *Cantata, Kvalite Boga (Praise the Lord), Op. 65*
*** Chan. 9698. (i) Kuznetsova, Russian State Symphonic Cappella; Russian State SO, Polyansky

The *Third Symphony* is said to be the composer's own favourite among his five essays in the genre. It has some of the pastoral charm of Glazunov's *Seventh*. While the ideas fall short of melodic distinction, they are sunny and genial, and the theme and variations that comprise the third movement have a delightful fairy-tale atmosphere. The cantata *Kvalite Boga* ('Praise the Lord') is earlier (1915) and, if the ideas in themselves are not strong, the overall effect of the piece is; it is endearing and quite touching. The performances are very good, as is the recording. A very enjoyable disc.

Symphony 5, Op. 153; (i) Missa occumenica, Op. 142
** Chan. 9845. Russian State SO, Polyansky; (i) with Sharova, Kuznetsova, Dolgov, Fadeyev, Symphonic Cappella

The *Fifth Symphony* of 1936 still sounds as if it could have been written by Rimsky-Korsakov, with whom Grechaninov studied. The *Missa occumenica* was also composed in the late 1930s before Grechaninov left France to settle in America. The *Mass* draws on Jewish and Catholic liturgical traditions, though for the most part it sounds very Russian. Despite sympathetic advocacy from Valéry Polyansky and his accomplished artists, neither work shows this often appealing composer at his best, and both works rather outstay their welcome.

(i) Cello Sonata in E min., Op. 113; (ii) Piano Trios 1 in C min., Op. 38; 2 in G, Op. 128
*** Hyp. CDA 67295. (i) Tsinman, Yampolsky; (ii) Moscow Rachmaninov Trio

The *First Piano Trio* comes from 1906 and was dedicated to Sergei Taneyev; the *Second* comes from 1930, by which time he had left Russia and settled in Paris. Their musical language is highly conservative and rooted in Tchaikovsky, Brahms and Rachmaninov, though no really distinctive voice surfaces here and the ideas fall short of memorability. Like the two piano trios, the *Cello Sonata* of 1927 is strongly lyrical and beautifully fashioned and played with tremendous ardour and conviction by the cellist, Mikhail Tsinman, and pianist, Viktor Yampolsky, both of the splendid Moscow Rachmaninov Trio. First-class recorded sound.

String Quartets 1 in G, Op. 2; 2 in D min., Op. 70
*** MDG 603 1157-2. Utrecht Qt

First Quartet was composed in 1894, a year after Tchaikovsky's death, and inhabits much the same world as Borodin or Glazunov, albeit without the rich fund of melody. The *Second* comes from 1913 and again belongs to this same world of Russian lyricism, although there is a greater use of chromaticism. Both pieces offer civilized discourse and are beautifully proportioned and expertly fashioned. They are played with great affection and conviction by the Utrecht Quartet and truthfully recorded. Grechaninov is not a highly individual figure, but his music gives much pleasure and enjoyment.

All-Night Vigil (Vespers), Op. 59; Nunc dimittis (Lord now lettest Thou Thy servant), Op. 34/1; The Seven Days of the Passion; (i) In Thy Kingdom, Op. 58/3. Now the Powers of Heaven, Op. 58/6
*** Hyp. CDA 67080. (i) Bowman; Holst Singers, Layton

Grechaninov's *All-Night Vigil* was composed in 1912, three years before Rachmaninov's celebrated setting. It is a work of great beauty; radiance might be a better word, particularly as presented here by Stephen Layton and the Holst Singers. Marina Rakhmanova speaks of its grand ('essentially epic') scale, and its handling of choral texture is masterly. The singing is strikingly idiomatic and the Temple Church, London, provides an ideal acoustic. There is an ideal balance,

too, between choir and the chant intoned by James Bowman in *In Thy Kingdom*. Really something of a triumph.

GREENE, Maurice (1696–1755)

Hearken unto Me, ye Holy Children (motet)
*** Hyp. CDA 67298. Blaze, Daniels, Harvey, King's Consort Ch. & O, King – HANDEL: *The Choice of Hercules* ***

Maurice Greene, Handel's contemporary and for many years his unfriendly rival, cannot compare with that master in originality of invention, but this extended motet makes an attractive and valuable fill-up for the rare Handel cantata, equally well performed by the King's Consort.

GREGORIAN CHANT

Mass Propers for Good Friday & Easter
(M) *** DG (IMS) (ADD) 447 299-2. Abteikirche Münsterschwarzach, Joppich
(BB) **(*) Naxos 8.550951. Nova Schola Gregoriana, Turco

Mass Propers for the Church Year
(BB) *** Naxos 8.550711. Nova Schola Gregoriana, Turco

The liturgy of the Catholic Church has the Mass as its central focus. The Ordinary of the Mass – those elements that are unchanging through the Church year – has been set by countless composers and includes the *Kyrie* ('Lord have mercy'), the *Gloria, Credo* and *Sanctus* ('Holy, holy, holy') and the *Agnus Dei* ('Lamb of God, who takes away the sins of the world, have mercy on us and grant us peace'). The Mass Propers are chants which change with the seasons of the year or the occasion of the celebration; they consist of Introit, Gradual, Alleluia, Tract, Offertory and Communion. These are amplified by Sequences (accretions to the liturgy) and Tropes (additions which amplify and heighten the meaning of the biblical text in prose or poetry). The changes brought about by the reforming Council of Trent in the sixteenth century removed many of these additions, but they are at the heart of medieval Church music.

To evaluate Gregorian Chant in a volume of this kind is hazardous and essentially subjective. However, DG's Archiv label offers a number of seasonal discs, such as the Gregorian chant for Good Friday and Easter from the Abteikirche Münsterschwarzach, led by Pater Godehard Joppich and recorded in 1981–2, while an inexpensive Naxos disc (with full texts provided, though no translations) by the Nova Schola Gregoriana, directed by the Italian scholar, Alberto Turco, covers this same area very effectively, and this choir is recorded in the Parish Church of Quatrelle, Mantua, which provides a suitably atmospheric setting.

This fine choral group are heard to even better effect in an excellently chosen 75-minute compilation of chants taken from different Sundays in the Church year. The singing has a firm profile and is well recorded, not seeking to create a purely atmospheric effect. It is a pity that texts and translations are not provided, but the back-up notes are very helpful.

'Liturgia defuntorum': Gregorian chant for the dead (from the Order of Burial and for All Souls' Day)
(BB) **(*) Naxos 8.553192. Aurora Surgit, Randon

To use a group of female voices in this repertoire (but with a male cantor) may not be completely authentic but the soaring monody gains a special character from the use of female trebles, and the added element of contrast in the responsories is also attractive. By no means all this music is solemn or dark in feeling: the closing group of chants, the *Libera me*, and especially the soaring *In paradisum – Chorus angelorum*, followed by the *Ego sum resurrectio*, are intended to give the Christian soul an eloquent send-off. Fine singing and atmospheric yet clear recording.

GREGSON, Edward (born 1945)

Blazon; (i) *Clarinet Concerto;* (ii) *Violin Concerto. Stepping Out* (for string orchestra)
*** Chan. 10105. (i) Collins; (ii) Charlier; BBC PO, Brabbins

Edward Gregson is Principal of Manchester's Royal Northern College of Music, but there is no suspicion of academia here; instead, a highly individual composer emerges who writes in the mainstream of twentieth-century English music.

The CD opens with *Blazon* (1992), a small-scale concerto for orchestra, brimful of energy and ideas. Opening and closing with royal brass fanfares, it features each orchestral group in turn, underwritten with a striking lyrical theme that acts as an anchor.

The splendid *Clarinet Concerto* (1994) opens with the soloist reflectively exploring the work's basic material, and the work's beautiful second half begins ethereally with *pianissimo* high strings and creates magical textures and an atmosphere of profound, moving serenity. But the dynamism of the first part returns, and from this previous material Gregson fashions a richly heart-warming melody, which becomes a satisfying resolution. The concerto is brilliantly, sensitively and exuberantly played by Michael Collins.

Each movement of the *Violin Concerto* (1999) is prefaced by lines of poetry, but these prove to be only a series of inspirational stepping-off points. Certainly the brashly, almost vulgarly sardonic waltz climax of the first movement does catch something of the decadent atmosphere of Oscar Wilde's *The Harlot's House.* But the kernel of the work is the Elysian, mystical slow movement, inspired by Paul Verlaine's *Chanson d'automne*, warmly and delicately played by Olivier Charlier. The Irish reel of the athletically vigorous finale is then at one with the words of W. B. Yeats ('And the merry love the fiddle, And the merry love to dance'). The soloist leads the dance uninhibitedly, even drawing on the blazing energy of the ideas we first heard at the climax of *Blazon*.

Stepping Out (1996) for string orchestra briefly visits the world of John Adams, but the work's succinct polyphonic second section brings a spontaneous lyrical momentum all Gregson's own, and the colourful individuality of the richly coloured orchestral detail in all three works proves the composer's orchestral resourcefulness, if directed as spontaneously as they are here by Martyn Brabbins. The recordings are vivid and warmly atmospheric; moreover Olivier Charlier's small, sweet violin-image is perfectly balanced in the *Violin Concerto.*

Concerto for Orchestra

(N) *** Classico CLASSCD 384. RLPO, Bostock – HODDINOTT; MCCABE: *Concertos for Orchestra* ***

Edward Gregson's *Concerto* springs from a striking four-note motto theme which we hear at the outset to set the *Intrada* aflame, and which reappears later as a haunting lyrical theme on the woodwind. It then dominates the central dirge-like *Elegy* and forms the basis of the rumbustiously vibrant

Toccata finale with its syncopations, bursting percussion and thundering drums, and plentiful use of brass sonorities. Indeed, vivid orchestration is Gregson's strong suit, alongside a recognizable melodic flow. The Liverpool performance is first class and the recording spectacular. This is part of a splendid triptych of orchestral concertos by contemporary British composers, all of whom are immediately communicative to the listener.

GRÉTRY, André-Ernest-Modeste (1741–1813)

Céphale et Procris (suite; ed. Mottl); *Lucile* (suite); Overtures: *L'Ami de la maison; L'Amitié à l'épreuve; L'Epreuve villageoise; Guillaume Tell; Le Huron; Le Jugement de Midas; Le Magnifique; Silvain; Le Tableau parlant; Zémire et Azor* (suite)
**(*) ASV CDDCA 1095. O de Bretagne, Stefan Sanderling

This is Beecham territory. He rightly loved the graceful and delectably scored music of *Céphale et Procris* and *Zémire et Azor*, and he played it with exquisite elegance. He would also have known how to handle these overtures, especially *Le Jugement de Midas* with its thunderous storm sequence (here not really very spectacular), the attractive *L'Ami de la maison* and *L'Amitié à l'épreuve*, the very winning *Le Magnifique* with its offstage drum beats, and the unexpected *Guillaume Tell* with its woodwind piping and bustling allegro. Here it is all well played, but that special Beechamesque touch is absent. One has only to compare the famous *Air (Pantomime)* from *Zémire et Azor*: under Beecham it is quite magical, whereas Stefan Sanderling brings to it a simple, innocent charm. The ASV recording is pleasing, too, especially in relation to the strings, but it has a rather dead, boomy bass and a lack of real sparkle. Given that the disc was engineered by Brian Culverhouse, the acoustic of the Rennes Opera House must have proved intractable. Worthwhile for much music that is otherwise unavailable.

L'Amant jaloux (complete)

(B) ** EMI (ADD) 5 75263-2 (2). Mesplé, Burles, Brewer, Bastin, Perriers, Chateau, Belgian R. & TV CO, Doneux

L'Amant jaloux has been described as a 'masterpiece of ironic humour', though without any texts or translations this will be hard for many to judge. The story concerns Lopez, a Spanish merchant who does his best to prevent – for the usual financial reasons – his widowed daughter Leonore from remarrying. Her suitor becomes suspicious that she has a lover but, after the familiar operatic contrivances, sub-plots and misunderstandings, all ends happily. The score has melody, elegance and wit. First performed in 1778, it was a big success, and at the time was considered the composer's masterpiece, though that mantle later passed to *Richard Coeur-de-Lion*. Jules Bastin is a rather gruff-sounding Lopez (though he is indeed a gruff character); Mady Mesplé is excellent as Leonore, her pert, French manner used to colourful effect. Her aria *Je romps la chaîne qui m'engage* is a delight: Grétry at his stylish best. Her lover, Don Alonzo, is sung by Bruce Brewer, who has a very light French voice and here sounds rather underpowered, but the style is right. Christiane Chateau, as the heroine's servant, Jacinte, is not so appealing, distinctly lacking in charm. Charles Burles as the officer, Florial, is more agreeable, and his charming serenade, *Tandis que tout sommeille*, accompanied by mandolin and pizzicato strings, is delectable. Edgard Doneux directs proceedings in a lively and positive manner, and the 1978 recording is vivid, if a bit dry. If the performance as a whole lacks polish, it is certainly enjoyable, although no libretto is included.

Richard Coeur-de-Lion (complete)

(B) **(*) EMI (ADD) 5 75266-2 (2). Mesplé, Burles, Perriers, Trempont, LMEP Ch., Belgian R. & TV CO, Doneux – ROUSSEAU: Le Devin du village (**)

Premièred in 1784, *Richard Cour-de-Lion* was considered Grétry's masterpiece, and it is curious that this is the only current recording. The libretto, by Michel Sedaine, centres on the imprisonment of Richard I in Austria (following the Third Crusade) and his subsequent – in the opera at least – rescue. Grétry here shows his mastery at writing memorable tunes with an appealing period flavour, and this, combined with a strong libretto, is the reason why this opera is held in such esteem. Much more than many operas of the period, the music is made central to the plot by the use of recurring themes: the main Romance, *Une fièvre brûlante*, is heard at least nine times, but always in different arrangements. With delightfully rustic-sounding choruses (the 'Ronde et choeur', *Ziz et zic et zigand*, is a joy) and attractive dances, all offset by piquant orchestration, the work is unfailingly entertaining. This 1975 performance brings an indigenous cast who are obviously at home in the *opéra-comique* tradition. Mady Mesplé's distinctive French timbre – even though it may not appeal to all listeners – is obviously suited to this work, attractively colouring her aria, *O Richard, O mon Roi!* Charles Burles is sometimes taxed in the high tessitura but otherwise makes a splendid Richard I, and he is well matched by characterful Michel Trempont in the role of Blondel, Richard's faithful servant. Like the others in this series, the recording is rather dry and if, like the performance as a whole, it seems a little rough around the edges, the set can certainly be recommended, even though, once again, no libretto is included in this bargain release. The coupling of Rousseau (whose house, incidentally, was bought by Grétry in 1798) is a charmer, too. Each opera occupies one CD.

Zémire et Azor (complete)

(B) **(*) EMI (ADD) 5 75290-2 (2). Mesplé, Bufkens, Louis, Orliac, Van Gorp, Simonka, Belgian R. & TV Ch. & CO, Doneux

Written in 1771, Grétry's *Zémire et Azor* is an attractive example of pre-revolutionary *opéra comique* in France, a charming adaptation of the 'Beauty and the Beast' fable. Though the recording is very over-reverberant and the orchestral playing could be more precise, this is a generally stylish performance, with Roland Bufkens fresh and firm in the high tenor role of the hero. Mady Mesplé as Zémire sometimes indulges in ugly portamento, but this is a sweeter and truer performance than many she has recorded. A synopsis is provided, but no texts or translations.

GRIEG, Edvard (1843–1907)

COMPLETE MUSIC WITH ORCHESTRA

(i) *Bergliot* (melodrama for orchestra), Op. 42; (ii) *Piano Concerto in A min. 2 Elegiac Melodies, Op. 34; Funeral March in Memory of Richard Nordraak; Holberg Suite,*

Op. 40; In Autumn, Op. 11; 2 Lyric Pieces, Op. 68; Lyric Suite, Op. 54; Norwegian Dances, Op. 35; 2 Norwegian Folk Melodies, Op. 53; 2 Nordic Melodies, Op. 63; Old Norwegian Romance with Variations, Op. 51; Sigurd Jorsalfar (suite) Op. 56; 4 Symphonic Dances, Op. 64; Symphony in C min.; Choral: (iii) Before a Southern Convent; Op. 30; (iv; v) Orchestral Songs: The First Meeting; From Monte Pincio; Henryk Wergeland; Spring; A Swan. (v; vi) Landkjenning, Op. 31; (v) The Mountain Thrall, Op. 32; (v; vii) Olav Trygvason (scenes), Op. 50; (viii) Peer Gynt (complete incidental music); (ix) Sigurd Jorsalfar (incidental music)

(B) *** DG 471 300-2 (6). Gothenburg SO (& Ch.), Järvi; with (i) Tellefsen (nar.); (ii) Zilberstein; (iii) Bonney, Stene, Women's Ch.; (iv) Bonney; (v) Hagegard; (vi) with Men's Ch.; (vii) Stene, Gjevang & Ch.; (viii) Bonney & Soloists

This comprehensive coverage of Grieg's 'music with orchestra', with many of the performances unsurpassed, would make an ideal basis for any Grieg collection. Most are discussed below, although not Lilya Zilberstein's account of the *Piano Concerto*, one of the few disappointments. It is a good narrative performance and could never be called routine, but her reading is comparatively conventional, with few fresh insights. This, incidentally, has just been issued separately on a DB Entrée disc coupled with the *Peer Gynt Suites* and *Norwegian Folk Melodies* (DB 477 500-2). The documentation is excellent but the surprise is the omission of texts and translations for the vocal music, with only synopses deemed necessary. But the standard of recording is consistently high, and this six-disc bargain box is still remarkable value.

At the Cradle, Op. 68/5; Country Dance; 2 Elegiac Melodies, Op. 34; Holberg Suite, Op. 40; 2 Melodies, Op. 53

⊶ (M) *** Virgin 2x1 5 62179-2 (2). Norwegian CO, Brown – BRITTEN: Lachrymae, etc. *** ●; NIELSEN: At the Bier of a Young Artist, etc. ***

The Norwegian Chamber Orchestra collect all of Grieg's music for strings. Very alert and responsive playing in a programme that offers lovely music-making of great feeling and sensitivity. The recording, made in the glorious acoustic of Eidsvoll Church in Norway, is in the demonstration bracket. This now comes as part of an outstanding Virgin Double.

Cello Concerto (arr. from Cello Sonata by Horovitz & Wallfisch); Elegiac Melodies: The Last Spring. Peer Gynt (excerpts): Solveig's Song; Ingrid's Lament (arr. Wallfisch). I Love but Thee; To Spring (arr. Freyhan)

*** Black Box BBM 1170. Wallfisch, LPO, Handley

No, Grieg did not write a cello concerto, but what Joseph Horovitz has brilliantly done here, abetted by Benjamin Wallfisch, is to orchestrate the magnificent Grieg *Cello Sonata*. Amazingly, with echoes of *Peer Gynt* and much else in the instrumentation, the result sounds more Grieg-like than the original, with Raphael Wallfisch as soloist giving a commanding performance, and with Vernon Handley drawing warmly committed playing from the LPO. Comparable cello arrangements of favourite Grieg pieces and songs make an ideal coupling.

(i) Piano Concerto in A min. (original 1868/72 version). Larviks-polka (1858); 23 Small Pieces (1859)

*** BIS CD 619. Derwinger, (i) Norrköping SO, Hirokami

This CD offers us a fascinating glimpse of how the concerto must have sounded to its contemporaries. Love Derwinger is the intelligent and accomplished soloist with the Norrköping orchestra, and he proves a sensitive guide in the collection of juvenilia that completes the disc. The *Larviks-polka*, written when Grieg was fifteen, is probably the very earliest of his piano pieces to survive, and the *Nine Children's Pieces* are all very slight in substance, but they fill out the picture of the young composer and the world in which he grew up. The concerto is well balanced and Love Derwinger's solo pieces are well recorded too.

Piano Concerto in A min., Op. 16

⊶ ✿ *** EMI 5 57562-2. Andsnes, BPO, Jansons – SCHUMANN: *Piano Concerto* *** ✿

⊶ (M) *** Ph. (ADD) 464 702-2. Kovacevich, BBC SO, C. Davis – SCHUMANN: *Concerto* ***

*** Sony 518810-2 [SK 92736]. Perahia, Bav. RSO, C. Davis (with MENDELSSOHN: *Concerto 2: Finale*) – SCHUMANN: *Concerto* ***

(B) *** Decca 433 628-2. Curzon, LSO, Fjeldstad – FRANCK: *Symphonic Variations* *** ✿; SCHUMANN: *Concerto* **(*)

*** EMI 7 54746-2. Vogt, CBSO, Rattle – SCHUMANN: *Concerto* ***

(M) *** Decca (ADD) 466 383-2. Lupu, LSO, Previn – SCHUMANN: *Concerto* ***

(B) **(*) EMI Red Line CDR5 69859. Ousset, LSO, Marriner – SCHUMANN: *Concerto* **(*)

(BB) (***) Dutton mono CDBP 9719. Lipatti, Philh. O, Galliera – SCHUMANN: *Concerto* ***

(BB) (***) Naxos mono 8.110683. Moiseiwitsch, Hallé O, Heward – SAINT-SAENS: *Piano Concerto 2*; LISZT: *Hungarian Fantasia* (***)

(B) (**(*)) EMI mono 5 74802-2. Lipatti, Philh. O, Galliera – CHOPIN: *Piano Concerto 1* (**)

(M) ** DG (ADD) 474 838-2. Anda, PO, Kubelik – BRAHMS: *Piano Concerto 2* **(*)

(i) *Piano Concerto in A min. 6 Lyric Pieces, Op. 65*

(M) *** Virgin 5 61996-2. Andsnes, (i) Bergen PO, Kitajenko – LISZT: *Piano Concerto 2* ***

(i) *Piano Concerto in A min.;* (ii) *Peer Gynt Suites 1–2*

(M) **(*) DG 439 427-2. (i) Anda, BPO, Kubelik; (ii) BPO, Karajan

It was with the Grieg *Piano Concerto in A minor*, coupled with a fine Liszt *A major Concerto*, that Leif Ove Andsnes, most celebrated of Norwegian pianists and among the most sensitive young artists, made his concerto début in 1990 on the Virgin label. This new version, recorded live in Berlin, is just as spontaneous-sounding, with soaring flights of imagination. The excellent performance is also a degree more urgent than in his 1990 recording, while the Berlin Philharmonic is at its warmest under Mariss Jansons. This is a conductor for whom any trace of routine is alien, and who so often illuminates familiar terrain; equally, the freshness of approach that distinguishes Andsnes's performances in the concert hall is also well in evidence here. His virtuosity is commanding, but it is never at the expense of tenderness and poetic feeling; he is an aristocrat among pianists and has the gift of bringing new and deeper insights (listen to the slow movement) without any loss of spontaneity or with the slightest trace of artifice. The Schumann too brings glorious playing from both soloist and orchestra, with both offering warm, clear sound. Even alongside Stephen Kovacevich's much admired coupling, this new issue stands

out: in short, this is a gramophone classic for the present decade.

Whether in the clarity of virtuoso fingerwork or the shading of half-tone, Kovacevich is among the most illuminating of the many great pianists who have recorded the Grieg *Concerto*. He plays with bravura and refinement, the spontaneity of the music-making bringing a sparkle throughout, to balance the underlying poetry. The 1972 recording has been freshened most successfully and this now reappears as one of Philips's '50 Great Recordings'.

Perahia revels in the bravura as well as bringing out the lyrical beauty in radiantly poetic playing. He is commanding and authoritative when required, with the blend of spontaneity, poetic feeling and virtuoso display this music calls for. He is given sympathetic support by Sir Colin Davis and the fine Bavarian Radio Symphony Orchestra, and there is no finer version of the Grieg recorded in the digital age than this, and it now comes at mid-price with the finale of the *Second Mendelssohn Concerto* as an encore.

Curzon's approach to Grieg is wonderfully poetic and this is a performance with strength and power as well as lyrical tenderness. This reading on the Decca label is second to none in distilling the music's special atmosphere and it is available coupled either with Franck and Schumann at bargain price.

Lars Vogt never allows his personality to obtrude; he colours the familiar phrases with great subtlety yet without the slightest trace of narcissism. He is very well supported by Rattle and the CBSO, and excellently recorded. An unusually sensitive player, his version, with the inevitable Schumann coupling, is eminently satisfying. Curzon and Kovacevich are top recommendations, but among newcomers this has strong claims to be put among them.

Decca's remastering of Radu Lupu's fine (1973) Kingsway Hall recording, one of Decca's very best of the period, suits the style of the performance, which is boldly compelling in the outer movements, but has warmth and poetry too, especially striking in the slow movement, where Previn's hushed opening is particularly telling. Indeed, the orchestral contribution is a strong one throughout, while Lupu's playing has moments of touching delicacy, and this Decca performance must stand high on the list of mid- and bargain-priced recommendations.

Virgin have now restored Andsnes's original coupling – an outstanding account of the Liszt *A major Concerto* – but have included Book VIII of the *Lyric Pieces* (Op. 65) with its touching *Melancholy* and lively *Wedding Day at Troldhaugen*, which Grieg later orchestrated. They are played with real imagination and finesse. In the *Concerto* Andsnes wears his brilliance lightly. There is no lack of bravura and display, but no ostentation either. Indeed, he has great poetic feeling and delicacy of colour, and Grieg's familiar warhorse comes up with great freshness.

Dinu Lipatti's classic 1947 version of the Grieg *Concerto*, intensely poetic, like the Schumann with which it is coupled, has been a staple of the catalogue from when it was made, but here in the superb Dutton transfer the sound is fuller and clearer than ever before, preferable to the EMI remastering, with the additional advantage that the disc comes at bargain price.

Géza Anda's account of the *Piano Concerto* is more wayward than some but is strong in personality and has plenty of life. Kubelik's accompaniment is good too, and the 1963 recording sounds well. However, Karajan's analogue *Peer Gynt Suites* are in a class of their own. They were also recorded – a decade later – in the Berlin Jesus-Christus-Kirche but, for some reason, the CD transfer seems very brightly lit, although the fullness and analogue ambience are retained. The alternative coupling with Brahms is less enticing.

Ousset's is a strong, dramatic reading, not lacking in warmth and poetry but, paradoxically, bringing out what we would generally think of as the masculine qualities of power and drive. Marriner gives persuasive support, the sound is full, firm and clear, and this reading gives a refreshingly individual slant on a much-played work.

Moiseiwitsch recorded the Grieg *Concerto* with the Philharmonia Orchestra and Otto Ackermann in the early days of LP, but the authors of *The Record Guide* were distinctly unenthusiastic, writing that while there were moments of delicacy from the pianist, the performance as a whole was insensitively conducted. No such caveat need be made here, and Moiseiwitsch generally is in excellent form.

(i) *Piano Concerto in A min., Op. 16;* **(ii)** *Symphony in C min.*

(N) **(BB)** ** Warner Apex 2564 60458-2. (i) Duchable, Strasbourg PO, Guschlbauer; (ii) Norwegian R. O, Rasilainen

Duchable's reading of the *Concerto* is a strong but charmless one which misses Grieg's gentle poetry. However, many may consider this inexpensive disc in order to sample Grieg's comparatively rare *Symphony*. No masterpiece this, but Rasilainen's is just about the best reading the work has received: it is a strong account with plenty of impetus and a notably eloquent *Adagio*, its coda particularly beautiful. Good sound, too.

2 Elegiac Melodies, Op. 34; Erotik; 2 Melodies, Op. 53; 2 Norwegian Airs, Op. 63

(BB) **(*) Naxos 8.550330. Capella Istropolitana, Leaper – SIBELIUS: *Andante festivo*, etc. ***

Adrian Leaper secures responsive and sensitive playing from the Capella Istropolitana in this Grieg collection, the recording is very good indeed and the balance natural.

(i) *2 Elegiac Melodies, Op. 34; Holberg Suite;* **(ii)** *In Autumn, Op. 11;* **(iii)** *Lyric Suite, Op. 54; Norwegian Dances, Op. 35;* **(iv)** *Old Norwegian Romance with Variations; Symphonic Dances, Op. 64;* **(iii)** *Sigurd Jorsalfar: Homage March;* **(Piano):** **(iv)** *Lyric Pieces, Op. 12 & Op. 28*

(N) **(BB)** *** EMI Gemini (ADD) 5 86513-2 (2). (i) N. Sinfonia, Tortelier; (ii) RPO, Beecham; (iii) Hallé O, Barbirolli; (iv) Bournemouth SO, Berglund; (iv) Adni

A most attractive bargain anthology, recorded over 25 years. Yet how well the very first recording, Beecham's *In Autumn*, still sounds. (It was made in the Kingsway Hall in 1955.) Tortelier gives most affecting performances of the *Elegiac Melodies* and *Holberg Suite*, very well recorded and still among the best in the catalogue. Barbirolli's three items are also available on a Dutton CD (see below). How delightfully he presents the *Allegretto tranquillo*, the second of the *Four Norwegian Dances*. Berglund's highly dramatic *Symphonic Dances* are also available on an Encore disc, but his highly sympathetic and imaginatively volatile performance of the delightful *Old Norwegian Romance with Variations* (all separately cued) are well worth having. Daniel Adni's *Lyric Pieces*, which act as an appendix, are most beautifully played and very well recorded indeed. All the CD transfers are excellent.

(i) *2 Elegiac Melodies;* **(ii)** *Holberg Suite;* **(iii)** *Lyric Suite; Peer Gynt Suites 1–2*

(BB) **(*) Warner Apex 0927 45510-2. (i) Ostrobothnian Chamber O, Kangas; (ii) Helsinki Strings; (iii) Norwegian R. O, Rasilainen

In the *Peer Gynt* suites, the Norwegian Radio Orchestra, under their Finnish conductor, Ari Rasilainen, are certainly enjoyable, while the recording is good but not outstanding. Similar comments apply to the lovely *Lyric Suite* (with the same forces) that follows. The *Holberg Suite* with the Helsinki Strings comes off very well: lots of life in the vital outer movements, matched by tenderness in the haunting *Andante religioso*.

(i) *2 Elegiac Melodies; Lyric Suite: Norwegian March & Nocturne. Norwegian Dance, Op. 35/2;* **(ii)** *Peer Gynt Suites 1–2 (including Solveig's lullaby);* **(i)** *Sigurd Jorsalfar: Homage March 56/3*

(B) *** Sony SBK 53257. (i) Phd. O, Ormandy; (ii) Söderström, New Philh. O, A. Davis

Andrew Davis offers freshly thought performances of the two *Peer Gynt Suites*, beautifully played and warmly recorded at Abbey Road in 1976. A special attraction is the singing of Elisabeth Söderström, not only in *Solveig's song* but also in *Solveig's lullaby*, which has been added to the second suite. The Ormandy recordings date from a decade earlier but they make up a most attractive anthology. The orchestral playing is very good indeed and Ormandy's warmth is obvious. The transfers are well managed.

Holberg Suite, Op. 40

(M) *** Decca (ADD) 470 262-2. ASMF, Marriner – TCHAIKOVSKY: *Serenade* ***; DVORAK: *Serenade* **(*)

(BB) *** Warner Apex 0927 43075-2. Norwegian R. O, Rasilainen – NIELSEN: *Little Suite;* STENHAMMAR: *Serenade* *** ●

Marriner's richly lyrical account of the *Holberg Suite* is outstanding in every way: the *Air* has a pleasing graciousness and the *Rigaudon* plenty of sparkle. The 1970 (Argo) recording remains splendidly fresh.

An unaffected account of the *Holberg Suite* from Ari Rasilainen and his Norwegian players that serves to enhance the attractions of the coupling, Stenhammar's glorious *Serenade for Orchestra*.

Holberg Suite, Op. 40; Peer Gynt Suites 1–2

*** DG 439 010-2. BPO, Karajan – SIBELIUS: *Finlandia*, etc. ***

Holberg Suite, Op. 40; Peer Gynt Suites 1–2; Sigurd Jorsalfar: Suite, Op. 56

●➔ **(B)** *** DG 2-CD (DDD/ADD) 474 269-2 (2). BPO, Karajan – SIBELIUS: *Finlandia*, etc. ***

Karajan's performance of the *Holberg Suite* is the finest currently available. The playing has wonderful lightness and delicacy, with cultured phrasing not robbing the music of its immediacy, while in *Peer Gynt* many subtleties of colour and texture are revealed by the vividly present recording, clear and full and with a firm bass-line, especially in the thrillingly gutsy *In the Hall of the Mountain King*. Grieg's perennially fresh score is marvellously played. *Anitra* dances with elegance, and the *Death of Aase* is movingly eloquent. The digital recording now proves to be one of the best to have emerged from the Philharmonie in the early 1980s.

For their 'Karajan Collection' reissue, DG have added the three pieces from *Sigurd Jorsalfar* and joined this CD economically to an equally outstanding Sibelius programme. This is Karajan and the BPO at their very finest, and the coupling is outstanding in every way. Very fine sound, too.

In Autumn Overture; Lyric Piece: Erotik, Op. 43/5; Norwegian Dances; Old Norwegian Romance with Variations

*** Chan. 9028. Iceland SO, Sakari (with SVENDSEN: *2 Icelandic Melodies* for strings ***)

The Icelandic orchestra play very responsively for their Finnish conductor, Petri Sakari, who gives very natural and straightforward accounts of this endearing music. Highly musical performances, with no lack of personality, truthfully recorded. Very recommendable.

Lyric Suite, Op. 54; Norwegian Dances, Op. 35; Symphonic Dances, Op. 64

**(*) BIS SACD 1291. Bergen PO, Ruud

This is rather less successful than the earlier Grieg disc from Bergen under Ole Kristian Ruud, devoted to music of 1864–8. The sound is first rate, well defined and full-bodied, and captures the excellent acoustic of the Grieg Hall with great realism. For the most part the Bergen orchestra play with the naturalness and eloquence we associate with this repertoire – and with them. But the phrasing in the second of the *Norwegian Dances* is a little too 'knowing' and *Shepherd Boy* in the *Lyric Suite* is too slow and affected. Neeme Järvi takes 4 minutes 14 seconds over this as opposed to Ruud's 5 minutes 31 seconds! All the same, Ruud draws some highly responsive playing from his fine orchestra, and the sound is quite sumptuous.

Lyric Suite; Norwegian Dances; Symphonic Dances. Sigurd Jorsalfar: Homage March

*** Barbirolli Society/Dutton Lab. (ADD) CDSJB 1012. Hallé O, Barbirolli

The set of four *Symphonic Dances* is the earliest recording here, dating from 1957. With Harold Lawrence leading a team of Mercury engineers, the sound is, if anything, even cleaner and brighter than the first-rate EMI quality for the rest, recorded in 1969–70. Sir John brings out all their drama and colour, and the orchestral wind soloists make an often memorable contribution. There are characteristic touches too in the rest of the programme, notably in the expressive warmth of the *Nocturne* in the *Lyric Suite*, and in the *Homage March* from *Sigurd Jorsalfar*. The *Norwegian Dances*, too, are affectionately done and very positively presented. As ever, Mike Dutton gives the sound plenty of body and weight, not least in the *Symphonic Dances* and finally in the *Homage March*, which rounds the selection off.

Sigurd Jorsalfar: Suite; Symphonic Dances. (i) *6 Songs for Voice and Orchestra (From Monte Pincio; Norway; Solveig's Cradle Song; Solveig's Song; Spring; A Swan)*

(M) **(*) Chan. 10287X. Royal Stockholm PO, Rozhdestvensky, (i) with Kringelborn

Responsive playing here from the Stockholm orchestra and sensitive and vital direction from Rozhdestvensky. Solveig Kringelborn sings beautifully enough, though her intonation is not always perfect. However, this is worth having for the *Symphonic Dances* and *Sigurd Jorsalfar*. Very good sound.

4 Symphonic Dances; Peer Gynt Suites 1–2

(BB) **(*) EMI Encore (DDD/ADD) 5 74566-2 [5 74731-2]. Bournemouth SO, Berglund (with ALFVEN: *Swedish Rhapsody 1*; JARNEFELT: *Praeludium* ***)

Berglund's attractive performances of the *Symphonic Dances* coupled with strongly characterized performances of the two *Peer Gynt Suites*. Here *Ingrid's Lament* is notably sombre, and very well played. But elsewhere there is some lack of charm, and the recording has artificial brilliance so that the upper string-sound is clear and vivid rather than rich-textured. However, the inclusion of two favourite encore pieces by Alfvén and Järnefelt – both based on catchy melodies – makes this disc quite enticing.

CHAMBER MUSIC

Cello Sonata in A min., Op. 36

**(*) CRD 3391. Cohen, Vignoles – FRANCK: *Cello Sonata* **(*)

Cello Sonata in A min.; Intermezzo in A min.; Piano Sonata, Op. 7

(BB) *** Naxos 8.550878. Birkeland, Gimse

Oystein Birkeland and Håvard Gimse give the sonata an alive and sensitive account, coupled with the early and unrepresentative *Intermezzo in A minor*. They are both imaginative players and are decently recorded. Given the modest outlay involved, this competes very strongly with its rivals, but even if it were at mid- or full price it would be highly recommendable. Gimse's performance of the early *Piano Sonata*, Op. 7, is also very good indeed. Altogether a first-rate bargain.

In the folk element Cohen might have adopted a more persuasive style, bringing out the charm of the music more, but certainly he sustains the sonata structures well. The recording presents the cello very convincingly. It has been most naturally transferred to CD.

(i) *Cello Sonata;* (ii) *String Quartet 1*

*** Virgin 5 45505-2. (i) Mørk, Gimse; (ii) Sigerland, Sponberg, Tomter, Mørk

Like Leif Ove Andsnes's recent set of *Lyric Pieces*, the *Cello Sonata* was recorded at Grieg's home, Troldhaugen, on his own piano. It is Truls Mørk's second recording (his earlier version was with Jean-Yves Thibaudet, also on Virgin) and he plays with characteristic sensitivity and refreshing ardour. Håvard Gimse is an impeccable partner: he has the keenest musical instincts and great keyboard finesse. This is arguably the best and most compelling account of the *Sonata* to be had. Apart from the *Ballade*, Op. 24, the *String Quartet*, also in G minor, is Grieg's most deeply felt instrumental piece, and it is more often than not coupled with the unfinished *F major Quartet* of 1890, which Julius Röntgen completed after Grieg's death. However, the four artists assembled for the excellent Virgin recording can hold their own with the best, and they bring an intensity, freshness and imagination to this fine score.

String Quartet 1 in G min., Op. 27

(BB) *** Warner Apex 0927 40601-2. New Helsinki Qt – SIBELIUS: *Quartet* ***

(M) (***) Biddulph mono LAB 098. Budapest Qt – SIBELIUS: *Quartet*; WOLF: *Italian Serenade* (***)

String Quartets 1–2 in F (unfinished)

(BB) *** Naxos 8.550879. Oslo String Qt – JOHANSEN: *String Quartet* ***

*** Hyp. CDA 67117. Chilingirian Qt

String Quartets 1–2; Fugue (1861)

*** Victoria VCD 19048. Norwegian Qt

**(*) BIS CD 543. Kontra Qt

The Naxos account of the quartets from the Oslo String Quartet, a relatively new group, proves the best of the lot – indeed it is the best version we have had since the Budapest. They would easily sweep the board even at full price, on account of their sensitivity, tonal finesse and blend, and the keenness of their artistic responses. They play only the first two movements of the *F major Quartet*, leaving room for a fine quartet by Grieg's biographer, David Monrad Johansen. The recording balance, made in the Norwegian Radio studios, is excellent, neither too forward nor too recessed.

The Chilingirians leave off where Grieg did, just as the Oslo Quartet do on Naxos. They have lavished much care on it and their disc is expertly engineered by Arne Kaselborg and Andrew Keener. Recommended alongside the Naxos.

The version of the *First Quartet* from the New Helsinki Quartet couples it with the Sibelius Quartet. It is dramatic, well shaped and vital, yet full of sensitivity, and can be strongly recommended among modern recordings, assuming price is no consideration. Apart from the excellence of the playing, the recording is also very present and well detailed and the disc now comes in the lowest price-range.

The Budapest Quartet's recording dates from 1936, but its attractions in terms of coupling here are strong. The Sibelius *Voces intimae* and the Hugo Wolf *Italian Serenade* are both superb performances and still remain unsurpassed. The Biddulph transfer is excellent.

The Norwegian Quartet may not be immaculate in terms of tonal blend or ensemble but the performances are decent and have plenty of spirit, and the recorded sound is excellent.

The Kontra play with much dramatic power and invest the music with great feeling; one would hesitate to speak of unforced eloquence. In this respect the Norwegians score, for their playing is somehow truer in scale. The BIS recording is excellent and, though not a first choice artistically, the disc is perfectly recommendable.

Violin Sonatas 1 in F, Op. 8; 2 in G, Op. 13; 3 in C min.

*** DG (IMS) 437 525-2. Dumay, Pires

*** Simax PSC 1162. Tonnesen, Smebye

*** Chan. 9184. L. and E. Mordkovitch

Like the *Piano Concerto*, the *Violin Sonatas* possess extraordinary resilience and survive countless repetition. The French violinist, Augustin Dumay, and his distinguished partner, Maria João Pires, give poised, animated accounts of all three sonatas. Their performances are exemplary in every way, and the recorded sound is also excellent in terms of both balance and realism.

In each sonata Terje Tonnesen plays with much sweetness of tone and tenderness of feeling. His virtuosity is disarmingly effortless and there is a lyric and expressive grace that is captivating. His partner, Einar Henning Smebye, is sensitive and responsive, and the balance is excellent. For many this will be a first choice, although Dumay and Pires are in some ways more individual.

Yet the same goes for Lydia and Elena Mordkovitch (*mère et fille*) on an admirably recorded Chandos CD. They, too, give splendidly fresh and well-shaped accounts of all three

sonatas which give much pleasure in music-making. Affectionate yet virile performances – thoroughly recommendable.

Violin Sonata 3 in C min., Op. 45

(B) *** EMI Début 5 72825-2. Zambrzycki-Payne, Presland – BRITTEN: *Suite for Violin & Piano*; SZYMANOWSKI: *Violin Sonata* ***

Rafal Zambrzycki-Payne is the young Polish-born player who was the 1996 'BBC Young Musician of the Year'. In the *C minor Sonata*, he has a youthful ardour that carries the listener with him. There is a strong musical personality here and his partner, Carole Presland, is hardly less impressive. The Abbey Road recording is expertly balanced and sounds very natural.

PIANO MUSIC

Einar Steen-Nøkleberg Complete Naxos Series

Einar Steen-Nøkleberg has recorded every note of music Grieg composed for the piano. He has impressive musical credentials and is, among other things, the author of a book on Grieg's piano music and its interpretations. His survey displaces earlier sets in quality: he is responsive to mood and is searchingly imaginative in his approach. A full listing will be included in the 2006/7 Yearbook.

(BB) *** Naxos 8.550881 Vol. 1: *Early and Late Pieces*

(BB) *** Naxos 8.550882 Vol. 2: *19 Norwegian Folksongs*

(BB) *** Naxos 8.550883 Vol. 3: *Ballade; Melodies of Norway*

(BB) *** Naxos 8.550884 Vol. 4: *17 Norwegian Peasant Songs*

(BB) **(*) Naxos 8.553391 Vol. 5: *Norway's Melodies 1–63*

(BB) **(*) Naxos 8.553392 Vol. 6: *Norway's Melodies 64–117*

(BB) **(*) Naxos 8.553393 Vol. 7: *Norway's Melodies 118–52*

(BB) **(*) Naxos 8.550394 Vol. 8: *Lyric Pieces, Books 1–4*

(BB) **(*) Naxos 8.550395 Vol. 9: *Lyric Pieces, Books 5–7*

(BB) **(*) Naxos 8.550396 Vol. 10: *Lyric Pieces, Books 8–10*

(BB) **(*) Naxos 8.550397 Vol. 11: *Orch. Transcriptions, I*

(BB) **(*) Naxos 8.550398 Vol. 12: *Orch. Transcriptions, II*

(BB) **(*) Naxos 8.550399 Vol. 13: *Orch. Transcriptions, III*

(BB) **(*) Naxos 8.550400 Vol. 14: *Sketches: Concerto; Sonata*

Steen-Nøkleberg does not proceed chronologically: the first disc couples early and late Grieg – the very earliest of his published pieces, written while he was still studying at Leipzig, the *Humoresques*, Op. 6, and the *E minor Piano Sonata*, Op. 7, alongside the *Stimmungen* ('Moods'), Op. 73, composed in the early years of the twentieth century (1901–5). Whether the music is early or late, Steen-Nøkleberg plays with total sympathy and dedication, and he is beautifully recorded throughout in the Lindeman Hall of the Norwegian State Academy of Music. Only in the *Sonata* does he suffer a trace of self-consciousness.

The second disc includes the remarkable *Nineteen Norwegian Folksongs*, Op. 66, which are contemporaneous with what many would see as Grieg's masterpiece, the song-cycle *Haugtussa*, which the composer himself spoke of as full of 'hair-raising' chromatic harmonies. (One of the folksongs appears in Delius's *On Hearing the First Cuckoo in Spring*.) But the earlier set, Op. 17, written not long after the first version of the Piano Concerto, is also full of delights.

The third CD includes the poignant *Ballade in G min.*, Op. 24, composed by Grieg on the death of his parents. Steen-Nøkleberg is highly imaginative and, even if some may find his rubato a little extreme, the keyboard colouring is subtle and rich. He conveys a splendidly rhapsodic spontaneity and there is much feeling. This and the companion disc, with the *Seventeen Norwegian Peasant Dances (Slåtter)*, Op. 72, deserve a particularly strong recommendation. These extraordinary pieces with their quasi-Bartókian clashes are most characterful in Steen-Nøkleberg's hands.

The next three discs are devoted to *Norges Melodier* ('Norway's Melody'), an anthology Grieg made in the mid-1870s for a Danish publisher, of 'easy to play' arrangements of tunes, some of them charming, others less so. Steen-Nøkleberg plays some on the house-organ or harmonium, some on the clavichord, some on a Graf piano to match those sonorities which would have been familiar in Norwegian homes in the 1870s, and some on a Steinway.

Volumes 8–10 survey the delightful *Lyric Pieces*. They are admirably fresh and are presented with the utmost simplicity, yet are obviously felt. These performances come into direct competition with Daniel Adni's not quite complete but otherwise excellent set on an EMI forte double CD. Many will like to have the coverage absolutely complete, and the three Naxos discs cost about the same. The EMI piano-sound is perhaps very slightly warmer and fuller, but the Naxos recording is wholly natural and believable. Einar Steen-Nøkleberg is totally idiomatic and authoritative, and readers wanting a complete set need not hesitate.

With the remaining four volumes we enter the realm of Grieg's transcriptions of his orchestral works and his juvenilia, as well as sketches for works that did not materialize. Most valuable are the *Waltz Caprices*, Op. 37, and the early *Agitato*, EG 106, and *Albumblad*, EG 109. Both these issues are recommendable but dispensable.

The last two volumes are another matter. Volume 13 brings rarities in the shape of the *Three Piano Pieces*, EG 105, and a further three, EG 110–12, all of which are otherwise available only on Love Derwinger's full-priced BIS record of the 1874 version of the *Piano Concerto*. The last volume is of particular interest in that it brings – in addition to various juvenilia – the sketches for a *Second Piano Concerto* – very Lisztian – and the first versions of the slow movement and finale of the Op. 7 *Sonata*.

Album Leaves, Op. 28; Ballade, Op. 24; The Dance goes on; Funeral March for Rikard Nordraak; Gnomes Tune; Holberg Suite, Op. 40; Humoresques, Op. 6; Improvisations on 2 Norwegian Folksongs, Op. 29; Lyric Pieces, Volumes 1–10; Moods, Op. 73; Nordic Folksongs & Dances, Op. 17; Norwegian Folkdances, Op. 66; Norwegian Peasant Dances, Op. 72; Pictures from Life in the Country, Op. 19; 4 Pieces, Op. 1; Pieces Based on the Composer's Songs, Opp. 41 & 52; Poetic Tone Pictures, Op. 3; Sonata, Op. 7
(N) (B) * RCA 82876 60391-2 (7). Oppitz

As you would expect from this accomplished pianist, Gerhard Oppitz's survey (described as the 'Complete Solo Piano Music') is not without its merits and insights; but, generally speaking, there is a certain want of grace, tenderness and poetry. In the *Lyric Pieces* and the *G minor Ballade* there is little of the freshness, delicacy of feeling and innocence this music should convey. There are occasional glimpses of poetry, but for the most part Oppitz is prosaic. His account of the *Sonata* does not begin to compare with Pletnev in lightness of touch and spirit. Admittedly this artist is not helped by the somewhat unglamorous quality of the recorded sound.

Carnival Scene, Op. 19/3; 7 Fugues, EG 184a–g. Lyric Pieces: Berceuse, Op. 38/1; Butterfly; To Spring, Op. 43/1 & 6;

Melody, Op. 47/3; March of the Trolls; Scherzo; Bell-ringing, Op. 54/3, 5 & 6; Brooklet, Op. 62/4; In Ballad Vein; Wedding Day at Troldhaugen, Op. 65/5 & 6; Grandmother's Minuet, Op. 68/2. Piano Sonata in E minor, Op. 7
🎧 ⚙ *** DG 459 671-2. Pletnev

There are fewer *Lyric Pieces* here than on Gilels's classic DG recording, which has held sway for more than a quarter of a century. But Pletnev finds room for the *E minor Sonata*, the *Carnival Scene*, and seven early *Fugues*. He brings great delicacy, control of keyboard colour and freshness to Grieg's youthful *Sonata*, which can be recommended alongside Andsnes (Virgin – see above). The *Fugues* are student exercises from Grieg's Leipzig years, but Pletnev succeeds in making them sound like music. This CD is likely to be to the next quarter of a century what Gilels was to the last.

Lyric Pieces: Op. 12/1; Op. 38/1; Op. 43/1–2; Op. 47/2–4; Op. 54/4–5; Op. 57/6; Op. 62/4 & 6; Op. 68/2, 3 & 5; Op. 71/1, 3 & 6–7
(M) *** DG (ADD) 449 721-2. Gilels

With Gilels we are in the presence of a great keyboard master whose characterization and control of colour and articulation are wholly remarkable. An altogether outstanding record in every way. This recording has been admirably remastered for reissue in DG's 'Originals' series and now sounds better than ever.

Lyric Pieces: Op. 12/1, 4 & 5; Op. 38/1–2, 5 & 7; Op. 43/1, 4 & 6; Op. 47, 1–4; Op. 54/1–4; Op. 57/6; Op. 62/3, 4 & 6; Op. 65/5–6; Op. 68/9; Op. 71/3 & 7
(BB) *** Naxos 8.554051 Steen-Nøkleberg

A compilation disc for those who do not want to invest in all three of this artist's discs of the *Lyric Pieces*. Very distinguished playing, though not to be preferred to Gilels's anthology in the DG 'Originals' series.

Lyric Pieces: Op. 12/1, 6; Op. 38/5; Op. 54/1, 4 & 5; Op. 57/4, 6; Op. 62/3, 4 & 6; Op. 65/1–4; Op. 68/2, 4 & 5; Op. 71/1
**(*) Naxos 8.550650. Szokolay

Lyric Pieces: Op. 12/3, 8; Op. 38/1; Op. 43/1, 3 & 6; Op. 47/3–7; Op. 54/3, 5–6; Op. 57/1–3; Op. 62/1–2, 5; Op. 65/6; Op. 71/7
**(*) Naxos 8.550557. Szokolay

Naxos are not always lucky with their piano recordings, but the two CDs that Balázs Szokolay has recorded are very good. Szokolay's playing is not as consistently subtle in colouring or as poetic in feeling as that of Leif Ove Andsnes, but it is pretty idiomatic. However, at super-bargain price it is without doubt very good value indeed, and although the balance is very slightly close, it is not oppressively so. Both CDs give pleasure.

Lyric Pieces, Op. 12/1, 2, 3 & 6; Op. 18/6–8; Op. 47/1; Op. 54/3–4; Op. 57/2, 3 & 6; Op. 62/1, 4–6; Op. 65/6: Wedding Day at Troldhaugen; Op. 68/3; Op. 71/2, 6–7
🎧 ⚙ *** EMI 5 57296-2. Andsnes

The Op. 65 *Lyric Pieces* on the Andsnes bargain recital derive from the young Norwegian pianist's début recordings of the Grieg *A minor* and Liszt *A major Concertos*, while the remainder come from the following year when he was 22 years old. The playing has great freshness, and Andsnes almost succeeds in making listeners feel that they have not heard such oft-played pieces as *Butterfly*, *Solitary Wanderer*, *To Spring* or *Shepherd Boy* before. Andsnes commands great tonal subtlety and a wonderful range of keyboard colour, yet there is no pursuit of surface beauty at the expense of artistic truth. At its price, this is outstanding. But the later recital, performed on Grieg's own piano at the composer's villa in Troldhaugen, is very special indeed.

Lyric Pieces: Op. 12/3, 5, 7 & 8; Op. 38/1, 3 & 6; Opp. 43, 47 & 54; Op. 57; Opp. 62, 65, 68 & 71
(B) *** EMI Double forte (ADD) 5 68634-2 (2). Adni

Daniel Adni has also made a complete recording but, in order to fit the majority of the works on to two CDs (with a total playing time of 155 minutes), some of the earlier pieces from Books I and II have been omitted. Adni plays with genuine feeling for their character and a strong sense of atmosphere, and the 1973 EMI recording is very good indeed.

Lyric Pieces, Opp. 12/8; 38/1 & 6; 43/1 & 2; 47/1, 3 & 7; 54/3–4; 57/4, 5 & 6; 62/4; 68/2; 71/2–3
(B) *** CDK CDKM 1003. Pletnev

It is good to see this masterly Grieg recital return to circulation, as it contains playing of great poetic feeling and keen sensibility. It was briefly available on Melodiya in the late 1980s and, though by no means the equal of Gilels's famous anthology on DG in terms of recorded sound, was artistically a worthy successor. His *Klokkeklang* ('Bell Ringing') has a remarkable range of colour and dynamics, even though it is not as slow and mysterious as his BBC broadcast of much the same period. There are many individual insights: the quality of the *pianissimo* tone in *Hemmelighed* ('Secrecy'), Op. 57, No. 4, is a case in point, and the poignancy of *Hjemve* ('Homesickness') is eloquently conveyed. As usual with Pletnev nothing is routine and there is a concentration that gives these miniatures a freshness and depth that few artists can match. Even if you have the Gilels and Andsnes anthologies, you should not miss this. One had forgotten just how good this revealing recital is. If the distinction of the playing is not matched by the quality of the recorded sound, it is still eminently serviceable.

25 Norwegian Folk-Songs and Dances, Op. 17 1, 5, 7–8, 10, 12, 18, 19, 22, 24–25; Norwegian Folk Dances, Op. 66 1, 7–8, 12, 14–15, 18–19; Norwegian Peasant Dances, Op. 72 2, 7, 8, 14–16; Songs, Op. 41 1, 4, 6; Op. 52, 1–3
(B) *** Naim CD 059. Gimse

Håvard Gimse is among the most impressive and imaginative of Norwegian pianists, and he offers an expertly chosen anthology of dances from the Op. 17 set of 1870 and a handful of pieces from the much later Op. 66 and Op. 72 collections from 1896 and 1902. He also gives us half a dozen of Grieg's own song transcriptions. The lifelike recording (if slightly closely balanced) is made on a well-regulated Steinway in the fine acoustic of the Sofienberg Church in Oslo, and this is a most distinguished and satisfying addition to the Grieg discography.

VOCAL MUSIC

A cappella choral music: (i) At the Halvdan Kjerulf monument; Ave maris stella; Dona nobis pacem; (ii) 4 Psalms, Op. 74; Holberg Cantata. Male-voice choruses: Election song; Impromptu; Inga Litamor; The late rose; Westerly wind
*** Simax PSC 1187. (i) Sandve; (ii) Vollestad; Oslo Ph. Ch., Skiöld

Grieg's *a cappella* output is among the least known. This disc by the Oslo Philharmonic Choir offers a generous helping of it and presents it persuasively. His last work, the *Four Psalms*, Op. 74, dates from 1906 and is based on traditional tunes of popular Norwegian origin. The Oslo Philharmonic Choir produce a beautiful and well-blended sound. Good recording.

Orchestral songs: Album lines, Departed; En svane (The swan); Eros (orch. Reger); Fra Monte Pincio (orch. Grieg); Spillemænd (Fiddlers); The mountain thrall, Op. 26; The Princess; 4 Songs, Op. 60; 6 Songs, Op. 48; To the motherland. A vision (orch. Byl); With a water-lily. Peer Gynt: Solveig's cradle song
*** Dinemec DCCD022. Farley, LPO or Philh. O, Serebrier

This anthology collects 23 Grieg songs, three in the composer's own orchestrations but the vast majority in transcriptions by the conductor, José Serebrier. Some of them, like *Prinsessan (The Princess)* do not gain in the process, but the vast majority do, and Serebrier's orchestrations are both expert and idiomatic. Carole Farley does not use the white-toned, vibrato-free style favoured by some of the younger generation of Norwegian singers, but her disc is none the worse for that. Only occasionally is her vibrato obtrusive. For the most part she commands a wide expressive range and exhibits considerable feeling for the character of each of the songs. Moreover the orchestral support is sensitive and the recording well balanced.

Songs: At Rodane; A bird song; The first primrose; From Monte Pincio; Hope; I love but thee; I walked one balmy summer evening; Last spring; Margreta's cradle song; On the water; The Princess; Spring showers; A swan; To her II; Two brown eyes; Upon a grassy hillside. 4 Poems from Bjørnstjerne Bjørnson's Fishermaiden, Op. 21; 6 Songs, Op. 48; Peer Gynt: Solveig's song; Solveig's cradle song
(BB) **(*) Naxos 8.553781. Arnesen, Eriksen

An inexpensive and, at 70 minutes, well-filled CD, beautifully recorded and pleasingly sung. Bodil Arnesen has a voice of great purity and radiance. She sings marvellously in tune, though some may find that in this repertoire she has something of a 'little-girl', innocent quality that does not give the whole picture. This perhaps is troubling when you are listening to all the songs straight off. Taken a group at a time, she will touch most hearts, particularly in the setting of Bjørnson's *Prinsessen* and *Det første møte*. Erling Eriksen is an excellent accompanist.

Den Bergtekne, Op. 32; 10 Songs from Poems by A. O. Vinje, Op. 33 (orch. Søderlind)
(N) **(*) Claves 50-2310. Wallén, Helsingborg SO, Lintu –
    MAHLER: *Lieder eines fahrenden Gesellen* **(*)

Herman Wallén is a Finnish baritone in his mid-twenties who caused a stir at the third annual Sommets Musicaux in Gstaad in 2003. He gives us 10 of the 12 Op. 33 Vinje settings, albeit in an orchestral version by Ragnar Søderlind, and *The Mountain Thrall (Den Bergtekne)*, for which Grieg himself had a particularly soft spot – and rightly. It is not dissimilar in theme to Keats's *La Belle Dame sans Merci*, with the poet's bewitchment by a troll's daughter when he loses his way in the forest and is pursued by trolls, a lone human in a hostile environment. In her book on the songs, Beryl Foster calls it 'more of a miniature cantata than a song', and its scoring is unusual too, for baritone, two horns and strings. *The Mountain Thrall* is also the first time Grieg ventured into anything other than standard Norwegian, as he was later on to do in his settings of Garborg's *Haugtussa*. In 1880 he was much taken with the poems of Aasmund Olavson Vinje and his setting of the *Twelve Poems*, Op. 33, must be numbered among his most poetic and finest. This gifted young singer conveys their intensity of feeling very well indeed. His vocal timbre reminds one just a little of the young Håkan Hagegård, and he receives attentive support by the Helsingborg orchestra under the excellent Hannu Lintu. Decent recording.

Songs in historic performances (1888–1924): *Det første møte (First meeting); Den gamle vise (The old song); Dulgte kjaerlighed (Hidden love); Eine Traume (A dream); En fuglevis (A bird-song); En Svane (A swan); Eros; Fra Monte Pincio; God Morgen; Jag elsker Dig (I love thee); Jag reiste en deilig sommerkvaeld (I walked out one balmy summer evening); Killingdans (Kids' dance); Kongekvadet (The king's song); Margretas Vuggesang (Margreta's cradle song); Mens jeg venter (On the water); Moderen synger (The mother's lament); Norønnafolket (The Northland folk); Og jeg vil ha mig en Hjertenskaer (Midsummer eve); Ragnhild; Solveig's song; Solveigs vuggevise (Solveig's lullaby); Stambogsrim (Album lines); Takk for dit råd (Say what you will); Trudom (Faith); Våren (Spring); Vaer hilset I Damer (Greetings, fair ladies)*

(*(**)) Simax mono PSC 1810 (3). Ackté, Anselmi, Barrientos, Bryhn-Landgaard, Bronnum, Burg, Burzio, Bye, Chaliapin, Clément, Cornelius, Destinn, Eide, Elwes, Elizza, Farrar, Flagstad, Forsell, Galli-Curci, Gates, Gerhardt, Graarud, Gulbranson, Grieg, Hedemark, Heim, Hempel, Herold, Hultgren, Jadlowker, Kernic, Kline, Kruszelnicka, Lehmann, Lütken, Lykseth-Schjerven, Monrad, Ohman, Olitzka, Rethberg, Schumann-Heink, Scheidemantel, Slezak, Stückgold, Schwarz, Tauber, Tetrazzini (various pianists)

As the cast-list shows, this is a veritable treasure-house of singing at the beginning of the twentieth century, not only in northern Europe but elsewhere. Naturally in the early years of the gramophone, singers tended to gravitate towards a handful of songs so that familiar numbers such as *Jag elsker Dig* and *En Svane* turn up in several versions, the former 11 times and the latter seven. There are no fewer than 16 different versions of *Solveig's song*, including a few bars sung without accompaniment by Nina Grieg in 1889 when she would have been forty-four, and, although she is barely audible through the deluge of background noise, the voice is obviously of great purity. The roll-call is pretty dazzling, ranging as it does from big names such as Aino Ackté (for whom Sibelius composed *Luonnotar*), to Chaliapin and Emmy Destinn (the copy of her *Mens jeg venter* is unfortunately pretty rough) and there are 47 singers in all; but the less familiar names also offer valuable insights into performance practice. There are nearly 80 performances altogether, and the quality of the recordings which have been subjected to the NoNoise system of reduction calls for more tolerance than many listeners will feel able to extend. This is a set for libraries, specialist collectors and students of song, and it is an invaluable resource into which to dip.

4 Songs, Op. 14; 6 Songs, Op. 49; Songs from Peer Gynt
**(*) Victoria VCD 19038. Hirsti, Sandve, Skram, Jansen

Marianne Hirsti possesses a voice of great purity; her intonation is spot-on, and the overall sound radiates a childlike innocence. She is heard at her best in, say, *Margreta's cradle song*, one of the four songs of Op. 15 and Grieg's very first setting of Ibsen. Characterization, on the other hand, is not always her strong suit; all the same, it's a beautiful voice. Knut Skram has lost some of the bloom his voice once possessed – though none of his artistry or musical intelligence. Good recordings throughout.

Haugtussa (song-cycle), Op. 67; 6 Songs, Op. 48; Songs: *Beside the stream; Farmyard song; From Monte Pincio; Hope; I love but thee; Spring; Spring showers; A swan; Two brown eyes; While I wait; With a waterlily* (sung in Norwegian)
➤━◖ ✿ (M) *** DG Dig. 476 18157. Von Otter, Forsberg

This recital of Grieg's songs by Anne Sofie von Otter and Bengt Forsberg is rather special. Von Otter commands an exceptionally wide range of colour and quality, and in Forsberg she has a highly responsive partner. Altogether a captivating recital, and beautifully recorded, too; it rightly won the *Gramophone* Solo Vocal Award in 1993 and was also the magazine's 'Record of the Year'. It now reappears in Universal's 'Gramophone Award Collection' at mid-price, with full documentation included.

Peer Gynt (incidental music), Op. 23 (complete); Sigurd Jorsalfar (incidental music), Op. 56 (complete)
(N) (M) *** DG (IMS) 475 5433-2 (2). Bonney, Eklöf, Sandve, Malmberg, Holmgren; Foss, Maurstad, Stokke (speakers); Gösta Ohlin's Vocal Ens., Pro Musica Chamber Ch., Gothenburg SO, Järvi

Neeme Järvi's recording differs from its predecessor by Per Dreier in offering the Grieg Gesamtausgabe *Peer Gynt*, which bases itself primarily on the 26 pieces he included in the 1875 production rather than the final, published score, prepared after Grieg's death by Halvorsen. This well-documented set comes closer to the original by including spoken dialogue, as one would have expected in the theatre. The CDs also offer the complete *Sigurd Jorsalfar* score, which includes some splendid music. The performances by actors, singers (solo and choral) and orchestra alike are exceptionally vivid, with the warm Gothenburg ambience used to creative effect; the vibrant histrionics of the spoken words undoubtedly add to the drama. Full texts and translations are included.

Peer Gynt: extended excerpts
(N) *** Virgin 5 45 722-2. Mattei, Tilling, Hellekant, Ellerhein Girls' Ch., Estonian Nat. SO & Male Ch., Paavo Järvi
(N) (M) *** Decca 476 7260. Haeggander, Mainberg, San Francisco Ch. & SO, Blomstedt
(B) *** Sony SBK 89898. Hendricks, Oslo PO Ch. & O, Salonen

Peer Gynt: extended excerpts; Bridal Procession, Op. 19/2; 4 Norwegian Dances
(N) (M) *** RCA 82876 65834-2. Dam-Jensen, L. Symphony Ch., RPO, Temirkanov

Paavo Järvi conducts his Estonian forces in warmly expressive, full-blooded readings of 20 items from Grieg's complete *Peer Gynt* music. There are several discs which offer more than the two popular orchestral suites, but Järvi's selection is more generous than most of them, simply omitting the items where spoken words predominate. His principal rival is his father, Neeme Järvi, whose DG set of the complete *Peer Gynt* music stands supreme, with actors playing an important part, and this has now been reissued at mid-price. If Järvi Sr is a degree cooler and more restrained and captures the folk element more vividly, Paavo compensates in the extra warmth of his performances, helped by full, forward sound, recorded in a rather reverberant acoustic. His account of the celebrated number, *In the Hall of the Mountain King*, is even more exciting than that of his father, with a wild accelerando and vigorous vocal contributions. Though their roles are limited, the three soloists are first rate, with the baritone, Peter Mattei, giving a virile portrait of Peer Gynt in his *Serenade*.

Blomstedt's selection on Decca makes yet another useful alternative. All but about 15 minutes of the complete score is here, and the spoken text is also included, all admirably performed. If the Estonian acoustic may be preferred to the Davies Hall, San Francisco, and if there is a marginally greater sense of theatre with Neeme Järvi, there is little to choose between them; the Decca recording approaches the demonstration class. Moreover, the Decca reissue (part of the 'Critics' Choice' series, as it was chosen on BBC Radio 3 for 'Building a Record Library') now comes with full documentation at mid-price.

Even though this repertoire is so well served on CD, Temirkanov's fine RCA disc should not be passed by. He seems to have an innate feeling for Grieg, and this is one of his very finest records. He offers 16 numbers from *Peer Gynt* and has a vigorous response from the London Symphony Chorus (who are enthusiastically angry trolls in *The Hall of the Mountain King*), while he conjures most sensitive playing from the RPO. There are also three lovely vocal contributions from Inger Dam-Jensen. Moreover, he also includes sprightly, colourful and dramatic accounts of the *Four Norwegian Dances*, while the delightful *Bridal Procession* is a closing lollipop. The resonance means that the choral focus is not absolutely sharp, but in all other respects the recording is excellent.

Salonen offers some 17 numbers in all, all those included in the suites plus various other shorter pieces. The orchestral playing is excellent, the style idiomatic and anyone wanting to invest in this inexpensive collection with Barbara Hendricks and the Oslo Philharmonic Chorus is unlikely to be disappointed. The recording is of very good quality.

(i) *Peer Gynt*: excerpts. *In Autumn* (overture)*; An Old Norwegian Romance with Variations; Symphonic Dance 2*
☛ ✪ (M) *** EMI 5 66914-2 [5 66966-2]. (i) Hollweg, Beecham Ch. Soc.; RPO, Beecham

Beecham showed a very special feeling for this score, and to hear *Morning*, the gently textured *Anitra's Dance* or the eloquent portrayal of the *Death of Aase* under his baton is a uniquely rewarding experience. Ilse Hollweg makes an excellent soloist. The recording dates from 1957 and, like most earlier Beecham reissues, has been enhanced by the remastering process. The most delectable of the *Symphonic Dances*, very beautifully played, makes an ideal encore after *Solveig's Lullaby*, affectingly sung by Hollweg. The *In Autumn* overture, not one of Grieg's finest works, is most enjoyable when Sir Thomas is so persuasive, not shirking the melodramatic moments. Finally for the present reissue, we are offered *An Old Norwegian Romance with Variations* (not previously released in its stereo format). It is a piece of much colour and charm, which is fully realized here.

Peer Gynt (incidental music): *Overture; Suites 1-2. Lyric Pieces: Evening in the Mountain; Cradle Song; Sigurd Jorsalfar: Suite, Op. 56; Wedding Day at Troldhaugen, Op. 65/6*
(BB) **(*) Naxos 8.550140. CSSR State PO, Košice, Gunzenhauser

A generous Grieg anthology on Naxos (70 minutes, all but 3 seconds) and the performances by the Slovak State Philharmonic Orchestra in Košice are very fresh and lively and thoroughly enjoyable. There is wide dynamic range both in the playing and in the recording, and sensitivity in matters of phrasing.

Peer Gynt Suite 1; Suite 2: Solveig's Song
*** Sony (ADD) **SACD** SS 89414. Cleveland O, Szell – BIZET: *L'Arlésienne: Suite 1*; MUSSORGSKY: *Pictures; Khovanshchina: Prelude* ***

The refinement of the orchestral playing under Szell is very striking. The *Death of Aase* is movingly done, with a superbly hushed *pianissimo* at the end; *Anitra's Dance* is no less impressive, with subtle control of light and shade, and *Solveig's Song* is ravishing. The early (1966) recording has been transferred to CD most skilfully: the upper range is very slightly restricted to add warmth and smoothness to the string-tone, but the ambient warmth and overall vividness remain.

GRIFFES, Charles Tomlinson
(1884–1920)

Bacchanale; Clouds; The Pleasure-Dome of Kubla-Khan; (i) *Poem for Flute and Orchestra. 3 Tone-Pictures (The Lake at Evening; The Vale of Dreams; The Night Winds); The White Peacock.* (ii) *3 Poems of Fiona McLeod (The Lament of Ian the Proud; The Dark Eyes to Mine; The Rose of the Night)*
☛ (BB) *** Naxos 8.559164. Buffalo PO, Falletta; with (i) Wincenc; (ii) Quintiliani

This invaluable disc gives a warm and colourful portrait of this late-romantic American composer, sadly short lived. It includes not only his three best-known orchestral works, but a clutch of rarities as well, otherwise unavailable on disc. Most of these started as piano pieces, which Griffes orchestrated, yet such was the composer's mastery over evocative tone-painting that one would never guess that. Griffes was the first US composer to respond to the call of Impressionism. In 1903 he studied in Berlin with Humperdinck, turned his main interest towards composition and returned four years later to the United States, taking a job as a music teacher. The shimmering beauty of his writing matches that of Debussy on the one hand, Delius on the other, with his inspiration regularly coming from English literature, Coleridge in *Kubla Khan*, Fiona McLeod (William Sharp) in *The White Peacock*, as well as in the three songs, and W. B. Yeats in the first of the *Three Tone Pictures*. Apart from Debussy and Ravel, Griffes was drawn to Mussorgsky and Scriabin, as well as to oriental music. *The White Peacock* (1915) comes from a suite for piano (*Four Roman Sketches*), which he later scored for orchestra. *The Pleasure-Dome of Kubla Khan* (1919) and the *Poem for Flute and Orchestra* (1918) are probably his masterpieces. Performances here are outstanding and very well recorded, with JoAnn Falletta as music director of the Buffalo Philharmonic drawing refined and atmospheric performances from her players, with Barbara Quintiliani as the bright soloist in the songs and Carol Wincenc, principal flute in the orchestra, a most sympathetic soloist in the *Poem*. This fine compilation fills an important gap in the catalogue.

GROFÉ, Ferde (1892–1972)

Death Valley Suite; Hollywood Suite; Hudson River Suite
(BB) *** Naxos 8.559017. Bournemouth SO, Stromberg

It is good to find a triptych of Grofé's descriptive orchestral suites which are more imaginative than usual. The *Hollywood Suite* (1938), originally conceived as a ballet, is a musical tribute to the Hollywood of the 1930s and has some unexpected cameos. *Carpenters and Electricians* depicts the flurry of activity involved in the building of sets, while *Production Number* genially reflects the work's balletic origins. In both the *Death Valley* and *Hudson River Suites*, Grofé's descriptive scoring is always telling, and the swirling Hudson river theme ebbs and flows quite powerfully, with the ensuing movements portraying various characters or scenes, including a vivid portrayal of *Rip Van Winkle*, while the evocative *Albany Night Boat* has its spell shattered by the *New York* finale. The *Death Valley Suite* (1949) shares the pictorial world of *Grand Canyon*. If not quite matching the latter's inspiration, it portrays the scorching heat of this notorious desert, while the *Forty-niner Emigrant Train*, with its opening screeching strings, melodramatically sets the scene: a group of settlers lost in the desert, dying of thirst and hunger, with menacing Indians lurking. Mercifully for them, the next movement is the *Desert Water Hole*, though – bad luck again – the finale is a *Sand Storm*. William Stromberg and his Bournemouth orchestra play with enthusiasm, and the engineers provide vivid and often spectacular sound. This may all be ingenuous, but much of it is diverting. Excellent documentation too.

Grand Canyon Suite
(N) (M) *** Telarc CD 80086 (with additional cloudburst, including real thunder). Cincinnati Pops O, Kunzel – GERSHWIN: *Catfish Row* ***
☛— (M) *** Sony **SACD** SS 89033; SMK 63086. NYPO, Bernstein – GERSHWIN: *An American in Paris*, etc. *** ✪

The Cincinnati performance is played with great commitment and fine pictorial splendour. What gives the Telarc CD its special edge is the inclusion of a second performance of *Cloudburst* as an appendix with a genuine thunderstorm laminated on to the orchestral recording. The result is overwhelmingly thrilling, except that in the final thunderclap God quite upstages the orchestra, who are left trying frenziedly to match its amplitude in their closing peroration.

Bernstein treats the music as if it was a masterpiece of orchestral impressionism, while the famous *On the Trail* (John Corigliano the solo fiddler) has never sounded more infectiously witty. The closing storm has real spectacle, powerfully generated by the orchestral playing itself. The recording has never sounded half as good is it does here, especially in the remastered SACD version.

Grand Canyon Suite; Mississippi Suite; Niagara Falls Suite
(BB) ** Naxos 8.559007. Bournemouth SO, Stromberg

These are well-played performances although they only emphasize that the music of the *Mississippi* and *Niagara Falls Suites* does not match *Grand Canyon*, and the only hit here is *On the Trail*. The recording is good but has nothing like the spectacular quality of Bernstein's version.

GRUENBERG, Louis (1884–1964)

Violin Concerto, Op. 47
(BB) (**) Naxos mono 8.110942. Heifetz, San Francisco SO, Monteux – PROKOFIEV: *Violin Concerto 2* (***)

Commissioned by Heifetz, Louis Gruenberg, best known for his opera, *The Emperor Jones*, wrote his *Violin Concerto* in 1943. A massive 40-minute work, it has some warmly attractive material in a slightly jazzy idiom, and formidably exploits violin technique to stretch even Heifetz. But it seriously outlasts its welcome with much empty doodling. A comfortable transfer of the limited (1945) sound.

GUERRERO, Francisco (1528–99)

Missa de la batalla escoutez; Conditor alme siderum; Duo Seraphim clamabant (motet); In exitus Israel; Magnificat octavi toni; Pange lingua gloriosi; Regina coeli laetari, Alleluia (instrumental version)
*** Hyp. CDA 67075. Westminster Cathedral Ch., His Majestys Sackbutts and Cornetts, O'Donnell

The performances here (even in the *Mass*) use brass instruments as well as voices, following the *alternatim* style, which was a particular feature of Guerrero's music, where plainchant regularly alternates with polyphony. The Trinity motet, *Duo Seraphim*, opening descriptively with two solo trebles, uses twelve voices in three choirs to create wide contrasts of dynamic and texture. The *Missa de la batalla*, for five voices, uses a chanson of Jannequin, *La guerra*, as its basis, indicated by including the French word '*escoutez*' in its title. *Pange lingua gloriosi* uses a popular melody, a gently swinging Iberian song, ornamented with counterpoint, and moving from voice to voice, in many ways like a primitive theme and variations. Throughout the disc, the eloquent singing and very well-balanced, never overwhelming brass choir make this a varied and highly enjoyable introduction to a remarkable composer, of whom we shall surely discover much more.

Missa pro defunctis (Requiem) & Burial Service
(N) *** Glossa GCD 920012. Vocal Ens., O of Renaissance, Noone
Missa pro defunctis; 5 Vespers Psalms for the Feast of All Saints; Magnificat; Motet: O Domine Jesu Christe
(N) *** Signum SIDCD 017. Chappelle du Roi

Guerrero's *Requiem* was first published in 1566, to be replaced by a revised version in 1582 which followed the liturgical reforms brought about by the Council of Trent. It is this later version which Michael Noone and his ensemble perform on this Glossa CD, seeking to re-create the complete Burial Service that might have been used for the composer himself in Seville Cathedral when he died in 1599. The additional plainsong is of course conjectural, and there are extra musical interpolations too, like the *Pater noster* of Josquin Desprez; and the whole ceremony ends with the plainchant antiphon, *In paradisum*. In accordance with late sixteenth-century practice in Seville, brass instruments are added to the sonority, and the effect in the echoing acoustic of St Jude-on-the-Hill, Hampstead, is magnificent, if rather extended.

For collectors preferring to have the *Requiem* without the considerable amount of additional plainchant, Alistair Dixon and his Chappelle du Roi offer a much plainer version, based on the original, unrevised score – and, of course, without the brass. This is very beautiful in a more austere way, but it is also much shorter, and means that they have space on their disc to offer Guerrero's lovely settings of the five *Vespers Psalms for the Feast of All Saints*. The fifth of these, *Laudate Dominum*, closes with a lovely *Gloria Patri* and then, to end the traditional celebration of Vespers, Dixon uses the hymn, *Christe redemptor omnium*, and Guerrero's climactic *Magnificat*, both haunting and joyful. The serene motet for Palm Sunday, *O Domine Jesu Christe*, then acts as a radiant interlude before the mood darkens for the *Missa pro defunctis*. Beautifully recorded, this is yet another imaginative enterprise of the Chappelle du Roi on Signum and it can be cordially recommended, even though one misses the additional brass.

Missa Sancta et immaculata; Hei mihi, Domine; Lauda mater ecclesia; Magnificat septimi toni; O lux beata Trinitas; Trahe me post te, Virgo Maria; Vexilla Regis
*** Hyp. CDA 66910. Westminster Cathedral Ch., O'Donnell

Guerrero's *Missa Sancta et immaculata* is based on the celebrated four-part motet of that name by his one-time master, Christóbal de Morales. It comes from his *Liber primus missarum* which was published in Paris in 1566. The two serene motets, *Hei mihi, Domine* and *Trahe me post te, Virgo Maria*, come from the second book of Masses (1582) and the three hymns, *Vexilla Regis*, composed for Passion Sunday, *O lux beata Trinitas* and the spirited *Lauda mater ecclesia*, are of striking quality and character. The Westminster Cathedral Choir and James O'Donnell give performances of quite outstanding eloquence and purity. The recording is first class and there are exemplary notes by Bruno Turner.

GUILMANT, Félix Alexandre
(1837–1911)

Symphony 1 for Organ & Orchestra, Op. 42
*** Chan. 9271. Tracey (organ of Liverpool Cathedral), BBC PO, Tortelier – WIDOR: *Symphony 5* ***; POULENC: *Organ Concerto* **(*)

This Guilmant *Symphony* (the composer's own arrangement of his *First Organ Sonata*) is a real find, with all the genial vigour of the famous work of Saint-Saëns. The first movement has a galumphing main theme and an equally pleasing secondary idea. It is followed by a tunefully idyllic *Pastorale* (with some delicious registration from Ian Tracey) and a rumbustiously grandiloquent finale. All great fun, and well suited to the larger-than-life resonance of Liverpool Cathedral with its long reverberation period.

Symphony 2 for Organ & Orchestra, Op. 91
*** Chan. 9785. Tracey (organ of Liverpool Cathedral), BBC PO, Tortelier – FRANCK: *Choral 2*; WIDOR: *Symphony 3* ***

Guilmant's *Second Symphony* is a hugely effective transcription of his *Eighth Organ Sonata*. It opens gently with an anticipatory, fanfare-like figure on the violins; then, after the grandiose organ entry with tutti, the allegro sets off with infectious vigour. The *Adagio con affetto* is romantic but still reminds us we are in a cathedral, as does the shorter *Andante sostenuto*, which follows the rumbustious Scherzo. The finale opens evocatively and then becomes instantly animated, working towards a splendidly grandiloquent ending. The performance has great gusto and, if the wide resonance of Liverpool Cathedral prevents any chance of internal clarity, it

certainly gives the music a superb impact. Full marks to the Chandos engineers.

GURNEY, Ivor (1890–1937)

Songs: *All night under the moon; An epitaph; Bread and cherries; By a bierside; The cloths of Heaven; Cradle song; Desire in spring; Down by the Salley Gardens; Epitaph in old mode; 5 Elizabethan Songs; Even such is time; The fields are full; The folly of being comforted; Hanacker mill; In Flanders; I will go with my father a-ploughing; Most holy night; Nine of the clock; Severn Meadows; The singer; You are my sky*
*** Hyp. CDA 67243. Agnew, Drake

Ivor Gurney was born in Gloucester and became a chorister at the cathedral, later studying composition under Stanford and (after his wartime service) Vaughan Williams. Soldiering in the trenches in the First World War ruined his physical health, and probably led to a later mental deterioration and eventually complete mental collapse. But during his comparatively short creative life he composed over 300 songs, the best of which are among the finest settings in the English language, their pervasive dolorous mood often drawing parallels with Dowland.

The *Five Elizabethan Songs* of 1913–14 are already establishing the melancholy quality of his melodic lines (even *Under the greenwood tree* is nostalgic in feeling). The wartime songs also include an intensely emotional Masefield setting, *By the bierside*, while *In Flanders* is full of longing for the Severn Hills. The rich lyricism of *The fields are full of summer* and *The cloths of Heaven* and the gentle evocation of *Down by the Salley Gardens* are touching in a very direct way, the music's aura consistent in its pastoral evocation. Paul Agnew moulds the melodic lines with great sensitivity, his use of vocal colour illuminating the words, and Julius Drake accompanies with natural understanding. The recording is excellent, and this is another fine addition to the Hyperion treasure-house of vocal recordings.

PIANO MUSIC

Nocturnes: in A flat; B. 4 Unpublished Pieces: Despair; The Sea; Sehnsuch (Longing); Song of the Summer Woods. Preludes 1–9
(N) (M) **(*) Somm CD038. Bebbington – FERGUSON: *Bagatelles; Sonata* ***

Ivor Gurney is remembered more for his songs (he was also a poet) than for his piano music. The four unpublished pieces written when he was in his late teens show a strong poetic feeling and, though the idiom is eclectic, there is a real emerging musical personality and a strong sense of Englishness. Most of these pieces cast a certain spell, despite a limited range of moods. Mark Bebbington plays them very sensitively.

GYROWETZ, Adalbert (1763–1850)

Symphonies: in E flat; F, Op. 6/2–3; in D, Op. 12/1
*** Chan. 9791. LMP, Bamert

The Bohemian composer Adalbert Gyrowetz, a talented contemporary of Haydn and Mozart, outlived both of them. The Gyrowetz symphonies are delightful, full of characterfully individual invention, with Gyrowetz adding *galant* touches of his own. The engaging bravura horn solo in the Trio of the Minuet of Op. 6/2 is truly Bohemian, as is the genial opening movement of Op. 6/3, while the *Andante* soon produces a winning arioso for the oboe, followed by a bouncing half Scherzo, half Ländler and a Haydnesque finale. There are catchy ideas too in the *Andante* of the later *D major Symphony* and again in the nicely scored finale. In short, these are most enjoyable works and they are played (on modern instruments) with great elegance and sparkle and are beautifully recorded. Well worth seeking out.

HADLEY, Henry Kimball (1871–1937)

The Culprit Fay (Rhapsody), Op. 62; The Ocean, Op. 99; Symphony 4 in D min., Op. 64

(BB) **(*) Naxos 8.559064. Ukraine Nat. SO, McLaughlin Williams

Another issue in Naxos's enterprising American Classics series. Hadley's music is very much in the European Romantic tradition, and the 1921 tone-poem, *The Ocean*, is full of melodrama, thundering timpani and sea effects (the poem on which it is based is included in the sleeve-notes). Though this style of writing is not too far away from a Hollywood film score of the 1930s or '40s, it is no less effective for that, especially when it is so colourfully orchestrated. *The Culprit Fay*, wth its evocative string-writing at the opening, portrays the magical, airy quality of Joseph Drake's poem depicting the adventures of a fairy. There is more attractive colouring in this delicate, animated score, and it sustains its 15 minutes remarkably well. The *Fourth Symphony* was composed for the Norfolk, Connecticut Festival and was first performed in 1911. It comes with a programme portraying different parts of America (the four movements are entitled *North, South, East* and *West*) though, curiously, the second movement is described as an 'Oriental tone-picture' and is predictably exotic. If far from a masterpiece, it is entertaining and ingenuously tuneful. The performances here are enthusiastic, and the recording vivid, though the violins tend to sound a bit under-nourished above the stave.

HADLEY, Patrick (1899–1973)

(i) *Lenten Cantata. The cup of blessing; I sing of a maiden; My beloved spake; A Song for Easter*

*** ASV CDDCA 881. (i) Mark Ainsley, Sweeney; Ch. of Gonville & Caius College, Cambridge, Webber; Hill or Phillips (organ) – RUBBRA: *Choral Music* ***

The most substantial piece here is the *Lenten Cantata* or *Lenten Meditations* for two soloists, choir and orchestra (here given in an organ transcription), composed in 1963. Not a strongly individual voice, Hadley is nevertheless a refined craftsman whose feeling for line and texture is highly developed. The performances are of high quality, and so is the recording.

HAHN, Reynaldo (1875–1947)

Le Bal de Béatrice d'Este (ballet suite)

(BB) *** Hyp. Helios CDH 55167. New L. O, Corp –
POULENC: *Aubade; Sinfonietta* ***

Le Bal de Béatrice d'Este is a charming pastiche, dating from the early years of the century and scored for the unusual combination of wind instruments, two harps, piano and timpani. Ronald Corp and the New London Orchestra play it with real panache and sensitivity. This is welcome back to the catalogue on Hyperion's budget label.

Piano Concerto in E

*** Hyp. CDA 66897. Coombs, BBC Scottish SO, Ossonce –
MASSENET: *Piano Concerto* ***

Entitled *Improvisation*, the opening movement of this charming work starts with a theme which surprisingly has an English flavour, easily lyrical, leading on to variations full of sharp, sparkling contrasts. A brief, light-hearted Scherzo leads to a combined slow movement (*Reverie*) and finale (*Toccata*). What Stephen Coombs's inspired performance demonstrates, most sympathetically supported by Jean-Yves Ossonce with the BBC Scottish Symphony, is that, though no deep emotions are touched, this is a delightful piece, well worth reviving, here perfectly coupled with another concerto also uncharacteristic of its composer and written late in his career.

CHAMBER MUSIC

Nocturne in E flat for Violin and Piano; Piano Quartet 3 in G; Romance; Si mes vers avaient des ailes (trans. for cello and piano); *Soliloque et Forlane for Viola and Piano; Violin Sonata in C*

*** Hyp. CDA 67391. Room-Music

Recent years have brought a welcome resurgence of interest in Reynaldo Hahn, for we have had generous attention paid not only to the songs but also to such chamber works as the *F sharp minor Piano Quintet* and the *String Quartets*. Stephen Coombs, who is the pianist of Room-Music, has proved a persuasive advocate of the composer in the *Piano Concerto* and the *Quintet* and here he plays with great sensitivity and intelligence. So, too, do his companions, the violinist Charles Sewart, violist Yuko Inoe and Philip de Groote, cellist of the Chilingirian Quartet. The *C major Violin Sonata* of 1926 breathes much the same air as the Fauré of the *Piano Quartets* and the *A major Sonata*; and much the same goes for the shorter pieces: the *Romance* and the *Nocturne*. Both come from the first decade of the last century and the charming *Soliloque et Forlane* from 1936.

The *Piano Quartet No. 3* was composed on the composer's return to France. He had been forced to flee Paris in 1940 as he was part-Jewish – though he was born in Venezuela – and he spent the war in the somewhat safer environment of Cannes. But this work reflects nothing of the darkness of the times. Its slow movement has all the enchantment of a balmy Mediterranean night. Jeremy Filsell's note speaks of the 'uncomplicated and radiant freshness' of Hahn's music. It has fluency and grace, and an innocent delight in life. Hahn's own transcription for cello and piano of the setting of Victor Hugo's *Si mes vers avaient des ailes*, which he had composed when he was thirteen, acts as a kind of encore to the recital.

Piano Quintet in F sharp min.

*** Hyp. CDA 67258. Coombs, Chilingirian Qt – VIERNE:
Piano Quintet ***

Hahn's *Piano Quintet* makes a striking contrast to its companion on this disc. Apart from the finale, which is a bit manufactured, its invention is both compelling and fresh, although the debt to Fauré (not so much the later music as the Fauré of the *A major Sonata* and the *Piano Quartets*) is pervasive. Civilized discourse, though not as deeply felt as the Vierne. Stephen Coombs and the Chilingirians play with conviction and character, and are given the benefit of present and vivid recorded sound.

(i) Piano Quintet in F min.; String Quartets 1 in A min.; 2 in F

**(*) Naïve V 4848. (i) Tharaud; Quatuor Parisii

The *Piano Quintet* is persuasively played here, particularly by the pianist, Alexandre Tharaud, who is well inside its sensibility, and it is a pity that the recording of the strings does not produce riper textures. The *Second Quartet*, ambitiously modelled on the Franck *Quartet*, was never published, but has a memorably atmospheric slow movement, the strings muted throughout. The *First Quartet* is a thoughtful, delicate evocation of considerable Gallic charm, with a yearning *Andantino* and a light-hearted finale. It is played most appealingly, and here the recording is better balanced and more naturally integrated.

Mélodies

L'Air; A Chloris; L'Automne; 7 Chansons grises; La Chère Blessure; D'une prison; L'Enamourée; Les Etoiles; Fêtes galantes; Les Fontaines; L'Incrédule; Infidélité; Offrande; Quand je fus pris au pavillon; Si mes vers avaient des ailes; Tyndaris

(BB) ******* Hyp. Helios CDH 55040. Hill, Johnson

If Hahn never quite matched the supreme inspiration of his most famous song, *Si mes vers avaient des ailes*, the delights here are many, the charm great. Martyn Hill, ideally accompanied by Graham Johnson, gives delicate and stylish performances, well recorded. The reissue on the Helios bargain label should tempt collectors to sample this attractive repertoire, particularly when full translations are included.

L'Air; Chansons grises; D'une prison; L'Enamourée; Les Fontaines; L'Incrédule; Je me metz en vostre mercy; La Nuit; Quand je fus pris au pavillon; Le Rossignol des lilas; Seule; Si mes vers avaient des ailes; Le Souvenir d'avoir chanté

(BB) ******* Virgin 2×1 5 61433-2. Yakar, Lavoix – FAURE: *Mélodies* *******

Rachel Yakar with her warm, very French-sounding timbre is an ideal interpreter of the songs of Hahn, Bizet and Chabrier (listed under the Fauré coupling) on this second disc of the well-conceived bargain-priced Double. It is a pity that in this reissue no texts are given, but Yakar's way of bringing out the subtleties of word-meaning goes with beautifully clear diction. Though Hahn cannot match the other composers in depth or imagination, his facile genius in 19 songs, including the seven *Chansons grises*, setting Verlaine, and the most popular of all, a teenage inspiration, *Si mes vers avaient des ailes*, brings many delights. Excellent (1988) recording from Radio France.

A Chloris; Au rossignol; Les Cygnes; D'une prison; Fêtes galantes; L'Heure exquise; Infidélité; Je me souviens; Mai; Ma jeunesse; Nocturne; La Nymphe de la Source; Offrande; Paysage; Le Plus Beau Présent; Puisque j'ai mis ma lèvre; Quand la nuit n'est pas étoilée; Rêverie; Le Rossignol des lilas; Séraphine; Seule; Si mes vers avaient des ailes; Sur l'eau; Trois jours de vendange. Ciboulette: C'est sa banlieue (Y a des arbres); Non avons fait un beau voyage. O mon bel

inconnu: C'est très vilain d'être infidèle. 10 Etudes Latines; 12 Rondels. Mozart (musical comedy): Air de la lettre. Une Revue: La Dernière (valse)

*** Hyp. CDA 67141/2. Lott, Bickley, Bostridge, Varcoe, L. Schubert Chorale, Layton, Johnson

This is the most comprehensive collection of Hahn songs ever recorded, including a number of items never available before and even items from stage works. As in his Schubert edition for Hyperion, Graham Johnson masterminds the project to give endless new insights, whether in his ideal choice of soloists, his inspired playing or his illuminating notes. Specially valuable are the ten *Etudes latines*, both pure and sensuous in their classical evocation. Fine, atmospheric sound.

'La Belle Epoque': Mélodies: A Chloris; L'Automne; D'une prison; L'Enamourée; Dans la nuit; Fêtes galantes; Les Fontaines; Fumée; L'Heure exquise; Infidélité; Je me souviens; Mai; Nocturne; Offrande; Paysage; Le Printemps; Quand je fus pris au pavillon; Quand la nuit n'est pas étoilée; Le Rossignol des lilas; Si mes vers avaient des ailes; Trois jours de vendange. Etudes Latines: Lydé; Phyllis; Tyndaris

*** Sony SK 60168. Graham, Vignoles

The solemnity of Susan Graham's first song, *A Chloris*, with its Bachian pastiche may surprise those who think of Hahn as merely a dilettante tunesmith, and Graham finds the fullest range of expression in this charming collection. Hahn may fail to bring out the poignancy behind the Verlaine poem, *D'une prison*, but within his limited range he is a master. A good single-disc choice, made the more attractive by the glowing beauty of Graham's voice, sensuous in the most famous song, *Si mes vers avaient des ailes*. Fine, sensitive accompaniment from Roger Vignoles.

HALÉVY, Jacques Fromental
(1799–1862)

La Juive (complete; DVD version)

(N) ******* DG **DVD** 073 4001 (2). Shicoff, Stoyanova, Ivan, Zhang, Fink, Daniel, V. State Op. Ch. & O, Sutej (V/D: Johannes Muller – described as the DVD Producer, no video director identified)

Recorded at the Vienna State Opera in 2003, Gunter Kramer's production of Halévy's most famous opera seeks to make the story of Jewish persecution in 1414 relevant to today by updating it broadly to the twentieth century. With Gentile characters and the chorus wearing Austrian traditional costume, '*Trachten*', the date becomes slightly ambiguous. The central character of Eleazar, the Jew, is very much a figure such as the Nazis might have condemned, a characterization that Neil Shicoff relishes (as he does in the earlier CD set), singing nobly. His daughter, Rachel (touchingly sung by Krassimira Stoyanova), is later revealed to be adopted and in fact a Gentile, daughter of Eleazar's enemy, Cardinal de Brogni, powerfully sung by Walter Fink. The love between Rachel and Prince Leopold, disguised as a Jewish painter, becomes central, with self-sacrifice a recurrent theme over the five Acts. Though Jianyi Zhang as Leopold is hardly a romantic figure, he sings with freshness and clarity, his tenor well contrasted with that of Shicoff. Simina Ivan as Princess Eudoxie sings with sweetness and poise, and Boaz Daniel is fine as Ruggiero, firm and dark. The production involves an upper stage set at an angle, with minimal scenery. Vjekoslav Sutej draws warmly expressive playing and singing from the orchestra and chorus, making the most of melodramatic situations even when backed by less than inspired music. Bright, forward sound. The second disc contains an hour-long bonus in two films, 'Finding Eleazar', a portrait of Shicoff, and a film of Shicoff singing one of his big arias as directed by Sidney Lumet in New York.

La Juive (opera): (complete; CD version)
** RCA 74321 79596-2 (3). Isokoski, Shicoff, Schorg, Todorovic, Gati, Miles, Vienna State Op. Ch & O, Young

La Juive ('The Jewess') was the piece that, along with the vast works of Meyerbeer, set the pattern for the epic French opera, so popular in the nineteenth century. Eléazar was the last role that the great tenor, Enrico Caruso, tackled.

Although there is some strong, stylish singing from the principals – Soile Isokoski in the title role, Neil Shicoff as her father, Eleazar, the welcome newcomer, Regina Schorg, as the Princess, and Alastair Miles as the Cardinal – this radio recording from the Vienna State Opera is no substitute for the deleted Philips set with Julia Varady and José Carreras. Such subsidiary roles as Leopold and Ruggiero, sung respectively by the strained Zoran Todorovic and the wobbly Istvan Gati, let the set down, with the conductor, Simone Young, less dramatic than Antonio de Almeida. The absence of a libretto is a serious flaw, particularly when it makes it harder to identify which passages are cut. RCA offers the Princess's aria in the opening scene but cuts the whole of the ballet music, part of which was included on Philips.

HALVORSEN, Johan (1864–1935)

Air norvégien, Op. 7; Danses norvégiennes
(BB) *** Naxos 8.550329. Kang, Slovak (Bratislava) RSO, Leaper – SIBELIUS: Violin Concerto; SINDING: Légende; SVENDSEN: Romance ***

Dong-Suk Kang plays the attractive Danses norvégiennes with great panache, character and effortless virtuosity, and delivers an equally impeccable performance of the earlier Air norvégien.

Askeladden: Suite; Gurre (Dramatic Suite), Op. 17; The Merchant of Venice: Suite
*** Simax PSC 1198. Latvian Nat. SO, Mikkelsen

Festival March; Kongen (The King): Suite; Tordenskjold (Suite); Vasantasena: Suite
*** Simax PSC 1199. Latvian Nat. SO, Mikkelsen

Halvorsen composed extensively for the stage. The suite from The Merchant of Venice on the first CD is second-rate salon stuff, but that is the only disappointment. The music to Holger Drachmann's play Gurre is not only expertly laid out for the orchestra but delightfully fresh. The idiom is indebted to Grieg but he obviously knew his Berlioz and Svendsen. Sommernatsbryllup ('Summer night's wedding') has much charm and brilliance and so has the opening Aftenlandskap ('Evening scene'), an atmospheric and appealing piece. Askeladden is a play for children, and the suite recorded here has abundant charm. The second disc brings music for Bjørnstjerne Bjørnson's play, Kongen ('The King'), whose delightful second movement, Hyrdepigernes Dans ('Dance of the Shepherdesses') is quite irresistible; it is difficult to get it out of your head. Vasantasena aspires to an oriental exoticism which

is quite endearing and charming. The Latvian National Orchestra play splendidly for Terje Mikkelsen, and the recording is state of the art, with beautifully transparent strings and with plenty of space round the sound.

Fossegrimen, Op. 21 (complete stage music); Norway's Greeting to Theodore Roosevelt, Op. 31
*** Simax PSC 1027. Bergset (hardanger fiddle), Blunck, Vollestad, Refsdal, Ginnungagap Ch., Latvian Nat. SO, Mikkelsen

Sigurd Eldegard's Fossegrimen, a 'troll-play in four parts', is partly based on the story of Torgeir Augundsson, better known as Myllarguten ('The Miller's Son'), Norway's celebrated folk fiddler who learned his art from Fossegrimen, musical master of all the underworld creatures, and who, Faust-like, 'pawned his soul' for his secrets. Halvorsen's music from 1904 has much charm and fluency, and is full of appealing folk-like ideas alongside some more conventional episodes. Some of it is so good that it seems curmudgeonly to say that, at over 50 minutes, it slightly outstays its welcome. The playing is very committed, particularly that of Arve Moen Bergset who not only handles the hardanger fiddle and the violin brilliantly but also contributes vocally. There are four other soloists including a boy soprano, and a mixed choir. Øivind Bergh recorded a 20-minute suite from it in the 1970s which left one wanting more; better compile one's own suites than play it all at one go. Norway's Greeting to Theodore Roosevelt was commissioned to mark the occasion of the former president's visit to Norway in 1910 to receive the Nobel Peace Prize and is occasional music. However, there is a lot here that rewards the enterprising listener.

HAMILTON, Iain (1922–2000)

Like Peter Racine Fricker, Iain Hamilton was a commanding figure in the British avant garde of the 1950s, but interest in his work seems to have fallen off since then. In 1961 he went to the United States and lectured at a number of universities. His output there included such stage works as The Royal Hunt of the Storm and Tamburlaine, as well as two more symphonies (in addition to the two he had already composed). His music has a haunting post-expressionist idiom that recalls Berg or early Henze, though he does not have the fantasy of the latter. He is a thoughtful composer, but there is no lack of imagination in his music, which is well worth getting to know.

(i) Violin Concerto. Sinfonia for 2 Orchestras
(N) (M) **(*) EMI (ADD) 5 86189-2. (i) Parikian, SNO, Gibson – GOEHR: Violin Concerto **

Hamilton wrote his Violin Concerto in 1952, at the beginning of his career, in memory of his father who had died the previous year, and before his music took on the craggy quality of his serial works. It is lyrical, with overtones from Sibelius and Walton, brooding melancholy alternating with red-blooded passion – very much young man's music, here persuasively presented. The Sinfonia for Two Orchestras is much later (1959), a fascinating work both in its intricate but clear-cut form, and in the highly original instrumental layout. The composer divides his orchestra into two, most unconventionally arranged groups, and their interplay in the 11 separate sections makes for some memorable effects. The idiom may be 12-note, but even unprepared listeners should find that the skill of the writing – and the committedness of the playing –

gives an immediate impact. The performance is excellent, as are both recordings, from 1971 and 1965 respectively.

HANDEL, George Frideric (1685–1759)

The Alchymist. Suite; Concerti a due cori 1–3; 2 Arias for Wind Band; Royal Fireworks Music; Water Music: Suites 1–3 (complete)

(B) **(*) O-L Double (ADD/DDD) 455 709-2 (2). AAM, Hogwood

A useful and attractive two-CD collection, bringing together rarities as well as the complete *Fireworks* and *Water Music*. The *Alchymist* suite is jolly music but, presented here spiritedly, is much more conventional than the consistently inspired invention for the two great royal occasions. It was the *Water Music* with which Hogwood's Academy of Ancient Music made its début at the Proms in 1978, and the joy of that occasion is matched by this performance. While it may still seem disconcerting to hear the well-known *Air* taken so fast – like a minuet – the sparkle and airiness of the invention have rarely been caught on record so endearingly. Hogwood's account of the *Fireworks Music*, recorded two years later, can also be counted among the best available. The *Concerti a due cori*, sharing musical material taken from familiar works (including *Messiah*), are scored for two groups of wind instruments with an accompanying string orchestra plus continuo. Horns are strongly featured in the *F major Concertos* (Nos. 1 and 3). The present (1983) performances are lively enough, but the recording is thinner. The two *Arias for Wind Band* include an arrangement of an actual operatic aria (from *Teseo*) and again are rather spoilt by the inaccurate tuning of the period horns.

Ballet Music: Alcina: Overture; Acts I & III: Suites. Il pastor fido: Suite. Terpsichore: Suite

(M) *** Warner Elatus (ADD) 2564 60335-2. E. Bar. Sol., Gardiner

John Eliot Gardiner is just the man for such a lightweight programme. He is not afraid to charm the ear, yet allegros are vigorous and rhythmically infectious. The bright and clean recorded sound adds to the sparkle and the quality is first class. A delightful collection, and very tuneful too.

Ariodante (suite): Overture; Sinfonia pastorale; Ballo. Il Pastor Fido (suite): Overture; March: Air pour les chasseurs I & II

(N) *** Australian Decca Eloquence (ADD) 476 2440. ASMF, Marriner – GLUCK: *Don Juan* ***

These two highly attractive suites are played with grace and fine rhythmic point by Marriner and his splendid orchestral group. Hopefully the gently rustic hunting music – a very leisurely hunt – which closes this collection escapes the new hunting ban. A fine bonus for the superb Gluck ballet, with vintage Argo (1971) sound.

2 Concerti a due cori, 2–3, HWV 333–4; Concerti grossi, Op. 3/1–6; Op. 6/1–12; Concerto grosso in C (Alexander's Feast); Music for the Royal Fireworks; Water Music (both complete)

(B) **(*) DG 463 094-2 (6). E. Concert, Pinnock

A generous bargain set of some of Handel's most famous orchestral music which Pinnock's admirers will not want to miss. His accounts of the *Fireworks* and *Water Music* have

tremendous zest and are among the best of the available period-instrument performances. The six Op. 3 concertos also find Pinnock and his English Concert at their freshest and liveliest. The twelve Op. 6 concertos however are not quite so recommendable: there is comparatively little sense of grandeur and few hints of tonally expansive beauty. But Pinnock's English Concert are never unresponsive and they offer much fine solo playing, helped by an attractively atmospheric acoustic, and, in spite of the above reservation, there is much to enjoy. The *Alexander's Feast Concerto grosso* also has vitality and imagination to recommend it, as have the *Concerti a due cori*, and all are well recorded.

Concerti grossi, Op. 3/1–6 (including) 4b, HWV 312–17

🔑 (BB) *** Hyp. Helios CDH 55075. Brandenburg Cons., Goodman

(M) *** Warner Elatus (ADD/DDD) 2564 6028-2. VCM, Harnoncourt

Roy Goodman's set achieves the best of both worlds by including the spurious (but very engaging) No. 4b and, like Hogwood (currently deleted), using an authentic version of No. 6, yet featuring the concertante organ at its close as a bonus. The playing is rhythmically spirited and enjoyably light and airy: this is period-instrument music-making at its most seductive, helped by some delightfully sensitive flute and oboe contributions from Rachel Brown and Katharina Arfken respectively. First-class recording, natural and transparent, with a pleasing ambience. A fine bargain.

This Elatus set is among the most endearing of Harnoncourt's earlier, authentic performances of baroque music. In Op. 3, tempi tend to be relaxed, but the performances are very enjoyable in their easy-going way; the ripe, fresh colouring of the baroque oboes, played expertly and expressively, is most attractive to the ear, and the string-sound is unaggressive. The recordings were made in the Vienna Casino Zögernitz between 1971 and 1981. Curiously, string tuttis are a little dry, although the overall effect is quite spacious and the inner detail excellent. Not a first choice perhaps, but the whole effect is distinctive.

Concerti grossi, Op. 3/1–6

(BB) *** Naxos 8.553457. N. Sinfonia, Creswick

*** DG (ADD) (IMS) 413 727-2. E. Concert, Pinnock

(BB) **(*) Warner Apex 0927 48682-2. E. Bar. Sol., Gardiner

Barry Creswick and his excellent Northern Sinfonia provide a most enjoyable modern-instrument version of Op. 3. They do not include No. 4b, nor give us the revised version of No. 6, but neither do most of their competitors, and with excellent playing throughout, freshly paced and most truthfully recorded, this is excellent value.

The six Op. 3 concertos with their sequences of brief jewels of movements also find Pinnock and the English Concert at their freshest and liveliest, with plenty of sparkle and little of the abrasiveness associated with 'authentic' performance.

Gardiner's analogue set from 1980 has transferred well to CD. Recorded in the Henry Wood Hall, textures are slightly more ample but still clear and admirably balanced. The starry cast-list includes Simon Standage and Roy Goodman among the violins, and the playing is both lively and stylish. There is a slight lack of finish in one or two places and some poor intonation in *No. 2 in B-flat* – yet one also notes the imaginative treatment of the *Largo e staccato* of Op. 3/3 and its following *Adagio*, with Lisa Beznosiuk the engaging flute soloist. Moreover this is now very inexpensive.

(i) *Concerti grossi, Op. 3* (including *4a*); (ii) *Coronation Anthem: Zadok the Priest. Dixit Dominus; Israel in Egypt; The Ways of Zion Do Mourn.*

(N) (BB) *** Warner (ADD/DDD) 2564 61757-2 (4). (i) E. Bar. Sol.; (ii) Soloists, Monteverdi Ch. & O, Gardiner

Gardiner's key early Handel recordings for Warner/Erato make an attractive budget box, but all are available separately and are individually reviewed. Here the CDs are presented in their original packaging with full texts.

Concerti grossi, Op. 6/1–10

(B) **(*) EMI double forte (ADD) 5 73344-2 (2). Bath Festival CO, Menuhin

(i) *Concerti grossi, Op. 6/11–12; Water Music* (Suites 1–3; complete); (ii) *Violin Sonatas, Op. 1/3, 10, 12–15*

(B) **(*) EMI double forte (ADD) 5 73347-2 (2). (i) Bath Festival CO, Menuhin; (ii) Menuhin, Malcolm, Gauntlet

Concerti grossi, Op. 6/1–12

☛ *** Chan. 9004/6. I Musici de Montréal, Turovsky

12 Concerti grossi, Op. 6/1–12; Concerto grosso in C (Alexander's Feast)

**(*) Chan. 0600 (*Nos. 1–5*); 0616 (*Nos. 6–9*); 0622 (*Nos. 10–12; Alexander's Feast*) (available separately). Coll. Mus. 90, Standage

I Musici de Montréal offer a refreshing and stimulating set of Handel's Opus 6. The group uses modern instruments and Yuli Turovsky's aim is to seek a compromise between modern and authentic practice by paring down vibrato in some of the expressive music. The concertino, Eleonora and Natalya Turovsky and Alain Aubut, play impressively, while the main group (6.3.1.1) produces full, well-balanced tone, and Handel's joyous fugues are particularly fresh and buoyant. Turovsky paces convincingly, not missing Handel's breadth of sonority and moments of expressive grandeur. This could now be first choice for this wonderful music.

Simon Standage's Chandos set with Collegium Musicum 90 has been much admired for its combination of delicately crisp rhythmic vitality and airy grace. Yet anyone looking for weight of Handelian sonority in the ripieno will not find it here. Even though the main orchestral group is not small in numbers (5.5.3.3.1) and includes Handel's optional oboes and bassoon, the tutti is very much that of a small chamber group. Clearly, robustness is not part of Standage's conception: fresh, refined transparency is his hallmark and this means no bold, full contrasts with the concertino. The playing is of high calibre, though there is a complete absence of geniality, notably in the fugal writing, where Handel is so different from Bach. The Chandos recording is first class.

Menuhin gave us the first complete stereo set of Op. 6 in the early 1960s, recording the later concertos first and working backwards. He used a modest body of strings, and during the sessions it was suggested to the artists that a double continuo might be used, as was Handel's practice. But this does not appear to happen until what was originally the third LP, containing Nos. 1, 2, 4, and 5 (in this reissue the works are presented in a straightforward numerical sequence). In consequence, the performances of the first two concertos – the last to be recorded – are the finest of the set, both buoyant and rich in expressive feeling; the harpsichord contribution comes through splendidly. In the later concertos the harpsichord continuo is too backwardly balanced. But they are still very enjoyable.

For the *Water Music* Menuhin used a new edition especially prepared by Neville Boyling, and his genial approach again demonstrates the humanity and freshness that always informed his music-making, with excellent playing and lively spontaneity throughout. Both recordings have been admirably transferred to CD. The Opus 1 *Violin Sonatas* were pioneering authentic versions, vital and stylish, using a well-balanced continuo (Ambrose Gauntlet, viola da gamba, and George Malcolm, harpsichord). But here the CD transfer makes Menuhin's violin-timbre sound slightly edgy. The 1963 Abbey Road recording is warm, fresh and clear in its new CD transfer.

Concerti grossi, Op. 6/1, 2, 6, 7 & 10

(B) **(*) HM HMA 1951507. Les Arts Florissants, Christie

For some reason Christie also never completed his set of Op. 6, the present selection dating from 1995. The performances are vivid and athletic, helped by clean, transparent recording, with no lack of body and with the concertino and ripieno clearly defined. The playing in slow movements is refined and there is no lack of expressive feeling, but the overall result is less involving than with Turovsky and, although allegros are spirited, there is more to this music than these performers discover.

Concerto grosso in B flat, Op. 6/7

*** Ara. Z 6723. San Francisco Ballet O, Lark Qt, Le Roux — SCHOENBERG: *Concerto for String Quartet & Orchestra after Handel's Op. 6/7*; ELGAR: *Introduction & Allegro for Strings*; SPOHR: *Concerto for String Quartet & Orchestra* ***

What a pleasure to hear a Handel *Concerto grosso* played for once on a full body of modern strings, emphasizing its warmth of sonority. But this is included as part of an imaginative concert of string music so that the listener can compare the original with Schoenberg's bizarre but aurally fascinating recomposed pastiche.

Concerto grosso in G min., Op. 6/6; (i) Il duello amoroso (HWV 2)

(M) *** DHM/BMG 82876 60157-2. Freiburg Bar. O, Von der Goltz; (i) with Argenta, Chance — PURCELL: *Dioclesian* excerpts. ***

As we know from their outstanding DVD of the Bach *Brandenburgs*, the Freiburg Baroque Orchestra is outstanding among period-instrument ensembles, and their account of the *G minor Concerto grosso* (using oboes as well as strings) is full of character. It acts here as an enticing prelude to Handel's Italian cantata, *Il duello amoroso*, probably written (in Rome) in 1708. Its engaging dialogue represents the efforts of the shepherd Daliso (Michael Chance) to win back his unfaithful beloved, the nymph Amarilli (Nancy Argenta). At the close she tells him abruptly, 'Don't beg for my love any more. No, you haven't got the torch to light my fire.' The performance of this light-hearted lovers' tussle is admirable and very well recorded.

(i) *Harp Concerto, Op. 4/6. Variations for Harp*

☛ ✪ (M) *** Decca (ADD) 425 723-2. Marisa Robles, (i) ASMF, Iona Brown — BOIELDIEU; DITTERSDORF: *Harp Concertos, etc. *** ✪

Handel's Op. 4/6 is well known in both organ and harp versions. Marisa Robles and Iona Brown make an unforgettable case for the latter by creating the most delightful textures, while never letting the work sound insubstantial. The ASMF accompaniment, so stylish and beautifully balanced, is a treat in itself, and the recording is well-nigh perfect.

(i) *Harpsichord Concerto, Op. 4/6. Suite 15: Air & Variations*
(**(*)) Biddulph mono LHW 032. Landowska; (i) with O, Bigot – BACH: *Concerto 1 in D min.* (**); HAYDN: *Concerto in D*, etc. (***)

We more usually hear this concerto on the organ or harp, but Wanda Landowska makes a fairly good case for the harpsichord, although her predilection towards grandeur means that her presentation is on the heavy side. The *Air and Variations* is played with much character and is made to be every bit as memorable as *The Harmonious Blacksmith*. The recording is vivid throughout and very well transferred.

Oboe Concertos 1, HWV 301; 2, HWV 302a; 3, HWV 287; Sonatas for Oboe & Continuo in B flat, HWV 357; in F, HWV 363a; in G min., Op. 1/6, HWV 364a; in C min., Op. 1/8, HWV 366; Sonata in G min. for Oboe, Violins & Continuo, HWV 404
☛ (BB) *** Regis RRC 1106. Francis, L. Harpsichord Ens.

Oboe Concertos 1–3; Air & Rondo (ed. Camden); (i) *Suite in G min.* (ed. Camden); *Otho: Overture*
(BB) *** Naxos 8.553430. Camden, (i) Girdwood; City of L. Sinfonia, Ward

Sarah Francis is a superb baroque oboist, at the same time directing the members of the London Harpsichord Ensemble with spirit and finesse. These performances are not only delightful but a model of style. In the sonatas Handel's ever-engaging contrapuntal interplay is beautifully clear (the harpsichord comes through in perfect balance with the continuo) so that for sheer pleasure these performances almost upstage the more familiar concertos. A collection that leads the field, not least for its excellent sound. At its new Regis price it is a remarkable bargain.

Anthony Camden, for years principal oboe of the LSO, here makes a very welcome solo appearance on disc, playing with typical point and style, using his attractively reedy tone. The regular oboe concertos are well supplemented by the *Suite in G minor* as edited by Camden, where he is joined by the prize-winning Julia Girdwood on the second oboe. The *Otho Overture* too features prominent roles for oboes in duet. Ward and the City of London Sinfonia are sympathetic accompanists using modern instruments. First-rate sound from All Saints, East Finchley.

Organ concertos

Organ Concertos, Op. 4/1–6; Op. 7/1–6; in F (The Cuckoo and the Nightingale), HWV 295; in A, HWV 296; in D min., HWV 304
☛ (BB) *** DG Trio 469 358-2 (3). Preston; Holliger (harp in Op. 4/6), E. Concert, Pinnock

Simon Preston's set of the major organ concertos returns to the catalogue, economically priced on a DG Archiv Trio. On the first CD, containing the six Op. 4 works, although the balance of the solo instrument is not perfect, the playing of both Preston and the English Concert is admirably fresh and lively. While, with alternative recordings of the *Harp Concerto*, Op. 4/6, available, many collectors might have preferred all the works to be played on the organ, Ursula Holliger's solo contribution on a baroque harp is memorable, for she creates some delicious sounds. The second and third discs contain

the six Op. 7 works, plus *The Cuckoo and the Nightingale* and the *A major* and *D minor Concertos*. All but the *A major* were recorded using the organ at St John's, Armitage in Staffordshire, and are even more attractive for the warmth and assurance of the playing. The *A major* which completes the set was recorded earlier with Op. 4. For those wanting a complete coverage of these engaging works this should serve admirably.

Organ Concertos, Op. 4/1–6
(BB) *** Naxos 8.553835. Lindley, N. Sinfonia, Creswick

A most enjoyable and inexpensive modern-instrument performance of Op. 4, rhythmically jaunty and warmly expressive by turns. Simon Lindley is an excellent soloist and the piping reeds of the organ at Holy Cross Church, Fenham, seem very apt for the music. Op. 4/6 is played and registered with appealing delicacy to remind us of the alternative version for harp. The recording balance is admirable. Not a first choice overall but an undoubted bargain.

Organ Concertos, Op. 4/1–6 (Chamber versions)
☛ (N) (M) *** Avie AV 2055. Halls, Sonnerie, Huggett

Although Handel's *Organ Concertos* are associated with his oratorios, they were afterwards given frequent concert performances, often using more modest-sized instruments. It must be remembered that Handel re-employed movements from his instrumental music for some of these works: the *F major Concerto*, HWV 393, sounds immediately familiar as it is a transcription of the *Recorder Sonata*, Op. 1/11. Matthew Halls is therefore entirely justified in presenting these works on a chamber organ, a Dutch Fama/Klop instrument, with a specification to meet all of Handel's demands. Monica Huggett's period-instrument accompaniments are similarly on a chamber scale, using a small string group, plus a pair of oboes (as used by Handel) in Nos. 1 and 4. The result is delightful. Matthew Halls is a superb soloist, improvising and decorating genially and stylishly without ever overdoing it. Sample the opening of No. 4 with his opening flourish, and the neatly managed contrapuntal finale of the same work, or the delicacy of the strings at the opening of No. 6, and the charming organ response. Moreover, the recording is beautifully balanced, the sound throughout wholly beguiling. A clear first choice, unless you insist on a larger scale. The documentation is first class.

Organ Concertos, Op. 4/2; Op. 7/3–5; in F (The Cuckoo and the Nightingale)
(M) *** DG 447 300-2. Preston, E. Concert, Pinnock

This is more generous than the previous (full-price) sampler from Preston's series with Pinnock. Both performances and sound are admirably fresh.

Organ Concertos: 4, Op. 4/4; 13 (The Cuckoo and the Nightingale)
(N) (B) ** CfP (ADD) 5 86046-2. Kynaston, Virtuosi of England, Davison (with chorus) – BACH: *Violin Concertos* **

Nicholas Kynaston offers spirited performances of two favourite concertos. The registration in *The Cuckoo and the Nightingale* is piquant, and to end the performance of Op. 4/4 Davison uses the rare choral finale (*Alleluia*), which comes as a pleasant surprise, making this something of a collector's item.

Organ Concertos 7–12, Op. 7/1–6; 13 in F (The Cuckoo and the Nightingale), HWV 295; 14 in A, HWV 296; 15 in D min., BWV 304; 16 in D, BWV 305a

*** Virgin 5 45236-2 (2). Van Asperen, OAE

Bob van Asperen's survey was originally complete, but now Op. 4 has been withdrawn. Nevertheless its combination of musicianship and scholarship gives this Virgin set a special feeling of authenticity. Although the accompanying group is comparatively modest there is no feeling that the scale of the music is minimized. The recording could hardly be bettered. He uses an appealing four-stop continuo organ by N. P. Mander Ltd. Also included here is the pair of concertos known as the 'Second set' (one is the famous *The Cuckoo and the Nightingale*) and the two final works, as published by Arnold in 1797. Throughout, in the places where Handel would have improvised, extra Handelian movements are interpolated (mainly from the keyboard suites and solo sonatas, and all listed in the synopsis), but van Asperen improvises shorter linking passages himself. A considerable achievement.

Organ Concertos 7–10, Op. 7/1–4 (HWV 306–9); 13 (The Cuckoo and the Nightingale)

(N) (BB) ** DG Eloquence (ADD) 4077 5033. Müller (organ of Tituskirche, Basle), Schola Cantorum Basiliensis, Wenzinger

Eduard Müller's collection with Wenzinger comes from the mid-1960s, and now sounds rather old-fashioned in using a full string ensemble and relaxed tempi. This is very noticeable at the opening of Op. 7/3, in which the main theme mirrors the opening '*Halleluja*' of Handel's most famous chorus. Yet the *Spiritoso* third movement is sprightly enough, and in their way these very well played, upholstered accounts are agreeable enough when they are given such full and well-balanced recordings. The documentation, however, is non-existent.

(i) *Piano Concerto in A* (arr. Beecham). *The Gods Go A-Begging* (ballet, arr. BEECHAM): excerpts. *The Origin of Design* (suite de ballet, arr. BEECHAM)

(***) Somm mono Beecham 7. (i) Humby Beecham; LPO or RPO, Beecham

This disc of Beecham's arrangements of Handel, like the companion issue of Delius recordings, draws on private discs in Beecham's own collection. The ten movements from the ballet, *The Origin of Design*, come from the very first recording sessions of Beecham's newly founded London Philharmonic in December 1932. They were never issued, when the following month he recorded some of the movements again. The performances are brilliant, with the players on their toes, not least the oboist, Leon Goossens. Seven of the movements from the later ballet, *The Gods Go A-Begging*, made between 1933 and 1938, did get published, but all the rest, including the six movements from the same ballet recorded with the RPO in 1949, have never appeared in any format, inexplicably so.

The oddity is the four-movement *Piano Concerto* which Beecham cobbled together from various Handel movements (unidentified here) for his then wife, the pianist Betty Humby. It makes a curious confection, starting with a nine-minute *Chaconne* in which grandly spacious sections punctuate energetic variations. The result is exuberant, sounding less like Handel than twentieth-century pastiche. As in the Delius disc, transfers bring satisfyingly full-bodied sound, if with obvious limitations.

The Faithful Shepherd Suite (arr. Beecham)

(M) *** Sony SMK 87780. RPO, Beecham – GOLDMARK: *Rustic Wedding Symphony, Op. 26* ***

The Faithful Shepherd ('Il pastor fido') *Suite* was the third of Beecham's arrangements of Handel and possibly the most attractive in its grace and diversity, with the *Musette* winningly quoting both from *Ariodante* and also *Messiah* ('And He shall feed his flock'). The playing here is characteristically warm, lively and elegant by turns, and the mono recording is excellent.

Music for the Royal Fireworks (original wind scoring)

*** Telarc CD 80038. Cleveland Symphonic Winds, Fennell – HOLST: *Military Band Suites* *** ✪

Music for the Royal Fireworks (original wind version; complete); *Water Music Suite* (arr. Harty); *Concerto a due cori in F; Concertos 1 in F; 3 in D*

✪ *** Testament SBT 1253. L. Wind Ens., Pro Arte O, LSO, Mackerras

Music for the Royal Fireworks (original version); (i) *Coronation Anthems* (see also below)

*** Hyp. CDA 66350. (i) New College, Oxford, Ch.; augmented King's Consort, King

For a recording well over forty years old, this historic Testament (originally Pye) account of Handel's *Fireworks Music* is astonishing. Charles Mackerras in 1959 followed up the adventurous idea of using a band of no fewer than 62 wind players plus nine percussionists, echoing Handel's original Hyde Park ensemble in 1749. The result hits you between the ears, especially the rasping horns in the overture, thanks to full and spacious sound with a wide stereo spread. This was a very early foray into the then unexplored world of period performance, with the recording made in the middle of the night, the only time when so many wind-players could be gathered together. But far from sounding jaded, these leading players were challenged to give an electrifying performance. As a supplement comes a mono recording of the *Minuets I* and *II* with fireworks and cannon effects as background, a fun item demonstrating how important stereo is. The other items, more traditional in style, find Mackerras also blowing away cobwebs. The composite *Concerto a due cori* (bringing together movements from two different works) again features bright, braying horns, while the two shorter concertos for wind and strings involve the theme Handel also used for the grand opening of the *Fireworks Music* but in a far more reticent way. Even the *Water Music Suite* as arranged by Harty sounds brighter and fresher than usual.

King also provides a period performance of Handel's *Royal Fireworks Music* using the full complement of instruments Handel demanded, assembling no fewer than 24 baroque oboists and 12 baroque bassoonists, 9 trumpeters, 9 exponents of the hand horn and 4 timpanists. It all makes for a glorious noise. King's Handel style has plenty of rhythmic bounce, and the recording in its warmly atmospheric way gives ample scale. The coupled performances of the four *Coronation Anthems* are not as incisively dramatic as some but still convey the joy of the inspiration.

In 1978, in Severance Hall, Cleveland, Ohio, Frederick Fennell gathered together the wind and brass from the Cleveland Symphony Orchestra and recorded a performance to demonstrate spectacularly what fine playing and digital sound could do for Handel's open-air score. The overall sound-balance tends to favour the brass (and the drums), but few will grumble when the result is as overwhelming as it is on the CD, with the sharpness of focus matched by the presence and amplitude of the sound-image.

Music for the Royal Fireworks, HWV 351 (original wind scoring); *Concertos in D* (arr. from *Fireworks Music, HWV 335a*; *in F* (arr. from *Water Music*), HWV 331/316; *Occasional Suite in D* (arr. PINNOCK); *Passacaille, gigue et menuet* (arr. *from Trio Sonata, Op. 5/4*)
*** DG 453 451-2. E. Concert, Pinnock

Pinnock's 1996 recording of the *Royal Fireworks Music* adds grandeur to vitality. It is superbly played, although fascinatingly the period horns do not quite produce the exciting edge that made Mackerras's early stereo Pye recording so memorable. The rest of the programme is agreeable occasional music, played with warmth and the new elegance which original-instrument performances have discovered recently, and the *Passacaglia, Gigue and Minuet* has the warmth of timbre one would expect from modern instruments. The two concertos have interpolated slow movements from other sources; the *Occasional Suite* (a pastiche in the manner of Beecham) draws on the *Overture* from the *Occasional Oratorio* (with a particularly beautiful oboe solo) plus excerpts from *Ariodante, Joshua* and *Alessandro Severo*. All most enjoyable in an unexpected way: almost old-fashioned in its colour and popular appeal.

Music for the Royal Fireworks; Water Music (complete)
☛— ✿ **(N)** (M) *** DG Entrée 474 168-2. Orpheus CO
*** Virgin 5 45265-2. LCP, Norrington
(M) *** Ph. 464 706-2. E. Bar. Sol., Gardiner
(M) *** Classic fM 75605 570442. Scottish CO, McGegan
(BB) *** Warner Apex (ADD) 0927 48685-2. Paillard CO, Paillard
(BB) *** Naxos 8.550109. Capella Istropolitana, Warchal
**(*) Telarc CD-80594. Boston Bar., Pearlman
(N) *(*) Sony (ADD) 516236-2. NYPO, Boulez (with *Berenice: Minuet*: Philh. CO)

The conductorless Orpheus Chamber Orchestra are always impressive, but here their playing and ensemble are little short of superlative in polished and alive performances that sweep the board. Although modern instruments are used, such is the Orpheus' sense of baroque style, so crisp and buoyant are the rhythms, that the effect has much in common with a period performance without any of the snags. How warmly and elegantly they play the colourful and more intimate dances in the central *G major Suite* of the *Water Music*, and they begin with a riveting account of the *Royal Fireworks Music*, catching its sense of spectacle. Strings are used as Handel wished, but the wind and brass dominate. The recording is in the demonstration bracket, and these performances are so fresh that it is like listening to this marvellous music for the very first time. This record has been out of the catalogue far too long, but now it makes its Entrée début – the finest single disc on this DG label intended to entice novice collectors. That it should certainly succeed in doing!

Norrington uses a full orchestra but highlights the bright trumpets and braying horns to give both works a vividly robust, open-air flavour. The dance movements have grace, but a lively grace, and it is the consistent vitality that makes these performances so stimulating. The overtures of both works bring the crispest double-dotting, while the outer movements of the *Fireworks Music* are as strong and rugged as you could want, without loss of polish or tuning.

Gardiner's earlier *Fireworks* and *Water Music* on Philips

were recorded eight years apart and have only now been combined on one CD. The *Royal Fireworks Music* brings an excellent response from the English Baroque Soloists, rhythms are alive and well articulated, and phrasing is musical. Tempi are a bit on the fast side, and rather more grandeur might have been welcome in the closing sections. But the result remains fresh, if comparatively lightweight. The *Water Music*, however (with the *F major Suite* played first), is brighter, more resilient, full of vitality and colour, although the famous *Air* trips along in sprightly fashion, more like a dance movement. But this is period-instrument playing at its most stimulating and the sound-picture is vivid and clear.

Nicholas McGegan and his excellent Scottish players, very well recorded in the Caird Hall, Dundee, use modern instruments but seek a style deriving from period-instrument experience, with brisk tempi and lifted rhythms, though somewhat more easygoing than Norrington. The Overture and finale of the *Royal Fireworks Music* are boldly expansive, and in the *Water Music* textures are attractively light, phrasing neat and stylish. At mid-price this Classic fM pairing is very competitive.

On Apex Jean-François Paillard offers a really first-class bargain combination of the *Fireworks* and *Water Music*, admirably played on modern instruments. There is both vitality and finesse and a genuine sense of style. The *Fireworks Music* is heard in its original wind scoring, and no one could complain about a lack of spectacle – the horns rasp splendidly in the *Overture* and one can really imagine a fiery backcloth for the grand closing Minuets, with the exuberant horns again contrasting well with the oboes. The CD transfer of spaciously resonant recordings made in 1973 and 1962 respectively is admirably fresh and robust.

Bohdan Warchal directs the Capella Istropolitana in bright and lively performances of the complete *Water Music* as well as the *Fireworks Music*, well paced and well scaled, with woodwind and brass aptly abrasive, and with such points as double-dotting faithfully observed. Textures are clean, with an attractive bloom on the full and immediate sound, to provide a strong bargain recommendation.

Martin Pearlman, with the period forces of Boston Baroque, offers yet another enjoyable pairing. Except in the Minuets, which tend to be slower than in most period performances, his speeds are on the fast side, and the intimacy of the approach is reflected in the recording, with brass set slightly backward. Rather restrained, he is not as flamboyant or as rhythmically invigorating as some. The *Fireworks Music* brings a performance notable for the winning lightness of the fast movements.

Boulez's direction of the *Fireworks Music* is disappointing, inappropriately heavy, and it is not helped by poor ensemble and indifferent recording. The *Water Music* is much more successful. Boulez uses his large-scale forces expertly and secures results that are both stylish and vigorous. There are many details of phrasing that excite unqualified admiration, and the NYPO responds with playing of both vigour and sensitivity. The recording is not particularly distinguished (the strings could sound more appealing) but is acceptable enough. The *Berenice Minuet* is well played and recorded by the Philharmonia group.

Music for the Royal Fireworks: Suite; Water Music: Suite (arr. Harty and Szell); *The Faithful Shepherd: Minuet* (ed. Beecham); *Xerxes: Largo* (arr. Reinhardt)
(BB) *** Belart (ADD) 450 001-2. LSO, Szell

Many readers will, like us, have a nostalgic feeling for the

Handel–Harty suites from which earlier generations got to know these two marvellous scores. George Szell and the LSO offer a highly recommendable coupling of them on a Belart super-bargain issue, with Handel's *Largo* and the *Minuet* from Beecham's *Faithful Shepherd Suite* thrown in for good measure. The orchestral playing from the early 1970s is outstanding, and the strings are wonderfully expressive in the slower pieces. The horns excel, and the crisp new transfer seems to add to the sheer zest of the music-making. A splendid bargain.

Water Music: Suites 1–3 (complete)

*** Hyp. CDA 66967. King's Cons., King – TELEMANN: *Water Music* ***

**(*) Telarc CD-80279. St Luke's O, Mackerras

(N) (BB) *** EMI Encore 5 86409. BPO, Muti

(M) **(*) Chan. 6642. SCO, Gibson

Water Music: Suites 1–3 (complete); *Il pastor fido: Overture*

*** DG 471 723-2. E. Concert, Pinnock

If you need a CD offering the complete *Water Music* without the *Fireworks Music*, Pinnock's first DG Archiv version remains one of the very finest on period instruments, with rhythms delectably sprung and with a degree of expressive warmth – as in the *Air* of the F major Suite – usually missing from period performances. Here it remains an engagingly gentle piece. He has an unsurpassed line-up of soloists, and the 1983 recording remains outstanding, with a wide separation that highlights the dramatic antiphonal contrasts between trumpets and horns in such a number as the *Alla Hornpipe* from the *Suite in D*. Speeds are consistently well chosen and are generally uncontroversial. You might perhaps think that the addition of just an overture for this reissue on DG Archiv's Blue label is ungenerous, but the Overture Handel provided for *Il pastor fido* is 24 minutes long, a work very similar in style to the *Water Music* but dating from five years earlier. There is, first, a brief French overture, then five following contrasted movements, very like those in the *Water Music* and, as Stanley Sadie comments in the accompanying note, 'giving the English Concert's accomplished woodwind [more] opportunities to shine'. The recording is beautifully balanced, full and clear.

Robert King's is above all a performance of contrasts – between the elegant lighter dance movement, the playing warmly refined, and the set-piece allegros where the baroque horns and trumpets burst forth exuberantly. They always play with joyful vigour, with as much weight and more brightness and bite than with modern instruments. The strings are never edgy and often quite mellow, as in the famous *Air*. The coupling with Telemann's *Water Music* works well.

Sir Charles Mackerras, though he uses modern, not period instruments, adopts many of the techniques of period practice, with speeds consistently on the fast side and textures crisp and clean, helped by the wide separation of the stereo sound, recorded in 1991 and still sounding impressive. However, with no coupling the disc offers rather short measure.

The playing of the Berlin Philharmonic under Muti is polished and elegant. In the *Overture* of the first suite, a small instrumental group is featured as a neat counterpoint to the main ripieno: throughout there is a strong emphasis on contrast, with instrumental solos often treated in a concertante manner. The playing is very responsive and the strings generally display a light touch, but the horns are almost aggressive in their spirited vigour in the famous fanfare tune.

With a full, vivid, yet clear sound-picture, this is very easy to enjoy.

The Scottish Chamber Orchestra re-emerges on Chandos with its head held high, due not only to the sense of style and polish, but also to the vigour and sparkle of the playing. Gibson's pacing of the allegros is brisk and he points rhythms with infectious zest. There is fine lyrical playing too, notably from the principal oboe, and the horns are robust without being too emphatic. This combination of energy and warmth comes as a welcome relief after prolonged exposure to period instruments. The ample acoustic of Glasgow City Hall is most attractive and the sound has fine clarity and firmness of definition. But the measure is short, and without the *Fireworks Music*, even at mid-price, this cannot carry a strong recommendation.

CHAMBER MUSIC

Complete chamber music

Sinfonia in B flat (for 2 flutes & continuo) (*HWV 338*); *Flute Sonatas, Halle 1–3* (*HWV 374/376; 378*), *Op. 1/1a* (*HWV 379*); *Oboe Sonatas in B flat* (*HWV 357*), *Op. 1/5 & 8* (*HWV 363a & 366*). *Recorder Sonatas, Op. 1/2, 4, 7, 8a & 11* (*HWV 360, 362, 365, 367a & 369*); *in B flat* (*HWV 377*). *Violin Sonatas in D min* (*HWV 359a*); *Op. 1/3, 6, 9, 10, 12–15* (*HWV 361, 364a, 367a, 368, 370/373*); *Fantasia in A* (for violin & continuo), *HWV 406*. *Trio Sonatas* (for flute, violin & continuo), *Op. 2/1–2* (*HWV 386b & 387*); (for 2 violins & continuo), *Op. 2/3* (*HWV 388*); (for recorder, violin & continuo), *Op. 2/4*; (for 2 violins & continuo), *Op. 2/5* (*HWV 390a*); (for 2 flutes & continuo), *Op. 2/6* (*HWV 391*); *3 Dresden Trio Sonatas* (for 2 violins & continuo), (*HWV 392/3*); *in E* (*HWV 394*). *Trio Sonatas in E min.*, (*HWV 395*); (for 2 oboes & continuo), *Op. 5/1* (*HWV 396*); *Op. 5/2* (for 2 violins & continuo); *Op. 5/3* (for flute, violin & continuo); *Op. 5/4–5* (for 2 violins & continuo) (*HWV 396/400*); *Op. 5/6* (for 2 oboes and continuo); *Op. 5/7* (for 2 violins & continuo) (*HWV 401/402*); *in C* (*Saul*) (*HWV 403*); *in F* (for 2 recorders & continuo) (*HWV 405*)

(B) *** Ph. (ADD/DDD) 470 893-2 (9). Academy Chamber Ens.

This remarkable achievement of Philips in recording virtually all Handel's chamber music in London between 1982 and 1984 with a group of outstanding instrumentalists has lain dormant in the catalogue for two decades. Yet it is an enterprise that can be compared with the Beaux Arts' set of Haydn's *Piano Trios* in both its enterprise and its excellence in terms of performance and outstandingly natural recording quality. As can be seen below, many of the wind concertos are available separately on a Duo set and are discussed there, but now the whole survey arrives in a bargain box, admirably documented. Those who want period performances can safely turn to the distinguished alternative survey from L'Ecole d'Orphée on CRD. But while the members of the Academy Chamber Ensemble (including artists of the calibre of William Bennett, the characterful Michala Petri and Neil Black) may use modern instruments, they achieve an excellent sense of period style and faultless intonation. As can be seen in the listings above, the *Trio Sonatas* are varied in instrumentation, but all have a refreshing vigour and warmth. In these sonatas Handel's invention seems inexhaustible, and it is difficult to imagine readers not responding to them. The use of the bassoonist, Joanna Graham, for the continuo in the *Oboe* and *Recorder Sonatas* brings an added touch of colour. In short, this set is an endless source of stimulation and pleasure and can be very strongly recommended.

Flute Sonatas; Oboe Sonatas & Violin Sonatas; Recorder Sonatas; Trio Sonatas (complete)
(BB) **(*) CRD (ADD) CRD 5002 (6). L'Ecole d'Orphée

The complete period-instrument recording by L'Ecole d'Orphée of Handel's chamber music involves outstanding artists like Stephen Preston (flute) and David Reichenberg (oboe), and the string players are led by John Holloway. The playing is distinguished, the recording excellent, and the new bargain box is handsomely packaged. The one great snag, carried over from the separate CD issues, is the absence of cues for individual movements, so these records are more difficult to delve into than the original LPs. They are very good value just the same, and the documentation cannot be faulted.

Volume 1: *Flute Sonatas: in E min., Op. 1a/b; in G, Op. 1/5; in B min., Op. 1/9; in D (HWV 378); Halle Sonatas 1–3*
(M) *** CRD (ADD) CRD 3373. L'Ecole d'Orphée (Preston, Sheppard, Toll, Carolan)

Volume 2: *Oboe Sonatas 1 in B flat (HWV 357); in F (HWV 363a); in C min., Op. 1/8 (HWV 366); Violin Sonatas: in D min.* (original version of Op. 1/1), HWV 359a; in A, Op. 1/3, HWV 361; in G min., Op. 1/6 (HWV 364a); in D, Op. 1/13 (HWV 371); Allegros for Violin & Continuo: in A min. (HWV 408); in C min., HWV 412*
(M) **(*) CRD (ADD) CRD 3374. L'Ecole d'Orphée (Reichenberg, Holloway, Sheppard, Carolan)

Volume 1 contains the seven sonatas for flute (three are the so-called 'Halle' *Trio Sonatas*, published in 1730 and thought to be the product of Handel's youth) as well as a sonata recently discovered in Brussels, for flute and continuo in D major (HWV 378). The playing is always spirited and intelligent, and if Stephen Preston's eighteenth-century flute timbre sounds a little watery, his phrasing is often beguiling. David Reichenberg's Hailperin oboe is full of ripe colour, and the playing of both artists is immaculate.

Volume 3: *Trio Sonatas, Op. 2: 1 for Flute, Violin & Continuo in B min.; 2 in G min.; 3 in B flat for 2 Violins & Continuo; 4 in F for Recorder, Violin & Continuo; 5 in G min.; 6 in G min. for 2 Violins & Continuo*
(M) **(*) CRD (ADD) CRD 3375. L'Ecole d'Orphée (Holloway, Comberti, Preston, Pickett, Sheppard, Wooley, Toll)

Volume 4: *Trio Sonatas, Op. 5 for 2 Violins & Continuo: 1 in A; 2 in D; 3 in E min.; 4 in G; 5 in G min.; 6 in F; 7 in B flat*
(M) **(*) CRD (ADD) 3376. L'Ecole d'Orphée (Holloway, Comberti, Sheppard, Carolan)

Volume 5: *Sinfonia in B flat (HWV 338); Trio Sonatas: in C min., Op. 2/1a; in F (HWV 392); in G min. (HWV 393); in E (HWV 394); in C (HWV 403)*
(M) **(*) CRD (ADD) CRD 3377. L'Ecole d'Orphée (Holloway, Comberti, Sheppard, Carolan)

The *Trio Sonatas* recorded by L'Ecole d'Orphée include the complete Op. 2 set, an alternative version of another sonata of Op. 2, the seven sonatas of Op. 5, and the three so-called 'Dresden' *Sonatas* (HWV 392–4). Only one of them (in F) is totally authentic, though whoever composed the remaining

two was no mean figure. In addition there is a very attractive *Sinfonia in B flat* (HWV 338), which is written in trio sonata form. There are many musical riches here and no want of accomplishment in the performances. The two violins in use by John Holloway and Micaela Comberti have markedly different tone-quality.

Volume 4 of the CRD set includes Op. 5. Here Handel frequently borrows from himself, and much of this material is also found in the overtures for the *Chandos Anthems* or in the dance music for his operas. No. 6 is familiar, as Handel himself re-used the material of the first and fourth movements for the *Cuckoo and the Nightingale Organ Concerto*.

Volume 6: *Recorder Sonatas, Op. 1: 2 in G min. (HWV 360); 4 in A min. (HWV 362); 7 in C (HWV 365); 11 in F (HWV 369); in G (HWV 358); in B flat (HWV 377); in D min. (HWV 367a); Trio Sonata in F (HWV 405)*
(M) *** CRD (ADD) CRD 3378. L'Ecole d'Orphée (Pickett, Beckett, Sheppard, Carolan)

In the final volume the CRD performances bring elegant and finished playing from the two recorder players and, besides the Op. 1 *Sonatas*, the programme includes a *G major Sonata*, first published in 1974, and the original D minor version of the *Flute Sonata*, Op. 9/1, which has an engaging second movement based on a minor-key variant of a famous allegro in the *Water Music*. Excellent, intimate recording, but again with the irritating drawback that individual movements are not cued, and the *D minor Sonata* has seven of them.

Sonatas for Flute, Oboe, Recorder or Violin & Continuo, Op. 1/1, 1a, 1b, 2–8, 9a, 9b, HWV 359 & b, 361/2; 363b, 364a, 365–6, 367a & b, 369, 371, 379; Halle Sonatas 1–3 (HWV 374–6); & HWV 357–8 & 377
*** Hyp. CDA 66921/3 Beznosiuk, Beckett, Tunnicliffe, Wallfisch, Nicholson

The Hyperion set concentrates on Opus 1 although, illogically, four of the violin sonatas previously counted as being part of Handel's opus have been omitted as spurious (HWV 368 and 372–3). The fine *Halle Sonatas* have been included, plus some other miscellaneous works now considered to be authentic. The performances use period instruments and have the advantage of current practice, so both flute and oboe timbres have a strong baroque flavour, but the violins are less raw-timbred than the quality offered by L'Ecole d'Orphée; on the other hand, the playing itself is mellower and perhaps at times slightly less vital than on the more comprehensive CRD set.

Flute Sonatas: Op. 1/a; Halle Sonatas 1–3; Oboe Sonatas 1–2, HWV 357, 363a; Op. 1/5 & ; Recorder Sonatas, Op. 1/2, 4, 7 & 11 & HWV 367a & 377; Sinfonia in B flat for 2 Violins & Continuo, HWV 338; Trio Sonatas for 2 Flutes & Continuo & 2 Recorders & Continuo, HWV 395 & 405
☞ (N) (BB) *** Ph. Duo (ADD) 446 563-2 (2). ASMF Chamber Ens.

This superb Philips Duo assembles virtually all the important *Sonatas* for wind instruments and continuo, plus a single (*Sinfonia*) *Trio Sonata* for two violins and continuo, on a pair of discs offered for the price of one. William Bennett uses a modern flute very persuasively in the *Flute Sonatas* and includes, besides the work from Opus 1 and the three *Halle Sonatas*, a more recent discovery from a Brussels manuscript. Nicholas Kraemer and Denis Vigay provide admirable support, and the recording is most realistic and present. In the

Recorder Sonatas Michala Petri plays with her customary virtuosity and flair, and Neil Black is marvellously accomplished in the *Oboe Sonatas*. Both artists share an excellent rapport with their continuo players, who include George Malcolm (harpsichord), Denis Vigay (cello) and Graham Sheen (bassoon), and again the sound is exemplary, natural and spacious. Only those seeking original instruments need look elsewhere.

Flute Sonatas: in E min., Op. 1/1–1a; 5; 9; Halle Sonatas 1–3; Sonata in D, HWV 378
*** Hyp. CDA 67278. Beznosiuk, Tunnicliffe, Nicholson

The playing of Lisa Beznosiuk (using an attractive period instrument), Richard Tunnicliffe and Paul Nicholson is delightful in every way, freshly spontaneous, warmly responsive and always aptly paced. There are excellent, extensive notes by Stanley Sadie. As he points out, the poetic *Adagio* which opens the most recent addition to the canon (HWV 378), which comes last in the programme, shares the nobility of line of the more familiar melody in the Largo of Op. 1/1a. Both are beautifully played here, and the closing jig-like finale of the *D major Sonata* ends the concert with sparkling felicity. The Hyperion recording is naturally balanced in an ideal acoustic.

Flute or Alto Recorder Sonatas: Op. 1/2, 4, 7, 9 & 11; in B flat
*** HM HMU 907151. Verbruggen, Koopman, Linden

Marion Verbruggen uses modern copies of two alto recorders from the early eighteenth century and a similar voice flute in D; the sounds here are appealingly mellow, with the continuo featuring cello, harpsichord and chest organ. The effect is intimate, expressive and lively by turns, but with no attempt at self-conscious bravura. The recording is beautifully balanced.

Recorder Sonatas, Op. 1/2, 4, 7, 11; HWV 367a, 377
(N) *** BIS CD 955. Laurin, Masaaki & Hidemi Suzuki
(N) (B) **(*) RCA 82876 65843-2. Petri, Jarrett (harpsichord)

Dan Laurin is a virtuoso recorder player to match Michala Petri (although with less charm), and his decoration is ever impressive. He is readily matched by Hidemi Suzuki on his baroque cello (their performance of the *Furioso* movement in HWV 367a is hair-raising), and Masaaki Suzuki completes the partnership on the harpsichord. The balance is excellent, within a pleasing acoustic. Need we say more, except that the content is ungenerous for a full-priced CD.

Michala Petri has recorded these sonatas before for Philips, with a full bass continuo involving members of the ASMF Chamber Ensemble (see above). The present performances are of high quality, and Keith Jarrett is an excellent harpsichordist. However, the Philips performances are even more authentic and are beautifully balanced and recorded.

Recorder Sonatas, Op. 1/2, 4, 7, 11; in D min. (Fitzwilliam), HWV 367a; Trio Sonata in F, HWV 405; Favourite Air (Lelio's Aria from 'Scipio'); Gavotte, HWV 604; Gigue, HWV 599; Minuet, HWV 603
(BB) *** Naxos 8.550700. Czidra, Harsányi, Pertis, Keleman

A particularly attractive and generous anthology. These Hungarian musicians are first-class players and their accounts of the sonatas from Op. 1 and the *Trio Sonata* (for two recorders and continuo) are second to none. The encores (for various combinations) are most engaging, especially the *Gavotte* and *Gigue*. The recording is excellent.

Trio Sonatas, Op. 2/1–6 (HWV 386–91) (complete)
(N) *** Avie AV 0033. Huggett, Benjamin, Crouch, Hazelzet, Halls

Handel's set of *Trio Sonatas*, Opus 2, was published by Walsh as being suitable for a pair of violins, oboes or flutes, but this was a publishing gambit to secure more sales, and they are best suited for a pair of violins. The *First Sonata* is available in an alternative version, often performed on oboes; however, here Wilbert Hazelzet plays the upper part on a flute, and this works admirably. Not surprisingly with this cast list, these period performances are of high quality, catching the Handelian sprightliness and nobilty of melodic line (especially when Matthew Halls choses an organ for the continuo) and yet retaining the character of the Corellian *Sonate da chiesa* which was Handel's compositional pattern. First-class recording.

(i) Trio Sonatas, Opp. 2/5; 5/4 & 7 for 2 Violins & Continuo; Italian cantatas: (i; ii) Notte placida e cheta; (i; ii; iii) Tra la fiamme
*** Chan. 0620. (i) Purcell Qt (members); (ii) Bott; (iii) with Kershaw, Downer, Amherst, Manson

An entirely delightful recital. The *Trio Sonatas* are full of attractive invention, notably an impressive passacaglia in Op. 5/4, and they are used to frame and act as an interlude between the two Italian cantatas, ravishingly sung by Catherine Bott. It is difficult to decide which of the two – *Tra la fiamme* (about Daedalus and Icarus) with its descriptive aria *Among the flames*, or *Notte placida e cheta* ('Calm and quiet night') – is the more enchanting. The recording is ideally balanced.

Violin Sonatas, Op. 1/3, 6, 10, 12–13; in G, HWV 358; D min., HWV 359a; Allegro in C min., HWV 408; Andante in A min., HWV 412
*** HM HMU 907259. Manze, Egarr (harpsichord)

Anyone looking for a complete set of Handel's *Violin Sonatas* on period instruments need look no further. The performances are buoyant and full of life. They have undoubted panache and easy virtuosity, and the eloquence of Andrew Manze's lyrical phrasing is immediately demonstrated by the opening *Affetuoso* of the D major, Op. 1/13, with which the programme begins. The period violin is vividly caught and the harpsichord is well placed in the attractively resonant sound-picture. Highly recommended.

KEYBOARD MUSIC

Keyboard Suites Sets 1 & 2: (i) 1 in A; (ii) 2 in F; 3 in D min.; (i) 4 in E min.; (ii) 5 in E; (i) 6 in F sharp min.; 7 in G min.; (ii) 8 in F min.
⊙–📻 ⊛ (BB) *** EMI Gemini (ADD) 5 86540-2 (2). (i) Gavrilov; (ii) Richter

Keyboard Suites. (i) 9 in G min.; (ii) 10 in D min.; 11 in D min.; (i) 12 in E min.; (ii) 13 in B flat; (i) 14 in G; (ii) 15 in D min.; (i) 16 in G min.
⊙–📻 ⊛ (BB) *** EMI Gemini (ADD) 5 86543-2 (2). (i) Richter; (ii) Gavrilov – BEETHOVEN: *Piano Sonata 17* *** ⊛

These superb recordings of the Handel *Keyboard Suites* were recorded by Sviatoslav Richter and Andrei Gavrilov at the Château de Marcilly-sur-Maulne during the 1979 Tours Festival. EMI have issued the set in first-class transfers, and in an economical format – two twin CDs packaged as one, available separately, and competitively priced – and with Richter's famous 1961 account of Beethoven's *D minor Sonata*, Op. 31, No. 2, thrown in for good measure. The serenity and tranquillity of the slow movements and the radiance of the faster movements have never before been so fully realized. Not to be missed, especially at Gemini price.

Harpsichord Suites, Set 1 (1720): 1–8
(N) **(*) CPO 999 940-2 (2). Rémy (harpsichord)

Harpsichord Suites, Set 1: 1–8, HWV 426/433; 6 Fugues or Voluntariess for Organ or Harpsichord, HWV 605/10; Fugues: in F; E, HWV 611/12
(N) (M) *** Hyp. CDD 22045 (2). Nicholson (harpsichord)

Paul Nicholson's playing is admirable, full of life yet with a degree of intimacy that is very appealing. He has an ideal (unnamed) harpsichord, which is perfect for this repertoire and which is superbly recorded. Nicholson's crisp and stylish ornamentation is never fussy, and he is generous with repeats. The most famous of the eight is, of course, No. 5 which has the variations known as *The Harmonious Blacksmith* as its finale, here ending in a blaze of bravura. Highly recommended, and unlikely to be surpassed in the near future.

It would be difficult to make these suites sound dull or uninteresting and Ludger Rémy clearly enjoys them, as we do his lively, sensitive performances with their attractive element of rhythmic boldness, as at the opening of the *Harmonious Blacksmith*, which is the closing 'Air' of the *Fifth Suite*. His harpsichord is a Dutch copy of a 1700 Mietke and it has plenty of personality, although the recording is just a shade over-resonant, especially when compared with Paul Nicholson's Hyperion set. That remains a first choice, and it also contains far more music.

Harpsichord Suites, Set 1 (1720): 1–8; Set 2 (1733) 7–8; 9: Preludio (only)
*** Chan. 0669 (Set 1 1–5); Chan 0688 (Set 1 6–8; Set 2 7–8; 9: Preludio). Yates (harpsichord)

Harpsichord Suites, Set 1 (1735): 1–6
*** Chan. 0644. Yates

Sophie Yates offers both sets of the *Harpsichord Suites*, Set 1 from 1720 and Set 2 from 1733, rather clumsily laid out on three separate discs. She plays with flair and vivacity and has the exuberance and bravura – and, above all, the sense of style – that this music calls for. These are vivacious and intelligent performances, very well recorded.

Harpsichord Suites, Sets 1 & 2: 3; 8; 11; 13; 14; 15
(M) *** Lyrichord LEMS 8034 (2). Wolfe (harpsichord)

The Texan harpsichordist Paul Wolfe was a pupil and protégé of Wanda Landowska. He had a harpsichord specially built for him by Frank Rutkowski of Stoney Creek, Connecticut. It is a magnificent creature, dubbed by its maker 'the *Queen Mary*' because of its length – nine feet! It has two manuals with a range of just over five octaves, and seven pedals to alter and mute the timbre, and it includes a buff (or lute) stop which creates a dry, pizzicato sound. The range of colour is aurally fascinating and Wolfe makes the very most of the tonal and dynamic contrasts possible in Handel's music, especially in the variations. The playing itself is infectiously full of life; one's only comment is that Wolfe usually chose to pace the *Allemandes* very slowly and grandly, even the *Sarabande variée* in the 11th Suite, which is based on *La folia*. The

deep bass stop (also favoured by Landowska) can be heard to its fullest effect in the *Prelude* of the *F minor Suite* (No. 8), which provides a lively end to the second disc. The two-CD set, which has 85 minutes of music, is offered at a special price.

Keyboard Suite, Set 2, 1 in B flat (HWV 434)
(N) (M) *** Warner Elatus 2564 61762-2. Schiff (piano) –
  BRAHMS: *Variations & Fugue on a Theme of Handel;* REGER: *Variations and Fugue on a theme of Bach* ***

This is the *Harpsichord Suite* from which Brahms drew the theme of Handel's third-movement *Aria con variationi* for his own *Variations and Fugue*. András Schiff plays the Handel very stylishly, and then moves with hardly a pause straight on to the opening of the Brahms, presumably to avoid any interruption of applause, as these performances are taken from a live recital at the Concertgebouw in 1994. Excellent recording.

VOCAL MUSIC

(i) Aci, Galatea e Polifemo; (ii) Recorder Sonatas in F; C & G (transposed to F)
(B) *** HM HMA 901253/4. (i) Kirkby, Watkinson, Thomas, L. Bar., Medlam; (ii) Piquet, Toll

Aci, Galatea e Polifemo proves to be quite a different work from the always popular English masque, *Acis and Galatea*, with only one item even partially borrowed. Charles Medlam directs London Baroque in a beautifully sprung performance with three excellent soloists, the brightly characterful Emma Kirkby as Aci, Carolyn Watkinson in the lower-pitched role of Galatea, and David Thomas coping manfully with the impossibly wide range of Polifemo's part. The three recorder sonatas are comparably delightful, a welcome makeweight. Excellent sound, full of presence. Particularly enticing at bargain price.

Acis and Galatea (complete)
*** Erato 3984-25505-2 (2). Daneman, Petibon, Agnew, Cornwell, Ewing, Sinclair, Piolino, Le Monnier, Les Arts Florissants, Christie
(N) (M) **(*) DG 476 2520 (2). Burrowes, Rolfe Johnson, Hill, White, E. Bar. Sol., Gardiner

Acis and Galatea; Il pastor fido: Hunting Scene
(B) *** Double Decca 452 973-2 (2). Tear, Gomez, Langridge, Luxon, Ch. & ASMF, Marriner – Tear: 'Baroque Recital' ***

(i) Acis and Galatea; (ii) Cantata: Look Down, Harmonious Saint
*** Hyp. CDA 66361/2. (i; ii) Mark Ainsley; (i) McFadden, Covey-Crump, George, Harre-Jones; King's Cons., King

Acis and Galatea was written in the early 1730s for the Duke of Chandos and includes such famous numbers as *O ruddier than the cherry* and *Love in her eyes sits playing*. The work is now remarkably well represented on CD.

William Christie's account on Erato is probably now a first recommendation alongside Robert King's Hyperion version. Christie gives us a chamber performance with forces similar to those Handel used for the Canons performances. Tempi are inclined to be brisk and rhythms crisp but he has marshalled expert singers; Alan Ewing's Polyphemus is particularly good, well characterized and spirited. Indeed, the whole performance is full of life and personality, and William

Christie holds everything together with finesse and grace. The sound, too, is well balanced and natural.

Robert King directs a bluff, beautifully sprung reading of *Acis and Galatea* that brings out its domestic jollity. Using the original version for five solo singers and no chorus, this may be less delicate in its treatment but it is just as winning. The soloists are first rate, with John Mark Ainsley among the most stylish of the younger generation of Handel tenors, and the bass, Michael George, characterizing strongly. Claron McFadden's vibrant soprano is girlishly distinctive. This Hyperion issue provides a valuable makeweight in the florid solo cantata, thought to be originally conceived as part of *Alexander's Feast*, nimbly sung by Mark Ainsley.

The refinement and rhythmic lift of the Academy's playing under Neville Marriner make for a lively, engaging performance, marked by characterful solo singing from a strong team. The choruses are sung by a quartet drawn from a distinguished vocal sextet (Jennifer Smith, Margaret Cable, Paul Esswood, Wynford Evans, Neil Jenkins and Richard Jackson) and, with warmly atmospheric recording, the result is a sparkling entertainment. Robert Tear's tone is not always ideally mellifluous (for instance in *Love in her eyes sits playing*) but, like the others, he has a good feeling for Handelian style; the sweetness of Jill Gomez's contribution is a delight. The 1977 (originally Argo) recording is of vintage quality and this Double Decca reissue is made the more attractive by the inclusion of a further solo recital from Robert Tear of rare English baroque repertoire – music by Arne, Boyce and Hook, as well as Handel. Before this, as an interlude, comes a sprightly (orchestral) *Hunting Scene* from *Il pastor fido* consisting of a *March* and a pair of *Airs pour les chasseurs*.

Agrippina condotta a morire; Armeda abbandonata; Lucrezia (Italian cantatas)
**(*) Virgin 5 45283-2. Gens, Les Basses Réunies

The only really well-known piece here is *Lucrezia*, which Dame Janet Baker has also recorded with distinction and whom Véronique Gens does not quite match. Nevertheless, she is convincingly and powerfully indignant at her violation, and in her closing suicidal aria, although at first touchingly vulnerable, she becomes really vehement as she determines vengeance '*nell' inferno*'. The abandoned Armida, against a bare accompaniment, laments her fate (*Ah crudele!*) to a particularly lovely melisma, and at the close she reveals her deep distress in a simple siciliana, movingly sung here. Agrippina, at her son Nero's mercy, contemplates her coming execution with all the volatile anger of her tempestuous character. Véronique Gens is here in her element, revelling in the dramatic mood changes and in the vocal bravura, where she is always in control. Her decoration is apt and she is persuasively accompanied.

Marian arias and cantatas: *Ah! Che troppo inequale; Donna, che in ciel; Haec est Regina;* G. B. FERRANDINI (attrib. HANDEL): *Il pianto di Maria*
*** DG (IMS) 439 866-2. Von Otter, Col. Mus. Ant., Goebel

Dating from his years in Italy, these Handel works, directly linked to the worship of the Virgin Mary, inspire von Otter to give radiant performances. Ironically, the longest work, *Il pianto di Maria*, long attributed to Handel, has been found to be by G. B. Ferrandini; but it has many beauties, not least in a measured cavatina, *Se d'un Dio*. Both *Haec est Regina* and *Ah! che troppo inequale* are strong, imaginative arias, and *Donna, che in ciel* is a superb, full-scale cantata with a fine overture and four splendid arias. Reinhard Goebel and his team give

sympathetic support, though the period string-playing is on the abrasive side. Warm, immediate recording, which captures von Otter's firm mezzo superbly.

Ah! crudel, nel pianto mio; Armida abbandonata (cantatas)
(B) *** EMI double forte (ADD) 5 74284-2 (2). J. Baker, ECO, Leppard – BACH: *Cantatas* ***

Dame Janet Baker delivers a strongly impassioned style for music which, though formal in layout, expresses far from normal emotions. Her singing is magnificent; even though the tessitura is a little high for a mezzo it brings a striking display of virtuosity as well as of incomparable tone-colour. Leppard's accompaniments are spirited and the recording is fresh, and this makes an admirable coupling for some of her equally beautiful Bach recordings.

Alexander's Feast; Concerto grosso in C (Op. 3/4b)
(M) ** Teldec (ADD) 3984 26796-2 (2). Palmer, Rolfe Johnson, Roberts, Stockholm Ch., VCM, Harnoncourt

Alexander's Feast was the first and greatest of the odes by Dryden which Handel set to celebrate St Cecilia's Day. The invention is consistently on the highest level, without a single poor number. Harnoncourt's 1978 recording is variably successful. The team of soloists is first rate, with Felicity Palmer, Anthony Rolfe Johnson and Stephen Roberts all stylish, although Palmer's line is not always even and Roberts is too light of voice for the magnificent Revenge, Timotheus cries. The Stockholm Choir is consistently lively, a splendid ensemble, and the Concentus Musicus play with excellent precision, but the edginess that comes with authentic performance of this vintage piece (the horns sound awkward) is often disconcerting, albeit generally well served by the recording. It also seems perverse to include the *Concerto grosso* from Op. 3 as a fill-up, rather than the obvious choice of the concerto that carries the name of the vocal work.

L'allegro, il penseroso, il moderato
(M) *** Erato (ADD) 2292 45377-2 (2). Kwella, McLaughlin, Smith, Ginn, Davies, Hill, Varcoe, Monteverdi Ch., E. Bar. Sol., Gardiner
(N) (BB) * Naxos 8.557057/8 (2). Perillo, Hannigan, Schoch, MacLeod, Junge Kantorei, Frankfurt Bar. O, Martini

Taking Milton as his starting point, Handel illustrated in music the contrasts of mood and character between the cheerful and the thoughtful. Then, prompted by his librettist, Charles Jennens, he added compromise in *Il moderato*, the moderate man. The sequence of brief numbers is a delight, particularly in a performance as exhilarating as Gardiner's, with excellent soloists, choir and orchestra. The recording is first rate.

Sadly, the Naxos recording, taken live from a concert at Kloster Eberbach, has very limited success. Many of the fast numbers bring agile playing and singing, but from the start the measured numbers bring limp, heavy-handed performances with poor ensemble, not helped by scratchy period violins. The soloists are clear and well focused, with the soprano, Linda Perillo, firm and bright but with poor diction. No texts, except via the Internet.

(i; ii) *Amarilli vezzosa (Il duello amoroso). Clori, mia bella Clori;* (i) *O come chiare e belle* (Italian Cantatas)
(BB) *** Hyp. Helios CDH 55136. Kwella, L. Handel O, Darlow; with (i) Fisher, (ii) Denley

The team that recorded the highly successful Hyperion issue

of Handel's *Aminta e Fillide* here tackles three more cantatas from Handel's Italian period. The most ambitious work here is *O come chiare e belle*, a half-hour piece with allegorical overtones using three voices and written to compliment Pope Clement XI during the War of the Spanish Succession. As in most of the cantatas, some of the ideas are familiar from later versions, as in the aria, *Tornami a vagheggiar*, later used in *Alcina*, and here brilliantly sung by Gillian Fisher. The two shorter cantatas are equally charming, *Clori, mia bella Clori* for solo voice, the other a duet for soprano and contralto, well sung by Patrizia Kwella and Catherine Denley. Though Denys Darlow does not always lift rhythms enough, the freshness of the music is well caught.

Aminta e Fillide (cantata)

⊙━ (BB) *** Hyp. Helios CDH 55077. Fisher, Kwella, L. Handel O, Darlow

In writing for two voices and strings, Handel presents a simple encounter in the pastoral tradition over a span of ten brief arias which, together with recitatives and final duet, last almost an hour. The music is as charming and undemanding for the listener as it is taxing for the soloists. This lively performance, beautifully recorded with two nicely contrasted singers, delightfully blows the cobwebs off a Handel work till now totally neglected. It is even more attractive on the bargain Helios label.

Apollo e Dafne (cantata); The Alchemist (incidental music)

(BB) *** Naxos 8.555712. Pasichnyk, Pomakov, European Union Bar. O, Goodman

Apollo e Dafne, one of Handel's most delightful cantatas, tells how the determinedly chaste heroine, after an unwelcome and persistent pursuit by her godly suitor, finally escapes a fate worse than death by being transformed into a laurel bush. It has two strikingly memorable numbers, a lovely siciliano for Dafne with oboe obbligato, and an aria for Apollo, *Come rosa in su la spina*, with unison violins and a solo cello.

Roy Goodman, an alert, stylish interpreter of Handel, draws from his baroque orchestra, with its team of international players, a lively reading of this dramatic cantata on a classical theme, written by Handel at the beginning of his career during his stay in Italy. The Overture used here is the *Allegro* from the *Concerto grosso* Op. 3, No. 1, with the brisk sequence of brief arias and duets culminating in the longest aria, *Cara pianta*, with its expansive phrases well sustained by the young baritone, Robert Pomakov. As Dafne, Olga Pasichnyk sounds fresh and girlish. Voices are balanced, forward with the orchestra cleanly focused behind, despite distantly distracting reverberation. But with the attractive suite of incidental music from *The Alchemist* thrown in for good measure this is a good Naxos bargain.

Athalia (complete)

(M) *** Decca 475 207-2 (2). Sutherland, Kirkby, Bowman, Jones, Rolfe Johnson, Thomas, New College, Oxford, Ch., AAM, Hogwood

(BB) *** Naxos 8.554364/5. Scholl, Schlick, Holzhausen, Reinhold, Brutscher, MacLeod, Junge Kantorei, Frankfurt Bar. O, Martini

Hogwood's splendid set is cast from strength, with Dame Joan Sutherland's richly vibrant singing contrasting with the pure silver of Emma Kirkby, not to mention the celestial

treble of Aled Jones in the role of the boy-king, Joas. Christopher Hogwood and his Academy are on top form too, and this recording is now deservedly reissued as winner of *Gramophone*'s 1987 Choral Award.

Very well cast and stylishly performed, using period instruments, the Naxos set makes an excellent bargain. Even if the playing is not quite as crisp or purposeful as on the rival (full-priced) set from Hogwood, the result is compellingly dramatic. Outstanding among the singers is Barbara Schlick as Josabeth, pure, sweet and expressive, and though Elisabeth Scholl in the title-role provides too little contrast with her rather boyish tone not really apt for this 'Jewish Clytemnestra', her attack is clean and fresh. The castrato role of Joad is taken by Annette Reinhold, who sounds uncannily like a low counter-tenor, firm and secure, with little vibrato. Good, undistracting recording.

Belshazzar (complete)

⊙━ (B) *** DG Trio 477 037-2 (3). Rolfe Johnson, Augér, Robbin, Bowman, Wilson-Johnson, E. Concert Ch. & O, Pinnock

(M) **(*) Teldec 0630 10275-2 (3). Palmer, Lehane, Tear, Esswood, Van der Bilt, Stockholm Chamber Ch., VCM, Harnoncourt

Handel modified *Belshazzar* over the years, and Pinnock has opted not for the earliest but for the most striking and fully developed text. The cast is starry, with Arleen Augér at her most ravishing as the Babylonian king's mother, Nitocris, Anthony Rolfe Johnson in the title-role, James Bowman as the prophet Daniel and Catherine Robbin as King Cyrus, all excellent. Full, well-balanced sound. This reissued Trio is a real bargain.

With authentic style and instruments set against a relatively intimate acoustic, Harnoncourt's opening of the fine overture to *Belshazzar* on this Teldec recording may initially seem gruff. The drama is the more pointed when the soloists, led by Felicity Palmer and Robert Tear, keep the story-line clearly in mind with their expressive enunciation of the words. The other soloists, too, are excellent, notably Paul Esswood with his fresh counter-tenor tone, and the bass, Peter van der Bilt. Most enjoyable of all is the singing of the fine Stockholm choir, delectably light and pointed in some of the end-of-scene choruses. Harnoncourt is at his best when given the chance to point a brisk number with lifted rhythms, but he is less effective in warmer music.

Caro sempre di gloria; La Lucrezia; Mi palpita il cor; Splenda l'alba in oriente (Italian cantatas). Trio sonata in G, Op. 5/4

(B) **(*) Virgin 2x1 5 61803-2 (2). Lesne, Il Seminario Musicale – A. SCARLATTI: *Cantatas* **(*)

Gérard Lesne's collection of Handel cantatas makes an admirable coupling for those of Scarlatti, even if the finest, *La Lucrezia* (a masterpiece), was intended for soprano voice. *Mi palpita il cor* is also very theatrical and operatic in feeling, while *Caro sempre* and *Splenda l'alba* pay homage to St Cecilia. All these works combine bravura florid passages (which bring no problems for this fine artist) with expressive passages, which Lesne sings with much feeling. Il Seminario Musicale provides admirable backing and offers a *Trio sonata* as a central interlude. The only considerable snag about this inexpensive reissue is the absence of vital texts and translations.

Caro sempre di gloria; Splenda l'alba in oriente; Tu fedel? Tu constante? (Italian cantatas)

**(*) Australian Decca Eloquence (ADD) 461 596-2. Watts, ECO, Leppard – A. SCARLATTI: *Cantatas* **(*)

These are sympathetic performances dating from the early 1960s. Helen Watts is direct in manner rather than being especially subtle in her use of vocal colouring, but the results are free from indulgence. Leppard's direction is stylish and alive, and the recording is warm and vivid.

Carmelite Vespers

(BB) *** Virgin 2×1 5 61579-2 (2). Feldman, Kirkby, Van Evera, Cable, Nichols, Cornwell, Thomas, Taverner Ch. & Players, Parrott

What Andrew Parrott has recorded here is a reconstruction by Graham Dixon of what might have been heard in July 1707 at the church of the Carmelite Order in Rome for the Festival of Our Lady of Mount Carmel. Dixon has put the motets and Psalm settings in an order appropriate for the service of Second Vespers, noting that it is not the only possible reconstruction. So *Dixit Dominus* is introduced by plainchant and a chanted antiphon, with similar liturgical links between the other Handel settings – in turn *Laudete pueri, Te decus Virgineum, Nisi Dominus, Haec est Regina Virginum, Saeviat Tellus* and *Salve Regina*. Of these, the only unfamiliar Handel piece is *Te decus Virgineum* – which makes this not quite the new experience promised but nevertheless an enjoyable way of hearing a magnificent collection of Handel's choral music. In a liturgical setting in 1707, women's voices would not have been used, but the sopranos and altos of the Taverner Choir produce an aptly fresh sound, as does the fine group of soloists, headed by an outstanding trio of sopranos: Emma Kirkby, Jill Feldman and Emily van Evera. The recording, made in St Augustine's, Kilburn, London, has a pleasant and apt ambience, which however does not obscure detail. At its modest price this reissue is well worth having.

Chandos Anthems 1–11, HWV 246–256 (complete)

(M) *** Chan. 0554/7. Dawson, Kwella, Partridge, Bowman, George, Sixteen Ch. & O, Christophers

Chandos Anthems 1: O be joyful in the Lord; 2: In the Lord put I my trust; 3: Have mercy on me
*** Chan. 0503. Soloists, Sixteen Ch. & O, Christophers

Chandos Anthems 4: O sing unto the Lord a new song; 5: I will magnify thee; 6: As pants the hart for cooling streams
*** Chan. 0504. Soloists, Sixteen Ch. & O, Christophers

Chandos Anthems 7: My song shall be alway; 8: O come let us sing unto the Lord; 9: O praise the Lord
*** Chan. 0505. Soloists, Sixteen Ch. & O, Christophers

Chandos Anthems 10: The Lord is my light; 11: Let God arise
*** Chan. 0509. Soloists, Sixteen Ch. & O, Christophers

It is appropriate that a record label named Chandos should record a complete set of Handel's *Chandos Anthems*. This is now available on four CDs in a box (still at full price) and marks one of the most successful and worthwhile achievements of The Sixteen on CD. From the first of these fine works, which Handel based on his *Utrecht Te Deum*, to the last with its exuberant closing *Alleluja* the music is consistently inspired; it has great variety of invention and resourceful vocal scoring. The recordings are well up to the house standard.

The Choice of Hercules (cantata)

*** Hyp. CDA 67298. Gritton, Coote, Blaze, King's Consort Ch. & O, King – GREENE: *Hearken unto Me* ***

The Choice of Hercules is unique among Handel's works, a dramatic cantata to an English text in a single Act lasting 50 minutes. It was in the summer of 1750, at the peak of his powers, that Handel decided to re-use material he had composed for a play by Smollett, never produced, on the subject of Alceste. He changed both the subject and the words in his customary way, and the result is a delightful sequence of two dozen brief numbers crisply telling the story of Hercules (taken by a counter-tenor, here the excellent Robin Blaze) making his choice between Virtue (the rich, firm mezzo, Anna Coote) and Pleasure (Susan Gritton, equally radiant). Robert King, in this work otherwise unavailable on disc, brings out the unquenchable freshness of invention that Handel retained even in his last years, with the choir and players of the King's Consort consistently responsive and resilient. The extended anthem by Handel's contemporary and rival, Maurice Greene, makes a valuable extra.

(i) *Coronation Anthems* (complete); (ii) *Concerti a due cori 2–3, HWV 333/4*
◑━ (M) *** DG 447 280-2. (i) Westminster Abbey Ch., Preston; (i–ii) E. Concert; (ii) Pinnock

(i) *Coronation Anthems* (complete); (ii) *Ode for the Birthday of Queen Anne*
*** Australian Decca Eloquence (ADD) 466 676-2. (i) King's College, Cambridge, Ch., ECO, Willcocks; (ii) Kirkby, Nelson, Minty, Bowman, Hill, Thomas, Christ Church Cathedral Ch., Oxford, AAM, Preston

Willcocks's famous 1961 recording of these four anthems sounds much better on CD than it ever did on LP, and is greatly enjoyable. They are coupled with a fine performance of the *Ode for the Birthday of Queen Anne*, recorded in the late 1970s, and sound very good indeed. An excellent CD from Australian Decca.

Those who like sparer, period textures will favour Preston in the *Coronation Anthems* where, although the result is less grand, the element of contrast is even more telling. To have the choir enter with such bite and impact underlines the freshness and immediacy, with characterful period playing. An exhilarating version. The new coupling of the two *Concerti a due cori* is welcome, with the performances full of rhythmic vitality.

Coronation Anthem: Zadok the Priest

(M) *** Decca (ADD) 458 623-2. King's College, Cambridge, Ch., ASMF, Marriner – HAYDN: *Nelson Mass*; VIVALDI: *Gloria, RV 589* ***

Many collectors will be glad to have a separate recording of this fine King's performance of *Zadok the Priest*, coupled with Vivaldi's most famous *Gloria* – to say nothing of the favourite among Haydn's late Masses. Moreover the current transfer has added to the impact of the choir, so that it soars out well over the orchestra.

Deborah (complete)

*** Hyp. CDA 66841/2. Kenny, Gritton, Denley, Bowman, George, New College Ch., Oxford, Salisbury Cathedral Ch., King's Consort, King

(BB) **(*) Naxos 8.554785/87 (3). Scholl, Ducret, Zazzo, Wolak, Junge Kantorei, Frankfurt Bar. O, Martini

Handel's 1733 oratorio, *Deborah*, only the second which he wrote in English (after *Esther*) is a work which readily sustains its length in telling a Biblical story, despite Handel's extensive borrowing from earlier works. The Hyperion version is based on a performance first heard at a 1993 Promenade Concert, opening spectacularly with a fine trumpet overture which borrows fom the *Fireworks Music*. The cast is strong, with clear, bright singing from Yvonne Kenny in the name-role and Susan Gritton as Jael. James Bowman as Barak and especially Michael George as Abinoam make impressive contributions, and Catherine Denley is even more striking as Sisera. But what gives the set its distinction is the fine singing from the combined choristers of Salisbury Cathedral and the Choir of New College, Oxford, although the resonance does take some of the edge off the sound. Nevertheless, Robert King's direction is assured and stylish and this is most enjoyable.

Recorded live in May 1999 in a reverberant German church, the Naxos version also gets off to a big, bold start, again with trumpets and drums adding to the impact. While rhythms tend to be too square, the choral singing is fresh and lively, but the soloists make a variable team. Best is the counter-tenor, Lawrence Zazzo, clear-toned and stylish as Barak, leader of the army of Israel, but both Elisabeth Scholl in the title-role and Natacha Ducret as Jael are edgy in tone and often not steady. The oratorio comes on three discs instead of the two for the rival Hyperion version, but there is the incidental advantage of having each of the three parts on a separate disc. That full-priced rival brings a much more sympathetic performance with soloists far finer. Even so, this Naxos set at super-budget price is valuable in spreading knowledge of a long-neglected work, and is worth its asking price.

Dettingen Te Deum; Dettingen Anthem
*** DG 410 647-2. Westminster Abbey Ch., E. Concert, Preston

The *Dettingen Te Deum* is a splendid work, continually reminding one of *Messiah*, written the previous year. Preston's Archiv performance with the English Concert makes an ideal recommendation, with its splendid singing, crisp but strong, excellent recording and a generous, apt coupling. This setting of *The King shall rejoice* should not be confused with the *Coronation Anthem* of that name. It is less inspired, but has a magnificent double fugue for finale. The recording is first class.

Dixit Dominus; Coronation Anthem: Zadok the Priest
⊶ (BB) *** Warner Apex 0927 48683-2. Palmer, Marshall, Brett, Messana, Morton, Thomson, Wilson-Johnson, Monteverdi Ch. & O, Gardiner

Dixit Dominus; Nisi Dominus; Silete venti
*** Chan. 0517. Dawson, Russell, Brett, Partridge, George, Sixteen Ch. & O, Christophers

Handel's *Dixit Dominus* divides into eight sections, and the setting, while showing signs of his mature style in embryo, reflects also the Baroque tradition of contrasts between small and large groups. The writing is extremely florid and requires bravura from soloists and chorus alike. John Eliot Gardiner catches all its brilliance and directs an exhilarating performance, marked by strongly accented, sharply incisive singing from the choir and outstanding solo contributions. In high contrast with the dramatic choruses, the duet for two sopranos, *De torrente*, here beautifully sung by Felicity Palmer

and Margaret Marshall, is languorously expressive, but stylishly so. Other soloists match that, and the analogue recording is first rate, making this reissue a real bargain.

Christophers's speeds tend to be more extreme, slow as well as fast, and the recorded sound, though full and well detailed, is less immediate. The Chandos issue gains from having a third item. *Silete venti* allows the silver-toned Lynne Dawson to shine even more than in the other items, ending with a brilliant *Alleluia* in galloping compound time.

Esther (1718 version)
(BB) *** Regis RRC 2025 (2). Russell, Randle, Padmore, Argenta, Chance, George, Sixteen Ch. & O, Christophers

Esther was the first of Handel's oratorios with a substantial role for the chorus, and this period performance opts for the 1718 version of the oratorio. It may be odd structurally compared with later revisions – with Esther appearing only after the halfway point – but the six compact scenes in a single Act are crisper, so suiting modern taste. Christophers with a small choir of 18 singers offers an aptly intimate view, light and fresh, helped by bright, immediate recording. Lynda Russell and Nancy Argenta are exceptionally sweet and pure in the soprano roles, with the two tenors sharply contrasted – Thomas Randle more heroic, Mark Padmore purer and more refined. Michael George gives fine Handelian thrust to the bass solos.

(i) Gloria in B flat; (ii) Dixit Dominus
(M) *** BIS CD 301235. (i) Kirkby, Royal Ac. of Music Bar. O, Cummings; (ii) Martinpelto, Von Otter, Stockholm Bach Ch.; Drottingholm Bar. Ens., Ohrwall

The existence of the *Gloria* has been known for some time, and there is a full score plus two sets of parts in London's Royal Academy of Music library. But only in September 2000 was it positively identified as a work by Handel, and an inspired one too. It was appropriate that Emma Kirkby, the reigning queen of baroque, was given the privilege of making the first recording, accompanied by an excellent modern-instrument chamber group. She sings the florid opening exultantly and is even more impressive in the heady bravura of the closing *Cum sancto spirito*. Yet it is the beauty of her lyrical singing which stands out even more, and indeed her stylish control of ornamentation. The recording is vividly forward.

The performance of *Dixit Dominus* also has very fine soloists, although none quite to match Kirkby in easy flowing lines. But the chorus is equally important here and the singing of the Stockholm Choir has splendid vigour and bite. The recording is set further back here than in the *Gloria*, and effectively so, for the period-instrumental accompaniment is without edginess.

Israel in Egypt (oratorio; with *The Lamentations of the Israelites for the Death of Joseph*)
(N) (BB) ** Virgin 5 62390-2 (4). Argenta, Van Evera, Wilson, Rolfe Johnson, Thomas, White, Taverner Ch. & Players, Parrott – *Messiah* **

(i) Israel in Egypt; (ii) Organ Concerto in F (The Cuckoo and the Nightingale), HWV 295
(BB) *(**) Regis RRC 2012 (2). (i) Jenkin, Dunkley, Trevor, MacKenzie, Evans, Birchall, The Sixteen; (ii) Nicholson; O of The Sixteen, Christophers

(i) *Israel in Egypt*; (ii) *Chandos Anthem 10: The Lord is my Light. Organ Concerto in F (The Cuckoo and the Nightingale)*

(B) *** Double Decca (ADD) 443 470-2 (2). (i) Gale, Watson, Bowman, Partridge, McDonnell, Watts, Christ Church Cathedral, Oxford, Ch., ECO, Preston; (ii) Cantelo, Partridge, King's College, Cambridge, Ch., ASMF, Willcocks

(i) *Israel in Egypt. Coronation Anthems: Zadok the Priest; The King shall Rejoice*

☛ (B) *** Ph. Duo 473 304 (2). (i) Holton, Priday, Deam, Stafford, Chance, Collin, Kenny, Robertson, Salmon, Tindall, Tusa, Clarkson, Purves; Monteverdi Ch., E. Bar. Sol., Gardiner

(i) *Israel in Egypt: Lamentations of the Israelites for the Death of Joseph*; (ii) *The Ways of Zion do Mourn (funeral anthem)*

*** Erato (ADD) 2292 45399-2 (2). (i) Knibbs, Troth, Greene, Priday, Royall, Stafford, Gordon, Clarkson, Elliott, Kendall, Varcoe, Stewart; (ii) Burrowes, Brett, Hill, Varcoe; Monteverdi Ch. & O, Gardiner

In his Philips Duo version of *Israel in Egypt* Gardiner secures subtler playing from his period instruments, not just more stylish and generally more lightly sprung than in the earlier, Erato version, but conveying more clearly the emotional and dramatic thrust. So the start is more mysterious, and such illustrative numbers as the hopping of the frogs during the Plague choruses are even more delightfully pointed than before. As before, first-rate soloists have been chosen from the chorus, and the digital recording is full and well balanced. The *Coronation Anthems* are also winningly performed. At Duo price, this is even more of a first choice.

Using modern instruments, Gardiner made his Erato recording in 1978. His style here, crisply rhythmic, superbly sprung, with dozens of detailed insights in bringing out word-meaning, is very much what has since become his forte in period performances of Handel and others. The singing both of the chorus and of the twelve soloists chosen from its members is excellent, though, like all other modern recordings, this one slightly falls down in resonance on the most famous number, the duet for basses, *The Lord is a Man of War*. In almost every way Gardiner gains by presenting the *Lamentations* not as an introduction to the main oratorio, but as a supplement, with the same music given in its original form, with text unamended, as written for the funeral cantata for Queen Caroline. Excellent, full-bodied, analogue sound.

Simon Preston, using a small choir with boy trebles and an authentically sized orchestra, directs a performance that is beautifully in scale. He starts with *The Cuckoo and the Nightingale Organ Concerto* – a procedure sanctioned by Handel himself at the first performance. Though Elizabeth Gale is not as firm a soprano as Heather Harper on Mackerras's (currently withdrawn) Archiv set, the band of soloists is an impressive one and the ECO is in splendid form. The 1975 recording (originally Argo), vividly transferred, is warmly atmospheric. This Double Decca set generously includes the tenth Chandos anthem, *The Lord is my Light*, remarkable for magnificent fugal writing, freshly performed by the King's College Choir under Sir David Willcocks.

Parrott directs a clean-cut, well-paced reading which wears its period manners easily. This may lack the distinctive insights of Gardiner's more sharply rhythmic versions, but with excellent choral and solo singing the performance is unlikely to offend anyone. Good, warm sound. Parrott follows the precedent of Handel's very first performance in using as the first part of the oratorio the cantata written on the death of Queen Caroline, *The Lamentations of the Israelites for the Death of Joseph*, with text duly adapted. This set is now attractively inexpensive, but comes in harness with a less recommendable *Messiah* (see below).

Christophers uses the *Lamentations* as a first part to the oratorio, and also – another nod towards Handelian performance-practice – adds the best-known of Handel's organ concertos, the *Cuckoo and the Nightingale*, between Parts One and Two. The playing and singing are bright, but sadly the (originally Collins) recording is so reverberant that there is a serious loss of inner detail.

Jephtha
*** Ph. 422 351-2 (3). Robson, Dawson, Von Otter, Chance, Varcoe, Holton, Monteverdi Ch., E. Bar. Sol., Gardiner

John Eliot Gardiner's recording was made live at the Göttingen Festival in 1988 and, though the sound does not have quite the bloom of his finest studio recordings of Handel, the exhilaration and intensity of the performance come over vividly, with superb singing from both chorus and an almost ideal line-up of soloists. Nigel Robson's tenor may be on the light side for the title-role, but the sensitivity of expression is very satisfying. Lynne Dawson, with her bell-like soprano, sings radiantly as Iphis; and the counter-tenor, Michael Chance, as her beloved, Hamor, is also outstanding. Anne Sofie von Otter is powerful as Storge, and Stephen Varcoe with his clear baritone, again on the light side, is a stylish Zebul. As for the Monteverdi Choir, their clarity, incisiveness and beauty are a constant delight.

Joshua (complete)
☛ ◉ *** Hyp. CDA 66461/2. Kirkby, Bowman, Mark Ainsley, George, Oliver, New College, Oxford, Ch., King's Consort, King

Emma Kirkby is here ideally sparkling and light in the role of Achsa, daughter of the patriarchal leader, Caleb (taken here by the bass, Michael George). Her love for Othniel, superbly sung by James Bowman, provides the romantic interest in what is otherwise a grandly military oratorio, based on the Book of Joshua. The brisk sequence of generally fresh arias is punctuated by splendid choruses, with solo numbers often inspiring choral comment. The singing is consistently strong and stylish, with the clear, precise tenor John Mark Ainsley in the title-role. Robert King and his Consort crown their achievement in other Hyperion issues, notably their Purcell series, with polished, resilient playing, and the choir of New College, Oxford, sings with ideal freshness. Warm, full sound.

Judas Maccabaeus (complete)
☛ (M) *** DG (ADD) 447 692-2 (3). Palmer, Baker, Esswood, Davies, Shirley-Quirk, Keyte, Wandsworth School Ch., ECO, Mackerras
**(*) Hyp. CDA 66641/2 (2). Kirkby, Denley, Bowman, MacDougall, George, Birchall, Ch. of New College, Oxford, King's Consort, King

Judas Maccabaeus may have a lopsided story, with a high proportion of the finest music given to the anonymous soprano and contralto roles, Israelitish Woman and Israelitish Man; but the sequence of Handelian gems is irresistible, the more so in a performance as sparkling as DG's reissued 1976 recording under Sir Charles Mackerras. Though not everyone will approve of the use of boys' voices in the choir (inevitably the tone and intonation are not flawless), it gives an extra bit of character. Hearing even so hackneyed a number as *See, the conqu'ring hero* in its true scale is a delightful surprise. The orchestral group and continuo sound splendidly crisp. Ryland Davies and John Shirley-Quirk are most stylish, while both Felicity Palmer and Janet Baker crown the whole set with glorious singing, not least in a delectable sequence, towards the end of Act I, on the subject of liberty. The recording quality is outstanding in its CD format, fresh, vivid and clear.

With some superb solo singing and refined instrumental textures, Robert King's performance can be recommended warmly, even though it is not as lively as some of his Purcell recordings. It is partly that the chorus is not as forward or as bright-toned as one wants in Handel; but there is much to enjoy, with Jamie MacDougall clean and bright if not always ideally firm in the title-role, and with the pure-toned Emma Kirkby well contrasted with the much warmer mezzo of Catherine Denley. Michael George gives splendid weight to the bass arias so central to Handel oratorio.

Sacred cantatas: Laudate pueri (Psalm 112); Coelestis dum spirat aura; O qualis de coelo sonus; Salve Regina. Trio Sonata in G min., HWV 27

⊗ ✸ *** BIS CD 1065. Kirkby, L. Baroque, Medlam

Emma Kirkby is in glorious voice throughout this splendid recital, floating the opening line of *Salve Regina* most beautifully, and then dashing away to a sparkling accompaniment in *Eja ergo*. Her closing *Alleluja!* in *O qualis de coelo sonus* is wonderfully nimble, as is the flowing *Felix dies* ('Happy day') of *Coelestis dum spirat aura*. Finest of all is the setting of *Psalm 112*, where she soars up to the heavens on a characteristic repeated phrase and sings flowingly and ravishingly against a particularly attractive accompaniment – in which the continuo with organ is delightfully conceived – capped by the spirited runs of the *Gloria Patri*. This is one of Kirkby's very finest Handel records. Her voice is caught with a lovely bloom, and the balance with the accompaniment is just about perfect. Not to be missed.

Messiah (complete)

⊶ (N) *** DG **SACD** Surround Sound 477 066-2; CD 453 464-3 (2). Röschmann, Gritton, Fink, Daniels, Neal Davies, Gabrieli Consort & Players, McCreesh ✓

*** DG 423 630-2 (2). Augér, Von Otter, Chance, Crook, Tomlinson, E. Concert Ch., E. Concert, Pinnock ✓✓

*** BIS CD 891/892 (2). Midori Suzuki, Mera, Elwes, Thomas, Bach Collegium Japan, Masaaki Suzuki

(M) *** Hyp. Dyad CDD 22019 (2). Dawson, Denley, Davies, George, Sixteen Ch. & O, Christophers

*** HM HMC 901498.99 (2). Schlick, Piau, Scholl, Padmore, Berg, Les Arts Florissants, Christie

*** Ph. 434 297-2 (2). Marshall, Robbin, Rolfe Johnson, Brett, Hale, Shirley-Quirk, Monteverdi Ch., E. Bar. Sol., Gardiner

*** Decca 414 396-2 (2). Te Kanawa, Gjevang, Lewis, Howell, Chicago Ch. & SO, Solti — DISLIKE

(M) *** Ph. Duo (ADD) 464 703-2 (2). Harper, Watts, Wakefield, Shirley-Quirk, L. Symphony Ch., LSO, C. Davis

(B) *** EMI (ADD) 5 69449-2 (2). Harwood, Baker, Esswood, Tear, Herincx, Amb. S., ECO, Mackerras ✓✓

(B) **(*) CfP (ADD) 575 7762 (2). Morison, Thomas, Lewis, Milligan, Huddersfield Ch. Soc., RLPO, Sargent

(M) **(*) EMI (ADD) 7 63784-2 (2). Trebles from King's, Bowman, Tear, Luxon, King's College, Cambridge, Ch., ASMF, Willcocks

(BB) **(*) Naxos 8.550667/8. Amps, Davidson, Doveton, Van Asch, Scholars Bar. Ens.

(N) (BB) ** Virgin 5 62390-2 (4). Kirkby, Van Evera, Cable, Bowman, Cornwell, Thomas, Taverner Ch. & Players, Parrott – *Israel in Egypt* **

DG's superb recording for Paul McCreesh's 1996 set is the first to appear on Surround Sound SACD – and very impressive it is. If the balance is correctly set between front and rear speakers, the sense of sitting within the warm acoustics of All Saints Church, Tooting, is very real indeed. Using the Foundling Hospital version of the score, McCreesh, in re-creating the sort of performance Handel supervised there in 1754, sought to present a 'thoroughly modern performance – A *Messiah* for the Millennium' as he puts it. It is a bright and individual reading, bringing out the drama of the music with extreme speeds in both directions. The chorus copes well with all his bracing tempi, and the result is both expressive and vital. He is lucky to have an excellent team of young soloists, with both sopranos singing with appealing freshness and the splendid contralto, Bernarda Fink, touchingly simple in *He was despised*. The golden-voiced tenor opens the performances with a warmly lyrical account of *Comfort ye my people*, and the resonant bass, Neal Davies, shakes with the best of them in *Thus said the Lord of Hosts*. It is altogether a most stimulating performance, and for collectors with surround sound facility will probably be a first choice, even before Pinnock and Suzuki.

Trevor Pinnock presents a performance using authentically scaled forces which, without inflation, rise to grandeur and magnificence, qualities Handel himself would have relished. The fast contrapuntal choruses, such as *For unto us a Child is born*, are done lightly and resiliently in the modern manner, but there is no hint of breathlessness, and Pinnock (more than his main rivals) balances his period instruments to give a satisfying body to the sound. There is weight too in the singing of the bass soloist, John Tomlinson, firm, dark and powerful, yet marvellously agile in divisions. Arleen Augér's range of tone and dynamic is daringly wide, with radiant purity in *I know that my Redeemer liveth*. Anne Sofie von Otter sustains *He was despised* superbly with her firm, steady voice. Some alto arias are taken just as beautifully by the outstanding counter-tenor, Michael Chance. The tenor, Howard Crook, is less distinctive but still sings freshly and attractively.

With his excellent Japanese singers and players, Masaaki Suzuki here excels himself. His crisp, sharp manner goes with transparent textures and sprung rhythms, and though modest forces are used the result has natural dramatic weight. The consistent alertness of the chorus is a delight but the fast speeds he tends to prefer never sound breathless, and he is never afraid to choose a spacious tempo, if the mood of the music demands it – as in the aria, *He was despised*, sung with seamless beauty by the male alto, Yoshikazu Mera. The soprano Midori Suzuki sings with radiant purity, notably in *I know that my Redeemer liveth*, and the two British soloists are excellent too, with John Elwes bright and eager and David Thomas caught at his warmest. This can readily be recommended alongside Pinnock, Christophers and Christie.

Harry Christophers consistently adopts speeds more relaxed than those we have grown used to in modern performances, and the effect is fresh, clear and resilient. Alto

Vanguard M. Price, Minton, Young
Somary 1970
McGegan – Lorraine Hunt Lieberson

Marriner – Elly Ameling

lines in the chorus are taken by male singers; a counter-tenor, David James, is also used for the *Refiner's fire*, but *He was despised* is rightly given to the contralto, Catherine Denley, warm and grave at a very measured tempo. The team of five soloists is as fine as that on any rival set, with the soprano, Lynne Dawson, singing with silvery purity. The band of 13 strings sounds as clean and fresh as the choir. Even the *Hallelujah chorus* – always a big test in a small-scale performance – works well, with Christophers in his chosen scale, through dramatic timpani and trumpets conveying necessary weight. The sound has all the bloom one associates with St John's recordings. Now offered as a two-for-one Dyad, this is a real bargain.

More than most period performances William Christie gives the impression of a live performance caught on the wing, even though it was recorded in the studio. His preference for fast, resilient speeds and light textures, not least in choruses, never prevents him from giving due emotional weight to such key numbers as *He was despised*. That is superbly sung, with touching simplicity, firm tone and flawless intonation, by the counter-tenor, Andreas Scholl. The other singers too sound fresh and young, with the two sopranos, Barbara Schlick and Sandrine Piau, delectably counterpointed, both pure and true, making light of the elaborate divisions in such a number as *Rejoice greatly*. The treble, Tommy Williams, also sings with beautiful, firm clarity in the Angel's narration, *There were shepherds abiding in the fields*. The tenor, Mark Padmore, and the bass, Nathan Berg, complete the pattern, light by old-fashioned standards but fresh and cleanly focused. Christie in his text opts for Handel's later versions of numbers. Excellent sound, though the chorus is placed a little backwardly.

John Eliot Gardiner chooses bright-toned sopranos instead of boys for the chorus and he uses, very affectingly, a solo treble to sing *There were shepherds abiding*. Speeds are fast and light, and the rhythmic buoyancy in the choruses is very striking, though idiosyncratically Gardiner begins *Hallelujah!* on a *pianissimo*. *Why do the nations* and *The trumpet shall sound* (both sung with great authority) come over dramatically, and the soloists are all first class, with the soprano Margaret Marshall finest of all, especially in *I know that my Redeemer liveth*. Other highlights include Marshall's angelic version of *Rejoice greatly*, skipping along in compound time.

Sir Georg Solti inspires a vital, exciting reading. The Chicago Symphony Orchestra and Chorus respond to some challengingly fast but never breathless speeds, showing what lessons can be learnt from authentic performance in clarity and crispness. Yet the joyful power of *Hallelujah* and the *Amen chorus* is overwhelming. Dame Kiri Te Kanawa matches anyone on record in beauty of tone and detailed expressiveness, while the other soloists are first rate too, though Anne Gjevang has rather too fruity a timbre. Brilliant, full sound.

The LSO recording conducted by Sir Colin Davis, in the 1960s the first of a new generation of *Messiah* recordings, fresh and urgent, has not lost its impact, remastered in bright sound. Textures are beautifully clear and, thanks to Davis, the rhythmic bounce of such choruses as *For unto us* is really infectious. Even *Hallelujah* loses little and gains much from being performed by a chorus of this size. Excellent singing from all four soloists, particularly Helen Watts who, following early precedent, is given *For He is like a refiner's fire* to sing, instead of the bass, and produces a glorious chest register.

With Sir Charles Mackerras the chorus is not so fresh as Davis's London Symphony Choir but has a compensating breadth and body. More than Davis, Mackerras adopts

Handel's alternative versions, so the soprano aria, *Rejoice greatly*, is given in its optional 12/8 version. A male alto is also included, Paul Esswood, and he is given some of the bass arias as well as some of the regular alto passages. Among the soloists, Janet Baker is outstanding. Her intense, slow account of *He was despised* – with decorations on the reprise – is sung with profound feeling. The recording is warm and full in ambience and, with the added brightness of CD, sounds extremely vivid.

It is good to have Sir Malcolm Sargent's 1959 recording restored to the catalogue on Classics for Pleasure. For, apart from the pleasure given by a performance that brings out the breadth of Handel's inspiration, it provides an important correction to misconceptions about pre-authentic practice. Sargent unashamedly fills out the orchestration (favouring Mozart's scoring where possible). Compared with Sir Colin Davis, his tempi are measured, but his pacing is sure and spontaneous, and with a hundred-strong Huddersfield group, no one will be disappointed by the weight or vigour of the choruses. There is some splendid singing from all four soloists, and Marjorie Thomas's *He was despised* is memorable in its moving simplicity. The success of the new CD transfer is remarkable: the old analogue LPs never sounded as clear as this. The only snag is the violin timbre, now better focused but still thin.

David Willcocks's recording, made in the Chapel at King's in 1971–2, has been described as the 'all-male *Messiah*', since a counter-tenor takes over the contralto solos, and the full complement of the trebles of King's College Choir sings the soprano solos, even the florid ones like *Rejoice greatly*; the result is enchanting, often light and airy. The bigger choruses do not lack robust qualities. The sound is vivid and atmospheric. A gimmicky version, perhaps, but one that many will find refreshing and involving.

On the bargain Naxos label the Scholars Baroque Ensemble presents the oratorio on the smallest possible scale, with individual singers from the small chorus coming forward to sing the arias. In keeping with this approach, the performance is directed by one of the basses, David van Asch, and characteristically the booklet seeks as far as possible not to highlight individual contributions but to emphasize teamwork. At brisk speeds, with rhythms well sprung, this will please those who fancy such an approach, though the period-instrumental sound is abrasive, and none of the singers has a voice of star quality. By their own definition, these are good choristers rather than great soloists.

Andrew Parrott assembled a fine team of performers, as well as his own Taverner Choir and Players, on his 1989 set. Emma Kirkby is even more responsive than she was on her earlier recording for Oiseau-Lyre; but, for all its merits, the performance lacks the zest and the sense of live communication that mark out a version like Pinnock's, another period performance that also dares to adopt slow, expressive speeds for such arias as *He was despised* and *I know that my Redeemer liveth*. Even at bargain price this is not a strong contender, and it now comes in a four-disc set, coupled with *Israel in Egypt*.

Messiah (reorchestrated by Sir Eugene Goossens)

⊛ (M) *** RCA (ADD) 09026 61266-2 (3). Vyvyan, Sinclair, Vickers, Tozzi, RPO Ch. & O, Beecham

This is a performance flamboyantly reorchestrated, both dramatic and moving, which at every point radiates the natural flair of the conductor. The use of the cymbals to cap the

[handwritten marginalia: 300]

[handwritten marginalia: SHE'S AWFUL & ruins the record my for overall choice]

[handwritten marginalia: yes]

[handwritten marginalia: still fabulous after all these years]

choruses *For unto us a Child is born* and *Glory to God* is unforgettable. Many of Beecham's tempi are slower than we expect today, but not the *Hallelujah Chorus*, which is fast and resilient. Jennifer Vyvyan and Monica Sinclair both sing freshly. Jon Vickers brings to his tenor arias a heroic quality that is often welcome and effective. Giorgio Tozzi's English is sound and his management of the tricky bass arias (especially *Why do the nations*) compels admiration. The 1959 recording of the chorus and orchestra is full and expansive in its CD transfer, and the soloists have remarkable presence and immediacy. The third disc with its 17-minute appendix of eight items – normally cut at the time this recording was made – comes as a bonus, as the set is priced as for two mid-range CDs.

(i) *Messiah* (complete); (ii) *Israel in Egypt*: 3 Choruses: *But for His people; Moses and the children of Israel; The Lord is a man of war. Amaryllis Suite* (arr. Beecham): *Gavotte; Scherzo*
(***) Biddulph mono WHL 059/61 (3). (i) Suddaby, Thomas, Nash, Antony, Luton Ch. Soc.; (ii) Leeds Festival Ch.; RPO, Beecham (with BACH: *Christmas Oratorio: Sinfonia* (***))

Issued only in the United States, never in Britain, this recording of 1947 is one of Beecham's rarest, an oddity but a fascinating one. Unlike his later, RCA version of *Messiah*, this one has no percussion trimmings in the orchestra, but, as he explains in a spoken introduction, he uses choirs of different sizes for different numbers. Speeds are often extreme, commendably so in brisk numbers, while his expansive slow speeds bring persuasive, Beechamesque moulding. A fine quartet of soloists includes the great tenor Heddle Nash. The *Israel in Egypt* excerpts date from 1934, celebrating Beecham's work at the Leeds Festival, the instrumental pieces from 1947. Beecham rarely conducted Bach, and in this brief bonus he makes the *Sinfonia* sound like one of his arrangements of Handel.

Messiah (slightly abridged)
✹ (BB) (***) Dutton Lab. mono 2CDEA 5010 (2). Baillie, Ripley, Johnson, Walker, Huddersfield Ch. Soc., Liverpool PO, Sargent

Sargent's first recording of Handel's *Messiah* is not complete. Following his usual performance practice, three numbers are cut from Part II and four from Part III. The recording venue was Huddersfield Town Hall in 1946, when that great Choral Society was still at its peak, and Handel's masterpiece is here brought vividly to life in a brilliant Dutton transfer from the 78s. What is so involving is the way this remarkably realistic and present recording (in many ways more vivid than the later, stereo set), made in a series of four-minute takes, comes over with the tension of a live performance. There may be strictures about the style, not least the slow tempi (especially in Part II) and the orchestration (Prout's edition, plus additions from Mozart's version) and of course its weight and scale. But the chorus sings throughout with enormous conviction and the four fine soloists obviously live their parts, with their enunciation making every word clear. The star of the performance is Isobel Baillie. Her first entry in *There were shepherds* is a moment of the utmost magic, and what follows is utterly ravishing, while her gloriously beautiful *I know that my Redeemer liveth* has never been surpassed on record. Gladys Ripley sings *He was despised* with moving simplicity and restraint, and she warmly introduces *He shall feed His flock*, sharing it with Baillie, who re-enters exquisitely. At

bargain price this is an essential investment for anyone who loves the English amateur choral tradition.

Messiah (sung in English): highlights
(M) **(*) Classic fM 75605 57057-2. Kwella, Denley, Ainsley, Terfel, London Musici & Chamber Ch., Stephenson
(M) *** EMI Red Line (ADD) 5 72431 (from above set, cond. Mackerras)
(BB) **(*) EMI Encore 5 74733-2. Battle, Quivar, Aler, Ramey, Toronto Mendelssohn Ch. & SO, A. Davis
(B) **(*) CfP (ADD) 762 0202. A. Morison, Thomas, Lewis, Milligan, Huddersfield Ch. Soc., RLPO, Sargent
(BB) **(*) Belart (ADD) 450 045-2 (from above Philips Duo set, cond. C. Davis)
(N) (B) *(**) Cala 2-CD CACD 0538. Soloists, L. Symphony Ch., LSO, Stokowski – VIVALDI: *Four Seasons* *(**)
(N) (M) ** Warner Apex (ADD) 0927 48726-2. (from complete recording with Palmer, Watts, Davies, Shirley-Quirk, ECO Ch. & O, Leppard)

Recorded for Conifer in 1989, Mark Stephenson's disc of favourite numbers offers fresh, bright performances vividly recorded in full, atmospheric sound. In style this follows the example of Colin Davis's vintage recording, using modern instruments but with choruses challengingly fast and with bright, crisp choral singing. It was recorded before Bryn Terfel became an international star, and his voice is gloriously dark and firm in his two solo passages. Sadly, *The trumpet shall sound* is not included. The others are impressive too, notably Patrizia Kwella at her most golden. A pity this is not the complete oratorio.

Otherwise Mackerras is first choice, while the great and pleasant surprise among the bargain selections is the Classics for Pleasure CD of highlights from Sir Malcolm Sargent's 1959 recording; no one will be disappointed with *Hallelujah*, while the closing *Amen* brings a powerful apotheosis.

Andrew Davis's 1987 performance of *Messiah* steps back a little in time to what was until recently considered a traditional style of performance; nevertheless his presentation uses current practice in using judicious decoration in *da capo* arias, and his tempi for choruses are lively, even though he uses a modern orchestra and a large amateur choral group. They are well trained and generally cope well with the demands he places on them. The special strength of this set of highlights lies in the soloists, a team without weakness, each of them getting a chance to shine, although the tenor only has the opening number, and the soprano gets the lion's share. Kathleen Battle's *I know that my Redeemer liveth* has mature expressive feeling and Florence Quivar's *He was despised* is comparably eloquent. The sound is first class, clear and well balanced and the selection runs for 75 minutes. Excellent value at budget price.

Although it is not generous, the Belart set of highlights from Sir Colin Davis's mid-1960s recording offers a dozen key items, including most of the favourites, but not *He was despised*.

Stokowski can hardly be counted a naturally idiomatic Handel interpreter, and his selection from *Messiah* (he chose the items himself) is arbitrary for, as he said about his choice: 'Each soloist has the finest music for his or her voice, and the tenor has three solos simply because the music is so great.' The soloists, all first rate, are forwardly balanced and Stokowski's tempi and style are inevitably idiosyncratic, as for instance his slow speed for *And the glory of the Lord*, and the warmly sensuous richness of the strings in the *Pastoral Symphony*. As Edward Johnson relates in his excellent historical note for this reissue, there was barely any rehearsal during the sessions. Sheila Armstrong (who sings gloriously in *He shall feed his flock* and *I know that my Redeemer liveth*) recalls that the conductor 'just wanted a beautiful line and heartfelt words, which is what I tried to do'. She certainly succeeds, as do her companions, and the LSO and London Symphony Chorus are well up to standard.

Raymond Leppard's set of highlights from an admirable 1976 complete set is generous (73 minutes), but the selection is arbitrary and omits key items including *For unto us a child is born*, *I know that my Redeemer liveth* and *He was despised*. The performance is a fine, enjoyable account with lively but not exaggeratedly fast tempi, except in *The trumpet shall sound*, which is very fast indeed, while *All we like sheep*, preceded by a delightful flourish from the organ, is engagingly jaunty. Both Helen Watts and Felicity Palmer are in excellent form, which makes the omissions all the more surprising. The chorus is admirably clear and precise.

Der Messias (arr. & orch. Mozart, K.572)

(N) **(*) Arthaus **DVD** 101 175. Donna Brown, Kallisch, Sacca, Miles, Stuttart Gäschinger Kanorei, Rilling (V/D: Helmut Rost)

It is curious that the first DVD of *Messiah* should be Mozart's German version, commissioned by Baron Gottfried van Swieten in 1789 and first performed at the Esterházy Viennese palace. It was intended to 'suit contemporary tastes', and the additional scoring for woodwind, horns and brass certainly gives the orchestra an eighteenth-century sound, while the three trombones add to the weight of the choruses. Ironically, in the truncated *Sie schalft die Posaun* the trumpet sounds only very modestly and much of the instrumental obbligato is given to the horn, for there were no solo performers readily available on high baroque trumpets in Mozart's time. Quite reasonably, the conductor here, Helmuth Rilling, has opted for a traditional rather than a period-style performance, and he deliberately opts for spacious, though not leaden, tempi. The result remains enjoyable and quite fresh.

Apart from providing a 'concise' edition, Mozart made a number of alterations to Handel's original, often giving parts of choruses to his solo group (with contrasts rather like a vocal *Concerto grosso*), and this is particularly striking in *For unto us a Child is born*. Rilling has a splendid team of soloists, and an excellent chorus. No one could complain of a lack of power and impact in *Hallelujah*, and the closing *Würdig is das Lamm* and *Amen* are equally impressive. The key solos all come off well. The tenor and bass are excellent, though, despite beautiful singing from Donna Brown and Cornelia Kallosch, neither *I know that my Redeemer liveth* nor *He was despised* are as moving sung in German as they are in English. In the latter case that is partly because the more richly scored orchestral accompaniment is less telling than the violins alone in echoing the singer at her final anguished words. Nevertheless, overall this is very enjoyable; the camera angles are not too fussy, and the backcloth of the Stadtkirche Ellwangen in Stuttgart is visually pleasing. However, as this is not a live performance, the empty hall resonance does tend slightly to blur the choral focus.

Nabal (compiled by John Christopher Smith)

(BB) **(*) Naxos 8.555276/77 (2). MacLeod, Boog, Schoch, Heijden, Perillo, Junge Kantorei, Frankfurt Bar. O, Martini

Given just two performances in 1764, five years after Handel's death, *Nabal* is a pasticcio oratorio with material drawn from a wide range of the composer's works. It was compiled by John Christopher Smith, Handel's favourite copyist as well as a composer, using material left to him in Handel's will. The story is drawn from the Old Testament, the book of Samuel, where the young David defies the rich and churlish Nabal, who promptly dies and whose wife, Abigail, then becomes one of David's wives. The libretto was written by Thomas Morell, who had collaborated with Handel on at least four of his oratorios, including *Theodora* and *Jephtha*. Here he had to fit words to music already written, with fluent results. It makes an attractive curiosity in a generally well-sung, alert performance, recorded live with occasionally intrusive applause. All five soloists have fresh young voices, with all three sopranos first rate and Knut Schoch as David clear and fluent. As Nabal, Stephan MacLeod is not weighty or old-sounding enough for a villainous role, but he sings well. The principal snag is that the chorus is dimly recorded, set behind the soloists and period orchestra. A valuable issue, just the same.

The Occasional Oratorio

**(*) Hyp. CDA 66961/2. Gritton, Milne, Bowman, Mark Ainsley, George, New College, Oxford, Ch., King's Consort Ch. & Ens., King

Handel's *Occasional Oratorio* offers a wonderful showcase of Handel at his most inspired and vigorous. The choruses in particular, some only a few seconds long, regularly punctuate the work to heighten the effect of the arias. The piece culminates in an adaptation of Handel's great coronation anthem, *Zadok the Priest*, with loyal cries of *God save the King* ringing out at the end. The whole performance is fresh and electrifying, with excellent singing from all the soloists. Susan Gritton and Lisa Milne, the clear-toned sopranos, are set against the increasingly dark counter-tenor tones of James Bowman, with John Mark Ainsley and Michael George both clear and fresh Handelian stylists. The chorus fares rather less well in a generally excellent recording for, though the ensemble is first rate, the backward balance takes some of the edge off the more dramatic choruses.

Ode for the Birthday of Queen Anne (Eternal source of light divine); Sing unto God (Wedding Anthem); Te Deum in D (for Queen Caroline)

*** Hyp. CDA 66315. Fisher, Bowman, Mark Ainsley, George, New College, Oxford, Ch., King's Consort, King

Handel's *Birthday Ode for Queen Anne* combines Purcellian influences with Italianate writing to make a rich mixture. Robert King's performance is richly enjoyable, with warm, well-tuned playing from the King's Consort and with James Bowman in radiant form in the opening movement. The other two items are far rarer. Warmly atmospheric recording, not ideally clear on detail.

Ode for St Cecilia's Day

⊕ *** ASV CDDCA 512. Gomez, Tear, King's College, Cambridge, Ch., ECO, Ledger

(M) *** DG Blue 474 549-2. Lott, Rolfe Johnson, Ch. & E. Concert, Pinnock

(M) *** Teldec (ADD) 0630 12319-2. Palmer, Rolfe Johnson, Stockholm Bach Ch., VCM, Harnoncourt

Ode for St Cecilia's Day; Cecilia volgi un sguardo

⊕ (N) *** Hyp. CDA 67463. Sampson, Gilchrist, Ch. & King's Consort, King

Robert King's outstanding version of the *St Cecilia's Day Ode* gains even over the finest rivals by also including as a generous fill-up a half-hour cantata, far less well-known but a fine piece, equally dedicated to St Cecilia. Helped by the recording, King's reading is crisp and clear, with textures transparent. Carolyn Sampson sings with radiant purity, not least in the lovely aria, *The soft complaining flute*, while James Gilchrist confirms his status as among the very finest British tenors of his generation, his clear, firm voice beautifully projected. The chorus of the King's Consort sings with comparable freshness. The same two soloists feature in the cantata, *Cecilia volgi un sguardo*, written in 1736 to be interpolated in a performance of the oratorio, *Alexander's Feast*. The two tenor arias are followed by one for the soprano in three sections. The piece ends triumphantly with a fine duet.

Those seeking a version with modern instruments will find Philip Ledger's ASV version a splendid one. With superb soloists – Jill Gomez radiantly beautiful and Robert Tear dramatically riveting in his call to arms – this delightful music emerges with an admirable combination of freshness and weight. Ledger uses an all-male chorus; the style of the performance is totally convincing without being self-consciously authentic. The recording is first rate: rich, vivid and clear.

Trevor Pinnock's account of Handel's magnificent setting of Dryden's *Ode* comes near the ideal for a performance using period instruments. Not only is it crisp and lively, it has deep tenderness too, as in the lovely soprano aria *The complaining flute*, with Lisa Beznosiuk playing the flute obbligato most delicately in support of Felicity Lott's clear singing. Anthony Rolfe Johnson gives a robust yet stylish account of *The trumpet's loud clangour*, and the choir is excellent, very crisp of ensemble. Full, clear recording with voices vivid and immediate.

Harnoncourt's Teldec version of the *Ode*, recorded in 1979, comes up well in its digital transfer to CD. It is only slightly less recommendable than Trevor Pinnock's Archiv version, though the non-British choir, for all its fluency, sounds less comfortable than its rival and sings less crisply. Anthony Rolfe Johnson is excellent on both versions, while Felicity Palmer as soprano sings most characterfully. One special point in favour of Harnoncourt is his own striking cello playing in the beautiful setting of Dryden's second stanza, *What Passion cannot Musick raise and quell!* Now reissued in Teldec's Das Alte Werk mid-priced series.

La Resurrezione

*** DG (IMS) 447 767-2 (2). Massis, Smith, Maguire, Mark Ainsley, Naouri, Les Musiciens du Louvre, Minkowski

In 1708, halfway through his four-year stay in Italy, the young Handel wrote this refreshingly dramatic oratorio. With opera as such prohibited in Rome, it served as a substitute, not solemn at all, but with dramatic and moving exchanges between the central characters. There is no chorus until the close, but Handel makes up for this with a wonderful palette of orchestral colour in his accompaniments, liberally featuring trumpets, recorders and oboes.

Marc Minkowski brings out the dramatic bite of this early Handel oratorio, often opting for extreme speeds, particularly fast ones, challenging his excellent soprano Annick Massis to the limit in the Angel's brilliant first aria. He may rarely relax in the way that Ton Koopman did on his earlier Erato version (currently withdrawn), but in this episodic piece there is much to be said for such a taut approach, with fine, clean-textured playing from Les Musiciens du Louvre.

Samson (complete)

*** Teldec 9031 74871-2 (2). Rolfe Johnson, Alexander, Kowalski, Miles, Prégardien, Venuti, Blasi, Arnold Schoenberg Ch., VCM, Harnoncourt

Harnoncourt here conducts a Handel performance in which Handelian grandeur shines out from the opening overture with its braying horns and genially strutting dotted rhythms. He is altogether warmer than before, and a fine team of singers, led by Anthony Rolfe Johnson in the title-role, is allowed full expressiveness, with speeds in slow numbers broader than one might expect. So the blind Samson's first aria, *Total eclipse*, is very measured, with Rolfe Johnson using the widest tonal and dynamic range. Though the recording catches some flutter in Roberta Alexander's voice as Dalila, she gives a characterful performance, well contrasted with Angela Maria Blasi, her attendant, who sings the lovely aria, *With plaintive note*, most beautifully. Maria Venuti in the climactic *Let the bright seraphim* at the end is not ideally pure-toned, but she sings strongly and flexibly. Other fine singers include Alastair Miles, magnificent in the bass role of the giant, Harapha, not least in *Honour and arms*, as well as the rich-toned counter-tenor, Jochen Kowalski as Micah and Christoph Prégardien in the tenor role of the Philistine. With the Schoenberg choir singing incisively, Harnoncourt presents the work not only with period instruments but on an authentic scale.

Saul (complete)

*** DG 474 510-2 (3). Neal Davies, Scholl, Padmore, Gritton, Argenta, Agnew, Lemalu, Gabrieli Consort and Players, McCreesh

(BB) **(*) Naxos 8.554361/63 (3). MacLeod, Cordier, Schuch, Schlick, McFadden, Beekman, Junge Kantorei, Frankfurt Bar. O, Martini

Central to the success of Paul McCreesh's version of *Saul* is the warmly characterful singing of the counter-tenor Andreas Scholl, in the role of David, in effect the central character in this dramatic oratorio even more than the king himself. McCreesh favours speeds on the fast side, only occasionally sounding too rushed, and his excellent cast responds well, with the chorus singing with crisp ensemble, strong and incisive. That said, none of the other soloists quite matches their counterparts on the rival Gardiner version on Philips (426 265-2), a recording made live in Gottingen in 1989 and still sounding well, with an acoustic less reverberant than that of All Saints, Tooting, where this DG Archiv recording was made. So Neal Davies as Saul is less cleanly focused than Alastair Miles on Philips, and Neil Mackie is fresher and firmer as the High Priest than Paul Agnew here, while even Nancy Argenta as Saul's daughter, Michal, sounds less sweet than usual, hardly a match for Lynne Dawson on Philips. The tautness of McCreesh's direction and the precision of the choral singing, all the crisper in a studio performance, make it a strong alternative, but the Gardiner version remains first choice.

Joachim Carlos Martini on Naxos offers a clear, fresh, lively reading using period instruments, very well recorded, making an excellent bargain version. Outstanding among the soloists is the creamy-toned Barbara Schlick, who sings the role of Michal, Saul's daughter and David's wife. Singers with fresh, young voices fill the other roles effectively, if not always very characterfully. Stephan McLeod as Saul is a clear, firm baritone rather than the dark bass the role ideally requires, and

David Cordier as David is a very English-sounding counter-tenor, clean and cultivated. Claron McFadden in the dual role of Merab and the Witch of Endor is rather edgy, better suited to the second of those roles. The chorus sing well, but are not ideally focused. Otherwise the sound is fresh and clear.

Solomon (complete) McCreesh 1999?

⊕– ✱ * Ph. 412 612-2 (2). Watkinson, Argenta, Hendricks, Rolfe Johnson, Monteverdi Ch., E. Bar. Sol., Gardiner

(M) **(*) Somm-Beecham 17-2 (2) (ed. & arr. Beecham). Cameron, Young, Morison, Marshall, Beecham Choral Soc., RPO, Beecham

(i) *Solomon* (ed. & arr. Beecham). *Love in Bath* (ballet music, arr. Beecham)

(N) (M) **(*) EMI Gemini (ADD) 5 86516-2 (2). (i) Cameron, Young, Morison, Lois Marshall, Beecham Choral Soc.; RPO, Beecham

This is among the very finest of all Handel oratorio recordings. With panache, Gardiner shows how authentic-sized forces can convey Handelian grandeur even with clean-focused textures and fast speeds. The choruses and even more magnificent double choruses stand as cornerstones of a structure which may have less of a story-line than some other Handel oratorios – the Judgement apart – but which Gardiner shows has consistent human warmth. The Act III scenes between Solomon and the Queen of Sheba are given extra warmth by having in the latter role a singer who is sensuous in tone, Barbara Hendricks. Carolyn Watkinson's pure mezzo is very apt for Solomon himself, while Nancy Argenta is clear and sweet as his Queen; but the overriding glory of the set is the radiant singing of Gardiner's Monteverdi Choir. Its clean, crisp articulation matches the brilliant playing of the English Baroque Soloists, regularly challenged by Gardiner's fast speeds, as in *The Arrival of the Queen of Sheba*; and the sound is superb, coping thrillingly with the problems of the double choruses.

In his revision and re-orchestration of *Solomon*, Sir Thomas Beecham boldly left out sections which hold up the central plot involving the Queen of Sheba, omitting the Judgement Scene but using the double chorus *From the censer curling rise* after the entertainment for the Queen. With Beecham magicking the music – however inauthentically – the performance can be warmly recommended to devotees of the conductor – and to Handelians too, as long as they are tolerant. Lois Marshall is effective enough as the Queen of Sheba, and the other soloists are first rate. The early (1955/6) stereo recording was made mainly at Abbey Road, but with final sessions in Kingsway Hall in May 1956, and the new CD transfer is eminently satisfactory.

However, the EMI Gemini set is not only less expensive but also finds room for *Love in Bath*, the title of which conceals the identity of Beecham's ballet, first performed just before the end of the war, called *The Great Elopement*. Beecham recorded a suite from this on 78s, but the present selection contains much more music – 19 numbers plus a *Rondeau* purloined from yet another Handel/Beecham suite – 47 minutes in all. Needless to say, the Royal Philharmonic Orchestra play like angels – if occasionally not perfectly disciplined angels. However, the transfer of *Solomon* produces rather fierce violin-sound in the *Overture*, and the spikiness is again noticeable in the *Arrival of the Queen of Sheba*; and there is a thinness too on the violins in the ballet suite. But for most of the time this is not really a problem and the choral sound is vivid.

Theodora (complete; DVD version)

(N) *** Warner **DVD** 0630-15481-2. Upshaw, Daniels, Olsen, Croft, Hunt-Lieberson, OAE, Christie (V/D: Peter Sellars)

The Glyndebourne staging of Handel's oratorio, *Theodora*, was recorded in June 1996, an exceptionally powerful production from the controversial but inspired Peter Sellars with a stellar cast under William Christie. Sellars himself has directed the video as well as acting as stage director, heightening the impact of this updated production. Though the original is set in AD 304, Sellars updates the story to the present day, with the Roman Governor, Valens, becoming an American-style President, and with the soldiers, notably the hero, Didymus, and his colleague, Septimius, wearing orange American combat fatigues and carrying firearms. At the end, when Theodora and Didymus are martyred, Sellars has them strapped down and lethally injected, a chilling dénouement. The staging involves a stylized set so as to cope with the changes of scene normal in a Handel oratorio. What makes the result so compelling is not just the richness of Handel's inspiration, with one memorable aria after another, and the inspired direction of William Christie with the Orchestra of the Age of Enlightenment, but above all a cast that it would be hard to match. Dawn Upshaw in the title-role is tenderly appealing, and her sweet, pure singing is matched by that of Lorraine Hunt-Lieberson as her friend, Irene, conveying a depth of feeling if anything even greater in wonderful arias. In the castrato role of Didymus, the counter-tenor David Daniels gives a masterly performance, brilliant technically and moving too, and the tenor, Richard Croft, is equally stylish as Septimius, with Frode Olsen powerful as the unyielding Valens. Generous measure, with three and a half hours of music on a single disc – though the documentation is sketchy, with no booklet and only a brief synopsis of the plot.

Theodora (complete; CD versions)

*** DG 469 061-2 (3). Gritton, Bickley, Blaze, Agnew, N. Davies, Gabrieli Cons. & Players, McCreesh

(M) *** MDG 332 1019-2 (3). Somer, Buwalda, Rasker, Schoch, Sol, Schweiser, Cologne Chamber Ch., Coll. Cartusianum, Neumann

Handel's penultimate oratorio, *Theodora*, initially a failure but one of his own favourites, has been fortunate in the age of CD, yet Paul McCreesh's version sweeps the board. Beautifully recorded in a sympathetic acoustic it offers an outstandingly sensitive, well-paced reading, ideally cast, using a text which gives alternative versions of numbers that Handel revised. Using a relatively large string section (26 players), McCreesh brings out the dramatic contrasts vividly in a work which, in its telling of the story of Theodora, the early Christian martyr, has its elements of grandeur. In the title-role Susan Gritton sings radiantly, unaffectedly compassing the widest range of expression, a moving central focus to the drama, with the even-toned counter-tenor, Robin Blaze, equally impressive as Didymus, the Roman officer who becomes her fellow martyr. The mezzo, Susan Bickley, sings with simple dedication as Irene, with Paul Agnew elegant in the role of Septimius and Neal Davies an authoritative Valens, President of Antioch.

Peter Neumann's version on MDG, well played and sympathetically paced, would be very welcome but for the formidable competition from both McCreesh on DG Archiv and McGegan on Harmonia Mundi. The German cast is first rate, admirably coping with an English text, led by the warm-toned Johanette Somer as Theodora and the excellent counter-tenor, Sytse Buwalda, as Didymus. The three discs come for the price of two.

The Triumph of Time and Truth

(N) (M) *** Hyp. Dyad CDD 22052 (2). Fisher, Kirkby, Brett, Partridge, Varcoe, L. Handel Ch. and O, Darlow

Darlow's performance of Handel's very last oratorio is broad and strong and very enjoyable. The soloists have all been chosen for the clarity of their pitching – Emma Kirkby, Gillian Fisher, Charles Brett and Stephen Varcoe, with the honey-toned Ian Partridge singing even more beautifully than the others, but with a timbre too pure quite to characterize 'Pleasure'. Good atmospheric recording, and especially welcome as a mid-priced Dyad.

Utrecht Te Deum & Jubilate in D – see below, under *Alceste*

OPERA

Admeto, re di Tessaglia (complete)

(M) *** Virgin (ADD) 5 61369-2 (3). Jacobs, Yakar, Gomez, Bowman, Cold, Dams, Van Egmont, Il Complesso Barocco, Curtis

Admeto is among the very greatest of Handel's operas, and this recording, made in 1977 in Holland, was one of the first complete recordings of a Handel opera to attempt an authentic approach, and the most successful up to that time. Though recitatives are on the slow side, it stands the test of time, a fine performance, very well cast, played with refinement on period instruments and excellently recorded. Handel wrote *Admeto* with the three greatest singers of the time in mind, the castrato, Senesino, in the title-role, and the rival prima donnas, Cuzzoni and Bordoni, as Antigona and Alceste. Here the counter-tenor René Jacobs gives an understanding and characterful performance in the title-role, but it is Jill Gomez as Antigona who steals first honours, with magnificent singing, sweet, pure and strong of tone, with ornamentation beautifully crisp. Rachel Yakar is not so sweetly caught by the microphones, but hers is a stylish performance too, and the rest of the cast has no weak link, with James Bowman outstanding as Admeto's brother, Trasimede.

(i) Alceste: Overture & Incidental Music; (ii) Anthem for the Foundling Hospital; Ode for the Birthday of Queen Anne; (iii) Utrecht Te Deum & Jubilate in D

(B) *** Double Decca 458 072-2 (2). (i; ii; iii) Kirkby, Nelson, D. Thomas, AAM; (i) Cable, Elliott, Ch., Hogwood; (ii) Minty, Bowman, Hill; (ii; iii) Christ Church Cathedral Ch., Preston; (iii) with Brett, Covey-Crump, Elliott

Handel left us much to enjoy in the impressively dramatic *Alceste Overture* in D minor and the *Grand entrée* for Admetus, Alceste and their wedding guests, which get the proceedings off to a fine start. There follows a series not just of solo items but also some simple tuneful choruses in which a small secondary vocal group participates. There is nearly an hour of freshly enjoyable music and Hogwood draws lively, sympathetic performances from his team. The *Ode* has its Italianate attractions and opens with a splendid counter-tenor aria from James Bowman, with an elaborate trumpet obbligato, superbly played here. But it is the much later *Foundling Hospital Anthem* that is the more memorable, not just because it concludes with an alternative version of the *Hallelujah Chorus*, but also because the other borrowed numbers are also superb. The Utrecht pieces were written just before Handel came to London and were intended as a sample of his work. Preston directs performances which are characteristically alert and vigorous, particularly impressive in the superb closing *Glory be to the Father* with its massive eight-part chords. Throughout the team of soloists regularly associated with the Academy give of their best, and the recordings, made in 1977 and 1979 are splendidly transferred, clean and clear yet not losing their analogue atmosphere.

Alcina (DVD version)

* Arthaus **DVD** 100 338. Nagelstad, Coote, Schneidermann, Smith, Romei, Mahnke, Ebbecke, Gerger, Stuttgart Op. Ch. & O, Hacker. Producers: Wieler, Morabito; Video director: Darvas

Alcina (CD versions)

B *** Erato 8573 80233-2 (3). Fleming, Graham, Dessay, Kuhlmann, Lascarro, Robinson, Naouri, Les Arts Florissants, Christie

(i) Alcina (complete); (ii) Giulio Cesare (Julius Caesar): highlights

(M) **(*) Decca 433 723-2 (3). Sutherland, M. Sinclair; (i) Berganza, Alva, Sciutti, Freni, Flagello, LSO; (ii) Elkins, Horne, Conrad, New SO; Bonynge

Alcina is thought to be among the finest of Handel's operas. The fine Erato set was recorded live at the Paris Opéra. Only in recitatives do stage noises ever intrude, and the tensions of a live recording help to minimize the drawback of an opera containing only one ensemble number (the Act III terzetto) in addition to the traditional brief choral finale. Christie too is masterly at avoiding any monotony in the long sequence of *da capo* arias, with recitative superbly timed and reprises beautifully decorated. It is striking that the star singers here are not just brilliant in tackling elaborate passage-work and ornamentation, but are stylishly scrupulous in avoiding unwanted aspirates. Renée Fleming is in glorious voice as Alcina, with Susan Graham characterizing well in the trouser-role of Ruggiero. Natalie Dessay as Alcina's sister, Morgana, relishes the challenge of the brilliant *Tornami a vagheggiar* (appropriated by Joan Sutherland in the inauthentic Decca set), helped by Christie's relatively relaxed tempo. He also sets relaxed speeds in some of the great slow arias such as *Verdi prati*, encouraging an expressive approach which yet remains within the bounds of period style.

Alcina represents the extreme point of what can be described as Sutherland's dreamy, droopy period. The fast arias are stupendous. But anything slow and reflective, whether in recitative or aria, has Sutherland mooning about the notes, with no consonants audible. Of the others, Teresa Berganza is completely charming in the castrato part of Ruggiero, even if she does not manage trills very well. Monica Sinclair shows everyone up with the strength and forthrightness of her singing. Both Graziella Sciutti and Mirella Freni are delicate and clear in their two smaller parts. Richard Bonynge draws crisp, vigorous playing from the LSO.

Not surprisingly, the *Giulio Cesare* highlights are used as a vehicle for Sutherland, and her florid elaborations of melodies turn *da capo* recitatives into things of delight and wonder. There is some marvellous singing from Marilyn Horne and Monica Sinclair too, and Bonynge conducts with a splendid sense of style. As a sample, try *V'adoro pupile*, Cleopatra's seduction aria. Full translations are provided in both works.

The Arthaus DVD performance is cut and runs to 159 minutes. Its strong points are the musical direction of Alan Hacker, who has a real feeling for the Handelian style, and some of the singers, most notably the Bradamante of Helene Schneidermann and Alice Coote's vibrant Ruggiero. However, the production, which was recorded at Stuttgart in 2000, is appalling and shows scant respect for, or interest in, Handel and a predisposition for sensational stage tricks. The set is grotty, and the tone of the whole production can be discerned during the course of the overture when the camera shows us an array of shoes, Second World War tin helmets, an electric light bulb and a bowl of cherries! Those who have the patience to go any further will find a great deal of intrusive and quite silly stage business, much tearing away at one another's clothing and a generally anti-musical approach to Handel's score. Don't waste your time or money!

Alcina: highlights

(M) *** Erato 8573 85356-2 (from complete recording, cond. Christie)

An excellent and generous (78 minutes) set of highlights centring on Act II but with well-chosen excerpts from the other two Acts and ending with the brief final chorus. This will suit those who want to sample Christie's splendid live version, made at the Paris Opéra in 1999.

Almira (complete)

(B) **(*) CPO 999 275-2 (3). Monoyios, Rozario, Gerrard, D. Thomas, Nasrawi, MacDougall, Elsner, Fiori Musicale, Lawrence-King

Almira was Handel's first opera, written in Hamburg in 1704. Even so, one regularly detects a genuine Handelian flavour in the themes, and he himself borrowed a fair measure of the material here in later works. This recording, with three discs offered for the price of two, was made after a staging presented in both Halle and Bremen in 1994. Andrew Lawrence-King secures a fresh and well-paced – if rather plain – performance, with deft playing from the German period orchestra. Ann Monoyios is a light, bright Almira, with Patricia Rozario, taxed a little by the high tessitura, equally stylish as Edilia. The two principal tenor roles are very well taken by Jamie MacDougall and Douglas Nasrawi, with the third tenor, Christian Elsner, taking the comic servant role. David Thomas sings with clean attack in the bass role of the Prince of Segovia. Good, undistracting and well scaled in an intimate acoustic.

Amadigi di Gaula (complete)

*** Erato 2292 45490-2 (2). Stutzmann, J. Smith, Harrhy, Fink, Musiciens du Louvre, Minkowski

Minkowski's electrifying performance is one of his sharpest, dominated vocally by the magnificent young French contralto (no mere mezzo) of Nathalie Stutzmann in the title-role. She sings Amadigi's gentle arias most affectingly, notably

the lovely *Sussurrate, onde vezzose*, and the two women characters, Amadigi's lover Melissa and Princess Oriana, are well taken by Eiddwen Harrhy and Jennifer Smith, with the brilliant arias for Prince Dardano of Thrace superbly sung by Bernarda Fink. It is a performance on an intimate scale, and the more involving for that.

Ariodante (complete)

*** DG 457 271-2 (3). Von Otter, Dawson, Podles, Croft, Musiciens du Louvre, Minkowski

(M) *** Ph. Trio (ADD) 473 955-2 (3). J. Baker, Mathis, Burrowes, Bowman, Rendall, Ramey, L. Voices, ECO, Leppard

Ariodante is among the most richly inspired of Handel's operas. On DG Archiv, with an outstanding, starry team of soloists, Marc Minkowski conducts a high-powered reading of *Ariodante*, urgently dramatic and a compelling set in every way. Though Anne Sofie von Otter in the title-role is not quite at her freshest, and Dame Janet Baker on the rival set gives an even more moving performance, her characterization is as strong as ever. Among the others Lynne Dawson and Ewa Podles are outstandingly fine.

In the colourful, urgent performance under Raymond Leppard, the castrato role of Ariodante is a challenge for Dame Janet Baker, who responds with singing of enormous expressive range, from the dark, agonized moments of the C minor aria early in Act III to the brilliance of the most spectacular of the three display arias later in the Act. Baker's duets with Edith Mathis as Princess Ginevra, destined to marry Prince Ariodante, are enchanting too, and there is not a single weak member of the cast, though James Bowman as Duke Polinesso is not as precise as usual, with words often unclear. Consistently resilient playing from the English Chamber Orchestra and refined, beautifully balanced (1978) analogue recording, vividly transferred to CD. However, this now returns as a mid-priced Trio, which means that it is without a translated text, and a cued synopsis is offered as a poor alternative. In all other respects it is an outstanding set.

Arminio (complete opera)

*** Virgin 5 45461-2 (2). Genaux, McGreevy, Labelle, Custer, Petroni, Buwalda, Ristori, Il Complesso Barocco, Curtis

Written at high speed in 1736, towards the end of Handel's career as opera-composer, *Arminio* starts in defiance of early-eighteenth-century convention with a duet for hero and heroine immediately after the Overture, and the sequence of brief arias brings changes of mood and voice, with one delightful number after another. Recitatives are reduced to modest proportions in obedience to London taste, so that the overall span over the three Acts fits neatly on to the two discs. Standing out in the cast is Geraldine McGreevy, winner of the 1996 Kathleen Ferrier Award, who takes the key role of the heroine, Tusnelda, daughter of the German prince, Segeste. Tusnelda has far more arias than anyone else, many of them vigorous, but including such deeply reflective numbers as the ravishing *Rendimi il dolce sposo*, which ends Act II. In Act III she has (in addition to another reflective aria) two charming duets with voices in chains of thirds. Vivica Genaux as Arminio is not caught quite so well by the microphone, but the whole cast, including Dominique Labelle, an excellent second soprano as Sigismondo, are commendably agile in the florid writing, with the fresh-toned period band, Il Complesso Barocco, ever-responsive. Clear, well-balanced sound.

Flavio (complete)

(B) *** HM HMX 2901312.3 (2). Gall, Ragin, Lootens, Fink, Högman, Fagotto, Messthaler, Ens. 415, Jacobs

Based on a staging of this unjustly neglected Handel opera at the 1989 Innsbruck Festival, René Jacobs's recording vividly captures the consistent vigour of Handel's inspiration. Handel's score was brilliantly written for some of the most celebrated singers of the time, including the castrato, Senesino. His four arias are among the highspots of the opera, all sung superbly here by the warm-toned and characterful counter-tenor, Derek Lee Ragin; almost every other aria is open and vigorous, with the whole sequence rounded off in a rousing ensemble. René Jacobs's team of eight soloists is a strong one, with only the strenuous tenor of Gianpaolo Fagotto occasionally falling short of the general stylishness. Full, clear sound, and text and translations included.

Giulio Cesare (complete)

⊕⊷ (B) *** HMX 2901 385.7 (3). Larmore, Schlick, Fink, Rorholm, Ragin, Zanasi, Visse, Concerto Köln, Jacobs

*** Astree E 8558 (3). Bowman, Dawson, Laurens, James, Visse, La Grande Ecurie et la Chambre du Roy, Malgoire

**(*) DG 474 210-2 (3). Mijanovic, Koženà, Von Otter, Hellekant, Bejun Mehta, Ewing, Bettini, Ankaoua, Musiciens du Louvre, Minkowski

The casting of the pure, golden-toned Barbara Schlick as Cleopatra on Harmonia Mundi proves outstandingly successful. Jennifer Larmore too, a fine, firm mezzo with a touch of masculine toughness in the tone, makes a splendid Caesar. Together they crown the whole performance on Harmonia Mundi with the most seductive account of their final duet. Derek Lee Ragin is excellent in the sinister role of Tolomeo (Ptolemy); so are Bernarda Fink as Cornelia and Marianne Rorholm as Sesto, with the bass, Furio Zanasi, as Achille. René Jacobs's expansive speeds mean that the whole opera will not fit on three CDs, but the fourth disc, at 18 minutes merely supplementary, comes free as part of the package, and includes an extra aria for the servant, Nireno, delightfully sung by the French counter-tenor, Dominique Visse. Firm, well-balanced sound. This now comes at bargain-price with texts and translations included.

The counter-tenor James Bowman in the Malgoire set is strongly contrasted against the firm and purposeful mezzo, Jennifer Larmore. Bowman cannot quite match Larmore in the brilliance of his florid singing, but the timbre is firm and rich at less demanding speeds, and the portrait of a hero is conveyed convincingly. The contrast between Lynne Dawson as Cleopatra and Barbara Schlick is a key one too, for Dawson, following Malgoire's general approach, concentrates on beauty and classical poise, whereas Schlick brings out greater depth of expression. The contrast is similar over Giullemette Laurens as Cornelia as against Bernarda Fink, the one poised, the other more deeply expressive, often at broader speeds. By contrast, the counter-tenor, Dominique Visse, is the more actively characterful as the villainous Tolomeo, where Derek Lee Ragin for Jacobs combines sharp characterization with cleaner vocalization. Malgoire's text is not quite as complete as Jacobs's, with cuts in recitative.

Minkowski's version of what is arguably Handel's greatest opera was recorded live at a concert performance in Vienna. That adds to the dramatic impact of a long and varied piece, helped by a strong and distinguished cast of soloists. As he establishes in the Overture, Minkowski prefers speeds on the fast side, sometimes very fast, with playing clear and clipped

from the Musiciens du Louvre. That regularly sets a challenge to his singers as well as the players, very well taken. So Cleopatra's first aria in Act I sounds rushed despite the brilliant, characterful singing of Magdalena Koženà, and sadly her second Act I aria is cut. Otherwise, hers is a commanding performance, deeply moving in her big lyrical numbers, V'adoro pupille and Piangero, for which Minkowski allows full warmth and tenderness at aptly spacious speeds. Marijana Mijanovic sings powerfully in the title-role, with Anne Sofie von Otter a poised Sesto and Charlotte Hellekant a firm, clear Cornelia. This now provides a fair alternative to the outstanding Jacobs version.

Julius Caesar (Giulio Cesare; complete, in English)

(*) Arthaus **DVD 100 308. Details as below. (Director: John Copley. V/D: John Michael Phillips.)

(M) *** Chan. 3019 (3). J. Baker, Masterson, Walker, D. Jones, Bowman, Tomlinson, ENO Ch. & O, Mackerras

Taken from Channel 4's TV presentation of the English National Opera production, the Arthaus DVD offers a studio performance with the original staging modified. Recorded in 1984, the same year that the audio recording was made at EMI's Abbey Road studio, it vividly captures the dramatic bite of John Copley's production, using Brian Trowell's fluent translation, with a cast of principals that would be hard to match. Janet Baker sings and acts commandingly in the title-role, with Valerie Masterson a sympathetic if hardly sensuous Cleopatra, and Sarah Walker as Pompey's widow, Cornelia, matching even Baker in the intensity of her singing and acting. Della Jones as Sextus, James Bowman as the scheming Ptolemy and John Tomlinson as Achillas are all ideal in their roles, with Michael Stennett's sumptuous costumes adding to the success of the production. Sir Charles Mackerras paces the music masterfully, but sadly the orchestral sound on DVD is thinner than in the audio recording, with an edge to it. So the CDs remain first choice. On CD the ravishing accompaniments to the two big Cleopatra arias amply justify the use by the excellent ENO Orchestra of modern rather than period instruments. The full, vivid studio sound makes this one of the very finest of the invaluable series of ENO opera recordings in English, now made available again by Chandos, sponsored by the Peter Moores Foundation.

Julius Caesar: Scenes (in English)

(N) (M) *** Chan. 3072 (from above recording, with Masterson, J. Baker, ENO; cond. Mackerras)

There are 75 minutes of well-selected excerpts here, and full texts are provided.

Giustino (complete)

*** HM HMU 907130/32. Chance, Röschmann, Kotoski, Gondek, Lane, Padmore, Minter, Cantamus Halle Chamber Ch., Freiburg Bar. O, McGegan

First heard in 1737 and never revived until 1967, the opera, Giustino, has been consistently underestimated. This splendid, lively set should do much to bring a full reassessment, for Nicholas McGegan, with his fast, crisp manner and fondness for extra decoration in da capo repeats, brings out the element of sparkle and irony implied in the improbable story, treated refreshingly in dozens of brief arias. Michael Chance is outstanding in the title-role originally written for a castrato, and Dorothea Röschmann sings most movingly in the key role of Arianna. Drew Minter, stylish and intelligent as he is, fails to give enough bite to the villainous role of Amanzio; but there are few other disappointments, and the tenor, Mark Padmore, sings with virtuoso flair in the military role of Vitaliano. The German string-players are more abrasive than one expects nowadays, but this is a set to delight all Handelians, filling in an important gap.

Hercules (complete)

*** DG 469 532-2 (3). Saks, Von Otter, Croft, Dawson, Daniels, Pujol, Ch. & Musiciens du Louvre, Minkowski

(M) *** DG 447 689-2 (2). Tomlinson, Walker, Rolfe Johnson, J. Smith, Denley, Savidge, Monteverdi Ch., E. Bar. Sol., Gardiner

Mark Minkowski conducts an urgently dramatic account of Handel's music-drama in English on a classical theme. It is a work strangely neglected, when it contains exceptionally fine and memorable inspirations, with two very striking central roles, not just Hercules but, even more deeply expressive, that of Dejanira, his wife. Anne Sofie von Otter may not float her voice quite as smoothly and easily as she once did, but hers is still a vividly characterful performance which, with fine gradation of tone and expression, brings out the full range of emotion implied. She is specially moving at the end when she realizes that her jealousy has brought the death of her husband. As Hercules, Gidon Saks sings with fine, clear focus, not as weighty as many a traditional Handel bass, but firm and dark. Excellent contributions too from Lynne Dawson as a bright, charming Iole, from the counter-tenor, David Daniels, peerless as the herald, Lichas, and from Richard Croft, elegant in the music of Hyllus, Hercules's son. The French chorus is not quite as idiomatic as the Monteverdi Choir in the rival Gardiner version, which dates from the early 1980s but still sounds well, and is more consistently paced. The new set brings fewer cuts in a work which presents textual problems that the composer failed to resolve.

Gardiner's brisk performance of Hercules using authentic forces may at times lack Handelian grandeur in the big choruses, but it conveys superbly the vigour of the writing, its natural drama; and the fire of this performance is typified by the outstanding singing of Sarah Walker as Dejanira. John Tomlinson makes an excellent, dark-toned Hercules. Fresh voices consistently help in the clarity of the attack – Jennifer Smith as Iole, Catherine Denley as Lichas, Anthony Rolfe Johnson as Hyllus and Peter Savidge as the Priest of Jupiter. Refined playing and outstanding recording quality make this most welcome at mid-price.

Imeneo (complete)

(B) *** CPO 999 915-2 (2). Hallenberg, Stojkovic, Thornhill, Stiefermann, Chung, Cologne Vocal Ens., Capella Augustina, Spering

This late opera by Handel, one of the last two Italian operas he ever wrote, has been inexplicably neglected on disc, and this lively version, recorded in Cologne in collaboration with West German Radio, admirably fills the gap, well sung and well played, even if Andreas Spering's direction brings some plodding continuo. The story is relatively simple, with Princess Rosmene saved from the pirates by Imeneo (the Italian for Hymen) and demanding her hand in reward, even though she is still in love with Tirinto. Gratitude prevails in the end over love, to the despair of Tirinto. The story inspires Handel to a sequence of fine numbers, notably for Rosmene and Tirinto. The scoring is light, with the story moving easily and with Rosmene in Act II given a fine, thoughtful arioso

and later a stormy aria. Johanna Stojkovic sings strongly, bright and clear in the most taxing divisions, while Anna Hallenberg as Tirinto is equally commanding with her warm, firm mezzo, rising superbly to the challenge of her big showpiece aria, Sorge nell'alma, which anticipates Why do the nations in Messiah. Finer still is her tragic minor-key aria in Act III, Pieno il core, by far the most extended number. Also impessive is the trio for Rosmene and the rival suitors, while Rosmene's final aria is the most original of all, with curious stops and starts, and bald octave writing in the accompaniment. The original version of the text is used, with the role of Imeneo taken by a baritone – impressively sung by Kay Stiefermann – where Handel's revision for Dublin uses a tenor instead. Clear, well-balanced sound.

Orlando (complete)

*** O-L 430 845-2 (3). Bowman, Augér, Robbin, Kirkby, D. Thomas, AAM, Hogwood

*** Erato 0630 14636-2 (3). Bardon, Mannion, Summers, Joshua, Van der Kamp, Les Arts Florissants, Christie

Handel's Orlando was radically modified to provide suitable material for individual singers, notably in the magnificent Mad scene which ends Act II on the aria, Vaghe pupille. That number, superbly done on Oiseau-Lyre by James Bowman, with appropriate sound effects, is only one of the virtuoso vehicles for the counter-tenor. For the jewelled sequences of arias and duets, Hogwood has assembled a near-ideal cast, with Arleen Augér at her most radiant as the queen, Angelica, and Emma Kirkby characteristically bright and fresh in the lighter, semi-comic role of the shepherdess, Dorinda. Catherine Robbin assumes the role of Prince Medoro strongly and David Thomas sings stylishly as Zoroastro. This is one of Hogwood's finest achievements on record, taut, dramatic and rhythmically resilient. Vivid, open sound.

William Christie's Erato recording of Orlando makes a valuable alternative. The most obvious difference is that, where Hogwood has a male alto singing the title-role, Christie here opts for a fine mezzo, Patricia Bardon. Her approach is more overtly dramatic than James Bowman's for Hogwood, with moods and passions more positively characterized. The celebrated Mad scene ending Act II illustrates the point perfectly, with Christie and Bardon more violent, using bigger contrasts, ending in a scurrying accelerando, whereas the Bowman/Hogwood approach keeps some classical restraint to the end, pointing the drama of the moment in thunder effects. The Erato recording is warm and full but not as transparent or well separated as the earlier one, with Christie often opting for marginally broader speeds. His other soloists are all excellent, readily matching their rivals, not least the contralto, Hilary Summers, as Prince Medoro.

Ottone, re di Germania (complete)

*** Hyp. CDA 66751/3. Bowman, McFadden, Smith, Denley, Visse, George, King's Cons., King

Robert King and his King's Consort offer a version on Hyperion with James Bowman as Ottone. The women principals do not have sufficiently pure, firm voices, but when it comes to the key castrato roles taken by counter-tenors, it is quite different. Bowman, with his rich tone, continues to sing with enormous panache and virtuoso agility. Dominique Visse as the duplicitous Adalberto on King's set tends to overcharacterize, but the singing is full of colour. Added to that is the richness and bloom on the instrumental sound.

Partenope (complete)

(N) *** Chan. 0719 (3). Joshua, Summers, Wallace, Zazzo, Streit, Foster-Williams, Early Op. Co., Curnyn

The musicologist Edward Dent said that the libretto for *Partenope* was perhaps the finest Handel ever set, with a spicing of wit and humour in this story of the founding Queen of Naples. Certainly Handel followed a long line of composers using it, including Caldara, whose *Partenope* Handel saw in Venice in 1708. Handel completed his version in 1730, soon after taking control of what became known as the 'Second' Academy of Music. It is a fine piece that moves swiftly in a story ranging wide from despair to witty innuendo, ending happily on a double wedding. Central to the success of Christian Curnyn's well-paced performance is the glorious singing of Rosemary Joshua in the title-role of Partenope. Set against her in the role of the mischievous Rosmira, Princess of Cyprus (for most of the time disguised as a man), is the ripe-toned contralto, Hilary Summers. Other principals in the excellent Early Opera Company cast include two outstanding counter-tenors, Stephen Wallace as Armindo and Lawrence Zazzo as Arsace, suitors to the Queen, with the warlike Emilio, the third suitor, strongly taken by the tenor, Kurt Streit. Handsomely packaged, with each of the three Acts complete on a single disc, it is among the most attractive of rarities among Handel operas.

Rinaldo (DVD version)

(*) Arthaus **DVD 100 388 (2). Daniels, York, Walker, Köhler, Silins, Nadelmann, Bav. State O, Bicket (Dir. David Alden; TV Dir. Brian Large)

Rinaldo (CD versions)

🔘 *** Decca 467 087-2 (3). Daniels, Bartoli, Fink, Finley, Orgonasova, Taylor, AAM, Hogwood

(M) *** Sony (ADD) SM3K 34592 (3). Watkinson, Cotrubas, Scovotti, Esswood, Brett, Cold, La Grande Ecurie et la Chambre du Roy, Malgoire

Recorded in the intimate Prinzregentheater in Munich in 2001, the Arthaus DVD offers a lively 'concept' production, directed by David Alden for the Bavarian State Opera, which incongruously mixes modern figures (mostly wearing trilbies) with characters wearing stylized costumes representing the period of the crusades, as specified in the libretto. It makes an odd, if not ridiculous mix, with surreal scenery as background, and makes one again lament that modern opera producers are so determined to promote their own eccentric ideas and submerge the composer's original intentions.

Musically, Harry Bicket directs a performance that is at once lively and stylish. The American counter-tenor David Daniels is superb in the title role of Rinaldo, using his exceptionally warm, varied tone with consistent imagination. He is joined by a formidable group of counter-tenors in other roles, notably David Walker as Goffredo, rather outshining the sterling contributions of the two basses and the edgily abrasive Noemi Nadelmann as the sorceress, Armida. As Almirena, the heroine, Deborah York is far sweeter in tone. Though it is easy to access subtitles, it does not help comprehension in this anti-realistic presentation that no synopsis of the plot is provided in the booklet, although Alden provides a very broad account of the story in the interview he gives in the 'special feature' material. That has Sir Peter Jonas, Intendant of the Bavarian State Opera, introducing a programme, 'Handel the Entertainer'. The two-disc format allows other extras to be included, though, irritatingly, they are not cued.

On CD it would be hard to devise a cast for this colourful and vigorous opera which would begin to match that on Hogwood's Decca set. The inspired and characterful counter-tenor, David Daniels, makes an ideal choice for the castrato role of Rinaldo, strong and imaginative in martial music, tenderly expressive in such a poignant aria as *Cara sposa*. Though the vibrant Cecilia Bartoli was considered for that role, she rightly preferred to tackle the gentler role of Rinaldo's wife, Almirena, and makes *Lascia ch'io pianga* one of the high points of the performance. Luba Orgonasova is wonderfully contrasted in the fire-eating role of the sorceress, Armida, with Bernarda Fink bringing character to the recessive role of Goffredo, the Christian captain-general, and Gerald Finley firm and positive as Argante, King of Jerusalem. Above all, Christopher Hogwood brings out not only the colour but the vigour of Handel's inspiration, with speeds on the fast side but never rushed, always sounding fresh. By contrast he allows full expansion on the big slow numbers, encouraging the expressiveness of his starry team, with brilliant, incisive playing from the Academy of Ancient Music.

The vigour of Malgoire's direction of an opera which plainly for him is very much alive, makes this another attractive set, with the one caveat that it has been reissued without a translation (the full libretto is in Italian only). The elaborate decorations on *da capo* arias are imaginatively done, but most effectively the famous *Cara sposa* is left without ornamentation, beautifully sung by the contralto Rinaldo, Carolyn Watkinson. The finest singing comes from Ileana Cotrubas, but the whole team is convincing. The bright but spacious recording adds to the projection, and the magic sounds associated with the sorceress, Armida, such as the arrival of her airborne chariot, are well conveyed, and Handel's invention throughout is a delight.

Rodelinda, Regina de Langobardi (complete)

(N) *** DG 477 5391 (3). Kermes, Mijanović, Davislim, Prina, Lemieux, Priante, Il Complesso Barocco, Curtis

*** Virgin 5 45277-2 (3). Daneman, Taylor, Thompson, Robbin, Blaze, Purves, Raglan Bar. Players, Kraemer

For the excellent DG Archiv version of *Rodelinda* the conductor, Alan Curtis, has prepared a version of the score primarily based on the original production in 1725 but with important additions from later versions, including the superb aria for the main castrato role of Bertarido, *Vivi Tiranno*. The ensemble of Il Complesso Barocco, recorded in association with the Festival of Viterbo in Italy, is clear and full-bodied, supporting a first-rate cast of soloists. In the title-role of Rodelinda, Simone Kermes copes splendidly with the enormous range demanded and the feats of coloratura, if with a slight edge at the top of the voice. For the castrato roles of Bertarido and Unulfo, Curtis has opted to have mezzos, with Marijana Mijanović and Marie-Nicole Lemieux both excellent, and with Mijanović singing nobly in the most celebrated number, *Dove sei*. Outstanding even in this cast is the Australian tenor, Steve Davislim, as Grimoaldo, betrothed to Eduige, sister of Bertarido, well taken by Sonia Prina. First-rate sound.

Rodelinda, dating from 1725, has a plot typically involving disguises and forced coincidences, which may be hard for the modern listener to accept. Yet the variety of Handel's invention triumphs over all complication in clearly defining each character, not least the two villains, tenor and bass respectively. Nicholas Kraemer, drawing refined playing from the Raglan Baroque Players, has a winningly light touch. The singers in this live recording work very effectively as a team, characterizing sharply. Sophie Daneman as Rodelinda, with vibrato stilled, produces sound of bell-like purity and crisp ornamentation. Daniel Taylor, as the hero, Bertarido, uses his refined counter-tenor with subtlety and point, not least in the most famous aria, *Dove sei*, while the mezzo, Catherine Robbin, is superb as his disappointed sister, Eduige.

Rodrigo (complete)

*** Virgin 5 45897-2 (2). Banditelli, Piau, Fedi, Müller, Invernizzi, Calvi, Il Complesso Barocco, Curtis

Rodrigo was Handel's very first Italian opera, written for the Medici court in Florence in 1707. It was not heard again until 1984, when Alan Curtis (the conductor here) directed a performance using a score he himself had prepared, with newly rediscovered material restored. This spirited performance has been neatly tailored to fit on two generously filled CDs, with cuts mainly of the *secco* recitatives. The freshness of the performance matches the freshness of Handel's youthful inspiration, with numbers generally more compact than in later Handel operas. Gloria Banditelli sings richly and firmly in the castrato role of Rodrigo, King of Spain, with Sandrine Piau sweet and bright as his wife Esilena, who is given many of the most memorable arias. Elena Cecchi Fedi sings edgily as Florinda but is well in character, and Rufus Müller is a strong Giuliano. A valuable first recording, with bright, fresh sound.

Semele (complete)

⊶ *** DG 435 782-2 (3). Battle, Horne, Ramey, Aler, McNair, Chance, Mackie, Amb. Op. Ch., ECO, Nelson

With its English words, *Semele* stands equivocally between the genres of opera and oratorio. DG's digital recording turns away from current fashion in using modern rather than period instruments, but the balance of advantage lies very much in its favour. If *Semele* – dating from 1744, three years after *Messiah* – is known as a rule only by its most celebrated aria, *Where'er you walk*, it contains many other superb numbers.

Semele (slightly abridged)

**(*) Pierre Vernay PV 704021/2 (2). De Niese, Miller, Innes, Laurens, Fournier, Agnew, Palacio, May, Opera Fuoco Ch. & O, Stern

This alternative set of *Semele* from the French label Pierre Vernay, with a strong cast and period orchestra directed by the American David Stern, by rights should fill an obvious gap, but it offers a cut text, with both of Athamas's arias cut, as well as a couple of choruses, Juno's aria in Act III and Cupid's delightful aria in Act II. Immediately in the Overture Stern reveals his preference for daringly fast speeds, with scampering triplets to challenge the players to the limit. It is very much the same with the vocal numbers following, when again high speeds are allied to a winning lightness of touch. This is helped by the intimate acoustic, with limited forces involved. One benefit is that the performance comes on two discs instead of the three for Nelson's DG version using modern instruments.

Stern's cast may not be as characterful as those of its rivals, and half of the singers are Francophone rather than English-speaking. Yet the mezzo, Guillemette Laurens, makes a most striking Juno, totally convincing. The bright, fresh-toned Danielle De Niese makes an innocent-sounding Semele. Though the microphone catches some shrillness in places, she is amazingly agile, apparently unfazed by Stern's hectic speeds. Paul Agnew as Jupiter offers similar virtuosity in coping with rapid divisions. Happily, as in Semele's sleep aria,

the conductor relaxes persuasively for *Where'er you walk*. The others in the cast are comparably agile, though Susan Miller as Iris is unpleasantly edgy. Jonathan May doubles as both Cadmus and Somnus, more convincing in the latter role. The Scottish soprano Louise Innes, light and fresh as Semele's sister, Ino, makes her mark positively, and the warm-toned counter-tenor Sebastien Fournier, stylish as Athamas, makes one regret the loss of his arias. The excellent chorus is only twelve singers strong. An interesting and always refreshing alternative to existing versions. First choice still goes to Nelson's DG set (see above).

Serse (Xerxes; complete)

*** Conifer 75605 51312-2 (3). Malafronte, J. Smith, Milne, Bickley, Asawa, D. Thomas, Ely, Ch. & Hanover Band, McGegan

(M) **(*) Sony (ADD) SM3K 36941 (3). Watkinson, Esswood, Wenkel, Hendricks, Rodde, Cold, Bridier Vocal Ens., La Grand Ecurie et la Chambre du Roy, Malgoire

Following Venetian fashion, Handel here wrote a piece, built on dozens of short numbers, which has humour and irony as part of the mixture. Even the most celebrated number, Xerxes' aria, *Ombra mai fù*, addressed to a plane tree, is hardly serious, rather illustrating the central character's quirky tastes. McGegan, with light textures and generally brisk speeds, gives necessary momentum while allowing his principals full expressiveness in such deeper numbers as the hero's Act II aria, *Il core spera e teme*, warmly sung by Judith Malafronte, as is *Ombra mai fù*. The counter-tenor Brian Asawa, in the role of Xerxes' brother, Arsamene, is equally expressive with rich, even tone and fine agility, and Jennifer Smith as the heroine, Romilda, is particularly effective in her dramatic arias. Lisa Milne as her sister, Atalanta, nicely catches an ironic tone, with Susan Bickley fresh and agile as Amastre. Characterful baritone contributions from David Thomas (as a comic servant) and Dean Ely, with the chorus's brief interjections adding brightness and sparkle. Full, open sound.

On Sony, Carolyn Watkinson may not be the most characterful of singers in the high castrato role of Xerxes himself, but it is good to have the elaborate roulades so accurately sung. The celebrated *Ombra mai fù* is most beautiful. Paul Esswood is similarly reliable in the role of Arsamene (originally taken by a woman) and the counter-tenor tone is pure and true. Barbara Hendricks and Anne-Marie Rodde are both outstanding in smaller roles, and the comic episodes (most unexpected in Handel) are excellently done. There are detailed stylistic points one might criticize in his rendering (for instance the squeeze effects on sustained string notes) but the vitality is never in doubt, and the close recording is vivid too. As in the rest of this series of Sony reissues, the snag is the absence of an English translation.

Silla (complete)

(M) *** Somm SOMMCD 227-8 (2). Bowman, Lunn, Marsh, Baker, Nicholls, Cragg, Dixon, London Handel O, Darlow

Handel's early opera, *Silla*, is a curiosity. It is not known precisely when it was written, probably in 1713, and it is not even certain that it was ever performed in Handel's lifetime. The story about the predatory Roman dictator, Sulla (spelt Silla in the eighteenth century), is bizarre, with a forced happy ending, but over its compact span – three Acts in under two hours – it has one delightful number after another, all relatively brief with no longueurs anywhere. Silla's slumber aria, *Dolce nume*, is ravishing, as is the touching aria for Silla's estranged wife, Metella, *Io noin chiedo più*, while Silla's aria, *La vendetta*, and that of his enemy, Claudio, *Con tromba guerriera*, with trumpets blazing, are fine examples of the martial Handel.

Denys Darlow conducts a fresh, stylish performance with his London Handel Festival forces, recorded live at the Royal College of Music. Textures are clean and rhythms light and resilient, with James Bowman in the title-role leading a consistently reliable team. Rachel Nicholls as Metella is not as steady as the rest, but everyone copes very well with florid vocal writing, and with a live occasion, well caught, adding to the magnetism.

Siroe, Re di Persia (complete)

(N) *** HM HMC 901826.27 (2). Hallenberg, Stojkovic, Im, Schmid, Noack, Jong, Cappella Coloniensis, Spering

Using a libretto adapted from Metastasio by Niccola Haym, Handel wrote *Siroe* in 1728, taking care to give equal prominence to the two soprano roles, to be taken by the two jealous prima donnas in the Royal Academy company, Francesca Cuzzoni to sing the role of King Cosroe's mistress, Laodice, and Faustina Bordoni to sing Princess Emira, secretly in love with Siroe (Cyrus). That title-role was taken by the leading castrato, Senesino, then nearing the end of his career. It is sung here with satisfyingly rich, firm tone by the contralto, Ann Hallenberg, with Johanna Stojkovic similarly firm as Emira and Sunhae Im as Laodice, light, bright and agile, with just a touch of rawness on top. The baritone, Sebastian Noack, sings Siroe's scheming father, Cosroe, given the first aria, and the soft-grained counter-tenor, Gunther Schmid, takes the second castrato role, Medarse. Neatly fitted on to two very well-filled discs, Andreas Spering's bright and well-paced reading with Cappella Coloniensis brings out the consistent freshness of Handel's inspiration, making it strange that after the first run of 18 performances, the piece is totally neglected until the twentieth century, though Handel re-used various numbers in later operas. Clear, well-balanced sound.

Tamerlano (complete)

☉➤ *** Arthaus **DVD** 100 702 (2). Bacelli, Randle, Norberg-Schulz, Pushee, Bonitatibus, Abete, E. Concert, Pinnock (V/D: Jonathan Miller)

**(*) Avie AV 0001. (Cast as above), E. Concert, Pinnock

(M) *** Erato 2292 454908-2 (2). Ragin, Ronson, Argenta, Chance, Findlay, Schirrer, E. Bar. Sol., Gardiner

Written in 1724, just after *Giulio Cesare* and just before *Rodelinda*, *Tamerlano* comes from one of the most fruitful periods of Handel's career, full of compelling inspiration, yet it has been relatively neglected on disc. This Avie recording was made live at Sadler's Wells in London in collaboration with the BBC in June 2001, marking a welcome return to disc of Trevor Pinnock and the English Concert. The result is delicate on a smallish scale, less sharply focused than Pinnock's Archiv recordings, but with unerring judgement on style and pacing. This is an instance where the DVD, recorded live in the small and ideal Goethe theatre in Bad Lauchstädt, is greatly preferable to the CDs, with solo voices naturally caught and strongly projected against the beautifully recorded and balanced orchestra. It is a strong team of soloists, with Monica Bacelli in the title-role controlling her full, firm contralto well, the counter-tenor, Graham Pushee, light and free as Andronico and Anna Bonitatibus a charming Princess Irene. Thomas Randle gives a vigorously resonant account of the role of Bazajet, and Elizabeth Norberg-Schulz is most resonant as

Bazajet's daughter, Asteria. The production is simple and very effective, and Judy Levine's vivid costumes create a colourful contrast. The DVD performance is totally gripping throughout, whereas on CD the stage noises tend to be obtrusive. The DVD set is splendidly documented, and includes a 'read the score' facility, with the action taking place behind the music – of course one can alternatively have the sub-titles. The additional features include a retrospective review of 50 years of the Handel Festivals, from which this comes, and rehearsal sequences of the present performance.

On CD John Eliot Gardiner's live concert performance of *Tamerlano* presents a strikingly dramatic and immediate experience. Leading the cast are two outstanding counter-tenors whose encounters provide some of the most exciting moments: Michael Chance as Andronicus, firm and clear, Derek Lee Ragin in the name-part equally agile and more distinctive of timbre, with a rich, warm tone that avoids womanliness. Nigel Robson in the tenor role of Bajazet conveys the necessary gravity, not least in the difficult, highly original G minor aria before the character's suicide; and Nancy Argenta sings with starry purity as Asteria. The only snag is the dryness of the sound, which makes voices and instruments sound somewhat aggressive.

Teseo (opera; complete)

*** Erato 2292 45806-2 (2). James, D. Jones, Gooding, Ragin, Napoli, Gall, Les Musiciens du Louvre, Minkowski

Using an Italian translation of a French libretto originally written for Lully 40 years earlier, Handel uniquely produced a hybrid between an Italian *opera seria* and a French tragédie lyrique, with the classical story of Theseus and Medea told in a brisk sequence of short arias. The score may not contain great Handel melodies, but it is characteristically fresh and imaginative. Marc Minkowski, among the liveliest of period-performance specialists, brings out the inventiveness, helped by an excellent cast, dominated by British and American singers. These include Della Jones as Medea, Eirian James in the castrato role of Teseo, Julia Gooding as Agilea and characterful counter-tenors, Derek Lee Ragin and Jeffrey Gall, as Egeo and Arcane.

VOCAL COLLECTIONS

Occasional songs: *7 Airs français, HWV 155; 4 Songs in Different Languages, HWV deest. 3 Theatre Songs, HWV 218 & 228; An answer to Collin's complaint; The beauteous Cloe; Di godere ha sperenza il mio core; The dream; From scourging rebellion; Hunting song; Je ne scai quoi (Yes, I'm in love); Molly Mog; The poor shepherd; Stephon's complaint of love; The unhappy lovers. 4 Minuets; March in G*

(M) **(*) Somm SOMMCD 226. Kirkby, Daniels, Instrumental Ens. & Ch., Nicolson

If not quite all of these 'occasional' songs are authentic, most of them have charm. Notably so the French songs, shared very colloquially by Emma Kirkby and Charles Daniels. The most interesting is *Nos plaisirs serant peu durables*, a chaconne with ground bass, later used in *Alexander's Feast*, while the German Lied in the following group has a nimble cello obbligato, and the Spanish item has a rather lovely tune which Handel was also to re-use later. Many of the English items are in a simple pastoral style. *The Dream (beneath a shady willow)* draws on the opening chorus of *Acis and Galatea* and *The beauteous Cloe* transforms a melancholy aria from *Ottone* into a lighthearted swain's praise of his beloved.

The theatrical songs would fit readily into a piece like *The Beggar's Opera*, and that especially applies to the strophic songs, notably the patriotic numbers with chorus, *Stand round my brave boys* and the lively closing *From scouring rebellion*. Both Emma Kirkby, who sings as sweetly as ever, and the fresh-voiced Charles Daniels have just the right, easy style for this undemanding repertoire, and the performances are pleasingly spontaneous. The instrumental items are slight, but used as intermezzi they are effective enough. The accompaniments are ever-spirited and the recording excellent. Full texts are included.

Arias from: *Acis and Galatea; Atalanta; Athalia; Esther; Jephtha; Judas Maccabaeus; Messiah; Ode for St Cecilia's Day; Ptolemy; Samson; Semele; Serse; Tamerlano; Il trionfo del Tempo e del Disinganno*

(*) Australian ABC Classics 472 151-2. Hobson, Cantillation, Sinf. Australis, Walker

David Hobson's voice is suave if relatively light-timbred, but its reedy sound gives it more of a penetrating quality of the kind one associated more readily with French tenors than with Australian ones, and his diction is crystal-clear. The coloratura is brilliant in such items as *Sound an Alarm* (from *Judas Maccabaeus*) and *The Trumpet's Loud Clangour* (from the *Ode for St Cecilia's Day*), and although Walker's tempi are at breakneck speeds, the results are exciting. In the slower arias, such as *Tune your Harps* (from *Esther*) and *Gentle Airs* (from *Athalia*), he is winningly elegant and able to produce a dark, grave timbre for slow arias like *Total Eclipse* (from *Samson*) which is really quite doleful. The odd transcription is included here, such as the tender arioso *Care selve* (from *Atalanta*). Although a modern orchestra and chorus are used, their approach acknowledges period-instrument manners, and they are certainly warmly recorded, with the voice emerging vividly. Full texts and translations are included, along with an interesting essay on the use of the tenor voice in nineteenth-century England.

Airs, 'scènes célèbres', sinfonias and instrumental music from: *Admeto; Alcina; Giulio Cesare; Radamisto; Rodelinda; Serse. Concerto grosso (Alexander's Feast)*

⊶ ✿ ******* HM HMC 901685. Scholl, Berlin Akademie für Alte Musik

Handel's most celebrated aria, *Ombra mai fù*, is radiantly sung here, with firm, golden tone, alongside the equally lovely *Chiudetevi, miei lumi* from *Admeto*, and the glorious *Dove sei* from *Rodelinda*, with the programme capped by an unforgettably beautiful *Verdi prati* from *Alcina*. There are lively moments too, notably the genial *Va tacito*, which has a jolly horn obbligato. The splendid period-instrument accompaniments by the Berlin Akademie für Alte Musik make the 76-minute programme doubly diverting by playing sinfonias and dance movements (including an engaging suite from *Radamisto*) in between the arias. They end the programme with a superb account of the *Alexander's Feast Concerto grosso*, light and airy. But it is Andreas Scholl's wonderfully stylish and moving singing that makes this record indispensable. The recording is full and immediate.

Arias from: *Agrippina; Orlando; Partenope; Rinaldo; Serse*

(BB) ****(*)** Warner Apex 2564 60519-2. Horne, Sol. Ve., Scimone

Here is a dazzling demonstration of Marilyn Horne singing a varied compilation of Handel arias to set beside her

wider-ranging collection listed in our Vocal Recitals section. The flexibility of her voice in scales and trills and ornaments of every kind remains formidable, and the power is extraordinary down to the tangy chest-register. The voice is spotlit against a reverberant acoustic. Purists may question some of the ornamentation, but voice-fanciers will not worry.

Arias from: *Agrippina: Pensieri, voi mi tormentate; Bel picere. Alexander Balus: Convey me to some peaceful shore . . . Calm thou my soul. Giulio Cesare: V'adoro pupille; Da tempeste il legno infranto. Lotario: Sommo rettor del cielo . . . D'una torbida sorgentel. Orlando: Quando spieghi. Rinaldo: Lascia ch'io pianga; Dunque lacci d'un volto . . . Ah! crudel. Rodelinda: Ritorno, caro e dolce. Samson: To fleeting pleasures; Let the bright Seraphim. Scipione: Scoglio d'immota fronte. Semele: Endless pleasure, endless love; O sleep why dost thou leave me. Serse: Ombra mai fù*

(N) *** Decca 475 6186-2. Fleming, OAE, Bicket

Until now, Renée Fleming has not been associated with this repertory, yet, as she explains in her note for this collection, 'Handel arias comprised the cornerstone of my undergraduate education'. Plainly, those early lessons were well learned by this most conscientious of singers, for her trills are flawlessly even, with other ornaments neatly enunciated. Accompanied by the fine period players of the Orchestra of the Age of Enlightenment under Harry Bicket, she has taken scholarly advice over such matters as ornamenting *da capo* repeats, not making them too intrusive. The 16 items range wide, with favourites like *Ombra mai fù, Let the bright seraphim* and Cleopatra's arias in *Giulio Cesare*, set against rarities like Adelaide's Act II aria in *Lotario* and, best of all, Cleopatra's touching aria, *Calm thou my soul*, from the oratorio, *Alexander Balus*.

Arias from *Alessandro; Amadigi; Arianna in Creta; Deidamia; Faramondo; Giulio Cesare; Orlando; Partenope; Rodelinda; Scipione; Tamerlano*

(N) *** Naïve E 8894. Piau, Les Talens Lyriques, Rousset

The French soprano, Sandrine Piau, has few rivals today in the phenomenal agility she brings to these 12 arias, each from a different *opera seria*, starting with a breath-taking display in Berenice's aria from *Scipione*. Her control of coloratura is complete, with never a hint of any intrusive aitches, and that goes with a voice that is bold, fresh and clear, beautiful in such darkly intense slow arias such as those from *Amadigi* and *Deidamia*. None of these arias is among the popular favourites, not even the excerpt from *Giulio Cesare*, yet with understanding support from Christophe Rousset and the instrumentalists of Les Talens Lyriques she makes them magnetic. The arias are each linked to a series of six great prima donnas of the eighteenth century, and Piau amply demonstrates that in every way she is a modern match for any of them.

Arias: *Alexander's Feast: The Prince, unable to conceal his pain; Softly sweet in Lydian measures. Atalanta: Care selve. Giulio Cesare: Piangerò. Messiah: Rejoice greatly; He shall feed his flock. Rinaldo: Lascia ch'io pianga. Samson: Let the bright Seraphim*

(*) Delos D/CD 3026. Augér, Mostly Mozart O, Schwarz — BACH: *Arias* **(*)**

Arleen Augér's bright, clean, flexible soprano is even more naturally suited to these Handel arias than to the Bach items with which they are coupled. The delicacy with which she tackles the most elaborate divisions and points the words is a delight.

Overtures and Arias (1704–1726) from *Almira; Amadigi di Gaula; Giulio Cesare in Egitto; Rinaldo; Rodelinda; Rodrigo; Scipione* (with *March*); *Silla; Tamerlano*
*** Hyp. CDA 66860. Kirkby, Brandenburg Cons., Goodman

Overtures and Arias (1729–1741) from: *Alcina; Ariana in Creta; Atalanta; Berenice, regina d'Egitto; Deidamia; Ezio; Lotario; Partenope; Sosarme, re di Media*
*** Hyp. CDA 67128. Kirkby, Brandenburg Cons., Goodman

It might be thought that a collection interspersing Handel arias and overtures would not be particularly stimulating, but Emma Kirkby (in glorious voice) and Roy Goodman directing invigorating playing by the Brandenburg Consort prove just how enjoyable such a concert, or pair of concerts, can be. The first disc covers the first half of Handel's operatic career. After opening with Handel's second overture to *Almira*, Kirkby clears her throat with the sprightly roulades of *Vedrai s'a tuo dispetto*, and then enchants us with the melancholy line of *Perché viva il caro sposo* from *Rodrigo*. *Desterò dall'ampia Dite*, from *Amadigi di Gaula*, then brings a superb trumpet (Robert Farley) and oboe (Katharina Arfken) obbligato duet, and the oboe is again prominent in the introduction to the famous *V'adoro pupille* (from *Giulio Cesare*) while the lovely *Ombre piante* brings an echoing flute. Both are ravishingly sung and the trumpet returns for the lively closing regal number from *Scipione*.

Volume 2 deals with Handel's later operas and opens with the virtually unknown overture to *Lotario* (1729). Queen Adelaide's feisty aria which follows shows Emma Kirkby at her nimblest, although she is hardly less dazzling in *Dite pace* from *Sosarme*. Other highlights include the lovely *Caro padre* from *Ezio* and the anguished recitative, *Ah! Ruggiero*, from *Alcina*, with its dramatic pauses, and a lovely flowing aria, *Ombre pallide*, both of which show Kirkby at her very finest. Perhaps the most delightful item here is *Chi t'intende?* from *Berenice*, where Kirkby clearly enjoys her continuing duet with the solo oboe. The closing number, *M'hai resa infelice*, comes from *Deidamia*. It opens with a touching lament and then its heroine curses Ulysses spectacularly for taking her lover Achilles away from her to the war against Troy.

Arias from: *Belshazzar; Jephtha; Messiah; Saul; Semele; Theodora*
*** Virgin 5 45497-2. Daniels, Ens. O de Paris, Nelson

Even David Daniels has rarely matched the brilliance, beauty and expressive intensity of this superb collection of arias from Handel oratorios, starting with two arias from *Belshazzar*, the one exuberant in vigour, a display aria for Cyrus with trumpets and timpani, the other noble and deeply felt for Daniel, *O Sacred Oracles of Truth*. Similarly a light and brilliant aria from *Semele* is set against one in a poignant minor key, while the four arias from *Theodora*, all for the character Didymus, similarly cover a wide range. Those from *Saul* have David singing his lament for Jonathan set against a noble prayer, while Hamor's arias from *Jephtha* lead to the noblest performance of all, *He was despised* from *Messiah*, the most ambitious and original of all the arias. Daniels's combination of flawless technique and expressive depth makes for magnetic performances, with elaborate divisions effortlessly thrown off. John Nelson draws electric playing from his period orchestra, starting brilliantly on the first *Belshazzar* aria.

Arias from: *Flavio:(i) Amor, nel mio penar. Giulio Cesare in Eggitto: Va tacito e nascosto. Hercules:(ii) Turn thee, youth*

to joy and love(with Chorus); (iii) *This manly youth's exalted mind; Mount, mount the steep ascent(with Chorus). Messiah:(iv;v) He shall feed his flock;(v) Rejoice greatly;(vi) Why do the nations?... Let us break(with Chorus); Orlando:(i) Fammi combattere. Rinaldo:(vii) Or la tromba in suon festante. Rodelinda: Vivi tirano.Xerxes: Frondi tenere... Ombra mai fù.(viii) 9 German Arias: Süsse Sille, sanfte Quelle.(ix) Silente venti* (Motet, with flute & Continuo)
🔊 ⚙ *** Capriccio **Surround Sound** SACD 71 024. (i) Axel Köhler; (ii) Hruba-Freiberger; (iii) Arleen Augér; (iv) Charles Humphries; (v) Max Emanuel Cencic; (vi) Robert Torday, V. Boys' Ch.; (vii) Jochen Kowalski; (viii) Ann Monoyios & Berlin Bar. Co.; (ix) Emma Kirkby; (with various orchestras & conductors)

[handwritten: out of print]

This is simply the most thrilling collection of miscellaneous Handel arias in the catalogue, and the Rosette must be shared equally by the perceptive unnamed compiler, the artists for their inspired contributions, and to Capriccio's Surround Sound for providing such an extraordinary communication of the artists' presence and of the feeling of actually sitting in the concert hall. It is not possible to do justice to the many fine performances here. Opening with resplendent trumpets, as only Handel knows how to write for them, the programme begins with the clarion call from *Rinaldo*, *Or le tromba in suon festante*, dramatically sung by Jochen Kowalski, who is later to be equally commanding in the bravura aria from *Rodelinda*, and then melts the listener with a glorious *Ombra mai fù*. In all three items, there are splendid accompaniments by the C. P. E. Bach Chamber Orchestra under Helmut Haenschen. The three excerpts from *Messiah* are memorable too, with the silvery voice of the remarkable male soprano, Max Emanuel Cencic, standing out. (His singing is also a highlight of the DVD of Haydn's *Creation* – see below.)

After Axel Köhler has sung the virtuoso aria from *Orlando* with alomb, she is joined in duet in the *Julius Caesar* excerpt by a remarkably characterful unnamed period-horn soloist. Our own Emma Kirkby is as ravishing as ever in the celestial motet, *Silente venti*, and Ann Monoyios shares her lovely German aria, *Süsse Stille*, with the flute d'amour. And it is the delicate opening and closing writing for flutes that helps to make Arleen Augér's first aria from *Hercules* so haunting. Then in the closing item, *Mount, mount the steep ascent*, she is followed by a thrilling burst of choral fervour by the combined Leipzig University and New Bach Collegium choirs. There are, alas, no texts and translations – but, for once, one is lost for words anyway.

Arias from: *Giulio Cesare; Rinaldo; Rodelinda; Serse; Tamerlano*
*** Virgin 5 45326-2 Daniels, OAE, Norrington

Here again, David Daniels stands out for the evenness and beauty of his voice, with an exceptionally rich lower register. Though the orchestra is not always as alert as it might be, his singing in this challenging group of arias, starting with *Ombra mai fù* from *Serse*, is warmly expressive in slow numbers and brilliantly dramatic in fast ones like *Al lampo dell'armi* from *Giulio Cesare*. Well-balanced sound.

Arias: *Judas Maccabaeus: Father of heaven. Messiah: O Thou that tellest; He was despised. Samson: Return O God of Hosts*
🔊 ⚙ (M) (***) Decca mono 433 474-2. Ferrier, LPO, Boult
– BACH: *Arias* (***)

Kathleen Ferrier had a unique feeling for Handel; these

performances are unforgettable for their communicative intensity and nobility of timbre and line. She receives highly sympathetic accompaniments from Boult, another natural Handelian.

Arias: *Partenope: Sento amor; Ch'io parta?; Furibondo spira il vento. Tolomeo: Stille amare*

*** Virgin 5 45365-2. Daniels, OAE, Bicket – GLUCK, MOZART: *Arias* ***

One of the *Partenope* arias provides the title for this third exceptional disc of counter-tenor arias, ranging widely in its expressiveness, with David Daniels using his extraordinarily beautiful voice, clear and pure with none of the usual counter-tenor hoot, with the keenest artistry. Whether in deeply expressive lyrical numbers or in brilliant florid passages, his technique is immaculate, with the voice perfectly placed.

Overtures and excerpts from *Jephtha; Joseph and His Brethren; Joshua; Solomon. Belshazzar: Let festival joy reign!*

**(*) Ara. Z 6720. Elwes, St Lukes CO

There are lots of good tunes here and each selection includes a key aria, strongly and dramatically sung by John Elwes. His manner is direct and forward, and he sings Handel's runs with gusto, using his vibrato with individuality. He tends to over-phrase in the lyrical music, yet can produce lovely tone in a number like *Waft her angels* (from *Jephtha*) which he does not attempt to decorate. Excellent recording, lively but with a nice degree of resonance.

HANSON, Howard (1896–1981)

Howard Hanson was the first American to win a Prix de Rome in 1920, studying orchestration and composition with Respighi. He can best be described as a neo-Romantic, with a strong lyrical vein to his make-up. His musical sympathies lay with Scandinavia (he was of Swedish descent) and, above all, Sibelius – though it was the Sibelius of the first two *Symphonies* rather than the *Fourth* and *Sixth* that left the strongest imprint on his musical language. If Hanson composed seven *Symphonies* in all, he was hugely productive in many other genres. As befits a student of Respighi, his musc is superbly scored and has a Korngold-like fluency and directness of appeal. Many of his bigger works were written on commission: *Mosaics* (1958) for George Szell and the Cleveland Orchestra, and the *Third Symphony* (1938) for Koussevitzky, whose recording of it is peerless.

Symphonies 1–7; (i) *Piano Concerto in G. Elegy in Memory of Koussevitzky; (i) Fantasy Variations on a Theme of Youth, Op. 40. Mosaics; Merry Mount Suite, Op. 31; Pastorale for Oboe, Harp & Strings, Op. 38; Serenade for Flute, Harp & Strings, Op. 38; (ii) Lament for Beowulf, Op. 25; Song of Democracy*

(M) *** Delos DE 3150 (4). Seattle SO, Schwarz; with (i) Rosenberger; (ii) Ch.

Symphonies 1 in E min., Op. 21 (Nordic); 2 in E min., Op. 30; 3 in A min., Op. 44; Elegy for Koussevitzky, Op. 44; For the First Time; Merry Mount Suite; Mosaics;(i) Song of Democracy; Lament for Beowulf;(ii) Piano Concerto, Op. 36

(N) **(*) Mercury 475 6867 (4). Eastman-Rochester SO, Hanson, with (i) Eastman-Rochester Ch.; (ii) Mouledous (**with talk by Hanson about** *Merry Mount Suite, Mosaics* & *For the First Time*)

Gerard Schwarz has proved himself a master of Hanson's Nordic idiom and a consistently convincing interpreter of his symphonies, in which he secures high commitment and playing of the highest quality from the excellent Seattle orchestra. Carol Rosenberger is an excellent soloist in the two concertante piano works; the other soloists are drawn from the orchestra, and all make admirable contributions. This is all music which is easy to enjoy, and these artists are afforded full, brilliant recording from the Delos engineers within an expansive acoustic.

The pioneering Mercury recordings, made in the late 1950s, are very characteristic of the Living Presence label: bright, well detailed, with a touch of glare. This is all music which benefits from the richer patina of modern stereo, so Schwarz's highly idiomatic Delos anthology must take pride of place. Even so, the composer's own accounts have a special niche in the catalogue; the performances are freshly spontaneous, concentrated and very well played. Hanson remained at all times true to himself and his music has a total honesty and an authenticity of feeling that has enabled him to hold his public when many of his more radical contemporaries have fallen from view.

Symphonies 1 in E min. (Nordic), Op. 21; 2 (Romantic), Op. 30; (i) Song of Democracy

(*) Mercury (ADD) **SACD 475 6181. Eastman-Rochester O, composer; (i) with Eastman School of Music Ch.

Hanson's own pioneering stereo recordings of his two best-known symphonies have a unique thrust and ardour. The *Song of Democracy* has plenty of dramatic impact and is also well recorded. The new format enhances the results afforded by the 'Living Presence' technology, but cannot disguise the thinness of violin timbre, especially in the *First Symphony*. An indispensable disc, just the same.

Symphony 1; Merry Mount (suite); Pan and the Priest, Op. 26; Rhythmic Variations on Two Ancient Hymns

(BB) **(*) Naxos 8.559072. Nashville SO, Schermerhorn

Schermerhorn gives a relaxed account of the *First Symphony*, notably slower than the composer's own thrusting Mercury account, but this warmer approach offers its own rewards, especially in some of the more lyrical passages. The two tone-poems are rarities: *Pan and the Priest*, written during 1925–6, begins quite mournfully on a solo cor anglais, and is passionate and reflective in turn, with the orchestra (including a piano) used colourfully. The *Rhythmic Variations* are melancholic and contemplative in nature, but appealing also, and the colourful *Merry Mount* suite (one of Hanson's best works) is splendidly done. The Nashville SO play well for Schermerhorn, and the sound is warm and reasonably vivid. Good value.

Symphonies 1; 3; 5 (Sinfonia Sacra), Op. 43; (i) Piano Concerto in G, Op. 36. Merry Mount: Suite; (ii) Lament for Beowulf

☞ (B) *** Delos Double DE 3709 (2). Seattle SO, Schwarz; (i) with Rosenberger; (ii) with Symphony Ch.

Hanson is of Swedish descent and his music has a strong individuality of idiom and colour. The *First Symphony* is very like the more famous *Second* – warmly appealing, held together with indelible ideas which appear in all three movements. After getting to know these two works (which are also available coupled together on D/CD 3073) the musical terrain of the *Third* will seem familiar: the string threnodies surge purposefully forward, there are similar rhythmic patterns and confident rhetorical gestures. The single-movement *Sinfonia Sacra* – inspired by Christ's Passion – is also very succinct, again showing the composer's Nordic inheritance. The four-movement *Piano Concerto* (1948) is also compressed. Carol Rosenberger is a brilliant and responsive soloist. The *Lament for Beowulf* is an eloquent, elegiac piece with chorus which does not outstay its welcome. These Seattle performances have plenty of breadth and ardour. The recording, made in Seattle Opera House, is gloriously expansive and the balance convincingly natural.

Symphonies (i) 2 (Romantic); 4 (Requiem); 6; (i–ii) 7 (Sea Symphony after Walt Whitman); (i) Elegy in Memory of Serge Koussevitzky; (i; iii) Fantasy Variations on a Theme of Youth (for piano and orchestra); (i) Mosaics; (iv) Serenade for Flute, Harp & Strings

⊕━ (B) *** Delos Double DE 3705 (2). (i) Seattle SO; (ii) Seattle Chorale; (iii) Rosenberger; (iv) Meredith, Jollies, NY Chamber Ens.; all cond. Schwarz

This second Delos Double includes his *Second Symphony*, melodically so memorable. Like this symphony, the *Fourth* has strong Nordic influences, and the *Sea Symphony* brings stirring choral writing to words of Walt Whitman. All three are superbly played in Seattle and Schwarz's powerful direction is thoroughly idiomatic and committed. The *Fantasy Variations* have a fine piano soloist in Carol Rosenberger. *Mosaics* is another set of variations, written in 1957 for Szell and the Cleveland Orchestra. The even briefer and delicately scored *Serenade* makes a delightful contrast, finely crafted. All this music is well worth getting to know, and much of it is very rewarding indeed. The recordings are in the demonstration bracket.

Symphony 3

(***) Biddulph mono WHL 044. Boston SO, Koussevitzky (with MUSSORGSKY: *Khovanshchina: Prelude.* LIADOV: *The Enchanted Lake.* RIMSKY-KORSAKOV: *Legend of the Invisible City of Kitezh: Entr'acte. Dubinushka.* FAURE: *Pelléas et Mélisande: Prélude; La Fileuse; Mort de Mélisande* (**(*))

With passionate playing from the Boston orchestra, Koussevitzky's reading is powerfully committed, immediately establishing the northern atmosphere of Hanson's sound-world and building the finale steadily to its final climax with gripping concentration. The Biddulph transfer is very good, with sonic inadequacies easily forgotten. The other pieces, which come before the symphony, are all played superbly, but the sound is more variable. Highlights include the Mussorgsky *Khovanshchina Prelude*, sombrely paced, and the Liadov *Enchanted Lake*, both highly evocative and the latter remarkably full and atmospheric. The excerpts from Fauré's *Pelléas et Mélisande* are delicately done, although here climaxes are less refined.

HARRIS, Roy (1898–1979)

(i) Violin Concerto; Symphonies 1; 5

** Albany (ADD) AR012. (i) Fulkerston; Louisville O, Smith; Mester or Whitney

The *First Symphony* is strong stuff, hardly less impressive than No. 3; but neither No. 5 nor the *Violin Concerto* adds greatly to our picture of its composer. Gregory Fulkerston gives a

persuasive account of the solo part, but the strings of the enterprising Louisville Orchestra are wanting in body and lustre. The recordings are serviceable rather than distinguished.

Symphony 2

(*) Albany **SACD TROY 515. Albany SO, Miller – HARRIS: *Symphony 3* **(*)

Here is something of special interest and value. It fills in the gap between Harris's *First Symphony* of 1933, which Koussevitsky premièred to such acclaim, and the celebrated *Third*. The work gave Roy Harris much anguish, and he was altering or cutting it right up to the first performance. Although Koussevitzky had commissioned it, the first performance was conducted by his concert-master, Richard Burgin, and Harris never attended it (Ormandy was giving the first performance of his *Prelude and Fugue* on the same day in Philadelphia). He subsequently seems to have disowned the piece, except for the middle movement, which is undoubtedly the finest. It is fascinating to hear the harmonic language of the *Third* taking shape and the sinewy counterpoint and Gregorian-like melodies unfold so naturally. One is occasionally reminded of Vaughan Williams. The first movement is less convincing, although Harris already shows his firmness of grip and purpose; the finale makes a strong ending. The orchestral playing is committed, though the string tone is lacking in weight. The SACD recording reproduces on normal CD players, it is perfectly acceptable, if not outstanding; but the sheer interest of the work carries the day.

Symphony 3

(M) **(*) Sony SMK 60594. NYPO, Bernstein – DIAMOND: *Symphony 4*; THOMPSON: *Symphony 2* **(*)

This Sony account comes from 1961 and is quite simply the best LP/CD version artistically; only his mentor Koussevitzky's pioneering 78s have greater concentration and fire, and Bernstein runs him pretty close, even if the forwardly balanced recording is less than ideal. It comes with another classic of the American discography, the Diamond *Fourth Symphony*.

Symphonies 7; 9; Epilogue to Profiles in Courage – J.F.K.

(BB) **(*) Naxos 8.559050. Nat. SO of Ukraine, Kuchar

Kuchar and the Ukraine orchestra offer powerfully idiomatic accounts of these two symphonies, and they are recorded vividly, though the upper strings are lacking real body and weight. The writing, open and strong, with antiphonal effects between massed strings and brass is recognizably from the same pen as the *Third*, well worth investigating. No. 7, like that celebrated work, is in a single 20-minute movement of contrasted sections, and builds up from a slowly monumental opening to a massive climax with powerful strings and brass, and relaxes at the end with tinkling percussion effects that are anything but monumental.

Commissioned for Philadelphia, No. 9 takes its inspiration from the American Constitution and is in three substantial movements, each with a quotation from the Constitution as a superscription. Surprisingly, the opening, '*We, the people*', brings a jolly waltz motif with whooping brass, and it is only in the second and third movements, much more extended, that the composer takes on a solemn mood, with the pavane-like second movement leading to a strong finale with martial overtones. The *Epilogue* in memory of President Kennedy is elegiac, dignified without quite becoming a funeral march, gritty at times, leading to a meditative close. A valuable addition to the Naxos 'American Classics' series.

Symphonies (i) 8 (San Francisco Symphony) for Orchestra with Piano; 9; Memories of a Child's Sunday
*** Albany TROY 350. Albany SO, Miller, (i) with Feinberg

The *Eighth Symphony* is a one-movement piece in five sections; although the melodic language and harmonic vocabulary are familar from the *Third* and *Seventh*, the scoring is different (apart from some inventive wind writing, Harris provides a virtuoso piano part, and tubular bells). Dan Stehman speaks of the chorale-like slow movement of the *Ninth Symphony*, along with the slow movement of the *Fifth*, as being Harris's finest. Its sound world is fresh and there is a Gallic transparency of texture. *Memories of a Child's Sunday* is a slight piece written much earlier, in 1945, for Rodzinski and the New York Philharmonic. The Albany Orchestra plays very well for David Alan Miller and in the *Ninth* they are to be preferred to their Ukrainian colleagues. The strings have greater weight and the orchestral performance overall has even greater conviction and eloquence. Very fine recorded sound.

HARTMANN, Karl Amadeus
(1905–63)

(i) Chamber Concerto for Clarinet, String Quartet & Strings; (ii) Concerto funèbre for Violin & Strings; Symphony 4 for Strings
*** ECM 465 779-2. Munich CO, Poppen, with (i) Meyer, Peterson Qt; (ii) Isabelle Faust

The *Concerto funèbre*, the lament for the betrayal of Czechoslovakia, is the best-known work here, and Isabelle Faust holds her own alongside all her rivals in previous recordings. The *Chamber Concerto* for the unusual combination of clarinet, string quartet and string orchestra (from 1935) is a rarity in which there are occasional touches of Bartók and at one point even Kodály. The performance of the *Fourth Symphony* comes off well. The playing here has eloquence, and the recording is absolutely first class. A well-filled disc which makes a more than serviceable calling-card for Hartmann's music.

Concerto funèbre
(BB) *** Warner Apex 0927 40812-2. Zehetmair, Deutsche Chamber Philharmonie – BERG: *Violin Concerto*; JANACEK: *Concerto* ***

As one of the two couplings for a highly sensitive version of the Berg *Concerto*, Zehetmair offers this strong, intense *Concerto funèbre* for violin and strings – very much reflecting in its dark moods the troubled period (1939) when it was written.

Symphonies 1–8
(M) *** EMI 5 56911-2 (3). Bamberg SO, Metzmacher

Ingo Metzmacher and his Bamberg orchestra have been exploring the Karl Amadeus Hartmann symphonies over the last half-dozen years, and EMI have now collected them on these three CDs. All eight have been issued before on Wergo in performances by Kubelik and Zdeněk Macal, but these are currently out of circulation, and in any event this set is more economical. All the Hartmann symphonies up to the *Sixth* (1951–3) have their origins in earlier work. The *Third* (1949) is

a conflation of movements from two different pieces written during the Second World War – the *Sinfonia tragica* (1940, revised 1943) and the *Klagegesang* (1944–5, revised 1946–7). The *Fourth* (1947), which is for string orchestra, was completed two years before the *Third*; it is sinewy and Bartókian but without the strong personality and memorability of the latter. The *Fifth*, subtitled *Symphonie concertante*, has its origins in a trumpet concerto from 1933. The *Sixth* is the most performed of all and was the first to be recorded, in the days of mono LP, but despite numerous recordings it has never gained more than a toe-hold on the repertory. Some find the post-expressionist language of Hartmann hard going, but he is a composer of both integrity and substance and is well worth the effort. This expertly recorded set is now a strong recommendation.

Symphonies (i) 1 (Versuch eines Requiem). 6; Miserae
*** Telarc CD 80528. LPO, Botstein; (i) with Van Nes

Leon Botstein gives very committed accounts of the two symphonies recorded here. Jard van Nes is a distinct asset in the *First Symphony*. Those who want to investigate this challenging and respected composer (and who do not want to embark on the Metzmacher cycle) should find this a satisfying buy.

String Quartet 1 (Carillon)
**(*) ECM 465 776-2. Zehetmair Qt – BARTOK: *Quartet 4* **(*)

The Hartmann *First Quartet* comes from 1933, and its subtitle, *Carillon*, alludes to the prize Hartmann's quartet won at a competition in Geneva in 1936. The Zehetmair gives an intense and dedicated account of this work and readers with an interest in this composer need not entertain any serious artistic doubts. Bartók's *Fourth Quartet* (1928), whatever its merits, makes for short measure. The disc runs to only 43 minutes.

HARTY, Hamilton (1879–1941)

A Comedy Overture; (i) Piano Concerto; (ii) Violin Concerto; (iii) In Ireland (Fantasy); An Irish Symphony; (ii) Variations on a Dublin Air. With the Wild Geese. (iv) The Children of Lir; Ode to a Nightingale. Arrangement: The Londonderry Air
(M) *** Chan. 10194X (3). (i) Binns; (ii) Holmes; (iii) Fleming, Kelly; (iv) Harper; Ulster O, Thomson

Bryden Thomson's reissued box gathers togther Harty's orchestral and concertante works with great success. The *Piano Concerto* has strong Rachmaninovian influences, and if the *Violin Concerto* is less individual it is often touched with poetry. Ralph Holmes gives a thoroughly committed account of the solo part and is well supported by an augmented Ulster Orchestra under Bryden Thomson. The *Irish Symphony*, built on traditional themes, is best known for its Scherzo, entitled *A Fair Day*, but it is brilliantly scored and enjoyable throughout. It is extremely well played by the Ulster Orchestra; while the *In Ireland Fantasy* is full of delightful Irish melodic whimsy. Melodrama enters the scene in the symphonic poem, *With the Wild Geese*, but its Irishry asserts itself immediately in the opening theme. All these performances are highly sympathetic and there is high standard of digital sound throughout. The three discs are no longer available separately.

An Irish Symphony; In Ireland; With the Wild Geese
(BB) *** Naxos 8.554732. Nat. SO of Ireland, O Duinn

The *Irish Symphony* has won great acclaim for its brilliant scoring and craftsmanship, with the Scherzo particularly engaging.The brief, dancing Scherzo entitled *The Fair Day*, which may here be less genial on Naxos than it can be, is the more exciting for being taken at breathtaking speed. The players of the National Symphony Orchestra of Ireland take up the challenge brilliantly, and bring all the necessary warmth to the other evocative movements, which, like the two tone-poems, a generous fill-up, are atmospheric programme–pieces inspired by Irish legends and places. Full, clear sound.

Music for cello and piano: *Butterflies; Romance & Scherzo, Op. 8; Wood-stillness*
(M) *** Dutton Epoch CDLX 7102. Fuller, Dussek –
 HURLSTONE: *Cello Sonata*; PARRY: *Cello Sonata* ***

Slight but quite pleasing pieces that are fill-ups for the two cello sonatas by Hurlstone and Parry. Effective and accomplished playing from Andrew Fuller and Michael Dussek – and very well recorded too.

3 Pieces for Oboe & Piano
(BB) *** Hyp. Helios CDH 55008. Francis, Rasumovsky Qt –
 BOUGHTON: *Pastorale*; HOWELLS: *Sonata*; RUBBRA: *Sonata* ***

Harty's three oboe *Pieces*, played here with piano, were written for Henry Wood's 1911 Proms with an orchestral accompaniment. They are utterly charming in this more intimate version, and both artists respond to their disarming melodiousness, especially in the very Irish tune of the closing *A la campagne*. The balance is too forward but the playing has delicacy of feeling and, if you turn the volume down, the effect is very pleasing.

VOCAL MUSIC

(i) *The Children of Lir; Ode to a Nightingale*; (ii) *Variations on a Dublin Air*. Arrangement: *Londonderry Air*
(M) *** Chan. 7033. Ulster O, Thomson, with (i) Harper; (ii) Holmes

Harty's setting of Keats's *Ode to a Nightingale* is richly convincing, a piece written for his future wife, the soprano, Agnes Nicholls. The other work, directly Irish in its inspiration, evocative in an almost Sibelian way, uses the soprano in wordless melisma, here beautifully sung by Heather Harper. The performances are excellent, warmly committed and superbly recorded. The *Variations on a Dublin Air*, for violin and orchestra, and Harty's arrangement of the *Londonderry Air* have been added for the reissue.

HARVEY, Richard (born 1953)

Concerto antico (for guitar and small orchestra)
⊕ *** Sony SK 68337. Williams, LSO, Daniel – GRAY: *Concerto* *** ⊕

Richard Harvey's highly atmospheric *Concerto antico* is easily the best concerto for the guitar since the work by Malcolm Arnold of several decades earlier, admirably written for the soloist and most imaginatively scored in the orchestra. As much a five-movement suite as a concerto, the piece uses old song- and dance-forms, but the composer's ideas are his own – and very tuneful they are, with an element of pastiche in their settings, yet nicely spiced with modern harmonic touches. In every way this is a masterly work, and it is played superbly by its commissioner and dedicatee, John Williams, splendidly accompanied by the LSO under Paul Daniel. The recording, ideally balanced, is of demonstration quality.

HASSE, Johann (1699–1783)

(i; ii) *Aria 'Ah Dio, ritornate'* from *La conversione di San'Agostino* for viola da gamba and harpsichord; (iii; i; ii) *Flute Sonata in B min., Op. 2/6*; (ii) *Harpsichord Sonata in C min. Op. 7/6*; (iv; i–iii) Cantatas: *Fille, dolce mio bene; Quel vago seno, O Fille;* Venetian ballads: *Cos e' sta Cossa?; Grazie agli inganni tuoi; No ste' a condanare; Si' la gondola avere', non crie'*
(M) *** CRD 3488. (i) Headley; (ii) Proud; (iii) Hadden; (iv) Baird

The cantatas here are written in a pastoral style, with important flute obbligatos (a legacy from Frederick II). They show much charm and distinct expressive feeling, and Julianne Baird has exactly the right voice for them, with a freshness of tone and purity of line matched by the right degree of ardour. The *Harpsichord Sonata*, alternating fast and slow movements, is inventive and good-humoured, and the *Aria* for viola da gamba readily shows the composer's operatic style, while the Venetian ballads that close this elegantly performed and very well-recorded concert are also full of character, cultivated rather than folksy in their more popular idiom.

HAYDN, Josef (1732–1809)

Cello Concertos 1 in C; 2 in D, Hob VIIb/1–2
(M) *** EMI (ADD) 5 66896-2 [566948]. Du Pré, ECO, Barenboim; or LSO, Barbirolli – BOCCHERINI: *Cello Concerto in B flat* (arr. GRUTZMACHER) ***
(BB) *** Naxos 8.550059. Kanta, Capella Istropolitana, Breiner – BOCCHERINI: *Cello Concerto* ***
**(*) Orfeo C080031A. Müller-Schott, Australian CO, Tognetti – BEETHOVEN: *Romances 1 & 2* **(*)
(M) **(*) EMI 5 67234-2 [5 67263-2]. Rostropovich, ASMF
(BB) **(*) EMI Encore 5 74734-2. Harrell, ASMF, Marriner – VIVALDI: *Concertos* **

(i) *Cello Concertos 1–2. Overture in G (Lo speziale)*
**(*) EMI 5 56535-2. (i) Chang; Dresden State O, Sinopoli

(i) *Cello Concertos 1–2. Sinfonia concertante in B flat*
(N) (B) *** DHM/BMG 74321 935482. (i) Hidemi Suzuki; La Petite Bande, Sigiswald Kuijken

(i) *Cello Concertos 1–2. Symphony 104* (arr. Salomon)
*** Channel Classics CCS 7395. (i) Wispelwey; Florilegium

Hidemi Suzuki is second to none as a soloist in the two concertos, playing with fine tone, sensibility and refinement, and producing electrifying bravura in the finales – especially the *First in C major*, which Kuijken takes exhilaratingly briskly. La Petite Bande provides the stylish soloists for the engaging *Sinfonia concertante*, and the balance is again just right.

Pieter Wispelwey is also an inspired soloist in the period performance with Florilegium, at times abrasive but always transparent in texture, with the soloist's clean articulation allowing fast speeds in outer movements with no feeling of rush. The central *Adagios* by contrast are surprisingly slow, not as elegant as some, but deeply felt. Salomon's arrangement of Haydn's last symphony for flute, string quartet and piano makes an unusual if lightweight coupling.

Jacqueline du Pré's recording of the *C major Concerto* in April 1967 was the first she made with her husband, Daniel Barenboim, and she gives a performance of characteristic warmth and intensity. Equally, with Barbirolli scaling his accompaniment to match the inspirational approach of his young soloist, the performance of the better-known *D major Concerto* is just as warm and expressive, and the romantic feeling is matched by an attractively full, well-balanced sound-picture.

Ludovít Kanta is a fine artist. The excellent Naxos recording is made in a bright, resonant acoustic in which every detail is clearly registered, though the players are perhaps forwardly placed. The accompaniments are alert and fresh. Kanta plays contemporary cadenzas. An excellent bargain.

The young Korean cellist Han-Na Chang gives warm but essentially refined readings of both concertos and in the beautiful slow movement of the *D major*, she draws out the melodic line exquisitely on a half-tone, and she conveys pleasure in what she does. Sinopoli affectionately fines down the orchestral accompaniment to match his soloist's delicacy, but some may prefer a more robust, more mature approach in eighteenth-century concertos. The Italian *Overture* (in effect a miniature sinfonia) is most deftly played and makes an engaging interlude between the two works.

Daniel Müller-Schott is in his late twenties and hails from Munich, but he has already appeared as a soloist with most of the major European orchestras as well as the Philadelphia Orchestra. He is obviously a thoughtful and intelligent musician and he gives highly accomplished accounts of the *C major* and *D major Concertos* with the Australian Chamber Orchestra, led by Richard Tognetti. In both concertos he plays cadenzas he has written in collaboration with Heinrich Schiff and Steven Isserlis, who has placed his 1740 Venetian instrument by Domenico Montagnan at Müller-Schott's disposal. We do not care for the exaggerated *pianissimos* in which he indulges, but in other respects he is very stylish. He plays his own transcription of the two Beethoven *Romances* with an appropriate lyrical ardour. The recordings, made in Nimbus's Monmouthshire studio, are very truthfully balanced.

Rostropovich's virtuosity is astonishing. True, there are moments of breathless phrasing, and Rostropovich's style has acquired a degree of self-indulgence in the warmth of expressiveness; and this is reflected in the accompaniment from the ASMF, which he also directed. Just the same, the solo playing is very compelling for all its romantic emphasis and slow movements are certainly beautiful.

The attractions of Lynn Harrell's super-bargain coupling are enhanced by the inclusion of two Vivaldi concertos interspersed with Haydn (although the recorded sound is strikingly different). Harrell, rather after the manner of Rostropovich, seeks to turn these elegant concertos into big, virtuoso pieces, helped by Marriner's beautifully played accompaniments. Although touches of romantic expressiveness tend to intrude, the result is enjoyable, even if cadenzas are distractingly long.

(i) *Cello Concertos 1–2*; (ii; iii) *Piano Concerto in D, Hob XVIII/11*. (iv) *Trumpet Concerto in E flat. Violin Concertos Nos.* (v) *1 in C*; (vi; iii) *4 in G, Hob XVIIa/1 & 4*. (vii) *Flute Trios (London), Hob IV/1–3*

(M) *** Sony (ADD/DDD) SM2K 89984 (2). (i) Ma, ECO, Garcia; (ii) Ax; (iii) Franz Liszt CO; (iv) Marsalis, ECO, Leppard; (v) Lin, Minnesota O, Marriner; (vi) Stern; (vii) Rampal, Stern, Rostropovich

☛ (N) (B) *** Sony 517 485-2. (i) Ma; (ii) Ax; (iv) Marsalis; (v) Lin (as above)

An excellent compilation, well worth collecting if you want all these works. In the *Cello Concertos* Ma's refinement of approach brings its own rewards, though some may prefer a bolder approach to music that belongs firmly to the classical eighteenth century. The well-transferred analogue recording is clean and full. Ax plays the finest of Haydn's piano concertos on a modern piano and does so with great style; he is splendidly accompanied and recorded. Marsalis's invigorating account of the *Trumpet Concerto* is second to none and, aided by Leppard and the ECO, the result is both brilliant and stylish. Cho Liang Lin's account of the *C major Violin Concerto* also has plenty of classical strength and drive; the slow movement is perhaps a little lacking in charm but is nevertheless enjoyable: the playing is by no means insensitive. Stern takes over for the *G major Concerto*, helped by another outstanding accompaniment from the Franz Liszt Chamber Orchestra. This must have been a recording made late in his career – we have not heard it before – for his tone is thinner than it once was, but there is no doubting his artistry. The *London Flute Trios* come as a surprising bonus, for neither Rampal nor Rostropovich is named on the front of the disc, nor pictured with the other artists on the back, and the word 'flute' is not mentioned in the listing of the music. But these are eminently winning performances of some charming if minor pieces of Haydn's London years, and the players convey a sense of enjoyment and much pleasure. The recording is again excellent.

However, the alternative bargain CD, offering four of Haydn's very finest concertante works in first-class performances, is even more tempting.

(i) *Cello Concertos 1–2*; (ii) *Violin Concertos 1, 3 & 4*; (ii; iii) *Double Concerto for Violin & Harpsichord in F, Hob XVIII/6*

(B) *** Ph. Duo (ADD) 438 797-2 (2). ECO, with (i) Walevska, De Waart; (ii; iii) Accardo; (iii) Canino

Christine Walevska presents the two cello concertos freshly, well partnered by Edo de Waart and the ECO. She is balanced almost within the orchestra, to give an agreeable chamberlike quality to the music-making. The three *Violin Concertos* are all early; the *C major*, written for Tomasini, is probably the best. The other two have come into the limelight fairly recently. Accardo plays with great elegance and charm. It would be idle to pretend that either they or the *Double Concerto for Violin and Harpsichord* are great music, in that the soloists are rather forward, but the 1980 recording has been well transferred.

(i) *Flute Concerto in D* (attrib., but probably by Leopold Hoffmann). *Scherzandi 1–6*

☛ ✹ *** EMI 5 56577-2. Berlin Haydn Ens., Schellenberger; (i) Pahud – M. HAYDN: *Flute Concerto* *** ✹

This is an enchantingly lighthearted record, displaying the supreme artistry of Emmanuel Pahud and also the stylish excellence of the Berlin Haydn Ensemble directed by Hansjörg Schellenberger, and it should be snapped up without delay, before it disappears. The *Flute Concerto in D*, with its shapely *Adagio* and spirited finale, has long been attributed to Haydn but is almost certainly by his prolific contemporary, Leopold Hoffmann. No matter, it is very agreeable and beautifully played and recorded. So too are the six *Scherzandi*, unexpected treasures, dating from Haydn's early Esterházy years. They are four-movement miniature symphonies, and all six are played here by a group representing the size of Haydn's original Esterházy orchestra, consisting of first and second violins, viola, cello, and pairs of horns and oboes, which are replaced by a single solo flute in the Trios of the Minuets. The first movements steadily become more elaborate as the series progresses. The slow movements are brief but often have surprising expressive depth; they are usually in the minor key and quite touching. That for No. 4 in G is introduced over a 'walking' pizzicato, but the lyrical *Adagio* of No. 6 is particularly touching. The naturally balanced recording makes this a very desirable collection indeed.

(i) *Harpsichord Concerto in D, Hob XVIII/11. Sonata 36 in C sharp min.; Minuet; German Dance 5 (Ballo tedesco)*
(***) Biddulph mono LHW 032. Landowska; (i) with O, Bigot – BACH: *Harpsichord Concerto 1 in D min.* (**); HANDEL: *Concerto, Op. 4/6, etc.* (**(*))

With neatly scaled playing from Landowska, and a crisp, clean accompaniment from Bigot, the Haydn concerto is much more attractive than its heavyweight Bach coupling, and the encores too are very pleasing, especially the sharply rhythmic *German Dance*. The recording is surprisingly good (a bit thin on violin timbre, but not unpleasantly so) and this is a most refreshing view of Haydn, dating from 1937.

Horn Concerto 3 in D, Hob VII/d3
*** Ara. Z 6750. Rose, St Luke's Chamber Ens. – FORSTER; LEOPOLD MOZART; TELEMANN: *Horn Concertos* ***
(BB) *** Teldec (ADD) 0630 12324-2. Baumann, Concerto Amsterdam, Schröder – DANZI; ROSETTI: *Concertos* ***

Stewart Rose plays the outer movements ebulliently and, like Dennis Brain, phrases the eloquent slow movement richly, yet sonorously relishing the passages where the melodic line dips down into the horn's lower register. He has the big, broad tone typical of a modern wide-bore instrument. The St Luke's Chamber Orchestra provide a lively, supportive accompaniment and the recording is excellent, as are the couplings. A first-rate disc in every way.

Baumann's 1969 account has firm classical lines. The *Adagio* is rather sombre here but brings some splendidly resonating low notes from the soloist, and the finale is attractively spirited. The recording has been attractively remastered and has more bloom than on its last appearance.

Horn Concertos 3 in D, Hob VII/d3; 4 in D, Hob VII/d4
(BB) *** Warner Apex 0927 40825-2. Clevenger, Franz Liszt CO, Rólla – M. HAYDN: *Concertino* ***

Dale Clevenger gives superb accounts of the two surviving *Horn Concertos* attributed to Haydn (the fourth is of doubtful lineage). He is especially good in slow movements, like Baumann a little solemn in No. 3, but eloquently so, with the *Adagio* of No. 4 given a gentle melancholy. The dotted main theme of the first movement, nicely pointed, is most engaging and the performance projects a *galant* charm of the kind

we associate with Hummel. The accompaniments are supportive, polished and elegant. These performances have fine spirit and spontaneity and the recording, made in a nicely judged and warm acoustic, approaches the demonstration class: when Clevenger plays his solo cadenzas, the tangibility of his presence is remarkable, yet the orchestra remains well in the picture.

Oboe Concerto in C, Hob VIIg/C1
(M) *** Dutton Lab./Barbirolli Soc. (ADD) CDSJB 1016. Rothwell, Hallé O, Barbirolli – CORELLI; MARCELLO: *Oboe Concertos* *** (with Instrumental Recital: C. P. E. BACH; LOEILLET; TELEMANN: *Sonatas, etc.* **)

Haydn's *Oboe Concerto* is of doubtful authenticity, but in this account played by Evelyn Rothwell, deftly accompanied by her husband, Haydn would surely have welcomed the attribution. The orchestra is given a very positive classicism by Barbirolli's firmness, and in the opening movement his wife's delicacy makes a delightful foil for the masculine orchestral presentation. The slow movement is well brought off and the delicacy of articulation returns in the finale. The 1958 recording is resonant and the skilful Dutton transfer almost entirely disguises its age.

Piano Concertos: in F; in G; in D, Hob XVIII/3, 4 & 11
*** EMI 5 56960-2. Andsnes, Norwegian CO
(BB) *** Arte Nova 74321 51635-2. Smirnova, Sinfonia Varsovia, Schmidt-Gertenbach

Leif Ove Andsnes gives inspired performances of the three Haydn piano concertos that are fully authenticated, not just the early *F major* and *G major*, here made to sparkle brightly, but the best known and finest of the series, *No. 11 in D*. Andsnes justifies his generally brisk speeds for outer movements in subtle pointing of rhythm and phrase, articulating crisply – always individual without being self-conscious. His preference is for speeds on the slow side in middle movements, more measured than eighteenth-century manners might allow, but rapt and naturally expressive; in his hands and those of the Norwegian Chamber Orchestra, which he directs from the keyboard, these concertos blossom. These are fresh, poetic and brilliant performances, recorded with exemplary clarity.

These works are also played with freshness and point by Lisa Smirnova and admirably accompanied with a sure sense of style and a nice feeling for light and shade by Volker Schmidt-Gertenbach and the excellent Sinfonia Varsovia. The recording is beautifully balanced.

Piano Concertos in G; F; D, Hob XVIII/4, 7 & 11
(BB) *** Virgin 2×1 5 61881-2 (2). Pletnev, Deutsche Kammerphilharmonie – *Piano Sonatas 33, 60 & 62, etc.* ***
(i) *Piano Concertos in G, F & D, Hob XVIII/4, 7 & 11. Piano Sonatas 33, Hob XVI/20; 60 (English), Hob XVI/50; 62, Hob XVI/52; Andante & Variations in F min., Hob XVII/6*
(BB) *** Virgin 4-CD 5 62259-2 (4). Pletnev; (i) Deutsche Kammerphilharmonie – MOZART: *Piano Concertos 9, 20, 23 & 24* ***

Of the three concertos recorded here, one is of doubtful authenticity: the *F major* (XVIII/7 in the Hoboken catalogue) is probably by Wagenseil; and not very much is known about the *G major*, which is very early. In both pieces, as well as in the well-known *D major Concerto*, Mikhail Pletnev offers playing of great character and personality. He obviously enjoys a splendid rapport with the Deutsche Kammerphilharmonie, and the colour and feeling Pletnev discovers in these pieces is a source of wonder, both distinctive and distinguished. This now comes inexpensively coupled on a Virgin Double with Pletnev's accounts of three key piano sonatas – a superb bargain.

The sonatas too are full of personality and character. The *C major*, the so-called *English Sonata*, is given with great elegance and wit, and the great *E flat Sonata*, Hob XVI/52, is magisterial. The playing has a masterly authority and Pletnev is well recorded throughout. Now coupled in an alternative super-bargain box with hardly less memorable accounts of four Mozart piano concertos, this is well worth considering, even if duplication is involved.

(i) *Piano Concerto in D, Hob XVIII/11*; (ii) *Violin Concertos: in C; in G; Hob VIIa/1 & 4*; (ii–iii) *Double Concerto for Violin & Harpsichord in F, Hob XVIII/6*

*** Sup. SU 3265-2. (i) Davidovich; (ii) Sitkovetsky; (iii) Hudeček; Prague CO, Sitkovetsky

Here is the most winning of Haydn's solo keyboard concertos together with two of the violin concertos, including the *C major* with its engaging, serenade-like, cantabile slow movement. They are impeccably played, with just the right degree of expressive feeling. The piano used by Bella Davidovich has a crisp, clean timbre, rather like a fortepiano, only with more colour. What clinches the appeal of this attractive collection is the delightful account of the *Double Concerto*. Here the interplay of piano and violin is perfectly balanced. This disc makes a splendid case for the use of modern instruments in this repertoire when Sitkovetsky directs the accompanying group so stylishly, with the overall effect pleasingly intimate.

Trumpet Concerto in E flat

☛ (B) *** Ph. Duo 464 028-2 (2). Hardenberger, ASMF, Marriner – HERTEL; HUMMEL; STAMITZ: *Concertos* *** (with Concert: '*Famous Classical Trumpet Concertos*' *** ✿)

✿ (N) (B) *** Sony 516 233 (2). Marsalis, Nat. PO, Leppard (with MICHAEL HAYDN: *Concerto in D*; VIVALDI: *Double Concerto, RV 537*. BACH: *Brandenburg Concerto 2*)

*** Sony SACD SS 57497. Marsalis, Nat. PO, Leppard – FASCH; HUMMEL; LEOPOLD MOZART: *Trumpet Concertos* ***

(B) *** CfP 573 4392. Balmain, RLPO, Kovacevich – MOZART: *Horn Concertos* ***

(i) *Trumpet Concerto in E flat. Sinfonia concertante*

(BB) *** DG (DDD/ADD) 474 567-2. COE, Abbado, (i) with Herseth – VIVALDI: *The Four Seasons* ***

Both the Hardenberger and Wynton Marsalis performances have been reissued within well-chosen collections, both worthy of their Rosette, and it is difficult to make a choice between them. Couplings will surely dictate the collector's choice and the Marsalis 2-disc set includes also concertos by Michael Haydn, Vivaldi and Bach's *Second Brandenburg*.

Hardenberger's playing of the noble line of the *Andante* is no less telling than his fireworks in the finale and with Marriner providing warm, elegant and polished accompaniments throughout, this is outstanding in every way.

But Marsalis is splendid too, his bravura no less spectacular, with the finale a tour de force, yet never aggressive in its brilliance. His way with Haydn is eminently stylish, as is Leppard's lively and polished accompaniment.

Marsalis's performance also comes on a non-compatible SACD, which undoubtedly offers superior sound quality but is much more expensive.

With Stephen Kovacevich as conductor, Ian Balmain favours extreme speeds for Haydn's delectable *Trumpet Concerto*, playing brilliantly. It makes an apt and attractive coupling for Claire Briggs's fine recordings of all four Mozart *Horn Concertos*, very well recorded.

Abbado conducts the Chamber Orchestra of Europe in a winning performance of the *Sinfonia concertante* – the violinist and cellist just as stylish as their wind colleagues who have appeared as soloists on several CDs – this issue even outshines other excellent versions from Vienna and London with more mature soloists. The *Trumpet Concerto* is not quite in the same class, lacking the last ounce of character; but it is spirited enough, is well played and recorded and is certainly enjoyable. The coupling is a highly distinguished account of Vivaldi's *Four Seasons*.

Violin Concertos 1 in C; 4 in G, HobVIIa/1 & 4; (i) *Double Concerto for Violin & Piano, HobVIII/6*

(BB) *** Hyp. Helios CDH 55007. Adelina Oprean, European CO; (i) with Justin Oprean

Violin Concertos 1 in C; 4 in G, Hob VIIa/1 & 4; (i) *Sinfonia Concertante in B flat for Violin, Cello, Oboe, Bassoon & Orchestra, Hob I/105*

(B) *** Virgin 2×1 5 61800-2 (2). Wallfisch, OAE; (i) with Watkin, Robson, Warnock – *Symphonies 26; 52; 53* ***

Elizabeth Wallfisch leads the Orchestra of the Age of Enlightenment from her bow and proves a highly sensitive soloist – these performances are if anything even more impressive than those of the Mozart concertos by the same soloist. Her serenely reflective account of the *Adagio molto* of the *C major* is memorable. In the *Sinfonia Concertante* the smiling interplay of the various wind and string soloists has never been bettered on record and the use of period instruments brings a pleasing intimacy and plenty of spirit. The recording is truthfully balanced and vivid. These performances now come on a Virgin Double, coupled with three symphonies admirably played by Kuijken's Petite Bande.

The Helios disc makes a good modern-instrument alternative for those interested in the well-crafted (and very well played) *Double Concerto for Violin and Piano*, which has a particularly striking dialogue between the two soloists in the central *Largo*. In the two solo concertos, Adelina Oprean proves a persuasive soloist with a dulcet but not over-opulent timbre. The central cantilena of the *G major Concerto*, with its pizzicato accompaniment, is delightful, and she directs the orchestra in outer movements with vigour and point. The sound is good too.

Violin Concertos 3 in A; 4 in G, HobVIIa/3–4

(BB) **(*) Virgin 2×1 5 61504-2 (2). Seiler, City of L. Sinfonia – BEETHOVEN; MENDELSSOHN: *Concertos* **(*)

Unlike the coupled Beethoven and Mendelssohn concertos on this Virgin bargain Double, the soloist Mayumi Seiler also directs the orchestra. The effect is very much of chamber performances: warm, polished and comparatively intimate. The result is musically enjoyable, if not distinctive, but this inexpensive two-disc set offers five concertos, all very well played and recorded, for the cost of a single medium-priced CD.

The Seven Last Words of Our Saviour on the Cross
(Orchestral Version)

(N) *** EMI **DVD** 5 99400-9. La Scala, Milan, PO, Muti (V/D: Pierre Cavassilas)

The performance of the orchestral version of the *Seven Last Words* by Riccardo Muti and the Filharmonica della Scala is recorded in the Chiesa di San Francesco, Arezzo, and sets Haydn's masterpiece against the backcloth of the frescoes of Piero della Francesca. A very well-shaped performance which Muti controls sensitively. The menu enables you to access descriptions of the various frescoes and also a commentary on the music. The full score can also be accessed, but it masks the performers and the other visual delights completely. A marvellous set.

Sinfonia Concertante in B flat for Violin, Cello, Oboe, Bassoon & Orchestra, Hob I/105

(M) *** DG (IMS) 463 078-2. Zukerman, Leonhard, Winters, Breidenthal, LAPO, Barenboim – BEETHOVEN: *Violin Concerto* ***

In Barenboim's enjoyably spontaneous performance the four soloists work splendidly together as a team and the *Andante* is particularly successful. The recording is well balanced and well transferred.

(i; ii) *Sinfonia concertante in B flat;* (i) *Symphonies 88 in G; 92 (Oxford); 94 (Surprise);* (iii–v) *Mass 7 (Missa in tempore belli): Paukenmesse;* (iii; v; vi) *The Creation (Die Schöpfung)*

(N) (M) **(*) DG 474 919-2 (4). Bernstein, with (i) VPO; (ii) Küchl, Bartolomey, Lehmayer, Werba; (iii) Bav. R. Ch. & SO; (iv) Fassbaender, Ahnsjö, Sotin; (v) Blegen; (vi) R. Moser, Moll, Popp, Ollmann

Bernstein had a genuine affinity with the music of Haydn, as this fine, if uneven, collection readily shows. The *Symphonies* receive warm, glowing accounts with the full strings of the VPO and richly upholstered recording. His humane approach has a warmth not always found in period performances. He observes the repeat of the development in the first movement of No. 88 and gives a romantic and really beautiful account of the *Largo*.

The *Surprise Symphony* was originally released with the *Sinfonia concertante* and is a characteristically lively reading. The Vienna sound as recorded is full-textured, but that doesn't stop Bernstein adopting fast tempi in the finales of both works, with his flair very apparent in the contrasting alternations of orchestra and solo violin in the *Sinfonia concertante*. The slow movements are relaxed, with the *Andante* of the *Sinfonia concertante* beautifully sustained over accompanimental figures that are elegantly lifted. Here Bernstein is at his most winning. The performances emanate from concerts in the Musikvereinsaal, but the audiences are mercifully silent. *The Creation* was recorded live in Munich. It uses a relatively large chorus, encouraging Bernstein to adopt rather slow speeds at times. What matters is the joy conveyed in the storytelling, with the finely disciplined chorus and orchestra producing incandescent tone, blazing away in the big-set numbers: the performance is compulsive from the very opening bars. At a very relaxed speed *The Heavens are telling* becomes majestic rather than urgent, but the joy is still intense. Bernstein's set also brings the advantage that five soloists are used instead of three, with the roles of Adam and Eve contrasting with the silvery, ethereal Gabriel of Judith Blegen, while Kurt Ollmann as Adam is lighter and less

magisterial than Kurt Moll as Raphael who, with his dark bass tone, produces the most memorable singing of all. Bernstein's tenor, Robert Moser, combines a lyrical flow with heroic weight, confirming this as an unusually persuasive if highly individual performamce, well recorded in atmospheric sound. The *Paukenmesse* (another live recording from 1984) is not so successful. In the fast numbers Bernstein's rhythmic flair and feeling for dramatic contrast add to the strength of the reading, However, muffled recording inflates the scale of the performance and in his dangerously romantic treatment of slow sections, such as the introduction to the bass's *Qui tollis*, and rough singing from the soloist (Hans Sotin, well below form), the good qualities are all but cancelled out.

SYMPHONIES

Austro-Hungarian Haydn Orchestra Series, cond. Adám Fischer

Symphonies: A in B flat; B in B flat; Nos. 1 in D; 2 in C; 3 in G; 4 in D; 5 in A; 6 in D (Le Matin); 7 in C (Le Midi); 8 in G (Le Soir); 9 in C; 10 in D: 11 in E flat; 12 in E; 13 in D; 14 in A; 15 in D; 16 in B flat; 17 in F; 18 in G; 19 in D; 20 in C; 21 in A; 22 in E flat (Philosopher); 23 in G; 24 in D; 25 in C; 26 in D min. (Lamentatione); 27 in G; 28 in A; 29 in E; 30 in C (Alleluja); 31 in D (Horn Signal); 32 in A; 33 in C; 34 in D min.; 35 in B flat; 36 in E flat; 37 in C; 38 in C (Echo); 39 in G min.; 40 in F; 41 in C; 42 in D; 43 in F (Mercury); 44 in E min. (Trauer-symphonie); 45 in F sharp min. (Farewell); 46 in B; 47 in G; 48 in C (Maria Theresa); 49 in F min. (La Passione); 50 in C; 51 in B flat; 52 in C min.; 53 in D; 54 in G; 55 in E flat (School-Master); 56 in C; 57 in D; 58 in F; 59 in A (Fire); 60 in C (Il distratto); 61 in D; 62 in D; 63 in C (La Roxelane); 64 in A; 65 in G; 66 in B flat; 67 in F; 68 in B flat; 69 in C (Laudon); 70 in D; 71 in B flat; 72 in D; 73 in D (La Chasse); 74 in E flat; 75 in D; 76 in E flat; 77 in B flat; 78 in C min.; 79 in F; 80 in D min.; 81 in G; (82–87 'Paris Symphonies') 82 in C (The Bear); 83 in G min. (La Poule); 84 in E flat; 85 in B flat (La Reine); 86 in D; 87 in A; 88 in G; 89 in F; 90 in C; 91 in E flat; 92 in G (Oxford); (93–104 'London Symphonies') 93 in D; 94 in G (Surprise); 95 in C min.; 96 in D (Miracle); 97 in C; 98 in B flat; 99 in E flat; 100 in G (Military); 101 in D (Clock); 102 in B flat; 103 in E flat; 104 in D (London)

Symphonies 1–20

(M) **(*) Nim. NI 5426/30 (5). Austro-Hungarian Haydn O, Fischer

The Nimbus project of recording all the Haydn symphonies on modern instruments in the Haydnsaal of the Esterházy Palace brings playing that is fresh yet warm, with the considerable reverberation adding to the weight and scale of the earlier symphonies in a manner that some ears will relish but others may find too opulent. In the accompanying notes the conductor, Adám Fischer, comments that the chosen orchestra, which is made up of players from Vienna and Budapest, carries forward the tradition of Austro-Hungarian music-making. The playing itself is warm and elegant, and time and again in these early symphonies the ear enjoys the finesse of this music-making and its ripeness of texture, with the rich-toned Viennese horns soaring out over the strings when given an opportunity to do so. The woodwind are sprightly and offer plenty of colour, and in Nos. 6–8 the various orchestral solos are taken with distinction. The conductor's speeds are moderate. Slow movements are gracious and phrasing is cultivated; minuets are courtly and finales lively and resilient, without being rushed. The sound itself is rich in ambience and easy to enjoy, for it does not cloud.

Symphonies 21; 22 (Philosopher); 23–5; 26 (Lamentatione); 28–9; 30 (Alleluja); 31 (Horn Signal); 32–7; 38 (Echo); 39; Symphonies A & B

⊕ (M) *** Nimbus NI 5683/7 (5). Austro-Hungarian Haydn O, Fischer

Adám Fischer's set of earlier Haydn symphonies caps his achievement for Nimbus in a series of astonishingly perceptive performances, very strongly characterized, played with great finesse, with Fischer showing a remarkable ear for detail. Many of these works cannot be dated with certainty, although we know that Nos. 21–4 were written in 1764. We can sense Haydn continually experimenting with his orchestral forces. Fischer gives all three on a chamber scale, slow movements are delicate and graceful, and allegros (taken fast) bubble over with vitality, notably the finales, with brilliant writing for horns and oboes. Indeed, so sharply pointed and vibrant are allegros throughout this set that at times one feels that Haydn's later Sturm und Drang period is being anticipated.

The best-known work in this group, subtitled Philosopher (with its potent scoring of pairs of cor anglais and horns), is outstanding, as is the later account of the remarkable Lamentatione (No. 26) with its raw emotional vitality and deeply expressive Adagio. Nos. 28–31 can be dated to 1765. Each is individual: there is brilliant trumpet playing to open the 'Alleluja' Symphony (the reason for the nickname obvious), while in the Horn Signal the four horns blaze away gloriously. There are more exuberant horn contributions in Nos. 35 and 36, and 37 is all but dominated by the timpani. No. 38 is a particularly fine work, with a charming Andante with delicate echo effects, and virtuoso oboe parts in the Minuet's Trio, against economical bowed string pizzicati.

Most striking of all is No. 39 (1766–7), with Haydn again using four horns dramatically. The opening movement with its false starts and a finale bursting with impetuous passion are clearly looking to the future. The superb orchestral playing throughout this set is something to revel in, and Adám Fischer's vital, imaginative approach ensures that there is not a dull bar anywhere. The transparent textures and sharp rhythmic springing (in the Minuets especially) bring a style of performance that has the best of both worlds, period and modern. The recording too is outstanding, full and clearly detailed.

Symphonies 40–54

(M) *** Nim. NI 5530/4 (5). Austro-Hungarian Haydn O, Fischer

In Volume 3 of his splendid series, Adám Fischer homes in on the Sturm und Drang works, but he is working in numerical order, so he includes one or two other symphonies, though none that is not full of stimulating ideas (the theme and variations that forms the Andante of L'Imperiale is sheer delight). The orchestral playing is consistently warm and committed and of course there is none of the astringency of texture one expects with Hogwood, or squeezed violin phrasing that Brüggen and others insist is authentic. The result is richly enjoyable, and slow movements in particular consistently gain from such a dedicated orchestral response. The Adagio opening of La Passione is gentle yet intensely concentrated in feeling, and the following Allegro di molto is crisp,

fast and biting. Minuets are faster and racier than with Dorati, with plenty of dynamic contrasts – and finales, if helter-skelter, still retain an elegant poise. The unnamed C major Symphony (No. 50) and the following B flat major work are among the finest performances here, splendidly characterful – and in the Adagio of the latter there is a glorious horn solo, followed by the graceful Allegretto finale. The Viennese elegance of phrasing, and polish combined with sparkle, often reminds one of Beecham in its friendly listener-appeal. The recording is first class, full and warm, with a natural concert-hall ambience.

Symphonies 43; 44; 49; 52 in C min.; 59; 64 (Tempora mutantur)

(B) *** Nim. NI 7072/3 (2). Austro-Hungarian Haydn O, Fischer

This Nimbus Double, centring on the Sturm und Drang era, makes a splendid sampler for Adám Fischer's Haydn cycle, played on modern instruments. Fischer is often at his most imaginatively persuasive in these works, and both orchestral playing and recording are first class. The slow movements of the Mercury and Trauer symphonies are both very beautiful, while the Adagio opening of La Passione is gentle yet intensely concentrated in feeling, and the following Allegro di molto is crisp, fast and biting. In the notes we are told by David Threasher that the nickname of No. 64 (Tempora mutantur) is based on a couplet by the Welsh epigrammist John Owen, which was used as an inscription on clocks and sundials.

Symphonies 55–69

(M) *** Nim. NI 5590/4 (5). Austro-Hungarian Haydn O, Fischer

With Adám Fischer a dedicated advocate, inspiring fresh, persuasive playing from his hand-picked orchestra, there is no slackening of standards in this fourth volume of Nimbus's Haydn cycle. This group of works follows up the Sturm und Drang sequence with symphonies regularly related to Haydn's theatre music, at times with eccentric effects, as in the six-movement Il distratto, No. 60, or No. 67 with its col legno and hurdy-gurdy effects. In the helpful acoustic of the Haydnsaal of the Esterházy Palace at Eisenstadt, the sound is at once warmly atmospheric and intimate, with high contrasts of dynamic and texture. Continuing to use modern rather than period instruments, but with limited string vibrato and with Viennese oboes and horns standing out distinctively, these are recordings to challenge the long-time supremacy of Dorati's pioneering Decca set. In important ways, not just in the extra fullness of the digital sound, the new performances improve on the old, notably in the brisker speeds for Minuets. Fischer generally tends to prefer speeds in slow movements a fraction more flowing than those of Dorati, while outer movements are regularly a degree more relaxed. Thanks to Fischer's springing of rhythm, speeds never drag, even if those dedicated to period practice might well prefer the more hectic Prestos and Prestissimos of the earlier set. These are performances that register Haydn's humour more clearly, even in the Sturm und Drang symphonies here, Nos. 58 and 59 (The Fire).

Symphonies 70–81

(M) *** Nim. NI 5652/5 (4). Austro-Hungarian Haydn O, Fischer

With the exception of No. 72, which probably dates from the 1760s, Volume 5 of Adám Fischer's ever more attractive survey contains works written more or less consecutively during a compact period of just over four years (1778–82). Robbins Landon has emphasized that generally these are much more courtly works than their *Sturm und Drang* predecessors, and No. 79 is a characteristically elegant example.

No. 70 is not. It opens very dramatically and bursts with energy, then changes mood completely, before its minor-key slow movement, which is a set of double variations. The brilliantly contrapuntal finale, based on a repeated note motif, also opens in the minor key and develops into a remarkable triple fugue. No. 71 brings another striking opening movement, which may have been written earlier than the other three, and also has a very beautiful *Adagio*.

Symphony No. 72 immediately recalls the *Horn Signal Symphony*, and the scoring for four horns is certainly virtuosic, with bravura upward scales and roulades in the first movement, which even today remain fiendishly difficult. The *Andante* is a concertante movement featuring solo violin and flute, and the finale, another *Andante*, offers more solo playing (including a double-bass contribution) within an enchanting set of variations. No. 73 is the best known. Its slow movement offers more variations, this time on a song, *Gegenliebe*. The finale with its main hunting theme on horns and trumpet gives the symphony its title (*La Chasse*).

But what will continually strike the non-specialist listener when listening through these ever-diverting works is their wide range of mood, particularly in the two minor-key symphonies (Nos. 78 and 80). Development sections give a flashing reminder of Haydn's most concentrated manner. Kaleidoscopic sequences of keys whirl the argument in unexpected directions (especially in No. 80), while slow movements are winningly diverse. The *Adagio cantabile* of No. 74, the *Poco Adagio (Andante con variazioni)* of No. 75, the *Adagio* of No. 76 and the memorable flowing melody of No. 77 are all highly rewarding examples.

Haydn was incapable of being boring, and some of these works are in every way remarkable in their forward-looking progressions, often anticipating Mozart's most visionary works. The modern-instrument performances here combine vitality, intensity and warmth in ideal proportions, and the recording reveals the full detail of Haydn's very felicitous scoring, besides having an attractive overall bloom.

Symphonies 82–87 (Paris Symphonies)

(B) **(*) Nim. NI 5419/20 (2). Austro-Hungarian Haydn O, Fischer

The expansive sound of the Austro-Hungarian Orchestra suits the *Paris Symphonies*. *La Poule* and *La Reine* (with its rhythmically powerful opening movement) both show Fischer and his players at their best, and finest of all is one of the least known, *Symphony No. 84 in E flat*, with another remarkably original first movement. Slow movements are warm and poised: the *Largo* of No. 86 is particularly successful, as is the light-hearted trio of its Minuet, with a vigorous finale, lightly articulated, to round the work off. The sound is always satisfyingly full-bodied, with the violins resonantly rich. The weighty bass is not always absolutely clean, but generally the effect is very believable.

Symphonies 88–92; Sinfonia concertante in B flat for Violin, Cello, Oboe, Bassoon & Orchestra

(B) ** Nim. NI 5417/8 (2). Austro-Hungarian Haydn O, Fischer

As with the other issues in this Nimbus series, the recording is full and pleasing, but here the warm resonance prevents sharpness of detail and also has the effect of blunting the string articulation. Too often one feels the need for more bite in *Allegros*. Tempi are almost always relaxed, so that the famous slow movement of *No. 88 in G*, warmly expressive as it is, very nearly drags, although Fischer brings off the *Adagio* of the *Oxford Symphony* beautifully. Throughout, Minuets are very stately indeed, but finales dance gracefully and opening *Adagios* are warmly expressive; yet in the end there is an absence of conveyed exhilaration. The *Sinfonia concertante* included on the second disc is a particularly pleasing performance, with most sympathetic solo playing.

Symphonies 93–104 (London Symphonies)

(M) **(*) Nim. NI 5200/4 (5). Austro-Hungarian Haydn O, Fischer

With three symphonies apiece on the first two discs of the five-disc Nimbus set, Fischer's cycle of all twelve *London Symphonies* makes a neat and attractive package, with consistently fresh, resilient and refined performances. Though these works were first given in the intimate surroundings of the Hanover Square Rooms in London, they were very quickly heard in this much grander setting, and the performances reflect the fact, with broad speeds and weighty tuttis made weightier by the reverberant Nimbus recording. Such a movement as the lovely *Adagio* of No. 102 with its soaring melody is given added beauty by the ambience and slow speed. The set can be warmly recommended to most who resist period performance when, even at broad speeds, rhythms are light and resilient. Never sounding breathless, Fischer's Haydn consistently brings out the happiness of the inspiration. These are very much performances to relax with.

Philharmonia Hungarian Series, cond. Dorati

Symphonies 1–104; Symphonies A; B. Alternative versions: Symphony 22 (Philosopher), 2nd version. Symphony 63 (La Roxelane), 1st version. Symphony 53 (L'Impériale): 3 alternative Finales: (i) A (Capriccio); (ii) C (Paris version, attrib. Haydn); D: Overture in D (Milanese version). Symphony 103: Finale (alternative ending). (i) Sinfonia Concertante in B flat for Oboe, Bassoon, Violin & Cello ◆
(B) *** Decca (ADD) 448 531-2 (33). (i) with Engl, Baranyai, Ozim, Rácz

Dorati was ahead of his time as a Haydn interpreter when, in the early 1970s, he made this pioneering integral recording of the symphonies. Superbly transferred to CD in full, bright and immediate sound, the performances are a consistent delight, with brisk allegros and fast-flowing *Andantes*, with textures remarkably clean. The slow, rustic-sounding accounts of Minuets are more controversial, but the rhythmic bounce makes them attractive too. The set includes not only the *Symphonies A* and *B* (Hoboken Nos. 106 and 108) but also the *Sinfonia Concertante in B flat*, a splendidly imaginative piece with wonderful unexpected touches. Dorati's account – not surprisingly – presents the work as a symphony with unusual scoring, rather than as a concerto. As H. C. Robbins Landon tells us in the accompanying notes, the *Symphonies A* and *B* were omitted from the list of 104 authentic symphonies by error, as the first was considered to be a quartet (wind parts were discovered later) and the second a divertimento. Dorati also includes as an appendix completely different versions of *Symphony No. 22* (*The Philosopher*), where Haydn altered the orchestration (a pair of flutes substituted for the cor anglais), entirely removed the first movement and introduced a new *Andante grazioso*; plus an earlier version of No. 63, to some extent conjectural in its orchestration, for the original score is lost. Of the three alternative finales for *L'Impériale* (No. 53), the first (A) contains a melody which, Robbins Landon suggests, 'sounds extraordinarily like Schubert'; the second (C) seems unlikely to be authentic; but the third (D) uses an overture which was first published in Vienna. 'In some respects,' Robbins Landon suggests, 'this is the most successful of the three concluding movements.' He feels the same about the more extended finale of the *Drum Roll Symphony*, which originally included 'a modulation to C flat, preceded by two whole bars of rests'. But Haydn thought that this made the movement too long and crossed out the whole section. Robbins Landon continues: 'Perhaps Haydn was for once in his life too ruthless here.'

Hanover Band Series, cond. Goodman

Symphonies 1–5
(BB) *** Hyp. Helios CDH 55111

Symphonies 6 (Le Matin); 7 (Le Midi); 8 (Le Soir)
(BB) *** Hyp. Helios CDH 55112

Symphonies 9–12
(BB) *** Hyp. Helios CDH 55113

Symphonies 13–16
⊶ (BB) *** Hyp. Helios CDH 55114

Symphonies 17–21
⊶ (BB) *** Hyp. Helios CDH 55115

Symphonies 22 (Philosopher); 23–25
⊶ (BB) *** Hyp. Helios CDH 55116

Symphonies 42; 43 (Mercury); 44 (Trauer)
⊶ (BB) *** Hyp. Helios CDH 55117

Symphonies 45 (Farewell); 46; 47
⊶ (BB) *** Hyp. Helios CDH 55118

Symphonies 70–72
⊶ (BB) *** Hyp. Helios CDH 55120

Symphonies 76–78
⊶ (BB) *** Hyp. Helios CDH 55122

Symphonies 82 (The Bear); 83 (The Hen); 84
(BB) **(*) Hyp. Helios CDH 55123

Symphonies 85 (La Reine); 86; 87
(BB) *** Hyp. Helios CDH 55124

Symphonies 90; 91; 92 (Oxford)
(BB) *** Hyp. Helios CDA 55125

Symphonies 93; 94 (Surprise); 95
(BB) *** Hyp. Helios CDA 55126

From the very outset of his Hyperion project, Goodman, who began at the beginning with the low-numbered symphonies, established a winning manner in early Haydn and, as the series progressed, he showed that his dramatic approach was being fruitful in the middle-period and later works. The recording is resonant, giving bloom to the strings, yet oboes and horns (and other wind and brass, when used) come through vividly.

The performances of the linked Esterházy works (Nos. 6–8) are predictably lively and fresh, bringing out the colour of all three works. Allegros never sound breathless and slow movements are relaxed enough to allow a winning expressiveness. The following four works are full of charm and imagination, fully realized by Goodman and his players. Excellent recording.

The chronology of these early Haydn symphonies is difficult to pin down. They were written between 1759 and 1764, but it is certain that the numbering here is only approximate in indicating the order of their composition, and it seems likely that Nos. 13–16 were in fact written in reverse numerical order. *No. 13 in D* is remarkably mature, being scored for four horns. Haydn uses them to fill out the rich sonority of the first movement, but they also state and restate in unison the very striking arpeggio main theme as well being featured in the Minuet and finale. The slow movement is an *Adagio cantabile* for solo cello (here sounding more like a gamba) and strings. The finale, more surprisingly still, anticipates the key four-note theme of the finale of Mozart's *Jupiter Symphony*.

The high horns return in No. 14, and Haydn introduces an oboe solo for the Trio of its Minuet. Nos. 15 and 16 are by no means predictable either, with the first movement of the former in the style of a French overture (slow–fast–slow) and the sprightly 6/8 finale of the latter wittily looking to the future.

The horns remain important in the first work on the next disc (No. 17) which has a gracious slow movement, and the opening *Andante* of No. 18 is even more stately, with a sparkling allegro to follow and a Minuet acting as finale. The *Andante* of No. 19, for strings alone, has a gentle melancholy offset by a vigorous closing movement, while the more festive No. 20 includes trumpets and drums, dating it to Haydn's pre-Esterházy years (for those forces were not available to the composer in his early Esterházy period); but again the wind are silent in the slow movement. No. 21 (which exists in an autograph score) dates from 1764. It has an eloquent opening *Adagio*, followed by a vigorously rhythmic following Presto, again bringing the horns to the fore, while the lively finale returns to the vibrant style of the second movement.

Goodman's account of the *Philosopher*, with its pair of cor anglais, is predictably bold and rhythmic, with an exhilarating finale (superb horn triplets!) to cap what has gone before. The dramatic contrasts of the first movement of No. 24 are offset by a delicate Adagio with a cantabile flute solo. No. 25 has a briefly pensive introduction but is most notable for its hectic final Presto. Again brilliant, highly persuasive performances and excellent recording.

Roy Goodman opens No. 42 energetically, in spite of Haydn's *Moderato e maestoso* marking, but his virility is infectious, and the rondo finale is equally catchy. No. 43 has a three-note linking figure, which unites the first three movements, and it is the finale that develops Mercurial vigour. The *Trauersinfonie*, the first of these works to be written (1770/1), opens tersely; but it is the contemplative *Adagio* that gives the symphony its sobriquet, followed by the powerfully cogent finale, which is full of nervous rhythmic energy.

All three symphonies on the following disc date from 1772. The famous *Farewell Symphony*, with its rare key of F sharp minor, follows on naturally after the *Sturm und Drang* of the finale of No. 44. The famous finale here opens vivaciously, then makes its abrupt change of mood and tempi so that the players can depart one-by-one, with Goodman himself relinquishing his place at the harpsichord at bar 205 to play the solo violin part in duet with his leader, Pavlo Beznosiuk.

The key of B major in No. 46 was also rarely used in the eighteenth century. Haydn produces a brisk, tightly constructed opening movement, with the horns gleaming in their upwards transposition. The tension relaxes in the graceful *Adagio* but increases, with the horns all but struggling at the very top of their compass, lighting up the Minuet and dancing finale.

The horns immediately play a strong role in No. 47, but this time crooked in G, opening and dominating the first movement with an arresting fanfare, answered engagingly by dancing strings and woodwind. There follows a slow movement with a cantabile theme and four variations, where the melody and bass line are later inverted. Even more ingenious is the 'reversible Minuet', in which each section is followed by its exact mirror image; the horns again feature in the *Trio*. The finale is a lively rondo, with sparkling strings to balance the opening movement. This pair of discs is among the finest in the series.

Haydn's *Symphonies 70* and *71* followed each other in 1779 and 1780 respectively. No. 70 is a vigorous, confident work, notable for its brilliant scoring, an (invertible) two-part canon slow movement and the concentrated triple fugue in the brief finale with its striking five-note motto theme. No. 71 opens somewhat pontifically but soon introduces a genial, swinging allegro. The essentially peaceful, muted *Andante* is interrupted by sforzando chords, ensuring that listeners remain awake, well worthwhile as the Minuet's Trio brings two solo violins heard against a pizzicato backing, and the finale (coloured by the high B flat horns) is racily exuberant, with a catchy second subject on the wind.

No. 72 is now known to have been written during the composer's earliest years at Eisenstadt, and its appearance in 1763 reflected the arrival of two additional horn players, so that the work becomes something of a display piece for the horn quartet, for which the *Horn Signal* (No. 31) was also written. From the very opening, the horns are spectacularly featured and return in the Minuet and are afforded antiphonal echo effects, and then they take a back seat for the agreeable theme and variations finale, until their flourishes in the coda.

Symphonies 76, 77 and *78* were composed as a group and published concurrently in London, Paris and Vienna in the early 1780s. Haydn described them to his Paris publisher as 'beautiful, elegant, and by no means over-lengthy ... they are all very easy, and without too much concertante'. So they are; but they are by no means inferior, being full of characteristic invention, especially the elegant *Adagio* of No. 76, which opens so persuasively on strings alone and follows with a contrasting wind chorale. The Rondo finale, too, is Haydn at his most endearing.

No. 77 has a vivace opening movement, but it is the sparkling, forward-looking Sonata-Rondo finale that reminds us that Haydn never rested on his laurels. No. 78, with its thrusting, boldly assertive minor-key opening, brings a taste of *Sturm und Drang*, but Haydn then lets the stress evaporate: the stately *Adagio* is richly scored and the lively finale returns confidently to the major key.

The toughness of Goodman's approach to Haydn comes out strikingly in the *Paris Symphonies*. Indeed, some listeners may resist his bold accents and gruff manner; in the *Hen Symphony* where a little more charm would have been welcome, even though the playing is always polished and neatly articulated. No. 84 fails to take off in the first movement and seems to come fully to life only in the dancing Minuet. The second disc, with *La Reine* and Nos. 86 and 87, is more successful: these are large-scale performances, often weighty, but slow movements are most elegantly played, especially the delightful *Capriccio Largo* of No. 86, while the Vivace finale of No. 87 is superbly spirited.

Symphonies 90–93 are engagingly lightweight performances, though full of character and vitality. But the first three *London Symphonies* are immediately weightier, as the first movement of 93 demonstrates, although first movement second subjects remain graceful and rhythmically lifted. In No. 94 the *Surprise* is beautifully prepared with a *pianissimo* repeat of the main theme before the *fortissimo* chord. The Minuet (more a scherzo) is then a real *Allegro molto*. The Hyperion recordings maintain the highest standard throughout.

Other miscellaneous symphonies

Symphonies 6 (Le Matin); 7 (Le Midi); 8 (Le Soir)

⊕ (BB) *** Naxos 8.550722. N. CO, Ward

(M) **(*) Warner Elatus 0927 49561-2. VCM, Harnoncourt

These were almost certainly the first works that Haydn composed on taking up his appointment as Kapellmeister to the Esterházys. The Northern Chamber Orchestra under Nicholas Ward has wind players who relish their solos, so that the flute chirps merrily and the bassoon immediately has a chance to shine in the Trio of the Minuet of No. 6. In the *Andante* of *Le Soir* the strings create a chamber-music atmosphere, and it is the intimate scale of these performances that is so attractive. Modern instruments are used, but textures are fresh and the ambience of the Concert Hall of New Broadcasting House, Manchester, adds the right degree of warmth.

Harnoncourt is nothing if not dramatic. He opens No. 6 with an impressively controlled crescendo, beginning from an almost inaudible *pianissimo*, while the opening of the main allegro is characteristically gruff. But this music-making bursts with vitality, and a soothing flute solo soon appears to calm the listener. The very opening of Harnoncourt's slow movement (of No. 6) is austere but the atmosphere lightens, and it is again a flute which gaily introduces the lively finale. So it is throughout, with tuttis edgily bold and with plenty of accents, yet with balancing passages of delicacy. The recording is as vivid as the playing; if Harnoncourt's eccentricities prevent an unreserved period-instrument recommendation, this will be welcomed by his admirers.

Symphonies 22 (Philosopher); 86; 102

(N) (M) *** EMI 5 62975-2 [5 62976-2]. CBSO, Rattle

It is refreshing to have a coupling of symphonies from different periods of Haydn's career. One of the most striking of the early works, the *Philosopher*, with its trudging chorale on two cor anglais, comes with one of the *Paris Symphonies*, No. 86, and one of the final *London* set. If only No. 102 had a nickname, it would be even more widely appreciated as a supreme masterpiece with its exhilarating outer movements and the most beautiful of all Haydn slow movements. Rattle's speeds are on the fast side but not extreme. Only in the final *Presto* of No. 86 does he opt for a hectic speed, making one marvel at the agility of the Birmingham horns in repeated triplets.

Symphonies 23; 24; 61

(BB) *** Naxos 8.550723. N. CO, Ward

The fresh, stylish approach of the Northern Chamber Orchestra is entirely suited to these three symphonies, and here Nicholas Ward makes a persuasive case for the use of modern instruments. No. 24 includes a leading semi-concertante flute part (nicely managed) and the *G major* has a wistful *Andante* for strings alone, and a vital *Presto* finale, well sprinkled with strongly accented quadruplets. The opening movement of No. 61 is obviously more mature and is presented with both character and charm. Excellent recording.

Sturm und Drang Symphonies 26; 35; 38; 39; 41; 42; 43 (Mercury); 44 (Trauer); 45 (Farewell); 46; 47; 48 (Maria Theresia); 49 (La Passione); 50; 51; 52; 58; 59 (Fire), 65

(B) *** DG 463 731-2 (6). E. Concert, Pinnock

Pinnock's forces are modest (with 6.5.2.2.1 strings), but the panache of the playing conveys any necessary grandeur. It is a new experience to have Haydn symphonies of this period recorded in relatively dry and close sound, with inner detail crystal clear (harpsichord never obscured) and made the more dramatic by the intimate sense of presence, yet with a fine bloom on the instruments. Some may find a certain lack of charm at times, and others may quarrel with the very brisk one-in-a-bar Minuets and even find finales a little rushed. However, at bargain price, it is certainly value for money.

Symphonies 26 (Lamentatione); 35; 49 (La Passione)

(BB) **(*) Naxos 8.550721. N. CO, Ward

Although enjoyable, this disc from Nicholas Ward and his Northern Chamber Orchestra is not quite as fresh-sounding as his first. The playing remains elegant and the horns (in B flat alto) are splendid in the Minuet of No. 35. But the opening *Allegro assai con spirito* of the *Lamentatione* could do with a shade more bite, and in the *Adagio* the warm resonance makes the finely played oboe solo almost a cor anglais and the melodic line like a Handel aria. The opening slow movement of No. 49 is not as intense as it might be, though the *Allegro di molto* which follows has plenty of energy. The resonance of the BBC's Studio 7 in Manchester brings a pleasingly mellow sound-picture, but the string detail is not sharply defined.

Symphonies 26 (Lamentatione); 52; 53 (L'Impériale)

(B) *** Virgin 2x1 5 61800-2 (2). La Petite Bande, Kuijken – *Violin Concertos 1 & 4; Sinfonia Concertante* ***

These are fresh, vital, cleanly articulated performances which wear their authenticity lightly and even indulge in speeds for slow movements that are more expansive and affectionate than many purists would allow. These three symphonies now appear on a Virgin Double, coupled with two key violin concertos and the *Sinfonia Concertante in B flat.*

Symphonies 30 in C (Alleluja); 53 in D (L'Imperiale); 69 in C (Laudon)

(BB) *** Warner Apex 2564 60520-2. VCM, Harnoncourt

Here is another outstandingly vibrant Harnoncourt triptych of named Haydn symphonies to set beside his Elatus disc of Nos. 31, 59 and 73 (see below). The first movement of No. 30 is based on an *Alleluja* that formed part of the Mass for Easter week. The work features unusually prominent writing for the trumpets in the outer movements, and in the charming *Andante* there are important solo parts for flute and oboes, played most delicately here. No. 53 has a vigorous first movement with dancing strings, and the *Andante* features characteristically inventive variations on one of the composer's most engaging themes. The finale recorded here, although effectively vigorous, is comparatively straightforward and (according to Robbins Landon) may not have been Haydn's own composition, but written by a pupil under the composer's surpervision. Yet in Harnoncourt's hands it makes a convincing conclusion.

The sobriquet of No. 69, *Laudon*, was appended by Haydn himself and celebrates a highly successful field marshal of that name. The vigorous rhythms of the opening movement certainly have a military flavour, yet the slow movement (*Un poco adagio, più tosto Andante*) has a contrasting elegant gentility. But it is the unpredictable finale with its fiercely contrasting dynamics (and a violin solo to introduce the return of the main theme) that gives the work its individuality. All three performances here are quite splendid, with outstandingly brilliant playing from the Vienna strings. This is music-making that makes an unanswerable case for playing Haydn on period instruments. The recording is first class, the resonant acoustic seems just right.

Symphonies 30 (Alleluja); 55 (Schoolmaster); 63 (La Roxelane)

(BB) *** Naxos 8.550757. N. CO, Ward

An entirely winning triptych of named Haydn symphonies, spanning a highly creative period from the three-movement *Alleluja* (1765), with its delightful woodwind contribution in the *Andante*, to *La Roxelane* (1780), where the *Allegretto* paints an engaging portrait of a flirtatious character in a play and the finale fizzes with energy. In between comes *The School-master*, whose *Adagio* brings a theme and variations of disarming simplicity. Alert and vivacious playing from all concerned; admirable pacing and first-class sound ensure a welcome for a disc that would be just as recommendable if it cost far more.

Symphonies 31 (Horn Signal); 59 (Fire); 73 (La Chasse)

(M) *** Warner Elatus 2564 60033-2. VCM, Harnoncourt

This is one of Harnoncourt's very best records. All three symphonies are notable for their spectacular horn parts. The playing here – using natural horns – is superb, with throatily exuberant braying at the opening of the *Horn Signal*, an equally striking contribution throughout the *Fire Symphony* (where the horns are crooked in A), and more cheerful hunting-calls in the spirited finale of *La Chasse*. The playing is not only extremely vital and polished but even has an element of charm (not something one can always count on from this source). The orchestra communicate their involvement throughout. We are glad to see this is now on Elatus at mid-price.

Symphonies 41 in C; 58 in F; 59 in A (Fire)

(BB) **(*) Naxos 8.557002. Cologne CO, Mühler-Brühl

Symphonies 43 (Mercury); 46–47

*** Naxos 8.554767. Cologne CO, Mühler-Brühl

Haydn's *Symphonies Nos. 41, 58* and *59* were written between 1768 and 1769, during the composer's early period as Kapell-meister at the Ersterháza, but they already display his imaginative thrust and feeling for orchestral colour. They are beautifully played here, but one feels that a work with the sobriquet 'Fire' might have been a bit firier in the opening Presto. However, the splendid horn playing in the finale more than compensates, and this is certainly an enjoyable disc, although it could hardly be further from the abrasive Roy Goodman approach.

The nickname 'Mercury' for No. 43 probably relates to a stage work, with a fine A flat slow movement opening on muted strings. No. 47 brings striking military horn-calls at the start, beautifully caught in this recording; but the most memorable of the three is No. 46, with its lilting B minor slow movement. Its extraordinary finale is then punctuated by sudden silences, with sharp modulations and an unexpected quotation from the preceding Minuet. Such quirkiness is what makes Haydn endlessly fascinating, from whichever period.

For over ten years this orchestra played on period instruments, so many of the lessons of period performance have been taken on board. Now using modern instruments, Mühler-Brühl's choice of speeds cannot be faulted, with allegros crisp and alert and slow movements kept flowing.

Symphonies 44–49
(N) (B) *** Artemis/Van. ATM-CD 1495 (3). Zagreb RSO, Janigro

Janigro's 1963 Vanguard collection of the six *Sturm und Drang Symphonies* stands as one of the early treasures of the bargain shelf, serving in the early stereo era to confirm what sharp, vital work Haydn was producing long before the famous symphonies written for London. Each of the *Sturm and Drang* works has its own hallmark, even the two unnamed symphonies, 46 and 47. Both Nos. 44 and 45 (the famous 'Farewell' *Symphony*) are in minor keys, and in itself that was an innovation for Haydn at the time. No. 44 is especially dramatic, and Janigro directs it with great stylishness. The *Adagio* first movement of *La Passione* (No. 49) is one of the most striking and poignant in all of Haydn's symphonies. With all four movements in F minor, this work in some ways looks backwards to the classical suite rather than forward to the full-blown symphony; but the music itself is violently original, revealing an 'inner' Haydn not normally observed in his symphonies. No. 48 (*Maria Theresia*) provides a complete contrast, happy enough for any ceremonial occasion involving an empress. Throughout, the modern-instrument performances with a modest-sized ensemble are exemplary; the first-rate analogue recording sounds excellent in this new CD transfer, and there are fine notes by Christa Landon, wife of H. Robbins Landon.

Symphonies 44 (Trauer); 88; 104 (London)
(BB) *** Naxos 8.550287. Capella Istropolitana, Wordsworth

Symphonies 45 (Farewell); 48 (Maria Theresia); 102
(BB) *** Naxos 8.550382. Capella Istropolitana, Wordsworth

Symphonies 82 (The Bear); 96 (Miracle); 100 (Military)
(BB) *** Naxos 8.550139. Capella Istropolitana, Wordsworth

Symphonies 83 (The Hen); 94 (Surprise); 101 (The Clock)
(BB) *** Naxos 8.550114. Capella Istropolitana, Wordsworth

Symphonies 85 (La Reine); 92 (Oxford); 103 (Drum Roll)
(BB) *** Naxos 8.550387. Capella Istropolitana, Wordsworth

Like Barry Wordsworth's recordings of Mozart symphonies, with the Capella Istropolitana on the Naxos label, this Haydn collection provides a series of outstanding bargains at the lowest budget price. The sound is not quite as clean and immediate as in the Mozart series, a little boomy at times in fact, and Wordsworth's preference for relatively relaxed speeds is a little more marked here than in Mozart, but the varied choice of works on each disc is most attractive. At their modest cost, these are well worth collecting.

Symphonies 44 (Trauer); 95 in C min.; 98 in B flat
✿ (N) (M) (***) DG mono 474 981-2. Berlin RIAS O, Fricsay

A superb disc, offered nostalgically in a facsimile of the original cream-and-yellow LP sleeve of 1954 (the only snag being that the listing on the front shows two symphonies, whereas of course there are three here). DG are justly proud of what they describe as 'the legendary Deutsche Grammophon sound of the 1950s', which is of course mono; and it is nowhere better illustrated than in this reissue. Fricsay, too, never made a finer classical disc than this. The *Trauersymphonie* is one of the most original of Haydn's whole cycle, and it was very little known in the early 1950s. The Minuet (*Canon in Diapasone*) for once becomes the second movement and the *Adagio* is as beautiful as the terse *Presto* finale is powerful. Here the brilliant, finely pointed string-playing of the Berlin RIAS Orchestra is electrifying. The *C minor Symphony* has a magnificent first movement, and Fricsay and his forces are again on the top of their form, both here and in the slow movement, a delightfully played set of variations. Lyrical and ornamental phrases are moulded with admirable plasticity, a feature which is true also of No. 98, another masterpiece, with a dignified *Adagio cantabile* which starts off like 'God save the Queen'. But this work also has one of Haydn's joke finales, which is neatly managed by Fricsay without loss of either vivacity or drama. This is still one of the best Haydn records in the catalogue.

Symphonies 54; 56; 57
(BB) *** Naxos 8.554108. Cologne CO, Müller-Brühl

In vivid, full-ranging recordings made by German Radio, Müller-Brühl conducts lively performances with his excellent chamber orchestra of three symphonies from around 1774. Müller-Brühl, using modern instruments, yet reflects period practice in asking for very limited vibrato and light articulation from the strings.

Symphonies 68 in B flat; 93 in D; 100 in G (Military)
(M) **(*) Warner Elatus 2464 60126-2. Conc. O, Harnoncourt

Harnoncourt's original 1986 pairing of Nos. 68 and 100 was apt for both works characterized by sharp, vivid effects, which are obviously relished. Taken at a measured speed, the slow movement of the *Military* erupts weightily in its martial music, while in the *Adagio cantabile* slow movement of No. 68 Harnoncourt similarly jabs home the curious *forte staccato* semiquavers that punctuate the main theme. In this symphony there is a curious idiosyncrasy in the Trio of the second movement Minuet, which Harnoncourt takes – without any evident justification – at double speed. Overall, these two symphonies present a tough, weighty view of Haydn that deliberately rejects charm but refuses to be dismissed, though most listeners will prefer versions that take more account of the composer's sense of humour.

However, No. 93, recorded six years later, is altogether more relaxed, and is one of Harnoncourt's most convincing Haydn performances. He finds all the geniality you could wish for in the neatly pointed second subject of the first movement, which he obviously relishes. The *Largo cantabile* is very beautifully played, the *fortissimo* interruptions are dramatic but not too forceful, and the Minuet is bounced enthusiastically, more like a Scherzo-Ländler, before the lively finale. Throughout the disc the sound is full and bright, clouding just a little in heavy tuttis.

Symphonies 69 (Laudon); 89; 91
(BB) **(*) Naxos 8.550769. Budapest Nicolaus Esterházy Sinfonia, Drahos

The resonance of the Reformed Church, Budapest, prevents the sharpest definition here. The orchestra is set back and the internal balance is natural: the strings have bloom without edginess. This is alert, thoroughly musical playing with apt tempi. The *Andante con moto* of No. 89 is elegantly done, and the variations of the *Andante* of No. 91 are neatly handled (with an elegant bassoon solo). All in all this gives pleasure, but more brightness on top would have been welcome.

Symphonies 72; 93; 95

(BB) *** Naxos 8.550797. Nicolaus Esterházy Sinfonia, Drahos

These performances are polished, warm and spirited and, if the Naxos recording is on the reverberant side, it does not cloud textures. Four horns are featured prominently in No. 72 and provide many bravura flourishes and virtuoso scales in the opening movement; the playing here is first class. The orchestral response is equally impressive in the fine slow movements of these later works, and throughout Béla Drahos's pacing is matched by the overall sense of spontaneity and style.

Symphonies 74–76

(BB) *** Naxos 8.554109. Cologne CO, Müller-Brühl

The three symphonies dating from the early 1780s make an attractive group, characteristically lively in outer movements but each with slow movements involving the use of mysterious muted strings. Müller-Brühl, as in his other Haydn recordings, favours broad adagios and Minuets that retain the idea of a stately dance. Yet the freshness and rhythmic resilience never fail to bring the performances to life. Like its companions, an excellent recommendation.

Symphonies 77–79

(BB) *** Naxos 8.553363. N. CO, Ward

For these three little-known but most engaging symphonies, written in 1782–3, Nicholas Ward could hardly be more persuasive. The colourful charm of Haydn's scoring in the *B flat Symphony* is most sensitively caught, the *Vivace* opening of No. 78 *in C minor* is highly dramatic, while both slow movements are eminently graceful. The Minuets, though not rushed, are suitably spirited and finales are deft and lively, especially the winning monothematic *Presto* of the *C minor* work, which includes some of the composer's genial pauses.

Symphonies 80; 81; 99

(BB) *** Naxos 8.554110. Cologne CO, Müller-Brühl

Müller-Brühl here couples two symphonies of 1783–4 with the first of the masterpieces which Haydn wrote for Salomon for the second of his two visits to London. No. 80 is remarkable for the dark intensity of the minor-key opening with its dramatic use of tremolo. Chromatic touches break in later too. In these later symphonies, unlike the earlier ones, Müller-Brühl does allow Minuets to acquire a hint of the Scherzo at brisker speeds. No. 99 is remarkable for Haydn's inclusion for the first time in a symphony of a pair of clarinets.

Symphonies 82 (The Bear); 83 (The Hen); 84; 85 (La Reine); 86; 87 (Paris)

⊕━ ✿ (BB) *** Virgin 2x1 5 61659 (2). OAE, Kuijken

(B) *** Double Decca (ADD) 473 801-2 (2). Philh. Hungarica, Dorati

Kuijken and his players wear their authenticity lightly and the slow movements are allowed to relax beautifully, while the one-in-a-bar treatment of the Minuets produces a delightful Ländler-like swing. With dynamic contrasts underlined, the grandeur of Haydn's inspiration is fully brought out, along with the rigour; yet Kuijken gives all the necessary sharpness to the reminiscence of *Sturm und Drang* in the near-quotation of the *Farewell* in the first movement of No. 85, *La Reine*. The magnificence of that movement is underlined by the observance of the second-half repeat. Above all, he and his players convey the full joy of Haydn's inspiration in every movement and the reissue at bargain price is surely irresistible.

Dorati's set of *Paris Symphonies* are well up to the high standard of his integral Haydn series, freshly stylish performances with plenty of vigour. The sinewy strength of the G minor opening of No. 83 for a moment brings a hint of *Sturm und Drang*, then yields its surprise as it gives way to the clucking of its titular *Hen*, while the variations which form its slow movement are matched in charm by those based on the French folksong (*La petite gentille et jeune Lisette*) which make up the *Romance: Allegretto* of No. 85. No. 84 has a first movement of the most delicate fantasy, while No. 87, after its sublime *Adagio*, ends in a mood of lithe high spirits. The only point of controversy here is Dorati's consistently slow tempi for the Minuets, nicely pointed as they are.

Symphony 83 in G min. (La Poule)

*** BBC (ADD) BBCL 4038. Hallé O, Barbirolli – LEHAR: *Gold and Silver;* JOHANN STRAUSS JR: *Emperor Waltz,* etc.; R. STRAUSS: *Der Rosenkavalier Suite* ***

This is one of Barbirolli's most cherishable records. The account of *Symphony No. 83* is delightful, with the 'Hen' clucking to the manner born. There is grace and simplicity in the *Andante* and exuberance in the finale, and the couplings are unmissable.

Symphonies 83 (La Poule); 88; 96 (Miracle)

(N) (BB) (***) Dutton mono CDBP 9750. Hallé O, Barbirolli

Barbirolli's mono recording of No. 83 (*The Hen*), made in 1949, was the very first in the catalogue. Characteristically, he gives it an energetic reading full of fun and high dramatic contrasts. So the clucking of the second subject has rarely been pointed with more wit. No. 96, with which *The Hen* was originally coupled on LP, has freer, more open sound. The playing is a degree more polished and elegant, with no diminution of energy or wit, and again the flute and oboe emerge as stars in the Hallé team. All three symphonies were originally recorded for EMI, although No. 88, dating from 1953, was never issued, perhaps for lack of a coupling. Barbirolli sustains the great, sensuously tuneful melody of the *Largo* at a slow speed, with elegance as well as warmth, and the fun of the finale is delightfully caught. Though in slow movements generally his speeds are very spacious by latter-day standards, Barbirolli has more concern for scholarly texts than most of his generation, and the wit and sparkle of the playing in fast movements is a delight. Michael Dutton's transfers are a model of their kind, full-bodied and warm.

Symphonies 85 in B flat (La Reine); 86 in D

(BB) **(*) Warner Apex 2564 60451-2. St Paul CO, Wolff

The excellent St Paul Chamber Orchestra give polished, animated accounts of two of the finest *Paris Symphonies*. No. 85 (*La Reine*) includes the slow-movement variations on *La petite gentille et jeune Lisette*, so admired by Queen Marie-Antoinette, here played most elegantly. The *Capriccio* slow movement of No. 86 is perhaps a little staid, but the finale is infectiously spirited. Excellent, natural recording with the concert-hall acoustic on the resonant side, adding to the weight of the first movement of the D major work.

Symphony 88
☗━ ✿ (N) (M) (***) DG mono 474 988-2. BPO, Furtwängler
– SCHUMANN: *Symphony 4* *** ✿

Even those who usually find Furtwängler's interpretations too idiosyncratic will be drawn to this glowing performance. The beauty of his shaping of the main theme of the slow movement is totally disarming, and the detail of the finale, lightly sprung and vivacious, is a constant pleasure. The Berlin Philharmonic plays marvellously well for him, and the 1951 recording in its remastered form sounds admirably fresh, yet has plenty of body.

However, DG have now reissued the original coupling, a uniquely inspired performance of Schumann's *Fourth Symphony*, which also has a Rosette, so collectors should seek this wonderful disc out without delay.

Symphonies 88; 92 (Oxford); 94 (Surprise)
(M) **(*) DG (IMS) 445 554-2. VPO, Bernstein

All three G major symphonies emanate from concerts at the Musikvereinsaal in the mid-1980s, using the full strings of the Vienna Philharmonic and given a richly upholstered recording. For all his idiosyncrasies, Bernstein is never more winning than in Haydn, with a romantic, beautiful account of the *Largo*. The slow movement of the *Surprise* is also taken relaxedly, and the speed of the finale is challengingly fast. Good sound.

Symphonies 88; 101 (Clock)
(N) (M) (**) Decca Heritage mono 475 6160. VPO, Münchinger

It is good that Decca has remembered Münchinger in its Heritage series. He is seen as a variable conductor, his reputation marred by some of his later Baroque recordings, several (but not all) of which were rather stodgy. His Haydn, however, was rather good (his *Creation*, also with the VPO, was superb). The two *Symphonies* here are presented with vigour, offering good, honest, polished playing which allows the music to speak for itself. The sound is a bit dry but is certainly vivid. With only two symphonies included, this is hardly exceptional value (the Heritage series only included the contents of the original LP) and the sleeve-notes are almost illegible. But this is a genuine collector's item.

Symphonies 88; 104 (London)
(M) *** CRD (ADD) CRD 3370. Bournemouth Sinf., Thomas

With an orchestra on a chamber scale, the playing has great freshness and vitality; indeed it is the urgency of musical feeling that Ronald Thomas conveys which makes up for the last ounce of finesse.

Symphonies 91 in E flat; 92 (Oxford); (i) Scena di Berenice
☗━ (N) *** HM HMC 901849. (i) Fink; Freiburg Bar. O, Jacobs

As in their exuberant account of Haydn's *Seasons*, René Jacobs and the Freiburg Baroque Orchestra (currently the finest of all period-instrument groups of this size) find a sense of joy, of carefree intensity in the playing of the two *Symphonies*. As in the oratorio, Jacobs is well aware of Haydn's sense of humour, pointing rhythms to bring it out in

such a movement as the *Andante* in No. 91. With the repeats observed in the second halves of the outer movements of the two *Symphonies*, there would have been no room for a third symphony, and outer movements readily sustain their extra length, thanks to the superb polish and resilience of the playing. Minuets are taken very fast, Scherzos in all but name, and the finales of both works have a winning lightness, with the *Presto* of No. 92 challengingly fast. The other distinctive point about this issue is the inclusion of Haydn's *Scena di Berenice* as a coupling, the most powerful bonus. Here Bernarda Fink is searingly dramatic, freely varying the pace and tone-colours of the recitatives to bring out the meaning of the words (included, along with translations, in the booklet) and rising superbly to the challenge of the two arias, slow and fast. This is one of the finest Haydn discs of recent years.

Symphonies 92 (Oxford); 94 (Surprise); La fedelta premiata: Sinfonia
(N) *** MDG SACD 1325-6. Austro-Hungarian Haydn O, Fischer

It was Adám Fischer who, with this orchestra, founded by him in 1986, made a formidable recording of the complete Haydn symphonies for Nimbus (see above). This coupling of Nos. 92 and 94, recorded live in Graz in 2004, demonstrates that they have lost none of their sparkle in exceptionally lively and alert performances which bring out the drama of each symphony in high dynamic contrasts. They are also marked by speeds on the fast side, so that the celebrated *Andante* of the *Surprise* with its sudden *fortissimo* on the timpani not only goes at a brisk walking pace, but has a drum stroke guaranteed to wake up anyone. The last two movements are also exceptionally fast, but cleanly articulated in reflection of period practice, even though modern instruments are used. The timpani are prominent throughout, with sharp attack in all four movements of the *Oxford*, bringing out the symphony's originality. What matters is the vitality, with the galloping rhythms of the *Overture* to *La fedelta premiata* exhilarating too. The Graz acoustic is generous rather than intimate, but textures are admirably clear in this excellent Hybrid SACD recording.

Symphonies 92 (Oxford); 104 (London)
(BB) *** Regis RRC 1084. E. Sinfonia, Groves – MOZART: *Symphony 31 (Paris)* ***

Sir Charles Groves's performances are robust yet elegant; both slow movements are beautifully shaped, with Haydn's characteristic contrasts unfolding spontaneously. In the last movement of the *Oxford* the dancing violins are a special delight in what is one of the composer's most infectious finales. Excellent recording, and this budget Regis reissue has an equally recommendable Mozart bonus.

Symphony 92 (Oxford); (i) Arianna a Naxos (Cantata); Scena di Berenice
(*) BBC Opus Art **DVD OA 0831 D. (i) Bartoli; VCM, Harnoncourt at the 2001 Syriarte Festival, Graz, Austria (includes discussion of the music of Haydn between Bartoli and Harnoncourt, and a brief depiction of the Festival) (TV Director: Brian Large)

We already have a Decca recording of *Arianna a Naxos* by Cecilia Bartoli with András Schiff, but this splendidly sung version with string accompaniment is even more telling, even though the orchestral transcription was not Haydn's own. Moreover, the performance is especially vivid in the singer's visual presence, while Harnoncourt accompanies with great sensitivity.

The equally inspired *Scena di Berenice* is set to a text taken from Metastasio's *Antigono*. It has a direct affinity with *Arianna*, as its heroine has to come to terms with the fatal wounding of her lover and asks God to increase her suffering so that death will claim her. Bartoli's performance is again very moving, and is most expressively accompanied. The two vocal items are preceded by a vibrant performance of Haydn's *Oxford Symphony* which, like *Arianna*, was very well received during Haydn's visits to London in the 1790s. This is a characteristic Harnoncourt performance with a rather gruff, even abrasive, first movement that not all will take to. He is more persuasive in the central movements, and the sparkling finale is a joy. Certainly the performance gains from watching the conductor, whose facial expressions are so mobile; and in Brian Large's directions the camerawork cannot be faulted. The bonuses include a fascinating dialogue between the conductor and singer, who discuss Haydn and his music, and a brief look at the Festival founded by Harnoncourt in Graz, with a little music from a novel instrumental group.

Symphonies 93–104
(B) **(*) Decca 475 551-2 (4). LPO, Solti

Symphonies 93; 94 (Surprise); 97; 99; 100 (Military); 101 (Clock) (London Symphonies)
— ✪ *** Ph. Duo (ADD)/DDD 442 614-2 (2). Concg. O, Davis

Symphonies 95; 96 (Miracle); 98; 102; 103 (Drum Roll); 104 (London) (London Symphonies)
— ✪ *** (B) *** Ph. Duo (ADD)/DDD 442 611-2 (2). Concg. O, Davis

Symphonies 93–98 (London Symphonies)
— (BB) *** EMI mono Gemini (ADD) 5 85770-2 (2). RPO, Beecham

Symphonies 99–104 (London Symphonies)
— (BB) *** EMI mono Gemini (ADD) 5 85513-2 (2). RPO, Beecham

Symphonies 93; 94 (Surprise); 103 (Drum Roll)
(M) (***) Sony mono SMK 89890. RPO, Beecham

(i) *Symphonies 93–104 (London Symphonies)*; with extra performances of Nos. (ii) *88 in G*; (iii) *91 in E flat*; (ii) *98 in B flat*
✪ *** (B) *** DG (ADD) 474 364-2 (5). (i) LPO; (ii) BPO; (iii) Bav. RSO, Jochum

Sir Colin Davis's Haydn series (recorded between 1975 and 1981) is one of the most distinguished sets he has given us over his long recording career, and its blend of brilliance and sensitivity, wit and humanity gives these two-for-the-price-of-one Duo reissues a special claim on the collector. There is no trace of routine in this music-making and no failure of imagination. The excellence of the playing is matched by Philips's best recording quality, whether analogue or digital. The Concertgebouw sound is resonant and at times weighty, but has good definition. The *Allegretto* of the *Military Symphony* is properly grand and expansive, balanced by vital, sparkling outer movements. Excellent notes from Robin Golding. A bargain in every sense of the word.

Jochum's exhilarating set of Haydn's *London Symphonies* (1972/3) has long been among the top recommendations. The playing is consistently stylish, and the challengingly fast

tempi in the outer movements bring an athletic exuberance, which is highly infectious. The conductor moulds the slow movements with a tenderness that never spills over to unstylish mannerisms and handles the sets of themes and variations to bring great diversity of atmosphere and mood, all of which combine to make these wonderfully satisfying readings. The recordings have never sounded better than in these new transfers, with sound that is both full and vivid. To make this set even more appealing, DG have added an extra disc containing an earlier recording. No. 98 is a performance of equal distinction, perhaps a degree more mellow (though surprisingly the slow movement is a little faster) while the 1962 sound is slightly richer. In No. 88 the Berlin orchestra is even more polished than the LPO, and Jochum brings his characteristic warmth and humanity to both these scores. No. 91, with the Bavarian orchestra, was recorded in 1958 and sounds only fractionally less full-bodied than its 1960s companions. The performance is a little less extrovert in the first movement, but enjoyably so, and the finale displays a lightness of touch that is quite captivating. The set comes in DG's handsome Collector's Edition packaging, and cannot be too highly recommended.

This first EMI collection is of Beecham's earlier mono recordings; they sound admirably full-bodied and have been transferred amazingly successfully, and we see no reason to put brackets round the stars. The performances are just as sensitive and invigorating as the later ones. The art of phrasing is one of the prime secrets of great music-making, and no detail in Beecham's performances of the *London Symphonies* goes unattended. They have also great warmth, drama too, and perhaps a unique geniality. The sound throughout is full and fresh (it's the 1992 remastering), with plenty of body, sweet violin-timbre and no edge. The performances possess an inner life and vitality that put them in a class of their own and are wonderful value in this bargain Gemini-double format.

Though Beecham was almost as devoted to Haydn as to his beloved Mozart, he had his firm favourites among the symphonies, concentrating almost exclusively on the last twelve, the *London Symphonies*, of which he recorded a complete cycle for EMI in 1957–8. These mono recordings from 1950–1 certainly deserve their place beside the EMI stereo versions. The ear quickly adjusts to the relative dryness of the mono sound, with good inner detail conveyed. The main *Allegros* in the first movements of each bring either triple or compound time, and it is there above all that Beecham's rare mixture of energy and charm comes over most distinctively, with slow movements and Minuets on the slow side by latter-day standards but beautifully lifted rhythmically, and the finales bringing the most exuberant conclusion in each, giving the feeling of live performance.

A very welcome return to Solti's survey of the *London Symphonies*. While Solti's way is very different from Beecham's and he can be a bit uptight for Haydn, some of these works really glow in his hands, with the coupling of Nos. 93 and 99 (recorded in 1987) proving the pick of the set. (They received a ✪ from us on their initial release.) Solti's manner in this pairing is sunny and civilized; there is no lack of brilliance – indeed, the LPO are consistently on their toes – but the music-making is infectious rather than hard-driven. The lovely slow movement of No. 93 has both delicacy and gravitas, and that of No. 99 is serenely spacious. The Minuets are shown to have quite different characters, and the finales sparkle in the happiest manner. However, the earliest symphonies recorded (1981) were the *Miracle* and the *Clock*, and, although brilliantly played, they were rather too taut to convey all Haydn's charm. Again, in Nos. 102 and 103, recorded a year later, even though the beauty and refinement of the LPO and the fine Decca recording cannot help but give pleasure, the tensions speak of the twentieth century rather than the eighteenth, with even the lovely *Adagio* of No. 102 failing quite to relax. In the *Surprise* and *Military Symphonies* (recorded in 1984), the conductor again stresses the brilliance and fire of the outer movements, which are a bit hard-driven, but there is no lack of *joie de vivre*. The recordings, hitherto excellent, here approach demonstration standard in fullness and transparency, and this is even more striking in Nos. 95 and 104. Here (in 1986), Solti found the perfect balance between energy and repose. The pacing is admirable and the LPO playing is smiling and elegant, yet full of bubbling vitality. No. 95 has a striking sense of cohesion and purpose, and there are few finer versions of No. 104. Throughout, Solti uses a full body of strings and all the resources of modern wind instruments with the greatest possible finesse, yet the spontaneity of the music-making is paramount. The final release, of Nos. 97 and 98, was in 1992, and maintained the balance between Solti's boundless energy and Haydn's warmth and humour. The twelve symphonies, now released in a bargain box (on four instead of five CDs), make a very attractive set, for the qualities of the playing outweigh the points of criticism, and this is music-making of strong personality.

Symphonies 94 (Surprise); 96 (Miracle); 103 (Drum Roll)
(M) **(*) Warner Elatus 2564 60337-2. Concg. O, Harnoncourt

Symphonies 95 in C min.; 97 in C; 98 in B flat
(M) *** Warner Elatus 2564 60438-2. Concg. O, Harnoncourt

Harnoncourt is nothing if not wide-ranging in his Haydn interpretations: the vigorous and polished Concertgebouw playing, with hard-driven allegros and contrasting moments of great delicacy, is certainly never dull. Although the readings bring characteristic gruffness, they have great character. Accents are stronger than ever, and in the *Andante* of the *Surprise*, after the orchestra has fined down to a *pianissimo* for the repetition of the opening phrase, not only is there one loud explosive interruption, but others follow, and the climax is spectacular. Then the Minuet whirls along at a forceful, rhythmic one-in-a-bar. If one accepts the sheer weight of the *fortissimo* tuttis, the *Miracle* is another impressive reading, with the secondary theme of the opening movement elegant enough. Here the Minuet is not pressed as hard, with the fizzing energy released in the finale. Nos. 97 and 98 are similarly compelling. The most notable eccentricity is at the opening of the *Drum Roll*, which is an arresting volley of 'drumshots', which return at the close of the movement, not at all what Haydn intended! Yet the performance overall combines characteristic vigour with moments of graciousness.

Symphonies 94 (Surprise); 96 (Miracle); 104 (London)
(M) **(*) DG (IMS) 463 083-2. BPO, Karajan
(BB) **(*) RCA 74321 68003-2. Philh. O, Slatkin

Karajan's *London Symphony* has impressive power and dignity with altogether splendid string-playing from the Berlin Philharmonic, with none of the interpretative self-indulgence which sometimes marred this conductor's later performances. Similar comments also apply to the *Surprise* and *Miracle* symphonies: these are beautifully played works,

weighty by modern standards, but not ponderous. With a playing time of 76 minutes, this is an excellent way to sample Karajan's plush approach to Haydn. Good recording.

Leonard Slatkin's series of Haydn *London Symphonies* brings fresh, refined readings at speeds that never sound breathless. Indeed, there is a certain urbane quality about these readings, especially when compared with Sir Colin Davis on Philips, which sometimes puts polish and eighteenth-century elegance before an earthier gusto. There is wit from the Philharmonia woodwind and the string phrasing always gives pleasure (particularly as Slatkin likes to divide his first and second violins on either side of the spectrum). But Davis finds an added tension – No. 104, for instance, is a work that can readily sound too easy-going, and with Davis there is more bite. However, the *Miracle* is both robust and genial, and if you want just these three symphonies this RCA disc is certainly worth its bargain price.

Symphonies 99 in E flat; 101 in D (Clock)
(M) **(*) Warner Elatus 2564 61175-2. Cong. O, Harnoncourt

An effective recoupling. Although the interpretations still have their eccentricities – the opening to the finale of the *Clock*, for instance, is surprisingly slack – this is Harnoncourt's Haydn at its most stimulating. In period-performance style, first movements are fierce and emphatic, and Minuets are treated as Scherzos with rhythms clipped, but their Trios are full of character. The *Adagio* of No. 99 is leisurely but well sustained and beautifully played (woodwind as well as strings distinguish themselves throughout both works), and the *Andante* of the *Clock* is genially relaxed. Excellent recording, with the Concertgebouw acoustic adding weight.

Symphonies 101 (Clock); 102 in B flat
(B) **(*) DHM/BMG 05472 77859-2. La Petite Bande, Kuijken

Kuijken is pretty well back on form for this fine coupling of two of the *London Symphonies*. The *Andante* of the *Clock* is ideally paced – indeed, tempi throughout are apt, with allegros full of life, especially the exuberant finale of No. 102. The *Adagio* is presented thoughtfully and with a degree of detachment, but remains pleasingly spontaneous. Excellent recording, but 53 minutes' content is ungenerous, even at bargain price.

Symphonies 102 in B flat; 104 in D (London)
(M) ** Warner Elatus 2564 60659-2. Concg. O, Harnoncourt

Harnoncourt's eccentricity again rears its head in this coupling of two of Haydn's late and great symphonies. In period-performance style, the first movements of both symphonies are fierce and emphatic, and the glorious *Adagio* of No. 102 is clipped and short winded. The Minuets of both symphonies are strongly accented and are treated briskly like Scherzos. Yet the opening of the Trio of No. 102 is surprisingly slack. While this is music-making of a powerful persuasion, very well played and recorded, it cannot receive a strong general recommendation.

Symphony 104 in D (London)
(M) *** Decca (IMS) (ADD) 470 256-2. VPO, Karajan –
BEETHOVEN: *Symphony 7* **(*)

A really noble account, powerful and forward-looking, of the *London Symphony* from Karajan and the Vienna Philharmonic on their finest form. At the time of its first issue *Gramophone* commented on the 'vigour and sense of proportion' of the interpretation. As in Karajan's later, DG account, the first-movement repeat is observed and detail is etched with loving care, the delicate passages perfectly balanced with the bold tuttis. The slow movement, without any self-conscious mannerisms, is shaped warmly and graciously, and the Minuet sparkles, taken at a brisk pace, while the outer movements have splendid life and impetus. The 1959 recording, produced by John Culshaw, is extremely fine for its period (indeed any period) and has been transferred to CD without loss of the ambient bloom of the Sofiensaal.

CHAMBER MUSIC

Baryton Trios 71 in A; 96 in B min.; 113 in D; 126 in C
*** ASV Gaudeamus CDGAU 109. Hsu, Miller, Arico

Baryton Trios 87 in A min.; 97 in D (Fatti per la felicissima nasetta de S:ai:S); 101 in C; 111 in G
*** ASV Gaudeamus CDGAU 104. Hsu, Miller, Arico

Our apologies are due not only to readers but also to Gaudeamus for omitting these two excellent CDs from recent volumes, particularly as this is rare repertoire. Prince Esterházy was particularly fond of the baryton, whose delicate sonorities much appealed to him. He was a keen amateur player himself, and during his years at Eisenstadt Haydn composed 126 trios for his delectation. As John Hsu puts it: 'The baryton is a kind of viola da gamba, with a broadened neck, behind which there is a harp … the metal harp strings are exposed within the open-box-like back of the neck so that they may be plucked by the thumb of the left hand.' These are most beguiling performances, which have subtlety and finesse, and the music itself is consistently inventive and attractive. Natural and well-balanced recorded sound, too. The second collection is no less desirable than the first. Well worth exploring.

Cassations in E flat & D, Hob II/21–22 (arr. for String Quartet, as Op. 2/3 & 5)
(BB) *** Naxos 8.555703. Kodály Qt – HOFFSTETTER: *String Quartets* ***

The original versions of these five-movement *Cassations* were scored for two horns and strings, and the arranger of the string quartet versions is unknown, but they transcribe very effectively. The *E flat Quartet* is notable for its charming serenade-like slow movement, pizzicato second Minuet and cheerful finale; the *D major* has a winningly energetic opening movement, another graceful slow movement and a racy finale. They are admirably played here and splendidly recorded.

8 Divertimenti (Feldparthie) (for Wind Sextet)
(N) **(*) Testament (ADD) SBT 1346. L. Wind Soloists, Brymer

Mozart's special gift in the writing of his *Wind Divertimenti* was a penchant for achieving inner parts that are not only a pleasure to play but which continually alter the colouring of texture by the instinctive placing of each note of the harmony in the right instrument. This is demonstrated on the highest level of genius in even the simplest of Mozart's occasional pieces. By comparison, Haydn's writing is much more earthy, suggesting (like the original title of these works, 'Feldparthie') that they were written for a private wind band. Moreover the bravura of the horn writing suggests the availability of local virtuosi of a high calibre, and this applies equally to the superb playing here. The music has elegance too, as the very

first of the series immediately displays; but it makes its effects more from the spirited brilliance of the playing (particularly in the vigorous 'hunting' finales of Nos. 1 to 3) than for subtlety of colour. Excellent (originally Decca) recording from 1968, immaculately transferred to CD.

(i) *Flute Trios for 2 Flutes & Cello 1–4 (London), Hob IV/1–4;* (ii) *Flute Quartets, Op. 5, 1 in D, Hob II/D9; 2 in G, Hob II/G4; 3 in D, Hob II/D10; 4 in G, Hob II/1; 5 in D, Hob II/D11; 6 in C, Hob II/11*
*** Accent ACC 9283/4 (2). (i) Bernard Kuijken, Mark Hantaï, Wieland Kuijken; (ii) Bernard, Siegfried & Wieland Kuijken, François Fernandez

The *London Trios* date from 1794 during Haydn's visit to England and the first two include variations on the song, *Trust not too much*. They are delightful works and receive felicitous performances from this authentic group on Accent who make the most winning sounds. The *Flute Quartets*, Op. 5, in the view of H. C. Robbins Landon may not all be by Haydn. It seems fairly certain, however, that the first two, also known as *Divertimenti*, are authentic, very early works from the 1750s. All the music is engaging when played with such finesse and warmth, although this is a set to be dipped into rather than taken in large doses. The recording is admirably fresh and realistic.

Flute Trios for 2 Flutes & Cello (London), Hob IV/1, 2 (Andante & Variations), 3–4; Flute Trios (for Piano, Flute & Cello): in D, F & G, Hob XV/15–17
(N) *** CPO 999 920-2. Camerata Köln

The Camerata Köln also offer captivating accounts of the four *London Trios* and add the three *Trios* from 1790 also recorded on Apex by the Finnish group, below. In the performances of the latter works there is little to choose between them, so it is a question of whether or not you want both sets, as the CPO disc is more expensive.

Flute Trios: in D, F & G, Hob XV/15–17
(BB) **(*) Warner Apex 0927 40602-2. Helasvuo, Hakkila, Kartunnen

These three *Flute Trios* were written together in the summer of 1790. They are slight but have a simple charm which is well caught by these unpretentious performances by this Finnish team, Mikael Helasvuo (flute), Tuija Hakkila (fortepiano), and Anni Kartunnen (cello). The recording is clear and truthful.

Piano Trios 1–46, Hob XV:1–41; Hob XIV:C1 in C; Hob XV:C1 in C; Hob XIV6/XVI6 in G; Hob XV:fl in F min.; Hob deest in D (complete)
❀ (B) *** Ph. 454 098-2 (9). Beaux Arts Trio

It is not often possible to hail one set of records as a 'classic' in quite the way that Schnabel's Beethoven sonatas can be so described. Yet this set can be described in those terms, for the playing of the Beaux Arts Trio is of the very highest musical distinction. The contribution of the pianist, Menahem Pressler, is inspired, and the recorded sound on CD is astonishingly lifelike. The CD transfer has enhanced detail without losing the warmth of ambience or sense of intimacy. Now offered in a bargain box of nine CDs, this is a set no Haydn lover should miss: it is desert island music.

Piano Trios: Hob XV/5; 18; 19; 20
(M) **(*) CPO 999 468-2. Trio 1790

Piano Trios, Hob XV, 6–10
(M) **(*) CPO 999 466-2. Trio 1790

Piano Trios, Hob XV, 11–14
(M) **(*) CPO 999 467-2. Trio 1790

The Beaux Arts Trio have long reigned supreme in this repertoire but those who are attracted by the idea of original instruments might well consider this expert group, Trio 1790, which is based in Cologne and was recorded there in the WDR studios. They are intelligent players, and their discs are priced economically. The performances sparkle; there is plenty of wit and character, and the Cologne Radio recordings are first class. All the same this will remain an adjunct rather than a replacement for the Beaux Arts and the sublime Menahem Pressler.

Piano Trios, Hob XV, 21–23
(M) **(*) CPO 999 731. Trio 1790

Piano Trios, Hob XV, 24–26; 31–32
(M) **(*) CPO 999 828-2. Trio 1790

The Trio 1790 continue their series with Nos. 21–23, which were composed in 1794–5 and published in London in 1795 as Haydn's Op. 71. They are fresh and pleasing, but not very different from their predecessors, although No. 21, unusually, has a slow introduction, and No. 23 has an attractive set of double variations for its D minor/D major first movement.

Trios Nos. 24–26 were dedicated to Rebecca Schroter, the English widow whom Haydn met on his first London visit in 1791 and who became his pupil (and probably more than that, for she was reputedly beautiful and the composer undoubtedly became emotionally attached to her). The *Trios* give little or no indication of his feelings, except perhaps that No. 25 includes the famous *Gypsy Rondo*, one of the composer's happiest and most genial movements. Nos. 31 and 32 are in two movements only, and there have been suggestions that No. 32 was originally intended as a violin sonata. The performances here are well up to standard, and many may respond to Harald Hoeren's crisp fortepiano contributions as being more authentic than versions using a modern piano.

Piano Trios, Hob XV, 18, 19; (i) *Andante with Variations in F min., Hob XVII;* (ii) *Cantata: The Battle of the Nile, Hob XXVIb4; 2 Italian Duets, Hob XXVa1–2; The Spirit's Song, Hob XXV1a41*
*** Gaudeamus CDGAU 219. Four Nations Ens., with (i) Appel; (ii) Monoyios, Nils Brown

The Battle of the Nile, from which the CD takes its title, was occasioned by Nelson and Lady Hamilton's visit to Esterháza. The Princess Esterházy arranged for Haydn and some musicians to entertain the guests and Haydn was persuaded to compose this cantata to words by Cornelia Knight, who accompanied them on the visit, celebrating Nelson's victory. This expert group play the two 1794 *Trios* with exemplary taste and vitality and Andrew Appel gives us a sensitive account of the *Andante with Variations in F minor* on a fine copy of an instrument by Anton Walter. *The Battle of the Nile* is a rarity and is currently available in only one alternative. An enjoyable, well-played and beautifully recorded disc.

Piano Trio, Hob XV, 25 in G (Gypsy)
(BB) (***) Naxos mono 8.110188. Thibaud, Casals, Cortot –
BEETHOVEN: *Kakadu Variations* (***); SCHUBERT: *Piano Trio 1* (***)

Few Haydn trios – apart from this one in G major, the

so-called *Gypsy* – were played in the 1920s and 1930s. This famous recording, made in 1927, has been lovingly restored by Ward Marston even if it undoubtedly shows its age.

String quartets

String Quartets 1 in B flat; 2 in E flat; 3 in D; 4 in G; 5 in E flat; 6 in C (Op. 1/1–6); 7 in A; 8 in E (Op. 2/1–2); 9 in F; 10 in B flat (Op. 2/4 & 6); 19 in C; 20 in E flat; 21 in G; 22 in D min.; 23 in B flat; 24 in A (Op. 9/1–6); 25 in E; 26 in F; 27 in E flat; 28 in C min.; 29 in G; 30 in D (Op. 17/1–6); 31 in E flat; 32 in C; 33 in D min.; 34 in D; 35 in F min.; 36 in A (Op. 20/1–6); 37 in B min.; 38 in E flat; 39 in C; 40 in B flat; 41 in G; 42 in D (Op. 33/1–6); 43 in D min. (Op. 42); 44 in B flat; 45 in C; 46 in E flat; 47 in F sharp min.; 48 in D (Op. 50/1–6); 50–56 (The Seven Last Words of Our Saviour on the Cross), Op. 51; 57 in G; 58 in C; 59 in E (Op. 54/1–3); 60 in A; 61 in F min.; 62 in B flat (Op. 55/1–3); 63 in C; 64 in B min.; 65 in B flat; 66 in G; 67 in D; 68 in E flat (Op. 64/1–6); 69 in B flat; 70 in D; 71 in E flat (Op. 71/1–3); 72 in C; 73 in F; 74 in G min. (Op. 74/1–3); 75 in G; 76 in D min.; 77 in C; 78 in B flat; 79 in D; 80 in E flat (Op. 76/1–6); 81 in G; 82 in F (Op. 77/1–2); 83 in D min. (Op. 103)

String Quartets 1–10; 19–83; String Quartet Fragments in D min. (Andante grazioso & minuet), Op. 103 (includes The Seven Last Words of Christ on the Cross, Op. 51/1–7, with readings selected by Reginald Barrett-Ayres)
(B) *** Decca 455 261-2 (22). Aeolian Qt

The first complete recording of the Haydn *String Quartets* in stereo was Decca's project parallel to Dorati's integral recording of the symphonies. The performances were recorded over a period of four years between December 1972 and December 1976, using the critical edition by Reginald Barrett-Ayres and H. C. Robbins Landon. The recordings were made in two London churches, beginning with Opp. 71 and 74, followed by Op. 2. Though the performances of these late works are vigorously enjoyable, the engineers let the ecclesiastical acoustic provide the four players with a degree of 'helpful' reverberation which in Opp. 71 and 74 made them sound a little like a string orchestra, although the microphone placing ensures clarity of part-writing as well as warmth. By the time Decca came to record Op. 2, the problem was solved, and for the remaining sessions the recording team moved to St John's, Smith Square, where an excellent and realistic presence was consistently achieved, the profile of the leader (Emanuel Hurwitz) bright without being edgy. The Op. 3 *Quartets* are now claimed to be by Romanus Hoffstetter, not by Haydn, and they have understandably been omitted from the present box.

The set is crowned by their admirable performances of the consistently inspired last quartets, Opp. 77 and 76. The straight, unmannered approach disguises consistent imaginative thoughtfulness, and the music's characteristic touches of humour (as in the genial bouncing opening *Allegro* of Op. 77/1) are not missed. *The Seven Last Words of Our Saviour* (Nos. 50–56, Op. 51) are treated as an appendix. The performances here avoid any risk of monotony by inserting poetry readings between movements. The texts (from John Donne, George Herbert, Robert Herrick and Edith Sitwell, among others) are aptly chosen and beautifully read by Sir Peter Pears. All told, this is a fine achievement. The documentation consists of an excellent essay by Lindsay Kemp, but analysis is confined to Opus number groupings.

String Quartets 1–10; 19–83 (complete)
(B) *** Ph. 464 650-2 (21). Angeles Qt
(BB) *** Naxos 8.502301 (23). Kodály Qt

This complete survey by the Angeles Quartet comes on 21 CDs and was made over a period of five years (1994–9). Both the playing and the sound quality are of a consistently high standard: generally speaking, the set is beautifully balanced without excessive reverberation and with great clarity; the players have warmth, intelligence and a refined tonal blend and their readings are full of character and wit. They leave you in no doubt that they have thought deeply about this music, but at the same time they never leave the impression that they are too studied or wanting in spontaneity. The internal balance is very good indeed, even if one might occasionally welcome greater projection from the cellist. Tempos are finely judged, and there is a keen awareness of Haydn's developing stature throughout. One never gets the feeling that one is hearing the earlier quartets through the eyes and ears of the later quartets. The group's sense of characterization is pretty unerring, and it leaves you marvelling anew at the quality of Haydn's musical invention.

It is difficult to generalize about so vast an output or so ambitious a recording enterprise, but the Angeles Quartet brings greater elegance and polish to this music than the Aeolian set on 22 CDs, which comes from the early 1970s, and greater transparency of texture than the Kodály on Naxos and arguably greater finish. The Kodály does not lack warmth or a sense of style, and the consistently friendly warmth of these players' approach to Haydn's music is always endearing. The result almost always sounds spontaneous and usually carries the feeling of 'live' music-making. The Kodály's playing was flattered by the warm acoustics of the Budapest Unitarian Church, which suited its mellow, civilized approach, although at times the engineers slightly miscalculated the microphone balance and captured a little too much resonance, bringing a degree of textural inflation. But the sound is always natural, the performances do not miss Haydn's subtleties or his jokes, and the group always communicates readily.

Those wanting to collect an inexpensive survey in instalments might prefer the Kodály set rather than the larger initial outlay of the Angeles Philips box. However, without forgetting or naming all the many excellent individual sets and collections by the Mosaïques (on period instruments), the Lindsays (especially in Op. 76) and others, the Philips set ranks alongside the very best. Its claims are enhanced by an impressive essay by Richard Wigmore. The Naxos discs (which come in a big slip-case in their original jewel-cases with excellent documentation) are all available separately, and as such are discussed below.

String Quartets: Op. 1/0; 43, Op. 42; 83, Op. 103
**(*) Mer. (ADD) ECD 88117. English Qt

These fine players rise to all the challenges posed by this music, and the recorded sound is eminently truthful. There would have been room for another quartet on this disc, which offers rather short measure at 43 minutes.

String Quartets 1–4, Op. 1/1–4
(BB) **(*) Naxos 8.550398. Kodály Qt

String Quartets 5–6, Op. 1/5–6; 7–8, Op. 2/1–2
(BB) **(*) Naxos 8.550399. Kodály Qt

The Opp. 1 and 2 quartets are in essence five-movement divertimenti scored for four string players. These earliest works have not quite the unquenchable flow of original ideas that the early symphonies have but, in such fresh performances as these, they make easy and enjoyable listening even if, with the performances generous in observing repeats, some movements outstay their welcome. The resonant ambience of the Unitarian Church in Budapest seems not unsuitable for works which lie midway between divertimenti and quartets, and the focus seems brighter and sharper on the second CD, recorded in June 1991, two months after the first.

String Quartets: 1 (La Chasse), Op. 1/1; 32, Op. 20/2; 35, Op. 20/5; 46, Op. 50/3; 57; 58; 59, Op. 54/1–3; 65; 66, Op. 64/3–4; 74 (Rider), Op. 74/3; 77 (Emperor), Op. 76/3; 78 (Sunrise), Op. 77/2
(**(*)) Testament mono SBT 3055 (3). Pro Arte Qt

String Quartets: 6, Op. 1/6; 16; 17 (Serenade), Op. 3/4–5 (Hoffstetter); 31; 34, Op. 20/1 & 4; 38 (Joke); 39 (Bird); 42 (How do you do?), Op. 33/2, 3 & 6; 49 (Frog), Op. 50/6; 60; 62, Op. 55/1 & 3; 68, Op. 64/6; 69, Op. 71/1; 72; 73, Op. 74/1–2; 81, Op. 77/1
(**(*)) Testament mono SBT 4056 (4). Pro Arte Qt

While LP and CD reissues have kept the name of the Busch Quartet alive, the Pro Arte is a less familiar one to modern collectors. In their hands the Haydn *Quartets* bring us a world of delight, wisdom and sanity, and few groups are better guides. They have great purity of style and an immaculate intonation and technique, while they seem always to hit on exactly the right tempo, which in turn enables phrasing to speak naturally. However, the actual sound of these recordings calls for a little tolerance. The violin, particularly above the stave, is wanting in bloom, and one would welcome more space between movements. Less than perfect sound, perhaps, as might be expected from their recording dates (1931–8), but impeccable Haydn playing.

String Quartets 1, Op. 1/1; 67 (Lark), Op. 64/5; 74, Op. 74/3 (Rider)
*** DG (IMS) 423 622-2. Hagen Qt

The Hagen are supple, cultured and at times perhaps a little overcivilized, but in these three Haydn quartets they play flawlessly and are wonderfully alert and intelligent.

String Quartets 9–10, Op. 2/4 & 6 (Le Matin); 35, Op. 42
(BB) **(*) Naxos 8.550732. Kodály Qt

The Unitarian Church, Budapest, continues to provide a warm, flattering tonal blend but a texture that is a little too ample for early Haydn, while the fairly close microphones reduce the dynamic range. However, the Kodály's friendly style and elegant finish suit early Haydn. These performers find exactly the right degree of expressiveness for the *Adagio* of Op. 2/4 and are equally at home in the engaging *Andante ed innocentemente* which opens the first movement of Op. 42, a splendid work, written a quarter of a century later.

String Quartets 15 in G, Op. 3/3; 16 in B flat, Op. 3/4; 17 in F (Serenade), Op. 3/5; 18 in A, Op. 3/6
String Quartets 19; 21–22, Op. 9/1, 3 & 4
☛ (BB) *** Naxos 8.550786. Kodály Qt

String Quartets 20; 23; 24, Op. 9/2, 5 & 6
☛ (BB) *** Naxos 8.550787. Kodály Qt

The Kodály Quartet are in excellent form throughout Opus 9. Their simple eloquence in all three slow movements on the first disc serves Haydn well: the *Largo* of Op. 9/3 is ideally paced and beautifully poised. The players then go on to give a captivating account of the finale. Indeed, all the finales here are superb, showing Haydn at full stretch. The last of the set in A major opens with a very attractive *Presto* in 6/8, which is delightfully buoyant here. Fortunately, the Naxos recording team (in December 1992 and January 1993) have mastered the acoustics of the Unitarian Church in Budapest. The microphones are in the right place and the sound is not inflated.

String Quartets 22, Op. 9/4; 35, Op. 20/5; 39 (Bird), Op. 33/3
(N) (M) ** Arte Nova 74321 77636-2. Quartet As fontes

The Quartet As fontes are a period-instrument group who match their timbres very closely indeed, to make a sonorous blend without a suspicion of edginess. They are a little solemn in slow movements, notably so in the thoughtful *Adagio* of Op. 20/5, but they find a suitably light touch in finales, particularly in the *Bird Quartet*. The recording is very close and somewhat opaque, but detail comes through well enough, although a little more sparkle would not have gone amiss.

String Quartets 25–26; 28, Op. 17/1, 2 & 4
(BB) * Naxos 8.550853. Kodály Qt**

The Kodály Quartet seem very much at home in this music, which they approach with affection, yet with an appealing directness which leads to playing which is perfectly integrated, yet fresh. The recording could hardly be bettered: the balance is most natural.

String Quartets 27; 29; 30, Op. 17/3, 5 & 6
(BB) * Naxos 8.550854-2. Kodály Qt**

While the other works here are also played with pleasing warmth and finesse, the highlight of the second Naxos disc of Op. 17 is the *D major Quartet* which has a searching, aria-like slow movement, dominated by the principal violin, which is played most eloquently here. This is the last of the set, and appropriately the last to be recorded in this highly distinguished Naxos series. The recording balance is quite admirable.

String Quartets 31–36, Op. 20/1–6
⊶ ❂ * Astrée E 8802 (2). Mosaïques Qt**

String Quartets 31–33, Op. 20/1–3
(BB) ** Naxos 8.550701. Kodály Qt

String Quartets 34–36, Op. 20/4–6
(BB) ** Naxos 8.550702. Kodály Qt

Using period instruments, the four players of the Mosaïques Quartet create individual timbres which are pleasing to the ear and which have body and transparency, are perfectly matched and never edgy. There is no squeezed phrasing, and the use of vibrato is as subtle as the control of colour and dynamic. Intonation and ensemble are remarkably exact. Such is the calibre of this music-making and the strength of insight of these players that the character of these fine, relatively early works is communicated with seemingly total spontaneity. This is playing of rare distinction which is immensely revealing and rewarding, helped by state-of-the-art recording of complete realism and presence within an acoustic that provides the necessary intimacy of ambience.

The Naxos Kodály series brings polished, sympathetic playing of considerable warmth. Allegros are lively, but the acoustics of the Unitarian Church, Budapest, though providing beautifully rich string-textures, here make the effect

almost orchestral and bring an element of blandness to the fine *Adagio* slow movements; throughout, the dynamic range of the playing is reduced by the microphone positioning. The theme and variations of the *Poco adagio e affettuoso* of the *D major Quartet*, Op. 20/4, are attractively characterized but badly need a wider dynamic contrast. This is even more striking in the *Fuga a quattro soggetti* which forms the finale of Op. 20/2.

String Quartets 31; 33; 34 (Sun), Op. 20/1, 3, & 4
**** (*) ASV CDDCA 1027. Lindsay Qt**

The Lindsays are at their finest in *No. 34 in D major* and make much of its theme and variations slow movement, brief Gypsy Minuet and scherzando finale. These recordings were apparently made under studio conditions and the playing in the slow movements of the other two quartets has slightly less concentration than one has come to expect from their 'live' recordings. The sound is first class, and the extra finish of the ensemble brings its own rewards.

String Quartets 32; 34; 35, Op. 20/2, 5 & 6
***** ASV CDDCA 1057. Lindsay Qt**

These are three of Haydn's very greatest mid-period quartets, and the Lindsays have their full measure, with the feeling of 'live' music-making persisting throughout. The rich-textured opening of *No. 32 in C major* is immediately inviting, and the *Capriccio* second movement is most sensitively done, as is the lovely, rocking siciliano *Adagio* of *No. 34 in F minor*. The *Allegro di molto e scherzando* character of the first movement of the *A major* is perfectly caught. All three finales are fugal, and the lightness and keenness of articulation here is a joy. Excellent, truthful recording. Very highly recommended.

String Quartets 34 (Sun), Op. 20/4; 38 (Joke), Op. 33/2; 39 (Bird), Op. 33/3; 61 (Razor), Op. 55/2; 67 (Lark), Op. 64/5; 77 (Emperor), Op. 76/3
⊶ (M) * ASV CDDCS 236 (2). Lindsay Qt**

All these performances show the Lindsays on top form; indeed the *Sun Quartet* is the finest performance on the full-priced CD from which it comes. Anyone wanting a grouping of these named quartets (all masterpieces) cannot go wrong here as the recordings are all vividly real: the *Emperor*, for instance, which was recorded live, is very present indeed. The only snag is that a compilation like this cuts across other collections which group together works of a single Opus number.

String Quartets 34, Op. 20/4; 47, Op. 50/4; 77 (Emperor), Op. 76/3
***** ASV CDDCA 731. Lindsay Qt**

The Lindsay's performances were again recorded at public performances, on this occasion in London's Wigmore Hall. The advantages this brings are twofold: higher spontaneity and a greater propensity to take risks. In all three performances the gains outweigh any loss, though the balance tends to cause some coarse-sounding tone in *fortissimo* passages.

String Quartets 35, Op. 20/5; 38 (Joke), Op. 33/2; 57, Op. 54/1; 67 (Lark), Op. 64/5; 74 (Rider), Op. 74/3; 76 (Fifths), Op. 76/2; 81, Op. 77/1
***(**) DG 471 327-2 (2). Emerson Qt**

Readers who admire the Emersons need not hesitate. They bring to this repertoire their usual phenomenal unanimity of ensemble and extraordinary precision and accuracy. At the same time, those who don't respond to them will know what to expect. There is no period sense; we are in Manhattan not Esterháza, and the surroundings are distinctly 21st century, gleaming and neon-lit. They certainly evoke admiration, but convey little of the civilized humanity which is the epitome of Haydn's chamber music.

String Quartets 37; 38 (Joke); 39 (Bird), Op. 33/1–3
*** Kingdom KCLCD 2014. Bingham Qt

String Quartets 37; 38 (Joke); 40, Op. 33/1–2 & 4
**(*) ASV CDDCA 937. Lindsay Qt

String Quartets 37–42, Op. 33/1–6
*** Astrée E 8801 (2). Mosaïques Qt

String Quartets 37–38 & 41, Op. 33/1–2 & 5
(BB) **(*) Naxos 8.550788. Kodály Qt

String Quartets 39–40 & 42, Op. 33/3–4 & 6
(BB) **(*) Naxos 8.550789. Kodály Qt

String Quartets 39 (Bird); 41 in G; 42, Op. 33/3, 5 & 6
*** ASV CDDCA 938. Lindsay Qt

String Quartets 40; 41; 42 (How do you do?), Op. 33/4–6
*** Kingdom KCLCD 2015. Bingham Qt

The Lindsays are vividly alert and their playing is full of tension, emphasized by the recording, where the microphones are close, giving striking presence and emphasizing the bite on the timbre of the leader, Peter Cropper. Fortunately, the superb ensemble stands up to such scrutiny. No one could say that the Lindsays miss the wit inherent in the finale of the *Joke*; yet, in spite of the gentle ending, the smile is weakened by the vibrant purposefulness. The performances here use the Henle Urtext edition, which differs quite substantially in phrasing and, in places, even in notes from the more familiar Peters Edition, especially at the opening of Op. 33/1. The second disc includes a Rosette-worthy account of Op. 33/3 with Haydn's birdsong exquisitely simulated.

Those wanting Op. 33 on period instruments can be recommended without reservation to the Mosaïques Quartet, whose performances are more penetrating than any of their competitors. Indeed the intensity of the playing is remarkable, with concentration held throughout the widest range of dynamic, and constantly uncovering hidden depths in these works, even in the *Joke Quartet*. There are touches of darkness, as well as serenity, in adagios; and finales dance with fairy lightness, while the crisply pointed *Allegretto* which ends Op. 33/6 has a Beechamesque rhythmic panache. Marvellous playing throughout, with every detail revealed in sound which is both transparent, yet never in the least textually meagre. The superb recording is perfectly balanced.

The tonal matching and ensemble of the Bingham Quartet are most impressive, with the leader, Stephen Bingham, a remarkably stylish player who really understands how to shape a Haydn phrase. Above all the Binghams convey their pleasure in the music, and every performance here sounds fresh. The recording was made at the Conway Hall, London, in 1990. The balance is a shade close, but the instruments are naturally focused, individually and as a group. Even if the range of dynamic is a little affected, the playing itself is full of light and shade so that if the volume level is carefully set one soon forgets this reservation in the sheer pleasure this music affords.

The Kodály Quartet play Op. 33 with an easy, relaxed warmth. Their style is low-key so that the 'Joke' finale of Op. 33/2 is rather gentle and muted; on the other hand, the

reason for the sobriquet of the *Bird Quartet* is affectionately conveyed and the finale is delightfully light-hearted. Slow movements are serene and quietly musical. Minuets are generally full of character, with the trios nicely realized, and this applies especially to the charming middle section of the Scherzo in the *Joke Quartet*. In short these are performances which convey the players' affection for this wonderful music with no possible desire to put their own personalities between composer and listener. The Naxos recording is wholly natural, with the acoustics of the Budapest Unitarian Church beautifully caught without any textural inflation.

String Quartet 39 in C (Bird), Op. 33/3
🎵➔ ✿ (BB) (***) Dutton mono CDBP 9702. Griller Qt –
   MOZART: *String Quartets 14–15 (Haydn Quartets)* *** ✿

This simply is one of the finest Haydn Quartet recordings ever put on disc, and the Dutton transfer from the 1946 Decca ffrr 78s miraculously provides a sound quality superior to many modern digital stereo recordings. The Griller were in their absolute prime at the time. You need only sample the grace and finesse of the first movement, with its engaging chirping, the serene blending of timbre in the *Adagio* and the elegance of the closing *Rondo* to realize that this playing is very special indeed, as is the recording.

String Quartets 44–49, Op. 50/1–6
🎵➔ (BB) *** Naxos 8.553983 *(Nos. 44–46)*; 8.553984 *(Nos. 47–49)* (available separately). Kodály Qt
🎵➔ (N) *** ASV Gold GLD 4007 (1–3); GLD 4008 (4–6). The Lindsays

The Kodály Quartet are back to their finest form in Op. 50 and they are most naturally recorded. These are mellow performances, warm and polished, with perfect blending of timbre, yet refined detail. Slow movements are beautifully shaped, with the leader, Attila Falvay, frequently distinguishing himself with the graceful finish of his phrasing. Allegros are spirited but unforced, Minuets have an affectionate modicum of wit, and finales are never rushed.

The Lindsays' set of Op. 50, superbly played and recorded, arrived just as we were going to press. Their approach is less mellow, less affectionate than that of the Kodály Quartet (Naxos 8.553983/4) who are not surpassed, but the playing is very stimulating indeed.

String Quartets 50–56 (The Seven Last Words of Our Saviour on the Cross), Op. 51
🎵➔ ✿ *** ASV CDDCA 853. Lindsay Quartet
*** Astrée E 8803. Mosaïques Qt

String Quartets: 50–56: The Seven Last Words of Our Saviour on the Cross, Op. 51
(N) **(*) DG 474 836-2. Emerson Qt

String Quartets 50–56 (The Seven Last Words of Our Saviour on the Cross), Op. 51; 83, Op. 103
(BB) *** Naxos 8.550346. Kodály Qt

No work for string quartet, not even late Beethoven, presents more taxing interpretative problems than Haydn's *Seven Last Words of Our Saviour on the Cross*. The recording by the Lindsay Quartet, while offering all the devotional gravity that Haydn demands, brings not just an illuminating variety but also a sense of drama, and the performance makes no compromise for, unlike some others, the Lindsays observe the first-half repeats in each movement, extending the work to a full 70 minutes, instead of under an hour. After the long sequence of slow movements, the Lindsays' account of the final, brief *Presto*, *Il terremoto*, then conveys the full, elemental force of the earthquake. It is thrilling with so elusive a work to have so complete an answer in a single recording, with sound both well defined and glowingly beautiful, set against an apt church acoustic.

The slightly austere style of the Mosaïques Quartet is perfectly suited to the sometimes withdrawn, expressive intensity of Haydn's collection of seven *Adagios*. The Introduction is immediately commanding, and throughout the playing combines strength with subtlety, with the fifth and sixth movements gaining from the lean timbre, delicacy of feeling and great concentration, and the seventh (which Haydn marks 'Pater in tuas manus commendo spiritum meum') finding a natural resolution. The final 'earthquake' could hardly be more forcefully telling. Excellent, vivid recording within a well-judged ambience.

The Kodály Quartet give a memorable performance, strongly characterized and beautifully played, with subtle contrasts of expressive tension between the seven inner slow movements. They also offer an appropriate bonus in Haydn's last, unfinished, two-movement *Quartet*. The recording is first rate, vividly present yet naturally balanced, like the other issues in this attractive Naxos series.

Flawless quartet playing from the Emerson Quartet, for which it would be curmudgeonly to withhold three stars, but the performance will be too wanting in inwardness of feeling, and too glossy for many collectors.

String Quartets 57–59, Op. 54/1–3
*** HM Aeon AECD 0313, Ysaÿe Qt
*** ASV CDDCA 582. Lindsay Qt
(BB) *** Naxos 8.550395. Kodály Qt
*** Hyp. CDA 66971. Salomon Qt

These Ysaÿe performances can rank with the very best. Playing and ensemble are first class and there is plenty of warmth: the *Adagio* of the *C major*, Op. 54/2, is particularly fine, and the finale is most impressively handled. The slow movement of the *E major*, too, is beautifully judged, and the finale is both graceful and spirited. Excellent, well-balanced recording and a friendly atmosphere to make this a most enjoyable disc.

The present works show Haydn at his most inventive and resourceful. The playing of the Lindsay Quartet is splendidly poised and vital, and the recording is very fine indeed.

The Kodály players enter animatedly into the spirit of the music; the leader, Attila Falvay, shows himself fully equal to Haydn's bravura embellishments in the demanding first violin writing. The Naxos sound is fresh and truthful.

The Salomon Quartet, led by Simon Standage, play on period instruments, but there is nothing anaemic or edgy about the body of tone they command, and the pervading feeling here is of freshness, with finales spirited without being rushed off their feet. This is one of the very best records from these excellent players, and the recording is first class.

String Quartets 57–59, Op. 54/1–3; 71; 73; 74, Op. 74/1–3
(BB) *** Virgin 2×1 5 61436-2 (2). Endellion Qt

The Endellion Quartet were recorded in The Maltings, Snape (in 1988 and 1990 respectively), which provides an ideal acoustic environment. The playing is bright-eyed, fresh and vital, and in both sets they prove a sound guide to this repertoire. The sound is strikingly immediate but is beautifully integrated, and there are many moments of musical

insight. With the two discs offered for the cost of a single mid-priced CD, this set is very competitive.

String Quartets 60; 61 (Razor); 62, Op. 55/1–3 (Tost Quartets)
*** ASV CDDCA 906. Lindsay Qt
(BB) **(*) Naxos 8.550397. Kodály Qt
**(*) Hyp. CDA 66972. Salomon Qt

Here the Lindsays are heard under studio conditions, but in Holy Trinity Church, Wentworth, and the results, on the second set of *Tost Quartets*, are marginally less chimerical than in their live recordings, but not less dedicated or less vital. There is of course greater polish, as the fizzing finale of Op. 55/3 readily demonstrates. The recording is lifelike and vivid without excessive resonance.

Opus 55 brings playing from the Kodály Quartet which is undoubtedly spirited and generally polished, but the music-making at times seems plainer than usual in the Naxos series. The recording is bright and clear, with a realistic presence.

Generally fine playing from the Salomon Quartet in Op. 55, although this record is not quite as memorable as was Op. 54. The *Razor*, the second of the set, comes off very well indeed; but the slow movements in the two works on either side of it sound a shade too precise. The recording is truthful but rather close.

String Quartets 63–5, Op. 64/1–3
⊕━ *** ASV CDDCA 1083. Lindsay Qt
*** Hyp. CDA 67011. Salomon Qt
(BB) *** Naxos 8.550673. Kodály Qt

String Quartets 66; 67 (Lark); 68, Op. 64/4–6
*** Hyp. CDA 67012. Salomon Qt
⊕━ (BB) *** Naxos 8.550674. Kodály Qt

Op. 64 are splendidly played by the Lindsays and are well up to the standard of their outstanding cycle. The slow movements of the *B minor* and *B flat major* are particularly searching. First-class recording.

The Salomon performances are well up to the standard of their versions of the earlier works. Their timbre is leaner than that of the estimable Kodály Quartet on Naxos but they blend beautifully and have their own insights to offer: their precise ensemble in no way inhibits commitment and feeling. The second of the two discs is particularly rewarding, with the famous opening movement of the *Lark* readily taking flight and the *Adagio* poised and intense. The Hyperion recording is admirably truthful.

These Kodály performances are all enjoyable, but the set seems to get better and better as it progresses. Op. 64/1–3 were recorded on 25–29 April 1992; the last to be done, the *B flat major*, is remarkably successful, with a vigorous opening *Vivace assai* and a rapt *Adagio*. The other three works were taped on 1–3 May, and clearly the group had found its top form. The *Adagio cantabile e sostenuto* of No. 4 finds them at their most concentrated: the *Lark* has never soared aloft more spontaneously and the Minuet and finale of No. 6 close the set in a winningly spirited fashion. The warm acoustics of the Budapest Unitarian Church provide a mellow and expansive sound-image, but not an orchestral one, and detail remains clear. A most enjoyable set.

String Quartets 63, 65 & 68, Op. 64/1, 3 & 6
*** Astrée E 8886. Mosaïques Qt

Immaculate period-instrument performances from the

Mosaïques, with absolutely no rough edges. They are beautifully played in every respect, but are a little cool by the side of the Lindsays. However, admirers of 'authentic' Haydn will find this well up to standard, and the recording is very lifelike.

String Quartets 67 in D (Lark), Op. 64/5; 76 in D min. (Fifths), Op. 76/2; 81 in G, Op. 77/1

☛ *** HM HMC 901823. Jesusalem Qt

The Jerusalem Quartet is a first-class group and they give outstanding performances of these three masterpieces. In the D major, the 'Lark' soars aloft sweetly and disarmingly, and after a beautifully played Adagio the finale has the lightest possible touch. The first movement of the Fifths is faster than usual, but convincingly so, and the following Andante is delightfully elegant. Similarly, the opening movement of the G major dances along with engaging rhythmic pointing, and the Adagio that follows is comparably searching. The recording is beautifully balanced and sounds very real in a most suitable acoustic. Highly recommended (alongside the Lindsays on ASV).

String Quartets 69–71 (Apponyi Quartets), Op. 71/1–3

(N) **(*) Chan. 9416. Chilingirian Qt
(N) **(*) ASV Gold GLD 4012. The Lindsays

The Chilingirian's opening of the first of the Apponyi Quartets is very positive. This is spick-and-span playing, highly musical and full of character. Slow movements are well shaped and expressive, and there are moments of wit, notably in the Minuet and Trio of No. 3. The recording is truthful. Yet this playing, although by no means plain, lacks something of the sunny quality that the Kodály Quartet bring to this music.

The first instalment of Op. 71 from the Lindsays is curiously disappointing. There is much here to admire: immaculate ensemble, fine phrasing, and tension; the two closing movements of Op. 71/2 are felicitous. Yet the effect, dedicated and serious, is only sporadically completely spontaneous-sounding, failing to exude the sparkle of a really involving set of 'alive' performances that we expect from this fine group.

String Quartets 69–71 (Apponyi Quartets), Op. 71/1–3; 72–74 (Rider), Op. 74/1–3

☛ (BB) *** Naxos 8.550394 (69–71); 8.550396 (72–74). Kodály Qt
(M) *** Arcana A 918 (2). Festetics Qt

The Naxos recordings by the Kodály Quartet are outstanding in every way and would be highly recommendable even without their considerable price advantage. The digital recording has vivid presence and just the right amount of ambience: the effect is entirely natural.

The Festetics Quartet continue their period-instrument Haydn series with beautifully judged performances of Opp. 71 and 74. The playing has the customary animation and finish, with detail perceptively observed, and well-blended yet beautifully transparent textures. As before, there is nothing vinegary here, and phrasing and line are impeccably musical. Minuets are pleasing, without heaviness (sample the Trio of Op. 71/3 for delectable articulation) and finales sparkle. These are three-star performances without a doubt, and the recording could hardly be better judged. One's only reservation concerns slow movements, sometimes a little solemn.

String Quartets 71, Op. 71/3; 72 in C, Op. 74/1

**(*) Hyp. CDA 66098. Salomon Qt

String Quartets 73; 74, Op. 74/2–3

**(*) Hyp. CDA 66124. Salomon Qt

The Salomon Quartet use period instruments, vibrato-less but vibrant; the sonorities, far from being nasal and unpleasing, are clean and transparent. There is imagination and vitality here, and the Hyperion recording is splendidly truthful. However, each disc offers short measure.

String Quartets 74–76, Op. 76/4–6

*** Praga PRD 250 070. Pražák Qt

The Pražák Quartet was founded in the 1970s, while its members were still students at the Prague Conservatoire. Now, nearly three decades later, the group's ensemble intercommunication and full tonal blending are as immaculate as their musicianship is sound. As the opening Allegro con spirito of the Sunrise Quartet immediately demonstrates, this is playing of fresh vitality and polish, and the slow movements of all three works bring a profound depth of feeling, without expressive exaggeration. In short, these performances are among the finest, and the recording is most real and present.

String Quartet 74 (Rider), Op. 74/3

(B) *** HM Cal. CAL 5698. Talich Qt – BOCCHERINI: Quartet, Op. 58/2; MENDELSSOHN: Quartet 2; MICA: Quartet 6 ***

The Quartet in G minor, Op. 74, No. 3, is one of Haydn's greatest quartets. It brings a very beautiful, serenely introspective Largo assai in which, in this searching Talich performance, one has the feeling of eavesdropping on private music-making. After the blithe Minuet, the finale is engagingly light and spirited. Superb playing and most natural recording, and the rest of the performances on this generously filled mid-priced CD (76 minutes) are equally distinguished.

String Quartets 75; 76 (Fifths); 77 (Emperor); 78 (Sunrise); 79; 80, Op. 76/1–6 (Erdödy Quartets)

☛ ✪ *** ASV CDDCA 1076 (75–77); CDDCA 1077 (78–80). Lindsay Qt
*** Astrée E 8665 (2). Mosaïques Qt
(BB) *** Naxos 8.550314 (75–77); 8.550315; (78–80). Kodály Qt

String Quartets 75; 79; 80, Op. 76/1, 5 & 6

(M) *** EMI 5 56826-2. Alban Berg Qt

String Quartets 76 (Fifths); 77 (Emperor); 78 (Sunrise), Op. 76/2–4

(BB) *** Naxos 8.550129. Kodály Qt
(M) *** EMI 5 56166-2. Alban Berg Qt
(BB) *** Warner Apex 0927 40824-2. Eder Qt

The Lindsays crown their series of Haydn recordings with this superb set of the supreme masterpieces from Op. 76, marvellously played and truthfully recorded. In their hands these quartets are made to sound among the greatest ever written, which of course they are. The Lindsays have covered three of these works before, in live recordings, but this time not only is the sound more refined, the performances are too, while keeping the strength and warmth which characterize all the Lindsays' playing. The later quartets are equally fine. Very highly recommended.

The Kodály Quartet too are fully worthy of the composer's inexhaustible invention and make a splendid bargain recommendation. Their playing brings a joyful pleasure in Haydn's inspiration and there is not the slightest suspicion of over-rehearsal or of routine: every bar of the music springs to life spontaneously, and these musicians' insights bring an ideal combination of authority and warmth, emotional balance and structural awareness.

The leonine style and comparatively spare textures that are the essential feature of the playing of the Mosaïques Quartet are immediately apparent at the opening of first of the *Erdödy* set and undoubtedly cast a new and different light on Haydn's supreme masterpieces in this genre. Every detail of the polyphonic emerges clearly, but with no sense of didacticism. The recording could hardly be bettered, transparent and beautifully focused within a pleasing ambience. If you already have a modern-instrument recording of these marvellous works, this is surely an essential supplement.

The Alban Berg Quartet's set of Op. 76 offers peerless playing, with poised slow movements, simply and beautifully played, yet with every note perfectly in place. At times one might venture a suspicion that everything is too perfectly calculated, but such a judgement would be unfair, for Haydn's spirit hovers over this music-making. Perhaps they could smile a little more here. Nevertheless this is playing of distinction, bringing impeccable blending and ensemble. Although the recording is brightly lit and the effect a shade too up-front, it is realistic and admirably balanced.

The Eder is a Hungarian Quartet which came to the fore in the early to mid-1980s, when these recordings were made. The players command a refined and beautiful tone, with generally excellent ensemble and polish. These are elegant performances that are unlikely to disappoint even the most demanding listener, save perhaps in the finale of the *Emperor*, which they take a little too quickly. They are unfailingly thoughtful players whose internal balance and tonal blend are practically flawless. The recording is altogether excellent and this reissue is a bargain.

String Quartets 75–80, Op. 76/1–6; 81–2, Op. 77/1–2; 83, Op. 103

(M) *** DG (ADD) Trio 471 762-2 (3). Amadeus Qt

Haydn's late quartets have much the same expansiveness and depth as the symphonies, and here the Amadeus succeed in conveying both their intimacy and their sense of scale. The recordings are bright and truthful. Those who invest in this Trio will find much to reward them, though in Op. 76 the Kodály Quartet are even finer. However, the Amadeus accounts of the two Op. 77 *Quartets* are outstanding, as is the unfinished *D minor*, Op. 103. They are on their finest form here. There is a sense of spontaneity as well as a genuine breadth to these readings. The recordings have a warm acoustic and plenty of presence.

String Quartet 76, Op. 76/2

(**(*)) Testament mono SBT 1085. Hollywood Qt – HUMMEL: *Quartet in G* *(*); MOZART: *Quartet 17* **(*)

The Hollywood Quartet were recorded at a memorable concert in London's Royal Festival Hall in September 1957, which also included the Mozart coupling and, in the second half of the programme, the Schubert *C major Quintet*. These recordings have never been available before. The playing can only be described as impeccable, not surprisingly so, given the tonal beauty and musical sophistication these artists commanded; and the sound is astonishingly good for the period. There are a couple of minutes of balance test and a brief exchange among the players.

String Quartet 79 in D, Op. 76/5

*** Telarc CD 80415. Cleveland Qt – CORIGLIANO: *Quartet* ***

This is a superb performance, the noble simplicity of the slow movement gravely and movingly caught, and the racy finale as spic and span as it is exhilarating. Outstandingly fine recording, too, and if the coupling is unexpected it is certainly rewarding.

String Quartets 81; 82, Op. 77/1–2; 83, Op. 103

*** Astrée E 8800. Mosaïques Qt
*** HM PRD 250 157. Kocian Qt
(N) *** Australian Decca Eloquence 476 2575. Takács Qt
*** Hyp. CDA 66348. Salomon Qt

String Quartets 81; 82, Op. 77/1–2

(BB) ** Naxos 8.553146. Kodály Qt

Using period instruments to totally convincing effect, the Mosaïques Quartet give outstanding performances of Haydn's last three quartets. They play with much subtlety of colour and dynamic and bring total concentration to every bar of the music. The *D minor Quartet*, Haydn's last, is beautifully judged. The recording is absolutely real: the sound is transparent as well as immediate. This is among the finest of all Haydn quartet records.

Those preferring modern-instrument performances could hardly do better than invest in the Kocian Quartet. Allegros sparkle, ensemble is clean and true, and slow movements are beautifully played, notably the eloquent variations of Op. 77/2, but also the *Andante grazioso* of Haydn's last quartet, where the hint of melancholy is nicely understated. The recording is very real, the players not too close in an attractive acoustic.

The Takács Quartet play with warmth, expressive refinement and vitality, and the Decca recording has clean, well-focused sound, with just about the right degree of resonance. Though this is not perhaps a first choice, their admirers need not hesitate.

The Salomon, recorded in a less ample acoustic, produce an altogether leaner sound but one that is thoroughly responsive to every shift in Haydn's thought. They seem to have great inner vitality and feeling.

The Kodály Quartet give comparatively robust performances of both works, made to seem even more robust by the close balance which reduces the dynamic range – not that the playing is notable for *pianissimo* contrast. This is warm, friendly music-making and in that respect (and in that respect only) preferable to the Mosaïques; but the latter's playing has considerably more subtlety, and they offer an extra work.

PIANO SONATAS

Keyboard Sonatas 1–62; Adagio in F, Hob XVII/9; Capriccio in G, Hob XVII/1; Fantasia in C, Hob XVII/4; 20 Variations in A, Hob XVII/2; 12 Variations in E flat, Hob XVII/3; 6 Variations in C, Hob XVII/5; Variations in F min., Hob XVII/6; 5 Variations in D, Hob XVII/7; (i) Partita for two harpsichords, Hob XVIIa

(N) (B) **(*) Capriccio 40 494 (14). Schornsheim (various keyboard instruments), (i) with Staier

Capriccio offer a useful, scholarly and exhaustive survey of the Haydn *Keyboard Sonatas*, made in collaboration with Westdeutschen Rundfunks, Cologne, and making use of appropriate period instruments, from a modern unfretted clavichord to a 1777 Kirckman harpsichord, a 1793 Dulcken fortepiano and a 1804 Broadwood pianoforte, among others. The last CD presents an interesting discussion of the six instruments in question. Christine Schornsheim has made a couple of records for Capriccio, but this is a major venture. She is a cultured musician and plays with an excellent sense of style, and she has a naturalness and freedom of expression that are very persuasive. The essays and documentation are as good as the recordings. Doubtless Ronald Brautigam's survey on BIS has the stronger profile and distinction, but this set is more than acceptable in its own right, and it enjoys a price advantage. Those who have invested in the Brautigam set can pass this by, and those who prefer the sonatas on the modern piano have the excellent McCabe survey and various individual discs to treasure. But the present set is far from uncompetitive.

Piano Sonatas 1–16; 17–19 (Hob Deest) 20; 28, Hob XIV/5; 29–62, Hob XVI/1–52 & G1; Hob XVII/D1; The Seven Last Words on the Cross; Adagio in F; Capriccio in G on the song 'Acht Sauschneider müssen sein'; Fantasia in C; 7 Minuets from 'Kleine Tänz für die Jugend'; Variations in F min.; 5 Variations in D; 6 Variations in C; 12 Variations in E flat; 20 Variations in A
(B) *** Decca (ADD) 443 785-2 (12). McCabe (piano)

John McCabe made the first successful complete survey of the Haydn *Sonatas* for Argo between 1974 and 1977, including also *The Seven Last Words on the Cross*, an arrangement not made by the composer but approved by him. It is remarkably successful here. Indeed two things shine through John McCabe's performances: their complete musicianship and their fine imagination. In presenting them as he does on a modern piano, McCabe makes the most of the colour and subtlety of the music, and in that respect his style is more expressive, less overtly classical than Jandó's (see below) while the recording is made to sound somewhat softer-grained by the acoustic of All Saints' Church, Petersham. Given phrasing so clearly articulated and alertly phrased, and such varied, intelligently thought-out and wholly responsive presentation, this set can be recommended very enthusiastically. The recordings are of the very highest quality, truthful in timbre and firmly refined in detail, and they must be numbered among the most successful of this repertoire ever to be put on disc, for the piano is notoriously difficult to balance in eighteenth-century music. The set is most reasonably priced and the pianist provides his own extensive and illuminating notes. To sample the calibre of this enterprise, begin with *The Seven Last Words* – playing of unexaggerated expressive feeling that almost makes one believe this was a work conceived in pianistic terms.

Keyboard (Divertimento) Sonatas 1–20, Hob XVI/1–16 & G1; D1; 17–18, Hob Es2 & 3; 19, Hob XVI/47; 20, Hob XVI/18
(M) *** BIS CD 1293/4 (3). Brautigam (fortepiano)

With this volume, the ninth in his Haydn survey, Ronald Brautigam turns to the early 'Divertimeno' sonatas that were written in the 1750s and 1760s for the clavichord or harpsichord. Brautigam uses a fortepiano, a copy by Paul McNulty of a mid-1790s instrument by Walter. Many of the earlier sonatas are of little consequence and Haydn did not include them in his list of complete keyboard works that he made for Breitkopf. The more individual sonatas, such as the *E minor*, No. 19, Hob XVI/47, and the *B flat*, No. 20, Hob XVI/18, come

from the 1760s and are played with imagination and delicacy. Overall, the short sonatas that predominate in this three-CD set are not the most substantial or satisfying of Haydn's keyboard output and the discs are primarily of value in completing the picture. Good playing and exemplary recording, but ultimately the set is for completists.

Piano Sonatas 1, Hob. XVI/8; 2, Hob XVI/7; 3, Hob XVI/9; 4, Hob XVI/G1; 5, Hob XVI/11; 6, Hob XVI/10; 7, Hob XVII/D1; 8, Hob XVI/5; 9, Hob XVI/4; 10, Hob XVI/1
(BB) *** Naxos 8.553824. Jandó

There are no autograph manuscripts of Haydn's earliest sonatas, which were all written before 1766. The authenticity of No. 1 (Hob. XVI/8) is certain, and many of the others of these three-movement works bear the same musical fingerprint and a characteristic simplicity of style. Doubts have been expressed about No. 8 (Hob XVI/5), but it is presented attractively enough here. Indeed Jenö Jandó seems in his element throughout: his freshness of approach and stylistic confidence are consistently striking. The recording too is excellent, and overall this Naxos series can be recommended with confidence.

Piano Sonatas 11, Hob XVI/2; 12, Hob XVI/12; 13, Hob XVI/6; 14, Hob XVI/3; 15, Hob XVI/13; 16, Hob XVI/14; 18, Hob XVI deest
(BB) *** Naxos 8.553825. Jandó

These early sonatas are all played freshly in Jandó's pleasingly direct style. All but one are simple, three-movement works; the exception is *No. 13 in G*, which has an appealing additional *Adagio* which Jandó treats simply but appealingly. The recording is truthful and this issue, Volume 8 in the series, cannot be faulted.

Piano Sonatas 20, Hob XVI/18; 30, Hob XVI/19; 31, Hob XVI/46; 32, Hob XVI/44
(BB) **(*) Naxos 8.553364. Jandó

Jandó continues his Haydn sonata series in his clean, direct style. The first movement of the *G minor Sonata* is particularly appealing, with its neat articulation and tight little runs, and the same might be said of the opening movement of the *A flat major* (No. 31), while its finale is similarly bright and sparkling. But first prize goes to the closing movement of the *D major*, which skips along delightfully and brings quite dazzling dexterity. The thoughtful *Adagio* of the *B flat major*, however, is just a little too studied; but this is not enough of a disadvantage to prevent a recommendation. The piano recording is very realistic.

Piano Sonatas 24, Hob XVI/26; 30, Hob XVI/19; 32, Hob XVI/44; 33, Hob XVI/20; 44, Hob XVI/29
☛ ✪ *** EMI 5 56756-2. Andsnes

Playing of great elegance and consummate artistry, the finest Haydn sonata recording to have appeared for a long time. Very different in approach from Pletnev's 1989 recital (see below) – the repertoire does not overlap – but no less individual or persuasive. The young Norwegian pianist plays with rare imagination and keyboard colour, and the EMI sound is first class. The recordings are all made in Abbey Road, save for the *E flat* (No. 44), which was recorded in Oslo.

Piano Sonatas 28 in D, Hob XVI/5a; 29 in E flat, Hob XVI/45; 30 in D, Hob XVI/19
*** BIS CD 1174. Brautigam

Piano Sonatas 31 in A flat, Hob XVI/46; 45 in A, Hob XVI/30; 46 in E, Hob XVI/31; 47 in B min., Hob XVI/32
*** BIS CD 1194. Brautigam

Piano Sonatas 32 in G min., Hob XVI/44; 34 in D, Hob XVI/33; 42 in G, Hob XVI/27; 43 in E flat, Hob XVI/28; 44 in F, Hob XVI/39
*** BIS CD 1093. Brautigam

Piano Sonatas 35 in A flat, Hob XVI/43; 36 in C, Hob XVI/21; 37 in F, Hob XVI/22; 38 in F, Hob XVI/23
*** BIS CD 1095. Brautigam

Ronald Brautigam continues his much and rightly admired Haydn odyssey. We can only re-echo our continued enthusiasm for this set. Brautigam has tremendous life and combines apparent spontaneity of expression and scholarship. Those who are rightly content with Haydn on the piano played by a great pianist should still investigate this wonderful series which apart from its exhilarating freshness and virtuosity brings us so close to Haydn's world. The recordings are altogether exemplary.

Piano Sonatas 29; 31; 34; 35; 49, Hob XVI/45, 46, 33, 43 & 36
☛ (N) *** Sony SK 89363. Ax

If you want Haydn *Sonatas* on a modern grand piano, you would have to go a long way to beat these elegant accounts by Emanuel Ax. They are fluent and unmannered, sensitive and vital, and they are very well recorded. An excellent sampler for some of the composer's most attractive keyboard works.

Piano Sonatas 29, Hob XVI/45; 33, Hob XVI/20; 34, Hob XVI/33; 35, Hob XVI/43
(BB) *** Naxos 8.553800. Jandó

Jandó is on very good form here. His style is a little plain and classical but never insensitive, and he is well recorded. A useful addition to a fine series.

Piano Sonatas 31, Hob XVI/46; 45–47, Hob XVI/30–32
*** BIS CD 1094. Brautigam

Piano Sonatas 32, Hob XVI/44; 34, Hob XVI/33; 42–4, Hob XVI/27–29
*** BIS CD 1093. Brautigam

These two recordings in Ronald Brautigam's ongoing Haydn cycle are devoted to the sonatas of 1776, and they are as refreshing and alive as earlier issues in this eminently collectable series. The high spirits are contagious, but nothing is ever driven too fast, and at no time does Brautigam step outside the sensibility of the period; the only reservation concerns the *A flat Sonata* (No. 31, Hob XVI/46), which is a shade judicious and without his usual sparkle. He uses a copy made in 1992 by Paul McNulty of a fortepiano by Anton Gabriel Walter from about 1795. Wonderful recorded sound.

Piano Sonatas 32 in G min., Hob XVI/44; 33 in C min., Hob XVI/20; 53 in E min. Hob XVI/34; 54 in G, Hob XVI/40; 58 in C, Hob. XVI/48
(M) *** Warner Elatus 2564 60677-2. Schiff

Piano Sonatas 59–62, Hob XVI/49–52; Fantasia in C, Hob XVII/4
(M) *** Warner Elatus 2564 60807-2. Schiff

András Schiff's Haydn recordings were much acclaimed when they first appeared in 1999. They are now released at mid-price. Recorded in the Berlin Teldec studios by Christopher Raeburn, one of Decca's most distinguished producers,

this is a collection issue of high quality – and it comes with the original essays by Misha Donat.

Piano Sonatas: 33, Hob XVI/20; 34, Hob XVI/33; 48–52, Hob XVI/35–9; 53, Hob XVI/34; 58–62, Hob XVI/48–52; Andante with Variations in F min., Hob XVII/6; Arietta with 12 Variations in E flat, Hob XVII/3; Variations on the hymn, 'Gott erhalte', Hob III/711
☛ (N) (B) *** DHM/BMG 82876 67376-2 (3). Staier (fortepiano)

In this competitively priced set Andreas Staier's collection of Haydn's middle and late *Sonatas* is one of the best collections on the market. He gives us the late sonatas and variations, including what must be one of the most searching accounts of the *F minor* set ever recorded. He uses two fine instruments modelled on fortepianos by Anton Walter from the early 1790s. He is a player of great imaginative flair, and these early 1990s performances are arguably unchallenged, even by Ronald Brautigam's full-priced survey on BIS. Staier proves a highly sensitive and imaginative interpreter. He brings a surprisingly wide dynamic range as well as a diversity of keyboard colour to these works (including the variations) and holds the listener throughout. He is very well recorded indeed.

Piano Sonatas 33, Hob XVI/20; 39, Hob XVI/39; 40, Hob XVI/25; 41, Hob XVI/26
*** BIS CD 1163. Brautigam (fortepiano)

Piano Sonatas 35, Hob XVI/43; 36, Hob XVI/21; 37, Hob XVI/22; 38, Hob XVI/23
*** BIS CD 1095. Brautigam (fortepiano)

With the present pair of CDs Brautigam reaches the *Esterházy Sonatas* (Nos. 36–41), dating from 1773. The additional sonatas, *No. 33 in C minor* (Hob XVI/20) and *No. 35 in A flat* (Hob XVI/43) come from 1771 and the period 1771–3 respectively, though doubt has been cast on the latter's authenticity. However, both Christa Landon and Georg Feder think it genuine.

Piano Sonatas 33, Hob XVI/20; 47, Hob XVI/32; 53, Hob XVI/34; 50, Hob XVI/37; 54, Hob XVI/40; 56, Hob XVI/42; 58–62, Hob XVI/48–52; Adagio in F, Hob XVII/9; Andante with Variations in F min., Hob XVII/6; Fantasia in C, Hob XVII/4
*** Ph. ADD/DDD 416 643-2 (4). Brendel

This collection offers some of the best Haydn playing on record – and some of the best Brendel, too. The eleven sonatas, together with the *F minor Variations* and the *C major Fantasia*, have been recorded over a number of years and are splendidly characterized and superbly recorded. The first is analogue, the remainder digital.

Piano Sonatas 33, Hob XVI/20; 60, Hob XVI/50; 62, Hob XVI/52; Andante & Variations in F min., Hob XVII/6
☛ (BB) *** Virgin 2x1 5 61881-2. Pletnev – *Piano Concertos, Hob XVIII/4, 7 & 11* ***

Pletnev's reading of the *Sonatas* is full of personality and character. The *C major* is given with great elegance and wit, and the great *E flat Sonata* is magisterial. This playing has a masterly authority, and Pletnev is very well recorded. Now coupled with his equally memorable accounts of Haydn's three finest piano concertos, this reissue is a splendid bargain and one not to be missed.

Piano Sonatas 36, Hob XVI/21; 37, Hob XVI/22; 38, Hob XVI/23; 39, Hob XVI/24; 40, Hob XVI/25; 41, Hob XVI/26
(BB) *** Naxos 8.553127. Jandó

The sonatas in Volume 5 of the Naxos series form a set of six, written in 1773 and dedicated to Prince Nikolaus Esterházy. They are all attractive works and they inspire Jandó to consistently fine performances, as the opening of No. 36 immediately shows. The finale of No. 37 is beautifully played, and the following two sonatas with their striking slow movements will not disappoint either. This is one of the most rewarding issues in this admirable series. Excellent piano sound.

Piano Sonatas 38, Hob XVI/23; 51, Hob XVI/38; 52, Hob XVI/39
*** Mer. (ADD) CDE 84155. Cload

Julia Cload's cool, unidiosyncratic style is heard at its best in her second group of sonatas. The piano image is bright and clear, with just a touch of hardness on *forte*s.

Piano Sonatas 42, Hob XVI/27; 43, Hob XVI/28; 44, Hob XVI/29; 45, Hob XVI/30; 46, Hob XVI/31; 47, Hob XVI/32
(BB) *** Naxos 8.550844. Jandó (piano)

The last work here, in B minor, opens with perhaps the most striking idea of all and, after the gracious central Minuet, ends in a flurry of precocious virtuosity, with Jandó clearly in his element. He shows himself a complete master of this repertoire, and the recording, crisp and clean but not too dry, is first class.

Piano Sonatas 47 in B min., Hob XVI/32; 53 in E min., Hob XVI/34; 56 in D, Hob XVI/42; Adagio in F, Hob XVII/9; Fantasia in C, Hob XVII/4
❂ (M) *** Ph. 476 1715-2. Brendel

Here is a Haydn recital about which we waxed enthusiastic when it first appeared in the 1980s. The disc was soon withdrawn (although the recordings remained available in a boxed set), but now happily Universal have reissued it at medium price as part of the 'Penguin ❂ Collection'. Brendel's performances are marvellously held together, self-aware at times, as many great performances are, but inspiriting and always governed by the highest intelligence. The *B minor Sonata* has a *Sturm und Drang* urgency, and Brendel's account has vitality and character. Moreover, the recording is splendidly realistic.

Piano Sonatas 48, Hob XVI/35; 49, Hob XVI/36; 50, Hob XVI/37; 51, Hob XVI/38; 52 in G, Hob XVI/39
(BB) *** Naxos 8.553128. Jandó

The sonatas in Volume 5 were part of a set of six published in 1780 and dedicated to the sisters Caterina and Marianna Auenbrugger, both proficient young players, admired by Leopold Mozart. Not all these works were newly written, and this shows in the writing; but their clear layout is obviously designed to attract talented amateurs. The opening movement of No. 49 and the memorable *Largo e sostenuto* of No. 50 (and its infectious finale) show Jandó in top form; in the other works his bright, stylish playing is always responsive to Haydn's direct, lively manner. We underrated this disc on its first appearance. The recording is well up to the high standard of this series.

Piano Sonatas 48, Hob XVI/35; 49, Hob XVI/36; 50, Hob XVI/37; 51, Hob XVI/38; 52, Hob XVI/39
*** BIS CD 992. Brautigam (fortepiano)

Piano Sonatas 53, Hob XVI/34; 54, Hob XVI/40; 55, Hob XVI/41; 56, Hob XVI/42; 57, Hob XVI/47; 58, Hob XVI/48
(M) *** BIS CD 300993. Brautigam (fortepiano)

Piano Sonatas 59, Hob XVI/49; 60, Hob XVI/50; 61, Hob XVI/51; 62, Hob XVI/52
*** BIS CD 994. Brautigam (fortepiano)

Ronald Brautigam's first disc here is given over to five of the so-called *Auenbrugger Sonatas*, Nos. 48–52 or Hob XVI/35–39, which Jandó has also recorded. Brautigam is hardly less vital and imaginative here than in Mozart. Apart from his technical virtuosity, his playing has tremendous flair and sparkle. This is spirited and life-loving music-making and almost ideally recorded. The second disc (CD 300993) includes the *Bossler Sonatas* (Nos. 54–6), so-called because they were published by the house of Bossler. Brautigam gives them with tremendous flair and, in the *Presto* of *G major* (No. 54, Hob XVI/40), great wit. The *B flat Sonata* (No. 55, Hob XVI/41) is played with conspicuous relish, and in fact the whole disc is a delight from beginning to end. The third (CD 994) brings the *Genzinger Sonata* (No. 59), so named because Marianne von Genzinger was its dedicatee, and three *London Sonatas*, composed in 1794–5, when Haydn was in his early sixties. The *E flat Major* (No. 62, Hob XVI/52) is the biggest and most symphonic of all. Exhilarating playing which augurs well for the rest of the series.

Piano Sonatas 50, Hob XVI/37; 54, Hob XVI/40; 55, Hob XVI/41; Adagio in F, Hob XVII/9
*** Mer. (ADD) ECD 84083. Cload

Julia Cload's playing is fresh, characterful and intelligent, and will give considerable pleasure. She has the advantage of very truthful recorded sound.

Piano Sonatas 53, Hob XVI/34; 54, Hob XVI/40; 55, Hob XVI/41; 56, Hob XVI/42; 58, Hob XVI/48; Variations in F min. (Sonata, un piccolo divertimento), Hob XVII/6
(BB) *** Naxos 8.550845. Jandó (piano)

These are appealing performances of the three *Sonatas*, Hob XVI/40–42, dedicated to Princess Marie Esterházy. All three are fine works and not as simple as they at first appear. Jandó also gives a splendid account of the more ambitious three-movement *Sonata in E minor*, Hob XVI/34. He is a true Haydn player, and this is in every way recommendable, particularly as the recording is so vivid and clean: just right for the repertoire.

Piano Sonatas 58–62, Hob XVI/48–52
(M) *(**) Sony SMK 87857. Gould

Glenn Gould recorded Haydn's last five *Piano Sonatas* in 1981/2 and his clean, classical style is often refreshing, but after a while his squeaky-clean articulation, although quite remarkably crisp, becomes a little wearing and the ear craves less staccato and a less percussive approach to allegros. This is not a fortepiano imitation but a pianoforte played with the most sparing sonority. Gould undoubtedly makes a sensitively expressive response to slow movements, but an air of eccentricity remains in the overall shaping of phrases, and the irritating vocalise is always there to disturb the otherwise silent background. The digital recording is clear and truthful. Aficionados will notice that this survey was originally on two discs; now, for the Anniversary Edition, the reissue is accommodated on one without difficulty.

Piano Sonatas 59–62, Hob XVI/49–52

(BB) *** Naxos 8.550657. Jandó

Without allowing himself stylistic idiosyncrasies, Jandó here shows himself a thoughtfully imaginative player as well as a bold one, and the finale of the great *E flat Sonata* has splendid, unforced bravura. The recording, made in the Unitarian Church, Budapest, provides an attractive ambience without an excess of ecclesiastical resonance.

Piano Sonatas 60 in C, Hob XVI/50; 62 in E flat, Hob XVI/52

(N) *** Channel Classics **SACD** CCSSA19703. Lazic –
   BEETHOVEN: *Piano Concerto 2* ***

There is a muscularity and bite in the Haydn performances of these two so-called 'English' *Sonatas*: without apology they make no attempt to charm, often leaning towards fierceness; yet, with the crispest possible articulation, they are electrically alive. They make an unusual and illuminating coupling for Lazic's live recording of the Beethoven *Concerto*.

Other piano music

Adagios: in G, Hob XV/22II & F, Hob XVII/9. Allegrettos: in G, Hob XVII/10 & Hob III/411V (authentic version of the finale of the String Quartet in G, Op. 33/5). Andante and Variations in: A, Hob XVII/A3; F min., Hob XVII/6; D, Hob XVII/7; B flat, Hob XVII/12. Andantino (Allegretto) with Variations in A, Hob XVII/8; Aria with Variations in C, Hob XVII/15; Ariettas with 12 Variations in E flat, Hob XV11/3 & A, Hob XVII/2. Capriccio in G, Hob XVII/1 'Acht Sauschneider müssen seyn'; 6 Easy Variations in C, Hob XVII/5; Fantasia in C, Hob XVII/4; 12 German Dances, Hob IX/12; Il Maestro e lo Scolare in F, Hob XVIIa/1; Kontretanz, Hob XXXI/c:17b; March, Hob. VIII/3/3bis; 2 Marches (for Sir Henry Harpur), Hob VIII/1; 12 Minuets: Hob IX/3, 8 & 11. Variations in G on the Hymn, 'Gott erhalte Franz, den Kaiser', Hob III/77II; 20 Variations in G, Hob XVII/2.

*** BIS CD 1323/4 (3). Brautigam (fortepiano)

This is the tenth and penultimate survey of Haydn's keyboard music by Ronald Brautigam (only the keyboard arrangement of *The Seven Last Words* remains). Its contents range from the remarkable *Andante con variazioni in F minor* with its wide range of feeling to the delightful *Deutsche Tänze*, which older collectors will remember from Mogens Wöldike's 78rpm set (now on the Dutton label). The diversity and range of Haydn's invention never fail to surprise and delight. As always, Brautigam's playing has an irresistible vitality and finesse – and Ingo Petry's recording (he also serves as the pupil in *Il Maestro e lo Scolare*) is excellently balanced.

Adagios: in F, Hob XVII/9; in G, Hob XV/22 (II); Allegrettos: in G after Hob III/41 (IV); in G, Hob XVII/10; Arietta with 12 Variations in A, Hob XVII/2; Fantasia in C (Capriccio), Hob XVII/4; Piano Sonatas 17, Hob deest; 19, Hob XVI/47bis; 28, Hob XVI/5a (incomplete)

(BB) *** Naxos 8.553826. Jandó

Jenö Jandó is at his best in the simple *Adagios* and *Allegrettos* (that in G, Hob III/41, is an arrangement of the engaging variations from the 'How do you do?' *Quartet*, Op. 33/5). He gives a strongly impulsive and exciting account of the *Fantasia in C*, which ends the recital boldly. The two complete sonatas are a shade on the literal side, but still fresh; however, he does not make much of the unfinished fragment of the

first movement of *No. 28 in D*, where he tends to rush his fences. The good things here outweigh reservations, there is much to enjoy, and the recording is up to standard.

VOCAL MUSIC

Arianna a Naxos (cantata)

*** Decca 440 297-2. Bartoli, Schiff – BEETHOVEN: *Che fa il mio bene?*, etc.; MOZART: *Ridente la calma;* SCHUBERT: *Da quel sembiante appresi*, etc ***

(B) *** EMI Début 5 85559-2. Coote, Drake – MAHLER: *Das Knaben Wunderhorn* (excerpts), etc.; SCHUMANN: *Frauenliebe und Leben.* ***

Arianna a Naxos; Fidelity; The mermaid's song; Pastoral song; Sailor's song; She never told her love; Spirit's song; Der verdienstvolle Sylvius

*** DG (IMS) 447 106-2. Von Otter, Tan (fortepiano) – MOZART: *Lieder* ***

To declare a preference between Cecilia Bartoli and Anne Sofie von Otter or indeed Arleen Augér (see below) in Haydn's extended scena is virtually impossible. With its double alternating recitative and aria, the first doubtful concerning a lover's faithfulness, the second expressing the despair and anger of known betrayal, Haydn's setting demands the widest range of mood and identification with the words; both singers rise to the occasion with passion and consummate artistry. Bartoli has the inestimable András Schiff as partner; Von Otter has Melvyn Tan's eloquent fortepiano. So in the end it depends on the couplings: the other Haydn songs on the DG disc are happily varied in mood, to bring either innocent simplicity (*Pastoral song*), histrionics (*Fidelity*) – with Tan very much rising to the occasion – or touching, unexaggerated pathos (*She never told her love* and *Der verdienstvolle Sylvius*). By comparison, the *Sailor's song* is suitably robust and the melancholy *Spirit's song*, which ends the recital, pensively nostalgic. The recording balance is just about ideal.

The mezzo Alice Coote offers a comparably stylish performance, which stands well against this formidable competition, with her wide range of dynamic and tone-colour adding to the drama. This is one of the very finest of EMI's admirable Début series, though – as with other EMI issues of Lieder at budget price – no texts or translations are given.

Arianna a Naxos (orchestral version); *Scena di Berenice; Miseri noi, miserata patria!; Son pietosa, son bonina; Solo e pensoso*

☛ (N) *** Avie AV 2066. Augér, Handel & Haydn Society O, Hogwood

Originally issued on the Handel and Haydn Society's own label, this 1988 recording of three cantatas and two arias is a valuable reminder of the beauty and brilliance of Arleen Augér's singing in the years before her untimely death from cancer in 1993. With Christopher Hogwood drawing fresh, alert playing from the Society's orchestra, Augér holds the contrasted sections of the two big cantatas, the *Scena di Berenice* and *Arianna a Naxos* firmly together. The latter is performed in an anonymous eighteenth-century orchestral arrangement – legitimately so, when Haydn himself expressed his intention of orchestrating the original keyboard part. The third cantata, *Miseri noi*, like the *Scena di Berenice*, is another jewel not published until well on in the twentieth century. Those and the two arias – *Solo e pensoso* is a setting of a Petrarch sonnet – inspire Augér to heartfelt singing, helped by immaculate recording, engineered by a Decca team. Full texts are provided.

Canzonettas, Book 1 (1794), Hob XXVIa:25–30; Book 2 (1795), Hob XXVIa:31–6

(N) (BB) **(*) Warner Apex 2564 61746-2. Griffett, Tracey (fortepiano)

Haydn composed these two groups of 'Canzonettas' in co-operation with Anne Hunter, the widow of a distinguished London surgeon. She wrote the verses herself for 11 of the 14 songs and selected lyrics by Shakespeare and Metastasio for the remaining three. Haydn responded with attractive settings of a fairly wide musical range, and although these are little more than drawing-room ballads there is some evidence that Haydn himself sang some of them for King George III on his second London visit to London in 1794/5. The best known are the catchy nautical numbers, the *Mermaid's Song* and the *Sailor's Song*, but the Pastoral, *My mother bids me bind my hair*, is attractive too, and perhaps the finest of all is *The Spirit's Song*, the penultimate number of the second set. If without quite the individuality of Von Otter, above, they are sung pleasingly and eloquently by James Griffett with supportive fortepiano accompaniments from Bradford Tracey. This is not momentous Haydn, but nearly all the songs have genuine character and charm; full texts are included and the disc is temptingly inexpensive.

The Creation (complete; in English)

*** EMI 7 54159-2 (2). Augér, Langridge, Thomas, CBSO & Ch., Rattle

**(*) Telarc CD 80298 (2). Upshaw, Humphrey, Cheek, Murphy, McGuire, Chamber Ch. & SO, Shaw

The English version may have its oddities – like the 'flexible tiger' leaping – but it is above all colourful, and Rattle brings out that illustrative colour with exceptional vividness: birdsong, lion-roars and the like. He has plainly learnt from period performance, not only concerning speeds – often surprisingly brisk, as in the great soprano aria, *With verdure clad* – but as regards style too. The male soloists sound none too sweet as recorded, but they characterize positively; and there is no finer account of the soprano's music than that of Arleen Augér. The weight of the Birmingham chorus is impressive, achieved without loss of clarity or detail in a full, well-balanced recording.

Robert Shaw with his keenly disciplined chamber choir conducts a strong, clean-cut performance, using an English translation modified from the traditional one. Though Shaw's generally broad speeds show little influence from period performance, his concern for clarity of texture is very different from old-style performances, and the Telarc engineers help with full, immediate sound, bringing out sharp dynamic contrasts. Dawn Upshaw adopts too romantically expressive a manner, but the solo singing is good, with Heidi Grant Murphy and James Michael McGuire brought in for the Adam and Eve numbers of Part 3.

The Creation (Die Schöpfung; complete in German) (DVD version)

⊕ (N) *** Capriccio Surround Sound **DVD** 93 507. Cencic, Schmidt, Bauer, Jankowitsch, V. Boys' Ch., Ch. Viennensis, V. Volksoper SO, Marschik (V/D: Axel Stummer)

A splendid 1994 DVD of Haydn's *Creation* can be most cordially recommended. It may not have soloists of quite the individuality of the top CD versions, notably Karajan's, but they are a fine team with the rich-voiced bass, Ernst Jankowitsch, dominating, first as a resonant Rafael, and in Part 3 as a fine, mature Adam, where he is an excellent match for Gertraud Schmidt. She is not a young Eve, but she has a lovely voice and sings impressively. Christian Bauer is a fresh-voiced Uriel who discards his glasses not long before the interval, and the male soprano, Max Emanuel Cencic, deals with Gabriel's coloratura with ease, even if he has a curious lip-vibrato. His voice is so like that of a woman's and he is costumed in male-styled evening dress, so that at his first solo entry one does a visual double-take, and it takes a while to adjust to such a beautiful high soprano voice emerging from an obviously masculine figure. The choral singing is first class and the conductor has the performance firmly in his grip: at the opening, the 'Representation of Chaos' is powerfully evoked. His concentration goes with a serious demeanour, and he smiles only a couple of times in the first two Parts of the oratorio. He then relaxes and obviously enjoys the warm lyricism of Part 3, and this gives the performance an added joyful lift at exactly the right moment, as Haydn radiantly celebrates the creation of mankind. The visual backcloth and the atmospheric acoustics of the Grosser Saal of the Musikverein add to one's pleasure, for the Surround Sound is full and vivid, well balanced, with an impressive dynamic range and good clarity. The camera moves around but is generally focused on the main events of the narrative – vocally or orchestrally. However, the video director has his favourite shots and returns to the very personable principal flautist for almost all her solos. All in all, a real success, with a feeling of participation for the viewer, and certainly a performance to return to. Subtitles should be available if required (and they are needed to appreciate Haydn's word-settings to the full), although on some players it seems difficult to get the English subtitles. The German-language booklet, however, is a disgrace: the English translation suddenly cuts off in the middle of the biographical note about the soloist, Max Emanuel Cencic, and does not mention the male soloists at all!

The Creation (Die Schöpfung; in German)

⊕ *** DHM/BMG 82876 58340-2 (2). Röschmann, Schade, Gerhaher, Arnold Schoenberg Ch., VCM, Harnoncourt

(N) (M) (***) DG mono 474 955-2 (2). Janowitz, Wunderlich, Prey, Borg, V. Singverein, VPO, Karajan

⊕ (M) *** DG (ADD) 449 761-2 (2). Janowitz, Ludwig, Wunderlich, Krenn, Fischer-Dieskau, Berry, V. Singverein, BPO, Karajan

(N) (BB) *** Naxos 8.557380/81 (2). Im, Kobow, Müller-Brachmann, Cologne Vocal Ens., Capella Augustina, Spering

*** DG 449 217-2 (2). McNair, Brown, Schade, Finley, Gilfry, Monteverdi Ch., E. Bar. Sol., Gardiner

(B) *** Sony SX2K 57965 (2). Monoyios, Hering, Van der Kamp, Tölz Boys' Ch., Tafelmusik, Weil

(B) *** DG Double (ADD) 453 031-2. Blegen, Popp, Moser, Ollman, Moll, Bav. R. Ch. & SO, Bernstein

*** DHM/BMG 05472 77537-2 (2). Kermes, Mields, Davislim, Mannov, Chung, Balthasar-Neumann Ch. & Ens., Hengelbrock

(BB) **(*) EMI double forte 5 75163-2 (2). Bonney, Blochwitz, Rootering, Wiens, Bär, SW German R. Ch. & O, Stuttgart, Marriner

(M) **(*) DG (IMS) 445 584-2 (2). Battle, Winbergh, Moll, Stockholm R. Ch. and Chamber Ch., BPO, Levine

(B) **(*) EMI double forte 5 69343-2 (2). Donath, Tear, van Dam, Philh. Ch. & O, Frühbeck de Burgos

(i) *The Creation (Die Schöpfung)*: complete (in German);
(ii) *Salve regina*

(B) *** Double Decca (ADD) 443 027-2 (2). (i) Popp, Hollweg, Moll, Döse, Luxon, Brighton Festival Ch., RPO, Dorati; (ii) Augér, Hodgson, Rolfe Johnson, Howell, L. Chamber Ch., Argo CO, Heltay

Celebrating their fiftieth anniversary at the Musikvereinsaal in Vienna, Nikolaus Harnoncourt and the Concentus Musicus give an incandescent account of Haydn's *Creation*, recorded live. This warm and dramatic reading is very different from the very scholarly and sometimes abrasive performances that marked much of the early work of the Concentus Musicus, admirable as it always was. Harnoncourt, benefiting from his wide experience conducting orchestras of every kind in a wide range of repertory, here inspires a natural warmth that infects all the performers, the outstanding Arnold Schoenberg Choir as well as the three splendid soloists, the soprano Dorothea Röschmann at once full and clear, the tenor Michael Schade heady and unstrained and the finely focused bass Christian Gerhaher plainly benefiting from his experience as a Lieder singer. The live atmosphere adds to the dramatic bite of the performance from the start, with period players in a substantial body bringing out the daring originality of such passages as the *Chaos Prelude*. The recording, well forward with weighty brass, adds to the drama, not least with the great entry of the chorus on the word, *Licht* ('Light'), thrillingly powerful. A triumphant celebration of 50 years' achievement.

As the last event of the 1965 Salzburg Festival, Herbert von Karajan conducted his Viennese forces in a performance of Haydn's oratorio, *Die Schöpfung, The Creation*, universally acclaimed as magnetic. Here we have glowing proof of that judgement in a live recording made by Austrian Radio, a valuable supplement to the two studio recordings which Karajan went on to record. The first of his studio versions, begun the following year, was sadly interrupted when the tenor, Fritz Wunderlich, was tragically killed, and another tenor was brought in for the missing passages. Here we have Wunderlich complete, singing superbly, not just heedily sweet of tone but dramatic too, while Gundula Janowitz, at the beginning of her career, never sounded more radiant, heart-stoppingly beautiful in her purity of tone. Excellent contributions too from Hermann Prey as Adam and Kim Borg as Raphael. The radio sound is in mono only, but gives splendid weight and contrast to choir and orchestra as well as to the soloists.

Among regular versions of *The Creation* sung in German, Karajan's 1969 set remains unsurpassed and at mid-price is a clear first choice, despite two small cuts (in Nos. 30 and 32). The combination of the Berlin Philharmonic at its most intense and the great Viennese choir makes for a performance that is not only polished but warm and dramatically strong too. The soloists are an extraordinarily fine team, more consistent in quality than those on almost any rival version.

Recorded in Cologne in July 2003 by German Radio, this Naxos issue offers another first-rate period performance of Haydn's masterpiece, lively and very well sung. When other issues of *Die Schöpfung* in the super-bargain category use modern instruments, it fills an important gap, particularly when the digital sound is so clear and transparent. The opening prelude representing Chaos is taken very slowly, but that brings out all the more the abrasiveness of Haydn's daring dissonances on the period strings of the Capella Augustina. After the extreme hush of that opening, the choral cry of *Licht!, Light!*, is then shattering in its impact, and in the following tenor aria for Uriel, Spering shows his true colours in a crisp, faster than usual *Andante* which is exhilaratingly carefree.

Generally, Spering's speeds are on the fast side, so that such a number as the great soprano aria, *Nun beut die Flur* ('With verdure clad'), an *Andante* in 6/8, is taken at a speed traditionalists might find alarmingly fast, yet with no feeling of rush. The chorus, the Cologne Vocal Ensemble, is a relatively compact body, incisive in its attack; it is set in a helpful but not over-large acoustic, but it has ample power for the dramatic moments. The three soloists too are all excellent and youthful-sounding. The Korean, Sunhae Im, has a sweet, bright soprano that she uses with style and extreme flexibility; the German tenor, Jan Kobow, has a clean-cut, well-focused voice, a touch baritonal in timbre but with no strain in the upper register; while Hanno Müller-Brachmann, also German, sings with similarly clean attack and fine focus. An outstanding bargain.

Characteristically, Gardiner takes a dramatic view, overtly expressive, vividly pointing the highlights of the Creation story. Gardiner may not always convey the relaxed joy of Weil's fresh and brisk version on Sony, but the exhilaration and power of Haydn's inspiration, as well as its lyrical beauty, have never been conveyed more tellingly in a period performance on disc, with the Monteverdi Choir singing with virtuoso clarity and phenomenal precision of ensemble. The soloists are outstanding too, though the silvery soprano, Sylvia McNair, does not always sing full out.

Bruno Weil conducts a brisk, clean-cut reading, using the period instruments of Tafelmusik and a bright-toned chorus, augmented by the Tölz Boys' Choir. If the intimacy at times seems to reduce the scale of this masterpiece, and Weil at times is fussy over detail, the urgent exuberance of the performance is most winning, with an outstanding trio of cleanly focused soloists. The chorus is finely focused too, providing sharp, dramatic contrasts, and the orchestral sound is so clean that one can hear the fortepiano continuo even in tuttis.

Dorati, as one would expect, directs a lively and well-sprung account. The very opening is magnetic and its imaginative touches and joyfulness of spirit more than compensate for any minor lapses in crispness of ensemble. The soloists are a splendid team. The chorus is as gusty as you like in *Die Himmel erzählen*, with the soloists nicely balanced. The set opens gloriously with Heltay's lovely (1979) recording of the *Salve regina*, an early work dating from 1771, comparable in its depth of feeling with his finest vocal music. The recording is most realistic and the CD transfer of *The Creation* is strikingly vivid and immediate.

Bernstein's DG version, recorded at a live performance in Munich, uses a relatively large chorus, encouraging him to adopt rather slow speeds at times. What matters is the joy conveyed in the story-telling, with the finely disciplined chorus and orchestra producing incandescent tone, blazing away in the big set-numbers, and the performance is compulsive from the very opening bars. Five soloists are used instead of three, with the parts of Adam and Eve sung by nicely contrasted singers, confirming this as an unusually persuasive version, well recorded in atmospheric sound.

Thomas Hengelbrock conducts a period performance of Haydn's great oratorio that, with sharply focused sound and clipped rhythms, is consistently refreshing, even if the result is at times severe rather than joyful. The clarity of detail is consistently revealing, exploiting the widest dynamic range, so that the epic quality of Haydn's vision of Creation as filtered from Milton by Baron van Swieten takes priority. Crisp and purposeful, Hengelbrock adopts consistently fast speeds, with freshness intensified by the excellent singing. These are all fresh-toned young artists, chorus as well as soloists, with Johannes Mannov as Raphael and Steve Davislim as Uriel ideally clean in attack and firmly focused, bringing out the meaning of the text with exceptional clarity, helped by the close balance. Simone Kermes as Gabriel has a bright, clear soprano, well suited to period performance, very boyish in timbre, though in the great aria, *Nun beut die Flur* ('With verdure clad') she tries a little too hard to sound expressive, hardly consistent with Hengelbrock's clipped accompaniment. Dorothee Mields, who sings the role of Eve in the third section of the oratorio, has a similarly clear, boyish voice, while Locky Chung as Adam is aptly lighter in timbre than Mannov as Raphael, but again youthfully fresh.

What distinguishes Sir Neville Marriner's 1989 Stuttgart recording is the truly outstanding contribution of the soloists. Each in turn enters singing most beautifully, Hans Peter Blochwitz as Uriel, Jan Henrik Rootering as Raphael, and Barbara Bonney a radiant-voiced Gabriel. And how delightfully they combine in their Trios in Part II. In Part III Edith Wiens is a hardly less delightful Eve, and her duets with the warm-voiced Adam of Olaf Bär are similarly memorable. The chorus is comparatively lightweight in *Die Himmel erzählen*, but they sing with vigour and conviction and the finale of Part III, *Sing dem Herrn*, combined with the soloists, is exhilarating. Throughout, the orchestral playing is first rate, and the recording excellent. A splendid bargain version that can be ranked alongside the best, let down only by the absence of a translation and instead an inadequate synopsis. Most enjoyable, just the same.

Though James Levine with his weighty forces is occasionally heavy-handed over both dynamics and rhythm, lacking rather in elegance, he conveys the joy of inspiration in this work with characteristic boldness. He is helped not just by the highly polished playing of the orchestra but by characterful singing from all three soloists and fresh, finely disciplined choral singing. The recording, made not in the Philharmonie but in the Jesus-Christus-Kirche, is weighty and satisfyingly full, with ample bloom.

Rafael Frühbeck de Burgos directs a genial performance, recorded with richness and immediacy. The soloists are all excellent and, though Helen Donath has a hint of flutter in her voice, she is wonderfully agile in ornamentation, as in the bird-like quality she gives to the aria, *On mighty pens*. The chorus might gain from a more forward balance but their singing is impressive. An enjoyable set.

Masses

Masses (i–iii) 1 *in F (Missa brevis), Hob XXII/1;* (i; iii–vi) *1a in G (Rorate coeli desuper), Hob XXII/3;* 3 *in C: Missa Cellensis in honorem Beatissimae Virginis Mariae (Missa Santae Caeciliae), Hob XXII/5;* (i; iii; v–viii) 4 *in E flat: Missa in honorem Beatissimae Virginis Mariae (Great Organ Mass), Hob XXII/4;* (i; iii; vi; ix; x) 6 *in G (Missa Sancti Nicolai), Hob XXII/6;* (xi–xv) 7 *in B flat: Missa brevis Sancti Joannis de Deo (Little Organ Mass);* (xi; xiii–xviii) 8 *in C: Mariazellermesse, Hob XXII/8;* (xiii–xv; xix; ix;

xxi–xxii) 9 *in B flat: Missa Sancti Bernardi de Offida (Heiligmesse), Hob XXII/10;* (xiii–xvi; xvii; xix; xx) 10 *in C: Missa in tempore belli (Paukenmesse), Hob XXII/9;* (xvi; xxiii–xxvi) 11 *in D min.: Missa in angustiis (Nelson Mass), Hob XXII/11;* (xiii–xv; xxv; xxvii–xxviii) 12 *in B flat: Theresienmesse, Hob XXII/12;* (xiii–xvii; xix; xxix) 13 *in B flat: Schöpfungsmesse (Creation Mass), Hob XXII/13;* (xiii–xvi; xxvii; xxx) 14 *in B flat (Harmoniemesse), Hob XXII/14*

(B) *** Decca (ADD) 448 518-2 (7). (i) Nelson; (ii) Kirkby; (iii) Christ Church Cathedral Ch., AAM, Preston; (iv) Cable; (v) Hill; (vi) Thomas; (vii) Watkinson; (viii) Hogwood (organ); (ix) Minty; (x) Covey-Crump; (xi) J. Smith; (xii) Scott (organ); (xiii) St John's College, Cambridge, Ch.; (xiv) ASMF; (xv) Guest; (xvi) Watts; (xvii) Tear; (xviii) Luxon; (xix) Cantelo; (xx) McDaniel; (xxi) Partridge; (xxii) Keyte; (xxiii) Stahlman; (xxiv) Wilfred Brown; (xxv) Krause; (xxvi) King's College, Cambridge, Ch., LSO, Willcocks; (xxvii) Spoorenberg; (xxviii) Greevy, Mitchinson; (xxix) Forbes Robinson; (xxx) Young, Rouleau

Decca's survey of the complete Masses of Haydn, which appeared originally on the Argo and Oiseau-Lyre labels, omits only the newly discovered fragmentary *Missa Sunt bona mixta malis*, Hob XXII/2, of 1768. Overall this achievement stands alongside Dorati's complete recording of the symphonies (and the Beaux Arts' *Piano Trios*) as one of the landmarks of the gramophone during the analogue LP era.

Starting in 1962 with Sir David Willcocks's King's version of the *Nelson Mass*, the production team then moved down the road to St John's for the five remaining magnificent Mass settings which Haydn wrote between 1796 and 1802 for his patron, Prince Esterházy, after his return from London. With changing soloists, of generally consistent quality, George Guest directed a series of performances notable for their fresh directness and vigour, with his St John's Choir showing itself a ready match for the more famous choir at King's College and the sound even more vivid. The recordings were made between 1965 and 1969, with the *Little Organ Mass* and *Mariazellermesse* following in 1977. The project was completed over the next two years with the early Masses. But the 'authentic' era had arrived and the orchestra changed from the Academy of St Martin-in-the-Fields to the Academy of Ancient Music. Simon Preston took over, and he directed his Christ Church Cathedral Choir with a comparable freshness and spontaneity to that established at St John's. The engineering team excelled themselves throughout, to produce a well-balanced and spacious yet clearly detailed sound, boldly projected against a nicely resonant acoustic. As with the companion Decca box of the symphonies, H. C. Robbins Landon has provided the notes with his usual spirited scholarship.

Hickox Chandos Recordings

Masses 1 in F (Missa brevis), Hob XXII/1; 11 in D min. (Nelson), Hob XXII/11; Ave Regina in A, Hob XXIIIb/3
*** Chan. 0640. Gritton, Stephen, Padmore, Varcoe, Coll. Mus. 90, Hickox

In his survey of the Haydn masses Richard Hickox offers performances which consistently bring out the freshness and originality of the writing, with crisp, bright singing from his excellent chorus, and first-rate soloists. The Chandos recording is well scaled too, with chorus and soloists set in a natural balance, not spotlit, and with the lively acoustic giving agreeable bloom to the voices as well as a sense of space, while conveying ample detail.

It is a great merit of this series that early Masses and shorter choral works are included as couplings for the late, great Masses written for the name-days of the Princess Esterházy, not least Haydn's last major work of all, the *Harmoniemesse* of 1802. Those extra items include some masterly works, and it is fascinating to hear Haydn's very first Mass – the coupling for the *Nelson Mass*, most popular of all – which he wrote in his teens, a wonderfully fresh, bright inspiration. It is good too as one of the couplings for the *Schöpfungsmesse* to have the alternative setting of the *Gloria*, with the quotation from Haydn's oratorio, *The Creation* ('*Schöpfung*'), removed in deference to an objection from the Austrian Empress.

Masses 1a in G (Rorate coeli desuper), Hob XXII/3; (i) 13 in B flat (Schöpfungsmesse), Hob XXII/13 (with Haydn's alternative Gloria)

*** Chan. 0599. (i) Gritton, Stephen, Padmore, Varcoe; Coll. Mus. 90, Hickox

Masses 2a: Sunt bona mixta malis; 3 in C: Missa Cellensis in honorem Beatissima Virginis Mariae

*** Chan. 0667. Gritton, Stephen, Padmore, Varcoe, Coll. Mus. 90, Hickox

Richard Hickox here tackles two of the earlier works, both problematic in their own way. The fragmentary *Missa Sunt bona mixta malis* consists only of a brief setting of the *Kyrie*, followed by a more expansive setting of the *Gloria* which is cut off after the *Gratias agimus tibi*. No orchestra is involved, just organ and string continuo in support of the choir. It makes a fascinating supplement to Hickox's superb account of what is, by a fair margin, the longest setting of the liturgy that Haydn ever composed, dating from 1766, five years after Haydn joined the service of Prince Esterházy.

The title, *Missa Cellensis* is misleading when there is another, later Mass also entitled *Cellensis*, although this one has generally been known as the *St Cecilia Mass*. Whereas in the Preston version, which does not include a fill-up, the boys' voices of the Christ Church Cathedral Choir have attractive freshness, the Collegium Musicum 90 choir has sopranos who are amply bright and boyish, while achieving crisper ensemble. The soloists, all associated with earlier issues in Hickox's series, make an outstanding, responsive team.

Masses 4 in E flat: Missa in honorem Beatissimae Virginis Mariae (Great Organ Mass); 8 in C (Mariazellermesse)

*** Chan. 0674. Gritton, Winter, Padmore, Varcoe, Watson, Coll. Mus. 90, Hickox

The *Great Organ Mass*, dating from 1768–9, is unique among Haydn's earlier Masses, with a pair of cor anglais instead of oboes bringing a darkness to the textures, and with the organ adding delicate baroque tracery, beautifully played with light registration by Ian Watson. A devout Catholic, Haydn's joy in the liturgy bubbles out, as in the wildly syncopated *Amen* at the end of the *Sanctus*.

The *Mariazeller Mass*, written in 1782, was the last Mass setting that Haydn composed before the final six masterpieces, in many ways anticipating the stylistic development that they represent. Adventurous modulations of key relate to Haydn's symphonic writing, leading to an exuberant setting of the final *Dona nobis pacem*, so syncopated it is almost

jazzy. There and throughout, Hickox, with bouncing rhythms, inspires performances that convey the pure joy of Haydn.

Masses 6 in G (Missa Sanctae Nicolai), Hob XXII/6; 9 in B flat (Missa Sancti Bernardi de Offida (Heiligmesse))

*** Chan. 0645. Anderson, Stephen, Padmore, Varcoe, Coll. Mus. 90, Hickox

The so-called *Heiligmesse*, dating from 1796, was the first of the great sequence of six Masses, written annually for the name-day of Princess Esterházy, that crowned Haydn's composing career. He had just returned from the second of his triumphant visits to London, universally acknowledged as the most famous composer in the world, and here demonstrated in choral music what he had learned in his last masterly symphonies, with adventurous chromatic progressions and high dramatic contrasts. The opening *Kyrie* with its slow introduction leading to a vigorous allegro is parallel to a symphonic first movement, and typically in these last masterpieces brisk music far outweighs the slow and meditative, notably in the final *Dona nobis pacem*. Hickox and his fine team of soloists, choir and period orchestra bring out the exuberance of inspiration that marks this and the other works in the series. Equally, the *St Nicolae Mass*, written in 1772, the year when Haydn, in the *Farewell Symphony*, had to remind Prince Esterházy that the musicians needed a break, points forward to his later achievements, though the conclusion on *Dona nobis pacem* more conventionally brings a radiantly lyrical close, all beautifully achieved here by Hickox and his team, vividly recorded.

Masses 7 in B flat: Missa brevis Sancti Joannis de Deo (Little Organ Mass); 12 in B flat (Theresienmesse)

*** Chan. 0592. Watson, Stephen, Padmore, Varcoe, Coll. Mus. 90, Hickox

What distinguishes Richard Hickox's version of the *Theresienmesse*, fourth in the series of the six final masterpieces, is the way he brings out the joyful exuberance of inspiration, with the old composer at the end of his career as inventive as ever. At each turn he surprises his listeners with new approaches, from the symphonic setting of the *Kyrie* with contrapuntal entries and side-slipping harmonies to the trumpets and drums of the final *Dona nobis pacem*. The fugue in triple time ends the *Credo* with happy skipping and elaborate key-changes, while the radiant G major of the extended setting of *Benedictus* shines out, never more so than in Hickox's outstanding performance. The excellent coupling is the *Little Organ Mass* – so-called because of the elaborate organ accompaniment for the soprano solo in the *Benedictus*, with Janice Watson a radiant soloist.

Mass 10 in C: Missa in tempore belli (Paukenmesse), Hob XXII/9; Alfred, König de Angelsachsen (incidental music): Aria of the Guardian Spirit; Chorus of the Danes. 2 Te Deums in C, Hob XXIIIc/1–2

⊙━ *** Chan. 0633. Argenta, Denley, Padmore, Varcoe, Coll. Mus. 90, Hickox

The impact of war is reflected not just in the title, *Missa in tempore belli*, of the second of Haydn's final choral masterpieces, but in the writing, with the hushed *Kyrie* dramatically interrupted by trumpets and timpani. Writing for timpani – *Pauken* in German – is prominent later too, with the baritone solo of *Qui tollis* in the *Gloria* bringing a warmly contrasting cello solo. The *Benedictus*, too, is distinctive, less flowing than usual in its lyricism, unsettling in a dark C minor. Hickox's outstanding performance offers fascinating couplings, not only the two brilliant settings of the *Te Deum*, with celebratory trumpets and timpani, but the two completed items that Haydn wrote for the production of a German play about Alfred the Great, written in the same year as the Mass and with similarities of style. The Guardian Spirit's aria brings spoken passages and a distinctive accompaniment for wind sextet, while the *Chorus of Danes* is much more vigorous in a triumphant triple time, again with prominent timpani. Exuberant performances under Hickox and brilliant recording.

Mass 14 in B flat (Harmoniemesse); Salve regina in E

🕪➔ *** Chan. 0612. Argenta, Stephen, Padmore, Varcoe,
    Coll. Mus. 90, Hickox

Hickox's superb disc aptly couples the *Harmoniemesse*, the last major work that Haydn ever wrote, with his first important work, the *Salve Regina*, written in his twenties, when he was still an assistant to the composer Porpora and echoing his style. Nonetheless, there are plenty of distinctive points in the young composer's vigorous writing, simple as it is compared with his mature work. The *Harmoniemesse* is a favourite with Hickox, with Haydn's final fling as a composer bringing more elaborate orchestral writing. That was thanks to Prince Esterházy hiring a full *Harmonie* (wind section), while in unflagging inspiration Haydn delivers characteristic surprises in the setting with Hickox fully relishing the composer's humour.

Other recordings

Masses (i) 1 in F (Missa brevis); (ii) 3 in C: Missa Cellensis in honorem Beatissimae Virginis Mariae; (iii) 4 in E flat: Missa in honorem Beatissimae Virginis Mariae (Great Organ Mass); (iv) 6 in G (Missa Sanctae Nicolai)

(B) *** O-L Double (ADD) 455 712-2 (2). (i) Kirkby; (i–iv)
    Nelson; (ii) Cable; (ii–iii) Hill; (ii–iv) Thomas; (iii)
    Watkinson; (iv) Minty, Covey-Crump; Christ Church,
    Oxford, Cathedral Ch., AAM, Preston

Haydn wrote the early *Missa brevis* when he was seventeen. The setting is engagingly unpretentious, some of its sections last for under two minutes and only the *Credo* takes slightly more than three and a half. The two soprano soloists, Judith Nelson and Emma Kirkby, match their voices admirably and the effect is delightful. By contrast the *Missa Cellensis* (which is split between the two discs, after the *Gloria*), at 68 minutes, is Haydn's longest setting of the liturgy. Preston directs an excellent performance with fine contributions from choir and soloists, set against a warm acoustic. The *Missa Sanctae Nicolai* has a comparable freshness of inspiration and the performance is first rate in every way, even finer than that of the earlier *Great Organ Mass*, beautifully sung, with spontaneity in every bar and a highly characterized accompaniment. Both are admirably recorded, and the CD transfers are first class.

Masses (i) 7 in B flat; (Little Organ Mass) (ii) 10 in C: (Paukenmesse); (iii) 11 (Nelson); (iv) 14 (Harmoniemesse)

(B) *** Double Decca (ADD) 455 020-2 (2). (i) Smith, Scott
    (organ); (ii) Cantelo, Watts, Tear, McDaniel; (iii) Stahlman,
    Watts, Brown, Krause; (iv) Spoorenberg, Watts, Young,
    Rouleau; (i–ii) St John's College, Cambridge, Ch., ASMF,
    Guest; (iii) King's College Ch., LSO, Willcocks

Three major *Masses* and one shorter work are combined here

to make a very tempting Double Decca for those not wanting the complete set listed above.

(i; ii) Mass 9 (Heiligmesse); (ii) Mare Clausum (fragment), Hob XXIVa/9; Motet: Insanae et varae curae, Hob XXI/1:13c; Motetti de Venerabili sacramento, Hob XXIIIc/5a–d; Te Deum for the Empress Marie Thérèse, Hob XXIIIc/2

🕪➔ ✪ *** Sony SK 66260. (i) Hering, (ii) Van der Kamp,
    soloists from Tölz Boys' Ch., Tölz Ch., Tafelmusik, Weil

Bruno Weil's inspired and inspiring new period-instrument set was recorded under the guidance of H. C. Robbins Landon, who provides the excellent notes. There could be no more thrilling version than this. The choral singing in the magnificent *Heiligmesse* has overwhelming momentum, yet is radiantly rich in expressive intensity, and the listener is carried through on a tide of exultant spiritual energy to a closing *Agnus Dei* of real grandeur. And in the *Credo* how touchingly the soloists from the Tölz Boys' Choir enter, one by one, at the *Et incarnatus est*, with just a simple clarinet accompaniment. Then comes a surprise. The *Mare Clausum* brings a jolly patriotic bass solo, sung in English, followed by a rousing chorus (all about preserving Britain's marine power!). The two affirmative sacred motets are hardly less vigorous, with the second using a solo group of trebles in alternation with the full chorus, and the programme ends with the even more dramatic Marie Thérèse *Te Deum*, which concludes with a thrilling, trumpet-laden climax. This is a superb collection, and the bright, spaciously resonant recording, with the words always clear, is in every way outstanding.

Mass 10 in C (Paukenmesse); Salve Regina

**(*) Teldec 0630 13146-2. Röschmann, Von Magnus,
    Lippert, Widmer, Arnold Schoenberg Ch., Harnoncourt
**(*) Eufoda EUF 1305. Grimm, Karhauser, te
    Brummelstroete, De Kegel, Sol, Namur Chamber Choir;
    Prima la musica, Vermeulen

Harnoncourt has the advantage of the gleaming-voiced Dorothy Röschmann and a really excellent tenor (Von Magnus). The four soloists also show their fine tonal matching in the *Salve Regina*. The choral singing in the Mass is excellent too, and as it is a live recording there is an added dimension of concentration, so that Harnoncourt can afford to be more relaxed in his tempi. On its own terms, Harnoncourt's reading is satisfying and is at its finest in the *Agnus Dei*. The recording is spacious but the chorus, although vivid, lacks something in edge. In any case this is upstaged by the Sony disc, which offers an extra work and a very attractive one too.

Dirk Vermeulen directs his Belgian forces in a distinctive account of the second of the six great settings of the Mass that Haydn wrote at the very end of his career. The title *Missa in tempore belli* reflects the troubled times of the Napoleonic wars, but musically the alternative title is even more informative: *Paukenmesse* reflects Haydn's dramatic use of the kettledrum together with military trumpets. This performance is remarkable, especially for the clarity of textures, with soloists sharply contrasted both with each other and with the chorus. The light, crisp attack adds to the clarity and bite, even if the result is less joyful than most. This is a reading of extremes, with sharply drawn dynamic contrasts and tempos that tend to be extreme in both directions, with andantes and adagios slower than usual in a period performance.

The rarer *Salve Regina in G minor* makes a welcome if not very generous coupling. This is the setting from 1771 that, with its adventurous harmonic scheme, dramatically reflects the biting manners of Haydn's *Sturm und Drang* period, baldly involving just four soloists, organ and strings and no choir. The baroque organ is attractively mellow toned.

Mass 11 in D min.: Missa in angustiis (Nelson)

(M) *** Decca (ADD) 458 623-2. Stahlman, Watts, Brown, Krause, King's College, Cambridge, Ch., LSO, Willcocks – HANDEL: *Coronation Anthem: Zadok the Priest;* VIVALDI: *Gloria, RV 589* ***

Mass 11 (Nelson); Te Deum in C, Hob XXIIIc/2

*** DG 423 097-2. Lott, Watkinson, Davies, Wilson-Johnson, Ch. & E. Concert, Pinnock

(i) *Mass 11 (Nelson);* (ii) *Arianna a Naxos* (orchestral version), *Hob XXVIb/2; Scena di Berenice (Berenice che fai?), Hob XXIVa/10*

(B) *** Decca 448 983-2. (i) Bonney, Howells, Rolfe Johnson, Roberts, L. Symphony Ch., Hickox; (ii) Augér, Handel & Haydn Society, Hogwood

The *Nelson Mass* (*Missa in angustiis*: 'Mass in times of fear') brings a superb choral offering from Trevor Pinnock and the English Concert. With incandescent singing from the chorus and fine matching from excellent soloists, Pinnock brings home the high drama of Haydn's autumnal inspiration. Similarly, the *Te Deum* leaps forward from the eighteenth century all the more excitingly in an authentic performance such as this. Excellent, full-blooded sound, with good definition.

It was Sir David Willcocks who made Argo's pioneering recording of the *Nelson Mass* in 1962, a work that is clearly among Haydn's greatest music. The solo singing is uniformly good, Sylvia Stahlman negotiating her florid music with great skill, while Willcocks maintains quite remarkable tension throughout. The splendid recording is admirably remastered and the added Handel and Vivaldi bonuses for this reissue on Decca's 'Legends' label make the reissue very competitive. It is characteristically well documented.

Richard Hickox's earlier recording of the most celebrated of Haydn's late Masses is most impressive in the vigorous, outward-going music which – with Haydn – makes up the greater part of the service; here the choral singing is little short of glorious. In serene moments the choral sound is slightly recessed, with inner parts less well defined than they might be. The soloists are very good, and Barbara Bonney's purity of line is impressive, although tonally she is a little thin. While in some ways the Willcocks version of 20 years earlier is even finer, in the work's more resplendent moments the London Symphony's choral focus is given greater impact by the more modern digital sound.

What makes Hogwood's contribution almost indispensable is the inclusion of Haydn's two major solo cantatas (a full half-hour of wonderful music) which he wrote for his two London visits in the 1790s. Arleen Augér was never more impressive in the recording studio than here. She is superbly dramatic in the cantata which tells of Ariadne abandoned by Theseus on Naxos, and – in melting voice – infinitely touching in the *Scena di Berenice*. Hogwood accompanies most sympathetically and the recording is perfectly balanced. Not to be missed.

Masses 11 (Nelson); 12 (Theresienmesse); Te Deum in C

☛ (B) *** DG Double 470 286-2 (2). Brown, Bruce-Payne, Butterfield, Finley, Monteverdi Ch., E. Bar. Sol., Gardiner

Haydn gloriously rounded off his long composing career with his last six settings of the Mass to complement his symphony sequence in thrusting energy and originality. No one on disc has brought out that originality more tellingly than Sir John Eliot Gardiner in this second instalment of a series planned to cover all six of the late Masses, each pair in a two-discs-for-the-price-of-one package. In both masses here, written respectively in 1798 and 1799, the background of the Napoleonic wars is vividly brought out in dramatic martial sounds on trumpets and timpani. Gardiner's performances tellingly underline that in superb, clearly separated sound. Each Mass ends, as a Haydn symphony would, not in a conventionally meditative setting of *Dona nobis pacem* 'Give us peace', but in joyful exhilaration, with Haydn at his most daringly original. Outstanding singing from the team of young soloists, with the Monteverdi Choir both polished and passionate.

Mass 13: Schöpfungsmesse (Creation Mass)

*** Teldec 3984 26094-2. Oelze, Von Magnus, Lippert, Finley, Arnold Schoenberg Ch., VCM, Harnoncourt – SCHUBERT: *Magnificat, D.486; Offertorium in B flat, D.963 (Intende voci)* ***

Like the Schubert couplings, Harnoncourt's period performance of Haydn's *Schöpfungsmesse*, set in a warm church acoustic, was recorded live, making the music sound fresh and new. Marked by lightness, resilience and transparency, this is a reading that consistently demonstrates how far Harnoncourt has travelled since his early days with the Concentus Musicus. Speeds are moderate in both directions, easily flowing with rhythms well sprung. That is, until the final *Dona nobis pacem*, where Harnoncourt opts for a very fast speed, rounding off this celebration of the Mass in exhilaration – as Haydn himself used to put it, *Laus Deo*, 'Praise to God'. The four soloists are excellent, as is the chorus. The recording is warmly atmospheric, though the backward balance of the choir prevents it from having quite the impact its incisive singing deserves. An unexpected coupling, but an illuminating one.

The Seasons (complete; in English)

☛ ✹ (B) *** Ph. Duo (ADD) 464 034-2 (2). Harper, R. Davies, Shirley-Quirk, BBC Ch. and SO, C. Davis

(B) *** Somm Beecham (ADD) 16-2 (2) (arr. and orch. Beecham). Morison, Young, Langdon, Beecham Choral Soc., RPO, Beecham

(N) (BB) *** EMI Gemini (ADD) 5 86118-2 (2). Morison, Young, Langdon, Beecham Choral Soc., RPO, Beecham

Sir Colin Davis directs a tinglingly fresh performance of Haydn's last oratorio which ranks alongside his great Haydn symphony performances (also on Philips Duo). The soloists are excellent and Davis's direction can hardly be faulted, even in our age of authentic enlightenment. This set makes a strong case for an English translation, and although no libretto is provided, the English generally comes over with clarity. The 1968 recording is exceptionally vivid and full, and this is another great bargain in the Philips Duo series.

Beecham recorded *The Seasons* in its entirety between 1956 and 1958, yet he had only once conducted a complete concert performance (at the Edinburgh Festival in 1950). He preferred instead to conduct individual movements, of which *Spring* was his favourite. But it is a work that suited his personality, and his interpretation combines vigour with an affectionate warmth.

Nevertheless, Beecham's approach to Haydn's score was somewhat cavalier. He used orchestrations of the keyboard accompaniments for the recitatives, and (as with his RCA recording of Handel's *Messiah*) added percussion effects, including cymbals. A bell was added to the horns striking eight o'clock in *Summer*, and extra shots to the bass's hunting aria in *Autumn*. Yet he obviously revelled in Haydn's expressive tone-painting and he chose a fine solo team, led by Elsie Morison, who sings with tender flexibility and charm. The fresh-voiced tenor, Alexander Young, and the vibrant bass, Michael Langdon, are equally strong, and the three singers match their voices very musically in the various trios. The choral singing is not as polished as we would expect today from an entirely professional chorus, but the hearty vigour and commitment carry the day, while the RPO, and especially the strings, play with both warmth and stylish delicacy of feeling. In short, this is as spirited and individual as one would expect from Beecham, and the early Abbey Road stereo is full and clear. The remastering on Somm cannot be faulted, and a full text is provided of Dennis Arundell's new translation, which was especially commissioned for this recording.

On the EMI budget Gemini set the recording has again been remastered quite splendidly, but there is no libretto.

The Seasons (*Die Jahreszeiten*; complete; in German)

(N) ✪ **** HMC 801829.30 (2). Petersen, Gura, Henschel, RIAS Chamber Ch., Freiburg Bar. O, Jacobs

*** DG 431 818-2 (2). Bonney, Rolfe Johnson, Schmidt, Monteverdi Ch., E. Bar. Sol., Gardiner

(B) *** Ph. 438 715-2 (2). Mathis, Jerusalem, Fischer-Dieskau, Ch. & ASMF, Marriner

(M) *** DG 457 713-2 (2). Janowitz, Schreier, Talvela, V. Singverein, VSO, Boehm

(N) (BB) **(*) Warner Apex 2564 62086-2 (2). Blasi, Protschka, Holl, Schoenberg Ch., VSO, Harnoncourt

(M) **(*) EMI 7 69224-2 (2). Janowitz, Hollweg, Berry, Ch. of German Op., BPO, Karajan

It is astonishing that Haydn, at the end of his career, could write with such youthful exuberance in his culminating masterpiece, *The Seasons*. More than any other version, this period performance under René Jacobs brings out the joy of this piece based on James Thomson's poem, as he nudges the music persuasively when Haydn has fun in imitating the lowing of cattle, the cry of the quail and the chirping of the cricket. With recording of ideal clarity and immediacy Jacobs also brings out the boldness of the writing for brass and timpani in the finales of each section, notably the drinking chorus which rounds off *Autumn*. Marlis Petersen is the fresh, agile soprano, Werner Gura the light, heady tenor and Dietrich Henschel the fine baritone, singing with a liedersinger's concern for detail. Excellent contributions too from the RIAS Chamber Choir and the splendid Freiburg Baroque Orchestra.

Gardiner here more than ever rejects the idea prevalent among period performers that slow, measured speeds should be avoided, and almost always gets the best of both worlds in intensity of communication, whatever the purists may say. Even more than usual, this studio performance conveys the electricity of a live event. The silver-toned Barbara Bonney and Anthony Rolfe Johnson at his most sensitive are outstanding soloists, and though the baritone, Andreas Schmidt, is less sweet on the ear, he winningly captures the bluff jollity of the role of Simon.

Marriner directs a superbly joyful performance of Haydn's last oratorio, effervescent with the optimism of old age. Edith Mathis and Dietrich Fischer-Dieskau are as stylish and characterful as one would expect, pointing the words as narrative. The tenor too is magnificent: Siegfried Jerusalem is both

heroic of timbre and yet delicate enough for Haydn's most elegant and genial passages. The chorus and orchestra, of authentic size, add to the freshness. The recording, made in St John's, Smith Square, is warmly reverberant without losing detail. The CD transforms the sound, with added definition for both chorus and soloists. Highly recommended – a remarkable bargain by any standards.

Boehm's performance enters totally into the spirit of the music. The soloists are excellent and characterize the music fully; the chorus sing enthusiastically and are well recorded. But it is Boehm's set. He secures fine orchestral playing throughout, an excellent overall musical balance and real spontaneity in music that needs this above all else. The CD transfer of the 1967 recording is admirably managed.

Harnoncourt's version is characteristically vibrant and his dramatization of the elements strong, with Robert Holl making a memorable contribution in *Winter*. On the other hand, Protschka's style is lighter than that of Siegfried Jerusalem on Philips with his honeyed elegance and heroic ring. Angela Maria Blasi has a sweet, small timbre and is consistently persuasive. The Arnold Schoenberg Choir sing with fine bite and fervour and are especially invigorating in the harvest celebrations of *Autumn*. Detail is perceptively observed throughout the work, and Harnoncourt brings his usual powerful rhythmic feeling to the music-making – accents are more readily stressed here than with Marriner, and the narrative flow is vividly maintained. The Warner Teldec recording is excellent, with good balance and realistic projection; if there is less charm than under Marriner – who captures the work's innocent pictorialism with pleasing naturalness – there is certainly no lack of drama, and at budget price this Apex reissue remains distinctly competitive.

Karajan's 1973 recording of *The Seasons* offers a fine, polished performance which is often very dramatic too. The characterization is strong, and in Karajan's hands the exciting Hunting chorus of *Autumn* (*Hört! Hört! Hört das laute Getön*) with its lusty horns anticipates *Der Freischütz*. The remastered sound is drier than the original but is vividly wide in dynamic range. Choruses are still a little opaque, but the soloists are all caught well and are on good form; and the overall balance is satisfactory. Highlights are available on a budget Encore disc (5 74976-2 [5 7497-2]).

Stabat mater

*** Griffin GCCD 4029. Bern, Ager, Carwood, Underwood, Christ Church Cathedral Ch., L. Musici, Darlington, Goode (organ)

(N) **(*) Australian Decca Eloquence (ADD) 476 2441. Augér, Hodgson, Rolfe Johnson, Howell, London Chamber Ch., Argo Chamber O, Heltay

**(*) Teldec 4509 95085-2. Bonney, Von Magnus, Lippert, Miles, Arnold Schoenberg Ch., VCM, Harnoncourt

Haydn's *Stabat mater* was the first of his vocal works to establish his reputation internationally, an ambitious cantata written in 1767 soon after Haydn took over responsibility for Prince Esterházy's church music. Even against strong competition, the Griffin issue finds a distinctive place. It uses an orchestra of modern instruments; but, far more than Heltay, Stephen Darlington takes note of period practice, lightening string textures and finding extra detail. He also tends to adopt fast speeds, at times challengingly so, as in the big tenor aria, *Vidit sum*, stylishly sung by Andrew Carwood. The other striking quality of this set, besides the use of a church choir with boy trebles, is the warmly atmospheric cathedral acoustic, which yet allows ample detail. The line-up of soloists may not be as starry as those on rival versions, but these are young singers with fresh, clear voices and, like Carwood, with keen experience of the choral repertory.

Heltay's reading conveys its essential greatness, helped by admirable soloists, led by Arleen Augér in excellent form, and atmospheric (1979) recording. But, although this is preferable to the Harnoncourt version, it would not now be a first choice.

Harnoncourt's is a spacious and eloquent account of the *Stabat mater*, with a good solo team (although the tenor has moments of insecurity). But when the splendid bass, Alastair Miles, enters arrestingly at the *Pro peccatis* and the *Flammis orci ne succedar*, there are bursts of energy from Harnoncourt and the orchestra too, and one realizes that the overall tension has been lower than one expects with this conductor. Yet the penultimate *Quando corpus morietur* brings lovely singing from soprano and mezzo together, and the closing contrapuntal *Paradisi gloria* makes a telling close, even if here the soloists are not entirely comfortable in their sudden bravura entries.

Te Deum in C, Hob XXIIIc/2

(BB) *** RCA Navigator (ADD) 74321 29238-2. V. Boys' Ch., Ch. Viennensis, VCO, Gillesberger – MOZART: *Requiem Mass* ***

A fine, vigorous account of the *Te Deum* by these Viennese forces, very vividly recorded, coupled to a not inconsiderable account of Mozart's *Requiem*. At super-bargain price it makes excellent value.

Folksong Arrangements

27 Scottish Songs for George Thomson
(N) (BB) *** Brilliant Classics 92278. Anderson, MacDougall, Haydn Trio Eisenstadt

With two fresh-voiced and imaginative singers, Lorna Anderson and Jamie MacDougall, this is the first disc in an ambitious project to record all of the folksong arrangements that Haydn made of Scottish songs, some 400 of them. The 27 songs chosen here come from those he did for the Edinburgh publisher, George Thomson. Like Beethoven in the British folksongs he arranged for the same publisher, the accompaniment is for piano trio, and though Haydn's tend to be rather less inventive than Beethoven's, they are unfailingly attractive, regularly displaying a spark of originality, demonstrating this as far from hack work. Amazingly, Haydn was given only the tunes, not the words, but he responsively captured many an apt mood. The texts of this selection are generally not from traditional sources, but from Scottish poets, notably Robert Burns. *Over the hills and far awa'* is well known from being included in *The Beggar's Opera*; one of the liveliest settings in galloping 6/8 time is of *Rattling Roaring Willie*, with words by Anne Grant. The excellent Austrian players of the Haydn Trio Eisenstadt add to the authenticity of the performances, recorded in the Haydn Hall of the Esterházy Palace at Eisenstadt. Full texts are given.

OPERA

L'anima del filosofo (Orfeo ed Euridice) (complete)
*** O-L 452 668-2 (2). Bartoli, Heilmann, D'Arcangelo, Silvestrelli, AAM, Hogwood

Haydn wrote his last and grandest opera for London in 1791 but, when the king refused to give the theatre a licence, it was never performed, and it was not until 1950 that the opera was heard complete.

Impressed by Handel oratorios and the English choral tradition, Haydn includes many choruses of comment. He also takes the opportunity of writing for a large orchestra, far beyond what he had been used to in Esterháza. Hogwood uses an enlarged Academy, with 12 first violins, and though at times his manner is severe, he paces the piece very effectively, making the most of the drama.

The very opening brings one of the most telling passages, a monologue when Euridice in distress flees into the forest. Cecilia Bartoli is in her element, passionately expressive, creating a larger-than-life character. Euridice's death scene, Orfeo's agony of lament (agitated, and very different from Gluck's *Orfeo* aria, *Che farò*), and a brilliant coloratura aria for the Sybil (dazzlingly done by Bartoli) bring other high points. Though Orfeo's death comes as an anticlimax, the final chorus for the Bacchantes is most memorable, in a minor key, dark and agitated, then fading away to the close. Uwe Heilmann is a most sympathetic Orfeo, musically stylish, even if the microphone catches the hint of a flutter, as it does too with the well-contrasted voices of Ildebrando d'Arcangelo as King Creonte, Euridice's father, and Andrea Silvestrelli as Pluto. The chorus, so important in this work, is fresh and well disciplined.

Armida (complete)

**(*) Teldec 8573 81108 (2). Bartoli, Prégardien, Petibon, Schäfer, Weir, Widmer, VCM, Harnoncourt

On Teldec, *Armida*, the last opera which Haydn wrote for the theatre at Esterháza, and arguably his finest, receives a period performance under Nikolaus Harnoncourt which brings out its freshness and vigour, helped by a strong cast. Cecilia Bartoli in the title-role gives a seductive portrait of the sorceress, strongly and characterfully sung. The tessitura is high for her, which means that the warmth of her tone tends to disappear above the stave, yet unlike Jessye Norman on Antal Dorati's outstanding version for Philips (in 1978 using modern instruments), she does not transpose down the big fury aria in Act II, *Odio furor*. What seals the strength of her performance is the vitality of the recitatives, with word-meaning electrically conveyed. Christoph Prégardien gives a sensitive, stylish performance as Rinaldo, but the tone is sometimes thin, and Patricia Petibon as Zelmira, bright and agile, becomes a little shrill in high coloratura. The others form a good cast, though not as satisfying as Dorati's. Though the Concentus Musicus is not so abrasive as in its early days, and the full recording gives the players plenty of weight, there is still an edge on the sound that most period-performance rivals have modified.

(i) *Armida;* (ii) *La fedeltà premiata;* (iii) *Orlando paladino;* (iv) *La vera costanza* (all complete)
(B) *** Ph. (ADD) 473 476-2 (10). (i) Burrowes, Ramey, Leggate; (i; iii; iv) Ahnsjö; (i; iv) Norman, Rolfe Johnson; (ii) Terrani, Landy, Von Stade, Titus, Cotrubas, Alva, Mazzieri, SRO Ch.; (ii; iv) Lövaas; (iii) Augér, Ameling, Killebrew, Shirley, Luxon; (iii; iv) Trimarchi; (iv) Donath, Ganzarolli; Lausanne CO, Dorati

(i) *L'incontro improvviso;* (ii) *L'infedeltà delusa;* (iii) *L'isola disabitata;* (iv) *Il mondo della luna* (all complete). (v) **Cantata:** *Miseri noi! misera patria; Petrarch's Sonnet from 'Il Canzionieri': Solo e pensoso.* (vi) *Terzetto and* (vii) *Aria*

from PASTICCIO: *La Circe, ossia L'isola incantata. Arias for:*
(viii) *Acide e Galatea.* (ix) SARTI: *I finti erede.* (x)
TRAETTA: *Ifigenia in Tauride.* (xi) BIANCHI: *Alessandro
nell'Indie.* CIMAROSA: *I due supposti conti.* GAZZANIGA:
L'isola di Alcina. GUGLIELMI: *La Quakera spiritosa.*
PAISIELLO: *La Frascatana*

(B) *** Ph. (ADD) 473 851-2 (10). (i) Luxon, M. Marshall, D.
Jones, Prescott; (i; ii; vi; x) Ahnsjö; (i; iii) Zoghby; (i, iv)
Trimarchi; (ii) Hendricks; (ii; iv; v; vii; xi) Mathis; (ii; vi; vii;
ix) Baldin; (ii; vi; viii) Devlin; (iii) Lerer; (ii; iv) Alva, Bruson;
(iv) Von Stade, Augér, Valentini, Terrani, Rolfe Johnson;
Lausanne CO, Dorati

Haydn is not celebrated as an operatic composer, yet in
many ways his contribution to this genre is underrated, and
for those drawn to Dorati's vintage series, these two boxes,
each of ten CDs, in the Philips bargain Collector's Edition,
provide an economical way to explore this repertoire. Each
opera is also available separately and is discussed individually in our forthcoming Yearbook. With fine soloists there
will be much here to delight the ear, and Dorati conducts
brightly and resiliently; although he tends to flag in the
recitatives, these performances still offer much to relish.
Indeed, after each fairly conventional overture, the vocal
writing flows forward enticingly, with many a sparkling
reminder of Mozart. One can imagine how much these
works must have been enjoyed at Esterházy. The presentation offers good documentation, but keyed synopses in place
of full libretti. Also included is an additional programme of
miscellaneous arias by Haydn and substitution arias by
other composers, the latter (for the most part) sung by
Edith Mathis. The analogue recording from the late 1970s is
excellent and the CD transfers first class. Try the first box
and you will surely want the second.

(i) *L'isola disabitata* (complete); (ii) Cantata: *Arianna a
Naxos*

*** Ara. Z 6717-2 (2). Mentzer, with (i) Huang, Aler,
Schaldenbrand, Padova CO, Golub; (ii) Golub (piano)

L'isola disabitata is a lightweight, relatively brief work, involving only four characters, performing seven arias and a final
quartet, with copious recitative in between. The set numbers
are typically fresh in their inspiration, and the final quartet is
a delight in offering solo roles not just to the three singers but
to a quartet of obbligato instruments echoing each character:
violin and flute for the women, cello and bassoon for the
men, with horns and timpani adding to the brilliance of the
orchestra. The economy of scale was influenced by the fact
that it was Haydn's first opera for Esterháza after the disastrous fire in the theatre in 1779.

David Golub and his orchestra from Padua give a warm,
relaxed reading, with speeds consistently slower than on the
rival Dorati version. The soloists are all first rate, with
Susanne Mentzer warm and firm as Costanza, Ying Huang
fresh and girlish as Silvia and John Aler clear-toned as Gern-
ando. Christopher Schaldenbrand jibs at singing trills but is
stylish otherwise. Well-balanced sound. *Arianna a Naxos* has
Mentzer accompanied by Golub at the piano (unidentified in
the booklet) to make a very welcome fill-up, to give a
substantial advantage over the Dorati set.

HAYDN, Michael (1737–1806)

Flute Concerto in D

⊶ ✿ *** EMI 5 56577-2. Pahud, Berlin Haydn Ens.,
Schellenberger – HAYDN: *Flute Concerto; Scherzandi ****
✿

Played with superb artistry by Emmanuel Pahud, Michael
Haydn's *Flute Concerto* is an enchanting little work, with an
elegant *Andante* and an irrepressibly lighthearted, perky
finale. Here it comes as an ideal coupling for another attractive concerto attributed to Joseph, plus some little-known but
equally engaging *Scherzandi*.

Horn Concertino in D

(BB) *** Warner Apex 0927 40825-2. Clevenger, Franz Liszt
CO, Rolla – J. HAYDN: *Horn Concertos 3 & 4 ****

Michael Haydn's *Concertino* is in the form of a French overture, beginning with a slow movement, followed by a fast one
and closing with a Minuet and Trio where the soloist is
featured only in the middle section. The music itself is attractive; the second-movement *Allegro* is played in fine style by
Dale Clevenger, whose articulation is a joy in itself. Rolla and
his excellent orchestra clearly enjoy themselves in the Minuet,
which they play with elegance and warmth, and in the absence
of the soloist, the unnamed continuo player embroiders the
texture gently and effectively. The recording, like the coupled
Concertos of Josef Haydn, is very realistic, especially during the
solo cadenzas which Clevenger provides for the first two
movements. An outstanding bargain coupling.

*Symphonies 1 in C, P.35; 2 in C, P.2; 3 (Divertimento) in G; 4
in B flat, P.51; 5 in A, P.3; 6 in C, P.4; 7 in E, P.5; 8 in D, P.38;
9 in D, P.36; 10 in F, P.45; 11 in B flat, P.9; 12 in G, P.7; 15 in
D, P.41; 16 in A, P.6; 18 in C, P.10; 25 in G, P.16; 26 in E flat,
P.17; 27 in B flat, P.18; 28 in C, P.19. Sinfonia (Divertimento)
in G, P.8*

(BB) **(*) CPO 999 591-2 (6). Slovak CO, Warchal

Michael Haydn's 41 symphonies were composed over three
decades from 1760 until 1789. The early three-movement
works are comparatively straightforward and seldom adventurous, usually simply scored for oboes, horns and strings;
sometimes flutes were added. The invention, too, though
often quite endearing, is not particularly individual. Even so,
almost all the symphonies written in the 1760s have at least
one memorable movement and sometimes two.

With No. 18 we move into the 1770s and find the most
ambitious work so far (36 minutes 34 seconds with repeats);
its scoring includes a solo cor anglais. For a long time, *No. 25
in G* (1783) was attributed to Mozart, and with some justice –
its slow movement is rather fine and the finale spirited and
graceful. Nos. 26 to 28 all date from 1783–4 and show the
composer at full stretch. Each has an outstanding slow movement. Finales too are infectious and very neatly scored. No. 27
has an extended slow introduction, but it is No. 28 which caps
the series so far. It is not for nothing that it is in C major, for
its impressive fugato closing movement has much in common with the finale of Mozart's *Jupiter Symphony*. The Slovak
Chamber Orchestra is an excellent modern-instrument
ensemble and performances throughout are lively in the
traditional sense, warm and committed. Warchal phrases
most musically, but generally observes repeats, which makes
some slow movements seem rather long. Occasionally one

might enjoy the brighter sound and brisker tempi of period-instrument manners, but overall this well-recorded and inexpensive set remains a fine achievement.

Symphonies 1c in E flat, P.1; 22 in D, P.43; 23 in F, P.14; 33 in D, P. deest

*** CPO 999 380-2. New German Chamber Ac., Goritzki

A delightful collection of Michael Haydn's symphonies: the earliest two here are No. 1c (1760) and, despite its numbering, No. 33 (around 1760). Both are fresh in spirit, classical in style. Not that the later two symphonies lack freshness: following the slow introduction to No. 23, the *Allegro* is exhilaratingly vivacious, likewise the delightfully bouncy strings, punctuated by the horns, in the *Allegro assai* of No. 22; the fugato *finale* of that symphony is unexpected but highly effective. This disc brims with melodic invention, with the high-spirited allegros contrasting well with the minuets and charming slow movements – this is life-affirming music that one associates with the composer's more famous brother. The performance and recordings are absolutely first rate.

Symphonies 11, P.9; 16, P.6; 25, P.16; 34, P.26; 40, P.32

☛— *** Chan. 9352. LMP, Bamert

Here are some performances of the Michael Haydn symphonies that really do them full justice. Moreover Bamert's programme is very well chosen and makes a fine sampler for this repertoire. None of this is great music, but all of it is enjoyable and the composer's penultimate F major work (1789) brings a strong, impressively constructed opening movement and a tender *Adagio* with muted strings. The well-detailed recording is pleasingly full and resonant.

Symphonies 21 in D, P.42; 30 in D, P.21; 31 in F, P.22; 32 in D, P.23

*** CPO 999 179-2. Deutsche CO, Neuss, Goritzki

For the later symphonies Michael Haydn remains faithful to the three-movement format, jettisoning the minuet. Both Nos. 21 and 30 have slow introductions. By now his orchestration has become much more sophisticated, using woodwind quite subtly for colouring and enriching the textures, and in the *Andante* of No. 21 (a particularly impressive work) the horns too. His melodic material is more refined and musical arguments are developed with much greater assurance, as in the quite excellent opening *Allegro assai* of No. 31 (1785). The following *Andante cantabile* uses orchestral soloists, including cor anglais, almost as in a sinfonia concertante. No. 32 (1786) is the only two-movement work in the series, and very delightful it is. The playing of the Deutsche Chamber Orchestra is first rate.

Symphonies 34 in E flat, P.26; 35 in G, P.27; 36 in B flat, P.28; 37 in D, P. 29; 38 in F, P. 30; 39 in C, P.31

(BB) *** CPO 999 379-2. Deutsche CO, Neuss, Goritzki

Michael Haydn wrote these six symphonies in a continuing burst of inspiration in seven weeks, at the beginning of 1788. He again chose the three-movement format and his invention is fecund and concentrated: all but No. 39 are under ten minutes in overall length. But they bring a bubbling torrent of ideas; and how much more skilfully they are scored than the early symphonies!

From its opening, No. 39 is strong and forward looking; the *Andante* uses the full orchestral palette, and in the final fugato there is mature use of counterpoint to knit the ideas convincingly together, with a brief, powerful coda. All these works are

superbly played, conveying an exhilarating mixture of verve and elegance. Again first-class sound.

Missa in honorem Sanctae Ursulae; Requiem pro defuncto Archiepiscopo Sigismondo

(N) (B) *** Hyp. CDA 67510 (2). Sampson, Summers, Gilchrist, Harvey, King's Consort & Ch., King

The *Requiem*, written on the death of Archbishop Siegmund of Salzburg in 1771, reflects not only the sadness Michael Haydn felt for a much-loved cleric, but his deep grief over the death of his daughter earlier in the year. The steadily treading setting of the *Requiem aeternam* and *Kyrie* is unusually sombre, a mood which recurs throughout the nine sections, with C minor the prevailing key. As an exception, the *Sanctus* brings a radiant outburst, soon extinguished. At 15 the boy Mozart is certain to have heard this remarkable piece, and scholars have pointed out the parallels between this and Mozart's last, unfinished *Requiem*. The *Mass*, dating from much later, 1783, was written for a Benedictine Abbey near Salzburg, a fine example of Michael Haydn's late style, with thematic links between the movements and sharply illustrative settings of the *Gloria* and *Credo*. In complete contrast with the *Requiem*, the opening *Kyrie* is an elegant piece expressing happiness, while the *Sanctus*, very brief, is gentle and reflective, expanding into joy for *Pleni sunt coeli*. The *Benedictus* is the longest movement, a soprano solo, beautifully sung by Carolyn Sampson, punctuated by the chorus. Like the Masses of Michael's brother Joseph, the *Dona nobis pacem* brings a brisk, joyful fugue. Robert King conducts a fresh, lively performance, with Hilary Summers and James Gilchrist also outstanding among the soloists, as they are again in the *Requiem*, though here the ensemble is not always as crisp as in the *Mass*. First-rate sound.

HEADINGTON, Christopher
(1930–96)

(i) *Piano Concerto;* (ii) *The Healing Fountain;* (iii) *Serenade for Cello & String Orchestra*

*** ASV CDDCA 969. Britten Sinfonia, Cleobury, with (i) Fergus-Thompson; (ii) Carwood; (iii) Baillie

The Healing Fountain was composed in 1978 'in memoriam Benjamin Britten' and is a 26-minute cycle for high voice and chamber orchestra, comprising settings of Auden, Sassoon, Wilfred Owen, Thomas Moore and Shelley. It is expertly fashioned and often imaginative, though it is perhaps a little too close for comfort to the Britten idiom – indeed it quotes from *Peter Grimes*, *Death in Venice* and the underrated *Nocturne*. The *Piano Concerto* was begun the following year but was put aside until 1991. Although it is not as haunting or personal as the *Violin Concerto*, Headington's masterpiece, it is a strong piece, well structured and rewarding. The composer was an excellent pianist and his writing for the instrument is exhilarating and adroit. Those who respond to, say, Prokofiev or Britten will find much to admire here. The *Serenade* is the most recent work, and was commissioned by Julian Lloyd Webber and premièred by him in 1995. Fine and committed performances and very good recording too.

Violin Concerto

☛— ⊛ *** ASV CDDCA 780. Wei, LPO, Glover –
   R. STRAUSS: *Violin Concerto* ***

The Headington *Violin Concerto* is a warmly lyrical, unashamedly tonal work in which a fiery central Scherzo is framed by two longer, more reflective movements. The finale is a spacious set of variations in which the last and longest acts as a movingly meditative summary. Xue Wei plays with passionate commitment, with Jane Glover and the London Philharmonic providing warmly sympathetic accompaniments. Excellent sound. Those looking for twentieth-century music that is accessible and rewards familiarity need not hesitate.

HEATH, Dave (born 1956)

The Frontier

(M) *** Virgin 5 61851-2. LCO, Warren-Green – ADAMS: *Shaker Loops* *** ❂; GLASS: *Company*, etc. ***; REICH: *8 Lines* ***

In *The Frontier* Heath's incisive rhythmic astringency is tempered by an attractive, winding lyrical theme which finally asserts itself just before the spiky close. The work was written for members of the LCO, and their performance, full of vitality and feeling, is admirably recorded.

HEINICHEN, Johann David

(1683–1729)

Dresden Concerti: in C, S 211; in G, S 213; in G (Darmstadt), S 214; in G (Venezia), S 214; in G, S 215; in F, S 217; in F, S 226; in F, S 231; in F, S 232; in F, S 233; in F, S 234; in F, S 235. Concerto movement in C min., S 240; Serenata di Moritzburg in F, S 204; Sonata in A, S 208

(M) *** DG 474 892-2 (2). Col. Mus. Ant., Goebel

Johann David Heinichen, a contemporary of Bach, was a Dresden court musician and the concertos here were intended for the (obviously excellent) Dresden court orchestra. It is the orchestral colour that makes these concertos so appealing rather than their invention, which is more predictable. Goebel's Cologne forces obviously relish the delicacy of Heinichen's wind scoring and his neat and busily vital allegros. The lollipop of the set is the *Pastorell* second movement of the *C major Concerto*, Seibel 211, with its piquant drone (track 5 of the second CD). It is immediately followed by a peaceful *Adagio* for flute and strings and a sparkling finale. This set is now re-issued at mid-price celebrating its winning *Gramophone* magazine's Non-Vocal Baroque Award in 1993.

Dresden Concerti: in A min., S 212; in E min., S 218; in E min., S 222; in D, S 225; in G min., S 237; in G min., S 238

**(*) CPO 999 637-2. Fiori Musicale, Albert

It is fortunate that the present issue from Thomas Albert and his Bremen group involves no duplication of items in the DG set, and so for those who have the Archiv recordings this will be a welcome supplement, though it must be said that the playing is by no means as accomplished or elegant as that of the Cologne group.

HELWEG, Kim (born 1956)

American Fantasy (A tribute to Leonard Bernstein)

** Chan. 9398. Safri Duo & Slovak Piano Duo – BARTOK: *Sonata for 2 Pianos & Percussion;* LUTOSLAWKI: *Paganini Variations* ***

The *American Fantasy* is a four-movement sonata and at the same time a set of variations on Bernstein's song, *America*, from *West Side Story*. But although it is obviously the work of a resourceful and intelligent musician, it is of insufficient individuality to reward repeated listening. Fine playing, stunning recording. The audience goes wild at the end of the performance.

HENSELT, Adolf von (1814–89)

Piano Concerto in F min., Op. 16; Variations de Concert on 'Quand je quittai la Normandie' from Meyerbeer's 'Robert le Diable', Op. 11

*** Hyp. CDA 66717. Hamelin, BBC Scottish SO, Brabbins – ALKAN: *Concerti da camera* ***

Henselt's *F minor Concerto* is fiendishly difficult (Egon Petri thought it one of the hardest pieces he had ever played) but it seems to present few problems for Marc-André Hamelin, who is more than equal to its challenges. The idiom, as one might expect, is greatly indebted to Mendelssohn and Chopin, but there is much to give delight, quite apart from the virtuosity of the playing. Stunning playing throughout from this remarkable Canadian pianist, and very good recorded sound.

HENZE, Hans Werner (born 1926)

'Henze: Portrait of an Outsider'; Requiem

☛ *** ❂ Arthaus **DVD** 100 360. Wiget, Hardenberger, Bostridge, Kaune, Drake, Frankfurt RSO, Stenz; CBSO, Rattle; Ens. Modern, Metzmacher. (Prod: Dennis Marks; Director: Barrie Gavin.)

The portrait of Hans Werner Henze, made by Hessischer Rundfunk to mark the composer's 75th birthday in 2001, is substantial and runs to almost 90 minutes. It is followed by a performance of the *Requiem* recorded in 1993. The portrait must be one of the best documentary productions of its kind committed to video. (Only the 2-hour Bavarian TV feature on Richard Strauss screened in the early 1980s can match it.) There are contributions from Simon Rattle, Oliver Knussen and (albeit briefly) William Walton, and excerpts from the *Third* and *Eighth Symphonies*, the haunting *La selva incantata*, the *Nachtstücken und Arien*, *Undine* (with Fonteyn in the first production) and the *Arabian Songs* he composed for Ian Bostridge. We follow him from the war years, his first German successes, through to his move to Italy where he speaks in the surroundings of his home and his spectacular garden. The programme is strongly atmospheric and never indulges in excessive explanation or talking down (it is indeed far more ambitious than anything we are likely to find on BBC TV nowadays). It is a reflective and moving programme, which brings us close to this remarkable composer. The *Requiem*, which is dedicated to the memory of his friend Michael Vyner of the London Sinfonietta, occupied him during 1990–92 and receives as definitive a performance as any can be. Henze himself spoke of the work as a search for 'a new key to these dark rooms we have to go to find our way and to find ourselves', and the work is among his most deeply felt and personal utterances.

(i) *Piano Concerto 2. Telemanniana*

*** CPO 999 322-2. NWD PO, Markson, (i) with Plagge

Henze's *Second Piano Concerto* is a complex, intricate work. Rolf Plagge gives a good account of it, even if his recording must yield in authority to the Eschenbach version which features Henze himself. However, it is important that there should be new and alternative versions, and this newcomer has much going for it. Plagge has great fluency and an impressive technical address. The concerto has the benefit of being coupled with the appealing and beautifully written *Telemanniana*, which does for Telemann what Casella did for Paganini. While this does not displace the Eschenbach, which is still in circulation, it is a very good and recommendable alternative.

Violin Concertos 1; (i) *2.3*
(N) *** MDG 601 1242-2 (2). Janicke, Madgeburg PO, Ehwald; (i) with Mädler

The three *Violin Concertos* of Hans Werner Henze provide a broad overview of his whole composing career from 1948 when, still studying, he wrote his first concerto, to 1997 when he completed his third. The *First Concerto* was written when Henze had worked out his combination of 12-tone serialism and neo-classicism. Though the orchestral textures have a Stravinskian clarity, the harmonic idiom echoes that of Berg over its four clearly defined movements. The *Second Concerto* of 1971 comes from the period when Henze was profoundly influenced by left-wing politics and, in a far wilder idiom over its six movements, with surreal diatonic passages, brings a linking of concerto form and music-theatre. It involves not just the solo violin and 33 instruments, but also recorded tape and a baritone soloist. After the instrumental introduction, the second movement has the soloist dressed as Baron Munchausen delivering cadenzas in comment on a poem about the baron, while the longest movement, a fantasia, introduces electronic distortion of the violin on tape, the whole work powerfully presented in Torsten Janicke's fine performance. The *Third Concerto* of 1997, here given in the composer's 2002, more elaborate revision, offers in its three movements portraits of characters in Thomas Mann's *Dr Faustus*, which is a novel about musical creation centring on the composer Adrian Leverkuhn. So the first movement portrays Esmeralda, who infects the composer with syphilis, the second picture is of his young nephew called Echo, who is a symbol of innocence, while the finale, warmer, richer and more brilliant, portrays his violinist friend Schwerdtfeger. First-rate performances, vividly recorded.

3 symphonische Etüden; (i) *Nachtstücke und Arien; Quattro Poemi; La selva incantata*
*** Wergo WER 6637-2. NDR SO, Ruzicka with (i) Kaune

It is strange that we have had to wait so long for a CD recording of the *Nachtstücke und Arien* of 1957, one of Henze's most seminal works. An earlier version, with Edda Moser and Cologne forces under Christoph von Dohnányi, was available only as part of a three-LP anthology of Contemporary West German Music. Three of the four pieces come from the 1950s, and the inspired *Nachtstücke und Arien* are beautifully given by Michaele Kaune and the NDR Orchestra under Peter Ruzicka. What a powerful spell the much later *La selva incantata* casts! It must be among Henze's most atmospheric and imaginative scores.

Symphonies (i) *1–5;* (ii) *6*
(N) 𝄞→ (M) *** DG (ADD) 476 7234 (2). (i) BPO; (ii) LSO; cond. composer

The *First Symphony*, with its cool, Stravinskian slow movement, was a remarkable achievement for a 21-year-old, and

there is a dance-like feel to the *Third*, written while Henze was attached to the Wiesbaden Ballet. The *Fourth* is meant to connote 'an evocation of the living, breathing forest, and the passing of the seasons'. There is at times an overwhelming melancholy and a strongly Mediterranean atmosphere to its invention. The *Fifth* embraces the most violent angularity, with passages of exquisite poignancy and tranquillity; the language is strongly post-expressionist. The *Sixth Symphony* was composed while Henze was living in Havana. The performances are brilliant and the vivid recordings do not sound their age; those of the first five symphonies are getting on for 40 years old. The set is now reissued as part of Universal's 'Critics' Choice' series.

INSTRUMENTAL MUSIC

Royal Winter Music: Guitar Sonatas 1 & 2
*** MDG MDGL 3110. Evers

These are 'sonatas on Shakespearean characters', the first ranging from Romeo and Juliet, Ariel, Ophelia and the malice and majesty of Richard III; the second encompassing Sir Andrew Aguecheek, Bottom's Dream from *A Midsummer Night's Dream* and a particularly compelling and effective portrait of Lady Macbeth. Henze exploits all the resources of the instrument with astonishing assurance, subtlety and imagination. Reinbert Evers dispatches its many challenges with great virtuosity and brilliance. The 1983 recording still sounds first class.

Music for 2 guitars: Memorias se El Cimarrón; Minette (Canti e rimpianti ariosi); 3 Märchenbilder from the Opera 'Pollicino'
*** MDG 304 0881-2. Ruck, Càsoli

Of the three pieces recorded here, *Memorias se El Cimarrón* (1995) is the most immediately striking. It retraces and paraphrases the course of his opera, *El Cimarrón*, and exploits an extraordinarily wide range of sonorities and expressive devices, which Jürgen Ruck and Elena Càsoli of the Ensemble Villa Musica bring vividly to life. Highly imaginative and resourceful writing, reproduced with exemplary subtlety and naturalness by the recording engineers. *Minette* (1997) returns to the theme of his opera *The English Cat* and reworks, re-creates and sometimes freshly composes its material. For the *Märchenbilder from 'Pollicino'* Henze returns to the children's opera he composed for Montepulciano, 'a delightful self-immersion in simple music for the purpose of escorting the younger generation into the world of today's musical language', as the composer himself put it. The whole programme is played with effortless mastery and imagination.

VOCAL MUSIC

(i) *3 Dithyramben;* (ii) *Ode to the Westwind;* (iii) *5 Neapolitan Lieder*
(BB) ** Arte Nova 74321 89404-2. Saarbrücken RSO; (i) Wich; (ii) Rivinius, Saarbrücken RCO, Skrowaczewski; (iii) Hermann, Halffter

Henze's music is not well served on bargain disc, so this issue should be welcome, even if the welcome must be qualified. The good news – in that it is not otherwise recorded and is also by far the best thing on the disc – is the *Drei Dithyramben* with its Italianate warmth and strong atmosphere. In the *Ode to the Westwind* the cellist is rather too far forward and in the *Neapolitanische Lieder*, one of Henze's most approachable and charming scores, Roland Hermann is less subtle and less varied in tonal colour than in the pioneering Fischer-Dieskau recording from the 1950s. The balance in all three pieces is less than ideal, and in the *Ode to the Westwind* the sound is opaque. Recommended at the price for the *Drei Dithyramben*.

Die Bassariden (opera; complete)

(M) (**(*)) Orfeo mono C605032I (2). Driscoll, Paskalis, Lagger, Melchert, Dooley, Meyer, V. State Op. Ch., VPO, Dohnányi

Although his orchestral and instrumental work is well represented in the catalogue, Henze's operas, which occupy a central position in his output, are not. *The Bassarids* comes from 1965, three years after his successful collaboration with Auden and Chester Kallman in *Elegy for Young Lovers*. It was recorded commercially with a strong cast, including Kenneth Riegel as Dionysus, Andreas Schmidt as Pentheus and Berlin Radio forces under Gerd Albrecht on Schwann Musica Mundi. It comes chronologically midway between the *Fifth* and *Sixth Symphonies* of 1962 and 1969. In many ways it represents a synthesis of Henze's symphonic and operatic writing, its single 2½-hour act being divided into four movements: a first-movement sonata form, a Scherzo, an *Adagio* and a passacaglia finale. The plot (after Euripides's *The Bacchae*) concerns the conflict between Pentheus, the new king of Thebes, and the god Dionysus, and the king's subsequent murder at the hands of Dionysus's drunken followers, among them Pentheus's own mother. It contains some of Henze's most imaginative and compelling invention. This Orfeo performance is of the première on 6 August 1966 and is an impressive one. Loren Driscoll's Dionysus is perhaps not quite as imposing as Kenneth Riegel's in the slightly later (deleted) recording made for Koch under Gerd Albrecht, but he is very good indeed, and the remainder of the cast could hardly be bettered. Christoph von Dohnányi gets first-class results from the Vienna Philharmonic. The recording is pretty monochrome but generally well balanced, and it makes an important contribution to the Henze discography.

Voices

*** Berlin Classics (ADD) 2180-2 BC (2). Trexler, Vogt, Leipzig RSO Chamber Ens., Neumann

This massive and wide-ranging song-cycle of 22 numbers, lasting over 90 minutes, is among Henze's most inspired and characterful works, even including ironic songs echoing Kurt Weill, several of them setting poems by Bertolt Brecht. The wonder is that, so far from seeming too disparate a sequence, *Voices* gathers in richness as it progresses, with instruments including ocarina, accordion, mouth-organ and electric guitar, as well as a large percussion section. Some of the episodes are violent, but the work is rounded off with the most beautiful and most extended piece, a duet, *Blumenfest* ('Carnival of flowers'), which seems to suggest a final ray of hope, with bitterness gone. This analogue recording, made in Germany in 1980, presents a sharply focused performance, strong and dramatic, with two excellent, clean-cut soloists.

HERBERT, Victor (1859–1924)

Cello Concerto 2 in E min., Op. 30

*** Sony (ADD) SK 67173. Ma, NYPO, Masur – DVORAK: *Cello Concerto* ***

**(*) Guild GMCD 7253. Kreger, Philh. O, Yu – DVORAK: *Cello Concerto; Silent Woods* **(*)

The Victor Herbert concerto, which sparked Dvořák into writing his masterpiece within the year, makes an apt and unusual coupling for that superb work. Yo-Yo Ma gives a compelling, high-powered performance. His use of rubato is perfectly judged, with that slow movement made the more tender at a flowing speed. The finale is then given a quicksilver performance, both brilliant and urgent.

James Kreger comes into direct competition with Yo-Yo Ma with Kurt Masur and the New York Philharmonic and, although there is much to be said for Kreger's naturalness of expression, Masur provides stronger support than Djong Victorin Yu.

HÉROLD, Ferdinand (1791–1833)

La Fille mal gardée (ballet; complete. Choreography: Frederick Ashton)

☞ *** Warner NVC Arts **DVD** 0630 19395-2. Collier, Coleman, Shaw, L. Edwards, Grant, Royal Ballet, ROHCG O, Lanchbery. (Design: Osbert Lancaster. V/D: John Vernon)

La Fille mal gardée (arr. Lanchbery): extended excerpts

(B) *** CfP 2-CD 586 1782 (2). RLPO, Wordsworth – MESSAGER: *Deux Pigeons; Isoline* ***

(M) *** Decca (ADD) 430 196-2. ROHCG O, Lanchbery

One of the jewels in the crown of the Royal Ballet, *La Fille mal gardée*, with costumes and scenery by Osbert Lancaster, is a visual delight from beginning to end. Frederick Ashton's ever-inventive choreography is both witty and charming, and Lesley Collier and Michael Coleman are a most engaging pair of lovers and dance with nimble grace. Brian Shaw's Widow Simone is the perfect foil, with the famous *Clog Dance* a captivating highlight, and Garry Grant is by no means outshone as the goofy Alain: he remains in our affections when his inept wooing comes to naught.

The orchestra is conducted by John Lanchbery who has arranged this complex score so that it naturally follows every move of the dancers, while his constant drawing on familiar passages by Rossini adds to the listener's pleasure. The recording too is excellent, and the slight touch of thinness on the violin timbre is not a problem when the overall sound is so rich and resonantly full. The imaginative production brings much to please the eye, including a spectacular storm which is a true *coup de théâtre*; and the ballet's closing visual flourish cannot but raise a smile with its ingenious parallel with the final moments of *Der Rosenkavalier*. A greatly entertaining DVD which wears well on repetition.

Barry Wordsworth's scintillating CD account of a generous extended compilation from the ballet, including all the important sequences, is no less recommendable and the EMI digital recording is still in the demonstration bracket. With playing from the Royal Liverpool Philharmonic that combines refinement and delicacy with wit and humour, this is very recommendable indeed, especially in its inexpensive CfP reissue, coupled with Messager's delectable *Two Pigeons Ballet*.

The earlier extended selection on Decca has a vintage Kingsway Hall recording. One cannot believe that it dates from 1962, for the combination of ambient bloom and the most realistic detail still places it in the demonstration bracket. The performance is also wonderfully persuasive and brilliantly played, displaying both affection and sparkle in ample quantity.

Overture: Zampa
*** Chan. 9765. RLPO Ch., BBC PO, Tortelier (with Concert: *French Bonbons* ***)

Hérold's famous bandstand overture is played here with fine panache and given first-class recording. The rest of the programme of 'French Bonbons' is equally diverting, part of a concert of French orchestral lollipops.

HERTEL, Johann (1727–89)

Trumpet Concerto in D
(B) *** Ph. Duo 464 028-2 (2). Hardenberger, ASMF, Marriner – HAYDN; HUMMEL; STAMITZ: *Concertos* *** (with concert: '*Famous Classical Trumpet Concertos*' *** ✿)

Johann Hertel's *D major Trumpet Concerto* is typical of many works of the same kind written in the Baroque era. Håkan Hardenberger clearly relishes every bar and plays with great flair. This now comes as part of a Philips Duo compilation of trumpet concertos which is outstanding value.

HERZ, Henri (1803–88)

Piano Concertos 1 in A, Op. 34; 7 in B min., Op. 207; 8 in A flat, Op. 218
(N) *** Hyp. CDA 7465. Shelley, Tasmanian SO

Few composers, regarded in their lifetimes as major figures, have had quite such a dramatic fall as the Frenchman Henri Herz, born in 1803. A piano virtuoso, he wrote much of his music, including his eight piano concertos, for himself to play, and not surprisingly they are showy in their brilliant passagework, light and effective. Herz's success – not just in Europe but during an extended stay in America – attracted the bitter envy of Robert Schumann, who as an active music critic took a malicious delight in exposing Herz's work as trivial and worthless. He was too harsh. There is little musical weight in these three well-made concertos, superbly performed by Howard Shelley, directing the excellent Tasmanian orchestra from the keyboard, but plenty of sparkle and charm, particularly in the dance-finales. In the nineteenth century no one would have worried that these are works simply designed to entertain. When Herz died in 1888 on the eve of his 85th birthday, they (understandably) said that his music had predeceased him by several decades.

HIGDON, Jennifer (born 1962)

Concerto for Orchestra; Cityscape
✆➠ ✿ *** Telarc CD 80620. Atlanta SO, Spano

Here, bursting upon us with her dazzling *Concerto for Orchestra*, is a new American composer with the kind of immediacy and communicative force that are all too rare in the concert hall today. Serialism is forgotten: this is music of immediate appeal in its melodic lines, its rich palette of colour and its

inherent vitality. Ned Rorem, Jennifer Higdon's teacher and mentor, has placed her foremost among today's American women composers, and it is no wonder that, when her *Concerto* was premièred by the Philadelphia Orchestra, it brought a roaring ovation from the audience. It is an astonishingly alive and fertile work in five movements, summoned by bells, and opening with a whirlwind on the strings, soon joined by woodwind, and introducing glowing brass sonorities. The second movement is a sprightly Scherzo, first with witty pizzicatos; then the strings take up their bows athletically, the animation undiminished. The third movement, which is most imaginatively scored, introduces each section of the orchestra in turn, with the string chords giving a distinct whiff of Copland (which is to return in the finale). The fourth belongs to the percussion. With sounds both exotic and ear-tweaking, it gathers momentum, helped by the drummers, to lead to the exhilarating finale with its stabbing rhythmic ostinato on the violins, which becomes more and more jubilant.

Cityscape, commissioned by the orchestra, is a portrait of Atlanta, first its vibrant *Skyline*, the centrepiece a haunting pastoral evocation as the 'river sings a song to the trees', and finally a kaleidoscopic evocation of the city's main thoroughfare – *Peachtown Street* – with its swiftly changing evocations and unrelenting, unstoppable energy, even including a dynamic fugato.

The performances here are outstanding, the *Concerto* resplendent with orchestral virtuosity, the *Cityscape* conveying an unmistakable American panorama. The Telarc engineers rise to the occasion, yet they have the advantage of the superb acoustics of Atlanta's Symphony Hall, which gives a radiance to the quiet strings and bloom to both woodwind and brass, within a realistically spacious overall sound-picture.

HILDEGARD of Bingen (1098–1179)

(i) *Ordo Virtutum*; (ii) *In Portrait*
✆➠ ✿ *** BBC **DVD** Opus Arte OA 0874 D (2). (i) Boothroyd, Hancorn, Mayfield, Chamber Op. Ch., Vox Animae, Fields, Adams, Devine (Directors: Michael Fields & Evelyn Tubb)

Hildegard was not only the most remarkable 'Renaissance woman' of the twelfth century, she was one of the most remarkable women (or men) of all time. Confidante of popes, she was a genius in almost every field – composer, playwright, author, poet, artist, theologian, philosopher, visionary and prophet. She believed in the 'web of creation to which all creatures belong'; she compared 'the great love of the Creator and creation to the same love and fidelity with which God binds man together'; and she taught that the world should be enjoyed by man and woman together – 'Only thus is the earth fruitful'. Her views were so remarkable in their time that it is a wonder they could be expressed and survive. Because her mystic visions (in which she believed that God was communicating directly to her) were accepted by the Church as genuine, her power was remarkable and far-reaching. Moreover, she could speak plainly to those in authority above her and her criticisms would be accepted.

Her extraordinarily sung and spoken mystery play, *Ordo Virtutum* ('The Play of the Virtues') celebrates her philosophy, based on the love of God and the enjoyment of life, alongside resistance to sin. Even with the music alone (which has been imaginatively recorded by Sequentia) this is a remarkable achievement, but to see it played out in glowing colours, imaginatively performed and beautifully sung, partly outside and partly inside, in splendidly chosen natural settings, adds an extra dimension to the drama, particularly in the dramatic passages in Scenes I and IV, where the Devil enters. He contests the value of the fear of God and the virtue of chastity, to receive the neat reply that chastity produced 'one man who bound himself to humankind'. The music, simple but soaring monody but with sparingly used harp, recorder and percussion accompaniments, is very beautiful in itself; its flowing lines haunt the memory and it is radiantly sung, while the drama of the piece comes over splendidly.

The accompanying second CD includes a compulsive BBC 'Omnibus' dramatization of Hildegard's early life, before she set up her own order; and no better choice for the role of Hildegard could have been found than Patricia Routledge, who conveys her humility in the face of God and her determination in the face of man (and woman) and the warmth and spiritual essence of her character. This is a film to watch more than once, so it makes an ideal counterpart to the music, which one can return to again and again. The additional items include 'A Real Mystic' (an interview and lecture with Professor Matthew Fox, author of *Illuminations*, supplemented with an illustrative art gallery tour), while Mary Grabowsky considers Hildegard's spiritual significance for the twenty-first century. This DVD Double is a truly remarkable achievement, but it also surely points the way to the manner of biographical publishing in the future.

Canticles of Ecstasy

⊕—⊛ *** DHM/BMG 05472 77320-2. Sequentia, Thornton

This first instalment makes a splendid introduction, a collection of Marian antiphons, sequences, and responsories, plus eulogies to the Holy Spirit where the poetic imagery is often drawn from nature. At speeds more spacious than those of the Gothic Voices, with women's voices alone, the elaborate monodic lines soar heavenwards even more sensuously, matching the imagery of Hildegard's poetry. For a meditative mood this outdoes Gregorian chant.

Hymns and sequences: *Ave generosa; Columba aspexit; O Ecclesia; O Euchari; O Jerusalem; O ignis spiritus; O presul vere civitatis; O viridissima virga*

⊕— *** Hyp. CDA 66039. Gothic Voices, Muskett, White, Page

This Hyperion CD by the Gothic Voices was the disc which put Hildegard firmly on the map. It draws widely on the Abbess of Bingen's collection of music and poetry, the *Symphonia armonie celestium revelationum* – 'the symphony of the harmony of celestial revelations'. These hymns and sequences, most expertly performed and recorded, have excited much acclaim – and rightly so. A lovely CD.

O Jerusalem; Voice of the Blood

(B) *** DHM/BMG 2-CD 74321 88689-2 (2). Sequentia Women's and Men's Vocal & Instrumental Ens., Thornton

RCA are now re-issuing the other CDs in the Sequentia series as bargain Doubles, and the present pairing offers two collections. The first is called 'O Jerusalem'.

On 1 May 1152 Hildegard's very own newly built church in Rupertsberg was dedicated, with considerable ceremony, to serve her personal Benedictine order, and this collection is devised as a conjectural programme of celebratory music to fit such an occasion. The bells of Bamberg Cathedral toll through the opening title-piece, which also has simple instrumental backing, and there is more purely instrumental music here than in previous collections, joining flute, rebec, organ and vielle (hurdy-gurdy). There follows a lively *Magnificat* for St Rupert and two very touching (and typical) melismas extolling his virtues. The following music, beginning with *O tu illustrata*, soaringly evokes a radiantly mystical image of the Virgin Mary, to stand as symbol for the consecration of the women who were to renounce the physical world and join Hildegard's order; but for the hymn to the Holy Spirit a male group enters impressively, before the closing rapturous Marian testament from the women.

The sequence of music included in *Voice of the Blood* is related to St Ursula who, in the company of a group of 11 virgin noblewomen, was reputedly slaughtered in Cologne on her return from a pilgrimage to Rome. (The telling of her story, in the course of time, increased the number of virgins to 11,000!) As leader of a spiritual community of women, Hildegard felt a strong identification with Ursula, and the opening lament of the cycle, *O rubor sanguinis*, immediately brings the imagery of flowing blood. It is sung unaccompanied, but the following responsory has a long instrumental pedal note over which the vocal melisma floats. The poetry draws on the natural world. *Favus distillans* pictures the saint as 'A honeycomb dripping honey' and later her purity is compared with apple-blossoms. After a reference to the Trinity, the fifth piece is an address to Ecclesia, a female personification of the heavenly community, and this symbolic (and vulnerable) figure is to return in the closing pieces, of which the antiphon, *Nunc gaudeant*, brings an extraordinary burst of spiritual energy. Two purely instrumental interludes (constructed by Elizabeth Gaver for fiddle and organ) add variety to a carefully planned collection which is, understandably, often rather sombre in its basic mood. Unfortunately, no texts or translations are offered.

Laudes of Saint Ursula

*** HM HMC 901626. Ens. Organum, Pérès

The sound of the Ensemble Organum directed by Marcel Pérès cannot fail to be stimulating. They sing at a lower pitch than usual, in a robustly vibrant style, darker than a normal West European vocal group. Pérès is concerned to present Hildegard's music alongside the Gregorian monody from which it springs, so it is heard in the context of a reconstruction of the liturgy for the office of Lauds (a celebration of the arrival of the sun and the end of night). The result is a great deal more chant than Hildegard, but the combination is certainly compelling.

The Origin of Fire (Music and Visions)

(N) *** HM Surround Sound **SACD** HMU 807327. Anonymous Four

Hildegard of Bingen's celestial music is well suited to SACD, offering the listener the ability to use the controls for the sound to float all around, while staying well focused. The present collection explores the theme of the 'fiery spirit' and climaxes with the extended hymn, *O ignee spiritus*, with the melismas of this central sequence and the following vision of Love particularly memorable. The Anonymous 4 are ideal exponents, blending together and soaring up and over Hildegard's curving lines, the effect at once ecstatic and serene in a well-judged, spacious ambience.

Saints
**(*) DHM/BMG 05472 77378-2 (2). Sequentia Vox Feminae, Sons of Thunder Men's Vocal Ens., Instrumental Ens., Thornton, Bagby

Apart from *Ordo virtutum*, the mystery play mentioned above, this two-disc set is Sequentia's most ambitious project so far. It covers a wide range of music created to be sung by monks as well as nuns in honour of the early Saints: Disibod, Eucharius and Maximin, Mattias (who joined the Apostles to replace Judas) and Saint Boniface. Sequentia's vigorous male group alternates with the Vox Feminae, sometimes with instrumental support. This is eloquent singing of stirring music, usually extrovert, with strong lyrical lines, more like Gregorian monody, less sensuous than much of Hildegard's output, except for the two tributes to Saint Ursula. It is all impressively sung, but is a survey to be recommended to the Hildegard enthusiast rather than the general collector.

Symphoniae (Spiritual Songs)
(M) *** DHM/BMG 82976 60152-2. Sequentia, Thornton; Bagby

This is a further reissue of Sequentia's very first collection, made in 1979. The collection divides into two groups – the first celebrating female divinities such as Mary, Ursula and her accompanying virgins, and even Wisdom, considered a type of feminine deity and for which Hildegard wrote one of her most eloquent tributes. The second group is of laudatory pieces – for the Apostles (a responsory, introduced with a plaintive flute solo), for the Holy Confessors, for the Patriarchs and Prophets, and for the Martyrs. In this last, remarkable piece the upper vocal line moves over a sustained lower note. The freshness of the singing here and the considerable instrumental interest makes this one of the most imaginatively conceived of the series.

HINDEMITH, Paul (1895–1963)

'Hindemith Conducts Hindemith' (complete DG recordings):

Amor und Psyche: Overture; Concerto for Orchestra, Op. 38; (i) The Four Temperaments (Theme and Variations for Piano and Strings); (ii) Konzertmusik for Harp, Piano & Strings, Op. 49. Symphonic Dances; Symphonic Metamorphoses on Themes of Carl Maria von Weber; Symphony (Die Harmonie der Welt); Symphony (Mathis der Maler)
⊶ (***) DG mono 474 770-2 (3). BPO, composer; with (i) Otte; (ii) Haas

Hindemith made a number of records for Deutsche Grammophon in the early 1950s, before transferring his allegiance to EMI. All of them are collected in this invaluable boxed set. Some of them have been in the CD catalogue, but works like the exhilarating *Symphonic Dances*, the *Konzertmusik for Harp, Piano and Strings*, and the *Harmonie der Welt Symphony* have not been in currency since the days of vinyl. DG certainly lavished first-class sound on them and the *Mathis Symphony* and the *Weber Metamorphoses* are impressively detailed and full-bodied, given their date. Those who have treasured their LPs of these pieces can rest assured that a great deal of trouble has been taken over these transfers, and it is particularly good to have Hindemith's own thoughts on the *Harmonie der Welt Symphony*, one of his greatest works. We must hope that EMI will be prompted to reissue the

Sinfonia serena and the *Clarinet Concerto* with the Philharmonia Orchestra. Meanwhile, do not hesitate or procrastinate! Get this while the opportunity still exists and before it succumbs to deletion.

Concert Music for Strings & Brass; (i) Violin Concerto. Symphonic Metamorphoses on Themes of Weber
*** Chan. 9903 (i) Kavakos; BBC PO, Tortelier
(N) (BB) *** EMI (ADD) 5 86095-2. Phd. O, Ormandy – BARTOK: *Miraculous Mandarin* ***

The *Concert Music for Strings and Brass* (1930) was commissioned by Koussevitzky for the fiftieth anniversary of the Boston Symphony. It is superbly played here. The *Violin Concerto* of 1939 has been memorably recorded by David Oistrakh and the composer but this newcomer by Leonidas Kavakos is without doubt the best since then. A first-class account in every way and, coupled with the post-war *Symphonic Metamorphoses on Themes of Weber*, makes up a highly attractive and worthwhile programme.

The *Concert Music for Strings and Brass* is also given a superb performance and recording by the Philadelphia Orchestra, who bring virtuosity and opulent tone to this rewarding score. In the *Symphonic Metamorphosis on Themes of Weber*, although these artists play with splendid panache and brilliance, the humour of the second movement is perhaps less effectively caught. In every other respect, this is first class, and the recording quality also does justice to the quality of sound this great orchestra produces. With its excellent coupling, this is a terrific bargain.

Cello Concertos 1 in E flat, Op. 3; 2 (1940); Kammermusik 3, Op. 36/2
(BB) *** CPO 999 375-2. Geringas, Queensland SO, Albert

The *Cello Concerto*, Op. 3, is naturally a derivative piece, with a lot of Reger and Strauss and not too much of the Hindemith we know. The 1940 *Second Concerto* is a fine piece, though not the equal of the *Violin Concerto* of the previous year, and the programme is completed by the little concerto from the *Kammermusik*. David Geringas is a generally impressive soloist and the orchestral response maintains the eminently respectable standard we have come to expect from this series.

Cello Concerto 2
(M) **(*) BBC mono BBCL 4133-2. Tortelier, BBC SO, Downes – SCHUMANN: *Cello Concerto* **(*)

(i) Cello Concerto 2; (ii) Clarinet Concerto
*** Etcetera KTC 1006. (i) De Machula; (ii) Pieterson; Concg. O, Kondrashin

(i) Cello Concerto 2; (ii) The Four Temperaments (theme and variations for piano and strings)
*** Chan. 9124. (i) Wallfisch; (ii) Shelley; BBC PO, Tortelier

Both the *Cello Concerto* and *The Four Temperaments* are vintage Hindemith and well worth adding to your collection. The four variations of the latter are ingenious and subtle and are splendidly realized by Howard Shelley and the BBC Philharmonic under Yan Pascal Tortelier. Raphael Wallfisch is the eloquent soloist in the *Cello Concerto*. The Chandos recording is very good indeed. These recordings set new standards in both works.

Paul Tortelier's account of the *Cello Concerto* comes from a 1967 TV broadcast from the BBC Maida Vale studios in which Tortelier gave a masterclass on the piece, an excerpt from which is included on this disc. Tortelier was a consistent champion of this concerto and played it with the composer himself. This is a highly persuasive account to which we would have accorded three stars, were it not for the rather opaque, monochrome sound of Maida Vale Studio 1. But this should be recommended for the artistry and conviction of both the soloist and the BBC Symphony Orchestra under Downes.

Tibor de Machula also proves an excellent protagonist in the *Cello Concerto No. 2*. The *Clarinet Concerto* is lyrical and eventful. The recordings (made in the Concertgebouw, Amsterdam) are public performances and emanate from the Hilversum Radio archives. But the Chandos disc is the one to go for.

(i) *Clarinet Concerto*; (ii) *Horn Concerto*; (iii) *Concerto for Trumpet, Bassoon & Strings*; (iv) *Concerto for Woodwinds, Harp & Strings*

(BB) **(*) CPO 999 142-2. (i; iv) Mehlhart; (ii) Neunecker; (iii) Friedrich; (iii–iv) Wilkening; (iv) Büchsel, Varcol, Cassedanne; Frankfurt RSO, Albert

The *Clarinet Concerto* was written for Benny Goodman; the *Horn Concerto* is comparatively familiar. The *Concerto for Woodwinds, Harp and Strings* is the more rewarding of the other two works and is more varied in texture. The *Trumpet and Bassoon Concerto* finds Hindemith in more routine mode. The soloist is rather too forward in the *Clarinet Concerto* and, though the recording quality is decent, it is possible to imagine more transparent orchestral textures. The performances throughout are eminently acceptable.

(i) *Horn Concerto. Concert Music for Brass and Strings*

(M) (***) EMI 5 67782-2 [5 67783-2]. (i) Brain; Philh. O., Sawallisch – R. STRAUSS: *Horn Concertos 1–2* (***) ◉

The Hindemith *Horn Concerto* at first seems lyrically much less voluptuous than its Strauss couplings, but it is very atmospheric and has a brief but witty central Scherzo which Brain articulates very winningly. Towards the close of the haunting palindromic finale the soloist imaginatively declaims a short poem – written by the composer – in such a way that the horn's note values match the syllables of the words (which are not intended to be spoken). Brain's performance is incomparable, with splendid support from Sawallisch, a superb Straussian, who also directs a fine account of the *Concert Music for Brass and Strings*. Both were recorded in the Kingsway Hall in 1956 and the early stereo is clear and full.

(i) *Organ Concerto*; (ii) *Organ Sonatas 1–3*

(BB) *** Warner Apex (ADD) 2564 60227-2. (i) Heiller, Austrian RSO, Hórvat; (ii) Ullmann

A most valuable reissue, particularly at so competitive a price. The *First* and *Second Organ Sonatas* come from 1937 and they are both exhilarating and masterly, and are beautifully laid out for the instrument. The *Third Sonata* was written shortly after Hindemith had settled in Yale. Apart from Messiaen, nobody composed more idiomatically for the instrument in the 1930s and '40s. The *Organ Concerto* is not to be confused with the last of the *Kammermusik* of 1927, but is the larger-scale four-movement score, commissioned by the New York Philharmonic in 1962 and which was to prove the composer's last work. The performance by Anton Heiller and Austrian Radio forces under Milan Hórvat is authoritative and well recorded, and the sonatas are also finely played on the organ of the Brucknerhaus, Linz. Very good value for money.

(i) *Piano Concerto; The Four Temperaments*

(BB) *** CPO 999 078-2. Mauser, Frankfurt RSO, Albert

The *Piano Concerto* (1945) is a rarity and has been unjustly neglected, for it is an often inspired and beautifully lucid piece. The slow movement is one of the most beautiful and imaginative of its period. The CPO recordings emanate from the early 1990s, and even if you are normally unattracted by Hindemith you should consider acquiring this coupling, as *The Four Temperaments* is one of the composer's most immediately approachable works and it is equally successful here.

Violin Concerto

⊕ (M) *** Decca (ADD) 476 7288-2 (2). D. Oistrakh, LSO, composer – MOZART: *Sinfonia concertante*, etc. **(*); BRUCH: *Scottish Fantasia* ***

David Oistrakh's 1962 reading of the *Violin Concerto* is still first choice. It was a revelation on its release: the work has never before or since blossomed into such rewarding lyricism on record. The orchestral contribution, under the composer himself, is strikingly passionate, with the soloist providing many moments when the ear is ravished by the beauty of phrasing and inflexion. The superb sound emerges finely in the transfer and this is an ideal choice for reissue in Decca's 'Critics' Choice' series, as it is a *Gramaphone* recommendation as well as one of the Penguin Guide's key recordings.

Concerto for Winds, Harp & Orchestra; Konzertmusik for Brass & Strings, Op. 50; Mathis der Maler: Symphony

*** Chan. 9457. Czech PO, Bělohlávek

The *Concerto for Winds, Harp and Orchestra* has never been heard to better effect on record. The *Konzertmusik for Brass and Strings* is hardly less imposing. Bělohlávek takes a broad and spacious view that is most impressive. Competition is of course much keener in the *Mathis der Maler Symphony*, and here Bělohlávek is a little more detached and wanting in intensity. The playing of the Czech Philharmonic is as expert and responsive as one might expect, and the Chandos engineers cope well with the reverberant acoustic.

Kammermusik 1 for 12 Instruments, Op. 24/1; (i) 2 (Piano Concerto), Op. 36/1; (ii) 3 (Cello Concerto), Op. 36/2; (iii) 4 (Violin Concerto), Op. 36/3; (iv) 5 (Viola Concerto), Op. 36/4; (v) 6 (Viola d'amore Concerto), Op. 46/1; (vi) 7 (Organ Concerto), Op. 46/2; Kleine Kammermusik for Wind Quintet, Op. 24/2

⊕ (B) *** Double Decca 473 722-2 (2). (i) Brautigam; (ii) Harrell; (iii) Kulka; (iv) Kaskhashian; (v) Blume; (vi) Van Doeselaar; Concg. O, Chailly

The Decca set is complete and includes the delightful little *Wind Quintet (Kleine Kammermusik)*. The playing of the distinguished soloists and the members of the Concertgebouw is beyond praise, so is the Decca recording, and this now has a considerable price advantage.

Kammermusik 2 for Piano & 12 Solo Instruments, Op. 36/1; Konzertmusik for Piano, Brass & Harps, Op. 49

(M) **(*) CPO 999 138-2. Mauser, Frankfurt RSO, Albert

Werner Andreas Albert's Hindemith survey continues to impress. The *Kammermusik No. 2* is well represented on disc but every newcomer serves to underline its originality of mind. Siegfried Mauser is the expert soloist, and he and his colleagues produce superb results in the imaginative second movement. The *Konzertmusik* is served less well (there is one alternative, albeit from the 1960s, on Supraphon with Panenka as pianist) and readers may well want this CD just for this. The work is as original as its instrumental setting might suggest. Good performances and clear studio recording from the early 1990s. But even at mid-price it is short measure at 47 minutes.

(i) *Kammermusik 4, Op. 36/3. Tuttifäntchen: Orchestral Suite;* (i) *Violin Concerto*
**(*) CPO 999 527-2. Queensland SO, Albert; (i) with Olding

The main work here is the *Violin Concerto* of 1939, in which Dene Olding acquits himself well. He is particularly impressive in the slow movement, which is thoughtful and inward-looking. There is a good, truthful balance between soloist and orchestra here, though in the *Kammermusik No. 4*, Op. 36/3, the balance is too close and claustrophobic and the results unpleasing. Hindemith's music needs all the help it can get from a flattering acoustic. Of good broadcasting standard rather than a first choice in the commercial record field.

Kammermusik 5, Op. 36/4; Konzertmusik for Viola & Orchestra, Op. 48; Viola Concerto (Der Schwanendreher)
*** ASV CDDCA 931. Cortese, Philh. O, Brabbins

Paul Cortese is the accomplished soloist in all three works, including the fifth of the *Kammermusik*. The Philharmonia respond with some enthusiasm to Martyn Brabbins's direction, and although there are finer recordings of *Der Schwanendreher* to be had (above all, Tabea Zimmermann on EMI) this disc gives undoubted pleasure. The recording is very good indeed, with great presence and body.

Kammermusik 5, Op. 36/4 (for viola and large chamber orchestra); Konzertmusik (for viola and large chamber orchestra), Op. 48; Der Schwanendreher (Viola Concerto); Trauermusik (for viola and strings)
*** CPO 999 492-2. Dean, Queensland SO, Albert

The viola was Hindemith's own instrument and he writes gratefully for it. The *Kammermusik No. 5* is generously represented on disc, while the *Konzertmusik*, Op. 48 (1929–30) (with no violins or violas in the string section, hence its rich sonorities at the bass-baritone end of the spectrum) is relatively neglected, and undeservedly so, for it has a particularly engaging first movement and an imaginative and deeply felt slow movement. It operates at a higher level of inspiration than the oft-recorded *Der Schwanendreher*, good though that is, or the *Trauermusik* that Hindemith composed at high speed on the death of George V. The Australian violist and composer Brett Dean gives masterly accounts of all four pieces, and the Queensland orchestra plays with excellent ensemble and precision for Werner Albert. Recommended with enthusiasm.

(i) *Kammermusik 6 for Viola d'amore, Op. 46/1;* (ii) *Kammermusik 7 for Organ, Op. 46/2; Organ Concerto* (1962)
(BB) **(*) CPO 999 261-2 (i) Dean; (ii) Haas; Frankfurt RSO, Albert

Although the *Kammermusik* are generously represented in the catalogue, the *Organ Concerto* of 1962, commissioned for the inauguration of the organ of the New York Philharmonic Hall, is a rarity. To be frank, it is a rather manufactured piece, not by any means vintage Hindemith. The earlier concerto, the *Kammermusik No. 7*, written for another inauguration, that of the Frankfurt Radio instrument, on which this performance was given, is infinitely more rewarding: its austere

contrapuntal slow movement is particularly impressive. Hindemith nursed a great affection for the viola d'amore, and the second movement of his *Kammermusik No. 6* shows the quality of feeling it aroused. Brett Dean plays with eloquence, as does the organist, Rosalinde Haas. Good recording, with well-defined and transparent orchestral detail.

Der Dämon; (i) *Hérodiade* (two versions)
(BB) *** CPO 999 220-2. (i) Gicquel; Mauser, Frankfurt RSO, Albert

Der Dämon (*The Demon*) (1922) is an early ballet; it has great resource in matters of colour and is full of imaginative, original textures. There is a prominent role for the piano, brilliantly and sensitively played by Siegfried Mauser. *Hérodiade* dates from 1944 and derives its inspiration from Mallarmé's poem. It is an excellent idea to let us have it first with the text, then again without it, and Annie Gicquel speaks it in exemplary fashion. *Hérodiade* is a beautiful score and Werner Andreas Albert gets excellent results from his Frankfurt forces. The Hessischer Rundfunk engineers produce recordings that are a model of good balance. Strongly recommended.

(i) *The Four Temperaments; Nobilissima visione*
⊶ *** Delos D/CD 1006. (i) Rosenberger; RPO, De Preist

The Four Temperaments, a set of variations, is one of Hindemith's finest and most immediate works. Carol Rosenberger gives a formidable reading of this inventive and resourceful score. James de Preist also secures responsive playing from the RPO strings and gives a sober, well-shaped account of the *Nobilissima visione* suite, doing justice to its grave nobility.

Mathis der Maler (symphony); *Nobilissima visione; Symphonic Metamorphoses on Themes by Weber*
⊶ *** EMI 5 55230-2. Phd. O, Sawallisch

Mathis der Maler (symphony); *Symphonic Metamorphoses on Themes by Weber; Neues vom Tage (News of the Day): Overture*
(B) ** Virgin 5 62047-2. Bamberg SO, Rickenbacher –
MAHLER: *Blumine; Totenfeier; etc.* **

It is good to hear the great Philadelphia Orchestra sounding itself again. Sawallisch draws a warm, rich-textured sound from them, and he also gives a performance of the *Nobilissima visione* that does justice to its breadth and dignity. His account of the *Symphonic Metamorphoses on Themes by Carl Maria von Weber* is not quite as sharp or fleet of foot as the older, Bernstein version, but it is still very well characterized. The *Mathis* scores over the rival Blomstedt on Decca in depth of characterization and orchestral opulence and, all things considered, should probably be the preferred recommendation.

Rickenbacher's are straightforwardly strong and very serious-minded performances, not helped by a recording that is well balanced but rather opaque. His lighter novelty is the brief overture to an early 'comic' opera, *Neues vom Tage*, which generates plenty of sardonic energy, introduces a melancholy lyrical theme, becomes more exotic, and ends rumbustiously, but heavily. The main interest of this reissue is the Mahler couplings.

Pittsburgh Symphony; Ragtime; Symphonic Dances
*** Chan. 9530. BBC PO, Tortelier

The *Symphonic Dances* is one of Hindemith's most inventive and enjoyable works and its present neglect in the concert hall and the recording studio is quite unaccountable. Dating from 1937, it is full of resource and imagination and deserves to be as popular as the *Symphonic Metamorphoses on Themes of Weber*. The *Pittsburgh Symphony* is a rewarding piece – not as high-spirited or poetic as the *Symphonic Dances* but hard-edged and full of good ideas. Yan Pascal Tortelier and the BBC Philharmonic give meticulously prepared and committed performances, and the Chandos sound is above reproach. Strongly recommended.

Sinfonia serena; Symphony (Die Harmonie der Welt)
🔓 ⚙ *** Chan. 9217. BBC PO, Tortelier

The *Sinfonia serena* (1946) is a brilliant and inventive score, full of humour and melody. The scoring is inventive and imaginative. There is plenty of wit in the Scherzo, which paraphrases a Beethoven march from 1809. The *Symphony, Die Harmonie der Welt* (1951), is another powerful and consistently underrated score. These well-prepared and finely shaped BBC performances are given state-of-the-art recording quality. An outstanding issue.

Symphonic Metamorphoses on Themes of Weber
(N) **(*) Telarc SACD 60648. Atlanta SO, Shaw – COPLAND: *Appalachian Spring*, etc. **(*)

Robert Shaw treats Hindemith's colourful variations almost neo-classically. His is a sharp, incisive performance that misses some of the bounce and charm but is very well recorded – although the SACD enhancement is marginal. A curious coupling for the three Copland ballet scores.

Symphony in E flat; Overture Neues vom Tage; Nobilissima visione
*** Chan. 9060. BBC PO, Tortelier

The *Symphony in E flat* is an inventive and resourceful score and is well worth investigating. Yan Pascal Tortelier gets excellent results from the BBC Philharmonic. Good, musicianly performances of *Nobilissima visione* and the much earlier *Neues vom Tage Overture* complete an admirable addition to the Hindemith discography.

CHAMBER MUSIC

(i) *Alto Saxophone Sonata;* (ii) *Bass Tuba Sonata;* (iii) *Bassoon Sonata;* (iv) *Morgenmusik;* (v) *Trio;* (vi) *Trombone Sonata;* (vii) *Trumpet Sonata*
**(*) BIS (ADD) CD 159. (i) Savijoki, Siirala; (ii) Lind, Harlos; (iii) Sonstevold, Knardahl; (iv) Malmö Brass Ens.; (v) Pehrsson, Jonsson, Mjönes; (vi) Lindberg, Pöntinen; (vii) Tarr, Westenholz

The *Alto Saxophone Sonata* and the *Alto Horn Sonata* are the same work. The *Recorder Trio* is expertly played, as is the exhilarating *Morgenmusik* for brass, not to mention the inventive *Bassoon Sonata*. However, the BIS recordings are rather closely balanced, though not disturbingly so.

Bassoon Sonata; Harp Sonata; Horn Sonata; Sonata for 2 Pianos; Sonata for Piano 4 Hands
*** MDG 304 0694-2. Ens. Villa Musica, with Thunemann, Storck, Vlatkovic, Piret, Randalu

Hindemith had an unfailingly resourceful musical mind, even if inspiration at times seems second place to sheer facility. These are not only well-fashioned but often very satisfying pieces. Klaus Thunemann is an expert and persuasive advocate of the *Bassoon Sonata* and its companions here receive

highly accomplished performances. Throughout the Ensemble Villa Musica's Hindemith series we have heard so far, the recording is very faithful and lifelike.

(i) Double-bass Sonata; (ii) Trombone Sonata; (iii) Tuba Sonata; (iv) Cello Sonata; Small Sonata for Violoncello; A Frog He Went A-courting
*** MDG 304 0697-2. Randalu, with (i) Güttler; (ii) Slokar; (iii) Hilgers; (iv) Ostertag

This collection is both artistically rewarding and technically excellent. The sound is very vivid and present and the programme intelligently laid out. Hindemith was enormously prolific and often composed on automatic pilot, but these pieces are fresh and inventive.

Horn Sonata
(N) (M) (**) BBC mono BBCL 4164-2. Brain, Mewton-Wood
  – BEETHOVEN: *Quintet* (**); JACOB: *Wind Sextet*;
  HINDEMITH: *Horn Sonata*; VINTER: *Hunter's Moon* (***)

Dennis Brain gives a masterly account of the lyrically unpredictable and at times marmoreal Hindemith *Sonata* which, like the *Concerto*, was written for him. His outstanding partner, Noel Mewton-Wood, is a strong musical personality in his own right: in the slow movement his delicate, bravura articulation is memorable, and elsewhere his playing is truly authoritative. The mono recording is well balanced.

Kleine Kammermusik for Wind Quintet, Op. 24/2
*** Nim. NI 5728. V. Quintet – LIGETI: *6 Bagatelles*;
  NIELSEN: *Wind Quintet* ***
(BB) **(*) Naxos 8.553851-2. Thompson Wind Quintet –
  BARBER: *Summer Music* **(*); JANACEK: *Mládí* **(*);
  LARSSON: *Quattro tempi* **

The Vienna Quintet fully convey the wit and lightness of touch that distinguish Hindemith's writing in this entertaining *Kleine Kammermusik*. We are well served in this repertoire, but the 'quintett.wien' as they call themselves are as good as the very best. The playing is a delight from first to last and is beautifully recorded in the Wiener Konzerthaus. The coupling, too, is logical in giving us an exact contemporary, the Nielsen *Wind Quintet*.

The Michael Thompson Wind Quintet give an excellently spirited and alert performance with plenty of wit. The playing is wonderfully accomplished and sensitive but the close balance is a distinct handicap. If you think this would not worry you, it is worth the modest outlay.

Octet
**(*) Nim. NI 5461. BPO Octet – BEETHOVEN: *Septet* **(*)

The *Octet* is well fashioned but a bit manufactured, and many of the ideas find the composer at his most routine. The exception is the central slow movement, which has considerable eloquence. The playing is expert, but the recording is closely balanced and upfront.

String Quartets 1 in C, Op. 2; 2 in F min., Op. 10; 3 in C, Op. 16; 4, Op. 22; 5, Op. 32; 6 in E flat; 7 in E flat
(N) ** Praga PRD 350 113-114. Kocian Qt

The Hindemith quartets are not generously represented in the catalogue, so this issue is (on the face of it) particularly welcome. They also include an early quartet (Op. 2) composed in 1915 and not recognized in the published order of the scores. Accordingly, what we have always known as the *Sixth Quartet in E flat* of 1945 becomes the *Seventh*, and each of its predecessors adds one. Recorded in Geneva at the time of the Hindemith centenary in 1995, these Kocian performances are eminently dedicated and serviceable. At the same time, the playing here falls a little short of real distinction and needs more bite. Recommendable, but essentially a stopgap until something rather better comes along.

String Quartet 3, Op. 22

⊙ (***) Testament mono SBT 1052. Hollywood Qt –
PROKOFIEV: *Quartet 2;* WALTON: *Quartet in A min.* (***) ⊙

The Hollywood Quartet possessed extraordinary virtuosity and perfection of ensemble, and it is difficult to imagine more persuasive advocacy. The transfer is excellent and, although the mono sound is less than ideal, the performance still sweeps the board.

Viola Sonata in F, Op. 11/4

(***) Biddulph mono LAB 148. Primrose, Sandromá – BAX:
Fantasy Sonata for Viola & Piano; BLOCH: *Suite* (***)

The classic 1938 Primrose recording of Hindemith's most lyrical sonata, with Jesús María Sandromá, probably remains unsurpassed for sheer style and refinement of tone. Given the date, the sound is very acceptable.

(Unaccompanied) Viola Sonatas 1; 2, Op. 11/5; 3, Op. 25/1; 4, Op. 31/4

*** ASV CDDCA 947. Cortese

(i) Viola Sonatas (for viola and piano) Op. 11/4; Op. 25/4; (Unaccompanied) Viola Sonatas: Op. 11/5; Op. 25/1; Op. 31/4

*** ECM 833 309-2 (2). Kashkashian, (i) with Levin

The solo sonatas are played with superb panache and flair – and, even more importantly, with remarkable variety of colour – by Kim Kashkashian, who has an enormous dynamic range. The performances of the sonatas with piano are hardly less imaginative and the recording is good.

Paul Cortese is a player of considerable accomplishments and he is persuasive in this somewhat forbidding repertoire. He is not perhaps always as imaginative or as poetic as Kim Kashkashian, but the disc is certainly recommendable.

Violin Sonatas 1 in E flat, Op. 11/1; 2 in D, Op. 11/2; 3 in E; 4 in C

*** BIS CD 761. Wallin, Pöntinen
**(*) Live Classics LCL 161. Kagan, S. Richter

As with most Hindemith, both the Op. 11 sonatas are well crafted and inventive. The finest of the four is the last, in C major, which is both individual and finely wrought. Ulf Wallin and Roland Pöntinen play this repertoire with real dedication and conviction, and the BIS recording is very lifelike and present. They include a fragment of an alternative finale for the *E flat Sonata*, Op. 11/1, that Hindemith subsequently discarded.

The Kagan/Richter performances were given in the Grand Hall of the Moscow Conservatory in May 1978. Some of the Soviet recordings of Oleg Kagan have suffered from inferior sound, but this is acceptable without being anywhere near top-drawer. A tough programme for a live concert, and there is the occasional minor blemish of intonation or colour to serve as a reminder that this great violinist was human. Admirers of Hindemith will want this.

PIANO MUSIC

Piano Sonatas 1–3

*** MDG 304 0693-2. Randalu

Hindemith's three piano sonatas, all written in quick succession in 1936 just before he fled from Hitler's Germany, are firmly in the grand German tradition. Long neglected but among the most satisfying piano sonatas of the century, they owe a direct debt not just to Beethoven but also to Bach's *Well-Tempered Clavier.* Hindemith's crisply contrapuntal piano writing brings a strong consistency to the three contrasted works. No. 1 is the most challengingly ambitious, with the compact No. 2 more easily lyrical. Yet it is No. 3, directly echoing the first of Beethoven's late sonatas, Opus 101, which is the clearest masterpiece. Built on strikingly memorable themes and ending with a formidable double fugue, it inspires the Estonian, Kalle Randalu, to a powerful performance, very well recorded.

Ludus tonalis; Suite (1922), Op. 26

**(*) Hyp. CDA 66824. McCabe

Hindemith's *Ludus tonalis* – comprising 25 sections – is, in total, not far short of an hour in length. It has been recorded before, but not with more concentration and authority than it is on Hyperion by John McCabe. As if not wishing to compromise himself, instead of coupling it with something a little less formidably intellectual, he offers also the *Suite 1922* which, if anything, is thornier still. So if you are a Hindemith addict, this is surely a disc you will want to explore.

Organ Sonatas 1–3

*** Chan. 9097. Kee – REGER: *4 Organ Pieces* ***

Piet Kee plays on the Müller organ of St Bavo in Haarlem, an instrument more suited to Hindemith than the somewhat spacious acoustic in which it is recorded. This small point apart, Kee plays with his customary distinction and character. All three sonatas are rewarding, and no one investing in this disc is likely to be disappointed on either artistic or technical grounds.

VOCAL MUSIC

When Lilacs Last in the Dooryard Bloom'd (Requiem)

(M) *** Telarc CD 80132. DeGaetani, Stone, Atlanta Ch. & SO, Shaw

This 'Requiem for those we loved' is one of the composer's most deeply felt works and one of his best. Shaw gives a performance of great intensity and variety of colour and nuance. Both his soloists are excellent, and there is both weight and subtlety in the orchestral contribution. Splendid recording.

OPERA

(i; ii) Sancta Susanna (complete). Das Nusch-Nuschi: Dances, Op. 20; Tuttifäntchen: Suite; (i) 3 Songs, Op. 9

*** Chan. 9620. (i) Bullock; (ii) D. Jones, Gunson & Soloists, Leeds Festival Ch.; BBC PO, Y. P. Tortelier

In the one-Act opera *Sancta Susanna* Hindemith's musical language is distinctly expressionist, lyrical and atmospheric, though with traces of Gallic influence (and in particular Debussy) and Puccinian elements happily intermingled. It is a far cry from the austere, monochrome contrapuntalist of the later symphonies. Written immediately after the end of the First World War, it scandalized its first audiences by its erotic-cum-blasphemous character. It is a short piece, some 23 minutes in length, but enormously intense and concentrated in feeling. The performance is gripping, splendidly sung and expertly played by Yan Pascal Tortelier and the BBC Philharmonic Orchestra.

The oriental elements in the *Nusch-Nuschi Dances* simply adorn a 1920s-style score, while the suite from the children's pantomime, *Tuttifäntchen*, of 1922 is delightful in its use of tunes from children's games, with ragtime introduced in the *Dance of the Dolls*. The Straussian *Drei Gesänge*, Op. 9, written earlier, in 1917, are luxuriant and rich, and again unlike anything we know from the mature composer. Susan Bullock sings them with great conviction and flair.

HODDINOTT, Alun (Born 1929)

Concerto for Orchestra

(N) *** Classico CLASSCD 384. RLPO, Bostock – GREGSON; MCCABE: *Concertos for Orchestra****

Part of a triptych of *Orchestral Concertos* by contemporary British composers, Hoddinott's work is notable for ever-changing textures, underpinned by 23 tuned and untuned percussion instruments. The opening movement's momentum is created against an atmospheric background whch becomes both 'elegiac and spectral' in the central *Adagio*. But the haunted spirits are vanquished in the vibrant, motoric finale, full of energy, confidence and excitement, before the pounding final coda. The performance is both brilliant and committed, and vividly recorded.

HOFFMANN, Leopold (1738–93)

(i) *Flute Concerto in D* (attrib. Haydn)

✿ *** EMI 5 56577-2. Pahud, Berlin Haydn Ens., Schellenberger – JOSEF HAYDN: *Scherzandi 1–6*; M. HAYDN: *Flute Concerto* *** ✿

(N) *** CPO 999 888-2. Gurtner, Wiener Akademia, Haselböck – W. F. BACH: *Flute Concerto in D*; C. P. E. BACH: *Flute Concerto in D* ***

Hoffmann's attractive *Flute Concerto* has long been attributed to Haydn, and Pahud's delightfully polished account should ensure its survival, irrespective of its true composer.

Hoffmann's best-known concerto is also very well played and recorded on CPO, part of an attractive collection, including felicitous works by two of Bach's sons.

(i) *Oboe Concertos: in C (Badley), C2; G, G1*; (i; ii) *Oboe and Harpsichord Concertos: in F, F1; C, C1*

(N) **(BB)** ** Naxos 8.553979. Nicolaus Esterházy Sinfonia, Drahos, with (i) Schilli; (ii) Jandó

This disc of Hoffmann's *Oboe Concertos* offers greater variety of invention than the flute concertos, especially in the *Double Concertos* including the harpsichord, which brings appealing added colour. The interplay of the solo instruments is often delightful, such as in the *tempo di giusto* movement of the *C major Concerto*. Good performances and recording, but not in the inspired league.

Violin Concertos: in B flat, Bb1; in A, A2; (i) *Double Concerto for Violin and Cello in G (Badley), G1*

(N) **(BB)** **(*) Naxos 8.554233. McAslan, N. Chamber O, Ward, (ii) with Hugh

Hoffmann's *Violin Concertos* offer more scope than you might think for the soloist, and Lorraine McAslan responds to the music's virtuosity with aplomb, and she plays with appealing warmth and expression too. Tim Hugh is the excellent soloist in the enjoyable *Double Concerto*, though his (too forward) balance is not ideal, with the cello not able to blend into the sound-picture as it might, but the performance is still enjoyable. Nicholas Ward and the Northern Chamber Orchestra are fresher and more lively in direction than the Esterházy group (see above) and the sound in general is very good.

HOLBORNE, Antony (c. 1560–1602)

Pieces for bandora: Almain: The Night Watch; Fantazia; A Ground; for cittern: A French Toy; A Horne Pype; The Miller; Praeludium; Sicke Sicke and Very Sicke; (i) *for cittern with a bass: Galliard; Maister Earles Pavane; Queenes Galliard; for lute: Almains: Almaine; The Choice. Fantasia. Galliards: As it fell on a holie yve; The Fairy-rownde; Holburns passion; Muy linda; Responce; The teares of the muses. Pavans: Heres paternus; Pavan, and Galliard to the same; Posthuma; Sedet sola. A French Toy. Variations: Il Nodo di gordio*

➲ ✿ *** Gaudeamus CDGAU 173. Heringman, (i) with Pell

An entirely delightful representation on CD of an Elizabethan lutenist, composer and poet, now totally overshadowed by Dowland. Indeed, his melancholy pavane, *Posthuma*, has as much 'dolens' as almost anything by Dowland. It is this meditative quality which Jacob Heringman catches to perfection and which makes this collection so appealing. He improvises his own divisions when needed, as was expected by the composer, and his playing is appealingly spontaneous. But there is lively writing too, like *The Miller* and *A French Toy*; and how well they sound on the cittern, a robust-timbred instrument favoured mainly by the lower classes, and which came to be much played in barber's shops. The composer took especial care over the four duet pieces for cittern with bass viol. Heringman is beautifully recorded in a most suitable ambience, providing the ideal CD for a late-evening reverie.

Lute pieces: Cradle Pavane; Countess of Ormond's Galliard; The Fairy Round; Fantasia 3; Galliards 2 & 17; Heres Paternus; Muy Linda; The Night Watch; Last Will and Testament Pavans 2 & 11; Wanton

(BB) **(*) Naxos 8.553974. Wilson (lute) – ROBINSON: *Lute Pieces & Duets ****

Christopher Wilson plays these pieces very well, notably the lively items like *The Fairy Round* and *Wanton*, with *Muy Linda* a highlight. But he does not penetrate the inner core of the ruminative pieces as touchingly as Jacob Heringman. However, there is not too much duplication here and this inexpensive Naxos disc is well worth obtaining for the coupled repertoire (including duets) by Holborne's contemporary, Thomas Robinson.

HOLBROOKE, Joseph (1878–1958)

*The Birds of Rhiannon, Op. 87; The Children of Don:
Overture, Op. 56; Dylan: Prelude, Op. 53*
** Marco Polo 8.223721-2. Ukraine Nat. SO, Penny

In Holbrooke's opera *The Children of Don* (the first of a
trilogy) neither overture nor prelude offers particularly
memorable or individual ideas and, generally speaking, inspiration is pretty thin. There are touches of Wagner in the
former but the musical language is predominantly diatonic,
particularly in the tone-poem, *The Birds of Rhiannon*. The
longest piece is the *Prelude* to *Dylan*, which is pretty undistinguished stuff. The performances sound a bit under-rehearsed
but are adequate (some may find the horn vibrato a bit
excessive) and the recording is decent.

Piano Concerto 1 (Song of Gwyn ap Nudd), Op. 52
*** Hyp. CDA 67127. Milne, BBC Scottish SO, Brabbins –
  HAYDN WOOD: *Piano Concerto* ***

Joseph Holbrooke had the misfortune to develop his high
romantic style just when it was being superseded on almost
every front. It has taken a long time for his star to rise again,
but this ambitious piano concerto provides a fair sample of
his writing, presenting both its strengths and its weaknesses.
The grandeur of the manner is not matched often enough by
memorable material, and when a melody does emerge to
catch in the mind it verges on the banal. The piano-writing
too often suggests a popular idiom, making this an apt
coupling for the fine concerto by a composer who did find his
success in light music, Haydn Wood. What makes this recording of the concerto most enjoyable despite the weaknesses is
not only the brilliance of the performance – with Hamish
Milne masterly in finding poetry in the Chopinesque figuration – but also the presentation. As in the score, the 22
index-points are linked directly to the text of the poem which
inspired the piece, telling the evocative story. Full, well-
balanced recording.

Eilean Shona
(BB) *** Hyp. Helios CDH 55105. King, Britten Qt – COOKE;
  FRANKEL; MACONCHY: *Clarinet Quintets*; HOWELLS:
  Rhapsodic Quintet ***

Joseph Holbrooke's *Eilean Shona*, a brief but evocative portrayal of one of Scotland's Western Isles, acts as an epilogue in
this outstanding collection of *Clarinet Quintets* following on
after the sublime closing movement of Frankel's work. It is
played equally beautifully.

HOLMBOE, Vagn (1909–96)

(i) *Cello Concerto, Op. 120;* (ii) *Brass Quintet, Op. 79;* (iii)
Triade, Op. 123; (iv) *Benedic Domino, Op. 59*
*** BIS ADD/DDD CD 78. (i) Bengtsson, Danish RSO,
  Ferencsik; (ii) Swedish Brass Quintet; (iii) Tarr,
  Westenholz; (iv) Camerata Ch., Enevold

Vagn Holmboe's magificent *Cello Concerto* is given an excellent performance here, and the account of the choral piece,
Benedic Domino, has an austere beauty and elevation of
feeling that are rare in contemporary music. The *Brass Quintet* is effective and stirring; and the *Triade* for trombone and
organ is hardly less striking. Only the *Quintet* is a digital
recording, but its companions here are also strikingly good as
sound.

*Chamber Concertos (i) 1 for Piano Strings & Tympani,
Op. 17; (ii) 2 for Flute, Violin, Strings & Percussion, Op. 20;
(iii) 3 for Clarinet & Chamber Orchestra, Op. 21*
*** dacapo 8.224038. (i) Oland; (ii) Ostergaard, Futtrup; (iii)
  Tomsen; Danish R. Concert O, Koivula

*Chamber Concertos (i; ii; iv) 4 for Piano Trio & Chamber
Orchestra, Op. 30; (iii) 5 for Viola & Chamber Orchestra,
Op. 31; (ii) 6 for Violin & Chamber Orchestra, Op. 33*
*** dacapo 8.224063. (i) Oland; (ii) Futtrup; (iii) Frederiksen;
  (iv) Ullner; Danish R. Sinf., Koivula

*Chamber Concertos (i) 7, for Oboe, Op. 37. 8 (Sinfonia
Concertante), Op. 38; (ii) 9 for Violin & Viola, Op. 39*
*** dacapo 8.224086. (i) Artved; (ii) Futtrup,
  Frederiksen; Danish R. Sinf., Koivula

*Chamber Concertos 10 for Wood–brass–gut & Orchestra,
Op. 40; (i) 11 for Trumpet & Chamber Orchestra, Op. 44; (ii)
12 for Trombone & Orchestra, Op. 52; (iii) 13 for Oboe, Viola
& Chamber Orchestra, Op. 67*
*** dacapo 8.224087. (i) Antonsen; (ii) Mauger; (iii) Artved,
  Frederiksen; Danish R. Sinf., Koivula

Vagn Holmboe's concertos are fresh, clean-textured pieces,
full of musical interest and a zest for life. A good point to
start is the third disc (Nos. 7–9) which covers the period
1944–6. The most substantial of the three is No. 8, the
Sinfonia Concertante, with its inventive set of variations,
which (along with No. 11) is the only one that made any
headway into the repertory outside Denmark in the 1950s. It
is somewhat Hindemithian in its stance yet is distinctive.
Holmboe is always very much his own man. No. 11 has been
the most widely recorded. Rewarding music, very well performed and decently recorded.

*Chamber Concertos (i) 1, Op. 17; (ii) 3, Op. 21; (iii) 7, Op. 37;
(iv) Beatus Parvo for Choir & Orchestra, Op. 117*
(N) *** BIS CD 1176. Aalborg SO, Hughes, with (i) Ogawa;
  (ii) Fröst; (iii) Hunt; (iv) Danish Nat. Op. Ch.

BIS here follow up their series of the later *Chamber Concertos*
(see below) with these fine recordings of the earlier concertos
for piano (1939), clarinet (1942) and oboe (1945). The *Beatus
Parvo* (1971), composed for an amateur music society in
southern Sweden, has the same clarity of texture and immediacy of response. Those who have the dacapo accounts of
the concertos will probably not want to duplicate the works,
but readers coming to this repertoire afresh will find the
present issue and its companions bring performances of real
distinction and very vivid recorded sound.

*Chamber Concertos 8 (Sinfonia concertante), Op. 83; 10
(Woodwind, Brass and Gut), Op. 40; Concerto giocondo e
severo, Op. 132; Den Galsindede Tyrk (The Ill-tempered
Turk): Ballet Suite, Op. 32b*
*** BIS CD 917. Aalborg SO, Arwel Hughes

The *Eighth Chamber Concerto* was one of the first of Holmboe's orchestral works to be given in England (by Harry
Newstone and the Haydn Orchestra). It belongs in a set of
twelve chamber concertos composed during 1939–50 (a thirteenth followed in 1955). There is a strongly neo-classical
flavour to both scores, and those who enjoy the exhilarating
Fifth Symphony will derive much pleasure from both, and
particularly the resourceful theme-and-variations that comprise the second movement of the *Eighth*. Good though the
complete survey by the Danish Radio Sinfonietta is on

dacapo (see above), these performances and above all the recordings are even finer.

In the *Concerto giocondo e severo* of 1977, Holmboe returned to the genre and produced a short work of just over ten minutes, which is scored for much larger forces than its predecessors but which has much of their ambience and spirit and is every bit as rewarding. Holmboe composed little for the stage, though there is an opera, *Kniven* ('The Knife') – and his ballet *Den Galsindede Tyrk* ('The Ill-tempered Turk'), based on a Thousand-and-One-Nights theme by the Danish author and illustrator Axel Salto, which occupied him in 1942–4, was never mounted. In 1970 Holmboe returned to the score and fashioned a five-movement work of quality from the original, recasting and rescoring much of it. In a tribute in the journal *Nordic Sounds* the Canadian scholar Paul Rapaport wrote of Holmboe as 'a noble and wondrous composer', and here is another disc to bear witness to that. As his BIS cycle of the symphonies has shown, Owain Arwel Hughes and his fine Aalborg musicians are completely attuned to Holmboe's world and the recording has all the realism, clarity and presence one has come to expect from BIS and Robert Suff. Recommended with all possible enthusiasm.

Chamber Concertos (i) 11 for Trumpet & Orchestra, Op. 44; (ii) 12 for Trombone, Op. 52; (iii) Tuba Concerto, Op. 152. Intermezzo Concertante, Op. 171

*** BIS CD 802. (i) Hardenberger; (ii) Lindberg; (iii) Larsen; Aalborg SO, Hughes

The noble neo-baroque *Concerto No. 11 for Trumpet* (1948) could hardly be better served than by Håkan Hardenberger's account with the Aalborg orchestra, and one is tempted to add that any newcomer will have to be pretty good to match Christian Lindberg's account of the *Twelfth Chamber Concerto*. These are inspiriting and inspiring pieces. The one-movement *Tuba Concerto* explores the virtuoso possibilities of this instrument as do few others; so does the *Intermezzo Concertante*. These are dazzling performances and the orchestral support under Owain Arwel Hughes is first class. The recording is state of the art. Highly recommended.

Epilog, Op. 80; Epitaph (Symphonic Metamorphosis), Op. 68; Monolith, Op. 76; Tempo variabile, Op. 108

☯➞ ✸ *** BIS CD 852. Aarhus SO, Hughes

The first of Vagn Holmboe's *Symphonic Metamorphoses* (Holmboe's title, *Epitaph*, Op. 68, was to be all too prophetic) brings musical ideas that unfold, change shape and assume new identities without losing sight of their individuality, in much the same way as does, say, the *Seventh Symphony* of Sibelius. Three like-minded successors followed in the next few years, all of them works of great concentration, cogency and power. The playing of the Aarhus orchestra is excellent and Owain Arwel Hughes is in total sympathy with these magnificent scores. The recording is state of the art.

Flute Concertos 1, Op. 126; 2, Op. 147; (i) Concerto for Recorder, Strings, Celesta & Vibraphone, Op. 122

☯➞ *** BIS CD 911. Wiesler, (i) with Laurin; Aarhus SO, Hughes

The *Flute Concertos* and the *Concerto for Recorder, Strings, Celesta and Vibraphone* are wonderfully inventive scores whose luminous, shining textures captivate the mind and reaffirm the conviction that Holmboe stands head and shoulders above his contemporaries in the North. Strong performances from all concerned, and splendid recording too. Don't miss this.

Preludes for a Sinfonietta Ensemble: To a Dolphin; To a Living Stone, Op. 172C/5; To a Maple Tree, Op. 168/3; To the Unsettled Weather, Op. 188/10; To the Victoria Embankment, Op. 184/8

*** dacapo 8.224123. Copenhagen Athelas Sinf., Bellincampi

The *Preludes* for a sinfonietta ensemble or chamber orchestra are miniature tone-poems, evocative and full of atmosphere and invention.

(i) Preludes for a Sinfonietta Ensemble, Vol. 2: To a Pine Tree, Op. 164/1; To a Willow Tree, Op. 170/4; To the Seagulls and the Cormorants, Op. 174/6; To the Pollution of Nature, Op. 180/7; To the Calm Sea, Op.187/9; (ii; iii) Music with Horn, Op. 148; (iii; iv) Trombone Sonata, Op. 172a

*** dacapo 8.224124. (i) Copenhagen Atlas Sinf., Bellincampi; (ii) Ekman; (iii) Steohr; (iv) Sørensen

The second issue includes the *Music with Horn* for piano, violin and horn and the *Trombone Sonata*. There is something cleansing about Holmboe's late music, and readers will find its rewards are rich: his music goes its own way without any thought of ephemeral fashion. Dedicated performances from these Copenhagen musicians and their Italian-born conductor, and very well recorded too.

Sinfonias 1–4 (Chairos), Op. 73

(N) *** dacapo 8.226017/18. Danish R. Sinfonia, Koivula

The *Four Sinfonias* for strings come from the period 1957–62, thus following on from the 13 *Chamber Concertos* (1939–56) and the *Eighth Symphony*. Apart from the *Fourth*, all the *Sinfonias* are in one continuous movement of just over ten minutes (No. 2 takes almost 20). The *Fourth* consists of a Prelude, two Interludes and a Postlude. When the *Sinfonias* are performed together as the composite collection '*Chairos*', the three one-movement pieces are enveloped in the fourth, so No. 1 is preceded by the Prelude, and the *Second* by the first Interlude. The second disc presents the work in this form, to spare the listener complicated track programming. *Chairos* means 'time' – but 'psychological time', as we sense it, not time as it is conceived in minutes and seconds (*Chronos*). The invention, as always in Holmboe, unfolds naturally and is fashioned with that distinction of mind we associate with this composer. Very dedicated playing by the members of the Danish Radio's chamber orchestra.

Symphonies 1, Op. 4; 3 (Sinfonia rustica), Op. 25; 10, Op. 105

*** BIS CD 605. Aarhus SO, Hughes

The general outlook of the *First Symphony* (*Sinfonia da camera*) is neo-classical and its proportions are modest, but one recognizes the vital current of the later Holmboe, the lucidity of thinking and the luminous textures. The last movement has an infectious delight in life; so, too, has the exhilarating finale of the *Third* (*Sinfonia rustica*), the first of his three wartime symphonies. The *Tenth* is dark, powerful and imaginative: altogether one of the Danish composer's most subtle and satisfying works. The performances and recordings are altogether first class.

Symphony 2, Op. 15; Sinfonia in memoriam, Op. 65

*** BIS CD 695. Aarhus SO, Hughes

The *Second Symphony* with its imaginative middle movement and its vital companions is a splendid piece. The *Sinfonia in memoriam* is a dark work of striking power and imaginative breadth and is masterly in every way. Owain Arwel Hughes and the Aarhus orchestra give a performance that is in every way worthy of it, and the recording is in the demonstration bracket.

Symphonies (i) 4 (Sinfonia sacra), Op. 29; 5, Op. 35
**(*) BIS CD 572. (i) Jutland Op. Ch.; Aarhus SO, Hughes

The *Fifth Symphony* makes a good entry point into Holmboe's world. The only word to describe its outer movements is exhilarating. The slow movement has a modal character, but an anguished outburst in the middle serves as a reminder that this is a wartime work, composed during the dark days of the Nazi occupation. The *Fourth* (*Sinfonia sacra*) is a six-movement choral piece. It encompasses a bracing vigour and underlying optimism alongside moments of sustained grief. Very good performances, though the strings are a little under-strength and the acoustic is on the dry side. But don't let this put you off this inspiriting music.

Symphonies 6, Op. 43; 7, Op. 50
**(*) BIS CD 573. Aarhus SO, Hughes

Holmboe's *Sixth Symphony* is a much darker piece than its predecessor. Its distinctively Nordic world is established by the brooding, slow-moving fourths of the long introduction; there is writing of great luminosity too. The one-movement *Seventh Symphony* is a highly concentrated score, individual in both form and content, which encompasses great variety of pace and mood. Owain Arwel Hughes acquits himself very well, and this is music that speaks with so strong and distinctive a voice that it is self-recommending.

Symphonies 8, Op. 56 (1951); 9 (1968)
⊶ ✿*** BIS CD 618. Aarhus SO, Hughes

This conductor has a real feeling for the composer and penetrates the spirit of the score of the *Eighth Symphony*. The *Ninth Symphony* is a dark, powerful work, among the finest Holmboe has given us. This is music which, one can feel with some certainty, future generations will want to hear. The Aarhus orchestra are equally persuasive in the *Ninth* as in the *Eighth*, and the recording is the best so far in the cycle.

Symphonies 11, Op. 141; 12, Op. 175; 13, Op. 192
*** BIS CD 728. Aarhus SO, Hughes

The *Thirteenth Symphony* is an astonishing achievement for a composer in his mid-eighties. It is a veritable powerhouse. The *Twelfth* is tautly structured and well argued, though less inspired than the *Eleventh Symphony*, which finds Holmboe at his most visionary. Every credit is owed to Owain Arwel Hughes and the Aarhus Symphony Orchestra for their fervent advocacy of this music and to the splendid BIS engineers for the vivid and superbly natural sound.

String Quartets 1, Op. 46; 3, Op. 48; 4, Op. 63
*** dacapo CDDC 9203. Kontra Qt

String Quartets 2, Op. 47; 5, Op. 66; 6, Op. 78
*** dacapo 8.224026. Kontra Qt

These quartets have a certain reserve: nothing is overstated, everything is quietly but cogently argued and, once one has broken through its reticence, its rewards are rich. This is easily the finest post-war quartet cycle from Scandinavia. The *Second Quartet* has a particularly engaging main theme and these artists play it with conviction. The *Fifth* and *Sixth* are both finely argued works. What a rewarding composer Holmboe is, and how well played and recorded these quartets are!

String Quartets 10, Op. 102; 11, Op. 111 (Quartetto rustico); 12, Op. 116
**(*) dacapo 8.224101. Kontra Qt

The *Tenth Quartet* in two movements is arguably the most concentrated in feeling and is powerfully structured. Its successor is the most relaxed and smiling. The *Twelfth* is a five-movement piece whose central slow movement has great eloquence. The performances are excellent and the Danish Radio recording acceptable in quality, though tone tends to harden a little above the stave.

String Quartets 13, Op. 124; 14, Op. 125; 15, Op. 135
*** dacapo 8.224127. Kontra Qt

The *Thirteenth Quartet* must be numbered among the most eloquent of Holmboe's works. Indeed, all three works here find him at the height of his intellectual powers. There is a certain severity and rigour about these pieces and the Kontras give them all with the concentration and dedication they require. The recordings, made in 1997–8, are excellent and without hardness. Strongly recommended to admirers of this composer.

String Quartets 16, Op. 146; 18 (Giornata), Op. 153; Sværm, Op. 190b; Quartetto sereno, Op. 197 (completed Per Nørgård)
*** dacapo 8.224131. Kontra Qt

String Quartets 17 (Mattinata), Op. 152; 19 (Serata), Op. 156; 20 (Notturno), Op. 160
*** dacapo 8.224128. Kontra Qt

As their titles show, the last four quartets form an entity on the theme of the times of the day from morning to evening. They were composed in quick succession between 1982 and 1985. Despite their titles, these works are pure music and share the same distinction of mind that we find in their contemporaries. Along with the quartets of Robert Simpson and of course Shostakovich, this is the most notable twentieth-century quartet cycle after Bartók.

PIANO MUSIC

Romanian Suite; Sonatina Briosa (symphonic suite); Suono da bardo; Suite, Op. 4
*** Danacord DACOCD 502. Blyme

Suono da bardo is Holmboe's most important piano piece and comes from the same period as the *Seventh Symphony*. Subtitled 'Symphonic Suite', it is undoubtedly more symphonic than pianistic. Holmboe's composer-pianist colleague, Niels Viggo Bentzon, gave its first performance, and Anker Blyme made its first LP recording a few years later, in 1956. He returned to it some four decades later to give this admirable account; the rest of the programme is equally impressive.

VOCAL MUSIC

Requiem for Nietzsche, Op. 84
⊶ ✿ *** dacapo 8.224207. Rønning, Reuter, Danish Nat. Ch. & SO, Schønwandt

The *Requiem for Nietzsche* is quite simply one of the most inspired choral works of the twentieth century. It is a work by which the composer set great store – and rightly so! Inspired by Torkhild Bjørnvig's sonnets on events in the life of Nietzsche, it has everything that we recognize from the finest of the symphonies: vision, subtlety, concentration, power and originality – particularly in the imaginative use of voices. It is good to welcome its appearance in so eloquent and committed a performance. An exceptionally rewarding work and altogether excellent sound.

HOLST, Gustav (1874–1934)

(i; ii) *Egdon Heath, Op. 47*; (iii) *A Fugal Concerto, Op. 40/2*; (iv) *A Moorside Suite*; (i; ii) *The Perfect Fool* (ballet suite), *Op. 39*; (iii) *St Paul's Suite, Op. 29/2*; (v; vi) *Choral Hymns from the Rig Veda, Op. 26/3*; (v) *The Evening Watch, Op. 43/1*; (vii; ii) *The Hymn of Jesus, Op. 37*; (v; viii) *7 Part Songs, Op. 44*; (v; vii; i; ix) *Savitri* (opera; complete)

(M) *** Decca (ADD/DDD) 470 191-2 (2). (i) LPO, (ii) Boult; (iii) St Paul CO, Hogwood; (iv) Grimethorpe Colliery Band, Howarth; (v) Purcell Singers, Imogen Holst; (vi) with Ellis; (vii) BBC Ch. & SO; (viii) ECO; (ix) with J. Baker, Tear, Hemsley

A fine collection of Decca's classic Holst recordings. The mystical element of *The Planets* is very apparent in *The Hymn of Jesus*, and the fine (1962) recording adds remarkable atmosphere to Boult's distinguished performance. The bleak, sombre portrayal of *Egdon Heath* is just as hauntingly evocative, while the brilliantly played and recorded *Perfect Fool* music flashes with colour. There are few chamber operas so beautifully scaled as *Savitri* and Imogen Holst could hardly be more imaginative, while Janet Baker in particular produces some of her most intense and expressive singing. The *Rig Veda Choral Hymns* are also from a Sanskrit source, and the composer himself suggested that the last of them could, if necessary, be used as a prelude to *Savitri*. The opening *Hymn to the Dawn*, and the fast and rhythmically fascinating *Hymn to the Waters* are even more attractive. The *Seven Part Songs* are hardly less inventive and, like the other Imogen Holst performances, are equally sympathetic. The Grimethorpe account of the *Moorside Suite* (in its original, brass-band form) is first class and given recording that approaches demonstration standard. Hogwood's digital *St Paul's Suite* and *Fugal Concerto* are excellent. Only the lack of texts mars this highly recommendable release.

Beni Mora (Oriental Suite); Egdon Heath; Fugal Overture; Hammersmith; (i) Invocation for Cello & Orchestra. Somerset Rhapsody
*** Naxos 8.553696. RSNO, Lloyd-Jones; (i) with Hugh

The six works here are neatly balanced, three dating from before the climactic period of *The Planets* and three after. So the generously lyrical *Somerset Rhapsody*, *Beni Mora* and the long-neglected *Invocation for Cello and Orchestra* (with Timothy Hugh a moving soloist) lead on to the tauter and more astringent post-war works: the Hardy-inspired *Egdon Heath*, the darkly intense prelude and fugue, *Hammersmith*, and the *Fugal Overture*. Fresh and idiomatic performances, superbly recorded in full and brilliant sound.

(i) *Brook Green Suite for String Orchestra*; (ii) *Fugal Concerto for Flute and Oboe*; *The Perfect Fool (Ballet Suite)*; *St Paul's Suite for String Orchestra*; *Somerset Rhapsody*,

Op. 21/2; (iii) *Six Choruses for Male Voices*, excerpts: *Good Friday; Love Song; Intercession; Before Sleep; Drinking Song. A Dirge for Two Veterans*
☛ (B) *** CfP (DDD/ADD) 575 9812. ECO, (i) Menuhin; (ii) with Snowden; Theodore; (iii) with Baccholian Singers, Humphries

There are a number of collections of Holst's shorter orchestral works currently available on CD, but none is better played or recorded than this and none is better value. Holst wrote for St Paul's Girls' School, Hammersmith, not just the *St Paul's Suite* but also the *Brook Green Suite* (one passes this pleasant grassy patch on the right, while driving between Hammersmith and Shepherd's Bush). Both sound very fresh, while the rarer *Somerset Rhapsody* is also very atmospherically presented. There is some delightful solo playing from Jonathan Snowden and David Theodore in the *Fugal Concerto*. Even if the suite from *The Perfect Fool* involves duplication, this is still a disc well worth having, the more so as EMI have now added a short but memorably beautiful collection of Holst's shorter choral pieces, beautifully sung and warmly recorded two decades earlier. Helen Waddell's *Medieval Latin Lyrics* provided the texts for the *Six Choruses for Male Voices and Strings*, of which five are included. Most memorable of all is the darkly compressed *A Dirge for Two Veterans*, a processional setting with brass and percussion, written in 1914.

Brook Green Suite; (i) *Double Violin Concerto, Op. 49*; (ii) *Fugal Concerto for Flute, Oboe & Strings, Op. 40/2*; (iii) *Lyric Movement for Viola & Small Orchestra; 2 Songs Without Words, Op. 22; St Paul's Suite, Op. 29/2*
*** Chan. 9270. (i) Ward, Watkinson; (ii) Dobing, Hooker; (iii) Tees; City of L. Sinfonia, Hickox

The most striking piece here, a fine example of Holst's later, sparer style, is the *Double Concerto* for two violins and small orchestra, very taut and intense. The delicacy of the solo playing in the central *Lament* of this fine work is matched by the ethereal *pianissimo* from Stephen Tees at the opening of the *Lyric Movement*. The woodwind playing is delightful here too, as is the gentle clarinet solo which opens the *Country Song*, the first of Holst's two *Songs Without Words*; the second, appropriately, is more robust. The *Brook Green Suite* is wonderfully fresh and there is a comparable lightness of touch at the opening of the delightful *Fugal Concerto*. What matters throughout this programme is the surging warmth that Richard Hickox draws from his modest forces. The recording is superb – very real indeed.

Cotswolds Symphony in F, Op. 8; A Hampshire Suite, Op. 28/2 (orch. Gordon Jacob); *The Perfect Fool* (ballet suite); *Scherzo for Orchestra* (1933/4); *Walt Whitman Overture*
*** Classico CLASSCD 284. Munich SO, Bostock

The work completely new to CD is the *Walt Whitman Overture*, written as early as 1899. It is a vigorous but untypical piece, its scoring strong on trombones. The rather jolly *Cotswolds Symphony* immediately shows the Holstian flair for colourful orchestration and has a folksy influence. The melancholy slow movement (*An Elegy for William Morris*) brings a few slight hints of the later Holst; its Scherzo has an attractive lumbering dance rhythm; and the finale brings quite a striking tune in 6/4 time. *A Hampshire Suite* is Gordon Jacob's orchestration of the *First Suite for Military Band*, and he skilfully ensures that wind and brass textures predominate. The independent *Scherzo* was the composer's final orchestral flourish. But it is the familiar suite from *The Perfect Fool* in which we hear the composer at his most inspired and, like the rest of the programme, it is most vividly played and recorded, with the slow movement especially persuasive. It is remarkable how well this fine Munich orchestra takes to English music under the expert guidance of Douglas Bostock.

(i) *Egdon Heath*; (ii) *Fugal Concerto, Op. 40/2*
(M) (***) BBC mono/stereo BBCB 8007-2. (i) LSO, Britten; (ii) Adeny, Graeme, ECO, I. Holst – BRITTEN: *The Building of the House Overture*; BRIDGE: *Enter Spring; The Sea* ***

Though the 1961 mono recording is dry, with the limited dynamic range sabotaging *pianissimo*s, the concentration of Britten interpreting *Egdon Heath*, one of Holst's most inspired works, makes this well worth hearing, particularly with such excellent couplings.

Imogen Holst's urgent, robust reading of her father's *Fugal Concerto* comes from 1969 in much finer sound, also recorded at the Aldeburgh Festival. She brings out a bluff honesty in Holst's very English neo-classical writing. Fine solo work, too, from Richard Adeney on the flute and Peter Graeme on the oboe.

Egdon Heath; The Perfect Fool (ballet suite)
●━ (M) *** EMI 5 62615-2 [5 626162]. LSO, Previn – BRITTEN: *Sinfonia da Requiem* etc. *** ◉

Previn's account of *Egdon Heath* is full of dark intensity and his *Perfect Fool* ballet suite makes a colourful, extrovert contrast. First-class recording makes this an excellent bonus for Previn's outstanding Britten coupling.

Hammersmith: Prelude & Scherzo, Op. 52; Marching Song, Op.22; Military Band Suites 1 in E flat; 2 in F, Op. 28/1–2; arr. of BACH (attrib.): Fugue à la gigue
*** Chan. 9697. Royal N. College of Music Wind O, Reynish – VAUGHAN WILLIAMS: *English Folksongs Suite*, etc. ***

Truly marvellous bravura playing from the Royal Northern College of Music's Wind Orchestra in the *Second Military Band Suite*. Timothy Reynish catches the jaunty quality of this attractive music and is especially perceptive in the way he sneaks the *Greensleeves* melody into the *Fantasia on the Dargason*. The only slight disappointment is the climax of the great *Chaconne*, at the opening of the *First Suite*, and the bass drum is submerged – not nearly as telling as on the Telarc recording. As a compensation we are given an inspired account of *Hammersmith*, the finest performance on record. The work's haunting atmosphere is fully captured. It is good, too, to have Holst's effective arrangement of the spirited *Fugue à la gigue*. Apart from the matter of the bass drum, the vivid Chandos recording is demonstration-worthy, with splendid range, detail and a rich underlying sonority. Most enjoyable!

Military Band Suites 1 in E flat; 2 in F
●━ ◉ *** Telarc CD 80038. Cleveland Symphonic Winds, Fennell – HANDEL: *Royal Fireworks Music* ***

Holst's two *Military Band Suites* contain some magnificent music. Frederick Fennell's Telarc versions have more gravitas though no less *joie de vivre* than his old Mercury set. They are magnificent, and the recording is truly superb – digital technique used in a quite overwhelmingly exciting way. The

Chaconne of the *First Suite* makes a quite marvellous effect here. The playing of the Cleveland wind group is of the highest quality.

The Planets (suite), Op. 32
(M) *** Decca 476 17242. Montreal Ch. & SO, Dutoit
●━ *** DG **SACD** 471 634-2; CD 445 860-2. Monteverdi Ch. women's voices, Philh. O, Gardiner – GRAINGER: *The Warriors* ***
(M) *** Decca (ADD) 452 303-2. VPO, Karajan – ELGAR: *Enigma Variations* ***
(M) *** EMI 5 67748-2 [567749]. Geoffrey Mitchell Ch., LPO, Boult – ELGAR: *Enigma Variations* ***
(BB) *** DG (ADD) 439 446-2. Boston SO, Steinberg – ELGAR: *Enigma Variations* ***
(M) *** DG (ADD) 463 627-2. Boston SO, Steinberg – R. STRAUSS: *Also sprach Zarathustra* ***
*** DG 439 011-2. Berlin Ch., BPO, Karajan
(B) **(*) LSO Live LSO 0029. LSO, C. Davis
(M) **(*) BBC (ADD) BBCM 5002-2. BBC SO, Sargent – ELGAR: *Enigma Variations* **(*)
(BB) **(*) EMI Encore 5 75868-2. Amb. S., Philh. O, Rattle – BRITTEN: *Sinfonia da Requiem* ***
(M) **(*) Chan. 6683. SNO & Ch., Gibson
(M) (***) Cala mono CACD 0526. NBC SO, Stokowski (with DEBUSSY: *Prélude à l'après-midi d'un faune; La Cathédrale engloutie* (**(*)); GOULD: *2 Marches* (***))
(M) ** RCA 74321 68018-2. Philh. O, Slatkin (with VAUGHAN WILLIAMS: *Fantasia on Greensleeves*, etc. **(*))

(i) The Planets; Beni Mora; (ii) The Perfect Fool (Ballet Suite)
(B) *** CfP 585 9132. (i) BBC SO; (ii) RPO; Sargent

The Planets (suite); Egdon Heath, Op. 47
(BB) *** Warner Apex 8573 89087-2. BBC SO, with women's chorus & organ, A. Davis

The Planets; The Perfect Fool (Suite)
(BB) **(*) Virgin 2×1 5 61510-2 (2). RLPO, with Ch., Mackerras – ORFF: *Carmina Burana* **(*)

Charles Dutoit's natural feeling for mood, rhythm and colour, so effectively used in his records of Ravel, here results in an outstandingly successful version of *The Planets*, both rich and brilliant, and recorded with an opulence to outshine almost all rivals. It is remarkable that, whether in the relentless build-up of *Mars*, the lyricism of *Venus*, the rich exuberance of *Jupiter* or in much else, Dutoit and his Canadian players sound so idiomatic. It won the *Gramophone* Engineering Award in 1987, as well it might, and now appears in Universal's 'Gramophone Awards Collection' at mid-price.

With speeds never exaggerated, John Eliot Gardiner avoids vulgarity, yet with his rhythmic flair he gives *The Planets* a new buoyancy. Outstandingly enjoyable are the two most extrovert pieces: *Jupiter, the Bringer of Jollity* has rarely sounded so joyful, with a hint of wildness at the start, and the dancing rhythms of *Uranus* have a scherzando sparkle, with timpani and brass stunningly caught in the full, brilliant recording. The offstage women's chorus at the end of *Neptune* has seldom been more subtly balanced. Gardiner's *Planets* stands alongside the other current highly recommendable versions, whereas on DG the unusual Grainger coupling, typically rumbustious, pays tribute to the conductor's great-uncle, the composer Balfour Gardiner, who promoted the first performances of both works. This is also available in compatible SACD surround sound.

With Karajan at his peak, this extraordinarily magnetic and powerful (1961) Decca account of *The Planets* is uniquely individual, bringing a rare tension, an extra magnetism, the playing combining polish and freshness. The superb Decca recording – produced by John Culshaw in the Sofiensaal – is fully worthy of reissue in Decca's 'Classic Sound' series. *Mars* is remorselessly paced and, with its whining Wagnerian tubas, is unforgettable, while the ravishingly gentle portrayal of *Venus* brings ardent associations with the goddess of love, rather than seeking a peaceful purity. The gossamer textures of *Mercury* and the bold geniality of *Jupiter* contrast with the solemn, deep melancholy expressed by the VPO strings at the opening of *Saturn*. *Uranus* brings splendid playing from the Vienna brass, given splendid bite.

With spectacularly brilliant and wide-ranging digital recording, engineered by Tony Faulkner, Andrew Davis's set of *Planets* is among the finest of modern recordings, and this Apex disc is a first choice among super-bargain versions. *Mars*, taken briskly, is both sinister and barbarous, followed by a translucently chaste *Venus*, while *Mercury* has sprightly daintiness and delicacy. *Jupiter* galumphs ruggedly but the highlight of the performance is *Saturn*, whose remorseless forward tread has remarkable sustained intensity, with the closing bass pedal notes (recorded by Davis on the organ at King's College) especially telling. The ethereal atmosphere of *Neptune* is sustained by a celestially delicate contribution from the women of the BBC Chorus and exquisite *pianissimo* orchestral tracery. *Egdon Heath* then follows on very effectively, another intense performance, but here the spectacular recording at climaxes sounds more uninhibited, less in character than in the older Boult and Previn versions.

Sir Adrian Boult with the LPO gives a performance at once intense and beautifully played, spacious and dramatic, rapt and pointed. The great melody of *Jupiter* is calculatedly less resonant and more flowing than previously but is still affecting, and *Uranus* as well as *Jupiter* has its measure of jollity. The spacious slow movements are finely poised and the recording, always excellent, has added presence and definition in its latest remastering.

The EMI engineers have freshened the quality of Sargent's early stereo recordings on Classics for Pleasure, made in Kingsway Hall in the late 1950s and Abbey Road in 1961, so that they hardly sound dated at all, and have still plenty of spectacle. Sir Malcolm introduced many of us to *The Perfect Fool* and, like *The Planets*, his performance is full of character. *Mars*, taken fast, like *Uranus*, has plenty of clarity and bite and the organ pedals come through well in the sombre portrayal of *Saturn*, while the central tune in *Jupiter* is given special dignity. Sargent is equally at home in *Beni Mora*, an attractively exotic piece that shows Holst's flair for orchestration in a different but equally vivid way. Altogether a splendid collection, showing Sargent at his most charismatic.

Steinberg's Boston set of *Planets*, offered in alternative couplings, is another outstanding version from a vintage analogue period. It remains one of the most exciting and involving versions and now sounds brighter and sharper in outline, though with some loss of opulence. *Mars* in particular is intensely exciting. At his fast tempo, Steinberg may get to his *fortissimos* a little early, but rarely has the piece sounded so menacing on record. The testing point for most will no doubt be *Jupiter*, and here Steinberg the excellent Elgarian comes to the fore, giving a wonderful *nobilmente* swagger.

Karajan's early (1981) digital DG recording is spectacularly wide-ranging, while the marvellously sustained *pianissimo*

playing of the Berlin Philharmonic – as in *Venus* and the closing pages of *Saturn* – is very telling indeed. *Mars* has great impact, and the sound, full and firm in the bass, gives the performance throughout a gripping immediacy and presence. *Jupiter*, at its climax, still seems a bit fierce: ideally it needs a riper body of tone, yet the big melody has a natural flow and nobility. *Venus* brings sensuous string-phrasing, *Mercury* and *Uranus* have beautiful springing in the triplet rhythms, and the climax of that last movement brings an amazing glissando on the organ. In short this is a thrilling performance and highly recommendable, but it remains at full price and without a coupling.

Sir Colin Davis's disc on the LSO's own label series offers a well-paced live recording that is marked by exceptionally clear textures, even though the sound is rather more recessed than most others recorded in the Barbican. *Jupiter* brings an incisive performance, and *Uranus* is clipped and precise, but the gentler, slower movements are the most impressive, with string *pianissimos* of exceptional refinement, with *Saturn* rapt and intense at a very measured tempo, and the end of *Neptune* bringing an offstage chorus very realistically balanced. Even at super-bargain price there are more flamboyant rivals, some with generous couplings, but this gains from the clarity of its modern digital sound.

For Simon Rattle, EMI's digital recording provides wonderfully atmospheric sound, and the quality in *Venus* and *Mercury* is also beautiful, clear and translucent. Otherwise it is not as distinctive a version as one might have expected from this leading conductor; it is sensibly paced but neither so polished nor so bitingly committed as Karajan or Boult, and *Jupiter* is disappointing, lacking in thrust and warmth. But it is fair value on EMI's budget Encore label coupled with Britten's *Sinfonia da Requiem*.

Sargent's BBC account of *The Planets* was recorded (like the coupled Elgar) in the Royal Albert Hall (in 1965), though the inner leaflet incorrectly suggests the Royal Festival Hall as the venue. Though this was a February performance, not one given at the Proms, the atmosphere is similarly electric, with the sequence of movements building warmly and atmospherically. Good, full-bodied if rather opaque sound.

Gibson's reading is characteristically direct and certainly well played. Other versions have greater individuality and are more involving, but there is no doubt that the Chandos recording has fine bite and presence, although there are moments when one would have expected a greater degree of transparency.

Mackerras's usual zestful approach communicates readily and the Liverpool orchestra brings a lively response, but the over-reverberant recording tends to cloud the otherwise pungently vigorous *Mars*, and both *Venus* and *Saturn* seem a little straightforward and marginally undercharacterized, while again in the powerful climax of *Uranus* there is some blurring from the resonance. *The Perfect Fool*, with its vivid colouring and irregular rhythms, has much in common with *The Planets* and makes a fine coupling, especially when played with such flair. This now comes on a bargain Virgin Double, coupled with an excitingly vivid account of Orff's *Carmina Burana*, rather let down by inadequate documentation.

Stokowski's personality is stamped on every note of his individual and exciting reading of *The Planets*, taken from an NBC broadcast in February 1943. The tempi, with the exception of a few exaggerated examples, are remarkably similar to Holst's own, though the performance is very individual. Each planet is vividly characterized, with plenty of atmosphere running through each of the seven movements. The sound calls for some tolerance: although basically full – the opening of *Mars* (which makes a thrilling impact) is particularly effective – there is a fair amount of distortion at the climaxes and the surface noise can at times make its presence felt. But not too much should be made of this as the performance tends to make one forget technical imperfections.

Slatkin's recording dates from 1996 and has the benefit of first-class orchestral playing and recording. He brings out much of the beauty and detail of the work if, ultimately, the reading does not convey the full magical qualities that the score possesses. *Mercury* is certainly fleet and light, but *Jupiter*, the 'Bringer of Jollity', feels a little earth-bound. *Saturn* and *Neptune*, too, seem just that bit too slow and uncelestial in Slatkin's hands, whereas in other accounts, Boult's for example, the otherworldly qualities of the score are conveyed much more mystically.

The Planets (including Colin Matthews: *Pluto*; with visualization by Rhodric Huw)
(N) BBC Opus Arte **DVD** OA 09162. BBC Nat O of Wales, Atherton (DVD Producer: Ferenc van Damme)

This 'lavish visualization' of *The Planets*, according to the blurb on the box 'features spectacular images which enhance the symbolic meaning attributed to each planet by the composer'. In fact, the result is an almost unmitigated disaster. The war imagery for *Mars* is only too predictable, *Venus* opens in Arctic wastes, *Mercury* provides animated computer graphics which soon weary the eye; *Jupiter*, the most English of the set, ends up in Latin America and even includes a glimpse of a bullfight; poor *Uranus* is given speeded-up urban images and telescopes, and *Neptune* washy colouristic patterns. Colin Matthews's additional *Pluto* comes off best, with bizarre images which almost fit his score which, although imaginative, is of a lesser calibre than Holst's. In between we are offered glimpses of the orchestra and Atherton, ill-focused and over-lit (only the solo cellist seems worthy of a clear picture!). Worst of all, it is all so *boring*, and the listener is robbed of the privilege of switching off the video and listening only to the music, for various sound-effects are laminated on, and in any case the orchestral recording, though full and well balanced, has a limited dynamic range. It is more of a soundtrack to a film than a performance in its own right. Watching this through makes one realize just how uniquely inspired was Disney's *Fantasia*.

The Planets (suite, including Colin Matthews: *Pluto* and *Neptune* with original ending); *Lyric Movement*
*** Hyp. CDA 67270. Hallé O, Elder

The Planets (suite; including Matthews: *Pluto*); *The Mystic Trumpeter*
⊕ (BB) ******* Naxos 8.555776; also **Audio DVD** 5.11004. RSNO, Lloyd-Jones

Mark Elder conducts the Hallé Orchestra in a warm rather than bitingly dramatic reading of *The Planets*, which ends in Colin Matthews's extra movement, *Pluto – The Renewer*. That epilogue celebrates the outermost planet discovered after Holst wrote his suite, though not before he died. It was the idea of Kent Nagano as Elder's predecessor with the Hallé to add such a movement, with Matthews proving the ideal composer for a seemingly impossible task. Though he makes no attempt at writing Holst pastiche, his atmospheric movement inhabits very much the same sound-world as the suite, with colourful orchestration and high dynamic contrasts used dramatically. Though the tempo is very fast, the rapid scurrying seems to move round in circles, evoking an atmosphere of mystery apt for the smallest, remotest planet.

Since it emerges out of Holst's last movement, *Neptune*, involving a slight modification of the score, Elder conducts a second performance of that movement with the original ending of offstage women's choir fading into nothing. The tender, reflective *Lyric Movement*, with Timothy Pooley a fine viola soloist, makes a generous bonus.

David Lloyd-Jones's reading with the Royal Scottish National Orchestra is even finer than Elder's, more spontaneous-sounding if not always quite so polished. Where Lloyd-Jones scores is in bringing out the contrasted character of each movement, starting with an account of *Mars* which in its urgency and menace contrasts strongly with the strangely relaxed view of Elder. *Mercury* is lighter and wittier, *Jupiter* jollier and *Uranus* more full of flair. Where Elder has for coupling a rare late work, Lloyd-Jones and Matthews have unearthed a very early work of Holst's that was never performed, a Scena to a text by Walt Whitman, which may reveal little of Holst's mature style, but which is colourful and atmospheric and well worth hearing. Full, vivid sound. This is also available on Audio DVD with the additional possibility of Advanced Resolution Surround Sound, but this costs considerably more.

(i; ii) The Planets (suite, arr. 4 hands), Op. 32; (i) *Christmas Day in the Morning; Jig; Nocturne; O! I Hae seen the Roses Blaw; The Shoemaker; Toccata*
*** Black Box BBM 1041. (i) John York; (ii) Fiona York

Holst's own arrangement of *The Planets* for piano duet may lack the atmospheric warmth and rich orchestral colours of the original, but in this alert reading by the York duo the clarity is refreshing and there is plenty of magnetism in the rhythmic writing. It follows that the fast movements are much more effective than the three slow movements, *Venus*, *Saturn* and *Neptune*, even if the fading of the alternating chords at the end, originally given to offstage women's chorus, is persuasively done. The delight of the disc is to have this major work preceded by six pieces for piano duet, which sparkle from first to last, ranging from the vigorous *Toccata* of 1924 to the tonally equivocal *Jig* of 1932, all brilliantly played and very well recorded.

St Paul's Suite
⊕ **(N)** (BB) ******* Warner Apex 2564 61437-2. RPO, Warren-Green – BRITTEN: *Simple Symphony;* BUTTERWORTH: *Banks of Green Willow;* ELGAR: *String Serenade;* VAUGHAN WILLIAMS: *Fantasia on a Theme of Tallis* *******

Warren-Green's strongly characterized performance is second to none, with the outer movements characteristically full of joyous energy and a wide range of dynamic used to charm the listener with the wistful delicacy of the engaging second-movement *Ostinato*. Fine playing and first-class recording.

Air & Variations; 3 Pieces for Oboe & String Quartet, Op. 2
*** Chan. 8392. Francis, English Qt – BAX: *Quintet;* MOERAN: *Fantasy Quartet;* JACOB: *Quartet* *******

The three pieces here are engagingly folksy, consisting of a sprightly little *March*, a gentle *Minuet* with a good tune, and a *Scherzo*. Performances are first class, and so is the recording.

VOCAL MUSIC

Part Songs: *Ave Maria; Bring us in good ale; Diverus and Lazarus; Home they brought her warrior dead; I love my love; In youth is pleasure; I sow'd the seeds of love; Jesu, Thou the Virgin-born; Light leaves whisper; Lullay my liking; Mae 'nghariad i'n Fenws; Matthew, Mark, Luke and John; Now sleeps the crimson petal; Of one that is so fair and bright; O spiritual pilgrim; O swallow, swallow; The Song of the Blacksmith; The splendour falls; Spring; Summer; Swansea Town; Sweet and low; Tears, idle tears; Terly, terlow; There was a tree; This have I done for my True Love; A Welcome Song*

🔕— (BB) *** Hyp. Helios CDH 55171. Holst Singers, Layton (with Theodore, Truman, Williams)

A wholly delightful collection: it has so many treasures and the music and singing (and recording) are of such quality that, as the original *Gramophone* review rightly commented, it is 'a joy to listen through without interruption'. The sheer technical excellence of the singing is remarkable, as is Stephen Layton's absolute control: the blending peeerless, partly because the choir's intonation is absolutely secure.

The programme opens with carols (the eight-part double-choir setting of *Ave Maria* has an extraordinarily rich interplay of harmony, and the two linked numbers – *A Welcome Song* and *Terlyi, terlow* – both with David Theodore (oboe) and Robert Truman (cello) – are enchanting). The programme then becomes more robust with *Bring us in good ale* and a strophic *Diverus and Lazarus*, the tune of which we know so well from the Vaughan Williams string-piece. Another passage which has been used elsewhere (this time by Holst himself, in one of the *Military Band Suites*) pictures the syncopated hammering of *The Song of the Blacksmith* with its refrain, *Kiki, kikki, kang, kang*, which sounds for all the world like 'Chitty, chitty, bang, bang', and with the same rhythm.

The group of settings from Tennyson's *The Princess* was written for schoolgirl singers, but you would never guess that. The radiant *Sweet and low* and *The splendour falls* have superbly evocative imitative effects, spectacularly echoing into the distance, the latter ending with the repeated word 'dying' fading away, rather like *Neptune* in *The Planets*. The lovely *Now sleeps the crimson petal* brings delightful overlapping of parts, and the unpronounceable Welsh folksong translates as 'My sweetheart's like Venus'. *There was a tree*, richly expanded, brings ever-varying tempo changes. Holst's imagination knows no bounds and this is altogether a superb reminder of his remarkable versatility.

(i) *Ave Maria, H.49*; (ii–iv; viii) *A Choral Fantasia, Op. 51 (H.177)*; (iii–iv; viii) *A Dirge for Two Veterans, H.121*; (v–viii) *The Cloud Messenger, Op. 30 (H.111)*; (i) *The Evening Watch, H.159*; (vi–viii) *The Hymn of Jesus, Op. 37 (H.140)*; (iv; vi; viii) *Ode to Death, Op. 38 (H.144)*; (i) *4 Partsongs*; (ii–iv; viii) *7 Partsongs, H.162*; (i) *This have I done for my true love, H.128*

🔕— (B) *** Chan. 2-for-1 241-6 (2). (i) Finzi Singers, Spicer; (ii) Rozario; (iii) Joyful Company of Singers; (iv) City of L. Sinfonia; (v) D. Jones; (vi) L. Symphony Ch.; (vii) L. Symphony Ch.; (viii) Hickox

Richard Hickox proves a passionate advocate of the shorter choral works of Holst, demonstrating that the two Whitman settings, *A Dirge for Two Veterans* and *Ode to Death*, are among his finest pieces for voices: the *Dirge*, written just after war had started in 1914, a grim processional for male voices,

brass and percussion, and the *Ode* in 1919 when it was over and his disillusion was even more intense. That second work is in very much the same vein of inspiration as his masterpiece, the *Hymn of Jesus*, and, with the larger forces of the London Symphony Chorus, brings the most powerful performance here. It easily outshines even Sir Adrian Boult's vintage version for Decca. Hickox secures tauter and crisper ensemble, as well as treating the sections based on plainchant with an aptly expressive freedom.

The long-neglected choral piece, *The Cloud Messenger*, may lack the concentration of the *Hymn of Jesus*, but it brings similarly incandescent choral writing. Warmly and positively realized by Hickox and his powerful forces, with Della Jones a fine soloist, it makes a major discovery. Both the later works, the *Seven Partsongs* of 1925 as well as the *Choral Fantasia* of 1930, set poems by Robert Bridges, with the choral writing fluently beautiful. Though Patricia Rozario is not on her finest form, the Joyful Company of Singers sing superbly in intense and moving performances, helped by rich and full Chandos sound.

A Choral Fantasia, Op. 51; Choral Symphony, Op. 41

(BB) **(*) Hyp. Helios CDH 55104. Dawson, Guildford Choral Society, RPO, Davan Wetton

Though the ensemble of the Guildford Choral Society is not ideally crisp, and one really wants more weight of sound, the originality of Holst's choral writing and the purposeful nature of the argument are never in doubt in this surprisingly rare coupling, with Lynne Dawson the radiantly beautiful soprano soloist in both works. Holst is nothing if not daring in using well-known texts by Keats in the *Choral Symphony*, adding a new dimension even to the 'Ode on a Grecian Urn'. This is well worth considering in its bargain-priced reissue.

(i) *A Choral Fantasia, Op. 51*; (ii) *Psalm 86*

(M) *** EMI (ADD) 5 65588-2. (i) Baker; (ii) Partridge; Purcell Singers, ECO, Imogen Holst – FINZI: *Dies natalis*; VAUGHAN WILLIAMS: *5 Mystical Songs*, etc. ***

In Holst's *Choral Fantasia* – a setting of words written by Robert Bridges in commemoration of Purcell – Dame Janet Baker once again shows her supreme quality as a recording artist. The recording, though not lacking ambient warmth, is admirably clear (indeed the organ pedals are only too clear). The sound could perhaps be more open, but there is no lack of projection and vividness. The setting of *Psalm 86*, with its expressive tenor part sung beautifully by Ian Partridge, is also included in this generous compilation. The recording here is outstanding, and the success of both these performances owes much to the inspired direction of the composer's daughter.

Choral Hymns from the Rig Veda (Group 3), *H. 99, Op. 26/3*
*** Hyp. CDA 66175. Holst Singers & O; Davan Wetton; Owen – BLISS: *Lie Strewn the White Flocks*; BRITTEN: *Gloriana: Choral Dances* ***

The third group of *Choral Hymns from the Rig Veda*, like the whole series, reveals Holst in his Sanskritic period at his most distinctively inspired. In this responsive performance, it makes an excellent coupling for the attractive Bliss and Britten items, atmospherically recorded.

The Evening Watch, H.159; Six Choruses, H.186; Nunc dimittis, H.127; 7 Partsongs, H.162; 2 Psalms, H.117
*** Hyp. CDA 66329. Holst Singers & O, Davan Wetton

Hilary Davan Wetton's performances of the comparatively

austere but no less inspired *Evening Watch* creates a rapt, sustained *pianissimo* until the very closing bars, when the sudden expansion is quite thrilling. The *Six Choruses* for male voices show the composer at his most imaginative, while the comparable *Partsongs* for women often produce a ravishingly dreamy, mystical beauty. The final song, *Assemble all ye maidens*, is a narrative ballad about a lost love, and its closing section is infinitely touching. The performances are gloriously and sensitively sung and unerringly paced.

OPERA

(i) *Savitri* (complete); (ii) *Dream City* (song-cycle, orch. Matthews)

(BB) **(*) Hyp. Helios CDH 55042. (i) Langridge, Varcoe, Palmer, Hickox Singers; (ii) Kwella, City of L. Sinfonia, Hickox

The simple story of *Savitri* is taken from a Sanskrit source – Savitri, a woodcutter's wife, cleverly outwits Death, who has come to take her husband – and Holst with beautiful feeling for atmosphere sets it in the most restrained way. With light texture and many slow tempi, it is a work which can fall apart in an uncommitted performance, but the Hyperion version makes an excellent alternative to Imogen Holst's earlier recording with Dame Janet Baker, bringing the positive advantage of fine digital recording. Felicity Palmer is more earthy, more vulnerable as Savitri, her grainy mezzo caught well. Philip Langridge and Stephen Varcoe both sing sensitively with fresh, clear tone, though their timbres are rather similar. Hickox is a thoughtful conductor both in the opera and in the orchestral song-cycle arranged by Colin Matthews (with Imogen Holst's approval) from Holst's settings of Humbert Wolfe poems. Patrizia Kwella's soprano at times catches the microphone rather shrilly.

HOLZBAUER, Ignaz (1711–83)

Holzbauer was an Austrian Kapellmeister to the courts of Vienna (1745), Stuttgart (1751) and the famous Mannheim Court (1753). In Mannheim, his operas were performed for many years, and in his symphonies one can hear in the bold and dramatic writing the influence of the theatre.

Symphonies: in A, Op. 2/4; E flat, Op. 3/1; D, Op. 3/4; D min.; G (Il figlio delle selve Overture)

✪ (N) *** CPO 999 585-2. L'Orfeo Barockorchester, Gaigg

CPO keep finding new names to record – some of them, such as Ignaz Holzbauer, unexpectedly exciting. From the word go, there is innovation in these works: a famous 'Mannheim crescendo' opens the *D major Symphony* (on oboes and strings), leading to some exceptionally lively writing, especially for the strings, who have to do some real scurrying around. But it is not all flashy brilliance, there is much charm, even humour, in this music, with some unexpectedly delicate writing: the *Minuetto* movement of the same *D major Symphony* has a gorgeous *Cantabile gratioso* section, where the orchestra relaxes beautifully, before the galumphing minuet is repeated, played with great élan. The short *D minor Symphony* is like Vivaldi on steroids, and again one is struck by the imaginative string-writing. Both the *A major* and *G major Symphonies* (the latter with four movements) have plenty of vigour (the opening snap of the strings of the *G major* is sharply arresting). Mozart admired this composer, and so do we. The performances and recording are superb, with all the dash and sparkle needed.

HONEGGER, Arthur (1892–1955)

Film Music: *Les Misérables* (complete)

(N) (BB) **(*) Naxos 8.557486. Slovak RSO, Adriano

Honegger's score to Raymond Bernard's 1934 black-and-white film of Victor Hugo's novel comprises 23 movements or 'cues', of which 17, lasting about an hour, are presented here (omissions comprise three dance pieces by another hand and some inconsequential bars elsewhere; other passages, cut from the film for editing reasons, are restored). The music is of considerable interest, for Honegger was a highly imaginative composer, though not all of it merits re-hearing out of context. (The scoring is interesting too: no double basses but saxophone, piano and harp.) Not essential Honegger, but worth having all the same. The playing of the orchestra is very acceptable, but the acoustic is wanting in bloom.

Pacific 231; Pastorale d'été; Rugby; (i) *Christmas Cantata (Cantate de Noël)*

(M) **(*) EMI (ADD) 7 63944-2. O Nat. de l'ORTF, Martinon; (i) with Maurane & Ch. d'Oratorio Maîtrise de l'ORTF

The Orchestre National de l'ORTF plays well for Jean Martinon, though we have heard more atmospheric accounts of *Pastorale d'été* (Martinon is not always responsive to *pianissimo* indications here). The *Cantate de Noël* is given a strong performance, though not even the expert French Radio choir manages the highly exacting demands of Honegger's difficult (and not always effective) choral writing. Generally these are good performances – although the programme offers short measure at 46 minutes.

Symphonies 1; 2 for Strings with Trumpet Obbligato; 3 (Symphonie liturgique); 4 (Deliciae Basilienses); 5 (Di tre re); 3 Symphonic Movements: 1, Pacific 231; 3. The Tempest: Prelude

(M) *** Sup. (ADD) 11 1566-2 (2). Czech PO, Baudo

Honegger's symphonies are currently much underrated. The *First* is a highly stimulating and rewarding piece: its level of energy is characteristic of the later symphonies. The *Second* is a probing, intense wartime composition that reflects something of the anguish Honegger felt during the German occupation. The *Third* (*Liturgique*) dates from the end of the war, while the *Fourth*, composed for Paul Sacher, makes use of Swiss folk material. Beneath its smiling surface there is a gentle vein of nostalgia and melancholy, particularly in the slow movement. The finale is sparkling and full of high spirits, though even this ends on a bitter-sweet note. The *Fifth* is a powerful work, inventive, concentrated and vital.

The Supraphon performances come from the 1960s, but they are more than merely serviceable. The sound comes up very well indeed and the playing of the Czech Philharmonic for Baudo is totally committed. The performance of the *Fifth Symphony* has never been surpassed (except possibly by the pioneering Munch recording) and has amazing presence and detail for its period.

Symphonies 1–5; Pacific 231

(BB) ** EMI Gemini (ADD) 5 85516-2 (2). Toulouse Capitole O, Plasson

Michel Plasson has the advantage of fine recordings from the late 1970s, and the spacious acoustics of the Toulouse Halle-aux-Grains seem right for the music. However, the performances do not have the panache and virtuosity that make Karajan's coupling of Nos. 2 and 3 so memorable, or the character of Munch's account of No. 4; at times, in the most searing music, one feels a lack of grip and emotional intensity. Nevertheless, there are some fine moments here, and Plasson finds much of the charm in *No. 4*, even if the Scherzo of the *Fifth Symphony* sounds rather tame. One other point: in the *Symphony for Strings* (the *Second*) the trumpet for which Honegger called to strengthen the chorale, but which he did not regard as mandatory, is omitted. The CD transfers are natural in balance and enhance the sound, which has plenty of ambience.

Symphony 2 for Strings & Trumpet

(M) *** EMI (ADD) 5 67595-2 [567597]. O de Paris, Munch – RAVEL: *Boléro*, etc. ***

*** Delos DE 3121. Seattle SO, Schwarz – R. STRAUSS: *Metamorphosen*; WEBERN, arr. SCHWARZ: *Langsamer Satz* ***

Honegger's wartime *Second Symphony*, scored for strings to which an obbligato trumpet is added at the very end of the work, commands a genuine intensity of feeling with a strong and vital imagination. Munch conducted the work's French première and made the pioneering set of 78s. The present version is his finest account of this dark and haunting score, and he secures first-class playing from the strings of the Orchestre de Paris. It surely deserves its place in the EMI annals of 'Great Recordings of the Century', for the naturally balanced recording is lively and has atmosphere as well as opulence, and it has been splendidly transferred to CD.

In terms of recording quality, Schwarz's account can hold its own alongside the very best, and the playing of the Seattle strings is splendidly responsive. He is just a bit too slow at the very beginning, and the same reservation could be made against the slow movement, but there is plenty of atmosphere. Although it does not displace the Munch or Karajan accounts or other recommendations, this performance is very fine indeed and will give much pleasure.

Symphonies 2 for Strings with Trumpet Obbligato; 3 (Symphonie liturgique)

☞ ✪ (M) *** DG (ADD) 447 435-2. BPO, Karajan – STRAVINSKY: *Concerto in D* ***

Karajan's accounts of these magnificent symphonies come from 1973 and still remain in a class of their own, luminous, incandescent and moving. It certainly deserves its place as one of DG's 'Legendary Originals'.

Symphony 3 (Symphonie liturgique); Rugby; Mouvement symphonique 3; Pacific 231; Pastoral d'été

(N) (BB) *** Naxos 8.555974. New Zealand SO, Yuasa

Karajan's account of the *Symphonie liturgique* is one of the classics of the gramophone and remains supreme. But this newcomer is far from undistinguished, even though the strings (of course) are not in the same class as Karajan's Berlin Philharmonic. Takuo Yuasa, currently principal conductor of the Ulster Orchestra, gets impressive results from the New Zealanders, and the recording has great presence and detail. In repertoire which can boast Jansons and Mravinsky, this is not perhaps a first choice but, taken on its own merits, is a perfectly viable one and at its modest price will give much satisfaction.

Symphonies 3; 5; Pacific 231

*** Chan. 9176. Danish Nat. R. O, Järvi

The *Symphonie liturgique* has stiff competition to meet in the classic Karajan account, but Neeme Järvi and the Danish orchestra serve it very well indeed, and the digital Chandos recording is even more detailed and present, and certainly fuller, than the DG version. Järvi's version of the *Fifth Symphony* is also masterly, even if it does not match the hell-for-leather abandon of Baudo's Supraphon version (see above). But that is now over 30 years old and, though it still sounds pretty amazing, this is undeniably superior.

VOCAL MUSIC

Une Cantate de Noël

(N) (B) *** CfP 586 1722. Sweeney, Waynflete Singers, Winchester Cathedral Ch., ECO, Neary – BERLIOZ *L'enfance du Christ* **(*); POULENC: *Mass; Motets* ***

At last a recording of Honegger's charming *Christmas Cantata* to do it full justice. It was the composer's last completed work and deserves to be more popular in the festive season outside France. The performance here is superior in every way and the recording is impressively wide-ranging and well defined.

La danse des morts

(N) **(*) Calliope 9526. Wilson (nar.), Schmidt, Brua, Claessens, French R. Ch., O de Picardie, Colomer – MILHAUD: *L'Homme et son désir* **(*)

La Danse des morts (1938) has not fared anywhere near as well as *Jeanne d'Arc au bûcher*, the composer's earlier collaboration with Claudel, though there was a memorable recording of it with Jean-Louis Barrault as the narrator and Charles Panzéra among the soloists, and with Charles Munch conducting. This is not exactly in that class but it has enthusiasm to commend it and, in the absence of an easily accessible rival, this is a useful addition to the catalogue.

Jeanne d'Arc au bûcher

☞ ✪ (M) *** DG 476 16502. Keller, Wilson, Escourrou, Lanzi, Pollet, Command, Stutzman, Aler, Courtis, R. France Ch., Fr. Nat. O, Ozawa

Honegger's 1935 setting of the Claudel poem is one of his most powerful and imaginative works, full of variety of invention, colour and textures. It is admirably served by these forces, and in particular by the Joan of Marthe Keller. The singers, too, are all excellent and the Choir and the six soloists of the Maîtrise of Radio France are as top-drawer as the orchestra. The DG engineers cope excellently with the large forces and the acoustic of the Basilique de Saint-Denis. This now reappears at mid-price among Universal's 'Penguin ✪ Collection'.

Le Roi David (complete)

(BB) **(*) Naxos 8.553649. Martin, Fersen, Borst, Todorovitch, Ragon, Guedj, Ch. Régional Vittoria d'Ile de France, O de la Cité, Piquemal

The Naxos set gives us the original scoring of *Le Roi David* for 17 instruments, the double bass being the only string instrument. In 1923, Honegger scored it in the familiar concert version, adding the narration which Naxos use here. Michel Piquemal's performance is a good one and, though there are certain weaknesses (the tenor's vibrato will not be to all tastes), there is a good feeling for the dramatic shape of the work. Piquemal keeps a firm grip on the proceedings and the instrumentalists play with real commitment, while the recording is very adequate.

HOVHANESS, Alan (1911–2000)

(i) *Symphonies 1 (Exile), Op. 17/2;* (ii) *22 (City of Light), Op. 236;* (iii) *Bagatelles 1–4;* (i) *Fantasy on Japanese Woodprints, Op. 211;* (iv) *The Flowering Peach, Op. 125;* (i) *Prayer of St Gregory;* (v) *A Rose Tree Blossoms, Op. 246/4;* (iii) *String Quartet 4 (The Ancient Tree), Op. 208/2*

(B) **(*) Delos Double DE 3700 (2). Seattle SO, (i) Schwarz; (ii) Hovhaness; (iii) Shanghai String Qt; (iv) Ohio State University Concert Band, Brion; (v) St John's Episcopal Cathedral Ch., Pearson

The music on this CD is all melodic and easy to come to terms with. The persecution of Armenians in Turkey in the 1930s was the inspiration for the *Symphony No. 1*: its modal, oriental tonalities set the scene quite hauntingly, while the violent outbursts sound distinctly gothic. *City of Light* is agreeable enough, if conventional, and the *Prayer of St Gregory*, essentially a chorale, has a certain innocent appeal. *The Flowering Peach* was a serio-comic retelling of the Noah's Ark story, performed on Broadway in 1954, for which Hovhaness wrote the incidental music; it has some atmosphere, but is not very interesting or memorable. *A Rose Tree Blossoms* is a short but charmingly simple choral work, and the *Bagatelles* are unassuming milk-and-water pieces. The *Fantasy on Japanese Woodprints* produces lots of bizarre sounds (horror-film-type noises), but to little effect. The performances and recordings are more than adequate and the two-for-the-price-of-one format makes this good value for the composer's admirers.

Symphonies (i) *2 (Mysterious Mountain); 50 (Mount St Helens), Op. 360;* (ii) *53 (Star Dawn), Op. 377; Alleluia & Fugue; And God Created Great Whales; Celestial Fantasy; Meditation on Orpheus, Op. 155; Prelude & Quadruple Fugue;* (iii) *String Quartet 3 (Reflections on My Childhood), Op. 208/1; Suite from String Quartet 2*

(B) *** Delos DE 3711 (2). (i) Seattle SO, Schwarz; (ii) Ohio State University Concert Band, Brion; (iii) Shanghai String Qt

The *Symphony No. 2* begins with pastoral, modal writing, leading to a central fugal climax and returning to rich, expressive serenity. More action-packed is the extravagant *Mount St Helens Symphony*, with an awe-inspiring volcano eruption in the finale (with some quite shattering orchestral effects), as well as the genuinely evocative *Spirit Lake* central movement. The *Star Dawn Symphony*, evoking travelling in space towards heaven, is quite effectively depicted, though after the allegro climax, the following slow movement lets the listener down.

The *String Quartets* are attractive, with some nice touches, without being really memorable. But the most sensational piece here is *And God Created Great Whales*, which reaches a hugely spectacular climax and interpolates tapes of the actual song of the humpbacked whale. The effect is very grandiose indeed and everyone rises to the occasion, including both the whales and the recording engineers. The performances are

dedicated and very well presented, so this is excellent value if the musical scenario appeals.

HOWELL, Dorothy (1898–1981)

(i) *Violin Sonata; Rosalind; The Moorings; Phantasy. Piano Sonata. Humoresque; 5 Studies*

(N) (M) *** Dutton Epoch CDLX 7144. (i) McAslan; Rahman

Dorothy Howell taught at the Royal Academy of Music throughout her long career (1924–70). Although Sir Henry Wood championed her tone-poem, *Namia*, in the post-war years, her music has fallen into total neglect (she is not listed in *Grove* or in the Blom edited Cummings *Everyman Dictionary*) and her work forgotten. This disc of three of her piano pieces and her music for violin and piano makes some belated amends. The music is finely crafted and her ideas are fashioned with fastidious taste. If no strong personality emerges, she is a composer of distinct culture, who is eminently well served by this impressive violinist and her excellent partner, and the recording does her proud. The *Phantasy* and *Violin Sonata* and the *Studies* for piano are well worth saving from virtual oblivion, and the Dutton label deserves praise for doing so and for the excellent recorded sound.

HOWELLS, Herbert (1892–1983)

(i) *Piano Concertos 1 in C min., Op. 4 (completed Rutter); 2 in C, Op. 39. Penguinski*

*** Chan. 9874. (i) Shelley; BBC SO, Hickox

Long buried, Herbert Howells's *First Piano Concerto*, with its final pages now restored by John Rutter, is a revelation. As one of Stanford's favourite pupils, Howells wrote this big, bravura work in 1913, but a poor first performance put it in limbo. With Grieg and Rachmaninov among the models, the piano writing is bold and powerful, full of strong themes, set in a warmly English idiom. Howard Shelley as soloist and Richard Hickox as conductor hold the expansive structure superbly together. The *Second Concerto* of 1925, more modest in scale but more advanced in idiom with its echoes of Debussy, Ravel and Stravinsky, is equally attractive, and the jolly occasional piece *Penguinski* makes a delightful encore.

Concerto for Strings; Elegy for Viola, String Quartet & Strings; Suite for String Orchestra; Serenade

⊶ ✪*** Chan. 9161. City of L. Sinfonia, Hickox

These three splendid and inspired works are all in the great and ongoing tradition of English string-writing. The *Concerto* (1938) opens with a great burst of energy, but the secondary theme is hauntingly nostalgic, and the elegiac character of the slow movement establishes the music's character. That it owes a debt to Elgar is no accident, for the work is dedicated jointly to him and to the composer's only son, whose loss is also remembered in the *Hymnus paradisi*. The viola *Elegy*, written much earlier (1917), is clearly modelled on Vaughan Williams's *Tallis Fantasia*, yet it is masterly in its own right and very moving. The delicate one-movement *Serenade*, which also features a solo quartet, dates from the same year. The *Allegro deciso* and *Rondo* which open and close the *Suite* (1938) are rhythmically extrovert in a Holstian 'St Paul's' manner, but then, after a gentle, rapturous *Siciliano*, the Minuet opens with a deeper-voiced pizzicato. The performances here are exemplary, superbly played and conducted by Hickox with deep commitment and understanding. The recording is warm, sonorous and clearly detailed.

(i) *Concerto for Strings;* (ii) *Hymnus paradisi*

(M) **(*) EMI (ADD) 5 67119-2. (i) LPO, Boult; (ii) Harper, Tear, Bach Ch., King's College Ch., New Philh. O, Willcocks

Boult's understanding and vigorous performance of the *Concerto for Strings* – a work dedicated to him – is coupled here with the *Hymnus paradisi*; both were written in memory of the composer's son. It is a dignified and beautifully wrought piece but also, and more importantly, it is both moving and powerful. Willcocks's performance is eloquent and warmly persuasive within the glowing Kingsway Hall acoustics, but even so it does not match Handley's later account on Hyperion (see below) in intensity of feeling.

The 'B's' (Suite for Orchestra); (i) 3 Dances for Violin & Orchestra; (ii) Fantasia; Threnody (both for cello & orchestra). The King's Herald; Paradise Rondel, Op. 40; (iii) In Green Ways (Song Cycle); Pastoral Rhapsody; Procession, Op. 36

☞ (N) (BB) *** Chan. 2 for 1 CHAN 241-20 (2). (i) Mordkovitch; (ii) Welsh; (iii) Kenny; LSO, Hickox

The inspired suite, *The Five 'B's*, celebrates the composer's musician friends and colleagues at the Royal College of Music at the beginning of the 1914–18 war. As such it has something in common with Elgar's *Enigma Variations*, although Howells clearly identified each dedicatee. Ivor Gurney is remembered with a movingly passionate *Lament*, and Frances 'Bunny' Warren is personified in a delicate *Minuet/Mazurka*, at times disconsolate, but with a blithe pastoral counterpart. 'Blissy' (Arthur Bliss) inspires a dainty, chimerical *Scherzo* on the first disc, with the piano an orchestral soloist. The shorter evocations are framed by an exuberant *Overture* with a *nobilmente* lyrical expansiveness representing the composer himself ('Bublum') and the finale ('Benjee' – Arthur Benjamin), which begins lightheartedly but ends grandiloquently, recalls the composer's own themes from the overture. The *Three Dances for Violin and Orchestra*, another wartime work (1915), are in the best English folk/pastoral tradition, with Lydia Mordkovitch as a brilliant violin soloist; and the song-cycle, *In Green Ways*, with Yvonne Kenny also includes poignant elegies. The English countryside is strikingly evoked in this group of five songs, using lyrics by Shakespeare and Goethe. Yvonne Kenny sings the whole group most affectingly and Richard Hickox and the LSO are ardent and communicative advocates of all this fine music. A most attractive bargain reissue, joining together two equally desirable discs.

The most personal works on the second disc are the *Fantasia* and *Threnody*, both for cello and orchestra, together forming a sort of rhapsodic concerto. Howells was reflecting his anguish over the death of his nine-year-old son, with flashes of anger punctuating the elegiac lyricism. The *Threnody*, simpler in its lyricism, was probably planned as the slow movement of a three-movement *Cello Concerto*. The other major piece is the *Pastoral Rhapsody*, written in 1923. Similarly pastoral but predominantly vigorous, the *Paradise Rondel* of 1925 is full of sharp contrasts, with one passage offering clear echoes of the *Russian Dance* from *Petrushka*. The collection opens with the boldly extrovert *King's Herald*, bright with Waltonian fanfares. *Procession* brings more echoes of *Petrushka*, again reflecting Howells's response to the Diaghilev Ballets Russes' appearances in London. Helped by rich, atmospheric sound, Richard Hickox draws performances that are both brilliant and warmly persuasive from the LSO, with Moray Welsh a movingly expressive soloist in the concertante works.

CHAMBER MUSIC

Clarinet Sonata; A Near-Minuet for Clarinet & Piano; Prelude for Harp; Rhapsodic Clarinet Quintet; Violin Sonata 3

(BB) *** Naxos 8.557188. Mobius

Howells's *Rhapsodic Quintet* for clarinet and string quartet is one of the most beautiful clarinet works of the twentieth century, a piece written in 1919 which brought the young composer immediate recognition. Robert Plane, the clarinet of the talented group Mobius, plays with a ravishing range of tone and natural warmth, well supported by the string quartet led by Philippe Honore. Plane is also the brilliant soloist in Howells's even more ambitious *Clarinet Sonata* of 1946, a work in two extended movements (one predominantly reflective, one fast), more angular and percussive than one expects from Howells. Honore is the violinist with the pianist Sophia Rahman in the powerful *Violin Sonata No. 3*, written for Albert Sammons in 1923 after a visit by the composer to Canada, inspired by the rugged grandeur of the Rockies. The *Prelude for Harp* and the *Near-Minuet for Clarinet and Piano* are attractive make-weights for a superb disc, compelling in every way and vividly recorded.

Oboe Sonata

(BB) *** Hyp. Helios CDH 55008. Francis, Dickenson – BOUGHTON: *Pastoral;* HARTY: *3 Pieces;* RUBBRA: *Sonata* ***

Howell's *Oboe Sonata* is a florid work, but Sarah Francis surmounts its complexities very musically, echoed by her pianist, Peter Dickenson. She provides a full, singing tone. The balance is forward, within a resonant acoustic, and it is important not to set the volume control too high.

In Gloucestershire (String Quartet 3)

(BB) *** Hyp. Helios CDH 55045. Divertimenti – DYSON: *3 Rhapsodies* ***

Howells's *Third String Quartet* had a chequered history. The first (1916) version was lost on a train. A second version then also disappeared but was reconstructed in the early 1960s. A third, definitive version (full score and parts) was discovered in the Library of the Royal College of Music and is here recorded. The music is permeated with the spirit of Vaughan Williams; the opening movement, treating the first violin as a soloist, mistily yet radiantly evokes the Gloucestershire countryside. After the wind-swept Scherzo, the slow movement is elegiac; but the finale, jauntily alive and folksy in flavour, is drawn back eventually to the gently atmospheric mood of the work's opening. The performance by Divertimenti is deeply expressive and beautifully played and recorded.

Rhapsodic Clarinet Quintet, Op. 31

(BB) *** Hyp. Helios CDH 55105. King, Britten Qt – COOKE: *Clarinet Quintet;* HOLBROOKE: *Eilean Shona;* HOWELLS: *Rhapsodic Quintet;* FRANKEL; MACONCHY: *Clarinet Quintets* ***

Howells's inspired single-movement *Rhapsodic Quintet,*

which dates from 1919, is one of his very finest works, opening arrestingly with rich string harmonies and based on two utterly haunting, very English themes. Thea King, who plays ravishingly and with great poetic feeling, reckons its closing section 'to be one of the loveliest moments in music – the peace of ages is in it'. The performance here is fully responsive to this mood, and the recording is first class.

Violin Sonatas 1 in E, Op. 18; 2 in E flat, Op. 26; 3 in E min., Op. 38; Cradle Song, Op. 9/1; 3 Pieces, Op. 28
⊕ (BB) *** Hyp. Helios CDH 55139. Barritt, Edwards

A truly outstanding disc, missed by us when it first appeared in 1993. The three *Violin Sonatas* come from an intensely creative period. The *First* (1917) was originally entitled *Phantasy Sonata* but was later (during 1919) revised. In four movements, it opens delicately and romantically, darkens a little in the *Meno mosso*, then, after a brief, unbridled Scherzo, ends in ravishing tranquillity. The *Second*, although in only three movements, is a bigger work both emotionally and in its overall span and bold forward impulse. Rhapsodically lyrical, with a lovely, simple, folk-like slow movement, it bursts into sparkling vitality in the finale. The *Third Sonata* maintains the English pastoral character in its underlying lyricism, but erupts with energy in the pizzicato centrepiece, which carries through into the restless finale: both are marked *assai ritmico*. The main theme of the delightful *Cradle Song* is rather like a Slavonic folk-tune, and while the first two of the *Three Pieces* are richly English in feeling, the haunting finale is actually based on a Russian folksong. Paul Barritt and Catherine Edwards are right inside this music and play together with a passionate and moving single voice; moreover, they are superbly balanced and recorded. The ⊕ is for the sheer pleasure this record brings when it is played straight through – such is the variety of the music, with the splendid *Second Sonata* rightly coming last.

VOCAL MUSIC

Canticles for Morning and Evening Services, Vol. 1: Settings of *Magnificat and Nunc dimittis: in G* (1918); for *Men's Voices and Organ* (performed by women's voices, 1941); *Collegium regale* (1945); *New College, Oxford* (1949); *Collegium Sancti Johannis Cantabrigiense* (1957); *Sarum* (1966); *York* (1973)
*** Priory PRCD 748. Collegiate Singers, Millinger, Moorhouse (organ)

Canticles for Morning and Evening Services, Vol. 2: Settings of *Magnificat and Nunc dimittis: Gloucester* (1946); *Worcester* (1951); *Collegiate Church of Saint Peter in Westminster* (1957); *Chichester* (1967); *Magdalen College, Oxford* (1970). *Nunc dimittis* (only, for unaccompanied choir, 1914). *Anthem: Behold O God our Defender; Hymn for St Cecilia; Salve Regina, Op. 9/4*
*** Priory PRCD 759. Collegiate Singers, Millinger, Moorhouse (organ)

Howells composed some 20 settings of the *Magnificat* and *Nunc dimittis* and, while it is not difficult to pick one's favourites, the amazing consistency of inspiration shines out again and again through these two collections, making his contribution to the Anglican Matins and Evensong uniquely special, astonishing when one realizes that he was himself an agnostic. The familiar examples from the *Collegium regale*, using a tenor soloist in the *Nunc dimittis*, have a natural

beauty and eloquence, while the *Sarum Magnificat* with its rich interplay of trebles, and the lyrically glowing male line in the *Nunc dimittis* which the upper voices then join resplendently, also stand out, as does the *York Magnificat* with its radiant opening, gleamingly anticipated by the organ.

The 1941 settings for men's voices and organ are here sung by women, with tonally lavish and at times radiantly ethereal effect. Similarly Howells's writing for the upper voices is richly harmonized for Oxford in 1970, showing that the composer's touch remained as sure as ever three decades later. Also included on the second CD is the brief but memorable *Hymn for St Cecilia* and the luminous unaccompanied *Salve Regina* which is so poignant in its emotional pull, for all its underlying serenity. The performances here are splendidly sung by the Collegiate Singers, who are based at Westminster Abbey, and their deep involvement can be felt throughout these invariably fine performances under Andrew Millinger, while Richard Moorhouse's organ contribution always makes its mark. The recording, made in Marlborough College Chapel, could hardly be bettered.

3 Children's Songs (Eight o'clock, the postman's knock; The days are clear; Mother, shake the cherry-tree); 3 Folksongs (I will give my love an apple; The brisk young widow; Cendrillon); 4 French Chansons, Op. 29; A Garland for de la Mare (group of 11 unpublished songs); In Green Ways (song-cycle), Op. 43; Peacock Pie (song-cycle), Op. 33; 2 South African Settings (Loneliness; Spirit of freedom); 4 Songs, Op. 22 (There was a maiden; Madrigal; The widow bird; Girl's song). Miscellaneous songs: An old man's lullaby; Come sing and dance; Flood; Gavotte; Goddess of the Night; Here she lies; King David; The little boy lost; Lost love; Mally O!; The mugger's song; O garlands, hanging by the doors; O my deir hert; Old Meg; Old skinflint; The restful branches
*** Chan. 9185/6 (2). Dawson, Pierard, Mark Ainsley, Luxon, Drake

This two-disc collection covers virtually all of Howells's completed songs. One of the driving forces behind the project is the pianist Julius Drake, who plays the accompaniments with a consistent rhythmic spring and a sense of fantasy. Two of the finest songs are among the best known, *King David* and *Come sing and dance*, and such a group of miniatures as *Peacock Pie*, settings of Walter de la Mare written early in Howells's career, have a characteristic point and charm. Far more searching are the 11 much longer settings of de la Mare poems. Among the other fascinating examples are two South African settings to words by the Afrikaner poet, Jan Celliers, including one still very topical, *Spirit of freedom*. The sopranos, Catherine Pierard and Lynne Dawson, both have aptly fresh, English-sounding voices, with John Mark Ainsley as the thoughtful tenor and Benjamin Luxon the characterful baritone; a fine team, even though the recording brings out some unevenness in the vocal production of both Mark Ainsley and Luxon.

Chichester Service: Magnificat; Nunc dimittis. A Hymn for Saint Cecilia; Like as the hart desireth the waterbrooks; My eyes for beauty pine; O salutaris Hostia; Salve Regina
(*) ASV CDDCA 851. Went, Ch. of The Queen's College, Oxford, Owens – LEIGHTON: *Crucifixus pro nobis*, etc. *

Howells is nearly always at his best in his choral work, and the pieces gathered here are all worth having. Neither in terms of ensemble nor intonation is The Queen's College, Oxford, choir in the first league, but the performances are committed and give pleasure, and they are well recorded. The disc has the advantage of a coupling rarely heard: music of quality by Kenneth Leighton.

3 Carol Anthems: A Spotless Rose; Sing lullaby; Here is the little door. Collegium regale: Magnificat; Nunc Dimittis. Hymn for St Cecilia; O love all beauteous things; O Pray for the Peace of Jerusalem; A Sequence for St Michael; Salve Regina. Service for New College, Oxford: Magnificat; Nunc dimittis. Service for St George's Chapel, Windsor: Te Deum; Benedictus
♦━ (N) *** Hyp. CDA 67494. Wells Cathedral Ch., Archer; M. Gough

Like the CRD New College, Oxford, collection below, this splendid programme from Wells Cathedral includes three of Howells's finest short choral works, and here Malcom Archer uses then to open his programme. *A Sequence for St Michael*, a supreme masterpiece, is underpinned emotionally by the resonance of the tragic death of the composer's child, whose name was also Michael. Yet Howells invokes the Archangel himself as he stands in both mystery and glory on the Western cliffe of Paradise. It is work of grandeur and passion as well as beauty, and this is marvellously conveyed in the profoundly fervent performance here. *A Hymn for St Cecilia* is more direct and hymn-like, but it gathers intensity as it proceeds; *O Pray for the Peace of Jerusalem* is, by contrast, meditative and is sung with affecting simplicity.

The anthem, *O love all beauteous things*, set to a poem of Robert Bridges, is another small-scale masterpiece, with characteristic moments of both sensuousness and passion, and there is to be a passionate response again from the choir in the rich St Georges *Te Deum* and the vibrant Oxford *Magnificat*. The three delightful and tender carol settings come towards the end of the recital, to be followed by the most famous of Howells's settings of the *Magnificat* and *Nunc dimittis*, drawn from the Collegium regale, less extrovert than those written for Oxford, but no less moving, with the *Nunc dimittis* ending the programme in a burst of glory. The choir is superbly recorded within the cathedral ambience, yet is not too backwardly placed, with words clear and plenty of edge to the climaxes. With a playing time of nearly 80 minutes, this must be a prime choice among collections of Howells's church music.

Collegium regale: canticles; Behold, O God our defender; Like as the hart; St Paul's Service: Canticles. Take him, earth, for cherishing. (Organ): Psalm prelude: De profundis; Master Tallis's testament
*** Hyp. CDA 66260. St Paul's Cathedral Ch., Scott, Dearnley

All the music here is of high quality and the recording gives it resonance, in both senses of the word, with the St Paul's acoustic well captured by the engineers. A fine representation of a composer who wrote in the mainstream of English church and cathedral music but who had a distinctive voice of his own.

Collegium regale: Office of Holy Communion; Requiem. St Paul's Service: Magnificat; Nunc dimittis. Motets: Like as the hart; Long, long ago; Take him, earth. Organ music: Paean; Rhapsody 3
♦━ (BB) *** Naxos 8.554659. St John's College Ch., Robinson, Farrington

No composer this century has surpassed Herbert Howells in the beauty and imagination of his Anglican church music.

Naxos here offers a generous selection, in seductive performances from the Choir of St John's College, Cambridge, that match and almost surpass any previous versions. This will have King's Choir down the road looking to its laurels, helped by immaculate sound, at once atmospheric and cleanly focused.

Collegium regale: Te Deum & jubilate; Office of Holy Communion; Magnificat & Nunc dimittis. Preces & Responses I & II; Psalms 121 & 122; Take him, earth; for cherishing. Rhapsody for Organ, Op. 17/3
♦━ ● (M) *** Decca 470 194-2. Williams, Moore, King's College, Cambridge, Ch., Cleobury, Barley (organ)

Here is an outstanding collection of the settings inspired by the greatest of our collegiate choirs, King's College, Cambridge, presented in performances of heart-warming intensity in that great choir's 1989 incarnation. The boy trebles in particular are among the brightest and fullest ever to have been recorded with this choir. The disc sensitively presents the sequence in what amounts to liturgical order, with the service settings aptly interspersed with responses, psalm-chants, anthems with organ introits and voluntaries all by Howells. Even those not normally attracted by Anglican church music should hear this.

Hymnus Paradisi; An English Mass
♦━ *** Hyp. CDA 66488. Kennard, Mark Ainsley, RLPO Ch., RLPO, Handley

In *Hymnus Paradisi* Handley conveys a mystery, a tenderness rather missing from the previous recording, made by Sir David Willcocks for EMI, as strong as that is. Handley's soloists bring a moving compassion, as in the haunting setting of the 23rd Psalm which makes up the third movement. The Hyperion digital recording is very warm, full and atmospheric. *An English Mass* is simpler yet also hauntingly beautiful.

Missa Sabrinensis
(N) (B) *** Chan. 2 for 1 241–27 (2). Watson, D. Jones, Hill, Maxwell, L. Symphony Ch., LSO, Rozhdestvensky – *Stabat Mater* ***

Rozhdestvensky here conducts a passionate account of what in many ways is the most powerful of all the composer's major works. There is little of the restraint that is typical of much of Howells's choral writing. Rather he exploits the lushest, most passionate elements in his richly post-impressionist style, and he hardly lets up over the whole span. It would be hard to imagine a more inspired performance than Rozhdestvensky's. Over the incandescent singing of the choir, the four excellent soloists give radiant performances, with the golden-toned soprano, Janice Watson, regularly crowning the mood of ecstasy in her solos. Full, glowing, atmospheric sound to match, and a superb coupling.

(Organ) De la Mare's Pavane; Flourish for a Bidding; Jacob's Brawl; St Louis Come to Clifton; Walton's Toye. (Choral): House of the Mind; Hymn for St Cecilia; King of Glory; New College Service: Magnificat & Nunc Dimittis; O Pray for the Peace of Jerusalem; A Sequence for St Michael
(N) (M) *** CRD CRD 3454. New College, Oxford, Ch., Higginbottom

Even finer than Higginbottom's companion collection below, this programme includes some of Howells's most celestial music. Higginbottom opens with the inspired *Sequence for St Michael*, a setting of a medieval lyric which was originally intended as part of *Hymnus paradisi* and is connected with the death of the composer's nine-year-old son. This beautiful and very dramatic motet is most movingly sung. The *Hymn to St Cecilia* is more direct yet, set to a poem by Ursula Vaughan Williams, and has increasing radiance. *O Pray for the Peace of Jerusalem* was written during the war, while Howells and his wife were snowbound in a cottage in the Cotswolds. It has a magnetic, tranquil stillness. These are all fine performances, beautifully sung, with the choir more recessed, less dramatically projected, than with the Wells Cathedral Choir on Hyperion. But the result is moving in a less extrovert way, more contemplative but hardly less affecting. Especially telling is the *House of the Mind*, one of three more motets from the 1940s, which has a mood of restrained rapture highly characteristic of the composer. The organ pieces act as contrasting interludes, *St Louis Come to Clifton* is based on a simple fifteenth-century French melody, and the more robust *Walton's Toye*, originally a clavichord piece and transcribed here by the conductor/organist, uses a sparky motif from *Crown Imperial* but transforms it with sustained organ sonorities. The programme ends with a thrillingly unrestrained setting of George Herbert's *King of Glory*. Howells believed there was no dividing line between spiritual tranquillity and God-given ecstasy, and this remarkable piece carries both expressions of human experience. The whole programme is very well sung, played and recorded, and shows the composer at his most inspirational.

(Organ) *Psalm-preludes, Set 1/1; Paen; Prelude: Sine nomine.* (Vocal): *Behold, O God our defender; Here is the door; Missa Aedi Christi: Kyrie; Credo; Sanctus; Benedictus; Agnus Dei; Gloria. Sing lullaby; A spotless rose; Where wast thou?*
(M) *** CRD 3455. New College, Oxford, Ch., Higginbottom (organ)

A further collection of the music of Herbert Howells, splendidly sung by Edward Higginbottom's fine choir, while he provides the organ interludes in addition. Among the shorter pieces, the carol-anthem *Sing lullaby* is especially delightful, and the programme ends with the motet *Where wast thou?*, essentially affirmative, in spite of the question posed at the opening. Beautifully spacious sound makes this a highly rewarding collection.

Requiem. Motets: *The House of the Mind; A Sequence for St Michael*
*** Chan. 9019. Finzi Singers, Spicer – VAUGHAN WILLIAMS: *Lord thou hast been our refuge*, etc. ***

Requiem; Take him, earth, for cherishing
*** United Recordings 88033. Barber, Field, Johnstone, Angus, Vasari, Backhouse – MARTIN: *Mass* ***

Howells's *Requiem* is the work which prepared the way for *Hymnus Paradisi*, providing some of the material for it. For unaccompanied chorus, it presents a gentler, compact view of what in the big cantata becomes powerfully expansive. The Finzi singers, 18-strong, give a fresh and atmospheric, beautifully moulded performance, well coupled with two substantial motets with organ by Howells, as well as choral pieces by Vaughan Williams.

On United the soloists and Vasari, a choir conducted by Jeremy Backhouse, are absolutely first class and give a well-nigh exemplary performance, possibly finer than its immediate rival. Doubtless couplings will resolve the matter of choice. The present disc offers the *Requiem* in harness with another Mass from the inter-war years by Frank Martin.

Stabat Mater
(N) (B) *** Chan. 2 for 1 247–27 (2). Archer, L. Symphony Ch., LSO, Rozhdestvensky – *Missa Sabrinensis* ***

The *Stabat Mater* was Howells's last major work. Though the ecstasy is not as consistently sustained as in the earlier *Missa Sabrinensis*, with which it is now coupled; with many more passages of hushed devotion, one registers with new intensity the agony of St John the Divine at the foot of the Cross, the companion of the Virgin Mary. The saint is personified in the tenor solos, here sung superbly by Neill Archer with a clear, heady tone, starting with his first thrilling entry on *O quam tristis*. As in the *Missa*, Rozhdestvensky proves the most passionate advocate, magnetically leading one through the whole rich score. Though ensemble sometimes suffers, it is a small price to pay for such thrusting, spontaneous-sounding conviction. Glowing, rich sound.

HUMFREY, Pelham (1647–74)

Verse Anthems: *By the Waters of Babylon; Have Mercy on Me, O God; Hear, O Heav'ns; Hear my Crying, O God; Hear my Prayer, O God; Lift up your Heads; Like as the Hart; O give thanks unto the Lord; O Lord my God*
☞ (BB) *** HM HMX 2907053. Deam, Minter, Covey-Crump, Potter, David Thomas, Clare Coll., Cambridge, Ch., Romanesca, McGegan

Here yet another name from the past emerges as a remarkably strong musical personality. Pelham Humfrey (or Humphrey) began his career as a chorister at the Chapel Royal, and he made such an impression that he was sent abroad at the expense of the royal purse of Charles II to study in France and Italy. After more than one visit he returned as a Gentleman of the Chapel Royal and, when the incumbent died in 1672, he took over as Master of the Choristers. He married, and his short life ended at the age of 27. He brought back from Italy (and from Lully in France) a thorough absorption of the operatic style, and his verse-anthems are remarkably dramatic and powerfully expressive, using soloists almost like operatic characters. *By the Waters of Babylon* and, especially, *O Lord my God* are very striking indeed. Nicholas McGegan's fine performances reflect this histrionic dimension, helped by his soloists who at times approach stylistic boundaries in their performance of what is essentially devotional music, even if intensely felt. Nevertheless, no one could say that these authentic performances are in any way dampened by scholarly rectitude. With a highly sensitive instrumental contribution from the excellent Romanesca, this collection (about half of Humfrey's surviving output) is very freshly recorded, and this bargain reissue is strongly recommended to the adventurous collector.

HUMMEL, Johann (1778–1837)

Bassoon Concerto in F
*** Chan. 9656. Popov, Russian State SO, Polyansky – MOZART; WEBER: *Bassoon Concertos* ***

A first-class modern recording of Hummel's genial *Bassoon Concerto* was needed, and Valeri Popov fits the bill, twinklingly good-natured and elegant, especially in the swinging 6/8 finale. His woody timbre (a French instrument perhaps) is most appealing, and Polyansky provides a warmly polished accompaniment, helped by the resonant, but not clouded, recording.

Piano Concerto in C, Op. 34; Rondos brillants in A, Op. 56 & B flat, Op. 98
(N) *** Chan. 10216. Shelley, LMP

It was in 1987, on the earlier Chandos issue below, that Stephen Hough transformed our ideas of Hummel piano concertos in a coupling of the B minor and A minor works. This new disc from Howard Shelley, every bit as fine, with full, open, well-balanced sound and sparkling performances, rounds off the series with the C major work, the earliest of Hummel's mature piano concertos, written in 1809, the year of Beethoven's *Emperor Concerto*, in coupling with two semi-concertos never previously recorded. The structure of the *C major Concerto* is as clear and forthright as the themes themselves, with fewer dalliances in empty passagework than one finds in the later concertos. Surprisingly for a composer who was also a leading piano virtuoso, Hummel, as in other concertos, avoids a solo cadenza, but there is enough display in the worked-out writing of the main structure. The two works labelled *Rondo brillant* were written later, in 1814 and 1822 respectively, each with a lyrical introduction of roughly five minutes leading on to a rondo finale, full of elaborate passagework for the soloist – both rather like concertos without a first movement.

Piano Concertos: in A min., Op. 85; B min., Op. 89
*** Chan. 8507. Hough, ECO, Thomson

The *A minor* is Hummel's most-often-heard piano concerto, never better played, however, than by Stephen Hough on this prize-winning Chandos disc. The coda is quite stunning; it is not only his dazzling virtuosity that carries all before it but also the delicacy and refinement of colour he produces. The *B minor*, Op. 89, is more of a rarity, and is given with the same blend of virtuosity and poetic feeling which Hough brings to its companion. He is given expert support by Bryden Thomson and the ECO – and the recording is first class.

Piano Concerto in A flat, Op. 113; Concertino in G, Op. 73; Gesellschafts Rondo, Op. 117
*** Chan. 9558. Shelley, LMP

The *Concertino* is an 1816 arrangement for piano and orchestra of the *Mandolin Concerto* of 1799. The music is slight and frothy but is played with elegance and virtuosity by Howard Shelley, who directs from the keyboard. The *A flat major Concerto* comes from 1827 and was written for the composer's concert tours of 1828–30. As Hummel was uncertain of the rehearsal time and the quality of some of the orchestras with which he would be playing, his orchestration errs on the side of caution. All the same, it is well scored and the solo part is brilliantly decorative. Some have found the final *Rondo alla Spagniola* prophetic of Chopin's *E minor Concerto*. The *Gesellschafts Rondo* (Society Rondo) from 1829 is a 12-minute piece consisting of a slow introduction and a dashing vivace. It is all fresh and delightful, even if it plumbs no depths. Brilliant playing from Shelley, whose artistry tends to be taken all too much for granted in his homeland. The 1997 recording still sounds as fresh and present as we thought first time round.

Trumpet Concerto in E
⊕ **(B)** *** Ph. Duo 464 028-2 (2). Hardenberger, ASMF, Marriner – HAYDN; HERTEL; STAMITZ: *Concertos* *** (with Concert: 'Famous Classical Trumpet Concertos' *** ✿).

Trumpet Concerto in E flat
(M) *** Sony SMK 89611. Marsalis, Nat. PO, Leppard – HAYDN: *Concerto* *** (with concert: *Trumpet Concertos*. *** ✿)
*** **SACD** SS 57497. Hardenberger, ASMF, Marriner – FASCH; HAYDN; L. MOZART *Concertos* ***

Both the Hardenberger and Wynton Marsalis performances have been reissued within well chosen collections and both are worthy of their Rosettes. But here there is a distinct choice between the two accounts of Hummel's *Concerto*. This is usually heard in the familiar brass key of E flat (which is the way Marsalis plays it), but the brilliant Swedish trumpeter, Håkan Hardenberger, uses the key of E, which makes it sound brighter and bolder than usual. Neither he nor Marsalis (and their respective accompanists) miss the genial lilt inherent in the dotted theme of the first movement, and the finale captivates the ear with its high spirits and breezy bravura.

Marsalis also gives a very fine account of this engaging work, but his approach is straighter, more classical, less *galant*. In matters of bravura, however, he matches Hardenberger at every turn: he relishes the sparkling finale. This is also available in a more expensive, less generous SACD.

(i) Violin Concerto in G; Adagio and Rondo alla Polacca in A (for violin & orchestra); Potpourri for Viola and Orchestra in G min., Op. 94. Variations, Op. 115 (for piano & orchestra).
(N) *** Chan. 10255. Shelley, LMP, (i) with Ehnes

The Hummel scholar Joel Sachs lists the composer's G major *Violin Concerto* among the 'doubtful or unverifiable works', but it has many characteristic touches, built as it is on warmly lyrical themes, starting with a clean-cut march tune marked by dotted rhythms. The first movement in a compact sonata form leads to a poignant *Adagio* slow movement in E minor, which promises deeper thoughts, until after two minutes it leads into the chatter of a *moto perpetuo* finale. The Canadian violinist, James Ehnes, is the brilliant and persuasive soloist. Though other composers may have had a hand in the work's composition, notably in the writing for solo violin, and the score (kept in the British Museum) is not quite complete (so that Stephen Haggard and Howard Shelley have had to fill in the gaps), it makes a very attractive addition to the expanding repertory of Hummel works on disc. In the *Variations in B flat* for piano and orchestra, you also have an indication of the way Hummel seems to shy away from any idea that threatens any depth of emotion. Evidently designed for his own display as a virtuoso pianist, it finds the soloist, Howard Shelley, in peak form, dazzlingly finger-perfect, and the result is a delight. The *Adagio and Rondo alla Polacca* for violin and orchestra is less elaborate, a simple, attractive showpiece, while the *Potpourri* for viola and orchestra brings another example of Hummel veering away from the gravity of an opening idea in the slow G minor introduction. That leads into a charming set of variations on Ottavio's *Il mio tesoro* from Mozart's *Don Giovanni*. Played and recorded like this, all these works are immensely enjoyable.

CHAMBER MUSIC

Amusement for Piano & Violin in F min., Op. 108; Violin Sonatas: in F, Op. 5/2; C, Op. 14; Variations 'alla Monferina' in D, Op. 54 for Piano & Cello

*** Mer. CDE 84439. Triangulus

The title *'Amusement'* for the first of the four works on this Meridian disc could not be more apt. This is in effect a compact sonatina for violin and piano, which brings out the open, unpretentious qualities of Hummel's writing at their most appealing The outer movements are built on tinkling tunes (the finale in jaunty polka-rhythm), while the slow movement is a song without words in all but name, with a reminder not just of Mendelssohn but of Bellini. Though longer and structurally more elaborate, the two *Sonatas* are hardly more ambitious, two works similarly designed to entertain without making too many demands on the listener. The Op. 5 work, an early piece, again has a song without words for its slow movement and another jaunty finale. The Op. 14 is just as charming, with the slow movement, similarly songful, this time in a yearning minor key.

The *Variations 'alla Monferina'* for cello and piano, varied and inventive, have a haunting little refrain in 6/8 which recurs at various points. After ten variations the piece is rounded off with a galloping 6/8 coda. Though Alison Moncrieff's cello is not helped by the recording, which underlines some minor flaws, this is another engaging example of Hummel's attractive and undemanding writing. In both the works with violin and those with cello, Lyn Garland at the piano is the prime mover, as Hummel would have expected, always fresh and lively.

Piano Quintet in E flat, Op. 87

(B) **(*) Hyp. Dyad CDD 22008 (2). Schubert Ens. of L. – SCHUBERT: *Trout Quintet*; SCHUMANN: *Piano Quintet; Piano Quartet* **(*)

A strong account of an impressive work from the Schubert Ensemble of London, who approach the piece as one in the classical mainstream rather than a *galant* entertainment. There is plenty of energy and commitment, and the brief *Largo* is made a touching interlude; only the finale (admittedly marked *Allegro agitato*) might seem too strongly driven and with not enough balancing elegance. The recording has fine immediacy.

Piano Quintet in E flat, Op. 87; Piano Septet in D min., Op. 74

(N) (B) *** Australian Decca Eloquence (ADD) 476 2447.
    Melos Ens. – WEBER: *Clarinet Quintet* ***

These two highly engaging works show the composer at his most melodically fecund and his musical craftsmanship at its most apt. One can see how Hummel charmed nineteenth-century audiences into regarding him as being a greater composer than he was, although recordings have certainly raised his claims in recent years. His skill at shaping and balancing a movement can be impressive: it is the ideas themselves (as in all music) that can make or break a structure, and here they are entirely appropriate to music designed to entertain. This these works certainly do in such spontaneous and polished performances – just try the opening movement of the *Septet* to sample the composer's felicity. The 1965 sound is warm, full and rich, and this is a vintage recording in every way; and this version of the *Piano Quintet* is preferable

to that on its Hyperion Dyad competitor. The Weber coupling is a charmer too.

Piano Trios 1–7

(M) *** MDG 3307/8 (2). Trio Parnassus

Piano Trios 1 in E flat, Op. 12; 2 in F, Op. 22; 3 in G, Op. 35; 7 in E flat, Op. 96

*** Mer. CDE 84350. Triangulus

Piano Trios 1 in E flat, Op. 12; 5 in E, Op. 83; 7 in E flat, Op. 96

*** Chan. 9529. Borodin Trio

Hummel's *Piano Trios* show the fluency, elegant craftsmanship and easy melodic flow for which he is admired in his better-known concertos. Comparing the first with the last of the trios shows no marked development of style of the kind one expects with the very greatest composers, but all seven works are individually rewarding in their diverse ways, and the composer's fund of ideas never dries up for a moment. The Trio Parnassus play throughout with consistent zest and spontaneity and they obviously enjoy the simple lyrical melodies. They are admirably recorded and this box can carry a strong recommendation.

Both these single-disc collections share the first and last of the *Trios*, each among the finest of the series, and each set of performances is enjoyable in different ways. Rostislav Dubinsky, leading the Borodin Trio, is a bolder, more temperamental player than Alison Kelly of Triangulus. Generally, the Triangulus performance is more relaxed than the Borodin's, and we are inclined to prefer the stronger pulse of the latter's first movement; but in the finale they tend almost to rush, and here Triangulus score a point or two. The opening movement of Op. 96 immediately produces the dotted rhythms which are Hummel's special trademark, while the simplicity of the melody at the heart of the *Poco Larghetto* is very winning in both performances; and in the closing *Rondo alla Russe*, the Borodin account is that bit stronger. The finale of Op. 85 (only included by Chandos) is also very catchy; however, Triangulus offer an extra work, and the closing Rondo of Op. 35 sparkles delightfully and shows the Meridian players at their most captivating.

Septet in D min., Op. 74

🕮 (M) *** CRD 3344. Nash Ens. – BERWALD: *Septet* ***

Hummel's *Septet* is an enchanting and inventive work with a virtuoso piano part, expertly dispatched here by Clifford Benson. A fine performance and excellent recording make this a highly desirable issue, particularly in view of the enterprising coupling.

Flute Sonatas 1 in G, Op. 2/2; 2 in D, Op. 50; 3 in A, Op. 64; (i) Flute Trio in A, Op. 78. Grand rondeau brillant for Flute & Piano in G, Op. 126

(BB) *** Naxos 8.553473. Daoust, Picard, with (i) Dolin

Hummel's elegant, easygoing melodic style seems custom-made for the flute, and his three lightweight sonatas are lacking in neither diversity nor charm. The *Grand rondeau brillant* is entertainingly like a Weber display piece. The performances on Naxos are both sunny and technically felicitous, and are warmly recorded. The *Trio* is an ingenuous set of variations on a Russian folk tune which lends itself to sparkling divisions. Here there is plenty of bustle before the work ends peacefully.

String Quartets: in C; in G; in E flat, Op. 30/1–3
☛ (N)(B) *** Hyp. Helios CDH 55166. Delmé Qt

Hummel's three quartets are closer to Haydn than Beethoven, though the first of the set in C major with its impressive opening *Adagio e mesto* in the minor key, and fine *Adagio*, obviously leans towards the influence of the later composer, while the audacious quotation of *Comfort ye* from Handel's *Messiah* in the preceding *Andante* brings yet another example of Hummelian sleight of hand. In short these are fascinating works, highly inventive, and crafted with the composer's usual fluent charm. They are splendidly played by the Delmé group, who provide plenty of vitality and warmth. The Hyperion recording is fresh and believable.

String Quartet in G, Op. 30/2
(*(*)) Testament mono SBT 1085. Hollywood Qt – HAYDN: Quartet 72; MOZART: Quartet 17 (**(*))

Hummel's charming *G major Quartet* comes with the first half of a 1957 Festival Hall concert. This performance was recorded two years earlier in a Hollywood studio and, though dazzlingly played, is a bit shrill.

Piano Sonatas 2 in E flat, Op. 13; 3 in F min., Op. 20; 5 in F sharp min., Op. 81
(BB) *** Naxos 8.553296. Chang (piano)

Hummel's piano sonatas at their best can match those of Haydn, and the *E flat major* work (1805) in Hae-won Chang's hands makes an attractive introduction to the genre. The more thoughtful first movement of the *F minor Sonata* (1807) is interrupted by a recurring brief *Adagio*; the central *Adagio maestoso* is more imposing, with the tension released in the bravura finale. The *F sharp minor Sonata* is a splendid work, nearer to Beethoven than to Haydn, its kernel a memorable *Largo con molto espressione*, to be followed by a vigorous bravura finale. This is the first of a Naxos series, and very welcome it is when this accomplished Korean pianist is right inside the music, which she plays very persuasively indeed. She is excellently recorded.

Piano Sonata 2, Op. 13; La bella capricciosa (Polonaise), Op. 55; Caprice, Op. 49; La contemplazione (Una fantasia piccola), Op. 107/3; Hungarian Rondo, Op. 107/6; Rondo, Op. 11; Variations on a Theme from Gluck's Armide, Op. 57
*** Chan. 9807. Shelley

Starting with a wittily pointed account of the *Rondo*, Opus 11, Hummel's best-known piece, Howard Shelley gives the most persuasive accounts of piano music by this leading virtuoso of his time, a composer so well thought of that he succeeded Haydn as Kapellmeister to Prince Esterházy. He may never have developed towards free romanticism as Beethoven, Schubert and Weber did, but such stylish performances as Shelley's, beautifully recorded, bring many delights, as in the sparkling *Gluck Variations*, the well-constructed *Sonata*, Opus 13, and the late, polka-like *Hungarian Rondo*.

Piano Sonatas 3 in F min., Op. 20; 4 in F sharp min., Op. 81; 6 in D, Op. 106
☛ *** Hyp. CDA 67390. Hough

Johann Nepomuk Hummel, renowned as one of the greatest pianists of his day, wrote a series of works to celebrate his own virtuosity – not just piano concertos (already recorded by a number of pianists, including Stephen Hough) but sonatas, of which nine are for solo piano. These three, argu-ably the finest of the series, generally avoid the empty passage-work which sometimes mars the concertos, and Hough gives the most characterful performances, beautifully recorded. The most radical of the three, written in 1819, is in F sharp minor, in which Hummel fully embraces the new romantic movement, with a first movement that brings a very free rendering of sonata form, full of contrasts and surprises, built on a striking, angular main theme. The slow movement after a weighty introduction then anticipates Chopin's *Noc-turnes*, leading to an energetic Slavonic dance finale. *No. 6 in D* marks a return to a more classical manner, at times like Weber, with a fast mazurka for Scherzo, while *No. 3 in F minor* of 1807 has a quirkiness typical of the composer, with a central slow movement marked to be played 'majestically'. In its way this makes as much of a discovery as Richard Hickox's revelatory recordings of Hummel *Masses*.

VOCAL MUSIC

Masses in B flat, Op. 77; D, Op. 111. (i) Alma Virgo
☛ *** Chan. 0681. Gritton, Collegium Musicum 90, Hickox; (i) with Gritton

Johann Nepomuk Hummel, who was born eight years after Beethoven, is one of those composers, celebrated in musical dictionaries rather than in live performance, who have had to wait until the age of CD to have their music meaningfully revived. This superb disc from Hickox not only fills an important gap but also demonstrates that the idea of Hum-mel as primarily a pianist-composer is quite misleading. It is astonishing that such fine works as these have been so neglected, not just on disc. Like Haydn's last six settings of the Mass they were written for the name-day of the Princess Esterházy, and they have inspired Hickox and his team to performances just as electrifying as those they have given of those Haydn Masses. These Hummel Masses, unlike Haydn's, are for chorus alone without soloists. The *Mass in D* (1808) begins in sombre mood with some adventurous harmonies, but Hummel in both Masses, like Haydn, prefers vigorous movement to meditation, often in fugal writing with sharply syncopated rhythms, which makes for exhilarating results.

As with Haydn, the settings of the final *Dona nobis pacem* in both Masses, far from conveying peace, are joyfully ener-getic, though, unlike Haydn, Hummel fades down to a gentle close in each. Distinctively, his settings of *Et resurrexit* in the *Credo*, instead of entering on an immediate *fortissimo*, build up in rising crescendo, as though bystanders are gradually appreciating the wonder of the event, one of many perceptive symbolic points in these inspired and sensitive settings of the liturgy. Susan Gritton is the pure-toned soloist in the fill-up, *Alma Virgo*, an aria in two sections, with the chorus joining in for the culminating *Alleluia* with whooping horns.

(i) Mass in E flat, Op. 80. Quod in urbe, Op. 88; Te Deum
(N) *** Chan. 0712. Coll. Mus. 90, Hickox, (i) with Gritton, Murray, Gilchrist, Varcoe

This, the second in Hickox's Hummel Mass Edition for Chandos, concentrates on works he wrote soon after being appointed Konzertmeister to Prince Esterházy in 1804. The *Mass in E flat*, dating from May of 1804, is the first Mass to follow on the great series of Haydn masterpieces celebrating the name-day of Princess Esterházy. Hummel's eagerness led him to complete it four months before the September dead-line. The result has a winning freshness, with a setting of the *Kyrie* which, after opening gently, promptly expands into a joyful *Allegro*. As in the first disc in Hickox's series, the performance consistently captures the joy of Hummel's inspiration, with clean attack and fine diction from the chorus as well as the soloists. That clarity extends to the superb setting of the *Te Deum*, written at high speed to celebrate peace with Napoleon in 1805. Each section of this elaborate text is strikingly characterized, without holding up the urgent impulse established in the opening fanfares. *Quod in urbe*, written as a gradual for inclusion in services, also starts strikingly, with timpani alone in fanfare rhythm, another fine work neglected for far too long. With full, clear sound, recorded in the Blackheath Concert Hall, Hickox must again be congratulated on what promises to be an outstanding series.

Missa Solemnis in C; Te Deum

(BB) *** Naxos 8.557193. Wright, McKendree-Wright, Power, Griffiths, Tower Voices, New Zealand SO, Grodd

Following Richard Hickox's brilliant Chandos issue of two Hummel Masses (see above) comes more evidence of the vigour that this neglected composer brought to his choral works. On the recommendation of Haydn he was carrying on the tradition of writing annual Masses for Prince Esterházy, demonstrating what a sense of drama he had in illustrating the liturgy, masterly in counterpoint and orchestration, never resorting to note-spinning, as he often does in his keyboard writing. Here with New Zealand forces, including the brilliant professional chamber choir, Tower Voices, we have the longest of Hummel's five Masses in coupling with an electrifying setting of the *Te Deum*. Both were written in 1806, and one is constantly reminded that this was the period of the Napoleonic wars, when each of these works so often features martial music with fanfares, trumpets and drums. Unlike most Anglican settings, this *Te Deum* ends on a grand *fortissimo*. A thrilling issue, all the more recommendable at super-bargain price.

HUMPERDINCK, Engelbert
(1854–1921)

The Canteen Woman (Die Marketenderin): Prelude. The Merchant of Venice: Love Scene. Moorish Rhapsody: Tarifa (Elegy of Summer); Tangier (A Night in a Moorish Coffee-house); Tetuan (A Night in the Desert). The Sleeping Beauty: Suite

**(*) Marco Polo 8.223369. Slovak RSO (Bratislava), M. Fischer-Dieskau

The Love scene from *The Merchant of Venice* ('On such a night') is beautiful but rather over-extended, and all three sections of the *Moorish Rhapsody* are much too long (the composite piece lasts some 32 minutes). The opening of the *Summer Elegy* begins with raptly ethereal writing for the violins, but the jolly Moorish coffee-house sequence sounds as if the restaurant has been leased from the owner of a Bavarian bierkeller. The Slovak performances under Martin Fischer-Dieskau (the famous Lieder singer's grandson) are not ideally polished but have freshness and vitality, while the Marco Polo recording is open and reasonably full.

Hänsel und Gretel (complete)

(N) (BB) (***) Naxos mono 8.110897/8. Schwarzkopf, Grümmer, Metternich, Ilosvay, Schürhoff, Felbermayer, Children's Ch., Philh. O, Karajan (with additional excerpts sung by Supervia, Ferraris, Hüsch, Seinemeyer, Jung)

(M) *** EMI mono 5 67061-2 [5 67145-2] (2). Schwarzkopf, Grümmer, Metternich, Ilosvay, Schürhoff, Felbermayer, Children's Ch., Philh. O, Karajan

(M) **(*) RCA (ADD) 74321 25281-2 (2). Moffo, Donath, Fischer-Dieskau, Berthold, Ludwig, Augér, Popp, Bav. R. Ch. & RSO, Eichhorn

(M) **(*) Decca 455 063-2 (2). Fassbaender, Popp, Hamari, Berry, Burrowes, Gruberová, Schlemm, V. Boys' Ch., VPO, Solti

Karajan's classic 1950s set of Humperdinck's children's opera, with Schwarzkopf and Grümmer peerless in the name-parts, is enchanting; this was an instance where everything in the recording went right. The original mono LP set was already extremely atmospheric. In most respects the sound has as much clarity and warmth as rival recordings made in the 1970s. There is much to delight here; the smaller parts are beautifully done and Else Schürhoff's Witch is memorable.

This is now reissued as one of EMI's 'Great Recordings of the Century', but there is no doubt that the alternative Naxos set is the one to go for. This is one of the finest transfers Mark Obert-Thorn has achieved to date. The glow on the horns at the opening of the Overture extends throughout the set, so that the sound, vocal and orchestral, is so gloriously warm and vivid, yet still clear, that one has the illusion of stereo. Moreover, as a bonus on the second disc we are offered a series of historical recordings of excerpts dating from 1928, with Conchita Supervia rattling away as Hansel, partnered by Maria Ferraris as Gretel singing the *Dance Duet* in Italian; Meta Seinemeyer and Helen Jung in 1929; Gerard Hüsch as Peter (in 1937); and three excerpts from 1935, with Elisabeth Schumann as the Sandman singing a duet with herself, accompanied by Ernest Lush.

There are some fine solo performances on the mid-priced 1971 RCA set, notably from Helen Donath as Gretel and Christa Ludwig as the Witch; and Kurt Eichhorn's direction is vigorous, with excellent orchestral playing and full, atmospheric recording. It is a pity that a more boyish-sounding singer than Anna Moffo could not have been chosen for the role of Hänsel but, all told, this is a colourful and enjoyable account of a unique, eternally fresh opera, well worth considering.

Solti with the Vienna Philharmonic directs a strong, spectacular version, emphasizing the Wagnerian associations of the score. Solti does the *Witch's ride* very excitingly, and the VPO are encouraged to play with consistent fervour throughout. The result, though rather lacking in charm, is well sung, with the two children both engagingly characterized. Edita Gruberová is an excellent Dew Fairy and Walter Berry is first rate as Peter. Anny Schlemm's Witch is memorable if vocally unsteady, and there are some imaginative touches of stereo production associated with *Hocus pocus* and her other moments of magic. The recording is even more vivid in its CD transfer.

Hänsel und Gretel: highlights

(BB) *** EMI Encore 5 86097-2 [5 86098-2]. Von Otter, Bonney, Lipovšek, Schwarz, Schmidt, Hendricks, Lind, Tölz Boys' Ch., Bav. RSO, Tate

It is good to have a set of highlights from the deleted Bavarian set conducted, fairly briskly but sympathetically, by Jeffrey Tate. Barbara Bonney as Gretel and Anne Sofie von Otter as Hänsel are hardly less fine than the exceptionally strong duos on rival sets, and the chill that Marjana Lipovšek conveys as the Witch, using the widest range of expression, is equally telling. The recording has plenty of warmth and atmosphere. A bargain.

Hansel and Gretel (complete; in English)

●━ (B) *** CfP (ADD) 5 75993-2 (2). Kern, Neville, Howard, Hunter, Herincx, Robinson, Sadler's Wells Op. O, Bernadi (with WAGNER: Siegfried Idyll: L. Sinf., C. Davis ***)

Hansel and Gretel (English version by Tom Hammond)

(N) *(*) Avie AV 0050 (2). Mentzer, Murphy, Forst, Taylor, Orth, Christy, Milwaukee SO, Delfs

This was the first full-length Sadler's Wells Opera recording in English, and it proved to be one of the finest of all the company's ventures into the recording studio. It was also the first complete foreign opera in English on record since way back in the days of early operatic 78s. EMI used their then (1964) new 'ambionic' technique with feedback, bringing extra reverberation to the comparatively dry No. 1 Studio at Abbey Road. The result is warm and atmospheric and not at all artificial sounding.

As for the performance, it is in every way successful, and the clear English words undoubtedly enhance one's enjoyment at every point, with no musical loss. The singing is full of zest, with Patricia Kern and Margaret Neville as the two children in splendid voice (and vocally well differentiated). Rita Hunter and the richly resonant Raimund Herincx are strongly cast as Mother and Father, and the smaller parts of the Dew Fairy (Jennifer Eddy) and Sandman (Elizabeth Robinson) are delightfully sung. Ann Howard makes a characterful and believable Witch. But the overall achievement relies much on the Canadian conductor, Mario Bernadi, who not only keeps the narrative flow sparklingly alive but also ensures that the orchestra consistently excels itself. The English text rises over the ripe orchestral sound, and altogether this is just as rewarding as any of the German-language versions, and altogether more accessible (for there is an excellent synopsis). With room to spare on the second CD, EMI remind us of the Wagnerian affinities of Humperdinck's score by including Colin Davis's 1960 Sinfonia of London recording of the Siegfried Idyll, a real performance and enjoyable for its simplicity and eloquence, although the sound is a little dated. The opera is not to be missed.

Recorded live at performances in Milwaukee in November 2003, the Avie version offers two star singers in the central roles, but little else to compete with the vintage Sadler's Wells version in English on CfP. With Andreas Delfs an uninspired conductor, too often stodgy rhythmically, it is strangely undercharacterized even from the two principals, with Heidi Grant Murphy not boyish enough, too womanly. The CfP also has Wagner's Siegfried Idyll for fill-up.

Königskinder (complete)

**(*) Calig CAL 50968/70 (3). Moser, Schellenberger, Henschel, Schmiege, Kohn, Munich Boys' Ch., Bav. R. Ch. & O, Luisi

The success of Hänsel und Gretel has completely overshadowed this second fairy-tale opera of Humperdinck, which contains much fine music.

It is good to have a new recording of a rich score, generally well sung and warmly conducted by Fabio Luisi, who uses the same choir and orchestra as the earlier, EMI set, recorded in 1976, with sound rather more spacious but not so immediate. An incidental shortcoming is that the libretto comes in German only, with the Calig libretto omitting even the stage

directions. The tenor of Thomas Moser, taking the central role of the Prince, is more heroic than that of his earlier EMI rival, Adolf Dallapozza, with the voice often shaded down beautifully. Though Dagmar Schellenberger as the Goosegirl lacks sweetness, hers is a feeling, well-characterized performance, and she finds a delicate mezza voce for the prayer to her parents. Marilyn Schmiege with her warm, firm mezzo makes rather a young Witch. All told, this is a performance marked by good teamwork, with the chorus bringing energetic echoes of Smetana's Bartered Bride in their brief contributions.

HURLSTONE, William (1876–1906)

Cello Sonata in D

(M) *** Dutton Epoch CDLX 7102. Fuller, Dussek – HARTY: Butterflies, etc.; PARRY: Cello Sonata in A ***

Hurlstone's Cello Sonata is as well fashioned and musicianly as you would expect from this gifted composer. It receives excellent advocacy from Andrew Fuller, who also writes the intelligent notes, and his fine pianist, Michael Dussek. At the same time it is not easy to discern a distinctive voice here beneath the Brahmsian veneer. The recording is excellent, well balanced and present.

(i) Piano Quartet in E min.; Piano Trio in G; Adagio (arr. from (i) Cello Sonata 2)

●━ (M) *** Dutton Epoch CDLX 7128 Dussek Piano Trio; (i) with Boyd

The tragedy of the early death of William Hurlstone at the age of 30 is underlined in this finely crafted chamber music. As a favourite pupil of Stanford, Hurlstone had already established himself as a fluently lyrical composer, pouring forth a stream of warm and striking tunes, such as provide the material here. The idiom in both the Piano Trio and the Piano Quartet is conservative, with echoes of Mendelssohn and Brahms as much as of Stanford. What raises them above the level of imitations is the fluent memorability of both the material and the arguments, as in the jig-like Scherzo and jaunty finale of the Trio and the sweetly tuneful Andante cantabile of the Quartet. The moving Adagio lamentoso slow movement of the Cello Sonata No. 2 was arranged for viola by Hurlstone's fellow composer, Frank Bridge, and it makes a fine supplement to the major works. It is played beautifully here by James Boyd, who also joins the excellent Dussek Trio for the Piano Quartet. When tunes sprang from Hurlstone's imagination so fluently, it would be good to hear some of his dozens of songs and the cantata, Alfred the Great.

IBERT, Jacques (1890–1962)

La Ballade de la Geôle de Reading; Féerique; 3 pièces de ballet (Les Rencontres); (i) Chant de folie. Suite Elisabéthaine

**(*) Marco Polo 8.223508. (i) Slovak Ph. Ch.; Slovak RSO (Bratislava), Adriano

The Suite Elisabéthaine is a nine-movement suite taken from the incidental music Ibert composed for Shakespeare's A Midsummer Night's Dream. It is largely pastiche and four of the movements draw on Blow, Purcell, Bull and Gibbons. More characteristic is La Ballade de la Geôle de Reading, an exercise in neo-impressionism and highly accomplished. The Chant de folie is an effective four-minute choral and orchestral piece inspired by the composer's experiences in the First

World War. Good performances and eminently serviceable recording.

La Ballade de la Geôle de Reading; (i) Persée et Andromède (opera; complete). Sarabande pour Dulcinée

(N) *** Avie AV 0008. (i) Massis, Rouillon, Beuron; Strasbourg PO, Latham-Koenig

When Ibert won the Prix de Rome in 1919 it led to a two-year residence in Rome, which proved a most fruitful period for him creatively, resulting in, among other pieces, the two main works on this Avie disc. The *Ballade de la Geôle de Reading*, inspired by passages from Oscar Wilde's poem, ignores the text in a purely orchestral evocation, with echoes of Ravel's *Daphnis et Chloé* hardly suggesting the rigours of prison life. *Persée et Andromède* is a miniature opera in two compact Acts, telling of Andromeda and the monster Cathos who eventually, after being slaughtered by Perseus, rises from his remains to become a handsome prince. The opening immediately establishes an exotic atmosphere, very French, with echoes of Ravel and Poulenc, and with Cathos's suppressed love for Andromeda, his prisoner, finding the beginnings of a response. Perseus does not arrive until Act II, riding on Pegasus, here depicted as a rather conceited figure. When Cathos is finally transformed, his music grows more sensuous too, culminating in a love duet. All three principal soloists are first rate, with fresh, youthful-sounding voices. The *Sarabande pour Dulcinée*, taken from Ibert's ballet *Don Quichotte*, is an attractive makeweight. Sensitive direction from Jan Latham-Koenig throughout and very well recorded, warmly responsive playing from the Strasbourg Philharmonic.

Concerto for Cello & Wind Instruments

(N) *** BBC (mono) BBCL 4156-2. Du Pré, Michael Krein Ens., Krein – DVORAK: *Cello Concerto* **(*)

Ibert's delightful concerto was pioneered on LP by André Navarra, and the seventeen-year-old Jacqueline Du Pré probably knew this account. In any event, she took it into her repertory for a BBC studio concert in 1962 with the Michael Krein Ensemble, whose enterprising and expert programmes were frequent at this period. A splendid performance and a worthwhile and welcome, if all too brief, supplement to her superb Prom performance of the Dvořák, superbly played, with the cello the first among many soloists.

Flute Concerto

*** EMI 5 57563-2. Pahud, Tonhalle O, Zinman – KHACHATURIAN: *Flute Concerto* ***

Emmanuel Pahud and the Zurich Tonhalle Orchestra under David Zinman give the most virtuosic and stylish account of Ibert's delightful *Flute Concerto*. No need to hesitate if you accept the coupling, for not only is the performance outstanding but so, too, is the recorded sound.

Divertissement

☛ *** Chan. 9023. Ulster O, Tortelier – MILHAUD: *Le Bœuf; Création; POULENC: Les Biches* ***
(***) Testament mono SBT 1309. Paris Conservatoire O, Désormière – IPPOLITOV-IVANOV: *Caucasian Sketches*; DOMENICO SCARLATTI (arr. Tommasini): *The Good-Humoured Ladies*; TCHAIKOVSKY: *Sleeping Beauty Suite* (***)

Yan Pascal Tortelier provides at last a splendid, modern, digital version of Ibert's *Divertissement*. There is much delicacy of detail, and the coupled suite from Poulenc's *Les Biches*

is equally delectable. Marvellous, top-drawer Chandos sound.

Désormière was a stylist, and it shows in every bar. This 1951 recording, produced (like the rest of the programme) by John Culshaw, remains unsurpassed in terms of sheer character and style, though there have been many since that have been played with greater polish and better recorded. Lovers of French music of the 1920s should not miss it.

Escales (Ports of Call)

☛ (M) *** RCA (ADD) **SACD** 82876 61387-2. Boston SO, Munch – DEBUSSY: *La Mer* **(*); SAINT-SAENS: *Symphony 3* *** ✪

Munch's *Escales* brings some ravishing textures from the Boston violins, and the finale, *Valencia*, has sparkling dance rhythms. The 1956 recording, if balanced rather closely, has brilliance and transparency; and it sounds much fuller in this new SACD transfer.

CHAMBER MUSIC

3 Pièces brèves

☛ (M) *** Chan. 6543. Athena Ens. – GOUNOD: *Petite symphonie in B flat; POULENC: Sextet* ***
(***) BBC mono BBCL 4066-2. Dennis Brain Wind Quintet (with instrumental recital (***))

Ibert's *Trois pièces brèves* could hardly be played with more polish, wit and affection than in this brilliantly realized performance by the Athena group, the effect enhanced when they are recorded so realistically.

The characterful blend of Dennis Brain and his colleagues in his Wind Quintet (Gareth Morris, Leonard Brain, Stephen Waters and Cecil James) is fully captured in the BBC mono recording, and the warm, spirited geniality of their ensemble brings a delightful bonhomie to the music's wit – the pastoral opening is captivating.

INCE, Kamran (born 1960)

Symphonies 3 (Siege of Vienna); 4 (Sardis); Domes

(N) **(BB)** *** Naxos 8.557588, Prague SO, composer

Born in Montana, of American-Turkish parentage, Kamran Ince was educated in Turkey and settled in the USA around 1980. He is a directly communicative avant-garde composer whose music is underlyingly melodic and who demonstrates a remarkably individual orchestral palette. Indeed, his music depends a great deal on exotic scoring and weirdly picturesque imagery, often looking to the distant past. Both symphonies are made up of a series of brief monolithic movements, which maintain their contrasting moods and atmosphere, so that after the first three violent sections of the *Siege of Vienna* (by the Ottomans in 1529 and 1683) we have a contrasting poignant evocation of those who perished. Similarly, *Sardis* evokes the history of an area (currently under excavation) north-east of Ephesus. Ince again creates a series of fascinating aural pictures, beginning with the *Hermus River* and ending with an evocation of the Tmolus Mountains, with stabbing storm chords and a haunting oboe theme representing the eternity of their existence. *Domes* has no programme, but its sensuously nocturnal mood is essentially melancholy and human in its expressive language. The performances, directed by the composer, could not be more authentic, and the powerful orchestral response and excellent recording ensure its vivid projection.

INDY, Vincent d' (1851–1931)

Jour d'été à la montagne, Op. 61; (i) Symphonie sur un chant montagnard (cévenole), Op. 25

(BB) **(*) Warner Apex 0927 49809-2. R. France PO, Janowski; (i) with Collard

This inexpensive Apex reissue is worth having for the sake of *Jour d'été à la montagne*, one of d'Indy's most inspired pieces. This version is artistically superior to most rivals, though the late lamented Catherine Collard's version of the *Symphonie sur un chant montagnard français*, sometimes known as the *Symphonie cévenole*, is handicapped by some unsympathetic accompanying from Janowski, while the 1991 recording's synthetic balance does not allow the sound to expand. Good playing from the Orchestre Philharmonic de Radio France makes this disc value for money.

Symphonie sur un chant montagnard français (Symphonie cévenole)

(BB) **(*) Naxos 8.550754. Thiollier, Nat. SO of Ireland, De Almeida – FAURE: *Ballade;* FRANCK: *Symphonic Variations* **(*)

On Naxos the French-born but American-trained François-Joël Thiollier gives an intelligent performance, perfectly well accompanied and decently recorded, and with an interesting coupling. It is worth the money, but there are finer accounts to be had.

(i) Symphonie sur un chant montagnard français; (ii) Symphony 2 in B flat, Op. 57

— (M) *** EMI (ADD) 7 63952-2. (i) Ciccolini, O de Paris, Baudo; (ii) Toulouse Capitole O, Plasson

Aldo Ciccolini gives a good account of himself in the demanding solo part of the *Symphonie*, and the Orchestre de Paris under Serge Baudo give sympathetic support. The recording is pleasing and with a convincing piano image. The *Second Symphony* remains one of the neglected masterpieces of turn-of-the-century French music. Michel Plasson proves a sympathetic and committed advocate, and his orchestra responds with enthusiasm and sensitivity to his direction. The recording too is spacious, full and well focused.

String Quartet 1

*** Hyp. CDA 67097. Chilingirian Qt – CHAUSSON: *String Quartet* (completed D'INDY)

Among the string quartets which French composers wrote in the last years of the nineteenth century – generally prompted by the example of César Franck – those of Vincent d'Indy are the most unjustly neglected, as this outstanding performance of No. 1 demonstrates. It is a striking work which in its bold thematic material often echoes Beethoven. A powerful first movement leads to an ecstatic slow movement, an elegant interlude and an exuberant finale. We now need the Chilingirians with their deep sympathy for the idiom to record d'Indy's other two quartets. The Chausson quartet makes a very apt coupling here, completed by d'Indy after the composer's tragic death in a road accident.

String Quartets 1 in D, Op. 35; 2 in E, Op. 45; 3 in B flat, Op. 96; (i) String Sextet, Op. 92

*** Cal. CAL 9891/2. Joachim Qt with (i) Mereaux, Poulet

String Quartets 1 in D, Op. 35; 2 in E, Op. 45

**(*) Marco Polo 8.223140. Kodály Qt

D'Indy greatly admired the Beethoven Quartets: in them he saw the perfect balance between formal strength and spirituality of content. His own *First Quartet* comes from 1890, the year in which his master, César Franck, died, and it leaves no doubt as to his indebtedness to both Beethoven and Franck, as indeed does the Second (1897), written not long after the *Istar Variations*. It is built almost wholly on a four-note motto and fashioned with great skill and refined craftsmanship. The *Third Quartet* comes from the other end of his life and was completed in 1929, a year later than the *Sextet*, and when d'Indy was 78. It is dignified in utterance, and there is nobility even if some of the ideas fall short of distinction. It is impossible to fault the excellent playing of the Joachim Quartet or the quality of the Calliope recording.

The excellent Kodály Quartet are recorded in the Italian Institute in Budapest, where the rather close balance tends to iron out dynamic extremes.

IPPOLITOV-IVANOV, Mikhail (1859–1935)

Armenian Rhapsody, Op. 48; Caucasian Sketches, Set II: Iveria, Op. 42; Jubilee March (Voroshilov), Op. 67; (i) Mtzyri, Op. 54. Turkish Fragments, Op. 62; Turkish March, Op. 55; (ii) Aria: Assya: I wonder if it is misfortune

— *** ASV CDDCA 1102. Armenian PO, Tjeknavorian; with (i) Hatsagortsian; (ii) Khachaturian

Tjeknavorian and ASV have turned up a second set of *Caucasian Sketches*, called *Iveria*, with a jubilant closing *Georgian March* that might become popular, like the *Procession of the Sardar*, given sufficient exposure. The sombre opening *Lamentation* is also rather telling, followed by a lazily sinuous *Berceuse* and a brightly scored, rhythmically catchy *Lezghinka*. The *Turkish Fragments* describe the progress of an Eastern caravan, opening with a processional, and including a nocturnal sequence with a sultry Rimskian oboe melody. The symphonic poem *Mtzyri* is most notable for its interpolated ballad from the nymph who finds the young hero of the story wounded by a leopard in the forest. This is touchingly sung by Hasmit Hatsagortsian, if with a very characteristic Russian vibrato. Vardouhi Khachaturian's performance of the mezzo scena from *Assya* has no lack of temperament or eloquence, and the other (*Turkish March*) is enjoyably ebullient. Very well recorded, this CD is worth exploring if you enjoy this kind of undemanding and tuneful Russian orchestral music.

Caucasian Sketches (suite), Op. 10

*** Chan. 9321. BBC PO, Glushchenko – KHACHATURIAN: *Symphony 3, etc.* ***

*** ASV CDDCA 773. Armenian PO, Tjeknavorian – KHACHATURIAN: *Gayaneh, etc.* **(*)

Once a popular repertory piece, the colourful *Caucasian Sketches* have fallen out of favour; only the final *Procession of the Sardar* is generously represented on CD. The present version by the BBC Philharmonic under Fedor Glushchenko is generally superior to the alternative on ASV.

The *Procession of the Sardar* is played by the Armenians with great brio. The other items rely mainly on picaresque oriental atmosphere for their appeal, which Tjeknavorian also captures evocatively in this brightly lit recording.

IRELAND, John (1879–1962)

Concertino pastorale; A Downland Suite (arr. composer and Geoffrey Bush); *Orchestral Poem; 2 Symphonic Studies* (arr. Bush)

☮– *** Chan. 9376. City of L. Sinfonia, Hickox

The valedictory *Threnody* of the *Concertino pastorale* and the lovely *Elegy* from the *Downland Suite* show the composer at his most lyrically inspired, and the rapt playing here does them full justice. The early *Orchestral Poem* (1904) is a surprisingly powerful work as presented here with great passion, with splendid brass writing at its climax. The two *Symphonic Studies* come from film music Ireland wrote for *The Overlanders*, not incorporated into the concert suites: the brass chromatics in the first have a familiar ring; the second has a wild momentum, recalling the cattle stampede in the film, but both stand up well as independent concert pieces.

Piano Concerto in E flat; Legend for Piano & Orchestra; Mai-Dun (symphonic rhapsody)

☮– *** Chan. 8461. Parkin, LPO, Thomson

Eric Parkin gives a splendidly refreshing and sparkling performance and benefits from excellent support from Bryden Thomson and the LPO. They are no less impressive in *Mai-Dun* and the beautiful *Legend for Piano & Orchestra*.

A Downland Suite; Elegiac Meditation; The Holy Boy

*** Chan. 8390. ECO, Garforth – BRIDGE: *Suite for Strings* ***

A Downland Suite was originally written for brass band. However, the present version was finished and put into shape by Geoffrey Bush, who also transcribed the *Elegiac Meditation*. David Garforth and the ECO play with total conviction and seem wholly attuned to Ireland's sensibility. The recording is first class, clear and naturally balanced.

A London Overture; Epic March; The Holy Boy; (i–ii)
Greater love hath no man; These things shall be; (i; iii)
Vexilla Regis

☮– (M) *** Chan. 7074. LSO, Hickox, with (i) L. Symphony Ch.; (ii) Terfel; (iii) Bott, Shaw, Oxley

Richard Hickox is a sympathetic interpreter of Ireland's music and he obtains sensitive results (and good singing) in *The Holy Boy* and *These things shall be* (surprisingly, the latter is not otherwise available on silver disc). The CD is of particular interest in that it brings a rarity, *Vexilla Regis*, for chorus, brass and organ, composed when Ireland was 19 and still a student of Stanford. First-class recorded sound.

MUSIC FOR BRASS

Comedy Overture; A Downland Suite (for Brass Band); The Holy Boy (arr. Cameron)

(N) (BB) **(*) Hyp. CDH 55070. L. Brass Virtuosi, Honeyball
 – ELGAR: *Severn Suite,* etc.; VAUGHAN WILLIAMS: *Prelude on 3 Welsh Hymns* **(*)

John Ireland's *Downland Suite* and what was later – in its orchestral form – to become the *London Overture* were both conceived for brass band. The two central movements of the suite (*Elegy* and *Minuet*) and indeed the main 'Piccadilly' theme of the *Overture* sound especially well on brass, as does David Cameron's arrangement of *The Holy Boy*. Excellent

performances and recording, but one could wish the ensemble was larger: these are first-rate players, but we need more of them.

CHAMBER MUSIC

(i) *Cello Sonata;* (ii) *Fantasy Sonata for Clarinet & Piano;* (i) *The Holy Boy* (for cello & piano); (iii) *Phantasie Trio; Piano Trios 2–3;* (iv) *Violin Sonatas 1–2*

*** Chan. 9377/8. (i; iii) Georgian; (i; iii–iv) I. Brown; (ii) De Peyer, Pryor; (iii–iv) Mordkovitch

Few British composers have written with quite such easy lyricism as John Ireland. The first two of the *Piano Trios*, well contrasted, are warmly appealing, but the masterpiece is the four-movement *Piano Trio No. 3* of 1938, passionately intense. The two *Violin Sonatas* are both superb works too, masterfully played here by Lydia Mordkovitch with Ian Brown, who also accompanies Karine Georgian in the *Cello Sonata*. Completing the set, the recording of the *Fantasie Sonata* of 1943 for clarinet dates from earlier, with Gervase de Peyer and Gwenneth Pryor playing with equal commitment.

(i) *Cello Sonata in G min.; The Holy Boy;* (ii) *Violin Sonata 1 in D min.;* (i; ii) *Piano Trio 2 in E*

(N) *** ASV Gold GLD 4009. McCabe; with (i) J. Lloyd Webber; (ii) Hope

In inspired performances, all with John McCabe at the piano, this ASV disc offers a fine cross-section of Ireland's warmly expressive chamber music, an excellent alternative to the more comprehensive two-disc collection on Chandos. The *First Violin Sonata*, with Daniel Hope a masterly violinist, may not be as well known as the *Second*, but it is just as skilfully written, with a tenderly meditative slow movement between powerful outer movements. In a single movement, compact but well varied, the *Piano Trio No. 2* is one of Ireland's tautest works, inspired by the horrors of the First World War, while the *Cello Sonata* of 1923 is stylistically more adventurous in its chromatic writing, rounded off with a vigorous finale that anticipates the jazzy rhythms of the comparable movement in Ireland's popular *Piano Concerto*. That and *The Holy Boy* in its cello version were recorded well before the rest, but the sound remains consistent, and the performances with Julian Lloyd Webber are characteristically sensitive.

Violin Sonatas 1 in D min.; 2 in A min.; Bagatelle; Berceuse; Cavatina; The Holy Boy

(BB) *** Hyp. Helios CDH 55164. Barritt, Edwards

Paul Barritt and Catherine Edwards make an effective partnership and give very persuasive accounts of both these fine sonatas. An excellent, well-balanced recording earns this a strong recommendation to those wanting just this repertoire alone on a single (budget) disc.

(i) *The Holy Boy;* (ii) *Phantasie Trio;* (iii) *Violin Sonatas 1–2*

(M) (***) Dutton Epoch mono CDLX 7103. (i–ii) Hooton; (i) Pratt; (ii–iii) Grinke; (ii) Taylor; (ii–iii) composer; (iii) Sammons

We have long treasured Frederick Grinke's 78-r.p.m. set of the *Violin Sonata No. 1* with the composer at the piano, and can confirm that the Dutton transfer of this 1945 recording brings its sound to life with striking effect. It is possible that there have been better recordings but not a more vibrant or more authoritative performance. The *Violin Sonata No. 2*, on the other hand, again with John Ireland at the piano but with its dedicatee, the legendary Albert Sammons, recorded in 1930, still sounds very well for its age, as does the *Phantasie Trio*, in which Grinke is joined by Florence Hooton and Kenneth Taylor. An invaluable and self-recommending set which readers should cherish. Outstanding transfers.

String Quartets 1 in D min.; 2 in C min.; The Holy Boy
**(*) ASV CDDCA 1017. Holywell Ens.

Both quartets come from 1897, when Ireland was 18, and were published posthumously. There is little sign of individuality but each work is beautifully crafted and gives much pleasure. The idiom is close to Dvořák and the ideas are fluent and pleasing. The Holywell Ensemble offer decent performances and are well recorded.

PIANO MUSIC

The Almond Tree; Decorations; Merry Andrew; Preludes (The Undertone; Obsession; The Holy Boy; Fire of Spring); Rhapsody; Sonata in E min.; Summer Evening; The Towing-Path
*** Chan. 9056. Parkin

Amberley Wild Woods; Ballad; The Darkened Valley; Equinox; For Remembrance; Greenways; In Those Days; Leaves from a Child's Sketchbook; London Pieces; 2 Pieces; Prelude in E flat; Sonatina
*** Chan. 9140. Parkin

Ballade of London Nights; Columbine; Month's Mind; On a Birthday Morning; 3 Pastels; 2 Pieces (February's Child; Aubade); 2 Pieces (April; Bergomask); Sarnia; A Sea Idyll; Soliloquy; Spring Will Not Wait
*** Chan. 9250. Parkin

Few British composers have matched John Ireland in the point and individuality of his piano music, with its offbeat melodies and tangy dissonances. It goes without saying that Eric Parkin is completely inside Ireland's idiom and he brings both dedication and sympathy to this repertoire. Moreover, the sound is clean, well-rounded and pleasing.

Aubade; February's Child; The Darkened Valley; Decorations; April; Leaves from a Child's Sketchbook; Merry Andrew; 3 Pastels; Rhapsody; Sonatina; Summer Evening; The Towing-Path
☛ (BB) *** Naxos 8.553889. Lenehan

Ballade; Columbine; In Those Days; London Pieces; Prelude in E flat; Sarnia
☛ (BB) *** Naxos 8.553700. Lenehan

John Lenehan is making a complete survey for Naxos and he too proves the most persuasive advocate, warmly expressive, using rubato in a totally idiomatic way. The four *London Pieces* are among his most colourful, not just *Ragamuffin*, played here with quicksilver lightness, but also the barcarolle-like *Chelsea Reach*, tenderly emotional. The most ambitious work is the three-movement suite, inspired by Guernsey, *Sarnia*, far more than a set of atmospheric colour pieces. This music shows Ireland's poetic imagination to particular advantage and its last movement has echoes of the *Piano Concerto in E flat*.

The second programme offers a score of miniatures, including two of Ireland's most hauntingly atmospheric pieces, *The Towing-Path* and *The Darkened Valley*, a Blake inspiration. The longest work here is the *Sonatina* in three short movements, with the opening *Moderato* bringing echoes of Ireland's colourful *Piano Concerto*, the second a dark meditation leading to a galloping finale. Impeccable performances, vividly recorded.

VOCAL MUSIC

Songs: Disc 1: *Earth's call; 5 Songs to Poems by Thomas Hardy; Great things; Hope the hornblower; If there were dreams to sell; If we must part; I have twelve oxen; Love is a sickness full of woes; Santa Chiara; Songs Sacred and Profane; Spleen; Spring Sorrow; 2 Songs; 3 Songs; 3 Songs to Poems by Thomas Hardy; Tryst; Tutto è sciolto; When I am old*

Disc 2: *Bed in summer; The bells of San Marie; During music; 5 XVIth-Century Poems;The journey; Mother and child; The heart's desire; Ladslove; Remember; The sacred flame; Sea fever; Songs of a Wayfarer; 3 Songs; The vagabond; We'll to the woods no more; What art thou thinking of ?; When I am dead, my dearest; When lights go rolling round the sky*
**(*) Hyp. CDA 67261/2 (2). Milne, Mark Ainsley, Maltman, Johnson

John Ireland's settings of English verse are among the most sensitive of the early twentieth century, as this welcome collection of 68 songs makes plain. They include one of the best-known of all songs of the period, his setting of John Masefield's *Sea fever*, a haunting tune that completely transcends the genre of the drawing-room ballad. Mostly, Ireland's songs are more sophisticated, and his gift of writing distinctively for the piano is consistently revealed in the accompaniments with their ear-catching harmonies.

Graham Johnson relishes the felicity of the piano-writing, but the singing is less consistently satisfying. Lisa Milne uses her light, bright soprano very sympathetically in the women's songs, while John Mark Ainsley, if not in his sweetest voice, is similarly sensitive in the tenor songs, just over a dozen of them. But almost half of the selection features Christopher Maltman, who (as caught here by the microphones) sings with fluttery tone, often undistracting, but regularly under pressure, making the sound gritty and unfocused, as in the late setting of William Cornish's *A thanksgiving*. Clear, well-balanced recording. In the excellent documentation, the lively commentary of Andrew Green adds greatly to the value of the set.

IVES, Charles (1874–1954)

'An American Journey': From the Steeples and the Mountains; Symphony 4: 3rd Movement: Fugue; Three Places in New England; The Unanswered Question. **Choral:** (i) *The Circus Band;* (i; ii) *General William Booth Enters into Heaven;* (i) *The Pond (Remembrance); Psalm 100; They are There!* **Songs:** (ii) *Charlie Rutlage; In Flanders Field* (orch. David Tredici); *Memories; Serenity* (orch. John Adams); *The Things our Fathers Loved; Tom Sails Away*
☛ ✿ *** RCA 09026 63703-2. (i) San Francisco Girls' Ch.; (ii) Hampson; San Francisco Symphony, Tilson Thomas

Michael Tilson Thomas follows up his superb CD of the three complete Copland ballets with this remarkable survey of the extraordinarily diverse music of Charles Ives. The programme opens with one of Ives's most succinct and evocative orchestral explosions of dissonant polyphony, *From the Steeples and the Mountains*, and ends with his most beautiful, enigmatic and visionary work, *The Unanswered Question* (with a haunting trumpet obbligato from Glenn Fischthal, and wonderfully quiet strings).

Tilson Thomas places Ives's other out-and-out masterpiece, *Three Places in New England*, at the centre of a collection of vocal music. The choral items range from the mystically brief evocation of *The Pond* (subtitled *Remembrance*) for female voices, and a heartfelt setting of *Psalm 100*, to the rumbustiously syncopated *Circus Band* and the enthusiastically patriotic but characteristically zany *They are There!*

The songs include rhythmically spirited, folksy numbers like *Memories* and *Charlie Rutlage* contrasting with the touchingly nostalic *Serenity* (sensitively orchestrated by John Adams) and *Tom Sails Away*. Thomas Hampson is obviously in his element in this repertoire. But the vocal highlight is *General William Booth Enters into Heaven*, where soloist and the excellent choruses exultantly combine in Ives's glorious portrayal of Booth and his Salvation Army leading his assembly of converted drunks and floozies into heaven, to the discomfiture of the angels. Not to be missed.

(i) *New England Holidays Symphony. Three Places in New England;* (i) *They are There!*

☛ ✹ (M) *** Decca 476 153-2. (i) Baltimore SO Ch.; Baltimore SO, Zinman

Opening with the exuberantly spectacular Sousa-esque choral march *They are There!* (a true lollipop if ever there was one), this is now the finest CD coupling of Ives's two key masterworks, the *New England Symphony* and *Three Places in New England*. The orchestral playing is splendid: the quiet, gentle evocations raptly sustained by the strings and woodwind, the multitude of quotations wittily evoked, and the polyphonic and polytonal clashes are all presented with great vigour and panache. The vivid Decca recording is truly in the demonstration class, handling the complicated sound-pictures with remarkable clarity, yet within a spacious ambience. The brief entry of the Baltimore Symphony Chorus at the close of *Thanksgiving and Forefathers' Day* is a truly arresting moment.

Central Park in the Dark; Country Band March; Holidays Symphony: Washington's March. Overture and March (1776); Symphony 3 (The Camp Meeting); The Unanswered Question

(BB) **(*) Naxos 8.559087. N. Sinf., Sinclair

There have been tauter, more warmly expressive versions of the major work in this enterprising collection, Ives's *Symphony 3*, which, with its quotations from hymn-tunes, here seems to meander. However, James Sinclair is a long-established Ives specialist, who has edited a number of the master's works, and in the rest of the disc he secures more concentrated playing, notably in the hushed writing of the two *Contemplations*, *The Unanswered Question* and *Central Park in the Dark*. The high contrasts and extrovert humour of *Washington's Birthday*, the *Country Band March* and the *Overture and March (1776)* are well caught, too, helped by full, colourful recording.

(i) *Central Park in the Dark;* (ii) *Holidays Symphony; Symphonies 2 & 3 (The Unanswered Question)* (original version for Trumpet, Flute Quartet & Strings)

(M) *** Sony (ADD) 516023-2 (2). NYPO, Bernstein; with (i) Ozawa & Peress (assistant conductors); (ii) Camerata Singers, Kaplan (with talk: 'Leonard Bernstein discusses Charles Ives')

Central Park in the Dark, as the title implies, provides a brilliant collection of evening sounds, evocative yet bewildering. The first three sections of the so-called *Holidays Symphony*, with their still-startling clashes of impressionistic imagery, are well enough known. The fourth – full title: *Thanksgiving and/or Forefathers' Day* – is more of a rarity, bringing in a full chorus to sing a single verse of a hymn at the close. The performance is red-bloodedly convincing yet has remarkably clear detail. *The Unanswered Question* is probably the most purely beautiful music Ives ever wrote, with muted strings (curiously representing silence) set against a trumpet representing the problem of existence. No need to worry about Ives's philosophy when the results are so naturally moving. Superb playing (the trumpeter is William Vacchiano) and vivid recording, but the forward balance means the lack of a true *pianissimo*, especially noticeable in *The Unanswered Question*.

Bernstein's earlier, CBS/Sony recordings of the *Symphonies* have characteristic conviction and freshness. The remastered sound is amazingly improved over the old LPs, full and atmospheric. The balance is too close, but the dynamics of the playing convey the fullest range of emotion. This reissue includes Bernstein's illustrated lecture on Ives (recorded in 1966).

(i) *Symphonies 1 in D min.;* (ii) *2; 3 (The Camp Meeting);* (i; iii) *4;* (i) *Central Park in the Dark; New England Holidays Symphony; The Unanswered Question* (original & revised scores). (iii) *Hymns*

(BB) *** Sony SB3K 87746 (3). Tilson Thomas, with (i) Chicago SO; (ii) Concg. O; (iii) Chicago Symphony Ch.

Symphonies (i) *1 in D min.;* 2; (ii) *3;* (iii; iv) *4;* (iii) *Orchestral Set 1;* (iii; iv) *Orchestral Set 2;* (iii) *Three Places in New England*

(B) **(*) Double Decca (ADD) 466 745-2 (2). (i) LAPO, Mehta; (ii) ASMF, Marriner; (iii) Cleveland O, Dohnányi; (iv) Cleveland Ch.

Michael Tilson Thomas is an impressive exponent of this repertoire. If the *Second* and *Third Symphonies* with the Concertgebouw Orchestra do not have quite the fervour of a Bernstein in this music, they remain strong and direct performances and are very well recorded (the revised edition is used in No. 3). The *New England Holidays Symphony* consists of four fine Ives pieces normally heard separately. Here, Tilson Thomas's Chicago forces are superb in every way, while the wide-ranging Sony sound provides admirable atmosphere. With two versions of the *Unanswered Question* (the original and revised editions) as well as *Central Park in the Dark* and *Hymns*, the latter a short choral work quoted in the *Fourth Symphony*, all very impressively done, this set is recommendable in every way.

Mehta's Los Angeles recordings of the first two symphonies are very well recorded indeed. The *First* is a charming work, much influenced by Dvořák and Tchaikovsky, but still with touches of individuality. It is superbly played, but the drawback here is a substantial cut in the last movement. The more uneven *Second Symphony* is given an equally committed performance, with the rich but brilliant Decca sound revealing every detail, though it is not over-lit or too analytical. Marriner's account of the *Third Symphony* is first rate in every way, just as successful as Bernstein's account, and much better recorded. For the *Fourth Symphony*, *Orchestral Sets Nos. 1 & 2* and the masterly *Three Places in New England* we move into the digital era with Dohnányi's Cleveland forces: these performances are very fine, and the sound is superb. In short, if you don't mind about the cut mentioned above, this is an inexpensive way of making a representative collection of Ives's major works at a modest outlay.

Symphony 1 in D min.
*** Chan. 9053. Detroit SO, Järvi – BARBER: *Essays 1–3* ***

Symphony 1 in D min.; Orchestral Set 2; Robert Browning Overture; The Unanswered Question
(BB) **(*) RCA (ADD) Navigator 74321 29246-2. Chicago SO, M. Gould

Symphonies 1; 4
*** Sony SK 44939. Chicago SO, Tilson Thomas

The RCA recording, the very first recording of the *First Symphony*, was made by Morton Gould in Chicago in 1965; it has that special quality of freshness almost always found in recording premières, with the mercurial spirit of Ives emerging every so often, so that the result is very enjoyable indeed. The *Orchestral Set No. 2* is similarly vivid in colour and detail. The *Robert Browning Overture* (at 20 minutes) has some good ideas but rather outstays its welcome, while *The Unanswered Question* is one of the composer's most beautiful and imaginative pieces. Gould's performances are sympathetic and very well played, if lacking the intensity that Bernstein and others brought to them, although they are still pretty magnetic. The mid-1960s recordings are basically warm and atmospheric, even if the violins are very brightly lit, and even fierce at times.

Neeme Järvi gives a very persuasive account of the *First Symphony*, and there is a fresh and unforced virtuosity from the Detroit orchestra. Excellent, very natural recorded sound, excellently balanced.

Tilson Thomas's strong and brilliant Chicago performances make a generous and apt coupling, the more valuable for providing first recordings of the revised editions of the composer's tangled scores, with bright, well-detailed sound and superb playing.

Symphony 2
*** Chan. 9390-2. Detroit SO, Järvi – CRESTON: *Symphony 2* ***

Symphony 2; Central Park in the Dark; The Gong on the Hook and Ladder; Hallowe'en; Hymn for Strings; Tone Roads 1; The Unanswered Question
*** DG 429 220-2. NYPO, Bernstein

Bernstein's DG disc brings one of the richest offerings of Ives yet put on record, offering the *Symphony No. 2* plus six shorter orchestral pieces. They include two of his very finest, *Central Park in the Dark* and *The Unanswered Question*, both characteristically quirky but deeply poetic too. The extra tensions and expressiveness of live performance here heighten the impact of each of the works. The difficult acoustic of Avery Fisher Hall in New York has rarely sounded more sympathetic on record.

The Chandos CD offers a very good performance, and has

the great advantage of also offering Neeme Järvi's account of Paul Creston's vital and invigorating *Second Symphony*.

Symphony 3 (The Camp Meeting)
*** Pro Arte CDD 140. St Paul CO, R. Davies – COPLAND: *Appalachian Spring*, etc. ***

Russell Davies does not use the new edition of Ives's score; nevertheless, he too gives a fine account of this gentlest of Ives's symphonies, with its overtones of hymn singing and revivalist meetings, and the beauty of the piece still comes over strongly.

Variations on America (orch. Schuman)
(BB) *** Naxos 8.559083. Bournemouth SO, Serebrier – SCHUMAN: *Violin Concerto*, etc. ***

Ives's *Variations on America* is an apt coupling for two outstanding works of William Schuman, who proves an infinitely imaginative colourist in orchestrating the former's brilliant and sometimes whimsical variations on the national melody, which has quite different words and implications in the USA and Britain. Serebrier's performance with the excellent Bournemouth orchestra has subtlety of detail as well as gusto, and the recording is first class.

(i) Hallowe'en; 5 Take-offs; (ii) 3 Quarter-tone Pieces (for 2 pianos); (iii) Duet: Aeschylus & Sophocles; Songs: The Housatonic at Stockbridge; On the Antipodes; Sunrise
(N) (BB) **(*) Naxos 8.559194. (i) Continuum; (ii) Seltzer, Sachs; (iii) Villamil and Schonbrun

Described as a 'Portrait of the Composer', this collection of shorter pieces, songs as well as instrumental pieces, some barely a minute long, presents Charles Ives at his wildest. The selection opens with a song drawn from his orchestral piece, *The Housatonic at Stockbridge*, a meditation that works up to a wild climax. It continues with songs and instrumental pieces for various combinations, which can only be described as weirdly expressionistic. In many of the pieces Ives's habit of including a phrase or two of deliberate banality amid the wildness adds piquancy, well caught in these performances from the New York-based group, Continuum. The instrumental piece *Hallowe'en* has a bass drum entry that takes you terrifyingly by surprise, helped by the vivid recording. The *Take-offs* (an expression Ives used as meaning improvisation) are simpler but just as original, while the *Quarter-tone Pieces*, written for two pianos tuned a quarter-tone apart, merely sound out of tune. The two excellent pianists are Joel Sachs and Cheryl Seltzer, and the sopranos, both projecting well, are Victoria Villamil and Sheila Schonbrun. This collection shows the composer as slightly off the beam at times, but endearingly so.

String Quartets 1–2
*** DG 435 864-2. Emerson Qt – BARBER: *Quartet* **(*)

The *First* of Ives's *String Quartets* comes from the composer's early twenties and makes liberal use of hymn-tunes in the first-movement fugue. The *Second* is made of sterner stuff with its high norm of dissonance. It is undeniably an extraordinary musical document and is well worth study. The Emerson Quartet give it a performance of stunning efficiency and brilliance. Full-blooded and very present DG recording.

Piano Sonata 1
*** Mode 93. Laimon – COPLAND: *Piano Fantasy* ***

Ives's five-movement *First Piano Sonata* was composed over a long period and finally put together in 1919. The structure is not readily ascertainable – Henry Cowell suggested pragmatically that Ives intended 'to create an underlying unity out of a large number of diverse elements', but whether he managed to do so is open to question. The result is a series of events, the piano writing is alternately lyrically expressive or hard-hitting, and often chromatically dense. It is also leavened with the usual popular quotations, including the hymn *Welcome Voice* in the second movement and a touch of 'revivalist ragtime' with the introduction of *Bringing in the Sheaves* in the fourth. The boldly discursive finale, the longest movement, recaptures some of the evocative mood of the opening, and the work ends enigmatically, as it began. Sara Laimon obviously has the full measure of the piece and certainly demonstrates its intractable nature and its compulsive originality. She is very well recorded.

Piano Sonata 2 (Concord, Mass., 1840–1860)

(N) *** Hyp. CDA 67469. Hamelin – COPLAND: *Piano Sonata ***

As with the Copland coupling, Marc-André Hamelin is completely at home in Ives's eccentric, discursive *Sonata* whose four movements are each inspired by key nineteenth-century literary figures in Concord, from Emerson to Thoreau. The second movement (Hawthorne), which brings oscillation between thunderous complexity and tender lyricism, is superbly played, so that the touching and boldly romantic picture of the Alcotts that emerges in the third movement leads easily into the finale, with its flute solo stealing in beguilingly. (When asked why he put in this interlude, Ives suggested that as no one was likely to play his sonata he saw no reason not to include a flute when required.) Well, he was wrong about the performances, and Hamelin's wonderful account of this fascinatingly eccentric and rewarding work shows why. The recording is first class.

Piano Sonatas: 2 (Concord, Mass.); Three-page Sonata

(N) (B) *** DG 2-CD 477 5439 (2). Szidon, LPO, Downes – GERSHWIN: *Piano Concerto in F*; MACDOWELL: *Piano Concerto 2*; VILLA-LOBOS: *Piano Music ***

Roberto Szidon, who charges into the formidable *Concord Sonata* with supreme confidence and later relishes its folksy moments, also offers the earlier and briefer *Three-page Sonata* of 1905. It is made of the same stuff, and its score bears the inscription 'Made mostly as a joke to knock the mollycoddles out of their boxes and to kick out Softy Ears'. There is the usual variety of ingredients (ragtime, chord clusters, polyrhythms, church bells and even a quote from Beethoven's *Fifth Symphony*). Good knockabout stuff, splendidly played and mercifully short.

Songs: Autumn; Berceuse; The cage; Charlie Rutlage; Down east; Dreams; Evening; The greatest man; The Housatonic at Stockbridge; Immortality; Like a sick eagle; Maple leaves; Memories: 1, 2, 3; On the counter; Romanzo di Central Park; The see'r; Serenity; The side-show; Slow march; Slugging a vampire; Songs my mother taught me; Spring song; The things our fathers loved; Tom sails away; Two little flowers

*** Etcetera KTC 1020. Alexander, Crone

Roberta Alexander presents her excellent and illuminating choice of Ives songs in chronological order, starting with one written when Ives was only fourteen, *Slow march*, already predicting developments ahead. Sweet, nostalgic songs predominate, but the singer punctuates them with leaner,

sharper inspirations. Her manner is not always quite tough enough in those, but this is characterful singing from an exceptionally rich and attractive voice. Tan Crone is the understanding accompanist, and the recording is first rate.

JACOB, Gordon (1895–1984)

Mini-Concerto for Clarinet & String Orchestra

⊶ **(BB)** *** Hyp. Helios CDH 55069. King, Northwest CO of Seattle, Francis – COOKE: *Concerto*; RAWSTHORNE: *Concerto ***

Gordon Jacob in his eighties wrote this miniature concerto for Thea King, totally charming in its compactness. She proves the most persuasive of dedicatees, splendidly accompanied by the orchestra from Seattle and treated to first-rate (1982) analogue sound, splendidly transferred. An enticing bargain reissue.

Symphony 2 in C; A Little Symphony; Festival Overture

*** Classico CLASSCD 204. Munich SO, Bostock

The *Second Symphony* (1944/5) is spirited and outgoing. The first movement, after its deceptively gentle introduction, is boisterously scored and full of energy. It is followed by an intense, searching *Adagio*, which opens plangently on high strings but later assumes the character of a threnody. The mood lightens with an engaging *Scherzo* and the final *Ground* is a passacaglia which reaches a boisterous, confident conclusion. The '*Little*' *Symphony* is perhaps an even finer work, more succinct and more introspective, but with a splendidly vigorous *Scherzo* whose rhythmic character is arresting, and with a jaunty, light-hearted finale, full of good humour. The *Festival Overture*, written for the Essex Youth Orchestra, combines Waltonesque rhythmic exuberance with a characteristic Jacobian lyrical strain. The performances here by the excellent Munich orchestra under Douglas Bostock are alive and thoroughly persuasive and in no way unidiomatic; the recording is vivid and quite spacious.

Clarinet Quintet in G min.

⊶ **(BB)** *** Hyp. Helios (ADD) CDH 55110. King, Aeolian Qt – SOMERVELL: *Clarinet Quintet ***

Gordon Jacob wrote his fine *Clarinet Quintet*, an ambitious work lasting over half an hour, in 1942 for Frederick Thurston. It is essentially pastoral, even autumnal, in feeling but has an engaging second movement Scherzo, a *Rhapsody* for slow movement and a chirpy *Theme and Variations* for finale. Thea King, Thurston's widow and former pupil, plays with deep understanding and much character, and she is strongly matched by the Aeolian Quartet, led by Emmanuel Hurwitz. The fine 1979 analogue recording, engineered by Bob Auger, is impeccably transferred to CD, and this reissue is a worthwhile bargain.

Divertimento for Harmonica & String Quartet

*** Chan. 8802. Reilly, Hindar Qt – MOODY: *Quintet; Suite ***

Gordon Jacob's set of eight sharply characterized miniatures shows the composer at his most engagingly imaginative and the performances are deliciously piquant in colour and feeling. The recording could hardly be more successful.

Oboe Quartet

*** Chan. 8392. Francis, English Qt – BAX: *Quintet*; HOLST: *Air & Variations*, etc.; MOERAN: *Fantasy Quartet ***

Gordon Jacob's *Oboe Quartet* is well crafted and entertaining, particularly the vivacious final Rondo. The performance could hardly be bettered, and the recording is excellent too.

Piano & Wind Sextet, Op. 3

(N) (M) (**) BBC mono BBCL 4164-2. Malcolm, Dennis Brain Wind Quintet – BEETHOVEN: *Quintet* (**); HINDEMITH: *Horn Sonata*; VINTER: *Hunter's Moon* (***)

Gordon Jacob's *Piano and Wind Sextet* is most delightfully scored and full of attractive invention. Composed in memory of Dennis Brain's father, Aubrey (who was for many years principal horn of the BBC Symphony Orchestra), all but one of its five movements is ingeniously constructed using the musical notes ABEBA, taken from Aubrey's name. The opening and closing of the work are elegiac, and there is a sparkling Scherzo for which the forward recording is very close indeed! The slow movement, a B flat minor *Cortège*, is imbued with a gentle melancholy; the Minuet is an engaging highlight, and the buoyant, syncopated finale is joyously zestful, but with a recurring lyrical horn theme, of which Dennis makes the very most.

JACQUET DE LA GUERRE, Elisabeth (1665–1729)

Pièces de clavecin: Premier livre (1687); Pièces de clavecin (1707): Suites: in D min.; G

*** Metronome METCD 1026. Cerasi (harpsichord)

Elisabeth Jacquet de La Guerre emerges as a major musical talent of her time, composing music of very high quality which can compare with and match the output of her more famous contemporaries. Carole Cerasi's recital includes all her solo keyboard works, and her CD won *Gramophone*'s 1999 Award for baroque instrumental music. It received the special accolade of Stanley Sadie, who commented that Cerasi 'plays all this music with real command: she knows where in the passionate pieces to press forward and where to linger, how to let the rhythms flow in the dances, how to shape the extended chaconnes and how to make the most of Jacquet's expressive harmony'. To this we would add her skill in giving an improvisatory impression in her freedom of line in the remarkable *Préludes*. We would add one proviso, and it is an important one. Her ornamentation is profuse and continuing, and it certainly affects the line of the music: some listeners may have problems with this, so an element of caution must accompany our otherwise strong recommendation. She plays a characteristic seventeenth-century Rückers harpsichord, rebuilt in 1763, and is excellently if fairly resonantly recorded.

JANÁČEK, Leoš (1854–1928)

Adagio for Orchestra; Ballad of Blaník; Cossack Dance; (i) Danube Symphony. The Fiddler's Child (ballad); Idyll for Strings; Jealousy Overture; Lachian Dances; (ii) The Pilgrimage of the Soul (Violin Concerto); (iii) Schluck und Jau (incidental music): excerpts: Andante & Allegretto. Serbian Kolo; Sinfonietta; Suite, Op. 3; Suite for Strings; Taras Bulba (rhapsody)

*** Sup. 11 1834-2 (3). Brno State PO, Jílek, with (i) Dvořáková; (ii) Zenatý; (i; iii) Beneš

(i) Danube Symphony. Sinfonietta; (ii) The Pilgrimage of the Soul (Violin Concerto); (iii) Schluck und Jau

*** Sup. 11 1422-2. Brno State PO, Jílek, with (i) Dvořáková; (ii) Zenatý; (i; iii) Beneš

Jílek's performance of the *Sinfonietta* can hold its own with the best in terms of atmosphere and authority, though the recording is admittedly not in the demonstration bracket. There is some invention of great imagination in the *Danube Symphony*, as, indeed, there is in the *Violin Concerto* (*The Pilgrimage of the Soul*). Ivan Zenatý is an aristocrat of the violin and his performance is poignantly affecting. The incidental music to *Schluck und Jau* is a two-movement piece about as long as the *Violin Concerto* and likewise full of characteristic ideas. Of the other two discs, the first, offering the *Lachian Dances*, the early *Suite for Strings* and its seven-movement companion, the *Idyll*, is well filled, and the other disc brings such valuable scores as *Blaník*, *The Fiddler's Child* and *Taras Bulba*. Good, idiomatic performances and very good, though not demonstration-quality, recordings.

Capriccio for Piano Left-hand & Wind; Concertino for Piano & Seven Instruments

⊕— (B) *** RCA 2-CD 74321 88683-2 (2). Firkušný ; with (i) Czech PO, Neumann; (ii) Ridge Qt – DVORAK: *Piano Concerto; Piano Quintets* ***

At the time of making these recordings Rudolf Firkušný (1912–94) was older than Janáček when he wrote these remarkable pieces, but he conveys a youthful fire that seems to burn almost as brightly as the earlier recordings he made in the 1950s and 1970s. A thoroughly worthwhile coupling with Dvořák.

(i) Capriccio for Piano & Wind; Concertino for Piano & Chamber Ensemble; (ii) Lachian Dances; (iii) Sinfonietta; (iv) Suite for String Orchestra; (iii) Taras Bulba; (v) Mládí (suite for wind)

(B) *** Double Decca (ADD) 448 255-2 (2). (i) Crossley, L. Sinf., Atherton; (ii) LPO, Huybrechts; (iii) VPO, Mackerras; (iv) LACO, Marriner; (v) Bell, Craxton, Pay, Harris, Gatt, Eastop

On this Double Decca, Paul Crossley is the impressive soloist in the *Capriccio* and the *Concertino*, performances that can be put alongside those of Firkušný – and no praise can be higher. This account of *Mládí* is among the finest available; the work's youthful sparkle comes across to excellent effect here. In Mackerras's VPO coupling of the *Sinfonietta* and *Taras Bulba* the massed brass of the *Sinfonietta* has tremendous bite and brilliance as well as characteristic Viennese ripeness. *Taras Bulba* is also given more weight and body than usual, the often savage dance-rhythms presented with great energy. The performance of the *Lachian Dances* under the Belgian conductor, François Huybrechts, is highly idiomatic and effective, and he is helped by fine playing from the LPO. The *Suite for String Orchestra* was Marriner's first recording with the Los Angeles Chamber Orchestra, and the sound is characteristically ripe. The *Suite* is an early and not entirely mature piece but, when played as committedly as it is here, its attractions are readily perceived, and it certainly does not want character. Excellent sound throughout.

(i; ii) Capriccio; Concertino; (iii) Lachian Dances; (iv) Sinfonietta; (v) Suite for String Orchestra; (iv) Taras Bulba; (vi; vii) Dumka (for violin & piano); (viii) Mládí; (ix; vi) Pohádka; Presto (for cello & piano); (vi; vii) Romance (for

violin & piano); (x) *String Quartets 1; 2;* (v; vi) *Violin Sonata;* (i) *In the Mist; On an overgrown Path; Teme con variations (Variations for Zdenka);* (xi) *Glagolitic Mass;* (xii) *Říkadla*

(N) (B) *** Decca (ADD/DDD) 475 523-2 (5). (i) Crossley; (ii) L. Sinf. (members); (iii) LPO, Huybrechts; (iv) VPO, Mackerras; (v) LAPO, Marriner; (vi) Atherton; (vii) Sillito; (viii) Bell, Craxton, Pay, Harris, Gatt, Eastop; (ix) Van Kampen; (x) Gabrieli String Qt; (xi) Urbanová, Beňaková, Bogachov, Novák, Slovak Phil. Ch., VPO, Chailly; (xii) London Sinf. Ch.

This set adds to the Double Decca collection of orchestral and concertante works above and proves a useful and inexpensive way of acquiring a lot of Janáček. The two *String Quartets* are among the composer's most deeply individual works and are profoundly impassioned utterances. The Gabrieli Quartet have the measure of this highly original music and give an idiomatic account of these masterpieces, playing with clarity as well as warmth, and with the advantage of vintage (1978) Decca sound. In the account of *Mládí*, the work's youthful sparkle comes across to excellent effect here. Crossley's survey of the piano music is both poetic and perceptive, and his mastery of keyboard colour and feeling for atmosphere are everywhere evident, while the sound that the engineers have achieved is very truthful and satisfying. The set brings a number of rarities, including the *Violin Sonata* and the *Říkadla* for chamber choir and ten instruments, both works very much worth getting to know. Finally, Chailly's strong and refined reading of the *Glagolitic Mass* makes a splendid finale, with fine detail emerging in the glowing Decca recording (1998), even if it is not as immediate as with Rattle or Mackerras. If the work's earthiness is a degree underplayed, the emotional depth is fully brought out, with fine, idiomatic singing and a virtuoso display from Thomas Trotter in the final organ solo.

(i; ii) *Capriccio for Piano & Wind; Concertino for Piano & Chamber Orchestra.* (ii) *3 Moravian Dances;* (iii; i) *Fairy Tale; Presto in E min.* (both cello & piano); (iv; i) *Violin Sonata; Street Scene;* (i) *On an Overgrown Path; Po zarostém chodnîcku*

(B) *** EMI Double forte 5 74843-2 (2). (i) Rudy, (ii) Paris Opéra O, Mackerras; (iii) Hoffman; (iv) Amoyal

(i) *Capriccio for Piano; Concertino. (Piano) Sonata (1.X.1905); Along an Overgrown Path I & II; In the Mist; Reminiscences; Zdenka Variations*

(M) *** DG (ADD) 449 764-2 (2). Firkušný; (i) Bav. RSO (members), Kubelik

Capriccio; Concertino; Mládí (Youth) for wind sextet; March of the Blue Boys for piccolo & piano; (i) *Nursery Rhymes (Říkadla) for chamber ch. & chamber ens.*

*** Chan. 9399. Berman, Netherlands Wind Ens., Fischer; (i) with Prague Music Ac. Ch.

Kubelik partners Rudolf Firkušný in his thoroughly idiomatic earlier account of the *Concertino*. Now reissued in DG's series of 'Originals', this collection is eminently recommendable. It again offers Firkušný in a discerningly sympathetic account of the *Capriccio*. Firkušný has long been regarded as the most authoritative exponent of the piano music. He recorded these pieces in the early 1970s, and he produces seamless legato lines, hammerless tone and rapt atmosphere. Kubelik then

partners him in the concertante works. The recordings are all of high quality.

Though Firkušný remains in a class of his own, Boris Berman is a good soloist in both the *Concertino* and *Capriccio*. The astonishing *Říkadla* are given with great character by the Netherlands Wind Ensemble and the Prague Academy Choir. Thierry Fischer directs the proceedings impressively: the playing throughout is full of life and sensitivity. Vibrant recorded sound – every detail tells.

A very good performance too from Mikhail Rudy, who is completely inside the quirky left-hand *Capriccio* and gives a totally idiomatic account of the *Concertino*. He does not eclipse Firkušný in either piece, but the EMI compilation is in every way recommendable and very good value.

(i) *Concertino for piano & seven instruments;* (ii) *Sinfonietta; Taras Bulba*

☞ ✹ (M) *** DG 476 2196. (i) Firkušný, Bav. RSO (members); (ii) Bav. RSO; Kubelik

A quite outstanding bargain triptych that would make a worthwhile addition to any collection, large or small. Kubelik has a special feeling for this repertoire, and he partners Rudolf Firkušný in a thoroughly idiomatic account of the *Concertino*, with the dialogue between keyboard and sparsely scored accompaniment both plangent and witty. *Taras Bulba*, with its unpleasant scenario of death and torture, is powerfully evoked, with a discerning balance between passion and subtlety. The organ part is integrated into the texture most delicately in the first section, yet adds grandiloquence to the work's triumphant apotheosis, with its vision of a triumphant Cossack future. Virtuoso playing from the Bavarian orchestra throughout, with much excitement generated in the last two sections. The orchestra is hardly less impressive in the *Sinfonietta* (and particularly so in the central movements), while at the opening and close of the work the spacious acoustic of the Munich Herculessaal is especially suited to the massed brass effects. The vintage (1970) recording has been superbly remastered and sounds amazingly fresh. It is now reissued as part of Universal's mid-price 'Penguin ✹ Collection'.

Violin Concerto (Pilgrimage of the Soul) (reconstructed Faltus & Stĕdrŭ)

☞ (BB) *** Warner Apex 0927 40812-2. Zehetmair, Philh. O, Holliger – BERG: *Violin Concerto;* HARTMANN: *Concerto funèbre* ***

(i) *Violin Concerto* (ii) *Violin Sonata*

(B) *** Virgin 2x1 5 62053-2 (2). Tetzlaff; (i) Philh. O, Pešek; (ii) Andsnes – BARTOK: *Violin Concerto 2; Violin Sonata;* WEILL: *Concerto* ***

This is highly original music, with some delightful lyrical ideas, imaginatively scored, albeit also with moments of top-heavy orchestral writing, searing in its intensity – particularly as played here by Thomas Zehetmair and the Philharmonia under Heinz Holliger. Excellent recorded sound. A most rewarding triptych, well worth exploring at budget price.

Christian Tetzlaff also gives an outstandingly sympathetic account of the short reconstructed *Violin Concerto*, in essence a series of seven brief vignettes lasting about 11 minutes. He is most sensitively accompanied by Pešek. In the equally attractive *Sonata* he is joined by Leif Ove Andsnes and they play with commitment and dedication. Theirs is an eloquent – indeed at times inspired – performance and in both works the recording is excellent. A thoroughly recommendable collection.

(i) The Fiddler's Child; (ii) Idyll for String Orchestra; (i) Jealousy: Overture. Sinfonietta; (ii) Suite for Strings; (i) Taras Bulba; The Cunning Little Vixen: Suite

(B) *** Chan. 2-for-1 241-7 (2). (i) Czech PO, Bělohlávek; (ii) Jupiter O, Rose

Idyll; Suite for String Orchestra

⊶ ✿ *** Chan. 9816. Norwegian CO, Brown – BARTOK: *Divertimento for Strings* *** ✿

(M) **(*) Panton 81 1437-2 131. Czech Chamber Soloists, Matyáš – MARTINU: *Sextet*

(i) Idyll for String Orchestra; (ii) Mládí for Wind Sextet

(BB) **(*) Warner Apex (ADD) 7559 79680-2. (i) LACO, Schwarz; (ii) LA Wind Ens.

In the *Idyll* the Norwegian Chamber Orchestra and Iona Brown sweep the board. Their playing is vibrant, full of enthusiasm and vitality, and yet finding also a touching nostalgia in the slow sections of the *Idyll* and an even more subtle and haunting espressivo in the two lovely *Adagio*s of the *Suite*. The recorded sound is absolutely state-of-the-art and the Bartók coupling quite outstanding.

The *Idyll* and the *Suite for Strings* are also ravishingly played by the Jupiter Orchestra under Gregory Rose, who shows himself completely at home in the lilting Czech idiom and who achieves rapt concentration in the touching slow movements. The rest of the Chandos programme is also very stimulating. There are more dramatic and fiery accounts available of *Taras Bulba*. Bělohlávek is perhaps less at home in this melodramatic piece than in the nature mysticism of the orchestral suite from *The Cunning Little Vixen* or the pathos of *The Fiddler's Child*. But his splendidly vivid account of the *Sinfonietta* is unsurpassed, and throughout all these performances the beauty of the orchestral playing, and opulence and detail of the recordings add to the attractions of a very well-chosen compilation.

The Czech Chamber Soloists led by Ivan Matyáš deliver straightforward and well-played accounts of these early pieces for string orchestra, but they are no match for Iona Brown and the Norwegian Chamber Orchestra on Chandos.

The *Idyll* is very persuasively played by the Los Angeles Chamber Orchestra under Gerard Schwarz, who is mindful of dynamic nuances and shapes phrases with imagination, while the sound is very lifelike and clean. The wind players of the Los Angeles orchestra play marvellously in *Mládí* with altogether superb ensemble and blend. The Los Angeles team are placed well forward, though the acoustic is warm and the detail remarkably clean. However, lasting under 45 minutes, this disc is not quite the super-bargain it first appears.

Sinfonietta

⊶ (M) *** EMI 5 66980-2 [566995]. Philh. O, Rattle – *Glagolitic Mass* ***

*** Chan. 8897. Czech PO, Bělohlávek – MARTINU: *Symphony 6*; SUK: *Scherzo* ***

(B) *** Sony SBK 89903. LSO, Tilson Thomas – *Glagolitic Mass* ***

**(*) Orfeo C 55201B. Bav. RSO, Kubelik – DVORAK: *Symphony 6* **(*)

Sinfonietta; Lachian Dances; Taras Bulba

(BB) *** Naxos 8.550411. Slovak RSO (Bratislava), Lenárd

(i) Sinfonietta; (ii) Taras Bulba

(B) ** Sony (ADD) SBK 62404. (i) Cleveland O, Szell; (ii) Toronto SO, A. Davis – KODALY: *Dances of Galánta; Dances of Marosszék* **(*)

Rattle gets an altogether first-class response from the orchestra and truthful recorded sound from the EMI engineers, and his coupling with the *Glagolitic Mass* is very attractive indeed.

Jiří Bělohlávek's exultant and imaginative account of the *Sinfonietta* is one of the best currently on offer and is coupled with an outstanding version of Martinů's *Sixth Symphony*; the recording, made in the Smetana Hall, Prague, is impressive.

A bold and brassy performance from Michael Tilson Thomas with the LSO at their virtuosic best, helped by very full recorded sound, bright as well as weighty. This makes a fine bargain alternative coupling to Rattle.

On Naxos we have the normal LP coupling of the *Sinfonietta* and *Taras Bulba*, but with the *Lachian Dances* thrown in for good measure, all played by musicians steeped in the Janáček tradition – and all at a very modest cost. These are excellent performances; the recording, made in a fairly resonant studio, is natural and free from any artificially spotlit balance.

Szell's 1965 recording of the *Sinfonietta* has long been admired for its orchestral virtuosity and control. It is a very spirited and colourful account, and the new transfer brings out the ambient effect of the Severance Hall recording, even if the dynamic range remains less expansive than it should be. But the real snag here is that Andrew Davis's *Taras Bulba* has an altogether lower voltage. What a pity that was included instead of Ormandy's *Háry János Suite*!

Kubelik's Orfeo broadcast is not quite as polished nor is the recording as finely focused as the 1970 DG account which is coupled with *Taras Bulba* and the *Concertino* for piano.

Sinfonietta; Taras Bulba; Jealousy Prelude; The Cunning Little Vixen: Suite. Káta Kabanová: Overture & Interludes. Sárka Overture. Schluck und Jau (incidental music): excerpts: Andante & Allegretto

*** Sup. SU 3739-2 (2). Czech PO, Mackerras

No one can match Sir Charles Mackerras as an inspired and dedicated advocate of the music of Janáček. Issued to celebrate the 150th anniversary of the composer's birth, this collection neatly encompasses the whole span of his career. *Sarka*, his first opera, is represented by the *Overture* in an excerpt from Mackerras's revelatory complete recording, issued two years ago, and the *Káta Kabanová* excerpts (including the two delightful little *Interludes* that Mackerras himself discovered in Prague) similarly come from his complete recording of 1997. The other items all come in completely new recordings, with the Czech Philharmonic responding warmly in what may well be Mackerras's very last Janáček recordings. Apart from *Jealousy*, the original prelude to *Jenůfa*, the rarity in the collection is the very last orchestral music that Janáček wrote, two pieces from the incidental music for a play by Gerhardt Hauptmann, *Schluck und Jau*. Mackerras describes it as 'a peculiar play whose subject matter bears a great resemblance to Beckett's *Waiting for Godot*'. The first of the two completed movements brings some intriguing echoes of the fanfares in the *Sinfonietta*, and the second in 5/8 time is equally original in its unexpected instrumentation, with deep trombones and stratospheric violins, light and exciting, with a brassy climax. The suite taken from *The Cunning Little Vixen*, consisting of virtually the whole of Act I without the voices, is here given in Janáček's own sharply original orchestration, whereas generally the smoothed-over version of Vaclav Talich is used. Best of all, the two central orchestral works, the *Sinfonietta* and *Taras Bulba*, come in live recordings which, spurred on by a Czech audience, are magnetic, flowing lightly and flexibly, building up in excitement. Mackerras has recorded both these works before with great success, but these latest versions are even warmer and more idiomatic, crowning the whole collection, helped by full and spacious recording.

Taras Bulba

*** Australian Decca Eloquence 467 602-2. Cleveland O, Dohnányi – KODALY: *Concerto for Orchestra*; BARTOK: *Concerto for Orchestra* ***

Dohnányi's warmly expressive reading of *Taras Bulba* is recorded in Decca's finest digital Cleveland style, and is imaginatively coupled on this excellent Australian Eloquence CD.

CHAMBER MUSIC

(i; iii) *Allegro; Dumka; Romance; Sonata* (for violin & piano); (ii; iii) *Pohádka (Fairy Tale); Presto* (for cello & piano); (iii) (Piano) *Along an Overgrown Path, Series I–II; In the Mists; 3 Moravian Dances; Paralipomena; Reminiscence; Piano Sonata in E flat min. (I. X. 1905); Theme & Variations (Zdenka's Variations)*
**(*) BIS CD 663/664. (i) Wallin; (ii) Rondin; (iii) Pöntinen

This excellent collection ranges from the *Romance* for violin and piano from the late 1870s, to the much later *Reminiscence* for piano. Pöntinen is an unfailingly intelligent player. Ulf Wallin proves a strong yet sensitive advocate of the *Violin Sonata*, and the cellist Mats Rondin is no less admirable in the *Pohádka (Fairy Tale)* and the *Presto* for cello and piano. Readers wanting this whole collection may rest assured that both playing and recording are of a generally high standard.

Concertino; Mládí

*** HM HMA 1901399. Walter Boeykens Ens. – DVORAK: *Serenade in D min. for Wind* ***

The Walter Boeykens Ensemble is a most distinguished group, and anyone wanting this coupling need have no qualms about investing in it. Both the *Concertino*, with Robert Groslot as the soloist, and *Mládí* are as fresh and compelling as any currently on disc. The 1991 recordings from Antwerp have worn well.

Mládí

(BB) **(*) Naxos 8.553851-2. Michael Thompson Wind Quintet – BARBER: *Summer Music* **(*); HINDEMITH: *Kleine Kammermusik* **(*); LARSSON: *Quattro tempi* **

Janáček's *Mládí* is superbly played by the Michael Thompson Wind Quintet, who are sensitive to every nuance of this glorious and haunting score. Wonderfully accomplished and sensitive though they are, they are let down by a close balance, which robs the music of atmosphere.

String Quartet 1 (Kreutzer Sonata)

*** Testament (ADD) SBT 1074. Smetana Qt – DVORAK: *Piano Quintet*, etc. ***

String Quartet 2 (Intimate Letters)

*** Testament (ADD) SBT 1075. Smetana Qt – DVORAK: *String Quartet 14*, etc. ***

The Smetana Quartet's account of the *First Quartet (Kreutzer Sonata)* is also one of the very best versions of the work ever committed to disc. There is a wonderful feeling that these players have lived with this music all their lives – and in fact live *for* it, so committed do they sound. Recommended with some urgency. Worth every penny of its full price.

Like its companion, the Smetana account of the *Intimate Letters* appears in Britain for the first time. It deserves the same accolade. In terms of subtlety, tonal finish and technical polish, this is absolutely flawless – and the 1960s sound is superb, and not just for its period. Strongly recommended alongside its companion.

String Quartets 1 (Kreutzer); 2 (Intimate Letters)

*** ASV CDDCA 749. Lindsay Qt – DVORAK: *Cypresses* ***
(BB) **(*) Warner Apex 0927 40603-2. New Helsinki Qt (with DVORAK: *Cypresses*: excerpts **(*))
(B) **(*) HM (ADD) HMT 790138o. Melos Qt

(i) String Quartets 1–2; (ii) Along an Overgrown Path: Suite 1

⊕ (M) *** Cal. CAL 5699. (i) Talich Qt; (ii) Kvapil

(i) String Quartets 1–2; (ii) Pohádka for Cello & Piano; (iii) Violin Sonata

(BB) *** Naxos 8.553895. (i) Vlach Qt; (ii) Ericsson, Maly; (iii) Vlachová

Pride of place must go to the Talich Quartet on Calliope, not because their recording is the best, but because of their extraordinary qualities of insight. They play the *Intimate Letters* as if its utterances came from a world so private that it must be approached with great care. The disc's value is much enhanced by a fill-up in the form of the *First Suite, On an Overgrown Path*. Radoslav Kvapil is thoroughly inside this repertoire.

The Lindsays on ASV are also eminently competitive and have the right blend of sensitivity and intensity. Theirs must certainly rank very highly among current recommendations. They play with the same concentration and sensitivity they bring to all they do, and are recorded with great naturalness.

The Vlach Quartet on Naxos give well-played, impassioned accounts of both Quartets and are warmly recorded. Moreover, the account of the *Violin Sonata* by Jana Vlachová and František Maly is very fine, and the *Pohádka for Cello and Piano* is given as touching and imaginative a performance by Mikael Ericsson as any in the catalogue. Good recordings and excellent value for money.

Without being a very first choice, the New Helsinki Quartet on Warner's budget Apex label is strongly competitive. The performances are characterful, and they come coupled with some of Dvořák's charming *Cypresses*.

The Melos Quartet offer nothing in addition to the two Quartets, but theirs are performances of considerable character and fire and, though the playing-time is ungenerous and the recording a bit fierce, they are worth consideration. The performances are very idiomatic and appealing, the recording far from inferior, and this record will give pleasure. At least they are now offered at bargain price.

Violin Sonata

*** Praga PRD 250 153. Remés, Kayahara – DVORAK: *Sonatina*; MARTINU, SMETANA: *Violin Sonatas* ***
(N) *** Analekta FL2 3191. Ehnes, Laurel – DVORAK: *Romantic Pieces; Sonatina in G; Humoresque*; SMETANA: *From the Homeland* ***

*** HM HMC 901793. Faust, Kupiec – LUTOSLAWSKI: *Partita; Subito*; SZYMANOWSKI: *3 Mythes* ***

**(*) Avie AV0023. Gleusteen, Ordonneau – PROKOFIEV: *Violin Sonata 1*; SHOSTAKOVICH: *19 Preludes* **(*)

This newest Praga account from Václav Remeš and the rich-timbred Sachito Kayahara is fiercely intense, yet warmly affectionate, the questing closing *Adagio* highly dramatic, and with the closing pages creating a mood of tender intensity. The playing itself is superbly assured and characterful, and the recording first class. The couplings are equally fine.

In the equally fine collection of violin and piano music by the three greatest Czech composers on Analekta, Ehnes and Laurel make light of the technical and interpretative problems of the Janáček *Sonata*, always an elusive work. Playing with ease and warmth, they are persuasively spontaneous-sounding, with Ehnes using the widest tonal range, as in an ecstatic *pianissimo* at the end of the second-movement *Ballada*.

The programme on the Harmonia Mundi disc may seem an odd mixture, but it works well. Quite apart from all three composers having a Slavonic background, the performances bring out unexpected similarities, not just between the Janáček and Szymanowski, both dating from 1915, but with the much more recent Lutoslawski *Partita* of 1984. There is a spontaneous sense of fantasy in all these performances which lightly brings out the quirky side of the Janáček, and also does similarly in some passages of the Lutoslawski *Partita*, while the pianist Ewa Kupiec matches Isabelle Faust in drawing out the atmospheric beauties of Szymanowski's *Three Mythes*. The Janáček makes a sharp opening item that in the hands of these performers flows on naturally as though they are improvising it with its potentially awkward tremolos and trills in the first movement and the odd, fragmentary interjections so typical of Janáček. In the lyrical *Ballata* second movement, Isabelle Faust's *pianissimo* playing is breathtaking.

The similarly mixed bag of Slavonic works on the Avie disc makes an impressive showcase for the talents of the Canadian-born violinist, Kai Gleusteen, and his French accompanist, Catherine Ordonneau. Their account of the quirky Janáček *Violin Sonata* is most compelling, though Faust brings out the fantasy more clearly in this highly original work. In a relaxed manner, with pure violin tone, Gleusteen brings the work closer than usual to the central repertory, finding fire in the energetically folk-based third movement. The recording, one of a series made in the 'inspirational and innovative working space' of Crear, on the west coast of Scotland, is on the reverberant side, thanks to the large, bare studio where it was made, but there is no lack of detail.

PIANO MUSIC

Along an Overgrown Path, Books I & II; In the Mists; Piano Sonata (I.X.1905); Reminiscence
🔊 (M) *** SOMMCD 028. Owen

Along an Overgrown Path: Books I & II; In the Mists; Sonata (I.X.1905); Souvenir
**(*) HM HMC 901508. Planès

Along an Overgrown Path: Suite 1; In the Mists; Piano Sonata (I.X.1905)
(M) *** Virgin 5 61839-2. Andsnes

It says much for Charles Owen and his understanding of

Janáček, that he should present this music with such a distinctive voice. As is evident from the first of the two movements of the *Sonata*, he is even more strikingly successful at bringing out the quirky side of Janáček's writing, with jagged little flurries of notes directly echoing his orchestral style. Here and throughout the disc Owen is helped by the clarity of the well-balanced recording. The subtle dynamic gradations in the second movement of the *Sonata* add to the thoughtfulness of the reading, tender in its lyrical simplicity. Janáček was impulsively inspired to write this moving work by the bayonetting of a protester in Brno, who was demonstrating in favour of a Czech University. The qualities that make Owen's performance of the *Sonata* so impressive recur in the other works here. So the two series of miniatures that make up *Along an Overgrown Path* – ten in the first series, five in the second – reflect the composer's folk influences in their lyrical freshness, whether in the songful pieces or the dances. In the four pieces in the suite *In the Mist* Owen conveys the impression of improvisations caught on the wing, again gaining from the extra clarity and range of the Somm recording. The tiny *Reminiscence*, product of the year the composer died, makes a moving supplement.

Leif Ove Andsnes gives us a very well-thought-out and imaginatively realized recital, including a highly sensitive account of *In the Mists*, which is second to none in conveying the pervasive melancholy and evocative atmosphere of these pieces. This is every bit as telling as Firkušný's account, and beautifully recorded, and while it includes less music it has now been reissued at mid-price.

Alain Planès is a sensitive and intelligent artist whose sympathy with this repertoire is evident. All the same he is not quite as authoritative musically or as distinguished pianistically as Andsnes (Virgin).

Piano Sonata (I.X.1905)

*** MDG 604 1141-2. Von Eckardstein – MESSIAEN: *La Rousserolle effarvatte*; PROKOFIEV: *Piano Sonata 8* ***

Severin von Eckardstein won a special prize for contemporary music at the last Leeds Piano Competition, and his searching account of the elegiac *Sonata* is a complete vindication of the jury's judgement. Of course the sonata is not contemporary but von Eckardstein's approach is extremely sensitive and thoughtful. As fine an account of the work as we have encountered.

VOCAL MUSIC

Glagolitic Mass (original version, ed. Wingfield)

*** Chan. 9310. Kiberg, Stene, Svensson, Cold, Danish Nat. R. Ch. & SO, Mackerras – KODÁLY: *Psalmus hungaricus* ***

The added rhythmic complexities of this original version, as interpreted idiomatically by Mackerras, encourage an apt wildness which brings an exuberant, carefree quality to writing which here, more than ever, seems like the inspiration of the moment. The wildness is also reinforced by having the *Intrada* at the very beginning, before the Introduction, as well as at the end. The chorus sings incisively with incandescent tone, and the tenor soloist, Peter Svensson, has a trumpet-toned precision that makes light of the high tessitura and the stratospheric leaps that Janáček asks for. The soprano Tina Kiberg, also bright and clear rather than beautiful in tone, makes just as apt a choice, and only a certain unsteadiness in Ulrik Cold's relatively light bass tone prevents this from being an ideal quartet. Recorded sound of a weight and warmth that convey the full power of the music.

Glagolitic Mass

⊕✈ (M) *** EMI 5 66980-2 [566995]. Palmer, Gunson, Mitchinson, King, CBSO & Ch., Rattle – *Sinfonietta* ***

(B) *** Sony SBK 89903. Beňačková, Palmer, Lakes, Kotcherga, L. Symphony Ch., LSO, Tilson Thomas – *Sinfonietta* ***

*** Australian Decca Eloquence (ADD) 466 902-2. Kubiak, Collins, Tear, Schöne, Brighton Festival Ch., RPO, Kempe – KODÁLY: *Laudes organi; Psalm 114* ***

Rattle's performance of the standard published score, aptly paired with the *Sinfonietta*, is strong and vividly dramatic, with the Birmingham performers lending themselves to Slavonic passion. The recording is first class and is now reissued as one of EMI's 'Great Recordings of the Century'.

Tilson Thomas directs a powerful, virtuoso performance of the normal published score, superbly played and sung, and helped by full, weighty recorded sound. The soprano solos are both idiomatic and beautiful as sung by Beňačková, unsurpassed by any rival, and Gary Lakes, though not quite so idiomatic, uses his clean-cut, firm Heldentenor tone in the important tenor solos with no strain whatsoever. The London Symphony Chorus is magnificent and the LSO plays brilliantly in every department, not least in the woodwind and brass, with the brightness of the sound adding to the impact. An excellent alternative to Rattle on EMI and a real bargain.

Kempe's interpretation and the singing of the Brighton Festival Chorus do not always have the snapping authenticity of Rattle's and Mackerras's versions. Instead Kempe stresses the lyrical elements of the score rather than going for outright fervour, but the orchestra and chorus are fully committed, and the solo singing is first rate too, with Teresa Kubiak particularly impressive. Everything is helped by the most realistic recording, which has transferred very well to CD. The unusual Kodály coupling is appropriate and adds to the interest of this reissue on Australian Decca's Eloquence label, which, however, becomes more expensive in the UK.

(i) Glagolitic Mass; (ii) The Cunning Little Vixen: Suite; Zárlivost: Overture

(M) *** Decca (ADD) 470 263-2. (i) Kubiak, Collins, Tear, Schöne, Brighton Festival Ch., RPO, Kempe; (ii) VPO, Mackerras

Kempe's 1973 *Glagolitic Mass* makes a welcome alternative issue on Decca's 'Legends' label. Written when the composer was over seventy, it is full of those strikingly fresh orchestral textures that make his music so distinctive. The text is taken from Croatian variations of the Latin, and indeed Janáček said that he had village services in mind when he wrote the work. Fine, colourful bonuses from Mackerras, also in excellent sound.

OPERA

The Cunning Little Vixen (complete; DVD version)

(*) Arthaus **DVD 100 240. Allen, Jenis, Minutillo, O de Paris, Mackerras

With Sir Charles Mackerras again bringing out the characteristic sharpness of Janáček's writing in this fantasy opera, the power of the score as well as its charm comes over strongly in this DVD production at the Châtelet Theatre in Paris with Nicholas Hytner as stage director. Central to the production's success are the designs of Bob Crowley which take one into a toy-town world with stylized, brightly coloured sets in angular shapes, and costumes to match. Musically, the singing of Thomas Allen as the Forester focuses the whole performance, strong and sympathetic in conveying this character's devotion to the life of the forest. He is one of the few singers who dominate the orchestra in a recording which favours instruments against voices. The bright, penetrating voices of Eva Jenis as the Vixen and Hana Minutillo as the Fox also defy the recording balance. With Czech titles for individual tracks it is not always easy to identify which character is singing.

The Cunning Little Vixen (complete; CD version); The Cunning Little Vixen (suite, arr. Talich)

*** Decca 417 129-2 (2). Popp, Randová, Jedlická, V. State Op. Ch., Bratislava Children's Ch., VPO, Mackerras

*** Sup. SU (ADD) 3071/2 612 (2) (without suite). Tattermuschová, Zikmundová, Kroupa, Hlavsa, Prague Nat. Ch. & O, Gregor

Mackerras's thrusting, red-blooded CD reading on Decca is spectacularly supported by a digital recording of outstanding, demonstration quality. The inspired choice of Lucia Popp as the vixen provides charm in exactly the right measure: sparkling and coquettish, spiteful as well as passionate. The supporting cast is first rate, too. Talich's splendidly arranged orchestral suite is offered as a bonus in a fine new recording.

Janáček's opera is given on Supraphon with plenty of idiomatic Slavonic feeling by the composer's compatriots, with the part of the little vixen here charmingly sung by Helena Tattermuschová. The recording is evocatively warm and atmospheric. While the digitally recorded Decca Mackerras set (with Lucia Popp) remains a more obvious first choice, this earlier Czech version can hold its own. While not missing the red-blooded nature of the composer's inspiration, Gregor also captures the woodland ambience with appealing warmth and colour.

The Cunning Little Vixen (sung in English)

(M) *** Chan. 3101 (2). Watson, Allen, Tear, Knight, Howell, ROHCG Ch. & O, Rattle

The Rattle set is ideal for anyone wanting the opera in English. It gains from having been recorded as a spin-off from a highly successful Covent Garden production with the same excellent cast. In interpretation, Rattle's approach provides a clear alternative to that of Sir Charles Mackerras on his classic Decca version with a Czech cast. Where Mackerras characteristically brings out the sharp, angular side of Janáček's writing, the distinctly jagged element, Rattle's manner is more moulded, perhaps more immediately persuasive, if less obviously idiomatic. The recording is beautifully balanced, with the new Chandos transfer a degree more open on top and cleaner in texture than the previous EMI issue of the same recording, and this is important in the ensembles. What matters is that the words are ideally clear, with excellent diction from everyone.

The Cunning Little Vixen (sung in German, Das schlaue Füchslein)

(N) (**) Immortal **DVD** IMM 960001. Arnold, Asmus, Enders, Berlin Comic Op. and O, Neumann (V/D: Walter Felsenstein)

One might well ask why any non-German viewer would want a presentation of Janáček's *The Cunning Little Vixen* in the radical German adaptation of Max Brod, recorded in the 1950s, not in black and white but in a fuzzy dark-green and white. The answer is that this film was directed by the legendary Walter Felsenstein, with evocative images adapted from the stage production at the Comic Opera in Berlin. The Brod adaptation involves the Cunning Little Vixen turning into a gypsy girl before the eyes of the Forester, though she reverts to her foxy self for the subsequent Acts. Irmgard Arnold sings characterfully in the title-role, very much in the style of comic opera or cabaret, with Rudolf Asmus powerful as the Forester. The sound, like the picture, is rather fuzzy, though Vaclav Neumann conducts an idiomatic performance. Under Felsenstein's direction the acting and staging very much reflect the traditions of the German cinema of earlier generations. Unhelpfully, there is no option for subtitles.

The Excursions of Mr Brouček (complete)

*** Sup. (ADD) 11 2153-2 (2). Přibyl, Svejda, Jonášová, Czech PO Ch. & O, Jílek

This performance comes over with real charm, thanks to the understanding conducting of Jílek, but also to the characterization of the central character, the bumbling, accident-prone Mr Brouček (literally Mr Beetle). Vilém Přibyl portrays him as an amiable, much-put-upon figure as he makes his excursions. The big team of Czech singers (doubling up roles in the different parts, with Vladimir Krejčik remarkable in no fewer than seven of them) are outstanding, bringing out both the warmth and sense of fun behind the writing. The result is a delight, as sharp and distinctive as any Janáček opera. The analogue recording, made in Prague in 1980, is full and atmospheric, with a fine sense of presence on CD.

(i) From the House of the Dead; (iii) Mládí (for wind sextet); (ii; iii) Říkadla (for chamber ch. & 10 instruments)

*** Decca DDD/ADD 430 375-2 (2). (i) Jedlička, Zahradníček, Zídek, Zítek, V. State Op. Ch., VPO, Mackerras; (ii) L. Sinf. Ch.; (iii) L. Sinf., Atherton

With one exception, the Decca cast is superb, with a range of important Czech singers giving sharply characterized vignettes. The exception is the raw Slavonic singing of the one woman in the cast, Jaroslav Janska, as the boy Aljeja, but even that fails to undermine the intensity of the innocent relationship with the central figure which provides an emotional anchor for the whole piece. The chamber-music items added for this reissue are both first rate.

Jenůfa (complete; DVD version)

🔗 *** Arthaus DVD 100 208. Alexander, Silja, Langridge, M. Baker, Glyndebourne Ch., LPO, A. Davis (V/D: Nikolaus Lehnhoff)

Jenůfa (complete; CD versions)

🔗 ✪ *** Decca 414 483-2 (2). Söderström, Ochman, Dvorský, Randová, Popp, V. State Op. Ch., VPO, Mackerras

*** Erato 0927 45330-2 (2). Mattila, Silja, Silvasti, Hadley, Randová, ROH Ch. & O, Haitink

The impact of Nikolaus Lehnhoff's production of Jenůfa was always strong and positive, with the stark yet atmospheric designs of Tobias Hoheisel adding to the sharpness. On DVD, with close-ups in this television film of 1989 adding to the impact, the result is even more powerful. This visual treatment exactly matches the sharp originality of Janáček's score, with its often abrasive orchestration heightened by passages of surging beauty, superbly realized by Andrew Davis and the LPO.

Roberta Alexander makes a warm, slightly gawky Jenůfa, with Philip Langridge as the frustrated lover, Laka, making this awkward character totally believable, an object for sympathy, finally fulfilled. Both sing superbly, and so do the rest of the cast, including Mark Baker as the wastrel, Steva, a tenor well contrasted with Langridge. Yet dominating the cast is the Kostelnicka of Anja Silja. This was the production which brought this characterful soprano, veteran of many years of singing Wagner at Bayreuth, to Glyndebourne for the first time, where she has since added an Indian summer to her long career, singing this and other Janáček roles with enormous success. The abrasiveness in her voice, which with Wagner heroines was often obtrusive, is here a positive asset, and her portrayal of this formidable character, positive and uncompromising yet ultimately an object of pity, is totally convincing in all its complexity. The way she delivers Kostelnicka's apprehensive cry at the end of Act II was 'as if death were peering into the house'. Full, vivid sound very well transferred, if with an edge that suits the music.

The Decca CDs bring a performance from Mackerras and his team which is deeply sympathetic, strongly dramatic and superbly recorded. Elisabeth Söderström creates a touching portrait of the girl caught in a family tragedy. The two rival tenors, Peter Dvorský and Wieslav Ochman as the half-brothers Steva and Laca, are both superb; but dominating the whole drama is the Kostelnicka of Eva Randová. Some may resist the idea that she should be made so sympathetic but the drama is made stronger and more involving.

Haitink's version, recorded live at Covent Garden in October 2001, is distinguished not only by the warm, intense conducting but by the fine singing of the principals, notably Karita Mattila in the title role. Any new version of this opera has to be matched against the masterly version on Decca under Sir Charles Mackerras, and here Mattila with her fresh, girlish tone combined with great emotional depth, outshines even Elisabeth Söderström, whose more mature voice is less appropriate for the role, warmly expressive as she is. Alja Silja, who as a veteran artist has made a speciality of the role of the Kostelnicka, at both Glyndebourne and Covent Garden, also gives a most memorable performance. She is not always as secure as Eva Randová on the Decca set, with some rawness at the top, but from first to last she is searingly intense and the more moving for bringing out the element of vulnerability in this fearsome character. Randová is masterly in the much smaller role of Grandmother Buryja, and both tenor roles are very well taken, too, with Jorma Silvasti as Laca rising most movingly to the challenge of the final scene and the reconciliation with Jenufa, while Jerry Hadley sings with comparable freshness as Steva. Though the sound on this live recording does not have the weight and power of the Decca digital studio recording and stage noises inevitably intrude at times, it is finely detailed, and the atmosphere adds to the compulsion of the performance, with refined playing from the orchestra. While the Decca set still has its unique place in the catalogue, this new Erato set is in some ways even more recommendable.

Jenůfa (sung in English)

(M) *** Chan. 3106 (2). Watson, Barstow, Wedd, Robson, Davies, WNO Ch. & O, Mackerras

Based on the acclaimed production of Jenůfa from Welsh National Opera, Sir Charles Mackerras's Chandos set offers an important alternative to the classic, prize-winning version he conducted in 1982 for Decca. The first obvious difference is the use of English in this issue in the Peter Moores Foundation's 'Opera in English' series. The translation by Edward Downes and Otakar Kraus works very well, even though the sumptuous Chandos recording places the voices a little further back than the Decca version does, with many words less clear. The benefit of the Chandos sound is that the colour and originality of Janáček's orchestral textures come over even more vividly than on the brilliant Decca set, at once opulent and well defined, with each strand clarified and the exotic percussion effects brought out. Helped by a few sound-effects, the result is generally more atmospheric.

In international terms the Welsh National Opera Orchestra may be no match for the Vienna Philharmonic on Decca, but their experience of this opera in the pit ensures not only that the playing is finely honed but that there is an extra idiomatic warmth, born of long experience, while reflecting the insights of the conductor. Using, as before, the original scoring of the so-called Brno version, without the radical re-orchestration imposed by Karel Kovarovic, Mackerras takes a marginally broader view than last time, remaining just as powerful and dramatic.

When it comes to the rival casts on CD, they are both very strong, with no weak links. If it was luxury casting to have Elisabeth Söderström in the title-role on Decca, Janice Watson on Chandos has just as beautiful a voice, sounding more aptly young, fresh and girlish, and deeply expressive too. As the Kostelnicka, Dame Josephine Barstow presents a striking contrast to her Decca opposite number, Eva Randová, Wagnerian in richness and power. Barstow's voice is edgier and more abrasive, and with that she conveys not only the obsessive side of this powerful character but an element of vulnerability, apt for the story. The two tenor roles are also very well taken, with Peter Wedd as Steva and Nigel Robson as Laca nicely contrasted, effectively bringing out the sharp differences of character between the half-brothers. Elizabeth Vaughan as Grandmother Buryja and Neal Davies as the Foreman complete a formidable line-up of principals. Not surprisingly, words are much clearer from the male singers than from the female. The Chandos set does not include the extra items on the earlier Decca – the discarded Prelude Jealousy and Kovarovic's version of the opera's conclusion – but the final duet between Jenůfa and Laca is even more tender than it was in the Vienna performance, bringing out all the subtlety of Janáček's evocative writing.

Káta Kabanová (complete; DVD versions)

⊕➥ *** Arthaus **DVD** 100 158. Gustafson, Palmer, R. Davies, McCauley, Graham-Hall, Winter, Glyndebourne Ch., LPO, A. Davis. (V/D: Nikolaus Lehnhoff)

(**) TDK Mediactive **DVD** DV-OPKK. Denoke, Kuebler, Henschel, Smit, Delamboye, Trost, Peckova, Slovak Phil. Ch., Czech PO, Cambreling

Káta Kabanová (complete; CD versions)

** Sup. SU 3291-2 632 (3). Vele, Straka, Randová, Kopp, Beňačková, Kundlak, Pecková, Harvánek, Bauerová, Burešová, Prague Nat. Theatre Ch., Czech PO, Mackerras

(i) *Káta Kabanová* (complete); (ii) *Capriccio for Piano & 7 Instruments; Concertino for Piano & 6 Instruments*

⊕➥ *** Decca (ADD) 421 852-2 (2). (i) Söderström, Dvorský, Kniplová, Krejčik, Márová, V. State Op. Ch., VPO, Mackerras; (ii) Crossley, L. Sinf., Atherton

First seen at Glyndebourne in 1988, this Arthaus DVD offers the ground-breaking production by Nikolaus Lehnhoff with

stark, striking designs by Tobias Hoheisel, which led to a whole sequence of memorable Janáček productions. It remains one of the most powerful, with Nancy Gustafson tenderly moving as the heroine starved of love, constantly frustrated by her implacable mother-in-law, the deeply unsympathetic Kabanicha, brilliantly portrayed and sung by Felicity Palmer, with a powerful cutting edge. The production, too, is exactly suited to the distinctive idiom of Janáček, with its contrasts of abrasiveness and rich beauty. Strong contributions too from Ryland Davies as Tichon, Káta's husband, Barry McCauley as Boris, and John Graham-Hall as Kudrjas, with characterful contributions too from such a veteran as Donald Adams as Boris's father, Dikoj. Bright, forward sound adds to the impact.

Recorded live at the 1998 Salzburg Festival, the TDK DVD of *Káta Kabanová* offers a starkly updated production by Christoph Marthaler with a permanent set by Anna Viebrock which puts the whole opera in a courtyard surrounded completely by high-rise apartment blocks. Such an urban setting may capture an appropriate feeling of claustrophobia, and the visual brutality chimes to a degree with the abrasiveness of the score, but, totally unatmospheric, it flies in the face of Ostrovsky's story in more than the period. So instead of throwing herself in the Volga at the end, Káta curls up among the tiny fountains dotted about a central flower-bed, and instead of gazing at the Volga in the opening scene Kudrjas is simply looking at a small painting. This is the sort of production that makes one despair of present-day opera presentation, and the stiffly stylized acting adds to the feeling of alienation, all the more so when musically the performance with the Czech Philharmonic and a Slovakian choir under Sylvain Cambreling is first rate. The whole opera is presented without intervals, adding to its concentration, with the title-role most movingly taken by Angela Denoke, singing with radiant, creamy tone. Among the others Jane Henschel stands out, characterful as the Kabanicha, looking less menacing than she might, with David Kuebler excellent as Káta's lover, Boris.

On Decca, Elisabeth Söderström dominates the cast as the tragic heroine and gives a performance of great insight and sensitivity; she touches the listener deeply and is supported by Mackerras with imaginative grip and flair. The other soloists are all Czech and their characterizations are brilliantly authentic. But it is the superb orchestral playing and the inspired performance of Söderström that make this set so memorable. The recording is vividly transferred to CD, with a double bonus added in the shape of the two concertante keyboard works, in which Paul Crossley is the impressive soloist.

Though Mackerras's Supraphon set offers digital sound and has an excellent Czech cast, it cannot match his earlier, Decca version in colour or bite. Though his speeds are a degree faster than before, the result is less violent and less involving, thanks partly to the low-level recording, set in a reverberant acoustic. Beňačková, rich and vibrant, is an exceptionally characterful Káta, arguably more idiomatic than Söderström on Decca, and the other principals are first rate too, but at every point this pales before its rival.

The Makropulos Affair (DVD version)

⊕➥ ✪ *** Warner **DVD** 0630 14016-2. Silja, Begley, Braun, Shore, LPO, A. Davis (Director: Nikolaus Lehnhoff; V/D: Brian Large)

The Makropulos Affair is Janáček's penultimate opera, and it is a masterpiece. It had an almost definitive performance on Decca with Elisabeth Söderström in one of her greatest roles as the 337-year-old heroine, Emilia Marty, and with the Vienna Philharmonic under Sir Charles Mackerras in superb form (see below). Now comes the 1995 Glyndebourne production by Nikolaus Lehnhoff, whose *Kát'a Kabanová* we so much admired, and with an astonishingly powerful account of the heroine from Anya Silja. In fact, it is difficult to flaw this production on any count. It is excellently cast, with Kim Begley as Gregor, Viktor Braun as Pruš and Andrew Shore as Dr Kolenaty, and it is conducted with a sense both of atmosphere and of pace by Sir Andrew Davis. He is hardly less idiomatic and sensitive than Mackerras. Those who were privileged to see this will not forget the excellence of the staging either, but above all the commanding portrayal of Emilia by Silja. As usual, Brian Large brings everything to the screen with scrupulous care and taste to make this a very special contribution to the Janáček DVD discography. A small but tiresome point: Warner's presentation is virtually non-existent and does not even run to a full cast-list.

(i) *The Makropulos Affair* (CD version): complete; (ii) *Lachian Dances*

*** Decca (ADD) 430 372-2 (2). (i) Söderström, Dvorský, Blachut, V. State Op. Ch., VPO, Mackerras; (ii) LPO, Huybrechts

Mackerras and his superb team provide a thrilling new perspective on this opera, with its weird heroine preserved by magic elixir well past her 300th birthday. Elisabeth Söderström is not simply malevolent: irritable and impatient rather, no longer an obsessive monster. Framed by richly colourful singing and playing, Söderström amply justifies that view, and Peter Dvorský is superbly fresh and ardent as Gregor. The recording, like others in the series, is of the finest Decca analogue quality. The performance of the *Lachian Dances* is highly idiomatic and makes a good bonus.

Osud (complete, in English)

(M) *** Chan. 3029. Langridge, Field, Harries, Bronder, Kale, Welsh Nat. Op. Ch. & O, Mackerras

Janáček's most unjustly neglected opera – richly lyrical, more sustained and less fragmented than his later operas – was for generations rejected as being unstageable, thanks to the oddities of the libretto, until, however, the English National Opera presented it at the Coliseum in London. Though this recording was made with Welsh National Opera forces, its success echoes the ENO production. Philip Langridge is again superb in the central role of the composer, Zivny, well supported by Helen Field as Mila, the married woman he loves, and by Kathryn Harries as her mother – a far finer cast than was presented on a short-lived Supraphon set. This performance, following ENO, uses Rodney Blumer's excellent English translation, adding to the immediate impact. Sir Charles Mackerras captures the full gutsiness, passion and impetus of the composer's inspiration, from the exhilarating opening waltz ensemble onwards, a passage that vividly sets the scene in a German spa at the turn of the century. The warmly atmospheric recording brings out the unusual opulence of the Janáček sound in this work, written immediately after *Jenůfa*, yet it allows words to come over with fine clarity.

Sarka (complete)

*** Sup. SU 3485-2. Urbanová, Straka, Kusnjer, Brezina, Prague Philharmonic Ch., Czech PO, Mackerras

Sarka, written originally in 1887, was Janáček's very first opera, a piece that was put aside when the author of the original play withheld his consent to its use. In 1916 Janáček rediscovered the score, was impressed, and made revisions until it was finally produced in 1925 in Brno. It was promptly dismissed as being inferior to Fibich's opera on the *Sarka* legend. Though the idiom has more echoes of Dvořák and Smetana than anticipations of the mature Janáček, its dramatic point comes over strongly, with the legend reduced to bare essentials to give it a dream-like quality, making it a Freudian fantasy before its time. Though the three Acts last little more than an hour, Janáček regarded this as his Wagnerian opera, ending as it does with the immolation of the formidable heroine, Sarka (an Amazonian figure sworn to avenge herself on man) on the funeral pyre of Ctirad, the hero-figure with whom, against her will, she falls in love. It is not just an immolation, but a Liebestod, or love-death. This first stereo recording could hardly be finer, with Mackerras inspiring his Czech singers and players to give an incandescent performance, with Eva Urbanová and Peter Straka ideally cast, both characterfully Slavonic and clean in attack. First-rate sound, with atmospheric choral effects beautifully caught.

JENKINS, John (1592–1678)

Consort Music: *Ayres a 4 in D min. & G min. (Ayre; Almaine; Couranto); Divisions for 2 Basses in C; Fantasia: in C min.; D; E min.; Fantasias in C min. (2); Fantasia in F (All in a Garden Green); Fantasy-suite in A min.; In nomine in G min.; Newarke Seidge (Pavan; Galliard); Pavan in F*

(B) *** Naxos 8.550687. Rose Consort of Viols, with Roberts

Consort Music: *Divisions for 2 Bass Viols in D; Fantasias: a 4 in D; in F (2); a 5 in C min. (2); & D; a 6 in A min. & C min.; In nomines: a 6 in E min. & G min.; Pavan for 2 Bass Viols; Pavan a 6 in F; Pieces for Lyra Viol; Suites 4 in C for 2 Trebles, Bass & Organ; 7 in D min., for Treble, 2 Basses & Organ in D min.*

*** Virgin 5 45230-2. Fretwork, with Nicholas

John Jenkins spent his life in Norfolk and lapsed into obscurity. Yet on the evidence of these two fine, complementary CDs his viol music is of high quality and well worth rediscovering. It does not seek great profundity, although the beautiful *Pavan in F major*, common to both discs, is memorable, and all the *Fantasias* are well crafted – their invention appealingly immediate. Where there are several in the same key, each differs from the others, yet uses the same basic theme. In terms of colour, Jenkins's combination of viols with organ is quite ear-tickling.

Although they overlap, both collections are thoroughly recommendable, with the difference between them accentuated by the difference in performance pitch, with Fretwork slightly higher, giving a brighter, fresher impression, whereas the Rose Consort have a somewhat warmer tonal blend, especially noticeable in that fine *Pavan*.

Consort Music for Violins in 6 Parts: Fantasies 1–11; Bell Pavan; In nomines 1–2

*** Astrée ES 9962. Hespèrion XX, Savall

Jenkins's set of six-part *Fantasias* appear to be early works. There is a twelfth, but it is not thought to be authentic and has been omitted here. The manuscripts include the pair of *In nomines* (based on plainsong), but the two *Pavans* have been added to give necessary variety to the programme, with the

Bell Pavan, so called as it quotes a sequence of notes supposedly used (until the Great Fire of London) in the clock of St Mary-le-Bow. The performances here are richly blended and bring out the full, expressive depth of this music. At times one feels that the playing of the faster pieces could have produced a brighter projection, but viols are not violins and have a more limited dynamic range, so this remains a highly recommendable anthology. The recording itself, warm and full and not too close, cannot be faulted.

JOACHIM, Joseph (1831–1907)

Violin Concerto 2 in D min. (In the Hungarian Style)

(B) **(*) Cedille Double CD 9000068 (2). Barton, Chicago SO, Kalmar – BRAHMS: *Violin Concerto* **(*)

In 1861, some 17 years before Brahms produced his masterpiece in the genre, Joseph Joachim as a young virtuoso wrote his *D minor Violin Concerto 'In the Hungarian Style'*. Later he was to collaborate with his composer-friend on perfecting the solo part of the Brahms concerto, but here in his own work the solo part is, if anything, even more formidable in its technical demands. It makes a good coupling to have the two works side by side in a two-for-the-price-of-one package from Cedille, even if the Brahms inevitably shows the inferiority of the Joachim work. Even longer than the Brahms, it challenges even the imagination of Rachel Barton to sustain its length, for the Chicago Symphony under Carlos Kalmar is again lacklustre. Fiery in the bravura passages, tenderly expressive in the many lyrical moments, she brings out the Hungarian flavour idiomatically in her shaping of phrases and pointing of rhythm, not least in the Hungarian dance of the finale, precursor of Brahms's Hungarian-flavoured finale.

Hamlet Overture, Op. 4

*** Simax PSC 1206. Oslo PO, Jansons – BRAHMS: *Symphony 1* ***

Though this first of Joachim's two Shakespearean overtures (the second being *Heinrich IV*) cannot compare in quality of material with the Brahms symphony, it makes an apt and enjoyable coupling, when the young Brahms admired it so much that he made a piano transcription. The *Moderato* introduction brings the main motif, but much of it is conventional bogey music, and the main meat comes in the following *Allegro*, where a sharply rhythmic main subject leads to a lyrical second theme, presumably characterizing Ophelia. After that symphonic exposition the piece grows increasingly free along Lisztian lines, ending on a mysterious *pianissimo*. Excellent performance and fine sound.

Heinrich IV Overture, Op. 7

*** Simax PSC 1205. Olso PO, Jansons – BRAHMS: *Symphony 4* ***

Joachim wrote the second of his Shakespearean overtures, based on Henry IV, over a prolonged period in 1853 and 1854, reacting to the adverse criticism of Schumann that it was too gloomy. Whether or not through Joachim's revisions, it is certainly not that, with its fanfares and marches a sharper, more inventive piece than the earlier *Hamlet Overture*, making an interesting coupling for the Brahms symphony, similarly well recorded.

JOHANSEN, David Monrad (1888–1974)

String Quartet, Op. 36

(BB) *** Naxos 8.550879. Oslo String Qt – GRIEG: *String Quartets* ***

David Monrad Johansen's *String Quartet*, composed in 1969 when in his early eighties, is persuasively played by the Oslo String Quartet and is impeccably recorded. It is a well-crafted piece but not as distinctively personal as *Pan* or the best of his mature works.

JOHNSON, Robert (c. 1563–1633)

Lute Pieces: Almaynes 1–4; Fantasia; The gipsies dance; My Lady Mildmay's Delight (Gallyard); Pavans 1–3; Songs: (i) As I walked forth; Away delights; Care-charming sleep; Come heavy sleep; Come hither you that love; Hark! hark! the lark; Have you seen the bright lilly grow?; How wretched is the state; Oh let us how; Tell me dearest; Where the bee sucks; With endless tears; Woods, rocks and mountains

(N) **(*) Avie 2053. (i) Sampson; Wadsworth, Levy

Robert Johnson, son of John Johnson, lutenist to Queen Elizabeth I, became in his turn lutenist to King James I, also serving under Prince Charles and remaining with him after he became Charles I. Johnson was later to provide songs for Shakespeare's plays, notably *The Tempest*. His writing has a wider range of mood than Dowland's, although he can certainly achieve movingly expressive dolour, as in *Care-charming sleep*, *With endless tears* and *Come heavy sleep*, which are as fine as any of Dowland's songs. The delightful *Have you seen the bright lily grow?*, with its upward leap, is a number that ought to be really famous. Carolyn Sampson has a sweet but full voice and sings most pleasingly and stylishly, and she is felicitously accompanied by Matthew Wadsworth (and occasionally by Mark Levy's bass viol); the lute solos are also attractively played. The one snag to the recording is the resonance of St Mary's Church, South Crake, Norfolk, which has not been fully controlled by the recording engineer and sometimes catches the voice slightly on louder climaxes.

JONES, Robert (1570–1615)

Lute Songs: Farewell dear love; Fly from the world; Go to bed sweet muse; Happy be; If in this flesh; Ite calsi sospiri; Lie down poor heart; Love is a bable; Love's god is a boy; Love wing'd my hopes; Might I redeem mine errors; Now what is love; O thread of life; What if I seek for love of thee; When I sit reading; When love on time; When will the fountain?

(N) (BB) *** Virgin 2x1 5 64210-2 (2). Kirkby, Rooley – DOWLAND: *Lute Songs* **(*)

Robert Jones was a younger contemporary of John Dowland of whom we know little, except that he never enjoyed the same acclaim. Yet his songs, if seldom exploring the greater depths of emotion (there is little or no despair in his amorous encounters), have great charm and are often very touching. No one could say that *Lie down poor heart*, *Fly from the world* or *When will the fountain?* are without a gentle sadness, and the thoughtful nostaglia of the closing *Might I redeem mine errors* is equally affecting as presented here. Indeed, these songs suit Emma Kirkby's voice and her simplicity of style to perfection. She catches their mood admirably and is especially delightful in the more optimistic celebrations of love from the Second Book: *Love wing'd my hopes, Love is a bable*, and *Love's god is a boy*, with its pretty refrain. In short, this recital is most rewarding, and it suggests that Robert Jones was a finer composer than his reputation suggests. Anthony Rooley accompanies most supportively, and voice and lute are admirably balanced.

JONGEN, Joseph (1873–1953)

Symphonie Concertante for Organ & Orchestra, Op. 81
*** Telarc CD 80096. Murray, San Francisco SO, De Waart –
  FRANCK: *Fantaisie*, etc. ***

Anyone who likes the Saint-Saëns *Third Symphony* should enjoy the Jongen *Symphonie Concertante*. Even if the music is on a lower level of inspiration, the passionate *Lento misterioso* and hugely spectacular closing *Toccata* make a favourable impression at first hearing and wear surprisingly well afterwards. Michael Murray has all the necessary technique to carry off Jongen's hyperbole with the required panache. He receives excellent support from Edo de Waart and the San Francisco Symphony Orchestra, and Telarc's engineers capture all the spectacular effects with their usual aplomb. A demonstration disc indeed.

JOSQUIN DESPREZ (died 1521)

Chansons: *Adieu mes amours; Allégez moy; Cueur langoreulx; Cueurs désolez; Déploration sur la mort de Ockeghem; En son saichant; El grillo; Faulte d'argent; J'ay bien cause de lamenter; Je me complains; Mille regretz; Nimphes, nappés; Parfons regretz; Petite camusette; Plaine de dueil; Plusiers regretz; Plus n'estes ma maitresse; Si congié prens; Tenez moy en vos bras; Vous l'arez s'il vous plais.* Instrumental pieces (viols or lute): *Adieu mes amours; Fors seulment; Fortuna desperata; Ile fantazies; Mille regretz; La plus des plus; Si j'ay perdu mon amy*
(N) (B) *** HM Musique d'Abord HMA 1951279. Ens.
  Clément Janequin

'*Un magnifique condensé de l'art de Josquin*', justly commented *Le Monde* about this disc. Of course it is not literally true, for there is no church music; but in surveying the wide range of delightful and touching chansons it could not be bettered. The vocal numbers are sung with dolour or vitality as required, and the blending of the two, three, four, five or even six voices is as admirable as the intonation is secure. Lute and viol pieces provide interludes. The programme ends with the sparkling six-voice *Allégez moy*, followed by the infinitely touching tribute to Ockeghem. A pity there are texts but no translations, but that is the French way. A marvellous disc just the same, and very well recorded.

Motetti de Passione … B (1503): *Ave verum corpus; Christem ducem/Qui velatus; Domine, non secundum; O Domine Jesu Christe; Tu solus, qui facis mirabilia. Missa faisant regretz*
🔔 ✿ *** Gaudeamus CDGAU 302. Clerks' Group, Wickham
  – FRYE: *Tut a par moy* ***

Josquin's compact but consistently fluent and appealing four-part Mass setting, *Faisant regretz*, is based on a four-note motif taken from Walter Frye's rondeau for three voices, *Tut a par moy*, which is also included on this CD. This dolorous

song must have been very famous in its day and Josquin ingeniously weaves the very striking motto theme (always easy to recognize) into his vocal texture with great imaginative resource – right through to the *Agnus Dei*. In his notes Edward Wickham wittily describes this fascinating work as a 'masterpiece of minimalism'.

But even more striking in this outstanding collection is the cycle of five motets largely based on the readings in Petrucci, *Motetti de Passione … B* of 1503. They are arrestingly chordal in style, the opening declamatory *Tu solus, qui facis mirabilia*, with its bare harmonies, arrestingly so, the *Ave verum corpus* similarly simple and affecting, *Domine, non secundum* more elaborate, and with women's voices soaring celestially in *O Domine Jesu Christe*. The extended *Christem ducem/Qui velatus* (a setting of Passiontide hymns by St Bonaventure) which Wickham rightly places last, is the most movingly expressive of all. Superb performances, given an uncanny presence in an ideal acoustic.

Motets: *Ave Maria, gratia plena; Ave, nobilissima creatura; Miserere mei, Deus; O bone et dulcissime Jesu; Salve regina; Stabat mater dolorosa; Usquequo, Domine, oblivisceris me*
*** HM HMC 901243. Chapelle Royale Ch., Herreweghe

The Chapelle Royale comprises some 19 singers, but they still produce a clean, well-focused sound and benefit from excellent recording. Their account of the expressive *Stabat mater* sounds thicker-textured than the New College forces under Edward Higginbottom, but there is a refreshing sense of commitment and strong feeling.

Motets: *Inter natos mulierum; Pater noster/Ave Maria; Planxit autem David; Recordare, virgin mater*
*** Hyp. CDA 67183. Binchois Cons., Kirkman (with:
  BAULDEWEYN: *Ave caro Christi cara*; CHAMPION (or
  JOSQUIN): *De Profundis*; FORESTIER (or JOSQUIN): *Veni
  sancte spiritus*; CRAEN: *Tota pulchra est*; WILLAERT:
  Verbum bonum et suave)

Entitled '*Josquin and his Contemporaries*', the Binchois Consort's excellent disc adds two formidable motets by Nicolaes Craen and Adrian Willaert to major items by Josquin himself, with the authenticity of three of them now questioned in favour of Noel Bauldewyn, Mathurin Forestier and Nicolas Champion. What the disc amply demonstrates is that, though Josquin's fame and reputation are securely based (a supreme master of the period – witness the lovely *Recordare* for upper voices), there was much superb music being written by less celebrated composers from the early sixteenth century. Willaert's six-part *Verbum bonum* is wonderfully inventive, and Forestier's *Veni sancte spiritus*, long thought to be by Josquin, is equally powerful. Under Andrew Kirkman the Binchois Consort sing with fine, beautifully matched ensemble, and are treated to finely balanced recording.

Antiphons, motets and sequences: *Inviolata; Praeter rerum serium; Salve regina; Stabat mater dolorosa; Veni, sancte spiritus; Virgo prudentissima; Virgo salutiferi*
*** Mer. (ADD) ECD 84093. New College, Oxford, Ch.,
  Higginbottom

The Meridian anthology collects some of Josquin's most masterly and eloquent motets in performances of predictable excellence by Edward Higginbottom and the Choir of New College, Oxford. An admirable introduction to Josquin, and an essential acquisition for those who care about this master.

Chanson: *Fortuna desperata* (probably by BUSNOIS); *Missa Fortuna desperata; Adieu mes amours; Bererette savoysienne; Consideres mes incessantes (Fortuna); La plus des plus*

*** Gaudeamus CDGAU 220 Clerks' Group, Wickham (with ISAAC: *Bruder Conrat/Fortuna;* SENFL: *Herr durch dein Bluet/Pange lingua/Fortuna;* ANON.: *Fortuna Zibaldone;* GREITER: *Passibus anbiguis/Fortuna valubis errat* ***)

The fascination of the collection from the Clerks' Group is the inclusion of not just the chanson on which Josquin's Mass was based, probably by Antoine Busnois (1430–92), but also eight further treatments and rearrangements of a song which in its time was obviously as popular as *L'Homme armé* – including four by Josquin himself. Most striking of all is the anonymous Florentine *Fortuna Zibaldone*, in which one really needs the provided translation, for the four voices sing three different light-hearted texts simultaneously, together with the original chanson, with the whole performance taking just over a minute! As usual, the singing here is admirable in its blending and clarity of line, and the recording quite excellent.

Chanson: *L'Homme armé; Missa l'homme armé super voces musicales; Missa l'homme armé sexti toni*

*** Gimell CDGIM 019. Tallis Scholars, Phillips

Josquin wrote two Masses using *L'Homme armé* as the cantus firmus, but in the later (though not much later) *Sexti toni* (sixth mode), the last note of the cantus is different – F, instead of G as favoured by most other composers including Du Fay. The character of the melody is thus given a more positive character with the major key implied. The Tallis performances are in their usual impeccable flowing style, and the performance of the later work undoubtedly brings out its greater complexity, although the closing *Agnus Dei* has a hauntingly beautiful bare simplicity.

Missa Hercules Dux Ferrariae; Miserere mei Deus. Motets: *Absolom, fili mi; Ave Maria gratia pleni; De profundis clamavi; In te Domine speravi per trovar pietà; Pater noster/Ave Maria; Tu solus qui facis mirabilia; Veni, Sancti Spiritus*. Chansons: *Le Déploration de la mort de Johannes Ockeghem (Nymphes de bois); El grillo; En l'hombre d'ung buissonet au matinet; Je me complains; Je ne me puis tenir d'aimer; Mille regretz; Petite camusette; Scarmella va alla guerra – Loyset Compère: Scaramella fa la galla.* GOMBERT (attrib. JOSQUIN): Motet: *Lugabet David Absalon*

(BB) *** Virgin 2×1 5 62346-2 (2). Hilliard Ens., Hillier

The Hilliard Ensmble find the full measure of Josquin's Mass, *Hercules dux Ferrariae*, probably written just before the composer's appointment to Ferrara in 1505, and featuring a cantus based on the letters of the work's title, paying homage to the composer's future employer, Duke Ercole d'Este. The performance revels in the rich flowing lyricism of the *Kyrie* and *Agnus Dei*, whose second section includes a fascinating three-in-one canon, yet bringing passionate ardour to the climaxes of the *Sanctus* and *Benedictus*.

Both the *Pater noster/Ave Maria* and the masterly *Miserere mei Deus* – a setting of Psalm 50, actually commissioned by the duke – are taken slowly and serenely. Some might feel that, particularly in the latter, the music might have been pressed forward more strongly, but the underlying intensity is well sustained and there is no lack of light and shade. One can understand, after listening to the dedicated Hilliard account, why the deeply expressive *Lugabet David Absalon*

was attributed to Josquin, although it was probably written by Nicolas Gombert, and the first disc ends with a gloriously blended and ideally paced performance of the beautiful *Tu solus qui facis mirabilia*.

The motets are sung with dignity and feeling, but the chansons display infinite variety and colour. *Petite camusette* ('Little Snubnose') has a winning charm to set against the deeply touching *Mille regretz*, while the sparkling Italian frottola, *Scaramella va' alla guerra* and the witty portrait of a cricket, *El grillo*, show Josquin in lighter vein. The disc ends movingly with an elegiac tribute to Ockeghem, who succeeded Josquin in Ferrara after only a year, only to perish later in the plague. The collection of motets and chansons was recorded in London's Temple Church in 1983, the Mass and other items in the Priory Church of St Mary and St Blaise in Boxgrove, Chichester, in 1989. Expertly balanced and eminently truthful, they make an admirable pair (at budget price) to kindle the enthusiasm of the uninitiated as will few other Josquin compilations. But it is a pity there are no texts and translations.

Missa l'homme armé sexti toni. Motets: *Absalom, fili mi; Ave Maria*

🔶 ✿ (BB) *** Naxos 8.553428. Oxford Camerata, Summerly – VINDERS: *Lament on the Death of Josquin* ***

Another interesting feature of the Josquin setting is his interpolation of a trope (*Laeta dies*) following the *Credo* and before the *Sanctus* using a non-liturgical text. The effect is undoubtedly dramatic at the centre of a work where the flowing lines of the polyphony have such a rich harmonic implication. The long *Credo* breaks free, with the polyphony becoming more animated, and so becomes the central focus of the whole Mass – and what a beautiful Mass it is; very beautifully sung and recorded here. The *Ave Maria* is used to create a tranquil mood before the Mass itself begins, and the very touching motet, *Absalom, fili mi*, makes a poignant coda. This is followed by the radiant elegy of Josquin's contemporary, Jheronimus Vinders, with its soaring treble line, surely a fitting tribute. With full texts provided, this CD is one of the very finest of this distinguished Naxos series.

Missa pange lingua; Missa la sol fa re mi

*** Gimell CDGIM 009. Tallis Scholars, Phillips

The Gimell recording of the *Missa pange lingua* has collected superlatives on all counts and was voted record of the year in the *Gramophone* magazine's 1987 awards. The tone the Tallis Scholars produce is perfectly blended, each line being firmly defined and yet beautifully integrated into the whole sound-picture. Their recording, made in the Chapel of Merton College, Oxford, is first class, the best of the *Missa pange lingua* and the first of the ingenious *Missa la sol fa re mi*. Not to be missed.

JOUBERT, John (born 1927)

Sinfonietta, Op. 38; Temps perdu (Variations for String Orchestra), Op. 99; (i) The Instant Moment, Op. 110

(N) ** British Music Society BMS 419CD. E. String O, Boughton; (i) with Herford

John Joubert was born in Cape Town but settled in Britain during the early years of apartheid. He taught at the Universities of Hull and Birmingham, but his large output has received scant recognition in the record catalogues. Now approaching his eighties, we must hope that he will receive some long overdue recognition. What a fine composer he is – a musician of culture and imagination. His *Variations* were inspired by his re-reading of Proust's *Swann's Way* and grew out of the proposition 'whether the process of memory could be made to work for music as it had obviously done for literature in the hands of Proust'. He returned to some short pieces for string orchestra from his youth, and a further connection with Proust comes in the shape of a little theme ('*la petite phrase*') from the *First Violin Sonata* of Saint-Saëns, which Joubert cleverly incorporates into his music. All three works are unfailingly inventive and don't waste notes. Those who feel at home in the worlds of Sibelius or Britten will respond to these fine scores. Joubert's is a quiet but distinctive voice. The performance, alas, is no more than adequate: the strings are lacking in body and tonal bloom. Nevertheless, this is recommended, for we are unlikely to have an alternative.

KABALEVSKY, Dmitri (1904–87)

Colas Breugnon: Overture & Suite; The Comedians (Suite); Romeo and Juliet (Suite)
*** ASV CDDCA 967. Armenian PO, Tjeknavorian
(BB) *** Naxos 8.553411. Moscow SO, Jelvakov

Kabalevsky speaks a patois akin to the language of Shostakovich and Prokofiev but without a scintilla of their depth and genius. The suite from *The Comedians*, music for a play called *The Inventor and the Comedian*, is cheap and cheerful, quite attractive and very well laid out for the orchestra – though, as in the score for *Romeo and Juliet* (which derives from 1956), some of its faster movements are tiresomely scatty. Still, there are others which are inventive and atmospheric.

However, Tjeknavorian's performances are characterized more sharply than Jelvakov's and in *Romeo and Juliet* these fine Armenian players find echoes of Prokofiev. Both *The Comedians* and *Colas Breugnon* are exceptionally vivid, for the ASV recording projects the orchestra in the brightest hues and with a striking presence.

The Comedians (suite), Op. 26

☛ (M) *** RCA (ADD) 09026 63302-2. RCA Victor SO, Kondrashin – KHACHATURIAN: *Masquerade Suite*; RIMSKY-KORSAKOV: *Capriccio espagnol*; TCHAIKOVSKY: *Capriccio italien* *** ✪

On the RCA collection the *Comedians' Galop* follows on almost immediately after the finale of Khachaturian's *Masquerade*, and the impetuous stylistic link is obvious. Kondrashin's performance is affectionate and colourful as well as lively, and the warm resonance of the recording helps to prevent the music from sounding too brash. The Tchaikovsky and Rimsky-Korsakov couplings are marvellous.

(i) Cello Concertos 1 in G min., Op. 49; 2 in C min., Op. 77. Spring (symphonic poem), Op. 65

(BB) **(*) Naxos 8.553788. (i) Rudin; Moscow SO, Golovschin

The enchanting *First Concerto in G minor* was written in 1949 for Kushevitzky, and it wears well. Alexander Rudin is a first-rate soloist who yields nothing to the majority of his full-priced rivals. The orchestral playing is decent and acceptable but falls short of distinction. Good recording; this Naxos disc is generally worth the money. The short, slight and charming symphonic poem is not otherwise available.

Cello Concerto 2, Op. 77

*** Chan. 8579. Wallfisch, LPO, Thomson – GLAZUNOV: *Chant du ménestrel*; KHACHATURIAN: *Concerto* ***
(BB) *** Virgin 5 61490-2 (2). Isserlis, LPO, Litton – BLOCH: *Schelomo*; ELGAR: *Cello Concerto*; R. STRAUSS: *Don Quixote*; TCHAIKOVSKY: *Rococo Variations*, etc. ***
**(*) BIS CD 719. Lindström, Gothenburg SO, Ashkenazy – KHACHATURIAN: *Cello Concerto* **(*)

Steven Isserlis on Virgin gives as compelling and ardent an account of the concerto as does Wallfisch on Chandos, since the LPO play as well for Andrew Litton as they did for Brydon Thomson, there is little to choose between them. As far as recorded sound is concerned, both are impressive; perhaps Virgin uses a slightly less resonant acoustic. The coupling will probably settle matters. Chandos offers two key Russian cello works; the Virgin bargain Double offers fine performances of concertante cello works by no fewer than five different composers!

Mats Lindström also proves an admirably sensitive soloist in Kabalevsky's *Second Concerto*. The recording is of high quality and well balanced but is a shade over-resonant, although the ear adjusts. Not a first choice, but an enjoyable performance, with no lack of spontaneity.

(i) Piano Concertos 2 in G min., Op. 23; 3 in D, Op. 50. Colas Breugnon: Overture. The Comedians, Op. 26; Suite

*** Chan. 10052. BBC PO, Sinaisky with (i) Stott

Kathryn Stott gives us two of Kabalevsky's four piano concertos, the *Second* in G minor, written in the mid-1930s and overhauled in 1973, and the *Third* in D major, premièred in 1953 (by the 17-year-old Vladimir Ashkenazy). The *Second Concerto*, which owes a great deal to Prokofiev, is extremely well crafted and proportioned. The *Third*, his 'Youth' Concerto, enjoyed the advocacy of Gilels, no less, in the mid-1950s; it is simple and direct in style, rather like the *Second Piano Concerto* of Shostakovich. Miss Stott brings both wit and charm to this slight if often predictable piece – not a work that many people will want to revisit very often – and gives a no less outstanding account of the *Second*. The BBC Philharmonic under Vassily Sinaisky give admirable support and lively and well-characterized accounts of the popular *Colas Breugnon* and *The Comedians Suite*, and the Chandos/BBC recording is first class.

Violin Concerto in C, Op. 48

☛ *** DG 457 064-2. Shaham, Russian Nat. O, Pletnev – GLAZUNOV: *Concerto*; TCHAIKOVSKY: *Souvenir d'un lieu cher*, etc. ***
*** Chan. 8918. Mordkovitch, SNO, Järvi – KHACHATURIAN: *Violin Concerto* ***

Kabalevsky's *Violin Concerto* has never enjoyed the same popularity among players as either of the cello concertos. However, its effortless invention and Prokofievian charm lend it a genuine appeal. Gil Shaham's brilliant account of the piece with Mikhail Pletnev and the Russian National Orchestra should win it many friends.

Lydia Mordkovitch also plays with great flair and aplomb and is given first-class recording. This is coupled with an equally fine version of the Khachaturian concerto, which collectors who already have the Glazunov might prefer.

Cello Sonata in B flat, Op. 71

*** Simax PSC 1146. Birkeland, Gimse – MARTINU: *Cello Sonata 1; Variations* ***

(M) *** Somm CD 029. Walton, Grimwood – MIASKOVSKY: *Cello Sonata 2*; PROKOFIEV: *Cello Sonata* ***

Instead of giving us the remaining Martinů sonatas, Øystein Birkeland and Håvard Gimse offer a Kabalevsky rarity: his *Sonata in B flat*, composed in 1962. It is one of Kabalevsky's better pieces. This new version is a first recommendation. Excellent, full-bodied and well-balanced sound, as well as being artistically impeccable. A rewarding issue.

Jamie Walton and Daniel Grimwood are young artists, and Somm deserve credit for giving them their début. Their playing is fresh and in every way unaffected.

KALINNIKOV, Vasily (1866–1901)

Intermezzos 1 in F sharp min.; 2 in G
*** Chan. 8614. RSNO, Järvi – RACHMANINOV: *Symphony 3* ***

These two colourful *Intermezzos* with a flavour of Borodin are charming.

Overtures: The Cedar and the Palm; Tsar Boris
(M) *** Chan. 7093. RSNO, Järvi – RIMSKY-KORSAKOV: *Scheherazade*, etc. ***

Kalinnikov's *Cedar and the Palm Overture*, his final work for orchestra, is an atmospheric piece (based on a Heine poem). It has eminently nostalgic Slavonic invention and, like its companion, *Tsar Boris*, vividly colourful scoring. Kalinnikov's portrayal of the Tsar, however, has none of the sombre desolation of Mussorgsky's opera and ends joyously with a resplendent fanfare. Järvi's performances with his responsive Scottish players are very sympathetic and the Chandos recording is in the demonstration class.

Symphonies 1 in G min.; 2 in A
*** Chan. 9546. RSNO, Järvi

Kalinnikov's *First Symphony* contains something akin to the flow and natural lyricism of Borodin, and the *Second* is also rewarding in a similar way if not quite as appealing as No. 1. Neeme Järvi and the Royal Scottish National Orchestra recorded these delightful works in 1987 and 1989 respectively. These are spacious, well-performed performances and exemplary recordings.

KÁLMÁN, Emmerich (1882–1953)

Countess Maritza (highlights; in English)
**(*) TER CDTER 1051. Hill-Smith, Remedios, Livingstone, Moyle, Rice, Martin, Barber, Bullock, New Sadler's Wells O, Wordsworth

Set in the Hungarian countryside, *Countess Maritza* gave Kálmán plenty of chances to display his skill in writing memorable numbers with a Hungarian flavour. The plot is slight, but the nostalgic *Luck is a Golden Dream*, sung by Lynn Barber as a gypsy girl, sets the scene, followed by the delightful *How Do You Do*, characterfully sung by Count Tassilo, the opera's hero, with children's chorus. But the score's highlight must be the evocative *Vienna Mine*, one of the composer's most catchy melodies, although Remedios has not quite the easy smoothness of a Tauber to make it as captivating as it might be. Marilyn Hill-Smith as the Countess, singing with her customary style, is charming in the sentimental duet with the Count, *Be Mine, My Love*, as well as in the aria, *Set the Gypsy Music Playing* – another popular hit. The opera ends

with a swinging waltz. Barry Wordsworth conducts securely and catches the spirit of Kálmán's world with a fair degree of success. The recording, though perhaps not ideally atmospheric, is reasonably full and bright. The English translation works with varying degrees of success, but operetta fans should not be too disappointed.

Die Csárdásfürstin (The Gypsy Princess)
(N) (BB) *** Naxos 8.660105/6 (2). Kenny, Roider, Erdmann, Kathol, Slovak Philh. Ch., Slovak RSO, Bonynge
(M) **(*) Oehms OC 201. Serafin, Ronald, Bothmer, Grotrian, Eröd, Mörbisch Festival Ch. & O, Bible

Die Csárdásfürstin tells an improbable tale of the mismatch between a showgirl, Sylva, and an aristocrat, Prince Edwin. During the First World War it was immensely popular in Vienna, when it pictured an imperial world on the verge of extinction. Richard Bonynge conducts a lively, beautifully sprung performance, made the more idiomatic by using an East European orchestra. Yvonne Kenny as Sylva gives a characterful, idiomatic performance, well supported by singers very much in the operetta tradition, and by Michael Roider as Edwin and Mojca Erdmann and Marko Kathol as the second couple. Well produced, the numbers are introduced by a sprinkling of dialogue. The first-rate sound brings out the beauty of Kálmán's orchestration.

Martina Serafin proves a spirited Sylva, and if at times she is a little shrill, the lively numbers such as *O jag dem Glück nicht nach* are dispatched with spirit. Edwin Ronald makes an attractive Prince with his light but secure tenor, and the rest of the cast provides ebullient support. The recording is warm and well balanced, but it is a little confined in the upper register, failing to open out as it should. Only a German text is provided (the dialogue is omitted in this recording) but the CD is offered at mid-price.

KANCHELI, Giya (born 1935)

Mourned by the Wind; Simi (both for cello & orchestra)
(N) *** Chan. 10297. Ivashkin, Russian State SO, Polyansky

Giya Kancheli was born in Tbilisi, Georgia, but moved to Berlin in 1991, and then in 1994 settled in Belgium. His music has undoubtedly absorbed influences from his homeland, yet it also shows awareness of the Western avant-garde, though it is productive and never nihilistic. *Simi* is subtitled 'Bleak reflections for cello and orchestra', yet its sustained desolation of mood is never barren but a threnody whose ruminative cello oscillations are part of a rhapsodical structure, imbued with much darkness of orchestral colour and punctuated by violent orchestral surprises, but never immolating itself in hopelessness.

Mourned by the Wind is similarly threnodic, a concertante liturgy remembering a close friend, and the writing is profoundly ruminative but even more thematically lyrical within a four-movement structure. For the most part it again becomes a slow, intense elegy, and is held together in this performance by the powerful concentration of the playing, with the soloist often moving gently and quietly into the upper range of the cello. The passages of surging forward momentum, in the finale hinting at a funeral dirge, are only sporadic. It is a remarkable work and distinctly original, but some listeners may find it too static. The recording, as usual from Chandos, is superbly full and atmospheric.

KARLOWICZ, Mieczyslaw (1876–1909)

Bianca da Molina (Symphonic Prologue); Rebirth Symphony; Serenade

*** Chan. 10171. BBC PO, Noseda

Mieczyslaw Karlowicz, killed in an Alpine avalanche at the age of 32, might well have developed into a major figure in Polish music. Though these are all early works, written or conceived when he was still studying in Berlin, they have an individuality and richness of invention that are immediately attractive. *Bianca da Molina*, the symphonic prologue for a play, opens magically with shimmering strings and brassy fanfares, anticipating Respighi's *Pines of Rome* by two decades. Karlowicz's orchestral mastery shines throughout. The four movements of the *Serenade* have a winning lightness of touch, with a haunting waltz as third movement, while the *Rebirth Symphony*, much weightier, relates to Tchaikovsky on the one hand, to Richard Strauss on the other, but remains individual in its structure, warmly lyrical, built on memorable themes. Those who feel at home in the musical world of Suk or Novák will respond to his musical language and will lose no time in investigating this successor. Under Gianandrea Noseda the BBC Philharmonic gives strong, persuasive performances, opulently recorded.

Violin Concerto in A, Op. 8

*** Hyp. CDA 67389. Little, BBC Scottish SO, Brabbins – MOSZKOWSKI: *Violin Concerto, etc.* ***

Like the works on Noseda's Chandos disc, this *Violin Concerto* demonstrates the mastery of this sadly short-lived composer. Written in 1902, it marked a turning point in Karlowicz's career, a piece which – in an inspired performance like this from Tasmin Little – emerges as a long-neglected masterpiece. It may bring echoes of Tchaikovsky, not least in the glowing horn motif at the very start (like the opening of the *First Piano Concerto* in reverse), but Karlowicz's personal tone of voice, strong and inventive, with one striking theme after another, is securely established in each well-constructed movement, all superbly orchestrated, not least for the brass section. Warm, vivid sound. With the Moszkowski works, a valuable addition to Hyperion's 'Romantic Violin Concerto' series.

Eternal Songs, Op. 10; Lithuanian Rhapsody, Op. 11; Stanislaw and Anna Oswiecim, Op. 12

*** Chan. 9986. BBC PO, Y. P. Tortelier

Mieczyslaw Karlowicz was only six years older than Szymanowski, but his life was cut short when he was only 32. He was born into a noble family and studied the violin in Prague, Dresden and Heidelberg. His music is steeped in the language of Wagner and Strauss, but there is a lively imagination at work here, and readers interested in composers like Suk and Novák will find his world congenial and rewarding. He is given the most committed advocacy from Yan Pascal Tortelier and the BBC Philharmonic and excellent recording. Not a fully formed master, perhaps, but a very likeable and interesting composer.

KERLL, Johann Casper (1627–93)

Battaglia; Canzonas 1–6; Capriccio sopra' il cucu; Ciaccona; Passacaglia; Ricercata; Toccatas 1–8

(N) *** Oehms OC 362. Kelemen (organ of Prömonstrate Abbey, Schlögl)

Johann Kerll was born in Saxony, and in his youth he entered the service of the Habsburg Archduke, Leopold Wilhelm, who sent him to Italy to study under Carissimi. On his return he became court organist in Brussels before being appointed Kapellmeister in the Munich Bavarian Court. In 1677 he moved to Vienna (where this music was probably composed) then back to Munich, where he spent the rest of his life. The young Bach knew Kerll's music, and Handel borrowed from his imitative 'Cuckoo' Capriccio for the famous organ concerto, which includes also a 'nightingale'. This collection contains all of Kerll's keyboard music that is suitable for the organ, here a modernized historic instrument that keeps or simulates the original sounds, often piquant with a 'throaty' tutti. Kerll's *Toccatas* and *Canzonas* are attractively inventive, extrovert pieces, not too complicated and often based on climbing or descending scalic figures: the *Canzona sesta* is very like a peal of bells. The ingenuous *Battaglia* uses all the organ's resources for its imitative effects, which Joseph Kelemen manages with aplomb. He also makes the most of the decorative figurations of the masterly closing *Passacaglia*, the longest and the most impressive work here. The recording is excellent.

KERN, Jerome (1885–1945)

Overtures: (i) *The Cat and the Fiddle; The Girl from Utah; Have a Heart; Leave It to Jane; O, Lady! Lady!;* (ii) *Show Boat;* (i) *Sitting Pretty; Sweet Adeline; Very Warm for May.* (i; iii) Film music: *Swing Time* (suite)

(B) ** EMI double forte 5 68589-2 (2). (i) Nat. PO; (ii) L. Sinf.; (iii) Ambrosian Ch.; McGlinn – GERSHWIN: *Broadway & Film Music* **(*); PORTER: *Overtures* ***

These Jerome Kern overtures, recorded from the original band-parts of musicals dating from between 1914 (*The Girl from Utah*) and 1939 (*Very Warm for May*), are musically unimpressive. They are all played with an infectious sense of style, but really memorable tunes are thin on the ground. In *Sweet Adeline*, instead of his own material, Kern uses a pot-pourri of period songs from the 1890s, including *Daisy, Daisy* and *The band played on*. By far the most attractive music comes in the film score from *Swing Time*, which includes *The way you look tonight*. For this reissue, the *Overture* from McGlinn's complete recording of *Show Boat* has been added, but that is not much more than a pot-pourri.

Songs from musicals: *Centennial Summer: All through the day. Cover Girl: Long ago and far away. High, Wide and Handsome: The folks who live on the hill. Lady be Good: The last time I saw Paris. Music in the Air: The song is you. Roberta: Yesterdays; Smoke gets in your eyes. Sally: Look for the silver lining. Show Boat: Can't help lovin' dat man. Swing Time: The way you look tonight. Very Warm for May: All the things you are. You were Never Lovelier: I'm old fashioned*

*** EMI 7 54527-2. Te Kanawa, L. Sinf., Tunick

Kiri Te Kanawa proves completely at home in these luscious and life-enhancing Kern favourites. Her rich vocal line is matched by a nice feeling for the wittier lyrics. But it's the tunes that count, and she revels in them. So does Jonathan Tunick, who has scored the accompaniments; and the London Sinfonietta obviously enjoy themselves too, yet there is also a sense of sophistication and style. Excellent recording.

Show Boat (complete recording of original score)

⊶ ✪ *** EMI 7 49108-2 (3). Von Stade, Hadley, Hubbard, O'Hara, Garrison, Burns, Stratas, Amb. Ch., L. Sinf., McGlinn

In faithfully following the original score, this superb set at last does justice to a musical of the 1920s which is both a landmark in the history of Broadway and musically a work of strength and imagination hardly less significant than Gershwin's *Porgy and Bess* of a decade later. The original, extended versions of important scenes are included, as well as various numbers written for later productions. As the heroine, Magnolia, Frederica von Stade gives a meltingly beautiful performance, totally in style, bringing out the beauty and imagination of Kern's melodies, regularly heightened by wide intervals to make those of most of his Broadway rivals seem flat. The London Sinfonietta play with tremendous zest and feeling for the idiom; the Ambrosian Chorus sings with joyful brightness and some impeccable American accents. Opposite von Stade, Jerry Hadley makes a winning Ravenal, and Teresa Stratas is charming as Julie, giving a heartfelt performance of the haunting number, *Bill* (words by P. G. Wodehouse). Above all, the magnificent black bass, Bruce Hubbard, sings *Ol' man river* and its many reprises with a firm resonance to have you recalling the wonderful example of Paul Robeson, but for once without hankering after the past. Beautifully recorded to bring out the piece's dramatic as well as its musical qualities, this is a heart-warming issue.

KHACHATURIAN, Aram (1903–78)

Cello Concerto in E min.

*** Chan. 8579. R. Wallfisch, LPO, Thomson – GLAZUNOV: *Chant du ménestrel;* KABALEVSKY: *Cello Concerto 2* ***
(*) BIS CD 719. Lindström, Gothenburg SO, Ashkenazy (with RACHMANINOV: *Vocalise* *) – KABALEVSKY: *Cello Concerto* **(*)

Khachaturian's *Cello Concerto* of 1946 has some sinuous Armenian local colour for its lyrical ideas, but none of the thematic memorability of the concertos for violin and piano and the *Gayaneh Ballet* score, on which Khachaturian's reputation must continue to rest. Raphael Wallfisch plays with total commitment and has the benefit of excellent and sympathetic support. The recording is of the high standard we have come to expect from Chandos.

The combined concentration of Lindström and Ashkenazy prevents the writing from sounding too inflated. The recording is a bit over-resonant, but otherwise faithful and well balanced. As an encore we are given a fine if restrained account of Rachmaninov's *Vocalise.* An enjoyable if not, in the last resort, memorable coupling.

(i) *Cello Concerto in E min.;* (ii) *Violin Concerto in D*

*** Chan. 9866. (i) R. Wallfisch, LPO, Thomson; (ii) Mordkovitch, RSNO, Järvi

On the face of it it would seem a sensible idea to re-couple Raphael Wallfisch's sympathetic and committed account of the *Cello Concerto* with Lydia Mordkovitch's even more fiery account of the *Violin Concerto*, particularly as they both have outstandingly realistic Chandos recordings. However, the music itself is uneven – the work for violin is an underrated masterpiece of great vitality, but the work for cello cannot match it in melodic inspiration. None the less, admirers of the composer should be well satisfied.

Flute Concerto (arr. of *Violin Concerto*)

*** EMI 5 57563-2. Pahud, Tonhalle O, Zinman – IBERT: *Flute Concerto* ***

Emmanuel Pahud and the Zurich Tonhalle Orchestra under David Zinman give a pretty dazzling account of Jean-Pierre Rampal's transcription of the Khachaturian *Violin Concerto.* If you like the concerto in this particular form, not only is the performance outstanding, so also is the recorded sound.

Piano Concerto in D flat

(B) (***) RCA Double mono 74321 845952 (2). Kapell, Boston SO, Koussevitzky – CHOPIN: *Sonata 2;* DEBUSSY: *Children's Corner;* PROKOFIEV: *Piano Concerto 3* (***); RACHMANINOV: *Rhapsody on a Theme of Paganini* (with SHOSTAKOVICH: *3 Preludes;* SCHUBERT: *Impromptu; Ländler; Moment musical; Waltzes* ***)
(BB) (***) Naxos mono 8.110673. Kapell, Boston SO, Koussevitzky – PROKOFIEV: *Piano Concerto 3* (***); SHOSTAKOVICH: *3 Preludes; Piano Concerto 3* (***)
(M) **(*) Hyp. CDA 66293. Servadei, LPO, Giunta – BRITTEN: *Piano Concerto* **(*)

(i) *Piano Concerto in D flat. Dance Suite; Polka & Waltz* (both for wind band)

⊶ *** ASV CDDCA 964. (i) Serviarian-Kuhn; Armenian PO, Tjeknavorian

(i) *Piano Concerto in D flat. Gayaneh* (ballet) *Suite; Masquerade: Suite*

**(*) Chan. 8542. (i) Orbelian; SNO, Järvi

(i) *Piano Concerto in D flat. Sonatina; Toccata*

(N) (BB) ** ASV Resonance RSN 037. Portugheis; (i) LSO, Tjeknavorian

There is not a great deal to choose between these two transfers of the legendary Kapell recording with Koussevitzky, although it is at least possible to read the notes with the Naxos. The RCA 'artwork' is dreadful and renders detail illegible: moreover, no recording dates are given. The performance is the greatest account of the Khachaturian – ever! Quite electrifying and inspiriting, although Koussevitzky's presence at the helm also has something to do with it. The same must also be said for the Prokofiev. The RCA transfer does not give us the Prokofiev but includes an extraordinary Rachmaninov *Paganini Rhapsody.*

The Armenian partnership of Dora Serviarian-Kuhn and Loris Tjeknavorian provides a clear first recommendation for a modern version of Khachaturian's somewhat uneven *Piano Concerto*, easily the finest account to have appeared on disc since the pioneering versions of William Kapell and Moura Lympany. The Russian dance finale has plenty of dash, but what makes the performance individual is the sense of quixotic fantasy Serviarian-Kuhn brings to her cadential bravura. The bright piano-timbre and comparatively lean orchestral textures are not a disadvantage in a work that can too easily sound inflated. The other pieces on the ASV disc are very slight but lively enough; easily the most memorable item is the second *Uzbek Dance* in the *Dance Suite*, quite extended and touchingly atmospheric.

The Chandos recording is splendid technically, well up to the standards of the house. Constantin Orbelian, an Armenian by birth, plays brilliantly, and Järvi achieves much attractive lyrical detail. Overall it is a spacious account, and though the finale has plenty of gusto, the music-making seems just a shade too easygoing in the first movement. The couplings, sumptuously played, are both generous and appealing.

Annette Servadei makes up in clarity and point for a relative lack of weight in the outer movements, which she takes at speeds marginally slower than usual. The slow movement brings hushed and intense playing, sympathetically supported by the LPO under Joseph Giunta in a digital recording that is well balanced and unaggressive. However, ideally this work needs a stronger grip than these artists exert – the first movement in particular could do with greater thrust.

Alberto Portugheis's time for the first movement of the *Concerto* is 15" 4', and the effect is to make the music sound rambling. The rest of the performance goes well (the flexitone is used with confidence to good effect) and the recording is admirably vivid. But the couplings are ungenerous: the *Sonatina* is an insubstantial piece and the more memorable *Toccata* is merely a spirited encore.

(i) *Piano Concerto in D flat;* (ii) *Violin Concerto in D min.;* (iii) *Masquerade Suite;* (iv) *Symphony 2*

(B) **(*) Double Decca (ADD) 448 252-2 (2). (i) De Larrocha, LPO, Frühbeck de Burgos; (ii) Ricci, LPO, Fistoulari; (iii) LSO, Black; (iv) VPO, composer

The key performance here is the composer's own – of the *Second Symphony*. His advocacy is passionate and the recording is spectacular. The slow movement of the *Piano Concerto* as interpreted by a Spanish pianist and a Spanish conductor sounds evocatively like Falla, and the finale is also infectiously jaunty. Not so the first movement, which is disappointingly slack in rhythm at a dangerously slow tempo. Ricci is a good deal more consistent in the *Violin Concerto*. He does not supply quite the demonic energy which the outer movements ideally call for, but his lyrical approach has its own attractions, and the closing pages of the slow movement are wonderfully atmospheric. The late-1950s recording does not have the projection we would expect today, but Ricci's fine playing is well focused. The *Masquerade Suite* is consistently alive and colourful and is vividly if forwardly recorded.

Violin Concerto in D min.

☛━ ✱ (M) *** RCA [ADD] 09026 63708-2. Kogan, Boston SO, Monteux – PROKOFIEV: *Alexander Nevsky* *** ✪

(N) *** Pentatone **SACD** PTC 5186 059. Fischer, Russian Nat. O, Kreizberg – GLAZUNOV: *Violin Concerto ***;* PROKOFIEV: *Violin Concerto 1 ***

*** HM Naïve V 4959. Sergey Khachaturian, Sinfonia Varsovia, Krivine – SIBELIUS: *Violin Concerto ***

*** Chan. 8918. Mordkovitch, SNO, Järvi – KABALEVSKY: *Violin Concerto ***

Violin Concerto in D min.; Concerto-Rhapsody for Violin & Orchestra

(BB) **(*) Naxos 8.555919. Martin, Ukraine Nat. SO, Kuchar

Leonid Kogan's powerfully direct approach to this once-popular concerto, aided by superlative playing from the Boston Symphony Orchestra under Monteux, is electrifying. Together, they make it sound like an unqualified masterpiece, and the astonishingly vivid (1958) recording puts many digital recordings to shame with its vivid presence. This is the most exciting performance of Khachaturian's underrated concerto that you can buy.

Julia Fischer offers the first Surround Sound SACD of this attractive concerto, made in May 2004 in Moscow – and very

impressive it is in its vividness and presence and in the clarity of the orchestral sound. The recording was a labour of love, the more attractive to her when she was able to choose the two other Russian concertos on the disc for a very generous coupling. The clarity and freshness of her performance of the Khachaturian are what immediately strike home in the chattering figuration at the start, with a rare tenderness developing in the lyrical second subject. The yearning tenderness of the slow movement confirms that this was one of the composer's most inspired works in a performance of high contrasts, while the biting clarity of Fischer's performance in the finale brings lightness and sparkle. The unique coupling of two more Russian violin concertos could hardly be more recommendable, and both are just as superbly recorded.

The young Sergey Khachaturian has already made his name with performances in Europe and Tokyo of this very underrated concerto. He has found an ideal partner in Emmanuel Krivine, who brings out all the colourfully imaginative orchestral detail to match the soloist's commanding lyrical flow, especially in the unforgettable, sinuous main theme of the first movement. The *Andante* produces another haunting Armenian melody, and the soloist phrases it exquisitely, then ruminates poetically until, with the reprise, Krivine produces the composer's thrillingly brash orchestral climax, and the movement ends gently. The finale sets off with tremendous gusto and, when the winding melody of the first movement reappears, soloist and orchestra are perfectly integrated. With splendid recording, spacious, open and wide-ranging, this highly spontaneous account now goes to the top of the list of modern recordings of this rewardingly melodic concerto.

Among other recent performances of this attractively inventive concerto, Lydia Mordkovitch is probably the most competitive. She plays with real abandon and fire, and Chandos balance her and the orchestra in a thoroughly realistic perspective.

The Romanian-born Mihaela Martin and the Ukraine National Symphony Orchestra, directed by Theodor Kuchar, also play the concerto very sympathetically. Martin has a rich timbre, and the sinuous melodies, especially that of the *Andante*, sit warmly on her bow, and there is no lack of impetus and energy in the finale. Orchestra and soloist are well balanced and recorded, but there is a studio-ish feel to the recording and the overall effect has less flair. However, she also gives us the much rarer 1992 *Concerto-Rhapsody*, written for Leonid Kogan. It has to be said that this is a less inspired work, with much less memorable invention; but Martin and Kuchar make as strong a case for the piece as possible, and their performance is very successful.

(i) *Gayaneh* (ballet; original, 1942 score), Op. 50; (ii) *Masquerade (Suite); Spartacus* (excerpts); *Russian Fantasy*

(N) (B) *** RCA 82876 65836-2 (2). (i) Nat. PO; (ii) LSO, Tjeknavorian

Khachaturian began his score for *Gayaneh* in 1939 but later revised it during the period which also produced the *Violin Concerto*. It was completed in 1942 and is among his finest works. Not all the music has the quality of invention of the best-known items but, taken as a whole, the ballet with its lively dance-rhythms and strong colours offers plenty to enjoy. It is admirably played here under a conductor (himself an Armenian, like the composer) who has a natural feeling for Khachaturian's music. However, that was not the end of the story, for the composer later reworked the score to fit a new scenario, as the earlier narrative (set on a collective farm and with an ingenuous wartime moral tone) had become embarrassing to the Soviets. The expanded version was published as Op. 89, and here the fresh inspiration of the original is often vulgarized – it is a case of all loss and no gain. So we must be grateful that this well-balanced recording of the original is now available again, coupled to naturally sympathetic performances of the *Masquerade Suite* and excerpts from *Spartacus* (with the great *Adagio* splendidly expansive and passionate), recorded a decade later. The *Russian Fantasy* is not memorable, but the set as a whole is indispensable.

Gayaneh (ballet; excerpts); *Spartacus* (ballet; excerpts)
☞ (M) *** Decca (ADD) 460 315-2. VPO, composer – GLAZUNOV: *The Seasons* **(*)
**(*) Chant du Monde RUS 288171. Bolshoi Theatre O, Svetlanov

Gayaneh (ballet): *Suite*; *Masquerade*: *Suite*; *Spartacus* (ballet): *Suite*
(*) ASV (ADD) CDDCA 773. Armenian PO, Tjeknavorian – IPPOLITOV-IVANOV: *Caucasian Sketches* *

Gayaneh (ballet): *Suite*; *Masquerade*: *Waltz & Mazurka*. *Spartacus* (ballet): *Suite*
(BB) *** Warner Apex 8573 89237-2. Bolshoi SO, Lazarev

Gayaneh (ballet; highlights); *Spartacus* (ballet; highlights)
(B) *** CfP (ADD) 767 7522. LSO, composer (with GLAZUNOV: *The Seasons: Autumn*: Philh. O, Svetlanov ***)

Khachaturian came to Vienna in 1962 to record these inspired performances of the most popular numbers from his two ballets, and this Decca record (reissued in Decca's 'Legends' series) is the one to go for. It is superbly remastered to restore and even improve on the demonstration quality of the original LP, recorded in the Sofiensaal. Like the sound, the performances are very fresh. The Glazunov coupling, if not quite so fine, is very well played and shows Ansermet at his best. As usual in this series, good documentation and photographs of both conductors.

The composer's later, EMI Classics for Pleasure selections from his two famous ballets offer one more item from *Gayaneh* than on his earlier, Decca coupling. The EMI sound, obviously more modern than the Decca, is a shade reverberant for the more vigorous numbers, but the present remastering presents a firmer focus than on LP. The LSO play excitingly throughout. The inclusion of only *Autumn* from Glazunov's *Seasons* decreases the appeal of this CD, when the competing Decca disc offers the whole ballet.

At the opening of Alexander Lazarev's Bolshoi CD, the famous *Sabre Dance* bursts into the room spectacularly, with thumping drums and blazing percussion, and the *Lezginka* is similarly vibrant and exciting. Yet *Ayshe's awakening* could not be more evocative with its growling bass clarinet. The two best-known *Masquerade* items are brightly done, but with plenty of dynamic shading to counter the ebullience. Then Lazarev opens his *Spartacus* selection with the famous *Adagio*, and the gentle oboe solo and languorous Bolshoi strings soon expand passionately. In short, with extremely spectacular, if reverberant, recording, this super-bargain reissue makes an easy first choice for those wanting a modern digital selection of this music.

The Armenians also clearly relish the explosive energy of this music. The *Masquerade Suite* relies rather more on charm for its appeal, but Tjeknavorian and his players bring a determined gusto, even to the *Waltz* and certainly to the

ebullient closing *Galop*. Then the vibrant Spartacus and his ardent lover Phrygia come on stage with a great flare of passion in a melody that is justly famous. One wishes the recording were more sumptuous here, but for the most part its burnished primary colours suit the dynamic orchestral style.

Svetlanov's recordings were made as recently as January 2000, and both he and the Bolshoi Theatre Orchestra are in very good form. His ear for detail is as perceptive as ever and his handling of phrasing and dynamics is ever-sensitive. The famous *Adagio* from *Spartacus* is both ardent and refined, and the genre dances are beautifully played, a potent mixture of sinuousness and charm. There is plenty of rhythmic energy and vitality in the *Gayaneh lezginka* and the *Sabre Dance*, but both Tjeknavorian and the composer play this music more vibrantly and passionately still. Yet with excellent recording these Bolshoi performances do not lack appeal. They are certainly never dull.

Masquerade Suite
☞ (M) *** RCA (ADD) 09026 63302-2. RCA Victor SO, Kondrashin – KABALEVSKY: *The Comedians Suite*; RIMSKY-KORSAKOV: *Capriccio espagnol*; TCHAIKOVSKY: *Capriccio italien* *** ●

Kondrashin certainly knows how to play this music, with warmth as well as sparkle, and even a touch of romantic elegance when Oscar Shumsky plays the violin solo in the *Nocturne*. Yet the final *Galop* is as boisterous as one could wish. The resonant recording gives the orchestra a pleasing ambience.

Spartacus (ballet): *Suites 1–3*
*** Chan. 8927. RSNO, Järvi

The ripe lushness of Khachaturian's scoring in *Spartacus* narrowly skirts vulgarity. Järvi and the RSNO clearly enjoy the music's tunefulness and primitive vigour, while the warmly resonant acoustics of Glasgow's Henry Wood Hall bring properly sumptuous orchestral textures, smoothing over the moments of crudeness without losing the Armenian colouristic vividness.

Symphonies 1 in E min.; 3 in C (Symphonic Poem)
*** ASV CDDCA 858. Armenian PO, Tjeknavorian

The *First Symphony* was Khachaturian's exercise on graduating from Miaskovsky's class in 1934. It is far from negligible and in some ways is superior to some of his later work – certainly to the bombastic *Third*. Now there is a modern account from Armenia under Loris Tjeknavorian which enjoys the advantage of good digital recording. The Armenian orchestra play well for Tjeknavorian, and his is a safe recommendation.

Symphony 2 in E min. (The Bell); Battle of Stalingrad (suite)
**(*) ASV CDDCA 859. Armenian PO, Tjeknavorian

Symphony 2 (original version); *Gayaneh: Suite* (excerpts)
*** Chan. 8945. RSNO, Järvi

The *Second Symphony* comes from 1943 but the composer subsequently made a number of revisions, the last in 1969, which Tjeknavorian has recorded. It acquired its nickname, 'The Bell', because of a motive heard on tubular bells, and in the slow movement makes fascinating use of the *Dies irae*.

Neeme Järvi and his Scottish forces give a very fine account of themselves and they enjoy the benefit of a superb recording. It runs to some 51 minutes, while Tjeknavorian's account of the final revision prunes the score down to 42 minutes 45 seconds. The suite from *The Battle of Stalingrad* is taken from a score composed for a patriotic film and is empty and inflated.

(i) Symphony 3 (Symphonic Poem); Triumphal Poem
*** Chan. 9321. BBC PO, Glushchenko, (i) with Lindley –
IPPOLITOV-IVANOV: *Caucasian Sketches* ***

If the *Third Symphony* was as strong on musical substance as it is on decibels, it would be something to reckon with. But, alas, it is garish and empty; there are no fewer than 18 trumpets in all! Analgesics and earplugs will be in brisk demand in its vicinity. The BBC Philharmonic, spurred on by their Russian conductor, play as if they believe in it, and the Chandos recording is in the demonstration category. The three stars are for the performance and the recording – not for the music!

The Valencian Widow (incidental music): Suite; Gayaneh (ballet): Suite 2
*** ASV CDDCA 884. Armenian PO, Tjeknavorian (with
TJEKNAVORIAN: *Danses fantastiques* **(*))

Khachaturian's early suite from his incidental music to the Spanish comedy *The Valencian Widow* (1940) is probably his first major score and, brimming over with striking tunes as it is, one is surprised that it has not been discovered by the gramophone before this. This is the Khachaturian of *Gayaneh*, so the coupling of seven lesser-known excerpts from that fine ballet score is very appropriate. Tjeknavorian and his orchestra play this music with great spirit and they relish its Armenian flavours; they are equally at home in Tjeknavorian's own suite of *Danses fantastiques*, full of energy and colour, if essentially sub-Khachaturian. Splendidly vivid, yet spacious sound.

PIANO MUSIC

10 Children's Pieces; 2 Pieces; Poem; Sonata; Sonatina; Toccata; Waltz (from Masquerade)
(N) (BB) **(*) Regis RR 1184. McLachlan

Apart from the *Toccata* (1932), which is a frequent encore, Khachaturian's piano music rarely features in piano recitals. At 80 minutes, this CD offers all of it with the exception of the *Scenes from Childhood* and the *Recitative and Fugues*. The early pieces, *Poem* (1927) and the *Valse-caprice* and *Dance* (1926), are much like the *Toccata*, pretty empty, but the later pieces including the *Sonatina* (1959), the *Ten Children's Pieces* (1964) and the *Sonata* (1961) are worth a hearing, even though they are limited in range and rely on a small vocabulary of musical devices. Murray McLachlan is a persuasive guide. His recording, made at All Saints' Church, Petersham, is eminently serviceable, though there are times when the attentions of a tuner would not have come amiss (particularly in the garrulous first movement of the *Sonata*).

KNUSSEN, Oliver (born 1952)

(i) Horn Concerto, Op. 28. Flourish with Fireworks, Op. 22; Music for a Puppet Court, Op. 11; Two Organa, Op. 27; '... Upon One Note' (Fantasia after Purcell); The Way to Castle Yonder, Op. 21a. (ii) Whitman Settings, Op. 25a
*** DG 474 322-2. L. Sinf., composer, with (i) Tuckwell; (ii) Shelton

This collection of seven of Oliver Knussen's shorter works, brilliantly performed and recorded under his own baton, consistently brings out his fascination with original and exotic orchestral sounds. The very opening *Flourish with Fireworks*, written for Michael Tilson Thomas's first concert as music director of the LSO, brings magical textures, with sidelong references to Stravinsky's early piece, *Fireworks*, a favourite of Tilson Thomas's. *The Way to Castle Yonder* re-cycles three evocative passages from Knussen's opera for children, *Higglety Piggelty Pop*, and the *Horn Concerto* that he wrote for Barry Tuckwell in 1994 exploits the solo instrument in gloriously ripe sounds, with the longest of the four compact movements, *Fantastico*, bringing the most exuberant fantasy, designed to make full use of the acoustic of the Sun Tory Hall in Tokyo, which sponsored the commission. Tuckwell's playing, recorded in 1995, is masterly. The two *Organa* exploit medieval techniques, and *Music for a Puppet Court*, using two antiphonal chamber orchestras, is developed from puzzle-canons attributed to the Tudor composer John Lloyd. Most challenging is the final item, the *Whitman Settings* written for Lucy Shelton, the soloist on this disc, with the angular vocal line obscuring rather than illuminating the four short poems on big themes. Brilliant playing from the London Sinfonietta, matched by full, immediate sound.

Higglety Pigglety Pop!, Op. 21; Where the Wild Things Are, Op. 20.
*** DG 469 556-2 (2) Buchan, Saffer, Hardy, Gillett, Wilson-Johnson, Richardson, King, London Sinf., composer

These two one-Act operas, based on the books of Maurice Sendak, will please children of all ages, reflecting child-fantasies that so delight youngsters, while giving adult listeners many musical insights both witty and searching. Originally intended as a double-bill, they were written in reverse order between 1979 and 1985, with *Higglety-Pigglety Pop!* revised in 1999. It follows the idiosyncratic fortunes of the Sealyham, Jennie, delightfully characterized by Cynthia Buchan. It is the more complex of the two operas, leading to a play within a play, marked by colourful fanfares.

Where the Wild Things Are, more compact, at times more violent, relates even more closely to the example of Ravel's *L'Enfant et les sortilèges*, involving Max, a boy in a wolf suit (Lisa Saffer excellent), who travels by boat to the land of the Wild Things and is there crowned king, only to return from his Rumpus-bound dream in time for supper. Oliver Knussen's evocation of a child-world is at once open and innocent in approach and charmingly sophisticated in expression. With consistently fine casts and brilliant playing from the London Sinfonietta he could not be more persuasive in performances recorded immediately after live concerts. Brilliant, atmospheric sound. The packaging adds to the charm of the issue.

KODÁLY, Zoltán (1882–1967)

Concerto for Orchestra
*** Australian Decca Eloquence (ADD) 467 602-2. Philh. Hungarica, Dorati – JANACEK: *Taras Bulba*; BARTOK: *Concerto for Orchestra* ***

Concerto for Orchestra; Dances of Marosszék; Symphony in C; Theatre Overture
*** Chan. 9811. BBC PO, Y. P. Tortelier

Concerto for Orchestra; Dances of Galánta; Dances of Marosszék; Háry János: Suite; Symphony in C; Summer Evening; Theatre Overture; Variations on a Hungarian Folksong (The Peacock)

(B) *** Double Decca (ADD) 443 006-2 (2). Philh. Hungarica, Dorati

Yan–Pascal Tortelier and the BBC Philharmonic prove a superb partnership here, while the Chandos and BBC engineering team have surpassed themselves to produce demonstration quality. Kodály's *Concerto for Orchestra* was written for the Chicago orchestra and Bartók actually took it with him to America in 1940. This, the *Dances of Marosszék* and the *Theatre Overture* leave no doubt that Kodály was a pastmaster of the orchestra, and these showpieces receive their full due on this highly recommendable issue.

The *Symphony* comes from the composer's last years and lacks real concentration and cohesion. Even so, in Dorati's hands the passionate *Andante* is strong in gypsy feeling and the jolly, folk-dance finale, if repetitive, is colourful and full of vitality. *Summer Evening*, too, is warmly evocative, but in the *Theatre Overture*, brightly and effectively scored, the invention is thin. The 1973 sound remains of vintage quality, and the CD transfers are first rate.

Dorati's warmly committed performance of Kodály's *Concerto for Orchestra* in fine analogue sound is also available in Australia with the more obvious coupling of Bartók's *Concerto*, while Janáček's *Taras Bulba* is equally worth having.

Dances of Galánta

(N) *** Linn CKD 234. Scottish CO, Mackerras – BARTOK: *Divertimento; Music for Strings, Percussion & Celesta* ***

On Linn, the *Dances from Galánta* make a valuable supplement for Sir Charles Mackerras's warm, refined readings of the two great Bartók works. In this genial work he brings out the dance element delectably, and the recording brings out the colourfulness of Kodály's orchestration.

Dances of Galánta; Dances of Marosszék

(BB) ** Warner Apex 0927 48732-2. St Paul Chamber O, Wolff – BARTOK: *Divertimento; Romanian Folk Dances* ***

Dances of Galánta; Dances of Marosszék; Háry János Suite; (i) Psalmus Hungaricus, Op. 13

(M) *** DG mono/stereo 457 745-2. Berlin R.I.A.S., Fricsay, (i) with Ernst Haefliger, St Hedwig's Cathedral Ch.

Dances of Galánta; Dances of Marosszék; (i) Háry János Suite, Instrumental Excerpts & Singspiel; Gergëly-Járás; (ii) Táncnóa; Túrót eszik a cigány

⊶ *** Ph. 462 824-2. Budapest Festival O, Fischer; with (i) Children's Ch. Magnificat, Budapest; (ii) Children's Ch. Miraculum, Kecskemét

(i) Dances of Galánta; (ii) Dances of Marosszék; Háry János Suite; (i) Variations on a Hungarian Folksong (The Peacock)

**(*) BIS CD 875. (i) Brno State PO; (ii) SWF SO, Baden-Baden; Serebrier

Dances of Galánta; Háry János Suite

*** Delos DE 3083. Seattle SO, Schwarz – BARTOK: *Miraculous Mandarin* **(*)

Dances of Galánta; Háry János Suite; Variations on a Hungarian Folksong (The Peacock)

**(*) Telarc CD 80413. Atlanta SO, Levi

Iván Fischer's Kodály is no less successful than his Bartók

records. His set has the advantage of totally idiomatic playing from a very fine orchestra and superbly well-defined recording from the Philips engineers. This is now the front-runner in the Kodály discography and the point from which lovers of this genial composer should set out. The extra items are very enticing.

The Seattle Symphony Orchestra play Kodály's music with great vividness and warmth. The *Háry János Suite* is more spaciously romantic in feeling than some versions – helped by the rich acoustics of the Seattle Opera House – and there is less surface glitter. But *The Battle and Defeat of Napoleon* and the *Entrance of the Emperor and His Court* have all the necessary mock-drama and spectacle, and it is good to hear the cimbalom again balanced so effectively within the orchestra. The *Galánta Dances* have splendid dash. The recording is outstandingly real.

José Serebrier gets very good playing from the Brno orchestra in both the *Dances of Galánta* and the *Peacock Variations*, and the remaining two works with the Südwestfunk Orchestra in Baden-Baden are, if anything, even better and the recording warmer. There is plenty of character in the orchestral playing of both ensembles, and the BIS recordings are up to house standard.

Robert Shaw in his Telarc recordings has repeatedly demonstrated what a fine orchestra the Atlanta Symphony is, and here Yoel Levi carries on the good work in a coupling of Kodály's three most popular orchestral works. The digital recording is full and well balanced, and the performances are brilliant and persuasive, with some fine, sparkling playing from the wind principals in particular. The snag is that this issue comes into direct competition with other versions that also offer the *Marosszék Dances*.

Fricsay's performances are crisp and exciting, the orchestra superbly on its toes, a notable passage being the beautifully managed horn solo in the central trio of the intermezzo in *Háry János*. The mono recording was demonstration-worthy in its day and is still pretty remarkable. The coupled performance of the *Psalmus Hungaricus* has characteristic electricity, and with fine soloists is effortlessly idiomatic and thrillingly alive. This disc is well chosen for DG's 'Originals'.

Hugh Wolff directs well-played but essentially relaxed performances of Kodály's well-known dance sets and brings out plenty of detail, if not always maximum bite. These readings are without the brilliance and character of the best available, although the recording is full and well balanced.

Háry János Suite

⊶ (B) *** Sony SBK (ADD) 48162. Cleveland O, Szell – MUSSORGSKY: *Pictures at an Exhibition*; PROKOFIEV: *Lieutenant Kijé: Suite* ***

(BB) *** Naxos 8.550142. Hungarian State O, Mátyás Antal (with Concert: 'Hungarian Festival' ***)

Szell – Budapest born – was in his element in *Háry János*. Superb Cleveland polish matches the vitality of the playing, with a humorous sparkle in Kodály's first two movements and the mock pomposity of the Napoleon episode wittily dramatized. The 1969 recording was one of the very finest from this source, bold with a too-forward cimbalom, but the engineers certainly capture the exhilaration of the playing in this way.

The Naxos Hungarian performance of the *Háry János Suite* is also wonderfully vivid, with the cimbalom – here perfectly balanced within the orchestra – particularly telling. The grotesque elements of *The Battle and Defeat of Napoleon* are pungently and wittily characterized and the *Entrance of the Emperor and His Court* also has an ironical sense of spectacle. The brilliant digital sound adds to the vitality and projection of the music-making, yet the lyrical music is played most tenderly.

(i) *Hungarian Rondo. Summer Evening; Symphony*
**(*) ASV CDDCA 924. (i) Warren-Green; Philh. O, Butt

The *Summer Evening* is a beautiful piece, eminently well served by Yondani Butt. It comes with a well-characterized account of the *Symphony*, not more impressive than Dorati's version but, of course, a more up-to-date recording. Very good indeed, albeit not quite three-star.

(Unaccompanied) *Cello Sonata, Op. 8*. (i) *Cello Sonata* (for cello and piano), *Op. 4*
⊕━ *** Sup. SU 3515-2. Barta, (i) with Cech – NOVAK: *Cello Sonata* ***

(Unaccompanied) *Cello Sonata, Op. 8*. *Cello Sonata, Op. 4*; *Adagio* (both for cello and piano)
(B) *** EMI Debut 5 75685-2. Yang, Moon

(Unaccompanied) *Cello Sonata, Op. 8*; (i) *Cello Sonata* (for cello & piano), *Op. 4*; *3 Chorale Preludes* (arr. from Bach, BWV 743, 747 & 762)
(BB) *** Naxos 8.553160. Kliegel, (i) with Jandó

(Unaccompanied) *Cello Sonata, Op. 8*; (i) *Duo for Violin & Cello, Op. 7*
*** Delos D/CD 1015. Starker, (i) with Gingold

Kodály's *Solo Cello Sonata* is among the strongest, most searching of all his works, arguably the finest of all works for unaccompanied cello since Bach's *Suites*, and here it receives a performance of exceptional power, precision and clarity from the Czech cellist Jiří Barta. More than most rivals, he is able to keep a steady tempo and to clarify textures with clean attack on double stopping, all seemingly without strain. Deeply reflective, the intensity of his performance never flags, with a rare depth of concentration in the darkly intense central *Adagio*. In the *Allegro* finale, with its folk-dance rhythms, he is volatile and thrusting, again using a formidable range of dynamic, well caught in the recording. In both movements of the Op. 4 *Sonata*, the opening *Fantasia* as well as the weighty finale, Barta and his pianist, Jan Cech, make the switches of speed seem natural as though part of an improvisation, and the folk element is aptly heightened by an element of rawness, with the players striking sparks off each other in fiery fantasy. The Novák *Sonata* makes a welcome and substantial supplement.

When, not long before the composer's death, Kodály heard Starker playing this *Cello Sonata*, he apparently said: 'If you correct the ritard in the third movement, it will be the Bible performance.' The recording is made in a smaller studio than is perhaps ideal; the *Duo*, impressively played by Janos Starker and Josef Gingold, is made in a slightly more open acoustic. There is a small makeweight in the form of Starker's own arrangement of the Bottermund *Paganini Variations*.

Maria Kliegel in Kodály's magnificent solo *Cello Sonata* offers a warm and fanciful performance, powerful and flowing. Jenö Jandó is an outstandingly sympathetic partner in the two-movement Op. 4 *Sonata*, a performance deeply introspective in the slow first movement and full of fantasy in the *Allegro con spirito* of the finale. The three *Chorale Preludes*

are romantic arrangements – with the cello generally underlining the chorale melodies – of organ pieces attributed to Bach but now thought spurious.

The two Korean musicians introduced on EMI's Debut label are very impressive, and Sung-Won Yang's account of the *Solo Cello Sonata* can withstand the most elevated comparisons and must receive the strongest recommendation, particularly as the disc includes the 1905 *Adagio for Cello and Piano*, which was originally intended to serve as a movement of the Op. 4 *Sonata* and is of considerable quality. The expertise and warmth of both players is matched by first-rate recording.

String Quartet 2, Op. 10
*** DG (IMS) 419 601-2. Hagen Qt – DVORAK: *String Quartet 12*, etc. ***
*** Testament (ADD) SBT 1072. Hollywood Qt – DVORAK; SMETANA: *Quartets* (***)

The Hagen give a marvellously committed and beautifully controlled performance of the *Second* – indeed as quartet playing it would be difficult to surpass. In range of dynamic response and sheer beauty of sound, this is thrilling playing and welcome advocacy of a neglected but masterly piece. The recording is well balanced and admirably present.

Although American readers will know the Hollywood Quartet's account of this piece, it will be new to collectors on this side of the Atlantic. It was recorded in 1958 and, unlike the Dvořák and Smetana with which it is coupled, is in stereo. Once a frequent item on concert and radio programmes, the Kodály has become something of a rarity. The present performance can only be described as masterly, enhancing the attractions of an already excellent issue.

VOCAL MUSIC

Laudes organi (Fantasia on a 12th-Century Sequence); Psalm 114 (from the Geneva Psalter)
*** Australian Decca Eloquence (ADD) 466 902-2. Brighton Festival Ch., Heltay, Weir – JANACEK: *Glagolitic Mass* ***

These works were written towards the end of Kodály's career; they are richly rewarding and show that even when the composer took on dramatic subjects, his was a relatively gentle art (in contrast to his friend Bartók). Heltay directs persuasive performances, with Gillian Weir brilliant as the organ soloist (the *Laudes organi* performance receives its CD début here). The recording is excellent, and these works make a fine bonus for the Janáček coupling.

Psalmus hungaricus, Op. 13
*** Chan. 9310. Svensson, Copenhagen Boys' Ch., Danish Nat. R. Ch. & SO, Mackerras – JANACEK: *Glagolitic Mass* ***
(M) *** Decca (ADD) 468 487-2 (2). Kozma, Brighton Festival Ch., Wandsworth School Boys' Ch., LSO, Kertész – DVORAK: *Requiem; Symphonic Variations* ***

As the unusual but refreshing coupling for the Janáček *Mass*, the *Psalmus hungaricus* is infected by Mackerras with an element of wildness that sweeps away any idea of Kodály as a bland composer. As in the Janáček, the tenor Peter Svensson is an excellent, clear-toned and incisive soloist, if here rather more backwardly balanced. The glory of the performance lies most of all in the superb choral singing, full, bright and superbly disciplined, with the hushed *pianissimos* as telling as the great *fortissimo* outbursts. It is a mark of Mackerras's understanding of the music that the many sudden changes of mood sound both dramatic and natural. Full, warm and atmospheric recording, with plenty of detail.

Kodály's *Psalmus hungaricus* is also splendidly vibrant in the hands of Istvan Kertész, but there is no doubt that the training of the Brighton Festival Chorus by their Hungarian chorus master, Lászlo Heltay, contributed much to the fluency of the outstanding performance, idiomatically presented in Hungarian, with Lajos Kozma an ideally chosen soloist. The vintage (1970) Kingsway Hall recording is excellent and here superbly transferred.

KOECHLIN, Charles (1867–1950)

Le Buisson ardent; The Jungle Book (Le Livre de la Jungle): La Course de printemps
*** Häns. CD 93.045. SWR Stuttgart SO, Holliger

La Course de printemps from *Le Livre de la Jungle* has already been recorded (Segerstam does the four purely orchestral pieces and Zinman includes all seven pieces). *La Course de printemps* is astonishingly atmospheric and its range of sonorities bold and forward-looking. Segerstam has also recorded *Le Buisson ardent* ('The Burning Bush'), another luminous and evocative score, the composer's last symphonic poem, which calls for a huge orchestra, including *ondes martenot*, five saxophones, piano and organ. It is an evocation of re-birth – at times ardently intense in the strings but with the *ondes martenot* later used to represent the incorporeal manifestation of the re-born spirit. The sense of ecstasy then gives way to the vigour and potency of life itself, first with the robust humanity of a country dance, but soon becoming much more elaborate, climaxing with a bold affirmation, but closing temperately but with an underlying feeling of gentle ecstasy. This new version under Heinz Holliger is every bit as good as its predecessor and more than acceptably recorded. Koechlin is one of the most remarkable figures in French music after Debussy, a master of the orchestra and completely original.

Les Heures persanes, Op. 65
*** Marco Polo 8.223504. Reinland-Pfalz PO, Segerstam

Koechlin's powers as an orchestrator are evident in these 16 exotic mood-pictures, which were originally composed for the piano in 1913. They evoke a journey recorded by Pierre Loti in 1900: 'He who wants to come with me to see at Isfahan the season of roses should travel slowly by my side, in stages, as in the Middle Ages.' The work is generally slow-moving, but this music has tremendous atmosphere and exotic colours and the very titles of the movements (*Les Collines au coucher du soleil, A l'ombre près de la fontaine marbre*, for example) conjure up some idea of its character. In the hands of Leif Segerstam and the Reinland-Pfalz orchestra this music casts a powerful spell. It is also beautifully recorded.

The Jungle Book (Le Livre de la jungle)
*** Marco Polo 8.223484. Reinland-Pfalz PO, Segerstam

(i) *The Jungle Book (Le Livre de la jungle);* (ii) *3 Songs (Seal Lullaby; Night-Song in the Jungle; Song of Kala Nag), Op. 18;* (iii) *Seven Stars Symphony, Op. 132; L'Andalouse dans Barcelone, Op. 13; 4 Interludes, Op. 214*
☞ (B) *** RCA 2 CD 74321 84596-2 (2). (i) Berlin RSO, Zinman; (ii) with Vermillion, Botha, Lukas & Ch.; (iii) Deutsches SO, Berlin, Judd

Koechlin's lifelong fascination with Kipling's *Jungle Book* is reflected in this extraordinary four-movement tone-poem whose composition extended over several decades. *La Course de printemps*, Op. 95, the longest of them, is extraordinarily imaginative and pregnant with atmosphere: you can feel the heat and humidity of the rainforest and sense the presence of strange and menacing creatures. *La Loi de la jungle* is the most static and the least interesting. Leif Segerstam is excellent in this repertoire and with his refined ear for texture distils a heady atmosphere and he is beautifully recorded. Anyone with a feeling for the exotic will respond to this original and fascinating music.

David Zinman and the Berlin Radio Symphony Orchestra also give a very well characterized performance, almost as atmospheric as their Marco Polo competitor, though the texture is more brightly lit and clearly defined. However, this RCA bargain Double not only includes the three Op. 18 *Songs* for soloists, chorus and orchestra, but also offers a very persuasive account under James Judd of the *Seven Stars Symphony*, the stars in question coming not from the heavens but from Hollywood. They include Douglas Fairbanks Sr and Greta Garbo, who is coolly depicted by an *ondes martenot*; a brilliant *scherzando* represents Clara Bow; Marlene Dietrich is personified by a luscious melody using her name as its basis; and finally Chaplin is portrayed with considerable depth as well as humour. The *Four Interludes* (not orchestrated by the composer) were written as links intended to make the symphony into a ballet; the delightful *L'Andalouse dans Barcelone* was conceived as gypsy dance music for a film, but was never used. The recording is excellent – to match these highly persuasive performances.

CHAMBER MUSIC

L'Album de Lilian, 1st Series, for Voice, Flute & Piano; 2nd Series, for Flute & Piano, Op. 149. Morceau de lecture, Op. 217; 14 Pièces, Op. 157b (both for flute & piano); (i) Sonata for 2 Flutes; Sonata for Piano & Flute, Op. 52
☞ (N) (BB) *** Hyp. Helios CDH 55107. Fenwick Smith, West, Amlin; (i) with L. Buyse

Charles Koechlin's writing for the flute is very French, very delicate and very special. The *Fourteen Pièces*, which open this programme, are enchanting and show his supreme gifts as a miniaturist. Only four of them last for more than a minute, yet all are perfectly formed, and the longest, a *Marche funèbre*, although dolorous is not to be taken at all seriously. The Première Série of *L'Album de Lilian* is slightly more substantial, but only slightly. Only two have lyrics, the first translates as 'Keep that schoolgirl complexion', the second, *Tout va bien*, suggests 'All is well because love's sorrow lasts but a moment'. The others are for piano solo and are slightly Satiesque, while the delicious *Skating – Smiling*, and *En route vers le bonheur* are for voice and piano, but without words. Two of the *Four Pièces* of the magical Second Series, *Swimming* and *Le Jeux du clown*, are worthy of Debussy in their simple impressionism, while *Le Voyage chimérique* could only be Koechlin himself. The *Flute Sonata* opens with tranquillity, moves on to a wistful *Sicilienne* and closes in vivid animation. The *Sonata for Two Flutes* begins very sadly, but after a cheerful little *Scherzando* moves to a perky allegro and then, inevitably, back to the mood of the opening. These top Boston musicians play all this music with supreme understanding and elegance: indeed, the performances here are little short of exquisite and full of life. They are beautifully recorded. Of this disc the critic of the *American Record Guide* wrote: 'Entrancing, enthralling, and entertaining – I shall not part with my copy until the Sheriff knocks on the door and then only grudgingly!' He is absolutely right. If you only buy one disc of the music of Charles Koechlin, this is the one to get.

Cello Sonata, Op. 66; Chansons bretonnes, Book 1, Op. 115
*** Hyp. CDA 66979. Lidström, Forsberg – PIERNE: *Cello Sonata* ***

Koechlin's sonata is pensive and introspective, ruminative in character, and Mats Lidström and Bengt Forsberg give a cultured, finely controlled performance of compelling subtlety. The sound is natural and lifelike. In every respect this is a disc of quality.

Chansons bretonnes* (for cello & piano), *Book 3
(N) *** Hyp. CDA 67244. Lidström, Forsberg – MAGNARD & WIDOR: *Sonatas* ***

Mats Lidström recounts a visit to the composer's son, Yves, when he presented him with the manuscript of the third book of the Koechlin *Chansons bretonnes*. They have the charm and imagination one associates with this composer. Lidström and Bengt Forsberg play all these pieces, which are quite short, with eloquence and flair. The sound is excellent.

Horn Sonata, Op. 70; 15 Pieces, Op. 180; Morceau de lecture* (for horn); *Sonneries
*** ASV CDDCA 716. Tuckwell, Blumenthal

The *Sonata* is a richly conceived three-movement work, linked by its evocative opening idea. The *Morceau de lecture* is freer, more rhapsodic, immediately stretching up ecstatically into the instrument's higher tessitura. The *15 Pieces* are delightful vignettes, opening with a rapturous evocation, *Dans la forêt romantique*. While some of them are skittish, notably the muted Scherzo (No. 4) or jolly *Allegro vivo* (No. 11), many explore that special solemn melancholy which the horn easily discovers in its middle to lower register, as in Nos. 10 and 12 (both marked *doux*). Two others are for hunting horns, and they robustly use the open harmonics which are naturally out of tune (an effect Britten tried more sparingly), while the 11 brief *Sonneries* are all written for cors de chasse in two, three or four parts, which Tuckwell plays by electronic means. This is a collection to be dipped into rather than taken all at once, but Tuckwell's artistry sustains the listener's interest; and the fine pianist, Daniel Blumenthal, makes the most of his rewarding part in the *Sonata*. The recording is excellent.

PIANO MUSIC

Les Heures persanes, Op. 65 (16 Pieces for Piano)
*** Chan. 9974. Stott

This is the original piano score of *Les Heures persanes* ('The Persian Hours') of which the orchestral version is praised above. It evokes a two-month journey through Persia in 1900 by the writer Pierre Loti, who recorded his visit in a diary. So the listener makes his musical journey filtered through the composer's own response to the diarist's exotic impressions in a series of 16 vignettes. Almost all this music is seductively unhurried. The listener is thus made to linger in scenery that is often picturesque in a gently evocative way, although *Á l'ombre près de la fontaine de marbre* does hint at a vision of trickling water and *Arabesques* suggests glittering reflections. Both the haunting *Chant du soir* and *Les Collines au coucher du soleil* inhabit a world that the composer directs must always be *très calme*. The closing number speaks for itself: *Derviches dans la nuit. Assez animé, nocturne mystérieuse – Variante – Clair de lune sur a place désert*, ending the journey mystically as it began, *after the legendary roses have blossomed*. Kathryn Stott's pianistic colours are sensuously warm and often exotic, and she is very atmospherically recorded.

KOKKONEN, Joonas (1921–96)

(i) ***Sinfonia da camera; Il paesaggio;*** (ii) ***'... durch einen Spiegel ...'***; (iii) ***Wind Quintet***
🔑 *** BIS CD 528. (i; ii) Lahti SO; (i) Vänskä; (iii) Söderblom; (ii) with Tiensuu; (iii) Lahti Sinf. Wind Quintet

Those coming new to Kokkonen's musical idiom should try the pretentiously titled but resourceful and imaginative '... *durch einen Spiegel ...*', subtitled *Metamorphosis* for 12 strings and harpsichord. There are some rewardingly individual sonorities. *Il paesaggio* is an evocative landscape study, and the earlier *Wind Quintet* is a lively piece. The early *Sinfonia da camera* is grey, general-purpose, modern music deriving from Bartókian-Hindemithian roots. Very good performances and splendid recording.

Symphony 1; Music for String Orchestra; (i) ***The Hades of the Birds*** (song-cycle)
*** BIS CD 485. Lahti SO, Söderblom; (i) Groop

The *Music for String Orchestra* is a rather powerful piece lasting almost half an hour, well wrought, its invention finely sustained if slightly anonymous. The colourings are dark. *The Hades of the Birds* is a short song-cycle which shows Monica Groop's talents to strong effect, but it is the *First Symphony* that is the strongest piece on the disc. It is serious in purpose and, as far as the orchestra is concerned, shows considerable mastery of colour.

Symphony 2; Inauguratio; Erekhtheion (cantata); ***The Last Temptations*** (opera): ***Interludes***
**(*) BIS CD 498. Vihavainen, Grönroos, Akateeminen Laulu Ch., Lahti SO, Vänskä

The *Second Symphony* is a work of some eloquence and its invention has a certain freshness and quality, even if it remains ultimately unmemorable. The interludes from his opera, *The Last Temptations*, make a strong impression. Not an essential purchase.

Symphony 3; (i) ***Opus sonorum;*** (ii) ***Requiem***
*** BIS CD 508. Lahti SO, Söderblom; with (i) Sivonen; (ii) Iskoski, Grönroos, Savonlinna Op. Festival Ch.

Söderblom's account of the *Third Symphony* has detail and atmosphere, and the same must be said of the *Requiem*. In the *Opus sonorum*, written in reaction to the sight of the vast battery of percussion so common in the 1960s, Kokkonen assigns all the percussion part to a piano, played with great delicacy here.

Symphony 4; (i) ***Cello Concerto. Symphonic Sketches***
*** BIS CD 468. (i) Thedéen; Lahti SO, Vänskä

The *Fourth Symphony* is the strongest work here: its ideas are symphonic, its structure organic and its atmosphere powerful. The *Cello Concerto* is a lyrical and accessible piece, just a shade mawkish. The Swedish cellist Torleif Thedéen gives a performance of great restraint, mastery and sensitivity. Good orchestral playing and recording.

(i) *Piano Quintet. String Quartets 1–3*
*** BIS CD 458. (i) Valsta; Sibelius Ac. Qt

The *Quintet* is a slight but not unpleasing work; the *First Quartet*, which sounds like any chamber work of the period, has more gravitas. Like its companions it is very well played, but even such eloquent advocacy cannot disguise a certain facelessness. But three stars for the performers and the engineers.

KOPPEL, Herman D. (1908–98)

Cello Concerto, Op. 56
*** BIS (ADD) CD 80. Bengtsson, Danish Nat. RSO, Schmidt – NORHOLM: *Violin Concerto* ***

Herman D. Koppel's idiom stems from Stravinsky and Bartók, but the opening of his *Cello Concerto* has something of the luminous quality of Tippett's *Midsummer Marriage*. Very good recording of an inventive and original piece that deserves to enter the wider international repertoire.

Symphonies 1, Op. 5; 2, Op. 37
**(*) dacapo 8.224205. Aalborg SO, Atzmon

The *First Symphony* (1929–30), composed when Koppel was in his early twenties, is pure Nielsen but well argued. There is a good feeling for line and a genuine sense of symphonic writing. The *Second* was written in 1943, during the Nazi occupation of Denmark but before the round-up of the Jews forced Koppel to take refuge in Sweden. It, too, is strongly Nielsenesque, and after its first performance, under Thomas Jensen, Koppel disowned it, as he did its predecessor. But there are too many good things in it and evidence of too lively an imagination to allow this verdict to stand. Neither work is inferior to, say, the symphonies of Lars-Erik Larsson, to name another exact contemporary, though they do not have the strong profile or concentration of Holmboe, Tubin or the best symphonies of Niels Viggo Bentzon. Those who feel at home in these latitudes will enjoy making the acquaintance of these two symphonies, derivative though they are, in these eminently serviceable performances and recordings.

Symphonies 3, Op. 39; 4, Op. 42
*** dacapo 8.226016. Aalborg SO, Atzmon

Herman D. Koppel was among those Danes who made the crossing to Sweden when the Nazis gave the order to round up the Jews. He spent the rest of the war in Sweden where the *Third Symphony* was written. He wrote his *First* in his early twenties and its successor in 1943 during the Nazi occupation, and subsequently disowned them. But they are well worth hearing for all that. He was enormously productive, with seven symphonies to his credit as well as five piano concertos, a highly imaginative cello concerto written for Erling Bløndal-Bengtsson, and five quartets. But Koppel is primarily a symphonist, as the two works recorded here show. There is a real sense of movement and a feeling that we have embarked on a voyage; there is breadth, a sense of organic cohesion and inevitability. There is a lot of Nielsen in the *Third Symphony* and, in the opening movement of the postwar *Fourth*, of Shostakovich too.

The *Fourth*, from 1946, is the longer work and the breadth of its first movement is impressive, though the following two

are less concentrated. If Koppel's imagination is not perhaps as rich nor his invention as strong in profile or as distinguished as the symphonies of his contemporaries, Holmboe and Bentzon, both these works are rewarding and will leave one keen to explore his other music. There is a strong sense of nature and of the North in both works. Moshe Atzmon gets good results from the Aalborg orchestra, though the upper strings are occasionally wanting in bloom. Very well-balanced recordings.

Sextet for Piano and Wind, Op. 36
*** dacapo 224208. Nikolaj Bentzon, Members of the Danish Nat. SO Wind Quintet – BENTZON: *Wind Quintet; Sextet* ***

Considering that Koppel's *Sextet for Piano and Wind* comes from the dark years of the Nazi occupation of Denmark, it is remarkably carefree. Its ideas are bright, and one is reminded of *Les Six* – particularly Milhaud – while the middle section of the first movement almost recalls the Constant Lambert of the *Concerto for Piano and Nine Instruments*. There is still a lot of Nielsen in the *Pastorale* movement, and if the high spirits of the finale may be scatty, the result is quite infectious. It is all rather delightful and very well played and recorded.

KOPYLOV, Aleksandr (1854–1911)

Concert Overture in D min., Op. 31; Scherzo in A, Op. 10; Symphony in C min., Op. 14
*** ASV CDDCA 1013. Moscow SO, Almeida

Aleksandr Kopylov, a pupil of Rimsky-Korsakov in St Petersburg, was more of a teacher than a composer, but all three of these works, the sum total of Kopylov's orchestral music, will delight devotees of the Russian Romantics. The *Concert Overture* has the strongest Russian flavour, with colourful themes and snapping rhythms in the main *Allegro*. The *Scherzo* too is fresh and open, with well-contrasted themes. The *Symphony* is more like Balakirev watered down, beautifully made with clean-cut structures. Persuasive performances under Antonio de Almeida, in one of the last recordings he made before his untimely death.

KORNGOLD, Erich (1897–1957)

'Erich Wolfgang Korngold – The Adventures of a Wunderkind': A Portrait; with Concert: (i) *Cello Concerto*; (ii) *Violin Concerto*; (iii) *Don Quixote*: excerpt; 2 *Fairytale Pictures, Op. 3*
*** Arthaus **DVD** 100 362. (i) Frankfurt RSO, Wolff; with (i) Viersin; (ii) Kavakos; (iii) Frey (Producers: Axel Hempel, Klaus Helmbold, Director: Barrie Gavi)

The feature on Korngold's career in Vienna and then Hollywood comes from Hessischen Rundfunk and is enriched with rare archive material from the family archives and Warner Brothers' films. It is intelligently directed. Korngold's life unfolds in a leisurely and effortless way and the biography includes musical illustrations by Anne Sofie von Otter, Bengt Forsberg and Mats Lindström. The *Cello* and *Violin Concertos* are expertly played and the Frankfurt orchestra responds well to Hugh Wolff's direction. Those with an interest in the composer or in music in pre-war Vienna should not hesitate to get this.

Baby Serenade, Op. 24; Sursum corda (Symphonic Overture), Op. 13; Der Schneemann: Prelude & Serenade. Die tote Stadt: Prelude. Das Wunder der Heliane: Interlude
*** ASV CDDCA 1074. Bruckner O, Richter

This is a delightful disc, centring on a work new to the catalogue, the *Baby Serenade*, providing a musical evocation of family life with a baby, charmingly unpretentious. The *Overture, Sursum corda*, is like Respighi with a German accent, and even the excerpts from *The Snowman*, an opera written when Korngold was only eleven, are rich and lush, though the orchestration is by Zemlinsky, a point not mentioned in the booklet. The other two operatic excerpts make up the warmly enjoyable programme, helped by excellent playing and recording.

(i) Cello Concerto in C, Op. 37; (ii) Piano Concerto in C sharp for the Left Hand, Op. 17. Symphonic Serenade for Strings, Op. 39; Military March in B flat
*** Chan. 9508. (i) Dixon; (ii) Shelley; BBC PO, Bamert

The *Cello Concerto* is an adaptation of a short piece Korngold composed in 1946 for the film *Deception* starring Bette Davis and Claude Rains. The *Concerto in C sharp for Piano Left Hand* (1924) is an altogether different matter. Composed, like Ravel's concerto, for the one-armed pianist Paul Wittgenstein, who had lost his right arm during the First World War, it is an extraordinarily imaginative and resourceful work. Although it springs from a post-Straussian world, it is full of individual touches. Howard Shelley gives it a radiant performance and is given splendid support. To complaints that the *Military March* (1917) was rather fast, Korngold is said to have replied that it was intended to be played for the retreat! The *Symphonic Serenade for Strings* is a very beautiful (as well as beautifully crafted) work with a highly inventive Scherzo and an eloquent, rather Mahlerian slow movement. First-rate playing and opulent, well-balanced recording. Well worth exploring.

Violin Concerto in D, Op. 35
(N) *** DG 474 874-2. Mutter, LSO, Previn – TCHAIKOVSKY: *Violin Concerto in D* ***
(M) *** EMI 5 62590-2. Perlman, Pittsburgh O, Previn – SIBELIUS: *Concerto;* SINDING: *Suite in A min.* ***
(BB) *** Naxos 8.553579. Tsu, Razumovsky Sinfonia, Yu Long – GOLDMARK: *Violin Concerto* ***

(i) Violin Concerto; (ii) Much Ado about Nothing (suite), Op. 11
*** DG 439 886-2. Shaham; (i) LSO, Previn; (ii) Previn (piano) – BARBER: *Violin Concerto* ***

The Israeli violinist Gil Shaham gives a performance of effortless virtuosity and strong profile. Shaham is warm and committed. There is greater freshness and conviction than in the Perlman. The recording helps, far clearer and more immediate than Perlman's EMI. It is true that Perlman finds an extra tenderness in such passages as the entry of the violin in the slow movement, but Shaham and Previn together consistently bring out the work's sensuous warmth without making the result soupy. The suite from Korngold's incidental music to *Much Ado about Nothing* provides a delightful and apt makeweight, with Shaham yearningly warm without sentimentality, clean and precise in attack.

In another outstanding performance, Mutter adopts a freely expressive style, almost improvisatory in the way she inflects the ripe melodies drawn from the composer's scores

for Hollywood films. Plainly, for her, this is the music of love, reflected in having her husband, André Previn, conducting. The inner depth of her playing at the end of the central slow movement is magical, and her dazzling virtuosity in the dashing finale is breathtaking.

Perlman, dashing and romantic, also gives a superlative account, and though he is placed too close to the microphone the recording overall is vivid, and the couplings are very recommendable.

Vera Tsu, born in Shanghai and trained in America, is another outstanding soloist in a coupling that directly challenges the EMI disc from Itzhak Perlman. In every way this ripely romantic version of the Korngold is a match for that and for other full-price rivals, thanks to Tsu's rich, ample tone and her flawless intonation, as well as her fearless attack in bravura writing. In the quality of sound the recording outshines most other versions, rich and free, both immediate and atmospheric, with fine dynamic range and with the Chinese conductor, Yu Long, drawing beautiful, refined playing from the Bratislava orchestra.

Film scores: Captain Blood; Elizabeth and Essex; The Prince and the Pauper; The Sea Hawk (all arr. Russ)
*** DG 471 347-2. LSO, Previn

As Previn points out, in his film music Erich Korngold used a style he had already established in his operas and symphonic works, so producing what was quickly recognized as the characteristic musical idiom for Hollywood epics. He thought of the ripely romantic film scores for these four swashbucklers starring Errol Flynn as 'operas without singing'. Considering how quickly he had to work, the complexity of the writing is astonishing, with Korngold closely supervising sumptuous orchestrations by associates such as Hugo Friedhofer and Milan Roder. The sequence culminates in *The Sea Hawk* of 1940, with over 100 minutes of music deftly compressed into a colourful 18-minute suite of highlights, the most substantial of the four here, each with scores reconstructed and reassembled by Patrick Russ. Such a haunting movement as *Sold into Slavery* from the *Captain Blood* suite fully matches in originality anything Korngold ever wrote. André Previn, nurtured in Hollywood and himself the winner of four Oscars for his film music, proves the ideal interpreter, with the LSO both brilliant and passionate.

(i) Much Ado About Nothing (Suite), Op. 11. (ii) Abschiedslieder (Songs of Farewell), Op. 14; Einfache Lieder (Simple Songs), Op. 9; (iii) Prayor; (ii) Tomorrow
*** ASV CDDCA 1131. Linz Mozart Female Ch., Bruckner O, Linz, C. Richter with (i) Hochstenbach; (ii) Mitchell-Velasco; (iii) Gould

The suite that Korngold provided for *Much Ado About Nothing* is richly orchestrated and includes the première recording of his *Garden Music*. The film *The Constant Nymph* (1942) centred on the life of a composer and needed an original composition for the climax. Korngold provided *Tomorrow*, a characteristically flamboyant work, in his lushest style, for large orchestra, female choir and mezzo soprano soloist, here the excellent Gigi Mitchell-Velasco. She also sings with great sensitivity in the two Mahlerian song-cycles, bringing much charm to the earlier – but by no means immature – Op. 9 set (the evocative *Night Wanderer* is another first recording), and she is no less successful in the moving *Songs of Farewell* of 1920–21. The *Prayor* is a short but effective liturgical work, dating from 1940, for female choir, organ and orchestra, though it is slightly marred by a solo tenor who is somewhat wobbly and not producing the sweetest of sounds. Otherwise, all the performances are warmly sympathetic, as is the sound, with a full amplitude and plenty of range to suit the music. Texts and translation are included.

Sinfonietta, Op. 5; Sursum corda, Op. 13
*** Chan. 9317. BBC PO, Bamert

Korngold's *Sinfonietta* is a four-movement symphony in all but name, betraying a prodigious expertise both in the organization of musical ideas and in the handling of the orchestra; and not only that, the ideas themselves are of real quality and individuality. At 43 minutes, it is an extraordinary achievement for a fourteen-year-old – an adolescent composer springing as it were fully equipped on to the musical scene. *Sursum corda*, an early virtuoso showpiece lasting 20 minutes, is finer than one might expect, an extraordinarily sumptuous piece that in its wide range of moods keeps suggesting that it will turn into the *Pines of Rome*. The present performance of the *Sinfonietta* is a clear front-runner, and the Chandos recording is altogether superb in terms of definition and opulence. A ripely enjoyable disc of beautifully played performances, with a sumptuous sound-picture.

Symphony in F sharp, Op. 40; (i) Abschiedslieder, Op. 14
*** Chan. 9171. (i) Finnie; BBC PO, Downes

The *Symphony* is a work of real imaginative power. It is scored for large forces – a big percussion section including piano, celeste, marimba, etc. – and the orchestra is used with resource and flair. The BBC Philharmonic play with enthusiasm and sensitivity for Edward Downes. The *Abschiedslieder* are much earlier and were completed in 1920; there is a great deal of Strauss, Mahler and Zemlinsky here. Linda Finnie is a persuasive soloist, and the balance is eminently well judged. The Chandos recording is wide-ranging and lifelike.

CHAMBER MUSIC

(i) *Piano Quintet in E, Op. 15*; (ii) *Suite for 2 Violins, Cello & Piano Left Hand, Op. 23*
*** ASV CDDCA 1047. (i) Schmolk; (ii) McFarlane; Schubert Ens. of London

The *Piano Quintet* is powerfully wrought and superbly laid out for the medium, and rightly enjoyed much exposure in the 1920s. Its resurrection in this fine new recording is more than welcome, for it reaffirms the fertility of Korngold's imagination and the quality of his invention. The *Suite*, Op. 23, one of six works written for Paul Wittgenstein, has some splendid ideas: the third-movement *Grotesquerie* is particularly striking.

String Sextet, Op. 10
*** Hyp. CDA 66425. Raphael Ens. – SCHOENBERG: *Verklaerte Nacht* ***

The Korngold *Sextet* is an amazing achievement for a seventeen-year-old. Not only is it crafted with musicianly assurance and maturity, it is also inventive and characterful. The Raphael Ensemble play it with great commitment and the Hyperion recording is altogether first class.

Piano Music, 4 Hands: (i) *Piano Trio in D, Op. 1.* Solo Piano Music: *Piano Sonatas 1–3. Don Quixote: 6 Character Pieces after Cervantes. 4 Little Caricatures for Children, Op. 19; Much Ado About Nothing (3 Pieces); Märchenbilder, Op. 3; Potpourri aus der Oper 'Der Ring des Polykrates'; The*

Snowman (Pantomime in 2 Scenes); Die tote Stadt: Schach Brugge; What the Woods Tell Me; 4 Waltzes; Das Wunder der Heliane: Intermezzo
(B) *** Nim. NI 5705/8 (4). Jones, (i) with McMahon

Martin Jones has always been one of the most exploratory of pianists and his four-CD set of the Korngold piano music is a valuable addition to the catalogue. The early music is of astonishing precocity and pianistic assurance – and some of it (such as the second of the *Four Waltzes*) touching. The *Four Little Caricatures for Children* in the style of Schoenberg, Bartók and others are quite elegant. The *Second Sonata*, composed when Korngold was 13, was given its first performance by Schnabel, no less, in Berlin in 1911, and is a finely wrought piece, played with great conviction by Martin Jones. The *Piano Trio*, written when he was only 12, is given in its transcription for piano, four hands (the original was premièred by Bruno Walter, Arnold Rosé and Friedrich Buxbaum). There are some delightful shorter pieces, such as *Heinzelmännchen* ('The Imps'), which are quite haunting. A worthwhile set with well-balanced and truthful recorded sound.

VOCAL MUSIC

3 Lieder, Op. 18. Lieder: *Alt-spanisch; Gefasster Abschied; Glückwunsch; Liebesbriefchen; Sonett für Wien; Sterbelied*
*** DG (IMS) 437 515-2. Von Otter, Forsberg – BERG: *7 Early Songs*; R. STRAUSS: *Lieder* ***

Inspired playing and singing in these rare and immediately attractive songs by Erich Korngold. Though a few date from his early, precocious years in Vienna, including some of the most sensuously beautiful, such a charming miniature as *Alt-spanisch* is taken from the film music he wrote in 1940 for the swashbuckling Hollywood film, *The Sea Hawk*. Singer and pianist draw out the intensity of emotion to the full without exaggeration or sentimentality. A fascinating programme.

5 Lieder, Op. 38; Songs of the Clown, Op. 29
*** Sony SK 68344. Kirchschlager, Deutsch – MAHLER: *Lieder und Gesänge* ***

These two song-groups, written after Korngold went to America – charming miniatures most of them – are tuneful in an innocent way. Even *Come away death* fails to draw from the composer a deep response (no doubt reflecting his title for the group), gravitating quickly to the major mode. With Op. 29 here receiving its first recording, they add a pointful element to the début recital of this talented, fresh-voiced singer; well worth exploring.

OPERA

Die Kathrin (complete)
*** CPO 999 602-2 (2). Diener, Rendall, Hayward, Watson, D. Jones, BBC Singers, BBC Concert O, Brabbins

Die Kathrin is a far warmer and more relaxed piece than Korngold's other operas. The opulent scoring and ripe lyricism go with a novelettish story of Kathrin, a servant-girl, and her wandering minstrel of a sweetheart. With echoes of Strauss's *Arabella*, Puccini's *Suor Angelica* and even Humperdinck's *Hänsel und Gretel*, Martyn Brabbins draws aptly sumptuous sounds from the BBC Concert Orchestra, in a recording taken from a BBC radio production. A characterful cast, including Della Jones and Lillian Watson in small roles, is headed by the radiant young German soprano, Melanie Diener, but with David Rendall rather strained as the hero, François.

Die tote Stadt (complete)
(M) *** RCA (ADD) GD 87767 (2). Neblett, Kollo, Luxon, Prey, Bav. R. Ch., Tölz Ch., Munich R. O, Leinsdorf

(N) **(*) Naxos 8.660060/1 (2). Sunnegardh, Dalayman, Bergstrom, Tobiasson, Royal Swedish Op. Ch. & O, Segerstam

At the age of twenty-three Korngold had his opera, *Die tote Stadt*, presented in simultaneous world premières in Hamburg and Cologne! The score includes many echoes of Puccini and Richard Strauss, but its youthful exuberance carries the day. Here René Kollo is powerful, if occasionally coarse of tone, Carol Neblett sings sweetly in the equivocal roles of the wife's apparition and the newcomer, and Hermann Prey, Benjamin Luxon and Rose Wagemann make up an impressive cast. Leinsdorf is at his finest.

Recorded live at the Royal Swedish Opera in 1996, the Naxos version offers a warmly expressive reading of Korngold's youthful opera, bringing out the ripeness of melodic writing and orchestration, with echoes of Puccini and Strauss. The recording too is admirably clear, with more orchestral detail than in the vintage first recording under Leinsdorf. The tenor, Thomas Sunnegardh, sings cleanly and freshly in the central role of Paul, with Anders Bergstrom youthfully convincing as his friend, Frank. Yet the glory of the set is the singing of Katarina Dalayman as Marietta – radiantly pure and tender in Marietta's song in Act I – which even outshines the model of Carol Neblett on RCA. The snag is that Segerstam observes various cuts in the score, omitting some 15 minutes of music. Naxos provide a detailed synopsis and a German libretto, but no translation.

KOZELUCH, Leopold (1747–1818)

Clarinet Concerto 2 in E flat
*** ASV CDDCA 763. Johnson, RPO, Herbig – CRUSELL; KROMMER: *Concertos* ***

Leopold Kozeluch's concerto is a highly agreeable work, especially when performed so magnetically by Emma Johnson. There is plenty of Johnsonian magic here to light up even the most conventional passage-work and the 'naturally flowing melodies' (the soloist's own description), and she is accompanied well and recorded admirably, with the slow movement made to sound recessed and delicate.

Symphonies in D; F; & G min.
*** Chan. 9703. LMP, Bamert

Kozeluch was born near Prague but established himself in Vienna in 1778, where he was appointed to the Imperial Court as official composer and director of the orchestra. These symphonies are pleasingly crafted, sub-Mozart; but each is distinguished by a graceful and appealing slow movement and a vigorous, light-hearted finale. They are very well played on Chandos, and the fairly resonant recording ensures their weight and substance.

KRAMÁŘ, František – see under Krommer, Franz

KRAUS, Joseph Martin (1756–92)

Symphonies: in A, VB 128; in F (Buffa), VB 129; in F, VB 130; C (Violin obbligato), VB 138
(BB) *** Naxos 8.554472. Swedish CO, Sundkvist

Symphonies: in C, VB 139; C min., VB 142; E flat, VB 144; Olympie Overture, VB 29
(BB) *** Naxos 8.553734. Swedish CO, Sundkvist

Symphonies: in C sharp min., VB 140; in E min., VB 141; in C min. (Funèbre), VB 148 in C; Overture in D min., VB 147
(BB) *** Naxos 8.554777. Swedish CO, Sundkvist

Symphonies in D, VB 143; F, VB 145; Riksdagsmusiken: Sinfonia per la Chiesa in D, VB 146 & Riksdagsmarsh, VB 15
(BB) *** Naxos 8.555305. Swedish CO, Sundkvist

Born in the same year as Mozart, Kraus was dubbed the 'Swedish Mozart', but these lively symphonies, freshly performed by the Swedish Chamber Orchestra, suggest that his music has more in common with that of Haydn, above all the *Sturm und Drang* period. Haydn, who met Kraus in both Vienna and Esterházy, praised his music highly. Unlike Mozart, Kraus was drawn to minor keys, not just in the *C minor Symphony*, and the tough streak in the writing is emphasized by the sharpness of syncopated rhythms. The *Olympie Overture* was written for a stage production of Voltaire's play of that name.

The major-keyed symphonies are marginally less striking, although *Allegros* still have plenty of vitality and VB 138 in C includes an important solo violin obbligato throughout all three movements. The hunting finales of VB 128 and 130 dance along merrily, while the last movement of the *Sinfonia buffa* is strikingly ambitious, much varied in mood and with passages of concertante flute writing.

Most individual of all are the minor-key symphonies on the third disc, especially the remarkable work in C sharp minor (1782), a symphony fully worthy of Haydn. The *Symphonie funèbre* opens and closes with muffled beats on the side-drum; the first movement is a sombre march, the third a funeral chorale, the finale an expressive *Adagio* which includes an eloquent central horn solo and an impressive double fugue. The *D minor Overture* (heard here in its original, darker scoring for strings with bassoons) brings a solemn Largo followed by a dignified fugue. It shares the mood of Haydn's *Seven Last Words* and was often played on Good Friday. Full, warm sound and excellent performances, involving a substantial string section with first-rate wind and brass playing, notably from the horns. Well worth exploring.

The fourth volume contains all the positive qualities that mark the other three volumes. Kraus's music is animated and inventive, with a *Sturm und Drang* flavour permeating his scores and giving them a compelling edge. The *Riksdagsmusiken* music was written for the convening of the Swedish parliament in March 1789, and here the attractively bright-eyed *Overture* and *Ceremonial March* are included. The two major-keyed, three-movement symphonies combine classical elegance with Kraus's more dramatic style, and if they are not as individual or as potent as his minor-keyed works, they are certainly enjoyable, with the spirit of Haydn strongly felt.

First-class recording and lively, fresh playing complete the picture.

KREBS, Johann Ludwig (1713–80)

Music for harpsichord: *Preludes 2 in D min.; 3 in E min.; 5 in G; 6 in A min.; Suites in B min.; in C min.; Organ chorales: Allein Gott in der Höh' sei Ehr; Auf meinen lieben Gott* (2 settings); *Christ lag in Todesbanden; Jesu meine Freude* (2 settings); *Jesus meine Zuversicht* (2 settings); *Sei Lob und Ehr dem höchsten Gut; Vater unser im Himmelreich; Von Gott will ich nicht lassen; Warum betrübst du dich, mein Herz?; Wass Gott will nicht lassen; Wass Gott tut, das ist wohlgetan* (2 settings); *Wer nur den lieben Gott lässt walten* (2 settings)

⊕ *** Mer. (ADD) CDE 84306. Gifford (harpsichord or chamber organ)

The title of this collection, 'The best crayfish in the brook', is a pun on the composer's name, often attributed to his mentor. Krebs (the fish) was a favourite pupil of Bach (the brook). On the evidence of this highly attractive recital he was also a very talented pupil, who obviously absorbed much of his master's contrapuntal style in his organ chorales, even if their expressive and imaginative range is more limited. But Krebs's clavier music has a strong personality in its own right. His harpsichord dance *Suites* and *Preludes* demonstrate a lively mixture of French and Italianate manners, and their invention is consistently attractive. Gerald Gifford plays with a vividly communicative yet scholarly style, alternating harpsichord and organ music to make a stimulating and diverting programme. His harpsichord is a copy of a Hemsch, his organ a modern copy of a small eighteenth-century instrument in Nuremberg. Both are beautifully recorded. This is a disc you might easily pass by. But don't. Professor Gifford is a highly persuasive advocate and his two instruments are perfectly recorded.

ORGAN MUSIC

Complete organ music

Vol. 1: Chorales: *Ach Gott, erhör mein Seufzen; Ach Herr mich armer Sünder; Allein in Gott in der Höh' sei Her'; Sei Lob und Ehr dem höchsten Gut; Wer nur den lieben Gott lässt walten; Fantasia sopra 'Freu dich sehr, o meine Seele'; Prelude & Fugue in C; Toccatas & Fugues: in A min.; E; Trio in E flat*

(BB) *** Naxos 8.553924. Gnann (Gabler organ, Weingarten Abbey)

Both Naxos and Priory are currently undertaking a complete survey of Krebs's organ music. Fortunately both organists are players of calibre.

For Volume 1, Gerhard Gnann has chosen the Gabler organ in Weingarten Abbey, built between 1737 and 1750. It is a superb example of a large baroque organ, with throaty reeds (obvious from the very opening of the *Toccata in E*) and boldly powerful pedals, demonstrated splendidly in the *Prelude in C major*. The organ's fine palette of colours is obvious in the slow chorales, where Gnann makes sure the cantus firmus is very clear. His playing reveals the power and contrast inherent in the large-scale pieces, yet finds all the charm in the *galant Trio*. There are 65 minutes of music here, and if the Naxos series continues on this level it will be hard to beat.

Vol. 1: *Chorales: Ach Gott, erhör mein Seufzen; Ach Herr mich armer Sünder; Christ lag in Totesbanden; Herzlich lieb hab ich dich, o Herr; Nun freut euch, lieben Christen gmein; Sei Lob und Ehr dem höchsten Gut; Von Himmel hoch; Was Gott tut, das ist wohlgetan. Fantasia à giusto italiano; Fugues: in A min.; C min.; F. Prelude in C; Prelude sopra 'Sei Lob und Ehr dem höchsten Gut'; Prelude & Fugue in F min.; Prelude sopra 'Christ lag in Todesbanden'; Prelude sopra 'Was Gott tut, das ist wohlgetan'; Trios: E flat; 1 & 2 in F*

*** Priory PRCD 734. Kitchen (organ of Canongate Kirk, Edinburgh)

The organ used by John Kitchen is a modern instrument, built by Frobenius of Denmark, in the Canongate Kirk in Edinburgh. It, too, has character, its reeds slightly less pungent than the German instrument used on Naxos, but not lacking edge in *fortissimo* and glowing with colour in the chorales. When Kitchen registers *pro organo pleno*, the richness of texture is all but orchestral. The pedals have plenty of weight and are telling, even though they blend more smoothly into the overall texture than with the baroque instrument.

In many cases Kitchen offers us two versions of the same chorale and in the *organo pleno* version of *Nun freut euch* the tutti is thrilling. Like Gnann, Kitchen has planned each collection in the form of a recital, and Volume 1 (78 minutes) ends with three fugues, of which the closing scalic piece in F makes a powerful coda.

Vol. 2: *Chorales: Freu dich sehr, o meine Seele; Jesu meine Zuversicht; Von Gott will ich nicht lassen; Wir glauben all an einen Gott, Vater; Wir glauben all an einen Gott, Schöpfer* (3-verse setting); *Fantasia & Fugue in F; Prelude sopra 'Von Gott will ich nicht lassen'; Prelude & Fugue in C min.; Toccata & Fugue in E; Trios: in D min.; E flat; A min. Fantasia sopra 'Freu dich sehr, o meine Seele'*

*** Priory PRCD 734. Kitchen (organ of St Salvator's Chapel, St Andrews University)

The St Andrews organ dates from 1974 and was built by Gregor Hradetzky. It has a slightly more baroque tang than the Edinburgh instrument, as John Kitchen demonstrates in the opening *Toccata and Fugue in E*. This opens with a virtuoso pedal solo and then exploits the antiphonal use of two manuals. The performance is properly grand, yet the instrument's pretty reed colouring comes to the fore in the three engaging *Trios*, which are placed at strategic points in the programme. In several cases we are invited to enjoy different settings of the same *cantus firmus*. Kitchen ends with a three-verse chorale setting of *Wir glauben*, and although the third verse is jubilant and ends with a powerful *Amen*, one is left with the feeling that this is a less substantial (73-minute) programme than Volume 1, although it suits the organ in St Andrews very well.

Complete Works for Organ & Instrumental Obbligato. Clavierübung, Books 1 & 2: 13 Chorale Preludes (complete)

(N) (M) *** MDG 614 971-2 (2). Rami (Gabler organ, Weingarten), with Dean, Westerman, Hartwich, Bruns

We are familiar with the solo organ music of Bach's favourite pupil, but here we find him exploring a field that he did not create but rather made his own, using well-known chorales as a basis for simple variations and allotting the cantus firmus to a wind or brass instrument. Here Krebs offers us eight *Fantasias* and 11 different *Chorale Preludes* with three different settings for *Wachet auf* (twice boldly stated by a trumpet, and once on the clarino), and the remainder given one setting each. *Trauer Gott, ich muss die klagen* is heard on the oboe (against piquant registration), and this same solo instrument is also used effectively for *Jesu, meine Freude* and *Wie schön leuchtet der Morgernstern*. Then a flute is featured in *Meine seele, ermuntre dich* and a corno da caccia is used for *Est ist gewisslich an der Zeit* and *Kommt her zu mir*, and so on. To complete the collection, MDG gives us both books of Krebs's *Clavierübung*, a further series of 13 *Chorale Preludes*, where the invention of the variants is of a higher order, as there is no solo wind instrument and the organist has to hold the listener's attention alone. This Franz Rami does admirably, while earlier his colleagues from the Hassler Consort, using period instruments, are equally expert in their solos. The recording and documentation are well up to MDG standard.

KREISLER, Fritz (1875–1962)

Violin Concerto in the Style of Vivaldi
*** DG (IMS) 439 933-2. Shaham, Orpheus CO – VIVALDI: *Four Seasons* ***

An amiable pastiche, which sounds almost totally unlike Vivaldi as we experience his music performed today. It is warmly played and clearly enjoyed by its performers, and the sumptuousness of the sound is the more striking, coming, as it does, immediately after Vivaldi's wintry winds.

Allegretto in the Style of Boccherini; Aucassin & Nicolette; Berceuse romantique; Caprice viennoise; La gitana; Liebesfreud; Liebesleid; Marche miniature viennoise; Menuett in the Style of Porpora; Polichinelle; Praeludium & Allegro in the Style of Pugnani; La Précieuse in the Style of Louis Couperin; Rondino on a Theme of Beethoven; Schön Rosmarin; Sicilienne & Rigaudon in the Style of Francoeur; Syncopation; Tambourin chinois; Tempo di Minuetto in the Style of Pugnani; Toy-Soldiers' March
(N) (B) *** Decca 2-CD 475 6715 (2). Bell, Paul Coker (with 'Violin Favourites': BLOCH: *Nigun (Baal Shem)*. BRAHMS: *Hungarian Dance 1* (arr. Joachim). FALLA, arr. Kreisler: *La vida breve: Spanish Dance*. GRASSE: *Wellenspiel*. NOVACEK: *Perpetuum mobile*. PAGANINI: *Cantabile, Op. 17*. SARASATE: *Carmen Fantasy, Op. 25*. SCHUMANN: *Vogel als Prophet*. SIBELIUS: *Romance, Op. 78/2; Mazurka, Op. 81/1*. WIENIAWSKI: *Scherzo-tarantelle, Op. 16; Thème original varié, Op. 15* (with Sanders))

As readily shown by the opening *Praeludium & Allegro*, Joshua Bell refuses to treat this music as trivial, and there is a total absence of schmaltz. *Tambourin chinois*, impeccably played, lacks something in charm, but not the neatly articulated *La Précieuse*. And what lightness of touch in *Schön Rosmarin*, what elegance of style in the *Caprice viennoise*, what panache in the paired *Liebesfreud* and *Liebesleid*, and how seductive is the simple *Berceuse romantique*, one of the novelties here, like the winning *Toy-Soldiers' March* and the unexpected, almost Joplinesque rag, *Syncopation*. The recording is completely realistic. This recital has now been reissued as a Double with a further disc of encores, of which the most substantial item is the luscious *Carmen Fantasy* of Sarasate. They are played with similar elegance and flair, and equally persuasively accompanied by Samuel Sanders. If you want 2 hours and 9 minutes of violin lollipops, very realistically recorded, this reissue could prove ideal.

Encores: *Andantino in the style of Martini; Caprice Viennoise; Liebesleid; Recitative & Scherzo capriccioso, Op. 6; Schön Rosmarin; Siciliano & Rigaudon in the Style of Francoeur; Tempo di minuetto in the Style of Pugnani. Syncopation; Toy Soldiers' March; Tambourin chinoise.* **Arrangements:** ALBENIZ: *Tango.* CHAMINADE: *Sérénade espagnole.* DVORAK: *Slavonic Dances 2 in E min.; 3 in G; Songs my Mother taught me.* GLUCK: *Mélodie.* GRAINGER: *Molly on the Shore.* GRANADOS: *Spanish Dance 5.* CHOPIN: *Mazurka 45 in A min., Op. 67/4.* LEHAR: *Frasquita: Serenade.* SCHUMANN: *Romance in A, Op. 94/2*
☛ (M) *** EMI (ADD/DDD) 5 62601-2. Perlman, Sanders

Drawn in the main from four separate recitals, recorded between 1972 and 1985, these *morceaux de concert* show Perlman in sparkling form, the selection not missing favourites like *Caprice Viennoise* and *Liebesleid*, while the pastiche items like the *Minuet in the Style of Pugnani* are played with elegant simplicity. Perlman's supreme mastery has rarely been demonstrated more endearingly than in the collection of arrangements, where the partnership with Samuel Sanders has the intimacy of equals rather than that of star soloist and accompanist. The original pieces here include such artless charmers as *Syncopation* (jauntily relaxed), and the inclusion of Grainger's *Molly on the Shore* in the transcriptions is both unexpected and successful. The recording is vivid and realistic, the balance placing Perlman well forward but with the piano well in the picture.

Aucassin et Nicolette; Caprice viennoise; La gitana; Marche miniature viennoise; 3 Old Viennese Dances (Liebesfreud; Liebesleid; Schön Rosmarin); Praeludium & Allegro in the Style of Pugnani; Preghiera in the Style of Martini; Sicilienne & Rigaudon in the Style of Francoeur; Slavonic Fantasie on Themes by Dvořák; Tambourin chinois. **Arrangements of:** CHAMINADE: *Sérénade espagnole.* DVORAK: *Slavonic Dance, Op. 72/2.* SCOTT: *Lotus Land.* TCHAIKOVSKY: *Chant sans paroles, Op. 2/3.* MENDELSSOHN: *Songs without Words: Andante espressivo in G, Op. 62/1.* RACHMANINOV: *Rhapsody on a Theme of Paganini: Variation.* LEHAR: *Frasquita: Serenade.* ANON.: *Londonderry Air.* ALBENIZ: *España: Tango, Op. 165/2.* HEUBERGER: *Midnight Bells*
☛ (M) *** Classic fM 75605 57020-2. Hattori, Seiger

Joji Hattori brings to these Kreisler trifles not only a brilliant technique and rich, firm violin-tone, but the rhythmic flair and naughty pointing of phrase which makes them sparkle. The 22 encores include not only original pieces by Kreisler, but his inspired violin arrangements of favourite pieces by such composers as Dvořák, Tchaikovsky, Rachmaninov, Lehár and others. Also a sequence of the pieces he wrote, originally attributing them to then-neglected eighteenth-century composers like Pugnani, Francoeur and Martini. The gently lyrical *Preghiera* after Martini inspires Hattori to hushed, meditative playing just as intense as his bravura fireworks in such pieces as *Tambourin chinois*. Joseph Seiger is a comparably inspired accompanist, relishing the *glissando* display in such a piece as *La gitana*. Warm, full recording. A best buy among mid-priced recordings of the repertoire.

Caprice viennoise; Chanson Louis XIII & Pavane in the Style of Couperin; La gitana; Liebesleid; Liebesfreud; Polichinelle; La Précieuse in the Style of Couperin; Rondino on a Theme by Beethoven; Scherzo alla Dittersdorf; Tambourin chinois; Schön Rosmarin. **Arrangements:** BACH: *Partita 3 in E, BWV 1006: Gavotte.* BRANDL: *The Old Refrain.* DVORAK:

Humoresque. FALLA: *La vida breve: Danza española.*
GLAZUNOV: *Sérénade espagnole.* HEUBERGER: *Midnight
Bells (Im chambre séparée).* POLDINI: *Poupée valsante.*
RIMSKY-KORSAKOV: *Sadko: Chanson hindoue.* SCHUBERT:
Rosamunde: Ballet Music 2. SCOTT: *Lotus Land.*
TCHAIKOVSKY: *Andante cantabile from Op. 11.* WEBER:
Violin Sonata 1 in F, Op. 10: Larghetto. TRAD.: *Londonderry
Air*

(M) (***) EMI mono 7 64701-2. Kreisler, Rupp or Rachelsein;
or (in *Scherzo*) Kreisler String Qt

Impeccable and characterful performances by Fritz Kreisler
of his own lollipops, including those 'in the style of' pieces
with which – until he owned up – he fooled his audiences
into believing were actually written by the composers in
question. Most of the recordings were made with Franz Rupp
in 1936 or 1938, and the transfers offer a convincingly realistic
if studio-ish balance and are of excellent technical quality; a
few (the *Polichinelle*, the pieces in the style of Couperin, the
Schubert *Rosamunde Ballet Music*, the Glazunov and Weber
arrangements, *The Old Refrain* (especially) and an indulgent
performance of Heuberger's *Im chambre séparée*) date from
1930, and here the piano-balance is poor, the piano badly
defined. However, these were recorded before Kreisler's accident and the violin timbre is noticeably more opulent. A
valuable document.

KREUTZER, Conradin (1780–1849)

*Septet (for clarinet, horn, bassoon, violin, viola, cello &
double-bass), Op. 62; (i) Trio in E flat (for piano, clarinet &
bassoon), Op. 43*

❀ (BB) *** Arte Nova 74321 54462-2. Mithras Octet
(members), (i) with Rivinius (piano)

A delightful performance to suggest that the *Septet* by Conra-
din Kreutzer is almost more infectiously enjoyable than the
Beethoven *Septet* on which it was modelled (in 1824). The
members of the Mithras Octet have the full measure of the
music, playing with grace and elegance and an infectious
charm, while the recording is excellent in every respect. The
Trio is a similarly amiable and inventive work, if less distinctive. It has a doleful *Andante grazioso* and is capped by
another memorably light-hearted finale. It is very well played
here; but unfortunately the piano, recorded too resonantly,
outbalances the pair of woodwind instruments, and this
reduces the listener's enjoyment. The Rosette is for the *Septet*,
which is not to be missed.

KREUTZER, Joseph (1778–1832)

Grand Trio for Flute, Clarinet & Guitar, Op. 16

*** Mer. CDE 84199. Conway, Silverthorne, Garcia –
BEETHOVEN: *Serenade;* MOLINO: *Trio* ***

Joseph Kreutzer, thought to be the brother of Rodolphe,
dedicatee of Beethoven's *A major Violin Sonata*, wrote many
works for the guitar, of which this is a delightful example.
The guitar, given at least equal prominence with the other
instruments, brings an unusual tang to the textures of this
charming piece, ending with a rousing *Alla polacca*. A nicely
pointed performance on Meridian, very well recorded in
warm, faithful sound.

KREUTZER, Rodolphe (1766–1831)

Grand Quintet in C

(BB) **(*) Hyp. Helios CDH 55015. Francis, Allegri Qt –
CRUSELL: *Divertimento;* REICHA: *Quintet* **(*)

This is the Kreutzer of the Beethoven sonata. The *Grand
Quintet* is thought to date from the 1790s; it is somewhat
bland but rather enjoyable when played as beautifully as it is
here. This is part of an attractive triptych, now offered by
Hyperion at bargain price. However, the CD plays for under
50 minutes.

KROMMER, Franz (Kramář, František) (1759–1831)

Clarinet Concerto in E flat, Op. 36

*** ASV CDDCA 763. Johnson, RPO, Herbig – CRUSELL:
Concerto 1; KOZELUCH: *Concerto 2* ***
(M) *** Warner Elatus 0927 49558-2. Kam, Württemberg CO,
Heilbronn, Faerber – MOZART: *Clarinet Concerto* ***

Emma Johnson is at her most winning in this attractive
concerto, which is made to sound completely spontaneous in
her hands, particularly the engaging finale, lolloping along
with its skipping main theme. The *Adagio* is darker in feeling,
its mood equally well caught. Excellent accompaniments and
warm, refined recording make this a most engaging triptych.

Sharon Kam's performance is also very attractive and full
of personality, and she is well accompanied by Faerber. If you
prefer the Mozart *Concerto* as a coupling, she plays that very
well too and with real charm.

Oboe Concertos in F, Op. 37 & 52

☛ (BB) *** Hyp. Helios CDH 55080. Francis, LMP, Shelley
– MOZART: *Oboe Concerto* ***

These two concertos were published in 1803 and 1805 respectively. Needless to say, Sarah Francis winningly essays all the
music's changes of mood and style: her exquisite timbre and
elegant phrasing would surely have delighted this attractively inventive Bohemian composer, as would Howard Shelley's polished accompaniments, delicate or full-blooded as
necessary.

Symphonies 2 in D, Op. 40; 4 in C min., Op. 102

*** Chan. 9275. LMP, Bamert

Collectors who acquired the *Harmonien* wind band music on
Naxos will know how infectiously high-spirited this composer
is; and they will not be disappointed by the two symphonies
played here by the London Mozart Players under Matthias
Bamert. They present a different picture of him: the *D major
Symphony* (1803) opens in something of the manner of *Don
Giovanni*, while much else conveys a distinctly Beethovenian
visage. The *C minor*, Op. 102, composed towards the end of the
second decade of the nineteenth century, already has a whiff of
the changing sensibility that we find in Schubert and Weber.
Very interesting and refreshing music, played with evident
enthusiasm, and well recorded.

Oboe Quartets 1–2, IX:21/2; 2 Oboe Quintets in C, VII:12/13

(N) (BB) *** Regis RRC 1201. Francis, Tagor String Trio, with
Barritt

Krommer's music was greatly admired in its day, and although
it is slight, its charm is as undeniable as its craftsmanship.

Sample the simple interplay of parts at the opening *Quintet in C* or the wistful *Adagio* of the *First Quartet* to be instantly won over, while the Rondo finales are engagingly light and vivacious in the hands of the stylish Sarah Francis. She dominates the performances without swamping her companions, and the recording has an agreeable intimacy.

Partitas: in E flat; in B flat, Op. 45/1–2; in E flat with 2 Horns, FVK 2d
☛ (BB) *** Naxos 8.553868. Michael Thompson Wind Ens.

Partitas: in F, Op. 57; E flat, Op. 71; B flat, Op. 78. Marches, Op. 31/3–5
☛ (BB) *** Naxos 8.553498. Budapest Wind Ens.

Franz Krommer specialized in music for wind instruments, of which the two *Partitas*, Op. 45, were always among his most popular works, exploiting the conventional wind band (or *Harmonie*) of flutes, oboes, horns and bassoons in pairs, plus trumpet on occasion. Even more striking – and not published till this century – is the third *Partita* here, with the two horns given virtuoso solo roles, a concerto in all but name. Vividly recorded, this Naxos issue offers masterly performances from the ensemble of leading London performers previously led by Barry Tuckwell.

The second Naxos disc is just as successful as its predecessor. The Budapest Wind, led by their exuberant clarinettist Kálmán Berkes, are a first-rate ensemble, full of spirit and personality. They yield nothing in terms of artistic excellence or recording quality to any rivals.

Octet-Partitas in B flat, Op. 67; in E flat, Op. 79
(M) *** CRD (ADD) CRD 3410. Nash Ens. – DVORAK: *Serenade for Wind* ***

The Nash Ensemble give excellent and lively accounts of both these attractive pieces. This is not great music, but it is highly agreeable (the main theme of the first movement of Op. 67 is engagingly ingenuous) and the Nash Ensemble readily demonstrate their charms in a direct way, for which the bright recording is admirably suited.

KUHLAU, Friedrich (1786–1832)

Overtures: Elisa; Elverhøj (The Elf's Hill); Hugo and Adelheid; Lulu; The Magic Harp; The Robber's Castle; The Triplet Brothers from Damask; William Shakespeare
*** Chan. 9648. Danish Nat. RSO, Schønwandt

Lulu is a fairy-tale opera from the same source as *Zauberflöte*, while *William Shakespeare* is based on the Bard's (alleged) youthful exploit of poaching deer. This delightful disc, brilliantly played and recorded, offers all seven of Kuhlau's opera overtures, plus his most famous work: the overture to the classic Danish play, *Elverhøj* (*Elf's Hill*).

Flute Quintets 1–3, Op. 51
*** ASV CDDCA 979. Stinton, Prospero Ens.
(BB) *** Naxos 8.553303. Rafn, Sjogren, Rasmussen, Andersen, Johansen

Kuhlau's *Flute Quintets* are charmingly amiable works, well crafted, with fresh invention, the slow movements having surprising expressive depth. We are marginally inclined to prefer the playing of Jennifer Stinton, and she gets excellent support from the Prospero Ensemble, but their Scandinavian competitors are also first class, and Eyvind Rafn is also a soloist of personality. Both recordings are vivid and present.

Violin Sonatas: 1 in F min., Op. 33; 2 in E flat, Op. 64; 3 in F; 4 in F min.; 5 in C, Op. 79/1–3
(BB) *** CPO 999 363-2. Bratchkova, Meyer-Hermann

This collection of Kuhlau's complete *Violin Sonatas* is a delightful surprise. Written between 1820 and 1827, they have much in common with the violin sonatas of Beethoven, and it is surprising how often one is reminded of that master when listening to these attractive and in no way superficial works. The slow movement of the *F minor* and also the finale bring the most striking echoes, but the composer's own personality also emerges strongly, notably in the attractive variations on a Danish folksong which form the slow movement of the *E flat* work and in the *Rondo* finale. The three Op. 79 works are undoubtedly masterpieces, full of life and with invention of a consistently high order. The performances by the Bulgarian violinist Dora Bratchkova and Andreas Meyer-Hermann are in every way first rate, and they are most naturally balanced and realistically recorded. If you enjoy the Beethoven violin sonatas, you will certainly enjoy these.

Lulu (opera; complete)
*** Kontrapunkt/HM 32009/11. Saarman, Frellesvig, Kiberg, Cold, Danish R. Ch. & SO, Schønwandt

This *Lulu* comes from 1824 and is surely too long: the spoken passages are omitted here – but, even so, the music takes three hours. The opening of Act II has overtones of the Wolf's Glen scene in *Der Freischütz* and the dance of the black elves in the moonlight is pure Mendelssohn – and has much charm. The invention is generally fresh and engaging, though no one would claim that it has great depth. The largely Danish cast cope very capably with the not inconsiderable demands of Kuhlau's vocal writing, the Danish Radio recording is eminently truthful and vivid, and Michael Schønwandt draws excellent results from the Danish Radio Chorus and Orchestra.

KUHNAU, Johann (1660–1722)

Der Gerechte kommt um (motet)
(M) *** O-L 443 199-2. Christ Church Ch., AAM, Preston – BACH: *Magnificat*; VIVALDI: *Nisi dominus*, etc. ***

Kuhnau was Bach's predecessor in Leipzig. He wrote this charming motet with a Latin text; it was later arranged in a German version, and there are signs of Bach's hand in it. The piece makes an excellent makeweight coupling for the original version of Bach's *Magnificat*.

Magnificat in C
(N) *** EuroArts DVD 2053419. York, Bartosz, Dürmüller, Mertens, Amsterdam Bar. Ch. & O, Koopman – BACH: *Magnificat, BWV 243a; Cantata 10* ***
*** BIS CD 1011. Persson, Tachikawa, Türk, Urano, Bach Coll., Japan, Suzuki – BACH: *Magnificat in D*; ZELENKA: *Magnificats in C & D* ***

Johann Kuhnau died the year before the Bach *Magnificat* came into being in its first (E flat) incarnation. Kuhnau's own setting is his most ambitious work and calls for large forces (a five-part chorus, three trumpets, timpani, two oboes, strings, including two viola parts and continuo) and is thought to have been composed for a Christmas service at Leipzig. It is not otherwise available on CD and any rival will have to be pretty stunning to match this version from Masaaki Suzuki and his largely Japanese forces. It is not as consistently inspired as the Zelenka (let alone the Bach) but it is well worth hearing. Apart from the excellence of his singers and instrumentalists, the recorded sound is quite exemplary.

Koopman's DVD has the added advantage of the visual imagery in the beautiful St Thomas's Church, Leipzig, where both this setting and Bach's follow-up version were first heard. In all respects the performance is first class, and the recording is wonderfully vivid. DVD collectors need not hesitate: it stands out among Bach recordings in this medium.

KULLAK, Theodor (1818–82)

Piano Concerto in C min., Op. 55
*** Hyp. CDA 67086. Lane, BBC Scottish SO, Willén –
DREYSCHOCK: *Piano Concerto* ***

Theodor Kullak, on the evidence of this most attractive concerto, was a very gifted composer, with melody coming easily to him. A strong march-like theme dominates the first movement and, when the piano enters, the glittering passagework lies somewhere between that in the Liszt and Chopin concertos, while the romantic secondary tune has a comparable heritage. The central movement is equally engaging, with bursts of energy, never languishing, and the glittering Weberian finale makes one smile with pleasure at the witty audacity of the main theme. The work is given a scintillating performance by Piers Lane, vigorously and sensitively supported by the BBC Scottish players under Niklas Willén. The recording is first class.

KURTÁG, György (born 1926)

Aus der Ferne III; Hommage à András Mihály (12 Microludes for String Quartet), Op. 13; Hommage à J. S. Bach; Ligatura y (both for String Trio); Officium breve in memoriam Andreae Szervánszky, Op. 28; Ligatura for 2 violins; Perpetuum mobile (for String Trio)
(N) (***) EuroArts **DVD** 2050759. Keller Qt (members) –
BACH: *Art of Fugue*, etc. (***)

György Kurtág studied in Paris with Milhaud and Messiaen, then returned to Budapest, and much of this music reflects the difficult political times in Hungary's recent history, which the composer himself experienced. Not one of it is easy listening, but the sheer concentration and dedication of the players ensure that it is all communicated. The three pieces for string trio are a good entry point into his spare sound-world, but the work dedicated to his friend Andreas Szervánszky has great emotional intensity, which comes over the more when one can both see and hear the players. The drawback is that each of these pieces alternates with *Contrapuncti* from Bach's *Art of Fugue*. However, they are, of course, accessible separately.

KUUSISTO, Jaakko (born 1974)

Between Seasons, Op. 7
*** Finlandia 8573 84714-2. Helsinki Strings, Csaba & Géza
Szilvay – VIVALDI: *Four Seasons* **(*)

The Finnish composer and violinist, Jaakko Kuusisto, wrote his suite of interludes so that they could be performed either in conjunction with the Vivaldi or on their own, prompting the eye-catching title of this disc, *The Seven Seasons*. The very titles of the movements bear out that role as links between each season: *May Day*, *Wind and Water* and finally *First Snow*. Partly designed to give the main violin soloist a rest, they make attractive, evocative interludes, with the harpsichord nicely integrated into the texture, with direct echoes mainly of Bartók but also of the Stravinsky of the string works. Vivid, immediate sound, very well balanced.

LALO, Edouard (1823–92)

Cello Concerto 1 in D min., Op. 33
*** ASV CDDCA 867. Rolland, BBC PO, Varga – MASSENET:
Fantaisie; SAINT-SAENS: *Cello Concerto 1* ***
*** EMI (ADD) 5 55528-2. Du Pré, Cleveland O, Barenboim –
R. STRAUSS: *Don Quixote* *** ✿
(B) *** EMI Début 5 73503-2. Phillips, Bav. Chamber O,
Plasson – CAPLET: *Epiphany;* FAURE: *Elégie* ***
*** DG 427 323-2. Haimovitz, Chicago SO, Levine –
SAINT-SAENS: *Concerto 1;* BRUCH: *Kol Nidrei* ***
(M) *** DG (ADD) 457 761-2. Fournier, LOP, Martinon –
BLOCH: *Schelomo;* BRUCH: *Kol Nidrei;* SAINT-SAENS:
Cello Concerto 1 ***

Sophie Rolland plays with effortless eloquence and is given responsive support from the BBC Philharmonic under Gilbert Varga, though he is a little brusque in the *Intermezzo*. An enjoyable and convincing performance. The excellence of the BBC/ASV recording makes for a strong recommendation.

Jacqueline du Pré's recorded repertory is thrillingly expanded in previously unpublished recordings of Strauss and Lalo. While the studio recording of *Don Quixote*, dating from 1968, has been pieced together from long-buried tapes, this recording of the Lalo *Concerto* was taken live from a broadcast in Cleveland in January 1973, right at the end of du Pré's playing career, in one of her last remissions from multiple sclerosis. It is a masterly performance and is totally involving, even though the cello is balanced rather more backwardly than in du Pré's studio recordings. In spite of that, her fire at the opening grabs the attention, leading on to a performance that is both passionate and poetic.

Emmanuel Plasson and his Bavarian Chamber Orchestra open Lalo's *Cello Concerto* with a bold dramatic flourish, and Xavier Phillips enters with a firm, full timbre, his line romantically strong. Yet he soon slips into gentle lyricism for Lalo's lovely secondary theme. The unusually clear (yet not unflattering) acoustic means that Lalo's scoring never congeals, and the cello focus is clean and truthful. In short, this version of a much-recorded work matches any of its competitors.

An outstandingly impressive début from Matt Haimovitz; the performance throughout combines vitality with expressive feeling in the most spontaneous manner. The recording is very well balanced indeed and highly realistic.

Fournier's performance has dignity and character and he is well supported by Martinon, who secures spirited playing from the Lamoureux Orchestra. The recording, from 1960, has never sounded better than in this new DG 'Originals' transfer. Excellent value.

(i) *Concerto russe; Violin Concerto in F. Scherzo; Le Roi d'Ys Overture*
*** Chan. 9758. (i) Charlier; BBC PO, Y. P. Tortelier

Yan Pascal Tortelier opens with a marvellously rumbustious account of *Le Roi d'Ys Overture*, with its melodramatic brass and luscious cello solo, and he includes also an equally fine account of the orchestral *Scherzo*. But the main value of this disc is Olivier Charlier's seductive accounts of the two concertante works (both written for Sarasate). The *Violin Concerto* is engagingly songful and ought to be better known, but the real find is the *Concerto russe*, in essence a sister work to the *Symphonie espagnole*, but with Slavonic rather than sultry Spanish inspiration. The *Intermezzo* has witty offbeat comments from the timpani, and there is a sparkling finale introducing two more striking ideas. Charlier is obviously in his element throughout both works, relishing their lyricism. Tortelier – with the help of Lalo – provides a vivid orchestral backcloth, and the opulent, well-balanced Chandos recording adds to the listener's pleasure.

Namouna (ballet): extended excerpts *(Suites 1–2 & Allegro Vivace; Tambourin; La Gitane; Bacchanale)*
**(*) Auvidis V 4677. Monte Carlo PO, Robertson

Namouna (ballet): *Suites 1–2; Valse de la cigarette*
**(*) ASV CDDCA 878. RPO, Butt (with GOUNOD: *Mors et Vita: Judex*)

There is no complete version available of Lalo's ballet, but David Robertson has added four more items to the content of Lalo's two *Suites*, plus the charmingly Gallic *Valse de la cigarette* (which the composer extracted as a separate number). He has also re-established the music in ballet-order, whereas in the *Suites* Lalo reassembled the items for concert performance. Robertson secures sensitive, polished playing from his Monte Carlo orchestra, who resound with warmth, and the recording has plenty of colour and ambience.

Yondani Butt achieves performances of the *Suites* and the *Valse de la cigarette* which have comparable colour and finesse, and the RPO play extremely well. Even so, they don't necessarily upstage their French competitors and they offer less music. Where they gain is in the *Prélude*, which is an unashamed crib from Wagner's *Das Rheingold*. The ASV disc offers a big *religieuse* Gounod tune as an encore, but more of *Namouna* would have been preferable.

Symphonie espagnole (for violin and orchestra), *Op. 21*
⌀━ *** EMI 5 55292-2. Chang, Concg. O, Dutoit –
VIEUXTEMPS: *Violin Concerto 5* ***
(M) *** Virgin 5 61910-2. Tetzlaff, Czech PO, Pešek –
DVORÁK: *Violin Concerto* ***
(M) *** DG (IMS) 445 549-2. Perlman, O de Paris, Barenboim – SAINT-SAENS: *Concerto 3*; BERLIOZ: *Rêverie et caprice* ***
*** Claudio CB 5256-2. Jin, LSO, Wordsworth – SARASATE: *Carmen Fantasy* ***; PROKOFIEV: *Solo Violin Sonata* *** (with KROLL: *Banjo and Fiddle* orch. BRADBURY; TARREGA: *Recuerdos de la Alhambra*, arr. RICCI **(*))
(B) **(*) Sony (ADD) SBK 48274. Zukerman, LAPO, Mehta – VIEUXTEMPS: *Concerto 5* **(*)
(BB) **(*) EMI Encore 5 74735-2. Mutter, O. Nat. de France, Ozawa (with MASSENET: *Thaïs: Meditation*) – SARASATE: *Zigeunerweisen* **(*)
(N) ** Decca 2-CD 475 6706 (2). Bell, Montreal SO, Dutoit (with CHAUSSON: *Poème*; MASSENET: *Thaïs: Méditation*; RAVEL: *Tzigane*; SARASATE: *Zigeunerweisen*; YSAYE: *Caprice*) – SAINT-SAENS: *Concerto 3* etc. **

Symphonie espagnole, *Op. 21* (omitting *Intermezzo*)
(M) (**(*)) RCA mono 09026 61753-2. Heifetz, RCA Victor SO, Steinberg – CHAUSSON: *Poème* **(*); SAINT-SAENS: *Havanaise*, etc.; SARASATE: *Zigeunerweisen* (***)

(**(*)) APR Signature mono APR 5506. Huberman, VPO, Szell – BEETHOVEN: *Violin Concerto* (***)

Sarah Chang's dazzling account of Lalo's five-movement feast of Spanish dance-rhythms goes readily to the top of the list. Dutoit provides a vigorous backing and the soloist's seductive lilt in the shimmering malaguena of the first movement is matched by the sparkling seguidilla rhythms of the *Scherzo* and the bouncing habanera of the *Intermezzo*. The *finale* scintillates. The orchestra readily echoes Chang's sparkle, and the expansively resonant recording is ideally balanced.

Tetzlaff's account of the Lalo is marked by playing of quicksilver lightness in passage-work, bringing out the element of fantasy. Equally the soloist's concentration makes for a sense of spontaneity, leading one on magnetically in this episodic work. As for Tetzlaff's accompanists – chosen no doubt specifically for the Dvořák – the Czech Philharmonic's playing under Pešek proves just as idiomatic in the Spanish dance-rhythms of Lalo as in Czech dances, with crisp ensemble and rhythms deliciously sprung and the advantage of the resonant ambience is to give a more expansive warmth to the overall sound than in Perlman's DG version.

Although the lively digital sound remains a trifle dry, Perlman's performance easily maintains its place near the top of the list. For the reissue in the Masters series, the Berlioz *Rêverie et caprice* makes an attractive if brief bonus.

Min Jin's essentially delicate approach is very appealing and it was with this Lalo work that she made her début at the age of twelve. Barry Wordsworth's spacious opening sets the mood for her warm yet gently lyrical entry, and how delicately and seductively she introduces the secondary theme. The *Scherzo* is again lightly pointed. The *Andante* then becomes the heart of the performance, with a noble breadth in the orchestral introduction and the soloist entering on an exquisite half-tone, managing the gentle rhythmic snaps very engagingly. The chirping woodwind opens the finale invitingly, and again she displays airily blithe phrasing in her lilting bowing. The Abbey Road recording is very well balanced and natural.

Among the encores the *Recuerdos* of Tárrega (arranged for solo violin by Min Jin's mentor, Ruggiero Ricci) is a distinct novelty, and is bowed with exquisite fragility; but the transcription is not really convincing. Kroll's *Banjo and Fiddle* (with orchestra) is more successful: good-humoured, and played with warmth as well as virtuosity.

Heifetz's 1951 account has superb panache and there are no complaints about the mono recording. Alas, he omitted the *Intermezzo* (a practice curiously common in his time), which is our loss, but the performance of the rest, like all the music on this CD, is dazzling.

Zukerman's performance is outstandingly successful. He plays with great dash and fire yet brings a balancing warmth. His couplings are more generous than Perlman's, but the effect of the DG recording is to give Perlman's account slightly more romantic finesse.

Anne Sophie Mutter's account brings a dazzling display of bravura in the outer movements. Many will find the delicacy of her phrasing in the second subject of the first movement refreshing, with its absence of schmaltz. Both in the *Intermezzo* and in the *Andante* there is solo playing of passionate eloquence, the timbre richly expansive. The balance, however, projects the violin well to the front, and the slightly-too-close microphones add a touch of shrillness to the upper range. As an encore, Massenet's *Méditation* from *Thaïs* is played gently and dreamily, and here Karajan's accompaniment sounds more sumptuous.

Joshua Bell is not at his finest in the Lalo Spanishry. Dutoit opens rather heavily, and Bell's reading of the secondary theme is rather bland, missing its Mediterranean languor. Overall, the performance lacks spontaneity and fire, until it springs to life in the finale. Splendidly glowing Montreal sound and a good balance hardly compensate, although the various shorter pieces offered as encores are much more successful, especially the rhapsodical Chausson *Poème* and the Ravel *Tzigane* and Ysaÿe *Caprice*, both of which are dazzling.

Huberman, like Heifetz, omits the central *Intermezzo*. Yet as a historic document this makes a welcome coupling for Huberman's classic reading of the Beethoven concerto with the same accompanists. Here more than in the Beethoven, Huberman indulges in surprising swoops of *portamento* – another sign of the times – though always with perfect control to match the sweetly expressive style.

Piano Trios 1 in C min., Op. 7; 2 in B min.; 3 in A min., Op. 26
*** ASV CDDCA 899. Barbican Piano Trio

As always with Lalo, this is the kind of unpretentious, inventive, well-crafted and delightful music which nineteenth-century civilization seemed able to foster and their composers to produce – and of which the late twentieth was conspicuously and lamentably bare. There is not much to say about the performances, except to note their excellence and poise.

LAMBERT, Constant (1905–51)

Apparitions (Ballet; arr. of Liszt); *Mars & Venus* (Ballet; arr. of Scarlatti)
(N) (M) *** Dutton CDLX 7149. Royal Ballet Sinfonia, Wordsworth (with LANCHBERY: *Tales of Beatrix Potter*: Excerpts) – L. BERKELEY: *Judgement of Paris: Suite* ***

Constant Lambert's delightful arrangements of four Scarlatti *Keyboard Sonatas*, chosen by Marie Rambert, for a ballet strangely entitled *Mars and Venus*, managed to retain much of the character and charm of the originals, to make entertaining listening. But finer still was *Apparitions*, created jointly with Gordon Jacob. Lambert's scenario was derived from Berlioz's *Symphonie fantastique*, for which he chose the music of Liszt with great skill, and it was brilliantly orchestrated by Jacob. The ballet itself was only a partial success, but the score itself is masterly, opening and closing with the romantic *D flat major Consolation*, and with all the Liszt pieces following on as if the work had been composed as an entity. Just sample the sequence of movements, including the Offenbachian *Galop*, leading to the *Elegy, Evening Bells* and *Carillon* to discover just how well Lambert dovetailed Liszt's ideas; and the finale, based on the *Mephisto Waltz No. 3* and *Venezia*, is very dramatic indeed. The music is superbly played and recorded, and this CD, which celebrates the choreography of Sir Frederick Ashton and includes also a suite from Lanchbery's *Tales of Beatrix Potter*, is far more than a nostalgic memento.

Aubade héroïque; (i) The Rio Grande; (ii) Summer's Last Will and Testament
☛ *** Hyp. CDA 66565. E. N. Philh. O, Lloyd-Jones; (i) with Gibbons; (ii) Burgess, Shimell, Ch. of Opera North & Leeds Festival

The Rio Grande, Lambert's jazz-based choral concerto setting of a poem by Sacheverell Sitwell, is one of the most colourful and atmospheric works from the 1920s. The *Aubade héroïque* is an evocative tone-poem inspired by Lambert's memory of a beautiful morning in Holland in 1940 when, with the Nazi invasion, it was far from certain whether he and his colleagues would be able to get back to England. *Summer's Last Will and Testament* is a big, 50-minute choral work, setting lyrics by the Elizabethan, Thomas Nashe, on the unpromising subject of the threat of plague. Lloyd-Jones and his outstanding team, mainly from Opera North, bring out the vitality and colour of the writing, with each of the nine substantial sections based on Elizabethan dance-rhythms. The recording in all three works is full, vivid and atmospheric.

The Bird Actors Overture; Pomona (ballet); Romeo and Juliet (ballet)
*** Chan. 9865 Victoria State O, Lanchbery

Pomona is well served by John Lanchbery and his Victoria State Orchestra, even if it does not quite command the elegance of the David Lloyd-Jones account on Hyperion. This present issue also brings *Romeo and Juliet*, which Lambert composed for Diaghilev, and which has not been recorded since Norman Del Mar's version on a Lyrita LP from the late 1970s (also coupled with *Pomona*). *The Bird Actors* is a short overture of some three minutes, originally intended for an earlier ballet called *Adam and Eve*. Recommended to all with a taste for this engaging composer.

(i) Piano Concerto (for piano & 9 players); (ii) Horoscope (ballet suite); (ii; iii) The Rio Grande
(M) **(*) Decca 473 424-2. (i) Stott; (ii) D. Jones, BBC Singers; BBC Concert O, Wordsworth

With bright, forward recording this account of *The Rio Grande* is rather more aggressive than the Hyperion one (see below) and is a degree more literal, less idiomatic in its interpretation of jazzy syncopations, but the power and colour of the writing come across with fine bite and clarity. In the ballet suite from *Horoscope* there is one more movement than Lambert ever recorded, the *Palindromic prelude*, less striking than the other movements but still beautifully written. Here again Wordsworth and the BBC Concert Orchestra are a degree more literal than Lambert himself was in jazz-rhythms. Kathryn Stott with members of the orchestra gives splendid point to the angular *Concerto* for piano and nine players, where the emotional element is much more severely repressed than in the other works on the disc. This is now reissued at mid-price in Decca's British Music Collection and is worth considering for the *Piano Concerto* alone.

(i) Piano Concerto (1924). Merchant Seamen (Suite); Pomona; Prize Fight
(M) *** ASV CD WHL 2122. BBC Concert O, Wordsworth, with (i) Owen Norris

The *Piano Concerto* of 1924 was composed three years before *The Rio Grande*. Lambert's preferred scoring was for two trumpets, strings and timpani. It is very characteristic, with something of the spirit of Milhaud, jazzy and entertaining. *Prize Fight*, also from 1924, is Lambert's first ballet and his earliest surviving orchestral score. It is a rumbustious work for the same forces as the concerto and lasts a mere nine minutes. Lambert's score for the documentary, *Merchant Seamen*, dates from 1940 and he drew on this for a five-movement suite two years later. The most familiar of the pieces here is the ballet *Pomona*, which receives a most sympathetic performance at the hands of the excellent BBC Concert Orchestra and Barry Wordsworth. In fact, the playing throughout is very good indeed, and so is the ASV/BBC recording.

Horoscope (complete ballet)

(N) *** ASV CDDCA 1168. BBC Concert O, Wordsworth –
   WALTON: *Wise Virgins* ***

Like *The Wise Virgins*, Lambert's *Horoscope*, a colourful work on an astrological theme, dates from a vintage period of the Sadler's Wells ballet company at the beginning of the Second World War. Until now it has appeared on disc only in truncated form as an orchestral suite, but on this ASV issue Barry Wordsworth has resurrected four extra items to make up the complete ballet. Though the newly restored movements are not as striking as those we already know, Wordsworth's warmly sympathetic readings make a strong case for the revival of the original ballets.

Horoscope: Suite

☛━◆ (BB) *** Hyp. Helios CDH 55099. E. N. Philh. O, Lloyd-Jones – BLISS: *Checkmate*; WALTON: *Façade* ***

The suite from *Horoscope* is sheer delight. David Lloyd-Jones is very sympathetic to its specifically English atmosphere. He wittily points the catchy rhythmic figure which comes both in the *Dance for the Followers of Leo* and, later, in the *Bacchanale*, while the third-movement *Valse for the Gemini* has a delectable insouciant charm. Excellent playing and first-class sound, perhaps a shade resonant for the ballet pit, but bringing plenty of bloom. A superb bargain.

Pomona (ballet); Tiresias (ballet)

*** Hyp. CDA 67049. E. N. Philh. O, Lloyd-Jones

Pomona, written for Diaghilev in 1927, finds Lambert deftly echoing the neo-classical Stravinsky and Les Six in his sequence of formal dances. *Tiresias*, completed not long before Lambert died, is more ambitious, the work of a composer steeped in the dramatic needs of ballet. The thematic material may not be so memorable as in Lambert's finest works, but with strong rhythmic invention and rich sounds – the piano often prominent – it is most attractive, only disappointing in the downbeat ending.

CHAMBER MUSIC

(i; ii) *Concerto for Piano & 9 Players*; (i) *Piano Sonata*; (iii; i) *8 Poems of Li-Po*; (iv; i) *Mr Bear Squash-you-all-flat*

*** Hyp. CDA 66754. (i) Brown; (ii) Nash Ens., Friend; (iii) Langridge; (iv) Hawthorne

Constant Lambert's remarkable qualities are in excellent evidence here in the Nash Ensemble's anthology which brings two of his most powerful works, the *Concerto for Piano and Nine Players* and the *Piano Sonata*, as well as one of his most delicately wrought, the *Eight Poems of Li-Po*, in a lovely performance from Philip Langridge. Ian Brown proves an equally exemplary advocate in the *Concerto* and the *Piano Sonata*, which is not generously represented on disc. *Mr Bear Squash-you-all-flat* is Lambert's first composition, an entertainment written at roughly the same time as Walton's *Façade*, when Lambert was still in his teens, and based on a Russian fairy story. Imaginative and accomplished but, hardly surprisingly, not first-class Lambert. It is not certain whether

Lambert meant the text to be spoken, but Sir Nigel Hawthorne speaks it excellently; he is balanced somewhat reticently (a fault on the right side).

Salome (incidental music): Suite

*** Hyp. CDA 67239. Nash Ens., Lloyd-Jones – WALTON: *Façade* ***

The three items drawn from Constant Lambert's incidental music for Oscar Wilde's *Salome* make a pleasing extra for the excellent Hyperion version of Walton's *Façade* entertainment. They were written for the first staging in English in 1931 of that controversial play, using four of the *Façade* instruments, clarinet, trumpet, cello and percussion. Long buried in the BBC Music Library, Lambert's score was discovered by Giles Easterbrook, who confected this suite of two atmospheric scene-setting fragments, followed by Salome's dance and sudden demise, a long way after Strauss. With Richard Hosford on clarinet and John Wallace on trumpet, the performance is exemplary and very well recorded.

LAMOND, Frederic (1868–1948)

Symphony in A, Op. 3; Overture: Aus dem schottischen Hochlande, Op. 4; Sword Dance

*** Hyp. CDA 67387. BBC Scottish SO, Brabbins – D'ALBERT: *Overture: Esther* ***

Frederic Lamond was one of the most distinguished interpreters of Beethoven's piano music in the early years of the last century, making a number of impressive recordings. Born in the Glasgow area, he came from a poor family but, thanks to the dedication of his father, a Scottish weaver who devoted himself to local music-making, and helped also by an older brother and sister, he was able to study in Germany and to get to know Liszt and Brahms among others. It is sad that, once he achieved success as a pianist, he never continued composing, for these are strong, inventive works, built on memorable themes, superbly orchestrated. Thanks to vigorous, finely judged performances by Brabbins and the BBC Scottish Orchestra, they make a powerful impact, with the four movements of the *Symphony* well contrasted. There are obvious influences – from Beethoven in the energetic Scherzo and, above all, from Brahms in the finale, which starts with a bare-faced crib from the *Second Symphony* – but the fluency and confidence of the writing with the occasional hint of a distinctive Scottish flavour make such echoes of little importance. The *Overture* is similarly inventive, with some glorious writing for the horns, and the *Sword Dance*, a Scottish reel using drone basses, makes one curious about the opera from which it is taken. Though these performances were recorded in the difficult acoustics of Usher Hall in Edinburgh, the engineers have produced excellent sound.

LANGLAIS, Jean (1907–91)

(i) *Messe solennelle*; (i; ii; iii) *Missa salve regina*; (Organ): (i) *Paraphrases grégoriennes, Op. 5: Te Deum. Poèmes évangéliques, Op. 2: La Nativité. Triptyque grégorien: Rosa mystica*

*** Hyp. CDA 66270. Westminster Cathedral Ch., Hill, (i) with O'Donnell; (ii) Lumsden; (iii) ECO Brass Ens.

Jean Langlais's organ music owes much to Dupré's example, and the two Masses are archaic in feeling, strongly influenced by plainchant and organum, yet with a plangent individuality that clearly places the music in the twentieth century. The style is wholly accessible and the music enjoys fervent advocacy from these artists, who are accorded sound-quality of the high standard one expects from this label.

LANNER, Joseph (1801–43)

Badner Ring'ln (Baden Round Dance). Ländler: Dornbacher; Neue Wiener. Hofballtänze; Steyrische Tänze. Waltzes: Abend-Sterne; Die Kosenden; Pesther; Die Romantiker; Die Schönbrunner; Die Weber

(M) **(*) RCA (ADD) 74321 84145-2. Berlin SO or VSO, Stolz

It was Joseph Lanner, rather than the Strausses, who fathered the Viennese waltz. This fascinating RCA collection dates from the beginning of the 1970s. Robert Stolz, using a full-bodied string section, conducts the whole programme liltingly and with gusto, and the reverberant recording, if not ideally refined, suggests the ambience of a large ballroom. The more robust *Ländler* of Opp. 1 and 9 were peasant dances, which Stolz makes clear by his bold rhythmic emphases. But we soon enter the Viennese upper-class ballroom with the much more sophisticated cyclic waltz, with an introducion and coda. *Die Weber*, for instance, begins with a fast introduction before the undulating waltz tune appears.

The *Styrian Dances* are particularly charming. *Pesther* opens with the brass in march time, but then lightens (with harp roulades) and the opening melody of *Abend-Sterne* ('Evening Stars') is quite seductive, sounding very like 'Under the lilac he played his guitar' while *Die Kosenden* ('The Lovers') has an agreeable rhythmic lift. The finale item, *Die Schönbrunner*, opens ruggedly on the brass, but the first waltz theme is the soul of delicacy, and this is another of Lanner's more sophisticated pieces, with a telling *rallentando* before the coda. All in all an excellent introduction to an underrated and very influential composer.

Galops: Amazonen; Jägers Lust; Malapou. Ländler: Neue Wiener. Polonaise: Bankett. Polka: Cerrito. Waltzes: Marien-Walzer; Steyrische Tänze; Die Weber

(BB) **(*) Naxos 8.555689. Vienna Tanzquartett – J.
STRAUSS: *Pariser-Polka; Wiener Blut Walzer*, etc. **(*)

The arrangements, for string quartet, would have been heard all over Austria's coffee-houses and restaurants in the 19th century, and the Tanzquartett Wien easily evoke that period. This CD sensibly mixes some energetic polkas with the more leisurely waltzes and a single Ländler to make a good representative programme. The recording and performances are both good, if not quite in the superlative league.

LARSSON, Lars-Erik (1908–86)

(i; ii) *Folkvisenatt; Liten marsch;* (iii) *Little Serenade; Pastoral Suite, Op. 19;* (iv) *Variations for Orchestra;* (v) *Winter's Tale;* (vi) (Piano) *Croquisiers: Espressivo*

**(*) Swedish Society (ADD) SCD 1051. (i) Stockholm SO, Westerberg; (ii) Orrebro CO, Hedwall; (iii) Stockholm CO; (iv) Swedish R. O, Ehrling; (v) Stockholm PO, Westerberg; (vi) Larsson

Most of these performances date from the 1960s, and this CD should be offered at a bargain price, particularly as the playing time is less than an hour. Best known is the celebrated *Pastoral Suite*, which Stig Westerberg recorded over 40 years ago and which sounds fresher than ever. Probably the most substantial piece is the *Variations for Orchestra*, Larsson's flirtation with serialism, from the 1960s, which is not just ingenious but full of fantasy and inspiration. Ehrling's account with the Swedish Radio Orchestra still comes up well, despite a rather dry acoustic. Much care has been taken over the transfers and the sound is excellent. The final item is Larsson himself playing one of his set of *Croquisiers*. An excellent introduction to this most likeable composer.

Förklädd Gud, Op. 24: Lyric Suite for Soprano, Baritone, Narrator, Chorus & Orchestra

(*) Marco Polo 8.225123. Inglebäck, Anders Larsson, Lindkvist, Amadel Chamber Ch., Swedish Chamber O, Sundkvist – ROSENBERG: *Den heliga natten (Holy Night)* *

Förklädd Gud is a product of a collaboration between the poet Hjalmar Gullberg and Lars-Erik Larsson in the enlightened days when radio stations broadcast poems with accompanying specially commissioned music. It is a charming and lyrical piece with a Nielsenesque directness of utterance. Sundkvist's performance holds its own against earlier competition and can be recommended to all with a feeling for and interest in Swedish music.

Symphonies 1 in D, Op. 2; 2, Op. 17

**(*) BIS CD 426. Helsingborg SO, Frank

The *First Symphony* is derivative but is a work of obvious promise, fluent and well put together. There are obvious echoes of the Russian post-nationalists as well as of Nielsen and Sibelius. Much the same could be said of the more mature *Second Symphony* (1936–7), which is genial and unpretentious. Good performances and recording, but the music itself is not Larsson at his strongest.

Symphony 3 in C min., Op. 34; (i) *Förklädd Gud (A God in Disguise), Op. 24*

** BIS (ADD) CD 96. (i) Nordin, Hagegård, Jonsson, Helsingborg Concert Ch., Helsingborg SO, Frykberg

A God in Disguise was a production for Swedish Radio. The choral suite for two soloists and narrator that Larsson fashioned from it has great freshness and charm. This 1978 performance has some fine singing from Håkan Hagegård, and the Helsingborg chorus and orchestra give a serviceable account of the score. The symphony is as diatonic as *A God in Disguise* and, though not completely successful, is strong enough to deserve rescue.

Quattro tempi (Divertimento for Wind Quintet)

(BB) ** Naxos 8.553851. Michael Thompson Wind Quintet –
BARBER: *Summer Music* **(*); HINDEMITH: *Kleine Kammermusik* **(*); JANACEK: *Mládí* **(*)

Lars-Erik Larsson's *Quattro tempi* are pleasing open-air pieces, written in 1968, which has not made their way into the repertoire. The Michael Thompson Wind Quintet give a most expert and sensitive performance, but the close balance is even more disturbing than in its couplings and seriously detracts from the pleasure this music should give. Disappointing.

Croquisier, Op. 38; 7 Little Fugues with Preludes in the Old Style, Op. 58; Sonatinas 1, Op. 16; 2, Op. 39; 3, Op. 41

*** BIS CD 758. Pålsson

Larsson's piano music is slight but far from insignificant. It is beautifully fashioned, always intelligent and often witty. Hans

Pålsson serves it with exemplary taste and expertise. It is well recorded, and those who like Larsson's music need not hesitate.

LA RUE, Pierre de (c. 1460–1518)

Missa Pascale a 5; Missa de Septem Doloribus beatissimae Marie Virginis a 5; Pater de caelis, Deus a 6; Vexilla Regis/Passion Domini a 4

(N) *(*) Naxos 8.554656. Ars Antiqua de Paris, Sanvoisin

Missa de Sancta Cruce; Motets: Considera Israel; Salve Regina III; Vexilla Regis

(N) *** ASV Gaudeamus CDGAU 307. Clerks' Group, Wickham (with Johann de QUADRIS: *Lamentations* ***)

Pierre de la Rue spent most of his career at the Burgundian court, where he became virtually a court composer. He travelled little and was not exposed to outside influences as was his more famous contemporary, Josquin. In his Masses his polyphony is complex and swift moving, the harmonic implications relatively plain, although the *Salve Regina* and *Vexilla Regis* are richer in texture. Edward Wickham and his Clerks' Group negotiate the intricacies of the imitative writing with skill, especially the triple-time writing in the *Gloria* and *Credo*. The two-part *Lamentations* of Johannes de Quadris are further examples of the spare vocal writing of the mid-fifteenth century, but this is a specialist collection rather than one for the general collector.

The Parisian group on the Naxos disc offers us two further Masses, but their singing is much less secure, and the more complicated textures of the writing bring problems of ensemble and intonation.

LASSUS, Orlandus (c. 1532–94)

Chansons and Morescas: Allala, pia Calia; Canta Giorgia; Cathalina; Chi chilichili?; Elle s'en va; En un chasteau; Fuyons tous l'amour le jeu; Hai, Lucia; Je l'ame bien; Las! me faut-il; Lucescit jam o socii; Lucia, celu; Mais qui pourroit estre celuy; La Nuict froide et sombre; O foible esprit; O Lucia; Si du malheur; Une Jeune Moine est sorti du couvent; Une Puce j'ay dedans l'oreille; Un Triste Coeur; Vignon, vignon, vignette. (i) *Lute pieces: J'ay un mary; Quand mon mary vient de dehors; Le Tems peult bien*

(B) **(*) HM Musique d'abord HMA 1951391. Ens. Janequin, Visse; (i) Bellocq (lute)

This delightful collection of chansons and morescas, with three short lute pieces acting as a central interlude, shows an entirely different Lassus from the more familiar composer of deeply devotional church music. Even though they were published in Paris as late as 1581, they were written in his youth, and are expressive and humorous by turns. *Si du malheur* and *Un Triste Coeur* are full of melancholy, while the title of *La Nuict froide et sombre* speaks for itself. But even in his mature years Lassus could be a humorist, and the light-hearted works, inspired by the spirit of the *commedia dell'arte*, show that readily. They include morescas – villanellas with texts parodying African dialect, characterized by quirky rhythms, a swift interplay of voices, and often sudden changes of tempo. *Cathalina* and *Hai, Lucia* are engaging examples, sung here with vivacious aplomb, while in *Lucescit jam o socii*, the four voices sing alternately in Latin and French. The great drawback to this reissue is that the texts are

provided without translations and the notes do not tell the listener what the songs are about. This is a quite unforgivable omission, when the performances are so idiomatic and lively. The recording too is vividly atmospheric.

Chansons from France; German Lieder; Italian Madrigals & Villanelles

(N) **(*) CPO 999 855-2. Die Singphoniker

This excellent Bavarian vocal sextet offers a well-contrasted collection of Lassus's lighter (unaccompanied) secular settings, including drinking songs, and love songs which are singularly explicit in their texts, with unsubtle metaphors about male desires and amorous intentions. There are seven German songs, eight French chansons and five Italian madrigals and villanelles. The group members blend together perfectly. They sing with feeling and vitality, and their intonation cannot be faulted. The snag is that, while their pronunciation is secure in all three languages, they are unable to project the colloquial inflexions of the French and Italian songs so that their national flavour is diluted. Full translations are included, so there is still much to admire and enjoy here, and this repertoire reveals another side to the composer, far away from the church altar.

Le lagrime di San Pietro a 7

(BB) *** Naxos 8.553311. Ars Nova, Holten

*** HM HMC 901483. Kiehr, Koslowsky, Berridge, Türk, Lamy, Koay, Peacock, Ens. Voc. Européen, Herreweghe

Le lagrime di San Pietro (*The Tears of St Peter*) is a late work, a setting of 21 verses of the poet, Luigi Transillo (1510–68), a Neapolitan best known for his lyrical love-sonnets. The music is rich in variety of expressive means: Howard Mayer Brown calls it a work of 'almost Baroque religious fervour'. The Naxos performance by a first-class Danish choir (6 sopranos, 2 altos, 2 counter-tenors, 4 tenors and 3 basses) is comparatively robust yet offers singing of great sensitivity and a wide dynamic range. The recording, made at the Copenhagen Grundtvigskirken, has a properly spacious ambience, yet is admirably clear.

The *Lagrime di San Pietro* is a work of great expressive purity and is also performed by Herreweghe's forces with dedication and perfection in the matter of intonation. Excellent recording.

9 lamentationes hieremiae

(BB) *** Regis RRC 1123. Pro Cantione Antiqua, Turner

*** HM HMC 901299. Paris Chapelle Royale Ens., Herreweghe

(i) *9 lamentationes hieremiae;* (ii) *Missa pro defunctis (Requiem) for 4 voices;* (i) *Aurora lucis rutilat;* (hymn for Lauds); *Magnificat on Aurora lucis rutilat. Motets: Christus resurgens; Regina coeli laetare; Surgens Jesus*

(B) *** Hyp. Dyad CDD 22012 (2). Pro Cantione Antiqua, (i) Turner, (ii) Brown

The competing Harmonia Mundi set of the *Lamentations* is available on a single, premium-priced disc, whereas for approximately the same cost this Hyperion Dyad offers much more music. Within this set, Bruno Turner's 1981 digital recording of the *Lamentations* is also now accommodated on a single CD, while the second includes a selection of music for Easter Sunday, including the glorious *Aurora lucis rutilat* for two five-part choirs and the *Magnificat* based on the motet, plus Mark Brown's fine performance of the four-part

Requiem. The performances under Bruno Turner are expressive and vital. The recording too is spacious and warm. So for that matter is the Harmonia Mundi recording for the Chapelle Royale and Philippe Herreweghe, whose performances of the *Lamentations* are hardly less admirable.

Like the Harmonia Mundi version, Bruno Turner's 1981 digital recording (originally Hyperion) of the *Lamentations* is now accommodated on a single CD. The performances are expressive and vital and the recording, too, is spacious and warm. So, for that matter, is the Harmonia Mundi recording for the Chapelle Royale and Philippe Herrewege, whose performances of the *Lamentations* are hardly less admirable. However, the Regis reissue has a considerable price advantage.

Missa bell'amfitrit'alterna

- (BB) *** Naxos 8.550836. Oxford Schola Cantorum, Summerly – PALESTRINA: *Missa hodie Christus natus est*, etc. ***
- (B) **(*) CfP 575 5602. St John's College, Cambridge, Ch., Guest – ALLEGRI: *Miserere* **(*); PALESTRINA: *Missa Veni sponsa Christi* **(*)

This magnificent Mass of Palestrina's great Flemish contemporary, Lassus, makes a superb coupling for the outstanding performances of Palestrina masterpieces on the Naxos disc. This is the full Schola Cantorum of Oxford, not just the smaller Camerata group, and arguably it is too large for the dedicated, intimate polyphony of Lassus; but the singing is superb and the recording is warm and atmospheric. Yet another outstanding Naxos issue of early music.

Amphrite was not only the mythological goddess of the sea but also a nickname for Venice, and this Mass is almost certainly connected with the city rather than with Poseidon's wife. It is a complex and varied piece of remarkable textural diversity, and it is finely sung at St John's, although perhaps a little more Latin fervour would have been in order. The digital recording is first class.

Missa osculetur me; Motets: Alma redemptoris mater; Ave regina coelorum; Hodie completi sunt; Osculetur me; Regina coeli; Salve regina; Timor et tremor

- *** Gimell CDGIM 018. Tallis Scholars, Phillips

Lassus learned the technique of double-choir antiphonal music in Italy. The Mass is preceded by the motet, *Osculetur me* (*Let him kiss me with the kisses of his lips*), which provides much of its motivic substance and is glorious in its sonorities and expressive eloquence. The singing of the Tallis Scholars under Peter Phillips is as impressive as it was on their earlier records, and the recording is beautifully present.

(i) Missa pro defunctis (Requiem) for 4 voices; (ii) Aurora lucis rutilat (hymn for Lauds); Magnificat on Aurora lucis rutilat. Motets: Christus resurgens; Regina coeli laetare; Surgens Jesus

- (BB) *** Regis RRC 1124. Pro Cantione Antiqua, Brown; (ii) Turner

Originally coupled with the *Lamentations* (see above), the Pro Cantione Antiqua's selection of music for Easter Sunday includes a glorious *Aurora lucis rutilat* for two five-part choirs and the *Magnificat* based on the motet, plus Mark Brown's fine performance of the four-part *Requiem*. The performances are of high quality, as is the recording.

Missa pro defunctis (Requiem) à 5; (i) Alma Redemptoris mater à 6; (i) Ave Maria à 5; (i; ii) Magnificat (Praeter rerum serium) à 6. O bone Jesu à 4

- (M) *** DHM/BMG (ADD) 82876 60153-2. L. Pro Cantione Antiqua, Turner; with (i) Hamburg Wind Ens. für Alte Musik; (ii) Coll. Aur. (members)

Lassus's *Requiem à 5* of 1580 stays close to the Gregorian chants for the *Missa pro defunctis*, with the setting often allotting a simple *cantus firmus* to the solo tenor. The choral contribution brings much rich homophony, reaching a celestial climax in the *Offertorium, Domine Jesu Christe*, with the following *Sanctus* serene and the rest of the Mass maintaining this deeply moving but tranquil mood.

The large-scale *Magnificat* of 1582 uses Josquin's motet, 'Praeter rerum serium' as its model: it is powerfully sustained and richly scored, here using cornets and trombones to fill out the textures. They are retained in the two motets, *Alma Redemptoris mater* and *Ave Maria*, with the comparatively gentle unaccompanied *O bone Jesu* providing an expressive interlude. Superb singing and playing throughout, under the wise directing hand of Bruno Turner, and wonderfully sonorous recording in an ideal ambience make this a collection to cherish.

Missa: Tous le regretz; Motets, Hymns & antiphons: Aurora lucis rutilat; Ave verum corpus; Domine convertere; Salve regina; Surgens Jesus; Timor et tremor; Tristis est anima meo; Veni creator

- (N) *** CRD CRD 3517. New College, Oxford, Ch., Higginbottom

The *Mass Tous les regretz* is based on a six-voice chanson by Nicholas Gombert, and in this performance the Mass movements are interspersed with some of Lassus's finest shorter pieces, including the Eastertide hymn and motet, *Aurora lucis rutilat* and *Surgens Jesus*, with its joyous 'Alleluias' stirringly sung here, while *Timor et tremor* and *Tristis est anima meo* show the despairing and apprehensive side of the composer's faith. However, after the lovely, serene *Benedictus* and *Agnus Dei* of the Mass, Higginbottom ends his programme with the Marian antiphon, *Salve regina*, and the Pentecostal hymn, *Veni creator*, with its glowing confidence in salvation. Whether liturgically correct or not, this musical sequence works well, and the performances could not be more dedicated or more beautifully sung. The recording, too, is first class.

LAWES, Henry (1596–1662)

Songs: *Amintor's welladay; The angler's song; Come sad turtle; Fairwell despairing hopes; Hark, shepherd swains; I laid me down; I prithee send me back my heart; The lark; My soul the great God's praises sings; O King of heaven and hell; Sing, fair Clorinda; Sitting by the streams; Slide soft you silver floods; Sweet stay awhile; Tavola; Thee and thy wondrous deeds; This mossy bank*
*** Hyp. CDA 66315. Kirkby, Consort of Musicke, Rooley

The Lawes songs were enormously popular in their time. Today their direct, declamatory style seems comparatively unsubtle alongside Purcell. The melancholy is tangible, but not overtly expressive. The brief but effective *Tavola* is like an arietta from an Italian opera. The Hyperion collection is fairly wide in its range: the title-number (*Sitting by the streams*) is a verse anthem. There are plenty of secular songs too, notably the engaging *Angler's song*, and admirers of Emma Kirkby – here in radiant voice – and Anthony Rooley's immaculately stylish Consort of Musicke will find much to enjoy.

LAWES, William (1602–45)

Consort Setts a 5 1–5; Consort Setts a 6, 1–5
*** Allia Vox AV 9823 (2). Hespèrion XXI, Savall

Consort Setts a 5 1–5; Consort Setts a 6 1–5; 2 Airs for Lyra Viol; Airs for 3 Lyra Viols; 5 Dances for Lyra Viol
(B) **(*) Virgin 2x1 5 62001-2 (2). Fretwork, Nicholson (organ)

The *Consort Sett*s reveal a distinct musical personality, not as strong as Purcell's, but with an individual lyrical gift, a propensity for moments of dissonance and the skill of a craftsman. Like Dowland, Lawes also had a penchant for melancholy.

The *Consort Sett*s in five and six parts are in three movements, usually consisting of a pair of *Fantazies* and an *Air*, or sometimes a plaintive *Paven*. Scored for viols with an underlying organ continuo, they are through-composed – each of the movements draws on the same thematic material, and Lawes weaves his part-writing to achieve the fullest possible sonorities. The *Fantazies* are searching, usually melancholy or sombre in feeling, while the *Air*s provide lighter contrast. Jordi Savall and Hespèrion XXI give well-paced, expressive performances, often intense, and the balance of the viols with the organ avoids making the texture opaque. However, unlike Fretwork, they offer no bonus items, which makes the Allia Vox issue less competitive, even though the Hespèrion performances would be a first choice for the complete set.

The Fretwork viols are closely balanced, which reduces the dynamic range of the playing, while the organ integrates so well with the vibrato-less string texture that there seems a lack of contrast in colour, if not in feeling. The pieces for lyra bring a livelier 'country dance' feel, but when one turns to the Concordia collection below, the effect is undoubtedly fresher.

Consort Setts a 6 in B flat; in F; in D; Lyra Viol Trios in D; in D min.; Catches; Come my Lads, Hark Jolly Lads; Whither go Ye?; The Wise Men were but Seven
⊙ *** Metronome METCD 1045. Concordia, Levey

Mark Levey and Concordia also give stylish and appealing performances of these three well-chosen *Consort Sett*s in six parts. The playing is alert and sensitive, and the recording is very successful. It was made in Orford Church, Suffolk, and the acoustics and microphone placing seem just right to bring a pleasing freshness of string texture (seventeenth-century viols are used), yet attractively underpinned by the organ. Incidentally, they play the *F major Fantasy* with the four movements in a different order from Jordi Savall's version (*Fantazy–Air–Fantazy–Air*, instead of the other way about). The pacing here is exceptionally well judged to reveal the full character of all these works. It is good to have the *Lyra Viol Trios*: the *D major*, with its central movement entitled *Humor* and with a closing *Saraband*, is a striking little work. The catches, which act as interludes, are paired, in each case alternating slow and fast examples. The curious title of the collection, *Knock'd on the Head*, refers to the composer's death at the siege of Chester; but as the 'knock' came from a bullet, it hardly seems an appropriate description, and the sobriquet could put some collectors off acquiring the disc, which is very recommendable.

Fantasia Suites for 2 Violins, Bass Viol & Organ 1–8
*** Chan. 0552. Purcell Qt

Lawes studied with Coperario, and Lawes's own *Fantasia Suites* are based on those of his mentor but are simpler, usually more extrovert works than the *Consort Suites*. They are in three movements, in each case a *Fantazy* followed by two *Aires*, in essence dance movements, *Alman* and *Galliard*, later *Corant* or *Saraband*. The organ does not just play a continuo role but is important in its own right. The music itself is lively in invention and by no means predictable, with surprise moments of passing dissonance, and the composer's individuality comes out in his special brand of lyricism. The performances here have plenty of life, and the recording balance is very successful: the result is enjoyably fresh.

Royal Consorts 1–10
*** Chan. 0584/5. Purcell Consort

Royal Consorts 1 in D min.; 3 in D min.; 6 in D; 7 in A min.; 9 in F
*** Gaudeamus CDGAU 146. Greate Consort, Huggett

Royal Consorts 2 in D min.; 4 in D; 5 in D; 8 in C; 10 in B flat
*** Gaudeamus CDGAU 147. Greate Consort, Huggett

The 10 *Royal Consorts*, even though they are in four rather than five or six parts like the *Setts*, in many ways represent Lawes's most ambitious undertaking. There is evidence that he conceived the works as simple quartets (two violins and two viols) around 1620, but a decade later theorbos (archlutes) were added, to provide a basic continuo and increase the range of textural colour. Each suite is in six or seven movements, the first of which is the most extended, sometimes taking as long as the remaining charming *Aires* and increasingly lively *Almans*, *Corants* and *Sarabands*, all put together. Indeed, these opening expressive *Fantazies* or *Pavanes* offer the kernel of the arguments and contain the most adventurous music, combining nobility of feeling with ear-catching contrapuntal lines.

The playing of the Purcell Consort is notably sprightly, the recording fresh and vividly clear, but within an open acoustic of some depth. The brightness and transparency of the sound, without loss of sonority, means that the individual instruments are cleanly delineated, although blending well together, never better demonstrated than in the splendidly managed *Echo* movement that ends the first work of the series.

Monica Huggett and her Greate Consort are very slightly recessed; their sound is warmer and the expressive music is given a fuller texture by the resonance. Some will feel that, presented in this way, this music is afforded more atmosphere. They also play at a slightly lower pitch, which means that the effect is inevitably mellower when compared directly with the brighter Chandos sound, although on ASV detail is by no means unclear. Both sets of performances are very rewarding, and if we are inclined, marginally, to favour the bright projection and added transparency of Chandos, many collectors will surely respond differently.

Collections

Consort Setts a 5: in A; C (2); F & G; Consort Pieces a 4: 2 Aires in C; 2 Aires in C min.; Aire (Fantazy) in C; Fantazy in C min. (VdGS 108/113)
⊙ *** Channel Classics CCS 15698. Phantasm

The playing of Phantasm explores a wide dynamic range and is beautifully blended in its delicacy and warmth, in no way edgy or acerbic. The group is most naturally recorded and this disc is as fine an introduction to Lawes's consort music as any in the catalogue.

Consort Setts a 5: in A min. & C; Divisions on a Pavan in G min. for 2 Bass Viols & Organ; Royal Consorts 1 in D min.; 6 in D; Sett a 4 in G min. (with 2 theorbos); Lute duets: Alman; 2 Corants

(BB) **(*) Naxos 8.550601. Rose Consort of Viols; Herigan, Miller (lutes), Roberts (organ)

Naxos provide an attractive cross-section of Lawes's instrumental music, using an all-viol texture for the string parts in the *Consorts* (with organ where appropriate). The group also include a fascinatingly bravura set of *Divisions for Viols and Organ* on the same *Pavane* which opens the four-part *Sett in G minor*. The pieces for two lutes could have been given more lively projection, although they are well enough played. The excellent balance helps to make this inexpensive sampler recommendable, which readers might well try.

LEBRUN, Ludwig (1752–90)

Oboe Concertos 1–6

(M) *** DG 471 724-2 (2). Holliger, Camerata Bern, Füri — MOZART: *Oboe Concerto* **(*)

Lebrun, a contemporary of Mozart, joined the Mannheim orchestra as oboist in the mid-1760s and soon rose to fame as one of the great virtuosi of the age. After 1778 he toured widely and his links with Mannheim weakened. He is more than an interesting historical figure, or a note spinner, like so many of his contemporaries. Although these six concertos do not have the depth of Haydn or Mozart, they are compositions of substance and imagination and well worth committing to disc, and the music is tuneful and elegant. The playing of Heinz Holliger and the Camerata Bern under Thomas Füri could hardly be more persuasive, and for this reissue on the Archiv Blue label DG have thrown in Holliger's earlier 1964 account of the Mozart *Oboe Concerto* for good measure (the second CD plays for 80 minutes).

LECLAIR, Jean-Marie (1697–1764)

Flute Concerto in C, Op. 7/3; Violin Concertos: in F; in A, Op. 7/4 & 6; in A, Op. 10/2

*** Chan. 0564. R. Brown; Standage, Coll. Mus. 90

Violin Concertos: in D min., Op. 7/1; in D; F; G min., Op. 10/3–4 & 6

*** Chan. 0589. Standage, Coll. Mus. 90

Violin Concertos: in D, Op. 7/2; in A min., 7/5; in B flat, Op. 10/1; in E min., Op. 10/5.

*** Chan. 0551. Standage, Coll. Mus. 90

The 12 concertos of Opp. 7 and 10 make up Leclair's complete orchestral output; generally speaking, they are underrated and their merits are considerable. Although one cannot include among these a strongly individual lyrical power, the *Aria gracioso* of No. 1 is quite ear-catching. The *Andante* of Op. 10/3 could well have been written by Vivaldi. Finales too are sprightly in their invention. Op. 7/3 is optionally for flute or oboe, and Rachel Brown makes a pleasing case for the use of a baroque flute, especially in the rather winning slow movement. Simon Standage is a stylish soloist of impeccable technique and Collegium Musicum 90 (4.4.2.2.1) provide authentic, spirited accompaniments. The recordings were

made either in St Jude's in northwest London or in All Saints', East Finchley, and textures are transparent and have good sonority.

Flute Sonatas (for flute & continuo), Op. 1/6; Op. 2/1, 3 & 11; Sonata for flute, viola da gamba & continuo, Op. 2/8; Sonata for 2 viola da gambas, Op. 12/1

⊖━ *** Mer. CDA 84381. Badinage

A well-planned collection that gives much pleasure. The *Flute Sonatas* are lightweight but consistently appealing, the *Sonata* for a pair of violas da gamba makes a good contrast, with its darker, lower sonorities very telling. In the *Sonata* that combines both solo instruments, the flute wins hands down in lightening the texture, even managing to make the gamba (very well played by Sally Givval) sound cheerful. Badinage is an excellent group: this is period-instrument playing at its most diverting; and the recording is very good, too.

Trio Sonatas: in D (Première récréation de musique d'une exécution facile), Op. 6; in A, Op. 14; Double Violin Sonata in D, Op. 3/6

**(*) Chan. 0582. Coll. Mus. 90 (Standage, Comberti, Coe, Parle)

The pair of *Trio Sonatas* prove to be elegant and tuneful French suites and, although the composer advertised the *D major* as making few technical demands on the players, it is by no means simplistic, and the extensive decorated *Chaconne* with which it ends (splendidly played here) is hardly music for beginners! The *Double Violin Sonata* opens with a tenderly melancholy *Andante* but proves a lively and engaging work with a dancing finale, even though the central *Largo* is again rather doleful. In short this is all highly attractive music with a consistently high standard of invention, and it is played on period instruments with fine style and much vitality. The recording cannot be faulted. The sole reservation, and it is not unimportant, is that Simon Standage's timbre has a characteristic cutting edge which some ears may find wearing after a time.

Violin Sonatas, Op. 9/2–3; 6–7

**(*) Hyp. CDA 67068. Convivium

Fine, stylish period-instrument playing here from Elizabeth Wallfisch, Richard Tunnicliffe and Paul Nicholson which has no lack of finesse and much vitality; but one wishes they could communicate a greater sense of warmth and enjoyment in the more expressive music. Such feelings really come over only in the (often dazzling) bravura passages, and Wallfisch's timbre really is spikey, so that after a while it becomes tiring to listen to.

LEHÁR, Franz (1870–1948)

Chinese Ballet Suite; Fata morgana; Korallenlippen; Marsch und Palótas; Ein Märchen aus 1001 Nacht; Peter and Paul in Cockaigne: Ballet Music; Preludium religioso; Resignation; Suite de danse; Zigeunerfest (ballet scene)

*** CPO 999 761-2. German (Berlin) RSO, Jurowski

A delightful concoction of unfamiliar Lehár, most of it stemming from his stage works. It is all highly tuneful and vivacious in the Viennese manner, with splashes of local colour – such as the delightful *Chinese Ballet Suite* and the very Hungarian-sounding *Fata morgana* – with lively orchestrations adding spice. Lehár's inventive ideas always engage the ear, helped by enthusiastic performances and a warm recording.

Gold and Silver Waltz, Op. 79

⊶ *** BBC (ADD) BBCL 4038. Hallé O, Barbirolli –
HAYDN: *Symphony 83 in G min. (La Poule)*; JOHANN
STRAUSS JR: *Emperor Waltz*, etc.; R. STRAUSS: *Der
Rosenkavalier Suite* ***

Lehár's finest waltz acts as an unforgettable encore for Barbirolli's 1969 Promenade Concert. He encourages the Prommers to hum along gently, yet not overwhelm the famous tune, and they even manage a *pianopianissimo* at the reprise. The result is magical.

Waltzes: *Eva; Gold and Silver; Gypsy Love. The Count of Luxembourg: Luxembourg. Giuditta: Where the lark sings. The Merry Widow: Ballsiren*

(BB) **(*) EMI Encore 5 74735-2. V. Johann Strauss O,
Boskovsky

Gold and Silver was Lehár's waltz masterpiece; the others are his arrangements, using melodies from the operettas. They are ravishingly tuneful and, given such warmly affectionate recordings and a digital recording which is sumptuous and has sparkling detail, this is easy to enjoy. Lehár's scoring is often imaginative, but in the last resort one misses the voices.

Overtures: *Clo-clo; Der Göttergatte. Die lustige Witwe.* Waltzes: *Adria; Altwiener; Grützner; Valse Boston (Wilde Rosen)*

**(*) CPO 999 891-2. Berlin RSO, Jurowski

These are large-scale performances of generally little-known Lehár, with the exception of the *Merry Widow Overture* (here in the composer's 1940 version). The less well-known concert waltzes are enjoyable, with a lovely robust theme in the *Altwiener Liebeswalzer Waltz*, with some felicitous writing throughout. It is hard to understand why the *Grützner Waltz*, with its beautiful opening building up to a fine waltz, very much in the Strauss tradition, was never published. The *Valse Boston* dispenses with the Strauss-like introduction and replaces it with a short *maestoso* to call the dancers to the floor. The overtures to *Clo-Clo* and *Der Göttergatte* are lively works and full of delightful ideas, as is the *Adria Waltz*, with a short but exhilarating introduction leading quickly to another good waltz tune (there is also an especially attractive minor-key waltz in this one). It is all very enjoyable, and the orchestra play to the manner born. The only reservation is the recording, which, although it allows details to emerge well, is just a bit too reverberant.

The Czarevitch (in English)

*** Telarc CD 80395. Gustafson, Hadley, Itami, Atkinson,
Carl, ECO, Bonynge

Though it lacks the really memorable melodies which make the finest Lehár operettas so winning, *The Czarevitch* is a delightful piece which, with Richard Bonynge as a most understanding conductor, is full of charm and sparkle, with Russian colour from balalaikas nicely touched in. Anyone wanting this in English translation will not be disappointed, with the second couple of principals readily matching up to Jerry Hadley and Nancy Gustafson.

(i) *Friederike;* (ii) *Giuditta;* (iii) *Der Graf von Luxemburg;* (iv) *Das Land des Lächelns;* (v) *Die lustige Witwe;* (vi) *Paganini;* (vii) *Der Zarewitsch* (all complete; in German)

(N) (BB) **(*) EMI (ADD/DDD) 585997-2 (13). (i) Kalenberg, Datz, Stadler, Fuchs, Donath, Dallapozza, Bav. R. Ch., Munich RSO, Wallberg; (ii) E. Moser, Hirte, Gedda, Baumann, Munich Conzert Ch. & R. O, Boskovsky; (iii) Gedda, Böhme, Litz, Brokmeier, Popp, Holm, Bav. State Op. Ch., Graunke SO, Mattes; (iv) Rothenberger, Gedda, Holm, Friedauer, Moeller, Bav. RSO Ch., Graunke SO, Mattes; (v) Lott, Hampson, Szmytka, Aler, Azesberger, Glyndebourne Ch., LPO, Welser-Möst; (vi) Rothenberger, Lenz, Gedda, Sachtleben, Dieberitz, Zednik, Bav. State Op. Ch., Bav. SO, Boskovsky; (vii) Gedda, Söhnker, Reimer, Streich, Friedauer, Relchart, Bav. State Op. Ch., Graunke SO, Mattes

This is a bumper bargain box for Lehár aficionados and, with the exception of *The Merry Widow*, all the performances here are recommendable. Unfortunately, for Lehár's most popular work, EMI opted to use the 1993 Welser-Möst recording, which is far from ideal for, though he has a fair idea of the idiom, his slowish speeds often diminish the sparkle, as in the *March Septet* in Act II. Thomas Hampson makes a handsome, swaggering Danilo, but he is not vocally at his sweetest, and the other three principals all sing with more uneven production than usual, so that their duets lose much of their appeal. Felicity Lott has both charm and dignity as the widow herself, but her voice is given an unpleasant edge at times. The applause is also intrusive, but the somewhat arch dialogue included with the original set (narrated by Dirk Bogarde) has been edited out.

There is plenty to enjoy in the lively and well-recorded (1980) version of *Friederike*, the Goethe operetta Tauber inspired Lehár to write. It is a delightful performance, with Helen Donath charming in the name-part, and Dallapozza, a light, heady tenor, perhaps a bit stressed by the weight in his title-role but rising to the great Tauber number *O Mädchen, mein Mädchen!*

Das Land des Lächelns dates from 1967, and after the rather thin-sounding overture the recording has plenty of theatrical presence. The cast is strong: Gedda is in excellent form and, besides Anneliese Rothenberger, Renate Holm makes a charming contribution as Mi. The most famous numbers, such as *You are my heart's delight*, are splendidly done.

Giuditta, another Tauber-inspired operetta, was the composer's own favourite work. With its distinctive Balkan atmosphere it is both charming and distinctive, even if without the degree of melodic inspiration of *The Merry Widow*. Recorded in 1980, Gedda hardly shows his years in the Tauber role, with half-tones honeyed as ever, but Edda Moser is disappointing in the name-part, rarely sounding seductive as Schwarzkopf and Gueden did in this role. Boskovsky conducts with his usual sympathy and the sound is decent.

Willy Mattes presents a bright and breezy version of *Der Graf von Luxemburg*, recorded in 1969. Gedda and Holm (who has many delightful numbers to sing) are once again on form, and most of the rest of the cast carry the lively spirit of the performance. The recording, only slightly lacking in richness, captures the atmosphere well. Recorded around the same time, Mattes's account of *Der Zarewitsch* is hardly less impressive. Gedda is once again in the lead and, with such delightful artists as Rita Streich (whose singing is as charming and stylish as ever), it is impossible not to enjoy this, even if it is not all top-rank Lehár, especially the music's dash of Russian colour.

Choosing the romanticized demon violinist Paganini as a subject for an operetta gave Lehár a chance to exploit a plot full of court intrigue, with the celebrated court violinist in love with the crown princess. All that is missing is a score overflowing with memorable musical ideas, though the piece is hardly tuneless. In this red-blooded performance from 1977 Boskovsky makes an excellent case for the work, especially as the singing is generally first rate, as is the recording.

The one snag for non-German speakers throughout these performances is the large amount of dialogue. Translations are not included, but there is a track-by-track outline included with the synopses, as well as the background for each opera as a guide. However, this is an inexpensive way to acquire all the composer's key works.

The Land of Smiles (in English)
☞ *** Telarc CD 80419. Gustafson, Hadley, Itami, Atkinson, ECO, Bonynge

Richard Bonynge proves as warmly understanding of the Lehár idiom as he is in Bellini, while Jerry Hadley winningly takes the Tauber role of Prince Sou-Chong. He also provides a new translation, with the hit-number, *You are my heart's delight*, becoming *My heart belongs to you*, with diction commendably clear. Nancy Gustafson makes a bright heroine, and Lynton Atkinson sings with winning lightness in the second tenor role. Recommended.

The Land of Smiles (Das Land des Lächelns); The Merry Widow (Die lustige Witwe) (both complete in German)
(M) (***) EMI mono 5 85822-2 (2). Schwarzkopf, Kunz, Gedda, Loose, Philh. Ch. & O, Ackermann

It was the Ackermann mono sets of *The Land of Smiles* and *The Merry Widow* in the early 1950s which established a new pattern in recording operetta, treating it with all the care for detail normally lavished on grand opera. The result brought heightened character, both dramatic and musical, with high polish and sharp focus the order of the day. As Hanna Glawari in *The Merry Widow* (which she was to record again in stereo) Schwarzkopf has both sparkle and youthful vivacity, and the *Viljalied* – ecstatically drawn out – is unique. Some may be troubled that Kunz as Danilo sounds older than the Baron (Anton Niessner), but it is still a superbly characterful cast.

The Land of Smiles has a comparably glamorous roster, and if here Gedda does not have quite the passionate flair of Tauber in his famous *Dein ist mein ganzes Herz*, his thoughtful artistry matches a performance which effortlesssly brings out the serious parallels without weighing the work down. Schwarzkopf and Kunz again sing delectably, and the CD transfers are lively and full of presence. Dialogue is included, but separately cued.

The Merry Widow (complete; DVD version; in English)
(N) *** Opus Arte **DVD** OA 0836 D. Kenny, Skovhus, Kirchschlager, Turay, San Francisco Op. Ch. & O, Kunzel (V/D: Gary Halvorson)

It would be hard to imagine a more extravagant production of *The Merry Widow* than Lotfi Mansouri's for the San Francisco Opera, recorded live on this DVD in December 2001. It was Mansouri's last production after his years as the Company's General Director and (as he explains in an interview included as a bonus, along with contributions from the

principal singers) he wanted to bring a new slant to this favourite operetta. Michael Yeargan's sets faithfully echo the 1890s designs at Maxim's in Paris, and Mansouri opts very effectively to set Act III in that venue, referred to throughout the piece. Thierry Bosquet's costumes are comparably lavish, and the text is unusually full, with a Lehár ballet included at the start of Act III, followed by Njegus's song, normally cut. The dialogue – with Christopher Hassall's translation expanded by Ted and Deena Puffer – is supplemented from the French version as being wittier and truer to the Parisian atmosphere than the original German. Mansouri explains that in the central role of Hanna Glawari he wanted a singer who has sung the role of the Marschallin in *Rosenkavalier*, and Yvonne Kenny not only sings beautifully but is both vivacious and provocative. Bo Skovhus makes a handsome Danilo, determined not to be putty in her hands, and their final reconciliation to the *Merry Widow Waltz* could not be more moving. Angelika Kirchschlager makes a charming Valencienne, opposite the Camille of Gregory Turay, with Carlo Hartmann as Baron Mirka, Valencienne's husband, strong and characterful, relishing the humour. Though some of the comic acting involves too much mugging, and though Pontevedrian accents from some of the characters can be irritating, this makes a delightful entertainment.

The Merry Widow (Die lustige Witwe; complete; in German)
*** DG 439 911-2. Studer, Skovhus, Bonney, Trost, Terfel, Monteverdi Ch., VPO, Gardiner
(M) *** EMI (ADD) 5 67370-2(2) [567367]. Schwarzkopf, Gedda, Waechter, Steffek, Knapp, Equiluz, Philh. Ch. and O, Matačić
(N) (BB) (***) Regis mono RRC 1163. Schwarzkopf, Gedda, Kunz, Loose, Philh. Ch. & O, Ackermann

A single-disc version of *The Merry Widow*, with full text and ample dialogue, neatly packaged with libretto, makes an attractive recommendation ahead of any rival. John Eliot Gardiner has the bonus of the Vienna Philharmonic very much on home ground, playing not only with a natural feeling for the idiom but with unrivalled finesse and polish. As Hanna Glawari, the widow of the title, Cheryl Studer gives her most endearing performance yet and the gentle half-tone on which she opens the soaring melody of the *Viljalied* is ravishing. Consistently she sings with sweet, firm tone and the Danish baritone, Boje Skovhus, as Danilo makes an animated, raffish hero. The second couple, Valencienne and Camille, are delectably taken by Barbara Bonney and Rainer Trost, clear and youthful-sounding, outshining all rivals. The rest make an outstanding team, with Bryn Terfel, ripely resonant, turning Baron Mirko into more than a *buffo* character, while the choristers of Gardiner's Monteverdi Choir, obviously enjoying their Viennese outing, bring to Lehár the point and precision they have long devoted to the baroque repertory.

Elisabeth Schwarzkopf was surely born to take the role of Hanna, and Matačić provides a magical set, guaranteed to send shivers of delight through any listener with its vivid sense of atmosphere and superb musicianship. It is one of Walter Legge's masterpieces as a recording manager, and the theatrical presence and ambience are something to marvel at, although at the very opening one might have welcomed a touch more sonic brilliance in the Decca manner. The new transfer certainly retains the full bloom of the original. This set is surely worthy of a place among EMI's 'Great Recordings of the Century'. However, the reissue, with an overall playing time of 79 minutes 40 seconds (the first CD, Act I, plays for just 29 minutes), is uneconomical, even at mid-price: it would surely have been possible to get the whole opera on a single disc, even if a line or two of the copious dialogue had to be cut. The documentation cannot be faulted, with a full translation included.

Those collectors wanting just Schwarzkopf's celebrated earlier mono recording of the *Merry Widow* will find the Regis transfer smooth and pleasing, with the voices truthfully caught. There is no translation but a good synopsis, and the dialogue is separately banded. A genuine bargain.

'Lehár Gala': Arias from: (i) *Eva*; (ii) *Frederike; Der Graf von Luxemburg; Das Land des Lächelns; Die lustige Witwe; Paganini; Schöne ist die Welt; Der Zarewitsch; (i) Zigeunerliebe*

(N) (B) **(*) Australian Decca Eloquence (ADD) 476 2702.
   (i) Lorengar, V. Op. O, Weller; (ii) Holm, Krenn, V. Volksoper, Paulik

Some 53 minutes of this hour-long CD come from a two-LP set of operetta excerpts that Renate Holm and Werner Krenn made together in the Sofiensaal in December 1970. They were both in splendid voice, and the opening *Merry Widow Waltz*, when they sing the famous melody together and then hum the reprise, is quite delightful. Songs like Krenn's title number, *Schöne ist die Welt*, and Holm's *Ich bin verliebt*, from the same operetta, are splendidly done, and their charming duet from *The Land of Smiles*, *Bei einem Tee à deux*, is matched by Krenn's heady *Dein ist mein ganzes Herz!* The seductive *Gern hab'ich die Frau'n geküsst* from *Paganini* and the *Wolgalied* from *Der Zarewitsch* are hardly less successful, while the following duet, *Kosende Wellen*, is ravishing, as is the justly famous *Bist du's, lachendes Glück?* from *Der Graf von Luxemburg*. The only slight snag is that there is too little variety in the programme – almost all the music is relaxed and lyrical. However, towards the end of the concert, Pilar Lorengar comes on stage and adds Hungarian gypsy flavour with a vibrant *Hör'ich Cymbalklünge* from *Zigeunerliebe*. The recording is warm and vivid throughout, and this is undoubtedly a very beguiling disc.

OPERA

Die Lustige Witwe (in German)
(N) ** Arthaus **DVD** 100451. Schellenberger, Gilfry, Gfrerer, Hartmann, Beczala, Zurich Op. Ch. & O, Welser-Möst (V/D: Anton Reitzenstein)

Recorded at the Zurich Opera House in 2004, the Arthaus DVD features a lavish production by Helmuth Lohner, involving sets and costumes by Rolf Langenfass with a Second Empire flavour. The timing is slick under Franz Welser-Möst, even if the singing is variable, the big ensembles none too tidy, with some of the fun missing. Rodney Gilfry makes a handsome Count Danilo with a big presence and voice, even if he resorts to sing-speech too often. Dagmar Schellenberger in the title-role is pretty and young, but anyone who feels that the role of the newly rich widow is best taken by a Marschallin figure will be disappointed by her shallow histrionics, particularly when her heavy vibrato becomes too insistent. As Valencienne, Ute Gfrerer has rather too shrill a soprano to convey the sweetness of her duets with Camille, not helped when Piotr Beczala in that role is loud and unsubtle. As Baron Mirka, Rudolf A. Hartmann skilfully brings out the humour.

LEIFS, Jón (1899–1968)

Baldr, Op. 34
*** BIS CD 1230/1. Gudbjörnsson, Schola Cantorum, Iceland SO, Kropsu

The Icelandic composer Jón Leifs studied in Germany and remained there with a Jewish wife and two daughters until he was able to take refuge in Sweden in 1944. *Baldr* is a 'choreographic drama in two acts' which draws on the *Prose Edda*, written in 1220 by Storri Sturluson. It relates the struggle between Baldr, the son of Odin and the fairest of the gods, and Loki, the personification of evil. Leifs began the score in 1943 when he was still in Nazi Germany (where Loki ruled), finishing it in 1947, the year in which Mount Hekla erupted: the final movement is called *Volcanic Eruption and Atonement*. In *Baldr* Leifs goes even further than he did in earlier works: the wind section includes *lurs* (primitive horns), and to the percussion he adds anvils, cannons, rocks, metal chains and so on – not to mention organ and carillons! Aspirins must have been in brisk demand in Reykjavik after this performance! Imposing though it is, Leifs's primitivism may strain the patience of some listeners: the brutal, repetitive pounding rhythms and the crude *fortissimos* prompt longing for some variety of pace and rhythm, but at the same time there are many imaginative and even beautiful episodes that reward perseverance. Enough of his music is recorded to leave no doubt that Leifs is distinctive – a maverick, no doubt, but powerful nevertheless, and as unlike anyone else as the Icelandic landscape is unlike anywhere else! The present performance is totally committed and convincing, while the recording is pretty amazing and of demonstration quality.

LEIGH, Walter (1905–42)

Concertino for Harpsichord & String Orchestra
☛ (M) *** BBC BBCM 5025-2. Malcolm, ASMF, Marriner – FINZI: *Clarinet Concerto; Introit* *** (with Concert: *English Music* ***)

Like George Butterworth, whose *Banks of Green Willow* is included on this disc, Walter Leigh was killed in action before his gifts could develop fully. His *Concertino for Harpsichord and String Orchestra*, with its heavenly slow movement, which dates from 1936, is an inventive and resourceful score whose delights remain undimmed. It has surely never been played more winningly than it is here by George Malcolm. The balance with Marriner and his Academy is perfectly judged, so that the appearance of so lively a performance (from 1972), expertly engineered by the late James Burnett, is most welcome. This is a highlight of a desirable bargain collection of English music, by Butterworth, Finzi, Vaughan Williams and Warlock.

Concertino for Piano & String Orchestra
(BB) (***) Dutton CDBP 9714. K. Long (piano), Boyd Neel String O., Boyd Neel – FAURE: *Ballade in F sharp*; MOZART: *Piano Concertos 15 & 24* (***)

Though this charming *Concertino* was primarily designed for harpsichord, the piano is given as an option, chosen here for the première recording in 1946. In subtlety and feeling Kathleen Long's reading has never been surpassed. It makes a fine supplement to the equally sensitive performances of Mozart and Fauré which provide the greater part of this tribute to a superb pianist long under-appreciated. The transfer is excellent.

Music for Strings; Air (for treble recorder & piano); *3 Movements for String Quartet; Reverie* (for violin & piano); *Recorder Sonatina; Romance* (for 2 violins, viola, cello & piano); *Trio for Flute, Oboe & Piano; Viola Sonatina*

(N) (M) *** Dutton CDLX 7143. Lochrian Ens., Student String Qt

Because of his early death, Walter Leigh did not realize the full potential of the splendid *String Quartet* of 1929, with its sinewy, Hindemithian influences. Earlier (in 1922) he wrote the easily communicative *Reverie*, while the *Romance* is even more appealingly languorous. But by 1930 Leigh was writing his *Three Movements* in an expressively direct style. The *Music for String Orchestra* is in the same popular vein and of warm appeal. If the *Viola Sonatina* of 1932 returns to more astringent, Hindemithian lyricism, the *Flute, Oboe and Piano Trio* is unashamedly genial, while the delectably tranquil recorder *Air* and 1939 *Recorder Sonatina* finally established the pastoral English neo-classicism that is the true hallmark of Leigh's style. A most attractive and varied collection, very well played and recorded.

LEIGHTON, Kenneth (1929–88)

Cello Concerto

☛ *** Chan. 9949. Wallfisch, RSNO, Thomson – FINZI: *Cello Concerto* ***

(i) *Cello Concerto;* (ii) *Symphony 3 (Laudes musicae)*

*** Chan. 8741. (i) Wallfisch; (ii) Mackie, RSNO, Thomson

Though not as powerful or deeply moving as the superb Finzi *Cello Concerto*, this Leighton work makes an excellent coupling, tautly argued and thoughtful. Raphael Wallfisch plays it as if his life depended on it. The work is available alternatively coupled, but while the *Symphony* draws the same complete dedication from its performers, many will opt for the pairing with Finzi. The recording is very immediate and has splendid clarity and definition.

Veris gratia (for cello, oboe & strings), *Op. 9*

*** Chan. 8471. Wallfisch, Caird, RLPO, Handley – FINZI: *Cello Concerto* ***

Finzi is the dedicatee of Kenneth Leighton's *Veris gratia*, and so it makes an appropriate coupling for his *Cello Concerto*, more particularly as its English pastoral style nods in his direction. The performance is highly sympathetic, George Caird the excellent oboist, and the naturally balanced recording is first class.

(i; iii) *Elegy for Cello & Piano, Op. 5;* (ii; iii) *Metamorphoses for Violin & Piano, Op. 48;* (ii; iii) *Partita for Cello & Piano, Op. 35;* (i–iii) *Piano Trio, Op. 46*

☛ (M) *** Dutton CDLX 7118. (i) Fuller; (ii) McAslan; (iii) Dussek

The *Piano Trio* (1965) is a work of real substance, which grows with repeated hearing. It has a powerfully argued, sinewy first movement and a brilliantly vital Scherzo, which has the occasional echo of Petrassi and Shostakovich. There is an eloquent and highly individual slow movement to bring the work to an end. The *Partita for Cello and Piano* (1959) is another searching, thoughtful piece with an impassioned opening *Elegy* and an inventive Scherzo. All three works are deeply felt and serious, concentrated in utterance, and all deserve to be more widely known. With the exception of the

Elegy, Op. 5, they are new to the catalogue. There are committed and powerful performances from all three artists, who are completely inside this fine music, and the cellist, Andrew Fuller, provides the excellent and informative notes. This is a first-rate recording, and the recorded sound is in the top flight.

Piano Quartet in 1 Movement (Contrasts & Variants), Op. 63; Piano Quintet, Op. 34; Piano Trio, Op. 46

*** Mer. CDE 84465. Markham, Edinburgh Qt

We have already had a fine recording of the *Piano Trio* of 1965, and the *Piano Quartet* and *Quintet* confirm what a strongly individual contribution Kenneth Leighton has made to mid-twentieth-century English chamber music. Both establish his concentrated polyphonic style and the structural unity of his conceptions, the early *Piano Quintet* of 1959 growing out of a four-note theme at the opening, which returns in the finale as a splendidly developed *Passacaglia*. The elegiac *Adagio* contrasts with a vibrant Scherzo to match that in the *Piano Trio*. The single-movement *Piano Quartet* of 1972 is a concentrated kaleidoscope of mood and tempo contrasts, yet ends in calm serenity, confirming the underlying lyricism of all Leighton's music. The performances are first class. These artists are thoroughly inside this music and their playing is deeply felt, displaying the virtuosity only possible from great familiarity, with the pianist Robert Markham making a strikingly brilliant contribution to the Scherzo.

PIANO MUSIC

(i) *Sonata for Piano, 4 Hands, Op. 92.* **(Solo Piano)** *4 Romantic Pieces, Op. 95*

(N) *** BMS CD 408R. Composer, (i) with Kingsley

Kenneth Leighton was a formidable pianist and wrote for the instrument with consummate mastery. Both the *Four Romantic Pieces* and the *Sonata for Piano, Four Hands* are late works, the former dating from the last year or so of his life and the *Sonata* from the mid-1980s. Both performances were recorded at the Wigmore Hall and are expertly engineered by Mike Skeet. This is approachable music, yet challenging and thoughtful, and these performances obviously enjoy a special authority. The opening of the *Sonata* has an almost Bartókian atmosphere, and the finale, a slow movement, has an individual and haunting eloquence.

Conflicts, Op. 51; Fantasia contrappuntistica, Op. 24; Household Pets, Op. 86; Sonatina 1; 5 Studies, Op. 22

**(*) Abacus ABA 402-2. Parkin

Kenneth Leighton was one of the most musical of pianists and wrote beautifully for the instrument. The *Household Pets* is a sensitive piece, refined in craftsmanship, and the *Fantasia contrappuntistica* is comparably powerful. Eric Parkin plays it with total sympathy, and the recording is eminently serviceable.

VOCAL MUSIC

Crucifixus pro nobis; An Easter Sequence; Evensong Services: Magnificat & Nunc Dimittis; Magnificat & Nunc Dimittis (Collegium Magdalenae Oxoniense); Give Me the Wings of

Faith; Rockingham: Chorale Prelude on 'When I Survey the Wondrous Cross'; Veni, creator spiritus; What Love of this is thine?

(BB) *** Naxos 8.555795. Durrant, Oxley, Steele-Perkins, Whitton, St John's College, Cambridge, Ch., Robinson

Leighton was steeped in the Anglican tradition in his youth as a cathedral chorister, and he contributed to its repertory throughout his life. There are two settings here of the Evening Canticles, framing the sequence, one for Magdalen College, Oxford (1959), and the *Second Service* (1971) composed in memory of the organist Brian Runnett, who died tragically in his mid-30s. They are among the most powerful since those of Herbert Howells, vividly and thoughtfully illustrating each verse, the *Second Service* ending with a hushed *Gloria*. The *Easter Sequence*, with trumpet obbligato, here played superbly by Crispian Steele-Perkins, is wonderfully written for trebles, and the cantata, *Crucifixus pro nobis*, using 17th-century texts by Patrick Carey and Phineas Fletcher, is a movingly spare and compressed setting of the Passion story. Composed for the Choir of New College, Oxford, it is a setting of four metaphysical poems, for tenor, choir and organ. With James Oxley the sensitive tenor soloist, it comes over as a work of real substance and deserves the widest dissemination. Christopher Whitton, the responsive organist, has his solo item in *Rockingham*, based on the hymn, *When I Survey the Wondrous Cross*. Leighton is a fine and unjustly neglected composer whose music has vitality and eloquence and impeccable craftsmanship. Robinson obtains very good singing from St John's College Choir and the acoustic of St John's College Chapel is splendidly captured in this fine Naxos recording.

Crucifixus pro nobis; Give me the wings of faith; O sacrum convivium; The second service: Magnificat; Nunc dimittis. Solus ad victimam

*** ASV CDDCA 851. Went, Ch. of The Queen's College, Oxford, Matthew Owens – HOWELLS: *Chichester Service*, etc. **(*)

A chorister in his youth, Kenneth Leighton wrote with an inborn sympathy for the voice and a natural feeling for line. These are beautiful pieces with an occasional reminder of Britten, and they are well sung, too, by the Choir of The Queen's College, Oxford, where Leighton was a student.

LEKEU, Guillaume (1870–94)

Adagio for Quartet & Orchestra (Les Fleurs pâles de souvenir ...) (arr. for quartet with piano by Gérard Inglésia); Molto Adagio for String Quartet (Commentaire sur les paroles du Christ); (i) Larghetto for Cello & Instrumental Septet; Piano Quartet (completed d'Indy). (ii) 3 Poèmes (Sur une tombe; Ronde; Nocturne)

(B) *** HM HMA 901455. Ens. Musique Oblique; (i) with Veyrier; (ii) Yakar, Adler

The Belgian composer Guillaume Lekeu left only a small number of works, all of which have a haunting post-Wagnerian *fin-de-siècle* atmosphere. Indeed, the slow movement of his unfinished *Piano Quartet*, the beautiful *Larghetto* for solo cello and instrumental septet with its voluptuous tenderness, and the (arranged) *Adagio* for string quartet and piano all resonate in the memory. In many ways the early extended *Molto Adagio for String Quartet*, with its strange 5/4 rhythmic pulse, inspired by Christ's lament in the Garden of Gethsemane, is most remarkable of all, not only in itself, but in having a germinal influence on the later works. The playing here by the Ensemble Musique Oblique catches the music's passionate feeling and at times almost despairing intensity. The recording, though closely observed, has plenty of ambience. The collection ends with three delightful contrasting *Poèmes* for soprano (the sensitive Rachel Yakar) and piano, where the sombre mood melts away in the central *Ronde*, but is felt again in the closing *Nocturne*.

Piano Quartet in B min.: 1st Movement: Très animé (only)

(N) (M) *** Virgin 482061-2 (2). Kandinsky Qt – CASTILLON; CHAUSSON; SAINT-SAENS: *Piano Quartets* ***

(i) *Piano Quartet. String Quartet; Molto Adagio*

(N) *** MDG 644 1266-2. Spiegel Qt, (i) with Michiels

The Belgian Guillaume Lekeu studied with Franck and d'Indy and tragically succumbed to typhoid at the age of 24. The *Piano Quartet*, which he left unfinished, made so strong an impression on d'Indy that he completed it. Lekeu's aim was to put all his soul into his music, and he seems to have achieved it. The *Piano Quartet* runs to two movements, though only the first is recorded on Virgin, even though the notes discuss it as if the whole piece was here! In any event, it is good to have it here, very well played and recorded and in such interesting company.

Unlike the Kandinskys above, Jan Michiels and the members of the Spiegel Quartet give us both movements of the *Piano Quartet*, coupling it with the *Quartet* he composed at the age of 17 and a deeply felt *Adagio* from the same year, which hints at his best-known work, the elegiac and eloquent *Adagio* for strings. The *Quartet* is in six movements and was obviously written during his studies of the late Beethoven *Quartets* with Franck and d'Indy. The slow movement is one of his most searching utterances, and although the *Quartet* is not expertly structured it is a work of quality and elevation of spirit. Very good performances and truthful recorded quality.

LEONCAVALLO, Ruggiero
(1858–1919)

I Pagliacci (complete; DVD version)

(N) *** Ph. **DVD** 070 428-9. Domingo, Stratas, Pons, Rinaldi, La Scala, Milan, Ch. & O, Prêtre (Dir: Franco Zeffirelli) – MASCAGNI: *Cavalleria rusticana*

Each half of this double bill is announced as 'A Film by Franco Zeffirelli', but where *Cavalleria rusticana* was recorded on location in Sicily, *Pagliacci* uses open sets as realistic as possible. Here, too, the singers mime to an audio recording, with Zeffirelli's camerawork generally helping to disguise any discrepancies between sound and vision. Juan Pons sings the Prologue – very powerfully – before a genuine audience including children, and that set reappears in the staging of Act II. The preliminary drama of Act I involves a more informal set, equally naturalistic, with the company of actors using an ancient van in this updating to the 1930s. Nedda's communing with the birds is introduced by offstage tweeting, as she plays with her children. Teresa Stratas sings brilliantly if with some edge at the top, and Alberto Rinaldi makes a very convincing Silvio. Yet it is Plácido Domingo who dominates, singing superbly in this 1981 recording.

I Pagliacci (complete; CD versions)

☞— **(N)** (M) DECCA 476 7217. Cura, Frittoli, Alvarez, Keenlyside, Castronovo, Netherlands R. Ch., Concg. O, Chailly

*** DG (IMS) (ADD) 419 257-2 (3). Carlyle, Bergonzi, Taddei, Panerai, La Scala, Milan, Ch. & O, Karajan – MASCAGNI: *Cavalleria rusticana* ***

(M) *** EMI (ADD) 7 63967-2 (2). Amara, Corelli, Gobbi, La Scala, Milan, Ch. & O, Von Matačić – MASCAGNI: *Cavalleria rusticana* **(*)

(M) *** RCA (ADD) 74321 50168-2 (2). Caballé, Domingo, Milnes, John Alldis Ch., LSO, Santi

(***) EMI mono 5 56287-2 (2). Callas, Di Stefano, Gobbi, La Scala, Milan, Ch. & O, Serafin – MASCAGNI: *Cavalleria rusticana* (***)

(M) **(*) EMI (ADD) 7 63650-2 (2). Scotto, Carreras, Nurmela, Amb. Op. Ch., Philh. O, Muti – MASCAGNI: *Cavalleria rusticana* **(*)

(B) **(*) Naxos 8.660021. Gauci, Martinucci, Tumagian, Dvorský, Skovhus, Slovak Philh. Ch., Czech RSO, Rahbari

(M) (**(*)) Nim. mono NI 7843/4. Gigli, Pacetti, Basiola, Nessi, Paci, La Scala Ch. & O, Ghione – MASCAGNI: *Cavalleria rusticana* **

The first big merit of the Chailly recording is the glorious playing of the Royal Concertgebouw Orchestra under their long-time musical director. The orchestral prelude instantly alerts one to the refinement of the playing, while letting one hear the piece with new clarity, making one marvel at the beauty and subtlety of Leoncavallo's orchestration. The incisive singing of the Netherlands Radio Choir also has one marvelling afresh at the complexity of the choral writing in the sparkling ensembles which frame the piece. Happily, Decca have lined up a first-rate cast to match. It is true that José Cura's voice has not quite the glowing freshness it once had, having acquired something of a baritonal quality, but there is little of the roughness that mars other relatively recent issues. The feeling for detail as well as the heroic power make this a strong, intense reading, and Cura reserves his finest singing of all for the climactic *No! Pagliacci non son.* Barbara Frittoli proves an excellent choice as Nedda, giving a finely detailed performance, with signs in almost every phrase that she has rethought the role, rather as Maria Callas did. Another rising star, Carlos Alvarez, with his big heroic baritone makes an impressive Tonio, from the Prologue onwards, even if he does not sound as menacing in scale and timbre as some. He is well contrasted with Simon Keenlyside as Nedda's lover, Silvio, lighter and more lyrical, while Charles Castronovo as Beppe in the final play scene sings with comparable refinement. The Decca recording is rich, spacious and brilliant, and this is now reissued at mid-price in Universal's Critics' Choice series, with full libretto and translation.

Karajan does nothing less than refine Leoncavallo's melodrama, with long-breathed, expansive tempi and the minimum of exaggeration. Karajan's choice of soloists was clearly aimed to help that – but the passions are still there; and rarely if ever on record has the La Scala Orchestra played with such beautiful feeling for tone-colour. Bergonzi is among the most sensitive of Italian tenors of heroic quality, and it is good to have Joan Carlyle as Nedda, touching it often rather cool. Taddei is magnificently strong, and Benelli and Panerai could hardly be bettered in the roles of Beppe and Silvio. The combined set remains available, but on three records at premium price – although, as well as *Cav.*, DG provide a splendid set of performances of operatic intermezzi as a filler.

The EMI (originally Columbia) recording under Von Matačić dates from the early 1960s and is especially notable for the contribution of the tenor, Franco Corelli, as Canio, which calls for some superlatives. He is not nearly as imaginative as some of the great tenors of the past, yet he shows a natural feeling for the phrases. It is not just a question of making a big, glorious noise – though of course he does that too – but of interpreting the music; and a performance like this puts several others, by more obviously starry names, in the shade. The coupled *Cav.* is dramatically not quite so striking, but this still makes a clear first choice in the mid-priced range for those who want the pairing with Mascagni.

For those who do not want that obvious coupling, the alternative RCA set is a first-rate recommendation, with fine singing from all three principals, vivid playing and recording, and one or two extra passages not normally included – as in the Nedda–Silvio duet. Milnes is superb in the Prologue.

It is thrilling to hear *Pagliacci* starting with the Prologue sung so vividly by Tito Gobbi. Di Stefano, too, is at his finest, but the performance inevitably centres on Callas and there are many points at which she finds extra intensity, extra meaning. Serafin's direction is strong and direct. The mono recording is greatly improved in the new transfer, with voices well forward, but this set is overpriced.

Under Muti's urgent direction both *Cav.* and *Pag.* represent the music of violence. In both he has sought to use the original text, which in *Pag.* is often surprisingly different, with many top notes eliminated and Tonio instead of Canio delivering (singing, not speaking) the final *La commedia è finita.* Muti's approach represents the antithesis of smoothness. Scotto's Nedda goes raw above the stave, but the edge is in keeping with Muti's approach, with its generally brisk speeds. Carreras seems happier here than in *Cav.*, but it is the conductor and the fresh look he brings that will prompt a choice here. The sound is extremely vivid.

Alexander Rahbari conducts his Slovak forces in a vigorous, red-blooded reading which with first-rate solo singing makes an excellent bargain recommendation, very well recorded, if with the chorus a little distant. Miriam Gauci is a warmly vibrant Nedda, with plenty of temperament, and Eduard Tumagian is an outstanding Tonio, not only firm and dark of tone but phrasing imaginatively. As Canio, Nicola Martinucci has an agreeable tenor that he uses with more finesse and a better line than many more celebrated rivals, even though his histrionics at the beginning and end of *Vesti la giubba* are unconvincing.

The Nimbus transfer of the classic (1934) recording with Gigli focuses the voices effectively enough, giving them a mellow bloom – though the orchestra, often rather recessed, is relatively muffled. Gigli is very much the centre of attention, with Iva Pacetti as Nedda clear and powerful rather than characterful.

I Pagliacci (in English; complete)

(M) *** Chan. 3003. Opie, Mannion, O'Neill, Bronder, Dazeley, Geoffrey Mitchell Ch., Peter Kay Children's Ch., LPO, Parry

David Parry conducts a powerful performance in the Peter Moores Foundation's 'Opera in English' series, building the drama persuasively. The cast is one of the finest in the series yet, with Rosa Mannion a touching Nedda, and Alan Opie and William Dazeley both outstanding and well contrasted in the baritone roles. Dennis O'Neill sings very well too as

Canio, but he faces greater problems with translating the tragic clown into an English-speaking hero. No longer *On with the motley* but '*Put on your costume*'. Warm, atmospheric sound, with voices beautifully focused.

Zaza (complete)

(N) ** Warner Fonit (ADD) 5050467 7799-2 (2). Petrella, Campora, Turtura, Buda, RAI O of Turin, Silipigni

Zaza, written at the turn of the 20th century, is the story of a music-hall star, Zaza, and her affair with Milio Dufresne, who she discovers is married. She sacrifices herself by rejecting him, contemplating a life of loneliness rather than disrupting his family. It gives Leoncavallo a chance to write fluently and brilliantly, not least in the music-hall scene at the start. Though over four brief Acts the music regularly leads up to moments calling for a big tune, the lyrical gift that makes *I Pagliacci* so memorable never emerges in any melody to remember. The role of Zaza is designed for a singing actress, but sadly Clara Petrella in this historic recording of 1969 falls short, with her shallow, fluttery soprano. The other principals are far better, notably the clear and sweet-toned Giuseppe Campora, one of the finest Italian tenors of his generation. The booklet pays tribute to him, noting his death in 2004.

LEONIN (c. 1163–90)

Organa: *Alleluya, Epulemur Azamis; Gaude Maria; Propter veritatem; Viderunt omnes*

*** Lyrichord LEMS 8002. Oberlin, Bressler, Perry –
PEROTINUS: *Organa* ***

Over eight centuries have passed since the construction of the Cathedral of Notre Dame began and Leonin, the cathedral's composer, was writing this music. It is in two parts, with the top voice moving in unison or octaves, over a sustained or only occasionally moving second part. Sometimes both voices sing in unison. The present performances are extraordinarily convincing and take us back in time to the very beginning of written music. Excellent recording.

Organa: *Alleluya, Dies sanctificatus; Alleluya, dulce lignum; Alleluja, inter natos mulierum; Alleluya, Pascha nostrum; Alleluja, Paraclitus Spiritus Sanctus; Alleluya, Spiritus Sanctus procedens; Priusquam te formarem; Viderunt omnes*
*** Hyp. CDA 66944. Red Byrd, Capella Amsterdam

This is a more extensive selection of Leonin's organa than the Lyrichord disc above. The recordings include compositions for the main feasts from the first part of the liturgical year. Much of the music brings elaborate, rhapsodic melodic lines which are quite haunting in these atmospheric and confidently sung performances, admirably recorded. Full texts, translations and good documentation, as we expect from Hyperion.

Organa for Christmas: *Ludea et Iherusalem; Descendit de celis;* **Easter:** *Et valde mane; Christus resurgens; Sedit angelus;* **Pentecost:** *Dum complerentur; Adventit ignis repleti sunt omnes; Benedictus Domino*
☛ *** Hyp. CDA 67289. Red Byrd & Yorvox

Red Byrd's first Hyperion disc of the music of Magister Leoninus is highly praised by us. But this second Leonin collection, containing some of the very first music for Christmas, Easter and Pentecost to be written down, is even

more compelling. The melismatic upper part of the plainsong weaves its way over the sustained pedal-like sonority below, never more passionately or floridly than in the Easter plainsong, *Et valde mane*, which tells of the discovery of Christ's empty tomb ('And very early in the morning, the first day of the week, they came to the sepulchre, the sun being now risen …'). A superb disc, gloriously sung in an ideal acoustic.

LIADOV, Anatol (1855–1914)

Baba-Yaga, Op. 56; Ballade, Op. 21b; The Enchanted Lake, Op. 62; From the Apocalypse, Op. 66; Intermezzo, Op. 8; Kikimora, Op. 63; Mazurka, Op. 19; Nénie, Op. 67; Polonaises, Opp. 49 & 55
(BB) **(*) Naxos 8.555242. Slovak PO, Gunzenhauser

Baba-Yaga, Op. 56; The Enchanted Lake, Op. 62; From the Apocalypse, Op. 66; Kikimora, Op. 63; Mazurka: Village Scene by the Inn, Op. 19; Polonaise, Op. 49; 8 Russian Folksongs, Op. 58; Scherzo in D, Op. 16
☛ *** Chan. 9911. BBC PO, Sinaisky

(i) *Baba-Yaga, Op. 56; The Enchanted Lake, Op. 62; Kikimora, Op. 63;* (ii) *8 Russian Folksongs*
(BB) **(*) Naxos 8.550328. Slovak PO, (i) Gunzenhauser; (ii) Jean (with Concert: '*Russian Fireworks*' ***)

Russian composers at the end of the 19th century and beginning of the 20th seem to possess the ability to evoke the world of the fairy-tale and of magic with unerring sympathy, and none more successfully than Liadov. *The Enchanted Lake* and *Kikimora* are wonderfully atmospheric, and the performances by Vassily Sinaisky and the BBC Philharmonic are pure magic. Although they are the best known, a piece like *From the Apocalypse* is hardly less inspired. Commentators always speak of Liadov's expertise and beautiful craftsmanship, but he is a master who creates a world quite unlike that of any other composer. The performances are matched by recording of equal richness and luminosity.

It is good that Gunzenhauser's comprehensive Liadov collection has been transferred from full-price Marco Polo to bargain-price Naxos. They are well played and recorded versions of this colourful and imaginative music, and certainly worth the very modest cost. The new full-price Chandos version under Sinaisky, with slightly different programming, offers more sophisticated playing and outstandingly atmospheric recording and is obviously preferable, though the Naxos has the brighter focus.

It is good to have inexpensive recordings of these key Liadov works, particularly the *Russian Folksongs*, eight orchestral vignettes of great charm, displaying a winning sense of orchestral colour. The Naxos performances are persuasive, and the digital recording is vivid and well balanced.

LIBERT (or LIEBERT), Reginaldus (born c. 1425/35)

Missa de Beata Virgine; Kyrie à 4
*** Lyrichord LEMS 8025. Schola Discantus, Moll

Like Du Fay's *Missa Sancti Jacobi*, Libert's Marian Mass has the distinction of being one of the earliest to survive that includes settings of both the Ordinary and Proper. Moreover, the Mass is made cohesive by being based on a very striking, melismatic cantus firmus, which is always recognizable as it usually appears in the upper voice, decorated with ornamental notes. The three-voiced counterpoint is comparatively simple, with the third voice subordinate to the upper parts, enriching the sonority. Even so, the *Credo* is powerful and ambitious, followed by a particularly fine *Sanctus*. In short, this is an appealing and memorable work, and the performance here is an eloquent one, with well-judged pacing. With the addition of the separate four-part *Kyrie*, this disc includes all the music positively attributed to Libert. The recording is first class, made in a spacious acoustic, and the documentation very good, except that for the text and translation of the *Kyrie* and *Gloria* we are referred to another Lyrichord issue (LEMS 8010), a curious proposition, as we are not told any more about this CD. The presentation also associates Libert's Mass with Jeanne d'Arc, and gives her biography, but although she was a contemporary of the composer and this music, there is no other connection.

LIGETI, György (born 1923)

(i) *Cello Concerto;* **(ii)** *Piano Concerto;* **(iii)** *Violin Concerto*
⊶ * DG 439 808-2. (i) Queras; (ii) Aimard; (iii) Gawriloff; Ens. InterContemporain, Boulez

This concertante triptych won the *Gramophone* magazine's Contemporary Music Award in 1996. The composer's imaginative inventiveness is never in doubt, but his musical purpose is not always easy to fathom. All the performers believe that this music has an underlying profundity; all three performances are musically and technically impressive and communicate strongly.

6 Bagatelles for Wind Quintet

*** Nim. NI 5728. V. Quintet – HINDEMITH: *Kleine Kammermusik;* NIELSEN: *Wind Quintet ***
*** Crystal CD 750. Westwood Wind Quintet – CARLSSON: *Nightwings;* MATHIAS: *Quintet;* BARBER: *Summer Music ***

Ligeti's folk-inspired *Bagatelles* are highly inventive and very attractive; and on Crystal they are played with dazzling flair and unanimity of ensemble by this American group.
The Vienna Quintet give a persuasive account of the lighthearted 1953 *Bagatelles* as any we have had in the past. They are subtle, witty and effervescent and a delight from first to last – and they are beautifully recorded in the Wiener Konzerthaus. Choice here will depend on couplings.

Horn Trio

*** Chan. 9964. Danish Horn Trio – BRAHMS: *Horn Trio ***

Ligeti entitled his Trio 'Homage to Brahms', and he follows Brahms's four-movement layout, though with a *Passacaglia-Lament* placed as the finale, rather than an eruption of exuberance. It would seem an obvious coupling, yet the composer said of his work that 'the only thing reminiscent of Brahms is perhaps a certain smilingly conservative comportment – with distinctly ironic distance' (whatever that implies). Calum MacDonald, who writes the extremely lucid notes, says: 'In the first movement the three instruments move almost independently of one another, forming harmonies that are tonal, indeed often triadic, and yet without traditional function, creating a continual sense of lyric ambivalence.' The movement is not very coherent, but the

Scherzo is wild and brilliant, even witty. The third movement's ironically brusque *Alla marcia* is angular and spiky; the finale then opens in a luminous, harmonic atmosphere to introduce an eerily intense five-bar sequence, which is (in the composer's words) a 'chromatic variation' of the first three movements. This sequence develops as a mysterious *Passacaglia-Lament*, which later becomes more passionate, with a wailing horn soliloquy, and the music finally dies away in a spirit of desolation. It is an individual and challenging work, played with extraordinary commitment and expertise, but one wonders whether many Brahms lovers will take to it!

Le Grand Macabre (complete opera)

*** Sony S2K 62312 (2). Ehlert, Clark, White, Nes, Ragin, Cole, Suart, L. Sinf. Voices, Philh. O, Salonen

It is the revised version of *Le Grand Macabre* that is recorded here under supervision from the composer, using an English text. Set in Breughland, this apocalyptic vision lightens its macabre theme – of the ending of the world – with humour, viciously satirical and anarchic, setting out from a witty prelude for tuned motor-horns, with tongue-in-cheek echoes of a baroque toccata. Salonen is a brilliant advocate, drawing colourful playing from the Philharmonia. Sibylle Ehlert is dazzling in the coloratura role of Gepopo, Graham Clark a characterful Piet the Pot, and Willard White aptly baleful as the *grand macabre* himself, the sinister Nekrotzar. This may be an off-beat piece, but as audiences have found, it has a sparkle which has one simultaneously laughing and thinking. Atmospheric sound, recorded live at the Théâtre du Chatelet.

LILBURN, Douglas (1915–2001)

Symphonies 1–3

⊶ (BB) *** Naxos 8.555862. New Zealand SO, Judd

Douglas Lilburn is one of New Zealand's leading composers and his music deserves to be better known. He could not be better served than by this splendid Naxos disc which gathers together the three symphonies which are at the very kernel of his output. He is a true symphonist: his structures are not inflated, and the orchestral colouring is an integral part of the musical argument. Inspired by the spacious landscapes and mountain ranges of his homeland, the first two are heavily influenced by Sibelius; indeed the slow movement of No. 1 (1949) includes a direct quotation. Vaughan Williams (under whom the composer studied in England) makes his presence felt in the slow movement of No. 2 and perhaps also in the folksy flavour of the Scherzos. In the *Third Symphony* (1961) Lilburn finds an even more individual voice. Lighter-textured than the others, often skittish, it is in one continuous movement that falls into five sections, all of which use a three-note rising motif, heard at the very opening. Although there are aspects of serialism here, one would hardly guess, so spontaneously appealing is the writing. Indeed, all three symphonies are splendid works, immediately drawing the listener in to their special world, and they could not have a more committed advocate. Judd's performances are vigorously alive, gripping, and splendidly played, and the Naxos recording is vividly detailed, with plenty of warmth and atmosphere. This now replaces their earlier disc on Continuum.

LINDBERG, Magnus (born 1958)

'Meet the Composer': (i) Action – Situation; Signification; (ii–iii) Kinetics; (i–ii; iv) Kraft; (v; iii) Rittrato; (vi–vii; iii) Zona; (Instrumental) (viii–ix) Ablauf; (x) … De Tartuffe, je crois (for piano quintet); (viii; xi) Linea d'ombra; (vi) Stroke; (Piano) (xii) Twine

🎵 (B) *** Finlandia Double 0630 19756-2 (2). (i) Toimili Ens.; (ii) Finnish RSO; (iii) Salonen; (iv) Swedish RSO; (v) Avanti! CO; (vi) Karttunen; (vii) L. Sinf.; (viii) Krikku; (ix) Aaltonen, Ohenoja; (x) Endymion Ens., Witfield; (xi) Ferchen, Pohjola, Virtanen; (xii) Hakkila

Magnus Lindberg belongs to the younger generation of Finnish composers now moving into their middle years. He studied with Paavo Heininen in Helsinki and with Bryan Ferneyhough at the Darmstadt summer courses in the early 1980s. He also studied with Franco Donati in Siena and with Vinko Globokar in Paris. His breakthrough as a composer came with Kraft (the second item on the first CD), which had its première in 1984 and brought him to international attention. This Finlandia Meet the Composer set of two CDs gives a good cross-section of his work during the 1980s, when he was still in his late 20s and early 30s. If you do not respond to avant-garde music, you may still find something to reward you here, for Lindberg is a composer of imagination and intelligence.

LINDBLAD, Adolf Fredrik (1801–78)

Symphonies 1 in C, Op. 19; 2 in D
*** Marco Polo 8.225105. Uppsala CO, Korsten

Lindblad is best known for his songs, of which there are some 250. Indeed, he is generally spoken of as 'the father of Swedish song'. Mendelssohn thought highly enough of the First Symphony to conduct it at Leipzig with the Gewandhaus Orchestra. Gérard Korsten and the Uppsala Chamber Orchestra give splendid accounts of both symphonies, extremely vital and spirited, with infectious high spirits in the first movement of the C major Symphony. And what delightful pieces these are, not strong on individuality perhaps but, like the Weber symphonies, highly attractive. Quite a find, and very good sound, warm and well focused.

LIPINSKI, Karol (1790–1861)

Violin Concertos 2 in D, Op. 21; 3 in E min., Op. 24; 4 in A, Op. 32
*** CPO 999 787-2. Breuninger, Polish RSO, Rajski

Karol Lipinski belongs to the generation before Chopin, but he was overshadowed in his lifetime by Paganini and, later, by Wieniawski. He became the Royal Concert-master at Dresden and was among the most brilliant and admired virtuosi of his day, earning generous praises from Berlioz and Schumann. The three concertos recorded here are very much in the Paganini tradition, though far from inferior to him. The opening ritornello in the first movement of the D major is overlong and although there is much that is pleasing, there is little real depth in any of the three, but they are dispatched with great aplomb and brilliance by Albrecht Breuninger and the Polish Radio Orchestra under Wojeiech Rajski and very well recorded.

LISZT, Franz (1811–86)

Piano Concertos 1–2; Fantasia on Hungarian Folksongs; Fantasia on Themes from Beethoven's 'Ruins of Athens'; Grande fantaisie symphonique on Themes from Berlioz's 'Lélio'; Malédiction; Polonaise brillante on Weber's Polonaise brillante in E (L'Hilarité); Totentanz (paraphrase on the Dies Irae); Schubert/Liszt: Wanderer Fantasia
🎵 (B) *** EMI (ADD) 5 69662-2 (2). Béroff, Leipzig GO, Masur

Michel Béroff's 1977 account of the two concertos can hold its own with the best of the competition: here there is nothing routine or slapdash, but instead excitement, warmth and spontaneity, along with his remarkable technical prowess. The piano timbre has plenty of body and colour, as well as sparkle. This is an exhilarating and rewarding set which can be given a strong recommendation on all counts.

Piano Concertos 1 in E flat; 2 in A; 3 in E flat, Op. posth. (ed. Rosenblatt); Concerto pathétique (orch. Reuss)
*** Chan. 9918. Lortie, Hague Residentie O, Pehlivanian

The so-called Third Concerto, first given in 1990, and the Concerto pathétique are reconstructions and of interest to Lisztians rather than to the wider musical public. Lortie's accounts of the concertos with the Hague Residentie Orchestra under George Pehlivanian are very impressive and can hold their own with all but the very best (only the likes of Zimerman, Brendel and Richter remain unchallenged, and, in No. 1, Arrau and Argerich). They are better recorded than any of their rivals and bring poetic insights as well as virtuosity. Highly recommendable.

Piano Concertos 1–2
(M) *** Ph. (ADD) 464 710-2. S. Richter, LSO, Kondrashin – BEETHOVEN: Piano Sonatas 10; 19–20 ***
(M) (***) DG mono 474 024-2 (5). Kempff, LSO, Fistoulari – BEETHOVEN: Piano Concertos 1–5; BRAHMS: Piano Concerto 1; MOZART: Piano Concertos 9 & 15; SCHUMANN: Piano Concerto (***)

(i) Piano Concertos 1–2; (ii; iii) Fantasia on Hungarian Folk Tunes; Malédiction; Totentanz; (ii; iv) Arr. of Schubert: Wanderer Fantasia (all for piano and orchestra)
(B) *** Double Decca (ADD) 458 361-2 (2). (i) Katchen, LSO, Argenta; (ii) Bolet; (iii) LSO, Fischer; (iv) LPO, Solti – DOHNANYI: Variations on a Nursery Tune, Op. 25 ***

Piano Concertos 1–2; Hungarian Fantasia
(***) BBC mono BBCL 4031-2. S. Richter, LSO, Kondrashin (with CHOPIN: Andante spianato & grande polonaise, Op. 22 (***))

(i) Piano Concertos 1–2; (ii) Hungarian Rhapsody 4; Les Préludes, G.97
(BB) *(**) DG Entrée (ADD/DDD) 474 563-2. (i) Berman, VSO, Giulini; (ii) VPO, Sinopoli

(i) Piano Concertos 1; 2; (ii) Malédiction; (iii) Dante Sonata (orch. Lambert)
(B) (***) Dutton mono CDBP 9742. (i) Sauer, Paris Conservatoire O, Weingartner; (ii) Osborn, Boyd Neel SO, Boyd Neel; (iii) Kentner, Sadler's Wells O, Lambert

Piano Concertos 1–2; Totentanz

⊛ ✿ *** DG 423 571-2. Zimerman, Boston SO, Ozawa

(N) (BB) *** Warner Apex 2564 62044-2. Berezovsky, Philh. O, Wolff

Krystian Zimerman's record of the two *Concertos* and the *Totentanz* is altogether thrilling, and he has the advantage of excellent support from the Boston orchestra under Ozawa. It has poise and classicism and, as one listens, one feels this music could not be played in any other way – surely the mark of a great performance! This record is outstanding in every way, and still remains a first choice for this repertoire.

Boris Berezovsky's thrillingly extrovert yet highly musical accounts of the two *Concertos* and the rumbustious *Totentanz* make a superb alternative super-bargain issue. Berezovsky plays throughout with enormous panache and bravura, yet with melting poetic feeling. Hugh Wolff proves a splendid partner, and the Philharmonia Orchestra play with great gusto. The full-blooded, resonantly spacious recording was made at Aldeburgh in 1994.

Sviatoslav Richter's 1961 performances on Philips are very distinguished indeed, and the recent remastering by Wilma Cozart Fine makes the very most of the recording, originally engineered by the Mercury team. Richter's playing is unforgettable and so is his rapport with Kondrashin and the LSO, whose playing throughout is of the very highest order. The sound is vivid and present but the acoustic is rather dry for full comfort. However, given playing of this calibre, one soon adjusts. The reissue is now available as one of Philips's '50 Great Recordings', curiously recoupled with three of Beethoven's least ambitious early piano sonatas, beautifully played and recorded.

Katchen is superb in the *E flat Concerto*, only slightly less successful with the changes of mood of the *Second*. But by any standard these are commanding performances, and he found an erstwhile partner in Ataulfo Argenta, who also died sadly young. Bolet is no less masterful in the splendid triptych of shorter concertante works, which thrillingly bring out all his characteristic bravura. The digital recording remains in the demonstration bracket. He and Solti also make out a fairly convincing case for Liszt's concertante arrangement of Schubert's *Wanderer Fantasia*.

Kempff recorded the two Liszt Concertos for Decca in 1954 in totally distinctive performances, remarkable for the diamond clarity of textures and rhythmic sparkle. The inflation so easily suggested in these works is completely avoided, so the results are uniquely fresh, helped by clean Decca sound engineered by Kenneth Wilkinson. Mono recordings too long unavailable.

This Dutton reissue is of special documentary interest. Emil Sauer and Felix Weingartner were the last surviving members of Liszt's circle so they knew his musical intentions well. Their recording of the two *Concertos* was made in two sessions in December 1938 in the somewhat unglamorous acoustic of the Rue d'Albert studios in Paris. The sound is a bit dry and wanting in transparency, but it affords a rare opportunity to relish the artistry of Sauer, then seventy-six but still a commanding, authoritative virtuoso. Franz Osborn (1905–55) gave us the very first recording of the *Malédiction*, which comes from 1945, his only appearance as a concerto soloist on records. (Egon Wellesz used to speak of his late Beethoven sonatas, Opp. 109–111, with awe – he was not a pupil of Schnabel for nothing – but, alas, he never recorded them.) The sound is very natural indeed for the period and the playing magisterial. So, too, is Louis Kentner's *Dante*

Sonata in the arrangement that Constant Lambert made of *Après une lecture de Dante*. Again, the 1940 recording wears its years lightly in this fine Dutton transfer. A valuable set that all Lisztians will want.

The BBC Legends CD is a memento of Richter's first major concert in London in the Royal Albert Hall in 1961. After playing the two Liszt concertos he took them into the studio for Philips. The BBC engineers here place Richter very much in the foreground and the mono recording is really rather good for its age, though the orchestral detail has less transparency than the studio versions. Broadly the interpretations, spontaneously poetic as well as powerful, reveal little difference between live and studio, with the important exception that the rush of adrenalin at the end of each finale brings speeds a fraction more urgent, with virtuosity even more daring. But the disc is a must for the *Hungarian Fantasia*. This is electrifying playing and even finer than the account he recorded at Budapest shortly afterwards with Ferencsik, with the music presented with power rather than wit. Moreover, the BBC CD captures a real sense of occasion. The Chopin, recorded at a concert two days earlier, provides a delightful bonus.

Lazar Berman's 1976 recording of the concertos has the advantage of Giulini's sensitive and masterly accompaniment with the Vienna Symphony Orchestra, and even if you feel that these scores hold no surprises for you, try listening to this CD. Berman's playing is consistently poetic and he illuminates detail in a way that has the power to touch the listener. Some of his rapt, quiet tone would not register without the tactful assistance of the DG engineers, who enable all the detail to 'tell', but the balance is most musical and well judged. A very thoughtful account of No. 1 and a poetic reading of No. 2 make this a desirable CD of this repertoire. Giulini keeps a strong grip on the proceedings and secures an excellent response from his players. If they don't eclipse the greatest performances of these works, they remain distinguished accounts.

Sinopoli offers highly polished accounts of the *Rhapsody* and tone-poem, often very beautiful but lacking the unbridled enthusiasm which this music ideally needs. In the *Hungarian Rhapsody*, the orchestra almost grinds to a halt in the passages leading up to the faster gypsy dancing music, in theory providing contrast, but in effect sounding mannered. That said, with the rich, bright, digital recording, and with superb orchestral playing, these performances are not without enjoyment – but Karajan and Stokowski really know how to make this music go.

Piano Concerto 1 in E flat

(M) *** DG (ADD) 449 719-2. Argerich, LSO, Abbado – CHOPIN: *Piano Concerto 1* ***

Martha Argerich (in 1968) recorded only Liszt's *First Concerto* and not the *Second*. However, there is an excellent partnership between the pianist and Abbado, and this is a performance of flair and high voltage which does not ever become vulgar. It is very well recorded, and in this reissue, coupled with Chopin, it sounds better than ever. The performance is also available on DG's bargain Classikon label, coupled with the *Sonata*, which Argerich recorded three years later.

(i; ii) *Piano Concerto 1 in E flat*; (iii; iv) *Hungarian Fantasia*; (iv) *Hungarian Rhapsodies 2, 4* & (i) *6*; (v)

Mephisto Waltz 1; (iv) *Les Préludes;* (i) *Piano Sonata in B min.;* (vi) *Bénédiction de Dieu dans la solitude;* (vii) *Feux follets; Harmonies du soir*

(BB) ** DG Panorama (ADD) 469 151-2 (2). (i) Argerich; (ii) LSO, Abbado; (iii) Cherkassky; (iv) BPO, Karajan; (v) Ashkenazy; (vi) Arrau; (vii) Richter

Argerich and Abbado are in very good form in the *E flat Concerto* and the recording is excellent. Equally compelling are Karajan's *Hungarian Rhapsodies Nos. 2* and *4* (the 6th is for piano solo, excitingly done by Argerich) and *Les Préludes* – all deservedly famous recordings. Cherkassky's glittering account of the *Hungarian Fantasia* is another highlight, and the solo items from Ashkenazy and Arrau are all worth having. The Richter performances are live and date from the late 1950s, but the much poorer sound and unbelievably noisy audience preclude much enjoyment.

Piano Concerto 2 in A

(M) *** Virgin 5 61996-2. Andsnes, Bergen PO, Kitaienko – GRIEG: *Piano Concerto; Lyric Pieces, Op. 65* ***

This reissue reverts to the original Virgin coupling for the Grieg concerto, and very fine it is. Leif Andsnes is a real musician who plays with great tenderness and poetic feeling, as well as bravura. First-class sound too, with a piano in perfect condition (not always the case on records) and an excellent balance.

Concert paraphrases (for piano & orchestra): *Fantasia on a Theme from Beethoven's 'Ruins of Athens'; Grande fantasie symphonique on Themes from Berlioz's 'Lélio'; Arr. of Schubert's Wandererfantasie; Arr. of Weber's Polonaise brillante*

*** Chan. 9801. Lortie, Hague Residentie O, Pehlivanian

In the 1940s Liszt's transcription of Schubert's *Wandererfantasie* for piano and orchestra was a familar item in the concert hall and on the radio, but it is now something of a rarity. It goes without saying that Louis Lortie is second to none; indeed his version would now be a first recommendation, particularly as the remainder of his programme – the *Fantasia on a Theme from Beethoven's Ruins of Athens*, the Weber *Polonaise brillante* and the *Grande fantasie symphonique on Berlioz's 'Lélio'* – is so desirable. Lortie's aristocratic pianism and the fine playing of the Residentie Orchestra of The Hague under George Pehlivanian make this an exhilarating record. Excellent Chandos recording.

Dante Symphony

☞— *** DG (IMS) 457 614-2. Dresden State Op. Ch. and State O. Sinopoli (with BUSONI: *Doktor Faust; Saraband und Cortège* ***

(i) *Dante Symphony;* (ii) *Années de pèlerinage, Book 2: Après un lecture du Dante (Fantasia Quasi Sonata)*

(N) (M) *** Warner Elatus 2564 61780-2. (i) Women's Voices of Berlin R. Ch., BPO, Barenboim; (ii) Barenboim (piano)

(i) *Dante Symphony;* (ii; iii) *A Faust Symphony, G.108;* (ii; iv) *Les Préludes; Prometheus*

(B) **(*) Double Decca (ADD) 466 751-2 (2). (i) Voltaire College Ch., SRO, Lopez-Cobos; (ii) Solti; (iii) Jerusalem, Chicago Ch. & SO; (iv) LPO

Liszt's *Dante Symphony* divides naturally into two very expansive, equally balanced halves – *Inferno* and *Purgatorio* – each

lasting about 21 minutes, with a relatively short choral *Magnificat* as a finale. The second movement is calming – some might say becalmed in its spacious paragraphs. Finally the heavenly chorus enters and lusciously proclaims salvation.

Sinopoli, on one of his very finest records, gives a grippingly inspired account. He draws a clear parallel, not only with Tchaikovsky's *Francesca da Rimini*, but also with the *Manfred Symphony*. The refined and beautiful playing of the Dresden orchestra easily sustains the long central *Purgatorio*, and the luminous and superbly sung choral entry in the finale creates a magical apotheosis. The DG recording is in the demonstration bracket, wonderfully spacious and clear. For an imaginative coupling we are offered the two pieces Busoni composed in 1918/19 as 'a reduced-size model' while working on his opera, *Doktor Faust*, well worth having when played so impressively.

Barenboim too really has the measure of this overextended but remarkable work and controls its rhapsodic structure admirably, holding the tension throughout the first movement and creating enormous visceral excitement at the close. He is helped by marvellous playing from the BPO, who really sound as if they believe in it all, and the radiant choral effects are superbly brought off. The resonant acoustic of Berlin's Schaulspielhaus lets everything expand with Wagnerian amplitude and the result is very impressive indeed. As an encore, Barenboim leaves the rostrum for the piano and offers the *Dante Sonata*, which has the same literary basis but offers a quite different musical treatment. The performance is flamboyantly arresting, but the piano recording is curiously shallow.

Lopez-Cobos's account of the *Dante Symphony* comes with Liszt's alternative conclusion, a sudden loud outburst of 'Hallelujahs' from the trebles after the usual *pianopianissimo* ending. It is most effective, crowning a performance which is more remarkable for its refinement of sound and balance than for its dramatic thrust. It is not underpowered, however, and the early digital recording is rich and full, while the SRO is on better form than it was in Ansermet's day. Solti's Liszt is almost always successful. His performance of the *Faust Symphony* is spacious, yet brilliant, with superb playing from his Chicago orchestra, though the bright recording underlines the fierce element in his reading and removes some of the warmth. The Mephistophelean finale brings the most impressive playing of all, with Solti's fierceness chiming naturally with the movement's demonic quality. The two tone-poems, recorded in the 1970s, are brilliantly played and recorded. Even with the reservations expressed, this is excellent value.

(i) *Fantasia on Hungarian Folk Tunes; Malédiction; Totentanz;* (ii) Arr. of Schubert: *Wanderer Fantasia* (all for piano and orchestra). *Années de pèlerinage* (complete); *Ballade 2; Concert paraphrases: Bellini: Réminiscences de Norma; 12 Schubert Songs; Mozart: Réminiscences de Don Juan; Verdi: Rigoletto. 2 Concert studies (Waldesrauschen; Gnomenreigen); 3 Concert studies (Il lamento; La reggierezza; Un sospiro); Consolations 1–6; 12 Etudes d'exécution transcendante; Etudes d'exécution transcendante d'après Paganini: La campanella. Grand galop chromatique; Harmonies poétiques et religieuses: Funérailles. Hungarian Rhapsody 12; Liebesträume 1–3; Mephisto Waltz 1; Sonata; Valse impromptu*

(B) *** Decca 467 801-2 (9). Bolet; with (i) LSO, Iván Fischer; (ii) LPO, Solti

The full range of the late Jorge Bolet's achievement for Decca in the music of Liszt is admirably surveyed in this bargain box, all splendidly recorded, and there are two other shorter surveys below. One or other should be in every representative collection.

Fantasia on Hungarian Folk Themes (for piano & orchestra)
(BB) (***) Naxos mono 8.110683. Moiseiwitsch, LPO, Lambert – GRIEG: *Piano Concerto*; SAINT-SAENS: *Piano Concerto 2* (***)

A useful reminder of Moiseiwitsch's virtuosity and Lisztian prowess. His account with Constant Lambert still gives much pleasure.

A Faust Symphony
(M) *** DG (IMS) (ADD) 447 449-2. Riegel, Tanglewood Festival Ch., Boston SO, Bernstein

(N) (BB) *** Warner Apex 2564 61460-2. Aler, Slovak Ch., Rotterdam PO, Conlon

**(*) Chan. 9814. Elsner, Danish Nat. R. Ch. and SO, Thomas Dausgaard

Bernstein on DG seems to possess the ideal temperament for holding together grippingly the melodrama of the first movement, while the lovely *Gretchen* centrepiece is played most beautifully. Kenneth Riegel is an impressive tenor soloist in the finale, there is an excellent, well-balanced choral contribution, and the Boston Symphony Orchestra produce playing which is both exciting and atmospheric.

James Conlon secures extremely good results in his Warner Apex version of the *Faust Symphony*. The Rotterdam orchestral playing is very alive and committed, and the recorded sound is altogether excellent, with the choral finale coming over impressively. This is an excellent recommendation at budget price, although Barenboim and Bernstein have more charisma, and Rattle's Berlin performance is closer to Beecham's pioneering set.

Chandos offer a performance that brings together the tenor Christian Elsner and the Danish Radio Chorus and Orchestra under Thomas Dausgaard. This is a finely paced and intelligent reading which has a good deal going for it. It does not in any way displace its competitors but those investing in it are unlikely to be greatly disappointed.

Hungarian Rhapsodies 1–6
(*) Mercury (ADD) **SACD 475 6185. LSO, Dorati – ENESCU: *Romanian Rhapsody 1* ***

Dorati's is undoubtedly the finest set of *Hungarian Rhapsodies*. He brings out the gypsy flavour and, with lively playing from the LSO, there is both polish and sparkle. The new SACD transfer further enhances the sound although the upper range betrays the age of the recordings.

Mephisto Waltz 1
*** BBC mono BBCL 4059-2. LSO, Stokowski – GABRIELI: *Sonata pian e forte*; NIELSEN: *Symphony 6*; TIPPETT: *Concerto for Double String Orchestra* ***

Stokowski's zestful and vibrant account of the first *Mephisto Waltz* comes with two rarities of the Stokowski discography, Nielsen's *Sixth Symphony* and the Tippett *Double Concerto*.

SYMPHONIC POEMS

Symphonic poems: *Ce qu'on entend sur la montagne (Bergsinfonie); Festklänge; Hunnenschlacht; Die Ideale; Von der Wiege bis zum Grabe;* (i) *Dante Symphony*
(B) *** EMI double forte (ADD) 5 68598-2 (2). Leipzig GO, Masur; (i) with Arndt, Leipzig Thomaskirche Ch.

(i) *Faust Symphony.* **Symphonic poems:** *2 Episodes from Lenau's Faust; Hamlet; Héroïde funèbre; Hungaria; Prometheus*
(B) *** EMI double forte (ADD) 5 68595-2 (2). Leipzig GO, Masur; (i) with König, Leipzig R. Ch.

On the whole, Masur's survey of Liszt's symphonic poems is the finest we have had so far. The performances have a dramatic vitality, and the Leipzig orchestra's playing is even finer than that of the LPO on Philips. Some of the earlier pieces, such as *Ce qu'on entend sur la montagne* and *Festklänge*, suffer not only from formal weakness but also from a lack of interesting melodic invention. However, these performances – and, whatever one may think of it, this music – cast a strong spell, and with rare exceptions Masur proves a most persuasive advocate. *Hamlet* has great dramatic intensity, and *Die nächtliche Zug*, the first of the *Two Episodes from Lenau's Faust*, strikes the listener immediately with its intent, brooding atmosphere. Masur's *Faust Symphony* can certainly hold its own against most of its rivals, although in the *Gretchen* movement he moves things on, though not unacceptably. It is the rich sonority of the lower strings, the dark, perfectly blended woodwind-tone and the fine internal balance of the Leipzig Gewandhaus Orchestra that hold the listener throughout.

Symphonic poems: *From the Cradle to the Grave (Von der Wiege bis zum Grabe); Hamlet; Die Ideale; Orpheus*
(BB) *(**) Naxos 8.553355. New Zealand SO, Halász

Michael Halász gets a vital and sensitive response from his fine New Zealand orchestra, with some beautiful string-playing at the opening of *From the Cradle to the Grave* – an elusive, extended work that he holds together very well – and the opening of *Orpheus* is most evocative. He does not shirk the melodrama in *Die Ideale*, and *Hamlet* too is powerfully done. Artistically this is very impressive, but the recorded sound brings problems. There is no lack of vividness but the balance is too close and, while all is well in *piano* and *pianissimo* passages, tuttis are less comfortable, with a degree of glare and congestion and a lack of space round the climaxes. Impressive just the same, and good value.

(i) *Hunnenschlacht; Mazeppa; Orpheus;* (ii) *Les Préludes* (symphonic poems)
*** Australian Decca Eloquence 466 706-2. (i) LAPO; (i) VPO; Mehta

Zubin Mehta is in his element here. The performances are red-blooded and tremendously exciting. Liszt's vulgarity is played up in a swaggeringly extrovert way, but there is plenty of character too. The rich, vibrant recording is an audiophile's delight – the staggered entries throughout the strings in *Mazeppa* are thrilling. Equally praiseworthy is the pastoral atmosphere Mehta creates in *Orpheus* – with real sensitivity from the Los Angeles orchestra. Those who like Liszt with all the stops out will certainly enjoy this Australian reissue, especially when the CD transfer is so vivid.

Les Préludes

(M) *** DG 463 650-2. BRSO, Fricsay – DVORAK: *Symphony 9 in E min. (New World)*; SMETANA: *Má vlast: Vltava* ***
(BB) **(*) EMI Encore (ADD) 5 85460-2. Phd. O, Muti – RAVEL: *Boléro* *(*); TCHAIKOVSKY: *1812* *(**)

Though it is unfashionable to say so, *Les Préludes* is easily the best of Liszt's symphonic poems, alongside *Mazeppa*, and Fricsay's performance is masterly. It has great impulse, coupled with engaging detail and freshness, and the climax has dignity, the vulgarity minimized.

Muti has the full measure of *Les Préludes*, catching its breadth as well as its exuberance, with the Philadelphia Orchestra on top form. This is the most successful of the three showpieces on this inexpensive reissued CD and, while the early digital recording shows that the engineers were striving for brilliance rather than sonority, the result is still impressive and certainly exciting.

Les Préludes; Mazeppa; Prometheus; Tasso, lamento e trionfo (symphonic poems)

☛ (BB) *** Naxos 8.550487. Polish Nat. RSO (Katowice), Halász

Michael Halász has the full measure of this repertoire, and this is one of the most successful collections of Liszt's symphonic poems to have emerged in recent years. He draws some remarkably fine playing from the Katowice Radio Orchestra. The brass playing is very impressive throughout, especially the trombones and tuba, who have the epic main theme of *Mazeppa*, but its grandiloquence is no less powerful in *Les Préludes*, weighty and never brash. The recording is spacious, with full, natural string-textures, but it is the resounding brass one remembers most.

Tasso, lamento e trionfo

**(*) Testament mono SBT 1129. Philh. O., Silvestri – TCHAIKOVSKY: *Manfred Symphony* *(*)

Silvestri's version of *Tasso* was one of his best recordings (second only perhaps to his account of Elgar's *In the South*). It comes up well in this new transfer but the Tchaikovsky coupling does not show the Romanian maestro at his best.

PIANO MUSIC

Complete piano music (57 volumes) and supplement
Hyperion. Leslie Howard

Leslie Howard's ambitious project to record all the piano music of Liszt is now complete and has been generally well received internationally, with several issues collecting a Grand Prix du Disque in Budapest. The set has great documentary interest and has been listed and discussed in several earlier editions. The performances are very capable and musicianly, and there are many moments of poetic feeling, but for the most part his playing rarely touches distinction. The kind of concentration one finds in great Liszt pianists such as Arrau, Kempff and Richter (and there are many younger artists whose names spring to mind) only surfaces occasionally. Howard's technique is formidable, but poetic imagination and the ability to grip the listener are here less evenly developed. However the coverage is remarkable and if this playing rarely takes the breath away by its virtuosity or its poetic insights, it is unfailingly intelligent and the Hyperion recordings are consistently first class.

A full listing and discussion of the merits of the series in detail is being carried forward to our 2006/7 Yearbook, meanwhile we would wish to draw readers' attention to some of the rarer and more outstanding issues, such as Liszt's transcription of the *Bunte Reihe* (originally for violin and piano) of Ferdinand David (1810–70) in Volume 16 (CDA 66506). Leslie Howard plays them beautifully, as he does the two Liszt Song-books of early Lieder in Volume 19 (CDA 66593).

Volume 26 (CDA 66771/2) is almost entirely devoted to music which Liszt wrote as a teenager, and has obvious interest, as has Howard's pioneering recording of the *12 Grandes Etudes* in Volume 34. They were pilot versions of the *Etudes d'exécution transcendante*, and Leslie Howard plays them with remarkably confident bravura (CDA 66973). Many of the Russian and Hungarian novelties in Volume 35 (CDA 66984) are also ear-tickling.

One of the most valuable discs of the series is Volume 47 (CDA 67187), which includes unpublished music which Liszt intended for a first cycle of *Harmonies poétiques et religieuses*, while Volume 51 (CDA 67233/4), which Howard calls 'Paralipomènes', has early drafts of other famous works including three different versions of the *Dante Sonata*. The eighteen *Hungarian Romances* presented on Volume 52 are equally fascinating, in essence a manuscript notebook of Hungarian themes, which in Volume 57 (CDA 67418/19), in their final form, became the 19 *Hungarian Rhapsodies*, growing out of those early collected ideas.

Alternative versions of six of those *Rhapsodies* appear in the penultimate volume (56), which consists of four CDs of 'Rarities, Curiosities, and Fragments' (CDA 67414/7) plus 23 *Album Leaves*, simple romantic pieces, which Liszt dedicated to his friends. And if you are drawn by a collection of rare operatic Concert Paraphrases, Volume 54 admirably features some rare examples (CDA 67406/7).

Crowning the whole series are the two volumes (53a/b) of the complete music for piano and orchestra (CDA 67401/2 and 67403/5) in which Howard tackles no fewer than 15 different works, admirably accompanied by the Budapest Symphony Orchestra. He plays them all with flair and dedication and is, as usual, very well recorded.

Other piano music

Années de pèlerinage: Book 1, 1st Year: Switzerland; 2nd & 3rd Years: Italy; Supplement: Venezia e Napoli (complete)

(B) *** DG (ADD) 471 447-2 (3). Berman

The *Années de pèlerinage* contain some of Liszt's finest inspirations, and Lazar Berman's 1977 recording is fully worthy of this complete survey. Berman's technique is fabulous, more than equal to the demands made by these 26 pieces. The playing is enormously authoritative and quite free of empty display or virtuoso flamboyance, even though its brilliance is never in question. Indeed Berman brings searching qualities to this music; much of the time he is thoughtful and inward-looking in pieces like *Angelus* and *Sunt lachrymae rerum*. The imaginative colour and flair he displays in *Les cloches de Genève* and the simple freshness of *Eclogue* are matched by the felicity of the watery evocations, *Au lac de Wallenstadt* and *Les jeux d'eau á la Villa d'Este*, while the power of the *Dante sonata* is equalled by the coruscating glitter of his articulation of the *Tarantella* from the *Supplément: Venezia e Napoli*. The recording is firmly and faithfully transferred to CD and does full justice to Berman's range of colour and dynamics. Moreover this box is remarkably inexpensive and well documented.

Années de pèlerinage, 1st Year (Switzerland)
(BB) *** Naxos 8.550548. Jandó

Even remembering his excellent Beethoven and Haydn recordings, Jandó's performances of the Liszt *Années de pèlerinage* are an impressive achievement. The solemn opening of *La Chapelle de Guillaume Tell* immediately shows the atmospheric feeling he can generate in this remarkable music, and its later, more grandiose rhetoric is handled with powerful conviction. First-class recording, and the feeling throughout is very much of the spontaneity of live music-making.

Années de pèlerinage, 2nd Year (Italy); Supplement: Venezia e Napoli
☞ ✪ (BB) *** Naxos 8.550549. Jandó

Jandó offers Lisztian playing of the highest order, confirming the *Années de pèlerinage* as being among the supreme masterpieces of the piano. *Sposalizio* is superbly evoked, and the three contrasted *Petrarch Sonnets* bring the most imaginatively varied characterization, with No. 123 especially chimerical. But clearly Jandó sees the *Dante Sonata* as the climactic point of the whole series. His performance has tremendous dynamism and power. One has the sense of Liszt himself hovering over the keyboard. Again first-class recording and the feeling of a continuous live recital. This is the disc to try first, and we have awarded it a token Rosette.

Années de pèlerinage, 3rd Year (Italy) (complete)
☞ (BB) *** Naxos 8.550550. Jandó

The opening *Angelus* shows Jandó at his most imaginatively expansive and commanding, while *Les Jeux d'eau à la Villa d'Este* sparkles and glitters: this is playing of great appeal. The secret of Jandó's success is that he is deeply involved in every note of Liszt's music.

Ballades 1 in D flat; 2 in B min.; Christmas Tree (Weinachtsbaum) (suite)
(M) **(*) Chan. 6629. Gillespie

The *Christmas Tree Suite* is a charming rarity which deserves recording, even if the music is simplistic by Lisztian standards. The composer wrote it for his granddaughter, Daniela von Bülow. Rhondda Gillespie plays with obvious dedication and is equally at home in the two very contrasted *Ballades*, the first chimerical, the second darker and more reflective. It is a pity that the piano recording of the suite is not out of Chandos's top drawer, though it is more impressive in the *Ballades*.

Concert Paraphrases of Beethoven's 'An die ferne Geliebte'; Mignon; Schumann Lieder: Widmung; Frühlingsnacht
*** Chan. 9793. Lortie – SCHUMANN: *Fantaisie in C, Op. 17* ***

Louis Lortie's Chandos recital appears under the title 'To the Distant Beloved', after Beethoven's song-cycle, *An die ferne Geliebte*, which he plays in Liszt's transcription (together with a pair of Schumann Lieder), and very impressively too. But collectors will want this for the Schumann *Fantasy*, which is the centrepiece of the recital and is given an outstanding performance.

Concert Paraphrases of Beethoven's Symphonies 2 & 5
(BB) *** Naxos 8.550457. Scherbakov

It is Scherbakov's achievement that he makes Liszt's piano transcriptions of these Beethoven symphonies sound so pianistic. With wonderfully crisp articulation and fluent passage-work, textures are clarified, and the freshness and energy of the writing are strongly brought out both in the exuberantly youthful No. 2 and the darkly dramatic No. 5. This is as imaginative as Cyprien Katsaris's Teldec accounts from the days of LP, and no one with a taste for keyboard heroism should overlook them. He is vastly superior to Leslie Howard's pedestrian set on Hyperion. He is, so to speak, more of a Weingartner than a Toscanini (as was Katsaris) but his *Fifth* still has that barnstorming quality that arrests your attention. At super-bargain price, well worth investigating even by those who shy away from transcriptions. Excellent, clear piano sound.

Concert paraphrases of Rossini: Soirées musicales; Overture William Tell
(BB) *** Naxos 8.553961. Gekić

Liszt made his Rossini transcriptions in 1836, and they are rarely heard in the recital room or on record. The only rival is Leslie Howard's set on Hyperion, and this performance by the Yugoslav-born Kemal Gekić at super-bargain price has infinitely more wit, lightness of touch and subtlety of articulation. Were the price-tags reversed, this would still be the preferred recommendation. In fact this is dazzling playing that sparkles when required and has an effortless brilliance that is quite captivating. Gekić has real flair and is very well recorded too, with natural, lifelike quality. One looks forward to returning to this disc.

Concert paraphrases of Schubert Lieder: Auf dem Wasser zu singen; Erlkönig; In der Ferne; Ständchen
☞ ✪ *** Sony SK 66511. Perahia – BACH/BUSONI: *Chorales*. MENDELSSOHN: *Songs without Words* *** ✪

Murray Perahia brings to these transcriptions a poetic finesse that is very much his own. Impeccable artistry and taste are blended with a wonderful naturalness.

Concert paraphrases of Schubert Lieder: Auf dem Wasser zu singen; Gretchen am Spinnrade; Der Müller und der Bach; Ständchen. Hungarian Rhapsody 12
(M) *** DG 445 562-2. Kissin – BRAHMS: *Fantasias*; SCHUBERT: *Wanderer Fantasia* **(*)

There is – as always – much to admire in Kissin's playing, and he is in good form in these Liszt–Schubert transcriptions. Both *Der Müller und der Bach* and *Ständchen* are beautifully done. The Brahms and the *Wanderer Fantasia* find him in good rather than outstanding form.

12 Etudes d'exécution transcendante
*(**) Naïve **DVD** DR 2104 AV103. Berezovsky. Recorded live at La Roque d'Anthéron, France, 6 August 2002 (V/D: Andy Sommer)

Boris Berezovsky's account of the *Transcendental Studies* is stunning. Ever since we first encountered him playing the Beethoven *G major Concerto* at Leeds, this pianist has never ceased to amaze by his sheer virtuosity, imagination and musicality. Although this is remarkable musically, the video direction greatly diminishes the listener's pleasure. The camera shots are often very close, concentrating on a narrow area of the keyboard, restlessly changing and generally attracting attention to the camera itself. It must have been a hot evening, as Berezovsky perspires profusely and the camera dwells on beads of sweat that gather on the pianist's nose. There is some tiresome mixing of images in *Feux follets*, and admiration for the sheer musical wizardry is tempered by exasperation at the unmusical production. Three stars and a bouquet for the playing but a brickbat for the visual direction. So intrusive and irritating is the latter that many will find it difficult to go on watching. However, fortunately, Berezovsky's complete CD recording of the *Etudes* is available on Warner Elatus.

12 Etudes d'exécution transcendante (complete)
⊶ (M) *** Warner Elatus 2564 60125-2. Berezovsky

Boris Berezovsky shows astonishing flair and technical assurance, yet in *Feux follets* he plays with the utmost delicacy, and the ruminative poetry of *Ricordanza* is melting. The piano is recorded boldly and brilliantly, not as full and sonorous as with Arrau, but there is no lack of pianistic colour in the gentler lyrical writing. The colour portrait of Liszt on the back of the accompanying booklet demonstrates why so many women succumbed to his physical charms!

(i) 12 Etudes d'exécution transcendante; (ii) 6 Etudes d'exécution transcendante d'après Paganini; (i) 3 Etudes de concert (Il lamento; La leggierezza; Un sospiro); 2 Etudes de concert (Waldesrauschen; Gnomenreigen)
(B) **(*) Ph. (ADD) (IMS) Duo 456 339-2 (2). (i) Arrau; (ii) Magaloff

Arrau always played with great panache and musical insight, which more than compensates for the occasional smudginess in the recorded sound. He produced a wonderfully distinctive tone, and his enormous range of keyboard colour was splendidly captured by the Philips engineers of the day. Arrau's playing is most masterly and poetic, and the recording, if too reverberant, is admirably truthful and rich in timbre. The three *Etudes de concert* are strongly characterized; indeed some might find Arrau's richly textured romanticism in *Un sospiro* a little overwhelming. However, his bravura in *Gnomenreigen* is riveting. So too is Nikita Magaloff's virtuosity in the *Paganini Studies*, and here the bright, less sumptuous piano-tone projects his digital dexterity with fine glitter. He gives scintillating accounts of *La campanella* and *Arpeggio* and tickles the ear with a delectably sparkling *La Chasse*. The set, of course, ends with variations on the famous theme used also by Brahms and Rachmaninov, also played with fine dash. Overall this is most impressive and can be recommended enthusiastically.

Collection: 12 Etudes d'exécution transcendante; Hungarian Rhapsodies 1–19; Rhapsodie espagnole; Sonata in B min. Recital: Années de pèlerinage: Les jeux d'eau à la Villa d'Este. Ballade 2; Etudes de concert: 1, Ronde des lutins; 2, Danse le bois; Grand études après Paganini: La campanella; La chasse. Grand galop chromatique; Harmonies poètiques et religieuse: Funérailles; 2 Légendes; Liebestraum 3; Mephisto Waltz; Polonaise 1; Valse-impromptu; Valse oubliée 1
(B) (***) EMI mono/stereo 5 74512-2 (5). Cziffra

12 Etudes d'exécution transcendante; Mephisto Waltz 1
(M) *** EMI mono 5 62799-2 [5 62801-2]. Cziffra

This five-disc set gathers together the recordings made by the celebrated virtuoso, Georges Cziffra, over three decades between the mid-1950s and the mid-1980s. He began with a chimerically brilliant set of the *Etudes d'exécution transcendante* and the equally legendary *Hungarian Rhapsodies*. Both were made in faithful if slightly restricted mono sound in the Hungaroton studio in Budapest in 1956. The result is strikingly fresh and the easy technical dexterity is astonishing. He

was to re-record both sets in stereo, in 1959 and in 1974–5 respectively; later both appeared on CD, but certainly they do not dwarf the earlier achievement and this is a predictable reissue to include in EMI's series of 'Great Artists of the 20th Century'. Much of the rest of the repertoire appears for the first time. Cziffra remained at the height of his powers throughout, and the shorter bravura pieces, most recorded in stereo, display the same enormous technical command and delectably clean, light articulation as the earlier sessions, the playing volatile and charismatic, the recordings clear and forward. The two *Legends* (1985) are played with full romantic power, rather than being subtle performances of the kind we expect from, say, Kempff, and the dashing account of the *Sonata* (1968) is flamboyantly romantic, although certainly not lacking delicacy of feeling or thoughtfulness in the gentler lyrical pages, with the closing section memorable. The recordings have been effectively remastered, the sound variable, often good, very good in the *Sonata*. But the panache of the playing triumphs over the early technology.

Collection: Disc 1: 6 Etudes d'exécution transcendante d'après Paganini; Années de pèlerinage: Au lac de Wallenstadt; Il penseroso; Les jeux d'eau à la Villa d'Este. Hungarian Rhapsody 13 in A min.

Disc 2: Piano Sonata in B min.; Bagatelle without Tonality; Concert Study in D flat (Un sospiro); En rêve; Etude d'exécution transcendante 10: Appassionata; Nuages gris; Schlaflos Frage und antwort; Valse oubliée 1
(B) *** EMI double forte 5 74846-2 (2). Watts

This EMI double forte reissue from 1986 combines two separate recitals, so we have listed them accordingly. On the first disc André Watts gives sensitively conceived, well-paced accounts of all these pieces, in which his virtuosity (sparkling vividly in the *Etudes d'exécution transcendante d'après Paganini*), though it can be taken for granted, does not dominate at the expense of sensibility. There are some minuscule miscalculations, which the artist, believing in the importance of truth and of the kind of playing one encounters in the concert hall, does not correct. These performances convey spontaneity and are well recorded.

On the second disc the performance of the *Sonata* has not the sheer dramatic power of such artists as Brendel, Bolet or Pletnev, but it is still very fine and undoubtedly grips the listener, as does the varied remainder of his programme with *Un sospiro*, *Nuages gris* and the *Bagatelle sans tonalité* standing out in their different ways. *En rêve*, too, is played with great delicacy. Again good recording, and this inexpensive set provides a well-planned survey of the composer's wide range of style, mood and colour.

Hungarian Rhapsodies 1–19; Rhapsodie espagnole
(B) *** DG Double (ADD) 453 034-2 (2). Szidon

Roberto Szidon offers Liszt playing of the highest order. He has flair and panache, genuine keyboard command and, when required, great delicacy of tone. He is well recorded too, and this DG Double is not only inexpensive but also provides (as does Cziffra on EMI) an excellent version of the *Rhapsodie espagnole*. Cziffra's performances are from an artist of an even more volatile personality, but Szidon is by no means upstaged: his style is equally valid and his approach is always imaginatively illuminating.

Hungarian Rhapsodies 2, 6, 8 (Capriccio), 9 (Carnival in Pest), 10 (Préludio), 12–15 (Rákoczy March)

(M) *** EMI (ADD) 5 67554-2 [567555-2]. Cziffra

As can be heard in the most famous *C sharp minor Rhapsody* (No. 2), Cziffra's reckless impulsiveness is matched by his breathtaking bravura in the closing section, and it was an excellent idea to issue a selection from his deleted complete set as one of EMI's 'Great Recordings of the Century'. The remastered recordings from the early 1970s have fine realism and presence.

Piano Sonata in B min.

(N) *(*) RCA 82876 64561-2. Luisada – CHOPIN: *Sonata 3**(*); SCRIABIN: *Sonata 9* *

Piano Sonata; Années de pèlerinage: Dante Sonata. Bagatelle without Tonality; Czárdás macabre; La lugubre gondola; Mephisto Waltz

(BB) ** Regis (ADD) RRC 1020. Brendel

Piano Sonata; Années de pèlerinage, 1st Year: Vallée d'Obermann. Concert Studies 1: Waldesrauschen; 2: Gnomenreigen. Harmonies poétiques et religieuses: Bénédiction de Dieu dans le solitude

(M) *** Ph. (ADD) 464 713-2. Arrau

Piano Sonata; Années de pèlerinage, 1st Year: Vallée d'Obermann; Concert Paraphrase of Wagner: Isoldens Liebestod; Nuages gris; Variations on 'Weinen, Klagen, Sorgen, Zagen'

(B) EMI *** Début 5 74233-2. Papadiamandis

Piano Sonata; Années de pèlerinage, 2nd Year: Après une lecture du Dante (Fantasia Quasi Sonata); Concert Study: Gnomenreigen; Harmonies poétiques et religieuses: Funérailles

☛ (N) (M) *** DG 476 7237-2. Pletnev

Piano Sonata; Années de pèlerinage, Supplement: Tarantella. Concert paraphrase on Verdi's Rigoletto. Etude d'exécution transcendante d'après Paganini: La Campanella. Liebeslied (Widmung); Liebestraum 3

*** DG 471 585-2. Li

Piano Sonata; Concert Paraphrase of Wagner: Isoldes Liebestod; La lugubra gondola 2; Mosonyis Grabgeleit; Romance oubliée; Variations on 'Weinen, Klagen, Sorgen, Zagen'

**(*) MDG 312 0957-2. Tanski

Piano Sonata; 3 Concert Studies

*** Chan. 8548. Lortie

Piano Sonata in B min.; En rêve; 4 Little Piano Pieces; La Lugubre Gondola; Nuages gris; Richard Wagner – Venezia; Schlaflos! Frage und Antwort; Trübe Wolken; Unstern!; Sinistre, disastro

(N) *** HM HMC 901845. Lewis

Piano Sonata; Grandes Etudes de Paganini 1–6

(BB) *** EMI Encore 5 85057-2. Ousset

Piano Sonata; 2 Legends (St Francis of Assisi Preaching to the Birds; St Francis of Paola Walking on the Waves); Scherzo & March

(N) (BB) *** Hyp. Helios CDH 55184. Demidenko

Piano Sonata; 2 Legends, G.175; La Lugubre Gondola 1 & 2

(N) (M) *** Ph. 4767 9424. Brendel

Piano Sonata in B min.; La Lugubre Gondola

(M) *** DG (IMS) 471 358-2. Pollini – SCHUMANN: *Fantasy in C; Arabesque* ***

Pletnev's earlier account of the *B minor Sonata*, made when he was in his 20s and briefly available on Olympia, had dazzling virtuosity and brilliance. This newcomer has even greater tonal finesse, articulation and control of keyboard colour; there is a tremendous grip, depth and majesty, and the breadth of the *Sonata* is deeply impressive. A performance of stature among the very best that this great pianist has yet given us. The remainder of the programme is hardly less gripping; reservations concerning the close balance do not obscure the artistry and distinction of this recital. This is now reissued in Universal's 'Critics' Choice' Series.

It is good that DG have restored Pollini's riveting 1989 account of the Liszt *B minor Sonata* to the catalogue for the 'Pollini Edition'. It is a performance of real vision, which combines powerful emotional feeling with astonishing bravura; moreover Pollini's structural grasp is consummate, moving unerringly to the closing pages, with the concentration never slipping. *La Lugubre Gondola* makes a curious encore but its darker atmosphere is well caught, and there are no complaints about the recording.

Paul Lewis's version of the Liszt *Sonata* stands out, even among the many dozens of rival recordings, for its power and clarity, enhanced by full, immediate sound. If many virtuosi impulsively treat this massive one-movement structure freely, like an extended improvisation, Lewis with masterly control brings out the structural strength. He regularly reminds one of the way in which Liszt drew inspiration from Beethoven's late quartets, giving shape and coherence to the great fugue instead of rushing through it. For coupling he has an illuminating group of late pieces, including two written as elegies for Wagner, not just *La Lugubre Gondola* (in the second and more extended version) but *RW – Venezia*, building up powerfully over the briefest span. Also two pieces, *Nuages gris* and *Unstern!*, works not published till 40 years after Liszt's death, which find the composer at his most adventurous.

Nikolai Demidenko's is a keenly dramatic and powerfully projected account of the sonata that has the listener on the edge of his or her seat. It must be numbered among the finest performances he has given us. The excitement and virtuosity are second to none and almost call to mind Horowitz: his playing can be measured against that of Brendel and Pletnev. He has the advantage of exceptionally vivid recorded sound, and the remainder of the recital goes equally well.

Brendel's recording of the Liszt *Sonata* for Philips won the *Gramophone* Solo Piano award in 1983 and has been out of the catalogue far too long. It is a more subtle and concentrated account than his earlier version made in the mid 1960s and must be numbered among his finest records. There is a wider range of colour and tonal nuance, and yet the undoubted firmness of grip does not seem achieved at any expense in spontaneity. Moreover he is very realistically recorded.

Louis Lortie gives almost as commanding a performance of the Liszt *Sonata* as any in the catalogue; its virtuosity can be taken for granted and, though he does not have the extraordinary intensity and feeling for drama of Pletnev, he has a keen awareness of its structure and a Chopinesque finesse that win one over. The Chandos recording, though a shade too reverberant, is altogether natural.

Cécile Ousset's account of the *Sonata* is also among the finest. A thoroughly integrated view of this piece, it is played with remarkable flair and forward drive. It is very impressive indeed. There is a steely timbre in the first of the *Paganini studies* but the others, like the *Sonata*, demonstrate her formidable musical personality. The 1974 recording is first class too, and this is superb value at budget price.

Arrau's performance of the *Sonata* has characteristic eloquence and power. His style, however, is somewhat deliberate, even pontifical, but this is still remarkable pianism. About the rest of the recital there are no reservations whatsoever. The *Bénédiction* is exceptionally imaginative and rewarding, the *Vallée d'Obermann* is hardly less fine, and the bravura in *Gnomenreigen* is riveting. The recording is resonant and full-blooded and makes a considerable impact.

This is Yundi Li's second recording for DG after winning the Warsaw Chopin Prize. His Liszt recital reaffirms the young Chinese pianist's artistry. He brings an impressive keyboard control, effortless and unostentatious technique and refinement of tone colour – and he has taste. The *Sonata* does not challenge the great recordings from the past of Horowitz, Richter and, more recently, Pletnev (above) but this does not diminish the value or interest of this well-recorded recital for aficionados of this repertoire.

The young French pianist Matthieu Papadiamandis has dazzling technique (but then so have so many young players) and a refined musical intelligence. His *B minor Sonata* may not have the transcendental mastery of a Pletnev, but it is quite an achievement; you will be surprised how well it stands up to the most exalted rivals. His *Vallée d'Obermann* is quite something too, as is the Wagner transcription. Fine, lifelike recorded sound makes this a compelling and enjoyable recital, as well as a most auspicious début.

Claudius Tanski also possesses formidable technical prowess and fine musicianship. Everything in his recital is musically satisfying and the claims of this well-recorded MDG version are quite strong. Unlike Matthieu Papadiamandis's account, however, the Tanski recording is at full price, which will not enhance its competitive status.

Readers unfamiliar with these Regis Vox recordings from the 1960s, originally issued in England on Turnabout, will be surprised at the impetuously volatile nature of the playing of the young Alfred Brendel in both sonatas. Of course, in the *B minor Sonata* he is obviously aware of the structural underlay, but here as in the other works his playing is more overtly emotional than it later became, indeed with an unexpected overflow of passionate bravura. The recording is a bit hard but, such is the interest of the playing and the imaginative programme, this recital remains of considerable appeal.

Jean-Marc Luisada's account of the *Sonata* is disfigured by disruptive rubati, and he pulls the musical argument out of shape. One critic of excellent judgement found it convincing and even mentioned it in the same breath as Pletnev, so some readers may find this more convincing than we do. For us, the interpretative distortions undermine the authority of this account.

Piano Sonata; Années de pèlerinage, 1st Year: Au bord d'une source; 2nd Year: Sonetto 104 del Petrarca; 3rd Year: Les Jeux d'eau à la Villa d'Este. Concert Paraphrases: Die Forelle; Erlkönig (Schubert); Réminiscences de Don Juan (Mozart); Rigoletto (Verdi). Consolation 3; Etudes d'exécution transcendante d'après Paganini: La campanella. Etudes de concert: Gnomenreigen; Un sospiro. Harmonies poétiques et religieuses: Funérailles. Hungarian Rhapsody 12 in C sharp min.; Liebestraum 3 in A flat; Mephisto Waltz 1

(B) *** Double Decca 444 851-2 (2). Bolet

The full range of Jorge Bolet's achievement for Decca in the music of Liszt is admirably surveyed here, ending with his commanding account of the *Sonata*, a performance combining power, imagination and concentration. He can be romantic without sentimentality, as in the *Consolation*, *Un sospiro* or the most famous *Liebestraum*, yet can dazzle the ear with bravura or beguile the listener with his delicacy of colouring, as in the *Années de pèlerinage*. All the recordings here, save the Mozart *Concert Paraphrase*, are digital and are as clear and present as one could wish.

Miscellaneous recitals

Années de pèlerinage, 2nd Year: Après une lecture du Dante. Ballade 2 in B min.; Harmonies poétiques et religieuses: Andante lagrimoso. Mephisto Waltzes 1, 2 & 4; Valse oubliée 4; Die Zelle in Nonnenwerth

⊖-- *** EMI 5 57002-2 Andsnes

Leif Ove Andsnes gives us an outstanding *Dante Sonata* and is hardly less impressive elsewhere, in a recital which strikes a good balance between well-known Liszt and the less familiar. There is no playing to the gallery and his virtuosity is always at the service of musical thought. He rarely puts a foot (or finger) wrong and he is aided by an eminently vivid and well-balanced recording.

Années de pèlerinages, 3rd Year: Aux cyprès de la Villa d'Este; Jeux d'eau à la Ville d'Este; Sunt lachrrymae rerum. Czárdás macabre; Mosonyi's Funeral Procession; Schlaflos! Frage, und Antwort; Unstern!; Valse oubliée 1; Schlumerlied

(N) (M) *** Ph. 4767 9431. Brendel

This collection which won a *Gramophone* Award is among the very best records Brendel has ever made, and it also has the benefit of extraordinarily lifelike sound. The progamme of both rare and unusual pieces is imaginatively chosen, and there is something stark and bitter about some of them. Brendel's playing is distinguished by a concentration and subtlety of nuance that are wholly convincing. This is a most distinguished issue and an obligatory purchase for admirers of this great pianist.

Années de pèlerinage: Au bord d'une source; Au lac de Wallenstadt; Les Jeux d'eau à la Villa d'Este. Harmonies poétiques et religieuses: Bénédiction de Dieu dans la solitude. Liebestraum 3; Mephisto Waltz 1; Hungarian Rhapsody 12; Variations on B-A-C-H

(BB) *** Virgin 2×1 5 61757-2 (2). Paik – *Recital of French Piano Music* ***

Kun Woo Paik is an outstanding Lisztian. Whether in the delicacy of Liszt's watery evocations from the *Années de pèlerinage*, the devilish glitter of the upper tessitura of the *Mephisto Waltz*, or the comparable flamboyance of the *Hungarian Rhapsody*, this is playing of a high order. The famous *Liebestraum* is presented more gently, less voluptuously than usual and the wide range of the *Bénédiction* is controlled very spontaneously; it is only at the climax of the *B-A-C-H Variations* that perhaps a touch more restraint would have been effective. Fine recording, and the coupled French repertoire is also very stimulating.

Années de pèlerinage, 2nd Year: 3 Sonetti di Petrarca (47, 104 & 123). Concert Paraphrase on the Quartet from Verdi's 'Rigoletto'; Consolations 1–5; Liebesträume 1–3

(M) *** DG (ADD) 435 591-2. Barenboim

Daniel Barenboim proves an ideal advocate for the *Consolations* and *Liebesträume*, and he is highly poetic in the *Petrarch Sonnets*. His playing has an unaffected simplicity that is impressive and throughout there is a welcome understatement and naturalness, until he arrives at the *Rigoletto Paraphrase*, which is played with plenty of flair and glitter. The quality of the recorded sound is excellent.

Recital I: *Années de pèlerinage, 3rd Year: Tarantella. Harmonies poétiques et religieuses: Pensées des morts; Bénédiction de Dieu dans le solitude; Legend: St Francis of Assisi Preaching to the Birds. Mephisto Waltz 1; Rhapsodie Espagnole*

Recital II: *Années de pèlerinage, 2nd Year: Après une lecture du Dante (Dante Sonata). 3rd Year: Aux cyprès de la Villa d'Este I & II; Les Jeux d'eau à la Villa d'Este. Ave Maria; Ave Maria (Die Glocken von Rom); La Lugubre Gondola (2 versions); Recueillement*

🔾➟ ✱ (BB) *** Virgin 2×1 Double 5 61439-2. Hough

Few pianists of the younger generation have quite such a magic touch as Stephen Hough, and this budget-priced Virgin Double rescues two of his finest recitals. The performances are all magnetic. On the first disc, he brings sparkle and wit to the fireworks of the *Mephisto Waltz* and the *Tarantella* from the third year of the *Années de pèlerinage* with phenomenal articulation, and he plays the extended slow movement of the *Bénédiction* with velvety warmth. The second collection is mainly of rarer music and is imaginatively chosen to include two different versions of both *Aux cyprès de la Villa d'Este* and the darkly original *La Lugubre Gondola*, in each case with the second version longer and more elaborate than the first. The cascades of *Les Jeux d'eau à la Villa d'Este* make a glittering centrepiece. The recording is excellent, but the documentation is abysmal, and even the frontispiece (a detail from Giordano's *L'Archange Michel écrasant les anges rebelles*) seems far less appropriate than the pictures of the actual fountains and cypresses at the Villa d'Este that illustrated the second recital when it first appeared at full price. Nevertheless the concentration of the playing here is unforgettable.

Ave Marias in D flat; G; E; d'Arcadelt; 6 Consolations; Harmonies poétiques et religieuses, 7–10; Ungarns Gott (left-hand)

(BB) *** Naxos 8.553516. Thomson

Concert paraphrases of sacred music: *Alleluja; Ave maris stella; 11 Chorales; Hungarian Coronation Mass: Benedictus; Offertorium. L'Hymne du pape; In festo transfigurationis; O Roma noblis; Sancta Dorothea; Stabat Mater; Urbi et orbi; Weihnachtslied; Zum Haus des Herrn ziehen wir*

(BB) *** Naxos 8.553659. Thomson

Harmonies poétiques et religieuses 1–6; Les morts; Resignazione; Ungarns Gott (two-hand)

(BB) *** Naxos 8.553073. Thomson

Philip Thomson is a Canadian pianist who has specialized in Liszt. He exhibits considerable artistry in the two discs listed above and commands not only the virtuosity which this repertoire calls for in abundance but also great poetic feeling. (He seems to be a remarkable all-rounder, having occupied teaching posts in both China and the United States, being an accomplished violinist, champion table-tennis player and even parachute jumper.) He commands a wide range of keyboard colour and refinement of *pianissimo* tone and has the benefit of very good recorded sound as well. All of his

Liszt recitals are touched by distinction and are a real bargain.

The transcriptions from the 1860s and 1870s are rarely heard in recital and, apart from Leslie Howard's survey, are seldom encountered on disc. Philip Thomson brings a wide dynamic range and a fund of keyboard colour to this repertoire. As in the earlier discs, the recording is eminently acceptable without being outstanding.

3 Recitals: (i) *Années de pèlerinage; Sonetti del Petrarcha 104 & 123; Ballade 2 in B min.; Concert paraphrase: Tarantella di bravura from Auber's 'La Muette de Portici'; Etudes d'exécution transcendante: 5, Feux follets; 9, Ricordanza. Grandes études de Paganini 3: La campanella.* (ii) *Concert paraphrases: Isolde's Liebestod from Wagner's 'Tristan und Isolde'; Reminiscences from Bellini's 'Norma'; 2 Concert Studies: Waldesrauchen; Gnomenreigen. Etude d'exécution transcendante 3, Paysage; Grande étude de Paganini 5: La Chasse; Rhapsodie espagnole (Folies d'Espagne et jota aragonesa).* (iii) *Concert paraphrases: Valse infernale from Meyerbeer's 'Robert le diable'; Polonaise from Tchaikovsky's 'Eugene Onegin'. Hexaméron (Grandes variations de bravoure on the March from Bellini's 'I Puritani' by Liszt, Thalberg, Pixis, Herz, Czerny & Chopin)*

(N) (BB) **(*) EMI Gemini (ADD) 5 86522-2 (2). (i) Wild; (ii) Wilde; (iii) Kersenbaum

Here are three impressive recitals from EMI's analogue archives, recorded in the late 1960s and early 1970s, all devoted to Lisztian bravura. Although in the first collection the sound is less than ideal (there is a certain dryness about the timbre), Earl Wild's contribution is enhanced by the presence of a *Tarantella* rarely heard in the recital room, which he despatches with great aplomb. Indeed, the playing is quite stunning, as it is in the glittering *La campanella* and *Feux follets.*

David Wilde's style is less immediately extrovert, but he too provides some impressive virtuosity, notably in the nimble-fingered *Gnomenreigen*. The dazzling *Rhapsodie espagnole* is a *tour de force*, followed with a powerful emotional climax in the Wagnerian *Liebestod*. His is a fully coloured timbre, whereas Sylvia Kersenbaum, successfully recorded in the Paris Salle Wagram, is given a striking presence, with a brilliant upper range highly suitable for the *Hexaméron*. This was the brain child of Princess Belgioioso, whose idea was to have the six most famous pianists of the day perform at one of her glittering social occasions. Although the event never took place, she managed, after months of hounding, to extract each composer's assignment, with Liszt acting as the binding force by composing the introduction and finale. It then became one of his favourite vehicles because of its fiendish difficulty. Yet it is contrasted enough to hold the listener, even though the Bellini march (which we have already heard in David Wilde's recital) is not the most subtle theme for variations. Kersenbaum's performance is remarkably assured, with sparkling bravura, and she manages to avoid banality. She then follows with the more elegant paraphrase of Meyerbeer and the rather over-elaborate arrangement of the Tchaikovsky *Polonaise*. All in all, a many-faceted portrait of Liszt as composer/performer.

Ballade 2; Harmonies poétiques et religieuses: Bénédiction de Dieu dans la solitude. Mephisto Waltz 1; Sposalizio; En rêve; Schlaflos!; Unstern!

(M) *** Oehms OCD 228. Perl

The Chilean pianist Alfredo Perl has already made a powerful impact on disc with his superb complete cycle of the thirty-two Beethoven sonatas for the midpriced label Oehms. Here, in playing equally commanding, he tackles Liszt, making an imaginative choice of pieces, four of them substantial, three of them miniatures. In his rapt concentration Perl brings weight to Liszt's sequential arguments, underlining the link between the magnificent *Ballade* over its 15-minute span and Liszt's sonata in the same key. Even more expansive is the surgingly lyrical *Bénédiction*, with the first *Mephisto Waltz* bringing virtuoso fireworks at the end. Excellent, well-balanced sound.

Concert paraphrases: on Mozart's Don Juan (Fantasia); Verdi's Rigoletto. Consolations 2 & 3; Étude d'exécution transcendante d'après Paganini: La campanella. Hungarian Rhapsodies 6 & 15; Legend: St Francis of Paola Walking on the Waves. Paganini Study 2; Polonaise 2; Valse impromptu
(M) (***) DG mono/stereo 474 423-2. Vásáry

In representing Tamás Vásáry in their series of 'Legendary Originals', DG have rightly returned to the very first Liszt recital he recorded for them in the late 1950s. The playing is consummate, technically very accomplished and happily combining sensitivity with brilliance. The mono sound is a little dry but is otherwise very good. The *Don Juan Fantasia*, *Legend* and sparkling *Paganini Study* come from the early 1960s and are in more variable stereo sound. But it is the earlier performances that are the most memorable.

Concert paraphrase of Wagner's Tannhäuser Overture; Etudes de concert, 1st Set, 3: Un sospiro; 2nd set, 1: Waldesrauschen; 2: Gnomenreigen. Etudes d'exécution transcendante d'après Paganini, 3: La campanella. Grand galop chromatique; Harmonies poétiques et religieuses: Funérailles. Liebestraum 3; Rhapsodie espagnole
(N) (M) *** RCA (ADD) 82876 63310-2. Bolet

Here is a real find, a recital recorded by Jorge Bolet in the early 1970s, when he was at the very peak of his form, a decade before he made his series of digital recordings for Decca, and just before his Carnegie Hall début in 1974. The playing in *Gnomenreigen* and the exuberant *Grand galop chromatique* is dazzling, while *La campanella* is articulated with crystal clarity, and there is more glittering fingerwork in the *Rhapsodie espagnole*.

The famous *Liebestraum* and *Un sospiro* are romantically charged, without a hint of sentimentality, while the darker atmosphere of *Funérailles* is powerfully caught. Even the almost unplayable finale of Liszt's arrangement of Wagner's *Tannhäuser Overture* is made coherent by the clear separation of the chorale from the decorative cascades – a *tour de force* of pianism. The analogue recording is excellent and the CD transfer faithful (perhaps a fraction hard) and gives him a most realistic presence.

ORGAN MUSIC

Concertstück in A; Fantasia and Fugue on 'Ad nos salutarem, undam'; Orpheus (Symphonic Poem); Prelude on 'Weinen, Klagen, Sorgen, Zagen'; Trauerode (Les Morts: Oraison)
☛ (BB) *** Naxos 8.554544. Rothkopf (Sauer organ, Evangelische Stadtkirche, Bad Homberg)

Consolations in D flat; E (Tröstung); & E (Andantino); Evocation à la Chapelle Sistine; Prelude and Fugue on the name 'BACH'; Legend: St Francis of Assisi Preaching to the Birds; Variations on 'Weinen, Klagen, Sorgen, Zagen'
☛ (BB) *** Naxos 8.555079. Rothkopf (Sauerorgan, St Petri Dom, Bremen)

The key Liszt works which were originally written for organ include the *Prelude* and *Variations on 'Weinen, Klagen, Sorgen, Zagen'* the *Prelude and Fugue on the name 'BACH'* and *Fantasia and Fugue on 'Ad nos salutarem, undam'*. Andreas Rothkopf opens the first disc with the last-named piece, and gives a magnificent account: the delayed entry of the pedals is a thrilling moment and the climactic fugue no less exciting. The *Prelude and Fugue on 'BACH'* and the *'Weinen, Klagen'* *Variations* are similarly spectacular and demand great virtuosity, which is fully forthcoming here. The other pieces are transcriptions, some made by the composer, some by others. But they all take full advantage of the rich palette of these two magnificent organs, from the dark-hued *Trauerode*, to the romantic *Consolations*. The *Concertstück* is in fact an arrangement of the most famous of these piano pieces (it was originally in D flat). The *Evocation à la Chapelle Sistine* is an elaborate fantasia on Allegri's *Miserere* and Mozart's *Ave verum*. But the most surprisingly effective transcription here is of the *Legend of St Francis Preaching to the Birds*, where the organ effects are more exotically descriptive than in the piano version, while the chorale sounds richly expansive on the organ. Throughout both CDs the performances are very fine indeed and the recording in the demonstration bracket. The back-up documentation, too, is excellent.

VOCAL MUSIC

Lieder (extended collection)
(M) *** DG 474 891-2 (3). Fischer-Dieskau, Barenboim

As in a number of other fields Liszt has been severely under-appreciated as a song composer. The reissue of this collection of 43 songs plus an accompanied declamation, which won the *Gramophone* Solo Vocal Award in 1981 and is now on three mid-priced CDs instead of four LPs, should do something to right the balance. Fischer-Dieskau, so far from making such an enormous project sound routine, actually seems to gain inspiration and intensity with the concentration; for example, the most famous of the songs, the *Petrarch Sonnets*, are here even more inspired than in his previous performances. The sheer originality of thought and the ease of the lyricism – not least in *O Lieb*, which everyone knows as the famous piano solo, *Liebestraume No. 3* – are a regular delight, and Barenboim's accompaniments could hardly be more understanding, though Liszt presented surprisingly few virtuoso challenges to the pianist. The recording is excellent.

Lieder: Comment, disaient-ils; Die drei Zigeuner; Ein Fichtenbaum steht einsam; Enfant, si j'étais roi; Es muss ein Wunderbares sein; Oh, grand je dors; S'il est un charmant gazon; Über allen Gipfeln ist Ruh; Vergiftet sind meine Lieder
(M) *** Decca 474 536-2. Fassbaender, Gage – R. STRAUSS: *Lieder* ***

Coupled with an equally characterful collection of Strauss songs, Brigitte Fassbaender's Liszt selection richly deserved to win the Solo Vocal prize in the *Gramophone* awards in 1987. This is singing which, in its control of detail, both in word and in note, as well as in its beauty and range of expression, is totally commanding. There are few women Lieder singers in any generation who can match this in power and intensity, with each song searchingly characterized. Fassbaender proves just as much at home in the four Victor Hugo settings in French as in the German songs. Sensitive accompaniment and well-placed recording.

Lieder: *Blume und Duft; Die drei Zigeuner; Der du von dem Himmel bist* (2 settings); *Ein Fichtenbaum steht einsam; Es muss ein Wunderbares sein; Es rauschen die Winde; Der Hirt; Ihr Auge; Ihr Glocken von Marling; Freudvoll und leidvoll; Die Lorelei; O komm im Traum; Des Tages laute Stimmen schweigen; Uber allen Gipfeln ist Ruh; Vergiftet sind meine Lieder*
*** Cap. 10 294. Shirai, Höll

There is only one collection of Liszt songs as searchingly persuasive as this, and none more beautiful. Provocatively the record starts with Shirai at her most vehement in *Vergiftet sind meine Lieder*, written when Liszt's long relationship with the Countess d'Agoult was breaking up. Regrettably, no English translations are provided with the text, only a commentary.

Lieder: *Du bist wie eine Blume; Die drei Zigeuner; Der du von dem Himmel bist; Es war ein König in Thule; Die Fischerstochter; Freudvoll und leidvoll; Im Rhein, im schönen Strome; Die Lorelei; S'il est un charmant gazon; Uber allen Gipfeln ist Ruh'; Die Vätergruft; Das Veilchen*
⊶ (B) *** EMI (ADD) double forte 5 73836-2 (2). Baker, Parsons – MENDELSSOHN: *Lieder;* SCHUMANN: *Liederkreis, Op. 39* ***

Dame Janet Baker's selection of songs – starting with one of the most beautiful and the most ambitious, *Die Lorelei* – brings out the wide range of Liszt in this medium. His style is transformed when setting a French text, giving Parisian lightness in response to Hugo's words, while his setting of *King of Thule* from Goethe's *Faust* leaps away from reflectiveness in illustrating the verses. The glowing warmth of Baker's singing is well matched by Geoffrey Parsons's keenly sensitive accompaniments. The recording is excellent, and the couplings admirably chosen, but there are no texts or translations.

Christus (oratorio)
(BB) *** Warner Apex 2564 61167-2 (3). Valente, Lipovšek, Lindroos, Krause, Slovak Philharmonic Ch., Rotterdam PO, Conlon

Liszt's *Christus* is less an oratorio than an episodic sequence of contrasted pieces, many of them very beautiful, inspired by the person of Christ. It is not part of the scheme to personify Christ in the way that Bach does in the Passions, but to intersperse devotional hymns – such as *The Three Kings* or the carol-like *O filii et filiae* – between atmospheric scene-paintings such as *The Beatitudes* or *The Miracle Depicting Christ Walking on the Waters*. James Conlon and his Rotterdam forces give a dedicated reading, full of warmth and understanding. The liveliness of the acoustic and the distancing of the sound may obscure some detail, but this is an account, recorded at a live concert, that brings out the beauties and expressiveness of the writing to the full. Tiny mishaps, inevitable in a live performance, are not likely to undermine enjoyment, and the reissue is very reasonably priced.

LITOLFF, Henri (1818–91)

Concerti symphoniques 2 in B min., Op. 22; 4 in D min., Op. 102
*** Hyp. CDA 66889. Donohoe, Bournemouth SO, Litton

The *Fourth Concerto Symphonique* is the source of the famous Litolff Scherzo, so often heard in the days of 78s. The first movement is rhetorical but opens with endearing flamboyance under the baton of Andrew Litton, while the passage-work scintillates in the hands of Peter Donohoe. The secondary material has both delicacy and charm. The famous Scherzo which follows is taken a fraction too fast and loses some of its poise, the articulation not always absolutely clean; but one adjusts to the breathless virtuosity, and it remains the work's finest inspiration. The *Adagio religioso* opens with some lovely horn-playing, its solemn mood nicely offset later by the pianistic decoration. The finale, marked *Allegro impetuoso*, is certainly all of that, with more twinkling bravura from Donohoe.

The *Second Concerto* is also well worth while. True, its opening *Maestoso* is hopelessly inflated, but in the Chopinesque secondary material Donohoe finds an engaging charm as well as brilliance. The second movement is another scintillating Scherzo and, if not quite as memorable as its more famous companion, it has a tripping centrepiece worthy of Saint-Saëns, especially as presented here. With a warm, naturally balanced recording, this entertaining Hyperion CD is very much worth having.

Concerti symphoniques 3 in E flat (National hollandais), Op. 45; 5 in C min., Op. 123
*** Hyp. CDA 67210. Donohoe, BBC Scottish SO, Litton

Overall, this pair of engaging works are much more consistently inspired than the more famous No. 4. Litolff incorporates two old Dutch tunes into No. 3 (hence the work's subtitle). After an opening movement with a zestful military flavour, the rollicking Scherzo includes one of these; the following nocturnal *Andante* makes a touching, songful interlude before the dazzling finale, which is to introduce the second in the form of a patriotic chorale. The brilliant dénouement is fully worthy of Liszt.

The opening mood of the *Fifth Concerto* seems darker, dispelled by another jauntily memorable Scherzo. The finale opens with a whiff of Beethoven and has unexpected weight, with the contrasting lyrical material moving into a world somewhere between Liszt and Mendelssohn. Both performances have great flair, with Donohoe playing brilliantly throughout, and Litton and his Scottish players giving splendid support. The recording is first class. A most enjoyable and recommendable coupling, notable for its ready fund of memorable melody.

Concerto symphonique 4: Scherzo
⊶ (M) *** Decca (ADD) 466 376-2. Curzon, LPO, Boult – BRAHMS: *Piano Concerto;* FRANCK: *Symphonic Variations* ***

Curzon provides all the sparkle Litolff's infectious Scherzo requires, and the 1958 Walthamstow Town Hall recording makes a delightful encore for the Brahms *Concerto* and the Franck *Symphonic Variations* in this reissue in Decca's 'Classic Sound' series. The fine qualities of the original sound, freshness and clarity, remain impressive.

LLOYD, George (1913–98)

(i) Cello Concerto. The Serf (opera): Orchestral Suite 1
⊶ *** Albany TROY 458. (i) Ross; Albany SO, Miller

Like the comparable work of Elgar, George Lloyd's poignant *Cello Concerto* was a late composition. It was completed in July 1997, a year before his death at the age of 85, and its ethos clearly reflects the composer's frustration at the rejection of his work by the musical establishment. The work is in seven continuing sections, all based on the opening lyrical theme. The variations which follow alternate fast, sometimes lighter-hearted writing, with deeply expressive, introspective slow sections. The penultimate movement, with its intense yearning, then moves into the closing 'epilogue' – a truly affecting coda. Anthony Ross is clearly very committed to this highly emotional work and, with strong support from the Albany Symphony Orchestra under David Miller, he gives a performance of moving eloquence.

The *Serf* is a colourful score, but its touches of melodrama are not wholly convincing, and the extended *Love Duet* is without a sufficiently memorable melodic line for its purpose. *Sicily* (which does not obviously relate to the opera's plot) is the most attractive movement, but this suite is not vintage Lloyd, although it is effectively played here. First-class recording throughout.

Piano Concerto 3
**(*) Albany TROY 019-2. Stott, BBC PO, composer

The *Third Piano Concerto* is very eclectic in style, with flavours of Prokofiev (with diluted abrasiveness) and even of Khachaturian – minus vulgarity – in outer movements which have a toccata-like brilliance and momentum. Kathryn Stott plays with a pleasing, mercurial lightness and makes the most of the music's lyrical feeling. But the slow movement is too long and its climax does not show Lloyd at his best. On the other hand, the wistful tune at the centre of the finale is rather appealing. The composer achieves a fine partnership with his soloist and the performance has undoubted spontaneity.

(i) Piano Concerto 4. The Lily-Leaf and the Grasshopper; The Transformation of That Naked Ape
*** Albany AR 004. Stott; (i) LSO, composer

The *Fourth Piano Concerto* is a romantic, light-hearted piece with a memorable 'long singing tune' (the composer's words), somewhat Rachmaninovian in its spacious lyricism contrasting with a 'jerky' rhythmic idea. The performance by Kathryn Stott and the LSO under the composer is ardently spontaneous from the first bar to the last. The solo pieces are eclectic but still somehow Lloydian. The recording is first rate.

Concerto for Violin & Strings; Concerto for Violin & Winds
⊶ *** Albany TROY 316. Anghelescu, Philh. O, Parry

George Lloyd's *Concerto for Violin and Strings* is very much in the great English tradition of writing for string orchestra, with or without a soloist. Its plaintive opening develops a plangent melancholy in the first movement. The rhythmically quirky Scherzo which follows is more cheerful, but the clouds do not lift entirely and it is left to the dancing finale to round off the work, but the closing bars are curiously equivocal. The *Concerto with Winds* is more robustly extrovert, neo-classical, acerbic, and brilliantly and originally scored. Its slow movement is bitter-sweet, very touching, but again producing an ambivalence of feeling, which strays into the initially light-hearted, dancing finale. In both works the Romanian soloist Cristina Anghelescu has just the right temperament for the music's quixotic changes of mood. David Parry directs, in partnership with his soloist, definitive recorded performances. The recording too is first class and most realistically balanced.

Symphonies 1 in A; 12
*** Albany TROY 032-2. Albany SO, composer

The pairing of George Lloyd's first and last symphonies is particularly appropriate, as they share a theme-and-variations format. The *First* is relatively lightweight. The mature *Twelfth* uses the same basic layout but ends calmly with a ravishingly sustained *pianissimo*, semi-Mahlerian in intensity, that is among the composer's most beautiful inspirations. At the beginning of the work, the listener is soon aware of the noble lyrical theme which is the very heart of the *Symphony*. The Albany Symphony Orchestra gave the work its première and they play it with enormous conviction and eloquence, helped by the superb acoustics of the Troy Savings Bank Music Hall, which produces sound of demonstration quality.

Symphonies 2; 9
*** Albany TROY 055. BBC PO, composer

Lloyd's *Second Symphony* is a lightweight, extrovert piece, conventional in form and construction, though in the finale the composer flirts briefly with polytonality, an experiment he did not repeat. The *Ninth* (1969) is similarly easygoing; the *Largo* is rather fine, but its expressive weight is in scale, and the finale, 'a merry-go-round that keeps going round and round', has an appropriately energetic brilliance. Throughout both works the invention is attractive, and in these definitive performances, extremely well recorded, the composer's advocacy is very persuasive.

Symphony 3 in F; Charade (suite)
*** Albany TROY 90. BBC PO, composer

The *Third Symphony* dates from the composer's 19th year, its idiom undemanding but agreeable. Although it is described as a one-movement piece, it clearly subdivides into three sections, and it is the central *Lento* which has *the* tune, a winding, nostalgic theme that persists in the memory. It is atmospherically prepared and eventually blossoms sumptuously. *Charade* dates from the 1960s and attempts to portray the London scene of the time, from aggressive *Student Power* and *LSD* to *Flying Saucers* and *Pop Song*. The ironic final movement, *Party Politics*, is amiable rather than wittily abrasive. The composer is good at bringing his music vividly to life, and he is very well recorded indeed.

Symphony 4
*** Albany AR 002. Albany SO, composer

George Lloyd's *Fourth Symphony* was composed during his convalescence after being badly shell-shocked while serving in the Arctic convoys of 1941/2. The first movement is directly related to this period of his life, and the listener may be surprised at the relative absence of sharp dissonance. After a brilliant Scherzo, the infectious finale is amiable, offering a series of quick, 'march-like tunes', which the composer explains by suggesting that 'when the funeral is over the band plays quick cheerful tunes to go home'. Under Lloyd's direction, the Albany Symphony Orchestra play with great commitment and a natural, spontaneous feeling. The recording is superb.

Symphony 5 in B flat
☛ *** Albany TROY 022-2. BBC PO, composer

The *Fifth Symphony* is a large canvas, with five strong and contrasted movements, adding up to nearly an hour of music. It was written during a happy period spent living simply on the shore of Lac Neuchâtel, during the very hot summer of 1947. In the finale, the composer tells us, 'everything is brought in to make as exhilarating a sound as possible – strong rhythms, vigorous counterpoints, energetic brass and percussion'. The symphony is played with much commitment by the BBC Philharmonic under the composer, who creates a feeling of spontaneously live music-making throughout. The recording is first class.

Symphonies (i) 6; (ii) 10 (November Journeys); (i) Overture: John Socman
**(*) Albany TROY 15-2. (i) BBC PO; (ii) BBC PO Brass; composer

The bitter-sweet lyricism of the first movement of *November Journeys* is most attractive, but the linear writing is more complex than usual in a work for brass. In the finale a glowing *cantando* melody warms the spirit, to contrast with the basic *Energico*. The *Calma* slow movement is quite haunting, no doubt reflecting the composer's series of visits to English cathedrals, the reason for the subtitle. The *Sixth Symphony* is amiable and lightweight; it is more like a suite than a symphony. Lloyd's performances are attractively spontaneous and well played, and the equally agreeable *John Socman Overture* also comes off well, although it is rather inconsequential.

Symphony 7
☛ *** Albany TROY 057. BBC PO, composer

The *Seventh Symphony* is a programme symphony, using the ancient Greek legend of Proserpine. The slow movement is particularly fine, an extended soliloquy of considerable expressive power. The last and longest movement is concerned with 'the desperate side of our lives – "Dead dreams that the snows have shaken, Wild leaves that the winds have taken" –' yet, as is characteristic with Lloyd, the darkness is muted; nevertheless the resolution at the end is curiously satisfying. Again he proves an admirable exponent of his own music. The recording is splendid.

Symphony 8
*** Albany TROY 230. Philh. O, composer

After his severe depression and nervous breakdown, Lloyd gave up composing entirely for many years, earning his living instead as a mushroom farmer, only gradually turning back to composition. The *Eighth Symphony*, written in 1961 – the first to be heard in public – is a product of that long recuperative period, and in the openness of inspiration (passionately English) it both belies earlier depression and testifies to the success of composition as therapy. Linked by a six-note leitmotif, the work holds well together. Even if the scherzando finale is arguably a little too long for its material, the elliptical first movement (opening and closing atmospherically and with a richly memorable secondary theme) and the eloquently sustained *Largo* both show the composer

at his finest. The recording, made in the spacious acoustics of Watford Town Hall, is first class.

Symphony 11
*** Albany TROY 060. Albany SO, composer

The urgently dynamic first movement of the *Eleventh Symphony* is described by the composer as being 'all fire and violence', but any anger in the music quickly evaporates, and it conveys rather a mood of exuberance, with very full orchestral forces unleashed. With the orchestra for which the work was commissioned, Lloyd conducts a powerful performance, very well played. The recording, made in the Music Hall of Troy Savings Bank near Albany, is spectacularly sumptuous and wide-ranging.

PIANO MUSIC

Music for piano duet

Aubade (fantasy suite); Eventide; The Road through Samarkand
*** Albany Troy 248. Goldstone and Clemmow (piano duet)

Aubade, written in 1971, is a substantial suite of some 38 minutes' length, a dream-like fantasy, with pictures flitting through his mind at dawn. Its evocations are impressionistic, its flavour distinctly Gallic. It is all brilliantly imagined and its colourful imagery is vividly realized in a bravura performance by Anthony Goldstone and Caroline Clemmow. *Eventide* is a touching re-presentation and elaboration of a carol from the composer's youth – a simple melody which is charmingly ingenuous and not sentimentalized. *The Road through Samarkand* is a virtuoso toccata dominated by a simple motto theme. It is full of rhythmic interest, often syncopated, and the players clearly relish the virtuosity it demands. In short these are first-rate performances of highly communicative music which shows the composer at his most successfully spontaneous. The recording is vivid but somewhat over-reverberant.

An African Shrine; The Aggressive Fishes; Intercom Baby; The Road through Samarkand; St Anthony and the Bogside Beggar
**(*) Albany AR 003. Roscoe

The most ambitious piece here is *An African Shrine*, in which the composer's scenario is linked (not very dissonantly) to African violence and revolution. *The Road through Samarkand* (1972) has travellers from the younger generation leaving for the East; while *The Aggressive Fishes* are tropical and violently moody, changing from serenity to anger at the flick of a fin. The two most striking pieces are the picaresque tale of the *Bogside Beggar* and the charming lullaby written for a baby whose mother is in another room listening with the aid of modern technology. Martin Roscoe's performances are thoroughly committed and spontaneous, and the recording is first class.

VOCAL MUSIC

A Litany
**(*) Albany TROY 200. Watson, White, Guildford Choral Soc., Philh. O, composer

A Litany is a setting of 12 verses from the John Donne poem. If anything, the recording is more successful than the first performance, with the choir enthusiastically at home in music which communicates readily, even if the soloists are less than ideal, both having rather wide vibratos. *A Litany* is not as inspired as the *Symphonic Mass*. It is unfortunate that the very opening brings a curious reminder of *The Phantom of the Opera* and *Belshazzar's Feast* with a whiff of Ketèlbey for good measure. But the music soon settles down and there is much fine choral writing in the first two sections, even if it is the third, unaccompanied, section, 'a song of thanks to the Virgin', that is the heart of the piece. The spacious recording is well up to Albany's usual high standard.

(i) *Requiem. Psalm 130*
⊕ ✪ * Albany TROY 450. (i) Wallace; Exon Singers, Owens

The *Requiem* was George Lloyd's final work and it represents the composer's infinitely touching farewell to life, which he always celebrated with vigour in spite of his many disappointments. It is written for counter-tenor and small chorus, although the choral writing is as rich in melody and harmony as anything in the *Symphonic Mass*. Indeed at 50 minutes the *Requiem* is hardly less ambitious, and one does not sense a smaller scale. Because of his realization that he would not have enough time to complete a large orchestral score, Lloyd turned to the organ, and that proved one of the work's principal strengths, for the organ writing is often thrilling and always imaginatively resourceful. The *Confutatis*, for instance, brings a surging bravura organ passage and then the *Dies irae* (using the medieval chant) makes its thrillingly exuberant choral entry. But the work is predominantly lyrical, and the serene mood of the opening of the *Kyrie* returns radiantly at the *Lacrimosa*. The jaunty, scalic *Hostias* and the following, comparably rhythmic *Sanctus* demonstrate that the vitality of Lloyd's inspiration was undiminished, and after a touching solo *Agnus Dei*, finely sung by Stephen Wallace, the work closes peacefully and optimistically with a seraphic *Lux eterna*, quoting the celestial rocking theme from the *Kyrie*. The work is splendidly sung and played (the organist, Jeffry Makinson, deserves his own Rosette). It is inspirational in feeling, with that special quality that almost always comes with a first recording. The simple *a cappella* setting of *Psalm 130*, written in 1995, makes an apt coupling. The recording itself, made in the Church of St Alban the Martyr, Holborn, is first class, but black marks for the documentation, which provides no translation of the Latin text of the *Requiem* and omits the words of the *Psalm* altogether.

A Symphonic Mass
⊕ ✪ * Albany TROY 100. Brighton Festival Ch., Bournemouth SO, composer

George Lloyd's *Symphonic Mass* is his masterpiece. Written for chorus and orchestra (but no soloists) on the largest scale, the work is linked by a recurring main theme, a real tune which soon lodges insistently in the listener's memory, even though it is modified at each reappearance. It first appears as a quiet setting of the words *Christe eleison*, nearly four minutes into the *Kyrie*. The climax of the whole work is the combined *Sanctus* and *Benedictus*, with the latter framed centrally. To the words, *Dominus Deus*, the great melody finds its apotheosis in a passage marked *largamente con fevore*. Then the *Sanctus* reasserts itself dramatically and, after a cry of despair from the violins, the movement reaches its overwhelmingly powerful and dissonant dénouement. Peace is then restored in the *Agnus Dei*, where the composer tells us

the words *Dona nobis pacem* became almost unbearably poignant for him. The performance is magnificent and the recording is fully worthy, spaciously balanced within the generous acoustic of the Guildhall, Southampton, and overwhelmingly realistic, even in the huge climax of the *Sanctus* with its shattering percussion.

The Vigil of Venus (Pervigilium Veneris)
(M) *** Decca 473 437-2. James, Booth, Welsh Nat. Op. Ch. & O, composer

As in the symphonies, Lloyd thumbs his nose at fashion in a score that both pulses with energy and cocoons the ear in opulent sounds. Delian ecstasy is contrasted against the occasional echo of Carl Orff, an attractive mixture, even if – for all the incidental beauties – there is dangerously little variety of mood in the nine substantial sections. The composer was not entirely happy with what he was able to achieve in this first recording; even so, his performance certainly does not lack intensity, and the recording (made by Argo engineers) is excellent, given the inherent problems of the recording venue in Swansea.

Iernin (opera; complete)
*** Albany TROY 121/3 (3). Hill Smith, Pogson, Herford, Rivers, Powell, BBC Singers & Concert O, composer

George Lloyd was only 21 when in the early 1930s he wrote this ambitious opera, and there is an open innocence in the warmly atmospheric, lyrical score. The piece was inspired by an ancient Cornish legend about ten maidens turned into a circle of stones, one of whom, Iernin (pronounced Ee-er-nin), returns in human form. Though this is ostensibly an old-fashioned opera, it deserves revival, and on the recording – taken from a BBC Radio 3 presentation in 1988 – the composer conducts a red-blooded, warmly expressive reading. Though some of the ensemble writing is less distinguished, the offstage choruses of faery folk are most effective. As to the soloists, Marilyn Hill Smith sings brightly in the title-role with all the agility needed, and the tenor, Geoffrey Pogson, copes well with the hero's role, if with rather coarse tone. The most distinguished singing comes from the rich-toned contralto, Claire Powell, as Cunaide. The third disc includes a half-hour interview with the composer, which makes up in part for the absence of background notes in the booklet with the libretto. Excellent, well-balanced BBC sound.

LLOYD WEBBER, William
(1914–82)

(i) *Aurora (tone-poem); Invocation; Lento; Serenade for Strings; 3 Spring Miniatures*; (ii) *Benedictus (for violin and organ)*; (iii) *Nocturne (for cello and harp)*; (iv) *Jesus, Dear Jesus*; (i; v) *Love divine, all loves excelling; Mass (Princeps pacis)*
*** Chan. 9595. (i) City of L. Sinfonia, Hickox; (ii) Little, Watson; (iii) Julian Lloyd Webber, Kanga; (iv) Cook, Arts Educational School, London, Jones; Antrobus (organ); (v) Westminster Singers

William Lloyd Webber demonstrates in ten short works that he wrote tunes every bit as fluently as his son, Andrew. Lloyd Webber senior, church organist and teacher, was yet an arch-romantic at heart, whose style sets English pastoral alongside Rachmaninov-like surges of passion. The most ambitious piece is the symphonic poem, *Aurora*, which starts like Bartók as smoothed over by Vaughan Williams, then develops in a colourfully orchestrated sequence of ideas. A forthright setting of the *Mass*, written for Westminster Cathedral, happily reconciles Roman and Anglican manners, yet every one of these unpretentious miniatures, beautifully performed and recorded, offers music of winning openness.

(i) *Air & Variations; Fantasy Trio; Frensham Pond (Aquarelle); The Gardens at Eastwell (A Late Summer Impression); Mulberry Cottage; Sonatina; A Song for the Morning; 3 Spring Miniatures;* (ii) *Songs: The call of the morning; The forest of wild thyme; How do I love thee; I looked out into the morning; Love, like a drop of dew; Over the bridge; Sun-Gold; To the Wicklow hills*
*** Hyp. CDA 67008. (i) Nash Ens.; (ii) Mark Ainsley, Brown

Lloyd Webber's chamber and piano pieces span a far wider period than the songs, starting with the *Fantasy Trio* of 1936, written when the composer was 22. The pieces inspired by particular places, like his very last known work, *The Gardens at Eastwell* for flute, are as freely lyrical as the songs. Very English in idiom, this music echoes not just early Bridge but occasionally Ireland too, as in the brisk, chattering piano piece, *Tree Tops*. The Nash Ensemble soloists are all outstanding, with the pianist, Ian Brown, an inspired linchpin in every item. Again, the gift of melody revealed in the eight songs included here is a rare one. In idiom rather like early Frank Bridge they have tunes ready to latch in the mind, largely predictable but with unexpected twists. John Mark Ainsley is a most sensitive interpreter, and again Ian Brown makes a fine contribution.

Aria; Chorale, Cantilena & Finale; Choral March; Elegy; Festal March; 3 Interludes on Christmas Carols; Intermezzo; Meditation on Stracathro; Prelude; Prelude on Winchester New; 3 Recital Pieces (Prelude; Barcarolle; Nuptial March); Slumber Song; Solemn Procession; Song without Words; Trumpet Minuet; Vesper Hymn
*** Priory PRCD 616. Watts (Willis organ of Salisbury Cathedral)

Like other discs of William Lloyd Webber's music, the Priory issue of organ pieces consistently reveals his fluent tunefulness, even if this is much more a specialist issue – the first recording made on the refurbished Willis organ at Salisbury Cathedral. Roughly half the 22 pieces here are typical examples of hushed and meditative organ music designed to fill in discreetly between items in a service, with five more designed as bright and energetic voluntaries for speeding congregations out of church. There are Franckian echoes in the chromaticism of the *Chorale, Cantilena and Finale*, but generally the style is very similar to that of the orchestral pieces. Sympathetic performances, very well recorded.

(i) *Missa Sanctae Mariae Magdalenae;* (ii) *Arias: The divine compassion: Thou art the King. The Saviour: The King of Love. 5 Songs;* (iii; iv) *In the half light (soliloquy); Air varié (after Franck);* (iv) *6 Piano Pieces*
*** ASV CDDCA 961. (i) Richard Hickox Singers, Hickox; Watson (organ); (ii) Hall, P. Ledger; (iii) Julian Lloyd Webber; (iv) Lill

William Lloyd Webber was a distinguished academic who, in a few beautifully crafted works, laid bare his heart in pure romanticism. In his varied collection, the *Missa Sanctae Mariae Magdalenae* is both the last and the most ambitious of his works, strong and characterful. John Lill is a persuasive

advocate of the *Six Piano Pieces*, varied in mood and sometimes quirky, and accompanies Julian Lloyd Webber in the two cello pieces, written – as though with foresight of his son's career – just as his second son was born. Graham Hall, accompanied by Philip Ledger, completes the recital with beautiful performances of a group of songs and arias. Recording, made in a north London church, is warm and undistracting.

LÔBO, Alonso (c. 1555–1617)

Motets: *Audivi vocem de coelo; Pater peccavi*
(BB) *** Naxos 8.553310. Ars Nova, Holten (with Concert of Portuguese Polyphony ***) – CARDOSO: *Motets;* MAGALHAES: *Missa O Soberana luz, etc.* ***

Lôbo's two beautiful motets, *Audivi vocem de coelo* ('I heard a voice from heaven') and *Pater peccavi* ('Father, I have sinned'), confirm the individuality of his writing. They are part of an outstandingly sung collection which is among the most desirable records of its kind in the catalogue.

LÔBO, Duarte (c. 1565–1646)

Missa pro defunctis
(BB) *** Naxos 8.550682. Oxford Schola Cantorum, Summerly – CARDOSO: *Missa pro defunctis* ***

Duarte Lôbo, Mestre de Capela at Lisbon Cathedral, was an almost exact contemporary of Manuel Cardoso, whose music we have already discovered and who provides an eloquent coupling for this splendid Naxos CD. As performed here, Lôbo's *Missa pro defunctis* for double choir is a work of beautiful flowing lines (following directly on from Palestrina), bold dramatic contrasts and ardent depth of feeling. The *Agnus Dei* is particularly beautiful. A solo treble briefly introduces each section except the *Kyrie*, which adds to the effect of the presentation. This is another triumph from Jeremy Summerly and his excellent Oxford group (38 singers), who catch both the Latin fervour and the underlying serenity of a work which has a memorably individual voice.

Motets: *Audivi vocem de coelo; Pater peccavi*
(BB) *** Naxos 8.553310. Ars Nova, Holten (with Concert of Portuguese Polyphony ***) – CARDOSO: *Motets;* MAGALHAES: *Missa O Soberana luz, etc.* ***

Lôbo's two beautiful motets, *Audivi vocem de coelo* ('I heard a voice from heaven') and *Pater peccavi* ('Father, I have sinned'), confirm the individuality of his writing. They are part of an outstandingly sung collection which is among the most desirable records of its kind in the catalogue.

LOCATELLI, Pietro (1695–1764)

L'Art del violino (12 violin concertos), *Op. 3*
*** Hyp. CDA 66721/3. E. Wallfisch, Raglan Bar. Players, Kraemer

Pietro Locatelli was a younger contemporary of Handel and Vivaldi. It was in 1733 that he wrote the present set of concertos, each of which in its outer movements includes an extended *Capriccio* of enormous technical difficulty with fast, complicated, sometimes stratospheric, upper tessitura. Elizabeth Wallfisch not only throws off the fireworks with ease but also produces an appealingly gleaming lyrical line. Although Locatelli has not as strong a melodic personality as his famous contemporaries, the invention here has rhythmic vitality (which at times mirrors Vivaldi) and, in the Largo slow movements, a series of flowing ideas that have an inherent Handelian grace. With excellent, vital and stylish support from Kraemer and his Raglan Baroque Players, this may be counted a stimulating authentic re-creation of a set of concertos which had a profound influence on the violin technique of the time. The very well-balanced recording (the soloist real and vivid) is admirably clear yet has plenty of ambience.

Concerti grossi, Op. 1/1–12

☞ (BB) *** Naxos 8.553445/6. Capella Istropolitana, Jaroslav Kreček

**(*) Hyp. CDA 66981/2. Raglan Bar. Players, E. Wallfisch, Kraemer

Locatelli's Op. 1, although indebted to Corelli (with the eighth of the set ending with a Christmas *Pastorale*), has a style and personality of its own. The invention is vigorous, the expressive range appealing. The Capella Istropolitana play with crisp attack, plenty of sparkle and resilient rhythms; the style of the slow movements reveals a keen identity with the lessons of period performances, even though modern instruments are used and phrasing is not exaggerated by bulges. The recording is admirable, with textures clear and with attractive, light sonorities. Most enjoyable and highly recommended.

The performances on Hyperion are lively enough, but there is at times an element of routine, a feeling of jogging along, as if the players are not convinced that this is a very distinctive Opus. Elizabeth Wallfisch leads the concertino and is fully up to the bravura demands placed on her, though in the lyrical music her 'authentic' style of phrasing seems slightly more intrusive than usual. The recording is bright and vivid, the ambience spacious.

Concerti grossi, Op. 1/2, 5 & 12; Il pianto d'Arianna, Op. 7/6; Sinfonia in F min. (composta per le esequie della sua Donna che si celebrarono in Roma)

*** Opus 111 OP 30-104. Europa Galante, Biondi

The composer himself set great store by his Op. 1 and they are remarkable works, full of individuality. The sonata subtitled *Il pianto d'Arianna*, from Op. 7, is even more ambitious, with ten brief movements, an occasional whiff of Vivaldi, and plenty of drama. Perhaps most striking of all here is the *Sinfonia 'for the Funeral of his Lady which Took Place in Rome'*, which opens with an accented *Lamento* of rare intensity, in which the composer could be suggesting a heartbeat. The performances here are full of cleanly articulated, bouncing rhythmic vitality and are also persuasively expressive. Fabio Biondi, who really knows his way about this repertoire, uses a triple rather than a double layout, with the concertino, a further tutti group still made up of soloists, plus the real tutti or ripieno. The organ continuo adds subtle extra colour. The recording is most vividly clear yet not too close, with plenty of natural ambience. Highly recommended.

6 Introduttioni teatrali, Op. 4/1–6; 6 Concerti grossi, Op. 4/7–12

*** Hyp. CDA 67041/2. Raglan Bar. Players, E. Wallfisch

There is simply no better introduction to the music of Locatelli than this superbly invigorating collection of his six

Theatrical Introductions. They are essentially (highly inventive) small-scale concerti grossi, with a concertino of four players, written in the fast–slow–fast manner of an Italian overture. Indeed, the finale of No. 5 reminds one of the fifth concerto grosso of Handel's Op. 6.

The Raglan Baroque Players offer also the other six *Concerti grossi* which make up the rest of Locatelli's Op. 4. They too show him at his finest form, particularly the *Concerto No. 8 in F à immitazione de Corni da caccia*, where the opening *Grave* is quite profound, and then in later movements the solo violin of the concertino uses double-stopping ingeniously to depict a pair of horns. The remaining works are not as novel as this, but No. 10 (*Da Camera*) is a reworking of the *Sixth Sonata* of Locatelli's Op. 8 (see below) and includes the remarkable *Minuetto* with extended bravura variations, which are superbly played here by Elizabeth Wallfisch. The final concerto of the set features four solo violins and was surely influenced by Vivaldi's famous work in this format which he included in *L'Estro armonico*. It deserves to be better known. The playing of the Raglan Baroque Ensemble, directed from the violin by the estimable Elizabeth Wallfisch, is supremely vital and expressively alive. The aural brightness is rather sharply etched, but the basic sonorities are full and the ambience is appealing.

CHAMBER MUSIC

12 Trio Sonatas, Op. 2

(M) ** Van. 99099 (2). Wentz, Musica ad Rhenum

The Vanguard set is fluent and highly musical, and the continuo group (including organ in Nos. 2, 4, 6, 9 and 11) is very effective; but Jed Wentz's period flute sounds a little pale. Even so, this is offered at mid-price and is very well recorded. Readers will note that the cueing goes wrong for the final double sonata (in which, presumably, Wentz plays a duet with himself), which starts at track 19 (not 18), since the previous sonata has four sub-divisions, not the indicated three.

6 Trio Sonatas, Op. 5

(M) **(*) Van. 99087. Wentz, Moonen, Musica ad Rhenum

Locatelli's Op. 5 Trio Sonatas are full of agreeable, singing melody and have plenty of lively invention too. It is optional to use a pair of flutes or two violins in their performance, and it might have been a good idea to vary the instrumentation, as two flutes used continually can prove too much of a good thing. However, Jed Wentz and Marion Moonen play with style and they blend nicely together; the continuo group includes a bassoon for added colour. Good performances, without any of the acerbities one associates with period performance, nicely recorded.

Violin Sonatas (for 1 or 2 violins) and continuo, Op. 8/1–10

*** Hyp. CDA 67021/2. Locatelli Trio

Locatelli's Op. 8 consists of six works for solo violin, of which the last is the most impressive with its closing *Aria di minuetto* with eight variations, demanding considerable bravura from the soloist. All the sonatas start with a slow, expressive introduction, with faster movements following. The remaining works are *Trio Sonatas*; with their format of (usually) four (or sometimes five) movements, they offer the composer even greater opportunities for variety and he is obviously intending to please his cultivated listeners. But the invention in these later works is deft in imaginative touches, and the contrapuntal writing is genially spirited. Provided you don't respond adversely to Elizabeth Wallfisch's tendency in playing to bulge very slightly on expressive phrasing, the performances are admirable, crisply detailed and refreshingly alive. The Hyperion recording is well up to standard.

LOCKE, Matthew (c. 1621–77)

Consort of Fower Parts: Suites 1 in D min.; 2 in D min./maj.; 3 & 4 in F; 5 in G min.; 6 in G
*** Astrée ES 9921. Hespèrion XX

Consort of Fower Parts: Suites 1–6. Flatt Consort a 3 'for my cousin Kemble'
*** Global Music Network GMNC 0109. Phantasm

Matthew Locke, born in Devon, was a choirboy at Exeter Cathedral, but when Charles II was restored to the throne of England, Locke became Master of the King's Music at the royal court; but he probably wrote the *Consort of Fower Parts* earlier, most likely in the 1650s. If they are not ambitious in instrumentation, they are much more so in musical achievement. Each suite opens with a *Fantazie* and then follows a standard sequence of *Courante*, *Ayre* and *Saraband*. Locke's suites were regarded at the time as being composed, 'after the old style', but the music itself is forward-looking and by no means predictable. It seems likely that they would have been performed with continuo, a practice followed sparingly in the Hespèrion performance which prefers a double harp to the lute.

Both sets of performances are highly musical, scholarly and well recorded, but there is a first choice. In the dance movements there is an extra rhythmic vigour and buoyancy with Hespèrion, and in the *Ayres* of the *First* and *Second Suites*, for instance, there is extra expressive warmth.

However, Phantasm also play this music delightfully. Their approach is intimate yet also reveals the music's expressive qualities as being considerable, while the dance movements are very sprightly. They are admirably recorded and they also include the ambitious suite of six movements which the composer wrote for his cousin which includes no fewer than three *Fantazies*.

The Tempest (incidental music); *Canon on a Plain Song by Mr William Brode of Hereford*
**(*) Teldec 3984 21464-2. Il Giardino Armonico (with ZELENKA: *Fanfare*; ANON.: *Tune for the Woodlark*; ONOFRI: *Ricercare for Viola da Gamba & Lute*) – BIBER: *Battaglia*, etc. **(*)

Matthew Locke wrote only the instrumental pieces for the 1674 London performance of *The Tempest*, which was a hybrid work, almost an opera, with contributions from various composers in addition to spoken dialogue. However, this collection of lively dances (often strikingly English in spirit), and the more expressive and sometimes piquant Act Tunes, works well as a suite. It is presented with great vitality by Il Giardino Armonico, although they tend to overdramatize music intended to divert, and their aggressive rhythmic and bowing style will appeal mainly to those who are totally won over to period-instrument practice. The recording is vivid but close.

LOEWE, Carl (1796–1869)

Ballads and Lieder (extended collection)
(M) *** DG (IMS) 449 516-2 (2). Fischer-Dieskau, Demus

For the most part this set was recorded in 1968–9, with a second group of songs added a decade later. With the great German baritone consistently in fine voice, it makes an ideal selection of some of Loewe's most memorable songs and ballads. Dietrich Fischer-Dieskau, admirably accompanied by Jörg Demus, gives performances which have the commitment and intensity of spontaneous expression while remaining flawlessly controlled and strongly thought through. This alternative setting of the *Erlkönig*, preferred by many in the nineteenth century, is in its way as dramatic as Schubert's, if musically less subtle. The following *Edward* is also extraordinarily dramatic, while the magnificent *Die Uhr* ('The Timepiece') opens lightly but develops an unexpected depth of feeling. It is an excellent feature of the set that the translations are provided in full. Splendidly vivid recording: if you enjoy Schubert, you can hardly fail to relish the best of Loewe.

LOMBARDINI, Maddelena Laura
– see under Sirmen, Maddelena

LORTZING, Albert (1801–51)

Die Himmelfahrt Jesu Christi (The Ascension of Jesus Christ)
**(*) CPO 999 837-2. Pfeffer, Fassbaender, Schneider, Hilz, Steifermann, Cologne Ch. & RSO, Fraschauer

In 1828, just as Lortzing was setting out on his highly successful career as an opera composer in Germany, he wrote this oratorio on the theme of Christ's Ascension for a performance in Munster. It is a well-mannered work, not specially original but nicely constructed over its hour-long span, starting directly with a chorus of Angels and ending with the Angel chorus joined by the quartet of soloists, representing not just Christ but St Peter, the Angel Gabriel and Eloa – *Blessed are they that call on God*. Christ (the tenor role) does not appear until the second half, first with a lyrical aria, then praying to God the Father for glorification on the completion of His work on earth. There is a naïvety about the text which is matched by the music, written in a post-Beethoven style that often comes close to Mendelssohn. Though the soloists are variable, with the light, agile soprano Anneli Pfeffer edgy and not always steady, Helmuth Fraschauer directs a capable performance, helped by a fresh-toned chorus.

Die Opernprobe
(M) *** CPO/EMI (ADD) 999 557-2. Marheineke, Gedda, Hirte, Litz, Lövaas, Berry, Bav. State Op. Ch. & O, Suitner

Best known for his opera *Der Wildschütz*, still popular in Germany today, Lortzing wrote this light-hearted satire in 1851, his very last piece, given its first performance on the day before he died. As a singer and actor himself, writing his own librettos, he had the gift of composing operas which, helped by his easy tunefulness, work well. *Die Opernprobe* ('The Opera Rehearsal') involves disguises and confusions of identity in the household of a music-loving Count who encourages his servants to perform. In a sparkling overture and ten numbers, mostly brief, it tells a simple story of true love triumphant, ending with a substantial finale in Mozartian style. Otmar Suitner directs a lively performance, very well sung and well produced in its dialogue, with first-rate (1974) EMI sound.

LOTTI, Antonio (c. 1667–1740)

Crucifixus

(B) *** Double Decca (ADD) 443 868-2 (2). St John's College, Cambridge, Ch., L. Philomusica, Guest – BONONCINI: *Stabat Mater* ***; PERGOLESI: *Magnificat in C; Stabat Mater* **(*); D. SCARLATTI: *Stabat Mater; A. SCARLATTI: Domine, refugium factus es nobis; O magnum mysterium; CALDARA: Crucifixus* ***

(B) *** Double Decca (ADD) 455 017-2. St John's College, Cambridge, Ch., L. Philomusica, Guest – CALDARA: *Crucifixus* ***; PERGOLESI: *Magnificat*, etc. **(*)

This short *Crucifixus*, which takes less than four minutes, may well have inspired the noble Caldara setting with which it frames Bononcini's beautiful *Stabat Mater* in this highly desirable collection of choral music. The Lotti setting is less elaborate in texture than Caldara's but it is hardly less noble or affecting. Performance and recording are excellent. Alongside the Caldara setting, this fine piece also comes as a filler for Decca's alternative compilation centring on Pergolesi.

LOVENSKIOLD, Herman (1815–70)

La Sylphide (ballet; complete)

(M) *** Chan. 6546. Royal Danish O, Garforth

La Sylphide (1834) predates Adam's *Giselle* by seven years. It is less distinctive than Adam's score, but it is full of grace and the invention has genuine romantic vitality – indeed, the horn writing in the finale anticipates Delibes. The wholly sympathetic playing is warm, elegant, lively and felicitous in its detailed delicacy, yet robust when necessary and always spontaneous. A most enjoyable disc, superbly recorded.

LUDFORD, Nicholas (1485–1557)

Masses; Magnificat benedicta & Motets (as listed below)

☛ ❂ (M) *** Gaudeamus CDGAX 426 (4). Cardinall's Musick, Carwood

Nicholas Ludford is one of the least familiar of the Tudor masters; he never enjoyed the fame of his older contemporary, Fayrfax, or the much younger Tallis. This four-CD box gathers together the four splendid discs of Ludford's music performed by Andrew Carwood and his excellent group of singers, who are individually as impressive as in the blended whole. This is music of remarkably passionate feeling, and it brings to life a composer who spent much of his working life in St Stephen's Chapel at St Margaret's, Westminster. He was an ardent Catholic and was very happily married – he paid for his wife to have her own pew and gave her an elaborate ceremonial burial. He then married again, and his second wife was instructed to prepare something more modest for his interment alongside his beloved first spouse. His music is little short of extraordinary, and we hope our Rosette will tempt collectors to explore it, either through this comprehensive box, which retails at just short of £40, or by trying one of the individual issues (CDGAU 131/3 and 140).

LULLY, Jean-Baptiste (1632–87)

Dies irae; Te Deum

(BB) **(*) Warner Apex 2564 61369-2. J. Smith, Bessac, Vandersteene, Devos, Huttenlocher, Vocal Ens. 'A Cœur Joie' de Valance, Paillard CO, Paillard

The *Dies irae* is written for double choir, and the antiphonal dialogue between the two groups is a vital part of Lully's musical architecture. Paillard makes no attempt to divide his forces, relying mainly on the contrast with the solo group. It is a noble piece, encapsulating a mood of dark melancholy, and it makes the strongest impression here. The performance itself is suitably restrained and dignified, with a totally dedicated contribution from the soloists. The effect has a striking elegiac beauty. The sudden choral interjections at a faster pace are convincingly managed. The coupled *Te Deum*, which dates from 1677, is probably Lully's best-known sacred piece. It is a creation of genuine splendour and breadth, rather than the general-purpose pomp often favoured by Lully and his followers. Like the *Dies irae*, the work makes effective use of the contrast between soloists, chorus and orchestra, and Jean-François Paillard and his vocal forces give a thoroughly committed and eloquent account of the piece, and the orchestra accompanies impressively. The analogue recording is eminently satisfactory in both works; the overall balance is good and the CD transfer is well managed. Paillard does not offer the last word on either work, but the record is worth having, especially at so modest a price. Incidentally, it was while conducting the *Te Deum* that Lully vigorously brought the heavy stick that served to mark the beat down on his right foot; gangrene eventually set in, and he died a couple of months later.

Armide; Isis (extracts)

(M) **(*) Erato (ADD/DDD) 2564 60578-2. Ch. Caillard, Jean-François Paillard O, Paillard – DELALANDE: *Premier Caprice* **(*)

A very pleasing selection from *Armide* and *Isis*, recorded in 1972. While the performances lack the bite one would undoubtedly get from an authentic performance today, under Paillard these do not lack life and character. There is a nice balance between the orchestral and choral writing, and all the music is of Lully's best inventive quality. *Le Sommeil de Renaud* from *Armide* is very much the sort of thing that Beecham might have selected as one of his lollipops, while the *Choeur des trembleurs* from *Isis*, with its staccato 'trembling' chorus echoed in the orchestra, makes an enjoyable novelty number, and it is followed by a charming if melancholy *Rondeau 'Plains de lo'*. The sound is good, if a little reverberant, slightly blunting some of the sharpness.

Motets: *Benedictus; Exaudi Deus; O dulcissime; Notus in Judaea Deus*

☛ (BB) *** Naxos 8.554389. Concert Spirituel, Nicquet

Master of the King's Music in the golden age of Louis XIV, Lully dominated French music for over 30 years, carefully keeping such composers as Charpentier in the background. Though in depth he may not quite match Charpentier, let alone Purcell, he was consistently lively and inventive. This excellent Naxos issue offers three of the larger-scale, multi-movement motets with choir and soloists, set against two of the best-known 'little' motets for soloists alone, including the beautiful *O dulcissime*. First-rate French performances, with no singers individually named.

Atys (opera; complete)

*** HM HMC 901257/9 (3). De Mey, Mellon, Laurens, Gardeil, Semellaz, Rime, Les Arts Florissants Ch. & O, Christie

Christie and his excellent team give life and dramatic speed consistently to the performance of *Atys*, and there are many memorable numbers, not least those in the sleep interlude of Act III. Outstanding in the cast are the high tenor, Guy de Mey, in the name-part and Agnès Mellon as the nymph, Sangaride, with whom he falls in love.

Atys (highlights)

☛ (B) *** HM HMA 1951249 (from above complete recording, with De Mey, Mellon; cond. Christie)

Atys remains one of Christie's greatest successes on record; it is full of good things, and many of them are also included on the single-disc highlights selection (notably the delightful Sleep scene of Act III). With consistently fine singing and superb recording, this disc contains about a third of the opera (68 minutes).

LUMBYE, Hans Christian (1810–74)

The complete orchestral works

Volume 1: *Amélie Waltz; Britta Polka; Artist Dreams Fantasia; Cannon Galop; Champagne Galop; Columbine Polka-mazurka; Copenhagen Steam Railway Galop; Dagma Polka; Deborah Polka Mazurka; King Christian IX's March-past; Otto Allin's Drum Polka; Queen Louise Waltz; Saecilie Waltz; Salute to August Bournonville Galop; A Summer Night at the Mön Cliffs Fantasia; (Berlin) Vauxhall Polka*

** Marco Polo 8.223743. Tivoli SO, Bellincampi

Volume 2: *Amanda Waltz; Camilla Polka; Crinoline Polka-mazurka; The Dream after the Ball; Goodnight Polka; King Carl XV's March-past; A Little Ditty for the Party Galop; Master Erik's Polka; Military Galop; Minerva Polka; Regatta Festival Waltz; Rosa and Rosita Waltz; Salute to Capri Polka; Victoria Bundsen Polka-mazurka; Victoria Galop; Wally Polka*

** Marco Polo 8.223744. Tivoli SO, Bellincampi

Volume 3: *Amager Polka, 2; Carnival Joys; Pictures from a Masquerade; Concert Polka for 2 Violins; Festival Polonaise in A; The Guardsmen of Amager: Finale-galop; New Year Greeting March; Ornithobolaia Galop; Sounds from Kroll's Dance Hall; Tivolis Concert Salon Galop; Tivoli Volière Galop; Torchlight Dance*

** Marco Polo 8.225122. Tivoli SO, Bellincampi

Following on from their monumental Strauss Edition, Marco Polo now turn their attention to the 'Strauss of the North', Hans Christian Lumbye. The first three volumes are sympathetically and enjoyably played, but the recordings are not ideal: they are too reverberant and backwardly balanced, taking away some of the warm intimacy, as well as the sparkle, this music should ideally have. But collectors who wish to explore this composer's output in depth will find much to enjoy here. Like the Strausses, Lumbye's fund of melody is seemingly inexhaustible, and the various novelty pieces are often delightful. Much of the writing has a robust quality which is most infectious, and the orchestration is always colourful. These Marco Polo discs, despite the too-resonant sound, will certainly give pleasure.

Volume 5: *Artist Carnival Locomotive Galop; Caroline Polka Mazurka; In the Dusk (Fantasy); Fountain Waltz; Hesperus Waltz; Jenny Polka; Marie Elisabeth Polka; Memories of Vienna, Waltz; The Night before New Year's Day (Polka Mazurka); Regards to the Ticket-Holders of Tivoli (March); Salute March of King Frederik VII; The Sleigh Ride (Galop); Telegraph Galop*

*** Marco Polo 8.225171. Tivoli SO, Vetö

Volume 5 in Marco Polo's Lumbye edition seems to offer marginally richer sound than earlier volumes, and the performances are excellent. There are plenty of things to delight here: the *Sleigh Ride* sounds suitably festive, with its dashing runs up and down the scale, whips and bells, while the full-length concert waltzes, such as *Memories of Vienna* and the *Hesperus Waltz*, provide more substantial fare as well as much charm and elegance. *The Night before New Year's Day* charmingly alternates the major and minor keys, while *In the Dusk* is a charming pastoral evocation of a peaceful evening, which gradually becomes more and more animated, though it ends, 'à l'invitation to the dance', as peacefully as it began. There are some novelties here, too: the *Telegraph Galop*, reflecting rivalry between two orchestras, opens with a couple of wallops on the bass drum and is a communication between both groups, who 'telegraph melodies' to each other, sometimes in different keys, though finally coming together – an amusing idea skilfully realized. This is one of the best CDs in the series.

Amelie Waltz; Britta Polka; Champagne Galop; Columbine Polka Mazurka; Concert Polka (for 2 violins and orchestra); Copenhagen Steam Railway Galop; Dream Pictures (fantasy); The Lady of St Petersburg (polka); The Guards of Amager: Final Galop. My Salute to St Petersburg (march); Napoli (ballet): Final Galop. Polonaise with Cornet Solo; Queen Louise's Waltz; Salute to August Bournonville; St Petersburg Champagne Galop

☛ (B) *** Regis RRC 1155. Odense SO, Guth

*** Chan. 9209. Danish Nat. RSO, Rozhdestvensky

The superb Regis collection (originally on Unicorn) offers 75 minutes of the composer's best music, with wonderfully spontaneous performances demonstrating above all its elegance and gentle grace. It opens with a vigorous *Salute to August Bournonville* and closes with a *Champagne Galop* to rival Johann junior's polka. In betweeen comes much to enchant, not least the delightful *Amelie Waltz* and the haunting *Dream Pictures Fantasia* with its diaphanous opening texture and lilting main theme. But Lumbye's masterpiece is the unforgettable *Copenhagen Steam Railway Galop*. This whimsical yet vivid portrayal of a local Puffing Billy begins with the gathering of passengers at the station – obviously dressed for the occasion in a more elegant age than ours. The little engine then wheezingly starts up and proceeds on its short journey, finally drawing to a dignified halt against interpolated cries from the station staff. Because of the style and refinement of its imagery, it is much the most endearing of musical railway evocations, and the high-spirited lyricism of the little train racing through the countryside, its whistle peeping, is enchanting. This is a superbly entertaining disc, showing the Odense Syphony Orchestra and its conductor Peter Guth as naturally suited to this repertoire as was the VPO under Boskovsky in the music of the Strauss family. The recording has a warm and sympathetic ambience which gives a lovely bloom to the whole concert. This reissue is a bargain if ever there was one.

The Chandos disc opens with an arresting fanfare and sets off into the *Champagne galop* with much brio. Throughout his programme, Rozhdestvensky's approach is extrovert, and the Danish orchestra, without loss of finesse, play almost everything here with great gusto. The Copenhagen Steam Railway engine becomes a mainline express and reaches an exhilarating momentum before slamming on its brakes, to be welcomed vociferously by the Danish porters as it arrives at its destination. One cannot but respond to the energy and vivacity of the playing here, while the lovely *Dream Pictures* creates a total contrast and is most poetically done. The recording is spectacularly resonant and adds to the impact.

LUTOSLAWSKI, Witold (1913–94)

(i) *Chain II*. (ii) *Piano Concerto*; (i) *Partita for Violin and Orchestra*

*** DG (IMS) 471 588-2. (i) Mutter; (ii) Zimerman; BBC SO, composer

Chain II, a 'dialogue for violin and orchestra', contrasts fully written sections with *ad libitum* movements, where chance plays its part within fixed parameters. The *Partita* is a development of a piece for violin and piano that Łutosławski originally wrote for Pinchas Zukerman, with the first, third and fifth movements now scored for violin and orchestra. With Mutter and the composer the most persuasive advocates, both these concertante pieces establish themselves as among the finest of Łutoslawski's later work. The *Piano Concerto* is also marvellously played by Zimerman and the BBC Symphony Orchestra, again under the composer. It is beautiful to listen to, but for all its diversity of aural incident and activity, one is left wondering whether there is much of enduring substance. First-rate recordings, which date back to 1988–9. The reissue is handsomely packaged but remains at full price.

Cello Concerto

☛ (M) *** EMI (ADD) 5 67867-2 [567868]. Rostropovich, O de Paris, composer – DUTILLEUX: *Cello Concerto* ***

The *Cello Concerto* was written in response to a commission by Rostropovich. As in some other Łutoslawski pieces, there are aleatory elements in the score, though these are carefully controlled. The sonorities are fascinating and are heard to good advantage on the EMI CD. The soloist is rather forward, but in every other respect the recording is extremely realistic. Rostropovich is in his element and gives a superb account of the solo role, and the composer's direction of the accompaniment is grippingly authoritative. This coupling with Dutilleux has rightly been reissued as one of EMI's 'Great Recordings of the Century'.

(i; ii; iii) *Cello Concerto*; (i; ii; iv) *Concerto for Oboe, Harp & Chamber Orchestra*; (v) *Concerto for Orchestra*; (i; ii; ix) *Dance Preludes*; (i; vi; vii) *Les Espaces du sommeil*; (v) *Funeral Music*; (i; vii) *Symphony 3*; (viii) *Variations on a Theme by Paganini*; (v) *Venetian Games*

(B) *** Ph. Duo (ADD) 464 043-2 (2). (i) composer; (ii) Bav. RSO; (iii) Schiff; (iv) H. and U. Holliger; (v) Nat. SO of Warsaw, Rowicki; (vi) Fischer-Dieskau; (vii) BPO; (viii) Argerich, Freire; (ix) Brunner

This is an excellent bargain-price introduction to Łutoslawski which includes many of his most important works. The *Third Symphony* is given an authoritative performance under the direction of the composer, while *Les Espaces du sommeil* is performed by its dedicatee, Dietrich Fischer-Dieskau, and more definitive versions could hardly be imagined. Recorded around the same time in equally impressive performances was the *Cello Concerto* with Heinrich Schiff, a fine work, while the *Concerto for Oboe, Harp and Chamber Orchestra* was written for the Holligers, who perform it here; it mingles charm, irony and intelligence in equal measures. The *Dance Preludes* date from 1953 and were later scored for clarinet and orchestra, as recorded here. They are more folk-like in idiom and are attractively presented by Eduard Brunner (clarinet). The *Paganini Variations*, a piano duo dating from 1941, is exhilarating and is played with great virtuosity by Martha Argerich and Nelson Freire. The Rowicki performances date from 1964. The *Funeral Music* is an angular work which makes some impression, but is rather empty. *Venetian Games* is music of wider appeal, while the famous *Concerto for Orchestra* – a brilliant and highly attractive work – is thoroughly idiomatic. All the Rowicki performances are excellently recorded and have transferred very well to CD. A bargain set in every way.

(i; ii) *Cello Concerto*; (ii) *Postlude 1*; (iii) *7 Preludes & Fugue for 13 Solo Strings*; (iv) *String Quartet*; (v; ii) *Paroles tissées*; (ii; vi) *3 Poèmes d'Henri Michaux*; (vii; ii) *5 Songs for Soprano & Orchestra (The Sea; Storm; Winter; Knights; Church Bells)*

☛ (B) *** EMI Gemini (ADD) 5 85773-2 (2). (i) Jablonski; (ii) Polish R. Nat. SO; (iii) Polish CO; all cond. composer; (iv) Alban Berg Qt; (v) Louis Devos; (vi) Kraków R. Ch.; (vii) Lukomska

This valuable collection was recorded under the auspices of the composer in the Polish Radio Studios in Kraków in 1976–7, with the *String Quartet* added much later, in 1995. Roman Jablonski's account of the *Cello Concerto* still stands up well against the competition, though it is not a first choice. The searching *Seven Preludes and Fugue for Strings* (1970–72) show the mature Łutoslawski and are vividly played by the Polish orchestra, as is the short, elliptical *Postlude* (1958). The choral *Poèmes d'Henri Michaux* date from the early 1960s. With their variety of effects, including whispering and syllabic monotones, the writing readily contrasts with the atmospheric *Paroles tissées* ('Woven Words') with its mystical feeling and remarkable word-imagery. The equally atmospheric *Five Songs* (written in 1957 and orchestrated the following year) find a highly sympathetic and idiomatic soloist in Halina Lukomska, with the texturally intriguing accompaniments catching the ear quite as much as the vocal line.

In his two-movement *String Quartet* Łutoslawski tells us that he uses 'chance elements to enrich the rhythmic and expressive character of the music without in any way limiting the authority of the composer over the final shape of the piece'. Whatever its merits, it has a highly developed and refined feeling for sonority and balance, the main movement sounding all but orchestral at times, and generally speaking it succeeds in holding the listener in a performance and recording as compelling as this. Altogether this inexpensive survey offers a well-conceived demonstration of the composer's breadth of achievement. As might be expected, performances are of a generally high standard and the analogue recordings have been transferred very well to CD.

Concerto for Orchestra; Jeux vénitiens; Livre pour orchestre; Mi-parti; Musique funèbre; Symphonic Variations; Symphonies 1–2

(B) *** EMI (ADD) double forte 5 73833-2 (2). Polish Nat. RSO, composer

Concerto for Orchestra; Mi-parti; Overture for Strings; (i) 3 Poems by Henri Michaux

(BB) *** Naxos 8.553779. (i) Camerata Silesia Ch., Szostak; Polish Nat. RSO, Wit

The eminently recommendable EMI set conducted by the composer is a 'retrospective', drawing many of the key orchestral works from an even more comprehensive six-LP set dating from the late 1970s. Opening with the enticing early *Symphonic Variations*, with their highly individual colouring and atmosphere (sparklingly recorded), the set includes not only the *Concerto for Orchestra* but also both symphonies. Even today some of this music, notably *Jeux vénitiens*, *Livre* and *Mi-parti*, sounds very avant-garde, but the latter piece is hauntingly atmospheric in the composer's hands. Indeed, with performances so obviously authoritative and of a high standard, and the recording exceptionally vivid, they show this composer's sound-world to good advantage.

This fifth volume of Naxos's excellent Łutoslawski series provides an excellent cross-section for anyone wanting to sample this inspired composer's work. The settings of the surrealist poet, Henri Michaux, dating from the early 1960s, are highly original in their use of choral textures, and *Mi-parti* in a single span, slow then fast, points forward in the brilliance and originality of its interplay of instruments to the later symphonies. Strong and purposeful performances, vividly recorded in full, immediate sound.

(i) Piano Concerto. Chain 3; Novelette

*** DG (IMS) 431 664-2. (i) Zimerman; BBC SO, composer

(i) Piano Concerto. Little Suite; Symphonic Variations; Symphony 2

(BB) *** Naxos 8.553169. (i) Paleczny; Polish Nat. RSO, Wit

The *Piano Concerto* is marvellously played by Zimerman and the BBC Symphony Orchestra under the composer. It is beautiful to listen to, but for all its diversity of aural incident and activity here one is left wondering whether there is much of enduring substance. The two remaining works are also very convincingly presented. Absolutely first-rate recording.

The early, tonal *Symphonic Variations* make an attractive introduction to the second of Naxos's discs in what aims to cover his complete orchestral music. The *Little Suite* is an approachable work too, before the much tougher and more substantial symphony and concerto, which make up the greater part of the disc. In two massive movements, *Hesitant* and *Direct*, the *Symphony No. 2* is an uncompromising piece, and here it is helped by a purposeful, very well-rehearsed performance. The *Piano Concerto* is even more elusive, often fragmentary, but again the performance is magnetic: Paleczny plays with a clarity and brilliance that sound totally idiomatic. Excellent sound, with good presence.

Dance Preludes (for clarinet & orchestra)

(BB) *** Hyp. Helios CDH 55068. King, ECO, Litton – BLAKE: *Clarinet Concerto*; SEIBER: *Concertino* ***
*** Chan. 8618. Hilton, SNO, Bamert – COPLAND; NIELSEN: *Concertos* ***

Łutoslawski's five folk-based vignettes are a delight in the

hands of Thea King and Andrew Litton, who give sharply characterized performances, thrown into bold relief by the bright, clear recording. An excellent bargain reissue.

Janet Hilton also emphasizes their contrasts with her expressive lyricism and crisp articulation in the lively numbers. Excellent recording.

Symphony 3; (i) Variations on a Theme of Paganini; (ii) Les Espaces du sommeil; (iii) Paroles tissées

(BB) *** Naxos 8.553423. (i) Glemser; (ii) Kruszewski; (iii) Kusiewicz; Polish Nat. RSO (Katowice), Wit

The earliest piece on Naxos, the *Paganini Variations* for two pianos, comes from 1941, but in 1978 the composer rearranged the piece for piano and orchestra. This and the *Third Symphony* from 1982 are well played and recorded. Less persuasive, perhaps, is *Les Espaces du sommeil* (the soloist is a bit forward, though he sings well). In the *Paroles tissées* the singer is less at ease both with the musical idiom and with the French language. All the same, this well-filled CD is recommendable in every other respect.

Symphony 4; (i) Chain II; Interlude; Partita. Musique funèbre

(BB) *** Naxos 8.553202. (i) Bakowski; Polish Nat. RSO, Wit

The *Symphony No. 4* is Łutoslawski's culminating masterpiece which, in its concentration over two linked movements, seems to echo Sibelius's *Seventh*. The darkly intense *Funeral Music* in memory of Bartók is another beautiful and concentrated work, while the two violin concertante works, *Chain II* and *Partita*, here come with the separating *Interlude*, similarly thoughtful, which Łutoslawski wrote as a link. In almost every way, not least in the playing of the violinist, Krzysztow Bakowski, these Polish performances match and even outshine earlier recordings conducted by the composer, helped by full, brilliant sound.

Paganini Variations (arr. Ptasazynska)

*** Chan. 9398. Safri Duo & Slovak Piano Duo – BARTOK: *Sonata for 2 Pianos & Percussion* ***; HELWEG: *American Fantasy* **

A slight piece from Łutoslawski's youth, dressed up by Marta Ptasazynska for the same forces as the Bartók *Sonata*. It is brilliantly played and no less remarkably recorded at a Danish Radio concert. There is enthusiastic applause, which is understandable, and whistling, which is unfortunate.

Partita; Subito

*** HM HMC 901793. Faust, Kupiec – JANACEK: *Violin Sonata*; SZYMANOWSKI: *3 Mythes* ***

Spicing up this Slavonic mixed bag, Łutoslawski's *Subito* is a showpiece full of manic energy, quirky and fragmentary, inspiring Isabelle Faust and Ewa Kupiec to a dazzling performance. The five-movement *Partita*, which Łutoslawski originally wrote for Pinchas Zukerman and Marc Neikrug, makes a powerful concluding item. Structurally, the composer may have had baroque models in mind, but stylistically this is well removed from regular neoclassicism, like the other pieces on the disc, making formidable technical demands in the quirkiness of the writing over the widest dynamic and tonal range.

LYAPUNOV, Sergei (1859–1924)

Piano Concertos 1 in E flat min., Op. 4; 2 in E, Op. 38.
Rhapsody on Ukrainian Themes, Op. 28
*** Hyp. CDA 67326. Milne, BBC Scottish SO, Brabbins

It is to the *Etudes d'éxecution transcendante* that one's thoughts turn when Lyapunov's name is mentioned. The *First Piano Concerto* of 1890 is much earlier and, although it was published in Berlin in the mid-1890s and was frequently played in the decade or so after its composition (its première was conducted by Balakirev and the pianists who took it up included Josef Hofmann), this is its first commercial recording. Like so much of the music of the post-nationalist generation, its debts are to Borodin and Balakirev, the keyboard writing showing the Lisztian sympathies of its composer. Along with the Rachmaninov *Second Concerto*, the Arensky *D minor Trio* and Scriabin's *Third* and *Fourth Sonatas*, it was awarded a Belaiev Glinka prize in 1904 and, although in terms of originality and musical substance it does not belong in their company, it is far too good to languish unplayed. Although Lyapunov never escaped the influence of Balakirev to develop a strong individual creative personality, his writing is unfailingly accomplished and satisfying. Both the remaining works have been recorded, the *Ukrainian Rhapsody* by Michael Ponti (Vox) and the *Second Concerto* of 1909 more recently by Howard Shelley (Chandos). All three pieces offer civilized pianistic discourse and will reward the interest of all who love Russian music of this period. Hamish Milne's aristocratic playing and effortless virtuosity give much delight, though in the *Second Concerto* (Chan. 9808) Shelley has perhaps greater dash and imagination. The orchestral playing under Martyn Brabbins is eminently supportive and the balance between soloist and orchestra could not be better judged. There are excellent and authoritative notes by Edward Garden.

(i) *Piano Concerto 2 in E, Op. 38; Symphony 1 in B min., Op. 12; Polonaise in D, Op. 16*
☛ *** Chan. 9808. (i) Shelley; BBC PO, Sinaisky

As far as the wider musical public is concerned, Lyapunov is remembered for the fiendishly demanding *Transcendental Studies*, modelled on Liszt, which Louis Kentner recorded so brilliantly after the war. Lyapunov was a pupil of Sergei Taneyev, and this shows in the exemplary craftsmanship that informs these pieces. The *First Symphony* comes from 1897 and belongs very much to the world of Glazunov, Tchaikovsky and Arensky, although Borodin is perhaps the most obvious model. Like Liadov and Rimsky-Korsakov he evokes a kind of fairy-tale world, and if, perhaps, the thematic substance is not particularly distinctive, it is highly attractive and the scoring has greater transparency than Glazunov. In the *Second Piano Concerto* of 1909, Liszt is again the model, though Lyapunov is very much his own man. David Brown's excellent notes speak of its opening as being 'especially ravishing [with] a touch of languor of a sort exploited especially by Lyapunov's idols, Balakirev and Borodin'. It is a short, one-movement work, like the Liszt *A major Concerto*, and highly engaging. Howard Shelley plays with impressive virtuosity, and the BBC Philharmonic respond to Vassily Sinaisky's direction with enthusiasm. Rightly so, for this music is quite a find. At a time when Taneyev is gaining advocacy in the concert hall from Isserlis and friends, Lyapunov deserves to come in from the cold. The recording is in the best traditions of the house.

LYATOSHYNSKY, Boris (1895–1968)

Symphony 1 in A min., Op. 2; Overture on 4 Ukrainian Themes, Op. 20; Poem of Reunification, Op. 40
*** Russian Disc RDCD 11055. Ukrainian State SO, Gnedash

Symphonies 2, Op. 26; 3 in B min., Op. 50
*** Marco Polo 8.223540. Ukrainian State SO, Kuchar

Symphonies 4 in B flat min., Op. 63; 5 in C (Slavonic), Op. 67
*** Marco Polo 8.223541. Ukrainian State SO, Kuchar

Lyatoshynsky began writing his *First Symphony* immediately after the First World War, and it is a well-crafted, confident score that inhabits the world of Russian post-nationalism, Strauss and Scriabin. It abounds in contrapuntal elaboration and abundant orchestral rhetoric. The *Second Symphony* followed in 1936, but its air of pessimism did not sit well in post-*Lady Macbeth* Russia. Although the *Third Symphony* (1951) tries hard to be a good Soviet symphony, it does not wholly ring true.

The *Fourth Symphony* (1963) is more directly Shostakovichian than its predecessors. Its middle movement depicts what must be a mysterious, chimerical city to a Ukrainian, namely Bruges. There is striking use of bells and celesta, and at times a suggestion of Messiaen. The *Fifth (Slavonic)* certainly pays tribute to his master, Glière, in using the *Rus* theme, *Il'ya Mourametz*, as well as a wide variety of Russian, Bulgarian and Serbian liturgical melodies. It aspires to explore the common roots of the Slavonic peoples; hence its title. There are many touches of colour and some token modernity, but basically this looks back to earlier masters.

Those with exploratory tastes will find much to interest them in these symphonies, provided they are not expecting masterpieces. As far as performances are concerned, the Ukraine orchestra obviously is inside this music, and none of the playing is second rate. The Marco Polo recordings are more than marginally superior, and the performances sound much better rehearsed than is usually the case with this label.

MCCABE, John (born 1939)

(i) *Flute Concerto; Symphony 4 (Of Time and the River)*
☛ *** Hyp. CDA 67089. BBC SO, Handley; (i) with Beynon

Celebrating the composer's 60th birthday, this is the finest disc yet of the music of John McCabe. Completed in 1994, his *Fourth Symphony*, entitled *Of Time and the River* after Thomas Wolfe's novel, is a magnificent work in two substantial movements – fast to slow, then slow to fast. The idiom is warmer and more approachable than in McCabe's earlier music, echoing in its atmospheric orchestration and some of the melodic lines Britten on the one hand and Sibelius on the other, while remaining distinctive and new. Superb performances and vivid recording, not just of the *Symphony* but of the large-scale *Flute Concerto* McCabe wrote for James Galway. Ideal notes as well.

Concerto for Orchestra
(N) *** Classico CLASSCD 384. RLPO, Bostock – HODDINOTT; GREGSON: *Concertos for Orchestra* ***

At the end of this triptych of post-Bartók orchestral concertos from three contemporary British composers there is a brief recorded discussion in which each emphasizes the importance of variety of orchestral colour in the structure of such music, with the percussion section 'an integral part of the texture'. The galaxy of sounds in John McCabe's extraordinary and inspired work more than bears this out. His *Concerto*, which opens very dramatically on percussion and brass, is a 25-minute piece divided into 10 sections. They range from an intensely expressive *Adagio* (the longest movement) which opens mysteriously and celestially on strings and flutes and leads on to a delicate *Scherzino* and *Romanze*. After a *Giocoso* Intermezzo comes the slow forward tread of a *Largo*, summoned by bells. Here McCabe uses a piano to underline the rhythm, and we reach a blazing *deciso* climax, with the tension excitingly sustained through to the closing *Pesante*, with its powerful interleaving brass and thundering drums, but whose tremendous driving energy finally ebbs away at the close. It is a truly individual orchestral excursion, heightened by superb playing from the RLPO under Douglas Bostock, who makes the most of every instrumental opportunity, while holding the myriad changes of mood and colour together as an entity. An outstanding recording of the widest range.

Edward II (ballet; complete)

B━ ******* Hyp. CDA 67135/6 (2). Royal Ballet Sinfonia, Wordsworth

This full-length ballet, in two Acts of nearly an hour each, is not only John McCabe's most ambitious work, it is among the most powerful as well as the most approachable of all his music. Taking as his starting point the Marlowe play, *Edward II*, McCabe (in a scenario devised in collaboration with the choreographer David Bintley) has also drawn on Brecht's rethinking of that play, as well as the satirical 14th-century *Le Roman de Fauvel* (which was itself inspired by the story of the English king and his weaknesses). That last source has helped him to introduce a contrasting element of humour. McCabe's score is at once colourfully atmospheric as well as symphonic in its thinking, vividly telling the story in mood and action, drawing on medieval sources for themes and for the 'tuckets and alarums' which add point to such a plot. Having abandoned the more severely serial stance of his earlier music, McCabe as in his superb *Third Symphony* (also issued on Hyperion) adopts a tonal idiom which is yet distinctively his, not at all derivative. There have been few full-length ballet scores as impressive as this since Prokofiev and Britten, inspiring Barry Wordsworth and the Royal Ballet Sinfonia to a strong and colourful performance, vividly recorded.

CHAMBER MUSIC

Concerto for Piano & Wind Quintet; Fauvel's Rondeaux; Musica notturna; Postcards for Wind Quintet

(M) ******* Dutton CDLX 7125. Fibonacci Sequence

The bold opening of the *Concerto* on *fortissimo* wind in unison on this vividly recorded Dutton disc has an astonishing impact, leading to a work built on sharply rhythmic, often angular material. This fresh and alert piece in four linked sections dates from 1969, early in McCabe's career, a concerto, he explains in his own illuminating note, as much for the members of the wind quintet as for the virtuoso piano soloist. The *Musica notturna*, dating from even earlier (1964), has a comparable sharpness in exploiting the changing moods and aspects of a great city at night, while the third of these works in linked sections dates from much more recently, *Fauvel's Rondeaux* of 1995. As a 'satellite work' to

McCabe's full-length ballet, *Edward II*, its eight sections, like the ballet, evoke sharply contrasted moods and emotions, with court entertainment set in the corrupt world of conspiracy and power-mania. *Postcards*, dating from 1991, is a set of eight striking miniatures, including a *bossa nova* and a *fugato*, reworked for wind quintet from *Eight Bagatelles* for two clarinets, originally written in 1965. The bite and brilliance of the performances by the Fibonacci Sequence are ideal for this music, helped by full, immediate sound.

Maze Dances; (i) Star Preludes

*** Metier MSV CD 92029. Sheppard Skaerved; (i) with Honma – RAWSTHORNE: *Violin Sonata*, etc. *******

These two substantial works by McCabe make an ideal coupling for the two fine violin pieces by Rawsthorne, a fellow composer he has long championed. *Maze Dances* is a brilliant and varied fantasia for unaccompanied violin, inventive and ingenious in exploiting this limited medium, while *Star Preludes* for violin and piano, just as varied in expression, equally reveals the composer's deep understanding of string technique. Flawless performances, beautifully recorded.

String Quartets 3, 4 & 5

*** Hyp. CDA 67078. Vanbrugh Qt

Few 20th-century string quartets have such a haunting opening as John McCabe's masterly *Third*, written in 1979; this indelibly simple phrase resonates throughout the *Variants* of the first movement which alternate between intense slow sections and quixotic and sometimes aggressive faster passages. Two chimerical Scherzos frame the central *Romanza*, passionate and restless, and the work ends with a *Passacaglia* which 'derives its overall shape and flow from the concept of a lakeland stream', tumbling down in irregular patterns until the return of that memorable opening motif leads to a wonderful sense of calm. The single-movement *Fourth Quartet* (1982) is hardly less compelling. It again uses variation form. Its treatment is at times serene, at others very vigorous indeed. Once again the close is comparatively peaceful, with an expressive cello soliloquy. The *Fifth Quartet* (1989) is programmatic and, as the very beginning makes plain, was inspired by a series of Graham Sutherland's aquatints called *The Bees*. We follow these small but energetic creatures through larval and hatching stages, the first flight, the partnership of bee and flower, a wild nest, the expulsion and killing of an enemy intruder, and finally a domestic fight between workers and drones, which ends brusquely and positively. The aural results are most intriguing and require much virtuosity from the players, which is readily forthcoming. Indeed, these three remarkable works could hardly be presented with greater concentration or more commitment, and the recording is first class.

5 Bagatelles; Haydn Variations; Studies 3 (Gaudi); 4 (Aubade); 6 (Mosaic); Variations, Op. 22

*** British Music Society BMS 424DC. Composer

The British Music Society have here published a major survey of McCabe's piano music, from the early *Variations* (1963) to the much more complex *Haydn Variations* of 1983, while the pianistically exploratory *Studies* span the decade between 1970 and 1980. The early *Variations* are not difficult to follow, but the later *Haydn Variations* are much more complex and individual, and made less approachable for the listener in that the Haydn theme (from the *Piano Sonata in G minor*, Hob XVI:44) does not appear until more than halfway into the work. The *Bagatelles*, five brief vignettes, in the words of the composer 'were written to a request for not-too-difficult 12-notes pieces', but the third and sixth *Studies* are extended works, architecturally inspired. McCabe is a formidable pianist and is obviously an ideal exponent of his own music, which is highly atmospheric in pianistic terms, but intellectually stimulating rather than lyrical in the melodic sense. Excellent recording.

3 Folk Songs, Op. 19: Johnny was gone for a soldier; Hush-a-by Birdie; John Peel (for tenor, clarinet & piano)
*** Campion Cameo 2001. Hindmarsh, Turner, Cuckson –
BUSH: *Prison Cycle*; RAWSTHORNE: *Songs* **(*)

The *Three Folk Songs*, by John McCabe, very well sung by Martin Hindmarsh, have a neatly tailored clarinet obbligato, and the recital closes with a droll arrangement of *John Peel*, with its witty hornpipe pay-off.

MACCUNN, Hamish (1868–1916)

Concert overture: *The Land of the Mountain and the Flood*
☛ (B) *** CfP (ADD) 767 7532. RSNO, Gibson (with
GERMAN: *Welsh Rhapsody*; HARTY: *With the Wild Geese*;
SMYTH: *Wreckers Overture* ***)

Concert overture: *The Land of the Mountain and the Flood; The Dowie Dens o'Yarrow; The Ship o' the Fiend*. Cantata: (i) *The Lay of the Last Minstrel: Breathes There the Man; O Caledonia!; Jeannie Deans* (opera; excerpts)
*** Hyp. CDA 66815. BBC Scottish SO, Brabbins; (i) with Watson, Milne, MacDougal, Sidholm, Gadd, Danby, Scottish Opera Ch.

For many years Hamish MacCunn's name has been kept alive by Sir Alexander Gibson's dramatically sympathetic account of his colourful and melodramatic concert overture, *The Land of the Mountain and the Flood*, written when he was only eighteen. It is a very well-constructed piece, with a memorable tune. Martyn Brabbins and the BBC Scottish Orchestra, in a brilliant new performance, give it fresh life, and the Hyperion recording has more range and sparkle than the (fully acceptable) CfP version. *The Dowie Dens o'Yarrow* is a very similar piece, with comparable rhythmic impetus and another attractive secondary theme, given to the oboe. The even more atmospheric *Ship o' the Fiend* introduces another endearing lyrical cello theme reminiscent of *The Land of the Mountain and the Flood*. Thus the three works are in many ways linked and are all worth hearing in performances as committed and convincing as these.

MacCunn's opera *Jeannie Deans* is a tuneful and colourful piece with plenty of musical vitality. One thinks at times of a Scottish Edward German, but sometimes of Boughton too. Effie's aria, *Oh that I again could see* (she is imprisoned in the Tolbooth), and the following *Lullaby* are touchingly sung here by Janice Watson, and the choral contribution is very spirited. Some of the singing is vibrato-afflicted, but the performance is thoroughly alive and freshly enjoyable. The excerpt from the cantata *The Lay of the Last Minstrel* brings a suitably vigorous closing chorus, *O Caledonia!*

Piano music: 6 Scottish Dances; Valse
*** Divine Art 2-5003. McLachlan – MCEWEN: *La Côte d'Argent*, etc. ***; MACKENZIE: *Chasse aux papillons*, etc. **(*)

The subtitle of this Scottish collection is 'Impressionistic piano works', but that hardly applies to these simple miniatures by Hamish MacCunn, engaging though they are. They include one real lollipop: the *Plaid Dance* (track 5) which, with its gentle Scottish snaps, haunts the memory beguilingly. Murray McLachlan plays most sympathetically and is well recorded.

MACDOWELL, Edward (1860–1908)

(i) *Piano Concertos 1–2; Witches' Dance, Op. 17/2*; (ii) *Romance for Cello & Orchestra, Op. 35*
(BB) **(*) Naxos 8.559049. (i) Prutsman; (ii) Byrne; Nat. SO of Ireland, Fagen

(i) *Piano Concertos 1–2. Second Modern Suite, Op. 14*
☛ *** Hyp. CDA 67165. Tanyel; (i) with BBC Scottish SO, Brabbins

Of MacDowell's two *Piano Concertos* the *First* is marginally the lesser of the two: the melodic content, though very pleasing, is slightly less memorable than in the *Second*. This is a delightful piece, fresh and tuneful, redolent of Mendelssohn and Saint-Saëns. Seta Tanyel gives sparkling performances of these attractive works, relishing the pianistic fireworks typical of this lyrical American composer. The fill-up, involving piano alone, offers a sequence of six colourful and unpretentious genre pieces, squibs that allegedly were written largely on MacDowell's train journeys for composition lessons. Tanyel's characterful playing, full of sparkle and imagination, is well matched by the playing of the BBC Scottish Orchestra under Martyn Brabbins, helped by full-bodied, well-balanced recording.

Stephen Prutsman is a powerful pianist who relishes the challenge of MacDowell's virtuoso demands, never overtaxed, yet who misses the degree of characterful individuality brought to this music by Amato and Tanyel. The coupling of two concertante works may not be as generous as that on Hyperion, but it is more apt, when the *Witches' Dance* is a delightful showpiece for piano and orchestra, and the *Romance*, rather less interesting, is a typically lyrical piece with cello. The Irish orchestra is most responsive, though not helped by sound which is slightly muffled at times.

Piano Concerto 2 in D min., Op. 23
(N) (B) *** DG 2-CD 477 5439 (2). Szidon, LPO, Downes –
GERSHWIN: *Piano Concerto in F*; IVES: *Piano Sonatas*;
VILLA-LOBOS: *Piano Music* ***

MacDowell's best-known concerto makes an unexpected appearance in this well-planned collection of 'Piano Music from the Americas'. Szidon's sparkling, alert qualities are here just as remarkable as in his stimulating couplings. The Mendelssohnian central movement, marked *Giocoso*, gives a physical thrill with its delicacy. The recording is remarkably good.

2 Fragments after the Song of Roland, Op. 30: The Saracens; The Lovely Aldä. Hamlet/Ophelia, Op. 22; Lancelot and Elaine, Op. 25; Lamia, Op. 29
*** Bridge 9089. RPO, Krueger

The two *Fragments from the Song of Roland* are the middle movements of what was intended as a programme-symphony, and *The Lovely Aldä* is a gentle portrait which has something in common with MacDowell's *Wild Rose*, if not as melodically memorable. The portraits of *Hamlet* and *Ophelia* are highly romantic and, like both the symphonic poems, the lyrical writing is very appealing. There is a distinct flavour of Tchaikovsky, and Lisztian hyperbole is absent from the more vigorous passages. *Lancelot and Elaine* (drawing on Tennyson's *Idylls of the King*) is particularly evocative.

Lamia is based on a poem by Keats. She is an enchantress in the form of a serpent, but changes into a lovely maiden in order to win the love of Lycius. MacDowell's music resourcefully varies the theme representing Lamia to indicate her changes of form and the events of the narrative, which ends badly for both characters. The performances here are very persuasive. Karl Krueger is a splendid and dedicated advocate and the RPO playing is warmly seductive and beautifully recorded.

Suites 1, Op. 42; 2 (Indian); Hamlet and Ophelia (tone-poem), Op. 22

(BB) *** Naxos 8.559075. Ulster O, Yuasa

MacDowell may have been a musical conservative but, in spite of the European flavour of his music, he thought himself a true 'American' composer – favouring the influences of 'the manly and free rudeness of the American Indian' rather than jazz, which he thought had too strong an eastern European, Bohemian inheritance.

The *Indian Suite* opens with a dramatic horn call and its first movement (*Legend*) is a grandiose evocation of the 'once-great past of a dying race' and draws on folk themes from the Iowas and Kiowas. The closing *Village Festival* expands energetically in the brass, finally returning to the mood of the opening movement.

The *First Suite* (actually the second in order of composition) is a comparable series of genre evocations, and the suite ends with a winning dance from the *Forest Spirits*.

The brooding atmosphere of the portrait of *Hamlet and Ophelia* soon gives way to melodrama in the manner of a Lisztian symphonic poem. The music has a rich lyrical strain and later a doom-laden ambience; although it is Ophelia rather than Hamlet who dominates the touchingly lyrical close. The performances here are outstanding in every way, full of colour, warmth and vitality, and the recording is state-of-the-art.

PIANO MUSIC

Fireside Tales, Op. 61; New England Idylls, Op. 62; Sea Pieces, Op. 55; Woodland Sketches, Op. 51

**(*) Marco Polo 8.223631. Baragallo

MacDowell's most famous piano piece opens this recital: *To a Wild Rose* (named by his wife) is the first of the 10 *Woodland Sketches*. They are all pleasant if not distinctive vignettes, most lasting a little over a minute. The other three suites are very similar. Not a CD to listen to all at once but to be dipped into; one can appreciate that James Baragallo is a thoroughly sympathetic exponent, and he is well recorded.

MCEWEN, John Blackwood (1868–1948)

Three Border Ballads: Coronach; The Demon Lover; Grey Galloway

*** Chan. 9241. LPO, Mitchell

These three *Border Ballads*, written between 1906 and 1908, are symphonic poems, well stocked with distinctive ideas, and with a strong Lisztian inheritance. *The Demon Lover*, the

most ambitious in scale (some might feel too ambitious), has a kind of luscious melodramatic post-Wagnerian chromaticism that isn't too far from the world of Scriabin. Even the first to be written, *Coronach*, has a sensuous feeling that one associates with more southern climes, yet the nobility of its main theme also suggests links with Parry and Elgar. The performances here are warmly sympathetic and very well played and recorded, and almost convince one that these works are masterpieces.

A Solway Symphony; (i) Hills o'Heather; Where the Wild Thyme Blows

𝄢 *** Chan. 9345. (i) Welsh; LPO, Mitchell

McEwen's highly evocative *Solway Symphony* is a triptych of seascapes marked by magically transparent orchestration and crisply controlled argument. He was influenced by the folksong movement – notably here in *Hills o'Heather* with its hints of reels – but the flavour is quite individual, with occasional echoes of Sibelius in the sparer moments. Above all, this is warm-hearted music. *Hills o'Heather* is a charming movement for cello and orchestra, while *Where the Wild Thyme Blows* uses slow pedal points to sustain harmonically adventurous arguments. The performances, conducted by Alasdair Mitchell, who edited the scores, are outstanding, a well-deserved tribute to a neglected composer who was far more than an academic. The recording is sumptuously atmospheric.

CHAMBER MUSIC

String Quartets 4; 7 (Threnody); 16 (Quartette provençale); 'Fantasia' for String Quartet, 17

*** Chan. 9926. Chilingirian Qt

McEwen remained true to his Scottish roots in marrying Scottish motifs into skilful quartet-writing which equally paid tribute to developments in Europe, whether Debussy and Ravel or, more radically, Bartók. By the time he died in 1948 he had written no fewer than 17 quartets. The *Fourth Quartet* in its chromatic writing yet brings in a Scottish flavour, while No. 7 is a moving response to the tragedy of the First World War. No. 16 is openly evocative in its often Debussian response to the countryside of Provence, and the *Fantasia Quartet*, No. 17, his last, written the year before he died, in a single substantial movement of five linked sections, reaffirms his romantic allegiances with echoes of Dvořák in the meditative central section. Superb, warmly expressive performances and full, warm Chandos sound.

Violin Sonatas 2; 5 (Sonata-Fantasia); 6; Prince Charlie – A Scottish Rhapsody

*** Chan. 9880. Charlier, Tozer

McEwen's *Second Violin Sonata* (1913–14) shows the influence of both Debussy and Chausson. All the works recorded here show him to be a polished craftsman and a composer of real culture. The *Fifth Sonata* (1921), written for Albert Sammons, said to be his finest in this genre, recalls John Ireland and, like everything on this disc, holds the listener. Very good playing from Olivier Charlier and Geoffrey Tozer, excellent and vivid sound from Chandos and informative notes by Bernard Benoliel.

Piano music: *La Côte d'Argent: 5 Vignettes. 3 'Keats' Preludes; On Southern Hills; 4 Sketches; Sonatina*

🎵 *** Divine Art 2-5003. McLachlan – MACKENZIE: *Chasse aux papillons*, etc. **(*); MACCUNN: *6 Scottish Dances* ***

Of the three composers included in this collection it is John Blackwood McEwen who is the true 'Scottish impressionist', showing distinct French influences in his piano music. Not so much in the *Four Sketches*, which includes a brief 5/4 'Minuet', and a dazzling closing *Humoresque*, or the *Sonatina* which, with its Celtic flavours, is very much his own – especially the charming central *Andante semplice* – but in the *Three 'Keats' Preludes* (each prefaced by a fragment of the poet's verse) and even more in the atmospheric triptych, *On Southern Hills*, the influences of Debussy and Ravel are clear. The *Five Vignettes*, written while on holiday in Cap Ferrat during May 1913, are lighter, but still evocative, especially the engaging *Petite chérie*, while the toccata-like finale is a bustling image of a motor boat on full throttle. Excellent performances from Murray McLachlan and good recording.

MACHAUT, Guillaume de

(*c*. 1300–1377)

Ballades, rondeaux, virelais

🎵 *** Hyp. CDA 66087. Kirkby, Gothic Voices, Page

Although (until recently) primarily celebrated for his church music, Guillaume de Machaut, poet-composer, canon and lover (even in his 60s), led the fullest secular life. He finally assembled his own poetry and music and arranged to have it elaborately illustrated and copied into a permanent anthology. The ballades and virelais included here are written imploringly, and in elaborate admiration, to ladies of great beauty and of all other virtues, except apparently a willingness to respond. The fluid part-writing of the ensemble pieces is unique, but the solo pieces are very appealing, especially when sung, as two of them are here, by an artist of the calibre of Emma Kirkby. One wishes she had played a larger part in the programme, but Rogers Covey-Crump, Colin Scott-Mason, Emily van Evera and Margaret Philpot all make sympathetic individual contributions. As a group the Gothic Voices certainly know how to shape the melancholy melismas of the concerted items: they blend beautifully together, giving effective, unexaggerated tweaks to the passing moments of dissonance. The closing four-part motet, a Triplum, celebrates the Virgin Mary and is perhaps the most beautiful work on the disc. Excellent recording.

Ballades, motets, rondeaux & virelais

(M) *** Virgin (ADD) 5 61284-2 (2). Early Music Cons. of L., Munrow (within Recital: 'The Art of Courtly Love' ***)

This collection is within 'Guillaume Machaut and His Age', which is itself part of David Munrow's wide-ranging collection, 'The Art of Courtly Love'. Treasures here include cantatas with James Bowman and Charles Brett beautifully matched as soloists. Everything reveals both the remarkable individuality of Machaut as a highly influential composer who spanned the first three-quarters of the 14th century, and the life and energy that Munrow consistently brought to early music. Excellent transfers.

Motets

Ivrea Codex: ANON. Mass Movements: *Sanctus (Sanans fragilia); Kyrie; Gloria; Credo; Sanctus.* ANON. Motets: *Clap, clap/Sus Robin; Post missarum sollempnia; Post misse modulamina*

(N) 🎵 *** Signum SIGCD 011. Clerks' Group, Wickham

This collection is doubly valuable, as it includes not only three-part motets from early in Machaut's career (1320–50), which he composed over French love-song melodies, but also a group of Latin motets which are later (1360) and are set in four parts to religious and more serious secular texts and are written over a plainchant melody. They use an isorhythmic style, that is regularly repeating combinations of rhythm and harmony, after each voice has entered singly. Moreover, Edward Wickham has also included five anonymous independent Mass movements, simple and beautiful in their austerity, taken from the Ivrea Codex. (This was found in Ivrea Cathedral in the 15th century, although containing music written much earlier, including several of the works here known to be by Machaut.) The performances are exemplary, enjoyably bold and melismatic, and full of rhythmic vitality, relishing Machaut's idiosyncratic twists and turns. Intonation has to be perfect in music in organum style with consecutive fourths and fifths as a harmonic basis, and it certainly is here. Splendid recording too.

Chansons (ballades, rondeaux, viralais)

**(*) DG (IMS) 457 618-2. Orlando Consort

The opening and closing four-part melismas here, *Tant doucement* ('So sweetly am I imprisoned') and *De toutes fleurs* ('If all the flowers'), are characteristic of Machaut's hypnotic flowing style. Moreover, the duet *Mors suis* ('I die if I do not see you') is a highlight, showing his writing at its most intensely melodic. The Orlando Consort blend beautifully together, led by Robert Harre-Jones whose richly coloured alto line is most appealing. But the snag is the basic sameness of colour inevitable with two, three or four unaccompanied male voices, however expressively they sing, and however pleasingly recorded. In that respect the Hyperion disc above is much more appealing.

Messe de Nostre Dame (with Plainsong for the Proper of the Mass of Purification for the Blessed Virgin (Candlemas))

**(*) HM HMC 901590. Soloists, Ens. Organum, Pérès

Messe de Nostre Dame; Le Lai de la Fonteinne (The Lay of the Fountain); Rondeau: *Ma fin est mon commencement (My End is my Beginning)*

**(*) Hyp. CDA 66358. James, Stafford, Covey-Crump, Potter, Padmore, Nixon, George, Hilliard Ens., Hillier

Messe de Nostre Dame; Le Livre dou Voir dit (excerpts): *Plourez dames; Nes qu'on porroit* (ballades); *Sans cuer dolens* (rondeau); *Le Lay de bonne esperance; Puis qu'en oubli* (rondeau); *Dix et sept cinq* (rondeau)

🎵 (BB) **(*) Naxos 8.553833. Oxford Camerata, Summerly

With his *Messe de Nostre Dame* (dedicated to the Virgin Mary), Guillaume de Machaut wrote the first known complete setting of the Ordinary of the Mass: *Kyrie, Gloria, Credo, Sanctus* and *Agnus Dei*. He chose to finish with his own simple interpolation: *Ite missa est*, which very briefly tells us, 'The Mass is ended; thanks be to God.' Machaut's writing is full of extraordinary, dissonant clashes and sudden harmonic twists which are immediately resolved, so the music is both serene and plangently stimulating: here is an epoch-making work of great originality. Both the Hilliard Ensemble and the Oxford Camerata present the Mass as it stands (and therefore they have room for extra items), whereas Marcel Pérès has inserted the plainsong for the Proper of the Mass, taken from the Candlemas liturgy for the Purification of the Virgin, which is presented in the same florid style as is Machaut's setting of the Ordinary.

Of the three performances here, Jeremy Summerly's account is undoubtedly the most eloquently serene; it is beautifully controlled and modulated, rather after the fashion of the famous Willcocks/King's College accounts of the Byrd Masses. The harmonic pungencies are cleanly presented but unexaggerated and – compared with Hillier and (especially) Pérès – the music's lines, although by no means bland, flow in relative tranquillity. The singers apparently experimented freely with plicas (notational signs indicating some kind of ornament), but there is none of the audacious decoration which is so striking on the Harmonia Mundi version.

Hillier's approach certainly does not lack repose or linear beauty, but he presses the music onwards with a much greater sense of drama than obtains in Oxford. His *Kyrie* is three minutes shorter than Summerly's, and the *Gloria* brings freely passionate accelerandos, which are highly involving but may or may not be authentic. The Hilliard group is superbly recorded with a strong presence, and there is no doubt that the music's unexpected dissonances are more dramatically brought out here than on Naxos.

However, the boldness of effect produced by the Ensemble Organum under Marcel Pérès in every way dramatically upstages its two competitors. In his words: 'The ornamentation ... creates the active force of the work.' The Ensemble Organum with the dark pungency of male timbre and twirling embellishments is powerfully resonant and the dissonances ring out boldly. The recording is splendid.

On Naxos the chansons were recorded, equally effectively, at the BBC's Maida Vale studio; they celebrate Machaut as poet/lover as well as composer and, at its modest price, the disc is worth having for these alone. Indeed *Le Livre dou Voir dit* is one of the most remarkable cycles of poems of the Middle Ages, inspired by the passionate love between the elderly composer (Machaut was in his 60s when he wrote all the music here) and his adolescent student admirer, Péronne d'Armetières.

The solo singing in the extra items on the Hyperion disc is very impressive indeed. *Le Lai de la Fonteinne* is another elaborate poem of 12 stanzas in praise of the Virgin, six polyphonic, six monodic, beautifully sung by Rogers Covey-Crump and John Potter, while the shorter rondeau, an expressive piece if restlessly so, is ingeniously constructed, and is a 'crab' canon by inversion, in that the imitating part, instead of being presented straightforwardly, is written backwards and upside down – appropriately so, to fit the text: 'My End is my Beginning.'

MACKENZIE, Alexander (1847–1935)

Benedictus, Op. 37/3; Burns – 2nd Scottish Rhapsody, Op. 24; Coriolanus* (incidental music): *Suite, Op. 61. The Cricket on the Hearth: Overture, Op. 62. Twelfth Night* (incidental music): *Overture/Suite, Op. 40

🔑 *** Hyp. CDA 66764. BBC Scottish SO, Brabbins

Mackenzie wrote in the Stanford/Elgar/Parry tradition rather than showing any strong Scottish traits. However, in the *Burns Rhapsody* he uses three Scottish folk tunes quite felicitously, notably '*Scots! wha hae*', which is very emphatic. The second movement has charm, and indeed Mackenzie's own lyrical gift is quite striking in the jolly, at times Sullivanesque *Cricket on the Hearth Overture* (which also shows his deft orchestral skill), and of course the *Benedictus* with a melody typical of its time. The incidental music for *Twelfth Night* is in the form of an overture, subdivided into six sections, with a Shakespeare quotation for each to identify its mood. These vignettes are attractively scored and have considerable character. The whole programme is presented with commitment and polish by the BBC Scottish Symphony Orchestra and makes a very agreeable 75 minutes of not too demanding listening. The recording is excellent.

Scottish Concerto, Op. 55

*** Hyp. CDA 67023. Osborne, BBC Scottish SO, Brabbins – TOVEY: *Piano Concerto in A* ***

Hyperion's imaginative series of Romantic piano concertos here offers two works by composers associated with Scotland. Unlike Tovey, Sir Alexander Mackenzie was Scottish by birth. Built on Scottish themes, Mackenzie's *Concerto*, premièred by Paderewski, centres round its lyrical slow movement, framed by a rhapsodic first movement and a dance finale based on *Green Grow the Rushes O*. The young Scottish pianist Steven Osborne is a brilliant advocate, Brabbins a natural partner.

Piano music: *Chasse aux papillons; Harvest Home; Odds and Ends: High Spirits; Refrain 3 Morçeaux*

(*) Divine Art 2-5003. McLachlan – MACCUNN: *6 Scottish Dances;* MCEWEN: *La Côte d'Argent*, etc. *

Mackenzie's genre piano vignettes are derivative but hardly draw on the French impressionist school, as their inclusion in this collection might imply. *Chasse aux papillons, High Spirits* and the closing *Harvest Home* are all bravura display pieces, and Murray McLachlan throws them off in virtuoso style, although not without a feeling that a fractionally slower tempo would have been even more effective. It is the music of the other two composers on this enterprising collection that makes it worth exploring.

MACMILLAN, James (born 1959)

(i) ***As others see us; 3 Dawn Rituals; Untold;*** (ii) ***Veni, veni, Emmanuel (Concerto for Percussion & Orchestra);*** (iii) ***After the Tryst (Miniature Fantasy for Violin & Piano)***

(N) 🔑 ✿ *** (M) RCA CATALYST 82876 65285-2. (i) Scottish CO (members), composer; (ii) Glennie, SCO, Saraste; (iii) Crouch, composer

In *Veni, veni, Emmanuel* MacMillan has written a concerto for percussion that in its energy as well as its colour consistently reflects both the virtuosity and the charismatic personality of Evelyn Glennie. Taking the Advent plainsong of the title as his basis, he reflects in his continuous 26-minute sequence the theological implications behind the period between Advent and Easter. The five contrasted sections are in a sort of arch form, with the longest and slowest section in the middle. The very close of the work brings a crescendo of chimes intended to reflect the joy of Easter in the Catholic service and the celebration of the Resurrection. In this superb recording the orchestra as well as Evelyn Glennie play with both brilliance and total commitment, if not with quite the

extra thrill that at the end is experienced in live performances. In the fill-up works – brief pieces marked by the same
dramatic intensity – MacMillan himself as conductor inspires
strong, positive performances from various groups of SCO
players. With first-rate, atmospheric sound (*Veni, veni,
Emmanuel* recorded in Usher Hall, Edinburgh, the rest in
City Hall, Glasgow) this is outstanding in every way.

(i) *Clarinet Concerto (Ninian)*; (ii) *Trumpet Concerto (Epiclesis)*
*** BIS CD 1069. RSNO, Lazarev, with (i) Cushing; (ii)
  Wallace

The *Clarinet Concerto* is a celebration of the early Scottish
Saint Ninian, with three of his miracles each inspiring a
movement. The third and last, much the longest, brings
another depiction of the Eucharist, with a joyful brassy
chorale as a final climax. The soloist has a virtuoso role, but
many of the most memorable moments come in hushed
lyrical passages, with the clarinet bringing a resolution after
orchestral violence. *Epiclesis*, the *Trumpet Concerto*, meaning
prayer or invocation, leads the composer to attempt a musical
equivalent to the Eucharist, the act of communion, in what
he describes as 'the transformation of musical substances'. As
ever, the orchestral writing is colourful and brilliant, with
elaborate use made of percussion, notably a thunder-sheet
often played *pianissimo*. The free-flowing, almost improvisatory writing for the solo trumpet, with much fluttering
figuration, is punctuated by big orchestral outbursts, leading
at the most moving moment to a simple chorale, played
pianissimo on the trumpet as though in purification. After
that the jazzy syncopations of the final section sound almost
like Charles Ives in brash contrast, leading finally to the most
powerful climax and a fading away as the soloist departs. The
performances of both works are not just brilliant but totally
committed in bringing out the drama of this music, with BIS
recording of demonstration quality.

Cumnock Fair; Sinfonietta; Symphony 2
*** BIS CD 1119. SCO, composer

MacMillan's *Second Symphony*, written in 1999, builds on
ideas from an early piano sonata. A massive central movement is flanked by an evocative prelude, with bird-twittering
ostinatos, a slow chorale and a reflective postlude, in which
the chorale returns. The central movement is often violent,
with sharp contrasts of mood and tempo. Typically full of
striking ideas, it is brilliantly orchestrated.

The *Sinfonietta*, written in 1991 and dedicated to MacMillan's wife, Lynne, starts mysteriously with a hypnotic slow
section, which is brutally interrupted by violent *fortissimo*
chords. It is almost Ives-like in its terracing of contrasted
ideas, while *Cumnock Fair* is even more so in its kaleidoscopic
quotations of dances with a Scottish flavour, wilder and
wilder. With a piano prominent in the texture, the mêlée
finally fades away to common chords. Strong, intense performances, flawlessly balanced.

The Confession of Isobel Gowdie; The Exorcism of Rio Sumpul; Tuireadh
*** BIS CD 1169. BBC Scottish SO, Vänskä

BIS continues its excellent series of MacMillan discs with a
coupling of the work which made him famous overnight in
1990, *The Confession of Isobel Gowdie*, and two other substantial works of the same period, similarly inspired by events
which moved the composer deeply. *Tuireadh* is a lament

inspired by the Piper Alpha oil-rig disaster. The writing,
originally for clarinet and string quartet, is here reassigned to
orchestral strings, with the clarinet vividly conveying the
agony of the bereaved. The *Exorcism of Rio Sumpul* was
inspired by an atrocity in El Salvador in 1986, with the music
illustrating the violence as well as the menace, and unexpectedly erupting into a final dance of joy and thanksgiving when
it was revealed that by some miracle no one was killed.
MacMillan's direct, intensely communicative style is well
illustrated in all three works, with Osmo Vänskä drawing
powerful performances from the BBC Scottish Symphony
Orchestra, very well recorded.

The Confession of Isobel Gowdie; Symphony 3
(N) *** Chan. 10275. BBC PO, composer

The Confession of Isobel Gowdie was the work that, at the
Proms in 1990, brought James MacMillan instant success with
a far wider audience than is normally attracted to new music.
As the composer describes it, it is the Requiem that Isobel
Gowdie, a Catholic martyr accused of witchcraft, never had.
In a single 25-minute span it begins in deep meditation, then
the central section, by far the longest, brings a violence
reflecting the brutality with which the martyr was treated.
The beauty of the final section, in which she seems to find
peace, with its references to plainsong is all the more affecting
here in the composer's own performance.

Symphony 3 (2002) follows a comparable pattern of slow,
inexorable build-up over a massive span, this time far bigger
still. The work's paradoxical subtitle, 'Silence', was inspired by
the work of the Japanese author Shusaku Endo, whose novel
with that title has had a profound influence on the composer.
In reflection of that and the fact that the piece was commissioned by the NHK Orchestra of Japan, MacMillan introduces ideas and timbres from oriental sources. The colour of
the writing and the dramatic impact of the high contrasts,
which are typical of the composer, hold the massive structure
together with many clear landmarks. The concentration of
the playing of the BBC Philharmonic under MacMillan adds
to the tautness in both works, and the performances are
brilliant in every way and superbly recorded. Sadly, the
different sections of each work are not marked by separate
CD tracks, making it far more difficult for the listener to
identify the geography of each structure, despite excellent
notes by Stephen Johnson.

(i) *I (A meditation on Iona); They Saw the Stone Had Been Rolled Away; Tryst*; (ii) *Adam's Rib for Brass Quintet*
*** BIS CD 101. (i) SCO, Swensen; (ii) SCO Brass

The central piece in this fine collection is *Tryst*, inspired by a
love poem in broad Scots by William Soutar. That poem has
provided the source for a sequence of MacMillan's works, of
which this is the most ambitious. Written in 1989, its five
linked sections bring a kaleidoscopic sequence of striking
ideas, brilliantly orchestrated, centring round a motto theme.
Adam's Rib (1995) uses a brass quintet to produce dark and
earthy sounds, underpinned by a growling tuba, and leading
to a ritual built on sharp contrasts of timbres.

In *They Saw the Stone Had Been Rolled Away*, MacMillan
conveys the exhilaration of Christ's resurrection with brilliant
fanfares and ominous drumbeats, while *I* (pronounced 'ee'),
written in 1996, in eight sections, is spare and less dissonant
than the rest, evoking a mood of profound meditation.
Dedicated performances, brilliantly recorded.

Triduum, an Easter Triptych, Part 1: (i) *The World's Ransoming* (for cor anglais and orchestra); Part 2: (ii) *Cello Concerto*

*** BIS CD 989.(i) Pendrill; (ii) R. Wallfisch; BBC Scottish SO, Vänskä

The World's Ransoming and the *Cello Concerto*, each self-contained, are the first two in a sequence of three related works representing MacMillan's response to Christ's Passion and the Easter story. *The World's Ransoming*, with its poignant writing for cor anglais set against violent interruptions, provides the emotional prelude and is intensely involving music, often wild in its expressionism. In its energy it mixes styles and idiom with abandon. This is religious inspiration at the farthest remove from that of John Tavener or Arvo Pärt, but just as likely to strike a chord with listeners of whatever faith, or of none. Christine Pendrill is the superb soloist, and though Raphael Wallfisch is just as expressive as the soloist in the *Cello Concerto*, conveying Christ's agony, sadly the balance sets him at a distance. This three-movement work, a response to Good Friday and the Crucifixion, is even more violent – using thunder-sheet amid heavy brass and percussion, the embodiment of earthquake and storm, both physical and spiritual. Brilliant performances, spaciously recorded.

Triduum, an Easter Triptych, Part 3: *Symphony (Vigil)*

*** BIS CD 900. Fine Arts Brass Ens., BBC Scottish SO, Vänskä

The *Symphony (Vigil)* in three movements – *Light*, *Tuba insonet salutaris* and *Water* – forms the climax of the *Triduum* triptych, longer than either of the preceding works. Predictably it moves from darkness to light, with violence at the start of the first movement echoing the music of the *Cello Concerto*. The second movement brings fanfares spread spaciously, the last trump graphically portrayed, while the resolution of the final movement, longer than the other two put together, brings no easy salvation. Even the meditative close still implies the memory of pain, ever more pauseful, fading into nothing. Here too, as in the companion disc, Vänskä draws brilliant, warmly committed playing from the BBC Scottish Symphony Orchestra, vividly recorded.

Veni, veni, Emmanuel; Tryst

🔊 (BB) *** Naxos 8.554167. Currie, Ulster O, Yuasa

With Colin Currie, the young prizewinning percussionist, matching his compatriot predecessor, Evelyn Glennie, in flair and panache, the Naxos version of the brilliant and dramatic percussion concerto, *Veni, veni, Emmanuel*, cannot be recommended too highly. Takuo Yuasa is a strong and persuasive conductor, not just in *Veni, veni, Emmanuel*, but in the earlier work, *Tryst*, an extended and colourful fantasy in five sections built on a setting of a Scottish song. Recorded in the helpful acoustic of the Ulster Hall, Belfast, the sound is exceptionally full and vivid, matching the excellent playing of the orchestra.

(i) *Piano Sonata; Barncleupedie; Birthday Present; For Ian;* (ii) *Raising Sparks* (cantata)

*** Black Box BBM 1067. (i) York; (ii) Rigby, Nash Ens., Brabbins

The *Piano Sonata* of 1985 in three movements is much the most demanding work here, far grittier than the rest, inspired by the extreme winter of that year and later the source of the *Second Symphony*. *For Ian* then brings total release into pure tonality and lyricism, a strathspey full of Scottish-snap

rhythms. *Birthday Present* seems a very sombre gift, musically striking nonetheless, and the final *Barncleupedie* (1990) rounds things off light-heartedly with a piece which in slow barcarolle rhythm supports the melody, *Will Ye No Come Back Again.*

Like so much of MacMillan's music, *Raising Sparks* has a profoundly religious base, this time from a Jewish inspiration. The opening incantation by the mezzo-soprano soloist, low and sustained in the chest register with occasional ornamentation, immediately makes the Jewish associations clear enough, leading to a sequence of five songs setting poems by Michael Symmons Roberts on the theme of creation and redemption. The striking imagery, with one simile piled on another, inspired MacMillan to musical ideas, comparably varied, often onomatopoeic in direct illustration, which are striking and dramatic within a taut musical structure. The vocal line, though taxing, is more lyrical than in many new works, superbly sung by Jane Rigby, while the instrumental accompaniment is endlessly inventive, with the piano (the masterly Ian Brown) generally the central instrument in the ensemble. In the penultimate song, spare and recitative-like, the question is asked 'Was the diaspora for this – to look in places no one else has looked, to send the sun home piece by piece?'

VOCAL MUSIC

Mass; A Child's Prayer; Changed; Christus vincit; A New Song; Seinte Mari moder milde; (i) *Gaudeamus*

*** Hyp. CDA 67219. Westminster Cathedral Ch, Baker; (i) Reid

It would be hard to think of any recent music that so intensely conveys religious ecstasy as James MacMillan's *Mass*, a liturgical setting, with text (in English) expanded from the Ordinary of the Mass, which he wrote for Westminster Cathedral for the Millennium celebrations in 2000. Closer in style to Britten than to Tavener, MacMillan is yet distinctive in his brilliant use of choral effects, with surging crescendos up to glowing *fortissimos* to stir the blood.

Two of the extra sections, taken from the Eucharistic Liturgy, largely involve solo chanting, but the fervour of MacMillan's inspiration as a devout Catholic himself makes for music of high voltage from first to last. Equally the shorter choral works on the disc, all written in the 1990s, have a rare freshness and concentration, often involving powerful slabs of sound.

The singing of the Westminster Cathedral Choir is electrifying, with Martin Baker directing his first recording as choirmaster. The solo singing, too, deserves special mention, with a solo treble negotiating a spectacular upward leap at the close of *Christus vincit*. *Gaudeamus* is a brief organ solo involving bird-noises, rather different from Messiaen's, beautifully played by Andrew Reid.

MACONCHY, Elizabeth (1907–94)

Clarinet Concertinos 1 (1945); *2* (1984)

(BB) *** Hyp. Helios CDH 55060. King, ECO, Wordsworth – ARNOLD: *Clarinet Concertos 1–2; Scherzetto;* BRITTEN: *Clarinet Concerto Movement* ***

The two Maconchy *Concertinos*, each in three movements and under ten minutes long, have a characteristic terseness, sharp and intense, that runs no risk whatever of seeming short-winded. Not only Thea King but the ECO under Barry Wordsworth bring out the warmth as well as the rhythmic drive, as in the other attractive works on this disc.

Clarinet Quintet

(BB) *** Hyp. Helios CDH 55105. King, Britten Qt – COOKE; FRANKEL: *Clarinet Quintets*; HOWELLS: *Rhapsodic Quintet*; HOLBROOKE: *Eilean Shona* ***

Elizabeth Maconchy's *Clarinet Quintet*, with its bright, acerbic wit, makes a perfect foil for the other works in Thea King's fine anthology, its dancing, racy finale contrasting with her special brand of poignant lyricism in the slow movement. King's sprightly playing is admirably supported by the Britten Quartet, and the recording is outstandingly vivid.

String Quartets 1–13

(N) (M) *** Regis Forum FRC 9301 (3). Hanson, Bingham or Mistry Qts

Elizabeth Maconchy has excited the admiration of musicians far and wide, from Tovey and Sir Henry Wood to Holst and Vaughan Williams. Hopefully this Regis reissue of a distinguished Unicorn series will introduce her to a wider audience. The first four *Quartets*, recorded by the Hanson Quartet, encompass the period 1932–43, while the second disc spans the years 1948–67 and the Bingham Quartet seem equally at home in this repertoire. The third CD moves on to 1968–79 and includes the final *Quartetto Corto*, a miniature piece, dating from 1984, all persuasively played by the Mistry Quartet. All these works testify to the quality of Maconchy's mind and her inventive powers. She speaks of the quartet as 'an impassioned argument', and there is no lack of either in these finely wrought and compelling pieces. Even if there is not the distinctive personality of a Bartók or a Britten, her music is always rewarding. Though the playing may occasionally be wanting in tonal finesse, each group plays with total commitment and is well recorded.

MADERNA, Bruno (1920–73)

Aura; Biogramma; Quadrivium (for 4 percussionists & 4 orchestral groups)

(N) *** DG 477 5383. N. German RSO, Sinopoli

This record usefully brings together three of Bruno Maderna's key works, among the last he wrote before his untimely death in his early 50s. Earliest is *Quadrivium*, a work spectacularly laid out and designed 'to entertain and to interest, not to shock the bourgeoisie'. In 1972 came *Aura* and *Biogramma*; the former won the composer (posthumously) the city of Bonn's Beethoven prize. These are excellent recordings of dedicated performances.

MADETOJA, Leevi (1887–1947)

Symphonies 1 in F, Op. 29; 2, Op. 35; 3 in A, Op. 55; Comedy Overture, Op. 53; Okon Fuoko, Op. 58; Pohjalaisia Suite, Op. 52

⊶ (M) *** Chan. 7097 (2). Iceland SO, Sakari

Comedy Overture, Op. 53; Kullervo (symphonic poem), Op. 15; Symphony 2, Op. 35

(BB) *** Finlandia Apex 0927 43074-2. Finnish RSO, Segerstam

Apart from Sibelius himself, with whom Madetoja briefly studied, there are many influences to be discerned in the *First Symphony* (1915–26) – figures like Strauss, the Russian post-nationalists, Reger and above all the French, for whom Madetoja had a lifelong admiration. The *Second Symphony* (1917–18), composed at about the same time as Sibelius was working on the definitive version of his *Fifth*, is expertly fashioned and despite the obvious debts there is some individuality too. The *Third* was written in the mid-1920s while Madetoja was living in Houilles, just outside Paris. Gallic elements surface most strongly in this piece. The *Comedy Overture* (1923) is an absolute delight, and both the suite from the opera *Pohjalaisia (The Ostrobothnians)* and the ballet–pantomime *Okon Fuoko* show an exemplary feeling for colour and atmosphere. Now that the excellent Chandos set under Petri Sakari has been transferred to the Double format at mid-price, it deserves to carry our first recommendation. Both the performances and the spacious natural recordings are exemplary and Sakari gets imaginative and sensitive playing from his Reykjavik forces.

No real grumbles about the Finlandia performances, which are well worth the money and will give pleasure, but the Icelandic is the more distinguished of the two and worth the extra cost.

'Meet the Composer': Complete Songs for Male Voice Choir (52 songs)

(B) *** Finlandia Double 0630 19807-2 (2). Helsinki University Ch., Hyökki

The present Finlandia Double assembles the contents of three previous issues, recorded 1990–91, devoted to Madetoja's output for male voice choir, and offers no fewer than 52 part-songs, many of them of signal quality. The male voice choir is a popular medium in both Finland and Sweden, and both countries have produced a rich repertory of songs and expert groups to sing them. The Helsinki University Choir is among the very finest, and they certainly sing these pieces with wonderful ensemble and fervour. The notes (by the conductor, Matti Hyökki) provide exemplary background information as well as the texts themselves. Many of the songs have something of the modal quality of Sibelius's output in this genre; and the later songs, which Madetoja composed in the 1940s when ill-health inhibited him from finishing a fourth symphony and a violin concerto, are striking. A rewarding set.

Songs, Vol. I

*** Ondine ODE 996-3 Suovanen, Djupsjöbacka

Madetoja composed fewer songs than did Sibelius, with whom he briefly studied, and far fewer than his contemporary, Yrjö Kilpinen. There are some 65 in all, the majority to Finnish texts, and in this respect he is unlike Sibelius who, in his solo songs, was primarily drawn to the lyric poets writing in Swedish. There are some in Danish (Opp. 44 and 58) including *Sang bag Ploven* ('Song at the Plough') set to the same poet, Ludvig Holstein, that Nielsen favoured. (Those using French texts will presumably follow in the next volume.) Only a few of his songs are currently available in recitals by Torju Valjukka and Yorma Hynninen, but it is evident right from the very first song that Madetoja had a strong lyrical talent with a good feeling for the atmosphere of the poem. Many have a distinct feeling for nature, for example *Winter Morning* and *The Starry Sky* (Op. 2/3–4). Although none of the songs here are as inspired as the best Sibelius or as concentrated in feeling or poetic insight as the finest

Kilpinen, Madetoja is obviously a talent to reckon with. Gabriel Suovanen is a fine and persuasive artist, though he rarely gives us much *pianissimo*, and Gustav Djupsjöbacka gives good support.

Songs, Vol. II
*** Ondine ODE 995-2. Juntunen, Djupsjöbacka

This companion volume of Madetoja songs is entrusted to the soprano, Helena Juntunen, still in her mid-20s, again with Gustav Djupsjöbacka as accompanist. All the songs are to Finnish texts, apart from Verlaine (the *Romance sans paroles*), and three to Danish texts. They are often of the utmost simplicity as in *Farewell*, Op. 26/1, and the *Lullaby*, Op. 16/3. Most of them take about two minutes or under and nearly all are of quality. *Talvikuutamolla* (*By Winter Moonlight*) is particularly haunting and atmospheric. Some have Gallic influences: *Hymyi Hypnos* (*Hypnos Smiled*) reminds one of early Debussy, and there is even a hint of Duparc in the Holstein setting, *The Golden-white Light of Heaven*. Madetoja's songs are not a patch on those of Sibelius or Kilpinen, but they are obviously the product of a cultured mind and a refined imagination. This is the more rewarding of the two discs and the contents are sung better. Djupsjöbacka plays with great subtlety and imagination. Good sound.

OPERA

The Ostrobothnians (Pohjalaisia) (complete); Suite from the opera, Op. 52a
(M) *** Finlandia 3984 21440-2 (2). Hynninen, Sirkiä, Groop, Auvinen, Finnish R. Ch.; Finnish RSO, Saraste

Madetoja's opera dates from the early 1920s and is set in the western Finnish plains of Ostrobothnia which Madetoja knew well, and its central theme is the Bothnian farmer's love of personal liberty and his abhorrence of authoritarian restraints. Against this background of tension, there is a simple love story. Antti, one of the farmers, is imprisoned after a stabbing incident; the first act centres on his relationship with Maija. In the second Antti escapes, and the opera ends with Jussi's death at the sheriff's hands. The opera is also interspersed with humorous elements that lighten the mood and lend the work variety. Madetoja's language springs from much the same soil as most Scandinavian post-nationalists. However, the score makes often imaginative use of folk material and Madetoja's sense of theatre and his lyrical gift are in good evidence. *Pohjalaisia* is effective theatre and this new recording completely supersedes the 1975 set under Jorma Panula – also with Hynninen as the hero – both artistically and technically. Like its predecessor it offers excellent teamwork from the soloists, and keen, responsive playing from the Finnish Radio forces under Saraste. The work lasts barely two hours, and the fill-up derives from a 1993 recording.

MAGALHÃES, Filipe de (1571–1652)

Missa O Soberana luz; Motets: Commissa mea pavesco; Vidi aquam
(BB) *** Naxos 8.553310. Ars Nova, Holten – CARDOSO; LOBO: Motets ***

Filipe de Magalhães was the youngest of the three great Portuguese composers who all became pupils of Manuel Mendes (c. 1547–1605) at Evora in eastern Portugal. The others, Cardoso and Lobo, are also represented in this outstanding concert, but Magalhães was reputedly the favourite pupil. One can see why, listening to his highly individual writing in both the Mass *O Soberana luz* and the two hardly less memorable motets, *Vidi aquam* ('I beheld the water') and *Commissa mea pavesco* ('I tremble at my sins') with its instantly poignant opening. In the Mass the *Sanctus* soars radiantly and the lovely *Benedictus* is equally affecting, only to be capped by the *Agnus Dei*. The Danish performances are wonderfully eloquent and the recording, made at Kasterskirken, Copenhagen, has an ideal ambience and is beautifully clear.

MAGNARD, Albéric (1865–1914)

Symphonies 1 in C min., Op. 4; 2 in E, Op. 6
☛ *** Hyp. CDA 67030. BBC Scottish SO, Ossonce

Symphonies 3 in B flat min., Op. 11; 4 in C sharp min., Op. 21
☛ *** Hyp. CDA 67040. BBC Scottish SO, Ossonce

Symphonies 1–4; Chant funèbre; Hymne à la justice; Ouverture
(B) *** EMI double forte (ADD) 5 72364-2 (3). Capitole Toulouse O, Plasson

Symphonies 1; 3
**(*) BIS CD 927. Malmö SO, Sanderling

Symphonies 2; 4
**(*) BIS CD 928. Malmö SO, Sanderling

The *First Symphony* (1889–90) was composed in the shadow of Magnard's friend and mentor, Vincent d'Indy, and follows more strictly cyclical principles. Yet its ideas still show individuality of character and, despite the debt to Wagner and Franck, the last two symphonies have distinct personalities; they are separated by 17 years. The *Fourth* has an impressive intellectual power and is well crafted, with no shortage of ideas. For all the appearance of academicism, there is a quiet and distinctive personality here, and dignity too. The *Chant funèbre* is an earlier work that has a vein of genuine eloquence.

The superb Hyperion set of his four symphonies, neatly fitted on two separately available CDs, easily outshines earlier rivals, with warm, cleanly focused sound.

The Toulouse Capitole Orchestra under Michel Plasson also play this music as if they believe every note, as indeed they should, and the recording is sonorous and well defined. Plasson spreads to three CDs but offers extra items, and the EMI set is at bargain price and is excellent value.

Generally speaking, Thomas Sanderling opts for broad tempi. Indeed, his leisurely tempi compel BIS to accommodate the *Second* and *Fourth Symphonies* on a separate CD, retailing them for the price of one. In the *Fourth* Sanderling is almost five minutes longer than his two rivals. He is the best recorded of the three, but both Plasson and Ossonce get a more powerfully concentrated response from their players. But in almost all respects the Hyperion set (using two full-priced discs) takes pride of place, with warm, cleanly focused sound.

Cello Sonata in A, Op. 20
*** Hyp. CDA 67244. Lidström, Forsberg – KOECHLIN: Chansons Bretonnes; WIDOR: Sonata ***

Magnard's music has an unfailing nobility as well as a distinction in terms of line and form. The *Cello Sonata*, which dates from 1910–11, is a big work lasting half an hour. Mats Lidström and Bengt Forsberg play it with eloquence and feeling, and are very well recorded.

MAHLER, Gustav (1860–1911)

Symphonies 1–9; 10 (Adagio)

(B) **(*) Ph. 442 050-2 (10). Concg. O, Haitink (with Ameling, Heynis & Netherlands R. Ch. in 2; Forrester, Netherlands R. Ch. & St Willibrod Boys' Ch. in 3; Ameling in 4; Cotrubas, Harper, Van Bork, Finnila, Dieleman, Cochran, Prey, Sotin, Amsterdam Choirs in 8)

(B) **(*) DG 463 738-2 (10). Arroyo, Mathis, Morison, Spoorenberg, Hamari, Procter, Marjorie Thomas, Grobe, Fischer-Dieskau, Crass, Bav. R. Ch., N. German R. Ch., W. German R. Ch., Regensburger Domchor, Munich Motteten Ch., Bav. RSO, Kubelik

Symphonies 1–9

(B) *** Decca (DDD/ADD) 430 804-2 (10). Buchanan, Zakai, Chicago Ch. in 2; Dernesch, Ellyn Children's Ch., Chicago Ch. (in 3); Te Kanawa (in 4); Harper, Popp, Augér, Minton, Watts, Kollo, Shirley-Quirk, Talvela, V. Boys' Ch., V. State Op. Ch. & Singverein (in 8); Chicago SO, Solti

(i) *Symphonies 1–9;* (ii) *Kindertotenlieder;* (iii) *Kindertotenlieder; 3 Rückert Lieder; Das irdische Leben*

(B) **(*) Sony (ADD) SX12K 89499 (12). Spoorenberg, Annear, Procter, Mitchinson, McIntyre, Venora, Tourel, Lipton, Israel PO, LSO or NYPO, Bernstein; (ii) J. Baker; (iii) J. Tourel

(i) *Symphonies 1–10; 6 Early Songs; Kindertotenlieder;* (ii) *Das Lied von der Erde;* (i) *Lieder eines fahrenden Gesellen; Das Klagende Lied*

(BB) **(*) DG 471 451-2 (15). Studer, Meier, Goldberg, Allen, Fassbaender, Plowright, Schwartz, Keikl, Gruberová, Terfel, Vermillion, Lewis; (i) Philh. O; (ii) Dresden Staatskapelle; all cond. Sinopoli

Solti's achievement in Mahler has been consistent and impressive, and this reissue is a formidable bargain that will be hard to beat. Nos. 1–4 and 9 are digital recordings, Nos. 5–8 are digitally remastered analogue. Solti draws stunning playing from the Chicago Symphony Orchestra, often pressed to great virtuosity, which adds to the electricity of the music-making; if his rather extrovert approach to Mahler means that deeper emotions are sometimes understated, there is no lack of involvement; and his fiery energy and commitment often carry shock-waves in their trail. All in all, an impressive achievement.

Haitink's set of Mahler *Symphonies* offers characteristically refined and well-balanced Philips recording. The performances bring consistently fine playing from the Concertgebouw Orchestra, but Haitink is not by nature an extrovert Mahlerian. While he is always sensitive and thoughtful – and this works well enough in Nos. 1 (his earlier recording is included) and 4 (with Elly Ameling a freshly appealing soloist) and they have an attractive simplicity of approach – Nos. 2 and 8 lack the necessary sense of occasion, and No. 8 also needs greater overall grip and a more expansive recording. No. 5 is fresh and direct (the *Adagietto* a little cool) but No. 6 has more refinement than fire. The finest of the set are the deeply satisfying accounts of No. 3 (with fine contributions

from both Maureen Forrester and the choristers) and the finely wrought and intensely convincing performance of No. 7. However, the series is capped by an outstanding performance of No. 9. Here Haitink is at his most inspirational and the last movement has a unique concentration, with its slow tempo maintained to create the greatest intensity of feeling. As usual from Philips, the original recordings are consistently enhanced by the CD transfers, and only No. 8 is technically disappointing.

The 12-disc Sony compilation includes not only Bernstein's historic pioneering cycle of the Mahler symphonies for CBS but a number of valuable supplements. With the nine completed symphonies recorded between 1960 and 1967 and the *Adagio* from No. 10 added in 1975, the cycle has never sounded fresher or clearer, with sound less coarse than originally. The venues range between the St George Hotel in Brooklyn (surprisingly free in No. 4) to Walthamstow Assembly Rooms in London for No. 8, sounding more open than originally. The recordings made in the Philharmonic Hall, New York (now Avery Fisher Hall), vary between the relative dryness of No. 1, recorded in 1963, to the far fuller sound of Nos. 6, 7 and 9, recorded later. Curiously, the live recording of the first movement of No. 8, made at the opening of the hall in 1962, is more open in sound than the slightly disappointing No. 5. Though Bernstein's later deleted cycle for DG brings more refined sound, these earlier interpretations, all but No. 8 with the New York Philharmonic, are generally more thrustful and dramatic. The reading of No. 9 is far less expansive in the last movement but is still deeply meditative, so that the whole symphony can be fitted on to a single disc. The valuable supplements include a live recording of the *Adagietto* of No. 5 played at the funeral of Robert Kennedy and two versions of *Kindertotenlieder*, not just the one recorded in Israel in 1974 with Dame Janet Baker, but the earlier studio recording of 1960 with Jenny Tourel, a favourite singer with Bernstein, brisker, less reflective, as well as Tourel in three of the *Rückert Lieder* and *Das irdische Leben* from *Des Knaben Wunderhorn*.

Giuseppe Sinopoli began his Mahler symphony cycle with the Philharmonia in January 1981, when he recorded the *Fifth*, and rounded it off six years later with No. 4. If the orchestra initially found it hard to respond to the subtleties of expression demanded by the conductor – more under the tight rehearsal schedules for London concerts than in recording sessions – there is no sign of it here. These are individual, sometimes wilful readings of Mahler, but ones which with full-blooded recording bring out the warmth as well as the power. One is never in doubt as to the greatness of the music, or the dedication with which the conductor approaches each work. Just occasionally Sinopoli chooses a tempo that is not just wilful but perverse – as in the snail-pace for the second *Nachtmusik* of No. 7, and he generally favours speeds on the broad side, but magnetism is a consistent quality, and so it is in the other Mahler works which make up this 15-disc set. *Das Klagende Lied* – with a starry quartet of soloists – is taken from a live concert which the Philharmonia gave in Tokyo in November 1990, while the song-cycles were recorded as adjuncts to the symphonies. *Das Lied von der Erde* is the odd one out, recorded in Dresden with the Staatskapelle five years after the rest had been completed, but just as persuasive in its Mahlerian manners, with Iris Vermillion and Keith Lewis strong and reliable soloists, if not as characterful as some. The brilliantly extrovert Solti or the more refined Haitink are a safer recommendation for the nine symphonies.

Kubelik's is a fastidious and generally lyrical view of Mahler, most persuasive in the delightful performances of the least weighty symphonies, Nos. 1 and 4. In much of the rest these sensitive performances lack something in power and tension, tending to eliminate the neurotic in Mahler; but there is a fair case for preferring such an approach for relaxed listening. As can be seen, he has excellent soloists and distinguished choral contributions in Nos. 2 and 8. Other sets more compellingly encompass the full range of Mahler's symphonic achievement, but with good sound and in a bargain box, this is worth considering if Kubelik's less flamboyant view seems appealing. The new transfers are strikingly fresh.

Symphonies 1–9; 10 (Revised Performing Edition by Derycke Cooke)

(N) (B) *** Decca 475 6686 (10). Concg. O (Berlin RSO in 10), Chailly; with Diener, Lang, Prague Philharmonic Ch. in 3; Bonney in 4; Eaglen, Fulgoni, Schwanewilms, Siezak, Larrson, Heppner, Mattei, Rootering, Prague Philharmonic Ch., Netherlands R. Ch., Children of Katthedrale Ch. St Bavo & Breda in 8

Chailly's Mahler box is the only cycle to include Derycke Cooke's performing edition of the *Tenth Symphony*, and if the performance does not hold the internal tension quite as powerfully as Rattle's account, it remains satisfying. What stands out through this series is the way Chailly's strong, satisfying overall approach to Mahler, without eccentricity, is supported by the superb playing of the Royal Concertgebouw Orchestra throughout and the demonstration quality of the Decca sound, never more remarkable than in the dedicated account of the *Resurrection Symphony*. The *Third* also has comparably weighty intensity, but the spacious account of *No. 4* has rather less depth of inner feeling. The *Fifth* more than compensates and is perhaps the highlight of the cycle, although the *Sixth* also conveys great concentration and is marvellously played. In the spectacular *Symphony of a Thousand* the Decca engineers more than rise to the challenge, as they do again in the *Ninth*. Chailly is lucky in his soloists, all of whom sing beautifully, and the choral contributions are of the highest quality too. Overall, this box is strongly recommendable, particularly if demonstration recording quality is a priority. It comes with full texts and translations.

Symphony 1 in D (Titan)

☛ (M) *** Decca 458 622-2. LSO, Solti

(B) *** Sony SBK 89783. VPO, Maazel

(B) *** CfP 573 5102. RLPO, Mackerras

*** Decca (IMS) 448 813-2. Concg. O, Chailly (with BERG: Sonata, Op. 1, orch. Verbey) ***

*** DG (IMS) 431 769-2. BPO, Abbado

**(*) Sony (ADD) SACD SS 7069. NYPO, Bernstein

(BB) **(*) EMI 5 74963-2. Phd. O, Muti

The London Symphony Orchestra play Mahler's *First* like no other orchestra. They catch the magical opening, with its bird sounds and evocatively distanced brass, with a singular ambience, at least partly related to the orchestra's characteristic blend of wind timbres. Throughout there is wonderfully warm string-playing and the most atmospheric response from the horns. Solti's tendency to drive hard is felt only in the second movement, which is pressed a little too much, although he relaxes beautifully in the central section. Especially memorable are the poignancy of the introduction of the *Frère Jacques* theme in the slow movement and the exultant brilliance of the closing pages, helped by the wide range of dynamic and the wonderfully clear inner detail of the newly remastered, 1964 Kingsway Hall recording. This is

another disc produced by John Culshaw which is rightly included among Decca's 'Legends'.

With superb playing and refined recording, Maazel's account of the *First* has an authentic Viennese glow. Though there are other versions which point detail more sharply, this performance has a ripeness and an easy lyricism that place it among the most sympathetic bargain versions. The sound too is full and atmospheric as well as brilliant. A fine bargain alternative to Solti.

Mackerras's version, now reissued on CfP, offers a performance that, with crisply sprung rhythms, brings out the youthful freshness of Mahler's inspiration. The natural warmth and spontaneity of the reading have one concentrating on Mahler's arguments rather than on points of interpretation. Speeds are consistently well chosen and, though the finale is not quite as biting as the rest, the joy of the inspiration comes over winningly, so that the whole performance hangs together magnetically, making this an outstanding choice, irrespective of price.

Helped by immaculate playing from the Concertgebouw, meticulous on detail and with sound of demonstration quality, Chailly's direct, positive reading is magnetic in its control of the long line. More subjective interpretations may characterize more strongly, but this is consistently satisfying, and it comes with an unusual coupling in an orchestration of the early Berg *Sonata* by the Dutch composer, Theo Verbey.

Abbado's Berlin reading, like others in his Mahler series, was recorded live and, though one or two coughs intrude, the sound is fresh and full, bringing out the beauty and clarity of the Berlin strings. Though Abbado occasionally exaggerates the pointing of rhythms and speed-changes (as in the Ländler), the high voltage of the whole performance makes it most compelling, if not an obvious first choice.

Bernstein's performance was recorded in the Avery Fisher Hall in 1966. It is an excellent, red-blooded version of considerable charisma and individuality, particularly in the central movements. The originally close-up sound is given more space and atmosphere in this new (non-compatible) SACD transfer, with a wider range of dynamic at the atmospheric opening, and the brass particularly impressive in the finale. But the thinner violins give away the age of the recording, and this remastered disc is currently very expensive.

Muti's 1984 version was the first recording made in the Philadelphia Orchestra's (then new) Memorial Hall venue, which did convey the richness of timbre typical of this orchestra. Muti, like other conductors prone to fierceness, manages to relax most persuasively for the gentler *Wunderhorn* inventions, contrasted sharply against extrovert outbursts, with rhythms crisply pointed and solo playing exceptionally fine. This is not the greatest performance of Mahler's *First Symphony* available, but at its new budget price it is certainly worth considering.

Symphony 1 in D (Titan) (with Blumine)

(M) **(*) HM HCX 3957118. Florida PO, Judd

(B) **(*) EMI Red Line 5 69816. Israel PO, Mehta

** EMI 7 54647-2. CBSO, Rattle

James Judd demonstrates the virtuoso qualities of the Florida Philharmonic in a warm, well-pointed, spontaneous-sounding performance, slightly marred by a slow and rather heavy reading of the second-movement Ländler, which yet includes a most delicate account of the central Trio. The atmospheric recording sets the orchestra at a slight distance, which may take away some of the bite but enhances the beauty of the string-tone, not least in a dedicated performance of *Blumine*, which comes as a supplement after the symphony.

Mehta's version with the Israel Philharmonic brings a hybrid – the regular four-movement version in its revised instrumentation, into which is inserted the lyrical *Blumine* movement from the original version, which Mahler later excised. Mehta's reading of the whole work, though not the most individual or illuminating, is satisfyingly warm and direct, helped by very full, forward recording, among the best in the difficult acoustic of the Mann Auditorium. A worthwhile reissue.

Recorded live in Symphony Hall, Birmingham, Rattle's account with the CBSO is rather lacking in the spontaneity one expects. Speed changes in the first movement sound self-conscious, as do the exaggerations of dotted rhythms in the Ländler movement. It remains an acceptable reading, well recorded, but hardly matches Rattle's achievement in other Mahler recordings. As a preface to the main work, the *Blumine* movement is given with a freshness and spontaneity that rather shows up the rest.

Symphonies 1; (i) 2 (Resurrection)

(B) *** Double Decca (ADD) 448 921-2 (2). (i) Harper, Watts, L. Symphony Ch.; LSO, Solti

(N) (B) *** Ph. Duo 475 6222 (2). BPO, Haitink; (i) with McNair, Van Nes, Ernst-Senff Ch.

(B) **(*) EMI double forte (ADD) 5 74182-2 (2). (i) Mathis, Soffel, LPO Ch.; LPO, Tennstedt

Symphonies (i) 1 (Titan); (ii) 2 (Resurrection); (iii) Lieder eines fahrenden Gesellen

(M) *** Sony (ADD) 516 025-2. (i) Columbia SO; (ii) Cundari, Forrester, Westminster Ch., NYPO; (iii) Miller, Columbia SO; Walter

Solti's 1964 LSO account of No. 2 remains a demonstration of the outstanding results Decca were securing with analogue techniques at that time, although on CD the brilliance of the *fortissimos* may not suit all ears. Helen Watts is wonderfully expressive, while the chorus has a rapt intensity that is the more telling when the recording perspectives are so clearly delineated. Coupled with his outstanding version of No. 1, it makes a genuine bargain at Double Decca price.

The Berlin Philharmonic Orchestra plays superbly for Haitink in his third and finest recording of Mahler's *First Symphony*. There is greater gravity in his view now, to bring out the full weight of this ambitious early work and a greater freedom of expression, though this conductor is hardly one to wear his heart on his sleeve or even inject charm into such a passage as the Ländler trio of the second movement. The purity and refinement of the Berlin string-tone is superbly caught, and the recorded sound of the 1987 recording is notably finer than in many previous recordings made in the Philharmonie, even if it is not entirely free from cloudiness. The *Resurrection Symphony* dates from six years later and brings another of Haitink's finest Mahler recordings, if anything even more weighty and powerful. The sound of the Berlin Philharmonic in the Philharmonie is projected with remarkable vividness and sense of presence. Above all, Haitink conveys the tensions of a live occasion, even though this was a studio performance, leading up to a glorious apotheosis in the Judgement Day finale. The soloists are outstanding, and the chorus immediately expands from rapt, hushed singing to incandescent splendour. Outstanding in

every way, this can be placed alongside Rattle's superb CBSO set.

Bruno Walter's stereo recording of the *First Symphony* was recorded in Hollywood in 1961, and in its remastered form the recording sounds better than ever, richer and fuller at the bottom end of the spectrum, and the dynamic range seemingly extended. Even more than the *First Symphony*, the 1958 set of the *Resurrection Symphony* is among the gramophone's indispensable classics. In the first movement there is a restraint and in the second a gracefulness which provide a strong contrast with a conductor like Solti. In the newest remastering, detail registers more clearly; while the sound is not sumptuous, in the finale the balance with the voices still gives the music an ethereal resonance, with the closing section thrillingly expansive. In the 1960 recording of the *Lieder eines fahrenden Gesellen* the superb orchestral detail glows as never before. Mildred Miller is perhaps not an inspirational soloist, but she sings well enough, and Walter ensures that the performance is dramatically alive.

Tennstedt's manner in the *First Symphony* is somewhat severe, with textures fresh and neat and the style of phrasing generally less moulded than under Solti. The concentration on precision and directness means that when the conductor does indulge in rubato or speed changes it does not sound quite consistent and comes as a surprise in the big string melody of the finale. Most Mahlerians will prefer a more felt performance than this, but the rich, warm Abbey Road recording is first class. Tennstedt's approach is more obviously dedicated in the *Resurrection Symphony*. The performance, if not quite as well played as the finest, conveys Mahlerian certainties in the light of day, underemphasizing neurotic tensions. The Kingsway Hall recording is excellent (with splendid perspectives), as are the soloists (especially Doris Soffel) and chorus, and both symphonies are given impressively full and clear new transfers. The snag is the absence of texts and translations.

Symphonies 1; 5 in C sharp min.

(B) **(*) DG Double 459 472-2 (2). Philh. O, Sinopoli

Symphonies (i) 1; (ii) 5; (ii; iii) Lieder eines fahrenden Gesellen

(BB) **(*) DG Panorama 469 154-2 (2). (i) Concg. O; (ii) VPO; Bernstein; (iii) with Hampson

On Panorama an inexpensive way to sample Bernstein's distinctive approach to Mahler. The *First* receives a vital performance with some splendidly alert and beautiful playing; the opening movement conveys the joys of spring with its *Wayfaring Lad* associations, while the second, with a relaxed Ländler tempo, sounds more rustic than usual. The finale has superb panache, and in all ways this performance is preferable to his 1966 Sony account. No allowances need be made for the live recording. The *Fifth* is hardly less compelling: it is a deeply personal account with the conductor's stamp apparent in every bar. The conception is certainly expansive, but it is utterly compelling, and ranks as one of his finest performances. Fine (live) recording.

Sinopoli's account of the *First Symphony* is warmly satisfying and passionately committed, with refined playing from the Philharmonia. He allows the fullest expressiveness, with bold theatrical gestures thrust home purposefully. In the *Fifth* he draws a sharp distinction between the dark tragedy of the first two movements, and the relaxed *Wunderhorn* feeling of the rest. He seems intent on not overloading the big melodies with excessive emotion. This comes out more clearly in the central movements, where relaxation is the key-note, often with a pastoral atmosphere. The celebrated *Adagietto* brings a tenderly wistful reading, songful and basically happy, not tragic. Warmly atmospheric recording throughout, though detail is not ideally clear in the *Fifth*; this is still a recommendable coupling.

Symphony 2 in C min. (Resurrection)

⊖━ ✪ *** EMI 7 47962-8 (2). Augér, Baker, CBSO Ch., CBSO, Rattle

⊖━ ✪ (M) (***) BBC Legends (mono) BBCL 4163-2. Woodland, Baker, BBC Ch. & Choral Soc., LSO, Stokowski

(M) (***) Testament (mono) SBT2 1320 (2). Stader, J. Baker, St Hedwig's Cathedral Ch., BPO, Barbirolli

(M) *** EMI (ADD) 5 57235-2 [567255]. Schwarzkopf, Rössl-Majdan, Philh. Ch. & O., Klemperer

(M) *** Chan. 6595/6. Lott, Hamari, Latvian State Ac. Ch., Oslo Philharmonic Ch., Oslo PO, Jansons

(N) *** DG 477 5082 (2). Gvazava, Larsson, Orfeon Donostiarra, Lucerne Festival O, Abbado – DEBUSSY: *La Mer* **(*)

(N) *** Avie **SACD** 821936 005-2. Bayrakdarian, Lieberson, San Francisco SO, Tilson Thomas

**(*) DG (IMS) 439 953-2 (2). Studer, Meyer, Arnold Schoenberg Ch., VPO, Abbado

(B) *** Conifer 76505 51337-2 (2). Valente, Forrester, Ardwyn Singers, BBC Welsh Ch., Cardiff Philharmonic Ch., Dyfed Ch., L. Symphony Ch., LSO, Kaplan

(N) ** DG 474 380-2 (2). Moore, Michael, V. Singverein, VPO, Kaplan

Symphony 2 (Resurrection); Totenfeier

*** Decca 470 283-2 (2). Diener, Lang, Prague Phil. Ch., Concg. O, Chailly

(i) Symphony 2 (Resurrection); (ii) Lieder eines fahrenden Gesellen; (iii) Lieder und Gesang aus der Jugendzeit (excerpts)

(M) *** DG (IMS) 445 587-2 (2). (i; ii) Fassbaender; (i) Plowright, Philh. Ch.; (iii) Weikl; Philh. O, Sinopoli

Simon Rattle's reading of Mahler's *Second* is among the very finest records he has yet made, superlative in the breadth and vividness of its sound and with a spacious reading which in its natural intensity unerringly sustains generally slow, steady speeds to underline the epic grandeur of Mahler's vision. The playing of the CBSO is inspired. The choral singing, beautifully balanced, is incandescent, while the heart-felt singing of Arleen Augér and Dame Janet Baker is equally distinguished and characterful.

For the first ever Prom performance of the *Resurrection Symphony*, William Glock, as BBC Controller of Music, made a shrewd choice in Leopold Stokowski (in 1963 then aged 81), still only an occasional visitor to his native country. It was a triumph, for here was a larger-than-life reading of an apocalyptic work. The response of the audience at the end was so prolonged and so enthusiastic that, against the strict Prom rule of the time, Stokowski gave an encore, repeating the final visionary choral sequence. Even critics who generally dismissed Stokowski as a publicity-seeker were bowled over, recognizing that here was music-making of exceptional power and intensity. Now at last on disc in this BBC Legends recording of the broadcast, we have the legend vividly confirmed, for though the sound is in mono the immediacy and sense of presence, as well as the atmosphere of the hall, are vividly caught: full, bright and clear, giving the illusion of

stereo. As issued on Testament, Barbirolli's rich and powerful reading of this same work with the Berlin Philharmonic is very compelling, yet the impact of the Stokowski performance is even greater, with Janet Baker again the dedicated mezzo soloist, this time joined by the fresh-toned Rae Woodland. Stokowski is more urgent than Barbirolli, lighter in the second-movement Andante, more sinister in the Scherzo, leading to a shattering rendering of the Judgement Day finale, with the BBC Chorus, Choral Society and attendant choirs as intense in their dedicatedly hushed singing as in the extrovert power of the climaxes. It makes an overwhelming experience, marred only slightly by inevitable audience noises.

Barbirolli's long-buried radio recording from Berlin will be a revelation even to the many admirers of this great Mahlerian. In 1965, a year after he had conducted a historic studio recording of Mahler's *Ninth Symphony*, he returned to the Berlin Philharmonic for this concert performance of the *Resurrection Symphony*, and the result is electrifying from beginning to end. Helped by full, vividly immediate sound, this is an impassioned, freely volatile performance, massively powerful in the outer movements while setting in contrast the '*Wunderhorn*' playfulness of the third movement against the darkness of the *Urlicht* slow movement, sung by Dame Janet Baker with heartfelt intensity. The vision of Judgement Day in the long choral finale is then cataclysmic, so shattering that one readily forgives the out-of-time chimes at the very end. Just too long for a single CD, this issue is offered on two discs for the price of one.

Beauty and refinement are the mark of Chailly's reading of the *Resurrection Symphony*. Until the choral finale, with its vision of Judgement Day, the performance has a degree of restraint, but then, with massed forces superbly recorded, it is rounded off as dramatically as one could want. It also has the unique merit of offering *Totenfeier* as a coupling, Mahler's first working of what later became the first movement of the *Symphony*. The differences between the two versions – mainly in the long development section – are fascinating but would have been made even clearer to the curious listener had that fill-up been placed before the *Symphony* on the same disc as the first movement. Petra Lang is the warm-toned soloist in *Urlicht*, and both soloists and chorus sing superbly in the great finale. A fine alternative to Rattle's excellent version.

Klemperer's performance – one of his most compelling on record – comes back to the catalogue on a single CD as one of EMI's 'Great Recordings of the Century', sounding better than ever. The remastering of the Kingsway Hall recording is impressively full and clear, with a real feeling of spectacle in the closing pages. The first movement, taken at a fairly fast tempo, is intense and earth-shaking; though in the last movement (which incidentally is generously cued) some of Klemperer's speeds are designedly slow, he conveys supremely well the mood of transcendent, heavenly happiness in the culminating passage, with the Philharmonia Chorus and soloists themselves singing like angels.

Sinopoli's *Resurrection* has the advantage of including the *Lieder eines fahrenden Gesellen*, beautifully sung by Brigitte Fassbaender, and the *Songs of Youth* ('*aus der Jugendzeit*'), skilfully orchestrated by Harold Byrns and well sung by Bernd Weikl, bringing extra anticipations of the mature *Des Knaben Wunderhorn* songs. In the symphony Sinopoli has meticulous concern for detail, yet he still conveys consistently the irresistible purposefulness of Mahler's writing, fierce at high dramatic moments and intense too, rarely relaxed, in moments of meditation, with *Urlicht* beautifully sung with warmth and purity by Fassbaender. The recorded sound, though not quite as full and vivid as that for Rattle, is among the most brilliant of any in this work. Rosalind Plowright is a pure and fresh soprano soloist, contrasting well with the equally firm, earthier-toned mezzo of Fassbaender.

The crisp attack at the start of the opening funeral march sets the pattern for an exceptionally refined and alert reading of the *Resurrection Symphony* from Jansons and his Oslo orchestra. During the first four movements, this may seem a lightweight reading, but the extra resilience of rhythm brings out the dance element in Mahler's *Knaben Wunderhorn* inspirations rather than ruggedness or rusticity, while at the finale the whole performance erupts in an overwhelming outburst for the vision of Resurrection. That transformation is intensified by the breathtakingly rapt and intense account of the song, *Urlicht*, which precedes it. In the finale, power goes with precision and meticulous observance of markings, when even Mahler's surprising diminuendo on the final choral cadence is observed. With the Oslo Choir joined by singers from Jansons's native Latvia, the choral singing is heartfelt, to crown a version which finds a special place even among the many distinguished readings on a long list.

Abbado's 2004 version of the *Resurrection Symphony* was recorded live at the Lucerne Festival, using an orchestra of specially chosen players, partly drawn from those in the conductor's Mahler Chamber Orchestra, but also including such distinguished soloists as the violinist Renaud Capuçon, the cellist Natalia Gutman and the horn-player Myron Bloom. The liveness gives it a rare intensity, putting it among the most powerful of all versions of the work. The thrust and tautness of the performance are established from the very start, with speeds faster than usual and generally faster than those which Abbado adopted in his two previous recordings of the work. The exception is the third-movement Ländler, where at a relatively relaxed speed he brings out the *Des Knaben Wunderhorn* associations. The mezzo soloist, Anna Larsson, gives a satisfyingly weighty performance, with warm contralto timbre in the chest register, and though the microphone brings out the vibrato of the soprano, Eteri Gvazava, she is a first-rate soloist too, while the choral singing is focused with exceptional clarity. The closeness of the well-detailed recording adds to the impact.

Michael Tilson Thomas's San Francisco version on Avie offers a spacious reading which builds up powerfully over the movements, until the choral finale crowns a performance which until then is more remarkable for refinement and lyricism than for drama. Spectacular sound reinforces the depiction of Judgement Day, with the alto solo more closely integrated than usual, thanks to the masterly, deeply moving singing of the soloist, Lorraine Hunt Lieberson. The soprano soloist, Isabel Bayrakdarian, is less intense but still sings well, and the chorus is first rate. A valuable addition to Tilson Thomas's emerging Mahler cycle.

Abbado's recording with the Vienna Philharmonic was made live in 1992 in the Musikverein, offering a predictably fine, beautifully paced performance, but one that rather suffers, compared with his Berlin version of the *Fifth*, recorded live six months later. The Vienna Philharmonic's ensemble is less refined than that of the Berliners, even in the strings, and the sound is less immediate and involving. Tensions are not helped when the audience is so noisy. Yet with powerful soloists and a superb choir, it is still a strong reading.

Kaplan's performance of the *Resurrection Symphony* is not only thoroughly idiomatic and full of enthusiasm but totally compelling. He gets keenly dramatic and highly responsive

playing from the LSO, and the recording is of demonstration quality, indeed second to none. The performance runs to just over 83 minutes so it has been issued in a Double format to compete with other full-priced versions on a single CD.

The conducting career of Gilbert Kaplan is a curious one. A wealthy businessman, he has concentrated almost entirely on this massive symphony, and on DG has made the first recording of the *Resurrection Symphony* using the revised score which his own Kaplan Foundation has sponsored in collaboration with the Universal Edition. The result is beautifully played and superbly recorded, with every note clearly in place. That the discs present the work on no fewer than 40 CD tracks means that analysis is made far clearer than usual, particularly in relation to Kaplan's own detailed description of the work, which is given in the booklet, taking the listener through it section by section. The performance may lack the full power of the finest versions but, until the massive finale depicting the Day of Judgement, tension is well maintained. There the sections tend to fall apart, though the choral singing of the Vienna Singverein helps to bring greater intensity. The soloists, Latonia Moore and Nadja Michael, are good but flawed.

(i–iii) *Symphony 2 (Resurrection) in C min.*; (i; iv–v) 3; (i; iv; vi) 4 (choral movements of symphonies only); (vii) *Kindertotenlieder*; (viii & i; iv; vi) *Des Knaben Wunderhorn* (2 versions); (i; ix) *Das Lied von der Erde*; (x) *Lieder eines fahrenden Gesellen*; (viii) *Lieder und Gesänge der Jugendzeit*; (xi) *Rückert Lieder*

(BB) *** EMI (ADD/DDD) 5 85024-2 (5). (i) LPO, Tennstedt; (ii) LPO Ch.; (iii) Mathis, Soffel; (iv) Wenkel; (v) Southend Boys' Ch., Ladies of LPO Ch.; (vi) Popp; (vii) Ludwig, Philh. O, Vandernoot; (viii) Fischer-Dieskau, Barenboim; (ix) König, Baltsa; (x) Allen, ECO, Tate; (xi) Baker, New Philh. O, Barbirolli

At budget price, this makes an unexpected but worthwhile compilation, bringing together all of Mahler's settings of *Des Knaben Wunderhorn*. Those who are primarily interested in Mahler's love of the German language and the folk-poems of *Des Knaben Wunderhorn* in particular will welcome this, when the versions chosen – some of them unexpected – are all good, with some outstanding, like Janet Baker's classic reading of the *Rückert Lieder* with Barbirolli.

Symphony 3 in D min.

*** Ph. (IMS) 432 162-2 (2). Van Nes, Tölz Boys' Ch., Ernst Senff Ch., BPO, Haitink

(N) *** Decca **SACD** 470 652-2. Lang, Prague Philharmonic Ch., Netherlands Children's Ch., Concg. O, Chailly

*** DG (IMS) 410 715-2 (2). Norman, V. State Op. Ch., V. Boys' Ch., VPO, Abbado

(M) *** Warner Elatus 0927 49618-2 (2). Pecková, Women of Berlin R. Ch. and Knabenchor Hannover, Berlin Deutsches SO, Nagano

(M) **(*) BBC (ADD) BBCL 4004-7. Meyer, Ladies of Hallé Ch., Boys of Manchester Grammar School, Hallé O, Barbirolli

(i) *Symphony 3. Kindertotenlieder*

**(*) Chan. 9117/18. Finnie, RSNO, Järvi; (i) with Royal Scottish Ch. & Junior Ch.

(i) *Symphony 3;* (ii) *Kindertotenlieder; Des Knaben Wunderhorn: Das irdische Leben; 3 Rückert Lieder: Ich atmet' einen linden Duft; Ich bin der Welt abhanden gekommen; Um Mitternacht*

(M) *** Sony (ADD) SM2K 61831(2). (i) Lipton, Schola Cantorum, Boys' Ch. of the Church of Transfiguration; (ii) Tourel; NYPO, Bernstein

(i) *Symphony 3;* (ii) *Des Knaben Wunderhorn: 8 Lieder*

☞ *** EMI 5 56657-2 (2). (i) Remmert, CBSO Women's Ch.; (ii) Keenlyside; CBSO, Rattle

Rattle conducts an outstanding version of No. 3, magnetic from the very start, rich, bold and opulent, and very well recorded with an exceptionally full bass. The subtlety of Rattle's phrasing and rubato not only brings out the work's deeper qualities, with the visionary intensity of the long finale superbly caught, but – far more than most – the joy and humour of the lighter movements. Simon Keenlyside's beautiful, finely detailed readings of the *Knaben Wunderhorn* songs make a very welcome bonus, with an extra song, *Ablösung im Sommer* (which is quoted in the third movement of the *Symphony*) aptly included in an arrangement by Berio.

With the Berlin Philharmonic producing glorious sounds, recorded with richness and immediacy, Haitink conducts a powerful, spacious reading. It culminates in a glowing, concentrated account of the slow finale, which gives the whole work a visionary strength often lacking. The mystery of *Urlicht* is then beautifully caught by the mezzo soloist, Jard van Nes.

Characteristically strongly characterized and brilliantly played, with the second and fourth movements even more sharply rhythmic than with Abbado, Chailly's account is among the finest. He has a warmly sensitive mezzo soloist in Petra Lang, and the reading is heightened by his dedicated account of the finale with its easy flowing tempo. The Decca SACD recording is among the finest this symphony has yet received.

Abbado's performance is sharply defined and deeply dedicated. The range of expression, the often wild mixture of elements in this work, is conveyed with extraordinary intensity, not least in the fine contributions of Jessye Norman and the two choirs. The spectacular recording has great presence and detail on CD.

On its own merits Nagano's performance too has much in its favour: there is a good sense of drama, a well-judged balance between beauty of detail and the overall architecture of the piece, and impressively realistic sound – as good as any around now. Nagano has a real affinity with Mahler's pantheism and the middle movements come off splendidly. It is not easy these days to speak of a 'best' version but this is certainly impressive. Now it is available on Elatus at mid-price.

Bernstein's 1961 account of Mahler's *Third Symphony*, strong and passionate, has few of the stylistic exaggerations that sometimes overlaid his interpretations. Here his style in the slow movement is heavily expressive, but many will respond to his extrovert involvement. The recording, made in New York's Manhattan Center, the venue of so many of the best of his early records, has added spaciousness and body in this very successful remastering for CD. The vocal contributions from Martha Lipton and the two choirs contribute to the success of this venture and the generous Lieder coupling is well worth having, and Jennie Tourel is in excellent voice.

Barbirolli's BBC *Third Symphony* was recorded at a concert at the Free Trade Hall, Manchester, in May 1969, the same year as Sir John's celebrated *Fifth* with the New Philharmonia. There is much of the fervour and warmth that characterized all he did, which compensates for various shortcomings. The recording is generally very good, though the cellos and double-basses are wanting in weight. Kerstin Meyer displays artistry but has an unwelcome and obtrusive vibrato. For some reason the engineers cut off the applause and the resulting edit on the last D major chord is ugly. The disc also includes an interesting conversation between Sir John and the critic C. B. Rees.

Järvi conducts a warmly expressive, spontaneous-sounding reading which brings out the joy behind Mahler's inspiration rather than any tragedy. This makes light of the epic qualities in this massive work. Though the ensemble of the Royal Scottish Orchestra is not as immaculate as that of some distinguished rivals, the bite of communication is always intense, helped by full, atmospheric Chandos recording. Järvi brings out the folk-like elements in the second and third movements, and Linda Finnie is a dedicated soloist who gives a felt, expressive reading of the *Kindertotenlieder*.

(i) *Symphonies 3;* (ii) *4 in G*

(B) *** EMI double forte (ADD/DDD) 5 74296-2 (2). LPO, Tennstedt, with (i) Wenkel, Southend Boys' Ch., Ladies of LPO Ch.; (ii) Popp

The *Third Symphony* receives an eloquent performance under Tennstedt (1979), the spaciousness underlined with measured tempi. With Ortrun Wenkel a fine soloist and the Southend boys adding lusty freshness to the bell music in the fifth movement, it is crowned by an impressively noble finale and splendid recording.

The *Fourth* is similarly spacious yet conveys an innocence entirely in keeping with this most endearing of Mahler symphonies. Tennstedt makes the argument seamless in his easy transitions of speed, yet he never deliberately adopts a coaxing, charming manner. The recording (1982) is splendid and this is a fine bargain in EMI's 'Double Forte' series.

Symphony 4 in G

(M) *** RCA (ADD) 82876 59413-2. Blegen, Chicago SO, Levine

*** EMI 5 56563-2. Roocroft, CBSO, Rattle

(N) (M) *** RCA **SACD** 82876 67901-2. Della Casa, Chicago SO, Reiner

(B) *** CfP 573 4372. Lott, LPO, Welser-Möst

(M) *** DG (ADD) 419 863-2. Mathis, BPO, Karajan

(M) *** BBC (ADD) BBCL 4014-2. Harper, BBC SO, Barbirolli (with BERLIOZ: *Overture: Le Corsaire, Op. 21*)

(BB) *** Naxos 8.550527. Russell, Polish Nat. RSO, Wit

(BB) *** Arte Nova 74321 46506-2. Kwan, Gran Canaria PO, Leaper

(*) Decca 466 720-2. Bonney, Concg. O, Chailly – BERG: *7 Early Songs* *

(*) Australian Decca Eloquence 467 235-2. Israel PO, Mehta – WAGNER: *Lohengrin: Preludes* *

(N) ** DG **SACD** 474 991-2. Banse, Cleveland O, Boulez

Symphonies 4; 5 (Adagietto)

(B) *** EMI Red Line CDR5 69817. Popp, LPO, Tennstedt

(i) *Symphony 4*; (ii) *Des Knaben Wunderhorn: Das irdische Leben; Wo die schönen Trompeten bläsen. Rückert Lieder: Ich atmet' einen linden Duft; Ich bin der Welt abhanden gekommen; Um Mitternacht*

(M) **(*) EMI (ADD) 5 67035-2. (i) Schwarzkopf; (ii) Ludwig; Philh. O, Klemperer

(i) *Symphony 4*; (ii) *Lieder eines fahrenden Gesellen*

☛━◉ (B) *** Sony (ADD) SBK 46535. (i) Raskin, Cleveland O, Szell; (ii) Von Stade, LPO, A. Davis

(i) *Symphony 4*; (ii; iii) *Lieder eines fahrenden Gesellen*; (iii; iv) *Des Knaben Wunderhorn: Das irdische Leben; Wer hat dies Liedlein erdacht?*

(M) **(*) BBC mono/stereo BBCB 8004-2. (i) Carlyle, LSO; (ii) Reynolds; (iii) ECO; (iv) with Ameling; Britten

Symphony 4; 4 Early Songs
*** RCA 75605 51345-2. Ziesak, RPO, Gatti

George Szell's 1966 record of Mahler's *Fourth* represented his partnership with the Cleveland Orchestra at its highest peak, and the digital remastering for CD brings out the very best of the original recording. The performance remains uniquely satisfying: the music blossoms, partly because of the marvellous attention to detail (and the immaculate ensemble), but more positively because of the committed and radiantly luminous orchestral response to the music itself. In the finale Szell found the ideal soprano to match his conception. An outstanding choice, generously coupled. In contrast with most other recorded performances, Frederica von Stade insinuates a hint of youthful ardour into her highly enjoyable account of the *Wayfaring Lad* cycle.

James Levine draws a superlative performance from the Chicago orchestra, one which bears comparison with the finest versions, bringing out not merely the charm but also the deeper emotions. The subtlety of his control of tempo, so vital in Mahler, is superbly demonstrated and, though he may not quite match the nobility of Szell's famous analogue Sony version in the great slow movement, he has the advantage of a more modern (1975) recording. Judith Blegen makes a fresh, attractive soloist, and this is a thoroughly worthwhile addition to RCA's mid-priced 'Classic Library' series, even if it does not replace Szell.

Daniele Gatti conducts a beautifully paced reading of the *Fourth* which is among the finest of recent digital versions, with the Royal Philharmonic playing superbly. It is a mark of Gatti's Mahlerian understanding that he can so perfectly time such a passage as the close of the first movement with its witty pay-off. That leads on to an account of the Scherzo which brings out its macabre humour, a dance of death. Gatti also paces the dedicated slow movement very impressively, with contrasts of tempo finely judged, and the finale too brings sharply defined contrasts, with Ruth Ziesak a sweetly girlish-sounding soloist. The *Four Early Songs* make an apt and generous coupling, also beautifully sung by Ziesak. Full, vivid sound.

Simon Rattle's performance begins with an idiosyncratic but valid reading of the opening bars, at first very slow then brisk for the main *Allegro*. It reflects the thoughtfulness on detail of his approach to Mahler, reflected in an unusually refreshing account, youthfully urgent, which rises to a spacious, songful reading of the long slow movement. Amanda Roocroft sings with warm, creamy tone in the finale. Refined recording to match. This also stands high among modern recordings of this beautiful symphony.

On RCA the SACD remastering has brought a glowing warmth to the 1958 Chicago recording. Reiner's performances is wayward, but lovingly so; and everything he does sounds spontaneous. There is a mercurial quality in the first movement and plenty of drama too; the second is engagingly pointed but with a balancing warmth, the Viennese element strong. The slow movement has striking intensity, and in its rapt closing pages leads on gently to the finale in which Lisa della Casa, in ravishing voice, matches Reiner's mood.

Welser-Möst's outer movements are fresh and beautifully shaped, with Felicity Lott a youthful-sounding soloist, and the Ländler second movement clean-cut and crisp. It is the third-movement *Adagio* that crowns the performance, hushed and intense from the start, with the emotional outbursts strongly controlled. At bargain price, with excellent modern digital sound, spacious like the performance, it makes an outstanding recommendation, a fine alternative to Szell.

Karajan's refined and poised, yet undoubtedly affectionate account remains among the finest versions of this lovely symphony, and Edith Mathis's sensitively composed contribution to the finale matches the conductor's meditative feeling. With glowing sound, this makes another outstanding mid-priced recommendation alongside Szell's renowned Cleveland CD.

With the orchestra very well drilled, responding warmly to the fluctuations of Barbirolli's expressive Mahler style, this is an account to set alongside Barbirolli's classic studio recording of the *Fifth* in its passionate generosity. As in the *Fifth*, he tends to prefer broad speeds, but controls them masterfully with all the familiar warmth and conviction one expects from this conductor. The glowing, seamless reading of the slow movement leads on to a spacious account of the finale, with Heather Harper a radiant soloist. Full, warm, well-balanced sound to match. The Berlioz overture, dashingly done and brilliantly played by this fine orchestra, is a welcome makeweight.

Tennstedt's reading conveys spaciousness and strength, yet brings an agreeably light touch in the outer movements. Lucia Popp is the pure-toned soloist in the finale. The peak of the work as Tennstedt presents it lies in the long slow movement, here taken very slowly and intensely. The 1982 digital recording, made in the Kingsway Hall, is among EMI's finest, full and well balanced. Tennstedt's account of the *Adagietto* makes a worthwhile bonus.

Antoni Wit conducts a fresh, spontaneous-sounding reading, beautifully played and recorded, that can be warmly recommended at Naxos's bargain price. Lynda Russell is a pure-toned soprano soloist in the finale, both fresh and warm, with Wit giving a good lilt to the rhythm. Excellent sound, which gives a good bite and focus to the woodwind, so important in Mahler.

Spaciously recorded, the Arte Nova version offers a fresh, crisply paced reading from Adrian Leaper, demonstrating what polished ensemble the Gran Canaria Philharmonic can achieve. Woodwind soloists are most imaginative, and most striking of all is the refinement of the strings, with the opening of the slow movement bringing the gentlest *pianissimo*, ravishingly sustained. The finale is then beautifully sprung, with the Korean soprano, Hellen Kwan, a golden-toned soloist, aptly young-sounding. Without being in the same class as the famous Szell version, this is thoroughly recommendable in the budget range.

Klemperer is slow in the first movement and, strangely, fractionally too fast in the slow movement. Yet the Philharmonia make some ravishing sounds, and one can easily fall under Klemperer's spell. The two highlights of the reading are the marvellously beautiful Ländler, which form the central section of the second movement, and the simplicity of Elisabeth Schwarzkopf's singing in the finale. This is a recording to enjoy, but perhaps not the one to buy as a single representation of Mahler's *Fourth* in a collection. In the Lieder other performers may find a deeper response to the words but the freshness of the singing, when Christa Ludwig's voice was in its early prime and at its richest, here gives much pleasure.

With rich, immediate recording, Chailly draws brilliant playing from the Concertgebouw. The detail and clarity are extraordinary, with solos regularly highlighted, though at times too much so, as in the eerie *scordatura* violin solo of the Scherzo. Speeds are on the broad side both in the outer movements and in the slow movement, with moulding of detail often meticulously underlined. Barbara Bonney is a delightfully girlish soloist in the *Wunderhorn* finale, both sweet and characterful, but she sounds even more appealing in the seven early Berg songs which come as a very generous coupling. Chailly, and the orchestra too, seem a degree more committed in Berg than in the Mahler.

Britten is brisker, more classical in approach, yet his feeling for this music always shines through. Though the very opening threatens chaos, when he launches the main *Allegro* at a very fast tempo, it is still a revelatory account, in some ways neo-classical in its freshness, edgy and abrasive in the Scherzo, tender in the slow movement and light and jaunty in the child–heaven finale, with Joan Carlyle the boyish soloist. The two songs from *Des Knaben Wunderhorn*, with Elly Ameling in radiant form, were recorded in 1969 and the *Lieder eines fahrenden Gesellen* with Anna Reynolds three years later at Snape Maltings. No one with an interest in Britten as interpreter should neglect this issue.

Fresh and spontaneous-sounding, with an apt hint of rusticity, sums up Mehta's 1979 reading with the Israeli orchestra. The digital recording is cleanly defined and sounds better than many recordings from this source. The slow movement is expansive but finely concentrated, and although Mehta occasionally indulges in exaggerated espressivo it is a performance which holds together in its amiability, not least in the finale, where Barbara Hendricks brings a hint of boyishness to the solo. With two very well-played *Preludes* from *Lohengrin* as fill-ups, this Australian release, while not a first choice, is worth considering, and it has the interest that these performances appear on CD for the first time.

Nothing could be further removed from the warmth of Fritz Reiner than Pierre Boulez's account of the *Fourth Symphony* with the Cleveland Orchestra and Juliane Banse as soloist in the finale. It is a generally brisk, rather understated performance that takes a cool, analytical view of Mahler. The result lacks spontaneity except in the slow movement, where Boulez's simple dedication conveys a depth of feeling rather missing in the rest. The new SACD transfer adds to the breadth of the sound but hardly affects the performance.

(i; ii) *Symphony 4*; (iii) *Das Lied von der Erde*; (i; iv) *Rückert Lieder*
(B) **(*) DG (ADD/DDD) 469 304-2 (2). (i) BPO, Karajan;
(ii) Mathis; (iii) Fassbaender, Araiza, BPO, Giulini; (iv) Ludwig

With playing of incomparable refinement – no feeling of rusticity here – Karajan directs a performance of compelling poise and purity, not least in the slow movement, with its pulse very steady indeed, most remarkably at the very end. Karajan's view of the finale is gentle, wistful, almost ruminative, with the final stanzas very slow and legato, beautifully so when Edith Mathis's poised singing of the solo is finely matched. Not that this quest for refinement means in any way that joy has been lost in this performance, and the 1979 recording is excellent. Karajan is no less sensitive in his 1975 recording of the *Rückert Lieder*, and his accompaniment is perfectly matched with Christa Ludwig's beautiful singing in these fine, positive performances.

Giulini's 1984 performance of *Das Lied von der Erde* is a characteristically restrained and refined reading. With Francisco Araiza a heady-toned tenor rather than a powerful one, the line 'Dunkel ist das Leben' in the first song becomes unusually tender and gentle, with rapture and wistfulness the keynote emotions. In the second song Brigitte Fassbaender gives lightness and poignancy rather than dark tragedy to the words 'Mein Herz ist müde'; and even the final *Abschied* is rapt rather than tragic, following the text of the poem. Not that Giulini fails to convey the breadth and intensity of Mahler's magnificent concept, and the playing of the Berlin Philharmonic could hardly be more beautiful. The only snag to this Panorama release is the absence of texts, but it is an inexpensive way to acquire some wonderful Mahler performances.

Symphonies (i) *4*; (ii) *5 in C sharp min.*
(B) ** Double Decca 458 383-2 (2). (i) Stahlman, Concg. O;
(ii) Chicago SO; Solti
(B) ** Ph. Duo 475 445-2 (2). BPO, Haitink; (i) with McNair

Symphonies (i; ii; iii) *4 in G*; (i; ii) *5 in C sharp min.*; (iii; iv) *Lieder und Gesänge aus der Jugendzeit*
(M) (**) Sony mono 515301-2. (i) NYPO; (ii) Walter; (iii) Halban; (iv) Walter (piano)

Solti's earlier Concertgebouw performance of the *Fourth Symphony* is disappointing. It is extremely well balanced as a recording, but the conductor is not altogether happy in the first movement and, besides a wilfulness of style, there are dull patches which he is unable to sustain with any richness of emotional expression. He does the finale best, and here Sylvia Stahlman sings charmingly. The opening *Funeral March* sets the tone of his reading of the *Fifth*. At a tempo faster than usual, it is wistful rather than deeply tragic, even though the dynamic contrasts are superbly pointed, and the string-tone could hardly be more resonant. In the pivotal *Adagietto* too, Solti secures intensely beautiful playing, but the result lacks the 'inner' quality one finds so abundantly in Barbirolli's interpretation. Full-bodied if slightly over-reverberant recording.

Recorded in New York in 1945, Bruno Walter's performance was – astonishingly – the first ever complete recording of Mahler's most popular symphony to be issued commercially. Interpretatively, the *Fourth* still has much to show any rival, with delicately pointed rhythms and easily flexible speeds that consistently sound idiomatic. He brings out the pure joy behind the inspiration, culminating in the child-heaven finale, performed with delicious jauntiness. The aptly boyish-sounding soloist, Desi Halban, is not well focused in the recording, but her voice is caught with more presence in the original fill-up, eight of Mahler's 'Youth' songs, *Aus der Jugendzeit*, with Walter accompanying on the piano. Recorded in a dry acoustic, Halban (daughter of the celebrated soprano, Selma Kurz) is made to sound a little edgy under pressure, but the latest transfer catches her voice freshly enough.

Walter's playing, however, is often rhythmically lumpy, not nearly as persuasive as his conducting. The closely balanced recording allows little dynamic range, with *pianissimos* eliminated and the high strings thin and peaky in the symphony. But the woodwind have lustre, and for its age it has reasonable body and clarity.

Walter followed up his recording of the *Fourth* with this account of the *Fifth*, another persuasive reading, marked by fine rhythmic pointing and natural expressiveness. It is transferred (evidently from the original 78s, not from tape) with a good body of sound, but again with a limited dynamic range. Even so, the celebrated *Adagietto* – taken much faster than has become customary – has an easy warmth, which makes one recognize it as idiomatic, naturally and unselfconsciously flexible in a song-like way. Mahler, one imagines, would have wanted it like this and might well have objected to the extra weight and depth which latter-day slow readings bring. The ensemble is not always perfect – as at the end of the finale – and the recording gives even more of an unwanted edge to the high violins; but this remains a classic reading that is welcome back in the catalogue.

Haitink's later (1992) Berlin Philharmonic recording of the *Fourth Symphony* is a warm, highly polished reading that can hardly be faulted, except that it rather misses the innocent freshness lying behind this of all Mahler's symphonies. In the slow movement this seems a poised rather than a rapt performance: very beautiful, but not as moving as it can be. The child-heaven finale too is smoother than usual, with Sylvia McNair the light and boyish soloist. The *Fifth* is also less than ideal: imposing, very expansive, especially the *Adagietto*, which is very slow, though offset by the bucolic flavour of the Scherzo, and the finale well controlled but somehow heavy-handed. Marvellous playing throughout, of course, and fine recording, but this Duo is not a top recommendation.

Symphony 4 (arr. for Chamber Orchestra by Erwin Stein, edited by Alexander Platt)

(N) *** Avie AV 2069. Royal, Manchester Camerata, Boyd

Erwin Stein transcribed Mahler's *Fourth Symphony* in 1920 at Schoenberg's request for use at a private concert, scoring for an ensemble of 15 players, plus soprano voice. This is not the original transcription (as the instrumental parts were lost), but an arrangement based on Stein's annotated copy of the full orchestral score, which has survived. The effect is extremely intimate, more like chamber music than symphonic music, with a greatly reduced dynamic range. This is emphasized by Douglas Boyd's performance here, relaxed, affectionate and beguiling, but totally undramatic, matched by the delightful simplicity of Kate Royal's vocal contribution to the finale.

Symphony 5 in C sharp min.

🔊 *** Decca 458 860-2. Concg. O, Chailly
*** EMI 5 57385-2. BPO, Rattle
*** DG 437 789-2. BPO, Abbado
⊕ **(M)** *** EMI (ADD) 5 66910-2 [566962]. New Philh. O, Barbirolli
(B) *** CfP 585 6222. RLPO, Mackerras
(B) *** DG (ADD) 439 429-2. BPO, Karajan
(BB) **(*) RCA (ADD) 74321 68011-2. Phd. O, Levine

Chailly excels himself in his strong, clear-sighted, but deeply felt reading of No. 5, with his concentration reflected in superlative playing from the Concertgebouw, caught with exceptional clarity in the full and brilliant Decca recording.

The beauty of Mahler's orchestration has rarely been conveyed so vividly, with the hushed intensity of the *Adagio* the more moving for its reticence, and with the joyful finale dazzling in its crisp detail. Other, more personal readings may be more distinctive, but none is more widely recommendable.

Taken from Sir Simon Rattle's historic first concert as music director of the Berlin Philharmonic in September 2002, his is also one of the outstanding recorded versions of Mahler's *Fifth Symphony* to have appeared recently, and some collectors may even prefer it to Chailly, superb though that is. One element which Rattle brings out more than his rivals is the exuberance of Mahler's writing. In this live recording one vividly registers the excitement of the occasion, with the players more freely expressive than they have generally been with their last two music directors, Herbert von Karajan and Claudio Abbado. Even the opening funeral march is more lyrical than usual, and from then onwards the joyfulness of Mahler's inspiration, the rhythmic spring, makes for exhilarating results. The emotional climax of the performance comes, as it should, in the great *Adagietto*, the penultimate movement in Mahler's five-movement scheme. Yet Rattle, looking at the evidence, treats it differently from most latter-day interpreters who make it expansively elegiac. By contrast he responds to it as love music, inspired by the composer's love for his young wife, Alma, with the music emerging tenderly, as though from another world. This above all is a songful vision full of tenderness, with phrasing affectionately moulded in spontaneous warmth.

Abbado's is also an outstanding version, recorded live in the Philharmonie, Berlin, with the dramatic tensions of a concert performance vividly captured. Abbado's view is clean-cut and taut, bringing out the high contrasts between movements, pointing rhythms not just precisely but with often-Viennese seductiveness. The great *Adagietto* is raptly done, wistful rather than openly romantic at a flowing tempo, and the *Wunderhorn* finale is at once refined and exuberant. With excellent sound, there are few versions to match this, presenting Abbado at his peak.

Barbirolli's famous analogue 1969 recording (made in Watford Town Hall) has now been splendidly remastered for EMI's 'Great Recordings of the Century' series and sounds fuller, clearer, more atmospheric than ever. On any count this is one of the greatest, most warmly affecting accounts ever committed to disc, expansive, yet concentrated in feeling: the *Adagietto* is very moving indeed. A classic version which many will prefer even to Abbado's newer digital account.

Mackerras in his well-paced reading sees the work as a whole, building each movement with total concentration. There is a thrilling culmination on the great brass chorale at the end, with polish allied to purposefulness. Barbirolli in his classic reading may find more of a tear-laden quality in the great *Adagietto*; but Mackerras, with fewer controversial points of interpretation and superb modern sound, makes an excellent alternative choice at bargain price.

Karajan's 1973 version makes a very welcome reissue on DG's Classikon label. This is one of the most beautiful and intense versions available, starting with a highly compelling account of the first movement which brings biting funeral-march rhythms. Karajan's characteristic emphasis on polish and refinement goes with sharpness of focus. This is a performance of stature and, with excellent sound, a genuine bargain.

Apart from a self-consciously slow account of the famous *Adagietto*, Levine directs a deeply perceptive and compelling performance, bringing out the glories of the Philadelphia Orchestra. The outer movements are beautifully paced and the 1977 recording has been transferred very successfully to CD, so this remains a distinctly recommendable budget version.

(i) *Symphony 5 in C sharp min.;* (ii) *Lieder und Gesänge aus der Jugendzeit*
(N) (BB) ((*))** Naxos mono 8.110896. (i) NYPO, Walter; (ii) Halban, Walter (piano)

This new transfer of Bruno Walter's pioneering 1947 recording of the *Fifth Symphony* is welcome, particularly as it comes with the *Lieder und Gesänge aus der Jugendzeit*, which Desi Halban recorded later the same year in Los Angeles, with Bruno Walter at the piano. Those who grew up with this set probably feel that it has never been surpassed in authenticity of feeling and emotional intensity. It is taut and concentrated: Walter takes 60 minutes 52 seconds, as opposed to the 75 minutes of Bernstein or 72 of Karajan. The Obert Thorn transfer is the best we have had so far.

Symphony 5; (i) *Das Lied von der Erde*
**(B) ** **EMI double forte (ADD/DDD) 5 74849-2 (2). LPO, Tennstedt, (i) with Baltsa, König

Tennstedt takes a ripe and measured view of Mahler's *Fifth* (recorded in 1978), and though his account of the lovely *Adagietto* lacks the fullest tenderness (starting with an intrusive balance for the harp), this is an outstanding interpretation, thoughtful on the one hand, impassioned and expressive on the other. The recording is warm and full. The coupling of *Das Lied von der Erde* is less successful. Though Tennstedt's interpretative insight is never in doubt, the tension behind the performance is relatively low, not helped by the recorded sound, which is lacking in bass and with a relatively narrow dynamic range. The moments of hushed intensity, of which there are many, notably in the long final *Abschied*, fail to create the necessary heart-stilling effect. In that the choice of Agnes Baltsa as mezzo soloist is in good measure to blame. Not only is her tone often made impure with pronounced vibrato, words are so heavily inflected that the oriental detachment implied in the poems is completely missing. For all the expressive weight of the mezzo songs, the singing should be poised if the full emotion is to be conveyed. Klaus König is a clear-toned Heldentenor, strained at times at the top but always well focused, though he too misses the Mahlerian magic. No texts are provided.

Symphony 6 in A min.
***** DG 445 835-2. VPO, Boulez
(B) * Sony (ADD) SBK 47654. Cleveland O, Szell
**(M) **(*) Sony (ADD) SMK 60208. NYPO, Bernstein
(B) * Naxos 8.550529 (2). Polish Nat. RSO (Katowice), Wit
(B) * Double Decca (IMS) (ADD) 444 871-2 (2). Concg. O, Chailly – ZEMLINSKY: *Maeterlinck Lieder* ***
**(***) Testament mono SBT 1342. BPO, Barbirolli
**(M) **(*) Decca (ADD) 425 040-2. Chicago SO, Solti
(B) **(*) EMI double forte (ADD) 5 69349-2. New Philh. O, Barbirolli – R. STRAUSS: *Ein Heldenleben* *
**(M) **(*) Telarc CD 80444. Atlanta SO, Levi

Symphony 6; (i) *Kindertotenlieder; 5 Rückert Lieder*
☛ (M) * DG (ADD) 457 716-2 (2). BPO, Karajan, (i) with Ludwig

With superlative playing from the Berlin Philharmonic, Karajan's reading of the *Sixth* is a revelation, above all in the slow movement, which emerges as one of the greatest of Mahler's slow movements. Though the outer movements firmly stamp this as one of the darkest of the Mahler symphonies, in Karajan's reading their sharp focus makes them both compelling and refreshing. The fine, mid-1970s DG recording, with its wide dynamic, adds enormously to the impact. Christa Ludwig's moving account of the *Kindertotenlieder* has been added to the previously coupled *Rückert Lieder*: fine, positive performances with comparative distinction and refinement in the orchestral playing.

Boulez conducts a performance of the most enigmatic symphony which in its power and sharpness of focus transcends almost any rival. Boulez's control of speeds is masterful, never rushed, even though this is a performance squeezed on to a single disc, and the slow movement brings hushed, ravishingly beautiful playing of a refinement it would be hard to match. The finale is rugged and weighty, with crisp pointing of rhythms, making this an outstanding recommendation alongside Karajan who, on two discs, also includes Christa Ludwig's five *Rückert Lieder*. Though R. L. found this a performance observed rather than felt at white heat, E. G. was totally involved.

Szell's powerful outer movements are masterfully shaped and unerringly paced, with the second-movement Scherzo beautifully sprung to bring out the grotesquerie. The *Andante moderato* then brings a uniquely delicate and moving account, hauntingly wistful, tender without a hint of sentimentality. The CD transfer gives a fuller, more atmospheric impression of what the orchestra sounded like in Severance Hall, Cleveland, than most of the studio recordings of the time. At budget price, squeezed on to a single disc, this is buried treasure and a fine counterpart to Szell's classic reading of Mahler's *Fourth*.

It is good that Sony have now separated Bernstein's enormously gripping NYPO account of the *Sixth* from the *Eighth* (see below). Now on a single, mid-priced disc it is highly competitive. The remastering has further improved the sound; although the close balance remains a drawback, actual sounds are impressive, and the performance itself is very compelling indeed.

The excellent quality of the Katowice Orchestra of Polish Radio is impressively demonstrated in all four movements of this difficult symphony. The ensemble can hardly be faulted, and the full, atmospheric recording enhances that quality with string-sound that is fresh and radiant. Wit conducts a spacious performance, clean and well sprung, with the varying moods sharply contrasted. On two full discs it becomes less of a super-bargain than some Naxos issues, but it stands comparison with any rival.

Chailly's version with the Concertgebouw offers brilliant playing and spectacular sound in a reading remarkable for its broad, rugged approach in the outer movements. There is relentlessness in the slow speed for the first movement, with expressive warmth giving way to a square purposefulness, tense and effective. The third movement brings a comparably simple, direct approach at a genuine flowing *Andante*. In its open songfulness it rouses *Wunderhorn* echoes. Anyone fancying the unexpected but attractive Zemlinsky coupling need not hesitate.

Testament here follows up its Barbirolli version of Mahler's *Second* with his 1966 account of the enigmatic *Sixth Symphony* in another radio recording, again with the Berlin Philharmonic in superb form. It is a reading markedly faster than Barbirolli's studio recording of the following year, and it builds to a full-blooded account of the long finale, bringing out its fantasy as well as its power. The mono sound cannot compare with that of the studio version (EMI 5 69349-2), but the impact of the whole is comparably great.

Solti draws stunning playing from the Chicago orchestra. The electric excitement confirms this, with brilliant, immediate but atmospheric sound. Solti's rather extrovert approach is here at its most impressive. His fast tempi may mean that he misses some of the deeper emotions, and the added brightness of the CD transfer perhaps emphasizes this, but it is still a very convincing and involving performance.

Barbirolli gives a characteristically expansive account with the New Philharmonic Orchestra, and there are many of the same fine qualities as in his version of the Fifth, recorded with the same orchestra a year later. But, particularly in the first movement, the slow tempo is allowed to drag a little, so that tension falls. Such wavering of concentration will not trouble everyone, but the 1967 Kingsway Hall recording has now lost some of its bloom. Moreover there is nothing like the same illusion of a live Barbirolli performance as there is with the earlier recording on Testament. The pairing with Ein Heldenleben has a superior CD transfer.

By dint of omitting the exposition repeat in the first movement Yoel Levi's mid-priced version is squeezed on to a single disc, despite an exceptionally spacious reading of the finale. His is generally an extrovert approach to Mahler, leading occasionally to heaviness, though with finely disciplined playing from the Atlanta orchestra, vividly recorded.

Symphony 7 in E min.

☞ (M) *** Decca (ADD) 425 041-2. Chicago SO, Solti

(M) *** DG 445 513-2. Chicago SO, Abbado

(N) *** Decca 444 446-2 (2). Concg. O, Chailly (with DIEPENBROCK: Im grossen Schweigen ***)

*** RCA 09026 63510-2 (2). LSO, Tilson Thomas

**(*) Telarc 2CD 80514 (2). Atlanta SO, Levi

**(*) EMI 7 54344-2. CBSO, Rattle

(B) **(*) Sony SB2K 89785 (2). VPO, Maazel

(BB) **(*) Naxos 8.550531. Polish Nat. RSO, Halász

In interpretation, Solti's version is as successful as his fine account of the Sixth Symphony, extrovert in display but full of dark implications. The tempi tend to be challengingly fast – at the very opening, for example, and in the Scherzo (where Solti is mercurial) and in the finale (where his energy carries shock-waves in its trail). The second Nachtmusik is enchantingly seductive, and throughout the orchestra plays superlatively. This is one of Solti's finest Mahler records, and the recording is brilliant and full – the CD transfer increases the brightness.

Abbado's command of Mahlerian characterization has never been more tellingly displayed than in this most problematic of the symphonies; even in the loosely bound finale Abbado unerringly draws the threads together. The precision and polish of the Chicago orchestra go with total commitment, and the recording is one of the finest DG has made with this orchestra.

Chailly's version, superbly played and recorded, has speeds on the slow side firmly maintained and with the lyrical element brought out. Both of the Nachtmusik movements are treated lightly, with a touch of irony conveyed in the first. The central Scherzo is turned into a nightmare fantasy, though the long Rondo finale lacks a little in tension. The two-disc

set brings as a substantial bonus a piece by Mahler's friend and contemporary, Alphons Diepenbrock.

Michael Tilson Thomas conducts a strong, purposeful reading of the Seventh, with polished and refined playing from the LSO and recording to match. His terracing of textures and dynamics is perfectly judged. The result may be less atmospheric and evocative than in some readings, but the relative coolness of the second Nachtmusik, for example, makes one appreciate the work the more keenly for its symphonic qualities. Although the fragmentary structure of the finale is in no way disguised, the pointedness of the playing holds it firmly together. A strong contender in a hotly competitive field.

Yoel Levi conducts a reading of the Seventh which gains in strength and purpose as it progresses. If the very slow tempo for the first movement makes it seem a degree subdued, the strong colouring of later movements, as in the nightmare quality he gives to the central Scherzo, makes an increasingly characterful impression, though the relatively fast tempo for the second Nachtmusik does not quite avoid a jog-trot. The sound is close and brilliant, overpowering in big tuttis, if not ideally clear on detail.

Rattle, as ever, proves a sensitive and persuasive Mahlerian in this most equivocal Mahler symphony. He made this recording live in The Maltings at Snape, disappointed with an earlier, studio version, which he did not want to have issued. Sadly, live or not, this performance does not have the biting tension and thrust that makes Rattle's recording of the Second Symphony so compelling, and the sound is not as full. The first movement suffers most, and the finale is the most successful. But as a single-disc version of the symphony – when most other versions take two CDs – this is still well worth considering.

Maazel's account comes from his Mahler cycle of the early 1990s. He always works well with the Vienna Philharmonic and this performance, very well played and spacious in conception, is no exception. The recording too is very good. However the effect is rather studio-bound and there is not the spontaneous feeling of a live occasion.

Very well played and treated to refined and well-balanced digital recording, the Naxos version offers excellent value on a single disc at super-bargain price. With well-chosen speeds, often brisk but unhurried, with crisp ensemble and good rhythmic point, the only snag is that, by the standards of the finest versions, it is undercharacterized, lacking both flamboyance and tragic weight. Even there one has an advantage in the haunting melody of the second Nachtmusik, which is the more moving for being treated in a restrained way.

Symphony 8 (Symphony of 1000)

☞ (M) *** Decca (ADD) 460 972-2. Harper, Popp, Augér, Minton, Watts, Kollo, Shirley-Quirk, Talvela, V. Boys' Ch., V. State Op. Ch. & Singverein, Chicago SO, Solti

(N) *** EMI 5 57945-2. Brewer, Isokoski, Banse, Rammert, Henschel, Villars, Wilson-Johnson, Relyea, L. Symphony Ch., CBSO Ch., Youth Ch. & O, Rattle

● (M) *** DG 476 2198. Studer, Blasi, Jo, Lewis, Meier, Nagai, Allen, Sotin, Southend Boys' Ch., Philh. Ch. & O, Sinopoli

(N) *** Decca 467 324-2. Eaglen, Schwarnewilms, Ziezak, Fulgoni, Larsson, Heppner, Mattri, Rootering, St Bavo's Cathedral Boys' Ch., Breda Sacraments Ch., Prague Philharmonic Ch., Netherlands R. Ch., Concg. O, Chailly

(B) *** Sony (ADD) SBK 48281. Robinson, Marshall, Heichele, Wenkel, Laurich, Walker, Stilwell, Estes, Frankfurt Kantorei, Singakademie, Limburger Boys' Ch., Op. & Museum O, Gielen

**(*) BBC (ADD) BBCL 4002-7. Barker, Hatt, Giebel, Meyer, Watts, Neate, Orda, Van Mill, BBC Ch. and Choral Soc., Goldsmith Ch. Union, Hampstead Ch. Soc., Emanuel School Boys' Ch., Orpington Junior Singers, LSO, Horenstein

(N) **(*) HM **SACD** 801858/59 (2). Greenberg, Dawson, Matthews, Koch, Manistina, Gambill, Roth, Rootering, Berlin R. Ch., MDR R. Ch, Windsbacher Children's Ch., Deutsches SO, Nagano

**(*) DG (IMS) 445 843-2 (2). Studer, McNair, Rost, Von Otter, Lang, Seiffert, Terfel, Rootering, Tölz Boys' Ch., Berlin R. & Prague Philharmonic Ch., BPO, Abbado

(N) (B) ** Sony (ADD) 517493-2 (2). Spoorenberg, G. Jones, Reynolds, Procter, Mitchinson, Ruzdjak, McIntyre, Leeds Festival Ch., Orpington Junior Singers, Finchley Children's Music Group, LSO, Bernstein (with *Kindertotenlieder*: J. Baker, Israel PO)

Solti's magnificent analogue version, recorded in Vienna, has the added advantage of being available on a single CD – now reissued in the Decca Legends series – which makes a strong first choice.

Recorded live in Symphony Hall, Birmingham, in June 2004, Rattle completes his Mahler symphony cycle with a powerful, urgent reading of the *Symphony of a Thousand*. The performance gains enormously from the liveness of the occasion, with high-voltage electricity generated from first to last. Added to that, his relatively fast tempi for the long expanses of the second movement, setting Goethe, mean that, as with Solti, the whole work is on a single disc, an obvious advantage. The soloists are an excellent team, headed by the superb American soprano Christine Brewer, and the massed choruses match the orchestra in the bite and power of their singing, leading up to a thrilling account of the final sequence. The recording is not quite as full or open in atmosphere as some rivals, but that never masks the power of the performance.

Giuseppe Sinopoli crowns his Mahler cycle with the Philharmonia in a ripely passionate account of this most extravagant of the series, recorded with a richness and body that outshine any digital rival. In vividness of atmosphere it is matched only by Solti's magnificent analogue version, recorded in Vienna (see above). Sinopoli, highly analytical in his methods and flexible in his approach to speed, here conveys a warmth of expression that brings joyful exuberance to the great outburst of the opening *Veni creator spiritus*. It builds into one of the most thrilling accounts ever, helped by a superb team of soloists and incandescent choral singing, recorded with fine weight and body. In the long second movement and its setting of the closing scene of *Faust*, Sinopoli's approach is almost operatic in its dramatic flair, magnetically leading from one section to another, with each of the soloists characterizing strongly. As in the first movement, the chorus sings with fine control and incandescent tone, from the hypnotic first entry through to a thrilling final crescendo on '*Alles vergängliche*'. It is now available at midprice on one CD, being part of Universal's 'Penguin ❂ Collection'.

Though it features multiple choirs and spectacular recording, Chailly's version is distinctive for underplaying the grandeur of the opening movement, *Veni creator spiritus*. He has

deliberately sought to make the long second movement with its Faust setting – a sequence of dramatic scenes culminating in the chorus, *Alles vergängliche* – the true climax of the work. The team of soloists is outstanding, with the recording vividly catching the detail and perspectives of the massive ensemble.

Recorded live at the opening of the Alte Oper in Frankfurt in August 1981, Gielen's version offers a direct, fresh reading, full of atmosphere, in which brisk speeds allow ample weight. The analogue recording is less full than some, but it is naturally balanced with plenty of presence, if with brass a little distant. The chorus sings with heartfelt intensity, and the soloists make a distinguished team, except that the ringing Heldentenor, Mallory Walker, develops a beat in the voice under stress as Dr Marianus. On a single disc at budget price in Sony's Essential Classics series, it makes an outstanding bargain.

Horenstein's reading conveys a thrilling sense of occasion, and though it does not challenge some of the later commercial recordings, it is the feeling that they were engaged in something special that makes this so memorable. Though audience noises are intrusive at times, the atmosphere is vividly caught, with the conductor's unforced, firmly paced reading magnetic from beginning to end, always natural, never exaggerated. Other readings may have a higher voltage or present a more distinctive view, but this has a special place in the Mahler archive. The sound the BBC engineers get from the Festival Hall holds up very well. The second disc includes a conversation between Horenstein and the critic Alan Blyth.

The great asset of Nagano's Berlin version for Harmonia Mundi is the quality of sound, which is full and open, with fine clarity and a sense of presence in the weightiest passages. This is a studio performance and, with relatively spacious speeds, particularly in the long second movement, the tension cannot match that of the finest versions. The opening of the second movement, for example, lacks the poignancy and chill which Rattle, among others, conveys, and the great violin melody, *Adagissimo*, introducing the solo of *Una Poenitentium*, lacks the ecstasy Rattle finds, while the tenor, Robert Gambill, as Dr Marianus, is not always steady. A good version nevertheless, if lacking the ultimate vision.

Claudio Abbado's 1994 recording, keenly analytical and precisely balanced, fails to capture the very quality one would expect in a live account: a sense of atmosphere. Except in the final chorus, *Alles vergängliche*, where the tension and slow momentum are irresistible, making a magnificent climax, this is too often a detached-sounding reading, clear and transparent rather than intense, relating the music more than usual to Mahler's *Knaben Wunderhorn* inspirations.

Bernstein recorded Mahler's epic *Symphony of a Thousand* at Walthamstow Town Hall in 1966, in the days immediately following a hazard-filled live performance at the Royal Albert Hall, in which emergency measures had to be taken to reinforce the choral strength. You would hardly know that from this fine recorded performance, though the hazards still left their mark. One of them was entirely to the good, the last-minute inclusion of John Mitchinson among the soloists, following his predecessor's indisposition. The Orpington Junior Singers too did valiant work in taking on more than their share of the children's choral music. In the final recorded account the Leeds Festival Chorus is strongly stiffened with professional choristers. The unfortunate point undermining much of the superb achievement of the performance is the closeness of sound and resulting lack of atmosphere in the recording quality. This of all symphonies needs spacious, reverberant sound, and here one seems to be among the very performers.

Dame Janet Baker made her 1974 recording of *Kindertotenlieder* after a sequence of performances in Israel with Bernstein conducting. The contrasts with her much earlier, EMI version are fascinating, the performance under Barbirolli generally more tender and beautiful, the one under Bernstein tougher and darker. The closeness of the recording sometimes exaggerates a slight beat in Dame Janet's voice, never there before, but it is a gloriously involving performance. In the fifth song the storm music is wonderfully sharp and biting, with the cradle-song resolution beautifully poised and steady. However, the dry closeness of the Israel recording prevents an ideally atmospheric ambience. Full texts and translations are included for both works.

Symphony 9 in D min.

(N) *** DG 471 624-2. BPO, Abbado

(M) *** DG 474 537-2. BPO, Karajan

*** DG (IMS) 439 024-2 (2). BPO, Karajan

*** EMI 5 56580-2 (2). VPO, Rattle – R. STRAUSS:
   Metamorphosen ***

*** DG (IMS) (ADD) 435 378-2. BPO, Bernstein

(M) *** EMI (ADD) 5 67925-2 [567926]. BPO, Barbirolli

(N) *** Decca **SACD** 475 6191 (2). Concg. O, Chailly

(M) *** Sony (ADD) SMK 60597. NYPO, Bernstein

(M) *** EMI (ADD) 5 67036-2 (2). New Philh. O, Klemperer –
   R. STRAUSS: *Metamorphosen;* WAGNER: *Siegfried Idyll* ***

(N) **(*) San Francisco SO 821936-0007-2 (2). San Francisco SO, Tilson Thomas

(B) **(*) Sony SB2K 89786 (2). VPO, Maazel

(B) (***) Dutton Lab. mono CDBP 9708. VPO, Walter

(N) **(BB)** ** Warner Apex 2564 62034-2. NYPO, Masur

Symphony 9 (with separate talk by the conductor on performing and listening to the symphony)

(M) **(*) Telarc 3CD 80527 (3 for cost of 1). Philh. O, Zander

Symphony 9; Symphony 10: Adagio

(M) *** Regis 2033 (2). Mahler-Jugend O or European Community Youth O, Judd

(B) *** EMI double forte (ADD) 5 75169-2 (2). LPO, Tennstedt

Symphony 9; (i) Kindertotenlieder; 5 Rückert Lieder

(B) *** DG Double (ADD) 453 040-2 (2). BPO, Karajan; (i) with Ludwig

Symphony 9; (i) Des Knaben Wunderhorn: excerpts: Das irdische Leben; Rheinlegendchen; Verlor'ne Müh; Wo die schönen Trompeten blasen. Lieder eines fahrenden Gesellen

(B) **(*) Double Decca (ADD/DDD) 473 274-2. Chicago SO, Solti, (i) with Minton

Symphony 9; (i) Das Lied von der Erde

(B) *** Ph. Duo (ADD) 462 299-2 (2). Concg. O, Haitink, (i) with Baker, King

Claudio Abbado had just recovered from a life-threatening illness when he made his live recording of Mahler's *Ninth*, far transcending not just his own earlier, Vienna version but almost every other current rival. Power and emotional warmth go with richness and refinement in the playing of the Berlin Philharmonic, with the great spans of the two outer movements firmly held together at easy-flowing speeds, allowing the whole work to be fitted on a single disc. The middle two movements are winningly pointed, and the *Adagio finale*, magnetic from first to last, has a rare tenderness, the expression of a composer doomed to die. The nearest rival is Karajan's live account with the same orchestra, but the extra weight of the 2002 sound easily outshines that earlier, digital recording, fine as it was, reinforcing the emotional thrust of Abbado's performance.

Fine as Karajan's other Mahler recordings have been, his two accounts of the *Ninth* transcend them. In the earlier, analogue version (453 040-2) it is the combination of richness and concentration in the outer movements that makes for a reading of the deepest intensity, while in the middle two movements there is point and humour as well as refinement and polish. Helped by full, spacious recording, the sudden *pianissimos* that mark both movements have an ear-pricking realism such as one rarely experiences on record, and the unusually broad tempi are superbly controlled. In the finale Karajan is not just noble and stoic; he finds the bite of passion as well, sharply set against stillness and repose.

Within two years Karajan went on to record the work even more compulsively at live performances in Berlin. The major difference in that later recording (474 537-2) is that there is a new, glowing optimism in the finale, rejecting any Mahlerian death-wish and making it a supreme achievement. The 'original-image' bit-processing has added to the projection, but the strings have plenty of body. Yet the earlier (1980) analogue performance makes a remarkable bargain alternative, reissued as a DG Double and costing half as much as the later, digital recording. Moreover the performances of the *Kindertotenlieder* and *Rückert Lieder* have a distinction and refinement of playing which stand out above all.

Rattle's reading, recorded live in the Musikverein in Vienna, consistently brings out the deeper qualities in No. 9, the hushed, tender intensity of the outer movements, erupting in monumental climaxes with dynamic contrast matched by emotional power. Equally the central movements are just as sharply characterized, with the fun and wit behind the writing conveyed with winning lightness, aptly Viennese. The sound is not as full or immediate as in some versions, but the beauty and subtlety of the Vienna Philharmonic's playing come over vividly. Strauss's *Metamorphosen* makes an excellent fill-up.

Tennstedt's *Ninth* is a performance of warmth and distinction, underlining nobility rather than any neurotic tension, so that the outer movements, spaciously drawn, have architectural grandeur. The second movement is gently done, and the third, crisp and alert, lacks just a little in adrenalin. The playing is excellent and the 1979 Abbey Road recording is full and well focused, with good detail. The *Adagio* from the *Tenth* makes an acceptable fill-up, although here the sound is slightly less sharply detailed. However, Tennstedt's admirers will surely count this good value.

Haitink, too, is at his very finest in Mahler's *Ninth*, and the last movement, with its slow expanses of melody, reveals a unique concentration. Unlike most other conductors he maintains his intensely slow tempo from beginning to end. This is a great performance, beautifully recorded at the end of the 1960s, and this will be for many Mahlerians a primary recommendation, particularly as it now comes generously recoupled in Duo format with Haitink's famous set of *Das Lied von der Erde* with Baker and King.

Bernstein's Berlin version of Mahler's *Ninth*, made live in 1979, was the solitary occasion when he was permitted to conduct Karajan's own orchestra, and the response is electric, with playing not only radiant and refined but also deeply expressive in direct response to the conductor. Highly spontaneous, with measured speeds superbly sustained in a tautly concentrated reading, Bernstein conveys a comparably hushed inner quality.

Barbirolli greatly impressed the Berliners with his Mahler performances live, and this recording reflects the players' warmth of response. He opted to record the slow and intense finale before the rest, and the beauty of the playing makes it a fitting culmination. The other movements are strong and alert too, and the sound remains full and atmospheric, though now even more clearly defined in its current remastering for reissue as one of EMI's 'Great Recordings of the Century'. An unquestionable bargain.

The great glory of the Chailly version is the spectacular SACD recording, which is very full-bodied and almost larger than life, with the widest dynamic range. The playing of the Royal Concertgebouw is spectacular too, with details clearly in place and rhythms crisp and sharp in the middle two movements. If, next to the finest live recordings, this studio account sounds a degree too metrical in the massive outer movements, the power of the work has never come over with greater impact.

Bernstein's New York Ninth – a lucky symphony on record – is undoubtedly also a great performance. Here Bernstein's sense of urgency has its maximum impact, though in the finale he does not quite achieve the visionary intensity of his later recording for DG with the Berlin Philharmonic. The recording, made in the Avery Fisher Hall at the same time as his equally successful Seventh, is forwardly balanced but has plenty of body.

Klemperer's refusal to languish pays tribute to his spiritual defiance, and the physical power is underlined when the sound is full-bodied and firmly focused. The sublimity of the finale comes out the more intensely, with overt expressiveness held in check and deep emotion implied rather than made explicit. Now recoupled both with the Strauss Metamorphosen and with Wagner's Siegfried Idyll, this is one of the more important reissues in EMI's 'Klemperer Legacy'.

Michael Tilson Thomas's reading with the San Francisco Symphony on the orchestra's own label is refined and lyrical, yet never lacks power. This is a live recording, yet the precision of the playing and the very steady speeds adopted seem to suggest a studio recording. Full-ranging, open sound.

Zander is a natural Mahlerian, and his is a powerful, red-bloodedly passionate, yet at times relatively intimate view of this visionary symphony. The concentration of the performance is immensely compelling throughout, with the hushed intensity of the final Adagio superbly caught, enhanced by an exceptionally spacious tempo, very well sustained. That said, while the orchestra is given great presence, the sound lacks full body as recorded in the difficult acoustic of the Barbican Hall. The illuminating and thoughtful extended talk on the third disc is a distinct bonus. The three discs come for the cost of one and, apart from the normal documentation, there is a folded facsimile of the first page of Mahler's score, with the conductor's markings.

On its original, full-priced issue, Maazel's superbly controlled Vienna version was coupled with a comparably powerful reading of the opening Adagio of the Tenth. Without it the second of the two discs only plays for just over 25 minutes, which all but negates the bargain aspect of this reissue! However, those prepared to accept this short measure will find the Ninth very impresssive. Maazel may not have quite the gravity and supreme control that mark the very finest versions – Karajan's for example – but with glorious

playing from the Vienna strings and unexaggerated speeds it is hard to fault him on any point. Though some may miss an element of temperament, this is one of the more satisfying of his mid-1980s Mahler series. It is very well recorded, although the transfer of the spectacular sound-quality to CD does bring a feeling in the climaxes that the microphones were very near the orchestra.

Solti's digital version of the Ninth Symphony, presented in brilliantly rich and forward sound, conveys the power of the piece with total conviction. What it lacks, especially in the outer movements, is a sense of mystery, and Solti is short on charm too in the central movements, which should present a necessary contrast. His earlier version with the LSO was warmer and more spontaneous-sounding, with the recording more naturally balanced. However, this is coupled with Yvonne Minton's colourful excerpts from Des Knaben Wunderhorn and her outstandingly successful account of the Wayfaring Lad cycle. They are impressive accounts from the early 1970s in very full, vintage Decca sound. Texts and translations are included.

Judd conducts the brilliant young players of the Mahler-Jugend Orchestra in a deeply moving account of the Ninth, recorded live in Bratislava in April 1990. With recording of spectacular range and vividness, this makes one of the most appealing of all versions. The searing emotional commitment of the players comes out consistently, and no allowance whatever need be made on technical grounds for their youth. The performance of the Adagio from the Tenth is not quite so distinguished, though warmly satisfying; it was recorded in August 1987 by the rival band from EEC countries, the European Community Youth Orchestra.

Bruno Walter's 1938 version with the Vienna Philharmonic was the first recording of this symphony ever issued. The opening is not promising, with coughing very obtrusive; but then, with the atmosphere of the Musikvereinsaal caught more vividly than in most modern recordings, the magnetism of Walter becomes irresistible in music which he was the first ever to perform. Ensemble is often scrappy in the first movement, but intensity is unaffected; even at its flowing speed, the finale brings warmth and repose with no feeling of haste. The new Dutton transfer (transferred direct from 78-r.p.m. shellac discs) can do little about the audience noises, but the sound-balance is further enhanced over the EMI transfer (7 63029-2), and the last movement in particular offers amazingly natural and believable string-sound.

Masur's New York version, recorded live in 1995, makes a good bargain on a single Apex disc. The opening in this live recording may sound almost casual, and Masur consistently takes an objective view of the work, less emotional than usual and missing the visionary quality of the writing, but the playing and recording are first rate.

Symphony 10 (incomplete); Andante-Adagio; Purgatorio
(*) Sony (ADD) **SACD SS 89415. Cleveland O, Szell –
  STRAVINSKY: Firebird Suite; WALTON: Partita ***

As we know, Mahler died leaving the sketches for his Tenth Symphony incomplete. It is now almost normal procedure to perform the work in the revised performance edition of Deryck Cooke – see below. But it is useful to have an outstanding performance of the two movements Mahler actually left in score. Szell and his Cleveland Orchestra (at their peak in 1958) play with passion and they are stylish too. The recording, enhanced in this SACD remastering, is full and rich; the only snag is the absence of pianissimos, caused by the close balance.

Symphony 10 in F sharp (Unfinished) (revised performing edition by Deryck Cooke)

⏻— *** EMI 5 56972-2. BPO, Rattle

(B) **(*) CfP 585 9012. Bournemouth SO, Rattle

In 1980, at the beginning of his recording career, Simon Rattle recorded this inspired realization of Mahler's five-movement concept. With the Bournemouth Symphony Orchestra, that remains an electrifying account, weightily recorded (EMI 7 54406-2), but his new version with the Berlin Philharmonic, recorded live, transcends it in almost every way. It is not only the extra refinement of the Berliners but also the extra detail that Rattle brings out in almost every phrase that goes with an even greater concentration. His interpretation remains broadly the same, though the slow outer movements are a shade more spacious than previously, with the finale and its brutal hammer blows – inspired by a funeral procession heard from afar – becoming a degree more consolatory than before, conveying hope after death. The contrast of the middle movements with their *Wunderhorn* echoes is also more strongly characterized.

With a digital recording of outstanding quality, Simon Rattle's vivid and compelling reading of the Cooke performing edition did much to convince that a remarkable revelation of Mahler's intentions was achieved in this painstaking reconstruction. The Bournemouth orchestra plays with dedication (marred only by the occasional lack of fullness in the strings) and this recording makes for an excellent and genuine bargain.

Symphony 10 in F sharp (revised performing edition by Joe Wheeler)

(BB) **(*) Naxos 8.554811. Polish Nat. RSO, Olsen

Simultaneously with Deryck Cooke, Joe Wheeler in the 1950s was producing his performing edition of Mahler's unfinished *Tenth Symphony*. He uses simpler, sparer scoring, which – so it is argued – is closer to Mahler's practice in his last works. Whatever the arguments, this recording demonstrates that the result sounds far less like genuine Mahler than the Cooke version, though the rugged strength of the full five-movement structure is convincingly brought out in this well-rehearsed and warmly recorded account.

VOCAL MUSIC

Kindertotenlieder

(M) (**) Decca mono (IMS) 425 995-2. Ferrier, Concg. O., Klemperer – BRAHMS: *Liebeslieder Waltzes* (***)

The Ferrier version with Klemperer is a live recording taken from a broadcast in July 1951, some two years after her EMI recording with Bruno Walter. Though the voice is caught vividly and the richness of her interpretation has, if anything, intensified, the surface-hiss is daunting. Unusually coupled with the Brahms in which Ferrier's role is only incidental.

(i) *Kindertotenlieder; Des Knaben Wunderhorn: Des Antonius von Padua Fischpredigt; Das irdische Leben; Urlicht;* (ii) *Das klagende Lied;* (i) *Lieder eines fahrenden Gesellen; 5 Rückert Lieder*

(B) *** Double Decca 473 725-2 (2). (i) Fassbaender, Berlin Deutsche SO; (ii) Dunn, Baur, Hollweg, Schmidt, Düsseldorf State Musikverein, Berlin RSO; Chailly

Fassbaender gives fearless, vividly characterized performances of *Kindertotenlieder*, the *Lieder eines fahrenden Gesellen*, the *Five Rückert Lieder*, and three songs from *Des Knaben Wunderhorn*. In the latter, *Urlicht* (usually heard as part of *Symphony No. 2*) finds her voice not as even as usual, and the orchestra slacker than elsewhere, but otherwise these are undoubtedly very fine performances. The strength of Chailly's *Das klagende Lied* lies with the splendid singing of the Düsseldorf choir and the demonstration-worthy Decca recording, full of presence. While not quite upstaging Rattle in revealing the music's imaginative detail, Chailly pulls one special trick out of the hat in *Waldmärchen* by using a boy alto (Markus Baur) to represent the voice from the grave, a tellingly sepulchral effect. Full texts and translations are provided, and this makes an impressive and generous Double Decca anthology.

Kindertotenlieder; Lieder eines fahrenden Gesellen

(M) ** Decca (ADD) 468 486-2. Flagstad, VPO, Boult –
WAGNER: *Wesendonck Lieder, etc.* ***

Flagstad sings masterfully in these two most appealing of Mahler's orchestral cycles, but she was unable to relax into the deeper, more intimate expressiveness that the works really require. The voice is magnificent, the approach always firmly musical (helped by Sir Adrian's splendid accompaniment), but this recording is recommendable for the singer rather than for the way the music is presented. The coupled *Wesendonck Lieder*, however, offers repertoire far more suited to her special artistry. The recording (late-1950s vintage) re-emerges with remarkable freshness.

Kindertotenlieder; Lieder eines fahrenden Gesellen; Lieder und Gesänge: 1, 3, 5, 10–13; 5 Rückert Lieder

(N) *** Hyp. CDA 67392. Gentz, Vignoles

Stephan Gentz gives sensitive, finely detailed readings of Mahler's three most popular cycles in their piano versions, adding for good measure seven of Mahler's Youth songs, *Lieder und Gesange*. It says much for Roger Vignoles's accompaniments that he finds such fantasy in the piano writing, with the sparer textures of the accompaniments for *Kindertotenlieder* made to reflect the pain of bereavement in their bareness. Though this comes in direct competition with Fischer-Dieskau's two-disc collection with Barenboim on EMI (see below), Gentz and Vignoles hold their own with their more vividly recorded, lighter, more delicate performances.

(i) *Kindertotenlieder; Lieder eines fahrenden Gesellen;* (ii) *5 Rückert Lieder*

⏻— ✿ (M) *** EMI (ADD) 5 66981-2 [5669962]. Baker, Hallé or New Philh. O, Barbirolli

(BB) **(*) Naxos 8.554156. Greevy, Nat. SO of Ireland, with (i) Fürst; (ii) Decker

(N) ** DG 477 5329. (i) Von Otter; (ii) Quasthoff; (iii) Urmana; VPO, Boulez

Dame Janet Baker's collaboration with Barbirolli represents the affectionate approach to Mahler at its warmest: intensely beautiful, full of breathtaking moments. The spontaneous feeling of soloist and conductor for this music comes over as in a live performance and brings out the tenderness to a unique degree. An indispensable CD.

Bernadette Greevy uses her opulent mezzo, firm and even, to bring out the lyrical beauty of Mahler's writing in all three of these orchestral song-cycles. She may lack a degree of vitality in such a song as the second of the *Wayfaring Lad* cycle, the song that gave Mahler his first theme in his *First*

Symphony, but her poise in such a great song as the Rückert setting, *Ich bin der Welt abhanden gekommen*, is most satisfying, readily compensating for any lack of emotional weight compared with the finest interpretations. The Irish National Symphony Orchestra play with rich, velvety tone in every section, helped by the warmly atmospheric recording, made in the National Concert Hall in Dublin.

On DG, instead of having the same soloist in all three works, Pierre Boulez has chosen three artists, all outstanding, who in their different ways bring out the contrasting character of each cycle: the clear-toned baritone Thomas Quasthoff in the *Wayfaring Lad* songs, the velvety soprano Violeta Urmana for the *Rückert Lieder* and the ever-perceptive mezzo Anne Sofie von Otter for the darkest of the three cycles on the death of children. The precision and clarity of these performances are exceptional, with each phrase meticulously pointed and with each singer shading tone as subtly as Boulez moulds the playing of the Vienna Philharmonic's superb soloists. Contrasts are sharply drawn, yet there is a shortage of Mahlerian warmth, with so much calculation undermining a sense of spontaneity. One admires without getting involved.

(i) *Kindertotenlieder*; (ii) *Lieder eines fahrenden Gesellen*; (iii) *Des Knaben Wunderhorn: Das irdisch Leben; Wo die schönen Trompeten blasen. Rückert Lieder: Ich atmet' einen linden Duft; Ich bin der Welt abhanden gekommen; Um Mitternacht*

(BB) *** EMI Encore (ADD) 5 74738-2. Ludwig, Philh. O; (i) Vandernoot; (ii) Boult; (iii) Klemperer

Here Ludwig's singing is intensely poetic and the Kingsway Hall recording gloriously atmospheric. In the two cycles, dating from 1958, her voice is in its early prime and equally rich. Other versions may find a deeper response to the words, but the freshness of the singing here gives much pleasure. It is a pity texts and translations are omitted, but this disc is well worth its modest price.

Kindertotenlieder; 3 Rückert Lieder: Ich atmet' einen linden Duft; Ich bin der Welt abhanden gekommen; Um Mitternacht

⊕━ ✹ (BB) (***) Regis mono RRC 1153. Ferrier, VPO, Walter – BRAHMS: *Vier ernste Gesang*; etc. (***)

Kathleen Ferrier's radiant *Kindertotenlieder* (from 1949) are wonderfully moving, and the three *Rückert Lieder* from 1952, heartfelt and monumental, are magically intense, with Bruno Walter and the Vienna Philharmonic Orchestra adding a special affectionate glow to the music-making. Indeed, the orchestra sounds far better here than on the original Decca LPs. These two artists worked wonderfully well together and this Regis coupling, transferred warmly and smoothly, is a very real bargain.

Das klagende Lied (complete: *Part 1, Waldmärchen; Part 2, Der Spielmann; Part 3, Hochzeitsstücke*)

⊕━ *** EMI 5 66406-2. Döse, Hodgson, Tear, Rea, CBSO Ch., CBSO, Rattle

Rattle brings out the astonishing originality of Mahler's cycle, but adds urgency, colour and warmth, not to mention deeper, more meditative qualities. So the final section, *Wedding Piece*, after starting with superb swagger in the celebration music, is gripping in the minstrel's sinister narration and ends in the darkest concentration on a mezzo-soprano solo, beautifully sung by Alfreda Hodgson. The ensemble of the CBSO has a little roughness, but the bite and commitment could not be more convincing. Dating from 1983–4, this is one of Rattle's earliest Mahler recordings, but it sounds excellent in what appears to be a new transfer.

Des Knaben Wunderhorn: excerpts and other Lieder, including *Lieder und Gesäng aus der Jugendzeit: Ablösung in Sommer; Aus! Aus!; Des Antonius von Padua; Fischpredigt; Frülingsmorgen; Lied des Verfolgten' im Turm; Lob des hohen Versandes; Revelge; Rheinlegendchen; Starke Einbildungskraft; Der Tambourg'sell; Zu Strassburg auf der Schanz; Wo die schönen Trompeten blasen; Das himmlische Leben; Das irdische Leben; Urlicht* (with Interviews)

(*) TDK **DVD DV-TTTH-EUR. Hampson, Rieger

This admirably sung recital, filmed live with six cameras in the elegant surroundings of the Théâtre Musical de Paris Châtelet, demonstrates once again the difficulty of presenting this kind of programme on DVD. Let it first be said that Thomas Hampson sings with great intensity, a natural feeling for the words and music, and he characterizes strongly. His performances of *Der Tambourg'sell* (darkly histrionic), *Wo die schönen Trompeten blasen* (touchingly tender) and *Das himmlische Leben* – which we know from the *Fourth Symphony* – (full of innocent charm) are instances of his identification with Mahler, which is shared by his superb accompanist Wolfram Rieger whose total absorption in the music is a pleasure to watch. But while the perspectives change, the principal camera dwells too often on the singer's face in close-up, and his highly dramatized facial expressions (obviously sincere, but often held self-consciously at the end of a song) become difficult to watch – one wishes one was at a greater distance, and sometimes needs to shut one's eyes.

The songs are imaginatively divided into three groups, 'Fables and Parables of Nature and Man', 'Humoresques and Ballads – Scenes of Separation and War' and 'Ballads and Allegories – Transcendence of Life'. Each group is introduced and analysed by the singer; moreover, he interrupts each section at least twice to make further intellectualized comments, and he is big on the 'transcendence of life'. Whether one would want to hear his remarks, however informed and thoughtful, more than once is open to doubt. Of course, they are separately cued and can be programmed out, but it would have been far better to have these dissertations at the beginning and end of the recital. One receives a far more intuitive feeling about the music by watching the pianist, who is extraordinarily expressive, especially when he is playing a prelude or a postlude to a song. The recording is technically and visually of high quality.

Des Knaben Wunderhorn

⊕━ (M) *** EMI 5 67236-2 [567256]. Schwarzkopf, Fischer-Dieskau, LSO, Szell

Des Knaben Wunderhorn; Das himmlische Leben; Urlicht

*** Decca 467 348-2. Bonney, Fulgoni, Winbergh, Goerne, Concg. O, Chailly

Szell's 1968 Kingsway Hall recording of *Des Knaben Wunderhorn* was a primary recommendation for three decades at premium price. Now it rightly joins EMI's 'Great Recordings of the Century' and the careful remastering plus the lower price will surely extend its catalogue life for a considerable time to come. The superb singing of Schwarzkopf and Fischer-Dieskau is underpinned by wonderfully sensitive playing from the LSO under Szell, who matches and even surpasses his achievement with his own Cleveland Orchestra in the *Fourth Symphony*.

Strongly characterized, Chailly's disc of the *Des Knaben Wunderhorn* songs provides a powerful supplement to his cycle of the Mahler *Symphonies*. In full, brilliant sound it is among the most distinctive versions available. The soloists are an outstanding team, with Matthias Goerne exceptionally perceptive in drawing out the dramatic contrasts between the songs, consistently heightening the words. Set against the seven songs allotted to him, the five sung by Barbara Bonney are equally individual in their characterization, with the Viennese associations in such a song as *Verlor'ne Müh* deliciously caught. Fresh and girlish, she also sings one of the two extra songs added to the usual 12, the child–heaven finale to the *Fourth Symphony*, *Das himmlische Leben*, with Chailly opting for extreme speeds, fast and slow. The other extra song is the meditative *Urlicht* from the *Resurrection Symphony*, with the rich-toned Sara Fulgoni as mezzo soloist. The late Gösta Winbergh is also brought in as tenor soloist, when Chailly opts for having the military song, *Revelge*, in a higher key than usual. He also presents the songs in an unusual order, generally effectively, even though *Der Schildwache Nachtlied* makes an awkward start. The illuminating note by Donald Mitchell, like the performances, brings out the close links between these songs and the Mahler symphonies.

Des Knaben Wunderhorn: Das irdische Leben; Nicht wiedersehen!; Rheinlegendchen; Urlicht. 4 Rückert Lieder

(B) *** EMI Debut 5 85559-2. Coote, Drake – HAYDN: *Arianna a Naxos*; SCHUMANN: *Frauenliebe und leben* ***

This is one of the finest issues in EMI's excellent Debut series, with the mezzo Alice Coote boldly choosing challenging repertory that will be widely associated with Janet Baker. The voice may not have the velvety warmth of the latter, but the range of tone and dynamic, down to breathtaking *pianissimos*, could not be more distinctive. Here, in four of the five *Rückert Lieder*, her performances are so magnetic that for once one hardly misses the orchestra, with Julius Drake the most sympathetic accompanist. A pity that, as in other EMI issues of Lieder in this series, no texts or translations are given.

Des Knaben Wunderhorn: 12 Lieder; Lieder eines fahrenden Gesellen; Lieder und Gesänge 1–14; 5 Rückert Lieder

(N) (BB) *** EMI 4 76780-2 (2). Fischer-Dieskau, Barenboim

The piano versions of Mahler's songs may not match in colour his orchestral versions, but with Daniel Barenboim imaginatively accompanying Dietrich Fischer-Dieskau the subtlety of Mahler's word-setting and of his piano writing is most compelling. This two-disc compilation at bargain price brings together a series of recordings they made in Berlin in 1978, classic performances, even if Fischer-Dieskau's baritone is not quite as fresh as it was earlier. Texts and translations are provided, though in minuscule type.

Lieder eines fahrenden Gesellen

(M) *** Orfeo C 522 991B. Ludwig, VPO, Boehm –
BEETHOVEN: *Symphony 4*; SCHUMANN: *Symphony 4* ***
(N) **(*) Claves 50-2310. Wallén, Helsingborg SO, Hannu Lintu – GRIEG: *Den Bergtekne*; *10 Songs from Poems by A. O. Vinje* **(*)

As the chosen soloist in an electrifying concert conducted by Karl Boehm in August 1969, Christa Ludwig excels herself in a deeply moving, strongly characterized reading of the *Wayfaring Lad* songs. The spontaneity of the performance makes up for any incidental flaws of the moment, with the voice

gloriously firm and rich. No texts or translations of the songs are given, but every word is clear in this helpfully balanced radio recording.

Herman Wallén is a Finnish baritone in his mid-twenties who came to wider notice at the third annual Sommets Musicaux in Gstaad in 2003. As in the Grieg pieces, he proves an intelligent and persuasive interpreter, though this repertory is hotly contested on disc. Highly promising (he sounds a bit like the youthful Håkon Hagegård), though not a first choice if you are only after the Mahler songs.

Lieder eines fahrenden Gesellen; Lieder und Gesänge (aus der Jugendzeit); Im Lenz; Winterlied

✪ *** Hyp. CDA 66100. J. Baker, Parsons

Janet Baker presents a superb collection of Mahler's early songs with piano, including two written in 1880 and never recorded before, *Im Lenz* and *Winterlied*; also the piano version of the *Wayfaring Lad* songs in a text prepared by Colin Matthews from Mahler's final thoughts, as contained in the orchestral version. The performances are radiant and deeply understanding from both singer and pianist, well caught in atmospheric recording. A heart-warming record.

(i) Lieder eines fahrenden Gesellen; (ii) 3 Rückert Lieder: Ich atmet' einem linden Duft; Ich bin der Welt abhanden gekommen; Um Mitternacht

(M) (***) BBC mono/stereo BBCL 4107-2. Christa Ludwig, with (i) Philh. O, Cluytens; (ii) Parsons (with: BRAHMS: *Ständchen; Wiegenlied* ***) – R. STRAUSS: *Four Last Songs* ***

These radio recordings from the BBC archives give a winning picture of Christa Ludwig, well coupled with a valuable recording of Sena Jurinac in Strauss's *Four Last Songs*. The mono recording for Ludwig's 1957 account of the Mahler *Wayfaring Lad* cycle captures the richness of the voice vividly, with changing emotions clearly conveyed. The other songs, with Geoffrey Parsons at the piano, come from a Wigmore Hall recital given 21 years later, with the glorious voice still flawless in poised legato.

Lieder eines fahrenden Gesellen; Lieder und Gesänge (aus der Jugendzeit); Im Lenz; Winterlied

✪ (BB) *** Hyp. Helios CDH 55160. J. Baker, Parsons

Janet Baker presents a superb collection of Mahler's early songs with piano, including two written in 1880 and never recorded before, *Im Lenz* and *Winterlied*; also the piano version of the *Wayfaring Lad* songs in a text prepared by Colin Matthews from Mahler's final thoughts, as contained in the orchestral version. The performances are radiant and deeply understanding from both singer and pianist, well caught in atmospheric recording. A heart-warming reissue.

Lieder und Gesänge

*** Sony SK 68344. Kirchschlager, Deutsch (with Alma MAHLER: *5 Lieder*) – KORNGOLD: *5 Lieder, Op. 38; Songs of the Clown* ***

In Mahler's youth songs, Angelika Kirchschlager may not have the subtlety of Janet Baker in the same repertory, with tonal contrasts far more limited, but the girlishness and direct approach are arguably more apt for these early songs with their folk flavours, often settings of *Des Knaben Wunderhorn*. The five additional songs by Alma Mahler were written in the early years of her marriage to Gustav: charming inspirations, tuneful and direct but full of subtle modulations, and quite unlike her husband's work. They make an attractive extra item in this impressive début recording.

Das Lied von der Erde

🎧— (M) *** Ph. (ADD) 432 279-2. Baker, King, Concg. O., Haitink

*** Audite 95.491. Baker, Kmentt, Bav. RSO, Kubelik

(M) *** BBC (ADD) BBCM 5012-2. Baker, Mitchinson, BBC N. SO, Leppard

(M) *** EMI (ADD) 5 66892-2 [5669442]. Ludwig, Wunderlich, Philh. & New Philh. O, Klemperer

**(*) BBC (ADD) BBCL 4042-2. Hodgson, Mitchinson, BBC N. SO, Horenstein

(N) (BB) ** Regis mono RRC 1146. Ferrier, LPO Ch. & O., Krauss – BRAHMS: *Alto Rhapsody* (***)

(i) *Das Lied von der Erde;* (ii) *Des Knaben Wunderhorn;* (iii) *Kindertotenlieder; Lieder eines fahrenden Gesellen*

(B) *** Ph. Duo (ADD) 454 014-2 (2). (i) Baker, King; (ii) Norman, Shirley-Quirk; (iii) Prey; Concg. O, Haitink

(i) *Das Lied von der Erde; 3 Rückert Lieder*

(M) (***) Decca mono 466 576-2. Ferrier; (i) Patzak, VPO, Walter

(BB) (***) Naxos mono 8.110871. Ferrier; (i) Patzak; VPO, Walter

(i; ii) *Das Lied von der Erde;* (i) *Rückert Lieder: Ich bin der Welt abhanden gekommen. Symphony 5 in C sharp min.: Adagietto*

(BB) (**) Naxos mono 8.110850. VPO, Walter, with (i) Thorborg; (ii) Kullman

(i; ii) *Das Lied von der Erde. Symphony 5: Adagietto;* Lieder: (i) *Ich bin der Welt abhanden gekommen;* (ii) *Ich atmet' einen linden Duft*

(BB) (**(*)) Dutton mono CDBP 9722. (i) Thorborg; (ii) Kullman; VPO, Walter

The combination of Janet Baker, most deeply committed of Mahler singers, with Haitink, the most thoughtfully dedicated of Mahler conductors, produces radiantly beautiful and moving results, helped by refined and atmospheric recording. James King cannot match his solo partner, but his singing is intelligent and sympathetic. However, this version – vividly re-transferred – is now additionally offered on a Philips Duo set, coupled with Mahler's three other key song-cycles, and as such is very tempting. In *Des Knaben Wunderhorn* the singing of both Jessye Norman and John Shirley-Quirk brings out the purely musical imagination of Mahler at his finest, while Haitink's accompaniments are refined and satisfying, especially when the 1976 analogue sound is vividly atmospheric. Hermann Prey's performances of *Kindertotenlieder* and the *Lieder eines fahrenden Gesellen* are fresh and intelligent, and the colour of the baritone voice brings a darkness of timbre which is especially poignant, as in the third song of the *Wayfaring Lad* cycle. The Philips recording (from 1970) is of very high quality – the effect is most beautiful.

Recorded live for radio in February 1970, Kubelik's version on the Audite label offers a magnetic reading which reveals both the conductor and the mezzo soloist, Dame Janet Baker, at their peak. Fine and fresh as Waldemar Kmentt's account of the tenor songs is, with positive characterization and no sense of strain, it is Baker who sets the seal on the performance. The tonal range which she uses is magical, velvety down to finely shaded *pianissimos*, vividly responding to the words.

With subtlety and warmth concentrated over the full span, the long *Abschied* culminates in Baker's heartfelt account of the final coda with its murmurs of 'ewig', ever tear-laden but with no hint of sentimentality, kept fresh by Kubelik. First-rate radio sound. However, Baker's earlier version with James King and the Concertgebouw Orchestra under Haitink still stands supreme.

Taken from a performance for radio in the Free Trade Hall, Manchester, the Leppard version offers Baker at her very peak in 1977, giving another of her moving and richly varied readings of the contralto songs. The final *Abschied* has a depth and intensity, a poignancy that sets it alongside Dame Janet's earlier recordings. John Mitchinson may not have the most beautiful tenor, but his voice focuses ever more securely through the work, with many cleanly ringing top notes. Raymond Leppard draws fine playing from the orchestra, now renamed the BBC Philharmonic, though the body of strings is thin for Mahler. Acceptable BBC sound, with the voices naturally placed, not spotlit.

The latest Decca remastering of the famous (1952) Ferrier–Patzak version of *Das Lied* is a revelation. At the very opening the orchestral strings are not ideally focused, but the edginess has been smoothed, and one is now made conscious of the ambience of the Grosser Saal of the Musikverein. Ferrier's voice is warmly and vividly caught, as is the characterful Patzak. At last Walter's classic recording comes into its own. Even more remarkable is the transfer of the three Rückert songs recorded at the same time (*Ich bin der Welt abhanden gekommen, Ich atmet' einen linden Duft* and *Um Mitternacht*). Here the recording is even more warm and atmospheric, and the richness of Ferrier's voice and the simplicity of her approach make for glorious listening. The brass at the close of *Um Mitternacht* is rather forward, but full-bodied. Full translations are provided.

Mark Obert-Thorn's transfers on Naxos are also admirable, slightly less open than the Decca in *Das Lied*, but somewhat smoother in focus. The *Rückert Lieder*, which come first, sound particularly beautiful. However, the Naxos disc, though it is less expensive than the Decca, unusually for this label does not include texts or translations.

The Regis transfer is well managed but is not as fine as Decca's own, and this disc is mainly recommendable for the *Alto Rhapsody* coupling.

Klemperer's way with Mahler is at its most individual in *Das Lied von der Erde* – and that will enthral some, as it must infuriate others. With slower speeds, the three tenor songs seem initially to lose some of their sparkle and humour; however, thanks to superb, expressive singing by the late Fritz Wunderlich – one of the most memorable examples of his artistry on record – and thanks also to pointing of rhythm by Klemperer himself, subtle but always clear, the comparative slowness will hardly worry anyone intent on hearing the music afresh, as Klemperer intends. As for the mezzo songs, Christa Ludwig sings them with a remarkable depth of expressiveness; in particular, the final *Abschied* has the intensity of a great occasion. Excellent digitally remastered recording.

As ever, Horenstein favours spacious speeds, sustaining them magnetically, not just over the meditative songs of the alto – with Alfreda Hodgson bringing echoes of Kathleen Ferrier, subtle and moving in her tonal shading – but also in the tenor's lighter songs, at once relaxed and crisply pointed. John Mitchinson is here at his finest, contrasting his firm, heroic tone in the first song against delicate half-tones, using his head-voice. Though the strings could be fuller and sweeter, the BBC Manchester recording is well balanced, even if it now sounds rather opaque. In a brief interview Horenstein talks of his experience of the work.

The Dutton Lab. CD offers the pioneering live recordings made in the mid-1930s by Bruno Walter with the Vienna Philharmonic. The soloists here are excellent, both with clear, firm voices that convey full expressiveness without strain. The recording is dry but voices are very well caught, and the Dutton transfer does wonders in improving the orchestral sound. The generous fill-ups are also welcome. *Ich bin der Welt abhanden gekommen* with Kerstin Thorborg was recorded from the same concert as the main work, while the other Rückert setting – using an English translation – was recorded by Charles Kullman in 1938 with Sargent conducting. Walter's 1938 studio recording of the *Adagietto* from the *Fifth Symphony* is fascinating for being so much faster than latter-day readings, while still conveying total repose.

Bruno Walter's 1936 recording of Mahler's *Das Lied von der Erde* was made live, with fine soloists, even if they do not quite match Kathleen Ferrier and Julius Patzak on Walter's later Decca recording. Warmly idiomatic, it atmospherically captures the feeling of a great occasion in this new transfer. The Naxos disc of Bruno Walter's pre-war Mahler recordings from Vienna duplicates the Dutton issue of the same live recordings, but the transfers give less body to the orchestral sound. It also lacks some of the clarity and immediacy of the Dutton issue and has higher background hiss. In addition, the Dutton offers an extra item, one of the other *Rückert Lieder, Ich atmet' einen Linden duft*, recorded by Charles Kullman in London with Sargent conducting, using an English translation.

MALIPIERO, Gianfrancesco
(1882–1973)

La cimarosiana; Gabrieliana; Stradivario; Symphonic Fragments from 3 Goldoni Comedies
**(*) Marco Polo 8.225118. Swiss Italian O, Christian Benda

The two pastiche suites, *La cimarosiana* and *Gabrieliana*, are well fashioned if inconsequential. The *Tre commedie goldoniane* (1925) have been described by John G. Waterhouse in his book on the composer as 'perhaps the richest expression of the comic side of his genius'. The ideas are drawn from episodes from the operas and are full of life and character.

The ballet *Stradivario* comes from 1947–8, when Malipiero was director of the Venice Conservatory. It tells how in the silence of the night all the instruments from the collection come alive and dance. It is all pleasing and inventive, more than adequately played by the Orchestre della Svizzera Italiana under Christian Benda and decently recorded. None of this music sets the pulse racing but at the same time it is far from negligible. Not for nothing did Malipiero command respect both in the Italian musical world and internationally during his lifetime.

String Quartets 1–8
*** ASV CDDCD 457 (2). Orpheus Qt

Malipiero's eight *String Quartets* are all modest in length: the longest being the *First* (*Rispetti e strambotti*) (1920), which runs to 20 minutes, while the *Eighth* (1963–4), written when the composer was in his early eighties, takes only 12. None falls below a certain level of distinction, all are beautifully crafted and there is much freshness and fertility of invention. They are all played with expertise and conviction by the

Orpheus Quartet, and very well recorded indeed.

I capricci di Callot (opera; complete)
** CPO 999 830-2 (2). Winter, Müller, Kjellevold, Valentin, Ulrich, Sabrowski, Kiel PO, Marschik

Malipiero wrote some 23 operas and it is surprising that, with the exception of the trilogy *L'Orfeide*, none has been previously recorded. Described as a 'comedy', *I capricci di Callot* is rather deeper than that, and might be described as bittersweet. Much of its narrative spell comes from the blurring of fantasy and reality, with the dull dressmaker's room contrasting with the colourful back-drop of palaces and carnivals in Rome. The story provided Malipiero with plenty of opportunity to use his imaginative orchestral palette, notably in the haunting 'Funeral dance' in Act III, as well as writing some fine if not memorably tuneful lyrical music for the voices. There are some striking moments, including Giacinta's 'Mad scene', where she imagines herself waiting for an imaginary prince in a glittering palace.

Martina Winter is securely sympathetic in the role of Giacinta, firm throughout her registers, while her lover, Giglio, is ably sung by Markus Müller, a light tenor whose line is only occasionally marred by a wobble. The rest of the cast is generally more than acceptable. This live performance captures the atmosphere of the opera well enough, although the recording is a bit dry and closely miked (the strings sound a little pinched in the upper register). With full texts and translations and excellent essays, curious collectors might find this worth exploring.

MANFREDINI, Francesco (1684–1762)

Concerti grossi, Op. 3/1–12
☞ ✿ (BB) *** Naxos 8.553891. Capella Istropolitana, Krček

This splendid set of 12 concertos, published in Bologna in 1718, was dedicated to Prince Antoine I of Monaco, with whose court orchestra Manfredini was associated. The most famous of them is No. 12, a *Christmas Concerto* in the style of Torelli and Corelli, opening with a delightful *Pastorale* in siciliano rhythm. And if there are other influences here too, of Vivaldi in particular, and even anticipations of Handel, the music has its own individuality and is endlessly inventive. *Allegros* are vital and buoyant, slow movements tenderly touching, often featuring one or two solo violins. The performances here are both fresh and penetrating, with bouncing outer movements and expressive *Adagios*. Moreover the playing is perfectly in style, demonstrating how using modern instruments can be just as authentic as period manners in baroque music. The recording is absolutely natural, very much in the demonstration bracket.

MANZONI, Giacomo (born 1932)

Masse: Omaggio a Edgard Varèse
(M) *** DG 471 362-2. Pollini, BPO, Sinopoli – NONO: *Como una ola de fuerza y luz; ... soffrte onde serene*

Manzoni might be broadly classified as a follower of Luigi Nono, a teacher and critic as well as a composer, so the present recoupling in the 'Pollini Edition' is very appropriate. *Masse* has nothing to do with church liturgy, but refers to measures or quantities, and in its tribute to Varèse follows up a scientifically based mode of thought which proves surprisingly dramatic and colourful. Only the piano part has much in the way of melodic interest, and Pollini exploits it for all he is worth, not least in the elaborate cadenza-like passages. Sinopoli too, in what (in 1982) was his first major recording, already revealed his feeling for texture and dynamic which has since made his conducting so memorable.

MARAIS, Marin (1656–1728)

Alcione: Suite des airs à joüer (1706)

(M) *** Astrée ES 8525. Le Concert des Nations, Savall

Marais is almost solely known as a performer/composer of viol music, and this collection of airs and dances from his opera *Alcione* is a revelation. The work was a great success in its day (1706). Its outrageous mythological plot has the gods intervening to rescue the pair of mortal lovers from the various disasters that continually befall them. Finally, Neptune rises out of the sea to provide a happy ending by bringing back to life the apparently drowned hero and his beloved (who has stabbed herself). He changes them into seabirds, commanding them to remain ever faithful in their love and calm the waves by charming the winds.

There is plenty of opportunity for divertissements, with dance music in the tradition of Lully, and Marais's delightfully elegant invention seems inexhaustible. There are dances for shepherds and shepherdesses, a symphony of *Sleep*, a famous *Sailors' March* and a highly spectacular *Tempête*, in which a double-bass was added to the score of a French opera for the first time. There is also a particularly fine closing *Chaconne for the Tritons*. Savall is here at his finest, directing the proceedings with great vitality, clearly relishing the music's grace and colour, and the playing has an endearing vivacity and elegance. Excellent recording too.

Pièces a deux viole, Book I (1686): *Chaconne in G; Suites in D min. & G*

(N) *** Astrée Naïve ES 9963. Savall, Coin, Koopman, Hopkinson Smith

Pièces de viole, Book II (1701)

(N) *** Astrée Naïve ES 9978. Savall, Gallet, Hopkinson Smith

Pièces de viole, Book II: Couplets de folies; Fantaisie pièces in D min.; E; Suite in E; Tombeau de Monsieur Ste Colombe

☞ (N) *** BIS CD 909. Luolajan-Mikkola, Haavisto, Palviaininen

Pièces de viole, Book II: Suite in D min.; Couplets de folies; Book III: Suites in G & A min.

(N) *** Glossa GCD 920406. Pandolfo, Balestracci, Boysen, Costoyas, Meyerson

Marais wrote his five books of *Pièces de viole* over four decades – between 1686 and 1725 – and their contents were slowly amended to reflect changing fashions. Marais was a strong personality and resisted sudden alterations in their contents, but as time went by he moved onward from the standard dance pattern of allemande, courante, sarabande, gigue, gavotte and minuet. The First Book introduces a fine *Chaconne*, an *Echo fantaisie*, and ends with a deeply expressive *Tombeau*. The Second Book is mainly famous for its *Follie d'espagne*, 32 bravura variations on an Iberian dance we know as *La folia*. But it also includes *La Voix humaine* and another *Tombeau*, remembering Lully. The Third Book includes a *Gigue à l'anglais*, a *Muzette*, a *Grand ballet* and another *Chaconne*.

There is no questioning Jordi Savall's authority in these pieces, and he leads a dedicated team. But his manner is somewhat austere, the colouring is comparatively dark, and some may well prefer the lighter touch and textures of Paolo Pandolfo and his colleagues. The Glossa issue is particularly well documented, and it includes *Folies d'espagne* separately on a bonus disc.

However, our favourite among these issues is the BIS CD, which is particularly attractively recorded. Markku Luolajan-Mikkola's full timbre is warmly caught, and he plays with plenty of expressive feeling and flexibility and a wide range of dynamic. In essence, this is very friendly playing which wins the ear without abrasiveness, and his continuo group is just as excellent.

Pièces de viole, Book IV, Part 2: Le Goût étranger: Suites in F, E min., G & D min.; Caprice ou sonata

(N) *** ASV Gaudeamus CDGAU 152. Charivari Agréable

By the time we come to Book IV, we meet a new concept. The second part of the Book brings a diverse Suite, subtitled *Le Goût étranger*, which represented everything that was non-Parisian, from *La Provençale* to a *Sarabande à l'espagnole*, *L'Américaine* and even an *Allemande la bizarre*. There are 33 pieces in all, and for practical purposes the collection is usually divided up into three separate suites, as in this excellent recording in which the players, led by Susanne Heinrich's nimble and attractively light-timbred gamba, make the most of Marais's remarkable range of picturesque invention. Indeed, the group have taken their name from the catchy final item, *Charivari*. Excellent recording: a most rewarding disc of its kind.

Pièces à violes: Book IV (1717): *Suite d'un goût étranger* (excerpts)

(M) *** Astrée (ADD) ES 9932. Savall, Koopman, Smith

Savall's selection of 11 items from Part II of the Marais Book 4 could not be more attractively chosen. The opening *Marche Tartare* is as bold as you could wish, contrasted with the charming *La Tartarine*. The swirling portrait of *Le Tourbillon* is matched by a lively Gigue and a fine Allemande – *La Superbe*. *La Rêveuse* is touchingly sombre. Most memorable of all is the superb account of the celebrated six-section fantasy, *Le Labyrinthe*, played with spontaneous bravura, yet convincingly structured. Ton Koopman (harpsichord) and Hopkinson Smith (guitar) provide a discreet continuo.

Pièces en trio pour les flûtes, violon & dessus de viole (1692): *Le Contrefaiseurs; 6 Suites* (edited into *10 Suites*)

(N) ** (BB) VIRGIN 2x1 5 62422-2. Musica Pacifica

The ten *Suites* have been arranged and extended by the performers here from the six original *Pièces en trio* as published by Marais in Paris in 1692. In order to do this, extra movements have been interpolated, taken from a manuscript collection of chamber trios by Lully and Marais (*Trios pour le coucher du Roy*) and including the vignette *Les Contrefaiseurs* ('The Counterfeiters'). The new arrangements feature a wider range of instrumentation than planned by the composer, including recorders, oboe, violin, two violas da gamba, archlute and harpsichord. The music is often doleful in its expressive feeling, but it needs all the advocacy it can get: it would be idle to pretend that it always commands attention. Unlike some of Marais's gamba writing, these suites are of limited musical interest and belong among that repertoire which is more rewarding to play than to hear. Some might feel that to stretch out the available music to fill a pair of CDs (136 minutes) was too much of a good thing! Aficionados can be assured of the refinement and expertise of both playing and recording.

Pièces en trio pour les flutes, violon & dessus de viole (3 Suites); Sonata à la Maraisienne for Violin & Continuo
(N) **(*) Opus 111 OP 30335. L'Assemblée des Honnêtes Curieux (with REBEL: Violin Sonata 9 ***)

Many collectors wishing to sample Marais's *Pièces en trio* will be satisfied with just three of them, and they are well played by the Honest and Curious group here. The snag is that the sound of the woodwind plus violin gels together somewhat in the resonance of the studio. But the special interest of this collection is the inclusion of the *Sonata for Violin*, the instrument which was reputedly the 'enemy' for Marais, as it threatened the future of the viola da gamba. We are given his model in the brilliant little *Ninth Sonata* of Rebel and then an attempted copy of the new sonata style by Marais himself. He does not quite match his far younger contemporary in virtuoso brilliance, yet the closing *Très vivement* and the catchy final *Gigue* are genuinely memorable. Both are splendidly played and recorded.

Collections

Pièces à violes: Suites for Viola da Gamba & Continuo: Book I: Tombeau de M. Meliton for 2 Viols; Book IV: Suite for 3 Viols in D
*** Virgin 5 45358-2. Hantaï, Uemura, Verzier, Hantaï – FORQUERAY: *Pièces for 3 Viols; Suite* ***

These works were both part of a larger collection of solo viol pieces which Marais published in 1686. Their ethos is comparatively austere, yet the nine-movement *Suite* of dances has plenty of variety: the central *Sarabande* has a noble dignity, followed by a lighter *Gigue* and an engaging *Petite paysanne*. The *Tombeau* for two bass viols – the composer's longest work in this form – sustains a mood of dark, profound melancholy and this fine performance holds the listener firmly in its spell. The recording is vividly real.

Pièces à violes: L'Arabesque; Le Badinage; Le Labyrinthe; Prélude in G; La Rêveuse; Sonnerie de Sainte-Geneviève du Mont de Paris; Suite in G; Tombeau pour Monsieur de Sainte-Colombe
☞ (BB) *** Naxos 8.550750. Spectre de la Rose – SAINTE-COLOMBE: *Le Retour*, etc. ***

Naxos have stepped in enterprisingly and chosen a programme that is not only most attractive in its own right, but which also includes the key items used in the fascinating film about the conjectural relationship between Marin Marais and his reclusive mentor, Sainte-Colombe (*Tous les matins du monde*). Spectre de la Rose consists of a first-rate group of young players, led by Alison Crum, who plays in a dignified but austere style which at first seems cool but which is very effective in this repertoire. *Le Badinage* is perhaps a little stiff and unsmiling, but the key item, Marais's eloquent lament for his teacher, *Tombeau pour Monsieur de Sainte-Colombe*, is restrained and touching. Good, bright, forward recording, vividly declaiming the plangent viola da gamba timbre. But be careful not to play this record at too high a volume setting.

Pièces à violes: Book I (1686): Tombeau de M. Meliton. Book II (1701): Couplet de folies; Les Voix humaines. Book III (1711): Suite in D. La Gamme et autres Morceaux de Simphonie (1723): Sonata à la Marésienne
☞ (BB) *** Naxos 8.553081. Spectre de la Rose

The second Naxos collection from Spectre de la Rose is even more attractive than the first, and it is even better recorded. It even includes a rare work in which the violin takes the lead (the *Sonata à la Marésienne*), although the embroidering gamba partner takes the lion's share of bravura. It is a most attractive work and is played here with real sparkle, while the following *Suite in D* also shows Marais at his most attractively inventive. *Les Voix humaines* is deeply pitched, and even the *Couplets de folies* is far from light-hearted. Spectre de la Rose are experts in this field and play most persuasively throughout.

MARCELLO, Alessandro (1669–1747)

6 Oboe Concertos (La cetra)
(M) *** DG (ADD) (IMS) 427 137-2. Holliger, Pellerin, Camerata Bern, Füri

The six concertos of *La cetra* reveal a pleasing mixture of originality and convention; often one is surprised by a genuinely alive and refreshing individuality. These performances are vital and keen, full of style and character, and the recording is faithful and well projected.

Oboe Concerto in C min. (arr. Rothwell)
☞ (M) *** Dutton Lab./Barbirolli Soc. CDSJB 1016. Rothwell, Hallé O, Barbirolli – CORELLI; HAYDN: *Oboe Concertos* ***(with Recital: C. P. E. BACH; LOEILLET; TELEMANN: *Sonatas*, etc. **

Sir John's subtlety in matters of light and shade within an orchestral phrase brings this music immediately alive, and at the same time prevents the rather jolly opening tune from sounding square. The exquisitely beautiful *Adagio* is followed by a gay finale, both showing the soloist at her finest, and the well-balanced (1969) recording and excellent transfer add to one's pleasure.

Oboe Concerto in D min.
(BB) **(*) Naxos 8.550556. Kiss, Erkel CO – C. P. E. BACH: *Concertos* **(*)

This enjoyable concerto, once attributed (in a different key) to Benedetto Marcello, is given a good performance here by József Kiss and is very well recorded. One might have preferred more dynamic contrast from the soloist, but his timbre is right for baroque music and he plays with plenty of spirit. This disc is well worth its modest cost for the C. P. E. Bach couplings.

10 Keyboard Sonatas, Op. 3; Labarinto sopra il clavicembalo; La stravaganza in C (ciaccona con variazione)
*** Chan. 0671 (2). Loreggian (harpsichord)

Marcello's 10 harpsichord sonatas, Op. 3, appear to date from between 1712 and 1717. As no complete set exists in print, Alessandro Boris, the editor of the edition recorded here, has drawn on five manuscripts held in the libraries of various European cities, centring on a Venetian source which appears to be the most reliable. He has chosen to group the movements of each sonata (using all five manuscripts) and the result is inevitably conjectural, yet always convincing.

Marcello's invention is usually common to all the movements of each sonata, and though infinitely varied in treatment the basic ideas remain intact and attractively recognizable throughout. The *Labarinto* (in two sections) is a free, fantasy-like piece, with the bold rhythms and repeated notes of the closing section catchily bizarre. The C major ciaccona, *La stravaganza*, was Marcello's most famous harpsichord piece, and its 38 variations produce an expansive 15-minute work which rather outstays its welcome. Not the fault of the performance, one hastens to say, for the playing here is full of life and sparkle. The instrument itself is a reconstruction of a late-seventeenth-century Italian harpsichord, and it is vividly recorded.

MARCELLO, Benedetto (1686–1739)

Arianna (complete)
**(*) Chan. 0656 (3). Chierichetti, Banditelli, Guadagnini, Foresti, Abete, Athesis Ch., Academia de li Musici, Bressan

Benedetto Marcello, as a rich, dilettante composer, may treat the legend of Ariadne, Theseus and Bacchus rather casually, with little or no attempt to plumb the heroine's depths of feeling, but this 'Play in music for five voices' brings a sequence of fresh and lively numbers, predominantly brisk, starting with a vigorous overture. Though the strings of the Academia de li Musici are more abrasive than we now expect of period instruments, that is obtrusive only in slow music, and the conductor, Filippo Maria Bressan, inspires a well-sprung performance, with the singers sympathetically supported. The recording brings out some unevenness in the voices of both Anna Chierichetti as Ariadne (Arianna) and Mirko Guadagnini as Theseus (Teseo), but they are aptly fresh and youthful, and the mezzo Gloria Banditelli is outstanding as Phaedra (Fedra), with a resonant chest-voice; and Sergio Foresti as Bacchus (Bacco) and Antonio Abete as Silenus are well focused too. Clear, well-balanced sound.

MARCHAND, Louis (1669–1732)

Te Deum
(BB) *** Arte Nova 74321 65413-2. Ens. Canticum, Erkens; Deutsch (Koenig organ, St Avold, France) – François
COUPERIN: *Messe pour les couvents* ***

Louis Marchand was a year younger than Couperin-le-grand and was among the most brilliant improvisers and virtuosi of the day. Like the Couperin organ masses, his *Te Deum* is interspersed with chant. A fine piece, it ends with a particularly magnificent *Grand jeu*. Helmut Deutsch plays with magisterial authority on the Koenig organ at the former St Nabor Abbey in St Avold, France. Very good and lifelike recordings and impressive playing. A most worthwhile issue.

MARENZIO, Luca (1553–99)

Madrigals (1580): Book I
*** Opus 111 OP 30245. Concerto Italiano, Alessandrini

Rinaldo Alessandrini here demonstrates the claims as a madrigalist of Luca Marenzio, born 14 years before Monteverdi, concentrating in his choice on the madrigals Marenzio wrote early in his life in a fresh, open style that attracted listeners with its sweetness. A good selection from those written later in the composer's brief career complete the picture. Very well

paced, with structures clearly presented, they make a superb sequence in these beautifully recorded, finely detailed performances. Adding to the variety, Alessandrini adds discreet instrumental continuo to many of the items.

MARINI, Biago (c. 1587–1663)

Affetti Musicali, Op. 1
(N) *** Chan. 0660. Il Viaggio Musicale

When in 1617 the Venetian musician Biago Marini published the 27 sinfonias, arias, canzonas, sonatas and ballettos that make up his *Affetti Musicali*, he was in the employ both of the city council and as a violinist at St Mark's, where Monteverdi had been maestro di cappella since 1613. One of the pieces was by Giacinto Bondioli, Marini's uncle, but they were all named after, and dedicated to, important Venetian families. The writing is in two or three parts with continuo, and their style is quite varied, as is the instrumentation here, where the composer's instructions are vaguely all-embracing. Il Viaggio Musicale have very successfully chosen instrumentation to suit each piece, whether lively or expressive and delicate. A mixture of violins, cornetti and tromboni bass dulcien (an early one-piece bassoon) is aptly blended, often with an elaborate continuo, and the result is aurally very appealing, for Marini's invention does not fail him, either rhythmically or melodically. Monteverdi's namepiece, a *balleto alemano*, is particularly fetching. The playing here is expert and well balanced and recorded, and this is altogether a surprisingly attractive, well-documented disc.

MARKEVITCH, Igor (1912–83)

(i) *Piano Concerto. Icare*; (ii) *Cantate*
**(*) Marco Polo 8.225076. Arnhem PO, Lyndon-Gee, with (i) Van den Hoek; (ii) Oostenrijk, Nederlands Concertkoor, Amsterdam (men only)

Before becoming a conductor in the years immediately after the Second World War Markevitch was known first and foremost as a composer who occasionally appeared as a conductor, primarily of his own music. As a youth he was Diaghilev's last protégé, and the great impresario brought the 17-year-old to London in 1929 to give the first performance of his *Piano Concerto*. This is derivative, with lots of Stravinsky and the motoric rhythms of Prokofiev in the outer movements; the slow movement is by far the most memorable. The soloist, Martijn van den Hoek, is a magnificent artist whose neglect by the gramophone companies has been puzzling. The *Cantate* for solo soprano, male chorus and orchestra was composed after Markevitch received news of Diaghilev's death. He asked Cocteau to compose the text and the work, given at the Théâtre de la Pigalle in 1930, was hailed by Henri Sauguet no less as a work of 'rare mastery'. As with the *Concerto*, its opening has something of the neo-classical concerto grosso about it and it is an individual and imaginative piece. *Icare* is the 1943 revision of *L'Envoi d'Icare* of 1932 written when the composer was twenty. It was written for Serge Lifar, who never danced the role or mounted the ballet. Again, it is an arresting work, full of imagination, though at times there is a certain awkwardness rhythmically; but readers who have any of the earlier discs in the series should get it. The music is of great interest and, although the orchestral playing lacks the last degree of polish, the recording is eminently acceptable.

Rébus; Hymnes
*** Marco Polo 8.223724. Arnhem PO, Lyndon-Gee

Rébus was written in 1931 for Massine, though he never mounted or danced it. No less an authority than Henri Prunières hailed it as a work of genius: it is certainly an interesting piece of immense talent. *Hymnes* was completed in 1933, though the final section, *Hymne à la mort*, was not added until 1936. There is much Stravinsky in the very imaginative *Prélude* and *Pas d'acier* in the first section, *Hymne au travail*, and a strong sense of atmosphere in *Hymne au printemps*. This CD gave us much pleasure and is well worth investigating; good recorded sound too.

(i) *The Flight of Icarus*; (ii) *Galop*; (iii) *Noces*; (iv) *Serenade*
*** Largo 5127. (i) Lyndon-Gee, Lang, Gagelmann, Haeger; (ii) Markevitch Ens., Köln; (i; iii; iv) Lessing; (iv) Meyer, Jensen

Noces, for piano, was composed in 1925 when Markevitch was only thirteen, and it was on the strength of this and a *Sinfonietta* that Diaghilev was prompted to take him up. The young composer-conductor was only 20 when he composed *L'Envoi d'Icare*, which Lifar commissioned but subsequently never produced. It is heard here not in its orchestral form but in the transcription for two pianos and percussion. *Noces*, neatly played by Kolja Lessing, is close to the world of Poulenc and Satie, and it is obvious that Markevitch knew his Ravel. The *Serenade* is akin to the Milhaud of the *Petites symphonies*, and there is tremendous energy and a lot of Stravinsky in *L'Envoi d'Icare*. This disc gives an insight into his talent and musicianship which will be of interest to all those who care about the Diaghilev years and Paris between the wars.

La Taille de l'Homme (Part 1)
*** Marco Polo 8.225054. Shelton, Arnhem PO, Lyndon-Gee

Markevitch was not a conductor-composer like Furtwängler or Weingartner, but a composer first and foremost who abandoned composition during the war and then (encouraged by Nadia Boulanger) turned to the baton. He composed the first part of *La Taille de l'Homme* in the autumn of 1939, between the outbreak of war and Christmas, but the work remains incomplete and the first part (lasting just under an hour) is all that exists. The war years, in which Markevitch served in the Italian resistance, brought his creative career virtually to an end.

La Taille de l'Homme is a strange and highly original piece, quite unlike anything else of the period; it is scored for chamber-music forces: four wind-players, horn, trumpet, piano and string quintet (enlarged in this recording to enrich the sonority). Once or twice one is reminded of other contemporaries (among them Koechlin) but both Markevitch's conception and his musical language are quite personal. The piece, a setting of C. F. Ramuz (of *L'Histoire du soldat* fame) takes the form of six movements: an instrumental Prelude, a *Choral orné* (ornamented chorale) for soprano, obbligato trumpet and strings, thirdly a Sonata, fourthly an *Andantino* for soprano, oboe, bass clarinet and strings, then a Scherzo and Finale, which includes a cadenza for solo piano. With each new recording this composer grows in interest and stature. Eminently serviceable performances and sound.

Vuca Lorenzo il Magnifico; Psaumes
*** Marco Polo 8.223882. Shelton, Arnhem PO, Lyndon-Gee

Markevitch's vocal symphony, *Lorenzo il Magnifico*, sets poems by Lorenzo de' Medici. It is said to be his masterpiece, and it is not only highly imaginative but quite masterly in its variety of pace and feeling of growth. *Psaumes* comes from 1933 when Markevitch was 21 and enjoyed a *succès de scandale* at the time. It is powerful stuff, rather Milhaudesque at times, but at the same time evidence of a distinctive and original mind. Lucy Shelton sings the demanding solo part well in both scores, and the playing and recording are eminently serviceable. Markevitch is a composer of substance and some distinction.

MARTIN, Frank (1890–1974)

Ballades for: (i) *Cello & Small Orchestra*; (ii) *Flute, Strings & Piano*; (iii) *Piano & Orchestra*; (iv) *Saxophone & Small Orchestra*; (v) *Viola, Wind, Harpsichord, Timpani & Percussion*; (vi) *Trombone & Piano*
*** Chan. 9380. (i) Dixon; (ii) Chambers; (ii–iii; v–vi) Elms; (iv) Robertson; (v) Dukes, Masters; (vi) Bousfield; LPO, Bamert

The *Ballades* are among Martin's most personal utterances. Only three are otherwise currently available, so the present issue is a most valuable addition to the Martin discography, particularly in view of the excellence and commitment of the performances. Subtle, state-of-the-art recording with no false 'hi-fi' brightness, but a natural and unobtrusive presence. An indispensable disc for admirers of this subtle and rewarding master.

(i) *Ballade for Piano & Orchestra. Piano Concertos 1*; (ii) *2*; (i; ii) *Danse de la peur for 2 Pianos & Small Orchestra*
⊕➝ ✿ *** ASV CDDCA 1082. (i) Sebastian Benda; (ii) Badura-Skoda; O della Svizzera Italiana, Christian Benda

The *Ballade for Piano and Orchestra* is a poignant and affecting score, written in the immediate wake of a bereavement, and its depth of feeling and imagination are never in doubt. The *First Piano Concerto* of 1933–4 is not quite as moving but anticipates many of the characteristic fingerprints of the *Petite symphonie concertante* and the *Concerto for Seven Wind Instruments*. The pale, haunting instrumental colourings of the slow movement evoke Martin's own special world. The ASV CD brings the *Danse de la peur*, also from the 1930s, a highly imaginative, dramatic and above all atmospheric score which is new to the Martin discography. Good performances and decently balanced recordings, which are recommended with the strongest enthusiasm.

(i) *Ballade for Piano & Orchestra*; (ii) *Ballade for Trombone & Orchestra*; (iii) *Concerto for Harpsichord & Small Orchestra*
**(*) Jecklin-Disco (ADD) JD 529-2. (i) Benda; (ii) Rosin; (iii) Jaccottet; Lausanne CO, composer

The *Harpsichord Concerto* is a highly imaginative and inventive piece, arguably the most successful example of the genre since the Falla *Concerto*. The orchestral texture has a pale, transparent delicacy that is quite haunting, and the atmosphere is powerful – as, indeed, it is in the fine *Ballade*. Christiane Jaccottet is a committed advocate and her performance has the authority of the composer's direction.

(i) *Ballade for Piano & Orchestra*; (ii) *Ballade for Trombone & Orchestra*; (iii) *Concerto for Clavecin & Small Orchestra*
(M) **(*) Jecklin (ADD) JD 529-2. Lausanne CO, composer, with (i) Benda; (ii) Rosin; (iii) Jaccottet

(i; ii) *Ballade for Cello & Piano;* (i; iii) *Ballade for Flute &
Piano;* (i) *8 Préludes pour le piano;* (i; iv) *Drey Minnelieder;*
(i; iv) *6 Monologues from Jedermann;* (ii; v) *3 Chants de
Nöel*

(M) **(*) Jecklin JD 563-2. (i) Composer; (ii) Honegger; (iii)
Willoughby; (iv) Rehfuss; (v) Ameling, Odé

As time goes on, the true stature of Frank Martin's music
emerges. On each occasion you return to it, the more interesting and individual his sensibility seems, and the more
rewarding are its depths and subtlety. Both discs give invaluable insights into this music. JD 529-2 brings the *Harpsichord
Concerto* with Christiane Jaccottet, who took part in the
première recording of the *Petite Symphonie Concertante* in
the early 1950s. Like the companion works, it derives from the
Swiss Radio Archives and comes from 1971. Sebastian Benda
gives just as powerful and imaginative account of the *Ballade
for Piano and Orchestra*. This is quintessential Martin: music
from another world.

JD 563-2 restores to circulation a memorable (1955) recording of the *Jedermann Monologues* with Heinz Rehfuss and the
composer, originally made for Decca, as well as a 1952 broadcast with Henri Honegger for the Süddeutscher Rundfunk,
Stuttgart. Martin is the pianist throughout this disc, and just
how formidable a player he is emerges in the eight *Préludes* he
wrote for Lipatti. An essential acquisition for all admirers of
the composer.

(i) *Piano Concerto 2;* (ii) *Violin Concerto*
** Jecklin-Disco (ADD) JD 632-2. (i) Badura-Skoda; (ii)
Schneiderhan; Luxembourg RSO, composer

The *Violin Concerto* is a score of great subtlety and beauty.
Don't be put off by the less than lustrous sound, for this is a
masterpiece and has the benefit of having Martin himself at
the helm. The *Second Piano Concerto* is not as lyrical as the
Violin Concerto but is still worth investigation for its thoughtful slow movement.

Concerto for 7 Wind Instruments, Percussion & Strings; (i)
Erasmi monumentum (for organ and orchestra); *Etudes for
Strings*
*** Chan. 9283. (i) Pearson; LPO, Bamert

Erasmi monumentum is a substantial piece of some 25 minutes. The first movement, *Homo pro se* ('The Independent
Man'), alludes to the name given to Erasmus by his contemporaries; the second is *Stulticiae Laus* ('In Praise of Folly'),
and the third is *Querela Pacis* ('A Plea for Peace'). The outer
movements are pensive and atmospheric; the middle movement is less convincing. Matthias Bamert's account of the
Concerto for Seven Wind Instruments is very assured, relaxed
and animated; although thoroughly persuasive, he makes
rather heavy weather of the *Etudes*.

*Concerto for 7 Wind Instruments, Timpani, Percussion and
Strings;* (i) *Petite symphonie concertante;* (ii) *6 Monologues
from Jedermann*
⊕— (BB) *** Warner Apex 0927 48687-2. (i) Guibentif,
Jaccottet, Riuttimann; (ii) Cachemaille; SRO, Jordan

The Chandos Martin series under Matthias Bamert has not
included the *Petite symphonie concertante* except in the transcription for full orchestra, when it is simply known as the
Symphonie concertante, coupled with the wonderful and
unaccountably neglected *Symphony* of 1937. Armin Jordan
has atmosphere and an unhurried sense of pace, and the
soloists and orchestra are very well balanced. It is excellently

played (with Christiane Jaccottet, who took part in the first
performance). The account of the *Concerto for Seven Wind
Instruments* is also a fine one. The *Six Monologues* from
Hofmannsthal's *Everyman,* written at the height of the Second World War, are subtle and profound. Their concentration of mood is well conveyed by Gilles Cachemaille, and the
orchestral detail is well captured. Eminently recommendable
and an inexpensive entry into Martin's world.

The Four Elements; (i) *In terra Pax*
⊕— *** Chan. 9465. (i) Howarth, Jones, Hill, Williams,
Roberts, Brighton Festival Ch.; LPO, Bamert

Les Quatre Eléments, written for Ansermet's 80th birthday in
1967, is a highly imaginative work which exhibits to striking
effect Martin's feeling for the orchestra and his subtle mastery
of texture. *In terra Pax* is a noble work, and this makes a
distinguished addition to the growing Martin discography.
The singers are not perhaps quite as impressive as in the
Ansermet set, but in every other respect the new recording is
superior.

Symphonie concertante (arr. of *Petite symphonie concertante*
for full orchestra); *Symphony; Passacaglia*
⊕— ✿ *** Chan. 9312. LPO, Bamert

The *Symphony* is a haunting and at times quite magical piece.
It has all the subtlety of colouring of the mature Martin and
is a piece of great imaginative resource. The slow movement
in particular has an otherworldly quality, suggesting some
verdant, moonlit landscape. The two pianos are effectively
used and although, as in the *Petite symphonie concertante,* lip
service is paid to the 12-note system, the overall effect is far
from serial. Its main companion here is the transcription
Martin made for full orchestra of the *Petite symphonie concertante* the year after its first performance. Harp and piano are
used for colouristic effects but completely relinquish any hint
of soloist ambitions. The *Passacaglia* is Martin's 1962 transcription for full orchestra of his organ piece. Sensitive playing from the LPO under Matthias Bamert and exemplary
Chandos recording.

CHAMBER MUSIC

(i) *Ballade for Cello & Piano;* (ii) *Ballade for Flute & Piano;
Piano Quintet;* (iii) *Violin Sonata;* (iv) *4 Sonnets à
Cassandre*
*** ASV CDDCA 1010. Burnside, Pears-Britten Ens.; (i)
Watkins; (ii) K. Jones; (iii) Jackson; (iv) Rearick

This rewarding issue brings us the rarely heard *Piano Quintet,*
in which Martin's debts to Ravel and Fauré are clearly evident. The *Violin Sonata* is a three-movement piece, much
indebted to the Debussy *G minor Sonata*. All these pieces,
save for the *Ballades* for flute and cello, pre-date the period in
which Martin found his true idiom – in such works as *Le Vin
herbé* and *Der Cornet*. The performances are as alert and
sensitive as one could wish, and the recordings are very good
too.

*Piano Quintet; String Quintet (Pavane couleur de temps);
String Trio; Trio sur des mélodies populaires irlandaises*
*** Jecklin-Disco (ADD) JD 646-2. Zurich Ch. Ens.

The *Piano Quintet* has an eloquence and an elegiac dignity
that are impressive; the short *String Quintet,* subtitled *Pavane
couleur de temps* (the title is taken from a fairy story in which

a young girl wishes for 'a dress the colour of time'), is a beautiful piece. The *Piano Trio on Irish Popular Themes* is full of imagination and rhythmic life. The *String Trio* is a tougher nut to crack; its harmonies are more astringent and its form more concentrated. To summarize: altogether a most satisfying disc, offering very good performances and recordings.

Piano Trio on Irish Folktunes
*** Simax PSC 1147. Grieg Trio – BLOCH: *3 Nocturnes;*
   SHOSTAKOVICH: *Piano Trios* ***

The *Piano Trio* is expertly played here and the interest of the couplings further enhances the value of this issue, arguably the best the Grieg Trio has given us. The Simax recording is first rate.

VOCAL MUSIC

Der Cornet
*** Orfeo S 164881A. Lipovšek, Austrian RSO, Zagrosek

Der Cornet or, to give it its full title, *Die Weise von Liebe und Tod des Cornets Christoph Rilke* ('The Lay Song of the Love and Death of Cornet Christoph Rilke'), is one of Martin's most profound and searching works. Martin's setting for contralto and small chamber orchestra was written at the height of the war and in the immediate wake of *Le Vin herbé*, his oratorio on the Tristan legend. The shadowy, half-real atmosphere often reminds one of the world of *Pelléas*; and the restrained, pale colourings provide an effective backcloth to the vivid and poignant outbursts which mark some of the settings. The performance by Marjana Lipovšek is remarkable. Sensitive orchestral playing and faithfully balanced, well-recorded sound. This music casts a powerful spell and is strongly atmospheric.

Golgotha (oratorio; complete)
*** Cascavelle VEL 3004. Locher, Graf, Dami, Fink, Brodard,
   Baghdassarian, Antoniotti, Ens. Voc. de Lausanne & Sinf.,
   Corboz

Martin's post-war oratorio, *Golgotha*, is a work of power and substance. It has nobility and elevation of feeling, and its inspiration runs at a high level. Some have argued that it is possibly the greatest Passion since Bach but, in contradistinction to Bach, the narrative passes freely between the various soloists and the body of the choir.

The Cascavelle performance is magnificent, admirably paced by Michel Corboz, and with some fine solo singing. Elisabeth Graf in the *Méditation* that opens the second half sings with much feeling though it is almost invidious to single out any of the fine soloists. The recording, made in Lausanne Cathedral in 1994, has greater presence and depth than its Erato predecessor, and there is plenty of space around the aural image. There are two Cascavelle booklets, one reproducing the text and the other the notes that Harry Halbreich wrote for the original Erato set, now deleted, made under the artistic supervision of Martin himself, and included in the CD transfer: indeed it even reproduces the note on the *Mass for Double Choir* which Erato used as a fill-up and which is not included here.

Mass for Double Choir
*** United Recordings (ADD) 88033. Vasari, Backhouse –
   HOWELLS: *Requiem,* etc. ***
**(*) Nim. NI 5197. Christ Church Cathedral Ch., Oxford,
   Darlington – POULENC: *Mass in G,* etc. ***

(i) *Mass for Double Choir;* (ii) *Passacaille for Organ*
B—ᴛ ✿ *** Hyp. CDA 67017. Westminster Cathedral Ch.,
   O'Donnell – PIZZETTI: *Messa di requiem; De profundis*
   *** ✿

(N) *** HM HMC 901834. RIAS Kammerchor, Reuss –
   MESSIAEN: *5 Rechants; O sacrum convivium* ***

The *Mass for Double Choir* is one of Martin's purest and most sublime utterances. The latest version from the Westminster Cathedral Choir under James O'Donnell is the most outstanding. The boys produce marvellously focused tone of great purity and expressive power, and the tonal blend that O'Donnell achieves throughout is little short of miraculous. This won *Gramophone* magazine's 'Record of the Year' award in 1998, and deservedly so. As a fill-up O'Donnell offers the *Passacaille* for organ, together with two magnificent Pizzetti works.

The RIAS choir under their Dutch conductor, Daniel Reuss, give a performance of great feeling and sensitivity. In terms of tonal blending and purity of intonation they are second to none, and the performance has real eloquence and nobility. They also give us the magical *Songs of Ariel*, not otherwise available since the deletion of the Harry Christophers version, which much enhances the value of this fine issue. The *Mass* is recommended alongside (though not necessarily in preference to) the Westminster Cathedral account.

Irrespective of the above competition, the United Recordings version is also quite masterly in every respect, and Vasari, a choir conducted by Jeremy Backhouse, get remarkably fine results. A very convincing performance and an exemplary recording.

The Choir of Christ Church Cathedral, Oxford, under Stephen Darlington also give a good account of themselves: their tone is clean and beautifully balanced. The boys' voices are moving in a different way from that of the Westminster choir, but Darlington's performance does not add up to quite as impressive or richly imaginative a musical experience. The Nimbus disc is eminently well recorded.

6 Monologues from 'Jedermann' (Everyman)
(M) *** Virgin 5 61850-2. Van Dam, Lyon Nat. Op. O,
   Nagano – IBERT: *4 Chansons de Don Quichotte;*
   POULENC: *Le Bal masqué;* RAVEL: *Don Quichotte à
   Dulcinée* ***

(i) *6 Monologues from Everyman;* (ii) *Maria Triptychon;* (i)
The Tempest (3 excerpts)
*** Chan. 9411. (i) Wilson-Johnson; (ii) Russell; LPO, Bamert

Kent Nagano directs powerfully sustained accompaniments for what is perhaps the most enterprising item in this imaginatively chosen quartet of French song groupings, all written around the third decade of the 20th century. Van Dam has major rivals here, of course, notably Fischer-Dieskau, whom he does not quite match. But he comes pretty near to doing so: his singing, like Nagano's orchestral backcloth, is impressively felt, and his darkness of colour in the penultimate monologue prepares the way movingly for the ardently sombre closing prayer. A full text and translation is provided, and this collection can be strongly recommended.

As with Fischer-Dieskau's earlier DG recording, Chandos couples the excerpts from *The Tempest* with the *Everyman Monologues*; it is a measure of David Wilson-Johnson's artistry here that in both instances one forgets the exalted comparison that the appearance of this new record invites. He sings with intense – but not excessive – dramatic feeling and total commitment and conviction. The extra rarity on this disc is the *Maria Triptychon*. The central movement, *Magnificat*, originally stood on its own, but Martin subsequently added the two outer movements, *Ave Maria* and *Stabat Mater*, and Linda Russell and the violinist Duncan Riddell give a totally dedicated account of it. Bamert and the LPO generate a keen sense of atmosphere, and the Chandos recording is every bit as good as the other issues in this splendid series.

Requiem

☸━ *** Jecklin-Disco (ADD) JD 631-2. Speiser, Bollen, Tappy, Lagger, Lausanne Women's Ch., Union Ch., SRO, composer

This is arguably the most beautiful *Requiem* to have been written since Fauré's and, were the public to have ready access to it, would be as popular. The recording, made at a public performance that the (then 83-year-old) composer conducted in Lausanne Cathedral, is very special. The analogue recording is not in the demonstration class, but this music and performance must have three stars.

Le Vin herbé (oratorio)

*** Newport Classics NPD 85670 (2). Tharp, Whyte, Osborne, I Cantori di New York and Ens., Shapiro

Le Vin herbé was commissioned in 1938 by the Swiss-German conductor, Robert Blum, who wanted a piece for his madrigal choir. It was finished in 1939 as *The Love Potion*, to which Martin eventually added two further sections as well as a short Prologue and Epilogue. It made a great impression on the young Hans Werner Henze when he heard it as a teenager in wartime Nazi Germany: 'So that's what 12-note music sounds like,' he thought. 'So beautiful and so tender. And such ravishing sounds.' (Of course its serialism is hardly even skin-deep, like the *Petite symphonie*.) The colours are delicate in shade, pastel and half-lit, and the whole piece strikes a strong, almost mesmeric spell. Both as soloists and as a choir the American singers are first class, as are the instrumentalists. The acoustic is warm and open, and the aural image well focused. *Le Vin herbé* is a haunting and powerful score, full of subtle beauties, and Mark Shapiro and his colleagues' love for this masterpiece is evident throughout.

MARTINI, Johannes (c. 1440–97/8)

Ave Maris stella; Magnificat terti toni; O beate Sebastiane; Salve regina

*** Gaudeamus CDGAU 171. Clerks' Group, Wickham – OBRECHT: *Laudes Christo; Missa Malheur me bat* ***

Though Martini cannot compare with Obrecht in imagination, the motets recorded here have a simple beauty, made the more compelling by the dedicated performances of the Clerks' Group, atmospherically recorded.

MARTINŮ, Bohuslav (1890–1959)

The Amazing Flight (Podivuhodný Let); On tourne! (Natáči se!); La Rêvue de cuisine (Kuchynska Revue)

☸━ *** Sup. SU 3749-2. Czech PO, Hogwood

Christopher Hogwood made an earlier record of *La Rêvue de cuisine* with the Saint Paul Chamber Orchestra on an all-Martinů record for Decca which lasted only a very short time

in the catalogue. The piece stands up rather well against *La Création du monde* or any other of Milhaud's jazz-inspired pieces, and Martinů's 'Charleston' is particularly infectious. The present CD arrived without any documentation, save for the bare titling in Czech. In his Grove VI article on Martinů Brian Large lists *Báječný let* of 1927 as a mechanical ballet without dancers: 'báječný' and 'podivuhodný' are synonyms (like 'incredible' and 'amazing'). The only other ballet from 1927 that he lists is *On tourne!*, whose Czech name is *Natáči se! La Rêvue* is well represented on CD, but the present performance is second to none, if not a first choice. The Czech Philharmonic play every note with great zest. Neither of the other 1927 ballets was performed at the time and both contain music of real quality, imaginative invention and outstanding charm even by Martinů's standards. *Natáči se!* is quite irresistible in its freshness and innocence, and its seventh movement, once played, is difficult if not impossible to get out of one's head. And what harmonic subtlety there is elsewhere in this wonderfully inventive and imaginative score. This is music which infectiously communicates its love of life and high spirits – and leaves you feeling better! Very good and well-detailed recorded sound.

La Bagarre; Half-Time; Intermezzo; The Rock; Thunderbolt

*** Sup. (ADD) 001669. Brno State O, Vronsky

La Bagarre and *Half-Time* are early evocations, the latter a Honeggerian depiction of a roisterous half-time at a football match that musically doesn't amount to a great deal. The three later works are much more interesting – *Intermezzo* is linked to the *Fourth Symphony* – and the collection as a whole will be of great interest to Martinů addicts, if perhaps not essential for other collectors. All the performances are alive and full of character, and the recording is vividly immediate.

(i) Concertino in C min. for Cello, Wind Instruments & Piano; (ii) Harpsichord Concerto; (iii) Oboe Concerto

*** Sup. 11 0107-2 031. (i) Večtomov, Topinka, members of Czech PO; (ii) Růžičková, Rehák; (iii) Krejči; (ii; iii) Czech Philharmonic Chamber O; (i, iii) Skvor; (ii) Neumann

Zuzana Růžičková has made a number of recordings of the *Harpsichord Concerto* but this is her most successful. The sound is agreeably spacious, though the balance is synthetic and the piano has equal prominence with the solo harpsichord. However, the playing is spirited and sympathetic; and the *Oboe Concerto* is heard to excellent advantage too, with very good playing and a well-laid-out sound-picture. The early *Concertino for Cello with Piano, Wind and Percussion* is more than acceptably played and recorded.

Cello Concertos 1–2

**(*) Sup. 1110 3901-2. May, Czech PO, Neumann

Cello Concertos 1–2; Concertino in C min. for Cello, Wind Instruments, Piano & Percussion

*** Chan. 9015. Wallfisch, Czech PO, Bělohlávek

The *Cello Concerto No. 1* was composed in 1930 but has been revised twice. The *Cello Concerto No. 2* is the bigger of the two. It opens with a very characteristic and infectiously memorable B flat tune, and there is much of the luminous orchestral writing one associates with the *Fourth* and *Fifth Symphonies*. It is a warm-hearted, lyrical score with a Dvořák-like radiance.

Angelica May, a Casals pupil, gives a good account of both scores and, in the absence of the Wallfisch, this is perfectly recommendable. But as both performance and recording, her version is outclassed by the Chandos, which has much greater definition and presence and also has the advantage of offering the *Concertino for Cello, Wind, Piano & Percussion* (1924).

(i) ***Concerto for Double String Orchestra, Piano & Timpani;*** (ii) ***Concerto for String Quartet & Orchestra;*** (i; iii) ***3 Ricercari for Chamber Orchestra & 2 Pianos***

(N) (BB) *** Warner Apex 2564 62035-2. (i) Heisser; (ii) Brandis Qt; (iii) Planès; O Nat. de France, Conlon

(i) ***Concerto for Double String Orchestra, Piano & Timpani;*** (ii) ***Concerto for String Quartet & Orchestra;*** (iii) ***Sinfonia concertante for Oboe, Bassoon, Violin, Cello & Orchestra***

(N) (BB) *** Virgin 2x1 5 62437-2 (2). (i) Alley, Fullbrook; (ii) Endellion Qt; (iii) Daniel, Reay, Watkinson, Orton; City of L. Sinfonia, Hickox – DVORAK; SMETANA: *String Quartets* **(*)

Concerto for Double String Orchestra, Piano & Timpani; Symphony 1

🔑 *** Chan. 8950. Czech PO, Bělohlávek

(i) ***Concerto for Double String Orchestra, Piano & Timpani, H. 271. Symphony 3, H 299***

(***) Sup. mono/stereo SU 1924-2 001. (i) Panenka, Hejduk; Czech PO, Sejna – DVORAK: *Suite in A, Op. 98b* (***)

The *Double Concerto* is one of the most powerful works of the present century, and its intensity is well conveyed in Bělohlávek's vital, deeply felt performance. His dedicated and imaginative account of the *First Symphony* is very good indeed. Bělohlávek is totally inside this music, and the recording, made in the agreeably resonant Spanish Hall of Prague Castle, is very natural. Strongly recommended for both works.

Although the Virgin collection is curiously coupled, the *Double Concerto* has splendid vitality in Hickox's hands (he is brisker than Jirí Bělohávek and has obvious sympathy for this repertoire). The *Sinfonia concertante* was inspired by (and written for) the same combination as the famous Haydn score for which Martinů, rightly, had great affection. It is more rewarding than the neo-Baroque *Concerto for String Quartet and Orchestra*, which is very manufactured. However, this set is well worth its modest cost, and Richard Hickox is an enthusiastic and expert guide in this terrain.

Karel Sejna's *Double Concerto* (recorded in 1958 and in stereo) is not the first recording, but the dark events that inspired it were sufficiently close to be vivid in the minds of all Czechs. His account of the *Third Symphony*, made in 1947, was a first recording and there is the vivid, intense quality about the performance which you often find in premières. The frequency range is naturally limited, and much effort has been made to brighten the sound. It is a wonderful performance. Both performances on Supraphon have a dimension that is not always completely realized in more recent and better-recorded versions.

On the Warner Apex disc the balance is close and synthetic. One soon becomes aware that the studio is simply not spacious enough. There is plenty of impact and some vigorous, spirited playing from the strings of the Orchestre National, but overall this is no match either technically or artistically for the Czech Philharmonic on Chandos. The *Concerto for Quartet and Orchestra* is again very forwardly balanced, and the perspectives are quite unnatural, though the performance by the Brandis Quartet and the French orchestra certainly sounds convinced. But both here and in the *Three Ricercari* the cramped acoustic diminishes the pleasure these performances would otherwise have given.

Concerto grosso; Overture for Orchestra; The Parables; Rhapsody for Large Orchestra; Sinfonia concertante for 2 Orchestras

*** Sup. SU 3743-2. Czech PO, Bělohlávek

These recordings come from the late 1980s: the *Overture, Rhapsody* and *Parables* were originally issued together, while the *Concerto grosso* and *Sinfonia concertante* came with another piece, the *Tre Ricercari* (on a not so well-filled disc). This coupling is much better value. The set of *Parables* is among the composer's last works and is vintage Martinů. It is some four years later than the more celebrated *Frescoes of Piero della Francesca* but is in no way inferior to them in terms of invention and fantasy. The *Rhapsody* of 1928 was written for Koussevitzky, but the *Sinfonia concertante* and the *Concerto grosso* are both from the 1930s and are good examples of Martinů's neo-baroque style. The *Overture* is much later and comes from the period of the *Sixth Symphony* (*Symphonies fantastiques*) though it is much less imaginative and inventive. It is something of a rarity, and this is the only recording currently available. The resonant acoustic of the Dvořák Hall of the Rudolfinum, Prague, slightly muddies detail, but this will not put off admirers of the composer, for the performances by the Czech Philharmonic under Jirí Bělohlávek are exhilarating and idiomatic. The artwork (including the CD label itself) has a childlike, paintbox quality that is highly attractive.

Concerto grosso; (i) ***Sinfonietta la jolla; Toccata e due canzoni***

*** Panton 71 0580-2. Prague CO, (i) with Hála

The Prague Chamber Orchestra recorded the *Sinfonietta la jolla* and the *Toccata e due canzoni* initially in the days of mono LP and again in 1974. This version adds the *Concerto grosso* for chamber orchestra (1937), and two pianos to make a coupling that is both logical and rewarding. Even though there is some want of the nervous tension so characteristic of the composer, this latest recording is the most recommendable (and certainly the sunniest) of the three.

Oboe Concerto

*** Nim. NI 5330. Anderson, Philh. O, Wright – FRANCAIX: *L'Horloge de flore;* R. STRAUSS: *Concerto* ***

The account by John Anderson, principal of the Philharmonia, is outstanding in every way, with the *Andante* quite ravishing when the soloist's timbre is so rich. The recording is first class and the couplings particularly attractive.

(i) ***Piano Concertos 2, 3 & 4 (Incantation).*** **Piano music:** ***Etudes and Polkas; Fantasy and Toccata; Julietta, Act II: Moderato. Les Ritournelles; Piano Sonata 1***

🔑 ✿ (M) *** RCA 2 CD 74321 88682-2 (2). Firkušný; (i) with Czech PO, Pešek

Rudolf Firkušný premièred all three *Concertos* here and was the dedicatee of No. 3; and his recordings are very special. The finest of them is No. 4 (*Incantation*), which here receives a performance that is unlikely to be surpassed. Its exotic colourings and luminous, other-worldly landscape, with its bird cries and extraordinary textures, have never been heard to better advantage. It is a work of strong atmosphere and mystery. Firkušný is its ideal advocate. In the *Fourth Concerto* nothing is hurried and every phrase is allowed to breathe – and the same goes for its two companions. The 1988 recording is very good indeed.

Firkušný also gave the first performances of many of these

solo piano pieces. The *Fantasy and Toccata* was written for him in the dark days of 1940. Had he recorded it when he was younger (he was in his late 70s at the time of the present sessions) no doubt the rhythmic contours would have been more sharply etched and would have more bite, but his playing could not be more delicate in its keyboard colouring, more authoritative or refined. The recording is not made in a large enough acoustic but is otherwise truthful, and this set is not to be missed, even though the presentation and documentation leave much to be desired. Firkušný was an aristocrat of the keyboard and a great pianist whose exclusion from the Philips 'Great Pianists of the Twentieth Century' series was unaccountable.

(i) *Piano Concerto 3*; (ii) *Bouquet of Flowers*

(M) *** Sup. stereo/mono SU 3672-2 901. (i) Páleníček; (ii) Domanínská, Cervená, Havlák, Mráz, Prague Philharmonic Ch., Kühn Children's Ch.; Czech PO, Ančerl

Martinů's highly eclectic *Third Piano Concerto* (1948) was commissioned by Firkušný, and it displays an infectious and lively facility, but (the slow movement especially) is rather too long for its content. Yet this work, one feels, would go down well at a live performance by its very vitality, and Páleníček is impressive, especially in the sparklingly rhythmic finale. The 1961 stereo recording has transferred well to CD. But what makes this disc special is the inclusion of the exuberant *Bouquet of Flowers* (1937). The text is taken entirely from Czech folk poetry, the music echoes the wild speech-rhythms, and the orchestration (with prominent parts for two pianos) is most colourful. The performance here is magnificent, each short movement gripping the attention and helping to form a natural part of the whole elaborate bouquet. No apologies whatsover need to be made for a 1955 mono recording which is very good indeed: atmospheric, yet with incisive choral tone.

(i) *Piano Concerto 4 (Incantations)*; (ii) *Symphony 4; Tre Ricercari*

(BB) *** Warner Apex 0927 49822-2. (i) Páleníček, Brno State PO, Pinkas; (ii) Czech PO, Turnovsky

These recordings were made in 1967/8 and derive from the Supraphon catalogue. The *Fourth Piano Concerto*, written in the mid-1950s for Firkušný, is a highly imaginative and original score, presented most persuasively here. The *Fourth Symphony* dates from 1945 and is written in a readily accessible style. The dichotomy of the first movement, with its swinging (lyrical) harmonic theme on the strings in contrast with the florid counter-subject on the wind, is particularly successful, and throughout the work one feels a strong thematic unity. The Scherzo is exhilarating, with an attractive middle section, and the *Lento* has a genuine depth of expression (again the characteristic, spacious harmony making its effect). The *Three Ricercari* are less substantial but attractive enough; the outer movements rattle along with characteristic toccata-like brilliance, the piano strongly featured in the rhythmically beguiling finale. The performances of both works, but especially the symphony, are first rate and the recording, one of Supraphon's best, has transferred vividly to CD with only slight loss of body.

Violin Concertos 1–2; Rhapsody-Concerto for Viola & Orchestra

(M) **(*) Sup. (ADD) 11 1969-2 Suk, Czech PO, Neumann

The *Second Violin Concerto* is an appealing and inventive score and of greater substance than its predecessor from the 1930s, and it finds Martinů very much in concerto grosso mode. By far the most poignant and eloquent of these three works is the *Rhapsody-Concerto* for viola and orchestra, in which Suk is also the soloist and which dates from the period of the *Fantaisies symphoniques*. Suk is an exceptionally masterly player, of course, and the Czech Philharmonic play with obvious pleasure. The recordings are analogue and inner detail is not quite as sharply focused as in the very best discs from the 1970s.

Violin Concerto 1; Suite concertante for Violin and Orchestra (2nd version; 1945)

**(*) Sup. SU 3653-2-031. Matousek, Czech PO, Hogwood

Both works on this disc were commissioned by Samuel Dushkin, for whom Stravinsky had composed his *Violin Concerto*. The *First Concerto* was written in Paris during 1932–3, though Dushkin never played it. Rather surprisingly, in view of this cavalier treatment, Martinů accepted a second commission from him in 1938, for a suite of Czech dances for violin and orchestra. The *Suite concertante* was the result, though Martinů completely revised it at the end of the war. This time Dushkin did play it, in St Louis with Vladimir Golschman conducting, but this is its first recording. The work is characteristic Martinů, neo-classical, fresh and vital. Its second movement is one of his most inspired and radiant pieces, and is as luminous as Dvořák. The third movement, too, is infectiously high-spirited. The disc runs to just under 48 minutes, so room could have been found for the *Second Violin Concerto*. All the same, devotees of this masterly composer should not overlook this CD, if only for the sake of the wonderful slow movement of the *Suite*. Charcterful performances from Bohuslav Matousek and the Czech Philharmonic, and Christopher Hogwood has shown himself a committed advocate of this composer. The recorded sound is a little glassy and reverberant, in the Supraphon manner, but very serviceable.

Spalíček (ballet; complete); Dandelion (Romance); 5 Duets on Moravian Folksongs

*** Sup. 11 0752-2 (2). Soloists, Kantilena Children's Ch., Kühn Mixed Ch., Brno State PO, Jílek

The original of Martinů's engaging ballet *Spalíček* dates from 1931–2. The dances, familiar from the suites, are interspersed with vocal episodes, both solo and choral. For the most part this music is quite captivating, particularly given the charm of this performance. Two shorter works complete the set: *Dandelion Romance* for mixed chorus and soprano, and *Five Duets on Moravian Folksong Texts* for female voices, violin and piano. Both of these pieces come from his last years. All in all, this is a delightful addition to the Martinů discography.

Symphonies 1–6

⊖— **(M)** *** BIS CD 1371/2. Bamberg SO, N. Järvi
(N) **(M)** **(*) Chan. 10316X (3). RSNO, Bryden Thomson
(M) *** Sup. 11 0382-2 (3). Czech PO, Neumann

Symphonies 1; 3; 5

*** Multisonic (ADD) 31 0023-2 (2). Czech PO, Ančerl

Martinů always draws a highly individual sound from his orchestra. On hearing the *First Symphony*, Virgil Thomson wrote, 'the shining sounds of it sing as well as shine', and there is no doubt this music is luminous and life-loving. The BIS recording is in the demonstration class yet sounds completely natural, and the performances under Neeme Järvi are totally persuasive and have a spontaneous feel for the music's pulse. BIS have now put Järvi's set of the six *Symphonies* in a box, with the three CDs offered for the price of two, making a clear first choice for modern recordings of this repertoire.

Neumann's set was recorded in the Dvořák Hall of the House of Artists, Prague, between January 1976 (No. 6) and 1978 (No. 5). The transfers to CD are excellently done: the sound is full, spacious and bright; it has greater presence and better definition than the original LPs.

Whether or not you have modern versions of these Martinů symphonies, you should also obtain Ančerl's powerful, luminous performances; they come from Czech Radio recordings made in 1963, 1966 and 1962 respectively. They are such superb and convincing readings that readers should not hesitate. The music glows in Ančerl's hands and acquires a radiance that quite belies its date.

Bryden Thomson's RSNO set has now reappeared at mid-price. The performances have a robust spirit and an enthusiasm which cannot be gainsaid, and they are accorded very good Chandos sound. The *Fourth* and *Sixth Symphonies* are not quite as subtle as those on the same label by Bělohlávek, though the recording is every bit as good.

Symphonies 2 & 4

(BB) ** Naxos 8.553349. Nat. SO of the Ukraine, Fagen

These are both radiant symphonies, life-enhancing and infectious in their rhythmic vitality and luminous textures. The playing of the Ukraine orchestra is lively, and the recording is well lit and full of inner detail. All the same, they are not in the same league as Järvi or, in the case of No. 4, Bělohlávek, which will give greater long-term satisfaction.

Symphonies 3 & 4

**(*) Sup. SU 3631-2. Czech PO, Bělohlávek

Jirí Bělohlávek has given us earlier versions of some of the symphonies on Chandos, but this looks set to challenge them, at least in terms of intensity. This new account of Nos. 3 and 4 is the opening of a fresh cycle of Martinů's symphonies, based on new editions of the scores. The *Third* is the darkest of the symphonies, and Bělohlávek gives an insightful account, and his Prague orchestra play with fire and enthusiasm. The *Fourth*, the most immediately appealing, is given a splendidly characterized and committed account by Martinů's countrymen. The recordings are the problem. Made in the Dvořák Hall, they are very resonant and tutti become coarsened. They are by no means as well detailed as the Bamberg set on BIS – but the playing is thrilling.

Symphony 4; Memorial to Lidice; (i) Field Mass

*** Chan. 9138. (i) Kusjner, Czech Ph. Ch.; Czech PO, Bělohlávek

There is a radiance about this work that is quite special, and Bělohlávek's account of it is quite the best that has appeared in recent years. The *Memorial to Lidice*, composed in response to a Nazi massacre, is a powerful and haunting piece, and so is the *Field Mass*, which receives its best performance until now – by far.

Symphonies 5; 6 (Fantaisies symphoniques)

*** BIS CD 402. Bamberg SO, Järvi

Symphonies 5–6 (Fantaisies Symphoniques); Memorial to Lidice

(N) (M) *** Sup. mono SU 3964-2. Czech PO, Ančerl

The *Fifth* is a glorious piece and Järvi brings to it that mixture of disciplined enthusiasm and zest for life that distinguishes all his work. Wonderfully transparent, yet full-bodied sound, in the best BIS manner.

These are pioneering recordings on Supraphon. The *Fifth Symphony* comes from 1955, the *Sixth* from 1956, and the *Memorial to Lidice* from 1957. The mono sound never detracts one moment from the stature of the performances, and the new transfers are full and clear. They have tremendous authority. An indispensable element in any Martinů collection, and the account of the *Sixth* is hauntingly powerful and still unsurpassed.

Symphony 6 (Fantaisies symphoniques)

*** Chan. 8897. Czech PO, Bělohlávek – JANACEK: *Sinfonietta*; SUK: *Scherzo* ***

This Chandos version of No. 6 has great dramatic strength and is fully characterized; undoubtedly these players believe in every note. It is an outstanding performance that does full justice to the composer's extraordinarily imaginative vision and is very well recorded.

CHAMBER MUSIC

Cello Sonatas 1 (1939); 2 (1942); 3 (1952)

☛ (N) (BB) *** Hyp. Helios CDH 55185. Isserlis, Evans

Cello Sonatas 1, H 277; 2, H 286; 3, H 340; 7 Arabesques, H 201a; Arietta, H 188b

(BB) **(*) Naxos 8.554502. Sebastian & Christian Benda

Martinů's three *Cello Sonatas* span the period 1939–52 and are full of rewarding musical invention. Steven Isserlis and Peter Evans offer very good playing and very acceptable recording, and this can be strongly recommended, especially at Helios price.

Christian Benda was a Fournier protégé and his playing, like that of his partner, is commendably direct in utterance, though these versions do not match the subtlety of Isserlis and Evans. Worth the money, but the performances are not as involving as those of their more expensive rivals.

Cello Sonata 1; Variations on a Theme of Rossini; Variations on a Slovak Theme

*** Simax PSC 1146. Birkeland, Gimse – KABALEVSKY: *Cello Sonata 2* ***

Diverting though they are, the two sets of *Variations* are not top-drawer Martinů even if they do sound at their freshest and most charming in the hands of this Norwegian partnership. The powerful *Cello Sonata No. 1*, however, is another matter and Oystein Birkeland and Håvard Gimse play it wonderfully, with splendid rhythmic vitality, lyrical fervour and abundant imagination. The recorded sound is exceptionally truthful and lifelike, as well as being sonorous and marvellously balanced. This is a most rewarding issue in every way.

(i) Madrigal Sonata for Flute, Violin & Piano; (ii) 5 Madrigal Stanzas for Violin & Piano; (i) Promenades for Flute, Violin & Harpsichord; (iii) Scherzo for Flute & Piano; Sonata for Flute & Piano; (i) Sonata for Flute, Violin & Piano

*** Fleurs de Lys FL 2 3031. (i–ii) Dubeau; (i–iii) Hamelin; (i; iii) Marion

The performances are as fresh and exhilarating as the music itself, delightfully inventive and vital. All three artists play with imagination and virtuosity, and the recording has exemplary clarity and presence. The jazz-like *Scherzo* from the late 1920s comes off particularly well.

4 Madrigals for Oboe, Clarinet & Bassoon; 3 Madrigals for Violin & Viola; Madrigal Sonata for Piano, Flute & Violin; 5 Madrigal Stanzas for Violin & Piano

*** Hyp. CDA 66133. Dartington Ens.

These delightful pieces exhibit all the intelligence and fertility of invention we associate with Martinů's music. The playing of the Dartington Ensemble is accomplished and expert, and the recording, though resonant, is faithful.

Nonet; Trio in F for Flute, Cello & Piano; La Revue de cuisine

*** Hyp. (ADD) CDA 66084. Dartington Ens.

Only one of these pieces is otherwise available on CD and all of them receive first-class performances and superb recording. The sound has space, warmth, perspective and definition. An indispensable issue for lovers of Martinů's music.

Oboe Quartet (for oboe, violin, cello & piano); Piano Quartet; String Quintet; Viola Sonata

⊶ (BB) *** Naxos 8.553916. Artists of 1994 Australian Festival of Chamber Music

The best thing here is the captivating *Oboe Quartet*, which is quite a discovery. Like the fine *Viola Sonata* and the early *String Quintet*, whose slow movement is crossed by the shadow of Martinů's master, Roussel, its appearance at budget price is doubly welcome in that the performances are lively and spirited and the recording eminently natural.

Piano Quintet 2

*** ASV CDDCA 889. Frankl, Lindsay Qt – DVORAK: *Piano Quintet* ***

Martinů's *Second Piano Quintet* is a remarkably successful piece, characteristically original in its content and rhythmic style. The Lindsays with Peter Frankl have its full measure. The recording is lively and present, with the piano well integrated, although there is just a touch of thinness on the strings. An outstanding coupling.

Sextet for Strings

(M) **(*) Panton 81 1437-2 131. Czech Chamber Soloists, Matyáš – JANACEK: *Idyll; Suite* **(*)

The *Sextet for Strings* (1932) is not one of Martinů's most inspired pieces. Even so, it is played well enough by the Czech Chamber Soloists under the direction of Ivan Matyáš.

String Quartets 1–7

**(*) Sup. (ADD) 110 994-2 (3). Panocha Qt

The *First* of the quartets is both the longest and the most derivative; it is heavily indebted to the world of Debussy and Ravel. The *Third* is by far the shortest (it takes barely 12 minutes) and has the nervous energy and rhythmic vitality characteristic of the mature composer. The *Fourth* and *Fifth* are close to the *Double Concerto for Two String Orchestras, Piano and Timpani*. The *Fifth* is the darkest of the quartets and in its emotional intensity is close in spirit to Janáček's *Intimate Letters*. The *Sixth* – and in particular its first movement – is a powerful and disturbing piece, and there is a sense of scale and a vision that raise it above its immediate successor. The Panocha set is eminently recommendable, even

though it is a bit steep to ask full price for it, and the recordings are a bit two-dimensional.

String Quartets 1–2; Tri jezdci (Three Horsemen)

(BB) **(*) Naxos 553782. Martinů Qt

The *First Quartet* lasts almost 40 minutes and is known as the '*French*' (the nickname was Martinů's own) and what it lacks in individuality it makes up for in craftsmanship. The *Second Quartet* (1925) is more concentrated and more complex, and its greater density of incident reflects the influence of Roussel, with whom Martinů was studying. The fill-up is a remarkably accomplished first recording of *Tri jezdci*, which was written when the composer was twelve. The Martinů Quartet play with spirit and the recording is decent: fresh and lifelike without being outstanding.

String Quartets 3, 4 & 5

*** BIS CD 1389. Emperor Qt

Using new, critically revised scores, the Emperor String Quartet present their interpretations of three works that give a fascinating picture of an exciting era in twentieth-century music. Composed between 1929 and 1937, these *Quartets* employ various styles and techniques. With its inventive sonorities and the focusing on rhythm rather than melody, the brief *Quartet No. 3* is more reminiscent of non-European music than of the normal canon of Western music of the period. In the neoclassical *Fourth Quartet* Martinů combined French *mesure* with Czech melodic invention. The combination of typical stylistic characteristics of Martinů, Roussel and Stravinsky makes this classically disciplined and moderate work a fascinating mixture of the styles which were common in Paris towards the end of the 1930s; the result, however, is extremely individual and homogeneous. Martinů's source of inspiration for *String Quartet No. 5* was Vítezslava Kaprálová, a talented composer 25 years his junior, who took private lessons from him in Paris and with whom he soon started an affair. In his informed and informative liner-notes, Ales Brezina (director of the Bohuslav Martinů Institute in Prague) proposes that this may have been why Martinů refrained from publishing the work until the very last year of his life, a fact all the more astonishing since there is no doubt that the quartet is one of the composer's most significant chamber works.

String Quartets 4–5; 7 (Concerto da Camera)

(BB) *** Naxos 8.553784. Martinů Qt

The *Fourth* and *Fifth Quartets* come from the period 1937–8 and are close to the *Double Concerto for two string orchestras, piano and timpani* – and, of course, are contemporary with the Munich crisis. The *Fifth* is the darker of the two, and in its emotional turbulence it comes closer in spirit to Janáček's *Second Quartet*. The *Seventh*, subtitled *Concerto da camera*, is less concentrated in feeling. It is finely crafted and very much in Martinů's neoclassical vein, if less memorable and spontaneous. Anyway, they are all well played and recorded and can be confidently recommended to those who are collecting this inexpensive cycle by the eponymous Martinů Quartet.

String Trio 2

*** Hyp. CDA 67429. Leopold String Trio – DOHNANYI: *Serenade in C*; SCHOENBERG: *Trio* ***

Martinů's *First String Trio* dates from 1923, when the composer was living in Paris, and it is seldom heard (it is not listed in the current catalogues). Its successor also comes from his Paris years, 1934 in fact, by which time he had made a name for himself in the musical world. Much of the writing is in the composr's neoclassical manner, and the Leopold String Trio make a strong case for the piece. Exemplary recorded sound.

Violin Sonata 1, H 182; Sonatas in C, H 120; D min., H 152; Concerto, H 13; Elegy, H 3; Impromptu, H 166; 5 Short pieces, H 184

(M) *** Sup. SU 3410-2 (2). Matoušek, Adamec

Violin Sonatas 2, H 308; 3, H 303; Sonatina in G, H 262; 7 Arabesques, H 201A; Arietta, H 188A; Czech Rhapsody, H 307; Intermezzo, H 261; 5 Madrigal Stanzas, H 297; Rhythmic Etudes, H 202

(M) *** Sup. SU 3412-2 (2). Matoušek, Adamec

Violin Sonatas 2–3; 5 Madrigal Sonatas

** Sup. 11 0099-2. Suk, Hála

Enormously prolific in most genres and combinations, Martinů's output for violin and piano is fairly extensive – 19 pieces in all. The two handsomely produced and well-recorded double-CD sets cover his whole output: from the age of nineteen when he composed the *Elegy*, and the *Concerto* from the following year, through to his mid-fifties and the *Sonata No. 3* (1944) and the *Czech Rhapsody* written for Kreisler (1945). At times, Martinů is given to self-imitation, and there are occasions when his muse is on autopilot but, for the most part, they are few and far between. The *Third Sonata* in particular is very impressive. Bohuslav Matoušek and Petr Adamec are completely inside the idiom, having played Martinů virtually from the cradle.

Josef Suk and Josef Hála give excellent accounts of all three pieces, though the 1987 recording is balanced less than appealingly. The sound is rather synthetic and too close.

Violin Sonata 3 in G, Op. 100

*** Praga PRD 250 153. Remés, Kayahara – DVORAK: *Sonatina; JANACEK, SMETANA: Violin Sonatas ***

Václav Remés and Sachito Kayahara combine to give a superb account of Martinů's passionate *Third Sonata*, fiery and intense, yet relaxing warmly for the composer's moments of gentler lyricism: the opening of the *Finale* has a lovely rapt serenity.

Sonata for 2 Violins & Piano

(*) Hyp. CDA 66473. Osostowicz, Kovacic, Tomes – MILHAUD: *Violin Duo, etc.* **(*); PROKOFIEV: *Violin Sonata *

Martinů's *Sonata for Two Violins and Piano* finds him full of invention and vitality. Krysia Osostowicz, Ernst Kovacic and Susan Tomes play it with all the finesse and sensitivity you could wish for, and they are excellently recorded. The disc would be even more recommendable if it had a longer playing time than 46 minutes.

PIANO MUSIC

Bagatelle (Morceau facile), H 323; Dumka 3, H 285 bis; Fantasia et toccata, H 281; The fifth day of the fifth moon, H 318; 8 Preludes, H 181; Piano Sonata, H 350

** Chan. 9655. Bekova

Martinů's piano music has been well served in the past, but the uniquely authoritative RCA disc by Rudolf Firkušný is at present out of circulation, so Eleonora Bekova's set fills a gap. The playing is more than serviceable without being really distinguished, and the recording is eminently truthful.

VOCAL MUSIC

The Butterfly That Stamped (ballet): 5 scenes (arr. Rybár)

** Sup. 11 0380-2. Women's voices of Kühn Ch., Prague SO, Bělohlávek

Martinů's choral ballet, *The Butterfly That Stamped*, is based on one of Kipling's *Just-So* stories. The five scenes have been put into a performing edition by Jaroslav Rybár. The score has a great deal of Gallic charm, and it is a pity that Supraphon market this slight but charming score (lasting only 41 minutes 47 seconds) at full price.

The Epic of Gilgamesh (oratorio)

*** Marco Polo 8.223316. Depoltová, Margita, Kusnjer, Vele, Karpíšek, Slovak Philh. Ch. & O, Košler

*** Sup. 11 1824. Machotková, Zahradníček, Zítek, Průša, Brousek, Czech Philh. Ch., Prague SO, Bělohlávek

The Epic of Gilgamesh comes from Martinů's last years and is arguably his masterpiece. It evokes a remote and distant world, full of colour and mystery. Gilgamesh is the oldest poem known to mankind. The work abounds with invention of the highest quality and of consistently sustained inspiration. The Marco Polo performance is committed and sympathetic and the recording very natural in its balance.

Bělohlávek's version can hold its own artistically with the excellent Marco Polo account. It does not displace it but can certainly be recommended alongside it.

OPERA

Ariane (complete; in French)

*** Sup. SU 3524-2 6312. Lindsley, Phillips, Doležal, Burun, Novák (bass), Czech PO & Ch., Neumann

As with his earlier operatic masterpiece, *Julietta*, Martinů based his one-act opera *Ariane* on a play, *Le Voyage de Thésée*, by his friend Georges Neveux. In making his adaptation Martinů treats it as baroque monody, interspersed with three sinfonias, three self-contained dramatic sequences and a closing aria. The pastiche elements have great lightness of touch; it seems that the bravura of Ariane herself, sung excellently by the American soprano Celina Lindsley, was inspired by Callas. Richard Novák's vibrato may be too wide for some, but generally speaking the performance is sung well (in French), and Václav Neumann gets alert and sensitive playing from the Czech Philharmonic. The recording (from 1987) is eminently serviceable. In order to accommodate its four-language libretto, the CD is housed in a jewel case that could happily encompass *Siegfried* or *Walküre* – somewhat bizarre as *Ariane* runs only to 43 minutes 44 seconds. But the opera has both freshness and charm and devotees of Martinů need not hesitate.

The Greek Passion (in English)

*** Sup. 10 3611/2. Mitchinson, Field, Tomlinson, Joll, Moses, Davies, Cullis, Savory, Kuhn Children's Ch., Czech PO Ch., Brno State PO, Mackerras

Written with much mental pain in the years just before Martinů died in 1959, this was the work he regarded as his musical testament. It tells in an innocent, direct way of a village where a Passion play is to be presented; the individuals

– tragically, as it proves – take on qualities of the New Testament figures they represent. Mackerras makes an ideal advocate, and the recording is both brilliant and atmospheric. With the words so clear, the absence of an English libretto is not a serious omission, but the lack of any separate cues within the four Acts is a great annoyance. Extraordinarily vivid recording.

Julietta (complete)

🔾 ☞ *** Sup. (ADD) 3626-2 612 (2). Tauberová, Zídek, Zlesák, Otava, Bednář, Mixová, Jedenáctík, Procházková, Hanzalíková, Soukupová, Jindrák, Veverka, Svehla, Zlesák, Lemariová, Berman, Prague Nat. Theatre Ch. & O, Krombholc

Described by the composer as a Dreambook, *Julietta* was given first in Prague in March 1938. This vintage Supraphon recording, made in 1964, captures that surreal quality vividly, for the ear is mesmerized from the very start, when the howling of a high bassoon introduces the astonishingly original prelude. The voices as well as the orchestra are then presented with a bright immediacy which reinforces the power and incisiveness of Krombholc's performance. The sharpness of focus adds to the atmospheric intensity, as when in the first Act The Man in the Window plays his accordion. Ivo Zídek gives a vivid portrait of the central character, Michel, perplexed by his dream-like search, and there is no weak link in the rest of the cast. The three CDs of the 1993 transfer are now reduced to two (the break coming at scene V of Act II) and the sound is brighter and more firmly focused, with a very marginal loss of the gentler sonority that distinguished the LP set. Informative notes and libretto come with multiple translations.

Les Larmes du couteau; The Voice of the Forest

*** Sup. SU 3386-3 631. Jonášová, Smidová, Janál, Prague Philharmonia, Bělohlávek

The two one-Act operas recorded here are both short, roughly half an hour each. With the Dadaist *Les Larmes du couteau* (or *The Knife's Tears*) we are close to the world of *L'Histoire du soldat*, Les Six and Kurt Weill. It is entertaining if insubstantial and diverts the listener. Good soloists and recording, with the musical and speech elements well balanced. *The Voice of the Forest* offers a more familiar Martinů. It is far more individual in style and, like the ballet *Spalíček*, draws on Czech folklore and melody. In it, Martinů's invention is unfailingly fresh and although one can see why it has never made waves it has much to offer. The set is packaged as one disc in a box for two, so as to accommodate the copious and handsomely produced documentation.

MASCAGNI, Pietro (1863–1945)

L'amico Fritz (complete)

🔾 ☞ (M) *** EMI 5 67376-2 [567373] (2). Pavarotti, Freni, Sardinero, ROHCG Ch. & O, Gavazzeni

The haunting *Cherry Duet* from this opera whets the appetite for more, and it is good to hear so rare and delightful a piece, one that is unlikely to enter the repertory of our British opera houses. The performance could not be more refined, and Freni and Pavarotti were both at their freshest in 1969 when it was recorded. While the dramatic conception is at the opposite end of the scale from *Cavalleria rusticana*, one is easily beguiled by the music's charm. The Covent Garden orchestra

responds loyally; the recording is clear, warm and atmospheric and has transferred beautifully to CD. Though perhaps not a 'Great Recording of the Century', this mid-priced reissue is very winning. The documentation includes a full libretto and attractive sessions photographs.

Cavalleria rusticana (complete; DVD version)

(N) *** Ph. **DVD** 070 428-9. Obraztsova, Domingo, Bruson, La Scala, Milan, Ch. & O, Prêtre (Director: Franco Zeffirelli) – LEONCAVALLO: *Pagliacci* ***

Franco Zeffirelli has here (in 1981) opted to film *Cavalleria rusticana* on location in Sicily, with wonderfully evocative results, helped by total freedom of movement between outdoor and interior scenes, fluid even within musical numbers. The camerawork brilliantly heightens the drama too, with long shots used for such key moments as the final fight between Turiddù and Alfio, which in the theatre always takes place off-stage. He also uses close-ups very effectively to bring out the conflicting emotions of Santuzza and Turiddù in their big duet. Authentic costumes augment the local colour, and the handling of the chorus adds to the realism. As in *Pagliacci*, Zeffirelli regularly conceals any problem of co-ordination between sound and vision as the singers mime their words. Plácido Domingo is in superb voice as Turiddù, singing and acting with total command, and Renato Bruson makes a strong, characterful Alfio. As Santuzza, Elena Obraztsova sings warmly, with a rich and fruity mezzo, if with too insistent a vibrato. Stealing the scene in the far smaller role of Mamma Lucia, the veteran mezzo Fedora Barbieri is superb, wonderfully characterful and still in fine voice.

Cavalleria rusticana (complete; CD versions)

🔾 ☞ (M) *** RCA (ADD) 74321 39500-2. Scotto, Domingo, Elvira, Amb. Op. Ch., Nat. PO, Levine

(M) *** DG (ADD) 457 764-2. Cossotto, Bergonzi, Allegri, Guelfi, Martino, Ch. & O of La Scala, Milan, Karajan

*** DG (ADD) 419 257-2 (3). Cossotto, Bergonzi, Guelfi, Ch. & O of La Scala, Milan, Karajan – LEONCAVALLO: *I Pagliacci* *** (also with collection of operatic intermezzi ***)

(***) EMI mono 5 56287-2 (2). Callas, Di Stefano, Panerai, Ch. & O of La Scala, Milan, Serafin – LEONCAVALLO: *I Pagliacci* (***)

(M) **(*) Decca (ADD) 458 224-2. Tebaldi, Björling, Bastianini, Maggio Musicale Fiorentino Ch. & O, Erede

(M) **(*) EMI (ADD) 7 63967-2 (2). De los Angeles, Corelli, Sereni, Rome Op. Ch. & O, Santini – LEONCAVALLO: *I Pagliacci* ***

(M) **(*) EMI (ADD) 7 63650-2 (2). Caballé, Carreras, Hamari, Manuguerra, Varnay, Amb. Op. Ch., Southend Boys' Ch., Philh. O, Muti – LEONCAVALLO: *I Pagliacci* **(*)

**(*) Decca (ADD) 444 391-2. Varady, Pavarotti, Bormida, Cappuccilli, Gonzales, Nat. PO, Gavazzeni

(BB) **(*) Naxos 8.660022. Evstatieva, Aragall, Tumagian, Di Mauro, Michalková, Slovak Philh. Ch., Czech RSO, Rahbari – LEONCAVALLO: *I Pagliacci* **(*)

(N) (M) ** Decca (ADD) 476 7216. Souliotis, Del Monaco, Gobbi, Rome Op. Ch. & O, Varviso

(M) (**) Nim. mono NI 7843/4. Gigli, Bruna Rasa, Marcucci, Bechi, Simionato, La Scala Ch. & O, composer – LEONCAVALLO: *I Pagliacci* (**(*))

Now reissued at mid-price (pleasingly presented in a slip-case with libretto), the Scotto–Domingo set now stands as a first recommendation for Mascagni's red-blooded opera, with Domingo giving a heroic account of the role of Turiddù, full of defiance. Scotto is strongly characterful too, and James Levine directs with a splendid sense of pacing, by no means faster than his rivals (except the leisurely Karajan) and drawing red-blooded playing from the National Philharmonic. The recording is vivid and strikingly present in its CD transfer.

It is good to see that Karajan's outstanding recording, hitherto linked to *Pagliacci*, is now available separately. Karajan pays Mascagni the tribute of taking his markings literally, so that well-worn melodies come out with new purity and freshness, and the singers have been chosen to match that. Cossotto quite as much as Bergonzi keeps a pure, firm line that is all too rare in this much-abused music – not that there is any lack of bite (except that the original recording could have made the chorus better defined). However, it has never sounded more vivid than on this Originals CD – which manages to squeeze just under 81 minutes on a single disc – with texts and translations. The recording remains available at full price, coupled with *Pagliacci*.

Dating from the mid-1950s, Callas's performance as Santuzza reveals the diva in her finest form, with edginess and unevenness of production at a minimum and with vocal colouring at its most characterful. The singing of the other principals is hardly less dramatic and Panerai is in firm, well-projected voice.

The early (1957) Decca recording with Tebaldi offers a forthright, lusty account of Mascagni's piece of blood and thunder and has the distinction of three excellent soloists. Tebaldi is most moving in *Voi lo sapete*, and the firm richness of Bastianini's baritone is beautifully caught. As always, Björling shows himself the most intelligent of tenors, and it is only the chorus that gives serious cause for disappointment; they are very undisciplined. The CD sound is strikingly bright and lively.

Though not as vibrant as Von Matačić's *Pagliacci* coupling, this beautifully sung, essentially lyrical Santini performance could give considerable satisfaction, provided the bitterness of Mascagni's drama is not a first consideration. Like the coupling, it shows Corelli in good form; both he and de los Angeles are given scope by Santini to produce soaring, Italianate singing of Mascagni's richly memorable melodies. The recording is suitably atmospheric.

There are fewer unexpected textual points in Muti's EMI *Cav.* than in *Pag.*, but the conductor's approach is comparably biting and violent, brushing away the idea that this is a sentimental score, though running the risk of making it sound vulgar. The result is certainly refreshing, with Caballé – pushed faster than usual, even in her big moments – collaborating warmly. So *Voi lo sapete* is geared from the start to the final cry of *Io son dannata*, and she manages a fine snarl on *A te la mala Pasqua*. Carreras does not sound quite so much at home, though the rest of the cast is memorable, including the resonant Manuguerra as Alfio and the veteran Astrid Varnay as Mamma Lucia, wobble as she does. The recording is forward and vivid.

With Pavarotti loud and unsubtle as Turiddù – though the tone is often most beautiful – it is left to Julia Varady as Santuzza to give the 1976 Decca recording under Gavazzeni its distinction, the sharpness of pain in *Voi lo sapete* beautifully conveyed, the whole performance warm and authentic. Cappuccilli's Alfio is too noble to be convincing, and the main claim to attention lies in the brilliant forward recording. This set remains at full price.

As in his parallel recording of *Pag.*, Alexander Rahbari conducts a red-blooded reading of *Cav.*, making it a first-rate super-bargain choice. Stefka Evstatieva is a warmly vibrant Santuzza, well controlled, no Slavonic wobbler, and Giacomo Aragall as Turiddù, not quite as fresh-sounding as he once was, yet gives a strong, characterful performance, with Eduard Tumagian excellent as Alfio, firm and dark. Well-focused digital recording.

Decca's 1966 set under Varviso was a curious selection for Universal's 'Critics' Choice' series, although it was apparently picked for the BBC's 'Building a Library' on Radio 3. Souliotis's can be an exciting voice on record, and here she gives a dramatic performance, but in many details it seems unfinished, and though the voice is characterful it is not always under complete control. If Souliotis was caught too early as Santuzza, Gobbi was caught just in time as Alfio – and for that many thanks. He turns the conventional figure of the carter into a real, three-dimensional character. Mario del Monaco is not at his best, but nor is he at his coarsest – a fair enough, big-voiced performance. Nor does Varviso's conducting emerge with any individuality, and it is the magnificent Decca analogue sound that saves the day: the result is undeniably dramatic.

EMI's vintage (1940) version of *Cav.*, conducted by the composer with Gigli as Turiddù, is again available from Nimbus, along with the curious little speech of introduction that Mascagni himself recorded. Yet the composer's sluggish speeds mean that this opera has to start awkwardly at the end of the *Pag.* disc. Nimbus's transfer captures the voices well, giving them a mellow bloom, though the focus is not nearly as sharp as on the old EMI transfer.

Cavalleria rusticana (complete; in English)

(M) **(*) Chan. 3004 (2). Miricioiu, O'Neill, Joll, Montague, Bainbridge, Geoffrey Mitchell Ch., LPO, Parry

David Parry gives a warmly atmospheric reading of the Mascagni score which, as well as bringing out its atmospheric beauty, brings home the high drama, as in the big duet between Turiddù and Santuzza at the very end. Nelly Miricioiu is an inspired choice to take the role of the heroine, her rich, vibrant voice firmly under control, with fine legato and passionately declaimed climaxes. Dennis O'Neill with his clear Italianate tone is also excellent as Turiddù, passionate and intense. It is good to hear the fruity and characterful Elizabeth Bainbridge as Mamma Lucia, and Diana Montague sings with creamy beauty in Lola's Song. The serious blot comes with the Alfio of Phillip Joll, most damagingly in the Carter's song, in which the voice is pitched so vaguely it is halfway to talking, with notes spreading under pressure. A pity, when the rest is so convincing.

MASSENET, Jules (1842–1912)

Le Carillon (ballet; complete)

(B) *** Double Decca 444 836-2 (2). SRO, Bonynge – DELIBES: *Coppélia* ***

Le Carillon was written in the same year as *Werther*. The villains of the story who try to destroy the bells of the title are punished by being miraculously transformed into bronze jaquemarts, fated to continue striking them for ever! The music of this one-Act ballet makes a delightful offering – not always as lightweight as one would expect. With his keen rhythmic sense and feeling for colour, Bonynge is outstanding in this repertory, and the 1984 Decca recording is brilliant and colourful. A fine bonus (37 minutes) for a desirable version of Delibes' *Coppélia*, at the cheapest possible price.

Le Cid: ballet suite

~ (B) *** Double Decca (ADD) (IMS) 448 095-2 (2). Nat. PO, Bonynge – DELIBES: *Sylvia* (complete) ***

(N) ✹*** Australian Decca Eloquence (ADD) 476 2742. Israel PO, Martinon – DVORAK: *Slavonic Dances*; MEYERBEER: *Les Patineurs* *** ✹

Bonynge's version is among the finest yet, with the most seductive orchestral playing, superbly recorded, with the remastering for CD adding to the glitter and colour of Massenet's often witty scoring, and made the more attractive at Double Decca price.

Over the years Decca have made a house speciality of recording the ballet music from *Le Cid* and coupling it with Constant Lambert's arrangement of Meyerbeer's *Les Patineurs*.

In Martinon's hands, Massenet's tunes fizz and effervesce like the best champagne, while the more reflective numbers have colourful, picture-postcard atmosphere. Equally remarkable is the astonishingly vivid Decca recording, the sort of brilliant yet warm sound for which the company became famous, and it is superbly transferred to CD. It is a pity that these Australian reissues are not more easily available in the UK; but they are available through the Internet, and this one is worth seeking out.

Piano Concerto in E flat

*** Hyp. CDA 66897. Coombs, BBC Scottish SO, Ossonce – HAHN: *Piano Concerto in E* ***

Massenet unexpectedly completed this substantial concerto at the age of 60. It regularly reveals his love of the keyboard, and in a performance like Stephen Coombs's the result is a delight, the writing full of attractive ideas. That is so, even when in the Slovak dance of the finale the main theme barely skirts banality, providing an extra challenge for Coombs to magic it with sparkling articulation. As in the Hahn concerto – an apt coupling, when it occupies a similar place in that composer's career – Jean-Yves Ossonce is a most sympathetic accompanist, drawing idiomatic playing from the BBC Scottish Symphony, helped by warm, well-balanced sound.

(i) Piano Concerto in E flat. Année passées, I–IV; 2 Berceuses; 6 Danses; Devant la Madonne; 7 Improvisations; 3 Marches; Musique pour bercer les petits enfants; Papillons noirs, Papillons blancs; Première suite; Toccata; Valse folle; Valse très lente; La Vierge: galiléenne

(BB) ** EMI Gemini (ADD) 585517-2 (2). Ciccolini, (i) with Monte Carlo Nat. Op. O, Cambreling

Massenet's *Piano Concerto in E flat* has perhaps the manners of Saint-Saëns. There are some nice things in it though, the Hungarian colourings of the first and last movements especially so. This performance is lively and enjoyable, a little dry in sound, but reasonably vivid. Stephen Coombs's newer Hyperion account is finer, however, but that is at full price and differently coupled. The bulk of this two-CD set comprises Massenet's piano works, most of it salon music. This is lightweight repertoire, but it has a certain charm running throughout the best pieces; with some lively character dances and nostalgic sentimental ones – including the lovely *Elégie* – it makes for excellent light listening. The piano image is well focused, if the acoustic is a bit dry.

Fantaisie (for Cello & Orchestra)

*** ASV CDDCA 867. Rolland, BBC PO, Varga – LALO: *Cello Concerto*; SAINT-SAENS: *Cello Concerto 1* ***

Massenet's *Fantaisie for Cello and Orchestra* is music for the sweet-toothed (and none the worse for that), though its ideas are not anywhere near as memorable as those of its two companions on this disc. The Canadian cellist, Sophie Rolland, and the BBC forces under Gilbert Varga play it with total commitment and fervour as if they believe every note. Excellent recording.

Hérodiade (ballet) Suite; Orchestral Suites 1; 2 (Scènes hongroises); 3 (Scènes dramatiques)

(BB) ** Naxos 8.553124. New Zealand SO, Ossonce

The ballet suite from *Hérodiade* comes in the final scene of the opera and the five movements are nicely scored, including flutes and harp, delicate dancing strings, a luscious tune in the middle strings, decorated by chirpy woodwind, and a vigorous dance finale. The other orchestral suites are also well worth hearing, offering a further series of sharply memorable vignettes, demonstrating Massenet's ready store of tunes and his charmingly French orchestral palette. The playing of the New Zealand orchestra is first class, polished and vivid, though it is a pity that the microphones are somewhat close. The wind have plenty of colour, but the string tuttis are made to sound a bit tight and fierce.

Scènes alsaciennes; Scènes dramatiques; Scènes de féerie; Scènes pittoresques; Don Quichotte: Interludes. La Vierge: The Last Sleep of the Virgin

(N) (BB) ** Warner Apex 2564 62085-2 (2). Monte Carlo Op. O, Gardiner

This linked pair of Apex discs gathers together four of Massenet's seven orchestral suites, plus a few encores, including one of Sir Thomas Beecham's favourites, *The Last Sleep of the Virgin*. In fact, this is all music that would respond to the Beecham touch. John Eliot Gardiner secures quite impressively characterized performances, and he finds suitable gravitas and breadth in the *Scènes dramatiques*; the *Scènes pittoresques* are bright and fresh, the horns tolling the Angelus with resonant impact. But the Monte Carlo orchestra produces a rather thin-bodied tutti, and although the full, atmospheric recording minimizes the effect, the ear remains conscious that the playing lacks the last degree of polish and elegance, while the sound itself is limited in range and colour alongside Frémaux. However, the set is inexpensive, and the music itself is well worth having.

Scènes alsaciennes; Scènes de féerie; Scènes napolitaines; Scènes pittoresques

~ (BB) *** Naxos 8.553125. New Zealand SO, Ossonce

Massenet's orchestral suites are in essence picture-postcard music, but they include plenty of tunes (perhaps not always first-rate ones) and the scoring has characteristic Gallic charm and colour. Best known are the somewhat ingenuous *Scènes pittoresques* and the *Scènes alsaciennes*. The most touching movement is the beautiful *Sous les tilleuls* ('Under the Lime Trees'), with its wilting dialogue between cello and clarinet, played here with an affectionate finesse worthy of a Beecham. With full, sparkling, yet warmly atmospheric recording, this is a first-class disc in every way. Why pay more?

La Vierge: Le Dernier sommeil de la vierge (The Last Sleep of the Virgin)

(M) (**(*)) BBC mono BBCL 4113. RPO, Beecham (with spoken introduction) – BERLIOZ: *The Trojans: Royal Hunt and Storm*; CHABRIER: *España; Gwendoline Overture*; DEBUSSY: *L'Enfant prodigue: Cortège et Air de danse*; DELIUS: *Brigg Fair*; SAINT-SAENS: *Le Rouet d'Omphale*. (with MOZART: *Divertimento in D, K. 131:* excerpts) (**(*))

This was one of Sir Thomas's most celebrated 'lollipops' and it comes from a live broadcast concert of 1956, complete with a characteristic spoken introduction. It is beautifully played but the recording, although warm and pleasing, is rather restricted.

(i) *Mélodie: Elégie* (arr. Mouton); *Les Erinnyes: Tristesse du soir;* (ii) *Thaïs: Méditation. La Vierge: Le Dernier Sommeil de la vierge*

*** Chan. 9765. (i) Dixon; (ii) Torchinsky; RLPO Ch.; BBC PO, Y. P. Tortelier (with Concert: *French Bonbons* ***)

This is Beechamesque material (especially *Le Dernier Sommeil de la vierge*) and beautifully played and recorded too. It is part of a particularly delectable collection of French music, including a number of familiar overtures.

OPERA

Don Quichotte (complete)
*** EMI 7 54767-2 (2). Van Dam, Fondary, Berganza, Toulouse Capitole Ch. & O, Plasson

Michel Plasson conducts a sumptuous account of Massenet's charming Cervantes-based opera, with José van Dam singing gloriously as the Don, producing consistently firm and velvety tone. Alain Fondary as Sancho Panza is equally strong and firm vocally, shadowing and matching his master instead of contrasting, never indulging in exaggeratedly comic effects. Teresa Berganza as Dulcinée adds to the sensuousness of the performance, with the Toulouse acoustic bringing out the richness and beauty of Massenet's orchestral writing. No one will be disappointed, but the deleted 1977 Decca set still has clear advantages.

Esclarmonde (complete)
(B) *** Decca Trio 475 50129 (3). Sutherland, Aragall, Tourangeau, Davies, Grant, Alldis Ch., Nat PO, Bonynge

Joan Sutherland is the obvious diva to encompass the demands of great range, great power and brilliant coloratura of the central role of *Esclarmonde*, and her performance is in its way as powerful as it is in Puccini's last opera. Aragall proves an excellent tenor, sweet of tone and intelligent, and the other parts are well taken too. Richard Bonynge draws passionate singing and playing from chorus and orchestra, and the recording has both atmosphere and spectacle to match the story, based on a medieval romance involving song-contests and necromancy. This has now been reissued on a Decca Trio, and although only a synopsis is included, it makes a fine bargain for those wanting to explore Massenet's lesser-known operas.

(i) *Le Jongleur de Notre-Dame;* (ii) *La Navarraise* (also includes excerpts from 1933 recording of *Le Jongleur* with Vezzani, O cond. Dumazert)

(N) (M) ** Gala (ADD; stereo/mono) GL 100.747 (2). (i) Vanzo, Massard, Bastin, Dupouy, Ch. & O de l'ORTF, Dervaux; (ii) Moizan, Vanzo, Mars, Lovano, Vigneron, Lyrique Ch. & O de la RTF, Hartemann

Few French tenors in the recent past can match Alain Vanzo for the beauty and imagination of his singing, and it is sad that he made relatively few studio recordings. That makes these radio recordings especially valuable, even though *La Navarraise*, recorded in 1963, is in mono only. *Le Jongleur de Notre-Dame*, written in 1900, is one of Massenet's most charming pieces. It centres on the juggler, Jean, who finds salvation through the miraculous intervention of the Virgin Mary when he performs in front of the altar, a sentimental story nicely spiced with a touch of humour in the character of the abbey's cook, Boniface. As a single-sex piece in a religious setting with the Virgin intervening, it evidently influenced Puccini's *Suor Angelica*. Though it has no grand Puccinian tunes, the writing is consistently inventive and beautifully crafted, with mock-medieval songs for Jean. Vanzo dominates this broadcast recording, but the others in the cast (as well as the mixed chorus) all sing well, with the 1973 sound nicely atmospheric. *La Navarraise* (1894) marks Massenet's response to the big success of Mascagni's *Cavalleria rusticana*. It is the tragic tale of Anita, who is passionately devoted to her heroic soldier-lover, Sergeant Araquil, but who, despite her own heroism, loses him through unfounded jealousy. Though this radio recording can hardly match stereo versions in sound, the performances (not just of Vanzo but of Geneviève Moizan in the title-role as well as of Jean Peyron as the second tenor) make it well worth hearing, particularly as it comes as a bonus on this two-disc set, which also includes historic recordings of both operas from the 1930s.

Hérodiade (complete)
*** EMI 5 55378-2 (3). Studer, Denize, Heppner, Hampson, Van Dam, Capitole Toulouse Ch. & O, Plasson

Massenet's opera about Salome and John the Baptist, completed in 1880, has little in common with either the Bible story or the violent Strauss opera based on Oscar Wilde's play, and the final scene, so far from involving Salome in asking for John's head, has an ecstatic duet for them both, 'hymning the chaste flame of their immortal love' – as the EMI synopsis graphically puts it. When John is executed, Salome then kills herself. What matters is that the opera offers five fat parts for well-contrasted voices.

Michel Plasson's studio recording offers well-balanced sound, opulent and firmly focused. His text is complete, using the final and fullest version of a work that Massenet revised several times. As Hérodiade herself, Nadine Denize sings with gloriously rich, firm tone, and Thomas Hampson's portrait of Hérode could hardly be richer either vocally or dramatically, with words brought out vividly. It would be hard to imagine a finer Phanuel than José van Dam, with his well-contrasted bass-baritone incisive in attack. As for Cheryl Studer as Salome, she has rarely sung with such expressive range and beauty of tone, with words crystal-clear. Ben Heppner as Jean confirms in his clear, firmly focused delivery earlier impressions of his development as a genuine heroic tenor with few rivals today. There are first-rate singers too in the small roles, and the Toulouse orchestra plays with glowing warmth and intensity, helped by the acoustic of the Halle-aux-Grains. A warmly enjoyable set from first to last, admirably filling a major gap in the catalogue.

Le Jongleur de Notre-Dame (complete)
(B) **(*) EMI (ADD) 5 75297-2 (2). Vanzo, Bastin, Vento, Raffali, Frémeau, Monte-Carlo Op. Ch. & O, Boutry

Le Jongleur de Notre-Dame, written in 1900, was composed entirely for male voices (with the exception of the chorus of angels). Even so, Mary Garden made the leading part of the Juggler a breeches role, somewhat to the irritation of its composer. Set in a Benedictine abbey in the fourteenth century, it provided Massenet with an opportunity to display his penchant for medieval musical pastiche. The juggler of the title, Jean (who is also an acrobat and minstrel), relies on his talents and his wits to earn a living, but, feeling he needs to give his life a spiritual dimension, he joins the Benedictine order. At the climax of the opera he steals into the Sanctuary and performs his skills in front of the statue of the Virgin. His supplication is successful, the Virgin is seen in a vision of glowing acceptance, angels are heard singing from above, and the opera culminates in Jean's death in religious ecstasy.

Despite the slight plot, the work is neither dull nor too religiose. The images of rustic village and abbey life are colourfully contrasted. Alain Vanzo as the juggler, Jean, is at his stylish best – his drinking song (an 'Alleluia' to wine!) with its rustic violin obbligato is a highlight. The rest of the French cast is idiomatic and convincing. In the comic role of the Abbey's cook, Boniface, the robust humour is brought out well by Jules Bastin. Roger Boutry provides sympathetic support with his Monte Carlo forces, and the 1978 sound is warmly atmospheric. There are no texts to help non-French speakers, but the set is inexpensive and has undoubted period charm.

Manon (complete; DVD version)
*** TDK **DVD** DVOPMANON (2). Fleming, Alvarez, Chaignaud, Sénéchal, Paris Nat. Op. Ch. and O, Lopez-Cobos (Dir.: Deflo, DVD Dir.: François Roussillon)

Manon (complete; CD versions)
➤ *** EMI 5 57005-2 (2). Gheorghiu, Alagna, Patriarco, Van Dam, La Monnaie Op. Ch. & O, Pappano

(***) Testament mono SBT 3203 (3). De los Angeles, Legay, Dens, Paris Opéra-Comique O, Monteux – BERLIOZ: *Les Nuits d'été*; DEBUSSY: *La Demoiselle élue*. (***)

**(*) EMI 7 49610-2. Cotrubas, Kraus, Quilico, Van Dam, Toulouse Capitole Ch. & O, Plasson

(N) (M) **(*) DG (ADD) 474 950-2 (3). Sills, Gedda, Souzay, Bacquier, Amb. Op. Ch., New Philh. O, Rudel

(B) (***) Naxos mono 8.110203/4 (2). Feraldy, Rogatchewsky, Guenot, Villier, Opéra-Comique Ch. & O, Cohen

Recorded in 2001, Gilbert Deflo's production for the National Opera in Paris offers no 'concept' pretensions and is refreshingly direct in its presentation of the story over the five acts, using apt in-period costumes set in contrast with the simple stylized sets, both designed by William Orlandi. The undistracting simplicity of the sets, merely suggesting the broad outlines of buildings and rooms, has the big advantage of allowing swift scene-changes in this long and complex piece. The casting of the three principals is outstanding. Renée Fleming not only sings superbly, she acts with total conviction, brilliantly making the transition from the vivacious seventeen-year-old of Act I, inexperienced yet wilful, to the

mature, even more wilful figure of the later acts, making one understand her dilemma over her love for Des Grieux. It is a commanding performance, well matched by the upstanding, slightly awkward Des Grieux of Marcelo Alvarez, also singing splendidly with a wide tonal range down to a fine head-voice in *Ah fuyez douce image*. Equally fine is the magnificent singing of the baritone Jean-Luc Chaignaud, a handsome, swaggering figure who sings with a virile firmness and no hint of strain, readily commanding the stage. With Jesus Lopez-Cobos drawing idiomatic playing and singing from chorus and orchestra, it makes a splendid addition to the DVD catalogue.

On CD the starry husband-and-wife team of Angela Gheorghiu and Roberto Alagna is ideally cast in Massenet's *Manon*, a favourite opera that in comparison with *Werther* has been neglected on disc. In Act I Gheorghiu instantly establishes the heroine as a vivacious, wilful character with a great sense of fun, and her singing is both imaginative and technically flawless. The aria, *Adieu, notre petite table*, is tenderly affecting, shaded down to a breath-taking *pianissimo* at the end. A fine actress, she develops the character too, while Alagna, always at his happiest in French-language opera, portrays Des Grieux as full of eager innocence as well as passion, impulsive in his responses before disillusion teaches him new lessons. The other La Monnaie soloists make a splendid team under Antonio Pappano, with José van Dam impressively cast as Des Grieux's father. Pappano himself is as understanding an interpreter of Massenet as he is of Puccini, drawing warmly committed playing and singing from the whole company. Well-balanced recording to match.

No one has recorded the role of Manon in Massenet's opera quite so bewitchingly as Victoria de los Angeles in this historic EMI recording of 1955, girlishly provocative at the start, conveying tragic depth later. The voice is at its most golden, and this vivid new transfer from Testament gives the mono sound extra warmth and immediacy. Henri Legay as Des Grieux also sings with honeyed tones, a believable young lover ensnared, and Pierre Monteux in one of his rare opera recordings is masterly in his timing and phrasing. As a splendid bonus you also have RCA recordings of Berlioz and Debussy, similarly persuasive, recorded in Boston, also in 1955.

The Plasson Toulouse set is a stylish performance, well characterized and well sung. Ileana Cotrubas is a charming Manon, more tender and vulnerable than De los Angeles was on the earlier mono set but not so golden-toned and with a more limited development of character, from the girlish chatterbox to the dying victim. Alfredo Kraus betrays some signs of age, but his is a finely detailed and subtle reading. Louis Quilico has a delightfully light touch as Lescaut, and José van Dam is a superb Comte Des Grieux. The warm reverberation of the Toulouse studio is well controlled to give bloom to the voices, and, although Plasson is rougher with the score than Monteux was, his feeling for French idiom is very good.

Beverly Sills scored an enormous success at the New York City Opera with this enchanting work, and she brings to this 1970 recording the benefits of intensive stage experience of the role. Her voice too was more naturally suited to the character of the flirtatious Manon than it was to some of her bigger roles, and there is much to charm and delight here. The other soloists are well cast, though neither Gedda nor Souzay is in his sweetest voice. Julius Rudel makes a strong and understanding conductor, and although finer versions have appeared since this set was first issued (on EMI in the

UK) there is no question that Sills is remarkably compelling. The set is reissued with full libretto and translation.

Recorded over a period of four months in 1928/9, the pioneering Opéra-Comique set of *Manon* on 18 short-playing 78-r.p.m. discs remained unchallenged until the arrival of LP. Very well transferred in Naxos's historical series, it makes a vivid reappearance on CD with the voices full and immediate and with the orchestra clear and dry behind them. It gives an excellent snapshot of standards at the Opéra-Comique between the wars, with Germaine Feraldy light, bright and vivacious in the title-role, very French in manner and timbre, singing with a tight vibrato. Though born in the Ukraine, Joseph Rogatchewsky, who had trained in Paris from the age of eighteen, also sounds very French as an ardent lover, again with a tight vibrato and clean focus. He manages the head voice traditionally required in the role of Des Grieux very beautifully, too rarely achieved latterly. Georges Villier, for long a favourite at the Opéra-Comique, makes a characterful Lescaut, with excellent teamwork from everyone under the conductor, Elie Cohen.

La Navarraise (complete)

(M) *** RCA (ADD) 74321 50167-2. Horne, Domingo, Milnes, Zaccaria, Bacquier, Davies, Amb. Op. Ch., LSO, Lewis

La Navarraise is a cross between *Carmen* and *Cavalleria rusticana*, with a touch of *Il tabarro*. To earn her dowry before marrying her beloved, the intrepid heroine penetrates the enemy lines in the Carlist wars and for money assassinates the royalist general's direct adversary. Following a misunderstanding, the hero follows her and is mortally wounded. In despair she promptly goes mad – a great deal of story for so short a piece. It says much for Massenet's dramatic powers that he makes the result as convincing as he does, and the score is full of splendid, atmospheric effects. Massenet originally had a heavyweight, 'Carmen' voice in mind, and Marilyn Horne seems an apt choice for the role of heroine. Even if her upper register is not as firm as it was, it remains an appealing performance, and Domingo is characteristically rich-toned. Henry Lewis conducts with a sense of the work's atmosphere and grandeur, and this is an opera ideally suited to the gramophone. The recording, made at Walthamstow in 1975, is appropriately spacious.

Le Roi de Lahore (complete)

✿ (M) *** Decca 476 1705 (2). Sutherland, Lima, Milnes, Ghiaurov, Morris, Tourangeau, L. Voices, Nat. PO, Bonynge

It is good to have this fine set restored to the catalogue at mid-price in Universal's 'Penguin ✿ Collection'. *Le Roi de Lahore* was Massenet's first opera for the big stage of L'Opéra in Paris and marked a turning point in his career, even introducing the supernatural, with one act set in the Paradise of Indra. The characters may be stock figures out of a mystic fairytale, but in the vigour of his treatment Massenet makes the result red-blooded in an Italianate way. This vivid performance under Bonynge includes passages added for Italy, notably a superb set-piece aria which challenges Sutherland to some of her finest singing. Sutherland may not be a natural for the role of the innocent young priestess, but she makes it a magnificent vehicle with its lyric, dramatic and coloratura demands. Luis Lima as the King is somewhat strained by the high tessitura, but his is a ringing tenor, clean of attack. Sherrill Milnes as the heroine's wicked uncle sounds even

more Italianate, rolling his 'r's ferociously; but high melodrama is apt, and with digital recording of demonstration splendour and fine perspective this shameless example of operatic hokum could not be presented more persuasively on CD.

Thaïs (complete)

🎧 *** Decca 466 766-2 (2). Fleming, Hampson, Sabbatini, Bordeaux Op. Ch. & O, Abel

(M) ** EMI 5 65479-2 (2). Sills, Milnes, Gedda, Van Allan, John Alldis Ch., New Philh. O, Maazel

The character of Thaïs in Massenet's opera, developing as she does from one moral extreme to another, is one of his most complex, and finds an ideal interpreter in Renée Fleming, a fine actress. The technical demands of the role too are comparably great, and again Fleming is ideal from first to last, at once powerful and delicate, with trills and other decorations meticulously placed in phrases of sweeping warmth. After making the heroine's unlikely conversion to virtue totally convincing, she crowns her performance with a deeply affecting account of her death scene, ending with a ravishing *pianissimo* top A. No soprano in a complete set has come near to matching her achievement, and though Thomas Hampson as Athanaël, a character working just as improbably in the opposite direction, cannot quite equal her in such total conviction he is vocally ideal. The others are well cast too, notably Giuseppe Sabbatini as Nicias, and though the Bordeaux Opera Orchestra is not quite as refined as some, Yves Abel draws warmly sympathetic playing from them throughout, with the young French virtuoso, Renaud Capuchon, luxuriously cast in the big violin solo of the *Méditation*. Excellent sound. A clear first choice, even finer than the EMI set with Gheorghiu and Alagna under Pappano.

Maazel's conducting is crisply dramatic (and he plays the violin solo himself most tastefully in the famous *Méditation*). The casting is good, except for the heroine. Beverly Sills has a bright, almost brittle voice, and here it sounds neither seductive nor idiomatic. She is at her best as the reformed Thaïs in the later scenes. Sherrill Milnes is a powerful but conventional Athanaël, and, though Nicolai Gedda sings Nicias with his usual intelligence, it is not a young enough voice for the role. A good, warm recording, well transferred on to CD, and with a complete text and translation.

Werther (complete)

🎧 *** EMI 5 56820-2 (2). Alagna, Gheorghiu, Hampson, Petibon, Tiffin School Children's Ch., LSO, Pappano

*** RCA 74321 58224-2 (2). Vargas, Kasarova, Schaldenbrand, Kotoski, Berlin Knabenchor & Deutsche SO, Jurowski

(B) *** Ph. 475 496-2 (2). Carreras, Von Stade, Allen, Buchanan, Lloyd, Children's Ch., ROHCG O, C. Davis

(M) **(*) EMI (ADD) 5 62627-2 [5 62630-2] (3). Gedda, De los Angeles, Soyer, Benoit, Grigoriou, Mallabrera, Mesplé, ORTF Children's Ch., O de Paris, Prêtre

(M) *** Orfeo C4 64972 (2). Domingo, Fassbaender, Seibel, Nöcker, Bav. State Op. Ch., Bav. State O, López-Cobos

*** Erato 0630 17790-2 (2). Hadley, Von Otter, Upshaw, Théruel, Lyon Opéra Ch. & O, Nagano

(BB) *** Naxos 8.660072/3 (2). Haddock, Uria-Monzon, Massis, Azzaretti, Delacluse, O Nat. Lille-Région N./Pas de Calais, J.-C. Casadesus

(N) ** Decca 475 6557 (2). Bocelli, Carolis, Giuseppini, Gertseva, Léger, Lefebvre, Ariostini, Teatro Comunale di Bologna Ch. & O, Abel

It makes a formidable line-up to have the starry husband-and-wife team of Roberto Alagna and Angela Gheorghiu joined by the ever-responsive Antonio Pappano. Though Alagna with his French background is an ideal choice for Werther himself, Gheorghiu with her bright soprano is a less obvious one for the role of the heroine, Charlotte, normally given to a mezzo. But as a magnetic actress she conveys an extra tenderness and vulnerability, with no lack of weight in such a solo as *Laisse couler mes larmes* in Act III. Alagna makes a characterful Werther, using his distinctive tone-colours most sensitively, with Thomas Hampson outstanding as Albert and Patricia Petibon a sweet-toned Sophie. As in Puccini, Pappano is subtle as well as powerful, using rubato idiomatically and with refinement to heighten the drama and point the moments of climax. Good warm sound.

The RCA set makes the perfect alternative to the EMI version. Here is casting of the two principals that in every way is centrally satisfying. With her vibrant mezzo, Vesselina Kasarova is a natural choice for Charlotte, full and intense at the big moments, even if the vibrancy, as caught by the microphone, turns into unevenness under pressure. Ramon Vargas with his clear, precise tenor is the perfect hero here. He may not be as distinctive as Alagna, but he sings such a solo as *Pourquoi me reveiller* with greater purity, shading the voice down most sensitively. The other principals are not so strongly cast, with Dawn Kotoski rather shrill as Sophie, but Jurowski's conducting is warm and dramatic, even if it lacks the distinctive subtleties of Pappano. The sound is brilliant and clear.

Sir Colin Davis's bargain alternative is also highly recommendable, with Frederica von Stade an enchanting Charlotte, matched by Thomas Allen as her husband, Albert, and Isobel Buchanan as her sister, Sophie. The recording was outstanding enough to win the *Gramophone*'s Engineering Award for 1981; but in this reissue the break between the two discs remains badly placed in the middle of a key scene in Act II between Werther and Charlotte. A full text and translation are still provided.

Victoria de los Angeles's golden tones, which convey pathos so beautifully, are ideally suited to Massenet's gentle melodies and, although she is recorded too closely (closer than the other soloists), she makes an appealing heroine. Gedda, too, makes an intelligent romantic hero, though Prêtre's direction could be more subtle. This set now reappears, excellently remastered, as one of EMI's 'Great Recordings of the Century', and while it has now been outclassed by EMI's newest recording with Gheorghiu and Alagna, it still has much going for it as a reminder of past glories.

Also at mid-price the Bavarian Radio recording on Orfeo makes another excellent alternative choice, with Plácido Domingo an ardent hero. Opposite him as Charlotte is Brigitte Fassbaender on peak form, rich and firm as well as passionately expressive. Marianne Seibel and Hans Günter Nöcker are first rate too, as Sophie and Albert. López-Cobos is an ardently red-blooded interpreter of Massenet, and though, in this live recording, stage noises are obtrusive at times and balances are not always perfect, they hardly detract from the impact of the whole.

With an excellent cast, Kent Nagano conducts his Lyon Opéra team in a warm, well-paced reading. With the orchestra backwardly placed, this is a relatively intimate performance,

with the two principals, Jerry Hadley and Anne Sofie von Otter, sounding youthful and characterizing well, with neurotic tensions implied. Dawn Upshaw is excellent too as a characterful Sophie.

With five first-rate versions of *Werther* already on the stocks it is bold of Naxos on its bargain label to offer yet another. Happily, the result is a great success. As with the excellent Naxos set of Debussy's *Pelléas et Mélisande*, the company went to Lille, and there in the impressive twentieth-century baroque opera-theatre recorded a series of performances live, editing the results together. As with *Pelléas*, the conductor is Jean-Claude Casadesus, drawing not just from the excellent line-up of soloists but from the whole ensemble an idiomatic performance that in its urgency leads you magnetically through the unconventional yet moving plot based on Goethe.

It is striking that, like other live recordings, this one adopts speeds generally faster than those in studio recordings, to its obvious gain, while suffering little from the perennial problem of intrusive stage and audience noises. In the title-role the American, Marcus Haddock, gives a youthfully ardent performance, using his clear, ringing tenor sensitively with a fine feeling for the idiom, never simply belting. The mezzo, Béatrice Uria-Monzon, one of the few French singers currently on disc in this role, is even more impressive, with her gorgeously sensuous voice vividly conveying the impression of a youthful heroine. Her richness contrasts well with the fresh tones of Jaël Azzaretti as Charlotte's teenage sister, Sophie. The baritone, René Massis, as Charlotte's husband, Albert, is convincingly youthful too, not the stolid figure often presented. Even in face of strong competition this latest Naxos set is far more than just a bargain alternative, offering a powerfully enjoyable experience, made the more involving by the tensions of a live staging. Though the recording level is rather low, the voices are very well balanced with words exceptionally clear and, unlike most bargain versions of opera, this one has a complete libretto in French, plus a detailed synopsis in English.

Werther's aria *Pourquoi me reveiller?* was among the highlights of Andrea Bocelli's first recital disc, which makes it disappointing that in this complete recording, made in Bologna following live performances, he sings so consistently loud, with little of the shading he displayed before, however distinctive the tenor sound. That goes with a performance, otherwise variably cast, which lacks subtlety in its up-front insistence as well as in its sound. Julie Gertseva sings well enough as Charlotte, but this does not begin to rival such outstanding sets as Pappano's with Alagna and Gheorghiu.

Werther (complete; in English)

(M) *** Chan. 3033 (2). Brecknock, Baker, Wheatley, Blackburn, Roberts, Tomlinson, ENO Ch. & O, Mackerras

Recorded live at the Coliseum in 1977 in vividly atmospheric sound, full of presence, Sir Charles Mackerras's version offers an exceptionally warm reading in English which is strong in dramatic thrust. The cast too is exceptionally strong, with John Brecknock clear, fresh and firm in the title-role. Yet it is the performance of Janet Baker as Charlotte that provides the linchpin, rising to great heights in the tragedy of Act IV. This is Baker at her very finest, singing with heartfelt fervour, using the full tonal range of her unique voice, always fresh and clear in attack. Joy Roberts is a bright, agile Sophie, and the other male singers can hardly be faulted. Remarkably, this was taken from a single performance, not edited from a series. Voices are close enough for every word of Norman Tucker's excellent translation to be heard.

MATHIAS, William (1934–92)

Summer Dances; Soundings

*** Nim. NI 5466. Fine Arts Brass Ens. – HODDINOTT: *Chorales, Variants & Fanfares*, etc. ***

Mathias's seven *Summer Dances* (1990) bring witty rhythmic quirkiness but, if the writing is consistently skilful, the invention is at times rather conventional. His *Soundings* (commissioned by the Philip Jones Brass and first performed in 1988) is much more entertaining with its kinky *March* (its humour agreeably lugubrious), a darkly nostalgic *Elegy* and a catchy but unpredictable final *Capriccio*. Fine playing and splendid recording in an ideal acoustic that brings plenty of sonority but provides firmly focused detail.

String Quartets 1–3

*** Metier MSVCD 92005. Medea Qt

Spanning the years 1967–86, Mathias's three string quartets make a fine sequence, illuminating his whole achievement. The *First Quartet*, in a single 20-minute movement, pithily argued, has a Stravinskian directness. The idiom brings momentary echoes of Britten, but might best be described as music by a composer who has thoroughly digested the Bartók *Quartets*. The *Second Quartet* dates from 1980–81, and in each of its four compact movements Mathias echoes medieval music in different ways. The result is stylistically as individual as the *First Quartet*, never sounding merely derivative. The *Third Quartet*, dating from 1986, brings together elements of both the earlier works, with the first of its three movements developing from a deceptively light opening into a taut, large-scale structure comparable with the *Quartet No. 1*. All three quartets, very well recorded, are outstandingly well performed by the young Medea Quartet, formed as recently as 1991 at the Royal Academy of Music.

Wind Quintet

*** Crystal CD 750. Westwood Wind Quintet – CARLSSON: *Nightwings*; LIGETI: *Bagatelles*; BARBER: *Summer Music* ***

Of the five movements of this spirited *Quintet* the Scherzo is particularly felicitous and there is a rather beautiful *Elegy*. The playing of the Westwood Wind Quintet is highly expert and committed, and the recording is very good indeed.

Piano Sonatas 1, Op. 23; 2 (in one movement), Op. 46

(N) *** Minerva Atheme ATH CD 15. Clarke – PICKARD: *Sonata*, etc. ***

Lux aeterna, Op. 88

*** Chan. 8695. Lott, Cable, P. Walker, Bach Ch., St George's Chapel Ch., Windsor, LSO, Willcocks; Scott (organ)

Just as Britten in the *War Requiem* contrasted different planes of expression with Latin liturgy set against Wilfred Owen poems, so Mathias contrasts the full choir singing Latin against the boys' choir singing carol-like Marian anthems, and in turn against the three soloists, who sing three arias and a trio to the mystical poems of St John of the Cross. Overall, the confidence of the writing makes the work far more than derivative, an attractively approachable and colourful piece, full of memorable ideas, especially in this excellent performance, beautifully sung and played, and atmospherically balanced.

Missa brevis; Rex gloriae; Anthems: Ad majorem Dei gloriam; Angelus; Alleluia; Doctrine of Wisdom; Except the Lord build the house; Hodie Christus natus est; The Lord is my Shepherd; Veni sancte spiritus

🔑 ✿ *** Paraclete Press GDCD 026. Gloriæ Dei Cantores, Patterson

This splendidly sung programme comes from Gloriæ Dei Cantores, a 44-voice choir from Cape Cod, Massachusetts, directed by Elizabeth Patterson. They have the advantage of the superb acoustics of the Methuan Music Hall and the use of its famous organ, which Mathias uses very orchestrally – and often in the *Missa brevis* to provide 'instrumental' obbligatos. The thrilling opening of *Sanctus* establishes this as the emotional kernel of the work, with the organ then creating darker woodwind colours to introduce the very touching *Agnus Dei*. The anthems are hardly less individual and inspired. Trumpets and percussion announce the exultant setting of *Except the Lord build the house* while the celestial *Angelus* brings a surprisingly effective use of the piano. *The Lord is my Shepherd* is very Welsh in feeling, a passionate declaration of faith; *The Doctrine of Wisdom* again uses the organ very atmospherically, and its melodic simplicity is telling. With singing of such commitment and intensity, yet exploiting the widest range of dynamics, every piece here is memorable. Mathias could hardly have hoped for more persuasive advocacy or finer recording. If you have difficulty in getting this disc, the Choir's web-site address is: www.paracletepress.com.

MATTEIS, Nicola (*c.* 1640–*c.* 1714)

Ayres for the Violin*, Book I: *Suite in C min.*; Book II: *Suite in G min.*; Book IV: *Suites in A; C; G min.; D min.

(B) *** HM HCX 3957067. Arcadian Academy

Not a great deal is known about Nicola Matteis. Born in Naples, he apparently came to England in 1670 and later had considerable success as a solo violinist/guitar player, then married a wealthy widow and 'took a great house' in Norfolk. His *Suites of Ayres for the Violin* date from the 1670s and 1680s and are either solo or trio sonatas. Each suite is in essence a set of variations, for the same musical material undergoes many melodic and rhythmic transformations with diverting results. In every case there is an opening *Preludio*; then follows a series of brief vignettes exploiting various dance movements – Giga, Minuet, Ricercata, Corrente, Sarabanda – plus slow and fast sections, grounds, fugues and *Arie amarosi*. McGegan and his Arcadian Players respond with spontaneous vitality and revel in the music's undoubted fantasy. The recording, although a bit edgy on top, is otherwise vivid.

MATTHEWS, Colin (born 1946)

Broken Symmetry; Sonata for Orchestra 4; Sun Dance

(M) *** Decca 474 316-2. L. Sinf., Knussen

These three fine works, given superb performances by Oliver Knussen and the London Sinfonietta, present a strong portrait of an outstanding and imaginative composer, each taken from a different period in his career. The *Fourth Sonata*, from the mid-1970s, presents Matthews's response to minimalism in its repetitive rhythms but with ideas kept continually alert in a well-planned structure. *Sun Dance*, from the mid-1980s, is a ballet for ten instruments which brilliantly transcends that limitation of forces. *Broken Symmetry*, from the early 1990s, is a Scherzo movement for large orchestra, leading to a dramatic conclusion. The excellent recording, originally from DG, brings both bloom and sharp focus, and the reissue is now offered at mid-price within Decca's 'British Music Collection'.

MAUNDER, John (1858–1920)

Olivet to Calvary (cantata)

(B) **(*) CfP (ADD) 575 7792 (2). Mitchinson, Harvey, Guildford Cathedral Ch., Rose; Morse (organ) – STAINER: *The Crucifixion* ***

It is easy to be patronizing about music like this but, provided one accepts the conventions of style in which it is composed, the music is effective and often moving. The performance has an attractive simplicity and genuine eloquence. Frederick Harvey is particularly moving at the actual moment of Christ's death; in a passage that, insensitively handled, could be positively embarrassing, he creates a magical, hushed intensity. The choir sing beautifully, and in the gentler, lyrical writing (the semi-chorus *O Thou whose sweet compassion*, for example) sentimentality is skilfully avoided. The 1964 recording is first class in every way, and it has been admirably transferred to CD. This now comes aptly paired with Stainer's *Crucifixion*.

MAW, Nicholas (born 1935)

Violin Concerto (1993)

*** Sony SK 62856. Bell, LPO, Norrington

Maw here excels himself in a work specifically written for Joshua Bell, who responds superbly with playing of heartfelt warmth as well as brilliance. The opening *Moderato* movement has something of the fervour of the Walton *Violin Concerto*, with Maw firmly establishing his personal approach to tonality in seamless lyricism, leading up to a grinding climax. Coming second, the Scherzo is the longest movement, with Walton again brought to mind in the spiky brilliance, set against a central section with a ripe horn solo. The third movement, *Romanza*, is then a calm interlude before the carefree surging thrust of the finale, leading to a bravura conclusion, not the slow fade so often favoured latterly by concerto composers. Roger Norrington and the LPO are strong and sympathetic partners, with warm, full recording to match.

(i) *Dance Scenes*; (ii) *Odyssey*

(M) *** EMI 5 85145-2 (2). (i) Philh. O, Harding; (ii) CBSO, Rattle

Spanning 100 minutes, Nicholas Maw's panoramic *Odyssey* has been counted the biggest continuous orchestral piece ever written, and its gestation came over a period of 13 years, between 1972 and 1985. As in Mahler, if not so readily, one comes to recognize musical landmarks in the six substantial movements. The slow movement alone lasts over half an hour, while the *Allegros* bring a genuine sense of speed, thrusting and energetic. It was at Rattle's insistence that this superb recording was made at live concerts. The result is astonishingly fine, with the engineers totally disguising the problems of recording in Birmingham Town Hall.

The *Dance Scenes* of 1995 could hardly be more different.

Lightweight but never trivial, it is a buoyantly spirited work, brilliantly scored and full of readily accessible melodic lines and ideas. The influence of Walton is predominant, but the four dances are full of personality and individually attractive. They obviously appealed to the Philharmonia players, whose advocacy has both polish and sparkle. The Abbey Road recording is first class.

(i) *Flute Quartet*; (ii) *Piano Trio*

*** ASV CDDCA 920. Monticello Trio, with (i) Pearce; (ii) Coletti

Commissioned by the Koussevitzky Foundation, the *Piano Trio* was written in 1991 for the Monticello Trio, who here record it in a warmly expressive performance, fiery where necessary. The *Flute Quartet* of 1981 was written for Judith Pearce of the Nash Ensemble, who plays it most beautifully here; it is another fine example of Maw's broad romanticism, powerful and lyrical, often sensuous, approachable yet clearly contemporary. Though the central slow movement opens as a fugue, it develops emotionally to become an atmospheric nocturne, leading to a scurrying finale. Excellent performances and sound.

MAXWELL DAVIES, Peter (born 1934)

(i) *Antechrist*; (i; ii) *Missa super 'L'Homme armé'*; (iii) *Second Fantasia on John Taverner's 'In nomine'*; (iv) *Seven In Nomine*; (v) *Lullaby for Ilian Rainbow*; (i; vi) *From Stone to Thorn*; *Hymn to St Magnus*; (vi) *O magnum mysterium*

🔗 (M) *** Decca (ADD) 475 6166 (2). (i) Fires of London, composer; (ii) V. Redgrave (speaker); (iii) New Philh. O, Groves; (iv) London Sin., Atherton; (v) Walker (guitar); (vi) Thomas (soprano); Cirencester Grammar School Ch. & O, composer

Much of Maxwell Davies's creative energy has been projected towards writing works for the two overlapping groups which he formed and directed, first the Pierrot Players and later the Fires of London. The latter recorded four characteristic works in 1973 (of which three are included here, *Hymnos* being omitted for reasons of space) which they regularly performed at their concerts, starting with *Antechrist*, a sort of exuberant overture. *L'Homme armé*, a more extended but comparable work, similarly working on a medieval motif, is also approachable, while *From Stone to Thorn*, a work much thornier in argument, directly displays the formidable talents of – among others – the soprano Mary Thomas. Two years later, the Fires of London recorded the *Hymn to St Magnus*, a powerful and uncompromising piece lasting over 36 minutes, one of the finest works inspired by the composer's flight to Orkney. Living there alone when he wrote this music, based on a twelfth-century hymn about St Magnus (martyred in 1137), he reflected the Orkney landscape and weather in his music. For all the complexity of its intellectual base, it has an immediacy of impact that is most compelling in this performance under the composer's direction. The soprano soloist, Mary Thomas, helps to build the concentration, particularly in the hypnotic repetitions of the plea, *St Magnus, pray for us* (in Latin), which punctuate the long third movement.

The original (1975) review of *The Second Fantasia on John Taverner's 'In nomine'* noted, 'In an age of crabbed inspiration on the one hand, uncharted wildness on the other, it is remarkable that a composer making no concessions should argue strongly, satisfyingly and movingly over a span of 40 minutes, using the conventional symphony orchestra but producing something totally original and new.' The first public performance required an introductory lecture from the conductor (Pritchard) but, on repeated hearing, the logic in its 13 sections is plain enough. Some of the music was used later in *Taverner*, the opera about the composer whose *In nomine* forms the basis of this work. Groves's 1972 performance, in good sound, is not ideally incisive or polished; but anyone willing to accept a challenge will find this work very rewarding. *O magnum mysterium* was written for the Cirencester Grammar School, where the composer once taught, and his pupils sing this brilliantly imaginative cantata with skill and enthusiasm, while the school orchestra provides an exotic accompaniment. Good (1962) sound.

This excellent Maxwell Davies anthology is especially valuable for including *Seven in Nomine*, released for the first time. It is an early work, starting life as a composition exercise when the composer was at Princeton University in 1963–4, but eventually forming this composition after a commission by the Melos Ensemble, who gave the work its première. Opening with a string quartet version of John Taverner's organ *In nomine*, followed by his own *In nomine*, its seven movements are full of the composer's fascinating experiments in textures and form, often reflecting and using music from the sixteenth and seventeenth centuries. The 1979 performance under David Atherton is excellent. All in all, this is an ideal introduction to Maxwell Davies's music, and represents superb value for money.

Salome (ballet)

(N) ***(B) EMI (ADD) 586184-2 (2). Danish R. Concert O, Fürst

Commissioned by the Danish choreographer Flemming Flindt, Peter Maxwell Davies wrote this, his first full-length ballet, in 1978. He worked out the scenario in close collaboration with Flindt and produced a score that vividly illustrates each dramatic development, from the arrest and enslavement of John the Baptist and Herod's rise to power, in music always colourful, often violent. His orchestration adds to the atmospheric effectiveness, as in his use of marimba in the sequence representing the waters of Jordan, when John baptizes his followers. Act II begins with a sinister movement representing Herod's 'dark night of the soul' and reaches a climax with the execution and apotheosis of John, leading finally – and unexpectedly – to the scene of John and Salome united in heaven. Since the Danish production, it is a piece that has been seriously neglected, but here it receives a warmly persuasive performance by well-recorded Danish forces. The set is made the more attractive by being offered at bargain price.

Sinfonia; Sinfonia concertante

(BB) *** Regis RRC 1148. SCO, composer

A welcome bargain reissue. In his *Sinfonia* of 1962 Peter Maxwell Davies took as his inspiration Monteverdi's *Vespers* of 1610, and the dedication in this music, beautifully played by the Scottish Chamber Orchestra, is plain from first to last. The *Sinfonia concertante* is a much more extrovert piece for strings plus solo wind quintet and timpani. In idiom this is hardly at all neo-classical and, more than usual, the composer evokes romantic images, as in the lovely close of the first movement. Virtuoso playing from the Scottish principals, not least the horn. Well-balanced recording too.

String Quartets 1 & 2

(N) (BB) *** Naxos 8.557396. Maggini Qt

Maxwell Davies's projected series of 10 *Quartets* on Naxos starts impressively in No. 1, with movements that combine structural and thematic ingenuity, typical of the composer, with emotional weight. The work is rounded off with a Scherzo that is light and ghostly in texture. The first of the four movements in *Quartet No. 2* opens with an impressive slow introduction, leading to an energetic *Allegro*. The middle two movements are linked as a pair, with the recitative in the first echoing ideas in *Quartet No. 1*, while the finale is slow and deeply meditative, a movingly serene conclusion. The Maggini Quartet, vividly recorded, fully respond to the challenge of the writing in powerfully committed performances.

String Quartets 3 & 4

(N) (BB) *** Naxos 8.557397. Maggini Qt

The very opening of the third of Maxwell Davies's *Quartets* on Naxos may be dauntingly thorny, schematically based on magic squares inside one other, but that leads quickly to meditative music which is plainly from the heart, inspired, so the composer explains, by his response to the Iraq War, which began while he was writing. The second movement, *In Nomine*, the longest of the four, is even more deeply intense, with plainsong an underlying element, leading to a sharply rhythmic Scherzo, full of brilliant effects, and a Fugue which starts in echo of late Beethoven and then develops as a *Fuga* in the Italian meaning of 'flight'. *No. 4*, lighter in tone and more direct, opens on a motif in simple octaves and was inspired by Brueghel's picture of children's games. In a single massive movement of 25 minutes it switches between passages of manic energy and dark meditation, with quirky twists and turns, reflecting underlying aggression and conflict in children's games. The superb performances are ideally recorded.

(i–iii) Leopardi Fragments; (ii; iv) Revelation & Fall; (v) 5 Pieces, Op. 2

(N) (B) *** EMI (ADD) 5 86187-2 (2). (i) Melos Ens., Carewe; (ii) Thomas; (iii) Philips; (iv) Pierrot Players, composer; (v) Ogdon – BIRTWISTLE: *Tragoedia* ***

Revelation and Fall is one of the most striking works written by Peter Maxwell Davies, when early in his career he was beginning to establish himself as one of the most distinctive composers of his generation. Setting words by Georg Trakl, it represents the composer in expressionistic style in music designed to shock. The soprano soloist, the superb Mary Thomas, is required not just to sing normally but to use *Sprechgesang* and even to scream through a loud-hailer. Daunting as the initial impact may be, it stands as a powerful, instantly memorable work. Here, performed by the musicians who gave the première in 1968, it receives a magnetic performance. The other works are far less abrasive, with an apt element of sensuousness in the setting of verse by the early nineteenth-century poet, Giacomo Leopardi, completed in 1962, while the *Five Pieces* for piano, dating from 1956, already demonstrate the skill and distinctiveness of Maxwell Davies's writing, even though his style was about to develop rapidly. Outstanding performances and recording throughout. The pieces are well coupled with the fine Birtwistle work.

(i; ii) *Mass*; (i) *Missa parvula. Dum complerentur; Veni Sancta Spiritus*. Organ pieces: (i) *Reliquit domum meum; Veni Creator Spiritus*

*** Hyp. CDA 67454. Westminster Cathedral Ch., Baker; with (i) Quinney; (ii) Houssart (organ)

Maxwell Davies wrote his two strongly contrasted settings of the Mass for Westminster Cathedral Choir in 2002 and 2003, both of them among his most approachable works. Where the *Missa parvula* is a setting for boys' voices in unison with organ accompaniment, the *Mass* is for full choir and with organ accompaniment involving a second instrument in two of the sections. The lyrical directness of the *Missa parvula*, with the final *Agnus Dei* sounding almost like a carol, is immediately attractive, touching in its simplicity. Maxwell Davies, with roots in medieval music, tends to avoid making the liturgy dramatic, so that even the setting of *Et resurrexit* in the *Credo* hardly stands out from the lyrical flow. Similarly, in the *Mass* for full choir, using a much more elaborate idiom, the composer even more strikingly draws on medieval techniques, basing it on two Whitsun plainsong chants. The result is altogether darker, even violent at times, thanks to powerful organ writing, with the *Gloria* the longest and most elaborate movement, and the *Sanctus* bringing a triumphant setting of *Hosanna*. Originally, Maxwell Davies intended to keep this as a *Missa brevis*, without a *Credo*, but then was persuaded to set the *Credo* after all, contrasting it with the rest with voices in forthright unison. In this setting, as in the *Missa parvula*, there is no change of pace for *Crucifixus* and *Et resurrexit*, but the simple dedication is most moving. Complementing the two settings of the Mass come two motets, *Veni Sancta Spiritus*, slow and devotional, and *Dum complerentur*, a Pentecostal piece involving triumphant 'Alleluias', and two organ pieces, the valedictory *Reliquit domum* and the penitential *Veni Creator Spiritus*. As in his previous Westminster recordings for Hyperion Martin Baker draws radiant singing from his fine choir, atmospherically recorded.

MAYER, Emilie (1812–83)

String Quartet in G min., Op. 14

(M) ******* CPO 999 679-2. Basle Erato Qt – Fanny MENDELSSOHN: *String Quartet;* SIRMEN: *Quartets 2–3* *******

We know comparatively little about Emilie Mayer. Op. 14 was the only string quartet included in her printed works and it was evidently valued, and rightly so. It is an ambitious, well-crafted work, romantic in feeling, with appealing ideas – the extended first movement opens with an engaging dialogue between violin and cello. The fine slow movement touchingly introduces the chorale, *Wer nur den lieben Gott lässt walten*, over a pizzicato accompaniment, before the reprise of the serene main theme. The busy finale has a Mendelssohnian lightness of touch, but overall the music has genuine individuality. The performance here is highly persuasive and naturally recorded.

MAYR, Giovanni (1763–1845)

Overtures: *Adelasia e Aleramo; Alonso e Cora; Ginrevra di Scozia; Medea in Corinto; La rosa bianca e la rosa rossa; Il segreto; Sisara; Un pazzo ne fa cento; I virtuosi a teatro*

⊙━ (M) ******* Warner Fonit 8573 87134-2. O Stabile di Bergamo, Renzetti

This delightful collection of overtures is a real find. They are very Rossini-ish in character, and if Mayr's tuttis are more conventional and his manipulation of key changes less witty than with Rossini, the music itself is full of charming ideas and felicitous scoring. *Adelasia e Aleramo* is one of the most striking, opening with a fully scored melody in 6/8, after which the main string theme soon leads to a piquant march, reminiscent of Auber, which is introduced by a solo violin.

Sisara (which begins the programme) immediately brings a cute secondary theme on the strings and the jocular main theme of *Un pazzo ne fa cento* leads to a similarly dainty secondary idea. *Il segreto*, after a grand beginning, relents immediately, with charming writing for the woodwind leading to a virtuoso bassoon solo. These three overtures are all four-minute pieces, but the others are rather more ambitious, and still remarkably inventive. *Alonso e Cora* opens grandly and is more rumbustious than the rest, including dramatic timpani rolls, but still has an elegant secondary tune, while *La rosa bianca e la rosa rossa* brings pizzicati and a charming woodwind introduction, leading to a succession of felicitous themes, with a rollicking clarinet solo as its highlight. The performances here by a modest-sized orchestra, using modern instruments, are nicely turned and well recorded. This is a disc with which to quiz your friends about the composer: they will almost certainly guess wrongly.

Ginevra di Scozia (complete)

⊙━ *** Opera Rara ORC 23 (3). Vidal, Barcellona, Siragusa, Lazzara, Grassi, Teatro Lirico di Trieste, Severini

Mayr wrote this opera for the opening in April 1801 of the Teatro Nuovo in Trieste – where, exactly 200 years later, performances were given from which this recording was taken. The reference to Scotland in the title is misleading in that the story, taken from Ariosto, is basically the one which Handel also used in his opera, *Ariodante*. The heroine, Ginevra, beloved of Ariodante, is wrongly accused by Ariodante's scheming rival, Polinesso, of losing her virginity to an unknown lover, while her brother invokes a law condemning a woman to death for unchastity. All is sorted out in the end, with Mayr inspired to write a characteristic score, varied in pace and (for the time) adventurous in structure, which largely justifies his reputation as providing a link between Mozart and Rossini, while offering a model for the *bel canto* school of Bellini and Donizetti.

Very well cast, this is a lively performance under the direction of Tiziano Severini which makes light of any longueurs. The coloratura singing of the French soprano, Elisabeth Vidal, is spectacular, with top E's in profusion flawlessly tackled; while the mezzo, Daniela Barcellona, in the castrato role of the hero sings with comparable warmth and flexibility, her tone gloriously rich and firm. To a modern ear it is misleading to find the role of the villain taken by a free-ranging tenor who is also given some of the best tunes, but Antonino Siragusa as Polinesso is aptly unctuous in his characterization, while all the lesser roles are also well taken, with the chorus fresh and vigorous. Mayr's imaginative orchestration, with strong principals regularly given solos, is well caught in an atmospheric live recording which, unlike many, includes the enthusiastic response of the audience.

Medea in Corinto (highlights)

⊙━ *** Opera Rara ORR 215. Eaglen, Ford, Giménez, Miles, Kenny, Philh. O, Parry

Recorded complete by Opera Rara in 1993, Mayr's Medea

opera deserves to be more widely known, and this generous, 76-minute selection of the highspots involving the heroine is very welcome. Since 1993 Jane Eaglen's international career has blossomed, not least on disc, but this relatively early recording reveals the voice at its freshest and firmest, with the big dramatic qualities that have made her reputation already in place. It is good to have not just the big solo numbers, but substantial sequences like the finale to Act I, with excellent support from the other soloists, including the two fine high tenors, Bruce Ford and Raul Giménez. As ever, David Parry draws warmly idiomatic playing from the Philharmonia, with full, well-balanced recording. Unlike most Opera Rara issues, this one does not provide texts, only a summary of plot for each item.

MAZZOCCHI, Domenico (c. 1592–1665)

Sacrae concertationes: *Concilio de' farisei;* (i-v) *Dialogo della cantica. Dialogo della Maddalena; Dialogo dell'apocalisse; Dialogo di Lazaro;* (i; iv; v) *Gaudebunt labia mea; Jesu, dulcis memoria. Lamento di David.* (i; iii) *Miseris omnium, Domine;* (i; ii; v) *Peccantem me quotidie. Vide, Domine, afflictionem nostram*

(M) *** HM (ADD) HMT 7901357. (i) Kiehr; (ii) Borden; (iii) Scholl; (iv) Türk; (v) Messthaler; Netherlands Chamber Ch., Jacobs; with Rousset, Swarts, Schröder

Domenico Mazzocchi almost certainly studied music in Rome, and the present *Sacred Concertantes* form part of his last work to be published, in 1664, though probably dating from much earlier. Whether writing for soloists, solo groups, chorus or a combination of them all, his part-writing is blended and interwoven with skill, and his invention is of high quality. His music includes deeply expressive solo melismas – as in the lovely *Peccantem me quotidie* ('Since daily I sin') – or choral writing (*Jesu, dulcis memoria*), or both (the deeply touching *Dialogo della Maddalena*) alternated with bursts of Italianate exuberance. The *Lamento di David* has a remarkable closing section which includes all these features. Performances here are wonderfully sympathetic. The soloists include outstanding contributions from Maria Cristina Kiehr and the bass, Ulrich Messthaler, who has some splendidly resonant low notes to sing, while we should not underpraise the other members of the solo team here, or the excellent choir, admirably accompanied by a continuo led by Christophe Rousset, and directed very persuasively indeed by René Jacobs. The recording, too, is first class.

MEDTNER, Nikolai (1880–1951)

(i) *Piano Concertos 1 in C min., Op. 33; 2 in C min., Op. 50; 3 in E min. (Ballade), Op. 60. (Piano) Sonata-ballade in F sharp, Op. 27*
*** Chan. 9040 (2). Tozer; (i) LPO, Järvi

(i) *Piano Concerto 1; Sonata-ballade*
*** Chan. 9038. Tozer, (i) LPO, Järvi

(i) *Piano Concerto 1;* (ii) *Piano Quintet in C, Op. posth*
**(*) Hyp. CDA 66744. Alexeev, with (i) BBC SO, Lazarev; (ii) New Budapest Qt

Piano Concertos 1; 3
☛ (BB) *** Naxos 8.553359. Scherbakov, Moscow SO, Ziva

(i) *Piano Concerto 2;* (ii) *Piano Quintet in C*
☛ (BB) *** Naxos 8.553390. Scherbakov, with (i) Moscow SO, Golovschin; (ii) Danel, Tedla, Bourová, Pudhoransk

Piano Concertos 2–3
*** Hyp. CDA 66580. Demidenko, BBC Scottish SO, Maksymiuk
*** Chan. 9039. Tozer, LPO, Järvi

Piano Concertos 2–3; Arabesque in A min., Op. 7/2; Tale in F min., Op. 26/3
(***) Testament mono SBT 1027. Composer, Philh. O, Dobrowen

Konstantin Scherbakov is highly sympathetic and offers very musical playing. He strikes us as more imaginative and subtle in both his range of dynamics and diversity of colour than any of his rivals. True, Geoffrey Tozer (Chandos) has the finer recording, but taken all round Scherbakov would make an eminently satisfactory first choice: artistically it is impeccable, as a recording it is very natural and well balanced and, not least, the price is right.

Tozer has obvious feeling for this composer and his playing has no lack of warmth and virtuosity. He has the advantage over his rivals of a richer, more transparent recording and a more sympathetic and responsive accompanist in Järvi and the London Philharmonic. Demidenko, on the other hand, has the greater fire and dramatic flair, and his performance with the BBC Scottish Orchestra under Jerzy Maksymiuk has one very much on the edge of one's chair. He is by no means as well recorded as Tozer: the sound of the piano is shallow and the orchestra lacks real transparency and is a bit two-dimensional in terms of front-to-back perspective.

Dmitri Alexeev also plays the *First Piano Concerto* with virtuosity, flair and sympathy, and the BBC Symphony Orchestra under Alexander Lazarev give excellent support. The recording is very good and generally well balanced, and overall gives better results than the coupling, the late *Piano Quintet in C major*. Alexeev plays it with dedication, but the New Budapest Quartet are conscientious rather than committed or inspired partners. The two-dimensional and rather congested recording does not help.

On Testament we have two of the celebrated set of Medtner concerto recordings which the Maharajah of Mysore funded in the late 1940s. Medtner was then in his sixties but his playing is still pretty magisterial. These two concertos and the early miniatures that make up the disc still possess an aristocratic allure and a musical finesse that it is difficult to resist. The performances were never reissued in the UK in the days of LP, and their reappearance at long last is as welcome as it is overdue. Good transfers.

Violin Sonatas 1 in B min., Op. 21; 2 in G, Op. 44
*** Chan. 9293. Mordkovitch, Tozer

The first two of Medtner's three *Violin Sonatas* come on a well-recorded Chandos release. Lydia Mordkovitch proves a most imaginative and thoughtful advocate of the sonata, betraying an effortless expressive freedom. Both she and her partner are well recorded.

Violin Sonata 3 (Sonata Epica), Op. 57
*** Erato 0630 15110-2. Repin, Berezovsky – RAVEL: *Violin Sonata* ***

Vadim Repin and Boris Berezovsky make a formidable partnership, and they give what is arguably the most sensitive and certainly the most persuasive account of the *Sonata Epica* since David Oistrakh and Alexander Goldweiser's celebrated Melodiya LP. They bring to it a wide range of colour and dynamics and infuse every phrase with life. Very natural recording-balance adds to the pleasure this CD gives.

PIANO MUSIC

Piano duet: *Russian Round Dance; Knight Errant, Op. 58/1–2*
*** Hyp. CDA 66654. Demidenko, Alexeev –
RACHMANINOV: *Suite,* etc. *******

The Russian round-dance or *khorovod* was written in 1946 and Medtner and Moiseiwitsch recorded it the same year for EMI. Here it is given with great lightness of touch, though this partnership loses beauty of tone-production above *fortissimo.*

Dancing Fairy Tale, Op. 48/1; Fairy Tale (1915); Fairy Tales in D min., Op. 51/1; in E min., Op. 34/2; in F min., Op. 26/3; in G sharp min., Op. 31/3. Funeral March, Op. 31/2; The Organ Grinder, Op. 54/3; Russian Fairy Tale, Op. 42/1; Sonata in G min., Op. 22; Sonata reminiscenza in A min., Op. 38/1
*** Chan. 9050. Tozer

Tozer takes much less time over the *Sonata reminiscenza* than Demidenko but he creates the illusion of unhurried calm. He allows the music to speak for itself without recourse to ostentation or flamboyance. The lifelike recording enhances the claims of this issue and bodes well for the enterprise (a complete survey of the keyboard music) as a whole.

Fairy Tales, Op. 51; Forgotten Melodies, Op. 38; Sonata Triad, Op. 11
**(*) Chan 9153. Tozer

Forgotten Melodies, Op. 39–40; Sonata in A min., Op. 30
**(*) Chan. 9692. Tozer

Sonatas in B flat min. (Sonata romantica), Op. 53/1; in F min., Op. 5; in F min. (Sonata minacciosa), Op. 53/2
**(*) Chan. 9691. Tozer

Complete piano music (as above)
*** Chan. 9723 (4). Tozer

Geoffrey Tozer has long championed Medtner, and his excellently recorded series for Chandos has put collectors in his debt. His playing is unfailingly reliable and scrupulously conscientious and often persuasive. Where, in the *Sonatas,* for instance, he duplicates repertoire recorded by Marc-André Hamelin, his imaginative and poetic limitations can be discerned. All the same, he has good fingers and a keen musical intelligence. The Chandos discs are all available separately, as well as in a box at a slightly reduced price.

Dithyrambe 3, Op. 10/3; 2 Elegies, Op. 59; Fairy Tales, Op. 20/1–2; Op. 26/1–4; Op. 48/2; Lyric Fragments, Op. 23; Theme & Variations, Op. 55
**(*) Chan. 9899. Tozer

The present CD in Geoffrey Tozer's Chandos series includes a very attractive account of the delightful Op. 55 *Theme and Variations,* and more of the *Fairy Tales,* in which he readily displays their diversity. The recital ends with Medtner's final piano works, the two *Elegies,* both opening with the same music, only in different keys. The recording was made at Snape Maltings concert hall with pleasing results.

3 Arabesques, Op. 7; 2 Fairy Tales, Op. 8; 2nd Improvisation, Op. 47; Romantic Sketches for the Young, Op. 54
(N) *** Chan. 10266. Tozer

Geoffrey Tozer continues his exploration of this neglected master whose 'traditional' yet subtle pianistic language belies a quietly individual creative personality. The *Second Improvisation* is a set of intricate and imaginative variations which are highly original and expertly played here. State-of-the-art recorded sound.

Dithyrambe, Op. 10/2; Elegy, Op. 59/2; Skazki (Fairy Tales): 1 (1915); in E min., Op. 14/2; in G, Op. 9/3; in D min. (Ophelia's Song); in C sharp min., Op. 35/4. Forgotten Melodies, 2nd Cycle, 1: Meditation. Primavera, Op. 39/3; 3 Hymns in Praise of Toil, Op. 49; Piano Sonata in E min. (The Night Wind), Op. 25/2; Sonata Triad, Op. 11/1–3
(M) *** CRD (ADD) CRD 3338/9. Milne

Improvisation 2 (in Variation Form), Op. 47; Piano Sonata in F min., Op. 5
(M) *** CRD (ADD) CRD 3461. Milne

3 Novelles, Op. 17; Romantic Sketches for the Young, Op. 54; Piano Sonatas in G min., Op. 22; A min., Op. 30; 2 Skazki, Op. 8
(M) *** CRD (ADD) CRD 3460. Milne

Medtner's art is subtle and elusive. He shows an aristocratic disdain for the obvious, a feeling for balance and proportion and a quiet harmonic refinement that offer consistent rewards. There is hardly a weak piece here, and Milne is a poetic advocate whose technical prowess is matched by first-rate artistry. The recording too is very truthful and vivid, and at mid-price is very competitive indeed.

Forgotten Melodies, Op. 39; 2 Skazki, Op. 48; Etude in C min.; I Loved Thee, Op. 32/4; Sonata minacciosa, Op. 53/2
(M) *** CRD (ADD) CRD 3509. Milne

4 Skazki, Op. 34; Sonata-Ballade in F sharp, Op. 27; Sonata romantica in B flat min., Op. 53/1
(M) *** CRD (ADD) CRD 3498. Milne

These are new performances, and such is the quality of Hamish Milne's playing that one is never tempted to think of this music as pale Rachmaninov. Milne has lived with Medtner for the best part of a lifetime, and this tells. His playing has refinement and authority, and the transcription he has made of the Pushkin setting, *I Loved Thee,* is quite magical. In the *Sonata minacciosa,* though Milne's playing might be more mercurial and incandescent, he brings valuable insights of his own. The *Sonata-Ballade* and *Sonata romantica* are also finely and perceptively played. Very good recording.

Forgotten Melodies, Opp. 38–9; 3 Marches, Op. 8; Sonata-Ballade in F sharp, Op. 27; Sonata Idylle in G, Op. 56; Sonata Skazka in C min., Op. 25/1; Sonata Triad, Op. 11; Sonatas in A min., Op. 30; in B flat min. (Sonata romantica), Op. 53/1; in E min. (Night Wind), Op. 25/2; in F min., Op. 5; in F min. (Sonata minacciosa), Op. 53/2; in G min., Op. 22
⌐ *** Hyp. CDA 67221-4 (4). Hamelin

Marc-André Hamelin's artistry is to be found at its most consummate in this four-CD set of the sonatas and miscellaneous piano music. If you find Medtner just a little bland or predictable, then try this set, for in Hamelin's hands it is neither. Playing touched by distinction.

MÉHUL, Etienne-Nicolas (1763–1817)

Overtures & Preludes: *Ariodant; Bion; La Chasse du jeune Henri; Les Deux Aveugles de Tolède; Horatius Cocles; Le Jeune sage et le vieux fou; Joseph; Mélidore et Phrosine; Le Trésor supposé*

☛ *** ASV CDDCA 1140. O de Bretagne, Sanderling

Méhul thrived over the period before and after the French Revolution, serving each regime in turn. Most of these colourful overtures and preludes for nine of his operas are new to the catalogue, but they include a favourite of Sir Thomas Beecham, *The Two Blind Men of Toledo*, in which a bouncy bolero rhythm establishes its Spanish flavour. There are anticipations of Weber and early Wagner in the slow prelude to *Ariodant*, as well as occasional likenesses elsewhere to Beethoven's *Egmont*. Méhul likes to begin his overtures with a solemn slow introduction, though he then moves on with rousing ideas, such as galloping hunting-rhythms and horn-calls, as in the two longest overtures, *La chasse du jeune Henri* and *Mélidore et Phrosine*. Though the Orchestre de Bretagne, based at Rennes in Brittany, is one of the newer French orchestras, it responds splendidly to its music director, Stefan Sanderling, with good string-playing and rich brass sounds.

Symphonies 1–4; Overtures: La Chasse de jeune Henri; Le Trésor supposé

*** Nim. NI 5184/5. Gulbenkian Foundation O, Swierczewski

The four symphonies recorded here come from 1808–10 (Nos. 3 and 4 have been discovered only in recent years by David Charlton, who has edited them) and are well worth investigating. The invention is felicitous and engaging, and in *No. 4 in E major* Méhul brings back a motif of the *Adagio* in the finale, a unifying gesture well ahead of its time. The performances are eminently satisfactory, even if the strings sound a shade undernourished.

Symphonies 1 in G min.; 2 in D

(BB) *** Warner Apex 0927 49535-2. Les Musiciens du Louvre, Minkowski

(BB) **(*) Naxos 8.555402. Rhenish PO, Rotter

Méhul's lively symphonies are familiar through Swierczewski's complete cycle on Nimbus. The Naxos recording dates from 1988, and the sound is warm and full, and the performances are lively enough. However, Minkowski and his period band, Les Musiciens du Louvre, have the edge on their competitors. Their clarity of texture and rhythmic bite bring exhilarating results. This is undoubtedly the disc to go for.

MELARTIN, Erkki (1875–1937)

(i) *Violin Concerto, Op. 60. Sleeping Beauty (Suite), Op. 22; Suite lyrique 3 (Impressions de Belgique)*

** Ondine (ADD) ODE 923-2. (i) Storgårds; Tampere PO, Segerstam

Ten years younger than Sibelius, Erkki Melartin's music shows a considerable lyrical talent and expertise in writing for the orchestra. The *Violin Concerto* (1910–13) has a lot going for it and John Storgårds takes its formidable difficulties in his stride. At one point its slow movement even brings Delius to mind. The atmospheric *Suite lyrique* is a set of six impressionistic sketches inspired by a visit the composer made to Bruges in 1914, and the incidental music to Topelius's

play, *The Sleeping Beauty*, dates from 1910. Decent recording, but the Tampere orchestra is a bit too raw-toned and ill-tuned to do this music full justice. Worth hearing all the same.

MENDELSSOHN, Fanny (1805–47)

Piano Trio in D, Op. 11

*** Hyp. CDA 66331. Dartington Piano Trio – Clara SCHUMANN: *Trio in G min ***

Like Clara Schumann's *G minor Trio* with which it is coupled, the *Piano Trio* has impeccable craftsmanship and great facility. Its ideas are pleasing, though not strongly individual. The Dartington Piano Trio play most persuasively and give much pleasure. Excellent recording.

String Quartet in E flat

(M) *** CPO 999 679-2. Basle Erato Qt – MAYER: *Quartet 14;* SIRMEN: *Quartets 2–3 ***

Fanny Mendelssohn's *String Quartet*, written in 1834, was influenced – notably in its layout and key sequence – by her brother's Op. 12, but the delectable Scherzo is the only movement that might be mistakenly assumed to be Felix's work; otherwise the music is wholly her own. The pervasive melancholy which permeates the opening movement and the *Romanze* is strikingly personal. But most remarkable of all is the forward-looking *Molto vivace* finale, with its determined energy, which is so like the finale of Tchaikovsky's *Souvenir de Florence* in its passionate forward impulse. The performance here is first class in every way, as is the recording; the couplings are stimulating too.

Lieder

*** Hyp. CDA 67110. Gritton, Asti

Fanny Mendelssohn's response to German poets from Goethe to Heine is at least the equal of her brother's, at once memorably tuneful and subtle in her illumination of the texts, adding distinctively to the Lieder tradition. Her writing is not just poetic but often vigorous, with fine accompaniments to match. Susan Gritton, sweet if just a little unvaried in tone, and Eugene Asti are refreshing, consistently sympathetic interpreters. They provide their own perceptive notes: Fanny's caustic comments on the poet Heine bring the man vividly to life.

MENDELSSOHN, Felix (1809–47)

(i; ii) *Capriccio brillant in B min. for Piano & Orchestra, Op. 22;* (iii) *Piano Concerto in A min. (for piano and strings);* (i; iv) *Piano Concertos 1 in G min., Op. 25; 2 in D min., Op. 40;* (iii; v) *Double Piano Concerto in E (for two pianos and strings);* (i; ii) *Rondo brillant in E flat for Piano & Orchestra, Op. 29;* (vi) *Rondo capriccioso in E, Op. 14*

(B) *** Double Decca 452 410-2 (2). (i) Katin; (ii) LPO, Martinon; (iii) Ogdon, ASMF, Marriner; (iv) LSO, Collins; (v) with Lucas; (vi) Bolet

Peter Katin's classic (1956) performances of the two best-known solo concertos have come up very freshly on CD. The two concertante pieces were recorded earlier (1954) and find Katin in sparkling form. Here a mono master is used; but this gives an impression of stereo. The ambitious and successful *A minor Concerto* and the *Double Concerto* have engaging ideas and are played with great verve and spirit by John Ogdon and his wife. The orchestral playing is equally lively and fresh throughout, and the vivid (originally Argo) 1969 Kingsway Hall recording has hardly dated. Jorge Bolet (recorded digitally in 1985) offers the solo *Rondo capriccioso* as a closing encore with the lightest of touch.

(i) *Capriccio brillant, Op. 22;* (i; ii) *Double Concerto for Violin & Piano;* (i) *Rondo brillant, Op. 29; Serenade & Allegro giocoso, Op. 43* (BIS CD 713); *Piano Concertos 1 in G min., Op. 25; 2 in D min., Op. 40; Piano Concerto in A min.* (BIS CD 718); (iii) *Double Piano Concertos: in A flat; E* (BIS CD 688); (ii) *Violin Concerto in D min.; Violin Concerto in E min., Op. 64 (1844 version); Octet, Op. 20: Scherzo* (orchestral version) (BIS CD 935)

(M) *** BIS CD 966/68. (i) Brautigam; (ii) Van Keulen; (iii) Derwinger, Pöntinen, Amsterdam New Sinf., Markiz

These are exemplary recordings of exemplary performances. Indeed it is difficult to flaw them. They are available separately (the individual catalogue numbers are listed within the titles above), but there is a price advantage in purchasing them all together. The interesting account of the *E minor Violin Concerto* in its original form (beautifully played by Isabelle van Keulen) is of particular interest. Mendelssohn spent seven years (1838–45) working over what is perhaps his most successful concertante work and this is its earlier draft. Its gestation is discussed in greater detail in the accompanying notes for the individual disc, but the notes here are still pretty copious.

(i) *Capriccio brillant* (for piano & orchestra); *Piano Concertos 1–2.* (ii) *Violin Concertos in D min. & E min. Overtures: Athalia; Calm Sea & Prosperous Voyage; The Hebrides (Fingal's Cave); The Marriage of Camacho; Ruy Blas; Trumpet Overture. Symphonies 1;* (iii; iv) 2 (Hymn of Praise); 3 (Scottish); 4 (Italian); 5 (Reformation); (iv; v) *Die erste Walpurgisnacht, Op. 60; Leise zieht durch mein Gemüth: 12 Songs for High Voice & Orchestra* (arr. Matthus); (iv; vi) *A Midsummer Night's Dream (Overture & Incidental Music)*

☛ **(N)** (B) **(*) RCA 82876 67885-2 (6). Bamberg SO, Flor, with (i) Edelmann; (ii) Takezawa; (iii) Popp, Protschka, Kaufmann; (iv) Bamberg SO Ch.; (v) Van De Walt, Rappé, Scharinger, Hölle; (vi) Popp, Lipovšek

Claus Peter Flor is a natural Mendelssohnian, and we have long praised his unsurpassed recordings of the key overtures and incidental music for *A Midsummer Night's Dream*. These are as desirable as ever and are still available on a two-CD set, together with the *Scottish, Italian* and *Reformation Symphonies* conducted by Munch, which are much less enticing (see below). Here they come in a six-CD box, with much more music, including all the symphonies very successfully conducted by Flor in essentially mellow readings, with sunnily romantic slow movements.

Nos. 1 and 5 again show him and the Bambergers at their best, with the *Andante* of No. 1 particularly beautifully played, and the outer movements of the *Reformation Symphony* given plenty of weight by the resonant Bamberg acoustic. Yet Flor opens the work atmospherically and treats the great chorale theme (*Ein' feste Burg*) most imaginatively, then finding much charm in the second movement.

Unfortunately, the recording lets down No. 2, the *Hymn of Praise*. In this work Flor has three outstanding soloists (Lucia

Popp, Julie Kaufmann and Josef Protschka), but the ill-focused, distantly balanced choral sound robs the performance of dramatic bite. It does not help that the string sound is thin.

In the *Scottish Symphony* Flor does not observe the exposition repeat (neither does Karajan) but he includes the 20-bar lead-back in the *Italian*. Even here his pacing never sounds rushed, and there is an engaging lightness of touch. The elfin horns in the Minuet are a highlight, while in the coda of the *Scottish* the horns ring out regally. Once more the Bamberg acoustic adds to the character of these unforced and beaming performances.

The soloist in the *Capriccio* and *Piano Concertos*, Sergei Edelmann, is an artist of considerable poetic insight, and the slow movement of the *G minor* (No. 1) is played with great delicacy of feeling and refinement of colour; but he needs to provide more dash and sparkle elsewhere. Not surprisingly, Flor gives excellent support, both here and in the *Violin Concertos*, which Kyoko Takezawa plays most winningly. Indeed, these are performances that consistently reflect the joy of the performers in the music. With a persuasive and resilient rather than a high-powered reading of the *E minor Concerto*, Takezawa relates that mature work more closely than usual to the often Mozartian invention of the 13-year-old Mendelssohn's *D minor Concerto*, with exceptionally neat articulation of rapid passage-work. Takezawa's reading of the *D minor* has each movement sharply characterized to make the piece sound more mature than it is.

The *Trumpet Overture* was not included in Flor's original collection. Mendelssohn wrote it in his youth but revised it to use as an introduction for a performance of Handel's *Israel in Egypt* which he conducted in 1833.

One of the greatest assets of the set is the fine performance of Mendelssohn's extraordinary cantata, *Die erste Walpurgisnacht*. While he was composing it in Rome, Mendelssohn wrote to his sister: 'It can be good fun: at the beginning there are songs of Spring and the like in abundance – then, when the guards make a noise with their pitchforks, and hay forks and trowels, the witches arrive on the scene, and you know that I am especially fond of them.' Flor paints the opening scene in the richest Mendelssohnian colouring, relishing the special effects, and the big choruses come off superbly, even if the Bamberg acoustic prevents absolute sharpness of choral focus. The soloists are very good, although the tenor, Deon Van der Walt, sounds a little strained at times.

The group of songs, arranged by Siegfried Matthus, includes favourites like *Auf Flügeln des Gesanges*, and the *Spring Song* is used as an orchestral interlude. But every number here is delightfully tuneful, and the scoring is felicitous and often recalls *A Midsummer Night's Dream*, while the horns are used very effectively, as in *Leise zieht durch mein Gemüth* and *In dem Mondenscheine im Walde*. The sequence closes with a stirring account from the tenor of Mendelssohn's *Hexenlied*. All in all, this is a very impressive budget collection, and it is a pity that no texts and translations are included for the vocal music.

(i) *Piano Concerto in A min.* (for piano and strings); (iv) *Piano Concertos 1 in G min; 2 in D min.*

(BB) *** Warner Apex 8573 89088-2. Katsaris; (i) Franz Liszt CO, Rolla; (ii) Leipzig G. O, Masur

It was a happy idea to couple the early *A minor Concerto* at budget price with the two major works in this form. The former is an extended piece lasting over half an hour, far longer than the two numbered concertos, an amazing work for a thirteen-year-old and endlessly inventive. It is impossible not to respond to Katsaris's vitality, even if at times there is a feeling of rushing his fences. He plays with enormous vigour in the outer movements of the later works and receives strong support from Masur. There is nothing heavy, yet the music is given more substance than usual, while the central slow movements bring a relaxed lyrical *espresso* which provides admirable contrast. The full, well-balanced recording has attractive ambience and sparkle.

Piano Concerto 1 in G min., Op. 25

*** DG 474 291-2. Lang Lang, Chicago SO, Barenboim – TCHAIKOVSKY: *Piano Concerto 1* **(*)

Lang Lang in his native China first tackled the Mendelssohn concerto when he was only seven, since when it has become a favourite work of his. As in the Tchaikovsky, the close balance of the piano establishes this as a big-scale performance, with the minor-key bite of the opening strongly presented. In the slow movement he opts for a tempo on the broad side, lessening its role as a song without words. With sparkling playing, the performance erupts into a winningly joyful account of the finale. A rare and attractive coupling for the distinctive account of the Tchaikovsky.

Piano Concerto 1, Op. 25; Capriccio brillant, Op. 22

(BB) *** Warner Apex 0927 99842-2. Huang, NYPO, Masur – MOZART: *Piano Concerto 21* ***

A fresh and pleasing account of No. 1 plus a sparkling *Capriccio* from Helen Huang, and the Mozart coupling is enjoyable, too. Excellent value.

Piano Concertos 1–2; Capriccio brillant

☛ ✿ *** Chan. 9215. Shelley, LMP

Piano Concertos 1–2; Capriccio brillant; Rondo brillant

(BB) *** Naxos 8.550681-2. Frith, Slovak State PO (Košice), Stankovsky

**(*) Ara. Z 6688. Hobson, Illinois Sinfonia da Camera

Piano Concertos Nos 1–2; Capriccio brillant; Rondo brillant; Serenade & Allegro Giocoso in B min., Op. 43

*** Hyp. CDA 66969. Hough, CBSO, Foster

(i) Piano Concertos 1–2. Prelude & Fugue, Op. 35/1; Rondo capriccioso, Op. 14; Variations sérieuses, Op. 54

(M) *** Sony (ADD) SMK 42401. Perahia; (i) ASMF, Marriner

(i) Piano Concertos 1–2. Songs without Words, Op. 19/1, 2, & 6 (Venetian Gondola Song); Op. 30/4 & 6; Op. 38/6; Op. 53/1; Op. 62/1 & 6 (Spring Song); Op. 67/4 (Spinning Song) & 6; Op. 85/6; Op. 102/5

(M) *** Decca 466 425-2. Schiff, (i) with Bav. RSO, Dutoit

Stephen Hough treats these compact minor-key works with a biting intensity. Yet with freer expressiveness and bigger contrasts he also brings out extra poetry, and in the finales a sparkling wit. He also has the advantage of the most generous and very apt couplings, three other, rare, concertante piano works by Mendelssohn. The point and delicacy of Hough's passage-work are a constant delight.

Howard Shelley offers marvellous playing in every respect: fresh, sparkling and dashing in the fast movements, poetic and touching in the slower ones. The London Mozart Players are a group of exactly the right size for these works and they point rhythms nicely and provide the necessary lift. Shelley dispatches the *Capriccio brillant* with similar aplomb, and the

recording-balance is admirably judged, with rich, truthful recorded sound.

Benjamin Frith on Naxos is a hardly less personable and nimble soloist: he is sensitively touching in the slow movements. The Slovak orchestra accompany with vigour and enthusiasm, and if the effect is at times less sharply rhythmic this is partly the effect of a somewhat more reverberant acoustic. What makes the Naxos disc very competitive is the inclusion of the *Rondo brillant*, which Frith dispatches with admirable vigour and sparkle. This disc is very good value indeed.

András Schiff also plays both concertos marvellously, with poetry, great delicacy and fluency, while his virtuosity is effortless. He is given excellent accompaniments by Dutoit and the Bavarian players, and the Decca recording is first class. His simplicity of style suits the *Songs without Words*, although some might find his approach a little cool. Yet the famous *Spring Song* shows him at his best. The recording is again most natural and realistic.

Murray Perahia's playing catches the Mendelssohnian spirit with admirable perception. There is sensibility and sparkle, the slow movements are shaped most beautifully and the partnership with Marriner is very successful, for the Academy give a most sensitive backing. The recording could be more transparent but it does not lack body, and the piano timbre is fully acceptable. At mid-price, a very recommendable issue.

As befits a Leeds prize-winner, these concertos are dispatched by Ian Hobson with consummate agility and fleetness of finger. He is nothing if not fluent, and he directs his Illinois players with expert musicianship. Recommendable enough – though there is, perhaps, not enough charm here to challenge the finest versions.

Double Piano Concertos: in A flat; in E

*** Hyp. CDA 66567. Coombs, Munro, BBC Scottish SO, Maksymiuk

(BB) *** Naxos 8.553416. Frith, Tinney, Dublin RTE Sinf., ODuinn

Mendelssohn's *Double Concerto in A flat* is the most ambitious of all his concertante works, and the work in E brings an expansive first movement too; they provide formidable evidence of the teenage composer's fluency and technical finesse. Stephen Coombs and Ian Munro prove ideal advocates, playing with delectable point and imagination, finding a wit and poetry in the writing that might easily lie hidden, with even the incidental passage-work magnetizing the ear. The recording of the pianos is on the shallow side, and the string-tone is thin too, but that is not inappropriate for the music.

The Naxos disc challenges the outstanding Hyperion issue coupling these same two charming double concertos. If the Irish players are not quite as persuasive as their Scottish counterparts on Hyperion, their playing is just as refined, and Frith and Tinney are a fair match for Coombs and Munro, less powerful but just as magnetic and even more poetic. The transparent recording helps, very appropriate for such youthful music.

Double Piano Concerto in E.

*** Chan. 9711. Güher and Süther Pekinel, Philh. O, Marriner – BRUCH; MOZART: *Double Concertos* ***

**(*) Ph. 432 095-2. K. and M. Labèque, Philh. O, Bychkov – BRUCH: *Double Concerto* **(*)

Mendelssohn wrote his *Double Piano Concerto* when he was only fourteen, yet it contains many ideas that are entirely characteristic of his mature style. In such a performance as this its freshness justifies the length, for unlike the rival version from the Labèque sisters on Philips – which has only the Bruch for coupling – this one brings an accompaniment from Marriner and the Academy, finely pointed, which does not inflate the piece. The Pekinel sisters, as in the other two works, give a fresh, alert performance with pin-point ensemble. Warm, full sound.

The Labèques play the ambitious *E major Double Concerto* with enthusiasm and flair, and Bychkov accompanies manfully. But, partly because of the resonant acoustic, the effect is rather inflated and the ear looks for more transparency and lightness of texture in such an amiable piece.

Violin Concertos in D min. (for Violin & Strings); in E min., Op. 64

(BB) **(*) Virgin 2x1 5 61504-2 (2). Seiler, City of L. Sinfonia, Hickox – BEETHOVEN: *Concerto* **(*)

It is good to have a recommendable bargain pairing of Mendelssohn's youthful and mature concertos. Mayumi Seiler is fresh and appealing in the one, and then gives a sparkling account of the famous *E minor* work with the slow movement serene in its simplicity, as with the coupled Beethoven concerto. Hickox is in good form and the recording is pleasingly balanced; although the timbre of the soloist is small, it is perfectly focused.

Violin Concerto in D min.; (i) Double Concerto in D min. for Violin, Piano & Strings; Violin Concerto in E min., Op. 64

(BB) *** Naxos 8.553844. Bisengaliev, N. Sinfonia, Penney; (i) with Frith

Two juvenilia are here dispatched with zest and freshness by these excellent musicians, even if in the *D minor Violin Concerto* Bisengaliev's finale is a bit headlong. Spirited playing from the Northern Sinfonia under Andrew Penney and a predictably stylish contribution from Benjamin Frith.

Violin Concerto in E min., Op. 64

(*) EMI **DVD 490445-9. Grumiaux, O. Nat. de l'ORTF, Rosenthal (with BACH: *Violin Partita 2, BWV 1004: Sarabande & Chaconne*. BLOCH: *Baal Shem: Il Nigun* (with André Chometon)) – BEETHOVEN: *Violin Concerto* **(*)

*** Sony SK 87740. Midori, BPO, Jansons – BRUCH: *Violin Concerto 1* ***

(M) *** Decca 460 976-2. Chung, Montreal SO, Dutoit – BRUCH: *Violin Concerto 1; Scottish Fantasy* ***

(M) *** Decca (IMS) 460 015-2. Chung, Montreal SO, Dutoit – ELGAR: *Violin Concerto* ***

*** EMI 5 56418-2. Chang, BPO, Jansons – SIBELIUS: *Violin Concerto* ***

(N) *** Virgin 545663-2. Capuçon, Mahler CO, Harding – SCHUMANN: *Violin Concerto in D min.* ***

*** Teldec 0630-15870-2. Perlman, Chicago SO, Barenboim – BRAHMS: *Double Concerto* ***

(M) *** EMI (ADD) 5 62591-2. Perlman, LSO, Previn – TCHAIKOVSKY: *Concerto* **(*)

(BB) *** Naxos mono 8.110977. Milstein, Philharmonic-Symphony O, New York, Barbirolli – BRUCH: *Violin Concerto 1*; TCHAIKOVSKY: *Violin Concerto* (***)

(BB) *** Naxos 8.550153. Nishizaki, Slovak PO, Jean – TCHAIKOVSKY: *Concerto* ***

(M) *** CRD (ADD) CRD 3369, R. Thomas, Bournemouth SO – BEETHOVEN: *Romances 1–2*; SCHUBERT: *Konzertstück* ***

(M) *** DG 445 515-2. Mutter, BPO, Karajan – BRAHMS: *Violin Concerto* ***

(M) *** DG 463 641-2. Mutter, BPO, Karajan – BRUCH: *Concerto 1* ***

*** EMI 7 49663-2. Kennedy, ECO, Tate – BRUCH: *Concerto 1*; SCHUBERT: *Rondo* ***

(M) *** EMI (ADD) 5 66906-2 [5-66958]. Menuhin, Philh. O, Kurtz – BRUCH: *Concerto 1* ***

(N) (M) *** EMI Legend (ADD) 5 57766 (with bonus **DVD**: MOZART: *Violin Concerto 3, K. 216*). Menuhin, Philh. O, Kurtz – BRUCH: *Violin Concerto* ***

(B) *** DG Double (ADD) 453 142-2 (2). Milstein, VPO, Abbado – BEETHOVEN: *Concerto* ***; BRAHMS: *Concerto* **(*); TCHAIKOVSKY: *Concerto* ***

(N) (M) *** RCA **SACD** (ADD) 82876 61391-2. Heifetz, Boston SO, Munch – BEETHOVEN: *Violin Concerto* ***

(M) **(*) RCA 09026 61743-2. Heifetz, Boston SO, Munch – TCHAIKOVSKY: *Concerto, etc.* **(*)

(N) (BB) *** Regis RRC 1152. Laredo, SCO – BRUCH: *Concerto 1* ***

(***) Testament mono SBT 1037. Martzy, Philh. O, Kletzki – BRAHMS: *Concerto* (***)

(M) (***) EMI mono 5 66975-2 [66990-2]. Menuhin, BPO, Furtwängler – BEETHOVEN: *Concerto* (***)

(***) Beulah (ADD) 1PD 10. Campoli, LPO, Boult – ELGAR: *Violin Concerto* (***)

(N) (B) **(*) Decca 475 6000 (2). Bell, ECO, Marriner – BRUCH; MOZART: *Violin Concertos* **(*)

**(*) Sony SK 89505. Bell, Camerata Salzburg, Norrington – BEETHOVEN: *Violin Concerto* **(*)

(B) **(*) Discover DICD 920122. Bushkov, Slovak New PO, Rahbari (with TCHAIKOVSKY: *Concerto* **)

(M) **(*) Sup. (ADD) SU 1939-2 011. Suk, Czech PO, Ančerl – BERG: *Concerto* ***; BRUCH: *Concerto* **

(*) Australian Decca Eloquence (ADD) 461 369-2. Ricci, LSO, Gamba – BRUCH: *Violin Concerto* **(*); SAINT-SAENS: *Havanaise, Op. 83, etc.* *

(BB) (**(*)) Naxos mono 8.110941. Heifetz, RPO, Beecham – MOZART: *Violin Concertos 4; 5 (Turkish)* (**(*))

(i) Violin Concerto in E min., Op. 64; (ii) Song without Words: May Breezes, Op. 62/1

(BB) (***) Naxos mono 8.110909. Kreisler; (i) Berlin State Op. O, Blech; (ii) Sàndor (piano) – BEETHOVEN: *Violin Concerto* (***) (with BACH: *Unaccompanied Violin Sonata 1, BWV 1001: Adagio* (***))

The Grumiaux DVD account of the Mendelssohn *Concerto* was made in the Palais de la Méditerranée in Nice in January 1961. In his day Grumiaux was an aristocrat of violinists, and his tonal refinement and selfless artistry made his achievement quite special. The sound is somewhat wanting in bloom and climaxes are wanting in transparency, but the essential qualities of this great violinist emerge in this work and in the various shorter pieces listed above. The Paganini was an encore at the Mendelssohn concert, while the Bach and Bloch pieces were recorded variously at the ORTF studios and in the Netherlands.

It is surprising that Midori has taken so long to record this traditional coupling, but the wait has been worth it when, in live performances with Jansons and the Berlin Philharmonic at their most inspired, the results are so distinctive, at once thoughtful and detailed yet youthful-sounding too. The moment in the first movement when the soloist for a moment relaxes on a downward arpeggio brings a breathtaking *pianissimo*, always a fine testing-point. Recorded live, Midori and Jansons convey urgency, heightening climaxes with a hint of *accelerando*, so that in all three movements Midori's overall timings are relatively fast, with the central *Andante* flowing freely. In the finale the urgency brings extra excitement, with a consistent sense of freely spontaneous expressiveness.

Kyung Wha Chung favours speeds faster than usual in all three movements, and the result is sparkling and happy, with the lovely slow movement fresh and songful, not at all sentimental. With warmly sympathetic accompaniment from Dutoit and the Montreal orchestra, amply recorded, the result is one of Chung's happiest records. The Elgar coupling works well, but the alternative of Bruch's *G minor Concerto* and *Scottish Fantasy* in Decca's 'Legends' series is more attractive still.

The lightness and resilience of Renaud Capuçon's playing at the very start of the Mendelssohn, matched by the transparent textures of the Mahler Chamber Orchestra under Daniel Harding, instantly establish the distinctive character of his version of a much-recorded concerto. The urgency of the main *Allegro* still allows the crystalline precision of Capuçon's playing of rapid passage-work to come over without any hint of rush. The chamber scale works well, but Capuçon's formidable virtuosity ensures that there is no feeling of a small-scale performance. With free, open sound, recorded in the Jugendstilltheater in Vienna, this makes an outstanding version of an apt and rare coupling.

Unlike the Sibelius with which it is coupled, Sarah Chang's account of the Mendelssohn was recorded under studio conditions in the Philharmonie, Berlin. Here too she offers an astonishingly mature reading, more restrained than some, but still magnetic in its thoughtfulness and spontaneous poetry. Warm, atmospheric sound.

Perlman's 1993 Chicago version, strong and volatile, was recorded live and originally issued in coupling with the second Prokofiev. It makes an excellent, more generous coupling in the new format with the powerful Perlman/Ma version of the Brahms *Double Concerto*.

Perlman's 1972 recording was very highly regarded in its day. He gives a performance as full of flair as almost any, and he is superbly matched by the LSO under Previn, at that time at their very peak. With ripe recording, this remains competitive in its mid-priced reissue in the 'Perlman Edition', although the Tchaikovsky coupling is not quite its match.

Milstein made four recordings of the Mendelssohn, and this Naxos reissue, his first, comes from May 1945, shortly after the war in Europe had come to an end. There is a sense of exhilaration and a freshness that is very persuasive and the engineers capture Milstein's tone with great fidelity. Just before (and through) the war American Columbia recorded on to 33⅓r.p.m. lacquer master discs, after which the approved takes were dubbed on to wax 78r.p.m. discs. Although the resultant 78s were not as impressive as direct-to-wax discs, when they were transferred to LP in the early 1950s there was a much wider frequency-range as well as quieter surfaces. The recordings sound as well as 1950s early tape masters. Mark Obert Thorn's transfers are exemplary; the performance, which (unless we are much mistaken) has not been available on LP or CD since the 1950s, should be snapped up, particularly at so competitive a price.

Takako Nishizaki gives an inspired reading of the concerto, warm, spontaneous and full of temperament. The central *Andante* is on the slow side, but well shaped, not sentimental, while the outer movements are exhilarating, with excellent playing from the Slovak Philharmonic. Though the forwardly placed violin sounds over-bright, the recording is full and warm. A splendid coupling at super-bargain price.

Ronald Thomas's account is in many ways the opposite of a dashing virtuoso approach, yet his apt, unforced choice of speeds, his glowing purity of intonation and the fine co-ordination with the orchestra he leads (an amazing achievement in this often complex, fast-flowing music) put this among the most satisfying versions available. It is intensely refreshing from first to last, and is helped by excellent recording and fine couplings.

The freshness of Anne-Sophie Mutter's approach communicates vividly to the listener, creating the feeling of hearing the work anew. Her gentleness and radiant simplicity in the *Andante* are very appealing, and the light, sparkling finale is a delight. Mutter is given a small-scale image, projected forward from the orchestral backcloth; the sound is both full and refined. This fine performance comes alternatively coupled with either Brahms or Bruch.

Kennedy establishes a positive, masculine view of the work from the very start, but fantasy here goes with firm control. The slow movement brings a simple, songful view of the haunting melody, and the finale sparkles winningly, with no feeling of rush. With a bonus in the rare Schubert *Rondo* and clear, warm recording, it makes an excellent recommendation.

The restrained nobility of Menuhin's phrasing of the famous principal melody of the slow movement has long been a hallmark of his reading with Efrem Kurtz, who provides polished and sympathetic support. The sound of the CD transfer is bright, with the soloist dominating but the orchestral texture well detailed.

Menuhin's coupling with Bruch also comes in EMI's new Legend series with a bonus DVD of Mozart's *Third (G major) Concerto*, which was filmed with the Orchestre de Chambre de l'ORTF in Paris in 1967 and makes an interesting, but not exceptional, bonus.

Milstein's later DG version is a highly distinguished performance, very well accompanied. His account of the slow movement is more patrician than Menuhin's and his slight reserve is projected by sound which is bright, clean and clear in its CD remastering. This now comes on a DG Double which also includes the Beethoven and Brahms concertos.

As one might expect, Heifetz gives a fabulous performance. His speeds are consistently fast, yet in the slow movement his flexible phrasing sounds so inevitable and easy that it is hard not to be convinced. The finale is a *tour de force*, light and sparkling, with every note in place, and Munch's accompaniment throughout is outstanding. The 1959 recording is very good for its period and sounds well on CD, where it is paired with Tchaikovsky. But the new SACD transfer brings an added warmth, and the new coupling, the Beethoven *Concerto*, is eminently recommendable.

Jaime Laredo's version on a budget CD brings an attractively direct reading, fresh and alert but avoiding mannerism, marked by consistently sweet and true tone from the soloist. The orchestral ensemble is amazingly good when you remember that the soloist himself is directing. Vivid recording.

It is not just the perfect sweetness and purity of Johanna Martzy's tone that are so impressive, but also her freely flexible rubato, which always sounds spontaneous, and the hushed tenderness of her *pianissimo* playing is breathtaking, as in the central *Andante*. The performance is also remarkable for the quicksilver energy of the finale and, with the soloist well forward, the mono sound is full and clear.

Menuhin's unique gift for lyrical sweetness has never been presented on record more seductively than in his classic, earlier version of the Mendelssohn *Concerto* with Furtwängler. The digital transfer is not ideally clear, yet one hardly registers that this is a mono recording from the early 1950s.

Kreisler's Mendelssohn is hardly less cherishable than the Beethoven coupling: richly lyrical, full of charm and with an unforgettably songful account of the *Andante*, with an exquisite coda and a beautifully judged transition to the sparkling, delectably articulated finale. Leo Blech accompanies persuasively and the orchestral ensemble follows the soloist impressively. The orchestral sound is backward, but Kreisler's violin is vividly present in Mark Obert-Thorn's first-class transfer. The *Song without Words*, played very simply, comes before the *Concerto*, following the Bach *Adagio*.

Campoli's perfectly formed tone and polished, secure playing are just right for the Mendelssohn *Concerto*. A delightful performance, notable for its charm and disarming simplicity. The 1958 (originally Decca) recording is marred by a degree of roughness in the orchestral focus; but no matter, this very inexpensive record gives much pleasure and is a fine reminder of a superb violinist, coupled with the Elgar concerto.

Joshua Bell is given a very forward balance by the Decca engineers, but he can still achieve a genuine *pianissimo* when he wants to, as in the lead-in to the first-movement cadenza, which is a moment of magic. Overall, this is a boldly romantic reading, full of warmth and not without poetry, but the spotlight on the soloist all but masks Marriner's fine accompaniment, a distinct drawback.

As in the Beethoven concerto with which it is coupled on Sony, Bell in the Mendelssohn uses his own cadenza in the first movement, suggesting that the published cadenza was mainly by Mendelssohn's friend, Ferdinand David, not by the composer himself. Perhaps more controversial is the coolness of the slow movement, very simple, pure and direct, totally avoiding sentimentality, though missing some of the warmth Bell brought to this movement in his earlier, Decca version of this work, a reading a shade more expansive in all three movements. The finale this time is very fast indeed, light and sparkling but with plenty of detail, again in a performance relatively small in scale in reflection of the chamber accompaniment.

Evgeny Bushkov is a pupil of Leonid Kogan, and he prepares and plays the secondary theme of the opening movement with appealing tenderness. The *Andante* has a matching simplicity and the finale no lack of bravura and fire. He is well accompanied, and the recording, made in the Concert Hall of Slovak Radio, Bratislava, is full and well balanced. Not a first choice, however, for the coupled Tchaikovsky *Concerto* sounds less spontaneous.

Suk's small, sweet timbre is particularly suited to the Mendelssohn *Concerto*. This is a highly congenial performance, not as individual as some, with a straightforwardly lyrical slow movement and a finale which gains from not being rushed off its feet. An excellent CD transfer, firm and full. However, Suk's style is less suited to the Bruch *Concerto*.

Ricci's account of the Mendelssohn *Concerto* is clean and sympathetic and technically brilliant, even if his characteristic timbre and use of vibrato is rather intense. Gamba conducts

with his usual vigour, and this 1958 performance, which sounds hardly at all dated, comes up as fresh as paint in its new transfer. The couplings are equally characterful.

Heifetz's 1948 version is among the most controversial of all his recordings, with breathtakingly fast accounts of the outer movements. If at first the impression is simply of rush for its own sake, there are contrasting passages where the Beecham influence brings total relaxation, as in the sweetness of the downward arpeggio leading into the second subject. In any case the results are undoubtedly exciting, and the sweet songfulness of the slow movement reveals Heifetz at his warmest. On Naxos, a good coupling with the two Mozart concertos, one also with Beecham, the other from 1934 – Heifetz's very first concerto recording.

Violin Concerto in E min. (1st movement only)

(N) (***) EMI **DVD** 492840-9. Heifetz, Bell Telephone Hour O, Voorhees (with bonus: DEBUSSY: *La Fille aux cheveux de lin*; DINICU: *Hora staccato*) – BEETHOVEN: *Piano Concerto 4* **; WALTON: *Cello Concerto* (***)

Heifetz, Rubinstein and Piatigorsky were called the million-dollar trio, though their ensemble was short-lived. They are all heard on this DVD, albeit not together, but not even the primitive (1949) sound can diminish the extraordinary tone Heifetz commands or the dazzling virtuosity he displays. The picture in all three pieces calls for some tolerance, though both eye and ear quickly adjust.

(i; ii) Violin Concerto in E min., Op. 64; (ii) Hebrides Overture, Op. 26; Symphony 4 in A, Op. 90 (Italian); (iii) A Midsummer Night's Dream: Incidental Music; (iv) Octet; (v) Songs without Words: Opp. 38/6, 62/5 & 6, 67/4

(B) *** DG Panorama (ADD) 469 157-2 (2). (i) Mutter; (ii) BPO, Karajan; (iii) Mathis, Boese, Bav. RSO, Kubelik; (iv) ASMF Chamber Ens.; (v) Barenboim

DG's Panorama double pack offers performances that would be a first choice at any price level. Karajan and the Berlin Philharmonic playing the *Hebrides Overture* and the *Italian Symphony* are difficult to surpass and so is the *Violin Concerto* with a 19-year-old Anne-Sophie Mutter. On the companion disc Kubelik's much-admired *Midsummer Night's Dream: Incidental Music* returns to the catalogue alongside the Academy of St Martin in the Fields' *Octet*. Given the blend of artistic excellence and good quality sound, this is a bargain.

2 Concert Pieces for Clarinet & Basset Horn: in F min., Op. 113; in D min., Op. 114

☛ *** EMI 5 57359-2. S. Meyer, W. Meyer, ASMF, Sillito – BAERMANN: *Clarinet Quintet 3*; WEBER: *Clarinet Quintet* ***

(B) *** Hyp. Dyad CDD 22017 (2). King, Dobrée, LSO, Francis (with Concert – see below ***)

*** Sup. SU 3554-2. Peterkova, Prague Philh. O, Bělohlávek – BRUCH: *Double Concerto*; ROSSINI: *Introduction, Theme and Variations*; *Variations in C* ***

These two delightful pieces for clarinet and basset horn are miniature concertos in all but name, each in three tiny movements. They are perfect vehicles for the brother-and-sister team of Sabine and Wolfgang Meyer, here opting for string orchestra accompaniment rather than the original piano. The perfect coupling for the Weber and Baermann *Quintets*, very well recorded.

They are also played with a nice blend of expressive spontaneity and high spirits by Georgina Dobrée, who proves a nimble partner for the ever-sensitive Thea King. This is part of an excellent two-disc set, including other attractive concertante works by Max Bruch, Crusell, Spohr and other less familar names.

Ludmila Peterkova also brings out the charm of these two miniature concertos as well as the wit, with Jiří Bělohlávek and the Prague Philharmonia sensitive partners. Excellent, full-bodied sound.

(i) Overtures: Athalia; Calm Sea and a Prosperous Voyage; The Hebrides (Fingal's Cave); The Marriage of Camacho; A Midsummer Night's Dream; Ruy Blas; (ii) Symphonies 3 (Scottish); 4 (Italian); 5 (Reformation)
⊕– (BB) **(*) RCA 2 CD 74321 84600-2 (2). (i) Bamberg SO, Flor; (ii) Boston SO, Munch

Claus Peter Flor's collection of overtures (which received a Rosette from us in its original format) remains the most desirable the catalogue has ever offered. The magically evocative opening of *Calm Sea and Prosperous Voyage*, followed by an allegro of great vitality, is a demonstrable example of the spontaneous imagination of these performances, and there is no finer or more atmospheric version of *Fingal's Cave*. The bold *Ruy Blas* and the nobly contoured *Athalia* are also greatly enjoyable, especially when played with such freshness and polish. The recording, made in the Dominikanerbau, Bamberg, has splendid bloom, for the hall ambience is just right for this repertoire. The *Midsummer Night's Dream* incidental music is recorded equally beautifully, glowing and radiant. The little melodramas are omitted, but the performance is otherwise complete. Flor's stylish yet relaxed control brings the kind of intimacy one expects from a chamber group. Again the Bamberg acoustic adds to the character of these outstanding performances, unforced and beaming.

Unfortunately, the Munch performances of the last three symphonies are disappointing. The *Scottish Symphony* is not insensitive, but both the *Italian* and *Reformation* are over-driven and charmless, and they are not helped by the coarse recording, which glares unattractively in *fortissimos* from the close microphone placing.

The Hebrides (Fingal's Cave) Overture
(M) (**) Beulah mono 3PD12. BBC SO, Boult – SCHUBERT: *Symphony 9 (**(*)); WAGNER: Die Meistersinger: Overture (**)*

Boult, recording the *Hebrides Overture* in 1933 with the recently founded BBC Symphony Orchestra, takes a fresh, generally brisk view, which allows a degree of flexibility in the build-up of ostinatos and in the lovely reprise of the second subject, but with no romantic excess. The Beulah transfer is dry, with no added reverberation, not helped by a high but even surface hiss; but the body of sound makes one readily forget the limitations.

Symphonies for Strings 1–12; 13 in C min. (single movement)
*** BIS CD 938/940. Amsterdam New Sinf., Markiz

Symphonies for Strings 1–12
⊕– (M) *** Hyp. CDS 44081/3. L. Festival O, Pople
(N) (B) *(*) RCA 82876 60427-2 (3). Hanover Band, Goodman

Symphonies for String Orchestra 1–6
(BB) *** Naxos 8.553161. N. CO, Ward

Symphonies for String Orchestra 7–9
(BB) *** Naxos 8.553162. N. CO, Ward

Symphonies for String Orchestra 10–13 (Sinfoniesatz)
(BB) *** Naxos 8.553163. N. CO, Ward

Mendelssohn's early symphonies for strings, lost for 150 years, were rediscovered in 1950. The first ten were student works and the last two, together with the virtually unknown *Symphony Movement in C minor* (No. 13), had all been completed before their young composer reached the age of fourteen. The playing of the Amsterdam New Sinfonietta is vibrant and alive, and the recording has a warmth and clarity that give the set the edge over almost all its current rivals. This music is full of charm, and the quality of Mendelssohn's youthful invention is little short of astonishing.

Originally issued in 1991/2 on three separate discs, Ross Pople's set is among his finest recordings. He achieves modern-instrument performances that are as polished and spirited as they are lyrically persuasive and dramatic. Slow movements are both gracious and with genuine gravitas and much depth of feeling, often elegiac (sample No. 9). The contrapuntal interplay of the *Allegros* has an attractive lightness of touch (as in the splendid opening movement of No. 12), yet the music is never made to sound trivial. The recordings, made between 1985 and 1990 in the Church of Edward the Confessor, Mottingham, Kent, are warm and natural, and detail is not clouded.

Nicholas Ward and the Northern Chamber Orchestra match rivals at whatever price. The freshness and incisiveness of the performances are enhanced by bright, clean recording, made in the Concert Hall of Broadcasting House in Manchester. Not only does Ward bring out the exhilarating sparkle and vigour of the fast movements – with Mendelssohn, even at the age of eleven, giving clear anticipations of his mature style – but he also gives apt emotional weight to such beautiful lyrical movements as the *Andante* of No. 2 or the darkly slow introduction to the one-movement *No. 10 in B minor*. All three discs can be warmly recommended to everyone.

Although Roy Goodman's complete set of Mendelssohn's delightfully inventive *String Symphonies* has the benefit of completeness, with the inclusion of the first movement of the *13th String Symphony*, it is in every other respect outclassed by Ross Pople's London Festival Orchestra account on Hyperion. Goodman's performances are not unappealing but they are doubly handicapped by being both backwardly balanced and set in a reverberant acoustic: the resultant washy sound blunts the music's sparkle.

Symphonies for Strings 1, 4, 6, 7 & 12
(M) **(*) Warner Elatus 2564 60353-2. Concerto Köln

Symphonies for Strings 2, 3, 5, 11 & 13
(M) **(*) Warner Elatus 2564 60440-2. Concerto Köln

Symphonies for Strings 8–10
(M) **(*) Warner Elatus 2564 60124-2. Concerto Köln

These are excellent period-instrument performances, very well recorded, but they would have been even more attractive on the budget Apex label.

Symphonies for String Orchestra 2 in D; 3 in E min.; 5 in B flat; 6 in E flat
(B) *** EMI double forte 5 69524-2 (2). Polish CO, Maksymiuk – JANIEWICZ: *Divertimento*; JARZEBSKI: *Chromatica; Tamburetta*; ROSSINI: *String Sonatas ***

This collection of four of the boy Mendelssohn's early *String Symphonies* is most invigorating. These earlier symphonies from the series of 13 may look to various models from Bach to Beethoven, but the vitality of the invention still bursts through. The slow movement of *Symphony No. 2*, for example, is a Bachian meditation that in its simple beauty matches later Mendelssohn. The Polish strings are set in a lively acoustic, giving exceptionally rich sound, but the playing also has plenty of dash.

Symphonies 1–5 (complete)
(BB) **(*) Arts 47620/2 (3). SO de Madrid, Maag (with Valente, Suárez, Calderon, Orfeón Donostiarra in 2)

Symphonies 1 in C min., Op. 11; (i) 2 in B flat, Op. 52 (Hymn of Praise); 3 in A min., (Scottish), Op. 56; 4 in A (Italian), Op. 91; 5 in D min. (Reformation), Op. 107
(B) *** Decca Trio 470 946-2 (3). (i) Banse, Rubens, Cole, Berlin R. Ch.; Deutsches SO, Berlin, Ashkenazy

Symphonies 1; (i) 2. (ii) Die erste Walpurgisnacht, Op. 60
(B) *** Double Decca (ADD) 460 236-2 (2). VPO, Dohnányi, with (i) Ghazarian, Gruberová, Krenn, V. State Op. Ch.; (ii) Lilowa, Laubenthal, Krause, Sramek, V. Singverein

Symphonies 3–5; Athalie: Overture & War March of the Priests; Overtures: Calm Sea and a Prosperous Voyage; The Hebrides (Fingal's Cave)
(B) *** Double Decca ADD/DDD 460 239-2 (2). VPO, Dohnányi

Symphonies 1–5; Overtures: Fair Melusina; The Hebrides; Meeresstille und glückliche Fahrt; A Midsummer Night's Dream; Ruy Blas; Trumpet Overture: Overture for Wind Instruments; Octet, Op. 20: Scherzo.
⊶ (B) *** DG 471 467-2 (4). LSO, Abbado

Symphonies 1–5; Overture: The Hebrides
(N) (M) *** Chan. 10224X (3). Philh. O, Weller (with Haymon, Hagley, Straka, Philh. Ch. in *Symphony 2*)

(i) *Symphonies 1; (i) 3, Overture: The Hebrides*
(B) *** Ph. Duo (ADD) (IMS) 456 071-2 (2). LPO; (i) Haitink; (ii) M. Price, Burgess, Jerusalem, LPO Ch., Chailly

(i) *Symphonies 4–5; Calm Sea and a Prosperous Voyage Overture; (ii–iii) Violin Concerto in E min.; (iii–iv) A Midsummer Night's Dream: Overture; Incidental Music*
(B) *** Ph. Duo (ADD) (IMS) 456 074-2 (2). (i) LPO; (ii) Grumiaux; (iii) Concg. O; (iv) with Woodland, Watts, Women of Netherlands R. Ch.; all cond. Haitink

Abbado's is an outstanding set in every way. It is his gift to distract you from any weaknesses of structure or thematic invention with the brightness and directness of his manner. In the *First Symphony*, the toughness of the piece makes one marvel that Mendelssohn ever substituted the third movement with the Scherzo of the *Octet* (as he did in London), but Abbado helpfully includes that extra Scherzo, so that on CD, with a programming device, you can readily make the substitution yourself. This set is now available at bargain price in DG's handsome Collector's Edition, with some extra overtures included which, like the symphonies, are superbly played and recorded. This set takes its place at the top of the list, irrespective of price.

Weller's set of the Mendelssohn symphonies can stand comparison with the finest alternatives, including Abbado. Certainly it is the most beautifully recorded, the Chandos sound richly full-bodied, though not sharply defined. He plays the *First Symphony* as if it were a mature work, not the inspiration of a fifteen-year-old. The *Scottish* and *Italian*

Symphonies convey the sense of live performances caught on the wing. These are warm, affectionate readings which include exposition repeats and build excitingly to climaxes. In the *Reformation Symphony* and in *Fingal's Cave*, which follows, there is an emotional thrust that is very involving, leading to a joyfully exultant conclusion in the finale. Again in the *Hymn of Praise* (No. 2) from the opening trombone solo onwards it is the warmth and weight of the recorded sound that tells, with a large chorus set against full-bodied, satisfyingly string-based orchestral sound. Though again speeds are often dangerously slow, the sense of spontaneity in the performance makes it compelling throughout. In the finale, Cynthia Haymon and Alison Hagley are warm-toned soloists, with Peter Straka an expressive if slightly fluttery tenor, but with a timbre which suits Mendelssohn. A considerable achievement.

The alternative tastefully presented Trio box collects Ashkenazy's Decca Mendelssohn symphonies, recorded at various times between 1993 and 1997 with the Deutsches Symphonie-Orchester, Berlin (the reborn Radio Symphony Orchestra). The set has a great deal going for it, particularly at this attractive price, with characterfully shaped phrasing and vital playing. Ashkenazy is unfailingly musical and fresh in his approach, and both the playing of this fine orchestra and the Decca recording are first rate. Although Abbado remains a first choice in this price range, this Trio set is eminently satisfying, very well recorded, and represents good value for money.

When Bernard Haitink in 1980 was prevented from rounding off his planned Mendelssohn symphony cycle with the *Symphony No. 2* (*Lobgesang – Hymn of Praise*), Riccardo Chailly stepped in to record it in his place. This compilation brings together what, despite the change of conductor, is another outstanding cycle, fresh and energetic, with a geniality that regularly puts a smile on Mendelssohn's face. Only in the first movement of the *Italian Symphony* does Haitink press too hard, and even then he has time to spring rhythms. Broadly, Chailly follows a similar pattern in the *Hymn of Praise*, another excellent performance with an outstanding trio of soloists, helped by full and vivid sound, though the fine chorus is backwardly balanced. The fourth disc contains Haitink's brilliant Concertgebouw version of the *Midsummer Night's Dream* incidental music – ten movements, including a dazzling account of the Overture – as well as the excellent Grumiaux version of the *Violin Concerto*, also with Haitink and the Concertgebouw, with 1960s sound still fresh and clear.

Dohnányi's pair of Double Deccas (which include two key overtures, lesser-known *Athalie* items and a half-hour cantata, as well as the symphonies) brings performances which are fresh and direct, often relying on faster and more flowing speeds than in Abbado's set. The most striking contrast comes in the *Hymn of Praise*, where Dohnányi's speeds are often so much faster than Abbado's that the whole character of the music is changed. Many will prefer Dohnányi in that, particularly when the choral sound is brighter and more immediate too. The *Reformation Symphony* comes off particularly well. The vintage recordings were made in the Sofiensaal between 1976 and 1978, and the two overtures and the *Italian Symphony* are digital, the Decca engineers producing sound which was among the finest of its period. The snag of the set is that Dohnányi, unlike Abbado, omits exposition repeats, which in the *Italian Symphony* means the loss of the substantial lead-back passage in the first movement. *Die erste Walpurgisnacht* makes an excellent contribution to the first of the two Doubles.

When Peter Maag conducted a vintage (1960) Decca version of the *Scottish Symphony*, long regarded as a classic, it is good that at the end of his career he was able to record a complete Mendelssohn symphony cycle. These are generally light, resilient performances that bring out the joy of Mendelssohn's inspiration, his youthful exuberance. On this showing the Madrid Symphony Orchestra has some impressive wind and brass soloists and refined strings, with rhythms elegantly pointed, and with everyone responding well to the challenge of Maag's very fast speed in such a movement as the *Saltarello* finale of the *Italian Symphony*, a genuine *Presto*. The recording also helps to clarify textures, with impressive weight given to the brass in the *Reformation Symphony*. Sadly, Mendelssohn's choral symphony, No. 2, *The Hymn of Praise*, is markedly less successful than the rest, partly because this is an ambitious work that needs full weight, but more particularly because the soloists are disappointing, with the first soprano edgy and the tenor strained. Even so, at bargain price this is a set well worth considering by collectors who have relished Maag's justly famous early Decca disc.

Symphonies 1; 5 (Reformation)

🔾 (BB) *** Warner Apex 256460370-2. Leipzig GO, Masur; (i) with Bonney, Schönheit, Leipzig R. Ch.

Masur's mastery in his later Mendelssohn recordings is due in good measure to his ability to adopt relatively fast speeds and make them sound easy and relaxed, not hurried and breathless, and in both symphonies here Masur is faster than his principal rivals on disc, not just in *Allegros* but in slower movements too. In Nos. 1 and 5 that works very well indeed, bringing an alert freshness with no hint of sentimentality.

Symphonies 1; 5 (Reformation); Octet, Op. 20: Scherzo

(M) *** DG 445 596-2. LSO, Abbado

The *First* and *Fifth* are Mendelssohn's least-played and least-recorded symphonies, so Abbado's coupling is very welcome. His version includes a sparkling version of the Scherzo from the *Octet* which Mendelssohn substituted for the original when he presented it in London, so that you can readily programme the substitution yourself. His direct manner suits the *Reformation Symphony* equally well. Brightly lit, early-digital recording (1984), but with the warm ambience of St John's, Smith Square, adding overall bloom.

Symphony 2 (Hymn of Praise)

*** DG (IMS) 423 143-2. Connell, Mattila, Blochwitz, L. Symphony Ch., LSO, Abbado

(M) *** DG (ADD) 431 471-2. Mathis, Rebmann, Hollweg, German Op. Ch., BPO, Karajan

*** Opus 111 OP 30-98. Isokoski, Bach, Lang, Ch. Musicus Köln, Das neue Orchester, Spering

(BB) **(*) Warner Apex 2564 60156-2. Bonney, Wiens, Schreier, Schönheit, Leipzig R. Ch. & GO, Masur

Karajan's recording of the *Hymn of Praise*, recorded in the Jesus-Christus-Kirche in 1972, brings outstanding sound; the very fine choral singing is caught vividly. The soloists make a good team, rather than showing any memorable individuality; but overall Karajan's performance is very satisfying.

In some ways Abbado's full-price digital version is even finer, if not more clearly recorded, brushing aside all sentimentality, both fresh and sympathetic and, though the recording is not ideally clear on inner detail, the brightness reinforces the conductor's view. The chorus, well focused, is particularly impressive, and the sweet-toned tenor, Hans-Peter Blochwitz, is outstanding among the soloists.

Spering presents a performance of the *Hymn of Praise* in period style. With clean, crisp textures this is most refreshing, full of incidental beauties. For example, the once-celebrated duet for the two soprano soloists, *Ich harrete des Herrn* ('I waited for the Lord'), is intensely beautiful in its simplicity, with Soile Isokoski (also in Herreweghe's *Elijah*) and Mechthild Bach both angelically sweet yet nicely contrasted. The tenor soloist, Frieder Lang, is also exceptionally sweet-toned, though his projection is keen enough to make the *Huter, ist die Nacht bald hin?* ('Watchman, what of the night?') episode very intense and dramatic. Though not always clear in inner definition, the freshness of the choral singing matches that of the whole performance.

Whereas Masur's brisk tempi suit his coupling of Nos. 1 and 5 well, in the big choral symphony they seem too extreme. Where Abbado on DG takes takes 29 minutes over the three instrumental movements which open the work, Masur takes only 21 minutes, an astonishing discrepancy. Nevertheless, as ever, Masur avoids breathlessness and, with excellent soloists and choir, freshly recorded with plenty of detail, this is still recommendable enough, especially at Apex price.

Symphony 3 (Scottish); Overtures: Calm Sea and Prosperous Voyage; The Hebrides; Ruy Blas

(BB) **(*) Naxos 8.550222. Slovak PO, Dohnányi

Symphony 3 in A min. (Scottish); (i) A Midsummer Night's Dream: Overture & Incidental Music

🔾 ✪ (M) *** Decca (ADD) 466 990-2. LSO, Maag; (i) with Vyvyan, Lowe, ROHCG female ch.

Maag's classic account of the *Scottish Symphony* rightly finds itself on the Legends label, for it is indeed legendary, remarkable for its freshness and natural spontaneity. The opening cantilena is poised and phrased very beautifully and sets the mood for what is to follow. A pity that the exposition repeat is not included, and though in the last movement the final *Maestoso* is measured, the effect remains most compelling, almost Klemperian in manner, with superb horn-playing.

The *Midsummer Night's Dream* excerpts date from 1957 and sound equally fresh, and the character of the playing is again superb; the recording includes a strong contribution from a fruity bass wind instrument (representing Bottom) which might possibly be Mendelssohn's ophicleide, but is probably a well-played tuba. The Kingsway Hall recording is warm, full and well projected, and this new Legends mastering includes the vocal and choral numbers on the original LP, which were not included on the previous reissue. Strongly recommended – a wholly delightful disc.

Oliver Dohnányi conducts a joyful account of the *Scottish Symphony* on Naxos, given the more impact by forward recording. Mendelssohn's lilting rhythms in all the fast movements are delightfully bouncy, and though the slow movement brings few hushed *pianissimos*, its full warmth is brought out without sentimentality. The three overtures, also very well done, not least the under-appreciated *Ruy Blas*, make an excellent coupling.

Symphonies 3 in A min. (Scottish); 4 (Italian)

(M) *** DG 427 810-2. LSO, Abbado

(BB) *** ASV Resonance CD RSN 3018. O of St John's, Lubbock

*** Mer. CDE 84261. Apollo CO, Cherniak

(M) *** Virgin 5 61735-2. LCP, Norrington

(B) *** Australian Decca Eloquence (ADD) 458 176-2. LSO, Abbado

*** Teldec 9031 72308-2. COE, Harnoncourt

(BB) **(*) Warner Apex 0927 49817-2. Leipzig GO, Masur

(M) **(*) DG (IMS) (ADD) 439 980-2. Israel PO, Bernstein

Symphonies 3 (Scottish); 4 (Italian); Hebrides Overture

☛ (M) *** DG (ADD) 449 743-2. BPO, Karajan

(M) *** Classic fM 75605 57013-2. Ulster O, Sitkovetsky

Karajan's 1971 account of the *Scottish* is justly included among DG's 'Originals', as it is one of his finest recordings. The coupling was originally the *Fingal's Cave*, a characterful and evocative account, but now the *Italian Symphony* has been added, recorded two years later. This is also played very beautifully and brilliantly but, good though the performance is, it does not quite match that of the *Scottish* and it is just a shade wanting in spontaneity and sparkle.

Dmitry Sitkovetsky draws superb performances of both symphonies as well as the overture from the Ulster Orchestra, helped by outstandingly full and rich recording, made in the Ulster Hall. With speeds beautifully chosen and with rhythms crisp and well sprung, his readings are full of light and shade, warmly dramatic, demonstrating an expressive freedom – notably in pressing ahead – which always sounds natural, never self-conscious. The strings in particular produce some magical *pianissimos*, reflecting Sitkovetsky's own mastery as an instrumentalist. A very generous and apt coupling, with the exposition repeat observed in the *Italian Symphony* but not in the *Scottish*.

Abbado's fine digital recordings of the *Scottish* and *Italian Symphonies*, coupled together from his complete set, make a splendid mid-price bargain. The recording is admirably fresh and bright – atmospheric, too – and the ambience, if not absolutely sharply defined, is very attractive. Both first-movement exposition repeats are included.

Lubbock's coupling of the *Scottish* and *Italian Symphonies* makes an outstanding super-bargain reissue, offering performances of delightful lightness and point, warmly and cleanly recorded. The string section may be of chamber size but, amplified by a warm acoustic, the result sparkles, with rhythms lifted exhilaratingly. The slow movements are both on the slow side but flow easily with no suspicion of sentimentality, while the *Saltarello* finale of the *Fourth*, with the flute part delectably pointed, comes close to Mendelssohnian fairy music.

The dynamic young American conductor, David Chernaik, gives performances of these two symphonies which in their vitality and freshness are second to none. Although the recording is live, the audience is notably quiet and shows its presence only by clapping perfunctorily at the end of each work, a distraction which could and should have been edited out. The London-based Apollo Chamber Orchestra, on its toes throughout, is exactly the right size for these two symphonies, and the recording (in St John's, Smith Square) has been beautifully balanced so that detail is transparently clear, yet a warm ambience remains. Chernaik includes the essential exposition repeats in both symphonies.

As in his comparable Schumann coupling (see below), Norrington opts for unexaggerated speeds in the outer movements, relatively brisk ones for the middle movements. The results are similarly exhilarating, particularly in the clipped and bouncy account of the first movement of the *Italian*. The *Scottish Symphony* is far lighter than usual, with no hint of

excessive sweetness. The Scherzo has rarely sounded happier, and the finale closes in a fast gallop for the 6/8 coda with the horns whooping gloriously. Good, warm recording, only occasionally masking detail in tuttis.

It is good to have Abbado's outstanding (1968) coupling with the LSO back in the catalogue again on Australian Decca's Eloquence label. His *Scottish Symphony* is beautifully played and the LSO respond to his direction with the greatest delicacy of feeling, while the *Italian Symphony* has comparable lightness of touch, matched with lyrical warmth. The only drawback is the absence of the first-movement exposition repeat in the *Scottish* (though not in the *Italian*).

As in Beethoven and Schubert, Nikolaus Harnoncourt's happy relationship with the Chamber Orchestra of Europe brings performances which on modern instruments might be counted 'historically aware', with shortened phrasing, limited string vibrato, rasping horns and clean-cut timpani. The cleanness of texture is enhanced by Harnoncourt's generally relaxed speeds, which allow Mendelssohnian rhythms to have an infectious spring. Natural, well-balanced sound.

Masur starts with many advantages. Unlike some versions of this favourite coupling, he observes exposition repeats in both symphonies, and he is an exceptionally understanding interpreter of this composer. His choice of speeds brings out the freshness of inspiration judiciously, avoiding any suspicion of sentimentality in slow movements, which are taken at flowing tempi. Conversely, the *Allegros* are never hectic to the point of breathlessness. The one snag is that the Leipzig recording tends to obscure detail in tuttis; the Scherzo of the *Scottish*, for example, becomes a blur, losing some of its point and charm. Otherwise the sound of the orchestra has all the characteristic Leipzig bloom and beauty.

Bernstein's expansive tempi run the risk of overloading Mendelssohn's fresh inspiration with heavy expressiveness, making the slow introduction and slow movement sound almost Mahlerian. The rhythmic lift of the Scherzo and finale makes amends; but it is a performance to bring out for an interesting change, rather than a version to recommend for repeated listening. The recording is well balanced and full. The sparkling account of the *Italian* was made a year earlier in the Mann Auditorium, Tel Aviv, but remains convincingly atmospheric if not ideally clear. It is also available at bargain price, coupled with the *Midsummer Night's Dream* incidental music – see below.

Symphony 4 (Italian)

☛ (M) *** Cala CACD 0531. Nat. PO, Stokowski –
BRAHMS: *Symphony 2* ***

(M) *** DG 445 514-2. Philh. O, Sinopoli – SCHUBERT: *Symphony 8* ***✪

(***) Testament mono SBT 1173. Philh. O, Cantelli –
BRAHMS: *Symphony 3* (***)

(B) (***) EMI mono 5 74801-2. Philh. O, Cantelli –
SCHUBERT: *Symphony 8;* SCHUMANN: *Symphony 4* (***)

Like the coupled Brahms, this was one of the last recordings Stokowski made, with a first-class orchestra of London's top musicians. The result is a fizzingly brilliant account of the *Italian Symphony*, exhilarating, yet with never any sense of the music being rushed. Stokowski observes the all-important first-movement exposition repeat, and the elegant *Andante* and the colourful Minuet, with delightful playing from the horns in the Trio, show him at his most beguiling. The new transfer of the 1978 recording is splendidly done.

Sinopoli's great gift is to illuminate almost every phrase afresh. His speeds tend to be extreme – fast in the first movement but with diamond-bright detail, and on the slow side in the remaining three. Only in the heavily inflected account of the third movement is the result at all mannered but, with superb playing from the Philharmonia and excellent Kingsway Hall recording, this rapt performance is most compelling. For refinement of detail, especially at lower dynamic levels, the CD is among the most impressive digital recordings to have come from DG.

A strong welcome for EMI's bargain reissue of Cantelli's finely characterized 1955 recording of the *Italian Symphony*. It has only rarely been equalled and even more rarely surpassed. But he recorded Mendelssohn's *Italian Symphony* twice with the Philharmonia and this 1951 version on Testament, the very first recording Cantelli made with the Philharmonia, was never issued. In fact, as close comparison reveals, it is even finer than the later version, a degree more biting and urgent in the first movement with more light and shade, more spontaneously expressive in the middle movements, and clearer and lighter in the *Presto* finale. In first-rate mono sound it makes a very welcome coupling for Cantelli's glowing account of the Brahms.

(i) Symphony 4 (Italian) in A, Op. 90; (ii) Hebrides Overture (Fingal's Cave)

(N) (B) (***) Hallé (mono) CDHLT 8002. Hallé O, (i) Harty; (ii) Sargent (with BRUCH: *Violin Concerto 1* ***)

Some valuable reminders of the pre-war Hallé and Sir Hamilton Harty. His account of the *Italian Symphony* has more character than the Sargent *Hebrides Overture*, though both are very good. The disc is of particular value as it gives us the incomparable Albert Sammons Bruch *G minor Concerto* from the 1920s.

Symphonies 4 (Italian; original & revised versions); 5 (Reformation)

*** DG 459 156-2. VPO, Gardiner

In both versions of the *Italian* and in the live recording of the *Reformation* – with all Victorian cobwebs blown away – John Eliot Gardiner brings out both the transparency and the urgency of Mendelssohn's inspiration, generally preferring fast but never breathless speeds. The *coup* is that the revised versions of the last three movements of the *Italian* have never been recorded before. The composer made the revisions in the year following the London première. Surprisingly for so discriminating a composer, he undermined the exuberant inspiration of the original, smoothing over melodic lines (as in the *Pilgrim's March*) and extending linking passages. Even so, a fascinating insight into the creative process and the danger of second thoughts on what was originally white-hot inspiration.

Symphony 4 (Italian); A Midsummer Night's Dream: Overture; (i) Incidental Music (complete)

(M) *** EMI (ADD) 5 67038-2. Philh. O, Klemperer, (i) with Harper, Baker, Philh. Ch.

(i) Symphony 4 in A (Italian); Overture, The Hebrides; (ii) A Midsummer Night's Dream: Overture; Scherzo; Nocturne; Wedding March

(B) *** DG (ADD) 439 411-2. (i) Israel PO, Bernstein; (ii) Bav. RSO, Kubelik

Symphony 4 (Italian); A Midsummer Night's Dream: Overture; Incidental Music: Scherzo; Over Hill and Dale; Allegro vivace; Intermezzo; Nocturne; Dance of the Clowns; Wedding March

(M) *** Virgin 5 61975-2. OAE, Mackerras

Klemperer takes the first movement of the *Italian Symphony* substantially slower than we are used to, but this is no heavily monumental and humourless reading. The Philharmonia playing sparkles and has an incandescence which outshines many other versions with more surface sparkle. There is again a slowish speed for the second movement, and it is the beautiful shaping of a phrase that makes the slow movement and finale so fresh and memorable. In the Overture and incidental music from *A Midsummer Night's Dream* the orchestral playing is again superb, the wind solos so nimble that even the *Scherzo*, taken more slowly than usual, has a light touch. The contribution of the celebrated soloists and the Philharmonia Chorus is first class and the quality of the remastered 1960 recording is full and fresh.

Mackerras directs fresh, resilient, 'authentic'-style performances of both the *Symphony* and the *Midsummer Night's Dream Overture*. The middle two movements of the *Symphony* are marginally faster than usual but they gain in elegance and transparency, beautifully played here, as is the *Midsummer Night's Dream* music. It is particularly good to have an ophicleide instead of a tuba for Bottom's music in the *Overture*, and the boxwood flute in the *Scherzo* is a delight.

Bernstein's performance of the *Italian Symphony* (exposition repeat included) is sparkling and persuasive. The 1978 recording was made at a public concert and, though speeds are often challengingly fast in outer movements, they never fail to convey the exhilaration of the occasion. *Fingal's Cave* is also a live recording, made a year later, and, while it has plenty of romantic warmth and Bernstein is slightly more indulgent, it too sounds spontaneously alive. In the items from *A Midsummer Night's Dream* the Bavarian orchestra are on top form, especially in the *Overture*, which is beautifully played. The recording, made in the Herkulessaal, Munich, still sounds excellent, and this bargain Classikon CD would grace any collection.

Symphony 5 (Reformation)

(M) *** DG (ADD) 449 720-2. BPO, Maazel – FRANCK: *Symphony in D min.* ***

The *Reformation Symphony* springs grippingly to life in Maazel's hands. The Berlin Philharmonic brass make an immediate impact in the commanding introduction and the orchestral playing throughout continues on this level of high tension. The finale is splendidly vigorous, the chorale, *Ein' feste Burg is unser Gott*, ringing out resplendently. Maazel's interpretation was aptly chosen for reissue in DG's series of 'Originals', and the Franck coupling is hardly less impressive. The recording is spacious and has been vividly enhanced by the DG CD transfer.

CHAMBER MUSIC

Cello Sonatas 1 in B flat, Op. 45; 2 in D, Op. 58

(B) *** EMI (ADD) 5 74333-2 (2). Tortelier, De la Pau – CHOPIN; FAURE; RACHMANINOV: *Cello Sonatas* ***

Cello Sonatas 1–2; Assai Tranquillo; Song without Words, Op. 109; Variations concertantes, Op. 17

(BB) *** Hyp. Helios CDH 55064. Lester, Tomes

Cello Sonatas 1–2; Songs without Words, Op. 19/1; Op. 109 (arr. Harrell); *Variations concertantes, Op. 17*

(N) (B) * Decca 475 6210 (2). Harrell, Canino – BRAHMS: *Cello Sonatas, etc. ***

Cello Sonatas 1–2; Song without Words, Op. 109; Variations concertantes, Op. 17

(BB) *** Naxos 8.550655 (without *Assai tranquillo*). Kliegel, Merscher

Cello Sonatas 1–2; Songs Without Words, Op. 19/1; Op. 109; Variations concertantes, Op. 17

*** RCA 09026 62553-2. Isserlis, Tan (fortepiano)

Susan Tomes, the inspired pianist of the group Domus, and her cellist colleague, Richard Lester, give performances full of flair on this ideally compiled disc of Mendelssohn's collected works for cello and piano, brimming with charming ideas. As well as the works with opus number they include a delightful fragment, *Assai tranquillo*, never previously recorded.

Naxos's star cellist, Maria Kliegel, together with Kristine Merscher also give enjoyably fresh and spontaneous accounts of the two *Sonatas*, and they certainly charm the ear with the *Variations concertantes*. Their naturally recorded Naxos disc is every bit as enjoyable as the Helios collection, except, of course, they omit the *Assai tranquillo*.

Steven Isserlis and Melvyn Tan also convey a freshness, delight and authenticity in music-making that rekindles enthusiasm for this delightful repertoire. They pace both sonatas expertly and are faithfully served by the RCA engineers. Like their colleagues, Richard Lester and Susan Tomes on Hyperion, they command poetry as well as virtuosity.

Big names in themselves are no guarantee of great music-making, but Lynn Harrell and Bruno Canino certainly do offer that; their playing has an ardour and expressive vitality that are totally compelling. Both *Sonatas* and *Variations concertantes* are played with a conviction that is completely persuasive, and the 1989 recording serves them well. The two items arranged from *Songs without Words* make an attractive bonus, and the Brahms coupling is hardly less recommendable, although this reissue involves two CDs.

Paul Tortelier is wholly in sympathy with these two sonatas, and even if he is partnered less expertly by his daughter Maria de la Pau this is still a thoroughly worthwhile collection. Good recording.

Octet in E flat, Op. 20

(B) *** Australian Decca Eloquence (ADD) 421 637-2. ASMF – BOCCHERINI: *Quintet for Cello & String Quartet ***

(BB) *** Hyp. Helios CDH 55043. Divertimenti – BARGIEL: *Octet ***

Octet in E flat, Op. 20; String Quintet 2 in B flat, Op. 87

☛ (B) *** Ph. 420 400-2. ASMF Chamber Ens.

The 1968 performance by the ASMF on Australian Decca is fresh and buoyant, and the recording wears its years lightly. It offers fine judgement in matters of clarity and sonority, and it is coupled with a highly desirable and much less well-known work by Boccherini. This Eloquence CD has full sleeve-notes.

The Philips account comes from just over a decade after the Academy's earlier record, and the playing has greater sparkle and polish. The recorded sound is also superior and sounds extremely well in its CD format. The *Second Quintet* is an underrated piece and it too receives an elegant and poetic performance.

Divertimenti give a very natural and unforced account of the celebrated *Octet* which, though it may not be the most distinguished in the catalogue, still gives great pleasure. Excellent recorded sound.

Octet in E flat, Op. 20; String Quintets 1 in A, Op. 18; 2 in B flat, Op. 87; String Quartet 2 in A min., Op. 13

(M) *** Virgin 2×1 5 61809-2 (2). Hausmusik

A highly desirable bargain set. The *Octet* and *String Quintet No. 1* were recorded in the Concert Hall of York University in 1989, and the recording, balanced by Mike Hatch, is outstanding, clear and transparent, with an attractively warm ambience giving extra weight to the lower lines. The period-instrument performance of the *Octet*, with Monica Huggett leading the violins and Anthony Pleeth the cellos, is most refreshing, as is the account of the *Second String Quintet*, another miraculous masterpiece of Mendelssohn's boyhood.

The coupling of the *Second Quartet* and *Second Quintet* was made four years later in an ecclesiastical acoustic, and the balance engineer, Mike Clements, had to put his microphones closer to the players. Paulo Beznosiuk leads the violins, and the fine cellist is Richard Lester. While the overall sonority at lower dynamic levels is finely blended, the *fortissimos* sound somewhat thinner. Yet the textural transparency remains, and these are two very well-characterized readings. Playing is alert and, above all, these players communicate delight in all this music, and their account of the *Octet* is second to none.

Piano Quartet 1 in C min., Op. 1; Piano Sextet in D, Op. 110

(BB) **(*) Naxos 8.550966. Bartholdy Piano Qt (augmented)

Piano Quartets 2 in F min., Op. 2; 3 in B min., Op. 3

(BB) **(*) Naxos 8.550967. Bartholdy Piano Qt

The Bartholdy Quartet have an excellent pianist in Pier Narciso Masi, and his mercurial style is just right for these early works. The string players are always fluent and show a light-hearted vivacity in Mendelssohn's scherzos (especially in the very winning *Allegro molto* of No. 3) and finales, and they play the simple slow movements gracefully. The *Piano Sextet* has an engaging immediacy. The recording was made in the fairly resonant Clara Wieck Auditorium in Heidelberg, which means that the microphones are fairly close to the strings and the balance is slightly contrived. Nevertheless the sound is good and the piano well caught.

Piano Trio 1 in D min., Op. 49

(N) *** Warner 2564 61492-2. Beaux Arts Trio – DVORAK: *Piano Trio 4 (Dumky) ***

(BB) (***) Naxos mono 8.110185. Thibaud, Casals, Cortot – SCHUMANN: *Piano Trio 1* (***)

When the Beaux Arts Trio made their début on LP, some fifty years ago, it was with this coupling and, although the personnel has changed, the youthfulness and grace of the playing has not. Menahem Pressler is every bit as mercurial and fleet-of-finger as he was in the mid-1950s. Though the original still sounds very acceptable, the new recording is, of course, far more realistic and wide-ranging. This splendidly balanced recording is a very happy tribute to this wonderful ensemble.

The partnership of Jacques Thibaud, Pablo Casals and Alfred Cortot was perhaps the most celebrated of its kind – and certainly the most famous pre-war trio. The Trio was formed in 1925 and made this set two years later so that the actual sound is wanting the body and colour of later recordings. For those growing up in the 1940s, this was *the* Mendelssohn Trio, so completely did the three masters seem attuned to its spirit. They are technically immaculate, supremely lyrical, and their apparent spontaneity of feeling is born of firm musical discipline. Ward Marston's transfer gives this exalted performance, with its miraculously characterized Scherzo, a new lease of life.

Piano Trios 1 in D min., Op. 49; 2 in C min., Op. 66
⊕— (BB) *** Naxos 8.555063. Gould Piano Trio
(M) *** CRD (ADD) CRD 3459. Israel Piano Trio
**(*) Chan. 8404. Borodin Trio

The young players of the Gould Trio give performances as fine as any on disc. Not just the violinist, Lucy Gould, but the cellist, Martin Storey, and above all the pianist, Benjamin Frith, prove to be inspired recording artists, offering passage-work of sparkling evenness and clarity. At Naxos price an outstanding bargain.

Very musical playing from the Israel Piano Trio, whose mood is comparatively serious, with the pianist, Alexander Volkov, contributing strongly. Some might look for greater lightness of touch. But the last movement of the C minor work is projected passionately to make a splendid finale. Slow movements are eloquent, both Scherzi come off vivaciously, and there is plenty to enjoy here. The acoustic of Rosslyn Hill Chapel in Hampstead is lively, which means that the reverberation is generally under control (the balance engineer was Bob Auger) and this reissued disc (from 1990) has much to recommend it.

The Borodin Trio are also recorded in a very resonant acoustic and are rather forwardly balanced. They give superbly committed but somewhat overpointed readings. All the same, there is much musical pleasure to be found here.

String Quartets 1–6
(N) (BB) *** EMI Encore 5 85693-2 (1 & 2); 5 85805-2 (3 & 4); 5 86104-2 (5 & 6). Cherubini Qt

Choice in this repertoire is very wide but, for those wanting the six Quartets alone, the members of the Cherubini Quartet consistently play with both warmth and intensity, even if they are occasionally guilty of a little self-consciousness and of slightly exaggerating dynamic markings at times. However, with a light touch they bring out the mercurial charm of Mendelssohn, as well as his vigour and high spirits. The pity is that, unlike many of their competitors, they fail to provide either the early E flat Quartet (without opus number), written when the composer was only 14, or the collection of four movements, Op. 81, that in shape and sequence group themselves satisfyingly together. One only wishes that the Cherubinis, consistently imaginative, had been persuaded to include these extra items as well. They are warmly and naturally recorded.

String Quartets: in E flat; 1–6; 4 Pieces, Op. 81
(N) (BB) *** Cal. 3311/3. Talich Qt
(M) *** Hyp. CDS 44051/3. Coull Qt

String Quartets 1–6; 4 Pieces, Op. 81
⊕— (M) *** Decca Trio 473 255-2 (3). Ysaÿe Quartet
(N) (BB) *** Arte Nova 82876 64009-2 (3). Henschel Qt

The fine Decca set from the Ysaÿe Quartet was recorded in two different venues between 1991 and 1994. In its new Trio box format it becomes a marginal first choice for the Quartets alone, though the three Naxos discs remain a highly recommendable alternative and they include more extra items (see below). In essence these Decca performances are warm, urbane and cultured, as befits this civilized and endearing

music, and the recording is eminently satisfactory, with fine presence set within a warm acoustic.

The three Henschel siblings were fortunate to find a cellist in Mathias Beyer Karlshøij to complete a prize-winning ensemble of distinction in both unanimity of ensemble and impressive tonal and dynamic finesse. Their Mendelssohn recordings rank with the very finest. On the first two discs they have happily chosen to couple early and late works, and they bring subtle differences of approach to each, so that, for instance, the Adagio and Intermezzo of Op. 13 have an endearing simplicity, and the Adagio of Op. 44/3 has a touching depth of feeling, readily contrasting with the dancing Scherzo and bravura virtuosity of the finale. The third disc pairs the remaining Op. 44 Quartets, adding the Four Movements of Op. 81, played with similar perception; and their readings have an appropriate warmth and delicacy of feeling. Decent sound and handsome packaging too. Recommended alongside the Ysaÿe.

The Coull survey is also eminently satisfactory and includes the early (1823) Quartet in E flat, the playing alive and spontaneous, well paced and musically penetrating. The quietly intense playing in slow movements shows the group's affinity with this repertoire. The recording is realistic and well balanced.

The Talich cycle is modern: the performances were recorded in Prague between 2000 and 2003. They include both the early Quartet in E flat and the Op. 81 Pieces. The sound is excellent, perhaps a little close, not always entirely flattering to the upper range but warm and naturally balanced. Not suprisingly, these are performances of distinction: their ensemble is still immaculate, their blend of timbre as impressive as ever, and the overall impression is of a combination of sensitivity and finesse with vitality. The three discs are available separately at mid-price: Cal 9311 (1 & 2); Cal 9302 (3–5); Cal 9313 (6, Quartet in E flat & 4 Pieces).

String Quartets: in E flat; 1 in E flat, Op. 12; 4 in E min., Op. 44/2
(BB) *** Naxos 8.550862. Aurora Qt

String Quartets 2 in A min., Op. 13; 5 in E flat, Op. 44/3; Scherzo in A min., Op. 81/2; Theme & Variations in E, Op. 81/1
(BB) *** Naxos 8.550863. Aurora Qt

String Quartets 3 in D, Op. 44/1; 6 in F min., Op. 80; Capriccio in E min., Op. 81/3; Fugue in E flat, Op. 81/4
(BB) *** Naxos 8.550861. Aurora Qt

At Naxos price, the new Aurora set of Mendelssohn's complete music for string quartet is a genuine bargain. The performances have a natural Mendelssohnian charm and elegance, but their strength and passion acknowledge the fact that the young composer in his teens wrote them under the influence of the Beethoven quartets. Indeed, the account of the F minor work, composed after his sister Fanny's death, is perhaps the highlight of the set. The Allegros are full of passionate angst and the Adagio expresses the composer's pain. The engaging early E flat Quartet of 1823, with its confident closing Fuga, written when the composer was only fourteen, is included, together with the four varied pieces of Op. 81 – notably the delightful Scherzo in A minor, here as light as thistledown. Slow movements throughout are beautifully shaped and played with warmth and feeling, never sentimentalized; Scherzios always sparkle; Allegros have vivacity and bite. The recording is first class.

String Quartets 1 in E flat, Op. 12; 2 in A min., Op. 13
*** MDG 307 1055-2. Leipzig Qt

String Quartets 3–4; Capriccio (1843); Fugue (1827)
*** MDG 307 1168-2. Leipzig Qt

String Quartets 5 in E flat, Op. 44/3; 6 in F min., Op. 80; Scherzo & Theme and Variations, Op. 81
*** MDG 307 1056-2. Leipzig Qt

String Quartet in E flat; Octet, Op. 20.
**(*) MDG 307 105-2. (Augmented) Leipzig Qt
*** EMI 5 57167-2. Alban Berg Qt
*** Auvidis E 8622. Mosaïques Qt
*** HM HMU 907245. Eroica Qt

String Quartet 2 in A min., Op. 13
(N) (M) *** CRD 2-CD CRD 2414 (2). Alberni Qt – SCHUMANN: *Quartets 1–3* *******
(M) *** HM Cal. (ADD) 5698. Talich Qt – BOCCHERINI: *Quartet, Op. 58/2;* HAYDN: *Quartet 74;* MICA: *Quartet 6* *******

String Quartets 3–4
*** HM HMU 907287. Eroica Qt

The excellent Leipzig Quartet, with their warm, richly blended tone and natural finesse, give superbly polished accounts of these delightful works. Their lightness of touch and elegance are balanced by great (but not exaggerated) depth of feeling. They also have a naturalness and warmth that is most satisfying. The third disc (coupling the superb *E flat Quartet*, the last of the Op. 44 series, and the *F minor*, Op. 80) is if anything even finer than its companions, and the Leipzig conveys its intensity and concentration with surpassing eloquence. Their performances serve as a reminder that this is great music which is all too often taken for granted by critics.

Not surprisingly, the Leipzig players also give a beautifully turned and graceful account of the remarkable early *Quartet in E flat* without opus number, but when they are joined by four undoubtedly excellent colleagues for the *Octet*, the effect is less refined. One can only describe the performance as rumbustious, with tremendous vigour and bustle in the outer movements, not helped by a recording which tends to emphasize both treble and bass at the expense of a detailed overall sound-picture. The central movements are the most successful, with the Scherzo fleet and delicate and the *Andante* appealingly phrased.

The Alban Berg versions are concert performances, recorded in the Mozartsaal in the Konzerthaus, Vienna, in 1999 and the Grosser Sendesaal of the Funkhaus, Hanover, in 2000. As with all this ensemble's performances, there is immaculate technical address and ensemble, but there is also greater spontaneity than we have had in some of their recent records. There is much delicacy of tone, even if the opening of the finale of the *A minor Quartet* is unduly aggressive. There is minimal audience noise, although applause is included.

Mendelssohn's *A minor Quartet* has a serene and remarkably searching slow movement, before its charmingly memorable *Intermezzo* which is linked to the lively but lyrical *Presto* finale, which has something of the character of a Mendelssohn *Scherzo*.

The Alberni Quartet are thoroughly at home here, giving a warm, understanding performance, well recorded and now appropriately re-coupled with the three Op. 41 *Quartets* of Schumann.

The *A minor Quartet* is also played with much warmth, spirit and cultivated elegance by the superb Talich group, who are also naturally recorded. If you prefer their couplings instead of Schumann, they are equally recommendable and more diverse.

The Mosaïques Quartet apply their delicacy of style and subtle grading of texture with winning results to the *A minor Quartet*, particularly in the delectable *Intermezzo*, which is as light as thistledown. They open the *B flat major* with great concentration, and the *Canzonetta* has an airy fragility. Some ears might prefer the fuller, suaver quality of modern instruments in the *Andante espressivo* and finale, but certainly these performances have a character of their own which aficionados will relish, and they are very well recorded.

The Eroica Quartet was formed in 1993 by four London period-instrument players who are committed to performing the nineteenth-century repertoire in nineteenth-century style. Their performances are distinguished by good ensemble, clean articulation and well-focused textures. Good recorded sound too.

The sparkling and spontaneous vitality of the playing of the Eroica Quartet is even more striking on their second disc, and is especially impressive in the brio of the outer movements of No. 3 and the joyful finale of No. 4. But why did they not include all three of the Op. 44 *Quartets*? Certainly what they do offer is consistently stimulating and strikingly well recorded (indeed the upper range is smoother than the Talich recordings on Calliope).

String Quartets 1–6; 4 Pieces, Op. 81; (with CD-ROM: Quartet in E flat (1823); Octet for Strings in E flat, Op. 20 and DVD documentary: Recording the Octet)
(N) *** DG 477 5370 (4). Emerson Qt

The Emerson Quartet are flawless in their unanimity of ensemble and tonal finesse. Indeed, in terms of technical prowess and sheer polish, all these Mendelssohn performances could hardly be bettered, and the DG recording is bright and well focused. If there is any reservation, it is a certain want of period sensibility. The playing is virtuosic – Manhattan rather than Weimar. The performances have the public profile of modern concert-giving and convey little sense of intimacy and too little sense of grace. But, of course, they are expert and masterly.

String Quintets 1 in A, Op. 18; 2 in B flat, Op. 87
⊕— *** SACD BIS-SACD 1254. Mendelssohn Qt with R. Mann

Anyone wanting modern-instrument recordings of two of Mendelssohn's finest chamber works could not better this SACD. The performances are full of sparkle and vitality: the outer movements have great spirit and energy while the finales with their brilliant contrapuntal writing are played with thrilling virtuosity, and the Scherzo of Op. 87 is like quicksilver. Yet the *Intermezzo* of the same work is touchingly simple in its natural warmth. Outstanding compatible recording which gives a very 'live' audio projection, naturally detailed if played on a normal CD player, although the first violin dominates in *fortissimos*. On a DVD/SACD player there is added fullness and resonance in the bass, at the same time producing a very slightly less transparent blend of timbre. Most ears, however, will prefer the marginal added depth.

Violin Sonatas: in F min., Op. 4; in F (1838)
(M) *** Decca 474 690-2. Mintz, Ostrovsky

Mendelssohn was only fourteen when he composed the *F minor Sonata*, but even so it is not wanting in individuality and is much more than a youthful exercise. The 1838 *Sonata* comes from Mendelssohn's productive Leipzig period. The performances are beyond reproach; the playing of both artists is a model of sensitivity and intelligence, the recording is absolutely first class, and the CD understandably won the *Gramophone* Chamber Award in 1988.

Violin Sonatas: in F (1820); in F min., Op. 4 (1823); in F (1838). Allegro in C; Andante in D min.; Fugues: in C min.; in D min.; Movement in G min.
(BB) *** Naxos 8.554725. Nomos Duo

Two of these *Sonatas* date from Mendelssohn's early years, but are attractively crafted. The mature work is notable for its brilliant *vivace* finale in which the Nomos Duo (Nicholas Milton and Nina-Margret Grimsdóttir) really let rip. Some may feel that a little more poise here would have been welcome, but that is the only reservation. They are a fine team and make a good case for the earliest work (more of a *Sonatina*), especially the closing moto perpetuo *Presto*, which is neatly paced. The shorter pieces come from a book of exercises but are rather pleasing miniatures. Excellent recording in a friendly acoustic.

PIANO MUSIC

Capriccio in F sharp min., Op. 5; 7 Characteristic Pieces, Op. 7; Fantasia (Sonata écossaise) in F sharp min., Op. 28; Prelude & Fugue in E min.; Sonata Movement in B flat
(BB) *** Naxos 8. 553541. Frith

This collection gives a very different idea of Mendelssohn's piano-writing from that in the *Songs without Words*. The *Characteristic Pieces* present fascinating evidence of the influence of Bach on the young composer, with some impressive contrapuntal writing in fugues both brilliant and thoughtful. Also some echoes of Scarlatti. The three-movement *Fantasia* and the *Capriccio*, as well, inspire Benjamin Frith to sparkling playing, vividly recorded.

Preludes & Fugues 1-6, Op. 35; 3 Caprices, Op. 33; Perpetuum mobile in C, Op. 33
(BB) *** Naxos 8.550939. Frith

Benjamin Frith offers a highly imaginative set of the Op. 35 *Preludes and Fugues*, full of diversity, from the flamboyant opening *Prelude in E minor* to the expansive *Prelude No. 6 in B flat*. The three *Caprices* are equally varied in mood and colour and are most sensitively presented. The *Perpetuum mobile* makes a scintillating encore. Acceptably full if not remarkable piano-sound.

Scherzo from A Midsummer Night's Dream, Op. 61 (trans. Rachmaninov)
*** Hyp. CDA 66009. Shelley – RACHMANINOV: *Variations*, etc. ***

Howard Shelley, with fabulously clear articulation and delectably sprung rhythms, gives a performance of which Rachmaninov himself would not have been ashamed.

Piano Sonatas: in E, Op. 6; in G min., Op. 105; in B flat, Op. 106. Rondo capriccioso, Op. 14
(N) (BB) *** HM HMX 395117. Chiu

Frederic Chiu is a delightful Mendelssohnian and he plays these three early *Piano Sonatas* with a winning mixture of brilliance and tranquillity. The *E major Sonata*, with its Beethovenian associations, written when the young composer was only 12, is played with just the right hint of gravitas, while

the *Presto* finale of Op. 105 and the Scherzo of Op. 106 are played with dazzling digital dexterity, and the more familiar *Rondo capriccioso* sparkles with wit. The recording is too close and a bit hard, but one can accept this at budget price when the playing is as remarkable as the control of colour.

Piano Sonata in G min., Op. 105; Capriccio in E, Op. 118; Etude in F min.; Fantasia on 'The Last Rose of Summer', Op. 15; 2 Pieces: Andante cantabile; Presto agitato. Scherzo a capriccio in F sharp min.; Variations in B flat, Op. 83
(BB) *** Naxos 8.553358. Frith

The *G minor Sonata*, Op. 105, is distinctly Haydnesque, and there is perhaps more charm than individuality. Although the *Fantasia on 'The Last Rose of Summer'* is pretty thin stuff, in such imaginative fingers, it sounds delightful and marvellously fresh. Naxos provide quite excellent recording, and the series so far is touched with distinction.

Piano Sonata in B flat, Op. 106; Albumblatt, Op. 117; Andante cantabile e presto agitato in B; 3 Fantasies et Caprices, Op. 16; Rondo capriccioso in E, Op. 14; Variations in E flat, Op. 82
(BB) *** Naxos 8.553186. Frith

The *B flat Sonata* has been called 'a comfortable and domestic' version of Beethoven's *Hammerklavier*. However, Benjamin Frith is so persuasive that he dispels this impression. His playing is nothing less than a delight, and in the celebrated *Rondo capriccioso* and the more conventional *Variations in E flat* of 1841 he is as light of touch as one could possibly wish.

Songs without Words, Books 1-8 (complete); 49 in G min., Op. posth.
(B) **(*) Hyp. Dyad CDD 22020 (2). Rév

Songs without Words, Books 1-8 (complete); Albumblatt, Op. 117; Gondellied; Kinderstücke, Op. 72; 2 Klavierstücke
(B) *** DG Double (ADD) 453 061-2 (2). Barenboim

Songs without Words (complete); Andante & Variations in E flat, Op. 82; Andante cantabile e presto agitato in B; Variations in B flat, Op. 83
(B) *** Ph. Duo (IMS) (ADD) 438 709-2 (2). Alpenheim

This 1974 set of Mendelssohn's complete *Songs without Words*, which Barenboim plays with such affectionate finesse, has dominated the catalogue for nearly two decades. The sound is first class. At DG Double price, this sweeps the board in this repertoire.

Ilse von Alpenheim's set of *Songs without Words* may not have quite the distinctive character of Barenboim, but she plays this music with an appealing spontaneous simplicity. The 1980 recording of the piano is natural and pleasing.

Lívia Rév's survey has charm and warmth, and she includes a hitherto unpublished piece. The set is handsomely presented and the recording is warm and pleasing. This might well now be seriously considered at its new price, especially by those who enjoy intimate music-making and want digital sound with its silent background.

Songs without Words, Opp. 19/1, 3, 5; 30/2, 4, 6; 38/2, 3, 6; 53/4; 62/2; 67/1–2, 4; 103/5
*** Sony SK 66511. Perahia – BACH/BUSONI: *Chorales*; LISZT: *Concert Paraphrases of Schubert Lieder* ***

As his earlier records have so amply demonstrated, Murray

Perahia has a quite unique feeling for Mendelssohn. He invests these pieces with a depth of poetic feeling that is quite special.

ORGAN MUSIC

Organ Sonatas 1–6, Op. 65/1–6

(N) (BB) ** Naxos 8.553583. Tharp (Casavant organ of St Clement's Church, Chicago)

Organ Sonatas 1–6; Preludes & Fugues 1–3, Op. 37/1–3; Andantes in D & F; Allegro in B flat; Allegro, Chorale & Fugue in D; Allegro maestoso in C; Fugues: (Allegro) in E min.; (Lento) in F min.

(B) *(*) Hyp. Dyad CDD 22029 (2). Scott (organ of St Paul's Cathedral)

John Scott's survey of Mendelssohn's organ music is pretty comprehensive, but the choice of the St Paul's Cathedral organ was a mistake. The ample sounds and blurring resonance prevent any kind of bite – particularly striking in the *Allegro con brio* which opens the *Fourth Sonata*. He is undoubtedly a master of this repertoire technically speaking (witness the closing *Allegro, Choral and Fugue in D*, which pays direct homage to Bach) but his style seems embedded in Victorian tradition.

Stephen Tharp is a fine organist, but the Casavant organ in Chicago seems no better suited to Mendelssohn's music than the instrument at St Paul's, but for a different reason. The sound is bright and well focused, but the throaty, reedy tuttis are inappropriate. We need Decca to reissue Peter Hurford's recordings of this repertoire.

VOCAL MUSIC

Lieder

(BB) *** Hyp. Helios CDH 55150. M. Price, Johnson

A wholly delightful collection, in many ways even more revealing than Dame Janet Baker's shorter survey (on EMI 5 73836-2, combined with songs by Liszt and Schumann) which is praised in our main *Guide*. Once again there is a delightfully light touch to the famous 'On Wings of Song', (*Auf Flügeln*). *Frühlingslied* ('Spring Song') is equally appealing, and *Minnelied* soars. The vivid portrayal of a witches' dance (*Hexenlied*) and *Neue Liebe* with its 'riding elves in the moonlight' are both very much in the spirit of the *Midsummer Night's Dream* music, even if the former, with the fiendishly complex piano part so brilliantly played by Graham Johnson, has a slightly sinister air. In between comes the lovely *Gruss*, a gentle 'Greeting'.

Perhaps the Goethe settings do not quite match those of Schubert, but the two *Suleika* settings are among the highlights of the recital and *Erster Verlust* is ravishing. It is followed by *Volkslied*, which is set with touching Mendelssohnian simplicity. The novelty is Graham Johnson's discovery of the two Byron settings in English, of which *Sun of the Sleepless!* is especially appealing. Then comes Mendelssohn's sole setting of Schiller, *Mädchens Klage*, showing the composer at his most imaginative, as do the four Eichendorf songs which end the recital (the piano introduction to the dramatic *Das Waldschloss* recalls Schubert's *Winterreise*). In short, this is a particularly rewarding collection, with Margaret Price and her partner Graham Johnson in splendid form and made vividly present by the recording. Even though this is a bargain reissue, full texts and translations are provided, plus excellent notes by Richard Wigmore.

Lieder

O– (B) *** EMI double forte (ADD) 5 73836-2 (2). Baker, Parsons – LISZT: *Lieder;* SCHUMANN: *Liederkreis, Op. 39* ***

Mendelssohn's songs, often dismissed as trivial ballads, bring repeated revelations from Janet Baker, with Geoffrey Parsons a comparably perceptive accompanist. Whether in the airy beauty of the most famous of the songs, *Auf Flügeln des Gesanges* ('On wings of song'), the golden happiness of *Morgengruss*, the darkness of *Reiselied* or the expressive narrative of *Hexenlied*, Dame Janet sings not only with rare intensity and acute sense of detail, but also with an unexpected heightening of expression in tone-colours, beautifully contrasted. Mendelssohn's songs, she tells us, are not just tuneful, they can communicate with the resonance of Schubert Lieder. Well-balanced recording and fair documentation, but no texts or translations.

Motets: *Aus tiefer Noth schrei'ich zu dir; 2 Geistliche Choere: Beati mortui; Periti autem, Op. 115; Heilig; Mitten wir im Leben sind, Op. 23;* (i) *3 Motets, Op. 39; 6 Sprüche, Op. 79*

**(*) Paraclete Press GDCG 107. Gloria Dei Cantores, Patterson; (i) with Jordan (organ) – BRAHMS: *Motets* **(*)

This excellent choir, based at Cape Cod, Massachusetts, is very much at home in Mendelssohn, and this rewarding repertoire is most persuasively presented and beautifully recorded in the ideal ambience of the Mechanics Hall in Worcester, Massachusetts, which shows the sonority and blend of this fine choir to moving effect. However, it is worth noting that the solo singing somewhat lets the side down, acceptable rather than distinguished, and in the three works for female voices with organ, Op. 39, the soloists (again from the choir) are insecure in *Surrexit pastor bonus*. But this is a relatively small blot on what remain eloquent performances, and the six brief *Sprüche* ('Sayings') make a splendid closing group. With the reservations noted, this remains a most rewarding collection. Full texts and translations are included.

Elijah (oratorio), Op. 70

O–▼ *** Chan. 8774/5. White, Plowright, Finnie, A. Davies, L. Symphony Ch., LSO, Hickox

(BB) *** EMI Gemini (ADD) 5 86257-2 (2). G. Jones, J. Baker, Gedda, Fischer-Dieskau, Woolf, Wandsworth School Boys' Ch., New Philh. Ch. & O, Frühbeck de Burgos

**(*) Decca 455 688-2 (2). Terfel, Fleming, Bardon, Mark Ainsley, Edinburgh Festival Ch., OAE, Daniel

(BB) **(*) Warner Apex 2564 60534-2 (2). Miles, Donath, Van Nes, George, Klein, Leipzig MDR Ch., Israel PO, Masur

**(*) Ph. 432 984-2 (2). Allen, Kenny, Dawson, Von Otter, Rigby, Rolfe Johnson, Begley, Connell, Hopkins, ASMF Ch., ASMF, Marriner

**(*) HM HMC 901463/4. Salomaa, Isokoski, Groop, Mark Ainsley, Collot, La Chapelle Royale, Coll. Voc., O des Champs-Elysées, Herreweghe

Richard Hickox with the London Symphony Chorus and the LSO secures a performance that both pays tribute to the English choral tradition in this work and presents it dramatically as a kind of religious opera. Willard White may not be ideally steady in his delivery, sometimes attacking notes from below, but he sings consistently with fervour. Rosalind Plowright and Arthur Davies combine purity of tone with operatic expressiveness, and Linda Finnie, while not matching the example of Dame Janet Baker in the classic EMI recording, sings with comparable dedication and directness in the solo, *O rest in the*

Lord. The chorus fearlessly underlines the high contrasts of dynamic demanded in the score. The Chandos recording, full and immediate yet atmospheric too, enhances the drama.

Frühbeck de Burgos proves an excellent Mendelssohnian. The choice of Fischer-Dieskau as the prophet is more controversial. His pointing of English words is not always idiomatic, but his sense of drama is infallible and goes well with this Mendelssohnian new look. Gwyneth Jones and Nicolai Gedda similarly provide mixed enjoyment, but the splendid work of the chorus and, above all, the gorgeous singing of Dame Janet Baker make this a memorable and enjoyable set, very well recorded (in the late 1960s) and spaciously and realistically transferred to CD. A real bargain.

The glory of Paul Daniel's Decca set is the fiercely dramatic portrayal of the central character by Bryn Terfel. This Elijah is the very personification of an Old Testament prophet. Renée Fleming sings most beautifully as the principal soprano, strong rather than reflective in *Hear ye, Israel.* There are no weak links among the others, even if there are no stars either, with Patricia Bardon's *O rest in the Lord* sounding rather matter-of-fact. Many will find it refreshing that with a period orchestra Paul Daniel takes a crisp, direct view of the work, helped by fresh, cleanly focused singing from the Edinburgh Festival Chorus. Yet Daniel is at times too metrical to conceal the squareness of some of the work's weaker passages. Clean, well-separated sound.

Masur as a Mendelssohnian consistently eliminates any hint of sentimentality, but in *Elijah* his determination to use a new broom involves many fast speeds that fail to let this dramatic music blossom, not least in the exuberant final chorus. Yet anyone wanting a fine, modern, digital recording, using the German text, crisply and urgently done, should not be too disappointed, particularly when Alastair Miles sings so freshly and intelligently in the title-role. Another incentive, too, is its new bargain price, complete with texts and translations.

Marriner in his line-up of soloists may look unmatchable, and there is much fine singing; but with the mellifluous Elijah of Thomas Allen balanced rather backwardly in the live recording, less dominant than he should be, the result is refined rather than dramatically powerful. Marriner and his splendid forces are in danger of sounding too well-mannered. He gives the quartets and double-quartets to the soloists, whereas Hickox, following the English tradition, has the chorus singing them.

Herreweghe's reading, using period forces, recorded live in Metz in February 1993, is predictably clean, fresh and light-textured. With a German text, this is as far removed from the English choral tradition as could be. Yet in its way it is quite compelling, thanks to the bright, clear choral singing. Petteri Salomaa is a lightweight Elijah, occasionally fluttery in timbre, and Soile Isokoski is less sweet-toned than in the Op. 111 recording of the *Hymn of Praise*, but John Mark Ainsley and Monica Groop are both excellent. Clear, atmospheric recording.

Hymn: Hor mein Bitten, Herr (Hymn of Praise); **Motets:** *Ehre sei Gott in der Höhe; Herr, nun lässest du deinen Diener in Frieden fahren; Mein Gott, warum hast du mich verlassen; Mitten wir im Leben sind; Warum toben die Heiden; 6 Sprüche, Op. 79*

(BB) *** HM (ADD) HMA 1951142. Paris Chapelle Royale, Coll. Voc. de Ghent, Herreweghe; Huys

Herreweghe's motet performances are splendidly fresh and vital, bringing out the composer's acknowledged debt to earlier models. *Mitten wir im Leben sind* features antiphonal alternation of male and female choirs and uses a chorale previously used by Bach. The part-writing is made admirably clear. Comparison with the recording by Gloria Dei Cantores of the *6 Sprüche,* Op. 79, shows the American choir rather more warmly expressive, but the slight reserve of the Herreweghe performances is enjoyable in a different way. Their account (in German) of the famous *Hymn of Praise* is very dramatic, shedding Anglican sentimental associations, with the excellent soloist, Greta de Reyghere, clear and true in the famous 'Oh for the wings of a dove'. The recording is excellent, cleanly focused within a non-blurring ecclesiastical ambience. The documentation is good, but the German texts and the English translations are not placed side by side. This now comes at budget price.

Psalms: 42: Wie der Hirsch schreit, Op. 42; 95: Kommt lasst uns anbeten, Op. 46; 98: Singet dem Herrn, Op. 91; 114: Da Israel aus Ägypten zog, Op. 151; 115: Nicht unserm Namen, Herr, Op. 31. Lass', o Herr, mich Hülfe finden, Op. 96; Lauda Sion, Op. 73

(N) (BB) *** Warner Apex Double (ADD/DDD) 2564 61692-2. Baumann, Brunner, Silva, Stutzmann, Ihara, Blaser, Ramirez, Huttenlocher, Gulbenkian Ch. & O, Lisbon, Corboz

These recordings were made a decade apart, but although the digital versions of Op. 151 and Op. 96 are that bit more brightly defined, the recording throughout is very good. Choral works like these may characteristically glide over the problems of religious faith in an easy and sweet setting (Psalm 42 begins with what is suspiciously close to a waltz), but in fine performances they are still worth hearing. Psalms Nos. 98 and 115 inspire Mendelssohn to some of his most effectively Bach-like writing. The text of No. 98 inspired Bach, too, and though austerity here periodically turns into sweetness both pieces are welcome in performances as fresh and alert as this. *Lauda Sion* is less varied in its expression, a persistent hymn of praise, but *Lass', o Herr, mich Hülfe finden* ('Let me find your help, O Lord'), a paraphrase of Psalm 13, is set in four contrasted sections, featuring contralto and chorus, and ending with a fugue. There are good soloists and the Lisbon choir responds to Corboz's dedicated direction.

Infelice; Psalm 47 (As pants the hart), Op. 42

(BB) *** Virgin 2x1 5 61469-2 (2). Baker, City of L. Sinfonia, Hickox – BERLIOZ: *Les Nuits d'été,* etc.; BRAHMS: *Alto Rhapsody,* etc.; RESPIGHI: *La sensitiva ****

The scena, *Infelice* – a piece that harks back to an earlier tradition – and the Psalm-setting both have the solos prescribed for soprano, but they suit Dame Janet well, here making a welcome foray out of official retirement for a recording. The voice is in superb condition, with the weight of expressiveness as compelling as ever. The Psalm sounds very like an extra item from *Elijah.*

A Midsummer Night's Dream (ballet; complete; choreography by George Balanchine)

☞ *** BBC Opus Arte **DVD** OA 0810D. Pacific Northwest Ballet, BBC Concert O, Steven Kershaw (Producer: Francia Russell; V/D: Nigel Shepherd)

Balanchine's 1962 ballet was created for the New York City Ballet, and based not only on the inspired score to Shakespeare's play of Mendelssohn's *A Midsummer Night's Dream* but also on other Mendelssohn scores, including the overtures *Athalia, Die schöne Melusine* and *Son and Stranger,* plus two

Have Rame Janet
w/ Psalm 42 ✓, Infelice & Alto Rhap.
Hickox Virgin ✓ w/out Berlioz

movements of the *Ninth* of his early symphonies for strings.

This performance was recorded in 1999 at the then newly reopened Sadler's Wells Theatre while the Pacific Northwest Ballet were on tour. It is a fine company with an enviable reputation and some altogether excellent principal dancers: Lisa Apple's Helena and Julie Tobiason's Hermia are particularly fine, and the scene between Titania and Bottom is most affecting. The fairy scenes are imaginatively handled and staged.

Mendelssohn's music is well served by the ever underrated BBC Concert Orchestra, who always excel when given a chance to play repertoire of quality – and Mendelssohn's score is always a source of wonder! The acoustic of the new Sadler's Wells does not have much warmth or space, but the engineers obtain a very good and well-defined sound. The camerawork and the quality of colour are very high. An enchanting ninety minutes.

A Midsummer Night's Dream: Overture, Op. 21; Incidental Music, Op. 61 (complete; with melodramas and text)
🔲➤ *** DG 439 897-2. Battle, Von Stade, Tanglewood Festival Ch., Boston SO, Ozawa (with excerpts from play spoken by Dame Judi Dench)

A Midsummer Night's Dream: Overture, Op. 21; Incidental Music, Op. 61 (complete)
🔲➤ (BB) *** EMI Encore (ADD) 5 74981-2. Watson, Wallis, Finchley Children's Music Group, LSO, Previn
(B) *** CfP 575 1422. Wiens, Walker, LPO Ch. & O., Litton (with GRIEG: *Peer Gynt*: excerpts; cond. Pritchard) **

A Midsummer Night's Dream: Overture, Op. 21; Incidental Music, Op. 61 (complete). *Overtures: Calm Sea and a Prosperous Voyage; The Hebrides; Ruy Blas.*
(N) (M) *** RCA 82876 60864-2. Popp, Lipovšek, Bamberg Ch. & SO, Flor

Ozawa's virtually complete performance presents Mendelssohn's enchanting incidental music – which is most beautifully played throughout by the Boston Symphony Orchestra – complete with the Shakespearean text, which is spoken over the melodramas by Judi Dench. With two excellent soloists and a fine choral contribution, the only omission here is the brief excerpt which is No. 6 in the score; but the fragmentary reprise of the *Wedding March*, and the two little comic snippets, the Bergomask (*Dance of the Clowns*) and ironic little *Funeral March*, intended for the Rude Mechanicals' 'Pyramus and Thisbe' playlet, are included, whereas they are missing in the competing Sony version with Kenneth Branagh. Judi Dench speaks the Shakespeare text in the simplest way, without any of Branagh's occasional exuberance of style, and in her performance Shakespeare's words seem to glow as magically as Mendelssohn's music. The recording is first class, and the balance, with Dench's narration quite intimate but with every word clear, is very well judged indeed. This DG alternative has no coupling and plays for only 56 minutes, but every one of them is delightful.

On EMI Previn offers a wonderfully refreshing account of the complete score; the veiled *pianissimo* of the violins at the beginning of the Overture and the delicious woodwind detail in the Scherzo certainly bring Mendelssohn's fairies to life. Even the little melodramas which come between the main items sound spontaneous here, and the contribution of the soloists and chorus is first class. The *Nocturne* (taken slowly) is serenely romantic and the *Wedding March* resplendent. The recording is naturally balanced and has much refinement of

detail. This is one of the very finest bargains on EMI's budget Encore label.

The RCA disc is Claus Peter Flor's finest record. His account of the incidental music omits the little melodramas, which is a pity, but otherwise this could be a first choice, particularly as the three Overtures are equally recommendable. Recorded in the warmly resonant acoustics of the Dominikanerbau, Bamberg, the orchestra is given glowingly radiant textures; but Flor's stylish yet relaxed control in *A Midsummer Night's Dream* brings the kind of intimacy one expects from a chamber ensemble. Lucia Popp's vocal contribution is delightful, especially when she blends her voice so naturally with that of Marjana Lipovšek in *You spotted snakes*. The Overtures are no less recommendable.

Andrew Litton also includes the melodramas and, like Previn, he uses them most effectively as links, making them seem an essential part of the structure. He too has very good soloists; in the *Overture* and *Scherzo* he displays an engagingly light touch, securing very fine wind and string playing from the LPO. The wide dynamic range of the recording brings an element of drama to offset the fairy music. Both the *Nocturne*, with a fine horn solo, and the temperamental *Intermezzo* are good examples of the spontaneity of feeling that permeates this performance throughout and makes this disc another bargain. However, Sir John Pritchard's account of the excerpts from *Peer Gynt*, although well played, is rather matter-of-fact.

St Paul, Op. 36
*** Chan. 9882 (2). Gritton, Rigby, Banks, Coleman-Wright, BBC Nat. Ch. & O of Wales, Hickox

Viciously attacked by Wagner and Bernard Shaw among others, *St Paul* – or *Paulus* in the original German, which is used here – has seriously suffered eclipse even in comparison with Mendelssohn's later and greater oratorio, *Elijah*. Yet Richard Hickox's version, recorded live in Cardiff with BBC Welsh forces, completely avoids sentimentality, finding a freshness in a score which effectively echoes the Bach *Passions* in punctuating the story of St Paul with chorales and the occasional 'turba' or crowd chorus. *St Paul* is not as dramatic as *Elijah*, but such a passage as the conversion of Paul (formerly Saul) on the road to Damascus is beautifully done, with the heavenly message bearing the words of Christ delivered by an ethereal women's chorus. The exuberance of the following chorus, like much else, then reflects the self-identification with Paul of a Jewish-born composer who was brought up as a Christian. In brushing any Victorian cobwebs away, Hickox tends to favour speeds on the fast side, never sounding hurried, as on occasion Kurt Masur can on his Philips version, but more importantly never sounding heavy or pompous as other German versions often do. Choral singing is excellent, and among the soloists Susan Gritton and Jean Rigby are first rate, though the tenor, Barry Banks, is a little strained, and Peter Coleman-Wright sounds rather gritty as recorded, though never wobbly as Theo Adam so often does on the Masur set. The warmth and clarity of the recording add to the freshness.

OPERA

Die beiden Pädagogen (complete)
(M) *** CPO/EMI (ADD) 999 550-2. Fuchs, Laki, Dallapozza, Fischer-Dieskau, Wewel, Hirte, Bav. Op. Ch. & O, Wallberg

Mendelssohn wrote this jolly piece, *Die beiden Pädagogen* ('The Two Pedagogues'), when he was only twelve. Starting with a brilliant overture, remarkable for deft woodwind writing, the musical ideas are charming, the manner light and sparkling in a way astonishing from a child, even one as talented as Mendelssohn. Solos are often superimposed on the choral writing with almost Mozartian skill. Under Heinz Wallberg, this CPO disc, very well recorded, offers a reissue of an EMI/Electrola recording made in 1978 with a first-rate cast. Fischer-Dieskau with great zest and style takes the *buffo* role of the schoolmaster, Kinderschreck, with Adolf Dallapozza clear and fresh in the principal tenor role of Carl, and with Krisztina Laki and Gabriele Fuchs well contrasted in the two soprano roles. A charming rarity. There is no libretto, only a detailed note and synopsis.

Die Heimkehr aus der Fremde (complete)
(M) *** CPO/EMI (ADD) 999 555-2. Donath, Schreier, Schwarz, Fischer-Dieskau, Kusche, Bav. Op. Ch. & O, Wallberg

It was at the time of his first visit to England in 1829 at the age of twenty that Mendelssohn wrote this lighthearted little one-Act *Singspiel*, *Die Heimkehr aus der Fremde* ('The Return from Abroad'). After the opening *Romanza* for the mother, a mezzo role, and a duet, the heroine Lisbeth is given a hauntingly beautiful aria in G minor, very sweetly sung here by Helen Donath. Hermann, the returning hero, also has a tender aria, more extended than the rest, with the young Peter Schreier perfectly cast. By that time an impostor, Kauz, has already made his mark in a jolly *buffo* aria referring to the *Dudelsack* (bagpipes), brilliantly sung by Fischer-Dieskau. The plot leads to a confrontation between the rivals, which brings an echo of Beethoven's *Fidelio*. A resolution is crisply achieved, leading to a mellifluous final ensemble very characteristic of the composer. Like *Die beiden Pädagogen*, this is a rarity well worth investigating in this vividly recorded, first-rate performance.

MENOTTI, Gian-Carlo (born 1911)

Apocalisse; (i) *Fantasia for Cello & Orchestra. Sebastian: Ballet Suite*
*** Chan. 9900. Spoleto Festival O, Hickox; (i) with Wallfisch

The *Sebastian Ballet Suite* dates from 1944, an attractive sequence of genre pieces that gives little idea of the seedy side of the story. Hickox's reading is refined and spacious, helped by the first-rate Chandos sound, recorded live in Spoleto. The orchestral triptych, *Apocalisse*, was written for Victor de Sabata in 1951-2, with the ambitious first movement, *Improperia*, inspired by the conflict between the goodness of Christ and His suffering from mankind. The striking fanfare motifs bring echoes of Hollywood film music and, as in the *Sebastian Suite*, there are many echoes of Stravinsky ballet in ostinato rhythms. The other two movements are shorter and simpler and similarly approachable rather than darkly apocalyptic, while the *Fantasia*, dating from 1976, is similarly full of striking ideas, with echoes of Walton in the virtuoso cello part, manfully tackled by Raphael Wallfisch. Good clear sound, giving no idea of the problems of live recording.

Piano Concerto in F
(M) **(*) Van. (ADD) 08.4029.71 [OVC 4071]. Wild, Symphony of the Air, Mester – COPLAND: *Concerto* ***

Menotti's *Piano Concerto*, like most of his music, is easy and fluent, never hard on the ear. Its eclectic style brings a pungent whiff of Shostakovich at the opening, and there are hints of Khachaturian elsewhere. Even if it is unlikely to bear repeated listening, the charisma and bravura of Earl Wild's playing make the music sound more substantial than it is.

(i) *Violin Concerto in A min.;* (ii) *Cantilena e Scherzo* (for harp & string quartet); (iii) *Canti della Lontananza; 5 Songs*
(N) **(*) ASV CDDCA 1156. (i) Shapira, Russian PO, Sanderling; (ii) Tingay, Vanbrugh Qt; (iii) Brewer, Vignoles

Ittai Shapira finds plenty of charm in Menotti's ever-tuneful *Violin Concerto*, and although her tone is thin as recorded, she comes into her own in the perkily rhythmic theme of the finale. The *Cantilena and Scherzo* too is completely beguiling, reminiscent of Ravel in its languorous textures for harp and string quartet. The recording here is over-resonant, but not unattractively so. Schwarzkopf commissioned the seven songs that make up the *Canti della Lontananza*, but, alas, Christine Brewer is not her match, producing squally climaxes; and the five English songs bring similar problems.

(i) *Violin Concerto; Cantatas:* (ii) *The Death of Orpheus;* (iii) *Muero porque no muero;* (iv) *Oh llama de amor viva*
*** Chan. 9979. (i) Koh; (ii) MacDougall; (iii) Melinek; (iv) Roberts; Spoleto Ch. & O, Hickox

Richard Hickox once more draws from his fine Spoleto team warmly persuasive readings of eclectic works which are powerfully convincing in committed performances like these. The young American violinist, Jennifer Koh, is the excellent soloist in the *Concerto*. The first movement with its sequence of flowing melodies might easily seem to meander, but Koh and Hickox between them give it a clear shape, with each new idea emerging seductively. The slow movement, played with hushed dedication, has a tender poignancy, while the vigorous finale with its jaunty main theme predictably ends with virtuoso fireworks.

The two cantatas, using Spanish texts by the mystics St Teresa of Avila and St John of the Cross, offer sensuous music closer to Puccini's opera, *Suor Angelica*, than to any religious model. The chorus in each dramatically enhances the meditative solos representing each saint. Julia Melinek is the vibrant soloist in the St Teresa cantata, though Stephen Roberts is sadly unsteady in the St John of the Cross setting. *The Death of Orpheus*, to an English text by Menotti himself, is similarly dramatic. Orpheus's song emerges as a broad diatonic melody, with choral writing of Delian sensuousness. Jamie MacDougall is the expressive soloist, with the chorus fresh and incisive in all three cantatas.

(i) *Sebastian* (ballet; complete); (ii) *Legend; Lyric Scene*
(M) ** Phoenix (ADD) PHCD 101. (i) LSO; (ii) Oslo PO; Serebrier

Serebrier's performance of *Sebastian* is lively and sympathetic, and the recording is vivid and detailed, but with a degree of dryness hinting that it is not recent (no date is given). But Menotti's vibrant score certainly comes fully to life. One irritating drawback, however, is that there are only two tracks for this 37-minute ballet. The two more reflective chamber works make a good contrast, though here the sound is just a bit too dry and up-front to be ideal. The sleeve-notes are quite comprehensive.

OPERA

Amahl and the Night Visitors (opera; complete)

🔊━ *** That's Entertainment CDTER 1124. Haywood, Dobson, Watson, Painter, Rainbird, ROHCG Ch. & O, Syrus

Recorded under the supervision of the composer himself, this is a fresh and highly dramatic performance, very well sung and marked by atmospheric digital sound of striking realism. Central to the success of the performance is the astonishingly assured and sensitively musical singing of the boy treble, James Rainbird, as Amahl, while Lorna Haywood sings warmly and strongly as the Mother, with a strong trio of Kings.

The Consul (complete)

🔊━ *** Chan. 9706 (2). Bullock, Otley, Kreitzer, Livengood, Austin, Broadbent, 1998 Spoleto Festival O, Hickox

This ripely red-blooded performance, recorded live at the Spoleto Festival in 1998, finds Richard Hickox a passionate interpreter of this early response to the Cold War and the human tragedies involved. In context today, it now emerges as a positive strength that Menotti unashamedly echoes Puccini in his emotional assault on the listener, whether in dramatic coups such as the very opening, which echoes the opening of *Tosca*, or in sweeping tunes that immediately catch in the memory. Hickox builds the structure masterfully, firmly controlling tension. He is helped by an excellent orchestra and a good cast, led by Susan Bullock in the central role of Magda. Her big outburst against bureaucracy at the end of Act II brings the emotional high point of the whole opera, an overwhelming moment worthy of Puccini. None of the others quite matches Bullock vocally, with some voices rather unsteady. Jacalyn Kreitzer is warmly affecting as the Mother, and Charles Austin sings strongly as the Secret Agent, giving a rounded portrait. Full-toned, vivid recording, with ample detail.

(i) Martin's Lie (complete); (ii) Canti della lontananza: Impossible Lovers; The Letter; Pegasus Asleep; Resignation; The Seventh Glass of Wine; Snowy Morning; The Spectre; (iii) 5 songs: The eternal prisoner; My ghost; The idle gift; The longest wait; The swing

*** Chan. 9605. (i) Tees Valley Boys' Ch., N. Sinfonia, Hickox; (ii) Leggate, Martineau; (iii) Howarth, Martineau

Martin's Lie was written as a follow-up to the children's piece for TV, *Amahl and the Night Visitors*, a sinister medieval story with a moral, fluently told in 45 minutes; warmly involving singing and playing. Judith Howarth and Robin Leggate are the singers in the two brief song-cycles, with Menotti's writing all the richer in the Italian settings.

The Saint of Bleecker Street (opera; complete)

*** Chan. 9971(2). Melinek, Richards, Stephen, Bindel, Zeltzer, Farrugia, Howard, Rozynko, Spoleto Festival Ch. & O, Hickox

Overlook the melodramatic plot, even forget the variable casting of solo singers – not Italianate enough with too many wobblers – for this pioneering recording of Gian-Carlo Menotti's opera, *The Saint of Bleecker Street*, demonstrates that this is one of the composer's most powerful scores, colourful, atmospheric and tuneful, with telling dramatic effects, often involving genuine Italian tunes. Set in New York's Little Italy, it revolves round the dying Annina, a would-be nun with a gift for faith-healing, and her boorish agnostic brother, Michele. For Menotti, a Catholic who lost his faith, the story aims to symbolize the clash between faith and doubt. In this performance, recorded live, the red-blooded feelings involved are passionately brought out by Richard Hickox, with talented young performers from the Festival Choir and Orchestra of Menotti's summer music festival at Spoleto. Full, brilliant sound.

MERBECKE, John (c. 1505–c. 1585)

Missa per Arma Iustitie; Antiphona per arma iustitie (plainsong); Ave Dei patris filia; Domine Ihesu Christe; A Virgin and Mother

*** Gaudeamus CDGAU 148. Cardinall's Musick, Carwood

The Tudor composer John Merbecke was a polyphonic master to bracket with his exact contemporary, Thomas Tallis, but his Latin church music has largely disappeared, perhaps destroyed by him after he became a devout Calvinist. This disc brings together all the major items that survive, a magnificent extended setting of the Mass and two splendid anthems, one early and direct in its polyphony, the other dauntingly complex. In the hands of Andrew Carwood and his fine choral group, Cardinall's Musick, the disc proves as revelatory and as beautiful as their previous, highly acclaimed issues of earlier Tudor masters, Nicholas Ludford and John Fayrfax.

MERCADANTE, Saverio (1795–1870)

Flute Concertos: in D; E; E min.

(N)(M) *** RCA 82876 60865-2. Galway, Sol. Ven., Scimone

These three *Flute Concertos* show Mercadante to be an excellent craftsman with a nice turn for lyrical melody in the slow movements with their simple, song-like cantilenas. Both the *Andante alla siciliana* of the *D major Concerto* and the *Largo* of the *E minor* are appealing, especially with Galway as soloist, while the *Rondo Russo* or *Polacca* finales are inventively spirited. Scimone makes the most of the often exuberantly florid tuttis of the opening movements, and elsewhere he accompanies Galway's silvery melodic line, sparkling and delicate by turns, with style and polish. The sound is excellent.

MERIKANTO, Aarre (1893–1958)

Andante Religioso; 4 Compositions for Orchestra; Lemminkäinen, Op. 10; Pan, Op. 28; Scherzo

** Ondine ODE 905-2. Tampere PO, Ollila

Lemminkäinen comes from 1916, when Merikanto was finishing his studies in Moscow, and is derivative (Russian post-nationalism, Sibelius and a dash of Scriabin). *Pan* is more radical and is highly imaginative with an evocative and powerful atmosphere. The *Four Compositions for Orchestra* come from the 1930s, as does the *Scherzo*. Good performances and decent recording, though the Tampere studio is a bit on the dry side.

(i) Piano Concertos 2 & 3; 2 Studies for Small Orchestra; 2 Pieces for Orchestra

** Ondine ODE 915-2. (i) Raekallio; Tampere PO, Ollila

Although neither of the piano concertos is the equal of the

Second Violin Concerto, they are both inventive and rewarding. The middle movement of the *Third Piano Concerto*, with its strong evocation of nature, is one of Merikanto's most haunting inspirations. The orchestral pieces are less interesting. Matti Raekallio is a very capable player, and the Tampere orchestra, though obviously a provincial band, copes well under Tuomas Ollila. The sound is synthetic, with little front-to-back perspective. Worth investigating all the same.

(i) *Concerto for Violin, Clarinet, Horn & String Sextet;* (ii) *Nonet;* (iii) *Works for Male Choir*

**(*) Ondine ODE 703-2. (i) Kagan, Brunner, Jolley, Erlich, Oramo, Hirvikangas, Mendelssohn, Sariola, Karttunen, Söderblom; (ii) Ens., Söderblom; (iii) Polytech Ch., Länsiö

The concerto's atmosphere is quite heady, and there is little sense of it being Nordic in feeling. The *Nonet* (1926) for flute, cor anglais, clarinet, piano, violins, viola, cello and double bass inhabits a similar world, and is an evocative piece with occasional reminders of the Ravel of the Mallarmé songs or *Aoua* from the *Chanson madécasses*. Good performances, but the recording is a trifle hard. The choral pieces are less adventurous in their harmonies except for *To the last living being*, but often quite haunting. Despite less than distinguished recording, this is strongly recommended for the sake of some extraordinary music.

MESSAGER, André (1853–1929)

Les Deux Pigeons

(N) (B) * Australian Decca Eloquence 476 2448. Welsh Nat. Op. O, Bonynge**

Messager's charming gypsy ballet was premièred at the Paris Opéra in 1886 on the same bill as Donizetti's *La Favorita*. But it swiftly established its independence, to remain on the repertoire and be revived (with new choreography by Frederick Ashton) by the Sadler's Wells Company in 1961. The music is light but cleverly scored, after the manner of Delibes; agreeably tuneful, it does not wear out its welcome. Bonynge secures playing from the Welsh Opera Orchestra that is consistently graceful and sparkling, and if the sound is vivid and naturally balanced, it is not quite out of Decca's very top drawer.

Les Deux Pigeons (complete ballet, arr. Lanchbery); *Isoline* (ballet suite).

(B) * CfP (DDD/ADD) 2-CD 586 1782. O de Paris, Jacquillat**
– HÉROLD: *La fille mal gardée* *

What an enchanting score Messager's *Two Pigeons* ballet is; and there is some lovely music in the ballet suite from *Isoline* too. This derives from an opera first heard in 1888 but rejected by the general public as the plot involved a (magical) sex-change (both ways) for the heroine! The ballet survives, and its seven movements are consistently delectable when played as lightly and spiritedly as this. The recording too is very successful, with plenty of colour and sparkle.

Les Deux Pigeons (ballet: excerpts)

(BB) **(*) EMI Encore (ADD) 5 75221-2. ROHCG O, Mackerras – DELIBES: *Coppélia; Sylvia* (excerpts); GOUNOD: *Faust: ballet music* **(*)

This delightful 20-minute suite from the ballet *Les Deux Pigeons* was recorded in stereo as early as 1956 and, despite a certain thinness, is remarkably vivid. The performance is

stylishly enjoyable, with Messager's melodic inspiration at its most felicitous. The numbers that employ 'local colour', such as the *Danse Hongroise*, are particularly piquant, as is the charming *Pas des deux pigeons*.

Véronique (opera; complete)

(BB) **(*) EMI (ADD) 5 74073-2 (2). Mesplé, Guiot, Benoit, Dens, Dunand, Pruvost, René Duclos Ch., LOP, Hartemann

Messager's gentle charms are well displayed in his 1898 opera, *Véronique*. The story of Hélène de Solanges, who works in disguise in a Parisian florist's in the 1840s under the assumed name Véronique, produces plenty of romantic complications, which are all sorted out by the end. There are several numbers that understandably became Edwardian favourites, including the two duets from Act I: the 'Donkey duet' (*De ci, de l'*) and the 'Swing duet' (*Poussez, poussez, l'escarpolette*). The Act I quartet with the refrain '*Charmant, charmant*' is another highlight of the utmost piquancy. The performance here is excellent, Mady Mesplé again showing her supremacy in this repertoire, while the rest of the cast and the conductor understand Messager's idiom perfectly. The 1969 recording has transferred very well to CD, with the voices clear and vivid. But as ever in this bargain operetta series, no texts or translations are provided, which will be a distinct drawback for many collectors.

MESSIAEN, Olivier (1908–92)

(i) *L'Ascension;* (ii) *Couleurs de la cité céleste; Et exspecto resurectionem mortuorum*

(N) * Erato (ADD) 2564 60225-2. (i) French R. & TV O, Constant; (ii) Loriod, Strasbourg Instrumental & Percussion Group, Boulez**

L'Ascension (an early work from 1933) may be static in feeling but it is highly personal in flavour. The performance from Marius Constant and the French Radio Orchestra is most persuasive, and they are admirably served by the engineers. The two coupled works date from the early 1960s, and *Et exspecto* draws liberally on the composer's beloved birdsong, ranging from Brazil to New Zealand as a source of inspiration. It withstands the test of the years and exerts a hypnotic grip over the listener for much of the time with its curiously inert yet strongly atmospheric world. *Les Couleurs de la cité céleste* represented the composer's ideal of 'stained-glass music' and 'ends no more than it begins, and turns on itself like a rose-window of blazing and invisible colours'. It sounds very impressive here in demonstrating the extraordinary sonorities the composer draws from piano, wind and percussion, with Boulez ensuring that every detail is clear.

Des Canyons aux étoiles

(M) * DG 471 617-2 (2). Muraro, Justafre, Fr. R. PO, Chung**

Myung-Whun Chung, who studied with the composer, conducts a warmly expressive, free-flowing reading of Messiaen's tribute to the United States on its bicentenary in 1976. Though the forces used, with only single strings, are relatively modest, the scale is massive, with 12 movements lasting over 90 minutes, and the DG recording underlines that in its fullness and richness of sound. The set offers a striking contrast with the now deleted Sony version under Salonen, which is more severe in its precise registering of Messiaen's evocation of birdsong in each movement. Chung, together with his brilliant soloists, is freer and therefore more evocative in his readings of movements directly inspired by a sequence of venues in the American south-west, mainly the deserts and canyons of Utah and Arizona. In most movements he is a degree more expansive, but the big exception comes in the spectacular sixth movement, *Interstellar Call*, for unaccompanied horn. In place of weight Jean-Jacques Justafre offers a volatile reading which spans an extraordinary tonal and dynamic range. Like the others, he brilliantly demonstrates that this is music to love and embrace. The Sony version offers substantial fill-ups, but in compensation the DG two-disc package comes at upper mid-price.

Eclairs sur l'au-delà (Illuminations of the Beyond)
*** DG 439 929-2. Paris Bastille Opéra O, Chung

Eclairs sur l'au-delà reveals an undoubted connection with the visionary *Turangalîla Symphony*, especially so in the longest movement, a haunting *Adagio* for strings, *Demeurer dans l'amour*. This magical sequence returns to close the work in translucent radiance, portraying *Le Christ, lumière du Paradis*. Of course the music features the composer's beloved birdsong. There are also evocations of constellations in the night sky 'in all their glory', and of 'seven angels with seven trumpets'. Myung-Whun Chung is at his most persuasive in holding this evocative score together, and this superbly played performance is even finer than his reading of *Turangalîla*; the DG sound is spaciously atmospheric yet beautifully clear.

Turangalîla Symphony
- (B) *** EMI (ADD) **Audio DVD** DVC 4 92398-9; CD double forte 5 69752-2 (2). Béroff, J. Loriod, LSO, Previn – POULENC: *Concert Champêtre; Organ Concerto* ***
- (M) *** RCA (ADD) 82876 59418-2. Yvonne & Jeanne Loriod, Toronto SO, Ozawa
- *** Decca 436 626-2. Thibaudet, Harada, Concg. O, Chailly
- *** Erato 8573 82043-2. Almard, Kim, BPO, Nagano
- **(*) Chan. 9678. Shelley, Hartmann-Claverie, BBC PO, Y. P. Tortelier
- (B) **(*) Sony SBK 89900. Crossley, Murail, Philh. O, Salonen

(i) Turangalîla Symphony; (ii) Quatuor pour la fin du temps; (iii) Le Merle noir
(N) (BB) *** EMI Gemini (DDD/ADD) 5 86525-2 (2). (i) Donohoe, Murail, CBSO, Rattle; (ii) Gruenberg, De Peyer, Pleth, Béroff; (iii) Zöller, Kontarsky

Messiaen's *Turangalîla Symphony* is on an epic scale, seeking to embrace almost the totality of human experience. *Turanga* is Time and also implies rhythmic movement; *Lîla* is love and, with a strong inspiration from the Tristan and Isolde legend, Messiaen's love-music dominates his conception of human existence. The actual love-sequences feature the ondes Martenot with its 'velvety glissandi'. The piano obbligato is also a strong feature of the score. Previn's vividly direct approach, helped by spectacular recording, has much electricity. He is at his best in the work's more robust moments, for instance the jazzy fifth movement, and he catches the wit at the beginning of the *Chant d'amour No. 2*. The idyllic *Garden of the Sleep of Love* is both serene and poetically sensuous, and the apotheosis of the love theme in the closing pages is jubilant and life-affirming. Previn's recording is also available much less expensively on a pair of CDs coupled with outstanding versions of two of Poulenc's finest concertos. The Audio DVD, like the others in the EMI series, is available in multi-channel surround sound or (by turning the disc over) in high-resolution stereo, in each case with enhanced dynamic range and definition. Because the sound-balance of the 1977 Abbey Road recording is comparatively unexpansive in the bass, the improvement in amplitude is less striking here than with some other Audio DVDs, yet the sound is still remarkably vivid and present.

Ozawa's performance comes from 1967, but you would never guess that from the brilliantly atmospheric sound, which is just as vivid as some of the newer versions, such as Nagano's Erato version, and has that bit more warmth and atmosphere. Yvonne Loriod's piano is placed too forward, but her contribution is undoubtedly seminal, and the overall balance is otherwise well managed. The performance itself is brilliantly played: it has plenty of electricity, and a warm sensuality too. It was and remains one of Ozawa's best recordings and is now economically reissued on a single CD as part of RCA's 'Classic Collection'. It is also available as a part of a bargain Double (24321 84601-2), coupled with Roussel's *Bacchus et Ariane* and *Third* and *Fourth Symphonies*.

Chailly's full-priced Decca account may have the advantage of even finer, digital recording, and it costs about the same; being (just) fitted on to a single CD; however, it is without Previn's considerable bonus: outstanding versions of two of Poulenc's finest concertos.

Simon Rattle conducts a winning performance of *Turangalîla*, not only brilliant and dramatic but atmospheric and convincing. The recording is warm and richly co-ordinated, while losing nothing in detail. Peter Donohoe and Tristan Murail play with comparable warmth and flair. Led by Aloys Kontarsky, the performance of the *Quartet for the End of Time* provides a contrasting approach to Messiaen from Rattle's, where atmospheric warmth is only an incidental.

The performance of the *Quatuor pour la fin du temps*, led by Erich Gruenberg and with Gervase de Peyer the inspirational solo clarinettist, is in the very highest class, the players meeting every demand the composer makes on them, and the fine, clear, Abbey Road recording gives the group striking presence while affording the proper background ambience. The bonus, *Le Merle noir*, exploits the composer's love of birdsong even more overtly and is splendidly played and recorded here.

The *Turangalîla Symphony* has never sounded more turbulently spectacular than in the live Berlin recording from Nagano. He seems determined to emphasize all the bizarre qualities of the score, including glissando whoops among the brilliant percussive effects. The *Joie du sang des étoiles* is jazzily, joyously extrovert, and this high level of tension (and noise) persists throughout. The *Final* is almost overwhelming in its energetic flamboyance and its culmination certainly has the sense of absolute finality. But although the sensuous aspects of the score are fully realized in the *Jardin du sommeil d'amour*, the contrasting element of repose seldom surfaces, and such a consistent clamour for most of the 73 minutes needs a fair degree of stamina. The recording itself has remarkable range and vividness.

Yan Pascal Tortelier's Chandos version opens excitingly, has undoubted grip, and the recording is exceptionally vividly detailed, with Howard Shelley's piano contribution always crystal clear. But the very positive characterization seems to give the work a more episodic nature, less overtly sensuous than Chailly. The reading overall is not particularly warm in its expressiveness, partly due to the effect of the sound-balance, and this is especially striking in the brilliant finale.

Esa-Pekka Salonen directs a performance in sharp focus. Relatively this is an account which minimizes atmospheric beauty and sensuousness, instead underlining the elements which look forward to later composers. This is emphasized by the close balance of the piano and ondes Martenot, which stand out instead of emerging as part of the rich orchestral texture. So the passage-work for piano, beautifully played by Paul Crossley, sounds angular in a very modern way rather than evoking birdsong. Significantly, the syncopated rhythms of the energetic fifth movement are pressed home very literally at a speed faster than usual, with little or no echo of jazz. The Philharmonia play brilliantly and the recording accentuates the sharp focus of the readings, while giving ample atmosphere.

Quatuor pour la fin du temps

☛— *** DG 469 052-2. Shaham, Meyer, Jian Wang, Chung

*** Decca 452 899-2. Mustonen, Bell, Isserlis, Collins —
SHOSTAKOVICH: *Piano Trio 2* ***

*** Delos D/CD 3043. Chamber Music Northwest —
BARTOK: *Contrasts* ***

(BB) **(*) Warner Apex 0927 48749-2. Brunner, Trio Fontenay

(i) *Quatuor pour la fin du temps;* (ii) *Theme & Variations for Violin & Piano*

(B) **(*) DG (ADD) 445 128-2. (i) Yordanov, Tetard, Desurmont, Barenboim; (ii) Kremer, Argerich

Messiaen's visionary and often inspired piece was composed during his days in a Silesian prison camp. Among his fellow-prisoners were a violinist, a clarinettist and a cellist, who, with the composer at the piano, made its creation possible.

The newest DG account of *Quatuor pour la fin du temps* must now take pride of place among its rivals. It is a performance of the highest quality, with a level of concentration and intensity that grips the listener from first to last, and is superbly recorded. There are notes by both Messiaen and the cellist Etienne Pasquier, who was interned with Messiaen and took part in the première at the German prisoner-of-war camp in January 1941.

Undoubtedly the new Decca version is also among the finest recent digital recordings. All four artists distinguish themselves, and Messiaen's other-worldly piece is beautifully played and has great concentration and atmosphere. The one snag is the wide dynamic range of the recording, although the clarinettist, Michael Collins, makes the very most of it with his *pianissimos*. It is difficult (but not impossible) to find a volume setting in which the gentler passages register, yet *fortissimos* do not become just a shade fierce, and the ear is conscious that the microphones are fairly close. Nevertheless this is very fine and, as on the earlier EMI version, the Abbey Road ambience is well judged.

David Shifrin, like his colleagues, fully captures the work's sensuous mysticism, while the solos of Warren Lash (cello) and Williams Doppmann have a wistful, improvisatory quality: both *Louange à l'éternité de Jésus* and the closing *Louange à l'immortalité de Jésus* are played very beautifully. The Delos recording is naturally balanced and very realistic, while the ambience is suitably evocative.

Edward Brunner is a fine clarinettist, and the Trio Fontenay are strongly committed, with Wolf Harden dominant. But this is a less resilient account than some, and the recording is less atmospheric. So, in spite of its modest cost, it is not a primary choice.

Barenboim and his colleagues recorded the *Quatuor pour la fin du temps* in the presence of the composer. Barenboim is a strong personality who carries much of this vibrant and atmospheric performance in his own hands and inspired his colleagues with his own commitment to the music. There are fine contributions from the cellist Albert Tetard and the clarinettist Claude Desurmont. But the CD transfer has added a degree of edginess to Luben Yordanov's violin timbre, making this less attractive than the original LP from which the recording derives. The *Theme and Variations* (a digital recording from 1990) is something of a rarity on disc but is in every way successful.

PIANO MUSIC

Catalogue d'oiseaux (complete); *La Fauvette des jardins*

(M) **(*) DG Trio 474 345-2 (3). Ugorski

It is good to have such a bold, powerful and essentially Slavonic approach to Messiaen's multi-faceted evocations of birdsong heard against graphically depicted landscapes, often rough-hewn, with all the extravagance of nature. It is impossible not to respond to such vivid pictorialism, even if Anatol Ugorski's approach is essentially extrovert and at times almost melodramatic in its dynamism and sense of contrast. This would make a spectacular impression at a live performance, but under domestic circumstances the greater intimacy and the less flamboyant, more subtle approach of Peter Hill on Regis and Håkan Austbø on Naxos are more satisfying. The DG recording is very immediate, which is not necessarily an advantage when Ugorski's playing creates its own presence.

Complete piano music

Disc 1: *Catalogue d'oiseaux, Books 1–3* (RRC 1108)

Disc 2: *Catalogue d'oiseaux, Books 4–6* (RRC 1109)

Disc 3: *Catalogue d'oiseaux, Book 7; Supplément: La fauvette des jardins; Petites esquisses d'oiseaux* (RRC 1110)

Disc 4: *20 Regardes sur L'Enfant-Jésus* (RRC 2055 (2))

Disc 5: *Cantéyodjaya; 4 Etudes de rythme; Fantaisie burlesque; Pièce pour le tombeau de Paul Dukas; Préludes; Rondeau;* (i) *Visions de l'Amen* (RRC 2056 (2))

☛— (BB) *** Regis RRC 7001 (7). Hill; (i) with Frith

Catalogue d'oiseaux

(BB) *** RRC 3008 (3). Hill (from above set)

Peter Hill made his outstanding collection of Messiaen's piano music between 1986 and 1992 for Unicorn. Those recordings now appear at bargain price on the Regis label, admirably documented. They come complete in a slip-case, but are available separately as listed above. The complete *Catalogue d'oiseaux* is also available as a separate collection.

Hill began his survey in 1986 with the vast *Catalogue d'oiseaux*, which derives its inspiration from Messiaen's beloved birdsong. Little of the piano writing is conventional, but there is no question as to the composer's imaginative flair, and the music is vivid and colourful to match the plumage of the creatures which he depicts so strikingly. Peter Hill prepared this music in Paris with the composer himself and thus has his imprimatur. He has great sensitivity to colour and atmosphere and evokes the wildlife pictured in this extraordinary music to splendid effect.

The *Oiseaux* sessions were completed in 1988–9 with *La fauvette des jardins*, another half-hour of music, composed in the summer of 1970, which the producer, Anthony Pople, describes as the perfect parergon to the cycle. The recording (by Bob Auger) was made in Rosslyn Hill Unitarian Chapel with the utmost clarity and definition.

The *Petites esquisses d'oiseaux*, written in 1985, formed a belated postlude to the series. Yvonne Loriod tells how she enticed her husband back to work with a commission for a miniature describing a robin. This led to the *Six esquisses*, with the first, third and fifth describing the robin, surrounded by the blackbird, song thrush and skylark, the latter particularly vividly represented. Again, Hill plays with total dedication and understanding; the recording was made much later, in 1992, at Brandon Hill, Bristol. However, the *Préludes* and shorter pieces were recorded at Rosslyn Hill in 1984 and 1985, where Peter Hill chose to use a Bösendorfer. With his inherent feeling for the colour and atmosphere of Messiaen's sound-world, he makes an excellent case for all this repertoire, save perhaps for the somewhat repetitive *Fantaisie burlesque* of 1932, which outstays its welcome. His playing is consistently sensitive and has great finesse, with the *Cantéyodjaya* (1948) particularly refined.

For the *Vingt regards sur L'Enfant-Jésus*, recorded in 1991 in St Paul's, Southgate, Peter Hill chose a Fazioli and his interpretation is surely enhanced by the special tonal qualities of the instrument, for he seeks to reveal the music's inner essence and colouring, its tranquil, unruffled moments of spiritual inspiration and subtlety of detail, rather than emphasize its inherent drama. In his hands it is the contemplative, lyrical writing that one remembers, the moments of calm, rather than the vibrant climaxes. Which is not to say that the playing is not vividly alive, but rather that bravura is never the first consideration, even though the pianism shows complete mastery. The composer himself has spoken with great warmth of the artist and he has every reason. Bob Auger's recordings, too, are a splendid memento of one of Britain's most musically perceptive sound-engineers.

Cantéyodjayâ; 4 Etudes de rythme; Préludes: Chant d'extase dans une paysage triste; Cloches d'angoisse et larmes d'adieu; La Colombe; Instants défunts; Le Nombre léger; Plainte calme; Un Reflet dans le vent; Les Sons impalpables du rêve
(BB) *** Naxos 8.554090. Austbø

Fantaisie Burlesque; La Fauvette des jardins; Les Offrandes; Pièce pour le tombeau de Paul Dukas; Prélude; Rondeau
(BB) *** Naxos 8.554655. Austbø

This impressive Norwegian pianist (who is domiciled in the Netherlands) is totally in sympathy with Messiaen's elusive idiom, and these latest additions to his discography are as recommendable as their predecessors (see below). Peter Hill's fine survey of Messiaen's keyboard music is listed above on Regis, also at bargain price. Austbø can certainly be recommended alongside him, though not in preference to him.

Catalogue d'oiseaux (complete); *Petites esquisses d'oiseaux*
(BB) *** Naxos 8.553532/4 (3). Austbø

The seven books of the *Catalogue d'oiseaux* occupied Messiaen between 1956 and 1958. The *Petites esquisses d'oiseaux* are much later. Whatever one's reactions to Messiaen's music, he creates a world entirely his own. Håkan Austbø is completely attuned to this sensibility, and the recording is exemplary. Aficionados of Messiaen need not hesitate.

Catalogue d'oiseaux: La Rousserolle effarvatte
*** MDG 604 1141-2. Von Eckardstein – JANACEK: *Sonata 1.X.1905*; PROKOFIEV: *Sonata 8* ***

Severin von Eckardstein's account of *La rousserolle effarvatte*, the seventh of the *Catalogue d'oiseaux*, is both sensitive and brilliant.

8 Préludes pour piano; 20 Regards sur l'Enfant-Jésus
(B) **(*) EMI (ADD) 5 69668-2. Béroff

The *Préludes* are early works but, like *Vingt regards*, they show Michel Béroff at his most inspired, generating the illusion of spontaneous creation. Clean, well-focused sound – but a little wanting in richness and sonority.

20 Régards sur l'Enfant-Jésus
*** Teldec **Audio DVD** 3984 26868-9; CD 3984 26868-2 (2). Aimard (piano)
*** Hyp. CDA 67351/2. Osborne
*** Erato (ADD) 4509 91705-2 (2). Y. Loriod
(N) (M) *** RCA 82876 62316-2 (2). Serkin
(BB) *** Naxos 8.550829/30. Austbø
(N) (M) **(*) Arte Nova 74321 85292-2. Zehn

Pierre-Laurent Aimard has received the composer's praise for his 'magnifique technique, sonorité claire et timbrée, et interprétations d'une rare intelligence'. Aimard's performance on disc is technically remarkable (although the virtuosity is always at the service of the music) and atmospherically perceptive. Fascinatingly, he is very relaxed at the opening, but evocation is in no doubt and the concentration steadily grows and with it the tension. The piano is very well recorded indeed, and this can be strongly recommended. This is also available on an Audio DVD.

Steven Osborne's performance has much in common with that of Pierre-Laurent Aimard. It too is deeply sensitive and full of atmospheric feeling. The Hyperion recording is first class, and to make a choice between these two versions is almost impossible: both are very distinguished indeed.

The 1973 recording by Yvonne Loriod – the composer's second wife – of *Vingt regards* has long been considered very special in its understanding and feeling for the composer's musical sound-world. The piano recording is full but is otherwise acceptable rather than outstanding – yet the magnetism of the playing overcomes the lack of the sharpest focus.

Peter Serkin's remains among the finest versions at midprice. He has an intense feeling for atmosphere and superb keyboard control. His recording is well lit and clear.

Håkon Austbø has excellent credentials in this repertoire. His is an individual view, with a wider range of tempi and dynamic than Loriod. His account of the opening *Regard du père* and the later *Regard du fils sur le fils* is paced much more slowly, but his playing has great concentration and evocative feeling so that he readily carries the slower tempo, and in *Par lui tout a été fait* articulation is bolder, giving the music a stronger profile, helped by the clearer, Naxos digital focus. This is undoubtedly a performance that grips the listener and can be strongly recommended as an alternative view.

Martin Zehn plays with a wide range of expressive dynamic and, with often bold articulation, varies his timbre with his wide dynamic contrasts, sometimes *sotto voce* and gentle (as at the opening of *Regard du temps*), at other times very forceful. He is flexible in matters of tempo, making, for instance, a steady acceleration to the climax of *Par lui tout a été fait*. His is a young man's interpretation, full of tension and impetus, and the piano is closely recorded. Not a first choice, but an engrossing and obviously dedicated account, undoubtedly spontaneous in feeling.

ORGAN MUSIC

Complete organ music (including unpublished works):
Monodie; Prélude; Offrande du Saint Sacrement
(M) *** DG 471 480-2 (6). Latry (organ of Notre-Dame de Paris)

Disc 1: *L'Apparition de l'église éternelle; Le Banquet céleste; La Nativité du Seigneur (9 Méditations)* (RRC 1086)

Disc 2: *L'Ascension (4 Méditations); Les Corps glorieux (7 Visions de la vie des ressuscités)* (RRC 1087)

Discs 3–4: *Livre d'orgue* (1951); *9 Méditations sur le mystère de la Sainte Trinité; Messe de la Pentecôte* (RRC 2051) (2)

Discs 5–6: *Diptyque (Essai sur la vie terrestre); (i) Livre du Saint Sacrement; Verset pour la fête de la dédicace* (RRC 2052) (2)

🔴 ✿ (B) *** Regis RRC 6001 (6). Bate (organ of Cathedral of Saint Pierre, Beauvais, or (i) L'Eglise de la Sainte-Trinité, Paris)

Volume 1: *Apparition de l'église éternelle; Le Banquet céleste; La Nativité du Seigneur*
(M) *** Priory PRCD 921. Weir

Volume 2: *Méditations sur le mystère de la Sainte Trinité*
(M) *** Priory PRCD 922. Weir

Volume 3: *Les Corps glorieux; Messe de la Pentecôte*
(M) *** Priory PRCD 923. Weir

Volume 4: *L'Ascension; Livre d'orgue*
(M) *** Priory PRDC 924. Weir

Volumes 5 & 6: *Livre du Saint Sacrement. Early Pieces: Diptyque; Monodie; Offrande au Saint Sacrement; Prélude; Verset pour la Fête de la Dédicace*
(M) *** Priory Double PRDC 925/6. Weir

'C'est vraiment parfait!' said Messiaen after hearing Jennifer Bate's recording of *La Nativité du Seigneur*, one of his most extended, most beautiful and most moving works, with the nine movements each hypnotically compelling in their atmospheric commentaries on the Nativity story. But the composer also gave his imprimatur to every one of these recordings, all but one of which were made between 1979 and 1981 on the Beauvais organ, endorsing the performances with great enthusiasm. He then sent Jennifer Bate the manuscript of his last masterpiece, *Livre du Saint Sacrement*, which she premièred at Westminster Cathedral in 1986 and went on to record at Sainte-Trinité in 1987. Of the other pieces, *Le Banquet céleste* and *Diptyque* are both early works, the former already intense in its religious feeling, the latter dedicated to Messiaen's teachers, Dukas and Dupré.

While much of this music is meditative, imbued with mysticism, *L'Apparition* builds directly to a great central climax, then recedes, while *L'Ascension* is in four movements specifically inspired by religious texts, joyfully proclaiming, in turn, the majesty of Christ and the serenity of heaven. The *Messe de la Pentecôte* brings together most tellingly the three principal elements of Messiaen's style – plainsong, birdsong and his own rich brand of harmony – in a particularly satisfying combination. The recordings were superbly engineered by the late Bob Auger and are all in the demonstration bracket, but the final disc is perhaps the most spectacular of

all. Jennifer Bate is completely at home in Messiaen's sound-world and readily identifies with the religious experience which has inspired all of the composer's organ music. In every way this inexpensive reissue of recordings originally made by Unicorn is definitive, marking the tenth anniversary of the composer's death. At the moment RRC 1086 and RRC 2052 are the only CDs available separately.

Gillian Weir's magnificently recorded coverage of Messiaen's organ music dates from 1994. It was recorded on the superb organ of Aarhus Cathedral, Denmark, in association with BBC Radio 3, and was originally issued on Collins – to be withdrawn only too swiftly when that label disappeared. On its original issue it received an extraordinary number of accolades, both for Gillian Weir's astonishing virtuosity and control, and indeed for the demonstration quality of the recording. Now it returns on Priory, and its excellence is confirmed. Like Jennifer Bate, Weir was a personal friend and confidante of the composer, and the authority and conviction of her playing shines out through the entire project: its concentration and power are immediately apparent in the opening *Apparition de l'église éternelle*, while *Le Banquet céleste* and the remarkably diverse *Le Corps glorieux* show the strength of her characterization. Only in the *Méditations sur le mystère de la Sainte Trinité* does one feel that, although she still holds the music in a firm grip, her approach is a little static. But this remains very compelling, if only for the rich and sometimes piquant palette of sound she commands on her Danish organ. The records are available individually at mid-price (with the fourth and fifth discs together, treated as a double), whereas Bate's recording is on the budget Regis label (see our main volume). But Gillian Weir's set is in every way a recommendable alternative, and it is well documented, including her personal reminiscences of the composer.

Three of the five early works (several only recently discovered), which have been added to Volume 6, were recorded as recently as 2003.

Olivier Latry's survey is also distinguished and is very well recorded indeed in Notre-Dame. The result has great atmosphere, especially effective in conveying the composer's spiritual mysticism which is at the heart of Latry's essentially thoughtful interpretations. Jennifer Bate is more vividly extrovert and this is clear when comparing the two accounts of *La Nativité du Seigneur*, which also demonstrates the special suitability of the Beauvais organ. Both approaches are valid, of course, and the DG set has the advantage of offering some more unpublished items. But it is offered on six mid-priced CDs, whereas Bate's Regis reissue is in the budget range.

L'Apparition de l'église éternelle; L'Ascension (4 Méditations); Le Banquet céleste; Le Corps glorieux (7 Visions de la vie des ressuscités); Diptyque (Essai sur la vie terrestre et l'éternité religieuse); Livre d'Orgue (Reprises par interversion; Première pièce en trio; Les Mains de l'abîme; Chants des oiseaux; Deuxième pièce en trio; Les Yeux dans les roues; Soixante-quatre durées). Messe de la Pentecôte; La Nativité du Seigneur (9 Méditations)
(M) *** EMI mono 7 67400-2 (4). Composer (Cavaillé-Coll organ of L'Eglise de la Sainte-Trinité, Paris)

In an intensive series of sessions which began at the end of May and continued through June and July of 1956, Olivier Messiaen returned to the organ in Sainte-Trinité, with which all his music is associated, and recorded everything he had written and published before that date. These performances not only carry the imprint of the composer's authority but also the inspiration of the occasion. The large-scale works have a concentration and compelling atmosphere that are unforgettable. No apologies at all need be made for the range, breadth and faithfulness of the recording, although some must be made for the organ itself, which is not always perfectly tuned. There is minor background hiss, which is not troublesome, and technically the CD transfers are a remarkable achievement.

VOCAL MUSIC

Cinq Rechants; O sacrum convivium
(N) *** HM HMC 901834. RIAS Kammerchor, Reuss –
  MARTIN: *Mass for Double Choir; Songs of Ariel* ***

The *Cinq Rechants* or 'Refrains' of 1948 is the last element in Messiaen's so-called Tristan trilogy, which includes *Turangalila*. It is his last *a cappella* work, and he thought of it as one of his very finest. It embraces elements of Peruvian folksong, the *alba* or dawn songs of the troubadours and the chansons of Claude le Jeune, as well as Indian rhythms. The Berlin Choir meet its formidable vocal demands with a performance of remarkable virtuosity, and add a serene account of the earlier *O sacrum convivium*. Superb and responsive singing throughout.

La Transfiguration de Notre-Seigneur Jésus-Christ
⌕ ✪ *** DG 471 569-2 (2). Instrumental soloists, R. France
  Ch. & PO, Chung

(i) *La Transfiguration de Notre-Seigneur Jésus-Christ;* (ii)
Réveil des oiseaux
(N) **(*) Häns. CD 93.078 (2). (i) SWR SO, Baden-Baden &
  Freiburg, Cambreling; (ii) Loriod, Rosbaud

La Transfiguration de Notre-Seigneur Jésus-Christ is an extraordinary work, on the largest scale, which gathers together everything with which we associate Messiaen: intangible mysticism, the power of light (here the blinding light shining on Christ's transfigured face), a sense of endless space and of eternity, balanced by the realism and vitality of the everyday world as embodied in birdsong. It is a remarkable conception structured in 14 sections, offering sounds that are ethereal, sensuous, bizarre and always uniquely imaginative. At the centre is the choir, celestial and sensuous, and with them and the orchestra is a vast array of percussion instruments, and of course the piano we associate with the composer's wife. The performance here is outstanding in every way. Myung-Whun Chung has shown how deeply sympathic he is to the composer's sound-world and this is undoubtedly his finest recording. The DG engineers have responded to this sonic galaxy to produce a wonderfully spacious recording to match.
  Cambreling's recording of *La Transfiguration* is very spectacular indeed, with the percussion condiment extremely vivid and sharply defined. But the effect of the DG set under Chung is that bit more atmospheric and spacious, so the DG version remains a clear primary choice, even though the Hänssler issue also includes Yvonne Loriod's definitive account of *Réveil des oiseaux*, which was recorded at the première in 1953 in remarkably clear and vivid mono sound.

OPERA

Saint François d'Assise (complete)
*** DG 445 176-2 (4). Van Dam, Upshaw, Aler, Krause,
  Arnold Schoenberg Ch., Hallé O, Nagano

It was a labour of love over a full eight years, writing this massive four-hour opera. The live recording, made in the Felsenreitschule in Salzburg during the 1998 Festival, is astonishingly vivid, with voices and orchestra clear and immediate but with ample bloom in the helpful acoustic. The discs actually improve on the live experience, not only in the extra clarity but in the audibility of words, with the libretto an extra help in following the measured progress of a work that tells the story of St Francis in eight tableaux that fight shy of conventional dramatic design, predominantly meditative at measured speeds. In such a performance as this the result is magnetic, with Nagano drawing inspired playing from the Hallé, with José van Dam masterly in the title-role and Dawn Upshaw radiant in the role of the Angel. The rest of the cast is comparably strong. Messiaen himself regarded this as his greatest achievement, a synthesis of what he represented musically and a supreme expression of his Catholic faith. His characteristic use of birdsong here reaches its zenith – aptly so with such a subject – when in his hypnotic patterning he claims to have used every example he had ever notated.

MEYER, Edgar (born 1960)

Violin Concerto
*** Sony SK 89029. Hahn, St Paul CO, Wolff – BARBER:
  Violin Concerto ***

Edgar Meyer wrote this *Violin Concerto* specially for Hilary Hahn, providing an unusual but apt coupling for the Barber *Concerto*, equally an example of American late romanticism. Unashamedly tonal and freely lyrical, it opens with a yearning folk-like melody that echoes Vaughan Williams, and there is also a folk-like pentatonic cut to some of the writing in both of the two substantial movements. The first is a free set of variations, leading to a virtuoso exercise in using a persistent pedal note, while avoiding monotony. The second movement, in clearly defined sections, easily erupts at times into a rustic dance, and ends on a dazzling coda. Hahn plays with passionate commitment, amply justifying her choice of coupling.

MEYERBEER, Giacomo (1791–1864)

Les Patineurs (ballet suite; arr. & orch. Lambert)
✪ **(N)** *** Australian Decca Eloquence (ADD) 476 2742.
  Israel PO, Martinon – DVORAK: *Slavonic Dances;* MASSENET:
  Le Cid Ballet Music *** ✪

This 1958 coupling of Meyerbeer and Massenet was justly famous in its day. The sheer vividness of the opening number, with its growling cellos, the swagger of the string rhythms and the thundering timpani strokes, are still startling – and praise be: the CD transfer is superb. No less astonishing is the quality of the playing, with Martinon inducing the Israeli orchestra to catch the full inflexion of the French ballet style: the performance overflows with colour, and the tunes come tumbling out, bursting with *joie de vivre*.

Il Crociato in Egitto (complete)

*** Opera Rara (ADD) OR 10 (4). Kenny, Montague, D. Jones, Ford, Kitchen, Benelli, Platt, Geoffrey Mitchell Ch., RPO, Parry

This was the sixth and last opera which Meyerbeer wrote for Italy. The musical invention may not often be very distinctive, but the writing is consistently lively, notably in the ensembles. With one exception – Ian Platt, ill-focused in the role of the Sultan – the cast is a strong one, with Diana Montague outstanding in the castrato role of the Crusader-Knight, Armando. Della Jones, too, in the mezzo role of Felicia, whom Armando has abandoned in favour of Palmide, the Sultan's daughter, sings superbly, with agile coloratura and a rich chest register. Yvonne Kenny is brilliant as Palmide. Bruce Ford, with his firm, heroic tone, and Ugo Benelli are very well contrasted in the two tenor roles. Though the chorus is small, the recording is clear and fresh.

Les Huguenots (complete)

(M) *** Decca (ADD) 430 549-2 (4). Sutherland, Vrenios, Bacquier, Arroyo, Tourangeau, Ghiuselev, New Philh. O, Bonynge

Sutherland is predictably impressive, though once or twice there are signs of a 'beat' in the voice, previously unheard on Sutherland records. The rest of the cast is uneven, and in an unusually episodic opera, with passages that are musically less than inspired, that brings disappointments. Gabriel Bacquier and Nicola Ghiuselev are fine in their roles and, though Martina Arroyo is below her best as Valentine, the star quality is unmistakable. The tenor, Anastasios Vrenios, copes with the extraordinarily high tessitura and florid diversions. Vrenios sings the notes, which is more than almost any rival could. Fine recording to match this ambitious project, well worth investigating by lovers of French opera. The work sounds newly minted on CD.

Margherita d'Anjou (complete)

(N) **(*) Opera Rara ORC 25 (2). Massis, Ford, Barcellona, Miles, Previati, LPO, Parry

Dating from 1820, *Margherita d'Anjou*, set on the Scottish borders in 1462, was a milestone in Meyerbeer's career, pointing forward not only to the last of his Italian operas, *Il Crociato in Egitto*, but to the grand historical epics of his Paris years. The heroine of the title is Margaret of Anjou, widow of Henry VI, a formidable role commandingly taken in this recording by Annick Massis. Starting with a military overture, the piece involves many lively choruses and ensembles, well controlled by David Parry, who has an excellent team. Opposite Massis as Lavarenne, Grand Senechal of Normandy, is the tenor Bruce Ford, exploiting his impressive vocal range, if sometimes with rough tone, while the mezzo Daniella Barcellona is strongly cast as Lavarenne's wife, and Alastair Miles is impressive too as the banished general, Belmonte. The full, clear sound is marred by piano continuo in recitative, set far too close.

MIASKOVSKY, Nikolay (1881–1950)

(i) *Cello Concerto; Symphony 27 in C min., Op. 85*

*** Chan. 10025. (i) Ivashkin; Russian State SO, Polyansky

At long last Miaskovsky's *Cello Concerto* is receiving the attention and recognition it deserves. Alexander Ivashkin's is an eloquent account which judges to perfection its melancholy and nobility, and the recording is very natural. As a coupling, Chandos offer the *Twenty-Seventh Symphony*, his last, completed in 1949, less than a year before he died. Yet it is a work which, far from reflecting the approach of death (he was already suffering from cancer), conveys an amiable warmth in the outer movements and a moving serenity in the lovely central slow movement, only briefly interrupted by a tender violin melody that is almost Elgarian in its nobility. It is steeped in the world of the past. Its slow movement at times seems to be wandering into the corresponding movement of Brahms's *Fourth*, while Miaskovsky paid necessary homage to his Soviet masters in the stirring march themes of the extrovert finale.

Violin Concerto

🔊 ⚫ *** Ph. 473 343-2. Repin, Kirov O, Gergiev – TCHAIKOVSKY: *Violin Concerto* ***

(BB) *** Naxos 8.557194. Grubert, Russian PO, Yablonsky – VAINBERG: *Violin Concerto* ***

Miaskovsky's *Violin Concerto* of 1939 is one of the most appealing and lyrical of all Russian concertos. Its neglect is quite unaccountable and, although it was recorded by David Oistrakh (now excellently transferred on Pearl), there has until recently been only one modern recording, by Gregor Feigin. In any event this version by Vladimir Repin and Valery Gergiev was well worth waiting for. They capture the sunny yet melancholy spirit of this wonderfully inventive score to perfection. Excellent recording and glorious music.

The Lithuanian violinist Ilya Grubert offers the Miaskovsky *Concerto* coupled enterprisingly with the Vainberg and at a remarkably competitive price. Grubert plays it with appropriate affection and grace, and he is well supported by his Russian players. At the price this must be self-recommending, and readers who have not acquired the even finer Repin version should lose no time in snapping this up.

Sinfonietta for Strings in B min., Op. 32/2; Theme & Variations; 2 Pieces, Op. 46/1; Napeve

*** ASV CDDCA 928. St Petersburg CO, Melia

The *Sinfonietta for Strings* will appeal to anyone of a nostalgic disposition. The players give an affectionate, well-prepared account of it and convey the wistful, endearing nature of the slow movement to perfection. The *Theme and Variations* (on a theme of Grieg) also has the same streak of melancholy. The first of the *Two Pieces*, Op. 46, No. 1, is a transcription and reworking for strings of the inner movements, reversing their order, of Miaskovsky's *Symphony No. 19 for Military Band*, composed in 1939. The St Petersburg Chamber Orchestra is an expert and responsive ensemble, and the ASV recording does them proud.

Symphonies (i) 1 in C min., Op. 3; (ii) 19 in E flat for Wind Band, Op. 46

**(*) Russian Disc (ADD) RDCD 11 007. (i) USSR MoC SO, Rozhdestvensky; (ii) Russian State Brass O, Sergeyev

Miaskovsky's *First Symphony* is a student work, very much in the received tradition. It is obvious from the very start that Miaskovsky was a composer who could think on a big scale. The *Nineteenth Symphony in B flat* for military band is a slighter piece, worth hearing for its inner movements, a wistful *Moderato* and a well-written *Andante*. The *First Symphony* is well played by the Ministry of Culture Orchestra under Gennady Rozhdestvensky, though the brass sound a bit raw, as indeed do the upper strings. The *Nineteenth* is played with great brio and genuine affection. The less-than-three-star recording-quality should not deter collectors from investigating this work.

Symphonies 2 in C sharp min.; 10 in F min., Op. 30
**(*) Orfeo C496991A. V. RSO, Rabl

The *Second Symphony* comes from 1912, when Miaskovsky was still a student (he turned to music at a relatively late stage), and breathes much of the same air as Scriabin, Rachmaninov and Glière (he was a pupil of the last). The *Tenth* (1927) is a more radical piece with greater contrapuntal density, which in its level of dissonance shows the influence of his lifelong friend, Prokofiev. The playing of the Austrian Radio Orchestra under Gottfried Rabl is serviceable rather than distinguished, and the recording is a bit resonant, but there are no alternative versions currently available.

Symphonies 5 in D, Op. 18; 9 in E min., Op. 28
**(*) Marco Polo 8.223499. BBC PO, Downes

The *Fifth Symphony* is a sunny, pastoral score dating from 1918, very much in the tradition of Glazunov and Glière. Downes's recording with the BBC Philharmonic, recorded in an admittedly over-resonant venue in Derby, is to be preferred both artistically and sonically to its earlier rival by the USSR Symphony Orchestra under Ivanov on Olympia (now deleted). The *Ninth Symphony* is somewhat better served than No. 5 so far as the sound is concerned. It is vintage Miaskovsky, more cogently argued and more interesting in thematic substance than the *Eighth*. Very good performances and good enough recording – just – to make three stars.

Symphony 6 in E flat min. (Revolutionary), Op. 23
*** DG 471 655-2. Gothenburg Ch. & SO, Järvi
(**(*)) Russian Disc mono RDCD 15008. Yurlov Russian Ch., USSR SO, Kondrashin

The *Sixth* is Miaskovsky's longest symphony (it takes nearly 65 minutes) and is arguably his masterpiece. The work occupied him over a two-year period (1921–3) and enjoyed spectacular success on its first performance in Moscow under Nikolai Golovanov. It encompasses a wide range of feeling and has dignity and an epic sweep reminiscent of Eisenstein. Miaskovsky subsequently re-touched its scoring and made further revisions in 1947. Neeme Järvi draws first-rate playing from the Gothenburg orchestra, and he is also helped by the celebrated acoustic of the hall and by the splendid DG recording. Järvi has a very good feel for the composer and he also uses the optional chorus in the finale. However, the 1959 Kondrashin recording had a special authority and dramatic intensity; it is still in circulation and remains a benchmark account.

Symphony 8 in A, Op. 26
** Marco Polo 8.223297. Slovak RSO (Bratislava), Stankovsky

Although the *Eighth* is not one of Miaskovsky's finest symphonies, it is still worth investigating. There are some characteristic ideas, and initially unfavourable impressions are soon dispelled as one comes closer to it. Neither the performance nor the recording is distinguished, but both are thoroughly acceptable; there is a lack of subtlety here, but not of vitality and commitment.

Symphony 12 in G min., Op. 35; Silence (symphonic poem after Poe), Op. 9
**(*) Marco Polo 8.223302. Slovak RSO (Bratislava), Stankovsky

The *Twelfth Symphony* is endearingly old-fashioned and has strong appeal. Although some of the big rhetorical gestures of the *Sixth Symphony* are to be found in the second movement, there are also some pre-echoes of things to come in the later symphonies. It is highly enjoyable, particularly when it is as well played as it is here by the Bratislava Radio Orchestra under their gifted young conductor, Robert Stankovsky. The tone-poem *Silence* draws for its inspiration on Edgar Allan Poe's *The Raven* and has a strongly atmospheric quality with a distinctly *fin-de-siècle* air: if you enjoy Rachmaninov's *Isle of the Dead*, you should investigate it. The orchestra play with enthusiasm and they are decently recorded.

Symphonies 24 in F min., Op. 63; 25 in D flat, Op. 69
(BB) *** Naxos 8.555376. Moscow PO, Yablonsky

Very worthwhile accounts of both symphonies from Dmitri Yablonsky and the Moscow Philharmonic. Yablonsky's account of *No. 25*, Miaskovsky's first post-war symphony, holds up well against Svetlanov's (coupled with *No. 1*). He is less expansive in the glorious first movement but no less heartfelt. This is particularly haunting and moving, full of the all-pervasive melancholy which is *echt*-Miaskovsky. The recording is decent and, although those collecting the Svetlanov cycle will want to complete it, those who cannot wait will find the modest outlay here well worth while.

Symphony 27 (see under *Cello Concerto*)

CHAMBER MUSIC

Cello Sonata 2 in A min., Op. 81
(M) *** Somm CD 029. Walton, Grimwood – KABALEVSKY: *Sonata in B flat*; PROKOFIEV: *Cello Sonata* ***

What a glorious work the *Second Sonata* of 1949 is! Its invention flows freely and naturally, and although the idiom was thought of as highly conservative (and it would have been for 1890, let alone the 1940s) the ideas are distinguished and have an eloquence that is most appealing. The trouble is that the opening tune is difficult to dislodge from the memory, as is the Fauréan contrasting idea. Impeccable playing from these little-known young artists, who more than repay the confidence Somm has placed in them. Good recording.

String Quartets 1 in A min., Op. 33/1; 4 in F min., Op. 33/4
(**) Russian Disc (ADD) RDCD 11013. Taneyev Qt

The *First Quartet* finds Miaskovsky more among the avant garde of Russian composers than the conservative figure he became, and it has a far higher norm of dissonance than we are used to. It is a surprisingly fascinating and powerful score. The *Fourth*, in F minor, is less challenging and more overtly lyrical and traditional in outlook. These imaginative and thought-provoking works are eminently well played, but the recording lets things down. The players are forwardly balanced, the sound is hard and vinegary and needs to be tamed above the stave. All the same, such is the interest of this disc that it must have a recommendation.

PIANO MUSIC

Piano Sonatas 6 in A flat, Op. 62/2; 7 in C, Op. 82; 8 in D min., Op. 83; 9 in F, Op. 84
(*) Marco Polo 8.223178. Hegedüs

The Marco Polo disc brings the last four sonatas. The young Hungarian pianist, Endre Hegedüs, is an imaginative interpreter: he colours the second theme of the *Barcarolle* section of the *Eighth Sonata* with great tenderness and subtlety. The sound is a little wanting in bloom.

MÍČA, Jan František Adam (1746–1811)

String Quartet 6 in C
(M) *** Cal. (ADD) 6698. Talich Qt – BOCCHERINI: *Quartet, Op. 58/2;* HAYDN: *Quartet 74;* MENDELSSOHN: *Quartet 2 ***

The Bohemian composer, Jan Míča, writes elegantly in the *galant* style, and this *C major Quartet* (his sixth) brings an enticing opening theme, then continues in a cultivated and courtly style. Throughout, the warmth and finesse of the Talich playing ensure our enjoyment of what is a slight but well-crafted little work.

MILANO, Francesco Canova da (1497–1543)

(i) *Lute duets: Canon; Fantasia quarta; Fantasia quinta; Fantasia sexta; Ricercar prima; Ricercar seconda; Ricercar terza; La spagna. Pieces for solo lute: Fantasias 30; 55–6; 63–7; 81–3; Ricercars 2; 10; 13; 69–70; 73; 76 & 79*
(BB) *** Naxos 8.550774. Wilson, (i) with Rumsey

During his lifetime Francesco Canova da Milano was known as 'Il Divino' and was, by all accounts, 'a miraculous lute player'. He was the most prolific lute composer of his day, even more so than his close contemporary, the Spanish vihuelist and composer, Luis de Milán. Christopher Wilson plays this collection of pieces, including duets with Shirley Rumsey, with a natural and unforced authority. Cultured playing of highly civilized music, recorded with admirable clarity, though it is advisable to reduce the level setting to get the most lifelike and natural result.

MILHAUD, Darius (1892–1974)

L'Apothéose de Molière, Op. 286; Le Bœuf sur le toit, Op. 58;
(i) *Le Carnaval d'Aix, Op. 83b; Le Carnaval de Londres, Op. 172*
(BB) *** Hyp. Helios CDH 55168. (i) Gibbons; New L. O, Corp

Le Carnaval d'Aix is a carefree work, full of high spirits, and is very expertly played by Jack Gibbons and the New London Orchestra under Ronald Corp. They also convey the Satie-like circus-music character of *Le Bœuf sur le toit* to excellent effect. What delightful music this is, and so expertly fashioned by this lovable composer. The Molière pastiche and the arrangement of melodies from *The Beggar's Opera* are not top-drawer Milhaud, but they are still worth having. Very good recording from the Hyperion team.

(i) *Ballade for Piano and Orchestra; Piano Concerto 4, Op. 295;* (ii) *Symphonies 4, Op. 281; 8 in D (Rhôdanienne), Op. 362*
(BB) *** Warner Apex 0927 49982-2. (i) Helffer, O Nat. de France, Robertson; (ii) Fr. R. & TV PO, composer

An immensely valuable budget reissue. The *Ballade* (1920) was composed for Roussel, and Milhaud made his piano début at its première in New York: its languorous opening seems to hark back to his days in Brazil. The *Fourth Piano Concerto* (1949), written for the virtuoso, Sadel Zkolowsky, is an inventive piece of some substance, with a particularly imaginative and evocative slow movement. Claude Helffer is an admirable exponent of both works, and he and David Robertson readily catch the music's special atmosphere.

The *Fourth Symphony* was commissioned by French Radio in commemoration of the centenary of the 1848 uprising and revolution, and its four movements offer a vivid portrayal of those events. It is scored for unusually large forces, including two saxophones and a vast array of percussion, all heard to good effect in the first movement, which depicts the uprising with massive polytonal and dissonant clashes; the second laments the fallen, the third describes liberty rediscovered, and the finale is almost festive. The *Eighth Symphony*, written in the late 1950s for a new concert hall at the University of California, is subtitled *Rhôdanienne* and evokes the course of the river Rhône from its beginnings in the Alps down to the Carmargue. Rich in instrumental resource, it is full of imaginative colours and textures, and the playing of the Orchestre Philharmonique de l'ORTF for Milhaud himself is absolutely first rate. These performances date from 1968, and the sound is much cleaned up for this CD, which commands an unqualified recommendation.

Le Bœuf sur le toit, Op. 58; La Création du monde, Op. 81
*** Chan. 9023. Ulster O, Y. P. Tortelier – IBERT: *Divertissement;* POULENC: *Les Biches ***

Le Bœuf sur le toit; La Création du monde; (i) *L'Homme et son désir. Suite provençale*
(N) (BB) *** Naxos 8.557287. Lille Nat. O, Casadesus; (i) with Makuuchi, Zhao, Vidal, Deletre

(i) *Le Bœuf sur le toit;* (ii) *La Création du monde;* (iii) *Saudades do Brasil; Suite provençale;* (iv) *Scaramouche (for 2 pianos)*
(***) EMI mono/stereo 7 54604-2. (i) Champs-Elysées Theatre O; (ii) Ens. of 19 soloists; (iii) Concert Arts O, composer; (iv) Meyer, composer

The Naxos issue, vividly recorded, makes an ideal Milhaud collection, surveying a wide range of his long career. It includes his two most popular works, the ballets *Le Bœuf sur le toit* (1919) and *La Création du monde*, both reflecting his dalliance with jazz and the music of South America. Jean-Claude Casadesus conducts the Lille orchestra in warmly idiomatic performances which combine refinement with rhythmic bite. The rarity is an even earlier ballet, *L'Homme et son désir*, written in 1917–18 to a scenario by Paul Claudel, set in the primeval Amazonian forest. The exotic scoring is for solo wind and strings, with a very large percussion section and four solo voices singing wordlessly. The atmospheric colours of the piece are brilliantly caught, with the eight brief movements of the *Suite provençale* as an attractive make-weight, taken in 1936 from incidental music to a play.

A most engaging account of *Le Bœuf sur le toit* from Yan Pascal Tortelier and his Ulster players, full of colourful detail, admirably flexible and infectiously rhythmic. Perhaps *La Création du monde* is without the degree of plangent jazzy emphasis of a French performance, but its gentle, desperate melancholy is well caught, and the playing has plenty of colour and does not lack rhythmic subtlety. The Chandos recording, although resonant, is splendid in every other respect, and so are the couplings.

Milhaud's own account of *La Création du monde* has a certain want of abandon but is otherwise well played, and this *Scaramouche* has an altogether special charm. The Capitol mono LP coupling of the captivating *Suite provençale* and the carefree and catchy *Saudades do Brasil* now appears for the first time in stereo, sounding very sprightly indeed. The 'Concert Arts' orchestra respond to the composer with evident delight, and they make this a most desirable issue. In addition there is *Le Bœuf sur le toit* that Milhaud made with a Champs-Elysées orchestra in 1958, which makes a welcome makeweight to an altogether delightful issue. However, it was curmudgeonly of EMI to put the disc in the full-price range.

(i; ii) *Le Carnaval d'Aix;* (ii) *Suite provençale; Suite française;* (iii) *Le Bal martiniquais;* (i; iii; iv) *Paris;* (iii) *Scaramouche*

(BB) **(*) EMI Encore (ADD). 5 74740-2. (i) Béroff; (ii) Monte Carlo PO, Prêtre; (iii) Ivaldi & Lee; (iv) with Collard

It is difficult to understand why Milhaud's *Le Carnaval d'Aix* does not enjoy greater popularity. It has immense charm and an engaging, easy-going Mediterranean sense of gaiety that never ceases to captivate. However, the present account proves something of a disappointment. Béroff rattles off the solo part without a trace of charm and without the tenderness that is at times called for. It comes here with the endearing *Suite provençale* and *Suite française* as companions, but the orchestral playing under Prêtre is fairly brash too, and the digital sound does not help very much either: it is inclined to be dry and close.

The charming music for two and four pianos fares much better. *Scaramouche* is the best-known piece and is extremely well played by Christian Ivaldi and Noël Lee, and they are joined by Béroff and Collard in the eight-handed *Paris* (for four pianos!). The recording here is fresh and lively. For all one's reservations this disc is worth its modest cost.

(i; ii) *Concertino de printemps* (2 versions); (iii) *Piano Concerto;* (ii) *Violin Concerto 2;* (iv) *Suite française;* (v) *Scaramouche* (suite for 2 pianos)

(BB) (***) Dutton mono CDBP 9711. (i) Astruc with O; (ii) Kaufman, French R. O (members); (iii) Long, O Nat. de France; NYPO; all cond. composer; (v) Sellick and Smith

Milhaud regarded melody 'as the only living element in music' and turned all his resources to the expression of melodic ideas, often spring-like in their freshness and charm. No more so than in the vivacious *Concertino de printemps* which, in a Dutton scoop, is given here, first in its brilliant (1933) première recording by Yvone Astruc, and also in an even more breathtaking later version (1949), dazzlingly played by Louis Kaufman. Yet both performances reveal the music's underlying expressive nostalgia, and this is found again in the 'Slow and sombre' middle movement of the *Second Violin Concerto,* which Kaufman also plays superbly, delivering the finale with sparkling virtuosity. He is recorded closely but truthfully.

Marguerite Long (in 1935) scintillates in the small-scale *Piano Concerto,* and the composer delivers the full bonhomie

of the *Suite française,* even if here the dated New York recording is brash and two-dimensional. For the most part, however, the splendid Dutton transfers make one forget the early provenance of these always vivid recordings. The performance of *Scaramouche* by Cyril Smith and Phyllis Sellick is unsurpassed, with the light-hearted Brazilian syncopations of the finale especially infectious, and here the 1948 Abbey Road recording sounds very realistic.

La Création du monde

🎵 (B) *** Virgin 2 CD 5 62050-2 (2). Lausanne CO, Zedda – DEBUSSY: *Danse; Sarabande* ***; PROKOFIEV: *Symphony 1 (Classical)* ***; SHOSTAKOVICH: *Chamber Symphony; Symphony 14* **

Milhaud's ballet, with its mixture of yearning melancholy and jazzy high spirits, comes off splendidly in Alberto Zedda's highly spontaneous account, its witty syncopations and brassy exuberance bringing an unbridled effervescence to offset the restrained blues feeling of the main lyrical theme. The performance does not miss the Gershwin affinities, and the very vivid recording makes a bold dynamic contrast between the work's tender and abrasive moments. It is a pity that this CD was not reissued separately instead of in harness with Shostakovich.

(i) *La Création du monde;* (ii) *Concertino de printemps;* (iii) *Piano Concerto 1;* (iv) *Suite française;* (v) *6 Chants populaires hebraïques;* (vi) *String Quartet 7 in B flat*

(***) Pearl mono GEM 0124. (i) O of 19 soloists, composer; (ii) Astruc, composer; (iii) Long, O. Nat.; (iv) NYPO, composer; (v) Martial Singher, composer (piano); (vi) Galimir Qt

Most of these performances are familiar from earlier transfers: both the *Concertino de printemps* and *La Création du monde* appeared on an earlier Pearl disc devoted to Milhaud and Honegger, and the *Seventh String Quartet,* which Milhaud supervised, appeared recently together with the Galimir Quartet's only other commercial records: the Berg *Lyric Suite* and the Ravel *Quartet* on Rockport. *La Création du monde* was recorded in 1931, the *Suite française* in 1946 and the remainder in the early 1930s in a rather dry studio acoustic. All the same, this has great period flavour and is an indispensable part of the Milhaud discography.

L'Homme et son désir

**(*) Calliope CAL 9526. Schmidt, Brua, Claessens, Fr. R. Ch., O de Picardie, Colomer – HONEGGER: *La Danse des morts* **(*)

L'Homme et son désir proves a logical make-weight for Honegger's *La Danse des morts.* It is here recorded in the version for soloists, 16 instruments and percussion, and is well performed and truthfully recorded.

Symphonies 1 (1939); 2 (1944); Suite provençale

⏺ (M) *** DG 476 2197. Toulouse Capitole O, Plasson

In the inter-war years Milhaud was known for his little three-minute symphonies, and it was not until he was in his late forties that he embarked on a full-scale essay in the form. This was in response to a commission from the Chicago Symphony Orchestra, and he subsequently recorded the work with the Columbia Broadcast Orchestra in the early days of LP. Those who possess that disc or the LP of the *Second* made by Georges Tzipine will not only know how richly imaginative, melodically inventive and rewarding these scores are;

they will also be puzzled as to why they have not entered the repertoire. Sample the fourth movement, *Avec sérénité*, of the *Second* and you will see just how sunny, relaxed and easy-going this music is; try also the slow movement of the *First* for its powerful, nocturnal atmosphere. The Orchestre du Capitole de Toulouse and Michel Plasson play these melodious scores with total commitment, and they convey their pleasure in rediscovering this music. The recording is very natural, with a refined tone and well-balanced perspective, by far the most successful sound to have been captured in the Salle-aux-Grains by any engineering team to date. The delightful *Suite provençale* is as good as a holiday in the south of France – and cheaper! It is now available at mid-price for the first time as one of Universal's 'Penguin ✿ Collection'.

Symphonies 2, Op. 247; (i) 3 (Te Deum), Op. 271
(BB) *** CPO 999 540-2. (i) Basel Theatre Ch.; Basel RSO, Francis

The central slow movement of the *Second Symphony* conveys some of the grief of the war years, but elsewhere (particularly in the captivating fourth movement) the carefree atmosphere that distinguishes Milhaud's music and its Mediterranean light are much in evidence. The *Third* (1946) was commissioned by the French Radio to celebrate victory over the Nazis. Particularly effective is the atmospheric slow movement with its wordless chorus. Good performances and a natural and well-balanced recording that holds its own with rival versions.

Symphonies 7, Op. 344; 8 (Rhôdanienne), Op. 362; 9, Op. 380
*** CPO 999 166-2. Basel RSO, Francis

Alun Francis makes sense of the slow movement of the *Seventh*, holding it together at a realistic tempo. It is a powerful and often searching movement, even if there is a fair amount of note-spinning in its companions. For that matter, so there is in the *Ninth*, though it begins splendidly with a short and lively *Modérément animé*. If the *Eighth Symphony* is full of colour, the scoring is also open to the charge of being a bit too dense. The Basel Radio Orchestra is a far from second-rate ensemble and in the *Seventh Symphony* hold up well.

CHAMBER MUSIC

La Cheminée du Roi René
(***) BBC mono BBCL 4066-2. Dennis Brain Wind Quintet (with instrumental recital (***))

The account by the Dennis Brain Wind Quintet of Milhaud's *Cheminée du Roi René*, with its pastiche Provençal flavour, is sheer delight, making it seem like a minor masterpiece. How beguiling are the *Aubade*, *La Maousinglade* and the finale, a *Madrigal-nocturne*. The sound too has a pleasing ambient glow.

Duo for 2 Violins, Op. 243; (i) Sonata for 2 Violins & Piano, Op. 15
**(*) Hyp. CDA 66473. Osostowicz, Kovacic, (i) with Tomes
– MARTINU: *Violin Sonata* **(*); PROKOFIEV: *Violin Sonata* ***

The *Sonata for Two Violins and Piano* of 1914 is beautifully crafted and has a charming slow movement but is very slight. Not as slight, though, as the *Duo*, the first two movements of which were composed at a dinner party; the finale was written the following morning. Elegant performances from

Krysia Osostowicz and Ernst Kovacic and, in the *Sonata*, Susan Tomes.

Music for wind: *La Cheminée du Roi René, Op. 105; Divertissement en trois parties, Op. 399b; Pastorale, Op. 47; 2 Sketches, Op. 227b; Suite d'après Corrette, Op. 161b*
(M) **(*) Chan. 6536. Athena Ens., McNichol

Though none of this is first-class Milhaud, it is still full of pleasing and attractive ideas, and the general air of easy-going, life-loving enjoyment is well conveyed by the alert playing of the Athena Ensemble. One's only quarrel is with the somewhat close balance.

String Quartets 1, Op. 5; 7 in B flat, Op. 87; 10, Op. 218; 16, Op. 303
*** Cybella CY 804. Aquitaine Nat. Qt

The *Seventh Quartet* speaks Milhaud's familiar, distinctive language; its four short movements are delightful, full of melody and colour. The *Tenth*, too, is attractive; the *Sixteenth* was a wedding anniversary present for his wife: its first movement has great tenderness and warmth. The Aquitaine Quartet have excellent ensemble, intonation is good and their playing is polished. The recording has a wide dynamic range and a spacious tonal spectrum.

String Quartets 5, Op. 64; 8, Op. 121; 11, Op. 232; 13, Op. 268
*** Cybella CY 805. Aquitaine Nat. Qt

The *Fifth Quartet* is not one of Milhaud's most inspired; the *Eighth*, on the other hand, has much to commend it, including a poignant slow movement. No. 11 has a splendid pastoral third movement and a lively jazzy finale; No. 13 has overtones of Mexico in its finale and a beguiling and charming *Barcarolle*. Both performance and recording are very good.

PIANO MUSIC

Music for 2 pianos: *Le Bal martiniquais, Op. 249; Le Bœuf sur le toit, Op. 58a; Carnaval à la Nouvelle-Orléans, Op. 275; Kentuckiana, Op. 287; La libertadora, Op. 236; Scaramouche, Op. 165b; Songes, Op. 237*
⊙-- *** Hyp. CDA 67014. Coombs, Pizarro

Hyperion assemble the bulk of Milhaud's music for two pianos from the popular and irresistible *Scaramouche* through to the duet arrangement of *Le Bœuf sur le toit*. An entertaining and delightful issue which brings some high-spirited pianism from these fine players and very good recorded sound.

MINKUS, Léon (1826–1917)

La Bayadère (complete; arr. Lanchbery)
*** Decca 436 917-2 (2). ECO, Bonynge

Lanchbery has provided the present score, and though officially he is responsible only for the orchestration, who knows, perhaps he also had a hand in its content, as in his vintage arrangement of Hérold's *La Fille mal gardée*. Whatever the case, the result is highly engaging. Unlike Adam's rather disappointing *Le Corsaire* (also recorded by the same forces), this work is full of attractive melody and sparkling orchestral effects. If you like late-nineteenth-century ballet music, then here is nearly two hours of it, played with much vivacity, elegance and drama, and given Decca's top-quality sound.

Don Quixote (ballet; original, 1869 version)
(BB) **(*) Naxos 8.557065/66 (2). Sofia Nat. Op. O, Todorov

As one would expect from a ballet by Minkus, *Don Quixote* is full of lively dances and attractive melodies, all of it well crafted and colourfully orchestrated, if without the genius of Tchaikovsky and Delibes. That said, it makes for undemanding, entertaining listening, with its dashes of Spanish colouring (the Spanish dances are especially attractive) and plenty of character dances, such as the *Sailor's Dance* in Act II, to enjoy. The performance is lively and sympathetic and the recording reasonably good (it lacks a certain richness), but they do not quite possess the flair which Bonynge and Decca brought to this repertoire. At the price, admirers of both light music and ballet should not hesitate: there is plenty to enjoy here.

MOERAN, Ernest J. (1894–1950)

(i) *Cello Concerto;* (ii; iii) *Violin Concerto;* (iii) *2 Pieces for Small Orchestra: Lonely Waters; Whythorne's Shadow*
〜 (M) *** Chan. 10168X. (i) Wallfisch, Bournemouth Sinf., Del Mar; (ii) Mordkovitch; (iii) Ulster O, Handley

The *Cello Concerto* (1945) is a pastoral work with elegiac overtones, save in its rather folksy finale. Raphael Wallfisch brings an eloquence of tone and a masterly technical address to this neglected piece, and he receives very responsive orchestral support from Norman Del Mar and the Bournemouth players. The *Violin Concerto* is also strongly lyrical in feeling. The first movement is thoughtful and rhapsodic, its inspiration drawn from Moeran's love of the west coast of Ireland; the middle movement makes use of folk music; while the finale, a ruminative elegy of great beauty, is the most haunting of the three. Lydia Mordkovitch plays with great natural feeling for this music and, quite apart from his sensitive support in the *Concerto*, Vernon Handley gives an outstanding account of *Lonely Waters*. Superb recording.

This a straight reissue of an outstanding coupling with the original superb recording sounding better than ever.

In the Mountain Country; Rhapsodies 1–2; Serenade in G; (i) *Nocturne*
(N) (M) *** Chan. 10235X. Ulster O, Handley, (i) with Mackey, Renaissance Singers – WARLOCK: *Capriol Suite*, etc. ***

The *Serenade in G* has a good deal in common with Warlock's *Capriol Suite*. Both use dance forms from a previous age and transform them with new colours and harmonic touches. Handley and the Ulster Orchestra present it with striking freshness and warmth in its original version. *In the Mountain Country* and the pair of *Rhapsodies* (the *First* Holstian in its quirky rhythms and colourful brass, the *Second* Irish in inflexion with a memorable main tune) are unashamedly folk-inspired and have great vitality and lyrical appeal. The *Nocturne*, a setting of a poem by Robert Nichols for baritone and eight-part chorus, much admired by Britten, receives a wholly sympathetic performance and recording here, and the resonant acoustics of the Ulster Hall, Belfast, provide a warmly atmospheric ambient glow.

(i) *Symphony in G min.; Lonely Waters; Whythorne's Shadow;* (ii) *Violin Sonata in E min.*
(N) (B) ** EMI (ADD) 5 85154-2. (i) E. Sinfonia, Dilkes; (ii) O'Grady, Lynch

Dilkes's fine, lusty performances of Moeran's eclectic but at the same time individually inspired symphony is not quite as powerful as the best versions around (especially Handley's Chandos account). With a relatively small band of strings, recorded quite closely, the sound is vivid and immediate, if lacking a little in atmosphere. But the reading remains a satisfying one, and it certainly does not lack urgency. The two lovely orchestral miniatures are most beautifully played and recorded and are well worth hearing. For this new British Composers issue, EMI have added the *Violin Sonata*. It is a good, fresh performance, but Mordkovitch on Chandos has far greater warmth and finds more colour in this score: the opening here is disconcertingly fast compared to the Chandos version, though it works as an overall concept. As Chandos now offer their Moeran recordings at mid-price, this is not quite the bargain it would once have been.

Symphony in G min.; Overture for a Masque; (i) *Rhapsody for Piano & Orchestra*
〜 (M) *** Chan. 10169X. (i) Fingerhut; Ulster O, Handley

Symphony in G min.; Sinfonietta
〜 (BB) *** Naxos 8.555837. Bournemouth SO, Lloyd Jones

Built confidently on strikingly memorable ideas, Moeran's *G minor Symphony*, first heard in 1937, is among the most attractive British symphonies of the period. To meet the competition from Naxos, Chandos have reissued at mid-price Vernon Handley's compelling performance with the exuberant, syncopated *Overture* thrown in for good measure. An outstanding disc in every way, with superb recording sounding better than ever.

The Naxos version, warmly and idiomatically conducted by David Lloyd Jones, could hardly be more persuasive, well played by the Bournemouth orchestra and treated to a full-range recording, with transparent textures bringing out the fine detail of the orchestration. The jolly, vigorous *Sinfonietta*, equally well played, makes an apt coupling. In the *Symphony*, Handley might be marginally more bitingly powerful, but this new version has a considerable price advantage and is certainly not second best.

Fantasy Quartet for Oboe & Strings
*** Chan. 8392. Francis, English Qt – BAX: *Quintet;* HOLST: *Air & Variations,* etc.; JACOB: *Quartet* ***

Moeran's folk-influenced *Fantasy Quartet,* an attractively rhapsodic single-movement work, is played admirably here, and the recording is excellent, well balanced too.

(i) *Fantasy Quartet for Oboe & Strings;* (ii) *String Quartet 2 in A min.;* (iii) *Violin Sonata*
(M) *** Chan. 10170X. (i) Francis, English String Qt (members); (ii) Melbourne Qt; (iii) Scott, Talbot

Sarah Francis's admirable account with the English String Quartet of Moeran's *Fantasy Quartet* is here re-coupled with the *String Quartet in A minor* of 1921, together with the more intense and forward-looking *Violin Sonata* (written a year later). The performance from Donald Scott and John Talbot is full of rough-hewn energy, with plenty of contrast in the central *Lento*. While the Maggini–Naxos coupling with the earlier *E flat Quartet* is more logical, the Chandos disc is very attractive in its own right.

String Quartets 1 in E flat; 2 in A min.; String Trio
〜 (BB) *** Naxos 8.554079. Maggini Qt

The *String Quartet in A minor* (1921) has a certain pastoral quality, with Irish echoes in the dance rhythms and ending on a flamboyant Rondo. The *String Trio* of 1931, beautifully written with no feeling of thinness, is even subtler, with the pastoral idiom more equivocal in its tonal shiftings. The Naxos CD also offers something of a discovery in the form of an earlier *Quartet in E flat*. Although it is not a masterpiece, there are some quite inspired things in it and the Maggini play throughout with great dedication and commitment. The recording is very life-like and present. A first-class bargain.

COMPLETE PIANO MUSIC

Bank Holiday; 3 Fancies (Windmills; Elegy; Burlesque); 2 Legends (Folk Story; Rune); On a May Morning; 3 Pieces (The Lake Island; Autumn Woods; At a Horse Fair); 2 Pieces (Prelude; Berceuse); Stalham River; Summer Valley; Theme and Variations; Toccata. Trad. arr. Moeran: Irish Love Song; The White Mountain
*** ASV CDDCA 1138. Hunt

Moeran was born in Middlesex but was buried in County Kerry in his beloved Ireland. Much of this music is unashamedly folksy. *Bank Holiday*, which opens the programme genially, 'tips its hat' to Percy Grainger, but most of the pieces are evocative and atmospheric, even the arrangement of the Irish tune, best known as 'Star of the County Down', which he called *The White Mountain*. The other arrangement, *Irish Love Song*, is simpler, a lovely melody which was later to become an *Irish Lament* for cello and piano. *On a May Morning* opens dreamily but has a lively central dance; on the other hand, the iridescent *Toccata* has a soft centre. *Summer Valley*, in lilting 6/8, has a Delian air. The most ambitious piece here is the *Theme and* (six) *Variations*. The theme is reminiscent of another folk tune, the variations flow into each other naturally and the work is in some ways more like a Fantasia. Fine, sensitive performances throughout from Una Hunt, well recorded. Generous measure too (77 minutes): a delightful disc to dip into rather than play all through.

MOLINO, Francesco (1775–1847)

Trio, Op. 45
*** Mer. CDE 84199. Conway, Silverthorne, Garcia –
BEETHOVEN: *Serenade*; JOSEPH KREUTZER: *Grand Trio*
***

Italian-born, Molino first settled in Spain before going on to London and Paris, where he built a reputation as a violinist and guitarist. Undemanding music to complete a charming disc for a rare combination. First-rate playing and recording.

MOMPOU, Federico (1893–1987)

COMPLETE PIANO MUSIC

Canciónes y danzas 1–12, 14; Cants Mágics; Chanson de berceuse; Charmes; Dialogues; Fêtes lointaines; Impresiones intimas; Musica callada, Books 1–4; Pessebres; Préludes; Scènes d'enfants; Souvenirs de l'Exposistion; Surburbis; 3 Variations; Variations sur un thème de Chopin
(B) **(*) Nim. NI 5724/7 (4). M. Jones

Martin Jones has already given us some fine recordings, including a first-rate set of the piano music of Percy Grainger.

Now he turns to another miniaturist. Born in Barcelona, Mompou studied in Paris and his music is a fascinating mixture of Catalan and French influences, though in its colouring and textures the French influence is strong. There are plenty of fine individual CDs of this composer's music, but for collectors who want to explore the entire repertoire, Jones is a sound guide, at home in its diverse moods and colours. One feels at times he could be more chimerical and seek more translucent textures, but his simplicity of approach is a plus point and, with truthful recording, this can certainly be recommended to musical explorers.

Canciónes y danzas 1–12; 14; Cants mágics; Suburbis
(BB) *** Warner Apex 8573 89228-2. Heisser

Jean-François Heisser displays a natural sympathy for Mompou's elusive world, and besides the *Canciónes y danzas* and *Cants mágics* he offers also the rarer early work, *Suburbis* (1916/17), which evokes the suburbs of Barcelona. The second and third of the five pieces are concerned with the gypsies, followed by a touching portrait of a little blind girl (*La ceguetta*), while the last is a lively picture of a street organ player. At its modest cost and very well recorded, this is well worth having.

Canciónes y danzas 1–12, 14; Charmes; Scènes d'enfants
(BB) *** Naxos 8.554332. Masó

In many ways Jordi Masó's excellent Naxos collection is not upstaged by the competition. Moreover this is to be the first of a continuing series. He gives us the complete *Canciónes y danzas* (except for No. 13, which is for guitar), plus the engagingly diverse, but at times almost mystical *Charmes*, and his playing is imbued with gentle poetic feeling. Masó's pianistic sensibility is never self-aware, always at the service of the composer, and the music's soft-hued colours are perceptively graduated. The unostentatious innocence of the *Scènes d'enfants* is beautifully caught. Excellent recording makes this a disc to recommend even if it cost far more than it does.

Canciónes y danzas 1, 3, 5, 7, 8–9; Cants mágics; Charmes; Dialogues I–II; Paisajes; Preludios 1, 5 (Palmier d'étoiles), 6 (for the left hand), 7, 9–10; 3 Variations
🇧 ➳ ✿ *** Hyp. CDA 66963. Hough

This exceptionally generous (77 minutes) and wide-ranging *Gramophone* Award-winning recital makes an obvious first choice for those wanting to explore, on a single CD, the fullest possible range of Mompou's piano music. Stephen Hough, who provides the illuminating notes, imaginatively describes this as 'the music of evaporation … There is no development of material, little counterpoint, no drama or climaxes to speak of; and this simplicity of expression – elusive, evasive and shy – is strangely disarming.' He is completely inside Mompou's fastidious, Satie-esque sound-world and understands the absorbed influences which make this music as much French as Spanish. The recording too is excellent if a little reverberant. Not even Mompou himself equalled, let alone surpassed, Hough in this repertoire.

Musica callada, Books I–IV; El pont; Muntanya (Dansa)
(BB) **(*) Naxos 8.554727. Masó

Jordi Masó's survey of Mompou's piano music continues with the *Musica callada* – 28 pieces which appeared in four volumes between 1959 and 1967. The title comes from the *Cántico espiritual* and means 'music without sound' although this is complemented with the additional description *Soledad sonora* ('insistent solitude'). The very first piece, *Angelico*, creates the work's atmosphere and other pieces are called *Placid*, *Tranquillo* – *trè calme*, *Luminoso* and so on. The problem for the performer is that almost all this music is slow and reflective (the Lento marking reappears frequently), and it has to be said that this is not entirely solved here. Jordi Masó is by no means insensitive, but although he is well recorded, the colouring remains monochrome. The two impressionistic pieces which close the recital are *El pont* ('The Bridge') and *Muntanya* ('Mountain'). They have not been recorded before and make successful encores.

MONDONVILLE, Jean-Joseph Cassanéa de (1711–72)

6 Sonates en symphonies, Op. 3

(M) *** DG Blue 474 550-2. Les Musiciens du Louvre, Minkowski

This entirely captivating set of *Symphonies* confirms Mondonville as a great deal more than a historical figure. They originated as sonatas for violin and obbligato harpsichord in 1734, but the composer later skilfully orchestrated them. Each is in three movements, with an expressively tuneful centrepiece framed by sprightly *Allegros*. Their invention is consistently fresh, and they are played here with great élan and spontaneity and are beautifully recorded. This now reappears competitively priced on DG's Archive Blue label. Highly recommended.

VOCAL MUSIC

Dominus Regnavit (Psalm 92); Venite Exultemus (Psalm 94)

(N) (BB) **(*) Warner Apex (ADD) 2564 60155-2.
Alliot-Lugaz, Borst, Goldthorpe, Huttenlocher, Vocal Ensembles: A Coeur joie de Lille, Animat de Valenciennes, De Chevreuse-Essonne, Adam de la Halle; Paillard CO, Paillard – CORRETTE: *Laudate Dominum* ***

Venite Exultemus dates from around 1740 and enjoyed considerable success in its day; given its attractive melodic lines and variety of moods, it is not hard to see why. *Dominus Regnavit*, dating from 1734, has all these qualities too, with some exciting writing for the chorus in the *Elevaverunt flumina Domine*, depicting the raging of the waves. There is much to enjoy here, including the lovely soprano duet, *Parata sedes*, and the majestic final chorus. The French performance is a decent, idiomatic one and more than a stop-gap, but it would be interesting to see what Minkowski would do with this repertoire. The sound is nothing special, but fair enough. Still, this is a bargain well worth exploring, and the Corrette bonus is a joy.

Grands motets: De profundis; Venite exultemus. Petits motets: Benefac Domine; In decachordo psalterio; Regna terrae

☛ (BB) *** Hyp. Helios CDH 55038. Fisher, Daniels, Varcoe, New College, Oxford, Ch., L. Bar. Ens., Higginbottom

Mondonville's *Grands Motets* were modelled on those of Delalande, but are even finer and more individual. This outstanding CD includes his *De profundis*, a remarkably diverse setting of verses 1–8 of Psalm 129. The performance is

of very high quality. The opening *De profundis clamavi* is wonderfully ethereal, with boy trebles set back in the atmospheric Oxford acoustic. Their refined approach is matched by the ravishingly pure soprano line of Gillian Fisher, while the closing *Requiem aeternam* floats celestially.

Higginbottom's Helios collection then offers another rather less grand motet, but one which alongside *De profundis* was greatly popular and frequently performed in its day. It is more lyrical, less dramatic and textually simpler – a radiant expression of praise. Both the counter-tenor and bass have major contributions to make which require virtuoso flexibility, and the work closes with a radiant display of vocal agility from the trebles in the final *Gloria Patri*, which tests the Oxford choir to their outer limits.

The three solo *Petits Motets* with their modest harpsichord and continuo accompaniments are altogether more intimate but no less valuable, each showing Gillian Fisher in glorious voice (indeed this CD is worth having for her contribution alone), while Edward Higginbottom exchanges his baton for the harpsichord keyboard. Altogether this is a delightful bargain collection, given state-of-the-art sound.

MONIUSZKO, Stanislaw (1819–72)

The Haunted Manor (opera; complete)

(M) *** EMI 5 57489-2 (2). Kruszewski, Hossa, Lubańska, Stachura, Nowacki, Toczyska, Polish Nat. Op. Ch. & O, Kaspszyk

Moniuszko, the leading Polish romantic after Chopin, is generally remembered, if at all, by his opera *Halka*, a tragic story set against a peasant background. Yet in almost every way *The Haunted Manor*, one of the hidden treasures of Polish opera, is more original, more inventive and, above all, more attractive with its tuneful sequence of ensembles.

Though ensembles predominate, each of the main characters is given a big showpiece aria. The one for Hanna is particularly impressive, with its Donizettian coloratura brilliantly sung by the bright-toned Iwona Hossa. Anna Lubańska with her firm, warm mezzo is also impressive as Jadwiga; but the casting of the two brothers is not so strong, with the lusty tenor Dariusz Stachura strained as Stefan, not attacking notes cleanly, and Piotr Nowacki as Zbigniev happier in fast music than sustained melody. Best of all is Adam Kruszewski in the central role of the host, Miecznik, the Sword-Bearer, a fine baritone with a timbre not unlike Sir Thomas Allen's. Add on a few *buffo* characters and a formidable aunt figure, strongly taken by Stefania Toczyska, and you have a splendidly successful entertainment, with superb playing and singing from the Polish National Opera Chorus and Orchestra, dynamically conducted from first to last by Jacek Kaspszyk.

MONN, George Matthias (1717–50)

Cello Concerto in G min.

(N) *** DG 474 236-2. Wang, Camerata Salzburg (with COUPERIN: *Pièces en concert* (arr. Bazelaire); FRESCOBALDI: *Toccata* (arr. Toister)) – BOCCHERINI: *Cello Concerto 9 in B flat* ***

Monn was one of the most interesting and forward-looking composers of his day, though he fell into some neglect after his death. He has the distinction of having composed the first four-movement symphony. The excellent sleeve-notes quote Sonnleithner's biographical sketch, which speaks of him as 'presumably of weak constitution, for he never drank wine – a rare phenomenon in a community of canons – and did not live to a great age. He was of gloomy disposition, never married and always dressed in black.' The *G minor Concerto* was restored to circulation in 1912 in an arrangement by Schoenberg, but his representation on CD remains meagre. The Chinese cellist Jian Wang uses a modern edition by Olivér Nagy and gives an eloquent account of this at times bold score. Excellent playing from the Salzburg orchestra too.

(i) *Cello Concerto in G min.*; (ii) *Harpsichord Concertos in D & G min.*; (iii) *Violin Concerto in B flat*
(N) *** CPO 999 391-2. La Stagione Frankfurt, with (i) Zipperling; (ii) Bauer; (iii) Utiger

George Monn, Austrian organist and composer, is not exactly the best-known composer of the pre-classical period, yet these works show him to possess a high degree of musicianship and originality. Arnold Schoenberg admired the *G minor Concerto* enough to make his own edition of the score. It is indeed an attractive work, stretching the instrument further than one expects from this period, and the finale, with its very appealing melodic line, nicely decorated, is a real winner. The *G minor Harpsichord Concerto* is an arrangement of that work, with the piquancy of the harpsichord giving the work a different kind of colour. The *D major Harpsichord Concerto* is positive and lively, as is the *B flat Violin Concerto*, both sunny works in Monn's tuneful *galant* style. Excellent sound and performances.

MONTEMEZZI, Italo (1875–1952)

L'amore dei tre re (complete)
(M) (**(*)) Warner Fonit mono 8573 87487-2 (2). Bruscantini, Petrella, Berdini, Capecchi, RAI Ch. & O of Milan, Basile

Recorded for Cetra in Milan in 1950 in collaboration with Italian Radio, the mono recording of Montemezzi's one operatic success brings a red-blooded, idiomatic account of a piece cherished in America as well as Italy, largely through the initial advocacy of Toscanini. It says much for the conductor, Arturo Basile, that he drives the piece so strongly through a tale of such improbable blood and thunder, helped by a strong cast. Central to the success of the performance is the singing of Sesto Bruscantini as the barbarian king, Archibaldo, who forces his daughter, Fiora, to marry the unfortunate Manfredo, before malevolently rooting out her passionate affair with her true love, Avito, with widespread carnage at the end. Bruscantini, only thirty-one at the time, sings with commanding power in this villainous role, cutting a very different figure from his classic Figaro, which became such a favourite at Glyndebourne. Clara Petrella sings sensitively as Fiora, well matched against her lover, Avito, sung by Amedeo Berdini, with the young Renato Capecchi making Manfredo into a believable character. The mono recording is very limited but catches voices well. The later stereo version with Moffo and Domingo is now deleted but must take priority, this one from a company of singers and players familiar with the music is both convincing and enjoyable in putting over such outrageous hokum. An Italian libretto is provided but no translation, only multi-lingual synopses.

MONTEVERDI, Claudio (1567–1643)

Monteverdi was for the late sixteenth and early seventeenth century what Haydn and Mozart together were for the eighteenth, a composer who completely dominated his era. Born in Cremona, he entered the service of Duke Gonzaga of Mantua, first as a violinist, then in 1601 becoming Court *maestro di capella*. But in 1612 he was dismissed. That turned out to be a blessing in disguise (not only for Monteverdi, but for us too). In 1613 (after the great success of his 1610 setting of the *Vespers*) he was placed in charge of the music at Saint Marco in Venice. Then yet another, even more propitious event was to mould his career, for it was in Venice, in 1637, that the first public opera house was established. In the ensuing few years Monteverdi virtually created the style of opera as we know it today, with recitatives and arias, even inventing orchestral devices for the orchestral pit, such as *tremolando*, for dramatic effect.

The quality of Monteverdi's extraordinarily original madrigal settings is lauded throughout our pages, but if he had only left us his two inspired opera ballets, *Il ballo delle ingrate* and *Il combattimento di Tancredi e Clorinda*, he would be celebrated as an uniquely innovative and imaginative composer. Nothing to match them came either before or after they were written. They encapsulate the entire spirit of dramatizing a simple narrative to maximum effect and with modest means, and creating a combination of music and drama that even Wagner's *Ring* could not eclipse.

Madrigals, Books 1 (1587); *2* (1590); *3* (1592); *6* (1614) (all complete); *7*, excerpts: *Tempo la cetra; Tirsi e Clori. 8: Madrigali guerrieri; Madrigali amorosi*; Opera-ballets: *Il ballo delle ingrate; Il combattimento di Tancredi e Clorinda; Volgendo il ciel* (1638) (complete)
(BB) **(*) Virgin 5 62268-2 (7). Kirkby, Tubb, Nichols, Agnew, King, Ewing and soloists, Cons. of Musicke, Rooley

Anthony Rooley recorded almost all the Monteverdi Madrigals between 1990 and 1996, mostly for EMI, but for Books 4–5 he turned to L'Oiseau-Lyre, and these recordings are now available on a reissued Double, together with two items from Book 7 and two from Book 8 (O-L 455 718-2 – see below). Rooley additionally recorded for L'Oiseau-Lyre ten further madrigals from Book 7 (1619) with instrumental accompaniments, under the title '*Madrigal erotici*'. These are currently withdrawn, but Regis have reissued a further collection of six more from Book 7, which first appeared on Carlton, including duets featuring Emma Kirkby and Evelyn Tubb (Regis 1060 – again, see below).

Two-thirds of the texts in Book 1 are concerned with love's disappointments, the words full of torments, which gives Monteverdi plenty of opportunity for expressive dolour. Though these early madrigals are usually brief and without the sharp poignancy of the later examples, there is much here that is imaginative and there is consistent lyrical beauty. This first disc also includes two excerpts from Book 7, including the charming pastoral ballet, *Tirsi e Clori*, written for the Mantuan court and extolling the the joys of requited love and faithfulness. Book 2 is also more simple in its appeal and imagery than the later writing but, like Book 1, it all comes to life freshly, including the very effective Tasso settings.

With Books 3 and 4 we move to some of Monteverdi's finest madrigals, often dazzling, in which his originality began to make itself felt to the full. Moreover these are masterly performances, the flexibility and control of dramatic contrasts conveying consistent commitment. Book 6 includes the five-part transcription of of the *Lamento d'Arianna* and *Zefiro torno*, two of the composer's masterpieces, and also works from Monteverdi's years at Mantua.

Monteverdi published his ambitious Volume 8 after a long gap in his madrigal output. It includes one of the very greatest examples in *Lamento della ninfa*, in what the composer described as the *stile rappresentativo* or theatre style, plus the well-known opera-ballets. The performances here continue to be polished and distinctive, and the cast-list is strong.

For the most part, however, this reissued collection represents a considerable achievement for Rooley and his singers and instrumentalists, with first-class recording throughout. The set is most inexpensive, but the documentation is sparse, with no texts and translations.

Madrigals, Book 2 (complete)

☙ *** Opus 111 OP 30-111. Concerto Italiano, Alessandrini

(N) *** Glossa GCD 920922. La Venexiana, Cavina

Rinaldo Alessandrini and his superb Concerto Italiano are singing their sunny Italianate way through Monteverdi's complete madrigal sequence. Apart from being of Italian birth, all the performers here have studied early Italian and therefore bring a special idiomatic feeling to the words. The Second Book, about half of whose five-part settings are from Tasso, demands and receives a simpler style of presentation than the later works, and there is radiant freshness about the singing here which is particularly appealing. The recording has the most pleasing acoustic.

The alternative performances from La Venexiana directed by Claudio Cavina have similar Italian flair and hardly less eloquence. They are particularly strong in bringing out the rich lyricism of the Second Book with its poetic evocations of nature, yet the love songs have a fine delicacy of passionate feeling (*Dolcemente, dormiva la mia Clori* is delightful), while the depth of distress expressed in *Crudel, perché mi fuggi?* is truly poignant. The generously expansive acoustic provides an admirable setting for a group in which individual voices can soar and blend with equal felicity. Excellent documentation and pleasing packaging.

Collection: (i) *Madrigals, Books 4–5* (complete); *Book 7: Con che soavità; Book 8: Mentre vaga; Ogni amante è guerrier.* Other Madrigals: (ii) *Altri canti di Marte; Ardo, avvampo; Hor ch'el ciel e la terra; Lagrime d'amante al sepolcro dell'amata; Ballo: Movete al mio bel suon; O ciechi, ciechi; Questi vaghi concenti;* (iii) *Vespro della Beata Vergine; Il ballo delle ingrate; I Combattimento di Tancredi e Clorinda; Tirsi e Clori;* (iii; iv) *L'Orfeo* (complete)

*** Decca (DDD/ADD) 470 906-2 (8). (i) Consort of Musicke, Rooley; (ii) Schütz Ch. & Consort, Norrington; (iii) Bott, Bonner, Robson, King, Mark Ainsley, George, Grant, New L. Consort, Pickett; (iv) with Gooding

The highlights of this eight-CD budget box are the unsurpassed account of *Orfeo*, boldly dramatic, with John Mark Ainsley outstanding in the title-role, and the trio of opera-ballets, *Il ballo delle ingrate, Combattimento di Tancredi e Clorinda* and *Tirsi e Clori*, to which we gave a ❂ on its original single-disc issue (now withdrawn). The star here is Catherine Bott, while John Mark Ainsley takes the narrative with distinction in *Tancredi e Clorinda*. Pickett presents Monteverdi's inspired triptych with sharp clarity and the same concern for dramatic impact that he found for *Orfeo*, and the result is unforgettable. The *Vespers* are given in a liturgical

context, with plainchant antiphons between the numbers. The sound is warm and well balanced, with clarini in the Consort particularly beautiful, but there is a serious snag in the heavily aspirated style of the tenors in the florid music.

Turning to the madrigals, Anthony Rooley offers the whole of the contents of Book 4 (dating from 1603) and Book 5 (1605), plus three other substantial accompanied madrigals which come from the composer's later, Venetian period. The Consort of Musicke, led by Emma Kirkby, give masterly performances of the Fourth Book which suits their style very well. But Book 5 marked a turning point in Monteverdi's madrigal output, for the last six works bring an obligatory continuo and are much freer in style than their predecessors, even semi-operatic in their use of freely individual vocal solos. This change is less marked in the singing from the Consort of Musicke than in their Italian competitors. Nevertheless the comparatively restrained approach of Rooley's group brings its own rewards, and their refinement is reflected in the delicate lute continuo in the later numbers, where their quixotic mood-changes are well caught.

The miscellaneous collection of madrigals comes from the 1970s and was among the pioneering recordings of the analogue LP era. Norrington directs crisp, well-drilled performances, not as relaxedly expressive as some, but refreshing in their clarity and eloquence, particularly the masterly *Hor ch'el ciel e la terra* and the ambitious *Lagrime d'amante al sepolcro dell'amata*, where the closing section, *Dunque, amate relique*, is very touching. The ample acoustic of St John's, Smith Square, adds agreeable atmosphere. Full texts and translations are included in the excellent accompanying booklet.

Madrigals, Book 4 (complete)

*** Opus 111 OP 30-81. Concerto Italiano, Alessandrini

Madrigals, Books 4–5 (complete). *Book 7: Con che soavità, labbra odorate; Tempro la cetra. Book 8: (Madrigali guerrieri et amorosi): Mentre vaga; Ogni amante è guerrier*

(B) *** O-L Double 455 718-2 (2). Consort of Musicke, Rooley

Madrigals, Book 5 (complete)

☙ ❂ *** Opus 111 OPS 30-166. Concerto Italiano, Alessandrini

The Fourth Book, published in 1603 and again for five voices, marks an added richness of expressive feeling over Monteverdi's earlier settings, well recognized by Rinaldo Alessandrini and his superbly blended vocal group. This series goes from strength to strength and can be strongly recommended. The recording continues to match the singing in excellence.

The Oiseau-Lyre Double offers exceptional value in including the whole of the contents of Book 4 (dating from 1603) and Book 5 (1605), plus four substantial accompanied madrigals which come from the composer's later, Venetian years. Under Anthony Rooley, the well-integrated singers of the Consort of Musicke, led by Emma Kirkby, give masterly performances of the Fourth Book, which suits their vocal style especially well. Book 5 marked a turning point in Monteverdi's madrigal output, for the last six works bring an obligatory continuo and are much freer in style than their predecessors, even semi-operatic in their use of freely individual vocal solos. It might be said that the change of style in the singing from the Consort of Musicke is less marked than in the competing (full-priced) collection of these works by the Concerto Italiano directed by Rinaldo Alessandrini, whose singing is distinctly Italianate and more extrovert. Nevertheless the comparatively restrained approach of Rooley's group brings its own rewards, and their refinement is reflected in the delicate lute continuo in the later numbers. However, the competing performances by Alessandrini's superb Italian vocal group, at one moment blending richly together, at another asserting solo individuality, cannot be praised too highly, and again they are beautifully recorded.

Madrigals, Book 7 (complete)

(N) *** Glossa GCD 920927 (2). La Venexiana, Instrumental Ens., Cavina

To describe the new style of his madrigals in Book 7 of 1619, Monteverdi coined the term *'stile concitato'* or concerto, and departed from his previous standard five-part format to embrace a wide variety of voicing: works for a solo voice are found alongside settings for two, three, four and six voices, with the duets often for two of the same genre: soprano, contralto or tenor. To introduce the listener to his use of instrumental accompaniments, he opens with a brief sinfonia, and to point to the future, he closes with a charming extended pastoral dance cantata, *Tirsi e Clori*, which is delightfully sung here. Indeed the enlarged La Venexiana and their accompanying instrumental group obviously relish the expanded style and the wide variety of mood, impassioned, joyful, dolorous and sensuous by turns; and again their standard of performance is consistently high, as is the quality of the warmly atmospheric recording. Full texts and translations are included.

Madrigals, Book 8: *Madrigali guerrieri et amorosi (Madrigals of War and Love)*

(BB) **(*) Virgin 2x1 5 61570-2 (2). Soloists, Consort of Musicke, Rooley

Madrigals, Book 8: *Madrigali guerrieri et amorosi:* Volume I: *Sinfonia: Altri canti d'amor; Lamento della Ninfa; Vago augelletto; Perchè t'en fuggi, o Fillide?; Altri canti di Marte; Due belli occhi fur l'ami; Ogni amante è guerrier; Hor che'l ciel e la terra; Gira il nemico, insidioso amore; Dolcissimo usignolo; Ardo, ardo avvampo*

*** Opus 111 OP 30-187. Concerto Italiano, Alessandrini

Rinaldo Alessandrini and his Concerto Italiano continue their superlative series of recordings of Monteverdi's madrigals with the first part of Book 8, *Madrigals of War and Love*. As before, the singing combines Italianate fire and lyricism in ideal proportions and the instrumental accompaniments could hardly be finer. The present disc includes famous items like the three-part *Lamento della Ninfa* and the two-part *Hor che'l ciel el la terra*. The recording too is first class.

The *Madrigali guerrieri* are very theatrical and include *Il ballo delle ingrate* and *Il combattimento di Tancredi e Clorinda*, which are also available separately in other individual versions (see below). The performances on Virgin are impressive, and anyone collecting Rooley's series should find this inexpensive Double well worth its modest cost. The cast list is strong, including Emma Kirkby and Evelyn Tubb, but Andrew King is the narrator in *Il Combattimento* and his approach is less than robustly full-blooded, while in both works the performances under Pickett (see above) and Christie (see below) are more dramatically arresting.

Madrigals, Book 8 (excerpts): *Madrigali guerrieri et amorosi: Altri canti d'amor; Altri cante di marte; Il Gira il*

nemico; Hor ch'el ciel e la terra; Lamento della Ninfa; 2 Sinfonias; Volgendo il ciel movete al mio bel suon (Ballo)

(M) *** Astrée ES 9944. Figueras, Tiso, Banditelli, Climent, Carnovich, Garrigosa, Costa, La Capella Reial de Catalunya, Savall

Savall's way with Monteverdi's Book 8 is, above all, theatrical and tremendously vital: his singers emphasize the strong rhythmic contrasts of the *Madrigali guerrieri*. There are some very fine voices in his team, none lacking individuality of character, yet blending splendidly, as at the opening of *Hor che'l ciel e la terra*. Montserrat Figueras, Lambert Climent (tenor) and Daniele Carnovich (bass) stand out, and Figueras is at her glorious best in the famous *Lamento della Ninfa*. This is an excellent anthology in all respects and full translations are included.

Madrigals, Book 8: Opera-Ballet

Altri canti d'Amor; Il ballo delle ingrate; Il combattimento di Tancredi e Clorinda; Volgendo il ciel (Ballo movt)

(N) (BB) *** Hyp. Helios CDH 55165. Red Byrd, Parley of Instruments, Holman

(i) *Il ballo delle ingrate;* (ii) *Il combattimento di Tancredi e Clorinda*

⊶ *** Opus 111 OP 30-196. (i) Ermolli, Dominguez, Carnovich, Franzetti; (ii) Franzetti, Ferrarini, Abbondanza; Concerto Italiano, Alessandrini

Il ballo delle ingrate; Il combattimento di Tancredi; Tirsi e Clori; Tempo la cetra

(N) (BB) *** Warner Apex 2564 6181-2. Tragicomedia, Stubbs

Il combattimento di Tancredi e Clorinda

(B) *** HM HMA 195 1626. Semeliaz, Brand, Rovenq, Les Arts Florissants, Christie

There is no more commandingly dramatic account of *Il combattimento* on record than this Italianate version from Rinaldo Alessandrini, with superb singing from all three principals. Roberto Abbondanza is a splendidly histrionic narrator, and in the death scene Elisa Franzetti, singing her farewell, is exquisitely moving. Franzetti returns at the end of *Il ballo delle ingrate* to bid an eloquent adieu on behalf of the ungrateful souls, condemned for rebelling against earthly love, to be echoed by Monteverdi's infinitely poignant closing chorus from her companions. The performance overall is cast from strength. Daniele Carnovich is a true basso profundo and makes a superb Pluto, but Francesca Ermolli and Rosa Dominguez are equally fine as Amor and Venus, respectively. The vivid recording is warmly atmospheric.

Red Byrd is an impressive vocal group and in *Il combattimento* John Potter narrates more colloquially than his competitors, yet builds up plenty of excitement in the heat of the battle, while Catherine Pierard as Clorinda sings her closing threnody very touchingly. *Il ballo* is also characterized most effectively. Richard Wistrech makes a striking Pluto, his low notes resonating tellingly, and at the close, after the beautiful lament from Pierard's Ungrateful Spirit, the charming little closing chorus is made to fade into the distance as the Lost Souls (who were 'so esteemed in the world' for their chaste purity) return to their dark abode in Pluto's kingdom. The major works are interspersed with two short but unexpectedly appealing works, written in praise of the Austrian Emperor Ferdinand III, 'Let others sing of Love . . . You whose immortal crown is woven from the laurels of Caesar' and a light-hearted ballet with a Poet as soloist and chorus: 'Turning in the sky along its immortal path the wheels of glorious and serene light, the sun brings back the age of peace under the new King of the Roman Empire.' Excellent recording, and full texts and translations.

Besides *Il ballo* and *Il combattimento*, Stephen Stubbs and Tragicomedia offer another opera-ballet written for the Mantuan court, *Tirsi e Clori*, a dialogue between two lovers celebrating both the spirit of love and the dance, while the solo madrigal, *Tempro la cetra*, eloquently sung by John Potter, acts as a dramatic prelude, 'I tune the lyre', though it lines up with *Il combattimento* rather than *Il ballo*. These two major works are strongly cast: the female dialogues are delightfully sung, and Harry van der Kempe is a dramatically commanding Pluto, with splendid lower tessitura. *Il combattimento* could not be more moving, with Douglas Nasrawi's narration rising to fever-pitch at the climax of the battle itself, then eloquently expressing the tragedy of the result. Excellent recording and full texts and translations make this irresistible at super-budget price.

Christie's account of *Il combattimento* is also very dramatic, with the storytelling vividly projected and with Françoise Semeliaz a touching Clorinda in the tragic closing scene. The recording is admirably vivid too. The libretto is in Italian and French only, but the narrative is easy enough to follow.

Other Madrigal collections

Madrigals: *Ab aeterno ordinata sum; Confitebor tibi, Domine* (3 settings); *Deus tuorum militum sors et corona; Iste confessor Domini sacratus; Laudate Dominum, O omnes gentes; La Maddalena: Prologue: Su le penne di venti. Nisi Dominus aedificaverit domum*
⊶ ✪ *** Hyp. CDA 66021. Kirkby, Partridge, Thomas, Parley of Instruments

There are few recordings of Monteverdi's solo vocal music as persuasive as this. The three totally contrasted settings of *Confitebor tibi* (Psalm 110) reveal an extraordinary range of expression, each one drawing out different aspects of word-meaning. Even the brief trio, *Deus tuorum militum*, has a haunting memorability – it could become to Monteverdi what *Jesu, joy of man's desiring* is to Bach – and the performances are outstanding, with the edge on Emma Kirkby's voice attractively presented in an aptly reverberant acoustic. The accompaniment makes a persuasive case for authentic performance on original instruments. The CD sounds superb.

Madrigals: *Addio Florida bella; Ahi com'a un vago sol; E cosi a poco a poco torno farfella; Era l'anima mia; Luci serene e chiare; Mentre vaga Angioletta ogn'anima; Ninfa che scalza il piede; O mio bene, a mia vita; O Mirtillo, anima mia; Partenza amorosa; Se pur destina; Taci, Armelin deh taci; T'amo mia vita; Troppo ben può questo tiranno amore*
(N) (B) *** HM (ADD) HMC 1951084. Concerto Vocale, Jacobs

A highly attractive collection of generally neglected items, briskly and stylishly performed. The most celebrated of the singers is the male alto, a fine director as well as a soloist. But since this disc was first issued in 1983, Barbara Schlick, Marius van Altena and Guy de Mey have also established themselves. With continuo accompaniment – the common factor in this programme, in which no *a cappella* madrigals are included –

the contrasting of vocal timbres is superbly achieved. An excellent recording, well transferred to CD.

Madrigals: *'Batto', qui pianse Ergasto; Gira, il nemico insidioso amore; Hor che'l ciel e la terra; O come sei gentile; Ogni amante è guerrir; Zefiro torna*
✪ (M) *** Virgin 5 61165-2. Chiaroscuro, L. Bar., Rogers – D'INDIA: *Madrigals* ***** ✪**

A hand-picked half-dozen of Monteverdi's finest madrigals, superlatively sung, consistently bringing out the expressive originality and the extraordinary variety of the settings, to say nothing of their inherent vocal bravura. *Zefiro torna* is justly famous, but *'Batto', qui pianse Ergasto* is hardly less remarkable, and the two *Madrigali guerrieri et amorosi* are very telling indeed. The engagingly lyrical *O come sei gentile* follows immediately after the d'India dramatized cycle from *Il pastor Fido* and makes a fascinating comparison. Accompaniments are nicely balanced and the recording has an exceptionally real and vivid presence.

Chamber Duets (complete); Trios: *Chi vol che m'innamori; Gira il nemico insidioso Amore; Perché te'n fuggi, o Fillide?; Spuntavi il di; Su, su su, pastorelli vezzosi; Quartet: Lamento della ninfa; Quintet: Voi ch'ascoltate; Sextet: Or, che 'l ciel*
(N) (BB) *(**) Virgin 2x1 5 62416 (2). Il Complesso Barocco, Curtis

This is a complete collection of Monteverdi's 24 *Chamber Duets*, plus five *Trios*, and a single *Quartet*, *Quintet* and *Sextet*. The consistent richness of Monteverdi's settings throughout is matched by the excellence of the performances from 11 singers from Alan Curtis's Il Complesso Barocco. Each number is strongly characterized, and each of the voices is able to blend and alternate naturally and persuasively. The famous opening duet, *Zefiro torna*, is a splendid example, here sung by a pair of tenors (Gian Paolo Fagotto and Luca Dordolo) with an infectious gusto, to be matched in vivacity immediately by a pair of bright-voiced sopranos (Elena Cecci Fedi and Roberta Invernizzi) in *Io son pur vezzosetta. Bel pastor* is a another lively dialogue number (between Aminta and Chlori). Roberta Invernizzi then joins with mezzo Gloria Banditelli to weave a richly coloured texture, first sustained thrillingly in the upper tessitura, and then alternating in the middle range in *Ohimè, dove il mio ben*.

The second disc opens with the quintet, *Voi ch'ascoltate*, both expressive and animated, and includes the delectably light-hearted *Su, su, su, pastorelli vezzosi* and the poignant *Lamento della ninfa* (a trio with an added soprano solo at its centre, one of Monteverdi's most beautiful settings). The programme ends with the outstandingly dramatic sextet, *Or, che'l ciel*.

Only Italian artists can sing this repertoire with this degree of idiomatic feeling and colloquial diction, and the accompaniments, usually effectively simple, but sometimes more ambitious (as in *Armato il cor*) could not be more appropriate. The recording, made in the Palazzo Giusti, Padua, has an appealingly warm atmosphere, yet splendid clarity. The one huge drawback to this set – one of the finest in the Monteverdi catalogue – is the complete absence of texts and translations, a crazy way of reissuing such distinguished music-making of which Virgin Records should be ashamed.

Chamber Duets: *Bel pastor; Non è di gentil core; O come sei gentile; Ohimè, dove il mio ben; Zefiro torna. Solos: Lamento*

d'arianna; Queste pungenti spine (Cantata spirituale).
L'Incoronazione di Poppea: Pur ti miro (Final Duet)
(N) (M) **(*) HM Suite HMT 7901129. Müller-Molinari,
Jacobs, Concerto Vocale

As can be seen below, *Zefiro torna*, which opens this collection, comes from the *Scherzi musicale*, a light-hearted chaconne in which the mezzo Helga Müller-Molinari matches
her voice (and vibrato) well to that of René Jacobs through all
the vocal intricacies. Their matching is less successful in
Ohimè, dove il mio ben, which is unwieldy it its operatic
intensity; they blend much better in the charming *Bel pastor*
and make a contrasted pair in the famous closing duet from
L'incoronazione di Poppea (which may not be by Monteverdi
at all!). But the finest items here are the solos, *Queste pungenti
spine* and the justly famous *Lamento d'arianna*, which is most
movingly sung. A plus point for this disc is the provision of
full texts and translations. Good recording too.

Madrigali concertati: *Augelin, che la voce; Eccomi pronta ai
baci; Ecco vicine, o belle tigre; Gira il nemico insidioso;
Lamento della ninfa; Mentre vaga Angioletta; Ninfa, che
scalza il piede; Ogni amante è guerrier; Perché fuggi; S'ei
vostro cor, Madonna; Soave libertate; Tornate, o cari baci;
Vaga su spina ascosa; Zefiro torna (Ciaccona)*
(N) (BB) *** Warner Apex 2564 60710-2. Soloists,
Tragicomedia, Stubbs

These concerted madrigals come from the Seventh and
Eighth Books. Those from the Seventh are written in from
one to six concerted parts, with the theme of love predominating. Such as *Eccomi pronta ai baci* ('Here I am ready for
kisses'), and of course the masterly vocal chaconne *Zefiro
torna* ('Summer breezes'), which seems to be in all such
collections. The madrigals from the Eighth Book include the
extended *Ogni amante è guerrier* ('Every lover is a warrior')
with its martial oratory, and the extended *Gira il nemico
insidioso* and the melancholy *Lamento della ninfa*, with its
stabs of dissonance at the loss of a beloved. *Mentre vaga
Angioletta* contrasts vocal bravura with a poignant dulcet
longing. The members of Tragicomedia never disappoint,
and this is a well-chosen collection, readily demonstrating the
amazing range of Monteverdi's madrigals. As the essential
texts and translations are included, this well-recorded disc is
a bargain.

Scherzi musicali a tre voci: *Amarilli onde m'assale; Amorosa
pupilletta; Clori amorosa; Damigella tutta bella; Deh chi
tace il bel pensero; De la bellezza le dovute lodi; Dispiegate
guance amati; Dolci miei sospiri Fugge'l verno; Giovinetta
ritrosetta; I bei legami; Lidia spina del mio core; Non così
tosto io miro; O rosetta che rosetta; La Pastorella; Quando
l'Alba in Oriente; Vaghi rai di cigli; La violetta*
(N) (BB) **(*) Naxos 8.553317. Concerto della Dame di
Ferrara, Vartolo

In 1607, two years after Book Five of Monteverdi's Madrigals
had appeared, the composer's brother published the eighteen
Scherzi musicali in three voices. However, they had been
written much earlier, around the turn of the century, when
Monteverdi had supposedly imported a French style (*canto
alla francese*) into Italy. Certainly the *Scherzi* are more simple
than the composer's earlier works. They have introductory
instrumental ritornelli and a simple melodic flow, with
underlying harmony and a recurring refrain. They also have a
guileless quality that is appealing in a less sophisticated way.
Dolci miei sospiri (one of the more memorable) even has the

string accompaniment creating a series of little sighs. While
they are concerned with love, either pastoral (*La violetta* and
Damigella tutta bella) or passionately sparkling (*Vaghira di
ardenti*), they are all essentially light-hearted and are set to
dance rhythms which obviously gave them considerable
popular appeal. They are sung and played brightly here,
although, pleasing as they are, they cannot compare with the
greatest concerted madrigals of Books Seven and Eight. Fine,
fresh performances, recorded in Verona by a group of Italian
singers and instrumentalists, sympathetically directed by Sergio Vartolo, but not an essential part of the Monteverdi
discography.

Madrigals (duets and solos): *Chiome d'oro, bel thesoro; Il
son pur vezzosetta pastorella; Non è gentil core; O come sei
gentile, caro augellino; Ohimé dov'é il mio ben?; Se pur
destina e vole il cielo, partenza amorosa.* **Sacred music:**
*Cantate Domino; Exulta, filia Sion; Iste confesse II; Laudate
Dominum in sanctis eius; O bone Jesu, o piissime Jesu;
Sancta Maria, succurre miseris; Venite, siccientes ad aquas
Domini.* **Opera:** *Il ritorno d'Ulisse in patria: Di misera
regina (Penelope's Lament)*
(BB) *** Regis 1060. Kirkby, Tubb, Consort of Musicke,
Rooley

Admirers of Emma Kirkby will surely revel in this collection,
mostly of duets, in which she is joined by Evelyn Tubb. The
two voices are admirably matched and both artists ornament
their lines attractively and judiciously. Tubb is given a solo
opportunity in Penelope's lament from *Il ritorno d'Ulisse*,
which she sings dramatically and touchingly. Anthony Rooley's simple accompaniments with members of the Consort
of Musicke are also imaginatively stylish. We are pleased to
report that this inexpensive reissue has been properly documented.

*Lamento d'Olympia; Maladetto sia l'aspetto; Ohimè ch'io
cado; Quel sdengosetto; Voglio di vita uscia*
*** Hyp. CDA 66106. Kirkby, Rooley (chittarone) – D'INDIA:
Lamento d'Olympia, etc. ***

A well-planned recital from Hyperion contrasts the two
settings of *Lamento d'Olympia* by Monteverdi and his
younger contemporary, Sigismondo d'India. The performances by Emma Kirkby, sensitively supported by Anthony
Rooley, could hardly be surpassed; this ranks among her best
records.

Church Music

Sacred Music, Vol. I: *Beatus vir I; Christe redemptor
omnium; Confitebor Primo; Dixit [Dominus] Primo;
Laudate Dominum omnes gentes; Laudate pueri Primo;
Magnificat Primo; Missa a 4*
*** Hyp. CDA 67428. Outram, Covey-Crump, Mulroy,
Auchincloss, Daniels, Gilchrist, Harvey, Evans, King's
Consort Ch. & O, King

When Monteverdi's Marian *Vespers* of 1610 have won such
wide appreciation, not least on disc, it is strange that his other
church music has been relatively neglected. Here Robert King
with his King's Consort follows up the success of his big
Purcell series with the first in a Monteverdi cycle, also for
Hyperion. The eight items offered here all come from the
great 1640 collection, *Selva morale e spirituale*, six Psalm
settings associated with Christmas Vespers (including the
haunting *Beatus vir*) plus the magnificent setting of the

Magnificat in eight parts and the *Mass in four parts 'da cappella'*, harking back to an earlier polyphonic style. In a recording made in St Jude's, Hampstead, King achieves a fine spread of vocal and instrumental sound as well as clarity, with instrumental accompaniment in the *Mass* as well as in the rest.

Motets: *Cantate domino a 6; Domine ne in furore a 6; Missa de cappella a 4; Missa de cappella a 6 (in illo tempore)*
(BB) *** Hyp. Helios CDH 55145. The Sixteen, Christophers; Phillips

Harry Christophers draws superb singing from his brilliant choir, highly polished in ensemble but dramatic and deeply expressive too, suitably adapted for the different character of each Mass-setting, when the four-part Mass involves stricter, more consistent contrapuntal writing and the six-part, in what was then an advanced way, uses homophonic writing to underline key passages. Vivid, atmospheric recording.

Motets for solo voice: '*Pianto della Madonna'*: *Confitebor tibi Domini (Missa a 4 voci e salmi, 1650). Currite populi; Ecce sacrum paratum; O quam pulchra es (Ghirlanda sacra, 1645). Exulta, Filia Sion (Sacri canti, 1629). Jubilet a voce sola in dialogo; Lamento dell'Arianna: Pianto della Madonna; Laudate Dominum (all from Selva morale e spirituale, 1640). Salve, O Regina (Sacre canti, 1624); Venite, videte (1625)*
🎵 ✿ (M) *** HM HMC 901680. Kiehr, Concerto Soave, Aymes (with MARINI: 2 *Sinfonias (from Church Sonatas);* Costanto ATEGNATI: *Ricercar;* Claudio MERULO: *Toccata con minute ***)*

Maria Cristina Kiehr's compilation is very beautiful. With the vocal items contrasted with short instrumental ritornellos by other musicians from the same period, we cannot praise this recital too highly. Every work is glorious and is ravishingly sung. *Currite populi* introduces a lovely flowing *Alleluia; O quam pulchra es* ('How fair thou art, my love') is permeated with an exquisite melancholy which returns in several later items, and especially the famous excerpt from the *Lamento dell'Arianna*, which gives the CD its title. The fresh, spring-like *Jubilet* has a delightful echo effect, with a nice touch of added resonance, and *Exulta, Filia Sion* is another joyful song, with florid runs and a jubilant closing *Alleluia*. The closing *Laudate Dominum* makes a wonderful apotheosis, with alleluias and echoing phrases adding to its paean of praise. Superb music, superb singing and playing, and warmly atmospheric recording all here combine to bring the listener the very greatest musical rewards.

Motets: *Ego flos campi; Ego sum pastor bonus; Exulta, filia Sion; Fuge, fuge anima mea, mundum; Iusti tulerunt spolia; Lapidabant Stephanum; Lauda, Jerusalem; Laudate Dominum; Nigra sum; O bone Jesu, illumina oculos meos; O bone Jesu; O piissime Jesu; O quam pulchra es; Pulchra es; Salve Regina; Spuntava al dì; Sugens Jesus, Dominus noster; Surge propera, amica mea; Veni in hortum meum (with*
PICCININI: *Toccata X)*
*** Virgin 59602-2. B. Lesne, G. Lesne, Benet, Cabré, Il Seminario Musicale, Tragicomedia

The music on this disc encompasses all periods of Monteverdi's career; the earliest comes from his first published collection, the *Sacrae canticulicae* (1582), composed when he was only fifteen. Other pieces, such as the *Salve Regina*, come from the *Selva morale* (1640), while *Pulchra es* and *Nigra sum*

are performed on instruments alone. The solo motet, *O quam pulchra es*, is preceded by a *Toccata* by Alessandro Piccinini about which the excellent notes are silent. The performances here are expert and totally committed. Excellent recording.

Selva morale e spirituale (complete)
*** HM HMC 901718/20 (3). Cantus Cöln, Concerto Palatino, Konrad Junghändel

Many of the 40 or so pieces which make up the *Selva morale e spirituale* – Monteverdi's last publication, a collection of sacred pieces, following up his eight books of madrigals – have often been recorded, but it is especially valuable that Junghändel and his talented performers have recorded the complete collection. These are performances marked by keen perception as well as energy. In his presentation Junghändel effectively solves one of the main problems of the whole: the very variety of the pieces, which range widely in their styles from pure polyphony to the latest developments of the mid-seventeenth century, plainly drawn from all periods of Monteverdi's career. The original publication also had them in higgledy-piggledy order, and Junghändel has perceptively reordered them to present the first and third of the three CDs roughly as *Vespers* collections, with miscellaneous items on the second disc. It works well, with the 12 singers of Cantus Cöln led by the superb soprano, Johanna Koslowsky, offering ample variety of colour and expression to keep concentration. A superb achievement, helped by fine, atmospheric recording.

Selva morale e spirituale: excerpts: *Adoramus te; Beatus vir a 6 voci; Chi vol che m'innamori; Confitebor terzo alla francese; Confitebor tibi Domine; E questa vita un Iampo; Gloria a 7 voci; Laudate Dominum; O ciechi ciechi*
(B) *** HM HMC 195 1250. Les Arts Florissants, Christie

Monteverdi's *Selva morale e spirituale* (1640) is a huge collection of nearly 40 separate works, written over three decades. Christie's programme here gives an idea of its range, from *Beatus vir*, the vivid large-scale Psalm-setting for six voices and violins, and the splendid seven-voiced *Gloria*, with its burst of vocal virtuosity at the opening, to the succinct *Adoramus te*, and the more modest *Laudate Dominum* for bass voice with continuo. All the performances here are imbued with a flowing vitality and combine breadth and devotional feeling with vocal and instrumental refinement. As usual from this source, the recording is admirably clear and spacious.

Vespro della Beata Vergine (Vespers)
🎵 ✿ *** DG **DVD** 073 035-9; CD 429 565-2 (2). Monoyios, Pennicchi, Chance, Tucker, Robson, Naglia, Terfel, Miles, H.M. Sackbutts & Cornetts, Monteverdi Ch., L. Oratory Ch., E. Bar. Sol., Gardiner
*** BIS CD 1071/2 (2). Midori Suzuki, Nonoshita, Hatano, Türk, Van Dyke, Taniguchi, MacLeod, Ogasawara, Bach Coll. Japan Ch. & O, Masaaki Suzuki
(BB) *** Hyp. Dyad CDD 22028 (2). The Sixteen, Christophers
(B) **(*) Teldec 4509 92629-2 (2). Marshall, Palmer, Langridge, Equiluz, Hampson, Korn, Tölz Boys' Ch., soloists from V. Hofburg Ch., Arnold Schönberg Ch., VCM, Harnoncourt
**(*) Erato 3984-23139-2 (2) Degor, Wieczorek, Stenowica, Schofrin, Agnew, Cornwell, Piolino, Felix, Bayley, Les Arts Florissants, Christie

(M) **(*) Teldec (ADD) 4509 92175-2 (2). Hansmann, Jacobeit, Rogers, Van t'Hoff, Van Egmond, Villisech, V. Boys' Ch. soloists, Hamburg Monteverdi Ch., Plainsong Schola of Munich Capella Antiqua, VCM, Jürgens

Vespro della Beata Vergine (Vespers). Selva morale e spirituale: Beatus vir; Confitebor tibi Domine; Dixit Dominus; Laudate pueri; Laudate Dominum; Salve Regina
(BB) *** Virgin 2x1 5 61662-2 (2). Kirkby, Rogers, Thomas, Taverner Ch., Cons. and Players, Parrott

When in 1989 John Eliot Gardiner made his live recording in the grand setting of St Mark's, Venice, this film was made for BBC television. If on CD the reverberation and occasionally the balances of voices do not suit every listener, the video version makes everything plain, and the beauty and grandeur of the setting exactly match the glories of the music, superbly interpreted. It is good to find the young Bryn Terfel among the soloists, one of an outstanding team. Among the bonus items is an illuminating 20-minute introduction by Gardiner himself, also filmed in Venice. He outlines the music and its composition, with a brief portrait of the composer, and emphasizes his own devotion to this of all works, which played a key part in his emergence as a conductor, evoking a sense of joy in him whenever he returns to it.

Gardiner's CD recording of the *Vespers* vividly captures the spatial effects that a performance in the Basilica of St Mark's, Venice, made possible. Gardiner made his earlier recording for Decca in 1974 using modern instruments (now withdrawn). Here, with the English Baroque Soloists and a team of soloists less starry but more aptly scaled, all of them firm and clear, he directs a performance even more compellingly dramatic. It would be hard to better such young soloists as the counter-tenor Michael Chance, the tenor Mark Tucker and the bass Bryn Terfel. Without inflating the instrumental accompaniment – using six string-players only, plus elaborate continuo and six brass from His Majesties Sackbutts and Cornetts – he combines clarity and urgency with grandeur. Gardiner (as before) does not include plainchant antiphons and so has room on the two discs for the superb alternative setting of the *Magnificat*, in six voices instead of seven, in another dedicated performance.

Suzuki's fine set aims to include not just the *Vespers*, complete with the grand *Magnificat* in seven voices, but the other items in the collection which Monteverdi published in 1610. Following the example of Andrew Parrott, Suzuki has chosen to transpose the music down a fourth not only for the two settings of the *Magnificat*, but for the *Mass* and the *Lauda Jerusalem*, each written in a combination of high clefs. He adds that this avoids the high scream of cornetts in the two settings of the *Magnificat*. It makes a satisfying and generous package, very well performed and warmly recorded. The scale is not as grand as in Gardiner's version nor as intimate as Philip Pickett's. The reverberation often obscures detail in the big choral numbers, but the balance is excellent between solo voices and choir, and the approach is characteristically lively and well sprung in the way one expects of this fine choral conductor. A first-rate recommendation, particularly with such generous bonuses.

Although Parrott uses minimal forces, with generally one instrument and one voice per part, so putting the work on a chamber scale in a small church setting, its grandeur comes out superbly through its very intensity. Far more than usual with antiphons in Gregorian chant, it becomes a liturgical celebration, so that the five non-liturgical compositions or concerti are added to the main *Vespers* setting as a rich glorification. They are brilliantly sung here by the virtuoso soloists, above all by Nigel Rogers, whose distinctive timbre may not suit every ear but who has an airy precision and flexibility to give expressive meaning to even the most taxing passages. With fine all-round singing and playing, and a warm, atmospheric recording which, despite an ecclesiastical ambience, allows ample detail through, this set is recommended. The other items, from the *Selva morale e spirituale*, are not quite so impressive – this singing is a bit bloodless – but are fully acceptable as a bonus. There are no texts or translations and minimal notes, but this is very inexpensive.

The Sixteen's version of Monteverdi's 1610 *Vespers* on Hyperion, beautifully scaled, presents a liturgical performance of what Graham Dixon suggests as Monteverdi's original conception. In practice the occasional changes of text are minimal; the booklet accompanying the set even includes an order of tracks if anyone wishes to hear the *Vespers* in traditional form. As it is, with a liturgical approach, the performance includes not only relevant Gregorian chant but antiphon substitutes, including a magnificent motet of Palestrina, obviously relevant, *Gaude Barbara*. The scale of the performance is very satisfying, with The Sixteen augmented to 22 singers (7.4.6.5) and with members of the group taking the eight solo roles. Christophers provides a mean between John Eliot Gardiner's unashamedly grand view and Andrew Parrott's vital, scholarly re-creation of an intimate, princely devotion.

Harnoncourt's admirers may well be attracted to his 1986 recording, particularly as it is now available as an Ultima bargain Double. It was recorded live and gives a keen sense of occasion, with the grandeur of the piece linked to a consciously authentic approach. There is an entirely apt ruggedness in the interpretation, which is lightened by the characterful refinement of the solo singing from an exceptionally strong team of soloists, not to mention the fine singing from all three choirs. Ample, atmospheric recording.

William Christie's version was recorded in 1997, following a live performance given in Sicily, and simply follows the pattern of the live event. Imaginatively Christie punctuates the sequence with instrumental numbers – two *Sonatas* by Monteverdi's contemporary, Giovanni Paolo Clima – and presents the whole performance with flair and dedication. The reverberation of the recording venue in Paris makes for washy sound, and many will miss having the six-part *Magnificat* as an alternative, but Christie's admirers will not be disappointed.

Recorded in Vienna in 1966/7 the Jürgens set is scholarly yet not without warmth. The liturgical sequence is respectful, and authentic instruments are used. The continuo tends to be somewhat lightweight, but there is a sure sense of style. The opening chorus is vivid with the colour of Renaissance trumpets and recorders, but the CD transfer cannot disguise a lack of sharpness of focus here and in the more complex analogue choral textures. At mid-price this is fair value, for the soloists are all fine artists and the choral singing is committed and polished. Documentation is excellent.

OPERA

L'incoronazione di Poppea (opera; DVD versions)
(N) *** Bel Air **DVD** BAC 004. Delunsch, Von Otter, Brunet, Hellekant, Sedov, Fouchécourt, Les Musiciens du Louvre, Minkowski (V/D: Vincent Bataillon)

(*) Arthaus **DVD 100 108. Schumann, Croft, Kuhlmann, Gall, Peeters, Brooks, Concerto Köln, Jacobs. (Dir: Michael Hampe; V/D: José Montes-Baquer)

L'incoronazione di Poppea (opera; CD versions)

☞ *** DG 447 088-2 (3). McNair, Von Otter, Hanchard, Chance, D'Artegna, E. Bar. Sol., Gardiner

(M) *** Virgin 5 61783-2 (3). Augér, D. Jones, Hirst, Reinart, Bowman, City of L. Bar. Sinfonia, Hickox

(M) **(*) Teldec (ADD) 2292 42547-2 (4). Donath, Söderström, Berberian, Esswood, VCM, Harnoncourt

Marc Minkowski's period performance of *L'Incoronazione di Poppea* was recorded at the Aix-en-Provence Festival in 2000 in the atmospheric courtyard of the Archbishop's Palace. With an outstanding cast, Klaus Michael Gruber's production offers a staging with stylized sets and timeless costumes, effectively clarifying the story of the love of Nero and Poppea. Minkowski has opted basically for the Venice version of the score, but has added three instrumental interludes by Monteverdi's associate, Biagio Marini, to facilitate scene-changes. He has chosen instrumentation with ample bass continuo to suit the venue, and the result is a moving and beautiful account, which heightens the love scenes between Poppea and Nero, not least the ecstatic final duet – when, curiously, they are not seen to embrace – and the monologues of the deserted wife, Ottavia, powerfully sung by Sylvie Brunet. She emerges as an equal star with Anne Sofie von Otter as Nero and Mireille Delunsch ravishing as Poppea. Other roles are strongly taken by Charlotte Hellekant as Ottone, Denis Sedov as a handsome, young-looking Seneca and Jean-Paul Fouché-court comically in drag as the nurse, Arnalta. A presentation that very effectively brings out the sharp contrasts of pathos and comedy in this masterpiece.

The Arthaus performance from the 1993 Schwetzingen Festival is far more severe, both artistically and as a visual experience. It suffers from a less than ideal Poppea in Patricia Schumann but both Kathleen Kuhlmann's Ottavia and Darla Brooks's Drusilla are expressive and intelligent singers, and the Seneca of Harry Peeters is exemplary. The performance as a whole is more compelling than the old Zurich alternative, which will presumably find its way on to DVD in the fullness of time. Subtitles are in English, French, German and Spanish.

With an exceptionally strong and consistent cast in which even minor roles are taken by star singers, Gardiner presents a purposeful, strongly characterized performance. He is helped by the full and immediate sound of the live recording, made in concert at the Queen Elizabeth Hall, London. Sylvia McNair is a seductive Poppea and Anne Sofie von Otter a deeply moving Ottavia, both singing ravishingly. Francesco d'Artegna, a robustly Italian-sounding bass, makes a stylish Seneca, and there are clear advantages in having a counter-tenor as Nero instead of a mezzo-soprano, particularly one with a slightly sinister timbre like Dana Hanchard. So in the sensuous duet which closes the opera, the clashing intervals of the voices are given a degree of abrasiveness, suggesting that, though this is a happy and beautiful ending, the characters still have their sinister side. The text has been modified with newly written ritornellos by Peter Holman, using the original, authentic bass-line, and aiming to be 'closer to what Monteverdi would have expected' than the usual flawed text.

On Virgin, the tender expressiveness of Arleen Augér in the title-role of Monteverdi's elusive masterpiece combines with a performance from Richard Hickox and the City of London Baroque Sinfonia which consistently reflects the fact that it was recorded in conjunction with a stage production in 1988. Hickox daringly uses a very spare accompaniment of continuo instruments, but he overcomes the problems of that self-imposed limitation by choosing the widest possible range of speeds. The purity of Augér's soprano may make Poppea less of a scheming seducer than she should be, but it is Monteverdi's music for the heroine which makes her so sympathetic in this oddly slanted, equivocal picture of Roman history, and one that has seldom sounded subtler or more lovely on record than this. Taking the castrato role of Nero, Della Jones sings very convincingly with full, rather boyish tone, while Gregory Reinart is magnificent in the bass role of Seneca. James Bowman is a fine Ottone, with smaller parts taken by such excellent singers as Catherine Denley, John Graham-Hall, Mark Tucker and Janice Watson. Linda Hirst sounds too raw of tone for Ottavia, making her a scold rather than a sympathetic suffering widow. Fitted on to three well-filled mid-priced CDs, the opera comes with libretto and translation and can be recommended alongside the Gardiner set.

Nikolaus Harnoncourt's well-paced and dramatic version makes a welcome reappearance at mid-price in Teldec's Harnoncourt series. First issued in 1974, it offers a starry cast, with Elisabeth Söderström as Nero (imaginative but not always ideally steady), Helen Donath pure-toned as Poppea and Cathy Berberian as the most characterful and moving Ottavia on disc. Others include Paul Esswood and Philip Langridge, and Harnoncourt's bold and brassy instrumentation adds to the bite. The snag is that, unnecessarily, the set stretches to four discs instead of three, which cancels out the price advantage over the excellent rival set from Richard Hickox.

(i) *L'incoronazione di Poppea* (abridged version, realized by Raymond Leppard); (ii) Madrigals: *Al lume delle stelle; A quest'olmo; Cor mio, mentre vi miro; Io mi son giovinetta; Lamento d'Arianna; Ohimè se tanto amaie; Volgendo il ciel* (ballo)

(B) **(*) EMI double forte (ADD) 5 73842-2 (2). (i) László, Bible, Lewis, Dominguez, Marimpietri, Cava, Alberti, Cuénod, Glyndebourne Festival Ch., RPO, Pritchard; (ii) Cantelo, Poulter, Watts, English, Tear, Keyte, ECO, Leppard

Raymond Leppard's edition of this equivocal masterpiece will probably shock baroque purists with sounds that are sumptuous rather than spare, while he makes use of two harpsichords, two organs, two cellos, lute, guitar and harp for the continuo group – a most generous array of instruments which certainly serve to colour the score in the best baroque manner. Even in this cut version, the honeyed warmth of the production comes over vividly, with Magda László and Richard Lewis fresh and dramatic. The bass, Carlo Cava, is a weighty Seneca, fully conveying the character of the noble and revered philosopher and statesman whose tragic suicide in this edition rounds off Act I. Throughout, his excellent low register never loses its flexibility. Nero's comic duet of rejoicing (with the unique Hugues Cuénod as Lewis's brilliant partner) could hardly be bettered as a musical picture of inebriation (hiccups and all), and this then sets the contrasted tone of Act II, leading to Nero and Poppea's ecstatic final duet. Frances Bible as Ottavia and Walter Alberti as Ottone portray the cast-off wife and lover with admirable skill. Vocally superior to these are Lydia Marimpietri, whose Drusilla is a marvel of characterization, and Orelia Dominguez, who plays the difficult and exacting role of

Poppea's nurse and confidante. John Pritchard coaxes from the Royal Philharmonic Orchestra a truly Monteverdian sound, and the Glyndebourne Chorus makes brief but significant contributions, notably in the scene of Seneca's farewell. The stars of the piece, Richard Lewis and Magda László, are on top of their form and their final love-duet comes as a magnificent end to a great opera. The recording is remarkably opulent.

This timely bargain issue is well supplemented by a collection of madrigals, recorded three years later with an entirely different cast. The singers here are all fine artists in their own right, but the choice of a group of soloists for this repertoire proves not to be the best way of ensuring a good blend between the parts, with individual voices tending to stick out at times from the overall texture. However, the performances certainly do not lack character and there are no complaints about the recording itself. In the opera no texts are given, but a detailed synopsis is related to the CD tracks, without however giving the Italian titles of each aria or excerpt, which are listed separately. There are no texts or translations for the madrigals.

Orfeo (opera; complete)

◎⊸ (N) (M) * Decca 476 7213-2 (2). Mark Ainsley, Gooding, Bott, Bonner, George, Grant, New L. Cons., Pickett

*** DG 419 250-2 (2). Rolfe Johnson, Baird, Dawson, Von Otter, Argenta, Robson, Monteverdi Ch., E. Bar. Sol., Gardiner

(N) (BB) *** Virgin 2x1 82070-2 (2). Rogers, Kwella, Kirkby, J. Smith, Chiaroscuro, L. Bar. Ens., L. Cornett & Sackbutt Ens., Medlam

** Virgin 5 45642-2 (2). Bostridge, Dessay, Coote, Gens, Ciofi, Maltman, Agnew, European Voices, Les Sacqueboutiers, Le Concert d'Astrée, Haïm

Pickett has not tried to treat *Orfeo* with kid gloves but has aimed above all to bring out its freshness. So, in the dark *Sinfonia* with its weird chromatic writing, which at the opening of Act III represents Orfeo's arrival in the underworld, Pickett cuts out strings and uses brass instruments alone. As Orfeo, John Mark Ainsley may have a less velvety tenor than Anthony Rolfe Johnson on the Gardiner set, but his voice is more flexible in the elaborate decorations of *Possente spirto*, Orfeo's plea to Charon. Outstanding among the others is Catherine Bott. In *Orfeo* she not only sings the elaborate role given to La Musica in the Prologue, sensuously beautiful and seductive in her coloration, but also the part of Proserpina and the key role of the Messenger who graphically describes the death of Euridice. This has now been re-issued in Universal's 'Critics' Choice' series with full documentation including text and translation.

John Eliot Gardiner very effectively balances the often-conflicting demands of authentic performance – when this pioneering opera was originally presented intimately – and the obvious grandeur of the concept. So the 21-strong Monteverdi Choir conveys, on the one hand, high tragedy to the full, yet sings the lighter commentary from nymphs and shepherds with astonishing crispness, often at top speed. However, Gardiner is strong on pacing. This is a set to take you through the story with new involvement. Though editing is not always immaculate, the recording on CD is vivid and full of presence.

In Medlam's re-issued Virgin version Nigel Rogers has the double function of singing the main part and acting as co-director. Rogers has modified his extraordinarily elaborate ornamentation in the hero's brilliant pleading aria before Charon and makes the result all the freer and more wide-ranging in expression. Euridice's plaint, beautifully sung by Patrizia Kwella, is the more affecting for being accompanied very simply on the lute. The other soloists make a good team, though Jennifer Smith as Proserpina, recorded close, is made to sound breathy. The brightness of the cornetti is a special delight, when otherwise the instrumentation used (largely left optional in the score) is modest. Excellent, immediate recording, making for a fine budget priced alternative to Gardiner. A cued synopsis is provided.

With an exceptionally starry cast led by Ian Bostridge in the title-role, Emanuelle Haïm's Virgin recording has much in its favour, recorded in the helpful acoustic of the Lebanese church in Paris. Directing from the continuo keyboards (harpsichord, organ and regal), Haïm is an energetic interpreter, tending to prefer fast speeds, while the singers characterize vividly. Impressive as Bostridge's virtuoso performance is in Orfeo's big Act III solo, *Possente spirto*, persuading Charon to let him cross the Styx, he is in danger of over-interpreting each word. Natalie Dessay, in the allegorical role of La Musica, the first solo singer one hears, adds to that impression with her fruity soprano, very different from the voices of most period singers. Patrizia Ciofi as Euridice, Véronique Gens as Proserpina and Alice Coote in the small but significant role of the Messenger are all strong artists too, technically perfect, but they too follow the same performing style, with the line-up of men also strong if not quite so characterful. Though the strings of Le Concert d'Astrée tend to be edgy in a way that most period bands have abandoned, the freshness of the whole set is certainly attractive. But first choice rests with Pickett's L'Oiseau-Lyre set with John Mark Ainsley in the title-role and Catherine Bott outstanding as La Musica and Prosperina.

Il ritorno d'Ulisse in patria (complete)

(M) **(*) Teldec (ADD) 2292 42496-2 (3). Eliasson, Lerer, Hansen, Baker-Genovesi, Hansmann, Equiluz, Esswood, Wyatt, Walters, Van Egmond, Mühle, Junge Kantorei, VCM, Harnoncourt

Harnoncourt's 1971 recording brings a sympathetic performance, square in rhythm and with a keen sense of repose, which is very important in Monteverdi. The solo singing is not as characterful as on Harnoncourt's *Poppea*, though Norma Lerer makes a touching Penelope, with Sven Olaf Eliasson a stylish Ulisse, not ideally pure of timbre. Highlights are also available (a generous 77 minutes) on Apex (2564 61508-2).

MONTSALVATGE, Xavier
(1912–2002)

Concerto brève for Piano & Orchestra

(N) *** Australian Decca Eloquence (ADD) 476 2971. Larrocha, RPO, Frühbeck de Burgos – ALBENIZ: *Rapsodia Española*; SURINACH: *Piano Concerto*; TURINA: *Rapsodia sinfónica* ***

Xavier Montsalvatge's *Concerto brève* is dedicated to Alicia de Larrocha, who plays it here with authority and conviction. While no masterpiece – there is no really memorable theme – it is nevertheless entertaining, especially with its colourful orchestration, which is well brought out by the first-class (1977) Decca engineering. The RPO under Frühbeck de Burgos are excellent, and this rarity makes a good bonus for the other concertante works offered here.

MOODY, James (1907–95)

(i) *Quintet for Harmonica & String Quartet*; (ii) *Suite dans le style français*

*** Chan. 8802. Reilly; (i) Hindar Qt; (ii) Kanga – JACOB: *Divertimento* ***

James Moody's *Suite in the French Style* may be pastiche but its impressionism is highly beguiling. The *Quintet* is more ambitious, less charming perhaps, but likely to prove even more rewarding on investigation, especially the very diverse theme and variations of the finale, the longest movement. The performance and recording are hardly likely to be bettered.

MORALES, Cristóbal de (c. 1500–53)

***Missa Mille regretz* (heard as part of the Mass for the Feast of St Isidore of Seville)**

(M) *** DG Blue 474 228-2. Gabrieli Consort & Players, McCreesh (with music by GUERRERO; CABEZON; ROGIER; GOMBERT; SANTA MARIA)

This is one of Paul McCreesh's less celebrated historical musical reconstructions, but it is hardly less rewarding than its more spectacular companions. Here McCreesh places Morales's Mass, *Mille regretz*, at the centre of an imaginary celebration in honour of St Isidore of Seville, on his Feast Day, 4 April. Because that date often falls within Lent, the choice of music 'corresponds to the introspective, penitent mood of that period of the church year'. *Mille regretz* is a 'parody Mass' and is based on a chanson about the pain of a lost love attributed to Josquin. Its easily recognizable melodic profile dominates the Mass movements, while the appropriate propers are also included. Further variety is achieved by interweaving organ voluntaries by Cabézon and other music by Guerrero (including two instrumental canciáns played on shawms). Later, a brief sung motet for the choir, with brass accompaniment, makes a further interpolation. Between the *Sanctus* and the *Agnus Dei*, the brass play Nicolas Gombert's arrangement of the original chanson, *Mille regretz*, and there are varied instrumental pieces by Philippe Rogier and others to accompany the imaginary pre-Mass processional and post-Mass recessional. The celebration ends with a beautiful closing motet by Morales, *Emendemus in melius* ('Let us amend for the better in those things in which we have sinned through ignorance'). McCreesh's re-creation works above all because the polyphony of the Morales Mass itself is so rich. The instrumental interludes too are attractively varied in instrumentation and are very well played, and the singing is very fine indeed, heard within the richly echoing acoustic of Brinkburn Priory in Morpeth. Even though this is a mid-priced reissue (on the Archiv Blue label) the full documentation, texts and translation are included.

Missa Si bona suseptimus

**(*) Gimell CDGIM 033. Tallis Scholars, Phillips (with CRECQUILLON: *Andreas Christi famulus*; VERDELOT: *Si bona suseptimus*)

The Spanish Renaissance master Cristóbal de Morales began and ended his career in Spain, but he spent the decade between 1535 and 1545 singing with the Sistine Chapel Choir in Rome. The *Missa Si bona suseptimus* was almost certainly composed during this period, and its opulence of line owes something to Italian influence, yet Morales retained his own fluid style, as comparison with *Mille regretz* shows. The present Mass is again a parody mass, using as its source Verdelot's motet, *Si bona suseptimus*, which is concerned with the theme of Job ('The Lord giveth and the Lord taketh away'), although Morales's texture and polyphony are richer than his model. The Tallis Scholars' performance is appropriately prefaced by its source motet and followed by another work long credited to Morales, but now thought to be by Thomas Crecquillon. It is the splendid eight-part motet, *Andreas Christi famulus*, but its layout is denser, less supple than that of Morales. These are fine performances, beautifully and passionately sung and recorded, but in the main work the lack of variety of dynamic (though not of tempo) is a drawback for the non-specialist listener.

MORENO TORROBA, Federico (1891–1982)

Sonatina for Guitar & Orchestra; Interludes I & II

*** Analekta Fleur de Lys FL 2 3049. Boucher, Amati Ens., Dessaints – ABRIL: *Concierto Mudéjar* ***

Moreno Torroba's *Sonatina* was written in the early years of the twentieth century for Segovia; the composer made the concertante arrangement of the solo work not long before he died. The outer movements, with their Castilian atmosphere, are gay and engaging, and the Romance, which forms the central *Andante*, is quite captivating, especially when the performance has such a simple spontaneity and is not too overladen with expressive feeling. The two *Interludes* are also both highly evocative and they are most winning in their present format. Rémi Boucher is a splendid soloist, and Raymond Dessaints gives him affectionate support. The warmth of the truthful and very well-balanced recording adds to the listener's pleasure.

***Luisa Fernanda* (complete)**

*** Valois V 4759. Domingo, Villaroel, Pons, Rodrigo, Madrid University Ch., Madrid SO, Marba

This is an ideal recommendation for anyone wanting to investigate the zarzuela, the Spanish genre of operetta. Moreno Torroba, best known for his guitar music, here offers in three compact Acts a sequence of catchily tuneful numbers, brightly orchestrated. Led by Domingo in glowing form as the hero, Javier, an army colonel, the cast is as near ideal as possible, with Veronica Villaroel in the title-role and Juan Pons as Javier's rich rival. Bright, immediate sound.

MORLEY, Thomas (1557–1602)

Ayres and Madrigals: *Absence, hear thou my protestation; Arise, awake; Besides a fountain; Deep lamenting; Fire and lightning; Hard by a crystal fountain; Hark! Alleluia; In every place; Mistress mine; No, no, no, Nigella; O grief ev'n*

on the bud; Phyllis I fain would die now; Singing alone; Sleep slumbr'ing eyes; Stay heart, run not so fast; With my love

(M) *** Decca 476 1971. Consort of Musicke, Rooley; or 476
7227 (2) – GIBBONS; WILBYE: *Madrigals* ***

Morley is generally thought of as a lesser figure than his contemporaries, even though he was the pioneering English madrigalist. This collection should do something to modify that picture of him, for although the lighter canzonetti and balletti based on Italian models (and in particular Gastoldi) are in evidence, there are more searching and thoughtful pieces. *Deep lamenting* and *O grief ev'n on the bud* are very touching, while Rooley himself provides lute accompaniments for Emma Kirkby's lovely *Sleep slumb'ring eyes* and the ambitious *Absence, hear thou my protestation*, the longest song in the whole programme, sensitively sung by Andrew King. *Mistress mine* is unexpectedly precocious, and there are others which make one feel that the range of Morley's musical personality has not been adequately reflected before. This is a rewarding recital and has the benefit of well-projected performances and very good recording. Full texts are provided. This reissue comes either as a single CD or as a 2-CD set in Universal's 'Critics' Choice' series.

MOSCHELES, Ignaz (1794–1870)

Piano Concertos 1 in F, Op. 45; 6 in B flat (Fantastique); 7 in C min. (Pathétique), Op. 93

*** Hyp. CDA 67385. Shelley, Tasmanian SO

The *First Piano Concerto* arrived in 1818. It is not a particularly flamboyant work, and is not really distinctive until the jolly finale. The *Sixth Concerto* (1834) is altogether more fluent and mature, with all three sections planned to be played without interruption, the gentle slow movement joined to the rollicking gypsy finale by an agitato bridge passage derived from the opening movement. The *Seventh Concerto* dates from the following year and is notable in that the central movement is a Scherzo with the slow movement ingeniously interwoven. The reason for the nickname *Pathétique* is not clear, but in Howard Shelley's hands it emerges as an attractively inventive work. Indeed, all the concertos are entertaining when the solo playing is so brilliantly persuasive, the orchestra supportive, and the recording excellent.

Piano Concertos 2 in E flat, Op. 56; 3 in G min., Op. 58; Anticipations of Scotland (Grand Fantasia), Op. 75

☛ *** Hyp. CDA 67276. Shelley, Tasmanian SO

Both these piano concertos appeared in 1825. *No. 2 in E flat* is particularly attractive, with one striking idea after another bubbling up in the substantial outer movements – the finale a Chopin-like Polacca – and with a deeply meditative central *Adagio*. Though the thematic material of *No. 3 in G minor* is not so memorable, with passage-work that involves notespinning reminiscent of a study by Czerny, the finale makes amends with a jolly Rondo in a galloping 6/8 time. *Anticipations of Scotland*, as the title suggests, was written before Moscheles ever visited the country. Scottish songs were freely available to him, however, and in this fantasia he uses three in particular, with characteristic Scottish snap-rhythms – *Kelvin Grove, Auld Robin Gray* and *Lord Moira's Strathspey* – for a sequence of variations. Again, this is a piece full of conventional passage-work, this time helped by the underlying melodies. Moscheles's writing is always winningly fluent, so

that even when it is at its most predictable, it sparkles away in the hands of a fine pianist like Howard Shelley, who draws lively playing from the Tasmanian orchestra, with vivid, immediate recording.

Piano Concertos 2 in E flat, Op. 56; 4 in E, Op. 64

*** Zephyr Z 116-99. Hobson, Sinfonia da Camera

The *E flat Concerto* opens with the timpani setting the mood for an imposing march, with a Hummelian dotted rhythm, and they later set off the jolly *Polonaise* of the finale. The E major work has a more expansively ambitious opening tutti, and its slow movement centres on a romantic horn solo. The horns then announce the closing set of bold variations on 'The British Grenadiers', which gives Ian Hobson plenty of opportunities for glittering bravura. He plays spiritedly throughout both works, yet obviously relishes their *galant* lyricism, while effectively directing the accompaniments from the keyboard. The recording is truthful and well balanced, and altogether this is a most enjoyable coupling.

MOSZKOWSKI, Moritz (1854–1925)

Piano Concerto in E, Op. 59

☛ *** Hyp. CDA 66452. Lane, BBC Scottish SO,
Maksymiuk – PADEREWSKI: *Piano Concerto* ***

(i) *Piano Concerto in E, Op. 59. From Foreign Lands, Op. 23*

(BB) *** Naxos 8.553989. (i) Pawlik; Polish Nat. RSO
(Katowice), Wit

It was Piers Lane's performance of this concerto, in partnership with the volatile Jerzy Maksymiuk, that inaugurated Hyperion's highly successful series, and anyone fancying a coupling with Paderewski will not be disappointed by this brilliant version, certainly full of vitality and both expressively sympathetic and subtle in detail. Excellent recording too.

The young German, Markus Pawlik, also proves a magnetic soloist, playing with the crispest articulation, readily matching the fine version from Piers Lane in Hyperion's parallel 'Romantic Piano Concerto' series. The fill-up, a suite of colourful orchestral pieces, is delightful.

Violin Concerto in C, Op. 30; Ballade in G min., Op. 16/1

*** Hyp. CDA 67389. Little, BBC Scottish SO, Brabbins –
KARLOWICZ: *Violin Concerto* ***

The Moszkowski *Violin Concerto*, first heard in 1883, may not be as inspired as the Karlowicz concerto with which it is coupled, but it delivers many striking ideas over its 34-minute span, from the attractively offbeat opening onwards. The jolly, gallumping first theme in compound time hardly sounds promising material for a 15-minute symphonic movement, but Moszkowski clearly demonstrates how unfair it is that he has regularly been dismissed as merely a composer of miniatures. As in the Karlowicz, Tasmin Little and Martyn Brabbins are most persuasive interpreters, with the playing from the BBC Scottish Orchestra both polished and warmly expressive, which no doubt reflects ample rehearsal time. The *Ballade*, Moszkowski's first orchestral work, developed from a piece for violin and piano, similarly ranging and wide in expression, makes an ideal filler. Full, warm sound, recorded in Caird Hall, Dundee.

Piano Music: *Air de ballet, Op. 36/5; Albumblatt, Op. 2; Au crépuscule, Op. 68/3; Barcarolle from Offenbach's 'Contes* *d'Hoffmann'; Chanson bohème from Bizet's 'Carmen'; Danse russe, Op. 6/4; En automne, Op. 36/4; Expansion, Op. 36/3; La Jongleuse, Op. 52/4; Minuetto, Op. 68/2; Nocturne, Op. 68/1; Poème de Mai, Op. 67/1; Près de berceau, Op. 58/3; Rêverie, Op. 36/2; Serenata, Op. 15/1; Tarantella, Op. 27/2; Valse mignonne*

(BB) **(*) Hyp. Helios CDH 55141. Tanyel

Pieces like *Au crépuscule* have a certain sub-Lisztian charm, *La Jongleuse* is an engaging *moto perpetuo*, and *Près de berceau* is the epitome of a salon piece. Seta Tanyel characterizes the music sympathetically, but she is hard put to sustain interest through a 69-minute recording of genre pieces that are heard most effectively as encores at the end of a more substantial programme. The *Air de ballet* is an ideal example, with its brilliant filigree at the close, which sparkles readily in her hands. Truthful recording.

Piano Music, Vol. 2: *3 Etudes de concert, Op. 24; Fantaisie impromptu, Op. 6; Grande valse de concert, Op. 88; Isoldens Tod; 3 Morceaux poétiques, Op. 42; 3 Morceaux, Op. 73*

(N) (BB) **(*) Hyp. Helios CDH 55142. Tanyel

Piano Music, Vol. 3: *Barcarolle, Op. 17/1; Etude, Op. 67/2; 6 Morceaux, Op. 83; 3 Morceaux, Op. 86; 3 Morceaux, Op. 87; Scherzo-Valse, Op. 40*

(N) (BB) *** Hyp. Helios CDH 55143. Tanyel

In the remaining two volumes Seta Tanyel continues to show her skill in seducing the ear with Moszkowski's sometimes ingenuous music with her delicacy of phrase and feeling, and genuine affection. The *Morceaux* of Opp. 42 and 73 are slight but have genuine charm, and the *Grande valse de concert* has a pleasing nostalgia for times past.

Every so often we are reminded of other composers, notably Mendelssohn in the *Scherzo-Etude* of Op. 86, and Chopin in the *Fantaisie impromptu* of Op. 6, the *Impromptu* of Op. 87 (an altogether attractive opus) and the *Barcarolle*. Quite a few of the *Morceaux* are engaging, and of the three Op. 24 *Etudes de concert* the second is surprisingly ambitious, if a little over-extended. As before, the recording is wholly natural.

MOZART, Leopold (1719–87)

Horn Concerto in D

*** Ara. Z 6750. Rose, St Luke's Chamber Ens. – FORSTER; HAYDN; TELEMANN: *Horn Concertos* ***

Leopold Mozart's *Horn Concerto* of 1755 is enormously demanding of its soloist – far more difficult than the later concertos of Wolfgang Amadeus. The first movement gambols in a sprightly 6/8, but soon takes the horn up into its highest register, where it remains for the expressive minor-key *Romanza*. The third movement then sets off lustily and demands that the soloist trill his way up a major arpeggio. Stewart Rose's trills, whether relaxed as in the slow movement, or buoyant as here, are impressively clean: he is a true virtuoso and establishes the difference between this essentially classical work and the earlier Baroque concerto of Telemann. A supplemental Minuet completes the piece traditionally and offers more opportunities for bravura. This performance will be hard to surpass, and the recording is excellent.

Trumpet Concerto in D

*** Sony **SACD** SS 57497. Marsalis, ECO, Leppard – FASCH; HAYDN; HUMMEL: *Trumpet Concertos* ***

Leopold Mozart's *Trumpet Concerto* contrasts a first movement with a long lyrical melisma, which lies very high up on the instrument, with a more robust and straightforward finale, still demanding considerable bravura. It is not a very original work and relies much on the expertise of the soloist to make an impression. Wynton Marsalis, playing a piccolo trumpet, is more than equal to the challenge and Leppard accompanies attentively. It is the Haydn and Hummel *Concertos* that make this SACD worth considering, although here the sound improvement over the CD is minimal.

MOZART, Wolfgang Amadeus
(1756–91)

Bargain Complete Mozart Edition, Vol. 2: (i) *Cassations*; (ii) *Contredanses; German Dances & Marches*; (ii) *Galimathias musicum; Marches (K.62, K.215, K.237, K.189, K.335, 1 & 2)*; (i) *Orchestral Serenades*

(B) *** Ph. (ADD) 464 790-2 (13). (i) ASMF, Marriner; (ii) V. Mozart Ens., Boskovsky

The Philips Complete Mozart Edition is no longer available in its original format, but it has been reissued in a bargain edition at a special price, much more simply packaged and with limited documentation. The discs are in cardboard sleeves within 17 boxes. This new 180-CD bargain set is available complete (on 464 660-2), but each of the new compilations is available separately. We have listed them concisely, although in many cases (as in the case of the *Dances, Marches* and major orchestral *Serenades*) the new compilations involve more than one of the original collections. Boskovsky's performances immediately set the manner for the whole series. The playing is marvellously alive and stylish, investing comparatively lightweight works with unexpected stature. The recording balance is flawless. Marriner and his Academy too are at their very finest here and make a very persuasive case for giving these works on modern instruments. The playing has much finesse, yet its cultivated polish never brings a hint of blandness or lethargy; it is smiling, yet full of energy and sparkle. In the concertante violin roles Iona Brown is an ideal soloist, her playing full of grace. Throughout this set the recording brings an almost ideal combination of bloom and vividness.

Cassations 1–3

☛ (BB) *** Naxos 8.550609. Salzburg CO, Nerat

All three early *Cassations* are given lively, nicely turned performances, very well – if resonantly – recorded. This admirable disc is certainly worth its modest cost and nicely fills a gap in the catalogue.

CONCERTOS

Bargain Complete Mozart Edition, Vol. 5: *Concertos for Bassoon; Clarinet; Flute; Flute & Harp; Horn (including Rondos). Violin Concertos 1–5; 7 in D, K.271; Adagio in E, K.261; Rondo in B flat, K.269; Rondo in C, K.373; Concertone, K.190; Double Concerto in D for Violin, Piano & Orchestra, K.315f; Sinfonie concertantes, K.297b; K.320e; K.364*

(B) *** Ph. (ADD/DDD) 464 810-2 (9). Various soloists, ASMF, Marriner

The principal wind concertos here are recent digital versions.

They are all well played and recorded. However, there is a slightly impersonal air about the accounts of the *Bassoon* and *Clarinet Concertos*, well played though they are; and there are more individual sets of the works for horn. The *Sinfonia concertante* is offered both in the version we usually hear (recorded in 1972, with the performance attractively songful and elegant) and in a more modern recording of a conjectural reconstruction by Robert Levin, based on the material in the four wind parts.

(i) ***Bassoon Concerto, K.191;*** (ii) ***Clarinet Concerto, K.622;*** (iii) ***Flute Concerto 1, K.313; Andante, K.315;*** (iii; iv) ***Flute and Harp Concerto, K.299;*** (v) ***Horn Concertos 1–4;*** (vi) ***Oboe Concerto, K.314. Divertimenti 2 in D, K.131; 11 in D, K.251; 12 in E flat, K.252; 14 in B flat, K.270; A Musical Joke, K.522; Serenades 6 (Serenata notturna); 10 in B flat, K.388; 12 in C min., K.388; 13 (Eine kleine Nachtmusik); Sinfonia concertante in E flat, K.297b***

(B) *** DG 471 435-2 (7). (i) Morelli; (ii) Neidich; (iii) Palma; (iv) Allen; (v) Jolley or Purvis; (vi) Wolfgang; Orpheus CO

(i) ***Bassoon Concerto, K.191;*** (ii) ***Clarinet Concerto, K.622;*** (iii) ***Flute Concerto 1, K.313; Andante, K.315;*** (iii; iv) ***Flute and Harp Concerto in C, K.299;*** (v) ***Horn Concertos 1–4;*** (vi) ***Oboe Concerto, K.314; Sinfonia concertante, K.297b***

(B) *** DG Trio 469 362-2 (3). (i) Morelli; (ii) Neidich; (iii) Palma; (iv) Allen; (v) Jolley or Purvis; (vi) Wolfgang; Orpheus CO

Frank Morelli chortles his way engagingly through the outer movements of the *Bassoon Concerto* and is contrastingly doleful in the *Andante*; Charles Neidich uses a basset clarinet in K.622 and his timbre is very appealing; Randall Wolfgang's plaintive, slightly reedy tone is especially telling in the *Adagio* of the *Oboe Concerto* and he plays the finale with the lightest possible touch, as does Susan Palma the charming Minuet which closes the *Flute Concerto*. The *Sinfonia concertante* for wind has three new soloists (Stephen Taylor, David Singer and Steven Dibner) plus William Purvis, and is pleasingly fresh; the players match their timbres beautifully in the *Adagio*, and again the last movement is delightful with its buoyant rhythmic spirit.

The *Divertimenti* and *Serenades* also bring highly admirable performances. Alert, crisply rhythmic *Allegros* show consistent resilience, strong, yet without a touch of heaviness, while slow movements are warmly phrased, with much finesse and imaginative use of light and shade. *Eine kleine Nachtmusik* is wonderfully light-hearted and fresh and among the finest on record; the *Serenata notturna*, which can easily sound bland, has a fine sparkle here, while the B flat *Wind Divertimento*, K.270, is notable for some felicitous oboe playing.

Impeccable in ensemble, this splendid playing has no sense of anonymity of character or style. All the works are given excellent recordings, and this is a very persuasive collection indeed, probably a 'best buy' for all wanting this music in a digital format.

The bargain-priced Trio is also highly recommendable.

Bassoon Concerto in B flat, K.191

*** Chan. 9656. Popov, Russian State SO, Polyansky – HUMMEL; WEBER: *Bassoon Concertos* ***

*** Caprice CAP 21411. Sönstevold, Swedish RSO, Comissiona – PETTERSSON: *Symphony 7* ***

Valeri Popov's playing has character and warmth. He is at his most personable in the Minuet Rondo finale. Polyansky's accompaniment is warmly supportive, and the Chandos recording is well up to standard.

Knut Sönstevold's performance of Mozart's concerto is a good, big-band performance which gives pleasure, and is very well recorded.

(i; ii) ***Bassoon Concerto;*** (iii; iv) ***Clarinet Concerto;*** (v) ***Flute Concerto 1*** (vi; iv) ***Horn Concertos 1–4;*** (vii; ii) ***Oboe Concerto***

🔑 *** (B) DOUBLE DECCA (DDD/ADD) 466 247-2 (2). (i) McGill; (ii) Cleveland O, Dohnányi; (iii) De Peyer; (iv) LSO, Maag; (v) Bennett, ECO, Malcolm; (vi) Tuckwell; (vii) Mack

These recordings readily demonstrate the ongoing excellence of the Decca coverage of the Mozart wind concertos over three decades. Gervase de Peyer is admirable in the *Clarinet Concerto*, and his account remains as fine as any available, fluent and lively, with masterly phrasing in the slow movement and a vivacious finale. Barry Tuckwell at the time was proving a natural inheritor of the mantle of Dennis Brain. His easy technique, smooth, warm tone and obvious musicianship command allegiance and give immediate pleasure. William Bennett a decade later, but again in the Kingsway Hall, is hardly less impressive in the *G major Flute Concerto*. Throughout, the recording is clean and well detailed, with enough resonance to add bloom to the sound. The CD transfers are immaculate. For the *Bassoon* and *Oboe Concertos* we turn to Cleveland. The oboist, John Mack, has an appealingly sweet (but not too sweet) timbre; then David McGill, in the work for bassoon, immediately establishes his keen individuality. He does not overdo the humour in the finale. Both performances are beautifully recorded and attractively balanced. All in all, very enjoyable music-making by musicians from both sides of the Atlantic who are equally at one with Mozart.

(i) ***Bassoon Concerto;*** (ii) ***Clarinet Concerto;*** (iii) ***Flute Concerto 1***

(M) *** DG 457 719-2. VPO, Boehm; with (i) Zeman; (ii) Prinz; (iii) Tripp

These are meltingly beautiful accounts. All three soloists perform with the utmost distinction under Boehm, who lets the music unfold in an unforced way, relaxed yet vital. Excellent mid-1970s sound makes this a highly recommendable DG 'Originals' disc.

(i) ***Bassoon Concerto;*** (ii) ***Clarinet Concerto;*** (iii) ***Oboe Concerto***

(BB) **(*) Naxos 8.550345. (i) Turnovskỳ; (ii) Ottensamer; (iii) Gabriel; V. Mozart Ac., Wildner

In the *Oboe Concerto* the soloist on Naxos, Martin Gabriel, is excellent. The clarinettist, Ernst Ottensamer, is also a sensitive player, his slow movement is full of feeling; and there is an accomplished performance of the *Bassoon Concerto* from Stepan Turnovskỳ, who has the measure of the work's character and wit. Recommendable.

(i) ***Bassoon Concerto;*** (ii) ***Flute & Harp Concerto. Sinfonia concertante, K.297b***

(M) *** Classic fM 76505 57038-2. (i) Andrews; (ii) Hill, Wakeford; soloists, Britten Sinfonia, Cleobury

Julie Andrews gives Mozart's droll *Bassoon Concerto* a genial lift-off, while the flautist, Kate Hill, and the harpist, Lucy Wakeford, create winningly delicate tracery in the *Concerto for Flute and Harp.* Both slow movements are beautifully phrased, and the team of soloists is no less persuasive in the *Sinfonia concertante*, not least in the light-hearted finale. The recording and balance are altogether first class.

Clarinet Concerto in A, K.622

*** DG 457 652-2. Collins, Russian Nat. O, Pletnev –
BEETHOVEN: *Clarinet (Violin) Concerto in D, Op. 61* ***

*** EMI 5 56832-2. Meyer, BPO, Abbado – DEBUSSY: *Première rapsodie*; TAKEMITSU: *Fantasma/cantos* ***

(i) *Clarinet Concerto*; (ii) *Flute Concerto 1 in G*; (ii; iii) *Flute & Harp Concerto*

*** EMI 5 57128-2. (i) Meyer; (ii) Pahud; (iii) Langlamet, BPO, Abbado

Michael Collins has here provided the weightiest, most challenging, if controversial, coupling in Mikhail Pletnev's arrrangement for clarinet of the Beethoven *Violin Concerto*. Collins uses a basset clarinet, relishing the extra downward range and richness of timbre. His speeds in the outer movements are fast, wonderfully agile and with the cleanest articulation and crisp rhythmic pointing, as well as fine detail. It is a reading not just elegant but powerful too, as well as deeply poetic in the slow movement. The playing of the Russian National Orchestra under Pletnev is refined and elegant to match.

Sabine Meyer's 1998 performance brings out how much her individual artistry has intensified even in the ten years between this and her first Dresden recording of this greatest of clarinet works, also for EMI (see below, where she chose to use the basset clarinet). She again opts for speeds faster than usual, but finds time to point phrasing and shade dynamics with keen imagination and a feeling of spontaneity. As before, where appropriate, she adds cadenza-like flourishes, as in the honeyed lead-back to the reprise in the central *Largo*.

Recorded live, she is even more inspired and imaginative than in her version of ten years earlier, with light, clear support from the orchestra which in the days of Karajan spurned her when she was proposed as principal clarinet. The two concertos with Pahud reveal him as an outstandingly individual artist, light and athletic, dominant over the rather reticent harpist in the *Double Concerto*. Though the original issue also had the *Flute Concerto No. 2*, that is less important, being an arrangement of a work for oboe, so the present triptych is highly recommendable.

(i) *Clarinet Concerto*; (ii) *Flute Concerto 1*; (iii) *Oboe Concerto*

(M) *** Classic fM 75605 57001-2. (i) Farrall; (ii) Hill; (iii) Daniel; Britten Sinfonia, Cleobury

In the *Clarinet Concerto* Joy Farrall's solo style lies somewhere between the freely spontaneous manner of Emma Johnson and the flexible, classical directness of Thea King. Nicholas Daniel is equally appealing in the stylishly infectious account of the *Oboe Concerto*. Kate Hill's *Flute Concerto* is hardly less delectable. Excellent balancing and fine recording make this mid-priced triptych from Classic fM hard to beat.

(i) *Clarinet Concerto*; (ii) *Flute & Harp Concerto*

(BB) *** REGIS RRC 1061. (i) Campbell; (ii) Davies, Masters; City of L. Sinfonia, Hickox

David Campbell's agile and pointed performance of the clarinet work brings fastish speeds and a fresh, unmannered style in all three movements. His tonal shading is very beautiful. The earlier work for flute and harp is just as freshly and

sympathetically done, with a direct, unmannered style sounding entirely spontaneous. A bargain.

(i) *Clarinet Concerto*; (ii) *Sinfonia concertante, K.297b*

(M) *** EMI 5 66897-2 [5669492]. (i) Meyer, Dresden State O; (ii) cond. Vonk

Using the original basset clarinet, in her earlier, Dresden account Sabine Meyer gives a highly seductive performance of Mozart's beautiful concerto and at the same time accompanies herself by directing a rich-textured modern-instrument backing. The solo playing has much warmth and great finesse. Indeed, some listeners may feel that this music-making has an element of self-consciousness, especially at the gentle muted reprise of the *Adagio*. But the finale trips along gracefully, and it is good to have a performance of such individuality paired with Vonk's persuasively stylish account of the *Sinfonia concertante*, with Meyer joining the team of soloists. The sound is excellent, but this coupling is a less than apt candidate for EMI's 'Great Recordings of the Century' series.

(i) *Clarinet (Basset-Clarinet) Concerto*; (ii) *Oboe Concerto*; (iii) *Sinfonia concertante for Violin, Viola & Orchestra, K.364*

(N) **(*) Guild GMCD 7181. (i) Lluna; (ii) Knights; (iii) Studt, Jvania; Bournemouth Sinf., Studt

(i) *Clarinet Concerto*; (ii) *Clarinet Quintet, K.581*

☛ *** Hyp. CDA 66199. King; (i) ECO, Tate; (ii) Gabrieli Qt

☛ (N) (M) *** RCA 82876 60866-2. Stoltzman; (i) ECO; (ii) Tokyo String Qt

(N) *** PentaTone **SACD** PTC 5186 048. Andrew Marriner; (i) ASMF, N. Marriner; (ii) ASMF Chamber Ens.

(i) *Clarinet Concerto*; (ii) *Clarinet Quintet*

(N) *** ASV Gold GLD 4001. Johnson; (i) ECO, Leppard; (ii) Takács-Nagy, Hirsch, Boulton, Shulman (with BAERMANN: *Adagio* ***) – WEBER: *Clarinet Concertino* ***

(i) *Clarinet Concerto. Overture: Die Entführung aus dem Serail* (arr. Sargent)

(N) (B) (***) BBC Classics mono BBCM 5014-2. (i) Brymer; BBC SO, Sargent (with MENDELSSOHN: *A Midsummer Night's Dream: Nocturne; Wedding March* (**)) – SCHUBERT: *Symphony 8 (Unfinished)* (**)

(i) *Clarinet Concerto, K.622*; (ii) *Clarinet Quintet, K.581*; (iii) *Exsultate, Jubilate, K.165*

(M) *** ASV Platinum PLT 8514. (i) Johnson, ECO, Leppard; (ii) Hilton, Lindsay Qt; (iii) Lott, LMP, Glover

Thea King's coupling brings together winning performances of Mozart's two great clarinet masterpieces. She steers an ideal course between classical stylishness and expressive warmth, with the slow movement becoming the emotional heart of the piece. The Gabrieli Quartet is equally responsive in its finely tuned playing. For the *Clarinet Concerto* Thea King uses an authentically reconstructed basset clarinet. With Jeffrey Tate an inspired Mozartian, the performance – like that of the *Quintet* – is both stylish and expressive, with the finale given a captivating bucolic lilt. Excellent recording.

Richard Stoltzman gives equally outstanding performances of both works. The *Concerto*, full of spontaneity, brings a comparatively brisk, sparkling tempo in the first movement and a contrasting, leisurely *Adagio*, deeply felt, in which Stoltzman produces the most beautiul timbre and gently embroiders the reprise of the main theme. The Rondo is high-spirited, with the clarinet roulades delightfully bucolic. By directing the ECO himself, the soloist controls the work's structure as he wants, and then in the *Quintet* the silky-toned Tokyo Quartet provide a seductive backing tapestry and a performance equally full of subtle light and shade, especially striking in the finale. The recording is first class, bright and glowing in both works and admirably balanced.

The smiling faces of Sir Neville and Andrew Marriner shine forth on the front of their SACD, which offers performances of a comparably gracious warmth, full of affectionate touches and tender nuances. Tempi are relaxed, the lovely *Larghetto* of the *Quintet* is exquisitely and balmily played; but the effect is never bland and the finale has a pleasingly light rhythmic touch. The producer, Andrew Keener, has made good use of the acoustic of the Henry Wood Hall, and the SACD envelops the listener in its friendly ambience. The overall musical tapestry is richly upholstered, not as bright and transparent as the RCA/Stoltzman version, but very beguiling.

This Platinum collection fascinatingly contrasts the styles of two young British clarinettists. Emma Johnson recorded her version of the *Clarinet Concerto* soon after winning the BBC's Young Musician of the Year in 1984. The result lacks some of the technical finesse of rival versions by more mature clarinettists, but it has a sense of spontaneity, of natural magnetism which traps the ear from first to last. There may be some rawness of tone in places, but that only adds to the range of expression, which breathes the air of a live performance, whether in the sparkle and flair of the outer movements or the inner intensity of the central slow movement, in which Emma Johnson plays magically in the delightfully embellished lead-back into the main theme. Leppard and the ECO are in bouncing form, and the recording is first rate.

This pairing has now been reissued on ASV's Gold label, re-coupled more generously with Baermann's lovely *Adagio* (once attributed to Wagner) and Weber's delightful *Concertino*.

Janet Hilton then gives a disarmingly unaffected account of the *Clarinet Quintet* and gets excellent support from the Lindsays. The recording is forward, but well balanced and vivid. There are many delights in Felicity Lott's *Exsultate, Jubilate*: her clean and stylish singing is well supported by Jane Glover's sympathetic conducting, which elicits poised playing from the LMP. Beautiful, if slightly distant, recording.

Recorded live at a Promenade Concert in the 1960s, Jack Brymer gives a characteristically luscious account of the *Clarinet Concerto*, with his chalumeau delectably rich. The Mendelssohn encores are well played too, although the *Wedding March* has much more spirit than the comparatively lethargic *Nocturne* (well recognized by the Promenaders). But the surprise here is what appears to be Sargent's own arrangement of the *Entführung Overture*, to which is added an elaborately extended coda, exciting enough but sounding more like Beethoven than Mozart.

Joan Enric Lluna's basset-clarinet sounds fascinatingly different from the clarinet in the hands of, say, Jack Brymer, with the lower chalumeau range drier and with more point on the articulation, the effect aurally intriguing. The slow movement sounds less romantic than usual, but not less fresh. Andrew Knights's *Oboe Concerto* is both nimble and full-timbred, enjoyably vivacious. But what makes this triptych especially attractive is the outstanding account of the *Sinfonia concertante*, with Richard Studt leading persuasively on the violin and Nodar Jvania a most sympathetic partner. The close of the *Andante* is memorably expressive and deeply

felt, and the finale is attractively jaunty. The Bournemouth Sinfonietta provide excellent accompaniments, but the one drawback here is the close balance, especially of the soloists, which robs the very present recording of a degree of refinement and inevitably reduces the dynamic range. But this remains a most enjoyable disc.

(i) *Flute Concertos 1–2; Andante, K.315*; (ii) *Flute & Harp Concerto, K.299*; (iii) *Sinfonia concertante, K.297b* (reconstructed R. Levin); (iv) *Flute Quartets 1–4*
(B) **(*) Ph. Duo (ADD) 442 299-2. (2) (i) Nicolet, Cong. O, Zinman; (ii) Barwahser, Ellis, LSO, C. Davis; (iii) Nicolet, Holliger, Baumann, Thunemann, ASMF, Marriner; (iv) Bennett, Grumiaux Trio

Aurèle Nicolet's performances of the *Flute Concertos* and *Andante for Flute and Orchestra* are very positive, and the solo playing throughout is expert and elegantly phrased. Barwahser and Ellis give a sparkling account of the *Flute and Harp Concerto* and Sir Colin accompanies them with the greatest sprightliness and sympathy. If these are not a top choice in this repertoire, the William Bennett accounts of the four *Flute Quartets* with the Grumiaux Trio certainly are. The wind *Sinfonia concertante*, in which the oboe and clarinet parts are replaced by flute and oboe respectively, is an interesting conjectural experiment rather than an essential part of a Mozart collection. The recordings throughout are smoothly remastered and sound fine.

Flute Concertos 1–2; Andante, K.315
(BB) **(*) Naxos 8.550074. Weissberg, Capella Istropolitana, Sieghart

Herbert Weissberg does not have the outsize personality of some of his rivals, but he is a cultured player, and the quality of the recording is excellent. In short, good value for money and very pleasant sound.

(i) *Flute Concertos 1–2*; (ii) *Flute & Harp Concerto*
(M) *** RCA 82876 59409-2. Galway; (ii) Robles; ASMF, Marriner
(M) *** Decca (ADD) 440 080-2. (i) Bennett, ECO, Malcolm; (ii) Tripp, Jellinek, VPO, Münchinger
(B) **(*) DG 469 553-2. Zöller; (i) ECO, Klee; (ii) Zabaleta, BPO, Märzendorfer
**(*) EMI 5 56365-2. Pahud; (ii) Langlamet; BPO, Abbado
(BB) **(*) Naxos 8.557011. Gallois, Swedish CO, (ii) with Pierre

James Galway and Marisa Robles take an expansive, warmly expressive view of the slow movement of the *Flute and Harp Concerto*; she also matches him in a delightfully bouncy account of the finale, sharper in focus than Pahud. In the solo concertos, too, Galway takes an expansive, expressive view of the slow movements and a winningly relaxed one of the *Allegros*.

William Bennett gives a beautiful account of the concertos, among the finest in the catalogue. Every phrase is shaped with both taste and affection, and the playing of the ECO under George Malcolm is fresh and vital. The earlier, Vienna recording of the *Flute and Harp Concerto* has also stood the test of time. Refinement and beauty of tone and phrasing are a hallmark throughout, and Münchinger provides most sensitive accompaniments.

Zöller is a superb flautist. K.313 is a little cool but is played most elegantly, with pure tone and unmannered phrasing.

The charming Minuet finale is poised and graceful. The performance of K.314 is more relaxed and smiling, and the *Andante* is admirably flexible. Bernhard Klee provides adept accompaniments. Zöller favours the use of comparatively extended cadenzas whenever Mozart provided space for them, and one wonders whether they will not seem too much of a good thing on repetition. In the *Flute and Harp Concerto* Zabaleta's composure and sense of line knit the texture of the solo-duet together most convincingly. Märzendorfer conducts with warmth yet with a firm overall control. In short, with pleasing analogue sound from the 1970s, well transferred, this is highly successful.

The fast speeds in the Berlin performance have a light, taut touch, with the ever-imaginative Emmanuel Pahud set against a modest-sized Berlin Philharmonic. Next to Pahud, the harp soloist, Marie-Pierre Langlamet is rather reticent in the *Flute and Harp Concerto*, though always sensitive.

Patrick Gallois is a delightful player, as is obvious in the Rondos of both solo concertos. But, surprisingly, the playing of the Swedish Chamber Orchestra is on the heavy side, not helped by the resonance of Örebro Concert Hall, which also affects the harp focus. So while these are stylish and enjoyable performances, they lack the lightness of touch that Galway, Robles and Marriner bring to them.

(i; ii) *Flute Concertos 1–2*; (i–iii) *Flute & Harp Concerto*; (iv) *Divertimento for Strings 1, K.136; 2 Marches, K.335; Serenades 6 (Serenata notturna); 9 (Posthorn)*; (v) *Symphonies 35 (Haffner); 36 (Linz); 38 (Prague); 39 in E flat, K.543; 40 in G min., K.550; 41 in C (Jupiter)*

☞ ⊛ (BB) *** Virgin Classics 5×1 5 61678-2 (5). (i) Coles; (ii) ECO; (iii) Yoshino; (iv) Lausanne CO; (v) Sinfonia Varviso; Menuhin

In many ways this is the outstanding Mozartian CD bargain of all time – five discs for the price of one. Moreover, the set would be highly desirable if it cost several times as much. Both the *Flute Concertos* are stylishly and pleasingly played by Samuel Coles, and when Naoko Yoshino joins him in the delectable *Flute and Harp Concerto* the interplay is fluently appealing. No complaints about the sound either and there is no doubting the character of these performances. The *Serenata notturna* and the *Divertimento* are graceful and fresh, and so is the *Posthorn Serenade*. Menuhin's approach is above all elegantly light-hearted and Crispian Steele-Perkins has his brief moment of glory as the posthorn soloist in the Minuet.

Yet when we turn to the last six symphonies, we encounter playing and interpretations of a very special order. The Sinfonia Varviso responds warmly to Menuhin as the group's chosen President. Though modern instruments are used, the scale is intimate, with textures beautifully clear, and the fresh, immediate sound highlights the refined purity of the string playing. In the last four symphonies speeds are on the fast side, yet he does not sound at all rushed. The *G minor* is especially memorable – among the finest ever recorded. With playing of precision, clarity and bite, one constantly has the feeling of live music-making. Exposition repeats are observed in both first and last movements of the *Jupiter* and this performance, like its partner, takes its place as a top recommendation for the two last symphonies, irrespective of cost. The five discs come in a pair of boxes (with accompanying booklet) in a slipcase, and are surely an essential purchase, even if some duplication is involved.

(i) *Flute Concertos 1–2*; (ii) *Flute Sonatas 4–6, K.13–15*

(N) (BB) *** Regis RRC 1151. Hall; (i) Philh. O, Thomas; (ii) Alexander-Max

We have long recommended Judith Hall's 1987 recordings of the *Flute Concertos* (originally on the Pickwick label). She produces a radiantly full timbre; moreover she is a first-class Mozartian, as she demonstrates in her cadenzas as well as in the line of the slow movement, phrased with a simple eloquence that is disarming. There is plenty of vitality in the allegros and Peter Thomas provides polished, infectious accompaniments to match the solo playing. The balance is most realistic and the sound overall is excellent, if perhaps not now quite in the demonstration bracket. For the Regis reissue, three of the *Flute Sonatas* have been added. Composed in 1764 when the Mozart family were staying in London, they are slight works, written when the very young composer was under the influence of Johann Christian Bach. Once again Judith Hall's instrumental personality dominates the music-making, and she is appropriately accompanied by Susan Alexander-Max on an Erard pianoforte (cc. 1846).

(i) *Flute Concertos 1 & 2. Symphony 41 (Jupiter)*

☞ (N) *** Telarc CD 80624. Boston Bar., Pearlman; (i) with Zoon

Jacques Zoon, formerly principal flute of the Royal Concertgebouw Orchestra and later of the Boston Symphony, here translates his style very convincingly to period performance. He gives readings of both works that it would be hard to match for both sheer virtuosity and imagination, making the baroque flute sound more like a flute and less like a recorder than usual. Stylishly, he adds substantial cadenzas in both works to slow movements as well as to the first, with Martin Pearlman and the Boston Baroque sympathetic accompanists. In the *Jupiter Symphony* they come into their own in a most refreshing performance, with the snapping rhythms of the opening motif given a dry, military flavour, and with a military flavour returning at the very end of the finale. The woodwind are cleanly defined, with the strings relatively reticent, but the reading is far from small-scale. An unusual coupling, but a highly enjoyable disc.

(i) *Flute Concerto 1; Andante, K.315*; (ii) *Flute & Harp Concerto*

(B) *** Ph. 420 880-2. C. Monteux; (ii) Ellis; ASMF, Marriner

First published in the early 1970s, these Philips performances with Claude Monteux as the principal soloist reappear on the bargain Virtuoso label. Exquisite playing from all concerned. The solo instruments sound larger than life as balanced, but in every other respect this splendidly remastered disc is highly recommendable.

(i; iv; v) *Flute Concerto 1 in G, K.313*; (i; ii; iv; vi) *Flute and Harp Concerto in C, K.314*; (iii; iv; v) *Oboe Concerto in C, K.314*

(B) **(*) CfP 575 1442. (i) Snowden; (ii) C. Thomas; (iii) Hunt; (iv) LPO; (v) Mackerras; (vi) Litton

Jonathan Snowden's account of the *Flute Concerto* is attractive, sprightly, stylish and polished (though some might not take to his comparatively elaborate cadenzas). The performance of the *Flute and Harp Concerto* is even more winning. Where Gordon Hunt in the *Oboe Concerto* seems a natural concerto soloist, Snowden, in collaboration with Caryl Thomas on the harp, is both sparkling and sensitive, regularly imaginative in his individual phrasing. The recording is life-like and this is good value although, in the final analysis, not a first choice.

Flute & Harp Concerto in C, K.299

(M) *** DG (ADD) 463 648-2. Zöller, Zabaleta, BPO, Märzendorfer – REINECKE: *Harp Concerto;* RODRIGO: *Concierto serenata* *** ●

Karlheinz Zöller is a most sensitive flautist, his phrasing a constant source of pleasure, while Zabaleta's contribution is equally distinguished. The 1963 recording is clear and clean, if not quite as rich as we would expect today. This performance is also available coupled with the solo flute concertos (see above).

(i) Flute & Harp Concerto in C, K.299; (ii) Oboe Concerto

*** Chan. 9051. (i) Milan, Kanga; (ii) Theodore; City of L. Sinfonia, Hickox – SALIERI: *Double Concerto* ***

A warmly elegant modern-instrument account of this beguiling concerto, with the delicate interweaving of flute and harp given a delightful bloom by the resonant recording. The *Oboe Concerto* is equally sensitive, again with the line of the *Adagio* delectably sustained by David Theodore, whose creamy tone is so enticing. Both soloists play their own cadenzas.

(i) Flute & Harp Concerto. Sinfonia concertante, K.297b

(BB) *** Naxos 8.550159. (i) Válek, Müllerová; Capella Istropolitana, Edlinger

Richard Edlinger's account of the *Flute and Harp Concerto* is thoroughly fresh and stylish, and the two soloists are excellent. Although the *Sinfonia concertante in E flat*, K.297b, is not quite so successful, it is still very impressive, and it gives much pleasure. Both performances are very decently recorded; in the lowest price-range they are a real bargain.

Horn Concertos 1 in D, K.412; 2–4 in E flat, K.417, 447 & 495

*** Crystal CD 515. Cerminaro, Seattle SO, Schwarz

(B) *** DG (ADD) 449 856-2. Seifert, BPO, Karajan

(M) **(*) Teldec (ADD) 0630 17429-2. Baumann, VCM, Harnoncourt

Horn Concertos 1 (with alternative versions of Rondo); 2–4; Allegro, K.370b & Concert Rondo in E flat (ed. Tuckwell); Fragment in E, K.494a

(B) *** Regis RRC 1007. Tuckwell, Philh. O

Horn Concertos 1–4; Concert Rondo in E flat, K.371 (ed. Civil or E. Smith)

*** Chan. 9150. Lloyd, N. Sinfonia, Hickox

(BB) *** Naxos 8.550148. Stevove, Capella Istropolitana, Kopelman

Horn Concertos 1–4; Concert Rondo, K.371 (ed. Tuckwell)

(M) *** EMI 5 72988-2. Vlatkovic, ECO, Tate – R. STRAUSS: *Horn Concerto 1* ***

Horn Concertos 1–4; Concert Rondo, K.371 (ed. Tuckwell); Fragment in E flat., K.494a

(BB) *** Virgin 2x1 Double 5 61573-2 (2). T. Brown (hand-horn), OAE, Kuijken – *Concert arias* ***

(BB) *** EMI Encore (ADD) 5 74966-2 [5749672]. Tuckwell, ASMF, Marriner

Horn Concertos 1–4; Concert Rondos: in E flat, K.371 (completed John Humphries); in D, K.514 (completed Süssmayr); Fragment for Horn & Orchestra in E flat, K.370b (reconstructed Humphries)

●→ (BB) *** Naxos 8.553592. Thompson, Bournemouth Sinf.

Horn Concertos 1 (including Rondo in D, K.514, completed Süssmayr); 2–4; Concert Rondos in E flat, K.371; in D (alternative finale to K.412, completed Humphries)

*** Häns. 98.316. T. Brown, ASMF, I. Brown

Horn Concertos 1–4; Concert Rondo in E flat, K.371 (reconstructed Greer); Rondo in D, K.485 (reconstructed Jeurisson)

(BB) *** HM HCX 3957012. Greer, Philh. Bar. O, McGegan

Horn Concertos 1–4; Concert Rondo, K.371; Fragments: in E, K.Anh.98a; in E flat, K.370b; in D, K.524 (all ed. Tuckwell)

(M) *** Decca 458 607-2. Tuckwell, ECO

As well as offering superb performances of the four regular concertos using revised texts prepared by John Humphries, the outstanding Naxos issue includes reconstructions of two movements designed for a horn concerto dating from soon after Mozart arrived in Vienna. The *Rondo* completed by Süssmayr is the version generally used as the second movement of K.412. The *Rondo* played here as the second movement of K.412 is Humphries's reconstruction from sources recently discovered. It is fascinating too to have extra passages in No. 4, again adding Mozartian inventiveness. Michael Thompson plays with delectable lightness and point, bringing out the wit in finales, as well as the tenderness in slow movements. He also draws sparkling and refined playing from the Bournemouth Sinfonietta, very well recorded in clear, atmospheric sound.

Another first-class super-bargain set comes from Lowell Greer, who uses a modern copy of a Raoux Parisian cor of 1818, which has a most attractive timbre. He plays with complete freedom, disguising the stopped notes skilfully, and his Mozartian line is impeccable. Slow movements are phrased with appealing simplicity and the rondo finales have splendid buoyancy. McGegan and his chamber orchestra accompany very stylishly and the recording is excellent.

For Hänssler, Timothy Brown chooses a modern instrument, and his persuasive lyrical line, imaginative phrasing and neat use of cadenzas show him as a true Mozartian. Another of the memorable features of this fine Hänssler disc is the warmth and finesse of Iona Brown's stylish accompaniments. The recording too is most natural in balance and sound-quality, and this CD stands high among modern versions of these ever-fresh concertos.

The Decca Ovation reissue (458 607-2) offers Barry Tuckwell's third set of four concertos in excellent digital sound, recorded in the Henry Wood Hall in 1983. He plays as well as ever and also directs the accompanying ECO. The orchestra provides crisp, polished and elegant accompaniments to make a perfectly scaled backcloth for full-timbred solo playing which again combines natural high spirits with a warmly expressive understanding of the Mozartian musical line. This reissue now includes the rest of Mozart's concertante horn music. Added to the *Rondo*, K.371, are three fragments which Tuckwell presents as Mozart left them but edited for concert performance.

Barry Tuckwell's Regis (originally Collins) CD, his fourth recording of the Mozart *Horn Concertos*, remains a splendid alternative choice. They are fresh, without a suspicion of routine, and are played with rounded tone and consistently imaginative phrasing. Moreover the collection is complete. Besides the *Fragment*, K.494a, Tuckwell includes both the familiar *Concert Rondo*, K.371, plus an *Allegro* first movement which Mozart wrote to go with it. Tuckwell also includes his own alternative *Rondo* finale of the *Concerto in D*, K.412, based directly on Mozart's autograph, placing the two alternative finales side by side.

Tuckwell's EMI Encore 1971 set offers strong, warm performances which have stood the test of time. If they do not quite have the magic of Dennis Brain's classic mono accounts (see below), they are still highly enjoyable, especially with Marriner's beautifully managed accompaniments. At budget price, with the two short fill-ups (the performance of the *Fragment* ends where Mozart left it at bar 91), this CD is well worth its modest cost.

In his earlier, Virgin recording Timothy Brown uses an open hand-horn without valves. He uses stopped notes with especially smart effect in the Rondos, and more sparingly and more subtly in the lyrical music. In short, these performances sound delightfully fresh, and give constant pleasure. Brown includes the additional *Rondo* and also the *Fragment*, which he leaves in mid-air, at the point at which the composer abandoned his manuscript. Kuijken's accompaniments are also pleasingly smooth and cultivated. But it seems a strange idea to couple this repertoire (even as a super-bargain Virgin Double) with concert arias.

Among the more recent versions is a fine Chandos set by Frank Lloyd, an outstanding soloist of the new generation. He plays these works with great character and poetic warmth; his phrasing is supple and his tone full, though never suave. Like Tuckwell, he uses a modern German double horn with great skill and sensitivity. Hickox provides admirable accompaniments, and the Chandos recording is well up to the high standards of the house.

Miloš Stevove on Naxos uses the slightest trace of vibrato but it is never obtrusive, and one has only to listen to the *Larghetto* of K.447 or the *Andante cantabile* of K.495 to discover his naturally warm feeling for a Mozartian phrase. *Allegros* are lively and the Rondos have agreeable lift. In short, with excellent, stylish accompaniments from the Capella Istropolitana this is enjoyably spontaneous.

John Cerminaro, at present principal with the Seattle orchestra, is a splendid soloist. His tone is rich and glowing (a little plump as recorded) and the hints of vibrato add to the individuality of his supple phrasing, for he shows a warmly elegant feeling for the Mozartian line. One of the highlights is the outstanding account of the *First Concerto*, into which he interpolates a soaring account of the slow movement of the *Horn Quintet*. He is warmly and persuasively accompanied by Schwarz – himself a brass player of distinction. But at full price, and without the *Concert Rondo*, this can hardly be a top recommendation.

Gerd Seifert has been principal horn of the Berlin Philharmonic since 1964, and his velvety, warm tone is familiar on many records. His articulation is light and neat here, and his nimbleness brings an effective lightness to the gay Rondos. The 1969 recording now brings just a hint of over-brightness on the *forte* violins, but this adds to the sense of vitality without spoiling the elegance.

Hermann Baumann successfully uses the original handhorn, without valves, and he lets the listener hear the stopped effect only when he decides that the tonal change can be put to good artistic effect. In his cadenzas he also uses horn chords (where several notes are produced simultaneously by resonating the instrument's harmonics), but as a complement to the music rather than as a gimmick.

Radovan Vlatkovic's tone is very full; there is also at times the slightest hint of vibrato, but it is applied with great discretion and used mostly in the cadenzas. His performances are full of imaginative touches and he has the perfect partner in Jeffrey Tate, who produces sparkling accompaniments. However, Vlatkovic only includes the *Concert Rondo*, K.371.

(i) *Horn Concertos 1–4;* (ii) *Horn Quintet, K.407*
(N) (M) **(*) Warner Elatus 0927 46723-2. Pyatt; (i) ASMF, Marriner; (ii) Sillito, Smissen, Tees, Orton

One expected much of David Pyatt's set of the four *Horn Concertos* with Marriner and the ASMF, recorded in 1996, not long after he came to fame as the BBC's 'Young Musician of the Year'. But for all his stylish playing, the result is very much studio-bound. Of course, the closing Rondos, nimbly articulated (especially those for K.447 and K.495), cannot fail to divert, but Marriner's accompaniments throughout fail to create a communicative spark with his celebrated soloist, even though they are quite elegant and smoothly recorded by Andrew Keener. The coupling, the engaging but less familiar *Horn Quintet*, is much more successful, with Kenneth Sillito leading the string group most expressively in the *Romanza*, and the finale vivaciously ebullient.

(i) *Horn Concertos 1–4;* (ii) *Piano & Wind Quintet in E flat, K.452*
(M) (***) EMI mono 5 66898-2 [5669502]. Brain; (i) Philh. O, Karajan; (ii) Horsley, Brain Wind Ens. (members)

Dennis Brain's famous (1954) mono record of the concertos with Karajan now rightly appears in EMI's 'Great Recordings of the Century' series. Brain's horn timbre was unique. As for the playing, Brain's glorious tone and phrasing – every note is alive – is life-enhancing in its warmth; the *espressivo* of the slow movements is matched by the joy of the Rondos, spirited, buoyant, infectious and smiling. Karajan's accompaniments, too, are a model of Mozartian good manners, and the Philharmonia at their peak play wittily and elegantly. Brain's distinguished earlier recording of the *Piano and Wind Quintet* has been added, with Colin Horsley making a fine contribution on the piano.

Oboe Concerto in C, K.314
(B) * Hyp. Helios CDH 55080. Francis, LMP, Shelley – KROMMER: *Oboe Concertos* ***

(M) **(*) DG 471 724-2 (2). Holliger, Camerata Bern, Füri – LEBRUN: *Oboe Concertos 1–6* *

Sarah Francis has already given us distinguished performances of oboe concertos by Handel and Telemann. Here she turns to Mozart with equal elegance and is persuasively accompanied by Howard Shelley and the London Mozart Players who, like their soloist, are completely satisfying in their stylish playing using modern instruments. The closing Rondo is particularly engaging.

Holliger phrases with fine musicianship, and his playing is impeccable. The performance is however overshadowed by a certain rigidity of approach; if the performers had been able to relax a little more they would have produced even finer results. However, there are no complaints about the recording, and Holliger is at his finest on the stimulating Lebrun coupling.

Keyboard concertos

(i) *Harpsichord Concertos 1–3, K.107. 2 Klavierstück, K.33b; Minuets, K.1–5; Sonatas: in E flat, K.26; in D, K.29 in B flat, K.31*

*** Opus 111 OPS 30-9003. Fernandez, (i) with Le Concert Français, Hantaï

Very slight pieces by the child Mozart, but very elegantly played and decently recorded.

Piano concertos

(with list of keys and Köchel numbers)

1 in F, K.37; 2 in B flat, K.39; 3 in D, K.40; 4 in G, K.41; 5 in D, K.175; 6 in B flat, K.238; 8 in C, K.246; 9 in E flat, K.271; 11 in F, K.413; 12 in A, K.414; 13 in C, K.415; 14 in E flat, K.449; 15 in B flat, K.450; 16 in D, K.451; 17 in G, K.453; 18 in B flat, K.456; 19 in F, K.459; 20 in D min., K.466; 21 in C, K.467; 22 in E flat, K.482; 23 in A, K.488; 24 in C, K.491; 25 in C, K.503; 26 in D, K.537 (Coronation); 27 in B flat, K.595; 2 Pianos: E flat, K.365; 3 Pianos: F, K.242; Concert Rondo in D, K.382; in A, K.386

Bargain Complete Mozart Edition, Vol. 4: *Piano Concertos; Rondos 1–2; Double Piano Concertos, K.242 & K.365; Triple Piano Concerto in F, K.242*

(B) ****(*)** Ph. (ADD/DDD) 464 800-2 (12). Koopman, Amsterdam Bar. O; Haebler, V. Capella Academica, Melkus; Brendel, ASMF, Marriner; Cooper; K. and M. Labèque, Bychkov, BPO, Bychkov

Piano Concertos 1–6; 8–9; 11–27; Rondo in D, K.382

(BB) ******* EMI (ADD) 5 72930-2 (10). Barenboim, ECO

Piano Concertos 1–6; 8–9; 11–27; Rondos 1–2, K.382 & 386

☛ ✿ (B) ******* SONY (ADD/DDD) SX12K 46441 (12). Perahia, ECO

(i) *Piano Concertos 1–6; 8–9, 11–27; Concert Rondos 1; (ii) 2; (iii) Double Piano Concerto in E flat, K.365; (iii; iv) Triple Piano Concerto in F, K.242*

(B) ******* Decca (ADD/DDD) 443 727-2 (10). Ashkenazy, with (i) Philh. O; (ii) LSO, Kertész; (iii) Barenboim, ECO; (iv) Fou Ts'ong

The Perahia cycle is a remarkable achievement; in terms of poetic insight and musical spontaneity the performances are in a class of their own. There is a wonderful singing line and at the same time a sensuousness that is always tempered by spirituality. About half the recordings are digital and of excellent quality and, we are glad to report, the earlier, analogue recordings have been skilfully remastered with first-class results, both in this complete set and in the separate issues below. This is an indispensable set in every respect.

Ashkenazy's set with the Philharmonia appeared over more than a decade. The account of the *E flat Concerto*, K.365, with Barenboim and the ECO, and the *Triple Concerto*, with Fou Ts'ong to complete the trio, is earlier still (1972). These performances have won golden opinions over the years, and the clarity of both the performances and the recordings is refreshing: indeed, the fine Decca sound is one of their strongest features.

The sense of spontaneity in Barenboim's EMI performances of the Mozart concertos, his message that this is music hot off the inspiration line, is hard to resist, even though it occasionally leads to over-exuberance and idiosyncrasies. These are as nearly live performances as one could hope for on record, and the playing of the English Chamber Orchestra is splendidly geared to the approach of an artist with whom the players have worked regularly. They are recorded with fullness, and the sound is generally freshened very successfully in the remastering. The set has been reissued in a handsomely produced super-bargain box, alongside his equally recommendable survey of the Beethoven piano sonatas. The recordings were made at Abbey Road between 1967 and 1974.

The Philips Bargain Mozart Edition *Piano Concertos* box is based on Brendel's set with the ASMF under Marriner. Throughout, his thoughts are never less than penetrating. The transfers are consistently of the very highest quality, as is the playing of the Academy of St Martin-in-the-Fields under Sir Neville Marriner. To make the set complete, Ingrid Haebler gives eminently stylish accounts of the first four *Concertos* on the fortepiano, accompanied by Melkus and his excellent Vienna Capella Academica; the sound is admirably fresh. However, on disc two the ear gets rather a shock when Ton Koopman presents the three works after J. C. Bach. Convincing though these performances are, it seems a strange idea to offer an authentic approach to these three concertos alone, particularly as at the end of the disc we return to a delightfully cultured performance on modern instruments of the alternative version for three pianos of the so-called *Lodron Concerto*, K.242, provided by the Labèque duo.

(i) *Piano Concertos 5–6; 8–9; 11–27; Rondo in D, K.382.*
Bonus DVD: (ii) *Double Piano Concerto in E flat, K.365; (ii; iii) Triple Piano Concerto in F, K.242*

(N) (B) ******* Warner 2564 61919-2 (8 + Bonus DVD). Barenboim; (i) BPO; (ii; iii) Solti; (iii) Schiff, with ECO

Barenboim recorded the *Piano Concertos* between 1986 and 1998, a number of them at live concerts. The performances are consistently of the highest quality, the earlier concertos made to sound both fresh and mature by the distinction of the playing, not only of Barenboim but also the Berlin Philharmonic Orchestra, which he directs from the keyboard. We gave a Rosette to the separate issue combining K.413, K.449 and K.451. In some of the later works the result is weighty in a way which sometimes makes the music look forward to Beethoven; indeed in the *D minor*, K.466 Barenboim plays Beethoven's cadenza, although elsewhere he often uses Mozart's, or provides his own. Occasionally there is a feeling of self-consciousness. The famous slow movement of the K.467 generates a certain languor, and similarly the lovely *Adagio* of K.488 misses something of the simplicity of Mozart's inspiration. However in K.482 the *Andante* is deeply felt and the finale, in which he chooses to play an abridged version of a cadenza by Edwin Fischer, is agreeably light-hearted. Overall these performances, which have rather more gravitas than his EMI series, yet remain spontaneous-sounding, are very satisfying in a different way, not least because of the expressive response of the Berlin Philharmonic and the very well balanced recordings. Moreover to make a very special bonus for this well documented boxed set Warner have provided a splendid DVD of the *Double* and *Triple Concertos* with Solti and András Schiff as Barenboim's excellent colleagues. Barenboim leads in the Double Concerto and Solti conducts, with delightful interchanges in the slow movement and a very brisk finale, sparkling rather than witty. Solti leads in the *Triple Concerto* and persuades the ECO to play very beautifully indeed. Excellent recording and effectively straightforward camera-work.

Piano Concertos 5–6; 8–9; 11–27

(M) *** Decca 448 140-2 (9). Schiff, Salzburg Mozarteum
    Camerata Academica, Végh

Piano Concertos 5–6; 8–9; 11; 13

(M) **(*) Ph. 473 889-2 (2). Uchida, ECO, Tate

*Piano Concertos 5–6; 8–9; 11–27; (i) Double Piano Concerto,
K.365; (i; ii) Triple Piano Concerto, K.242. Concert Rondos
1–2*

(B) *** DG 463 111-2 (9). Bilson (fortepiano), E. Bar. Sol.,
    Gardiner; with (i) Levin; (ii) Tan

András Schiff's cycle with the Salzburg Mozarteum Camerata
Academica under Sándor Végh proves to be one of the most
satisfying and – along with the new Shelley series on Chandos
– arguably the finest since Murray Perahia's cycle of the late
1970s. Schiff plays a Bösendorfer piano, and its relatively
gentle, cleanly focused timbre has something of the precision
of a fortepiano without any loss of the colour which comes
with a more modern instrument. The recording is consistently more beautiful than in Perahia's Sony set. For some
listeners, in certain works the warm resonance may offer a
problem. This is agreeably relaxed music-making, though not
in the least lacking in intensity or weight. Just occasionally
Schiff dots his 'i's and crosses his 't's a little too precisely, but
for the most part he is so musicianly and perceptive that this
seems unimportant. In short, these are lovely performances,
enhanced by the quality of the accompaniment under Végh,
who is unfailingly supportive. For the most part Schiff plays
his own cadenzas, but in the first movement of K.466 he uses
a cadenza by Beethoven, and the finale of K.488 brings one by
George Malcolm.

Malcolm Bilson is an artist of excellent musical judgement
and good taste and his survey is still the only one at present
available on the fortepiano. The overall musical standard is
very high, and the concentration and vitality of the music-
making are very compelling – especially so in Nos. 20 in D
minor and 21 in C (K.466–7). These originally received a
Rosette for their separate issue which is unfortunately now
deleted.

Mitsuko Uchida, following up her stylish and sensitive
accounts of the *Piano Sonatas*, began a cycle of the concertos
in 1985 which set the style for the series (recorded over a
period of nearly five years) with playing of considerable
beauty and performances guaranteed never to offend and
most likely to delight. There is some lovely playing, although
her cultured approach at times offers more than a glimpse of
Dresden china. She is unfailingly elegant but a little over-
civilized; some will find a faint hint of preciosity here and
there. Uchida is eminently alive and imaginative, although at
times one would welcome a greater robustness of spirit, a
lively inner current. Throughout, Jeffrey Tate draws splendid
playing from the ECO, and these artists have the benefit of
exceptionally good recorded sound; although the perspective
favours the piano, the timbre of the solo instrument is
beautifully captured.

Piano Concertos 5, K.175; 9, (Jeunehomme), K.271; 16, K.451

♦⸻ (M) *** Warner Elatus 0927 49827-2. Barenboim, BPO

Barenboim continues his cycle with the Berlin Philharmonic
with these three comparatively early concertos which show
him at his very finest form, free from affectation, both at the
keyboard and in directing the Berlin Philharmonic, who are

also on top Mozartean form. They sound very fresh and the
orchestral sonority is pleasingly well nourished. The recording is a bit forward but not excessively so and the whole disc
radiates pleasure.

Piano Concertos 5, K.175; 25, K.503

*** Sony SK 37267. Perahia, ECO

Murray Perahia has the measure of the strength and scale of
the *C major*, K.503, as well as displaying tenderness and
poetry; while the early *D major*, K.175, has an innocence and
freshness that are completely persuasive. The recording is
good, but the upper strings are a little fierce and not too
cleanly focused.

Piano Concertos 6, K.238; 8, K.246; 19, K.459

(BB) *** Naxos 8.550208. Jandó, Concentus Hungaricus,
    Antal

No. 19 in F is a delightful concerto and it receives a most
attractive performance, aptly paced, with fine woodwind
playing, the finale crisply sparkling. No. 6 is hardly less
successful; and if No. 8 seems plainer, it is nevertheless
admirably fresh. With excellently balanced recording this is a
genuine bargain.

Piano Concertos 6, K.238; 17, K.453; 21, K.467

(M) *** DG (ADD) 447 436-2. Anda, Salzburg Mozarteum
    Camerata Academica

Géza Anda's poetic account of the *C major Concerto*, K.467, is
one of the most impressive from his cycle, notably for a
beautifully poised account of the slow movement. In the *G
major*, K.453, there is both strength and poetry, while the
recording is excellent in both balance and clarity. The Deutsche Grammophon *B flat Concerto*, K.238, is played simply
and eloquently. The recording is not quite so cleanly transferred in the early work, but this nevertheless remains a most
enjoyable triptych.

*Piano Concertos (i) 9 in E flat (Jeunehomme), K.271; (ii) 12
in A, K.414; (i) 17 in G, K.453; (ii) 19 in F, K.459; Rondos: in
D, K.382; A min., K.511*

(B) *** Erato (ADD) 0927 41397-2 (2). Pires, with (i)
    Gulbenkian Foundation O, Guschlbauer; (ii) Lausanne CO,
    Jordan

Piano Concertos 12, K.414; 19, K.459

(BB) *** Warner Apex 2564 60161-2. Pires, Lausanne CO,
    Jordan

Maria João Pires recorded these Mozart concertos in the
1970s, before fame had overtaken her. They are refreshingly
musical and full of character, and no allowances need be
made for the sound. Readers wanting bargain accounts of
these concertos can rest assured that these are far more than
serviceable – indeed, they have style as well as the accomplished musicianship one expects from her. Eminently recommendable.

Piano Concertos 9, K.271; 14, K.449

(N) (M) *** Van. Compatible **SACD** ATM-SC-1587. Brendel, I
    Solisti di Zagreb, Janigro

For some time Brendel's Vanguard coupling of 1965 has been
available on Regis at budget price. Now it reverts to its parent
label on SACD, remastered from the original three channels,
and sounds very good indeed. Brendel's performance of No. 9

is quite outstanding, elegant and beautifully precise. The classical-sized orchestra is just right, and the neat, stylish string-playing finds real depth in both slow movements. Indeed, the performance of K.449 is also first rate, with a strong first movement and an equally memorable, vivacious finale.

Piano Concertos 9 (Jeunehomme), K.271; 14, K.449; 15, K.450; 17, K.453; 18, K.456; Rondo in D, K.382

(B) **(*) Ph. 473 313-2 (2). Uchida, ECO, Tate

Mitsuko Uchida's Mozart concerto recordings are, in general, elegantly faithful readings which will give pleasure, though they are not as memorable as the very finest versions. Here and there, there are some distractions which may irritate some listeners more than others: there is sometimes a hint of Dresden china in her playing, such as in the slow movement of K.449, which seems rather over-civilized. The slow movement of K.453, too, is mannered, and here, as in one or two other instances, her little touches of beautification sweeten and thus diminish the purity of the music. The ECO under Tate provide fine support, and the recording is full and rich.

Piano Concertos (i) 9 (Jeunehomme), K.271; (ii) 14, K.449; (iii) 22, K.482; (iv) 27, K.595. Serenade 13 (Eine kleine Nachtmusik), K.525

(***) Pearl mono GEMS 0167 (2). Perpignan Festival O, Casals, with (i) Hess; (ii) Istomin; (iii) Serkin; (iv) Horszowski

A welcome two-CD set of four Mozart concertos from the 1951 Perpignan Festival with Horszowski and Dame Myra Hess both inspired, with Casals conducting. Casals brought humanity and wisdom to all his music-making.

Piano Concertos 9, K.271; 15, K.450

(M) (***) DG mono 474 024-2 (5). Kempff, SRO, Munchinger – BEETHOVEN: Concertos 1–5; BRAHMS: Concerto 1; LISZT: Concertos 1–2; SCHUMANN: Concerto (***)

These long-forgotten mono recordings, made in 1953 for Decca, provide a valuable supplement to DG's limited-edition box of Kempff's 1950s concerto recordings. The clarity and sparkle of his playing, making for consistently transparent textures, is matched by the tender poetry of such movements as the C minor slow movement of K.271.

Piano Concertos 9, K.271; 15, K.450; 22, K.482; 25, K.503; 27, K.595

(B) *** Ph. Duo (ADD) 442 571-2 (2). Brendel, ASMF, Marriner

A first-class follow-up to Brendel's first Duo collection of Mozart piano concertos (see below). The account of the opening Jeunehomme is finely proportioned and cleanly articulated, with a ravishing account of the slow movement. The finale has great sparkle and finesse and the recording has exemplary clarity. Brendel is hardly less fine in K.450, and the E flat Concerto has both vitality and depth. Brendel's first movement has breadth and grandeur as well as sensitivity, while the Andante has great poetry. No. 25 (there is well-deserved applause at the close) was recorded at a live performance and has life and concentration, and a real sense of scale. Here as elsewhere the playing of the ASMF under Marriner is alert and supportive. K.595 is also among Brendel's best Mozart performances, with a beautifully poised

Larghetto and a graceful, spirited finale. Highly recommended.

Piano Concertos 9, K.271; 17, K.453

(M) *** Chan. 9068. Shelley, LMP

Howard Shelley's playing is a delight and is possessed of a refreshing naturalness which should win many friends. There is spontaneity and elegance, a strong vein of poetic feeling and extrovert high spirits. His G major Concerto belongs in the most exalted company and can withstand comparison with almost any rival. But both performances are touched by distinction, and they are beautifully recorded too.

Piano Concertos 9 (Jeunehomme); 18 in B flat, K.456

(N) ✪ *** EMI 5 57803-2. Andsnes, Norwegian CO

Outstanding Mozart playing from Leif Ove Andsnes and the Norwegian Chamber Orchestra, and first-rate sound too. If this were to prove the first in a complete cycle, it would be a cause for celebration. As it is, this is one of the most natural in style and completely musical accounts of Mozart that we have had recently.

Piano Concertos 9 in E flat (Jeunehomme), K.271; 20 in D min., K.466; 23 in A, K. 488; 24 in C min., K.491

⊶ (BB) *** Virgin 4-CD 5 62259-2 (4). Pletnev, Deutsche Kammerphilharmonie – HAYDN: Piano Concertos & Sonatas ***

Pletnev and the Deutsche Kammerphilharmonie have obviously established a close rapport, and each of these performances is individually and positively characterized. The Jeunehomme certainly sounds youthful, bringing crisp, precise articulation in the first movement and a poised Andante, yet with real expressive depth, followed by a brisk, attractively jaunty finale. The cadenzas are Mozart's own.

The uneasy, sotto voce opening of the D minor, K.466, is full of underlying tension, which is maintained throughout the strong tuttis, yet Pletnev relaxes completely for the delicate lyrical secondary theme and again in the Romance, bringing some exquisite articulation to the outer sections and a perfectly judged centrepiece. In this concerto he uses Beethoven's cadenzas, which bring a sudden striking change of mood in the finale, otherwise light-hearted, and with some fine wind playing from the orchestra. In Pletnev's hands the slow movement of K.488 is among the most beautiful on record, the finale the most rushed. Here he returns to Mozart's cadenzas. But in the C minor Concerto (K.491) he is again intensely dramatic, Beethovenian in feeling and powerful in conception: his own first-movement cadenza looks even more forward into the nineteenth century; and there is commanding playing from all concerned. Excellent recording throughout. This now comes recoupled in a budget box with equally impressive performances of piano concertos and sonatas of Haydn. It makes a fascinating set, well worth exploring, even if this involves duplication.

Piano Concertos 9, K.271; 21, K.467

(N) (M) *** Sony (ADD) 518808-2 [SK 92734]. Perahia, ECO

Perahia's reading of K.271 is wonderfully refreshing and delicate, with diamond-bright articulation, urgently youthful in its resilience. The famous C major Concerto is given a highly imaginative performance. Faithful, well-balanced recording.

Piano Concertos 9, K.271; 25, K.503

*** None. 7559 79454-2. Goode, Orpheus CO

*** Ph. **SACD** 470 616-2; CD 470 287-2. Brendel, SCO, Mackerras

Richard Goode, having given us an outstanding set of the Beethoven sonatas, is now embarking on a Mozart concerto series, like Murray Perahia before him, working with a first-class, modern-instrument chamber orchestra. The Orpheus Chamber Orchestra are consistently at one with him in matters of phrasing and style, and they immediately establish the boldly expansive character of the great *C major Concerto*, K.503. These are performances of much character, beautifully recorded. Mozart's cadenzas are used in K.271, but Goode uses his own in K.503.

Both the *Jeunehomme* and *C major Concertos* with Brendel have been greeted with acclaim and the three stars are there to reflect this widely held opinion. Needless to say, his playing is highly intelligent and impeccably executed but, by the side of the earlier records he made with Neville Marriner in the 1970s, it seems rather studied and calculated. Excellent sound, whether on CD or surround-sound-compatible SACD.

Piano Concertos 11, K.413; 12, K.414; 13, K.415

(B) *** EMI Debut 5 72525-2. Dechorgnat, Henschel Qt

The interplay between the stylish Patrick Dechorgnat and the polished and sympathetic Henschel Quartet is heard at its most appealing in the *Larghetto* of the *F major Concerto*, K.413, yet the touching *Andante* of K.414 is hardly less appealing, and the recording throughout is so expertly balanced that all three works are a great success. A first-rate début for soloist and string quartet alike.

Piano Concertos 11 in F, K.413; 12 in A, K.414; 13 in C, K.415 (chamber versions)

*** Hyp. CDA 67358. Tomes, Gaudier Ens.

Mozart himself arranged the orchestral parts of these concertos for chamber forces, the first three of the masterly sequence of piano concertos that he wrote for Vienna. These works have been recorded in chamber form before, but this time, even though a double-bass is added to the usual string quartet, the result is lighter and more intimate than in previous versions, helped by a clear, dry, recording acoustic. There are few recording pianists to match Susan Tomes in clarity of articulation, and here she leads performances which sparkle from beginning to end, with every note cleanly defined. Speeds are relatively fast, with slow movements kept moving to bring out their soaring lyricism.

Piano Concertos 11, K.413; 12, K.414; 14, K.449

*** Sony (ADD) SK 42243. Perahia, ECO

These performances remain in a class of their own. When it first appeared, we thought the *F major*, K.413, the most impressive of Perahia's Mozart concerto records so far, its slow movement wonderfully inward; and the *E flat Concerto*, K.449, is comparably distinguished. The current remastering is very successful.

Piano Concertos 11, K.413; 14, K.449; 15, K.451

⊕–➤ ✪ (M) *** Warner Elatus 2564 60116-2. Barenboim, BPO

The *F major Concerto*, K.413, is at the centre of a group of three outstanding early works which Mozart composed in Vienna in 1782/3. It has a tranquil and idyllic *Larghetto* and a Minuet finale, both of which are played most winningly here. The other two concertos followed on, composed within a few weeks of each other (beginning in February 1784). All three works show Barenboim in his very finest Mozartian style,

both at the keyboard and in directing the Berlin Philharmonic. The orchestral contributions in opening movements are imposing without being too heavy, and they bring much grace to slow movements. Finales are no less engaging, particularly in K.413; and witness the string-playing at the opening of the superb Rondo of K.449. The *B flat Concerto* is a live performance, but the others are by no means studio-bound. Barenboim's keyboard articulation is a constant joy, as is his pearly tone; and somehow he manages to give the first movement of the *F major*, K.413, an extra youthful freshness that places it before the others in the development of the composer's style. But it is the joyous spontaneity of the music-making throughout that makes this triptych so cherishable.

Piano Concerto 12, K.414 (version for piano and string quartet); Piano Quartet 2 in E flat, K.493

*** EMI 5 56962-2. Brendel, Alban Berg Quartet

Breaking the bonds of his exclusive recording contract, Alfred Brendel joins the Alban Berg Quartet in live recordings made in the Konzerthaus in Vienna. Together they give electrifying performances to match the quartet, while the four string players respond to his example with Mozart playing more flexible than usual, warmly expressive. The rapt *Andante* slow movement of the concerto brings playing of Beethovenian gravity, intensified still further on the entry of the piano. The concerto works surprisingly well in this chamber version, in which Mozart makes no changes to the score but simply points out that the wind parts can be omitted, and that those for strings can be played by four solo instruments. Brendel is here more relaxed than in his Philips recording of the full concerto, with delightful interplay between piano and quartet. The *Piano Quartet* brings a performance equally illuminating with Brendel at his most sparkling in the finale, playing with wonderfully clear articulation. The recording is bright, immediate and well balanced to match.

Piano Concertos 12, K.414; 14, K.449; 21, K.467

(BB) *** Naxos 8.550202. Jandó, Concentus Hungaricus, Ligeti

In Jenő Jandó's hands the first movement of K.449 sounds properly forward-looking; the brightly vivacious K.414 also sounds very fresh here, and its *Andante* is beautifully shaped. The excellent orchestral response distinguishes the first movement of K.467: both grace and weight are here, and some fine wind-playing. An added interest in this work is provided by Jandó's use of cadenzas provided by Robert Casadesus. Jandó is at his most spontaneous throughout these performances and this is altogether an excellent disc, well recorded.

(i) Piano Concertos 12 in A, K.414; 14 in E flat, K.449; 20 in D min., K.466; (ii; iii) Sinfonia concertante in E flat, K.364; (iii) Symphony 41 (Jupiter); (iv) Requiem Mass

(M) *** Andante 4993/5 (3). VPO; with (i) Pollini (piano & cond.); (ii) I. & D. Oistrakh; (iii) D. Oistrakh (cond.); (iv) Popp, Lilowa, Dermota, Berry, Wiener Singakademie, Krips

The most revealing disc of the three here has Maurizio Pollini directing the orchestra from the keyboard, magnetically spontaneous-sounding, playing with a freedom that as a rule in his studio recordings he rarely matches. Pollini draws a clear distinction between the three works: K.414, one of the lightest of all, K.449, weightier with its contrapuntal finale, and K.466, almost Beethovenian in its minor-key drama. By today's standards Pollini's speeds for slow movements are very measured, but the refinement and elegance make them anything but sentimental.

It is good too to have Josef Krips's account of the Mozart *Requiem*, given in the Musikverein in December 1973, his last public concert before he died less than a year later. The performance is irresistible, bitingly fresh from first to last and often brisk, with the chorus full-bodied and with a superb, characterful quartet of soloists.

The Oistrakh father-and-son duo, Igor on violin and David on viola, recorded the *Sinfonia concertante* a number of times, and there is a winning spontaneity about this reading, as there is in the *Symphony*, with the outer movements forthright and incisive, though it is a pity that Oistrakh does not observe the repeats in either half of the great finale. The quality of the original Austrian Radio recordings has here been faithfully captured on the French-made CD transfers.

Piano Concertos 12, K.414; 19, K.459

☛ (M) *** Chan. 9256. Shelley, LMP

Another fine disc in Howard Shelley's musically rewarding and beautifully recorded series. Admirers of this artist need not hesitate in investing here, with the music's expressive range fully encompassed without mannerism, slow movements eloquently shaped and outer movements aptly paced and alive with vitality.

Piano Concertos 12, K.414; 20, K.466; Rondo in D, K.382

*** RCA 09026 60400-2. Kissin, Moscow Virtuosi, Spivakov

The *D major Rondo*, K.382, has an elegance and delicacy worthy of the greatest Mozart players of the day. The *A major Concerto*, K.414, shows the same immaculate technical finesse and musical judgement (save, perhaps, in the slow movement, which some could find a little oversweet). There are perhaps greater depths in the *D minor Concerto* than Kissin finds but, even so, the playing is musical through and through and gives unfailing pleasure. The recorded sound is very good and the disc as a whole deserves the attention of any Mozartian.

Piano Concerto 13 in C, K.415

☛ ✿ *** TDK **DVD** DV-VERSA. Barenboim, BPO (with CONCERT ***)

This outstanding DVD brings a captivating account of this early concerto, greatly enhanced on video, with the empathy between pianist/conductor and his players communicating directly and magically to the viewer. The other works in the programme are Ravel's *Le tombeau de Couperin* and Beethoven's *Eroica Symphony*, also very finely played.

Piano Concertos 13, K.415; 14 in E flat, K.449; 23 in A, K.488

(BB) *** Warner Apex 2564 60448-2. Pires, Gulbenkian Foundation CO of Lisbon, Guschlbauer

Maria João Pires, in a triptych of her earliest recordings (1973–4) for Erato, plays with spirit and taste as well as immaculate small-scale fingerwork. She plays the lovely slow movement of K.488 delicately and gently, yet she sparkles in the finale. Her playing at that time reminds one a little of Ingrid Haebler's earliest records for Vox, and she offers many personal insights. Barenboim, for instance, may inflect the second theme of the first movement of K.415 with greater imagination, but Pires holds her own elsewhere. Guschlbauer

gives her most musical support and provides robust orchestral tuttis in the outer movements of the two early concertos. The recording can hardly be faulted, for the engineers provide a realistic balance and the sound is warm and pleasingly intimate. An enjoyable bargain.

Piano Concertos 13, K.415; 20, K.466

(BB) **(*) Naxos 8.550201. Jandó, Concentus Hungaricus, Ligeti

These performances set a high standard in their communicative immediacy, and if they have not quite the individuality of Perahia or Ashkenazy, they are worth a place in any collection and are very modestly priced. Jandó uses Beethoven's cadenzas with impressive authority. The balance and recording are most believable and there is good documentation throughout this series.

Piano Concertos 13, K.415; 24, K.491

☛ (M) *** Chan. 9326. Shelley, LMP

Howard Shelley has immaculate keyboard manners and his strong, natural musicianship is always in evidence. An instinctive yet thoughtful Mozartian whose consummate artistry places his cycle among the very finest now on the market.

Piano Concertos 14, K.449; 27, K.595

☛ (M) *** Chan. 9137. Shelley, LMP

Admirable performances, stylish and with a fine Mozartian sensibility. This is altogether most refreshing, and the recording is very good indeed.

Piano Concertos 15, K.450; 16, K.451

*** Sony SK 37824. Perahia, ECO

Perahia's are superbly imaginative readings, full of seemingly spontaneous touches and turns of phrase very personal to him, which yet never sound mannered. His version of the *B flat Concerto*, K.450, has sparkle, grace and intelligence; both these performances are very special indeed. The recording is absolutely first rate, intimate yet realistic and not dry, with the players continuously grouped round the pianist.

Piano Concertos 15, K.450; 21, K.467; 23, K.488

(M) *** Ph. (ADD) 464 719-2. Brendel, ASMF, Marriner

Brendel's versions of Nos. 21 and 23 are already available (see below). Now Philips add his equally distinguished account of the *B flat Concerto*, K.450, with Brendel at his very finest in the noble slow movement and releasing the tension delightfully in the finale. Marriner's supportive accompaniments are admirable.

Piano Concertos (i) 15 in B flat, K.450; (ii) 23 in A, K.488; 24 in C min., K.491

☛ ✿ (***) Testament mono SBT 1222. Solomon, Philh. O; (i) Ackermann, (ii) Menges

All three concertos were recorded in 1955, not long before this great pianist suffered the cruel stroke that silenced him. This is quite exceptional Mozart playing: it has depth and serenity, impeccable grace and wit, and an incomparable sense of style. Almost half a century has passed since these recordings were made, and they have been out of circulation most of that time. They are in a class of their own: only Perahia has come remotely close to them. Remarkably good sound.

Piano Concertos (i) *15, K.450;* (ii) *24, K.491*
(BB) (***) Dutton mono CDBP 9714. Kathleen Long; (i) Nat.
SO, Boyd Neel; (ii) Concg. O, Van Beinum – FAURE:
Ballade; LEIGH: *Concertino* (***)

These two vintage recordings of Mozart concertos, together
with the works by Fauré and Walter Leigh, provide a superb
memorial to a British pianist who has not been given credit
for her inspired artistry. Born in 1896, she lived until 1968, but
her recording career was all too short, even though she was
very highly regarded in France above all, where the subtlety of
her playing was much appreciated. In Mozart the pearly
clarity of her articulation is a delight throughout, not least in
the lilting finale of K.450. The natural, thoughtful gravity of
her playing comes out in the slow movements of both works,
with the C minor no less intense for being presented without
Beethovenian grandeur on a deliberately limited scale, with
Van Beinum and the Concertgebouw understanding partners. Excellent Decca sound, superbly transferred.

Piano Concertos 16, K.451; 24–5; 26 (Coronation); 27
(B) **(*) Ph. Duo 468 918-2 (2). Uchida, ECO, Tate
(B) **(*) Double Decca 475 181-2 (2). Schiff, Camerata
Academica des Mozarteum, Salzburg, Végh

Mitsuko Uchida's cycle with Jeffrey Tate has outstandingly
natural recording quality; if the perspective favours the
piano, one can only say in justification how beautifully the
timbre of the solo instrument is captured. But tonal refinement and delicacy are sometimes in stronger evidence than a
sense of scale. Tate draws fine playing from the ECO and the
soloist is unfailingly elegant. But this very refinement is a bit
too much of a good thing and at times one would welcome a
greater robustness, a more lively inner current. Uchida is
eminently imaginative through the slow movement of the C
major (No. 25, K.203), although the tempo may strike some
listeners as a bit too measured. But the slow movement of No.
27, K.595, is not free from preciosity, and one only has to
think of Gilels or Perahia in this work to put the undoubted
tonal beauties the playing offers into a true Mozartian perspective. As one would expect from two artists of this calibre,
there are many felicities; but individually none of the performances of the major works here would be a first choice, and
No. 16 is split between the two CDs, after the first movement.

András Schiff's recordings with Sándor Végh and the
Camerata Academica of the Salzburg Mozarteum were made
at various times between 1989 and 1994. The playing has
exemplary taste and is distinguished by refined musicianship,
though the recording balance tends to place Schiff's Bösendorfer rather distantly in an acoustic that may perhaps be a
touch too resonant for some collectors. Schiff eschews a wide
range of dynamics and conveys splendid intimacy in his
dialogue with Végh and his players. There is a wonderful
unanimity of phrasing and musical thinking from the strings
and some superb wind playing, every note finely placed and
every phrase shaped with keen sensitivity. One snag is that
the rare D major Concerto, K.451, is split between the two
CDs.

Piano Concertos 16, K.451; 25, K.503; Rondo in A, K.386
(BB) *** Naxos 8.550207. Jandó, Concentus Hungaricus,
Antal

Jenö Jandó gives a very spirited and intelligent account of the
relatively neglected D major Concerto, K.451, in which he
receives sensitive and attentive support from the excellent
Concentus Hungaricus under Mátyás Antal. The players

sound as if they are enjoying themselves and, although there
are greater performances of the C major Concerto, K.503, on
record, few are at this extraordinarily competitive price.

Piano Concertos 17, K.453; 18, K.456
(N) (M) *** Sony 518 809-2 [SK 92733]. Perahia, ECO
(BB) *** Naxos 8.550205. Jandó, Concentus Hungaricus,
Antal

The *G major Concerto,* K.453, is one of the most magical of
the Perahia cycle and is on no account to be missed. The *B
flat,* too, has the sparkle, grace and finesse that one expects
from him. Even if you have other versions, you should still
add this to your collection, for its insights are quite special.

This is also one of the finest in Jandó's excellent super-
bargain series. Tempi are admirably judged and both slow
movements are most sensitively played. Jandó uses Mozart's
original cadenzas for the first two movements of K.453 and
the composer's alternative cadenzas for K.546. Excellent
sound.

Piano Concertos (i) *17, K.453; 20, K.466; 21, K.467; 23, K.488;*
(ii) *24, K.491*
☛ (M) *** RCA (ADD) 09026 63061-2 (2). Rubinstein, RCA
Victor SO, (i) Wallenstein; (ii) Krips

Rubinstein's accounts of these favourite concertos could not
be further removed from current period-instrument manners using the fortepiano. Here the orchestral sound is rich
and glowing (almost lush), and Rubinstein has seldom been
caught so sympathetically by the microphones. In each concerto the slow movement is the kernel of the interpretation,
and Rubinstein's playing is meltingly lovely, notably in the
three middle concertos, which are the finest of the set, where
the hushed orchestral playing catches the intensity of the
pianist's inspiration. K.488 is especially beautiful, while in
K.491 crystal-clear articulation is allied to aristocratic feeling
characteristic of vintage Rubinstein, and Krips's accompaniment acts as a foil to the tragic tone of this great and
wonderfully balanced work. It is a pity, however, that K.467
had to be split between the two CDs.

Piano Concertos 17, K.453; 21, K.467
*** DG 439 941-2. Pires, COE, Abbado

Maria João Pires's playing, both in the mercurial *G major
Concerto* and in its more ceremonial *C major* companion, is
elegant, searching and intelligent. She has taste and fine
musicianship, and the Chamber Orchestra of Europe under
Abbado give excellent support. Good recording.

Piano Concertos 17, K.453; 27, K.595
(N) (B) *** Regis (ADD) RRC 1154. Brendel, V. Volksoper O,
Angerer

Brendel was an inspired Mozartian when he made his earlier
Mozart recordings for the Vox Turnabout label at the end of
the 1950s and beginning of the 1960s; these performances
have a radiant freshness and spontaneity which he did not
always match in his later, Philips versions. The recording is
thin in the matter of violin-tone, though it has good ambience, and at Brendel's first entry one forgets this fault, for the
piano is realistically recorded and convincingly balanced in
relation to the orchestra. Brendel is helped by a vivacious
orchestral contribution in both works. No. 27 is very distinguished and can be spoken of in the same breath as Gilels's
version. It is beautifully proportioned and the lyrical phrasing is most winning, with Brendel's sure feeling for nuance

and tempo lighting up the *Andante*, and the final *Allegretto* is engagingly nimble.

Piano Concertos 18, K.456; 19, K.459
*** HM HMX 3957138. Tan (fortepiano), Philh. Bar. O, McGegan

Piano Concertos 18 in B flat, K.456; 19 in F, K.459; Rondo in D, K.382
✪—▼ ✿ (M) *** Warner Elatus 2564 60810-2. Barenboim, BPO

Barenboim immediately puts his personal seal on this CD with his captivating account of the *D major Rondo*, a work of much charm but also repetitive, which lends itself to flexibility. Here, by imaginative variation of tempo and dynamic, it sounds wonderfully fresh. But so do both the Concertos. They are brimming over with Barenboim's joy in the music, with delightfully sprung rhythms and winningly felicitous slow movements, especially that for K.456 with its reminder of Barbarina's little aria in *Le nozze di Figaro*. The totally infectious finales end each work in a mood of blissful happiness, especially the *B flat major Concerto*, which is a live performance of special zest. The Berlin Philharmonic respond to Barenboim's flair and affectionate elegance with especially elegant woodwind playing, and the recording balance could not be improved on. A treasure of a disc – and Barenboim uses Mozart's own cadenzas.

No one is more convincing on the fortepiano than Melvyn Tan. The pointedly rhythmic main theme of the *F major Concerto* suits the fortepiano particularly well – which is not to say that the *Allegretto* isn't equally winning, with some delightful wind-playing from these characterful period instrumentalists. The *B flat Concerto* is hardly less successful. McGegan and his players are clearly completely at one with their soloist. The recording is more intimate, slightly drier than in Malcolm Bilson's DG series, and the result is most persuasive.

Piano Concertos 18, K.456; 20, K.466
✪—▼ *** None. 7559 79439-2. Goode, Orpheus CO

(BB) **(*) Arte Nova 74321 80784-2. Kirschnereit, Bamberg SO, Bermann

Yet another entirely captivating coupling in Richard Goode's outstanding series with the Orpheus Chamber Orchestra. The lightly sprung opening movement of the *B flat Concerto*, K.456, is sheer delight and the interplay between soloist and orchestra in the central theme and variations wonderfully light-hearted, matched by the infectiously spirited *opera-buffa* closing Rondo. There is no finer performance in the catalogue. The mood then changes completely for the dark opening of the *D minor Concerto*, at first ominously *sotto voce* but soon expanding with forceful rhythmic drama. The piano enters simply, but then engages in a dialogue which readily hints at the music's histrionic associations with *Don Giovanni*. After a serene opening, the central *Romance* brings comparable drama in its turbulent central section, and the dynamic finale is suitably impassioned. Goode uses Mozart's second cadenza in the first movement of K.456 and Beethoven's in the equivalent movement of K.466, composing one of his own for the finale. A superb disc, splendidly balanced and recorded.

Matthias Kirschnereit will be a new name to most collectors. This coupling of the *B flat* and *D minor Concertos* shows him to be a Mozartian of no mean order. Well worth the money, though not a first choice.

Piano Concertos 19, K.459; 20, K.466; 21, K.467; 23, K.488; 24, K.491; Concert Rondos 1–2, K.382 & 386
✪—▼ ✿ (B) *** Ph. (ADD) Duo 442 269-2. (2) Brendel, ASMF, Marriner

This must be the Mozartian bargain of all time, five piano concertos and two concert rondos – all for the cost of one premium-price CD. A Rosette then for generosity, to say nothing of the distinction of the performances. Indeed, the playing exhibits a sensibility that is at one with the composer's world and throughout the set the Philips sound-balance is impeccable.

Piano Concertos 19, K.459; 23, K.488
✿ *** Sony SK 39064. Perahia, ECO

Murray Perahia gives highly characteristic accounts of both *Concertos* and a gently witty yet vital reading of the *F Major*, K.459. As always with this artist, there is a splendidly classical feeling allied to a keenly poetic sensibility. His account of K.488 has enormous delicacy and inner vitality, yet a serenity that puts it in a class of its own.

Piano Concertos 19 in F, K.459; 27 in B flat, K.595
*** None. 7559 79608-2. Goode, Orpheus CO

Richard Goode follows up the success of his two earlier Mozart concerto discs with another nicely contrasted pair of works, superbly done. What shines out is the illusion of live performance, even though these come from the studio. Goode's approach is purposeful and direct, as well as magnetically individual, with natural weight and gravity reflecting his equivalent mastery as a Beethovenian. At such a moment as the hushed B minor opening of the development in the first movement of K.595, Goode has you marvelling afresh at a modulation that is quite extraordinary for a movement in B flat major. Not that Goode's Mozart has anything heavy about it, with the finales of both works marked by lightness, wit and sparklingly clear passage-work. The piano-tone is firm and full, though the orchestra could be more forwardly placed after the opening tuttis.

Piano Concerto 20 in D min., K.466
(M) *** DG (ADD) 463 649-2. S. Richter, Warsaw PO, Wislocki – BEETHOVEN: *Piano Concerto 3; Rondo* *(*)

(B) **(*) EMI double forte 5 73329-2 (2). Egorov, Philh. O, Sawallisch – BEETHOVEN: *Symphony 9; Piano Concerto 5* **(*)

Richter proves his virtuosity by restraint, and this is the quality running right through his extremely fine performance of the *D minor Concerto*. He lets Mozart's music speak for itself, but whether in the choice of tempo, a touch of rubato or some finely moulded phrase, his mastery is always apparent. The slow movement is beautifully shaped, its opening theme phrased with perfect grace, and the closing pages are exquisite. The buoyancy of the finale is a joy. Wislocki and the Warsaw orchestra provide an accompaniment of character, and although the recording sounds dated in the matter of string-tone, the piano image remains realistic. This reissue is fully worthy to take a place among DG's 'Originals', and it is a pity that the coupling is so disappointing.

It seems a curious idea to couple this concerto (albeit inexpensively) with part of Sawallisch's Beethoven symphony cycle. But Egorov is stylish enough and Sawallisch finds plenty of drama in the outer movements, and the slow movement, too, is elegantly shaped. Good, bright (1985) recording, made at Abbey Road.

Piano Concertos 20, K.466; 21, K.467; 23, K.488; 24, K.491; 25, K.503
(B) *** Double Decca (DDD/ADD) 452 958-2 (2). Ashkenazy, Philh. O

This Double Decca set, reissued for Ashkenazy's sixtieth birthday, now includes both the D minor and C minor masterpieces, but not K.595 (No. 27), which, however, remains available on a slightly different permutation at a similar cost – see below. K.491 and K.503 are among the finest in his series, so the present grouping is particularly attractive. The Kingsway Hall recordings cannot be faulted. They were made between 1977 and 1983; Nos. 20, 23 and 25 are digital.

(i) *Piano Concertos 20–21; 23; 27. Sonata 17 in D; Rondo in A min., K.511*
(B) *** Double Decca (ADD/DDD) 436 383-2 (2). Ashkenazy, (i) Philh. O

This alternative set, with slightly different contents, is also highly recommendable on all counts, with the four favourite Mozart *Piano Concertos* included, plus a splendid *Sonata* and a charming *Rondo*. Ashkenazy's performance of the *B flat Concerto* is as finely characterized as one would expect. The *Sonata* and *Rondo* were recorded earlier (in 1967); the playing is equally fine.

Piano Concertos 20–21; 25; 27, K.595
(B) **(*) DG Double (ADD) (IMS) 453 079-2 (2). Gulda, VPO, Abbado

Abbado had much greater luck in his Mozartian partnership with Gulda than he was to experience with Serkin a decade or so later. Gulda uses a Bösendorfer and in Nos. 20 and 21 his tone is crisp and clear with just a hint of a fortepiano about it, admirably suited to these readings, which have an element of classical restraint. In Nos. 25 and 27, however, Gulda is strangely cool, though he disciplines his responses impressively and there is no basic want of feeling or finesse, but overall there is a lack of charm. There are felicitous moments elsewhere, but the account of K.595 does not compare with the finest available, despite very good playing from the Vienna Philharmonic. The digital transfer is bright and clear, but there is also a certain shallowness of sonority.

Piano Concertos 20, K.466; 23, K.488
⊶ (M) *** Chan. 8992. Shelley, LMP

Those wanting this coupling with modern instruments will find Howard Shelley's performances immensely rewarding. Characterization is strong, yet the slow movement of K.488 is very beautiful and touching. Splendid Chandos recording.

Piano Concertos 20; 23–4; 25 in C, K.503
(BB) *** Virgin 2x1 5 62343-2 (2). Tan (fortepiano), LCP, Norrington

Melvyn Tan radiates delight in what he is doing, and the playing here has both imagination and poise. The fortepiano may be less able than a modern concert grand to convey the dark *Don Giovanni* colourings of the *D minor Concerto*, K.466, and the tragic overtones of the slow movement of the *C minor* (No. 24), where Tan does not help himself by adopting a rather brisk tempo; but these readings have an impressive flair. He tries not to see the *C minor Concerto* through Beethovenian eyes and approaches it with great freshness, shaping the finale with subtlety and finesse, and he is equally thought-provoking in the *C major* (No. 25). The

London Classical Players under Norrington are generally supportive, playing with poise and grace, and the naturally balanced EMI recording does justice to their artistry.

Piano Concertos (i) 20; (ii) 23; 24; 26 (Coronation); (i) 27
⊶ (M) *** Decca (ADD) 468 491-2 (2). Curzon, (i) ECO, Britten; (ii) LSO, Kertész

As Cyrus Meher-Homji's excellent notes for this reissue make abundantly clear, Curzon's recordings of the late Mozart concertos for Decca, made between 1967 and 1970, were fraught with issue problems. Always a perfectionist and especially so in Mozart, the great pianist was seldom satisfied with his performances, always feeling he could do better. Initially only K.466 and K.491 were approved by the soloist for release, yet K.595 was hardly less distinguished, while K.488 and K.491 were eventually released together. Even if they are slightly less fine and as such bear out Curzon's doubts, by any normal standards this is pianism of distinction. The additional attraction of the present set is the inclusion of K.537 (hitherto unavailable on CD) where Curzon is completely seductive in the *Larghetto* and sparkles happily in the finale. Strong support from the LSO, although Kertész perhaps proved a rather less imaginative accompanist than Britten. The recordings, made in the Kingsway Hall or the Maltings, are up to Decca's highest standards, and reservations must be swept aside, for this 'Legendary' reissue is certainly treasurable.

Piano Concertos 20, K.466; 24, K.491
*** Ph. 462 622-2. Brendel, SCO, Mackerras
(M) **(*) Ph. (IMS) (ADD) 464 718-2. Haskil, LOP, Markevitch

Brendel recorded this coupling with Neville Marriner in 1974 and now, more than a quarter of a century later, he gives accounts that are hardly less thoughtful without being wanting in spontaneity and which, if anything, are more searching and articulate. Moreover, in Mackerras he here has a partner who is one of the most experienced of Mozartians. This is a popular coupling: it is recorded with great realism and can be accommodated among top recommendations.

Clara Haskil's recordings were made shortly before her death in 1960. The poise she brought to Mozart and her effortless sense of style, with no straining after effect, are still a source of wonder. Comparing these latest CD transfers with their last incarnation on LP, one finds much greater body and clarity of detail – and, of course, greater range. The image is firmly in focus and if the sound from the Lamoureux Orchestra is certainly beefier than we are used to nowadays, the solo playing remains rather special.

Piano Concertos 20, K.466; 25, K.503 (arr. Hummel)
*** BIS CD 1147. Shiraga, with Wiese, Clemente, Benyi

Odd as it may seem to record such arrangements as these when there are so many recordings of these great concertos in their original form, these fine performances from Fumiko Shiraga, fresh and perceptive, give us important insights into performance practice in Mozart's time and after. These arrangements by Hummel are quite different from Mozart's own arrangements of his concertos, K.413, 414 and 415, which with string accompaniment retain the feeling of concertos; these Hummel arrangements are in effect self-sufficient piano transcriptions of the whole work, with flute, violin and cello added simply as trimmings. The piano enters instantly and is never silent for a single bar, the other instruments often simply doubling the lines in the piano part. The big loss is that there is no sense of a new arrival when the piano takes up the solo part after the opening tutti; one simply hears two versions of the exposition section. The slow movements of both works give the most striking instances of Hummel's performance practice, when he radically elaborates what is in the published scores with ornamentation and modified passage-work. Hummel's modifications of the solo part of K.503 are particularly relevant when, as a boy, he was studying with Mozart at the very time the concerto was written; and for many years after that it became a favourite party-piece for him in his career as a virtuoso pianist. The modifications to the solo part in the fast outer movements are fascinating but less striking, and it is worth noting how elaborate are the cadenzas which Hummel provides, longer than many. With clear sound tending to favour the piano rather than the attendant instruments – all very well played by distinguished performers – these are consistently refreshing performances.

Piano Concertos 20, K.466; 27, K.595
*** Sony (ADD) **SACD** SS 42241; SK 42241. Perahia, ECO

Perahia produces wonderfully soft colourings and a luminous texture in the B flat Concerto, yet at the same time he avoids underlining too strongly the valedictory sense that inevitably haunts this magical score. In the D minor Concerto none of the darker, disturbing undercurrents go uncharted, but at the same time we remain within the sensibility of the period. An indispensable issue, well recorded and excellently transferred. This is also available on one of Sony's Super Audio CDs but you need a special player to reproduce it. The sound is particularly impressive in K.595.

Piano Concerto 21 in C, K.467
(BB) *** Warner Apex 0927 99842-2. Huang, NYPO, Masur – MENDELSSOHN: Piano Concerto 1, etc. ***

Helen Huang gives a fresh, unmannered account of Mozart's most popular concerto and receives fine, expressive support from Masur in the beautiful slow movement. If you fancy a coupling with Mendelssohn, this is excellent value, for the recording cannot be faulted.

Piano Concertos 21, K.467; 22 in E flat, K.482
*** Chan. 9404. Shelley, LMP
☛ (M) *** EMI (ADD) 5 62750-2 [5 62767-2]. Fischer, Philh. O, Sawallisch

Howard Shelley's cycle continues to delight, and the C major has dignity, intelligence and poetic feeling. The E flat has poise and breadth, and the winds of the London Mozart Players are heard to good advantage. These performances can be confidently recommended alongside the very finest rivals.

Annie Fischer's vintage coupling was much treasured when it first appeared in 1959 on a mono LP and, while the general style of performance of Mozart concertos in recent years has tended to become more robust, Miss Fischer's gentle, limpid touch, with its frequent use of half-tones, still gives much pleasure. The slow movements of both concertos are beautifully done, and the pianist's intimate manner is often shared by the Philharmonia wind soloists, who offer playing of polish and delicacy. Sawallisch's contribution is also considerable, and his firm directing hand ensures that neither performance becomes effete. These are essentially small-scale readings, and the refined approach does not reduce the opportunities for displaying sparkle in finales. Fischer's silken

touch is highly persuasive and the recording is nicely balanced, the piano full in tone, and the orchestra does not sound too dated. An obvious candidate for EMI's 'Great Recordings of the Century'.

Piano Concertos 21, K.467; 23, K.488
(M) *** Virgin 5 61852-2. Pommier, Sinfonia Varsovia

Piano Concertos 21; 23; Rondos for Piano & Orchestra 1 in D, K.382; 2 in A, K.386
(M) *** Sony (DDD/ADD) SMK 89876. Perahia, ECO

(i) Piano Concertos 21; 23. Piano Sonata in A, K.331
(M) *** RCA 09026 63977-2. De Larrocha; (i) ECO, C. Davis

Both concertos capture Perahia's very special Mozartian sensibility and are beautifully recorded. The C major, K.467, is given delicacy and charm, rather than strength in the way of Brendel or Kovacevich, but the opposite is true of the exquisite slow movement (with very beautiful orchestral playing) and spirited finale. The slow movement of K.488 has an elevation of spirit that reaffirms one's conviction that this is indeed a classic recording. The finale, however, has a robust quality, with lively but controlled spontaneity. The digital recording is particularly fresh and natural. This very generous collection is completed by the two Concert Rondos which, when recorded in 1983, incorporated for the first time on record the closing bars newly rediscovered by Professor Alan Tyson.

Alicia de Larrocha was also on her finest form when she made her recordings in 1989, and she has a splendid partner in Sir Colin Davis, who provides vital, elegant accompaniments. He sets the scene in K.467 impressively and de Larrocha's articulation has fine character. Both slow movements are beautifully played, and finales have fine sparkle. In short, this is first rate in every way, and the recording is well balanced, warm and clear. The Sonata is a considerable bonus, with the first-movement grazioso theme and variations delightfully done. If the Alla Turca finale might have been more robust, many will like de Larrocha's delicacy of manner.

Both Virgin performances have plenty of sparkle in outer movements – the first movement of K.467 is particularly arresting – and both slow movements are played simply and beautifully. Jean-Bernard Pommier's Adagio in K.488 compares favourably with Brendel's, and the string playing at the famous opening of the Andante of K.467 is ravishing in its transparent delicacy and gentle warmth. The finale of the same work is brisk but never sounds rushed. The sound is first class.

Piano Concertos 21, K.467; 24, K.491
☛ (BB) *** Regis RRC 1067. Shelley, City of L Sinfonia

Howard Shelley's delightfully fresh and characterful readings of these fine concertos are outstanding value at budget price.

Piano Concertos (i) 21 in C; (ii) 24 in C min., K.481
(N) (M) (*(**)) EMI mono 4 76884-2. (i) Lipatti, Lucerne Festival O; (ii) Gieseking, Philh. O; both cond. Karajan

Lipatti's performance derives from a broadcast from the 1960 Lucerne Festival; the orchestral sound is not well focused and there is some discoloration and distortion at climaxes. However, nothing can detract from the distinction of Lipatti's playing or its immaculate control. This was originally coupled with Lipatti's account of the Schumann Concerto but is now reissued as part of the 'Karajan Collection' with Giesek-ing's poised, aristocratic (1953) account of the *C minor Concerto*, K.481. Here the Kingsway Hall recording is excellent. But it would surely have been better to keep this an all-Lipatti CD.

Piano Concertos 21, K.467; 26 (Coronation)
(M) *** DG Entrée 471 738-2. Pires, COE or VPO, Abbado

Pires's playing in the *C major Concerto* is elegant, searching and intelligent. She has taste and fine musicianship, and the Chamber Orchestra of Europe under Abbado give excellent support. The *Coronation Concerto* is, if anything, even finer. Recorded at a live performance (with a virtually silent, spell-bound audience), this is completely captivating, especially the slow movement. The balance favours the piano unduly, but so delightful is the playing (and otherwise the recording is faithful) one simply cannot cavil. This is one of the most recommendable of the DG Entrée series.

(i) Piano Concertos 21, K.467; 26 (Coronation), K.537; (ii) 12 Variations on 'Ah, vous dirai-je, Maman', K.265
●━ ✿ (B) *** Sony SBK 67178. (i) Casadesus, Columbia SO or Cleveland O, Szell; (ii) Previn (piano)

The ravishing slow movement of K.467 has never sounded more magical than here, and Robert Casadesus then takes the finale at a tremendous speed; but, for the most part, this is exquisite Mozart playing, beautifully paced and articulated. Casadesus's Mozart may at first seem understated, but the imagination behind his readings is apparent in every phrase.

Piano Concertos 21, K.467; 27, K.595
*** Sony SK 46485. Perahia, COE

Murray Perahia gives performances of characteristic under-standing and finesse with the Chamber Orchestra of Europe. There are new and different insights into both works, though neither reading necessarily displaces his earlier accounts with the ECO, which may have a slight edge over the newcomer in terms of freshness and spontaneity.

(i) Piano Concerto 22, K.482. Adagio & Fugue in C min., K.546; (ii) Sinfonia concertante, K.364
(M) *** BBC (ADD) BBCB 8010-2. (i) Richter; (ii) Brainin, Schidlof; ECO, Britten

With Britten as partner, Sviatoslav Richter gives an inspired reading of the Mozart concerto, for which Britten specially wrote new cadenzas, which are in use here. Though the sound is not as cleanly focused as in a studio recording, it is warmly atmospheric, as it is in the other two works. In the *Sinfonia concertante* Britten equally charms his two soloists from the Amadeus Quartet, making them relax in spontaneously expressive playing, with the lightness of the finale a special delight.

Piano Concertos 22, K.482; 23, K.488
(M) **(*) Warner Elatus 2564 61174-2. Barenboim, BPO

These come from Barenboim's digital re-recordings of the key Mozart Concertos with the Berlin Philharmonic, directed from the keyboard in the early 1990s, playing most expres-sively for him. The *E flat major Concerto* is the more reward-ing of the two performances here, the *Andante* obviously deeply felt, and the finale, in which Barenboim chooses to play an abridged version of a cadenza by Edwin Fischer, agreeably lighthearted. However, the lovely *Adagio* of the *A*

major, which is very leisured, is self-conscious and this per-formance is less spontaneous-sounding overall. Both record-ings are very well balanced.

Piano Concertos 22, K.482; 24, K.491
*** Sony SK 42242. Perahia, ECO

Not only is Perahia's contribution inspired in the great *E flat Concerto*, K.482, but the wind players of the ECO are at their most eloquent in the slow movement. Moreover, the *C minor Concerto* emerges here as a truly Mozartian tragedy, rather than as foreshadowing Beethoven, which some artists give us. Both recordings are improved in focus and definition in the CD transfer.

Piano Concertos 22, K.482; 27, K.595
*** Ph. 468 367-2. Brendel, SCO, Mackerras

These recordings were made in September 2000. Brendel's playing is peerless, and the bold, big-boned orchestral tapes-try against which he is admirably balanced ensures that the music-making looks forward, even while its Mozartian poise is secure. These are both concertos which were among the finest of Brendel's earlier recordings with Marriner, but many listeners will feel that these new readings have even greater breadth. His delightful performance of the finale of K.482 is wonderfully spirited, and the slow movement of K.595 shows him at his most eloquent. Mackerras proves a splendid part-ner, vital and supportive, and the orchestral playing is con-sistently alive and elegant.

Piano Concerto 23, K.488
(M) *** DG (IMS) 471 351-2. Pollini, VPO, Boehm –
BEETHOVEN: *Piano Concerto 5 (Emperor)* ***

This is one of the finest CDs in the 'Pollini Edition'. He gives a superbly poised account of the *A major Concerto*, with a vibrant sense of line. Every phrase here seems to speak, and everything is admirably paced. He is given excellent support from Boehm and the Vienna orchestra and the analogue recording is warm, well detailed and finely balanced, and has transferred very well to CD.

(i) Piano Concerto 23 in A, K.488. Adagio in B min. K.540; Rondo in D, K.485
(M) (**(*)) BBC mono BBCL 4111-2. Hess, (i) with LPO, Boult – BEETHOVEN: *Piano Concerto 4* **(*)

These broadcast performances of Mozart, well coupled with Beethoven's *Piano Concerto No. 4*, are specially valuable, when Dame Myra Hess recorded disappointingly little commer-cially. Dating from October 1961, the Mozart concerto per-formance was her very last in public, following her decision after a stroke to retire. You would never know that she was in anything but the most robust health from the vigour of her performance, with the finale taken at such a lick that the LPO under Boult finds it hard to keep up. Even when she was not on her most exalted form, Hess was always an artist from whom one could learn, and so it proves both in the concerto and in the two solo pieces. This may not be flawless playing, but it has a magnetic freshness and spontaneity, with power and purposefulness as well as poetry. It matters little that the balance in the limited mono recording favours the piano to a degree that prevents *pianissimos* being registered. The Festival Hall acoustic is not ideal, but most of the detail comes across clearly enough. The two separate solo pieces, which come as a valuable makeweight, are taken from studio recordings made in 1958.

Piano Concertos 23, K.488; 24, K.491

⊖‐ *** None. 7559 79489-2. Goode, Orpheus CO

*** Virgin 7 59280-2. Pletnev, Deutsche Kammerphilharmonie

Richard Goode gives an outstandingly fresh and satisfying account of Mozart's most lovable *A major Concerto*, the slow movement serenely beautiful and the finale delightfully vivacious. The opening tutti of K.491 is formidably strong and forward-looking, but the movement unfolds with a natural Mozartian flexibility, and Goode's playing in the *Larghetto* has a ravishing simplicity. The jaunty finale is nicely paced and gets attractively bolder as it proceeds. Throughout both works, the ear notices the sensitive contributions of the Orpheus woodwind as well as the elegant finish and warmth of the strings. Goode uses Mozart's cadenza in K.488 and, enterprisingly, one by Paul Badura-Skoda in K.491. These recordings are being made at the Manhattan Center, and very good they are too, with a most attractive ambient bloom.

Pletnev and the Deutsche Kammerphilharmonie have obviously established a close rapport. In Pletnev's hands the slow movement of the *A major Concerto* is among the most beautiful on record, the finale the most rushed. In the *C minor Concerto* he is intensely dramatic, Beethovenian in feeling and powerful in conception: his own first-movement cadenza looks forward even more into the nineteenth century. There is nothing bland here: commanding playing from all concerned.

Piano Concerto 24 in C min., K.491

(**(*)) VAI mono VAIA 1192-2 (2). Tureck, Oslo PO, Güner-Hegge – BACH: *Clavier Concertos 1, 5 & 7; in D min.* **(*)

Needless to say, Rosalyn Tureck's account, recorded live, is full of character, as is the accompaniment, although the actual orchestral playing could be more polished. Her style is both direct and flexible. She plays her own cadenzas and overall this is certainly an enjoyable account, the solo part beautifully articulated, if not as distinctive as her Bach. The finale is particularly strong. The mono recording is in every way excellent and well balanced too.

Piano Concerto 25, K.503

**(*) EMI (ADD) 5 56974-2. Argerich, Netherlands CO, Goldberg – BEETHOVEN: *Piano Concerto 1* **(*)

Martha Argerich is an inspirational pianist whose finest flights of imagination come in live performance. Like the Beethoven, recorded at the Concertgebouw 14 years later, this 1978 live recording offers a performance of the weighty *C major Concerto* magnetic in its spontaneity. This is muscular, positive playing which sparkles in the outer movements and finds a natural gravity in the central *Andante*. The recording is on the thin side, but never prevents one from enjoying a unique performance.

(i) Piano Concerto 25, K.503. Symphony 38 (Prague); (i; ii) Concert aria: Ch'io mi scordi di te

⊖‐ *** MDG 340 0967-2. (i) Zacharias (piano); Lausanne CO, Zacharias; (ii) with Fink

This is a delightful disc, offering a nicely balanced Mozart group of symphony, aria and concerto. Christian Zacharias, in consistently refreshing performances, relishes his multiple roles, not just conducting a fresh and lively account of the *Prague Symphony*, but also acting as piano soloist; in the *Concerto*, he directs the weighty K.503 from the keyboard and also provides a crisply pointed obbligato in the most taxing of

Mozart's concert arias, *Ch'io mi scordi di te*. Bernarda Fink with her firm, creamy voice, officially a mezzo, is untroubled by the soprano tessitura, giving the most characterful interpretation, imaginatively pointing words and phrases. The sense of freedom and spontaneous enjoyment is here enhanced by the clarity of the recording, made in the Metropole, Lausanne.

Piano Concerto 26 (Coronation), K.537

*** BBC (ADD) BBCL 4020-2. Curzon, BBC SO, Boulez – BEETHOVEN: *Piano Concerto 5 (Emperor)* ***

Curzon and Boulez in this 1974 Prom performance of the *Coronation Concerto* make rewarding partners. The combination of introspection and intellectual rigour results in an inspired reading of one of the more problematic Mozart piano concertos, fresh, bright and resilient in the outer movements with pearly passage-work, and thoughtfully unmannered in the slow movement. Full-bodied sound, set in the warm acoustic of the Royal Albert Hall.

Piano Concertos 26, K.537; 27, K.595

⊖‐ (M) *** Warner Elatus 2564 60679-2. Barenboim, BPO

This 1988–9 coupling from Barenboim is first class in every way, beautifully played, with warm, vigorous accompaniments from the Berlin Philharmonic which do not sound inflated. There is a hint of sobriety in both slow movements, but they are both memorable and each is perfectly offset by the light-hearted contrast of the finale which follows. A most enjoyable coupling, drawn from a highly distinguished cycle.

Piano Concerto 27; (i) Double Piano Concerto, K.365

⊖‐ ✿ (M) *** DG (ADD) 463 652-2. Emil Gilels, VPO, Boehm, (i) with Elena Gilels (with SCHUBERT: *Fantasy in F min., D. 940*)

Gilels's is supremely lyrical playing that evinces all the classical virtues. No detail is allowed to detract from the picture as a whole; the pace is totally unhurried and superbly controlled. All the points are made by means of articulation and tone, and each phrase is marvellously alive, while Boehm and the Vienna Philharmonic provide excellent support. The performance of the marvellous *Double Concerto* is no less enjoyable. Its mood is comparatively serious, but this is not to suggest that the music's sunny qualities are not brought out. The quality on CD is first class, refining detail yet not losing ambient warmth. The Schubert bonus has been added for the CD's rightful reissue as one of DG's 'Legendary Originals'.

(i; iv) Piano Concerto 27, K.595; (i; ii; iv) Double Piano Concerto, K.365; (i; iii) Double Piano Sonata in D, K.448

(***) BBC (ADD) stereo/mono BBCL 4037-2. (i) Curzon; (ii) Barenboim (piano); (iii) Britten; (iv) ECO, Barenboim

The two concertos, set in the warm Royal Albert Hall acoustic, come from a Prom concert in 1979, with Barenboim directing from the keyboard in the *Double Concerto* and conducting in Mozart's last *Piano Concerto*, K.595, Curzon's favourite. This is Mozart at his most joyous, with Curzon losing any of the inhibitions that sometimes dogged him in the studio, warmly supported by his younger colleague in both roles. Speeds in outer movements are broad enough to allow the most elegant pointing, not least in the jaunty finales. Slow movements are warmly expressive at broad speeds, concentrated and sustained. The *Duo Sonata* finds Curzon in 1960 in a partnership with Britten at Jubilee Hall, Aldeburgh, and though the mono sound is far drier, it is firm and immediate, letting one appreciate another exuberant performance, this time with the outer movements challengingly fast, and the middle movement bringing delectable interplay between the players.

(i; ii) *Piano Concerto 27, K.595*; (iii) *Piano Quartet in G min., K.478*; (iv; ii) *Exsultate, jubilate, K.165*

(M) *** BBC (ADD) BBCB 8005-2. (i) S. Richter; (ii) ECO, Britten; (iii) Britten, Sillito, Aronowitz, Heath; (iv) Ameling

Britten as conductor in Richter's reading of K.595 is warmer in his Mozart style than his soloist, just as persuasive as he is in his recording with Clifford Curzon. Best of all is the *Piano Quartet*, where Britten's expressiveness even in the simplest scale passage has one magnetized, a great performance. Though the string sound in the concerto is a little thin, the other two recordings are excellent. As an encore Elly Ameling has never sounded more sweetly radiant on disc than in this account of *Exsultate, jubilate*, technically immaculate.

Double Piano Concerto in E flat, K.365

*** Chan. 9711. G. and S. Pekinel, Philh. O, Marriner – BRUCH; MENDELSSOHN: *Double Piano Concerto* ***

This unique coupling of *Double Piano Concertos*, devised by the Pekinel sisters, is an inspired one, even though the Mozart is the only masterpiece among the three works. It receives a fresh, alert reading, marked by superb ensemble from the two soloists, helped by vivid Chandos sound.

(i) *Double Piano Concerto in E flat, K.365*; *Triple Piano Concerto in F (Lodron), K.242* (arr. for 2 pianos). *Andante & Variations in G, K.501*. *Fantasia in F min., K.608* (arr. Busoni)

(N) (M) *** Sony 518811 [SK 92735]. Perahia, Lupu; (i) with ECO

Murray Perahia and Radu Lupu are in good form in both concertos. The performances emanated from public concerts at The Maltings, Snape, between 1987 and 1990, and they have much of the excitement and spontaneity of live music-making. The two pianists are beautifully matched in both works, and again in the *Variations* and Busoni's transcription of the *F minor Fantasy*, originally written for a musical clock.

Violin concertos

Adagio for Violin and Orchestra in E, K.261; Rondo for Violin and Orchestra in C, K.373

(BB) (***) Naxos mono 8.110975. Milstein, RCA Victor SO, Golschmann – DVORAK; GLAZUNOV: *Violin Concerto* (***)

These Mozart pieces are given with all the elegance and finesse – and purity – that Milstein commanded, and make a splendid foil to the Dvořák and Glazunov *Concertos*.

Violin Concertos 1–5; Adagio in E, K.261; Rondo in C, K.373; Rondo Concertante in B flat, K.269

(B) *** O-L Double 455 721-2 (2). Standage, AAM, Hogwood

(M) *** Virgin 5 61841-2 (*1, 3 & 5*); 5 61842-2 (*2 & 4*; *Adagio Rondos*). Tetzlaff, Deutsche Kammerphilharmonie

(M) **(*) DG 445 535-2 (2). Perlman, VPO, Levine

(BB) **(*) EMI Encore (ADD) 5 74743-2 (*1-3*; *Rondo*); 5 74744-2 (*4-5*; *Adagio*; *Rondo concertante*). D. Oistrakh, BPO

(i) Violin Concertos 1–5; (ii) Adagio in E, K.261; Rondo in C, K.373; (i; iii) Sinfonia concertante, K.364

♦━ (B) *** Ph. (ADD) Duo 438 323-2 (2). Grumiaux, (i) LSO, C. Davis; (ii) New Philh. O, Leppard; (iii) with Pellicia

Violin Concertos 1–5; Adagio in E, K.261; Rondo Concertante in B flat, K.269

(BB) *** Virgin 2x1 Double 5 61576-2 (2). Huggett, OAE

Violin Concertos 1–5; (i; ii) Concertone in C, K.190; (i) Sinfonia concertante for Violin, Viola & Orchestra, K.364

♦━ (M) *** Avie AV 2058 (3). Mintz, with (i) Shaham; (ii) Anderson; ECO

Violin Concertos 1–5; Rondos 1–2, K.269 & K.373

(M) *** Sony SM2K 89983 (2). Lin, ECO, Leppard

Violin Concertos 1–5; (i) Sinfonia concertante, K.364

(BB) **(*) EMI Seraphim (ADD) 5 68530-2 (2). Menuhin, Bath Festival O; (i) with Barshai

Violin Concertos 1–5; (i) Sinfonia concertante for Violin, Viola & Orchestra, K.364

(N) (BB) ** EMI Gemini (ADD) 5 86528-2 (2). Spivakov, ECO; (i) with Bashmet

(i) Violin Concertos 1–5; (ii) Violin Sonatas 32 in B flat, K.454; 34 in A, K.526

(M) *** Ph. (ADD) stereo/mono 464 722-2 (2). Grumiaux, (i) LSO, C. Davis; (ii) Haskil

An outstanding new complete set from Shlomo Mintz on Avie makes a clear first choice for the five *Violin Concertos*. His naturally flowing classical simplicity of line and gleaming tone are a joy throughout, yet these performances are deeply felt, and he is not afraid to blossom into a full G-string richness when stylishly and musically appropriate. Mintz directs the ECO himself from the bow, and they provide the most polished, elegant and supportive accompaniments, with bouncing rhythms in *Allegros* and lovely, warm phrasing of slow movements. (One notices in passing the glowing contribution of the horns.) The famous *Tempo di Menuetto* finale of the *Fifth*, so-called 'Turkish', *Concerto*, with its middle section both jaunty and sparkling, brings a chimerical contrast characteristic of the whole series. The *Concertone*, with a delightful oboe contribution from John Anderson, is captivating, agreeably lightweight, while both here and in the lyrically flexible account of the inspired *Sinfonia concertante* Hagai Shaham proves an admirable violin partner. Mintz chooses himself to take the viola part in the latter, leading to a serenely beautiful solo interchange in the glorious slow movement which brings an almost improvisatory feeling. The high-spirited and debonair mood of the finale then completes the performance to perfection.

Overall, it would be hard to find a more genial set of Mozart's string concertos. Joy in the music-making brims out from every performance, with unexaggerated speeds chosen to bring a feeling of relaxation, with sprung rhythms, consistently sweet tone from Shlomo Mintz and alert playing from the English Chamber Orchestra, responding most sympathetically to direction from the soloist. The recordings were made in the Air Studios in Hampstead, a venue that has sometimes brought rather dry sound. Here, with engineering by Mike Hatch, there is a clarity and intimacy as well as warmth in the sound which, thanks to clean separation, never feels constricted.

Grumiaux's accounts of the Mozart *Violin Concertos* come from the early 1960s and are still among the most beautifully played in the catalogue at any price. The orchestral accompaniments have sparkle and vitality, and Grumiaux's contribution has splendid poise and purity of tone. For this generous reissue on their bargain Duo label, Philips have added the *Adagio*, K.261, and *Rondo*, K.373, recorded later in 1967, and also a fine performance of the great *Sinfonia concertante*, K.364, with Arrigo Pellicia proving a sensitive partner for Grumiaux, especially in the *Andante*. The new CD transfers are brightly lit but still faithful. Grumiaux's set comes alternatively with two late *Violin Sonatas*, where he is admirably partnered by Clara Haskil. This was a celebrated partnership and these classic vintage accounts are of the highest calibre. The recordings from the late 1950s are mono, and although the sound is remarkably vivid and true, this is not made clear on the packaging. Nevertheless these are treasurable performances.

Anyone seeking period-instrument performances need look no further than Standage's superb Oiseau-Lyre set. Standage's beautifully focused, silvery tone is a constant joy. Hogwood's accompaniments are beautifully sprung, with no lack of warmth, the orchestral violins articulating neatly and gracefully to match the soloist and the transparent textures revealing every detail of the orchestral scoring. The shorter pieces are also given fine performances and are never treated just as encores. The 1990 Abbey Road recording is first rate throughout, beautifully balanced and with not a trace of edginess anywhere.

Monica Huggett provides an admirable alternative. She directs from the bow and she is a superb soloist: spontaneous, vital, warm and elegant. She plays her own cadenzas, and very good they are too. Orchestral textures are fresh and transparent, ensemble is excellent, and the solo playing is without even a drop of vinegar; indeed, the violin timbre, if not opulent, is firm, well focused and sparkling. The Virgin Double omits the *Rondo in C*, but costs somewhat less than its Oiseau-Lyre competitor.

Christian Tetzlaff is a first-class player and an equally first-class Mozartian. He plays all five concertos with great freshness and he simultaneously directs the Deutsche Kammerphilharmonie in polished and sympathetic accompaniments. His pacing of *Allegros* is brisk, but exhilaratingly so, and his expressive phrasing in slow movements matches the clean, positive style of his contribution to faster movements. However, for a somewhat lower cost on a Philips Duo one can get Grumiaux, who is unsurpassed; and that set includes also the *Sinfonia concertante in E flat*.

Cho-Liang Lin creates a ready partnership with Leppard and the ECO, and his persuasive style brings a combination of effervescence and delicacy matched by the orchestra, with appealing tenderness in slow movements and plenty of dash in finales. Lin is full of fancy and imagination; there is an element of youthful lightness running through these performances, though there is no lack of bite or point either. But this is essentially sweet, elegant playing in a traditional but uninflated style. First-class recording.

Perlman gives characteristically assured, virtuoso readings with Levine, a fresh and undistracting Mozartian. The virtuoso approach sometimes involves a tendency to hurry, and the power is emphasized by the weight and immediacy of the recording. Warmth is here rather than charm; but Perlman's individual magic makes for magnetic results all through, not least in the intimate intensity of slow movements. Those of the first two concertos are particularly graceful, but at times (and notably in the two most popular concertos, Nos. 3 and 5) he treats the works rather more as bravura showpieces

than is common. However, Perlman's virtuosity is effortless and charismatic, and the orchestral playing is first class. The DG recording is well balanced, with the soloist close but not excessively so, and the perspective is on the whole well judged.

Menuhin uses cadenzas of his own, and many may feel that they are not Mozartian. Otherwise the style is sensibly exploited, and these performances give an engaging sense of musicians making intimate music together for the joy of it. One is always conscious that this is the phrasing of a master musician who can also provide the lightest touch in finales, which are alert and extrovert. In the *Sinfonia concertante* Menuhin and Barshai make a splendid team with happily similar views. Throughout, the stereo has a bright sheen and, with the remastering, the orchestral violins are made to sound glassy above the stave, but the ear adjusts when the music-making is so distinctive and the acoustic is basically warm.

David Oistrakh proves predictably strong and positive as a Mozartian, and he is well accompanied by the Berlin Philharmonic. But there are too many touches of unwanted heaviness to make this an ideal cycle. Needless to say, the performances have their fine moments. The slow movements of the *G major* and *D major* (Nos. 3 and 4) are memorably expressive, and the *Rondo concertante* is played with real sparkle. The recordings are consistently lively, with the soloist balanced well forward. Good value at Encore price.

Vladimir Spivakov is a highly accomplished Soviet master, still young at the time these recordings were made in the late 1970s and early 1980s. His admirably fluent playing throughout is very polished, yet he projects little sense of great personality. Although he is an alert and sensitive artist with a good sense of style, his partner in the *Sinfonia concertante*, Yuri Bashmet, is an artist of greater warmth. Well-balanced recording throughout the set, but even at the modest Gemini price, this playing is not quite memorable enough to displace any of the first recommendations.

Violin Concertos 1; 2; Rondo in B flat, K.269; Andante in F (arr. Saint-Saëns from *Piano Concerto 21, K.467*)

(BB) **(*) Naxos 8.550414. Nishizaki, Capella Istropolitana, Wildner

This was the last disc to be recorded of Takako Nishizaki's fine survey of the *Violin Concertos*. The opening movement of K.207 is brisk and fresh, although this is the least individual of Nishizaki's readings. The *Second Concerto*, K.211, has rather more flair, the *Andante* touchingly phrased, and the finale has a winning lightness of touch. The *Rondo* is also an attractively spontaneous performance, and as an encore we are offered Saint-Saëns's arrangement of the famous 'Elvira Madigan' theme from the *C major Concerto*, K.467.

Violin Concertos (i) 1 in B flat, K.207; (ii) 2 in D, K.211; 4 in D, K.218; (i) Adagio in E, K. 261

(M) *** EMI 5 62825-2. Mutter; (i) ASMF, Marriner; (ii) Philh. O, Muti

Anne-Sophie Mutter made her Mozartian début with Karajan on DG with a famous youthful coupling of the *G major* and *A major Violin Concertos* (K.216 and K.219). She then went on, in 1981, to record the two *D major Concertos* for EMI with a different orchestra and conductor, and the results were hardly less successful. A decade later, changing conductors once again, she provided a delightful successor, offering the *B flat Concerto*, with a quicksilver finale, and an exquisite account of the *Adagio in E major*. Throughout these performances she was given very sensitive support from both Muti and Marriner. Her playing combines purity and classical feeling, delicacy and incisiveness, and is admirably expressive. Its freshness is also most appealing. Moreover, the digital recording is consistently good, the images clearly defined and the balance very satisfactory. This reissue in EMI's 'Great Artists of the Century' series is a record to treasure.

Violin Concertos 1 in B flat, K.207; 3 in G, K.216; 5 in A, K.219

(N) *** Australian Decca Eloquence (ADD/DDD) 476 2748. Brown, ASMF

Violin Concertos 2 in D, K.211; 4 in D, K.218. (i) Sinfonia concertante in E flat, K.364

(N) *** Australian Decca Eloquence (ADD/DDD) 476 2747. Brown, ASMF; (i) with Suk

Iona Brown's accounts of the Mozart *Violin Concertos* (originally on Argo) have the advantage of including another fine account of the great *Sinfonia concertante*, in which she is joined by Josef Suk. The performances of the solo concertos have a freshness and vigour that are winning, and, like the newer Avie set, the participants convey a sense of pleasure in what they are doing. There is a spring-like quality to this music-making, such as in the outer movements of No. 3, with a sultry, Mediterranean warmth in the middle movement. No. 2 is very classical in spirit, with a striking vitality in the outer movements; but all these performances have an engaging liveliness and are very well integrated. The only slight reservation concerns the *Sinfonia concertante*, where there is an element of restraint in the slow movement, which does not quite blossom here as it does in the finest versions. Nevertheless, these two CDs fully deserve a three-star recommendation, and we hope Decca may decide to reissue them in the UK. Excellent recordings: Nos. 1, 2, 5 and the *Sinfonia concertante* are digital.

Violin Concertos 2 in D, K.211; 3 in G, K.216; 5 in A (Turkish), K.219

(M) *** Warner Elatus 0927 49559-2. Repin, VCO, Y. Menuhin

The finest performance on the 1997 Elatus disc is No. 5, the so-called 'Turkish', which springs to life from the opening bars and has an ethereal slow movement. Vadim Repin also plays exquisitely in the *Adagio* of the G major, K.216, and is matched by Menuhin. No. 2, K.211, has plenty of life, too; Repin is still very impressive, and there is some outstanding playing here too. Very good recording. Excellent value.

Violin Concerto 3 in G

(B) *** EMI double forte (ADD) 5 69331-2 (2). D. Oistrakh, Philh. O – BEETHOVEN: *Triple Concerto*; BRAHMS: *Double Concerto*; PROKOFIEV: *Violin Concerto 2* ***

(BB) *** EMI Encore 5 85455-2. F. P. Zimmermann, BPO, Sawallisch – BRAHMS: *Violin Concerto* **

(N) *** Warner 2564 61561-2. Rachlin, Bav. RSO, Jansons – BRAHMS: *Violin Concerto in D* ***

David Oistrakh's supple, richly toned yet essentially classical style suits the melodic line of this youthful work and gives it the stature of maturity. The orchestral contribution is directed by the soloist himself and is eminently polished. EMI provide admirably smooth yet vivid sound, and this is just one of four marvellous performances which make up this superb double forte compilation.

With the string complement of the Berlin Philharmonic aptly reduced and with Sawallisch at his most sparkling, Zimmermann's studio recording of Mozart's *G major Concerto* is a delight, with a quicksilver lightness in the outer movements and a compelling repose and concentration in the central *Adagio*. In its own right this is superb music-making, but the fact that it is coupled with Brahms rather than with other violin concertos of Mozart will not appeal to all collectors.

In Rachlin's version of K.216 it is striking that, though a full symphony orchestra is involved, Jansons keeps it in scale with the music. Even before the soloist enters, the brisk tempo and the lightness of texture establish the qualities of the reading, and despite the speed there is no feeling of rush, just of a persuasively taut interpretation. The central *Adagio* is marked by ultra-refined playing from soloist and orchestra alike. The finale, like the first movement, is fast, light and transparent, with a winning lilt.

Violin Concertos 3; 5 (Turkish)

⌀— (M) *** DG (ADD) 457 746-2. Mutter, BPO, Karajan

(BB) *** Naxos 8.550063. Nishizaki, Capella Istropolitana, Gunzenhauser

Violin Concertos 3 & 5; Adagio, K.251; Rondo, K.373

(N) **(*) Decca 475 6000. Bell, ECO, Maag – BRUCH; MENDELSSOHN: *Violin Concertos* **(*)

Extraordinarily mature and accomplished playing from Anne-Sophie Mutter, who was a mere fourteen years old when her recording was made. The instinctive mastery means that there is no hint of immaturity: the playing has polish, but fine artistry too and remarkable freshness. Karajan is at his most sympathetic and scales down the accompaniment to act as a perfect setting for his young soloist. The recording has been transferred brilliantly to CD, though some might feel that the orchestral strings are a shade too brightly lit.

This is the finest of Nishizaki's three discs of the Mozart *Violin Concertos* on Naxos. The readings are individual and possess the most engaging lyrical feeling and the natural response of the soloist to Mozartian line and phrase. A good balance, the soloist forward, but convincingly so, and the orchestral backcloth in natural perspective. A real bargain.

Joshua Bell is lucky in having the excellent Peter Maag to provide stylishly turned accompaniments and to phrase the slow movement cantilena so exquisitely on the violins, to prepare for the solo line, which is comparatively romantic. Bell is on excellent form, and he and Maag are especially good in handling the 'Turkish' interlude in the finale of K.219. Indeed, these are fine, assured readings, if perhaps not absolutely distinctive, although they have a very generous sprinkling of cadenzas. The recordings, made in the Blackheath Concert Halls in 1991, are resonantly warm, but orchestral tuttis are not absolutely clean in focus.

Violin Concerto 4, K.218

(BB) (***) Naxos mono 8.110946. Szigeti, LPO, Beecham – BEETHOVEN: *Violin Concerto* (***)

Szigeti's account of this Mozart concerto has appeared many times before, most recently in harness with the Prokofiev *D major*, which he recorded at much the same time. Now it comes in harness with his memorable Beethoven with Bruno Walter. Szigeti was in his prime when this was made, and his individuality shines through.

Violin Concerto 4; (i) Sinfonia concertante, K.364

(BB) **(*) Naxos 8.550332. Nishizaki, (i) Kyselak; Capella Istropolitana, Gunzenhauser

A fine account of No. 4, with Takako Nishizaki's solo playing well up to the high standard of this series and with Stephen Gunzenhauser's perceptive pacing adding to our pleasure. The *Sinfonia concertante* is very enjoyable too, if perhaps slightly less distinctive. The finale is infectious in its liveliness, its rhythms buoyantly pointed. Again, a good balance and excellent sound.

Violin Concertos (i) 4, K.218; (ii) 5 (Turkish) K219

(B) *** Nim. NI 1735 (3). Shumsky, SCO, Y. P. Tortelier –
    BACH: *Concertos*; YSAYE: *Sonatas* ***
(BB) (**(*)) Naxos mono 8.110941. Heifetz, (i) RPO, Beecham; (ii) LPO, Barbirolli – MENDELSSOHN: *Violin Concerto in E min.* (**(*))

Shumsky's performances are of the highest calibre. They are totally unaffected, spontaneous, and full of character. He has an excellent rapport with Yan Pascal Tortelier, who secures a warm, very alive and musical response from the Scottish Chamber Orchestra, with the players themselves conveying enthusiasm and pleasure. The recording is natural and nicely balanced. This now comes as part of a memorial box to profile the three major recordings which Shumsky made for Nimbus before he died in 2000. It is inexpensive and with good documentation; it is well worth acquiring.

Heifetz's EMI recording, now retransferred by Naxos, first appeared in 1934. The flair and elegance of his playing, as well as the hushed purity of the slow movement, reflect the violinist's devotion to the work, well matched by Barbirolli's beautifully sprung accompaniments with the recently founded LPO. The reading of the *D major Concerto*, recorded in 1947, has similar qualities, with Beecham's accompaniments intensifying the elegance. Well coupled with the Heifetz–Beecham Mendelssohn *Concerto*. Good transfers, if with surface hiss at times intrusive.

Violin Concerto 5 (Turkish)

(M) *** DG (ADD) 447 403-2. Schneiderhan, BPO, Jochum –
    BEETHOVEN: *Violin Concerto* *** ✪
(***) Testament mono SBT 1228. Kogan, Conservatoire O, Vandernoot – BEETHOVEN: *Violin Concerto* (***)

This was perhaps the finest of the complete set of Mozart's *Violin Concertos* which Schneiderhan recorded with the Berlin Philharmonic in the late 1960s. The recording is realistically balanced, and this makes a generous coupling for his famous record of the Beethoven, made six years earlier.

Matching the outstanding account of the Beethoven *Concerto* with which it is coupled, Kogan's 1957 version of Mozart, recorded later in the same month, is comparably strong and purposeful in the first movement, positive in the expressive contrasts. The slow movement is sweet and tender, poetic without self-indulgence, and the finale sparkles in its contrasting sections. Excellent transfer to make one forget the absence of stereo.

Double Concerto for Violin, Piano and Orchestra, K.315f; (i) Sinfonia concertante in E flat, K.364

*** Sony SK 89488. Midori, N. German RSO, Eschenbach (piano & cond.); (i) with Imai (viola)

The Mozart scholar, Alfred Einstein, described the 120 bars that have survived of Mozart's *Double Concerto for Piano,*

Violin and Orchestra as 'a magnificent torso', the most promising of starts to a work. The mystery is what happened to the rest. The reconstruction recorded here stems from the detective work of Philip Wilby, who has deduced that the *Violin Sonata in D*, K.306, grander in scale and manner than its fellow sonatas, was a reworking of the concerto.

The première recording with Iona Brown and Howard Shelley as soloists was issued as part of Volume 8 of the Philips Complete Mozart Edition, an excellent account, also coupled with K.364, as well as another reconstructed sinfonia concertante movement. In sound the Sony version is marginally fuller, with a more airy acoustic, while interpretatively Midori takes a more freely expressive, even romantic view, notably in the central *Andantino* of the *Double Concerto*, which is two minutes longer than the Brown/Shelley performance. The contrasts are similar in the familiar masterpiece, K.364, with Nobuko Imai magnificent in both versions, at once individual and classically pure. This is well worth exploring for those collectors without the Mozart Edition.

(i) Concertone in C.; K.190; (ii) Sinfonia concertante, K.364

☛ ✪ (M) *** DG 476 1651. Perlman, Zukerman, Israel PO, Mehta

The DG version of the *Sinfonia concertante* is in a special class and is an example of 'live' recording at its most magnetic, with the inspiration of the occasion caught on the wing. Zubin Mehta is drawn into the music-making and accompanies most sensitively. The *Concertone* is also splendidly done; the ear notices the improvement in the sound-balance of the studio recording of this work. But the *Sinfonia concertante*, with the audience incredibly quiet, conveys an electricity rarely caught on record. An outstanding addition to Universal's 'Penguin ✪ Collection'.

DANCES AND MARCHES

Contredanses: La Bataille, K.535; Das Donnerwetter, K.534; Les Filles malicieuses, K.610; Der Sieg vom Helden Koburg, K.587; It trionfo delle donne, K.607. Gallimathias musicum (quodlibet), K.32; 6 German Dances, K.567; 3 German Dances, K.605; German Dance: Die Leyerer, K.611. March in D, K.335/1. A Musical Joke, K.522

*** DG (IMS) 429 783-2. Orpheus CO

A splendid sampler of the wit and finesse, to say nothing of the high quality of entertainment, provided by Mozart's dance music, which kept people on their feet till dawn at masked balls in the 1780s and early 1790s. The playing of the Orpheus group is winningly polished, flexible and smiling, and they bring off the *Musical Joke* with considerable flair, both in the gentle fun of the *Adagio cantabile*, which is exquisitely played, and in the outrageous grinding dissonance of the 'wrong notes' at the end. First-class sound, fresh, transparent and vividly immediate.

12 German Dances, K.586; 6 German Dances, K.600; 4 German Dances, K.602; 3 German Dances, K.605

☛ (BB) *** Naxos 8.550412. Capella Istropolitana, Wildner

Fresh, bright, unmannered performances of some of the dance music Mozart wrote right at the end of his life. The playing is excellent and the recording is bright and full. An excellent super-bargain.

DIVERTIMENTI

Divertimenti and serenades

Complete Bargain Mozart Edition, Vol. 3: (i) *Divertimenti for Strings & Wind;* **(ii)** *Serenades & Divertimenti for Wind*
(B) *** Ph. 464 790-2 (11). (i) ASMF, Marriner; (ii) Hollinger Wind Ens.; Netherlands Wind Ens.; De Waart; ASMF, Marriner or Laird

This is one of the most attractive of all the boxes in the Philips Mozart Edition. The music itself is a delight, the performances are stylish, elegant and polished, while the digital recording has admirable warmth and realistic presence and definition.

Divertimenti for Strings 1–3, K.136-8; Serenades 6 in D (Serenata notturna), K.239; 13 in G (Eine kleine Nachtmusik), K.525
(M) **(*) Classic fM 75605 57024-2. City of L. Sinfonia, Watkinson

These are delightful performances from the City of London Sinfonia: fresh, warm and polished. *Eine kleine Nachtmusik* is elegant, graceful and nicely paced, and the same can be said of the three engaging *String Divertimenti*. The *Serenata notturna* features the leaders of each section (two violins, viola and double bass) as a solo concertino group, and with the timpani not over-dominant. The resonance of the recording is rather excessive but, if you don't mind that, this Classic fM programme is very recommendable.

Divertimenti for Strings 1–3, K.136/8; Serenade 13 (Eine kleine Nachtmusik; (i) Bassoon Concerto in B flat
(B) **(*) CfP 575 1432. LMP, Glover, (i) with Nakanishi

Jane Glover is an excellent Mozartian and she directs here a most elegant and stylish account of the famous *Night Music*, full of nice touches of light and shade. She is perhaps not as dashing as some in the opening *Allegro* of the most often played of the three *String Divertimenti*, K.136 in D major, but she has the gift of making the other two seem equally attractive. Yoshiyuki Nakanishi is a personable and fluent soloist in the *Bassoon Concerto*, but this account is enjoyable rather than distinctive. Good, natural recording.

Divertimenti 2 in D, K.131; 15 in B flat, K.287
(BB) *** Naxos 8.550996. Capella Istropolitana, Nerat

The playing of the Capella Istropolitana under Harald Nerat is beautifully turned and polished. They phrase elegantly; the sound is full and transparent, bringing the sweetest modern violin-timbre, yet the effect is as refreshing as any period performance. The *D major Divertimento* is charmingly scored for flute, oboe, bassoon, four horns and strings, but it has a gracious second-movement *Adagio* cantilena of disarming simplicity for strings alone. The *B flat Divertimento* was written five years later, in Salzburg, and is scored more simply for two horns and strings.

Divertimento 10 in F, K.247; March in F (Erste Lodron'sche Nachtmusik), K.248
(M) **(*) Orfeo (ADD) C589021B. V. Chamber Ens. – BARTOK: *Violin Concerto 2* **(*)

These performances from a Salzburg concert in 1983 offer an excellent example of Gerhart Hetzel as a leader of the Vienna Chamber Ensemble and provide an excellent foil for his Bartók *Concerto*. This is playing of real style, and the Vienna

Radio recording is eminently serviceable without being distinguished.

Divertimenti 10 in F, K.247; 11 in D, K.331
**(*) Cap. 10 203. Salzburg Mozarteum Camerata Academica, Végh

The playing has striking freshness and vitality; these are chamber orchestral performances on modern instruments, but the scale is admirable and the resonance adds a feeling of breadth. Although slow movements tend to be on the slow side, while not lacking grace, *Allegros* sparkle and have dash without ever seeming hurried, even if ensemble isn't always absolutely immaculate.

Divertimento 17 in D, K.334
(*) Sony **DVD SVD 46388. BPO, Karajan – Richard STRAUSS: *Also sprach Zarathustra* ***

By the time Karajan conducted these two celebratory concerts he was already ailing, as one registers from his painful progress to the podium each time; but, once there, the electric intensity of his conducting is as striking as ever. This last of the *Divertimenti* that Mozart wrote for Salzburg – for two horns and strings – was the first of the two items in a Berlin Philharmonic concert celebrating the city's 750th anniversary. Karajan gives brightly refreshing accounts of the outer movements, and determinedly traditional readings of the three middle movements omitting the march movement, K.445, latterly thought to belong to the piece. The celebrated Minuet, which comes third, prompts Karajan to a reading so slow and moulded one is reminded of Beecham's more eccentric interpretations of Mozart. The orchestra responds with total loyalty, and the wit and exhilaration of the finale make a delightful conclusion.

Divertimento 17 in D, K.334; Serenades 6 (Serenata notturna); 13 (Eine kleine Nachtmusik); Symphonies 39–41 (Jupiter)
(B) **(*) DG 2-CD (ADD) 474 272-2 (2). BPO, Karajan

A mixed bag of Mozart here, reassembled for DG's 'Karajan Collection', all showing the conductor's strong personality, if in different ways. The recordings come from a decade apart, the *Divertimento* and *Serenades* from the mid-1960s, the last three *Symphonies* from a decade later. The former are cultured and effortless readings, beautifully played and phrased, but excessively smooth. Indeed, the melodic line in the *Divertimento* is often lovingly caressed, as in the seductively slinky but hardly Mozartian phrasing of the famous Minuet. The *Serenata notturna* is a little square, but the performance of *Eine kleine Nachtmusik* is first rate, lithe, with the *Romanze* not over-indulged. The last three symphonies are even more vitally alert readings, admirably proportioned, gripping and finely paced. The opening of *No. 40 in G minor* may not be quite dark enough for some tastes, but it is certainly dramatic; the orchestra plays superbly, and the *Jupiter* has weight and power as well as surface elegance. The sound is first class, and if you enjoy Mozart on a full-sized orchestra these performances show the conductor at his greatest.

Wind divertimenti and serenades

Complete Wind Divertimenti & Wind Serenades
(B) *** CPO 999 822-2 (7). Consortium Classicum, Klöcker

Mozart's wind music, whether in the ambitious *Serenades* or the simpler *Divertimenti*, brings a naturally felicitous blending of timbre and colour unmatched by any other composer.

It seems that even when writing for the simplest combination of wind instruments, Mozart is incapable of being dull.

Between 1973 and 1986 the clarinettist, Dieter Klöcker, with his talented wind group, Consortium Classicum, recorded over 30 of Mozart's works for wind instruments that had been designed originally for party entertainment, outdoor as well as in. These recordings, made originally for German EMI and here reissued by CPO, form a valuable collection, starting with the three greatest works, the *Serenades Nos. 10, 11 and 12*, which transcend the limits of the genre, and including many delightful rarities, not just *Divertimenti* but *Duos* and a *Cassation*, all of which are listed in the Philips Complete Mozart Edition. Klöcker is a thoughtful artist and he provides an interesting note on the scholarship involved. Like most groups, this one opts for using a double-bass to reinforce the bass line of many of the pieces, notably the big *Serenade for 13 Wind Instruments*. Though charm is not a major factor in these performances, their freshness and direct expressiveness make for compulsive listening, with imaginative solos from the oboist, Gernot Schmalfus, as well as from Klöcker himself. The recordings, mostly made in various radio studios, are bright and clear. It is fascinating to find the *Divertimento No. 6 in C*, K.188, with three trumpets in C and two in D, plus timpani, sound so light in texture.

Adagios: in F, K.410; in B flat, K.411. Divertimenti for Wind 3 in E flat, K.166; 4 in B flat, K.186; 8 in F, K.213; 9 in B flat, K.240; 12 in E flat, K.252; 13 in F, K.253; 14 in B flat, K.270; 16 in E flat, K.289; in B flat, K.Anh. 226; in B flat, K.Anh. 227. Serenades 10 in B flat, for 13 Wind Instruments, K.361; 11 in E flat, K.375; 12 in C min., K.488

(B) **(*) Decca (ADD) 455 794-2 (3). L. Wind Soloists, Brymer

Divertimenti for Wind 3, K.166; 4, K.186; 8, K.213; 9, K.240; 12, K.252; 13, K.253; 14, K.270; Serenades 10, K.361; 11, K.375; 12, K.388

(M) *** Auvidis E 8627/29 (3). Zefiro Ens.

The Decca coverage is remarkably comprehensive and the playing here of the highest order, and the only drawback is the too-close balance for the large-scale *B flat major Serenade*. In this work the effect is rather dry; the digital remastering has taken much of the ambient bloom from the sound. However, Brymer's group gives a strong, stylish performance with plenty of imagination in matters of phrasing. Elsewhere there is presence and bloom in equal measure. There are countless felicities: all the finales have a wonderfully light touch, but one remembers especially the engaging three-movement *Divertimento in F*, K.253, with its charming first-movement theme and variations and its slow Minuet with its playful Trio.

Astrée Auvidis offer a digital set at mid-price (three records for the cost of two), offering the same three major *Serenades* as Jack Brymer, plus seven of the *Divertimenti*, played on period instruments by a highly sensitive Italian group. The performances are very recommendable on all counts. The sounds of the period instruments are delightfully fresh and the blending of timbres most felicitous. The playing itself brings a characteristic Italianate sunny quality to Mozart yet is remarkably subtle in detail. The *Gran Partita* is particularly seductive, with only one tiny flaw. At the opening of its eloquent *Adagio* the initial oboe entry begins a little below the note: some ears might find this disturbing on repetition. Otherwise intonation is impeccable and the brilliant playing on natural horns by Raul Diaz and Dileno Baldin is most

infectious. In the *C minor Serenade* with its darker sonorities, the Italians miss the sombre touch which the English players manage so adroitly, but overall the Zefiro group play with such glowing finesse and spontaneity that this Auvidis set must marginally take pride of place.

Divertimenti in B flat, K.Anh.227 (K.196f); 12 in E flat, K.252; 13 in F, K.253; Serenade 12 in C min., K.388

❡— (BB) *** Naxos 8.555943. Oslo PO Wind Ens.

These 1997 performances show the Oslo Philharmonic wind on top form. They give the two Salzburg *Divertimenti* with finesse and grace, and bring great intensity to the *C minor Serenade*. The recording, made at the Lommedalen Church at Baerun, has splendid presence and bloom. An outstanding bargain.

6 German Dances, K.571; Les petits riens: ballet music, K.299b; Serenade (Eine kleine Nachtmusik)

❡— (BB) *** Warner Apex 0927 48691-2. SCO, Leppard

An eminently desirable collection from 1984 which has been absent from the catalogue too long; it now returns at a most enticing price. The performance of *Les petits riens* is delightful, spirited and polished, and the *German Dances* are no less lively and elegant; the famous *Nachtmusik* is nicely proportioned and very well played. The sound too is most believable, giving a tangible impression of the players sitting together out beyond the speakers.

Overtures

Overtures: Apollo et Hyacinthus; Bastien und Bastienne; La clemenza di Tito; Così fan tutte; Don Giovanni; Die Entführung aus dem Serail; La finta giardiniera; Idomeneo; Lucio Silla; Mitridate, re di Ponto; Le nozze di Figaro; Il re pastore; Der Schauspieldirektor; Die Zauberflöte

❡— (BB) *** Naxos 8.550185. Capella Istropolitana, Wordsworth

Barry Wordsworth follows up his excellent series of Mozart symphonies for Naxos with this generous collection of overtures, no fewer than 14 of them, arranged in chronological order and given vigorous, stylish performances. In Italian overture form, *Mitridate* and *Lucio Silla*, like miniature symphonies, have separate tracks for each of their three contrasted sections. Very well recorded, the disc is highly recommendable at super-bargain price.

Overtures: Bastien und Bastienne; La clemenza di Tito; Così fan tutte; Don Giovanni; Die Entführung aus dem Serail; La finta giardiniera; Idomeneo; Il re pastore; Lucio Silla; Le nozze di Figaro; Der Schauspieldirektor; Die Zauberflöte

(BB) *** RCA 74321 68004-2. Dresden State O, C. Davis

A self-recommending set of Mozart overtures from Colin Davis. They are thoroughly musical and have both drama and warmth, with much felicity of orchestral detail emerging from the superb Dresden orchestra throughout the programme. Davis perfectly balances the full weight of the dramatic moments with the sparkle of the lighter ones, and the dynamic contrasts are very well judged. The recording is good. If occasionally the tuttis can seem a little bass-heavy because of the resonant Dresden acoustic, this is not a serious problem, and anyone wanting a budget collection of Mozart overtures on modern instruments in digital sound cannot go far wrong here.

Overtures: La clemenza di Tito; Così fan tutte; Don Giovanni; Die Entführung aus dem Serail; La finta giardiniera; Idomeneo; Lucio Silla; Le nozze di Figaro; Der Schauspieldirektor; Die Zauberflöte

(M) *** Warner Elatus 2564 60122-2. Zurich Opera House O; or Concg. O; or VCM; Harnoncourt

(BB) *** EMI Encore 5 85060-2. ASMF, Marriner (without La finta giardiniera)

Harnoncourt is just the man to direct a collection of Mozart Overtures, for he plays each with individuality and zest, characterizing strongly. He draws splendidly polished and spirited playing from all these orchestras, and the result is consistently dramatic and satisfying, even if the CD is played straight through. And although the most familar overtures (Don Giovanni and Così fan tutti for instance) come up freshly, the lesser-known ones, for example La clemenza di Tito and the three-part Lucio Silla, are among the most stimulating. Of course, because many of these performances derive from his opera recordings, some are without their concert endings. But no matter; this is an excellent disc, and consistently well recorded too.

Like Harnoncourt, Marriner's collection emphasizes the spirit of the opera house, offering plenty of drama in Don Giovanni and Idomeneo and a sense of spectacle with the percussion effects in Die Entführung. Così fan tutti and Figaro bring a lighter touch; throughout the ASMF playing is spirited and stylish with the string detail nicely clean and polished. The digital recording is bright and bold and, even though La finta giardiniera is omitted, this is excellent value at budget price.

Serenades

Serenades 1 in D, K.100; 10 in B flat for 13 Wind Instruments (Gran Partita), K.361
*** BIS CD 1010. Tapiola Sinf., Kantorow

The Tapiola Sinfonietta under Jean-Jacques Kantorow gives a finely paced and splendidly phrased account of the great Wind Serenade and a delightfully vital account of the D major Serenade, K.100, lightly accented and full of character and wit. They make more of this piece than many of their rivals, and they get superb recording from the BIS team. Very recommendable.

Serenades 3, K.185; 4 (Colloredo), K.203
(BB) *** Naxos 8.550413. Salzburg CO, Nerat

Well-played, nicely phrased and musical accounts on Naxos, recorded in a warm, reverberant acoustic, but one in which detail clearly registers. The Salzburg Chamber Orchestra has real vitality, and most readers will find these accounts musically satisfying and very enjoyable.

Serenades (i) 6 (Serenata notturna), K.239; 7 (Haffner), K.250; 9 (Posthorn), K.320
*** Telarc CD 80161. Prague CO, Mackerras

Serenades 6 (Serenata notturna) K.239; 7 (Haffner), K.250 (with March in D, K.249); 9 (Posthorn), K.320 (with March in D, K.335/1); 13 (Eine kleine Nachtmusik), K.525
☞— ✿ (B) *** Ph. Duo DDD/ADD 464 022-2 (2). ASMF, Marriner

Marriner's accounts of the Haffner and Posthorn are cultured, warm, spacious and marvellously played. Iona Brown makes a superb contribution in the concertante violin role of the Haffner. The performance of the Serenata notturna, too, is

first class, crisply rhythmic in the first movement, with the drums clearly focused. As for the most famous work of all, Sir Neville's polished and elegant account of Eine kleine Nachtmusik is clearly designed to caress the ears of traditional listeners wearied by period performance. Throughout, the Philips engineers provide a natural sound-balance, with rich, full textures.

In Mackerras's coupling the playing is lively and brilliant, helped by warm recorded sound, vivid in its sense of presence, except that the reverberant acoustic clouds the tuttis a little. The violin soloist, Oldrich Viček, is very much one of the team under the conductor rather than a virtuoso establishing his individual line. By omitting repeats in the Haffner, Mackerras leaves room for the other delightful Serenade, just as haunting, with the terracing between the solo string quartet (in close focus) and the full string band aptly underlined.

Serenade 7 (Haffner), K.250; March, K.249
(BB) **(*) Naxos 8.550333. Nishizaki, Capella Istropolitana, Wildner

The K.249 March is given twice, both as prelude and postlude to the main Serenade in the authentic manner. Wildner brings out the vigour rather than the charm of the fast movements, with the Minuets on the heavy side, but with the big final Allegro superbly articulated and erupting in rustic jollity. The important violin solos in earlier movements are played superbly by Takako Nishizaki. Bright, full recording. Even with the above reservations, this is an excellent bargain.

Serenade 7 (Haffner), K.250; Symphony 35 (Haffner), K.385
*** Häns. CD 98.173. ASMF, I. Brown

The coupling of the Haffner Symphony and Haffner Serenade, especially apt, is surprisingly rare. In the Symphony Iona Brown, unlike Marriner, follows the autograph in omitting an exposition repeat. Brown herself is the virtuoso soloist in the Serenade, as she was in the Marriner version on Philips, lighter than ever in the moto perpetuo scurryings of the fourth movement Rondo. Hänssler describe this issue and the companion disc of the Posthorn Serenade as part of their Academy series, and such refreshing discs, vividly recorded, could not be more promising.

Serenades 9 (Posthorn), K.320; 13 (Eine kleine Nachtmusik), K.525
**(*) Telarc CD 10108. Prague CO, Mackerras

(i) Serenades 9 (Posthorn), K.320; 13 (Eine kleine Nachtmusik), K.525; (ii) 6 German Dances, K.509; Minuet in C, K.409
(B) **(*) Sony (ADD) SBK 48266. (i) Cleveland O, Szell; (ii) LSO, Leinsdorf

Serenade 9 (Posthorn), K. 320; Symphony 33, K. 319
*** Häns. CD 98.129. ASMF, I. Brown

Challenging earlier recordings by the Academy under Sir Neville Marriner, Iona Brown neatly offers another popular Serenade alongside a symphony contemporary with it. The sound is outstandingly good, with plenty of bloom but with no excessive reverberation. These are attractively fresh Mozart performances, using modern instruments, which have concern for the crisper manners encouraged by period performance. Speeds are consistently brisker than those of the Marriner versions which we have used for comparison. The finale of Symphony 33, for example, brings a hectic speed which does not sound at all breathless, with feather-light triplets, and similarly in the finale of the *Posthorn Serenade* with which it is coupled.

The Prague strings have great warmth and Mackerras gets vital results from his Czech forces. Rhythms are lightly sprung and the phrasing is natural in every way. The Telarc acoustic is warm and spacious with a wide dynamic range (some might feel it is too wide for this music), though most ears will find the effect agreeable.

Marvellously vivacious playing from the Clevelanders in the *Posthorn Serenade*, especially in the exhilarating *Presto* finale, yet there is no lack of tenderness in the *concertante* third movement. *Eine kleine Nachtmusik* is similarly polished and vital, and in both works the Severance Hall acoustic provides a full ambience, but it is a pity that the close balance means a reduced dynamic range. Even so, this is music-making of great character. Leinsdorf's *German Dances* make a lively bonus, if not as distinctive as the Szell performances.

Serenade 10 for 13 Wind Instruments, K.361
(BB) **(*) Hyp. Helios CDH 55093. Albion Ens.

**(*) Accent ACC 68642D. Octophorus, Kuijken

Serenade 10 in B flat (Gran Partita), K.361; Adagio in B flat for 2 Clarinets and 3 Basset Horns, K.484a
*** MDG 301 1077-2. Consortium Classicum

The Consortium Classicum's performance of the *Gran Partita* is among the finest on disc. The CD begins with a rarity, the *Adagio in B flat for Two Clarinets and Three Basset Horns*, K.484a, and K.361 is a serenade with a difference. The 12 wind instruments, including basset horns, plus double bass would not have been easy to assemble outside Vienna, and Franz Gleissner (1759–1818) arranged it for more conventional forces. There are unusual touches: the first trio of the second movement and the theme in the variation movement are for strings alone. They are very well recorded, too.

The Albion Ensemble give a most enjoyable account of Mozart's large-scale *Serenade*, finely blended and polished, and with the outer movements enjoyably robust and spirited. There is some very fine oboe-playing, and Andrew Marriner's clarinet is noticeably elegant in the penultimate *Theme and Variations*. Elsewhere there are moments when the mellifluous playing has rather less character, although it never becomes bland.

On period instruments Barthold Kuijken directs his talented team in an authentic performance where the distinctive character of eighteenth-century instruments brings a sparer, lighter texture, as it should. Speeds tend to be on the cautious side but the liveliness of the playing makes up for that. The recording adds to the clarity but, again, there is no coupling.

Serenades 10, K.361; 11, K.375; 12, K.388; Wind Divertimenti: K.240; K.252; K.253; K.270
⟶ (B) *** Double Decca 458 096-2 (2). Amadeus Winds, Hogwood

Anyone wanting period performances of Mozart's three supreme *Serenades for Wind* will find that this collection offers a fascinating aural comparison. K.375 and K.388 were recorded first in 1985 in New York, and the effect is undoubtedly more plangent than in the later performances recorded in Boston in 1987 (K.361) and 1989 (the four *Divertimenti*). In the *C minor Serenade* the extra darkness of colour adds to the character of the music. Both here and in K.375 speeds are on the leisurely side, except in the finales, though well lifted both rhythmically and in phrasing. The speeds are perhaps a recognition of the players' technical problems, coping with

intonation and less sophisticated mechanisms, a point brought home in the clear, full, digital recording, with much clicking of keys. By the time they came to record the *Gran Partita*, two years later, the group's integration was much smoother and the effect is much more sophisticated. Indeed, this is an outstandingly characterful account, preferable to the Brymer version on modern instruments (see above), not lacking finesse, and making the strongest possible case for authenticity. Both the *Adagio* and *Romance* are lyrically mellow, and the *Theme and Variations* is almost Schubertian in its innocent charm. The jocular finale goes like the wind, pressed home with a virtuosity surmounting almost all difficulties. The four *Divertimenti* are also very successful, with the vivid colouring preventing any possible feeling of blandness.

Serenades 11, K.375; 12, K.388
(**(*)) Testament mono SBT 1180. L. Bar. Ens., Haas – DVORAK: *Serenade* (**(*))

Serenades 11, K.375; 12, K.388; Overtures: Le nozze di Figaro (arr. Vent); Don Giovanni (arr. Triebensee); Die Zauberflöte (arr. Heidenreich)
⟶ (BB) *** Hyp. Helios CDH 55092. E. Concert Winds

Both *Serenades* on Helios are among the finest on disc and the *Overtures* are great fun. Fresh, spirited playing throughout, firmly focused and well-blended sound, both from the players and from the engineers. A delight.

This historic reissue of pioneering recordings from Karl Haas and the London Baroque Ensemble of three of the greatest of all wind works is valuable for performances that are ahead of their time in their brisk, no-nonsense manners and fast speeds, with the works often tackled impromptu. There is a brisk, military flavour in allegros, yet the mastery of individual players still defies the idea of over-rigid performances, with delectable interplay between the principals. Vivid and immediate transfers of recordings, set in a dry acoustic.

Serenade 13 (Eine kleine Nachtmusik), K.525
*** Ph. (IMS) 410 606-2. I Musici (with Concert of Baroque music ***)

I Musici play the music with rare freshness, giving the listener the impression of hearing the work for the first time. The playing is consistently alert and sparkling, with the *Romanze* particularly engaging. The recording is beautifully balanced.

Sinfonias Concertantes and Epistle Sonatas
Sinfonia concertante for Violin, Viola & Orchestra, K.364
**(*) EMI DVD 490449-9. I. Oistrakh, D. Oistrakh, Moscow PO, Menuhin – BACH: *Double Violin Concerto*, etc.; BRAHMS: *Double Concerto* **(*)

(M) **(*) RCA (ADD) 09026 63531-2. Heifetz, Primrose, RCA Victor SO, Izler Solomon – BACH: *Double Concerto*; BRAHMS: *Double Concerto* ***

(***) BBC (ADD) BBCL 4019-2. D. and I. Oistrakh, Moscow PO, Menuhin – BEETHOVEN: *Violin Concerto in D, Op. 61* (***)

(N) (BB) (***) Naxos mono 8.110957. Sammons, Tertis, LPO, Harty (with: ELGAR: *Violin Sonata in E min., Op. 82* (with Murdoch). SCHUBERT: *Rosamunde: Entr'acte*. DVORAK: *Humoresque, Op. 101/7*. MASSENET: *Thaïs: Méditation*. NACHEZ: *Passacaglia on a theme of Sammartini*. SAMMONS: *Bourrée*. TRAD.: *Londonderry Air* (all with Moore))

Mozart's heavenly *Sinfonia concertante* is wonderfully played by Oistrakh *père et fils* at the Royal Albert Hall in September 1963 when the Moscow Philharmonic was on tour here, and in this item Menuhin rather than Kondrashin conducts. It is a valuable document and is splendidly produced by Anthony Craxton with appropriately discreet camerawork. David Nice's notes speak of 'the elegance and focused tone David Oistrakh draws from the viola', and this is a joy in itself. A moving record, in spite of the inevitable limitations of the sound.

The Heifetz/Primrose partnership is too closely balanced and the brisk pace of the finale may not suit all tastes, but the crisp interchange is fresh and joyful, and in the slow movement the warmly responsive interchange between the two great soloists is genuinely moving, with the cadenza outstanding.

With David Oistrakh playing the viola and his son, Igor, the violin, the Mozart *Sinfonia concertante* under Menuhin's baton is a most spontaneous and vivid performance, and the BBC recording gives us truthful and natural sound. Self-recommending.

Albert Sammons was the greatest English violinist of his day, and he possessed a wonderful breadth of phrasing and sensitivity. His account of the *E flat Sinfonia concertante*, K.364, remains one of the greatest performances of this masterpiece on record. It comes closer to Mozart than most subsequent recordings, particularly in the rapt, inward exchanges between the two soloists in the slow movement. Quite wonderful in fact. The fill-ups complete a splendid further tribute to Sammons's artistry.

(i) *Sinfonia concertante, K.364*; (ii) *Sinfonia concertante, K.297b*

*** DG (IMS) 429 784-2. (i) Phillips, Gallagher; (ii) Taylor, Singer, Purvis, Dibner, Orpheus CO

(M) **(*) DG (ADD) 474 424-2. (i) Brandis, Cappone; (ii) Steins, Leister, Seifert, Piesk; BPO, Boehm

In the ideal coupling of Mozart's paired *Sinfonias concertantes*, the performances from members of the Orpheus Chamber Orchestra have an appealing warmth and intimacy. The dialogue between the violin and viola soloists in K.364 is both lively and very sensitive, and the finale is buoyant. This is most satisfying, and the comparable work with wind soloists gives a similar feeling of a chamber performance. The recording is very truthful and the warm acoustic gives pleasing inner definition.

Boehm's introduction for K.364 is characteristically sunny, and the performance is stylish and sure; but in fairness one must point out that other versions offer more individual solo playing than Brandis and Cappone provide. However, the work for wind instruments is excellent in every way. Here the soloists all shine, and Boehm's apt tempi and spontaneous feeling add to one's pleasure. The recordings, made in the Berlin Jesus-Christus-Kirche in 1964 and 1966 respectively, are well balanced in an agreeable ambience, and in their remastered form sound only very slightly dated in the matter of orchestral string-timbre.

(i; ii) *Sinfonia concertante in E flat, K.364*; (ii) *Duo for Violin and Viola in G, K.423*

(M) **(*) Decca (ADD) 476 7288-2 (2). D. Oistrakh; (i) Moscow PO, Kondrashin; (ii) I. Oistrakh – BRUCH: *Scottish Fantasia*; HINDEMITH: *Violin Concerto* ***

The performance by the Oistrakh duo is not notable for its relaxed manner. Everything is shaped most musically, but sometimes the listener may feel that the performers in their care for detail and concern for the balance are less involved in the music itself. However, with solo playing of a high calibre the music-making is still rewarding, and the 1963 recording sounds well in this new transfer. This is now reissued in Universal's 'Critics' Choice' series.

Sinfonia concertante, K.297b

(M) (***) Cala mono CACD 0523. Tabuteau, Portnoy, Schoenbach, Jones, Phd. O, Stokowski – BEETHOVEN: *Symphony 6 (Pastoral)* (***)

Stokowski recorded the *Sinfonia concertante* in December 1940; it was his first and only Mozart recording made in his quarter-century directing the Philadelphia Orchestra. The result is sheer joy. His graceful string-phrasing may have romantic elements, but the warmth is ever persuasive. His expert group of orchestral soloists (balanced forwardly and clearly) blend well together – with the single proviso that the bassoonist at times produces a rather close vibrato. The transfer is excellent and the sound, though a bit subfusc, is always fully acceptable, with a wider dynamic range than on the coupled Beethoven. A disc to treasure for all Stokowskians.

(i) *Sinfonia concertante, K.297b*; (ii) *Piano & Wind Quintet in E flat, K.452*

☞ ✪ (***) Testament mono SBT 1091. (i) Brain, James, Sutcliffe, Walton, Philh. O, Karajan; (ii) Gieseking, Philh. Wind Ens. – BEETHOVEN: *Piano & Wind Quintet* (***) ✪

The Mozart *Quintet* is one of the classic chamber-music recordings of all time. Gieseking and members of the Philharmonia Wind (Dennis Brain, Sidney Sutcliffe, Bernard Walton and Cecil James) recorded it over 40 years ago, and in terms of tonal blend and perfection of balance and ensemble it has few rivals. To the original quintet coupling Testament have added the *Sinfonia concertante* for wind, which these distinguished players recorded with Karajan in 1953, a performance of comparable stature. Not to be missed. The mono sound comes up wonderfully fresh in this Testament transfer. This is a full-price reissue and is worth every penny of the asking price.

Sonatas 1–17 (Epistle Sonatas)

(BB) **(*) Naxos 8.550512. Sebestyén, Budapest Ferenc Erkel CO

The *Epistle Sonatas* derive their name from the fact that they were intended to be heard between the Epistle and Gospel in the Mass. Admittedly they are not great music or even first-class Mozart; however, played with relish they make a strong impression. The final *Sonata*, K.263, becomes a fully fledged concerto.

While it is understood that, apart from *No. 16 in C*, K.329, which has a specific solo part, the organ is not intended as a solo instrument in these *Chiesa Sonatas*, it seems perverse to balance the instrument so that it blends in completely with the orchestral texture, as the Naxos engineers have done. Otherwise these alert, polished and nicely scaled performances could hardly be improved on and, apart from the controversial matter of the relationship of the organ to the orchestra, the recording is first class.

SYMPHONIES

Complete Bargain Mozart Edition, Vol. 1: *Symphonies* (complete)

(B) **(*) Ph. (ADD) 464 770-2 (12). (i) ASMF, Marriner; (ii) Concg. O, Krips

Marriner's recordings confirm the Mozartian vitality of the performances and their sense of style and spontaneity. The Philips engineers respond with alive and vivid recording. Except perhaps for those who insist on original instruments, the finesse and warmth of the playing here is a constant joy. The Dutch players for Krips also bring warmth, as well as proving characteristically stylish in phrasing and execution. Quick movements can be bracingly vigorous. Both the previously underrated *No. 28 in C* and the first great masterpiece in A major, both aptly paced, are very persuasively done, with an almost ethereal delicacy from the strings in the beautiful *Andante* of No. 29 and the horns thrusting exuberantly in the coda of the finale. Although Krips's Mozartian sensibility never deserts him, the readings of some of the later symphonies are somewhat wanting in character, however, and do not do full honour to the fine Mozartian that Krips was, although No. 39 goes well enough. The ample Concertgebouw sound, with its resonant bass, emphasizes the breadth of scale of the music-making, yet the digital remastering gives an attractive freshness to the violins, although the Minuets sound well upholstered.

Symphonies 1 in E flat, K.16; in F, K.19a; 5 in B flat, K.22; in G, K.45a; 6 in F, K.43; 7 in D, K.45; 8 in D, K.48; 9 in C, K.73; in F, K.76; in B flat, K.45b; in D, K.81; in D, K.97; in D, K.95; 10 in G, K.74; 11 in D, K.84; in B flat, K.Anh.214; in F, K.75; in C, K.96; 12 in G, K.110; 13 in F, K.112; 14 in A, K.114; 15 in G, K.124; 16 in C, K.128; 17 in G, K.129; 18 in F, K.130; 19 in E flat, K.132; 20 in D, K.133; 21 in A, K.134; 22 in C, K.162; 23 in D, K.181; 24 in B flat, K.182; 25 in G min., K.183; 26 in E flat, K.184; 27 in G, K.199; 28 in C, K.200; 29 in A, K.201; 31 in D (Paris), K.297; 32 in G, K.318; 33 in B flat, K.319; 34 in C, K.338; 35 in D (Haffner), K.385; 36 in C (Linz), K. 425; 38 in D (Prague), K.504; 39 in E flat, K.543; 40 in G min., K. 550; 41 in C (Jupiter), K. 551

(B) *** DG 471 666-2 (7). E. Concert, Pinnock

Pinnock's Mozartian enterprise has the advantage of some years' experience of authentic performance, and certain exaggerated elements have been absorbed into a smoother, but not less vital, playing style. In the invigorating 'Salzburg' Symphonies (Nos. 16–29) the playing has polish and sophistication, fine intonation, spontaneity and great vitality, balanced by warm, lyrical feeling in the slow movements. Indeed, the account of *No. 29 in A* is among the finest available and the earlier *A major* work (No. 21) is very impressive too, as is the *G minor*, K.183, and the very 'operatic' *No. 23 in D*. In the later symphonies, the masterpieces from the *Paris* to the *Jupiter* can be warmly recommended, and not only to period enthusiasts. It is the joy and exhilaration in Mozart's inspiration that consistently bubble out from these accounts, even from the dark *G minor* or the weighty *Jupiter*. The rhythmic lift which Pinnock consistently finds is infectious throughout, and it is a measure of his mastery that when in a slow movement such as that of the *Prague* he chooses an unusually slow speed, there is no feeling of dragging. These performances are billed as being 'directed from the harpsichord', but that continuo instrument is never

obtrusive, and one can only register surprise that such subtlety and exuberance have been achieved without a regular conductor. Clear, well-balanced sound throughout the series makes this set an obvious primary recommendation for those wanting period-instrument performances, especially at its new bargain price.

Symphonies 1–41

(B) **(*) DG (ADD) 453 231-2 (10). BPO, Boehm

All the earlier symphonies were recorded in intensive sessions in March and November 1968, a real voyage of discovery, with performances warm and genial, with bold contrasts of dynamic and well-sprung rhythms. This latest CD reissue, on ten discs instead of twelve, also brings the advantage of fuller and more forward transfers, with good body and presence. The new bargain box, unlike the previous one, has essays on Boehm as Mozartian by Peter Cosse and Mozart as symphonist by Heinz Becker. An excellent bargain, and not just for the historical specialist, but for all Mozartians.

Symphonies 1; 4; in F, K.19a; 5; in G, K.45a; 6-36; 38–41

(M) *** Telarc CD 80300 (10). Prague CO, Mackerras

Mackerras's is an outstanding series, with electrifying performances of the early as well as the later symphonies. There is not a suspicion of routine, with the playing full of dramatic contrasts in rhythm, texture or dynamic. Mackerras has a keen feeling for Mozart style, not least in the slow movements and minuets, which he regularly takes faster than usual. His flowing *Andantes* are consistently stylish too, with performances on modern instruments regularly related to period practice. An outstanding instance comes in the G minor *Andante* of *No. 5 in B flat*, K.22, where Mackerras, fastish and light, makes others seem heavy-handed in this anticipation of romanticism, underlining the harmonic surprises clearly and elegantly. Consistently Mackerras finds light and shade in Mozart's inspirations, both early and late, though some may feel that, with warm reverberation characteristic of this Prague orchestra's recording venue, the scale is too large, particularly in the early symphonies. Harpsichord continuo, where used, is usually well balanced.

Symphonies 13–18

(B) **(*) DG (IMS) 469 552-2. BPO, Boehm

These 1968 recordings were part of Boehm's pioneering complete survey of the Mozart symphonies (see above). The playing is warm, elegant and polished, and has the freshness of new discovery by a great orchestra much more familiar with the later works. The recording was made in the Jesus-Christus-Kirche and wears its years lightly, the transfers full-bodied and immediate. In spite of the changes brought about by period-instrument performances, this disc holds its place in the catalogue, for Boehm was a true Mozartian.

Symphonies 14–18

🎜 *** Telarc CD 80242. Prague CO, Mackerras

No. 14 in A is a particularly fine work (as indeed are all Mozart's A major symphonies) and, like the others here, it receives an invigorating account with brisk *Allegros* and a strong, one-in-a-bar tempo for the Minuet (this suits the Minuet of *No. 18 in F* even better as it is very folksy). Slow movements, however, are very direct and are pressed onwards slightly unbendingly; here some might find Mackerras's approach too austere. The bright recording is resonant, which prevents absolute clarity, but the clean lines of the playing ensure plenty of stimulating impact.

Symphonies 15–18
(BB) **(*) Naxos 8.550874. N. CO, Ward

Symphonies 19; 20; 37 in G: Introduction only (with remainder of the symphony by Michael Haydn)
☛ (BB) *** Naxos 8.550875. N. CO, Ward

Nicholas Ward's stylish Mozart series here offers six symphonies written in 1772. The orchestral string-phrasing is particularly elegant in slow movements (notably the wistful *Andante* of *No. 15 in G* and the charming melody which forms the centre-piece of No. 17), while the lively first movement of *No. 18 in F* effervesces neatly. Elsewhere *Allegros* are alert and strong. Excellent, full and well-balanced recording, though not ideally sharply detailed. No. 19 is scored for four horns, two in E flat *alt*, and they give added weight and character to the orchestral texture in outer movements. No. 20 is given extra brightness by a pair of trumpets. But it is the delectable *Andante* that catches the ear with its charming flute solo over muted violins. Mozart contributed just the rather grand opening *Adagio maestoso* to the symphony once mistakenly regarded as his No. 37. It is played most persuasively: this disc is well worth having on all counts.

Symphonies 18 in F, K.130; in D, K.141a; 19 in E flat, K.132; 20 in D, K.133; 21 in A, K.134; in D, K.135; 26 in E flat, K.161a; 27 in G, K.161b; 22 in C, K.162; 23 in D, K.162b; 24 in B flat, K.173dA
(M) *** Decca (ADD) 476 1718 (3). AAM, Schröder; Hogwood

This was the first box of the Academy of Ancient Music's recording of Mozart symphonies using authentic texts and original instruments – and very invigorating it proved. The variety of scale as well as of expression makes it a very refreshing collection, particularly as the style of performance, with its non-vibrato tang, sharply picks out detail of texture rather than moulding the sound together. The recording is excellent, and the CD transfers are bright and clean. The set won the *Gramophone's* Early Music Award in 1979 and now reappears in the *Gramophone* Awards Collection at mid-price.

Symphonies 19–23
☛ *** Telarc CD 80217. Prague CO, Mackerras

Mackerras is equally lively in these early works from Mozart's Salzburg period. The surprising thing is how fast his speeds tend to be. In one instance the contrast is astonishing, when at a very brisk *Andantino grazioso* Mackerras turns the slow middle movement of No. 23 into a lilting Ländler, quite different from other performances. The recording is reverberant, as in the later symphonies, giving relatively weighty textures; with such light scoring, however, there is ample clarity, with braying horns riding beautifully over the rest.

Symphonies 24, K.173; 26, K.161a; 27, K.161b; 30, K.202
☛ *** Telarc CD 80186. Prague CO, Mackerras

Where in later symphonies Mackerras chooses more relaxed speeds, here he tends to be more urgent, as in the finale of No. 26 or the *Andantino grazioso* slow movement of No. 27, where he avoids the questionable use of muted strings. The reverberation of the recording gives the impression of a fairly substantial orchestra, without loss of detail, and anyone

fancying this particular group of early Mozart symphonies need not hesitate.

Symphonies 24–7; 32, K.318
(BB) *** EMI Encore 5 86422-2. ASMF, Marriner

Symphonies 31 (Paris), K.297; 33, K.319; 34, K.338
(B) *** EMI Red Line 5 69819. ASMF, Marriner

Symphonies 36 (Linz); 40 in G min.
(N) (BB) *** EMI Encore 5 86107-2. ASMF, Marriner

Symphonies 38 (Prague); 39
(N) (BB) **(*) EMI Encore 5 85813-2. ASMF, Marriner

Marriner's third set of Mozart symphony recordings for EMI is the most beautifully recorded of all. In the early symphonies the playing is graceful and elegant, with bracing rhythms and brisker pacing than in his earlier, Philips set. The 1984 ASMF pairing of Nos. 38 and 39 brings characteristically polished and stylish readings of both works in full, well-defined sound; the smoothness and polish of the string-tone in the sweetly lyrical account of the slow movement of the *Prague* even suggest that that section had been reinforced. Outer movements are brisk, the style rather plain yet well sprung. With no hint of overpointing or mannerism, they could be more positively characterful.

The coupling of the *Linz* and No. 40 brings an even keener sense of spontaneity, of conductor and players enjoying themselves. Brisk speeds and resilient rhythms go with subtle phrasing and refined ensemble. In No. 40 Marriner's view of the last two movements is markedly more dramatic than before, with crisper articulation and faster speeds, and this time in the slow movement he observes the first-half repeat.

Symphonies 25, K.183; 32, K.318; 41 (Jupiter), K.551
(BB) *** Naxos 8.550113. Capella Istropolitana, Wordsworth

Symphonies 27, K.199/161b; 33, K.319; 36 (Linz), K.425
(BB) *** Naxos 8.550264. Capella Istropolitana, Wordsworth

Symphonies 28, K.200; 31 (Paris), K.297; 40, K.550
(BB) *** Naxos 8.550164. Capella Istropolitana, Wordsworth

Symphonies 29, K.201; 30, K.202; 38 (Prague), K.504
(BB) *** Naxos 8.550119. Capella Istropolitana, Wordsworth

Symphonies 34, K.338; 35 (Haffner), K.385; 39, K.543
(BB) *** Naxos 8.550186. Capella Istropolitana, Wordsworth

Symphonies 40, K.550; 41 (Jupiter), K.551
(BB) *** Naxos 8.550299. Capella Istropolitana, Wordsworth

The Capella Istropolitana consists of leading members of the Slovak Philharmonic Orchestra of Bratislava; though their string-tone is thinnish, it is very much in scale with the clarity of a period performance but tonally far sweeter. The recording is outstandingly good, with a far keener sense of presence than in most rival versions and with less reverberation to obscure detail in tuttis. Wordsworth observes exposition repeats in first movements, but in the finales only in such symphonies as Nos. 38 and 41, where the movement particularly needs extra scale. In slow movements, as is usual, he omits repeats. He often adopts speeds that are marginally slower than we expect nowadays in chamber-scale performances; but, with exceptionally clean articulation and infectiously sprung rhythms, the results never drag, even if No. 29 is made to sound more sober than usual. In every way these are worthy rivals to the best full-priced versions, and they can be recommended with few if any reservations. Anyone wanting to sample might try the coupling of Nos. 34, 35 and 39 – with the hard-stick timpani sound at the start of No. 39 very dramatic. The *Linz* too is outstanding. For some, the option of having the last two symphonies coupled together will be useful.

Symphonies 25, K.183; 28, K.200; 29, K.201
♦— *** Telarc CD 80165. Prague CO, Mackerras

If you want performances on modern instruments, these are as fine as any, fresh and light, with transparent textures set against a warm acoustic and with rhythms consistently resilient. Mackerras's speeds are always carefully judged to allow elegant pointing but without mannerism, and the only snag is that second-half repeats are omitted in slow movements, and also in the finale of No. 29.

Symphonies 25; 29; 31 (Paris); Adagio & Fugue, K.546; Overture: Così fan tutte
(M) **(*) EMI (ADD) 5 67331-2. Philh. O or New Philh. O, Klemperer

Symphonies 33; 34; 40; Masonic Funeral Music, K.477
(M) **(*) EMI (ADD) 5 67332-2. Philh. O or New Philh. O, Klemperer

Symphonies 35 (Haffner); 36 (Linz); 38 (Prague); Overture: Die Zauberflöte
(M) **(*) EMI (ADD) 5 67333-2. Philh. O or New Philh. O, Klemperer

Symphonies 39; 41 (Jupiter); Serenade 13 in G (Eine kleine Nachtmusik)
(M) **(*) EMI (ADD) 5 67334-2. Philh. O or New Philh. O, Klemperer

Symphonies 38 (Prague); 39; Serenata notturna
(***) Testament mono SBT 1094. Philh. O, Klemperer

Symphonies 29; 41 (Jupiter); Serenade 13 (Eine kleine Nachtmusik)
(***) Testament mono/stereo SBT 1093. Philh. O, Klemperer

Klemperer's 1954 Mozart symphony recordings of Nos. 29 and 41 on Testament, unavailable for many decades, marked the turning-point in his accident-prone career. They were the very first recordings which he made with the Philharmonia Orchestra. Only the first movement of No. 29 bears out the later image of Klemperer as slow and rugged. After that, all is exhilaration, with superlative playing from the Philharmonia, with rhythms beautifully sprung and phrases elegantly turned. The *Jupiter* in particular is electrifying, one of the very finest versions on disc, both powerful and polished, while *Eine kleine Nachtmusik* (in stereo) for once is made to sound like late Mozart, both strong and elegant. Outstanding transfers.

The mono version of the *Prague Symphony* is strong and rugged, but finely sprung and phrased, with the *Don Giovanni* relationship firmly established. This mono version of No. 39 too is fresher than the stereo remake, while the *Serenata notturna* brings a typical Klemperer contrast, with the orchestra providing four-square support for the soloists, who by contrast are allowed their measure of charm and elegance.

The later, monumentally characterful stereo readings can still hold a place in the catalogue. If initially a Klemperer account of, say, the first movement of the great *G minor Symphony*, No. 40, sounds heavy, rhythmic subtleties are there, so that the hidden power makes its impact. The account of No. 33 is strikingly fresh, and No. 38 (the *Prague*) is

among the greatest ever recorded. No. 39 has a strength and virility in the first movement that anticipates Beethoven, and Klemperer lifts the finale out of its usual Mendelssohnian rut and gives it a Beethovenian power without losing any of the instrumental charm. Almost all the *Allegros* here are measured and meticulous, slow movements forthright rather than hushed, but power and purpose are never lacking. It is good that some of the shorter works are included, particularly the magnificent *Adagio and Fugue* and *Funeral Music*, while *Eine kleine Nachtmusik* is certainly not lacking in elegance, nor any lightness of touch in the finale.

Symphonies 29 in A, K.201; 35 (Haffner); 36 (Linz)
(N) (M) ** EMI 4 76890-2. BPO, Karajan

Symphonies 38 (Prague); 39 in E flat, K.453; (i) Bassoon Concerto
(N) (M) ** EMI 4 76891-2. BPO, Karajan; (i) with Piesk

Symphonies 40 in G min.; 41 (Jupiter); (i) Oboe Concerto
(N) (M) ** EMI 4 76892-2. BPO, Karajan; (i) with Koch

Reissued as part of EMI's 'Karajan Collection', the original rehearsal sequences have been removed and two concertos added. Günter Piesk gives a predictably fine account of the *Bassoon Concerto*, and Lothar Koch is also an estimable soloist in the work for oboe, but the richly homogeneous orchestral accompaniments without much analytical detail, although pleasingly warm and elegantly phrased, tend to rob the music of vitality. The symphonies, too, are large-orchestra Mozart, recorded in the Jesus-Christus-Kirche, Berlin (which the EMI recording team never handled as well in eighteenth-century music as their DG counterparts), giving considerable breadth and impact but also a cushioned thickness of orchestral texture. The interpretations have plenty of weight, although Karajan also shows poise and grace: the opening of the *Linz* is especially fine. Undoubtedly the best of the set is No. 39, in which the playing has superb polish and refinement of tone. The same might be said, if perhaps to a lesser extent, of No. 40 and certainly of the *Jupiter*. Again the playing of the orchestra is a joy in itself, and the interpretations are purposeful and considered, even if they do not have the sparkle and naturalness of the very finest performances of these works. No. 29, however, was not part of the original LP set: it was made in the Grünewaldkirche in 1960, and here the sound is fresher. It is a warm, polished performance and has plenty of life. Yet in the last analysis this music-making is wanting in the final touch of spontaneity and fire; for all the magnificent orchestral playing, the listener is sometimes left vaguely dissatisfied, and not only by the lack of transparency in the orchestral textures.

Symphonies 25 in G min., K.183; 29 in A, K.201; 35 (Haffner); 36 (Linz); 38 (Prague); 39 in E flat; 40 in G min.; 41 in C (Jupiter)
♦— (M) *** DG Trio 474 349-2 (3). VPO, Bernstein

Bernstein's recordings of Mozart's last and greatest symphonies were taken from live performances between 1984 and 1986, although the two early masterpieces now included in this Trio, which are equally successful (especially the beautifully played No. 29), date from 1990. All have the added adrenalin that is expected (but not always achieved) in live performances. Besides the electricity, Bernstein's Mozart also has breadth and style; only occasionally (as in No. 39) does a suspicion of self-consciousness affect the interpretation. But pacing is consistently well judged, except sometimes in finales, where the VPO are kept very much on their toes with speeds that are perilously brisk. For those not seeking the astringencies of 'authenticity' this is a fine, modern set, with more vitality and charisma than most alternatives. The sound is full and well balanced. The separate issue of Nos. 40 and 41 receives a ◉ (see below).

Symphonies 25 in G min., K.183; 29 in A, K.201; Serenade 6 in D (Serenata notturna), K.239
(N) (M) * Decca (ADD) 476 7102. ECO, Britten**

Several years before his untimely death Benjamin Britten recorded (in 1971) these exhilarating performances of the two greatest of Mozart's early symphonies. Inexplicably, the record remained unissued, finally providing a superb codicil to Britten's recording career and in 1978 winning the *Gramophone* Orchestral Award. It is striking that in many movements his tempi and even his approach are very like those of Sir Neville Marriner on his earlier Argo disc, but it is Britten's genius, along with his crisp articulation and sprung rhythms, that provides the occasional touch of pure individual magic. Britten's slow movements offer a clear contrast, rather weightier than Marriner's, particularly in the little *G minor*, where Britten – with a slower speed and more expressive phrasing – underlines the elegiac quality of the music. The recording is admirable, rich and well balanced, and the *Serenata notturna*, recorded three years earlier and hardly less individual, has been added for this reissue.

Symphonies 25 in G min., K.185; 31 (Paris); 41 (Jupiter)
(N) (BB) **(*) Warner Apex 0927 49045-2. Amsterdam Bar. O, Koopman

The highlight here is the early *G minor Symphony*, where original instruments, with their extra cutting edge, are ideal for expressing the *Sturm und Drang* neurosis of the first movement with its thrilling octave upward thrusts, and this degree of tension is maintained throughout the work. In comparison, the *Paris Symphony* lacks the balancing elegance that modern instruments can bring, but the *Jupiter* receives another powerfully energetic reading, with all important repeats included. When the finale reaches its vibrant apotheosis, the enthusiastic applause confirms that this has the vigour and spontaneity of live music-making. Good (rather than outstanding) recording, but this is excellent value.

Symphonies 26–8; 30; 32
*** ASV CDDCA 762. LMP, Glover

Jane Glover's generous coupling of five symphonies brings typically fresh and direct readings, marked by sharp attack and resilient rhythms, at speeds on the fast side. With tuttis a little weightier than with most rivals, these are brightly enjoyable performances.

Symphony 29 in A, K.201
(**(*)) Testament mono SBT 2242 (2). Royal Danish O, Klemperer – BEETHOVEN: Symphony 3; Leonore 3; BRAHMS: Symphony 4 (**(*))
**(*) Testament SBT2 1217 (2). BPO, Klemperer – BACH: Suite 3 in D; BEETHOVEN: Symphony 6 (Pastoral) **(*)

In Klemperer's live recording of No. 29 with the Royal Danish Orchestra, made in 1954, the opening *Allegro moderato* is characteristically slow and square, heavy despite the thin orchestral sound. But the last three movements are quite different, with the *Andante* refined and beautifully moulded at a flowing tempo, the Minuet light and tripping and the

finale exhilarating in its energy. However, as in the other two items from the same concert on the first of the discs in this set, the coughing of the audience is distracting.

In May 1964 Otto Klemperer, aged 79, returned to Berlin to conduct the Berlin Philharmonic in three works that were favourites with him, and he won a rapturous reception. It was over 40 years since his first appearance with the Berlin Philharmonic, and he seemed determined above all to get Karajan's orchestra to produce a distinctive Klemperer sound. Though the Mozart brings characteristically broad speeds, it erupts into an exuberant account of the finale. First-rate transfers of radio sound.

Symphonies 29; 31 (Paris); 34
(BB) (***) Dutton Lab. mono CDEA 5008. LPO, Beecham

These incomparable performances date from between 1937 and 1940. Beecham's are elegant and cultivated accounts which in many ways are unique, though No. 29 brings one of his most controversial readings, where the pace of the opening movement is eccentrically slow, even if Beecham is very persuasive in his pointing. In the finales, by contrast, Beecham prefers really fast speeds, exhilarating in all three here. The superb new transfers are fuller and have much finer presence, transparency and, above all, body than the earlier, EMI versions that appeared some years ago.

Symphonies 29; 32; 33; 35 (Haffner); 36 (Linz); 38 (Prague); 39; 40; 41 (Jupiter)
⌐ (N) (B) * DG 476 7238 (3). BPO, Karajan**

With Nos. 29, 32 and 33 added to the original DG double box (see below), these are beautifully played and vitally alert readings; and the recordings, made between 1966 and 1979, are well balanced and given full, lively transfers to CD. This is now one of Universal's 'Critics' Choice' series.

Symphonies 29; 35 (Haffner); 38 (Prague)
(***) BBC mono BBCL 4027-2. RPO, Beecham

It is good to have these broadcast performances from the 1950s, with the characterful bonus of Beecham's spoken introductions to No. 29 and the *Prague*. Interpretatively, it is fascinating to note the contrasts between these performances and those he recorded for EMI with the LPO – No. 29 in 1937, the *Haffner* in 1938/9 and the *Prague* in 1940. The extra elegance of these later RPO performances – with playing more lightly sprung and a degree more refined (the odd mishap apart) and with speeds less extreme than before – is what comes out most clearly. That impression is enhanced, when the BBC sound is rather more spacious and airy than the pre-war EMI.

Symphony 31 in D (Paris), K.297
(BB) * Regis RRC 1084. E. Sinfonia, Groves – HAYDN: Symphonies 92 (Oxford); 104 (London) *****

Sir Charles Groves's account of the *Paris Symphony* is mellow and relaxed, with a beautifully played slow movement and finely observed detail. The playing is alert, but the unhurried pacing brings out the music's breadth. The Abbey Road recording is excellent: warm yet clear.

Symphonies 31 (Paris); 33; 34
**(*) Telarc CD 80190. Prague CO, Mackerras

Mackerras and the Prague Chamber Orchestra give characteristically stylish and refined performances, clean of attack and generally marked by brisk speeds. As in their accounts of the later symphonies, all repeats are observed – even those in the *da capos* of Minuets. However, the reverberant Prague acoustic, more than in others of the Telarc series, clouds tuttis: the *Presto* finale of the *Paris* brings phenomenal articulation of quavers at the start, which then in tuttis disappear in a mush.

Symphonies 31 (Paris); 36 (Linz); 38 (Prague)
☛— *** ASV CDDCA 647. LMP, Glover

Jane Glover and the London Mozart Players offer a particularly attractive and generous coupling in the three Mozart symphonies associated with cities. Happily, exposition repeats are observed in the outer movements. The performances are all fresh and vital in traditional chamber style, with little influence from period performance. Tuttis are not always ideally clear on inner detail; but the result is nicely in scale, not too weighty, with the delicacy beautifully light and airy.

Symphonies (i) 31 in D (Paris); (ii) 40 in G min., K.550
(N) **(*) Arthaus **DVD** 100 073. (i) Salzburg Mozarteum O, Tate; (ii) Stuttgart RSO, Gelmetti (V/D: Jànos Darvas)

These two live performances were recorded two years apart, the *Paris Symphony*, in the beautiful Mozarteum, at the Salzburg Festival in 1989, the *G minor* in the Rokokotheatre, Schloss Schwetzinger, where the backdrop is plain but the acoustics far superior. Indeed, the performance of the *40th Symphony* is quite glorious; so beautiful is the playing on modern instruments and so warmly appealing and musically detailed is Gianluigi Gelmetti's interpretation that one realizes afresh as one listens that this is one of Mozart's supreme masterpieces. Gelmetti's conducting technique is strange. At first he appears to gesture very little (and more for the camera than for the players), but his control of light and shade is absolute, and as the music continues his style becomes more dramatic, and it is obvious that as he turns over the pages of the score he is totally within the music, and his little smiles of pleasure at the response of his fine orchestra communicate to us.

This is a traditional performance (with exposition repeat included), relaxed but beautifully shaped and with tempi ideally interrelated, so that after the warmth of the *Andante* and the strongly rhythmic Minuet, with its fine horn contribution in the Trio, the vivacious finale takes the work to its sparkling, joyful conclusion.

Needless to say, Jeffrey Tate also gives a very fine account of the symphony Mozart wrote for a comparatively large orchestra (55 strong) to impress the jaded Parisians in 1778, with its strong tutti opening and tenderly playful secondary theme, which Tate and his orchestra contrast so effectively. But they are not helped by the comparatively opaque acoustic of the Mozarteum when it is packed with a large audience, especially in the middle range of the sound. Tate's conducting technique is infinitely more athletic than that of his colleague, and it suits the brilliance of Mozart's writing. But the three-movement *Paris Symphony*, while showing the composer at his most elegant and resourceful, is a less inspired masterpiece than the *G minor*. It needs sharper definition, and it should have been first in the programme.

Symphonies 35 (Haffner); 36 (Linz); 38 (Prague); 39; 40; 41 (Jupiter)
(B) *** DG Double (ADD) 453 046-2 (2). BPO, Karajan
(M) **(*) DG (ADD) 447 416-2 (2). BPO, Boehm

Here is Karajan's big-band Mozart at its finest. Although there may be slight reservations about the Minuet and Trio of the *Linz*, which is rather slow (and the other minuets are also somewhat stately), overall there is plenty of life here, and slow movements show the BPO at their most graciously expressive. The opening of the *G minor* may not be quite dark enough for some tastes. The *Jupiter*, although short on repeats, has power as well as surface elegance. The remastered sound is clear and lively, full but not over-weighted. The separate issue makes a good sampler.

Karl Boehm's way with Mozart in the early 1960s was broader and heavier in texture than we are used to nowadays, and the exposition repeats are the exception rather than the rule; but these Berlin Philharmonic performances are warm and magnetic, with refined and strongly rhythmic playing, and there is an attractive honesty and strength about them. The *Linz*, for instance, is an example of Boehm at his finest, with an agreeable, fresh vitality; but overall there is a comfortable quality of inevitability here, perpetuating a long Mozart tradition. The recordings sound full, vivid and well balanced in the new transfers.

Symphonies 32; 35 (Haffner); 36 (Linz); 39; 41 (Jupiter)
☛— (BB) *** Virgin 2×1 5 61451-2 (2). SCO, Saraste

More than most other versions on modern instruments, Saraste's vividly alive accounts of the three earlier symphonies reflect the new lessons of period performance. These are more detached, less sostenuto than many modern-instrument chamber-orchestra versions and, with all repeats observed, are highly stimulating in their resilience. The recording, helpfully reverberant, yet gives lightness and transparency to textures, conveying an apt chamber scale for two of the finest accounts of the two late symphonies available on any disc. Wordsworth and the Capella Istropolitana may have more weight in these works, but Saraste has extra polish and refinement, with generally brisker speeds, notably in slow movements and Minuets.

Symphonies 32, K.318; 35 (Haffner), K.385; 39, K.543
*** Telarc CD 80203. Prague CO, Mackerras

On Telarc, Mackerras is fresh rather than elegant, yet with rhythms so crisply sprung that there is no sense of rush. His whirling one-in-a-bar treatment of Minuets may disconcert traditionalists, but brings exhilarating results. The third movements of both the *Haffner* and No. 39 become Scherzos, not just faster but fiercer than regular Minuets, and generally his account of No. 39 is as commanding as his outstanding versions of the last two symphonies. The clanging attack of harpsichord continuo is sometimes disconcerting, but this music-making is very refreshing.

Symphony 33 in B flat, K.319
(N) **(*) DG **DVD** 073 4017. Bav. State O, Kleiber (Producer: Harald Gerick) (with BEETHOVEN: *Overture Coriolan* ***) – BRAHMS: *Symphony 4* **(*)

Carlos Kleiber's account comes from a 1996 live concert in the Herculessaal. Kleiber's reading is a direct, classical one, firm in contour, and the Bavarian orchestra play very stylishly and responsively, though it is the genial finale that remains most vividly in the memory. The camera moves around the orchestra discerningly but often stays to watch the conductor, who seems very relaxed (but at times obviously conscious that he is being observed).

Symphonies 33 in B flat, K.319; 35 in D (Haffner), K.385
(M) *** Häns. CD 94.003. ASMF, I. Brown

These are spirited, sparkling performances, full of life and warmth. They were recorded in the Henry Wood Hall in 1997, and Andrew Keener has succeeded in getting a very good, natural and well-balanced sound. This CD delights, though it is short measure at 40 minutes even at mid-price. There are no liner notes.

Symphonies 34; 35 (Haffner); 39
🏵 *** ASV CDDCA 615. LMP, Glover

Tackling three major works, Jane Glover provides freshly imaginative performances that can compete with any in the catalogue, given the most vividly realistic recorded sound; Nos. 34 and 39 are especially striking. This collection can be recommended with enthusiasm.

Symphonies 35–36; 38–41 – see under Flute Concertos 1–2 (above)

Symphony 35 (Haffner)
(M) *** BBC BBCL 4076-2. Hallé O, Barbirolli –
  BEETHOVEN: *Symphony 7* ***; WAGNER: *Siegfried Idyll* (***)

(**) BBC mono BBCL 4016-2 (2). BBC SO, Toscanini –
  BEETHOVEN: *Missa solemnis; Symphony 7* (**(*));
  CHERUBINI: *Anacréon Overture* ***

Barbirolli's view of the *Haffner Symphony* is just as characterful as the Beethoven *Seventh* with which it is coupled on this BBC Legends issue. Recorded at the Royal Albert Hall during the Prom season, the sound is rather thick and dull, due in part to the string section being larger than we might expect today. Even so, Barbirolli's characteristic pointing of phrase and rhythm remains very compelling, leading to an effervescent account of the finale. The Wagner item also adds to this striking portrait of the conductor.

  Mozart's *Haffner Symphony* was always a favourite with Toscanini, and this live performance, recorded in London, is warmer and more sympathetic than either his early version with the New York Philharmonic or his later performance with the NBC Symphony. Though the recording is rather rougher than on the rest of the two-disc set, it makes a valuable bonus to the Beethoven items.

Symphonies 35 (Haffner), K.385; 38 (Prague), K.504; 39, K.543; 40, K.550; 41 (Jupiter), K.551
(B) *** Ph. Duo 470 540-2 (2). Dresden State O, C. Davis

These performances date from 1981 (Nos. 39 and 41) and 1988 (Nos. 35, 38 and 40). Though Colin Davis favours big-scaled Mozart, he opts for fastish allegros, and the refinement of the playing helps to make up for the bass-heavy thickness of the Dresden sound as recorded by the engineers. The dramatic opening of the *Haffner* is made very weighty indeed. In the slow movements of both the *Haffner* and *Prague*, Davis is less detached than he sometimes used to be in Mozart, more obviously affectionate, yet without sentimentality. Davis has recorded the *Jupiter* more than once and this version is all one would expect: alert, sensitive, perceptive and played with vitality and finesse by the Dresden orchestra. The *E flat Symphony* was one of the finest on the market at the time of its release, and there is no reason to modify that view. If the *G minor* may seem a little weighty to some, its relaxed manner and the superbly refined and elegant playing ensure the full power of the work is fully conveyed. The warm, reverberant

(though detailed) Dresden acoustic throughout suits Davis's conception of this music.

Symphonies 35 (Haffner); 40; 41 (Jupiter)
🏵 (B) *** Sony (ADD) SBK 46333. Cleveland O, Szell

As in his companion triptych of late Haydn symphonies, Szell and his Clevelanders are shown at their finest here. The sparkling account of the *Haffner* is exhilarating, and the performances of the last two symphonies are equally polished and strong. Yet there is a tranquil feeling to both *Andantes* that shows Szell as a Mozartian of striking sensibility and finesse. He is at his finest in the *Jupiter*, which has great vigour in the outer movements and a proper weight to balance the rhythmic incisiveness; in spite of the lack of repeats, the work's scale is not diminished. Here the sound is remarkable, considering the early date (late 1950s), and the remastering throughout is impressively full-bodied and clean.

Symphony 36 in C (Linz), K.425
(N) **(*) Ph. **DVD** 070 161-9. VPO, Kleiber (Director: Horant Hohlfeld) (with BEETHOVEN: *Overture Coriolan* ***) –
  BRAHMS: *Symphony 2* **(*)

Rather like the performance of No. 33, but with the Vienna Philharmonic, who always have something special to contribute to Mozart, the *Linz* is a similarly direct account, not as individual as one might expect, but even better recorded. The performance of *Coriolan* is especially fine.

Symphonies 36 (Linz); 38 (Prague); 39; 40; 41 (Jupiter)
(B) *** Ph. (ADD) Duo 438 332-2 (2). ASMF, Marriner

Symphonies 36 (Linz); 38 (Prague); 40; 41 (Jupiter)
(B) *** EMI double forte 5 74185-2 (2). ECO, Tate

Tate directs characteristically strong and elegant readings of both the *Linz* and *Prague Symphonies*, bringing out the operatic overtones in the latter, not just in the *Don Giovanni*-like progressions in the slow introductions, but also in the power of the development section and in the wonder of the chromatic progressions in the slow movement, as well as the often surprising mixing of timbres. In the *Linz*, Tate is again attractively individual, putting rather more emphasis on elegance and finding tenderness in the slow movement, taken (like the *Adagio* of the *Prague*) at a very measured speed. The last two symphonies are hardly less impressive, although those who prefer a plain approach may find the elegant pointing in slow movements excessive. Tate's account of the *Jupiter* has the clarity of a chamber performance, yet, with trumpets and drums, brings a full weight of expression which never underplays the scale of the argument. In both symphonies, exposition repeats are observed in outer movements and Tate's keen imagination in relation to detail, as well as over a broad span, consistently conveys the electricity of a live performance.

  In terms of finesse and elegance of phrasing, the orchestral playing on the Philips Duo is of very high quality and Marriner's readings are satisfyingly paced, full of vitality and warmth. There is not a whiff of original-instrument style here, but those who enjoy the sound of Mozart in a modern orchestra of a reasonable size should be well satisfied.

Symphonies 36 (Linz); 41 (Jupiter)
(N) *** Arthaus **DVD** 100 081. ECO, Tate (V/D: Jànos Darvas)

This the finest of the three Arthaus DVDs of Mozart symphonies. Once again the two symphonies are placed in the wrong order, but in this instance Tate's affectionate reading of the *Linz*, full of Beechamesque Mozartian detail in the woodwind (which the camera delights to pick up), is engaging in a quite different way from the powerful *Jupiter*. Warmly recorded in the Grosse Galerie Schloss Schönbrunn, Vienna, (in 1991) it is in no way an anticlimax. Tate plays repeats in the outer movements, and there is little sense of a smaller scale. The lovely *Andante cantabile* and buoyant Minuet are both memorable, and the *Molto allegro* finale is tremendously spirited.

But it is the *Jupiter* that stands out. It is on the largest scale (35 minutes, with all essential repeats included) and, as it happens, the sound here is more immediate and vivid to suit the music. Like Gelmetti's DVD account of the *G minor Symphony* (see above), it is among the finest performances on record, commandingly rhythmic in the first movement and with a tremendous head of steam built up in the finale. The central movements create first cantabile repose and then a good-humoured dance spirit in the bouncing Minuet. Once again the richness and colour of the ECO woodwind and the elegance and vitality of their playing make one appreciate how splendid this work sounds on modern instruments, with the camera helping the ear to savour Mozart's ever-imaginative scoring, not forgetting the bassoon or the horns when they firmly take up that four-note theme in the finale.

Incidentally, one pleasure of this Arthaus Mozart series is that you can start the DVD player (either at the beginning or halfway through) and then sit back and relax, and the music-making will continue onwards until the end of the programme.

Symphonies 37, K.444: Introduction (completed by M. Haydn); 40; 41 (Jupiter)
*** ASV CDDCA 761. LMP, Glover

Jane Glover does not skimp on repeats, as she might have done. She omits them – as most versions do – in the slow movements, but includes exposition repeats in the finales as well as in first movements, particularly important in the *Jupiter*, with its grandly sublime counterpoint. There Glover's speed is exceptionally fast, with ensemble not quite as refined or crisp as in some rival versions, but still making for a strong and enjoyable reading.

Symphonies (i) 38 (Prague); (ii) 39 in E flat, K.543
(N) **(*) Arthaus DVD 100 083. Deutsche
  Kammerphilharmonie, (i) Albrecht; (ii) Zinman

Again a pair of performances that are uneven in appeal. Gerd Albrecht directs an enjoyably polished but essentially direct and straightforward account of the *Prague,* recorded in the Christian Zaiss Saal, Wiesbaden, where the acoustic provides a well-integrated but not very transparent sound-picture. One's pleasure comes from the superb response of the Deutsche Kammerphilharmonie. But then we have a chance to observe David Zinman at the helm, a wholly different visual and musical experience. Since 1991 (when this DVD was recorded) he has made so many outstanding discs, not least an outstanding set of the Beethoven symphonies. Now we can see how he does it. His communication with the members of the Deutsche Kammerphilharmonie commands not only a superb, unforced discipline but also a smiling convey-ance of pleasure at the many felicities of their playing. He offers every possible repeat, and his characterization of every movement of this masterpiece is ever stimulating. The *Andante* is quite lovely, the Minuet is sheer joy, and the finale is a *tour de force* of virtuosity – no matter how many times we

hear that unforgettable group of seven notes on which the whole movement is based, it lights up. Moreover, Mozart never scored a finale more colourfully than this (it is almost Mendelssohnian), and his instrumentation glows richly throughout. The recording, made in the Munich Sophiensaal, is excellent, vivid, with far more range than its companion.

Symphonies 38 (Prague); 39; 40; 41 (Jupiter)
(N) (BB) *** Virgin 2x1 5 62428-2 (2). Sinfonia Varsovia, Y.
  Menuhin

Menuhin with this hand-picked modern-instrument orchestra (of which he was principal conductor at the end of the 1980s) brings the tangible benfits of an authentic approach without sacrificing sweetness of string-tone, and offering playing of precision, clarity and bite. Throughout all four symphonies the string tuning and refinement of expressive nuance match that of a fine string quartet. Menuhin reveals himself as very much a classicist, with speeds on the fast side, notably in the *Andante* of the *Prague*. Yet even here he does not sound at all rushed, giving the movement a free, song-like lyricism. He treats the third movement of No. 39 as a brisk Ländler, almost hurdy-gurdy-like, refusing – after consultation with the autograph – to allow a rallentando at the end. Otherwise the only other oddity is his omission of the exposition repeat in the first movement, when as a rule he is generous with repeats, observing them in both the first movement and finale of the *Jupiter*. With such vivid sound, this is a strong recommendation for those collectors wanting all four symphonies.

Symphonies 38 (Prague); 40 in G min., K.550
☙ *** Sony (ADD) **SACD** SS 6494. Columbia SO, Walter

Bruno Walter's recordings were made in 1959 and represent a cherishable tradition of Mozart performance that has not in any way been eclipsed by the later, authentic movement. His interpretation of Mozart's *G minor Symphony* has long been prized as one of the finest on record, bearing in mind the enormous latitude available in the choice of tempi for the first movement. Walter's is one of the few modern-instrument recordings that perfectly strike the happy medium. His slow movement spells enchantment and the Minuet takes on an added measure of dignity under his direction. In the finale he is careful not to obscure details by hurrying, and the result is a great performance. The *Prague*, too, is one of Walter's finest Mozart performances. He achieves the right balance of tempi in the two sections of the first movement, and he draws from the slow movement all the sweetness and power of which it is capable. The finale is brilliantly played but the pace is never forced, and if there are times now and then when the tempo is slightly relaxed, the reasons are drawn from the music itself. As with Walter's other SACD reissues (Beethoven's *Pastoral* and Brahms's *Fourth*) the new transfer brings rich, natural sound with an enhanced middle and bass response.

Symphonies 39–41 (Jupiter)
(N) (M) **(*) RCA 82876 65842-2. N. German RSO, Wand

Wand's performances were recorded live, No. 39 and the *Jupiter* in 1990 and No. 40 four years later. Yet his interpretations are curiously inconsistent. In some ways they are old-fashioned performances, without exposition repeats, and with speeds beautifully judged. Slow movements are lovingly moulded, never dragging, and with rhythms, phrasing and finely detailed dynamic shading always leading the ear onwards. In the *G minor Symphony*, however, the refinement of approach means that, even in the first-movement development, he seems reluctant to find menace in the music; rather, he concentrates on beauty, and that without any lack of intensity. Here the surprise is that, in contrast to the other two works, where Minuets tend to be slow and rather heavy, the Minuet of No. 40 is taken at a whirling one-on-a-bar tempo, with a lightness and speed to match any authenticist. Yet throughout, the performances bring immediate communication, and the warm recording has a vivid sense of presence, so the conductor's admirers should find this reissue an excellent bargain.

Symphony 40 in G min., K.550

(***) BBC mono BBCL 4120-2. Hallé O, Barbirolli – SCHUBERT: *Symphonies 5 & 8 (Unfinished)* (***)

Recorded in 1962 in the BBC studios, Barbirolli conducts a strong, finely shaped performance of the *G minor Symphony*. The middle two movements are rather broader than one would expect today, and there is no repeat of the first-movement exposition, but this is a fine example of the Hallé Orchestra's playing as Barbirolli developed it. The mono sound is limited but undistracting.

Symphonies 40; 41 (Jupiter)

⊕–▾ ✹ (M) *** DG 445 548-2. VPO, Bernstein

(M) *** DG Blue 474 229-2. E. Concert, Pinnock

*** Telarc CD 80139. Prague CO, Mackerras

Bernstein's electrifying account of No. 40 is keenly dramatic, individual and stylish, with the finale delightfully airy and fresh. If anything, the *Jupiter* is even finer: it is exhilarating in its tensions and observes the repeats in both halves of the finale, making it almost as long as the massive first movement. Bernstein's electricity sustains that length, and one welcomes it for establishing the supreme power of the argument, the true crown in the whole of Mozart's symphonic output. Pacing cannot be faulted in any of the four movements and, considering the problems of making live recordings, the 1984 sound is first rate, lacking only the last degree of transparency in tuttis. This mid-price reissue on DG's Masters label now takes its place again at the top of the list of recommendations for this coupling.

It is joy and a sense of exhilaration in Mozart's inspiration that consistently bubble out from Pinnock's performances, both the darker *G minor* and the weighty, energetic and imposing *Jupiter*. The playing is first class, the concert-hall balance is most convincing and Pinnock is very generous with repeats, scoring over Gardiner in including the second repeat in the finale of the *Jupiter*. For those wanting period-instrument performances, this is now a clear first choice.

On Telarc, with generally fast speeds, so brisk that he is able to observe every single repeat, Mackerras takes a fresh, direct view which, with superb playing from the Prague Chamber Orchestra, is also characterful. On the question of repeats, the doubling in length of the slow movement of No. 40 makes it almost twice as long as the first movement, a dangerous proportion – though it is pure gain having both halves repeated in the magnificent finale of the *Jupiter*.

By its side Boehm sounds mellow and cultivated but still magnetic and strong. He, of course, is much less generous in the matter of repeats, but the Berlin Philharmonic play very beautifully and the recording is agreeably warm and full, the reissue inexpensive. *Eine kleine Nachtmusik* was recorded a

decade and a half later, and the VPO playing is polished and fresh, with a neat, lightly pointed finale.

THEATRE AND BALLET MUSIC

Complete Bargain Mozart Edition, Vol. 17: 'Rarities & Surprises': Theatre Music: Ballet music: *Idomeneo; Les Petits Riens;* Incidental music: *Thamos, King of Egypt.* Music for Pantalon and Columbine; Sketches for a Ballet Intermezzo

(B) *** Ph. (IMS) (ADD) 464 940-2 (5). Various artists including ASMF, Marriner & Netherlands CO, Zinman

Zinman and his Netherlanders give a neatly turned account of the ballet from *Idomeneo*, musical and spirited. Marriner takes over with modern, digital sound for *Les Petits Riens* and the two novelties, and the ASMF playing has characteristic elegance and finesse. *The Sketches for a Ballet Intermezzo* survive only in a single-line autograph, but Erik Smith's completion and scoring provide a series of eight charming vignettes, most with descriptive titles, ending with a piquant *Tambourin*. The music for *Pantalon and Columbine* (more mime than ballet) survives in the form of a first violin part, and Franz Beyer has skilfully orchestrated it for wind and strings, using the first movement of the *Symphony*, K.84, as the overture and the last movement of *Symphony*, K.120, as the finale. Beautifully played as it is here, full of grace and colour, this is a real find and the digital recording is first rate. *Thamos, King of Egypt* is marvellous music which it is good to have on record, particularly in such persuasive hands as these. The choral singing is impressive and the orchestral playing is excellent.

CHAMBER MUSIC

Adagio & Fugue in C min., K.546 (see also under Clarinet Quintet)

(BB) (***) Dutton Lab. mono CDBP 9713. Griller Qt – BLOCH: *String Quartet 2; Night;* DVORAK: *String Quartet 12 (American)* ***

Played by a string quartet, Mozart's masterly *Adagio and Fugue* are if anything even tauter and stronger than when played by full strings. The Griller Quartet, at the peak of their form in 1948, give a fresh, purposeful reading, very well recorded, a welcome supplement to the equally fine readings of popular Dvořák and neglected Bloch.

Adagio & Rondo for Flute, Oboe, Viola, Cello & Piano, K.617; (i) Clarinet Trio (Kegelstatt); (ii) Flute Quartets 1–4; (iii) Horn Quintet; (iv) Oboe Quartet

⊕–▾ (BB) *** Virgin 2×1 5 61448-2 (2). Nash Ens., with (i) Collins; (ii) P. Davies; (iii) Lloyd; (iv) Hulse

This inexpensive Virgin Double offers two CDs which pair naturally together. In the *Adagio and Rondo*, originally written for glass harmonica, the wind instruments blend together most felicitously. Michael Collins proves a winningly personable soloist in the *Clarinet Trio*. Gareth Hulse plays exquisitely in the *Oboe Quartet* and the Nash Ensemble blend in most sensitively, and give excellent support to Frank Lloyd's warmly lyrical account of the *Horn Quintet*. The second disc contains the four *Flute Quartets*, with Philippa Davies both a nimble and a highly musical flautist. She is very well balanced with her Nash colleagues and these are pleasingly warm, intimate performances.

Complete Bargain Mozart Edition, Vol. 6: *Clarinet Quintet* and *Trio; Flute Quartets; Horn Quintet; Oboe Quartet; Piano Quartets & Piano Trios;* **10 movements and fragments for chamber ensemble**

(B) *** Ph. (ADD/DDD) 464 820-2 (8). ASMF Chamber Ens; Beaux Arts Trio, etc.

These are highly praised performances of the major chamber works featuring modern wind instruments. The rest of the items are by no means inconsequential offcuts and provide music of high quality. The performances here are all polished and spontaneous and beautifully recorded.

Clarinet Quintet in A, K.581

☛ (BB) *** Warner Apex 0927 44350-2. Leister, Berlin Soloists – BRAHMS: *Clarinet Quintet* ***

(B) *** HM HMN 911 691. Carbonare, Hery, Binder, Bone, Pouzenc – BRAHMS: *Clarinet Quintet* ***

(B) *** Decca Eclipse 448 232-2. Schmidl, V. Octet (members) – BEETHOVEN: *Septet* ***

(N) (**(*)) Testament (ADD) SBT 1282. Boskovsky, V. Octet (members) – BRAHMS: *Clarinet Quintet* ***

Simplicity is the keynote of Karl Leister's 1988 performance, but in the lovely slow movement he finds a gentle reflective serenity that creates a mood of elysian rapture, with his string group supporting him most sensitively. The Minuet makes a strong rhythmic contrast so that the final variations can again charm the ear with their combination of lyricism and high spirits. The coda is then presented as a light-hearted culmination. Very good recording and a modest price make this coupling, with an equally fine account of the Brahms, very recommendable indeed.

With talented young performers in Harmonia Mundi's bargain series, Les Nouveaux Interprètes, this apt coupling is most welcome. Alessandro Carbonare, principal clarinet of the Orchestre National de France, produces exceptionally beautiful, liquid tone-colours over the widest dynamic range. Clear and fresh as the outer movements are, the high point is the *Larghetto*, magically gentle and with the main melody tastefully elaborated on its reprise. The four string-players, also members of the Orchestre Nationale, are not quite so distinctive yet provide most sympathetic support.

Peter Schmidl, using a basset clarinet, is sometimes just a little cool, but his intimate approach has its own appeal. He phrases with imagination and much delicacy in matters of light and shade. Of course, these Viennese players use modern instruments, and the sound they make is consistently full and smooth. The 1989 Decca recording is state-of-the-art, and while this would not necessarily be a clear first choice for the *Quintet*, it is very distinguished, and the splendid Beethoven coupling makes this Eclipse reissue an outstanding bargain.

Alfred Boskovsky's account, with members of the Vienna Octet, of the *Clarinet Quintet* is fresh but relaxed, glowing with Viennese warmth and with the intimacy of home music-making. The vivid 1954 mono sound has been well transferred by Testament, but it is a bit close.

Clarinet Quintet in A, K.581; Fragment in B flat, K.516c

(*) ASV CDDCA 1079 [id]. Johnson, Takacs-Nagy, Hirsch, Boulton, Shulman – WEBER: *Clarinet Quintet* *

Clarinet Quintet; Clarinet Quintet Fragment in B flat, K.516c; (i) *Quintet Fragment in F for Clarinet in C, Basset Horn & String Trio, K.580b* (both completed by Druce)

☛ *** Amon Ra/Saydisc (ADD) CD-SAR 17. Hacker, Salomon Qt, (i) with Schatzberger

This is a superb recording by Alan Hacker with the Salomon Quartet, using original instruments. Hacker's gentle sound on his period instrument is displayed at its most ravishing in the *Larghetto*. Tempi are wonderfully apt and the rhythms of the finale are infectious, the music's sense of joy fully projected. The recording balance is near perfect. Hacker includes a fragment from an earlier projected *Quintet* and a similar sketch for a work featuring C clarinet and basset horn with string trio. Both are skilfully completed by Duncan Druce.

The coupling of Weber's and Mozart's *Clarinet Quintets* is surprisingly rare, with Emma Johnson here also offering a fragment of a further quintet which Mozart wrote some time after 1790 just before his death, and which frustratingly breaks off just after the end of the exposition. Johnson gives characterful readings, warmly expressive in the first movement of the main work, dashing in the last two movements. The close balance of the clarinet means that the slow movement is less poised than it can be, with some tonal unevenness. Sensitive support from four formidable chamber-players, but this is a less impressive account than the sparkling Weber coupling, where the soloist returns to her most spontaneous form.

(i) *Clarinet Quintet;* (ii) *Clarinet Trio (Kegelstatt)*

(N) *** Praga Compatible Surround Sound **SACD** PRD/DSD 250 200. Moraguès; with (i) Pražák Qt; (ii) Braley, V. Mendelssohn

The fine Czech clarinettist Pascal Moraguès subtly varies his timbre in this pair of performances, comparatively limpid in the *Quintet* – seductively so in the slow movement – and slightly more robust in the *Trio* to match the style of the excellent pianist, Frank Braley. Moreover, the *Quintet* has a subtlety of dynamic and a nicely judged variety of tempi that, together with a feeling of natural spontaneity, create what is a virtually ideal performance. The finale is especially enticing, with an infectious burst of bubbling bravura just before the coda. Moreover, the SACD transfer gives the players a natural presence within a most attractive acoustic. Highly recommended, especially to those collectors with full surround-sound facilities, but sounding pretty impressive as a normal CD.

(i; iii) *Clarinet Quintet;* (i; ii) *Clarinet Trio (Kegelstatt);* (iii) *Adagio & Fugue, K.546*

(N) *** HM Aeon AECD 0422. (i) Portal; (ii) Pennetier; (iii) Ysaÿe Qt

A truly distinctive collection. The clarinettist, Michel Portal, has a ravishing tone, and although his style in the famous *Quintet* is plainer, less garnished with nuanced idiosyncrasy than usual, his natural musical phrasing and sense of line captivate the ear throughout; the limpid beauty of the slow movement is truly memorable. He is admirably supported by the ever-sensitive members of the Ysaÿe Quartet and, in the equally rewarding account of the *Clarinet Trio*, by his pianist partner, Jean-Claude Pennetier. Moreover the account of the *Adagio and Fugue* is one of the most concentrated on disc, moving steadily to a powerful climax.

(i) *Clarinet Quintet, K.581;* (ii) *Horn Quintet, K.407*

(N) **(*) MDG 304 1184-2. (i) Rodenhäuser; (ii) Vlatkovic; Ens. Villa Musica

MDG have a very seductive way of recording chamber music, and this coupling is no exception. The richness of Ulf Rodenhäuser's timbre in the *Clarinet Quintet* combines with beautifully blended string-playing to provide a result to captivate any listener, with sheer beauty of timbre and limpid phrasing. Tempi are consistently relaxed, and although in that respect there is perhaps not enough variety, the result never quite becomes bland. The performance of the *Horn Quintet* has similar finesse, but Radovan Vlatkovic's horn-playing is robust enough to create a contrast between the two performances.

(i) *Clarinet Quintet;* (ii) *Horn Quintet;* (iii) *Oboe Quartet, K.370*

🔂 (M) ***** Ph. 422 833-2. (i) Pay; (ii) T. Brown; (iii) Black; ASMF Chamber Ens.

* Nim. NI 5487. (i) Leister; (ii) Seifert; (iii) Koch; Brandis Qt

Antony Pay's earlier account of the *Clarinet Quintet*, played on a modern instrument, with the Academy of St Martin-in-the-Fields players must be numbered among the strongest now on the market. Neil Black's playing in the *Oboe Quartet* is distinguished, and again the whole performance radiates pleasure, while the *Horn Quintet* comes in a well-projected and lively account with Timothy Brown. The recording is of Philips's best.

Karl Leister provides an essentially light-hearted account of the *Clarinet Quintet*, with the slow movement tranquil and beautifully poised. Gerd Seifert is just as lively and sensitive in the work for horn, even if his tone is a little plump. Lothar Koch is equally personable in the *Oboe Quartet*, although perhaps just a trifle studied in sustaining the *Adagio* (so beautifully opened by the Brandis Quartet). The recording, comparatively forward, is vividly present.

(i) *Clarinet Quintet. String Quartet 18 in A, K.464*

*(*) ASV CDDCA 1042. (i) Hilton; Lindsay Qt

Janet Hilton gives a disarmingly simple, unaffected account of the *Clarinet Quintet* and gets excellent support from the Lindsays. The performance of the *A major Quartet* is characteristically perceptive and vital, with the *Andante* on the whole beautifully played, although some may find dynamics a little overstressed. The balance is forward and vivid.

(i) *Clarinet Quintet;* (ii) *Violin Sonatas in F, K.376; E flat, K.481*

(M) ***** HM Cal. 5628. (i) Zahradnik, Talich Qt; (ii) Messiereur, Bogunia

The *Clarinet Quintet* is exquisitely done. Bohuslav Zahradnik's contribution has much delicacy of feeling and colour; he is highly seductive in the slow movement, and even in the finale the effect is gentle in the most appealing way without any loss of vitality. The recording balance is exemplary. The two *Violin Sonatas* are also beautifully played in a simple, direct style that is wholly persuasive. The recording is clearly detailed and well balanced, if slightly more shallow.

(i) *Clarinet Trio (Kegelstatt). Piano Trios 3–4, K.502 & K.542*

(N) (M) ***(*)** Warner Elatus 2564 61733-2. (i) Schmid; Schiff (fortepiano), Shiokawa, Höbarth, Perényí

If you need these works played on original instruments, this is worth considering. In the *Clarinet Trio* Elmar Schmid has a full, glowing timbre, but otherwise the balance, with the fortepiano at the back and Yuuoko Shiokawa's sharply focused lead violin dominating throughout, is less well integrated. But the performances are strong and András Schiff's contribution on the fortepiano is as ever distinctive, especially in slow movements.

Clarinet Trio (Kegelstatt); Piano & Wind Quintet, K.452

(N) ***(*)** CPO 777 010-2. Consortium Classicum – BEETHOVEN: *Piano & Wind Quintet* ***(*)**

On CPO the usual coupling of the *Piano and Wind Quintets* of Mozart and Beethoven, while perhaps not a first choice for these works, is enhanced by a fine account of the *Clarinet Trio*, with an excellent clarinettist in Dieter Klöcker. But the star of the proceedings overall is the fine pianist, Werner Genuit, who ensures that all three performances are enjoyable, with both the *Larghetto* and finale of the *Quintet* played most appealingly. Good, well-balanced recording.

(i) *Divertimento in E flat for String Trio, K.563;* (ii) *Duos for Violin & Viola 1–2, K.423/4;* (i) *6 Preludes & Fugues for String Trio, K.404a;* (iii) *Sonata (String Trio) in B flat, K.266*

(B) ***** Ph. Duo (ADD) 454 023-2 (2). (i) Grumiaux, Janzer, Szabo; (ii) Grumiaux, Pelliccia; (iii) ASMF Chamber Ens.

Complete Bargain Mozart Edition, Vol. 8: (i) *Duos & String Trios;* (ii) *Violin Sonatas; Sonatinas;* etc. (complete)

(BB) ***** Ph. (ADD/DDD) 464 840-2 (9). (i) Grumiaux Trio or ASMF Chamber Ens.; (ii) various artists

Grumiaux's 1967 recorded performance of the *Divertimento in E flat* remains unsurpassed; he is here joined by two players with a similarly refined and classical style. In the *Duos*, which are ravishingly played, the balance is excellent, and Arrigo Pelliccia proves a natural partner in these inspired and rewarding works. The *Sonata for String Trio* is well played by the ASMF Chamber Ensemble and it has a modern, digital recording. Of the six *Preludes and Fugues*, the first three derive from Bach's *Well-tempered Clavier*, the fourth combines an *Adagio* from the *Organ Sonata*, BWV 527, with *Contrapunctus 8* from the *Art of Fugue*, the fifth is a transcription of two movements from the *Organ Sonata*, BWV 526, and the sixth uses music of W. F. Bach. The performances here are sympathetic and direct, the recorded sound bold, clear and bright.

Divertimento in E flat for String Trio, K.563; Duo for Violin and Viola in B flat, K.424

🔂 ***** Hyp. CDA 67246. Leopold String Trio

Here is a completely natural performance of Mozart's *E flat Divertimento* and the first for some years that can come close to approaching the celebrated Grumiaux Trio version, which has served us so well for the past three decades. Marianne Thorsen and Scott Dickinson give a first-rate account of the *B flat Duo*, K.424. Very lifelike recording, totally at the service of Mozart and the musicians.

Flute Quartets 1 in D, K.285; 2 in G, K.285a; 3 in C, K.285b; 4 in A, K.298

🔂 ***** EMI 5 56829-2. Pahud, Poppen, Schlicht, Queras

(i) *Flute Quartets 1–4;* (ii) *Andante for Flute & Orchestra in C, K.315*

(B) ***** DHM (ADD) 05472 77442-2. B. Kuijken; (i) Coll. Aur. (members); (ii) La Petite Bande

Emmanuel Pahud gives inspired performances of the four Mozart *Flute Quartets*. These are all early works, generally lightweight, but with one movement of deep emotional feeling, the B minor *Adagio* of the *First Quartet*, K.285. In that songful piece Pahud finds new mystery through his subtly shaded phrasing. Otherwise this is a fun disc, full of youthful high spirits, charming and witty. Even more than his earlier disc of Mozart concertos for EMI, this signals the arrival of a new master flautist.

The Collegium Aureum set is the only bargain version using period instruments. Barthold Kuijken plays a beguilingly soft instrument from Dresden, made by August Grenser in 1789, and the effect has great charm. The playing of the three string instruments is also very smooth and accomplished, and the ensemble is beautifully recorded in a warm acoustic. The pitch is lower by a semitone, but few listeners will mind this. The *Andante for Flute and Orchestra* makes an engaging encore.

Horn Quintet in E flat, K.407

(BB) *** Warner Apex 8573 89080-2. Vlatkovic, Berlin Soloists
  – BEETHOVEN: *Septet* ***

(i) *Horn Quintet in E flat, K.407*; (ii) *Horn Duos in E flat, K.487/496a*

☛ (B) *** EMI Debut 5 72822-2. Clark (waldhorn); (i) Ens. Galant; (ii) Montgomery – BEETHOVEN: *Horn Sonata*, etc.; BRAHMS: *Horn Trio* ***

Radovan Vlatkovic is a most musical soloist, and his companions provide a warmly affectionate backing, most naturally recorded. The *Andante* is beautifully phrased by soloist and string group alike and the finale is appropriately perky. Excellent value.

On EMI's bargain Debut label Andrew Clark uses a waldhorn and displays considerable panache. As in the Brahms *Trio*, his virtuosity is well matched by his partners, also using period instruments. The two rare Mozart *Duos* are guaranteed to win the listener. Strongly recommended.

Horn Quintet, K.407; Oboe Quartet, K.370; Piano and Wind Quintet, K.452; Quintet Movement, K.580b

☛ *** Hyp. CDA 67277. Gaudier Ens.

The Gaudier Ensemble here offers an ideal Mozart coupling of four wind-based chamber works. The oboist, Douglas Boyd, brings out the depth in the D minor slow movement of the *Oboe Quartet* as well as the fun of the outer movements, while Jonathan Williams is brilliant in the *Horn Quintet*, with the more ambitious *Piano and Wind Quintet*, in which Susan Tomes is the outstanding pianist, providing the anchor point. The rarity is the *Quintet Movement* for the unusual grouping of clarinet, basset horn and string trio, a magnificent piece, left unfinished at Mozart's death and here completed by Duncan Druce.

(i) Horn Quintet; String Quartet 19 in C (Dissonance), K.465; (ii) String Quintet 4 in G min., K.516

(BB) (***) Dutton mono CDBP 9717. (i) Brain; (ii) Gilbert (viola); Griller Qt

This further outstanding disc of Mozart chamber music from the Griller Quartet offered in the Dutton bargain series, superbly transferred, demonstrates again the strength and refinement of this leading quartet of the post-war period, largely neglected by record companies during the age of the LP. The *G minor Quintet* is outstanding, with excellent sound, while it is also good to have the *Horn Quintet* in another vintage performance with Dennis Brain as soloist.

Piano Quartets 1 in G min., K.478; 2 in E flat, K.493

☛ *** TDK **DVD** DV-PQWAM. Zacharias, Frank & Tabea Zimmermann, Wick (Producer: Dietrich Mack; V/D: János Darvas)

(BB) *** EMI Encore 5 75874-2. Zacharias, F. & T. Zimmermann, Wick

*** Hyp. CDA 67373. Lewis, Leopold String Trio

(N) (M) *** Sony 517 484-2 [SK 93071]. Ax, Stern, Laredo, Ma

(N) (BB) *** HM Classical Express HMX 3957018. Mozartean Players

The TDK DVD, filmed and recorded at Ludwigsburger Schlossfestspiele in November 1988, offers the ideal way to present a chamber concert in video format. The players walk on and play Mozart's music in front of an attentive but quiet audience, and the whole effect is live and spontaneous and presented in front of a most attractive background. One can sit in one's armchair and in no time at all be transported into Mozart's sound-world, as if being present at a live performance. The camera is unfussy, focusing on the pianist very effectively at moments when the listener might well be drawn to look at him, and otherwise generally taking a broader view. Christian Zacharias and his colleagues give altogether delightful accounts of both works. Zacharias is on his best form and leads his team elegantly and with plenty of vitality. Pacing cannot be faulted, there is delicacy of detail, a nice rhythmic impetus and a pleasing overall combination of warmth and finesse. The sound is first class.

Whether or not the performances on the EMI Encore disc are identical is difficult to say; they are certainly very similar, no less pleasing and warmly spontaneous, and the recording is first class to make this a strong budget CD alternative, if you are not yet hooked on the added appeal of DVD.

The newest Hyperion coupling is equally recommendable, the performances a shade more intimate in style and texture, and refined in a most attractive way, with much that is felicitous from all concerned. Paul Lewis plays most nimbly and takes his colleagues with him. Most enjoyable in all respects, not least the natural recording with clear inner detail.

The grouping of star names by Sony offers performances of keen imagination and insight. Speeds are beautifully chosen and in both works the performances consistently convey a sense of happy spontaneity. It is striking that Emanuel Ax, in the many passages in which the piano is set against the strings, establishes the sort of primacy required, pointing rhythms and moulding phrases persuasively. The recording, made in the Manhattan Center, New York, in 1994, is a degree drier than in many previous versions, suggesting a small rather than a reverberant hall. This has now been reissued at mid-price, which increases its claims to be considered a front-runner among several other excellent accounts.

Those seeking early-instrument versions need look no further than these 1989 American accounts by the excellent Stephen Lubin, fortepiano, and his New York Mozartean group. Their sonority is pleasingly warm and well integrated, yet detail is naturally clear. Slow movements are admirably expressive and there is plenty of life and spontaneity in the playing throughout. In short, these are most rewarding accounts, making a completely convincing case for period instruments.

(i) Piano Quartets 1–2; (ii) Horn Quintet in E flat

☛ 🌑 (M) (***) Decca mono 425 960-2. (i) Curzon, Amadeus Qt; (ii) Brain, Griller Qt

All versions of the Mozart *Piano Quartets* rest in the shadow of the recordings by Clifford Curzon and members of the Amadeus Quartet. No apologies need be made for the 1952 mono recorded sound. The performances have a unique sparkle, slow movements are elysian. One's only criticism is that the *Andante* of K.478 opens at a much lower dynamic level than the first movement, and some adjustment of the controls needs to be made. The *Horn Quintet* coupling was recorded in 1944 and the transfer to CD is even more miraculous. The slight surface rustle of the 78-r.p.m. source is in no way distracting and Dennis Brain's performance combines warmth and elegance with a spirited spontaneity, and the subtleties of the horn contribution are a continuous delight. A wonderful disc that should be in every Mozartian's library.

Piano Quartet 1 in G min., K.478
*** Ph. 446 001-2. Brendel, Zehetmair, Zimmermann, Duven – SCHUBERT: *Trout Quintet* ***
(N) **(*) EMI 5 57506-2. Brakhman, Schwarzberg, Romanoff-Schwarzberg, Drobinsky – BEETHOVEN: *Piano Trio 4* **(*)

Brendel's performance of the *G minor Piano Quartet* has vigour and sensitivity and, not surprisingly, an admirable sense of style. It very well recorded too and, although most collectors will prefer a disc containing both *Piano Quartets*, this is a sizeable bonus for an outstanding account of Schubert's *Trout Quintet*.

Evgheny Brakhman and his companions were recorded at Martha Argerich's festival in Lugano in 2002, and they give a vigorous and spontaneous account of the *G minor Piano Quartet*, with well-judged tempi and intelligent phrasing. Brakhman, Argerich's protégé, is an elegant player, and there is fine rapport among the four players. Good though it is, it is not memorable enough (or, in the case of the middle movement, thoughtful enough) to prompt one to return to it in preference to the finest of those performances listed above.

Piano Trios 1 in B flat, K.254; 2 in G, K.496; 3 in B flat, K.502; 4 in E, K.542; 5 in C, K.548; 6 in G, K.564
☛ (N) (BB) *** Warner Apex 2564 62189-2 (2). Trio Fontenay
*** Chan. 8536/7 (2). Borodin Trio

Piano Trios 1–6; 3 Movements, K.442
(N) *** MDG 303 0373-2 (2). Trio Parnassus

The Trio Fontenay have already given us excellent accounts of the Brahms and Dvořák *Piano Trios* and they are equally happy in the music of Mozart. As before, the splendid pianist Wolf Harden dominates the music-making by strength of personality, although the others are well in the picture, and the contribution of the cellist, Niklas Schmidt, is notable. The playing of this group is consistently fresh and spontaneous and has the advantage of modern digital recording and a very reasonable cost.

The Parnassus have another outstanding pianist in Chia Chou and the advantage of particularly natural and beautifully balanced recording. As it happens, they put the very first Trio (described as a *Divertimento*) to open the second disc and as it is among the most spontaneous of the performances here, this is the place to begin listening. Moreover, MDG includes as a delightful bonus the three movements for the same instrumentation completed by Abbé Stadler and published in 1797. They are well worth having, with the finale acting as a sparkling encore, and their inclusion gives this set a strong claim on the collector, even though it is more expensive than the Trio Fontenay.

The Borodin Trio are slightly weightier in their approach and their tempi are generally more measured, very strikingly so in the *Allegretto* of the *G major*. All the same, there is, as usual with this group, much sensitive playing and every evidence of distinguished musicianship. The Chandos balance, recorded at The Maltings, Snape, produces a pleasingly integrated sound.

Piano & Wind Quintet in E flat, K.452
(M) *** Sony SMK 42099. Perahia, members of ECO – BEETHOVEN: *Quintet* ***
*** CBC MCVD 1137. Kuerti, Campbell, Mason, Sommerville, McKay – MOZART; WITT: *Quintets* ***
(M) **(*) Warner Elatus 2464 60445-2. Barenboim, Soloists of Chicago SO – BEETHOVEN: *Quintet* **(*)

An outstanding mid-priced account of Mozart's delectable *Piano and Wind Quintet* on Sony, with Perahia's playing wonderfully refreshing in the *Andante* and a superb response from the four wind soloists, and in particular Neil Black's oboe. Clearly all the players are enjoying this rewarding music, and they are well balanced, with the piano against the warm but never blurring acoustics of The Maltings at Snape.

The performance by this excellent group of leading Canadian instrumentalists is hardly less captivating. They share this wonderful music as a perfectly matched team. This is playing of great freshness and striking spontaneity, given a perfectly balanced recording of vividness and presence. Moreover, the CBC issue scores by including also the quintet of Friedrich Witt, closely modelled on the present work.

Barenboim shares Mozart and Beethoven with members of his Chicago orchestra, and the result is undoubtedly fresh and vital. But his comparatively brisk approach to the first movement misses the feeling of relaxation that this music ideally needs, and although the players work very well together elsewhere, and especially in the pert finale, this well-recorded performance is not a first choice.

Piano & Wind Quintet in E flat, K.452; Adagio in B flat, K.411; Adagio in C, K.580a; Adagio & Allegro in F min., K.594; Adagio & Rondeau in C min., K.617; Andante for a Small Organ Cylinder in F, K.616; Piece for Musical Clock in F min., K.608
*** BIS CD 1132. Hough, Berlin Philharmonic Wind Quintet

The *Quintet for Piano and Wind* finds Stephen Hough and the Berlin Philharmonic Wind Quintet in splendid form. They have lightness and wit to commend them, as well as an impeccable feeling for style. This recording is as good as any in the catalogue and survives the most exalted comparisons. The remaining pieces are all sensitive arrangements written by the flautist on this disc, Michael Hasel. However, do not expect two clarinets and three basset-horns in K.411, as there is a conventional wind quintet. Hough does his best to sound like the musical glasses for which Mozart wrote K.608. Good playing and recording throughout.

String quartets

Complete Bargain Mozart Edition, Vol. 7: (i) *String Quartets* (complete); (ii) *String Quintets* (complete)
(B) *** Ph. (ADD) 464 830-2 (11). (i) Italian Qt; (ii) Grumiaux, Gérecz, Janzer, Lesueur, Czako

The earliest recordings by the Italians now begin to show their age (notably the six *Haydn Quartets*, which date from 1966): the violin timbre is thinner than we would expect in more modern versions. But the quality is generally very satisfactory, for the Philips sound-balance is admirably judged. As a set, the performances have seen off all challengers for two decades or more; one is unlikely to assemble a more consistently satisfying overview of these works, or one so beautifully played. They hold a very special place in the Mozartian discography.

String Quartets 2 in D; 3 in G; 4 in C; 5 in F; 6 in B flat; 7 in E flat; K.155/160
(M) *** Cal. CAL 5246. Talich Qt

String Quartets 3, K.156; 14, K.387; 15, K.421
☞ (M) *** Cal. Approche (ADD) CAL 5241. Talich Qt

String Quartets 8–12, K.168–72
☞ (M) *** Cal. Approche (ADD) CAL 5247. Talich Qt

String Quartets 16, K.428; 17 (Hunt), K.458
☞ (M) *** Cal. Approche (ADD) CAL 5242. Talich Qt –
   HAYDN: String Quartet 74 ***

The prize-winning recordings by the Talich Quartet are here reissued in their previous couplings. As we have commented before, their playing is immaculate in ensemble and they have a special kind of shared intimacy which yet is immediately communicative. They are the soul of finesse and make music with expressive simplicity, while bringing vitality to Allegros and conveying a consistent feeling of spontaneous vitality throughout. They are naturally balanced. The analogue recordings have not been further remastered and remain beautiful, very warm and smooth on top, slightly middle- and bass-orientated. There are few records of Mozart's Quartets to match these.

String Quartets 14, K.387; 15, K.421; 16, K.428; 17 (Hunt), K.458; 18, K.464; 19 (Dissonance), K.465 (Haydn Quartets); 20 (Hoffmeister), K.499; 21, K.575; 22, K.589; 23, K.590 (Prussian Quartets 1–3)
☞ (M) *** Teldec 4509 95495-2 (4). Alban Berg Qt
(BB) *** CRD (ADD) CRD 5005 (5). Chilingirian Qt

The Teldec recordings were made by the Alban Berg in the latter half of the 1970s; the performances have not since been surpassed, and now they make one of the most distinguished sets of Mozart's late quartets currently available. The playing is thoroughly stylish and deeply musical; it is entirely free from surface gloss and there are none of the expressive exaggerations of dynamics and phrasing that marred this group's later records for EMI. The Haydn Quartets are consistently successful; the Hunt (1979) is still possibly the finest on the market and the Dissonance too is first class, with a wonderfully expressive account of the slow movement.

The splendid Chilingirian recordings on modern instruments have long been praised by us and rank among the freshest and most spontaneous performances in the catalogue. They are still second to none among versions using modern instruments, and at budget price this well-documented box is very highly recommendable.

String Quartets 14–19 (Haydn Quartets)
(M) *** Auvidis (14 & 15: E 8843; 16 & 17: E 8844; 18 & 19: E 8845). Mosaïques Qt
*** Hyp. CDS 44001/3. Salomon Qt
(i) String Quartets 14–19 (Haydn Quartets); also 3, K.156;
(ii) Violin Sonata 18 in G, K.301
(M) *** HM Cal. 3241/3. (i) Talich Qt; (ii) Messiereur, Bogunia (with HAYDN: String Quartet 74 in G min., Op. 74/3 **(*))

As with their previous award-winning performances of Haydn, Mosaïques Quartet offer playing of great distinction which offers new insights in every one of the six quartets.

Phrasing is wonderfully musical, textures are elegantly blended, there is great transparency yet a full sonority, and this music-making unfolds freshly and naturally. Slow movements have great concentration, yet Allegros are alert and vital and finales are a joy. The recording is first class. The three CDs are packaged in a slip-case and now they are also available separately, most attractively packaged.

The playing of the Salomon Quartet is highly accomplished and has a real sense of style; they do not eschew vibrato, though their use of it is not liberal, and there is admirable clarity of texture and vitality of articulation. There is no want of subtlety and imagination in the slow movements. The recordings are admirably truthful and lifelike, and those who seek 'authenticity' in Mozart's chamber music will not be disappointed.

The performances by the Talich Quartet are immaculate in ensemble and they have a special kind of shared intimacy which is yet immediately communicative. The analogue recordings are beautiful, very smooth on top, the balance slightly middle- and bass-orientated. The set has now been issued complete on three mid-priced discs with a pair of bonuses. The Violin Sonata comes after the Dissonance Quartet; the Haydn quartet, Op. 74/3, after the Hunt, K.458, at a disconcertingly higher level. This too is a fine performance – but be prepared!

String Quartets 14–19 (Haydn Quartets); 20–21 (Hoffmeister); 22–3 (Prussian)
☞ (M) *** Warner Elatus (ADD) 2-CD 2564 60678-2 (2) (14–17 & 20); 2564 60809-2 (2) (18–19; 21–3). Alban Berg Qt

These splendid recorded performances derive from the set made by the Alban Berg Quartet in the latter half of the 1970s, available on four CDs and highly praised by us above. This pair of separate reissues is most welcome.

String Quartets 14–15
☞ ✹ (BB) *** Dutton mono CDBP 9702. Griller Qt –
   HAYDN: String Quartet 39 *** ✹
*** MDG 307 1035-2. Leipzig Qt
(N) (M) ** Virgin 5 62201-2. Smithson Qt

Even more than the Adagio and Fugue (above) the playing of Nos. 14, K.387, and 15, K.421, by the Grillers reveals their supreme musicianship in Mozart, their warmth and above all the spontaneous feeling of their playing. Moreover, the miraculous Dutton transfers of these superb Decca ffrr recordings are so natural and beautiful that the sound is preferable to many modern digital recordings. Just sample their fizzing account of the Molto allegro finale of K.387 or the simple beauty of the Andante of K.421 to discover quartet playing of a very rare calibre indeed.

Those preferring first-class digital recordings played on modern instruments with greater tonal warmth than that afforded by the Smithson group will find the Leipzig Quartet second to none. As in their recordings of the last three quartets (see below), these performances also combine warmth and finesse with a natural spontaneity, and their music-making has much in common with the Grillers. They play repeats omitted on the earlier recordings. A lovely disc.

The Smithson Quartet, led by Jaap Schröder and using early instruments, are a strikingly well-integrated group, and they play immaculately and musically together. They are truthfully balanced and recorded, yet their very plain music-making fails to charm the ear and engage the listener's attention in the way that the Griller and Leipzig Quartets do.

String Quartet 14; (i) String Quintet 4 in G min., K.516

*** ASV CDDCA 923. Lindsay Qt, (i) with Ireland

This is what chamber-music playing is about. The Lindsays radiate a delight in their music and judge the character of each piece of music exactly; and one has only to sample the finale of K.387, played with enormous vitality and sparkle, to sense immediately that the music-making is a world apart. The slow movement of the *G minor String Quintet* is very touching in its gentle intensity. These are among the finest modern recordings of either work. The disc must be recommended with enthusiasm.

String Quartet 15 in D min., K.421

(B) *** EMI Début 5 85638-2. Atrium Qt – SHOSTAKOVICH: *String Quartet 7*; TCHAIKOVSKY: *String Quartet 3* ***

The present disc is part of the invaluable EMI Début series and serves as a visiting card for the young Atrium String Quartet. They hail from St Petersburg and were the winners of the 2003 London International String Quartet; they were coached by Iosif Levinzon, the cellist of the Taneyev Quartet. Their programme is intelligently chosen, not just as a vehicle for their artistry, but as repertoire useful for the collector. They play Mozart K.421 – the only one of his *Haydn Quartets* in a minor key – with much understanding and sympathy, and they penetrate the underlying melancholy of the *Andante* to telling effect. Throughout their recital they play with great finesse and tonal beauty, and EMI have given them first-rate recorded sound.

String Quartets 15 in D min., K.421; 16 in E flat, K.428; 17 in B flat (Hunt); 18 in A, K.464; 19 in C (Dissonance); 20 in D (Hoffmeister), K.499; 21 in D, K.575; 22 in B flat, K.589; 23 in F, K.590 (Prussian 1–3); (i) String Quintets 2 in C, K.515; 3 in G min., K.516; 5 in D, K.593; 6 in E flat, K.614

✿ (M) (***) DG Westminster mono/stereo 474 000-2. Amadeus Qt, (i) with Aronowitz

These legendary recordings were made for the Westminster label in the early days of mono LP, beginning in 1951 – three years after the Amadeus Quartet's Wigmore Hall début – and continuing in 1954, 1955 and 1957 (the *D major Quintet*, which is stereo). The venues chosen – London's Conway Hall, Hampstead Parish Church, Abbey Road Studios, the Beethovensaal in Hanover and the Hamburg-Blankenese Studio – each provided a pleasing acoustic, and the sound is real and vivid, a little forward, but not excessively so. The performances are very distinguished – indeed thrilling – wonderfully natural and spontaneous. The group's cellist, Martin Lovett has commented: 'They were probably the best of us because we were so fresh and keen.' That is certainly true; later recordings by this group may show keener insights gained from experience, but here the response to the music is instinctive and wonderfully vibrant. Even if tempi are sometimes pressed hard, the effect is often inspired, and that applies equally to the warmth and delicacy of the relaxed slow movements. The vibrato which always characterized their playing is never overdone. Indeed these performances, to quote Tully Potter, who wrote the accompanying biographical notes, 'still have the power to amaze'. The box is described as a 'limited edition' so an early purchase is essential.

String Quartets 15; 16; 18

(***) Testament mono/stereo SBT 1117. Smetana Qt

These are performances of a singular distinction, supremely classical in every way. The slow movement of K.428 has rarely sounded more affecting. This quartet appears in stereo for the first time. The *A major*, K.464, has not been issued before, and gives equal satisfaction. A very special record.

String Quartets 16, K.428; 18, K.464

*** MDG 307 1160-2. Leipzig Qt

The Leipzig performances of the Mozart *Quartets* continue to be second to none, and they are beautifully recorded.

String Quartet 17 (Hunt)

(**(*)) Testament mono SBT 1085. Hollywood Qt – HUMMEL: *Quartet in G* *(*); HAYDN: *Quartet 76* **(*)

The Hollywood Quartet's performance was recorded at a memorable concert in London's Royal Festival Hall in September 1957, and also included the Haydn coupling. The performance is as impeccable as one would expect from these artists, and the sound is astonishingly good for the period.

String Quartet 17 (Hunt); (i) String Quintet 3 in G min., K.516

(N) (**) EMI Classic Archive mono **DVD** DVB 5996839. Amadeus Qt, (i) with Aronowitz – BEETHOVEN: *String Quartets 4 & 6; 16: Lento assai* (only). (Bonus: BRAHMS: *Clarinet Quintet*: 3rd movt: Andantino; BARTOK: *Quartet 4: Allegretto Pizzicato*; SCHUBERT: *Quartet 14 (Death and the Maiden)*: 4th movt) (***)

The performance of the *G minor String Quintet* shows the Amadeus in good form in 1971 and is quite respectably recorded. Alas, the *Hunt Quartet* suffers from unacceptable harmonic distortion. There are also severe reservations about the two recordings of the Beethoven Op. 18 *Quartets*; the bonuses are the highlight of this DVD and are discussed under the Beethoven couplings.

String Quartets 17 (Hunt); 19 (Dissonance)

✿ (BB) *** Warner Apex (ADD) 0927 40828-2. Alban Berg Qt

*** MDG 307 1107-2. Leipzig Qt

(BB) **(*) Naxos 8.550105. Moyzes Qt

The Alban Berg Quartet recorded the *Hunt* in 1979 and it still ranks among the very finest accounts on disc. It has much greater polish and freshness even than the Italian Quartet, and well withstands all the competition that has come since. The *Dissonance* is of similar vintage. It, too, is first class, with a wonderfully expressive account of the slow movement. Although dynamic gradations are steep, there is no sense of exaggeration – on the contrary, there is only a sense of total dedication about these wholly excellent performances, which are recommended with enthusiasm. No reservations about the transfers either, and this Apex reissue is a marvellous bargain.

The Leipzig Quartet continue their excellent performances of Mozart's 'Haydn' quartets by pairing the two most famous works. As with their equally fine coupling of Nos. 14 and 15, these are most musicianly performances, strikingly fresh and free from the slightest trace of affectation, and full of vital musical feeling. This series ranks alongside the finest modern-instrument performances, for the recording, although fairly close, is naturally balanced.

The Moyzes Quartet come from Bratislava and are an accomplished ensemble, distinguished by a generally sweet and light tone, and decently recorded in the clean acoustic of the Concert Hall of Slovak Radio. The performances are very well prepared and neatly played; phrasing is musical and often sensitive, even if the overall effect is just a little bland.

But the performances still have a lot going for them and can be recommended.

String Quartets 17 (Hunt); 19 (Dissonance); Adagio & Fugue in C min., K.456.

☛ (M) *** Somm SOMMCD 040. Coull Qt

The Coull Quartet, who have already given us a fine set of the Mendelssohn *Quartets*, are now embarking on a Mozart survey, and their splendid coupling of the *Hunt* (spick and span and full of sparkle) and the *Dissonance*, with its arrestingly atmospheric opening, bodes well for the series. Both slow movements combine depth with a warm, expressive feeling. They are generous with repeats so that the vivacious finale of the *Dissonance* plays for just over 11 minutes. The *Adagio and Fugue*, too, is full of concentration, yet not exaggerated in intensity. First-rate recording, crisply focused and transparent.

String Quartet 19 (Dissonance); (i) String Quintet 6 in E flat, K.614

*** ASV CDDCA 1069. Lindsay Qt, (i) with Williams

The Lindsays continue their combined series of Mozart's *String Quartets* and *Quintets* with one of the finest discs in the series so far. The striking harmonic atmosphere at the opening of K.465 immediately registers why it was nicknamed 'Dissonance', yet the following *Allegro* is sunny and the *Andante* has both serenity and depth of feeling to make a foil for the delightful Minuet and light-hearted finale. The *Quintet* is hardly less successful, with its witty finale brought off in a true Haydnesque spirit. The recording is real and immediate.

String Quartets 20 (Hoffmeister); 21–3 (Prussian Quartets 1–3)

(M) *** CRD (ADD) CRD 3427/8. Chilingirian Qt

The Chilingirian Quartet give very natural, unforced, well-played and sweet-toned accounts of the last four *Quartets*. They are very well recorded too, with cleanly focused lines and a warm, pleasing ambience; indeed, in this respect these two discs are second to none.

String Quartets 20 (Hoffmeister), K.499; 21 (Prussian 1); K.575; (ii) Violin Sonata 17, K.296

☛ (M) *** Cal. Approche CAL 5244. Talich Qt

String Quartets 22 in B flat (Prussian 2), K.589; 23 in F (Prussian 3), K.590; Adagio & Fugue in C min., K.546

☛ (M) *** Cal. Approche CAL 5245. Talich Qt

The Talich couplings of the *Hoffmeister* and *Prussian Quartets* are digital and the recording is brighter and more present than in the earlier *Quartets*. The playing has comparable sensibility and plenty of vitality.

String Quartets 20 (Hoffmeister), K.499; 22, K.589

(BB) *** Hyp. Helios CDH 55094. Salomon Qt

The Salomon Quartet have impeccable ensemble and a real sense of style; they use vibrato judiciously and with taste. There is no lack of finesse or vitality, and if you want period-instrument performances of these two works, the present inexpensive CD could be a good choice. The recording is real and shows the transparency of texture these instrumentalists achieve, while blending beautifully together.

String Quartets 21–3 (Prussian Quartets 1–3)

☛ (B) *** MDG Double MDG 307 0936-2 (2). Leipzig Qt

String Quartets 21–2 (Prussian 1–2)

*** Nim. NI 5351. Franz Schubert Qt

(BB) *** Warner Apex 0927 49575-2. Lotus Qt

String Quartets 21; 23 (Prussian)

*** Astrée E 8659. Mosaïques Qt

String Quartets 22–3 (Prussian)

*** Delos DE 3192. Shanghai Qt

The Leipzig performances of Mozart's last three quartets are second to none and have all the spontaneity of live music-making. They fill up the rest of the space on the second CD by ingeniously creating a 'sampler' composite quartet. This combines the opening Allegro of Schubert's D.353 with the glorious *Lento assai* of Beethoven's Op. 135, followed by the Scherzo from Brahms's Op. 51/2 and the finale from Beethoven's Op. 59/3. In principle one would resist such an idea, but all four movements are played superbly, and the amalgam works astonishingly well.

The Franz Schubert Quartet play with refreshing lack of affectation and with great sweetness of tone. There is perhaps more sweetness than depth in the slow movements; but at the same time it must be said that there is nothing narcissistic about the playing, and the listener is held from start to finish. They are very well recorded too.

On Apex most enjoyable performances by the Lotus Quartet, polished, well paced, fresh, bright, clearly and naturally recorded. If you want to sample the Lotus Quartet's feeling for a Mozartian line, sample the opening of No. 22. Excellent value at Apex price.

Even those collectors who do not normally respond to period-instrument performances should be swayed by the warmth and finesse of the playing of the Mosaïques Quartet and by their lightness of touch in the finale of K.590. The closing *Allegretto* of K.575 is revealing in quite a different way, and both slow movements have a searching intensity; yet there is an underlying lyrical feeling which often brings the sun out from behind the clouds. The thoughtful subtlety of this playing is matched by a spontaneous response to Mozart at his most penetrating. The recording is extremely lifelike.

The New York-based Shanghai Quartet, who use modern instruments, have won glowing opinions from the American press and elsewhere, and no wonder. Their accounts of Mozart's last two quartets are second to none. They create a beautifully blended sound, warm and refined. Slow movements have a natural expressive flow, and there is all the delicacy of articulation needed for the dancing finales. They are recorded most naturally in a pleasingly spacious ambience.

String quintets

Complete Quintets: String Quintets 1 in B flat, K.174; 2 in C min., K.406; 3 in C, K.515; 4 in G min., K.516; 5 in D, K.593; 6 in E flat, K.614

☛ ⊙ (M) *** HM Cal. (ADD) CAL 3231/33. Talich Qt, Rehák, (i) Clarinet Quintet with Zahradnik

*** MDG 304 1031-2 (1 & 6); 304 1032-2 (2 & 3); 304 1106-2 (4 & 5). Ens. Villa Musica

(N) (M) ** DG (ADD) 477 5346 (2). Amadeus Qt, with Aronowitz

String Quintets 1 (with original version of Trio of the Minuet & Finale); 2–6

(BB) **(*) Naxos 8.553103 (1–2); 8.553104 (3–4); 8.553105 (5–6). Eder Qt, with Fehérvári

(i) *String Quintets 1–6; Divertimento for String Trio in E flat, K. 563*

(B) *** Ph. Trio (ADD) 470 950-2 (3). Grumiaux Trio, (i) with Gérecz, Lesueur

The six Mozart *String Quintets* played by the Talich Quartet and Karel Rehák are available in a mid-priced box, together with a radiant account of the *Clarinet Quintet* (with Bohyslav Zahradnik the sensitive soloist), on three Calliope discs which cost approximately the same as the pair of Duos above. The Calliope set will in the long run prove a far better investment.

On the bargain-priced Trio, Grumiaux's distinguished (1973) set of the *String Quintets* is coupled with his unsurpassed (1967) version of the rather less well-known but equally inspired *Divertimento for String Trio* – an ideal linking. The remastering of these fine analogue recordings is outstandingly natural – a tribute to the Philips engineers, for the bloom on the original LPs remains on CD, yet detail is enhanced.

The augmented Eder Quartet also offer a complete set of the *String Quintets*, and the first disc displays their unexaggerated Mozartian style, a fine blend of tone and musicianship. While not a match for the Talich, these performances are eminently recommendable to those with limited budgets. The last two quintets come off very well indeed. The recording is close but very realistic.

Another fine modern-instrument set of the Mozart *Quintets* comes from the Ensemble Villa Musica, led by Rainer Kussmaul, each disc available separately. The first, with the *B flat* and *E flat Quintets*, is particularly fine; the third includes a very impressive account of the *G minor*. The recording is real and present, although the balance lets Kussmaul's principal violin rather dominate the proceedings. The older recordings by the Grumiaux ensemble and the Talich are not surpassed.

The Amadeus is a distinguished team, and this set will give pleasure to their admirers. They play beautifully and are very well recorded; but other versions, notably the Grumiaux account on Philips, are fresher and purer in utterance.

String Quintets 3–6

(B) **(*) Hyp. Dyad CDD 22005 (2). Salomon Qt, Whistler

The Salomon Quartet use period instruments and are at their very best in the *G minor Quintet*, with the beauty of the *Adagio* sensitively caught. The final work is also splendidly played, but the *C major* and *D major Quintets* are cooler. The Hyperion recording is excellent, and this Dyad costs the same as a single premium-priced CD; but other modern- instrument performances find greater depth in this music.

Violin sonatas

Violin Sonatas 17–28; 32–4; Sonatina in F, K.547

(B) *** DG 463 749-2 (4). Perlman, Barenboim

(B) *** Decca (ADD) 448 526-2 (4). Goldberg, Lupu

Violin Sonatas 17–25; 12 Variations in G on 'La Bergère Célimène', K.359

☛ (B) *** Ph. Duo (ADD) 462 185-2 (2). Szeryng, Haebler

Violin Sonatas 17–20

(BB) **(*) Naxos 8.553111. Nishizaki, Jandó

Violin Sonatas 21–3; 25

(BB) **(*) Naxos 8.553110. Nishizaki, Jandó

Violin Sonatas 26–8

(BB) **(*) Naxos 8.553112. Nishizaki, Jandó

Violin Sonatas 32–3

(BB) **(*) Naxos 8.553590. Nishizaki, Jandó

Perlman and Barenboim form a distinguished team, with alert, vital playing and a sense of spontaneous music-making which pervades their four CDs. There is much attention to detail (though never fussy-sounding) which makes these come over as strikingly fresh accounts. Those who invest in this set will not be disappointed, and the recordings are vividly realistic.

Radu Lupu plays with uncommon freshness and insight, while Szymon Goldberg brings a wisdom, born of long experience, to these sonatas which is almost unfailingly revealing. Lupu gives instinctive musical support to his partner and both artists bring humanity and imagination to their performances. In short, very distinguished playing from both artists. The recordings were made in the Kingsway Hall in 1974 and were expertly balanced by Christopher Raeburn.

Ingrid Haebler brings an admirable vitality and robustness to her part. Szeryng's contribution is altogether masterly, and all these performances find both partners in complete rapport. The analogue recordings from the mid-1970s provide striking realism and truthfulness, and they have been transferred immaculately to CD. The *Variations* included in the set are managed with charm. The intimate atmosphere of these performances is particularly appealing.

The partnership of Takako Nishizaki and Jenö Jandó is very successful. In the earlier of the more mature sonatas, which date from 1778, the violin often takes a subsidiary role, and here the balance and Jandó's strong personality emphasize the effect. This is slightly less striking in K.379–80 (on the third disc) which are later (1781) and in which the part-writing is more equal. On the fourth CD of the series we move on to K.454 and K.481, which date from 1785 and 1786, respectively. The two instruments now form a much more equal partnership. Nishizaki's tone is small and at times a little thin and uncovered (rather like a period instrument) but seems perfectly scaled for Mozart; her playing is highly musical, and these artists strike a Mozartian symbiosis that is appealing in its fresh simplicity of approach.

Violin Sonatas 23 in D, K.306; 26 in B flat, K.378; 27 in G, K.379 & Sonata in B flat, K.372 (unfinished); Andante & Allegretto in C, K.404

(BB) **(*) EMI double forte (ADD) 5 74293-2 (2). Kagaan, Richter – BEETHOVEN: *Violin Sonatas 4 & 5* **(*)

These live (1974) accounts have all the excitement of being present at a concert, with very few irritations. The sound is vivid – a little dry, but more than acceptable. These are strong, vibrant performances, never rushed but always sparkling. A bargain with a fine coupling.

PIANO MUSIC

London Sketchbook (1764–5)

(BB) ** Naxos 8.554769. Kreuels, Vorarlberg Conservatory Ens. (members)

The 39 tiny pieces here come from the sketchbook containing the compositions of the eight-year-old Mozart on his visit to London, lumped together as K.15 in the Köchel catalogue. There are no masterpieces, but each of these miniatures has the nugget of a good idea, sharply expressed, the sort of material that, as he grew to maturity, Mozart was able to develop more elaborately. The pianist Hans-Udo Kreuels plays with an apt brightness and is well recorded by Austrian Radio. He himself has provided completions to two of the pieces which the boy left unfinished, a *Minuet* and a *Fugue*, in which he is joined by string-players from the Vorarlberg Conservatory Ensemble. An ideal disc for dipping into rather than playing all through at one go.

Complete works for piano

Complete Bargain Mozart Edition, Vol. 9: (i) *Complete Music for 2 Pianos and Piano Duets;* (ii) *Piano Sonatas 1–18; Fantasia in C min.;* (iii) *Variations, Rondos;* miscellaneous music for keyboard

(BB) **(*) Ph. (ADD/DDD) 464 850-2 (12). Haebler, Hoffmann, Demus, Badura-Skoda; (ii) Uchida; (iii) Haebler, Koopman

The highlight here is Uchida's complete set of the *Piano Sonatas* – her finest achievement on record. Not all the other performances are of this calibre, but they are all discussed below.

Piano duets

(i) *Andante with 5 Variations, K.501; Fugue in C min., K.426; Sonatas for Piano Duet: in C, K.19d; G, K.357; B flat, K.358; D, K.381; Sonata in D for 2 Pianos, K.448; F, K.497; C, K.521* (both for piano duet)

☛ **(N)** (BB) *** Warner Apex 2564 62037-2 (2). Güher & Süher Pekinel

This excellent duo are in their element in Mozart. Their playing is full of life and spirit, yet their vigour never rides roughshod over Mozart. The *Andante* of K.381 is beautifully poised, while the *molto allegro* finale of its D major companion (for two pianos) is memorably bold, rhythmic and infectious. Excellent modern digital recording makes this a first recommendation for this reportoire, even if the documentation is a little sparse.

Adagio & Allegro in F min., K.594; Andante & 5 Variations in G, K.501; Fantasia in F min., K.608; Sonatas in: C, K.19d; B flat, K.358; D, K.381; F, K.497; C, K.521; Sonata in D for 2 Pianos, K.448

☛ **(B)** *** DG Double 459 475-2 (2). Eschenbach, Frantz

(i) *Andante with 5 Variations, K.501; Fugue in C min., K.426; Sonatas for Piano Duet: in C, K.19d; D, K.381; G, K.357; B flat, K.358; F, K.497; C, K.521; Sonata in D for 2 Pianos, K.448;* (ii) *Larghetto & Allegro in E flat* (reconstructed Badura-Skoda)

(B) **(*) Ph. (ADD) Duo 454 026-2 (2). (i) Haebler, Hoffmann; (ii) Demus, Badura-Skoda

The Eschenbach/Frantz accounts of the Mozart piano duets were made between 1972 and 1975. They play with exemplary ensemble and fine sensitivity, and although finer performances of individual pieces may have come one's way, the standard maintained by these artists remains high throughout. The recordings are clean and well balanced, if occasionally a shade dry, but this is without doubt an excellent DG bargain Double.

The Philips two-CD set includes all the music Mozart composed for piano duet or two pianos, in elegant (if at times a little too dainty) performances by Ingrid Haebler and Ludwig Hoffmann in recordings dating from the mid-1970s. Also included is a Mozart fragment, the *Larghetto and Allegro in E flat*, probably written in 1782–3 and completed by Paul Badura-Skoda, who recorded it in 1971 for the Amadeo label

with Jörg Demus. Despite the occasional distant clink of Dresden china, all these performances give pleasure and are very decently recorded.

Andante with 5 Variations, K.501; Sonata in D, K.448

*** Chan. 9162. Lortie, Mercier – SCHUBERT: *Fantasia in F min.* ***

Andante & Variations in G, K.501 (for piano, 4 hands); *Sonata in D, K.448; Fantasia for Mechanical Organ in F min., K.608* (arr. Busoni for 2 pianos)

☛ **(N)** (M) *** Sony 517490-2. Perahia & Lupu – SCHUBERT: *Fantasia in D min.* ***

The partnership of two such individual artists as Murray Perahia and Radu Lupu produces magical results, particularly when it was set up in the context of the Aldeburgh Festival, playing at The Maltings concert hall. The *D Major Sonata*, like the Schubert *Fantasia*, was recorded live. With Perahia taking the primo part, his brightness and individual way of illuminating even the simplest passagework dominate the performance, challenging the more inward Lupu into comparably inspired playing. For this reissue two more works have been added, recorded at Abbey Road in 1990. The performance of the *Andante and Variations* is full of felicity and charm, but the transcribed *Fantasia* is another matter. All thoughts of the original instrumentation disappear in this remarkably arresting performance with its powerfully motivated outer movements and delicate but never flimsy *Adagio*. (Incidentally, Busoni's original arrangement omitted certain sections of Mozart's original, which have been restored here.) Very good recording makes this a reissue not to be missed.

The Louis Lortie–Hélène Mercier partnership also gives one of the most sensitive accounts of the *D major Sonata*, K.448, currently available on disc, and their account of the *Andante and Variations* is equally fine. The Schubert coupling is also recommendable. Very good recording.

Sonatas: in D, K.448; in C, K.521

(M) *** Decca (ADD) 466 821-2. Richter; Britten – SCHUBERT: *Andantino varié*; DEBUSSY: *En blanc et noir* ***

Characteristically, Britten and Richter in these magnificent Mozart works adopt phenomenally fast speeds in outer movements, with the finale of K.448 almost beyond belief, wonderfully clean in articulation. The sparkle of those movements is then set against broad, expressive treatments in the two slow movements. It is good to find the scale of the piano duet *Sonata*, K.521, reinforced by the observance of every single repeat, including the second half of the first movement, and with minor-key passages given heightened intensity in all three movements.

Sonatas: in F, K.497; in C, K.521. Pieces for mechanical organ: Adagio & Allegro in F min., K.594; Adagio & Allegro in F min., K.608

☛ ❂ *** Ottavio OTR C129242. Cooper, Queffélec

Above all, these performances convey a sense of joy in the music. The *Sonatas* – both highly inspired – are framed by the two works for mechanical clock, which here sound both thoughtful and unusually commanding: the opening *Adagio* of K.594 is wonderfully serene. The first movement of the *C major Sonata* sets off with great spirit, yet detail is always imaginatively observed. The slow movement of K.497 is a lovely, flowing melody, persuasively presented, while the finale has a most engaging lilt. Altogether this is playing of great distinction. Everything is marvellously fresh. Very strongly recommended.

Solo piano music

Piano Sonatas 1–18 (complete)
(B) *** EMI (ADD) 7 67294-2 (5). Barenboim

Piano Sonatas 1–18; Fantasia in C min., K.475; Variations, K.24–5; 54; 179–80; 264–5; 353–4; 398; 455; 500; 573; 613
(B) **(*) EMI 5 73915-2 (8). Barenboim

Piano Sonatas 1–18; Fantasia in C min., K.475
⊙━✿ (N) (B) PH. 468 356-2 (5). Uchida
(B) *** Decca (ADD) 443 717-2 (5). Schiff

Piano Sonatas 1–18; Fantasias: in D min., K.397; C min., K.475
*** DG (IMS) 431 760-2 (6). Pires

Piano Sonatas 1; 2; 9; 18
*** DG (IMS) 435 882-2. Pires

Piano Sonatas 3–4; 15: Andante & Allegro, K.533; Rondo, K.494
*** DG (IMS) 437 546-2. Pires

Piano Sonatas 5–6; 10
*** DG (IMS) 437 791-2. Pires

Piano Sonatas 7; 12; 17
*** DG (IMS) 439 769-2. Pires

Piano Sonatas 8; 13; 16
*** DG (IMS) 427 768-2. Pires

Piano Sonatas 11; 14; Fantasias: in C min., K.475; in D min., K.397
*** DG (IMS) 429 739-2. Pires

Piano Sonatas 1–18; Fantasias, K.457 & K.396; Variations, K.353; Variations, K.398 & K.460; Allegro, K.312; Minuet, K.355; Rondo, K.511; Adagio, K.540; Gigue, K.574
(M) (***) Music & Arts mono (ADD) CD-1001 (5). Kraus

Piano Sonatas 1–18; Sonatas in C, K.46d; in F, K.46e; Fantasia in C min., K.475
(B) *** DG (ADD) 463 137-2 (5). Eschenbach

Piano Sonatas 1–3
*** BIS CD 835. Brautigam (fortepiano)

Piano Sonatas 4–6
*** BIS CD 836. Brautigam (fortepiano)

Piano Sonatas 7–9
*** BIS CD 837. Brautigam (fortepiano)

Piano Sonatas 10–12
*** BIS CD 838. Brautigam (fortepiano)

Piano Sonatas 13–14; Fantasia in C min., K.475
*** BIS CD 839. Brautigam (fortepiano)

Piano Sonatas 15–18
*** BIS CD 840. Brautigam (fortepiano)

Adagio in B min., K.540; Eine kleine Gigue, K.574; Fantasy Fragment in D min., K.397; Klavierstücke in F, K.33b; Kleiner Trauermarsch, K.453a; Modulation Prelude in F/E min., K.6 Deest; Overture; Prelude in C, K.284a; Prelude and Fugue in C, K.394; Rondos, K.485 & K.511; Variations: K.24; K.25; K.180; K.264; K.265; K.352; K.353; K.354; K.398; K.455; K.457; K.460; K.573; K.613
(B) *** BIS CD 1266/676 (4). Brautigam (fortepiano)

Maria João Pires is a stylist and a fine Mozartian. She is

always refined yet never wanting in classical feeling, and she has a vital imagination. She strikes an ideal balance between poise and expressive sensibility, conveying a sense of spontaneity in everything she does. Moreover, the DG recording is full, and the slight dryness to the timbre suits the interpretations, which are expressively fluid and calm, without a trace of self-consciousness. While Uchida's much-praised versions are full of personal intimacy, Pires's more direct style with its tranquil eloquence is no less satisfying.

Ronald Brautigam's set is bursting with life and intelligence. He uses a 1992 copy (made in his native Amsterdam) of a fortepiano by Anton Gabriel Walter from about 1795. It is a very good instrument and he is a very good player. Dip in anywhere in this set and you will be rewarded with playing of great imagination and sensitivity – not to mention sureness and agility of mind and fingers, and he is completely inside the Mozartian sensibility of the period. Even if you prefer Mozart's keyboard music on the piano, you should investigate this set without delay. It brings Mozart to life in a way that almost no other period-instrument predecessor has done. This series has given great pleasure, and it is beautifully recorded too. It could not be more recommendable, now that the four CDs have reappeared offered for the price of two in a box, and very well documented.

Barenboim, while keeping his playing well within scale in its crisp articulation, refuses to adopt the Dresden china approach to Mozart's *Sonatas*. Even the little *C major*, K.545, designed for a young player, has its element of toughness, minimizing its 'eighteenth-century drawing-room' associations. Though – with the exception of the two minor-key *Sonatas* – these are relatively unambitious works, Barenboim's voyage of discovery brings out their consistent freshness, with the orchestral implications of some of the *Allegros* strongly established. The recording, with a pleasant ambience round the piano sound, confirms the apt scale.

EMI now also offer an alternative choice of a complete coverage of *all* the important solo piano music. The *Variations* were recorded – more forwardly – in Munich in 1991. As before, Barenboim's positive, direct approach brings all this music fully to life. But compared with the *Sonatas* the music is much more variable in interest, and this is a set to dip into with a degree of discretion, for Mozart occasionally seems almost on auto-pilot, writing for comparatively unsophisticated tastes.

Uchida's set of the Mozart *Sonatas*, with the *C minor Fantasia* thrown in for good measure, brings playing of consistently fine sense and sound musicianship. Every phrase is beautifully placed, every detail registers, and the early *Sonatas* are as revealing as the later ones. The piano recording is completely realistic, slightly distanced in a believable ambience.

András Schiff's earlier, Decca recordings now also reappear, in a bargain box. Schiff, without exceeding the essential Mozartian sensibility, takes a somewhat more romantic and forward-looking view of the music. His fingerwork is precise yet mellow, and his sense of colour consistently excites admiration. He is slightly prone to self-indulgence in the handling of some phrases, but such is the inherent freshness and spontaneity of his playing that one accepts the idiosyncrasies as a natural product of live performance. The piano is set just a little further back than in the Philips/Uchida recordings, and the acoustic is marginally more open, which suits his slightly more expansive manner.

Christoph Eschenbach gives consistently well-turned, cool and elegant performances without affectation or mannerism. Those looking for an unidiosyncratic, direct approach to Mozart should find this poised, immaculate pianism to their taste. The famous *Andante grazioso* variations which form the first movement of the *Sonata in A*, K.331, are entirely characteristic, played very simply and directly. Other pianists are gentler, more romantic, but Eschenbach's taste cannot be faulted.

Lili Kraus, born in Budapest in 1905, recorded this cycle of the Mozart *Sonatas*, as well as shorter pieces, in New York for the Haydn Society in 1954. Compared with her later recording, issued by Sony, the closeness of the sound allows one to appreciate more the diamond clarity of Kraus's playing with its high dynamic contrasts, even if *pianissimos* are not as hushed as they might be. These earlier performances are not only more dramatic but more spontaneous-sounding too, with firmer technical control. The mono sound is well transferred to make it firm and vivid. In both recordings Kraus omits the composite *Sonata in F*, K.533/494, which Mozart created by adding to two late movements an earlier *Rondo* in less complex style.

Piano Sonatas 3; 10; 13; Adagio, K.540; Rondo, K.485

☞— (M) *** DG 445 517-2. Horowitz

Playing of such strong personality from so great an artist is self-recommending. With Horowitz there were astonishingly few reminders of the passage of time and the artistry and magnetism remain undiminished. The recordings were made in the pianist's last vintage period, between 1985 and 1989, in either a New York studio, the pianist's home, or an Italian studio in Milan (K.333). Remarkable playing, not always completely free from affectation; but for variety of articulation just sample the *Allegretto grazioso* finale of K.333 and, for simply expressed depth of feeling, the *Adagio*, K.540.

Piano Sonatas 7–10, K.309/11 & K.331

☞— (N) (BB) *** Regis (ADD) RRC 1207. Walter Klien

Walter Klien's set of the Mozart sonatas, dates from 1964. The discs were originally issued in Vox Boxes (three LPs at a time). But they eventually found their way individually on to the celebrated Turnabout label. Now they are reintroduced into the British catalogue on Regis. Klien's playing is fresh, strongly characterized and with constant sensitivity; he is determined to show that there are no favourites, just a succession of masterpieces. Even so in this sampler the exquisite *Andante cantabile* of the *A minor* (K.310) and the spirited opening *Allegro* of the *D major* (K.311) are particularly memorable. On CD the recording is clean and clear, a little dry perhaps, but these performances are special.

Piano Sonatas 8–9, K.310/311; in F, K.533/494; Fantasy in D min., K.397

**(*) Ph. 473 689-2. Brendel

The three stars signify that this is a highly acclaimed Mozart recital which will give much satisfaction to admirers of this great pianist. But we find Brendel's playing here too studied and wanting in real spontaneity. It does not speak with the naturalness of line that distinguished his Mozart in the 1970s. You should note that it has been showered with plaudits and, unlike us, you may not be disturbed by the exaggerated staccatos and other idiosyncratic touches. Wonderfully natural recorded sound.

Piano Sonatas 8 in A min. K.310; 10 in C, K.330; 11 in A, K.331; 14 in C min., K.457; 16 in C, K.545

*(*) Sony (ADD) SMK 87860. Gould

These recordings were made between 1967 and 1973, but Glenn Gould's eccentricities persist throughout most of the music, as does the vocalise. As with his Haydn recordings, made at end of his recording career, Gould often makes a sensitively expressive response to slow movements, the *Andante cantabile* of K.310 *in A minor*, for instance; but he charges into the first movement breathlessly, and the finale is similarly rushed. Probably the finest performance here is *No. 14 in C minor*, K.457; *No. 10 in C major*, K.330, is clean and classical. But what is the listener to make of the perversely mannered and deliberate presentation of the opening *Andante grazioso* theme of the *A major*, K.331? And the staccato Minuet and slow, very precise *Alla turca* finale are equally exasperating. This sounds like the playing of a very talented child. So would the sharp articulation of the famous *C major*, K.545 – which is almost a caricature – if the fingerwork were not so dazzling. This recital is therefore strictly for Gould fans only. The piano-tone has the usual sparing sonority, but the recording is quite faithful.

Piano Sonatas 8; 11; 13; 14; Adagio, K.540; Fantasia, K.475; Rondo, K.511; 9 Variations in D on a Minuet by Dupont, K.573

(B) **(*) Ph. Duo (ADD/DDD) 454 244-2 (2). Brendel

The recordings of the *A major Sonata*, K.331, and the *B flat*, K.333, come from 1971 and 1975 respectively and they show Brendel at his very finest, while the *B minor Adagio* is also memorable. K.331, with its engaging opening theme and variations and justly famous *Alla turca* finale, is a joy. The analogue recording, too, is most realistic. However, the *A minor*, K.310, and the *C minor*, recorded digitally in the following decade, are more controversial. The first movement of the *A minor* has immaculate control but is more than a little schoolmasterly, particularly in the development. Brendel seems unwilling to seduce us by beauty of sound, and the result is self-conscious playing, immaculately recorded. Fortunately, he is back on form in the *Fantasia in C minor*, the *Rondo* and the *Variations*.

Piano Sonatas 8; 11; 15

☞— ✪ *** Sony SK 48233. Perahia

Such is Murray Perahia's artistry that one is never consciously aware of it. Nothing is beautified, nor does he shrink from conveying that hint of pain that fleetingly disturbs the symmetry of the slow movements. The Sony engineers provide excellent sound.

Piano Sonatas 10; 11; 12

(BB) **(*) EMI Encore 5 74893-2. Zacharias

EMI have chosen well from Christian Zacharias's series of the Mozart *Sonatas*, for all three works here show him in very good form. Even if at times he is a shade self-aware, both K.331 (with its sparkling *Alla turca* finale) and the *F major*, K.332, are played with real character. This gifted artist is an intelligent, cultured player with an immaculate technique, and he is most naturally recorded.

Piano Sonatas 10; 11; 16; Rondo, K.511

☞— *** Ph. 462 903-2. Brendel

Although for the most part recorded 'live', Brendel's performances here have an appealingly thoughtful intimacy, as if he were hardly conscious of the audience. Yet one still has the sense of being in Brendel's presence. Interestingly, the studio recording of the *C major Sonata*, K.330, seems very slightly less spontaneous in feeling than the rest of the programme.

But altogether this is playing of distinction. Audience noises are minimal (although applause is included), and the recording, although fairly closely observed, is very natural.

Piano Sonatas 15 in F, K.533/494; 16 in C, K.545; 17 in B flat, K.570; 18 in D, K.576

**(*) Avie AV 0025. Haefliger

Andreas Haefliger is an artist of calibre who gives splendidly vital accounts of these sonatas. He does not bring the same variety of keyboard colour and dynamic nuance or poetic feeling as do the likes of Perahia or Pletnev, but he has sobriety and an undoubted sense of style and unfailing musicianship. However, these four works are not otherwise available together on a single CD, and it remains a satisfying collection and benefits from excellent recorded sound.

Piano Sonata 17

(***) Testament mono STB 1089. Gilels – CHOPIN: Sonata 2; SHOSTAKOVICH: Preludes & Fugues Nos 1, 5 & 24 (***)

The *B flat Sonata* was recorded in Paris at the Théâtre des Champs-Elysées in March 1954. The sound is a little dry and close, but the playing has a simplicity and poetry that completely transcend sonic limitations.

ORGAN MUSIC

Andante in F, K.616; Adagio & Allegro in F min., K.594; Fantasia in F min. (Adagio & Allegro), K.608 (all for musical clock); Allegro in G (Veronese), K.72a; Gigue in G, K.574; (i) Epistle Sonatas: in F, K.244; in C, K.328

(BB) ** Teldec (ADD) 0630 17371-2. Tachezi (organ of Basilika Maria Treu, Vienna); (i) with Alice and Nikolaus Harnoncourt and Pfeiffer

Mozart is never really thought of as a composer for the organ, but he loved its challenge and, whenever he travelled, always made a point of seeking out a local instrument. The problem for us was that he liked best of all to improvise and seldom wrote anything down. Until now, the only 'organ works' we have had on record have been the three pieces he wrote for Count Deym's mechanical organ attached to a clock. Mozart had no opinion of the mechanism for which his music was commissioned and is known to have wished the pieces were intended for a large instrument. To these Herbert Tachezi adds a brief *Allegro* and an attractive *Gigue*, plus two of the *Epistle Sonatas*, in which he is joined by the Harnoncourt Trio. The performances overall are acceptable and well registered, but there is nothing distinctive about this record, although the sound is excellent.

VOCAL MUSIC

Complete Bargain Mozart Edition, Vol. 11: Adagio & Fugue, K.456; Apollo et Hyacinthus, K.38; Ave verum corpus; Benedictus sit Deus, K.117; La Betulia liberata, K.118; Cibavit eos, K.44; Davidde Penitente, K.469; Dir, Seele des Weltalls, K.429; Dixit Dominus & Magnificat, K.193; Ergo interest ... Quaere superna, K.143; Exsultate jubilate, K.165; Gesellenreise, K.468; God is our refuge, K.20; Grabmusik, K.42; Inter natos mulierum, K.72; Kleine deutsche Kantata; Kommet her, ihr freshen Sünder, K.146; Kyries: K.33, K.80, K.91, K.322/3 & K.341; Lasst uns mit geschlungen Händen, K.623a; Laut verkünde unsre Freude, K.623; Litaniae Laurentanae de BMV, K.109 & K.195; Litaniae de venerabili

altaris sacramento, K.125 & K.243; Lobgesang auf die feierliche Johannisloge, K.148; Der Maurerfreude, K.471; Miserere, K.85; Misericordias Domini, K.222; Quaerite primum regnum Dei, K.86; Regina coeli, K.108, K.127 & K.276; Sancta Maria, mater Dei, K.273; Scandal coeli limina, K.34; Die Schuldigkeit des ersten Gebots, K.35; Sub tuum presidium, K.198; Te Deum in C, K.141; Veneti populi, K.260; Veni, Sancte Spiritus, K.47; Vesperae de Dominica, K.321; Vesperae solennes de confessor, K.339; Züm Schluss der Freimaurerelloge, K.484; Zür Eröffnung der Freimaurerelloge, K.483

(B) *** Ph. (ADD/DDD) 464 870-2. Soloists, Dresden State O, Schreier; Salzburg Mozarteum O & Ch., Leipzig R. Ch. & O, Hager; L. Symphony Ch. & LSO, C. Davis; Stuttgart RSO; Frankfurt R. O, Marriner

It is fascinating to find that the boy Mozart's very first religious piece is an unaccompanied motet, written in London to an English text, *God is our refuge*. Herbert Kegel with the Dresden Staatskapelle and his Leipzig Radio Choir are responsible for the great majority of the pieces here, fresh and alert, if on occasion rhythmically too rigid. The big exception is the great setting of the *Solemn Vespers*, K.339, for which Sir Colin Davis's 1971 version has understandably been preferred, when the young Kiri Te Kanawa sings the heavenly soprano setting of *Laudate Dominum* so ravishingly. She is also the soloist in the early cantata, *Exsultate, jubilate*, with its brilliant *Alleluia*. Those 1971 recordings, made in London, are bass-heavy, but the rest bring very fresh and clean recording, with the choir generally more forwardly placed than in the recordings of Mozart's Masses, made by the same forces.

The two big oratorios are both early works, *La Betulia liberata* and (even earlier, dating from his twelfth year) *Die Schuldigkeit des ersten Gebots* ('The Duty of the First Commandment'). *Davidde penitente* is the cantata largely derived from the torso of the *C minor Mass*, while the sixth disc, in many ways the most inspired of all, contains the Masonic music, vividly done in Dresden under the direction of Peter Schreier. For convenience that disc also includes the purely instrumental Masonic music, the *Maurerische Trauermusik* and the *Adagio and Fugue in C minor*. Directed by Leopold Hager, *La Betulia liberata* is a plain, well-sung performance that does not quite disguise the piece's excessive length. Sir Neville Marriner is the conductor both of *Die Schuldigkeit* and of *Davidde penitente*, giving sparkle to the early oratorio and vigour to the cantata, a fine piece. Full texts are given, and informative notes on individual works.

Complete Bargain Mozart Edition, Vol. 12: Canons; Concert arias; Vocal ensembles; Lieder; Notturni; Alternative opera arias

(B) *** Ph. (IMS) (ADD/DDD) 464 880-2 (10). Soloists; Netherlands Wind Ens. Salzburg Mozart O; ASMF; Dresden PO; Bav. RSO; Munich R. O; Dresden State O; Hager; Marriner; Boehm; Harrer; Mancusi; Schreier; Weigle; C. Davis

This Philips set offers not just a collection of a dozen or so ensembles and a whole disc of 35 canons (some of them instrumental) but also some fascinating alternative versions and substitute arias for different Mozart operas, from *La finta semplice* and *Mitridate* through to the three Da Ponte masterpieces. It is fascinating to have Bryn Terfel, for example, as Figaro in a varied recitative and slightly extended version of the Act I aria, *Non piu' andrai*. Eva Lind is vocally a less happy choice for the items involving Susanna and Zerlina, and generally the sopranos chosen for this collection, stylish Mozartians as they are, have less sumptuous voices than those on the Decca set.

In the Lieder Elly Ameling is the ideal soprano for such fresh and generally innocent inspirations, with her voice at its purest and sweetest when she made the recordings in 1977. In the 1973 recordings of the *Notturni* (setting Italian texts by Metastasio) she is well matched by her soprano and baritone partners, though these are mostly plainer, less distinctive miniatures. Included are two hymns with organ and two tiny songs with mandolin, while aptly the very last of the series, K.598, is one of the lightest of all, *Children's Games*, sparklingly done. The recordings come up with fine freshness and presence.

51 Concert Arias

(B) *** Decca (ADD/DDD) 455 241-2 (5). Te Kanawa, Gruberová, Berganza, Laki, Hobarth, Winbergh; VCO, Fischer; or LSO, Pritchard; Fischer-Dieskau, V. Haydn O, Reinhard Peters; Corena, ROHCGO, Quadri

This very comprehensive coverage is based on a five-LP Decca set of the complete concert arias for female voice, published in 1981, to which those for male voice have subsequently been added. Berganza's collection includes the most demanding soprano aria of all, *Ch'io me scordi di te?*, recorded (with Pritchard and the LSO) a decade earlier than the rest. Te Kanawa opens the programme memorably. Her disc is available separately – see below. Gruberová's contribution is hardly less brilliant and charming, her singing full of sparkle and character, and superbly articulated. The others, Elfrieda Hobarth and Krisztina Laki, are less individual personalities but do not disappoint vocally. Laki shows impressive coloratura in her opening aria, the little-known *Fra cento affanni*, K.88, and she is equally impressive in the lyrical flow of *Non curo l'affetto*, which again demands comparable bravura. Hobarth's style is more operatic and she becomes a veritable Queen of the Night in tackling the fearsome upper tessitura of *Ma che vi fece, o stelle*, K.368, and *Mia speranza adorata!*, K.416, both of which are accomplished with confident bravado.

The digital recordings by Gösta Winbergh, an exceptionally stylish Mozart tenor, were added later; he rises splendidly to the challenges of such splendid arias as *Per pietà non ricercate*, K.420, and *Aura che intorno spiri*, K.431, using his clean, heady tenor very effectively if without the final degree of personal charisma. Fischer-Dieskau's contribution was a separate undertaking, recorded in 1969, and it includes a beautiful aria from 1787, *Mentre ti lascio*, which reveals Mozart's inspiration at its keenest. The other items too bring their delights. Fernando Corena's three contributions are among the first of any Mozart arias to be recorded in stereo, in 1960. In *Alcandro, lo confesso ... Non so d'onde viene*, K.512, and *Per questa bella mano*, K.612, he is less than ideally stylish and in the latter not always absolutely secure in intonation. Admittedly, some of the florid passages are fiendishly difficult for a bass to cope with but, when strained, Corena has a tendency to slide between the notes to ungainly effect. Yet he is at his very finest in the *buffo* aria, *Rivolcete a lui lo sguardo*, K.584, originally written for *Così fan tutte* and later cut because of its length. It is a superb piece and it suits Corena's voice well, so that the full power is brought out magnificently. The CD transfers throughout are of high quality, and full translations are included, but the accompanying essay by Kenneth Chalmers documents the music only sketchily, because of limited space.

Concert arias

(M) *** DG (ADD) 449 723-2. Janowitz, VSO, Boettcher

In 1966 when this recording was made (in the Grosser Saal of the Vienna Musikverein) Gundula Janowitz's voice combined a glorious tonal beauty with a surprising degree of flexibility so that Mozart's cruelly difficult divisions – usually written deliberately to tax the original ladies involved – present no apparent difficulty. Janowitz is helped by a flattering, reverberant acoustic, but there is no mistaking the singer's ability to shade and refine the tone at will. An excellent collection of delightful concert arias that are too often neglected nowadays, thanks to the vagaries of modern concert-planning.

Concert arias: Opera arias: (ii) *Le nozze di Figaro: Porgi amor; E Susanna non vien! ... Dove sono*; (iii) *Der Schauspieldirektor: Bester Jüngling!*

(M) *** Decca 440 401-2. Te Kanawa; (i) V. CO, Fischer; (ii) LPO, Solti; (iii) VPO, Pritchard

Kiri Te Kanawa's Decca set of Mozart's concert arias for soprano, recorded in 1982, makes a beautiful and often brilliant recital. Items range from one of the very earliest arias, *Oh temerario Arbace!*, already memorably lyrical, to the late *Vado, ma dove?*, here sung for its beauty rather than for its drama. The arias from *Figaro* and *Schauspieldirektor* come from the complete Decca sets and show the singer at her finest.

Concert arias:

🔊 (M) *** EMI mono/stereo 5 74803-2. Schwarzkopf, Gieseking, Brendel, LSO, Szell

Schwarzkopf's classic recital of the Mozart songs with Gieseking was recorded in 1955 and includes the famous *Das Veilchen*. With such inspired performances, one hardly worries about the mono sound. The coupling includes Schwarzkopf's much later recordings (1968) of four concert arias with Szell conducting – including the most taxing of all, *Ch'io mi scordi di te*. Though the voice is not quite so fresh here, the artistry and imagination are supreme, and the stereo recording helps to add bloom. Thankfully, full texts and translations are included in this mid-price release.

Concert arias

(BB) *** Virgin 2x1 5 61573-2 (2). Lootens, Prégardien, La Petite Bande, Kuijken – *Horn Concertos* ***

This is a highly authentic collection of concert arias, several comparatively rare, divided between two fine artists who not only have appealing voices but understand about period style, and ornamentation. Lena Lootens produces nimble coloratura (as in the engaging *Voi avete un cor fedele*) and can be dramatic or provide a lovely legato line, and in both respects Christoph Prégardien is consistently her equal. The accompaniments are fresh, the recording is vivid; but it was a curious idea to couple this programme with the *Horn Concertos*, even though they are also first-rate period performances.

Concert aria: *Ch'io mi scordi di te?, K.505*

(***) Testament mono SBT 1178. Schwarzkopf, Anda, Philh. O, Ackermann – BACH: *Cantatas 199; 202* ***

As John Steane points out in his most illuminating note, there is a fascinating contrast between this account of *Ch'io mi scordi di te?*, recorded in 1955 with Géza Anda playing the difficult piano obbligato, and Schwarzkopf's classic recording with Alfred Brendel and George Szell of 1968. The voice may be fuller in the later one, but this is uniquely fresh and urgent, with Schwarzkopf's vehement side given freer rein. A splendid and valuable supplement to the Bach recordings, which have also remained unissued for far too long.

Concert arias: (i) *Ch'io mi scordi di te?; Nehmt meinen Dank, ihr holden Gönner!, K.383; Voi, avete un cor fedele. Il re pastore: Aer tranquillo e di sereni;* (ii) *L'amerò sarò costante; Ah, lo previdi; Zaïde: Ruhe sanft, mein holdes Leben; Trostios schluchzet Philomele*

- (B) *** Double Decca (ADD) 458 084-2 (2). Kirkby, AAM, Hogwood; (i) with Lubin (fortepiano); (ii) Hirons (violin) – (with Recital ***)

This delightful recital, recorded in 1988–9, is admirably suited to Emma Kirkby's sweetly confident line and dazzling coloratura. She is ideally cast as Amita (originally a castrato role) in *Il re pastore* and as the heroine of *Zaïde*. Indeed, her rapturous line in *L'amerò, sarò costante* is fully worthy of Mozart's imaginative accompaniment (including violin obbligato). She is a compellingly passionate Andromeda in projecting the pain and rage of *Ah, lo previdi*, and very touching in the equally ambitious but more expressive *Ch'io mi scordi di te?* Here Stephen Lubin contributes the fortepiano accompaniment which Mozart himself played at its first performance in Vienna by Nancy Storace (who created the role of Susanna in *Le nozze di Figaro*). Hogwood's accompaniments are both stylish and warmly, dramatically supportive, and the Walthamstow recording has a fine, spacious bloom.

Concert aria: *Ombra felice, K.255; Opera arias: Ascanio in Alba: Ah di si nobil alma; Mitridate: Venga pur, Gia dagli occhi*

*** Virgin 5 45365-2. Daniels, OAE, Bicket – GLUCK; HANDEL: *Arias* ***

Under the title '*Sento amor*', David Daniels offers one of the finest of counter-tenor recitals. In the arias from early Mozart operas, the brilliance of his singing is what stands out above all, giving beauty and energy to the florid writing, as well as a deeper expressiveness to the lyrical passages than one might expect. At once pure and warm, completely avoiding the usual counter-tenor hoot, placing his voice flawlessly, Daniels is exceptional even in an age which has produced many outstanding rivals.

Concert aria: *Ridente la calma, K.152*

*** Decca 440 297-2. Bartoli, Schiff – BEETHOVEN: *Che fa il mio bene?*, etc.; HAYDN: *Arianna a Naxos*; SCHUBERT: *Da quel sembiante appresi*, etc. ***

Ridente la calma is invested with much innocent charm by Cecilia Bartoli within an interesting collection of Italian songs by German composers.

Lieder: *Abendempfindung; Als Luise die Briefe; An Chloe; Die betrogene Welt; Dans un bois solitaire; Komm, liebe Zither; Oiseaux, si tous les ans; Sehnsucht nach dem Frühling; Der Zauberer*

*** DG (IMS) 447 106-2. Von Otter, Tan (fortepiano) – HAYDN: *Songs* ***

A delightful recital in all respects. There is a winning charm in the opening *Komm, liebe Zither*, and *Oiseaux, si tous les ans* is hardly less appealing. Melvyn Tan accompanies most sensitively and – as so often with this artist – makes one feel that nothing other than a fortepiano could have been used to give

these songs the right lift. The balance seems just about ideal, and the Haydn couplings are equally pleasing.

Masonic music

Masonic Funeral Music (Maurerische Trauermusik), K.477; Die ihr des unermesslichen Weltalls Schöpfer ehrt (cantata), *K.619; Die ihr einem neuen Grade, K.468; Dir, Seele des Weltalls* (cantata), *K.429; Ihr unsre neuen Leiter* (song), *K.484; Lasst uns mit geschlungnen Händen, K.623a; Laut verkünde unsre Freude, K.623; O heiliges Band* (song), *K.148; Sehen, wie dem starren Forscherange, K.471; Zerfliesset heut', geliebte Brüder, K.483*

(M) *** Decca (ADD) (IMS) 425 722-2. Krenn, Krause, Edinburgh Festival Ch., LSO, Kertész

This Decca reissue contains the more important of Mozart's Masonic music in first-class performances, admirably recorded. Most striking of all is Kertész's strongly dramatic account of the *Masonic Funeral Music*; the two lively songs for chorus, *Zerfliesset heut'* and *Ihr unsre neuen Leiter*, are sung with warm humanity and are also memorable. Indeed, the choral contribution is most distinguished throughout, and Werner Krenn's light tenor is most appealing in the other items, which he usually dominates.

Sacred Vocal Music

Ave verum corpus, K.618; Exsultate, jubilate, K.165; Kyrie in D min., K.341; Vesperae solennes de confessore in C, K.339

- *** Ph. 412 873-2. Te Kanawa, Bainbridge, R. Davies, Howell, L. Symphony Ch., LSO, C. Davis

This disc could hardly present a more delightful collection of Mozart choral music, ranging from the early soprano cantata, *Exsultate, jubilate*, with its famous setting of *Alleluia*, to the equally popular *Ave verum*. Kiri Te Kanawa is the brilliant soloist in the cantata, and her radiant account of the lovely *Laudate Dominum* is one of the highspots of the *Solemn Vespers*, here given a fine, responsive performance. The 1971 recording has been remastered effectively, although the choral sound is not ideally focused.

(i–ii) *Ave verum corpus, K.618;* (iii–iv) *Exsultate, jubilate, K.165; Masses Nos. (i–iii; v) 10 in C (Missa brevis): Spatzenmesse, K.220; (ii–iii; vi) 16 in C (Coronation), K.317*

(M) *** DG (IMS) (ADD) 419 060-2. (i) Regensburg Cathedral Ch.; (ii) Bav. RSO, Kubelik; (iii) Mathis; (iv) Dresden State O, Klee; (v) Troyanos, Laubenthal, Engen; (vi) Procter, Grobe, Shirley-Quirk, Bav. R. Ch.

Kubelik draws a fine, vivid performance of the *Coronation Mass* from his Bavarian forces and is no less impressive in the earlier *Missa brevis*, with excellent soloists in both works. Then Edith Mathis gives a first-class account of the *Exsultate, jubilate* as an encore. The concert ends with Bernard Klee directing a serenely gentle account of the *Ave verum corpus* (recorded in 1979).

(i) *Exsultate, jubilate, K.165;* (ii) *Litaniae Lauretanae in D, K.195; Mass 16 (Coronation), K.317;* (iii) *Requiem Mass (No. 19) in D min., K.626*

(B) **(*) Double Decca (ADD) 443 009-2 (2). (i) Spoorenberg; (ii; iii) Cotrubas, Watts, Tear, Shirley-Quirk; (ii) Oxford Schola Cantorum; (iii) ASMF Ch; (i-iii), ASMF, Marriner

It is good to have Marriner's 1971 (Argo) recordings of two of

Mozart's most appealing early choral works, the *Litaniae Lauretanae* and the *Coronation Mass*, back in the catalogue on this Double Decca set. The solo work is particularly good (notably Ileana Cotrubas in the two lovely *Agnus Dei* versions) and the Academy Choir is on its best form. Erna Spoorenberg's impressive *Exsultate, jubilate* was recorded earlier (1966). However, Marriner generates less electricity than usual in the coupled (1977) *Requiem Mass*. It is interesting to have a version which uses the Beyer Edition and a text which aims at removing the faults of Süssmayr's completion. Solo singing is good, and some of the choruses (the *Dies irae*, for instance) are vibrant, but at other times they are less alert and the tension slackens. The sound is excellent, well balanced and vivid.

(i) *Litaniae Lauretanae in D, K.195;* (ii; iii) *Litaniae de venerabili altaris sacramento, K.243;* (iii; iv) *Mass 12 in C (Spaur), K.258; Vesperae solennes de confessore, K.339;* (ii; iii) *Vesperae solennes de Domenica, K.321*

(B) *** Double Decca (ADD) 458 379-2 (2). (i) Cotrubas, Watts, Tear, Shirley-Quirk, Oxford Schola Cantorum, ASMF, Marriner; (ii) Marshall, Cable, Evans, Roberts; (iii) St John's College, Cambridge, Ch., Wren O, Guest; (iv) Palmer, Cable, Langridge, Roberts

Readers will note that Marriner's performance of the *Litaniae Lauretanae in D*, K.195, is also available on another Double Decca (see above). Mozart made four settings of the Litany of which the *Litaniae de venerabili altaris sacramento* is the last, written in 1776. It is ambitiously scored and is Mozart at his most imaginative and vital; the artists here rise to the occasion and give a highly responsive performance, with Margaret Marshall outstanding among the soloists. The *Spaur Mass* is not among Mozart's most inspired, but its directness is appealing and the *Benedictus* offers a fine Mozartian interplay of chorus and soloists. In Guest's vigorous performance it is very enjoyable. The vibrant *Vesperae solennes de Domenica* opens with a series of brilliant choral settings. Margaret Marshall is appropriately agile in the lively soprano solo of the *Laudate Dominum*, and the work closes with an ambitious *Magnificat*, in which all the participants are joined satisfyingly together. The collection is completed with the masterly *Vesperae solennes de confessore*, and although Guest's account does not always match Sir Colin Davis's Philips version (see above under *Ave verum corpus*) – with Felicity Palmer a less poised soloist than Kiri Te Kanawa – the Decca has the advantage of authenticity in the use of boys in the chorus. Moreover the CD transfer of these (originally Argo) recordings offers a brighter, sharper focus than the less well-defined Philips sound.

Complete Bargain Mozart Edition, Vol. 10: (i) *Masses 1 (Missa brevis), K.49; 2 (Missa brevis), K.65; 3 (Dominicus), K.66; 4, K.139; 5 (Pastoral), K.140; 6 (Missa brevis), K.192; 7 (Missa in honorem Ssmae Trinitatis), K.167; 9 (Missa brevis), K.194; 10 (Spatzenmesse), K.220; 11 (Credo), K.257; 12 (Spaur), K.258; 13 (Organ Solo), K.259; 14 (Missa longa), K.262; 15 (Missa brevis), K.275; 16 (Coronation) K.317; 17 (Missa solemnis), K.337; 18 (Great), K.427 (rev. Schmitt & Gardiner); 19 (Requiem), K.626 (completed Süssmayr).* (ii; iii) *Epistle Sonatas for Organ & Orchestra 1-17;* (ii) *Andante in F, K.616; Fantasia in F min., K.606.*

(B) ***Ph. (DDD/ADD) 464 820-2 (11). (i) Soloists; Leipzig R. Ch. & SO, or Dresden PO, Kegel; V. Boys' Ch., Ch. Viennensis, VSO, Harrer; Alldis Ch., LSO, C. Davis;

Monteverdi Ch., E. Bar. Sol., Gardiner; Leipzig R. Ch., Dresden State O, Schreier; (ii) Barenboim; (iii) German Bach Soloists, Winschermann

In the Complete Bargain Mozart Edition only the *Great C minor Mass* has period performers. John Eliot Gardiner's inspired reading, with superb soloists as well as his Monteverdi Choir and English Baroque Soloists, has rightly been chosen, and the *Requiem* comes in another outstanding modern version, with the Dresden Staatskapelle and Leipzig Radio Choir conducted by Peter Schreier, as imaginative a conductor as he is a tenor. That same choir and orchestra under the choir's regular conductor, Herbert Kegel, is responsible for the great bulk of the rest of the Masses. With the chorus tending to be placed a little backwardly, it does not always sound its freshest, but performances – with consistently clean-toned soloists, including latterly Mitsuko Shirai – are bright and well sprung. Sir Colin Davis and the LSO in the earliest recording here, dating from 1971, take a weightier view than any in the *Credo Mass*, K.257, with sound bass-heavy, but again his vigour and freshness are very compelling. Two favourite Masses, the *Coronation Mass* and the *Spatzenmesse* (Sparrow Mass), come in performances conducted by Uwe Christian Harrer with the Vienna Symphony Orchestra and the Vienna Boys' Choir; boys also distinctively take the soprano and alto solos. Though Harrer's speeds tend to be slow, the rhythmic buoyancy is most compelling, with choral sound full and forward.

The *Epistle Sonatas* make a curious supplement for the Masses but they are played here with conviction, and in the two solo works Barenboim's registration is particularly appealing.

Masses: 2 (Missa brevis), K.65; 3 (Dominicus), K.66; 4 (Waisenhaus), K.139; 7 (Missa in honorem Ssmae Trinitas); 10 (Spatzenmesse), K.220; 11 (Credo), K.257; 12 (Spaur), K.258; 13 (Organ Solo), K.259; 16 (Coronation Mass), K.317; 17 (Missa solemnis), K.337; 18 (Great), K.427; 19 (Requiem), K.626; Ave verum corpus, K.618

(BB) **(*) Virgin 2x1 5 61769-2 (5). Frimmer, Kwella, Monoyios, Montague, Schlick, Graf, Groenewold, Chance, Pfaff, Prégardien, Schäfer, Mertens, Selig, Cologne Chamber Ch., Coll. Cartusianum, Neumann

As can be seen from our comments about the Virgin Double of Masses Nos. 16–18 below, Peter Neumann's performances are fresh, stylish, warmly enjoyable and very well sung. Most importantly, these artists give a very fine, dramatic account of the *Requiem* (not included below), and the recording here is excellent, clear and vivid. The soloists are all very good throughout, and the other Masses, early and late, have plenty of character. The backward balance of the chorus is not enough of a problem to make this other than a worthwhile collection of some of Mozart's finest non-operatic vocal music for those not wanting to stretch to the complete Harnoncourt edition.

Mass 3 in C (Dominicus), K.66; Vesperae de Domenica, K.321

(M) *** Teldec 2292 46469-2. Margiono, Bonney, Von Magnus, Heilmann, Cachemaille, Arnold Schoenberg Ch., V. Hofburgkapelle Ch. Scholars, VCM, Harnoncourt

Harnoncourt is at his finest in this splendidly lively Mass, which the thirteen-year-old Mozart wrote for a personal friend ten years his senior when he took holy orders, and the direct Harnoncourt style, with its strong accents and positive characterization, brings it vividly to life. The more ambitious

Vesperae de Domenica, written a decade later, forms a neat and joyful *Missa brevis*, here refreshingly alive and brimful of variety of invention. Again the singing of chorus and soloists alike is highly stimulating, and Harnoncourt's affection brings a committed and vivacious approach which is entirely successful. The recording is first rate.

Mass 4 in C min. (*Waisenhausmesse*), K.139

(M) *** DG (IMS) (ADD) 427 255-2. Janowitz, Von Stade, Moll, Ochman, V. State Op. Ch., VPO, Abbado

By any standards this Mass is a remarkably sustained example of the thirteen-year-old composer's powers, with bustling *Allegros* in the *Kyrie*, *Gloria* and *Credo*, as well as at the end of the *Agnus Dei*, while the *Gloria* and *Credo* end with full-scale fugues. This far from negligible piece sounds at its very best in Abbado's persuasive hands.

Masses (i–ii) 4 (*Waisenhaus*); (iii) 7 (*Missa in honorem Ssmae Trinitatis*); (i–ii) 11 (*Credo*); (ii; iv) 16 (*Coronation*); 17 (*Missa solemnis*)

(B) **(*) Double Decca (ADD) 455 032-2 (2). (i) Mentzer, Manca di Nissa, Mackie, Roberts; (ii) King's College, Cambridge, Ch., ECO, Cleobury; (iii) V. State Op. Ch., VPO, Münchinger; (iv) with Marshall, Murray, Covey-Crump, Wilson-Johnson

Mozart's early *C minor Mass* was composed for the dedication of a new orphanage church, the Waisenhauskirche am Rennweg, in 1768, and it is notable both for its rich choral writing and for the fine *Benedictus*, a dialogue between soprano and chorus, with the trumpets entering resplendently for the *Amen*. It is presented here most effectively by Cleobury and his team. The *Missa Trinitas*, written in Salzburg five years later, is even more ambitious, using a big orchestra with copious brass (four trumpets and three trombones) as well as oboe, strings and organ. Münchinger offers a strong, direct account, but the disappointment of this 1974 recording, made in the Sofiensaal, is how little is made of the trumpets, which, even in the *Credo*, are backwardly balanced. The other recordings are digital and were made a decade later. Stephen Cleobury is perhaps at his finest in the *Credo Mass* and, with the help of his excellent soloists, gives a vividly exuberant performance of a work that shows its composer at his most sunnily high-spirited throughout. The *Missa solemnis in C major*, K.337, was the very last of the 15 settings that Mozart wrote for Salzburg, another work that is just as inspired as the better-known *Coronation Mass*. Though Cleobury's direction here could be rhythmically more lively, both performances are of high quality, with excellent soloists and fresh choral singing.

Masses (i) 10 (*Spatzenmesse*), K.220; (ii) 18 (*Great*), K.427; (iii) 19 (*Requiem*), K.626

(B) **(*) DG Double (ADD/DDD) 459 409-2 (2). (i) Mathis, Troyanos, Laubenthal, Engen, Regensburg Cathedral Ch., Bav. RSO, Kubelik; (ii) Battle, Cuberli, Seiffert, Moll, V. State Op. Konzertvereinigung, VPO, Levine; (iii) Tomowa-Sintow, Baltsa, Krenn, Van Dam, V. Singverein, VPO, Karajan

Kubelik's direct but lively account of the *Spatzenmesse* does not disappoint: his soloists, led by Edith Mathis, make a good team and the recording from the early 1970s is fresh and clear. (This is also available coupled with the *Ave verum corpus* and *Coronation Mass* – see above.) Karajan's 1975 analogue

recording of the *Requiem* is outstandingly fine, deeply committed, with incisive playing and clean-focused singing from the chorus, not too large and set a little behind. The fine quartet of soloists too is beautifully blended. The reading has its moments of romantic expressiveness but nothing is smoothed over, and with splendidly vivid recording such a passage as the *Dies irae* has exceptional freshness and intensity. Levine's recording of the *C minor Mass* is digital and dates from 1987. There are reservations about the tremulous soprano line in the chorus, which otherwise sings powerfully. The soloists are individually impressive (Kathleen Battle shines in the *Laudamus te*), but the ensemble of the *Quoniam* is less than ideally polished, and the performance overall is a little rough round the edges. Yet the music's emotional power is never in doubt, for Levine's reading has a compelling, spontaneous vigour. The recording, too, is very live and vivid.

Mass 16 in C (*Coronation*), K.317

(M) **(*) DG (IMS) (ADD) 457 744-2. Stader, Dominguez, Haefliger, Roux, Brasseur Ch., LOP, Markevitch – CHERUBINI: *Requiem Mass 2 in D min.* ***

(M) **(*) DG (IMS) 445 543-2 (2). Battle, Schmidt, Winbergh, Furlanetto, V. Singverein, VPO, Karajan – BEETHOVEN: *Missa solemnis* **(*)

(B) **(*) DG Double (ADD) 453 016-2 (2). Tomowa-Sintow, Baltsa, Krenn, Van Dam, V. Singverein, BPO, Karajan – BEETHOVEN: *Missa solemnis* ***

Markevitch's performance, though not always completely refined, is incisively brilliant and its sheer vigour is infectious. This is not to say that its lyrical moments are not equally successful. He has an impressive team of soloists and they are well matched in ensemble as well as providing very good individual contributions. The *Agnus Dei* is especially fine. The brightly remastered recording has plenty of life and detail, but it is the coupled Cherubini that makes this disc especially attractive.

Karajan's 1985 recording of Mozart's *Coronation Mass* is certainly vibrant, with fine choral singing and good soloists. Kathleen Battle sings beautifully in the *Agnus Dei*, and the recording is bright, if not ideally expansive.

Karajan's earlier (1976) recording is a dramatic reading, lacking something in rhythmic resilience perhaps; but, with excellent solo singing as well as an incisive contribution from the chorus, there is no lack of strength and the score's lyrical elements are sensitively managed. The current remastering has further improved the sound.

Masses (i) 16 (*Coronation*); 17 (*Missa solemnis*); (ii) 18 (*Great*); Kyrie in D min., K.341

(BB) **(*) Virgin 2x1 5 61665-2 (2). Cologne Chamber Ch., Coll. Cartusianum, Neumann; with (i) Kwella, Groenewold, Prégardien, Selig; (ii) Schlick, Frimmer, Prégardien, Mertens

Masses (i; ii) 16 (*Coronation*); (i; iii) 18 (*Great*); (i; iv) 19 (*Requiem*)

(B) **(*) Ph. (ADD) Duo 438 800-2 (2). (i) Donath, R. Davies; (ii) Knight, Dean; John Alldis Ch., LSO; (iii) Harper, Dean, L. Symphony Ch., LSO; (iv) Minton, Nienstedt, Alldis Ch., BBC SO; C. Davis

These very successful Philips CD transfers demonstrate the best features of the original Philips recordings, which date from between 1967 and 1971. Sir Colin Davis's vital account of the *Coronation Mass* is given with a fine team of soloists; and in the so-called *'Great' Mass in C minor* the use of the Robbins Landon edition – which rejects the accretions formerly used to turn this incomplete torso of a work into a full setting of the liturgy – prompts him to a strong and intense performance which brings out the darkness behind Mozart's use of the C minor key. Again he is helped by fine soprano singing from Helen Donath, and from Heather Harper too. The *Requiem*, with a smaller choir, is more intimate and the soloists are more variable, yet with his natural sense of style Davis finds much beauty of detail. While the scale is authentic and the BBC orchestra is in good form, this reading, enjoyable as it is, does not provide the sort of bite with which a performance on this scale should compensate for sheer massiveness of tone.

Neumann directs an enjoyable account of the *Coronation Mass*, as well as the much rarer *Missa solemnis*, which is on a similar scale and is also very well sung. The singers, a well-blended team, are balanced somewhat backwardly within an ecclesiastical acoustic, which takes a little of the life from the chorus too, but the effect remains vivid. The *C minor Mass* has much to commend it: fine soloists – with Barbara Schlick always fresh and captivating in the *Laudamus te* – spacious choral singing (if, again, somewhat backwardly balanced) and excellent playing from an authentic-sized orchestra on original instruments. The only caveat is that the chorus again lacks the bite to make the performance really gripping, though the recording is partly to blame. The rather solemn *Kyrie* has plenty of character, with the performance darkly lyrical rather than dramatic. A good super-bargain set (if without texts or translations), which has much to recommend it.

Masses (i) *16 in C (Coronation)*; (ii) *19 in D min. (Requiem)*; *Ave verum corpus*
☛ (M) *** Ph. 464 720-2. (i) M. Price, Schmidt, Araiza, Adam; (ii) Mathis, Rappé, Blochwitz, Quasthoff; Leipzig R. Ch., Dresden Staatskapelle, Schreier

Schreier's 1982 version of the *Requiem* is here supplemented by the *Coronation Mass* and *Ave verum corpus*, recorded a decade later with the same choir and orchestra. By latter-day standards the opening *Introitus* of the *Requiem* is rather heavy, but that is the exception in this intensely dramatic and purposeful reading, with Dame Margaret Price singing ravishingly. The quartet of soloists is impressive too in the *Coronation Mass*, and in both the Leipzig Radio Choir sings with superb attack, if occasionally resorting to an aspirated style. Full, well-refurbished sound.

Mass 18 in C min. (Great), K.427
☛ *** DG 439 012-2. Hendricks, Perry, Schreier, Luxon, V. Singverein, BPO, Karajan
*** Ph. 420 210-2. McNair, Montague, Rolfe Johnson, Hauptman, Monteverdi Ch., E. Bar. Sol., Gardiner

(i) *Mass 18 (Great). Meistermusik* (1785 original choral version of *Masonic Funeral Music*), K.477
**(*) HM HMC 901393. (i) Oelze, Larmore, Weir, Kooy; Chapelle Royale Coll. Voc., O of Champs Elysées, Herreweghe

In his (1982) digital recording of the *C minor Mass* Karajan gives Handelian splendour to this greatest of Mozart's choral works and, though the scale is large, the beauty and intensity are hard to resist. Solo singing is first rate, particularly that of Barbara Hendricks, the dreamy beauty of her voice ravishingly caught. Woodwind is rather backward, yet the sound is

both rich and vivid – though, as the opening shows, the internal balance is not always completely consistent.

John Eliot Gardiner, using period instruments, gives an outstandingly fresh performance of high dramatic contrasts, marked by excellent solo singing: both the sopranos pure and bright-toned and Anthony Rolfe Johnson in outstandingly sweet voice. With the recording giving an ample scale without inflation, this too can be warmly recommended.

Herreweghe directs a satisfying and very well-recorded period performance, if not as vital as those of Gardiner and Karajan. He opens somewhat squarely, but the performance soon opens out. The choral singing is always vivid, and both soprano soloists are outstanding: Christine Oelze sweetly nimble in the *Et incarnatus est* and Jennifer Larmore giving a brilliant and moving account of the *Laudamus te*. The fill-up is the original choral version of the *Masonic Funeral Music*, and here Herreweghe achieves just the right feeling of sombre ceremonial.

Mass 19 (Requiem) in D min., K.626
*** DG **SACD** 471 639-2; CD 439 023-2. Tomowa-Sintow, Müller Molinari, Cole, Burchuladze, V. Singverein, VPO, Karajan
(BB) *** RCA Navigator (ADD) 74321 29238-2. Equiluz, Eder, V. Boys' Ch., V. State Op. Ch. & O, Gillesberger – HAYDN: *Te Deum ***
(***) BBC mono BBCL 4119-2. Harper, Hodgson, Pears, Shirley-Quirk, Aldeburgh Festival Ch., ECO, Britten (with Britten in conversation)
(M) **(*) Chan. 7059. Kenny, Walker, Kendall, Wilson-Johnson, St John's College, Cambridge, Ch., ECO, Guest
(B) **(*) EMI Red Line 5 69867. Donath, Ludwig, Tear, Lloyd, Philh. Ch. & O, Giulini
** Avie AV 0047. Jette, Larmore, Taylor, Owens, St Olaf Ch., St Paul CO, Delfs – SUSSMAYR: *Requiem ***

Mass 19 in D min. (Requiem) (ed. Maunder)
(M) **(*) O-L 411 712-2. Kirkby, Watkinson, Rolfe Johnson, Thomas, Westminster Cathedral Boys' Ch., AAM Ch. and O, Hogwood

(i) *Mass 19 (Requiem). Adagio & Fugue, K.546*
☛ (M) *** Decca 475 205-2. M. Price, Schmidt, Araiza, Adam, Leipzig R. Ch., Dresden State O, Schreier

(i; ii) *Mass 19 (Requiem) (ed. and revised Druce)*; (ii) *Ave verum corpus. Maurerische Trauermusik, K.477*
(M) **(*) Virgin 5 61520-2. (i) Argenta, Robbin, Mark Ainsley, Miles; (ii) L. Schütz Ch.; LCP, Norrington

Mass 19 (Requiem); (i) Grabmusik, K.42: Beatracht dies Herz; Vesperae solennes de confessore, K.339: Laudate Dominum
*** DG 463 181-2. (i) Harnisch; Mattila, Mingardo, Schade, Terfel, Swedish R. Ch.; BPO, Abbado

Mass 19 (Requiem); Kyrie, K.341
*** HM HMC 901620. Rubens, Markert, Bostridge, Müller-Brachmann, La Chapelle Royale Coll. Voc., O des Champs Elysées, Herreweghe
*** Ph. 420 197-2. Bonney, Von Otter, Blochwitz, White, Monteverdi Ch., E. Bar. Sol., Gardiner

(i) *Mass 19 (Requiem). Maurerische Trauermusik, K.477*
(BB) *** Virgin 2x1 5 61501-2 (2). (i) Kenny, Hodgson, Davies, Howell, L. Sinfonia Ch., N. Sinf. Ch. & O, Hickox – BRUCKNER: *Missa solemnis; Psalms ***

(B) *** Auvidis ES 9965. Soloists, La Capella Reial de Catalunya; Le Concert des Nations, Savall

Recorded live in July 1999 in Salzburg Cathedral, Abbado's performance of the traditional score with the Berlin Philharmonic was given to commemorate the tenth anniversary of the death of Herbert von Karajan. The dedicated atmosphere of such an occasion is powerfully caught, with the DG engineers clarifying the sound to a remarkable degree, with fine detail as well as ample weight. With the brilliant Swedish Radio Choir singing with exceptionally clear focus, such choruses as the *Dies irae* are thrillingly intense, and the starry yet youthful line-up of soloists – none of whom Karajan would ever have heard – makes an outstanding team. In the two extra items, among Mozart's loveliest soprano solos, Rachel Harnisch sings with warmth and refinement. This can be recommended to those wanting a traditional, modern-instrument account of Mozart's choral masterpiece.

Herreweghe is arresting from the very dramatic opening bars, and in the work's central *Sequenz* (*Dies irae*; *Tuba mirum*; *Rex Tremendae*; *Recordare*; *Confutatis* and the moving *Lacrimosa*) he achieves a remarkable emotional thrust. The orchestra gives weighty support, and one is hardly aware that this is a period-instrument performance, with the horns and trumpets capping climaxes forcefully. The soloists make an excellent team, singing with individuality (especially Ian Bostridge) but also blending together. The sound is spacious, but there is no feeling that the choral impact is blunted.

Richard Hickox's excellent bargain version of the *Requiem Mass* on the Virgin label matches almost any in the catalogue. With generally brisk speeds and light, resilient rhythms, it combines gravity with authentically clean, transparent textures in which the dark colourings of the orchestration, as with the basset horns, come out vividly. All four soloists are outstandingly fine, and the choral singing is fresh and incisive, with crisp attack. The voices, solo and choral, are placed rather backwardly; otherwise the recording is excellent. This now comes as part of a super-bargain Virgin Double, aptly coupled with the rare Bruckner *Missa solemnis*, which is also very well sung, the only drawback being sparse documentation and an absence of texts.

Peter Schreier's outstanding 1984 recording won a *Gramophone* Choral Award. Since then his performance has not been surpassed and is now most welcome back into the catalogue. It is a forthright reading, bringing strong dramatic contrasts and marked by superb choral singing and a consistently elegant and finely balanced accompaniment. The recording is exceptionally well balanced and the orchestral detail emerges with natural clarity. Margaret Price in the soprano part is as fine as any yet heard on record, and the others make a first-rate team, if individually more variable. Only in the *Kyrie* and the final *Cum sanctis tuis* does the German habit of using the intrusive aitch intrude. Altogether this is the most satisfying modern-instrument version now available of the standard Süssmayr score of Mozart's valedictory choral work, and it is splendidly recorded.

John Eliot Gardiner with characteristic panache also gives one of the most powerful performances on record, for while the lighter sound of the period orchestra makes for greater transparency, the weight and bite are formidable. The soloists are an outstanding quartet, well matched but characterfully contrasted too, and the choral singing is as bright and luminous as one expects of Gardiner's Monteverdi Choir. The superb *Kyrie in D minor* makes a very welcome and generous fill-up, to seal a firm recommendation.

The performance by La Capella Reial de Catalunya and Le Concert des Nations directed by Jordi Savall is both gutsy and expressive; at times tempi have great urgency – witness the thrilling *Dies irae* and the strong accents of the opening of the *Confutatis*, then contrasted by the angelic soprano line, with Montserrat Figueras a blissfully serene soloist. The trombones make a remarkable contribution throughout, and especially in the *Benedictus* and *Agnus Dei*. The recording is absolutely first class and, certainly, no other version of the *Requiem* makes more impact on the listener. It is aptly introduced by the plangent timbres of the *Maurerische Trauermusik*.

Karajan's 1987 digital version of the *Requiem* is a large-scale reading, but one that is white-hot with intensity and energy. The power and bite of the rhythm are consistently exciting. The solo quartet is first rate, though Helga Müller Molinari is on the fruity side for Mozart. Vinson Cole, stretched at times, yet sings very beautifully, and so does Paata Burchuladze with his tangily distinctive, Slavonic bass tone. The close balance adds to the excitement. This is now available on a compatible SACD.

Hogwood's version uses the edition of Richard Maunder, which aims to eliminate Süssmayr's contribution to the version of Mozart's unfinished masterpiece that has held sway for two centuries. So the *Lacrimosa* is completely different, after the opening eight bars, and concludes with an elaborate *Amen*, for which Mozart's own sketches were recently discovered. This textual clean-out goes with authentic performances of Hogwood's customary abrasiveness, very fresh and lively to underline the impact of novelty.

Norrington also uses an entirely new score, by Duncan Druce, rejecting Süssmayr and other additional editorial material. Druce's revisions are considerable, even presenting recomposed music, with alterations as early as the *Recordare* and *Sanctus*. Norrington certainly believes in it, and his account is both vibrant and compelling, with unpredictable tempi at times, but never eccentric. The soloists too are very impressive and so is the recording. As bonuses Norrington offers a tranquil (though not dallying) *Ave verum corpus* and a strongly characterized version of the *Maurerische Trauermusik*, moved forward with more drive than usual. This acts as a rather effective prelude to the main work.

The surprise version is Gillesberger's. Using treble and alto soloists from the Vienna Boys' Choir, who sing with confidence and no little eloquence, this performance also has the advantage of a dedicated contribution from Kurt Equiluz. Gillesberger's pacing is well judged and the effect is as fresh as it is strong and direct. The 1982 recording is excellent, vivid yet full, and the result is powerful but not too heavy.

Recorded in June 1971 at the Snape Maltings during the Aldeburgh Festival, Britten's live recording from the BBC archives brings an electrifying performance, with an outstanding quartet of soloists long associated with the Festival and with the chorus powerfully presented in full, immediate sound. It is a pity that it is in mono only, but the high voltage of Britten's conducting, even at a time when his health was beginning to fail, comes over vividly. Not all the choral singing is immaculate, but the bite of attack makes ample amends, and Britten's preference for speeds faster than were common in traditional performances adds to the magnetism. The bonus is a 27-minute conversation that Britten had in 1969 with Donald Mitchell, full of fascinating remarks, notably on the composition process. He reveals that though he always had a clear idea of the shape of a work in advance, it was invariably necessary to allow for an element of chance, of improvisation as the work progressed.

Guest has the advantage of first-class singing from his St

John's choristers, strong and eloquent, and an outstanding Chandos recording, full, vivid and clear. The performance is vigorous and positive, and well held together. The soloists, however, though making an excellent team and never letting the performance down, are not individually memorable, and altogether this cannot quite match Hickox.

Giulini directs a large-scale performance which brings out both Mozartian lyricism and Mozartian drama, and anyone who fancies what by today's standards is an inauthentic approach may consider this version. The choir is in excellent, incisive form, and the soloists are a first-rate quartet. As one would expect, what Giulini's insight conveys is the rapt quality of such passages as the end of the *Tuba mirum* and the *Benedictus*. The recording is warm rather than brilliant.

The great point in favour of the Avie version is not just the incisive singing of the St Olaf Choir but the unique coupling: what is claimed to be the first ever modern performance of the long-forgotten *Requiem* by the friend and composer whose completion of the Mozart has, as here, been generally used. Apart from a rather gruff bass, the team of soloists is strong and clear, but Andreas Delfs' direction in this live recording is too rhythmically square in slow music and too rigidly metrical in fast. Yet with full, well-balanced sound this is still an issue worth investigating.

Requiem Mass (revised Levin)

**(*) Dorian DOR 90310. Gauvin, Lemieux, Tessier, Berg, La Chapelle de Québec, Les Violons du Roy, Labadie

While Süssmayr's completion of the unfinished Mozart *Requiem* has long been criticized, there have been many rethinkings in new editions, some even excluding everything that cannot be proved to be genuine Mozart and some involving substantial recomposition. The baroque scholar and fortepianist, Robert Levin, takes a sympathetic line which he explains in his detailed note for this fine account with French-Canadian forces, recorded live in Troy, New York, in September 2001. His approach is that, thinking that Süssmayr knew more about Mozart's plans than is often assumed, he has tried to retain as much as possible of the established version, thinning down the instrumentation when needed and correcting such passages as the *Amen* Chorus at the end of the Sequenz, which Levin claims would never have included a modulation. Although the result is inevitably controversial, the result, well recorded, is fresh and bitingly alert under the direction of Bernard Labadie, with clean period textures in the orchestra and excellent singing from both the chorus and the young soloists.

OPERA

Complete Bargain Mozart Edition, Vol. 13: Early Italian Operas: Ascanio in Alba; La finta semplice; Lucio Silla; Mitridate, re di Ponte; Il sogno di Scipione

(B) **(*) Ph. 464 890-2 (13). Soloists; C. P. E. Bach CO, Schreier; or Salzburg Mozarteum O, Hager

In *Ascanio in Alba* Hager makes an excellent start with an exceptionally lively account of the delightful overture, but then the choruses seem relatively square, thanks to the pedestrian, if generally efficient, singing of the Salzburg choir. Hager's speeds are sometimes on the slow side, but the solo singing is excellent, with no weak link in the characterful cast, though not everyone will like the distinctive vibrato of Lilian Sukis as Venus. The 1976 analogue recording is full and vivid. The digital recording of Schreier's *La finta semplice* is wonderfully clear, with a fine sense of presence, capturing the fun of

the comedy. Ann Murray has never sung more seductively in Mozart than here as Giacinta, and the characterful Barbara Hendricks is a delight in the central role of Rosina. The castrato roles in *Lucio Silla* are splendidly taken by Julia Varady and Edith Mathis, and the whole team could hardly be bettered. The direction of Leopold Hager is fresh and lively, and the only snag is the length of the *secco* recitatives. However, with CD one can use these judiciously. Hager's fresh and generally lively performance of *Mitridate* (the rather heavy recitatives excepted) also brings illumination to the long-hidden area of the boy Mozart's achievement, with Arleen Augér the ravishing soprano. Ileana Cotrubas is outstanding as Ismene, and the soloists of the Salzburg orchestra cope well with the often important obbligato parts. The CD transfer is vivid and forward and a little lacking in atmosphere.

Ascanio in Alba (complete)

(BB) *** Naxos 8.660040-2 (2). Windsor, Chance, Feldman, Milner, Mannion, Paris Sorbonne University Ch., Budapest Concerto Armonico, Grimbert

Mozart at the age of fifteen wrote this charming, ever-inventive 'festa teatrale' for the coronation of the Archduke Ferdinand to an Italian princess in Milan in 1771. A court entertainment rather than an opera proper, it designedly identifies characters in a classical story, with the bride and bridegroom taking part in a delightful and original closing trio. The Naxos version easily outshines previous recordings with a lightly sprung, stylishly conducted performance featuring an outstanding cast. The counter-tenor, Michael Chance, sings flawlessly in the castrato role of Ascanio, son of Venus, even-toned and brilliantly flexible. The others are fresh-toned too. Lorna Windsor, bright and clear as Venus, is nicely contrasted with the girlish-sounding Silvia of Jill Feldman, who sings with fine assurance in one of the two extended arias. The other, even more extended and demanding, is given to Fauno, with Rosa Mannion arguably the most accomplished soloist of all. The excellent tenor taking the role of Aceste is Howard Milner. Well recorded with transparent textures, if with chorus backwardly balanced, this makes an outstanding bargain in every way, rare Mozart that for most will be a delightful discovery.

Complete Bargain Mozart Edition, Vol. 16: German Operas: Bastien und Bastienne; Die Entführung aus dem Serail; Die Gärtnerin aus Liebe; Zaïde; Der Schauspieldirektor; Die Zauberflöte

(B) ** Ph. (ADD/DDD) 464 930-2 (11). Soloists; VSO, Harrer; N. German RSO, Schmidt-Isserstedt; Dresden State O or LSO or ASMF, C. Davis

Among these Davis recordings *Die Entführung aus dem Serail* and *Die Zauberflöte* are disappointing, especially the latter, which makes this bargain compilation less attractive than it seems.

Complete Bargain Mozart Edition, Vol. 15: Late Italian Operas: La clemenza di Tito; Così fan tutte; Don Giovanni; Le nozze di Figaro

(B) *** Ph. (ADD) 464 920-2 (11). Soloists; BBC SO or ROHCG O, C. Davis

Sir Colin Davis's superb set of *La clemenza di Tito* is among the finest of his many Mozart recordings. Not only is the singing of Dame Janet Baker in the key role of Vitellia formidably brilliant; she actually makes one believe in the emotional development of an impossible character, one who progresses from villainy to virtue with the scantiest preparation. The two other mezzo-sopranos, Minton as Sesto and Von Stade in the small role of Annio, are superb too, while Stuart Burrows has rarely if ever sung as stylishly on a recording as here. Davis's swaggering manner transforms what used to be dismissed as a dry *opera seria*. Excellent recording. *Così fan tutti*, *Don Giovanni* and *Le nozze di Figaro* are all highly successful in every respect and are praised below in their alternative bargain box re-issue.

La clemenza di Tito (complete)

*(**) Arthaus **DVD** 100 406. Langridge, Putnam, Montague, Mahe, Szmytka, Rose, Glyndebourne Festival Ch., LPO, A. Davis (Producer: Nicholas Hytner)

*** DG 431 806-2 (2). Rolfe Johnson, Von Otter, McNair, Varady, Robbin, Hauptmann, Monteverdi Ch., E. Bar. Sol., Gardiner

*** Teldec 4509 90857-2 (2). Langridge, Popp, Ziesak, Murray, Ziegler, Polgár, Zurich Op. Ch. & O, Harnoncourt

**(*) O-L 444 131-2 (2). Heilmann, Bartoli, D. Jones, Montague, Bonney, Ch. & AAM, Hogwood

Recorded at Glyndebourne during the 1991 festival, this Arthaus DVD version of Mozart's last opera is superbly sung by an outstanding cast, with conducting by Andrew Davis that brings out the charm as well as the power of this *opera seria*. Among the soloists there is no weak link. The singing is consistently firm, clear and stylish, with Philip Langridge masterly in the title-role, Ashley Putnam superb as Vitellia and Diana Montague most moving as Sesto. In place of the usual recitatives (not by Mozart) new ones have been provided by Stephen Oliver, though some of them seem very long, notably the five-minute stretch immediately after the overture and before the first duet between Sesto and Vitellia. However, as so often with modern opera productions, Nicholas Hytner's staging, with stylized geometric sets by David Fielding, will not be to all tastes, and the flat backdrops, often decorated with torn wallpaper effects, have their bizarre side. The Roman costumes are relatively conventional, even if the long swirling skirts for male characters sung by women are very questionable. Excellent sound, but this can be recommended only with considerable visual reservations.

Again, with his vitality and bite, Gardiner turns the piece into a genuinely involving drama. Anthony Rolfe Johnson is outstanding in the title-role, matching the vivid characterization of both Anne Sofie von Otter as Sesto and Julia Varady as Vitellia. Sylvia McNair is an enchanting, pure-toned Servilia and Catherine Robbin a well-matched Annio, though the microphone catches an unevenness in the voice, as it does with Cornelius Hauptmann in the incidental role of Publio. More seriously, DG's vivid, immediate recording picks up a distracting amount of banging and bumping on stage in the Süssmayr recitatives.

Nikolaus Harnoncourt uses modern, not period, instruments. Even so, he has not forgotten his early devotion to period performance, making this a very viable account for anyone wanting a half-way approach. Though recorded in association with Zurich Opera, this is a studio, not a live recording like Gardiner's. It gains from not having stage noises in recitatives. Ann Murray is at her finest as Sesto, if not quite as firm or dominant as von Otter for Gardiner. Philip Langridge is a splendid Tito, and it is good to have Lucia Popp so affecting in her very last recording. Ruth Ziesak and Delores Ziegler complete a strong team which will not disappoint anyone, even if it cannot quite compare with Gardiner's, singer for singer.

With clean, crisp manners Hogwood draws transparent textures from the players in the Academy, pointing rhythms and phrases more lightly and almost as imaginatively as Gardiner. Sesto as portrayed by the characterful Cecilia Bartoli is clearly established as the central figure in the drama, with Della Jones as Vitellia comparably positive. Diana Montague as Annio and Barbara Bonney as Servilia both weigh in favour of Hogwood, but Uwe Heilmann with his slightly fluttery tenor conveys nothing like the heroic strength of Anthony Rolfe Johnson in the title-role for Gardiner. Clean, well-balanced studio sound.

Così fan tutte (complete; DVD versions)

⊕– *** DG **DVD** 073 026-9 (2). Roocroft, Mannion, Gilfry, Trost, James, Nicolai, Monteverdi Ch., E. Bar. Sol., Gardiner (Dir: Gardiner/Medcalf; TV Director: Mumford)

(N) *** Arthaus **DVD** 101081. Doese, Lindenstrand, Perriers, Allen, Glyndebourne Ch., LPO, Pritchard (V/D: Dave Heather)

(N) **(*) Opus Arte **DVD** OA LS 3006. Dessi, Ziegler, Corbelli, Kundlak, Scarabelli, Desderi, La Scala Ch. and O, Muti (Dir: Michael Hampe; V/D: Ilio Catani)

(N) **(*) TDK **DVD** DV OPCFT. Röschmann, Kammerloher, Müller-Brachmann, Güre, Bruera, Terkel, Berlin State Op. Ch. & O, Barenboim (Dir: Doris Dörrie; V/D: Michael Beyer)

(N) ** Arthaus **DVD** 100 012. Bartoli, Nikiteanu, Sacca, Widmer, Baltsa, Chausson, Zurich Op. Ch. and O, Harnoncourt (Dir: Jurgen Flimm; V/D: Brian Large)

The DVD version of John Eliot Gardiner's recording of *Così fan tutte* was recorded live simultaneously with the audio recording issued on CD. The staged production at the Théâtre du Châtelet in Paris was the work of Gardiner himself in collaboration with Stephen Medcalf, involving pretty sets and handsome costumes by Carlo Tomassi. The traditional approach to staging nicely matches the freshness and imagination of the period performance, with uniforms from the Napoleonic period and Ferrando and Guglielmo in disguise dressed identifiably as Albanians, even if as usual one wonders how Fiordiligi and Dorabella fail to recognize their lovers. Visually, the whole production consistently heightens the impact of the opera, with video direction by Peter Mumford. Though the performance spreads on to two discs, the only extras are promotional, including a survey of Gardiner's recordings of Mozart operas.

Recorded at the Glyndebourne Festival in 1975, Adrian Slack's production, with sets and costumes by Emanuele Luzzati, harks back to the period before Sir Peter Hall and John Bury did their classic productions of the three da Ponte operas. With the opening scene set domestically in what looks like a kitchen–dining room, the approach is intimate, apt enough for the old theatre at Glyndebourne, which is atmospherically presented at the end, when the audience is seen applauding. The singing is first rate and the acting good, and Slack's production brings out the fun of the piece, even though he rarely provides the sort of detailed illumination of words and character that mark the Peter Hall *Figaro*. The conductor, Sir John Pritchard, is at his most animated and magnetic, though in some of the ensembles he rushes his singers and players. Helene Doese as Fiordiligi and Sylvia Lindenstrand, a tall, imperious Dorabella, are both ideally steady and clear, and Doese's *Come scoglio* is brilliantly articulated, even though her Act II aria, *Per pietà*, could be more moving. The youthful Thomas Allen is a superb

Guglielmo, and the American tenor, Anson Austin, is a handsome, open-toned Ferrando, with Frantz Petri a splendid Alfonso and Daniele Perriers a light, agile Despina.

Recorded at La Scala in April 1989, Muti's DVD is very well paced and generally well cast and offers an attractive traditional production by Michael Hampe, with costumes and designs involving baroque arches by Mauro Pagano. Daniela Dessi sings with freshness and clarity as Fiordiligi, and Delores Ziegler is a handsome, finely projected Dorabella. The men, rather mature for young lovers, sing well, with Josef Kundlak a finely controlled Ferrando and Alessandro Corbelli a strong Guglielmo. Best of all is the veteran Claudio Desderi as Don Alfonso, in splendid voice. On only a single disc, the sound is thinner than most, a little veiled on the orchestra.

The Deutsche Oper production of *Così* conducted by Daniel Barenboim brings updated designs by Christian Sedelmeyer, with an aggressively modern sitting room at the start and a 1960s car in the on-stage garage, evidently indicating the date of this concept production. Though Barenboim does not always spring the rhythms as infectiously as he might, using rather a large orchestra, it is a lively performance, at times too fussy in its use of stage-business, but generally well cast, with Dorothea Röschmann an impressive Fiordiligi, not least in a brilliant *Come scoglio*, and *Per pietà* presented as a prayer of dedication. The inspired touch in Doris Dörrie's production is that Ferrando and Guglielmo return, not as Albanians, but as 1960s hippies, who promptly install themselves on camp-beds in the girls' flat. It is also a novel touch that at the end, when all four lovers separate, Alfonso and Despina fall into each other's arms. Roman Terkel is an unusually incisive Alfonso, and Daniela Bruera a lively Despina. The performance, like many versions, spreads on to two discs.

Nikolaus Harnoncourt with his Zurich Opera House company uses modern instruments but adopts many of the characteristics of a period performance. Speeds tend to be extreme in both directions, often uncomfortably so, with slow numbers sometimes stagnating and fast ensembles sounding rushed. Jurgen Flimm's production sets the whole opera in a school, reflecting the subtitle, 'School for Lovers', with Don Alfonso very much a schoolmaster type and the character simply play-acting. The heavyweight basic set gives way to simple drop curtains for scene-changes effectively enough. Cecilia Bartoli makes a powerful if hardly vulnerable Fiordiligi, with Liliana Nikiteanu a reliable Dorabella, and the veteran Agnes Baltsa a rough-voiced harridan of a Despina. The men sing well enough but tend to overact.

Così fan tutte (complete; CD versions)
*** DG 437 829-2 (3). Roocroft, Mannion, Gilfry, Trost, James, Feller, E. Bar. Sol., Gardiner
● (M) *** EMI (ADD) 5 67382-2 (3) [567379]. Schwarzkopf, Ludwig, Steffek, Kraus, Taddei, Berry, Philh. Ch. & O, Boehm
*** Decca 444 174-2 (3). Fleming, Von Otter, Lopardo, Bär, Scarabelli, Pertusi, COE, Solti
● (M) (***) EMI mono 5 67064-2 (3) [567138]. Schwarzkopf, Otto, Merriman, Simoneau, Panerai, Bruscantini, Philh. Ch. & O, Karajan
(M) *** Ph. (ADD) 422 542-2. Caballé, J. Baker, Cotrubas, Gedda, Ganzarolli, Van Allan, ROHCG Ch. & O, C. Davis
(B) **(*) Double Decca (ADD) 455 476-2 (2). Della Casa, Ludwig, Loose, Dermota, Kunz, Schoeffler, V. State Op. Ch., VPO, Boehm

(M) *** Erato (ADD) 4509 98494-2 (3). Te Kanawa, Stratas, Von Stade, Rendall, Huttenlocher, Bastin, Rhine Op. Ch., Strasbourg PO, Lombard
**(*) EMI 5 56170-2 (3). Martinpelto, Hagley, Murray, Streit, Finley, Allen, OAE, Rattle

On CD as well as DVD, the full flavour of *Così*, its effervescence as well as its deeper qualities, come over the more intensely with Gardiner. Though Amanda Roocroft and Rosa Mannion do not sound quite as sweet and even as they can, few tenors on disc can rival the German Rainer Trost in the heady beauty of his voice, above all in Ferrando's aria, *Una aura amorosa*. The poise and technical assurance of all the singers, not least Rodney Gilfry as Guglielmo, put this among the finest versions of *Così*.

Boehm's classic set has been splendidly remastered as one of EMI's 'Great Recordings of the Century' and remains a clear first choice, despite the attractions of the Solti version. Its glorious solo singing is headed by the incomparable Fiordiligi of Schwarzkopf and the equally moving Dorabella of Christa Ludwig; it remains a superb memento of Walter Legge's recording genius and remains unsurpassed by any other recordings made before or since. The documentation is generous and includes a full libretto and sessions photographs.

Solti takes a fast and light approach which yet has none of his old fierceness. The speeds may challenge the singers, notably in the many ensembles, but Solti gives his performers every consideration in moulding the arch of phrases or in allowing time for elaborate decorations. Though such meditative passages as the lovely little trio, *O soave sia il vento*, and the opening of Fiordiligi's aria, *Per pietà*, are taken at flowing speeds, faster than usual, they have a poise that holds one rapt. Much is owed to the superb playing of the Chamber Orchestra of Europe. Renée Fleming as Fiordiligi, brought in as substitute at the last minute, sings with a firm, full voice that is yet brilliant and flexible, ranging down to a satisfyingly strong chest register. Frank Lopardo, too, as Ferrando most sensitively uses his distinctive tenor over an unusually wide dynamic range, so that in the lovely aria, *Una aura amorosa*, he sings the reprise in a gentler, more beautiful half-tone than anyone else on disc. Anne Sofie von Otter predictably makes a characterful Dorabella, well contrasted with Fleming, and Olaf Bär a keenly intelligent Guglielmo, while two Italian singers, less well known but well chosen, Adelina Scarabelli and Michele Pertusi, complete the team in the manipulative roles of Despina and Alfonso. Altogether Solti's finest Mozart recording, outshining even his *Figaro*.

Commanding as Schwarzkopf is as Fiordiligi in the 1962 Boehm set, the extra ease and freshness of her singing in the earlier (1954) version under Karajan makes it even more compelling. Nan Merriman is a distinctive and characterful Dorabella, and the role of Ferrando has never been sung more mellifluously on record than by Leopold Simoneau. The young Rolando Panerai is an ideal Guglielmo, and Lisa Otto a pert Despina; while Sesto Bruscantini in his prime brings to the role of Don Alfonso the wisdom and artistry which made him so compelling at Glyndebourne. Karajan has never sparkled more naturally in Mozart than here, for the high polish has nothing self-conscious about it. The recording has been impressively remastered for reissue as another of EMI's 'Great Recordings of the Century'.

The energy and sparkle of Sir Colin Davis are set against inspired and characterful singing from the three women soloists, with Montserrat Caballé and Janet Baker proving a winning partnership, each challenging and abetting the other all the time. Cotrubas equally is a vivid Despina, never merely arch. Though Gedda has moments of rough tone and Ganzarolli falls short in one of his prominent arias, they are both spirited, while Richard van Allan sings with flair and imagination. Sparkling recitative and recording, which has you riveted by the play of the action.

Boehm's 1955 Decca stereo set is not as polished a performance as his later one for EMI, and the cutting of brief passages from the ends of arias may worry those who know the opera very well. But it remains a captivatingly spontaneous account of the frothiest of Mozart's comedies. Lisa della Casa is strong and sweet-toned, Christa Ludwig is admirably fresh-voiced, and the rest are sparklingly good, especially Emmy Loose's deliciously knowing portrayal of Despina. Paul Schoeffler in the role of Don Alfonso is most appealing. This was one of Decca's early stereo experiments, but the sense of the singers acting out the comedy just beyond the speakers is uncannily realistic. Decca's new-style synopsis – with the narrative first given briefly 'in a nutshell', followed by suggested highlights, and listener-friendly cueing of the action – is a distinct asset.

On Erato, Kiri Te Kanawa's voice sounds radiant, rich and creamy of tone; she is commanding in *Come scoglio*, and tenderly affecting in *Per pietà*, which is more moving here than with Levine. Lombard is a sympathetic accompanist, if not always the most perceptive of Mozartians; some of his tempi are on the slow side, but his sextet of young singers make up a team that rivals almost any other, giving firm, appealing performances. With warm recording of high quality, this is most enjoyable and could be a first choice for any who follow the singers in question.

Sir Simon Rattle offers a sizzling account of *Così*, recorded live, with the period instruments of the Orchestra of the Age of Enlightenment. In its often hectic speeds from the overture onwards, it may miss some of the sparkle of the piece, but Rattle knows how to bring out the emotional high points, so that the superb Fiordiligi, Hillevi Martinpelto, at a measured speed sings with aching beauty in *Per pietà*. Thomas Allen is a masterly Alfonso, Kurt Streit a clear-toned Ferrando and Gerald Finley a youthfully ardent Guglielmo. It is refreshing too to have a soprano Dorabella, particularly when the lovely timbre of Alison Hagley's voice is clearly contrasted with the brighter tones of Martinpelto. As ever, Ann Murray is a characterful Despina. The acoustic of Symphony Hall, Birmingham, adds brightness to the sound, though this is not focused quite as well as Birmingham recordings made without an audience.

Così fan tutte (excerpts)

(***) Testament mono SBT 1040. Jurinac, Thebom, Lewis, Kunz, Borriello, Glyndebourne Festival O, Busch; Noni, Philh. O, Susskind

The superb Testament transfer of excerpts from *Così fan tutte* in the 1950 Glyndebourne production gives a vivid idea of the way that even in the first year when the re-established Glyndebourne Festival was recovering its pre-war format, standards were never higher. Sena Jurinac as Fiordiligi, clear and vibrant, provides the central glory, with both her two big arias included, as well as six of her ensemble numbers, and three substantial rehearsal 'takes'. Blanche Thebom too, as Dorabella, sings with clarity and freshness, and the others make a splendid team. Alda Noni, the Despina, was not recorded at the Glyndebourne sessions but later, at Abbey Road, with Susskind and the Philharmonia. The recording brings out a flutter in her voice, less steady than the others. As

in pre-war days, a piano is used instead of harpsichord for recitatives.

Così fan tutte (highlights)

(N))(BB) **(*) Warner Apex 2564 61498-2 (from complete recording, with Margiono, Van der Walt, Ziegler, Cachemaille, Steiger, Hampson, Concg. O, Harnoncourt)

As in his other Mozart opera recordings, Harnoncourt here favours an orchestra of modern instruments while adopting aspects of period style with speeds eccentric in both directions. So while the lovely terzetto *O soave sia il vento* is raced along, Fiordiligi's great Act II aria, *Per pietà*, is taken impossibly slowly. Even so, Charlotte Margiono sustains the line immaculately, and she is similarly accommodating over another of Harnoncourt's eccentricities, making the emphatic opening of Fiordiligi's other big aria, *Come scoglio*, into a hushed meditation. With Deon van der Walt sweetly caught as Ferrando and Dolores Ziegler an outstanding Dorabella, the casting has no weak link. But this is a performance for which a 74-minute bargain highlights disc seems more desirable than the complete set.

(i) Così fan tutte; (ii) Don Giovanni; (iii) Le nozze di Figaro

(B) *** Ph. (ADD) 456 375-2 (9). (i–iii) Ganzarolli; (i) Caballé, J. Baker, Cotrubas, Gedda; (i–ii) Van Allan, ROHCG Ch. & O; (ii) Arroyo, Te Kanawa, Burrows, Roni; (ii–iii) Wixell, Freni; (iii) Norman, Minton, Casula, Grant, Tear, BBC Ch., BBC SO; all cond. C. Davis

Philips wisely decided to omit Sir Colin Davis's recording of *Die Zauberflöte* from this very tempting bargain box; it was the least successful of his Mozart opera series. The other three performances are sheer delight. The sparkling *Così fan tutte* brings a superb female trio in Caballé, Janet Baker and Cotrubas, and the men fall only slightly short of this very high standard. In *Don Giovanni* the very consistency of the whole cast is its major asset, led by Kiri Te Kanawa as Donna Elvira and Mirella Freni's engaging Zerlina, while Ingvar Wixell and Wladimiro Ganzarolli strike sparks off each other as the Don and Leporello; and the same comment applies to *Nozze di Figaro*, where those same two male singers are equally successful in the comparable master and servant roles. Throughout all three operas Davis's lively pacing brings a flowing spontaneity as at live performances. The Philips sound, from clean CD transfers of recordings made between 1971 and 1974, is always fresh and immediate.

Don Giovanni (complete; DVD versions)

(N) **(*) TDK **DVD** DVW-OPDG. Alvarez, Pieczonka, Antonacci, Schade, D'Arcangelo, Kirschlager, Regazzo, V. State Op. Ch. & O, Muti (V/D: Brian Large)

(*) Sony **DVD SVD 46383. Ramey, Tomowa-Sintow, Varady, Battle, Winbergh, Furlanetto, Malta, Burchuladze; V. State Op. Ch., VPO, Karajan (Dir: Michael Hampe; V/D: Claus Viller)

Don Giovanni (complete; CD versions)

➤— (M) *** EMI 5 67869-2 (3) [567873]. Waechter, Schwarzkopf, Sutherland, Alva, Frick, Sciutti, Taddei, Philh. Ch. & O, Giulini

*** DG 445 870-2 (3). Gilfry, Organasova, Margiono, James, D'Arcangelo, Prégardien, Clarkson, Silvestrelli, Monteverdi Ch., E. Bar. Sol., Gardiner

➤— ✿ (M) *** Decca (ADD) 466 389-2 (3). Della Casa, Danco, Siepi, Corena, Dermota, V. State Op. Ch., VPO, Krips

*** DG (IMS) 419 179-2 (3). Ramey, Tomowa-Sintow, Baltsa, Battle, Winbergh, Furlanetto, Malta, Burchuladze, German Op. Ch., Berlin, BPO, Karajan

(M) *** EMI (ADD) 7 63841-2 (3). Ghiaurov, Watson, Ludwig, Freni, Gedda, Berry, Montarsolo, Crass, New Philh. Ch. & O, Klemperer

(M) (***) EMI mono 5 66657-2 (3). Gobbi, Schwarzkopf, Welitsch, Seefried, Kunz, Dermota, Poell, Greindl, V. State Op. Ch., VPO, Furtwängler

(M) (***) EMI mono 7 63860-2 (3). Siepi, Schwarzkopf, Berger, Grümmer, Dermota, Edelmann, Berry, Ernster, V. State Op. Ch., VPO, Furtwängler

(M) (***) Orfeo mono C624 043D (3). Siepi, Schwarzkopf, Grümmer, Berger, Edelmann, Dermota, Arié, V. State Op. Ch., VPO, Furtwängler

(M) **(*) DG 463 629-2 (3). Fischer-Dieskau, Jurinac, Stader, Seefried, Haefliger, Kohn, Sardi, Kreppel, Berlin RIAS Chamber Ch. & R. O, Fricsay

(BB) (**(*)) Naxos mono 8.110013/14. Pinza, Novotna, Bampton, Sayão, Kullman, Kipnis, Harell, Cordon, NY Met. Op. Ch. & O, Walter

(M) **(*) Ph. Trio 473 959-2 (3). Allen, Sweet, Mattila, Alaimo, Araiza, Lloyd, McLaughlin, Otelli, Amb. Op. Ch., ASMF, Marriner

On TDK, Riccardo Muti conducts Vienna State Opera forces at the smaller Theater an der Wien in a recording made in June 1999. Muti's approach is traditional, except that his *Allegros* are often very fast, racing the singers off their feet, though Carlos Alvarez, splendid in the title-role, looking the perfect roué, masterfully defies the conductor's challenge in the hectic but finely articulated performance of the Champagne Aria. Adrienne Pieczonka's full, warm soprano makes her an impressive Donna Anna opposite the honey-toned Ottavio of Michael Schade, while Angelika Kirchschlager as Zerlina and Lorenzo Regazzo are both superb as the peasant pair, with Ildebrando d'Arcangelo as a loud but well-focused Leporello. In this company, Anna Caterina Antonacci makes a disappointing Donna Elvira, often squally. Roberto de Simone's production is remarkable for the frequency of the scene and costume changes, which become distracting when Zaira Vincentiis is so lavish in her many costume designs. Leporello appears initially as a white-faced clown, but quickly returns to conventional, eighteenth-century servant's garb. Donna Elvira first appears dressed as a man, but quickly returns with a massive pannier skirt, before donning many other creations. Don Giovanni, initially seen in an enormous periwig, is quickly given less elaborate hairstyles. Curiously, in the epilogue Zerlina and Masetto emerge in twentieth-century peasant costume. A mixed success, however well the orchestra plays.

The Sony DVD offers one of Karajan's final productions at Salzburg and was recorded during a performance at the 1987 Festival. It first appeared on video and on LaserDisc, where it occupied three sides as opposed to a single double-sided DVD here. There are some impressive things here. The Donna Anna of Anna Tomowa-Sintow and the Donna Elvira of Julia Varady are splendidly matched and, both vocally and dramatically, are commanding: it is probably worth having solely for them. The Leporello of Ferruccio Furlanetto is vivacious, and has a dramatic flair that seems to elude Samuel Ramey's Don. Kathleen Battle's Zerlina is better sung than acted but for the most part this is a satisfying performance, certainly superior to the *Don* that Karajan recorded in Berlin

for DG two years earlier with an almost identical cast (save for the Elvira, who was Baltsa). Some have found Karajan a little stiff, but there is no question as to the tonal splendour of the Vienna Philharmonic or the dignity and spaciousness of his reading. The visual presentation is excellent, as indeed is the well-balanced sound. There are subtitles in English, German and French.

On CD the classic Giulini EMI set, lovingly remastered, sets the standard by which all other recordings have come to be judged, and is now reissued as one of EMI's 'Great Recordings of the Century'. Elisabeth Schwarzkopf, as Elvira, emerges as a dominant figure to give a distinctive but totally apt slant to this endlessly invigorating drama. The young Sutherland may be relatively reticent as Anna but, with such technical ease and consistent beauty of tone, she makes a superb foil. Taddei is a delightful Leporello, and each member of the cast – including the young Cappuccilli as Masetto – combines fine singing with keen dramatic sense.

John Eliot Gardiner's set was recorded mainly live, and the result is vividly dramatic, beautifully paced and deeply expressive, with little or none of the haste associated with period practice. The performance culminates in one of the most thrilling accounts ever recorded of the final scene, when Giovanni is dragged down to hell. Gardiner opts for a text that is neither that of the original Prague version nor the usual amalgam of Prague and Vienna. Dramatically the result is tauter, and the numbers omitted are here included in an appendix. Sometimes lightness goes too far, as when Charlotte Margiono as Donna Elvira sings *Ah fuggi il traditor* in a half-tone; but increasingly Gardiner encourages his soloists, particularly Anna and Elvira, to sing expansively, bringing out the full weight of such arias as *Mi tradi* and Anna's *Non mi dir*. Fine as Margiono is, Luba Organasova is even more assured and characterful as Anna, and the agility of both is exemplary. Rodney Gilfry excels himself, on one side tough and purposeful, on the other a smooth seducer, with the clean-toned voice finely shaded. Ildebrando d'Arcangelo is suitably darker-toned as Leporello, lithe and young-sounding, hardly a *buffo*. Julian Clarkson makes a crotchety Masetto, and Eirian James a warmer, tougher Zerlina than usual, aptly so for her extra scene. The Commendatore of Andrea Silvestrelli, though recessed on the recording, is magnificently dark and firm, not least in the final confrontation. A recording that sets new standards for period performance and vies with the finest of traditional versions.

Krips's version, recorded in 1955 for the Mozart bicentenary, has remained at or near the top of the list of recommendations ever since. Freshly remastered, it sounds better than ever. Its intense, dramatic account of the Don's disappearance into hell has rarely been equalled, and never surpassed on CD, though there are many equally memorable sequences: the finale to Act I is also electrifying. As a bass Don, Siepi is marvellously convincing, but there is hardly a weak link in the rest of the cast. The early stereo recording is pretty age-defying, full and warm, with a lovely Viennese glow which is preferable to many modern recordings.

Even if ensemble is less than perfect at times in the Karajan set and the final scene of Giovanni's descent to hell goes off the boil a little, the end result has fitting intensity and power. Though Karajan was plainly thinking of a big auditorium in his pacing of recitatives, having Jeffrey Tate as continuo player helps to keep them moving and to bring out word-meaning. The starry line-up of soloists is a distinctive one. Samuel Ramey is a noble rather than a menacing Giovanni, consistently clear and firm.

Most of the slow tempi that Klemperer regularly adopts, far from flagging, add a welcome breadth to the music, for they must be set against the unusually brisk and dramatic interpretation of the recitatives between numbers. Added to that, Ghiaurov as the Don and Berry as Leporello make a marvellously characterful pair. In this version the male members of the cast are dominant and, with Klemperer's help, they make the dramatic experience a strongly masculine one. Nor is the ironic humour forgotten with Berry and Ghiaurov about, and the Klemperer spaciousness allows them extra time for pointing. Among the women, Ludwig is a strong and convincing Elvira, Freni a sweet-toned but rather unsmiling Zerlina; only Claire Watson seriously disappoints, with obvious nervousness marring the big climax of *Non mi dir*.

The 1950 EMI set with Tito Gobbi in the title-role should not be confused with the later Furtwängler recording, also made at the Salzburg Festival and issued by EMI, with Schwarzkopf as Elvira. The speeds, spacious by most standards, are here a degree faster than they became four years later. Gobbi, not usually a Mozartian, yet gives a commanding, keenly characterful portrayal of the Don, very much the centre of the drama, swaggering and snarling, a menacingly dangerous seducer. Schwarzkopf as ever is a comparably commanding and characterful Elvira, no wilting flower, and Ljuba Welitsch in 1950 was at her peak, a radiant Anna, with Irmgard Seefried a magical Zerlina and Anton Dermota a honeyed Ottavio. Erich Kunz is the vintage Leporello, and if neither Alfred Poell as Masetto nor Josef Greindl as the Commendatore can match the others vocally, the team could otherwise hardly be stronger. The sound is rough on the orchestra but improves after the overture, while voices are very well caught, though stage balances vary.

The alternative EMI Furtwängler performance was recorded live by Austrian Radio at the 1954 Salzburg Festival, barely three months before the conductor's death. Though speeds are often slow by today's standards, his springing of rhythm never lets them sag. Even the very slow speed for Leporello's catalogue aria is made to seem charmingly individual. With the exception of a wobbly Commendatore, this is a classic Salzburg cast, with Cesare Siepi a fine, incisive Don, dark in tone, Elisabeth Schwarzkopf a dominant Elvira, Elisabeth Grümmer a vulnerable Anna, Anton Dermota a heady-toned Ottavio and Otto Edelmann a clear and direct Leporello. Stage noises often suggest herds of stampeding animals, but both voices and orchestra are satisfyingly full-bodied in the CD transfer, and the sense of presence is astonishing.

Recorded in July 1953, the Orfeo issue of Furtwängler's performance of *Don Giovanni* at the Salzburg Festival makes a valuable supplement to the two EMI issues of his performances there in 1950 and 1954. Elisabeth Schwarzkopf as Donna Elvira and Anton Dermota as Ottavio are common to all three, superb each time. This 1953 performance otherwise has an identical cast to the one in 1954, with the exception that the clear, firm Rafaele Arié sings the role of the Commendatore instead of the wobbly Deszo Ernster in 1954. The recording is less forwardly balanced than the 1954 version but is enjoyable enough, and the performance is magnetic.

As he has shown in his recording of *Die Zauberflöte*, Fricsay is a forceful, dramatic Mozart conductor, but here the absence of charm is serious. This is mainly felt in some ridiculously fast speeds. Seefried being the superb artist she is, her charm comes through. The cast is generally strong, but unfortunately there is a serious blot in the Donna Elvira of Maria Stader; she is made to sound shrill and some of her

attempts to get round the trickier florid passages leave a good deal to be desired. Yet most of the singing is very stylish. Haefliger shows himself as one of the finest Mozart tenors of the time, Karl Kohn is a fine, incisive Leporello, Ivan Sardi an exceptionally rich-voiced Masetto, and Seefried a truly enchanting Zerlina. As so often on records, Sena Jurinac is not quite as thrilling here as one remembers her in the flesh. Fischer-Dieskau is a particularly interesting choice of Don; his characterization proves powerful and forwardly projected.

The vintage Bruno Walter recording, made live at the Met. in New York in March 1942, is one of the most desirable of the Naxos historic issues. Walter's brisk speeds may not allow the sort of detailed expressiveness one finds in any of the Furtwängler versions, but the bite of the drama is irresistible. Ezio Pinza is an engagingly characterful Don, a commanding performance vocally, matched by the rest of the cast. Few Annas equal Rose Bampton for her combination of purity and power, with every note cleanly in place; though Jarmila Novotna as Elvira is less polished, it is a strong performance, and Bidu Sayão makes a charming Zerlina. Charles Kullman is a clear-toned Ottavio, and though Alexander Kipnis as Leporello is not at his best in Act I, the biting clarity of his performance is magnetic. The 1942 sound, one of the better recordings from this source, has voices forwardly balanced. Elvira's aria, *Mi tradi*, is omitted.

Marriner's Trio reissue has the benefit of outstandingly fine recorded sound, full and well balanced. His direction is well paced and resilient, with far keener feeling for dramatic pacing than his earlier recording of *Figaro*. Vocally, the star is Thomas Allen as the Don, even more assured than he was for Haitink in the EMI Glyndebourne version. The others make a strong team, with Simon Alaimo an attractive, young-sounding Leporello, though Sharon Sweet is occasionally raw-toned as Donna Anna. There is no libretto, only a keyed synopsis, and overall this is far from being a primary choice.

Don Giovanni (highlights)

(M) *** EMI (ADD) 5 65567-2 (from above complete recording, with Sutherland, Schwarzkopf, Waechter; cond. Giulini)

Not surprisingly, the Giulini EMI selection concentrates on Sutherland as Donna Anna and Schwarzkopf as Donna Elvira, so that the Don and Leporello get rather short measure, but Sciutti's charming Zerlina is also given fair due.

Don Giovanni (complete; in English)

(M) **(*) Chan. 3057 (3). Magee, Cullagh, Shore, Tierney, Plazas, Banks, Robinson, Bayley, Geoffrey Mitchell Ch., Philh. O, Parry

Vividly recorded, David Parry's well-paced reading breaks new ground in offering the masterpiece in English, and very successful it is, even though the casting is not as starry as in many versions. The lively translation of Amanda Holden is used and, particularly from the men, every word is clear, with voices well balanced against the full-bodied orchestra, set in the helpful acoustic of the Blackheath Concert Hall. Parry, on the grounds of its greater cohesion, firmly opts for the original, Prague version of the score, which may disappoint some when Elvira's *Mi tradi* and Ottavio's *Dalla sua pace* are omitted. Garry Magee as the Don makes a believably virile lover, vigorous and youthful, articulating the *Champagne* aria cleanly at a crisp, well-chosen tempo. Andrew Shore also characterizes well as Leporello, bringing out the comedy but not guying it. Clive Bayley as the Commendatore, Barry

Banks as Ottavio, more heroic than usual, and Dean Robinson complete a strong team of men. Among the women the most satisfying performance comes from Mary Plazas as Zerlina, less soubrettish than usual but charming. Majella Cullagh is a warm-toned Donna Anna, only occasionally gusty, and Vivian Tierney a clear, reliable Elvira, whose voice is not flattered by the microphone.

Die Entführung aus dem Serail (complete; DVD version)

(N) *** DG **DVD** 073020-9. Holtzmann, Araiza, Gruberová, Grist, Orth, Talvela, Bav. R. Ch. & O, Boehm (V/D: Karlheinz Hundorf)

Karl Boehm conducted this beautifully paced account of *Entführung* at the Bavarian State Opera in April 1980, just over a year before he died. It was always a favourite opera with him, and the performance has a winning glow, with an excellent cast of soloists. Edita Gruberová as Constanze is at her freshest: clear and agile, tender in *Traurigkeit*, brilliant in *Martern aller Arten*. Though Reri Grist as Blonde has an edge on the voice, hers is a charming and characterful assumption, most of all when confronting the powerful Osmin of Martti Talvela, a giant of a figure with a voice to match. Francisco Araiza too is at his peak, with Norbert Orth exceptionally strong as Pedrillo. August Everding's stylized production, with smoothly sliding scenery by Max Bignens, sets each scene deftly and atmospherically in the Pasha's palace. The 1980 sound is exceptionally bright and clear for its age.

Die Entführung aus dem Serail (complete; CD versions)

(N) (M) *** DG 477 5593-2 (2). Organasova, Sieden, Olsen, Peper, Hauptman, Minetti, Monteverdi Ch., E Bar. Sol., Gardiner

(M) *** DG (ADD) 429 868-2 (2). Augér, Grist, Schreier, Neukirch, Moll, Leipzig R. Ch., Dresden State O, Boehm

(M) *** Oehms OCD 249 (2). Haberman, Ellen, Bezcala, Kalchmair, Ringelhahn, Linz Landestheater Ch., Linz Bruckner O, Sieghart

*** Erato 3984 25490-2 (2). Schäfer, Petibon, Bostridge, Paton, Ewing, Les Arts Florissants, Christie

(M) *** EMI (ADD) 7 63263-2 (2). Rothenberger, Popp, Gedda, Unger, Frick, V. State Op. Ch., VPO, Krips

(B) *** Double Decca 473 804-2 (2). Dawson, Hirsti, Heilmann, Gahmlich, Von Kannen, Hinz, AAM & Ch., Hogwood

(M) *** Teldec 2292 44184-2 (2). Kenny, Watson, Schreier, Gamlich, Salminen, Zurich Op. Ch. & Mozart O, Harnoncourt

Gardiner's *Entführung* was not recorded live but in the studio immediately after a concert performance. The overture immediately establishes the extra zest of the performance. So Konztanze's great heroic aria, *Martern aller Arten*, has tremendous swagger; thanks also to glorious singing from Luba Organasova, at once rich, pure and agile, the close is triumphant. Curiously, Gardiner exaggerates the ad lib. markings in the first half of that climactic aria. Organasova sounds far richer than Lynne Dawson, the outstanding Konstanze for Hogwood; and in the other great aria, *Traurigkeit*, she is warmer too, less withdrawn. As Belmonte, Stanfor Olsen for Gardiner is firmer and more agile than the fluttery Uwe Heilmann for Hogwood, and though Cornelius Hauptman, Gardiner's Osmin, lacks a really dark bass, he too is firmer

and more characterful than the unsteady Günther von Kannen for Hogwood. Altogether this now makes a fine mid-priced recommendation.

Boehm's is a delectable account, superbly cast and warmly recorded. Arleen Augér proves the most accomplished singer on record in the role of Konstanze, girlish and fresh, yet rich, tender and dramatic by turns, with brilliant, almost flawless coloratura. The others are also outstandingly good, notably Kurt Moll, whose powerful, finely focused bass makes him a superb Osmin, one who relishes the comedy too. The warm recording is beautifully transferred, to make this easily the most sympathetic version of the opera on CD, with the added attraction of being at mid-price.

With an excellent cast of young singers the Oehms (originally Arte Nova) set offers an outstanding version of *Entführung* to rival almost any in the catalogue. With Martin Sieghart a crisp and urgent conductor, stylistically impeccable, drawing fine playing from the Linz Bruckner Orchestra, the performance gains from having been recorded in conjunction with live performances on stage, a point consistently reflected in the interplay between the soloists. Ingrid Haberman is a formidable Konstanze, fresh and clear, bright in coloratura yet creamy of tone in lower registers, undaunted by the demands of *Martern aller Arten*. The American Donna Ellen is a lively Blonde with clear, unstrained top register. The Polish tenor Piotr Bezcala is a stylish, honey-toned Belmonte, with power as well as lyric beauty, only occasionally lachrymose in attack, while Oliver Ringelhahn is a well-contrasted Pedrillo, though pushed to the limit in his big Act II aria, *Frisch zum Kampfe*. Best of all is the Osmin of Franz Kalchmair, whose firm, dark bass copes masterfully with every demand of the role, cleanly focused from top to bottom. Still youthful-sounding, he yet conveys a compelling portrait of this prickly character. Good sound, though the spoken dialogue (well edited) is not consistent. Now at mid-price, the set comes with full libretto, including English translation.

William Christie's speeds are consistently on the fast side, even imperilling articulation in the overture and allowing less spring to rhythms than in the finest rival period performances. Christine Schäfer makes a ravishing Konstanze, powerful in *Martern aller Arten* and touchingly tender in *Traurigkeit*, though Christie's flowing speed prevents it from having the poignancy which more spacious treatment allows. Ian Bostridge, in the context of a light performance, is ideal as Belmonte, finely detailed in both words and musical treatment, always individual. Patricia Petibon is a light, bright, minxish Blonde, Iain Paton a clear Pedrillo. Most controversial is the choice of the velvet-toned Alan Ewing as Osmin, singing beautifully, but generally avoiding *buffo* characterization. The chorus is fresh and incisive, though at high speed the Janissaries at their entry are very rushed.

Recorded in 1966, the Krips EMI version brings an amiable and highly enjoyable performance with a formidable line-up of soloists. The team of Popp, Gedda, Unger and Frick could hardly have been bettered at the time, each of them singing beautifully and with vivid characterization. Anneliese Rothenberger, potentially the weak link as Konstanze, not only sounds amply powerful as recorded, but she sings with a purity and sweetness rarely caught on her discs. This is arguably her finest recording ever. The stereo sound is warm and well balanced, with spoken dialogue well presented. Act I comes on the first disc, with Acts II and III fitted complete on the second.

Christopher Hogwood, in what was the first (originally Oiseau-Lyre) period recording of *Die Entführung*, offers a bonus number discovered as the result of keen detective work. It is a march which precedes the chorus of janissaries, very useful for producers wanting to get supernumeraries on stage. Hogwood has rarely sounded so relaxed on record, though the excellent cast is let down by one unwise choice, the ill-focused Osmin of Günter von Kannen. Otherwise Lynne Dawson is a dazzling Konstanze, relying on fine projection rather than weight in the big tuttis, and contrasting well with the soubrettish Blonde of Marianne Hirsti. The tenor, Uwe Heilmann, as Belmonte here completely avoids the fluttery tone which mars his performance as Tamino on the Solti set of *Zauberflöte*. Altogether excellent value at Double Decca price. No libretto, but a good cued synopsis.

Harnoncourt's version establishes its uniqueness at the very start of the overture, tougher and more abrasive than any previous recording, with more primitive percussion effects than we are used to in Mozart's Turkish music. It is not a comfortable sound, compounded by Harnoncourt's often fast *Allegros*, racing singers and players off their feet. Slow passages are often warmly expressive, but the stylishness of the soloists prevents them from seeming excessively romantic. The men are excellent: Peter Schreier singing charmingly, Wilfried Gamlich both bright and sweet of tone, Matti Salminen outstandingly characterful as an Osmin who, as well as singing with firm, dark tone, points the words with fine menace. Yvonne Kenny as Konstanze and Lilian Watson as Blonde sound on the shrill side, partly a question of microphones. A bargain Apex CD of highlights (73') is also available (2564 61509-2).

'Mozart in Turkey' (*Die Entführung aus dem Serail*; sung in German; film interviews & narration in English)

(N) **(*) Opus Arte **DVD** OA 0891 D. Groves, Kodalli, Rancatore, Atkinson, Rose, Tobias, Scottish CO and Ch., Mackerras (V/D: Elijah Moshinsky)

Over 90 minutes *Mozart in Turkey* offers an abbreviated version of *Die Entführung aus dem Serail*, staged in the atmospheric setting of the Topkapi Palace in Istanbul. The excellent performance under Sir Charles Mackerras is introduced and punctuated by interviews and explanations, notably by the director, Elijah Moshinsky, which both tell the story and provide the background to the production. All the soloists are first rate under Mackerras's masterly direction, and Moshinsky's analysis of motive is most illuminating, making one wish that this was a complete performance and not just a collection of excerpts, particularly when many of the selected numbers are severely truncated.

The Abduction from the Seraglio (*Die Entführung aus dem Serail*; complete; in English)

⊙— ✹ (M) *** Chan. 3081 (2). Dobbs, Eddy, Gedda, Fryatt, Mangin, Kelsey, Amb. S., Bath Festival O, Y. Menuhin

Menuhin's set of *The Abduction from the Seraglio* in English stemmed directly from a staged production at the 1967 Bath Festival, of which Menuhin was then the musical director. He makes the performance sparkle from first to last, favouring brisk, well-lifted *Allegros*, so that the fun of the piece comes over vividly. The acting of the principal singers is exceptionally fine too, with Noel Mangin superb as Osmin, commandingly comic yet believable too, not least when in duo with John Fryatt, an outstanding Pedrillo. Their drinking duet is hilarious as well as musically sparkling. Mangin sings magnificently, firm and dark over the widest register. Nicolai Gedda, brought in as an international star, fully lives up to

expectation, giving one of his finest Mozart performances, poised and stylish, his English accent flawless. The American soprano, Mattiwilda Dobbs, similarly brought in as a star, uses her bright, agile coloratura brilliantly. Jennifer Eddy makes an enchanting Blonde, perfect as a defiant English girl.

When it comes to style, it is the Menuhin touch which makes all the difference: his pointing of the music is equivalently subtle and refined, besides anticipating the scale of later period performances. There is a generous – but not too generous – allocation of dialogue, and as it is separately banded on CD it can be dispensed with if one wants the music alone; for the score is absolutely complete, with all Belmont's arias included (and the full text given in the booklet). What completes this as wonderful entertainment is the quality of the 1967 recording, as full and vivid as if it was recorded yesterday, the sound-stage cleanly and atmospherically focused.

Complete Bargain Mozart Edition, Vol. 14: Middle period Italian Operas: *La finta giardiniera; Idomeneo; L'oca del Cairo; Il re pastore; Lo sposo deluso*

(BB) **(*) Ph. (IMS) (ADD/DDD) 464 910-2 (9). Soloists; Salzburg Mozarteum O, Hager; ASMF, Marriner; Bav. RSO or LSO, C. Davis; C. P. E. Bach CO, Schreier

Leopold Hager has a strong vocal team in *La finta giardiniera*, with three impressive newcomers taking the women's roles – Jutta-Renate Ihloff, Julia Conwell (in the central role of Sandrina, the marquise who disguises herself as a garden-girl) and Lilian Sukis (the arrogant niece). Brigitte Fassbaender sings the castrato role of Ramiro, and the others are comparably stylish. It is a charming – if lengthy – comedy which here, with crisply performed recitatives, is presented with vigour, charm and persuasiveness. The recording, made with the help of Austrian Radio, is excellent. However, Sir Colin Davis's *Idomeneo* is very flawed in its casting, while his reading has grown smoother and less fresh and incisive with the years. We owe it to the Mozart scholar and Philips recording producer, Erik Smith, that these two sets of Mozartian fragments, *L'oca del Cairo* and *Lo sposo deluso*, have been prepared for performance and recorded. *L'oca del Cairo* ('The Cairo goose'), containing roughly twice as much music as *Lo sposo deluso*, involves six substantial numbers, most of them ensembles, including an amazing finale to the projected Act I, with contrasted sections following briskly one after the other. It is very well conducted by Peter Schreier, who also takes part as one of the soloists. Dietrich Fischer-Dieskau takes the *buffo* old-man role of Don Pippo, and Anton Scharinger is brilliant in the patter aria in tarantella rhythm for the major-domo, Chichibio, bringing a foretaste of Donizetti. Fresh, bright, digital recording. *Il re pastore* is not exactly a music drama but it is still a splendid example of Mozart's youthful genius at work. The version by Marriner and the Academy, with a first-rate cast and with plenty of light and shade, and superbly played, does not efface memories of the 1979 DG version conducted by Leopold Hager, which offered even purer singing. Here Angela Maria Blasi, despite a beautiful voice, attacks notes from below, even in *L'améro*. Excellent sound.

Idomeneo (complete; DVD versions)

(N) **(*) Warner **DVD** 5050467 3922-2-9. Kenny, Hadley, Vaness, Hemsley, Langridge, Roden, Kennedy, Glyndebourne Ch., LPO, Haitink (Dir: Trevor Nunn; V/D: Christopher Swann)

(N) ** Arthaus **DVD** 101 079. Lewis, Goeke, Betley, Barstow, Glyndebourne Ch., LPO, Pritchard (V/D: Dave Heather)

Dating from 1983, the Warner DVD of *Idomeneo* from Glyndebourne offers a fine production by Trevor Nunn, with handsome, stylized sets and classical Greek costumes designed by John Napier. They match the stylization behind this greatest *opera seria*, at once formal yet so original in its defiance of the conventions of the time, as in the dramatic close to Act II, with the chorus melting away in darkness on the most atmospheric diminuendo, leaving Idomeneo crouching alone, centre-stage. Bernard Haitink is a powerful Mozartian, directing an excellent cast. The controversial point is that even in 1983 Glyndebourne used the version with Idamante as a tenor rather than a mezzo, as Mozart originally conceived it, upsetting the balance in the great quartet of Act III. Even so, the young Jerry Hadley in that role offers a lightly stylish contrast with the darkly intense Idomeneo of Philip Langridge. First-rate contributions too from Yvonne Kenny as Ilia and Carol Vaness as Elettra. One serious drawback is the limited background material provided, with no booklet and simply a synopsis of the plot inside the cover. It is confusing, too, that each track begins on recitative and not on the set numbers, making identification of items difficult.

Recorded for Southern Television in 1974, John Cox's vintage Glyndebourne production, with handsome sets and costumes by Roger Butlin, is strongly cast and conducted by John Pritchard to bring out the drama of the piece. The snags are that, to suit television, much of Act I is omitted and the orchestral sound is thin, with edgy violins. Pritchard, following earlier Glyndebourne practice, opts for having the role of Idamante sung by a tenor instead of following Mozart's original scheme of making it a castrato role. Richard Lewis, at the end of his career, still makes a stylish Idomeneo, even though his voice is strained at times, with Leo Goeke well contrasted as a fresh-voiced Idamante. Bozena Betley sings freely and sweetly as Ilia, and the young Josephine Barstow makes a striking Vitellia, coping fiercely with the challenge of her Act III aria. The staging, with concentric circles stretching back, tunnel-like, is most atmospheric, with a mysterious sea-monster appearing all too close at the end of Act II, making one wonder why the chorus, when they sing *Fuggiamo* ('Let us flee'), don't do it. As they say of the policemen in *The Pirates of Penzance*, 'But dammit they don't go!'

Idomeneo (complete; CD versions)

🎵— *** EMI 5 57260-2 (3). Bostridge, Hunt Lieberson, Milne, Frittoli, Rolfe Johnson, SCO, Mackerras

*** DG 431 674-2 (3). Rolfe Johnson, Von Otter, McNair, Martinpelto, Robson, Hauptmann, Monteverdi Choir, E. Bar. Sol., Gardiner

*** DG 447 737-2 (3). Bartoli, Domingo, Vaness, Grant-Murphy, Hampson, Lopardo, Terfel, Met. Op. Ch. & O, Levine

(M) *** DG 429 864-2 (3). Ochman, Mathis, Schreier, Varady, Winkler, Leipzig R. Ch., Dresden State O, Boehm

(B) (***) EMI double forte mono 5 73848-2 (2). Lewis, Simoneau, Jurinac, Udovick, Milligan, McAlpine, Alan, Glyndbourne Festival Ch. & O, Pritchard

Ian Bostridge with his heady tenor may seem too light a choice of singer for the title-role in Mozart's great *opera seria*, but with his ever-illuminating feeling for words and

his sensitive response to each phrase he brings the character vividly to life, with never a hint of strain. It is a magnetic performance, helped by the stylish and perceptive conducting of Sir Charles Mackerras, who gives a very full text, even if, unlike Gardiner on his DG Archiv version, he does not give alternatives in an appendix. The result is a performance, strong, dramatic and expressive, which brings out the originality of instrumentation, a point that Mackerras highlights. The others in the cast are first rate, with Lorraine Hunt Lieberson a bright, strong Idamante and Lisa Milne a charming, sweet-voiced Ilia and Barbara Frittoli a powerful Elettra. It is good too to have Anthony Rolfe Johnson, who takes the title-role in the Gardiner version, singing very stylishly as Arbace, here given both his arias, often cut. This new set is probably a marginal primary recommendation, especially for those preferring modern instruments, but the Gardiner version must be enthusiastically recommended alongside it.

With its exhilarating vigour and fine singing, Gardiner's aim has been to include all the material Mozart wrote for the original (1781) production, and he recommends the use of the CD programming device for listeners to select the version they prefer. Gardiner's Mozartian style is well sprung and subtly moulded rather than severe. The principals sing beautifully, notably Anne Sofie von Otter as Idamante and Sylvia McNair as Ilia, while Anthony Rolfe Johnson as Idomeneo is well suited here, with words finely projected. The electrifying singing of the Monteverdi Choir adds to the dramatic bite.

From the very opening of the overture it is clear what tense dramatic control James Levine has over this masterpiece of an *opera seria*, reflecting in the recording his experience in the opera house. It stands as his finest Mozart opera performance on disc. The text is roughly that of the Munich first performance, with Elettra given her culminating aria and Arbace both of his, and with recitatives given nearly complete. The cast is not just starry but stylish, with Plácido Domingo a commanding Idomeneo, giving a noble, finely controlled performance, which makes it a pity that the shorter version of his big aria, *Fuor del mar*, is preferred. Carol Vaness is a powerful, dramatic Elettra, well focused, and Cecilia Bartoli characterizes well as Idamante, wonderfully pure-toned in the Trio, while Heidi Grant-Murphy is a charmingly girlish Ilia with a light, bright soprano. Completing this team, you have Thomas Hampson as a superb Arbace and Bryn Terfel commanding in the brief solo given to the Oracle. The Met. chorus, like the orchestra, is incisively dramatic.

Boehm's conducting is a delight, often spacious but never heavy in the wrong way, with lightened textures and sprung rhythms which have one relishing Mozartian felicities as never before. As Idomeneo, Wieslaw Ochman, with tenor tone often too tight, is a comparatively dull dog, but the other principals are generally excellent. Peter Schreier as Idamante also might have sounded more consistently sweet, but the imagination is irresistible. Edith Mathis is at her most beguiling as Ilia, but it is Julia Varady as Elettra who gives the most compelling performance of all, sharply incisive in her dramatic outbursts, but at the same time precise and pure-toned, a Mozartian stylist through and through.

The very first 'complete' recording of *Idomeneo*, made in 1955 with Glyndebourne forces under John Pritchard, makes a timely reappearance on EMI's double forte label. Though it uses a severely cut text and the orchestral sound is rather dry, it wears its years well. The voices still sound splendid, notably Sena Jurinac as a ravishing Ilia, Richard Lewis in the title-role, and Léopold Simoneau so delicate he almost reconciles one to the casting of Idamante as a tenor (from Mozart's compromised Vienna revision). The cuts mean that the whole opera is fitted on to two discs instead of the usual three. A cued synopsis is provided, but as usual in this double forte series there is no aria or ensemble title with each cue.

Idomeneo (sung in English)

(M) *** Chan. 3103 (2). Ford, Montague, Evans, Patterson, Davies, Gedda, Bayley, Opera N. Ch. & O, Parry

On Chandos, the performance of Idomeneo in English works surprisingly well. The translation has been done very capably by David Parry, whose conducting brings out both the power and the originality of this great example of an opera seria which in every way transcends the limitations of the genre. The overture instantly establishes the vigour and weight of the performance, which yet allows clean textures, so that the excellent wind-playing of the Opera North Orchestra is caught vividly. The text is basically that of the original Munich production, with the role of Idamante taken by a high voice, but with substantial cuts to allow the whole opera to be fitted on two very well-filled discs. Both of Arbace's arias disappear (a pity, when Ryland Davies is strongly cast as the High Priest) as well as one of Idamante's and one of Idomeneo's in Act III.

In the title-role, Bruce Ford's distinctive tenor is powerfully expressive, even if his rapidly flickering vibrato does tend to obtrude in the more lyrical passages. The cast of women is outstanding, with Rebecca Evans as Ilia and Diana Montague as Idamante as mellifluous a duo as one could imagine, deeply expressive, too. Susan Patterson is well contrasted as Elettra, with her rather harder soprano suiting the aggressive side of the character. The drama of the piece is consistently brought out, not least in the thrilling close of Act II with its storm music, and in the climactic quartet of Act III. Having the veteran Nicolai Gedda in the cameo role of the Voice of Neptune is also a welcome plus-point. The vivid Chandos recording brings excellent balances between voices and orchestra, with words admirably clear. Mozart's score has never sounded fresher.

Lucio Silla (slightly abridged)

*** Teldec 2292 44928-2 (2). Schreier, Gruberová, Bartoli, Kenny, Upshaw, Schoenberg Ch., VCM, Harnoncourt

The sixteen-year-old Mozart wrote his fifth opera, on the subject of the Roman dictator Sulla (Silla), in double-quick time. What Harnoncourt has done is to record a text which fits on to two generously filled CDs, not just trimming down the recitatives but omitting no fewer than four arias, all of them valuable. Yet his sparkling direction of an outstanding, characterful team of soloists brings an exhilarating demonstration of the boy Mozart's genius, with such marvels as the extended finale to Act I left intact. As in the earlier set, Schreier is masterly in the title-role, still fresh in tone, while Dawn Upshaw is warm and sweet as Celia, and Cecilia Bartoli is full and rich as Cecilio. The singing of Edita Gruberová as Giunia and Yvonne Kenny as Cinna is not quite so immaculate but is still confident and stylish. The Concentus Musicus of Vienna has rarely given so bright and lightly sprung a performance on record. Excellent digital sound.

Mitridate, re di Ponto (complete; DVD version)

(N) *** EuroArts DVD 2053609. Blake, Kenny, Putnam, Boozer, Rozario, Papis, Dubosc, Lyon Op. O, Guschlbauer (V/D: Bernard Maigrot)

Strongly cast, the 1986 Lyon Opera production of Mitridate makes a powerful case for Mozart's early opera, written when he was 14. Though modern instruments are used, Theodor Guschlbauer paces the music well. Not only does the tenor, Rockwell Blake, in the title-role cope splendidly with the enormous vocal range demanded, Yvonne Kenny, firm and agile, is magnetic in the role of Aspasia. Ashley Putnam is bright and clear as Sifare, and Brenda Boozer's rich mezzo is ideal for the role of Farnace. Patricia Rozario as Ismene and Catherine Dubosc as Arbate are first rate too, making one wish that Mozart had given them more to sing. The sets are simple and stylish, and the costumes are traditional in Arab style.

Mitridate, re di Ponto (complete; CD version)

*** Decca 460 772-2 (3). Bartoli, Dessay, Sabbatini, Asawa, Piau, Les Talens Lyriques, Rousset

This Decca set is only the second recording to be issued, but it completely outshines the first (part of the Philips Bargain Mozart Edition). One big advantage is that Christophe Rousset conducts his period forces with a panache that disguises the weaknesses, pointing rhythms infectiously. Though the cast in the earlier set is an excellent one, the new line-up is even more characterful, with Cecilia Bartoli outstanding as the hero, Sifare, in love with Aspasia. In that prima donna role, Natalie Dessay is both rich of tone and brilliantly agile in coloratura, a match even for Arleen Augér on the earlier set. The counter-tenor, Brian Asawa, is firm and characterful as the predatory Farnace, and though in the title-role Giuseppe Sabbatini is overstrenuous at times, his is a heroic performance, clean in attack. The softer-grained Sandrine Piau as Ismene is well contrasted with the others. Vivid, well-balanced sound. An excellent set, unlikely to be easily supplanted.

Le nozze di Figaro (complete; DVD versions)

(N) *** Arthaus DVD 101 089. Skram, Cotrubas, Te Kanawa, Luxon, Stade, Rintzler, Condo, Glyndebourne Ch., LPO, Pritchard (V/D: Dave Heather)

(N) ** Arthaus DVD 100 410. Furlanetto, Watson, Szmytka, Provvisionato, Tramonti, Hoffmann, Tezier, Lyon Nat. Op. Ch. & O, Olmi (Dir: Jean-Pierre Vincent; V/D: Mate Rabinowski)

(N) (**) TDK DVD (ADD) DV CLOPNDF. Wixell, Watson, Grist, Berry, Thaw, Kelemen, Bence, Mathis, Hirte, V. State Ch., VPO, Boehm (Dir: Gunther Rennert)

☛ *** DG DVD 073 018-9. Terfel, Hagley, Gilfry, Martinpelto, Monteverdi Ch., E. Bar. Sol., Gardiner

☛ (B) *** Warner NVC DVD 0630-14013-2. Finley, Hagley, Fleming, Schmidt, LPO, Haitink (Producer: Stephen Medcalf; V/D: Derek Bailey)

* TDK DVD DV-OPNDF (2). Gilfry, Mei, Rey, Chausson, Nikiteanu, Von Magnus, Holl, Vogel, Larsson, Zurich Op. House Ch. & O, Harnoncourt (Producer: Jurgen Flimm)

Le nozze di Figaro (complete; CD versions)

*** Decca 410 150-2 (3). Te Kanawa, Popp, Von Stade, Ramey, Allen, Moll, Tear, LPO & Ch., Solti

(M) *** EMI (ADD) 7 63266-2 (2). Schwarzkopf, Moffo, Cossotto, Taddei, Waechter, Vinco, Philh. Ch. & O, Giulini

(B) *** EMI double forte (ADD) 5 73845-2 (2). Sciutti, Jurinac, Stevens, Bruscantini, Calabrese, Cuénod, Wallace, Sinclair, Glydebourne Ch. & Festival O, Guilini ?

*** DG 439 871-2 (3). Terfel, Hagley, Martinpelto, Gilfry, Stephen, McCulloch, Feller, Egerton, Backes, Monterverdi Ch., E. Bar. Sol., Gardiner

(M) **(*) Decca (ADD) 466 369-2 (3). Gueden, Danco, Della Casa, Dickie, Poell, Corena, Siepi, V. State Op. Ch., VPO, Kleiber

*** Teldec 4509 90861-2 (3). Scharinger, Bonney, Margiono, Hampson, Lang, Moll, Langridge, Netherlands Op. Ch., Concg. O, Harnoncourt

(M) *** DG (ADD) 449 728-2 (3). Janowitz, Mathis, Troyanos, Fischer-Dieskau, Prey, Lagger, German Op. Ch. & O, Boehm

**(*) DG (IMS) 445 903-2 (3). McNair, Gallo, Studer, Skovhus, Bartoli, V. State Op. Ch., VPO, Abbado

**(*) Telarc CD-80388 (3). Miles, Focile, Vaness, Corbelli, Mentzer, Murphy, R. Davies, R. Evans, SCO & Ch., Mackerras

(M) (**(*)) EMI mono 5 67068-2 (2) [5 67142]. Schwarzkopf, Seefried, Jurinac, Kunz, Majkut, London, V. State Op. Ch., VPO, Karajan

(BB) **(*) Arte Nova 74321 92759-2 (3). Youn, Steinberger, Schörg, Schmeckenbecher, Donose, Muraro, V. RSO & Ch., De Billy

(BB) (**(*)) Naxos mono 8.110206/7. Mildmay, Helletsgruber, Rautawaara, Domgraf-Fassbänder, Henderson, Nash, Glyndebourne Festival Ch. & O, Busch

(BB) *(*) EMI (ADD) 5 85520-2 (2). Evans, Fischer-Dieskau, Harper, Blegen, Berganza, Finnilä, Fryatt, John Aldis Ch., ECO, Barenboim

(N) (B) (**) Walhall WLCD 0083 (3). Schwarzkopf, Seefried, Jurinac, Panerai, Petri, Maionica, La Scala Ch. and O, Karajan

Recorded in 1973, Sir Peter Hall's production of *Figaro* at Glyndebourne is a model of its kind. Here is a traditional production that, far from being unimaginative, brings endless new perceptions and illuminations of the complicated plot devised by Lorenzo da Ponte from the original Beaumarchais play. John Bury's designs are solidly realistic yet comparably imaginative in the way that each scene is set diagonally on stage, giving interesting perspectives. The setting of the last Act is magically atmospheric, far more open than is usual, with a distant view of the Almavivas' palace, with its lights twinkling. The use of close-ups in the direction regularly clarifies the story.

The musical performance is comparably satisfying, with Sir John Pritchard pacing the piece superbly and directing a vintage Glyndebourne cast. It is led by three stars in their early prime: Ileana Cotrubas as a sparkling Susanna, Frederica von Stade as a wonderfully boyish Cherubino and, above all, Kiri te Kanawa as the Countess, commanding yet tenderly affecting in her vulnerability. They are matched by the lively Figaro of Knut Skram, rightly a favourite Glyndebourne singer, with clean, incisive delivery, Benjamin Luxon at his finest as the Count, Marius Rintzler as a dark, firm Bartolo and John Fryatt as a brilliant, witty Basilio, with Hall's production consistently enhancing their acting both in detail and overall. Fryatt as Basilio and Nucci Condo as Marcellina are each given their arias in Act IV, fully justifying their inclusion.

Like John Eliot Gardiner's CD version with the same forces, this DG DVD was recorded for video live, although at a different venue. Where the CDs were recorded at the Queen Elizabeth Hall in London, this staged version was made at the Théâtre du Châtelet in Paris, with economical but evocative sets. Simple screens illustrating each scene are dropped in front of a panoramic backcloth with trees and the Almaviva Palace in black silhouette against blue. Props as well as scenery are minimal but succeed in pointing the humour without distracting. The performance follows the splendid pattern of the CD version, with Terfel superb in the title-role, already at his peak in 1993, leading a young and consistently attractive cast. As on CD, the revised Moberly/Raeburn order of numbers for Act III is observed, and Gardiner's scholarly note arguing for an order reflecting key-relationships is also repeated from the CD set. Regrettably, no doubt for reasons of length, Marcellina's and Basilio's arias are omitted from Act IV, but otherwise this makes for an outstanding, consistently exhilarating presentation of the Mozart/Da Ponte masterpiece.

The Warner version must be one of the great bargains of DVD. At the time of writing it retails at £19.99, and you would not find it easy to get a CD version of any distinction at this price. And this *is* a performance of distinction, wonderfully conducted by Bernard Haitink and with four first-class principals. Gerald Finley's Figaro is expertly characterized and beautifully sung, and the same goes for both Renée Fleming's Countess and Alison Hagley's Susanna. The sets and staging are admirable in every way. It was with this production that the Glyndebourne Opera House reopened in May 1994 after its successful renovation. The three hours nine minutes are contained on one double-sided DVD, which accommodates two Acts per side. There are subtitles in English, French and German, together with cast and character screens. The quality of the colour and the sharpness of focus are in the demonstration bracket and so, too, is the vivid, well-balanced sound. Musically a satisfying set and one of the handful of DVDs that should be in every serious collection.

Recorded at the Lyon Opera in 1995, Jean-Pierre Vincent's production with economical designs by Jean-Paul Chambas in a broadly realistic style gives the impression that the Almaviva household was short of money, with bare walls and sparse furniture and with no one to smooth the Countess's rumpled bed in Act II. The team of young singers under Paolo Olmi is good if rarely exceptional, led by Giovanni Furlanetto as a strong, upstanding Figaro. Outstanding too is Janice Watson as the Countess, shading her big arias superbly, though the production tends to present her as a slightly sluttish figure. Elzbieta Szmytka is a bright, clear Susanna, and Ludovic Tezier a firm, young-looking Count. With limited use of close-ups, the direction does little to illuminate the acting in detail.

Gunther Rennert's 1966 Salzburg Festival production conducted by Karl Boehm, filmed in black and white, gives a good idea of the fine standards of the period. Ludwig Heinrich's designs are broadly realistic, with some distorted perspectives and designed to fill in a large stage. Quite apart from Boehm's idiomatic conducting, central to the success of the performance is the superb Figaro of Walter Berry, then at his peak, while Reri Grist makes a bright, pert Susanna, with the voice as recorded slightly shallow. Claire Watson is a reliable if rarely inspired Countess, and Ingvar Wixell is a strong if rather gruff Count, with Edith Mathis a charming Cherubino, Zoltan Kelemen an incisive Bartolo, and David Thaw an oily Basilio. Extravagantly, the performance spreads on to a second disc, even though Marcellina's and Basilio's arias are omitted from Act IV.

Dating from 1996, the TDK version on two DVDs offers a live recording of *Figaro* from the Zurich Opera House with Nikolaus Harnoncourt proving surprisingly expansive – not what one expects of a conductor who initially worked in the field of period performance. Not only are his speeds slow from the overture onwards, with the Countess's *Porgi amor* depressingly so, the recitatives are so pauseful that the action often fails to catch fire. It does not help that the staging by Jurgen Flimm is so bizarre, updated to the nineteenth century with bald and ugly sets by Erich Wonder. So Susanna (Isabel Rey) pours tea over the very young-looking Marcellina (Elisabeth von Magnus) in their duet of insults, and instead of having a chair in Act I Cherubino and the Count hide on and under a bare bedstead. The garden scene of Act IV is then dotted inconsequentially with modern deckchairs and garden furniture. The television direction by Felix Breisach compounds the problem by using more distance shots of the stage than usual. The singing and acting are variable, too. Rodney Gilfry makes an upstanding Count, as he does for John Eliot Gardiner, but Eva Mei is an undistinguished Countess, too often tremulous, and Rey a shrill Susanna, with Carlos Chausson a stiffly unfunny Figaro. The only advantage of the two-disc format is that it allows the arias of Marcellina and Basilio in Act IV, often omitted, to be included. The recorded sound puts an edge on all the women's voices. Not recommended.

Solti opts for a fair proportion of extreme speeds, slow as well as fast, but they rarely if ever intrude on the quintessential happiness of the entertainment. Samuel Ramey, a firm-toned baritone, makes a virile Figaro, superbly matched to the most enchanting of Susannas on record, Lucia Popp, who gives a sparkling and radiant performance. Thomas Allen's Count is magnificent too, tough in tone and characterization but always beautiful on the ear. Kurt Moll as Dr Bartolo sings an unforgettable *La vendetta* with triplets very fast and agile 'on the breath', while Robert Tear far outshines his own achievement as the Basilio of Sir Colin Davis's amiable recording. Frederica von Stade is a most attractive Cherubino, even if *Voi che sapete* is too slow; but crowning all is the Countess of Kiri Te Kanawa, challenged by Solti's spacious tempi in the two big arias, but producing ravishing tone, flawless phrasing and elegant ornamentation throughout. With superb, vivid recording this now makes a clear first choice for a much-recorded opera. However, in view of the strong competition, Decca should find a way of reducing its price.

Like others in EMI's series of Mozart operas, Giulini's set has been pleasingly re-packaged and has a cleanly printed, easy-to-read libretto, giving it an advantage over the competing double forte set. It remains a classic, with a cast assembled by Walter Legge that has rarely been matched, let alone surpassed. Taddei with his dark bass-baritone makes a provocative Figaro; opposite him, Anna Moffo is at her freshest and sweetest as Susanna. Schwarzkopf as ever is the noblest of Countesses, and it is good to hear the young Fiorenza Cossotto as a full-toned Cherubino. Eberhard Waechter is a strong and stylish Count. On only two mid-priced discs it makes a superb bargain, though – as in the other EMI two-disc version, the Gui – Marcellina's and Basilio's arias are omitted from Act IV.

Gui's effervescent Glyndebourne set has been promoted from Classics for Pleasure to EMI's own bargain double forte label. It costs a little more, but is worth every penny. It remains a classic set with a cast that has seldom been bettered, and the only regret is that there is a (very minor) cut to fit the recording on to two discs. There is no libretto, but the cued synopsis follows the narrative in detail, yet not giving the Italian titles of each item, only telling the listener what the character or characters are singing about. A pity, for this makes the set less easy to dip into.

Gardiner's CD version was recorded live, and this brings disadvantages in occasional intrusive stage noises, but it also offers a vividly dramatic and involving experience. In one instance the effect of the moment goes too far, when Cherubino (Pamela Helen Stephen) sings *Voi che sapete* for the Countess in a funny, nervous voice. That is very much the exception, for Gardiner's approach is lively and often brisk, with period manners made more genial and elegant. One of the most consistent and characterful of modern casts is led superbly by Bryn Terfel as Figaro, already a master in this role, with the enchanting, bright-eyed Alison Hagley as Susanna. Rodney Gilfry and Hillevi Martinpelto are fresh and firm as the Count and Countess, aptly younger-sounding than usual. Carlos Feller is a characterful *buffo* Bartolo, and Francis Egerton a wickedly funny Basilio. In Act III Gardiner adopts the revised order, suggested by Robert Moberly and Christopher Raeburn, with the Countess's aria placed earlier. More controversially, in Act IV he divides the recitative for Figaro's aria so that part of it comes logically before Susanna's *Deh vieni*.

Erich Kleiber's famous set was one of Decca's Mozart bicentenary recordings of the mid-1950s. It remains a memorably strong performance with much fine singing. Few sets since have matched its constant stylishness. Hilde Gueden's Susanna might be criticized but her golden tones are certainly characterful and her voice blends with Lisa Della Casa's enchantingly. Suzanne Danco and Della Casa are both at their finest. A dark-toned Figaro in Cesare Siepi brings added contrast and, if the pace of the recitatives is rather slow, this is not inconsistent within the context of Kleiber's overall approach. The closing scene of Act II is marvellously done.

Harnoncourt on Teldec makes the Royal Concertgebouw Orchestra produce fresh, light and transparent sounds, close to period style. The excellent cast has Thomas Hampson as a dominant Count, Charlotte Margiono as a tenderly sweet Countess, with Barbara Bonney a charmingly provocative Susanna and Anton Scharinger a winning Figaro, both tough and comic. Recitative at flexible speeds conveys the dramatic confrontations and complications vividly. A version that gets the best of both interpretative worlds, new and old. A generous budget Apex CD of highlights (76') is also available (2564 61514-2).

Boehm's version of *Figaro* is also among the most consistently assured performances available. The women all sing most beautifully, with Gundula Janowitz's Countess, Edith Mathis's Susanna and Tatiana Troyanos's Cherubino all ravishing the ear in contrasted ways. Hermann Prey is an intelligent if not very jolly-sounding Figaro, and Dietrich Fischer-Dieskau gives his dark, sharply defined reading of the Count's role. All told, a great success, with fine playing and recording, here impressively remastered.

Claudio Abbado adopts a surprisingly metrical, unyielding approach, failing to bend rhythms and phrases to suit the needs of words or plot or the natural expressiveness of singers. Sylvia McNair as Susanna, Cheryl Studer as the Countess and Cecilia Bartoli as Cherubino are all characterful and musically imaginative enough to overcome much of the dulling effect of this, but the character-roles of Dr Bartolo,

Marcellina and Basilio are all displayed colourlessly, with young voices unable to present the characters convincingly. Lucio Gallo is a dark-voiced Figaro who finds it hard to point comedy, similar in tone to the Count of Boje Skovhus, who however has a less pleasing, grittier voice. Most disappointing of all are the big ensembles where, with unexpectedly slow speeds and metrical rhythms, the comedy evaporates. Happily, the final resolution on *Contessa, perdono* is done ravishingly, with Studer crowning a totally radiant performance. McNair also sings enchantingly and Bartoli is ideally cast. It is worth hearing the set for these three alone. The recording, faithful to voices, is slightly cavernous.

The big advantage of the Telarc version is that Sir Charles Mackerras with the Scottish Chamber Orchestra provides some 34 minutes of alternative items and variants. It is fascinating, for example, to have two alternative versions of the Count's Act III aria, with the difficult triplets largely removed, and there is also a heavily ornamented version of Cherubino's *Voi che sapete*. Mackerras also encourages his singers to provide ornamentation in their arias and, more than his rivals, he inserts appoggiature, avoiding 'blunt endings'. Orchestrally, this is an exceptionally characterful reading, more so than for the singing of the arias and ensembles. Alastair Miles as Figaro sings superbly with clean focus but, next to his main rivals, he is straight-faced, and similarly the Susanna of Nuccia Focile is a little lacking in charm and humour, while Carol Vaness as the Countess is perhaps stressed by Mackerras's slow speeds (an exception) for her two big arias. The Count of Alessandro Corbelli is rather rough in tone, and Alfonso Antoniozzi is too light and unsteady as Bartolo, but Ryland Davies is a superb Basilio and Susanne Mentzer a strong Marcellina, both given their arias in Act IV, which comes complete on disc 3, along with the appendices.

Recorded in 1950, Herbert von Karajan's first recording of *Figaro* offers one of the most distinguished casts ever assembled; but, curiously at that period, they decided to record the opera without the *secco* recitatives. That is a most regrettable omission when all these singers are not just vocally immaculate but vividly characterful – as, for example, Sena Jurinac, a vivacious Cherubino. The firmness of focus in Erich Kunz's singing of Figaro goes with a delightful twinkle in the word-pointing, and Irmgard Seefried makes a bewitching Susanna. Schwarzkopf's noble portrait of the Countess – not always helped by a slight backward balance in the placing of the microphone for her – culminates in the most poignant account of her second aria, *Dove sono*. The sound, though obviously limited, presents the voices very vividly.

Though there are no star names in the cast on Arte Nova, these young singers form an excellent team with no seriously weak link. Standing out is the characterful Figaro of the Korean, Kwangchoul Youn, resonant and full of fun but with a hint of menace in the voice. Like the others, he responds well to the decision of the conductor, Bertrand de Billy – chief conductor of the Austrian Radio Orchestra in Vienna – to encourage extra elaborations and ornamentation in arias. So even *Non più andrai* includes little cadenzas, thrown off as though spontaneously, a pattern followed throughout the performance. As Susanna, Birgit Steinberger has an edge to the voice but generally manages to control it convincingly, and Regina Schörg as the Countess similarly controls her rapid vibrato to produce tender accounts of her key numbers, not least her two big arias, taken at aptly flowing speeds. Jochen Schmeckenbecher's Count is rather gruff, but

the Cherubino of Ruxandra Donose is excellent, with the ornamentation on her arias crisp and stylish. De Billy keeps the music moving, even refusing to relax in the Countess's crucial entry in the finale of Act IV, which is a rare misjudgement. A fortepiano is used for continuo instead of a harpsichord, and the studio recording is very full and well balanced. With both Marcellina's and Basilio's arias included in Act IV, the third of the three discs is devoted entirely to that final Act.

At the beginning of June 1934, only a few weeks after the very first Glyndebourne Festival, work was started on this pioneering recording of *Figaro*, reissued on Naxos. It was recorded and later issued by HMV on short-playing 78-r.p.m. discs in batches, arias separate from ensembles, and surprisingly the finished set omitted *secco* recitatives. Even so, with a classic cast the performance is well worth hearing, for, though in the Naxos transfer the orchestra is relatively dim, the voices come over well. Willi Domgraf-Fassbänder, father of Brigitte, is the most characterful Figaro, a dominant personality, even if his Italian is idiosyncratic. Audrey Mildmay, wife of John Christie, founder of Glyndebourne, is a charming, refined Susanna, nicely contrasted with Aulikki Rautawaara as the Countess. It is good too to have Heddle Nash in the comic role of Basilio, not a side of his work generally heard on disc, and Roy Henderson is characterful too as the Count, if a little stiff, stressed as he is by the high tessitura of his big aria and, like the others, by the often hectic speeds demanded from the overture onwards by the inspired Fritz Busch. A historic document well worth investigating at Naxos price.

For so lively a Mozartian, Barenboim takes a strangely staid view of *Figaro*. This EMI set was recorded soon after live performances at the Edinburgh Festival in 1976 and with substantially the same cast. Though recitatives are sharp enough, the result lacks sparkle, despite the characterful – if at times unsteady – Figaro of Sir Geraint Evans, in a classic characterization. The others too, on paper a fine, starry team, fail to project at full intensity, often thanks to slow speeds and unlifted rhythms. Those interested in individual singers might consider this set (especially at bargain price), but there are far finer versions than this. A synopsis is included, but nothing else.

The Karajan reading of 1954 with a near-ideal cast is taken from an Italian Radio broadcast, but sadly it offers rough, edgy sound with ill-focused voices. Added to that, Karajan seems intent on racing his singers off their feet to the point where the humour is undermined and ensembles tend to get scrambled. The exception is for the Countess of Elisabeth Schwarzkopf in her big arias, which are done spaciously with peerless command. The moment of forgiveness, too, *Contessa perdono*, finds Karajan at last relaxing. Yet many will find it fascinating to eavesdrop on such an occasion, whatever its faults, with Irmgard Seefried as Susanna, Rolando Panerai as Figaro, Sena Jurinac as Cherubino and Mario Petri as the Count all in superb voice.

Le nozze di Figaro (highlights)

(B) *** DG (ADD) 439 449-2 (from above complete recording, with Janowitz, Mathis, Prey, Fischer-Dieskau; cond. Boehm)

Boehm's selection includes many of the key numbers but, with a little over an hour of music, it is less than generous and inadequately documented; however, the singing is first class and the sound vivid.

The Marriage of Figaro (in English)

(N) **(*) Chan. 3113 (3). Kenny, Evans, Montague, Purves, Dazeley, Geoffrey Mitchell Ch., Philh. O, Parry

Even those who normally resist the idea of opera recordings in English should seriously consider this set, when the result using Jeremy Sams's lively translation is so refreshing. Arguably, *Figaro* gains more from being heard in English than any other opera, with the fun of the piece heightened; Parry's timing of the comedy here is impeccable, helped by light, clean textures and imaginative continuo-playing in recitatives, using fortepiano. The full, well-balanced recording helps too in sorting out the complications of the plot, even in such passages as the incident in Act I of Cherubino and the chair or the final dénouement in Act IV.

Most of the principals have had long experience of singing their roles on stage: Rebecca Evans as a golden-voiced Susanna for Welsh National Opera, Yvonne Kenny as a feisty, defiant Countess for Washington Opera (having graduated from the role of Susanna elsewhere), Diana Montague as a glowing Cherubino at Covent Garden, Christopher Purves as a powerful Figaro with Scottish Opera, and John Graham-Hall as a characterful Basilio at Glyndebourne. Williams Dazeley is the upstanding Count, and Jonathan Veira a rather young-sounding Bartolo. The one blemish is that Basilio's and Marcellina's arias are omitted in Act IV.

Der Schauspieldirektor (complete)

(M) **(*) Ph. (ADD) 422 536-2 (2). Welting, Cotrubas, Grant, Rolfe Johnson, LSO, C. Davis – *Zaïde* ***

There is no contest whatsoever between the two rival prima donnas presented in the Philips recording. *Ich bin die erste Sängerin* ('I am the leading prima donna'), they yell at each other; but here Ileana Cotrubas is completely in a world apart from the thin-sounding and shallow Ruth Welting. Colin Davis directs with fire and electricity a performance which is otherwise (despite the lack of spoken dialogue) most refreshing and beautifully recorded (in 1975) in a sympathetic acoustic.

Il sogno di Scipione

(*) Astreé E 8813 (2). Hartelius, Larsson, Brandes, Ford, Workman, Ovenden, Cremonesi, Louvre Ch. & O, Freiburger Bar. O, Goltz

Described as an 'azione teatrale', *Il sogno di Scipione* was first performed at the installation of Hieronimus Colloredo as Prince-Archbishop of Salzburg in 1772, having first been conceived as a celebratory piece for his predecessor, who promptly died. Like most early Mozart operas, it is an attractive trifle that only occasionally reveals the full individuality of the genius who was emerging. Sadly, this live recording, made in the Stravinsky Auditorium in Montreux in September 2000, is far too flawed to recommend beside the set about to be reissued in the Philips Mozart Edition. This new one uses period instead of modern instruments, but the style is rough and abrasive, and it is made worse by the unpleasantly dry acoustic. That also affects the voices, with only two of the soloists rising above the elimination of bloom, the radiant Malin Hartelius as Costanza and Christine Brandes as Licenza. All the others, including the distinguished tenor Bruce Ford, sound gritty or unsteady. The lumpish conducting of Gottfried von der Goltz really does not help either.

Zaïde (complete)

(M) *** Ph. (ADD) 422 536-2 (2). Mathis, Schreier, Wixell, Hollweg, Süss, Berlin State O, Klee – *Der Schauspieldirektor* **(*)

Zaïde, written between 1779 and 1780 and never quite completed, was a trial run for *Entführung*. Much of the music is superb, and melodramas at the beginning of each Act are strikingly effective and original, with the speaking voice of the tenor in the first heard over darkly dramatic writing in D minor. *Zaïde*'s arias in both Acts are magnificent: the radiantly lyrical *Ruhe sanft* is hauntingly memorable, and the dramatic *Tiger aria* is like Konstanze's *Martern aller Arten* but briefer and more passionate. Bernhard Klee directs a crisp and lively performance, with excellent contributions from singers and orchestra alike – a first-rate team, as consistently stylish as one could want.

Die Zauberflöte (DVD versions)

(*) Arthaus **DVD 100 188. Sonntag, Frei, Van der Walt, Mohr, Hauptmann, Connors (speaker), Ludwigsburg Festival Ch. & O, Gönnenwein (Dir: Axel Manthey; V/D: Ruth Kärch)

(*) DG **DVD 073 003-9. Battle, Serra, Araiza, Hemm, Moll, Schmidt (speaker), Met. Op. Ch. & O, Levine (Producers: Guus Mostart/John Cox; V/D: Brian Large)

Die Zauberflöte (CD versions)

*** DG 449 166-2 (2); Video VHS 072 447-3. Oelze, Schade, Sieden, Peeters, Finley, Backes, Monteverdi Ch., E. Bar. Sol., Gardiner

*** Erato 0630 12705-2 (2). Mannion, Blochwitz, Dessay, Hagen, Scharinger, Les Arts Florissants, Christie

⊛ (M) (***) DG mono 476 1752 (2). Stader, Streich, Fischer-Dieskau, Greindl, Haefliger, Berlin RIAS Ch. & SO, Fricsay

(M) *** EMI (ADD) 5 67388-2 (2) [567385]. Janowitz, Putz, Popp, Gedda, Berry, Frick, Schwarzkopf, Ludwig, Hoffgen (3 Ladies), Philh. Ch. & O, Klemperer

(M) (***) EMI mono 5 67071-2 (2) [567165]. Seefried, Lipp, Loose, Dermota, Kunz, Weber, V. State Op. Ch., VPO, Karajan

*** Telarc CD-80302 (2). Hadley, Hendricks, Allen, Anderson, Lloyd, SCO & Ch., Mackerras

(BB) *** Naxos 8. 660030/31 (2). Norberg-Schulz, Kwon, Lippert, Leitner, Tichy, Rydl, Hungarian Festival Ch., Failoni O, Budapest, Halász

(M) **(*) DG (ADD) 449 749-2 (2). Lear, Peters, Wunderlich, Fischer-Dieskau, Crass, Hotter, BPO, Boehm

(B) (***) Dutton mono 2CDEA 5011 (2). Lemnitz, Rosvaenge, Hüsch, Berger, Strienz, BPO, Beecham

The cast is less starry and the production less glamorous on the Arthaus DVD than the DG discussed below, but it has a good deal more style and gives more pleasure. None of the singers with the exception of Andrea Frei's Queen of the Night, who is inclined to be a little squally, falls seriously short of the highest standards and some are touched by considerable distinction – notably Ulrike Sonntag's Pamina and the Tamino of Deon van der Walt. Musically there is not much wrong and a great deal right about this performance, which is well paced and sensitively conducted by Wolfgang Gönnenwein. It comes from the Ludwigsburg Festival of 1992. The staging has great simplicity and the sets and costumes are all in bright primary colours. And no production detail gets in the way of Mozart.

The DG *Zauberflöte* is also pretty impressive. It derives from the Met.'s Mozart Bicentennial celebrations in 1991, and was issued on both video and LaserDisc but not on CD. It is not in the same league as the performances under Marriner, Gardiner, Boehm, Fricsay, Beecham and Karajan, under whom Araiza sang Tamino. The best performances, however, are Kathleen Battle's Pamina, Manfred Hemm's Papageno and Kurt Moll's magisterial Sarastro. David Hockney's sets are an absolute delight, and though Levine does not always get a light or transparent texture with his players, there is still a lot of pleasure to be had. Guus Mostart's adaptation of John Cox's production is pleasingly unobtrusive and Brian Large's visual direction up to his usual high standard. Though the quality of the picture does not match the definition and clarity of the BBC DVD of *Coppélia*, it is still very impressive.

John Eliot Gardiner rounds off his outstanding series for DG Archiv of Mozart's seven great mature operas with an electrifying account of *Zauberflöte*, even though the generally inspired casting is marred by the underpowered and uneven Sarastro of Harry Peeters. The recording was made in studio conditions over the same period as staged performances at the Ludwigsburg Festival, getting the best of both worlds. Gardiner is helped enormously by his choice of singer as Pamina, a young German soprano with a ravishingly pure and sweet voice, flawlessly controlled, Christiane Oelze. In the agonized Act II aria, *Ach, ich fühl's*, she conveys a depth of emotion rarely matched. Also superb is the American soprano who takes the role of Queen of the Night, with a voice as full and silvery as it is flexible, Cyndia Sieden. The Tamino of Michael Schade has youthful freshness combined with keen imagination; though there are more characterful Papagenos than Gerald Finley, few sing as freshly and cleanly as he. With recording clear and well balanced, the set offers an incidental practical advantage in putting the spoken dialogue on separate tracks.

Based on a production at the Aix-en-Provence Festival, and recorded in 1995 in collaboration with Radio France, William Christie's Erato set otherwise sweeps the board for recordings using period instruments, with Les Arts Florissants firm and full. More than his rivals, Christie wears his period manners easily and amiably, with fast speeds crisp and light, and with some numbers – such as Papageno's first aria – relaxedly expansive. There is no weak link in the cast, with Rosa Mannion a warm, touching Pamina, able to bring out deeper feelings as in *Ach, ich fühl's*, and Hans-Peter Blochwitz is an imaginative, sweetly expressive Tamino, while Natalie Dessay as Queen of the Night is unusually warm-toned for the role, not so much a frigid figure as a fully rounded character, with the coloratura display dazzlingly clear. Anton Scharinger is a genial, rich-toned Papageno, and Reinhard Hagen a Sarastro satisfyingly clean of focus. Above all, the joyful vigour of Mozart's inspiration captures one from first to last.

Fricsay's recording has been treasured by us since the early days of LP. It is an outstandingly fresh and alert *Die Zauberflöte*, marked by generally clear, pure singing and well-sprung orchestral playing at generally rather fast speeds which yet never sound rushed. It deserves its place within Universal's 'Penguin ❂ Collection'. Maria Stader and Dietrich Fischer-Dieskau phrase most beautifully, but the most spectacular singing comes from Rita Streich as a dazzling Queen of the Night, and the relatively close balance of the voice gives it the necessary power such as Streich could convey less readily in the opera house. Ernst Haefliger, too, is at his most honeyed in tone as Tamino, and only the rather gritty Sarastro of Josef Greindl falls short – and even he sings with a satisfying dark

resonance. This was the first version to spice the musical numbers with brief sprinklings of dialogue, just enough to prevent the work from sounding like an oratorio. Even including that, DG have managed to put each of the acts complete on a single disc.

Klemperer's conducting of *The Magic Flute* is one of his finest achievements on record; indeed, he is inspired, making the dramatic music sound more like Beethoven in its breadth and strength. The dialogue is omitted, but he does not miss the humour and point of the Papageno passages, and he gets the best of both worlds to a surprising degree. The cast is outstanding – look at the distinction of the Three Ladies alone – but curiously it is that generally most reliable of all the singers, Gottlob Frick as Sarastro, who comes nearest to letting the side down. Lucia Popp is in excellent form, and Gundula Janowitz sings Pamina's part with a creamy beauty that is just breathtaking. Nicolai Gedda too is a firm-voiced Tamino. The new transfer is managed expertly, and like Klemperer's set of Beethoven's *Fidelio*, this recording has reverted to mid-price and has been repackaged for its reissue as one of EMI's 'Great Recordings of the Century'.

The Vienna State Opera cast of Karajan's mono version of 1950 has not since been matched on record: Irmgard Seefried and Anton Dermota both sing with radiant beauty and great character, Wilma Lipp is a dazzling Queen of the Night, Erich Kunz as Papageno sings with an infectious smile in the voice, and Ludwig Weber is a commanding Sarastro. There is no spoken dialogue; but on two mid-priced CDs instead of three LPs, it is a Mozart treat not to be missed, with mono sound still amazingly vivid and full of presence. This is now another of EMI's 'Great Recordings of the Century'.

Though the recording puts a halo of reverberation round the sound, Mackerras and the Scottish Chamber Orchestra find an ideal scale for the work. His speeds are often faster than usual, not least in Pamina's great aria of lament, *Ach, ich fühl's*, but they always flow persuasively. Jerry Hadley makes a delightfully boyish Tamino, with Thomas Allen the most characterful Papageno, singing beautifully. Robert Lloyd is a noble Sarastro, and though June Anderson is a rather strenuous Queen of the Night, it is thrilling to have a big, dramatic voice so dazzlingly agile. Barbara Hendricks is a questionable choice as Pamina, not clean enough of attack, but the tonal quality is golden.

The Naxos set offers a very satisfying performance, well conducted and well recorded, with some very stylish solo singing and with a fair measure of German dialogue included (but on separate tracks to allow it to be programmed out if preferred). As Tamino, Herbert Lippert is a good, clean-cut Germanic tenor, hardly ever strained, with fine legato in *Dies Bildnis*. The young Norwegian, Elisabeth Norberg-Schulz, is a bright, girlish Pamina, who sustains a slow speed for *Ach, ich fühl's* very effectively, tenderly making it an emotional high point. Kurt Rydl is a powerful Sarastro, if not always perfectly steady, and Georg Tichy is a delightful Papageno, defying Halász's uncharacteristically stodgy tempo for his first aria, and from there consistently conveying characterful humour without vocal exaggeration. Hellen Kwon is an outstanding Queen of the Night, using full, firm tone with bright attack in her two big arias. The recording is clear and well balanced, with the Queen's thunder vividly caught.

One of the glories of Boehm's DG set is the singing of Fritz Wunderlich as Tamino, a wonderful memorial to a singer much missed. Fischer-Dieskau, with characteristic word-pointing, makes a sparkling Papageno on record and Franz Crass is a satisfyingly straightforward Sarastro. The team of women is well below this standard – Evelyn Lear taxed cruelly in *Ach, ich fühl's*, Roberta Peters shrill in the upper register (although the effect is exciting), and the Three Ladies do not blend well – but Boehm's direction is superb, light and lyrical, but weighty where necessary to make a glowing, compelling experience. Fine recording, enhanced in this new transfer.

Beecham's magical pre-war set of *Zauberflöte* has had three earlier CD transfers, all of them seriously flawed, which makes it especially welcome that Mike Dutton comes up with a transfer which at last does justice to the original sound, full and vivid; and the two discs are offered at bargain price. There is glorious singing from Tiana Lemnitz as Pamina, brilliant coloratura from Erna Berger as Queen of the Night, and sharp characterization from Gerhard Hüsch as Papageno. Helge Rosvaenge is a Germanic Tamino and Wilhelm Strienz a firm but lugubrious Sarastro. No spoken dialogue, but much warmth and sparkle.

Die Zauberflöte (highlights)

(M) *** EMI (ADD) 5 65568-2 (from above complete recording, with Janowitz, Putz, Popp, Gedda; cond. Klemperer)

(BB) *** EMI Encore 5 74770-2. (from complete recording with Popp, Jerusalem, Gruberová, Lindner, Brendel, Bracht, Bav. R. Ch. & SO, cond. Haitink)

Those looking for a first-rate set of highlights from *Die Zauberflöte* will find the mid-priced Klemperer disc hard to beat. It makes a good sampler of a performance which, while ambitious in scale, manages to find sparkle and humour too. A synopsis details each individual excerpt, and in this case the inclusion of the overture is especially welcome. The remastered sound has plenty of presence, but atmosphere and warmth too.

The selection from the Haitink set makes a fine bargain on the Encore label, including many favourites. Jerusalem makes an outstanding Tamino, Popp the most tenderly affecting of Paminas, and Gruberová has never sounded more spontaneous in her brilliance than here as Queen of the Night. The gravitas of Haitink's approach does not miss the work's charm, and the quality of the singing is matched by outstanding, wide-ranging digital sound.

The Magic Flute (complete; in English)

(N) *** Chan. 3121 (2). Evans, Vidal, Banks, Keenlyside, Tomlinson, Graham-Hall, Mitchell Ch., LPO, Mackerras

In superb sound, vivid and immediate, Sir Charles Mackerras conducts an exceptionally fresh and lively reading of *The Magic Flute* which is very well cast and an outstanding addition to Sir Peter Moore's Opera in English series. In his own note, the conductor explains his approach to tempo, arguing that in Mozart's time speeds faster than we are used to would have been preferred; and here, with no sense of rush, he regularly opts for brisk and flowing speeds, most strikingly in Pamina's great G minor aria, *Ach, ich fühls* ('Now I know that love can vanish' in Jeremy Sams's translation). Rebecca Evans sings passionately, as Mackerras suggests, coping splendidly with the florid writing. So does the French coloratura, Elisabeth Vidal, in the Queen of the Night's two big arias, bright and agile. That she betrays a hint of a foreign accent in the spoken dialogue (well edited in helpful links) is only apt. Standing out is the masterly portrayal of Papageno by Simon Keenlyside, vividly acted and flawlessly sung, and though Barry Banks as Tamino has his moments of roughness in dramatic passages, he sings very well in the lyrical

numbers. John Tomlinson as Sarastro gives necessary weight to the role, even if he is not always quite as steady as he once was, while John Graham-Hall sings and acts vividly as Monostatos, unfazed by Mackerras's hectic speed for his aria. Luxury casting too when singers of the calibre of Diana Montague (Third Lady) and Lesley Garrett (Papagena) are chosen for incidental roles. Defying the fast speeds, the vocal ensembles are wonderfully crisp, as is the playing of the LPO. As well as the well-delivered dialogue, the vivid sound-effects regularly add to the dramatic impact.

RECITALS

Arias and Duets from: *Così fan tutte; Davidde Penitente; Don Giovanni; Die verstellte Gärtnerin.* Arias: *Mentre ti lascio, o figlia; Misero! O Sogno ... Aura che intorno spiti; Per pietà, non ricercate; Si mostra la sorte; Un bacio di mano*
*** DHM/BMG 82876 55782-2. Christoph Genz, Stephan Genz, La Petite Bande, Kuijken

The tenor Christoph Genz and his baritone brother Stephan are among the most interesting young German singers of their generation; here, in a recording made in Spain, they offer a series of eleven arias, tricked out with the only two duets that Mozart wrote for tenor and baritone, both from *Così fan tutte*, shorter than most of the items here. The selection ranges wide, including not only popular favourites like Ferrando's *Un'aura amorosa* from *Così*, elegantly done, and Don Giovanni's Serenade, but rarities like the more extended aria that Mozart gave to Guglielmo in *Così* and *Per pietà*, an aria that Mozart wrote to be inserted in an opera by Pasquale Anfosso. Excellent as the performances are, the snag is that the closeness of the recording takes away some of the bloom on the voices, occasionally bringing a hint of roughness.

Arias from: (i) *La clemenza di Tito;* (ii) *Così fan tutte; Don Giovanni;* (i) *Lucio Silla; Mitridate, rè di Ponto;* (i) *Le nozze di Figaro; Zaïde; Die Zauberflöte*
(B) *** CfP 585 9022. SCO, with (i) Murray; cond. Leppard; (ii) Allen; cond. Armstrong

Dating from 1984, when both singers were in their prime, this is one of the most delectable collections of Mozart arias ever assembled on a single disc. Sir Thomas Allen has the lion's share, and he is in superb form in the four *Figaro* arias and in Papageno's pair from *Die Zauberflöte*. His honeyed legato in *Deh vieni alla finestra* from *Don Giovanni* is matched by the sheer gusto of *Finch'han dal vino*. To conclude, there are two rarer excerpts from *Zaïde*, and the engaging *Un bacio di mano*, an insertion aria which Mozart wrote for Pasquale Anfossi's *Le gelosie fortunate* in 1788. Ann Murray then takes over for splendidly sung excerpts from *La clemenza di Tito* (*Parto parto*, with the clarinet obbligato stylishly played by Lewis Morrison) and the spectacular *Lungi da te, mio bene* from *Mitridate, rè di Ponto*, with a fine horn obbligato from Frank Lloyd, who also stays around to contribute similarly to the Handelian encore, *Va tacito e nascosto* from Act I of *Giulio Cesare*, which is equally impressive. With stylish accompaniments from the Scottish Chamber Orchestra under Sir Richard Armstrong or Raymond Leppard, and warm, natural recording, which (because of the skill of the balance engineer, Stuart Eltham) is kind to both voices. At Classics for Pleasure price this is quite irresistible.

Arias: *La Clemenza di Tito; Don Giovanni; Die Entführung aus dem Serail; Idomeneo; Le nozze di Figaro; Il re pastore.* Concert Arias: *Ah, conte, partite, K.418; Resta o cara, K.528; Vado, ma dove?, K.583*

(N) (M) *** RCA 82876 65841-2. Margaret Price, ECO or LPO, Lockgart

An impressive disc of display arias. Margaret Price shows her versatility by singing excerpts from all three soprano roles in *Figaro*, but her most impressive performances remain those which demand coloratura brilliance combined with dramatic power. Strong accompaniments and good recording.

Arias from: *La clemenza di Tito; La finta giardiniera; Idomeneo; Le nozze di Figaro*

*** DG 471 334-2. Kožená, Prague Philh. O, Swierczewski – GLUCK: *Arias*; MYSLIVECEK: *Arias* ***

The Czech mezzo, Magdalena Kožená, glamorous of voice as well as of appearance, is an outstanding stylist in whatever she sings, seemingly untroubled by any of the formidable technical challenges in this fascinating collection of arias. The familiar Mozart arias are superbly done, all made to sound fresh and new, even Cherubino's aria from *Figaro*. An outstanding disc, with the valuable coupling of arias by Gluck and the under-appreciated Myslivecek. Under Swierczewski the Prague Philharmonia equals the Czech Philharmonic in the refinement of their playing.

Arias from: *La clemenza di Tito; Idomeneo; Lucio Silla; Le nozze di Figaro*

*** Erato 8573 85768-2. Graham, OAE, Bickett – GLUCK: *Aria* ***

This is a glorious recital of Mozart and Gluck, with Susan Graham radiant and characterful in arias she has sung on stage, highlighting the distinctive points of each character. So from *La clemenza di Tito* she contrasts Sesto's purposeful first aria with the far gentler second, producing a breathtaking *pianissimo* on the reprise. Cherubino's two arias from *Figaro* are made to sound new and intense, with the last and longest item, Cecilio's big, taxing number from *Lucio Silla*, *Il tenero momento*, providing the title of the whole recital, making a superb climax. Fine, sympathetic accompaniment and perfect sound.

Arias from: *La clemenza di Tito; Così fan tutte; Don Giovanni; Idomeneo; Lucio Silla; Mitridate; Le nozze di Figaro*

*** RCA 09026 68661-2. Kasarova, Dresden State O, C. Davis

The young Bulgarian, Vesselina Kasarova, with her tangy, sharply projected mezzo, is both characterful and magnetic. Here in a formidable collection of Mozart arias, much enhanced by Colin Davis's accompaniment, she demonstrates not only her stylishness and technical prowess – with not a single intrusive aitch allowed – but her musical flair. At the very start, she launches into the recitative before Dorabella's aria in *Così fan tutte* with a vehemence that takes the breath away, and vehemence is a quality that draws many of these portrayals together, whether as Donna Elvira in *Don Giovanni* (giving way to tenderness when required), Vitellia in *Clemenza* or a whole range of trouser-roles, including those in the early *Mitridate* and *Lucio Silla*.

Arias from: *Don Giovanni; Die Entführung aus dem Serail; La finta giardiniera; Le nozze di Figaro; Il re pastore; Il sogno di Scipione; Zaïde; Die Zauberflöte.* Concert aria: *Nehmt meinen Dank*

*** Decca 452 602-2. Fleming, O of St Luke's, Mackerras

Renée Fleming has rarely sounded quite so beautiful on disc as in this wide-ranging collection of Mozart arias, one of the finest available. If it is disappointing not to have her singing the role of the Countess in *Figaro*, the two Susanna items are both welcome – *Deh vieni* bringing out her most golden tone and the big alternative aria, *Al desio*, challenging her to her most brilliant singing. Her account of La Fortuna's aria from *Il sogno di Scipione* is commanding too, and her ornamentation is phenomenally crisp and brilliant throughout, not least in *Ach ich liebte* from *Entführung*. The only reservations come with the brisk treatment, period-style, of Pamina's *Ach, ich fühl's* and the lovely aria from *Zaïde*, both of which could be much more tenderly expressive. Excellent, stylish accompaniment and first-rate recording.

Arias: *Don Giovanni; Die Entführung aus dem Serail; Idomeneo; Le nozze di Figaro; Die Zauberflöte*

(M) (***) EMI mono 7 63708-2. Schwarzkopf (with various orchestras & conductors, including John Pritchard)

Just how fine a Mozartian Schwarzkopf already was early in her career comes out in these 12 items, recorded between 1946 and 1952. The earliest are Konstanze's two arias from *Entführung*, and one of the curiosities is a lovely account of Pamina's *Ach ich fühl's*, recorded in English in 1948. The majority, including those from *Figaro* – Susanna's and Cherubino's arias as well as the Countess's – are taken from a long-unavailable recital disc conducted by John Pritchard. Excellent transfers.

ANTHOLOGIES

'*Fifty Years of Mozart Singing on Record*': (i) *Concert Arias;* Excerpts from: (ii) *Mass in C min., K.427;* (iii) *La clemenza di Tito;* (iv) *Così fan tutte;* (v) *Don Giovanni;* (vi) *Die Entführung aus dem Serail;* (vii) *La finta giardiniera;* (viii) *Idomeneo;* (ix) *Le nozze di Figaro;* (x) *Il re pastore;* (xi) *Zaïde;* (xii) *Die Zauberflöte*

(M) (***) EMI mono 7 63750-2 (4). (i) Rethberg, Ginster, Francillo-Kaufmann; (ii) Berger; (iii) Kirkby-Lunn; (iv) V. Schwarz, Noni, Grümmer, Hahn, Kiurina, Hüsch, Souez, H. Nash; (v) Vanni-Marcoux, Scotti, Farrar, Battistini, Corsi, Leider, Rosvaenge, D'Andrade, Pinza, Patti, Maurel, Renaud, Pernet, McCormack, Gadski, Kemp, Callas; (vi) Slezak, L. Weber, Tauber, Lehmann, Nemeth, Perras, Ivogün, Von Pataky, Hesch; (vii) Dux; (viii) Jurinac, Jadlowker; (ix) Stabile, Helletsgruber, Santley, Gobbi, Lemnitz, Feraldy, Schumann, Seinemeyer, Vallin, Rautawaara, Mildmay, Jokl, Ritter-Ciampi; (x) Gerhart; (xi) Seefried; (xii) Fugère, Wittrisch, Schiøtz, Gedda, Kurz, Erb, Kipnis, Galvany, Hempel, Sibiriakov, Frick, Destinn, Norena, Schöne, Kunz

This is an astonishing treasury of singing, recorded over the first half of the twentieth century. It begins with Mariano Stabile's resonant (1928) account of Figaro's *Se vuol ballare*, snail-like by today's standards, while Sir Charles Santley in *Non più andrai* a few tracks later is both old-sounding and slow. The stylistic balance is then corrected in Tito Gobbi's magnificently characterful 1950 recording of that same aria. Astonishment lies less in early stylistic enormities than in the wonderful and consistent purity of vocal production, with wobbles – so prevalent today – virtually non-existent. That is partly the result of the shrewd and obviously loving choice of items, which include not only celebrated marvels like John McCormack's 1916 account of Don Ottavio's *Il mio tesoro* (breaking all records for breath control, and stylistically surprising for including an appoggiatura), but many rarities. The short-lived Meta Seinemeyer, glorious in the Countess's first aria, Germaine Feraldy, virtually unknown, a charming Cherubino, Johanna Gadski formidably incisive in Donna Anna's *Mi tradi*, Frieda Hempel incomparable in the Queen of the Night's second aria – all these and many dozens of others make for compulsive listening, with transfers generally excellent. There are far more women singers represented than men, and a high proportion of early recordings are done in languages other than the original; but no lover of fine singing should miss this feast. The arias are gathered together under each opera, with items from non-operatic sources grouped at the end of each disc. Helpfully, duplicate versions of the same aria are put together, irrespective of date of recording, and highly informative notes are provided on all the singers.

MUNDY, William (c. 1529–c. 1591)

Vox Patris caelestis

☛ *** Gimell CDGIM 339. Tallis Scholars, Phillips –
ALLEGRI: *Miserere*; PALESTRINA: *Missa Papae Marcelli* ***

Mundy's *Vox Patris caelestis* was written during the short reign of Queen Mary (1553–8). The work is structured in nine sections in groups of three, the last of each group being climactic and featuring the whole choir, with solo embroidery. Yet the music flows continuously, like a great river, and the complex vocal writing creates the most spectacular effects, with the trebles soaring up and shining out over the underlying cantilena. The Tallis Scholars give an account which balances linear clarity with considerable power. The recording is first class and the digital remastering for CD improves the focus further.

MUSSORGSKY, Modest (1839–81)

The Capture of Kars (Triumphal March); St John's Night on the Bare Mountain (original score); Scherzo in B flat; Khovanshchina: Prelude to Act I; (i) Introduction to Act IV. The Destruction of Sennacherib; (i; ii) Joshua; (i) Oedipus in Athens: Temple Chorus. Salammbô: Priestesses' Chorus (operatic excerpts all orch. Rimsky-Korsakov)

(M) *** RCA (ADD) 09026 61354-2. (i) L. Symphony Ch.; (ii) Zehava Gal; LSO, Abbado

It is particularly good to have so vital and pungent an account of the original version of *Night on the Bare Mountain*, different in all but its basic material from the Rimsky-Korsakov arrangement. Mussorgsky's scoring is so original and imaginative that the ear is readily held. Best of all are the four choral pieces; even when they are early and atypical (*Oedipus in Athens*, for example), they are immediately attractive and very Russian in feeling, and they include such evocative pieces as the *Chorus of Priestesses* (intoning over a pedal bass) from a projected opera on Flaubert's novel. The recording is first rate, and this is one of the most attractive Mussorgsky records in the catalogue.

Night on the Bare Mountain (orch. Rimsky-Korsakov)

(BB) **(*) EMI Encore (ADD) 5 74763-2. Philh. O, Cluytens –
RIMSKY-KORSAKOV: *Capriccio espagnol*, etc.; BORODIN: *In the Steppes of Central Asia* **(*)

An impressively dramatic performance from Cluytens, full of imaginative touches, dating from 1958 yet sounding astonishingly well in this transfer; only a touch of thinness by modern standards betrays its age, but the sound is beautifully balanced. Part of a highly attractive budget CD of Russian showpieces.

Night on the Bare Mountain; St John's Night on the Bare Mountain (original score); Pictures at an Exhibition (orch. Ravel); Khovanshchina: Golitsïn's Departure. Sorochinsky Fair: Gopak

☛ (BB) *** Naxos 8.555924. Nat. SO of Ukraine, Kuchar

It was an imaginative idea to record both Mussorgsky's original score – *St John's Night on the Bare Mountain* – alongside Rimsky's finished orchestral tone-poem, for in most respects they are entirely different works. Theodor Kuchar makes this plain by his contrasting interpretations, and he demonstrates that, however inspired and original Mussorgsky's draft may be in its rough-and-ready conception, the far more integrated Rimsky-Korsakov piece is the finer work overall. With a superbly rasping opening from the heavy brass, Kuchar demonstrates its malignant force, deftly amalgamating Rimsky's interpolated, very Russian, brass fanfares, then producing a serenely peaceful close, with lovely playing from the strings and woodwind. *St John's Night* begins in a comparable atmosphere of malevolence, but the witches' jamboree which follows is bizarrely grotesque rather than evil. Yet Kuchar sustains the tension through the composer's weird sequential repetitions before the brief, unearthly coda, which of course is without Rimsky's radiant apotheosis.

Mussorgsky's jolliest Russian dance, the Sorochinsky 'Gopak', is engagingly spirited, to be followed by a moving performance of the darkly mournful orchestral description of Prince Golitsïn's exile from Khovanshchina. Ravel's incomparable orchestration of *Pictures at an Exhibition* then proves an excitingly vivid showpiece for this superb Russian orchestra which paints the *Tuileries* and the cheeping *Unhatched Chicks* in glowing colours, while the solo saxophone sings his melancholy serenade touchingly outside the *Old Castle*. The massed lower strings show the fullest body of tone in depicting *Samuel Goldenberg*, and the sudden, bold brass entry in *Catacombs* has the richest underlying sonority. The percussion really make their mark in *The Hut on Fowls' Legs*, and the bass drum adds dramatic impact, both here and in the triumphant climax of the closing *Great Gate of Kiev*, which is thrillingly expansive, with Kuchar broadening the final statement of the great chorale to produce a frisson of weighty spectacle, helped by the demonstration sound-quality. An outstanding disc in every way which is strongly recommendable, quite irrespective of its modest price.

Night on the Bare Mountain; Khovanshchina: Prelude (both orch. Rimsky-Korsakov); Pictures at an Exhibition

(B) ** EMI double forte 5 75172-2 (2). Oslo PO, Jansons –
RIMSKY-KORSAKOV: *Scheherazade; Capriccio espagnol* **(*)

The highlight of Jansons's recording is the haunting *Khovanshchina Prelude*, which is played most beautifully, yet produces a passionate climax. *Night on the Bare Mountain* is diabolically pungent, but here, as in the *Pictures*, the fiercely brilliant EMI recording, with its dry bass and lack of sumptuousness, brings dramatic bite and sharply etched detail, but less in the way of expansiveness.

Night on the Bare Mountain; Khovanshchina Prelude (both orch. Rimsky-Korsakov); Pictures at an Exhibition (orch. Ravel); Sorochinsky Fair: Gopak

**(*) SACD 470 619-2; CD 468 526-2. VPO, Gergiev

Gergiev's *Pictures* are often vivid and very well played, but take a while to warm up, and the closing pages do not match Kuchar on Naxos in excitement and spectacle. The finest performance here is *Night on the Bare Mountain*, the *Gopak* too has plenty of spirit. The recording is sumptuous (especially on SACD) and this suits the *Khovanshchina Prelude*. But overall the Ukrainian Naxos collection is far more recommendable.

Night on the Bare Mountain (arr. Rimsky-Korsakov); Pictures at an Exhibition (orch. Ravel)

☛ ***** DG (IMS)** 429 785-2. NYPO, Sinopoli — RAVEL: *Valses nobles et sentimentales* ****(*)**

(N) (M) *** RCA SACD (ADD) 82876 61394-2. Chicago SO, Reiner (with TCHAIKOVSKY: *Marche slave; Marche miniature*; BORODIN: *Polovtsian March*; KABALEVSKY: *Colas Breugnon Overture*; GLINKA: *Ruslan and Ludmilla Overture* *******)

(B) **(*) Decca 448 233-2. Montreal SO, Dutoit — RIMSKY-KORSAKOV: *Capriccio espagnol*, etc. ****(*)**

(BB) ** Virgin 2×1 5 61751-2 (2). RLPO & Ch., Mackerras — BORODIN: *Prince Igor: Overture & Polovtsian Dances* *******; RIMSKY-KORSAKOV: *Scheherazade* ****(*)**; TCHAIKOVSKY: *The Tempest* *******

Sinopoli's electrifying New York recording of Mussorgsky's *Pictures at an Exhibition* again displays the New York Philharmonic as one of the world's great orchestras, performing with an epic virtuosity and panache that recall the Bernstein era of the 1960s. The playing of violins and woodwind alike is full of sophisticated touches, but it is the brass that one remembers most, from the richly sonorous opening *Promenade* to the malignantly forceful rhythms of *The Hut on Fowl's Legs*, with the playing of the trombones and tuba often assuming an unusual yet obviously calculated dominance of the texture. The finale combines power with dignified splendour. *A Night on the Bare Mountain* is comparably vibrant, with the Rimskian fanfares particularly vivid and the closing pages full of Russian nostalgia. The splendid digital recording was made in New York's Manhattan Center.

Reiner's 1957 *Pictures* is another demonstration of vintage stereo using simple microphone techniques to achieve a natural concert-hall ambience. The sound-balance is full and atmospheric, and Reiner's approach is evocative to match – the sombre picture of *The Old Castle*, the lumbering *Ox-Wagon*, the unctuous picture of *Samuel Goldenberg* (powerfully drawn in the strings) and the superb brass playing in the *Catacombs* sequence are all memorable. The final climax of *The Great Gate of Kiev* is massively effective. The Chicago brass is again very telling in *Night on the Bare Mountain*, made two years later, a performance that is just as strongly characterized. The rest of the orchestral items go splendidly, with the sparkling *Colas Breugnon Overture* one of the highlights. The charming *Marche miniature* is played with much delicacy, and there is no lack of energy in the *Ruslan and Ludmilla Overture*, with its superbly pointed strings and crisp

brass. Those with SACD playback facilities will find even greater warmth and spread of sound.

Dutoit's *A Night on the Bare Mountain* is strong and biting. His *Pictures* have each movement strongly characterized and there is a sense of fun in the scherzando movements, but overall this is less involving than with Reiner, and the brilliant recording is not as sumptuous as some other versions, although it has the bloom characteristic of the Montreal sound.

Mackerras's characterization of Mussorgsky's picture gallery comes over at a lower voltage than expected and it is not until *Limoges* that the performance springs fully to life; then *The Hut on Fowl's Legs* is powerfully rhythmic, with an impressive tuba solo. *The Great Gate of Kiev* is not as consistently taut as some versions, but is it properly expansive at the close, with the recording, always full-bodied, producing an impressive breadth of sound. *A Night on the Bare Mountain*, although vivid enough, lacks satanic bite and its closing pages fail to wrench the heartstrings.

(i) Night on the Bare Mountain (arr. Rimsky-Korsakov); Pictures at an Exhibition (arr. Funtek); (ii) Songs & Dances of Death (arr. Aho)

*** BIS CD 325. (i) Finnish RSO, (i) Segerstam; (ii) Järvi, with Talvela

This CD offers an orchestration by Leo Funtek, made in the same year as Ravel's (1922). The use of a cor anglais in *The Old Castle* mirrors Stokowski, while the soft-grained wind scoring makes the portrait of *Samuel Goldenberg and Schmuyle* more sympathetic, if also blander. The performances by the Finnish Radio Orchestra under Leif Segerstam both of this and of the familiar Rimsky *Night on the Bare Mountain* are spontaneously presented and very well recorded. The extra item is no less valuable: an intense, darkly Russian account of the *Songs and Dances of Death* from Martti Talvela with the orchestral accompaniment plangently scored by Kalevi Aho.

Night on the Bare Mountain; Pictures at an Exhibition; Khovanshchina, Act IV: Entr'acte. Boris Godunov: Symphonic Synthesis (all arr. and orch. Stokowski)

*** Chan. 9445. BBC PO, Bamert
*** DG 457 656-2. Cleveland O, Knussen

Oliver Knussen is a devotee both of Mussorgsky's music and of the conducting of Leopold Stokowski, who was a family friend when Oliver was a boy. That makes him an ideal interpreter of these colourful Stokowski arrangements, recorded in 1995–6, but not issued until 2004. Koussevitzky, who commissioned the Ravel transcription of the *Pictures*, retained exclusive performance rights for a number of years, so Stokowski created his own score, leaving out *Tuileries* and *The Market-Place at Limoges* for not very convincing reasons. Although he draws on Ravel in using a squeaking solo trumpet in *Samuel Goldenberg and Schmuyle*, much else is different and he opens the first *Promenade* with strings and low woodwind, in place of the brass. Knussen makes sure the effect has dignity and that the score's richness of colour is displayed throughout, for example in the serenade of *The Old Castle*, where the solo is given to the melancholy cor anglais.

As we discovered in Walt Disney's *Fantasia*, Stokowski's *Night on the Bare Mountain* is malevolently spectacular. He said that he went back to the 'original orchestration' – but which is that? Rimsky's version was based on Mussorgsky's revision for use in *Sorochinsky Fair*, which is vocal. Anyway,

Stokowski's transcription is splendidly played here, with a tolling bell left resonating at the close.

The *Symphonic Synthesis* from *Boris Godunov* fully captures the dramatic essence of the opera; the portrayal of the monks chanting may be romanticized, but it is genuinely evocative, and the two closing scenes (featuring the Idiot's warning and the death of Boris) also come off with moving narrative effect on the orchestra alone. But perhaps the most telling of Stokowski's Mussorgsky 'operatic scenas' is the entr'acte to *Khovanshchina*, scored with glowing richness. Knussen's performances are both powerful and polished, but a direct comparison with the Chandos disc of the identical coupling reveals how much fuller the Chandos sound is, weightier and more immediate with exceptionally powerful brass. One of the few marked interpretative contrasts is in *Bydlo*, the Polish ox-cart movement of *Pictures*, which Knussen takes unusually fast (too fast?), making the ox-cart move briskly, where Bamert makes it lumber along, as one expects it to do.

Pictures at an Exhibition (orch. Ravel)

(M) *** DG (ADD) 447 426-2. BPO, Karajan – DEBUSSY: *La Mer*; RAVEL: *Boléro* ***

(B) *** Sony (ADD) SBK 48162. Cleveland O, Szell – KODALY: *Háry János Suite*; PROKOFIEV: *Lieutenant Kijé Suite* ***

⊶ (M) *** RCA (ADD) 09026 61401-2. Chicago SO, Reiner – RESPIGHI: *Fountains of Rome*; *Pines of Rome* *** ☯

*** DG Gold (IMS) 439 013-2. BPO, Karajan – RAVEL: *Boléro, etc.* ***

(BB) *** EMI Encore 5 74581-2 [574742]. Phd. O, Muti – STRAVINSKY: *Rite of Spring* ***

(M) *** Decca (IMS) 417 754-2. Chicago SO, Solti – BARTOK: *Concerto for Orchestra* ***

(BB) *** DG Entrée (ADD/DDD) 474 564-2. Chicago SO, Giulini – RIMSKY-KORSAKOV: *Scheherazade* *

(B) **(*) RCA 74321 88692-2 (2). Chicago SO, Ozawa – DEBUSSY: *Images: Ibéria. La Mer* *** ☯; RAVEL: *Alborada, etc.* ***

(**(*)) BBC mono BBCL 4023-2. Philh. O, Giulini – TCHAIKOVSKY: *Symphony 6* (**(*))

(BB) (**(*)) Naxos mono 8.110154. Boston SO, Koussevitzky – RAVEL: *Boléro, etc.* (**)

(N) ** Australian Decca Eloquence 476 2452. Concg. O, Chailly – RAVEL: *Boléro* **(*); DEBUSSY: *Danse, etc.* **(*)

Pictures at an Exhibition (orch. Ravel); Khovanshchina: Prelude

(N) *** Sony SACD SS 89414. Cleveland O, Szell – BIZET: *L'Arlésienne: Suite*; GRIEG: *Peer Gynt Suite* ***

(N) (B) **(*) Sony (ADD) 516238-2 [SK 93018]. Cleveland O, Szell (with LIADOV: *The Enchanted Lake.*; BORODIN: *Polovtsian Dances*; RIMSKY-KORSAKOV: *Capriccio espagnol*)

(N) (M) **(*) Van. (ADD) Surround Sound SACD ATMCD 1504. New Philh. O, Mackerras

Among the many fine versions of Mussorgsky's *Pictures* on CD, Karajan's 1966 record stands out. It is undoubtedly a great performance, tingling with electricity from the opening *Promenade* to the spaciously conceived finale, *The Great Gate of Kiev*, which has real splendour. The remastered analogue recording still sounds marvellous, and this reissue, in DG's 'Originals' series of legendary recordings, includes a uniquely evocative performance of Debussy's *La Mer* as well as a very exciting account of Ravel's *Boléro*.

Szell's 1963 Cleveland performance also remains among the greatest of all recordings of Ravel's vividly inspired orchestration. Even if the recording has a somewhat less expansive dynamic-range, the character of each portrait is firmly drawn with vivid strokes of orchestral colour. The portrayal of *Goldenberg and Schmuyle* brings superbly full articulation from the lower strings, and *Baba-Yaga* makes the most incisive impact. Whether in the cheeping and chattering of the unhatched chicks, the bravura swirl of the *Limoges Market*, or the dignified grandiloquence of that final great gateway of Kiev, the controlled brilliance of the recording projects everything with extraordinary vividness.

As can be seen, Szell's performance is available in various formats. The most impressive of all is the SACD, which adds Szell's ravishing performance of the *Khovanshchina Prelude*, dating from 1968. But the warmly expansive quality disguises the recording's age, as it does indeed of the *Pictures*. The original bargain CD is apparently still available, coupled with outstanding accounts of Kodály's *Háry János Suite* and Prokofiev's *Lieutenant Kijé Suite*; there is also now an alternative CD bargain reissue, coupled with the *Capriccio espagnol* and *Polovtsian Dances*. They are also superbly played, and the Liadov tone-picture, *The Enchanted Lake*, is quite magically beautiful in its atmospheric sheen, the sound here again warmly atmospheric.

With the advantage of the rich acoustics of Symphony Hall, the RCA sound-balance of Reiner's 1957 Chicago performance is highly atmospheric, if less sharply focused. The finale climax of *The Great Gate of Kiev* shows the concentration of the playing. The remastering is fully worthy, and there is excellent documentation.

Karajan's 1986 recording is one of the most impressive of DG's digital recordings. The tangibility of the sound is remarkable, with the opening brass *Promenade* and the massed strings in *Samuel Goldenberg and Schmuyle* notable in their naturalness of sonority. With superb Berlin Philharmonic playing and the weight of the climaxes contrasting with the wit of *Tuileries* and the exhilaration of *The Market at Limoges*, this is certainly now among the top recommendations.

Muti's reading, given the excellence of its recorded sound, more than holds its own, although the balance is forward and perhaps not all listeners will respond to the brass timbres at the opening. The lower strings in *Samuel Goldenberg and Schmuyle* have extraordinary body and presence, and *Baba-Yaga* has an unsurpassed virtuosity and attack, as well as being of a high standard as a recording. The coupling is no less thrilling, and this is very reasonably priced.

Solti's performance is fiercely brilliant rather than atmospheric or evocative. He treats Ravel's orchestration as a virtuoso challenge, and with larger-than-life digital recording it undoubtedly has demonstration qualities, and the transparency of texture, given the forward balance, provides quite startling clarity.

Giulini's successful (1977) account of the *Pictures* was made with the Chicago Symphony Orchestra – the orchestra with which Reiner made his classic account. While not quite in that league, this is certainly excellent by any standards, with a vivid and atmospheric recording. Unfortunately, it is coupled with a lumbering (digital) *Scheherazade*.

The 1973 Vanguard recording was made on eight tracks in Surround Sound, but it is possible to balance the sound to get a forward orchestral placement with the percussion behind, including a spectacular bass drum which can make you jump. Many will enjoy being enveloped by the orchestra, and Mackerras certainly points a characteristically vivid set of pictures, obviously enhanced by the new technology. Although the overall quality is still slightly dated, the brass sonorities are impressive and there is plenty of life and impact. The orchestral playing does not bring the ultimate in refinement but has ample verve and colour. *Limoges* shows Mackerras at his most excitingly imaginative, the teeming market scene brilliantly drawn, and the remaining pictures produce some very dramatic brass playing, even if the final climax is not as overwhelming as in the very finest versions. The *Khovanshchina Prelude* is well played but is not as evocative as the versions with Szell or Abbado.

Above all, Ozawa shows his feeling for orchestral colour in his undoubtedly successful version. Moreover, the orchestra is on top form; yet the virtuosity is always put to the service of the music's pictorialism and atmosphere. Ozawa does not force the pace or make unnecessary underlining; he lets the work unfold naturally, though with excellent incidental detail, and the climax of *The Great Gate of Kiev* has all the spectacle you could want. The current transfer is first class and the 1967 recording has plenty of atmosphere and a natural focus. Yet why did RCA not choose Reiner's version for this reissue? That is finer still.

Though the initial impact of the dry mono sound of 1961 is disconcerting, made striking by the unhelpful acoustic of the Usher Hall, Edinburgh, there are ample compensations for losing the full beauty of Ravel's orchestration in Giulini's characterful BBC version. The bite and impact of a performance under Giulini at his most electrifying is intensified, so that in such a movement as *The Hut on Fowl's Legs* one even begins to think of this as a precursor of the *Rite of Spring*. The fast, light articulation of *Limoges* is very exciting, and the *Catacombs* brass fiercely sepulchral. Solo playing is immaculate too, despite the lack of bloom, and the closing *Great Gate of Kiev* makes a spectacularly spacious impact, with a fine contribution from the tam-tam. A generous coupling.

Naxos offers the very first recording of Ravel's transcription of *Pictures at an Exhibition* under the baton of its 'onlie begetter'. Koussevitzky commissioned Ravel's score, and his reading has obvious authority and imaginative intensity. The 1930 recording is not ideal: the lustrous Boston strings sound a little hard and climaxes are at times congested, but Mark Obert-Thorn has improved on earlier transfers.

Chailly's brilliant (1986) Concertgebouw recording – one of his first discs with the orchestra after he was appointed music director – takes an unusually metrical view of the score. That means that the *Promenade* links sound square and plodding, while the final *Great Gate of Kiev*, at a very slow and steady speed, is shattering in the wrong way as well as in the right one. But the light, brilliant numbers are delightfully done and, as part of a fascinating group of works demonstrating the genius of Ravel as orchestrator, this disc still has its place. Ripely brilliant sound of spectacular range.

Pictures at an Exhibition (incomplete; orch. Ravel)

(**(*)) Naxos mono 8. 110105. Boston SO, Koussevitzky –
BARTOK: *Concerto for Orchestra* (***)

Koussevitzky's 1943 reading of *Pictures* is an exciting one, prompting wild applause at the end. This is a performance white-hot with passion, with Koussevitzky challenging his players to the very limit, as in the hectic account of the *Tuileries* movement. Even with limited radio sound it makes an attractive supplement to the historic performance of the Bartók, though, sadly, Koussevitzky omits the two most evocative movements, the *Old Castle* and *Bydlo* (the Polish ox-cart), together with the *Promenades* that frame them.

Pictures at an Exhibition (orch. Cailliet)

(***) Biddulph mono WHL 046 Phd. O, Ormandy –
TCHAIKOVSKY: *Symphony 6* (***)

This 1937 recording offers the only version yet of Lucien Cailliet's orchestration of *Pictures*, specially commissioned by Ormandy from the orchestra's 'house arranger' and principal bass clarinet. Surprisingly for a wind-player, Cailliet uses full strings markedly more than Ravel in his orchestration, so that the result is more conventional. One bonus is that Cailliet includes the long *Promenade*, after *Goldenberg* and before *Limoges*, which Ravel omits. The transfer is clear and fresh, with remarkably little feeling of limitation.

(i) Pictures at an Exhibition (arr. Leonard for piano and orchestra). 3 Pictures from the Crimea (orch. Goehr); A Night on the Bare Mountain (arr. & orch. Rimsky-Korsakov); Scherzo in B flat (orch. Rimsky-Korsakov); From my Tears (orch. Kindler); Khovanshchina: Prelude (orch. Rimsky-Korsakov); Golitsin's Journey (orch. Stokowski). Sorochinsky Fair: Gopak (orch. Liadov)

(M) *** Cala CACD 1030. (i) Ungár; Philh. O, Simon

Lawrence Leonard's arrangement of Mussorgsky's *Pictures* for piano and orchestra is remarkably effective and very entertaining. The concertante format works admirably, especially powerful in *Gnomus* and *The Hut on Fowl's Legs*, charmingly depicting the *Unhatched Chicks* (a piquant mixture of keyboard and woodwind, spiced with xylophone). There are many added touches of colour. The other pieces are all well worth having, notably Rimsky's chimerical scoring (following the composer's orchestral sketch) of the *Scherzo in B flat*. The three *Pictures from the Crimea* are darkly nostalgic, and the lively *Gopak*, like the *Khovanshchina* excerpts (Stokowski's arrangement of *Golitsin's Journey* is sombrely characterful), is very welcome. All Geoffrey Simon's performances have plenty of life, and Tamás Ungár makes an exciting contribution and is fully equal to all the technical demands of the revised piano-part. The recording is warm, full and expansive, but not always sharply defined.

Pictures at an Exhibition (orch. Ellison; Gorchakov; Goehr; Naoumoff; Van Keulen; Ashkenazy; Simpson; Cailliet; Wood; Leonard; Funtek; Boyd; Ravel; Stokowski; Gamley)

(N) *** Warner 2564 61954-2. BBC SO & Ch., Slatkin –
RESPIGHI: *Pines of Rome* **(*)

This is the most original orchestral version of Mussorgsky's picture gallery on record. Leonard Slatkin conceived the idea of performing the work at the Proms using orchestrations by 15 different composers, reserving *Cum mortis in lingua mortua* for Ravel's own dramatic scoring. Byrwec Ellison opens with tolling bells, unpredictable percussion and a galaxy of colours, following (in microcosm) the style of Britten's *Young Person's Guide to the Orchestra*. Sergey Gorchakov's *Gnomus* is starkly primitive, and Goehr's following *Promenade* is contrastingly gentle, leading to Emile Naoumoff's melancholy minstrel's song outside *The Old Castle*, unexpectedly given a piano obbligato, while Cailliet's *Unhatched Chicks* trill vociferously. From there on the scoring becomes more and more exotic and extrovert, and none more so than Ashkenazy's larger-than-life *Bydlo*, using full-throated unison horns, and Henry Wood's *Goldenberg and Schmuyle*, with a surprise flourish at the latter's appearance, followed by guttural, protesting trombones. Lawrence Leonard's following *Promenade* (omitted by Ravel) is in piano concertante format. We are already familiar with the outrageous hyperbole of Stokowski's *Baba-Yaga*, and its spectacle prepares the way for Douglas Gamley's over-the-top, very Russian *Great Gate of Kiev*, using full chorus and bells and, finally, the thundering Albert Hall organ. The result, expanded by the hall's resonant acoustics, is quite overwhelming.

(i) *Pictures at an Exhibition* (orch. Ravel); (ii) *Pictures at an Exhibition* (original piano version)

(M) *** Sony SMK 89615. (i) BPO, Giulini; (ii) Bronfman

(N) *** Capriccio Surround Sound **SACD** 71 047. (i) Berlin RSO, Levine; (ii) Várjon

**(*) Australian Decca Eloquence (ADD) 467 127-2. (i) LAPO, Mehta; (ii) Ashkenazy

(M) **(*) Ph. 442 650-2. (i) VPO, Previn; (ii) Brendel

Giulini's account of the orchestral score can be considered among the best accounts of the 1990s. Recorded in the Jesus-Christus-Kirche, Berlin, the sound is rich and spacious, the orchestral playing superb. The reading has a pervading sense of nostalgia which haunts the delicate portrayal of *The Old Castle* and even makes the wheedling interchange between the two Polish Jews more sympathetic than usual. In the lighter pieces the scherzando element brings a sparkling contrast, with the unhatched chicks cheeping piquantly, and there is sonorous solemnity for the *Catacombs* sequence. A powerful and weighty *Baba-Yaga*, yet with the bizarre element retained in the subtle rhythmic pointing in the middle section, leads naturally to a majestic finale, with the Berlin brass full-bloodedly resplendent and the tam-tam flashing vividly at the climax.

Yefim Bronfman's account of the original piano score then matches Giulini's approach surprisingly closely. *The Old Castle*, beautifully graduated, is most poignant, there is strong characterization throughout and plenty of picaresque detail. Bronfman finds an added sense of fantasy in *Baba-Yaga* and the massive closing spectacle of *The Great Gate at Kiev* is viscerally thrilling, to give a genuine frisson when the piano recording is so full-bodied, and the playing so grand and powerful.

Anyone with surround-sound playback facilities will surely choose the Capriccio SACD as an excellent alternative choice for the coupling of Ravel's orchestral and Mussorgsky's original piano versions. The performances may not have quite the subtlety of detail of the Sony CD, but both performances are in every way first class, the individual pictures strongly characterized. Dénes Várjon's account of the piano score brings the boldest virtuosity throughout and reaches a powerful climax, matched by the splendid playing of the Berlin Radio Symphony Orchestra under Gilbert Levine, in which the brass, both at the opening and close of the work, has tremendous brilliance, sonority and immediacy. Curiously, the tam tam flashes more brilliantly in the coda on Giulini's CD; on the Capriccio SACD it is comparatively backward; with that single reservation, the Capriccio performances and recordings are second to none, and the concert-hall effect is very convincing indeed.

Zubin Mehta's Decca recording of *Pictures at an Exhibition* is brilliantly played and exciting, if not quite as imaginative as the very best. The sound has few rivals – it is exceptionally vivid and still packs a punch: the bass drum knocks spots off many modern digital recordings, and the whole orchestra sounds rich and full, with all departments clearly defined,

within a realistic balance. Ashkenazy's account of the original piano version is distinguished by a strong poetic feel, if not with the extrovert flair pianists like Richter or Berman brought to this music.

Obviously the Philips engineers had problems with the acoustics of the Musikvereinsaal, as the bass is noticeably resonant and inner definition is far from sharp. Otherwise the balance is truthful; but the orchestral performance, though not lacking spontaneity, is not distinctive, and there is a lack of the kind of grip which makes Karajan's version so unforgettable.

Brendel's performance of the original piano score has its own imaginative touches and some fine moments. He keeps the music moving but effectively varies the style of the *Promenades*. The closing pages, however, need to sound more unbuttoned: Brendel is weighty but fails to enthral the listener. The recording is faithful.

Night on the Bare Mountain (trans. Tchernov for piano)
⌐ ❂ *** Teldec 4509 96516-2. Berezovsky – BALAKIREV: *Islamey* *** ❂

This remarkable transcription by Konstantin Tchernov sounds hardly less dazzling in Berezovsky's hands than the outstanding *Islamey* with which it is coupled. The engineers capture very good piano sound.

Pictures at an Exhibition (original piano version)
⌐ ❂ (N) (BB) *** Virgin 2 x 1 4 82055-2 (2). Pletnev – TCHAIKOVSKY: *The Seasons; Sleeping Beauty: Suite; Pieces* *** ❂

(M) (***) Ph. mono 464 734-2. S. Richter (with 1958 live recital of CHOPIN; LISZT; RACHMANINOV; SCHUBERT (***))

Pictures at an Exhibition (piano version, ed. Horowitz)
⌐ (B) (***) RCA 2-CD mono 74321 84594-2 (2). Horowitz – (with CLEMENTI: *Sonatas, Op. 14/3; Op. 34/2; Op. 47/2: Rondo* (***) – SCRIABIN: *Etudes; Preludes; Sonatas* (***))

There are remarkable effects of colour and of pedalling in Pletnev's performance, which is easily the most commanding to have appeared since Richter's and, one is tempted to say, a re-creation rather than a performance. Pletnev does not hesitate to modify the odd letter of the score in order to come closer to its spirit. *The Ballet of the Unhatched Chicks* has great wit and *The Great Gate of Kiev* is extraordinarily rich in colour. With its new couplings this is a truly outstanding reissue.

Horowitz's famous (1951) recording, made at a live performance at Carnegie Hall, is as thrilling as it is perceptive. Mussorgsky's darker colours are admirably caught and the lighter, scherzando evocations are dazzlingly articulated. In *The Great Gate of Kiev* Horowitz embellishes the texture to make the result even more spectacular. The performances of the Clementi *Sonatas*, also from the 1950s, are hardly less electrifying, and though the piano-sound is again shallow, the quality is a great improvement on their previous vinyl transfers.

The Philips reissue offers Sviatislav Richter's 1958 Sofia recital, rightly included among their '50 Great Recordings'. The mono recital has been remastered using the latest background-noise-reduction technology. While this cannot suppress the audience's bronchial afflictions, the previously very troublesome tape roar has been considerably mitigated. It has never before sounded as vivid as this: the magnetism of Richter's playing comes over splendidly, and his enormously wide dynamic range brings a riveting final climax. The piano is backwardly positioned, and some of the *pianissimo* playing could ideally be more present; but the focus is improved, the piano timbre itself has more body and substance than previously, and does not lack colour. One can certainly forget the technical limitations and respond to this marvellous, indeed uniquely charismatic performance. Besides the Mussorgsky, the 76-minute recital offers a generous programme including two Schubert *Impromptus* (D. 899/2 & 4) and the *C major Moment musical* (D. 780/1), Chopin's *E major Etude*, Op. 10/3, two Liszt *Valses oubliées* plus a pair of *Transcendental Studies (Feux follets)* and *Harmonies du soir*, where there is more fabulous virtuosity. The recital closes with Rachmaninov's *Prelude in G sharp minor*, Op. 32/13. An indispensable disc for all lovers of great pianism.

VOCAL MUSIC

Songs

Song-cycles: (i) *The Nursery;* **(ii)** *Songs and Dances of Death;* **(i)** *Sunless. Songs: Darling Savishna; Hopak; King Saul; Lullaby;* **(ii)** *Mephistopheles' Song of the Flea.* **(i)** *Where are you, little star?; The wild winds blow*

⊕ (M) (***) EMI mono 5 67993-2. Christoff, with (i) Labinsky; (ii) Fr. R. & TV O, Tzipine

Between 1955 and 1957 the great Bulgarian bass, Boris Christoff, recorded for EMI a pioneering set of the complete Mussorgsky songs, 63 of them. This well-filled disc in EMI's 'Great Recordings of the Century' series offers a very well-chosen selection, including the three great Mussorgsky song-cycles: *The Nursery* (with Christoff, amazingly for a bass, imitating the sound of a child singing), *Sunless* and, greatest of all, the *Songs and Dances of Death,* using the orchestral arrangement of the accompaniment by Glazunov and Rimsky-Korsakov. The selection starts with the earliest of Mussorgsky's songs, *Where are you, little star?,* and includes the lovely *Lullaby* to words by Ostrovsky (with Christoff producing a seamless legato), the setting of Byron in translation, *King Saul,* and the most popular of all Mussorgsky songs, *The Song of the Flea,* also in orchestral form. Christoff is in superb voice throughout, with his dark bass perfectly focused and steady as a rock. The orchestral sound is thinner than that of the rest, but what matters is the vividness of the voice.

Songs and Dances of Death

*** EMI **DVD** DVA 4901209. Vishnevskaya, Rostropovich – PROKOFIEV: *Sinfonia concertante;* SHOSTAKOVICH: *Cello Concerto 1* ***

Vishnevskaya's classic performance with her husband at the piano was filmed in 1970, and it comes as a bonus for a stunning DVD of Rostropovich playing key cello works by Prokofiev and Shostakovich which were specially written for him.

Songs and Dances of Death (orch. Shostakovich)

(N) *** Warner 2564 62050-2. Hvorostovsky, St Petersburg PO, Temirkanov – RACHMANINOV: *Symphonic Dances* ***

(B) *** EMI double forte 5 75178-2. Lloyd, Phd. O, Jansons – SHOSTAKOVICH: *Piano Concerto 1; Symphonies 1 & 10* **(*)

Recorded live in the Albert Hall, Hvorostovsky's powerful and moving performances of these dark (but not depressing)

songs, with their mixture of irony and grief, now clearly lead the field. Termirkanov's accompaniments are idiomatic and supportive, and the recording is both atmospheric and well balanced.

Robert Lloyd gives a commanding and sonorous account of the Shostakovich transcription of Mussorgsky's gripping song-cycle. But this is a fill-up for three Shostakovich performances, only one of which (an intense and powerful reading of the *Tenth Symphony*) is of a similar calibre.

OPERA

Boris Godunov (complete)

⊕— *** Ph. **DVD** 075 089-9 (2). Lloyd, Borodina, Steblianko, Leiferkus, Kirov Op. Ch. & O, Gergiev (Producer: Andrei Tarkovsky; V/D: Humphrey Burton)

*** Ph. **DVD** 075 099-9 (6). As above – BORODIN: *Prince Igor,* GLINKA: *Ruslan & Ludmilla*

In 1990 the Covent Garden production of *Boris Godunov,* directed by the Russian, Andre Tarkovsky, and rehearsed by Stephen Lawless, was adopted by the Mariinsky Theatre in St Petersburg. This two-disc DVD offers the resulting film, originally shown on BBC Television, a magnificent presentation of the opera in the edition prepared by David Lloyd Jones using the original (1872) version of the score. Valery Gergiev conducts an outstanding Kirov Opera cast, joined in the title-role by Robert Lloyd from Covent Garden, giving one of his greatest performances ever, strong and resonant and movingly acted. It is astonishing how the different incidental parts are cast from strength with star singers, each rising superbly to the challenge of a major scene – Pimen, Varlaam, Rangoni and the Simpleton (who sings his pathetic solo twice – in the first scene of Act IV and at the end). Olga Borodina is magnificent as Marina in the Polish scenes opposite the powerful Grigory of Alexei Steblianko, and even such a small part as Feodor, Boris's young son, is taken with passionate intensity by a then-rising star, Larissa Diadkova. Musically it would be hard to imagine a finer performance, even though the recording balance sometimes has voices too distant and unrelated to close-up pictures. Visually it is superb too, with the complex, episodic story told with extraordinary clarity, set on a simple but very grand stage, with a floor in false perspective adding to the grandeur. Costumes are authentic and often colourful, with Tarkovsky's often stylized production bringing unforgettable moments, as when Rangoni comes and sits centre-stage at the end of the love scene between Marina and Grigory, and turns to give the most sinister stare as the curtain falls. This DVD set is now included in an attractive package with two other classic productions (presumably at an attractive discount) to mark Valery Gergiev's 25th anniversary at the Kirov, and those who do not have these performances should take advantage of this. All three performances are outstanding.

Boris Godunov ((i) 1869 & (ii) 1872 versions))

⊕— (M) *** Ph. 462 230-2 (5). (i) Putilin, Lutsuk, (ii) Borodina; Vaneev, Galusin; (i; ii) Ohotnikov, Kuznetsov, Trifonova, Bulycheva, Pluzhnikov, Akimov, Kirov Op. Ch. & O, Gergiev

It makes a fascinating contrast on CD in Gergiev's St Petersburg set (five discs for the price of three) to have the original (1869) version of seven scenes set against the 1872 revision with its amplification in the extra Polish Act and elsewhere.

Gergiev's incisive, keenly dramatic readings bring out the differences very effectively, and the casting of Boris in each heightens that. In 1869 the character is more direct, more of a villain, less of a victim – reflected in Nikolai Putilin's virile and firm singing – where in the expanded (1872) portrait the character is more equivocal, more self-searching, clearly verging on madness, and there you have Vladimir Vaneev bringing out the element of thoughtfulness and mystery over a wider expressive range. The role of Grigory, the Pretender, brings alternative casting too, but it is only in the 1872 version that the character plays a full part, very well taken by the ringing and clear, very Russian-sounding tenor, Vladimir Galusin. The others make a first-rate team, individually strong and idiomatic, and all enhancing the drama, obviously experienced on stage. Outstanding are Olga Borodina as Marina and Konstantin Pluzhnikov as a sinister Shuisky. The sound is fresh and forward, with voices set in front of the orchestra, more powerful in wind and brass than in the strings. The Abbado set on Sony (see below) offers a more starry cast and a more spacious reading, often more warmly expressive, but the practical advantages of the Gergiev set make it even more recommendable.

Boris Godunov (original version; complete)

*** Sony S3K 58977 (3). Kotcherga, Leiferkus, Larin, Lipovšek, Ramey, Nikolsky, Langridge, Slovak Philharmonic Ch., Bratislava, Tölz Boys' Ch., Berlin RSO, Abbado

**(*) EMI (ADD) 7 54377-2 (3). Talvela, Gedda, Mróz, Kinasz, Haugland, Krakow Polish R. Ch., Polish Nat. SO, Semkow

Claudio Abbado recorded Boris Godunov in its original version with speeds that regularly press ahead, and the urgency of the composer's inspiration is conveyed without reducing the epic scale of the work or its ominously dark colouring. Abbado inserts the beautiful scene in front of St Basil's at the start of Act IV, but then omits from the final Kromy Forest scene the episode about the Simpleton losing his kopek, which would otherwise come in twice – as it does in the Semkow (EMI) set. Vocally, the performance centres on the glorious singing of Anatoly Kotcherga as Boris. Rarely has this music been sung with such firmness and beauty as here. Kotcherga may not have as weighty a voice as Talvela on EMI, but the darkly meditative depth of the performance is enhanced without loss of power. The other principal basses, Samuel Ramey as the monk, Pimen, and Gleb Nikolsky as Varlaam, are well contrasted, even if Ramey's voice sounds un-Slavonic. The tenor, Sergei Larin, sings with beauty and clarity up to the highest register as the Pretender, not least in the Polish Act, while Marjana Lipovšek is a formidably characterful Marina, if not quite as well focused as usual. Having Philip Langridge as Shuisky and Sergei Leiferkus as Rangoni reinforces the starry strength of the team. The sound is spacious, more atmospheric than usual in recordings made in the Philharmonie in Berlin, and allowing high dynamic contrasts, with the choral ensembles – so vital in this work – full and glowing.

The EMI version offers (at full price) an analogue recording of 1977, but its warmth and richness go with a forward balance and a high transfer-level. The voices have an extra bite, not least the firm, weighty bass of Martti Talvela as Boris or of Aage Haugland, magnificent as Varlaam. Nicolai Gedda is excellent as the Pretender, if not as free on top as Larin in the Abbado set. The other soloists, as well as the chorus, make up a formidable Polish team, with hardly a weak link. Bozena Kinasz as Marina is particularly impressive. Jerzy Semkow may not convey as much bite and beauty as Abbado, but in his rugged, measured way he conveys more intensity at moments of high drama than the other Sony rival, Tchakarov, helped by the firm, full sound. If this were reissued at mid-price it would be a strong contender.

Boris Godunov (arr. Rimsky-Korsakov)

(B) **(*) Decca (ADD) 472 495-2 (3). Ghiaurov, Vishnevskaya, Spiess, Maslennikov, Talvela, V. Boys' Ch., Sofia R. Ch., V. State Op. Ch., VPO, Karajan

(M) ** EMI 5 67877-2 (3) [567881-2]. Christoff, Lear, Lanigan, Alexieva, Sofia Nat. Op. Ch., Paris Conservatoire O, Cluytens

With Ghiaurov in the title-role, Karajan's superbly controlled Decca version, technically outstanding, came far nearer than previous recordings to conveying the rugged greatness of Mussorgsky's masterpiece. Only the Coronation scene lacked something of the weight and momentum one ideally wants. Vishnevskaya was far less appealing than the lovely non-Slavonic Marina of Evelyn Lear on EMI, but overall this Decca set had much more to offer. However, Gergiev's recording of the original version makes a clear first choice for this opera, so Decca have now sensibly reissued this at bargain price, although with only a synopsis; the text and translation is available only on a CD-ROM.

The EMI set is chiefly valuable for the resonant contribution of Boris Christoff, for a generation unmatched in the role of Boris. Here he takes the part not only of the Tsar but of Pimen and Varlaam, relishing the contrast of those other, highly colourful bass roles. It is good that his glorious voice is so vividly caught on CD, but sadly the overall performance under Cluytens does not add up to the sum of its parts as the earlier, mono recording did. That would surely have been a more apt choice as one of EMI's 'Great Recordings of the Century'. However, it appears to still be available as a Références reissue (EMI mono 5 65192-2).

Boris Godunov (original, 1869 version): excerpts: Coronation Scene; Varlaam's Song; Apartment Scene; St Basil Scene; Death Scene (sung in English)

🔊 ⊛ (M) *** Chan. 3007. Tomlinson, Kale, Bayley, Rodgers, Best, Opera N. Ch., E. N. Philh. O, Daniel

This generous, 75-minute selection of excerpts from Boris Godunov is highly recommendable even when compared with current Russian versions of Mussorgsky's masterpiece. John Tomlinson has never been in finer voice on disc than here, with his dark bass-baritone perfectly focused. This is an exceptionally lyrical view of the self-tortured tsar, both dramatically powerful and warmly expressive, letting one appreciate the beauty of Mussorgsky's melodies. Tomlinson is helped by Paul Daniel's inspired direction and opulent recorded sound, with excellent support from singers in the vintage Opera North production, including Stuart Kale as Prince Shuisky, Clive Bayley as Varlaam, Joan Rodgers as Xenia and Matthew Best as Pimen. Anyone who supports the idea of opera sung in English should not miss this highly compelling disc.

Boris Godunov: Selected Scenes

(M) (***) Cala mono CACD 0535. Rossi-Lemeni, San Francisco Ch. and SO, Stokowski – WAGNER: Parsifal: Good Friday Spell; Symphonic Synthesis of Act 3 ***

In December 1952 in San Francisco, Stokowski conducted a series of concert performances of highlights from Boris Godnov in the Rimsky-Korsakov version, and promptly recorded for RCA the same brilliantly chosen group of favourite passages. The result is spectacular, as CALA's superb CD transfer demonstrates. The sound is so full, vivid and immediate, with an impressive spread – not least in the Coronation Scene with its bells– that it is hard to believe it is in mono. Matching this, Stokowski's conducting inspires performances of the highest voltage, electrifying from first to last. Both the chorus and orchestra are incandescent, and the Russian-Italian bass, Nicola Rossi-Lemeni – then at the beginning of his career – sings with a firmness of focus that later deserted him, at least on disc. He is wonderfully characterful, not just as Boris, but in a wildly exciting account of *Varlaam's Song*. Well-coupled with selections from Act III of *Parsifal*, another opera specially dear to Stokowski.

Khovanshchina: Prelude

*** BBC (ADD) BBCL 4123-2. Philh. O, Giulini – BRUCKNER: *Symphony 7*; FALLA: *Three-Cornered Hat* (excerpts) ***

In his live recording Giulini draws refined, evocative playing from the Philharmonia, an atmospheric supplement to the Bruckner *Symphony*, the main work.

Khovanshchina (complete)

☛ *** Arthaus **DVD** 100 310 (2). Ghiaurov, Atlantov, Marusin, Shaklovity; Burchuladze, Shemchuk, Slovak Phil. Ch., V. Boys' Ch.; V. State Op. Ch. & O, Abbado (Stage/Video Dir: Kirchner)

☛ *** DG 429 758-2 (3). Lipovšek, Burchuladze, Atlantov, Haugland, Borowska, Kotcherga, Popov, V. State Op. Ch. & O, Abbado

**(*) Ph. 437 147-2 (3). Minzhilkiev, Galusin, Steblianko, Ohotnikov, Borodina, Kirov Theatre Ch. & O, Gergiev

This DVD recording was made at the same time as the DG three-CD set, namely in September 1989. There are some differences in cast: to name the most important, the late Aage Haugland who was Ivan Khovansky is sung (wonderfully, too) by Nicolai Ghiaurov, Vladimir Popov's Prince Golitsin is replaced by Yuri Marusin and the Marfa of Marjana Lipovšek by Ludmila Shemchuk. Otherwise the performance does not differ from the rightly admired CD set. Those who know the rival Gergiev set made in 1991 (or who saw the production during the Kirov season at Covent Garden in 2002) should still investigate the present issue as they differ textually. Abbado's version is essentially the Shostakovich version (based on Pavel Lamm's 1929 edition) though he lightens some of the scoring and discards the triumphant ending in Act V with the return of the *Preobrazhensky March* in favour of the finale prepared by Stravinsky. Rimsky-Korsakov's marvellous orchestration is rejected as too sumptuous these days, and his corrections of Mussorgsky's harmony are seen as too academically correct. And with the beautiful, tragic music of Abbado's ending the strength and dignity of the Old Believers is reinforced. Gergiev's version occupied four LaserDisc sides and three CDs, and it cannot be long before it is transferred to DVD. His production is traditional (and none the worse for that) and has an outstanding Ivan Khovansky in the late Bulat Minzhilkiev, a superb Prince Golitsin in Vladimir Galusin and a gloriously refulgent Marfa in Olga Borodina. It has splendid tension, and Gergiev is masterly. However, Abbado, who has for so long been Mussorgsky's most eloquent champion among Western conductors of his generation, is even more electrifying. There is an intensity here, and a mastery both of pace and of climax. The playing of the Vienna orchestra is exquisite in the quieter episodes and

sumptuous in tone throughout. There is simply no question of its superiority over the Kirov orchestra (though the choral singing in the Gergiev version is arguably superior). The recording for Abbado, too, is superbly balanced and defined. Above all, the performance has a commanding assurance and compelling power: sample the first act, and the next 3½ hours are gone. The presentation was a very strong element of the DG set, with a remarkable survey by Richard Taruskin of the historical background to the work and a careful table of the manuscript sources. None of this is to be found in the DVD package, but there is a short essay and a synopsis of the plot. Visually the production is good to look at, and the camera is expertly directed and always where the viewer wants it. This is a mandatory choice for all lovers of Russian opera. And if the Gergiev set appears on DVD during the lifetime of this book, get that too for the sake of Bulat Minzhilkiev's Prince Khovansky – and much else besides!

Abbado's live recording also brings the most vivid account of this epic Russian opera yet on CD. He uses the Shostakovich orchestration (with some cuts), darker and harmonically far more faithful than the old Rimsky-Korsakov version. Yet Abbado rejects the triumphant ending of the Shostakovich edition and follows instead the orchestration that Stravinsky did for Diaghilev in 1913 of the original subdued ending as Mussorgsky himself conceived it. When the tragic fate of the Old Believers, immolating themselves for their faith, brings the deepest and most affecting emotions of the whole opera, that close, touching in its tenderness, is far more apt. Lipovšek's glorious singing as Marfa, the Old Believer with whom one most closely identifies, sets the seal on the whole performance. Aage Haugland is a rock-like Ivan Khovansky and, though Burchuladze is no longer as steady of tone as he was, he makes a noble Dosifei. Stage noises sometimes intrude and voices are sometimes set back, but this remains a magnificent achievement.

Gergiev does not disguise the squareness of much of the writing and his performance lacks the flair and brilliance of Abbado. He stays faithful to the Shostakovich version of the score to the very end. There he simply adds a loud version of the *Old Believers' Chorale* on unison brass – hardly a subtle solution! The Kirov soloists make a fine team, but on almost all counts Abbado is more persuasive.

MYSLIVEČEK, Josef (1737–81)

Symphonies: F26 in C; F27 in A; F28 in F; F29 in D; F30 in B flat; F31 in G

☛ *** Chan. 10203. LMP, Bamert

The symphonies of the Czech composer Josef Mysliveček have been almost completely neglected on disc. This delightful set of six, never previously recorded, was published in London in 1772, having been written for an expatriate British nobleman, Earl Cowper, living in Florence. Mysliveček left his native Prague in 1763 in his mid-twenties, having earlier worked in his family's milling business. He remained in Italy for most of the rest of his life, writing not only some 45 symphonies, many concertos and copious chamber music, but nearly 30 operas. All six of the present set of symphonies are in conventional three-movement form, fast–slow–fast, each lasting around ten minutes. What distinguishes all six from dozens of symphonies of the period is the liveliness and memorability of each movement, with the music never for a moment outstaying its welcome or falling into routine. The scoring is for two oboes, two horns and strings, with the last of the set in particular bringing some striking horn-writing. Fresh, lively performances, recorded in full, atmospheric sound.

La Passione di Nostro Signore Gesu Cristo

(N) *** Capriccio 71 025/6 (2). Kurtäuser, Waschinski, Berg, Karasiak, Ch. Musicus Cologne, Neue O, Spering

This Catholic version of the Passion comes as a shock after the dedicated solemnity of the great German Passion settings. Mysliveček, always at his most imaginative in vigorous music, has little time for meditation in his setting of a libretto by Metastasio which was used by many composers before him. Numbers are brief, with the two longest given to Mary Magdalene, though she also has a brilliant coloratura aria too, well sung by Sophie Kartäuser. The role of Jesus was originally for castrato and is taken here by an excellent male soprano, Jorg Waschinski, while the role of St John is taken by an alto, Yvonne Berg, and that of Joseph of Arimathea by a tenor, Andreas Karasiak. Christoph Spering conducts a fresh, well-sprung performance with a first-rate chorus, though the libretto involves surprisingly few choruses, the last two in six parts. Well-balanced sound.

Arias from: *Abramo ed Isacco; L'Olimpiade*

*** DG 471 334-2. Ko),ená, Prague Philh. O, Swierczewski – GLUCK; MOZART: Arias ***

The Czech mezzo, Magdalena Kožená, an outstanding artist in every way, boldly offers four nicely contrasted arias by Mysliveček as a welcome fill-up for her disc of Mozart and Gluck arias. One of the most talented as well as most seriously neglected of Mozart's older contemporaries, Mysliveček writes with consistent alertness and imagination, with Swierczewski and the Prague Philharmonia sensitive accompanists.

NANCARROW, Conlon (1912–97)

2 Pieces for Small Orchestra; String Quartet 1; Toccata for Violin & Player Piano; Trio Movement; (Piano) Prelude & Blues; Sonatina; Study 15 (both transcribed for piano, 4 hands by Yvar Mukhashoff)

(N) (BB) *** Naxos 8.559196. Continuum (members), Seltzer, Sachs

Conlon Nancarrow might be regarded as America's mid- to late-20th-century equivalent of Charles Ives; instead of drawing on hymnal melodies and popular band tunes he embraced jazz. But he also greatly admired György Ligeti, so not surprisingly his melodic writing is fragmented. Nevertheless, it is genuinely melodic, aurally fascinating and very American in feeling. The two *Pieces for Small Orchestra* are haunting and are alone worth the modest price of this disc. (The performance of the second is a *tour de force*.) The brief *Toccata* is wildly unpredictable, as is much of the chamber and instrumental music here. The *Prelude and Blues* is both jazzy and exhilaratingly virtuosic. The *Trio Movement* is piquantly original, while in the *String Quartet* the central *Andante* shows the composer at his most stringently expressive before the wild finale. The performances are remarkably confident, and the recording is excellent. If you are interested in original but accessible avant-garde music try this. It is genuinely unforgettable. The members of Continuum and their directors, Cheryl Seltzer and Joel Sachs, deserve congratulations for reviving Nancarrow's music so enjoyably and expertly.

NICOLAI, Carl Otto (1810–49)

The Merry Wives of Windsor (Die lustigen Weiber von Windsor): complete

(B) *** Double Decca (ADD) (IMS) 460 197-2 (2). Ridderbusch, W. Brendel, Malta, Donath, Schmidt, Bav. R. Ch. & SO, Kubelik

(M) **(*) EMI (ADD) 7 69348-2 (2). Frick, Gutstein, Engel, Wunderlich, Lenz, Hoppe, Putz, Litz, Mathis, Ch. & O of Bav. State Op., Heger

Kubelik's performance may be slightly lacking in dramatic ebullience, but its extra subtlety has perceptive results – as in the entry of Falstaff in Act I, where Kubelik conveys the tongue-in-cheek quality of Nicolai's *pomposo* writing. Ridderbusch portrays a straight and noble Falstaff. Although as an opera this may not have the brilliant insight of Verdi or all the atmosphere of Vaughan Williams, it has its own brand of effervescence which is equally endearing and is well caught here. The dialogue is crisply edited, and the recording, while fairly reverberant, is vividly atmospheric. *Faute de mieux*, it should receive a strong recommendation. This is particularly welcome as a Decca Double, although the documentation includes only a cued synopsis.

As Falstaff, Gottlob Frick is in magnificent voice, even if he sounds baleful rather than comic. It is good too to have the young Fritz Wunderlich as Fenton opposite the Anna Reich of Edith Mathis. Though the others hardly match this standard – Ruth-Margret Putz is rather shrill as Frau Fluth – they all give enjoyable performances. The effectiveness of the comic timing is owed in great measure to the conducting of the veteran, Robert Heger. From the CD transfer one could hardly tell the age of the recording, with the voices particularly well caught.

NIELSEN, Carl (1865–1931)

Aladdin (suite); An Imaginary Journey to the Faeroe Islands (Rhapsodic Overture); Helios Overture; Maskarade: Overture; Prelude to Act II; Dance of the Cockerels. Pan and Syrinx; Saga-drøm

*** DG 447 757-2. Gothenburg SO, Järvi

Of the anthologies of Nielsen's orchestral music other than the symphonies, this is now the best on offer. The performances are vital and affectionate, with the orchestra playing with their usual finesse and enthusiasm. Both *Pan and Syrinx* and *Saga-drøm* are atmospheric. One minor reservation: the *Helios Overture* is too swiftly paced (the sun rises over the Aegean in fast-forward mode). The recording is very fine indeed.

(i) Aladdin Suite, Op. 54. (ii) 3 Motets, Op. 55; (i–iii) Springtime in Fünen

(BB) *** Regis 1134. (i) Odense SO, Vetö; (ii) Klint Little Muko University Ch., St Klemens School Children's Ch.; (iii) with Nielsen, von Binzer

Another fine budget reissue from the Unicorn label on Regis offers a well-played account of the engaging *Aladdin Suite* by the Odense orchestra under Tamás Vetö, and the choral *Springtime in Fünen*, which is one of those enchanting pieces to which everyone responds when they hear it yet which is hardly ever performed outside Denmark. To make up the playing time Regis have now added the *Three Motets*, Op. 55.

This disc is well worth its modest cost and will give many hours of delight.

At the Bier of a Young Artist; Little Suite for Strings, Op. 1

(B) *** Virgin 2 × 1 5 62179-2 (2). Norwegian CO, I. Brown – GRIEG: *At the Cradle*, etc. ***; BRITTEN: *Lachrimae*, etc. *** ✿

The Norwegian Chamber Orchestra are an excellent group and their account of Nielsen's first opus, the *Little Suite for Strings*, is about the best in the catalogue. His moving elegy, the *Andante lamentoso* (*At the Bier of a Young Artist*), is equally eloquent in their hands. The recording, made in the glorious acoustic of Eidsvoll Church in Norway, is very real and tangible. This now comes as part of an outstanding Virgin Double. Very strongly recommended.

Clarinet Concerto, Op. 57

*** Chan. 8618. Hilton, SNO, Bamert – COPLAND: *Concerto*; LUTOSLAWSKI: *Dance Preludes* ***

Janet Hilton gives a highly sympathetic account of the Nielsen *Concerto*, but it is characteristically soft-centred and mellower in its response to the work's more disturbing emotional undercurrents than Olle Schill's splendid account on BIS - see below. The Chandos recording is first class.

(i) Clarinet Concerto; (ii) Flute Concerto; (iii) Violin Concerto, Op. 33

*** Chan. 8894. (i) Thomsen; (ii) Christiansen; (iii) Sjøgren; Danish RSO, Schønwandt

Niels Thomsen's powerfully intense account of the late *Clarinet Concerto* is completely gripping. Michael Schønwandt gives sensitive and imaginative support, both here and in the two companion works. Toke Lund Christiansen is hardly less successful in the *Flute Concerto*. Kim Sjøgren and Schønwandt give a penetrating and thoughtful account of the *Violin Concerto*; there is real depth here, thanks in no small measure to Schønwandt. The recording is first class.

(i) Clarinet Concerto; (ii) Flute Concerto; (iii) Violin Concerto. An Imaginary Journey to the Faeroe Islands (Rhapsodic Overture); Helios Overture, Op. 17; Pan and Syrinx, Op. 49; Saga-drøm, Op. 39; Symphonic Rhapsody

☛ (B) *** EMI double forte (ADD) 5 69758-2 (2). (i) Stevennson; (ii) Lemmser; (iii) Tellefsen; Danish RSO, Blomstedt

Arve Tellefsen is a first-class soloist in the *Violin Concerto* and Kjell-Inge Stevennson is pretty stunning in the *Clarinet Concerto*. The charm and subtleties of the *Flute Concerto* are hardly less well realized by Frantz Lemmser's nimble and sensitive account. Moreover, since the orchestra is Danish, the other works (such as the marvellous *Pan and Syrinx* and the atmospheric *Helios Overture*) are played with authentic accents. The collection also includes a novelty in the *Symphonic Rhapsody* (1889), composed before the *First Symphony*. Throughout the EMI engineers secure a natural sound-balance. In its economical new format this is a most attractive proposition, and the recordings still sound very warm and fresh.

(i) Clarinet Concerto; (ii; iii) Violin Concerto; (ii; iv) Little Suite for Strings, Op. 1

(BB) *** Warner Apex 0927 48311-2. (i) Kojo, Finnish RSO, Sarasate; (ii) Norwegian R. O, (iii) with Hannisdal, cond. Mikkelsen; (iv) cond. Rasilainen

A fine performance of the *Clarinet Concerto* from Kullervo Kojo, whose timbre has plenty of colour. He responds to the sudden bursts of bravura with aplomb and does not miss the work's gently musing, improvisatory quality, while Tim Feerce keeps the dramatic percussive interruptions in proportion, helped by a good balance. Henrik Hannisdal is equally at home in the *Violin Concerto*, and Ari Rasilainen's account of the *Little Suite* is most persuasive. This delightful work has the same kind of charm and appeal as early Sibelius and ought to be better known, and this inexpensive Apex disc is thoroughly recommendable.

(i) Clarinet Concerto; (ii) Symphony 3 (Sinfonia espansiva). Maskarade Overture

*** BIS CD 321. (i) Schill; (ii) Raanoja, Skram; Gothenburg SO, Chung

Olle Schill brings brilliance and insight to what is one of the most disturbing and masterly of all modern concertos. The young Korean conductor secures playing of great fire and enthusiasm from the Gothenburgers in the *Third Symphony* and he has vision and breadth – and at the same time no want of momentum. Two soloists singing a wordless vocalise are called for in the pastoral slow movement, and their contribution is admirable. Myung-Whun Chung also gives a high-spirited and sparkling account of the *Overture* to Nielsen's comic opera, *Maskarade*. The BIS recording is marvellous, even by the high standards of this small company.

(i) Clarinet Concerto; (ii) Serenata in vano; (iii) Wind Quintet, Op. 43

(***) Clarinet Classics mono CC 002. (i) Cahuzac, Copenhagen Op. O, Frandsen; (ii) Oxenvad, Larsson, Sorensen, Jensen, Hegner; (iii) Royal Chapel Wind Quintet

These are pioneering recordings. The *Clarinet Concerto* was to have been recorded by its dedicatee, Aage Oxenvad, who is heard in both the *Quintet* and the *Serenata in Vano*, but death intervened and the eminent French clarinettist Louis Cahuzac filled the breach. This lovely performance of the *Quintet* is so full of character that in some ways it remains unsurpassed. These transfers are a great improvement on the earlier ones on Danacord LPs, a bit dry but eminently clean and well detailed in the case of the *Concerto*, which Cahuzac plays with great feeling.

(i) Flute Concerto. Symphony 1; Rhapsody Overture (An Imaginary Journey to the Faeroe Islands)

*** BIS CD 454. (i) Gallois; Gothenburg SO, Chung

The *Flute Concerto* is given a marvellous performance by Patrick Gallois, and Myung-Whun Chung and the Gothenburg orchestra have an instinctive feeling for Nielsen. They play with commendable enthusiasm and warmth, and Chung shapes the *Symphony* with great sensitivity to detail and a convincing sense of the whole. The *Rhapsody Overture (An Imaginary Journey to the Faeroe Islands)* is not the composer at his strongest, but it has a highly imaginative opening.

(i) Flute Concerto. Symphony 5, Op. 50; Aladdin: Entrance March

(N) ***(M) HALLÉ CDHLL 7502. Hallé O, Elder; (i) with Nicholson

Mark Elder has a good feeling for this glorious repertoire and brings to the *Fifth Symphony* the epic sweep this great score needs. Anthony Nicholson, too, proves an eloquent soloist in the *Flute Concerto*, and the Hallé respond in both scores with enthusiasm and discipline, and offer the *Entrance March* from *Aladdin* as a nice little bonus. Good sound.

Violin Concerto, Op. 33

✿ **(N) (M) *** Sony SMK 89748.** Lin, Swedish RSO, Salonen
  – SIBELIUS: *Violin Concerto* *** ✿

(i) *Violin Concerto, Op. 33;* (ii) *Symphony 1, Op. 7*
(BB) **(*) Warner Apex 0927 40622-2. (i) Hannisdal;
  Norwegian RO, Rasilainen, or (ii) Mikkelsen

(i) *Violin Concerto. Symphony 5*
****** BIS CD 370.** (i) Kang; Gothenburg SO, Chung

Cho-Liang Lin brings as much authority to Nielsen's *Concerto* as he does to the Sibelius and he handles the numerous technical hurdles with breathtaking assurance. His perfect intonation and tonal purity excite admiration, but so should his command of the architecture of this piece; there is a strong sense of line from beginning to end. Salonen is supportive here and gets good playing from the Swedish Radio Symphony Orchestra.

Dong-Suk Kang too is more than equal to the technical demands of this concerto and is fully attuned to the Nordic sensibility. He brings tenderness and refinement of feeling to the searching slow movement and great panache and virtuosity to the rest. The *Fifth Symphony* is hardly less successful and is certainly one of the best-recorded versions now available. Myung-Whun Chung has a natural feeling for Nielsen's language and the first movement has real breadth.

The Norwegian Radio Orchestra is very good indeed, even if they do not match the excellence of the Oslo Philharmonic. Under their Finnish conductor, however, they turn in a very natural and unaffected account of the *First Symphony* and a hardly less appealing version of the *Violin Concerto*. Henrik Hannisdal's playing gives consistent pleasure, particularly when the recorded sound is so well balanced. If you want the pairing this is worth considering on this bargain reissue, but neither of these performances displaces the top recommendations with other couplings.

En aften paa Giske: Prelude (1889); *Bøhmiske-dansk folketone; Helios Overture, Op. 17; Paraphrase on 'Nearer my God, to thee' for Wind Band; Rhapsodic Overture (An Imaginary Journey to the Faeroe Islands); Saga-drøm, Op. 39; Symphonic Rhapsody* (1888)
*(*) Chan. 9287. Danish Nat. RSO, Rohzdestvensky

The *Paraphrase on the Psalm, 'Nearer, my God, to thee', for Wind Band* is both noble and individual. Rozhdestvensky gives musicianly, well-prepared and often poetic accounts of the more familiar pieces, though his *Helios Overture* must be the slowest ever – over 14 minutes! His account of *Saga-drøm* ('The Dream of Gunnar') is also spacious. Very good recording, but in the last analysis these performances are a little deficient in zest.

Little Suite for Strings, Op. 1

(BB) * Warner Apex 0927 43075-2.** Norwegian R. O,
  Rasilainen – GRIEG: *Holberg Suite*; STENHAMMAR:
  Serenade *** ✿

An unaffected, well-played account of Nielsen's Op. 1 from Ari Rasilainen and the Norwegian Radio Orchestra, also available above coupled with the *Clarinet* and *Violin Concertos*, is here an attractive bonus for the Stenhammar *Serenade*.

Symphonies (i) *1–2;* (i–ii) *3;* (iii) *4;* (i) *5;* (iii) *6;* (i; iv) *Clarinet Concerto;* (i; v) *Flute Concerto;* (i; vi) *Violin Concerto*
(M) * BIS CD 614/6 (4).** Gothenburg SO; (i) Chung; (ii) with Raanoja, Skram; (iii) Järvi; (iv) with Schill; (v) Gallois; (vi) Kang

Symphonies 1–2; (i) *3;* (ii) *Aladdin* (suite). *Maskarade Overture*
◑━ (B) * Double Decca 460 985-2 (2).** San Francisco SO, Blomstedt; (i) with Kromm, McMillan; (ii) San Francisco SO Ch.

(i) *Symphonies 4–6.* (ii) *Little Suite;* (ii–iii) *Hymnus amoris, Op. 12*
◑━ (B) * Double Decca 460 988-2 (2).** (i) San Francisco SO, Blomstedt; (ii) Danish Nat. RSO, Schirmer; (iii) with Bonney, Pedersen, Mark Ainsley, M. & B. Hansen, Danish Nat. R. Ch., Copenhagen Boys' Ch.

Symphonies 1–6

(B) * RCA 74321 20290-2 (3).** Royal Danish O, Berglund (with soloists in 3)
(BB) **(*) Regis (ADD) RRC 3002 (3). LSO, Schmidt
(N) (B) **(*) DG Trio 477 5514 (3). Gothenburg SO (with Isokoski & Hynninen in 3), Järvi
*(*) (M) DA CAPO 8.203130 (3). Danish Nat. RSO, Schønwandt
((*)) Danacord mono DACOCD 351/3.** Danish RSO; Tuxen; Grøndahl; Jensen

Symphonies 1–4; Bohemian–Danish Folk Tune; At the Bier of a Young Artist
(B) **(*) EMI double forte (ADD) CZS5 74188-2 (2). Danish RSO, Blomstedt

(i; ii) *Symphonies 5–6;* (iii) *Wind Quintet, Op. 43;* (i; iv; v) *Hymnus amoris, Op. 12; Søvnen (Sleep), Op. 18*
(B) * EMI double forte (ADD) 5 74299-2 (2).** (i) Danish RSO; (ii) Blomstedt; (iii) Melos Ens.; (iv) cond. Wöldike; (v) with Copenhagen Boys' Ch. & Danish R. Ch.

Blomstedt's complete Decca set of the symphonies is pretty well self-recommending. All six performances are among the finest available: the *First Symphony* has vitality and freshness, and there is a good feel for Nielsen's natural lyricism. Nos. 2 and 3 are possibly the finest of the cycle: Blomstedt finds just the right tempo for each movement. The two soloists are good and the orchestra play with all the freshness and enthusiasm one could ask for. The opening of Blomstedt's *Fourth* has splendid fire: this must sound as if galaxies are forming. The *Fifth Symphony*, too, is impressive: it starts perfectly and is almost as icy in atmosphere as those pioneering recordings of the 1950s. In the *Sixth Symphony* there is no want of intensity, though a broader tempo would have helped generate greater atmosphere in the first movement. However, the performance is undeniably impressive and like the rest of the series enjoys the advantage of first-class recording.

The fill-ups are also very recommendable. Blomstedt is an eminently reliable guide to the *Aladdin Suite*. Ulf Schirmer, too, shows a natural affinity for Nielsen. On the second of the two Doubles, he gives us Nielsen's early cantata, *Hymnus amoris*, one of his warmest and most open-hearted scores, and there is also a persuasive account of Nielsen's first published opus, the endearing *Little Suite for Strings*. To put it briefly, this remains the best all-round modern set of the symphonies and can be purchased with confidence.

Myung-Whun Chung's accounts of the *First* and *Second* symphonies can also hold their own against the best, and his version of the *Sinfonia espansiva* is one of the *very* best – and can be recommended alongside Blomstedt. The concertos are all excellent – some may even prefer them to the rival collection on Chandos. The package as a whole with four records for the price of three is eminently competitive.

Berglund's set with the Royal Danish Orchestra was recorded between 1987 and 1989. The ever-fresh *First Symphony* is given a thoroughly straightforward account and the *Sinfonia espansiva* (No. 3) is perhaps the finest of his cycle. His two soloists, though unnamed, are very good and the general architecture of the work is well conveyed. The *Fourth* (*Inextinguishable*) is more problematic. In his desire to convey the sense of drama and urgency, Berglund tends to be impatient to move things on, particularly in the closing paragraphs. The *Fifth* opens with a strong sense of atmosphere and the second movement's complex structure is well controlled and satisfyingly resolved. In the *Sinfonia semplice* (No. 6) Berglund again proves a perceptive guide. Here as elsewhere, the playing of the Royal Danish Orchestra is beautifully prepared and full of vitality and the RCA engineers produce a recording of splendid body and presence.

Blomstedt's EMI Nielsen symphony cycle comes into direct competition with his later and superior Decca series. These earlier accounts of the symphonies are variable. At the time it was issued No. 1 was arguably the best since Jensen's Decca mono version, with tempi excellently judged. Nos. 2 and 3 are less well characterized, yet are thoroughly alive. No. 4 is very successful, full of vitality, with a thrilling finale, and there is some fine wind playing from the Danish orchestra. The elegiac *Andante lamentoso* (*At the Bier of a Young Artist*) makes a touching epilogue. Neither of the lovely choral cantatas is otherwise available at mid-price and both are eminently worth acquiring. The performances have an appealing freshness. The 1960s Melos account of the *Wind Quintet* still ranks among the best and is also very well recorded.

The second double forte disc includes the fine Melos performance of the *Wind Quintet* and also two choral works from Nielsen's first period that had not been available before. They have subsequently been recorded on Chandos (see below), but the performances under Mogen Wöldike are authoritative and committed, though not enough is made of dynamic markings, with the result that the texture seems occasionally bland. In the *Symphonies* the sound is well balanced and clear, but lean textured – nothing like the original quadraphonic LPs.

Ole Schmidt's 1976 survey was the first one-man overview of the canon. It had the benefit of a first-rate orchestra, and in Ole Schmidt it had an intuitive interpreter. Musically these performances remain strong and, though the orchestral playing is not free from blemish, Schmidt has a keen authenticity of spirit. The *Fifth* is very impressive and the *Sixth* (*Sinfonia semplice*) remains the most searching of the set. The *First* and *Second Symphonies* would be better if their unforced and unaffected lyricism was allowed to speak for itself but they still have much going for them. Some trouble has been taken over these transfers, even if there is still not enough air around the aural image and the horns and brass are still too prominent. Yet the sound is certainly better focused now, and it is good to have these spirited and likeable performances back so inexpensively, even if Blomstedt has the benefit of better balanced recording and a finer orchestral response.

Neeme Järvi's cycle from 1991–2 has much to commend it: absolutely first-class recording with a completely natural balance, which enables the strings to sound rich and sonorous in *fortissimo* passages but delicate and transparent in lightly scored writing; the wind are ideally placed, with no hint of spotlighting, yet every detail registers clearly; and the brass and percussion are captured equally successfully. The Gothenburg orchestra play with great enthusiasm and responsiveness. At the same time, not all the performances can be wholeheartedly recommended. Järvi does not allow the atmosphere and mystery of the *Fifth Symphony*'s first movement to register fully; he is far too intent on moving things along. In the *First Symphony* he is a shade too brisk in the outer movements, though not unacceptably so, and the inner movements are played with real eloquence. The inner movements of the *Second Symphony* have plenty of character, though Järvi does make a little too much of the *allargando* markings in the *Third*, which becomes a little overblown. The finale is rather rushed off its feet, particularly at the very end. The *Sinfonia espansiva* is well paced, and the slow movement features some particularly sensitive singing from Hynninen. But the finale is let down by some uncharacteristic moments of bombast.

As a complete set, Schønwandt's cycle has much to recommend it, even apart from the authoritative edition the conductor uses. The performances are level-headed, occasionally a little too measured and cautious (No. 1), and in No. 2 without the fire of a Thomas Jensen. But his *Sixth* is really outstanding. All the same, as a collection Blomstedt on Decca remains a first recommendation.

The Danacord set of three CDs tells us more about Nielsen than almost any later performances. Only one commercial disc is included: Thomas Jensen's masterly account of the *Sixth Symphony*. Launy Grøndahl's version of the *Second Symphony* (*The Four Temperaments*) has tremendous fire, and Jensen's accounts of the *Third* (*Sinfonia espansiva*) and *Fourth* (*Inextinguishable*) are pretty electrifying. Although allowances must be made for the poor quality of sound in some instances, these performances radiate an authenticity of atmosphere and love of the scores that is quite infectious.

Symphonies 1 in G min., Op. 7; 2 in B min. (Four Temperaments), Op. 16
*** Chan. 8880. RSNO, Thomson

Strong, vigorous accounts of both symphonies from the Royal Scottish Orchestra under Bryden Thomson, with a particularly well-characterized reading of *The Four Temperaments*. The second movement is perhaps a shade too brisk, but in most respects these performances are difficult to fault.

Symphonies 1; 6 (Sinfonia semplice)
*** dacapo 8.224169. Danish Nat. RSO, Schønwandt
*** BIS CD 1079. BBC Scottish SO, Vänskä
(BB) **(*) Naxos 8.550826. Nat. SO of Ireland, Leaper

Michael Schønwandt's account of the *Sixth Symphony* shows a good grasp of structure, and in the inspired first movement he is particularly successful in conveying its atmosphere and sense of mystery. The *First* is sound and well proportioned, but does not carry all before it on an irresistible forward current. Both recordings have excellent sound with a wide dynamic range and vivid detail. As in earlier issues the new Carl Nielsen Edition is used. The *First* is noteworthy, but the *Sixth* is now a first recommendation.

Osmo Vänskä's *First Symphony* comes up fresh, though some expressive point-making does inhibit the onward flow in the first movement. The slow movement, perhaps, also needs to move forward a little more. The *Sixth Symphony* has a great deal going for it and, in intensity and freshness of approach, makes a real challenge to Schønwandt. The BBC Scottish Symphony Orchestra give keenly responsive playing in all departments. Recommended, though not in preference to Blomstedt or (in No. 6) to Schønwandt.

Very good performances indeed of Nielsen's first and last symphonies from Adrian Leaper and the National Symphony Orchestra of Ireland. The sound is exceptionally well balanced, with exemplary detail and good perspective. The playing is well prepared, full of vitality, phrasing is always intelligent and the Naxos disc remains very good value for money.

Symphony 2 (Four Temperaments); Aladdin Suite
*** BIS CD 247. Gothenburg SO, Chung

Symphonies 2 (Four Temperaments); (i) 3 (Sinfonia espansiva)
(BB) *** Naxos 8.550825. Nat. SO of Ireland, Leaper
*** dacapo 8.224126. Danish Nat. SO, Schønwandt; (i) with Elming

Symphonies 2 (Four Temperaments); 5
*** Classico CD296. RLPO, Bostock

Myung-Whun Chung has a real feeling for this repertoire and his account of the *Second Symphony* is among the best, while the *Aladdin Suite* is particularly successful. The Gothenburg Symphony Orchestra proves a spirited and responsive body of players. The recording is impressive, too, and can be recommended with enthusiasm.

Adrian Leaper gets vibrant and involved playing from the Dublin orchestra in *The Four Temperaments*, which is as good as any in the catalogue (save for the Jensen), and the *Espansiva* is well paced, with tempi well judged throughout. The orchestra sounds better rehearsed and more accustomed to the Nielsen idiom than they did in their earlier disc, and they are certainly well enough recorded. Not necessarily a first choice but highly competitive.

Both Michael Schønwandt and Douglas Bostock use the new scholarly Complete Edition. In the *Second Symphony*, Nielsen made minor corrections in the orchestral parts after the first printing and these are restored. Schønwandt gets very cultured playing from his fine orchestra, and judges tempi to excellent effect. There is breadth and nobility in *The Four Temperaments* and his account of the *Espansiva* is equally well paced. Its attractions are greatly enhanced by the fine singing of both soloists. This can hold its own with the best.

Bostock's account of *The Four Temperaments* has tremendous character. In the *Fifth*, he really inspires his players, who convey enthusiasm and freshness. Bostock has real identification with Nielsen and, though the playing has some rough edges and does not match the finesse or bloom of Blomstedt's San Francisco orchestra, it more than compensates in fire and intensity.

(i) Symphonies 3 (Espansiva); 4 (Inextinguishable)
(M) **(*) Warner Elatus 2564 60432-2. (i) Kaappola, Kortekangas; Finnish RSO, Saraste

Saraste and the Finnish Radio Orchestra capture to perfection the explosive character of the opening of No. 4 and, although there are moments when one feels that the current could flow with a higher charge, for the most part the performance is splendidly shaped and impressively executed. The *Sinfonia espansiva*, too, opens with a powerful impetus, and the first movement maintains its forward impulse, while

Saraste finds Sibelian affinities in the *Andante pastorale*. The vocal soloists are not too forwardly balanced, although some might find the soprano's vibrato a little too prominent. The finale opens nobly and closes with fierce eloquence. While not perhaps a first choice, this coupling is certainly compelling throughout.

(i) Symphonies 3 (Sinfonia espansiva); (ii) 5
*** Chan. 9067. (i) Bott, Roberts; RSO, Thomson
(M) **(*) Sony (ADD) SMK 47598-2. (i) Guldbaeck, Moller, Royal Danish O; (ii) NYPO; Bernstein

Bryden Thomson's chosen tempi in the *Sinfonia espansiva* are just right, particularly in the finale. In the slow movement Catherine Bott and Stephen Roberts are excellent, and the performance has a refreshing directness that is most likeable. The *Fifth Symphony* is equally committed and satisfying. The recordings are very good indeed.

Bernstein's genial *Espansiva* with the Royal Danish Orchestra has a lot going for it. And yet, for all the excellence of the orchestral playing, this performance misses something of the music's innocence. Bernstein is at his finest in the *Fifth*, giving an immensely powerful reading, and the passion of the string cantilena and the following movement through into the finale are indicative of the spontaneous feeling which pervades the whole symphony. The well-detailed, resonant recording adds to the impact of the performance.

Symphony 4 (Inextinguishable), Op. 29
(B) ** Australian Decca Eloquence (ADD) 466 904-2. LAPO, Mehta – SCRIABIN: *Le Poème de l'extase* ***

Symphony 4 (Inextinguishable); Amor og digteren (Cupid and the Poet): extracts; Symphonic Rhapsody; (i) Genrebillede (Genre Picture), Op. 6/1; Ariel's Song; Hjemlige Jul
*** Classico CD298. RLPO, Bostock; (i) Lund

Symphony 4 (Inextinguishable); Pan and Syrinx
(M) *** EMI (ADD) 7 64737-2. CBSO, Rattle – SIBELIUS: *Symphony 5* ***

Symphonies 4 (Inextinguishable), Op. 29; 5, Op. 50
(M) *** Warner Elatus 0927 49424-2. Finnish RSO, Saraste
**(*) dacapo 8.224156. Danish RSO, Schønwandt

Symphonies 4 (Inextinguishable); 6 (Sinfonia semplice)
✪ *** Chan. 9047. RSO, Thomson

The late Bryden Thomson's coupling of the *Fourth* and *Sixth Symphonies* is by far the most successful of his Nielsen cycle and possibly the finest recording of his career. The *Fourth Symphony* has great sweep and excitement and this account of the *Sixth Symphony* is quite simply the finest version now before the public, and arguably the most penetrating since Thomas Jensen's first recording. Indeed no one brings us closer to the spirit of this music than Thomson, and the recording is very good too. Recommended with enthusiasm.

Simon Rattle's version of the *Inextinguishable* dates from the late 1970s and is very fine indeed: it deserves a strong recommendation, particularly given the fact that it comes with an altogether outstanding account of *Pan and Syrinx* (the best ever on record) and his classic account of Sibelius's *Fifth Symphony*. Excellent sound.

In the *Fourth Symphony* Douglas Bostock uses the newly published score in the Complete Nielsen Edition. The reading has tremendous character, and both tempos and phrasing are just right. Bostock includes the early *Symphonic Rhapsody* (1888), using a new scholarly edition, as well as various songs, the *Overture* and four new excerpts from the incidental music to *Amor og digteren*. The orchestral version of the *Genre-billede (Genre Picture)* is also new to the catalogue. Although the *Fourth Symphony* is not a first recommendation, it is certainly among the most fiery and committed accounts to have appeared in recent times. Good, though not outstanding sound.

There can be no doubting the extraordinary energy of Mehta's performance of the *Fourth Symphony* nor the brilliance of the 1974 Decca recording. Though he fails to penetrate the music's fullest depths and disclose all its subtleties, this is still an exciting performance, and the coupling is superb.

Saraste and his Finnish orchestra capture the explosive character of the opening of No. 4 to perfection, and although there are moments when one feels the current could flow with a higher charge, for the most part this performance is splendidly shaped and impressively executed. The *Fifth* is hardly less successful: the conception is spacious yet there is no want of movement. The recorded sound has clarity, though the acoustic is a shade dry.

Saraste's coupling of the *Fourth* and *Fifth Symphonies* also come separately on a mid-priced Elatus disc.

Michael Schønwandt continues his fine survey in the newly published Carl Nielsen Edition with a magisterial *Fifth*. The orchestral playing is sensitive and cultured, but in fire and spirit Schønwandt's *Fifth* must yield pride of place among modern versions to Donald Bostock's rougher but wonderfully characterized account from Liverpool; this also draws on the new Nielsen Edition.

Symphony 6 (Sinfonia semplice)

*** BBC mono BBCL 4059-2. NPO, Leopold Stokowski – GABRIELI: *Sonata pian e forte*; LISZT: *Mephisto Waltz 1*; TIPPETT: *Concerto for Double String Orchestra* ***

Although Stokowski conducted the *Second Symphony* in Copenhagen, he never recorded any of the symphonies commercially. This studio performance from Maida Vale makes one think again about this absorbing and in some ways puzzling score. The first movement comes off marvellously, not that its companions fare less well. Meticulous playing, expertly prepared and thought through, which leaves one regretting that Stokowski never recorded the *Fifth*. The sound is very good and balanced beautifully.

CHAMBER MUSIC

Canto serioso; Fantasias for Oboe & Piano, Op. 2; The Mother (incidental music), Op. 41; Serenata in vano; Wind Quintet, Op. 43

**(*) Chan. 8680. Athena Ens.

This reissue gathers together Nielsen's output for wind instruments in chamber form, with everything played expertly and sympathetically. The recording is balanced very close; nevertheless much of this repertoire is not otherwise available, and this is a valuable disc.

String Quartets 1 in G min., Op. 13; 2 in F min., Op. 5

(BB) *** Naxos 8.553908. Oslo Qt

String Quartets 3 in E flat, Op. 14; 4 in F, Op. 44

(BB) *** Naxos 8.553907. Oslo Qt

String Quartets 1–4; (i) String Quintet in G (1888); (ii) Andante lamentoso (At the Bier of a Young Artist) (1910)

*** BIS CD 503/4. Kontra Qt; (i) Naegele; (ii) Johansson

String Quartets 1–4; 5 Quartet Movements, FS2

*** Kontrapunkt 32150-1 (2). Danish Qt

The performances by the Oslo Quartet are spirited, sensitive and very alive. There is a touch of fierceness in the recording quality (they are rather closely balanced) but artistically they are a first recommendation. They also enjoy a hefty price advantage over their Danish rivals.

The Danish Quartet are sensitive to the shape of the phrase, they produce a wide dynamic range, including really soft *pianissimo* tone when required. They are not always the last word in polish, but everything they do is musical, which makes one forgive the occasional rough edge and the somewhat dry quality and rather close balance of the recording. The set also includes five short movements that Nielsen wrote in his late teens and early twenties.

There is an ardour and temperament to the playing by the Kontra Quartet, which most listeners will find very persuasive. In addition we are given the finest account yet recorded of the *G major String Quintet*, where they are joined by the American violist Philipp Naegele, and the only current account of the *Andante lamentoso (At the Bier of a Young Artist)* in its chamber form. The BIS recordings, made in the Malmö Concert Hall, have plenty of presence and clarity, and are rather forwardly (but not unpleasingly) balanced.

String Quintet in G (1888), FS5

*** Chan. 9258. ASMF Ens. – SVENDSEN: *Octet* ***

The *String Quintet in G major* is very well fashioned and owes more to Svendsen, under whose baton the composer was to play, than to his teacher, Gade. It makes both an agreeable and an appropriate companion for Svendsen's early and delightful *Octet*. It receives a three-star performance and recording.

(i) Violin Sonatas 1 in A, Op. 9; 2 in G min., Op. 35. Prelude & Presto, Op. 52 (for solo violin); Prelude & Theme with Variations, Op. 48 (for solo violin)

*** BIS CD 1284. Demertzis, with (i) Asteriadou

The *Violin Sonatas* are relatively neglected, though they are both fine works; the *G minor*, composed just before the First World War, is one of his best pieces. Nielsen, himself an accomplished violinist, spent some time as a young man in the Royal Danish Orchestra. In addition to these two sonatas, we have two other works for violin alone. It was when he was shown the *First Sonata* that the Hungarian violinist Emil Telmányi made contact with the composer and later became his son-in-law. Nielsen composed two extended works for solo violin for him, the *Prelude and Theme with Variations* from 1923 and the *Prelude and Presto*, composed five years later. Georgios Demertzis and Maria Asteriadou do the sonatas justice and the former tackles the formidable difficulties of the two solo works with aplomb. This well-recorded CD fills an important gap in the Nielsen discography.

Violin Sonata 2 in G min., Op. 35

*** Virgin 5 45122-2. Tetzlaff, Andsnes – DEBUSSY; JANACEK; RAVEL: *Sonatas* ***

Nielsen's *G minor Sonata* is a transitional work in which Nielsen emerges from the geniality of the *Sinfonia espansiva* into the darker and more anguished world of the *Fourth Symphony*. It has much of the questing character of the latter and much of its muscularity. Christian Tetzlaff and Leif Ove Andsnes give a very distinguished – at times inspired – performance, and are accorded excellent recording.

Wind Quintet, Op. 43
*** Nim. NI 5728. V. Quintet – HINDEMITH: *Kleine Kammermusik;* LIGETI: *6 Bagatelles* ***

The Vienna Quintet – or, to give it its chosen website name, the 'quintett.wien' – give us a totally fresh and delightful account of the Nielsen, which proves, as do its two companions, a delight from start to finish. Beautifully cultured playing which reveals their affection for this piece. Perhaps the earthiness of some of the finale's variations eludes them, but this is a small reservation. There is no harm in seeing Nielsen attired in his Sunday best or having black Copenhagen coffee with schlagobers. The recording, made in the Wiener Konzerthaus, is first class. This displaces the Athena Quintet and the various Scandinavian ensembles from Bergen to Jutland who have recorded it, though the pioneering Copenhagen Wind Quintet, for whom Nielsen wrote the piece, is in a special category.

PIANO MUSIC

Chaconne, Op. 32; Humoresque-bagatelles, Op. 11; 5 Pieces, Op. 3; 3 Pieces, Op. 59; Suite luciferique, Op. 45
🔴➤ ✪ *** Virgin 5 45129-2. Andsnes

Nielsen's piano music is unmissable! The early pieces have great charm and the later *Suite* and the *Three Pieces*, Op. 59, great substance. Now at last they have found a princely interpreter in the Norwegian, Leif Ove Andsnes, who has a natural feeling for and understanding of this music. Indeed these are performances of eloquence and nobility that are unlikely to be surpassed for some years to come, and the recorded sound is vivid and lifelike.

VOCAL MUSIC

Songs: Æbleblomst; Den første Laerke; 5 Strophic Songs; Studie efter Naturen
*** EMI 5 68842-2. Hendricks, Pöntinen – GRIEG; RANGSTROM; SIBELIUS: *Songs* ***

In this fine collection of Nordic songs, Barbara Hendricks seems equally at home in the artless simplicity of Nielsen's *Strophic Songs*, Op. 21, as in the better known songs of Sibelius, and this recital can be cordially recommended.

Songs, Op. 4; 6; 10; Bow Down Your Head Now; Bright are the Leaves in the Woods Now; Flower; Maskarade: Duet. Nature Study; Italian Pastoral Aria; Oft am I Glad; Oh, Strange Evening Breezes
*** dacapo 8.224218. Dam-Jensen, Lassen, Stærk

Nielsen's songs may not have the psychological subtlety of Kilpinen or the nature mysticism of Sibelius, but within this repertory they have been surpassed in neither artistry nor beauty and subtlety of vocal colour. They stem from the directness and simplicity of Danish folksong and the songs of Nielsen's precursor, C. F. E. Weyse. All of them are strophic and fresh, touching and heart-warming. No doubt the wonderful records made in the 1940s by Aksel Schiøtz served to inhibit Danish singers from trespassing on this repertory, for the LP and CD eras have done nothing like justice to their genius, though all the Nielsen songs have been recorded at one time or another. But now at long last comes a new record that presents these captivating songs in a worthy manner and

well recorded. Inger Dam-Jensen captures their special character splendidly, and she has excellent support from the pianist Ulrich Stærk. Her choice ranges over the whole of Nielsen's career, from the Opp. 4 and 6 collections of 1891 through to the *Italian Pastoral* of 1931. There is also a short duet from the opera *Maskerade* in which she is partnered by Morten Ernst Lassen. Strongly recommended.

Amor and the Poet; An Evening at Giske; Cosmus; Sir Oluf He Rides; Tove; Willemoes (incidental music)
**(*) BIS CD 641 Bonde-Hansen, Persson, Lund, Vigant, Danish Nat. Op. Ch., Aalborg SO, Vetö

The music to *Herr Oluf han rider* (*Sir Oluf He Rides*) was written at high speed (in one number Nielsen even presses one of his early piano pieces, Op. 3, into service). The overture is very imaginative and deserves to enter the repertoire, but for the most part the music is slight. *An Evening at Giske* (*En aften paa Giske*), the earliest piece on the disc, is well held together. The overture, *Love and the Poet* (*Amor og Digtaren*), is not dissimilar in style or quality to *An Imaginary Journey to the Faeroe Islands*. More engaging than the Kontrapunkt collection with *Hagbarth og Signe*, but of specialist rather than general interest.

(i) *Hymnus amoris;* (ii) *3 Motets, Op. 55; The Sleep, Op. 18;* (iii) *Springtime in Fünen, Op. 43*
*** Chan. 8853. Soloists; (i) Copenhagen Boys' Ch.; (ii–iii) Danish Nat. R. Ch.; (iii) Skt. Annai Gymnasium Children's Ch., Danish Nat. RSO; (i; iii) Segerstam; (ii) Parkman

Hymnus amoris is full of glorious music whose polyphony has a naturalness and freshness that it is difficult to resist, and which is generally well sung. The harsh dissonances of the middle *Nightmare* section of *Søvnen* ('The Sleep') still generate a powerful effect. Segerstam gets very good results in the enchanting *Springtime in Fünen*, and the solo singing is good. The three motets actually contain a Palestrina quotation. Generally excellent performances and fine recorded sound.

6 Songs, Op. 10
*** Virgin 5 45273-2. Kringelborn, Martineau – GRIEG; RANGSTROM; SIBELIUS: *Songs* ***

Solveig Kringelborn's anthology includes a half-dozen songs by four composers from each of the Nordic countries. The most neglected are Nielsen's, perhaps because of their uniformly strophic folk-like character. The Op. 10 set is among the most delightful and she sings them with great purity and does them full justice. Only in *Lake of Memory* does she falter (she is a little under the note). But this apart, this is a lovely group and we are not well endowed with alternative readings. Malcolm Martineau is superb throughout. Excellent recorded sound too.

STAGE WORKS

Aladdin (complete incidental music), *Op. 34*
*** Chan. 9135. Ejsing, Paevatalu, Danish R. Chamber Ch. & SO, Rozhdestvensky

Until now the *Aladdin* music has been known only from the 20-minute, seven-movement suite, but the complete score runs to four times its length. Some numbers are choral, and there are songs and a short piece for solo flute. Thirteen of the movements are designed to accompany spoken dialogue and, although not all of it is of equal musical interest and substance, most of it is characteristically Nielsenesque, and much of it is delightful. The two soloists, Mette Ejsing and Guido Paevatalu, are very good and the Danish Radio forces respond keenly to Rozhdestvensky's baton. This is not top-drawer Nielsen but, given such a persuasive performance and excellent recording, one is almost lulled into the belief that it is.

OPERA

Maskarade (complete)

⊶ (M) *** Decca 475 214-2 (2). Haugland, Resmark, Henning, Jensen, Skovhus, Kristensen, Ravn, Bonde-Hansen, Rørholm, Danish Nat. R. Ch. & SO, Schirmer

(N) *** MVD DACAPO (ADD) **SACD** 6.220507/8 (2). Hansen, Plesner, Landy, Johansen, Serensen, Bastian, Brodersen, Haugland, Danish R. Ch. & SO, Fransden

Ulf Schirmer's outstanding recording of this neglected but appealing opera won the *Gramophone*'s 20th-Century Opera Award in 1999, so it now reappears at mid-price. It is an ideal work for enjoying on disc. The plot is the classic one of young lovers being coerced into arranged marriages by heavy-handed fathers, with the masquerade as the symbol of freedom. The result in the opera is a charming mixture, with echoes of Verdi's Falstaff as well as of Johann Strauss's Fledermaus. With eighteenth-century flavours invading the idiom, Nielsen has also learnt from Mozart's da Ponte operas. Central to the success of the recording is the weighty performance of the bass, Aage Haugland, as the heavy father, Jeronimus. Though the tenor, Gert Henning Jensen, is light-weight as the son, he characterizes well, as do the rest of the cast, including Susanne Resmark as the wife, Henriette Bonde-Hansen as the heroine, Leonora (who appears only in the second half of the opera), and above all, Bo Skovhus as the servant, Henrik, a key commentator. Ulf Schirmer draws sparkling and idiomatic playing from the Danish Radio Orchestra, recorded in warm, opulent sound.

Originally recorded in 1977 and issued in the UK by Unicorn, this alternative version of Nielsen's second and last opera now comes more realistically remastered on SACD and must be considered a triumphant success in its new format, with the rear speakers (used discreetly) adding to the atmospheric feeling. But it still sounds admirable through a normal stereo set-up. *Maskarade* is a buoyant, high-spirited score, full of strophic songs and choruses, making considerable use of dance and dance rhythms and having the unmistakable lightness of *buffo* opera. It is excellently proportioned: no Act outstays its welcome, one is always left wanting more, and the scoring is light and transparent. Fransden's performance is distinguished by good – sometimes very good – singing and alert orchestral support. The sound is well focused, and the singers are well blended; on the SACD the balance between singers and orchestra is very convincing. Above all, the sound is musical, the images are well located and firm, and the overall presentation is vivid. But the Decca set remains first choice.

Saul and David (complete)

✿ *** Chan. 8911/12. Haugland, Lindroos, Kiberg, Westi, Ch. & Danish Nat. RSO, Järvi

Nielsen's first opera is here sung in the original language, which is as important with Nielsen as it is with Janáček, and it has the merit of an outstanding Saul in Aage Haugland. The remainder of the cast is very strong and the powerful choral writing is well served by the Danish Radio Chorus. The opera abounds in wonderful and noble music, the ideas are fresh and full of originality. It convinces here in a way that it rarely has before, and the action is borne along on an almost symphonic current that disarms criticism. A marvellous set.

NIELSEN, Ludolf (1876–1939)

Symphony 1 in B min., Op. 3; Fra Bjærgene (From the Mountains: Symphonic Suite), Op. 8
** da capo 8.224093. Danish PO, Cramer

Ludolf Nielsen was eleven years younger than his famous namesake and, like his exact contemporary, Hakon Børresen, a pupil of Svendsen. His *First Symphony* (1903) has real symphonic feeling and a natural grasp of form. The ideas have a touch of Bruckner and of Carl Nielsen too, and it is obvious that Ludolf possessed an original mind. The Danish Philharmonic is the South Jutland Orchestra, based at Odense, and the playing under the German conductor Frank Cramer is perfectly acceptable, though the recording is not top-drawer. Both the *Symphony* and the *Suite*, Op. 8, are well worth investigating.

Symphony 3 in C, Op. 22; Hjortholm, Op. 53
** da capo 8.224098. Bamberg SO, Cramer

There are six Nielsens other than the famous Carl in the record catalogues, and even one who shares his first name. Like his colleague Hakon Børresen, who has been receiving attention of late, Carl Henrik Ludolf Nielsen was eleven years younger than his celebrated countryman. He was both eclectic and prolific, with some 200 works to his credit, and he served for a time in the viola section of the Tivoli Orchestra and later as its conductor. From 1926 until his death in 1939 Nielsen was with the Danish Radio, planning the programmes of its newly founded orchestra. Whatever his limitations, he has the breadth of a symphonist. His *Third Symphony* (1913) is generally post-romantic with touches of Bruckner and the occasional reminder of the late Dvořák tone-poems and of Wagner. However, the work is overlong and not free from bombast. Nielsen was not a great original, but his craftsmanship is expert and his discourse civilized. The tone-poem *Hjortholm*, written in the early 1920s, does not fulfil the promise of its opening. Well-prepared performances and acceptable recording, even if it is wanting the last ounce of transparency.

String Quartets 2 in C min., Op. 5; 3 in C, Op. 41
**(*) CPO 999 698-2. Aros Qt

Ludolf Nielsen formed and played in a string quartet in his younger days, and his *Second Quartet* of 1903–4 is beautifully crafted and effortlessly fluent. It is cyclic in layout, its language owes much to Svendsen and shows a natural feeling for form. There is a certain dignity and nobility that compensate for a lack of personality and depth. The slow movement of the *Third*, however, is a moving and eloquent lament, written on the death of the composer's parents in 1919. Civilized and cultured music, which gives pleasure, even though the Aros Quartet are not the last word in polish or tonal blend. Still, these are very acceptable performances, and very well recorded.

NONO, Luigi (1924–90)

(i) *Como una ola de fuerza y luz* (for soprano, piano, orchestra & tape). ... *soffrte onde serene* (for piano & magnetic tape)

(M) *** DG (ADD) 471 362-2. Pollini; (i) with Slava Taskova, Bav. RSO, Abbado) – MANZONI: *Masse: Omaggio a Edgard Varèse* ***

Like Henze, Nono was much influenced by the Cuban revolution. *Como una ola de fuerza y luz*, a large-scale work involving sumptuous sound, is among the direct inspirations. It involves electronic devices, with blocks of sound and a hammering piano soloist (what a waste to use Pollini!) subjected to electronic treatment – not music in the conventional sense at all, but, with superb recording, it certainly makes an impression.

... *soffrte onde serene* represents Nono's personal response to the playing of Pollini, his sympathy and admiration heightened by family bereavements suffered by composer and pianist. The concentration of the performance helps one to make light of the difficulty of the idiom. This repertoire is not for everyone, but it is well worth investigating by those for whom the possibilities of electronic exploration are of interest. Certainly there are no complaints about the skill and dedication of the recording producer and engineers.

NORBY, Erik (born 1936)

The Rainbow Snake

*** BIS (ADD) CD 79. Danish Nat. RO, Frandsen – BENTZON: *Feature on René Descartes*; JORGENSON: *To Love Music* **

The Rainbow Snake is an American Indian fable which tells how drought had produced infertility in the land. The snake heard of this and let itself be thrown, coiled up, into the sky where it uncoiled until it touched the earth at both ends. It then arched its back and scraped down the blue ice which had given rise to the drought, thus restoring life to the earth. Every time the sun and rain meet, the snake stretches its luminous body across the heavens. The scoring is highly colourful, the harmonic language impressionist. All highly atmospheric, with kaleidoscopic changes of harmony against an almost static rhythmic background. It is very well played and recorded.

NØRGÅRD, Per (born 1932)

Symphony 1 (Sinfonia austera); Symphony 2

*** Chan. 9450. Danish Nat. RSO, Segerstam

Per Nørgård is the leading Danish composer of his generation. The *Sinfonia austera*, Nørgård's *First Symphony*, comes from 1955 and has a strong atmosphere with something of Holmboe's sense of power and forward movement; impressive and compelling. The *Second* (1970) is different in kind, static in feeling and hypnotic in effect. The 'infinite series' which shaped his *Voyage into the Golden Screen* dominates the whole piece. There are some striking and imaginative effects here. Very good performances too from Leif Segerstam and the Danish National Radio Symphony Orchestra.

Symphony 6 (At the End of the Day); Terrains vagues

*** Chan. 9904. Danish Nat. SO, Dausgaard

Written in 1998–9 to celebrate the millennium in the Danish Orchestra's first concert in January 2000, Nørgård's *Sixth Symphony* is a powerful and violent piece that makes no compromises. One takes it on trust even at a first hearing that, as the composer claims, it is tautly structured, for from the opening onwards it demonstrates a vivid feeling for orchestral colour presented with an energy too often missing in new music of the late twentieth-century. Nørgård has said that this is to be the last of his symphonies, and the hushed close suggests something valedictory, but the vitality of invention not just in the symphony but in the substantial orchestral work with which it is coupled, written even more recently, suggests that he may change his mind. Neither work makes for easy listening, but in a superbly engineered recording the power of the writing comes over most persuasively, demanding attention.

NØRHOLM, Ib (born 1931)

Violin Concerto, Op. 60

*** BIS (ADD) CD 80. Hansen, Danish Nat. RSO, Blomstedt – KOPPEL: *Cello Concerto* ***

Ib Nørholm's *Violin Concerto* not only evinces considerable imaginative powers but contains some music of real beauty and is expertly laid out for the orchestra. The Danish Radio recording, while not state of the art, is more than acceptable, and it comes with a rewarding coupling.

NOVÁK, Vitězslav (1870–1949)

(i) Symphonic poems: *About the Eternal Longing, Op. 33; In the Tatras, Op. 26*; (ii) *Moravian-Slovak Suite, Op. 32*

*** Virgin 5 45251. RLPO, Pešek

(M) **(*) Sup. (ADD) 11 0682-2. (i) Czech PO; (ii) Brno State PO; Sejna

In the Tatras (1902), an opulent Straussian tone-poem, and *About the Eternal Longing* (1903–4) were inspired by unrequited love for a beautiful young pupil, Růžna. The *Slovak Suite* is a heavenly score. *Two in Love*, its third movement, could well become as widely popular as any piece of music you care to think of. *In the Church*, the opening movement, has something in common with Mozart's *Ave verum corpus*, though more obviously romantic, and the closing *At Night* is beguilingly atmospheric. Libor Pešek and the Liverpool orchestra put us firmly in their debt with this Virgin issue. Both performance and recording are first rate. All three works here are also persuasively played on Supraphon. The recording of the two symphonic poems is atmospheric and clear but a bit pale in the more expansive tuttis; the suite has slightly more body and colour.

De profundis, Op. 67; Overture: Lady Godiva, Op. 41; Toman and the Wood Nymph, Op. 40

⊶ *** Chan. 9821. BBC PO, Pešek

De profundis, Op. 67; Overture: Lady Godiva, Op 41; South Bohemian Suite, Op. 64

(***) Sup. mono 11 1873-2 011. Brno State PO, Vogel

Anyone familiar with *The Storm* should be in no doubt as to Novák's stature. A contemporary of Suk, he has been overshadowed understandably by Janáček and Martinů. Not even such an enchanting a work as the *South Bohemian Suite* is heard in the concert hall. *Lady Godiva* and *Toman and the*

Wood Nymph come from 1906–7. There is a lot of Dvořák in these pieces and a considerable debt to both Strauss and Mahler, plus an obvious awareness of French musical culture. *Lady Godiva* has something of the opulence of Strauss or the Elgar of *In the South*. It is full of dramatic fire, and its ideas are bold and orchestrated marvellously. Both *Lady Godiva* and *De profundis* are already available, but *Toman and the Wood Nymph* is new to the catalogue. It has the same lush orchestral palette and rich harmonic language. The dark and anguished *De profundis* was written in 1941 at the height of the Nazi occupation for a large orchestra with piano and organ. Stunning recorded sound from Chandos and admirably vivid and idiomatic playing from the BBC Philharmonic under Libor Pešek.

The classic Supraphon performances all come from 1960, except for the *De profundis*, which Jaroslav Vogel recorded two years later. The recordings still sound very good for their period and the performances are very fine. What attractive music it is, too. Recommended.

In the Tatra Mountains (symphonic poem)
**(N) (M) **(*) Sup. mono SU 3688-2. Czech PO, Ančerl –
SLAVICKY: *Moravian Dance Fantasias*; etc. **(*)

Another rewarding issue in the series devoted to the recorded legacy of Karel Ančerl. Novák's eloquent impression of the Tatras was composed at the beginning of the last century and finds him at his most resourceful in terms of orchestral colour. Ančerl's classic performance was recorded in 1950 and is an indispensable part of any collection of Czech music. In many ways it still surpasses the later recordings by Karel Sejna, Stupka, and more recently, Libor Pešek. The digital remastering produces vivid results.

Pan (symphonic poem), Op. 43
*** Marco Polo 8.223325. Slovak PO, Bílek

Novák's five-movement symphonic poem, *Pan*, has some lovely music in it, and there is a pantheistic sensibility here. The scoring has great delicacy and imaginative resource, and there is a distinctly Gallic feeling to much of it. Lyrical, often inspired (occasionally a bit overlong – particularly the last movement) and rewarding, this score is beautifully played by the Slovak Philharmonic under Zdeně Bílek, and no less beautifully recorded.

Cello Sonata, Op. 68
*** Sup. SU 3515-2. Barta, Cech – KODALY: *Cello Sonatas* ***

As a powerful supplement to Kodály's two cello masterpieces, Jiří Barta and Jan Cech offer one of Vitězslav Novák's late works, written in 1941 during the Nazi occupation of Czechoslovakia. As Novák explained, it represented an eruption of hatred against the invaders and their tyranny. Though it may not quite match the two Kodály works in emotional power, the darkness and intensity of the writing over the closely argued single movement – bringing together elements of a multi-movement sonata structure – are most impressive, particularly in a performance as commanding as this.

The Storm, Op. 42
(M) * Sup. (ADD) SU 3088-2 211. Soloists, Czech PO Ch. & O, Košler

The Storm is a work of great beauty and imagination, scored with consummate mastery and showing a lyrical gift of a high order. It has warmth and genuine individuality; the idiom owes something to Richard Strauss as well as to the Czech tradition, and there is an impressive command of both melody and structure. The performance is fully worthy and has splendid dramatic feeling, helped by good soloists and a fine chorus. The recording, too, is admirably balanced, and there is depth, and plenty of weight, even if the soloists are rather too forward. This is one of the best Supraphon reissues for some time.

NYMAN, Michael (born 1948)

(i) Piano Concerto; (ii) MGV
*** Argo 443 382-2. (i) Stott, RLPO; (ii) Nyman Band & O; composer

Michael Nyman's brand of minimalism has been most effective in illustrating a whole sequence of films, including the Oscar-winning *The Piano*, in which this concerto was evocatively used. Kathleen Stott's account of the concerto is as fine as one would expect, and the coupling on the Argo CD, *Musique à grande vitesse*, was commissioned for the inauguration of the high-speed TGV train from Paris to Lille. Not surprisingly, it relies on train rhythms, with all their unexpected syncopations. The Michael Nyman Band, heavily amplified, is set as a ripieno group alongside the orchestra, giving the piece what the composer thinks of as concerto grosso associations. Powerful, forward recording.

NYSTROEM, Gösta (1890–1966)

(i) Viola Concerto (Hommage à la France); Ishavet (Arctic Sea); (ii) Sinfonia concertante for Cello & Orchestra
*** BIS CD 682. (i) Imai; (ii) Ullner; Malmö SO, P. Järvi

Niels Ullner is a fine cellist with an opulent tone and eloquent phrasing and his is a thoughtful, well-integrated performance of the *Sinfonia concertante*, and the music has both quality and depth. The *Viola Concerto* has a neo-classical and eminently Gallic *joie de vivre*, as well as poignancy. Nobuko Imai plays it superbly and, throughout the whole programme, the Malmö orchestra are in excellent form under Neeme Järvi's son, Paavo. The recording is transparent and has excellent presence and definition.

(i) Sinfonia del mare; Sånger vid havet (Songs by the Sea); (ii) The Tempest: Prelude
*** Phono Suecia CD 709. (i) Hellekant; (ii) Swedish R. Ch. & SO, Svetlanov

The *Sinfonia del mare* (1948) is for a large orchestra and includes a wordless role for soprano which is beautifully sung here by the Swedish-born, America-trained mezzo-soprano Charlotte Hellekant. It was quite in vogue in Sweden during the early 1950s, although this performance under Evgeni Svetlanov has a stronger atmosphere and greater concentration than any of his previous recordings. The *Symphony* itself is distinctly short on thematic invention, and its main semi-tone idea overstays its welcome. *Songs by the Sea* is much stronger and more rewarding. Honegger was a major influence on Nystroem, and his *Tempest* prelude no doubt acted as a model for Nystroem's own *Prelude* (1934), although the Honegger work was written for women's voices as well as large orchestral forces. Those who warm to the *Sinfonia del mare* should get this dedicated performance under Svetlanov. It supersedes its predecessors and has excellent and natural recorded sound.

Sinfonia espressiva; Sinfonia seria

*** BIS CD 782. Malmö SO, P. Järvi

Along with the *Sinfonia concertante* for cello and orchestra, the *Sinfonia espressiva* is probably Nystroem's finest work; finely crafted and purposeful. The fires of inspiration burn less brightly in the *Sinfonia seria* of 1963, though its opening, which recalls Honegger a little, has a certain promise. Paavo Järvi and the Malmö orchestra give committed accounts of both pieces and the BIS engineers produce excellent results.

Sinfonia tramontana; Symphony 4 (Sinfonia Shakespeariana)

*** BIS CD 1082. Malmö SO, Andersson

The *Sinfonia Shakespeariana* was first performed in March 1955, together with Berwald's *Sérieuse* and Wiklund's *Second Piano Concerto*, with Sixten Ehrling as soloist and conductor of the rest of the concert. It is difficult to imagine such adventurous programming nowadays. R.L. was there and thought the Nystroem symphony would never end – it took about 40 minutes – and it would seem that the composer himself was not happy with the results. In its revised form it takes some 25 minutes and is a much happier experience. The *Sinfonia tramontana* of 1965 was his *Sixth* and last. Written in France, where Nystroem had spent so much of his life (he was an accomplished painter and studied in Paris in the 1920s), it is a well-argued piece which is well worth hearing. Whatever his faults (a certain paucity of melodic invention, for example, in the *Sinfonia del mare*, and a certain garrulousness in the *Ouverture symphonique* of 1945), Nystroem has a voice of his own and speaks with a distinct and vital accent. Good performances from the Malmö orchestra and superb BIS recording.

OBRECHT, Jacob (1457–1505)

Benedictus in Laude; Plainchant: Sub tuum Praesidium; Missa sub tuum Praesidium; Beata est Maria; Factor orbis; Mille quingentis; Salva Crux; Salve Regina a 3

(N) *** ASV Gaudeamus CDGAU 341. Clerks' Group, Wickham

The plainchant – with its Marian associations – on which Obrecht's *Missa sub tuum Praesidium* is based (and which follows it here, after the *Benedictus in Laude*) is then repeated unaltered in the top voice to dominate every movement of the Mass. This creates a flowing melodic unity in the music; but the writing, which opens in three parts, then expands, adding a voice at each section, so that the extended *Agnus Dei* brings increasing complexity in its seven parts yet retains its serenity. The collection here includes two other Marian motets, *Beata est Maria*, richer in harmonic feeling, and the plainer three-part *Salve Regina*. However, *Salve crux*, sombrely descriptive, and the closing penitential *Factor orbis* were both written for five voices. *Mille quingentis*, which is in a more confident mood, commemorates Obrecht's father, and the text was probably written by the composer himself. Overall, this splendidly sung and recorded collection gives an excellent survey of both Obrecht's compositional skills and his restrained but profound religious conviction.

Laudes Christo; Missa Malheur me bat

*** ASV Gaudeamus CDGAU 171. Clerks' Group, Wickham –
MARTINI: *Motets & Magnificat* ***

The Dutch composer, Jacob Obrecht, was one of the pioneers in developing a new, more closely organized polyphonic style, notably in his use of segmentation. This is well illustrated in this fine *Mass*, with the theme on which the work is based successively fragmented. There is a sublime summation at the end when the theme is restored to its original form, radiantly performed by the Clerks' Group, and with warmly atmospheric sound. The coupling is apt – Obrecht ended up as *Maestro di capella* at the court of Ferrara, where Martini had spent his career.

Missa Caput; Salve Regina: in 4 parts; in 6 parts. Venit ad Petrum

☛ (BB) *** Naxos 8.553210. Oxford Camerata, Summerly

The *Missa Caput* survives in a manuscript at the court of Ferrara but could possibly have been compiled in Bruges. Both of the *Salve Regina* settings are based on plainchant melody and are *alternatim* settings, the music alternating between a polyphonic treatment of the chant and the unadorned chant itself. Jeremy Summerly and his Oxford Camerata, recorded in the Chapel of Hertford College, Oxford, give expert and committed accounts of this music and they are accorded first-class sound.

OCKEGHEM, Johannes (c. 1410–97)

Alma redemptoris mater; Missa Mi-Mi; Salve Regina

☛ *** ASV Gaudeamus CDGAU 139. Clerks' Group, Wickham (with motets by BUSNOIS, ISAAC and OBRECHT)

Ockeghem's *Salve Regina*, the motet *Alma redemptoris mater* and the *Missa Mi-Mi* are contrasted here with motets by three of his contemporaries. The *Missa Mi-Mi* is so named because of the recurring descending fifth, both named 'mi' in the natural and soft hexachords. These performances have a refreshing enthusiasm and the approach to rhythm is remarkably free. An outstanding disc.

Ave Maria; Intemerata Dei Mater; Missa ecce ancilla Domina

*** ASV Gaudeamus CDGAU 223. Clerks' Group, Wickham
(with OBRECHT: *Salve Regina*; JOSQUIN DESPREZ: *Déploration sur la mort de Ockeghem* ***)

Ecce ancilla Domina is a middle-period mass (c. 1470), but its polyphonic richness and unpredictable rhythmic impetus make for compelling listening in a performance so aptly paced and involvingly spontaneous. The *Ave Maria* is relatively familiar (see below), but *Intemerata Dei Mater* (from the 1480s) has a poignant atmosphere all its own which matches the expressive power of Obrecht's six-part *Salve Regina* from the same period. Josquin's valedictory musical farewell in the plaintive Phrygian mode also has links to Ockeghem's moving supplication to the mother of God. This beautifully recorded disc is well up to the high standard of ASV's admirable series.

Missa caput; Ma maistresse; Missa Ma maistresse: Kyrie & Gloria

*** ASV Gaudeamus CDGAU 186. Clerks' Group, Wickham
(with ANON: Hymn: *O solis ortus cardine*; Motets: *O sidus Hispanie; Gaude Marie*. SARUM CHANT: Antiphon: *Venit ad Petrum*)

Only two movements survive of the *Missa Ma maistresse*, but very fine they are, bright and extrovert in feeling, making ingenious use of the song material. The song itself is solo-led, ravishingly sung: Ockeghem's lovely setting is fully worthy of the words: '*My mistress and my greatest love, perfect in attributes as ever woman was*'. The cantus firmus of the *Missa Caput* is derived from the long melisma on the word 'caput' which we have already heard at the end of the Sarum Antiphon, *Venit ad Petrum*. It is perhaps an awkward basis for a mass, but Ockeghem's polyphony rises to the challenge, and the work is both texturally and aurally intriguing, yet moves forward on a seemingly inevitable course, in spite of Ockeghem's frequent use of cadences. The three anonymous motets can be found in the same manuscript which is the earliest source of this mass and it is possible that *O sidus Hispanie*, a eulogy for St Anthony of Padua, was written by Du Fay, who greatly admired this saint. All the performances here are of the highest order and the recording is first-class too.

Missa de plus en plus. Chansons: *Autre Vénus estes sans faille; Mort tu as navré de ton dart; O rosa bella; Prenez sur moy vostre exemple amoureux; Presque transi; S'elle m'amera je ne sçay; Tant fuz gentement resjouy*
(M) *** DG Blue 471 727-2. Orlando Consort

It is difficult to make a choice between two recordings of the *Missa de plus en plus*. Remarkably, the beautifully recorded Orlando Consort, with fine tonal blending create the richest sonorities with only four singers. But what makes this Archiv reissue in DG's Blue series especially enticing is the inclusion of the varied love songs, touching and stimulating by turns. The selection opens and closes in melancholy, with the final lament, *Mort tu as navré ('Death you have wounded')* very moving, but in between comes lighter fare, including the lively canon *Prenez sur moy* and the richly harmonious *O rosa bella* and *Autre Vénus*, one in praise of a rose, the other a seductive beloved. They are sung with great character, and fortunately both texts and translations are included. Highly recommended.

Missa de plus en plus; Missa Fors seulement
*** Lyrichord LEMS 8029. Schola Discantus, Moll

This Lyrichord disc joins the beautiful middle-period four-part *Missa de plus en plus* with a later five-part work, *Missa Fors seulement*, based on one of the composer's own chansons, which is unfortunately not included here as it is on Edward Wickham's ASV disc (see below). However, the performances are finely sung and blended and have an appealing simplicity. Ken Moll's varied pacing is convincing. The *Missa Fors seulement* (which only consists of *Kyrie*, *Gloria* and *Credo*) is especially notable for its use of two basses, which darkens the texture very strikingly, although Moll takes care not to provide an exaggerated balance.

Missa l'homme armé; Alma redemptoris mater; Ave Maria
☞━ ✿ (BB) *** Naxos 8.554297. Oxford Camerata, Summerly (with DESPREZ: *Memor esto veri tui* ***)

Missa l'homme armé; Missa Sine nomine; Salve Regina (probably by Philippe Basiron)
*** Gaudeamus CDGAU 204. Clerks' Group, Wickham (with MORTON (attrib.): *Rondeau: Il sera pour vous (L'Homme armé)* ***)

On Naxos the soaring opening *Ave Maria*, gloriously sung, immediately sets the seal on the inspirational power of Ockeghem's music. It is followed by the plainchant, *Alma redemptoris mater*, and then its polyphonic setting, simple and flowing and harmonically rich. The robust ballad, *L'Homme armé*, follows ('The armed man must be feared'), sounding vigorously jolly, like a carol. It must have been hugely popular in its day since so many composers used it as a basis for a mass. While the polyphony in the *Gloria* and *Credo* moves onward inventively, the work's dramatic and emotional peak is readily found in the extended *Sanctus* (by far the longest section) and resolved in the sublime melancholy of the *Agnus Dei*. In short, this is a work of striking individuality and beauty, and it is sung superbly here, and marvellously paced. Josquin's setting of sixteen verses from Psalm 119, *Memor esto verbi tui*, with its expressively fertile imitative devices, makes an eloquent postlude, and the recording, made in the Chapel of Hertford College, Oxford, could hardly be bettered. It dates from February 1997, thus aptly celebrating the 500th anniversary of Ockeghem's death.

Ockeghem's striking *L'Homme armé* mass is always easy to follow as its cantus firmus is so characterful. On ASV it is quoted first in a rondeau, attributed to Ockeghem's contemporary, Robert Morton, where it is used mockingly; it is surprising that no translation is given, although it is provided for the other music. Both the *Missa sine nomine* and the *Salve Regina* are dubiously attributed to Ockeghem, but he would surely have been glad to acknowledge the rich polyphony of the latter.

The *Sine nomine mass* for three voices, however, is much less characteristic, although to our ears its flowing lines are very attractive. The performances here are well up to the standard of this excellent group, but the Naxos recording of the *Missa l'homme armé* by the Oxford Camerata is even more attractively coupled.

Missa Prolationum
*** ASV Gaudeamus CDGAU 143. Clerks' Group, Wickham (with BUSNOIS: *Gaude coelestis Domina; In hydraulis*; DESPREZ: *Illibata dei Virgo nutrix*; OBRECHT (attrib.): *Humilium decus*; PULLOIS: *Flos de spina* ***)

Missa Prolationum; Alma redemptoris mater; Ave Maria; Intemerata Dei Mater; Salve Regina (2 settings)
(M) **(*) Virgin 5 61484-2. Hilliard Ens.

Missa Prolationum; Requiem; Intemerata Dei Mater
(BB) **(*) Naxos 8.554260. Musica Ficta, Holten

Ockeghem was a mathematician as well as a composer, and his *Missa Prolationum* is famous for its intellectually complex polyphony based on double canons, while the rhythmic discipline is also carefully calculated. To all but the most analytical listener this will not matter too much, for the resulting music has a seemingly effortless flow, although the eight-voiced Clerks' Group, without losing melismatic sonority, certainly don't miss the special rhythmic relationships. They support the mass with five diverse motets by Ockeghem's contemporaries (nearly all set to Marian texts), to make a stimulating introduction to other Franco-Netherlands composers of this period. Excellent recording.

The performances by the first-class Danish choir under Bo Holten on Naxos use a larger group (fourteen in all) and one in which the rich-voiced women singers refine their tone to sound very like boy-trebles when required. The account of the *Missa Prolationem* is particularly rich-textured, and beautifully balanced: the *Sanctus* and *Benedictus* strikingly so. The *Requiem* is also superbly sung, if with the rough edges smoothed off. The *Intemerata Dei Mater* opens the programme. It is sung with considerable feeling and immediately shows the splendid inner blend commanded by this group.

Holten moves the polyphony forward with just the right degree of momentum. The choir is very beautifully recorded, but the disc (unusually for Naxos) is let down a little by the absence of English translations.

The *Mass*, famous for its polyphonic complexities, is sung with perfect vocal blend and immaculate ensemble, but the characteristic austerity of the Hilliard approach now sounds a little cool alongside the newer version by the Clerks' Group under Edward Wickham on ASV. However, the added attraction of the Hilliard programme is that it also includes similarly flowing accounts of all the known motets of Ockeghem, although the shorter of the two *Salve Regina* settings is now re-attributed to Philippe Basiron. Full texts and translations are provided, so this remains a valuable reissue.

Masses for 3 voices: *Missa Sine nomine; Missa Quinti toni*
*** Lyrichord LEMS 8010. Schola Discantus, Moll

The very austerity of Ockeghem's part-writing, with its serenely flowing polyphony, adds to the potency of his music for modern ears. It is very beautifully sung by a vocal quartet of high quality whose tonal matching and fine tuning are ideal. The recording, too, is clear yet has a perfectly judged ambience.

Requiem *(Missa pro defunctis)*
*** HMC 901441. Ens. Organum, Pages de la Chapelle, Pérès

Requiem; *Motet and Missa Fors seulement*
⊖━ *** ASV Gaudeamus CDGAU 168. Clerks' Group, Wickham

Requiem; *Missa Mi-Mi (Missa Quarti toni)*
(M) *** Virgin 5 61219-2. Hilliard Ens., Hillier

Ockeghem's *Requiem* remains one of the riddles of medieval liturgical music. Its various surviving movements are very different in style, notation and part-writing, and (rather like the Du Fay *St Anthony Mass*) it was long thought that the manuscript might be a collection of fragments from a number of different works. Even so the *Requiem* holds together with a convincing unity. Of all the available recordings, that by Marcel Pérès and the Ensemble Organum carries the darkest medieval feeling. The conductor's reconstruction is a quite arbitrary one. He even sings the solo plainchants himself, lugubriously but resonantly. Later he adds the (missing) *Sanctus* and *Communion* from a Mass by Antonius Divitis, emphasizing the change by the inclusion of trebles (Les Pages de la Chapelle). Inevitably this must be a controversial account, but it is both gripping and aurally stimulating.

Certainly every bar of the music is memorable in such a dedicated performance as we have from the Clerks' Group under Edward Wickham, who offer fine blending and tuning, clearly detailed inner parts and a richly flowing line which is seemingly ideally paced. In addition we are offered the *Kyrie*, *Gloria* and *Credo* of the *Missa Fors seulement*, plus the rondeau on which it is based, and further arrangements of the latter by Pierre de la Rue and Antoine Brumel, which offer more splendid music to intrigue the inquisitive ear.

The performances reissued on Virgin Veritas have the expertise, secure intonation, blend and ensemble that one expects from these singers, and the music itself has an austere and affecting simplicity. Although alongside the account of the *Requiem* by the Clerks' Group it has a certain blandness, it would be curmudgeonly not to welcome such generally persuasive accounts of both works.

OFFENBACH, Jacques (1819–80)

Concerto militaire; *Concerto rondo;* 4 Impressions: *(ii) Deux âmes au ciel – Elégie; (iii) Introduction et valse mélancolique; Rêverie au bord de la mer; (ii) La Course en traineau*
(N) *** CPO 777 069-2. Schiefen, WDR R. O, Köln, with (i) Froschauer; (ii) Villiers; (iii) Oskamp

Ofra Harnoy's deleted RCA recording made Offenbach's delightful *Concerto rondo* a famous novelty. Guido Schiefen's performance offers greater exuberance, but Harnoy offered greater elegance. However, Schiefen gives us the longer *Concerto militaire*, where there's plenty of sparkle throughout, especially in the irrepressibly catchy finale. The *Four Impressions* find Offenbach in more reflective mood and are lightly sentimental works of much charm, written for the instrument that he adored. Although Schiefen's timbre isn't always as ideally rounded as it might be, there is nothing to deter Offenbachians. Accompaniments are well managed under three different conductors, and the recording is well balanced.

Gaîté parisienne *(ballet, arr. Rosenthal; complete)*
⊖━ ✿ (M) *** RCA SADC 82876 66419-2. Boston Pops O, Fiedler – ROSSINI/RESPIGHI: *Boutique fantasque* *******
(B) ** EMI Encore (ADD) 5 85066-2. Monte Carlo Op. O, Rosenthal – WALDTEUFEL: *Waltzes* *******

Fiedler's *Gaîté parisienne* is irresistible – one of his very finest records. The orchestra are kept exhilaratingly on their toes throughout and are obviously enjoying themselves, not least in the elegantly tuneful waltzes and in the closing *Barcarolle*, which Fiedler prepares beautifully and to which the generous acoustic of Symphony Hall affords a pleasing warmth without in any way blunting or coarsening the brilliance. The percussion, including bass drum in the exuberant *Can-can*, adds an appropriate condiment and John Pfeiffer's superb SACD transfer makes the recording sound remarkably fresh and full. Unbelievably it dates from 1954, one of the very first of RCA's 'Living Stereo' records and still one of the finest.

As in his later version for Naxos, Rosenthal's mid-1970s EMI recording, though sometimes idiomatically persuasive, has not the glamour and verve of the finest versions, notably those of Fiedler and Karajan. However, those attracted to the four Waldtefeul *Waltzes* may well prefer this EMI coupling to *Offenbachiana*.

Gaîté parisienne *(ballet; extended excerpts, arr. Rosenthal)*
(B) *** DG (ADD) 429 163-2. BPO, Karajan – CHOPIN: *Les Sylphides* ***** ✿**; DELIBES: *Coppélia:* suite *******

Karajan's selection is generous. On the DG disc, only Nos. 3–5, 7 and 19–21 are omitted. The remastering of the 1972 recording is highly successful; textures have been lightened to advantage, and the effect is to increase the raciness of the music-making, while its polish and sparkle are even more striking.

Overtures: *Barbe-bleue; La Belle Hélène; Le Grande Duchesse de Gérolstein; Le Mariage aux lanternes; Orfée aux Enfers*
(N) ✿ (***) Australian Decca Eloquence mono 476 2757. LPO, Martinon (with ADAM: *Si j'étais roi.* BOIELDIEU: *Le Calife de Bagdad; La Dame blanche.* HEROLD: *Zampa********)

Martinon's celebrated mono LP collection of Offenbach overtures – quite the best ever committed to disc – has been out of the catalogue for far too long but now, at last, has made it to CD. Under Martinon these overtures explode like a suddenly shaken bottle of ice-cold champagne. The LPO strings play with polish as well as fizz, so the *cancan* finales of *Orfée* and *La Grande Duchesse* are both elegant and sparkling. While no one captures the whirlwind Offenbach impetus quite as Martinon does, one relishes this collection also for the charm of the playing, with the engaging tunes of *Barbebleue* beautifully phrased and so gentle that the sharply pointed rhythms of the finale seem even more racy. But nowhere is Martinon's rhythmic vitality and lift more apparent than in the deliciously crisp closing section of the rare *Le Mariage aux lanternes*; here one understands why Rossini dubbed Offenbach 'the Mozart of the Champs-Elysées'. Among the other delights here is the delicate oboe tune in *La Belle Hélène*, enchantingly played, while during the lilting waltz theme you can understand how Offenbach once beat Johann Strauss in a waltz-writing competition! A genuine Gallic wit runs through these performances, with the rollicking tune in *La Grande Duchesse Overture* (at 1'27") a prime example.

Australian Decca have coupled the Offenbach items with Martinon's accounts of other French overtures which we described in the original Penguin review as 'four French soufflés served up by a conductor who obviously relishes every moment and the orchestra giving of their very best'. *La Dame blanche* is especially enjoyable, with the bravura bassoon accompaniment to the second subject as perky as can be. The early 1950s sound is certainly vivid, although still a shade too bright. The original LXT (before it was re-cut) was undoubtedly warmer and sounded better balanced, but the sound of this transfer is miles ahead compared with the Ace of Clubs and Eclipse LP versions, which were last heard around 30 years ago! A unique disc and well worth any effort to obtain.

Overtures: *La Belle Hélène; Bluebeard; La Grande-Duchesse de Gérolstein; Orpheus in the Underworld; Vert-vert.* Barcarolle from *Contes d'Hoffmann*
**(*) DG (IMS) 400 044-2. BPO, Karajan

Other hands besides Offenbach's helped to shape his overtures. Most are on a pot-pourri basis, but the tunes and scoring are so engagingly witty as to confound criticism. Karajan's performances racily evoke the theatre pit. The Berlin playing is very polished and, with so much to entice the ear, this cannot fail to be entertaining. However, the compact disc emphasizes the dryness of the orchestral sound; the effect is rather clinical, with the strings lacking bloom.

Overture: *La Belle Hélène* (arr. Haensch); (i) *Les Contes d'Hoffmann*: Entr'acte et Barcarolle
*** Chan. 9765. (i) RLPO Ch.; BBC PO, Y. P. Tortelier (with Concert: *French bonbons* ***)

Haensch's *Overture La Belle Hélène* is a far better piece than the more famous overture to *Orpheus in the Underworld*. A stylish pot-pourri, it includes two of the opera's best tunes, the disarmingly seductive waltz, and a delightfully songful siciliano given to the oboe; it then ends with a brief, infectious can-can. Tortelier has its full measure, shaping it with great style and affection, and reminding us of Martinon's justly famous LPO mono Decca version (which needs a Dutton Lab. reissue). The *Barcarolle*, too, is very seductive,

and both are given state of the art recording. This is part of an unmissable concert of '*French bonbons*'.

***Le Papillon* (ballet: complete)**
(N) (B) *** Decca (ADD) 476 7220 (2). Nat. PO, Bonynge – TCHAIKOVSKY: *Nutcracker* ***

Le Papillon is Offenbach's only full-length ballet and it dates from 1860. The quality of invention is high and the music sparkles from beginning to end. In such a sympathetic performance, vividly recorded (in 1972 in the Kingsway Hall), it cannot fail to give pleasure. Chosen by the BBC CD Review this is now reissued in the Universal's 'Critics Choice' series.

Cello Duos, Op. 54: Suites 1–2
(B) *** HMA 1901043. Pidoux, Péclard

Offenbach was himself a very accomplished cellist, and these two works are tuneful and imaginatively laid out to exploit the tonal possibilities of such a duo. Offenbach's natural wit is especially apparent in the *First Suite in E major*. The performances are excellent and so is the recording.

PIANO MUSIC

***Bella notte* (Barcarola); *Décaméron dramatique* (Album du Théâtre français); *Dernier souvenir* (Valse de Zimmer); *Les Roses du Bengale* (6 Valses sentimentales)**
(N) *** CPO 777 079-2. Sollini

Offenbach's piano music is essentially salon music, tuneful and undemanding, and not terribly pianistic. Not all of it shows Offenbach in the best light, but there are some moments of charm, and his effervescent spirit certainly comes through. There is a nice story attached to the engaging *Valse de Zimmer*. Its tune – or at least the first eight bars of it – was hummed to Offenbach as a child, and it came to represent for him a nostalgic reminder of his childhood. At the time, his father had mentioned in passing the name of the composer of the melody, and many years later, after a great deal of detective work, Offenbach found him in a sadly reduced state in Vienna. He was half-starved and had lost his way since the death of his fiancée. Offenbach gamely came to his rescue and in return was bequeathed a lock of the fiancée's hair, her engagement ring – and the complete waltz, which Offenbach later published at his own cost. Excellent performances and recording, and guaranteed to bring a sentimental tear when the Waltz appears.

OPERA

***La Belle Hélène* (complete)**
☛ *** TDK **DVD** DV-OPLBH; CD *** Virgin 5 45477-2 (2)). Lott, Beuron, Sénéchal, Le Roux, Naouri, Todorovitch, Ch. & Musiciens du Louvre, Grenoble, Minkowski (Stage director: Laurent Pelly)
(*) Arthaus **DVD 100 086. Kasarova, Van der Walt, Chausson, Vogel, Widmer, Zurich Op. Ch. & O, Harnoncourt (Producer: Helmut Lohner; V/D: Hartmut Schottler)
*** EMI (ADD) 7 47157-8 (2). Norman, Alliot-Lugaz, Aler, Burles, Bacquier, Lafont, Capitole Toulouse O, Plasson

The new production of *La Belle Hélène* staged by Laurent Pelly, with costumes by Chantal Thomas, retains all the mythological characters, but they appear to Helen as in a dream – of being the most beautiful woman in the world and falling in love with the virile young Paris. Her double bed, to which she retires at the beginning, becomes the focus of the action until Act III, which takes place on the beach at Naples, from which she finally sails away with Paris. The whole production fizzes and has touches of romantic naughtiness which only the French can bring off with real style. There is an additional 'Behind the Scenes' sequence narrating the background to this brilliantly successful production.

Favouring brisk speeds and light textures, using the period instruments of Les Musiciens du Louvre, Marc Minkowski gives a winning sparkle to this delectable send-up of the classical story. He also has the benefit of offering a more complete, more authentic text than any predecessor. It was recorded after the highly successful stage production at the Châtelet Theatre in Paris in September 2000, when Felicity Lott was hailed as an outstanding star in the role of Hélène. That is true, even if vocally there are moments when her voice is not at its sweetest, not as rounded as it might be, but her feeling for the idiom and her characterization are unerring. Outstanding in the cast is the seductively honeyed tenor of Yann Beuron as Paris. His 'Judgement of Paris' solo in Act I has rarely been matched, with exquisite pianissimo singing in the final stanza, enhanced by Minkowski's persuasive rubato. An excellent supporting cast including such stalwarts of the repertory as Michel Sénéchal and François Le Roux. But although the CDs are in every way recommendable, the live performance on DVD is sheer delight, adding an extra dimension to Offenbach's scintillating score.

The roster in the alternative 1997 Arthaus production at the Zurich Opera is a strong one and Kasarova makes a positive impression here, as for that matter do the remainder of the cast. Harnoncourt gets lively results from his players but crisper and more lightly accented rhythms would have been welcome. He is a touch heavy-handed. The production is inventive and flows smoothly and the evening is thoroughly enjoyable: this can certainly be recommended, particularly for Vessalina Kasarova's Hélène. The French of the principals is wonderfully clear but the Minkowski set is a clear first choice.

On the earlier EMI audio recording the casting of Jessye Norman in the name-part of La Belle Hélène may seem too heavyweight, but the way that great soprano can lighten her magisterial voice with all the flexibility and sparkle the music calls for is a constant delight, and her magnetism is irresistible. John Aler, another American opera-singer who readily translates to the style of French operetta, makes a heady-toned Paris, coping superbly with the high tessitura in the famous 'Judgement' couplets and elsewhere. The rest of the cast is strong too, not forgetting Colette Alliot-Lugaz as Oreste, who had such a dazzling success in the central role of Chabrier's L'Etoile in John Eliot Gardiner's brilliant recording. Michel Plasson here produces similarly fizzing results, with excellent ensemble from the chorus and orchestra of the Capitole. Excellent, lively recording.

Highlights from: (i) La Belle Hélène; (ii) Orpheus in the Underworld; (iii) La Vie parisienne (all sung in English)
☛ ✿ (B) *** CfP (ADD) 5 75999-2 (2). (i) Blackham, Fryatt; (i; ii) Miller; (i) Crofoot (ii; iii) Bronhill; Shilling, Weaving; (iii) Steele, Sadler's Wells Op. Ch. & O, cond. (i; ii) Faris; (iii) Pollack, Matheson

These sparkling recordings of Sadler's Wells Offenbach productions from the early 1960s remain among the most convincing examples of operetta (or opera) sung in English on record. The offering, too, is generous – between them the two discs play for 151 minutes, all delightful entertainment. The English versions by Geoffrey Dunn are excellent examples of how French operetta can be brought to an English audience without losing the Gallic wit of the orginals. La Belle Hélène is a highly infectious performance, catching the comedy without overdoing things. Especially good is the Patriotic Trio from the third act; Kevin Miller's Paris and Joyce Blackham's Hélène are also excellent, and the conductor's touch is not too heavy, while the orchestral playing is crisp and well disciplined.

With a single reservation, Orpheus in the Underworld is the most successful of the three. Without visual help the recording manages to convey the high spirits and genuine gaiety of the piece, plus – and this is an achievement for a non-Parisian company – the sense of French poise and precision. June Bronhill, who sings most engagingly as Eurydice in the Concerto Duet, is infectiously provocative about her poor suitor's music. One's only complaint is that Alan Crofoot's King of Boeotians number at the opening of Act III is needlesssly cruel vocally.

In La Vie parisienne the vocal standards may sound thinner on record than they did on stage – even Anna Pollack sounds over parted – but the production is as imaginative as ever, and it is the Sadler's Wells teamwork that matters, so much of the effervescence of this Second Empire romp comes over well. Throughout, the CD remastering shows how vivid and clear were the original recordings, projecting the words admirably against a warm theatrical acoustic, even though the recordings were made at Abbey Road.

Les Brigands (complete)
**(*) EMI 7 49830-2 (2). Raphanel, Alliot-Lugaz, Raffalli, Trempont, Le Roux, Lyon Opera Ch. & O, Gardiner

Les Brigands has a Gilbertian plot about brigands and their unlikely association with the court of Mantua, with the carabinieri behaving very like the police in The Pirates of Penzance. The tone of the principal soprano, Ghislaine Raphanel, is rather edgily French, but the rest of the team are splendid. Outstanding as ever is the characterful mezzo, Colette Alliot-Lugaz, in another of her breeches roles. Warm, well-balanced recording.

Les Contes d'Hoffmann (The Tales of Hoffmann; complete)
*** Warner **DVD** 0630 19392-2. Domingo, Serra, Baltsa, Cotrubas, Evans, Nimsgern, Ghiuselev, Lloyd, ROHCG Ch. & O, Prêtre (V/D: Brian Large)
☛ ✿ *** Decca (ADD) 417 363-2 (2). Sutherland, Domingo, Tourangeau, Bacquier, R. Suisse Romande & Lausanne Pro Arte Ch., SRO, Bonynge
**(*) Ph. (IMS) 422 374-2 (3). Araiza, Lind, Studer, Norman, Von Otter, Ramey, Dresden Ch. & State O, Tate

The Warner DVD offers a 1981 performance at Covent Garden with Plácido Domingo ideally cast in the name-part, singing and acting superbly in John Schlesinger's production, here imaginatively directed for video by Brian Large. Georges Prêtre conducts an idiomatic performance, using the traditional score, with the climactic sextet as part of the Venice Act, which comes second in the sequence, leaving the Antonia Act till last and making the epilogue the briefest of afterthoughts.

Like the production, sets and costumes, the casting is lavish, with separate star singers for roles normally doubled up between the acts. Effective as all the performances are, the very length of the cast list makes it most regrettable that the box contains no booklet and little information, not even a cast list. One simply has to rely on the visual credits at the end. Luciana Serra is bright and agile as the doll, Olympia, though edgy as recorded, while Agnes Baltsa is an imperious Giulietta in the Venice Act, tough and characterful with her tangy mezzo, and Ileana Cotrubas is charming and touching as Antonia. Among those outstanding in the character roles are Geraint Evans as Coppelius, Robert Tear as Spalanzani, and Nicola Ghiuselev as Dr Miracle. The sound is a little dry and is distracting in the context.

On Decca Joan Sutherland gives a virtuoso performance in four heroine roles, not only as Olympia, Giulietta and Antonia but also as Stella in the *Epilogue*. Bonynge opts for spoken dialogue, and puts the Antonia scene last, as being the more substantial. His direction is unfailingly sympathetic, while Sutherland is impressive in each role, notably as the doll Olympia and in the pathos of the Antonia scene. As Giulietta she hardly sounds like a *femme fatale*, but still produces beautiful singing. Domingo gives one of his finest performances on record, and so does Gabriel Bacquier. It is a memorable set, in every way, much more than the sum of its parts.

Jeffrey Tate in this textually troubled work uses a new expanded edition prepared by Michael Kaye, where dialogue replaces all the recitatives written by Ernest Guiraud. The Prologue is more extended, showing the transformation of the Muse into Nicklausse, with extra material in the Olympia and Antonia Acts too. Jessye Norman, the Antonia of the new set, cunningly lightens her voice, making it sound as girlish as she can, but it is still hard to imagine her as the fragile young girl destined to die. Tate's determination to adopt an authentic text leads him to reject the wonderful septet, based on the *Barcarolle* theme, not even including it in an appendix. Nor is Dapertutto's *Scintille, diamant* included, drawn originally from another Offenbach work, when the authentic *Tourne, tourne miroir* is restored at that point. Samuel Ramey sings very well in all four villainous roles, with satisfyingly firm, dark tone, but principal vocal honours go to Anne Sofie von Otter as a superb Muse and Nicklausse, making one relish all the extra music given the character in this version. Eva Lind is bright and clear, if a little edgy and shallow, as Olympia, perfectly doll-like in fact; and Cheryl Studer is technically very strong and confident, even if she does not quite sound in character. Francisco Araiza makes an agreeable Hoffmann, but he lacks the flair of his finest rivals.

Les Contes d'Hoffmann: highlights
(M) *** Decca (ADD) 458 234-2 (from above set, cond. Bonynge)

The Decca highlights disc is one of the finest set of excerpts of its kind from any opera. With about 70 minutes of music, it offers a superbly managed distillation of nearly all the finest items and is edited most skilfully, including both the vocal and orchestral versions of the famous *Barcarolle*.

The Tales of Hoffmann (fairly complete; sung in English)
(M) (***) Somm mono 13-2 (2). (Recording made for the soundtrack of the Michael Powell and Emeric Pressburger film) Rounseville, Bond, Grandi, Ayars, Dargavel, Sinclair, Brannigan, Clifford, Sadler's Wells Ch., RPO, Beecham. (Includes Beecham at the piano, playing and singing through the score)

Somm have acquired the rights, not just to the Decca recording of the opera, but also to excerpts from Beecham's

fascinating private introduction of the music to Michael Powell and Emeric Presburger before the film was made. This was accomplished at an informal session with Beecham sitting at the piano, playing through the whole score and providing the vocalizations himself with passionate and sometimes bizarre enthusiasm.

None of the singers chosen by Beecham were famous, but all justified his confidence in them, and this new transfer brings plenty of bloom to their voices. Robert Rounseville is a warmly lyrical Hoffmann and, as one would expect, Monica Sinclair a superb Nicklausse, while Dorothy Bond makes a charmingly petite Olympia. Margherita Grandi may be a bit over the top in her sultry portrayal of Giulietta, but Ann Ayars is fully equal to the role of Antonia in the demanding final Act. The smaller parts are all characterfully sung, with Grahame Clifford excellent as both Spalanzani and Franz, and Owen Brannigan ready to change roles as Schlemil, Crespel and Hermann. But the surprise choice was Beecham's own discovery, Bruce Dargavel, who takes the three villanous roles, Coppelius, Dapertutto and Dr Miracle, and his richly resonant bass-baritone is wonderfully caught by the microphone in the celebrated *So Gleam with Desire* and of course in the finale. Franz's sole aria, *Day and Night I am Always Slaving*, included here, was cut from the film when the last Act was in danger of longueurs.

Most productions of Offenbach's finest opera are too long, but this performance is if anything too short. It is not for those expecting French finesse, but with Beecham in charge there is much to be said for British lustiness and the orchestral playing is splendid, especially in the *Barcarolle*. In short this is very enjoyable indeed, for the words are crystal clear, and we hope that Lady Beecham can be persuaded to organize the release of the film as a DVD, using the present remastering of the soundtrack.

Les Fées du Rhin (complete)
*** Accord 472 920-2 (3). Schörg, Gubisch, Beczala, Jenis, Klaveness, Pepper, R. Letton Ch., Montpellier Nat. O, Layer

When, in 1863, Offenbach was commissioned to write an opera by the director of the Hofoper in Vienna (Offenbach's operettas were hugely popular in Vienna at that time) he leapt at the chance, always wishing to write something more serious than operettas. The result was *Les Fées du Rhin*, or *Die Rheinnixen*, of which this CD set (sung in German) is its first recording. Into this work Offenbach poured everything that embodied German romanticism: from ruined castles by midnight, to soldiers, village maidens, the Rhine, of course (with its water-sprites, pixies and elves) – and even psychic shock is included! Add to this elements of grand opera, French and Italian opera, and just about everything else you can think of, and the result is a Weber-cum-Offenbach mélange. If the story is a typical example of operatic hokum, one forgives its excesses for the sake of the music, which contains some excellent Offenbach tunes; and if the spirit of operetta is never too far away, there is more dramatic writing than you might expect from this source – some of the arias and duets are really quite impressive; with plenty of splendid ensembles and vibrant choruses (as well as a delightful ballet and *grande valse*) there is plenty of spectacle too. The cast in this live (2002) recording is generally very good. The heroine, Armgard, sung by Regina Schörg, copes well with the coloratura passages: her aria in Act I, *There, where the ancient oaks and dark pine trees grow*, is a good example of Offenbach creating a gently eerie effect with wordless coloratura passages appearing throughout the song. It is curiously memorable; later, when she is forced to sing for the soldiers, she delivers some even more impressive coloratura, before dropping down dead – or at least appearing to do so. The hero, Franz, a light tenor sung by Piotr Beczala, has an attractive voice, coping reasonably well in the high passages and singing with sensitivity when called for; he is well contrasted with the baritone of Dalibor Jenis, his rival, in splendid full-blooded voice. Armgard's mother, Hedwig, sung by Nora Gubisch, is a fine mezzo, and the rest of the cast is good. That the whole thing works is a tribute to Friedemann Layer, who draws an excellent response from his orchestra. The sound is very acceptable too, with very little noise from the audience; and full texts and translations are provided.

La Fille du tambour major (complete)

(B) **(*) Accord/Universal (ADD) 461 673-2 (2). Harbell, Arnaud, Musy, Pondeau, Mallabrera, Light, Ch. & O, Blareau

La Fille du tambour major was one of Offenbach's best later works, closer to the spirit of a light *opéra-comique* than some of his more savage *opéras-bouffes* (the spirit of Donizetti's *La fille du Régiment* is also echoed here). It fizzes with good tunes and wit, and so does this 1962 performance. As one might expect, it is full of 'military' numbers, with plentiful use of snare drum and the like; the finales build up to a frenzy of excitement, with Acts II and III ending with the exhilarating opening tune of the *Overture*. (On the opening night, the audience rose to its feet when, in the finale, the exciting brassy *Chant du départ* – a patriotic song indelibly linked with Napoleonic victories – was thundered out on the stage, causing the audience to go wild with excitement: a brilliant *coup de théâtre* of which Offenbach was master.) Character numbers abound, such as a 'Donkey' song in which the owner sings of the virtues of the animal that pulls her cart: he had a good heart ('there are few men on earth that can say as much'), and an undefiled heart ('there are few women who can boast that'), all supported by 'Hee-haws' from the chorus; there is a splendid waltz, well up to Offenbach's best standard, and a dashing *Tarantella* which opens Act III; there is even a 'migraine' song! The drawback for non-French speakers is that there are no texts and translations, not even a synopsis, and there is quite a bit of spoken dialogue (performed with exceptional liveliness). The soloists are excellent, full of character, with Richard Blareau keeping the fun going all the way through. The sound, considering its provenance, is excellent: bright and vivid, only lacking the depth of a modern recording. A must for Offenbachians.

La Grande Duchesse de Gérolstein (complete)

(B) ** Accord/Universal (ADD) 465 871-2 (2). LaFaye, Raynaud, Aubert, Bedex, Asse, Terrasson, Ch. & O, Hartemann

Along with *Orphée aux enfers* and *La Vie parisienne*, *La Grande Duchesse de Gérolstein* represents the best of Offenbach's exhilarating satires, this time its target being the military. It is crammed full of his best tunes, sparkling ensembles and arias, with rousing choruses and with the score laced with piquant wit and sparkle; it is in many ways the most consistently enjoyable of all his *opéras-bouffes*. This performance dates from 1966 and has the obvious advantage of an all-French, idiomatic cast. The recording is a good one, though it does not quite possess the fizz of *La Fille du tambour major* on the same label. The rather dry, unflattering

sound does not help matters, although everything is reasonably vivid, especially the (lively) spoken dialogue, which sounds dubbed on afterwards. One drawback for non-French speakers is that there are no texts and translations, not even a synopsis, and there's quite a bit of spoken dialogue: one really does need to know what is going on to appreciate fully this marvellous piece of froth. The version ideally to wait for, not currently available, is Sony's glittering version with the delicious Régine Crespin in the title-role, conducted by Plasson. Until that arrives, this makes a serviceable stop-gap.

Orphée aux enfers (Orpheus in the Underworld; 1874 version)

*** EMI (ADD) 7 49647-2 (2). Sénéchal, Mesplé, Rhodes, Burles, Berbié, Petits Chanteurs à la Croix Potencée, Toulouse Capitole O, Plasson

Plasson recorded his fizzing performance – the first complete set in French for 30 years – using the far fuller four-act text of 1874 instead of the two-act version of 1858, so adding such delectable rarities as the sparkling *Rondo* of Mercury and the Policemen's chorus. Mady Mesplé as usual has her shrill moments, but the rest of the cast is excellent, and Plasson's pacing of the score is exemplary. The recording is brightly atmospheric and the leavening of music with spoken dialogue just enough. The newer recording by Minkowski of the alternative version is a disappointment (in spite of an impressive cast), over-driven and without the effervescence of the Plasson set.

Orphée aux enfers (complete; 1858 version)

(*) Arthaus **DVD 100 402. Badea, Vidal, Duesing, Macias, Jung, Quaille, Callatat, Théâtre de la Monnaie Ch. & O, Davin (Producer: Herbert Wernicke)

**(*) EMI 5 56725-2 (2). Dessay, Beuron, Naouri, Fouchécourt, Lyon Nat. Op. O, Grenoble CO, Minkowski

Although the Arthaus DVD performance, recorded in the Brussels Théâtre de la Monnaie in 1997, has been updated to the twentieth century, the setting of Mount Olympus in the famous *fin de siècle* café La Mort Subite, with the gods wearing evening dress, ensures that there is less of a visual jolt of the kind which often affects modern productions of Offenbach. There are a few curiosities here which may irritate the DVD collector, notably the use of a honky-tonk piano in the finale of the Act I *Can-can*. However, the ensuing journey down to Hell, conveyed spectacularly by a steam train plummeting through the surface of Heaven into the Underworld, with great whooshes of steam, is considerable compensation.

The cast is a good one: Alexandru Badea is a younger, more ardent Orpheus than might be expected, but his well-focused tenor and convincing acting is certainly engaging, whilst his coquettish wife, Eurydice, is well characterized by Elizabeth Vidal, though her voice is less well caught by the microphones and is a little harsh at times. Both Dale Duesing and Reinaldo Macias in the roguish roles of Jupiter and Pluto sing with plenty of character. André Jung's drunken John Styx is amusing to watch – though it would be less of a pleasure just to hear – and most of the incidental parts are well done. The conducting is efficient rather than inspired: Plasson's new EMI recording shows how much heady effervescence there is in Offenbach's music. However, there is plenty to enjoy here and a good deal more so than in many recent productions of this work.

The Minkowski version of Offenbach's first great success is based on the original 1858 version, with additions from the expanded 1874 score (used in Plasson's recording), including much of the delightful ballet music. Both the 'earthly' leads are superb: Natalie Dessay's secure, clear coloratura is well employed as the nagging wife, Eurydice, and one genuinely feels sorry for her hapless husband, Orphée, amiably characterized by Yann Beuron. Jean Paul Fouchécourt as Pluto oozes deceptive charm in his pastoral aria, though his true devilish character is revealed in some grotesque falsetto at the end, and Cupid's kissing song is charmingly sung by Patricia Petibon. From the opening bars, Minkowski's approach is apparent in the sparkling, crystal-clear textures, and he propels the opera along at a tremendous pace and with a bouncing rhythmic bite, matched by the exceptionally lively cast. The recording is superbly vivid and clear and adds to the immediacy of the drama.

La Périchole (complete)

(M) ******* Erato (ADD) 2292 45686-2 (2). Crespin, Vanzo, Bastin, Lombard, Friedmann, Trigeau, Rhine Op. Ch., Strasbourg PO, Lombard

**(*) EMI 7 47362-8 (2). Berganza, Carreras, Bacquier, Sénéchal, Trempont, Delange, Toulouse Capitole Ch. & O, Plasson

Though both Régine Crespin in the title-role and Alain Vanzo as her partner, Piquillo, were past their peak at that time, their vocal control is a model in this music, with character strongly portrayed but without any hint of vulgar underlining. Crespin is fresh and Vanzo produces heady tone in his varied arias, some of them brilliant. Jules Bastin is characterful too in the subsidiary role of Don Andres, Viceroy of Peru. Lombard secures excellent precision of ensemble from his Strasbourg forces, only occasionally pressing too hard. The recorded sound is vivid and immediate. A set of highlights is available at budget price (Apex 2564 61500-2).

Though the sound in Toulouse is over-reverberant, the CD remastering has sharpened the impact, and diction is surprisingly clear against the full orchestral sound. The incidental roles are superbly taken, but it is odd that Spaniards were chosen for the two principal roles. José Carreras uses his lovely tenor line to fine effect but is often unidiomatic, while Teresa Berganza – who should have made the central character into a vibrant figure, as Régine Crespin used to – is surprisingly heavy and unsparkling. The CD disc-break is well placed between the Acts, but cueing might have been more generous.

Robinson Crusoe (sung in English)

*** Opera Rara ORC 7 (3). Brecknock, Kenny, Kennedy, Hartle, Hill Smith, Oliver, Browne, Geoffrey Mitchell Ch., RPO, Francis

More ambitious than Offenbach's operettas, *Robinson Crusoe* offers a sequence of fresh and tuneful numbers with many striking ensembles. The plot is derived less from Daniel Defoe than from the British pantomime tradition. Characterization is strong and amusing, with a secondary couple shadowing Crusoe and his beloved Edwige. The casting is also from strength, with John Brecknock and Yvonne Kenny outstanding as Crusoe and Edwige, while Man Friday, as in the original Paris production, is sung by a mezzo, Sandra Browne. On the three discs are 3 hours of music, covering numbers which the composer cut even from the original production. The witty English translation, very freely adapted from the French text, with some changes of plot, is by Don White, and words are admirably clear.

La Vie parisienne (complete)

*** EMI (ADD) 7 47154-8 (2). Crespin, Mesplé, Masson, Sénéchal, Trempont, Benoit, Chateau, Lublin, Toulouse Capitole Ch. & O, Plasson

Hardly less effervescent than the parallel version of *Orpheus in the Underworld*, also conducted by Michel Plasson for EMI, *La Vie parisienne* is a scintillating example of Offenbach's work, an inconsequential farce around the heady days of the International Exhibition in Paris. Though the EMI recording is not quite as consistent as the one of *Orphée aux enfers*, the performance and presentation sparkle every bit as brilliantly, with the spoken dialogue for once a special attraction. Régine Crespin, in a smaller role, is most commanding and, though the cast lacks the excellent Vanzo and Massard, the style is captivatingly authentic. The CD transfer is vivid, without loss of ambient atmosphere.

Arias, Duets and Ensembles from: *Barbe-Bleu; La Belle Hélène; Les Contes d'Hoffmann; Fantasio; La Fille du Tambour-Major; La Grande-duchesse de Gerolstein; Lischen et Fritzchen; Madame l'Archiduc; La Périchole; La Vie parisienne. Ouverture à Grande Orchestre: Le Carneval des Revues*

*** DG 471 501-2. von Otter, Les Musiciens du Louvre et Ch., Minkowski

This sumptuously presented disc may be entitled 'Von Otter sings Offenbach', but it is far more than that, when it contains a wide range of duets and ensembles, too, with the Overture, a surreal, heavy-handed Wagner parody, the 'Symphony of the Future' (*Le Carneval des Revues*), as a supplement to von Otter's solo items. There are some of the usual favourites, like the *Barcarolle* from *Hoffmann* and the tipsy song from *La Périchole*, strongly characterized by von Otter, if not very funnily, but the most valuable items are the rarities, which consistently expand one's appreciation of the composer. Fluent and brilliant throughout, with splendid support from her colleagues, both vocal and instrumental, the result is playful and sparkling rather than comic. Highly enjoyable.

'The World of Offenbach': Overtures: (i–ii) *La Belle Hélène;* (iii–iv) *La Fille du tambour-major;* (i–ii) *Orpheus in the Underworld;* (iii–iv) *Le Papillon: Pas de deux* (excerpt); *Valse des rayons. Les Contes d'Hoffmann:* (v; i; iv) *Ballad of Kleinzach; O Dieu! De quelle ivresse* (vi; i; iv) *Doll song* (vi–vii; i; iv) *Barcarolle* (2 versions). *La Grande Duchesse de Gérolstein:* (viii–x) *Portez armes ... J'aime les militaires. La Périchole:* (viii; i; x) *O mon cher amant (Air de lettre); Ah! quel dîner.* (vi; i; iv) *Robinson Crusoé: Conduisez-moi vers celui que j'adore (Waltz Song).* (xi; iv) *Valse tyrolienne*

🔊 ✪ (M) ******* Decca ADD/DDD 452 942-2. (i) SRO; (ii) Ansermet; (iii) LSO; (iv) Bonynge; (v) Domingo; (vi) Sutherland; (vii) Tourangeau; (viii) Crespin; (ix) V. Volksopernorchester; (x) Lombard; (xi) Jo, ECO

This 'lucky-bag' of Offenbachian goodies which Decca have expanded for CD from the original LP selection is bursting with lollipops to make a marvellously entertaining 74 minutes. The programme now opens and closes with the *Barcarolle*. Ansermet and Bonynge offer much character in the overtures; even if the former takes the famous can-can which closes the *Orpheus* overture more slowly than usual, he invests it with much rhythmic vigour. Bonynge has another scintillating can-can to offer in *La Fille du tambour-major*, which opens with an arresting side-drum, and he now also includes two items from Offenbach's only ballet, *Le Papillon.*

The various excerpts from Bonynge's complete *Contes d'Hoffmann* are matched by Régine Crespin's delightful contribution as *La Périchole*, and Sutherland returns to sing the *Waltz Song* from *Robinson Crusoé*. The other additional item is Sumi Jo's sparkling *Valse tyrolienne*. With splendidly vivid recording this is an unmissable sampler, to match and even surpass '*The World of Borodin*'.

ONSLOW, Georges (1784–1853)

Symphonies 1 in A, Op. 41; 3 in F min.

(N) *** CPO 999 747-2. NDR Radiophilharmonie, Goritzki

This CD follows CPO's successful recording of the *Second* and *Fourth Symphonies*. The *First Symphony* (1831) is not lacking in good ideas, with the allegro dramatically compelling, and the opening of the slow movement is slightly reminiscent of the slow movement of Beethoven's *Seventh*. The *Third Symphony* is even more striking: after the slow introduction, there are some particularly fetching ideas in the jaunty first movement. The *Allegro impetuoso* Scherzo maintains the impetus with its rhythmic bounce and after the expressive slow movement, the vigorous finale – almost a tarantella – makes a lively conclusion. The recordings and performances are excellent.

Symphonies 2 in D min., Op. 42; 4 in G, Op. 71

*** CPO 999 738-2. Hannover R. PO, Goritzki

Georges Onslow wrote four symphonies between 1831 and 1846, though the two recorded here had limited success at the time. It is hard not to respond to the *Second Symphony*, which launches into its opening Allegro with tremendous gusto and one is swept away by the momentum. The second movement has a graceful charm, the Minuetto is energetic, more of a Beethovian Scherzo, whilst the finale is an enjoyably lively Presto.

The *Fourth Symphony* has a rather dramatic Largo introduction before being propelled into another vital Allegro which has both wit and energy. A vigorous Scherzo follows, with plenty of dash (even a hint of Berlioz is felt here), whilst the slow movement has a more dramatic minor-keyed central section flanked by cantabile writing. The finale, subtitled 'Souvenir de Rhim' brings trills and scurrying, chromatic glissandi alternating between the strings and woodwind. Whilst these are hardly profound works, they are thoroughly entertaining, and well worth investigating by anyone interested in rare symphonies. The recordings and performances are excellent, and the sleeve notes are copious and fascinating.

Grand Septet, Op. 79 (for flute, oboe, clarinet, horn, bassoon, double-bass & piano); Grand Sextet, Op. 77b (for flute, clarinet, bassoon, horn, double-bass & piano)

(BB) **(*) Warner Apex 0927 49536-2. Nielson Quintet, with Marder, Hubeau

These two works were written during Onslow's last creative period, both dating from 1849, though the *Sextet* was a transcription of the *Nonet*, Op. 77, for strings, published the previous year. Both are quite substantial works, lasting over half an hour, and are eminently entertaining in their bright and breezy way. The 1992 performance is good one, though occasionally it is possible to imagine more polished accounts. The recording is vivid, if a little unyielding – it's a tad dry and also quite closely miked, thus limiting the full dynamic range of the performance. However, these are comparatively minor points overall, and this disc, at its low price, is worth considering.

String Quintets in B flat, Op. 33; in E min., Op. 74

**(*) MDG 603 1233-2. Ens. Concertant Frankfurt

String Quintets in A min., Op. 34; G, Op. 35

*** MDG 603 1253-2. Quintett Momento Musicale

Georges Onslow was one of the few French composers of his generation who wrote a substantial amount of chamber music, which represents his largest body of work. His quartets and quintets were published in his lifetime and reached a wide audience in their day, although they were sometimes criticized for a certain emotional coolness, even blandness. The Ensemble Concertant are not quite as sweet-sounding as the Quintett Momento Musicale and don't seem to have the music quite under their belts as do their rivals. They still make a good case for the Op. 33 (1827–8) and Op. 74 (1847) *Quintets*, the latter being the more seductive. However, all these works, and especially those in the hands of the Quintett Momento Musicale, emerge as fresh, well-constructed pieces, generally in classical tradition, not always strikingly individual but unfailingly enjoyable. The *Adagio* movements are beautifully poised, while the lively outer movements have plenty of life – the *Presto* of the Op. 35 is especially enjoyable and inventive. Both CDs are beautifully recorded by MDG.

ORFF, Carl (1895–1982)

Carmina Burana

*** RCA DVD 74321 852859. Popp, Van Kesteren, Prey, Bavarian R. Ch., Munich R. O, Eichhorn (Video Producer: Jean-Pierre Ponnelle)

☛ *** EMI 5 57197-2. Dessay, Hampson, Lesne, Chœur d'enfants de Midi-Pyrénées, Orféon Donostiarra, Toulouse Capitole O, Plasson

*** Decca 430 509-2. Dawson, Daniecki, McMillan, San Francisco Boys' & Girls' Choruses, San Francisco Symphony Ch. & SO, Blomstedt

(M) *** Ph. 464 725-2. Gruberová, Aler, Hampson, Shinyukai Ch., Knaben des Staats & Berlin Cathedral Ch., BPO, Ozawa

*** EMI (ADD) 5 66899-2 [566951]. Armstrong, English, Allen, St Clement Danes Grammar School Boys' Ch., L. Symphony Ch., LSO, Previn

☛ ✿ *** Sony SACD SS 6163; (B) CD (ADD) SBK 47668. Harsanyi, Petrak, Presnell, Rutgers University Ch., Phd. O, Ormandy

(BB) *** Regis RRC 1136. Walmsley-Clark, Graham-Hall, Maxwell, Southend Boys' Ch., LSO Ch., LSO, Hickox

*** Guild GMCD 7227. Herrera, Holt, Kelly, Guadalope Basilica Boys' Ch., Mineria Academy of Music Ch. & O, De La Fuente

(M) *** DG 447 437. Janowitz, Stolze, Fischer-Dieskau, Schöneberger Boys' Ch., Berlin German Op. Ch. & O, Jochum

(M) *** RCA 09026 63981-2. Hendricks, Aler, Hagegård, St Paul's Cathedral Boys' Ch., L. Symphony Ch., LSO, Mata

(M) *** RCA (ADD) 82876 59417-2. Mandac, Kolk, Milnes, New England Conservatory Ch. & Children's Ch., Boston SO, Ozawa

(BB) **(*) Virgin 2x1 5 61510-2 (2). Watson, Bowman, Maxwell, Highcliffe Junior Ch., Waynflete Singers, Bournemouth Symphony Ch. & SO, Hill – HOLST: *The Planets; Perfect Fool* (suite) **(*)

(BB) **(*) Warner Apex 0927 41377-2. Jo, Kowalski, Skovhus, L. Philh. Ch. & O, Southend Boys' Ch., Mehta

(BB) **(*) EMI Encore (ADD) 5 74747-2 [574747]. Popp, Unger, Wolansky, New Philh. Ch. & O, Frühbeck de Burgos – STRAVINSKY: *Circus Polka; Fireworks* **(*)

(BB) **(*) Arte Nova 74321 34048-2. Liebeck, Hill, Barrell, New L. Children's Ch., Tallis Chamber Ch., L. Festival O, Pople

(BB) **(*) EMI Encore 5 86428. Augér, Van Kesteren, Summers, Southend Boys' Ch., Philh. Ch. & O, Muti

This fine RCA recording of *Carmina Burana*, conducted by Kurt Eichhorn with outstanding soloists in 1975, has been issued previously on CD, and here is treated to an imaginative staging for DVD by Jean-Pierre Ponnelle. The main background set is a ruined church against which the singers are seen in medieval costume, with action, sometimes surreal, invented to illustrate each section of the work, a technique which seems to anticipate the virtual reality of our digital age. So the roasted swan episode is introduced by a drunken monk, with a large swan in the background actually being roasted on a spit, and Lucia Popp in a medieval wimple looking and sounding enchanting. Hermann Prey is a superb baritone soloist, taking the main burden, and the choir is bright and lively. Not a first choice sonically, although the recording is very impressive, but there is an added dimension here. As a supplementary item comes a long interview with Orff himself – in German with English subtitles – in which he talks animatedly about key childhood experiences and how he came to write *Carmina Burana*, with many dozens of illuminating photographs and illustrations.

Michel Plasson's EMI performance, recorded in Toulouse, is rather special. Not only is the choral singing extraordinarily vivid, it is as seductively warm in *pianissimos* as it is incisively vibrant in *fortissimos*. The three soloists are the finest on record. Thomas Hampson's tender first entry, *Omnia sol temperat* ('*The Sun Rules Over All*'), is matched by his great vigour in the *Tavern Scene*, and Gérard Lesne's alto timbre is uniquely suited to the *Song of the Roast Swan*. The trebles open *Amor volat undique* with knowing Gallic delicacy, and Lesne and Hampson combine to make the sequence *Si puer cum puella* ('*If a Boy with a Girl*') quite delectable, topped by Natalie Dessay's tenderly ravishing *Stetit puella*. The choral *Tempus est iocundum* brings the fullest expression of sexual rapture, into which the trebles from the Midi-Pyrénées enter with enthusiasm, if without quite the knowing exuberance which English boy-trebles bring to it. But Plasson's closing *Ave formosissima – O Fortuna* has splendid grandeur, and this outstanding version must go straight to the top of the list.

Blomstedt's is also among the finest modern versions of Orff's exhilaratingly hedonistic cantata. Throughout the choral singing, men, boys and girls all enjoy themselves hugely – as they should, with such stimulating words to sing. They generate great passion and energy and all three soloists are equally outstanding. John Daniecki's use of vocal colouring is entertainingly diverse, while Kevin McMillan is a splendidly unctuous Abbot, and Lynne Dawson portrays the girl in the red tunic with sensuous innocence. Blomstedt's reading is full of imaginative touches of light and shade, yet the flow of passionate energy is paramount. He is helped by the remarkable range and sonority of the Decca recording, very much in the demonstration bracket.

Ozawa's digital recording of Orff's justly popular cantata carries all the freshness and spontaneity of his earlier successful Boston version. The *Cours d'amours* sequence is the highlight of his reading, with the soprano, Edita Gruberová, highly seductive; Thomas Hampson's contribution is also impressive. Ozawa's infectious rubato in *Oh, oh, oh, I am Bursting Out all Over*, interchanged between male and treble chorus towards the end of the work, is wonderfully bright and zestful, with the contrast of the big *Ave formosissima* climax which follows made to sound spaciously grand. Taken overall, this Philips version holds its position near the top of the list alongside Ormandy, and it has the additional advantage of spectacular, demonstration-worthy, digital recording.

Previn's 1975 analogue version, vividly recorded, is even more sharply detailed than Ozawa's. It is strong on humour and rhythmic point. The chorus sings vigorously, the men often using an aptly rough tone; and the resilience of Previn's rhythms, finely sprung, brings out a strain not just of geniality but of real wit. This is a performance which swaggers along and makes you smile. Among the soloists, Thomas Allen's contribution is one of the glories of the music-making, and in their lesser roles the soprano and tenor are equally stylish. The digital remastering is wholly successful: the choral bite is enhanced, yet the recording retains its full amplitude. This is now included among EMI's 'Great Recordings of the Century'.

Ormandy and his Philadelphians have just the right panache to bring off this wildly exuberant picture of the Middle Ages by the anonymous poets of former days, and there is no more enjoyable analogue version. It has tremendous vigour, warmth and colour and a genial, spontaneous enthusiasm from the Rutgers University choristers, men and boys alike, that is irresistible. The soloists are excellent, but it is the chorus and orchestra who steal the show; the richness and eloquence of the choral tone is a joy in itself. This is quite splendid, one of Ormandy's most inspired recordings and, even if you already have the work in your collection, this exhilarating version will bring additional delights. The sound on the non-compatible SACD is remarkably expanded, but this costs a great deal more than the CD.

Richard Hickox, on his brilliantly recorded Regis CD, uses the London Symphony Chorus but adds the Southend Boys' Choir, which makes sure we know all about sexual abandon – their *Oh, oh, oh, I am Bursting Out all Over* is a joy. Penelope Walmsley-Clark, too, makes a rapturous contribution: her account of the girl in the red dress is equally delectable. The other soloists are good if less individual, but the chorus rises marvellously to climaxes, and the sharp articulation when the singers hiss out the words of *O Fortuna* in the closing section is a highlight. The documentation provides a vernacular narrative for each band, which works well enough when there is no translation. A most successful disc in every way.

It is surprising that Orff's *Carmina Burana* has not been recorded live more often, for the presence of an audience can stimulate an extra tautness, immediately apparent on the Guild version in the genial vigour with which the chorus welcomes spring (*Ecce gratum*). The warm ambience of the Sala Mezahualcoyotl in Mexico City has already enveloped the listener, providing a sense of space and perspective. Even if the quieter choral enunciation is less sharp than it would be in the studio, the rich orchestral tapestry, capped with percussion, makes a splendid backcloth, while Herrera de la

Fuente's zestful pacing ensures a vigorously spontaneous forward flow. The singing of the Mineria Chorus is first class, with the boys' voices especially fresh and full of bounce in *Veni, veni, venias*. The Mineria Academy Orchestra, too, add characterful wind and brass colours: their comments lacing the tenor's *Tale of the Roasted Swan* are engagingly grotesque. Ben Holt gives a spirited personification of the Abbot, and the male tavern chorus follows on with gleeful, uninhibited impetus. However, it is the soprano, Gabriella Herrera, who stands out, nostalgically chaste in *Siqua sine socio*, radiantly feminine in *Stetit puella* and soaring celestially in *Dulcissime*, her rapturous moment of submission. The closing choral *Ave formosissima* has exultant grandeur, and the tension builds to a remarkable final climax (helped by a splendid bass drum). No wonder the audience bursts into applause even before the final words have died away.

Jochum's 1968 recording of *Carmina Burana* has never sounded better than it does in this reissue. The choral *pianissimos* lack the very last degree of immediacy, but the underlying tension of the quiet singing is very apparent. Fischer-Dieskau's singing is refined but not too much so, with the kind of tonal shading that a great Lieder singer can bring; he is suitably gruff in the Abbot's song – so much so that for the moment the voice is unrecognizable. Gerhard Stolze too is very stylish in his falsetto *Tale of the Roasted Swan*. The soprano, Gundula Janowitz, finds a quiet dignity, rather than an overt sensuality for her contribution and this is finely done. The closing scene is moulded by Jochum with wonderful control, most compelling in its restrained power.

Mata's splendid 1980 digital recording now comes at super-bargain price and is highly recommendable on all counts. It is a joyously alive and volatile reading, not as metrical in its rhythms as most; this means that at times the London Symphony Chorus is not as clean in ensemble as it is for Previn. The choristers of St Paul's Cathedral sing with purity and enthusiasm but are perhaps not boyish enough, though the soloists are first rate (with John Aler coping splendidly, in high, refined tones, with the Roast Swan episode). There is fine warmth of atmosphere and no lack in the lower range; indeed in almost every respect the sound is superb. This is unbeatable value for those wanting a bargain-priced version.

Ozawa's earlier version of *Carmina Burana* is strong and incisive, bringing out the bold simplicity of the score with tingling immediacy, rather than dwelling on its subtlety of colour. The soloists, too, are all characterful, especially Sherrill Milnes. The tenor Stanley Kolk sounds a little constrained with his *Roast Swan*, but otherwise the solo singing is always responsive. Overall, this is a highly effective account, if not a first choice. Full texts and translations have now been included in this mid-price release (unlike previous incarnations), making it now fully recommendable in RCA's mid-priced 'Classic Library' series.

David Hill's Bournemouth recording has a choral bite and an exhilarating rhythmic zest that carries the music thrustfully forward. Among the soloists Donald Maxwell makes a strenuously boisterous Abbot, his solo punctuated with spectacular percussion; but one wonders whether a countertenor was a good choice for the song about the roasting swan. Here a falsetto can have a more piquant edge. Janice Watson sings with enticing femininity: her red shift is obviously just a temporary covering. The boys' chorus are as pubescently eager as you could wish. This is excitingly vivid, and it is a pity that this reissue is so poorly documented. There are no texts or translations included, indeed virtually no information whatsoever to inform the listener of the meaning of the Latin titles of the work's 25 cued sections.

Mehta's 1992 Apex recording is often enjoyably vigorous, it has good soloists and an excellent choral response, with the Southend boys thrusting throatily, enjoying their pubescent spree. Sumi Jo is a seductive if rather knowing Girl in the Red Shift who submits willingly, rising nimbly up her ascending scale to a spectacularly floated *pianissimo*. But Boje Skovhus makes a strongly vibrant rather than subtle contribution. The recording, made at The Maltings, Snape, is resonantly spectacular, but the quieter choral passages are a little recessive. Mehta's direction is not as imaginative or as spontaneously exuberant as that of his finest competitors, but this is excellent value at budget price.

While the New Philharmonica performance under Burgos has no lack of vitality, it is in the more lyrical pages that Burgos scores, with his imaginative care for detail and obvious affection. The sheer gusto of the singing is the more remarkable when one considers the precision from both singers and orchestra alike. The brass, too, brings out the rhythmic pungency which is such a dominating feature of the work, helped by a very bright CD transfer. Lucia Popp's soprano solo, *Amor volat*, is really ravishing and Gerhard Unger, the tenor, brings a Lieder-like sensitivity to his lovely singing of the very florid solo in the tavern scene. The new coupling of early works by Stravinsky is hardly apt, but they are well played and this Encore disc is certainly worth its very modest cost.

With brilliant and atmospheric modern digital recording, Ross Pople's super-bargain version has a lot going for it, including vibrant singing and clear enunciation from the modest-sized but excellent Tallis Chamber group and the highly animated New London Children's Choir. Much of it is very enjoyable, but in *Tempus es iocundum* Pople's constant fluctuations of tempi detract from the feeling of unbuttoned sexual abandon. Among the solo contributions, Martin Hill's *Tale of the Roasted Swan* is suitably bizarre, and David Barrell makes an unctuous Abbot. The soprano, Anne Liebeck, sings sweetly and with virginal freshness, though her *Dulcissima* leap is dramatic rather than rapturous, and when the chorus follows, their *Ave formosissima* is very broad indeed. It is certainly jubilant, but Pople almost loses the forward impetus, fortunately regaining it in the closing *O Fortuna*. However, this account does not have the overwhelming impact of the new Mexican version. And it was a pity that Arte Nova have supplied the Latin texts only – without translation.

Muti's is a reading which underlines the dramatic contrasts, both of dynamic and of tempo, so the nagging ostinatos as a rule are pressed on at breakneck speed; the result, if at times a little breathless, is always exhilarating. The soloists are first rate; the Philharmonia Chorus is not quite at its most polished, but the Southend Boys are outstandingly fine. However, the digital remastering of the 1980 analogue recording is disappointing. The chorus and soloists seem to have lost a degree of immediacy.

The Telarc version is recorded in exceptionally full and brilliant digital sound for its time (1980). Robert Shaw prefers speeds on the fast side, though his manner is comparatively metrical. In the *Court of Love* one wants more persuasive treatment, though the choral singing – recorded rather close in analytical sound – is superb. The soloists are good, but the Atlanta boys cannot quite match their rivals on most European versions. The recording has eight dividing bands but is minutely indexed.

Carmina Burana; Catulli Carmina

(N) (B) *** Sony (ADD) 516026-2 (2). Soloists, Ch., Phd. O, Ormandy

If you want both the fine Ormandy performances, they are available together on this two-CD set, costing slightly less than the individual discs.

Catulli Carmina

(M) *** DG (IMS) (ADD) 449 097-2. Augér, Ochman, Berlin Op. Ch., 4 pianos & percussion, Jochum – EGK: *The Temptation of St Anthony* ***

(B) **(*) Sony (ADD) SBK 61703. Blegen, Kness, Temple University Ch., Phd. O, Ormandy – STRAVINSKY: *Symphony of Psalms* ***

Catulli Carmina; Trionfo di Afrodite

☛– ☼ *** EMI 5 55517-2. Schellenberger, Odinius, Linz Mozart Ch., Munich R. O, Welser-Möst

Orff's sequel to *Carmina Burana* (using much the same formula, but with the accompaniment scored for four pianos and percussion) cannot match its predecessor in memorability, but for anyone hypnotized by the composer's vital rhythmic ostinatos this is the work to recommend next, and certainly so in Franz Welser-Möst's vibrant performance, complete with enthusiastic crowd noises and superlative choral singing that in its sharpness and precision lifts the music clear of banality. The soloists, too, are excellent, the soprano, Dagmar Schellenberger, revelling in the sensuous upper tessitura which is so like the music for the Girl in the Red Tunic in *Carmina Burana*.

Trionfo di Afrodite is scored for large orchestra, including three pianos and plentiful percussion; with more nagging rhythmic repetitions it pays its hedonistic tribute to the pleasures of love in a similarly exhilarating manner. The vibrant *Invocation to Hymenaeus* brings a curious reminder of *Petrushka* but stirringly returns us to Orff's world of ostinatos until the arrival of the bride at the wedding chamber brings a series of spoken exhortations by the leader of the guests with vehement choral interruptions. The work ends dramatically with a vision of Aphrodite, which brings an immensely bold closing chorus and a final explosion of enthusiasm from the assembled guests. It is an extraordinary dramatization, and it is brought thrillingly to life by Welser-Möst and his combined soloists, singers and orchestra, working splendidly as a team and superbly recorded.

Until the arrival of the Welser-Möst version, Jochum's performance of *Catulli Carmina* was never surpassed. His chorus sings with sharp, rhythmic point and, if imagination is called for in such music, Jochum matches flexibility with a spark of humour in his control of mechanistic rhythms. His soloists are individual and sweet-toned. The recording is very fine, although even on CD evocative *pianissimos* sound a little recessed.

The exotic colours and rhythmic ostinatos are also well brought out by the Temple University Choir, and Ormandy's vigorous performance produces an altogether rougher experience than Jochum's version, for all the virtuosity of the players and singers. But the bluff humour of the piece comes out boldly. The 1967 recording is generally good, a little thin by modern standards, particularly at the top end, but nothing too serious. An undoubted CD bargain with the excellent Stravinsky coupling.

Trionfi (Trittico Teatrale): Carmina Burana, Catulli Carmina, Trionfi di Afrodite

(M) (***) DG mono 474 131-2 (2). Kupper, Lindermeier, Trotschel, Wiese-Lange, Delorko, Holm, Kuen, Braun (baritone), Boehme Bavarian R. Ch. & SO, Jochum

Eugen Jochum's stereo recording of *Carmina Burana*, made under the supervision of the composer, has long been a classic of the CD catalogue, but here, from the early 1950s, are Jochum's three pioneering recordings of all three of the works linked by their Latin texts. Neither *Catulli Carmina*, with texts drawn from the Roman poet Catullus, nor *Trionfi di Afrodite*, with varied texts not just from Catullus but also from Sappho and Euripides, can match *Carmina Burana* in sharp memorability, but they emerge very freshly in performances as lively as these. They are well played and sung, even if the trio of soloists in *Carmina Burana*, Trotschel, Kuen and Braun, cannot equal the starry team on Jochum's stereo version of 1963. Jochum may be best known for his readings of traditional repertory, but here, as a friend of Orff, he brings out the originality and often the beauty of the writing with winning directness. The mono recordings – respectively from 1952, 1954 and 1955 – are clear and well-balanced in first-rate transfers. The packaging is attractive, but no texts are given in the booklet, only detailed synopses.

OPERA

(i) Die Kluge; (ii) Der Mond

(M) *** EMI (ADD) 7 63712-2 (2). (i) Cordes, Frick, Schwarzkopf, Wieter, Christ, Kusche; (ii) Christ, Schmitt-Walker, Graml, Kuen, Lagger, Hotter; Philh. Ch. & O, Sawallisch

Sawallisch's pioneering Orff recordings of the mid-1950s are vivid and immediate on CD, with such effects as the thunderbolt in *Der Mond* impressive still. Elisabeth Schwarzkopf is characterful and dominant as the clever young woman of the title in *Die Kluge*. It is good too to hear such vintage singers as Gottlob Frick and Hans Hotter in unexpected roles. Musically, these may not be at all searching works, but both short operas provide easy, colourful entertainment, with Sawallisch drawing superb playing from the Philharmonia. No texts are provided, but the discs are very generously banded.

ORR, Robin (born 1909)

Symphony in One Movement

(M) *** EMI (ADD) 5 75789-2. RSNO, Gibson – SIMPSON: *Symphony 1* (***); FRICKER: *Symphony 2* (***)

Now a nonagenarian, Robin Orr studied with Casella and Nadia Boulanger before entering on an academic career at Cambridge. After the war, he was successively professor of music at the universities of Glasgow and Cambridge. His musical language is tonal and easily assimilated, and although the symphony is not of striking individuality, it is very well wrought and moves with a genuine sense of purpose. Alexander Gibson gets good results from the Scottish Orchestra, and the 1965 stereo recording comes up very freshly. It is coupled with pioneering recordings of two other notable British symphonies of the early 1950s.

PACHELBEL, Johann (1653–1706)

Canon and Gigue in D; Partita (Suite) 6 in B flat; Suite in G

(BB) **Warner Apex 0927 49980-2. Paillard CO, Paillard –
  FASCH: *Concerto; Symphonies* **(*)

Pachelbel's famous baroque lollipop is given a warm, nicely
paced performance, which brings out its noble progress
admirably, but the pair of suites (containing the usual introduction – here brief – plus groups of dances) offer writing
that is amiable but no more than that, although two *Sarabandes* are agreeably expressive. Good playing and pleasing
sound, but this is not memorable music like the *Canon*.

Keyboard Suites 25–6; 28–9; 32–3; 33b; 34; 36

(N) *** BIS CD 809. Payne (harpsichord)

The *Suites* were not found among the larger body of Pachelbel's keyboard works but were attributed to him by their
publisher on 'circumstantial evidence'. Never mind. They are
very attractive works and are written in the usual clavecin
French style, always beginning with an *Allemande*, then a
Courante, an agreeably expressive *Sarabande* and, usually, a
lively closing *Gigue*. The invention, especially in the *Sarabandes*, is of high quality, and the *Suites* make entertaining
listening, especially when they are played with such spontaneous feeling as they are by Joseph Payne, and quite ideally
recorded.

*Easter Cantatas: Christ ist erstanden; Christ lag in
Todesbanden; Deus in adjutarium; Halleluja! Lobet den
Herrn; Jauchzet den Herrn; Magnificat in C*

☛ (N) *** CPO 999 916-2. Soloists, La Capella Ducale,
  Musica Fiata, Wilson

On the evidence of the above keyboard suites (if they are
authentic) and these Easter cantatas, there is a great deal
more to Johann Pachelbel than his (justly famous) *Canon*.
Indeed, his confident skill in writing for soloists, chorus and
orchestra is comparable with that of Buxtehude. The opening
Deus in adjutarium is quite short, but it blazes with trumpets
and is splendidly written for the paired soprano soloists.
Moreover, the *Gloria patri* brings a commanding use of the
timpani. *Christ lag in Todesbanden* is essentially a chamber
cantata with fine expressive writing for the four soloists. Five
trumpets come to the fore in the exultant *Halleluja! Lobet den
Herrn*, and again there is glorious duet singing from the two
sopranos here, Monika Mauch and Constanze Backes, while
the confident alto solo is given a trombone obbligato. *Christ
ist erstanden* is a solo cantata, with the silvery-voiced Monika
Mauch in her element in the florid writing, while the violin
soloist in the continuo provides a bravura obbligato. *Jauchzet
den Herrn* uses all the soloists as a group, and the accompaniment is enriched with oboes, while the splendid closing
Magnificat is celebrated by the full ensemble, with brass and
timpani at their most spectacular. The performances are first
class, and the recording, made in the Klosterkirche Ensdorf,
Oberpfalz, is very well managed. A disc not to be missed.

PACINI, Giovanni (1796–1867)

Maria, Regina d'Inghilterra (complete)

*** Opera Rara ORC 15. Miricioiu, Ford, Fardilha, Plazas,
  Miles, Bickley, Geoffrey Mitchell Ch., Philh. O, Parry

With an outstanding cast, full, well-balanced recording and
powerful, well-paced conducting, this long-neglected opera

about Mary Tudor emerges as a surprisingly strong and
enjoyable piece, far finer than most conventional Ottocento
operas from the contemporaries of Donizetti and Bellini. The
admittedly improbable story is loosely based on a Victor
Hugo play, centring on the love of Mary for Fenimoore (high
tenor), her scheming favourite, also loved by Clotilde, who in
turn is loved and protected by Ernesto (baritone). Add to that
the Chancellor (bass), who is determined to unmask Fenimoore's evil-doing, and you have an operatic plot that gives
ample scope for confrontation in duets and ensembles, skilfully and imaginatively exploited by Pacini.

Nelly Miricioiu sings with warmth and character as the
suffering Queen, not least in her final agonized aria on
Fenimoore's execution. She is well contrasted with the lighter
Mary Plazas as Clotilde, with José Fardilha as Ernesto, distinctive with his flickering vibrato. Alastair Miles sings powerfully as the Chancellor, but it is the prowess of Bruce Ford
in the demanding role of Fenimoore that more than anything
holds the piece together, from his first evocative off-stage
entry in Act I. David Parry draws strong, idiomatic playing
from the Philharmonia, with the Geoffrey Mitchell Choir
intensifying the big ensembles.

PACIUS, Fredrik (1809–91)

The Princess of Cyprus

(N) *** BIS CD-1340. Wentzel, Åman, Eichenholz, Rantanen,
  Storgård, Jubilate Ch., Tapiola Sinf., Söderblom

Pacius is 'the father of Finnish music'. Even Sibelius paid
tribute: 'Everything we musicians do here now is based on the
life's work of Fredrik Pacius.' Pacius was a pupil of Spohr in
Kassel before going to Stockholm as leader of the Royal
Orchestra (1828–34); he was then lecturer at Helsinki University and director of its music. He transformed the city's
musical life and introduced such repertoire as Spohr's *The
Last Judgement*, Handel's *Messiah* and other choral works,
and he composed the first Finnish opera to a libretto by
Topelius, *King Charles's Hunt* (1852), and his collaboration
with the poet continued eight years later in the present work.
The *Princess of Cyprus* has been variously described as a
Singspiel and sometimes even as an opera, but it is more
accurately billed here as 'incidental music to Zopelius's play'.
In this version the plot is summarized and spoken by a
narrator. For all his undoubted importance as a pioneering
and inspiring force in Finland's musical life, Pacius's music is
not in the least Finnish or Nordic in character, nor is the
idiom particularly individual. The musical language is
indebted to Weber, Spohr and Mendelssohn, and the texture
is beautifully transparent. But what it lacks in individuality, it
makes up for in charm, and both performance and recording
are excellent.

PADEREWSKI, Ignaz (1860–1941)

Piano Concerto in A min., Op. 17

*** Hyp. CDA 66452. Lane, BBC Scottish SO, Maksymiuk –
  MOSZKOWSKI: *Piano Concerto* ***

Paderewski's *Piano Concerto* opens with strong thematic
promise, and the secondary lyrical material is attractive too.
The central *Romanza* brings another very winning theme,
and throughout the invention has genuine vitality. Even if
some of the passage-work is relatively conventional, the work
is well worth having back in the catalogue, especially when

Piers Lane gives a performance that is poetic and subtly coloured, as well as vivacious. The accompaniment from the BBC Scottish Orchestra under Maksymiuk is as alert as it is spirited.

Symphony in B min. (Polonia), Op. 28

**(*) Hyp. CDA 67056. BBC Scottish SO, Maksymiuk

Paderewski's *Symphony in B minor* is a mammoth affair. Its first movement alone takes half an hour, and the finale is almost as long. It occupied him for five years (1903–8) and runs to 74 minutes. It would have been longer had he added a Scherzo as he had originally planned. Although some of the ideas are unmemorable and the symphony is undoubtedly overblown, it is far from negligible. Moreover it has a certain sweep and is very well laid out for the orchestra. It is far more interesting than the admittedly much earlier *Piano Concerto*. If, for example, you enjoy the Glière symphonies, you should try it. The BBC Scottish Symphony Orchestra play well for Jerzy Maksymiuk and the only minor reservation is the recording quality, which is a bit opaque.

PAGANINI, Niccolò (1782-1840)

Andante amoroso; Balletto campestre (Variations on a Comic Theme; orch. Tamponi); Larghetto con passione; Moto perpetuo in C, Op. 11; Polacca with Variations in A; Sonata for Grand Viola; Sonata Maria Luisa in E; Sonata Varsavia; Variations on The Carnival of Venice; Variations on a Theme from Rossini's Mosè

(B) *** EMI (ADD) 7 67567-2 (2). Accardo, COE, Tamponi

Salvatore Accardo here explores the by-ways of Paganini's concertante music for violin and orchestra (with one piece for viola), and much of the virtuosity is stunning – sample the *Moto perpetuo*. As can be seen from the listing, Paganini's favourite device was a set of variations on a simple, often ingenuous theme, alternating *galant* lyricism with fiendish bravura. Accardo is equally at home in both. The orchestral accompaniments are of minimal interest but they are warmly supportive; the flattering ambience of the recording and the good balance ensure that the sounds reaching the listener are pleasingly believable. There are, however, no notes about the music.

Violin Concertos 1–6; 24 Caprices, Op. 1; Duo merveille; Introduction & Variations on 'Di tanti palpiti' from Rossini's Tancredi; Introduction & Variations on 'Nel cor più non mi sento' from Paisiello's La molinara; Maestoso sonata sentimentale; Perpetuela; La primavera; Sonata with Variations on a Theme by Joseph Weigl; Sonata Napoleone; Le streghe (Variations on a Theme by Süssmayr), Op. 8; Variations on 'God save the King'; Variations on 'Non più mesta' from Rossini's La Cenerentola

(B) *** DG 463 754-2 (6). Accardo, LPO, Dutoit

A self-recommending set. The Accardo/Dutoit Paganini cycle remains a secure first choice: the concertos are brilliantly and imaginatively played and well-recorded. Indeed, these accounts do not fall down in any department. The individual discs are contained in an excellently packaged DG bargain box.

Violin Concertos (i; ii) 1 in D, Op. 6; (iii; iv) 2 in B min., Op. 7; (v) 3 in E; (i; ii) 4 in D min.; (i; vi) Introduction & Variations on 'Di tanti palpiti' (arr. Kreisler); Le streghe,

Op. 8 (arr. Kreisler); (iii; vii) Caprices, Op. 1, 13 & 20 (arr. Kreisler); 24 (arr. Auer); (viii) Moto perpetuo, Op. 11

(B) ** Ph. (ADD) Duo 462 865-2 (2). (i) Grumiaux; (ii) Monte Carlo Op. O, Bellugi; (iii) Gitlis; (iv) Warsaw Nat. Philharmonic SO, Wislocki; (v) Szeryng, LSO, Gibson; (vi) Castagnone (piano); (vii) Janopoulo (piano); (viii) ASMF, Marriner

This set is a mixed success. The first CD contains Grumiaux's 1972 recordings of the *First* and *Fourth Concertos*, which are extremely good performances, full of bravura, yet highly musical. Grumiaux really comes into his own in the slow movements, and the outer movements tingle with excitement. The orchestra plays with passion, and the recording, albeit within the characteristic Monte Carlo acoustic, is warm and full. In the *Third Concerto*, Szeryng is not so well recorded, and Gibson's accompaniments, whilst fully acceptable, lack flair. The snag with this set is the *Second Concerto*: the performance is undistinguished and the sound thin. At bargain price, the set is worth considering for Grumiaux's readings alone, and the various fill-ups are a bonus.

Violin Concerto 1 in D, Op. 6

(M) *** EMI (ADD) 5 62594-2. Perlman, RPO, Foster – SARASATE: *Carmen Fantasy etc.* ***

*** DG (IMS) 429 786-2. Shaham, NYPO, Sinopoli – SAINT-SAENS: *Concerto 3* ***

**(*) EMI 5 55026-2. Chang, Phd. O, Sawallisch – SAINT-SAENS: *Havanaise; Introduction & Rondo capriccioso* **(*)

(M) **(*) Warner Elatus 2564 60013-2. Vengerov, Israel PO, Mehta – SAINT-SAENS: *Havanaise; Intro & Rondo Capriccioso* ***; WAXMAN: *Carmen Fantasy* **(*)

(i) *Violin Concerto 1; Introduction & Variations on 'Nel cor più non mi sento' (from Paisiello's La molinara); (ii) Cantabile; La campanella; Moses Fantasia*

🕪 ✪ *** BIS CD 999. Gringolts; with (i) Lahti SO, Vänskä; (ii) Ryumina

Violin Concerto 1 in D, Op. 6; I palpiti; Perpetuela; Sonata Napoleone

(M) *** DG (ADD) (IMS) 439 981-2. Accardo, LPO, Dutoit

The seventeen-year-old Russian violinist Ilya Gringolts plays the Paganini *D major Concerto* and the remainder of this recital not only with quite astonishing virtuosity but also with impeccable taste. Like Salvatore Accardo in the 1970s, he brings a refinement and noblesse to this repertoire, and indeed manages to make some of these display pieces really sound like music. There is an ardent quality to the playing, and a natural finesse that silences criticism. In the *Violin Concerto* and the *Introduction and Variations on 'Nel cor più non mi sento'* (from Paisiello's *La molinara*), the Lahti orchestra under Osmo Vänskä give excellent support, and the BIS recording is in the highest traditions of the house – natural and lifelike.

Perlman's famous 1971 recording returns at mid-price in the 'Perlman Edition', with two extra Sarasate items added. Provided one does not feel strongly about the traditional cuts in the Paganini, this performance remains unsurpassed. He demonstrates a fabulously clean and assured technique and, with the help of the EMI engineers, he produces a gleamingly rich tone, free from all scratchiness. Lawrence Foster matches the soloist's warmth with an alive and buoyant orchestral accompaniment.

Accardo's account is second to none in its sense of lyrical style, finesse and easy bravura. It is available at mid-price with attractive, shorter concertante pieces, of which the *Perpetuela* is quite dazzling and *I palpiti* is like an operatic air with variations.

Gil Shaham's technical ease in the histrionics of Paganini's stratospheric tessitura, harmonics and all, is breathtaking, and he can phrase an Italianate lyrical melody – and there are some good ones in this concerto – with disarming charm and ravishing timbre. His dancing spiccato in the finale is a joy and, however high he ascends, there is never a hint of scratchiness. Sinopoli's finely graduated and often dramatic accompaniment could hardly be more sympathetic.

Sarah Chang recorded this famous bravura concerto in Philadelphia. The slow movement is fresh and direct rather than romantic, but she knows how to charm the ear gently. The finale is dazzling. Chang can bounce her bow with aplomb and never fails to entice the ear. Sawallisch gives her admirable support, but the recording is flattering neither to soloist (balanced close) nor to orchestra, which lacks sumptuousness.

Maxim Vengerov gives a strongly extrovert account, egged on by Mehta, whose fast opening tutti sets the scene without poise. In spite of this, however, the solo contribution has much warmth and some infectious fireworks in the finale.

Violin Concertos 1; 2 in B min. (La campanella), Op. 7

(BB) *** Naxos 8.550649. Kaler, Polish Nat. RSO, Gunzenhauser

(B) *** DG (IMS) (ADD) 429 524-2. Ashkenasi, VSO, Esser

Ilya Kaler is fully equal to Paganini's once-devilish technical demands and the phrasing of warm Italianate melody. In every respect his technique is commandingly secure. Stephen Gunzenhauser is a sympathetic accompanist throughout, and the Polish Radio Orchestra play with suppleness and bring a sense of elegance and style to this music. There is no lack of dazzle in the fireworks, and no damp squibs here. With very good notes, this is an excellent example of a Naxos super-bargain at its best.

Shnuel Ashkenasi's coupling of the two favourite Paganini concertos is also good value. He surmounts all the many technical difficulties in an easy, confident style and, especially in the infectious *La campanella* finale of No. 2, shows how completely he is in control. The microphone is close, but his timbre is sweet and the high tessitura and harmonics are always cleanly focused.

Violin Concertos 3 in E; 4 in D min.

(BB) **(*) Naxos 8.554396. Rózsa, Slovak RSO, Dittrich

Ernö Rózsa is a first class soloist, fully equal to all Paganini's pyrotechnical demands, and on his bow the characteristic cantabile tunes (often over pizzicato accompaniments) sing out very winningly. He also plays his own cadenzas, which are perhaps rather too much of a good thing when these two concertos are quite long enough already! Michael Dittrich opens the first movement of No. 3 at an agreeable jog-trot, but then follows his soloist who relaxes for the lyrical passages. The result is that the movement lasts for just over 22 minutes, and the bass-heavy orchestral tuttis do not help to give the music a great deal of lift. The acoustic is not ideal but the recording of the orchestra (and the scoring) in No. 4 seems fresher, and the performance cannot be faulted when the soloist plays so enticingly and with such easy bravura, especially in the attractive Rondo finale.

CHAMBER MUSIC

Allegro di concert (Moto perpetuo) in C, Op. 11; Cantabile in D, Op. 17; Centone si sonate: in D; in A, Op. 64/2 & 4; Guitar & Violin Sonatas: in A; A min.; E min., Op. 3/1, 4 & 6; Grand Sonata for Violin & Guitar in A, Op. posth.; Sonata concertata in A, Op. 61; Sonata a preghiera (arr. Hannibal)

*** DG (IMS) 437 837-2. Shaham, Söllscher

The atmosphere of much of this repertoire is comparatively intimate, something these artists readily appreciate, and their playing is immaculate and amiably easy-going. Perhaps at times here the style of performance could with advantage have been more extrovert, but the present hour-long recital will make attractive late-evening entertainment (not taken all at once, of course). The recording has a realistic balance and fine presence.

Cantabile & Valse; 6 Sonatas for Violin & Guitar, Op. 2; Sonata for Grand Viola & Guitar; Variations di bravura on Caprice 24

(BB) **(*) Naxos 8.550759. St John, Wynberg

Cantabile in D; 6 Sonatas for Violin & Guitar, Op. 3; Sonata concertata in A; Variations on Barucabà, Op. 14

(BB) **(*) Naxos 8.550690. St John, Wynberg

Scott St John plays with flair and considerable virtuosity: his approach has more extrovert dazzle and rather less charm than the performances on DG, and he dominates the performances strongly. The recording venue is resonant, which means close microphones, but the violin timbre is bright without being edgy.

24 Caprices, Op. 1

↦ (N) (M) *** DG 476 7249-2. Accardo

(M) *** EMI 5 67237-2 [567257]. Perlman

(M) *** EMI 5 67986-2 [56789]. Rabin

(BB) *** Naxos 8.550717. Kaler

(M) *** Decca (IMS) (ADD) 440 034-2. Ricci

*** Telarc CD 80398. Ehnes

(M) **(*) Teldec 9031 76259-2. Zehetmair

Accardo succeeds in making Paganini's most routine phrases sound like the noblest of utterances and he invests these caprices with an eloquence far beyond the sheer display they offer. There are no technical obstacles and, both in breadth of tone and in grandeur of conception, he is peerless. He observes all the repeats and has an excellent CD transfer. This is now reissued in Universal's 'Critics' Choice' series.

Perlman's superbly played 1972 set now returns to the catalogue at mid-price as one of EMI's 'Great Recordings of the Century'. The transfer is immaculate, the violin image very real and vivid, and this can now be recommended without reservation alongside Accardo on DG.

Michael Rabin was a shooting star from New York who died sadly young. He recorded the Paganini *Caprices* in 1958 when he was 22 years old, and his consistent and astonishing dexterity is heard at its most electrifying in *No. 5 in A minor*, his sure sense of rhythmic style in *No. 9 in E major* and his delicious glissandi in *No. 13*, while he plays the most famous closing number with assured panache. His impeccable technique informs the whole set, and he is most vividly recorded. EMI now add his CD to their 'Great Recordings of the Century' alongside Perlman.

Those looking for a bargain will surely not be disappointed with the Russian fiddler, Ilya Kaler, on Naxos. A pupil of

Leonid Kogan, his playing is technically very assured, the lyrical bowing vibrant in a Slavic way, and, like Ricci, he projects a strong profile. The 1992 Naxos recording is truthful and real.

Ricci's Decca recording dates from 1959 but it is remarkably vivid and present. Ricci's playing often offers a breathtaking display of bravura and, oddly enough, his very occasional imperfections (usually minor slips of intonation) come at points where they are least expected – in the easier rather than the more difficult parts. The playing has great personality and the quicksilver articulation is often dazzlingly precise, conveying enormous dash, for instance in *No. 5 in A minor*. However, Perlman and Accardo are even more polished.

James Ehnes is Juilliard-trained and has technique to burn. He tosses off these pieces with great bravura and aplomb. His playing has real personality, even if others have managed to find greater subtlety and delicacy. All the same, there is much to relish in his youthful ardour and the splendid sound the Telarc engineers give us.

Thomas Zehetmair has a somewhat more reticent personality and seems to want to avoid virtuosity for its own sake. His style of articulation in the faster passages at times has an almost throwaway quality, but he soars most agreeably in the lyrical writing and his timbre above the stave is richly caught by the recording. There is much to appreciate and enjoy in these performances, but in the last resort Zehetmair projects less charisma than his competitors.

Caprice 24, Op. 1/24; Grand Sonata in A

(B) *** Sony (ADD) SBK 62425. Williams (guitar) –
 GIULIANI: *Variations on a Theme by Handel;*
 D. SCARLATTI: *Sonatas;* VILLA-LOBOS: *5 Preludes* ***

Grand sonata in A

(B) **(*) Decca 448 709-2. Fernández – GIULIANI;
 VIVALDI: *Concertos* **(*)

John Williams is in excellent form in the *Grand Sonata*, with its charming central *Romanza* and ingenuous closing *Andantino variato* (originally a duo for guitar and violin), and the famous *Caprice*, for violin solo, both arranged by Williams. The recording is only marginally balanced too forwardly and is otherwise truthful. Most enjoyable.

Fernández's playing is rightly much admired by fellow guitarists. His technique is immaculate and his somewhat self-effacing approach always puts the composer first. He is beautifully recorded and the effect is engagingly intimate to suit the gentle, improvisatory nature of his playing, especially the pensive central *Romanza*. Some might feel that the finale needs more extrovert feeling, but there is certainly no lack of dash or bravura.

PALESTRINA, Giovanni Pierluigi da (1525–94)

Giovanni Pierluigi da Palestrina was perhaps the key musical figure of the Italian Renaissance. Certainly his influence on Italian church music was profound. After beginning his career as a chorister at S. Maria Maggiore, he spent most of his life in Rome and in 1551 became director of music at St Peter's. However, as he was married, the enforcement of celibacy for members of the Sistine Chapel under Pope Paul IV led to his dismissal, and he moved to lead the music at St John Lateran. His main claim to fame is associated with the Council of Trent in 1545, which was assembled to bring about a reformation of church musical liturgy and a possible return to the use of simple plainchant. Supposedly, his *Missa Papae Marcelli* demonstrated to the Pope and his advisers that a polyphonic Mass setting could be intelligible, of the highest musical quality and without unwonted secular associations. Certainly his Masses are among the most beautiful and dedicated church music of his time.

Ad Dominum cum tribularer; Ad te levavi oculos meos; Alma Redemptoris; Dum complerentur; Magnificat & Nunc dimittis; Recordare; Stabat Mater; Veni sancte spiritus; Victimae Paschali

 (M) *** CRD (ADD) CRD 3519. New College, Oxford, Ch., Higginbottom

A particularly satisfying and beautiful collection of motets and canticles from the New College Choir singing with glorious, yet restrained feeling under Edward Higginbottom. The programme is arranged to give the kind of contrast that Palestrina himself achieves between the paired Vespers and Compline canticles, *Magnificat* and *Nunc dimittis*. Much of this music was written for a double choir – four voices expanding to eight – which meant that antiphonal effects were possible in the spacious baroque churches. But the *Magnificat* and *Stabat Mater* were written for the Papal Choir, and in the Sistine Chapel all the singers were placed in the balcony cut into the right-hand side wall, so spatial separation was not possible. Higginbottom and his choir achieve their contrasts in sound without attempting extreme left–right effects, and their recording engineer, Mike Clements, has produced a full, relatively homogenous, yet detailed sound picture in the Chapel, which is very telling when all these works are texturally so rich and often radiant, as at the opening of *Ad te levavi oculos meos*. The concert opens with the celebratory and thankful Easter sequence, *Victimae Paschali*, and closes with *Veni sancte spiritus*, where the triple time signature gives the music a jaunty bounce. Palestrina collections don't come any better than this and full texts and translations are included in the excellent documentation

Ardens est cor meum; Congratulamini mihi omnes; Crucem santam subiit; Crux fidelis; Fratres, ego enim accepi; Dominus Jesus; Haec Dies a 6; Improperium; Magnificat terti toni a 6 (with Plainsong: Et respicientes); Popule meus; Pueri Hebraeorum (with introductory Plainsong: Hosanna filio David); O Domine, Jesu Christe a 6; Stabat Mater a 8; Terra tremuit; Victimae paschali laudes a 6

(N) *** ASV Gaudeamus CDGAU 333. Cardinall's Musick, Carwood

Beautifully recorded in the Fitzalan Chapel of Arundel Castle, this outstanding collection is yet another example of the sublime singing of the Cardinall's Musick, directed by Andrew Carwood, in this case a well-planned programme of Palestrina's beautiful music for Holy Week. Although the noble *Stabat Mater* dominates the frontispiece of the disc, it is only one of the many memorable works offered here, which include the lofty setting of the grand *Magnificat* with its framing plainsong and the less imposing *Popule meus*, which has a sublime simplicity, as has the companion *Crux fidelis*. It was an inspired idea to follow the *Magnificat* with a group of motets that tell the Resurrection story, and the programme ends exultantly with the joyous Easter motet for double choir, *Victimae paschali laudes*.

Canticum canticorum Salomonis (Book 4 of motets for 5 voices from the *Song of Songs*)

🔦 (BB) *** Hyp. Helios CDH 55095. Pro Cantione Antiqua, Turner

The *Canticum canticorum Salomonis* is one of Palestrina's most sublime and expressive works, possibly wider in its range than anything else he composed, and certainly as deeply felt. The ten members of the Pro Cantione Antiqua under Turner bring an appropriate eloquence and ardour, tempered by restraint. They are accorded an excellently balanced and natural-sounding recording. Now reissued in the budget range, this can be recommended even more highly.

Lamentations for Good Friday, Book 3. *Crux fidelis/Pange lingua; Vexilla regis*

(N) *** Chan. 0652. Musica Contexta, Ravens

A contemporary source observed that Palestrina's settings of the Good Friday Improperia 'are for two choirs and are recited slowly and with solemn voice, since their sweetest harmonies render an inner devotion and contrition'. That could well describe the performances here by Simon Ravens and his Musica Contexta. Palestrina's *Tenebrae* music survives in two manuscripts with different time-values; in one, the music is notated in equal values; in the other, stressed and unstressed syllables are allotted long and short notes accordingly. The present performance draws on both manuscripts with scholarly and eminently musical understanding. At the end of the service, the hymn *Vexilla regis* marked the recession from the Sistine Chapel, and it is used to close the performance here.

Lamentations and Responsories for Holy Saturday; Book 3, 1–3; Benedictus for Holy Week; Sicut cervus; Stabat Mater

*** Chan. 0679. Musica Contexta, Ravens

In his perceptive note Simon Ravens points out that Holy Saturday has inevitably tended to be overshadowed in the church calendar by the days immediately before and after Good Friday and Easter Day. Yet in this fine collection, superbly performed by his group, Musica Contexta, and vividly recorded, he demonstrates what inspired music Palestrina wrote for this in-between occasion. Like the other sets of *Lamentations*, this third of the four has the first two motets using Hebrew letters as an introduction, leading on in the third to a magnificent setting of the Prayer of Jeremiah. More than usual, Palestrina's polyphony here has a biting edge, beautifully achieved in this performance. The *Stabat Mater* for double choir, one of Palestrina's best-loved works, follows up in its dedication, leading to the *Benedictus for Easter Saturday* and finally to the motet *Sicut cervus*, which prepares the way as a concluding liturgical act for the celebrations of the following day. Using texts transcribed from early editions, Ravens draws direct and dedicated performances from his fine group of singers.

Lamentations of Jeremiah, Book 4 (complete)

🔦 (M) *** Regis RRC 1038. Pro Cantione Antiqua, Turner

Many composers have set the Lamentation Lessons for the Tenebrae services on Maundy Thursday, Good Friday and Holy Saturday but, remarkably, Palestrina did so on five different occasions, the present (fourth) setting was discovered only at the beginning of the nineteeth century, and it is recorded here complete for the first time. The music has a serene but poignant simplicity, which Bruno Turner captures

admirably with spacious tempi. The concentration is obvious and the quality of the singing from a group of eight (including several famous names) is of a high order. So is the recording, which is very well balanced in the warm acoustic of St Alban's Church, Brook Street, London.

MASSES

Missa Aeterna Christi munera; Missa Papae Marcelli

(BB) **(*) Naxos 8.550573. Oxford Camerata, Summerly

Summerly's are bold, flowing performances, lacking something in mysticism and ethereal dynamics, but sung very confidently, with textures clear and the performances alive and compelling. The Oxford Camerata consists of twelve singers, of whom a third are female, and the blend is impressive. The account of the lesser-known *Missa Aeterna Christi munera* is particularly compelling. The recording was made in Dorchester Abbey, so the ambience is flattering, although the balance is fairly close.

Missa Assumpta est Maria (including *Gregorian Chant Proper for the Feast of the Assumption*); Missa Papae Marcelli

🔦 (BB) *** Regis RRC 1025. Pro Cantione Antiqua, M. Brown

Mark Brown and his Pro Cantione Antiqua made a series of Palestrina recordings (which last appeared on Carlton), and for this reissue Regis have re-coupled two of the finest. They give accounts of these celebrated pieces that aspire to total authenticity in that the forces used are those Palestrina himself would have known: no boys' voices, no women and just one-to-a-part, with the mass sections interspersed with plainchant. The Pro Cantione Antiqua sing with eloquence and power against the background of a resonant acoustic. The mid-1980s recording is splendidly balanced. Whatever other versions you might have of either work, this has special claims, and its outward severity does not preclude depth of feeling – rather the reverse.

'The Essential Palestrina': Missa Assumpta est Maria (with Plainchant: *Assumpta est Maria*). Motet: *Assumpta est Maria*. Missa brevis. Missa Papae Marcelli. Missa Sicut lilium inter spinas. Motet: *Sicut lilium inter spinas*

(N) (B) *** Gimell (ADD/DDD) CDGIM 204 (2). Tallis Scholars, Phillips

This highly recommendable and well-documented box joins together two CDs recorded by the Tallis Scholars between 1981 and 1989. As is their practice, this group records the Masses together with the motets on which they are based, even if they are by other composers. Their account of the most famous of Palestrina's works, the *Missa Papae Marcelli*, brings a characteristically eloquent performance.

Missa Assumpta est Maria; Missa Sicut lilium

*** Gimell CDGIM 020. Tallis Scholars, Phillips

After the *Missa Papae Marcelli*, the *Missa Assumpta est Maria* is one of Palestrina's most sublime works. Its companion on this CD is based on the motet, *Sicut lilium inter spinas* ('Like a lily among thorns'). As is their practice, the Tallis Scholars record the Masses together with the motets on which they are based, and sing with their customary beauty of sound and well-blended tone. They are superbly recorded in the Church of St Peter and St Paul in Salle, Norfolk.

Mass & Motet: *Assumpta est Maria*. Motets: *Ave Maria; Beata es, Virgo Maria; Hodie gloriosa semper Virgo Maria; Regina coeli; Magnificat septimi toni*

(B) **(*) EMI 5 69703-2. Clare College, Cambridge, Ch., T. Brown

This is an exceptionally well-chosen collection, mainly of shorter works, but also including the splendid *Missa Assumpta est Maria*. The programme ends with an equally fine *Magnificat* setting. We are familiar with the excellent Clare College Choir and their rich sound, partly achieved by using women's voices, from earlier recordings. This EMI Debut CD introduces their new conductor, Timothy Brown, and the choir responds expressively to his melismatic direction. The choir is beautifully recorded, and the only minor criticism is the relatively restricted dynamic range. But this remains a thoroughly worthwhile bargain disc, although it is a pity that the documentation has so little to say about the music.

Missa de Beata Virgine I (1567)

(N) (BB) *** Naxos 8.553313. Soloists of the Cappella Musicale di S. Petronio di Bologna, Vartolo

The special value of this Naxos performance by an Italian male-voice group is that Sergio Vartolo, the director of the Cappella Musicale di S. Petronio di Bologna, has sought to place the Mass within a liturgical sequence recalling early performance traditions. Thus it opens with the plainchant introit *Gaudeamus omnes in Domino* (intended for a major feast of the Virgin Mary) and after the *Gloria* comes a Gradual and an organ paraphrase of the hymn *Ave maris stella* (by Girolamo Cavazzoni), very well played by Vartolo himself. Then comes the plainchant *Alleluia* and, following the *Credo*, the Gregorian Offertory, *Beata ex Virgo Maria*, which leads on to the *Sanctus*; the communion verse precedes Palestrina's very beautiful double *Agnus Dei*. The performance has striking character and powerful devotional feeling and is very well recorded in the Church of St Zeno, Cavalo, Verona.

Missa: Benedicta es (with Plainchant)

*** Gimell CDGIM 001. Tallis Scholars, Phillips (with JOSQUIN: Motet: *Benedicta es*)

Palestrina's Mass is coupled with the Josquin motet, *Benedicta es*, on which it is based, together with the plainchant sequence on which both drew. It would seem that this Mass was the immediate predecessor of the *Missa Papae Marcelli* and was composed while the music of *Benedictus es* was still at the forefront of the composer's mind. The Tallis Scholars and Peter Phillips sing with impressive conviction and produce an expressive, excellently blended sound.

Missa dum complerentur; Motet: Dum complerentur; Magnificat sexti toni; Spiritus Sanctus replevit totam domum; Veni Creator Spiritus: Veni Sancte Spiritus (Alleluia, Sequence & Motet)

*** Hyp. CDA 67353. Westminster Cathedral Ch., Baker

When James O'Donnell moved as choirmaster from Westminster Cathedral to Westminster Abbey, Martin Baker, deputy at the Abbey, went in the opposite direction to succeed O'Donnell. Baker's first recording with the choir was a splendid account of James MacMillan's fervent new

Mass celebrating the millennium, and here he reinforces his reputation and that of the choir in fresh, energetic accounts of music by Palestrina celebrating Pentecost. The disc starts with the magnificent motet *Dum complerentur*, with its vivid portrayal of the rushing of winds. The magnificent parody Mass based on that motet, which Palestrina wrote some 30 years later, follows naturally, and so do three brilliant motets in eight voices, as well as the glorious *Magnificat sexti toni* with its graphic illustrations of the Virgin's prayer.

Missa Ecce ego Johannes; Cantantibus organis; Laudate pueri; Magnificat quarti toni; Peccantem me quotidie; Tribulationes civitatum; Tu es Petrus

*** Hyp. CDA 67099. Westminster Cathedral Ch., O'Donnell

Even among the Westminster Cathedral Choir's superb records this disc stands out. Perfect chording and ensemble, natural and musical phrasing, spot-on intonation and a glorious tonal blend, make this issue one to treasure. The recording serves the choir well and there are scholarly notes by Ivan Moody.

Missa Hodie Christus natus est; Motet: Hodie Christus natus est; Stabat Mater

(BB) *** Naxos 8.550836. Oxford Schola Cantorum, Summerly – LASSUS: *Missa Bell' Amfitrit' alterna* ***

Where in their account of Palestrina's *Missa aeterna Christi munera* Summerly's group are restrained in their devotional manner, this celebrated Mass for Christmas has them joyful and exuberant. The choir, over 30 strong, brings out both the beauty and the drama of the writing, and equally so in the brief motet setting the Christmas words. The magnificent *Stabat Mater* is wisely given to a smaller group of 16 singers, two to a part, with added clarity in the complex polyphony. Well coupled with one of Lassus's best-loved Masses, Palestrina's close contemporary from Flanders, this CD represents the work of two supreme polyphonic masters who died in the same year.

Missa: Nasce la gioia mia; Missa brevis (with PRIMAVERA: Madrigal: *Nasce la gioia mia*)

*** Gimell CDGIM 008. Tallis Scholars, Phillips

The *Missa: Nasce la gioia mia* is a parody Mass, modelled on the madrigal, *Nasce la gioia mia* by Giovan Leonardo Primavera. The Tallis Scholars and Peter Phillips give expressive, finely shaped accounts of both the *Missa brevis* and the *Mass*, which they preface by the madrigal itself. A most rewarding disc: no grumbles about the recording.

Missa: Nigra sum (with motets on *Nigra sum* by L'HERITIER; VICTORIA; DE SILVA)

*** Gimell CDGIM 003. Tallis Scholars, Phillips

Palestrina's *Missa: Nigra sum* is another parody Mass, based on a motet by Jean L'Heritier, and follows its model quite closely; its text comes from the Song of Solomon. On this record, the plainchant and the L'Heritier motet precede Palestrina's *Mass*, plus motets by Victoria and Andreas de Silva, a relatively little-known Flemish singer and composer who served in the Papal chapel and later in Mantua. The music is inspiring and the performances exemplary. This is a most beautiful record and the acoustic of Merton College, Oxford, is ideal.

Missa Papae Marcelli
*** Gimell (ADD) CDGIM 939-2. Tallis Scholars, Phillips –
ALLEGRI: *Miserere;* MUNDY: *Vox Patris caelestis* ***

*Missa Papae Marcelli; Alma redemptoris Mater; Magnificat 1
toni; Nunc dimittis; Stabat Mater; Surge illuminare*
**(*) Gimell CDGIM 994-2. Tallis Scholars (with ALLEGRI:
Miserere ***)

Missa Papae Marcelli; Missa brevis
⊕—★ *** Hyp. CDA 66266. Westminster Cathedral Ch., Hill

Missa Papae Marcelli; Tu es Petrus (motet)
*** DG (IMS) (ADD) 415 517-2. Westminster Abbey Ch.,
Preston (with ANERIO: *Venite ad me omnes;*NANINO: *Haec
dies;*GIOVANNELLI: *Jubilate Deo* ***) – ALLEGRI:
Miserere **(*)

David Hill and the Westminster Cathedral Choir give an
imposing and eloquent *Missa Papae Marcelli* that many collectors may prefer to the finely sung Gimell issue from the
Tallis Scholars. They, too, have the advantage of a spacious
acoustic and excellent recording.

The account by the Westminster Abbey choristers is a
performance of great fervour, married to fine discipline, rich
in timbre, eloquent both at climaxes and at moments of
serenity. The singing is equally fine in the hardly less distinctive motet, *Tu es Petrus*. Felice Anerio, Giovanni Bernardino
Nanino and Ruggiero Giovannelli represent the following
generation of composers. Their contributions to this collection are well worth having, particularly Giovannelli's *Jubilate
Deo* which makes a splendid closing item. The digital recording is first class.

The earlier Gimell alternative is an analogue recording
from 1980. The singing has eloquence, purity of tone, and a
simplicity of line which is consistently well controlled.

For their second, digital recording, the Tallis Scholars were
recorded in the Basilica of Maria Maggiore in Rome, where
Palestrina was a choirboy and, later, master of the choristers.
The most celebrated of Palestrina's Masses, *Missa Papae
Marcelli*, receives as eloquent an account as any in the
catalogue. The Tallis Scholars have wonderful fluidity and
the sense of movement never flags in this finely tuned,
well-paced reading. Much the same goes for the remaining
motets here and, of course, for the Allegri *Miserere*, which
had a unique association with the Sistine Chapel. As the
recording was made before an audience, there is applause,
which is quite inappropriate and very tiresome. In every
other respect this is a first-class issue and can be warmly
recommended.

Missa Veni sponsa Christi (with *Motet*)
(B) **(*) CfP 575 5602. St John's College, Cambridge, Ch.,
Guest – ALLEGRI: *Miserere;* LASSUS: *Missa
super'Bell'Amfitrit' alterna'* **(*)

Every section of the *Veni sponsa Christi* Mass is introduced by
the same idea with much subtle variation, and this impressive
work ends with two *Agnus Dei* settings, the second with an
additional tenor part. It receives an eloquent, imaginatively
detailed and finely shaped performance here, and the relative
restraint of the Anglican choral tradition suits Palestrina's
flowing counterpoint better than it does the Lassus Venetian
coupling.

COLLECTIONS

Music for Advent and Christmas: *Missa Hodie Christus
natus est.* **Motets:** *Alma redemptoris mater; Canite tube;
Deus tu converses; Christus, redemptor omnium; Hodie
Christus natus est; Magnificat Primi toni; O admirabile
commercium; O magnum mysterium; Tui sunt coeli*
*** Hyp. CDA 67396. Westminster Cathedral Ch., Baker

Westminster Cathedral Choir under its latest choirmaster,
Martin Baker, goes from strength to strength. This is a
thrilling recording of Palestrina's music for the Christmas
season, centring not just on the Mass, *Hodie Christus natus
est*, but on the motet on which the Mass is based. Vividly set
against the cathedral acoustic, warm but clear, it brings out
better than most rival versions the exuberance of the cries of
Noe ('Noel') that dramatically punctuate the piece, reflecting
individual joy in welcoming the birth of Christ. The eight
other items, all relating to Advent and Christmas, culminate
in the *Magnificat Primi Toni* with its rich textures, framed
before and after by the plainsong antiphon, *Hodie Christus
natus est.*

*Officium defunctorum: Ad Dominum cum tribularer
clamavi; Domine quando veneris; Heu mihi Domine; Libere
me, Domine* (with Plainchant taken from *Graduale
Romanum*)
**(*) ECM 1653. James, Covey-Crump, Potter, Jones –
VICTORIA: *Responsories* **(*)

This CD combines music by Palestrina and Victoria, for the
Office and Matins for the Dead and the Burial service,
including one text, *Libera me Domine*, set by both composers.
These 'composed pieces' are surrounded by the appropriate
plainchant, of which there is a great deal. But it could hardly
be more convincingly or beautifully sung. Indeed the four
singers blend their voices beautifully and sing with eloquence, and are beautifully recorded. However, the pervasive
mood of doom and gloom will not suit all tastes!

*Hodie Beata Virgo; Litaniae de Beata Virgine Maria in 8
parts; Magnificat in 8 parts (Primi Toni); Senex puerum
portabat; Stabat Mater*
(M) *** Decca (ADD) 466 373-2. King's College Ch.,
Willcocks – ALLEGRI: *Miserere* ***

The flowing melodic lines and serene beauty which are the
unique features of Palestrina's music are apparent throughout this programme, and there is no question about the
dedication and accomplishment of the performance. The
recording is no less successful, sounding radiantly fresh and
clear as remastered for Decca's Legend series.

PANDOLFI MEALLI, Giovanni
Antonio (*fl.* 1620–69)

Violin Sonatas, Op. 3, 1 (*La stella*); 2 (*La cesta*); 3 (*La
melana*); 4 (*La castella*); 5 (*La clemente*); 6 (*La sabbatina*);
Op. 4, 1 (*Laernabea*); 2 (*La viviana*); 3 (*La monella
romanesca*); 4 (*La biancuccia*); 5 (*La stella*); 6 (*La
vinciolina*)
*** HM HMU 907241. Manze, Egarr

Apart from being registered as an employee at the Hapsburg
Court, nothing is known of Pandolfi. The manuscripts of
his Opp. 3 and 4 were found in the Civico Museo of

Bologna. These twelve sonatas (published in 1660) are written in a highly individual and certainly unpredictable improvisatory style which moves from gentle expressive lyricism to bursts of more plangent virtuosity, allowing the kind of latitude in performance ('a Pandora's box of possibilities') which Andrew Manze and Richard Egarr obviously relish. *La biancuccia* and the passionate final sonata *La vinciolina* (the only work dedicated to a woman) are particularly remarkable. They are named after their dedicatees, who range from composers to Kapellmeisters, violinists and even castrati.

These remarkably spontaneous re-creative period-instrument performances won a *Gramophone* Baroque Music Award, and no wonder. They are superbly recorded. But in his notes Andrew Manze offers good advice: 'Only the more discerning palates will be able to appreciate more than one or two (sonatas) at a sitting. Indulge the chef by not over-indulging.'

Violin Sonatas: La cesta; La castella; La clemente; La sabbatina, Op. 3/2, 4–6; La bernabea; La biancuccia; La vinciolina, Op. 4/1, 4 & 6; (i) Anon.: *Harpsichord Suites in A, C & D*
*** Channel CCS 5894. Manze; (i) Egarr, Jacobs

Giovanni Antonio Pandolfi Mealli's reputation rests on a single surviving copy of two sets of violin sonatas, six sonatas in each. Seven are recorded here, interspersed with three anonymous, French-influenced harpsichord suites, very different in style. These are all rewarding and interesting scores, marvellously played by all concerned, and very well recorded too.

PANUFNIK, Andrzej (1914–91)

Cello Concerto
*** NMC Single D 0105. Rostropovich, LSO, Wolff

Panufnik's *Cello Concerto* was his very last work, completed only days before his death in September 1991. The recording is even more successful at conveying the purposefulness of the writing than the first performance, bringing out the tautness of the palindromic structure, with the two movements, each in arch form, a mirror-image of the other, slow then fast. The result is not a drily schematic work, as one might expect, but a piece that in its warmth reflects the player who inspired it, strong and eventful with a more open lyricism than in many previous Panufnik compositions.

(i) Piano Concerto. Symphony 9 (Sinfonia della speranza)
(N) (M) *** RCA 82876 64280-2. (i) Poblocka; LSO, composer

In a massive single movement of 41 minutes Panufnik's *Ninth Symphony* brings a formidable example of the composer's fascination with translating geometric concepts into notes. The visual analogy here is with light travelling through a prism, and the accompanying booklet provides a diagram illustrating how this formula works, using a three-note cell refracted in various ways. The result has similarities with a gigantic passacaglia and there is no denying the music's strength.

Panufnik's *Piano Concerto* is not so extended, but it carries comparable weight. The opening *Entrada* has a neoclassical flavour in its ostinatos for the solo instrument, leading to a bald, spare, central slow movement. The mood is rather like

that of some of Bartók's night music. By contrast the finale is violently rhythmic, with jazzy syncopations. Though the piano writing gives the soloist relatively little chance for conventional keyboard display, her playing adds to the power of the composer's purposeful interpretation. The piano tone is a degree too clangy, but otherwise the recording is spacious and full.

Symphony 8 (Sinfonia votiva)
(BB) *** Hyp. Helios CDH 55100. Boston SO, Ozawa –
   SESSIONS: *Concerto for Orchestra* ***

The *Sinfonia votiva* has a strongly formalistic structure, but its message is primarily emotional. Though Panufnik's melodic writing may as a rule reflect the formalism of his thought rather than tapping a vein of natural lyricism, the result is most impressive, particularly in a performance of such sharp clarity and definition as Ozawa's. Very well recorded, and excellent value.

PARRY, Hubert (1848–1918)

Piano Concerto in F sharp min.
*** Hyp. CDA 66820. Lane, BBC Scottish SO, Brabbins –
   STANFORD: *Piano Concerto* ***

The *Piano Concerto in F sharp minor* may at first seem rather naive in the way it embraces a grand manner but, written in 1880, it is a relatively early work which appeals openly with its directness and lyricism. The Brahmsian echoes are supplemented in the finale by clear if momentary echoes of Bizet's *Carmen*, then a very new work. Piers Lane plays with feeling and brilliance, helped by beautiful sound.

Concertstück in G min.; Elegy for Brahms; From Death to Life; Symphonic Variations
(M) *** Chan. 6610. LPO, Bamert

The eloquent *Concertstück*, literally a 'concert piece' without a soloist and with a strong Wagnerian flavour, is the least known work here. The *Elegy for Brahms* conveys grief, but its vigour rises above passive mourning into an expression of what might almost be anger. *From Death to Life* consists of two connected movements – hardly Lisztian as the title implies but exuberantly melodic, with a theme in the second that echoes Sibelius's *Karelia* and is at the same time Elgarian in its sweep. But the finest work of all is the *Symphonic Variations*, with its echoes of Brahms's St Anthony set and its foretastes of *Enigma*. Shorter than either, it does not waste a note: a big work in a small compass. The performances could hardly be more sympathetic, and the Chandos sound is suitably rich and clear.

Lady Radnor's Suite
*** Nim. NI 5068. E. String O, Boughton – BRIDGE: *Suite*;
   BUTTERWORTH: *Banks of Green Willow*, etc. ***

Parry's charming set of pastiche dances, now given an extra period charm through their Victorian flavour, makes an attractive item in an excellent and generous English collection, one of Nimbus's bestsellers. Warm, atmospheric recording, with refined playing set against an ample acoustic.

Symphonies 1–5; Symphonic Variations in E min.
☛ *** Chan. 9120-22 (3). LPO, Bamert

Bamert takes us convincingly through the symphonic terrain of a highly influential composer about whom Elgar declared,

'He is our leader – no cloud of formality can dim the healthy sympathy and broad influence he exerts upon us. Amidst all the outpourings of modern English music the work of Parry remains supreme.' Bamert's set, discussed in detail below, is offered here complete on three CDs and includes also Parry's best-known orchestral work, the *Symphonic Variations*.

Symphony 1 in G; Concertstück in G min.
*** Chan. 9062. LPO, Bamert

Bamert immediately demonstrates his response to the composer's muse in the way the opening Con fuoco sails off with a powerful thrust in the first movement. His control of the overall structure with its interrelated thematic material is most convincing, through the eloquent Andante and the Scherzo with its double trio, until he brings the finale to an impressively up-beat conclusion. He also offers the earlier *Concertstück for Orchestra*, though here the Wagnerian influences remain incompletely absorbed. The spacious Chandos recording seems exactly right for this pre-Elgarian opulence of symphonic thought.

Symphony 2 in F (Cambridge); Symphonic Variations
*** Chan. 8961. LPO, Bamert

Symphony 2 (Cambridge); Overture to an Unwritten Tragedy; Symphonic Variations
(BB) **(*) Naxos 8.553469. RSNO, Penny

The *Second Symphony* opens confidently (with distinct Mendelssohnian associations) and Brahms's influence appears in the main lyrical idea of the finale. In between there are reminders of Dvořák and Schumann but for all its eclecticism and occasional longwindedness, notably in the finale, Parry finds his own voice and the music has a genuinely vital flow. Bamert's advocacy certainly holds the listener's attention and the orchestra responds with obvious relish. The *Symphonic Variations* makes an admirable makeweight. Excellent, full-bodied sound of the best Chandos vintage.

Naxos here offers a very acceptable alternative to the *Symphony No. 2*, similarly coupled with the *Symphonic Variations* and with an extra item in the *Overture*. The playing of the Royal Scottish National Orchestra is just as polished as that of the LPO on Chandos, but Penny's manner is less warmly expressive at speeds generally a little faster, and the recorded sound is rather less opulent.

Symphonies 3 in C (English); 4 in E min.
*** Chan. 8896. LPO, Bamert

No. 3 is the most immediately approachable of the symphonies, with its bold melodies, often like sea-shanties, and its forthright structure. Yet it is No. 4 which proves the more rewarding, a larger-scale, ambitious work. The bold opening, in its dark E minor, echoes that of Brahms's *First Piano Concerto*, leading to an ambitious movement lightened by thematic transformation that can take you in an instant into infectious waltz-time. The elegiac slow movement and jolly and spiky Scherzo lead to a broad, noble finale in the major key. Bamert again proves a masterly interpreter, bringing out the warmth and thrust of the writing. The sound is rich and full to match the outstanding playing.

Symphony 5; Elegy for Brahms; From Death to Life
*** Chan. 8955. LPO, Bamert

The *Fifth* and last of Parry's symphonies is in four linked movements, terser in argument than the previous two, and often tougher, though still with Brahmsian echoes. After the minor-key rigours of the first movement, *Stress*, the other three movements are comparably subtitled *Love*, *Play* and *Now*, with the Scherzo bringing echoes of Berlioz and the optimistic finale opening with a Wagnerian horn-call. The *Elegy for Brahms* conveys grief, but its vigour rises above passive mourning into an expression of what might almost be anger. *From Death to Life* consists of two connected movements, exuberantly melodic, with a theme in the second which echoes Sibelius's *Karelia*. It would be hard to imagine finer, more committed performances than those on Chandos, or richer sound.

Cello Sonata in A
(M) *** Dutton CDLX 7102. Fuller, Dussek – HARTY: *Butterflies; Romance & Scherzo, Op. 8; Wood-Stillness;* HURLSTONE: *Cello Sonata in D* ***

Parry's *Cello Sonata* is finely wrought, though it does not wear its debt to Brahms lightly – understandably, perhaps, since it is a fairly early piece dating from 1879. It is designed on an almost symphonic scale – particularly the sinewy *Allegro* first movement. A splendid performance and recording.

Nonet in B flat
(BB) *** Hyp. Helios CDH 55061. Capricorn – STANFORD: *Serenade (Nonet)* ***

Parry's *Nonet* is for flute, oboe, cor anglais and two each of clarinets, bassoons and horns. Although the finale is perhaps a little lightweight, it is a delight from beginning to end. If one did not know what it was, one would think of early Strauss, for it is music of enormous accomplishment and culture as well as freshness. An excellent performance and recording, the more attractive at bargain price.

(i) Piano Quartet in A flat; Piano Trio 1 in E min.
**(*) Mer. CDE 84248. Deakin Piano Trio; (i) with Inoue

The *E minor Piano Trio* is both shorter and more direct than the *Piano Quartet*, which is more ambitious, with a darkly meditative slow introduction echoing late Beethoven. Though the performance on the disc is not as polished as one would like, Parry's melodic writing is more than distinctive enough to rebut the charge of mere imitation, with such a movement as the dashing tarantella-like Scherzo of the *Piano Quartet* very effective indeed. The recording balances the piano rather behind the rest, which is a pity when Catherine Dubois so often takes the lead.

Piano Trios 2 in B min.; 3 in G
*** Mer. CDE 84255. Deakin Piano Trio

In the two *Piano Trios* the English element in Parry's invention is more clearly identifiable, with some themes bringing anticipations of Elgar. Equally, the healthy outdoor feel of the triple-time main themes of the finales of both trios has a hint of English folk music. Both works are richly enjoyable, with the warm, open lyricism of the slow movement of No. 2 particularly attractive. The players of the Deakin Piano Trio seem more happily adjusted to the rigours of recording than in the first volume, with rather better matching and intonation.

Violin Sonata in D, Op. 103; Fantaisie-sonata in B, Op. 75; 12 Short Pieces
*** Hyp. CDA 66157. Gruenberg, Vignoles

The *Fantaisie-sonata* provides a fascinating example of cyclic sonata form, earlier than most but also echoing Schumann. The three-movement *Sonata in D* is another compact, meaty piece, the strongest work on the disc. The *Twelve Short Pieces*, less demanding technically, are delightful miniatures. Gruenberg and Vignoles prove persuasive advocates, and the recording is first rate.

PIANO MUSIC

Hands Across the Centuries (suite); *10 Shulbrede Tunes; Theme & 19 Variations in D min.*
*** Priory PRCD 451. Jacobs

Shulbrede Priory was the remains of a substantial twelfth-century Augustinian settlement, turned into a country house, where the composer's married daughter lived with her family. Parry was captivated by its charm and atmosphere and he published a set of ten delightful miniatures which showed this affection and the strong spell the house wielded over him. The mock-baroque *Hands Across the Centuries* is hardly less diverting, and its invention equally varied. The more ambitious *Theme and Variations* is rather prolix but is very well organized. Peter Jacobs, obviously enjoying himself, plays all this music with flair and there is never a dull bar here. Excellent natural recording, too.

ORGAN MUSIC

Chorale Fantasies on: 'When I survey the wondrous cross'; The Old Hundredth; 7 Chorale Preludes, Sets I & II; Elégie; Elegy; Fantasia & Fugue in G (2 versions); *Toccata & Fugue (The Wanderer). A Little Organ Book in Memory of Sir Hubert Parry*
(N) **(*) Priory PRCD 682 AB (2). Lancelot (organ of Durham Cathedral)

Although Parry is not now remembered for his organ music, he was fascinated by the instrument. Like Bach, he loved to try out every organ he came into contact with, and he had a fine knowledge of their strengths and weaknesses. His two versions of the *G major Fantasia and Fugue*, which frame the programme here, demonstrate the confident, traditional style of his writing. But it is his familiarity with different organ specifications and the possible contrasting of registrations that make his two sets of *Chorale Preludes* so attractive, as they make full use of the changing colours and contrasting registrations. A simple piece like *Melcome* is treated as a guileless pastoral, and, in the second set, *St Mary*, the engaging *Eventide* and the piquant *St Cross* are all aurally diverting. Equally, the swirls of decoration around *Hanover* make for a fine display piece, with the cantus firmus always clear. The spectacular *Toccata and Fugue* (*The Wanderer* – the composer's yacht, stirringly seaborne) also offers plentiful opportunities for bravura, as do the opening and closing sections of his *Fantasia on the Old Hundredth*, where Parry really lets himself go. But it is in the more lyrical central sections that he makes full use of the organ's palette; the most admired work here, the *Fantasia on 'When I survey the wondrous cross'*, deeply expressive, was highly praised by Gerald Finzi. For the Appendix, James Lancelot has added an engaging series of miniatures written in the composer's memory, and often in his gentle style. A *Chorale Prelude* by Stanford, Brewer's charming *Carillon*, and pieces by Frank Bridge, Harold Darke and Charles Wood are all melodically striking, but Walford Davies's *Jesus dulcis memoria* caps them all as a quite perfect closing memento. James Lancelot is thoroughly at home in all this repertoire and plays with flair and understanding. The organ of Durham Cathedral seems well chosen, although, as with many English cathedrals, the resonance prevents absolute internal clarity in the recording.

VOCAL MUSIC

Blest Pair of Sirens; I Was Glad (anthems)
*** Chan. 8641/2. L. Symphony Ch. & LSO, Hickox – ELGAR: *Dream of Gerontius* ***

Parry's two finest and most popular anthems make an attractive coupling for Hickox's fine, sympathetic reading of Elgar's *Dream of Gerontius*. The chorus for Parry is rather thinner than in the main work but is very well recorded.

(i) *Blest Pair of Sirens; I Was Glad; Judith: Long Since in Egypt's Plenteous Land; Jerusalem;* (ii) *Songs of Farewell: My Soul, There is a Country.* (iii) **English Lyrics:** *And Yet I Love Her; Blow, Blow, thou Winter Wind; Bright Star; From a City Window; Looking Backward; Love is a Babel; Marion; No Longer Mourn for Me; O Mistress Mine; On a Time the Amorous Silvy; Take, O Take those Lips Away; There; There Be None of Beauty's Daughters; Thine Eyes Still Shine for Me; Weep You no More; A Welsh Lullaby; When Comes my Gwen; When Icicles Hang by the Wall; When Lovers Meet Again; When We Two Parted*
(M) **(*) Decca (ADD/DDD) 470378-2. (i) Winchester Cathedral Ch., Waynflete Singers, Bournemouth SO, Hill; (ii) Canterbury Cathedral Ch., Wicks; (iii) Tear, Ledger

The bulk of this CD is drawn from Robert Tear's 1979 (Argo) LP of Parry songs. The music is of fine quality, showing judicious use of texts, all distinctively set, and offering variety of mood, from the jaunty *Love is a Babel*, to the haunting, even a touch unnerving, *From a City Window*. Tear is on good form; if very occasionally he seems just a bit too stylized, his diction is superb, and the accompaniments are excellent, though the piano timbre is not as rich and full as the voice. The splendid David Hill performances of the popular anthems provide strong contrast to the songs and are strikingly full and resonant in sound. *I was Glad*, in Gordon Jacob's colourful orchestration, is almost overwhelming at its final climax. Elgar's orchestration of *Jerusalem*, with its sweeping strings after the words 'arrow of desire' is thrilling. Another excellent mid-price CD in Decca's 'British Collection', and although no texts are provided, you barely need them when Tear's diction is so clear.

Evening Service in D (Great): Magnificat; Nunc Dimittis. Hear My Words, ye People; I Was Glad when They Said Unto Me; Jerusalem; Songs of Farewell
*** Hyp. CDA 66273. St George's Chapel, Windsor, Ch., Robinson; Judd (organ)

Everyone knows *Jerusalem*, which highlights this collection resplendently. In the *Songs of Farewell* trebles are used and the effect is less robust than in Marlow's version, but undoubtedly very affecting. Perhaps the stirring coronation anthem, *I Was Glad*, needs the greater weight of an adult choir, but it is still telling here. The excerpts from the *Great Service in D* are well worth having on record, as is the anthem, *Hear My Words, ye People*. Excellent recording, the chapel ambience colouring the music without blunting the words.

I was glad (from *Psalm 122*)

(M) *** EMI (ADD) 5 85148-2. Cambrige University Music Society, King's College, Cambridge, Ch., New Philh. O, Ledger – ELGAR: *Coronation Ode* etc. ***

This expansive version of Parry's most popular church anthem makes an excellent coupling for Elgar's patriotic ceremonial music. Splendid recording too.

Job (oratorio)

**(*) Hyp. CDA 67025. Coleman-Wright, Spence, Davies, Hitchcock, Guildford Choral Soc., RPO, Davan Wetton

Though Parry, as a Victorian, sidesteps the problem of conveying the pain and bitterness in the story of Job, this is a warm, beautifully written oratorio which is most welcome on disc, very English and optimistic. It would be even better, had Hilary Davan Wetton drawn a more biting response from the chorus and had Peter Coleman-Wright in the title role, clear and direct as he is, sounded less respectful. The other soloists are first-rate, notably Toby Spence in the tenor part of Satan, and the recording is warm and atmospheric, though with the chorus rather backwardly placed. For all its limitations a highly enjoyable curiosity.

The Soul's Ransom (Sinfonia sacra); The Lotos Eaters

*** Chan. 8990. Jones, Wilson-Johnson, LPO & Ch., Bamert

Using a biblical text *The Soul's Ransom*, with its sequence of solos and choruses, forms a broadly symphonic four-movement structure with references back not only to Brahms and the nineteenth century but to much earlier choral composers, notably Schütz. This 45-minute piece is generously coupled with *The Lotos Eaters*, a setting for soprano, chorus and orchestra of eight stanzas from Tennyson's choric song of that name, with Della Jones again the characterful soloist. Full and atmospheric recording to match the incandescent performances.

PÄRT, Arvo (born 1935)

(i) *Arbos* (2 performances); (ii) *Pari Intervallo;* (iii) *An den Wassern zu Babel; De Profundis;* (iv; v) *Es sang vor langen Jahren;* (iii) *Summa;* (iii; v; vi) *Stabat Mater*

*** ECM 831 959-2. (i) Brass Ens., Stuttgart State O, Davies; (ii) Bowers-Broadbent; (iii) Hilliard Ens., Hillier; (iv) Bickley; (v) Kremer, Mendelssohn; (vi) Demenga

All the music recorded here gives a good picture of Pärt's musical make-up with all its strengths and limitations. *Arbos*, which is heard in two different versions, 'seeks to create the image of a tree or family tree'. It does not modulate and has no development, though pitch and tempi are in proportional relationships. The *Stabat Mater* (1985) for soprano, counter-tenor, tenor and string trio is distinguished by extreme simplicity of utterance and is almost totally static. This music relies for its effect on minimal means and invites one to succumb to a kind of mystical, hypnotic repetition rather than a musical argument. The artists performing here do so with total commitment and are excellently recorded.

(i) *Cantus in Memory of Benjamin Britten* (for string orchestra and bell); *Festina lente* (for string orchestra & harp); (ii) *Fratres* (Version VI for strings & percussion; (i) *Summa* (for strings); (i; iii) *Tabula rasa: Silentium.* (iv; v)

The Beatitudes; (vi) *Cantata Domino; De profundis;* (v) *Magnificat;* (vi) *7 Magnificat Antiphons; Memento; Missa syllabica; Solfeggio; Statuit ei Dominus*

(N) (BB) *** Virgin 2x1 5 61434-2. (i) Bournemouth Sinf., Studt; (ii) LPO, Welser-Möst; (iii) Little, Studt, Roscoe; (iv) Johnston; (v) King's College, Cambridge, Ch., Cleobury; (vi) Estonian Philh. Chamber Ch., Kaljuste

Although a few of the items here are included in the Classics for Pleasure collection below, this Virgin Double now seems first choice for a compilation of the music of Arvo Pärt, instrumental as well as vocal, and excellent performances all of them. The second disc is given over entirely to vocal music which the Estonian Philharmonic Chamber Choir sings very beautifully within an ideally atmospheric acoustic. The seven *Magnificat Antiphons* are all brief yet remarkably contrasted, and the programme ends with a particularly haunting sequence of works, the solemn *De Profundis*, followed by the radiant *Memento*, the engaging *Cantata Domino* and finally the echoing, overlapping *Solfeggio* which returns the music gently to silence.

(i) *Cantus in memory of Benjamin Britten;* (ii) *Festina lente;* (i) *Fratres* (for string orchestra & percussion); *Summa* (for string orchestra) (iii) *Fratres; Spiegel im Spiegel* (both for violin & piano); (iv) *The Beatitudes for Choir & Organ; Magnificat;* (iv) *7 Magnificat Antiphons; Summa*

(B) *** CfP 585 9142. (i) Estonian Nat. SO, Järvi; (ii) Bournemouth Sinf., Studt; (iii) Little, Roscoe; (iv) King's College, Cambridge, Ch., Cleobury; (v) Varsai Singers, Backhouse

An admirable and enterprising compilation from Classics for Pleasure, gathered from a number of sources to tempt those who have not sampled this Estonian composer's highly individual sound-world with its tintinabulation (ringing bells). In the two works for violin and piano, Tasmin Little holds the listener's attention by the intensity of her commitment and the powerful projection of her playing. *Summa* is heard in two versions, the choral one being a fresh and carol-like setting of the Creed, and this leads naturally into the brief but concentrated *Magnificat Antiphons*, with the Seventh the longest and most telling. Pärt's comparatively static *Magnificat* relies on intensity of sonority rather than movement; his better-known *Beatitudes*, gentle and rippling, is regularly pierced by dissonance, with the organ entering briefly and unexpectedly at the end to add a florid postlude and then disappear into infinity. Fine, idiomatic performances throughout and excellent recording.

Cantus in memoriam Benjamin Britten; Festina lente; Fratres (6 versions)

☛ *** Telarc CD 80387. Manning, Springuel, Gleizes, I Fiamminghi, Werthen

(N) (BB) *** Naxos 8.1553950 Hungarian State Op. O, Benedek (without *Festina lente*)

For all the repetitions involved in Pärt's minimalist progressions there are no more hypnotic examples of his curiously compelling, ritualistic writing than this sequence of six settings of a very simple monastic chorale which he calls *Fratres*. We hear it first slowly swelling up from a *piano-pianissimo* on strings, with unobtrusive decorative percussion, then sinking away again. Then follow variants featuring first a solo violin, then for a carefully blended wind octet, for eight cellos used in their higher register, then returning to a string group and quickening to achieve the flavour of an elegant baroque dance, further adapted to the more economical texture of a string quartet, and finally rustling on the cello with the piano tolling a bell-like accompaniment until a closing climax builds and abates. The Britten tribute and *Festina lente for Strings and Harp ad libitum* are used as interludes. The playing here has great atmosphere and concentration, while Telarc's glowing sound adds to the sensuous physical beauty.

However the Naxos Hungarian performance is also very fine, splendidly played and richly recorded. *Festina lente* is omitted; instead the *Cantus* is used as a powerful apotheosis to end the disc with a thrilling climax.

(i) *Fratres*; (ii) *Magnificat; 7 Magnificat Antiphons*
*** Sony SK 61753. (i) Welsh, Blayden, Stirling; Tavener Ch., Parrott – TAVENER: *Canticle*, etc. ***

It may be considered an advantage or a disadvantage in that in coupling the hypnotic and often static music of Pärt and Tavener, the ear is drawn to the similarity of the style of the two composers. *Fratres*, which exists in many versions, is heard here in its comparatively spare instrumental scoring to make a centrepiece in what is essentially a choral programme. The simplicity of the *Magnificat* setting is its prime virtue, but the *Antiphons* are more varied, although still very compelling when so beautifully sung and recorded.

Fratres; Summa (string quartet versions)
*** Virgin 5 45023-2. Chilingirian Qt – TAVENER: *Last Sleep of the Virgin*, etc. ***

Like the Tavener works with which they are generously coupled on this 74-minute CD, these are both atmospheric works with a liturgical basis, using sparse basic material, which try to convey a sense of eternity. The performances here, obviously felt, make an interesting comparison with the alternative versions discussed above. But it must be admitted that, as music, they are less potent than the Tavener pieces.

CHORAL MUSIC

And One of the Pharisees; (i) *The Beatitudes; Cantate Domino (Psalm 95); (ii) De Profundis (Psalm 129); Magnificat; 7 Magnificat Antiphons; (i) Missa Sillabica; Solfeggio; Summa (Credo)*
*** HM HMU 907182. Theatre of Voices, Hillier; (i) with Bowers-Broadbent (organ); Kennedy (percussion)

The cover of this CD indicates that it includes just *De Profundis*, whereas this 76-minute collection covers a very wide range of Pärt's choral output, from the short *Solfeggio* of 1964, which seems to float in space, to *The Beatitudes* (1990) of which this is the recording première. This work opens in stillness and calm but, as so often with this composer, leads on to a great climax, here over an organ pedal; then, after an exultant 'Amen', the organ has a brief but prolix postlude. *De Profundis* (1980) brings a similarly elliptical structure, based on a simple climbing phrase in the bass; it again uses an organ pedal to underpin the climax. The *Missa Sillabica* (1977), heard here in a slightly revised version, is a fine example of Pärt's use of the simplest means to communicate his expression of the liturgical text, the repetitions within the 'Credo' a characteristic example. *And One of the Pharisees* is a setting for three voices of a text from Chapter 7 of St Luke's Gospel and its powerful medieval atmosphere, including solo chants, reminds us of the link which Pärt's litugical music has

with the distant past. The performances here could hardly be more powerful or atmospheric, yet they are firmly controlled. They are magnificently recorded.

St John Passion
*** (BB) Naxos 8.555860. Macdonald, Anderson, Tonus Peregrinus, Pitts

*** ECM 837 109-2. George, Potter, Hilliard Ens., Western Wind Chamber Ch. (Instrumental group), Hillier

Since it appeared in the late 1980s, the spare ritual of Arvo Pärt's setting of the *Passion According to St John* has established itself far more widely than could ever have been predicted, reflecting the hypnotic quality of this characteristic example of spiritual minimalism in music. Such a recommendable super-budget version as this is very welcome. Antony Pitts draws a magnetic performance from his newly founded choir, Tonus Peregrinus, and the soloists taking the roles of Christ and Pilate, and they are atmospherically recorded in bright, clear sound. It helps to sustain tension that the performance at just over an hour is some ten minutes shorter than its previous rival though that too is a dedicated performance, impeccably recorded.

PENDERECKI, Kryszstof (born 1933)

(i) *Anaklasis*; (ii; iii) *Capriccio for Violin & Orchestra*; (iii; iv) *Cello Concerto*; (iii) *De natura sonoris I & II; The Dream of Jacob; Emanationen for 2 String Orchestras; Fonogrammi*; (iii; v) *Partita for Harpsichord & Orchestra*; (iii) *Threnody for the Victims of Hiroshima*; (i) *Symphony*; (vi) *Canticum canticorum Salomonis*
*** (B) *** EMI double forte (ADD) 5 74302-2 (2). (i) LSO; (ii) Wilkomirska; (iii) Polish Nat. RSO; (iv) Palm; (v) Blumenthal; (vi) Kraków Phil. Ch.; all cond. Composer

For those who admire such athematic music, this inexpensive anthology, in authoritative performances under the composer's own direction, makes a splendid introduction to Penderecki's music.

Anaklasis is an inventive piece for strings and percussion and *De natura sonoris* is also brilliant in its use of contrasts. Wilkomirska proves a superb soloist in the *Capriccio* and so does Palm in the *Cello Concerto*. The beautiful and touching *Threnody* for 53 strings is the composer's best-known piece, and it is here given a magnificent performance. *The Dream of Jacob* of 1974 is as inventive as the rest, but sparer and more cogent.

Penderecki's music relies for its appeal on its resourceful use of sonorities and his sound world is undoubtedly imaginative, albeit limited. The choral work is a setting of a text from the *Song of Solomon* for large orchestra and sixteen solo voices. But the *Symphony* is the most ambitious work here. It was commissioned by a British engineering firm and first performed in Peterborough Cathedral. That setting influences the range of sumptuous orchestral colours devised by the composer, though you could argue that this work is a series of brilliant orchestral effects rather than a symphonic argument. However, with such a committed performance, it is certainly memorable. The 1970s recordings are excellent, and this EMI double forte is an undoubted bargain.

CHORAL MUSIC

Benedictus; Benedicamus Domine; Magnificat: Sidcut locutus est. Polish Requiem: Agnus Dei. Saint Luke's Passion: Stabat Mater; In pulverem mortis; Miserere. Veni creator; Song of Cherubim

⊶ (BB) *** Warner Apex 8573 88433-2. Tapiola Chamber Ch., Kulvanen

This superbly sung collection inexpensively monitors Penderecki's changing style of vocal writing beginning with the excerpts from the *St Luke's Passion* (1962) for three mixed choruses, using dramatic spoken utterance as well as powerfully sustained block choral sonorities. The *Sicut locutus est* from the *Magnificat* (1974) works in a similar way. Then with the lovely, plaintive *Agnus Dei* (for eight-part mixed chorus) of 1981 there is much more movement, and a surge of romantic feeling, with a dissonant climax of real angst. The new, freer romantic style reaches its peak in the powerful and often seraphic *Song of Cherubim* (1986) with its gentle closing Alleluias, the finest work here. But the remarkable setting of *Veni creator* (1987) returns to the spoken murmurings and interjections, while climaxing with a passionate affirmation, before the ethereality of the closing Amen. By 1992 the *Benedictus Domine* for five-part male choir is looking back to organum, and the closing *Benedictus*, based on the text of the medieval *Sanctus* trope is linked to liturgical chant, yet romanticized and brought into our own time. The Tapiola Choir sings passionately, with fine blending and a bright firm line in an atmospheric but never blurring acoustic. With texts and translations included, this is a real bargain.

PERGOLESI, Giovanni (1710–36)

Confitebor tibi Domine

✪ (M) *** DHM/BMG 82876 60145-2. Monoyios, Landauer, Balthazar-Neumann Ch., Freiburg Bar. O, Hengelbrock – DURANTE: *Magnificat in B flat*; D'ASTORGA: *Stabat Mater* *** ✪

Pergolesi's little-known setting of Psalm 110 immediately arrests the attention with its richly eloquent choral opening, but later it depends upon the solo soprano, who has a dialogue with the chorus in the *Confessio*, and the solo alto, whose *Sanctum et terrible* and *Intellectus bonus* create the work's expressive climax. Both Ann Monoyios and Bernhard Landauer rise to the occasion here, as does the chorus in the closing *Gloria Patri* and *Sicut erat*. The excellent period-instrument Freiburg Baroque Orchestra are notable for their characterful contribution to the *Sanctum*. In short, this performance, directed with life and spirit by Thomas Hengelbrock, is first class in every way, and so is the recording. Highly recommended.

(i) *Magnificat in C*; (ii) *Stabat Mater*

(B) **(*) Double Decca 443 868-2 (2). (i) Vaughan, J. Baker, Partridge, Keyte, King's College Ch., ASMF, Willcocks; (ii) Palmer, Hodgson, St John's College, Cambridge, Ch., Argo CO, Guest – BONONCINI: *Stabat Mater*; D. SCARLATTI: *Stabat Mater*; A. SCARLATTI: *Domine, refugium factus es nobis; O magnum mysterium*; CALDARA: *Crucifixus*; LOTTI: *Crucifixus* ***

This well-planned Double Decca collection centres on three different settings of the *Stabat Mater dolorosa*. Pergolesi's version dates from 1735 and, subsequently, settings were made

by many other composers, including Vivaldi and Haydn. Pergolesi conceived a work which has secular and even theatrical overtones, and its devotional nature is unexaggerated. George Guest directs a sensible, unaffected performance, simple and expressive, with relaxed tempi, not overladen with romantic sentiment. The *Magnificat* – doubtfully attributed, like so much that goes under this composer's name – is a comparatively lightweight piece, notable for its rhythmic vitality. The King's College Choir under Willcocks gives a sensitive and vital performance, and the recording matches it in intensity of atmosphere.

Stabat Mater

(N) *** EMI **DVD** 5 99404 9. Frittoli, Antonacci, Filharmonica della Scala, Muti (DVD Producer: Carlo Assalini)

⊶ (N) (B) ✪ *** Opus III 30406. Bertagnolli, Mingardo, Concerto Italiano, Alessandrini – A. SCARLATTI: *Stabat Mater* ***

*** DG 415 103-2. Marshall, Terrani, LSO, Abbado

(N) (B) *(**) HM Musique d'abord HMA 195119. Hennig, Jacobs, Concerto Vocale

(B) (**) Dutton 2CDAX 2005 (3). Taylor, Ferrier, Oriana Ch., Henderson – BACH: *St Matthew Passion* (**(*))

(i; ii) *Stabat Mater*; (ii) *In coelestibus regnis*; (i) *Salve Regina in A*

*** Hyp. CDA 66294. (i) Fisher; (ii) Chance; King's Consort, King

(i; ii) *Stabat Mater*; (ii) *Salve Regina in A min.*; (i) *Salve Regina in F min.*

*** Decca 466 134-2. Scholl, Bonney, Les Talens Lyriques, Rousset

Recorded and filmed in the beautiful surroundings of the Santuario della Beata Vergine del Miracoli in Saronno, Muti's dedicated performance matches his equally fine account of Haydn's *Last Words*. He has two first-class soloists in Barbara Frittoli and Anna Caterina Antonacci, who make a fine team, both in their expressive vocal interchanges and in matching their vibratos. Muti's tempi are spacious, and the use of modern instruments and the resonant acoustic ensure a warm and beautiful sound from the comparatively modest-sized orchestral group, while the soloists are clearly focused and well balanced in relation to the overall visual imagery. This moving performance is greatly enhanced by the back-cloth of the beautiful cupola frescoes of Gaudenzio Ferrari, on which the camera frequently dwells with poignant effect to illustrate the crucifixion, and the poignant image of Mary standing at the foot of the Cross.

Subtitles are available if required, and there is also an option to follow the score, with the visual images forming a shadowy backcloth. Bonuses include a long and intellectual exposition of the historical development of Italian music by Muti which not many collectors will want to hear more than once, and a whimsical commentary, 'Pergolesi and his Double', confirming that a great deal of music attributed to Pergolesi was written by others hoping to take advantage of his reputation. But the *Stabat Mater* is authentic and is splendidly performed here.

Both the soprano, Gemma Bertagnolli, and the contralto, Sara Mingardo (with her remarkably resonant lower register) have extraordinarily colourful voices, which blend beautifully at the work's sustained opening, but which only display their full richness in their solos, notably *Cujus animam gementem* and *Fac ut portem Christi mortem*. This is a totally Italianate performance of both high drama and moving pathos. The closing *Quando corpus morietur*, in which both singers join in sustained legato, is very moving indeed, followed by a passionately final affirmation of faith. Alessandrini's instrumental support could not be more telling and the recording is made in an ideal acoustic.

Abbado's account brings greater intensity and ardour to this piece than almost any rival, and he secures marvellously alive playing from the LSO – this without diminishing religious sentiment. The DG recording has warmth and good presence and the perspective is thoroughly acceptable. But there is no coupling.

The combination of Andreas Scholl's alto and Barbara Bonney's soprano makes a well-matched and certainly individual tonal blend and they often sing exquisitely, both solo and in tandem. Their *Stabat Mater* has plenty of drama as well as a fine expressive intensity and the closing *Quando corpus* is movingly restrained and beautiful. Both settings of the *Salve Regina* are authentic: Andreas Scholl sings the *A minor*, Barbara Bonney the *F minor*. Throughout, Christophe Rousset's period-instrument accompaniments are outstandingly fine and full of life, and the Decca recording is splendidly real. But this version of the *Stabat Mater* needs to be sampled before purchase: you may be captivated by it or not. Our vote still goes to the Bertagnolli/Mingardo account mentioned above.

The Hyperion recording also makes a very good case for authenticity in this work. The combination of soprano and male alto blends well together yet offers considerable variety of colour. Gillian Fisher's *Salve Regina* is quite a considerable piece in four sections, whereas Michael Chance's motet is brief but makes an engaging postlude. Excellent sound.

Sebastian Hennig is advisedly described in the Musique d'abord documentation as a soprano (*garçon*), for his piping timbre is fuller in tone than that of the customary boy treble; it also blends remarkably well with René Jacobs's countertenor, whose two alto solos are among the highlights of the performance. The result aims primarily at simplicity and, for the most part, serenity, and one which is more French in feeling than Italianate. In its way it is impressive and certainly does not lack inner feeling, while the Concerto Vocale provide a stylishly authentic accompaniment. But in essence this is a specialized approach which is not as moving as its finest competitors; moreover, the disc, though on a bargain label, offers no coupling.

The 1946 Decca recording of the *Stabat Mater* (in its Dutton transfer) makes a welcome fill-up to the Bach *St Matthew Passion*, thanks to the contribution of Kathleen Ferrier. The rest is less distinguished, with Joan Taylor a fluttery soprano soloist.

PEROTINUS, Magister (*c.* 1160–1225)

Organa: *Alleluya, Nativitas; Sederunt principes*
*** Lyrichord (ADD) LEMS 8002. Oberlin, Bressler, Perry, Barab – LEONIN: *Organa* ***

Perotinus extended the simple polyphony of Leonin from two to three and four parts, and the ear is very aware of the intervals which characterize the organum: unison, octave, fourths and fifths. This music is more florid, freer than the coupled works written several decades before. The performances here are totally compelling and the recording excellent.

PETERSON-BERGER, Wilhelm (1867–1942)

Symphony 1 in B flat (The Banner); Last Summer (suite)
*** CPO 999 561-2. Saarbrücken RSO, Jurowski

The Swedish composer Wilhelm Peterson-Berger is essentially a miniaturist, a watercolourist, whose ideas are not ideally suited to the symphonic canvas. His *First Symphony* (*Banéret* or *The Banner*) is heavily indebted to Grieg and Wagner, and has some appealing moments. As a symphony it is pretty flimsy in structure. In the quieter, pastoral moments the scoring is fresh but elsewhere it is far from expert. The suite, *Last Summer*, is the better piece. Both receive sympathetic and persuasive performances, and excellent recording.

Symphony 3 (Lapland); The Doomsday Prophets: Chorale & Fugue; Earina Suite
*(**) CPO 999 632-2. Norrköping SO, Jurowski

In the *Third Symphony* the ideas are still pretty thin but Peterson-Berger scores with some skill. His is a modest talent whose strengths lie in his songs and piano pieces, which are permeated by Swedish folk music and Grieg-like harmonies. The Norrköping Orchestra and Mikhail Jurowski give a very good account of themselves. One star only for the music but three for the performers.

Flowers from Frösö: Book I, Op. 16; Book II; Book III (Humoresques & Idylls for Piano)
*** BIS CD 925. Ogawa
(BB) *** Naxos 8.554343. Sivelöv

Frösölomster is variously described on these discs as *Frösöflowers* and *Flowers from Frösö Island* but they are the same pieces, and these miniatures, though not earth-shattering in any way, have a pallor and charm that is all their own. Norika Ogawa plays them with charm, grace and much sensitivity – and the BIS recording is exemplary.

Niklas Sivelöv is hardly less successful in conveying the fineness of these pieces. There is a Grieg-like salon quality about them redeemed by a certain freshness, and Sivelöv plays with style and elegance, He is recorded in St George's, Brandon Hill, Bristol and the sound is excellent. Price apart, there is nothing to choose between his set and Norika Ogawa on sonic or artistic grounds.

PETRASSI, Goffredo (1904–2003)

Concerti for Orchestra (i) 1 & 2; (ii) 3 (Récréation concertante); 4 for Strings; (iii) 5 & 6 (Invenzione concertato); (i) 7 & 8
(M) **(*) Warner Fonit 8573 83274-2. (i) BBC SO; (ii) Philh. Hungarica; (iii) SO di Milano della RAI, Peskó

Petrassi is scantily represented on disc, and this is the only version of his eight *Concertos for Orchestra*. The *Primo Concerto* comes from 1934 and was the only one of the eight to have been recorded before on a mono Decca LP (by Fernando Previtali and the Orchestra of the Accademia di Santa Cecilia in Rome, of which Petrassi was long director). The influences are neo-classical, namely Casella, Hindemith and Stravinsky, and it is a work that wears well, particularly its strongly atmospheric slow movement. The *Secondo Concerto* (1951) and the *Récréation concertante* (No. 3) (1952–3) continue the same line. They have a strong sense of forward movement and of musical purpose that impresses. In a way, they can be compared with the kind of writing favoured by Vagn Holmboe or Hilding Rosenberg further north. The *Quarto Concerto per orchestra d'archi* (1954) is closer to Bartók than its companions but again serious and purposeful – and also beautiful. The *Quinto Concerto* (1955), commissioned by the Boston Symphony Orchestra, is imaginative and thoughtful; its opening has its roots in Bartók but is suffused with Italian light. The *Sesto Concerto* (1956–7) (*Invenzione concertato*) was one of the works commissioned by the BBC to commemorate the foundation of the Third Programme (others were Tippett's *Second Symphony* and Holmboe's *Epitaph for Orchestra*); it is eventful and holds the listener. The *Settimo Concerto* (1964) and *Ottavo Concerto* (1972), the latter written for the Chicago Symphony, are tougher nuts to crack but, like everything this composer has done, are worth taking trouble with.

The performances were all recorded in the 1970s, Nos. 1 and 8 in the BBC Maida Vale studios, 2 and 7 in the more ample acoustic of St Pancras Town Hall; the former have the more opaque string quality and less transparent orchestral detail. Nos. 3 and 4 were recorded in Hungary, and Nos. 5 and 6 in the Milan Conservatory in 1979. Two LPs were issued on the Fonit Cetra label but not released in the UK. This is an important and rewarding set that goes some way at least in redressing the neglect this composer has suffered in recent years. It would be good if we had new recordings of the pre-war *Partita* that put him on the map and the fine *Piano Concerto*, which Pietro Scarpini and Nino Sanzogno introduced to Britain in the late 1950s.

PETTERSSON, Allan (1911–80)

(i) *Viola Concerto. Symphony 5*
*** BIS CD 480. (i) Imai; Malmö SO, Atzmon

Allan Pettersson's *Fifth* is a one-movement work and begins well. However, invention flags and the brooding, expectant atmosphere and powerful ostinatos arouse more promise of development than fulfilment. The *Viola Concerto* comes from the last year of Pettersson's life and is pretty amorphous. Both pieces lack the concentration and quality of Tubin or Holmboe. The three stars are for the performers and the recording team.

Symphony 7
*** Caprice CAP 21411. Swedish RSO, Comissiona –
    MOZART: *Bassoon Concerto* ***

Symphonies 7; 11
*** BIS CD 580. Norrköping SO, Segerstam

Symphonies 7; (i) 16
**(*) Swedish Soc. (ADD) SCD 1002. Stockholm PO, Doráti;
    (i) Ahronovitch

To some extent the success of Allan Pettersson's *Seventh Symphony* in Sweden was a reaction against the unremitting diet of serial and post-serial music. It enjoyed something of a cult following in the 1970s. Here was a tonal work which sounded much more human than Blomdahl and had a certain cumulative effect for all its debt to Mahler. Doráti is a persuasive advocate and achieves a good performance from the fine Stockholm Orchestra. The *Sixteenth Symphony* is not among his best works, although Yuri Ahronovitch does his best with it.

The *Seventh Symphony* is a long, dark work which wears an anguished visage and packs a considerable emotional punch.

Its musical substance is less weighty than appears to be the case on first acquaintance, and the ideas seem static and thinly spread; but it has a strong emotional appeal for many music-lovers and its atmosphere is quite powerful. Sergiu Comissiona gives a dedicated and sensitive account of the score that is every bit as fine as Doráti's première recording. The rather bizarre coupling is unlikely to sway the collector one way or the other.

Segerstam and his fine Norrköping players bring great feeling to the *Seventh* and give the somewhat shorter *Eleventh Symphony* the most sympathetic advocacy. If you want to explore further, you could try the *Fifth Symphony*, but the BIS disc seems the best possible place to start.

Symphonies 8; 10
*** BIS CD 880. Norrköping SO, Segerstam

The *Eighth Symphony* is long, often static, at times powerful and at others totally wanting in any kind of symphonic coherence. The *Tenth* is shorter but, good though this performance is, it does not dispel the impression made by an earlier LP account that this work is still essentially empty: the music of gesture not substance, and deficient in thematic vitality. Those who are on Pettersson's wavelength need not have any hesitations about either the performances or recordings on this BIS CD.

Symphony 9
(B) *** CPO 999 231-2. Berlin RSO, Francis

Pettersson's *Ninth Symphony* (1970) was composed in the valley of the shadow of death. Life being short and sweet, one can only say that the 70 minutes which it takes to unfold seem an eternity. The three stars are for the performance and recording, so that admirers of the composer can proceed accordingly.

(i; ii) *7 Sonatas for 2 Violins;* **(i; iii)** *Andante espressivo; 2 Elegies; Romanza* (all for violin & piano); **(iii)** *Lamento* (for piano)
*** BIS CD 1028. Duo Gelland: (i) M. Gelland & (ii) C. Gelland; (iii) L. Wallin

Pettersson wrote the *Seven Sonatas for 2 Violins* in 1951, after years in the viola section of the Stockholm Philharmonic, at roughly the time when he was studying in Paris with René Leibowitz. The music is indebted to Bartók, who was a cult figure in Sweden during the 1950s, and to folk music. Although expertly conceived for this demanding medium, it is somewhat anonymous. The performances are exemplary, as is the splendid BIS recording.

PFITZNER, Hans (1869–1949)

String Quartets: in D, Op. 13; in C min., Op. 15
(B) *** CPO 999 072-2. Franz Schubert Qt

We think of Pfitzner primarily as a composer of opera and Lieder, but this first-class CPO string quartet coupling serves to show him as a composer of fine chamber music in the mainstream of the German romantic tradition. Altogether these are two thoroughly rewarding works, finely crafted, with a ready flow of appealing variations and subtly individual harmonic progressions. They are splendidly played by the richly blended Schubert Quartet, whose chording is immaculate and who respond to the bittersweet, *fin de siècle* flavour of the writing. Excellent, realistic recording.

OPERA

Der arme Heinrich (complete)
** Capriccio 60 087 (2). Schmittberg, Killmeier, Markovich, Dortmund Ch. & PO, Rumpf

Der arme Heinrich is the first of Pfitzner's five operas, and astonishingly accomplished it is, too. Its musical language is much indebted to *Tristan* and (perhaps more particularly) *Parsifal*. Its sound world and melodic ideas reek of Bayreuth, but there are a mastery of the orchestra and a restraint that are impressive for so young a composer. (Pfitzner was in his early twenties when he composed it.) Despite the heavy Wagnerian mantle, there are some individual and imaginative moments, particularly in the very opening. Taken overall, the opera is lacking in variety, and the invention does not sustain so large a canvas. It was recorded live at the Dortmund Opera House in February 2000, and the performance is *very* well conducted, though none of the soloists is really distinguished: indeed, Norbert Schmittberg as Heinrich shows signs of strain. The radio recording has a certain warmth and naturalness, though there is a want of transparency.

Palestrina (complete)
(M) *** DG (ADD) 427 417-2 (3). Gedda, Fischer-Dieskau, Weikl, Ridderbusch, Donath, Fassbaender, Prey, Tölz Boys' Ch., Bav. R. Ch. & SO, Kubelik

Though Pfitzner's melodic invention hardly matches that of his contemporary, Richard Strauss, his control of structure and drawing of character through music make an unforgettable impact. It is the central Act, a massive and colourful tableau representing the Council of Trent, which lets one witness the crucial discussion on the role of music in the church. The outer Acts – more personal and more immediately compelling – show the dilemma of Palestrina himself and the inspiration which led him to write the *Missa Papae Marcelli*, so resolving the crisis, both personal and public. At every point Pfitzner's response to this situation is illuminating, and this glorious performance with a near-ideal cast, consistent all through, could hardly be bettered in conveying the intensity of an admittedly offbeat inspiration. This CD reissue captures the glow of the Munich recording superbly and, though this is a mid-price set, DG has not skimped on the accompanying booklet.

PHILIPS, Peter (c. 1561–1628)

Peter Philips, alongside William Byrd, was one of the two great English-born Catholic musicians and composers of the late 16th and early 17th centuries. Yet while Byrd's life and music are familiar, as he was able to remain in England as a favourite of Queen Elizabeth I, we know much less about his contemporary, who, though London-born and a chorister at St Paul's Cathedral, was forced to leave England in the early 1580s because of his religious beliefs. He first went to the English College in Rome, during the time of Palestrina's fame, and then entered the household of another Catholic recusant, Lord Thomas Paget, and travelled with him in Europe, before marrying and settling in Antwerp. After a visit to Amsterdam to meet Sweelinck, on his return he was imprisoned on suspicion of complicity in plotting against the queen, but was eventually cleared and later released. For the final stage of his career he is found in the safer haven of Brussels as organist at the vice-regal chapel.

KEYBOARD MUSIC

Almande Tregian; Aria del Gran Duca (Variations); 5 Intabulations: *Bon jour mon coeur; Chi fara fed'al cielo; Fece da voi partita; Tirsi morir volea – Freno Tirsi il desio – Così morirò. Fantasia in G; Galliard; 1st Pavan (1580); Passamezzo Pavan & Galliard; Pavan & Galliard Paget; Pavan & Galliard Doloroso Tregian. Veni sancte spiritus*
⊶ (N) *** Hyp. CDA 66734. Nicholson (harpsichord or virginals)

Because of Philips's émigré status, little of his keyboard music found its way into permanent printed editions (on either side of the English Channel) until the publication of the English Virginal Book in the 1890s. But what attractive music it is – both cosmopolitan and with English roots – and full of character, as the *First Pavane*, which dates from the composer's early years at St Paul's, immediately shows. The *Pavan and Galliard Paget* is rather more dolorous and probably commemorates Philips's employer in Rome. Like the other pavanes and galliards, this is paired, using the same musical material throughout. But perhaps the most individual music here is the series of 'intabulations', a term probably unfamiliar to most readers. It indicates an elaborate transcription, usually of a vocal piece by another composer, and with added decorations. Among those included are *Chi fara* (a five-part madrigal by Alessandro Striggio), *Bon jour mon coeur*, using a four-part romantic chanson of Lassus, and, most remarkably, a three-section intabulation of a five-part madrigal by Marenzio. The normal variation form is also skilfully and winningly used in the *Aria del Gran Duca* (from a ballo by Emilio de Cavalieri). The performances here by Paul Nicholson are little short of superb; he manages all the decorative detail with great skill, never obscuring the basic musical lines, and his easy bravura is invigorating. He is superbly recorded too, and this is a most stimulating collection in every respect.

VOCAL MUSIC

Cantiones Sacrae Quinis Vocibus (Antwerp 1612): excerpts
(N) *** ASV Gaudeamus CDGAU 217. Sarum Consort, Mackay
⊶ (N) (BB) *** Naxos 8.555056. Tudor Consort, Walls

The *Cantiones Sacrae Quinis Vocibus* was Peter Philips's first important publication of sacred music in 1612, dedicated to the Virgin Mary for the 'confirmation and amplification of the Catholic, Apostolic and Roman Faith'. The texts are liturgical, devotional and full of passionate feeling. *O Crux splendidior, Salve Regina* and *Ave verum corpus* are serenely beautiful, but the settings can be lighter, at times almost madrigal-like in feeling (*Cantatibus organis*), which the Sarum Consort bring out very effectively. The sombre *Mulieres sedentes* draws a picture of the women sitting by the tomb, weeping, yet there is an underlying feeling of hope. *O Nomen Jesu* is a simple portrait, while *Christus resurgens* has all the joy of the celebration of the Resurrection. There is great variety here, and these splendidly sung performances confirm that this is wonderful music which should be much better known.

Very little is duplicated between the two discs (there are 69 motets in the total collection, all five-part settings), but the presentations are very different. The Sarum Consort is a group of five solo voices, but the acoustic of Milton Abbey richly expands their sound. The Tudor Consort, from Wellington, New Zealand, is a much larger choir and is very spaciously recorded in an ecclesiastical acoustic. While Peter Walls favours a more ardent approach, including accelerandos (as in *Alma Redemptoris Mater*), both groups sing with great feeling, and certainly there is no lack of intensity in Andrew Mackay's Gaudeamus performances. If you buy one of these CDs you will surely go on to buy the other.

PICHL, Václav (1741–1805)

Symphonies in D, Z16; C, Z21; G, Z22; B flat, Z23; E flat, Z24
*** Chan. 9740. LMP, Bamert

Czech composer Wenzel Pichl is another of those classical composers who suffered the fate of not being Haydn and Mozart, and whose music has been largely forgotten. His symphonies – he wrote just under 90! – are close in style to those of Dittersdorf and middle-period Haydn. They are engagingly melodic, with the *allegros* bustling with energy: the finale of the *E flat Symphony* zips along in a most enjoyable way, while the more dramatic first movement of the *C major Symphony*, with timpani, is certainly effective and one of the most listenable movements here. There is plenty of elegantly attractive writing, but it is the bubbling geniality of the *allegros* that one enjoys most. There is lively, stylish playing from Bamert and his London Mozart Players, in full and rich sound, characteristics found on all of Chandos's excellent 'Contemporaries of Mozart' series.

PICKARD, John (born 1963)

String Quartets, 2–4
(M) *** Dutton CDLX 7117. Sorrel Qt

These are warmly expressive works in a vigorous post-Bartókian idiom, played with passion by the Sorrel Quartet, to whom No. 4 is dedicated. No. 2, written in 1993, is a single, extended movement in three distinct sections, at once establishing Pickard's gift for exploiting weighty quartet textures, with a richly lyrical 'second subject' on the viola leading to the long central slow section, also warmly expressive, and on to an urgent final section. In No. 3, written in 1994, the energetic first movement starts abrasively with scrunching discords, followed by a middle movement marked *intensivo* and a finale, also predominantly slow, which maintains a meditative mood. No. 4 was written for the Sorrel Quartet in 1997–8, the vigorous, positive first movement is entitled *Sinfonia*, almost a symphonic allegro, leading to a middle movement which brings four concertante sections, one for each quartet instrument starting with the viola and ending with a scurrying gallop in which the first violin finally is allowed to lead the pack. The third movement, marked *Fantasia of Four Parts*, brings a conscious reflection of the great string fantasias of Gibbons and Purcell, with a deeply felt slow first half leading to a fast, sharply syncopated final section. The Sorrel Quartet bring out the powerful emotional thrust of this closely organized music to the full, almost as though they are composing it on the spot, and are superbly recorded.

PICKER, Tobias (born 1954)

(i) *Cello Concerto*; (ii) *And Suddenly It's Evening; Keys to the City*
*** Chan. 10039. (i) Watkins, (ii) Denk; Russian PO, Sanderling

Tobias Picker's most celebrated work, *Keys to the City*, the first item on this disc, won the competition to celebrate the centenary of Brooklyn Bridge in 1982. It takes the form of a piano concerto, his second, a journey from the dark key of B major to a final resolution on the 'key of light', B flat major, although tonality tends to be elusive in this single, kaleidoscopic movement. It is amiable music – Picker himself acknowledges a debt in spirit to Gershwin's *Rhapsody in Blue*, even though the idiom is very different – but one would welcome a big tune of the kind that keeps promising to emerge and never does. The *Cello Concerto* too is lyrical rather than dramatic in its outer movements, the last one a lament, without leaving much thematic material in the memory. Contrast is provided in the two scherzando central movements. *And Suddenly It's Evening*, commissioned by a group of leading youth orchestras, was inspired by a poem of Salvatore Quasimodo. Rhythmically complex, it makes no concessions to young players, and the challenge is well taken in this and the other two works by the Russian Philharmonic under Thomas Sanderling.

Thérèse Raquin (opera: complete)
*** Chan. 9659 (2). Soviero, Fulgoni, Gietz, Bernstein, Woods, Andrasy, Kazaras, Dallas Op. O, Jenkins

This is Tobias Picker's third opera, and he confidently compresses the story. The first Act in three scenes leads to the murder by drowning of Camille, Thérèse's husband, by her lover, Laurent, ending on an orchestral coda in which *Psycho*-style chopping sounds mark the dramatic moment. The second Act, picturing the rising guilt and bitter quarrels of Thérèse and Laurent, ends with the deaths of both; Thérèse stabbing herself, Laurent drinking the poison he had prepared for her. The eight brief scenes accelerate the gathering tensions of the story. Picker's style is broadly lyrical if often abrasive, with heightened passages to mark emotional climaxes, and with ensembles playing an important part in punctuating the drama, a device too often avoided by modern composers. The orchestral writing is colourful and positive, and Graeme Jenkins, music director of the Dallas Opera, formerly of Glyndebourne Touring Opera, draws warmly committed playing and singing from the whole company. Outstanding among the singers is the fine British mezzo Sara Fulgoni in the title role who, following the composer's wishes, inspires more sympathy for Thérèse as victim than the novel may have intended. One oddity is that Picker defies convention in his allocation of voices, with Laurent, Thérèse's lover, a bass baritone, and Camille, her husband, a tenor (Richard Bernstein and Gordon Gietz respectively, both with fresh, clear voices). The role of Camille's sinister mother, who after her stroke cannot reveal the truth to her friends, is also allotted not to a mezzo as one might expect, but to a soprano, the characterful Diana Soviero. The live recording is a composite of four performances in December 2001, the world première, with atmospheric sound. The trilingual booklet provides not just the libretto but helpful essays and an analysis with musical illustrations.

PIERNÉ, Gabriel (1863–1937)

Cello Sonata in F sharp min., Op. 46
*** Hyp. CDA 66979. Lidström, Forsberg – KOECHLIN: *Cello Sonata; etc.* ***

Pierné was an interesting and cultured composer. His sonata is finely wrought with touches of real individuality, and well worth getting to know. Mats Lidström and Bengt Forsberg play with great intelligence and refinement and are well served by the engineers.

PIGGOTT, Patrick (1915–90)

Fantasia quasi una Sonata (No. 1); Sonata 2; 8 Preludes and a Postlude (3rd Set)

(N) *** British Music Soc. BMS 430CD. Malcolm Binns

Born in Dover, Patrick Piggott developed first as a brilliant pianist, then as a composer, studying first at the London Royal Academy, then in Europe with Nadia Boulanger, Emile Bosquet and, back in England, with Julius Isserlis. The *Fantasia quasi una Sonata* is one of the few works from his earlier years that he acknowledged. Not surprisingly, for his complex individual musical language is firmly stamped upon it, though also with outside influences, English and French, perhaps not always fully absorbed. After the improvisatory feeling of the first movement, with its distinct harmonic idiom, and the brilliance of the second, the closing *De Profundis*, though still prolix, makes a powerful extended epilogue. The *Second Sonata* and *Third Set of Preludes* date from his later years; both were dedicated to Malcolm Binns. The *Preludes* unpredictably contrast fast and slow tempi (and sections) and, while the central *Presto Commodio* and following *Con Moto* both demand considerable bravura, the repose of the intervening sections makes for a satisfying emotional sequence; and the work ends with a dignified, contemplative *Postlude – In Tempo di Corteo*.

The mature *Second Sonata* sums up Piggott's musical language, with its complex, all but obsessive figurations and its ambiguity of mode. The argument of the first movement is structurally enigmatic; then comes a restless *Andante*, characteristically marked *Un poco agitato, improvisando*. The finale is a solemn *Sarabande*, in which the theme itself is decorated with four variations, including a Minuet and Scherzo, before the summing up: *Brioso (senza misura); Tempo Misurato*, and closing *L'istesso tempo*. This is all fascinating music by a highly individual musician and, though not easy to get to grips with, it undoubtedly blossoms with repeated listening. It is played persuasively and expertly by an artist who really understands its inherent ruminative intricacies, and very naturally recorded.

PINTO, George Frederick (1785–1806)

Fantasia & Sonata in C min. (completed Joseph Woelfl); Grand Sonatas 1 in E flat; 2 in A, Op. 3/1–2; in C min.; Minuetto in A flat; Rondo in E flat; Rondo on an Irish Air, 'Cory Owen'

*** Chan. 9798. O'Rorke (piano)

This unmissable Chandos collection reveals another forgotten composer of distinction, who might have become a very considerable figure had he not died prematurely at the age of twenty-one. He was born in London within a musical family and began playing in public at the age of eleven. His first two *Grand Sonatas* were published in 1801 when Pinto was sixteen and already a very accomplished composer indeed, with a distinct individuality, yet writing in a forward-looking lyrical style, that sometimes reminds us of the young Schubert. The *C minor Sonata*, however, is dedicated to John Field and delightfully identifies with that composer's melodic simplicity. But most striking of all is the *Fantasia and Sonata in C*

minor, left unfinished at the composer's death, the opening quite worthy of Mozart, with a following *Adagio–Fugato* which has all the serenity of Bach, followed by a Beethovenian finale, which yet still has a personality of its own. Míceál O'Rorke plays all this music very persuasively indeed and is beautifully recorded.

PISTON, Walter (1894–1976)

(i) *Capriccio for Harp & String Orchestra. 3 New England Sketches; Serenata; Symphony 4*

⊶ ⊛ **(BB)** *** Naxos 8.559162. Seattle SO, Schwarz, with (i) Wunrow

The *Fourth* is Piston's most radiant and appealing symphony, one of the masterpieces of American – and not only American – symphonic writing. This and the three *New England Sketches* are among the composer's strongest and most attractive scores, and they come here in outstanding performances under Gerald Schwarz, originally issued on the Delos label, and here made doubly attractive at super-bargain price. The four movements of the symphony are all strongly characterized, with the gentle *piacevole* opening of the first movement leading to tough counterpoint, strongly syncopated, and the second movement *Ballando* rather like a hoe-down, vigorous, open-air music, with the evocative slow movement leading to a jaggedly rhythmic finale. The *New England Sketches* are more specifically evocative, set in contrast like a symphony, with a delicate picture of a *Summer Evening* placed between the opening picture of the seaside and the final rugged picture of *Mountains*. Even so, the musical argument is cogent, and although the *Capriccio* is less tautly constructed, it has an element of fantasy beautifully realized here by the excellent harpist, Therese Elder Wunrow. First-rate sound.

Violin Concertos 1–2; Fantasia for Violin & Orchestra

⊶ ⊛ **(BB)** *** Naxos 8.559003. Boswell, Ukraine Nat. SO, Kuchar

It is quite extraordinary that a work as inspired as Piston's *First Violin Concerto* (1939) should not already be in the standard repertoire alongside the Barber, with which it has much in common, including a comparable profusion of individual, lyrical melody. The second subject of the first movement persists in the memory until, most engagingly, it is rhythmically transformed to become the secondary theme of the riotous Rondo finale. The *Second Concerto* is more elusive, but its opening is no less haunting. The first movement is a two-part structure, developing two ideas, one sinuously 'expressible', the other pungently rhythmic and angular. The extended *Adagio* introduces a calm and very beautiful theme which is later to form a canonic duet with the flute. The *Fantasia* is a late work, first performed in 1973. Ruminative and searching, its language is more dissonant. It may seem remarkable that these works should be given their CD début by a Ukrainian orchestra, but they play the music with security, splendid commitment and feeling. James Boswell, who studied at Juilliard, is a superbly accomplished, dedicated and spontaneous soloist, and the recording is first class.

Symphonies 2; 6

⊶ **(BB)** *** Naxos 8.559161. Seattle SO, Schwarz

Make no mistake, these are superb works and they are interpreted here with total dedication and eloquence.

Michael Tilson Thomas's Boston account of the *Second Symphony* for Deutsche Grammophon is no longer in circulation. Even so, this competitively priced coupling makes as good an entry point into Piston's musical world as any – almost as good as the *Fourth*. On its original Delos release an additional work, the *Sinfonietta*, was included but is omitted here.

Symphonies 5; (i) 7 & 8
** Albany AR 011. Louisville O, Whitney; (i) Mester

The *Fifth Symphony* has a sureness of purpose and feeling for organic growth that are the hallmark of the true symphonist. The *Seventh* and *Eighth Symphonies*, though not quite the equal of the finest Piston, are powerful and rewarding works which will speak to those who are more concerned with substance than with surface appeal. The Louisville performances are thoroughly committed and good, without being outstanding. The recordings sound better than they did on LP.

Flute Quartet; Piano Quartet; Piano Quintet; String Sextet
(BB) *** Naxos 8.559071. Shylayeva, Gurt, Munrow, Buswell, Walsh, Hall, Gault, Kuchar, Kelly, Glyde, Ou

Piston's chamber music is less well served than his symphonies. The *Piano Quintet* is not only one of his finest works but one of the great quintets of the twentieth century, with a master's understanding of the medium and the musical material most effective and natural to it. It is a gripping and powerful piece, and the *Flute Quartet* and *Piano Quartet* are also well worth getting to know when the performances here are so sympathetic and the recording very good.

PIZZETTI, Ildebrando (1880–1968)

La pisanella; 3 Preludii sinfonici (per L'Edipo Re); Preludio a un altro giorno; Rondò Veneziano
**(*) Hyp. CDA 67084. BBC Scottish SO, Vänskä

This well-filled programme makes an excellent introduction to Pizzetti. The *Rondò Veneziano* of 1929 was first performed by Toscanini; the three preludes from the opera *L'Edipo Re* are full of interest and *La pisanella* is a sunny and glorious work, which dates from 1913. Osmo Vänskä plays all these pieces with appropriate feeling but the string sound lacks real body and richness, particularly at the bass end of the spectrum.

String Quartets 1 in A; 2 in D
**(*) Marco Polo 8.223722. Lajtha Qt

The *A major Quartet*, which comes from 1906, owes something to Brahms and Dvořák. The *D major*, which comes from 1932–3, is a work of substance and quality. One's thoughts occasionally turn to late Beethoven and even Fauré, but it has a quiet personality all its own. The Lajtha Quartet play decently, though there could be greater variety of tone colour. There is no alternative version, but there should be, for this quartet deserves wider dissemination.

Messa di requiem. De profundis
🔑 ✿ *** Hyp. CDA 67017. Westminster Cathedral Ch., O'Donnell – MARTIN: *Mass for Double Choir*, etc. *** ✿

Messa di Requiem; 2 composizioni corali: Il giardino dia Afrodite; Piena sorgeva la luna; 3 composizioni corali: Cade la sera; Ululate; Recordare, Domine
**(*) Chan. 8964. Danish Nat. R. Chamber Ch., Parkman

Pizzetti's 'serene and lyrical Requiem' (as his biographer, Guido Gatti, puts it) is a work of surpassing beauty which will be a revelation to those who have not encountered it before, particularly in this fervent and inspired performance. It comes with the *De profundis* he composed in 1937 to mark the healing of his breach with Malipiero. Fine though the performance by the Danish Radio Chamber Choir under Stephen Parkman is coupled with other Pizzetti choral pieces, this Westminster Cathedral version completely supplants it.

PLANQUETTE, Robert (1848–1903)

***Les Cloches de Corneville* (operetta: complete)**
(B) **(*) EMI (ADD) 5 74091-2. Mesplé, Sinclair, Stutzmann, Burles, Giraudeau, Benoit, Paris Opéra-Comique Ch. & O, Doussard

Les Cloches de Corneville was undoubtedly Planquette's most successful work. The plot (a cross between *La Dame Blanche* and *Martha*), with its action eerily set in an old, supposedly haunted castle, is agreeable enough, but it is the strongly melodic music that has made the work so durable. So much so that in 1877, when the original Paris production at the Théâtre des Folies-Dramatiques ran for 461 performances, the management made the unprecedented gesture of serving every member of the audience with free rolls and beer!

The operetta is crammed with good tunes, and not just the famous *Legende des cloches* and the simple but very charming *Chanson du mousse* (a lovely rondeau-valse), but also plenty of jolly choruses, comic numbers and rustic songs. This flavourful performance dates from 1973, with Mady Mesplé's agile French soprano ideally suited to the role of the heroine, Germaine. The only drawback for non-French speakers is the high proportion of dialogue, which is delivered with panache but without any supporting texts or translations. The recording is vivid if a touch raucous, but this set remains strongly recommendable at its modest cost.

PLEYEL, Ignaz (1757–1831)

(i) ***Sinfonia concertante in F, B.115; Symphony in D, Op. 3/1; Symphony périodique in F, B.140***
**(*) CPO 999 759-2. Zurich CO, Griffiths, with (i) Dzialak, Bobino

Pleyel's elegantly attractive if relatively conventional symphonies are given first-rate performances here. There is an infectious bounce to the playing, the minuets are nicely pointed, and the finales have plenty of vitality. The *Sinfonia concertante*, with piano and violin soloists, brings many attractive episodes and the finale is irrepressibly jolly. The only real criticism of this CD is the recording, which lacks expansive richness, with the orchestra rather too backwardly balanced, but not enough to seriously diminish the wit of the music.

Symphonies in C min. (Ben 121); C (Ben 128); F min. (Ben 138)
(BB) *** Naxos 8.554696. Capella Istropolitana, Grodd

Symphonies in D min. (Ben 147); C, Op. 66 (Ben 154); G, Op. 68 (Ben 156)
*** Chan. 9525. LMP, Bamert

It was Pleyel who gave the rival series of London concerts to Haydn and Salomon in 1792. He later settled in Paris, founding the celebrated Pleyel piano factory. The earliest of the three symphonies on the Naxos disc was composed in 1778, when the composer was twenty-one; it is actually in C major but has a dramatic C minor introduction leading to a very lively *Allegro* with trumpets and drums lacing the tuttis. The *Adagio* is rather fine, with horns echoing the string theme, but the trumpets and drums return in the bold minuet and add zest to a spirited moto perpetuo finale

The other two symphonies date from 1786 and follow a similar pattern, but Pleyel's minor-key works are the most strikingly inventive, and the *F minor* has an *Andante grazioso* of Boccherinian charm, using gently muted strings against a persistent repeated accompanying figure in the second violins.

The fast Minuet with its Laendler-like Trio is no less individual. The performances from the excellent Capella Istropolitana are crisply stylish, expressively persuasive, and very well recorded.

On the companion Chandos disc the playing of the London Mozart Players under Matthias Bamert has much charm and grace, and the recording is in the best traditions of the house. The earliest of this second group of symphonies, the *D minor*, has hints of *Don Giovanni* and the *C major* has Rossinian undertones. In short, both these CDs explain why Pleyel, pupil of Haydn from the age of fifteen to twenty (under the patronage of Count Erdödy), was such a successful composer in the early years of the nineteenth century.

PLUMMER, John (died *c.* 1487)

Missa Sine nomine
*** Signum SIGCD 015. Clerks' Group, Wickham (with
BEDYNGHAM: *Myn hertis lust; Fortune alas; Mi verry joy;*
ANON.: *Kyrie; Song; Pryncesse of youthe.* ***) – FRYE: *Missa Flos Regalis*, etc. ***

We know very little about the English composer, John Plummer, whose mass only survives in a Brussels manuscript. His setting is rather bare and primitive in its part-writing, less inspired than its coupling by Walter Frye, but it makes a fascinating aural glimpse into an unfamiliar period of English polyphony. The coupled songs by Bedyngham are delightful and this whole collection, beautifully sung and recorded, is treasurable.

PONCE, Manuel (1882–1948)

Folia de España (Theme & Variations with Fugue)
(B) *** Sony (ADD) SBK 47669. Williams (guitar) –
BARRIOS: *Collection* ***

Ponce's *Variations on 'Folia de España'* are subtle and haunting, and their surface charm often conceals a vein of richer, darker feeling. The performance is first rate and the sound admirably clean and finely detailed, yet at the same time warm.

PONCHIELLI, Amilcare (1834–86)

La Gioconda (complete)
⊕━ *** EMI 5 57451-1 (3). Urmana, Domingo, d'Intino, Fiorillo, Scandiuzi, Ataneli, Bavarian R. Ch., Munich R. O, Viotti

*** EMI (ADD) 5 56291-2 (3). Callas, Cossotto, Ferraro, Vinco, Cappuccilli, Companeez, La Scala, Milan, Ch. & O, Votto

(N) (M) *** Decca 475 6670 (3). Caballé, Baltsa, Pavarotti, Milnes, Ghiaurov, Hodgson, L. Op. Ch., Nat. PO, Bartolletti

(M) (***) Fonit mono 3984 29355-2 (3). Callas, Barbieri, Amadini, Silveri, Neri, Poggi, Turin R. Ch. & O, Votto

It was not until the summer of 2002 that Plácido Domingo finally had the chance to record the role of Enzo Grimaldo in *La Gioconda*, one of the only important roles in his vast repertory that he had never put on disc. The result here is a miracle, making this set an essential choice for admirers of this great singer. Though he was 61 by the time of the sessions, you would never know that from his singing, which is full and rounded with no hint of strain, rising to a performance of the big tenor aria, *Cielo e mar*, that is beautiful, deeply felt and finely shaded. He is well matched by the soprano, formerly a mezzo, Violeta Urmana, in the title role of La Gioconda. She may not have the temperament of such leading rivals on disc as Maria Callas and Montserrat Caballé, but the firm, rich focus of her voice is consistently satisfying. She brings out the musical qualities of Ponchielli's writing, with the big Act IV aria, *Suicidio*, offering a formidable range of tone and expression. Similarly, others in the generally excellent cast, such as Luciana d'Intino as Laura, Elisabetta Fiorillo as La Ciece and Lado Ataneli as the scheming Barnaba, may not be as characterful as some on the finest rival sets (none recent), but they tackle the vocal problems of this demanding score most satisfyingly. A clear choice among digital versions.

Maria Callas gave one of her most vibrant, most compelling, most totally inspired performances on record in the title-role of *La Gioconda*, with flaws very much subdued. The challenge she presented to those around her is reflected in the soloists – Cossotto and Cappuccilli both at the very beginning of distinguished careers – as well as the distinctive tenor Ferraro and the conductor Votto, who has never done anything finer on record. The recording still sounds well, though it dates from 1959.

The casting of Decca's 1980 *La Gioconda* could hardly have been bettered in its day, with Caballé just a little overstressed in the title-role but producing glorious sounds. Pavarotti, for long immaculate in the aria *Cielo e mar*, here expands into the complete role with equally impressive control and heroic tone. Commanding performances too from Milnes as Barnaba, Ghiaurov as Alvise and Baltsa as Laura, firm and intense all three. Bartolletti proves a vigorous and understanding conductor, presenting the blood-and-thunder with total commitment but finding the proper charm in the most famous passage, the *Dance of the Hours*. The colourfully atmospheric melodrama of this opera gives the Decca engineers the chance to produce one of their first digital blockbusters, with sound that gives both voices and orchestra vivid and warm presence. Full texts and translation are included in this mid-priced Classic Opera release.

Like the companion Callas set of *La Traviata*, this Fonit set was recorded (for Cetra in 1952) very early in the diva's career. She was to re-record the opera in 1959, again with Votto, but, as in the remake, the present set shows her dramatic powers at their peak and the voice fresher than ever. The famous *Suicidio* is sung with an intensity that has rarely if ever been equalled and the closing scenes of both Acts I and IV (with Maria Amadini and Paolo Silveri respectively) are memorable. Barbieri and Neri also make fine contributions and Poggi's contribution is suitably ardent. Votto conducts with understanding, maintaining a spontaneous dramatic flow and the remastering of the old mono recording is surprisingly good.

La Gioconda: Dance of the Hours
*** Testament (ADD) SBT 1327. Philh. O, Mackerras –
VERDI: *Overtures and ballet music;* WOLF-FERRARI:
Overtures, Intermezzi & Dances (***)

With the Philharmonia Orchestra in superb form, Mackerras brings refinement and point to his performance of Ponchielli's *Dance of the Hours*, without loss of sparkle.

PORTER, Cole (1891–1964)

Overtures: *Anything Goes; Can-Can; Gay Divorce; Kiss Me, Kate. Night and day* (from *Gay Divorce*)
(B) *** EMI double forte 5 68589-2 (2). L. Sinf., McGlinn –
GERSHWIN: *Broadway & Film Music* **(*); KERN:
Overtures **

These overtures were not put together or scored by the composer but by the professionals of the day. As *Gay Divorce* does not include the most famous number from the show, a separate arrangement of *Night and Day* has been included, richly scored. The performances here are definitive and the bright recording fits the music like a glove.

POTTER, A. J. (1918–80)

Finnegans Wake; Fantasia Gaelach 1; Overture to a Kitchen Comedy; Sinfonia de profundis; Variations on a Popular Tune
✪ *** Marco Polo 8.225158. Nat. SO of Ireland, Houlihan

Archibald James Potter's imaginative gift for enlivening folksongs might be compared to that of Percy Grainger. But he also had the ability to work on a larger canvas, and his five-movement *Sinfonia de profundis* is very impressive indeed. Although it is based on a serial theme (heard at the very outset), one would hardly suspect it, for the music is clearly tonal.

The eloquent and moving *Adagio* brings powerful writing for strings and the *Sinfonia* closes with an ethereal *Epilogue*, resolved with a chorale of affirmation over hammering timpani. It is an altogether remarkably communicative work, well worth getting to know.

Among the folk songs, *Finnegans Wake*, which is brilliantly scored for wind and percussion, reminds one a little of Vaughan Williams's *Folksongs Suite*, only it is far wittier. The *Fantasia Gaelach No. 1*, which features both *My Lagan Love* and *The Fair Child*, makes a ravishing lyrical contrast. The seven *Variations on a Popular Tune* (*The Wild Colonial Boy*), given out first by a solo violin, are brilliantly diverse and most entertaining, especially when Potter lapses into boisterous, trumpet-led vulgarity.

The *Overture to a Kitchen Comedy* (1956) was the composer's first orchestral work and bustles with energy and orchestral exuberance, but also has a nice lyrical strain. It is perhaps a trifle over-extended, but still very enjoyable. First-class performances and splendid recording make this CD unmissable.

POULENC, Francis (1899–1963)

EMI Centenary Edition, Vol. 1: Concertos, orchestral and sacred music: (i–iii) *Aubade (Concerto chorégraphique);* (ii; iii) *Les Animaux modèles;* (iv; v; iii) *Les Biches* (ballet: complete); (iv; iii) *Bucolique;* (vi; ii; vii) *Concert champêtre*
(for Harpsichord & Orchestra); (viii; ii; iii) *Concerto in G min. for Organ, Strings & Timpani;* (i–iii) *Piano Concerto in C sharp min.;* (ix; ii; vii) *Double Piano Concerto in D min.;* (x) *Gnossienne 3* (Satie, orch. Poulenc); (xi; iii) *2 Marches et un intermède (for Chamber Orchestra); Les Mariés de la Tour Eiffel;* (iv; iii) *Matelote provençale; Pastourelle;* (xi; iii) *Suite française; Sinfonietta.* Vocal: (xii) *Ave verum corpus; Exultate Deo;* (xiii; xiv; iii) *Gloria;* (xv) *Laudes de Saint Antoine de Padoue;* (xvi) *Litanies à la Vierge Noire;* (xvii) *Mass in G; 4 Motets pour le temps de Noël;* (xiv; xviii) *4 Motets pour un temps de pénitence;* (xix) *4 Petites prières de Saint François d'Assise;* (xx; iii) *7 Répons des ténèbres;* (xii) *Salve Regina;* (xxi; ii; iii) *Stabat Mater*
(M) **(*) EMI stereo/mono (ADD/DDD) 5 66837-2 (5). (i) Tacchino; (ii) Paris Conservatoire O; (iii) Prêtre; (iv) Philh. O; (v) Amb. S.; (vi) van der Wiele; (vii) Dervaux; (viii) Duruflé; (ix) Février, composer; (x) Toulouse Capitole O, Plasson; (xi) O de Paris; (xii) Groupe Vocal de France, Alldis; (xiii) Cateri; (xiv) French R. & TV Ch. & O; (xv) The Sixteen, Christophers; (xvi) French R. Children's Ch., Joineau, Roget; (xvii) Winchester Cathedral Ch., Neary; (xviii) Resnel; (xix) The King's Singers; (xx) Carpentier, various choirs, New PO of R. France; (xxi) Crespin, René Duclos Ch.

The composer's own recording of the *Double Piano Concerto* with Jacques Février goes back to 1957, a high-spirited account, at times unpolished; and so does the *Concert champêtre* with Aimée van der Wiele, made all the more effective thanks to a clangorous Pleyel harpsichord of the kind intended by the composer. The *Organ Concerto*, with the original soloist, Maurice Duruflé, brings some suspect intonation, but the performance is lively and dramatic. *Les Biches* comes in the full ballet version with chorus, not the usual suite. Readers will note that this, and much of the other orchestral and concertante music, are also available separately on the two-disc set below. In the religious music, the choral singing is variable, with the British choirs and groups generally setting a higher standard than the French, although the Groupe Vocal de France under John Alldis is the exception. For all the unevenness and occasional roughness of sound, a valuable and enjoyable collection. As in the rest of the series, the five CDs come in stout cardboard inners within a stylish box. There are excellent notes, with original texts provided (in French or Latin), but no translations.

EMI Centenary Edition, Vol. 2: Chamber and piano music: (i; ii) *Bagatelle for Violin & Piano;* (ii; iii) *Cello Sonata;* (ii; iv) *Clarinet Sonata;* (iv; v) *Sonata for 2 Clarinets;* (vi; vii) *Sonata for Clarinet & Bassoon;* (ii; vii) *Elégie for Horn & Piano;* (ii; viii) *Flute Sonata;* (vii; ix) *Sonata for Horn, Trumpet & Trombone;* (x) *3 Mouvements perpétuels for Chamber Ensemble;* (xi) *Sarabande for Guitar;* (ii; xii) *Oboe Sonata;* (ii; xiii) *Sextet for Piano, Flute, Oboe, Clarinet, Bassoon & Horn;* (xiv) *Suite française for Cello & Piano;* (ii; xv) *Trio for Piano, Oboe & Bassoon;* (xvi) *Villanelle for Flute & Piano;* (xvii) *Violin Sonata.* Piano duets: (xviii; ii) *Capriccio; Elégie; L'Embarquement pour Cythère; Sonata for Piano, 4 Hands; Sonata for 2 Pianos.* Solo piano: (xviii) *Badinage; Bourrée au Pavillon d'Auvergne; 3 Feuillets d'album; Française; Humoresque; 5 Impromptus; 15 Improvisations; 3 Intermezzi; Mélancolie; Pastourelle; 3 Mouvements perpétuels;* (ii) *Napoli;* (xviii) *8 Nocturnes; 3 Novelettes; 3 Pièces; Pièce brève; Presto in B flat;*

Promenades; (ii) *Les Soirées de Nazelles*; (xviii) *Suite française; Suite in C*; (ii) *Thème varié*; (xviii) *Valse in C; Valse improvisation; Villageoises*

(M) ** EMI (ADD/DDD) 5 66831-2 (5). (i) Grimal; (ii) Février; (iii) Fournier; (iv) Portal; (v) Gaal; (vi) Wallez; (vii) Civil; (viii) Debost; (ix) Wilbraham, Iveseon; (x) Members of O de la Garde Républicaine, F. Boulanger; (xi) Ghiglia; (xii) Bourgue; (xiii) Wind Ens.; (xiv) Phillips, Strosser; (xv) Casier, Faisandier; (xvi) Pottier, Strosser; (xvii) Zimmermann, Lonquich; (xviii) Tacchino

This is a pretty comprehensive collection of Poulenc's chamber music, but not all the performances are equally distinguished. It is good to have Fournier's elegant account of the *Cello Sonata* and Zimmermann's more recent one of the *Violin Sonata*; Bourgue's performance of the *Oboe Sonata* is also very enjoyable, and the other wind sonatas are effective enough, if less individual. Both the *Trio for Piano, Oboe and Bassoon* and the *Sextet* are rather dryly recorded; however, although the playing could have more elegance, there is a high-spirited, knockabout quality here that is eminently likeable. The brass trio is one of the highlights, very entertainingly played and given good sound. Most of the recordings date from the 1970s but one or two are more modern. Jacques Février's pianism, both in the sonatas and the two-piano works, does not always have the finish such repertoire ideally demands. Tacchino's playing of the solo piano music is often technically brilliant and strongly characterized (perhaps at times a shade too strongly), but it does not have the degree of charm or the gamin quality which are ideally required. The recording too, closely balanced, is a bit hard and lacking bloom.

EMI Centenary Edition, Vol. 3: Mélodies and chansons: *Airs chantés; A sa guitare; Banalités; Le Bestiare ou Cortège d'Orphée* (with unpublished supplement: *La Colombe; Le Serpent; La Puce). Calligrammes* (cycle); *Bleuet; Ce doux petit visage; Chanson à boire; 3 Chansons de Federico Garcia Lorca; Chansons gailliardes; 7 Chansons for Mixed Choir, a cappella; 8 Chansons françaises; 8 Chansons polonaises; 4 Chansons pour enfants; Une chanson de porcelaine; Chansons villageoises; Les Chemins de l'amour; Cocardes; Colloque; La Courte Paille* (cycle); *Dernier poème; Le Disparu; Epitaphe; Fancy; Fiançailles pour rire; La Fraîcheur et le feu* (cycle); *La Grenouillère; Hymne; Main dominée par le coeur; Mazurka; 2 Mélodies: Le Souris; Nuage; 2 Mélodies de Guillaume Apollinaire; Métamorphoses; Miroirs brûlants; Nos souvenirs qui chantent; Paul et Virginie; Petites voix* (cycle); *Pierrot; 2 Poèmes de Guillaume Apollinaire* (2 sets); *4 Poèmes de Guillaume Apollinaire; 3 Poèmes de Louise Lalanne; 3 Poèmes de Louis de Vilmorin; 4 Poèmes de Max Jacob; 5 Poèmes de Max Jacob; 2 Poèmes de Louis Aragon; 5 Poèmes de Paul Eluard; 5 Poèmes de Pierre de Ronsard; Le Portrait; Priez pour la paix; Rapsodie nègre; Rosamonde; Tel jour telle nuit* (cycle); *Toréador; Le Travail du peintre* (cycle); *Vive Nadia; Vocalise*

(M) *** EMI stereo/mono (ADD/DDD) 5 66849-2 (5). Benoit, Rivenq, Fouchécourt, Le Roux, Van Dam, Streich, Souzay, Ameling, Gedda, Mesplé, Bernac, Berton, Sénéchal, Parker, Bacquier, Norman, Develieraeu, French R. Children's Ch., Besson, The Sixteen, Christophers, Stockholm Chamber Ch., Erikson. Accompanists include Collard, Baldwin, Parsons, Tacchino, composer, Février

A fine gallery of singers is presented here, in vintage performances covering the full span of Poulenc's work as a song

composer, with his cabaret style happily set alongside deeper songs. There is an immense variety here and though there have been more refined performances on rival discs, there are none more idiomatic than these, with each singer characterizing vividly. Rita Streich, Jessye Norman and Elly Ameling are very well represented alongside native French singers ranging back to the composer's friend and associate, Pierre Bernac. The close-up sound, transferred with fine immediacy, hardly shows its age. Entirely new are the a cappella choral recordings, very well performed by The Sixteen and the Stockholm Chamber Choir. An indispensable collection.

EMI Centenary Edition, Vol. 4: Vocal works ('*Oeuvres lyriques*'): (i) *Le Bal masqué*; (ii) *Les Chemins de l'amour*; (iii) *La Dame de Monte-Carlo*; (iv) *Dialogues des Carmélites*; (v) *Esquisse pour une fanfare*; (vi) *Figure humaine*; (vii) *Le Gendarme incompris*; (viii) *L'Histoire de Babar le petit éléphant*; (ix) *L'Invitation au château*; (x) *Les Mamelles de Tirésias*; (xi) *Sécheresses*; (vi) *Un soir de neige*; (xii) *La Voix humaine*

(M) (***) EMI mono/stereo (ADD/DDD) 5 66843-2 (5). (i) Benoit, Charpentier, Paris Conservatoire O (Soloists), Prêtre; (ii) Printemps, O, Cariven; (iii) Mesplé, Monte-Carlo PO, Prêtre; (iv) Duval, Crespin, Scharley, Berton, Gorr, Depraz, Finel, Paris Op. O, Dervaux; (v) Toulouse O (members), Cardon; (vi) The Sixteen, Christophers; (vii) Rivenq, Fouchécourt, Benoit, Garde Républicaine Soloists' O, F. Boulanger; (viii) Ustinov, Paris Conservatoire O, Prêtre; (ix) Strosse, Grimal, Guyot; (x) Duval, Giraudeau, Opéra-Comique Ch. & O, Cluytens; (xi) New O of R. France, Prêtre; (xii) Duval, Opéra-Comique O, Prêtre

Although not everything here has been satisfactorily re-recorded, the vintage performances in this collection of Poulenc's stage works may not measure up to more recent rivals in opulence of recording, but the immediacy, intensity and feeling for idiom have never been surpassed, and the singers are all well chosen, firm and true even in face of the close-up sound favoured by the French EMI engineers. So the *Dialogues des Carmélites*, much the longest work, lacks atmospheric beauty, but makes its dramatic point with overwhelming force, and Poulenc's favourite soprano, Denise Duval, could not be more characterful, both there and in *Les Mamelles de Tirésias* and *La Voix humaine*. Peter Ustinov narrates the story of *Babar the Elephant* charmingly in French. Totally new and beautifully done by The Sixteen under Harry Christophers are the secular cantatas at the end, *Figure humaine* and *Un soir de neige*. Texts in French are provided but no translations.

ORCHESTRAL MUSIC

(i) *Les Animaux modèles*; (ii; iii) *Les Biches* (ballet: complete); (ii) *Bucolique*; (i; iv) *Concert champêtre* (for harpsichord & orchestra); (i; v) *Double Piano Concerto in D min.*; (vi) *2 Marches et un intermède* (for Chamber Orchestra); *Les Mariés de la Tour Eiffel* (*La Baigneuse de Trouville; Discours du général*). (ii) *Matelote provençale; Pastourelle*; (vi) *Sinfonietta; Suite française*

(B) *** EMI Rouge et Noir (ADD/DDD) 5 69446-2 (2). (i) Paris Conservatoire O; (ii) Philh. O; (iii) Amb. S.; (iv) van der Wiele; (v) composer; Février; (vi) O de Paris; all cond. Prêtre

Les Biches comes here in its complete form, with the choral additions that Poulenc made optional when he came to rework the score. The music is a delight, and so too is the group of captivating short pieces, digitally recorded at the same time (1980): *Bucolique, Pastourelle* and *Matelote provençale*. High-spirited, fresh, elegant playing and sumptuous recorded sound enhance the claims of all this music. The *Suite française* is another highlight. It is well played and recorded in a pleasing, open acoustic. Poulenc himself was a pianist of limited accomplishment, but his interpretation with Jacques Février of his own skittish *Double Concerto* is infectiously jolly. In the imitation pastoral concerto for harpsichord, Aimée van der Wiele is a nimble soloist, but here Prêtre's inflexibility as a conductor comes out the more, even though the finale has plenty of high spirits. The *Sinfonietta*, too, could have a lighter touch. *Les Animaux modèles* is based on the fables of La Fontaine, with a prelude and a postlude, but here the recording is rather lacking in bloom, and the *Deux marches* are also a trifle overbright. With nearly 156 minutes' playing time, these CDs are well worth exploring.

Aubade; Piano Concerto; (i) *Double Piano Concerto in D min.*

☙ *** RCA 82876 60308-2. Le Sage, Liège PO, Denève; (i) with Braley

After the ambivalent mood of the opening *Toccata*, Poulenc's *Aubade* ('an allegory of women and feminine solitude') is a series of brief vignettes, witty, audacious and melancholy by turns, and at the close the plaintive *Variation for Diana* (the unwillingly chaste heroine of the piece) leads on to a gentle, melancholy *Adieu*, which almost becomes a *marche funèbre*.

The easy-going charm of the opening of the *Piano Concerto* is also admirably caught, the *Andante* wistfully romantic and the skittish finale making a perfect foil. Both are played with style and panache by Eric le Sage, persuasively accompanied by Stéphane Denève.

Frank Braley enthusiastically joins the team for the *Double Piano Concerto*, which opens at high speed, with exhilarating, almost reckless dash, so the contrast of the gentle quasi-Mozartian pastiche of the *Larghetto* is the more enticing. More fireworks in the finale, which brings virtuosic precision of articulation from the soloists, yet keeps its élan. All in all, a very successful, consistently diverting triptych, very well (if resonantly) recorded.

(i) *Aubade;* (i; ii) *Double Piano Concerto in D min.; Sinfonietta*

(M) *** Virgin 5 61907-2. (i) Pommier; (ii) Queffélec; City of L. Sinf., Hickox

Jean-Bernard Pommier gives a thoroughly idiomatic and incisive account of the *Aubade*, and both he and Anne Queffélec play the *Concerto for Two Pianos* to the manner born. They have the measure of the pastiche Mozart slow movement and the quasi-Gamelan first. Hickox gives an affectionate and charming account of the *Sinfonietta* that matches – almost – the splendid account from the Orchestre National under Dutoit. Very recommendable, especially at mid-price.

(i) *Aubade. Sinfonietta*

(BB) *** Hyp. Helios CDH 55167. New L. O, Corp – HAHN: *Le Bal de Béatrice d'Este* ***

The *Sinfonietta* is a fluent and effortless piece, full of resource and imagination, and Ronald Corp and the New London

Orchestra do it proud. Julian Evans is an alert soloist in the *Aubade*: his is a performance of real character and, though less well balanced than the *Sinfonietta*, his account can hold its own artistically with the competition. The Hahn rarity with which it is coupled enhances the interest and value of this reissue.

Les Biches (ballet: suite)

☙ *** Chan. 9023. Ulster O, Y. P. Tortelier – IBERT: *Divertissement;* MILHAUD: *Le Bœuf; La Création* ***
(***) Testament mono SBT 1294. Paris Conservatoire O, Désormière (with DELIBES: *Coppélia & Sylvia Suites* (***))

Yan Pascal Tortelier and the Ulster Orchestra give an entirely winning account of Poulenc's ballet suite. Here the opening has delightfully keen rhythmic wit, and the playing is equally polished and crisply articulated in the gay *Rag-Mazurka* and infectious *Finale*. The lovely *Adagietto* is introduced with tender delicacy, yet reaches a suitably plangent climax. Top-drawer Chandos sound and splendid couplings ensure the overall success of this admirable compilation.

Désormière's pioneering 1951 mono set of the orchestral numbers from *Les Biches* has been out of circulation for almost four decades, but in terms of style and character it has never been surpassed. The 1955 edition of the Shawe-Taylor/Sackville-West *Record Guide* put it perfectly when it wrote that 'the present performance captures with affectionate irony the atmosphere of the period in which this music was conceived', and although at the time the recording was less than 'wonderfully realistic' (to quote the *Guide* again) – it was more than a shade top-heavy – the present restoration makes it sound very good indeed. The original LP was coupled with *The Good-humoured Ladies*, but this is replaced with the two Delibes *Ballet Suites* that Désormière recorded in 1950 on 78-r.p.m. discs. 'Charming and delicate performances,' was the *Guide*'s verdict, and so they seem now. Recommended with enthusiasm for those who care about real flair and a genuine sense of style.

Bucolique (from *Variations sur le nom de Marguerite Long*); (i) *Concert champêtre. 2 Marches et un intermède; Fanfare; Pièce brève sur le nom d'Albert Roussel; Sinfonietta; Suite française*

☙ ❂ (M) *** Decca 476 2181. (i) Rogé; French Nat. O, Dutoit

The major works here are the *Sinfonietta* and the *Concert champêtre*. The *Sinfonietta*, commissioned to mark the first anniversary of the BBC's Third Programme and dedicated to his fellow composer, Auric, comes off marvellously. For those who entertain doubts as to its quality, this version by Charles Dutoit and the Orchestre National de France should be mandatory listening; it is certainly among the most persuasive accounts in the catalogue. In the *Concert champêtre* Pascal Rogé proves as fine a clavecinist as pianist and his account, equally strong on charm and elegance, ranks high among present recommendations. The smaller pieces greatly enhance the already strong attractions of this disc. All of them are imaginative, none more so than *Bucolique* from the *Variations sur le nom de Marguerite Long*. The excellence of the performances is matched by first-rate and meticulously balanced Decca sound. It now returns to the catalogue at mid-price with Universal's 'Penguin ❂ Collection'.

(i; ii) *Concert champêtre for harpsichord & piano*; (i; iii) *Double Piano Concerto in D min.*; (i–iv) *Organ Concerto in G min.*

(M) (***) EMI mono/stereo 5 62647-2 [5 62649-2]. Paris CO, cond. (i) Dervaux; with (ii) Van de Wiele; (iii) Février; composer (iv) Duruflé; cond. Prêtre

This is the première recording of the *Organ Concerto* (which first appeared on LP in harness with the *Gloria*) and the very first LP account of the *Concerto champêtre* (written in the late 1920s for Landowska) with Aimée van de Wiele, and the *Concerto for Two Pianos* with Jacques Février, both recorded in 1957. This was briefly available to special order and was chosen for inclusion in the four-CD box of Poulenc's complete works that EMI issued to mark the centenary of his birth in 1999. It was rapidly superseded by the 1962 stereo version with the same soloists but with Georges Prêtre conducting, and the latter was chosen for reissue during the LP years. To be frank, apart from the greater amplitude of stereo there is not a great deal to choose between them, and in some ways Van de Wiele's first recording has marginally greater character. In any event this present issue with Duruflé's authoritative account of the *Organ Concerto*, made in the presence of the composer, is thoroughly recommendable in every way and the sound, exceptional in its day, is still first class. A worthy addition to EMI's 'Great Recordings of the Century'.

Concert champêtre (for Harpsichord & Orchestra); *Concerto in G min. for Organ, Strings & Timpani*

(B) *** EMI (ADD) double forte 5 69752-2 (2). Preston, LSO, Previn – MESSIAEN: *Turangalîla Symphony* ***

On EMI double forte each of the recordings is realistically balanced, and Simon Preston, who plays the solo parts in both concertos, produces readings of great fluency and authority, to say nothing of wit in the work for harpsichord. Previn too has a genuine feeling for the music: the orchestral playing is always musical, often sparkling, and the recording is first class. It set new standards in its day (1977).

(i) *Concert champêtre* (for harpsichord); (ii) *Concerto in G min. for Organ*; (iii) *Piano Concerto*

(M) **(*) Virgin 5 61979-2. (i) Cole; (ii) Weir; (iii) Pommier; City of L. Sinf., Hickox

The *Piano Concerto* receives rather laid-back treatment at the hands of Jean-Bernard Pommier, who misses the *gamin*-like charm of the opening. The instrument is also a bit backward and has a slightly resonant halo. The *Concert champêtre* is charming, though the perspective is not good. The harpsichord occupies an appropriately small space, but the wind and, more particularly, the percussion are far too prominent. Maggie Cole and the City of London Sinfonia produce a splendidly idiomatic performance, as does Gillian Weir in the *Organ Concerto*.

Concerto in G min. for Organ, Strings & Timpani

(⌐) (N) (BB) *** Warner Apex 2564 61912-2. Alain, Bamberg SO, Kantorow – ALAIN: *Sarabande for Organ, String Quintet & Timpani*; DURUFLE: *3 Dances*; *Prélude et Fugue* ***
(*) Chan. 9271. Tracey (organ of Liverpool Cathedral), BBC PO, Tortelier – GUILMANT: *Symphony 1*; WIDOR: *Symphony 5* *

Marie-Claire Alain's 1997 Bamberg recording is second to none. The unnamed organ in the Sinfonie an der Regnitz is

eminently suitable, and she plays with her usual flair. Kantorow accompanies her with comparable élan, and the recording is excellent. The couplings too are highly desirable.

The wide reverberation period of Liverpool Cathedral produces gloriously plush textures (the orchestral strings are radiantly rich in colour) but little plangent bite, and some may feel that the effect is too overwhelmingly sumptuous for Poulenc's *Concerto*. Yet it is easy to wallow in the gloriously full sounds, and the performance itself, spacious to allow for the resonance, is certainly enjoyable.

(i) *Organ Concerto in G min.* (ii) *Gloria*

(N) (M) *(*) Telarc CD 80643. (i) Murray; (ii) McNair, Atlanta Ch.; Atlanta SO, Shaw – STRAVINSKY: *Symphony of Psalms* *(*)

Although Michael Murray's fine account of the *Organ Concerto* is offered as a tempting bonus and the Telarc recording is characteristically brilliant and well balanced, Robert Shaw's brightly sung and well-disciplined performance of the *Gloria* misses both the electricity and the necessary lightness of Poulenc's vision. Moreover, Sylvia McNair is a disappointingly unsteady soloist.

The Story of Babar the Elephant (orch. Jean Françaix)

⌐ ✿ (BB) *** Naxos 8.554170. Humphries, Melbourne SO, Lanchbery – BRITTEN: *Young Person's Guide to the Orchestra*; PROKOFIEV: *Peter and the Wolf* ***

Barry Humphries adopts an engagingly cultivated male persona to tell *The Story of Babar* with an elegance and a sense of innocence which make the narrative seem completely believable, within a children's world where elephants can assume human vanities and aspirations. He is genial, gently touching and animated by turns, but always stylish; and so is Lanchbery's matching orchestral accompaniment, which catches the moments of nostalgia and joy with equal sensitivity and flair. The dance after the wedding (in Jean Françaix's uninhibited scoring) momentarily recalls *Les Biches*. The effect here is infinitely more involving than the composer's rather bald, original piano version. Jean de Brunhoff's tale has never been presented more effectively on record, or better recorded. A delight and very highly recommended, as the couplings are first rate too.

CHAMBER MUSIC

Complete chamber music: *Cello Sonata; Clarinet Sonata; Sonata for 2 Clarinets; Sonata for Clarinet & Bassoon; Elégie for Horn & Piano (in Memory of Dennis Brain); Flute Sonata; Oboe Sonata; Sarabande for Guitar; Sextet for Piano, Flute, Oboe, Clarinet, Bassoon & Horn; Sonata for Horn, Trumpet & Trombone; Trio for Piano, Oboe & Bassoon; Villanelle for Piccolo* (pipe) *& Piano; Violin Sonata*
*** Hyp. CDA 67255/6. Nash Ens., with I. Brown (piano)

Poulenc's delightful chamber music has done well in recent years: the set by various British artists on Cala has strong claims on the collector. Poulenc (or 'Poolonk', as he is called on BBC Radio 3 these days) is quintessential Nash territory and their Hyperion survey is of predictable excellence. Common to most of these works is the pianist Ian Brown, a stylist if ever there was one, whose playing lends such character to the proceedings. There are few performances that fail to delight and fewer that are surpassed elsewhere. Very good recorded sound makes this an excellent recommendation.

(i) *L'Invitation au château (for Clarinet, Violin & Piano)*; (i–ii; iv–vii) *Mouvements perpétuels for Flute, Oboe, Clarinet, Bassoon, Horn, Violin, Viola, Cello & Bass*; (i; ix–x) *Rapsodie nègre for Flute, Clarinet, String Quartet, Baritone & Piano*; (i; iv–vii; xi) *Sextet for Flute, Oboe, Clarinet, Bassoon, Horn & Piano*; (i; vi) *Sonata for Clarinet*; *Sonata for Clarinet & Bassoon*; (i) *Sonata for 2 Clarinets*; (iv; ix) *Sonata for Flute & Piano*; (v; x) *Oboe Sonata*; (iv–v; x) *Trio for Oboe, Bassoon & Piano*; (iv–ix) *Villanelle for Piccolo & Piano*

(B) *** Cala CACD 1018 (2). (i) Campbell; (ii) Carter; (iii) York; (iv) Bennett; (v) Daniel; (vi) Gough; (vii) Watkins; (viii) Tapping, Schrecker, West; (ix) Allegri Qt, Sidhom; (x) Drake; (xi) Benson – RAVEL: *Introduction & Allegro*, etc. ***

These Cala discs are a terrific bargain. The Poulenc accounts for the bulk of the two CDs (two hours' music in fact), all of it full of sparkle and freshness of invention. The discs comprise the complete chamber music for woodwind by Ravel and Poulenc, with the exception of works written primarily for the voice. The performances have great elegance and finesse. Poulenc has the rare gift of being able to move from the most flippant high spirits to the deepest poignancy, as in the *Oboe Sonata*, expressively played by Nicholas Daniel. His pianist, Julius Drake, is highly sensitive, though the piano is not always ideally focused in the excessively resonant acoustic. Elsewhere, in the captivating incidental music to a play by Jean Cocteau and Raymond Radiguet, *L'Invitation au château*, the playing is expert, tasteful and stylish. The *Mouvements perpétuels*, the *Sextet* and the various wind sonatas are beautifully played with great relish and spirit. This is a most attractive set, which deserves the widest dissemination.

Sextet (for Piano and Wind)

(M) *** Chan. 6543. I. Brown, Athena Ens. – GOUNOD: *Petite Symphonie in B flat*; IBERT: *3 Pièces brèves* ***

From Ian Brown and the Athena Ensemble a bravura and responsive performance of Poulenc's many-faceted *Sextet*, catching its high spirits as well as its wit, and the gentle melancholy which intervenes at the close of the boisterous finale. The recording is excellent, slightly dry, yet with a nice ambience. Even though the programme is short measure, every minute is enjoyable.

Sextet for Piano & Wind; Trio for Piano, Oboe & Bassoon; (i) Le Bal masqué; Le Bestiaire

(M) *** CRD CRD 3437. (i) Allen; Nash Ens., Friend

Thomas Allen is in excellent voice and gives a splendid account of both *Le Bal masqué* and *Le Bestiaire*. The Nash play both the *Trio* and the *Sextet* with superb zest and character. The wit of this playing and the enormous resource, good humour and charm of Poulenc's music are well served by a recording of exemplary quality and definition. Not to be missed.

PIANO MUSIC

Piano duet

Capriccio; Elégie; L'Embarquement pour Cythère; Sonata for Piano, 4 Hands; Sonata for 2 Pianos
*** Chan. 8519. Tanyel, J. Brown

These two artists have a very close rapport and dispatch this

repertoire with both character and sensitivity. The Chandos recording is excellent, very vivid and present.

(i) Music for piano, 4 hands: *L'Embarquement pour Cythère; Sonata*. Solo piano music: *Bourrée au Pavillon d'Auvergne; Française; Humoresque; 3 Intermezzi; Mélancolie; 3 Mouvements perpétuels; 3 Novelettes; Pastourelle; 3 Pièces; Presto in B flat; Suite in C; Suite française; Valse in C; Villageoises*

(BB) ** EMI Encore (ADD/DDD) 5 85457-2. Tacchino, (i) with Février

This is all delightful music and it is crisply played by Gabriel Tacchino, although he tends to favour brisk tempi. He is at his best in the six *Villageoises*, which are witty and brittle and with a general feeling of pastiche. The three *Intermezzi* are agreeably romantic, while much of the other music, although slight, is curiously haunting. Many of the pieces (the *Suite française* for instance) have a delicately observed period flavour as well as Poulenc's sophisticated harmonic sense. The piano-sound, whether analogue or digital, is acceptable but a bit shallow. Tacchino characterizes strongly and the piano timbre does not help. He is joined by Jacques Février in the four-handed music, which is thoroughly idiomatic but less strong on charm. This is fair value, but there are finer versions of this repertoire available if you pay a little more.

Solo piano music

Complete Solo Piano Music: *Badinage; Les Biches: 3 excerpts, including Adagietto. Bourrée, au pavillon d'Auvergne; Caprice; Feuillets d'album; Française; Humoresque; 5 Impromptus; 15 Improvisations; Intermède; Intermezzi 1–3; Mélancolie; Mouvements perpetuelles; Napoli (Suite); Nocturnes Nos.1–8; 3 Novellettes; Pastourelle; 3 Pièces; Pièce brève sur le nom d'Albert Roussel; Presto in B flat; Promenades; La Soirée de Nazelles (Suite); Suite; Suite française; Thème varié; Valse; Valse impromptu sur le nom de Bach; Villageoises*

(M) *** Chan. 10014 (3). Parkin

Eric Parkin is a much underrated artist who has never really received his due. He is a stylist and plays this music with elegance and taste. There is perhaps a gamine-like quality that eludes him, and it must be said that Rogé, who understands this repertoire so well, finds a much greater range of keyboard colour. But Parkin is still very rewarding and is to be preferred to Eric le Sage's RCA set, which has great clarity and intelligence but, good as it is, is sometimes a bit short on charm.

Badinage; Bourrée, au pavillon d'Auvergne; Humoresque; Suite Française d'après Claude Gervaise; 15 Improvisations; 5 Impromptus; Intermède en ré mineur; 3 Intermezzi; Pastourelle; Presto en si bémol; Mélancolie; 3 Mouvements perpétuels; Napoli (suite); 8 Nocturnes; 3 Novellettes; 3 Pièces; Les Soirées de Nazelles; Suite; Suite française; Valse; Valse improvisation sur le nom de Bach

(B) *** RCA 2 CD 74321 84603-2 (2). Le Sage

Eric le Sage is a virtuoso of a high order, as he immediately demonstrates in the opening *Presto en si bémol* (marked by Poulenc to be played as fast as possible), and later with the most precisely delicate articulation in *Les Soirées de Nazelles*, and in the second disc the amazingly varied *Improvisations* and the *Impromptus*, which are presented with great élan.

Sometimes his tempi seem a fraction fast, as in the most famous of the *Mouvements perpetuelles*, but he can readily charm the ear, as in the lovely *Pastourelle*, the *Novellettes* and *Suite française*. There is wit, too, and the flimsy little *Valse* is most delicate. In short, the playing here is full of character and certainly does not lack spontaneity of variety of style and timbre. The closing group of *Nocturnes* are exquisite. The recording is very real and vivid. Excellent value.

Improvisations 1–3; 6–8; 12–13; 15; Mouvements perpétuels; 3 Novellettes; Pastourelle; 3 Pièces; Les Soirées de Nazelles; Valse

☀—🔊 ✪ *** Decca 475 042-2. Rogé

On its first issue in 1988 this collection won the *Gramophone's* Instrumental Award and a ✪ from us – which we now restore. This music is absolutely enchanting, full of delight and wisdom; it has many unexpected touches and is teeming with character. Pascal Rogé is a far more persuasive exponent of it than any previous pianist on record; his playing is imaginative and inspiriting, and the recording is superb.

3 Mouvements perpétuels; Napoli: Suite

(B) *** Decca Eloquence 467 471-2. Rogé – SAINT-SAENS: *Piano Concertos 2 & 4* ***

The *Mouvements perpétuelles* are among Poulenc's most seductive piano miniatures and the *Napoli Suite* also has much charm. These pieces could hardly be better played or recorded and this makes an attractive bonus for two favourite Saint-Saëns *Piano Concertos*.

CHORAL MUSIC

Sacred Music: *Ave verum corpus; Exulate Deo; Laudes des Saint Antoine de Padoue;* (i) *Litanies à la vierge noire. 4 Motets pour un temps de Noël; 4 Motets pour un temps de Pénitence; Salve Regina;* Secular Music: *Chanson à boire; 7 Chansons* (1936); *8 Chansons françaises* (1945); *Figure humaine; Un Soir de neige*

(BB) **(*) EMI Gemini 5 85776-2 (2). Groupe Vocal de France, Alldis; (i) with Alain (organ)

Recognizing the need for a French chamber choir to match the great international choirs, the Groupe Vocal de France was formed in 1976 by the City of Paris and the French Ministry of Culture, under Marcel Couraud. The result was these two recorded collections: the sacred, recorded in 1981 in L'Eglise Saint Germain, and the secular, recorded six years later in the Salle Wagram. This is all music that ideally needs French voices, and John Alldis has trained his French group splendidly so that they combine precision and fervour with a natural feeling for the words.

In the sacred concert the soaring *Ave Verum* is matched by the exhilaration of the *Exultate Deo* and the originality of the *Litanies* with its stabbing bursts of organ tone. The *Salve Regina* is very fine too, and the four *Christmas Motets* which close the first disc have the right extrovert joyfulness and sense of wonder. The recording is made within an ecclesiastical ambience, yet the definition is admirable.

Alas, the secular music was balanced less satisfactorily and the effect sounds rather synthetic. Nevertheless the performances are expert enough and, although the acoustic is dryish, this shorter selection is worth having at so modest a cost, even if no texts and translations are included.

Ave verum corpus; 7 Chansons; Chanson à boire; 8 Chansons françaises; Exultate Deo; Figure humaine; Laudes de Saint Antoine de Padoue; Mass in G; 4 Motets pour le temps de Noël; 4 Motets pour un temps de pénitence; 4 petites Prières de Saint François d'Assise; Un soir de neige

(N) (BB) *** Virgin 2x1 5 62431-2 (2). The Sixteen, Christophers

A splendid anthology, which justaposes the cantata for double choir, *Figure humaine*, the dramatically contrasted *Mass in G*, and the exultant *Exultate Deo* with some of Poulenc's most celebrated *a cappella* motets for both mixed choir and men's voices alone. Also included are the lovely *Ave verum corpus* for female voices, and some secular (choral) chansons. Among these *La belle se sied au pied de la tour* is particularly beautiful, while *Clic, Clac, dansez sabots* ('Dance, clogs!') is irresistible. The petite cantata, *Un soir de neige*, is also delightful, and the closing settings of Apollinaire and Paul Éluard are lively, peaceful and voluptuous by turns. These performances can more than hold their own with most of Poulenc's choral music and they can be strongly recommended both on artistic grounds and for the excellence of the sound. It is a great pity that there are no texts and translations.

Le Bal masqué (cantata)

(M) *** Virgin 5 61850-2. Van Dam, Lyon Nat. Op. O, Nagano – IBERT: *4 chansons de Don Quichotte;* MARTIN: *6 Monologues from 'Jedermann';* RAVEL: *Don Quichotte à Dulcinée* ***

Kent Nagano and the Lyon orchestra set the scene vivaciously for Poulenc's 'cantata profana', and present the *Intermède* and reckless *Bagatelle* with the sharpest rhythmic felicity. José Van Dam is in his element, singing with all the necessary point in the opening *Préambule* and entering fully into the unpredictably changing moods of *Malvina*, with its touching lyrical strain. The spirited finale, with a prominent solo piano role (and even a momentary burst of falsetto from Van Dam), confirms the feeling that this is a kind of 'Divertissement' with vocal obbligato. It could hardly be more winningly presented. The accompanying notes do not include a translation, suggesting instead that Max Jacob's poems are 'best appreciated in their original French, as they rely for much of their effect on word associations – those of sound and suggestion rather than sense'. First-rate recording.

Gloria

(B) *** Decca (ADD) 448 711-2. Greenberg, SRO Ch., Lausanne Pro Arte Ch., SRO, López-Cobos – DURUFLE: *Requiem;* FAURE: *Pavane* ***

The *Gloria* is one of Poulenc's last compositions and is among his most successful. López-Cobos gives a fine account, expansive yet underlining the Stravinskian elements in the score. The recording is first class, full-bodied and with clean definition.

(i; ii) *Gloria; Ave verum corpus; Exultate Deo;* (ii) *Litanies à la Vierge Noire; 4 Motets pour le temps de Noël; 4 Motets pour un temps de pénitence; Salve Regina*

(N) (M) *** Coll. CSCD 506. (i) Deam, Cambridge Singers; (ii) City of L. Sinfonia, Rutter

A generous selection of Poulenc's choral music, much of it of great beauty and simplicity, in very fresh-sounding performances and well-focused sound. The performance of the *Gloria* is particularly fine and this disc is now offered at mid-price.

(i) *Gloria; Litanies à la Vierge Noire;* (i) *Stabat mater*
⊶ (M) *** Virgin 5 61843-2. (i) Dubosc; Westminster
Singers, City of L. Sinf., Hickox

Richard Hickox's quite outstanding version of Poulenc's *Glo-ria* brings singing of great freshness and bite. The ear is immediately struck, not only by the security of the Westminster Singers and the excellent playing of City of London Sinfonia, but also by the remarkably well-judged balance and detail of the recording. The *Stabat mater* is hardly less memorable, intensely dramatic and movingly lyrical by turns. Catherine Dubosc, who has already sung ravishingly in the *Dominus Deus* of the *Gloria*, is ethereally radiant in *Vidit suum* and soars heavenwards in *Fac ut portem*. The Westminster Singers are heard at their most subtle in the expressive contrasts of the *Litanies à la Vierge Noire*, singing of much clarity and delicacy of feeling. Throughout this splendid disc the recording is demonstration-worthy, with the orchestral woodwind glowing luminously. Full translations are included.

(i) *Gloria;* (ii) *Stabat Mater*
(N) *** Australian Decca Eloquence 476 2947. (i) Greenberg,
Lausanne Pro Arte Ch., Swiss R. Ch., SRO, López-Cobos;
(ii) Pollet, R. France Ch. & O, Dutoit – BIZET: *Te Deum* **(*)

López-Cobos's account of the *Gloria* is here coupled with an equally fine performance of the *Stabat Mater*, where Dutoit brings out both its lyrical and its dramatic qualities with characteristic flair. In his hands it is a work full of character and memorable ideas, much helped by the atmospheric recording. The choir is excellent, as is the soloist.

(i) *Mass in G. Exultate Deo;* (ii) *Litanies à la Vierge Noire.
Salve Regina*
(B) *** Double Decca (ADD) 436 486-2 (2). St John's
College, Cambridge, Ch., Guest; (i) with Bond; (ii) Cleobury
– FAURE; DURUFLE: *Requiems* ***

Mass in G; 4 Petites prières de Saint François d'Assise; Salve Regina
*** Nim. NI 5197. Christ Church Cathedral Ch., Oxford,
Darlington – MARTIN: *Mass for Double Choir* **(*)

The shadow of Stravinsky hovers over the *Mass in G*, which is a work of strong appeal and greater dramatic fire than the *Salve Regina* or the more intimate *Quatre petites prières de Saint François d'Assise* for men's voices. The choir of Christ Church Cathedral, Oxford, under Stephen Darlington sing with clean tone and excellent balance, and the Nimbus recording is very good indeed.

As an extraordinarily generous bonus for the two great *Requiems* of Fauré and Duruflé, this Double Decca set offers the Poulenc *Mass in G* together with two motets, *Exultate Deo* and *Salve Regina*, finely wrought pieces in performances of great finish. Then, together with Stephen Cleobury, they give us the cool, gently dissonant *Litanies à la Vierge Noire*, a dialogue between voices and organ in which the voices eventually take dominance. It is beautifully done and the St John's College forces cope with the delicacy and sweetness of Poulenc's chromatic harmony throughout. The (originally Argo) recording is eminently realistic and truthful.

4 Motets pour le temps de Noël
(N) (B) *** CfP 586 1722 (2). Winchester Cathedral Ch., ECO,
Neary – BERLIOZ: *L'enfance du Christ* **(*); HONEGGER: *Une Cantate de Noël* ***

Martin Neary gets excellent results from the Winchester Cathedral Choir in the delightful *Christmas Motets*, and the EMI recording is also first rate. The couplings are apt, and this is a very worthwhile CfP Double.

Stabat Mater; Litanies à la Vierge Noire; Salve Regina
*** HM HMC 905149. Lagrange, Lyon Nat. Ch. &O, Baudo

In the *Stabat Mater* Serge Baudo certainly makes the most of expressive and dynamic nuances; he shapes the work with fine feeling and gets good singing from the Lyon Chorus. Michèle Lagrange has a good voice and is an eminently expressive soloist. The coupling offers the short *Salve Regina* and the *Litanies à la Vierge Noire*, an earlier and somewhat more severe work.

SONGS

Banalités; Les Chemins de l'amour; 2 Mélodies de Guillaume Apollinaire
*** Virgin 5 45360-2. Gens, Vignoles – DEBUSSY; FAURE:
Mélodies ***

Véronique Gens possesses a delightful voice of much beauty, and is very much at home in Poulenc's world. As with the Debussy, she is both imaginative and characterful. She receives sensitive support from Roger Vignoles, and Virgin give her excellent and natural sound.

Mélodies: Banalités: Hôtel; Voyage à Paris. Bleuet. Calligrammes: Voyage. 4 Chansons pour enfants: Nous voulons une petite soeur. Les Chemins de l'amour; Colloque; Hyde Park; Métamorphoses; Miroirs brûlants: Tu vois le feu du soir. Montparnasse; 2 Poèmes de Louis Aragon; 3 Poèmes de Louise Lalanne; Priez pour paix; Tel jour, telle nuit; Toréador
*** Hyp. CDA 66147. Songmakers' Almanac: Lott, Rolfe
Johnson, Murray, Jackson

Felicity Lott sings the great majority of the songs here, joyful and tender, comic and tragic by turns. The other soloists have one song apiece, done with comparable magnetism, and Richard Jackson joins Felicity Lott (one stanza each) in Poulenc's solitary 'song for two voices', *Colloque*. First-rate recording, though Lott's soprano is not always as sweetly caught as it can be.

OPERA

Dialogue des Carmélites (complete)
⊶ ✹ *** Arthaus **DVD** 100 004. Schmidt, Fassbender,
Petibon, Henry, Dale, Chœurs de l'Opéra du Rhin,
Strasbourg PO, Latham-Koenig
*** Virgin 7 59227-2 (2). Dubosc, Gorr, Yakar, Fournier, van
Dam, Viala, Dupuy, Lyon Op. O, Nagano

Poulenc set great store by this opera and this DVD is a remarkably gripping and wholly convincing production which may well serve to persuade those who have not seen the light about this piece. In Anne-Sophie Schmidt it has a Blanche who looks as good as she sounds, and a cast which has no weak member. The production conveys the period to striking effect and the claustrophobic atmosphere of the nunnery. The camerawork is imaginative without ever being intrusive and the production so well managed that the *longueurs* that normally afflict the closing scene in the opera house pass unnoticed. Of the other roles Hedwig Fassbender (Mère Marie de l'Incarnation), Patricia Petibon (Sœur Constance), Didier Henry (Le Marquis de la Force) and Laurence Dale (as the Chevalier de la Force) are exemplary both as singers and as interpreters.

This production is excellent dramatically – and *looks* good. The stage director is Marthe Keller, who was the eponymous heroine of Honegger's *Jeanne d'Arc au bûcher* on DG. The Strasbourg Orchestra play well for Jan Latham-Koenig and, even apart from its compelling visual presence, it has the strongest musical claims as well. Subtitles are in English, German and Flemish.

Much is owed in the Virgin audio set to the dynamic Nagano, who gives an extra momentum and sense of contrast to a work that with its measured speeds and easily lyrical manner can fall into sameness. That the male casting is so strong, with the principal roles taken by José van Dam and the tenor, Jean-Luc Viala, compensates for any lack of variety in having women's voices predominating in an opera about nuns. Catherine Dubosc in the central role of the fear-obsessed, self-doubting Blanche is fresh and appealing, with Brigitte Fournier charming as the frivolous nun, Constance, and the veteran Rita Gorr as the old Prioress and Rachel Yakar as the new Prioress both splendid. The vivid recording, helped by a stage production in Lyon, culminates in a spine-chilling rendering of the final execution scene, with the sound of the guillotine ever more menacing.

La Voix humaine

(M) *** Warner Elatus 2564 60680-2. Migenes, O Nat. de France, Prêtre

Julia Migenes's dramatic and moving performance of Poulenc's theatrical telephone monologue, *La Voix humaine*, is the finest modern version on record, and this separate issue is most welcome.

PRAETORIUS, Michael (1571–1621)

Dances from Terpsichore: Ballet des coqs; Ballet des feus; Ballet des matelotz; Ballet du Roy pour sonner après; La Bourrée; Bransle de villages; La Canarie; 3 Courantes; Pavane de Spaigne; La Sarabande; Spagnoletta.
Arrangements: CAROUBEL: *Bransles.* VALLET: *Suite of Dances.* CAROUBEL: *Bransle simple.* BESARD: *Ballo des Gran Duca; Bransles de village; Une jeune fillette.* DOWLAND: *Courante;* CAMPION: *Courante.* ANON: *Ballet; Ballet des Baccanales; 2 Courantes*
*** Hyp. CDA 67240. Parley of Instruments, Renaissance Violin Band, Holman

Terpsichore is a huge collection of some 300 dance tunes used by the French-court dance bands of Henri IV. They were enthusiastically assembled by the German composer, Michael Praetorius, who also harmonized them and arranged them in four to six parts; however, any selection is conjectural in the matter of orchestration.

This 70-minute collection from Peter Holman and his various instrumental groups must be regarded as the most authentic and comprehensive now available. Praetorius makes it clear in the preface to *Terpsichore* that he regards these as French dances, and Holman convincingly suggests that they were intended primarily for performances on a French-style violin band, or a lute combination (a group of

four lutes play together here), and that is the instrumentation that he very refreshingly offers.

Among his other discoveries are a particularly lively group of *Courantes*, which he did not realize had an English source, of which the most attractive is Thomas Campion's *I Care Not for These Ladies*.

The programme here is very enjoyable in its undemanding way, even if the instrumentation itself is comparatively restricted. However, two engaging exceptions are Praetorius's own *Bransle de villages*, which are exotically scored for five-part violin band, pipe, tabor and bagpipe, and the Anonymous *Courante (Battaglia)*, which closes the programme in a very rhythmic arrangement for violins, lutes, guitar and – when it enters – a dominating drum. Excellent recording and documentation.

Dances from Terpsichore: Suite de ballets; Suite de voltes. (i) Motets: Eulogodia Sionia: Resonet in laudibus; Musae Sionae: Allein Gott in der Höh sei Ehr; Aus tiefer Not schrei ich zu dir; Christus der uns selig macht; Gott der Vater wohn uns bei; Polyhymnia Caduceatrix: Erhalt uns, Herr, bei deinem Wort

**(*) Virgin (ADD) 5 61289-2. Early Music Cons. of L., Munrow; (i) with boys of the Cathedral and Abbey Church of St Alban

Munrow's style is more robust than his competitors' but is always imaginatively scored: the third item, a *Bourrée* played by four racketts (a cross between a shawm and comb-and-paper in sound), is fascinating. The collection is a delightful one. After this stimulating aural feast, Munrow offers six of the composer's eloquent motets, the finest of which is *Erhalt uns, Herr, bei deinem Wort* for four choirs, each with its own accompanying instrumental group, although the shorter *Gott der Vater wohn uns bei* for double choir is hardly less resplendent, and the joyful *Allein Gott in der Höh sei Ehr* (for counter-tenor and triple choir) is also most stimulating, with crumhorns added to the third accompanying group. The only snag is the lack of a really clean focus in the CD transfer, especially in the exultant closing *Christus der uns selig macht*. The Abbey Road acoustic is reverberant, creating a wide amplitude, and the remastering has not altogether been a success in trying to sharpen up the focus. But the result remains rich in timbre, and this inspired music, which often reminds the listener of Giovanni Gabrieli, is sung superbly by the choir.

Christmas motets and chorale concertos: In dulci jubilo; Joseph, lieber Joseph mein; Der Morgenstern ist aufgedrungen; Nun komm der Heiden Heiland; Omnis mundus jocundetur; Psalitte; Puer natus: Ein Kind geborn zu Bethlehem; Singet und klinget; Vom Himmel hoch; Wachet auf, ruft uns die Stimme; Wie schön leuchtet der Morgenstern. Missa gantz Teudsch: Kyrie eleison

**(*) MDG 614 0660-2. Hassler Consort, Rami

The skill of Praetorius as a polyphonist is readily demonstrated in the more ambitious works here, with the settings varying within the chorale concertos between three and fifteen parts. Indeed the busy contrapuntal textures of the opening *Wachet auf* stretch up to nineteen different lines. They are full of interest, and *Nun komm der Heiden Heiland* is similarly lively and inventive. *Puer natus est* (à 3, 7 and 11) alternates slow and jolly, energetic sections very appealingly, while the two movements from the *Mass* show the composer at his most unconventionally individual. But it is the simpler and more lyrical settings that one remembers most affectionately. *In dulci jubilo* for double choir with solo lines simply embellished is quite delightful, and *Joseph, lieber Joseph mein* is equally lovely. *Der Morgenstern* is first heard in a simple evocative presentation and then in the chorale variations which follow. Of the two closing items *Omnis mundus jocundetur* is appealingly carol-like, pastoral in feeling, in spite of its complexity of texture. *Singet und klinget* reintroduces the melody, so associated with this composer, which we have heard before as the basis for *Joseph, lieber Joseph mein*. The performances here are on a chamber scale, with solo voices well matched and blended, if lacking something in individuality. But the freshness of the music-making is never in doubt and, although the balance is immediate, the recording is very good.

Christmas music: *Polyhymnia caduceatrix et panegyrica 9–10, 12 & 17. Puericinium 2, 4 & 5. Musae Sionae VI, 53: Es ist ein Ros' entsprungen. Terpsichore: Dances 1; 283–5; 310*
*** Hyp. CDA 66200. Westminster Cathedral Ch., Parley of Instruments, Hill

Praetorius was much influenced by the polychoral style of the Gabrielis; these pieces reflect this interest. The music is simple in style and readily accessible, and its performance on this atmospheric Hyperion record is both spirited and sensitive.

Christmas music: *Polyhymnia caduceatrix et panegyrica 10, Wie schön leuchtet der Morgenstern; 12, Puer natus in Bethlehem; 21, Wachet auf, ruft uns die Stimme; 34, In dulci jubilo*
☛ (M) *** Virgin (ADD) 5 61353-2. Taverner Cons. Ch. & Players, Parrott – SCHUTZ: *Christmas Oratorio* ***

This is the finest collection of Praetorius's vocal music in the current catalogue. The closing setting of *In dulci jubilo*, richly scored for five choirs and with the brass providing thrilling contrast and support for the voices, has great splendour. Before that comes the lovely, if less ambitious *Wie schön leuchtet der Morgenstern*. Both *Wachet auf* and *Puer natus in Bethlehem* are on a comparatively large scale, their combination of block sonorities and florid decorative effects the very essence of Renaissance style. The recording is splendidly balanced, with voices and brass blending and intertwining within an ample acoustic, and all the more welcome in this mid-priced Veritas reissue.

Lutheran Mass for Christmas Morning (1620)
*** DG 439 250-2. Soloists, Boys' Ch. and Congregational Ch. of Roskilde Cathedral, Gabrieli Consort & Players, McCreesh

Following on after Paul McCreesh's hypothetical re-creation of Schütz's *Christmas Day Vespers* of 1664 (see below), this is an even more stimulating and enjoyable liturgical Feast-day celebration. It is also a most attractive way to present a great deal of Praetorius's music within a Lutheran Mass, as it might have been heard at one of the churches in central Germany around 1620.

Opening with a choral processional to a simply harmonized Lutheran melody, we pass straight into the *Introit, Puer natus in Bethlehem*, for three soloists and three choirs; and after the *Alleluia* comes a spectacularly fast choral entry, *Singet jubilliret triumphant'*. The *Kyrie* follows, set for pairs of soloists, and then the brilliantly florid *Gloria*, where the singers (solo and choral) are again joined by brass and organ

This alternation sets the pattern for much that is to follow. The congregation participates richly in the *Gradual* hymn, *Vom Himmel hoch*, and as the Mass proceeds, there are also organ interludes and even a five-part brass sonata by Schein. After the jaunty closing hymn, *Puer nobus nascitur*, the Mass ends with the thrillingly exultant setting of *In dulci jubilo* for five choirs, including organ, six trumpets and drums, which is also used by the Taverner Consort to close their collection of Christmas music (see above). But here, magnificently sung and played in the echoing acoustic of Denmark's Roskilde Cathedral, the effect is even more spectacular.

PREVIN, André (born 1929)

Violin Concerto
*** DG 474 500-2. Mutter, LSO, composer – BERNSTEIN: *Serenade after Plato's 'Symposium'* ***

André Previn wrote his *Violin Concerto* in 2001 on commission from the Boston Symphony Orchestra for the violinist Anne-Sophie Mutter in the months leading up to their marriage. Starting with a melody as luscious as anything in the Korngold *Concerto*, a work they had already performed together, he makes it clear in the lyricism which invades each of the three movements that this is love music. Mutter responds accordingly with magical playing, making each phrase distinctive while also relishing the challenge of the bravura writing. The hushed ending of the third movement, a set of variations on a nursery theme that Previn as well as Mutter knew in childhood, is breathtaking. At 40 minutes the Previn work may be dangerously expansive, but the performance is magnetic, and the coupling of Bernstein's *Plato Serenade* makes an excellent foil, most persuasively done.

(i) *Diversions for Orchestra;* (ii) *3 Emily Dickinson Songs; The Giraffes Go to Hamburg;* (iii) *Sallie Chisum Remembers Billy the Kid;* (iii; iv) *Vocalise*
*** DG (IMS) 471 028-2 (i) VPO, Previn; (ii) Fleming, Previn (piano); (iii) Bonney, LSO, Previn; (iv) Welsh

The opening item, *Diversions*, written for the Vienna Philharmonic, is a compact four-movement work which with brilliant orchestration aims to exploit the solo talents of a range of the orchestra's leading players – woodwind, including piccolo, and trumpet and horn. The jaunty lighthearted mood of the *Prologue* leads finally to a deeply expressive slow finale which echoes Previn's opera, *A Streetcar Named Desire*. The two works for Renée Fleming come with Previn at the piano. *The Giraffes Go to Hamburg* sets an improbable passage from Karen Blixen's *Out of Africa*, a surreal prose-poem, strangely affecting, while the Emily Dickinson settings find Previn at his most warmly lyrical and approachable, lovely songs exactly reflecting the masterly innocence of the poems. Barbara Bonney earlier recorded the two vocal works written for her in the original piano versions, but the orchestral versions are even more richly expressive, particularly the *Vocalise* with Moray Welsh as cello soloist. Excellent sound.

(i) *Peaches for Flute & Piano; Trio for Piano, Oboe & Bassoon;* (ii) *Triolet for Brass;* (i) *Wedding Waltz for 2 Oboes & Piano;* (iii) (Piano) *Variations on a Theme by Haydn*
*** Ara. Z 6701. (i) Previn (piano), with Mann, Taylor, Godburn, Field; (ii) Philip Jones Brass Ens.; (iii) Han

These works bring out the fluency of Previn's writing in a lighter vein. The *Trio for Piano, Oboe and Bassoon* begins and ends as fun music, with a deeply emotional slow movement between. The *Triolet* is a display piece written for the Philip Jones Brass ensemble, and the piano *Variations*, using the slow movement theme from Haydn's *Symphony No. 82 (The Bear)*, set grittily purposeful writing against two warmly expressive slow variations. The two little occasional pieces, *Peaches* and the *Wedding Waltz*, also bring out Previn's lyrical side. A charming collection, very well performed and recorded.

A Streetcar Named Desire (opera: complete)

*** Arthaus **DVD** 100 138. Fleming, Futral, Forst, Gilfry, Griffey, San Franscisco Op. O, composer (V/D: Colin Graham)

*** DG (IMS) 459 366-2 (3). Fleming, Futral, Gilfry, Griffey, San Francisco Op. Ch. & O, Previn

André Previn's ambitious project to turn Tennessee Williams's ground-breaking play into an opera has resulted in one of the richest, most moving American works in the repertory. The approach may be more conventional in operatic terms than the operas of leading American minimalists, and Colin Graham's richly evocative production with ingenious sets by Michael Yeargan follows that approach, yet the power of the result is undeniable.

Previn himself draws passionate playing from the orchestra of the San Francisco Opera, leading an exceptionally strong cast of soloists, each establishing a distinctive character as laid down in the play.

Central to the opera's success is the moving and powerful assumption of the central role of Blanche by Renée Fleming, relishing music that was specially tailored for her. The big melody of her solo '*I can smell the sea air*' inspires her to producing ravishing sounds, leading to the final scene, where she is led away to the asylum, which is made the more poignant by the sheer beauty of her singing.

Rodney Gilfry admirably copes with the problem of singing freshly and clearly, while making Stanley necessarily a slob. This DVD offers a video recording of the world première, a historic occasion, even more vivid when seen as well as heard.

The live audio recording, also conducted by Previn himself, confirms this as by far his most powerful score yet, not just colourful and atmospheric but agonizingly intense in its portrait of the central character, Blanche. That role was specifically created for the soprano, Renée Fleming, and in the recording she responds magnificently. The inbred tensions created by Blanche's arrival in the home of her sister and the coarse Stanley Kowalski, build up relentlessly over the first two acts. They erupt in Act III in a sequence of solos for Blanche as she loses her mind, that have an overwhelming impact, at once sensuous and sinister. The whole is a great operatic concept, brilliantly achieved, distinctive in its lyricism and subtle in its orchestration. Fleming gives a heart-rending performance, well supported by Elizabeth Futral as Blanche's sister (if rather too close in timbre to Fleming), Rodney Gilfry as Stanley and Anthony Dean Griffey as the wimpish Mitch. Warm, atmospheric recording, with voices well caught and good detail in the orchestral sound.

'The Kindness of Strangers': A Portrait by Tony Palmer

*** Arthaus **DVD** 100 150

Tony Palmer, second to none in portraying great musicians, made this film in 1988 to coincide with the world premiere of Previn's opera, *A Streetcar Named Desire*. Starting with that as a news item, together with a tempting sample of Renée Fleming in the central role of Blanche, the film offers a wide-ranging survey of Previn's achievements, covering his career since boyhood.

It is a measure of his breadth of achievement, not just as a classical conductor, composer and pianist but as a jazz performer and an Oscar-winning Hollywood film composer, that the 90 minutes is crammed with so much rich material. That includes early and rare archive film, not just of Previn himself, but of clips of his early film-successes, *On an Island with You* and *The Sun Comes Out*.

Previn himself is the most engaging of musicians, full of sharp remarks, as when he turned down the idea of an opera as suggested by a German company: 'I can't write an opera where everyone's wearing a toga.' Or on gymnastic conducting: 'An orchestra does not play any louder if you jump, so why jump?' A film full of treasurable material about a fascinating and engaging musician.

PRIN, Yves (born 1933)

(i-iii) *Dioscures (Concerto grosso for Flute, Violin, Clarinet and Chamber Orchestra)*; (ii) *Ephémères (Capriccio for Violin and Chamber Orchestra)*; (iii) *Le Souffle d'Iris (Concerto for Flute and Orchestra)*

(BB) *** Naxos 8.555347. (i) Post; (ii) Graffin; (iii) Artaud; French RPO, Farrandis

Yves Prin studied piano with Yves Nat and conducting with Louis Fourestier, becoming director of the Orchestre Philharmonique des Pays de la Loire and, for a time, the Nouvel Orchestre Philharmonique de Radio France in the early 1980s. Although *Ephémères* has its origins in a solo piece composed in 1974, it has undergone several revisions, most recently in 1992; it is a beautiful and inventively scored work. *Le Souffle d'Iris*, a concerto for flute and orchestra, comes from the mid-1980s and was also revised in 1992. All three pieces on this disc are inventive and full of original sonorities, which spring from a rich imagination. Structurally they do not always convince, but the music mostly proceeds purposefully.

PROKOFIEV, Serge (1891–1953)

Andante for Strings, Op. 50 bis; Autumn (symphonic sketch), Op. 8; Lieutenant Kijé: Suite, Op. 60; The Stone Flower: Suite, Op. 118; Wedding Suite, Op. 126

*** Chan. 8806. SNO, Järvi

The *Andante* is a transcription for full strings of the slow movement of the *First String Quartet*, and its eloquence is more telling in this more expansive format. *Autumn*, on the other hand, is an early piece, much influenced by Rachmaninov and full of imaginative touches. Järvi takes it at a fairly brisk tempo but it remains appropriately atmospheric. The *Wedding Suite* is drawn from *The Stone Flower* and complements the Op. 118 suite from Prokofiev's last full-length ballet. The performances and recording are in the best traditions of the house.

Autumnal, Op. 8; Egyptian Nights, Op. 61; Hamlet (incidental music), Op. 77. (i) Flourish, Mighty Land, Op. 114; Hail to Stalin, Op. 85

*** Chan. 10056. Russian State SO, Polyansky

Autumnal is an early piece, which Prokofiev later revised, but his own personality is already in evidence. The *Egyptian Nights* comes from incidental music composed in 1934, soon after Prokofiev's return to the Soviet Union, and the suite was made four years later, the year in which he also wrote a score for Sergei Radiov's production of *Hamlet*. There are good things in both works, though neither is of the same order as his scores for *Nevsky* or *Ivan*. But still, Prokofiev at second best is better than most of his contemporaries on top form. Despite its naïve touches, the *Stalin Cantata* is far from negligible. An interesting disc, well performed and recorded.

Boris Godunov, Op. 70 bis: Fountain Scene; Polonaise. Dreams, Op. 6; Eugene Onegin, Op. 71: Minuet, Polka, Mazurka. 2 Pushkin Waltzes, Op. 120; Romeo and Juliet (ballet): *Suite 2, Op. 64*
*** Chan. 8472. SNO, Järvi

Järvi's second suite from *Romeo and Juliet* has sensitivity, abundant atmosphere, a sense of the theatre, and is refreshingly unmannered. A fuller selection of the music Prokofiev wrote for a production of *Eugene Onegin* is available; but what is offered here, plus the *Two Pushkin Waltzes*, are rather engaging lighter pieces. The performances are predictably expert, the balance finely judged and detail is in exactly the right perspective.

Chout (ballet; complete), Op. 21
☛ *** CPO 999 975-2. WDR SO, Cologne, Jurowski

Mikhail Jurowski and the Cologne Radio Orchestra continue their survey of the Prokofiev ballets with one of the most neglected and rewarding. *Chout* ('The Buffoon'), which Diaghilev mounted in 1921, did not enjoy the success its score deserved, though the music was not slow to reach the gramophone. It is a deliciously scored and inventive work with relatively few longueurs. Albert Wolff recorded a suite from it before the war, and in 1962 Rozhdestvensky did the most extensive recording up to that time, omitting some of the entr'actes. His version ran to just over 37 minutes while Jurowski's newcomer runs to nearly 57. He and his team maintain the high standards that he achieved in *The Stone Flower*, and Prokofiev admirers who want every note and every repeat need not hesitate. The NordWestDeutscher Rundfunk recording is to a very high standard in terms of clarity and definition.

Chout (ballet): *Suite, Op. 21a; The Love for Three Oranges: Suite, Op. 33a; Le Pas d'acier: Suite, Op. 41a*
*** Chan. 8729. SNO, Järvi

Järvi has a natural affinity for this repertoire and gets splendid results from the SNO; and the recording is pretty spectacular.

Cinderella (ballet; complete), Op. 87
☛ (B) *** Double Decca 455 349-2 (2). Cleveland O, Ashkenazy – GLAZUNOV: *The Seasons* ***

Cinderella (ballet; complete), Op. 87; *Summer Night: Suite, Op. 123*
☛ ✪ (M) *** DG 476 2233 (2). Russian Nat. O, Pletnev

Cinderella (ballet: complete); *Symphony 1 in D (Classical), Op. 25*
(B) *** EMI (DDD/ADD) double forte 5 68604-2 (2). LSO, Previn

Pletnev's account brings playing of terrific life, lightness of touch, poetic feeling and character. Quite simply the best-played, most atmospheric and affecting *Cinderella* we have

ever had on disc. We found its effect tremendously exhilarating and have had difficulty in stopping playing it! Don't hesitate – it is on every count one of the great recordings of the 1990s and is now available at mid-price, for the first time, in Universal's 'Penguin ✪ Collection'.

Otherwise artistic honours are very evenly divided between the Ashkenazy and Previn recordings. Some dances come off better in Previn's EMI version and there is an element of swings and roundabouts in comparing them. Ashkenazy gets excellent results from the Cleveland Orchestra. On CD, the recording's fine definition is enhanced, yet not at the expense of atmosphere, and the bright, vivid image is given striking projection. The appeal of the Double Decca is greatly increased by the inclusion of Ashkenazy's splendid account of Glazunov's finest ballet score. However, the EMI engineers have a more spacious acoustic within which to work and yet lose no detail. Moreover the CD reissue adds a splendid account of the *Classical Symphony*, sunlit and vivacious and hardly less well recorded five years previously.

Cinderella: Suite 1, Op. 107; Lieutenant Kijé: (suite); The Love for Three Oranges: March; Scherzo; The Prince and Princess. Romeo and Juliet: Madrigal; Dance of the Girls with Lilies
(BB) *** Naxos 8.550381. Slovak State PO, (Košice), Mogrelia

The calibre of this excellent Slovak orchestra is well demonstrated here, and its perceptive conductor, Andrew Mogrelia, is at his finest in his gently humorous portrait of *Lieutenant Kijé*, the three 'best bits' from *The Love for Three Oranges* and the charming items from *Romeo and Juliet*. Excellent recording.

Concertino in G min. for Cello & Orchestra (original version); *Cello Concerto in E min., Op. 58*
*** Chan. 9890. Ivashkin, Russian State SO, Polyanski

This Chandos disc is called 'The Unknown Prokofiev' and offers the *Cello Concerto* in its original form, before Prokofiev reworked it for Rostropovich. Starker's record from the 1960s was cut, whereas this is complete. Chandos's claim that this is its first recording is not strictly speaking true: Roger Aubin recorded it in the late 1950s and Rostropovich has recorded the *Cello concertino in G minor*, albeit not in this edition by Vladimir Blok and the cellist himself. These quibbles apart, the performances are very good indeed and splendidly recorded. There is much to be said for the original version of this piece: Prokofiev's second thoughts were not in every case improvements and he cut some inventive ideas.

(i) *Concertino in G min. for Cello & Orchestra, Op. 132* (completed and orch. Kabalevsky & Rostropovich); (ii) *Piano Concertos 1–5;* (iii) *Violin Concertos 1–2;* (i) *Sinfonia concertante for Cello & Orchestra, Op. 125*
☛ (M) *** Decca Trio (ADD/DDD) 473 259-2 (3). (i) Harrell, RPO, Ashkenazy; (ii) Ashkenazy (piano), LSO, Previn; (iii) Bell, Montreal SO, Dutoit

The *Cello Concertino*, inspired by Prokofiev's collaboration with Rostropovich in Op. 125, is a comparatively slight piece, but it is very well played by Lynn Harrell. He gives an even more impressive account of the *Sinfonia concertante* and he sounds as if he is relishing the numerous challenges to his virtuosity that this score poses. His playing of the cadenza in the middle movement (fig. 18 in the score and the ensuing paragraphs) is pretty stunning and Ashkenazy draws strongly characterized playing from the RPO. Turning to the keyboard, Ashkenazy then offers vintage, authoritative accounts of the five *Piano Concertos*, which have been much praised by us. (These are also available separately – see below.)

Employing a measure of emotional restraint and an exceptionally pure tone, Joshua Bell completes this outstanding anthology with ravishingly beautiful accounts of both *Violin Concertos*, heightening the light and shade in the great lyrical passages to contrast with the formidable bravura writing, which finds him at his most commanding. Others, like Chung, may find darker emotions here but, with outstanding recording throughout, this compilation is very recommendable indeed.

Concertino in G min. for Cello & Orchestra; Symphony-Concerto in E min. for Cello & Orchestra, Op. 125; 2 Pushkin Waltzes, Op. 120

(BB) *** Naxos 8.553624. Rudin, Ukraine Nat. SO, Kuchar

The Russian cellist, Alexander Rudin, proves a powerful interpreter of these two concertante works. Rudin can match and even outshine most other rivals, not least in the beauty of his half-tones, as in the slow movements of both works. He and the conductor, Theodore Kuchar, inspire the Ukraine orchestra to play with similar incisiveness, helped by vivid, immediate sound. The two charming Pushkin-based *Waltzes* make an attractive fill-up, winningly pointed.

Piano Concertos 1–5

(B) *** Double Decca (ADD) 452 588-2 (2). Ashkenazy, LSO, Previn

*** Ph. (IMS) 462 048-2 (2). Toradze, Kirov O, Gergiev

*** Chan. 8938 (2). Berman (in 1, 4 & 5); Gutiérrez (in 2 & 3), Concg. O, Järvi

(N) (BB) **(*) Warner Apex 2564 61694-2 (2). Krainev, Frankfurt RSO, Kitaenko

Piano Concertos 1 in D flat, Op. 10; 3 in C, Op. 26; 4 in B flat, Op. 53

(BB) *** Naxos 8.550566. Paik, Polish Nat. RSO (Katowice), Wit

Piano Concertos 2 in G min., Op. 16; 5 in G, Op. 55

(BB) *** Naxos 8.550565. Paik, Polish Nat. RSO (Katowice), Wit

(i) Piano Concertos 1–5; (ii) Overture on Hebrew Themes. Visions fugitives, Op. 22

(B) **(*) EMI (ADD) 5 69452-2 (2). Béroff; (i) with Leipzig GO, Masur; (ii) with Portal, Parrenin Qt

Ashkenazy is a commanding soloist in both the *First* and *Second Concertos*, and his virtuosity in the *First* is quite dazzling. If he is curiously wayward in the opening of the *Second*, there is no question that this too is a masterly performance. The *Third Concerto* is keen-edged and crisply articulated, and the only reservation here concerns the slow movement which at times is uncharacteristically mannered. Ashkenazy is authoritative in No. 4 and gives an admirable account of No. 5: every detail of phrasing and articulation is well thought out, and yet there is no want of spontaneity or any hint of calculation. Throughout, Previn and the LSO accompany sympathetically, and the recently remastered recording makes the most of the vintage mid-1970s Kingsway Hall sound.

The merit of the Berman single disc is discussed below. Gutiérrez gives vital and brilliant accounts of the solo parts of the remaining two concertos (2 and 3) and is keenly responsive to the shifting moods and extreme dynamics of Prokofiev's writing. The Concertgebouw Orchestra under Neeme Järvi play magnificently throughout. As a package, their claims are strong, both artistically and in terms of recording quality.

Kun Woo Paik's playing throughout these five concertos has exhilarating bravura. Tempi are dangerously fast at times and occasionally he has the orchestra almost scampering to keep up with him, but they do, and the result is often electrifying. The famous theme and variations central movement of the *Third Concerto* is played with great diversity of mood and style and the darkly expressive *Larghetto* of No. 5 is very finely done. The *First Concerto*, which comes last on the first CD has great freshness and compares well with almost any version on disc. In short, with vivid recording in the Concert Hall of Polish Radio, which has plenty of ambience, this set is enormously stimulating and a remarkable bargain. It has far better sound than the remastered Decca recording for Ashkenazy.

Alexander Toradze is a powerful pianist in whose musical armoury virtuosity is not in short supply. Superb recorded sound of impressive clarity and presence enhances the appeal of these performances, which are spirited, big-boned and powerful. As in the Scriabin *Prometheus* (coupled with Stravinsky's *Firebird*), this is a formidable partnership.

Vladimir Krainev and the Frankfurt Radio Orchestra under Dmitri Kitaenko are also formidable contenders in their Apex Double format. The recordings were made in 1992 and offer sound of considerable warmth and naturalness. Krainev is a virtuoso of the first order and, apart from the *Third*, which has greater brilliance than poetic feeling, his accounts of these concertos have much to recommend them. Though not quite the equal of Ashkenazy, these are eminently worthwhile accounts that will give pleasure.

A satisfying Rouge et Noir set from Michel Béroff, who plays masterfully and is a pianist of genuine insight where Prokofiev is concerned; Masur gives him excellent support. Béroff is free from some of the agogic mannerisms that distinguish Ashkenazy in the slow movement of the *Third*, and he has great poetry. The balance is good; although the overall sound-picture is not wholly natural, it is certainly vivid, and the timbre of the piano is captured sympathetically. However, in the transfer to CD, a degree of hardness and opaqueness has crept in.

(i) Piano Concertos 1–5. (ii) Violin Concerto 1 in D, Op. 19

(N) **(*) Testament (ADD) SBT2 1376. Boston SO, Leinsdorf with (i) Browning; (ii) Friedman

John Browning (1933–2003) was a pupil of Josef and Rosina Lhévinne, and one of the most brilliant of American virtuosi. Best known for his championship of Samuel Barber's *Piano Sonata*, as well as the *Concerto* that Barber wrote for him, he was the first pianist to record the cycle of all five Prokofiev concertos in the late 1960s. They were soon overtaken by the Ashkenazy and Béroff cycles and were (as far as we know) never transferred to CD, at least not in Britain. Browning gives pretty magisterial accounts of all five, but his *Second* is particularly imposing in its breadth and grandeur, and he is very persuasive in the enigmatic but rewarding *Fourth* for the left hand alone. Although Prokofiev had perhaps the most original keyboard style of his contemporaries after Bartók and Ravel, perhaps his greatest concertos are for stringed instruments. The *First Violin Concerto* inhabits a totally different world from the first two piano concertos. There is poetry, great tenderness and a fairy-tale quality that on Erick Friedman's bow immediately draws the listener into its world. He is a pupil of Heifetz and Milstein and came to prominence in the mid-1960s, but we have heard little of him since this fine Boston recording. Excellent transfers, though the recorded sound was never the equal of the Ashkenazy on Decca.

Piano Concertos (i) *1 in D flat*; (ii; iii) *2 in G min.*; (iii) *Symphony 1 (Classical)*
(M) (**(*)) Sup. mono/stereo SUA 3670-2 011. (i) Richter, Prague SO; (ii) Baloghová; (iii) Czech PO; Ančerl

Sviatoslav Richter gives a bold yet scintillating account of the *First Concerto*, with a delectable central movement and a glittering finale. The mono recording, if orchestrally not too refined, is fully acceptable, for the piano is crisp and clear and there is no lack of body. This performance is probably unsurpassed on record. Dagmar Baloghová proves a sensitive player in the *Second*, but slow tempi detract a little from this account, especially by comparison with Richter in No. 1. However, Ančerl gives a colourful, light-hearted performance of the *Classical Symphony*, which is played most elegantly by the Czech Philharmonic: the high violin entry in the *Larghetto* is exquisitely precise. The mono recorded sound here, if limited, with an emphasis on the middle and bass, is pleasantly warm.

Piano Concertos *1; 3*
*** DG 439 898-2. Kissin, BPO, Abbado
**(*) EMI 5 56654-2. Argerich, Montreal SO, Dutoit –
BARTOK: *Piano Concerto 3* **(*)

(i) *Piano Concertos 1; 3. Piano Sonata 7 in B flat, Op. 83*
*** ASV CDDCA 786. Kodama; (i) with Philh. O, Nagano

Yevgeni Kissin gives a virtuosic, dashing account of both concertos and is given highly sensitive and responsive support from the Berlin Philharmonic under Abbado. It is unfailingly brilliant, aristocratic in feeling and wonderfully controlled pianism, and the recording is very good. It is a pity that DG did not offer a fill-up, as this CD offers only 42 minutes 27 seconds of playing time.

Mari Kodama is a vital and imaginative player and the performances are wonderfully alert and fresh-eyed; there is splendid rapport between soloist and conductor (not surprisingly since they are husband and wife) and they benefit from first-class recording. A strong recommendation not only for newcomers to Prokofiev but for the experienced collector.

Argerich is pretty dazzling in the *First Concerto*, though there is perhaps more grace than fire. Indeed some will find it just a shade underpowered. The *Third*, too, has many felicitous touches and great refinement though it does not supersede the earlier version she made in Berlin for DG with Abbado (see below).

Piano Concertos *1; 4 for the Left Hand; 5*
*** Chan. 8791. Berman, Concg. O, Järvi
*(*) Hyp. CDA 67029. Demidenko, LPO, Lazarev

Boris Berman has established an enviable reputation in this repertoire, and he plays with great panache and dazzling virtuosity. He holds the music on a taut rein and has the nervous energy and ebullience this music needs. The superb recording quality will sway many collectors in his favour.

Nikolai Demidenko possesses formidable technical address but his musical personality is too intrusive for this to be the kind of recommendation his virtuosity should ensure. Tone

above *forte* is not always beautiful, *pianissimo* markings are not always observed, and though there is much to admire, it is the pianist rather than the composer to whom one's attention is too often drawn.

Piano Concerto *3 in C, Op. 26*
(M) *** DG (ADD) 447 438-2. Argerich, BPO, Abbado –
RAVEL: *Piano Concerto in G;* etc. ***
(N) (M) ***Mercury (ADD) **SACD** 475 6607. Janis, Moscow PO, Kondrashin (with MENDELSSOHN: *Song without Words, Op. 61/1;* PINTO: *3 Scenes from Childhood;* PROKOFIEV: *Toccata;* SCHUMANN: *Variations on a theme by Clara Wieck*) – RACHMANINOV: *Piano Concerto 1* ***
(**(*)) Testament mono SBT 1300. Katchen, SRO, Ansermet – BARTOK: *Piano Concerto 3,* etc. **(*)
(BB) (***) Naxos mono 8.110673. Kapell, Dallas SO, Dorati – KHACHATURIAN: *Piano Concerto* (***); SHOSTAKOVICH: *3 Preludes; Piano Concerto 3* (***)
(B) (***) RCA Double mono 74321 845952 (2). Kapell, Dallas SO, Dorati – BEETHOVEN: *Piano Concerto 2;* CHOPIN: *Piano Sonata 2;* DEBUSSY: *Children's Corner;* KHACHATURIAN: *Piano Concerto;* RACHMANINOV: *Rhapsody on a Theme of Paganini* (with SHOSTAKOVICH: *3 Preludes;* SCHUBERT: *Impromptu; Ländler; Moment musical; Waltzes*) (***)
*(**) Chan. 9913. Judd, Moscow PO, Lazarev – TCHAIKOVSKY: *Piano Concerto 1* *(**)

(i) *Piano Concerto 3. Conte de la vieille grand-mère, Op. 31/2–3; Etude, Op. 52; Gavotte, Op. 32/3; Paysage, Op. 59/2; Sonata 4, Op. 29: Andante assai. Sonatine pastorale, Op. 59/3; Suggestion diabolique, Op. 4/4; Visions fugitives, Op. 22/3, 5–6, 9, 10–11, 16–18*
(BB) (***) Naxos mono 8.110670. Composer; (i) with LSO, Coppola

Martha Argerich made her outstanding record of the Prokofiev *Third Concerto* in 1967, while still in her twenties. There is nothing ladylike about the playing, but it displays countless indications of sensuous feminine perception and subtlety, and Abbado's direction underlines that from the very first, with a warmly romantic account of the ethereal opening phrases on the high violins. This is a much more individual performance of the Prokofiev than almost any other available and brings its own special insights. The 1967 recording, always excellent, sounds even more present in this new transfer.

Byron Janis's account of the Prokofiev *Third Concerto* is outstanding in every way, soloist and orchestra plainly challenging each other in a performance full of wit (particularly in the delightfully managed slow-movement variations), drama and warmth. Even though it was made four decades ago, the Mercury recording sounds amazingly faithful (especially the piano). In the new SACD transfer with its added warmth only the thinness in the far upper range of the violins dates the sound. The recital (recorded in Russia the following year) is comparatively low key, except perhaps for the captivating *Scenes from Childhood* of Octavio Pinto, which combines charm with glittering bravura.

In the 1930s and 1940s the *Third Piano Concerto* was represented in the catalogue solely by Prokofiev's own records on 78s, and Katchen's 1953 account was the first LP version to be issued in Britain. The 1955 edition of the *Record Guide* called his playing 'immaculate, deliciously fanciful but never merely superficial,' and even now, half-a-century later, it sounds fresh and spontaneous. The transfer by Paul Baily is also immaculate.

Kapell's fabulously played and electrifying account of the Prokofiev concerto is a *must*. He outstrips even the composer himself – and most others who came after him. Not to be missed. Choice will depend on coupling, but the difficult-to-read sleeve material counts against the RCA version. Naxos promises a complete Kapell, and that may well be the best version to choose.

Recorded live when the late Terence Judd was competing in the 1978 Moscow Tchaikovsky Competition, this urgent and dynamic account of the Prokofiev *Third Concerto* makes up in impulse and conviction for what it lacks in refinement. The recording favours the piano. Like the coupled Tchaikovsky performance this is a valuable and compelling reminder of a talent tragically cut off. Limited sound, and while this reissue is welcome it ought to have been at mid-price.

Pearl issued this coupling of the Prokofiev *Third Concerto*, plus the recordings of piano music the composer made in the 1930s, some years ago, and the present Naxos transfer is a useful and cheaper alternative. However, readers should remember that Dutton have also issued the concerto in an impeccable transfer, coupled with Koussevitzky's unsurpassed account of the *Fifth Symphony* (see below).

(i) *Piano concerto 3*; (ii) *Symphony 5*

(BB) (***) Dutton Lab mono CDBP 9706. (i) Composer, LSO, Coppola; (ii) Boston SO, Koussevitzky

Two classic performances from the days of shellac, Prokofiev's own pioneering and exhilarating account of his then relatively new *Third Piano Concerto* from 1932 coupled with the superb 1946 Boston version of the *Fifth Symphony* under Koussevitzky. Both are indispensable and both have never sounded better.

(i) *Piano Concerto 5. Piano Sonata 8 in B flat, Op. 84; Visions fugitives, Op. 22/3, 6 & 9*

(M) *** DG (ADD) 449 744-2. Richter; (i) with Warsaw PO, Rowicki

Richter's account of the *Fifth Piano Concerto* is a classic. It was recorded in 1959, yet the sound of this excellent CD transfer belies the age of the original in its clarity, detail and vividness of colour. Richter then plays the *Eighth Sonata* and the excerpts from the *Visions fugitives* with comparable mastery, the latter deriving from a live recital. In both cases the recording is surprisingly good.

Violin Concerto 1 in D, Op. 19

(N) *** DG 464 814-2. Gringolts, Gothenburg SO, Järvi – SIBELIUS: *Violin Concerto; Humoresques* ***
(N) *** Pentatone SACD PTC 5186 059. Fischer, Russian Nat. O, Kreizberg – GLAZUNOV: *Violin Concerto*; KHACHATURIAN: *Violin Concerto* ***
✪ (BB) *** Naxos mono 8.110973. Szigeti, LPO, Beecham – BARTOK: *Portrait*; BLOCH: *Violin Concerto* (***) ✪
(M) *** Warner Elatus 0927 49014-2. Mutter, Nat. SO, Rostropovich – GLAZUNOV: *Violin Concerto, Op. 82*; SHCHEDRIN: *Stihira* ***

Ilya Gringolts gives one of the best accounts of the *D major Concerto* to have appeared in recent years, and DG present a perfect balance between soloist and orchestra and a wonderfully transparent orchestral texture. If you want the Sibelius couplings, this is highly recommendable.

On Pentatone the unique triptych of three warmly compelling concertos from this brilliant young German virtuoso, Julia Fischer, superbly recorded in full, bright, clear sound, could hardly be bettered. Central to her choice is her love of the Khachaturian, but her approach to the Prokofiev is just as warm. With fine shading, she takes a thoughtful, meditative view of the yearning melodies, the element in the work that, as she says, most attracts her, but her bravura playing is just as impressive.

Szigeti's pioneering version of the Prokofiev *D major Concerto* with Sir Thomas Beecham and the LPO captures the bitter-sweet intensity of this magical score to perfection. The demonic brilliance of the Scherzo has never been surpassed, even by such great soloists as Oistrakh and Milstein, and the sense of character throughout is superb. Szigeti was a strongly individual artist, and the partnership with Sir Thomas and the LPO brings altogether special results.

As in the Glazunov, Anne-Sophie Mutter gives a warmly sympathetic account, responding to the inspirational direction of Rostropovich. The great melodies of the outer movements are tenderly expressive and the central Scherzo delightfully witty. The Washington recording, airy and spacious, has the soloist forwardly balanced.

Violin Concertos 1, Op. 19; 2, Op. 63

(M) *** Warner Elatus 0927 49567-2. Vengerov, LSO, Rostropovich – GLAZUNOV: *Concerto* ***
(BB) *** Virgin 2x1 5 61633-2 (2). Sitkovetsky, LSO, C. Davis – SHOSTAKOVICH: *Concertos* ***
(N) (M) *** Decca (ADD) 476 7226-2. Chung, LSO, Previn – STRAVINSKY: *Concerto* ***
*** Chan. 8709. Mordkovitch, RSNO, Järvi

Violin Concertos (i; ii) 1; (ii; iii) 2; (iv) Love for Three Oranges (Suite), Op. 33a

(N) **(*) Australian Decca Eloquence (ADD/DDD). LPO, with (i) Belkin; (ii) Kondrashin; (iii) Barshai; (iv) Weller

Vengerov's account of the *First Concerto* was originally coupled with the Shostakovich *First* and as such not only won the *Gramophone*'s Concerto Award in 1995 but was also voted 'Record of the Year'. Now it re-appears at mid-price, joined to a hardly less fine account of the *Second Concerto*. Vengerov's magnetism in both is in no doubt: his playing is full of life and spontaneous feeling, helped by Rostropovich's highly supportive accompaniments. In the *Second Concerto* Vengerov opens the *Andante* magically on a thread of tone, and the playing and orchestral backing are quite ravishing. The finale has splendid vigour and bite. This now becomes the primary recommendation for these two works, and the Glazunov is no less remarkable.

The Virgin two-for-one Double makes an amazing bargain in offering first-class versions of both the paired concertos of Prokofiev and Shostakovich. Dmitri Sitkovetsky conveys the demonic side of the *First Concerto* more effectively than any other player, without losing sight of its lyricism or sense of line. His version of the Scherzo touches an ironic, almost malignant nerve, while he has the measure of the ice-maiden fairy-tale element at the opening. He has a sympathetic collaborator in Sir Colin Davis and the *Second Concerto* is hardly less powerful, and the internal orchestral balance is very natural.

Kyung Wha Chung's performances emphasize the lyrical quality of these concertos with playing that is both warm and strong, tender and full of fantasy. Previn's accompaniments are deeply understanding, while the Decca sound has lost only a little of its fullness in the digital remastering, and the soloist is now made very present. The Stravinsky coupling is equally stimulating. This is now reissued in Universal's 'Critics' Choice' series.

Lydia Mordkovitch gives readings of strong personality and character. She is well supported by the RSNO and Järvi, and more than holds her own with rival versions. There are some splendidly malignant sounds in the Scherzo of No. 1, and both performances make a very satisfying alternative and have first-class sound.

Boris Belkin's warmly expressive readings, from 1982, naturally responsive as they are (with the half-tone opening of the slow movement of No. 2 outstandingly beautiful), are less positive in their characterization than the finest available. However, in their warm digital sound they are still most attractive. Weller's lively and brightly recorded (1977) *Love for Three Oranges* is very successful.

(i) *Violin Concertos 1–2. Symphony 5 in B flat, Op. 100; Romeo and Juliet, Op. 64: Suite (Nos. 1–10); Scythian Suite, Op. 20*

(M) **(*) Decca (ADD) 466 996-2 (2). (i) Ricci; SRO, Ansermet

Ansermet's Prokofiev is always characterful, and if one accepts the less than ideally polished playing of the Swiss orchestra, there is much to enjoy here. The *Fifth Symphony* was one of Ansermet's finest performances, straight and unaffected, and the recording as brilliant as you could wish. The *Scythian Suite* comes off very well too: it is a grossly underrated score because of its parallels with *The Rite of Spring*. The aggressive passages are particularly threatening, largely due to the brilliant recording (wonderful timpani and bass drums), though the performance as a whole is not quite forceful enough. The *Romeo and Juliet Suite* is also rather impressive, though it is the conductor's attention to detail, rather than orchestral virtuosity, which impresses. The *Violin Concertos* are new to CD – and how good they sound. They are hardly top recommendations (intonation on the part of the soloist as well as the orchestra is not immaculate), but they have plenty of character and are not dull. A collection which will be of particular interest to Ansermet admirers, particularly as the vintage sound has been so vividly transferred to CD.

(i) *Violin Concertos 1–2; (ii) Sonata for 2 Violins*

(M) *** EMI (DDD/ADD) 5 62592-2. Perlman, with (i) BBC SO, Rozhdestvensky; (ii) Zukermann

Perlman's 1980 performances bring virtuosity of such strength and command one is reminded of the supremacy of Heifetz. Though the EMI recording has warmth and plenty of bloom, the balance of the soloist is unnaturally close, which has the effect of obscuring important melodic ideas in the orchestra behind mere passagework from the soloist, as in the second subject of the *First Concerto's* finale. Nevertheless, in their slightly detached way these performance are impossible to resist as, apart from the balance, the recording is excellent. The *Double Violin Sonata* (added for this reissue) dates from 1932, when Prokofiev was still living in Paris and is lyrical in feeling, offering both depth and charm. The playing is excellent – as one has every right to expect from this partnership.

(i) *Violin Concertos 1-2; (ii) Violin Sonatas 1-2; 5 Mélodies, Op. 35 bis*

(N) (B) *** Decca 475 6712 (2). Bell; (i) Montreal SO, Dutoit; (ii) Mustonen – SHOSTAKOVICH; *Piano Trio. 2* ***

Employing a measure of emotional restraint and an exceptionally pure tone, Joshua Bell gives a ravishingly beautiful account of both concertos, heightening in the great lyrical passages the light and shade contrasts with the formidable bravura writing, which finds him at his most commanding. Others like Chung may find darker emotions here but, with recording outstanding even by Decca's Montreal standard, these performances are made the more attractive by their coupling on a Double with the *Violin Sonatas* and the charming *Cinq Mélodies*. They give a highly intelligent reading of all three works and their playing carries a full three-star rating. If the recording balance at St George's, Brandon Hill in Bristol unduly favours the piano at the expense of the violin, this is still a very enticing coupling.

(i) *Violin Concertos (i) 1; (ii) 2; (iii) Violin Sonata 2 in D, Op. 94*

(BB) *** EMI Encore 5 85458-2. Zimmermann, with (i) BPO, Maazel; (ii) Philh. O, Jansons; (iii) Lonquich

(N)(M) (***) EMI mono/stereo 5 62888-2. Oistrakh, with (i) LSO, Matačić; (ii) Philh. O, Galliera; (iii) Yampolsky

These famous Oistrakh performances from the 1950s are among the most memorable Prokofiev concertos ever and fully deserve their classic accolade. The *First*, with Lovro von Matačić and the LSO, is from the mid-1950s (like the *D major Sonata*), and only the *Second* (with Galliera and the Philharmonia) of 1959 is in stereo. But this is incomparable playing, and the transfers by Andrew Walter are immaculate.

These Zimmermann performances were recorded in 1987 and 1991 and the disc is drawn from a two-CD set in which he played all Prokofiev's output for the violin, including the sonata for solo violin and for two violins. Zimmermann gives strong, eloquent accounts of the concertos, and they have no want of character. Those who know either of Heifetz's accounts of the *G minor Concerto* will find this just a bit lacking in sarcasm and bite, but there is no doubting the fine musicality and accomplishment of this performance and its companions. Not to be preferred to Oistrakh, Milstein or Kyung-Wha Chung where these are available, but well worth considering, given the competitive price and the excellence of the sound.

Violin Concerto 2 in G min., Op. 63

(N) (M) *** RCA (ADD) **SACD** 82876 66372-2. Heifetz, Boston SO, Munch – GLAZUNOV; SIBELIUS: *Concertos* ***

(B) *** EMI double forte (ADD) 5 69331-2 (2). D. Oistrakh, Philh. O, Galliera – BEETHOVEN: *Triple Concerto;* BRAHMS: *Double Concerto;* MOZART: *Violin Concerto 3* ***

(N) (M) *** Warner Elatus 2564 61572-2. Perlman, Chicago SO, Barenboim – STRAVINSKY: *Violin Concerto* ***

(***) Testament mono SBT 1224. Kogan, LSO, Cameron – TCHAIKOVSKY: *Violin Concerto etc.* (***)

(BB) (***) Naxos mono 8.110942. Heifetz, Boston SO, Koussevitzky – GRUENBERG: *Violin Concerto, Op. 47* (**)

In the *arioso*-like slow movement, Heifetz chooses a faster speed than is usual, but there is nothing unresponsive about his playing, for his expressive rubato has an unfailing inevitability. In the spiky finale he is superb, and indeed his playing is glorious throughout. The recording is improved on SACD, and it has been made firmer in the current RCA remastering. No one is going to be prevented from enjoying this ethereal performance because the technical quality is dated.

David Oistrakh's is a beautifully balanced reading which lays stress on the lyricism of the concerto, and the orchestral support he receives could hardly be improved upon. The 1958 recording is admirably spacious and atmospheric, with finely focused detail and great warmth. The CD transfer is immaculate. An altogether marvellous performance, and this double forte compilation of four very distinguished recordings is extraordinary value for money.

Though Perlman's coupling of Prokofiev's *Second Concerto* and the Stravinsky is ungenerous, this performance, recorded live, is more compelling than his earlier studio recording, with Barenboim adding to the urgency and energy.

Leonid Kogan's mono recording from 1955 has never been reissued on CD and its reappearance here gives us a welcome chance to reassess it. No doubt some will find it cooler than Oistrakh, but Kogan is very aristocratic and has tremendous grip and energy. Basil Cameron proves how supportive an accompanist he could be.

Heifetz's 1937 recording of the second Prokofiev concerto has extraordinary bite and intensity, tough and purposeful in the outer movements, flowing and lyrical in the lovely central slow movement, despite a recording that does not allow a true pianissimo. Otherwise the sound is good, well transferred in this Naxos edition. It is a pity that here it is coupled with the empty and overlong Gruenberg concerto.

Divertimento, Op. 43; The Prodigal Son, Op. 46; Symphonic Song, Op. 57; Andante (from Piano Sonata 4)
*** Chan. 8728. RSNO, Järvi

The *Divertimento* is a lovely piece: its first movement has an irresistible and haunting second theme. Its long neglect is puzzling since it is highly attractive and ought to be popular. So, for that matter, should *The Prodigal Son*, some of whose material Prokofiev re-used the following year in the *Fourth Symphony*. Another rarity is the *Symphonic Song*, a strange, darkly scored piece. The recording is first class – as, indeed, are the performances. An indispensable item in any Prokofiev collection.

Divertimento, Op. 43; Sinfonietta, Op. 5/48; (i) Sinfonia concertante, Op. 125
(N) (M) *** Chan. 10312X. SNO, Neeme Järvi; (i) with Wallfisch

The engaging *Divertimento* now comes additionally recoupled with the *Sinfonia concertante*, in which Wallfisch has the measure of the leisurely first movement and gives a thoroughly committed account of the Scherzo and the Theme and Variations which follow. Neeme Järvi lends him every support. It is inevitable that the cello should be given a little help by the microphones (as is the case with previous versions) but it does seem a shade too forward. The early *Sinfonietta* is offered as a highly attractive bonus (what a sunny and charming piece it is), and the recording throughout has great range, with no complaints about the balance elsewhere.

(i) Dreams, Op. 6; (ii) Lieutenant Kijé (suite); Love for Three Oranges (suite); (iii) The Stone Flower, Op. 118 (ballet; excerpts); (iv) Visions fugitives, Op. 22 (arr. Barshai). (ii; v) Alexander Nevsky, Op. 78
(BB) **(*) Double Decca (ADD/DDD) 473 277-2 (2). (i) Concg. O, Ashkenazy; (ii) Montreal SO, Dutoit; (iii) SRO, Varviso; (iv) ASMF, Marriner; (v) van Nes, Montreal Ch.

Dutoit's Prokofiev, as one would expect, is more than competent and is worth hearing, though he is not uniformly successful here. *Alexander Nevsky* opens atmospherically and, with characteristically good St Eustache sound, Prokofiev's abrasive scoring ensures that the effects are suitably ominous. But overall Dutoit's reading lacks the necessary pungency, and the *Battle of the Ice* sequence fails to grip, despite the spectacular Decca engineering. The highlight of the performance is Jard van Nes's moving solo contribution, and the closing section produces the proper grandeur and sense of triumphant exultation. The *Lieutenant Kijé* and *Love of Three Oranges suites* find the conductor back on form and are very enjoyable. Varviso's excepts from *The Stone Flower* are highly enjoyable too, even if the Swiss orchestra is hardly the last word in orchestral brilliance; it has plenty of character and the 1966 sound is exceptionally warm and vivid. *Dreams* was composed in 1910 while Prokofiev was still a student. It is an atmospheric piece, indebted to Debussy and early Scriabin; it is very well played by Ashkenazy and is recorded in warm, digital sound. New to CD is Marriner's 1972 account of Barshai's brilliant string arrangements of Prokofiev's piano pieces for his Moscow Chamber Orchestra. The ASMF clearly relish the ingenuity of the transcription, which makes them sound like original string music, and the sound is warm and atmospheric.

The Gambler: 4 Portraits, Op. 49; Semyon Kotko: Symphonic Suite, Op. 81 bis
*** Chan. 8803. RSNO, Järvi

Prokofiev's *Four Portraits* enshrine the best of the opera and are exhilarating and inventive. *Semyon Kotko*, though not top-drawer Prokofiev, is still thoroughly enjoyable. Järvi gives a thoroughly sympathetic reading in vivid and present sound.

Lieutenant Kijé (incidental music): Suite, Op. 60
⊶ (B) *** Sony (ADD) SBK 48162. Cleveland O, Szell –
KODALY: *Háry János Suite;* MUSSORGSKY: *Pictures at an Exhibition* ***

Lieutenant Kijé: Suite; The Love for Three Oranges: Suite; Symphony 1 (Classical)
(B) **(*) Ph. 426 640-2. LSO, Marriner

Szell is on his highest form. Seldom on record has the *Lieutenant Kijé* music been projected with such drama and substance, and Szell is wonderfully warm in the *Romance* without a suggestion of sentimentality. The recording, like the couplings, is balanced too closely, but the orchestral playing is so stunning one hardly minds, for the opening and closing trumpet-calls are properly distanced.

This bargain Philips disc offers good playing and recording and there is nothing to disappoint. Individually these works are available in other versions that are as good as (or better than) this compilation, but these are lively performances, and the remastered sound is fresh and open.

The Love for Three Oranges: Suite, Op. 33
*** BBC (ADD) BBCL 4056-2. BBC SO, Kempe –
BEETHOVEN: *Overture: Leonore 3.* DVORAK: *Symphony 9* *** ❁

(i) The Love for Three Oranges: Suite; (ii) Le Pas d'acier: Suite, Op. 41 bis; (i) Scythian Suite, Op. 20
(B) (**) EMI mono 5 69674-2 (2). (i) French Nat. R. O; (ii) Philh. O; Markevitch – STRAVINSKY: *Le Baiser de la fée, etc.* (***)

The Prokofiev suite, strikingly intense, finds Kempe at home in a sharply characterized performance full of grotesquerie. With well-defined contrasts of light and shade, bite and tenderness, it becomes more than a sequence of genre pieces. Vivid transfer of the 1975 radio recording, with high dynamic contrasts.

Sharply characterized performances from Markevitch, brilliantly played. No apologies need be made for the mono sound, which is both brilliant and atmospheric and is transferred to CD without added edge or thinness. However, it is the Stravinsky coupling which makes this reissue distinctive. The pair of CDs are now offered in EMI's French 'two for the price of one' series.

On the Dnieper, Op. 51 (ballet); (i) Songs of Our Days, Op. 76

*** Chan. 10044. Russian State SO, Polyansky with (i) Smolnikova, Tarasov, Russian State Symphonic Cappella

On the Dnieper or Sur le Borysthène was composed immediately after The Prodigal Son and was the last ballet to be commissioned by Diaghilev. It did not reach the stage until 1932, when it was choreographed by Lifar. It was not well received and was soon dropped from the repertory. Prokofiev himself called it 'lyrical and soft, with some energetic flashes'. It takes 40 minutes, and though its invention is not as strong as The Prodigal Son nor is it as imaginative as Chout, it is well worth hearing. Prokofiev at second best is better than most others on top form. Songs of Our Days comes from 1937 and is simple in language and patriotic in sentiment: it was unperformed in the 1950s and 1970s, thanks to Krushchev's ban on any references to Stalin. There are some appealing and (in the case of A Twenty-year-old and the Lullaby) touching ideas. It is an attractively naïve and enjoyable piece splendidly sung by the soloists and chorus. Good playing from Valéry Polyansky and his Moscow forces and very musically balanced recorded sound.

The Prodigal Son, Op. 46; Le Pas d'acier, Op. 41 (ballets; complete)

*** CPO 999 974-2. West German RSO, Cologne, Jurowski

Mikhail Jurowski made a strong impression with his recording of The Stone Flower ballet, recorded with the Hanover orchestra (see below) and the present release is no less satisfying. The Prodigal Son, on which Prokofiev drew for the Fourth Symphony, is a fine work which the Royal Ballet revived early in 2004 as part of its Balanchine triple bill. Le Pas d'acier is a little earlier and is an inventive and characterful work, designed to shock Paris audiences in the manner of the Second Symphony. Neither work is generously represented in the catalogue, so this well-played and -recorded newcomer deserves a welcome. It is as good as any of the (admittedly few) alternatives.

Peter and the Wolf, Op. 67

➤ (BB) *** Naxos 8.554170. Dame Edna Everage, Melbourne SO, Lanchbery – BRITTEN: Young Person's Guide ***; POULENC: The Story of Babar *** ☉

(N) (B) **(*) CfP 586 1752. Rushton, LPO, Edwards (with DEBUSSY: Children's Corner: 3 Pieces) – BRITTEN: Young Person's Guide ***; RAVEL: Ma Mère l'Oye **

(***) Pentatone PTC 5186. Sophia Loren, Russian Nat. O, Nagano (with BEINTUS: Wolf Tracks (narrated Bill Clinton); includes spoken prologue and epilogue in Russian by Mikhail Gorbachev)

(i) Peter and the Wolf; (ii) Lieutenant Kijé: Suite

(M) **(*) Decca Phase Four (ADD) 444 104-2. (i) Connery (nar.), RPO; (ii) Netherlands R. PO; Dorati – BRITTEN: Young Person's Guide **(*)

(i; ii) Peter and the Wolf; (iii) Lieutenant Kijé: Suite; (iv) The Love for Three Oranges: Suite; (ii) Symphony 1 in D (Classical)

➤ ☉ (B) *** Decca (ADD) 433 612-2. (i) Richardson; (ii) LSO, Sargent; (iii) Paris Conservatoire O, Boult; (iv) LPO, Weller

Sir Ralph Richardson brings a great actor's feeling for words to the narrative; he dwells lovingly on their sound as well as their meaning, and this genial preoccupation with the manner in which the story is told matches Sargent's feeling exactly. Sir Malcolm Sargent's direction of the accompaniment shows his professionalism at its very best. The original coupling, Sargent's amiable, polished account of the Classical Symphony, has now been restored. All the tempi, except the finale, are slow but Sir Malcolm's assured elegance carries its own spontaneity. The sound is vivid. Boult's Paris recording of Lieutenant Kijé offers more gusto than finesse, but the result is exhilaratingly robust and the very early (1955) stereo comes up remarkably well. Weller's Love for Three Oranges is a first-class performance, given top-drawer 1977 recording. But our Rosette is for Peter and the Wolf.

If you react adversely to Dame Edna Everage's exuberantly eccentric persona, the Naxos version cannot be recommended. But for those willing to be included among her possums it is a highly entertaining and very dramatic narrative, with the orchestral accompaniment splendidly paced to match the gripping onward flow of the story. The wolf-horns positively snarl, the flute-bird chirps merrily and the cat-clarinet has a certain elegant insouciance, while the hunter's guns are like thunder. There are twee moments, but children will readily respond to Dame Edna's very positive involvement with her characters, and so will most parents. At the close she throws away the humour of Grandfather's grumble but not the childish delight on discovering that the duck is still alive after all, inside the wolf. The couplings are equally splendid.

Although the narrative and orchestral commentary were recorded separately on the CfP disc, it is remarkable how well the two fit together. But the flair and professionalism of Sian Edwards meant that William Rushton was able to add his story-telling to a vividly colourful orchestral tapestry which had its momentum already established. He is a personable narrator, adding touches of his own like 'a vast grey wolf' and 'nothing to report' from the bird, and, while he does not match Sir Ralph Richardson in his relish for the words, overall this is a fine, sparkling presentation, brightly and realistically recorded, which cannot fail to entertain.

Sophia Loren's most engaging narration of Peter and the Wolf has universal appeal. Children will surely love its warmth and innocence, and adults will appreciate the way this fine actress identifies so charmingly with the story. She keeps closely to the text, yet her little personal touches add to the friendliness of her story-telling. She is helped by Kent Nagano's attentive yet relaxed pacing, and some strikingly picaresque characterizations by the orchestral soloists, especially the cat – so feline and sneaky on the clarinet. (The solo describing the dash up the tree, with its closing cadential near-'miaow', is a winning touch.) Grandfather too is chipper yet persuasive in his authority on the bassoon, and the oboe's melancholy is very affecting at the very close when Sophia's last words are so gentle and sympathetic. She will make any child face the situation that the duck alive inside the wolf brings a dilemma virtually impossible to resolve.

The coupling offers an anodyne retelling of the story in a completely new narrative by Walt Kraemer to suit 'wolf-friendly' sensibilities, backed with a pleasant but wishy-washy score by Jean-Pascal Beintus which adds virtually nothing to the narrative. The narration of the tale by Bill Clinton, though undoubtedly sympathetic, becomes increasingly and embarrassingly sentimental, and the otherwise admirable moral, 'The time has come to leave the wolves alone', is underlined *ad nauseam*. Mikhail Gorbachev provides a (fortunately brief) Prologue, Intermezzo and Epilogue in Russian, which is then spoken in translation by Sergei Markov. These cliché-ridden comments are pointless, and one wonders why the Russian ex-president could not have managed to speak his political benedictions in English. Each of the major participants is donating his or her royalties to the charity of choice, including of course the Wolf Conservation Center. Indeed, the Wolf himself is quoted in the booklet as saying, 'Everyone, including you dear listener, has made a contribution to a better future for wolves, and all the noble creatures on our planet'. Even so, this part of the CD is quite impossible to recommend.

Sean Connery uses a modern script by Gabrielle Hilton which brings a certain colloquial friendliness to the narrative and invites a relaxed style, to which the actor readily responds. If you can accept such extensions as 'dumb duck' and a pussy cat who is 'smooth, but greedy and vain', you will not be disappointed with Connery's participation in the climax of the tale, where Dorati supports him admirably. Both *Peter and the Wolf* and *The Young Person's Guide to the Orchestra* start with the orchestra tuning up, to create an anticipatory atmosphere, and the introductory matter is entirely fresh and informal. In *Lieutenant Kijé* Dorati is characteristically direct, with everything boldly characterized, and he secures excellent playing from the Netherlands orchestra. As with *Peter and the Wolf*, the extremely vivid Decca Phase Four recording (not unnaturally balanced but ensuring every detail is clear) gives the performance a strong projection.

***Romeo and Juliet* (ballet; complete. Choreography by Kenneth MacMillan)**

🔑 ❁ *** **DVD** TDK DV-BLRAJ. (Choreography further adapted by Monika Parker, Georgina Parkinson & Julie Lincoln.) Ferri, Corelli, Ghisleni, Villanova; La Scala, Corpo di Ballet; with La Scala O, cond. Garforth. (Set Designer: Ezio Frigerio. Producer; Nini Perno. V/D Tina Protasoni)

***Romeo and Juliet* (ballet: complete. Choreography and staging by Rudolf Nureyev)**

*** Warner NVC Arts **DVD** 0630 15154-2. Legris, Loudières, Jude, Delanoe, Carbonnel, Martinez, Paris Opéra O, Pähn. (Director: Alexandre Tarta. Producers: François Duplet and Damien Mathieu)

Kenneth MacMillan's classically choreographed *Romeo and Juliet* shows him at his very finest, endlessly imaginative both visually and dramatically. The magnificent set designs are by Ezio Frigerio, who also provided the backcloths for the 1995 Paris Opéra Ballet production discussed below. But La Scala is La Scala, and here the eye is almost overwhelmed by the scale of the backgroud opulence and the lavish traditional costumes. The present live recording was made in January 2000, with Alessandra Ferri an enchanting, waif-like Juliet, partnered by the charismatic, boyish Romeo of Angel Corelli. Not only is their dancing magically graceful, but their complete identification with the key roles brings a wonderful spontaneity of feeling. The great love scene in the garden is as full of shared joy as it is of passion, and when Juliet is left alone to face her parents' demands that she accept Paris, she conveys a hauntingly desparate vulnerability, which anticipates the joint despair of the tragic ending of the story.

Earlier, the scene of the death of Mercutio, most sensitively portrayed by Michele Villanova, is profoundly moving, so that one is totally gripped when Romeo takes up the sword to fight the second fatal duel. Yet there are many charming light-hearted moments too, as when Romeo delightedly receives his letter from Juliet. The large La Scala Corps de Ballet means that the crowd scenes are spectacular and danced with panache. But all the smaller individual cameos are beautifully drawn, and the many dances and divertissements that create the backgound to the story are visually entrancing. David Garforth conducts the La Scala Orchestra with a passionate commitment to Prokofiev's inspired score, yet he shows a wonderful ear for detail, making the music totally at one with the stage action. The recording is first class, and watching and listening to this superb DVD is a truly memorable experience.

Rudolf Nureyev famously created the role of Romeo for the Royal Ballet in 1965 with Margot Fonteyn as Juliet. In 1977 he revised the choreography for his own London Festival Ballet production, and in 1984 reworked the entire ballet for the Paris Opéra Ballet. The present live performance dates from 1995, with Manuel Legris dancing the role of Romeo with great distinction and Monique Loudières a delightful, elegantly graceful and passionate Juliet. Their love scenes together, at first romantic and finally erotically ardent, are among the ballet's highlights. But so too are the scenes with Tybalt (Charles Jude) and Mercutio (Lionel Delanoe) on whom Nureyev's choreography places special emphasis as 'champions' of the younger generation of the two rival families.

The confrontations between Mercutio and Tybalt are thrillingly visceral, the choreography for the electrifying duel with Romeo and the death of Tybalt a *coup de theâtre*, well matched by Prokofiev's vibrant music. The earlier panorama, with spectacularly spacious set designs by Ezio Frigerio, presents a brilliant, large-scale fresco of a turbulent Verona, full of colour and movement. Yet the simpler background for Friar Lawrence's chapel is equally memorable. Mauro Pagano's vivid costume designs give a vivid survey of the Italian Quattrocento, borrowing from paintings by Uccello, Piero Della Francesca, Pisanello and others.

In short, the production offers an ideal backcloth for superb dancing from the principals and a totally gripping projection of the narrative. At the anguished climax, Romeo's angry dispatch of Paris is more like murder than a duel. But by the ballet's close, which is not protracted, 'all are punished'. There is some intrusive audience applause, notably in Acts I and III, but it is a price well worth paying for the electricity of a live performance, and there are plenty of entry points on the DVD (which has an excellent booklet). The orchestra plays Prokofiev's infinitely inspired score very well indeed, and the recording, too, is very good (it seems to gain range and impact as the ballet proceeds). But it is not up to the superb demonstration quality provided by Decca for Ashkenazy's RPO audio recording (see below), which is surely an essential supplement to the DVD.

Romeo and Juliet (ballet), *Op. 64* (complete)

⊶ (M) *** Decca 436 078-2 (2). RPO, Ashkenazy

(M) *** Double Decca (ADD) 452 970-2 (2). Cleveland O, Maazel

(B) *** EMI double forte (ADD) 5 68607-2 (2). LSO, Previn

(B) **(*) Ph. 464 726-2 (2). Kirov O, Gergiev

Vladimir Ashkenazy's outstanding version of *Romeo and Juliet* was recorded as long ago as early 1991 yet did not appear until the Prokofiev centenary in 2003. That delay is all the more a mystery, when this version sets new standards: it is a full and rich digital recording of a reading that at once combines brilliance, warmth and a feeling of fantasy, with crisply sprung rhythms at speeds that are fresh and alert. The result is lighter and more idiomatic than the much earlier Decca analogue version from Lorin Maazel, and more sparkling than the Gergiev version on Philips, two rival sets from the Universal stable that may have unfairly delayed the new set's issue.

Previn and the LSO made their recording in conjunction with live performances at the Royal Festival Hall, and the result reflects the humour and warmth which went with those live occasions. Previn's pointing of rhythm is consciously seductive, whether in fast, jaunty numbers or in the soaring lyricism of the love music. The Kingsway Hall recording quality is full and immediate, yet atmospheric too.

Maazel by contrast will please those who believe that this score should above all be bitingly incisive. The rhythms are more consciously metrical, the tempi generally faster, and the precision of ensemble of the Cleveland Orchestra is little short of miraculous. The recording is one of Decca's most spectacular, searingly detailed, but atmospheric too. With the reissue of the Maazel set as a Double Decca, honours are even between both sets: if you want the finest sound and a gripping sense of drama, choose Maazel; if you prefer a more genial manner, Previn is your man.

Gergiev secures beautifully polished playing from the Kirov Ballet Theatre Orchestra. Indeed it is graceful to the point of being over-cultivated. There is much delicacy of effect, rhythms are crisp and clean and there is plenty of energy, while the brass sonorities are without the rough edges one expects from Russian orchestras. But this is a very romantic view, at its finest in the captivating portrayal of *The Young Juliet*, and *Juliet Alone*, while the picaresque numbers like the engaging *Dance with Mandolins* and the charming *Aubade* and *Dance of the Girls with Lilies* are beautifully played. The *Death of Mercutio* certainly brings a moment of red-blooded drama, but when it comes to the Balcony scene the lovers' ardour has little sexuality and elsewhere Prokofiev's pungency is muted. The opening of Act III is powerful, but the anguish and tragedy of the climax of the story has intensity without stark despair. The recording, made on location in Leningrad by a Philips team, is of the very highest quality, so this is a performance to enjoy primarily for the lyricism of Prokofiev's inspiration.

Romeo and Juliet, *Op. 64*: (ballet; highlights)

(B) *** Sony SBK 89740. BPO, Salonen

(M) *** Virgin 5 61977-2. RLPO, Pešek

With magnificent playing from the Berlin Philharmonic Orchestra, Esa-Pekka Salonen's set of excerpts – now reissued at bargain price – is probably a 'best-buy' for those wanting a single disc of highlights from Prokofiev's masterly score. The orchestral playing has an enormous intensity and a refined felicity in the score's more delicate evocations. One is touched

and deeply moved by this music-making, while the selection admirably parallels the ballet's narrative. The recording, made in the Philharmonie, matches sumptuousness with a potent clarity of projection, and the dynamic range is dramatically wide.

Pešek's selection follows the narrative line, and one feels that the conductor and his players are highly involved in the course of events; in the closing numbers Pešek tightens the screws so that the *Death of Juliet* is devastating. The Royal Liverpool Philharmonic Orchestra play very well indeed and achieve great freshness and spontaneity; they are given a satisfying concert-hall balance. This Virgin CD offers 71 minutes from Prokofiev's inspired score, and every minute is stimulating and enjoyable.

Romeo and Juliet (ballet): excerpts, (including *Suite 2*)

(M) *** Classic fM 75605 57047. RPO, Gatti –
  TCHAIKOVSKY: *Romeo and Juliet (Fantasy Overture)* ***

Romeo and Juliet (ballet): *Suites 1 & 2, Op. 64*

(B) **(*) Double Decca (ADD) 440 630-2 (2). SRO, Ansermet
  – TCHAIKOVSKY: *Swan Lake* **(*)

Romeo and Juliet (ballet): *Suites 1 & 2*: excerpts

⊶ (M) *** Telarc CD 80089. Cleveland O, Levi

Romeo and Juliet (ballet): *Suites 1 & 3*

(N) (B) *** DG Entrée 477 5011. Concg. O, Chung

After a bitingly pungent opening (*Montagues and Capulets*), Daniele Gatti's 50-minute selection effectively encapsulates the ballet's dramatic narrative in nine key numbers. The RPO characterizes very strongly indeed and, with generally brisk tempi, the strongest contrast is made between the bold, pungent rhythms of the more vigorous dances and the exquisite delicacy of the gentler, romantic evocation with its wonderfully translucent orchestral colouring. The portrait of *Friar Laurence* is touchingly gentle, but the ballet's passionate climax could not be more heart-rendingly plangent. The recording is superb, very much in the demonstration bracket, and the coupling with Tchaikovsky's fantasy overture is made the more apt by Gatti's highly romantic approach to that quite different response to Shakespeare's tragedy.

Yoel Levi also seems to have a special affinity with Prokofiev's score, for pacing is unerringly apt and characterization is strong. There are some wonderfully serene moments, as in the ethereal introduction of the flute melody in the first piece (*Montagues and Capulets*). The quicker movements have an engaging feeling of the dance and the light, graceful articulation in *The Child Juliet* is a delight; but the highlights of the performance are the *Romeo and Juliet Love Scene* and *Romeo at Juliet's before Parting*, bringing playing of great intensity, with a ravishing response from the Cleveland strings. The rich Telarc recording is in the demonstration class, and if this offers less music than several of its competitors it is now at medium price.

Myung-Whun Chung draws playing of great atmosphere, virtuosity and dramatic fire from the Royal Concertgebouw Orchestra, and DG provide a recording of great range and presence, comparable with the best now available. A pity that they did not include the second suite, for which there would have been room; this handicaps a record that should enjoy – and certainly deserves – the widest exposure. However, at its new price it is still very tempting, and those who use it for an entrée to Prokofiev's greatest ballet score will not be disappointed.

Ansermet's performances have both atmosphere and passion (notably *Romeo with Juliet Before his Departure*). After the ominous introduction, the playing is rhythmically a bit sluggish. But *Juliet As a Young Girl* and the *Madrigal* are charming, and the love scene of *Romeo and Juliet* is genuinely touching; the *Death of Tybalt* bursts with energy, and *Masks* is nicely pointed. If the Suisse Romande Orchestra in 1961 was not one of the world's greatest ensembles, Ansermet was very persuasive and he brings everything vividly to life. The dramatically vibrant recording is well up to Decca's vintage standard of the early 1960s.

Romeo and Juliet (excerpts); Lieutenant Kijé: Suite, Op. 60

(N) **(*)** Testament SBT 1394. Boston SO, Leinsdorf

In his book *The Composer's Advocate* Leinsdorf speaks of his love for *Romeo and Juliet* but recounts how the concert suites came to dissatisfy him, He then devised from the ballet a suite of his own, which continues uninterrupted, making a chronological sequence that conveys the dramatic narrative of Prokofiev's masterpiece. This he recorded in Boston in 1967, together with a fine account of *Lieutenant Kijé*. He is not perhaps as subtle as some of his rivals, but there is plenty of dramatic tension and atmosphere here and very good recorded sound.

Romeo and Juliet (ballet): Suite 1: (excerpts); Suite 2 (complete); Peter and the Wolf

(M) **(*)** Sup. (ADD) SU 3676-2 011. Czech PO, Ančerl

This 1959 Supraphon set of excerpts from Prokofiev's *Romeo and Juliet* was one of the first to appear in stereo, and it has much of the freshness of new discovery. Ančerl immediately grasped the style of this angular, yet inventive and highly characteristic writing, and the orchestral playing is superb. Moreover, the early stereo expands magnificently before our ears in the big romantic climaxes, and with such an impressive orchestral response and outstanding recording, this remains highly recommendable.

Eric Shilling's 1963 narration of *Peter and the Wolf* has a period charm, with its unselfconscious avuncular style and clear BBC English. There is just a twinkle of humour too, and with a fine orchestral response, this is most enjoyable – a good bonus, if not quite in the class of the finest versions.

Romeo and Juliet: Suite 2

(N) (BB) (***) Dutton mono CDBP 9754. Moscow State PO, composer – GLAZUNOV: *The Seasons* (***)

Recorded in Moscow in 1943 at the height of the Second World War, when the city was under threat from Nazi forces, Prokofiev's own recording of music from his *Romeo and Juliet* ballet – at that time not yet recognized as a masterpiece – brings some rough ensemble in playing, not helped by the dry acoustic. Yet the warmth and energy of the playing under the composer make this a valuable document, with the Dutton transfer greatly improving the original 78-r.p.m. sound. It is a pity that in the notes so little information is given on the backgrounds, either to this or to the Glazunov.

Russian Overture, Op. 72; Summer Night: (suite from The Duenna), Op. 123; War and Peace (suite, arr. Palmer)

*** Chan. 9096. Philh. O, Järvi

The *Russian Overture* is determinedly popular in appeal, and it teems with ideas, both lyrical and grotesque, and has plenty of vitality. The *Summer Night Suite* is notable for its delicate *Serenade* and a charmingly romantic movement called *Dreams*. But the finest music here is Christopher Palmer's suite of interludes from *War and Peace*, full of splendid ideas. It ends triumphantly with the magnificent patriotic tune associated with Marshal Kutuzov, the architect of the Russian victory. Järvi and the Philharmonia Orchestra are thoroughly at home in these scores, and the Chandos recording is characteristically spectacular.

Scythian Suite, Op. 20 (with rehearsal)

*** Arthaus **DVD** 100 314. Rotterdam PO, Gergiev (with DEBUSSY: *Le Martyr de Saint-Sébastien*) (Director: Rob van der Berg; V/D: Peter Rump) – STRAVINSKY: *Piano Concerto*, etc. *******

Apart from performing it, Gergiev here discusses the *Scythian Suite* and its composer, championing the score with much eloquence. There are few pieces in twentieth-century music that are as imaginative as its third movement, *Night*, or as inventive as the first, *The Adoration of Vélèss and Ala*, with its extraordinary lush contrasting group. Gergiev's performance has great fervour and eloquence, and it is good to hear him speak of the music with such warmth in the accompanying hour-long documentary. This includes some valuable archive material of Prokofiev himself and a contribution from his second son, the painter Oleg (who is also now no longer with us). The camera-work is unobtrusive and intelligent, though – as so often – one could do without some of the aerial shots of the orchestra. The *Scythian Suite* is difficult to balance, and some of the detail emerges in greater prominence than the main lines; but for the most part the sound balance is vivid and very present. The Debussy excerpts from *Le Martyr de Saint-Sébastien* are also most impressively played and recorded. This is an outstanding and invaluable DVD that is hugely enjoyable.

Scythian Suite, Op. 20; (i) Alexander Nevsky, Op. 78

⌐ *** Ph. 473 600-2. Kirov O, Gergiev, with (i) Borodina, Kirov Ch.

Recorded live at the first Moscow Easter Festival in May 2002, Gergiev's reading of the *Alexander Nevsky* cantata is larger than life, powerful and thrusting, rugged rather than refined or polished. The earthy qualities of a score linked to a patriotic film are heightened, with the *Battle on the Ice* wildly energetic and Olga Borodina making the *Lament for the Dead* a great public utterance. The sound, recorded in the Moscow Conservatory, is full and immediate, with good detail. DVD collectors may already have sampled Gergiev's superb *Scythian Suite* (see above), which the conductor – rightly – regards as one of Prokofiev's most imaginative and extraordinary inspirations. Recorded in the Martti Talvela Hall in Finland, the present performance has similar qualities to the cantata, a thrusting, powerful performance, which also finds warmth and colour in this early but remarkable Prokofiev score that some listeners wrongly regard as just brutal.

Sinfonia concertante for Cello & Orchestra, Op. 125 (see also above under Divertimento and Concertino)

⌐ ✿ *** EMI **DVD** DVA 4901209. Rostropovich, Monte Carlo Nat. Op. O, Kamu – SHOSTAKOVICH: *Cello Concerto 1*. Bonus: MUSSORGSKY: *Songs and Dances of Death* *******

(M) **(*)** Ph. 470 250-2 (2). Schiff, LAPO, Previn – DVORAK: *Cello Concerto*; SCHUMANN: *Cello Concerto*; R. STRAUSS: *Don Quixote* **(*)**

(M) ** Sup. (ADD) SU 3696-2. Navarra, Czech PO, Ančerl – *Alexander Nevsky* **(*)

The Prokofiev *Sinfonia concertante*, which reputedly inspired the coupled Shostakovich concerto, is an altogether more romantic, essentially lyrical work. But it has an extraordinarily manic Scherzo which Rostropovich plays with such breathtaking virtuosity that the audience breaks into applause at the end of the movement. The work then moves back to warm lyricism and on to a characteristic *Allegro marcato* theme, which the cellist shares joyfully with the orchestra, glancing towards other orchestral soloists when they take up the theme from him. Throughout both works the camera frequently focuses closely on the solo cello, which makes Rostropovich's playing intensely involving. The live communication between soloists and orchestra, projected out to the watcher/listener, is marked, with the work's close leaving one with the feeling that there is no more to be said. This is a DVD that is a historical treasure and also offers a performance that in its own right can surely never be surpassed and is here caught on the wing. The very dry Monte Carlo acoustic does not help the orchestra, but one soon adjusts to the unexpansive orchestral sound when the solo playing is so electrifying.

No grumbles about Heinrich Schiff's playing in the *Sinfonia concertante* (or *Symphony-Concerto*, as it is sometimes called) which Prokofiev composed for (and with) Rostropovich. The composer had originally planned to call it 'Cello Concerto No. 2', but it is so closely related to the thematic material of his pre-war *Cello Concerto* as to be a re-working. Schiff's is an impassioned, red-blooded and eminently well-recorded account which will give pleasure. Previn gets good results from the orchestra but this is not a first choice.

Navarra's performance with Ančerl is strong and committed, and the atmospheric recording has been greatly improved over the original LP. However, this is a curious coupling for *Alexander Nevsky*.

(i) *Sinfonia concertante for Cello & Orchestra, Op. 125*; (ii) *Cello Sonata in C, Op. 119*

☛ *** EMI 5 47438-2. Chang, with (i) LSO, Pappano; (ii) Pappano (piano)

Both the *Sinfonia concertante* (or *Symphony-Concerto*) and the *Cello Sonata* are well represented on CD, though not elsewhere coupled together. Han-Na Chang, in warm partnership with Pappano and the LSO, gives a rich, heartfelt, urgently impulsive reading, powerful as well as polished, with the element of fantasy brought out in the central *Allegro giusto* and the pawky humour nicely pointed. The late *Cello Sonata* makes an ideal coupling. Han-Na Chang again brings a youthful ardour and vigour to her performance, with Pappano at the piano proving a warmly sympathetic accompanist, even though the instrument is placed well behind the cello. Although Rostropovich himself is a mandatory acquisition in any self-respecting Prokofiev collection, this young cellist can more than hold her own with the current competition. First-rate and natural recorded sound.

The Stone Flower (ballet: complete)

☛ *** Chan. 10058 (2). BBC PO, Noseda
*** CPO 999 385-2 (3). Hanover R. PO, Jurowski

Conceived in 1948, during Stalin's worst artistic crackdown, but not staged until 1954, after the composer's death, *The Stone Flower* is a massive ballet built on folk stories in 46 numbers lasting two and a half hours. The freshness of invention, with one striking idea after another, demonstrates Prokofiev's astonishing ability to work under the most severe mental stress and yet remain his highly individual self. As in other late works, he eked out his ideas with material drawn from earlier pieces, but a warm, colourful performance, brilliantly recorded, such as this from the BBC Philharmonic under Gianandrea Noseda, makes one appreciate that this deserves to be in the ballet-theatre repertory alongside *Romeo and Juliet* and *Cinderella*. The variety of mood is a delight, with incidental divertissements developing naturally in the telling of the story of the hero, Danilo, in search of the stone flower – symbolic, no doubt, of the artist's search for an otherworldly goal. The chain of numbers over four acts ends in a triumphant *Adagio* in characteristically flamboyant ballet style; then follows a bold epilogue with a touch of Hollywood in it, all vividly presented in this opulent Chandos recording.

The version from Hanover under Mikhail Jurowski has a lot going for it. The orchestral playing is polished and characterful, and the CPO recording is fresh and well detailed, though it is expensive on three mid-price discs. Incidentally, the 1991 Kirov video production (Teldec 9031-76401-3) is not to be missed: a joy to the eye, very well danced and well worth buying; but the score is not complete.

SYMPHONIES

Symphonies 1–7
*** Chan. 8931/4. RSNO, Järvi

Symphonies 1–7; Overture russe, Op. 72; Scythian Suite, Op. 20
(B) **(*) Decca (ADD) 430 782-2 (4). LSO or LPO, Weller

These Chandos recordings from the mid-1980s are of the highest quality. They have been shorn of their couplings in this box, the only important loss being the delightful *Sinfonietta*. Both versions of the *Fourth Symphony* are included: the 1947 revision appears with the *Classical* on the first disc, while the 1930 original is coupled with the *Third*. Nos. 2 and 6 are on the third disc, and 5 and 7 on the last, so no side-breaks are involved. As performances, these are the equal of the best.

Weller's performances are polished and very well played, though at times they are emotionally a little earthbound. Transfers are well managed, though there is some loss of naturalness in the upper range. The finest of the set is No. 2. Elsewhere, the bitter tang of Prokofiev's language is again toned down and the hard-etched lines smoothed over. The *Seventh* suits Weller's approach readily and he catches the atmosphere of its somewhat balletic second movement particularly well. The *Russian Overture* has plenty of energy but the *Scythian Suite*, too, needs more abrasiveness.

Symphony 1 in D (Classical), Op. 25
*** TDK **DVD** DV-VPOVG. VPO, Gergiev (includes Gergiev talking on Prokofiev and Stravinsky) (V/D: Brian Large) – SCHNITTKE: *Viola Concerto*; STRAVINSKY: *Firebird Complete Ballet* ***
(B) *** Virgin 2×1 5 62050-2 (2). Lausanne CO, Zedda – DEBUSSY: *Danse; Sarabande* ***; MILHAUD: *La Création du monde* ***; SHOSTAKOVICH: *Chamber Symphony; Symphony 14* **

As the opening scenic view discloses, Gergiev's splendid performance, admirably paced and very well played, was recorded at the 2000 Salzburg Festival. The orchestra is perceptively photographed (the video director is Brian

Large), although curiously, among the many effective instrumental spotlights, the camera misses the bassoon's genial solo in the first movement. Gergiev, although he looks as if he might need a shave, is always fascinating to watch; facial communication and hand movements equally expressive. Excellent sound, too.

Zedda's account of the *Classical Symphony* is highly persuasive, the violins exquisitely gentle at their poised entry in the *Larghetto* and the outer movements spirited, with the finale mercurial in its zestful progress. The fairly resonant sound, with the orchestra slightly recessed, adds to the feeling of warmth without blunting the orchestral articulation.

Symphonies 1 (Classical); 4 in C, Op. 112 (revised, 1947 version)
*** Chan. 8400. RSNO, Järvi

Järvi succeeds in making out a more eloquent case for the revision of the *Fourth Symphony* than many of his predecessors. He also gives an exhilarating account of the *Classical Symphony*, one of the best on record. The slow movement has real douceur and the finale is wonderfully high-spirited. On CD in the *Fourth Symphony* the upper range is a little fierce in some of the more forceful climaxes.

Symphonies 1 (Classical); 5, Op. 100
⊛━ (M) *** DG (ADD) 437 253-2. BPO, Karajan
(BB) **(*) Naxos 8.550237. Slovak PO, Gunzenhauser
(N) *(*) EMI 557854-2. Munich PO, Celibidache

Karajan's 1969 recording of the *Fifth* is in a class of its own. The playing has wonderful tonal sophistication and Karajan judges tempi to perfection so that proportions seem quite ideal. It is coupled with his 1982 digital recording of the *Classical Symphony*, in which his performance is predictably brilliant and the playing beautifully polished, with grace and eloquence distinguishing the slow movement.

The Naxos coupling is very good value indeed. The recording is altogether first class: there is splendid detail and definition, and the balance is extremely well judged. Moreover the American conductor, Stephen Gunzenhauser, gets very good playing from the excellent Slovak Philharmonic and the performances have the merit of being straightforward and unaffected. The first movement of the *Classical Symphony* is a bit sedate and wanting in sparkle; the finale comes off best.

Celibidache gives us the Larghetto from the *Classical Symphony* in slow motion – and the effect is quite intolerable, as for that matter are the overblown distortions of the *Gavotte*. Nor is his 1988 account of the *Fifth Symphony* free from agogic distortion (the lead into the Scherzo's Trio being a case in point), and the *Adagio* is pretty slow too and will strain the patience of anyone who heard it under Ormandy or Karajan. There is some good playing from the Munich orchestra, but this is far too quirky to be a serious contender.

Symphonies 1 (Classical); 7, Op. 131; The Love for Three Oranges: Suite
(B) *** CfP (ADD) 762 7752. Philh. O, Malko

All the performances on CfP are quite excellent, and the *Seventh Symphony*, of which Malko conducted the UK première, is freshly conceived and finely shaped. What is so striking is the range and refinement of the 1955 stereo recording: the excellence of the balance and the body of the sound are remarkable.

Symphony 2 in D min., Op. 40; Romeo and Juliet (ballet): Suite 1
**(*) Chan. 8368. RSNO, Järvi

The *Second Symphony* reflects Prokofiev's avowed intention of writing a work 'made of iron and steel'. Neeme Järvi produces altogether excellent results from the Scottish National Orchestra and the Chandos recording is impressively detailed and vivid. The *Romeo and Juliet* suite comes off well; the SNO play with real character.

Symphonies 2; 6 in E flat min., Op. 111
(N) *** Testament (ADD) SBT 1395. Boston SO, Leinsdorf

The Boston Symphony had a close relationship with Prokofiev. Their great conductor Koussevitzky conducted the première of the *Second Symphony* in Paris, he commissioned the *Fourth* for the orchestra's fiftieth anniversary, and he made a recording of the *Fifth* that remained unsurpassed for many years. And so it was natural that in the 1960s they should have embarked on (though never completed) a Prokofiev cycle under their then conductor, Erich Leinsdorf. Only four symphonies were recorded, and this CD couples one of the rarest (No. 2) with the greatest (No. 6). The *Second* has a layout similar to that of Beethoven's *C minor Sonata*, Op. 111, a powerful, concentrated sonata-form movement followed by a theme and variations, and it is in the latter that its most inspired invention is to be found. The quality of its invention and its fantasy and poetic feeling make its neglect hard to explain. The *Sixth* is the darkest and most concentrated, and Leinsdorf gives a powerful reading that (for its day) has an outstanding recorded sound. It still sounds very impressive.

Symphonies 3; 4 in C, Op. 47 (original, 1930 version)
*** Chan. 8401. RSNO, Järvi

Neeme Järvi's account of the *Third* is extremely successful. In many ways the original of the *Fourth Symphony* seems more like a ballet suite than a symphony: its insufficient tonal contrast tells – yet the Scherzo, drawn from the music for the Temptress in *The Prodigal Son* ballet, is particularly felicitous.

Symphonies 3, Op. 44; 5 in B flat, Op. 100
(N) **(*) Testament (ADD) SBT 1396. Boston SO, Leinsdorf

Three stars for the *Third Symphony* and two and a half for the *Fifth*. Leinsdorf's account of the *Third* does not have the subtlety that Abbado brought to his LSO account which enjoyed currency at the same time. All the same, Leinsdorf gets a strong atmosphere and a fine sonority from the Boston orchestra in this highly imaginative score. The *Fifth* is a well-shaped account, though not everyone will care for the ritenuto Leinsdorf makes between the Trio section and the return of the Scherzo in the second movement. All the same, these performances make one regret that Leinsdorf never went on to complete his Prokofiev cycle. Exemplary transfers.

Symphony 4 in C (revised, 1947 version), Op. 112; The Prodigal Son (ballet: complete), Op. 46
(BB) *** Naxos 8.553055. Ukraine NSO, Kuchar

It makes an ideal coupling having the *Symphony No. 4* alongside the ballet score from which Prokofiev drew most of the material. The 1947 revision of the symphony, now generally preferred, is richer in both structure and instrumentation. Kuchar's readings are both powerful and idiomatic, with crisply disciplined playing from the Ukraine orchestra bringing home the weight and violence of much of the writing.

These are performances to match and even outshine current rivals at whatever price; the Naxos recording is satisfyingly full-bodied, not least in vivid brass and percussion sounds, with the piano both clear and well integrated in the symphony.

Symphony 5 in B flat, Op. 100

(M) *** DG (ADD) 463 613-2. BPO, Karajan – STRAVINSKY: *Rite of Spring* **(*)

*** Chan. 8576. Leningrad PO, Jansons

Symphony 5; Waltz Suite, Op. 110

*** Chan. 8450. RSNO, Järvi

Karajan's reading of the *Fifth Symphony* is outstanding in every way. It is a totally unaffected, beautifully played account, with the Berlin Philharmonic on top form, and the DG engineers at their best. The recording is a model of its kind, allowing all the subtleties of the orchestral colouring to register without any distortion of perspective. It has splendid range and fidelity and is wholly free from any artificial balance. It is here paired with his highly individual version of *The Rite of Spring* to make an intriguing coupling in DG's Originals series.

Jansons goes for brisk tempi – and in the slow movement he really is too fast. The Scherzo is dazzling and so, too, is the finale, which is again fast and overdriven. An exhilarating and exciting performance, eminently well recorded, recommended to those willing to accept the ungenerous measure.

Järvi's direction is unhurried, fluent and authoritative. His feeling for the music is unfailingly natural. The three *Waltzes* which derive from various sources are all elegantly played. The Chandos recording is set just a shade further back than some of its companions in the series, yet at the same time every detail is clear.

Symphonies 5 in B flat, Op. 100; 7 in C sharp min., Op. 131

**(*) Testament (ADD) SBT 1296. Paris Conservatoire O, Martinon

These performances appeared in 1959–60 on the RCA label, but the *Fifth Symphony* was soon to be overshadowed by the sumptuous Karajan account with the Berlin Philharmonic, and the *Seventh* was not as well played as Malko's finely recorded version with the Philharmonia on CfP coupled with No. 1 (see above). All the same, Martinon was a conductor of some stature (much underrated in his Chicago days), and both accounts have strong character and are well worth considering, particularly in such excellently refurbished transfers.

Symphony 6. Waltz Suite, Op. 110/1, 5 & 6

*** Chan. 8359. RSNO, Järvi

The *Sixth Symphony* goes much deeper than any of its companions; indeed it is perhaps the greatest of the Prokofiev cycle. Neeme Järvi shapes its detail as skilfully as he does its architecture as a whole. These artists have the measure of the music's tragic poignancy more than almost any of their predecessors on record. The fill-up is a set of waltzes, drawn and adapted from various stage works.

Symphony 7 in C sharp min., Op. 131; Sinfonietta in A, Op. 5/48

*** Chan. 8442. RSNO, Järvi

Neeme Järvi's account of the *Seventh Symphony* is hardly less successful than the other issues in this cycle. He draws very good playing from the RSNO and has the full measure of this repertoire. The early *Sinfonietta* is a highly attractive coupling (what a sunny and charming piece it is!). The digital recording has great range and is excellently balanced.

CHAMBER MUSIC

Music for Cello & Piano: *Adagio (Cinderella), Op. 97b; Ballade in C min., Op. 15; Cello Sonata in C, Op. 119; Solo Cello Sonata, Op. 134 (unfinished); Concertino, Op. 132: Andante. Chout: Fragments, Op. 21*

**(*) Chan. 10045. Ivashkin, Lazareva

Music for cello and piano: *Adagio (Cinderella), Op. 97b; Ballade in C min., Op. 15; Cello Sonata in C, Op. 119; Solo Cello Sonata, Op. 134; 5 Mélodies, Op. 35 bis (arr. Wallfisch); The Love for Three Oranges: March. The Tale of the Stone Flower: Waltz*

*** Black Box Music BBM 1027. Wallfisch, York

Adagio (Cinderella); Ballade, Op. 15; Cello Sonata, Op. 119

*** HM Chant du Monde LDC 2781112. Hoffman, Bianconi – SHOSTAKOVICH: *Cello Sonata; Moderato* **(*)

Cello Sonata in C, Op. 119

*** Virgin 2x1 4 82067-2 (2). Mørk, Vogt – MIASKOVSKY; RACHMANINOV; SHOSTAKOVICH: *Cello Sonatas;* STRAVINSKY: *Suite italienne* ***

(M) *** Somm CD 029. Walton, Grimwood – KABALEVSKY; MIASKOVSKY: *Cello Sonatas* ***

*** Chan. 8340. Turovsky, L. Edlina – SHOSTAKOVICH: *Sonata* ***

☛ (BB) *** Double Decca 473 807-2 (2). Harrell, Ashkenazy – RACHMANINOV: *Cello Sonata, etc.;* SHOSTAKOVICH: *Cello Sonata, etc.* ***

Prokofiev's *Cello Sonata* is the product of his last years and, like the *Sinfonia concertante*, was inspired by the playing of the young Rostropovich. The excellent account from 1988 remains one of the top recommendations; readers will find Lynn Harrell and Vladimir Ashkenazy wholly satisfying on all accounts. The rest of the programme is equally fine.

In addition to the *Cello Sonata* Raphael Wallfisch and John York give us the early *Ballade*, Op. 15, as well as Wallfisch's own transcription of the enchanting *Cinq mélodies*, Op. 35, and the *Solo Sonata* which Prokofiev began just before his death and whose first movement Vladimir Blok put into shape some years later. Wallfisch plays with superb golden tone and with great expressive eloquence. John York is a sensitive and intelligent partner. Their account can rank with the best.

Truls Mørk and Lars Vogt give a perceptive and thoughtful account of the *Sonata* and are expertly recorded in the Eidsvoll Church, Norway. This is among the best of recent versions and in addition to the Shostakovich has the advantage of equally fine couplings of the Miaskovsky and Rachmaninov *Sonatas* and an additional item, the Stravinsky *Suite italienne.*

Jamie Walton and Daniel Grimwood are new to the artists' catalogue, and their intelligently planned programme is a splendid visiting card. The Prokofiev *Sonata* is given with great character and musicality, and can hold its own with most of the competition. Moreover, the coupling with the Miaskovsky *Sonata* is a considerable plus point. It is an exact contemporary of the Prokofiev and a beautifully lyrical piece, which they also play with naturalness and affection. Good recording, too.

Gary Hoffman and Philippe Bianconi are hardly less fine than their distinguished rivals and are every bit as well recorded. Indeed, there is more air round the aural image in their recital. They opt for the more traditional Shostakovich coupling but do offer the early *Ballade*.

Yuli Turovsky and Luba Edlina are also eloquent advocates of this *Sonata* and the balance is particularly lifelike.

Enthusiasm for Ivashkin is tempered a little by the balance, which seems at times to favour his pianist. We are so well served in this repertoire by the Black Box collection that this issue loses its competitive edge.

Flute Sonata in D, Op. 94

*** EMI 5 56982-2. Pahud, Kovacevich – DEBUSSY: *Syrinx; Bilitis*, etc.; RAVEL: *Chansons madécasses* ***

(M) *** RCA (ADD) 09026 61615-2. Galway, Argerich – FRANCK; REINECKE: *Sonatas* ***

Prokofiev's *Flute Sonata* (1943) is one of his sunniest and most serene wartime compositions. Played as it is on EMI, it is quite captivating. Emmanuel Pahud and Stephen Kovacevich set ideal tempi in each movement and their characterization is perfect as a result. The familiar ideas sound completely fresh and novel. Easily a first recommendation. A perfectly balanced recording.

With its combination of effortless virtuosity and spontaneity of feeling, every detail of the Galway/Argerich version falls naturally into place. The RCA recording is most sympathetic.

(i) String Quartets 1–2; (ii) Cello Sonata

(BB) *** Naxos 8.553136. (i) Aurora Qt; (ii) Grebanier, Guggenheim

String Quartets 1 in B min., Op. 50; 2 in F (Kabarda), Op. 92; (i) Overture on Hebrew Themes, Op. 34

(B) **(*) Hyp. Helios Dig. CDH 55032. Coull String Qt.; with (i) Malsbury, Pettit

The Aurora Quartet give thoroughly straightforward, unaffected accounts of both *Quartets*. They are recorded in a warm, resonant acoustic. The *Cello Sonata* is a thoroughly musical account, not perhaps as strongly characterized as some, but eminently satisfying, and well recorded. This CD is well worth the money.

The eminently serviceable performances on Helios give pleasure, though the ensemble, ultimately, lacks the zest and authority of some of its rivals, though the Coull produce a clean, well-blended sonority. The nickname of No. 2 derives from Kabarda in the Caucasus whose musical folklore Prokofiev had encountered when he was evacuated there during the Second World War.

String Quartet 2 in F, Op. 92

⊙ (***) Testament mono SBT 1052. Hollywood Qt – HINDEMITH: *Quartet 3*; WALTON: *Quartet in A min.* *** ⊙

The pioneering Hollywood Quartet version of the *Second Quartet* is a stunning performance which has an extraordinary precision and intensity (as well as repose when this is required). The transfer sounds excellent.

Violin Sonata (for solo violin), Op. 115

*** Claudio CB 5256-2. Jin – LALO: *Symphonie espagnole*; SARASATE: *Carmen Fantasy, Op. 25*. *** (with KROLL: *Banjo and Fiddle*, orch. Bradbury; TARREGA: *Recuerdos de la Alhambra*, arr. Ricci **(*))

Violin Sonata (for solo violin), Op. 115; Sonata for 2 Violins

*** Chan. 8988. Mordkovitch, Young – SCHNITTKE: *Prelude*; SHOSTAKOVICH: *Violin Sonata* ***

Violin Sonata (for solo violin) Op. 115; (i) Violin Sonatas 1 & 2; 5 Mélodies, Op. 33b; Cinderella: 5 Dances (arr. Fichtenholz)

(B) *** Virgin 2×1 5 61887-2 (2). Sitkovetsky; (i) Gililov (with Recital: DVORAK: *Slavonic Dance, Op. 72/2*. BRAHMS: *Hungarian Dance 6*. BARTOK: *Rumanian Folk Dances*. WIENIAWSKI: *Polonaise in D*. KREISLER: *Liebesfreud; Liebesleid; Schön Rosmarin*. GRANADOS: *Spanish Dance 5*. ALBENIZ: *Malagueña, Op. 71/6*. RAVEL: *Valses nobles et sentimentales 6–7*. KHACHATURIAN: *Gayaneh: Aisha's Dances; Sabre Dance*)

Violin Sonatas (i; ii) 1 in F min., Op. 80; (iii; iv) 2 in D, Op. 94; (i; iii) Sonata for 2 Violins, Op. 56

(BB) *** Warner Apex 2564 60623-2. (i) Jaakko Kuusisto; (ii) Paananen; (iii) Pekka Kuusisto; (iv) Kerppo

Violin Sonatas: 1; 2. 5 Melodies, Op. 35; March, Op. 12/1; Love for 3 Oranges: March. Romeo & Juliet: Masks (all trans. Heifetz)

(B) *** Artemis Vanguard CD 1555 (2). Gil & Orli Shaham

Sonata for 2 Violins, Op. 56

*** Hyp. CDA 66473. Ososstowicz, Kovacic – MARTINU: *Violin Sonata*; MILHAUD: *Violin Duo*, etc. **(*)

The solo *Violin Sonata in D, Op. 115*, is a crisply characteristic piece in three short movements. The *Sonata in C for Two Violins*, written much earlier, is just as effective. The warmth of Lydia Mordkovitch is well matched by her partner, Emma Young.

Min Jin's disarmingly direct approach to the *Solo Sonata* is most appealing, crisply so in the opening Moderato, seductively simple in the *Tema con variazioni*, buoyantly rhythmic and certainly *Con brio* in the closing *Allegro precipitato*, where she brings out the lyrical underlay. She is truthfully recorded and not balanced too closely. An unexpected but welcome coupling for an equally fresh approach to Lalo's *Symphonie espagnole*.

Both Jaakko and Pekka Kuusisto produce playing with a youthful ardour and vitality that is refreshing. This (originally Finlandia) Apex reissue ranks among the best, yet it is now very inexpensive. Anyone investing in it is unlikely to be disappointed.

Gil and Orli Shaham (*frère* and *soeur*) form a mutually understanding partnership to present Prokofiev's three key works for violin and piano, interlaced with a trio of transcriptions by Heifetz, including a rhythmically gutsy account of *Masks* from *Romeo and Juliet* and an engaging presentation of the charming little March, Op. 12/1, originally written for the piano. The major works are strongly characterized and are played with a nice balance between ardent boldness and lyrical delicacy. The *Five Melodies* are made strikingly diverse, and the account of the *Second, D major, Sonata* is particularly compelling. Clear, forward, if slightly dry recording, but a good balance, with the violin dominating, but the piano well in the picture.

The two *Violin Sonatas* with Dmitri Sitkovetsky and Pavel Gililov on Virgin were recorded in 1990 and ranked among the best. With the *5 Mélodies* and the *Sonata for Solo Violin* they occupy the first disc – as they did originally. It is a pity that they were not coupled with the award-winning account of the two violin concertos that Sitkovetsky recorded with Sir Colin Davis, which would have greatly enhanced the value of the present set. The other virtuoso pieces and arrangements come from 1988; they are eminently well played but are not in any way more than *bonnes bouches*.

The *Sonata for Two Violins* gives the impression of being vintage Prokofiev, as performed by Krysia Osostowicz and Ernst Kovacic. The slow movement is played with exceptional imagination and poetry.

Violin Sonata 1 in F min., Op. 80

*** Orfeo (ADD) C489981B. D. Oistrakh, S. Richter –
   BRAHMS: *Sonata 2* ***

**(*) Avie AV0023. Gleusteen, Ordronneau – JANACEK:
   Violin Sonata; SHOSTAKOVICH: *19 Preludes from Op. 34*
   **(*)

This Orfeo disc records the Oistrakh–Richter partnership in a live concert at the 1972 Salzburg Festival at the very top of their form. The playing, as one might expect, silences criticism and the recording from ORF (Austrian Radio) is perfectly serviceable.

Even more than in the Janáček and Shostakovich works, Kai Gleusteen is in his element, and so is Catherine Ordronneau, bringing out the often violent contrasts in the writing, as well as the fantasy of the *Andante* third movement and the power and ebullience of the two fast movements, the second and the finale. It is a pity that Gleusteen and Ordronneau did not devote themselves entirely to Prokofiev and give a complete survey of his violin-and-piano music. The recording, one of a series made in Crear on the west coast of Scotland, is on the reverberant side, thanks to the large, bare studio in which it was made, but there is no lack of detail.

Violin Sonata 2 in D, Op. 94a

(N) *** New Note Quartz QTZ 2002. Liebeck, Apekisheva –
   CHAUSSON: *Poème*; SAINT-SAENS: *Sonata 1*; YSAYE: *Sonata 3* ***

Jack Liebeck's performance of the *D major Sonata*, admirably partnered by Katya Apekisheva, is second to none among modern recordings. The opening is exquisitely played, and the Scherzo crackles with rhythmic vitality. The wry, wistful quality of the *Andante* is perfectly caught and is followed by a gutsy, irresistibly spirited finale. The recording is vividly real, with the violin perhaps a little too close, and the couplings are equally good.

PIANO MUSIC

Cinderella: 3 Pieces, Op. 95; 3 Pieces, Op. 97; Romeo and Juliet: 10 Pieces, Op. 75; War and Peace: 3 Pieces, Op. 96

(BB) *** HM HCX 3957150. Chiu

Prokofiev's transcriptions of the ballet music from *Romeo and Juliet* are better known than *Cinderella* or the three pieces from the opera *War and Peace* (which include the delectable *Grand Waltz*). Frederic Chiu, who has already given us a first class set of the sonatas, plays with vivid colouring, often dazzling with his bravura. He is rather closely balanced, but the bright piano image is real enough, and this can be strongly recommended. Excellent value for money.

Piano Sonatas 1–9 (complete); Lieutenant Kijé (suite, transcribed Chiu)

*** Chan. (as listed below). Berman
**(*) HM HMU 907086/8 (3). Chiu

Piano Sonata 1 in F min., Op. 1; 4 Pieces, Op. 4; Prelude & Fugue in D min. (Buxtehude, arr. Prokofiev); *2 Sonatinas, Op. 54; Gavotte (Hamlet, Op. 77 bis); 3 Pieces, Op. 96.* (Chan. 9017)

Piano Sonata 2 in D min., Op. 14; Cinderella: 3 Pieces, Op. 102; Dumka; 3 Pieces, Op. 69; Waltzes (Schubert, arr. Prokofiev). (Chan. 9119)

Piano Sonata 3 in A min., Op. 28; Cinderella: 6 Pieces, Op. 95; 10 Pieces, Op. 12; Thoughts, Op. 62. (Chan. 9069)

Piano Sonata 4, Op. 29; Music for Children, Op. 65; 6 Pieces, Op. 52. (Chan. 8926)

Piano Sonata 5 in C, Op. 38/135; 4 Pieces, Op. 32; The Love for Three Oranges: Scherzo & March. Romeo and Juliet: 10 Pieces, Op. 75. (Chan. 8851)

Piano Sonatas 5 in C, Op. 38; 6 in A, Op. 82; 10 in E min., Op. 137 (fragment); *Gavotte (from Classical Symphony, Op. 25); Juvenilia; Toccata, Op. 11.* (Chan. 9361)

Piano Sonata 7; Sarcasms, Op. 17; Tales of an Old Grandmother, Op. 31; Visions fugitives, Op. 22. (Chan. 8881)

Piano Sonata 8; Cinderella: 10 Pieces, Op. 97; 4 Pieces, Op. 3. (Chan. 8976)

Piano Sonata 9; Choses en soi, Op. 45; Divertissement, Op. 43 bis; 4 Etudes, Op. 2. (Chan. 9211)

Boris Berman always plays with tremendous concentration and control. He commands a finely articulated and vital rhythmic sense as well as a wide range of keyboard colour. In the *Second Sonata in D minor* Berman is quite magnificent and full of panache. The *Third* remains one of the most desirable of the set. The *Fourth Sonata*, like its predecessor, takes its inspiration from Prokofiev's earlier notebooks. The Op. 52 *Pieces* are transcriptions of movements from other works. Berman plays them incisively, with marvellous articulation and wit. He plays the post-war revision of the *Fifth Sonata*, and its crisp, brittle inner movement is heard to splendid advantage. The other works are presented with equal perception.

Of course with the *Sixth Sonata* Berman is traversing hotly contested ground. Yet his cooler and more collected reading remains eminently recommendable. He then gives us the original (1923) version of the *Fifth Sonata* (generally to be preferred to the revision) but also the minute or so that survives of a *Tenth Sonata*. Berman is completely inside the astringent idiom and subtle character of the *Seventh Sonata*, and his playing in the *Sarcasms* could scarcely be bettered.

In the expansive *Eighth Sonata*, there is pianistic refinement in Berman's account, though it is in the ten numbers from *Cinderella* and the Op. 3 *Pieces* that Berman's command of atmosphere and character tells most.

Berman plays the *Ninth Sonata* with tremendous concentration and control. The *Choses en soi* (*Things in themselves*) comes from the period of the *Third Symphony*, though there is a momentary hint of *The Prodigal Son*. The *Divertissement* is a delightful piece in Prokofiev's most acerbic manner which derived from the ballet, *Trapeze*. Berman couples them with the brilliant Op. 2 *Etudes* of 1909. First class recording throughout.

Exciting playing too from Frederic Chiu. His tempi can be a little extreme, and there are greater extremes of dynamics and colours. The *Seventh* is brilliant and can be ranked along with the best, and the *Sixth*, though not superior to either of the Kissin accounts, is pretty dazzling. Throughout the cycle he impresses with his marvellous fingers, abundant energy and good musical taste. Unfortunately the recording lets him down: the tone is shallow and the balance a bit too close. Otherwise this would have been a strong three-star recommendation.

Piano Sonatas 1, 3–4; 10 Pieces from Romeo and Juliet, Op. 75
(BB) **(*) Naxos 8.554270. Glemser

This is more than serviceable, both for performances and recordings, for those with limited budgets and makes a good individual collection, but it makes no real challenge to the rival series now on offer (Berman on Chandos, Chiu on Harmonia Mundi).

Piano Sonatas 1; 6–7; Toccata in C, Op. 11
*** BIS CD 1260. Kempf

Freddy Kempf's Prokofiev has a lot going for it and finds him totally inside the idiom. He has all the technical address, flair and temperament this music needs. At present the sonatas are uncommonly well served on record. Kempf doesn't displace any of them, but his playing is satisfying and his admirers need not hesitate.

Piano Sonatas 2; 7–8
*** DG 457 588-2. Pletnev

Pletnev's 1997 account of the *Seventh Sonata* seems broader and deeper than his earlier version, and it is the mastery of pacing and characterization that gives this impression. The variety of keyboard colour and the control of voicing is stunning both here and in the *Eighth Sonata*. Stunning playing and good recording.

Piano Sonatas 3 (from the old notebooks); 7–8
(M) *** DG (IMS) 459 312-2. Gavrilov

Andrei Gavrilov's account of the *Seventh Sonata* is exciting and exhilarating and is totally devoid of any exaggeration. In the *Eighth* he is equally, if not more, successful and can withstand the most exalted comparisons. He rushes his fences in the *Third*, though as virtuoso playing it is pretty dazzling. Moreover, he was given (in 1992) impressive recorded sound, well balanced and not too close.

Piano Sonatas 4; 6; 10 Pieces from 'Romeo and Juliet', Op. 75
⬤ *** Warner 2564 61255-2. Lugansky

Dazzling playing from Nikolai Lugansky, performances that stand out even in exalted company. The *Sixth Sonata* is the most exciting and authoritative now before the public and supersedes the likes of Pogorelich and Kissin in musical insight and virtuosity. The *Romeo and Juliet Pieces* have equal mastery and fascination. Remarkable Prokofiev playing, wonderful in terms of characterization and effortless virtuosity.

Piano Sonata 6 in A, Op. 82
🔗 ⬤ (M) *** DG 463 678-2. Pogorelich – RAVEL: *Gaspard de la nuit* *** ⬤

Pogorelich's performance of the *Sixth Sonata* is quite simply dazzling; indeed, it is by far the best version of it ever put on record. It remains Pogorelich's most brilliant record so far and can be recommended with the utmost enthusiasm in its new mid-priced CD format.

Piano Sonatas 6; 8
*** Naive V 4898. Guy

Prokofiev's wartime trilogy of piano sonatas comprises Nos. 6

through to 8, and it is a pity that the present disc does not include No. 7. Be that as it may, these are electrifying performances of virtuosity and great musical intelligence. This ranks among the best Prokofiev sonata discs in the current catalogues along with the likes of Richter (within a recital collection), Pollini and Pletnev.

Piano Sonata 7 in B flat, Op. 83
🔗 (M) *** DG (ADD) 447 431-2. Pollini – *Recital* ***

This is a great performance by Pollini, well within the Horowitz or Richter category. It is part of a generous CD of twentieth-century music.

Piano Sonatas 7; 8; Romeo and Juliet: Romeo and Juliet before Parting; Masks
(M) *** Decca (IMS) (ADD) 468 497-2. Ashkenazy – LISZT: *Impromptu (Nocturne); Mephisto Waltz 1* ***

Ashkenazy's commanding performances of these two sonatas, recorded in 1967, have great authority and conviction and the present recordings are rather special. The rhapsodical excerpts from *Romeo and Juliet* are also memorable and the Liszt couplings are hardly less impressive, the *Mephisto Waltz* is predictably dazzling.

Piano Sonata 8 in B flat, Op. 84
*** MDG 604 1141-2. Eckardstein – JANACEK: *Sonata 1.X.1905*; MESSIAEN: *La Rousserolle effarvatte* ***

Severin von Eckardstein won a special commendation at the Leeds Piano Competition for his advocacy of twentieth-century music. His performance of the *Eighth Sonata* is beautifully shaped and expertly controlled. A fine début CD.

VOCAL MUSIC

Alexander Nevsky (cantata), Op. 78 (in English)
🔗 ⚙ (M) *** RCA (ADD) 09026 63708-2. Elias, Chicago SO & Ch., Reiner – KHACHATURIAN: *Violin Concerto* ***
(M) **(*) Sup. (ADD) SU 3696-2. Soukupová, Prague Philh. Ch., Czech PO, Ančerl – *Symphony-Concerto for Cello* **

Reiner's gripping account of *Alexander Nevsky* offers astonishingly vibrant and atmospheric sound from 1959. Even now these early stereo Chicago recordings can astonish the listener, while Reiner's performance is among the most exciting accounts available, with the music for the Teutonic invaders as sinister as the *Battle on the Ice* is thrilling. No less effective is the scherzando-like middle section of the battle music, which Reiner points in the most sparkling manner. The fervour of the choral singing is matched by the eloquence of Rosalind Elias's *Lament*.

The strength of the Supraphon performance lies in the magnificent singing of the Prague Philharmonic Choir, richly resonant and clear. The closing chorus for Alexander's entry into Pskov is thrilling, sung in Russian (like the rest of the work), which adds much to its character. Vera Soukupová gives her elegiac tribute to the dead on the field of battle very movingly, if without the passion of a traditional Russian reading. Ančerl conducts a reading which is lyrically strong. Even if he misses much of the sinister quality of those menacing Teutonic Knights in Eisenstein's great film, the *Battle on the Ice* is still powerful, helped by the spectacular Supraphon recording, which sounds newly minted here. It is a pity that the coupling, although well played, is not more appropriate.

(i) *Alexander Nevsky, Op. 78. Hamlet* (incidental music), *Op. 77: The Ghost of Hamlet's Father. Ivan the Terrible: Dance of the Oprichniks, Op 116; Pushkiniana* (ed. Rozhdestvensky)

(BB) *** Naxos 8.555710. (i) Gelahova, Stanislavsky Ch.; Russian State SO, Yablonsky

(i) *Alexander Nevsky* (cantata), *Op. 78;* (ii) *Ivan the Terrible, Op. 116* (film music, arr. in oratorio form by Stasevich)

(B) *** EMI double forte (ADD) 5 73353-2 (2). (i) Reynolds, LSO & L. Symphony Ch., Previn; (ii) Arkhipova, Mokrenko, Morgunov (narr.), Amb. Ch., Philh. O, Muti – RACHMANINOV: *The Bells*

(i) *Alexander Nevsky, Op. 78;* (ii) *Lieutenant Kijé, Op. 60; Scythian Suite, Op. 20*

(M) *** DG (ADD) 447 419-2. (i) Obraztsova; L. Symphony Ch., LSO; (ii) Chicago SO, Abbado

(i) *Alexander Nevsky, Op. 78. Scythian Suite, Op. 20*

*** Chan. 8584. (i) Finnie, RSNO Ch.; RSNO, Järvi

Abbado's performance of *Alexander Nevsky* culminates in a deeply moving account of the tragic lament after the battle (here very beautifully sung by Obraztsova), made the more telling when the battle itself is so fine an example of orchestral virtuosity. The chorus is as incisive as the orchestra. The digital remastering of the 1980 recording has been all gain, and the sound is very impressive indeed. A fine account of *Lieutenant Kijé* and what is probably the best version of the *Scythian Suite* to appear in many years make this a very desirable reissue.

The bitter chill of the Russian winter can be felt in the orchestra at the very opening of Järvi's reading and the melancholy of the choral entry has real Slavic feeling. His climactic point is the enormously spectacular *Battle on the Ice*, with the recording giving great pungency to the bizarre orchestral effects and the choral shouts riveting in their force and fervour. Linda Finnie sings the final lament eloquently and Järvi's apotheosis is very affecting. As coupling, Järvi also chooses the *Scythian Suite*.

Previn's direct and dynamic manner ensures that the great *Battle on the Ice* scene is powerfully effective. Anna Reynolds sings the lovely *Lament for the Dead* most affectingly. The sound is sharply defined, with plenty of bite. Like Rostropovich, Muti uses the version of *Ivan the Terrible* with spoken narration (in Russian), and this could well prove irritating on repetition when no texts are provided. Nevertheless, with fine playing and choral singing, there is much here to relish, not least those broad, folk-like melodies. The Kingsway Hall recording is admirably spacious and though the histrionic style of the narrator, Boris Morgunov, is unappealing, the two other soloists are excellent in their limited roles. The remastering has been successful and the effect is often thrillingly vivid, with the chorus especially telling.

Dmitri Yablonsky gives a strongly atmospheric account of *Alexander Nevsky*, with plenty of dramatic feeling and fire. The short movements from *Onegin* included in *Pushkiniana*, which Rozhdestvensky scored in the 1960s, and the excerpts from *Hamlet* are very well played. Good recording, too, and no one opting for this Naxos CD will be disappointed.

Cantata for the 20th Anniversary of the October Revolution, Op. 74; Stone Flower Suite

*** Chan. 9095. Rozhdestvensky (speaker), Philh. Ch. & O, Järvi

Even Prokofiev rarely wrote so wild and totally original a piece as this cantata. The key movement, centrally placed and the longest, uses such exotic percussion as rattles and sirens, with shouting from the chorus, in a graphic description of the revolution in St Petersburg. Järvi, here with his fellow-conductor Gennadi Rozhdestvensky as narrator, has made a first complete recording with the Philharmonia Chorus and Orchestra. As a valuable fill-up comes a suite of excerpts from the folk-tale ballet of 1948, *The Stone Flower*.

Ivan the Terrible (complete film score)

*** Ph. (IMS) 456 645-2. Sokolova, Putilin, Kirov Op. Ch., Rotterdam PO, Gergiev

Prokofiev's vividly colourful music for the Eisenstein film of *Ivan the Terrible* has never sounded quite so bitingly dramatic on disc as under Gergiev – as electrifying as any of his opera recordings with the Kirov Company. Here he has the advantage of excellent sound, recorded in the Rotterdam hall, De Doelen, with his 'other' orchestra, thrustful and earthy. Like competing versions, this one is based on Abram Stasevich's editing of the music into an 'oratorio', but without the spoken narration – hardly necessary on disc, when notes and text are provided. The two soloists, Liubov Sokolova and Nikolai Putilin, vibrantly Slavonic, add to the drama, as do the Kirov Chorus.

5 Poems of Anna Akhmatova, Op. 27; 2 Poems, Op. 9; 5 Poems of Konstantin Balmont, Op. 36; 3 Romances, Op. 73

**(*) Chan. 8509. Farley, Aronov

The Akhmatova settings are quite beautiful. The *Three Romances*, Op. 73, to words of Pushkin, are full of the wry harmonic sleights of hand that are so characteristic of his musical speech. The American soprano, Carole Farley, responds to the different moods and character of the poems and encompasses a rather wide range of colour and tone, although at times her voice is rather edgy and uneven in timbre. The accompaniments of Arkady Aronov are highly sensitive and perceptive. The recording is completely truthful.

OPERA

L'Amour des trois oranges (The Love for Three Oranges; sung in French)

*** Arthaus **DVD** 100 404. Bacquier, Viala, Perraguin, le Texier, Gautier, Henry, Reinhart, Lagrange, Caroli, Fournier, Dubosc, Bastin, Uria-Monzon, Lyon Opéra Ch. & O, Nagano (Producer: Erlo; V/P: Jung)

Although it contains some of Prokofiev's most popular orchestral interludes, the opera is in some ways less successful than its companions. As in *The Gambler* and *The Fiery Angel*, there are no set-pieces for the singers and there is scant thematic development. Indeed, the familiar orchestral March and Scherzo are practically the only elements that reappear. There is, however, no want of invention and exuberance, and the opera is ideal for DVD as it is very visual. The cast here is excellent, and so is the video recording. It offers subtitles in English, German, Italian, Spanish and the French in which it is sung. Recommended.

The Fiery Angel (complete; DVD)

➤– ❂ *** Arthaus **DVD** 100 390; CD Ph. 446 078-2 (2). Gorchakova, Leiferkus, Pluzhnikov, Ognovanko, soloists; Kirov Op. Ch. & O, Gergiev

The presence of vision in the finely directed DVD serves to underline an implicit ambiguity in the opera – whether

Madiel and the spirits conjured up in Act II are real or are just Renata's paranoid delusions. Here the use of mimed figures, unseen by the protagonists but perceived by the audience, was a brilliant solution. The frenetic, highly charged atmosphere of the final Convent scene benefits by vision particularly in this splendid production. The sound has marvellous presence and detail.

The Fiery Angel (CD versions)

☉ (M) *** Ph. 476 1826 (2). Gorchakova, Leiferkus, Pluzhnikov, Ognovanko, Kirov Op. Ch. & O, Gergiev

(N) (M) *** DG 477 5596 (2). Secunde, Lorenz, Zednik, Moll, Gotheburg SO, Järvi

Impressive as was Neeme Järvi's 1990 recording for DG of this elusive but powerful opera, Gergiev's with Kirov forces is even finer. From the very outset the style is declamatory in a way that recalls Mussorgsky. The vocal line is largely heightened speech, but Prokofiev does provide a series of leitmotivs which are identified with characters or situations in the opera. Indeed, in terms of fantasy and sheer imaginative vision, The Fiery Angel reaches heights which Prokofiev never surpassed, and its atmosphere resonates for a long time. This Philips live recording, with full, forward sound, avoids most of the snags of a recorded stage-performance. Above all, it offers in the singing and acting of Galina Gorchakova in the central role of Renata, the hysterical woman obsessed by demons, one of the most compelling operatic performances in years, with the timbre of the voice often sensuously beautiful, even when stretched to the limit. Sergei Leiferkus as Ruprecht with his clear, firm baritone is also ideally cast; the remainder of the cast, from the Landlady of Evgenia Perlasova to the resonant Inquisitor of Vladimir Ognovanko, are absolutely first class, while the Kirov team provides outstanding, always idiomatic and individual performances in smaller roles. Gergiev proves an inspired conductor who secures orchestral playing of great dramatic eloquence. There are the inevitable stage noises, but any snag is quickly forgotten.

With Järvi, the final scene with the Inquisitor (Kurt Moll, ever sinister) and chattering nuns does not quite rise to the expected climax. Nadine Secunde sings passionately as Renata and she is well supported by Siegfried Lorenz as Ruprecht. With such warm advocacy once can fully appreciate the work's mastery, even if the reasons for its failure to get into the repertory remain very clear.

The CD set won the 1996 *Gramophone* Opera Award and is now re-issued at mid-price in Universal's *Gramophone* Awards Collection, representing supreme value as texts and translations are included.

The Fiery Angel (complete; in French)

(***) Accord mono 472 723-2 (2). Rhodes, Depraz, Kolassi, Giraudeau, French R. & TV Ch., Paris Opera O, Bruck

Appropriately in the Prokofiev year, Accord restored the pioneering recording of The Fiery Angel (or L'Ange de feu, since it is sung in French) in a libretto based on the composer's own translation. It is particularly worth having for the extraordinarily intense account of Renata given by Jane Rhodes, who seems totally possessed. It remains a *tour de force*, and though the Ruprecht of Xavier Depraz is not in the same class, the cast is an impressive one, including, as it does, Irma Kolassi and Jean Giraudeau. Charles Bruck has terrific drive and gives an astonishingly atmospheric and demonic account of the score. Even if you have Gergiev's powerful account, either on CD or DVD, you should get this, despite its

dated sound. It has not been available since Decca issued it in their Ace of Diamonds series in the 1960s.

The Love for Three Oranges (complete; in Russian)

*** Ph. 462 913-2 (2). Akimov, Kit, Diadkova, Morozov, Pluzhnikov, Gerello, Shevchenko, soloists, Kirov Op. Ch. & O, Gergiev

Gergiev adds to his formidable Kirov series of Russian opera recordings with a brilliant reading of this fantasy fairy-tale. It was recorded not in St Petersburg but live in concert performances at the Concertgebouw in Amsterdam, with warmer, more consistent sound. Using the Russian text this is earthier, tougher and more biting than the smoother French version offered on Virgin by Kent Nagano and his Lyon Opera team. The satirical element of the piece with its wry humour comes over the more sharply, with more sparkle, and though not all the Kirov cast can quite match their Lyon counterparts in vocal beauty, they are on balance more characterful, notably the formidable mezzo, Larissa Diadkova, as Princess Clarissa.

Ivan the Terrible, Parts I and II (complete)

(***) Eureka **DVD** EKA 40018 (2). Cherkassov, Tselikovskaya, Birman (Film director: Sergei Eisenstein)

When Sergei Eisenstein sought to follow up the brilliant success of his film *Alexander Nevsky* with an even more ambitious epic, *Ivan the Terrible*, he naturally turned again to Prokofiev to provide the music, whose score for *Nevsky* is uniquely memorable.

The subject of Ivan the Terrible equally inspired Prokofiev to write a powerful and distinctive score, which can stand on its own as a concert work. Yet over two films (94 and 85 minutes respectively) the result is necessarily more diffuse.

Eisenstein's astonishingly striking and beautiful images in black and white have remarkable impact on DVD, based on an excellent copy of the original film, but sadly, the soundtrack is depressingly crumbly and ill-focused. Though it makes it hard to enjoy Prokofiev's music, its power is still very clear, enhancing the heavyweight treatment of history.

Olivier's *Henry V* with Walton's music was made at exactly the same period, but offers infinitely finer sound than this. It is a pity that it was not possible to superimpose a modern recording of the music, as has been effectively done in live concert-showings of the film.

Semyon Kotko (complete)

(M) (***) Chan. mono 10053 (3). Gres, Gelovani, Yanko, Troitsky, Penchekhin, USSR R. Ch. & O, Zhukov

Semyon Kotko was the fifth of Prokofiev's eight operas and the first on a Soviet theme. Conceived and written during the period of Stalin's purges, it is based on a blatantly propagandist novel by Valentin Katayev, *I am the Son of Working People*. It is a story of love and heroism in the Ukraine during the disturbed period after the 1917 Revolution, when the Bolsheviks were only just establishing their authority, bitterly opposed by the Haydamaks, who were in league with the invading German army. As for the music, it demonstrates once again that even when he was saddled with a propagandist Soviet theme, Prokofiev's fluent originality could not be submerged, any more than it is in the later propagandist opera, The Story of a Real Man, also issued by Chandos for the composer's centenary.

The libretto, which Prokofiev wrote in collaboration with the author of the novel, tells a complicated story crisply, with plenty of contrasts of mood, including Mussorgsky-like passages of rustic humour. Semyon Kotko is a virtuous peasant, a gunner first in the tsarist army, then in the Red Army. He is an enthusiastic communist, keen to liberate the peasants from the oppressive control of the greedy landowners, good to his ageing mother and so on. His sweetheart is the daughter of a rich landowner, opposed to the communists (and naturally Semyon), and this simple conflict is the basis of the plot.

Its easy melodic style with hints of Russian folk music relates it to the music that Prokofiev wrote for the film *Alexander Nevsky*. The only disappointment is that it lacks the big surging melodies that make Prokofiev's masterpiece, *War and Peace*, so memorable, though some of the choruses come close.

This first really complete recording on Chandos stems from a studio performance for Moscow Radio in 1960, which in mono sound captures the voices vividly, with words exceptionally clear. It has the authority of being conducted by Mikhail Zhukov who was responsible for the 1940 première and would have known Prokofiev's intentions. It scores surprisingly well alongside the 1999 Philips version with Kirov soloists in concert conducted by Valery Gergiev, containing some 45 minutes more of music omitted from that later set.

The Moscow cast is strong too, with Slavonic wobblers excluded. The tenor, N. Gres, in particular is magnificent in the title-role, firmer and more heroic than his opposite number on Philips. While most collectors will opt for the modern stereo version, this earlier recording is by no means outclassed.

Semyon Kotko (slightly abridged)

*** Ph. 464 605-2 (2). Lutsiuk, Pavlovskaya, Savoya, Bezzubenkov, Nikitin, Chernomortsev, Solovieva, Markova-Mikhailenko, Karasev, Akimov, Kirov Ch. & O, Gergiev

Semyon Kotko grips the listener from start to finish. The characters are one-dimensional as one would expect from this period, and the anti-German tenor of the work was suddenly an embarrassment when the Nazi–Soviet pact was signed in 1939. All the same there is a lot of good music, not counting the orchestral excerpts already in the catalogue, and although there are no big numbers, there is some consistently inventive writing. Viktor Lutsiuk as Semyon and Tatiana Pavlovskaya as his fiancée Sofya are both first class; however, the real hero is Gergiev who phrases sensitively and paces the music with all his dramatic expertise and gets an enthusiastic response from his Kirov forces. The recording is excellent.

The Story of a Real Man (opera; complete)

(M) *** Chan. (ADD) 10002(2). Kibkalo, Deomidova, Leonova, Pankov, Rezhetin, Maslennikov, Bolshoi Ch. & O, Ermler

Prokofiev's last opera, *The Story of a Real Man*, written just after the Second World War at the time of Stalin's most rigorous purge of the arts, was based on a novel by Boris Polevoy that, reflecting a true story, tells of a Soviet pilot, Alexei, who is shot down behind the German lines and who, for 18 days, crawls to find safety. So severely wounded that his feet have to be amputated, he at first despairs but later as a Soviet hero, returns to flying and a glorious career as a fighter pilot. Stalin greatly approved the novel, and a film followed. Prokofiev, prompted by his wife, Mira Mendelson, chose this unlikely story for his new opera, secure in the knowledge that the subject, at least, could not be condemned. Even so, it was not until 1960, long after Prokofiev's death, that the opera was

finally produced. This first CD version brings a transfer of the 1961 Soviet recording based on that first stage production at the Bolshoi, and the sound is astonishingly full and vivid, with the voices clear and immediate.

Even when Prokofiev is writing blatant propaganda music for his Soviet masters, his sharp originality rarely fails to shine through, though even his genius could not make the central characters much more than cardboard figures. Yet with clever timing – helped, one suspects, by the judicious cutting of the score sanctioned by Mira Mendelson – and a sequence of sharply memorable musical ideas typical of Prokofiev, it makes a compelling experience, despite the propagandist moments. Like Prokofiev's epic adaptation of Tolstoy's *War and Peace*, the opera starts with a choral epigraph, a rousing patriotic hymn, after which the long monologue following Alexei's crawl to safety is cleverly paced to avoid monotony, including a dream-sequence duet with his fiancée, Olga, as he looks longingly at her photo. Cunningly, Prokofiev uses the techniques of cinema, learned while working with his friend and colleague Sergei Eisenstein on the films *Alexander Nevsky* and *Ivan the Terrible*, with a barrage of gunfire and the arrival of a plane bringing strikingly atmospheric passages. There is also a direct echo of *Nevsky* in the haunting solos for the Nurse, that punctuate the opera, as the *Lament for the Dead* does in the film. Other echoes of *War and Peace* and the ballet *Romeo and Juliet* come in the haunting waltz, when Alexei demonstrates that he can now dance again, and that, in turn, leads to rumbustious popular numbers, including a riotous rumba.

Central to the success of this recorded performance is not just the inspired conducting of Mark Ermler, but also the brilliant singing of Yevgeny Kibkalo as Alexei, satisfyingly firm and dark, and rising to the challenge of the arioso passages of heightened lyricism, notably when his rehabilitation monologue leads to a duet with the great Russian bass, Mark Rezhetin, as the head surgeon. Other Bolshoi basses in the cast are splendid too, as is the tenor, Alexei Maslennikov, as a pilot colleague, though Glafira Deomidova in the surprisingly small role of the heroine, Olga, is disappointingly edgy.

War and Peace (DVD versions)

(N) *** Arthaus **DVD** 100 370-9. Gergalov, Prokina, Volkova, Sonya, Kanunnikova, Alexashkin, Gregoriam, Borodina, Bezukhova, Marusin, Morozov, Kit, Okhotnikov, Gerelo, Kirov Ch. and O, Gergiev (Director: Graham Vick, V/D: Humphrey Burton)

(N) *** TDK **DVD** DV OPWP (2). Guryakova, Gunn, Brubaker, Kotcherga, Obraztsova, Gerello, Zaremba, Margita, Poretsky, Paris Nat. Op. Ch. & O, Bertini (Director: Zambello, Hugues R. Gall)

We now have two versions of Prokofiev's monumental opera to choose between on DVD. Bertini's account was recorded at the Opéra Bastille in March 2000 and was the opera's first (and much heralded) staging in France. It has plenty in its favour, including a good cast, with an excellent Natasha in Olga Guryakova. (Prokina in the Gergiev set also has much tenderness and vulnerability, but she is not always 100 per cent secure.) There is a fine Bolkonski in Nathan Gunn and an ideal Pierre Bezhukov (Robert Brubaker), who both looks and sounds exactly right. Perhaps Anatoli Kotcherga is not quite as memorable a Kutuzov as Nikolai Okhotnikov on the Kirov set, but he is commanding nevertheless. The cast for *War and Peace* is huge (some 62 singers for the 72 parts in the Paris version) and the staging poses formidable problems, which are well handled. Gary Bertini conducts his fine chorus and orchestra well and, generally speaking, there are few serious weaknesses. It is impossible to suppress some sympathy for the Russian aristocratic classes who in this production seem to have no furniture for their names and no paintings on their walls – and, indeed, seem to live in pretty austere straits! (Things are not much better in the Kirov version, and the 'aristos' could do well to drop in at Moscow's equivalent of Harrods.) In addition to the 210 minutes of the opera itself, the Paris recording includes two features on the production, running to 79 minutes or so. No one investing in the set is likely to be greatly disappointed, for the viewer is held from start to finish. The range of camera positions is a little unvaried and stilted, and there are rather too many close shots that give too little idea of the space of the stage.

The alternative 1991 Kirov production was directed by Graham Vick with simple – but, on the whole, effective – designs and costumes. The opera runs to 248 minutes in all (including applause and credits), and its musical merits are outlined below in discussing the CDs alone. The Bolkonsky (Alexandr Gergalov), Pierre (Gegam Gregoriam) and Kutuzov (Nikolai Okhotnikov) are impressive, though the production, particularly in the first half, is not as distinguished as everyone said it was. However, it is in the quality of Gergiev's conducting – War and Peace was the first opera he conducted, a quarter of a century ago – and the magnificent choral forces he has at his command that would probably in the end tip the scales in favour of the St Petersburg set, were we forced to choose. However, we would be happy with either.

War and Peace (CD versions)

⊕ ☞ *** Chan. 9855 (4). Morozova, Williams, Lavender, Balashov, Dupont, Stephen, Ionova, Ewing, Opie, Russian State Symphonic Cappella, Spoleto Fest. O, Hickox

(M) *** Erato (ADD) 2292 45331-2 (4). Vishnevskaya, Miller, Ciesinski, Tumagian, Ochman, Ghiuselev, Smith, Paunova, Petkov, Toczyska, Zakai, Gedda, Fr. R. Ch. & Nat. O, Rostropovich

*** Ph. 434 097-2 (3). Gergalov, Prokina, Gregoriam, Borodina, Gerelo, Bogachova, Okhotnikov, Morozov, Kirov Theatre Ch. & O, Gergiev

Recorded live at the 1999 Spoleto Festival in full and open Chandos sound, Richard Hickox's formidable version of Prokofiev's epic opera offers a strong, thrustful performance with a cast more consistent than those on rival sets. With a warm understanding of the idiom, helped by a substantial Russian element among the singers, not least the chorus, Hickox keeps the thirteen scenes moving well at speeds often on the fast side. Pointing the dramatic contrast between personal tragedy and great public events, the surging lyricism of Prokofiev's inspiration is sharply set against bitingly rhythmic writing, whether in the party scenes of the first part or the wartime scenes of the second half. The glorious tunefulness of the patriotic numbers has just the gulp-in-throat quality needed, whether General Kutuzov's big aria, nobly sung by Alan Ewing, or the big choruses fervently sung by the Russian choir.

Ekaterina Morozova is a moving Natasha, Slavonic in timbre, weighty but still girlish enough, with an edge to the voice that rarely turns squally. She is well matched in the beautiful opening scene by Pamela Helen Stephen as her cousin, Sonya, while Roderick Williams is a fresh, virile Andrei, and Justin Lavender a vulnerable-sounding Pierre, who convincingly erupts in anger.

Alan Opie is a characterful Napoleon, with the battle scene of Borodino thrillingly vivid, not least in shattering cannon shots.

Other versions may have starrier individual contributions, but this one has no weak link, and the recording is not just full and brilliant, but, beautifully balanced, captures the sweetness of the Spoleto strings very persuasively. The four-disc layout (for the price of three) means breaks come at the ends of scenes.

In Rostropovich's powerful reading one revels – thanks also to the lively Erato recording – in the vividness of the atmosphere, both in the evocative love scenes and ball scenes of the first half (Peace) and in the high tensions of the battle scenes in the second (War). The opera culminates in a great patriotic chorus, using the most haunting tune of all, earlier sung by General Kutuzov after the Council of Fili, and the emotional thrust is overwhelming. The French Radio Choir sings that chorus with real Russian fervour. It was natural that Rostropovich's wife, Galina Vishnevskaya, should sing the central role of Natasha, as she did in the earlier, much-cut, Bolshoi recording. It is extraordinary how convincingly this mature soprano in her early sixties characterizes a young girl; there may be raw moments, but she is completely inside the role. The Hungarian baritone, Lajos Miller, not flawless either, is a clear-voiced Andrei, and Wieslaw Ochman is a first-rate Pierre, with the veteran, Nicolai Gedda, brought in as Kuragin. Katherine Ciesinski is a warm-toned Sonya, but Dimiter Petkov is disappointingly unsteady as Natasha's father, Count Rostov. The small role of Napoleon is strongly taken by Eduard Tumagian, while Nicola Ghiuselev is a noble Kutuzov, in some ways the most impressive of all. The libretto contains French and English translations, but no Russian transliteration, only the Cyrillic text in a separate section.

The Kirov performance under Valery Gergiev, at rather more urgent speeds than Rostropovich's, may be less warmly expressive and atmospheric, but it brings the advantage of having in the principal roles younger voices. Many will prefer the Kirov Natasha, Yelena Prokina, to the controversially cast Vishnevskaya on the Rostropovich set. The voice is fresher as well as younger-sounding, though the tone becomes hard under pressure, losing any sweetness. Alexander Gergalov, Prince Andrei in the Kirov performance, is attractively young-sounding too, lighter and more lyrical than Rostropovich's principal, also good, the Hungarian baritone, Lajos Miller. Otherwise the Kirov principals, including Nikolai Okhotnikov as Kutuzov, are almost all as characterful and assured as their generally starrier rivals on Erato, and the sense of purpose from a very large company, well drilled in the music, counter-balances in part, though not entirely, the unhelpful dryness of the sound. The economical layout on three CDs may seem to favour Philips, but there is no price-advantage, when Rostropovich's Erato comes at mid-price in the Libretto series.

PUCCINI, Giacomo (1858–1924)

Adagietto; Preludio; Scherzo (all for orchestra); Corazzata Sicilia; Scossa elettrica (both for wind). Vocal music: (ii) Cessato il suon' dell'armi (cantata); (i) Ecce Sacerdos Magnus; Inno a Roma; (i; iii) Motetto per San Paulino; Requiem; (i; iv) Salve Regina; (i; v) Vexilla Regis; Manon Lescaut, Act II: Prelude. (vi) Turandot, Act III: Finale (ed. Berio).

*** Decca 478 320-2. Giuseppe Verdi SO, Chailly, with (i) Giuseppe Verdi Ch.; (ii) Calleja; (iii) Mastromarino; (iv) Taigi; (v) De Thierry (organ); (vi) Urbanova, Fantosh, Volonte, Luperi

All but one of the items on this 'Discovery' disc are pieces incidental to Puccini's career, whether from his early years as a student, or short, occasional pieces written later for specific purposes; all of them are fascinating for giving us fresh insights into the composer's development. The final item on the disc is by far the most important, Luciano Berio's completion of Act III of the unfinished last opera, *Turandot*. Like Franco Alfano, who made the regular completion, Berio used the composer's sketches for that unfinished ending, but the results are very different, not least in having a hushed, downbeat ending. That ending may be totally justified dramatically, but it is unsatisfying compared with Alfano's knock-out blow in the choral reprise of *Nessun dorma*. Surprisingly, though the orchestral accompaniment is quite different, with a substantial orchestral interlude in the middle, the vocal lines of Turandot and Calaf in their duet are remarkably close to those in the Alfano, both following Puccini's sketches. Turandot's solo, *Del primo pianto*, then begins with the same melodic line, but quickly becomes impassioned, and Calaf's *Il mio mistero* also keeps the same vocal line. After Turandot and Calaf's final brief exchange, there is only a gentle easing into silence.

Seven of the 13 remaining items also come in première recordings. They include Puccini's first two surviving works, both written during his schooldays, the *Preludio a orchestra*, which charmingly turns into a Viennese-style waltz, and the *Motetto per San Paulino*, bold and brassy, with a long baritone solo in the middle (rather roughly sung by Alberto Mastromarino). *Vexilla Regis* for men's chorus and organ also dates from the composer's schooldays. At the other end of Puccini's career comes the untypical *Inno a Roma* of 1919, his last completed work, later notoriously adopted by Mussolini's fascists using different words. The *Scherzo* of 1882–3 and the *Salve Regina*, from his student years in Milan, both provided material for his first opera, *Le Villi*, and the tenderly beautiful *Adagietto for Small Orchestra* from the same period was used for Fidelia's aria in Act III of his second opera, *Edgar*.

Other little gems include two pieces for wind band, *Corazzata Sicilia*, a development of the march at the end of Act II of *La Bohème* using material from earlier in the act (the work of a bandmaster) and *Scossa elettrica* ('Electric Shock'), a lively fragment of 1899 with jaunty syncopations, written for a convention of telegraphists. By far the weakest piece, the cantata of 1877, *Cessato il suon*, discovered only in 2003, is one for which the vocal line had to be invented.

Chailly draws excellent performances from his various artists, with generally fresh, alert singing from soloists and chorus, and the one complaint is that, though the notes by Dieter Schickling (author of the comprehensive Puccini catalogue) are very informative, the lack of texts for the vocal items is a serious omission.

Crisantemi for String Quartet
(M) *** CRD (ADD) CRD 3366. Alberni Qt – DONIZETTI: *Quartet 13*; VERDI: *Quartet* ***

Puccini's brief essay in writing for string quartet dates from the late 1880s; three years later he used the main themes in his first fully successful opera, *Manon Lescaut*. The piece is given a warm, finely controlled performance by the Alberni Quartet and makes a valuable makeweight for the two full-scale quartets by fellow opera-composers. The sound is excellent.

Crisantemi; Fugues 1–3; Minuets 1–3; Scherzo in A min.; String Quartet in D
*** ASV CDDCA 909. Puccini Qt – CATALANI: *String Quartet in A, etc.* ***

Puccini's three *Fugues* and the *Quartet Movement in D* (with

the jolliest, most trivial of main themes) are mere student exercises, technically adept and charming but with no stylistic personality. The *Minuets*, more developed, are hardly identifiable as by Puccini. Then suddenly the full Puccini emerges in the beautiful *Crisantemi* of 1890. It is strange that though Puccini's musical personality began to emerge early in his choral and orchestral works, this sparer genre found him more anonymous, even in his melodies. Nonetheless, a delightful disc, warmly played and atmospherically recorded, with Catalani's quartet music providing an ideal coupling.

(i) *Messa di Gloria*. (ii) *Preludio sinfonico; Crisantemi*
☛ *** EMI 5 57159-2. (i) Alagna, Hampson, LSO Ch.; LSO, Pappano

(BB) *** Warner Apex (DDD/ADD) 0927 48692-2. (i) Carreras, Prey, Amb. S., Philh. O; (ii) Monte-Carlo Op. O; Scimone

(i) *Messa di gloria; Crisantemi; Prelude sinfonico*
(BB) *** Naxos 8.555304. Palombi, Lundberg, Hungarian R Ch. & Op. O, Morandi

Puccini's *Messa di gloria*, by far the most ambitious of his early works, is much more than a student exercise, full of anticipations of the mature opera-composer. He even uses material from the *Agnus Dei* in *Manon Lescaut*, yet the piece has been unfairly neglected on disc, when particularly the extended setting of the *Gloria* is so memorable, starting with a swaggering march such as Rossini might have put into a religious work

Antonio Pappano easily outshines his rivals on disc, enhancing the operatic element, including obvious echoes not just of the Verdi *Requiem*, but of *Otello*. Ideal soloists in Alagna and Hampson, with the London Symphony Chorus and LSO in incandescent form. The two bonuses are welcome, aptly chosen and very well played.

The return of Scimone's second (1983) digital version on the super-bargain Apex label makes this version much more attractive, particularly as he includes the same two orchestral pieces as Pappano as makeweights. Scimone's fine team are brisker and lighter than their predecessors on record, yet effectively bring out the red-bloodedness of the writing. José Carreras turns the big solo in the *Gratias* into the first genuine Puccini aria. His sweetness and imagination are not quite matched by the baritone, Hermann Prey. Excellent, atmospheric sound.

The Naxos recording from Budapest brings bright, urgent singing and playing under Pier Morandi. The early orchestral works (*Crisantemi* also provided material for *Manon Lescaut)* make an attractive bonus. An outstanding bargain.

OPERA

Collection: Renata Tebaldi: '*The Classic Puccini Recordings*': *La Bohème; Madama Butterfly; Manon Lescaut; Turandot; La Fanciulla del West; Tosca* (with soloists, Ch. & O of Rome Santa Cecilia Academy)
(B) (**(*)) Decca mono/stereo (ADD) 473 045-2 (12)

Here are the LP sets that not only revealed Renata Tebaldi as one of the supreme twentieth-century sopranos, at her very finest in Puccini, but that also helped to establish Decca as a major source of opera recordings. Listening through these remarkable recordings not only gives pleasure but also excites nostalgia for a period of recording history when the long playing record (and later stereo) transformed the operatic medium for home-listening. The booklet offers good cued synopses for each opera, an excellent historical note by Raymond McGill, but no texts and translations.

La Bohème (with Prandelli, Gueden, Inghilleri, Corena, Arié; cond. Erede)

The recording of *La Bohème* dates from 1951 and is still a lovely performance, more than fifty years later. Gueden is a most characterful Musetta, if not always in style vocally; Prandelli is a light-voiced but ardent and likeable Rodolfo; and Inghilleri is old-sounding but still interesting as Marcello. The main weakness lies in Erede's conducting, which is not terrible inspired and has a very fast speed for the opening of Act II at the Café Momus. But even that is no serious drawback when the singing is so consistently compelling. The balance is still remarkably realistic, and the thin, edgy violins (for which early Decca LPs became notorious) have been satisfactorily contained in this vivid new transfer.

Madama Butterfly (with Campora, Rankin, Inghilleri; cond. Erede)

Madama Butterfly was also recorded in 1951, and astonishingly this set was made before Tebaldi ever sang the part in the opera house. Once again, the orchestral strings now offer little to worry the ear and generally sound much more full-bodied than previously; indeed, such is the overall warmth and three-dimensional depth of the staging, that at times one almost has the illusion of stereo.

Manon Lescaut (with del Monaco, Borielli, Corena; cond. Molinari-Pradelli)

Manon Lescaut followed in 1954 and was recorded in stereo. The recording still sounds very well, with good detail, and this set is by no means outclassed by many more recent versions. While Tebaldi is not quite the little woman of Puccini's dreams, she still produces a flow of gorgeous, rich tone. Only the coarseness of Mario del Monaco as Des Grieux mars the set, but this is exciting, red-blooded singing, and he does not overwhelm Tebaldi in the duet sequences.

Turandot (with Borkh, del Monaco; cond. Erede)

Turandot, recorded a year later in 1955, proved to be the one near-failure of the series. The recording has a glitter and brilliance to match even the fabulous court of the emperor of China, yet somehow the performance lacks atmosphere and sheer vitality. Tebaldi opted for the part of Liù and sings beautifully, but Inge Borkh proved not the most biting of princesses, and the recording is not kind to her upper register, bringing out its unevenness. Monaco is his own loud-voiced self as the stranger prince. What a wonderfully heroic voice it is, yet how consistently he seeks to use it with blundering lack of restraint. The Ping, Pang, Pong of Fernando Corena, Mario Carlin and Renato Ercolani are excellent, and in consequence the performance brings a good deal to enjoy, but Erede's conducting seems too careful in passages that should have the most barefaced oriental panache.

La Fanciulla del West (with del Monaco, MacNeil, Tozzi; cond. Capuana)

Such was the success of *La Fanciulla del West*, made three years later in the summer of 1958, that it has remained unsurpassed until this day. It is discussed more fully below. Sufficient to say that both Tebaldi and del Monaco were at their finest, and Tozzi as Jake Wallace proved another outstanding asset. The Decca producers, James Walker and Christopher Raeburn, again demonstrated Decca's imaginative production values at their most impressive.

Tosca (with del Monaco, London; cond. Molinari-Pradelli)

It is Tebaldi's performance alone that redeems the 1959 *Tosca*. Apart from the sheer beauty of her singing, she is often splendidly dramatic, especially in the scene of the death of Scarpia, and she is unmatched in conveying the proud femininity of this character (perhaps Puccini's strongest heroine). Where Callas may bring more of the snarling of a tigress, Tebaldi's performance has a dimension of dignity and self-assurance, and it is a great pity that the other two principals do not match her.

The principal drawback is the Scarpia of George London. The voice is rough and uncontrolled, and the interpretation is completely out of style. When this is added to singing from del Monaco that rings out gloriously but is hardly subtle, the impression of coarseness is hard to avoid. The recording has a fine acoustic, with the orchestra sounding rich and full-blooded, but overall this remains a sadly flawed account.

Other Recordings

La Bohème (DVD versions)

(*) DG **DVD 073-027-9. Freni, Martino, Raimondi, Panerai, La Scala Ch. & O, Karajan (Director: Franco Zeffirelli)
(*) Warner **DVD 4509 99222-2. Cotrubas, Shicoff, Allen, Zschau, Howell, Rawnsley, ROHCG Ch. & O, Gardelli (Producer: John Copley; V/D: Brian Large)
(N) **(*) Arthaus **DVD** 100 046. Freni, Pavarotti, Pacetti, Quilico, Ghiaurov, San Francisco Ch. & O, Severini (V/D: Brian Large)
(N) **(*) TDK **DVD** DV-OPBOH. Gallardo-Domas, Hong, Alvarez, Servile, Carolis, Parodi, La Scala Ch. & O, Bartoletti (V/D: Carlo Battistoni)

La Bohème (CD versions)

●— *** EMI 5 56120-2. Vaduva, Alagna, Swenson, Hampson, Keenlyside, Ramey, L. Voices, boys from L. Oratory School, Philh. O, Pappano
*** Decca (ADD) 421 049-2 (2). Freni, Pavarotti, Harwood, Panerai, Ghiaurov, German Op. Ch., Berlin, BPO, Karajan
*** Decca 466 070-2 (2). Gheorghiu, Alagna, Scano, Keenlyside, D'Arcangelo, La Scala, Milan, Verdi Ch. & O, Chailly
(B) *** Double Decca (ADD) 448 725-2 (2). Tebaldi, Bergonzi, Bastianini, Siepi, Corena, D'Angelo, St Cecilia Ac. Ch. & O, Serafin
(B) (***) Double Decca (IMS) mono 440 233-2 (2). Tebaldi, Prandelli, Gueden, Inghilleri, Corena, Arié, Luise, Santa Cecilia Ac., Rome, Ch. & O, Erede
(***) EMI mono 5 56295-2 (2). Callas, Di Stefano, Moffo, Panerai, La Scala, Milan, Ch. & O, Votto
(M) **(*) EMI (ADD) 7 69657-2 (2). Freni, Gedda, Adani, Sereni, Mazzoli, La Scala, Milan, Ch. & O, Schippers
(M) **(*) RCA (ADD) 74321 39496-2 (2) [09026 61725-2]. Caballé, Domingo, Milnes, Raimondi, Alldis Ch., Wandsworth School Boys' Ch., LPO, Solti

Based on Zeffirelli's spectacular 1963 production at La Scala, Milan, this Karajan DVD version of *La Bohème* gives no idea of stage limitations. Indeed by completely avoiding shots of the full stage, Acts II and III give the illusion of being out of doors. One snag is that with the singers miming to recorded voices, often distant, there is sometimes little relationship between what one hears and what one sees in close-up. Nonetheless, with Karajan second to none as a Puccini interpreter, pointing the great emotional climaxes unerringly, and with Freni a meltingly beautiful Mimì, the combination of vividly atmospheric settings and a high-powered performance have one forgiving any discrepancies. Gianni Raimondi is a forthright Rodolfo with his ringing, unstrained tenor, while Panerai is an outstanding Marcello, and Adriana Martino a spunky Musetta.

Recorded for television in February 1982 with Brian Large directing, the alternative Warner DVD gives a vivid idea of John Copley's classic production of La Bohème at Covent Garden when it was new, with its evocative sets by Julia Trevelyan Oman. Traditionally realistic, the stage pictures are yet imaginatively fresh, at once grand to suit the opera-house, yet true to life. Though Lamberto Gardelli's conducting is relatively relaxed, veering towards expansive speeds, the results are keenly idiomatic with an excellent cast of soloists. With voices balanced relatively close, Neil Shicoff may be too loud at times, but this is yet a warmly sympathetic portrayal, never coarse, and Ileana Cotrubas at the peak of her career makes a charming Mimì, if at times with a beat in her voice. Thomas Allen, at his full maturity, is superb as Marcello, commanding in every way, but, for all her vivacity, the Musetta of Marilyn Zschau, suffering from a very slow speed in the Waltz Song, is often too tremulous. Excellent singing and acting from Gwynne Howell and John Rawnsley as the other two Bohemians.

Recorded in 1988, the San Francisco Opera production with Pavarotti and Freni offers a traditional production by Francesca Zambello, with the great tenor at his peak as Rodolfo and Freni still a tenderly moving Mimì, even though the voice is not as pure and even as it had been. She rises splendidly to the challenge of her big moments, such as Mimì's Farewell, like Pavarotti happily sustaining the lusciously measured speeds often allowed by the conductor, Tiziano Severini. Sandra Pacetti as Musetta is bright and characterful, and Gino Quilico as Marcello and Nicolai Ghiaurov as Colline are both excellent. The recording generally wears well, though the balance of voices in this live recording is sometimes odd.

Franco Zeffirelli's production of La Bohème for La Scala, Milan was first seen in 1963 and was used by Karajan (see above). It quickly came to be regarded as a classic, with its extraordinarily wide-spanning sets and hundreds of extras on stage in Act II. It was repeatedly revived at La Scala and elsewhere, and here is filmed in a 2003 revival, celebrating its fortieth anniversary. In an interview, Zeffirelli marvels at its longevity, noting that many in the excellent team of singers had not even been born when the production was new. Marcelo Alvarez proves an outstanding Rodolfo from the younger generation, opposite the fresh and girlish Mimì of Cristina Gallardo-Domas. Hei-Kyung Hong is a charmingly petite Musetta with a surprisingly strong character, and Roberto Servile as Marcello is powerful if rough at times. Bruno Bartoletti conducts a warm, well-paced and well-recorded reading, but it is the spectacle of Zeffirelli's lavish production that commands first attention, particularly in the split-level setting of Act II, with Musetta and Alcindoro arriving in a horse and carriage on the lower level and the soldiers' parade appearing on the upper level.

Pappano's CD recording of Bohème is conducted with ever-fresh imagination, bringing out not just subtle emotions alongside high passion, but also the fun of the piece in lightly sprung rhythms. Yet the exchanges when Mimì arrives have the most moving intimacy at the gentlest pianissimo, with the singers given full expressive freedom within a purposeful frame. The great set-piece numbers at the end of Act I, Che gelida manina, Mi chiamano Mimì and O soave fanciulla, then have the freshness of genuine emotion swelling in a radiant, towering crescendo. Alagna's tenor may not be velvety, but it has a fine tonal range with a heroic ring and Vaduva is similarly characterful rather than just sweet. The others make a superb team, virtually incomparable today – Ruth Swenson using her dramatic timbres most delicately even in the outburst of the waltz song, Thomas Hampson a swaggering Marcello, with Samuel Ramey and Simon Keenlyside characterfully contrasted as the other two Bohemians, all relishing the fun. With the Philharmonia inspired to playing of consistent flair, notably the woodwind soloists, this is a version to stand alongside the classics of the past.

On Decca, Karajan takes a characteristically spacious view of La Bohème, but there is an electric intensity which holds the whole score together as in a live performance. Pavarotti is an inspired Rodolfo, with comic flair and expressive passion, while Freni is just as seductive as Mimì. Elizabeth Harwood is a charming Musetta. Fine singing throughout the set. The reverberant Berlin acoustic is glowing and brilliant in superb Decca recording, with the clean placing of voices enhancing the performance's dramatic warmth.

The husband-and-wife partnership of Gheorghiu and Alagna is formidably demonstrated in Decca's more recent recording, though with Chailly in taut control and speeds consistently on the fast side, this is a performance that misses some of the tenderness in the score, as well as some of the fun. Gheorghiu's glorious singing is powerfully matched by the heroic tones of Alagna, culminating in a deeply moving death scene. With voices well forward and with words exceptionally clear, in an acoustic more open than in most Milan recordings, the brilliance of Chailly's reading is enhanced. Roberto Alagna as Rodolfo is more impulsive here than in EMI's Pappano recording, made four years earlier, responding no doubt to Chailly's fast speeds, but the manner is less affectionate. These are performances for a big opera-house, with shading less subtle than with Pappano. The notable casting among the rest is that of Simon Keenlyside, promoted to Marcello this time from Schaunard in the EMI set, again consistently responsive and alert. Elisabetta Scano is a light, bright Musetta, strongly contrasted with Gheorghiu, if a little shrill on top. Roberto di Candia makes a positive Schaunard, but Ildebrando d'Arcangelo as Colline is not helped by the close vocal balance, with a flutter emerging in the Act IV Coat Song.

Tebaldi's Decca set with Bergonzi dominated the catalogue in the early days of stereo, and it still sounds astonishingly vivid, with a very convincing theatrical atmosphere. At Double Decca price, it is one of the great operatic bargains in the current catalogue. Vocally the performance achieves a consistently high standard, with Tebaldi as Mimì the most affecting. Carlo Bergonzi is a fine Rodolfo; Bastianini and Siepi are both superb as Marcello and Colline, and even the small parts of Benoit and Alcindoro (as usual taken by a single artist) have the benefit of Corena's magnificent voice. The veteran Serafin was more vital here than on some of his records. The set comes with a perfectly adequate cued synopsis, for La Bohème is an exceptionally easy opera to follow.

The 1951 Decca set immediately won glowing praise, above all for Tebaldi's radiant and rich-voiced portrayal of Mimì.

The effect is still extraordinarily atmospheric in its sense of stage perspective. The one drawback was the whistly sound of the violins. The CD transfer has improved the violin focus, but the effect is still emaciated above the stave. Yet one soon adjusts to this, for the acoustic is basically warm and evocative. It is still a lovely performance, and there are no appreciable weaknesses in the cast. Erede keeps the music flowing; he controls the great love duet of Act I spaciously. The atmospheric opening of Act III at the Paris toll-gate is remarkably evocative. Indeed, at times here one could almost think stereo had already arrived.

Callas, flashing-eyed and formidable, may seem even less suited to the role of Mimì than to that of Butterfly, but characteristically her insights make for a vibrantly involving performance. Though Giuseppe di Stefano is not the subtlest of Rodolfos, he is in excellent voice here, and Moffo and Panerai make a strong partnership as the second pair of lovers. Votto occasionally coarsens Puccini's score but he directs with energy. The comparatively restricted dynamic range means that the singers appear to be 'front stage', but there is no lack of light and shade in Act II, and the sound of the new transfer is greatly improved.

In the Schippers version, the beauty of Freni's voice is what one remembers, with a supremely moving account of the Death scene. Nicolai Gedda's Rodolfo is not rounded in the traditional Italian way, but there is never any doubt about his ability to project a really grand manner of his own. Schippers quickly shows his genuinely Italianate sense of pause, giving the singers plenty of time to breathe and allowing the music to expand. The resonant, 1964 recording has transferred vividly to CD and the set has been attractively re-packaged with an excellently printed libretto.

The glory of Solti's set of *La Bohème* is the singing of Montserrat Caballé as Mimì, an intensely characterful and imaginative reading, the voice at its most radiant. Domingo is unfortunately not at his most inspired. *Che gelida manina* is relatively coarse, though here as elsewhere he produces glorious heroic tone, and he never falls into vulgarity. The rest of the team is strong, but Solti's tense interpretation of a work he had never conducted in the opera house does not quite let either the full flexibility of the music or the full warmth of romanticism have their place. The recording, however, is both vivid and atmospheric.

La Bohème (complete; in English)

*** Chan. 3008 (2). Haymon, O'Neill, McLaughlin, Miles, Dazeley, Geoffrey Mitchell Ch., Peter Kay Children's Ch., Philh. O, Parry

The magic mixture of humour and pathos in this unsinkable masterpiece is brought all the closer for having it in translation, even if the occasional line may ring false. Dennis O'Neill reinforces his high reputation as the regular tenor in the series, despite some intrusive vibrato under pressure, and Cynthia Haymon as a touching Mimì has never sounded more beautiful on disc, with the widest range of expression and tone. Marie McLaughlin is a warm-toned Musetta, temperamental rather than just flighty, and the other three Bohemians are ideally cast. Voices are vividly caught in the atmospheric recording, with the crowd scenes of Act II beautifully clarified. Highest praise too for David Parry who knows how to relax in tenderness, as well as when to press home hard. Warm, refined playing from the Philharmonia. Highly recommended to all who enjoy opera in English.

La Bohème: highlights. Arias from: Gianni Schicchi; Manon Lescaut; Turandot; Suor Angelica

(M) *** Decca (ADD) 458 248-2. Tebaldi, Bergonzi, d'Angelo, Bastianini, St Cecilia Ac. Ch. & O, Serafin

This is a well-chosen if not particularly generous selection of Serafin's highly involving 1959 *Bohème*, retaining all the fine qualities for which that set is famous. The handsomely packaged Opera Gala CD (texts and translations included) contains five primarily solo tracks of famous Puccini arias featuring Tebaldi, taken from Decca's complete opera recordings (from 1955 to 1962) and make an enjoyable bonus. The sound generally is astonishingly warm and vivid. The overall playing time is nearly 70 minutes.

Edgar (complete)

*** Naïve V4957. Varady, McCormick, Tanner, Jenis, Cigni, R. France Ch. & O, Levi

(M) ** Sony (ADD) M2K 79213 (2). Scotto, Bergonzi, Sardinero, Killibrew, NY Schola Cantorum and Op. O, Queler

After the success of his first opera, *Le Villi*, Puccini's publisher, Giulio Ricordi, kept faith with his young discovery, even though it was five years before he completed his next opera, *Edgar*. Puccini's big mistake was to retain the services of the same librettist, Ferdinando Fontana. Where the story of *Le Villi* is very simply told, telescoping much of the action and with motivation clear and direct despite the supernatural element, *Edgar* has a much more elaborate story, with absurd developments that no composer could make convincing. So the hero, Edgar, at the climax of Act I, for no evident reason burns down his own house, and in Act III, just as implausibly, he stages his own funeral, with a suit of armour in place of the body.

Where the faithful heroine, Fidelia, is a tenderly sympathetic character, her rival, Tigrana, as the name might suggest, is a fire-eater, modelled on Carmen. Evil through and through, she remains one-dimensional, making Edgar's sudden passion for her seem at best capricious. However, the score of *Edgar* brings important developments in Puccini's technique as a composer, through-composed, merging arias and ensembles.

Like the recording of *Le Villi*, also from French Radio (see below), this one of *Edgar* scores in the refinement of the sound. Julia Varady as Fidelia and Carl Tanner in the title-role of Edgar are both outstanding, allowed a range of expression largely denied to their rivals on Queler's Sony version, which suffers from aggressively close-up sound. Mary Ann McCormick as Tigrana is well contrasted with Varady, with her firm, clear mezzo finely controlled. Clean-cut singing too from Dalibor Jenis as Frank and Carlo Cigni as Gualtiero, with excellent choral work from the Choir of Radio France, whose choirmaster is the great Norbert Balasch. Yoel Levi proves a warmly understanding Puccinian, pointing rhythms and phrases with natural sympathy.

There is much to enjoy in the alternative Sony version. The melodies are not quite vintage Puccini, but Scotto as Fidelia, Killibrew as Tigrana and Bergonzi as Edgar give them compelling warmth. Eve Queler proves a variably convincing conductor, with Act III in need of more rehearsal. But this set, edited from live performances at Carnegie Hall, and commendably well recorded, makes a welcome alternative.

La Fanciulla del West (DVD versions)

(N) *** DG **DVD** 073 4023. Daniels, Domingo, Milnes, Yannissis, Metropolitan Op. Ch & O, Slatkin (V/D: Brian Large)

(N) *** Warner **DVD** 5050466-8356-2-8. Neblett, Domingo, Carroli, Lloyd, Howell, ROHCG Ch. & O, Santi (V/D: John Vernon)

(N) *** Opus Arte **DVD** OA LS 3004 D. Zampieri, Domingo, Pons, Roni, Salvadori, La Scala Ch. and O, Maazel (Executive producer: Hans Petri)

Leonard Slatkin conducts a bitingly dramatic account of Puccini's American opera with an outstanding cast in Giancarlo del Monaco's ultra-realistic production for the Met. in New York. In 1992 Sherrill Milnes was still an outstanding Rance, at once handsome and sinister, while Plácido Domingo is just as warmly expressive, both lyrical and heroic, as he is in the Covent Garden DVD of nine years earlier. As Minnie, the pretty and buxom Barbara Daniels with her bright, big soprano gives a characterful performance, even if her cheating in the poker game of Act II is no more convincing than usual. As Jake Wallace, the camp minstrel, Yanni Yannissis in his Act I solo is strong if a little tremulous. It is a measure of the lavishness of the Met. production with its grand sets by Michael Scott that through the open door of the Polka Bar in Act I you see a horse-drawn stage-coach arrive, and in Act II Minnie's cabin takes up only the left-hand side of the stage, with the rest given over to the snowy scene outside, letting you see the gunman who shoots Dick. Bright, clear recording, bringing out the emotional tug behind Slatkin's reading, powerfully so at the very end.

Recorded live at Covent Garden in 1983, Piero Faggioni's production with realistic sets by Ken Adam offers a similar cast to that on the vintage DG audio recording made in the studio, except that Silvano Carroli replaces Sherrill Milnes as Rance and Nello Santi replaces Zubin Mehta as conductor. Plácido Domingo is in superb voice as Dick Johnson, the reformed bandit who falls in love with Minnie, Girl of the Golden West; and Carol Neblett as the Girl sings freshly with an appealing directness, untroubled by the formidable demands of the role. Carroli makes an aptly sinister Rance, with Robert Lloyd forthright as Ashby and Gwynne Howell as the Minstrel shining in his brief appearance at the start of Act I. Faggioni's production has its symbolic moments, as when Minnie concedes her very first kiss to Dick and the door of her hut flails wildly back and forth.

Jonathan Miller's production for La Scala, Milan, was recorded in 1991 with costumes by Sue Blane and sets by Stefanos Lazaridis half-stylized, half-realistic. So in Act I the Polka Bar is extraordinarily high, with dozens of large sash windows, far grander than any likely bar. What matters is that the singing cast is strong, and Lorin Maazel's conducting is persuasive, despite a tendency to dawdle in grand moments. As at Covent Garden eight years earlier, Plácido Domingo makes a heroic Dick Johnson, and though Mara Zampieri cannot match Kiri Te Kanawa in glamour of voice or presence, with occasionally hooty tone, it is a strong, positive performance, as is Juan Pons as Rance. It is a colourful and striking presentation, with realistic sets and in-period costumes that take the melodrama seriously. It even manages to bring off the improbable scene in Act II when Sheriff Rance finds Dick Johnson's blood dripping down from the loft of Minnie's cabin. Domingo is in superb voice and rightly wins ovations for each of his big solos. Juan Pons too is wonderfully firm and dark of tone as Jack Rance, and Mara Zampieri

as Minnie sings with fine, clear focus with no suspicion of a wobble. The booklet gives no list of chapters, but otherwise the documentation is fuller than usual in DVD booklets, with a facsimile of the opera house's cast list on the back; it also contains a complete libretto in Italian and a translation.

La fanciulla del West (The Girl of the Golden West; CD versions)

☛ ✪ (M) *** Decca (ADD) 421 595-2 (2). Tebaldi, Del Monaco, MacNeil, Tozzi, St Cecilia Ac., Rome, Ch. & O, Capuana

☛ (M) *** DG (ADD) 474 840-2 (2). Neblett, Domingo, Milnes, Howell, ROHCG Ch. & O, Mehta

Tebaldi here gives one of her most warm-hearted and understanding performances on record, and Mario del Monaco displays the wonderfully heroic quality of his voice to great – if sometimes tiring – effect. Cornell MacNeil as the villain, Sheriff Rance, sings with great precision and attack, but unfortunately has not a villainous-sounding voice to convey the character fully. Jake Wallace's entry and the song *Che faranno i vecchi miei* is one of the high spots of the recording, with Tozzi singing beautifully. Capuana's expansive reading is matched by the imagination of the production, with the closing scene wonderfully effective in spectacular sound.

On DG, Mehta's manner – as he makes clear at the very start – is on the brisk side, even refusing to let the first great melody, the nostalgic *Che faranno i vecchi*, linger into sentimentality. Sherrill Milnes as Jack Rance makes that villain into far more than a small-town Scarpia, giving nobility and understanding to the Act I arioso. Domingo, as in the theatre, sings heroically, disappointing only in his reluctance to produce soft tone in the great aria, *Ch'ella mi creda*. The rest of the team is excellent, not least Gwynne Howell as the minstrel who sings *Che faranno i vecchi miei*; but the crowning glory of a masterly set is the singing of Carol Neblett as the Girl of the Golden West herself, gloriously rich and true, with formidable attack on the exposed high notes. Full, atmospheric recording to match, essential in an opera that is full of evocative offstage effects. With its new 'Originals' transfer and at a new mid-price, with texts and translations included, this set deserves upgrading to a full three stars.

Gianni Schicchi (DVD version)

(N) *** Opus Arte **DVD** OA 0918 D. Corbelli, Matthews, Giordano, Palmer, McLaughlin, LPO, Jurowski (V/D: Francesca Kemp)

Recorded at Glyndebourne in the 2004 Festival as the second half of a double bill with Rachmaninov's rarely performed one-act opera, *The Miserly Knight*, Puccini's comic masterpiece comes in a production by Annabel Arden that determinedly underlines the black side of this sparkling farce. The conductor, Vladimir Jurowski, also emphasizes that point, suggesting that Puccini's construction anticipates that of the modern film in its timing and cutting of scenes. The claustrophobic side of the piece is underlined by the heavily enclosed set of Vicki Mortimer, backing up the updating of the story from medieval to Edwardian times and largely eliminating the uplifting background of Florence. On the musical side, perfection of ensemble – for which Glyndebourne has long been famed – is at the root of this performance's success, with such characterful singers as Felicity Palmer and Marie McLaughlin among the mixed group of grasping relations. Alessandro Corbelli proves a masterly Schicchi, at once characterful, funny and sinister, and the two lovers are well taken by the tenor, Massimo Giordano, and the young soprano, Sally Matthews, with her fresh, flickering vibrato. Interviews with Jurowski, Arden and Corbelli come as extras, as well as a comment on the other opera in the double bill, *The Miserly Knight*, which Jurowski and Arden regard as the perfect counterpart in its contrasted treatment of the sin of avarice.

Gianni Schicchi (CD versions)

☛ (M) *** EMI 5 62777-2. Gobbi, De los Angeles, Del Monte, Montarsolo, Rome Op. Ch. & O, Santini – VERDI: *Don Carlo; Simon Boccanegra* excerpts ***

(M) *** RCA 74321 25285-2. Panerai, Donath, Seiffert, Bav. R. Ch., Munich R. O, Patanè

Tito Gobbi's classic assumption of the role of Gianni Schicchi has dominated the catalogue (as part of a complete recording of *Il Trittico*) since the earliest days of LP and it was a splendid idea for EMI to reissue it separately to represent Gobbi in their 'Great Artists of the Century' series. He gives an amazing performance. Though his incomparable baritone is not by nature comic-sounding, he is unequalled as Schicchi, sardonically manipulating the mourning relatives of Buoso Donati as he frames a new will for them. Puccini, the master of tragedy, here emerges as a supreme master of comic timing too. De los Angeles is charmingly girlish as Lauretta and the supporting cast is excellent. The early (1959) stereo is remarkably vivid and atmospheric, and there is a good cued synopsis.

The RCA (formerly Eurodisc) recording of *Gianni Schicchi* brings a co-production with Bavarian Radio, and the recording is vivid and well balanced. Central to the performance's success is the vintage Schicchi of Rolando Panerai, still rich and firm. He confidently characterizes the Florentine trickster in every phrase, building a superb portrait, finely timed. Peter Seiffert as Rinuccio gives a dashing performance, consistently clean and firm of tone, making light of the high tessitura and rising splendidly to the challenge of the big central aria. Helen Donath would have sounded even sweeter a few years earlier, but she gives a tender, appealing portrait of Lauretta, pretty and demure in *O mio babbino caro*. Though Italian voices are in the minority, it is a confident team.

Madama Butterfly (DVD versions)

(*) Decca **DVD DG 073 4037. Freni, Ludwig, Domingo, Kerns, Sénéchal, VPO, Karajan (Director: Jean-Pierre Ponnelle)

** Warner **DVD** 4509-99220-2. Kabaivanska, Antinori, Jankovic, Saccomani, Arena di Verona Ch. & O, Arena (Director: Giulio Chazalettes; V/D: Brian Large)

Madama Butterfly (CD versions)

☛ *** Decca (ADD) 417 577-2 (3). Freni, Ludwig, Pavarotti, Kerns, V. State Op. Ch., VPO, Karajan

*** DG 423 567-2 (3). Freni, Carreras, Berganza, Pons, Amb. Op. Ch., Philh. O, Sinopoli

(B) *** Double Decca (ADD) 452 594-2 (2). Tebaldi, Bergonzi, Cossotto, Sordello, St Cecilia Ac., Rome, Ch. & O, Serafin

(M) *** EMI (ADD) 5 67885-2 [567888] (2). Scotto, Bergonzi, di Stasio, Panerai, de Palma, Rome Op. Ch. & O, Barbirolli

(***) Testament mono SBT 2168 (2). De los Angeles, di Stefano, Gobbi, Rome Op. Ch. & O, Gavazzeni

(M) **(*) EMI (ADD) 7 63634-2 (2). De los Angeles, Björling, Pirazzini, Sereni, Rome Op. Ch. & O, Santini

(***) EMI mono 5 56298-2 (2). Callas, Gedda, Borriello, Danieli, La Scala, Milan, Ch. & O, Karajan

(B) (**(*)) Double Decca mono 440 230-2 (2). Tebaldi, Campora, Inghilleri, Rankin, St Cecilia Ac., Rome, Ch. & O, Erede

(M) **(*) Sony (ADD) SM2K 91135 (2). Scotto, Domingo, Knight, Wixell, Amb. Op Ch., Philh. O, Maazel

Recorded for television in 1974 in the same period as he recorded the opera for audio disc, Karajan's DVD of *Butterfly* is similarly magical in its evocation of Puccini's most atmospheric score. As on CD the title role is taken by Mirella Freni, as tenderly appealing to see as to hear, but where for audio the role of Pinkerton was taken by Luciano Pavarotti, here you have the much more telegenic Plácido Domingo, singing with similar fervour, responding to the inspired stage direction of Jean-Pierre Ponnelle to make this cad of a hero more complex than usual. Butterfly's house is set in fields on a misty hill-top, in the period around 1900, though Pinkerton is initially seen off-duty wearing a modern-looking T-shirt, and Butterfly demonstrates her American status in Act II by abandoning her kimono for blouse and skirt, before she returns to traditional dress at the end of the act. She uses no telescope to identify the 'Abramo Lincoln' entering Nagasaki harbour, but otherwise the setting is conventional and effective, with a comic portrait of Goro given by Michel Sénéchal, politically incorrect in its Japanese send-up, and the Bonze rather like a caricature from *Turandot*. The sound is full and atmospheric, though there is a curious pitch-problem in the middle of the *Flower Duet*, one of the few flaws in a fine issue.

The Warner DVD offers an atmospheric evocation of a performance, directed for video by Brian Large at the open-air Arena di Verona, complete with shots of the crowd outside beforehand and with curtain-calls at the end of each act. In such a setting the performance is lusty rather than subtle, with voices amplified reasonably well, but with the principals tending to belt things out, notably the tenor, Nazzareno Antinori. Raina Kabaivanska is more responsive, though her acting is rather stiff. In *Un bel di* she looks rather like a schoolmistress, implacable rather than tender, not helped by her likeness to Dame Maggie Smith in imperious mood.

Karajan's Decca CD set is extravagantly laid out on three discs instead of two as for most of the rival sets – slow speeds partly responsible. However, he inspires singers and orchestra to a radiant performance which brings out all the beauty and intensity of Puccini's score, sweet but not sentimental, powerfully dramatic but not vulgar. Freni is an enchanting Butterfly, consistently growing in stature from the young girl to the victim of tragedy, sweeter of voice than any rival on record. Pavarotti is an intensely imaginative Pinkerton, actually inspiring understanding for this thoughtless character, while Christa Ludwig is a splendid Suzuki. The recording is one of Decca's most resplendent, with the Vienna strings producing glowing tone.

However expansive his speeds, Sinopoli is never sentimental or self-indulgent. Puccini's honeyed moments are given, not sloppily, but with rapt intensity, through to the final aria, tough and intense. As she was for Karajan in his classic Decca set, Freni is a model Butterfly; though the voice is no longer so girlish, she projects the tragedy even more weightily than before. José Carreras is similarly presented as a large-scale Pinkerton. Juan Pons is a virile Sharpless and Teresa Berganza an equally positive, unfruity Suzuki.

Serafin's sensitive and beautifully paced reading finds Tebaldi at her most radiant. Though she was never the most deft of Butterflies dramatically, her singing is consistently rich and beautiful. The excellence of the Decca engineering in 1958 is amply proved in the CD transfer, the current remastering now providing full, atmospheric sound from the very beginning, opening out further as the orchestration grows fuller, with voices very precisely and realistically placed. At Double Decca price this is a pretty formidable bargain.

Under Sir John Barbirolli, players and singers perform consistently with a dedication and intensity rare in opera recordings made in Italy, and the whole score glows more freshly than ever. There is hardly a weak link in the cast. Bergonzi's Pinkerton and Panerai's Sharpless are both sensitively and beautifully sung; Anna di Stasio's Suzuki is more than adequate, and Renata Scotto's Butterfly has a subtlety and perceptiveness in its characterization that more than make up for any shortcoming in the basic beauty of tone-colour. This now rightly returns to the catalogue as one of EMI's 'Great Recordings of the Century'.

The *Butterfly* set with Victoria de los Angeles on Testament is her mono recording, made in 1954, when the voice was at its fullest and most golden, meltingly beautiful, bringing out the tender vulnerability of Puccini's heroine. Giuseppe di Stefano is also at his very finest as Pinkerton, with Tito Gobbi giving unexpected depth to the role of Sharpless, and Gavazzeni's timing heightening the pathos. The superb transfer is clearer and more forward than EMI's earlier CD version.

Victoria de los Angeles' 1960 recording also displays her art at its most endearing, her range of golden tone-colour lovingly exploited. Opposite her, Jussi Björling produces a flow of rich tone to compare with that of the heroine. Mario Sereni is a full-voiced Sharpless, but Miriam Pirazzini is a disappointingly wobbly Suzuki; Santini is a reliable, generally rather square and unimaginative conductor who rarely gets in the way.

Callas's view, aided by superbly imaginative and spacious conducting from Karajan, gives extra dimension to the Puccinian little woman, and with some keenly intelligent singing too from Gedda as Pinkerton this is a set which has a special compulsion. The performance projects the more vividly on CD, even though the lack of stereo in so atmospheric an opera is a serious disadvantage, and the new transfer is full and fairly spacious. However, it is at full price.

The Decca mono set was made in 1951. In the last resort Tebaldi lacks temperament but there is much magnificent singing. Campora is a fine Pinkerton. Erede's conducting is strong and dramatic, and there is much to relish, not least the amazingly atmospheric Decca recording, which is very kind to the voices, although the orchestra sounds thinner. The two CDs come in a single jewel-case with an independent plot summary unrelated to the 40 cues.

Eleven years after her EMI recording of *Butterfly* with Barbirolli, Renata Scotto recorded the role again, this time with Maazel, and the years brought nothing but benefit. The voice – always inclined to spread a little on top at climaxes – had acquired extra richness by the late 1970s and was recorded with a warmer tonal bloom. In perception too, Scotto's singing is far deeper, most strikingly in the heroine's *Un bel dì*, where the narrative leads to special intensity on the words 'Chiamerà Butterfly, della lontana'. Maazel is warmly expressive without losing his architectural sense; he has not quite the imaginative individuality of Barbirolli, but this is both powerful and unsentimental, with a fine feeling for Puccini's subtle orchestration. Other contributions are incidental, even Plácido Domingo, who sings heroically as Pinkerton, but arguably makes him too genuine a character for such a cad. Wixell's voice is not ideally rounded as Sharpless,

but he sings most sensitively, and Gillian Knight makes an expressive Suzuki. Among the supporting cast, Malcolm King as the Bonze is outstanding in a good team. The recording is rich and warm without having the bloom of Karajan's Decca set, and the voices are balanced relatively (though not uncomfortably) close. But the main snag of this reissue is the incredibly sparse documentation, without either libretto or cued synopsis – just a list of track titles!

Madam Butterfly (complete; in English)

(M) **(*) Chan. 3070 (2). Barker, Clarke, Rigby, Yurisich, Kale, Geoffrey Mitchell Ch., Philh. O, Abel

With Cheryl Barker a warm, fresh heroine, bringing out the girlish shyness at the beginning, and singing with radiant tone, this set of *Butterfly* in English, sponsored by the Peter Moores Foundation, fills an important gap (as do many other operas in English). Cheryl Barker as a pupil of Dame Joan Hammond, for long celebrated in this role, has plainly learnt from that experience, and she is helped by the expressive conducting of Yves Abel which consistently brings out the beauty of Puccini's orchestration, helped by full-bodied Chandos sound. As Pinkerton, the tenor, Paul Charles Clarke, is a disappointment with his gritty, tight tone, penetrating and un-Italianate, but he characterizes sensitively, and Gregory Yurisich is a splendid Sharpless and Jean Rigby a fine Suzuki. The old Elkins translation is used with a few necessary modifications.

Madama Butterfly: highlights

(M) *** Decca (ADD) 458 223-2 (from above complete set, with Tebaldi, Bergonzi, cond. Serafin)

The Decca selection is quite generous (68 minutes), and singing and recording are splendid; moreover the documentation includes a full translation. But with only a little more outlay one can get this version of the complete opera on a Double Decca, which seems a far more sensible investment.

(i) Madama Butterfly: highlights; (ii) Tosca, Act I: Love Duet: Mario! Mario! (sung in English)

⊶ (B) *** CfP (ADD) 585 0092. (i; ii) Craig; (i) Collier, Robson, Griffiths, Sadler's Wells Op. O, Balkwill; (ii) Hammond, RPO, Tausky

These recordings from the early 1960s celebrate the rich-timbred voice and dramatic stage personality of Charles Craig, one of the most impressive English operatic tenors since the war. He is as fine a Pinkerton as one can find anywhere today, and he is at his best here, not only in this selection from the 1960 Sadler's Wells production of *Madama Butterfly*, but in the Act I love duet from *Tosca* with Dame Joan Hammond – a partnership that is so fruitful that, when the music ends, one is left wondering why more was not recorded. As Butterfly, Marie Collier has a big, full voice and gets inside the part most convincingly. Her pronounced vibrato may trouble some ears, but one hopes the majority will find it nothing more than a natural colouring of the voice. Certainly her great closing aria, *You? You? Beloved Idol* ('Tu? tu? piccolo iddio!') is very powerful. As for the choice of extracts. the one omission that is at all serious is the entry of Butterfly. As it is, the duet of Pinkerton and Sharpless cuts off just as she is about to come in. But this is a most rewarding disc, for Puccini translates into English better than any other operatic composer. The recording is excellent, helping the listener to hear every word more clearly than would be possible in the theatre, and this is done without balancing things excessively in favour of the voices.

Manon Lescaut (DVD version)

(N) *** Warner **DVD** 5050466-7174-2-9. Domingo, Te Kanawa, Allen, ROHCG Ch. & O, Sinopoli (V/D: Humphrey Burton)

Götz Friedrich's production with solidly realistic sets by Gunther Schneider Siemssen was filmed at Covent Garden in 1983 with an ideal cast of principals and passionate, idiomatic conducting by Giuseppe Sinopoli. With voices well forward of the orchestra, the glorious singing of Plácido Domingo as Des Grieux comes over heroically, and Kiri Te Kanawa as Manon is both girlish and provocative, carefully modifying her tone between the open freshness of *In quelle trine morbide* in Act II and the darkened tone for her despairing final monologue in Act IV, *Sola, perduta, abbandonata*. Thomas Allen is equally strong and characterful as Lescaut, and the rest of the cast has no weak links. For a realistic presentation it would be hard to find any rival. No booklet is provided, with the full cast list given only on the film itself.

Manon Lescaut (CD versions)

🎵 *** Decca 440 200-2 (2). Freni, Pavarotti, Croft, Taddei, Vargas, Bartoli, NY Met. Op. Ch. & O, Levine

*** DG 413 893-2 (2). Freni, Domingo, Bruson, ROHCG Ch., Philh. O, Sinopoli

(B) *** Double Decca 460 750-2 (2). Te Kanawa, Carreras, Coni, Tajo, Matteuzzi, Ch. & O of Teatro Comunale di Bologna, Chailly

*** Naxos 8.660019/20 (2). Gauci, Sardinero, Kaludov, BRT Philh. Ch. & O, Rahbari

(***) EMI mono 5 56301-2 (2). Callas, di Stefano, Fioravanti, La Scala, Milan, Ch. & O, Serafin

(M) **(*) EMI (ADD) 7 64852-2 (2). Caballé, Domingo, Amb. Op. Ch., New Philh. O, Bartoletti

(BB) (**(*)) Naxos mono 8.110123/24 (2). Kirsten, Björling, Valdengo, Baccaloni, Hayward, Met. Op. Ch. & O, Antonicelli

** DG 463 186-2 (2). Guleghina, Cura, Gallo, Roni, La Scala, Milan, Ch. & O, Muti

With Luciano Pavarotti as a powerful Des Grieux, James Levine conducts a comparably big-boned performance of *Manon Lescaut*, bringing out the red-blooded drama of Puccini's first big success, while not ignoring its warmth and tender poetry. The impact is enhanced by exceptionally full, vivid sound, with the voices balanced close, well in front of the orchestra, and, though the closeness of balance exposes some inevitable blemishes of age in the voice, its fullness and warmth are more faithfully captured in a performance even warmer and more relaxed.

Pavarotti tackles his little opening aria, *Tra voi belle*, with a beefy bravado that misses the subtlety and point of Domingo, for example. But then he characteristically points word-meaning with a bright-eyed intensity that compels attention, and there is little harm in having so passionate a portrait of Des Grieux as Pavarotti's. The rest of the cast is strong too, with Dwayne Croft a magnificent Lescaut who brings out the character's wry humour. The veteran Giuseppe Taddei is superbly cast as Geronte, very characterful and still full-throated, while Cecilia Bartoli makes the unnamed singer in the Act II entertainment into far more than a cipher.

Plácido Domingo's portrait of Des Grieux on DG is far subtler and more detailed, with finer contrasts of tone and dynamic, than in his earlier, EMI recording opposite Caballé. Freni proves an outstanding choice: her girlish tones in Act I rebut any idea that she might be too mature. Of the others, a first-rate team, Renato Bruson nicely brings out the ironic side of Lescaut's character, and having Brigitte Fassbaender just to sing the *Madrigal* adds to the feeling of luxury, as does John Tomlinson's darkly intense moment of drama as the ship's captain. The voices are more recessed than is common, but they are recorded with fine bloom, and the brilliance of the orchestral sound comes out impressively.

The digital Chailly set dates from as recently as 1988 and makes a splendid bargain as a Decca Double. It comes with a 'listening guide' which offers good documentation and a simple cued synopsis. Dame Kiri gives an affecting characterization of Manon, at times rather heavily underlined but passionately convincing in the development from innocent girl to fallen woman. The playing from Chailly's Bologna orchestra cannot quite match that of the Philharmonia for Sinopoli, yet Chailly is a degree more idiomatic in his pacing. Carreras is in good form, but sounds a little strained at times. The Decca sound, with the voices well forward is characteristically vivid.

On the Naxos issue, Miriam Gauci gives one of the most sensitive performances of this role on any set. The young Bulgarian, Kaludi Kaludov, is a clean-cut, virile Des Grieux, opening up impressively in his big moments. Vincente Sardinero makes a powerful Lescaut, and Rahbari is a red-blooded interpreter of Italian opera, generally pacing well, even if at the very start he is disconcertingly hectic. This is the least expensive *Manon Lescaut* in the catalogue but, even if it cost more, it would still be very recommendable.

It is typical of Callas that she turns the final scene into the most compelling part of the opera. Serafin, who could be a lethargic recording conductor, is here electrifying, and Di Stefano too is inspired to one of his finest complete opera recordings. The cast-list even includes the young Fiorenza Cossotto, impressive as the singer in the Act II *Madrigal*. The recording – still in mono, not a stereo transcription – minimizes the original boxiness and gives good detail.

The EMI version conducted by Bartoletti is chiefly valuable for the performance of Montserrat Caballé as the heroine, one of her most affecting, with the voice alluringly beautiful. Otherwise the set is disappointing, with Plácido Domingo unflattered by the close acoustic, not nearly as perceptive as in his much later, DG performance under Sinopoli. The new transfer to CD, however, has improved the sound.

Dorothy Kirsten was a favourite lyric soprano at the Met. in New York for over 30 years, yet with hardly any commercial recordings to her name she is little known outside the United States. That makes this brilliant, well-cast version of *Manon Lescaut* especially welcome, recorded live on Christmas Eve, 1949. Kirsten's may not be a specially distinctive voice, but it is a pure, clear, beautiful one, perfectly controlled, as her portrayal here makes plain in her tender, affecting accounts of Manon's big moments. It is a pity that her final solo, *Sola, perduta, abbandonata* is severely cut. Björling as Des Grieux is even more ardent here than he is in his commercial recording opposite Albanese on RCA, a great tenor ideal for the role, and Giuseppe Valdengo is a powerful Lescaut, with Salvatore Baccaloni a characterful Geronte. Antonicelli sometimes rushes the fast music, Toscanini-style, but draws out the lyrical warmth perfectly. Clear, if limited sound, only occasionally marred by surface noise.

The problems of recording live at La Scala weigh heavily in the Muti recording for DG. The stage noises are often intrusive; the orchestral sound lacks body, and choral ensemble is often poor. Muti too is encouraged to underline too heavily such big dramatic moments as the end of Act III. Though Maria Guleghina sings affectingly as the heroine, the lovely soprano tone tends to spread under pressure in the upper register. José Cura sings strenuously from his very first aria, *Tra voi belle*, onwards, though he too characterizes well and is occasionally persuaded to modify his strong, heroic tone.

La Rondine (complete)

(M) **(*) Sony M2K 37852 (2). Te Kanawa, Domingo, Nicolesco, Rendall, Nucci, Watson, Knight, Amb. Op. Ch., LSO, Maazel

(i–iii) *La Rondine (complete)*. **(i; iii)** *Le Villi: Prelude, L'abbandono; La tregenda; Ecco la casa … Torna al felice.* **(i; iv)** Song: *Morire!*

☛ *** EMI 5 56338-2 (2). (i) Alagna; (ii) Gheorghiu, Mula-Tchako, Matteuzzi, Rinaldi; (iii) L. Voices, LSO, Pappano; (iv) Pappano (piano)

Pappano on this EMI issue transforms the work, revealing it to be another masterpiece. He is aided by the partnership of Angela Gheorghiu, most moving in the Violetta-like role of the heroine, Magda, and of Alagna as the ardent young student she falls in love with. Consistently Gheorghiu makes you share the courtesan's wild dream of finding her young student. As Ruggero, the hero, Alagna winningly characterizes in his freshest voice. What will specially delight Puccinians in this set is that he is given an extra aria about Paris, *Parigi e un citta*, which transforms his otherwise minimal contribution to Act I. The role of the poet, Prunier, is also transformed thanks to the casting of the clear-toned William Matteuzzi in what is normally a comprimario role. Inva Mula-Tchako is equally well cast in the soubrette role of Lisette, bright, clear and vivacious, with Alberto Rinaldi making the sugar-daddy, Rambaldo, the dull dog intended. The excerpts from *Le Villi*, warm and dramatic, include two orchestral showpieces. Alagna also gives a ringing account of Roberto's aria, as he does of the song, *Morire!* – with Pappano at the piano – the source of the extra aria for Ruggero included in the main opera.

Maazel's is a strong, positive reading, crowned by a superb and radiant Magda in Dame Kiri Te Kanawa, mature yet glamorous. Domingo, by age too mature for the role of young hero, yet scales his voice down most effectively in the first two Acts, expanding in heroic warmth only in the final scene of dénouement. Sadly, the second pair are far less convincing, when the voices of both Mariana Nicolesco and David Rendall take ill to the microphone.

Suor Angelica (complete)

(M) **(*) RCA (ADD) 74321 40575-2. Popp, Lipovšek, Schiml, Jennings, Bav. R. Ch., Munich R. O, Patanè

Patanè's performance is idiomatic and consistently well placed. Neither Lucia Popp as Angelica nor Marjana Lipovšek as the vindictive Zia Principessa is ideally cast – the one overstressed, the other sounding too young – but these are both fine artists who sing with consistent imagination, and the recording is pleasingly atmospheric. There is a libretto/translation provided, and the only snag is the lack of cueing: only two tracks are indicated, one 28 minutes into the opera and the second 12 minutes later.

Tosca (complete; DVD versions)

*** TDK **DVD** DV-OPTOS. Guleghina, Licitra, Nucci, Parodi, Mariotti, La Scala Milan Ch. & O, Muti (V/D: Pierre Cavasillas)

(N) *** Opus Arte **DVD** OA 0883 D. Gheorghiu, Alagna, Raimondi, ROHCG O, Pappano (Director: Benoit Jacquot)

(N) *** NVC Arts **DVD** 4509 99219-2. Marton, Aragall, Wixell, Ch. & O, of the Verona Arena, Oren. V/D Brian Large

(*) VAI **DVD VAI 4217. Tebaldi, Tobin, London, Stuttgart Staatsoper Ch. & O, Patanè

(N) ** Opus Arte **DVD** OA 0901 D (2). Dessi, Armiliato, Raimondi, Teatro Real, Madrid, Ch. & O, Benini (Director: Nuria Espert; TV director: Angel Luis Ramirez)

(N) ** Hardy **DVD** HCD 4011. Olivero, Misciano, Fioravanti, Foiani, Badioli, Cesarini, Torino della RAI R. Ch. & O, Vernizzi

Tosca (complete; CD versions)

(N) ☛ (M) (***) EMI mono 5 62890-2 [5 62893-2] (2). Callas, Di Stefano, Gobbi, Calabrese, La Scala, Milan, Ch. & O, De Sabata

☛ (BB) (***) EMI mono 5 85644–2 (2). Callas, Di Stefano, Gobbi, Calabrese, Mercuriali, La Scala, Milan, Ch. & O, De Sabata

*** EMI 5 57173-2 (2). Gheorghiu, Alagna, Raimondi, ROHCG Ch. & O, Pappano

(M) *** Decca (ADD) 466 384-2 (2). L. Price, di Stefano, Taddei, V. State Op. Ch., VPO, Karajan

*** DG 431 775-2 (2). Freni, Domingo, Ramey, Terfel, ROHCG Ch., Philh. O, Sinopoli

(B) *** Ph. (ADD) 464 729-2 (2). Caballé, Carreras, Wixell, ROHCG Ch. & O, C. Davis

(M) *** RCA (ADD) 74321 39503-2 (2). L. Price, Domingo, Milnes, Plishka, Alldis Ch., Wandsworth School Boys' Ch., New Philh. O, Mehta

*** DG (ADD) 413 815-2 (2). Ricciarelli, Carreras, Raimondi, Corena, German Op. Ch., BPO, Karajan

**(*) Decca (IMS) 414 597-2 (2). Te Kanawa, Aragall, Nucci, Welsh Nat. Op. Ch., Nat. PO, Solti

(M) **(*) EMI 5 66504-2 (2). Scotto, Domingo, Bruson, Amb. Op. Ch., St Clement Danes School Boys' Ch., Philh. O, Levine

(BB) (**) EMI mono 5 62675-2 (2). Callas, Cioni, Gobbi, ROHCG Ch. & O, Cillario

(BB) (**) Naxos mono 8.110096-97 (2). Caniglia, Gigli, Borgioli, Dominici, Tomei, Rome Op. Ch. & O, Fabritiis

In March 2000 Riccardo Muti conducted a staged performance of *Tosca* for the very first time, and as this DVD powerfully reveals he emerged as the hero of a great occasion. The high-voltage electricity is unflagging, with the drama timed to perfection, magnetically compelling from first to last. Having been the music director at La Scala since 1986, Muti knows unerringly how to pace his singers, letting them phrase expansively where needed, yet holding the structure firmly together. Maria Guleghina makes a formidable Tosca, at her finest in the great scene with Scarpia in Act II, leading up to a radiant account of *Vissi d'arte* and a chilling murder. The veteran Leo Nucci, tall, thin and mean, is most compelling as the police chief, at times a smiling villain, though the voice has its occasional roughness. As Cavaradossi Salvatore Licitra may be an unromantic figure, and he is heavy-handed at the start in *Recondita armonia*, but he develops from there and in Act III sings superbly, with fine shading of tone. The production, directed by Luca Ronconi, consistently heightens the dramatic conflicts. In period it is updated by roughly half a century from the Napoleonic era, with handsome costumes by Vera Marzot, though the sets of Margherita Palli bring a surreal contradiction between realism and fantasy. They look like conventional sets that have been hit by an earthquake, with uprights at all angles. Sections of scenery are retained from act to act, with an increasing pile of debris left behind. That makes the battlements of the Castell Sant'Angelo look like a bomb-site, which Tosca has to climb to fling herself to her death.

Using the outstanding EMI recording of *Tosca* conducted by Antonio Pappano for a soundtrack, the French film director Benoit Jacquot has created what he describes as a mixture of fiction and documentary. Clips of the recording sessions at Abbey Road in black and white punctuate elaborate stagings of the opera in full colour, filmed on location and with the singers miming to the music. In places – as when Scarpia voices his own thoughts while in conversation with Tosca – you hear Ruggero Raimondi singing without his lips moving. With shots of the action regularly taken from imaginative angles, and with Angela Gheorghiu the most masterful actress – herself very near the character, as Jacquot suggests – and Raimondi the most believably sinister of Scarpias, the mix works well, though reproduction of the EMI recording is not always perfect. Though Roberto Alagna as Cavaradossi is not at his most lyrical, the visuals certainly reinforce the judgement that this is the finest among recent versions of the opera, electrifyingly conducted by Antonio Pappano, who, along with Gheorghiu and Jacquot, contributes an interview.

It is not often one has a live performance of Tosca in which the key performers are so equally matched, as in the traditional NVC Arts production, filmed in the spectacular Roman ampitheatre in Verona. The producer, Sylvano Busotti and designer, Fiorenzo Giorgi have made the most of the spectacular natural backcloth, a dramatic setting to all three acts, and with a fine acoustic for the solo voices, chorus and orchestra, so that the big *Te deum* scene at the close of Act I is very effective indeed. Eva Marton is perhaps not as glamorous a Tosca as Gheorghiu, but she is a handsome woman with fine presence. She and Giacomo Aragall are a well matched pair of lovers, both in strong, unstrained vocal form, and the only drawback is that the key arias (very well sung) bring extended ovations from the audience which interrupt the continuity. However their presence undoubtedly adds to the tension. Wixell is a superb Scarpia, dignified as well as evil, and he sings magnificently throughout Act II. The murder scene with Tosca, and the close of the opera itself are handled powerfully but without melodrama. Throughout Daniel Oren conducts his excellent chorus and orchestra with fine lyrical Puccinian ardour and Brian Large ensures that the camera is close to the principals whenever needed, so that the listener/viewer is closely involved. If you can accept the occasional intrusive applause, this is very enjoyable indeed and does Puccini full justice on every count.

Filmed in black and white at a performance in the Stuttgart Staatsoper in June 1961, the VAI DVD offers a sound, conventional production with in-period costumes and realistic sets by Max Fritzsche. Its special value is the assumption of the title-role by Renata Tebaldi. With her firm, creamy tone perfectly controlled, Tebaldi seems to represent the very essence of the prima donna, grand in a traditional way, and who better to play the part of an operatic prima donna in *Tosca*? She rises magnificently to the challenge of *Vissi d'arte* in Act II, with fine shading of tone and flawless legato in that moment of repose, and the Stuttgart audience rewards her

with tumultuous applause. Yet this Tosca is not so much passionate as stately. Philip Hope-Wallace, reviewing one of her performances at Covent Garden, remarked that when she threw herself off the battlements, it was rather like watching an elderly matron entering a swimming-bath at the shallow end, though here she simply exits along the battlements to perform her leap out of sight.

Extravagantly, the Opus Arte Spanish DVD stretches to two discs instead of one. The conductor, Maurizio Benini, adopts excessively slow speeds, but otherwise the only reason for the length is the inclusion of a 50-minute supplement of interviews in Spanish and Italian with the director, Nuria Espert, and the principal singers. Espert's production, recorded in Madrid in 2004, injects an ecclesiastical element, with Scarpia dressed as a cardinal, and his office in Act II set out with his desk and altar. Daniella Dessi is impressive enough as Tosca, and Ruggero Raimondi retains much of his characteristic power, but Fabio Armiliato is an underpowered Cavaradossi. A distinctive version, but not a first choice.

Long before she retired from performing, Magda Olivero became an iconic figure in the world of opera, a status enhanced by the relative rarity of her recordings. The Hardy set of *Tosca* offers a vivid performance of her in the title-role of Puccini's opera, filmed in 1960 in fuzzy black-and-white. It was a role for which she was justly famed, suiting her both vocally and dramatically. Though both the camerawork and the style of acting recall the cinema's silent era, it makes a fine historical document which will delight more than her devotees, despite the crumbly sound. A second disc has clips of an interview with her when she was in her nineties, as well as films of informal performances she gave long after her retirement from the theatre. They include one of the heroine's final monologue, *Sola, perduta, abbandonata*, from Puccini's *Manon Lescaut*, made (with piano) when she was 83, and one of her singing alongside her pupil, Danilo Formaggio, in Franck's *Panis angelicus* when she was 92, an amazing achievement.

Eugene Tobin as Cavaradossi, like many tenors, starts lustily, and then gets more expressive as he goes along, never betraying signs of strain. George London makes a handsome Scarpia, imperious and vehement both in his acting and in his singing, though often gritty of tone. Franco Patanè as conductor is reliable but at times overemphatic, again presenting a conventional view. The television direction, like that of the stage director, is conventional, relying on the full stage picture rather more than usual. Optional English subtitles are provided but no other extras.

There has never been a finer recorded performance of *Tosca* than Callas's first, with Victor de Sabata conducting and Tito Gobbi as Scarpia. Gobbi makes the unbelievably villainous police chief into a genuinely three-dimensional character, and Di Stefano, as the hero Cavaradossi, was at his finest. The conducting of De Sabata is spaciously lyrical as well as sharply dramatic, and the mono recording is superbly balanced in Walter Legge's fine production. The recording now rightly takes its place as one of EMI's 'Great Recordings of the Century' and the new transfer brings enhanced sound that could almost be stereo, with the voices caught gloriously, and the mid-priced set includes a full libretto and translation.

EMI's super-bargain transfer of the classic Callas–Gobbi set with de Sabata conducting is designed to outclass the rival set from Naxos. As well as being packaged much more attractively, it brings a transfer which, taken from the original tapes, has the voices brighter and more immediate than on the Naxos set. Though painstakingly transferred from a series of different LPs, with minor imperfections ironed out, the Naxos set brings few advantages (8.110256/7). Though it is claimed that the EMI transfers have been made at the wrong pitch, there is no evidence that La Scala was using a relatively high pitch, such as is normal in the United States (where the transfers were made), and most ears will hardly detect a difference. The immediate impact of the voices on EMI will for most be the deciding factor. Neither set has a libretto, but both helpfully provide a detailed synopsis linked to the index points on the disc.

With all three principals the clarity of words adds to the power of this Pappano performance, most strikingly with Gheorghiu, who constantly sheds new light on one phrase after another. When Cavaradossi attempts to explain the black eyes of the Madonna he is painting, Gheorghiu, responding in the half-tone phrase '*Ah, quegli occhi*' ('Ah, those eyes') conveys her doubt with heart-stopping intensity. In Act II, when Scarpia is all-dominant, Gheorghiu, instead of being defiant from the outset is plainly frightened out of her wits, so that we then movingly witness the build-up of resolve that will lead to murder, punctuated by an account of the aria *Vissi d'arte* of velvet beauty. Gheorghiu's is a great performance, significantly expanding on what we already know of her, as magnetic as Callas's, rich and beautiful as well as dramatic. The EMI sound is superb, full, clear and atmospheric, making this a classic among the many versions of this opera.

Karajan's 1962 Vienna *Tosca* is rightly now assigned its place in Decca's Legends series. It was previously available on a Double Decca and now costs more, but as it includes a libretto/translation it is well worth its mid-price bracket. Karajan deserves equal credit with the principal singers for the vital, imaginative performance, recorded in Vienna. Taddei himself has a marvellously wide range of tone-colour, and though he cannot quite match the Gobbi snarl he has almost every other weapon in his armoury. Leontyne Price is at the peak of her form and di Stefano sings most sensitively. The sound is quite marvellous in its digitally remastered format, combining presence with atmosphere.

Even more than the Puccini operas he had previously recorded – always with spacious, finely moulded treatment – *Tosca* seems to match Sinopoli's musical personality, helped by DG recording of spectacular weight and range. Ramey's is not a conventional portrait of the evil police-chief, but the role has rarely been sung with more sheer beauty, with such a climax as the *Te Deum* at the end of Act I sounding thrilling in its firmness and power. Domingo's heroic power is formidable too, and unlike many of his opera recordings for DG this one presents him in close-up, not distanced. Freni's is not naturally a Tosca voice, but it is still a powerful, heartfelt performance.

Pacing the music naturally and sympathetically, Sir Colin Davis proves a superb Puccinian, one who not only presents Puccini's drama with richness and force but gives the score the musical strength of a great symphony. In this the quality of the singing from a cast of unusual consistency plays an important part. Caballé may not be as sharply jealous a heroine as her keenest rivals, but with the purity of *Vissi d'arte* coming as a key element in her interpretation, she still presents Tosca as a formidable siren-figure ('*Mia sirena*' being Cavaradossi's expression of endearment). Carreras reinforces his reputation as a tenor of unusual artistry as well as of superb vocal powers. Though Wixell is not ideally well focused as Scarpia, not at all Italianate of tone, he presents a completely credible lover-figure, not just the lusting ogre of

convention. The 1976 analogue recording is full as well as refined, bringing out the beauties of Puccini's scoring. An unexpected but worthy choice for the Philips selection of '50 Great Recordings'.

Leontyne Price made her second complete recording of *Tosca* (for RCA) ten years after the first under Karajan, and the interpretation remained remarkably consistent, a shade tougher in the chest register – the great entry in Act III a magnificent moment – and a little more clipped of phrase. That last modification may reflect the relative manners of the two conductors – Karajan more individual in his refined expansiveness, Mehta more thrustful. On balance, taking Price alone, the preference is for the earlier set, but Mehta's version also boasts a fine cast, with the team of Domingo and Milnes at its most impressive. The recording, too, is admirable, even if it yields to the Decca in atmosphere and richness.

On Karajan's DG version the police chief, Scarpia, seems to be the central character, and his unexpected choice of singer, a full bass, Raimondi, helps to show why, for this is no small-time villain but a man who in full confidence has a vein of nobility in him. Katia Ricciarelli is not the most individual of Toscas, but the beauty of singing is consistent. Carreras gives a powerful, stylish performance. The recording is rich and full, with the stage picture clearly established and the glorious orchestral textures beautifully caught.

Rarely has Solti phrased Italian melody so consistently *con amore*, his fiercer side subdued but with plenty of power when required. Even so, the timing is not always quite spontaneous-sounding, with transitions occasionally rushed. But the principal *raison d'être* of the set must be the casting of Dame Kiri as the jealous opera-singer. Her admirers will relish the glorious sounds, but the jealous side of Tosca's character is rather muted.

Levine directs a red-blooded performance which underlines the melodrama. Domingo here reinforces his claim to be the finest Cavaradossi today, while the clean-cut, incisive singing of Renato Bruson presents a powerful if rather young-sounding Scarpia. Renata Scotto's voice is in many ways ideally suited to the role of Tosca, certainly in its timbre and colouring; as caught on record, however, the upper register is often squally. The digital recording is full and forward.

Recorded at Covent Garden two years after Callas's classic studio recording of *Tosca* conducted by de Sabata, this alternative set, recorded live in 1954, makes a fascinating supplement but cannot in any way compare in quality. EMI make an apology for the technical imperfections of the sound, often cloudy and with odd balances and inevitable audience noises; and that will deter many. Yet Callas heard live, free and imaginative in one of her finest roles, is certainly worth an airing, and though Cillario cannot compare with de Sabata, he directs a powerful performance with Gobbi also at his finest and Renato Cioni a competent if not inspired Cavaradossi.

It is rare for a recording of *Tosca* to centre round the tenor taking the role of Cavaradossi, rather than round Scarpia or Tosca herself, yet here Gigli at the height of his fame in 1938 is manifestly the main focus. He does not disappoint, making the hero a more rounded, more human character than is common, with fun and playfulness well caught as well as pathos. Maria Caniglia was a last-minute choice when Iva Pacetti proved unavailable, and though it is not a searching portrayal of the jealous opera-singer, it is a vocally strong and purposeful one, with the occasional edge on the voice apt enough. Armando Borgioli as Scarpia is reliable vocally rather than characterful, with Oliviero de Fabritiis pacing the score well in a full, red-blooded reading. Excellent CD transfers, mastered by Ward Marston, with voices very well caught indeed. The two discs include a 50-minute supplement taken from a version of *Tosca* recorded in French in 1931, an abridged version on seven 78rpm discs chiefly valuable for the enchanting portrayal of Tosca by Ninon Vallin, very feminine and seductive. The others are no match for her – Enrico de Mazzei self-indulgent as Cavaradossi and Paul Payan as Scarpia not remotely sinister. One does not regret that the hero's two big arias are both omitted from this supplement.

Tosca (complete; in English)

(M) *** Chan. 3000 (2). Eaglen, O'Neill, Yurisich, Mitchell Ch., Kay Children's Ch., Philh. O, Parry

David Parry with Jane Eaglen, in one of her finest performances on disc, directs a gripping account of Puccini's red-blooded drama, sung in English. With the help of opulent, atmospheric Chandos sound, the bite and energy of the Philharmonia bring out the expressive warmth of the score, not least in the love music, whether in the power of the big tuttis or in magical, whispered *pianissimos*. What above all seals the success of the set is the power and command of Jane Eaglen as Tosca. The confident sureness with which she attacks every top note is a delight, so that in Act I she expresses her jealousy with the vehemence of a Wagnerian, while singing with warm, rounded tone. She is well matched by Dennis O'Neill as Cavaradossi, aptly Italianate, and Gregory Yurisich makes a powerful Scarpia, younger-sounding than most and therefore a plausible lover. The others are well cast too, notably Peter Rose as a fresh-voiced Angelotti. The Geoffrey Mitchell Choir and children's choir are superb in the crowd scenes of Act I.

Tosca: highlights

*** EMI 5 57364-2 (from complete set with Gheorghiu, Alagna, Raimondi, ROHCG Ch. & O, Pappano)

This EMI Gheorghiu, Alagna highlights follows the progress of the opera over a generous 78 minutes of excerpts well covered by the detailed synopsis.

Tosca: highlights (in English)

(M) *** Chan. 3066 (from above complete recording with Eaglen, O'Neill, Yurisich; cond. Parry)

A generous selection (74 minutes), centring on Jane Eaglen's magnificently sung portrayal of Tosca. The recording is superbly rich and this singing can stand alongside any international competition. A hugely enjoyable disc.

Il Trittico: (i) Il Tabarro; (ii) Suor Angelica; (iii) Gianni Schicchi

🎵 *** EMI 5 56567-2 (3) (i; iii) Gheorghiu, Alagna; (i) Guelfi, Guleghina, Shicoff; (ii) Gallardo-Domas, Manca di Nissa; (ii-iii) Palmer; (iii) Van Dam, Roni; (i-ii) L. Voices; (ii) Tiffin School Boys' Ch., LSO or Philh. O, Pappano

(M) (***) EMI mono/stereo 7 64165-2 (3). (i) Gobbi; (i) Pradelli, Mas; (ii-iii) de los Angeles; (ii) Barbieri; (iii) Canali, Del Monte, Montarsolo; Rome Op. Ch. & O; (i) Bellezza; (ii) Serafin; (iii) Santini

No previous recordings of the three one-acters in Puccini's triptych bring quite such warmth or beauty or so powerful a drawing of the contrasts between each – in turn Grand Guignol melodrama, pure sentiment and high comedy. Pacing each opera masterfully, Pappano heightens emotions fearlessly to produce at key moments the authentic gulp-in-throat, whether for the cuckolded bargemaster, Michele, for sister Angelica in her agonized suicide and heavenly absolution, or for the resolution of young love at the end of *Gianni Schicchi*.

Angela Gheorghiu and Roberto Alagna, as well as making a tiny cameo appearance in *Il Tabarro* as the off-stage departing lovers, sing radiantly as Lauretta and Rinuccio in *Gianni Schicchi*, with the happy ending most tenderly done. Maria Guleghina, well known for her fine Tosca, makes a warm, vibrant Giorgetta, and the touch of acid at the top of the voice adds character. Even more remarkable is the singing of the young Chilean soprano, Cristina Gallardo-Domas as Sister Angelica. This is a younger, more tender, more vulnerable Angelica than usual. As with Gheorghiu, the dynamic shading brings *pianissimos* of breathtaking delicacy, not least in floated top-notes. The casting in the middle opera is as near flawless as could be. The Zia Principessa is sung with chilling power by Bernadette Manca di Nissa, her tone firm and even throughout. Felicity Palmer with her tangy mezzo tone is well contrasted as the Abbess, and she is just as characterful as the crabby Zita in *Gianni Schicchi*. Among the men, Carlo Guelfi makes a superb Michele in *Il Tabarro*, incisive, dark and virile. Neil Shicoff makes a fine Luigi, his nervy tenor tone adding character. As Gianni Schicchi, José van Dam is in fine voice, with his clean focus bringing out the sardonic side of Schicchi, and his top Gs wonderfully strong and steady still. The recording is comfortingly sumptuous and atmospheric, very wide in its dynamic range, with magical off-stage effects.

The classic pioneering EMI set of *Il Trittico* has dominated the catalogue since the earliest days of LP, with Tito Gobbi giving two of his ripest characterizations. The central role of the cuckolded bargemaster, Michele, in the mono *Il Tabarro* inspires him to one of his very finest performances on record. The central leaf of the triptych, *Suor Angelica*, brings a glowing performance from Victoria de los Angeles, giving a most affecting portrayal of Angelica, with Fedora Barbieri formidable as her unfeeling aunt, the Zia Principessa. De los Angeles reappears, charmingly girlish as Lauretta, in *Gianni Schicchi*, where the high comedy has never fizzed so deliciously outside the opera house. Though Gobbi's incomparable baritone is not by nature comic-sounding, he is unequalled as Schicchi. Only *Gianni Schicchi*, recorded last in 1958, is in genuine and excellent stereo; *Il Tabarro* (1955) and *Suor Angelica* (1957) are mono, but all the transfers are expert, clear and convincingly balanced.

Turandot (complete)

(*) Arthaus **DVD 100 088. Marton, Sylver, Mazzaria, Langan, San Francisco Op. Ch. & O, Runnicles (Production/Design: David Hockney; Director: Peter McClintock; V/D: Brian Large)

🎵 *** Decca (ADD) 414 274-2 (2). Sutherland, Pavarotti, Caballé, Pears, Ghiaurov, Alldis Ch., Wandsworth School Boys' Ch., LPO, Mehta

(M) *** EMI (ADD) 7 69327-2 (2). Nilsson, Corelli, Scotto, Mercuriali, Giaiotti, Rome Op. Ch. & O, Molinari-Pradelli

*** DG 423 855-2 (2). Ricciarelli, Domingo, Hendricks, Raimondi, V. State Op. Ch., V. Boys' Ch., VPO, Karajan

(***) EMI mono 5 56307-2 (2). Callas, Fernandi, Schwarzkopf, Zaccaria, La Scala, Milan, Ch. & O, Serafin

(M) **(*) EMI (ADD) 5 65293-2 (2). Caballé, Carreras, Freni, Plishka, Sénéchal, Maîtrise de la Cathédrale, Ch. of L'Opéra du Rhin, Strasbourg PO, Lombard

(BB) (**(*)) Naxos mono 8.110193/4. Cigna, Olivero, Merli, Neroni, Turin R. Vh. & O, Ghione (includes historic recordings of key excerpts from *Turandot*)

The Arthaus DVD comes from a 1994 San Francisco production and has Eva Marton in the title role, which she has, of course, sung in Vienna under Maazel for Sony (1983), Roberto Abbado (RCA) and James Levine (DG). Thus the merits and shortcomings of her Turandot are well known: hers is a big, dramatic voice, but with far too little expressive variation in tone and she is content to sing loudly and leave it at that. However, there are other things in its favour: a decent Calaf in Michael Sylver, a good Ping (Theodore Baerg), Pang (Dennis Peterson) and Pong (Craig Estep). We have heard more moving accounts of Liù than Lucia Mazzaria's, but generally speaking the cast are more than acceptable. The orchestral and choral forces are very well harnessed by Donald Runnicles, who fires on all cylinders and visually the designs by David Hockney are vivid and bold (some might think them garish, and they have had a dismissive press) but they will strike most readers as effective. The sound is rather forward and bright, and detail is very well captured by the engineers. Brian Large, as always, makes sure that the camera is where you would want it to be, and although there are more subtle Turandots to be found than Marton, the performance is thoroughly gripping. (There are sub-titles in English, French, Dutch and German.)

Joan Sutherland gives an intensely revealing and appealing interpretation, making the icy princess far more human and sympathetic than ever before, while Pavarotti gives a performance equally imaginative, beautiful in sound, strong on detail. To set Caballé against Sutherland was a daring idea, and it works superbly well; Pears as the Emperor is another imaginative choice. Mehta directs a gloriously rich and dramatic performance, superlatively recorded, still the best-sounding *Turandot* on CD, while the reading also remains supreme.

The EMI set brings Nilsson's second assumption on record of the role of Puccini's formidable princess. As an interpretation it is very similar to the earlier, RCA performance, but its impact is far more immediate, thanks to the conducting of Molinari-Pradelli. Corelli may not be the most sensitive prince in the world, but the voice is in glorious condition. Scotto's Liù is very beautiful and characterful too. With vividly remastered sound, this makes an excellent mid-priced recommendation, though the documentation, as yet, does not include an English translation.

In Karajan's set, Hendricks is almost a sex-kitten with her seductively golden tone, and one wonders how Calaf could ever have overlooked her. This is very different from the usual picture of a chaste slave-girl. Ricciarelli is a far more vulnerable figure than one expects of the icy princess, and the very fact that the part strains her beyond reasonable vocal limits adds to the dramatic point, even if it subtracts from the musical joys. By contrast, Plácido Domingo is vocally superb, a commanding prince; and the rest of the cast present star names even in small roles.

With Callas, the character seems so much more believably complex than with others, and this 1957 recording is one of her most thrillingly magnetic performances on disc. Schwarzkopf provides a comparably characterful and distinctive portrait as Liù, far more than a Puccinian 'little woman', sweet and wilting. Eugenio Fernandi sounds relatively uncharacterful as Calaf, but his timbre is pleasing enough. By contrast, Serafin's masterly conducting exactly matches the characterfulness of Callas and Schwarzkopf, with colour, atmosphere and dramatic point all commandingly presented. With such a vivid performance, the 1957 mono sound hardly seems to matter, and the sound is much more expansive in the new transfer.

From the very start Caballé conveys an element of mystery while Freni underlines the dramatic rather than the lyrical side of Liù's role. The pity is that the EMI recording is unflattering to the voices – allowing Caballé less warmth and body of tone than usual, while setting Freni so close that a flutter keeps intruding. Lombard, so alert and imaginative in French music, proves a stiff and unsympathetic Puccinian so that the tenor, José Carreras, for example, is prevented from expanding as he should in the big arias. A good CD transfer and excellent back-up documentation.

The Naxos transfer of the very first complete recording of *Turandot*, made under Franco Ghione in 1938, is remarkably faithful on voices, if necessarily restricted over the sumptuous orchestration. Gina Cigna is a wonderfully incisive Turandot, Francesco Merli a thrillingly clear Calaf, and Magda Olivero a characterful Liù, with her distinctive, fluttering timbre. The historic recordings of supplementary items include not just Eva Turner's classic version of *In questa reggia* but rarities from 1926 onwards.

Turandot (complete; sung in English)
*** Chan. 3086 (2). Eaglen, O'Neill, Plazas, Bayley, Gedda, George Mitchell Ch., Philh. O, Parry

The glory of the Chandos set of *Turandot* is not just the spectacular, wide-ranging sound, bringing out details never heard before, but the singing of Jane Eaglen in the title role. Eaglen is a leading singer who has regularly been let down in her recordings for big international companies. Too often her powerful voice has been made to sound raw and ungainly, but here the voice is recorded with a satisfying firmness and precision apt for the Icy Princess. Her command is instantly established in her big entry aria in Act II, *In questa reggia*, in English translation becoming 'Within this palace'. The total absence of strain, even in the most taxing passages above the stave, and the magnetic sense of purpose reflect Eaglen's experience singing this role at Covent Garden (in Italian), while the gentler moments point forward to the resolution when, against all the odds, the Icy Princess is made to melt in the face of love, normally an unconvincing transformation (as Puccini himself evidently felt), but here in total conviction as she retains concentration through Alfano's completion to the grand choral reprise of the *Nessun dorma* theme at the end.

As Calaf Dennis O'Neill (who also appeared with Eaglen at Covent Garden) is strong and positive, even if the voice is no longer fresh and shows signs of strain. Mary Plazas is a charming, tender Liù and Clive Bayley a superb Timur, while Nicolai Gedda, sounding aptly old, takes on the cameo role of the ancient emperor. David Parry, as in his previous recordings for this Opera in English series, brings out the red-blooded thrust of the score, with the orchestral detail revealed as never before.

Turandot: highlights
(M) *** Decca (ADD) 458 202-2 (from above complete recording, with Sutherland, Pavarotti; cond. Mehta)

A generous and shrewdly chosen 70-minute collection of

excerpts from the glorious full-priced Decca set of *Turandot*. *Nessun dorma*, with Pavarotti at his finest, is here given a closing cadence for neatness. The vintage Decca sound is outstandingly full and vivid. The reissue in Decca's Opera Gala series is neatly packaged in a slipcase and includes a full translation.

Le Villi (complete)

*** Naïve V4958. Diener, Machado, Tézier, David, French R. PO, Guidarini

*** Sony (ADD) MK 76890. Scotto, Domingo, Nucci, Gobbi, Amb. Op. Ch., Nat. PO, Maazel

Puccini wrote his first opera, *Le Villi*, using a story similar to that of Adam's ballet, *Giselle*: the faithless lover finally destroyed by the ghostly spirit of the beloved who has died of a broken heart. Puccini composed it in 1883 for the Sonzogno competition for one-act operas, an annual event later won by Mascagni with *Cavalleria rusticana*. Puccini's effort was instantly rejected, largely because his manuscript score, written in haste, was so hard to read. Luckily, he was given a second chance, and the first performance in 1884 was an instant success, winning him a contract with Italy's leading publisher, Giulio Ricordi.

This French Radio recording scores impressively over Maazel's Sony version in the refinement of the sound, which in turn brings out the subtleties of the fine singing from all the principals. Where the Sony set has the characterful Tito Gobbi as the male narrator, the new one has a woman, Sylvie David, lighter and more conversational. Marco Guidarini proves a very convincing Puccinian, bringing out the dramatic bite of the orchestral showpieces, as well as moulding the big melodies affectionately. The Sony set has Lorin Maazel conducting, but he is not helped by the closeness of the Sony sound, which at times makes him sound too aggressive. Equally Renata Scotto is not flattered by the closeness, and though both she and Plácido Domingo as Roberto are more characterful than Melanie Diener and Aquiles Machado on the new disc, the refinement of sound helps to make the fresh, sensitive singing of the newcomers just as enjoyable. Equally Ludovic Tezier is clear and direct as Anna's father Guglielmo. A delightful bonus on the Sony set is Tito Gobbi's contribution, reciting the verses which link the scenes; he is as characterful a reciter as he is a singer.

COLLECTIONS

(i) *Crisantemi*; *Minuets 1–3*; *Quartet in A min.*: *Allegro moderato*; *Scherzo in A min.*; (ii) *Foglio d'album*; *Piccolo tango*; (iii; ii) Songs: *Avanti Urania*; *E l'uccellino*; *Inno a Diana*; *Menti all'avviso*; *Morire!*; *Salve regina*; *Sole e amore*; *Storiella d'amore*; *Terra e mare*

*** Etcetera KTC 1050. (i) Raphael Qt; (ii) Crone; (iii) Alexander

It is fascinating to find among early, rather untypical songs like *Storiella d'amore* and *Menti all'avviso* a charming little song, *Sole e amore*, written jokingly for a journal, *Paganini*, in 1888, which provided, bar for bar, the main idea of the Act III quartet in *La Bohème* of eight years later. The two piano pieces are simple album-leaves; among the six quartet pieces, *Crisantemi* is already well known; the rest are student pieces, including a delightful fragment of a Scherzo. Performances are good, though Roberta Alexander's soprano is not ideally Italianate. The recorded sound is vivid and immediate against a lively hall ambience.

'The Essential Puccini': *Preludio sinfonico*; Famous arias, duets and choruses from: *La Bohème*; *La fanciulla del West*; *Gianni Schicchi*; *Madama Butterfly*; *Manon Lescaut*; *La Rondine*; *Suor Angelica*; *Tosca*; *Turandot*

(B) **(*) Double Decca ADD/DDD 444 555-2 (2). Caballé, Chiara, Freni, Te Kanawa, Sutherland, Tebaldi, Bergonzi, Bjoerling, Carreras, Pavarotti, Corena, Ghiaurov, Krause, Milnes, Siepi (with various orchestras & conductors)

Many collectors will welcome a sampler of the vintage set of *La Bohème* with Tebaldi and Bergonzi at the height of their powers. Five items are included here, including the love scene from Act I. Tebaldi is also at her most seductive in *Madama Butterfly*, which is generously represented with well over half an hour of excerpts, including the whole of the Act I Love duet. She also provides the key arias from *Gianni Schicchi* and *La Rondine*, while Suor Angelica's ravishing *Senza mamma, o bimbo, tu sei morto* comes from Maria Chiara's glorious 1971 début recital. Dame Kiri gives a movingly passionate if comparatively unsubtle characterization of *Manon Lescaut*; with three numbers included, her partner, Carreras, recorded just before his illness, sounds a little strained. It was a pity that Rescigno's recording was chosen for the 30 minutes or so of *Tosca* excerpts. Freni as Tosca is below her best form and, though Sherrill Milnes does not disappoint as Scarpia, Pavarotti's *E lucevan le stelle* is the high point. Joan Sutherland's assumption of the role of the formidable *Turandot* is justly esteemed, as is Caballé's melting *Liù*, while Pavarotti delivers a splendid *Nessun dorma*. With Bjoerling on hand to provide a superb *Ch'ella mi creda* from *Fanciulla del West*, this is something of a (143-minute) Puccini feast, with the ripely expansive Decca sound fairly consistent throughout. The snag is that the documentation is totally inadequate.

'Gala': La Bohème: (i) *Che gelida manina*; *Sì, mi chiamano Mimì*; (ii) *Quando m'en vo*; (iii) *Donde lieta usci*. (iv) *La fanciulla del West*: *Ch'ella mi creda*. (v) *Gianni Schicchi*: *O mio babbino caro*. (i) *Madama Butterfly*: *Un bel dì*; *Addio fioriti asil*. (iii) *Manon Lescaut*: *In quelle trine morbide*; (vi) *Donna non vidi mai*. (v) *La Rondine*: *Sogno di Doretta*. (iii) *Suor Angelica*: *Senza mamma*. (vii) *Tosca*: *Recondita armonia*; *Vissi d'arte*; *E lucevan le stelle*. (viii) *Turandot*: *Signore ascolta!*; *Non piangere Liù!*; *Ah! Per l'ultima volta!*; *In questa reggia*; *Tu che di gel sei cinta*; *Nessun dorma!*

(M) *** Decca (ADD) 458 212-2. (i) Freni, Pavarotti; (ii) Harwood; (iii) Chiara; (iv) Milnes; (v) Tebaldi; (vi) Carreras; (vii) Corelli, Nilsson; Sutherland, Caballé, Pavarotti, Ghiaurov

This generous (71-minute) 'Gala' collection, with 22 items, opens predictably with Freni and Pavarotti in the Act I love scene from Karajan's 1972 *La Bohème*, and they sing again Karajan's 1974 *Butterfly*. The programme closes ambitiously, with six major excerpts from Mehta's *Turandot* with Sutherland, Caballé, and Pavarotti. Tebaldi is at her most ravishing in arias from *La Rondine* and *Gianni Schicchi*, and imaginatively, the 1966 Nilsson/Corelli/Maazel recording is chosen for the three items from *Tosca*. Decca are skilled at this kind of anthology, and particularly welcome is the inclusion of three arias from Maria Chiara's magical 1971 début recital, including lyrically very beautiful accounts of *In quelle trine morbide* (*Manon Lescaut*) and *Senza mamma* (*Suor Angelica*), recorded when her voice sounded wonderfully young and fresh. The documentation is excellent and full translations are included.

Arias and excerpts from: (i) *La Bohème;* (ii, iii or iv)
Madama Butterfly; (i; v) *Manon Lescaut;* (i; ii) *La Rondine;*
(vi) *Suor Angelica;* (ii) *Tosca;* (ii) *Turandot*

(B) *** RCA 2-CD 74321 88687-2 (2). Price, (i) New Philh. O,
Downes; (ii) Rome Opera O, De Fabritiis; (iii) with Tucker,
Elias, RCA Italiana O, Leinsdorf; (iv) with Horne & Met. O,
Levine; (v) Domingo, LSO, Santi; (vi) RCA Italiana O,
Molinari-Pradelli – RICHARD STRAUSS: *Arias & Lieder*
***

This collection is a formidable demonstration of the art of
Leontyne Price, with many of the items recorded early in her
career. The reissue draws on two previous collections and also
from her complete RCA opera sets. There is some glorious
singing from the 1960s – notably her recital with the Rome
Opera Orchestra with De Fabritiis. *Un bel dì* is thrilling, with
sharp contrasts of tone between the incisiveness of the opening and the delicacy of *Chi sarà, chi sarà.* The other major
excerpts from *Madama Butterfly* are taken from her complete
1962 set with Leinsdorf. He is not the most resilient of Puccini
conductors, and Richard Tucker is not the most refined
Pinkerton, but her contribution is gloriously rich. If in *Vissi
d'arte* from *Tosca* she forces her tone a little too hard, the two
Turandot arias are very beautiful, and Magda's aria *Ora dolci e
divine* from *La Rondine* is sweet, charming and lyrical. The
later excerpts are drawn from a collection called 'Puccini
Heroines' and recorded in London with Downes and Santi,
consistently show her at a vocal peak. The coupled CD of
Richard Strauss excerpts is equally recommendable.

Arias: *La Bohème: Quando m'en vo' soletta. Gianni Schicchi:
O mio babbino caro. Madama Butterfly: Un bel dì. Manon
Lescaut: In quelle trine morbide. La Rondine: Chi il bel
sogno di Doretta; Ore dolci e divine. Tosca: Vissi d'arte. Le
Villi: Se come voi piccina*

(M) *** Sony (ADD) SMK 60975. Te Kanawa, LPO, Pritchard,
or LSO, Maazel – VERDI: *Arias* *** (with MOZART: *Don
Giovanni: Ah! fuggi il traditor; In quali eccessi … Mi tradì;*
HUMPERDINCK: *Der kleine Sandmann bin ich;* DURUFLE:
Requiem: Pie Jesu ***)

In a recital recorded in 1981 the creamy beauty of Kiri Te
Kanawa's voice is ideally suited to these seven lyrical Puccini
arias including the little waltz-like song from *Le Villi.* The
other excerpt from this opera comes from the complete set
made around the same time. Throughout, expressive sweetness is more remarkable than characterization, but in such
music it is difficult to complain. Kiri was also in top form in
her 1978 assumption of the role of Elvira in Mozart's *Don
Giovanni* (again with Maazel), and the delightful Sandman
aria from *Hänsel und Gretel* and Duruflé's beautiful, serene
Pie Jesu again show the voice at its most appealing.

Arias: (i) *La Bohème: Sì mi chiamano Mimì; Donde lieta
uscì. Gianni Schicchi: O mio babino caro. Madama
Butterfly: Un bel dì; Con onor muore. Manon Lescaut: In
quelle trine morbide; Sola perduta. Suor Angelica: Senza
mamma. Turandot: Signore ascolta!; In questa reggia; Tu che
del sei cinta.* Duets: (ii; iii) *La Bohème: O soave fanciulla;*
(ii; iv) *Madama Butterfly: Vogliateme bene;* (ii; v) *Tosca:
Non la sospiri.* Aria: *Vissi d'arte*

(M) (***) EMI mono/stereo 5 62794-2. Callas; with (i) Philh.
O, Serafin; (ii) La Scala, Milan O; (iii) Votto; with Di
Stefano; (iv) cond. Karajan, with Gedda; (v) De Sabata;
with Di Stefano

The first eleven items here formed Callas's first EMI recital,
recorded in mono in Watford Town Hall in September 1954.
Now reissued to represent the diva among EMI's 'Great
Artists of the Century', it brings a classic example of her art.
She was vocally at her peak. Even when her concept of a
Puccinian 'little woman' has eyes controversially flashing and
fierce, the results are unforgettable, never for a moment
relaxing on the easy course, always finding new revelation,
whether as Turandot or Liù, as Manon, Mimi or Butterfly.
The other items, mostly duets, come from her complete sets,
including her famous and indispensable portrayal of Tosca,
conducted by Victor de Sabata. The transfers are excellent,
well balanced but with the voice always vividly projected.

Arias and Duets: *La Bohème: Donde lieta usci; Si,mi
chiamano Mimì.* (ii) *Canto d'anime.* (i) *Gianni Schicchi: O
mio babbino caro. Madama Butterfly: Intermezzo Atto II,
Parte seconda; Un bel dì vedremo. Manon Lescaut: In quelle
trine morbide; Intermezzo Act III; Sola perduta,
abandonnata.* (ii) *Morire.* (i) *La Rondine: Ch'il bel sogno di
Doretta.* (ii) *Sole e amore.* (i) *Suor Angelica: Senza Mamma,
o bimbo. Tosca: Vissi d'arte. Turandot: Signore ascolta; Tu
che di gel sei cinta. Le Villi: Se come voi*

(M) *** Warner Elatus 2564 60681-2. Te Kanawa; (i) Nat. Op.
de Lyons, Nagano; (ii) Vignoles (piano)

This is a Puccini disc with a difference. Besides the usual
operatic excerpts, it includes three Puccini songs of which
one, *Sole e amore,* is particularly enticing. Rightly Dame Kiri
sings it not as an opera excerpt *manqué* but – encouraged by
Roger Vignoles's imaginative accompaniment – as the trivial
album-leaf intended. Those three songs with piano provide a
welcome variety in a Puccini collection which, avoiding Minnie and Turandot, might have lacked contrast. Tosca's *Vissi
d'arte* comes as an introduction, but then the ordering is
chronological. The orchestra interludes from *Manon Lescaut*
and *Butterfly* are beautifully done, but more songs with piano
would have been preferable. With a recording lacking in
bloom on top, the voice is not quite as creamy as it once was,
if still very beautiful.

Arias: *Madama Butterfly: Un bel dì; Tu? tu? piccolo Iddio!
(Death of Butterfly). La Rondine: Che il bel sogno di
Doretta. Tosca: Vissi d'arte. Turandot: Signore ascolta; Tu
che di gel sei cinta*

(N) (M) **(*) RCA (ADD) SACD 82876 61395-2. L. Price,
Rome Op. O, De Fabritiis or Basile – VERDI: *Arias* ***

There is some glorious singing in this recital from the beginning of the 1960s. Perhaps Leontyne Price does not always get
right inside each heroine at this stage in her career, but *Un bel
dì* is thrilling, with a sharp contrast of tone between the
incisiveness of the opening and the delicacy of *Chi sarà, Chi
sarà.* In *Vissi d'arte* she forces a little too hard so that her
vibrato becomes a wobble, but the two *Turandot* arias are
very beautiful. Most welcome of all is Magda's aria from *La
Rondine,* sweet, charming and lyrical. The recording was
always very good indeed, and it sounds even more vivid in
this SACD transfer.

PUCCINI, Giacomo Sr (1712–81)

*Messa di Requiem. Overtures: Lucio Giunio Bruto; Marzio
Coriolano*

(BB) *** Arte Nova 74321 98497-2. Morgan, Kenny, Cornwell,
Thomas, Kantorei Saarlouis, Ens. UnaVolta, Fontaine

The celebrated Giacomo Puccini was the last in a line of composers, starting with another Giacomo, born in 1712, his great-great-grandfather. As this fine setting of the *Requiem* demonstrates, he was a notable figure in eighteenth-century Italian music, one who (like his descendant) was not afraid to cherry-pick his ideas. Here his elaborate contrapuntal writing for double choir harks back to an earlier generation, with clashing discords based on suspensions, such as one finds in Purcell's choral music, and chromatic sequences refreshing to the modern ear, all set against elegant baroque solos, well sung by the stylish quartet of British-based soloists. The two overtures, too, written for the secular oratorios celebrating the city of Lucca's annual elections, are lively and refreshing, with vigorous performances, cleanly recorded.

PURCELL, Henry (1659–95)

CHAMBER MUSIC

Chaconne in G min.; Overtures in D min.; G; & G min.; 3 Parts on a Ground in D; 2 Pavans in A; Pavan in A min.; 2 Pavans in B flat; 2 Pavans in G min.; Sonatas 6 in G min.; 7 in E min.; 12 in D; Suite in G

(B) **(*) HM HMT 7901 327. L. Baroque

Most of the music here was composed at the same time as his four-part *Fantasias*, and shows the young composer exploring the various instrumental styles available to him. The *Three Parts on a Ground* has some quite unexpected harmonies, while the *Pavan à 4 in G minor* uses some haunting and forward-looking minor-keyed progressions. But all these overtures, suites and sonatas are rewardingly inventive. The London Baroque perform them well, though lack a little in dynamic range. It may also have been better to have arranged the programme differently (with four pavans playing one after another), but one can reprogramme the order, and this bargain CD is certainly worth having.

Sonatas of 3 Parts 1–12, Z.790–801; Sonatas of 4 Parts 1–10, Z.802–810; Chacony in G min., Z.730; Pavans, Z.438–52; 3 Parts upon a Ground in D, Z.731
*** Chan. 0572/3. Purcell Qt

Sonatas of 3 Parts 1–7, Z.790–6; Pavans: in A min.; B flat; G min., Z.749, Z.750, Z.752
*** Chan. 8591. Purcell Qt

Sonatas of 3 Parts 8–12, Z.797–801; Sonatas in 4 Parts 1–2, Z.802–3; Chacony in G min., Z.751; Fantasia on a Ground in D & F; Pavans in A, Z.748; G min., Z.751
*** Chan. 8663. Purcell Qt

Sonatas of 4 Parts 3–10, Z.804–811; Prelude for Solo Violin in G min., Z.773; Organ Voluntaries 2 in D min.; 4 in G, Z.718 & 710
*** Chan. 8763. Purcell Qt

In these *Sonatas* Purcell turned to the new, concerted style which had been developed in Italy. Interspersed among the *Sonatas* are three earlier and highly chromatic *Pavans*, composed before Purcell embraced the sonata discipline. If anything, the second volume is more attractive than the first, for it includes the indelible *Chacony in G minor*. The third leaves room for a solo violin *Prelude* and two *Organ Voluntaries*, both admirably presented and, like the *Sonatas*, offering very realistic sound. The Purcell Quartet give a first-class account of themselves: their playing is authoritative and idiomatic,

and the artists are firmly focused in a warm but not excessively reverberant acoustic. Strongly recommended. These authoritative and thoroughly enjoyable accounts of Purcell's *Sonatas* have also been gathered together on two CDs without the miscellaneous items which filled out a third. Whichever format is chosen, this set can be thoroughly recommended.

KEYBOARD MUSIC

Harpsichord Suites 1–4, Z.660/663 (with alternative Preludes for Suites 1 & 4); Suites 5–8, Z.666/669; Transcriptions: A New Ground in E min., ZT.682; Theatre Music: Abdelazar: Round O, Z.684. Bonduca: Overture in C, Z.574/1. The Fairy Queen: Overture in D, ZT.692. King Arthur: Overture in D min., Z.628/2. Timon of Athens: Chaconne in G min., ZT.680. The Virtuous Wife: Overture in gamut flat, ZT.693
☛ (BB) *** Naxos 8.553982. Charlston (harpsichord)

This is both an enjoyable and a valuable collection, which not only includes the eight *Harpsichord Suites* deriving from Purcell's *Choice Collection of Lessons for the Harpsichord* but also some of the transcriptions of popular pieces from the theatre music. Purcell left this keyboard collection as a legacy for his wife, and they were posthumously published in 1696. The *Suites* are usually in four short movements, featuring a *Prelude, Almand, Corant* and *Sarabande* or *Hornpipe*. They are through-composed, using the same basic material throughout, but with attractive variants, and there are quite a few catchy 'lollipops' among their movements. The Transcriptions were thought to have been made by others, but modern scholarship suggests that they were possibly made by the composer himself, and each is used as a closing encore for one of the Suites, including the piece from *Abdelazar* made famous by Britten. Terence Charlston, who is thoroughly musical and consistently spontaneous, gives first-class performances, with apt tempi. He uses a modern harpsichord made by Bruce Kennedy in 1993: it seems ideal for the scale of the music and is perfectly recorded in a warm but not too resonant acoustic. For once, if anything, one has to turn up (rather than hastily turn down) the volume in playback. Highly recommended.

VOCAL MUSIC

Anthems & Services, Vols 1–11 (complete)
(M) *** Hyp. CDS 44141/51 (11). Soloists, King's Cons., King

Anthems & Services, Vol. 1: *It is a good thing to give thanks; Let mine eyes run down with tears; My beloved spake; O give thanks unto the Lord; O praise God in his holiness; O sing unto the Lord; Praise the Lord, O Jerusalem*
*** Hyp. CDA 66585. Witcomb, Finnis, Hallchurch, Bowman, Daniels, George, Evans, King's Cons., King

Anthems & Services, Vol. 2: *Behold now praise the Lord; Blessed are they that fear the Lord; I will give thanks unto Thee, O Lord; My song shall be alway; Te Deum & Jubilate*
*** Hyp. CDA 66609. Bowman, Covey-Crump, George, New College, Oxford, Ch., King's Cons., King

Anthems & Services, Vol. 3: *Begin the song, and strike the living lyre; Blessed Virgin's expostulation: Tell me, some pitying angel. Blow up the trumpet in Zion; Hear my prayer, O Lord; Hosanna to the highest; Lord, I can suffer thy rebukes; The Lord is King, be the people never so impatient;*

O God, Thou has cast us out; O Lord, our governor; Remember not Lord our offences; Thy word is a lantern unto my feet

*** Hyp. CDA 66623. Dawson, Bowman, Daniels, George, Evans, King's Cons. Ch., King's Cons., King

Anthems & Services, Vol. 4: *Awake ye dead; Behold I bring you glad tidings; Early, O Lord, my fainting soul; The earth trembled; Lord, not to us but to thy name; Lord, what is man?; My heart is inditing of a good matter; O all ye people, clap your hands; Since God so tender a regard; Sing unto God; Sleep, Adam and take thy rest; The way of God is an undefiled way*

*** Hyp. CDA 66644. Witcomb, Finnis, Hallchurch, Kennedy, O'Dwyer, Gritton, Bowman, Covey-Crump, Daniels, George, Varcoe, R. Evans, New College, Oxford, Ch., King's Cons., King

Anthems & Services, Vol. 5: *Awake, and with attention hear; How long, great God; Let the night perish (Job's Curse); O God, the king of glory; O God, Thou art my God; O, I'm sick of life; O Lord, rebuke me not; Praise the Lord, O my soul, and all that is within me; Rejoice in the Lord alway; We sing to him, whose wisdom form'd the ear; When on my sick bed I languish; With sick and famish'd eyes*

*** Hyp. CDA 66656. Witcomb, Finnis, Hallchurch, Kennedy, Gritton, Bowman, Covey-Crump, Daniels, George, Evans, King's Cons. Ch., King's Cons., King

Anthems & Services, Vol. 6: *Great God and just; Hear me, O Lord, the great support; I will love Thee, O Lord; Lord, who can tell how oft he offendeth?; My heart is fixed, O God; O Lord, grant the King a long life; O praise the Lord, all ye heathen; Plung'd in the confines of despair; Thou wakeful shepherd that dost Israel keep; Who hath believed our report?; Why do the heathen so furiously rage together?*

*** Hyp. CDA 66663. Witcomb, Kennedy, O'Dwyer, Bowman, Covey-Crump, Daniels, Agnew, George, New College, Oxford, Ch., King's Cons., King

Anthems & Services, Vol. 7: *Beati omnes qui timent; In the black dismal dungeon of despair; I was glad (2 settings: coronation anthem & verse anthem); Jubilate in B flat; O consider my adversity; Music for the Funeral of Queen Mary; Save me O God; Te Deum in B flat; Thy way O God is holy*

❂ *** Hyp. CDA 66677. Kennedy, O'Dwyer, Goodman, Gritton, Bowman, Short, Covey-Crump, Daniels, Milhofer, George, R. Evans, King's Cons. Ch., King's Cons., King

Anthems & Services, Vol. 8: *Be merciful unto me; Benedicte in B flat; Blessed is the man that feareth the Lord; Bow down thine ear, O Lord; Full of wrath, his threatening breath; In Thee, O Lord, do I put my trust; Jehova, quam multi sunt hostes mei; Magnificat & Nunc Dimittis in G min.; They that go down to the sea in ships*

*** Hyp. CDA 66686. O'Dwyer, Kennedy, Bowman, Covey-Crump, Daniels, Padmore, Milhofer, George, King's Cons. Ch., King's Cons., King

Anthems & Services, Vol. 9: *Blessed be the Lord my strength; Blessed is he whose unrighteousness is forgiven; Full Service, Z.230: Cantate Domine and Deus misereatur. Let God arise; The Lord is King, the earth may be glad thereof; The Lord is my Light; O Lord God of Hosts; O Lord, our Governor; In Guilty Night (Saul and the Witch of Endor)*

*** CDA 66 Covey-Crump, Daniels, George, Burrowes, O'Dwyer, Bowman, Padmore, Goodman, Milhofer, Webber, Kennedy, Gritton, King's Consort Ch., King's Consort, King

Anthems & Services, Vol. 10: *Blessed is he that considereth the poor; Full Service in B flat, Z.230: Benedictus in B flat; Kyrie eleison in B flat; Nicene Creed. Hear my Prayer; How have I stray'd; I will give thanks unto the Lord; I will sing unto the Lord as long as I live; The Lord is King and hath put on glorious apparel; Out of the deep have I called; Unto Thee will I cry*

*** CDA 66707. O'Dwyer, Goodman, Kennedy, Nickless, Webber, Gritton, Bowman, Covey-Crump, Daniels, Padmore, Milhofer, Campbell, George, King's Consort Ch., King's Consort, King

Anthems & Services, Vol. 11: *Awake, awake, put on Thy strength; Close thine eyes and sleep secure; Full Service in B Flat, Z.230: Hear me O Lord; Magnificat in B flat; Nunc dimittis in B flat. Hear me O Lord; Lord, how long wilt Thou be angry?; Now that the sun hath veiled his light (Evening Hymn); O Lord, Thou art my God; Praise the Lord, O my soul, O Lord my God; Turn Thou to us, O good Lord*

*** CDA 66716. Kennedy, O'Dwyer, Webber, Gritton, Bowman, Covey-Crump, Daniels, Padmore, George, King's Consort Ch., King's Consort, King

The different categories of work here, Services, Verse Anthems, Motets (or Full Anthems) and devotional songs, cover the widest range of style and expression, with Robert King's own helpful and scholarly notes setting each one in context. Generally the most adventurous in style are the Full Anthems, with elaborate counterpoint often bringing amazingly advanced harmonic progressions. Yet the Verse Anthems too include some which similarly demonstrate Purcell's extraordinary imagination in contrapuntal writing. So though Volume 6 is confined to Verse Anthems and devotional songs, they too offer passages of chromatic writing which defy the idea of these categories as plain and straightforward. As the title suggests, the devotional song, *Plung'd in the Confines of Despair*, is a particularly fine example. Although all the earlier volumes are full of good things, Volume 7 (to which we award a token Rosette for the extraordinary achievement of this series) is the one to recommend first to anyone simply wanting to sample Purcell's church music. Not only does it contain the *Music for the Funeral of Queen Mary* in 1695, with drum processionals, the solemn *March* and *Canzona for Brass* and *Funeral Sentences*, it has the *B flat Morning Service*, two settings of the Coronation anthem, *I Was Glad*, (one of them previously unrecorded), a magnificent Full Anthem, three Verse Anthems and two splendid devotional songs. Volume 8, too, is full of fine music. The opening Verse Anthem, *In Thee, O Lord, Do I Put my Trust*, opens with a very striking, slightly melancholy *Sinfonia*, with a six-note figure rising up from a ground bass, which sets the expressive mood. The closing anthem, so appropriate from an island composer, *They that Go Down to the Sea in Ships*, is characteristically diverse, with Purcell helping the Lord 'maketh the storm to cease' and at the end providing a joyful chorus of praise. King's notes and documentation closely identify each item, adding to one's illumination. An outstanding series, full of treasures, with King varying the scale of forces he uses for each item. Often he uses one voice per part, but he regularly expands the ensemble with the King's Consort Choir or turns to the full New College Choir, which includes trebles.

There are plenty of key items in the final three volumes including (in Volume 9), *In Guilty Night*, the dialogue cantata *Saul and the Witch of Endor*, with Susan Gritton, Rogers Covey-Crump and Michael George. Those who want to dive in at the deep end should invest in the complete set, with all eleven CDs neatly packaged in cardboard sleeves in a box with a booklet containing excellent extended documentation and full texts taken from the individual discs, which are, of course, all available separately.

Anthems: *Blow up the Trumpet in Zion; My Heart is Inditing; O God, Thou art my God; O God, Thou has Cast me out; Remember not, Lord, our Offences; Rejoice in the Lord Alway; Chaconne in G min. for 2 Violins & Continuo*
(BB) *** Warner Apex (ADD) 2564 60821-2. Bowman, Rogers, Van Egmond, King's College, Cambridge, Ch., Leonhardt Consort, Leonhardt

An attractive collection from the late 1960s, which happily blends scholarship and spontaneity. The instrumental ensemble uses period instruments and playing style, and the character of the sound is very distinctive. Not all the anthems have instrumental accompaniments – Purcell sometimes uses the organ, at others bass continuo – but they are all very well sung, with the characteristic King's penchant for tonal breadth and beauty. Excellent recording.

Anthems & Sacred Songs: *Bell Anthem (Rejoice in the Lord alway); Hear my prayer, O Lord; I was glad; My heart is inditing; Now that the sun hath veiled his light (Evening Hymn); Praise the Lord, O my soul; Remember not, Lord, our offences*
(N) **(*) Warner Teldec 2564 60290-2. Chanticleer, Jennings; with Capriccio Stravagante, Sempé

This disc is entitled *Evening Prayer*, and these are comparatively intimate, small-scale performances of eight favourite choral works, refined rather than rugged. Some might feel that the opening *Bell Anthem* might have been more robust, but *Remember not, Lord, our offences*, the beautiful *Evening Hymn* and, especially, *Hear my prayer, O Lord* are particularly appealing in their simple, expressive style, while *My heart is inditing* makes a rather more vigorous closing item. Finely balanced recording adds to the appeal of this disc.

Anthems: *Man that is born of woman; O God, thou has cast us out; Lord, how long wilt thou be angry?; O God, thou art my God; O Lord God of hosts; Remember not, Lord, our offences; Thou knowest, Lord, the secrets of our hearts.* Verse anthems: *My beloved spake; My heart is inditing; O sing unto the Lord; Praise the Lord, O Jerusalem; They that go down to the sea in ships. Morning Service in B flat: Benedicite omnia opera; Cantate Domino; Deus miscreatur; Magnificat; Nunc dimittis. Evening service in G min.: Magnificat; Nunc dimittis. Latin Psalm: Jehovah, quam multi sunt hostes mei. Te Deum & Jubilate in D*
(B) *** DG Double (ADD) 459 487-2 (2). D. Thomas, Christ Church Cathedral, Oxford , Ch., E. Concert, Preston

Recorded in the Henry Wood Hall in 1980, this admirable collection of Purcell's church music is self-recommending. Apart from David Thomas's fine contribution (in the verse anthems) the soloists come from the choir, and very good they are too, especially the trebles. The performances are full of character, vigorous, yet with the widest range of colour and feeling, well projected in a recording which is both spacious and detailed. The sound is excellent in its current transfer, and as a DG Archiv Double this is even more attractive.

Odes & Welcome Songs Vols. 1–8 (complete)
*** Hyp. CDS 44031/8. Soloists, New College, Oxford, Ch., King's Cons., King

Odes & Welcome Songs, Vol. 1: *Arise my muse (1690); Now does the glorious day appear (Odes for Queen Mary's Birthday; 1689); Ode for St Cecilia's Day: Welcome to all pleasures (1683)*
*** Hyp. CDA 66314. Fisher, Bonner, Bowman, Chance, Daniels, Ainsley, George, Pott, King's Cons., King

Odes & Welcome Songs, Vol. 2: *Ode on St Cecilia's Day (Hail! bright Cecilia!; 1692). Ode for the Birthday of the Duke of Gloucester: Who can from joy refrain (1695)*
*** Hyp. CDA 66349. Fisher, Bonner, Bowman, Covey-Crump, Ainsley, George, Keenlyside, New College, Oxford, Ch., King's Cons., King

Odes & Welcome Songs, Vol. 3: *Ode for Queen Mary's Birthday: Celebrate this festival (1693). Welcome Song for Charles II (1683): Fly, bold rebellion (1683). Welcome Song for James II: Sound the trumpet, beat the drum (1687)*
*** Hyp. CDA 66412. Fisher, Bonner, Bowman, Kenny, Covey-Crump, Müller, George, Pott, King's Cons., King

Odes & Welcome Songs, Vol. 4: *Ode for Mr Maidwell's School: Celestial music did the gods inspire (1689). Ode for the Wedding of Prince George of Denmark & Princess Anne: From hardy climes and dangerous toils of war (1683). Welcome Song for James II: Ye tuneful muses (1686)*
*** Hyp. CDA 66456. Fisher, Bonner, Bowman, Kenny, Covey-Crump, Daniels, George, Pott, King's Cons., King

Odes & Welcome Songs, Vol. 5: *Ode for the Birthday of Queen Mary: Welcome, welcome, glorious morn (1691). Ode for the Centenary of Trinity College, Dublin: Great parent, hail to thee (1694). Welcome Song for King Charles II: The Summer's absence unconcerned we bear (1682)*
*** Hyp. CDA 66476. Fisher, Tubb, Bowman, Short, Covey-Crump, Ainsley, George, Pott, King's Cons., King

Odes & Welcome Songs, Vol. 6: *Ode for Queen Mary's Birthday: Love's goddess sure was blind (1692). Ode for St Cecilia's Day: Laudate Ceciliam (1683). Ode for St Cecilia's Day: Raise, raise the voice (c. 1685). Welcome Song for Charles II: From those serene and rapturous joys (1684)*
*** Hyp. CDA 66494. Fisher, Seers, Bowman, Short, Padmore, Tusa, George, Evans, King's Cons., King

Odes & Welcome Songs, Vol. 7: *Welcome song for Charles II: Swifter Isis, swifter flow (1681). Welcome Song for the Duke of York: What shall be done in behalf of the man? (1682). Yorkshire Feast Song: Of old, when heroes thought it base (1690)*
*** Hyp. CDA 66587. Fisher, Hamilton, Bowman, Short, Covey-Crump, Daniels, George, Evans, King's Cons., King

Odes & Welcome Songs, Vol. 8: *Ode for the Birthday of Queen Mary: Come ye sons of Art, away (1694). Welcome Song for Charles II: Welcome, viceregent of the mighty king (1680). Welcome Song for King James: Why, why are all the Muses mute?*
*** Hyp. CDA 66598. Fisher, Bonner, Bowman, Chance, Padmore, Ainsley, George, Evans, Ch. of New College, Oxford, King's Cons., King

Just what a wealth of inspiration Purcell brought to the occasional music he wrote for his royal and noble masters comes out again and again in Robert King's splendid collection of the odes and welcome songs. It is sad that for three centuries this fine music has been largely buried, with just a few of the odes achieving popularity. In those, King's performances do not always outshine the finest of previous versions, but with an outstanding team of soloists as well as his King's Consort the performances achieve a consistently high standard, with nothing falling seriously short. Being able to hear previously unrecorded rarities alongside the well-known works sets Purcell's achievement vividly in context, helped by informative notes in each volume, written by King himself. Volume 1 includes the shorter of the two *St Cecilia Odes* and immediately – among the fine team of soloists – it is a delight to hear such superb artists as the counter-tenors James Bowman and Michael Chance in duet. Volume 3 with the 1693 *Birthday Ode* and Volume 7 with the fascinating *Yorkshire Feast Song* are two more CDs that would make good samplers. Those who want to dive in at the deep end should invest in the complete set, where all eight CDs are offered in a slip-case. First-rate sound throughout.

Gardiner Purcell Edition

(i) Disc 1: *Come, Ye Sons of Art Away; Funeral Music for Queen Mary (1695).* (ii) Disc 2: *Ode on St Cecilia's Day (Hail! Bright Cecilia).* (iii) Disc 3: *The Indian Queen* (incidental music). (iv) Disc 4: *The Tempest* (incidental music)

☯— (M) *** Erato 5046 68281-2 (4). (i) Lott, Brett, Williams, Allen, Equale Brass Ens.; (ii) Gordon, Elliott; (ii; iii) Stafford, (ii; iii; iv) Jennifer Smith, Varcoe, Elwes, Thomas; (iii) Fisher, Hill; (iii; iv) Hardy; (iv) Hall, Earle; (i–iv) Monteverdi Ch. & O, Gardiner

Originally issued to commemorate the tercentenary of Purcell's death, Gardiner's distinguished early series of Erato recordings from the 1970s and 1980s now reappear as a four-disc set, with each disc packaged separately in its jewel-case (the choral works with texts) and presented together in a slip-case. The individual CDs are not available separately any longer.

Come, Ye Sons of Art, the most celebrated of Purcell's birthday odes for Queen Mary, is splendidly coupled here with the unforgettable funeral music he wrote on the death of the same monarch. With the Monteverdi Choir at its most incisive and understanding the performances are exemplary, and the recording, though balanced in favour of the instruments, is clear and refined. Among the soloists Thomas Allen is outstanding, while the two counter-tenors give a charming performance of the duet, *Sound the Trumpet*. The *Funeral Music* includes the well-known *Solemn March* for trumpets and drums, a *Canzona* and simple anthem given at the funeral, and two of Purcell's most magnificent anthems setting the *Funeral Sentences*. Recording made in 1976 in Rosslyn Hill Chapel, London.

Gardiner's characteristic vigour and alertness in Purcell come out superbly in the delightful record of the 1692 *St Cecilia Ode* – not as well known as some of the other odes he wrote, but a masterpiece. Soloists and chorus are outstanding even by Gardiner's high standards, and the recording is excellent. Recording made in 1982 in the Barbican Concert Hall, London.

The Indian Queen is fully cast and uses an authentic accompanying baroque instrumental group. The choral singing is especially fine, with the close of the work movingly expressive. John Eliot Gardiner's choice of tempi is apt and the soloists are all good, although the men are more strongly characterful than the ladies; nevertheless the lyrical music comes off well. The recording is spacious and well balanced,

and was made in 1979 in Henry Wood Hall, London. Highlights are available on a budget Apex CD (2564 61501-2).

Whether or not Purcell wrote this music for *The Tempest* (the scholarly arguments are still unresolved), Gardiner demonstrates how delightful it is, a masterly collection, in performances both polished and stylish and with excellent solo and choral singing. At least the overture is clearly Purcell's, and that sets a pattern for a very varied collection of numbers, including three *da capo* arias and a full-length masque celebrating Neptune for Act V. The 1979 recording, made in London's Henry Wood Hall, is full and atmospheric; the words are beautifully clear, and the transfer to CD is admirably natural.

Pinnock Purcell Collection

(i) *Ode for the Birthday of Queen Mary* (1694): *Come, Ye Sons of Art Away; Ode for St Cecilia's Day: Welcome to All the Pleasures. Of Old when Heroes Thought it Base (The Yorkshire Feast Song).* (ii) *Dido and Aeneas* (complete); (iii) *Dioclesian* (masque); (iv) *King Arthur* (complete); (v) *Timon of Athens* (masque)

(B) *** DG 474 672-2 (5). (i) J. Smith, Chance, Wilson, Richardson, Mark Ainsley, George; (ii) Von Otter, Dawson, Varcoe, Rogers; (iii) Monoyios, Agnew, Edgar-Wilson, Gadd, Birchall, Wallington, Foster; (iii; iv) Argenta, Bannatyne-Scott; (iv) Perillo, Gooding, MacDougall, Tucker, Finley; E. Concert & Ch., Pinnock

Pinnock's is a somewhat arbitrary collection, but the standard of performance and recording is very high and this set represents excellent value. He directs exuberant performances of Purcell's two most celebrated odes; the weight and brightness of the choral sound go with infectiously lifted rhythms, making the music dance. The soloists are all outstanding, with the counter-tenor duetting of Michael Chance and Timothy Wilson in *Sound the Trumpet*, delectably pointed. The coupling, the neglected *Yorkshire Feast Song*, is full of wonderful inspirations, like the tenor and counter-tenor duet, *And Now When the Renown'd Nassau* – a reference to the new king, William III.

The performance of *Dido and Aeneas* is more controversial, presented as a court entertainment rather than as a school-sized entertainment in Dr Josias Priest's girls' establishment in Chelsea; but though the reading is not as inspired as many that Pinnock has given us, the scale is attractive. Both Anne Sofie von Otter and Lynne Dawson have voices that are at once warm and aptly pure for authentic performance. Von Otter as Dido, both fresh and mature-sounding, sings her two big arias with a combination of weight, gravity and expressive warmth which is yet completely in scale. The final lament, while faster than in traditional performances, still conveys the full tragic intensity of this epic in microcosm.

Much more questionable is the casting on the male side, and that includes a tenor taking the role of the Sorceress. Nigel Rogers, not in his sweetest voice, takes that role as well as that of the Sailor. Confusingly, almost immediately after the Sailor's jolly song at the start of Act III, Rogers reappears as the Sorceress in a quite different mood, making much too quick a change. Stephen Varcoe is a rather unheroic-sounding Aeneas, but the chorus of the English Concert produces fresh, alert singing. Instead of a repetition of the final chorus, Pinnock opts for an instrumental reprise to provide an epilogue.

Dioclesian and *Timon of Athens*, both sets of theatre music including masques, were recorded in tandem. Pinnock presents both works on a slightly larger (but not inflated) scale than Hickox on Chandos, often more weighty to match a bigger, warmer (though not over-reverberant) acoustic. In keeping with this, he is more warmly expressive, and often adopts broader speeds, which allow him to spring rhythms the more infectiously, more clearly introducing an element of sparkle and humour. He includes the extra song in Act III of *Dioclesian*, 'When I First Saw', and certainly here the effervescence of Purcell's inspiration in one of his finest collections of theatre music is consistently compelling.

King Arthur follows on after *Dido and Aeneas*, opening with the *Chaconne* and making a break between CDs at the end of Act I. Linda Perillo makes a charming Philidel; Brian Bannatyne-Scott and Nancy Argenta are equally memorable, and the chorus and orchestra sing and play throughout with consistent vitality.

Odes for Queen Mary's Birthday: Come ye Sons of Art; Love's Goddess sure was Blind

(N) (BB) **(*) CfP 586 0502. Burrowes, Bowman, Lloyd, Brett, York, Skinner, Hill, Shaw, Early Music Consort, Munrow

While *Come ye Sons of Art* is the richest of the sequence of ceremonial odes Purcell wrote for the birthday of Queen Mary, *Love's Goddess sure*, though not quite so grand, brings more Purcellian delights. The late David Munrow's early (mid-1970s) examples of the authentic approach deliberately opt for an intimate scale, using antique instruments and a matching style of string playing. The intimacy clearly detracts from the sense of grandeur and panoply apt for this music, but Munrow inspires fine playing and singing from his excellent forces, and the result is altogether joyous.

Ode on the birthday of Queen Mary (1694); Come, ye sons of art away; Funeral Music for Queen Mary (1695); Funeral Sentences; Odes for St Cecilia's day: Hail! bright Cecilia; Welcome to all the pleasures

(BB) *** Virgin 5 61582-2 (2). Kirkby, Chance, K. Smith, Covey-Crump, Elliott, Grant, George, Thomas, Taverner Ch. & Players, Parrott

A most inexpensive collection of key Purcell works on Virgin with many individual touches in Andrew Parrott's essentially intimate performances. Parrott takes the view that Purcell would have used a high tenor and not a second counter-tenor in *Sound the Trumpet*, and it works well, with John Mark Ainsley joining the counter-tenor, Timothy Wilson. In his pursuit of authenticity Parrott has eliminated the timpani part from the well-known solemn march for slide trumpets (performed here on sackbutts) in the *Queen Mary Funeral Music* – a pity when it becomes far less effective. The central anthem is beautifully done, and it is good also to have the three *Funeral Sentence Anthems*, written a few years earlier. *Hail! Bright Cecilia* is also relatively reticent, but brings another performance full of incidental delights, particularly vocal ones from a brilliant array of no fewer than twelve solo singers, notably five excellent tenors. With pitch lower than usual, some numbers that normally require counter-tenors can be sung by tenors. Interestingly, Parrott includes the *Voluntary in D minor* for organ before the wonderful aria celebrating that instrument and St Cecilia's sponsorship of it, *O Wondrous Machine*. And, if you feel it holds up the music's flow on, it can easily be omitted.

Ode for Queen Mary's birthday; Come, ye sons of art away; Funeral Music for Queen Mary (1695)

(BB) *** Warner Apex 0927 48593-2. Soloists, Monteverdi Ch. & O., Equale Brass Ens., Gardiner

Come, ye Sons of Art is splendidly paired here with the unforgettable funeral music he wrote on the death of the same monarch. With the Monteverdi Choir at its most incisive and understanding the performances are exemplary, and the recording, though balanced in favour of the instruments, is clear and refined. Among the soloists Thomas Allen is outstanding, while the two counter-tenors give a charming performance of the duet, *Sound the Trumpet*. The *Funeral Music* includes the well-known *Solemn March* for trumpets and drums, a *Canzona* and simple anthem given at the funeral, and two of Purcell's most magnificent anthems setting the *Funeral Sentences*. Recording made in 1976 in Rosslyn Hill Chapel, London. These works now come, coupled very economically together, on an Apex disc.

Ode for Queen Mary's Birthday: (i) Come ye Sons of Art (1694); Odes for St Cecilia's Day; (ii) Hail bright Cecilia (1692); (iii) Welcome to all Pleasures (1683). Anthems: (iv) My beloved spake; (v) Rejoice in the Lord alway (Bell Anthem)

(N) (B) **(*) Artemis Vanguard ATM-CD 1520 (2). Alfred Deller, Maurice Bevan, Deller Consort with (i) Mark Deller, Mary Thomas, Oriana Concert Ch. & O., Deller; (ii) Wilfred Brown, Salmon, Frost, Amb. S., Kalmar CO, Tippett; (ii; iii; iv) Cantelo; (iii) McLoughlin, English, Grundy, Kalmar CO, Deller; (iv) English; (iv; v) Oriana Concert O., Deller; (v) Thomas, Sheppard, Tear, Worthley

A welcome and enjoyable Vanguard anthology from the late 1950s and early 1960s, originally recorded by the Bach Guild, and showing Deller at his finest, both singing and conducting. The other soloists are good too, especially April Cantelo, and the tenor, Gerald English. Sir Michael Tippett's tempi in *Hail bright Cecilia* are more measured than we would expect today with original instruments, as are the warm, expressive accompaniments. The two anthems make a fine centrepiece on the second disc, responding to the demands of Charles II for composers 'not to be too solemn' and to 'add symphonies etc., with instruments' to their sacred vocal music. The *Bell Anthem* is so called because of the repeated descending scales in the introduction. The recordings, made at Cricklewood Church, Walthamstow or (more surprisingly) Vienna, are balanced closely, but are quite spacious and pleasingly full in the present transfers. Full texts are included.

(i) Ode on St Cecilia's Day; (ii) Dido and Aeneas (complete)

(N) **(*) DG (ADD) 477 5350 (2). (i) Woolf, Esswood, Tatnell, Young, Rippon, Shirley-Quirk, Tiffon Ch., Amb. S., ECO; (ii) Troyanos, Armstrong, Johnson, McDaniel, Hamburg Monteverdi Ch., NDR CO; Mackerras

It seems a strange idea to couple these two works for a reissue in DG's series of Legendary Originals, because the only thing they share, apart from their general excellence, is Sir Charles Mackerras. The famous *Ode* comes in a splendid all-male performance with an exceptionally incisive and vigorous choral contribution matched by fine solo singing. The treble soloist, Simon Woolf, has an amazing technical and musical range, and he is ideally cast here. The recording is very good, although the balance between soloists and tutti does not make much distinction in volume between the smaller and larger groups.

Mackerras's direction of *Dido and Aeneas* is also satisfying, for besides being scholarly it is very vital, with tempi varied more widely and – as he himself suggests – more authentically than in many versions. There is also the question of ornamentation, and as a whole Mackerras manages more authentically than most of his earlier rivals. Even so, his ideas for ornamenting Dido's two big arias are marginally less convincing than on Anthony Lewis's classic Decca version, with many appoggiaturas and comparatively few turns and trills. He has the advantage of using Neville Boyling's edition, which is based on the Tatton Park manuscript, and he adds brief extra items from suitable Purcellian sources to fill in the unset passages of the libretto. Tatiana Troyanos makes an imposing, gorgeous-toned Dido, and Sheila Armstrong as Belinda, Barry McDaniel as Aeneas and Patricia Johnson are all first rate; but ultimately the Dido of Janet Baker is so moving that it more than compensates for any relative shortcomings, and Thurston Dart's continuo playing on the Decca set is much more imaginative than the Hamburg harpsichordist's.

Funeral Music for Queen Mary: March, Anthem & Canzona; 3 Funeral Sentences; 2 Elegies; 2 Coronation Anthems; Anthem for Queen Mary's Birthday, 1688: Now does the glorious day appear

🕭— *** Sony SK 66243. Kirkby, Tubb, Chance, Bostridge, Richardson, Birchall, Westminster Abbey Ch., New L. Consort, Neary (with music by TOLLETT; PAISIBLE; MORLEY; BLOW)

Funeral Music for Queen Mary: March & Canzona in C min.; Funeral Sentences: Man that is born of a woman; In the midst of life we are in death; Thou knowest Lord the secrets of our hearts (2 settings). Anthems: Give sentence with me, O Lord; Hear my prayer, O Lord; Jehovah quam multi sunt hostes mei; My beloved spake; O God Thou art my God; O, I'm sick of life; Rejoice in the Lord alway (Bell anthem); Remember not Lord our offences; Organ voluntaries: in C; A Double Verse in G

(M) **(*) Decca 475 050-2. Winchester Cathedral Ch., L. Bar. Brass, Brandenburg Consort, Hill; Dunnett (organ)

Funeral Music for Queen Mary (with (i) Queen's epicedium); March & Canzona on the Death of Queen Mary. Funeral sentences: Man that is born of a woman; In the midst of life are we in death; Thou knowest, Lord, the secrets of our hearts. Anthems: Hear my prayer; Jehova quam multi sunt. (ii) 3 (Organ) Voluntaries: in D min.; in G; in C

(BB) *** Naxos 8.553129. Oxford Camerata, Summerly; with (i) Lane; (ii) Cummings

In the ample acoustic of Westminster Abbey, where the music was first performed in 1695, Martin Neary restores the original sequence of musical numbers given at the funeral of Queen Mary. The well-known *March* and *Canzona*, as well as the beautiful anthem, *Thou Know'st, Lord, the Secrets of Our Hearts*, are presented along with the settings of the remaining funeral sentences by Thomas Morley, equally inspired, as well as marches by James Paisible and Thomas Tollett. He adds a generous collection of other works inspired by Queen Mary. The result is not ideally clear, with the sound of traffic murmuring in from outside, but is undeniably atmospheric, conveying a weighty devotional intensity. One has a genuine sense of a great ceremonial, not just in the funeral music but

in the other works too, including the glorious 1688 birthday ode, *Now Does the Glorious Day Appear*, the first that Purcell composed for the new Queen. The boy trebles of the Abbey Choir are authentic and beautifully tuned. The soloists are outstanding, notably the counter-tenor, Michael Chance, and the tenor, Ian Bostridge.

The Naxos CD follows a similar sequence. This glorious, darkly intense funeral music is here given an outstandingly fresh and clear rendition, vividly recorded, matching even the finest rival versions. The sharpness of focus in the sound means that Purcell's adventurous harmonies with their clashing intervals are given extra dramatic bite in these dedicated performances, marked by fresh, clear soprano tone in place of boy trebles. The choice of extra items – full anthems with their inspired counterpoint rather than verse anthems – is first rate, including as it does the magnificent *Jehova, quam multi sunt* and the wonderfully compressed *Hear My Prayer*, both beautifully done. Aptly, the extended solo song for soprano (with simple organ accompaniment), *The Queen's Epicedium*, is also included with the funeral music, sung with boyish tone by Carys-Ann Lane.

In the *Queen Mary Funeral Music* David Hill and the Winchester Choir, plus instrumentalists, opt – like most previous interpreters – to have the drum recessionals simultaneously with the *March*. The brass group incidentally uses authentic 'flat trumpets', equipped with a slide similar to that found on a sackbut (trombone), which were developed in England in 1691. These instruments are used here on the two upper parts, sackbuts on the more technically demanding lower parts, to fine effect. Though the boy trebles in Winchester are attractively fresh-toned, the ensemble is not ideally polished, but the choice of other items includes a number of Purcell's most celebrated anthems, eloquently sung, as well as a pair of organ voluntaries.

Jubilate Deo in D; The Noise of Foreign Wars; Ode for St Cecilia's Day; Raise, Raise the Voice; Te Deum; (i) Trumpet Sonata

(BB) *** Naxos 8.553444. Bern, Bisatt, Robson, Purefoy, Honeyman, Guthrie, The Golden Age Ch. & O, Glenton; (i) with Staff

These superb examples of Purcell's choral music, both church music and secular cantatas, as well as a brief, joyful trumpet sonata, make an attractive collection, well recorded. The singing is excellent from a group which includes such distinguished singers as the counter-tenor, Christopher Robson, though the instrumental group is lacking in bite in the string section, hardly matching the wind. But this is not enough to detract from the pleasure of the music-making overall. David Staff on the trumpet is outstanding, in both the *Sonata* and the choral works too. Specially fascinating is the première recording of the *Noise of Foreign Wars*, a substantial fragment of a cantata only recently identified as being by Purcell.

The Complete Secular Solo Songs:

Volume 1: *Ah, how pleasant 'tis to love; Amidst the shades and cool refreshing streams; Beneath a dark and melancholy grove; Beware, poor shepherds; Cease anxious world, your fruitless pain; Draw near you lovers; How I sigh when I think of the charms of my swain; I loved fair Celia; Farewell, all joys; If music be the food of love; Let each gallant heart; Love, thou canst hear, tho' thou art blind; Musing on cares of human fate; My heart, whenever you appear; O! fair Cedaris, hide those eyes; On the brow of Richmond Hill;*

Pastora's beauties when unblown; Rashly I swore I would disown; See how the fading glories of the year; Since the pox of the plague; They say you're angry; A thousand sev'ral ways I tried; This poet sings the Trojan wars; Urge me no more; What hope for us remains now he has gone; While Thirsis, wrapp'd in downy sleep; Whilst Cynthia sung, all angry winds lay still; Ye happy swains, whose nymphs are kind (CDA 66710)

Volume 2: Ah! cruel nymph; Celia's fond, too long I've lov'd her; Farewell ye rocks, ye seas and sands; Fly swift ye hours; Gentle shepherds, you that know the charms (Pastoral elegy on the death of John Playford); How delightful's the life of an innocent swain; If grief has any pow'r to kill; Hears not my Phyllis how the birds (The knotting song); High on a throne of glitt'ring ore; If music be the food of love; Incassum, Lesbia (Queen's Epicidium); In vain we dissemble; I love and I must; I resolve against cringing and whining; I take no pleasure in the sun's bright beams; Love arms himself in Celia's eyes; Love's pow'r in my heart shall find no compliance; Not all my torments can your pity move; Phyllis, talk no more of passion; Scarce had the rising sun appear'd; She that would gain a faithful lover; She who my poor heart possesses; Through mournful shades and solitary groves; Since one poor view has drawn my heart; Sylvia, now your scorn give over; What a sad fate is mine; When all her languishing eyes said love; When first my shepherdess and I; When my Aemelia smiles; Who but a slave can well express (CDA 66720)

Volume 3: Amintas, to my grief I see; Amintor, heedless of his flocks; Ask me to love no more; Bacchus is a pow'r divine; Corinna is divinely fair; Cupid, the slyest rogue alive; The fatal hour comes on apace; From silent shades; He himself courts his own ruin; I came, I saw and was undone; If music be the food of love (3rd version); If pray'rs and tears; In Cloris all soft charms agree; Let formal lovers still pursue; Let us, kind Lesbia, give way; Love is now become a trade; Lovely Albina's come ashore; No, to what purpose should I speak?; O solitude, my sweetest choice; Olinda in the shades unseen; Phyllis I can ne'er forgive it; Pious Celinda goes to prayers; Sawney is a bonny lad; Spite of the godhead; Sylvia, 'tis true you're fair; When Stephen found his passion vain; Who can behold Florella's charms; Young Thirsis' fate (CDA 66730)

Volumes 1–3 (complete)

⊕━ (M) *** Hyp. CDS 44161/3 (3). Bonney, Gritton, Bowman, Covey-Crump, Daniels, George, King's Consort, King

Originally issued on three separate CDs, this boxed collection brings obvious advantages, not least in the alphabetical index provided of the 87 songs. It is good, for example, to be able instantly to compare the three different settings of *Music for a while*, each on a different disc. The second and best-known version is a revision of the first (both for tenor, elegantly sung here by Rogers Covey-Crump), whereas the third is quite different, a free-ranging arioso setting of the same text by Henry Heveningham, taking the first line from Shakespeare's *Twelfth Night*. Barbara Bonney sings it exquisitely, and all the soloists here are excellent, with Robert King with his Consort, notably on bass viols and theorbo, providing most sympathetic accompaniment. Not included are Purcell's bawdy songs and catches, usually for multiple voices.

Songs: *Ask me to love no more; Beneath a dark and melancholy grove; Evening Hymn; The fatal hour comes on apace; If music be the food of love; If pray'rs and tears; Incassum Lesbia (Queen's Epicidium); In Chloris all soft charms agree; O solitude; A thousand sev'ral ways I tried to hide; What a sad fate is mine; While Thirsis wrapp'd in downy sleep; Young Thirsis's fate ye hills and groves deplore.* **Instrumental:** *Airs from The Indian Queen & Intermède; Soft tune*

(N) ** Naïve Astree E 8882. Lesne, Il Seminario Musicale

We are admirers of Gérard Lesne, but this repertoire, although freshly delivered, seems not to suit him in the way it does a voice like Alfred Deller's. Moreover, the continuo accompaniments are very resonantly recorded and too dominant. The solo instrumental pieces suffer from this same problem.

Songs: *The fatal hour comes on apace; Lord, what is man?; Love's power in my heart; More love or more disdain I crave; Now that the sun hath veiled his light; The Queen's epicedium; Sleep, Adam, sleep; Thou wakeful shepherd; Who can behold Florella's charms.* **Arias:** *History of Dioclesian: Since from my dear Astrea's sight. Indian Queen: I attempt from love's sickness to fly. King Arthur: Fairest isle. Oedipus: Music for a while. Pausanias: Sweeter than roses. The Rival Sisters: Take not a woman's anger ill. Rule a wife and have a wife: There's not a swain*

*** Etcetera KTC 1013. Dalton, Uittenbosch, Borstlap

Andrew Dalton has an exceptionally beautiful counter-tenor voice, creamy even in its upper register to make the extended 'Hallelujahs' of *Lord, What is Man?* and *Now that the Sun* even more heavenly than usual. A delightful disc, well recorded.

Airs & Duets: *Arise my Muse: Hail, gracious Gloriana, hail! Fly Bold Rebellion: Be welcome, then, great sir. Come ye Sons of Art: Sound the trumpet. The Fairy Queen: Let the fifes and the clarions; Hark! the ech'ing air; One charming night. Hail Bright Cecilia: In vain the am'rous flute. If ever I more riches did desire: Here let my life; Me, O ye Gods. Love's goddess sure: Many, many such days; Sweetness of nature.* **Other songs:** *If music be the food of love; Lord, what is man (Divine Hymn); Lovely Albina's come ashore; Saccharissa's grown old*

⊛ (N) *** Lyrichord LEMS 8024. Dooley, Crook, Instrumental Ens., Brewer (harpsichord)

This reissue is a real find. It originally appeared in the late 1970s, when it created something of a sensation in the USA. Now remastered for CD, it deserves once more to catch the Purcell-lover's attention. Jeffrey Dooley (counter-tenor), a pupil and protégé of the late Alfred Deller, has a truly beautiful voice and takes naturally to this repertoire. Among his solo items *Be welcome, then, great sir* and the *Divine Hymn* (*Lord, what is man*) are quite ravishing, while *Hark! the ech'ing air* is delectably sprightly. Particularly engaging is *One charming night* from *The Fairy Queen*, with a pair of recorders. The tenor Howard Crook also has a disarmingly personable vocal line, and his solos, including *Beauty, thou scene of love* and the sombre *Here let my life*, are hardly less memorable, with the famous *If music be the food of love* splendidly sung. But it is when these two voices join together in duet that one's senses are truly ravished, from the opening *Let the fifes and the clarions* and the similarly light-hearted *Sacharissa's grown old* to *Many, many such days* (with its bassoon obbligato), and not forgetting *Sound the trumpet*. The celebration of the queen, *Hail, gracious Gloriana, hail!*, makes a well-chosen finale. The simple instrumental accompaniments are managed most stylishly, and this concert cannot be too highly recommended.

Songs and duets for counter-tenor: *Bonduca: Sing, sing ye Druids. Come, ye sons of art: Sound the trumpet. Elegy on the death of Queen Mary: O dive custos Auriacae domus. The Maid's last prayer: No, resistance is but vain. Ode on St Cecilia's Day: In vain the am'rous flute. O solitude, my sweetest choice. The Queen's epicedium: Incassum, Lesbia rogas. Timon of Athens: Hark how the songsters*

*** Hyp. CDA 66253. Bowman, Chance, King's Cons., King – BLOW: *Ode, etc.* ***

A sparkling collection of solos and duets which show both the composer and these fine artists in inspirational form. The performances are joyous, witty and ravishing in their Purcellian melancholy, with often subtle response to word meanings, and King's accompaniments have plenty of character in their own right. Excellent recording.

Songs and dialogues: *Go tell Amynta; Hence fond deceiver; In all our Cinthia's shining sphere; In some kind dream; Lost is my quiet; Stript of their green; What a sad fate is mine; What can we poor females do; Why my poor Daphne, why complaining.* **Theatre music:** *Amphitryon: Fair Iris and her swain. Dioclesian: Tell me why. King Arthur: You say 'tis love; For love every creature is formed by his nature. The Old Bachelor: As Amoret and Thyrsis lay*

⊶ (BB) *** Hyp. Helios CDH 55065. Kirkby, Thomas, Rooley

This nicely planned Hyperion collection has one solo apiece for each of the singers, but otherwise consists of duets, five of them from dramatic works. These near-ideal performances, beautifully sung and sensitively accompanied on the lute, make a delightful record, helped by excellent sound. Now reissued on the bargain Helios label, this disc is more attractive than ever.

Other collections

(i) *Abdelazar: Suite;* (i; ii) *Cibell for Trumpet & Strings;* (i) *Dioclesian: Dances from the Masque; Overtures: in D min.; G min.;* (i; ii) *Sonata for Trumpet & Strings;* (i) *Staircase Overture; Suite in G, Z.770; Timon of Athens: Curtain Tune;* **Keyboardworks:** (iii) *New Irish Tune; New Scotch Tune; Sefauchi's Farewell; Suite 6 in D;* **Songs:** (iv; i) *Hark How All Things; If Love's Sweet Passion;* (iv; iii) *If Music Be the Food of Love; Lord What is Man (Divine Hymn);* (iv; i) *See Even Night Herself is Here; Thus the Ever Grateful Spring*

*** Chan. 0571. (i) Purcell Qt; (ii) Bennett; (iii) Woolley; (iv) Bott

Catherine Bott opens this 72-minute concert with a glorious account of one of Purcell's most famous Shakespearean settings, most artfully decorated: *If Music Be the Food of Love;* if anything, the later song, *See, Even Night Herself is Here,* is even more ravishing, given an ethereal introduction by the string group. The instrumental items are most rewarding, notably the attractive unpublished suite of dances in G, while the three overtures are full of plangent character. Robert Woolley's harpsichord contribution is most infectious (the *New Irish Tune,* incidentally, is *Lillibulero*) and he is beautifully recorded, the harpsichord set back in an intimate acoustic and perfectly in scale. There are few better Purcell anthologies than this, and overall the CD gives an ideal introduction to the music of one of the very greatest English

composers. The Chandos recording is first class, well up to the standards of the house.

'*Music for Pleasure and Devotion*' Disc 1: *Fantasia VIII; 3 Parts upon a Ground;* Anthem: *Rejoice in the Lord, alway.* Funeral sentences: *Man that is born of woman; In the midst of life; Thou knowest Lord.* (Keyboard) *Organ Voluntary in D min.* Songs: *Close thine eyes; If music be the food of love;* Duets: *Close thine eyes; Of all the instruments. Suite of Theatre Music. The Fairy Queen: Masque of the Four Seasons*

Disc 2: *Pavans 1–4; Beati omnes qui timent Dominum; In Guilty Night (Saul and the Witch of Endor); Jehova, quam multi sunt hostes mei; My beloved spake; Te Deum & Jubilate (for St Cecilia's Day, 1694); Te Deum; When on my sick bed I languish*

(B) *** Virgin 2x1 5 62164-2 (2). Taverner Ch., Cons. & Players, Parrott

This attempt at an authentic 'Pocket Purcell' nearly comes off. If perhaps it tries to do too many different things in the space of a pair of CDs, it certainly shows the composer's breadth and variety of achievement. Opening with a four-movement *Suite of Theatre Music* brightly played (and including the inevitable *Rondeau* from *Abdelazar* which Britten borrowed for his *Young Person's Guide*). There is also a touching *Fantasia for Viols,* a delightful set of keyboard divisions on a *Ground in Gamut,* admirably played by John Toll, and an equally engaging joke-duet for two tenors, *Of All the Instruments That Are.* The first collection then closes with the *Masque of the Four Seasons* from *The Fairy Queen.* Fine, vivid recording.

The second CD opens with an exceptionally brisk and compelling account of the *Te Deum and Jubilate,* Parrott and his team provide a refreshing and illuminating survey of Purcell's vocal music, punctuated by four of the adventurous, intense *Pavans* which Purcell wrote in his youth, at about the same time as the great sequence of string *Fantasias.* In the relatively brief span of 70 minutes Parrott ranges wide, with the elaborately contrapuntal Latin anthem, *Jehova, quam multi sunt,* one of Purcell's finest, made the more moving, if less grand, with one voice per part, and with the scena about the Witch of Endor, *In Guilty Night,* thrillingly dramatic. Well-matched singing and playing, atmospherically recorded.

STAGE WORKS AND THEATRE MUSIC

Dido and Aeneas (complete)

⊶ ● (M) *** Decca (ADD) 466 387-2. Baker, Herincx, Clark, Sinclair, St Anthony Singers, ECO, Lewis

*** Erato 4509-98477-2. Gens, Berg, Marin-Degor, Brua, Fouchécourt, Les Arts Florissants, Christie

(BB) *** Teldec 4509 91191-2. D. Jones, Harvey, Dean; Bickley, Murgatroyd, St James's Singers & Bar. Players, Bolton

*** Chan. 0586. Ewing, Daymond, MacDougall, R. Evans, Burgess, Bowman, Coll. Mus. 90, Hickox

*** Ph. 416 299-2. Norman, McLaughlin, Kern, Allen, Power, ECO and Ch., Leppard

*** Chan. 0521. Kirkby, Thomas, Nelson, Noorman, Rees, Taverner Ch. & Players, Parrott

*** Virgin 5 45605-2. Graham, Bostridge, Tilling, De Boever, Palmer, Daniels, Agnew, European Voices, Le Concert d'Astrée, Haïm

(B) **(*) HM HMC 2901683. Dawson, Joshua, Finley, Bickley, Clare Col. Chapel Ch., OAE, Jacobs

(BB) **(*) Naxos 8.553108. Scholars Bar. Ens.

Janet Baker's 1962 recording of *Dido* is a truly great performance. The radiant beauty of the voice is obvious enough, but the opening phrase of *When I Am Laid in Earth* and its repeat a few bars later is a model of graduated mezza voce. Then with the words *Remember Me!*, delivered in a monotone, she subdues the natural vibrato to produce a white tone of hushed, aching intensity. Anthony Lewis and the ECO (Thurston Dart a model continuo player) produce the crispest and lightest of playing, which never sounds rushed. Herincx is a rather gruff Aeneas, but the only serious blemish is Monica Sinclair's Sorceress. She overcharacterizes in a way that is quite out of keeping with the rest of the production. Like most vintage Oiseau-Lyre recordings, this was beautifully engineered, and it is a welcome reissue on the Decca Legends label.

On Erato the scale is intimate, with one instrument per part, and one voice per part in choruses, yet Christie cunningly varies the pace to intensify the drama. Though speeds are generally fast, he points an extreme contrast in Dido's two big arias, giving them full expressiveness at measured speeds. In the final exchanges between Dido and Aeneas the hastening speed of the recitative directly reflects the mounting tensions. What then sets this above other period performances is the tragic depth conveyed by Veronique Gens in Dido's great *Lament*, taken very slowly, with the voice drained and agonized in a way that Janet Baker supremely achieved. The young Canadian baritone, Nathan Berg, dark and heroic of tone, is outstanding as Aeneas, making this thinly drawn character for once more than a wimp. Textually this version is interesting for supplying two very brief extra numbers to fill in the music missing from the end of Act II, as indicated in the suriviving libretto. Together they last less than 90 seconds.

Ivor Bolton and the St James's Singers and Players present another period performance, intimately scaled, which avoids the snags of earlier versions, with Della Jones as Dido giving one of her finest recorded performances yet. She has a weightier mezzo than her rivals in other period performances, yet her flexibility over ornamentation is greater, and Dido's lament is the more moving when she is restrained over expressive gestures, keeping a tender simplicity. She shades her voice tonally very much as Dame Janet Baker did in her classic recording with Sir Anthony Lewis. There is no weak link, with Peter Harvey as Aeneas, Susan Bickley as a clear-toned Sorceress, Donna Dean as a characterful Belinda, and Andrew Murgatroyd as the Sailor, a tenor who plays no stylistic tricks. Setting the seal on the performance's success, the choir is among the freshest and liveliest, and the use of the guitar continuo, as well as brief guitar interludes (suggested by the original libretto), enhances the happy intimacy of the presentation. Moreover, this reissue is very reasonably priced.

Richard Hickox's version was linked to a striking television presentation revolving round the magnetically characterful portrayal of the central role by Maria Ewing. In the event her performance, as recorded, is both distinctive and stylish. Combined with Hickox's lively direction, unmarred by intrusive re-allocation of voices, it makes an impressive version, with Karl Daymond making Aeneas a more complex character than usual, with Rebecca Evans a radiant Belinda, matching Ewing in emotional intensity, and with Sally Burgess a characterful, unexaggerated Sorceress. Add the excellent contributions of James Bowman and Jamie MacDougall, and it makes a strong contender, certainly for admirers of Maria Ewing.

Authenticists should keep away, but the security and dark intensity of Jessye Norman's singing make for a memorable performance, heightened in the recitatives by the equally commanding singing of Thomas Allen as Aeneas. The range of expression is very wide – with Norman producing an agonized whisper in the recitative just before *Dido's Lament*. Marie McLaughlin is a pure-toned Belinda, Patrick Power a heady-toned Sailor, singing his song in a West Country accent, while Patricia Kern's performance as the Sorceress uses conventionally sinister expression. Leppard's direction is relatively plain and direct, with some slow speeds for choruses. Excellent recording.

Andrew Parrott's concept of a performance on original instruments has one immediately thinking back to the atmosphere of Josias Priest's school for young ladies where Purcell's masterpiece was first given. The voices enhance that impression, not least Emma Kirkby's fresh, bright soprano, here recorded without too much edge but still very young-sounding. It is more questionable to have a soprano singing the tenor role of the Sailor in Act III; but anyone who fancies the idea of an authentic performance need not hesitate. The sound is well focused, with analogue atmosphere yet with detail enhanced.

With an exceptionally strong line-up of soloists, Emmanuelle Haïm directs a most distinctive period performance of *Dido and Aeneas*, with even the tiny role of the Spirit taken by a star singer, the counter-tenor David Daniels. The instrumental accompaniment is weightier than usual, helped by the immediate recording-balance, and that matches the thrustful manner of Haïm, strong and purposeful if occasionally challenging her singers and players uncomfortably. By contrast, in the brief chorus, *Cupid only throws the dart*, she is curiously slow and laboured. More aptly, she also adopts broad speeds in Dido's two big arias, *Ah Belinda* and the final *Lament*. There and throughout, Susan Graham as Dido sings with warm, full tone, and though some may resist the idea of a tenor taking the role of Aeneas, Ian Bostridge too characterizes strongly and darkens his voice more than usual. More controversially, as in Haïm's Virgin recording of Monteverdi's opera *L'Orfeo*, she encourages these and other soloists to lean into notes and phrases in search of expressive warmth, rather than attacking cleanly, as one expects in a period performance. It is a mannerism that many will welcome rather than resist, and Felicity Palmer as a larger-than-life Sorceress quickly makes one forget any expressive idiosyncrasy in the vividness of her characterization. Camilla Tilling as Belinda and Paul Agnew as the Sailor both sing strongly too, and the chorus, European Voices, under the direction of Simon Halsey, is crisp and alert.

René Jacobs directs a characterful and dramatic reading of *Dido and Aeneas*, with Lynne Dawson a pure and refined heroine leading an excellent cast. Speeds tend to be extreme in both directions, with Dido's *Lament* and final chorus very slow indeed, with some heavy underlining. Happily Dawson sustains her line very well in the *Lament*, deeply affecting in her noble dedication. What is more controversial is Jacobs's tendency in choruses not just to underline individual notes – as in the final chorus – but to pull the tempo around outrageously, particularly in the Witches' choruses. So both

Harm's Our Delight and *Destruction's Our Delight* start very slowly indeed, and then have sudden bursts at high speed, with phrasing pulled around too. Many will accept such quirks as part of a characterful experience, particularly when the Sorceress (Susan Bickley) and the two counter-tenors who take the roles of the first two witches (Dominique Visse and Stephen Wallace) are hilariously characterful in a way that Purcell would certainly have relished. Rosemary Joshua as Belinda, golden in tone, and Gerald Finley as a virile Aeneas are also ideally cast. Well-balanced recording, if with a reverberation that gives some of the choruses a religious flavour.

Using minimum forces, with one-to-a-part strings, the Scholars Baroque Ensemble offer an intimate view of Purcell's compressed epic. Though the instrumental sections are rather rough in ensemble, the performance is vigorous and compelling, with Dido's two great ground-bass arias both given necessary emotional weight. Kym Amps is a warmly expressive heroine, singing with moving restraint in the *Lament*, while Anna Crookes as Belinda sings with fresh, clear tone, and Sarah Connolly with her rich mezzo makes an impressive Sorceress. Though David van Asch is a dry-toned Aeneas, he compensates by his expressiveness. Two improvised guitar dances and an interlude for two violins are added to the surviving musical text where the libretto suggests. Clear, immediate recording.

(i) *Dido and Aeneas* (ed. Britten; complete). (ii) Evening hymn: *When Night her Purple Veil had Softly Spread*
(B) (**(*)) BBC mono/stereo BBCB 8003-2. Watson, Pears, J. Sinclair, Mandikian, Clark, Allister, Phillips, Hahessy, Ronayne, Purcell Singers, EOG O, Britten; (ii) Fischer-Dieskau; Davies; Pople; Britten

Britten's own performance of *Dido and Aeneas*, using the edition he and Imogen Holst prepared for the English Opera Group, was recorded in mono in the Maida Vale studio in 1959. The distinctive point about the text is that three brief Purcell items are added at the end of Act II, setting the passage in the libretto missing from the score. Britten's direction is alert, with rhythms crisply articulated and speeds on the slow side only in choruses. Though the EOG's strings are relatively sumptuous, he is ahead of his time in use of ornamentation. What is disappointing is the casting. Claire Watson is a reliable soprano but hardly a characterful one, even though she puts great feeling into the *Lament*. Peter Pears is an expressive Aeneas, treating recitative in a Lieder-like way, though in a low-lying role his tone is sometimes gritty. Arda Mandikian repeats the performance she gave earlier as the Witch in the Flagstad recording, characterful but at times ungainly, and Jeannette Sinclair, a fresh, bright Belinda, has moments of shrillness. Following the Britten edition, boy-trebles are used for the roles of Spirit and the Sailor, with often disconcerting results. Britten's edition of Purcell's extended *Evening Hymn* makes a valuable bonus, triumphing over current stylistic fashion when it inspires Fischer-Dieskau to give such a moving and intense performance.

(i) *Dido and Aeneas* (arr. Britten/I. Holst); (ii) *The Fairy Queen* (adapted Britten)
(B) *** Double Decca (ADD) 468 561-2 (2). (i) Baker, Pears, Burrowes, Reynolds, Lott, Palmer, Hodgson, Tear, L. Op. Ch., Aldeburgh Fest. Strings, Bedford; (ii) Vyvyan, Bowman, Pears, Wells, Partridge, Shirley-Quirk, Brannigan, Amb. Op. Ch., ECO, Britten, Ledger (harpsichord)

Both these productions were planned by Britten, but in the event it was Steuart Bedford who stepped in to conduct the Decca recording of the Britten/Holst edition of *Dido and Aeneas*, with Dame Janet Baker returning (in 1975) to the area of her earliest major success in the recording studio. Her portrait of Dido is even richer than before, with more daring tonal colouring, and challengingly slow tempi for the two big arias.

Many will prefer the heartfelt spontaneity of her youthful performance under Anthony Lewis, but the range of expression on the newer version is unparalleled, and the richer, more modern Kingsway Hall recording adds to the vividness of the experience. With Norma Burrowes a touchingly youthful Belinda, with Peter Pears using Lieder style in the unexpected role (for him) of Aeneas, with Anna Reynolds an admirable Sorceress, and other star singers in supporting roles, there is hardly a weak link, and the London Opera Chorus relishes Bedford's often unusual tempi (that suggest earlier consultation with Britten).

Britten's edition of *The Fairy Queen* grouped Purcell's music into four sections, *Oberon's Birthday*, *Night and Silence*, *The Sweet Passion* and *Epithalamium*. This version was first heard at the Aldeburgh Festival in 1967, and here the authentic glow of a Maltings performance (1971 vintage) is beautifully conveyed in the playing, the singing and the recording. Philip Ledger's imaginative harpsichord continuo is placed too far to one side, but otherwise the sound can hardly be faulted. The cast is consistently satisfying, with Peter Pears and Jennifer Vyvyan surviving from an earlier 'complete' mono recording directed by Anthony Lewis. At Double Decca price this is well worth exploring.

Dioclesian; Timon of Athens (masque)
*** Chan. 0569/70. Pierard, Bowman, Ainsley, George, Coll. Mus. 90, Hickox
Dioclesian; Timon of Athens (masques only)
*** Chan. 0568. (as above)

Richard Hickox on Chandos offers the apt coupling of *Dioclesian* and *Timon of Athens*, both sets of theatre music involving masques. Hickox takes a light view, at times detached, often adopting fast speeds and using on balance a consistent team of soloists, including in smaller roles such outstanding younger singers as Ian Bostridge and Nathan Berg. On the other hand, he does not include the overture to *Timon*. The single Chandos CD contains the masque music only.

Dioclesian: Overture and excerpts
(M) *** DHM/BMG 82876 60157-2. Argenta, Chance, Freiburg Bar. O, Von der Goltz – HANDEL: *Concerto grosso, Op. 6/6 etc.* ***

Those not wanting the entire masque shold be well satisfied with this overture and set of songs and dances, presented with great zest by the superb Freiburg Baroque Orchestra, with excellent soloists in Michael Chance and Nancy Argenta. The *Chaconne* is beautfully played and the Second Music, which ends the selection, is particularly lively. Excellent couplings and first-class recording make this a highly recommendable reissue.

The Fairy Queen (complete; DVD version)
*** Arthaus **DVD** 100 200. Kenny, Randle, Rice, Van Allan, ENO Ch. & O, Kok (Director: David Pountney)

The Fairy Queen (complete; CD versions)

🎧 *** DG 419 221-2 (2). Harrhy, J. Smith, Nelson, Priday, Penrose, Stafford, Evans, Hill, Varcoe, Thomas, Monteverdi Ch., E. Bar. Sol., Gardiner

*** HM HMC 901308/9. Argenta, Dawson, Daniels, Loonen, Correas, Les Arts Florissants, Christie

(BB) *** Naxos 8.550660-1 (2). Atherton, Amps, Davidson & Soloists, Scholars Bar. Ens., Van Asch

(M) **(*) Virgin 5 61955 2 (2). Bickley, Hunt, Pierard, Crook, Padmore, Wilson-Johnson, Wistreich, L. Schütz Ch., L. Classical Players, Norrington

Recorded live at the Coliseum in London in 1995, this DVD ENO production of *The Fairy Queen*, conducted by Nicholas Kok, turns an entertainment which can, under modern conditions, seem cumbersome into a sparkling fantasy, thanks to the brilliant stage direction of David Pountney and choreography of Quinny Sacks. The sequence of masques is treated as a series of circus turns, and thanks also to the fantastic costumes of Dunya Ramicova the atmosphere of the circus is never far away, helping to hold together an episodic sequence of scenes, originally designed to back up a garbled version of Shakespeare's *A Midsummer Night's Dream*.

The result is as much a surreal ballet as an opera, with Nicholas Kok drawing stylish playing from the ENO Orchestra, echoing period practice, using a realization prepared by Clifford Bartlett. So the scene of the Drunken Poet proves genuinely funny, with Jonathan Best (identified only in the final credits on film) doing a jolly imitation of a 1950s poet with scruffy sports jacket and pullover.

By contrast Titania – Yvonne Kenny at her finest – and Oberon – the exotic Thomas Randle – stand out the more sharply as otherworldly figures thanks to their glamorous costumes. More equivocal is the presentation of Puck by Simon Rice, lively as he is. A fun entertainment, as unstuffy a presentation of Purcell's problematic masterpiece as could be, vividly filmed and recorded.

Gardiner's CD performance is a delight from beginning to end, for, though authenticity and completeness reign, scholarship is worn lightly and the result is consistently exhilarating, with no longueurs whatever. The fresh-toned soloists are first rate, while Gardiner's regular choir and orchestra excel themselves, with Purcell's sense of fantasy brought out in each succeeding number. Beautifully clear and well-balanced recording.

William Christie uses a far bigger team of both singers and instrumentalists than Gardiner, allowing a wider range of colours. The bite of the performance is increased by the relative dryness of the recorded sound. Among Christie's soloists, Nancy Argenta and Lynne Dawson are outstanding, and the whole team is a strong one. The number of singers in solo roles allows them to be used together as chorus too – an authentic seventeenth-century practice. This makes a vigorous and refreshing alternative to the fine Gardiner set; but the Harmonia Mundi booklet is inadequate.

For Naxos at bargain price the Scholars Baroque Ensemble offer an outstanding version, stylishly presented with a refreshing vigour in its scholarly approach. The recording too is exceptionally bright and immediate, regularly giving the illusion of a dramatic entertainment on stage. Logically this version, unlike previous ones, presents the purely instrumental numbers designed as interludes for *A Midsummer Night's Dream* as an appendix, rather than including them during the course of the musical entertainment of five separate masques. The humour of the Scene of the Drunken Poet is touched on

delightfully without exaggeration, thanks to David van Asch, as is the Dialogue between Corydon and Mopsa, though the counter-tenor, Angus Davidson, has a flutter in the voice that the recording exaggerates. Outstanding among the sopranos are Diane Atherton, singing most beautifully in the Night solo of Act II, and Kym Amps, not only bright and agile in *Hark! The Ech'ing Air* but making the plaint, *O ever Let Me Weep*, of Act V into the emotional high-point of the whole performance. Instrumental playing on period instruments is first rate, and the chorus sings consistently with bright, incisive attack.

Roger Norrington recorded *The Fairy Queen* following a 'Purcell Experience' weekend, which culminated in a concert performance of this inspired but disjointed semi-opera. There is a refinement and polish about the solo singing and the ensemble which reflects the intensive preparation. Where William Christie's earthier reading with Les Arts Florissants reflects the experience of a stage production – bold, jolly and intense – Norrington's wears its polished manners in a crisp, lightly rhythmic way, helped by the finely honed playing of the London Classical Players. Speeds are often brisk, with rhythms lightly sprung, and the impressive line-up of soloists brings distinctive characterization from such singers as David Wilson-Johnson as the Drunken Poet, Mark Padmore in the tenor songs of Act IV and Lorraine Hunt in *Hark! The Echo'ing Air*, which is taken very fast and lightly. There is less fun and less dramatic bite here than in Christie's or Gardiner's versions, but recorded in a spacious acoustic, Norrington's light, clean approach never diminishes Purcell's bubbling inspiration.

The Indian Queen (complete; with Daniel Purcell (c. 1661–1717): The Masque of Hymen)

(M) *** Decca 475 052-2. Kirkby, Bott, Ainsley, D. Thomas, Finley, Williams, AAM Ch. & O, Hogwood

(BB) **(*) Naxos 8.553752. Soloists, Ch., Scholars Bar. Ens.

Hogwood's recording of Purcell's fourth and last semi-opera, left incomplete at his death, was the first to include the Wedding cantata which the composer's brother, Daniel, wrote to round off the entertainment. It makes an attractive if inconsistent addition to a score which contains vintage Purcell inspirations, notably the solo with chorus, *All Dismal Sounds*, which was the last part of the work completed by Purcell himself. The elaborate chromatics in that confirm the continuing vigour of Purcell's genius to the end. With John Mark Ainsley, Emma Kirkby and Catherine Bott all making outstanding solo contributions, and with clean-cut period playing from the orchestra, this performance on a relatively grand scale is consistently convincing, by turns lively and moving. It is now reissued in Decca's British Music Collection.

The Naxos version also comes with the added bonus of the concluding *Masque of Hymen*, which Daniel Purcell added after his brother's death, making a celebratory instead of a tragic conclusion. The work overall suits the lively style of the Scholars Baroque Ensemble admirably, on a scale rather more intimate than you find on most rival versions, with one instrument per part. Bright, clear recording to match, with dances and trumpet-tunes well sprung. The choral work is first rate; but when the singers come to their solos, the voices (mostly unidentified as to who sings what) are uneven, often with delivery rather unsteady. The fresh-toned soprano, Anna Crookes, makes an honourable exception. Yet solos are usually short, and what matters is the overall freshness, vigour and intensity.

(i) *The Indian Queen* (incidental music); (ii) *King Arthur* (complete)

♦— ☼ ◉ (M) *** Decca 476 1552 (2). (i) Cantelo, W. Brown, Tear, Partridge, Keyte, St Anthony Singers, ECO, Mackerras; (ii) Morison, Harper, M. Thomas, Whitworth, W. Brown, Galliver, Cameron, Anthony, Alan, St Anthony Singers, Philomusica of L., Lewis

It was a happy idea of Decca to pair these comparatively early but outstanding Purcell recordings to include in their 'Penguin ◉ Collection'. *The Indian Queen* (originally issued on L'Oiseau-Lyre) dates from 1966, and the recording from a vintage era remains first rate. With stylish singing and superb direction and accompaniment (Raymond Leppard's harpsichord continuo playing must be singled out), this is an invaluable reissue. Charles Mackerras shows himself a strong and vivid as well as scholarly Purcellian. The Rosette, however, is for the pioneering 1959 set (also Oiseau-Lyre) of *King Arthur*, fully worthy to stand alongside the companion recording of *Dido and Aeneas*, made three years later. Here the success of the interpretation does not centre on the contribution of one inspired artist, but rather on teamwork among a number of excellent singers and on the stylish and sensitive overall direction of Anthony Lewis. Oiseau-Lyre's excellent stereo also plays a big part. A very happy example is the chorus *This Way, That Way*, when the opposing spirits (good and evil) make a joint attempt to entice the King, while the famous freezing aria will surely send a shiver through the most warm-blooded listener.

King Arthur (complete)

*** Erato 4509 98535-2 (2). Gens, McFadden, Padmore, Best, Salomaa, Les Arts Florissants, Christie

(M) *** Erato 4509 96552-2 (2). J. Smith, Fischer, Priday, Ross, Stafford, Elliot, Varcoe, Monteverdi Ch., E. Bar. Sol., Gardiner

*** DG (IMS) 435 490-2 (2). Argenta, Gooding, Perillo, MacDougal, Tucker, Bannatyne-Scott, Finley, Ch. & E. Concert, Pinnock

Christie's Erato recording of the musical numbers consistently reflects stage experience. Some may not like the crowd noises in the more rollicking numbers but, more than his rivals, Christie brings out the jollity behind much of the piece. Even the pomposo manner of some of the Act Tunes (or interludes) has fun in it, with the panoply of the ceremonial music swaggering along genially. Few will resist the jollity of *Your Hay it is Mow'd* when the chorus even includes 'gentlemen of the orchestra' in the last verse. Christie's soloists are generally warmer and weightier than Pinnock's, notably Véronique Gens as Venus, sustaining Christie's exceptionally slow speed for *Fairest Isle*. Otherwise speeds are generally on the fast side, with *Shepherd, Shepherd, Cease Decoying* deliciously light and brisk. The vigour of Purcell's inspiration in this semi-opera has never been more winningly conveyed in a period performance on disc, with full-bodied instrumental sound set against a helpful but relatively dry acoustic, giving immediacy to the drama.

Gardiner's solutions to the textual problems carry complete conviction, as for example his placing of the superb *Chaconne in F* at the end instead of the start. Solo singing for the most part is excellent, with Stephen Varcoe outstanding among the men. *Fairest Isle* is treated very gently, with Gill Ross, boyish of tone, reserved just for that number. Throughout, the chorus is characteristically fresh and vigorous, and

the instrumentalists beautifully marry authentic technique to pure, unabrasive sounds.

Pinnock opens with the *Chaconne*, which is placed before the *Overture*. His performance is consistently refreshing and can be recommended alongside, though not in preference to Christie's. Linda Perillo makes a charming Philidel. Brian Bannatyne-Scott is superb in Aeolus's *Ye Blust'ring Brethren*, and in his *Frost Aria* he achieves an unusual if controversial effect by beginning his series of shakes from slightly under the note. Not surprisingly, Nancy Argenta sings beautifully in the double roles of Cupid and Venus and her *Fairest Isle* will not disappoint; both chorus and orchestra sing and play throughout with consistent vitality. The DG recording is first class, but why no coupling? The second CD plays for only 39 minutes.

Theatre Music (collection)

Disc 1: Abdelazar: Overture & Suite. Distressed Innocence: Overture & Suite. The Gordian Knot Untied: Overture & Suite; The Married Beau: Overture & Suite. Sir Anthony Love: Overture & Suite

Disc 2: Bonduca: Overture & Suite. Circe: Suite. The Old Bachelor: Overture & Suite. The Virtuous Wife: Overture & Suite

Disc 3: Amphitrion: Overture & Suite; Overture in G min.; Don Quixote: Suite

Disc 4: Overture in G min. The Double Dealer: Overture & Suite. Henry II, King of England: In Vain, 'Gainst Love, in Vain I Strove. The Richmond Heiress: Behold the Man. The Rival Sisters: Overture; 3 Songs. Tyrannic Love: Hark my Damilcar! (duet); Ah! How Sweet it is to Love. Theodosius: excerpts. The Wives' Excuse: excerpts

Disc 5: Overture in D min.; Cleomenes, the Spartan Hero: No, no, poor suff'ring heart. A Dialogue between Thirsis and Daphne: Why, my Daphne, why Complaining?. The English Lawyer: My wife Has a Tongue: excerpts. A Fool's Preferment: excerpts. The History of King Richard II: Retir'd from any Mortal's Sight. The Indian Emperor: I Look'd and Saw Within. The Knight of Malta: At the Close of the Ev'ning. The Libertine: excerpts. The Marriage-hater Match'd: As Soon as the Chaos ... How Vile are the Sordid Intregues. The Massacre of Paris: The Genius Lo (2 settings). Oedipus: excerpts. Regulus: Ah Me! to Many Deaths. Sir Barnaby Whigg: Blow, Blow, Boreas, Blow. Sophonisba: Beneath the Poplar's Shadow. The Wives' Excuse: excerpts

Disc 6: Chacony; Pavans 1-5; Trio Sonata for Violin, Viola de Gamba & Organ. Aureng-Zebe: I See, She Flies Me. The Canterbury Guests: Good Neighbours Why?. Epsom Wells: Leave these Useless Arts. The Fatal Marriage: 2 Songs. The Female Virtuosos: Love, Thou art Best. Love Triumphant: How Happy's the Husband. The Maid's Last Prayer: excerpts. The Mock Marriage: Oh! How you Protest; Man is For the Woman Made. Oroonoko: Celemene, Pray Tell Me. Pausanius: Song (Sweeter than roses) & Duet. Rule a Wife and Have a Wife: There's Not a Swain. The Spanish Friar: Whilst I with grief

(N) (B) *** Decca 475 529-2 (6). Kirkby, Nelson, Lane, Roberts, Lloyd, Bowman, Hill, Covey-Crump, Elliott, Byers, Bamber, Pike, Thomas, Keyte, Shaw, George, Taverner Ch., AAM, Hogwood

Most of the music Purcell wrote for the theatre is relatively little heard and much of the music comes up with striking freshness in these performances using authentic instruments.

As well as the charming dances and more ambitious overtures, as the series proceeds we are offered more extended scenas with soloists and chorus, of which the nine excerpts from *Theodosius*, an early score (1680), are a particularly entertaining example. Before that, on Disc 3 we have already had the highly inventive *Overture and Incidental Music* for *Don Quixote*, with much enchanting singing from both the soprano soloists, Emma Kirkby and Judith Nelson. Disc 4 also includes a delightful duet from *The Richmond Heiress*, representing a flirtation in music. There are other attractive duets elsewhere, for instance the nautical *Blow, Blow, Boreas, Blow* from *Sir Barnaby Whigg*, which could fit admirably into *HMS Pinafore* (Rogers Covey-Crump and David Thomas) and the jovial *As Soon as the Chaos* from *The Marriage-hater Match'd*. In *Ah Me! to Many Deaths* from *Regulus*, Judith Nelson is at her most eloquent while, earlier on Disc 5, she sings charmingly the familiar *Nymphs and Shepherds*, which comes from *The Libertine*, a particularly fine score with imaginative use of the brass. The equally famous *Music for a While*, beautifully sung by James Bowman, derives from *Oedipus*. The last disc also includes a splendidly boisterous *Quartet* from *The Canterbury Guests*. The collection is appropriately rounded off by members of the Academy giving first-class performances of some of Purcell's instrumental music, ending with the famous *Chacony*. The discs are re-released at bargain price, comprehensively documented and with full texts included.

QUILTER, Roger (1877–1953)

(i) *A Children's Overture*; (ii) *3 English Dances; Where the Rainbow Ends* (Suite). (iii) *The Fuchsia Tree; Now sleeps the crimson petal; Weep you no more*. (iv) *Come away, death*; (v) *7 Elizabethan Lyrics*; (vi; vii) *Go, lovely rose. It was a lover and his lass* (two versions, with viii; ix & x); (viii; ix) *Love's Philosophy*; (xi) *Non nobis, Domine*; (iv) *Now sleeps the crimson petal*; (vi; ix) *O mistress mine*

☐── (M) *** EMI (ADD/DDD) 5 85149-2. (i) Light Music Soc. O, Dunn; (ii) N. Sinf., Hickox; (iii) Hough; (iv) Bostridge, Drake; (v) Allen, Parsons; (vi) Harvey; (vii) Byfield; (viii) J. Baker; (ix) Moore; (x) Lott, Murray, Johnson; (xi) Finchley and Barnet & District Ch. Societies, Central Band of the RAF, Wallace

Beginning with Quilter's masterly *A Children's Overture*, in Sir Vivian Dunn's bright if not distinctive performance from 1969, this well-planned anthology is a worthy tribute to this master of unpretentious composition. Richard Hickox's digital accounts of the *Three English Dances* and *Where the Rainbow Ends* are charmingly done, fully revealing all the rustic qualities of 'olde England'. There are some real gems among the vocal items: Janet Baker bringing characteristic vocal richness to *Love's Philosophy*, and *It was a lover and his lass*, which is also heard in a quite different and equally delightful version with Felicity Lott and Ann Murray in duet. Baritone Trevor Harvey invests passion rather than finesse in *O mistress mine*, but sings *Go, lovely rose* with more tenderness. In Ian Bostridge's two numbers, the sheer beauty of his tenor makes one readily forgive any reservations concerning over-interpretation – and what lovely songs they are, too. With three very attractive piano pieces, finely played by Stephen Hough, and a rousing performance of *Non nobis, Domine*, this CD is thoroughly recommendable. The sound-quality throughout is excellent, only the Frederick Harvey items from the mid-1960s sounding a bit dated.

A Children's Overture; Country Pieces; 3 English Dances; As You Like It: Suite; The Rake: Suite; Where the Rainbow Ends: Suite

(*) Marco Polo 8.223444. Slovak RSO (Bratislava), Leaper

Adrian Leaper plays the enchanting *Children's Overture* with the lightest touch, and the transparency of the recording ensures that all the woodwind detail comes through nicely, even if his performance could ideally have had a shade more momentum. One might also have wished for a bigger band with a more opulent string sheen, but the texture here well suits the suites of incidental music, an agreeable mixture of the styles of Edward German (especially the *Country Dance* from *As You Like It*), Eric Coates and sub-Elgar of the *Nursery Suites*. All this nicely scored and amiably tuneful music is freshly and spontaneously presented and the recording is nicely resonant.

RABE, Folke (born 1935)

Sardinsarkofagen (Sardine Sarcophagus)

*** BIS CD 1021. Hardenberger, Malmö SO, Varga – BORTZ: *Trumpet Concerto*; SANDSTROM: *Trumpet Concerto 2* ***

The Swedish composer Folke Rabe is now seventy and he writes effectively for brass, though such earlier pieces as we have heard leave us unpersuaded that his is a notable creative gift. His *Sardinsarkofagen* alludes to the fact that in Seville a sardine is buried as part of the passion ritual, so rather appropriately the piece was commissioned by the Music Factory in Bergen, a lively group based in an old sardine factory! Despite Håkan Hardenberger's electrifying performance, the music remains pretty feeble, and the rather pointless quotes from Mahler serve to highlight the emptiness of the surroundings. The stars are for the performance and recording.

RACHMANINOV, Sergei (1873–1943)

Caprice bohémien, Op. 12; The Isle of the Dead, Op. 29; Prince Rostislav; The Rock, Op. 7; Scherzo in D min.

*** Chan. 10104. Russian State SO, Polyansky

All these orchestral pieces turn up from time to time as couplings for the symphonies, though the tone-poem, *Prince Rostislav*, is more of a rarity. The *Scherzo* is Rachmaninov's earliest orchestral score, dating from 1888, when he was sixteen, while *The Isle of the Dead* is one of his greatest. In the latter Polyansky does not displace Pletnev (DG) among modern recordings or the composer himself, but he is certainly competitive and has this music in his blood. The recording is perhaps a bit too reverberant, but no reader wanting this repertoire should be put off, for the performances are all vivid.

Piano Concertos 1–4

☐── (B) *** Double Decca (ADD) 444 839-2 (2). Ashkenazy, LSO, Previn

(BB) *** EMI 5 73765-2 (3). Rudy, St Petersburg PO, Jansons
 – TCHAIKOVSKY: *Piano Concerto 1* ***

Piano Concertos (i) 1 in F sharp min.; (ii) 2 in C min.; (iii) 3 in D min.; (i) 4 in G min.; (ii) Rhapsody on a Theme of Paganini, Op. 43

(N) *** Hyp. CDA 67501/2 (2). Hough, Dallas SO, Litton
(M) *** Chan. 7114 (2). Wild, RPO, Horenstein

(B) **(*) EMI double forte (ADD) 5 68619-2 (2). Anievas, New Philh. O; (i) Frühbeck de Burgos; (ii) Atzmon; (iii) Ceccato

(M) **(*) Danacord DACOCD 582-583 (3). Marshev, Aarhus SO, Loughran

Piano Concertos 1; 3 in D min., Op. 30
☸– (N) *** Warner 0927 47941-2. Lugansky, CBSO, Oramo

Piano Concertos 2 in C min., Op. 18; 4 in G min., Op. 33
☸– (N) *** Warner 2564 61946-2. Lugansky, CBSO, Oramo

It is not easy to think of any recent CDs of these marvellous concertos that surpass these by Nicolai Lugansky except those by Stephen Hough. Lugansky's account of the *First* is the finest since Pletnev's Virgin CD from the early 1990s, and the *Third* is even more impressive than his earlier version, coupled with the *Fourth* (Vanguard 99091). The *Second*, too, ranks alongside Ashkenazy's outstanding version.

The Double Decca set of the four Rachmaninov is admirable, fully capturing the Kingsway Hall ambient warmth yet not lacking brilliance and clarity, and with the *Third Concerto* better focused than when it first appeared on LP. The vintage 1972 performances, with their understanding partnership between Ashkenazy and Previn, have achieved classic status. The *Second Concerto*'s slow movement is particularly beautiful; it is almost matched by the close of the first movement of the *Third* and the restrained passion of the opening of the following *Adagio*. The individuality and imagination of the solo playing throughout, combined with the poetic feeling of Previn's accompaniments and the ever-persuasive response of the LSO, provide special rewards. An outstanding bargain in every way.

Mikhail Rudy and the St Petersburg Philharmonic under Mariss Jansons consistently demonstrate that extrovert bravura is not everything in Rachmaninov piano concertos, and that poetry and refinement can offer exceptionally rewarding results in works which emerge here as far more than conventional warhorses. There is plenty to admire and relish. The results are fresh and unhackneyed from first to last, with Rudy's light, clean articulation adding sparkle. Not that he lacks weight, and the strong support of Jansons and the St Petersburg Philharmonic intensifies the idiomatic warmth, with mystery alongside passion in Rachmaninov's writing. This account of the *Fourth Concerto* is especially valuable in offering the original, uncut version of the finale, as well as the usual revised text.

Recorded live in Dallas, Stephen Hough's prize-winning Rachmaninov set offers magnetic performances that reflect the thoughtfulness and care with which this masterly pianist approaches even the most frequently performed works. So the opening of the *Second Concerto*, taken much faster than usual but at a very steady pace, is quite different from most interpretations, firmly based on indications in the score rather than performing tradition, and that is typical of Hough's refreshing approach to each of these works. With Andrew Litton equally a devotee of the composer, these are unique readings, marred only slightly by rather clangorous piano-tone and orchestral textures that are far less detailed than in many rival versions.

The Earl Wild set with Horenstein was recorded at the Kingsway Hall in 1965. They worked marvellously together, with Horenstein producing an unexpected degree of romantic ardour from the orchestra. Earl Wild's technique is prodigious and sometimes (as in the first movement of the *Fourth*

Concerto) he almost lets it run away with him. What is surprising is how closely the interpretations here seem to be modelled on the composer's own versions – not slavishly, but in broad conception. This applies strikingly to the *First Concerto* and the *Rhapsody*. In terms of bravura, the *Third Concerto* is in the Horowitz class. However, he makes the three cuts Rachmaninov sanctioned, one in the second movement and two in the third, a total of 55 bars. All in all, this is a first-class and very rewarding set, and the sumptuousness of the sound belies the age of the recording.

Anievas cannot match Ashkenazy as a searching and individual interpreter of Rachmaninov, but his youthful freshness makes all these concerto performances highly enjoyable. With three Mediterranean conductors to help him, and with bright, vivid EMI recording, not as atmospheric as the quality Decca provide for Ashkenazy, the result brings a combination of brilliance and romanticism which never lets go, even if it rarely produces the moments of magical illumination that mark the most inspired interpretations. Like Ashkenazy, Anievas gives the *Third Concerto* absolutely uncut and uses the longer, more difficult version of the first-movement cadenza. It is a strong, direct interpretation, though at the very end of the finale the presentation of the big melody nearly goes over the top.

Oleg Marshev was born in Baku, a Russian-trained virtuoso who earlier recorded a whole series of adventurous discs for Danacord. These are broad-brush readings in many senses. The speeds are generally broader than usual – with No. 2 taking over five minutes longer than in some vintage versions – but with his weight and power Marshev sustains broad tempi well, only occasionally letting the music run the risk of sounding plodding, as in the slow movement of No. 2 and at the start of the *Third Concerto*. Yet the thrust and intensity of his performances consistently carries one along, with full, forward recording-balance adding to the power. It also allows one to appreciate Marshev's clarity of articulation in Rachmaninov's brilliant passage-work. The downside is that the weight of the recording in heavy-textured passages tends to obscure inner detail. It also tends to downplay the poetic side of these heartfelt warhorses. Marshev's control of rubato is always fluent and idiomatic, conveying spontaneity of feeling, but others are even freer, and the absence of a true *pianissimo* makes the slow movements in particular sound a little heavy-handed in comparison with the finest versions. Loughran draws comparably powerful playing from the excellent Aarhus Symphony Orchestra, with a fine sheen on the strings, its most outstanding section. The broad speeds mean that the set has had to spread to three discs, but they come at mid-price.

(i) *Piano Concertos 1–4; Rhapsody on a Theme of Paganini, Op. 43.* (ii) *Music for 2 pianos: Suites 1–2, Opp. 5 & 17; Russian Rhapsody; Symphonic Dances, Op. 45. Solo piano: Etudes-tableaux, Opp. 33 & 39; 24 Preludes (complete); Piano Sonata 2 in B flat min., Op. 36; Variations on a Theme by Corelli, Op. 42*
🏵 (B) *** Decca (ADD/DDD) 455 234-2 (6). Ashkenazy; (i) LSO, Previn; (ii) with Previn (piano)

(i) *Piano Concertos 1–4; Rhapsody on a Theme of Paganini. Piano Sonata 2 in B flat, Op. 36; Variations on a Theme of Corelli, Op. 42*
(M) *** Decca Trio (ADD) 473 251-2 (2). Ashkenazy, (i) with LSO, Previn

All these performances are very distinguished indeed. The

vintage Decca recordings (made over a decade and a half between 1971 and 1986, mostly in the Kingsway Hall, but also at Walthamstow and All Saints', Petersham) are fully worthy of the quality of the music-making. Ashkenazy's readings, with Previn an admirable partner (whether conducting or at the keyboard), are unsurpassed on CD, except by the composer's own historic versions; while they are also available on a series of Double Deccas, any collector not involved in too much duplication will find either of these bargain boxes will make an ideal linchpin for a Rachmaninov collection.

(i) *Piano Concertos 1–4; Rhapsody on a Theme of Paganini;*
(ii) *Cello Sonata. Etudes-tableaux, Opp. 33 & 39; Moment musical, Op. 16/3; Preludes, Op. 3/2; Op. 23/1, 2 & 4; Op. 32/12; Piano Sonata 2* (1913 version);*Variations on a theme of Corelli*

(N) (BB) **(*) EMI (ADD/DDD) 5 86134-2 (5). Collard, with (i) Capitole Toulouse O, Plasson; (ii) G. Hoffman

Jean-Philippe Collard's recordings of the Rachmaninov concertos date from the late 1970s and find him completely at home in this repertoire: his account of the *First* has splendid fire and can hold its own with allcomers (even Pletnev and Ashkenazy), and much the same goes for its companions. The slow movement of the *Second*, though not wanting in romantic ardour, has less in the way of romantic delicacy, and so misses the balancing sense of repose that illuminates Ashkenazy's version; but the *Rhapsody* responds readily to this degree of charismatic brilliance with strong characterization throughout, and the eighteenth variation is played with passionate fervour. Perhaps the *Third Concerto* is the least incandescent in his hands, but readers wanting an inexpensive set of the concertos and much else besides will find all this playing of quality and the recording, though not up to Decca standard, is vivid enough. The *Cello Sonata*, too, is beautifully played, but Gary Hoffman's timbre is small and his style somewhat recessive alongside Collard, who very much dominates the proceedings. The *Second Piano Sonata* and *Corelli Variations* are both very successful. Collard negotiates their not inconsiderable difficulties with genuine aplomb, and he is very well recorded. The *Études-tableaux* are also superbly played and strongly characterized, lyrical and commanding by turns, as are the five favourite *Préludes*, although the otherwise truthful piano recording hardens a little in *fortissimos*. But this remains an admirable survey overall, even if, as with the rest of these French EMI boxes, the notes are sparse and in French only. But this is a super-super-bargain set with the five discs offered for the price of one premium-priced disc.

Piano Concerto 1 in F sharp min., Op. 1
(N) (M) *** Mercury **SACD** 475 6607. Janis, Moscow PO, Kondrashin – PROKOFIEV: *Piano Concerto 3, etc.* ***

As in the Prokofiev coupling, the occasion of the first Western-engineered recordings made in the USSR at the beginning of the 1960s, soloist and orchestra plainly challenged each other to the limit, and the American technical team brilliantly captured the warmly romantic and chimerical interpretation that resulted. The solo playing stands alongside that of Horowitz in this repertoire, scintillating in the finale, yet never offering virtuosity simply for its own sake. Even now the recording is impressive for its clarity of texture, excellent piano sound and warm acoustic, made that bit more full and spacious by the new SACD transfer.

Piano Concertos 1–2
*** DG 459 643-2. Zimerman, Boston SO, Ozawa

Krystian Zimerman is an aristocrat among aristocrats of the piano and his playing is never less than awesome. These performances have been showered with so many plaudits and critical accolades that they must be regarded as self-recommending. Of course, like everything Zimerman does, they are touched by distinction, but for all the admiration they inspire, there is just a trace of self-possession about them: one would welcome greater emotional abandon. Feeling does not always seem to arise spontaneously. But this is playing at an exalted level and many readers may not respond in this way – and most critics we have read certainly have not. Good orchestral support from Ozawa and the Boston orchestra, and very vivid and present recording.

Piano Concertos (i) *1;* (ii; iii) *2;* (ii; iv) *Rhapsody on a Theme of Paganini*
(BB) (***) Naxos (mono) 8.110676. Moiseiwitsch; with (i) Philh. O, Sargent; (ii) RLPO; cond. (iii) Goehr; or (iv) Cameron

Rachmaninov used to say that his friend Moiseiwitsch was an even finer interpreter of some of his works than himself, and from this vintage collection one can understand why. Moiseiwitsch recorded No. 2 in 1937 for HMV on four budget-label 78s, undercutting the composer's classic version by half in price, yet the performance is if anything more electrifying. The sound is limited, with the piano close, but in Ward Marston's masterly transfer one quickly forgets the limitations, as one does in the other pre-war recording of the *Rhapsody on a Theme of Paganini*, a sparkling performance, again urgent in its expression, with the celebrated eighteenth variation all the warmer for going at a flowing speed. The rarity is the post-war, 1948 account of No. 1, in which the sound is full and clear with Moiseiwitsch still at the peak of his form, both passionate and sparkling, powerful and poetic.

Piano Concertos (i) *1;* (ii) *2;* (iii) *5 Preludes, Op. 3/2; Op. 23/2 & 5; Op. 32/2*
(N) (BB) *** EMI HMV 5 86754-2. (i) Pletnev, Philh. O, Pešek; (ii) Tirimo, Philh. O, Levi; (iii) Alexeev

Pletnev's *F minor Concerto* is a performance of classic status, strong in personality and musicianship, and with especially vivid sound. Tirimo's *C minor* is no less brilliant and again is highly individual (see below, where it is also available coupled to the *Paganini Rhapsody*) and has a memorably expressive slow movement. Alexeev's bonus of five of the most popular of the *Preludes* offers more masterly playing to make this well-recorded disc very desirable in the budget range.

Piano Concertos 1; 4 in G min.; Rhapsody on a Theme of Paganini
(BB) *** Naxos 8.550809. Glemser, Polish Nat. RSO, Wit

Bernd Glemser has a boldly impetuous way with Rachmaninov and, with excellent support from the Polish National Radio Orchestra under Antoni Wit, he generates plenty of excitement and expressive fervour in all three works. If Janis and Kondashin are that bit more characterful in the *F sharp minor Concerto*, and Pletnev is even more charismatic in the *Rhapsody*, Glemser is by no means unimaginative or wanting in poetic feeling, and he gives a very enjoyable account of the more elusive *Fourth Concerto*.

Piano Concerto 2 in C min., Op. 18
*** Häns. CD 98.932. Ohlsson, ASMF, Marriner –
TCHAIKOVSKY: *Piano Concerto 1* ***

☛ (N) (M) *** RCA **SACD** (ADD) 82876 61392-2. Cliburn,
Chicago SO, Reiner – TCHAIKOVSKY: *Piano Concerto 1* ***

(M) *** DG (ADD) 447 420-2. S. Richter, Warsaw PO,
Wislocki – TCHAIKOVSKY: *Piano Concerto 1* (**)

(M) (**) BBC BBCL mono 4074-2. Moiseiwitsch, BBC SO,
Sargent – BEETHOVEN: *Piano Concerto 5* (***)

Ohlsson and Marriner combine to give a satisfyingly romantic account of this favourite concerto. The climax of the first
movement is broad and very powerful, and the finale, while
not lacking brilliance, makes the very most of Rachmaninov's
great secondary melody with a gorgeously expansive final
presentation. The *Adagio* is equally persuasive with the
reprise tenderly beautiful, rapt in its gentle concentration.
The recording is full-bodied and natural and is admirably
balanced. If you want a modern, digital recording of this
coupling, this Hänssler CD is hard to beat.

With Reiner making a splendid partner, Van Cliburn's
1962 account of the Rachmaninov *C minor Concerto* is
second to none. The pacing of the first movement is
comparatively measured, but the climax is unerringly paced,
remaining relaxed yet enormously telling. The finale too
does not seek to demonstrate runaway bravura but has
sparkle and excitement, with the lyrical element heart-
warming to match the very beautiful account of the central
Adagio, full of poetry and romantic feeling. The recording is
wonderfully rich, with the Chicago acoustic adding glorious
ambient glow, while the piano, though forwardly balanced,
has unexpected body and fullness of timbre. In the finale the
cymbals demonstrate an excellent upper range, and this new
transfer makes it seem as though it were recorded yesterday.
The SACD offers an extra degree of warmth and spread to
the sound.

With Richter the long opening melody of the first movement is taken abnormally slowly, and it is only the sense of
mastery that he conveys in every note which prevents one
from complaining. The slow movement too is spacious –
with complete justification this time – and the opening of the
finale lets the floodgates open the other way, for Richter
chooses a hair-raisingly fast allegro, so this is a reading of
vivid contrasts. The sound is very good. It's a great pity that
the performance chosen as the new coupling should be
Tchaikovsky's *First Concerto*, with Karajan and the Berlin
Philharmonic, an example of a performance where two great
artists pull simultaneously in different directions.

Rachmaninov thought Moiseiwitsch one of his finest interpreters, and this performance from a 1956 Prom serves as a
reminder of his stature. Moiseiwitsch was seventeen years
younger than the composer and grew up in his shadow. He is
certainly steeped in both his spiritual and sound world, even
if, in the heat of live performance, he was prone to the odd
split note. But by this time, when he was in his sixties, he
unaccountably appeared less in the concert hall than he had
during the 1940s, and this inevitably took its toll. There are
plenty of insights into this piece that the gladiatorial virtuosi
of the present day do not bring, and he is given excellent
support from Sir Malcolm Sargent, a fine concerto accompanist. Unfortunately, the sound is wanting in transparency and
range and comes close to distortion in climaxes. All the same,
this is an invaluable musical document, which all who care
about the piano should investigate.

Piano Concertos (i) 2; (ii) 3
(M) **(*) Decca (ADD) 466 375-2. Ashkenazy, (i) Moscow
PO, Kondrashin; (ii) LSO, Fistoulari

(N) (M) **(*) Naxos **Audio DVD** 5.110013. (B) CD 6.110013.
Scherbakov, Russian State SO, Yablonsky

(BB) **(*) RCA (DDD/ADD) 82876 55269-2. (i) Douglas,
LSO, Tilson Thomas; (ii) Janis, Boston SO, Munch

Ashkenazy's first (1963) recording of the *C minor Concerto* is
more successful than his much later, digital account with
Haitink, but less compelling than his version with Previn,
which remains uniquely beautiful. But the performance with
Kondrashin offers superb Walthamstow sound and, though
Kondrashin does not hold the first movement at a consistent
level of tension, the close of the *Andante* is ravishing and no
one should be disappointed with the passionate climax of the
finale. The *Third Concerto* is another matter. Anatole Fistoulari proved a splendid partner, and this reading is the freshest
and most spontaneous of Ashkenazy's four recordings. Both
CD transfers are outstandingly successful and the vintage
(again Walthamstow) sound-balance is very satisfying.

Konstantin Scherbakov has shown us in his fine set of the
Medtner concertos and in much else besides that he is not
only a pianist of formidable technical prowess but also a real
artist. He never strives after effect or mere display but has a
refined and profound musicianship that makes this music
seem uncommonly fresh. Of course, competition in this
repertoire is so strong that even at so modest an outlay it is
not possible to speak of first preferences. Suffice it to say
that no one investing in this SACD is likely to feel short-
changed.

The main interest on the RCA disc is Byron Janis's very
fine first (1958) recording of the *Third Concerto* with Munch.
He was to re-record it later even more successfully with
Dorati for Mercury, and the earlier account produces a
somewhat less full-bodied piano image; but the balance is
acceptable within the warm Boston acoustic, and somehow
the timbre seems right for Janis's comparatively brisk tempo
for the main theme of the first movement. His approach is
often impetuous, spontaneously so, but the contrast with the
second subject is convincingly made and the reading has an
underlying lyricism. Munch is a sympathetic partner. He
contributes a strong surge of romanticism to the *Adagio*, and
the performance brings some dazzling solo playing in the last
movement with a particularly exciting close.

Unfortunately, Barry Douglas's digital recording of the *Second Concerto* (made 34 years later) does not take off in the
same way. It would be an exaggeration to call it prosaic, but it
is less imaginative or tonally refined than one would expect
from a Tchaikovsky Competition winner. No quarrels with
the excellent orchestral playing or the fine recorded sound.

Piano Concertos (i) 2; (ii) 3 (**transfers use alternative takes**)
(***) Biddulph mono LHW 036. (i) Composer, Phd. O,
Stokowski; (ii) Horowitz, LSO, Coates

Two classics of the Rachmaninov discography: the 1929
account of the *C minor Concerto* the composer recorded with
the Philadelphia Orchestra, coupled with the first (and in
some ways most exciting) of Horowitz's recordings of the
Third, made in London the following year with Albert Coates
conducting. An electrifying performance. The Biddulph
transfers made by Mark Obert Thorn are first-rate and in the
C minor, use is made of alternative takes made at the original

sessions. An invaluable supplement to RCA's Complete Rachmaninov Edition and a mandatory purchase for collectors of this repertoire.

Piano Concertos (i) 2; (ii) 3. Preludes: in C sharp min., Op. 3/2; in E flat, Op. 23/6

(N) (M) *** Mercury **SACD** (ADD) 470 639-2. Janis, with (i) Minneapolis SO; (ii) LSO; Dorati

In No. 2 Byron Janis has the full measure of the music: his shapely, lyrical phrasing and natural response to the ebb and flow of the melodic lines are a constant source of pleasure. In the finale there is all the sparkling bravura one could ask for, but the great lyrical tune is made beguilingly poetic. Although the 1960 recording has plenty of ambience, the Minneapolis violins lack the richness of the LSO strings, recorded at Watford in 1961. The simple opening of the *Third Concerto* benefits from the extra warmth, and Janis lets the theme unwind with appealing spontaneity, and in the great closing climax of the finale the passion is built up – not too hurriedly – to the greatest possible tension. Janis makes two cuts (following the composer's own practice), one of about 10 bars in the second movement and a rather long one in the finale. Two favourite *Preludes*, with the E flat coming first, most persuasively played, make some compensation. The sound retains all its best qualities in this new SACD transfer.

Piano Concerto 2; Rhapsody on a Theme of Paganini

(BB) *** Naxos 8.550117. Jandó, Budapest SO, Lehel

(B) *** CfP CD-CFP 9017. Tirimo, Philh. O, Levi

(N) ** DG 477 5231; **SACD** 477 5499. Lang, Mariinsky Theatre O, Gergiev

(i) Piano Concerto 2 in C min., Op. 18; (ii) Rhapsody on a Theme of Paganini, Op. 43. Prelude in C sharp min., Op. 3/2

(BB) (***) Naxos mono 8.110692. Kapell, Robin Hood Dell O, Philadelphia; (i) Steinberg or (ii) Reiner

Jandó has the full measure of the ebb and flow of Rachmaninov's musical thinking, and the slow movement is romantically expansive and the finale has plenty of dash and ripe, lyrical feeling. The *Rhapsody* is as good as almost any around. The digital recording is satisfyingly balanced, with a bold piano image and a full, resonant orchestral tapestry. A splendid bargain.

Concentrated and thoughtful, deeply expressive yet never self-indulgent, Tirimo is outstanding in both the *Concerto* and the *Rhapsody*, making this another of the most desirable budget versions. Speeds for the outer movements of the *Concerto* are on the fast side, yet Tirimo's feeling for natural rubato makes them sound natural, never breathless, while the sweetness and repose of the middle movement are exemplary. The digital recording is full, clear and well balanced.

Kapell's are exceptionally urgent readings, notably in No. 2, where the first movement gets you off to an electrifying start, pressing on at a far faster speed than usual. Yet there is nothing perfunctory about Kapell's fast speeds, just a demonstration of mastery, both in the *Concerto* and in the *Variations*. Significantly, each of the 'takes' in the many 78 sides involved was the first, with no retakes needed, demonstrating the spontaneous, white-hot quality of Kapell's playing, which yet did not rule out poetry. The Ward Marston transfers are vivid and full, both in the *Concerto* (1950) and in the *Rhapsody* (1951). The *Prelude*, recorded in 1945, is dimmer, and curiously the recording of that relatively simple piece comes from the fifth retake.

Thanks to his sensitivity, musicianship and flair (as well as

a brilliant publicity machine), Lang Lang has captured the public imagination. His playing is both cultured and often subtle but is surprisingly wanting in fire and momentum. Good playing from the Mariinsky Orchestra under Gergiev and well-balanced sound, but this performance really does not carry all before it as the best Rachmaninov performances do.

(i, iii) Piano Concerto 2; (ii, iii) Rhapsody on a Theme of Paganini; (iv) Suite 2 in C, Op. 17

(M) (***) Dutton Lab. mono CDCLP 4004. C. Smith; with (i) Liverpool PO; (ii) Philh. O; (iii) Sargent; (iv) Sellick

Cyril Smith's version of the *C minor Concerto*, made with the Liverpool Philharmonic in the Abbey Road Studios in 1947, has the real Rachmaninov sound and a great deal of feeling (Sir Malcolm Sargent too is an exemplary and supportive accompanist). Well worth investigating – as are the *Paganini Rhapsody*, again with Sargent, and the Op. 17 *Suite* which Cyril Smith recorded with his wife the following year. The sound is remarkably good for its day and the transfer in the best traditions of the house.

(i) Piano Concertos 2; 3. Rhapsody on a Theme of Paganini. Elégie, Op. 3/1; Etudes-tableaux, Op. 39/3 & 5; Moments musicaux, Op. 16/3–6. Preludes, Op. 23/1, 2, 5 & 6; Op. 32/12

(B) **(*) EMI Gemini 5 85779-2 (2). Gavrilov; (i) with Phd. O, Muti

Andrei Gavrilov recorded the solo items together in Moscow in 1984, the *Third Concerto* in Philadelphia in 1986, following on with the *Second* and the *Paganini Rhapsody* three years later. There is some pretty remarkable solo playing here, especially in the stormy *B flat major Prelude*, while the *G sharp minor* from Op. 32 has a proper sense of fantasy. More prodigious bravura provides real excitement in the *F sharp minor Etude-tableau*, Op 39/3, and in the *E minor Moment musical*, while Gavrilov relaxes winningly in the *Andante cantabile* of Op. 16/3 and the *Elégie*. Sometimes his virtuosity almost carries him away, and the piano is placed rather near the listener, so that we are nearly taken with him, but there is no doubt about the quality of this recital.

Before this, EMI had issued a remarkable Melodiya LP of Gavrilov's incandescent first recording of the *Third Concerto*, made at the time of the Tchaikovsky competition, which was rightly acclaimed as a truly memorable reading, strong and passionate, with the finale offering a thrilling display of bravura. The new account with Muti still offers some dazzling playing, with Gavrilov again using the longer, more complex first-movement cadenza to powerful effect and creating a thrilling climax to the finale. But overall the reading is more idiosyncratic and, although the lyrical waywardness is warmly sustained, the end result is less authoritative than the earlier version.

In neither the *C minor Concerto* nor the *Rhapsody on a Theme of Paganini* does Gavrilov bring the distinction he commanded in his earlier recordings. There is plenty of flamboyant virtuosity and all these Philadelphia performances have a finely shaped orchestral response from the Philadelphia Orchestra under Muti, and the recording is excellent. But there is a self-regarding brilliance from the pianist (noticeable immediately at the opening of the *Paganini Rhapsody*) that is not wholly pleasing. There is certainly no lack of adrenalin or charisma, but his account of the *D minor Concerto*, made in the 1970s, has a naturalness of utterance that is less apparent here.

(i) *Piano Concertos 2–3; Rhapsody on a Theme of Paganini. Preludes: in C sharp min., Op. 3/2; in B flat & G min., Op. 23/2 & 5; in B min. & D flat, Op. 32/10 & 13; Etudes-tableaux, Op. 39/1, 2 & 5*

(B) *** Double Decca (ADD) 436 386-2 (2). Ashkenazy, (i) with LSO, Previn

This pair of Decca CDs includes outstanding performances of Rachmaninov's three greatest concertante works for piano and orchestra, plus five favourite *Preludes* and three of the Op. 39 *Etudes-tableaux*. The digital remastering offers first-class transfers, full and well-balanced, with the Kingsway Hall ambience casting a pleasing glow over the proceedings. This is very highly recommendable.

(i) *Piano Concerto 2;* (ii) *Rhapsody on a Theme of Paganini;* (iii) *Symphony 2; Vocalise;* (iv) *The Bells, Op. 30*

**(*) DG (ADD) Panorama 469 178-2 (2). (i) Richter, Warsaw PO, Wislocki; (ii) Ashkenazy, LSO, Previn; (iii) BPO, Maazel; (iv) Soloists, Concg. O, Ashkenazy

This DG Panorama compilation brings together Richter's classic performance of the *Second Piano Concerto*, made on his visit to Warsaw in 1959, with Ashkenazy's reading of the *Paganini Rhapsody* from the early 1970s and his Amsterdam recording of *The Bells*. Less successful is Lorin Maazel's recording from 1983 of the *Second Symphony*, in which less than justice is done to the sumptuous tone of the Berlin Philharmonic.

Piano Concerto 3 in D min., Op. 30

*** Ph. 446 673-2. Argerich, Berlin RSO, Chailly – TCHAIKOVSKY: *Piano Concerto 1* ***

(N) (BB) (***) Naxos mono 8.110696. Horowitz, LSO, Coates – Recital: CHOPIN, DEBUSSY, LISZT, SCARLATTI

(B) (***) RCA mono 82876 56052-2 (2). Horowitz, RCA Victor SO, Reiner– TCHAIKOVSKY: *Piano Concerto 1; Recital: 'Legendary Recordings'* (***)

(***) Testament mono SBT 1029. Gilels, Paris Conservatoire O, Cluytens (with SHOSTAKOVICH: *Prelude & Fugue in D*) – SAINT-SAENS: *Piano Concerto 2* (***)

(*(**)) VAI mono VAIA IPA 1027. Kapell, Toronto SO, MacMillan – KHACHATURIAN: *Piano Concerto* (**)

(i) *Piano Concerto 3. Elegy, Op. 3/1; Polichinelle; Preludes: in C sharp min., Op. 3/2; in B flat; G min.; E flat, Op. 23/2, 5 & 6; in G; G sharp min., Op. 32/5 & 12*

⊕–⇥ ✿ *** Elan CD 82412. Rodriguez; (i) with Lake Forest SO, McRae

(i) *Piano Concerto 3. Etudes-tableaux, Opp. 33/1–3; 39/6*

(M) **(*) EMI 5 62837-2 [5 62838-2]. Andsnes; (i) with Oslo PO, Berglund

(i) *Piano Concerto 3. Piano Sonata 2, Op. 36*

(M) *** RCA (ADD) 82876 59411-2. Horowitz; (i) NYPO, Ormandy

(i) *Piano Concerto 3;* (ii) *Suite for 2 Pianos 2, Op. 17*

(M) *** Ph. 464 732-2. Argerich; (i) Berlin RSO, Chailly; (ii) Freire

Santiago Rodriguez is Cuban by birth but like Bolet has made his home in the United States. There is no doubt from the opening bars of the *Third Concerto* that he is a Rachmaninov interpreter of outstanding calibre, whose playing withstands the most exalted comparisons. Indeed, as one plays this disc, one's thoughts turn only to the greatest exponents of this repertoire – Horowitz, Rachmaninov himself and William

Kapell. Rodriguez, too, has dazzling virtuosity at his command and also fine musicianship and a rare keyboard authority. He plays the first-movement cadenza (and how!) that Rachmaninov himself favoured rather than the alternative one that came into fashion with Vladimir Ashkenazy. The eight remaining pieces are of the same exalted standard. A most exciting issue.

There are few finer examples of live recording than Martha Argerich's electrifying performance of Rachmaninov's *Third Concerto*, recorded in Berlin in 1982. Her volatility and dash are entirely at one with the romantic spirit of this music, and her interpretation is so commanding that individual eccentricities seem a natural part of the musical flow. Moreover she plays with great tenderness (well supported by Chailly) in the *Adagio* and the lyrical theme of the finale. The overall sound-picture satisfyingly demonstrates the skill of the Philips engineering team.

Those not wanting the coupling with Tchaikovsky will find the performance of the *Second Suite* for two pianos equally exciting. Argerich and Nelson Freire give it a dazzling virtuoso account, rushing the waltzes off their feet (the movement is marked *presto* but they play it *prestissimo*). They are as fresh, idiomatic and thoughtful as their Decca rivals (Ashkenazy and Previn – see below) and their performance is thoroughly exhilarating and well recorded too.

The first of the three commercial recordings Horowitz made of the *D minor Concerto* comes from 1929 (the others were with Fritz Reiner in 1951 and Ormandy in 1978), and for many collectors it is the finest. (Actually, one is tempted to say that of whichever was the last one you have heard.) However, it is still tremendously impressive and sounds better than ever in this new transfer.

Horowitz's 1951 RCA account with Reiner now reappears, coupled with his earlier (1941) version of the Tchaikovsky *First Concerto* with Toscanini. The Rachmaninov performance is full of poetry yet, like the Tchaikovsky, it is electrifying in its excitement. In spite of its dated sound (restricted but within a much warmer acoustic than the Tchaikovsky coupling) and a less than ideal balance, its magic comes over, and it is to be preferred to his later performance with Ormandy. The recital added to make a two-disc bargain double is assembled from various individual mono records mainly from the same era, but with a few items from the 1970s and 1980s.

Gilels's classic account of the *Concerto* with André Cluytens and the Paris Conservatoire Orchestra comes from 1955 and also belongs among the 'greats'. The piano-sound is a bit shallow and at times the balance favours the soloist unduly – but what lovely playing. This should still be in the collections of all who have an interest in Rachmaninov and piano playing.

Leif Ove Andsnes offers cultivated playing in the *D minor Concerto*, which was recorded at a public concert in Oslo in 1995. As always, he brings finesse and a refined musicianship to all he does, and the *Etudes-tableaux* are touched with distinction. Berglund is supportive and free from egotism, but he does not draw from the Oslo players the refined sonority which Jansons commands. Nevertheless, the many admirers of the young Norwegian pianist will feel that this is a worthy representation of his art in EMI's 'Great Artists of the Century' series.

During his short life William Kapell was closely identified with this concerto, and this performance was recorded in Toronto at a public concert in 1948. He is one of the very few pianists who can be compared to Horowitz and Rachmaninov himself. He plays the same cadenza as they did. The sound is very poor indeed, but the playing is absolutely electrifying.

In 1978 Horowitz re-recorded the *D minor Piano concerto* in stereo with Ormandy and the New York Philharmonic Orchestra, this time at a live concert. Perhaps just a little of the old magic is missing in the solo playing, but it remains prodigious, and Horowitz's special insights, which the composer acknowledged, are very apparent. The recording was made in Carnegie Hall, but certain portions of the work were remade following the concert. The result is that the sound is not completely stable; at times it seems to recede. But one adjusts when the music-making is so magnetic and the newest transfer makes the most of the sound and captures the hall ambience faithfully. The *Sonata* comes from two live recitals in 1980 and is also pretty electrifying. Horowitz plays the conflation he made (and which Rachmaninov approved) of the 1913 original and the 1931 revision, plus a few further retouchings he subsequently added.

(i) *Piano Concerto 3 in D min.*; (ii) *Rhapsody on a Theme of Paganini*
(N) (BB) *** EMI HMV 5 86755-2. (i) Rudy, St Petersburg PO, Jansons; (ii) Pletnev, Philh. O, Pešek

The performance of the *D minor Concerto* from Mikhail Rudy (drawn from the complete set above) is very fine indeed and, like Pletnev's classic account of the *Rhapsody*, is distinguished not only by quite stunning virtuosity and unobtrusive refinement but also by great feeling. The orchestral support is admirable, as is the recorded sound. A genuine bargain.

Piano Concerto 4 in G min., Op. 40
⊕- ✪ (M) *** EMI (ADD) 5 67238-2 [567258]. Michelangeli, Philh. O, Gracis – RAVEL: *Piano Concerto in G.* *** ✪

There are few records in the catalogue more worthy of being described as a 'Great Recording of the Century' than Michelangeli's superb coupling of Rachmaninov and Ravel. It has been with us for four decades and time has not diminished its unique appeal from the commanding opening onwards. The current remastering has been expertly managed and at mid-price it should be included in even the most modest collection.

The Isle of the Dead, Op. 29; The Rock, Op. 7; Symphonic Dances, Op. 45
(BB) **(*) Warner Apex 2564 60958-2. Royal Stockholm PO, A. Davis

Sir Andrew Davis gets good results from the Royal Stockholm Philharmonic Orchestra, who play very well indeed, and the recordings have admirable clarity and warmth. If neither *The Isle of the Dead* nor the *Symphonic Dances* – though eminently enjoyable – are really as distinguished as the best of their rivals, the bargain price-tag is very much in their favour.

The Isle of the Dead, Op. 29; Symphonic Dances, Op. 45
(N) (M) *** LPO 0004. LPO, Jurowski
(M) *** Decca 430 733-2. Concg. O, Ashkenazy
(BB) **(*) Naxos 8.550583. RPO, Bátiz

The LPO are now following the example of the LSO and the Concertgebouw Orchestra in launching their own label, and the orchestra's dynamic young principal guest conductor,

Vladimir Jurowski, makes an impressive first contribution. The high-voltage electricity he can generate is clearly established in the *Symphonic Dances*, leading up to a thrilling close, and if the hushed sequence of the *Isle of the Dead* is not a work to bring such a rush of adrenalin, the mystery of this piece, inspired by Hölderlin's great painting (reproduced in the booklet), is caught perfectly. These performances, recorded at the Royal Festival Hall in 2003 and 2004, can hold their own in the most exalted company and are marked by clean textures which gain in tension from being recorded live. Indeed, the sound in both is very well defined and wide-ranging, the aural perspective is truthful, and there is striking presence. (A trivial point: the sleeve gives an inaccurate total playing time – 50'45" instead of 60'19".)

Ashkenazy's too is a superb coupling, rich and powerful in playing and interpretation, *The Isle of the Dead* relentless in its ominous build-up, while the *Symphonic Dances* have extra darkness and intensity too. The splendid digital recording highlights both the passion and the fine precision of the playing.

Bátiz gives the *Symphonic Dances* an attractively spontaneous performance, full of lyrical intensity, with some splendid playing from the RPO strings. The vivid recording helps give the feeling that Bátiz almost goes over the top in his extremely passionate climax for *The Isle of the Dead*. The performance certainly does not lack darker feelings, and at super-bargain price this remains well worth considering.

(i) *Rhapsody on a Theme of Paganini*, Op. 43
(M) *** RCA (ADD) 09026 68886-2. Rubinstein, Chicago SO, Reiner (with CHOPIN: *Andante spianato & Grand polonaise*; FALLA: *Nights in the Gardens of Spain* ***)

Rubinstein's early stereo (1956) account of Rachmaninov's romantic showpiece is new to the British catalogue. There is no finer version. Rubinstein's playing is dazzling and it continually delights with its poetic sensibility and flair. Reiner is with him in every bar, orchestral detail persuasively delineated, and the warm Chicago acoustic ensures a glorious blossoming of string-tone at the *Eighteenth*. Both pianist and conductor relish the *Dies irae* each time it appears, and the closing pages reach a high pitch of excitement. The recording, with the piano forward but not unattractively so, sounds little short of ideal in Richard Mohr's splendid new remastering.

(i) *Rhapsody on a Theme of Paganini*, Op. 43.
Etudes-tableaux, Opp. 33 & 39; Piano Sonata 2, Op. 36; Moment musical, Op. 16/3; Preludes: Op. 3/2; Op. 23/1, 2 & 4; Op. 32/12; Variations on a Theme of Corelli, Op. 42
(B) *** EMI (ADD) 5 69677-2 (2). Collard; (i) Capitole Toulouse O, Plasson

In the *Rhapsody on a Theme of Paganini* Collard can hold his own with the finest, though he is not as well recorded as Ashkenazy. His account of the *Variations on a Theme of Corelli* is exemplary and the *Second Sonata* is no less powerful. Collard plays the 1913 version but, like Horowitz, incorporates elements of the revision. Playing of real distinction and very competitively priced.

(i) *Rhapsody on a Theme of Paganini*, Op. 43. (ii) Preludes Op. 3/2; Op. 23, 1, 2 & 4; Op. 32 10 & 12; Variations on a Theme of Corelli, Op. 42
(M) **(*) DG 457 906-2. (i) Vásáry, LSO, Ahronovitch; (ii) Berman

A competitive and welcome reissue, and even if Pletnev's

Paganini Rhapsody and those of Ashkenazy, Rubinstein and Collard are not eclipsed, Vásáry's is a more than respectable account. Lazar Berman's *Corelli Variations* are superlative and as good as any on or off record.

(i) Rhapsody on a Theme of Paganini; Variations on the Theme of Chopin, Op. 22; Variations on a Theme by Corelli, Op. 42

(N) *** Warner 2564 60613-2. Lugansky, (i) with CBSO, Oramo

Magisterial and excellently recorded performances from Nikolai Lugansky: an account of the *Paganini Rhapsody* that can be set alongside the Pletnev and a *Chopin Variations* to challenge the much-admired Berezowsky version. Those who want these pieces all on one CD need not hesitate.

Symphonic Dances, Op. 45

(N) *** Warner 2564 62050-2. St Petersburg PO, Temirkanov
 – MUSSORGSKY: *Songs & Dances of Death* ***

Temirkanov is at his best in front of an audience, and he characterizes the *Symphonic Dances* colourfully and idiomatically, securing fine playing from his St Petersburg orchestra, especially in the engaging central waltz. The three-part third dance is less easily held together, but if he does not quite manage the forward impetus of Jurowski (see above), he explores the music's detail and has the closing pages firmly in his grip. The live recording, balanced by Mike Hatch, is excellent, and the Mussorgsky coupling (which is the reason for being drawn to this CD) is outstanding in every way.

Symphonic Dances, Op. 45; (i) The Bells, Op. 35

**(*) Chan. 9759. (i) Lutsiv-Ternovskaya, Bomstein, Pochapsky, Russian State Cappella; Russian State SO, Polyansky

Valeri Polyansky is a bit self-indulgent in the *Symphonic Dances* and lingers, particularly in the middle movement, while the *Lento assai* section of the finale nearly crawls to a stop. The playing of the Russian State Orchestra is very fine and the recording is little short of spectacular in its clarity, definition and warmth. Artistically this is not a first choice. However, *The Bells* comes off well and is much helped by good soloists and the glorious recorded sound.

SYMPHONIES

Symphonies 1–3

(M) *** Virgin 5 62037-2 (2). RPO, Litton

(M) **(*) Double Decca 448 116-2 (2). Concg. O, Ashkenazy

Symphonies 1–3; The Isle of the Dead, Op. 29; Symphonic Dances, Op. 45; Vocalise, Op. 34/14; Aleko: Intermezzo & Women's Dance

(M) *** EMI (ADD) 7 64530-2 (3). LSO, Previn

Symphonies 1–3; The Isle of the Dead; Symphonic Dances; (i) The Bells, Op. 35

(B) *** Decca 455 798-2 (3). Concg. O, Ashkenazy; (i) with Troitskaya, Karczykowski; Concg. Ch.

Symphonies 1–3; The Rock, Op. 7

(M) **(*) DG (IMS) 445 590-2 (2). BPO, Maazel

Symphonies 1–3; Vocalise, Op. 34/14

(B) *** Sony SB2K 63257 (2). Phd. O, Ormandy

Ormandy pioneered the recording of the three Rachmaninov symphonies in stereo, and in many ways his performances remain unsurpassed. Certainly they have never sounded as good as they do in these splendid new transfers. The *Second Symphony* has great intensity of feeling and passion. The *First Symphony* was the work's first stereo version, an exceptionally strong performance it is too. Ormandy's thrustful view of the outer movements is supported by superbly committed Philadelphia playing, with the orchestra on top form. The balance has woodwind solos spotlighted, but the spacious acoustic of Philadelphia Town Hall provides the necessary ambient warmth. In some ways the *Third Symphony* is even more distinguished and now that the artificial brilliance of the old LP has been tamed one can at last appreciate the body of tone this great orchestra commanded in its heyday. The playing itself is marvellous, and this warmth of feeling carries over into the touchingly shaped *Vocalise* which acts as a final encore. A bargain set not to be missed, even if you have more modern versions of these splendid works.

Andrew Litton's mid-priced box is highly competitive alongside the Previn set, especially as all three symphonies are encompassed by a pair of CDs. They offer first-class digital sound with a beauty of orchestral texture ideal for Rachmaninov, and in this respect are superior to Previn.

In No. 1, Litton is most persuasive in his free use of rubato and his performance combines power and ripeness of romantic feeling with tenderness, bringing out the refinement of Rachmaninov's scoring. In the *Second Symphony* he readily sustains the observance of the exposition repeat in the first movement, making it a very long movement indeed at just over 23 minutes. But the moments of special magic are those where, as in his lightly pointed account of the Scherzo or, most of all, the lovely clarinet melody of the slow movement, subtlety of expression gives Rachmaninov's romanticism an extra poignancy. In the *Third Symphony*, the gentleness of his treatment of the great second subject melody means that the transparent beauty of Rachmaninov's scoring is brought out luminously, and though the opening of the finale may not sound urgent enough, it is crisply pointed and leads on to a superbly brisk, tense conclusion.

The Ashkenazy digital set of the three symphonies now comes either as a Double Decca or in a bargain box of three discs, one symphony to each CD and coupled respectively with *The Isle of the Dead*, *Symphonic Dances* and the dramatic cantata, *The Bells*, outstanding in every way. The performances of the symphonies, passionate and volatile, are intensely Russian; the only possible reservation concerns the slow movement of the *Second*, where the clarinet solo is less ripe than in some versions. Elsewhere there is drama, energy and drive, balanced by much delicacy of feeling, while the Concertgebouw strings produce great ardour for Rachmaninov's long-breathed melodies. The vivid Decca sound within the glowing Concertgebouw ambience is ideal for the music.

Previn's LSO set at mid-price offers some alternative couplings. His 1973 account of the *Second Symphony* – a passionately committed performance, with a glorious response from the LSO strings – has been remastered for CD again, with great improvement in the body of the string timbre. No. 1 is a forthright, clean-cut performance, beautifully played and very well recorded. It may lack some of the vitality that one recognizes in Russian performances (Ashkenazy is more volatile and remains first choice in this work) but is still very enjoyable. Previn's account of the *Third*, however, is outstanding: the LSO's playing again has enormous bravura and ardour, and the performances of the two shorter works have plenty of atmosphere and grip. With the *Aleko* excerpts and the *Vocalise* also included, this EMI box remains very competitive.

Maazel's set offers superb playing from the Berlin Philharmonic. However, the DG engineers secured a less sumptuous sound in the Berlin Philharmonie than their Decca colleagues in Amsterdam. The climaxes of the *Second Symphony* in particular would have been enhanced by a warmer middle and lower range. Maazel's readings are not to be dismissed: the *First Symphony* is particularly fine, with Rachmaninov's often thick orchestration beautifully transparent. The *Third* too is distinctive, unusually fierce and intense. The result is sharper and tougher than one expects, less obviously romantic, and the finale for all its brilliance lacks joyful exuberance.

Symphony 1; 5 Etudes-tableaux (orch. Respighi)
*** Chan. 9822. Russian State SO, Polyansky

Symphony 1; The Isle of the Dead
⊕━ ✿*** DG 463 075-2. Russian Nat. O, Pletnev
(BB) *** EMI Encore 5 85459-2. St Petersburg PO, Jansons

In the *First Symphony* Mikhail Pletnev produces a range of sonority and clarity of articulation that we recognize from his keyboard playing, and there is poetic vision alongside a splendid command of architecture. The symphony is quite outstanding in his hands and so is *The Isle of the Dead* which has the sense of inevitability and forward movement that recall Rachmaninov himself, Koussevitzky and Reiner.

Good playing and particularly good recording make Polyansky's Chandos CD a competitive issue, even though Pletnev, coupled with *The Isle of the Dead*, is not challenged artistically. A worthwhile addition to the catalogue, particularly in view of the Respighi transcription of the *Etudes-tableaux*.

Mariss Jansons and his St Petersburg musicians do not wear their hearts on their sleeves, but they give a totally committed and finely shaped performance of the *First Symphony*. Jansons maintains a firm hold over the architecture of the piece and produces playing of great poetic feeling. *The Isle of the Dead* is highly atmospheric, a convincing and indeed haunting performance. The recording is beautifully natural, with transparent string-sound and plenty of space around the instruments and with no want of presence. A very satisfying reissue and a real bargain.

Symphony 2 in E min., Op. 27
⊕━ ✿ (M) (***) DG mono 449 767-2. Leningrad PO, K. Sanderling
(N) (BB) *** Regis RRC 1210. LSO, Rozhdestvensky
(M) **(*) Chan. 6606. SNO, Gibson
**(*) Ph. (IMS) 438 864-2. Kirov O, Gergiev
**(*) BIS CD 1279. RSNO, Arwel Hughes
(B) **(*) CfP (ADD) 575 5652. Hallé O, Loughran –
TCHAIKOVSKY: *Romeo and Juliet* **(*)

Symphony 2; The Isle of the Dead
(M) **(*) DG 457 913-2. BPO, Maazel

Symphony 2; The Rock
**(*) DG 439 888-2. Russian Nat. O, Pletnev

Symphony 2; Scherzo in D min.; Vocalise, Op. 34/14
(BB) *** EMI Encore 5 85075-2. St Petersburg PO, Jansons

Symphony 2; (i) Vocalise
(N) *** Channel Classics **SACD** CCS SA 21698. Budapest Festival O, Fischer
**(*) Telarc CD 80312. (i) McNair; Baltimore SO, Zinman

Symphony 2; Vocalise, Op. 34/14; Aleko: Intermezzo & Women's Dance
(BB) *** EMI HMV (ADD) 5 86753-2. LSO, Previn

Previn's 1973 recording of the *Second Symphony* dominated the catalogue for over a decade in the analogue era. Its passionate intensity combines freshness with the boldest romantic feeling, yet the music's underlying melancholy is not glossed over. With vividly committed playing from the LSO and a glorious response from the strings, this remains a classic account, not even surpassed by Sanderling's, now that the recording has such opulence and weight in the bass. The addition of the engaging *Aleko* excerpts, plus a fine lyrical account of the *Vocalise*, makes for a generous reissue playing for nearly 75 minutes. In EMI's budget HMV Classics series, this is a bargain of bargains.

Kurt Sanderling's famous mono recording dates from 1956, but one would never guess, so voluptuously full is the sound of this current DG re-transfer and so remarkably refined the detail. Here is a great Russian orchestra at their very peak, obviously inspired by their conductor, Kurt Sanderling, and carried away on a tide of passion, underpinned by the very Russian melancholy of the slow movement, and especially at its close. The string playing throughout is glorious, reaching its apotheosis in the tremendous climaxes of the finale. A great performance and, astonishingly, the mono sound is fully worthy of it.

Rozhdestvensky gives a very Tchaikovskian reading of Rachmaninov's *E minor Symphony*. There is plenty of vitality but, with the big string melodies blossoming voluptuously, the slow movement, after a beguiling opening clarinet solo from Andrew Marriner, has a climax of spacious intensity, its power almost overwhelming. The finale is flamboyantly broadened at the end, and the feeling of apotheosis is very much in the Tchaikovsky mould. With the LSO responding superbly, this is a most satisfying account, and the richness, brilliance and weight of the recording add to the compulsion of the music-making. This is an easy first choice in the budget range.

Jansons's 1993 St Petersburg account offers a strong, warm reading in which climaxes are thrust home powerfully, even if occasionally over-moulded, and the recording gives fine body and immediacy to the sound, outshining most latter-day rivals. In Russian fashion, the clarinet in the slow movement sounds like an organ stop. But this is an exciting reading, which stands among the best modern versions. The coupling, in addition to the *Vocalise*, beautifully done, offers the early orchestral *Scherzo* of 1887.

A red-blooded account of the *Second Symphony* from Iván Fischer and the fine Budapest Festival Orchestra has much to commend it. It has splendid breadth and sweep, and Fischer generates admirable excitement. While it does not necessarily displace the finest alternatives, it may well be considered alongside them. Gergiev and the Kirov orchestra on Philips remains recommendable too, and the finely controlled, aristocratic feel of the Pletnev (DG) version repays repeated hearing. All the same, no one who chooses this newcomer will feel short-changed.

Pletnev brings a fresh mind to this symphony, with his approach very much controlled, giving a strong sense of onward current and producing none of the heart-on-sleeve emotion in the slow movement. The clarity and lightness of articulation that distinguish his piano playing seem to be in ample evidence and, throughout the work, feeling is held in perfect control. It is a performance of quality, though the recording, while good, could be cleaner-detailed in the lower end of the range. Ensemble is endangered by some frenetically fast speeds – as in the finale. *The Rock* makes a generous coupling.

Gibson and the Scottish National Orchestra have the advantage of an excellent digital recording. The brass sounds are thrilling, but the slightly recessed balance of the strings is a drawback. But this is a freshly spontaneous performance and overall the sound is admirably natural, even if it includes some strangely unrhythmic thuds at climaxes (apparently the conductor in his excitement stamping on the podium).

From the brooding opening Maazel moves the *Allegro* away very swiftly (ignoring the composer's marking of *moderato*), and the powerful forward impulse creates considerable electricity. The *Scherzo* is crisp and brilliant, while the *Adagio*, with its long-breathed phrasing, reaches a powerful climax, only to be capped in the exhilaratingly brilliant finale with an apotheosis of even greater fervour. The brightly lit digital recording enhances the excitement, but in this work one ideally needs a warmer, more sumptuous sound. Again choosing a fast speed, Maazel's view of *The Isle of the Dead* is less sombre than usual, but the climaxes are certainly powerful and the result is intense and compelling.

As in his opera recordings, Gergiev gives a strong and well-paced reading, if lacking a little in individuality. Although he takes what one might think of as a more traditional approach, he brings an appropriate warmth and also possesses considerable command of the architecture.

Owain Arwel Hughes on BIS offers an exceptionally expansive reading of Rachmaninov's *Second Symphony*. It is expansive not only in the tempos he chooses and in his expressive style, but in his decision to observe the rarely performed exposition repeat in the first movement. Inevitably the tensions and thrust are markedly less than in the finest rival versions, a point brought out the more when the BIS recording balance sets the orchestra at a slight distance. With fine discipline from the Royal Scottish National Orchestra the result is refined and thoughtful rather than fervently passionate, emphasizing the beauty of sound.

Although Loughran's performance takes a little while to warm up, the reading does not lack intensity, with a fine slow movement, and the orchestral playing is excellent. He plays the work uncut (something that could not be taken for granted in 1973 when the record was made). The recording is vivid and refined in detail and the equally impressive coupling gives this bargain disc a playing time of 79 minutes.

After a slack start Zinman builds the symphony persuasively, if with less character than some, helped by first-rate playing from the Baltimore orchestra. Good, clean sound. The coupling is an attraction when, unlike most rivals, Zinman has *Vocalise* with soprano soloist, the radiant Sylvia McNair. Even with that extra, Zinman manages to observe the exposition repeat in the first movement of the symphony.

Symphony 3 in A min., Op. 44
(M) **(*) Decca (ADD) 468 490-2. LPO, Boult – VAUGHAN
WILLIAMS: *Symphony 8* ***

Symphony 3; Symphony in D min. (Youth); Vocalise
*** BIS CD 1299. RSNO, Arwel Hughes

Symphony 3; Symphonic Dances
(M) *** EMI 5 62809-2 [5 62810-2]. St Petersburg PO,
Jansons

(N) (M) *** Chan. 10234X. LSO, Järvi

**(*) DG 457 598-2. Russian Nat. O, Pletnev

(i) *Symphony 3*; (i-iii) *Spring* (cantata), *Op. 20*; (iii) *3
Unaccompanied Choruses*
⌚ *** Chan. 9802. (i) Russian State SO; (ii) Martyrosyan;
(iii) Russian State Symphonic Capella; Polyansky

Jansons's account of the *Third Symphony* is arguably the finest of the three (though his version of the *First* runs it close). Jansons has the merit of superb recorded sound and a competitive price-tag. The *Symphonic Dances* are masterly. In any event, the Jansons is strongly recommended.

A splendid, very Russian account of the *Third Symphony* from Polyansky, volatile but convincingly so, with some glorious playing from the strings, especially in the lovely, nostalgic secondary theme of the first movement which is so very Slavic in feeling. The choral works too are superbly done, with the widest range of dynamic in the masterly unaccompanied choruses, while Tigram Martyrosyan is a richly resonant bass soloist in the cantata. The singers are helped by the resonant acoustic which creates the richest vocal sonorities. For the symphony, competition is strong, but with state-of-the-art Chandos sound this new version is well worth considering.

Owain Arwel Hughes, following up his thoughtful reading of Rachmaninov's *Second Symphony*, draws from the Scottish National Orchestra a comparably well-played account of the *Third*, also brilliantly recorded with textures exceptionally clear. Again speeds are on the broad side in a reading less red-bloodedly emotional than most, with the BIS sound again slightly distanced. Yet while in the *Second Symphony* that brought a lessening of emotional thrust, the degree of restraint in the *Third Symphony* brings advantages. That is especially so in the central *Adagio*, where the lovely horn solo at the start and the sweet solo violin entry at a full *pianissimo* have a tenderness that is most moving. Though in the finale the treatment is exceptionally expansive, Hughes holds the structure together well to bring an exciting close with its wildly syncopated rhythms in the coda.

The symphonic movement in D minor, written in 1891, Rachmaninov's *Youth Symphony*, may merely hint at his mature style, but it makes an attractive coupling, while *Vocalise* brings a touchingly refined and restrained reading of a popular piece that has often prompted much heavier-handed accounts.

Järvi in his weighty, purposeful way misses some of the subtleties of this symphony (although not the *Symphonic Dances*), but with superb playing from the LSO – linking back to André Previn's unsurpassed reading with them – the intensity is magnetic, with even a very slow *Adagio* for the outer sections of the middle movement made to sound convincing, and with the finale thrusting on at an equivalently extreme tempo. The *Dances* too are superbly done, with the changes of tempo and mood in the third section both subtle and passionate. Outstanding recording too.

The Russian National Orchestra and Mikhail Pletnev also couple the symphony with the late *Symphonic Dances*. If you have acquired Pletnev's CD of the *Second Symphony* you will know that he has a special feeling for this composer and is completely steeped in his spiritual climate. Thus, he can persuade you that his interpretative idiosyncrasies – the very slow tempo he adopts for the interlude in the finale, just about seven minutes in, or his phrasing of the second subject of the first movement – are right. The opulent sound world of this wonderful score is beautifully served by his players (and in particular the strings). However, this is not a first choice.

For Sir Adrian Boult's early stereo (1956) recording of the *Third Symphony* the Walthamstow recording has come up vividly – it is remarkably well detailed, the stereo warm-toned and colourful. A greater breadth of tone from the higher strings would have been welcome, but the LPO play passionately for him and create a touching mood of very Russian nostalgia in the *Adagio*, particularly at the close, which is very haunting. The original *Gramophone* review mentioned Boult's 'splendid sense of movement', and this is very striking in the *Scherzo* section of the central movement, which is very successful, and in the lively finale. It is overall a most sympathetic performance. Boult does not let his own personality intrude, but he captures the idiom with conviction, and the remastered sound is certainly impressive. The coupling with Vaughan Williams is unexpected but works well.

CHAMBER MUSIC

Cello Sonata in G min., Op. 19
(M) *** Somm SOMMCD 026. Walton, Owen – CHOPIN: *Cello Sonata* ***

(B) *** EMI (ADD) 5 74333-2 (2). P. Tortelier, Ciccolini – CHOPIN; FAURE; MENDELSSOHN: *Cello Sonatas* ***

**(*) EMI 5 57505-2. Capuçon, Zilberstein – FRANCK: *Violin Sonata* **(*)

Cello Sonata in G min.; Lied; Melody on a Theme by Rachmaninov (arr. Altschuler/Hayroudinoff); *2 Pieces, Op. 2; Prelude, Op. 23/10; Vocalise*
**(*) Chan. 10095. Ivashkin, Hayroudinoff

Cello Sonata in G min.; Lied (Romance) in F min.; Mélodie in D; 2 Pieces, Op. 2; Romance in F, Op. 4/3; Vocalise
☛ (BB) *** Naxos 8.550987. Grebanier, Guggenheim

Cello Sonata in G min.; 2 Pieces, Op. 2; Vocalise, Op. 34/14
(N) (BB) *** Virgin 2x1 4 820867-2 (2). Mørk, Thibaudet – MIASKOVSKY; PROKOFIEV; SHOSTAKOVICH: *Cello Sonatas*; STRAVINSKY: *Suite Italienne* ***

Cello Sonata in G min.; 5 Pieces for Cello & Piano: Oriental Dance, Op. 2/2; Prelude, Op. 2/1; Romance; Vocalise, Op. 34/14 (with ALTSCHULLER: *Mélodie*)
☛ (BB) *** Double Decca 473 807-2 (2). Harrell, Ashkenazy – PROKOFIEV: *Cello Sonata*; SHOSTAKOVICH: *Cello Sonata*, etc. ***

Lynn Harrell and Vladimir Ashkenazy give an impassioned, full-throated account of the glorious *Cello Sonata* and they capture its melancholy perfectly. They are very well attuned to its sensibility and to the affecting drama of the smaller pieces. The Decca recording is in the high traditions of the house; the balance and perspective are completely natural. An outstanding bargain in the Double Decca series.

Michael Grebanier too gives it a powerful, richly expressive reading, with Janet Guggenheim an incisive partner, very clearly focused if not always as warm. The slow movement is most moving, the headlong finale thrilling in its clarity. The shorter pieces make up an excellent bargain disc to match rivals at premium price.

A first-class account from Jamie Walton and Charles Owen – warm, passionate and refined, with fine lyrical impetus in the finale. A good recording balance too, although the otherwise attractive acoustic does not offer the clearest separation.

Tortelier is at his finest here: Rachmaninov's passionate lines are shaped with the right degree of nervous tension, and if Ciccolini sounds rather more like an accompanist than a full participant, his playing is technically secure. Excellent recording.

The gifted Norwegian cellist Truls Mørk plays with a restrained eloquence that is totally compelling. The demanding (and commanding) piano part is given with authority and conviction by Thibaudet, and they handle the companion pieces excellently. The value of this well-recorded and well-balanced issue is enhanced by the attractive Miaskovsky, Prokofiev, Shostakovich and Stravinsky couplings, and this set is a remarkable bargain.

Alexander Ivashkin and Rustem Hayroudinoff give us the complete works for cello and piano, though it is only the *Sonata* that really counts. The *Two Pieces* of Op. 2 (a *Prelude* and *Danse orientale*) are very appealing, as is the slightly earlier *Lied*, written when Rachmaninov was seventeen. But the remainder are arrangements. Ivashkin produces a beautifully burnished, lustrous tone, and the playing of this duo is highly cultured. One would at times welcome more abandon in the second movement. One respected critic wrote that 'everything on this CD is mahogany brown and as mellow as a fine brandy' – nothing wrong with that, one might think. It is all thoroughly enjoyable and well (if forwardly) recorded, but for those wanting just the *Sonata* this is probably not a first choice.

The cellist Gautier Capuçon, less well known than his violinist brother, Renaud, gives a bold, big-scale performance of the Rachmaninov *Sonata*, with the big exposition repeat observed. Even though the reading is extrovert rather than thoughtful, with the piano-playing splashy at times, this is a most warmly enjoyable version, helped by being recorded live.

Trio élégiaque 1 in G min., Op. 8
☛ *** BIS CD 1302. Kempf Trio – TCHAIKOVSKY: *Piano Trio* ***

Rachmaninov's first *Trio élégique*, Op. 8, was written in 1892 and remained unpublished during the composer's lifetime. Although obviously drawing on the inspiration of the Tchaikovskian model, which Rachmaninov was to use again a year later for the *Second Trio*, the first is in a single movement. Its mood is tinged with melancholy throughout, surging to moments of ardour less extrovert than with Tchaikovsky, but with a characteristic Rachmaninovian ebb and flow of feeling, which is captured most spontaneously by these players. The performance here comes into competition with that by the superb Borodin Trio on Chandos, whose coupling is more logical; but on performance grounds, Kempf and his colleagues are by no means second best and are very well recorded.

Trios élégiaques 1 in G min., Op. 8; 2 in D min., Op. 9
*** Chan. 8431. Borodin Trio
*** Tavros EPT 4516. Koo, Sakharova, Arnadóttir

The *Trios* are both imbued with lyrical fervour and draw from the rich vein of melancholy so characteristic of Rachmaninov. The performances by the Borodin Trio are eloquent and masterly, and the recording is admirably balanced.

Korean pianist Yung Wook Koo, Russian violinist Julia Sakharova, with the warm-toned Icelandic cellist, Margarét Arnadóttir, make a fine team and give performances that are as passionate as they are lyrically spontaneous. The long elliptical first movement of Op. 8 is admirably shaped, and the pianist emerges with special distinction in the following even more extended set of variations. The *D minor Trio* is an elegy for Tchaikovsky and its atmosphere of Russian melancholy (the composer's marking is *lento lugubre*) is richly caught, notably by the cellist. The recording is vividly up front – on one occasion the bass end of the piano is made to seem right on top of the listener – but the performances are so committedly vivid and alive that this debut CD must be welcomed with enthusiasm. (The disc is available from Tavros Records, 1187 Coast Village Road, 1-288, Santa Barbara, California 93108, USA. Fax: 00-1-805-969-5749. E-mail: info@tavrosrecords.com)

Trios elégiaques 1 & 2, Opp. 8–9; 2 Pieces for Cello & Piano, Op. 2; 2 Pieces for Violin & Piano, Op. 6
*** Hyp. CDA 67178. Moscow Rachmaninov Trio

Apart from two incomplete string quartets and the *Cello Sonata*, Op. 19, the four works here comprise Rachmaninov's complete chamber output. The Moscow Rachmaninov Trio (Viktor Yampolsky, Mikhail Tsinman and Natalia Savinova) are superb artists and play this music with feeling and sensitivity. This can be strongly recommended alongside the Tavros issue from the Koo/Sakharova/Arnadóttir Trio, although the Hyperion disc has the advantage of including much more music.

PIANO MUSIC

Piano duet

Music for 2 pianos: (i) *Suites 1–2, Opp. 5 & 17; Symphonic Dances, Op. 45; Russian Rhapsody. For solo piano: Etudes-tableaux, Op. 33; Variations on a Theme by Corelli, Op. 42*
(B) *** Double Decca (ADD) 444 845-2 (2). Ashkenazy, (i) with Previn

Suites 1–2, Opp. 5 & 17; Symphonic Dances Op. 45
** Sony SK 61767. Ax, Bronfman

Suite 2; Russian Rhapsody, Op. posth.; Symphonic Dances
**(*) Hyp. CDA 66654. Demidenko, Alexeev — MEDTNER: *Russian Round Dance, etc.* **(*)

The colour and flair of Rachmaninov's writing in the two *Suites* (as inspired and tuneful as his concertos) are captured with wonderful imagination on Double Decca. The two-piano version of the *Symphonic Dances* is masterly and dazzling, and they are hardly less persuasive in the early *Russian Rhapsody*. Ashkenazy's superb solo performances of the *Etudes-tableaux* and the *Corelli Variations* (a rarity and a very fine work) cap the appeal of this bargain. The recording throughout is superb, with a natural presence and a most attractive ambience.

There are some beautiful things on the Alexeev-Demidenko disc. They shape the second group of the first of the *Symphonic Dances* with exquisite sensitivity and colour, and there are many other felicities elsewhere. However, even allowing for the hazards of two pianos, there is some ugly *fortissimo* tone. All the same there is much to delight the listener, even though Previn and Ashkenazy are to be preferred in this repertoire.

Emanuel Ax and Yefim Bronfman have impressive technical address, but they are curiously unresponsive to the atmosphere engendered by these glorious pieces. These artists relish the bright surfaces without penetrating much further.

Solo piano music

Andante ma non troppo in D min.; Canon in E min.; Fragments (1917); *Fughetta; Lento in D min. (Song Without Words; 1866–7); Moment musical, Op. 16/2 (rev. version, 1940); Morceau de fantaisie in G min.; Oriental Sketch* (1917); *Prelude in F* (1891); *Variations on a Theme of Chopin, Op. 22*
(BB) *** Naxos 8.554426. Biret

Idil Biret's Rachmaninov recital here brings a powerful yet poetic reading of the *Chopin Variations*, one of Rachmaninov's finest piano works, coupled with miniatures and rarities including many rare early pieces. Biret's reading of the *Variations*, a work seriously neglected, brings out the high dramatic contrasts, cleanly establishing the character of each section and setting the whole structure (overall almost sonata-like) in relief. The fill-ups include an unpretentious little piece, *Lento*, that Rachmaninov wrote at thirteen, and demonstrations of his prowess in writing counterpoint, untypical but crisply refreshing. Excellent sound to bring out the subtleties of Biret's tonal shading.

Elégie, Op. 3/1; Etudes-tableaux, Op. 39/3 & 5; Moments musicaux, Op. 16/3–6; Preludes, Op. 23/1, 2, 5 & 6; Op. 32/12
(B) *** EMI (ADD) Red Line 5 69869. Gavrilov (with RAVEL: *Gaspard de la nuit*) — SCRIABIN: *Preludes* ***

There is some pretty remarkable playing here, especially in the stormy *B flat major Prelude*, while the *G sharp minor* from Op. 32 has a proper sense of fantasy. More prodigious bravura provides real excitement in the *F sharp minor Etude-tableau*, Op. 39/3, and in the *E minor Moment musical*, while Gavrilov relaxes winningly in the *Andante cantabile* of Op. 16/3 and the *Elégie*. Sometimes his impetuosity almost carries him away, and the piano is placed rather near the listener so that we are nearly taken with him, but there is no doubt about the quality of this recital.

Etudes-tableaux, Opp. 33 & 39; Fragments; Fughetta in F; Mélodie in E; Moments musicaux; Morceaux de fantaisie; Morceaux de salon; 3 Nocturnes; Oriental sketch; 4 Pieces; Piece in D min.; 25 Preludes (complete); Sonatas 1–3 (including original & revised versions of 2); Song Without Words; Transcriptions (complete); Variations: On a Theme of Chopin; On a Theme of Corelli
(M) *** Hyp. CDS 44041/8 (8). Shelley

Hyperion have collected Howard Shelley's exemplary survey of Rachmaninov into a mid-price, eight-CD set, and very good it is, too. Shelley can hold his own against most rivals not only in terms of poetic feeling but in keyboard authority and virtuosity. The recordings are variable in quality but mostly excellent.

Etudes-tableaux, Opp. 33 & 39
*** Hyp. CDA 66091. Shelley
(N) (BB) *** EMI Encore 5 85817-2. Ovchinnikov

The conviction and thoughtfulness of Shelley's playing, coupled with excellent modern sound, make this convenient coupling a formidable rival to Ashkenazy's classic versions, which in any case are not coupled together on CD.

Impressive and authoritative performances of all the *Études-tableaux* from Vladimir Ovchinnikov, whose playing cannot be faulted on any level and has the advantage of excellent recorded sound. These were recorded in 1989 at Abbey Road, not long after he performed the memorable feat of playing all 17 pieces straight through in London's Wigmore Hall. A genuine bargain.

Etudes-tableaux, Opp. 33 & 39; 6 Preludes, Op. 23/1–2, 4–5, 7–8; 7 Preludes, Op. 32/1–2, 6–7, 9–10, 12
(BB) *** Regis (DDD/ADD) RRC 1022. Richter

Although he played them in public, Sviatoslav Richter did not record all the *Preludes*, only the ones he liked best. Those here were recorded in 1971 but the *Etudes-tableaux* are later digital recordings. The playing is of a rare order of mastery and leaves strong and powerful resonances. Richter's conception goes far beyond the abundant virtuosity this music calls for and the characterization is very strong and searching. The sound quality is less than ideal, a bit hard and two-dimensional, but fully acceptable when the playing is so riveting. This reissue (of the original Olympia CD) is unique and not to be missed.

Moments musicaux; Morceaux de salon, Op. 10
*** Hyp. CDA 66184. Shelley

Howard Shelley has a highly developed feeling for Rachmaninov and distinguishes himself again here both by masterly pianism and by a refined awareness of Rachmaninov's sound-world. The recording is eminently realistic and natural.

Moments musicaux, Op. 16; Preludes, Op. 3/2; Op. 23/1–10
*** Erato 8573 85770-2. Lugansky

Nikolai Lugansky belongs to the same generation as Andsnes and Kissin, and those who acquired his Chopin *Etudes* on Erato will know that he is an artist of impeccable technique and taste. He was a protégé of Tatiana Nikolayeva and won the Tchaikovsky Prize, whose winners have included Pletnev (under whose baton he appeared in London). His musicianship in this repertoire is no less impressive; there is plenty of virtuosity but none of his playing is too ostentatious. As impressive an account of this repertoire as we have had since Ashkenazy and Shelley, and warmly recommended.

Morceaux de fantaisie, Op. 3; Sonata 2 in B flat min., Op. 36 (revised, 1931 version); Variations on a Theme of Corelli, Op. 42
*** Danacord DACOCD 525. Marshev

Oleg Marshev possesses the grand manner, and has won golden opinions for his Russian repertoire. Listening to his Rachmaninov, one can see why, for apart from flawless technical address and sensitivity, he has an innate feeling for this repertoire. His account of all three pieces belongs up there with the finest, though in the *Corelli Variations* Pletnev is in a class of his own. The dryish recording, if not ideal, is perfectly serviceable and should not deter readers from investigating some superbly idiomatic Rachmaninov playing.

Morceaux de fantaisie, Op. 3; Sonata 2 in B flat min., Op. 36; Variations on a Theme of Chopin, Op. 22
⊶ ❂ *** Elan 82248. Rodriguez

Préludes, Op. 32/1–13 ; Sonata 1 in D min., Op. 28
⊶ ❂ *** Elan 82244. Rodriguez

This is some Rachmaninov playing! Santiago Rodriguez is the real thing. For a moment one imagines that Rachmaninov himself is at the keyboard. Rodriguez has something of Pletnev about him: wonderful authority and immaculate technical control, tremendous electricity as well as great poetic feeling. Outstanding in every way.

24 Preludes (complete); Piano Sonata 2
(M) Decca 443 841-2 (2). Ashkenazy
⊶ (M) *** Decca (ADD) 467 685-2. Ashkenazy (without *Sonata*)

24 Preludes; Preludes in D min. & F; Morceaux de fantaisie, Op. 3
*** Hyp. CDA 66081/2 (available separately). Shelley

24 Preludes, Op. 23/1–10; Op. 32/1–13; in D min. Mélodie; 6 Moments musicaux, Op. 16; Morceaux de fantaisie, Op. 3; Oriental Sketch; Song Transcriptions: Daisies; Lilacs
(B) *** Virgin 2x1 5 61624 (2). Alexeev

There is superb flair and panache about Ashkenazy's playing and his poetic feeling is second to none. For its Legends reissue the whole set has been accommodated on a single mid-priced CD playing for just over 80 minutes, and as such sweeps the board, for the new transfer offers a most realistic piano image.

Shelley is a compellingly individual interpreter of Rachmaninov. Each one of the *Preludes* strikes an original chord in him. These are very different readings from those of Ashkenazy but their intensity is well caught in full if reverberant recording.

Dmitri Alexeev's 1989 two-CD set of the *Preludes* and various other works brings us formidable and powerful pianism. His mastery is evident throughout, and although there are occasions, such as in the *B minor Prelude*, Op. 32, No. 10, where one misses the depth and poetic feeling of some rivals, the recital is a satisfying one and value for money.

Piano Sonatas 1 in D min., Op. 28; 2 in B flat min., Op. 36 (revised 1931)
*** Hyp. CDA 66047. Shelley

Piano Sonata 2 in B flat min., Op. 36 (original version); Fragments in A flat; Fughetta in F; Gavotte in D; Mélodie in E; Morceau de fantaisie in G min.; Nocturnes 1–3; Oriental Sketch in B flat; Piece in D min.; 4 Pieces; Prelude in E flat min.; Romance in F sharp min.; Song Without Words in D min.
*** Hyp. CDA 66198. Shelley

Piano Sonata 2, Op. 36 (original version); Etudes-tableaux, Op. 39; trans. of KREISLER: *Liebesleid*
*** BIS CD-1042. Kempf

On CDA 66047, Howard Shelley offers the 1931 version of the *B flat Sonata*. He has plenty of sweep and grandeur and an appealing freshness, ardour and, when required, tenderness. He is accorded an excellent balance by the engineers.

Shelley then on CDA 66198 gives us the original version of Op. 36 and his performances here show unfailing sensitivity, intelligence and good taste. They have the merit of excellent recorded sound.

Freddy Kempf has a real feeling for this composer, and the authority and technical prowess to go with it. He is also a narrative pianist – from the very beginning he has you in the palm of his hand. The *Second Sonata* in the original, 1913 version is as good as any now before the public, and the *Etudes-tableaux* come off equally well. Vivid, realistic piano sound.

Piano Sonata 2, Op. 36 (rev. 1931); Preludes, Op. 3/2; Op. 23/1–2, 4–5, 10; Op. 32/2, 12; Siren, Op. 21/5; Margaritiki, Op. 38/3; Transcriptions: Scherzo from 'A Midsummer Night's Dream' (Mendelssohn); Flight of the Bumblebee (Rimsky-Korsakov); Lullaby (Tchaikovsky)
(N) ❂*** EMI 5 57943-2. Trpčeski

Simon Trpčeski's début recital last year (Prokofiev's *Sixth Sonata*, Scriabin's *Fifth* and *Petrushka*) collected some enthusiastic reviews, including one from us. This dazzling Rachmaninov recital reaffirms the arrival on the piano scene of a young keyboard master. His is an exciting talent, and this is wonderful Rachmaninov playing, expertly recorded in Potton Hall, Suffolk.

Transcriptions: *Daisies; Lilacs; Polka de W. R.; Vocalise.* BACH: *Prelude; Gavotte; Gigue.* BIZET: *Minuet from L'Arlésienne.* KREISLER: *Liebesleid; Liebesfreud.* MENDELSSOHN: *Midsummer Night's Dream: Scherzo.* MUSSORGSKY: *Sorochinsky Fair: Gopak.* RIMSKY-KORSAKOV: *Flight of the Bumblebee.* SCHUBERT: *Wohin?.* TCHAIKOVSKY: *Lullaby*
*** Hyp. CDA 66486. Shelley

Shelley plays with an authority and sensitivity that is wholly persuasive and dispatches the virtuoso transcriptions to the manner born. The transcription of the *Vocalise* is by Zoltán Kocsis, but otherwise all are Rachmaninov's own.

Variations on a Theme of Chopin, Op. 22; Variations on a Theme of Corelli, Op. 42; Mélodie in E, Op. 3/3
*** Hyp. CDA 66009. Shelley — MENDELSSOHN: *Scherzo* ***

Howard Shelley gives dazzling, consistently compelling performances, full of virtuoso flair. First-rate piano sound.

Recitals

'A Window in Time': Barcarolle, Op. 10/3; Elégie; Mélodie, Op. 3/3; Etudes-tableaux, Op. 39/4 & 6; Humoresque, Op. 10/6; Polinchinelle; Polka de V.R.; Preludes, Op. 3/2 & 4; Op. 23/5; Lilacs. Transcriptions: RIMSKY-KORSAKOV: *Flight of the Bumblebee.* KREISLER: *Liebesfreud; Liebesleid.* SCHUBERT: *Wohin?.* BIZET: *L'Arlésienne: Minuet.* MUSSORGSKY: *Sorochinsky Fair: Gopak.* TRAD.: *Star-Spangled Banner*
✹ (N) *** Telarc CD 80489. Rachmaninov

For once we award a Rosette out of sheer astonishment as well as admiration. There have been previous attempts to realize piano-roll recordings in LP and CD terms, but none to compare with this. As he explains in the accompanying note, Wayne Stahnke has re-created these recordings made by Rachmaninov between 1919 and 1929, using Ampico music rolls, only he has used modern computer technology via a Bösendorfer piano, then re-recorded digitally. The realism and sense of the composer's presence is amazing. There is no problem here about catching the most varied and subtle rubato or variations of dynamic, and in a transcription like the *Flight of the Bumblebee* the bravura is electrifying. *Lilacs* is captivating in its nuances of colour and Bizet's *Minuet* delicately entrancing. The freedom of style in the two Kreisler transcriptions, and indeed the famous *Prelude in C sharp minor*, which opens the programme dramatically, is remarkable. Needless to say the sound of the piano itself is very real and three-dimensional. Even after reading these comments we guarantee a surprise when you hear the disc itself!

VOCAL MUSIC

Songs: *All passes; All was taken from me; At my window; Before the icon; By a fresh grave; Christ is risen; Fate; The fountain; Night; Fragments from A. Musset; How pained I am; How peaceful; I am again alone; I am not a prophet; I*
beg for mercy; Lilacs; Let us leave, my sweet; Melody; Night is sorrowful; On the death of a siskin; The ring; There are many sounds; They replied; To my children; Twilight; Two farewells; We shall rest; Yesterday we met
*** Chan. 9451. Rodgers, Popescu, Naoumenko, Leiferkus, Shelley

Fluent in Russian, Joan Rodgers with her richly expressive voice makes a perfect interpreter of Rachmaninov songs, ideally partnered by the pianist, Howard Shelley. This generous selection of those for soprano ranges through the whole of the composer's songwriting career up to his exile from Russia in 1917, when in rejection of his roots he stopped completely. Loveliest of the songs is the extended wordless *Vocalise*, here set against its neighbour in Op. 34, the dramatic song, *Dissonance*. Most distinctive are the six forward-looking songs, Op. 38, to words by symbolist poets.

The Bells, Op. 35
☛ ✿ *** DG 471 029-2. Mescheriakov, Larin, Chernov, Moscow State Ch., Russian Nat. O, Pletnev – TANEYEV: *John of Damascus* ***
(B) *** EMI (ADD) double forte 5 73353-2 (2). Armstrong, Tear, Shirley-Quirk, LSO & Ch., Previn – PROKOFIEV: *Alexander Nevsky; Ivan the Terrible* ***
*** Telarc CD 80363. Fleming, Dent, Ledbetter, Atlanta Ch. & SO, Shaw – ADAMS: *Harmonium* ***

From Pletnev comes a performance and recording that shows *The Bells* in an entirely new light. He has his finger on the composer's pulse and always has special insights to bring to his music. He goes beyond the music's vivid colours and lush sonorities, and without in any way indulging in over-characterization gets singing and playing of impressive quality, much subtlety and intensity. With Rachmaninov, as with Tchaikovsky, Pletnev seems to have great affinity of temperament and spirit. The recording is first class.

The late Robert Shaw conducts a colourfully expansive performance of Rachmaninov's cantata. The special melancholy of the finale is touchingly conveyed, with a fine orchestral response as well as an ardent contribution from the choir. All three soloists are impressive and if Renée Fleming, who sings beautifully, is not especially Slavonic, in the closing *Lento lugubre* the baritone, Victor Ledbetter, catches the darkly expressive mood admirably. Anyone wanting the spectacular Adams work should be well satisfied with Shaw's Rachmaninov.

In *The Bells*, Previn's concentration on purely musical values as much as on evocation of atmosphere produces powerful results, even when the recording has lost just a little of its original ambient warmth in favour of added presence and choral brilliance. The soloists are excellent.

6 Choruses for Women's Voices, Op. 15
(N) *** Chan. 10311. Russian State Symphony Cappella & SO, Polyansky – SCRIABIN: *Symphony 1* ***

The *Choruses* for children's or women's voices come from the period just before the disastrous première of the *First Symphony*, when the composer was in his early twenties and teaching at the Mariinsky Ladies' School. And they are as appealing as they are demanding, the most haunting being the Lermontov setting, *The pine tree*, and *Dreaming waves*, both of which cast a distinct spell. A small point, since Chandos claims a première recording: there have been earlier versions, by Andrey Zaboronok and the Bolshoi Theatre Children's Choir (Chant du Monde) and the USSR Radio

Chorus with Svetlanov at the piano (Melodiya). But neither of these versions is now current, and collectors attracted to this CD need not hesitate.

Liturgy of St John Chrysostom, Op. 31

☞ ✿ (B) *** EMI double forte (ADD) 5 68664-2 (2). Maximova, Zorova, Vidov, Stoytsov, Petrov, Bulgarian R. Ch., Milkov

*** Hyp. CDA 66703. Corydon Singers, Best

Rachmaninov's *Liturgy of St John Chrysostom*, written in 1910, is an even fuller setting than Tchaikovsky's of 1878, and listening to this glorious performance by the Chorus of Bulgarian Radio, recorded in the spacious acoustics of the Alexander Nevsky Memorial Cathedral in Sofia, one can be in no doubt that the work's powerful expressive feeling has an underlying deep spirituality, while the performance itself conveys great religious fervour. Apart from the continuing dialogue between cantor (Ivan Petrov) and chorus (in which the soloists also participate), there are moments of overwhelming simple beauty, as in the sublime, sustained *Cheroubikon* ('*Cherubic hymn*'). It would be difficult to imagine this superbly recorded performance being bettered and, although the spacious tempi (which are sustained with continuing concentration) mean that the work runs to 97 minutes, the set is offered in EMI's forte series so that the two discs are offered for the price of one. It is a pity that a full text with translation is not included, but the presentation is otherwise fully acceptable.

The fine Hyperion alternative is a sharper, more cleanly enunciated account – the choral sound is without that misty focus which is so much part of the character of Slavic a capella singing. It is immensely stimulating, and very well recorded and documented. However, the Corydons curiously omit the prayer dialogue which is the centrepiece of the *Cherubic Hymn* and which in Sofia brings such a strikingly exhilarating response from the chorus. There are various other versions in the catalogue, including a superbly sung and deeply moving account from the St Petersburg Chamber Choir under Nikolai Korniev (Philips 442 776-2). But this has been cut to fit on to a single CD. If you have already succumbed to the *Vespers*, you won't be disappointed with *St John Chrysostom's Liturgy*.

3 Russian Songs, Op. 41

(N) *** Warner 2564 61992-2. Latvian Ch., Nordic SO, Tali – SIBELIUS: *The Wood-Nymph*; TUUR: *Zeitraum*; *Action, Passion, Illusion* ***

These glorious songs were composed for Stokowski and the Philadelphia Orchestra, who gave the first performance in 1928. They are sung by these Baltic forces with feeling, though memories of Kondrashin's full-blooded, intoxicating account from the mid-1960s are not banished. But we are not spoilt for choice in this repertoire, and the enterprising coupling is well worth the money.

Vespers, Op. 37

☞ (M) ✿ *** HM Chant du Monde RUS 788050. St Petersburg Capella, Chernuchenko

(M) *** Virgin 5 61845-2. Emman, Björsund, Höglund, Swedish R. Ch., Kaljuste

*** Hyp. CDA 66460. Corydon Singers, Best

*** EMI 5 56752-2. King's College Ch., Cleobury

Rachmaninov's *Vespers* – more correctly the '*All-night Vigil*' – rank not only among his most soulful and intensely powerful music but are also the finest of all Russian choral works. The St Petersburg Capella is in fact the Mikhail Glinka Choir and their lineage goes back to the fifteenth century. Their earlier recording of the piece was pretty impressive. Even so, this newcomer surpasses it and offers singing of an extraordinarily rapt intensity. The dynamic range is enormous, the perfection of ensemble and blend and the sheer beauty of tone such as to exhaust superlatives. The recording does them justice and is made in a suitably atmospheric acoustic.

Under Tõnu Kaljuste the Swedish Radio Choir's account of the *Vespers* shows that they have lost nothing of their sensitivity or command of sonority. They can produce a wonderful range of colour from the darkest to the most luminous. Their Russian sounds totally authentic too. This is undoubtedly one of the finest versions available, with its own special character.

Though Matthew Best's British choir, the Corydon Singers, lacks the dark timbres associated with Russian choruses and though the result could be weightier and more biting, theirs is still a most beautiful performance, very well sung and recorded in an atmospheric, reverberant setting.

It also makes a moving experience having the Anglican tradition, as ideally represented by the choir of King's College, Cambridge, meeting the Russian Orthodox tradition, represented by Rachmaninov's supremely beautiful setting of the *All-night Vigil*. Against the warm acoustic of King's College Chapel, beauty and refinement are the keynotes. The precision of ensemble and subtlety of dynamic shading – remarkable from a choir of young singers – are given extra freshness with the high dramatic contrasts. However, of the English versions, Matthew Best has the more authentic ring.

OPERA

(i) *Aleko;* (ii); *Francesca da Rimini;* (iii) *The Miserly Knight*

☞ (B) *** DG Trio 477 041-2 (3). Levitsky, Kotscherga, Von Otter; (i; ii) Guleghina, Leiferkus; (ii; iii) Larin, Aleksashkin; (iii) Chernov, Caley, Gothenburg SO, Järvi

DG recorded all three of Rachmaninov's operas in 1996, issuing them in a box, then followed up with three separate issues at full price. Now, they return to the catalogue as a bargain Trio, but without texts and translations. Rachmaninov wrote the one-act *Aleko* (based on Pushkin) when he was still a teenager, completing it (with orchestration) in only seventeen days. It is rather like a Russian-flavoured *Cavalleria rusticana*, with the hero murdering his unfaithful sweetheart and her lover, but musically it brings echoes of Borodin, notably in evocative choruses like Polovtsian dances. Distinctive Rachmaninov fingerprints are few, but the result is most attractive, particularly in a performance like this, ideally cast, with Sergei Leiferkus a commanding Aleko and Neeme Järvi a warmly persuasive conductor.

Francesca da Rimini comes from 1906 and, like *The Miserly Knight*, shows something of the effect Bayreuth had on him. The opera is encumbered by an unsatisfactory libretto by Modest Tchaikovsky, but there is some glorious music and some fine singing from Maria Guleghina as Francesca and Sergei Leiferkus as Lanciotto Malatesta, the jealous husband. Sergei Larin makes a convincing Paolo, and the Gothenburg Orchestra and Chorus again respond magnificently to Neeme Järvi. The recording quality is quite outstanding.

The Miserly Knight, to a Pushkin text, contrasts the old knight, whose devotion to gold is total, and his son, who eyes his father's fortune enviously. The famous soliloquy, arguably Rachmaninov's finest dramatic scena, is powerfully done by Sergei Aleksashkin, who succeeds in winning us over to the Knight. Sergei Larin is hardly less convincing as his son, Albert. The outstanding recording and the fine orchestral playing make this a most desirable set.

The Miserly Knight (DVD version)

(N) ✪ *** Opus Arte **DVD** oA 0919D. Leiferkus, Berkeley-Steele, Mikhailov, Voynarowsky, Schagidullin, LPO, Jurowski (Producer: Annabel Arden; V/D: James Whitbourn)

Though it is now represented on CD, readers need look no further than this DVD of the 2004 Glyndebourne production of *The Miserly Knight*, filmed at the performance on 11 June. Visually it is sumptuous, musically it is superlative. Composed in 1906 for Chaliapin, this production has a magnificent successor in Sergei Leiferkus, who dominates the stage. Apart from his magnificent voice and compelling acting, he has tremendous presence. It is difficult to find any flaw with the other members of the cast either. There is an almost symphonic feel to the opera, and Vladimir Jurowksi gets a thoroughly idiomatic sonority from the London Philharmonic. The production is a fine one, refreshingly unobtrusive and free from the egotism that mars so much that goes on in the opera house these days, and the camera direction is equally distinguished. There are subtitles in English, French, German, Spanish and Italian, as well as excellent documentation from Dennis Marks. There is an illustrated synopsis on the disc as well as interviews with those taking part in the production. Recommended with enthusiasm.

(i) *Monna Vanna* (incomplete opera: Act I, orch. Buketoff); (ii) *Piano Concerto 4* (original version)
**(*) Chan. 8987. (i) Milnes, McCoy, Walker, Karoustos, Thorsteinsson, Blythe; (ii) Black; Iceland SO, Buketoff

Monna Vanna is the fragment of an opera based on Maeterlinck. Rachmaninov thought so well of the fragment that it was the one score he brought away from Russia after the Revolution. Igor Buketoff, who knew the composer, has rescued this Act I score and orchestrated it very sensitively to make an interesting curiosity. In its ripely romantic manner the writing has lyrical warmth and flows freely, thrusting home climactic moments. Buketoff's performance with the Iceland Symphony is warmly convincing, but the singing is flawed, with Sherrill Milnes, as Monna Vanna's jealous husband, standing out from an indifferent team, otherwise thin-toned and often wobbly. Buketoff's resurrection of the original score of the *Fourth Piano Concerto* is rather more expansive than the text we know. William Black is the powerful soloist, though the piano sound, unlike that of the orchestra, lacks weight.

RAID, Kaljo (born 1922)

Symphony 1 in C min.
*** Chan. 8525. SNO, Järvi – ELLER: *Dawn; Elegia*, etc. ***

Raid's *First Symphony* shows a genuine feel for form and a fine sense of proportion, even though the personality is not fully formed. Well worth hearing. Neeme Järvi gets very committed playing from the Scottish National Orchestra and the recording is warm and well detailed.

RAMEAU, Jean Philippe (1683–1764)

Anacréon: Suite; Daphnis et Eglé: Suite
☛ (BB) *** Naxos 8.553746. Capella Savaria, Térey-Smith

The *Suite* from *Anacréon* is essentially lighthearted music, particularly vivid in its scoring, piquantly using sopranino recorders, notably in the *Premier et deuxième air vif*, the infectious *Premier et deuxième tambourin*, but even more strikingly in the penultimate *Bacchanales*. The *Suite* from *Daphnis et Eglé* is much longer and more varied including a gracious *Sarabande très tendre*, a *Gigue*, a *Gavotte*, a touching *Musette* and a sprightly *Contredanse très vive* to end. The Capella Savaria, using period instruments with fair panache, play all this music with considerable finesse and much spirit, and they are very well recorded.

Les Boréades (suite of dances); Le Naissance d'Osiris: Suite
(BB) **(*) Naxos 8.553388. Capella Savaria, Térey-Smith

The two suites on the second disc from Capella Savaria are also inventive, but, with a few exceptions, the various dances and interludes are less ear-tickling than those on the companion CD. The playing is lively and robust, with plenty of colour (including the use of horns in *Les Boréades*).

Dardanus: Suite; Les Indes galantes: Suite
(BB) *** DHM/BMG 05472 77420-2. Coll. Aur.

Any abrasiveness here deriving from the use of original instruments is countered by the generous acoustics of the Cedernsaal in the Schloss Kirchheim. But the playing has both life and elegance and the sound, though warm and full, is by no means bland: the flutes and oboes (and trumpets in *Les Indes galantes*) bring plenty of added colour. The selection from *Les Indes galantes* is shorter than that provided by Herreweghe, but many will welcome the coupling with *Dardanus*. At super-bargain price this is very recommendable.

Ballet music: Les Fêtes d'Hébé; Hippolyte et Aricie
*** Erato 3984 26129-2. Les Arts Florissants, Christie – M.-A. CHARPENTIER: *La Descente d'Orphée aux Enfers*, etc. ***

These extended selections from two of Rameau's ever-inventive and charmingly scored opera-ballets were recorded to celebrate the twenty-fifth anniversary of William Christie and Les Arts Florissants. This is all delightfully fresh and inventive music and Rameau's scoring is ever-resourceful and as presented here constantly sparkling and ear-tickling. Most entertaining and beautifully recorded.

Hippolyte et Aricie: Orchestral Suite
(N) (B) *** DHM/BMG 74321 935542. La Petite Bande, Sigiswald Kuijken

This CD collects all the orchestral music from *Hippolyte et Aricie*, with a long introductory Prologue and a section for each of the five Acts. The melodic invention is fresh and its orchestral presentation ingenious. Sigiswald Kuijken draws delightful results from his ensemble. In every way this is an outstanding reissue – and not least for the quality of the recorded sound.

Les Indes galantes: Suites for Orchestra
(B) *** HM (ADD) HMA 1951130. Chapelle Royale O, Herreweghe

Besides the harpsichord arrangements listed below, Rameau

also arranged his four 'concerts' of music from *Les Indes galantes* for orchestra. The result makes nearly three-quarters of an hour of agreeable listening, especially when played so elegantly – and painlessly – on original instruments, and very well recorded (in 1984) by Harmonia Mundi.

Naïs: Orchestral Suite. Le Temple de la gloire: Orchestral Suite
*** HM HMU 907121. Philh. Bar. O, McGegan

There is much delightful music here and the playing by the Philharmonia Baroque Orchestra has ravishing finesse, showing original instruments at their most persuasively delicate, textures always transparent; the ear is continually beguiled by this warm and polished playing, beautifully recorded. A quite lovely disc.

CHAMBER MUSIC

Pièces de clavecin en concert 1–5
(N) (B) *** HM Musique d'abord HMA 195 1418. Rousset, Terakado, Uemura

(BB) *** Virgin 2×1 5 61872-2 (2). Trio Sonnerie –
   FORQUERAY: *Harpsichord Suites* ***
**(*) BIS CD 1385. L. Baroque, Medlam

The instrumental *Pièces de clavecin* usually include a flute, but they are equally valid in the alternative format on Harmonia Mundi with baroque violin and viola da gamba. The playing is attractively spirited and rhythmically buoyant; the effect with period instruments brings a slightly abrasive edge at times, but not disagreeably so. The star here is Christophe Rousset, whose very imaginative contribution lights up this music-making. The recording is realistic and the balance excellent. At bargain price, well worth considering.

The Trio Sonnerie (Monica Huggett, Mitzi Meyerson and Sarah Cunningham) are also perfectly attuned to the sensibility of the period and its requirements. Theirs is a performance which exhibits a sense of style and a quality of feeling that outweigh any shortcomings. They too choose to limit the instrumental colours available to them by confining themselves to string instruments, excluding the flute which is usual in this repertoire. The Virgin recording is of great naturalness and presence and this reissue, with its excellent coupling, is a strong contender.

London Baroque also play with style, expressive feeling and much vitality. The BIS recording, too, is notable for its inner clarity, balancing the harpsichord very well with the strings. The snag for some listeners is that Ingrid Seifert's violin tone is thin and edgy and will not appeal to those who are not completely converted to period-instrument timbre at its most abrasive.

KEYBOARD MUSIC

Music for Harpsichord: *Book I* (1706); *Pièces de clavecin* (1724); *Nouvelles Suites de pièces de clavecin* (c. 1728); *5 Pièces* (1741); *La Dauphine* (1747)
☛ (M) *** Decca 475 493-2 (2). Rousset (harpsichord)

Christophe Rousset's coverage of Rameau's keyboard music deservedly won the *Gramophone*'s Baroque Non-Vocal Award in 1992. Rousset's playing is marvellously persuasive and vital, authoritative and scholarly, yet fresh and completely free from the straitjacket of academic rectitude. The recording is

excellent and this is most welcome, back in the catalogue at mid-price.

Pièces de clavecin, Book I: Suite in A min. (1706); *Suites in E min.; D min.* (1724, rev. 1731)
*** Chan. 0659. Yates (harpsichord)

Sophie Yates gives us Book I complete and plays it very appealingly indeed. Her ornamentation has flair and she is especially winning in the named pieces (notably the delightful *Vénétienne* in the *A minor* suite and the cascading *La Joyeuse* in the *D minor*). She uses a copy by Andrew Garlick of a 1749 Goujon harpsichord which has a most attractive palette, and she is very well recorded.

Pièces de clavecin, Book I: Suite in A min.; L'Agaçante; La Dauphine; L'Indiscrète; La Livri; La Pantomime: La Timide
(M) *** CRD (ADD) CRD 3320. Pinnock

Harpsichord Suites: in A min. (1728); *in E min.* (1724)
(M) *** CRD (ADD) CRD 3310. Pinnock

Harpsichord Suites: in D min./maj. (1724); *in G maj./min.* (1728)
(M) *** CRD (ADD) CRD 3330. Pinnock

Trevor Pinnock chose a mellow instrument here, making his stylish, crisply rhythmic performances even more attractive. The first selection includes *La Dauphine*, the last keyboard piece which Rameau wrote, brilliantly performed. Pinnock is restrained in the matter of ornamentation, but his direct manner is both eloquent and stylish. The harpsichord is of the French type and is excellently recorded.

Suite de clavecin in E min. (1724)
(BB) *** HM Solo HMS 926018. Christie (harpsichord)

Rameau's *E minor Suite* is one of his most inventive, from the bursting birdsong of *Le Rappel des oiseaux* to the charming portrait of *La Villageoise*, while the penultimate movement, a tender *Musette en rondeau*, is splendidly contrasted with the rumbustious closing *Tambourin*. William Christie plays the whole suite with infectious spontaneity and in fine style, and his Goujon-Swanen harpsichord is vividly recorded.

OPERA-BALLET AND OPERA

Les Boréades (complete)
(M) *** Erato (ADD) 2292 45572-2 (3). Smith, Rodde, Langridge, Aler, Lafont, Monteverdi Ch., E. Bar. Sol., Gardiner

Though the story – involving the followers of Boreas, the storm god – is highly artificial, the music, involving many crisp and brief dances and arias, is as vital and alive as anything Rameau ever wrote. Gardiner here directs an electrifying performance with generally first-rate singing, except that Jennifer Smith's upper register, in the central role of Alphise, Queen of Baltria, is not sweet. Chorus and orchestra are outstanding and the recording excellent. Bizarre copyright problems prevented a libretto from being included, which makes it hard to follow the plot because the synopsis is not cued. However, the set is very welcome.

Castor et Pollux (complete)
*** HM HMC 901435/7. Crook, Corréas, Mellon, Gens, Schirrer, Brua, Piau, Les Arts Florissants Ch. & O, Christie

William Christie's performance of Rameau's second *tragédie en musique* uses the original 1733 text, quite different from the 1754 text recorded by Charles Farncombe. Christie's performance consistently benefits from the dramatic timing, not least in the fluently alert and idiomatic exchanges in recitative, as well as in the broad, expressive treatment of set numbers like Telaire's lament, *Tristes apprets*, beautifully sung by Agnès Mellon. With such fine sopranos as Véronique Gens and Sandrine Piau in relatively small roles, the cast has no weakness. Howard Crook has the clear tenor needed for the role of Castor (who appears very late in the drama), with Jérôme Corréas a stylish Pollux. The sound is fresh and immediate and has plenty of body, with military percussion beautifully caught. This is now a clear first choice.

Dardanus (complete)

⊙➖ **(N)** **(M)** *** DG 476 7250 (2). Mark Ainsley, Gens, Naouri, Delunsch, Courtis, Smythe, Ko_ená, Masset, Bindi, Ch. & Musiciens du Louvre, Minkowski

(M) **(*) Erato (ADD) 4509 95312-2 (2). Gautier, Eda-Pierre, von Stade, Devlin, Teucer, Soyer, van Dam, Paris Op. Ch. & O, Leppard

Strongly cast and characterfully conducted, Minkowski's version offers a magnetic, lively reading of one of Rameau's finest *tragédies lyriques*. For reasons Minkowski explains, he opts for the earlier 1739 version of the score, but includes the most inspired passage from the 1744 revision, incompatible when its second half involves quite a different plot. So Dardanus' extended prison monologue, *Lieux funestes*, from 1744 is included as a moving prelude to Act IV. The striking combination of thrustful vigour and refinement in Minkowski's direction is instantly established in the Overture, and marks the whole performance, including the colourful dance movements which round off each act. The soloists are excellent, with Mireille Delunsch singing with beauty and biting dramatic power as Venus, and with Véronique Gens similarly beautiful yet subtly contrasted as the heroine, Iphise. In the title role John Mark Ainsley is in exceptionally sweet voice, light and clear, while Russell Smythe as Teucer, Iphise's father, is similarly fresh and well focused, with no weak link among the others. This was recorded live from a French Radio studio broadcast, with the double advantage of studio conditions and the flow of adrenalin from a live occasion. The storm sequence of Act IV could hardly be more dramatic, with vivid stage effects. The complete opera in prologue and five acts is neatly fitted on two very well-filled discs now offered at mid price as part of Universal's 'Critics' Choice' collection.

Though the French chorus and orchestra (using modern instruments) here fail to perform on Erato with quite the rhythmic resilience that Leppard usually achieves on record, the results are refreshing and illuminating, helped by generally fine solo singing and naturally balanced (if not brilliant) 1980 analogue recording, smoothly transferred to CD, with the choral sound quite vivid. José van Dam as Ismenor copes superbly with the high tessitura, and Christiane Eda-Pierre is a radiant Venus. The story may be improbable (as usual), but Rameau was here inspired to some of his most compelling and imaginative writing. Well documented and well worth exploring.

Dardanus (orchestral suite); Platée (orchestral suite)

(N) **(M)** *** RCA 74321 93580-2. Philh. Bar. O, McGegan

McGegan offers rather less music from *Dardanus* than Gardiner on his deleted Erato CD, but includes a charmingly Beechamesque *Air gracieux pour les Plaisirs*, omitted in the Erato suite. This makes room for the more extended suite from *Platée*, a *'ballet bouffon'* dating from 1745, written as an entertainment at a royal wedding between the king's son and a princess noted for her plain appearance! Platée herself is an unlovely nymph who rules over a swamp full of frogs and insects (we hear them croaking in the *Passepieds* and *Tambourins*). However, she fancies herself as a catch for the roving eye of the amorous Jupiter. The mock nuptials are finally interrupted by Folie and Momus (the God of Ridicule). McGegan and his period-instrument orchestra are if anything more crisply resilient than Gardiner and not a whit less graceful. Moreover the originally Conifer recording is first-class and the suite from *Dardanus* is given a warmer ambience, notably in the lovely *Le Sommeil*. The music for *Platée* has plenty of character and charm and, like *Dardanus*, ends with a memorable *Chaconne* for which – as it is interrupted in the ballet – McGegan provides a concert ending.

La Guirlande; Zéphyre

*** Erato 8573 85774-2 (2). Daneman, Méchaly, Agnew, Bazola, Ockended, Decaudaveine, WDR Capella Coloniensis, Les Arts Florissants Ch. & O, Christie

Rameau, as he was growing old in the 1740s, turned to writing such short operas, or ballets as they were called, as these. On classical pastoral themes, they have been described as 'Dresden-china Rameau', but that is to underestimate the bubbling inventiveness and warmth of expression which Rameau brought to these artificial stories. *La Guirlande*, the tale of a shepherd and shepherdess whose love is restored, appeared in 1751, but *Zéphyre*, telling the story of the Wind God, infatuated with the wood nymph Cloris, seems never to have been performed in Rameau's lifetime.

Though it is more limited in scale, in having only soprano soloists, it is even more inventive musically, with a sequence of striking numbers, as when the goddess, Diana, briefly appears at the denouement, accompanied by braying horn-fanfares.

The duet which follows, with the voices of Zephyr and Cloris interweaving, is also one of the loveliest in this double bill. Not that *La Guirlande* is at all lacking in invention, with extended monologues and dialogues punctuated by brief set numbers not just for the soloists but for the chorus. In all this Christie and his team are at their most inspired, consistently fresh and lively, though the Capella Coloniensis of West German Radio is not quite as polished a period band as Christie's own in Paris. With excellent soloists, notably Sophie Daneman and the pure 'haute-contre', Paul Agnew, this is a delightful set, giving new perspectives on the composer.

Hippolyte et Aricie (complete)

*** Erato (ADD) 0630 15517-2 (3). Padmore, Panzarella, Hunt, Naouri, James, Les Arts Florissants, Christie

*** DG (IMS) 445 853-2 (3). Gens, Fouchécourt, Fink, Feighan, Massis, Naouri, Smythe, Sagittarius Vocal Ens., Musiciens du Louvre, Minkowski

Christie has the benefit of using the text specially prepared for the complete Rameau Edition by Sylvie Bouissou, restoring fully the original (1733) edition. Marc Minkowski in his fine, crisply alert DG Archiv recording uses a text substantially similar, and both of them include the Prologue. The contrasts with Minkowski are striking, for Christie, using rather larger forces to produce warmer textures and timbres, consistently brings out the sensuous beauty of much of the writing as well as its dramatic point. At speeds fractionally broader, he bounces rhythms more infectiously and allows himself more flexible phrasing without undermining the classical purity of style. Though Anna Maria Panzarella as Aricie is not as golden in tone as Véronique Gens for Minkowski, she is fresh and bright, responding immediately to Christie's timing which more consistently seems geared to stage presentation, with a conversational quality given to passages of recitative. Mark Padmore is a more ardent Hippolyte than his opposite number and Lorraine Hunt a weightier, more deeply tragic Phèdre, with Eirian James a warm Diana and Laurent Naouri as Thésée weightier than Russell Smythe. The Erato sound too is warmer and more immediate than the DG Archiv.

Mark Minkowski is helped by an excellent cast, with the two young lovers of the title ideally taken by the sweet, silver-toned Véronique Gens, enchantingly girlish, and the light, very French-sounding tenor, Jean-Paul Fouchécourt, similarly conveying depth of feeling in formal melodic lines. Also central to the set's success is the powerful performance of Bernarda Fink as Phèdre, firm and rich, well contrasted with Gens, as memorable in its way as Dame Janet Baker's on the original Argo set conducted by Anthony Lewis. Though in the other major role of Thésée Russell Smythe's baritone is not always sweet, he sings with clear focus and expression, with Luc Coadou aptly sinister as Tisifone and Laurent Naouri sepulchral as Pluton. In the formal scheme the longest, most sustained aria, which comes at the very end, celebrating the nightingale, is given to an incidental character, a shepherdess, and is sung here sweetly and charmingly by Annick Massis. Minkowski also draws crisp, alert performances from his chorus and well-tuned orchestra.

Les Indes Galantes

(N) *** Opus Arte **DVD** OA 0923 D (2). Panzarella, Agnew, Berg, Croft, Petibon, Les Arts Florissants Ch. & O, Christie (V/D: Thomas Grimm)

Described as an Opera-Ballet in four Acts, Les Indes Galantes was Rameau's biggest stage success in his own lifetime, and one can understand why from this spectacular production, staged at the Paris Opéra in 2004. The director, Andrei Serban, presents the piece with the sort of lavish effects and movement that would have delighted eighteenth-century audiences. Sets are stylized and costumes are basically in-period, but with random updatings for members of the chorus, as when they appear as French sailors. Act II, set in Peru at the time of the Incas, brings the most striking spectacle with the eruption of a volcano – cue for the backcloth of Andean peaks to wobble and sway amid fiery lighting – for which Rameau devises vividly descriptive music. His inspiration is at white heat throughout, with William Christie and a large and stylish team of singers and players revelling in each number, often deliberately overacting in the more melodramatic moments of this fantastic drama. Outstanding among the soloists are Nathan Berg as Huascar (crushed by a boulder from the sky after his Act II aria), Anna Maria Panzarella as Emilie and Paul Agnew as Valere, with Loao Fernandez memorably in drag as Bellone. The final curtain brings an exuberant encore after the credits, with Christie hilariously joining in the dance. Extras include a feature about Rameau with Christie, Serban and the choreographer, Bianca Li, among those interviewed.

Platée (complete)

** Erato 2292 45028-2 (2). Ragon, Smith, De Mey, Le Texier, Gens, Ens. Vocale Françoise Herr, Musiciens du Louvre, Minkowski

Platée, written in 1745 and described as a 'ballet bouffon', is in fact a comic opera, based on a classical theme. With such a send-up of classical tradition, the performers here understandably adopt comic expressions and voices, which in a recording, as opposed to a stage performance, become rather wearing on the listener. Also almost all the soloists aspirate heavily in florid passages. Within that convention this is a lively, brisk performance, very well conducted by Marc Minkowski, but marred by the dryness of the recording.

Pygmalion (Acte de ballet). Le Temple de la gloire (excerpts): Air gay; Ces oiseaux par leur doux ramage

(M) **(*) Virgin 5 61539-2. Fouchécourt, De Reyghere, Fournié, Piau

Pygmalion falls in love with a female statue he has sculpted. The statue is then (by courtesy of Venus) brought to life by that very love – a moment of sheer orchestral magic in Rameau's delightful score. The Virgin Veritas version is robustly operatic, immediately obvious in the Overture, with its boldly repeated notes, superbly articulated which may (or may not) have been intended by Rameau to simulate the sculptor's chisel. Jean-Paul Fouchécourt gives a strong characterization of Pygmalion and, apart from Sandrine Piau as the Statue, her two female colleagues are more histrionic but less sweet-voiced than their rivals on Harmonia Mundi. Moreover, the excerpts from Le Temple de la gloire are quite brief (about 8 minutes), and while the Virgin reissue includes good notes and a libretto in French, there is no English translation.

Zoroastre (complete)

☛ *** Erato 0927 43182-2 (3). Padmore, Berg, Mechaly, Panzarella, Les Arts Florissants, Christie

William Christie and Les Arts Florissants add to their formidable list of baroque operas, not least those of Rameau, with this superb account of Zoroastre, described as one of the composer's most uncompromising music-dramas. Although the central character is the ancient Persian philosopher and founder of the Magian religion, the themes are the very human ones of love, jealousy and vengeance. Opposite Zoroastre is the evil magician, Abramane, whose ally, Princess Erinice, has been spurned by Zoroastre in favour of the good Princess Amelite. This typical story inspired Rameau to write an unusual fluid sequence of numbers, with recitative, arias and ensembles merging into one another in a rich kaleidoscope of ideas.

Christie directs a lively, beautifully paced performance, helped by a first-rate team of soloists. Standing out is Mark Padmore in the title role, with his natural high tenor totally unstrained and perfectly contrasted with the darkly sinister Abramane of Nathan Berg. Gaëlle Mechaly is ideally bright and agile as Amelite, and although Anna Maria Panzarella too often characterizes the malicious Erinice by attacking notes from below, her voice, too, is bright and agile. The recording presents the opera as Christie and his team gave it in concert in France, but the third disc gives as a supplement the eight dances and one Ariette omitted in the main performance. First-rate sound.

RANGSTRÖM, Ture (1884–1947)

Symphonies 1 (August Strindberg in memoriam); 2 in D min. (My Country); 3 in D flat (Song Under the Stars); (i) 4

(Invocation): Symphonic Improvisations for Orchestra &
Organ; Dithyramb; Intermezzo drammatica; Vårhymn
(Spring Hymn)
(M) **(*) CPO 999 748-2 (3). Norrköping SO, Jurowski; (i)
Fahlsjö

The performances by the Norrköping Symphony Orchestra
under Mikhail Jurowski are eminently acceptable. The package comes at a discount and those who enjoy the symphonies
of Alfvén or Atterberg may well be tempted to investigate this
set, although it must be said that neither as a symphonist nor
as a man of the orchestra is Rangström their equal.

Symphonies (i) 1 in C sharp min. (August Strindberg in
memoriam); (ii) 3 (Song under the Stars)
** Sterling (ADD) CDS 1014-2. (i) Swedish RSO, Segerstam;
(ii) Helsingborg SO, Fürst

Rangström's *First Symphony* dates from 1914, two years after
the death of Strindberg, to whose memory it is dedicated, as
indeed is the *Vårhymn* (*Spring Hymn*) of 1942 on the deleted
CPO set. This also includes his very first orchestral work, the
Dithyramb of 1909. Rangström was basically self-taught, and
the prime influences were Franck and early Sibelius. There
are some individual things in the slow movement but elsewhere, and particularly in the finale, the rhetoric is overblown and the ideas second-rate.

Of the two performances, Mikhail Jurowski is the more
persuasive and he gets very good playing from the Norrköping orchestra (see above). Leif Segerstam draws an
accomplished performance from his players and is decently
recorded in good analogue sound. It is difficult to work up
much enthusiasm for the Sterling coupling, the *Third Symphony* (*'Song Under the Stars'*), which is also rather corny. No
grumbles about the playing of the Helsingborg Symphony
Orchestra under Janos Fürst.

RATHAUS, Karol (1895–1954)

Symphonies 1; 2, Op. 7; 3, Op. 50
(N) *** CPO 777 031-2. Brandenburgisches Staats O,
Frankfurt, Yinon

The Polish-born Karol Rathaus enjoyed a short-lived success
in Germany during the 1920s. Bruno Walter championed one
of his operas, and both Furtwängler and Horenstein took him
up. Sensing the way things were going, he left Germany just
before Hitler came to power and wrote for films and composed a ballet for Paris and London before eventually settling
in America. The *First Symphony* was included in Decca's
'Entertate Music' series and now comes with its two companions of 1933 and 1943 in dedicated performances by the
Frankfurt orchestra. Rathaus remained something of a name
in the immediate post-war years but he was rarely played or
recorded. Like Ernst Toch, he ended his days revered as a
distinguished teacher rather than as an eminent composer.
The idiom is far from 'atonal' as the anti-Semitic 1930s press
had maintained: there are hints of his teacher Schreker and of
Mahler, but the overall impression is of a highly gifted and
inventive composer unafraid of dissonance but working well
within the discipline of classical tonality. Music very much of
its time, like a Teutonic Honegger, perhaps, whose argument
carries you along with conviction. It is powerful and often
disturbing music, which is well worth investigating, particularly in these dedicated performances. Good sound.

RAUTAVAARA, Einojuhani (born
1928)

Anadyomene (Adoration of Aphrodite); (i) Flute Concerto,
Op. 63; (ii) On the Last Frontier
*** Ondine ODE 921-2. Helsinki PO, Segerstam; with (i)
Gallois; (ii) Finnish Philharmonic Ch.

Anadyomene or the *Adoration of Aphrodite* comes from 1969,
and is highly atmospheric and compelling. The *Flute Concerto*, subtitled *Dances with the Winds*, employs bass flute, alto
flute and piccolo. It is one of Rautavaara's most imaginative
and resourceful scores, and its many hurdles are effortlessly
despatched by the distinguished French soloist. *On the Last
Frontier*, a fantasy for chorus and orchestra, is inspired by
Edgar Allan Poe's description of Antarctica, at the end of *The
Narrative of Arthur Gordon Pym.* Vaughan Williams occasionally comes to mind in its pages. All three pieces are expertly
performed by these Helsinki forces under Leif Segerstam and
superbly recorded.

Angels and Visitations; (i) Violin Concerto. Isle of Bliss
🕮 ✪ *** Ode ODE 881-2. (i) Oliveira; Helsinki PO,
Segerstam

Rautavaara's wholly original *Violin Concerto* is hauntingly
accessible and grips the listener completely. It moves from an
ethereal opening cantilena, through a series of colourful
events and experiences until, after a final burst of incandescent energy, it makes a sudden but positive homecoming. The
lively opening of the *Isle of Bliss* is deceptive, for the music
centres on a dreamy, sensual romanticism and creates a rich
orchestral tapestry with a sense of yearning ecstasy, yet overall it has a surprisingly coherent orchestral structure. *Angels
and Visitations* is close to the visions of William Blake and (as
the composer tells us) brings a sense of 'holy dread'. The
extraordinary opening evokes a rustling of angels' wings,
which is then malignantly transformed, becoming a ferocious
multitude of bumblebees. It is a passage of real imaginative
power, in some ways comparable to the storm sequence in
Sibelius's *Tapiola.* The work is in a kind of variation form and
moves from the ethereal nature of angels to demons quite
readily, while later taking on board forceful rhythmic influences from Stravinsky's *Rite of Spring* and *Petrushka.* Its
orchestration and impact are spectacular, hardly music for a
small flat! Elmar Oliveira is the inspired soloist in the *Violin
Concerto*, floating his line magically and serenely in the
opening *Tranquillo* and readily encompassing the work's
adventurous shifts of colour and substance. Segerstam provides a shimmering backing and directs a committed and
persuasively spontaneous orchestral response throughout all
three works. The recording is superbly balanced, spacious
and vivid in detail.

Angels and Visitations; Symphony 7 (Angel of Light)
(BB) *** Naxos 8.555814. RSNO, Koivula

The Royal Scottish National Orchestra under Hannu Koivula
are vividly recorded and have impressive body and refinement, and, while this does not displace the BIS version of
Angels and Visitations, which offers two couplings, for those
unwilling to make the outlay, this Naxos performance offers a
very desirable three-star alternative, including a fine performance of the *Seventh Symphony.*

Apotheosis

**(*) Ondine ODE 1002-2. Swedish RSO, Franck –
TCHAIKOVSKY: *Symphony 6* *

The title of this short piece, *Apotheosis*, would suggest that it could be a suitable prelude for a performance of Tchaikovsky's *Pathétique Symphony*, particularly as it is based on the concluding movement of Rautavaara's *Sixth Symphony*. In the event, although it is colourfully romantic, it does not really live up to its name, and in any case Mikko Franck's coupled performance of the Tchaikovsky is much too mannered and indulgent to be recommendable.

Cantus arcticus (Concerto for Birds & Orchestra), Op. 61; (i) Piano Concerto, Op. 45. Symphony 3, Op. 20

◑ (BB) *** Naxos 8.554147. (i) Mikkola; RSNO, Lintu

The *Cantus arcticus* (1972) uses taped Arctic bird-cries against an evocative orchestral background. The *Third Symphony* (1959–60) has genuine breadth and space. Rautavaara speaks of it as being 'freely constructed and emphatically tonal'. It has a strong feeling for nature. The later *Piano Concerto No. 1* (1969) has a certain neo-romantic feel to it. Laura Mikkola is a fervent exponent of it, and the Royal Scottish National Orchestra under Hannu Lintu play with real commitment and are well recorded.

(i) Harp Concerto. Symphony 8

*** Ondine ODE 978-2. (i) Nordmann; Helsinki PO, Segerstam

The *Concerto* (2001) is predominantly reflective and highly imaginative in its use of texture. In addition to the soloist, Rautavaara adds two harps in the orchestra in order, as he puts it, to create 'a really full and lush harp sound when needed'. The French soloist, Marielle Nordmann, a pupil of Lily Laskine, gives a performance of great distinction and subtlety. The *Eighth Symphony* was commissioned by the Philadelphia Orchestra, which premièred it in April 2000 under Sawallisch. Rautavaara speaks of its musical growth as characterized by slow transformation, a strong narrative element and 'the generation of new, different aspects and perspectives from the same premises, the transformation of light and colour'. As always with this composer there is a strong feeling for nature. Perhaps the most haunting movement is the third, whose quiet radiance stays with the listener. Excellent playing from the Helsinki Philharmonic under Leif Segerstam and state-of-the-art recording.

Piano Concertos 2; 3 (Gift of Dreams). Isle of Bliss

(BB) **(*) Naxos 8.557009. Mikkola, Netherlands RSO, Klas

Neither concerto is new to the catalogue and No. 3 has been recorded by Vladimir Ashkenazy, who commissioned it. It takes as a starting point the composer's 1978 Baudelaire setting, *La Mort des pauvres*, in which the words 'le don des rêves' occur: hence the subtitle. Both here and in the *Isle of Bliss*, written three years earlier and inspired by the Finnish poet Aleksis Kivi, one is reminded a lot of Honegger: Rautavaara's use of triads moving in contrary motion and his refined harmonic sense have more parallels with the French/Swiss master than with the Sibelius tone-poems to which it has been compared. But even if the music unfolds effortlessly and envelops the listener in its world, there is little real melodic distinction. The *Second Piano Concerto* comes from the late 1980s and is imaginative. The rippling piano figuration of the opening is effective, though the middle movement is lacking in concentration. All the same, this is good value for those wanting to sample these pieces.

Piano Concerto 3 (Gift of Dreams); Autumn Gardens

*** Ondine 950-2. Helsinki PO, Ashkenazy

The *Third Piano Concerto* is predominantly meditative and unconcerned with conventional bravura. It gets its subtitle from a Baudelaire setting, *La Mort des pauvres*, which Rautavaara made in the late 1970s and in which the words 'le don des rêves' appear. *Autumn Gardens*, from 1999, also has a dreamlike feel to it. The performances are exemplary and the recording is in the demonstration class. The disc also includes a conversation between Rautavaara and Vladimir Ashkenazy.

Symphonies 1–3

*** Ondine ODE 740-2. Leipzig RSO, Pommer

Einojuhani Rautavaara is a symphonist to be reckoned with. Ideas never outstay their welcome and there is a sense of inevitability about their development. Those with a taste for Shostakovich or Simpson should find these pieces congenial. Good performances by the Leipzig Radio Orchestra under Max Pommer and very decent recorded sound too.

Symphony 6 (Vincentiana); (i) Cello Concerto, Op. 41

*** Ondine ODE 819-2. (i) Ylönen; Helsinki PO, Pommer

The *Sixth Symphony* draws on material from the opera, *Vincent* (1985–7), based on the life of Van Gogh. There is, appropriately enough, no lack of colour, though the score tends to be both eclectic and amorphous. The orchestral scoring itself is quite sumptuous and there is no lack of incident. It comes with a much earlier and more cogently argued piece, the *Cello Concerto* of 1968, which is expertly played by Marko Ylönen. The recording is very impressive, well detailed and present, and is in the demonstration bracket.

Symphony 7 (Angel of Light); (i) Annunciations

*** Ondine ODE 869-2. (i) Jussila; Helsinki PO, Segerstam

Symphony 7; (i) Cantus arcticus; (i) Dances with the Winds (Concerto for Flutes & Orchestra)

◑ *** BIS CD 1038. (i) Alanko; Lahti SO, Vänskä

The *Seventh Symphony* is the more substantial piece and is both powerful and atmospheric. There is a good deal of Sibelius in its first movement and there is a pervasive sense of nature. Rautavaara betrays some affinities with the minimalists but offers greater musical substance. *Annunciations* for organ, brass quintet, winds and percussion, written in 1976–7, strikes a more dissonant note but it is brilliant and well thought out. Kari Jussila is the virtuoso soloist, and the Helsinki orchestra under Segerstam are eminently well served by the Ondine engineers.

The new BIS version of the *Seventh Symphony* is every bit as good as its Ondine competitor, both artistically and as a recording. The sound is pretty state-of-the-art, though its rival has the deeper perspective. But Vänskä's performance has impressive power and atmosphere; he keeps the music moving and casts the stronger spell. Both shorter pieces, the familiar *Cantus arcticus* and the *Dances with the Winds*, a concerto in which the solo flautist plays four members of the flute family (though not at the same time), are from the 1970s, and these fine performances have appeared before in other couplings.

PIANO MUSIC

Etudes, Op. 42; Icons, Op. 6; Partita, Op. 34; Preludes, Op. 7; Piano Sonatas 1 (Christus und die Fischer), Op. 50; 2 (The Fire Sermon), Op. 64

(BB) *** Naxos 8.554292. Mikkola

These admirably lucid performances by Laura Mikkola fill an important gap. The *First Sonata* (*Christus und die Fischer*) comes from 1969, the same year as the *First Piano Concerto*, which this artist has also recorded with such success, and the *Second* (1970) is also most convincingly done. She is given first-class recorded sound. An excellent and economical way of filling in your picture of this fine composer.

VOCAL MUSIC

Ave Maria; Magnificat; Canticum Mariae Virginis; Missa Duodecanonica

*** Ondine ODE 935-2. Finnish R. Chamber Ch., Nuoranne

The *Ave Maria* (1957) for male voices and the *Missa Duodeca-nonica* (1963) for female voices are both serialist, albeit in much the same way as was Frank Martin at one time. The *Magnificat* of 1979, the first Finnish setting of the text, has dignity and eloquence. The singing of the Finnish Radio Chamber Choir under Timo Nuoranne has security of pitch, subtle colouring and purity of tone. Expert, well-balanced Ondine recording.

(i) *Canción de nuestro tiempo.* (ii) *In the Shade of the Willow.* (i; iii) *True and False Unicorn*

*** Ondine ODE 1020-2. (i) Kortekangas, Rissanen, Salomaa; (ii) Huhta; Finnish R. Chamber Ch., (iii) with SO, Nuoranne

The three works on this disc are all from the last decade, the earliest being the *Canción de nuestro tiempo* from 1993, and the setting of James Broughton's *True and False Unicorn*, though first planned in 1971, was not finally realized until 2000. It is a 45-minute work, often inventive and imaginative, and nearly always compelling (one or two passages called to mind the Frank Martin of *The Tempest* in its harmonic language and colouring), though the *Horn and Hounds* section with its quotations including 'God save the Queen' does not really come off. However, the writing is always effective and the Holstian opening of *Mon seul désir*, the closing section of the piece, is rather haunting. The other two pieces are for voices alone and exhibit much command of vocal resource and colour. The *Canción de nuestro tiempo*, to three Lorca poems, is highly inventive, and the Aleksis Kivi settings, *In the Shade of the Willow*, prove admirable vehicles for the virtuosity of the Finnish Radio Chamber Choir and their soloists. Rautavaara's later music is always approachable (occasionally to the point of blandness). These pieces invariably hold the attention without necessarily striking the resonances that compel you to revisit it often. A worthwhile issue.

Hymnus; Independence Fanfare; Octet for Winds; Playgrounds for Angels; Requiem in our Time, Op. 3; A Soldier's Mass; Tarantara

*** Ondine ODE 957-2. Soloists, Finnish Brass Symphony, Lintu

A *Requiem in our Time* for brass and percussion put Rautavaara on the map. While he was in his mid-20s, before he began his studies with Copland, it won an American competition (1953). Rautavaara speaks of *A Soldier's Mass* (1968) as 'a companion work', although the forces involved are larger (it demands a full wind section) and the mood lighter. The *Octet for Winds* (1962) is mildly serial, but in no way inaccessible. Both the *Requiem* and the ingenious *Playgrounds for Angels*, the virtuoso piece written for the Philip Jones Brass Ensemble, are also available in a stunning BIS anthology by the German group, Brass Partout (BIS CD 1054) which is not easily eclipsed. The rest of the programme is not otherwise available: *Hymnus*, for trumpet and organ, was written recently for the Wagner scholar and critic, Barry Millington; *Tarantara* is for solo trumpet and played brilliantly by Pasi Pirinen, as for that matter is the rest of the programme. The Ondine recording is of demonstration quality.

RAVEL, Maurice (1875–1937)

Alborada del gracioso; Une barque sur l'océan; Boléro; (i) *Daphnis et Chloé* (complete ballet). *L'Eventail de Jeanne: Fanfare;* (ii) *Introduction & Allegro for Harp, Flute, Clarinet & String Orchestra. Ma Mère l'Oye* (complete ballet); *Menuet antique; Pavane pour une infante défunte; Rapsodie espagnole; Shéhérazade: Ouverture de féerie. Le Tombeau de Couperin; Trio in A min.* (orch. Tortelier); (v) *Tzigane* (for violin and orchestra). *La Valse; Valses nobles et sentimentales.* Song-cycles: (iii) *Don Quichotte à Dulcinée;* (iv) *Shéhérazade*

(N) (M) **(*) Chan. 10251X (4). Ulster O, Tortelier; with (i) Renaissance Singers, Belfast Philharmonic Soc.; (ii) Masters; (iii) Roberts; (iv) Finnie; (v) Tortelier (violin)

These are fine performances, and all with the advantages of excellent Chandos engineering. Tortelier's *Daphnis et Chloé* soon puts you under its spell: he conveys much of the sense of ecstasy and magic of this score and colours so richly hued and vivid that they belong to the world of the imagination rather than reality. Phrasing is sensitive, and there are some gorgeous sounds throughout. All the same, this version does not have quite the ecstatic quality of the old Munch version or Dutoit on Decca.

Ma Mère l'Oye has a more balletic feel than usual, bringing out the affinities with *Daphnis et Chloé*. The exotic orchestration associated with *Laideronnette, Empress of the Pagodas* glitters vividly, while the lovely closing *Jardin féerique* begins serenely before moving to a joyous climax. Tortelier's *Rapsodie espagnole* is not quite as gripping as some celebrated accounts (Reiner, Karajan, for instance), but it is highly atmospheric all the same.

Whether or not Ravel approved of full strings, the *Introduction and Allegro* loses some of its ethereal quality when given in this form, although the playing of the harpist, Rachel Masters, is impeccable. The validity of Tortelier's own transcription of the *Piano Trio* begs the question that Ravel was himself rather good at orchestration, and had he thought it worthwhile he might have had a shot at it himself! Some of the orchestral effects are idiomatic, but others (particularly the climax in the finale) are more questionable.

To most ears something quite essential is lost in the process; the soul as well as the scale of this music lies in the sonorities Ravel chose, and although Tortelier's skill and musicianship are not in question, this transcription is not one to which many will want to return. Tortelier directs the *Tzigane* from the bow, as it were, and plays very well, and this and the performances of *Le Tombeau de Couperin, La Valse* and *Valses nobles* have plenty of appeal.

The Ulster Orchestra certainly plays consistently well, and the top quality Chandos sound is a considerable bonus. The *Ouverture de féerie* is impressive, as is Linda Finnie's account of the *Shéhérazade* song-cycle, although it must be admitted that in neither vocal beauty not interpretative insight does it challenge classic accounts by Crespin or Baker. No grumbles about Stephen Roberts's fine singing in the *Don Quichotte* songs, but overall this set has uneven appeal and will best suit those for whom outstanding recorded quality is paramount.

Alborada del gracioso; Une barque sur l'océan; Boléro; (i) *Piano Concerto; Concerto for Piano, Left Hand.* (ii) *Daphnis et Chloé (complete Ballet). L'Eventail de Jeanne: Fanfare. Ma Mère l'Oye (complete Ballet); Menuet antique; Pavane pour une infante défunte; Shéhérazade: Ouverture de féerie. Rapsodie espagnole; Le Tombeau de Couperin; La Valse; Valses nobles et sentimentales;* (iii) *Shéhérazade (Song Cycle);* (iv) *L'enfant et les sortilèges (complete)*

(N) (B) ******* Decca 475 6891 (4). Montreal SO, Dutoit; with (i) Rogé; (ii) Ch.; (iii) Dubosc; (iv) Alliot-Lugaz, Lefort, Beaupré Carlson, Gautier, Henry, Sarrazin

Decca have now managed to squeeze all Dutoit's Ravel recordings (including the contents of the Double Decca below) into a bargain-priced 4-CD set which is truly remarkable value. The two *Piano Concertos* are now included. Pascal Rogé finds gracefulness as well as vitality for the *G major* work, and if there is less dynamism in the *Left-hand Concerto*, there is no lack of finesse. Catherine Dubosc is a fresh-voiced, girlish-sounding soloist in *Shéhérazade*, characterful but not sensuous, and the rare *Ouverture de féerie* is also included.

However, the most important addition is *L'enfant et les sortilèges*, a poetic reading of Ravel's fantasy-opera on childhood, helped by warm, evocative sound. Voices are balanced forwardly on the sound-stage, which lets words be heard, and the delicacy and point of Colette's offbeat libretto is nicely caught. Compared with Maazel's vivid and immediate reading on DG, this is a version for those who are looking for the beauty of the score to be brought out rather than the sharper qualities. Alliott-Lugaz is superb as the Child, with the rest of the French-speaking cast equally idiomatic, though voices are not always totally pure or firm.

Alborada del gracioso; Une barque sur l'océan; Boléro; Daphnis et Chloé (Suite 2); L'Eventail de Jeanne: Fanfare. Menuet antique; Ma Mère l'Oye (complete); Pavane pour une infante défunte; Rapsodie espagnole; Le Tombeau de Couperin; La Valse; Valses nobles et sentimentales

⌛ ✿ ******* Double Decca 460 214-2 (2). Montreal SO, Dutoit

Anyone beginning a Ravel collection, or coming fresh to most of this repertoire and willing to duplicate, will find this Double Decca unbeatable value, including as it does all the key orchestral works, though not the piano concertos. The orchestral playing is wonderfully sympathetic and the recording ideally combines atmospheric evocation with vividness. The balance is most musically judged and very realistic; indeed the sound remains in the demonstration class.

(i) *Alborada del gracioso; Une barque sur l'océan; Boléro.* (ii) *Daphnis et Chloé: Suite 2.* (i) *L'Eventail de Jeanne: Fanfare. Menuet antique; Pavane pour une infante défunte; Rapsodie*

espagnole; Shéhérazade: Ouverture de féerie. Le Tombeau de Couperin; La Valse; Valses nobles et sentimentales

(B) ******* DG Double (IMS) (DDD/ADD) 459 439-2 (2). (i) LSO; (ii) Boston SO, with New England Conservatory Ch.; Abbado

Abbado's feeling for the music's atmosphere is matched by his care for detail, and the glowing analogue recording was one of the best made in Symphony Hall in the analogue era. *Ma Mère l'Oye* is omitted, yet the early overture to *Shéhérazade* is included alongside the *Alborada* and *Une barque sur l'océan*. Abbado gets delicious sounds in all three, as he does in the *Valses nobles et sentimentales*. The sultry atmosphere of *Rapsodie espagnole* is very evocative, the *Pavane* has a grave, withdrawn melancholy and the characteristically polished and refined playing is matched by sound with a wide dynamic range, a fine focus, and yet plenty of ambience and warmth. *Boléro* and the exquisitely played *Le Tombeau de Couperin* are also included on another single-disc anthology, below.

Alborada del gracioso; Une barque sur l'ocean; Boléro; (i) *Daphnis et Chloé (ballet: complete). L'Eventail de Jeanne (fanfare); Menuet antique; Ma Mère l'Oye; Pavane pour une infante défunte; Rapsodie espagnole; Shéhérazade: Overture de féerie. Le Tombeau de Couperin; La Valse; Valses nobles et sentimentales*

(B) ****(*)** DG Trio 469 354-2 (3). LSO, Abbado; (i) with L. Symphony Ch.

Much of this collection is already available on a DG Double (459 439-2 – see above). But by using three CDs (offered for the cost of a pair of mid-priced discs) *Ma Mère l'Oye* has now been included plus the complete *Daphnis et Chloé*. Here the brilliant playing of the LSO is helpd by an exceptionally analytical DG recording which has the widest possible dynamic range – so that the *pianissimo* at the very opening is barely audible for almost 30 seconds. For all the refinement and virtuosity this is a performance to admire rather than love, lacking the atmosphere of the rest of the programme which is altogether more evocative, beautifully played and recorded without dynamic exaggeration. So the DG Double mentioned above is preferable, unless *Ma Mère l'Oye* is essential.

Alborada del gracioso; Une barque sur l'océan; Boléro; Ma Mère l'Oye (complete); Menuet antique; Shéhérazade: Ouverture de féerie; Pavane pour une infante défunte; Rapsodie espagnole; Le Tombeau de Couperin; La Valse; Valses nobles et sentimentales

(B) ******* EMI double forte (ADD) 5 68610-2 (2). O de Paris, Martinon

Like his version of *Daphnis et Chloé*, Martinon's *Ma Mère l'Oye* is exquisite, among the finest ever put on record. Although the *Valses nobles et sentimentales* and *La Valse* do not eclipse the 1961 Cluytens versions (see below) and the present *La Valse* has a rather harsh climax, there is much ravishing delicacy of orchestral playing, notably in *Le Tombeau de Couperin* and the rare *Ouverture de féerie* (*Shéhérazade*). The sound is warm and luminously coloured and the refined virtuosity of the Orchestre de Paris is a constant source of delight. Excellent value.

(i; iii) *Alborada del gracioso;* (ii; iii) *Boléro;* (iv) *Piano Concerto in G;* (ii; iii) *Daphnis et Chloé: Suite 2; Pavane pour une infante défunte*

(N) (BB) *** EMI HMV (DDD/ADD) 5 86756-2. (i) RPO; (ii) LSO; (iii) Previn; (iv) Collard, French Nat. O, Maazel

Previn's three LSO performances included here were among EMI's very first digital recordings, and they were also on one of that company's very first CDs (the RPO *Alborada* followed later). They provided remarkably rich, full and atmospheric sound for performances full of sparkle and flair. *Daphnis et Chloé* is sensuously beautiful and *Boléro*, at a slow and very steady tempo rather like Karajan's, sounds splendidly relentless. Originally there were no dividing bands within the *Daphnis Suite*, but there are now, and Collard's cultivated and brilliant account of the *G major Concerto* has extended the playing time (about which we originally complained) satisfactorily. A fine, inexpensive reissue with a certain historical as well as artistic interest.

Alborada del gracioso; Boléro; (i) *Daphnis et Chloé* (complete). *Ma Mère l'Oye* (suite); *Pavane pour une infante défunte; Rapsodie espagnole; La Valse; Valses nobles et sentimentales*

(B) ** Double Decca (ADD) 468 564-2 (2). SRO, Ansermet; (i) with Lausanne R. Ch.

Any comprehensive stereo Ravel discography would be incomplete without Ansermet's pioneering recordings, made between 1957 and 1965 in the excellent acoustics of the Victoria Hall, Geneva. But although Ansermet's ear for detail brought undoubted insights, the playing of the Suisse Romande Orchestra was distinctly variable in quality, and seldom matched the superb contribution of the Decca recording team, which included as producers James Walker and Michael Bremner, and as balance engineers Roy Wallace and, later, James Lock.

It was the vividness of the Decca sound which made these recordings famous; nevertheless two of the earliest works to be recorded, the *Rapsodie espagnole* and *Ma Mère l'Oye*, both from 1957, earned our praise in their day when we commented (concerning the latter) on the 'gauze-like textures of the quieter music, spun with the utmost delicacy, the sound at once vivid and iridescent'.

The strings sound a bit dated now the recordings have been remastered, but the ambient glow remains. Ansermet's coolness suits the *Pavane*, while *La Valse*, a piece which roused him and which he always performed well, is spectacular and atmospheric. The outstanding *Boléro*, one of the last works to be recorded (in 1965), has held its place as top recommendation up to the present day.

But the complete *Daphnis et Chloé*, from the same sessions, although again magnificently served by the engineers, misses the rapture and magic which Monteux for one so readily found, and the Swiss orchestra does not play with the virtuosity and sensitivity that this masterly score demands. Ansermet aficionados will surely want this generously full Double Decca, but the general collector would do better to look elsewhere.

Alborada del gracioso; Boléro; Daphnis et Chloé (ballet): *Suite 2; Pavane pour une infante défunte; Rapsodie espagnole*

(M) **(*) Warner Elatus 2564 60025-2. Chicago SO, Barenboim

Like Previn (see below), Barenboim's approach to Ravel is above all sultry, but in the *Rapsodie espagnole* comparison with Reiner is even more fascinating. The acoustics of Chicago Symphony Hall have changed irrevocably in the three and a half decades between the Reiner and Barenboim recordings, and not to advantage. We are told that the installation of air conditioning is partly the cause, but the hall itself has been renovated, and the result is the loss of the natural glow and, especially, the transparency of sound that made Reiner's recording so magical. Here the microphones are closer and the orchestra more firmly tangible. Yet Barenboim's *Rapsodie* is still seductive, with the *Prélude* dream-like, though not quite so measured and balmy as with Reiner. Similarly, *Daphnis* combines atmosphere with sensuous passion. There is some marvellous playing – from the principal flute, especially – and the *Danse générale* is even more intoxicatingly brilliant than the *Féria* in the *Rapsodie*. The *Pavane* is warmly languorous, while the following *Alborada* brings sharp, guitar-like transients to contrast with the ruminatively played central section, where the solo bassoon seems almost to be improvising. *Boléro* is direct and straightforward, the tempo maintained consistently throughout. It is not quite as compelling as Karajan's version, but still impressive. Providing one accepts the current hall ambience and the fairly close microphones, the 1992 digital recording is very good, full and well detailed.

Alborada del gracioso; Boléro; Pavane pour une infante défunte; La Valse; (i) *Shéhérazade* (song-cycle); *Vocalise en forme de habanera* (orch. Hoérée)

(BB) *** Virgin 2x1 5 61742-2 (2). (i) Augér; Philh. O, Pešek – CANTELOUBE: *Chants d'Auvergne ***

This is a particularly attractive programme, brilliantly recorded. The Philharmonia are in exuberant form. The *Alborada* glitters, the *Boléro* is built steadily to a splendid climax, and among the solos the flamboyant trombone is particularly memorable. The *Pavane* has a noble dignity and *La Valse* liltingly generates plenty of adrenalin. Arleen Augér's lovely voice is ideally suited to a languorous account of *Shéhérazade*, which she makes entirely her own, opening *Asie* gently and seductively but expanding to a passionate climax, while *La Flûte enchantée* is more intimate, with some delicately refined playing from the Philharmonia solo flute. If you also want the (excellent) coupling, this is a fine bargain.

Alborada del gracioso; Boléro; Rapsodie espagnole; Le Tombeau de Couperin; La Valse

(N) (M) *** EMI (ADD) 4 76859-2. O de Paris (or, in *Boléro*, BPO), Karajan

(BB) *** RCA 74321 68015-2. Dallas SO, Mata

These are superb performances (all but *Boléro* recorded in 1974), and this is a worthy disc to represent Karajan as one of EMI's 'Great Artists of the Century'. The Orchestre de Paris responds splendidly to the conductor's sensuous approach to these scores, and only the saxophone-like quality of the French horns gives cause for complaint. The dynamic range is extremely wide and the acoustic resonant. There is no doubt about the mastery of *La Valse*, which is extremely fine, or the *Rapsodie espagnole*, the best account since Reiner's. The *Alborada* is a bit too slow; doubtless the reverberant acoustic prompted this and also brought a degree of mistiness in *pianissimo* detail (noticeably at the opening of *La Valse*). But the overall focus is impressive, and the climaxes expand excitingly. *Boléro*, recorded three years later with the BPO, is superbly done and has even more presence than Karajan's highly praised DG version.

In the late 1970s Eduardo Mata helped to build the Dallas orchestra into a splendid band, and their excellence and his stylish conducting (helped by the splendid acoustics of the Dallas auditorium) was demonstrated by a series of outstanding Ravel recordings made in the early 1980s. The *Alborada* flashes, the *Rapsodie espagnole* shimmers and there is a balmy underlying patina of sensuous colour. Mata and his players are at their most impressive in *Le Tombeau de Couperin*, which has pleasing elegance and finesse and the expansive climaxes of *Boléro* and *La Valse* are very compelling. The recording has the most spectacular dynamic range and at bargain price this collection is most recommendable, standing up well to all the competition.

(i) Alborado del gracioso; Boléro; Rapsodie espagnole; Le Tombeau de Couperin; (ii) Valses nobles et sentimentales
(B) **(*) Sony (ADD) SBK 48163. Phd; O, (i) Ormandy; (ii) Munch

Ormandy was a first-class Ravel conductor. These performances are eminently well worth the money at bargain price, even if the recording is not three-star by present-day standards.

Alborada del gracioso; (i) Daphnis et Chloé: Suites 1 & 2; Une barque sur l'océan. Menuet antique
(**(*)) Testament mono SBT 1238. French Nat. R.O., Cluytens; (i) with Ch. – BIZET: *La Jolie fille de Perth* **(*) ROUSSEL: *Le Festin de l'araignée* ***

Cluytens' recording of these Ravel pieces is thoroughly idiomatic even if his later stereo versions sound better and are arguably superior artistically. The earlier versions come from 1953 and the *Daphnis* suites are unusual for that period in including the chorus. *Une barque sur l'océan* sounds eminently fresh though the later Conservatoire Orchestra version has the benefit of stereo. The coupling brings *Le Festin de l'araignée*, a magical account of Roussel's inspired score which has never been surpassed.

Alborada del gracioso; Daphnis et Chloé: Suite 2
❂ (M) *** EMI 5 62746-2 [5 627592]. Philh. O, Giulini – DEBUSSY: *La Mer; Nocturnes* *** ❂

Giulini's 1959 accounts of these two key works are justly celebrated. They are not only among the most polished Ravel performances on record (the solo flute playing in *Daphnis* is quite ravishing), but they are also richly sensuous, with the most refined detail and an exquisite feeling for atmosphere. The *Alborada* has great rhythmic flair and the sumptuous Kingsway Hall recordings reveal remarkable inner clarity as well as giving the orchestra a glowing overall bloom, which the CD transfer captures perfectly. The Debussy couplings are no less distinguished, and this is truly a 'Great Recording of the Century'.

Alborada del gracioso; Ma Mère l'Oye (complete ballet); Le Tombeau de Couperin; Valses nobles et sentimentales
⊶ ❂ (M) *** Decca 475 043-2. Montreal SO, Dutoit

As we commented when this CD was first issued (without the *Alborada*) to win the *Gramophone* Engineering Award in 1985, a few bars of *Ma Mère l'Oye* leave no doubt as to its quality. The sound is transparent and refined, the textures beautifully balanced, with translucent detail and firm focus. The performances, too, are wonderfully refined and sympathetic. *Ma*

Mère l'Oye is ravishingly beautiful, its special combination of sensuousness and innocence perfectly caught. The *Alborada*, recorded at the same time, glitters: within the St Eustache acoustic it has a clarity and depth of perspective to match the elegant *Tombeau de Couperin* and a no less distinguished account of the *Valses*. An outstanding reminder of Decca's supreme technical and musical achievement in the early days of the compact disc (two decades ago!).

Alborada del gracioso; Pavane pour une infante défunte; Rapsodie espagnole; Le Tombeau de Couperin; Valses nobles et sentimentales
(BB) **(*) EMI Encore 5 85078-2. RPO, Previn

Opening with a provocatively languorous account of *Valses nobles et sentimentales*, lazy of tempo and affectionately indulgent, Previn's whole 1986 collection is imbued with sentient warmth. It even pervades *Le Tombeau de Couperin*, although, with some delectable oboe playing, this retains its neoclassical lightness of character. The *Rapsodie espagnole* is unashamedly sultry and the effect throughout is helped by the glowing EMI recording.

Alborada del gracioso; Pavane pour une infante défunte; Rapsodie espagnole; Valses nobles et sentimentales
⊶ ❂ (B) *** RCA 74321 88692-2 (2). Chicago SO, Reiner – DEBUSSY: *Images: Ibéria. La Mer* ❂; MUSSORGSKY: *Pictures* **(*)

These performances are in an altogether special class. In the *Rapsodie espagnole* the *Prélude à la nuit* is heavy with fragrance and atmosphere; never have the colours in the *Féria* glowed more luminously, while the *Malagueña* glitters with iridescence. In the years since it first appeared on LP, this is the recording we have turned to whenever we wanted to hear the work for pleasure. No one captures its sensuous atmosphere as completely as did Reiner, and the recorded sound, with its natural concert-hall balance, still sounds pretty amazing. The recording is improved in terms of clarity and definition, even if with the digital remastering the *fortissimo* upper range of the violins has become sharper and less natural in focus.

Boléro
(M) *** DG (ADD) 447 426-2. BPO, Karajan – DEBUSSY: *La Mer*; MUSSORGSKY: *Pictures* ***
(N) ** Australian Decca Eloquence 476 2452. Concg. O, Chailly – DEBUSSY: *Danse*; MUSSORGSKY: *Pictures at an Exhibition* **
(BB) *(*) EMI Encore 5 85460-2. Phd. O, Muti – LISZT: *Les Préludes* **(*); TCHAIKOVSKY: *1812* *(**)

Boléro; Daphnis et Chloé: Suite 2
(M) *** DG (ADD) 427 250-2. BPO, Karajan – DEBUSSY: *La Mer; Prélude* ***

Karajan's 1964 *Boléro* is a marvellously controlled, hypnotically gripping performance, with the Berlin Philharmonic at the top of its form. It is available either with a superb suite from *Daphnis et Chloé*, or among DG's Legendary Recordings series of 'Originals'; the couplings on both discs show Karajan at his very finest.

Chailly uses *Boléro* as the introduction to a collection demonstrating the genius of Ravel as orchestrator, leading to his transcriptions of Debussy and Mussorgsky. Chailly's view of *Boléro* is strictly metrical, light and classical at the start, increasingly relentless as the crescendo develops. Though this is not the most sympathetic of versions, it has all the brilliance you could wish for, both in the playing and in the recording, which has spectacular range.

Muti sets a measured tempo and almost lingers in his expressive treatment of the opening statements of the theme, against the clear side-drum snares. But by the time the climax is in sight, the upper range has harshened and the strings are glassy: the final *fortissimo* is very fierce indeed.

Boléro; (i) Daphnis et Chloé (ballet: complete). La Valse

⊕▬ ✿ *** EMI **Audio DVD** DVC4 92395-9. O de Paris, Martinon; (i) with Ch.

Martinon's complete *Daphnis et Chloé*, recorded in the Salle Wagram, Paris, in 1974, was the most sensuous and magical to have appeared on disc since Munch's celebrated RCA Boston account, and in some ways it even surpasses it. Its intoxicating atmosphere, sense of ecstasy and Dionysian abandon are altogether captivating. *La Valse* is very fine too, though Cluytens's 1963 performance is every bit as good. *Boléro* is impressively graduated and stands alongside Karajan's BPO account on DG. Altogether this DVD is outstanding in every way, the sound wonderfully atmospheric, yet clearly defined, the dynamic range and amplitude enhanced, with an expansive lower range. As usual with this series, there is a choice between multi-channel surround sound (here remixed) or high-resolution stereo on alternate sides of the disc. The results are spectacular in either instance.

Boléro; Daphnis et Chloé: Suite 2. Ma Mère l'Oye: suite. Pavane pour une infante défunte; La Valse

⊕▬ *** Telarc CD 80601. Cincinnati SO, Järvi

An outstanding collection in every way, gloriously recorded in the rich ambience of Cincinnati's Music Hall. Paavo Järvi secures performances which are beautifully played, affectionately detailed, warmly sensuous and radiantly textured (especially *Ma Mère l'Oye*, which is more romantic than usual). The brightly paced *Boléro* and the expansive but equally magnetic *La Valse* both move to thrilling climaxes, the former with a characteristically spectacular bass drum. The wide dynamic range increases the drama of the interpretations – and indeed the spectacle of the demonstration-standard sound. Highly recommended.

(i) Boléro; Daphnis et Chloé: Suite 2. Ma Mère l'Oye: Suite; (ii) Rapsodie espagnole. La Valse

**(*) Australian Decca Eloquence 466 667-2. (i) LAPO, Mehta; (ii) LSO, Monteux

Mehta's Ravel is very high powered, but the visceral excitement he produces is most compelling. *La Valse* is full of tension, and the *Daphnis Suite* builds up to a splendid climax. *Ma Mère l'Oye* is brilliantly played too, although here the music's sense of gentle rapture is less fully realized. Not surprisingly, *Boléro* is a great success. Throughout, one marvels at the vivid Decca sound and the brilliance of the playing of the Los Angeles orchestra, and one feels that this period (late 1960s and 1970s) was Mehta's golden recording era. Monteux's LSO account of the *Rapsodie espagnole* is justly famous; it is a memorably glowing account, drenched in atmosphere, and, despite some tape hiss, it still sparkles.

Boléro; (i) Daphnis et Chloé: Suite 2. Ma Mère l'Oye (suite); Valses nobles et sentimentales

(BB) *** Naxos 8.550173. (i) Slovak Philharmonic Ch.; Slovak RSO (Bratislava), Jean

The Slovak Radio Orchestra, which is a fine body and is superbly recorded, respond warmly to Kenneth Jean. At the price, this is very good value indeed; the *Ma Mère l'Oye* can hold its own alongside all but the most distinguished competition: indeed *Les Entretiens de la belle et de la bête* is as keenly characterized as Dutoit at mid-price, and *Le Jardin féerique* is enchanting. For those wanting these pieces this is a real bargain.

Boléro; Daphnis et Chloé: Suite 2. Rapsodie espagnole

(M) *** EMI (ADD) 5 67595-2 [567597]. O de Paris, Munch – HONEGGER: *Symphony 2* ***

Munch recorded these Ravel pieces in 1968, shortly before his death on tour with the newly founded Orchestre de Paris. They bear the hallmark of his personality, intensity of expression and wonderful finesse. Apart from the excellence of the Ravel, the disc is of particular value in bringing his final thoughts on the Honegger symphony, of which he had made pioneering records in the war and with which he had a life-long association. Excellent sound.

Boléro; Jeux d'eau (orch. Viacava); Ma Mère l'Oye: Suite; (i) Tzigane. La Vallée des cloches (orch. Grainger); La Valse; (ii) 5 Mélodies populaires grecques

(M) **(*) Cala CACD 1004. (i) Chase; (ii) Burgess; Philh. O, Simon

The test of good orchestration is to convey the illusion that the music could have existed in no other form, and it is a tribute to Viacava's cunning and expertise that he succeeds as well as he does (albeit not completely) to disguise the keyboard origins of *Jeux d'eau*. Percy Grainger's *La Vallée des cloches* is quite remarkable, calling as it does on an exotic array of glockenspiel, vibraphone, marimba, celeste and dulcitone plus the strings of a piano struck by a mallet. It is not perhaps wholly Ravel in sensibility, but it is highly effective in its own right. Geoffrey Simon directs good performances from the Philharmonia: his two soloists in the *Cinq mélodies populaires grecques* and *Tzigane* are excellent, and the recording is very good indeed.

Boléro; Ma Mère l'Oye (complete); Pavane pour une infante défunte; Rapsodie espagnole; La Valse

(M) *** Ph. (ADD) 464 733-2. LSO, Monteux
(M) **(*) DG Entrée (ADD) 474 172-2. Boston SO, Ozawa

For this Philips reissue Polygram have taken the opportunity to combine recordings from two separate sources. Monteux's 1964 version of the complete *Ma Mère l'Oye* is a poetic, unforced reading, given naturally balanced sound. *La Valse* is impressive too, and *Boléro* has well-sustained concentration, even though some will raise an eyebrow at the slight quickening of pace in the closing pages. These three recordings are taken from a Philips original which has responded well to its digital remastering, retaining its warmth while obtaining a clearer profile. The *Pavane* and *Rapsodie espagnole*, however, come from a Decca source and date from two years earlier, yet the sound has strikingly more range and an added lustre. The *Pavane* is warm and poised; the *Rapsodie espagnole* can be spoken of in the same breath as Reiner's version. Monteux moves naturally and spontaneously from the exotic nocturnal atmosphere of the opening *Prélude à la nuit* to the flashing brilliance of the closing *Féria*.

Ozawa's disc is generously full (77 minutes), and the 1974 recording is of outstanding DG analogue quality. It is both refined and full-textured, and vividly focused. But the performances themselves, although played with distinction, do not display a very high voltage. *Boléro* is without a compulsive forward thrust, *Ma Mère l'Oye* is beautifully polished, but ultimately not as magical as Previn or Monteux; although *La Valse* has atmosphere, it lacks exuberance, and the *Rapsodie* is rather under-characterized, though it is excitingly recorded and the effect has fine glitter. Indeed, it is the translucent sound that makes this record appealing, demonstrating the wonderful acoustics of Boston's Symphony Hall.

Boléro; Ma Mère l'Oye; Rapsodie espagnole

(BB) (**) Naxos mono 8.110154. Boston SO, Koussevitzky – MUSSORGSKY: *Pictures at an Exhibition* (**(*))

Koussevitzky's feeling for Ravel is second to none and we wish Naxos had included his magical post-war account of the second suite from *Daphnis et Chloé*. There is a certain want of enchantment in the first two movements of *Ma Mère l'Oye*, but for the most part criticism is silenced.

Boléro; Rapsodie espagnole

*** DG (IMS) 439 013-2. BPO, Karajan – MUSSORGSKY: *Pictures* ***

Karajan's later versions of *Boléro* and *Rapsodie espagnole* find the Berlin Philharmonic in characteristically brilliant form, recorded in very wide-ranging digital sound; the thrust of *Boléro* and the sensuousness of the *Rapsodie* are conveyed with unerring power and magnetism, and the close of the *Féria* of the *Rapsodie espagnole* is spectacular indeed!

Boléro; Rapsodie espagnole; La Valse

(N) (M) **(*) RCA (ADD) **SACD** 82876 66374-2. Boston SO, Munch – DEBUSSY: *Images* ***

Munch's recordings originally appeared together on a single LP which was reviewed by us in the very first *Stereo Record Guide* in 1960. We found the sound in *Boléro* 'full-blooded yet well separated, the harp beautifully balanced in the opening music and the side-drum clear as a bell at the beginning and dominating the climax. The Boston trombone soloist does not slur his tune with glissandi (as on the recording which the composer himself supervises). Munch used the *Rapsodie* to show the orchestra's prowess in the many sparkling coloured effects it contains, with the percussion section marvellously captured and the string glissandi also. The Spanish condiment is not missing and the whole thing is highly entertaining.' We were much less happy with Munch's *La Valse* and thought it 'an unsubtle performance, for he presses the music to a frenzy in its final climax'.

Piano Concerto in G

☛ ✿ (M) *** EMI (ADD) 5 67238-2 [567258]. Michelangeli, Philh. O, Gracis – RACHMANINOV: *Piano Concerto 4* *** ✿

(*) Sup. SU 3714- 2 031. Moravec, Prague Philh., Bělohlávec– BEETHOVEN: *Piano Concerto 4*; FRANCK: *Symphonic Variations* *

Ravel's masterpiece is well served on CD but this reissue in EMI's 'Great Recordings of the Century' is second to none. Michelangeli's slow movement is ravishing, and the sparkle of the outer movements is underpinned by a refined Ravelian sensitivity. The remastering of the early stereo master (1957) is wholly beneficial, the sound full yet remarkably transparent in revealing detail.

The lightness and clarity typical of the veteran Czech pianist Ivan Moravec brings out the neo-classical element in the Ravel *G major Concerto*. In the first movement the contrast is heightened between the rapid passage-work of the main *allegro* sections and the lyricism of the broadly expressive *andante* passages, with Bělohlávek colourfully touching in the jazz influences. The slow movement is at once poised, rapt and poetic, the more moving for the degree of understatement, and Moravec characteristically manages a velvety legato with only the lightest use of the pedal. In the reprise of the main melody the cor anglais is then far too backward when it takes up the theme, an inconsistency untypical of a generally well-balanced recording. In the extrovert finale Bělohlávek more than ever relishes the jazz element, while Moravec brings his usual clarity to the rushing figuration.

Piano Concerto in G; Piano Concerto in D for the Left Hand

(BB) *** Warner Apex (ADD). 8573 89232-2. Queffélec, Strasbourg PO, Lombard – DEBUSSY: *Fantaisie for Piano & Orchestra* ***

(N) *** Australian Decca Eloquence (ADD) 476 235-2. De Larrocha, LPO, Foster – FAURE: *Fantaisie for Piano & Orchestra* ***; FRANCK: *Symphonic Variations* ***

(*) Chan. 8773. Lortie, LSO, Frühbeck de Burgos – FAURE: *Ballade* *

(i–ii) Piano Concerto in G; Piano Concerto for the Left Hand; (ii) La Valse; (i) Valses nobles et sentimentales (for piano)

(B) *** CfP (ADD) 568 029-2. (i) Fowke; (ii) LPO, Baudo

(i) Piano Concerto in G; Piano Concerto for the Left Hand. Jeux d'eau; (ii) La Valse (for 2 pianos)

(BB) *** EMI Encore 5 74749-2. Collard, (i) O Nat. de France, Maazel; (ii) Béroff

(i; ii) Piano Concerto in G; (i; iii) Piano Concerto for the Left Hand; (ii) Valses nobles et sentimentales

☛ ✿ *** DG 449 213-2. (i) Zimerman; (ii) Cleveland O; (iii) LSO; Boulez

(i) Piano Concerto in G. Gaspard de la nuit

(M) *** DG (ADD) 447 438-2. Argerich; (i) BPO, Abbado – PROKOFIEV: *Piano Concerto 3* ***

Zimerman's *G major Concerto*, the *Valses nobles et sentimentales* and the *Left-hand Concerto* are well nigh perfect in every respect. Boulez's account of the *Valses nobles* is quite wonderfully atmospheric, indeed magical, and in the concertos the delicacy and finesse of Krystian Zimerman's pianism is dazzling, his refinement of nuance and clarity of articulation a source of wonder. Beautifully balanced and finely detailed recording.

Argerich's half-tones and clear fingerwork give the *G major Concerto* unusual delicacy, but its urgent virility – with jazz an important element – comes over the more forcefully by contrast. The compromise between coolness and expressiveness in the slow minuet of the middle movement is tantalizingly sensual. Her *Gaspard de la nuit* abounds in character and colour. The remastered recordings sound first class.

Jean-Philippe Collard's coupling offers splendidly vivid recording quality, and Collard gives a meticulously refined and sparkling account of the *G major Concerto* and a brilliant and poetic account of the *Left-Hand Concerto*. Maazel's thoroughly sympathetic support shows how keenly attuned he is to this composer, and the Orchestre National play superbly. The solo account of *Jeux d'eau* is touched with the same sensitivity, and the other bonus is a rare two-piano version of *La Valse* in which Collard is admirably partnered by Michel Béroff. This is a real bargain.

Anne Queffélec's accounts of both Ravel concertos are less extrovert than Collard's, thoughtful and imaginative and often bringing an enticing languor, yet without loss of sparkle in the outer movements of the *G major*. She is a thorough musician with a considerable technique and no mean sense of poetry, and her approach is refreshing. The excellent Strasbourg orchestra under Alain Lombard give her admirable support, and the recording is well balanced in a warm acoustic. Again excellent value and proof that there are different ways of approaching these highly engaging works.

The performances of both the *Concertos* by Philip Fowke with Baudo and the LPO are particularly attractive in the way they bring out the jazzy side of Ravel's inspiration with winning results. In the slow movement of the *G major Concerto* the Spanish overtones also come out strongly, and Fowke's solo playing in the *Valses nobles et sentimentales* is clean, bright and rhythmic in a muscular way, without ever becoming brutal or unfeeling; nor does he lack poetry. Baudo and the orchestra also give a strongly characterized reading of *La Valse*. Excellent 1988 recording – irresistible at bargain price.

Alicia de Larrocha's 1972 recordings of the Ravel piano concertos have been somewhat elusive on CD, making this Australian release very welcome indeed. The performances are excellent, with de Larrocha, in her distinctive way, finding plenty of colour and sparkle in these wonderful concertos; and she is very well supported by Lawrence Foster and the Decca recording. The couplings are excellent too, and this disc is well worth seeking out, if the couplings are also wanted.

Louis Lortie's account of the two *Concertos* on Chandos has the advantage of altogether outstanding recording. In the *G major* he is often highly personal without becoming unduly idiosyncratic, with a fastidious sense of colour at his command. In the *Left-hand Concerto* he really takes his time over the cadenzas and his agogic hesitations are sometimes overindulgent. Immaculate playing as such, and superb recording.

(i) *Piano Concerto in G; Piano Concerto for the Left Hand in D. A la manière de Borodine; A la manière de Chabrier; Gaspard de la nuit; Jeux d'eau; Menuet antique; Menuet sur le nom de Haydn; Miroirs; Pavane pour une infante défunte; Prélude; Sonatine; Le Tombeau de Couperin; Valses nobles et sentimentales*

(B) **(*) Ph. Duo (ADD) 438 353-2 (2). Haas; (i) Monte-Carlo Opéra O, Galliera

Werner Haas has a genuine Ravel sensibility and he plays with delicacy and a fine feeling for the music's colour and its moments of gentle rapture. The performances of the two *Concertos* match the rest, refined and satisfying. Perhaps the playing here is a little strait-laced (elsewhere Haas is often pleasingly flexible) but Galliera's fine accompaniments add to the authority of these performances, and the 1968 recording is well balanced. These are performances one could live with.

Daphnis et Chloé (ballet: complete)

☛ ✿ (N) (M) *** RCA (ADD) **SACD** 82876 61388-2. New England Conservatory & Alumni Ch., Boston SO, Munch

(N) (M) *** EMI (ADD) 4 76853-2. Choeur René Duclos, Paris Conservatoire O, Cluytens (with DEBUSSY: *Jeux* ***)

Daphnis et Chloé (complete); *Boléro*

(BB) *** EMI Encore 5 74750-2. CBSO & Ch., Rattle

Daphnis et Chloé (complete); *Pavane pour une infante défunte; La Valse*

(M) *** Decca 458 605-2. Montreal SO & Ch., Dutoit

Charles Munch's Boston account is one of the great glories of the 1950s. The playing in all departments of the Boston orchestra is simply electrifying. The sound here may not be as sumptuous as the Dutoit on Decca, but the richness of colour lies in the playing, and there is a heady sense of intoxication that at times sweeps you off your feet, and the integration of the chorus is impressively managed. Try the *Danse de supplication de Chloé* and the ensuing scene in which the pirates are put to flight, and you will get a good idea of how dazzling this is, with the ballet ending in tumultuous orchestral virtuosity. The SACD transfer offers a little more ambience than the CD and the effect is quite glorious.

Reissued in EMI's 'Great Artists of the Century' series, Cluytens's splendidly vivid account of this great score projects the music with extreme brilliance, yet the effect is warmly atmospheric too in this splendidly remastered CD. With this 1962 recording you are confronted with the orchestral tradition Ravel himself would have known (including the saxophone-like horns and the sweet-sour, almost scented woodwind) and although the orchestral virtuosity in Paris is no match for, say, the 1955 Boston Symphony Orchestra under Munch, the playing has a voluptuousness all its own. The *Danse de Pan* is wonderfully played and *Lever du jour* gloriously expansive, with the analogue stereo beautifully open and natural. *Jeux*, delicate, luminous and transparent (recorded a year later), makes a fine bonus. This supersedes the Testament reissue which offered *Ma Mère l'Oye* instead of *Jeux* (SBT 1128).

Dutoit adopts an idiomatic and flexible style, observing the minute indications of tempo change but making every slight variation sound totally spontaneous. The final *Danse générale* finds him adopting a dangerously fast tempo, but the Montreal players – combining French responsiveness with transatlantic polish – rise superbly to the challenge, with the choral punctuations at the end adding to the sense of frenzy. The digital recording is wonderfully luminous, with the chorus ideally balanced at an evocative half-distance, fully worthy of Decca's 'Legends' series. The CD is now generously cued.

Simon Rattle conducts the CBSO in a most warmly expressive reading of Ravel's great ballet score. The sensuous beauty of the slow sequences is enhanced by the mistily evocative recording, though the dynamic range is extreme. Such showpiece numbers as the *Danse guerrière* and the final *Danse générale* have a winning resilience and energy. *Boléro* is relatively slow and easily expressive, not as hard-edged as it can be. Excellent value.

Daphnis et Chloé: Suite 2

**(*) BBC (ADD) BBCL 4039-2. Philh. O, Boult – BIZET: *Jeux d'enfants*; SCHUBERT: *Symphony 8 (Unfinished)*; SIBELIUS: *Symphony 7* **(*)

R.L. recalls hearing Sir Adrian conduct *Daphnis* in the early 1950s and being astonished by his slow tempo in *Lever du jour*. He subsequently learnt that Boult had adopted Ravel's tempo, after Boult had heard the composer conduct the piece in the 1920s. It really feels too slow all the same, but his account has a finely controlled sensuousness that is very persuasive. Excellent sound.

Daphnis et Chloé: Suite 2; Pavane pour une infante défunte
(***) Testament mono SBT1017. Philh. O, Cantelli –
   CASELLA: *Paganiniana;* DUKAS: *L'Apprenti sorcier;* FALLA:
   Three-Cornered Hat (***)
(M) *** Häns. CD 93013. Stuttgart SW RSO, Prêtre – BIZET:
   Symphony in C ***

Prêtre shapes the opening of *Daybreak* with an ecstatic richness of line, the Stuttgart strings gloriously expansive. There
is some radiant woodwind playing too in the *Pantomime* and
the principal flute of this fine orchestra plays his famous solo
with scintillating brilliance leading on to a thrillingly zestful
Danse générale. *La Valse* rises out of the mists and Prêtre's
string phrasing is again passionately seductive, the final climax thrillingly impulsive yet still controlled. This is 'live'
music-making at its finest, and the warm ambience of the
digital recording is just right for it.
   Cantelli's account of *Daphnis* was among his last – and
finest – records. It sounds remarkably good in this splendid
transfer and has classic status.

Ma Mère l'Oye (Suite)
(B) *** CfP 586 1752. LPO, Edwards (with DEBUSSY: *Children's
   Corner: 3 Pieces*) – BRITTEN: *Young Person's Guide* ***;
   PROKOFIEV: *Peter and the Wolf* **(*)

Warm and beautiful playing from the LPO under Sian
Edwards, but Ravel's magical score does not yield all its
secrets here; its sense of gentle, innocent ecstasy is missing.
But the recording is excellent.

Ma Mère l'Oye: Suite (with narration)
(BB) *** Naxos 8.554463. Morris (nar.), Slovak RSO, Jean –
   DUKAS: *L'Apprenti sorcier;* SAINT-SAENS: *Carnival of the
   Animals* **(*)

Ma Mère l'Oye is exquisite music and it is most beautifully
played by the Slovak orchestra under Kenneth Jean. Johnny
Morris provides a friendly spoken introduction for each
fairy-tale number which has been admirably and concisely
written by Keith and Anthony Anderson. To link them with
Ravel's music is surely a marvellous way of familiarizing
younger children with the music.

Ma Mère l'Oye: Suite; La Valse
⊕— *** MDG **SACD** 9371099-2; CD 337 1099-2. Orchester
   der Beethovenhalle, Bonn, Soustrot – DEBUSSY: *Le
   Martyre de Saint-Sébastien* ***

Soustrot gives a simple, dedicated reading of *Ma Mère l'Oye*,
with the tender delicacy of Ravel's score glowingly revealed by
the warm sensitivity of the players. The opening of *La Valse*,
too, has an almost ethereal quality, but there is no lack of
drama later. Indeed, Soustrot's approach, with careful attention to detail, allows the dramatic elements of the score to
emerge without the exaggerated point-making one sometimes encounters in this score. The recording is beautifully
balanced, with the natural concert-hall acoustic combining
clarity with a warm ambience. On SACD it sounds even more
beautiful.

**Menuet antique; Pavane pour une infante défunte; Le
Tombeau de Couperin; (i) Shéhérazade**
(N) *** DG 471 614-2. Cleveland O, Boulez, (i) with Von
   Otter – DEBUSSY: *Danses; Le Jet d'eau; 3 Ballades de
   François Villon* ***

Even those who do not always admire Boulez tend to respond

to his Ravel, and there is no reason not to do so in this
well-planned release. The delicacy and elegance of *Le
Tombeau* are well conveyed, and Anne Sofie von Otter gives a
beautiful account of the magical *Shéhérazade*, one of the best
to appear in recent years. The recorded sound and the
balance are first class.

Le Tombeau de Couperin; Valses nobles et sentimentales
** Testament mono SBT 1236. French Nat. RO, Cluytens –
   DEBUSSY: *La Boîte à joujoux; Children's Corner* **(*)

Cluytens's performance and recording of *Le Tombeau de
Couperin* are less satisfactory than his 1962 account with the
Conservatoire Orchestra which Testament reissued on vinyl
some while back. The recording was made in the Théâtre des
Champs-Elysées in 1953, a year before its companions on this
disc. Like the Debussy, the *Valses nobles et sentimentales* were
recorded in the Salle de la Mutualité and have slightly more
air around the aural image. This is well worth having all the
same: Cluytens never re-recorded *La Boîte à joujoux*, which
has great charm, and the sound is very good for the period.

**(i) Le Tombeau de Couperin; (ii) String Quartet in F; (iii)
Introduction and Allegro for Harp, Flute, Clarinet & Strings;
(iv) Valses nobles et sentimentales**
(M) **(*) ASV Platinum PLT 8517. (i) ASMF, Marriner; (ii)
   Lindsay Qt; (iii) Prometheus Ens.; (iv) Fergus-Thompson

Marriner's *Le Tombeau de Couperin* is, as one would expect,
extremely well played and recorded, and there is plenty to
enjoy on the way. But next to the classic French accounts of
Cluytens, Paray and others, it lacks that last ounce of character which would put it amongst the very best. The Lindsays
give a highly accomplished and finely etched performance of
the *Quartet*, played with their usual aplomb and panache.
There are splendid things here, notably the youthful fire of
the opening movement and the vivid finale, but they do not
always catch all the work's delicate poetic feeling. However,
this is far from a negligible account and it is well recorded.
Gordon Fergus-Thompson's performance of *Valses nobles et
sentimentales* cannot be faulted while the *Introduction and
Allegro* is an atmospheric, sensitive account, not quite in the
league of the classic Decca Melos Quartet recording, but a
good deal more than serviceable.

Tzigane (for violin and orchestra)
(M) *** EMI (ADD) 5 66058-2. Perlman, O de Paris,
   Martinon – SAINT-SAENS: *Havanaise;* VIEUXTEMPS:
   Violin Concertos 4 & 5 ***
(M) *** EMI (ADD) 5 62599-2. Perlman, O de Paris,
   Martinon (with MASSENET: *Thaïs: Méditation*) – CHAUSSON:
   Poème; SAINT-SAENS: *Havanaise etc.* ***
(M) *** DG 447 445-2. Perlman, NYPO, Mehta – BERG;
   STRAVINSKY: *Concertos* ***

Perlman's classic (1974) account of Ravel's *Tzigane* for EMI is
marvellously played; the added projection of the CD puts the
soloist believably at the end of the living-room and the
orchestral sound retains its atmosphere. There are alternative
couplings.
   Perlman's later digital version is very fine and the recording
is obviously modern. But the earlier, EMI performance has
just that bit more charisma.

Valses nobles et sentimentales
**(*) DG (IMS) 429 785-2. NYPO, Sinopoli – MUSSORGSKY:
   Night, etc. ***

With Sinopoli, Ravel's *Valses nobles et sentimentales* is perhaps a shade too idiosyncratic, even though it is played superbly by the New York Philharmonic.

CHAMBER MUSIC

Berceuse; Pièce en forme de habanera; Tzigane
*** DG (IMS) 445 880-2. Dumay, Pires – DEBUSSY; FRANCK: *Violin Sonatas* ***

Polished and elegant performances of these Ravel pieces. There would, of course, have been room on this disc for the 1922 *Sonata*, which at premium price would have made better sense as well as value for money. However, no complaints about these performances or the recording quality.

Introduction & Allegro for Harp, Flute, Clarinet & String Quartet
(***) Testament mono SBT 1053. Gleghorn, Lurie, Stockton, Hollywood Qt – CRESTON: *Quartet*; DEBUSSY: *Danse sacrée*, etc.; TURINA: *La oración del torero*; VILLA-LOBOS: *Quartet 6* (***)

(i) Introduction & Allegro; (ii) Pièce en forme de habanera
🎵— (B) *** Cala CACD 1018 (2). Campbell; (i) Bennett, Jones, Allegri Qt; (ii) York – POULENC: *L'Invitation au château*, etc ***

The Cala performances are recommendable in their own right, but they come in a particularly valuable two-CD set for the price of one, which includes over two hours of music for wind instruments by Poulenc. It is sheer delight from start to finish and cannot be too strongly recommended.

The Hollywood Quartet's version of the *Introduction and Allegro* gives us an example of the exquisite flute playing of Arthur Gleghorn as well as the artistry of Mitchell Lurie and Ann Mason Stockton. A fine performance, sounding remarkably fresh for a 1951 recording.

(i; ii) Introduction & Allegro for Harp, Flute, Clarinet & String Quartet; (ii–iv) Piano Trio; (v) String Quartet; (ii; iii) Violin Sonata; (vi) Sonata for Violin & Cello; (vii) Chansons madécasses
(B) ** Calliope (ADD) CAL 3822.4 (3). (i) Jamais & Ens.; (ii) Barda; (iii) Carracilly; (iv) Heitz; (v) Talich Qt; (vi) Hanover String Duo; (vii) Herbillon, Larde, Degenne, Paraskivesco – DEBUSSY: *Chamber Music* **(*)

The *String Quartet* was recorded in 1972 and very good it is too. The remaining performances in the repertoire date from 1974 and are decent rather than distinguished. The recordings are all analogue – and none the worse for that! But this is serviceable rather than special.

Piano Trio in A min.
🎵— *** Hyp. CDA 67114. Florestan Trio – DEBUSSY; FAURE: *Piano Trios* ***
(N) (B) *** Decca 2-CD 475 6709 (2). Thibaudet, Bell, Isserlis – CHAUSSON: *Concerto in D for Piano, Violin & String Quartet*; DEBUSSY; FAURE; FRANCK: *Violin Sonatas* **
*** Chan. 8458. Borodin Trio – DEBUSSY: *Violin & Cello Sonatas* ***
(BB) **(*) Naxos 8.550934. Joachim Trio – DEBUSSY: *Piano Trio in G*; SCHMITT: *Piano Trio: Très lent* **(*)

Led by the masterly pianist Susan Tomes, the Florestan Trio give an outstanding account of the Ravel masterpiece. They generally adopt speeds on the fast side, but with no feeling of

haste, thanks to playing at once highly polished and flexibly expressive. The couplings are unique and apt, with each composer represented at a different period of his career. Vivid sound.

Joshua Bell, Jean-Yves Thibaudet and Steven Isserlis show keen responsiveness in their account of the Ravel *Piano Trio*, the finest performance offered in this Decca anthology. These gifted players are second to none in sensitivity, and both Bell and Isserlis play with great tonal finesse and artistry. They are recorded with great clarity and presence, and it is a pity that the couplings are not equally recommendable.

The Borodin Trio are excellently recorded and their playing has great warmth and is full of colour. Some may find them too hot-blooded by the side of the Beaux Arts.

The Naxos version by the Joachim Trio who comprise Rebecca Hirsch, Caroline Dearnley and the pianist John Lenehan is worth any collector's notice. They play with sensitive musicianship and finesse. Their performance is imaginative and beautifully recorded, and it is far from uncompetitive.

Piano Trio in A min.; Violin Sonata in G; Violin Sonata posth.; Sonata for Violin & Cello
*** Virgin 5 45492-2. R. & G. Capuçon, Braley

Both the Capuçon brothers are first-rate players, and the pianist, too, is excellent – very sensitive in *pianissimos*, though once or twice a little too overpowering in louder passages. However, this does not detract from what are by any standards first-class readings, splendidly characterized and imaginative performances from all three artists, which can hold their own with any in the current catalogue. The characterization of these brilliant performers is just a shade exaggerated, but such is the quality and accomplishment of this playing that criticism should be silenced – or very nearly so! This is brilliantly thought out and executed playing, and readers wanting all these pieces, including the rare *Sonata posthume*, on one CD will not be disappointed.

Piano Trio in A min.; Sonata for Violin & Cello; (i) Chansons madécasses; 3 Poèmes de Stéphane Mallarmé (song-cycle)
(BB) **(*) Virgin 2×1 5 61427-2 (2). Nash Ens. (members); (i) with Walker – DEBUSSY: *Chamber music* **

The *Sonata for Violin and Cello* is expertly played by Marcia Crayford and Christopher van Kampen – as good an account as any – and in the *Piano Trio* Ian Brown joins them in a performance of real stature and eloquence. In the *Chansons madécasses* and the exquisite *Trois poèmes de Stéphane Mallarmé* Sarah Walker is *primus inter pares* rather than a soloist, though she is not balanced as reticently by Andrew Keener's team as is Delphine Seyrig in the Debussy *Chansons de Bilitis*. This is a pity, but it is not an insuperable obstacle to an apt and inexpensive Ravel collection.

(i) Piano Trio in A min.; (ii) String Quartet in F; (iii) Violin Sonata in G
(M) **(*) Ph. (ADD) 454 1342-2. (i) Beaux Arts Trio; (ii) Italian Qt; (iii) Grumiaux, Hajdu

Ravel's *String Quartet* is offered here as part of a triptych of Ravel's key chamber-works. The performance by the Quartetto Italiano has long been praised by us. The Beaux Arts give a predictably fine account of the *Trio*, though the violinist, Daniel Guilet, is a shade wanting in charm. In the *Violin*

Sonata Grumiaux's playing has great finesse and beauty of sound. The recordings date from 1966 and are very naturally balanced, but the CD transfer demonstrates their age by a degree of shrillness of the *fortissimo* string-timbre.

(i) *Pièce en forme de habanera;* (ii–iii) *Violin Sonata;* (iv; i) *Violin Sonata (Posthume);* (iv–v) *Sonata for Violin & Cello;* (ii–iii) *Tzigane*

(N) (BB) *** Praga (ADD) PR 54016. (i) Hála; (ii) Oistrakh; (iii) Bauer; (iv) Suk; (v) Navarra

These performances have appeared from time to time since they were recorded between 1957 and 1968, save for the *Sonata posthume,* which Suk and Hála recorded in 1979 for Prague Radio. This is a beguiling piece, and Suk fully conveys its charms. Oistrakh recorded the *Violin Sonata* with Frida Bauer for Philips in the late 1950s or early 1960s, and their Czech recording was made a few years later. The *Tzigane,* recorded in 1957, still sounds wonderfully persuasive. The 1967 *Sonata for Violin and Cello* with Suk and Navarra is pretty magisterial. This is not generously represented in the catalogue, so it enhances the undoubted value of this competitively priced reissue.

String Quartet in F

*** DG (IMS) 437 836-2. Hagen Qt – DEBUSSY; WEBERN: *Quartets* ***

(BB) *** EMI Début 5 74020-2. Belcea Qt – DEBUSSY: *String Quartet in G min.;* DUTILLEUX: *Ainsi la nuit* ***

☛— (M) *** DG (ADD) 463 082-2. Melos Qt – DEBUSSY: *String Quartet in G min.* *** ◉

(M) *** Ph. 464 699-2. Italian Qt – DEBUSSY: *Quartet* ***

(BB) *** Naxos 8.554722. Ad Libitum Qt – FAURE: *Quartet* *** ◉

(B) *** CfP 568 1472. Chilingirian Qt – DEBUSSY: *Quartet* ***

(B) *** Calliope (ADD) CAL 5893. Talich Qt – DEBUSSY: *String Quartet* **(*)

(*) ASV CDDCA 930. Lindsay Qt – DEBUSSY: *String Quartet* **(*); STRAVINSKY: *3 Pieces* *

(M) (**(*)) BBC mono BBCL 4063-2. Borodin Qt – BORODIN: *Quartet 2* (**(*)); SHOSTAKOVICH: *Quartet 8* **(*)

(M) **(*) Chan. (ADD) 9980. Borodin Qt – DEBUSSY: *String Quartet* **(*)

(M) **(*) EMI 5 67550-2 [567551]. Alban Berg Qt – DEBUSSY: *String Quartet* **(*); STRAVINSKY: *Concertino; Double Canon; 3 Pieces* ***

(B) **(*) Sony (ADD) SBK 62413. Tokyo Qt – DEBUSSY: *Quartet* **(*); FAURE: *Piano Trio* (*)

String Quartet in F; (i) Introduction & Allegro for Harp, Flute, Clarinet & String Quartet

(BB) *** Naxos 8.550249. Kodály Qt; (i) with Maros, Gyöngyössy, Kovács – DEBUSSY: *Quartet* **(*)

The Hagen Quartet give a performance of great finesse and tonal refinement, and are beautifully recorded to boot, very well served by an excellent balance from one of DG's best engineers, Wolfgang Mitelehner.

The Belcea Quartet sounds as if it is completely inside the music, but its responses are still fresh and felt keenly. As in the Debussy, it is scrupulous in detail and tempos could not be judged better. A performance of real finesse that can be recommended along with the best; at budget price it also enjoys a strong competitive edge.

The Melos playing is perfect in ensemble, has fine attack

and great beauty of tone. The slow movement offers the most refined and integrated matching of timbre; in terms of internal balance and blend it would be difficult to surpass, and the reading has great poetry. In both the *Scherzo* and finale the Melos players evince the highest virtuosity, with complete identification with Ravel's sensibility. The (1979) sound remains excellent in its Galleria transfer, and this disc remains among the primary mid-priced recommendations for this coupling.

For many years the Italian Quartet held pride of place in this coupling. Their playing is perfect in ensemble, attack and beauty of tone, and their performance remains highly recommendable, one of the most satisfying chamber-music records in the catalogue. However, it has now reverted to mid-price from its previous bargain incarnation.

The ensemble and intonation of the Romanian Ad Libitum Quartet are perfect, and their tone is silken. They couple the quartet with the late *E minor Quartet* by Ravel's teacher, Gabriel Fauré, one of the most persuasive and most haunting accounts in the catalogue and given a Rosette by us. Their Ravel is also refined and sophisticated (some may find it just a shade over-characterized), but all the same, this is most distinguished playing and can be confidently recommended given the excellence of the recorded sound, which is natural and lifelike, and the appeal of the coupling.

The Chilingirian recording has plenty of body and presence, and also has the benefit of a warm acoustic. The players give a thoroughly committed account, with well-judged tempi and very musical phrasing. The *Scherzo* is vital and spirited, and there is no want of poetry in the slow movement. At bargain price this is fully competitive and the sound is preferable to that of the Italian Quartet on Philips.

The Talich recorded their Debussy–Ravel coupling in 1984, the Debussy in the studio and the Ravel at a public concert. It goes without saying that they are distinguished by refinement, perfect ensemble and warmth. The tempi are well judged, and the playing is completely free from idiosyncratic or egocentric touches. The recording is not in the first flight but is very acceptable.

The Kodály version can more than hold its own. Artistically and technically this is a satisfying performance which has the feel of real live music-making. The *Introduction and Allegro* is not as magical or as atmospheric as that of the Melos Ensemble from the 1960s, nor is it as well balanced (the players, save for the harp, are a bit forward), but it is still thoroughly enjoyable.

A highly accomplished and finely etched performance from the Lindsays, who play with their usual aplomb and panache. There are splendid things here, notably the youthful fire of the opening movement and the vivid finale. They do not always match the poetic feeling and the *douceur* which some rivals find, but this is not a negligible account, and it is well recorded.

The sheer tonal finesse and subtlety of colouring that the Borodin Quartet bring to the score in their BBC version serve to make it a performance to remember. It is not quite as polished as their later studio version, but it is eminently fresh and the 1962 sound is well balanced.

The Borodin Chandos version was probably recorded in the late 1960s, and after the memorable performance from the Edinburgh Festival captured on BBC Legends. The playing is distinguished by their customary finesse and impeccable tonal aplomb, but there are even finer accounts available at mid-price.

Superb, indeed incomparable playing from the Alban Berg Quartet, and splendidly full and sonorous recording from the

EMI engineers. Yet while this is marvellously polished and has such excellence in terms of ensemble and tonal blend, there is a want of spontaneity that ultimately weighs against it, so that one is unable to forget the physical aspects of the music-making and become totally absorbed in the music itself.

The Tokyo Quartet play with great finesse and tonal beauty, especially in the warm yet refined account of the *très lent*. They certainly observe the marking of the finale, *vif et agité*, and perhaps elsewhere there could be a touch more poise. But their music-making is thoroughly alive. The sound is very good.

(i; ii) *Violin Sonata* (1897); *Violin Sonata in G*; *Tzigane*; (i; iii) *Sonata for Violin & Cello*; (i; ii) *Berceuse sur le nom de Gabriel Fauré*; *Kaddish*; *Pièce en forme de habanera*
— (M) *** Decca 475 486-2. (i) Juillet; (ii) Rogé; (iii) Mørk

This highly distinguished reissue won the *Gramophone* Chamber Music Award in 1997. These performances are predictably cultured and beautifully recorded, and the *Tzigane* is a version with a difference in that Rogé uses a piano luthénal (an instrument modified to sound like a cimbalom, which was used in the first performance in 1922). Strongly recommended, and the more so at mid-price.

Violin Sonata in G
*** Erato 0630 15110-2. Repin, Berezovsky – MEDTNER: *Sonata 3 (Sonata epica)* ***

(N) *** EMI 5 57679-2. Chang, Vogt – FRANCK; SAINT-SAENS: *Violin Sonatas* ***

(N) (M) *** DG 477 5448 (2). Mintz, Bronfman (with Recital of encores by ALBÉNIZ; COUPERIN; GLAZUNOV; GRANADOS; KREISLER; WEBER; WIENIAWSKI) – DEBUSSY; FAURE; FRANCK: *Violin Sonatas* ***

Sarah Chang and Lars Vogt give a brilliant and finely characterized account of the *Sonata* and in particular its blues movement. This has strong claims on the allegiance of the collector and can certainly be recommended if the couplings are suitable. Good recorded sound, too.

Shlomo Mintz and Yefim Bronfman's account offers highly polished playing, even if it is perhaps not so completely inside Ravel's world in the slow movement. The glorious sounds both artists produce are a source of unfailing delight, and they are beautifully recorded. At mid-price and coupled with fine performances of three other French violin sonatas, plus an enticing programme of encores, this is very recommendable.

Vadim Repin and Boris Berezovsky on Erato offer an unusual coupling. These two artists command a wide range of colour and dynamics, infuse every phrase with life, and have the full measure of the 'Blues' movement. Repin plays the Guarneri with which Isaac Stern delighted us for almost half a century and it sounds magnificently responsive in his hands. Very good and completely natural recording.

Violin Sonata (1897); *Tzigane*
(N) *** Avie AV 2059. Graffin, Désert – DEBUSSY: *Violin Sonata; Nocturne et Scherzo;* ENESCU: *Impressions d'enfance* ***

Philippe Graffin and Claire Désert give an entirely delightful account of the early *Sonata posthume*, playing with much delicacy and subtlety to make it sound like mature Ravel. Their *Tzigane*, too, is played with refinement as well as sparkle: it has plenty of gypsy feeling but is not treated as just a virtuoso display piece.

Tzigane (for violin and piano)
(BB) (***) Dutton mono CDBP 9710. G. & J. Neveu – BRAHMS: *Violin Concerto;* SUK: *4 Pieces; Encores* ***

Ginette Neveu's account of the *Tzigane* is full of gypsy temperament and fire, with some dazzling pyrotechnics at the close. She dominates the proceedings, although her brother, Jean, accompanies supportively. Also offered are some delectable encores including Chopin's *Nocturne in C sharp minor*, its cantilena sounding for all the world like a violin piece, and dazzling versions of Falla's *Spanish Dance* from *La vida breve* and Dinicu's gutsy *Hora Staccato*. The transfers of these 1946 Abbey Road sessions are vividly realistic.

PIANO MUSIC

Piano duet
Boléro; Introduction & Allegro; Ma Mère l'Oye; Rapsodie espagnole; La Valse
⌖ *** Chan. 8905. Lortie, Mercier

Louis Lortie's recital for piano (four hands and two pianos) with his Canadian partner, Hélène Mercier, is quite magical; these artists command an exceptionally wide range of colour and dynamic nuance. The acoustic is that of The Maltings, Snape, and the result is quite outstanding sonically: you feel that you have only to stretch out and you can touch the instruments. Ravel's transcriptions are stunningly effective in their hands, even, surprisingly, *Boléro*.

Entre cloches; (i) *Frontispiece. Introduction and Allegro; Ma Mère l'Oye; Rapsodie espagnole; Shéhérazade: Ouverture de féerie. La Valse*
(M) *** Somm SOMMCD 025. Micallef, Inanga; (i) with Sterling

The young, prize-winning duo of Micallef and Inanga are warmly responsive, naturally in sympathy with the idiom. They quickly make one appreciate the merits of these alternative versions. Their subtle and persuasive use of rubato comes out very clearly, as in the *Malagueña* from *Rapsodie espagnole*, a piece written earlier than the other three movements. That work was originally coupled with the much squarer *Entre cloches* (also included here) under the title, *Sites auriculaires*. Bell-sounds appear again in the fragment *Frontispiece*, written in 1918 as the introduction to a collection of war-poems. Lasting barely more than a minute, it brings some extraordinary polytonal writing, totally un-Ravelian. The other major item, *Shéhérazade*, with hard keyboard textures, is less evocative than tough, sounding more modern than the orchestral version. Best of all is *La Valse*, a brilliant transcription already a favourite with two-piano duos. Micallef and Inanga, instead of emerging from formless clouds of notes at the start, at once establish hints of the waltz rhythm, and go from strength to strength.

Music for Piano Duet and Two Pianos
Frontispiece (for 2 pianos & one hand); *Ma Mère l'Oye* (Suite; for piano, 4 hands); *Rapsodie espagnole; Sites auriculaires: Entrecloches* (only). *La Valse* (for 2 pianos)
(N) (BB) **(*) EMI Gemini (ADD/DDD) 5 86510-2 (2).
Collard, Béroff – DEBUSSY: *Music for 2 pianos;* BIZET: *Jeux d'enfants;* DUKAS: *L'Apprenti sorcier* **(*)

Jean-Philippe Collard, arguably the greatest French pianist of his generation, is here joined by Michel Béroff, and their playing never falls below distinction. Although the recordings, made in the Paris Salle Wagram, are too closely miked – there is a shallow quality at higher dynamic levels – the sound here is generally more amenable than in the Debussy couplings, particularly in *Ma Mère l'Oye* and the superb account of the *Rapsodie espagnole*, which loses surprisingly little in the composer's piano format. (This, of course, includes the *Malagueña*, the missing second movement of the *Sites auriculaires*.) In the brief *Frontispiece* Katia Labèque provides the fifth hand! A set not to be missed, not least because of the Bizet and Dukas bonuses.

Solo piano music

A la manière de Borodine; A la manière de Chabrier; Gaspard de la nuit; Jeux d'eau; Menuet antique; Menuet sur le nom de Haydn; Miroirs; Pavane pour une infante défunte; Prélude; Sérénade grotesque; Sonatine; Le Tombeau de Couperin; Valses nobles et sentimentales
*** Hyp. CDA 67341/2. Hewitt
(N) (BB) *** EMI Gemini (ADD) 5 86061-2 (2). Collard
*** Decca 433 515-2 (2). Thibaudet
(N) (M) *** Chan. 10142X (2). Lortie
(M) *** CRD CRD 3383/4. Crossley
(N) (BB) **(*) Virgin 5 62363-2 (4). Quefélec – SATIE: Collection ***

A la manière de Borodine; A la manière de Chabrier; Gaspard de la nuit; Jeux d'eau; Menuet antique; Menuet sur le nom de Haydn; Miroirs; Pavane pour un infante défunte; Prélude; Sonatine; Le Tombeau de Couperin; Valses nobles et sentimentales
➳ (B) (***) EMI mono 5 74793-2 (2). Gieseking

Ravel's solo piano music has been well served in the last couple of decades but this newcomer from Hyperion is second to none and will now probably be a first choice for most collectors. We associate Angela Hewitt with Bach, but the clarity she brought to that repertoire serves to illuminate Ravel's textures without ever entailing any loss of atmosphere. Her performances are characteristically full of the searchingly imaginative approach she takes to everything she plays. The playing is impeccable, in both technique and taste. Altogether this is a fascinating new look at these inspired pieces, so perfect in their detail, and one continually has the sense of coming to this music afresh.

Jean-Philippe Collard is a stylist and a master, and Ravel playing doesn't come much better than this. These recordings were made between 1977 and 1980. There are so many beautiful things here that it would be curmudgeonly to complain. What a beautiful sense of line he achieves in *Ondine*, the first of the *Gaspard de la nuit*, though it must be admitted that the right-hand ostinato is far from the *pianopianissimo* that Ravel marks. For the most part, however, this playing silences criticism. *Le Gibet* is wonderfully atmospheric, as is so much else, particularly the superb *Noctuelles*. The recording, made in the Salle Wagram, is not wholly sympathetic: there is a glassy, shallow quality, particularly on the upper part of the spectrum.

Jean-Yves Thibaudet's collected Ravel is quite outstanding playing on all counts; Thibaudet exhibits flawless technique, perfect control, refinement of touch and exemplary taste. He distils just the right atmosphere in *Oiseaux tristes* and *Une*

barque sur l'océan – but then, one might as well choose any other piece from *Miroirs*, and his *Gaspard* can hold its own with any in the catalogue. The recording is of real distinction too.

The fine Canadian pianist Louis Lortie made a strong impression with the two Ravel *Concertos* and with this survey of the piano music when it first appeared in the 1980s. We found his *Gaspard de la nuit*, with its chilling and atmospheric account of *Le Gibet*, particularly impressive. The recordings, made at The Maltings, Snape, have great clarity and presence, and the performances have proved very persuasive over the years.

Paul Crossley's accounts of all these works are aristocratic, with an admirable feeling for tone-colour and line, and rarely mannered. His version of *Le Tombeau de Couperin* has a classical refinement and delicacy that are refreshing. The CRD recording is very good indeed.

No quarrels with Anne Queffélec's playing. There are some masterly and enjoyable interpretations here, but it is all far too closely observed, as if one were in the front row of the concert hall; as a result not all the atmosphere registers to full effect, once the dynamics rise above *mf*. However, this is now one of the least expensive ways of collecting a complete digital survey of the solo piano music in really distinguished performances, if you want the Satie coupling.

Gieseking's classic recordings were made in 1954, with Walter Legge and Geraint Jones acting as producers. Gieseking's special affinity for this repertoire shines through, and no one with a serious interest in the French master should neglect these readings. Of course, the age of stereo has brought impressive modern successors, but nearly half a century on these performances speak with a specially idiomatic accent. Here are a pianist with a limpid, translucent tone and a piano with no hammers.

A la manière de Borodine; A la manière de Chabrier; Menuet antique; Menuet sur le nom de Haydn; Miroirs; Pavane pour une infante défunte; Prélude; Sérénade grotesque; Sonatine
**(*) ASV CDDCA 809. Fergus-Thompson

Gaspard de la nuit; Jeux d'eau; Le Tombeau de Couperin; Valses nobles et sentimentales
**(*) ASV CDDCA 805. Fergus-Thompson

Turning to Gordon Fergus-Thompson's Ravel immediately after Thibaudet is to enter a different imaginative world. There is an ample and rich colour-palette, and he exhibits considerable personality and imagination. Not to be preferred to the Decca set, but readers considering it can be assured that it is very well recorded.

A la manière de Borodine; A la manière de Chabrier; Menuet antique; Prélude; Le Tombeau de Couperin; Valses nobles et sentimentales
**(*) Nim. (ADD) NI 5011. Perlemuter

Gaspard de la nuit; Jeux d'eau; Miroirs; Pavane
**(*) Nim. (ADD) NI 5005. Perlemuter

Though Perlemuter's technical command is not as complete as it had been, he gives delightful, deeply sympathetic readings; the sense of spontaneity is a joy. There may be Ravel recordings which bring more dazzling virtuoso displays, but none more persuasive. Nimbus's ample room acoustic makes the result naturally atmospheric on CD.

Gaspard de la nuit

- ⊕ (M) *** DG (IMS) 463 678-2. Pogorelich –
  PROKOFIEV: *Sonata 6* *** ⊕
- (M) (***) BBC mono BBCL 4064-2. Michelangeli –
  BEETHOVEN: *Sonatas 4 & 12;* DEBUSSY: *Hommage à Rameau* (**(*))

Pogorelich's *Gaspard* is out of the ordinary. In *Le Gibet*, we are made conscious of the pianist's refinement of tone and colour first, and Ravel's poetic vision afterwards. But for all that, this is piano playing of astonishing quality. The control of colour and nuance in *Scarbo* is dazzling and its eruptive cascades of energy and dramatic fire have one sitting on the edge of one's seat.

Michelangeli's *Gaspard* comes from a recital given in the Concert Hall of Broadcasting House in 1959, and those who were fortunate enough to be there were electrified by Michelangeli's playing. The very opening of *Ondine* is not as hushed (the marking is *pianopianissimo*) as it seemed at the time, but everything else is magical. *Le Gibet* is fantastically controlled and full of atmosphere and *Scarbo* is dazzling and sinister – it must be one of the greatest performances it has ever received. The mono sound is strikingly well transferred and infinitely better than earlier, unauthorized LP versions that have been in currency.

Valses nobles et sentimentales (complete); *Le Tombeau de Couperin; Forlane; Miroirs; La Vallée des cloches*

- (B) *** RCA 2CD (ADD) 74321 846062. Rubinstein –
  CHABRIER: *Pièces Pittoresques: Scherzo-Valse;* DEBUSSY: *Estampes,* etc.; FAURE: *Nocturne 3;* FRANCK: *Symphonic Variations for Piano and Orchestra; Prélude choral et fugue;* SAINT-SAENS: *Piano Concerto 2* ***

These pieces (including the Fauré and Chabrier) appear to derive from an LP called 'A French Programme' which appeared in mono in the mid-1960s, and later in stereo. The playing is eminently aristocratic, and the sound greatly improved in these new transfers. Rubinstein could be a magician in French music just as he was in Chopin. A reissue of distinction.

VOCAL MUSIC

Chansons madécasses

*** EMI 5 56982-2. Karnéus, Pahud, Mørk, Kovacevich –
  DEBUSSY: *Syrinx; Bilitis,* etc.; PROKOFIEV: *Flute Sonata, Op. 94* ***

This EMI version of *Chansons madécasses* is primarily a vehicle for the virtuosity – or rather artistry – of Emmanuel Pahud, for there is no egotism in his playing, the virtuosity is merely by the by. He and Kovacevich are joined by Katerina Karnéus and Truls Mørk. Great sensitivity, powerful atmosphere, lucidity of diction and clarity of texture. This is an outstanding recital.

'Chant d'amour': 4 Chansons populaires; 2 Mélodies hébraïques; Tripatos; Vocalise-étude en forme de habanera

*** Decca 452 667-2. Bartoli, Chung – BIZET; BERLIOZ; DELIBES: *Mélodies* ***

Cecilia Bartoli is just as much at home in the music of Ravel as she is with the songs of the other composers represented in this outstanding recital of French songs. Myung Whun-Chung, too, proves himself a natural accompanist.

Don Quichotte à Dulcinée (song-cycle)

- (N) (***) Testament mono SBT 1312. Souzay, Paris Conservatoire O, Lindenberg – CHAUSSON: *Mélodies;* DEBUSSY: *Trois Ballades;* DUPARC: *12 Songs* (***)
- (M) *** Virgin 5 61850-2. Van Dam, Lyon Nat. Op. O, Nagano – IBERT: *4 Chansons de Don Quichotte;* MARTIN: *6 Monologues from 'Jedermann';* POULENC: *Le Bal masqué* ***

Souzay's 1951 record of *Don Quichotte à Dulcinée* with the Paris Conservatoire Orchestra is part of an outstanding recital. This recording, however, is just a bit too closely balanced: the orchestra is very much in the background. Nevertheless, this Testament reissue remains indispensable.

José van Dam's approach to Ravel's *Quichotte* triptych has an operatic flair, yet he closes the opening eulogy to Dulcinée very touchingly, while the central *Epic Song* has poignant nobility of line to contrast with the lighter closing number. Kent Nagano makes the very most of the scintillating orchestration, setting the scene admirably, and in the final song finding ready parallels with the *Rapsodie espagnole*. Excellent atmospheric recording, and full texts and translations make this imaginative collection more than the sum of its parts.

Histoires naturelles

- (N) (***) Testament mono SBT 1311. Souzay, Bonneau – FALLA: *7 canciones populares españolas;* FAURE: *Après un rêve,* etc. *** ⊕

Souzay made this record of the *Histoires naturelles* in 1951, only half a dozen years after his début in Paris, and it still remains arguably the finest recorded account of Ravel's imaginative cycle. Magnificently transferred, the sound belies its age and comes with some Fauré songs that are among the classics of the gramophone.

Shéhérazade (song-cycle)

- ⊕ (M) *** Decca 460 973-2. Crespin, SRO, Ansermet – BERLIOZ: *Les Nuits d'été* *** (with *Recital of French Songs* ***)
- (N) *** Warner 2564 61938-2. Graham, BBC SO, Tortelier – CHAUSSON: *Poème de l'amour et de la mer;* DEBUSSY: *Poèmes de Charles Baudelaire* ***
- (B) **(*) Sony SBK 87797. Von Stade, Boston SO, Ozawa – BERLIOZ: *Les Nuits d'été; Arias* **

Crespin is right inside these songs and Ravel's magically sensuous music emerges with striking spontaneity. She is superbly supported by Ansermet who, aided by the Decca engineers, weaves a fine tonal web round the voice. Her style has distinct echoes of the opera house; but the richness of the singer's tone does not detract from the delicate languor of *The Enchanted Flute*, in which the slave-girl listens to the distant sound of her lover's flute playing while her master sleeps. The new transfer of the 1963 recording adds to the allure of the remarkably rich and translucent Decca sound.

Susan Graham chooses wide contrasts for her performance of Ravel's inspired triptych, boldly operatic in line for *Asie*, tenderly languorous in the lovely *La Flûte enchantée* (with sensuous flute playing to match) and finding a delicate melancholy for *L'Indifférent*. Yan Pascal Tortelier's accompaniments are expressively ardent, and the recording is first class.

Ozawa is an experienced and sympathetic advocate of Ravel, and he and the Boston orchestra provide a seductive web of sound for von Stade's beguiling account of this most sensuous of French song-cycles. The centrepiece, *La Flûte enchantée*, is warm and atmospheric; it is a pity that the coupled *Nuits d'été* is so much less successful.

OPERA

L'Enfant et les sortilèges

➤ (M) *** DG 474 890-2. Ogéas, Collard, Berbié, Sénéchal, Gilma, Herzog, Rehfuss, Maurane, Fr. R. Ch. & Boys' Ch., Fr. R. O, Maazel

➤ ✿ (***) Testament mono SBT 1044. Sautereau, Vessières, Michel, Scharley, Le Marc'Hadour, Peyron, Angelici, French Nat. R. Ch. & O, Bour

(i) *L'Enfant et les sortilèges* (complete). *Ma Mère l'Oye* (ballet: complete)

*** DG (IMS) 457 589-2. (i) Stephen, Owens, Lascarro, Johnson, Soloists New L. Children's Ch., L. Symphony Ch.; LSO, Previn

It is good that DG have reissued Maazel's delightful recording of *L'Enfant et les sortilèges* as a separate disc, as it won the *Gramophone* Award for Remastered CDs in 1989. However, those seeking the companion CD of *L'Heure espagnole* will find that DG's two-disc set includes also Maazel's outstanding recordings of Rimsky-Korsakov's *Capriccio espagnol* and Stravinsky's *Le Chant du rossignol*, two classics of the gramophone from the early days of stereo.

With opulent recording heightening the sumptuousness of Ravel's orchestration, and with Previn infectiously pointing rhythms at generally spacious speeds, this evocative one-acter could not be more persuasive, with the atmospheric magic beautifully captured. Though a French-speaking cast might have sounded more idiomatic, characterizations here are exceptionally vivid, with Pamela Helen Stephen as the Child easily outshining her predecessor on Previn's EMI version, and the others making a strong team. The apt and substantial fill-up, the complete *Mother Goose* ballet, also beautifully done, makes a welcome bonus.

Testament here offer a superlative transfer of the unsurpassed first (1947) recording of Ravel's charming one-acter under Ernest Bour. There is a magic about this performance that completely captivates the listener. Each part, from Nadine Sautereau's Child, Yvon Le Marc'Hadour's Tom-Cat and Clock, and Solange Michel's touching squirrel, to Denise Scharley as the Dragonfly and the Mother, could not be improved upon in character, subtlety and style. The singing and playing of the French Radio forces are vital and imaginative. Ravel's exquisite score is heard to best advantage in this extraordinary transfer with voices firm and immediate. With no stars but with no weak link, the singers make an outstanding team, helped by sound which, with background hiss eliminated, has astonishing presence. No other version casts quite such a strong spell.

(i) *L'Enfant et les sortilèges*; (ii) *L'Heure espagnole* (both complete)

(M) *** DG (ADD) (IMS) 449 769-2 (2). (i) Ogéas, Collard, Berbié, Sénéchal, Gilma, Herzog, Rehfuss, Maurane, RTF Ch. & Boys' Ch., RTF Nat. O; (ii) Berbié, Sénéchal, Giraudeau, Bacquier, Van Dam, Paris Opera O; Maazel – RIMSKY-KORSAKOV: *Capriccio espagnol;* STRAVINSKY: *Le Chant du rossignol* *** ✿

Maazel's recordings of Ravel's two one-act operas were made in the early 1960s and, though the solo voices in *L'Enfant* are balanced rather closely, the remastered sound in both operas is wonderfully vivid and atmospheric and each performance is splendidly stylish. The singing is delightful: neo-classical crispness of articulation goes with refined textures that convey the ripe humour of one piece, the tender poetry of the other. The inclusion of Maazel's superb early stereo accounts of Rimsky's *Capriccio* (with the Berlin Philharmonic) and *Le Chant du rossignol* glitteringly played by the Berlin Radio Orchestra, two classics of the gramophone, is particularly welcome.

RAWSTHORNE, Alan (1905–71)

(i) *Concertante pastorale for Flute, Horn & Strings. Concerto for String Orchestra; Divertimento for Chamber Orchestra; Elegiac Rhapsody for String Orchestra; Light Music for Strings* (based on Catalan tunes); (ii) *Suite for Recorder & String Orchestra* (orch. McCabe)

(BB) *** Naxos 8.553567. Northern CO, Lloyd-Jones; with (i) Marshall, Goldberg; (ii) Turner

Though the melodic writing is rarely as memorable as that of, say, Walton, all the works here are beautifully crafted, not least the *Concerto for String Orchestra*, with two dark movements followed by lightness and open intervals. The *Concertante* is most evocative with beautiful solos for flute and horn. The neoclassical *Recorder Suite* has been deftly arranged by John McCabe from an original with piano. Finest of all is the *Elegiac Rhapsody*, written in memory of the poet Louis MacNeice, touching a deeper vein, erupting from lamentation into anger. Outstanding performances, vividly recorded.

(i) *Cello Concerto;* (ii) *Oboe Concerto. Symphonic Studies*

(BB) *** Naxos 8.554763. RSNO, Lloyd-Jones; with (i) Baillie; (ii) Rancourt

The *Cello Concerto* of 1966 is both imaginative and resourceful, though perhaps a little amorphous. Its first two movements are rewarding, though the finale sounds a bit manufactured. The post-war *Oboe Concerto* is less ambitious but full of good things. Alexander Baillie gives a masterly account of the *Cello Concerto*, and Stéphane Rancourt is hardly less persuasive in its companion. First-class orchestral playing under David Lloyd-Jones and excellently balanced and vividly present recording.

The *Symphonic Studies* is arguably Rawsthorne's masterpiece and one of the most ingenious works of its period. Astonishingly, apart from Constant Lambert's pioneering set with the Philharmonia Orchestra, there has been only one other recording, by Nicholas Braithwaite on Lyrita. All Rawsthorne's music is crafted superbly and highly personal, so that the idiom is immediately recognizable as his.

Clarinet Concerto

(BB) *** Hyp. Helios CDH 55069. King, Northwest CO of Seattle, Francis – COOKE: *Concerto;* JACOB: *Mini-Concerto* ***

Though the *Clarinet Concerto* is an early work of Rawsthorne's it already establishes the authentic flavour of his writing, the more obviously so in a performance as persuasive as this from soloist and orchestra alike. Excellent recording, and very good value.

Piano Concertos 1–2; (i) Double Piano Concerto
*** Chan. 9125. Tozer, LPO, Bamert; (i) with Cislowski

(i) *Piano Concertos 1–2; Improvisations on a Theme of Constant Lambert*
☙ (BB) *** Naxos 8.555959. Donohoe, Ulster O, Yuasa

The *First Piano Concerto* was a wartime work and the *Second* was composed for the Festival of Britain and is also rewarding. The *Concerto for Two Pianos* is likewise stimulating. Geoffrey Tozer gives a good account of the concertos. The opening of No. 1 is a bit rushed; Tamara-Anna Cislowski is an excellent partner in the 1968 concerto. Matthias Bamert and the LPO are very supportive and the recording is in the best traditions of the house.

In the new Naxos recording Peter Donohoe presents the first movement in an effervescent scherzando style, and in the *Chaconne* the dialogue between piano and orchestra has an engaging delicacy. The *Tarantella* finale is infectiously spirited, and Donohoe's brilliant solo contribution has all the sparkle you could want.

In the *Second Concerto* the opening flute solo is perhaps a little backward, otherwise the overall balance is admirable. The surge of ardour, from soloist and orchestra alike, carries the music forward, while again there is some delightful woodwind detail. In the finale Rawsthorne almost immediately introduces his catchy main theme, which is in a two-four/three-eight metre, and the movement as a whole is played with gusto and wit, producing a blaze of virtuosity at the close. The orchestral *Improvisations* which come as a bonus, are based on a seven-note theme from Lambert's last ballet, *Tiresias*. They are widely varied and listener-friendly and easy to follow. With excellent recording, this can be strongly recommended on all counts.

(i) *Violin Concertos 1–2. Fantasy Overture: Cortèges*
☙ (BB) *** Naxos 8.554240. (i) Hirsch; BBC Scottish SO, Friend

The Naxos recording brings the accomplished Rebecca Hirsch as soloist, with excellent orchestral support from the BBC Scottish Symphony under Lionel Friend. Her performances hold their own, and the value of the disc is enhanced by another première recording, that of Rawsthorne's *Cortèges*. It is an imaginative and at times haunting piece, very well played and recorded here.

Film music: *Burma Victory* (suite); *The Captive Heart* (suite; both arr. Gerard Schurmann); *The Cruel Sea: Main Titles & Nocturne. The Dancing Fleece: 3 Dances* (both scores arr. & orch. Philip Lane). *Lease of Life: Main Titles & Emergency. Saraband for Dead Lovers: Saraband & Carnival* (both arr. Schurmann). *Uncle Silas: Main Titles & Opening Scene; Valse Caprice; End Titles. West of Zanzibar: Main Titles. Where No Vultures Fly: Introduction; Main Titles & Opening Scene. Surveying the Game* (all arr. & orch. Philip Lane)
*** Chan. 9749. BBC PO, Gamba

Between 1937 and 1964 Rawsthorne wrote music for twenty-seven British films. He was not a ready melodist like Malcolm Arnold, but he could write memorable paragraphs, imaginatively and powerfully scored, and Gerard Schurmann's two suites from *The Captive Heart* and the fine documentary *Burma Victory* demonstrate his remarkable ability to characterize situations in music.

He is very good at flamboyant, Hollywoodian title music, yet the charming delicacy of the *Valse caprice* from *Uncle Silas* shows the other side of his musical nature and makes for a number well worth preserving independently. Gerard Schurmann had worked with the composer in preparing the original scores, and Philip Lane demonstrates his skills of reconstruction using the original soundtracks when the manuscripts are missing. The music is splendidly played and given Chandos's top-quality sound.

Symphonies 1; (i) 2 (A Pastoral Symphony). 3
(BB) *** Naxos 8.557480. (i) Ellett; Bournemouth SO, Lloyd-Jones

Why is Rawsthorne, whose centenary falls in the year of publication of our 30th anniversary *Guide*, so neglected? His language is individual and is immediately recognizable as his. And anyone who responds to Walton will feel at home in his world. The *First Symphony* (1950) is a haunting and powerfully wrought piece, which grows in stature on every hearing. The *Second* comes from 1959, and its finale includes a setting of Henry Howard, Earl of Surrey, in praise of summer, with a soprano soloist. Charlotte Ellett proves an excellent soloist. The impressive *Third* (1964), which Norman Del Mar recorded with the BBC Symphony Orchestra for Lyrita three years later, is equally well served here by David Lloyd-Jones and his Bournemouth forces. This conductor directs all three works with total conviction and real imagination. Powerful music then, splendidly played and vividly recorded, and all for a modest outlay. Good though the Lyrita recordings were, they are displaced by this newcomer.

Clarinet Quartet
*** Redcliffe RR 010. Cox, Redcliffe Ens. – BLISS; ROUTH: *Clarinet Quintets* ***

Rawsthorne's *Clarinet Quartet* is more ambivalent in feeling than the Bliss *Quintet*, but its quirky opening movement is appealing and the darker *Poco lento* hardly less striking. With Nicholas Cox a most winning soloist, the performance here could hardly be improved upon, and the recording is first class.

(i) *Violin Sonata; (ii) Theme & Variations for 2 Violins*
*** Metier MSV CD 92029. Skaerved; (i) Honma; (ii) Sohn – MCCABE: *Maze Dances*, etc. ***

Alan Rawsthorne's *Theme and Variations for Two Violins*, one of his earliest works, stands among the finest pieces ever written for this daunting medium, with the interplay between the two instruments bringing a kaleidoscopic sequence of ideas, sharply defined. The *Violin Sonata* of over 20 years later is tougher in its idiom with the four movements tautly argued within a compressed span, not a note wasted. Peter Sheppard Skaerved gives flawless performances, very well matched by Christine Sohn in the *Variations* and Tamami Honma in the *Sonata*. Clear, immediate sound.

4 Bagatelles; Ballade; 4 Romantic Pieces; Sonatina; Theme & 4 Studies
**(*) Paradisum PDS-CD2. Clegg – LENNOX BERKELEY: *6 Preludes* **(*)

On this CD John Clegg presents the whole of Rawsthorne's output for the piano (apart from the two concertos). Inventive and civilized music, every bar bearing his personal stamp, and persuasively played. The only snag is the rather claustrophobic acoustic in which it is recorded.

(i) Piano pieces: *Ballade in G sharp min.; Valse.* Songs: (ii) *Carol; 2 Fish;* (iii) *3 French Nursery Songs; Precursors; Prison Cycle* (with Alan Bush); (iv) *Scena Rustica* (for soprano & harp); (ii) *2 Songs for tenor & piano: (Away delights; God Lyaeus);* (iii) *Tzu-Yeh Songs*

(*) Campion Cameo 2001. (i) Cuckson; (ii) Hill; (iii) Wells; (ii; iii) Swallow; (iv) Buckle, Wakeford – BUSH: *Prison Cycle (3 Songs)* **(*); MCCABE: *3 Folk Songs* *

As Trevor Holst suggests in the accompanying notes, one thinks of Rawsthorne primarily as an orchestral and instrumental composer, so it is not remarkable that although all these settings bring appealingly melodic vocal lines, the musical kernel of each song is usually within the piano accompaniments, here so responsively played by Keith Swallow. The evocative opening *Prison Cycle*, with the settings shared by Rawsthorne and Bush, sets poems by the German Socialist poet Ernst Toller, who was imprisoned by the Nazis and who committed suicide in 1939. The soprano soloist Alison Wells (singing in German) sombrely evokes his claustrophobic imprisonment ('Six steps forward, Six steps back'), and the pleasure of seeing a pair of swallows perching on the barred window of his cell – before they are shot by the prison guards.

The mood is then lightened by five *Tzu-Yeh Songs*, translations from the Chinese, which have minimal oriental musical influence but much charm, as indeed have the *Three French Nursery Songs*, all of which show Alison Wells at her best, as does the richly lyrical MacNeice setting, *Precursors.* But the *Scena Rustica*, which offers an intimate dialogue for soprano and harp, suits Judith Buckle's voice less well, mainly because of an intrusive vibrato.

Of the tenor songs the gentle *Carol* and the boisterous medieval *Two Fish* ('the adult'rous Sargus' and 'the constant Cantharus') show Martyn Hill in good form. Two early piano pieces, played simply by Alan Cuckson, act as an interlude, before the sparkling tenor triptych, *Three Folk Songs* by John McCabe, closes the recital. Good recording, but made in a less than ideal ecclesiastical acoustic with the microphones fairly close and not always flattering the singers.

REGER, Max (1873–1916)

Ballet Suite, Op. 130; 4 Böcklin Tone-Pictures, Op. 128; Variations & Fugue on a Theme by Beethoven, Op. 86

*** BIS CD 601. Norrköping SO, Segerstam

Segerstam gets a very good response from the Norrköping Orchestra and obviously cares for this music and makes the most of it without succumbing to the expressive exaggeration which spoils some of his other work. Both the *Ballet Suite* and the *Beethoven Variations* are well served, and very well recorded.

4 Böcklin Tone-Pictures, Op. 128; Variations on a Theme by Hiller, Op. 100

🔑 *** Chan. 8794. Concg. O, Järvi

Of the four *Tone Poems* on Chandos, textures in *Der geigende Eremit* ('*Hermit playing the violin*') are unexectedly transparent, and *Im Spiel der Wellen* has something of the sparkle of the *Jeu de vagues* movement of *La Mer* photographed in sepia; while the *Isle of the Dead* is a lovely and often very touching piece. The *Hiller Variations* are gloriously inventive. These works are beautifully recorded and Neeme Järvi's performances have the combination of sensitivity and virtuosity that this composer needs.

Symphonic Prologue to a Tragedy; Variations & Fugue on a Theme of Mozart

*** BIS CD 771. Norrköping SO, Segerstam

Segerstam's obvious dedication to the spirit and the letter of these scores rises to their challenge admirably. The BIS recording is of demonstration standard.

Variations & Fugue on a Theme of Beethoven, Op. 86

(M) *** Chan. 7080 (2). LPO, Järvi – BRUCKNER: *Symphony 8* **(*)

Terminally ill, in his last years Reger concentrated on composition, here orchestrating eight of the twelve variations of a work he originally scored for two pianos. The result is a brilliant, sharply characterized piece with obvious echoes of Brahms, a fine companion for Reger's two better-known sets of variations on themes of Mozart and Hiller, and an attractive coupling for Järvi's warm-hearted reading of the Bruckner, now at mid-price. Rich 1986 Chandos sound.

Variations on a Theme by Mozart, Op. 132

(**N**) (M) (***) DG mono 474 989-2. BPO, Boehm – BRAHMS: *Symphony 2* **(*)

Boehm made the first 78-r.p.m. recording of Reger's masterpiece with the Saxon State Orchestra before the war, and this Berlin recording, completed a few days after the Brahms (in December 1956), was its LP première. It is a very fine performance, tastefully recorded and musically very satisfying, even after the passage of half a century.

CHAMBER MUSIC

(Unaccompanied) *Cello Suites 1 in G; 2 in D min.; 3 in A min., Op. 131c*

(M) *** Oehms OC 235. Schiefen

A pupil of Maurice Gendron and Siegfried Palm, Guido Schiefen is now in his early thirties and proves an authoritative and persuasive advocate of the three Reger *Cello Suites*, Op. 131c. These were composed immediately before the *Variations and Fugue on a Theme by Mozart* and were modelled on Bach, whom they at times paraphrase. Not essential listening perhaps, but played like this they are quite impressive and they are well recorded too.

(i) *Clarinet Quintet in A, Op. 146. String Quartet in E flat, Op. 109*

*** Nim. NI 5644. (i) Leister; Vogler Qt

The mellifluous *Clarinet Quintet*, his very last work, has never found its rightful place in the concert hall or the record catalogues. Karl Leister's artistry and eloquence are very persuasive, as indeed are those of the wonderful Vogler Quartet. The Nimbus engineers place us rather too close to the artists and we would welcome rather more space round the sound, but there is no doubt that these are very distinguished performances that call for a strong recommendation.

Piano Trios in B min., Op. 2; E minor, Op. 102

*** MDG 303 0751-2 Trio Parnassus

The *B minor Trio* is for piano, violin and viola and is very derivative. There are faint hints of things to come, but for the most part Brahms is the pervasive influence. The *E minor Trio* is another matter: there are some striking harmonic sleights of hand and a reminder of the first of the *Böcklin Portraits*, which bear a slightly later opus number. Fine performances, very well recorded too, and well worth taking the trouble to hear.

ORGAN WORKS

Aus tiefer Not schrei ich zu dir, Op. 67/3; Intermezzo in F min., Op. 129/7; Introduction & Passacaglia in D min., Op. posth.; Prelude in D min., Op. 65/7.
*** Chan. 9097. Kee – HINDEMITH: *Organ Sonatas* ***

The Müller organ of St Bavo in Haarlem seems ideally suited to this repertoire, as is the slightly reverberant acoustic which rather softens the textures and contours of the Hindemith. Piet Kee plays with his customary authority and distinction. A rewarding and satisfying issue.

Chorale fantasia on 'Straf' mich nicht in deinem Zorn', Op. 40/2; Chorale Preludes, Op. 67/4, 13, 28, 40, 48; Introduction, Passacaglia & Fugue in E min., Op. 127
*** Hyp. CDA 66223. Barber (Klais organ of Limburg Cathedral)

The *Introduction, Passacaglia and Fugue* is bold in conception and vision and is played superbly on this excellently engineered Hyperion disc by Graham Barber. The five *Chorale Preludes* give him an admirable opportunity to show the variety and richness of tone-colours of this instrument.

PIANO MUSIC

5 Humoresques, Op. 20; Improvisations, Op. 18; In der nacht; Träume am Kamin, Op. 143
(BB) *** Naxos 8.553331. Pawlik

Markus Pawlik is a most musical and sensitive player who captures the intimacy of the *Träume am Kamin* to perfection. They are predominantly poetic and gentle pieces, but elsewhere in the *Humoresques* he shows formidable virtuosity. Very acceptable sound – and those with a taste for music off the beaten track will find this well rewards the modest outlay.

5 Humoresques; Variations & Fugue on a Theme of Johann Sebastian Bach, Op. 81; Variations & Fugue on a Theme of Georg Philipp Telemann, Op. 134
⊖━ ✪ *** Hyp. CDA 66996. Hamelin

Variations & Fugue on a Theme of Bach, Op. 81
(N) (M) *** Warner Elatus 2564 61762-2. Schiff (piano) –
  HANDEL: *Keyboard Suite in B flat (HWV 434);* BRAHMS: *Variations & Fugue on a Theme of Handel* ***
(BB) **(*) Naxos 8.550469. Harden – SCHUMANN: *Humoreske* **(*)

Like Brahms, Reger was one of the greatest masters of the variation form. The Bach and Telemann sets are generally acknowledged to be among his finest keyboard works, and Marc-André Hamelin's playing has enormous eloquence and imagination as well as a wide range both of dynamics and tonal colour. This has an elegance and refinement that never calls attention to itself. Superbly natural recorded sound too.

Wolf Harden's account of the Reger *Variations and Fugue*

on a *Theme of Bach*, Op. 81, is also very fine. The piano sounds much drier here than in the Schumann coupling. Yet the compelling quality of his playing is in no doubt.

Reger's Op. 81 *Variations* date from 1904 and take as their basis the contralto/tenor duet *Seine Allmacht zu ergründen* from Bach's *Cantata 123*; they offer great variety of invention and the widest range of expressive dynamic, finally leading to a powerful contrapuntal climax: two large-scale, four-part fugues, with Bach's original theme reappearing near the close of the second fugue, before Reger's monumental conclusion. Schiff's performance is splendidly equal to all Reger's demands, yet it never overwhelms the listener with rhetoric, and the linked Brahms and Handel couplings make this live recital, excellently recorded in the Concertgebouw in 1994, very recommendable.

VOCAL MUSIC

3 geistliche Gesänge, Op. 110; 3 Gesänge, Op. 39
*** Chan. 9298. Danish Nat. R. Ch., Parkman

Stefan Parkman and the Danish National Radio Choir are the most persuasive advocates of Reger's *a cappella* music. The chromaticism and dense polyphony hold no fears for them and their finely blended tone is in itself a source of pleasure. The Op. 110 *Motets* can be heavy-going but not in these clearly delineated and eloquent performances. Those who are intimidated by Reger's reputation should try this excellently recorded disc.

REICH, Steve (born 1936)

Steve Reich received his initial training as a composer at Juilliard School of Music at the end of the 1950s, later studying under Milhaud and Berio. But he spent some of this time investigating the works of Stockhausen, Boulez and Cage and, in his own words, discovered that this music was unstimulating for him as it was 'nonpulsatile – there was no regular beat'. He realized that if he were to compose anything that had the least emotional resonance for himself, he 'had to reinstate the pulse, front and center'. In 1970 he went to Ghana and spent a period investigating drumming at the Instutute of African Studies, which proved to be the springboard for his whole future musical development. In the event his music proved greatly influential in encouraging other composers either to embrace or to circumvent this apparently unlimited ostinato-like musical technique.

'Works': Disc 1: *It's gonna Rain* (1965); *Come out* (1966); *Piano Phase*: (i) *Double Edge* (1967); (ii) *Four Organs* (1970)

Disc 2: *Drumming* (1971)

Disc 3: (iii) *Clapping Music* (1972); *Music for Mallet Instruments, Voices and Organ* (1973); (iv) *6 Marimbas* (1973–86)

Disc 4: *Music for 18 Musicians* (1976)

Disc 5: (v) *Eight Lines* (Octet) (1976); (vi) *Tehillim for Voices and Ensemble* (1981)

Disc 6: (vii) *The Desert Music* (1984)

Disc 7: (viii) *New York Counterpoint*; (ix) *Sextet* (1985); (x; xi) *The Four Sections: Strings* (with Winds and Brass); *Percussion; Winds and Brass* (with Strings); *Full Orchestra* (1987)

Disc 8: (xi) *Three Movements* (1986); (xii) *Electric Counterpoint* (1987); (xiii) *Different Trains* (1988)

Disc 9: (xiv; xv; xvi) *The Cave* (excerpts) (1993)

Disc 10: (xv; xvii) *City Life*; (xviii) *Nagoya Marimbas* (1994); (xv; xvi; xix) *Proverb* (1995)

(N) (M) ** Nonesuch 7559 79451-2 (10). Steve Reich & his musicians, with (i) Nurit Tiles & Edmund Niman (pianos); (ii) Michael Gordon, Lisa Moore, Mark Stewart, Evan Ziporyn; James Preiss, percussion; (iii) Russell Hartenberger & Composer; (iv) Marimba Quartet; (v) Ens., cond. Bradley Lubman; (vi) Schoenberg Ens., Hague Percussion Group, Reinbert de Leeuw; (vii) Members of Brooklyn Philharmonic & Chorus, Tilson Thomas; (viii) Evan Ziporyn (clarinets); (ix) Nexus; (x) Edward Niemann & Nuril Tillis (pianos); (xi) Percussion Soloists, LSO, Tilson Thomas; (xii) Paul Metheny (guitar); (xiii) Kronos Quartet; (xiv) Rowe, Beckenstein, Bassi, Mundau; (xv) Steve Reich Ens.; (xvi) cond. Paul Hillier; (xvii) cond. Bradley Lubman; (xviii) Bob Becker, James Preiss; (xix) Theatre of Voices

John Adams, in acknowledging his own debt to Steve Reich, has said that Reich 'participated in one of the most significant revolutions in twentieth-century music. It seems hard to believe that an artistic movement so single-mindedly dedicated to the act of reduction and simplification could have such a pervasive effect on the way we listen to and think about music.'

This invaluable Nonesuch 10-disc anthology traces the steady development of Reich's writing over three decades, beginning with the pure rhythm of the spoken voice alone, with the seemingly interminable repeated word-phrases, 'It's gonna rain' and 'Come out', which by an electronic phasing process overlap and echo ('It's gonna/it's gonna, rain rain'). This led him logically to musical equivalents, a repeated four-note *Piano Phase* and a single chord, reiterated continually on *Four Organs*. *Clapping Music* speaks for itself, while *Drumming*, Reich's best-known piece, which involves tuned drums, is here heard in a revised version, lasting just under an hour. The *Six Marimbas* follow a similar pattern of repetition. *Music for 18 Musicians* and *Tehillim* mark a further exploration, with an extension of the key rhythmic pattern, and with voices adding depth of colour to the latter piece.

Scored for just clarinets, *New York Counterpoint* (one of the composer's most genial later works) is in three sections, of which the finale is a piquantly witty jazz riff. But Reich returns to tuned percussion in the *Sextet*, extending its dimensions to five movements, with even more complex variation of timbres and rhythms.

But is is with *Desert Music* that we experience a marked expansion of the composer's minimalist horizons. It is set to a philosophical text by William Carlos Williams, and voices are now a major part of the texture; moreover, rhythms change between the three movements, harmonies are flexible, and there is a strong melodic element: the result is intriguing and attractive.

In *Three Movements* and *Four Sections* (1986/7) Reich turns to the resources of a full orchestra (though still, for the most part, used sectionally) and the second of the three movements develops a motif very like a folk tune, which is taken on into the finale.

Different Trains brings an excursion into descriptive evocation, opening with an obvious pulsing railway rhythm. Intoned dialogue forms a backing to the variety of imagery from the Kronos Quartet who, in the second movement (*Europe during the war*), even provide an impressive simulation of an air-raid siren.

The Cave is a unique kind of opera/oratorio, and easily Reich's most ambitious achievement. With the narrative based on Genesis, it tells the story of Abraham, God's refusal of the sacrificial offering of Isaac, and the equally dramatic rescue in the desert of Ishmail, Abraham's other son, born to him by his slave, Hagar. The Cave was the family burial place. The narrative is given a political significance by being laced with questions and comments from a cast of Israeli, Palestinian and American interviewees who, through their genealogy, feel themselves linked to these distant events.

The final disc sums up Reich's achievement, first with his vivid picture of *City Life* in New York, then with a nostalgic look back to his beloved marimbas, and finally the lovely *Proverb*, a floating vocal melisma. Beautifully sung by the Theatre of Voices, this somehow takes Reich into the mainstream of late-twentieth-century music, the world of Arvo Pärt and John Tavener.

(i; ii) *City Life*; (i; iii) *Eight Lines for Octet*; (iv) *New York Counterpoint* (for clarinets); (v) *Violin Phase*
*** RCA 74321 66459-2. (i) Ens. Modern, (ii) Rundel; or (iii) Lubman; (iv) Diry; (v) Mistry

For his portrait of *City Life* Steve Reich took his tape recorder out on the streets of New York to record its background noises, from police sirens and a hammering pile-driver, to rush-hour traffic, with its subway trains, alarm systems set off in parked cars, human heartbeats and various spoken street dialogues. The end result is not as daunting as it sounds, for musically this is the most imaginative work here, with the musical sounds varied, including instrumental chorale interludes and riff-like solos, into which the various real-life vignettes and spoken dialogues are seamlessly fitted.

New York Counterpoint is scored for nine B flat clarinets and three bass clarinets, in which the soloist himself plays, using his own pre-recordings of the other eleven parts. The sounds are extremely minimalist, including Reich's characteristic gentle throbbing and see-saw figurations. *Violin Phase* also brings four separate, amalgamated parts played by a single fiddler in the same way, and is even more naggingly repetitive.

The original version of *Eight Lines*, the most celebrated piece here, was scored for two pianists, string quartet and two woodwind players (who had to switch quickly between a variety of instruments). The revised version still uses the eight lines of the title, but now the strings underpin the counterpoint. All this sounds very complicated, but what the listener hears is the usual series of throbbing sounds, in which the harmonic changes are as minimal as the ideas. The performances are expert.

Drumming (original version)
(N) (B) *** DG (ADD) 474 323-2 (2). Composer and musicians

Written between 1970 and 1971, *Drumming* was one of Reich's key early works, firmly establishing the basic style of minimalism. This four-part work, played without a break, in this instance lasts for about an hour and a half and features only one basic rhythmic pattern throughout.

Part I is for four pairs of tuned bongo drums, played with sticks, together with a male vocal; Part II is for three marimbas and a modest contribution from female voices; Part III uses a trio of glockenspiels and a condiment of piccolo and whistling (here the composer himself); Part IV uses all the instruments and voices combined. Throughout, the voices attempt to sound entirely instrumental in timbre.

The composer tells us that the instruments playing the repeated 'melodic' pattern move gradually out of syncronization with each other; timbres change, while pitch and rhythm remain constant; beats are gradually substituted for rests (or vice versa) within a constantly repeating cycle. For the aficionado, the result induces an increasing musical hypnosis; for the uninitiated, nothing very important appears to change. The present performance under the composer's direction was faithfully recorded in 1974 and is seemingly spontaneous.

8 Lines

(M) *** Virgin 5 61851-2. LCO, Warren-Green – ADAMS:
 Shaker Loops *** ✪; GLASS: *Company*, etc. ***; HEATH:
 Frontier ***

Steve Reich's *8 Lines* is minimalism in its most basic form, and, although the writing is full of good-humoured vitality, the listener without a score could be forgiven for sometimes thinking that the music was on an endless loop. The performance is expert.

Music for 18 Musicians
*** RCA 09026 68672-2. Ens. Modern

Dating from 1974–6, *Music for 18 Musicians* derives from and returns to a pulsing eleven-chord cyclic 'theme', framing twelve connected sections, which have comparatively simple additional material superimposed upon them, as the music proceeds. As the recording is cued into fourteen separate tracks, the listener can readily isolate the changes within the basic structure. In his accompanying notes, Frank Oteri draws a parallel between Reich's sonic architecture and Beethoven's *Eroica Symphony*. This is going a bit far, but there is no doubt that this is a hypnotic performance of a key work in Reich's continuing odyssey in musical minimalism.

(i) Music for Mallet Instruments, Voices and Organ; (ii) Variations for Winds, Strings and Keyboards; (iii) 6 Pianos

(M) *** DG 471 591-2. (i) Instrumental & Vocal Ens., directed composer; (ii) San Francisco SO, De Waart; (iii) Chambers, Preiss, Hartenberger, Becker, Velez, composer

Easily the most attractive work here is the *Variations*, which was commissioned by the San Francisco Symphony Orchestra but is underpinned by the keyboard instruments (two pianos and three electric organs). The orchestral strings are used to double the harmony played by the organs, and the more active keyboard music is doubled by the woodwind. Only the brass act independently in the first and third of the work's three sections. However, the overall sonority has the woodwind predominant, and the repeated throbbing figure is brightly hued and aurally attractive. Much more happens here than is usual with this composer, for that *ostinato* theme has a constantly varying chaconne bass, except that, as the composer suggests, the 'bass is in the middle register'. For the patient listener this work is well worth exploring.

Music for Mallet Instruments, Voices and Organ (1973) deals with two simultaneous, interrelated rhythmic processes, which purposely get out of sync (or 'phase' as the composer describes the process). *Six Pianos* opens with three of the six

players sharing the same eight-beat rhythmic pattern, but with different notes for each pianist. The others then join in, again to produce a complicated rhythmic texture as the instruments get out of phase, substituting rests for notes. Both these works bring the seemingly endless repetitions for which Reich is famous, but the performance here cannot be faulted, neither can the recording, and there is excellent documentatiom.

Tehillim
*** ECM 827 411-2. Composer & musicians, Manahan

Steve Reich is listed among the percussion players in *Tehillim*, with George Manahan conducting. The central focus, in this Hebrew setting of Psalms 19 and 18 (in that order), is on the vocal ensemble of four voices. The result – with clapping and drumming punctuating the singing – has an element of charm rare in minimalist music. With jazzy syncopations and Cuban rhythms, the first of the two movements sounds like Bernstein's *Chichester Psalms* caught in a groove. The second starts slowly but speeds up for the verses of praise to the Lord and the final *Hallelujahs*. Clear, forward, analogue recording.

REICHA, Antonín (1770–1836)

(i) Sinfonia concertante in G for Flute, Violin & Orchestra. Symphony in E flat, Op. 41; Overture in D
*** MDG 335 0661-2. (i) Bieler, Gérard; Wuppertal SO, Gülke

The first movement of Reicha's *Sinfonia concertante* brings engaging textures but is otherwise relatively conventional. The galant *Andante*, however, brings a charming little violin melody over a tick-tock flute accompaniment; later the two instruments change roles. The *Overture in D minor* is, remarkably, in 5/8 time and its nagging ostinato main theme is at first quite catching. The snag is that, despite its variety of colour, it is a shade over-long. The *Symphony* is a different matter. Its main *Allegro* is very confidently constructed. The *Andante un poco adagio* doesn't disappoint, while in the lively finale the composer keeps a card or two up his sleeve until the very end. A real discovery, which invites repeated hearings. The orchestra is a fine ensemble and, with two first-class soloists here, offers a rewarding collection, well recorded.

Flute Quartets 1 in E min.; 2 in A; 3 in D, Op. 98/1–3
*** MDG 311 0630-2. Hünteler, R. & J. Küssmaul, Dietiens

In the opening *Quartet*, a particularly fine piece, one thinks often of Mozart, and Reicha's invention is seldom inferior. The piquant opening of the *Second Quartet* has a charming insouciance, and in the *Third Quartet* the quaint little tune, marching along slowly and elegantly, is again Bohemian in spirit. Throughout all three works the solo flute part demands, and receives, the utmost virtuosity from its performer, here Konrad Hünteler, who either dominates or blends with his colleagues, all excellent players. The vivid recording completes the listener's pleasure.

Oboe Quintet in F, Op. 107

(BB) *** Hyp. Helios CDH 55015. Francis, Allegri Qt –
 CRUSELL: *Divertimento* (with R. KREUTZER: *Grand Quintet*) **(*)

Antonín Reicha's *F major Quintet* is unmemorable but always amiable. The present performance is of high quality and very well recorded.

Wind Quintets: in F (1811); in E flat; in B flat, Op. 88/2 & 5; in D; in A, Op. 91/3 & 5

☛ (B) *** Hyp. Dyad CDD 22006 (2). Academia Wind Quintet of Prague

Czech wind-playing in Czech wind music has a deservedly high entertainment rating, and the present performances are no exception. The music itself has great charm and geniality; it is ingenuous yet cultivated, with some delightful, smiling writing for the bassoon. The players are clearly enjoying themselves, yet they play and blend expertly. The sound too is admirable.

Wind Quintets in B flat, Op. 88/5; C, Op. 99/1

(N) (BB) *** Naxos 8 554227. Michael Thompson Wind Quintet

The Michael Thompson Wind Quintet give expert accounts of these attractive pieces. Their playing is very fresh and alive, and Reicha can be both rewarding and interesting – it is finely wrought and pleasing. Very good sound.

Wind Quintets in A & C min., Op. 91/5–6

(N) *** Crystal CD 266. Westwood Wind Quintet

The American Westwood Quintet are an excellent group and are recording all Reicha's *Woodwind Quintets*. Their performances of the two Op. 91 works, both considerable pieces, are excellent and well recorded. This is music of much facility and charm.

REINCKEN, Johann (1623?–1722)

(i) *Partitas 1–6 (Hortus musicus)*: excerpts; (ii) *Keyboard pieces: Ballet (Partite diverse) in E min.; Toccata in G; Suite in G*

*** Chan. 0664. (i) Purcell Qt; (ii) Woolley

Johann Reincken reigned over Hamburg's musical scene before Telemann. He was organist at the Katharinenkirche from 1663 onwards, and his improvisational skills were greatly admired. Indeed, the young Bach came to hear him play; on a second visit in 1720 and improvising himself on the great organ, he received in return Reincken's admiration. These six *Partitas* (for two violins, viola da gamba and continuo) juxtapose movements in the styles of Italian church and chamber sonatas. It seems that Reincken did not intend that each partita should be played through in its entirety, so in these admirable performances the Purcell Quartet have selected movements from each of them. Reincken's invention is lively and his expressive writing quite touching. But what makes this collection especially attractive is the harpsichord music, full of winningly attractive ideas. Sample, for instance, the delightful closing Gigue of the *Suite in G major*. Most entertaining of all is the *Toccata in G*, a virtuosic piece, alternating free and fugal textures. It reminds one of Bach's bouncing *Fugue à la gigue*: the improvisatory sections use the *stylus phantasicus*, and Robert Woolley clearly revels in the dashing opportunities he is offered. Excellent recording.

REINECKE, Carl (1824–1910)

Harp Concerto in E min., Op. 182

(M) *** DG (ADD) 463 648-2. Zöller, Zabaleta, BPO, Märzendorfer – MOZART: *Flute & Harp Concerto in C, K. 299* ***; RODRIGO: *Concierto serenata* *** ⊙

This is an attractive work, Zabaleta's performance is an outstanding one, and it is truthfully recorded. If the couplings are suitable this is a highly recommendable disc.

Symphonies 2 in C min., Op. 134; 3 in G min., Op. 227

*** Chan. 9893 Tasmanian SO, Shelley

Few forgotten nineteenth-century composers so richly deserve revival as Carl Reinecke, in his time a leading teacher as well as a successful composer. Almost ten years older than his friend Brahms, he lived on until 1910, prolific into his eighties. His style is conservative but never bland, like a cross between Mendelssohn and Brahms, with memorable themes strongly developed, and with refined orchestration regularly revealing his Brahmsian love of the horn and oboe. *Symphony No. 2* is the more relaxed, leading to a warmly Mendelssohnian finale, while *No. 3 in G minor* is sharper and more dramatic, vigorously belying the idea that this was by a composer in his mid-seventies. You could hardly find more persuasive advocates than Howard Shelley and the brilliant Tasmanian Symphony Orchestra, vividly recorded.

Flute Sonata (Undine), Op. 167

(M) *** RCA (ADD) 09026 61615-2. Galway, Argerich – FRANCK; PROKOFIEV: *Sonatas* ***

Some of Reinecke's invention here is quite striking (as in the *Sonata's* first movement). His writing, which has sudden florid bursts, makes an engaging vehicle for an artist of Galway's calibre, and this makes a fine bonus for the coupling of two masterly works by Prokofiev and Franck.

String Trio in C min., Op. 249

*** MDG 634 0841-2. Belcanto Strings – FUCHS: *Trio in A, Op. 94* ***

This *C minor Trio* comes from around 1898 and is conservative in style, finely crafted and cultured music, superbly played and recorded.

RESPIGHI, Ottorino (1879–1936)

Adagio con variazioni (for cello & orchestra)

(M) *** Sup. (ADD) SU 3667-2. Navarra, Czech PO, Ančerl – BLOCH: *Schelomo*; SCHUMANN: *Cello Concerto* **(*)

Respighi's short but charming set of variations shows the composer on top form. It is an Italianate equivalent of Tchaikovsky's *Rococo Variations* and has a burst of almost Russian romantic expressiveness to make a sunset-like ending. Navarra plays it very beautifully, and both his timbre and the orchestra are greatly enhanced by the current remastering.

(i) *Adagio con variazioni (for cello & orchestra); The Birds; 3 Botticelli Pictures;* (ii) *Il tramonto*

*** Chan. 8913. (i) Wallfisch; (ii) Finnie; Bournemouth Sinf., Vásáry

Raphael Wallfisch is very persuasive in Respighi's *Adagio*. *The Birds* brings lovely playing and the luminous recording gives much pleasure. The lambent Italianate evocation of the *Three Botticelli Pictures* is also aurally bewitching. But what caps the success of this Chandos Respighi anthology is Linda Finnie's ravishing account of *Il tramonto*, even finer than Carol Madalin's on Hyperion – see below. Again very responsive orchestral playing and the recording is in the demonstration class throughout this CD.

Ancient Airs & Dances: Suites 1–3
(N) (M) *** Mercury **SACD** (ADD) 470 637-2. Philharmonia Hungarica, Dorati

(i) *Ancient Airs & Dances: Suites 1–3;* (ii) *Belfagor: Overture;* (ii) *The Birds* (suite); (iii) *The Fountains of Rome; The Pines of Rome;* (ii) *3 Botticelli Pictures (Trittico botticelliano)*
(N) (BB) **(*) EMI Gemini 5 865490-2 (2). (i) LACO, or (ii) ASMF; Marriner; (iii) LSO, Gardelli

Ancient Airs and Dances: Suites 1 & 3; The Birds (suite); 3 Botticelli Pictures
(BB) **(*) Warner Apex 0927 48694-2. Sol. Ven., Scimone

(i) *Ancient Airs and Dances: Suites 1–3; The Birds (Gli Ucceli): Suite;* (ii) *Feste Romane; The Pines of Rome*
(N) (B) *** Artemis Vanguard ATM-CD 1227 (2). (i) Australian CO, Lyndon-Gee; (ii) Baltimore SO, Comissiona

Ancient Airs & Dances: Suites 1–3; 3 Botticelli Pictures (Trittico botticelliano)
*** Telarc CD 80309. Lausanne CO, López-Cobos

Many collectors will feel that the reissue of Dorati's celebrated Mercury recording of Respighi's *Ancient Airs* without a fill-up is upstaged by the outstanding Vanguard Double, which includes Christopher Lyndon-Gee's treasurable coupling on the second disc. His performance of *The Birds* is a complete delight, opening and closing vigorously, yet providing the most refined portraits of the dove, nightingale and cuckoo, with particularly lovely oboe playing in *The Dove*. The opening of the first suite of *Ancient Airs and Dances* has a comparable grace and delicacy of feeling; throughout, Lyndon-Gee's response to Respighi's imaginative orchestration is wonderfully fresh, with the oboe (again) and bassoon distinguishing themselves among the many fine wind solos. The strings produce lovely, translucent textures at the beginning of the *Third Suite*; yet, when a robust approach is called for, the players respond admirably. The bitter-sweet combination of nobility and nostalgia that often haunts this music, especially in the *Second Suite*, permeates the expressive playing, which has an affecting eloquence. The digital recording, made at the ABC Studios at Chatsworth, Sydney, is in the demonstration class.

Feste Romane and *The Pines of Rome* were recorded a decade earlier in Washington DC's National Presbyterian Church and they take full advantage of the building's expansive acoustics, especially in the 'October Festival' sequence of the *Feste Romane* , with its echoing fanfares. The splendid Baltimore orchestra plays superbly and Comissiona generates plenty of adrenalin in the Epiphany finale of *The Pines* and in the spectacle of the Roman legions marching down the Appian Way. The only snag is that the *pines* have been assembled in the wrong order, with the finale second and the opening number third! However, one can easily reprogramme to have the movements in the correct order, and the descriptive notes make it plain which is which.

Dorati's famous and very distinguished Mercury recording of 1958 displays a remarkable feeling for the colour and ambience of Renaissance dances on which Respighi's three suites (the last for strings alone) are based. The refinement and warmth of the playing are very striking, particularly in the *Third Suite*, and the touch of astringency in the recording increases the piquancy (the sound is slightly more spread when heard through an SACD system). Dorati finds in this music a nobility and graciousness that make it obstinately memorable. While there have been excellent modern

accounts of this work, Dorati's has unique atmosphere and character. Indeed this disc remains very special indeed.

Opening brightly and comparatively robustly, the Lausanne performance of the *Ancient Airs* yet has both warmth and finesse. The rhythmic pulse is lively without being heavy, and there is much engaging woodwind detail; at the graceful beginning of the *Third Suite* textures are agreeably light and transparent. The Telarc recording is first rate and even more impressive in the *Botticelli Pictures*, with *La primavera* burgeoning with the extravagantly exotic spring blossoming, and *The Birth of Venus* rapt in its radiantly expansive ecstasy.

Marriner's account of the suites of dances is attractively light and gracious, offering an almost French elegance, with pleasingly transparent textures. *The Birds* and *Trittico botticelliano* are no less delightful, and they are beautifully recorded. So far so good; but Lamberto Gardelli's performances of *The Pines* and *Fountains of Rome*, though warmly sympathetic and finely played, bring less of a feeling of drama, and generate neither the atmospheric magic nor electricity experienced in the competing versions from Reiner or Karajan. The *Belfagor Overture* is an acceptable bonus, a dramatic and lively piece, strongly characterized and vivid.

Scimone omits the second suite of *Ancient Airs and Dances*. The playing is warmly sympathetic and graceful, and the 1988 recording has plenty of bloom and is full-bodied. but its resonance at times tends to inflate the string textures. Nevertheless this Apex compilation is enjoyable and inexpensive, and it is a pity that the second suite of airs was not included.

Ancient Airs & Dances: Suite 3 for Strings; The Fountains of Rome; The Pines of Rome
(M) *** DG (ADD) 449 724-2. BPO, Karajan (with BOCCHERINI: *Quintettino;* ALBINONI: *Adagio in G min.* (arr. Giazotto) ***)

In the symphonic poems Karajan is in his element, and the playing of the Berlin Philharmonic is wonderfully refined as well as exciting. The opening of the *Ancient Airs* brings ravishing tone from the strings, and they sound even more lavish in Giazotto's famous arrangement of Albinoni's *Adagio*, while Boccherini's *Quintettino* makes an engaging additional lollipop.

Le astuzie di Colombina; La pentola magica; Sèvres de la vieille France
*** Marco Polo 8.223346. Slovak RSO (Bratislava), Adriano

Sèvres de la vieille France is based on seventeenth- and eighteenth-century airs, scored with great elegance and charm; *La pentola magica* makes use of Russian models. *Le astuzie di Colombina*, described as a 'Scherzo Veneziano', uses popular Venetian melodies among other things. The scores contain some winning and delightful numbers. Decent performances and good recording.

Ballata delle Gnomidi; (i) *Concerto gregoriano; Poema autunnale*
*** Chan. 9232. (i) Mordkovitch; BBC PO, Downes

The *Concerto gregoriano* is a meditative, lyrical outpouring making free use of Gregorian modes. Apart from some moments of brilliant display, the slightly later *Poema autunnale* for violin and orchestra is also predominantly lyrical and has moments of a Delius-like mysticism. Lydia Mordkovitch gives most affecting accounts of both pieces and is very well supported by Downes and the BBC Philharmonic. The *Ballata delle Gnomidi* (1920) finds Respighi in his most exotic *Roman Trilogy* mode: it is a dazzling exercise in colour and orchestration.

Belfagor Overture; 3 Corali; (i) *Fantasia slava for Piano & Orchestra; Toccata for Piano & Orchestra*
*** Chan. 9311. (i) Tozer; BBC PO, Downes

The best thing here is the *Toccata for Piano and Orchestra*. It is better argued and structured, more inventive and novel, as well as more musically rewarding, than either of the piano concertos, and Tozer plays it with considerable bravura and panache and the BBC Philharmonic under Sir Edward Downes are admirably supportive. The *Fantasia slava* is shorter and less interesting, and the same goes for the three chorale arrangements. The *Belfagor* is a re-composition based on themes from his opera, and not the curtain-raiser heard in the theatre. Excellent in every way, and with recording of first-class quality.

Belkis, Queen of Sheba: Suite; Dance of the Gnomes; The Pines of Rome
*** Reference RR 965CD. Minnesota O, Oué

The Minnesota (formerly Minneapolis) Orchestra celebrates its latest music director with colourful performances of three Respighi showpieces, two of them rarities. Even by Respighi's standards the suite from the full-length ballet, *Belkis, Queen of Sheba*, is brazen to the point of vulgarity, with maximum decibels allied to minimal argument. The *Dance of the Gnomes* (1920) is a set of four pieces inspired by a deeply unpleasant poem of Carlo Clausetti, involving Amazon-like gnomes who first torture their newly acquired husbands and then kill them. The orchestral writing – with the shrieks of the victims illustrated – is yet subtler and more atmospheric than in *Belkis*, with a fascinating trial-run for the opening of *The Pines of Rome* (1924) at the start. Oué draws playing at once powerful and refined from his orchestra, and refinement is one of the elements in his reading of *The Pines of Rome*, generally light and transparent in its textures.

Belkis, Queen of Sheba: Suite; Metamorphosen Modi XII
*** Chan. 8405. Philh. O, Simon

The ballet-suite *Belkis, Queen of Sheba*, is a score that set the pattern for later Hollywood biblical film music; but *Metamorphosen* is a taut and sympathetic set of variations. It has been ingeniously based on a medieval theme, and though a group of cadenza variations relaxes the tension of argument in the middle, the brilliance and variety of the writing have much in common with Elgar's *Enigma*. Superb playing from the Philharmonia, treated to one of the finest recordings that even Chandos has produced, outstanding in every way.

The Birds (Gli uccelli); Church Windows (Vetrate di chiesa)
(B) **(*) Sony (ADD) SBK 60311. Phd. O, Ormandy –
    SCARLATTI: *The Good-Humoured Ladies* **(*)

In *Church Windows* the picture of the baby Jesus in *The Flight into Egypt* has a Latin intensity of feeling which suits Ormandy and the rich-textured Philadelphia sound, while the following evocation of St Michael, sword in hand, is spectacularly painted with broad strokes of the orchestral brush. The finale, a papal blessing scene, is on the largest scale. Ormandy rises to the occasion and the spectacular recording is a match for the Philadelphia big guns – although subtlety is not the keynote here and the listener is all but overwhelmed. *The Birds* is slighter, but the playing is full of charm, especially the delicate tracery of the final cuckoo evocation.

Brazilian Impressions; Church Windows (Vetrate di chiesa)
*** Chan. 8317. Philh. O, Simon

Geoffrey Simon is sympathetic and he secures very fine playing from the Philharmonia. On CD, the wide dynamic range and a striking depth of perspective create the most spectacular effects.

Burlesca; Overture Carnevalesca; Prelude, Chorale & Fugue; Suite in E; Symphonic Variations
**(*) Marco Polo 8.223348. Slovak RSO (Bratislava), Adriano

The *Symphonic Variations*, an early work, is very well crafted, with a lot of Brahms and Franck – though the scoring already betrays Respighi's future expertise. In the *Suite in E major* the influences are mainly Slavonic; primarily Dvořák and Rimsky-Korsakov, but in the *Burlesca* of 1906 with its whole-tone scale one can discern a whiff of Debussy. The release discovers no masterpieces but does afford a valuable insight into Respighi's creative development. Good performances from Adriano and the Slovak Radio Orchestra and decent recording.

Piano Concerto in A min.; Concerto in modo misolidio
**(*) Chan. 9285. Tozer, BBC PO, Downes

In Respighi's *Piano Concerto in A minor* of 1902, the influences of Rachmaninov and Grieg are strong. It is aptly coupled with a much later and more ambitious concertante work with piano, the *Concerto in modo misolidio* ('In the Mixolydian Mode'), which reflects Respighi's fascination with early Church music which is rather too diffuse a work for its material. The impact of Geoffrey Tozer's playing in both works is undermined by the backward balance of the piano, with only the A minor work taking fire.

Piano Concerto in A min.; Fantasia slava; Toccata for Piano & Orchestra
(BB) *** Naxos 8.553207. Scherbakov, Slovak RSO
    (Bratislava), Griffiths

Concerto in modo misolidio; (i) Concerto a cinque
(BB) *** Naxos 8.553366. Scherbakov, Slovak RSO, Griffiths;
    (i) Capella Istropolitana, Danel

The first Naxos CD misses out the *Concerto in modo misolidio* and includes instead the much finer if rather extended *Toccata* and the concise and rather engaging *Fantasia slava*. The Russian pianist, Konstantin Scherbakov, is a persuasive and at times dazzlingly brilliant soloist and he is accompanied persuasively by the Slovak Radio Symphony Orchestra (Bratislava) under Howard Griffiths. The recording is excellent and this disc is well worth its modest cost.

Scherbakov's account of the *Concerto in modo misolidio* is superior in every way (except recorded quality) to Tozer's on Chandos – and a third of the price. The *Concerto a cinque* makes a delightful and inventive makeweight.

Feste romane; The Fountains of Rome; The Pines of Rome (symphonic poems)
🕭 (N) (M) *** RCA 82876 60869-2. Santa Cecilia Ac., Gatti
*** Delos DE 2387. Oregon SO, DePreist
(BB) *** Naxos 8.550539. RPO, Bátiz
*** EMI 7 47316-2. Phd. O, Muti
(B) **(*) Sony (ADD) SBK 48267. Phd. O, Ormandy

The Fountains of Rome

(***) Testament mono SBT 1108. St Cecilia Ac., Rome, O, De Sabata – DEBUSSY: *La Mer; Jeux; Nuages; Fêtes* (***)

The Fountains of Rome; The Pines of Rome

⊕ (M) *** RCA (ADD) 09026 61401-2. Chicago SO, Reiner – MUSSORGSKY: *Pictures at an Exhibition* *** ⊕

The Pines of Rome

*** BBC (ADD) BBCL 1007-2. Bournemouth SO, Silvestri – TCHAIKOVSKY: *Manfred Symphony* **(*)

Daniele Gatti brings something special to all three works: a rapt intensity and an extraordinary feeling for atmosphere and a total dedication to Respighi's glowing, richly coloured scoring that is completely involving. The Santa Cecilia orchestra plays wonderfully for him, and the RCA recording challenges the very best of the competition and is very well detailed. The wide dynamic range needs some help in some of the *pianissimo* sections, at the end of the *Fountains* for example, where you may need to adjust the volume control. However, except for this, these Gatti performances could ultimately be a first choice.

The first great merit of the Delos version from Oregon is the spectacular sound which has a sensuously velvety, wrap-around quality that is both warmly atmospheric and finely detailed. The sharp terracing of textures also enhances the sound, making it both immediate and vividly realistic. De-Preist, over the years since he became music director of the Oregon Orchestra in 1980, has shaped it into a virtuoso band more than capable of holding its own in any international company, and these showpieces are presented with just the sort of panache that they need. Often they gain from the extra weight of the bass response, as in the second movement of *The Fountains, The Triton Fountain in the Morning*, when the pedal-notes from the organ have the tummy-wobbling quality usually experienced only in live performance.

Reiner's legendary recordings of *The Pines* and *Fountains of Rome* were made in Symphony Hall, Chicago, on 24 October 1959, and the extraordinarily atmospheric performances have never been surpassed since for their sultry Italian warmth. Yet the turning on of the Triton fountain brings an unforced cascade of orchestral brilliance. RCA's new generation of transfer engineers have put it all on CD with complete fidelity.

The Naxos recording, engineered by Brian Culverhouse in St Barnabas, Mitcham, is also in the demonstration bracket. The climax of *The Fountain of Trevi at Midday*, when Neptune parades across the heavens, is enormously spectacular, and here a computer organ was used to provide the underlying sustained pedal. The *Pines* and *Fountains* bring extremely fine playing with much warmth and finesse from the RPO. The sharp focus of the Naxos recording brings an extra degree of brazen splendour to the tumultuous popular crowd sequences in the *Circus* and *Jubilee* scenes of the *Feste romane*, while at the close of the *October Festival* the mandolin serenade emerges more tangibly.

Muti gives warmly red-blooded performances of Respighi's Roman trilogy, captivatingly Italianate in their inflexions. With brilliant playing from the Philadelphia Orchestra and warmly atmospheric recording, these are exceptional for their strength of characterization.

Ormandy's Sony *Feste romane* has great electricity and enormous surface excitement, and it is a pity that the sound-quality is fiercely brilliant. In the other two works the effect is more opulent, and the Philadelphia playing is fabulous, while

the recording has come up astonishingly well. This is still a very exciting example of the Ormandy/Philadelphia regime at its most spectacularly compelling.

Victor de Sabata's 1947 account of *The Fountains of Rome* was the earliest post-war set and superseded Albert Coates's early 1930s version with the LSO, also on HMV. It is a magical performance with many touches that, though different from Reiner and Karajan, are of comparable subtlety and atmosphere.

Silvestri's account of the *Pines* comes from the Colston Hall, Bristol, and 1967. It sounds remarkably good technically and the performance is very fine indeed. Atmospheric and evocative, and well worth considering. Not as subtle nor as masterly as Reiner but far from negligible. Unfortunately the *Manfred Symphony* is not so competitive, given the outstanding versions now available.

The Fountains of Rome; The Pines of Rome; Metamorphosen modi XII: Theme & Variations for Orchestra

*** Telarc CD 80505. Cincinnati SO, López-Cobos

This impressive new Telarc disc springs a surprise in making a new pairing with the *Theme and Variations for Orchestra*. This suffers from the somewhat ungainly title of *Metamorphosen modi XII*, but as those who know the earlier Chandos recording will testify, it is a marvellously inventive and resourceful score. Expert and sympathetic playing by the excellent Cincinnati orchestra under Jesús López-Cobos and (not unexpectedly from Telarc) altogether excellent recording which is spectacular, but also both natural in perspective and impressively detailed, with splendid range.

La Pentola magica (ballet); arr. of BACH: *Prelude and Fugue in D*; arr. of ROSSINI: *La Boutique fantasque* ***

*** Chan. 10081. BBC PO, Noseda

As his orchestral showpieces demonstrate, Ottorino Respighi was among the greatest orchestrators ever, and here, showing off his brilliance, he sumptuously transforms other composers' music. His sparkling arrangements of Rossini's late inspirations, the 'Sins of Old Age', which make up the ballet *La Boutique fantasque*, have long been popular, here inspiring an exhilarating performance from Gianandrea Noseda and the BBC Philharmonic, richly recorded. *La Pentola magica* ('The Magic Pot'), is a ballet score which remained unpublished until after the composer's death, drawing on rare Russian sources in a gentle sequence of ten brief movements, again beautifully orchestrated. The *Prelude and Fugue in D*, the most spectacular item, is an exuberant realization of Bach's organ original, which, far from imitating the organ, pulls out all the orchestral stops in a resounding display.

The Pines of Rome

(N) **(*) Warner 2564 61954-2. BBC Nat. O of Wales, Otaka – MUSSORGSKY: *Pictures at an Exhibition* ***

A brilliant, finely played account from the BBC National Orchestra of Wales, with some lovely, luminous sounds in *The Pines of the Janiculum* and the nightingale trilling to order. However, the resonant acoustic of the Royal Albert Hall, while creating a sinister atmosphere for the closing evocation of the marching Roman legions and an overwhelmingly thrilling climax, tends to blur orchestral detail.

Sinfonia drammatica

*** Chan. 9213. BBC PO, Downes

Respighi's *Sinfonia drammatica* (1914) is a work of ambitious proportions: epic in scale, it lasts just over an hour, the first movement alone taking 25 minutes. Yet it proves rich in incident and lavish in its orchestral colours and virtuosity; even if it is not organic in conception or symphonic in the classical sense, it is an immensely worthwhile addition to the catalogue. If you enjoy the *Alpine Symphony*, you should try this. An excellent performance and outstanding recording.

CHAMBER MUSIC

String Quartet in D; Quartetto dorico; (i) Il tramonto (The Sunset)

⊕━ ✪ (M) *** Van. 99216. Brodsky Qt, (i) with Von Otter

Il tramonto, a setting of Shelley, is relatively familiar: a number of great singers have recorded it. Anne Sofie von Otter is a match for any of them. However, the little-known early *Quartet in D major* and the *Quartetto dorico* are quite a find. Respighi was in his late twenties when he wrote the *D major*. His facility as a musician is legendary: he played the viola in the Imperial Orchestra in St Petersburg, took composition lessons from Rimsky-Korsakov and was also a violin maker! He was still a member of the Quartetto Mugellini at the time of this piece, so one would expect the music to be crafted beautifully. There is the occasional whiff of Brahms and even Debussy and at the beginning of the slow movement a fleeting suggestion of late Strauss, and there are moments of serene beauty throughout. The *Quartetto dorico*, which is hardly less rewarding, comes from the 1920s, when Respighi was at the height of his enthusiasm for Gregorian melody. Sensitive playing, finely blended tone and a magisterial authority distinguish the playing, and the recording team deserve congratulations on its truthfully balanced and natural sound.

Violin Sonata in B min.

⊕━ (M) *** Decca 474 558-2. Chung, Zimerman – R. STRAUSS: *Violin Sonata* ***

Winner of *Gramophone*'s Chamber Music Award in 1990, these performances have never been surpassed. Kyung-Wha Chung is at her best, and Krystian Zimerman brings an enormous range of colour and dynamics to the piano part – the clarity of his articulation in the *Passacaglia* is exceptional. Excellent recording, too.

PIANO MUSIC

Ancient Airs & Dances; 6 Pieces; 3 Preludi sopra melodie gregoriane; Sonata in F min.

(BB) *** Naxos 8.553704. Scherbakov

Respighi followed his famous orchestral set of *Antiche danze ed arie* (transcriptions from lute tablature) with some for the piano. He also transcribed others: the first by the Genovese, Simone Molinaro, *Balletto detto il Conte Orlando* bears a strong resemblance to the first movement of *The Birds*, as does the *Gagliarda* by Vincenzo Galileo (father of the famous scientist). Of the other pieces, the *Notturno* from the *Six Pieces* has a distinctly Rachmaninovian feel. The *F minor Sonata* (1897–8) is a rarity, and it is difficult to imagine a performance that is more persuasive than this – at any price level. Konstantin Scherbakov is a pianist of quality, combining the highest musicianship with sensitivity and refinement. He is excellently recorded too.

VOCAL MUSIC

(i) La primavera; (ii) 4 Liriche su poesie popolari armene (1921; arr. Adriano)

**(*) Marco 8.223595. (i) Lednárová, Valásková, Slepkovská, Dvorský, Haan, Kubovčic, Slovak Ph. Ch., Slovak RSO (Bratislava); (ii) Geriová, Ens., Adriano

La primavera is an ambitious cantata for six soloists, chorus and orchestra. It takes 45 minutes and is not vintage Respighi. But, although it has moments of bombast and periodically finds his muse on automatic pilot, it has some music of real quality, in particular the sixth of the seven movements; there are evocative and opulently scored orchestral interludes. The *Quattro liriche su poesie popolari armene* are simple and affecting. They are given here in Adriano's arrangement for flute, oboe, clarinet, bass clarinet, bassoon, trombone and harp. The performances throughout are more than adequate and are acceptably recorded.

La sensitiva

(BB) *** Virgin 2x1 5 61469-2 (2). J. Baker, City of L. Sinf., Hickox – BERLIOZ: *Les Nuits d'été*, etc.; BRAHMS: *Alto Rhapsody*, etc.; MENDELSSOHN: *Infelice*, etc. ***

Tautly structured over its span of more than half an hour, Respighi's setting of Shelley's poem, *The Sensitive Plant* (in Italian translation), is a most beautiful piece which Janet Baker and Richard Hickox treat to a glowing first recording. The vocal line, mainly declamatory, is sweetly sympathetic and the orchestration is both rich and subtle. Altogether this makes a quite outstanding anthology.

Il tramonto

*** Hyp. CDA 66290. Madalin, ECO, Bonavera – MARTUCCI: *Le canzone dei ricordi; Notturno* ***

Respighi's *Il tramonto* (*The Sunset*) is a glorious work which at times calls to mind the world of late Strauss. A most lovely record. Recommended with all possible enthusiasm.

REVUELTAS, Silvestre (1899–1940)

La Coronela (ballet; orch. Moncada; arr. Limantour); La noche de los Mayas (arr. Limantour); Sensemayá

(BB) *** Naxos 8.555917. Aguascalientes SO, Mexico, Barrios

The Mexican composer and violinist Silvestre Revueltas is essentially remembered for his colourful tone-poems, which are strongly influenced by Mexican folk music. His music is approachable: rhythmic, vibrant, even gaudily orchestrated, often with strong elements of popular Hispanic–American cultures in scores which also have strands of Stravinsky, Prokofiev and Chavez. The popular *Sensemayá* (1938), based on a poem by the Afro-Cuban revolutionary Nicolás Guillén, is about the killing of a snake. It is an exciting work, notable for its battery of drums and terrific rhythmic drive, building up to a huge climax, and here heard in its orchestral (as opposed to the original vocal and orchestral) form. *La noche des los Mayas* ('The Night of the Mayas') was written for a 1939 film; it forms the colourful 30-minute suite assembled by the composer José Yves de Limantour in 1960 recorded here. In the (unfinished) ballet *La Coronela*, written in 1940, Revueltas's obvious rhythmic flair produces some excellent, spikily balletic numbers, with the emphasis on rhythm and bold colour rather than long melodic lines. Not that there are no tunes: *Don Ferruco's Nightmare* starts out as a lovely Waltz and gets gradually more quirky as it goes on. Vibrant recording to match the performances.

REZNIČEK, Emil von (1860–1945)

Raskolnikov (Phantasy Overture); (i) *Schlemihl (A Symphonic Life Story)*

*** CPO 999 795-2. WDR SO, Cologne, Jurowski, (i) with Yamamasu

It is good to hear more music from the composer of the brilliant *Donna Diana Overture*, and it is immediately striking to hear Richard Strauss parallels (a composer who often entrusted performances of his tone-poems to Rezniček), notably in *Schlemihl (A Symphonic Life Story)*, first performed in 1912. It is loosely autobiographical, and the sleeve-note writer at one point suggests that it might be titled 'Not a Hero's Life'. The events of this 45-minute work (which contains plenty of hints of Mahler, Wagner and Shostakovich, along with Strauss) are written out in exhaustive detail, down to the last minute, and are included in the extensive booklet. In its way it makes enjoyable listening, especially with Rezniček's gift for bright orchestration, and with seemingly every conceivable emotion and orchestral gesture contriving to make an appearance. This committed performance makes a good case for it, though Nobuaki Yamamasu is a little unsteady in his short solo. The 22-minute *Raskolnikov Overture* (1932) has some good passages in it, but in its meandering way it does not always sustain interest. However, the performance is excellent. Good recording.

Der Sieger (Symphonic Poem)

(N) *** CPO 999898-2. Koepp, West German RSO and Ch. of Cologne, Jurowski

First heard in December 1913, *Der Sieger* ('The Victor') is a massive symphonic poem in three movements, involving an enormous orchestra with quadruple woodwind, as well as chorus and soloist. From an aristocratic background Rezniček represented a very different strand of society from his much more successful friend and rival, Richard Strauss, fuelling the rivalry, and though he disclaimed the idea, this vast piece was regarded by some as a parody of that master's big symphonic poems. In its own right it stands as a formidable work, rich in ideas, closely argued, with orchestral effects brilliantly handled to have maximum impact, a point superbly realized by Jurowski's performance with the Cologne Radio Orchestra. Though it was praised at the time, it was a work which failed to stay even in the German repertory in the post-war period of economy in music. This disc, spectacularly recorded, fills an important gap.

OPERA

Donna Diana (complete)

(N) *** CPO 999 991-2 (2). Uhl, Sadnik, Wittlieb, Pauly, Schluter, Wittges Kiel Op. Ch. and O, Windfuhr

This live recording of a comic opera known till now only from its sparkling overture fills an intriguing gap. The overture is one of the most scintillating in the whole repertory, and the rest of the piece is written just as skilfully, with many ensembles in compound time, inevitably echoing the music we know. The story involves a lovesick prince, Don Cesar, who despairs when his beloved princess, Donna Diana, daughter of the ruling Count of Barcelona, remains cold,

repelling all suitors. He himself is regularly the victor in tournaments, and many of the most striking moments in the score involve fanfare motifs. Needless to say, after many complications, Cesar finally wins Diana's love, with two other pairs also happily coupled. The score moves swiftly, with few set numbers of any length, and arias are generally avoided in favour of duets and ensembles. It is remarkable how skilfully Rezniček writes for a big orchestra without as a rule masking the singers. This recording from the Kiel Opera brings lively performances from everyone, with the tenor Roman Sadnik excellent as Don Cesar. The casting of Manuela Uhl in the title-role is more problematic, when in Act I the beat in her rich soprano is very obtrusive. Happily, in Acts II and III the voice comes into firm focus with clarity, power and warmth, with exposed top notes satisfyingly steady, and subtle shading of *pianissimos*. Warm, atmospheric recording.

RHEINBERGER, Joseph (1839–1901)

Organ Concerto 1 in F, Op. 137

*** Telarc CD 80136. Murray, RPO, Ling – DUPRE: *Symphony* ***

Rheinberger's *Concerto* is well made, its invention is attractive and it has suitable moments of spectacle that render it admirable for a coupling with the Dupré *Symphony*, with its use of the massive Albert Hall organ. The performance here is first rate. A fine demonstration disc.

Masses: in E flat (Cantus missae), Op. 109; in G min., for Female Voices & Organ, Op. 187; in F for Male Voices & Organ, Op. 190; Hymn: Tribulationes. Motets: Anima nostra; Laudate Dominum; Meditabor

**(*) Paraclete Press Gloria de Cantores GDCD 108. Gloria Dei Cantores, Patterson

Having given us a stimulating collection of the music of William Mathias, the Cape Cod-based choir Gloria Dei Cantores turn their attention to Reinberger, best known for his oratorio, *The Star of Bethlehem*. But he composed his first Latin Mass in 1847, when he was just eight years old.

The finest work here is the E flat *Cantus missae* for double chorus, dating from 1878. It is eloquently performed, with the sequence of *Credo*, *Sanctus*, *Bendictus* and *Agnus Dei* inspiring the singers to considerable expressive fervour. Among the motets the Offertory for Lent in D minor, *Meditabor*, is the most appealing.

The divided choirs seem slightly less confident, although the men are on the whole impressive in the *F major Mass*, with the rather sombre *Credo* the highlight. The women, however, have occasional moments of insecurity in the *G minor* work (dedicated to Brahms) although they still convey its linear beauty. Excellent recording (made in 1994) and an enterprising programme that deserves support. (Your supplier can obtain the disc via: www.paraclete-press.com.)

RICHAFORT, Jean (c. 1480–c. 1547)

Requiem Mass

🔊 *** Signum SIGCD 005. Chapelle du Roi, Dixon (with GUERRERO: *Gradual & Tract.* GOMBERT: *Dicite in magni.* INFANTAS: *Domine ostende.* JOSQUIN DESPRES: *Nimphes nappés.* LOBO: *Versa est in luctum; Libera me*)

This superbly recorded collection is entitled '*Music for Philip*

[II] of Spain', and it gathers together music that might have been sung at the spectacular Royal Exequies which was celebrated at San Jerónimo, Madrid, on 18 October 1598, five weeks after the King had died. It is not certain which music accompanied the celebrations, but scholarly detective work suggests that the *Missa pro defunctis* for six voices, composed by Jean Richafort around 1532, might have been chosen, supplemented here by Guerrero's *Gradual* and *Tract*. As a prelude, Alistair Dixon presents Gombert's motet written to celebrate Philip's birth in 1527, and he has also interpolated Josquin's great song of mourning, *Nimphes nappés*. Richafort's setting of the *Missa pro defunctis* is in a darkly solemn, chordal polyphonic style which has a grave beauty. So when, after the *Sanctus*, we hear Alonso Lobo's radiant motet *Versa est in luctum* (for the elevation of the Host) it is like a light shining down from heaven, and it is Lobo's equally beautiful Respond, *Libera me*, which concludes this remarkable vocal memento of the death of a long-dead monarch. Whether or not these actual settings were used in 1598, this enterprise achieves a satisfying linking together of some remarkable music, all sung with devotion and with the beautiful tonal blending for which the Chapelle du Roi are renowned.

RIDOUT, Alan (1934–96)

(i; ii) *Cello Concerto 1 for Cello, Strings and Percussion;* (i; iii) *2: Concerto for Cello and Voices;* (i; ii) *3: The Prisoner* (for cello solo & 8 cellos); (iv) *The Emperor and the Bird of Paradise*
☦— *** Black Box BBM 1037. (i) Leclerk; (ii) ECO, Barlow; (iii) Laudibus; (iv) Lumley, Edmund-Davies

Alan Ridout is another fine English composer whose concert music has fallen by the wayside, unheard during the last few decades. He studied at the Royal College of Music under Gordon Jacob and Herbert Howells and later, privately, with Michael Tippett. The *First Cello Concerto* was completed in 1984 yet has remained unperformed until the present recording. It is a work of distinction, richly lyrical and valedictory in feeling, especially in the third and final movements; the latter is very movingly played here. The *Second Concerto for Cello and Voices* is another valedictory work in three movements (*Threnody, Estampie* and a touching *Sarabande*) associated in the composer's mind with Hiroshima (which he recalls hearing about as a ten-year old). Some may feel that the use of voices instead of an orchestra gives a gimmicky feel to the piece, but Ridout's sincerity is in no doubt, and the work certainly communicates readily again, ending nobly and in tranquil mood. In the *Third Concerto* the setting of a solo cello against 'an orchestra of cellos' provides a depth and darkness of texture that is used to mirror Ridout's conception of the stress suffered by a political prisoner. But the music reflects also the suffering and final release of Christ: 'The captive world awakened and found the prisoner loose, the jailer bound.' The performances are persuasively dedicated. Just occasionally the intonation of the solo cellist, Gérard Leclerk, is a little insecure in its highest range, but he plays with such warmth of lyrical feeling and finds such bravura for the scherzando passages, that this seems a minor flaw.

As a gentle postscript, the tale of *The Emperor and the Bird of Paradise*, told simply by Joanna Lumley, is also about a caged prisoner being freed. As the narrator clearly recognizes, the piece has much in common with *Peter and the Wolf*, but here the flute obbligato, which serves for the acompaniment,

is simple and unpretentious. It is very well played by Paul Edmund-Davies.

RIES, Ferdinand (1784–1838)

Symphonies 1 in D, Op. 23; 2 in C min., Op. 80
*** CPO 999 716-2. Zürich CO, Griffiths

Ferdinand Ries was a pupil and protégé of Beethoven. The latter entrusted the second performance of his *Third Piano Concerto* to the youngster and also allowed him to write his own cadenza. Ries was in his mid-twenties when he wrote the first of his eighteen symphonies in 1809 (the year of the Siege of Vienna) and the *Second in C minor* was written and first given in 1814 in London, where Ries spent the best part of a decade. It enjoyed much exposure during Ries's lifetime, and although the shadow of his master (and especially the *Eroica*) is strikingly in evidence, it is by no means wanting in quality. Ries is a fine craftsman and has good taste and an inventive lyrical vein. This music serves to show that if Beethoven loomed head and shoulders above his contemporaries, they were still far from negligible. Both symphonies are the product of a fine musical intelligence and offer civilized discourse. Persuasive performances and decent recording from the Zürich orchestra under Howard Griffiths.

Symphonies 4 in F, Op. 110; 6 in D, Op. 146
*** CPO 999 836-2. Zürich CO, Griffiths

Another excellent find from MDG, who have been kindly resurrecting composers obscured in the shadow of Beethoven: Fesca, Onslow, Spohr and now Ferdinand Ries. Ries, composer, pianist and conductor, wrote some eighteen symphonies, of which the two recorded here make a good coupling. He was a pupil of Beethoven, who is alleged to have remarked that Ries 'imitates me too much', a remark – whether it was made or not – which has some justification; it would be pretty strange if there were not an element of imitation from a pupil of Beethoven, so powerful his influence was (and is!): the Scherzo of the *Fourth Symphony* is pure Beethoven, almost a crib. Even if no masterpieces have been uncovered, with their lively and melodic writing it is hard not to enjoy these two works, written in 1818 and 1822 respectively, both coming up freshly in these enthusiastic and sympathetic performances. Curiously, in the *Sixth Symphony*, Ries employs a *Menuetto* rather than more 'modern' Scherzo – and a very attractive one it is too; in the finale (which has a lovely, jaunty recurring tune), a battery of 'Turkish' instruments is recruited – bass drum, cymbals and triangle – to give an extra splash of colour, very exotic for its day. The sound is excellent and, as usual with CPO, the sleeve-notes are highly informative.

Horn Sonata in F, Op. 34
*** HM HMC 90 5250. Müller, Torbianelli – BEETHOVEN; DANZI: *Horn Sonatas ***

The *Horn Sonata* of Ferdinand Ries opens assertively but immediately relents into a cantabile. Yet as the movement proceeds one can hear his Beethoven model showing its strong influence. The greater composer (justly) accused him of imitation. The opening of the *Andante* is theatrically evocative, and this is the most original movement. The finale attractively follows Danzi in gallantry and bravura. This is a first-rate performance, with Thomas Müller playing his hand horn with great skill and Edoardo Torbianelli a fine partner, his fortepiano timbre always pleasing. The recording balance is excellent and catches Müller's full timbre most naturally.

RIHM, Wolfgang (born 1952)

Gesungene Zeit (Time Chant)
*** DG 437 093-2. Mutter, Chicago SO, Levine – BERG: *Violin Concerto* ***

Under the title *Gesungene Zeit* ('Time Chant'), Rihm has written what in effect is an extended lyrical meditation for the soloist, heightened and illustrated by the orchestra in the most discreet way. As in the Berg, Mutter is inspired, playing with an inner hush that used only rarely to mark her recordings.

RIISAGER, Knudåge (1897–1974)

(i) *Concertino for Trumpet & Strings, Op. 29. Darduse, Op. 32; Slaraffenland (Fools' Paradise): Suites 1 & 2; Tolv med Posten, Op. 37*
*** Marco Polo 8.224082. (i) Hardenberger; Hälsingborg SO, Dausgaard

Knudåge Riisager is best known for his neoclassical works from the 1930s, and all the music on this CD comes from that decade. *Fools' Paradise* has a fair amount of circus-like music à la manière de Satie and Milhaud, but the touching lyricism of *Prinsesse Sukkergodt* ('Princess Sweets') is captivating. The whole work has bags of charm and deserves the widest currency. Håkan Hardenberger is in good form in the *Concertino*, though the orchestral support could have greater lightness of touch and finesse. *April* from *Tolv med Posten*, on the other hand, has much elegance. Readers who investigate this CD will find little depth but much to entertain them. Generally good performances under Thomas Dausgaard but rather bass-light sound.

Erasmus Montanus Overture, Op. 1; Etudes (ballet: complete); *Qarrtsiluni, Op. 36*
*** Chan. 9432. Danish Nat. RSO, Rozhdestvensky

Both the *Etudes* and *Qarrtsiluni* are classics of the Danish ballet. Knudåge Riisager's admiration for *Les Six* is evident in the elegance and wit that distinguish the *Etudes* (1948), a pastiche based on Czerny, and *Qarrtsiluni* (1938). There is a zest and sparkle about his music, though it neither aims for nor has any great depth. The attractive *Erasmus Montanus Overture* is a highly accomplished first opus, neatly performed and superbly recorded.

RILEY, Terry (born 1935)

The Heavenly Ladder, Book 7; The Walrus in memoriam
*** Telarc CD 80513. Cheng-Cochran – ADAMS: *China Gates; Phrygian Gates* ***

The five pieces which make up *The Heavenly Ladder* were written in 1994 and represent the composer's move away from an aleatory improvisational style into written 'paper music'. The jazz element remains and is never more effectively interpolated than in the third piece, the polyphonic *Ragtempus fugatum. Venus in '94* is a bizarre waltz-scherzo and the *Fandango on the Heavenly Ladder* (the most extended movement) intriguingly combines melancholy with energy. Its three themes are then gently re-explored in the closing

Simone's Lullaby, a set of variations marked pianissimo throughout, and dedicated to the composer's newly arrived granddaughter. *The Walrus in memoriam* is a witty ragtime encore piece ending more reflectively, as it is intended as a memorial to John Lennon. The performances here are persuasive: Gloria Cheng-Cochran is very sensitive to the composer's eclectic but very personal pianistic excursions, and with the stimulating Adams couplings (dating from the late 1970s) this is an important issue for those interested in the way minimalism is developing.

RIMSKY-KORSAKOV, Nikolay (1844–1908)

Capriccio espagnol, Op. 34
⌐ (M) *** RCA (ADD) 09026 63302-2. RCA Victor SO, Kondrashin – KABALEVSKY: *The Comedians Suite*; KHACHATURIAN: *Masquerade Suite*; TCHAIKOVSKY: *Capriccio italien* *** ●
(M) *** DG (IMS) (ADD) 449 769-2 (2). BPO, Maazel – RAVEL: *L'Heure espagnole; L'Enfant et les sortilèges* ***; STRAVINSKY: *Le Chant du rossignol* *** ●

Kondrashin's 1958 performance is among the finest ever recorded, ranking alongside Maazel's famous Berlin Philharmonic account, but with the advantage of slightly more sumptuous string textures. Like the coupled Tchaikovsky *Capriccio* it has great flair and excitement, with glittering colour and detail in the variations and the *Scena e canto gitana*. The orchestral zest is exhilarating, yet there is warmth too and the resonant recording still sounds very good indeed.

Maazel's 1960 recording of the *Capriccio espagnol* is memorable in every way, and remains one of his finest recorded performances. With gorgeous string and horn playing and a debonair, relaxed virtuosity in the *Scena e canto gitana*, leading to remarkable bravura in the closing sequence, every note in place, this is unforgettable. The remastering has restored the recording's analogue allure and, although the *fortissimo* violins are a little thin above the stave, the ear readily adjusts when the playing is so exciting.

(i) *Capriccio espagnol;* (ii) *Le Coq d'or: Suite; Dubinushka;* (iii) *May Night Overture;* (iv) *Russian Easter Festival Overture; Scheherazade;* (ii) *Snow Maiden: Suite;* (v) *Tsar Saltan: Suite;* (i) *Flight of the Bumblebee*
(B) **(*) EMI (ADD) 5 69680-2 (2). Philh. O; with (i) Cluytens; (ii) Kurtz; (iii) Silvestri; (iv) Von Matačić; (v) Kletzki

These recordings were made at Abbey Road between 1956 and 1963, and although some of the allure in the treble has been lost with the CD remastering, the bright colouring remains, and the Philharmonia are on top form, as they immediately demonstrate in an exciting *Scheherazade*. Matačić's direction has plenty of drive in the opening movement, and the silky strings in the slow movement are matched by the lustre of the woodwind solos. The finale is really exciting. The *Russian Easter Festival Overture* wrings every ounce of colour from the music, and the famous trombone solo is played with great dignity. Efrem Kurtz is thoroughly at home in *Le Coq d'or* and *The Snow Maiden*, and Kletzki is vibrant in *Tsar Saltan*. Cluytens closes the first disc and opens the second with virtuoso accounts of the *Capriccio espagnol* and *Flight of the Bumblebee* respectively; in the former the sound is brilliant but lacking in voluptuousness.

Capriccio espagnol, Op. 34; Le Coq d'or: Suite; Russian Easter Festival Overture, Op. 36

(N) (M) *** Mercury **SACD** (ADD) 475 6194. LSO, Dorati – BORODIN: *Prince Igor: Polovstian Dances* **(*)

Dorati's 1959 *Capriccio espagnol* brings glittering bravura and excitement from the LSO players, and the *Russian Easter Festival Overture*, recorded at Walthamstow at the same sessions, is equally dynamic and colourful. Even more remarkably, the rich-hued and vibrant *Le Coq d'or* dates from as early as 1956, yet it hardly sounds dated – the finale is very exciting, with the bass drum stretching the recording technology to its limit! The SACD transfer brings the finest sound yet.

(i; ii) *Capriccio espagnol;* (iii) *Le Coq d'or: Suite. Russian Easter Festival Overture, Op. 36;* (i; iv) *Scheherazade, Op. 35;* (v) *Symphony 2 (Antar), Op. 9;* (vi) *Tsar Saltan: Suite, Op. 57. The Flight of the Bumblebee*

(BB) **(*) DG Panorama (ADD) 469 187-2 (2). (i) BPO; (ii) Maazel; (iii) LOP, Markevitch; (iv) Karajan; (v) Gothenburg SO, Järvi; (vi) Philh. O, Ashkenazy

On the whole, a good Panorama selection here. You get Karajan's exciting, and superbly played (if uneven) *Scheherazade*; vibrant accounts of the *Russian Easter Festival Overture* and *Le Coq d'or Suite* from Markevitch (from the late 1950s, and sounding slightly dated in the matter of string timbre); Ashkenazy's beautifully played and sumptuously recorded (Decca) *Tsar Saltan Suite*, and an excellent reading of *Antar* by Järvi (even if it could do with a bit more Russian bite). Best of all is Maazel's glittering *Capriccio espagnol*, a classic account which shows just how this repertoire should be played.

Capriccio espagnol; Russian Easter Festival Overture

(B) **(*) Decca Eclipse 448 233-2. Montreal SO, Dutoit – MUSSORGSKY: *Night on the Bare Mountain*, etc. **(*)

(i) *Capriccio espagnol, Op. 34;* (ii) *Russian Easter Festival Overture, Op. 36; Tsar Saltan: The Flight of the Bumblebee*

(BB) **(*) EMI Encore (ADD) 5 74763-2. (i) Philh. O; (ii) Paris Conservatoire O; Cluytens – MUSSORGSKY: *Night on the Bare Mountain;* BORODIN: *In the Steppes of Central Asia* **(*)

Cluytens imbues his *Capriccio espagnol* with more of a sultry atmosphere than is often the case, rather than simply treating the work as a brilliant show-piece. Not that excitement is lacking: it is a splendid performance and the recording is excellent for its period (1958), if a little thin by modern standards. Cluytens coaxes more sensitive playing from the Paris orchestra as well as drama (and a jet-propelled bumblebee) although the distinctive French sound (in particular, the vibrato on the brass) may not be to all tastes. Still, this is worth investigating at the price.

Dutoit's *Capriccio espagnol* is comparatively genial and relaxed; the *Russian Easter Festival Overture* is strong, with a fine climax. In both works the Montreal recording is full, with iridescent detail.

(i) *Christmas Eve (Suite); Le Coq d'or: Suite.* (ii) *Fantasia on Serbian Themes, Op. 6; Fairy-Tale (Skazka), Op. 29; Overture on Russian Themes, Op. 20;* (i) *Sadko, Op. 5; Scheherazade, Op. 35; Song of India (from Sadko);* (ii)

Symphonies 1, Op. 1; 2 (Antar); 3, Op. 32; (i) The Tale of Tsar Saltan: Suite & Flight of the Bumblebee; (ii) The Tsar's Bride: Overture

(BB) **(*) Brilliant 99934 (4). (i) Armenian PO, Tjeknavorian; (ii) Philh. O or LSO, Butt

This inexpensive Brilliant compilation is on the face of it a most attractive survey of Rimsky's orchestral works, but in the event it is uneven in appeal. Two of the four CDs, which include a seductive *Scheherazade* and lustrous, sparkling accounts of many of the shorter works, are played with much élan by the Armenian Philharmonic Orchestra under Loris Tjeknavorian and given first-class sound. The other pair of discs features the Philharmonia or London Symphony Orchestra, directed by Yondani Butt. Here the orchestral playing itself is refined and colourful, but the lack of vitality or a powerful forward drive in the *First* and *Third Symphonies* is a drawback, while in *Antar* it is only the central movements that spring powerfully to life. The shorter pieces are more successful, but the Armenian performances have far more red-blooded Russian character. The two CDs conducted by Tjeknavorian on ASV will perhaps be later reissued in a lower price range.

Christmas Eve: Suite; Le Coq d'or: Suite; Legend of the Invisible City of Kitezh: Suite; May Night: Overture; Mlada: Suite; The Snow Maiden: Suite; The Tale of the Tsar Saltan: Suite

*** Chan. 8327/9 (3). SNO, Järvi

Apart from the feast of good tunes here, the composer's skilful and subtle deployment of the orchestral palette continually titillates the ear. Neeme Järvi draws the most seductive response from the SNO; he consistently creates orchestral textures which are diaphanously sinuous. Yet the robust moments, when the brass blazes or the horns ring out sumptuously, are caught just as strikingly and the listener is assured that here is music which survives repetition uncommonly well.

Christmas Eve: Suite; Dubinushka, Op. 62; May Night Overture; Russian Easter Festival Overture, Op. 36; Sadko (musical picture), Op. 5; (i) Scheherazade, Op. 35; The Snow Maiden: Suite. Tsar Saltan (Suite), Op. 57; Tsar Saltan (opera): The Flight of the Bumblebee

(B) **(*) Double Decca (IMS) (ADD) 443 464-2 (2). SRO, Ansermet; (i) with Geneva Motet Ch.

This is all repertoire for which Ansermet was famous in the early stereo era, and *Scheherazade* must be counted a historic recording. It dates from 1960, and the sound still offers quality regarded as demonstration standard in its day and not very far short of it now. Ansermet's skill as a ballet conductor comes out persuasively. The outer movements with their undoubted sparkle are the finest: the first is dramatic and the last is built steadily to a climax of considerable impact. The music's sinuous qualities are not missed and every bar of the score is alive. *May Night* was recorded a year earlier and the strings have far less lustre; but the *Tsar Saltan Suite*, also made in 1959, shows Ansermet and the Decca engineers in glittering form, especially in the recording of brass and woodwind. The *Flight of the Bumblebee* is rather leisurely, but Ansermet is at his finest in the *Christmas Eve Suite*, played with much affection, plus that mixture of spontaneity and a remarkably graphic orchestral palette which made Ansermet's performances special. *Dubinushka* has some typical brass fanfare writing and Ansermet is (again in 1958) well served here by the engineers, as he is in *Sadko*, an exotic fairy-tale handled with characteristic aplomb. The earliest recording offered here is *The Snow Maiden Suite* (1957) and once again the sound is remarkably warm and richly coloured. This set can certainly be recommended at Double Decca price, especially to Ansermet aficionados.

Christmas Eve: Polonaise. Mlada: Procession of the Nobles. Snow Maiden: Dance of the Tumblers. Tsar Sultan: Farewell of the Tsar

(N) (B) *** Sony (ADD) 517482-2. Phd., Ormandy – TCHAIKOVSKY: *Nutcracker Suite* **

These four Rimsky lollipops are marvellously played and brightly recorded, with exhilarating brass in the closing excerpt from *Tsar Saltan*.

Concert Fantasy on Russian Themes for Violin & Orchestra in B min., Op. 33

**(*) Globe GLO 5174. Lubotsky, Estonian Nat. SO, Volmer – ARENSKY; TCHAIKOVSKY: *Violin Concertos* **(*)

The *Concert Fantasy in B minor on Two Russian Themes* is a slight but colourful piece, and it is persuasively performed here. It makes an admirable fill-up to Arensky's endearing *Violin Concerto* and the Tchaikovsky which inspired it. Good orchestral playing under Arvo Volmer and naturally balanced sound.

Piano Concerto in C sharp min., Op. 30

*** Hyp. CDA 66640. Binns, E. N. Philh. O, Lloyd-Jones – BALAKIREV: *Concertos 1–2* ***

Malcolm Binns proves a sensitive and intelligent exponent in the Rimsky-Korsakov concerto, which comes aptly coupled with Balakirev's two essays in the form. The Northern Philharmonia under David Lloyd-Jones give excellent support and the Hyperion recording is first class.

Le Coq d'or: Suite

(M) (***) BBC Legends mono BBCL 4084-2. RPO, Beecham – BALAKIREV: *Symphony 1*; BORODIN: *Polovtsian Dances* (***)

This live broadcast performance has all the swagger and panache that one would expect of Beecham in this music, compensating for the lack of stereo. A welcome fill-up for the outstanding account of the Balakirev *Symphony No. 1*.

Le Coq d'or; The Maid of Pskov; Pan Voyevoda: suites

☛ ☀ *** Kontrapunct 32247. Odense SO, Serov

Serov is complete master of the repertoire, and the playing of the Odense orchestra is glorious, the glowing woodwind palette matched by the most seductive and transparent string textures. Serov's performance of *Le Coq d'or* is every bit as fine as Maazel's, and the recording here is even more luxuriant. Indeed it is very much in the demonstration bracket. In *The Maid of Pskov* suite *The Tsar Hunting in the Wood and Tempest* has much of the imaginative pictorial evocation and imagery of Berlioz's *Royal Hunt and Storm*. Again it is superbly presented, as is the hardly less attractive *Pan Voyevoda* which opens with a pastoral evocation rather like Wagner's *Forest Murmurs* and includes three brilliantly scored *Russian Dances*.

Scheherazade (symphonic suite), Op. 35

☛ *** Ph. **SACD** 470 618-2; CD 470 840-2. Kirov O, Gergiev – BORODIN: *In the Steppes of Central Asia*; BALAKIREV: *Islamey* ***

☀ ☛ (M) *** RCA **SACD** 82876 66377-2. Chicago SO, Reiner – STRAVINSKY: *Song of the Nightingale* ***

(M) *** Ph. (ADD) 464 735-2. Concg. O, Kondrashin – BORODIN: *Symphony 2* *(*)

(M) *** EMI 5 66983-2 [CDM 566998]. RPO, Beecham (with BORODIN: *Polovtsian Dances* ***)

(M) (***) Cala (ADD) CACD 0536. LSO, Stokowski (with rehearsal sequence) – TCHAIKOVSKY: *Marche slave* **(*)

*** DG (IMS) 437 818-2. O de l'Opéra Bastille, Chung – STRAVINSKY: *Firebird Suite* ***

(BB) **(*) EMI Encore 5 74751-2. Phd. O, Muti – TCHAIKOVSKY: *1812* **(*)

(BB) **(*) Virgin 2×1 5 61751-2 (2). LPO, Litton – BORODIN: *Prince Igor: Overture & Polovtsian Dances* ***; MUSSORGSKY: *Night on the Bare Mountain; Pictures at an Exhibition* **; TCHAIKOVSKY: *The Tempest* ***

(M) **(*) DG (ADD) 463 614-2. BPO, Karajan – TCHAIKOVSKY: *Capriccio italien; 1812 Overture* **(*)

(B) ** EMI double forte (ADD) 5 69361-2 (2). LSO, Svetlanov – ARENSKY: *Variations on a Theme by Tchaikovsky*; GLAZUNOV: *The Seasons; Concert Waltzes* ***

(**) Testament mono SBT 1139. Philh. O, Stokowski – STRAVINSKY: *Petrushka* (***)

(BB) * DG Entrée 474 564-2. BPO, Maazel – MUSSORGSKY: *Pictures at an Exhibition* ***

(i) Scheherazade; (ii) Capriccio espagnol, Op. 34

*** Telarc CD 80208. LSO, Mackerras

**(*) Australian Decca Eloquence 466 907-2. (i) LAPO; (ii) Israel PO; Mehta

(B) **(*) EMI double forte 5 75172-2 (2). LPO, Jansons – MUSSORGSKY: *Night on the Bare Mountain; Khovanshchina: Prelude; Pictures at an Exhibition* **

(i–ii) Scheherazade; (iii–iv) Capriccio espagnol; (i; iv) Russian Easter Festival Overture, Op. 36

(M) *** Ph. (ADD) 442 643-2. (i) Concg. O; (ii) Kondrashin; (iii) LSO; (iv) Markevitch

Scheherazade; Dubinushka, Op. 62; Tale of Tsar Saltan: Flight of the Bumblebee

(M) *** Chan. 7093. RSNO, Järvi – KALINNIKOV: *Overtures* ***

(i) Scheherazade; (ii) Fairy Tale (Skazka)

(BB) (**) Dutton mono CDBP 9712. (i) Paris Conservatoire O, Ansermet; (ii) Philh. O, Lambert (with BORODIN: *Polovtsian Dances* arr. Rimsky-Korsakov (**))

Scheherazade; Fairy Tale (Skazka), Op. 29; Sadko, Op. 5; Song of India, from Sadko (arr. Tjeknavorian)

*** ASV CDDCA 771. Armenian PO, Tjeknavorian

Scheherazade; Mlada: Procession of the Nobles

(M) *** BBC (ADD) BBCL 4121-2. Georgiadis, LSO, Svetlanov – SCRIABIN: *Poème de l'extase* ***

(i) Scheherazade; (ii) Russian Easter Festival Overture

(N) (B) **(*) RCA 82876 65843-2. (i) RPO; (ii) Chicago SO; Stokowski

Scheherazade; Russian Easter Festival Overture

(BB) **(*) RCA 74321 68014-2. NYPO, Temirkanov

Scheherazade; Russian Easter Festival Overture; The Maid of Pskov: Hunt and Storm

(M) (***) Biddulph mono WHL 010. Phd. O, Stokowski

Scheherazade; Tsar Saltan: Orchestral Suite

(BB) *** Naxos 8.550726. Philh. O, Bátiz

Gergiev's Kirov performance is the most exciting, most red-blooded account of Rimsky-Korsakov's orchestral warhorse in many years, electrifying from beginning to end, with sound of a fullness and brilliance never before heard in Russian recordings. It even outshines previous benchmark recordings, culminating in the final climax of the fourth movement, where the motto theme returns *fortissimo* on heavy brass with an irresistible thrust. From the start Gergiev, magnetically sustaining the musical narrative, dispels any idea that this programme piece stops and starts too frequently. The recording has been enhanced with added reverberation, pinning you back in your seat, necessary because the acoustic is basically rather dry. The effect is even more spacious on SACD, and even though purists may disapprove, it works believably enough. The two shorter pieces, the atmospheric Borodin tone poem and Lyapounov's brilliant orchestration of Balakirev's virtuoso piano piece, *Islamey*, are welcome makeweights.

Reiner's magnificent (1956) *Scheherazade* stands out among the many superb RCA recordings made in Chicago in the 1950s. In the new SACD transfer the feeling of sitting in the concert hall is uncannily real, and the recording itself has extraordinary lustre. Mark Donahue shows how truthful and wide-ranging the original recording was, produced by Richard Mohr and engineered by Lewis Layton. Reiner's first movement opens richly and dramatically and has a strong forward impulse. Sidney Harth, the orchestral leader, naturally balanced, plays most seductively. Reiner's affectionate individual touches in the gloriously played slow movement have much in common with Beecham's version and they sound similarly spontaneous. Reiner told his players 'to play with glow, not perspiration', and they do: the string cantilena in the slow movement is quite ravishing. The finale, brilliant and exciting, was recorded in a single take and has a climax of resounding power and amplitude, and the acoustics throughout provide the orchestra with plenty of body and arresting brass sonorities. Above all, Reiner's is a virtuoso reading, with phenomenally crisp ensemble that has one relishing not just the brilliance but the individual finesse of the orchestral playing. Yet it is a romantic reading too, and the strings retain all their bloom in the third movement. The new Stravinsky coupling also shows the conductor and his orchestra at their finest, and this is a disc that should find a place in every collection. (The accompanying notes, incidentally, give full technical details of how this astonishing recording was made.)

Mackerras's reading combines gripping drama with romantic ardour, subtlety of colour with voluptuousness; he is helped by a wonderfully beguiling portrait of Scheherazade herself, provided by his orchestral leader, in this case Kees Hulsmann. After an appropriate pause, Mackerras then delivers a thrilling, bravura account of *Capriccio espagnol*, lushly opulent in the variations, glittering in the exotic *Scena e canto gitana*, and carrying all before it in the impetus of the closing *Fandango asturiano*. Telarc's digital recording is very much in the demonstration class.

Kondrashin's version of *Scheherazade* with the Concertgebouw Orchestra has the advantage of splendidly glowing (1980) analogue recorded sound. Hermann Krebbers' exquisitely seductive portrayal of Scheherazade is cleverly used by Kondrashin to provide a foil for the expansively vibrant contribution of the orchestra as a whole, and he creates an irresistible forward impulse, leading to a huge climax at the moment of the shipwreck. Markevitch gives an excellent account of the *Russian Easter Festival Overture* with the same

orchestra; the *Capriccio espagnol*, too, is brilliantly played by the LSO, and in both the sound also has considerable allure, with the present CD transfer much more vivid than the original LP.

Kondrashin's account is also available alternatively coupled with an unrecommendable account of Borodin's *Second Symphony*.

Beecham's 1957 *Scheherazade* is a performance of extraordinary drama and charisma. Alongside the violin contribution of Stephen Staryk, all the solo playing has great distinction; in the second movement Beecham gives the woodwind complete metrical freedom. The sumptuousness and glamour of the slow movement are very apparent and the finale has an explosive excitement, rising to an electrifying climax. This could well be first choice for some collectors, although the *fortissimo* massed strings in the first movement are on the thin side and show the age of the recording.

The BBC disc brings a welcome reminder of the highly charged and intense playing that Svetlanov could achieve in the concert hall. These two pieces, which come from a concert in London's Royal Festival Hall in 1978, find the LSO responding with enthusiasm and virtuosity to his direction. The ebullient *Procession of the Nobles* from *Mlada* sets the scene for a brilliant and sensuously individual reading with a strong Russian accent. The LSO are kept on their toes throughout, with John Georgiadis seductive in his storytelling. After a bold opening section, with plenty of thrust and momentum, the inner movements are flexible and relaxed, bringing out the maximum orchestral colour, yet with expansive ardour from the strings, then capped in the finale by a thrilling climactic shipwreck. The recording is wider ranging and has more sparkle than is usual from this source, and this must be placed well up on the recommended list if you want the powerful Scriabin coupling.

On his visits to England in the 1960s, Leopold Stokowski, always adventurous over recording techniques, became fascinated with the Phase Four system developed by the Decca engineers, and in 1964 he went to Kingsway Hall to make this spectacular recording of a favourite work of his. At 82 he was still at the height of his powers, and the result is even more thrillingly high-powered than the multiple versions he had already put on disc and the one which (11 years later) he was to make for RCA. The warmth and drama of this evocative programme piece have never been conveyed more vividly, and in this excellent CD transfer, using original material, the sound never for a moment betrays its age. This Cala version comes with fascinating couplings: the thrilling live performance of Tchaikovsky's *Marche slave* that Stokowski conducted as an encore at his ninetieth birthday concert in London, with a spoken introduction by himself, and, fascinatingly, four substantial clips from the rehearsals the conductor took in the Phase Four sessions on *Scheherazade*. As he says, 'Music is not mechanism,' and every note he conducted confirms that.

On ASV a refreshing and totally gripping *Scheherazade* from Eastern Russia. Yuri Boghosian immediately presents a seductively slight and sinuous image for the heroine-narrator and throughout the central movements one is made aware of the lustrous oriental character of Rimsky's melodies. The finale, with its spectacular storm and shipwreck, has exhilarating animation and bite. Tjeknavorian shows great imaginative flair in the two shorter folk tales and also offers his own gently luscious arrangement of the *Chant hindue*, which caresses the ear beguilingly. The brilliant recording has great vividness and projection, but relatively little sumptuousness. But it suits the performances admirably.

Järvi's version of *Scheherazade* with the RSNO is given one of Chandos's most sumptuous and spectacular digital recordings and, as with Kondrashin, Järvi's reading generates a vivid narrative feeling. The playing is no less fine, and this is well worth considering, and it offers a smiliarly brilliant account of the colourful *Dubinushka*, plus a buzzing, convincingly scaled *Bumblebee*. The coupled overtures by Kalinnikov are also well worth having.

There is a certain freshness about the Paris account under Myung-Whun Chung; nothing is routine and the playing has a certain enthusiasm. Very fast and effective tempo in the finale. The sound has warmth and perspective, though the timpani resonate perhaps a bit too much. All the same, a very enjoyable newcomer.

Bátiz's reputation for spontaneity in the recording studio is demonstrated at its most telling. His performance is impulsive, full of momentum and seductively volatile. David Nolan's picture of Scheherazade is rhapsodically evanescent and in the key second movement the lilting Philharmonia wind solos are a constant pleasure. The slow movement combines refinement with its sensuous patina, and the finale has fine zest and excitement. The colourful *Tsar Saltan Suite* is comparably dramatic and vivid. In short, with first-class recording, both clear in detail and full-bodied, at super-bargain price this is hard to beat.

Mehta's *Scheherazade* was considered a demonstration disc in its day (mid-1970s) and still sounds impressive. Though it is a high-powered performance, there is affection too, and despite the odd mannerism, it is very enjoyable, and the orchestral leader, Sydney Harth, offers a sinuously seductive image for Scheherazade herself. The Israeli version of *Capriccio espagnol* is not quite so successful in terms of sound or performance, but still entertains, and makes a fair bonus for the main work, which is more exciting than many more recent digital versions.

Jansons gives us a very well-played and warmly characterful account with much to recommend it. What distinguishes this from other versions is the way he points rhythms in all four movements – lilting, bouncy and affectionate – before bringing a satisfying resolution at the great climax towards the end of the finale, with Joakim Svenheden a warmly expressive soloist. The *Capriccio espagnol* brings a similar combination of warmth and exuberance. This is now reissued in EMI's bargain double forte series, coupled with Mussorgsky.

Muti's reading is colourful and dramatic in a larger-than-life way that sweeps one along. The bravura has one remembering that this was the orchestra which in the days of Stokowski made this a party-piece. The great string theme of the slow movement has all the voluptuousness one expects of Philadelphia strings in one of the best of HMV's latter-day Philadelphia recordings, more spacious than usual, though not ideally balanced. There is a glare in the upper range to which not all ears will respond, even if the racy finale, with its exciting climax, carries all before it. However, the brightness in the treble, especially in climaxes, is much less congenial than the Philips sound for Kondrashin.

Litton's first movement brings strong dramatic contrasts and the violin soloist, David Nolan, plays seductively. The *Andantino* has a Beechamesque languor and the freedom given to the woodwind soloists also recalls the Beecham version, which is also coupled with the Borodin *Polovtsian Dances*. Litton's finale is less than overwhelming, indeed less

exciting than Beecham's, and although the Virgin recording is opulent as well as brilliant, the RPO performance brings a greater sense of spontaneity, although Litton's version has more modern sound and is certainly enjoyable in its spaciousness.

In Karajan's account it is the brilliance and prowess of the Berlin Philharmonic which is immediately apparent from the sensitive opening violin solo from Michel Schwalbé onwards. The recording is full-blooded and vivid, but is a little light on bass – although in the present remastering this is less obvious. The first movement is hard driven but has plenty of excitement; the finale (a resounding success) has even more, but the inner movements do not glow as you would ideally expect them to. A typically individual Karajan account then, and if he is not quite at his best it is still impressive.

The collection of Leopold Stokowski's recordings of Rimsky-Korsakov on Biddulph centres on the first of his five versions of *Scheherazade*. Made in 1927, it is wilder and more passionate than later ones; fascinatingly, an alternative version of the first movement, never issued before, is included as a supplement. At a slightly broader speed, spreading to an extra 78-r.p.m. side, it is even more persuasive. Equally impressive is Stokowski's intense, volatile account of the *Russian Easter Festival Overture*, dating from 1929, while the *Hunt and Storm* sequence from the *The Maid of Pskov* comes from ten years later, with the sound drier and marginally less full. The Biddulph transfers are excellent, with plenty of body.

Though Ansermet's 1948 recording of *Scheherazade* cannot match his later stereo version with the Suisse Romande Orchestra in power and polish, let alone in sound, its lighter manner gives it an attractively balletic quality, building up gradually rather than packing a punch. The usual reservations need mentioning about the playing of the Paris orchestra – with brass vibrato and a sugary solo violin among them. As transferred, this is not one of the most vivid of early Decca mono *ffrr* recordings. The rarity, *Skazka*, conducted by Constant Lambert, is taken from a 1946 EMI recording, here transformed, with Gregor Fitelberg's reading of the *Polovtsian Dances* a welcome bonus.

Svetlanov's 1978 version with the LSO is disappointing, despite John Georgiadis's subtly seductive image of Scheherazade herself. The broad, powerful opening movement, taken very spaciously indeed, is balanced by a finale which is almost aggressively brilliant. The inner movements are extremely volatile and less contrasted than usual. The LSO wind solo playing is impressive, but the strings sometimes have an almost febrile timbre which is less than glamorous.

Stokowski and the RPO, recorded at Abbey Road in 1975, make some sensuously beautiful orchestral sounds. With Erich Gruenberg providing a sweet-toned commentary, the first and second movements are almost linked, with only the shortest of pauses. Stokowski is at his most characteristic in the slow movement, and his nudgings of rubato are not always spontaneous, despite the rich sheen of string-tone he creates. There is no lack of drama, and the finale is exciting, although here there is some resonant muddiness (and here the bass drum does not help the clarity). However, the Chicago performance of the *Russian Easter Festival Overture* is a very considerable bonus. Recorded a decade earlier, it is broad and sympathetic, with plenty of colour and excitement. The recording is rich, and if it lacks something in sparkle in the upper register it has an attractive bloom.

The highlight of the Temirkanov RCA account lies in the richly languorous slow movement, with the warmest, most sensuous string playing at the opening and a delightfully wistful, almost elegiac close. But the spacious opening movement lacks real tension, and the colourful events of the second movement are also very relaxed. The finale brings alert playing and vivid detail with an explosively climactic shipwreck, where the bold tam-tam stroke is followed by a hammering nemesis from the timpani. But overall this cannot compete with the finest bargain versions. The *Russian Easter Festival Overture*, too, takes a while to warm up properly, though again the climax is impressive.

Stokowski's 1950s Philharmonia recording of *Scheherazade* on Testament offers some superb playing – what performances under his baton did not! – but it is actually less likeable than his pre-war Philadelphia set. His rubati are intrusive in the slow movement and he pulls phrases out of shape elsewhere. Good sound and an excellent transfer.

There is nothing to detain the collector in Maazel's digital DG version. The playing of the Berlin Philharmonic Orchestra is, of course, peerless, and in the slow movement they make some gorgeous sounds, though the the acoustics of the Philharmonie are not entirely flattering on CD. But Maazel's spacious reading is simply lacking in electricity. A pity, as the coupling is a good one.

Symphonies 1, Op. 1; 2 (Antar), Op. 9; 3, Op. 32. Capriccio espagnol; Russian Easter Festival Overture

(M) *** DG 459 512-2 (2). Gothenburg SO, Järvi

Symphonies 1 in E min., Op. 1; 2 (Antar), Op. 9; 3 in C, Op. 32; Capriccio espagnol, Op. 36; (i) Piano Concerto in C sharp min., Op. 30. Russian Easter Festival Overture, Op. 36; Sadko, Op. 5

(M) **(*) Chan. 6613 (2). (i) Tozer; Bergen PO, Kitaienko

Whatever Rimsky-Korsakov's symphonies may lack in symphonic coherence they make up for in colour and charm. Some of the material is a little thin but there is some highly attractive invention as well. *Antar* is not quite as strong as some of its protagonists would have us believe, but it should surely have a stronger presence in the concert and recorded repertoire than it has. The performances under Neeme Järvi have considerable merit and the Gothenburg orchestra is excellently recorded; moreover, the addition of the *Capriccio* and *Russian Easter Festival Overture* make the DG set a very attractive proposition, particularly as it is now reissued at mid-price. A clear first choice.

Kitaienko draws very good playing from the Bergen Philharmonic throughout and the first two symphonies are generally successful. In the *Third Symphony* the lustrous colours of the secondary material glow appealingly, but the *Scherzo* lacks sparkle. He gets very lively results in the *Capriccio espagnol*, but *Sadko* takes a while to warm up, although it has a spectacular close. With Tozer at the keyboard he shares a warmly lyrical view of the *Piano Concerto* but, partly because of the resonant sound, the finale again lacks something in sparkle, and Malcolm Binns on Hyperion (see above) is preferable. However, this Chandos set is value for money.

Symphony 2 (Antar); Russian Easter Festival Overture

☛ (BB) *** Hyp. Helios CDH 55137. Philh. O, Svetlanov

It goes without saying that the Philharmonia Orchestra under Svetlanov produce an excellent account of Rimsky-Korsakov's colourful score and there is no want of atmosphere or spirit in their playing. Moreover, they are given excellent recorded sound by the Hyperion team. The performances themselves are not superior to those on the

two-CD set from the Gothenburg orchestra under Neeme Järvi, but at its new budget price this reissue can receive an unreserved recommendation, even if the playing time is still a bit short – a mite under 50 minutes.

Tsar Saltan: Suite

*** Belair BAM 9724. New Russian O, Poltevsky – BORODIN: *Symphony 2 in B min.* *(*)

The young Russian, Oleg Poltevsky, conducts this handpicked Russian orchestra in an electrifying account of the colourful *Tsar Saltan* music, well recorded. An excellent, if ungenerous coupling for a rather ponderous reading of the Borodin.

Piano & Wind Quintet in B flat

(BB) *** Hyp. Helios CDH 55173. Capricorn – GLINKA: *Grand Sextet in E flat* ***
*** CRD (ADD) 3409. Brown, Nash Ens. – ARENSKY: *Piano Trio 1* ***

Capricorn's sparkling account of Rimsky's youthful *Quintet* for piano, flute, clarinet, horn and bassoon is all the more welcome at budget price, particularly as it is very well recorded.

The Nash Ensemble also give a spirited and delightful account of it on CRD that can be warmly recommended for its dash and sparkle and full, naturally balanced sound.

VOCAL MUSIC

Cantatas: (i) Inz Gomera, Op. 60; The Song of Alexis, Man of God, Op. 20; (ii–iii) The Song of Oleg the Wise, Op. 58; (iii–iv) Switsezianka (or The Girl in the Lake), Op. 44

✪ *** Chant du Monde RUS 288175. (i) Fedotova, Sizova; (ii) Didenko; (iii) Kortchak; (iv) Mitrakova, Moscow Academy Ch., Moscow SO, Ziva

These splendid secular choral cantatas are a real find, and show an endearing new facet to Rimsky's genius. Try the opening *Song of Alexis, Man of God*, superbly sung by a fine Russian chorus, and you will surely immediately be hooked. The composer re-uses music written to accompany pilgrims in *The Maid of Pskov*, to evoke the legend of Saint Alexis, who renounced marriage with a princess in order to lead a hermit's life. Its noble melody is based on a Russian folk song. *The Song of Olga the Wise*, to a poem by Pushkin, for tenor (who tells the story) and bass (Oleg) is melodramatically operatic, and *Inz Gomera*, based on Homer, even more so with its powerful orchestral *Prelude* depicting Poseidon's tempest, before the luminously seductive writing for the female voices.

Switsezianka (set to a poem by Lev May) is the familiar folk tale of the watery nymph who captivates her young swain and insists on his fidelity, with a dire penalty if he forgets her. She then returns in an even more beautiful form to test his faithfulness and 'as she spoke the wind disturbed her raiment, uncovering her milk-white breast'. Needless to say, he immediately forgets his vows, succumbs to temptation, realizing only too late that 'the young girl was none other than his former beloved', and he is swallowed up by the frothing waters of the lake. Rimsky's highly atmospheric scena, using soprano and tenor soloists, climaxes a splended quartet of performances, with fine Russian singers throughout. The recording is first class and so is the documentation, with full translations included, which are easy to follow even without the original Russian.

OPERA

The Legend of the Invisible City of Kitezh (complete)

*** Ph. 462 225-2 (2). Gorchakova, Galuzin, Putilin,
Ohotnikov, Marusin, Minjilkiev, Ognovienko, Kirov Opera
Ch. & O, Gergiev

Recorded live at the Mariinsky Theatre in St Peterburg, this
long fairy-tale piece (lasting almost three hours) relies above
all on the cadences of Russian folk song. As usual with
Russian folk-tales the plot brings a curious mixture of jollity
and bitterness. Though the Prince dies in battle in the middle
of Act III – illustrated in an interlude – he is resurrected in
Act IV, when the disappearing City of Kitezh is magically
transformed into Paradise, with hero and heroine united in
life after death. What adds spice to the plot is the equivocal
character of the drunkard, Grishka, comic only in part, who
initially is prompted to attack Fevroniya, but who later is
befriended by her. Galina Gorchakova sings powerfully as
Fevroniya and Yuri Marusin is a strong, idiomatic Prince,
whose distinctive tenor is well contrasted with that of
Vladimir Galuzin as an incisive Grishka, characterizing splendidly. Despite moments of strain, the rest of the Kirov cast
make an excellent team. Live recording inevitably brings
intrusive stage noises and odd balances, but this is another
warmly recommendable set in Gergiev's excellent Philips
series.

The Tsar's Bride (complete)

*** Ph. 462 618-2 (2). Bezzuhenkov, Shaguch, Hvorostovsky,
Alexashlin, Akimov, Borodina, Kirov Ch. & O, Gergiev

Gergiev firmly establishes The Tsar's Bride as a most richly
enjoyable opera, full of outstanding set numbers, such as the
banqueting song in the party scene of Act I, which uses the
Tsar's Hymn in opulent counterpoint. The story itself, set at
the time of Ivan the Terrible, is a curious mixture of darkness
and light, of fairy-tale fantasy and melodramatic realism.
Jealousy is the dominant emotion, when the sinister adven-
turer, Gryaznoy, and the scheming Lyubasha take priority
over even the hero and heroine. In the casting here, that
priority is a great source of strength, when Dmitri Hovoros-
tovsky as Gryaznoy and Olga Borodina as Lyubasha give
superb performances, not just singing with rich, firm tone
but characterizing powerfully. Marina Shaguch is fresh and
clear as Marfa the heroine, if edgy under pressure, and
Evgeny Akimov with his typically Slavonic tenor sings idiomatically if with forced tone. In Act IV, with the plot turning
sour, Rimsky is prompted to round the work off with a
sequence of remarkable numbers, including a splendid quintet with chorus, when Gryaznoy stabs Lyubasha to death, and
a mad-scene for Marfa. A rich offering, strongly recommended.

ROBINSON, Thomas (fl. 1589–1609)

Lute pieces: Bonny Sweet Boy; A Galliard; A Gigue; Go from
My Window; A Toy. Lute duets: (i) A Fantasy for 2 Lutes;
Pazzamezzo Galliard; A Plaine Song for 2 Lutes; The Queen's
Goodnight; A Toy for 2 Lutes; Twenty Ways upon the Bells

(BB) *** Naxos 8.553974. Wilson (lute); (i) with Rumsey –
  HOLBORNE: Lute Pieces **(*)

Thomas Robinson taught the future Queen Anne in Denmark before she married King James. He liked to write and
play duets with his pupils and the 'Goodnight' here is obviously addressed to her. All the duets here are delightful,

particularly Twenty Ways upon the Bells with its two players
ingeniously ringing the changes. The solo pieces, too, are full
of character, notably the melancholy solo Toy, worthy of
Dowland. But Robinson has a personality in his own right
and it is good to have his music rediscovered. Christopher
Wilson and his pupil Shirley Rumsey play everything intimately and spontaneously, readily conveying their pleasure in
the music. They are truthfully recorded (not too close) in a
pleasant acoustic.

ROCHBERG, George (born 1918)

Symphony 5; Black Sounds; Transcendental Variations

☛ ⊕ (BB) *** Naxos 8.559115. Saarbrücken RSO,
  Lyndon-Gee

George Rochberg was born in New Jersey, became an accomplished pianist and worked his way through college playing in
jazz bands. While serving in the Second World War he was
seriously wounded, and that experience undoubtedly underpins his early music, especially Black Sounds. After the war he
studied at the Curtis Institute in Philadelphia, and, like many
of his generation, he began composing as a serialist, eventually returning to tonality.

His magnificent Fifth Symphony (1984–5) is expressive yet
never indulgent, passionate yet stringently argued. Opening
boldly and assertively, it is continuous and in seven major
sections. The music is both hard-driven and evocatively
lyrical while the otherworldly finale brings a dreamily withdrawn cello solo, until in the closing section reality takes over.

The formidable Black Sounds (1965) is based on an earlier
composition, Apocalyptica, for large wind ensemble, piano
and percussion, whose score is headed by a Shakespeare
quotation, calling up the tempest from King Lear. Stark and
emotionally spare, it makes a powerful statement about
human violence. After the climax, the epilogue closes the
work gently in muted cries of anguish.

But it is with the masterly Transcendental Variations for
string orchestra that the newcomer to Rochberg's music
should begin any exploration. Written in 1975, it was the
composer's first work to embrace tonality without reserve,
and it is derived from his Third String Quartet, written three
years earlier.

All three performances here are marvellously played by the
Saarbrücken Radio Orchestra under Christopher Lyndon-
Gee, who seems to find a total affinity with the composer.
The recording is first class, too, and this is a record not to be
missed by anyone who cares about real twentieth-century
music.

RODÓ, Gabriel (1904–63)

Symphony 2

*** ASV CDDCA 1043. Gran Canaria PO, Leaper –
  OBRADORS: El poema de la jungla ***

Gabriel Rodó was a cellist and conductor who spent his last
years as conductor of the Gran Canaria Filarmónica (1951–
62) and subsequently as first cellist in Bogotá where he died.
His Second Symphony was composed in 1957 following the
death of Sibelius. It is a powerful and well-argued piece and
though not highly individual, it is well worth investigating,
particularly in such a good performance and recording.

RODRIGO, Joaquín (1901–99)

A la busca del más allá; (i) *Concierto Andaluz* (for 4 guitars); (ii) *Concierto de Aranjuez* (for guitar); (iii) *Concierto de estío* (for violin); (iv) *Concierto en modo galante* (for cello); (v) *Concierto heroico* (for piano); (vi) *Concierto madrigal* (for 2 guitars); (vii) *Concierto pastoral* (for flute); (viii) *Concierto serenata* (for harp). (ii) *Fantasia para un gentilhombre. Música para un jardín; Per la flor del Iliri blau; 5 Piezas infantiles; Soleriana; Zarabanda lejana y Villancico*

(M) *** EMI 7 67435-2 (4). (i) Moreno, Garibay, López, Ruiz; (ii) Moreno; (iii) Léo Ara; (iv) Cohen; (v) Osorio; (vi) Moreno, Mariotti; (vii) Hansen; (viii) Allen; LSO, or Mexico State PO, or RPO; Bátiz

The present EMI recordings are of excellent quality, although the early digital technique often brings an overlit sound to the treble, perhaps appropriate for music drenched in Spanish sunshine. The *Summer Concerto* for violin ('conceived in the manner of Vivaldi') was the composer's own favourite, and Augustin Léo Ara catches its neo-classical vitality admirably. The *Cello Concerto* is given a masterly performance by Robert Cohen; the *Concierto serenata* for harp has both piquancy and charm. Nancy Allen consistently beguiles the ear with her gentleness. The opening of *Concierto pastoral* is far from pastoral in feeling, but Rodrigo's fragmented melodies soon insinuate themselves into the consciousness. Rodrigo's *Piano Concerto* has a programmatic content, with the four movements written 'under the sign of the Sword, the Spur, the Cross and the Laurel'. The performers give a strong, extrovert account of the piece. The *Concierto madrigal* has its weaknesses but remains engaging if a trifle inflated. A similar comment might be made about the effect of the duo *Concierto Andaluz*, but the four guitar soloists here do not achieve the strongest profile, and this is also one reason why Alfonso Moreno's account of the famous *Concierto de Aranjuez*, though bright and sympathetic, is in no way outstanding.

The symphonic poem, *A la busca del más allá*, is evocative and powerfully scored; *Música para un jardín* is a quartet of cradle songs. The *Five Children's Pieces* are equally delightful, while the two neo-classical evocations of eighteenth-century Spain (*Soleriana*) are also unostentatiously appealing. *Per la flor del Iliri blau* is based on a Valencian legend, and Rodrigo is more impressive in moments of gently atmospheric detail than in the melodrama. The *Zarabanda lejana* was Rodrigo's first work for guitar. He later orchestrated it and added the *Villancico* to make a binary structure, the first part nobly elegiac, the second a gay dance movement.

Naxos Complete Rodrigo Edition

Complete Orchestral Works, Vol. 1: *Soleriana* (ballet, arr. from Soler's keyboard music); *5 Piezas infantiles; Zarabanda lejana y Villancico*

(BB) **(*) Naxos 8.555844. Asturias SO, Valdés

Complete Orchestral Works, Vol. 2: (i) *Concierto Andaluz for 4 Guitars and Orchestra*; (ii) *Concierto de Aranjuez; Fantasia para un gentilhombre*

(BB) **(*) Naxos 8.555841. Asturias SO, Valdés, with (i) EntreQuatre Guitar Qt; (ii) Gallén

Complete Orchestral Works, Vol. 3: (i) *Concerto in modo galante* (for cello & orchestra); *Concierto como un divertimento* (for cello & orchestra); (ii) *Concierto de estío* (for violin & orchestra); *Cançoneta* (for violin & string orchestra)

(BB) *** Naxos 8.555840. Castile and León SO, Darman, with (i) Polo; (ii) Ovrutsky

Complete Orchestral Works, Vol. 4: (i) *Concierto para piano y orquesta* (rev. Achúcarro). *Homenaje a la tempranica; Juglares; Música para un Jardín; Preludio para un poema a la Alhambra*

(BB) **(*) Naxos 8.557101. Castile and León SO, Darman, (i) with Ferrandiz

Complete Orchestral Works, Vol. 5: *Concierto Madrigal; Concierto para una fiesta*

(BB) **(*) Naxos 8.555842. Gallén, Clerch, Asturias SO, Valdés

Complete Orchestral Works Vol. 6: *A la busca del más allá; Dos danzas españolas; Palillos y panderetas; Per la flor del Iliri blau; Tres viejos aires de danza*

(BB) ** Naxos 555962. Castile and León SO, Darman

Complete Orchestral Works, Vol. 7: *Cántico de San Francisco de Asis; Himnos de los neófitos de Qumrán; Música para un códice salmantino; Retable de Navidad*

(BB) ** Naxos 8.557223. Lojendio, Prieto, Marchante, Allende, Rubiera, Comunidad Ch. & O, Encinar

Complete Orchestral Works, Vol. 8: (i) *Concierto pastoral* (for flute & orchestra); *Fantasía para un gentilhombre* (arr. Galway for flute & orchestra). *Dos miniaturas andaluzas; Adagio para instrumentos de viento*

(BB) ** Naxos 8.557801. Asturias SO, Valdés, (i) with G'froerer

Naxos has embarked on the most comprehensive survey of Rodrigo's music available today and is now up to Volume 8. These Naxos recordings are all good, to varying degrees, though the most popular works are usually available in superior performances. However, for the serious Rodrigo collector, the series represents value for money, and the sound is usually full and vivid, although occasionally the orchestral playing proves not quite as fine as it might be, even at budget price. The CDs will be discussed individually in our 2006/7 Yearbook.

Other Recordings

(i; iv) *Concierto Andaluz* (for 4 guitars); (ii; iv) *Concierto de Aranjuez* (for guitar); (ii–iv) *Concierto madrigal* (for 2 guitars); (ii; iv) *Concierto para una fiesta; Fantasia para un gentilhombre; Sones en la Giralda;* (v) *Concierto serenata* (for harp)

(B) *** Ph. Duo (ADD) 462 296-2 (2). (i) Los Romeros; (ii) P. Romero; (iii) A. Romero; (iv) ASMF, Marriner; (v) Michel, Monte Carlo Op. O, Almeida

This Duo includes all Rodrigo's splendid concertante guitar works, plus the *Concierto serenata* for harp and orchestra, a delectable and unaccountably neglected work in which Catherine Michel is a seductive soloist, neatly accompanied by Almeida. La Giralda, the ancient tower of Seville Cathedral, obviously stimulated Rodrigo's imagination so that the first of its two sections is eerily atmospheric; then the clouds clear away and the finale sparkles with the flamenco dance rhythms of the *Sevillanas*. Pepe Romero and Marriner show an immediate response to its evocation and spirit, and the result is memorable, helped by the first-class recording which pertains throughout these two generously filled CDs.

(i) *Concierto Andaluz;* (ii; iii) *Concierto de Aranjuez;* (ii–iv) *Concierto madrigal;* (v) *Concierto pastoral;* (vi) *Concierto serenata;* (ii; vii) *Fantasia para un gentilhombre;* (ii) *Entre olivaras*

(B) ** DG Panorama (ADD/DDD) 469 190-2 (2). (i) Los Romeros, San Antonia SO, Alessandro; (ii) Yepes; (iii) Philh. O, Navarro; (iv) with Monden; (v) Gallois, Philh. O, Marin; (vi) Zabaleta, Berlin RSO, Märzendorfer; (vii) ECO, Navarro

The duet *Concierto madrigal,* with Yepes and Monden, is most enjoyable, with each of the twelve miniatures which make up the work springing readily to life. Yet Yepes's account of the *Concierto de Aranjuez* – the most famous piece here – lacks sparkle in the outer movements, and the DG sound is rather lacklustre. Yepes's *Fantasia para un gentilhombre* has more character and refinement, and the *Concierto Andaluz* for four guitars, recorded much earlier, is immediately more vivid and open, if a bit astringent, the performance more spontaneous. The *Concierto pastoral* is brilliantly played and recorded (digitally), but the highlight of the set is the delightful *Concierto serenata,* given an ideal performance and recording.

Concierto de Aranjuez (for guitar & orchestra)

❀ (M) *** Decca 430 703-2. Bonell, Montreal SO, Dutoit – FALLA: *El amor brujo,* etc. ***

*** Guild GMCD 7176. Jiménez, Bournemouth Sinf., Frazor – ANGULO: *Guitar Concerto 2 (El Alevín);* VILLA-LOBOS: *Guitar Concerto* ***

(BB) *** Naxos 8.550729. Kraft, N. CO, Ward – CASTELNUOVO-TEDESCO: *Concerto* ***; VILLA-LOBOS: *Concerto* **(*)

Concierto de Aranjuez; (i) *Concierto madrigal* (for 2 guitars). *Fantasia para un gentilhombre*

(M) *** Ph. (ADD) 432 828-2. P. Romero; (i) A. Romero; ASMF, Marriner

(i) *Concierto de Aranjuez;* (ii) *Fantasia para un gentilhombre*

(B) *** Decca 448 243-2. Bonell, Montreal SO, Dutoit – ALBENIZ: *Rapsodia española;* TURINA: *Rapsodia sinfónica* ***

(BB) *** Virgin 2×1 5 61627-2 (2). Isbin, Lausanne CO, Foster – SCHWANTER: *From Afar* (fantasy) **; Recital: '*Latin Romances*' ***

(B) **(*) Sony (ADD) SBK 61716. Williams; (i) Phd. O, Ormandy; (ii) ECO, Groves – DODGSON: *Concerto,* etc. **(*)

(i) *Concierto de Aranjuez; Fantasia para un gentilhombre. Elogio de la guitarra*

(BB) **(*) EMI Encore (ADD) 5 85063-2. A. Romero; (i) with LSO, Previn

(i) *Concierto de Arajuez; Fantasia para un gentilhombre. Piezas españolas: Fandango; Zapateado.* (ii) *Tonadilla* (for guitar duo)

(BB) **(*) Warner Apex 8573 89243-2. Santos; (i) Monte Carlo Op. O, Scimone; (ii) Caceres

(i) *Concierto de Aranjuez;* (ii) *Fantasia para un gentilhombre. En los trigales; Invocation & Dance (Hommage à Manuel de Falla); 3 Piezas españolas*

(N) (M) *** RCA 82876 60870-2. Bream; (i) COE, Gardiner; (ii) RCA Victor CO, Brouwer

(i) *Concierto de Aranjuez. Invocación y danza, Hommage à Falla*

(M) *** Sony (ADD) SMK 89753. Williams, ECO, Barenboim – CASTELNUOVO-TEDESCO: *Guitar Concerto 1;* VILLA-LOBOS: *Concerto* ***

The Bonell/Dutoit *Concierto,* a clear first choice, was originally paired with the *Fantasia para un gentilhombre.* In the *Fantasia,* the balance between warmly gracious lyricism and sprightly rhythmic resilience is most engaging. The coupling is with Dutoit's *El amor brujo* and Alicia de Larrocha's poetic account of *Nights in the Gardens of Spain.* There is another, even more generous coupling on Decca's Eclipse bargain label which is well worth considering, as the Albéniz and Turina concertante works for piano are also given dazzling, sultry performances by De Larrocha and Frühbeck de Burgos.

The differences between Bream's two earlier RCA readings of the *Concierto,* the first (analogue) with Colin Davis in 1963 (now deleted), the second (digital) with Gardiner in 1982, are almost too subtle to analyse and perhaps depend as much on the personalities of the two conductors as on that of the soloist. The Gardiner version has a little extra dash and, for those who prefer an all-Rodrigo programme, this could be a good choice and the famous *Adagio* is played in a very free, improvisatory way, with some highly atmospheric wind solos in the orchestra. In the *Fantasia para un gentilhombre* Leo Brouwer, himself a guitarist, brings plenty of orchestral vitality to the later sections of the score. The *Tres piezas españolas* add to the value of the disc, and both this and the *Hommage à Falla* show Bream at his most inspirationally spontaneous.

Sharon Isbin's recordings of Rodrigo's two most popular works with the Lausanne Chamber Orchestra under Lawrence Foster received the imprimatur of the composer before he died, and justly so. They are both played with flair and the orchestral detail could not be more vivid, while the famous slow movement of the *Concierto* is most atmospherically done. The recording is in the demonstration bracket. The snag is that the Schwanter coupling is a good deal less tangible.

What makes John Williams's 1974 recording of the *Concierto* particularly enticing is his bravura performance of Rodrigo's solo *Invocación y danza, Hommage à Falla* which opens the programme. Williams's style is not strikingly Spanish in its evocation, but the performance is full of charisma and the closing section brings electrifying virtuosity: indeed his digital dexterity is astonishingly clear and clean. The performance of the *Concierto* is superior to his earlier version with Ormandy. The playing again has marvellous point, the *Adagio* played with poetic spontaneity.

Pepe Romero's performance of the *Concierto de Aranjuez* has plenty of Spanish colour, the musing poetry of the slow movement beautifully caught. The account of the *Fantasia* is warm and gracious, with the Academy contributing quite as much as the soloist to the appeal of the performance. Angel joins Pepe for the Renaissance-inspired duet, *Concierto madrigal,* which is very attractive indeed, making this a very viable alternative to the Decca couplings.

Rafael Jiménez and the Bournemouth Sinfonietta under Terence Frazor make a fine partnership. The slow movement brings an appealing, ruminative intimacy to contrast with its bold, passionate climax, and the finale also has a neat delicacy of touch from the soloist, with buoyant rhythmic pointing from the orchestra. The recording is very good too.

Norbert Kraft is a soloist of personality and he receives spirited, sensitive accompaniments from the Northern Chamber Orchestra under Nicholas Ward. Indeed the work sounds remarkably fresh using a smaller-sized orchestral group. The recording is very well balanced, with the guitar given a most convincing relationship with the orchestra and the sound itself vividly realistic.

With Ormandy providing a rich orchestral tapestry Williams's earlier version is a distinctly romantic reading of the *Concierto*. If the later recording is maturer and has greater subtlety of detail, this performance, taken a little bit faster, remains fresh and enjoyable. Groves and the ECO take over for the *Fantasia*, and once again the interpretation is a shade brisker than the later, digital version.

On EMI Encore Angel Romero does not emerge as a very strong personality, but the skill and Spanish sensibility of the playing are in no doubt, and Previn is obviously so delighted with the orchestration that he communicates his enthusiasm with loving care for detail. The famous slow movement is very beautifully played, the opening especially memorable. Previn's approach to the *Fantasia* is vividly direct, and although it misses some of the music's noble graciousness, its infectious quality is more than enough compensation, and the warmly spacious 1977 Abbey Road recording has been admirably remastered. Away from the stimulus of the orchestra and conductor, the manner of Romero's playing seems even more withdrawn, but his thoughtful style suits the musing central *Andante* of the solo *Elogio*, which he recorded the following year in the USA. One can imagine more sparkling, extrovert accounts of the outer movements of this quarter-of-an-hour-long work, but it is still a worthwhile bonus.

Santos does not project as strongly individual a personality as Bonell, Bream or Williams, but he is a very musical player and his thoughtfully improvisatory approach to the *Adagio* is not unappealing. The resonant Erato recording gives the whole proceedings a pleasing glow, and if inner detail is less sharply focused than on Decca, it brings a sumptuously rich quality to the opening string melody in the *Fantasia*. For his encores Santos not only dances a lilting solo *Fandango* and lively *Zapateado*, but joins with a colleague, Oscar Caceres, in the more relaxed three-part *Tonadilla*, where the engaging central *Minuetto pomposo* leads to the busy interweave of the finale. Good value.

Concierto serenata (for harp & orchestra)

☊ ✿ (M) *** DG (ADD) 463 648-2. Zöller, Zabaleta, BPO, Märzendorfer – MOZART: *Flute & Harp Concerto in C, K.299*; REINECKE: *Harp Concerto* ***

We have always had a special regard for Zabaleta's pioneering version of Rodrigo's *Concierto serenata*, which has an unforgettable piquancy and charm both in its invention and in its felicity of scoring. The performance has great virtuosity and flair, and our Rosette is carried over from the original LP. It is excellently recorded, with the delicate yet colourful orchestral palette tickling the ear in charming contrast to the beautifully focused timbre of the harp. A worthy addition to DG's series of legendary 'Originals'.

(i) *Fantasia para un gentilhombre* (arr. Galway for flute & orchestra). *Juglare*; (*symphonic essay*); *Palillos y panderetas*; *Pavana Real* (complete ballet); *2 Piezas caballerescas*; *3*

viejos aires de danza; Soleriana (Suite); (ii) *Sones en la Giralda (Fantasia sevillana for harp & orchestra)*

(N) (BB) *** EMI 5 87030-2 (2). Mexico State SO, Bátiz; with (i) Hansen; (ii) Ieuan Jones

A most attractive budget set. Lisa Hansen plays Sir James Galway's transcription of the *Fantasia* most winningly and with great charm, and it all but upstages the arranger's own version. The two neo-classical ballets, *Pavana Real* and *Soleriana* (drawing on the keyboard works of Soler), are delightful and are piquantly scored. *Sones en la Giralda* also has a fine soloist in Ieuan Jones: it is a less focused piece than the *Concierto serenata* but is colourful and atmospheric. *Juglares* ('Minstrels') has an exotic, medieval feeling and is characteristically melodic; the shorter pieces are no less attractive. *Dos Piezas caballerescas*, inspired by Don Quixote, includes a melachoy madrigal featuring four solo cellos. The performances are first class: the Mexican orchestra is on top form and Bátiz can be relied on for spontaneity. The recording too is of quality.

Soleriana (ballet, arr. from Soler's keyboard music); 5 Piezas infantiles; Zarabanda lejana y Villancico

(BB) **(*)** Naxos 8.555844. Asturias SO, Valdés

Valdés includes Rodrigo's delightful eighteenth-century picture of Spain in his ballet *Soleriana*, which is based on the keyboard works of Antonio Soler and consists of eight dances lasting some 40 minutes in all. The *Pastoral* has a lovely melancholy beauty, though most of the movements are relatively lively and well portray a picturesque, rococo image of eighteenth-century Spain in music of great charm and piquancy. The *Zarabanda lejana* ('*Distant Sarabande*') is a haunting work, its two movements displaying some lovely string writing, and the highly engaging *Cinco Piezas infantiles* are characteristically brightly coloured. The performances are good, if perhaps not quite so imaginative as Bátiz on EMI (see above), who also benefited from more vivid sound. Here, the massed strings sound a bit thin above the stave (especially noticeable in the *Zarabanda lejana*), but the overall sound-picture is very acceptable, and this disc is well worth its modest price.

SOLO GUITAR MUSIC

Bajando de la Meseta; Elegio de la guitarra; En los trigales; En tierras de Jerez; Invocaciòn y danza (Homenaje a Manuel de Falla); Junto al Generalife; 3 Piezas españolas; Zarabanda lejana

(N) *** MDG 305 0834-2. Bungarten

Frank Bungarten, born in Cologne in 1958, was awarded the first prize at the International Guitar Competition in Granada when Segovia was president of the jury, so his credentials for this repertoire are impeccable. His brusque chords at the opening *Fandango* of the *Three Spanish Pieces* contrast with a thoughtful account of the noble central *Passacaglia*, and in *En tierras de Jerez* and the atmospheric *Bajando de la Meseta* his playing is masterly. The *Junto al Generalife*, the *Homenaje a Manuel de Falla* and the deliciously nuanced *Zarabanda lejana* are most all highly evocative. He is given a fine, natural presence here, and this collection will be hard to beat.

PIANO MUSIC

Music for 2 pianos: (i) *5 Piezas infantiles* (piano, 4 hands): *Atardecer; Gran marcha de los subsecretarios; Sonatina para dos Muñecas.* Solo piano: *Air de ballet sur le nom d'une jeune fille; Album de Cecilia; A l'ombre de Torre Bermeja; Bagatela; Berceuse d'automne; Berceuse de printemps; Danza de la Amapola; 3 Danzas de España; 4 Estampas andaluzas; 3 Evocaciones; Pastoral; 4 Piezas (Caleseras: Homenaje a Chueca; Fandango del Ventorrillo; Plegaria de la Infanta de Castilla; Danza Valenciana); Preludio de Añoranza; Preludio al gallo mañanero; Serenata española; Sonata de adiós (Hommage à Paul Dukas); 5 Sonatas de Castilla, con toccata a modo de Pregón: 1–2 in F sharp min.; 3 in D; 4 in B min. (como un tiento); 5 in A. Suite; Zarabanda lejana*

✪ *** Bridge BCD 9027 A/B. Allen; (i) with Nel

Air de ballet sur le nom d'une jeune fille; Album de Cecilia; A l'ombre de Torre Bermeja; Bagatela; 2 Berceuses; Canción y danza; Danza de la Amapola; 3 Danzas de España; 4 Estampas andaluzas; 3 Evocaciones; Pastoral; 4 Piezas; 5 Piezas del siglo XVI; Preludio de Añoranza; Preludio al gallo mañanero; Serenata española; Sonata de adiós (Homage to Paul Dukas); 5 Sonatas de Castilla con toccata a modo de Pregón; Suite; Zarabanda lejana

*** Sony S2K 89828 (2). Marianovich

Rodrigo's keyboard music is all but unknown and, as this first-class and comprehensive survey shows, for all its eclecticism it is well worth exploring. In his earliest piano work, the *Suite* of 1923, with its sprightly *Prelude*, cool *Sicilienne* and Satie-ish minuet, the link with the French idiom is obvious, while the glittering brilliance of the *Preludio al gallo mañanero* is unmistakably Debussian. The *cinco Sonatas de Castilla* look back further in time and draw continually on the keyboard writing of Scarlatti. But they are spiced with piquant dissonances which the Italian composer would have disowned. The *Serenata española* marks Rodrigo's positive adoption of an overtly Andalusian style, while the *Cuatro piezas* and the *Cuatro estampas andaluzas* are as sharply Spanish in character as any of the similarly picaresque miniatures of Granados or Albéniz. The darker side of Rodrigo's nature, sometimes brooding, sometimes nostalgic, is at its most expressive in the nocturne, *Atardecer*, an ambitious piece for two players; but it also colours some of the miniatures, not least the austere yet deeply felt *Plegaria de la Infanta de Castilla* from the *cuatro Piezas*. The recording is uncommonly real and has great presence. In the duo works Gregory Allen is admirably partnered by Anton Nel.

Sara Marianovich knew Rodrigo personally and played for him, learning a great deal, so that her performances received his imprimatur. She is indeed completely at home in this attractive repertoire, the early works with their distinct Gallic flavour, the comparable influence from Scarlatti, and the later interpolation of glittering Andalusian dance rhythms. The music is attractively arranged, as far as possible in order of composition, and ends nostalgically with Rodrigo's last piano work, the *Preludio de Añoranza* of 1987. But besides her ready bravura and feeling for the Spanish as well as the French pianistic palette, Sara Marianovich is also at her finest in the simpler pieces, the charming early *Suite*, the *Pastoral* (a captivating siciliana), the pair of *Berceuses*, the touching 'Adios' to Paul Dukas, the children's album, written for the composer's daughter, Cecilia, and the *Five Pieces from the Sixteenth Century* – transcriptions of Spanish renaissance miniatures. Also included is an impressive first recording of the rare *Canción y danza* of 1925 which opens musingly, but slowly becomes more passionate. This does not appear in the previous outstanding coverage of this repertoire by Gregory

Allen. However, joined by Anton Nel, he *does* include the repertoire for two pianos, which the Sony set omits. So that probably remains a primary choice. But Sara Marianovich's playing is so compellingly persuasive that her new set must also receive the strongest possible advocacy. She is vividly and truthfully recorded, and this highly rewarding music is undeservedly neglected.

Air de ballet sur le nom d'une jeunne fille; A l'ombre de Torre Bermeja; Bagatela; 2 Berceuses; 4 Estampas andaluzas; Fantasía que contrahace la harpa de Ludovico; Pastoral; 4 Piezas; Préludio de Añoranza; Serenata española; Sonata de adiós; Zarabanda lejana; 5 Piezas del siglo XVI

☛ (N) (BB) *** Naxos 8.557272. Pizarro

For most collectors, this excellent single-CD budget-priced collection from the highly sympathetic Artur Pizarro will prove an admirable introduction to Rodrigo's piano music. From the brilliant opening *A l'ombre de Torre Bermeja* onwards he brings out the music's ready associations with the guitar. The *Four Piano Pieces* include a bravura *Fandango* and a touchingly gentle *Prayer of the Princess of Castile*, while within the *Four Andalusian Pictures*, the *Twilight over the Guadalquivir River* makes an evocative contrast with the sparkling *Seguidillas*. The guileless *Nostalgic Prelude*, the charming *Pastoral* and the *Air de Ballet on a Girl's Name* are all highly beguiling, while the three transcribed *Pavans* (by Luis de Milán and Valderrábano) included among the sixteenth-century pieces are presented with a gentle nobility. Pizarro plays spontaneously and perceptively and proves very much at home in this repertoire; he is vividly recorded, and there is an excellent commentary on the music by Graham Wade.

ROMAN, Johan Helmich (1694–1758)

(i) *Violin Concertos in D min.; E flat; F min. Sinfonias in A; D & F*

*** BIS CD 284. (i) Sparf; Orpheus Chamber Ens.

Of the five *Violin Concertos*, the three recorded here are certainly attractive pieces, particularly in such persuasive hands as those of Nils-Erik Sparf and the Orpheus Chamber Ensemble, drawn from the Stockholm Philharmonic. None of the *Sinfonias* have appeared on disc before. Very stylish and accomplished performances, which are scholarly in approach.

Drottningholm Music; Little Drottningholm Music

(BB) *** Naxos 8.553733. Uppsala CO, Halstead

Little Drottningholm Music; Sjukmans Music; (i) *Piante amiche*

*** Musica Sveciae MSCD 417. (i) Nilsson; Stockholm Nat. Museum CO, Génetay

In 1744 Johan Helmich Roman wrote 24 pieces celebrating the marriage of the future King of Sweden to a daughter of Frederick the Great of Prussia. From first to last they are full of delightful invention, starting with a swaggering *Allegro* (which, like other movements, owes something to the example of Handel's *Water Music*), and ending with a bouncy *vivace* Jig. Halstead also includes eight extra pieces, written to be used in reserve at the wedding, under the title *Little Drottningholm Music*. Unlike the recording on Musica Sveciae, Halstead's Naxos version – just as exhilarating, often at brisker speeds – uses period instruments to bring out the great variety of instrumental colour. Fresh, lively performances and excellent sound.

Génetay offers all 17 dances of the *Little Drottningholm Music* plus the somewhat earlier *Sjukmans-musiquen*, which has no less appeal. The performances by the Stockholm National Museum Orchestra convey real pleasure in the music-making. The disc includes a short cantata probably (but not certainly) by Roman, *Piante amiche*, which is attractive whatever its authenticity, and nicely sung too by Pia-Maria Nilsson. The recorded sound is well balanced and truthful.

6 *Assaggi* (solo violin)
*** Nytorp 9902. Ringborg

As a young violinist in the Swedish Royal Orchestra, Roman was sent to study in England, where he played briefly in Handel's opera orchestra at the King's Theatre. He possessed much individuality and resource, even though here he is much indebted to Geminiani, Tartini and, above all, Handel. Tobias Ringborg is the first to record all six of the *Assaggi* ('essays' or 'attempts') for solo violin, which leave no doubt as to his familiarity with and mastery of contemporary technique, multiple stopping, etc. Technical matters apart, he reveals the extent of his inventive resource and imagination. He plays with great authority, and we doubt that his compelling accounts of these suites will be surpassed easily. They are excellently recorded.

(i) *Assaggi for Violin in A, in C min. & in G min., BeRI 301, 310 & 320; (i; ii) Violin & Harpsichord Sonata 12 in D, BeRI 212; (ii) Harpsichord Sonata 9 in D min., BeRI 233*
*** Cap. (ADD) 21344. (i) Schröder; (ii) Sönnleitner

The *Assaggi* ('essays') recorded here often take one by surprise, particularly when played with such imagination as they are by Jaap Schröder. The *Harpsichord Sonata* is also more inward-looking than many others of Roman's pieces, and the only work that one could possibly describe as fairly predictable is the opening *Sonata for Violin and Continuo*. Excellent performances and recording, as well as exemplary presentation.

ROMBERG, Andreas (1767–1821)

Clarinet Quintet in E flat, Op. 57
(BB) *** Hyp. Helios CDH 55076. King, Britten Qt –
   STANFORD: 2 *Fantasies* *******

Andreas Romberg (a violinist) settled in Hamburg in the early 1800s, where he wrote this enchanting *Quintet*, scored for clarinet, violin and a pair of violas plus a cello. From the very opening he reminds us how well he remembers the illustrious Mozart *Clarinet Quintet*, and he makes gentle allusions to its atmosphere and ideas throughout. But these gentle reminders only serve to enhance the charm of the music. The *Minuet* comes second, then the *Larghetto* cribs from its Mozartian model outrageously before the finale, which adds a Bohemian flavour. Obviously the performers here, and Thea King especially, relish the Mozartian associations, yet they give the piece an identity in its own right. Their performance is captivating, and the recording is very good indeed. At Helios price this is not to be missed.

String Quartets, Op. 1/1–3
**(*) MDG 307 0963-2. Leipzig Qt

String Quartets, Op. 2/2; Op. 16/2; Op. 30/2
*** MDG 307 1026-2. Leipzig Qt

Romberg was a celebrated violinist, admired by both Haydn and Beethoven. His three Op. 1 *Quartets* date from between 1794 and 1796 and are very much after the style of Haydn. Although they leave no doubt as to his expertise, next to the Viennese masters this is small talk – amiable and pleasing, but unmemorable. The Leipzig Quartet is such a superb ensemble and so thoroughly musical that the disc gives pleasure nonetheless.

The Op. 2 *Quartets* come from 1797–9 and show an intimate knowledge of, and admiration for, Haydn's quartets, and indeed are dedicated to 'l'homme de génie à l'immortel Haydn'. The Op. 16 *Quartets* come from 1804–6 and the Op. 30 set from 1806–10. After Romberg's death, his quartets fell into oblivion, for they do not blaze a trail as those of Haydn and Beethoven did. But they are none the less urbane, inventive and civilized, and well worth getting to know, particularly in these unforced and musical performances. Exemplary recording.

ROPARTZ, Joseph Guy (1864–1955)

(i) *Le Miracle de Saint-Nicolas.* (ii) *Psalm 136; Dimanche; Nocturne; Les Vêpres sonnent*
(BB) *** Naxos 8.555656. (i) Solistes de la Maîtrise de R. France, Lebrun (organ); (ii) Papis, Henry, Le Texier, Ile de France Vittoria Régional Ch., O Symphonique et Lyrique de Nancy, Piquemal

Ropartz has been rather overshadowed by Magnard, and while neither is in the front rank of French masters, both are rewarding. The longest piece on the disc is *Le Miracle de Saint-Nicolas* of 1905 for soloists, children's voices (here the excellent Solistes de la Maîtrise de Radio-France), organ, piano and orchestra. The *Psalm 136* dates from 1897 and the *Nocturne* and *Les Vêpres sonnent* from 1926–7. They are dignified and rather beautiful pieces with more than a touch of d'Indy and Fauré to commend them, and in the case of *Les Vêpres sonnent* echo the *Sirènes* of Debussy's *Nocturnes*. This recording from the mid-1990s first appeared on Marco Polo but its competitive price renders it much more attractive. The performances are eminently serviceable, though the Choeur Régional Vittoria d'Ile de France is at times a little vulnerable in terms of focus and blend. The repertoire will be new to most readers and will delight many who do not realize how touching and appealing this music is.

RORE, Cipriano da (c. 1515–65)

Missa Praeter rerum seriem. Motets: *Ave regina; Descendit in hortum meum; Infelix ego; Parce mihi*
☛ *** Gimell CDGIM 029. Tallis Scholars, Phillips (with
   JOSQUIN DESPRES: Motet: *Praeter rerum seriem* *******)

Cipriano da Rore was Josquin's successor at the Italian Court d'Este at Ferrara. His *Missa Praeter rerum seriem* is appropriately preceded by the richly textured six-part Josquin motet based on the same melodic sequence. Rore's piece was intended as a tribute to his illustrious predecessor and is a worthy accolade, lyrically powerful, contrapuntally fascinating, spiritually serene and beautifully sung by these highly experienced singers, whose director knows just how to pace and inflect its linear detail and shape its overall structure. The four motets are hardly less impressive, and Gimell's recording, as ever, is virtually flawless.

ROSENBERG, Hilding (1892–1985)

Piano Concertos 1 & 2
*** Daphne DR 1006. Widlund, Swedish RSO, Sundkvist

The *First Piano Concerto* is a recent discovery. When the *Second* (1950) was premièred, Rosenberg hinted at the existence of an earlier concerto. The two movements of the *First* were then discovered together with sketches for the finale. One can understand Rosenberg's doubts: the orchestral writing occasionally swamps the texture, and the range of keyboard devices is very limited. The *Second Concerto* is the more rewarding and the keyboard writing more interesting with some highly imaginative invention. There is some particularly atmospheric writing for strings and wind in the central *Andante tranquillo*. The score is rewarding and serves to fill in our picture of an underrated composer. Mats Widlund is the excellent soloist and Petter Sundkvist impresses with his sensitivity and musicianship. The recordings have good definition and the balance between soloist and orchestra is very well judged.

Concertos for Strings 1; 4; Suite on Swedish Folk Tunes for Strings, Op. 36
⊶ (B) *** CPO 999 573-2. Deutsche Kammerakadmie Neuss, Goritzki

The *First Concerto* for strings is one of Rosenberg's most inventive and engaging scores. Johannes Goritzki and his superb Deutsche Kammerakademie Neuss couple it with the early and often charming *Suite on Swedish Folk Songs* from 1927 and the much later *Fourth Concerto* also for strings from 1966. The latter is persuasively played here by these artists and the balance is eminently truthful. Those who are on Rosenberg's wavelength need not hesitate.

Orfeus i sta'n (Orpheus in Town; ballet suite); (i) Sinfonia concertante for Violin, Viola, Oboe, Bassoon & Orchestra; (ii) Violin Concerto 1. Symphony 3 (The Four Ages of Man; 1939 version); (iii) 4 (Johannes Uppenbarelse: The Revelation of St John the Divine): excerpts; (iv) 5 (Ortagårdsmästaren); (v) Den heliga natten (The Holy Night); (vi) Suite in D: Pastorale
(***) Caprice mono CAP 21510 (3). Swedish R.O or Stockholm PO, composer; with (i) Barter, Berglund, Lännerholm, Lavér; (ii) Barkel; (iii) De Wahl, Swedish R. Ch.; (iv) Lail, Swedish R. Ch.; (v) Björker, Lail, Lindberg-Torlind, Nilsson, Ohlson, Saedén, Widgren, Chamber Ch.; (vi) Andriesson

The majority of these Archive recordings were made between 1940 and 1947. The suite from the ballet, *Orpheus in Town*, shows the sophisticated man-about-town side of the composer and is inventive and witty, while his inspiration in the oratorio, *The Holy Night*, is spread rather thin – despite some memorable singing from the baritone, Erik Saedén. There is nothing thin about the *Third Symphony*, based on Romain Rolland's novel, *Jean Christophe*, and interspersed with narration before each of the four movements, read by the composer. His pacing, particularly in the first movement, is expansive and, above all, convincing, and the same measured style emerges in the excerpts from the *Fourth Symphony* (*The Revelation of St John the Divine*), recorded in 1940 with narrator rather than baritone. The *Fifth Symphony*, for

soprano, chorus and orchestra, has a serenity, eloquence and strength which are very striking. The *Sinfonia concertante* is a good piece in neo-classical idiom (sounding like a Swedish Martinů) but the *Violin Concerto No. 1* is of lesser interest and finds the composer in manufactured mode. It is good to hear him as pianist, accompanying Lotte Andriesson in 1935 in the *Pastorale* movement from his *Suite in D* for violin and piano. The documentation could not be more comprehensive or researched more scrupulously. A valuable issue of great interest.

(i) Symphonies 3; (ii) 6 (Sinfonia semplice)
*** Phono Suecia (ADD) PSCD 100. (i) Stockholm PO, Blomstedt; (ii) Stockholm SO, Westerberg

The *Third Symphony* originally bore the subtitle, *The Four Ages of Man* and was inspired by Romain Rolland's novel, *Jean Christophe*. Originally there was narration between each of the four movements. After this Rosenberg had second thoughts about the symphony, withdrawing the literary programme and excising a fugal section in the *Scherzo*. It is strong, purposeful music and its slow movement shows the composer at his best. Blomstedt and the Stockholm Philharmonic are persuasive advocates and the 1966 recording sounds well. The *Sinfonia semplice* radiates the poetic feeling and sense of melancholy that pervade the Swedish summer nights. The 1960 recording made by the augmented Swedish Radio Orchestra, here called the Stockholm Symphony, under Stig Westerberg is very good and the performance excellent. It would be more competitive at mid- rather than full price but nevertheless this CD is strongly recommended.

Symphony 4 (Johannes Uppenbarelse: The Revelation of St John the Divine)
*** Caprice CAP 21429. Hagegård, Swedish R. Ch., Pro Musica Ch., Rilke Ens., Gothenburg SO, Ehrling

Rosenberg's remarkable 80-minute symphony-oratorio to texts from the Bible and by the Swedish poet, Hjalmar Gullberg, is for large forces and is a powerful work of real vision. Its opening fourths recall the world of Walton's *Belshazzar's Feast* or of Hindemith, and one's thoughts occasionally turn to Honegger's *King David*. The biblical text inspires the most vividly expressive music, while the Gullberg poems are in an archaic and often serene style. Despite occasional longueurs, the overall impact of this score is very powerful. A splendid performance, very well recorded.

ROSETTI, Antonio (c. 1750–92)

Bassoon Concertos in B flat, C.69, C.73 & C.74; in F, C.75
(BB) *** Naxos 8.555341. Holder, New Brandenburg PO, Pasquet

Antonio Rosetti, a near contemporary of Mozart, was a working musician, born in Bohemia, who for professional reasons adopted an Italian form of his birth-name of Anton Rösler. He was much admired for a wide range of compositions, notably his works for woodwind and horn, which are well represented in this delightful collection of four of his five bassoon concertos, only one of which, C.74, has been recorded before. In form they are totally conventional, but the inventiveness of the thematic material makes for sparkling results in performances as lively as these.

(i) Clarinet Concertos 1–2; (i) Double Horn Concerto in F
**(*) CPO 999 621-2. (i) Klöcker; (ii) Wallendorf, Willis; SW RSO, Baden-Baden & Freiburg, Schröter-Seebeck

These two clarinet concertos are very Bohemian in flavour; both are melodically quite attractive, with the *Rondo* of the *First* and the *Romanze* and *Rondo scherzante* of the *Second* all equally striking. Dieter Klöcker certainly finds the light-hearted Bohemian spirit of this music and is a sympathetic soloist with a luscious tone. The *Double Horn Concerto* is less memorable musically, but demands considerable virtuosity in its solo interplay and certainly receives it here, especially in the buoyant finale. With sympathetic accompaniments and a pleasing recording this is all enjoyable, if not distinctive.

Flute Concertos in C, RWV C16; F, RWV C21; G, RWV C22; G, RWV C25
*** Orfeo C095 031A. Meier, Prague CO

These flute concertos, agreeably elegant and melodic, each lasting 18 or 19 minutes, with lively outer movements flanking slow movements of pastoral charm, receive their première recording here. The performances (on modern instruments) are as unselfconscious as the music itself and give unfailing pleasure.

4 Horn Concertos: in E flat (K.III:35 & 40; Murray C40 & 47); in E (K.III:45; Murray C52); in E flat (Kaul Deest; Murray C43Q)
(N) (BB) *** Arte Nova 74321 92764-2. Baborek, Bav. CO, Moesus

Rosetti wrote prolifically for the horn and it is good to have a representative selection splendidly played by his countryman, Radek Baborek, and given excellent, stylish accompaniments by the Bavarian Kammerphilharmonic, spiritedly directed by Johannes Moesus. These works are not of the calibre of Mozart – their harmonic progressions are much more conventional – but they are skilfully scored and full of attractive invention: taken one at a time, they are most entertaining. The first movement of the opening *E flat major Concerto* (C43Q) has an agreeable Hummelian second subject, and the E major work which follows (only recently rediscovered) has much charm throughout, and a perky finale based on a catchy scalic figure. Elsewhere there are plenty of opportunities for solo virtuosity, which are taken with aplomb by Baborek, and a ready supply of good tunes. The recording is excellent, with the horn boldly balanced forward, the orchestra well caught in a resonant acoustic .

Horn Concerto in E, K. III:42
(BB) *** Teldec (ADD) 0630 12324-2. Baumann, Concerto Amsterdam, Schröder – DANZI; HAYDN: *Concertos* ***

This *Concerto*, galant in style, is characteristic of the taxing melodic lines Rosetti provides for the soloist, with lyrical upper tessitura contrasting with florid arpeggios. He was especially good at jolly rondo finales and the present work shows him at his melodically most exuberant. Baumann plays with elegance and aplomb and is well accompanied. The remastered recording now sounds warmer with more ambience than on its last appearance, and altogether this is a very pleasing triptych.

Sinfonias: in D, K.I:12; in C, K.I:21; in G, K.I:22; in A, K.I:24
**(*) Chan. 9567. LMP, Bamert

As a court composer, first in south and later in north Germany, Rosetti composed a fair number of symphonies, and those recorded here come from the 1780s. In the hands of the London Mozart Players under Matthias Bamert they are amiable works, engagingly melodic and nicely scored for the normal classical orchestra. The Chandos recording is well up to standard, as is the playing of the London Mozart group, polished and nicely turned, if a little lacking in characterization and bite.

ROSSINI, Gioachino (1792–1868)

La Boutique fantasque (ballet; complete; arr. Respighi)
&—☉ ✪ (M) *** Somm mono SOMMCD 027. LSO, Ansermet – STRAVINSKY: *Petrushka* (***)
*** Chan. 10081. BBC PO, Noseda – RESPIGHI: *La Pentola magica*, etc. ***

Ansermet's classic 'complete' version (there are some fairly minor cuts) of *La Boutique fantasque* was outstanding among early LPs. It was recorded in the Kingsway Hall in 1950, which lends its ambient richness to the proceedings, and was one of the rare occasions on which Ansermet conducted the LSO. They play wonderfully for him, especially the woodwind, and in particular the distinguished principal oboe, whose phrasing and tone are exquisite. The whole orchestra are clearly on their toes and the exhilarating can-can and brilliantly executed finale have tremendous vivacity. But the disc is especially famous for its magical opening which has an extraordinary aura, with the gentle pizzicatos of the lower strings answered by glowing horn chords. There is a crescendo and decrescendo which Ansermet graduates perfectly, and the disc is worth having for this section alone. Fortunately, David Henning's digital remastering miraculously reflects the outstanding quality of those early Decca LXTs (before the recording was re-cut and given horridly thin violin timbre for its Ace of Clubs reissue). As it now stands the sound has fine range and bloom, almost like stereo at times. This is one of Ansermet's finest ballet records, if not the finest of all. What a pity he made so few recordings with the London orchestra.

Noseda's sparkling account of the famous Rossini/Respighi ballet is complete and is splendidly recorded. It is discussed under Respighi above, where it is combined with other spectacular Respighi arrangements.

La Boutique fantasque: extended suite
(M) *** RCA (ADD) **SACD** 82876 66419-2. Boston Pops O, Fiedler – OFFENBACH: *Gaîté parisienne* *** ✪
(M) **(*) Chan. 6503. SNO, Gibson – DUKAS: *L'Apprenti sorcier*; SAINT-SAENS: *Danse macabre* **(*)

Fiedler offers nearly half an hour of the ballet, not missing out much of importance. The performance sparkles, the playing has warmth and finesse and the Boston acoustics add the necessary atmosphere at the magically evocative opening. Mark Donahue's remastering of this 1956 recording for SACD leaves little to be desired and the coupling is indispensable.

Gibson's version of the suite is strikingly atmospheric. Helped by the glowing acoustics of Glasgow's City Hall, the opening has much evocation. The orchestra is on its toes and plays with warmth and zest, and the 1973 recording has transferred vividly to CD.

Introduction, Theme & Variations in C min. for Clarinet & Orchestra
*** ASV CDDCA 559. Johnson, ECO, Groves – CRUSELL: *Concerto 2* *** ✪; BAERMANN: *Adagio* ***; WEBER: *Concertino* ***

Introduction, Theme & Variations in B flat; Variations in C (for clarinet & orchestra)

*** Sup. SU 3554-2. Peterkova, Prague Philh., Bělohlávek – BRUCH: *Double Concerto.* MENDELSSOHN: *2 Concert Pieces* ***

The Czech clarinettist Ludmila Peterkova is an artist who is not only warmly expressive, but sparkles in everything she plays, bringing out the pure fun of the two sets of Rossini variations, warmly accompanied by Bělohlávek and the Prague Philharmonia. A delightful fill-up for an outstanding disc of rare clarinet pieces.

As in all her recordings, Emma Johnson's lilting timbre and sensitive control of dynamic bring imaginative light and shade to the melodic line. Brilliance for its own sake is not the keynote, but her relaxed pacing is made to sound exactly right. Vivid recording.

String Sonatas 1–6 (complete)

☛ (BB) *** Double Decca (ADD) 443 838-2 (2). ASMF, Marriner (with CHERUBINI: *Etude 2 for French Horn & Strings* (with Tuckwell); BELLINI: *Oboe Concerto in E flat* (with Lord) ***) – DONIZETTI: *String Quartet* ***
*** ASV (ADD) CDDCA 767. Serenata of L. (members)
(N) (BB) *** Hyp. Helios CDH 55200. OAE (members): Wallfisch, Marcus, Tunnicliffe, Nwanoku

String Sonatas 1–3; (i) Andante & Theme with Variations in E flat for Clarinet & Orchestra; (ii) Une Larme for Double Bass

(BB) ** Naxos 8.554418. Hungarian Virtuosi, Benedek; with (i) Szepesi; (ii) Buza

String Sonatas 4–6; (i) Variations in C for Violin & Small Orchestra

(BB) ** Naxos 8.554419. Hungarian Virtuosi, Benedek; with (i) Szenthelyi

We have a very soft spot for the sparkle, elegance and wit of these ASMF performances of the Rossini *String Sonatas,* amazingly accomplished products for a twelve-year-old. Marriner offers them on full orchestral strings but with such finesse and precision of ensemble that the result is all gain. The 1966 recording still sounds remarkably full and natural, and the current CD transfer adds to the feeling of presence. The new Double Decca format has other music added. Apart from the Donizetti *Quartet,* which has an appropriately Rossinian flavour, the two minor concertante works are well worth having, with both Barry Tuckwell (in what is in essence a three-movement horn concertino) and Roger Lord in excellent form.

The Serenata of London, working as a string quartet, and a comparably sized group from the Orchestra of the Age of Enlightenment, playing period instruments, each manage to include all six of the *String Sonatas* on one CD. As might be expected, the Serenata, playing modern instruments and led by the easily brilliant Barry Wilde, give the warmer, more sunny bouquet to Rossini's string textures; their competitors, led by the dazzling Elizabeth Wallfisch, offer a slightly drier vintage, though their approach is by no means unsmiling. On both discs the recording is truthful and naturally balanced. However, the OAE members' performance now reissued on Helios has a distinct price advantage.

The Naxos performances are very well played, warm and elegant enough, but surprisingly, with a Hungarian virtuoso group, have neither fizz not wit. Of the extra items the *Variations* for clarinet has an attractively jocular finale. There

are no complaints about the recording, but first choice rests with Marriner.

String Sonatas 1 in G; 2 in A; 3 in C; 6 in D

(M) **(*) DG (ADD) (IMS) 457 914-2. BPO, Karajan – BOCCHERINI: *Quintet: La ritirada di Madrid* ***

Rossini's delightful *String Sonatas* cannot fail to entertain, and nor do they here. Karajan's examples are sumptuously played, but are too suave to bring out all the wit and sparkle of Rossini's youthful inspiration. The 1972 recording is as rich as can be imagined.

VOCAL MUSIC

Cantata: *Giovanna d'Arco.* Songs: *L'âme délaissée; Ariette à l'ancienne; Beltà crudele; Canzonetta spagnuola (En medio a mis colores); La grande coquette (Ariette pompadour); La légende de Marguerite; Mi lagnerò tacendo (5 settings including Sorzico and Stabat Mater); Nizza; L'Orpheline du Tyrol (Ballade élégie); La pastorella; La regata veneziana (3 songs in Venetian dialect); Il risentimento; Il trovatore*

*** Decca 430 518-2. Bartoli, Spencer

The songs of Rossini's old age were not all trivial, and this brilliantly characterized selection – with the pianist as imaginative as the singer – gives a delightful cross-section. Bartoli's artistry readily encompasses such a challenge, a singer who, even at this early stage of her career, is totally in command both technically and artistically. The recording, too, has splendid presence.

Missa di Milano; Petite messe solennelle (1867 orchestral version)

(B) *** Ph. Duo 475 230-2 (2). Mentzer, Giménez, Bostridge, Alaimo, Ch. & ASMF, Marriner

This reissued 1995 recording of Rossini's *Missa di Milano* is a real find. It is not really a complete Mass but the assembly of a *Kyrie, Gloria* and *Credo* probably composed independently before 1808. They are three separate manuscripts held in the Milan Conservatory (hence the title) but they fit together convincingly. They are well sprinkled with the musical fingerprints of the youthful, zestful Rossini, notably the crescendo in the *Gloria in excelsis Deo,* the nimble *Laudamus,* the lighthearted *Domine Deus,* and the *Qui tollis* with violin obbligato, very well sung here by Susanne Mentzer, who is even more impressive than the full-toned operatic soprano, Susann Mentzner. The closing repeated *Amen* has an irresistible exuberance. The performance could hardly be better, full of jubilation, with the chorus singing lustily and the excellent soloists, including an early recorded contribution by Ian Bostridge, whose vocal personality comes over more robustly than we expect now.

Comparable praise applies to Marriner's account of the orchestral version of the *Petite messe solennelle,* which may not be as winningly coloured as the original score for two pianos and harmonium, but is very enjoyable in its own right. Marriner strikes a happy balance between the swingingly exuberant *Cum sancto spiritus,* and the more serious mood of the closing *Agnus Dei* – beautifully sung here. Excellent recording makes this a reissue to cherish.

Petite messe solennelle

(M) **(*) Decca 444 134-2 (2). Dessì, Scalchi, Sabbatini, Pertusi, Bologna Teatro Comunale Ch. & O, Chailly

(i) *Petite messe solennelle;* (ii) *Stabat Mater*

(B) **(*) EMI double forte 5 68658-2 (2). (i) Popp, Fassbaender, Gedda, Kavrakos, King's College Ch., K. & M. Labèque, Briggs, Cleobury; (ii) Malfitano, Baltsa, Gambill, Howell, Maggio Musicale Fiorentino Ch. & O, Muti

Rossini's *Petite messe solennelle* must be the most genial contribution to the church liturgy in the history of music. Sawallisch's recording of Rossini's original score of this work – originally Ariola, later Eurodisc, remains the finest on record, but perversely it remains out of the catalogue. The use of the refined trebles of King's College Choir brings a timbre very different from what Rossini would have expected from boys' voices – but, arguably, close to what he would have wanted. That sound is hard to resist when the singing itself is so movingly eloquent. The work's underlying geniality is not obscured, but here there is an added dimension of devotional intensity from the chorus which, combined with outstanding singing from a fine quartet of soloists and beautifully matched playing from the Labèque sisters, makes for very satisfying results. The recording, too, attractively combines warmth with clarity. Rossini loses nothing of his natural jauntiness in his setting of the coupled *Stabat Mater*, but Muti's view is a dramatic one, and it is sad that he did not record it with the Philharmonia or with the Vienna Philharmonic. As it is, the Florence Festival forces are sometimes rough – notably the orchestra – and the singing at times unpolished, though the solo quartet is a fine one. Warm but rather unrefined recording.

Chailly chooses Rossini's orchestral version (made in 1867), although Rossini himself preferred his original, as do we. Nevertheless, with a fine solo team, Daniella Dessì and Gloria Scalchi both singing beautifully (and ravishing in their *Qui tollis* duet), and with the bass rising to the occasion in the *Quoniam tu solus sanctus*, this is a very considerable account. The Bologna Chorus are not helped by a somewhat backward balance which, within the warmly resonant acoustic, does not provide an ideal sharpness of focus. But they sing with much ardour, especially in the *Gloria* and *Credo*, and Chailly ensures that the *Et resurrexit* caps the performance ebulliently. Apart from the choral balance (and that is not a real problem when the performers are so committed), the recording is glowing and vivid.

Soirées musicales (excerpts); *La partenza; La pesca; La promessa; La regatta veneziana*

*** BBC (ADD) BBCB 8001-2. Harper, Baker, Britten – BRAHMS: *Liebeslieder Waltzes, Op. 52;* TCHAIKOVSKY: *4 Duets* ***

Both the tongue-in-cheek humour and the outright fun (as in the gondolier race of *La regatta veneziana*) are vividly caught in this BBC recording from the 1971 Aldeburgh Festival. Heather Harper and Janet Baker match beautifully, while remaining characterfully distinct, yet Britten at the piano remains master of ceremonies in family music-making idealized.

Stabat Mater

⊕ ✪ *** Chan. 8780. Field, D. Jones, A. Davies, Earle, L. Symphony Ch., City of L. Sinfonia, Hickox

Richard Hickox rightly presents Rossini's *Stabat Mater* warmly and with gutsy strength. All four soloists here are first rate, not Italianate of tone but full and warm, and the London Symphony Chorus sings with fine attack as well as

producing the most refined *pianissimos* in the unaccompanied quartet, here as usual given to the full chorus rather than to the soloists. Full-bodied and atmospheric sound.

OVERTURES

Overtures: *Armida; Il barbiere di Siviglia; Bianca e Faliero; La cambiale di matrimonio; La Cenerentola; Demetrio e Poblibio; Edipo a Colono; Edoardo e Cristina;* (i) *Ermione. La gazza ladra; L'inganno felice; L'Italiana in Algeri; Maometto II; Otello.* (i) *Ricciardo e Zoraide. La scala di seta; Semiramide; Le siège de Corinthe; Il Signor Bruschino; Tancredi; Il Turco in Italia; Torvaldo e Dorliska; Il viaggio a Reims; William Tell. Sinfonia al Conventello; Sinfonia di Bologna*

(M) *** Ph. Trio (ADD) 473 967-2 (3). ASMF, Marriner; (i) with Amb. S.

Marriner's reissued Trio spans all Rossini's overtures, but one must remember that the early Neapolitan operas, with the exception of *Ricciardo e Zoraide* and *Ermione*, make do with a simple Prelude, leading into the opening chorus. *Ricciardo e Zoraide*, however, is an extended piece (12 minutes 25 seconds), with the choral entry indicating that the introduction is at an end. *Maometto II* is on a comparable scale, while the more succinct *Armida* is an example of Rossini's picturesque evocation, almost like a miniature tone-poem. Twenty-four overtures plus two sinfonias make a delightful package in such sparkling performances, which eruditely use original orchestrations. Full, bright and atmospheric recording, spaciously reverberant, admirably transferred to CD, with no artificial brilliance.

Overtures: *Il barbiere di Siviglia; La cambiale di matrimonio; La Cenerentola; La gazza ladra; L'Italiana in Algeri; La scala di seta; Semiramide; Il Turco in Italia; William Tell*

(M) *** Classic fM 75605 57031-2. Sinfonia Varsovia, Menuhin

Mehuhin and his Polish group, the Sinfonia Varsovia, present a stylishly enjoyable collection of nine favourite Rossini overtures. There is a nice balance between wit and finesse, geniality and grace. Tempi are often brisk, but when there is a surge of vivacity there is no loss of poise. The wind solos are elegantly done and the string phrasing combines neatness with graceful warmth. Above all there is spontaneity here, and even at times a Beechamesque twinkle. The recording, made in the No. 1 Studio of Polish Radio in Warsaw, is full and resonant but not excessively so.

Overtures: *Il barbiere di Siviglia; La cambiale di matrimonio; La gazza ladra; L'Italiana in Algeri; Otello; La scala di seta; Semiramide; Le siège de Corinthe; Il Signor Bruschino; Tancredi; Torvaldo e Dorliska; Il Turco in Italia; Il viaggio a Reims; William Tell*

(B) *** Double Decca 443 850-2 (2). Nat. PO, Chailly

In 1981 Chailly and the National Philharmonic made the first compact disc of Rossini overtures and these performances are here combined with their further compilation, recorded in 1984, to make a desirable bargain double. At times on the first disc there is a degree of digital edge on tuttis, but the bustle from the cellos is particularly engaging. The solo playing is fully worthy of such clear presentation, demonstrating that this is an orchestra of London's finest musicians. Under

Chailly the spirit of the music-making conveys spontaneous enjoyment too. Incidentally, *Il viaggio a Reims* had no overture at its first performance, but one was cobbled together later, drawing on the ballet music from *Le siège de Corinthe*. The other novelties, *Otello* – played with great dash – and *Torvaldo e Dorliska*, with its witty interchanges between woodwind and strings, are among the highlights, and overall the performances are undoubtedly as infectious as they are stylish.

Overtures: *Il barbiere di Siviglia; La cambiale di matrimonio; L'inganno felice; L'Italiana in Algeri; La scala di seta; Il Signor Bruschino; Tancredi; Il Turco in Italia*
⊖— (N) (B) *** DG Entrée 477 501-2. Orpheus CO

The Orpheus Chamber Orchestra displays astonishing unanimity of style and ensemble in this splendid and imaginatively chosen collection of Rossini overtures, played with Charles Neidlich leading but without a conductor. Not only is the crispness of string phrasing a joy, but the many stylish wind solos have an attractive degree of freedom. These are performances that in their refinement and apt chamber style give increasing pleasure with familiarity. The DG recording is marvellously real with the perspective perfectly judged and this is an ideal Entrée into the world of Rossini.

Overtures: *Il barbiere di Siviglia; La Cenerentola; La gazza ladra; L'Italiana in Algeri; La scala di seta; Semiramide; Il Signor Bruschino; William Tell*
(N) (BB) *** EMI HMV (ADD) 5 86759-2. Philh. O, Giulini
**(*) Australian Decca Eloquence 460 590-2. Montreal SO, Dutoit

Recorded in two separate batches in the early 1960s, these performances offer characteristically refined Philhamonia playing of impressive brilliance, matched by a bold, resonant recording of wide dynamic range. Giulini's careful attention to detail is balanced by a strong sense of drama, and although these are not the most genial performances on disc they are strong in personality. *La scala di seta* has a very fast introduction which sacrifices a little poise for brilliance, but the string-playing is deliciously neat and the account of *William Tell* is quite outstanding for the warmth of its opening and the affectionate detail of the pastoral section. A highly enjoyable reissue, very well transferred to CD.

From Dutoit a good collection of popular Rossini overtures, very well played, and decently recorded, though it lacks something in character and sparkle.

Overtures: *Il barbiere di Siviglia; La Cenerentola; La gazza ladra; L'Italiana in Algeri; Le siège de Corinthe; Il Signor Bruschino*
(M) *** DG (IMS) (ADD) 419 869-2. LSO, Abbado

Brilliant playing, with splendid discipline, vibrant rhythms and finely articulated phrasing – altogether invigorating and bracing. There is perhaps an absence of outright geniality here, but these are superb performances and this remains one of the very finest collections of Rossini overtures ever, for the wit is spiced with a touch of acerbity, and the flavour is of a vintage dry champagne which retains its bloom, yet has a subtlety all its own.

Overtures: *Il barbiere di Siviglia; La Cenerentola; La gazza ladra; L'Italiana in Algeri; La scala di seta; Semiramide; Il Signor Bruschino; Tancredi; William Tell*
(M) *** EMI (ADD) 5 62802-2 [5 62804-2]. Philh. O, Giulini

Giulini's performances, recorded between 1959 and 1964, derive from two LP sources and now appear on a single CD (77 minutes 33 seconds) for the first time. They offer characteristically refined Philharmonia playing, with the conductor's careful attention to detail balanced by a strong sense of drama. Although they are not the most genial accounts on record, they are strong in personality. The performance of *William Tell* is outstanding for the beauty of the cello playing at the opening and the affectionate shaping of the pastoral section, while the introduction to *La scala di seta* is very fast indeed, and the following allegro is also swiftly paced, but the Philharmonia playing is always immaculate. Bright, vivid sound, with the date of the earlier recordings showing in the rather thin upper-string *fortissimos*. But the ear soon adjusts when the performances are so characterful.

Overtures: *Il barbiere di Siviglia; La Cenerentola; La gazza ladra; La scala di seta; Il Signor Bruschino; William Tell*
(N) ⊖— (M) *** RCA (ADD) 82876 65844-2. Chicago SO, Reiner

Reiner's classic collection from 1958 here emerges as sparkling and vivacious as ever. A fine set of performances, with *La Cenerentola* in particular offering superb orchestral bravura. The recording has good range, and the acoustic of the Chicago Hall casts a pleasing bloom. Everything sounds fresh, and after lovely, refined cello playing at the opening of *William Tell*, the blaze of brass tone announcing the galop reminds us that the Chicago orchestra was always famous in this department.

Overtures: *Il barbiere di Siviglia; La gazza ladra; L'Italiana in Algeri; La scala di seta; Semiramide; William Tell*
(B) **(*) DG (ADD) 439 415-2. BPO, Karajan

Karajan's virtuoso performances are polished like fine silver. The main *Allegro* of *La scala di seta* abandons all decorum when played as fast as this, and elsewhere bravura often takes precedence over poise. However, with the Berlin Philharmonic on sparkling form, there is wit as well as excitement; but the remastering casts very bright lighting on the upper range, which makes sonic brilliance approach aggressiveness in some climaxes.

Overtures: *Il barbiere di Siviglia; La gazza ladra; L'Italiana in Algeri; La scala di seta; Semiramide; Il Signor Bruschino; William Tell*
⊖— ✪ (M) *** Virgin 5 61900-2. LCP, Norrington

It is the drums that take a star role in Norrington's Rossini collection. They make their presence felt at the beginning and end of an otherwise persuasively styled reading of *Il barbiere*; at the introduction of *La gazza ladra*, where the snares rattle spectacularly and antiphonally; creating tension more distinctly than usual at the beginning of *Semiramide*, and bringing tumultuous thunder to the Storm sequence in *William Tell*. Of course the early wind instruments are very characterful too, with plenty of piquant touches: the oboe colouring is nicely spun in *L'Italiana in Algeri* and properly nimble in *La scala di seta*, a particularly engaging performance, mainly because of the woodwind chirpings. The brass also make their mark, with the stopped notes on the hand horns adding character to the solo quartet in *Semiramide*, and both horns and trumpets giving a brilliant edge to the announcement of the galop in *William Tell*. The strings play with relative amiability and a proper sense of line and are obviously determined to please the ear as well as to stimulate; altogether these performances offer a very refreshing new look over familiar repertoire. The recording is first-class and this is one of the most characterful of all available collections of Rossini overtures, and irresistible at mid-price.

Overtures: *Elisabetta, Regina d'Inghilterra; La scala di seta; Semiramide; Tancredi; Il Turco in Italia; William Tell*

(BB) *** RCA 74321 68012-2. LSO, Abbado – VERDI: *Overtures* ***

The *Overture Elisabetta, Regina d'Inghilterra* is in fact our familiar friend, *The Barber of Seville Overture*, and is listed as such on this reissued CD. But there is a subtle change here which surely implies the use of the proper title – a triplet in the first theme of the *Allegro* which is repeated each time the theme reappears. This adds a touch of novelty to these zestful performances from Abbado, with exhilaratingly fast tempi, the LSO players kept constantly on their toes and obviously enjoying themselves. The effect is more genial than on Abbado's earlier DG collection with the same orchestra (see above). The exuberance comes to the fore especially in *Tancredi* – there is even a brief clarinet glissando – heard in a revised version by Philip Gosset. But some might feel that *La scala di seta* would be more effective if a fraction more relaxed and poised. *William Tell* opens with elegant cellos, then offers an unashamedly over-the-top storm sequence and a final galop taken at breakneck speed. The remastered recording is vividly bright, but it matches Abbado's approach and has plenty of supporting weight and a concert hall ambience.

Overtures: *La gazza ladra; L'Italiana in Algeri; Semiramide; Il Signor Bruschino; William Tell*

(B) **(*) EMI double forte (ADD) 5 69364-2 (2). RPO, C. Davis – BEETHOVEN: *Symphony 7* *** ✪; SCHUBERT: *Symphony 9* ***

(N) *** BBC (ADD) BBCL 4159-2 (2). Philh. O, Giulini – DVORAK: *Symphony 8* (**(*)); BRUCKNER: *Symphony 8* ***

Sir Colin Davis's 1962 collection, recorded at Abbey Road, brings playing that is admirably stylish with an excellent sense of nuance. *Semiramide* is superb, reminding one of Beecham, as does the spunky opening of *The Thieving Magpie*. *William Tell* is pretty good too, the opening beautifully played. In *Il Signor Bruschino* it seems as if the bow-tapping device is done by the leader alone, which is rather effective. The CD transfer is vivid, but very brightly lit, with some loss of the body of the original; but the orchestral balance is natural.

A sparkling bonus from Giulini for impressive performances of Dvořák's and Bruckner's *Eighth Symphonies*.

Semiramide: *Overture*

(***) Testament mono SBT 1015. BBC SO, Toscanini – BRAHMS: *Symphony 2* (***); MENDELSSOHN: *Midsummer Night's Dream*: excerpt (**)

Toscanini's famous concerts with the BBC Symphony Orchestra were obviously very special. This overture from a 1935 concert has one on the edge of one's seat. Quite electrifying. The sound calls for tolerance – but what playing!

OPERA

Il barbiere di Siviglia (complete)

**(*) Arthaus DVD 100 090. Bartoli, Quilico, Kuebler, Feller, Lloyd, Cologne City Op. Ch., Stuttgart RSO, Ferro (Director: Michael Hampe)

☛ *** Decca 425 520-2 (3). Bartoli, Nucci, Matteuzzi, Fissore, Burchuladze, Ch. & O of Teatro Comunale di Bologna, Patanè

*** EMI 5 56310-2 (2). Callas, Gobbi, Alva, Ollendorff, Philh. Ch. & O, Galliera

(N) (BB) *** Warner 9031 74885-2 (2). Hagegård, Larmore, Giménez, Corbelli, Ramey, Lausanne CO, López-Cobos

(M) *** EMI 5 67762-2 [567765] (2). De los Angeles, Alva, Cava, Wallace, Bruscantini, Glyndebourne Festival Ch., RPO, Gui

(***) Testament mono SBT 2166 (2). De los Angeles, Monti, Bechi, Rossi-Lemeni, Milan Ch. & SO, Serafin

(BB) *** Naxos 8.660027/29 (3). Ganassi, Serville, Vargas, Romero, De Grandis, Hungaria R. Ch., Failoni CO, Budapest, Humburg

Recorded live at the Schwetzingen Festival in a very pretty theatre in 1988, this DVD version of *Il barbiere* centres around the superb performances of the two principals, Cecilia Bartoli, already dominant, with voice and technique fully developed even before she became a superstar, and Gino Quilico as Figaro, wonderfully winning in his acting with voice magnificently firm.

David Kuebler with his rather gritty tenor is far from winning as the Count, Robert Lloyd is an imposing Basolio and Carlos Feller a characterful Bartolo. Gabriele Ferro springs the rhythms persuasively, and Michael Hampe's production works well, using realistic sets by Ezio Frigerio and costumes by Mauro Pagano. Excellent, cleanly separated sound.

On CD, Cecilia Bartoli's rich, vibrant voice not only copes brilliantly with the technical demands but she also gives a winningly provocative characterization. Like the conductor, Bartoli is wonderful at bringing out the fun. So is Leo Nucci, and he gives a beautifully rounded portrait of the wily barber. Burchuladze, unidiomatic next to the others, still gives a monumentally lugubrious portrait of Basilio, and the Bartolo of Enrico Fissore is outstanding, with the patter song wonderfully articulated at Patanè's sensible speed. The snag is that this Decca set is on three CDs; other recommended versions manage with two.

Gobbi and Callas were here at their most inspired and, with the recording quality nicely refurbished, the EMI is an outstanding set, not absolutely complete in its text, but so crisp and sparkling it can be confidently recommended. Callas remains supreme as a minx-like Rosina, summing up the character superbly in *Una voce poco fa*. The early stereo sound comes up very acceptably in this fine new transfer, clarified, fuller and more atmospheric, presenting a uniquely characterful performance with new freshness and immediacy.

López-Cobos directs a scintillating performance, helped by brilliant esnsembles, generally taken at high speed, with rhythms sprung delectably. Though Håkan Hagegård is a dry-toned Figaro, the recording sets him in a helpful ambience, which equally helps to enhance the comic atmosphere, with the interplay of characters well managed. There are few more stylish Rossini tenors today than Raúl Giménez, and though his voice is not as youthful as some, his musical imagination goes with fine flexibility and point. As for Jennifer Larmore, she is is an enchanting Rosina, both firm and rich of tone. Crisply consistent, this makes a strong contender among modern digital versions, even next to the delectable Decca set featuring Cecilia Bartoli. An excellent collection of highlights is available on a budget Apex disc, playing for 76 minutes (2564 61502-2).

Gui's 1962 Glydebourne production has been remastered for EMI's 'Great Recordings of the Century', and the bloom on voices and orchestra is even more apparent. The charm of Victoria de los Angeles's Rosina matches the unforced geniality of the production as a whole, strongly cast and easy to enjoy. Good documentation too. Not perhaps a first choice against competition like Bartoli, but that involves three full-priced CDs, making this a good mid-priced recommendation.

The Testament issue, superbly transferred, brings out of EMI's archive the long-buried set which Victoria de los Angeles recorded with Serafin in mono in 1952, when her voice was at its fullest and most golden. Though the orchestral playing is often rough, and Serafin is relaxed rather than sparkling, the performance of de los Angeles could not be more seductive. Not as light as her later account with Gui in stereo, this is even sunnier and more glowing. Gino Bechi is a strong if gruff Figaro, Nicola Monti a heady-toned Almaviva and Nicola Rossi-Lemeni a characterful Basilio.

Though the cast is not as starry as with most full-price rivals, the Naxos set makes a first-rate bargain. The singing is hardly less stylish, with Sonia Ganassi a rich-toned Rosina, controlling vibrato well, and with Ramon Vargas an agile and attractively youthful-sounding Almaviva. Roberto Servile as Figaro conveys the fun of the role brilliantly. The *buffo* characters are strongly cast too, with Basilio's *La calunnia* (Franco de Grandis) delightfully enlivened by comments from Bartolo (Angelo Romero), both very much involved in their roles. Will Humburg's often brisk speeds, with crisp recitative matched by dazzling ensembles, never prevent the music (and the singers) from breathing.

Il barbiere di Siviglia: highlights
(M) *** EMI (ADD) 5 66671-2 (from above complete recording, with Gobbi, Callas; cond. Galliera)

The EMI highlights disc offers most of the key solo numbers from Act I, while in Act II it concentrates on Rossini's witty ensembles, including the extended Second Act *Quintet*. The *Overture* is included and, while it is stylishly played, it would have been better to have offered more of the vocal music. The overall playing time is only 57 minutes 26 seconds.

The Barber of Seville (in English)
(M) **(*) Chan. 3025 (2). Jones, Ford, Opie, Rose, Shore, ENO Ch. & O, Bellini

Chandos here offers at mid-price this *Barber* in English, using the bright translation of Amanda and Anthony Holden. Strongly cast, it is a genial performance, very well played and recorded. The only reservation is over the relaxed conducting of Gabriele Bellini which lacks dramatic bite. Compensating for that, the principal singers not only characterize vividly but together form a lively ensemble. Alan Opie is a strong, positive Figaro, while Della Jones as Rosina both exploits her rich mezzo tones and brings sparkle to the coloratura. It is good too to have so accomplished a Rossini tenor as Bruce Ford singing Almaviva. Peter Rose as Basilio and Andrew Shore as Dr Bartolo, both young-sounding for these roles, are

fresh and firm too. Excellent documentation includes a full English libretto.

La cambiale di matrimonio (complete)
* Claves CD 50-9101. Praticò, Rossi, Comencini, De Simone, Facini, Baiano, ECO, Viotti

Here, while the voices have fair bloom on them, the recessed orchestra sounds washy, a significant flaw in such intimately jolly music, with ensembles suffering in particular. Viotti is a relaxedly stylish Rossinian, drawing pointed playing from the ECO, but the singing is poor. The tenor Maurizio Comencini sounds unsteady and strained, while Alessandra Rossi as the heroine, agile enough, is too shrill for comfort. The best singing comes from the *buffo* baritone, Bruno Praticò, as the heroine's father.

La Cenerentola (DVD versions)
☺━ *** Decca DVD 071 444-9. Bartoli, Dara, Giménez, Corbelli, Pertusi, Houston Grand Op. Ch. & Symphony, Campanella (V/D: Brian Large)
*** Arthaus DVD 100 214. Murray, Berry, Araiza, Quilico, Schöne, V. State Op. Ch., VPO, Chailly (Director: Michael Hampe; V/D: Claus Viller)

La Cenerentola (CD versions)
☺━ *** Decca 436 902-2 (2). Bartoli, Matteuzzi, Corbelli, Dara, Costa, Banditelli, Pertusi, Ch. & O of Teatro Comunale di Bologna, Chailly
(N) (M) *** Teldec 4509 94553-2 (2). Larmore, Giménez, Quilico, Corbelli, Scarabelli, ROHCG Ch. & O, Rizzi
(B) ** DG Double (ADD) 459 448-2 (2). Berganza, Alva, Montarsolo, Capecchi, Scottish Op., Ch., Abbado

Few Rossini operas have such fizz as Decca's Houston Opera production of *La Cenerentola*, a part Cecilia Bartoli was born to play. The rest of the cast is the same as the CD set, except that Raúl Giménez takes the part of Don Ramiro. Bruno Campanella conducts very spiritedly. Visually the production could not be more winning, and the camera placing is a great credit to Brian Large.

Riccardo Chailly (who directed the Decca CDs) conducts the alternative version, which comes from the 1982 Salzburg Festival, and had the Bartoli set not been available it would have been a very strong recommendation, for Ann Murray is delightful in the principal role and the rest of the cast is excellent. If in Act I Don Magnifico's castle looks run down and needing a coat of paint, the glamour of the Palace more than compensates. The recording is bright and sparking but has plenty of bloom and the camerawork is always well managed. Most enjoyable, with a dazzling *Non più mesta* and a particularly infectious finale. But Chailly is at his finest throughout and so are the chorus and orchestra.

On the Decca CDs Cecilia Bartoli again makes an inspired Cenerentola. Her tone-colours are not just more sensuous than those of her rivals: her imagination and feeling for detail add enormously to her vivid characterization, culminating in a stunning account of the final rondo, *Non più mesta*. William Matteuzzi is an engaging prince, sweeter of tone and more stylish than his direct rivals, while the contrasting of the bass and baritone roles is ideal between Alessandro Corbelli as Dandini, Michele Pertusi as the tutor, Alidoro, and Enzo Dara as Don Magnifico. Few Rossini opera-sets have such fizz as this, and the recording is one of Decca's most vivid.

Carlo Rizzi's mid-priced Teldec version, with Covent Garden forces, has been beautifully repackaged with full texts and translation. Jennifer Larmore makes an enchanting heroine, with her creamily beautiful mezzo both tenderly expressive in cantilena and flawlessly controlled through the most elaborate coloratura passages. She may not be the fire-eating Cenerentola the vibrant Cecilia Bartoli is on Chailly's outstanding Decca version, but this is a more smiling character, not least in the final exuberant rondo, *Non più mesta*, which sparkles deliciously, more relaxed than with Bartoli. As Ramiro, Raúl Giménez sings with a commanding sense of style, less youthful but more assured than his rival, while Alessandro Corbelli is far more aptly cast here as Don Magnifico than as Dandini in the Decca set. Here the Dandini of Gino Quilico is youthful and debonair, and Alastair Miles is a magnificent Alidoro. Though the Covent Garden forces cannot quite match the close-knit Bologna team in underlining the comedy as in a live performance, as directed by Carlo Rizzi they are consistently more refined, with more light and shade, bringing out the musical sparkle all the more. Excellent, well-balanced sound. A generous highlights disc (75 minutes) is available on a budget Apex CD (2564 61503-2).

Abbado's 1971 DG set lacks the extrovert bravura and sparkle of an ideal performance. The atmosphere in places is almost a concert performance, helped by fine analogue recording. Berganza, agile in the coloratura, seems too mature, even matronly, for the fairy-tale role of Cinderella. Alva sings well enough but is somewhat self-conscious in the florid writing. Abbado, although hardly witty in his direction, inspires delicate playing throughout. The CD transfer is admirably fresh.

Le Comte Ory (complete; DVD version)
(N) *** Warner **DVD** 0630 18646-2. Laho, Massis, Montague, Shaulis, Tezier, Robbins, Glyndebourne Ch., LPO, A. Davis (V/D: Brian Large)

Le Comte Ory, written for Paris in 1828, was Rossini's very last comic opera, and one which finds him at his most sparkling, relying not on big arias but on witty ensembles reflecting the humour of Eugène Scribe's libretto. It prompted a classic Glyndebourne production in the mid-1950s; here, in a 1997 production by Jerome Savary with colourful sets and costumes by Ezio Toffolutti, the fun is just as exuberant. That is so both in Act I, when the predatory Count Ory disguises himself as a hermit, intent on waylaying the Countess Adele in her castle while her brother is away at the Crusades, and in Act II when Ory and his followers disguise themselves as nuns and inveigle their way into the castle. Their drinking chorus – punctuated by pretended devotions when approached by strangers – is a delight, and the comic bed-scene when Ory thinks he is fondling the Countess when in fact it is the page, Isolier, is brilliantly handled. The cast, led by Marc Laho as Ory, Annick Massis as the Countess and Diana Montague as Isolier, has no weak link, with ensembles delectably timed and pointed by the conductor, Andrew Davis.

Le Comte Ory (CD versions)
(N) ☛ *** DG 477 5020 (2). Flórez, Miles, Bonfadelli, Todorovitch, De Liso, Pratico, Prague Ch., Bologna Theatre O, López-Cobos

(N) (M) *** Decca 475 7014-2 (2). Sumi Jo, Aler, Montague, Cachemaille, Quilico, Pierotti, Lyon Op. Ch. & O, Gardiner

This is one of the most delectable of all Rossini's comic operas, an essay in French that set a new pattern for the composer. Jesus López-Cobos, the most skilled of Rossini

conductors, directs a sparkling performance, recorded at the Rossini Festival in Pesaro in 2003. He even matches in rhythmic lift and comic timing the magic example of Vittorio Gui in the classic Glyndebourne recording of the 1950s. The big ensemble that ends Act I is taken even faster than with Gui, yet it is just as effervescent. The presence of an audience plainly helps, and the performance gains enormously too from the brilliant characterization of the central character of the predatory Count himself by Juan Diego Flórez. Not only does he invest every phrase with character, he sings with a fluency that stands out even among the current crop of excellent Rossini tenors, tackling the most formidable florid passages with ease and imagination. As the object of his desires, the Countess Adele, whose husband is away at the crusades, Stefania Bonfadelli sings with equal fluency, a coloratura soprano with a mezzo-ish tinge in the lower register who can reach a top E flat with ease. Alastair Miles as the Count's Tutor sings strongly, making him rather a severe character, with Marina De Liso light and sparkling as the page, Isolier. The closely focused recording is full and firm, if not always kind to the orchestra, with the voices very well caught, and vociferous applause at the end of each Act adding to the sense of presence.

The alternative Gardiner set, now reissued at mid-price in Decca's Classic Opera series is also beautifully sung, with ensembles finely balanced, as in the delightful Act II Trio. Gardiner tends to be rather more tense than López-Cobos or Gui on EMI (currently withdrawn), with speeds on the fast side, and he allows too short a dramatic pause for the interruption of the Nuns' drinking choruses. But the precision and point are most winning. Though John Aler hardly sounds predatory enough as the Count, the lightness of his tenor is ideal, and Sumi Jo as Adele and Diana Montague as the page, Isolier, are both stylish and characterful. So is the clear-toned Gino Quilico as the tutor, Raimbaud. With good and warm, if not ideally crystal clear recording, this set takes its place as a fine mid-price alternatative to the López-Cobos version.

La donna del lago (complete)
(B) *(*) Ph. Duo 473 307-2 (2). Anderson, Merritt, Dupuy, Blake, La Scala, Milan, Ch. & O, Muti

Recorded live at La Scala, Milan, in June 1992, the Philips account of this opera, freely adapted from Scott's novel, *The Lady of the Lake*, is no match for the earlier, Sony version with the COE under Pollini (currently withdrawn). Muti may be a more powerful conductor here, but the ensemble work of both chorus and orchestra is rough by comparison. The dry Scala sound is also unkind to the solo voices, exaggerating any unevenness. Rockwell Blake as Umberto (King James V) is made to sound strangulated as well as wobbly, and Chris Merritt in the other tenor role of Rodrigo (Roderick di Dhu) is powerful but coarse next to his Sony rival. With sweetness undermined by uneven production, June Anderson is no match for Katia Ricciarelli at her finest; Giorgio Surjan pales next to Samuel Ramey, and none of the Scala soloists outshines their predecessors. Limited sound completes the disappointment.

Elisabetta, Regina d'Inghilterra (complete)
* Hardy **DVD** HCD 4007. Cuberli, Dessi, Savastano, Blake, Teatro Regio Ch. & O, Ferro (V/D De Bosia)
☛ *** Opera Rara ORC 22 (3). Larmore, Ford, Cullagh, LPO, Carella

The Hardy DVD of this rare Rossini opera was recorded live in November 1985 at the Teatro Regio in Turin with an impressive cast conducted by the Rossini scholar, Gabriele Ferro. Lella Cuberli as the Queen and Daniela Dessi as Matilde, secretly Leicester's wife, both sing superbly, with coloratura brilliantly clear, and both Antonio Savastano as Leicester and Rockwell Blake as Norfolk are first rate, too. The snag lies both with the creaking production, updated from Elizabethan to Napoleonic times with faded pastel shades in sets and costumes, and with the recorded sound, which is depressingly dim. The documentation is paltry too.

Elisabetta d'Inghilterra, produced in 1815, like Walter Scott's novel, Kenilworth, of five years later, deals with the love of Queen Elizabeth for Leicester, but with the added gloss that Mary Queen of Scots had given birth during her captivity to two unacknowledged children by the Duke of Norfolk, one of whom married Leicester. The overture is the one that Rossini re-used in the Barber of Seville, and Elisabetta's first aria brings material later developed in the Barber as Rosina's Una voce poco fa. What matters is the vigour of the writing and many marvellous ensembles, beautifully performed on Opera Rara by a strong cast led by Jennifer Larmore, Bruce Ford and Majella Cullagh, with Giuliano Carella the idiomatic conductor. This can be strongly recommended.

L'equivoco stravagante (complete)
(BB) **(*) Naxos 8.660087/8 (2). Petrova, Felice, Vinco, Schmunck, Minarelli, Santamaria, Czech Chamber Ch. & Chamber Soloists, Zedda

L'equivoco stravagante ('The Bizarre Deception'), is one of Rossini's earliest operas, written when he was only 19. Already the Rossini fingerprints are firmly in place, with the music regularly sparkling from the Overture, with its brilliant horn triplets, onwards. The story of this dramma giocoso involves a scheming servant, Frontino, who deceives the stupid suitor, Buralichio, into believing that the girl he is wooing, the heroine, Ernestina, is in fact male and whose nouveau riche father, Gamberotto, has had 'him' castrated so that he could become a high-earning opera-singer. The complications are many, until Ernestina is safely united with Ermanno, the impecunious tutor whom she loves. After three performances in 1811 the piece was banned for being too licentious. Rossini cut his losses, using material from it in his subsequent operas. It makes an attractive rarity, generally well sung and very well conducted in this live recording by the Rossini scholar Alberto Zedda – if unhelpfully punctuated by tepid applause.

Guglielmo Tell (William Tell: complete, in Italian)
*** Decca (IMS) (ADD) 417 154-2 (4). Pavarotti, Freni, Milnes, Ghiaurov, Amb. Op. Ch., Nat. PO, Chailly

Rossini wrote his massive opera about William Tell in French, but Chailly and his team here put forward a strong case for preferring Italian, with its open vowels, in music which glows with Italianate lyricism. Chailly's is a forceful reading, particularly strong in the many ensembles, and superbly recorded. Milnes makes a heroic Tell, always firm, and though Pavarotti has his moments of coarseness he sings the role of Arnoldo with glowing tone. Ghiaurov too is in splendid voice, while subsidiary characters are almost all well taken, with such a fine singer as John Tomlinson, for example, ripely resonant as Melchthal. The women singers too are impressive, with Mirella Freni as the heroine Matilde providing dramatic strength as well as sweetness. The recording, made

in 1978 and 1979, comes out spectacularly, with the Pas de six banded into its proper place in Act I.

Guillaume Tell (William Tell; in French)
(M) *** EMI (ADD) 7 69951-2 (4). Bacquier, Caballé, Gedda, Mesplé, Amb. Op. Ch., RPO, Gardelli

The interest of the 1973 EMI set is that it is sung in the original French. Gardelli proves an imaginative Rossini interpreter, urging his formidable team to vigorous and sensitive performances. Bacquier makes an impressive Tell, developing the character as the story progresses; Gedda is a model of taste, and Montserrat Caballé copes ravishingly with the coloratura problems of Mathilde's role. While Chailly's full-price Decca set puts forward a strong case for using Italian with its open vowels, this remains a fully worthwhile alternative, with excellent CD sound. Indeed the current remastering is first class in every way and the choral passages, incisively sung, are among the most impressive; moreover the set now comes with full translation.

L'inganno felice (complete)
*(*) Claves CD 50-9211. De Carolis, Felle, Zennaro, Previato, Serraiocco, ECO, Viotti

L'inganno felice is stylishly and energetically conducted by Viotti with sprung rhythms and polished playing, but with a flawed cast. As the heroine, Amelia Felle is agile but too often raw-toned, even if on occasion she can crown an ensemble with well-phrased cantilena. As the hero, Bertrando, Iorio Zennaro has an agreeable natural timbre, but his tenor is not steady enough and strains easily. The buffo, Fabio Previato, is the soloist who comes closest to meeting the full challenge. The recorded sound has a pleasant bloom on it, but the orchestra is too recessed, and though the recitatives are briskly done, with crisp exchanges between the characters, the degree of reverberation is a serious drawback.

L'Italiana in Algeri (complete; DVD version)
** Arthaus DVD 100 120. Soffel, Gambill, Von Kannen, Bulgarian Male Ch., Stuttgart RSO, Weikert

This DVD production from the 1987 Schwetzingen Festival was available in the early 1990s on a Pioneer LaserDisc and looks even better on this DVD with its sharper, steadier focus and good colour – and subtitles in English, French and German.

Doris Soffel is a vivacious Isabella and the Mustafá of Günter von Kannen is characterized with great zest. Michael Hampe's direction is witty and well paced, and the set design and costumes of Mauro Pagano colourful.

The stage is small (as is the theatre itself) and despite the merits of the singing and playing leaves the impression of being cramped and provincial with little sense of back-to-front perspective. But there is a lot to enjoy here, particularly the final ensemble of the first Act, and much that is of quality. The Südwestfunk Orchestra plays well for Ralf Weikert and the sound is well balanced and has good presence.

L'Italiana in Algeri (complete; CD versions)
(N) ☞ *** Teldec 0630 17130-2 (2). Larmore, Giménez, Del Carlo, Corbelli, Grand Theatre Ch., Lausanne CO, López-Cobos

☞ ✹ *** DG (ADD) 427 331-2 (2). Baltsa, Raimondi, Dara, Lopardo, V. State Op. Konzertvereinigung, VPO, Abbado

(M) *** Erato 2292 45404-2 (2). Horne, Palacio, Ramey,
Trimarchi, Battle, Zaccaria, Prague Ch., I Sol. Ven.,
Scimone

The Teldec recording offers a near-ideal account, superbly
sung, sparklingly conducted and brilliantly recorded. Jennifer
Larmore in the title-role is both youthfully seductive and
ripely characterful, with her firm, fresh voice beautifully
caught, at once easily flexible on top and rich in the chest
register. Her big Rondo in Act II is one of the high spots of
the set, stylishly ornamented. Raúl Giménez as Lindoro
makes a perfect counterpart, establishing his comparable
brilliance in his elaborate Act I aria and investing everything
he sings with character and a sense of fun, not just singing
the notes. He is wonderfully fluent in the brilliant patter duet
with Mustafa, Bey of Algiers, characterfully sung by John Del
Carlo. Alexander Corbelli too makes the most of the humour
in the role of the put-upon servant, Taddeo. In a fascinating
appendix, Giménez also sings Lindoro's alternative aria in Act
II with its clarinet obbligato. A clear first choice among CD
versions.

Abbado's brilliant version was recorded in conjunction
with a new staging by the Vienna State Opera, with timing
and pointing all geared for wit on stage to make this the most
captivating of all recordings of the opera. Agnes Baltsa is a
real fire-eater in the title-role, and Ruggero Raimondi with
his massively sepulchral bass gives weight to his part without
undermining the comedy. The American tenor, Frank Lopardo, proves the most stylish Rossinian, singing with heady
clarity in superbly articulated divisions, while both *buffo*
baritones are excellent too. This uses the authentic score,
published by the Fondazione Rossini in Pesaro.

Scimone's highly enjoyable version is beautifully played
and recorded with as stylish a team of soloists as one can
expect nowadays. The text is complete and alternative versions of certain arias are given as an appendix. Marilyn
Horne makes a dazzling, positive Isabella, and Samuel Ramey
is splendidly firm as Mustafa. Domenico Trimarchi is a
delightful Taddeo and Ernesto Palacio an agile Lindoro, not
coarse, though the recording does not always catch his tenor
timbre well. Nevertheless the sound is generally very good
indeed.

Maometto II (complete)

(B) *** Ph. Trio 475 50921-2 (3). Anderson, Zimmermann,
Palacio, Ramey, Dale, Amb. Op. Ch., Philh. O, Scimone

Claudio Scimone's account of *Maometto II* has Samuel
Ramey magnificently focusing the whole story in his portrait
of the Muslim invader in love with the heroine. The other
singing is less sharply characterized but is generally stylish,
with Margarita Zimmermann in the *travesti* role of Calbo
and June Anderson singing sweetly as Anna. Laurence Dale is
excellent in two smaller roles, while Ernesto Palacio mars
some fresh-toned singing with his intrusive aitches. Excellently recorded, this is well worth exploring at bargain price,
even though only a synopsis is included.

L'occasione fa il ladro (complete)

(M) ** Claves CD 50-9208/9. Bayo, De Carolis, Zennaro,
Provvisionato, Previati, Massa, ECO, Viotti

On two discs, this is one of the longer one-Acters in the
Claves series, bringing one of the more recommendable
performances, with Viotti at his most relaxed. Maria Bayo as
the heroine sings warmly and sweetly, with no intrusive
aspirates in the coloratura. The soubrette role of Ernestina is

also charmingly done, and the *buffo* characters sing effectively, though the tenor, Iorio Zennaro, is hardly steady
enough for Rossinian cantilena. The two discs come in a
single hinged jewel-box at upper mid-price.

Otello (complete)

*** Opera Rara ORC 18 (3). Ford, Futral, Matteuzzi,
D'Arcangelo, Lopera, Philh. O, Parry
(B) *** Ph. Duo (ADD) 475 448-2 (2). Carreras, Von Stade,
Condò, Pastine, Fisichella, Ramey, Amb. S., Philh. O,
López-Cobos

Justifiably overshadowed by Verdi's masterpiece, this early
opera of Rossini, written in 1816 for Naples, is a piece very
much of its time, with the changes in Shakespeare's story
making the drama more conventional: a love-letter is substituted for the fatal handkerchief, and Desdemona is stabbed
instead of being smothered, while she also acquires a new
father, Elmiro. Even so, Rossini is inspired by a serious subject
to produce a striking series of arias and ensembles, which
culminate in what was then a revolutionary course in Italian
opera, a tragic ending. Significantly, later, in 1820 and pres-
sured by the authorities, Rossini provided a happy ending,
when Otello is finally convinced of Desdemona's innocence.
That alternative close is the first of three important appendices included in this very well-documented Opera Rara set.
Where the previous Philips recording, more starrily cast,
provided a badly cut text on two CDs merely, this one
stretches to three very well-filled discs.

It is a credit to Opera Rara that three formidable Rossini
tenors are here involved, not just Bruce Ford in the title role,
strong and stylish if a little gritty as recorded, but also Juan
José Lopera, impressive as Iago, and, singing even more
sweetly, William Matteuzzi as Rodrigo, here given a relatively
big role. Elizabeth Futral is a strong, dramatic heroine, rising
superbly to the challenge of the final Act, which, coming
closer to Shakespeare, brings the most memorable music,
including a lovely *Willow Song*. Enkeljda Shkosa sings most
beautifully as Emilia, as she does too in the alternative
Malibran version of the Act II duet, in which she sings Otello,
transformed into a breeches-role. David Parry excels himself
in drawing powerful, sensitive playing from the Philharmonia, dramatically paced, with some outstanding solo work
from the wind. Vivid, well-balanced sound.

It is some tribute to the Philips performance, superbly
recorded and brightly and stylishly conducted by López-
Cobos, that the line-up of tenors is turned into an asset, with
three nicely contrasted soloists. Carreras here is at his finest –
most affecting in his recitative before the murder, while
Fisichella copes splendidly with the high tessitura of Rodrigo's role, and Pastine has a distinct timbre to identify him as
the villain. Frederica von Stade pours forth a glorious flow of
beautiful tone, well matched by Nucci Condò as Emilia.
Samuel Ramey is excellent too in the bass role of Elmiro. It
makes an undoubted bargain at its new price – its cost, alas,
precluding the possibility of including text and translation.

La scala di seta (complete)

*** Claves 50-9219/20. Corbelli, Ringholz, Vargas, De Carolis,
Provvisionato, Massa, ECO, Viotti

The Overture is among the best known of all that Rossini
wrote, and here Viotti establishes his individuality with an
unusually expansive slow introduction leading to a brisk and
well-sprung *Allegro*, scintillatingly played by the ECO. The
cast here is stronger vocally than those in the rest of the

Claves series, with Teresa Ringholz delightful as the heroine, Giulia, warm and agile, shading her voice seductively. She and the *buffo*, sung by Alessandro Corbelli, have the biggest share of the solo work, and he is also first rate. The tenor Ramon Vargas sings without strain – rare in this series – and the mezzo, Francesca Provvisionato, sings vivaciously as the heroine's cousin, with a little aria in military rhythm a special delight. Warm sound with good bloom on the voices.

Semiramide (complete, but with traditional cuts)

⊕☛ *** Arthaus **DVD** 100 222 (2). Anderson, Horne, Olsen, Ramey, Met. Op. O and Ch., Conlon (Dir. John Copley; TV Dir.: Brian Large)

(M) *** Decca (ADD) 425 481-2 (3). Sutherland, Horne, Rouleau, Malas, Serge, Amb. Op. Ch., LSO, Bonynge

Grand opera presented unapologetically on a monumental scale in traditional style typifies this 1990 production of *Semiramide* at the Met in New York. The casting is very strong, centring as much around the commanding Arsace of Marilyn Horne as the powerful but less characterful June Anderson in the title role, both of them wonderfully agile in coloratura. Yet on DVD, with Brian Large as video director, it is the fine production of John Copley, using very grand sets by John Conklin and sumptuous costumes by Michael Stennett, that stands out. The tenor, Stanford Olsen, is impressive as Idreno, and Samuel Ramey is handsome of voice and presence as Assur, setting the seal on this supremely confident presentation of a difficult opera, purposefully conducted by James Conlon.

Rossini concentrates on the love of Queen Semiramide for Prince Arsace (a mezzo-soprano), and musically the result is a series of fine duets, superbly performed here by Sutherland and Horne (in the mid-1960s when they were both at the top of their form). In Sutherland's interpretation, Semiramide is not so much a Lady Macbeth as a passionate, sympathetic woman and, with dramatic music predominating over languorous cantilena, one has her best, bright manner. Horne is well contrasted, direct and masculine in style, and Spiro Malas makes a firm, clear contribution in a minor role. Rouleau and Serge are variable but more than adequate, and Bonynge keeps the whole opera together with his alert, rhythmic control of tension and pacing.

Il Signor Bruschino (complete)

(N) (BB) *** Naxos 8.660128. Codeluppi, Leoni, Rossi, Giorgelè, Marani, Giangaspero, Barbolini, Martino, I Virtuosi Italiani, Desderi

Il Signor Bruschino is the last of the five one-act operas in which the teenage Rossini first began to demonstrate his operatic genius. Latterly it has been remembered mainly for its distinctive overture, with orchestral violins asked to tap their bows on their music stands. Yet, as this lively account demonstrates, vigorously conducted by the former baritone Claudio Desderi, Rossini's style was already fully developed in such characteristic numbers as the patter-duet between the hero, Florville, and the guardian of his beloved, Gaudenzio. The involved plot is typical of the genre, with the Naxos booklet providing a detailed synopsis as well as a full libretto in Italian. The singing is stylish, led by Alessandro Codeluppi as Florville, and with Elena Rossi as the heroine, Sofia, bright and agile if rather unvaried in tone. An outstanding bargain.

Tancredi (complete)

⊕☛ (B) *** Naxos 8.660037/8. Podles, Jo, Olsen, Spagnoli, Di Micco, Lendi, Capella Brugensis, Brugense Coll. Instrumentale, Zedda

(M) *** Warner Fonit (ADD) 5050466-1814-2-8 (3). Cossotto, Cuberli, Hollweg, Ghiuselev, WDR Ch. Cologne, Cappella Coloniensis of WDR, Ferro

Tancredi, which was based on Tasso's epic poem *Gerusalemme Liberata* and was first heard in 1813, is most widely remembered for its overture, but this excellent Naxos set makes a strong case for the piece. It completely displaces the previous versions from Sony and RCA, and the eminent Rossini scholar and conductor, Alberto Zedda, proves a far more resilient, generally brisker and lighter Rossini interpreter than his predecessors. Sumi Jo is superb as the heroine, Amenaide, in dazzlingly clear coloratura, as well as imaginative pointing of phrase, rhythm and words. The mezzo, Ewa Podles, is less characterful, yet the voice is firm and rich as well as flexible; but it is the tenor, Stanford Olsen, previously heard as Belmonte on John Eliot Gardiner's recording of *Entführung*, who offers some of the freshest, most stylish and sweetly tuned singing from a Rossini tenor in recent years. The recording is a little lacking in body, but that partly reflects the use of a small orchestra, and the voices come over well. An Italian libretto is provided but no translation. Instead, a helpful synopsis is geared to the different tracks on the discs; had there been a libretto, this could well have received a Rosette.

The (1979) Warner Fonit version is a formidable competitor for the excellent Naxos set, generally using weightier voices and with an excellent orchestra of period instruments, whereas on Naxos there are modern instruments played in period style. Fiorenza Cossotto sings powerfully in the breeches role of Tancredi, and Lella Cuberli, then at her peak, is a most winning Amenaide, full and pure of tone as well as wonderfully agile. Werner Hollweg's headily light tenor is very apt for the role of Argirio, and Nicola Ghiuselev is a weighty Orbazzano. Though not digital, the recording is full and well balanced, with the scholar Gabriele Ferro drawing fresh, stylish playing from his period orchestra. As on Naxos, an Italian libretto is provided but no translation; unlike Naxos, there is no English synopsis. The three-disc format contrasts with the two of Naxos, but that brings only one break in Act II instead of two.

The Thieving Magpie (complete; in English)

(M) *** Chan. 3097 (2). Cullagh, Banks, Bickley, White, Smythe, Purves, Geoffrey Mitchell Ch., Philh. O, Parry

This is one of the very finest of the many Opera in English recordings promoted by the Peter Moores Foundation. David Parry draws sparkling performances from his excellent cast of singers, as well as from the Philharmonia Orchestra. Using a lively translation by Jeremy Sams, the performance makes light of the improbablities of the plot, which has its unpleasantly dark element when the heroine is threatened with death after being accused of stealing one of her mistress's silver spoons. The culprit is of course the magpie of the opera's title, and all turns out well in the end. The set gains enormously from having been made in the wake of a stage production at Garsington Manor in 2002, also conducted by Parry. As he points out in a note, the full score is unmanageably long, which has entailed some cutting of the piano recitative (almost certainly not by Rossini) and of some inessential numbers, no doubt originally included to placate certain solo singers. As Parry claims, the arias that are dramatically less essential tend to be those least interesting musically. As it is, the piece moves swiftly along, with the Irish soprano Majella Cullagh as the heroine, Ninetta, and Christopher Purves as the Mayor, her employer, outstanding both musically and dramatically with cleanly focused singing. It helps no doubt that they both took part in the Garsington production, but the others are first rate too, with the tenor Barry Banks as the hero, Giannetto, Susan Bickley as the Mayor's wife Lucia, Russell Smythe as Ninetta's father and John Graham-Hall as the pedlar, Isacco. Full, well-balanced sound, recorded in the Blackheath Concert Halls.

Il Turco in Italia (complete)

**(*) Decca 458 924-2 (2). Bartoli, Corbelli, Pertusi, Vargas, Ch. & O of La Scala, Milan, Chailly

(***) EMI mono 5 56313-2 (2). Rossi-Lemeni, Callas, Gedda, Stabile, Ch. & O of La Scala, Milan, Gavazzeni

Chailly's Decca version centres round the brilliantly characterful singing of Cecilia Bartoli as a fire-eating Fiorilla. The tessitura is high for a mezzo, but she copes with sparkling confidence. Chailly paces the many ensembles most effectively, with a first-rate team of soloists to back up Bartoli, agile and sparkling.

Callas was at her peak when she recorded this rare Rossini opera in the mid-1950s. As ever, there are lumpy moments vocally, but she gives a sharply characterful performance as the capricious Fiorilla, married to an elderly, jealous husband and bored with it. Nicola Rossi-Lemeni as the Turk of the title is characterful too, but the voice is ill-focused, and it is left to Nicolai Gedda as the young lover and Franco Calabrese as the jealous husband to match Callas in stylishness. It is good too to have the veteran Mariano Stabile singing the role of the Poet in search of a plot. Walter Legge's production has plainly added to the sparkle. On CD the original mono recording has been freshened and given added bloom, despite the closeness of the voices. It is a vintage Callas issue, her first uniquely cherishable essay in operatic comedy.

Il viaggio a Reims (complete)

⊖ ➤ ✿ *** DG 415 498-2 (2). Ricciarelli, Terrani, Cuberli, Gasdia, Araiza, Giménez, Nucci, Raimondi, Ramey, Dara, Prague Philh. Ch., COE, Abbado

This DG set is one of the most sparkling and totally successful live opera recordings available, with Claudio Abbado in particular freer and more spontaneous-sounding than he generally is on disc, relishing the sparkle of the comedy, and the line-up of soloists here could hardly be more impressive, with no weak link. Apart from the established stars the set introduced two formidable newcomers in principal roles, Cecilia Gasdia as a self-important poetess and, even finer, Lella Cuberli as a young fashion-crazed widow. Abbado's brilliance and sympathy draw the musical threads compellingly together with the help of superb, totally committed playing from the young members of the Chamber Orchestra of Europe.

Zelmira (complete)

(N) **(*) Opera Rara ORC 27 (3). Futral, Ford, Custer, Siragusa, Scottish Ch. & CO, Benini

Zelmira was the last but one opera that Rossini wrote before going off to live in Paris, and it has regularly been dismissed, unfairly when it contains much fine music. It was recorded in 1989 under Claudio Scimone for Erato, but that first-rate set has been deleted. This one, promoted by Opera Rara and recorded live at a concert performance given at the Edinburgh Festival in 2003, admirably fills the gap. Maurizio Benini may not have the finesse of Scimone, but he directs a lively, well-sprung performance, and though the cast cannot quite match the excellent one on Erato, the singing is consistently stylish and often brilliant. The wild applause for the astonishing Act I aria of Ilo, Zelmira's returning husband, and of the comparably challenging Act II aria of Zelmira's handmaid, Emma, is well deserved, for Antonino Siragusa as Ilo has both flexibility and an astonishing upper range, and Manuela Custer as Emma has fine vocal control, with crisp ornamentation and flawless trills. So too has the excellent Elizabeth Futral in the title-role, while Bruce Ford as the usurping Antenore, with a baritonal quality in his tenor tone, is well contrasted with the higher, lighter Ilo of Siragusa. The set takes up three discs instead of the two on Erato, but it brings a fuller text, with an extra half-hour of music.

COLLECTIONS

Arias from: Armida; L'assedio di Corinto; La donna del lago; Otello; Stabat Mater; Tancredi

(N) (M) *** RCA (ADD) 82876 62309-2 (2). Caballé, RCA Italiana Op. Ch. & O, Cillario – DONIZETTI; VERDI: Arias ***

Originally entitled 'Rossini Rarities', much of the music here, taken from a 1967 LP, is not over-familiar even today. It does, however, show Caballé displaying some of her finest qualities; indeed, there is tonal beauty and brilliance in equal measure. If the Italian orchestra is not the most refined in the world, Cillario achieves lively results, and the sound is suitably theatrical. The recording has transferred well to CD – full and vivid – and texts and translations are included.

'Rossini Gala': arias from: Armida; Aureliano in Palmira; Bianca e Falliero; Elisabetta, Regina D'Inghilterra; Mosè in Egitto; Semiramide; Vallace; Zelmira

*** Opera Rara ORR 211. Miricioiu, Ford, Magee, Banks, ASMF, Parry

Nelly Miricioiu, Romanian-born and British-based, is a soprano who deserves to be recorded far more. This wide-ranging, imaginatively devised recital of rare Rossini arias admirably fills a gap with Miricioiu strongly supported by a range of singers, including the Rossini tenors Bruce Ford and Barry Banks. Miricioiu's is a warm, characterful voice, which she uses with a fine feeling for dramatic point, bringing to life even the most conventional of operatic numbers. She also has the merit, very necessary in Rossini, of coloratura flexibility, which she relishes brilliantly in the cabalettas to arias. Strong support from David Parry and the Academy, with full, brilliant recording.

'Serious Rossini': excerpts from: Armida; Mosè in Egitto; Otello; Ricciardo e Zoraide; Ugo, Re d'Italia

*** Opera Rara ORR 218. Ford, Miricioiu, Matteuzzi, Kelly, Soloists, Geoffrey Mitchell Ch., Phil. O or ASMF, Parry

Here is a further glorious recital of Rossini excerpts, this time centring on the excellent tenor Bruce Ford, but including many memorable ensemble items. All are vividly projected by this outstanding cast of singers. Highlights include the duet of Agorante and Ricciardo (William Matteuzzi) in Riccardo e Zoraide, and the quintet from the finale of Act I. The trio In quale aspetto imbello (from Armida) and the quartet Mi *manca la voce* (from *Mosè in Egitto*) also stand out, as does the supremely dramatic finale of *Otello*, where Bruce Ford is powerfully partnered by Nelly Miricioiu. David Parry keeps the tension high and the chorus and orchestra give admirable support. The recording is splendidly vivid.

Arias from: *Il barbiere di Siviglia; La Cenerentola; La donna del lago; La gazza ladra; L'Italiana in Algeri; Otello; Semiramide; Zelmira*

*** Decca 470 024-2. Flórez, Verdi O Sinfonica di Milano, Chailly

Even in a generation that has thrown up some remarkable Rossini tenors, the Peruvian, Juan Diego Flórez, stands out with his clean-cut, wonderfully flexible voice, with not a suspicion of an intrusive aitch in the extraordinarily elaborate divisions of these challenging arias and with top Cs thrown off with consistent ease. The authority is never in doubt, and it is good to have such brilliant performances mainly of little-known arias, yet one hopes that Flórez will develop a gentler touch in hushed passages, with half-tones and a diamond bright timbre regularly dominating. Yet there are few recent discs of Rossini's tenor arias that begin to match this in excitement, with Chailly and the Milan Orchestra the most understanding partners. Full, clear sound.

Arias from: *Il barbiere di Siviglia; La Cenerentola; La donna del lago; L'Italiana in Algeri; Maometto II; Semiramide; Tancredi*

(BB) *** Naxos 8.553543. Podles, Hungarian State Op. Ch. & O, Morandi

The Hungarian mezzo, Ewa Podles, earlier the star singer in the complete set of Rossini's *Tancredi* on Naxos, is here even more impressive in one of the finest Rossini recitals in years. Hers is a rich and even voice which is not only weighty throughout its range but is also extraordinarily agile, dazzling in the elaborate divisions in all these coloratura numbers. She may find it hard to convey the fun and sparkle in Rossini, but the bright-eyed intensity provides fair compensation even with Cinderella or Rosina, and the cabaletta of Cinderella's final aria is breathtaking in its bravura at a formidably fast tempo. By contrast, this great voice is an ideal vehicle for the *opera seria* arias here, with the male characters very well characterized. First-rate accompaniment too.

Arias: *La Cenerentola: Nacqui all'affano. Guglielmo Tell: S'allontano alfin!; Selva opaca. Semiramide: Bel raggio lusinghier*

(M) **(*) EMI (ADD) 5 66464-2. Callas, Paris Conservatoire O, Rescigno – DONIZETTI: *Arias* **

If these performances from 1963–4 show a degree of cautiousness that rarely marked Callas's earlier work, this only goes to show how conscious she was of all the criticisms and how she did her utmost to avoid any real blots. In general she succeeds, often producing golden tone. Yet there is something less positive about the end result than in her earlier recordings of this repertory, and, more seriously, the performances do not have that refinement of detail which at her peak lit up so many phrases and made them unforgettable. Good documentation and full translations are provided.

Arias: *La Cenerentola: Non più mesta. La donna del lago: Mura felici … Elena! O tu, che chiamo. L'Italiana in Algeri: Cruda sorte! Amor tiranno! Pronti abbiamo … Pensa all*

patria. Otello: Deh! calma, o ciel. La pietra del paragone: Se l'Italie contrade … Se per voi lo care io torno. Tancredi: Di tanti palpiti. Stabat Mater: Fac ut portem

*** Decca 425 430-2. Bartoli, A. Schoenberg Ch., V. Volksoper O, Patanè

Cecilia Bartoli's first recital of Rossini showpieces brings a formidable demonstration not only of Bartoli's remarkable voice but of her personality and artistry, bringing natural warmth and imagination to each item without ever quite making you smile with delight. Yet there are not many Rossini recitals of any vintage to match this. Vocally, the one controversial point to note is the way that Bartoli articulates her coloratura with a half-aspirate, closer to the Supervia 'rattle' than anything else, but rather obtrusive. Accompaniments are exemplary, and Decca provided the luxury of a chorus in some of the items, with hints of staging. Full, vivid recording. Recommended.

'*Rossini Heroines*': **arias from:** *La donna del lago; Elisabetta, Regina d'Inghilterra; Maometto II; Le nozze di Teti e Peleo; Semiramide; Zelmira*

*** Decca 436 075-2. Bartoli, Ch. & O of Teatro la Fenice, Marin

Cecilia Bartoli follows up the success of her earlier Rossini recital-disc with this second brilliant collection of arias, mostly rarities. The tangy, distinctive timbre of her mezzo goes with a magnetic projection of personality to bring to life even formal passage-work, with all the elaborate coloratura bright and sparkling. The rarest item of all is an aria for the goddess Ceres from the classically based entertainment, *Le nozze di Teti e Peleo*, making a splendid showpiece. The collection is crowned by a formidably high-powered reading of *Bel raggio* from *Semiramide*, with Bartoli excitingly braving every danger.

ROTA, Nino (1911–79)

(i) *Castel del Monte (Ballad for Horn & Orchestra);* (ii) *Bassoon Concerto;* (iii) *Harp Concerto;* (iv) *Trombone Concerto*

🔗 *** Chan. 9954 (i) Corti; (ii) Carlini; (iii) Prandina; (iv) A. Conti; I Virtuosi Italiani, M. Conti

This is a delightful disc in every way, a collection of three concertos and one concertante work for horn demonstrating the unforced mastery of Rota, a composer remembered almost entirely for his film scores. Both in the *Harp Concerto* of 1947 and the three other works from much later in his career the outer movements regularly display a sparkle more often associated with French composers of the inter-war period, with chattering ostinato rhythms supporting jaunty melodies, and slow movements striking deeper, darker moods. In each Rota gives important solos to rival instruments, varying textures. This is fun music in the best sense, regularly concealing the ingenuity of the writing in the overall light-heartedness. The *Trombone Concerto* – the only one of the four works to have been recorded before – has exuberant outer movements framing a much longer *Lento* movement with a powerful climax. The *Bassoon Concerto* is the most original in structure, while the *Ballad for Horn and Orchestra, Castel del Monte* (a title taken from a medieval castle built by the Emperor Frederick II) builds up passionately over sharply contrasted sections. With brilliant playing from all the Italian soloists as well as the orchestra, this is a celebratory disc to parade the gifts of a long-neglected but warmly approachable composer, helped by full, well-balanced sound.

Piano Concertos in C; E min.
**(*) Chan. 9681. Palumbo, I Virtuosi Italiani, Boni

The *E minor Concerto* (1960) is new to the catalogue. It begins (*Allegro tranquillo*) in an attractively melancholy way, somewhere between film music and Rachmaninov, and goes on in a similar vein for some 16 minutes, with occasional lively outbursts. It is all attractive, but goes on too long; it doesn't help that another melancholy movement follows, lacking the necessary contrast. The finale is lively enough and brings the work to a jolly conclusion. The performances and recording are good.

Film music: Il gattopardo; Guerra e pace; La strada; Waterloo
(BB) *** EMI Encore 5 74987-2. Monte Carlo PO, Gelmetti

Nino Rota's film music is arranged here into four entertaining orchestral suites. His late-romantic style is appealing and interesting enough to stand on its own. The brooding drama of *Il gattopardo* is rather telling, as is the often quirky music to *La strada*, which includes among its eight diverse numbers a lively *Rhumba* and a circus sequence with a 'madman's violin'. The finale, *Zampano Alone in Tears*, brings some particularly vivid writing, and when the solo trumpet enters the effect is quite haunting, while the opening of *Zampano's Anger* sounds curiously like *The Rite of Spring*. La Rosa di Novgorod from *Guerra e pace* has an attractive, melancholy beauty, and the lilting waltz from *Waterloo* is another highlight. The performances and recordings are first class, and this inexpensive CD is tempting enough for those wanting to explore this composer's film music.

Symphonies 1 in G; 2 in F (Tarantina – Anni di pellegrinaggio)
*** BIS CD 970. Norrköping SO, Ruud

The *First Symphony* (1935–9) shows the imprint of Stravinsky, Copland, Hindemith and even Sibelius. It is well scored and often inventive. The *Second* (subtitled *Tarantina – Anni di pellegrinaggio*, alluding to the period he spent in Taranto, southern Italy, as a teacher) is even more indebted to Copland. They are thoroughly accessible pieces which engage the interest not only of the listener but also the Norrköping players and their Norwegian conductor. Good sound.

ROTT, Hans (1858–84)

Symphony in E
(BB) *** Hyp. Helios CDH 55140. Cincinnati Philh. O, Samuel

It is astonishing to encounter in Hans Rott's *Symphony* ideas that took root in Mahler's *First* and *Fifth* symphonies. Structurally the work is original, each movement getting progressively longer, the finale occupying nearly 25 minutes. But the music is full of good ideas and, anticipations of Mahler apart, has a profile of its own. The Cincinnati Philharmonia are a student orchestra who produce extraordinarily good results under Gerhard Samuel. The recording is good. Readers should investigate this bargain reissue.

ROUSE, Christopher (born 1949)

(i) Flute Concerto; Phaeton; Symphony 2
☛ *** Telarc CD 80452. (i) Wincenc; Houston SO, Eschenbach

The remarkable five-movement *Flute Concerto*, commissioned by the present soloist, followed two years after Rouse's *Trombone Concerto*. The beautiful first and last movements, with their serene, soaring solo line, are connected thematically, and share the Gaelic title *Anhran* ('Song'). They frame two faster, much more dissonant and rhythmically unpredictable movements. The kernel of the work is the gripping central *Elegia*, written in response to the terrible murder of the two-year-old James Bulger by two ten-year-old schoolboys. Rouse introduces a rich, Bach-like chorale, which moves with a wake-like solemnity towards a central explosion of passionate despair. Throughout, the solo writing demands great bravura and intense emotional commitment from the flautist, which is certainly forthcoming here.

The *Second Symphony* is a three-part structure, with the outer movements again using identical material to frame the anguished central slow movement. In the composer's words that forms a 'prism' through which the mercurial opening material is 'refracted' to yield the angry, tempestuous finale. The desperately grieving *Adagio* is another threnody for a personal friend and colleague, Stephen Albert, killed in a car accident in 1992. *Phaeton* is a savage, explosive early work (1986), which could hardly be more different from the tone poem of Saint-Saëns. Helios's sun chariot, immediately out of his son's control, charges its way across the heavens with horns roistering, and is very quickly blown out of the sky by Zeus's thunderbolt. Performances here are excellent, very well played and recorded, and the *Flute Concerto* is unforgettable.

(i) Violin Concerto; (ii) Der Gerettete Alberich (Fantasy for Solo Percussion and Orchestra). Rapture
(N) **(*) Ondine ODE 1016-2. (i) Lin; (ii) Glennie; Helsinki PO, Segerstam

This is all music which, one feels, would work far better in a large concert hall than reproduced for domestic listening. At a first hearing, the opening of *Der Gerettete Alberich* brings a brief Wagnerian double-take before Evelyn Glennie makes her entry. If not offering the visual spectacle of James MacMillan's *Veni, veni, Emmanuel*, and not to be taken too seriously, Rouse eagerly laminates Glennie's virtuosity into a spectacular biographical backcloth, with Alberich portrayed as a tragic figure in the central 'tableau' and a frenzied finale suggesting his physical and mental collapse, which unleashes a wild virtuoso percussion cadenza-break. *Rapture* begins in a glow of pastoral euphoria, but the mood becomes increasingly ecstatic, with a gradual increase of tempo used to create another big climax. Rouse's ambitious *Violin Concerto*, which comes last on the disc, then immediately confronts the listener with the diminutive solo voice of the violin singing a gentle barcarolle, but soon enveloped in a hugely dramatic, very loud, percussion-laced orchestral tutti. This contrast is the more disconcerting as Cho-Liang Lin's solo timbre as recorded here is so small, though his playing is tonally exquisite. The *Toccata* second movement is a Rondo demanding great solo bravura (and orchestral virtuosity too). Here the scoring is more economical, but the orchestral outbursts, boldly rhythmic, regularly return and, after a brief return to the elegiac mood of the barcarolle, it is the orchestra which has the last word. The performances are obviously expert and powerfully dedicated, and the recording is wide-ranging and spacious, but this is not a collection for aural fainthearts.

ROUSSEAU, Jean-Jacques (1712–78)

Le Devin du village (complete)
(B) *** EMI 5 75266-2 (2). Micheau, Gedda, Roux, Ch.
Raymond St-Paul, Louis de Froment CO, Froment –
GRETRY: *Richard Coeur-de-Lion* **(*)

The one-act Intermezzo, *Le Devin du village* (*The Village Soothsayer*), is Rousseau's most celebrated musical work, written in 1752, an unpretentious piece in what he conceived as the Italian style of the day, which he vigorously supported against the French, even though he here uses a French text. Starting with an overture in the Italian style, fast-slow-fast, it is charming in a plain and straightforward style, hardly original, and the baldness of the writing is rather underlined in this performance with continuo in bare chords. The 25 sections, mostly very short indeed, last well under an hour, offering a simple story of the soothsayer reconciling the estranged lovers, for a price. All three soloists are first rate, with Micheau at her most seductive, and the young Gedda heady-toned. This now returns to the EMI label coupled with Grétry but with no texts provided.

ROUSSEL, Albert (1869–1937)

Bacchus et Ariane, Op. 43: Suites 1 & 2; (i) Aeneas (ballet; complete)
☛ ✪ (M) *** Erato (ADD) 2564 60576-2. O Nat. de l'ORTF, Martinon, (i) with Ch.

Praise be! Erato have at last released Martinon's classic (1969) version of *Bacchus et Ariane* on CD. It is a thrilling performance and, compared with Dutoit's version on the same label, finds the latter sounding tame by comparison. Martinon's energy and momentum do not smudge Roussel's dense orchestration, and there is both inner life and outer drive here: the quiet passages are held raptly, with both tension and atmosphere. Splendid remastered sound, too, much better than it ever was on LP. The coupling of *Aeneas* (a much rarer work) is ideal. It was composed after *Bacchus* and based on a libretto by the Belgian poet Joseph Weterings, depicting the destiny of the founder of Rome; it is hardly less compelling and is undeniably powerful. It is laid out in Roussel's characteristic rich textures and orchestrated sumptuously, with the chorus playing an important role. There is no lack of vigorous imagination, both rhythmically and harmonically during its 40 minutes, ending with a triumphant hymn 'to his glory and the glory of Rome'. The only reservation is that *Aeneas* has only one cue. But, along with Munch's accounts of the *Third* and *Fourth Symphonies* on Erato, this is a must for anyone remotely interested in this composer.

Bacchus et Ariane (complete ballet), Op. 43; Le Festin de l'araignée (The Spider's Feast), Op. 17
☛ ✪ *** Chan. 9494. BBC PO, Tortelier

Tortelier offers the best *Bacchus et Ariane* yet – and what a marvellously inventive and resourceful score it is. The BBC Philharmonic play with tremendous zest and give a sensitive and atmospheric account of *Le Festin de l'araignée*. They offer us the complete banquet, not just the chosen dishes on the set menu! Splendid recording and performances of rewarding

and colourful music that deserves to be more widely heard.

Bacchus et Ariane: Suite 2; Sinfonietta for Strings, Op. 52; Symphonies 3 in G min., Op. 42; 4 in A, Op. 53
*** Testament (ADD) SBT 1239. Paris Conservatoire O, Cluytens

These recordings from the mid-1960s still sound very good and in some ways remain unchallenged. The sound is reverberant but detail emerges clearly. Cluytens has a splendid grasp of the energy and character of both symphonies, and in *Bacchus et Ariane* is scarcely less impressive than in his magical *Le Festin de l'araignée* reviewed below. Strongly recommended – for many this will be a first choice.

Le Festin de l'araignée (The Spider's Feast), Op. 17
*** Testament (ADD) SBT 1238. Paris Conservatoire O, Cluytens – BIZET: *La Jolie Fille de Perth*; RAVEL: *Daphnis*, etc. **(*)

Cluytens's 1963 recording of *Le Festin de l'araignée* remains in a class of its own: it has never been surpassed. There is tremendous atmosphere and delicacy of feeling. The recording was made in the rather reverberant Salle Wagram, but every strand is beautifully transparent and the orchestral texture expertly balanced with a lifelike perspective. This magical score strikes a strong spell, and this is one of Cluytens's finest recordings.

Le Festin de l'araignée, Op. 17; Symphony 2 in B flat, Op. 23
☛ (M) *** Erato (ADD) 2564 60577-2. O Nat. de l'ORTF, Martinon

Martinon fully captures the brooding atmosphere of Roussel's *Second Symphony*, and from the very opening bars the listener's attention is caught and held. This is one of the most gripping accounts available, with the richness of the writing and its inner vitality fully realized, ensuring total conviction. The lighter scoring of the magical *Le Festin de l'araignée* provides the perfect contrast, and the ballet receives a similar, totally idiomatic performance, with all the subtleties and nuances vividly caught. The remastered sound is very good for its date (1969) and this CD should be snapped up quickly: for some reason these outstanding Martinon performances never seem to stay in the catalogue for long.

Suite in F, Op. 33
(N) (M) *** Mercury **SACD** (ADD) 475 6183. Detroit SO, Paray – CHABRIER: *Bourrée fantasque*, etc. ***

The Mercury recording dates from 1957. With Paray on top form, the music generates plenty of adrenalin, with the closing *Gigue* especially lively and exciting. The new SACD transfer brings the benefit of greater warmth, and undoubtedly the sound overall is enhanced.

Symphonies 3 in G min.; 4 in A
(M) **(*) Warner Elatus 0927 46730-2. LOP, Munch

Another Erato disc from the LP era that makes a most welcome return to the catalogue, here on CD for the first time. Munch's coupling with the Lamoureux Orchestra dates from 1965 and had the benefit of infinitely better orchestral playing and greater commitment than its earlier Decca rival (Ansermet and the SRO, made in the earliest days of stereo). These are invigorating performances, well worth the money, and although the recording is not as rich or as refined as the finest modern discs, it is perfectly acceptable at mid-price. Although Munch's performances do not eclipse memories of

Bernstein in No. 3 and Karajan in No. 4, they are marvellously exhilarating and powerful.

(i) *Symphonies 3–4;* (ii) *Bacchus et Ariane: Suite 2*
(B) (**(*)) RCA 2-CD (ADD; mono) 74321 84601-2 (2). (i) R.
    France PO, Janowski; (ii) Boston SO, Munch – MESSIAEN:
    Turangalîla Symphony ***

Symphonies 3; 4 in A, Op. 53; Bacchus et Ariane: Suite 2;
Sinfonietta for String Orchestra, Op. 52
(N) (M) **(*) Chan. 10217X. Detroit SO, Järvi

Neeme Järvi's account of the *Third Symphony* has an engaging vitality and character, and the playing of the Detroit orchestra is highly responsive. In the slow movement he indulges in a rather steep accelerando after the fugal section. Likewise his finale feels too fast. But it is a committed performance. Some may find the acoustic a shade too resonant, but the overall balance is very natural and pleasing and this is certainly very recommendable, given the superior sound and Järvi's obvious enthusiasm for this repertoire.

Janowski has a natural feeling for the Roussel idiom, and his performances of the symphonies are well worth having. Perhaps the *Scherzo* of the *Third* is a shade too fast, but in all other respects his readings cannot be faulted. The digital recording has plenty of presence, body and detail and this coupling is definitely preferable to Järvi on Chandos. As for the new transfer of Munch's 1952 mono account of the *Second Suite* from Roussel's ballet, the sound is little short of amazing in its colour and ambient bloom. The Boston Orchestra was still under Koussevitzky's spell at the time and the playing is quite electrifying. Munch re-recorded it twice during the 1960s, but never with greater brilliance and luminosity than here. A few bars are missing, perhaps due to the original tapes being damaged, or Munch himself may have made a cut in performance.

ROUTH, Francis (born 1927)

Clarinet Quintet
*** Redcliffe RR 010. Redcliffe Ens. – BLISS: *Clarinet*
    Quintet; RAWSTHORNE: *Clarinet Quartet* ***

Routh's *Quintet* was written for Nicholas Cox, who plays it with great skill and understanding. Its variety of mood makes up for the melodic fragmentation, and its invention is lively throughout. Excellent recording.

PIANO MUSIC

(i) *Celebration; Elegy;* (ii) *Scenes for Piano: III, Angels of*
Albion, Op. 64; IV, Bretagne, Op. 68
*** Redcliffe RR 018. (i) Jacob; (ii) Dimitrova

Francis Routh has sought to combine a serial element in his music with a tonal centre, and in the earliest piece here, *Celebration* (1984), and the two sets of scenes for piano, he achieves this by using the whole tone scale with the addition of the perfect fourth. *Celebration* is a complex but exhilarating pianistic showpiece. Brilliantly played by Jeffrey Jacob, the relentless toccata-like vigour of the outer sections moderates in the semi-lyrical middle section, but the rhythmically insistent writing predominates. The result is pianistically dazzling, but wearing. *Elegy* (1985) is a transcription of a movement of an earlier *String Trio* (1972). The music is dedicated to the memory of the composer's infant son, who

died from rheumatoid arthritis. Its impetus derives from a single, hauntingly recurring melodic fragment. The composer acknowledges the obvious association with Chopin's *Berceuse*, and Jeffrey Jacob plays it with simple dedication.

The earlier *Scenes for Piano III, Angels of Albion* (1995) is inspired by the poetry of William Blake, and each of the five movements is prefaced by a brief quotation from Blake, Victor Hugo or Siegfried Sassoon. Although concerned with the conflict of the First World War, the last three sections – *To the Evening Star, Night Music* and *Berceuse* – are imbued with serenity and consolation. Yet the central interlude of the *Berceuse* erupts into martial violence, as the composer remembers the Christmas scene in 1914, when the soldiers threw down their arms and, during a brief respite, sang carols together in no-man's land. Then the killing began again.

The *Scenes for Piano IV*, subtitled *Bretagne*, is much more immediate in its colouristic appeal. The rather angular theme proves very fruitful. Much of the music is atmospheric, and the fourth movement, *Jour de Marché*, has something in common with the market scene in Mussorgsky's *Pictures*. In the *Cortège folklorique à Carnac* the composer moves into a more popular idiom, and the closing *Jour de fête* combines impressionistic and popular elements. Lora Dimitrova characterizes persuasively, and the recording is real and vivid.

ROWLEY, Alec (1892–1958)

Piano Concerto in D, Op. 49 (for strings & percussion)
(N) (BB) *** Naxos 8.557290. Donohoe, Northern Sinfonia –
    DARNTON; GERHARD; FERGUSON: *Piano Concertos* ***

Alec Rowley, best known for his educational music, also wrote more ambitious works, including this miniature *Concerto for Piano, Strings and Optional Percussion*. The writing is fluent and attractive, with sharp harmonies and cluster chords and a fanfare motif in the first movement, leading to open-air freshness in the slow movement and a jocular, easy-going finale. The addition of percussion adds piquancy to the writing. A welcome and rare addition to Peter Donohoe's imaginatively conceived collection of British piano concertos, brilliantly played and recorded.

RÓZSA, Miklós (1907–94)

(i) *Cello Concerto, Op. 32;* (ii) *Violin Concerto, Op. 24;* (i; ii)
Theme & Variations for Violin, Cello & Orchestra, Op. 29a
*** Telarc CD 80518. Atlanta SO, Levi; with (i) Harrell; (ii)
    McDuffie

These are splendid new recordings of Rózsa's highly romantic *Violin* and *Cello Concertos*, plus an enjoyable set of *Variations* in which both soloists join. The performances are superb and the recording is warm and detailed. Recommendable in every way.

(i) *String Quartets 1, Op. 22; 2, Op. 38;* (ii) *Sonata for 2*
Violins, Op. 15a
*** ASV CDDCA 1105. (i) Flesch Qt; (ii) Ibbotson, Gibbs

The *First String Quartet* was written in the late 1940s and revised and shortened in 1950. It is dedicated to Peter Ustinov, who was playing Nero in the film *Quo vadis* for which Rósza composed the score. It is a rewarding score, finely wrought and civilized, which improves as you get to know it better. There are reminders of Rózsa's kinship with Bartók and with Debussy in the slow movement. The *Second Quartet* is much later, completed in 1981, again the product of a cultured musical mind. Perhaps not as distinctively individual as, say, the Kodály *Second Quartet* but again eminently well worth getting to know. The *Sonata for Two Violins* is an early piece from 1933, which Rósza overhauled in 1973 and which the leader and violist of the Flesch play with spirit. Altogether an interesting and worthwhile issue, very well played and well if perhaps forwardly recorded.

RUBBRA, Edmund (1901–86)

(i) *Sinfonia concertante, Op. 38; A Tribute, Op. 56;* (ii) *The Morning Watch, Op. 55;* (iii) *Ode to the Queen, Op. 83*

*** Chan. 9966. BBC Nat. O of Wales, Hickox; with (i) Shelley; (ii) BBC Nat. Ch. of Wales; (iii) Bickley

Originally issued in harness with the *First Symphony*, the *Sinfonia concertante* was composed just before it, though the form in which we know it is the revision Rubbra made in the 1940s. Its beautiful opening almost anticipates the *Piano Concerto in G major*, but it is the searching and thoughtful finale, a prelude and fugue dedicated to the memory of Rubbra's teacher Gustav Holst who had died in 1934, which makes the strongest impression. Howard Shelley is a superb advocate and it is difficult to imagine a better performance. *The Morning Watch* is Rubbra at his most inspired. The text comes from the seventeenth-century metaphysical poet Henry Vaughan, and the music matches its profundity and eloquence. It dates from 1946, and so comes roughly half way between the *Fourth* and *Fifth Symphonies*. (It originally appeared in harness with the *Ninth*.)

The *Tribute* is to Vaughan Williams, one of three commissions (the others were Constant Lambert's *Aubade* and *One Morning in Spring* by Patrick Hadley), and the *Ode to the Queen* was commissioned by the BBC to celebrate the Coronation of the present Queen and is Rubbra's only song-cycle with full orchestra. He set three poems by Richard Crashaw, Sir William d'Avenant and Thomas Campion, in which inspiration runs high. Susan Bickley is the excellent soloist and Hickox is as always a dedicated interpreter of music that obviously means much to him.

Symphonies 1–8 *(Hommage à Teilhard de Chardin)*; (i) 9 *(Sinfonia Sacra)*. 10–11

*** Chan. 9944 (5). BBC Nat. O of Wales, Hickox; (i) with Dawson, D. Jones, Roberts, BBC Nat. Ch. of Wales

As can be seen, Chandos have collected all eleven Rubbra symphonies in a box of five CDs offered for the price of four, which can be strongly recommended to those collectors who have not already begun investing in the individual records. No doubt the couplings on those earlier issues will also reappear separately.

Symphony 1, Op. 44; (i) *Sinfonia concertante for Piano & Orchestra, Op. 38. A Tribute, Op. 56*

*** Chan. 9538. BBC Nat. O of Wales, Hickox; (i) with Shelley

The first movement of the symphony is fiercely turbulent; a French dance tune, a *Perigourdine*, forms the basis of the middle movement, but the pensive, inward-looking finale, which is as long as the first two movements put together, is the most powerful and haunting of the three. The *Sinfonia concertante* is no less symphonic in character and substance. The opening *Fantasia* begins with a reflective lento passage which anticipates the tranquility of the *G major Piano Concerto*, though it is the final *Prelude and Fugue*, composed in

memory of his teacher, Gustav Holst, which lingers longest in the memory. Howard Shelley is an inspired soloist and the sometimes thick textures of the symphony sound remarkably lucid in Richard Hickox's hands. The BBC National Orchestra of Wales play splendidly and the Chandos sound is in the best traditions of the house.

Symphonies 2 in D, Op. 45; 6, Op. 80

*** Chan. 9481. BBC Nat. O of Wales, Hickox

Richard Hickox and his fine players do make the score of the *Second Symphony* more lucid than Handley's Lyrita recording from the 1970s. The performance is meticulously prepared and yet flows effortlessly, and the slow movement speaks with great eloquence. The heart of the *Sixth Symphony* is the serene *Canto* movement which is not dissimilar in character to the *Missa in honorem Sancti Dominici*. It is arguably the finest of the cycle after No. 9, and Hickox and his fine players do it proud. So, too, do the Chandos engineers.

Symphonies 3; 7 in C, Op. 88

☞ ✿ *** Chan. 9634. BBC Nat. O of Wales, Hickox

The *Third Symphony* (1939) once enjoyed repertory status – at least in BBC programmes – but completely fell out of establishment favour from the 1960s through to the late 1980s. It has a pastoral character and a certain Sibelian feel to it (woodwind in thirds), though Rubbra is always himself. In the final movement there is even a hint of Elgar in the fourth variation. Hickox's is a more eloquent and ultimately more convincing account than the older Philharmonia version under Norman Del Mar on Lyrita.

The *Seventh Symphony* (1956) receives a performance of real power from Hickox and his Welsh orchestra. This is music that speaks of deep and serious things and its opening paragraphs are among the most inspired that Rubbra ever penned. Noble performances and excellent recorded sound.

Symphonies 4; 10 *(Sinfonia da camera), Op. 145; 11, Op. 153*

*** Chan. 9401. BBC Nat. O of Wales, Hickox

Richard Hickox offers a particularly imaginative account of the *Eleventh Symphony* in one movement (1979), which is new to the catalogue. Like so much of Rubbra's music, it has an organic continuity and inner logic that are immediately striking, and in common with the *Tenth Symphony*, also in one movement, its textures are spare and limpid. Hickox's account of the *Fourth Symphony* is totally convincing. The Chandos recording is excellent in every respect, with plenty of warmth and transparency of detail.

Symphony 5 in B flat, Op. 63

(M) *** Chan. 6576. Melbourne SO, Schönzeler – BLISS: *Checkmate* ***; TIPPETT: *Little Music* **(*)

Symphonies 5; 8 *(Hommage à Teilhard de Chardin), Op. 132;* (i) *Ode to the Queen, Op. 83*

*** Chan. 9714. BBC Nat. O of Wales, Hickox; (i) with Bickley

Richard Hickox's reading of the *Fifth Symphony* is easily the finest and most penetrating; the slow movement has depth and, thanks to a magnificent recording, a greater clarity than either of its predecessors. Tempi are unerringly judged and he brings great breadth and gravitas to the very opening of the work. He gives, too, a more intense account of the *Eighth (Hommage à Teilhard de Chardin)* than we have had before. *Ode to the Queen*, commissioned by the BBC for the Coronation in 1953, is a setting of three poems, variously by Richard Crashaw, Sir William d'Avenant and Thomas Campion, for mezzo-soprano and full orchestra and is strong in inspiration. Excellent performances and outstanding recorded sound from the Chandos/BBC team.

Although the Melbourne orchestra is not in the very top division, they play this music for all they are worth, and the strings have a genuine intensity and lyrical fervour that compensate for the opaque effect of the octave doublings. Altogether, though, this is an imposing performance which reflects credit on all concerned. The recording is well balanced and lifelike; but the ear perceives that the upper range is rather restricted.

(i) Symphony 9 (Sinfonia sacra), Op. 140. The Morning Watch for Chorus & Orchestra, Op. 55

☞ 🎧 *** Chan. 9441. (i) Dawson, Jones, Roberts; BBC Nat. Ch. & O of Wales, Hickox

The Ninth Symphony, arguably Rubbra's greatest work, is an unqualified masterpiece. Subtitled The Resurrection, it was inspired by a painting of Donato Bramante and has something of the character of the Passion, which the three soloists relate in moving fashion. The Morning Watch, a setting of Henry Vaughan for chorus and orchestra, which was originally to have formed part of a choral fifth symphony, is another score of great nobility, which has taken even longer (half a century) to be recorded. Both works are superbly served here by all these fine musicians, and the Chandos recording is no less magnificent.

Symphony 10 (Sinfonia da camera), Op. 145; Improvisations on Virginal Pieces by Giles Farnaby, Op. 50; A Tribute to Vaughan Williams on his 70th Birthday (Introduction & Danza alla fuga), Op. 56

(M) *** Chan. 6599. Bournemouth Sinf., Schönzeler

Rubbra's Tenth Symphony is a short, one-movement work, whose opening has a Sibelian seriousness and a strong atmosphere that grip one immediately. Schönzeler is scrupulously attentive to dynamic nuance and internal balance, while keeping a firm grip on the architecture as a whole. The 1977 recording has been impressively remastered. It has a warm acoustic and reproduces natural, well-placed orchestral tone. The upper range is crisply defined. The Farnaby Variations is a pre-war work whose charm Schönzeler uncovers effectively, revealing its textures to best advantage. Loth to Depart, the best-known movement, has gentleness and vision in this performance. Strongly recommended. Even though this CD plays for only 40 minutes, it remains indispensable.

CHAMBER MUSIC

The Buddha (incidental music: suite, arr. Croft); Duo for Cor Anglais & Piano, Op. 156; Meditazioni sopra 'coeurs désolés', Op. 67b; Phantasy for 2 Violins & Piano; Oboe Sonata in C, Op. 100; Piano Trios 1, Op. 68 (one movement); 2, Op 138

(M) *** Dutton Lab. CDLX 7106. Endymion Ens. (members)

Rubbra had a lifelong interest in the East, and his incidental music for Clifford Bax's radio play on the life of the Buddha makes a strong impression. The Duo for Cor Anglais and Piano is a late work, written in 1980 after the Eleventh Symphony, with a deeply felt, elegiac and valedictory character. The Meditazioni sopra 'coeurs désolés' (1949), originally for recorder and harpsichord, is a set of variations on Josquin's chanson. The wonderful Oboe Sonata, written in 1958 for

Evelyn Rothwell (Lady Barbirolli), is the best known of the seven pieces on this disc, and Melinda Maxwell and Michael Dussek successfully capture its nobility of spirit. The Phantasy for Two Violins and Piano (1927) was Rubbra's first published work and is finely wrought in every way. The First Piano Trio was written in 1950 and has the quiet seriousness of late Fauré and the same naturalness of speech; there is no trace of rhetoric or expressive emphasis, qualities which hold true of this dignified and selfless performance. No. 2 was composed 20 years later and is sparer than its predecessor. A thoroughly recommendable anthology, admirably recorded.

(i) Cello Sonata in G min.; String Quartets 1 in F min., Op. 35; 3, Op. 112. Improvisation for Unaccompanied Cello

☞ *** Dutton CDLX 7123. Dante Qt (members); with (i) Dussek

String Quartets 2 in E flat, Op. 73; 4, Op. 150. (i) Lyric Movement for String Quartet and Piano, Op. 24. Meditations on a Byzantime Hymn 'O Quando in Cruce', Op. 117a

☞ *** Dutton CDLX 7114. Dante Qt, with (i) Dussek

The G minor Cello Sonata of 1946 is one of Rubbra's finest chamber works, and it is beautifully played here, but it is the inclusion of the four String Quartets that is particularly valuable. They have been shamefully neglected on record, and cover an even longer period of Rubbra's creative career than the symphonies. The first version of the F minor Quartet comes from 1933, before the First Symphony, while the Fourth dates from 1977. The First pays homage to Vaughan Williams, 'whose persistent interest' in the original 1933 version led to a complete revision of the piece in 1946, while the Fourth is dedicated to Robert Simpson. There is a nobility and breadth of line that make these pieces resonate in the memory. The Third, written in 1963, moves with a tremendous sense of purpose and expressive substance, as does the elegiac Fourth. Dutton deserves many congratulations in making them available in such excellent performances together with other chamber pieces, some of which, such as Lyric Movement for Piano Quintet and the Meditations on a Byzantine Hymn for two violas, will be new to most collectors. Recommended with enthusiasm.

Oboe Sonata in C, Op. 100

(B) *** Hyp Helios CDH 55008. Francis, Dickenson –
BOUGHTON: Pastoral; HARTY: 3 Pieces; HOWELLS: Sonata ***

Rubbra's Oboe Sonata in C, Op. 100 has a songful, rhapsodic opening movement, which leads naturally into the soulful central Elegie; the fluent finale is a rondo with a semi-oriental melodic line. The performance here is of quality, but these artists are not helped by the forward balance and the background resonance. It is important not to have the volume level set too high.

(i) Violin Sonatas 1, Op. 11; 2, Op. 31; 3, Op. 133; 4 Pieces, Op. 29. Variations on a Phrygian Theme for Solo Violin, Op. 105

(M) *** Dutton Lab. CDLX 7101. Osostowicz; (i) with Dussek

The Second Violin Sonata, with Albert Sammons and Gerald Moore, was the first Rubbra work to reach the gramophone. Although Frederick Grinke and the composer himself recorded it for Decca in the early days of LP, there has been no decent modern recording. Krysia Osostowicz and Michael Dussek are worth waiting for, since not only the recording but also, surprisingly, the performance eclipses both its distinguished predecessors. The *First Sonata*, Op. 11, from the 1920s, is heavily indebted to Debussy and Rubbra's teacher, Gustav Holst. The *Third* is a sinewy work from 1963, formidably argued and finely laid out for the medium. The Op. 29 *Pieces* are really teaching material, as is the set of *Variations* for violin alone.

PIANO MUSIC

Fantasy Fugue, Op. 161; Fukagawa (Deep River); Introduction & Fugue, Op. 19; Introduction, Aria & Fugue, Op. 104; Invention on the Name of Haydn, Op. 160; Nemo Fugue; Prelude & Fugue on a Theme of Cyril Scott, Op. 69; 8 Preludes, Op. 131; 4 Studies, Op. 139; (i) 9 Teaching Pieces, Op. 74
(M) *** Dutton CDBP 9712. M. Dussek; (i) with R. Dussek

Considering that he was an outstanding pianist, Rubbra wrote relatively little for his instrument. Apart from the seraphic *Piano Concerto in G major*, of which we badly need a new recording, and the *Sinfonia concertante* the present disc contains the lot. Although all these pieces do exist in various other versions, Michael Dussek's fine survey is undoubtedly the one to have. Artistic matters apart, it also has the benefit of vivid and truthful recorded sound.

VOCAL MUSIC

(i) *Advent Cantata: Natum Maria Virgine, Op. 136. Inscape, Op. 122;* (i) *4 Mediaeval Latin Lyrics, Op. 32; Song of the Soul, Op. 78; Veni, creator spiritus, Op. 130*
☛ ✿ *** Chan. 9847. ASMF Ch., City of L. Sinf., Hickox; (i) with Varcoe

Having put us in their debt with their survey of the symphonies, Richard Hickox and Chandos now turn to the choral music. Three of the pieces here are first recordings. *Natum Maria Virgine* comes from the late 1960s when Rubbra was working on the *Sinfonia sacra*. As with all his vocal music it is beautifully crafted, its polyphony growing effortlessly and inevitably. *Song of the Soul* comes from 1951, the year of the *Second String Quartet*, and has dipped under the horizon as far as both concert and recorded performances are concerned, as has the *Veni, creator spiritus*, another late and inspiring piece. The only work otherwise available, now that John Carol Case's Decca account of *Inscape* (1966) has disappeared from view, is the *Four Mediæval Latin Lyrics* with David Wilson-Johnson as soloist and the late Hans-Hubert Schönzeler conducting (EMI). Although that has done sterling service, Stephen Varcoe and Hickox are to be preferred. The Abelard setting, the fourth of the *Mediæval Latin Lyrics*, sounds more beautiful. *Inscape*, which is set to the words of Gerard Manley Hopkins, has a quiet eloquence and depth that puts it among Rubbra's most memorable works in any genre. Hickox has real feeling for the mystical side of Rubbra and conveys his elevation of feeling. The recording has amplitude yet clarity and is expertly and naturally balanced. A very special disc.

The Beatitudes, Op. 109; 4 Carols; Lauda Sion, Op. 110; 5 Madrigals, Op. 51; 2 Madrigals, Op. 52; Mass in Honour of St Teresa of Avila; Missa à 3 voci, Op. 98; 5 Motets, Op. 37
*** ASV CDDCA 1093. Voces Sacrae, Martin

This CD is devoted to Rubbra's *a cappella* music and ranges from the early *Motets* of 1934, settings of Herrick, Donne and Vaughan, through to his last Mass, the *Mass in Honour of St Teresa of Avila*, which was composed in 1981, five years before his death. It also includes the spare and austere *Missa à 3 voci* from the early 1960s; both these Masses are new to the catalogue. When you think that Rubbra belongs to the same generation as Tippett, Walton and Shostakovich, you realize just how original a voice he has. His music is not of our time but could come from any other, and the two Masses recorded here have a sense of the eternal verities. The most important work here is the *Mass in Honour of St Teresa of Avila*, a work of haunting beauty and directness. The *Lauda Sion* (1960) is another work that leaves one feeling cleansed. Judy Martin and Voces Sacrae give sympathetic and idiomatic accounts of all these pieces, and the sound is natural and present.

(i) *Festival Gloria, Op. 94. Magnificat and Nunc Dimittis in A flat, Op. 65; Missa in honorem Sancti Dominici, Op. 66; Salutation, Op. 82; Tenebrae, Op. 72*
**(*) Paraclete Press Gloria Dei Cantores GDCD 024. Gloria Dei Cantores, Patterson; (i) with Jordan (organ). Available from: www.paraclete-press.com

It is good to see Rubbra's sacred music receiving the advocacy of an American choir and a very good one, too. Gloria Dei Cantores ('*Singers to the glory of God*') come from Cape Cod, Massachusetts, and have already given us an outstanding CD of the music of William Mathias (GDCD 026). With the exception of the *Salutation*, Op. 82, written for the Queen's accession, and the *Festival Gloria*, Op. 94, the repertoire is duplicated on the Naxos disc from St John's College, Cambridge.

However, Gloria Dei Cantores offer dedicated, well-prepared performances, although the sopranos do not have the accuracy and tonal purity of the boys' voices of St John's, nor their breadth of dynamic range and colour. Good though the *Missa in honorem Sancti Dominici* is (it has a mystical dedication that is impressive), it is outclassed by the Cambridge Choir, not only in the security of the soprano lines but also in the quality of tonal blend. In the *Magnificat and Nunc Dimittis in A flat* it is rather overpowering. The balance, which is mostly excellent, compares unfavourably with the more discrete relationship between singers and organ in Cambridge. But both the *Salutation* and the *Festival Gloria* are of great beauty, and the disc is worth acquiring for these works alone. But for those wanting the glorious *Tenebrae* and the *Dominican Mass*, the St John's College, Cambridge, CD is the one to have; for a third of the price the collector also has the bonus of the *Missa Cantuariensis*.

Songs: (i; ii) *A Hymn to the Virgin; The Jade Mountain; Jesukin; Mystery; Orpheus with his Lute; Rosa mundi.* Instrumental pieces: (ii; iii) *Discourse, Op. 127;* (iii) *Fukagawa; Improvisation, Op. 124.* (ii) Harp pieces: *Pezzo ostinato, Op. 102; Transformations, Op. 141*
*** ASV CDDCA 1036. (i) Chadwell; (ii) Perrett; (iii) Gill (with L. BERKELEY: *Nocturne for Harp;* HOWELLS: *Prelude ***)

The CD reflects Rubbra's lifelong interest in the Orient from the early *Fukagawa* (1929), an arrangement of a Japanese melody, to *The Jade Mountain* songs (1962). The two pieces for harp, the *Pezzo ostinato* and the *Transformations*, both reflect the fascination that Indian music exercised. They are both impressive – indeed, exalted is the word that springs to mind. Some of the very early pieces reflect the spell cast by Holst and Cyril Scott but the bulk of the music here finds him at his most individual. Tracy Chadwell sings ethereally though there is perhaps a little too much echo round her voice, but the harp pieces are both exquisitely played and could hardly be more authoritative. A most rewarding and recommendable issue.

Magnificat & Nunc Dimittis, Op. 65; Missa Cantuariensis, Op. 59; Missa in honorem Sancti Dominici; Tenebrae Motets, Op. 72: Nocturnos 1–3; (i) (Organ) Meditation, Op. 79; Prelude & Fugue, Op. 69

⊕ (BB) *** Naxos 8.555255. Ch. of St John's College, Cambridge, Robinson; (i) Houssart

The present inexpensive recording by Christopher Robinson and the Choir of St John's College, Cambridge, makes an excellent entry point into Rubbra's sacred music. The *Missa Cantuariensis* was composed for Canterbury Cathedral, whereas the *Missa in honorem Sancti Dominici* (1948) was written for the Catholic Rite. Both are crafted beautifully and elevated in feeling. The first *Nocturn* (which comprises three motets) of the *Tenebrae* was written in 1951, and a further two *Nocturnes* followed ten years later. They are anguished and eloquent expressions of faith. Do go on to explore the *Mass in Honour of St Teresa of Avila* and the *Mass for Three Voices* (on ASV) as they are among the most inspired works he wrote. This deeply satisfying recording is completed by the *Meditation* for organ, which was written for James Dalton, and Bernard Rose's transcription of the *Prelude and Fugue on a Theme of Cyril Scott*, a seventieth-birthday tribute to Rubbra's first teacher. The performances are quite outstanding and well recorded.

(i) Magnificat & Nunc Dimittis in A flat, Op. 65. Missa in honorem Sancti Dominici, Op. 66; 3 Hymn Tunes, Op. 114; 3 Motets, Op. 78

*** ASV CDDCA 881. Ch. of Gonville & Caius College, Cambridge, Webber; (i) Phillips (organ) – HADLEY: *Lenten cantata*, etc. ***

The most important work here is the *Missa in honorem Sancti Dominici* (1948), written at about the time of the *Fifth Symphony* and one of the most beautiful of twentieth-century *a cappella* choral pieces written in this or any other country. None of the other works on the disc is its equal. The performance by the Choir of Gonville & Caius College, Cambridge, under Geoffrey Webber is dedicated and sensitive. Excellent balance, though the organ is obtrusive, particularly so in the first of the Op. 78 *Motets*.

RUSSO, William (born 1928)

3 Pieces for Blues Band & Symphony Orchestra; Street Music, Op. 65

(M) ** DG (ADD) 463 665-2. Siegel-Schwall Band, San Francisco SO, Ozawa – GERSHWIN: *An American in Paris* **

William Russo has been an assiduous advocate of mixing jazz and blues traditions with the symphony orchestra, and *Street Music* has its attractive side. But despite the presence of Corky Siegel on harmonica, it is no more successful at achieving genuine integration than other pieces of its kind, and its half-hour span is far too long for the material it contains. The 1976 recording is excellent, though the close focus for the harmonica makes for some unattractive sound from Mr Siegel. *Three Pieces for Blues Band* represents another vigorous attempt at barrier-leaping and will appeal

to those who like such mixtures. To others it is likely to seem both over-sweet and over-aggressive (rather like the 1972 sound, which is both rich and fierce). Still, this is rare repertoire, although a curious choice for DG's 'Originals' label.

RUTTER, John (born 1945)

(i; ii) Suite antique (for flute and orchestra); (iii) 5 Childhood Lyrics (for unaccompanied choir); (ii; iii) Fancies; When Icicles Hang (for choir and orchestra)

*** Coll. COLCD 117. (i) Dobing, Marshall; (ii) City of L. Sinfonia; (iii) Soloists, Cambridge Singers; Composer

This whole collection is imbued with Rutter's easy melodic style and the touches of offbeat rhythm which he uses to give a lift to his lively settings. The *Antique Suite* (for flute, harpsichord and strings) opens with a serene *Prelude*, but includes a typically catchy *Ostinato*, a gay *Waltz* and a chirpy closing *Rondeau*. *Fancies* has a delightful *Urchins' Dance*, after the fairy style of Mendelssohn, and its *Riddle Song* has a most appealing lyrical melody. But the mood darkens for the closing *Bellman's Song*. Among the *Childhood Lyrics*, the settings of Edward Lear's *Owl and the Pussy-cat* and *Sing a Song of Sixpence* are particularly endearing.

The evocative *When Icicles Hang* brings characteristically winning scoring for the orchestral woodwind (Rutter loves flutes) and another fine melody in *Blow, Blow Thou Winter Wind*. The work ends happily in folksy style. Splendid performances throughout. Rutter is currently the most performed (by amateur choirs) of any living English composer, and no wonder. The performances here are excellent and so is the recording.

Anthems: All Things Bright and Beautiful; For the Beauty of the Earth; A Gaelic Blessing; God Be In My Head; The Lord Bless You and Keep You; The Lord is My Shepherd; O Clap Your Hands; Open Thou My Eyes; Praise Ye the Lord; A Prayer of St Patrick; (i) Gloria

*** Coll. COLCD 100; Cambridge Singers; (i) Philip Jones Brass Ens.; City of L. Sinfonia; composer

Rutter has a genuine gift of melody and his use of tonal harmony is individual and never bland. The resplendent *Gloria* is a three-part piece, and Rutter uses his brass to splendid and often spectacular effect. The anthems are diverse in style and feeling and, like the *Gloria*, have strong melodic appeal – the setting of *All Things Bright and Beautiful* is delightfully spontaneous. It is difficult to imagine the music receiving more persuasive advocacy than under the composer, and the recording is first class in every respect.

Christmas carols: Angels' Carol; Candlelight Carol; Carol of the Children; Christmas Lullaby; Donkey Carol; Dormi Jesu; Jesus Child; Love Came Down at Christmas; Mary's Lullaby; Nativity Carol; Sans Day Carol; Second Amen; Shepherd's Pipe Carol; Star Carol; There is a Flower; The Very Best Time of Year; What Sweeter Music; Wild Wood Carol.
Arrangements: Angel Tidings; Away in a Manger; I Wonder as I Wander; Silent Night

⊕ *** Hyp. CDA 67245. Polyphony, City of L. Sinfonia, Layton

John Rutter's larger-scale choral works, including the *Gloria*, *Requiem* and *Te Deum*, are among the most performed (by amateur choral societies throughout Britain and in America too) of any vocal works by a living British composer; but it is for his delightful carols that the composer will be especially remembered. 'They were my calling cards,' he says. 'You have to remember that the Christmas carol is one of the very few musical forms which allows classically trained musicians to feel it's permissible to write tunes!' And, as is shown again and again here, Rutter never had difficulty in coming up with a memorable melodic line, whether it be the *Shepherd's Pipe Carol*, with its characteristic flute writing, which opens the programme, or the deliciously perky *Donkey Carol*, with its catchy 5/8 syncopated rhythm, which closes it.

The twenty-two carols included here were composed in a steady stream over a period of three decades, with the charming *Dormi Jesu* dating from as recently as 1999. Rutter's writing is notable not only for its tunefulness and winning use of choral textures, but also for his always engaging orchestrations. I. M. has been playing Rutter's own Clare College recordings every Christmas since the 1970s, yet the present collection is the most comprehensive on record, and it is beautifully sung, played and recorded. But they were not written to be heard in a continuous sequence, rather to be juxtaposed with other carols; so to enjoy them at their best one needs to play them in small groups, or their melodic sweetness may tend to cloy. (Even so, this is perfect background music for Christmas Eve.)

(i; ii) *The Falcon*; (ii) 2 *Festival Anthems: O praise the Lord in Heaven; Behold, the Tabernacle of God*; (ii; iii) *Magnificat*
*** Coll. COLCD 114. (i) St Paul's Cathedral Choristers; (ii) Cambridge Singers, City of L. Sinfonia; (iii) with Forbes; all cond. composer

The Falcon was Rutter's first large-scale choral work. Its inspiration was a medieval poem, which is linked to the Crucifixion story, but the core of the piece is the mystical central *Lento*. The *Magnificat* has the usual Rutter stylistic touches, with a syncopated treatment of the opening *Magnificat anima mea*, and a joyous closing *Gloria Patri*. The two anthems are characteristically expansive and resplendent with brass. Fine performances and recording in the best Collegium tradition.

(i) *Mass of the Children. A Clare Benediction; I will sing with the Spirit; Look at the World; To Every thing there is a Season; Wings of the Morning; A cappella settings: Come down, O Love Divine; I my Best Beloved's am; Musica Dei dominum*
*** Coll. CSCD 129. (i) Lunn, Williams, Cantatas Youth Ch., Cambridge Singers, City of L. Sinfonia, composer

John Rutter's *Mass of the Children* has a characteristic simplicity of style and it immediately establishes his identity with the easily flexible musical phrase he has devised for the repetitions of the words '*Kyrie eleison*'. The light-hearted *Gloria* similarly is well conceived for a work designed for children's participation alongside adults. The *Sanctus* brings tripping flute arpeggios to decorate a flowing melodic line, the *Agnus Dei* is contrastingly sombre, and in the finale, in which each soloist interpolates a sung medieval prayer, children and adults again join together for the *Dona nobis pacem*. It is a work of genuine charm, yet not lacking substance, designed for wide popularity.

The other songs all have the immediacy of melodic flow and skilful orchestral colour we expect from Rutter's carols, with *Wings of the Morning* rhythmically catchy, *I will sing with the spirit* glowing with '*Alleluias*', and the *Clare Benediction* touchingly serene and tuneful. The three *a cappella* items

also show the composer at his most rewarding, notably the lovely *Musica Dei Dominum* with its flute obbligato and *Come down O Love Divine* for double choir, a richly harmonized setting of a fifteenth-century English text. Not surprisingly, performances are of the highest quality and the recording is finely balanced in a warm acoustic

3 *Musical Fables*: (i) *Brother Heinrich's Christmas*; (ii) *The Reluctant Dragon; The Wind in the Willows*
**(*) Coll. COLCD 115; City of L. Sinfonia; with (i) Kay, Cambridge Singers, composer; (ii) R. Baker, King's Singers, Hickox

Brother Heinrich's Christmas is a musical narrative with choir, telling the story of how one of the most famous of all carols was introduced late at night by the angels to Brother Heinrich, just in time for it to be included in the monks' Christmas Day service. It is all highly ingenuous but engagingly presented, and should appeal to young listeners who have enjoyed Howard Blake's *The Snowman*. The settings of the two famous Kenneth Grahame stories are no less tunefully communicative and include simulations of pop music of the 1940s (among other derivations), notably a Rodgers-style ballad which sentimentalizes the end of *The Wind in the Willows* episode, after Toad's escape from prison. All the music is expertly sung and played and blends well with the warmly involving narrative, splendidly done by Richard Baker.

Gloria; As the Bridegroom to His Chosen; Clare Benediction; Come Down, O Lord Divine; Go Forth into this World; I My Best-beloved's Am; Lord Make Me an Instrument of Thy Peace; Psalmfest: I Will Lift Up Mine Eyes; The Lord is My Light and My Salvation; Praise the Lord O My Soul. Te Deum; To Everything There Is a Season
*** Hyp. CDA 67259. Polyphony, Wallace Collection, City of L. Sinfonia, Layton

Framed by superb accounts of the *Gloria* and *Te Deum*, each with a magnificent brass contribution from the Wallace Collection, and given demonstration-standard sound-quality, this is one of the most attractive Rutter collections yet. Brass are used again to introduce the first of the three psalm settings taken from the nine-movement *Psalmfest*, followed by *I Will Lift Up My Eyes* introduced serenely by woodwind, which has much in common with Vaughan Williams's *Serenade to Music*. The third, *The Lord is My Light and My Salvation*, opens with a clarinet solo and has one of Rutter's most beguiling melodies. But everywhere here there is melody. *As the Bridegroom to His Chosen* has a chaste lyrical beauty and *Thy Perfect Love* soars gently, like one of Rutter's carols. Polyphony sing rapturously, with lovely blended tone, and the warmly persuasive accompaniments are ideally balanced within a pleasingly resonant but not blurring acoustic.

(i–iv) *Requiem*. Anthems: (i; iv) *Arise, shine*; (i) *Come down, O Love Divine*; (ii; v) *Musica Dei donum*; (i; iv) 2 *Blessings for Choir & Organ*; Organ Pieces: (iv) *Toccata in 7*; (iv; vi) *Variations on an Easter Theme for Organ Duet*
🎵 ✿ (BB) *** Naxos 8.557130. (i) Clare College, Cambridge, Ch.; (ii) L. Sinfonia; (iii) with Thomas; (iv) Rimmer (organ); (v) Jones; all cond. Brown; (vi) with Collon

(i) *Requiem*; (ii) *Magnificat*
(M) *** Coll. CSCD 504. (i) Ashton, Dean; (ii) Forbes; Cambridge Singers, City of L. Sinfonia, composer

(i) *Requiem. Cantata Domino;* (ii) *Cantus. Hymn to the Creator of light; Veni sancte spiritus; What Sweeter Music;* (ii) *Te Deum*

*** EMI 5 56605-2. King's College, Cambridge, Ch., Cleobury; with (i) Saklatvala, Harries, City of L. Sinfonia; (ii) The Wallace Collection

(i) *Requiem. Cantata Domino; Choral Fanfare; Draw on Sweet Night;* (ii) *Gaelic Blessing. God Be In My Head; Hymn to the Creator of Light; My True Love Hath My Heart;* (ii) *The Lord Bless You and Keep You. Open Thou Mine Eyes; A Prayer for Saint Patrick*

*** Hyp. CDA 66947. Polyphony, Layton; with (i) Manion; (ii) Bournemouth Sinf.

John Rutter's melodic gift, so well illustrated in his carols, is used in the simplest and most direct way to create a small-scale *Requiem* that is as beautiful and satisfying in its English way as the works of Fauré and Duruflé. The penultimate movement, a ripe setting of *The Lord is my Shepherd* with a lovely oboe obbligato, sounds almost like an anglicized *Song of the Auvergne.*

The newest Naxos recording of the *Requiem* tends to trump all previous versions, even the composer's own very fine account. Recorded in the expansive acoustic of Douai Abbey, Berkshire, it is very beautifully sung indeed, joyful in the *Sanctus* and darkly dramatic in the *Agnus Dei* with its steady drum beat. Elin Manahan Thomas is an ideal soloist singing the *Pie Jesu* with touching simplicity, and rising up celestially in the *Lux aeterna.* Christopher Hooker's oboe obbligato in *The Lord is my Shepherd* is comparably sensitive. The extra items are equally successful, the exultant Advent anthem, *Arise, Shine* contrasting with the opulent Howells-like piece for double choir, *Come down O Love Divine,* and the soaring Latin anthem, with its pastoral flute, Rutter's favourite woodwind instrument. The *Two Blessings,* with their easy melodic flow, are rather like Rutter's carols, and the pair of thematically linked organ voluntaries, the first immediately rhythmically catchy, the duet *Variations,* sonorous and unpredictable, round off the programme most satisfyingly. Both are very well played, indeed, and the recording is first class.

On Collegium Caroline Ashton's performance of the delightful *Pie Jesu* is wonderfully warm and spontaneous, most beautifully recorded on CD, with the equally glorious *Magnificat* setting (see above) making a superb bonus on this mid-priced reissue.

Both the EMI and Hyperion recordings are of high quality and both bring first-class digital sound. On EMI there is something special about hearing this music within the King's acoustic, and using boy trebles in the choir as well as for the two solos. At times there is an ethereal resonance here, although climaxes emerge strongly.

Polyphony uses women's voices (as does Rutter himself) in a choir of 25 voices. The balance is slightly more forward, and the result brings a radiant richness of sound which is hardly less enjoyable. Both choirs complete their programmes with some of Rutter's shorter choral works. Three of them – the memorable *Veni sancte spiritus, What Sweeter Music* and the *Cantus,* with its resonant brass accompaniment – were written for King's, but both choirs give us the refreshingly lively *Cantate Domino* and the remarkable *Hymn to the Creator of Light* for double chorus, which was written in memory of Herbert Howells but reminds one also of Tavener. The King's programme ends with the exultant *Te Deum;* Polyphony include the lovely *Gaelic*

Blessing and *Draw On Sweet Light,* plus Rutter's beautiful setting of the *Benediction,* which introduces one of his friendliest tunes.

RYBA, Jakob Jan (1765–1815)

Czech Christmas Mass; Missa pastoralis

☛ (BB) *** Naxos 8.554428. Soloists, Czech Madrigalists Ch. & O, Thuri

The Czech composer, Jakob Jan Ryba, contemporary with Mozart, wrote these *Christmas Masses* – one long, one short – as seasonal cantatas. With only token references to the liturgy, obvious enough in the *Gloria,* they relate the story of the shepherds visiting the baby Jesus to the various sections of the Mass. Understandably, with their simple folk-like tunes and harmonies, they have long been part of traditional Czech celebrations at Christmas, and they here receive winningly fresh and direct performances, atmospherically recorded.

SÆVERUD, Harald (1897–1992)

(i) *Oboe Concerto, Op. 15. Symphony 5 (Quasi una fantasia), Op. 16; Entrata regale, Op. 41; Sonata Giubilata, Op. 47*

*** BIS CD 1162. (i) Hunt; Stavanger SO, Ruud

Sæverud used to show his visitors newspaper caricatures of himself as a drayhorse, and this note of self-mockery can be clearly discerned in his music. RL was privileged to visit him from time to time and, apart from showing this caricature, he liked to give his visitors a small cow-bell! In this continuation of the BIS survey of Sæverud's music the *Fifth Symphony* (1941), composed a year after the Nazi invasion, is coupled with the *Oboe Concerto* of 1938 and a couple of later occasional pieces. The *Concerto* was first given in 1939 at Gothenburg, the most enterprising and outward-looking of the Scandinavian music centres, but the composer revised it in 1953, when the two outer movements were shortened. It is an inventive and spirited work, excellently played by Gordon Hunt and the Stavanger orchestra, and this CD supplants the earlier (1983) version with Erik Niord Larsen and the Oslo Philharmonic under Mariss Jansons, once available on Norwegian Philips. The *Fifth Symphony* is perhaps the least satisfying of the wartime trilogy: the powerful, lyrical *Sixth Symphony* (*Sinfonia dolorosa,* 1942) and its successor, *Salmesymfoni* (1944–5), both display a stronger feeling for structure and sense of the Norwegian landscape. Although it caused a great stir at its first performance under the composer's own baton, the *Fifth* is too short-breathed to carry symphonic conviction, even though it is unfailingly vital. This and the two occasional pieces that complete the disc are well served by Ole Kristian Ruud and his Stavanger players.

Just a reminder that there is a rival account by the Bergen orchestra and Dmitri Kitajenko on Simax PSC 3124, a two-CD set which offers symphonies (Nos. 4, 6, 7 and 8) plus the irresistible *Galdreslåtten* and the far from irresistible *Rondo Amoroso.* Three stars for the recorded sound and the performances, but not for the symphony itself.

(i) *Cello Concerto, Op. 7; Symphony 8 (Minnesota), Op. 40*

*** BIS CD 972. (i) Mørk; Stavanger SO, Ruud

The *Cello Concerto* was first performed in April 1999 and although Sæverud had intended to revise it he never got round to finishing it. The present score has been prepared by Robert Rennes. Although Sæverud writes gratefully for the cello, the invention is less memorable or imaginative than in the *Lucretia* or *Peer Gynt* suites.

The *Eighth Symphony* is full of imaginative things, particularly the mysterious opening pages, and the invention often takes you by surprise. Its four movements all have their rewards though the whole is ultimately less than the sum of its parts. Nevertheless, this is a world well worth exploring and to which you will want to return. Sæverud has a strong personality and creates his own distinctive sound world. In the concerto Truls Mørk is masterly and plays with a glorious tone, and the Stavanger Orchestra does well throughout. The recording is superb.

Symphony 6 (Sinfonia dolorosa), Op. 19; Galdreslåtten, Op. 20; Kjæmpevise-slåtten, Op. 22; Peer Gynt Suites 1 & 2
☞— *** BIS CD 762. Stavanger SO, Dmitriev

The *Sixth Symphony* (*Sinfonia dolorosa*) is a short but intense piece from the war years, dedicated to a close friend who perished in the resistance, and the *Kjæmpevise-slåtten* ('Ballad of Revolt') comes from the same years. It is an inspiriting work, an outraged, combative reaction to the sight of the Nazi occupation barracks near his Bergen home. The *Peer Gynt* music, written for a post-war production of Ibsen's play, could not be further removed from Grieg's celebrated score. It is earthy and rambunctious and makes Grieg sound positively genteel. So, too, does the delightful, inventive and wholly original *Galdreslåtten*. Eminently satisfactory performances from the Stavanger orchestra under Alexander Dmitriev, brought vividly to life by the BIS recording team.

Symphony 7 (Salme), Op. 27; (i) Bassoon Concerto, Op. 44. Lucretia (suite), Op. 10
*** BIS CD 822 (i) Rønnes; Stavanger SO, Dmitriev

The one-movement *Seventh* (1945) is the last of Sæverud's wartime symphonies, *Salme-symfoni*, a deeply felt work, a hymn of thanksgiving for peace. It has never sounded better than it does in this recording. The *Lucretia Suite* derives from the incidental music Sæverud wrote in 1936 for André Obey's play. Much of it is highly imaginative (the evocation of night in the fourth movement, for example), and the charming middle movement, *Lucretia Sleeping*. The second movement portrays Lucretia spinning. The *Bassoon Concerto* (1965) was revised towards the end of his long life in collaboration with Robert Rønnes, the soloist here. Absolutely first-class performances and recordings.

Symphony 9, Op. 45; (i) Piano Concerto, Op. 31. Fanfare & Hymn, Op. 48
*** BIS CD 962. Stavanger SO, Dmitriev (i) with Ogawa

Alexander Dmitriev and the Stavanger Orchestra are very persuasive in the *Ninth Symphony*. There is a strong sense of the Norwegian landscape here and the BIS recording conveys it all with striking clarity and presence. The *Piano Concerto* of 1950 is a delightful piece, full of quirky, robust humour. It is a work that haunts and fascinates, and the farmyard noises of the finale together with the strongly atmospheric slow movement linger in the memory. Norika Ogawa is an alert, sensitive player who has the measure of this piece, and Alexander Dmitriev and the Stavanger Orchestra are eminently supportive. The short *Fanfare and Hymn* was commissioned by

the City of Bergen to celebrate its 900th anniversary. The sound is in the demonstration bracket.

SAINT-SAËNS, Camille (1835–1921)

(i) Africa Fantasy for Piano & Orchestra, Op. 89. Ascanio: Valse-finale; Parysatis: Airs de ballet. Sarabande et Rigaudon, Op. 93; Suite algérienne, Op. 60: Marche militaire française. (ii) Tarantelle for Flute, Clarinet & Orchestra, Op. 6; (iii) Messe de Requiem, Op. 54
(M) **(*) Cala CACD 1015. LPO, Simon, with (i) Mok; (ii) Milan, Campbell; (iii) Olafimihan, Wyn-Rogers, Roden, Kirkbride, Hertfordshire Ch., Harlow Ch., East London Ch.

La jota aragonesa, Op. 64; (i) La Muse et le poète. La Princesse jaune: Overture; (ii) Symphony 3 in C min.; (iii) Danse macabre (original vocal version). Grande fantaisie on Themes from Samson et Dalila (arr. Luigini)
(M) ** Cala CACD 1016. LPO, Simon, with (i) Chase, Truman; (ii) O'Donnell; (iii) Roden

Geoffrey Simon is an amiably persuasive advocate of these Saint-Saëns novelties and his affectionate approach emphasizes the music's surface elegance. The nicely scored *Airs de ballet* are certainly enticing. But it is the lively and charming *Tarantelle* for flute, clarinet and orchestra which is the vivacious highlight of the first CD. It is winningly played by Susan Milan and James Campbell. The rich sonority of the sound suits the melodically catchy *Marche militaire française*, with its resplendent brass, but the exotically oriental *Africa Fantasy for Piano and Orchestra* loses some of its point and glitter when the acoustic is so resonant. Even so Gwendolyn Mok plays with flair. The *Messe de Requiem* is a real find, even if here the focus of the choral sound needs to be sharper. Pretty good choral singing, a well-matched team of soloists, and the recording gives the work a fine, sonorous impact, even if more bite is needed.

The undoubted highlight of the second disc is the fascinating original vocal version of *Danse macabre*, very much shorter than the familiar tone-poem. The effect is semi-operatic, interrupted by the cock-crow. *La Muse et le poète* is an extended duo for violin and cello with orchestra. Stephanie Chase and, especially, the cellist Robert Truman are good if not distinctive soloists. The *Jota aragonesa* is very like the Glinka fantasy and needs a recording with more glitter. The *Grande Fantaisie on Samson et Dalila* arranged by Luigini is rather inflated but is not helped by Geoffrey Simon's very leisurely tempo for *Softly Awakes My Heart*, even though there is some lovely warm string-playing. The *Overture: La Princesse jaune* is presented with real charm, but Geoffrey Simon then chooses to end his second CD with the *Organ Symphony* – an agreeable account, but no more than that.

Carnival of the Animals (with narration)
(BB) **(*) Naxos 8.554463. Morris (nar.), Slovak RSO, Lenárd – DUKAS: *L'Apprenti sorcier* **(*); RAVEL: *Ma Mère l'Oye* ***

This Naxos collection is clearly aimed at younger children, and many adults could find Johnny Morris's very personal (and often eccentric) descriptions and rhymes, which adorn this performance, too much to take. But the playing of the Slovak orchestra, with a persuasively spontaneous contribution from the two anonymous pianists, is most attractive. If Morris's friendly delivery and the lazy timing of his own text bring children to the music, all to the good, especially if they remember the musical association past childhood. They will surely not mind Morris's singing along in a quavery fashion with the Tortoise, and in the Aquarium, even though he drowns the music.

(i; ii) *Carnival of the Animals;* (iii) *Cello Concerto;* (i; iv) *Piano Concertos 1–5;* (v) *Caprice andalou; Violin Concertos 1–3; Le Déluge: Prélude. Havanaise; Introduction & Rondo Capriccioso; Morceau de concert;* (v; vi) *La Muse et le poète, Op. 132;* (v) *Romances , Opp. 37 & 48; Valse-Caprice en forme de valse* (arr. Ysaÿe); (vii) *Piano Quintet, Op. 14; Trumpet Septet, Op. 65;* (i) (Piano) *Etude en forme de valse, Op. 52/6*

(N) (BB) **(*) EMI 5 86128-2 (5). (i) Ciccolini; (ii)
  Weissenberg, Paris Cons. O, Prêtre; (iii) Tortelier, CBSO,
  Frémaux; (iv) O de Paris, Baudo; (v) Hoelscher, New Philh.
  O, Dervaux; (vi) with Kirschbaum; (vii) Groupe
  Instrumental de Paris

This makes an immensely enjoyable super-super-bargain concertante collection which at its very low price is hard to beat. The Paris recording of the *Carnival of the Animals* with Ciccolini and Weissenberg (who makes a contribution of some distinction) offers a refreshingly brilliant account of Saint-Saëns's *jeu d'esprit.* It opens a little heavily but the characterization is nicely managed, with some very good orchestral playing. Ciccolini is equally enjoyable in the five diverse *Piano Concertos* (also available separately – see below), and Paul Tortelier gives an assured account of the *Cello Concerto.*

The *Septet,* with its important trumpet part, has the composer's usual melodic facility, though the curious instrumentation does not quite gel here in a rather dry acoustic. It is well played and shows the composer at his most genially vivid, especially the closing *Gavotte et Final,* which brings some characteristically scintillating piano roulades. The equally rare *Piano Quintet* is cleanly recorded (like the *Septet*) at Abbey Road, but again lacks textural warmth. It is a lively work, the first movement has an engaging lyrical secondary theme, and the touching *Andante sostenuto* is rather like a gentle song without words. The Scherzo brings bravura running passages for the piano, then the finale opens *Allegro assai ma tranquillo* but moves to a passionate climax. The weaving of the part-writing here is engaging, while the piano continues its virtuoso role, and it is a pity that the string timbre is so dry. Nevertheless this work deserves to be much better known, and Cicciloni provides a brilliant account of the *Etude en forme de valse* as an encore. The last two discs collect the concertante music for violin and orchestra, with Hoelscher the principal soloist, and this is also available on a separate two-disc set (see below). As with the rest of these French EMI boxes, the notes are sparse and in French only, but musically this is remarkable value.

(i) *Carnival of the Animals;* (ii) *Piano Concerto 2 in G min., Op. 22;* (iii) *Violin Concerto 3 in B min., Op. 61;* (iv) *Danse macabre, Op. 40;* (v) *Havanaise, Op. 83; Introduction & rondo capriccioso, Op. 28;* (vi) *Symphony 3 in C min. (Organ), Op. 78. Samson et Dalila:* (vii) *Air et danse bacchanale;* (viii) *Mon cœur s'ouvre à ta voix*

(B) **(*) Double Decca (ADD) 444 552-2 (2). (i) Ortiz; (i; ii)
  Rogé; (iii) Bell; (v) Chung; (vi) Priest; (viii) Horne; (i) L.
  Sinf.; (ii; v) RPO; (iii; vii) Montreal SO; (iv) Philh. O; (i–v;
  vii) cond. Dutoit; (vi) LAPO, Mehta

Mehta's Los Angeles account of the *Third Symphony* is among the more recommendable versions of this much-recorded work, for he draws a well-disciplined and exuberant response from all departments of the orchestra. Joshua Bell's performance of the *Violin Concerto* is very attractive indeed: the pianissimo opening is full of atmosphere and the *Andantino* has a pleasingly lyrical simplicity. The disappointment is Dutoit's *Carnival of the Animals* – in a crisp, clean, digital recording with very bright sound – which is lacking characterization and charm. *The Swan* is played in a very matter-of-fact way. Dutoit shows himself in a better light in his deft account of the *Danse macabre,* while Kwung Wha Chung is on top form, playing with flair in both the famous violin showpieces. Marilyn Horne's ripe characterization of Saint-Saëns's most famous aria, 'Softly awakes my heart', will not disappoint, and nor will the excerpts from *Samson et Dalila.* Pascal Rogé's account of the favourite Saint-Saëns *Second Piano Concerto* is second to none.

(i) *Carnival of the Animals* (chamber version); (ii) *Piano Concerto 2 in G min.;* (iii; iv) *Danse Macabre;* (v) *Havanaise; Introduction et rondo capriccioso;* (vi) *Le Rouet d'Omphale;* (vii; viii; iv) *Symphony 3 in C min.; Samson et Dalila:* (vi; iv) *Bacchanale* & (ix) *Mon coeur s'ouvre à ta voix*

(B) **(*) DG Panorama (ADD/DDD) 469 310-2 (2). (i)
  Argerich, Freire, Kremer, Keulen, Maisky et al; (ii) Rogé,
  RPO, Dutoit; (iii) O de Paris; (iv) Barenboim; (v) Perlman,
  NYPO, Mehta; (vi) O Nat. de France, Bernstein; (vii)
  Litaize; (viii) Chicago SO; (ix) Bumbry, Berlin RSO, Kulka

A generally excellent DG Panorama collection. Barenboim's inspirational 1976 performance of the *Third Symphony* glows with warmth from beginning to end, even if the strings have lost some of their expansive quality in the CD remastering. Rogé's natural elegance brings out the warmth and sparkle of the *Second Piano Concerto* – which 'starts off like Bach, and ends like Offenbach' – in this (Decca) 1981 performance, and the tone-poems are also highly successful. The reservations concern the chamber performance of the *Carnival of the Animals:* the combination of Martha Argerich and Nelson Freire playing the piano duo ensures plenty of character and sparkle, as well as some extreme tempi, but overall this account is rather short on charm and is not helped by the dry sound, which at times is aggressive. However, at the price, this collection is certainly worth considering, and the rest of the recordings give no cause for complaint.

(i) *Carnival of the Animals;* (ii) *Le Cygne; Piano Concertos* (iii) *2;* (iv) *4 in C min., Op. 44;* (v) *Violin Concerto 3;* (vi) *Danse macabre; Introduction & rondo capriccioso;* (vii) *Symphony 3 in C min. (Organ)*

(B) **(*) Ph. Duo (ADD) 442 608-2 (2). (i) Villa, Jennings,
  Pittsburgh SO, Previn; (ii) Gendron, Gallion; (iii)
  Davidovich, Concg. O, Järvi; (iv) Campanella, Monte Carlo
  Op. O, Ceccato; (v) Szeryng, Monte Carlo Op. O,
  Remoortel; (vi) Concg. O, Haitink; (vii) Chorzempa,
  Rotterdam PO, De Waart

The inexpensive Duo collection is described as 'The Best of Saint-Saëns'. Notable here is Previn's 1980 *Carnival of the Animals,* as fine as almost any available (see above). (Philips have also included a second performance of *Le Cygne* by the inestimable Maurice Gendron.) Bella Davidovich gives a most sympathetic account of the *G minor Piano Concerto* and draws pleasing tone-quality from the instrument, even if she lacks the last degree of brilliance and flair. She has the advantage of excellent orchestral support from the Concertgebouw Orchestra, who also give a lively account of the *Danse macabre* under Haitink. In the *C minor Concerto* (which is analogue) the effect is harder, partly because Michele Campanella is a more boldly extrovert soloist; but this account has undoubted vitality and no lack of *espressivo*. Henryk Szeryng gives clean, immaculate performances of the *B minor Violin Concerto* and the *Introduction and Rondo capriccioso*. His approach is aristocratic rather than seductive. The contribution of the Monte Carlo orchestra is adequate. Edo de Waart's 1976 recording of the *Organ Symphony* is not among the most exciting versions available but, with polished orchestral playing and refined Philips sound, it is certainly enjoyable.

(i) *Carnival of the Animals;* (ii) *Danse macabre, Op. 40;*
Suite algérienne, Op. 60: Marche militaire française. Samson et Dalila: Bacchanale. (ii; iii) *Symphony 3 in C min., Op. 78*
(M) *** Sony (ADD) SBK 47655. (i) Entremont, Casadesus, Pasquier, Tortelier, Caussé, Ma, Lauridon, Marion, Arrignon, Cals, Cerutti; (ii) Phd. O, Ormandy; (iii) with E. Power Biggs

(i) *Carnival of the Animals;* (ii) *Danse macabre;* (iii) *Symphony 3;* (iv) *Wedding-Cake* (caprice-valse for piano and orchestra), *Op. 76*
**(*) ASV CDDCA 665. (i) Guillermo Salvador Snr & Jnr, Mexico City PO; (ii) Mexicana State SO; (iii) Rawsthorne, LPO; (iv) Osorio, RPO; Bátiz

It would be churlish to bracket the third star for the generous Sony collection because the opening of the *Carnival of the Animals*, performed in its original chamber version, is a bit lacklustre. The ear adjusts to the rather dry effect. It is a starry cast: Yo-Yo Ma personifies *The Swan* gently and gracefully. Ormandy and his splendid orchestra play the other orchestral lollipops with fine panache. No complaint about the 1962 sound in the *Symphony*. The performance is fresh and vigorous, with Ormandy at his most involved.

The *Carnival of the Animals* and *Danse macabre* also have plenty of genial vitality on ASV but are less strong on finesse, and the forwardly balanced recording adds to the robust feeling. Jorge Federico Osorio, however, dispatches the charming *Wedding-Cake caprice-valse* with a winning sparkle. Bátiz's version of the spectacular *Organ Symphony* was the first digital success for this work. The orchestral playing is exhilarating in its energy, while the organ entry is an impressive moment and the sense of spectacle persists in the closing pages.

(i) *Carnival of the Animals;* (ii) *Danse macabre;* (iii) *Symphony 3 (Organ), Op. 78;* (iv) *Samson et Dalila: Bacchanale*
(N) (BB) *** EMI HMV (ADD) 5 86760-2. (i) Nel, Snel, Ac. of L., Stamp; (ii) CBSO, Frémaux; (iii) Gavoty, Fr. Nat. R. O, Martinon; (iv) Paris Op. O, Prêtre

A thoroughly worthwhile anthology. Richard Stamp directs an outstanding version of the *Carnival of the Animals*, full of affectionate humour. Throughout one responds to the polished presentation overall and the sense of fun; although some may feel that the recording is rather resonant, it adds a genial warmth to the vitality of the proceedings. With the

Danse macabre and *Bacchanale* acting as a central interlude, Martinon's account of the *Symphony* is in every way distinguished, the first movement alert and sparkling, the *Poco Adagio* warmly romantic, yet with a touch of nobility at the close. The organ entry in the finale is massively buoyant, but detail registers admirably, so that both here and in the vivacious Scherzo the rippling piano figurations are clearer than usual. In fact, the recording with its ambient glow is very well balanced.

Cello Concertos 1 in A min., Op. 33; 2 in D min., Op. 119; Allegro appassionato in B min., Op. 43; Suite in D min., Op. 16; Carnival of the Animals: The Swan (orch. Vidal)
(BB) **(*) Naxos 8.553039. Kliegel, Bournemouth Sinf., Monnard

Maria Kliegel proves a most sympathetic soloist, technically immaculate, undeterred even by the relatively ungrateful writing for the cello in the *Second Concerto*, so much less striking a work than No. 1. It is good to have the early *Suite*, a colourful collection of genre pieces, and the dashing *Allegro appassionato*, both originally with piano accompaniment and here arranged by the composer himself. Saint-Saëns's most celebrated cello piece, *The Swan*, makes an attractive supplement, played in an orchestral arrangement by Paul Vidal, which adds strings to the usual harp accompaniment.

Cello Concertos (i; ii) *1, Op. 33;* (i; iii) *2, Op. 119. Piano Concertos* (iv; v; vi;) *1 in D, Op. 17;* (iv; v; vii) *2 in G min., Op. 22;* (iv; v; viii) *3 in E flat, Op. 29;* (iv; v; vi) *4 in C min., Op. 44;* (iv; v; vii) *5 in F, Op. 103. Violin Concertos* (v; ix; x) *1 in A, Op. 20;* (ix; xi; xii) *3 in B min., Op. 61.* (v; ix; vii) *Havanaise; Introduction et Rondo capriccioso;* (v; xiii) *Carnival of the Animals;* (v; vi) *Danse macabre; La Jeunesse d'Hercule; Marche héroïque; Phaéton; Le Rouet d'Omphale;* (v; x; xiv) *Symphony 3 (Organ) in C min., Op. 78*
(N) (B) *** Decca (ADD/DDD) 475 465-2 (5). (i) Harrell; (ii) Cleveland O, Marriner; (iii) German RSO, Chailly; (iv) Rogé; (v) Dutoit; (vi) Philh. O; (vii) RPO; (viii) LPO; (ix) Kyung Wha Chung; (x) Montreal SO; (xi) LSO; (xii) Foster; (xiii) L. Sinf.; (xiv) Hurford

Exceptional value here, with quantity and quality, and with a myriad of orchestras involved to make this a Saint-Saëns feast. Pascal Rogé brings delicacy, virtuosity and sparkle to the *Piano Concertos* (recorded in the late 1970s or early 1980s). Chung presents the short *First Violin Concerto* (recorded digitally in 1980) delightfully and gets similarly admirable accompaniments from Dutoit. She gives a passionate account of the *B minor Concerto*, so intense that even a sceptical listener will find it hard not to be convinced that this is a great work, with excellent support from Foster and the 1975 Decca recording. Both the *Havanaise* and *Introduction and Rondo capriccioso* have beauty and bravura in plenty, and they come up as fresh as paint. Harrell's account of the *First Cello Concerto* is an extrovert reading, and one which makes light of any idea that this composer always worked on a small scale. The opening is positively epic, and the rest of the performance is just as compelling, with the minuet-like *Allegretto* crisply neo-classical. The *Second Cello Concerto* has an attractive spontaneity and its ideas are memorable, notably the strikingly rhythmic opening theme of the first movement – which returns to cap the finale – and the very engaging melody of the *Andante* (which is linked to the opening movement). It is beautifully played and recorded: at its close, Harrell refines his timbre to an exquisite half-tone and the effect is ravishing, with a gently muted horn decoration. In Dutoit's collection of tone-poems, the works are beautifully played and recorded, with the 1979 Kingway Hall sound giving it all an appropriate atmosphere. Dutoit shows himself an admirably sensitive exponent, revelling in the composer's craftsmanship and revealing much delightful detail in the manner of Beecham. *La Jeunesse d'Hercule* is the most ambitious piece, and its lyrical invention is both sensuous and elegant. The *Marche héroïque* is flamboyantly enjoyable, and *Phaéton*, a great favourite in the Victorian era, is enjoyable in its old-fashioned way. But the delightful *Omphale's Spinning Wheel* and the familiar *Danse macabre* show the composer at his most creatively imaginative. The *Organ Symphony* was one of the first demonstration digital recordings (1982), with its bright sound and luminous detail, with the strings sounding thrilling above the stave. The reading combines lyricism with passion. In the finale, Hurford's entry in the famous chorale melody is more pointed, less massive than usual, although Dutoit generates a genial feeling of gusto to compensate, and there is a good final burst of adrenalin at the end. Only in the under-characterized version of the *Carnival of the Animals* does this set fall below a high standard, but it in no way detracts from its supreme value for money.

Cello Concertos (i; ii) *1, Op. 33*; (i; iii) *2, Op. 119*; *Suite for Cello & Orchestra, Op. 16*; (i; iv) *Prière* (for cello & organ). (i; iii; v) *La Muse et le Poète, Op. 132*

(N) (B) *** RCA 82876 65845-2. (i) Isserlis; (ii) LSO, Tilson Thomas; (iii) N. German RSO, Eschenbach; (iv) F. Grier; (v) Bell

Steven Isserlis's recording of the *First Concerto* is among the finest on record, and here RCA have made some valuable additions, not least the *Second Concerto*, which comes from the end of the composer's long career. If not so hauntingly lyrical as the *First*, it is equally strong and purposeful. The *Suite* is a very early work (1862) and looks over its shoulder stylistically with its *Gavotte, Romance, Serenade* and *Tarantelle*. With Isserlis masterly in bringing rarities back to life, they draw dedicated playing from him, full of high contrasts. The engaging *Prière*, for cello and organ, was written as late as 1919, while the lovely *La Muse et le Poète*, inspired by de Musset's *La Nuit de mai* is a haunting piece for violin (the warmly sympathetic Joshua Bell), cello and orchestra, which has an affecting directness of utterance. Throughout, the recorded sound is very good indeed and this disc is thoroughly recommendable on all counts.

Cello Concerto 1 in A min., Op. 33

☛ *** EMI 5 56126-2. Han-Na Chang, LSO, Rostropovich – BRUCH: *Kol Nidrei* ***; FAURE: *Elégie* ***; TCHAIKOVSKY *Rococo Variations* *** ✹

*** Teldec 8573-85340-2. Du Pré, Phd. O, Barenboim – DVORAK: *Cello Concerto* ***

*** ASV CDDCA 867. Rolland, BBC PO, Varga – LALO: *Cello Concerto in D min.*; MASSENET: *Fantaisie* ***

(M) *** DG (ADD) 457 761-2. Fournier, LOP, Martinon – BLOCH: *Schelomo*; BRUCH: *Kol Nidrei*; LALO: *Cello Concerto* ***

(i) *Cello Concerto 1, Op. 33*; (ii) *The Swan*; (iii) *Allegro appassionato, Op. 43*; *Cello Sonata 1, Op. 32*; *Chant*

saphique, Op. 91; Gavotte, Op. posth.; Romances 1 in F, Op. 36; 2 in D, Op. 51; (iv) *Prière* (for cello & organ)

*** RCA 09026 61678-2. Isserlis; (i) LSO, Tilson Thomas; (ii) Tilson Thomas, Moore; (iii) Devoyon; (iv) Grier

Han-Na Chang's delicacy of feeling, natural sense of line and wide range of dynamic show an instinctive musicianship and a mastery of her instrument that recall the young Menuhin, while the sophistication of the performance is extraordinarily mature, helped in no small part by Rostropovich's always supportive accompaniment and the superb playing of the LSO. The EMI Abbey Road recording is first class in every way and beautifully balanced.

The Saint-Saëns, recorded live in Philadelphia in 1971, makes a good coupling for du Pré's warmly expressive account of the Dvořák with Celibidache. Though this came right at the end of du Pré's playing career, before the onset of multiple sclerosis, the performance is typically magnetic in its high-powered intensity, full of manic energy, faster and wilder than her studio account, if not quite so cleanly recorded.

Steven Isserlis's account of the *Cello Concerto in A minor* is among the best on record. Of particular interest too is the *Cello Sonata No. 1 in C minor*, composed in the same year, in which he is accompanied with elegance and finesse by Pascal Devoyon. Isserlis himself plays with the musicianship and virtuosity one has come to expect from him. Most of the remaining pieces are both worthwhile and entertaining, particularly the *Allegro appassionato*. The *Prière*, Op. 159, for cello and organ, is a small but affecting addition to the Saint-Saëns discography. The recorded sound is very good indeed.

Sophie Rolland takes its technical hurdles in her effortless stride and is very well supported by the BBC Philharmonic under Gilbert Varga. Perhaps their opening is marginally too fast for an *Allegro non troppo*, but the performance is in every respect a highly enjoyable one. The excellence of the BBC/ASV recording makes for a strong recommendation.

Fournier brings his customary nobility to the concerto, and is well supported by Martinon, who provides stylish support with the Lamoureux Orchestra. The recording from 1960 has never sounded better than on this new DG Originals transfer, and the collection is excellent in every way.

(i) *Cello Concerto 1*; (ii) *Piano Concerto 2*; (iii) *Violin Concerto 3*

☛ ✹ (M) *** Sony SMK 89873. (i) Ma, O Nat. de France, Maazel; (ii) Licad, LPO, Previn; (iii) Lin, Philh. O, Tilson Thomas

Three outstanding performances from the early 1980s are admirably linked together in this highly desirable CBS mid-price reissue. Yo-Yo Ma's performance of the *Cello Concerto* is distinguished by fine sensitivity and beautiful tone, while Cécile Licad and the LPO under Previn turn in an eminently satisfactory reading of the *G minor Piano Concerto* that has the requisite delicacy in the Scherzo and seriousness elsewhere. Cho-Liang Lin's account of the *B minor Violin Concerto* with the Philharmonia Orchestra and Michael Tilson Thomas is exhilarating and thrilling. Indeed, this is the kind of performance that prompts one to burst into applause – his version is arguably the finest to have appeared for years.

Piano Concertos 1 in D, Op. 17; 2 in G min., Op. 22; 3 in E flat, Op. 29; 4 in C min., Op. 44; 5 in F (Egyptian), Op. 103

(B) *** Double Decca (ADD) 443 865-2 (2); 443 865-4. Rogé, Philh. O, RPO or LPO, Dutoit

(BB) *** EMI (ADD) Gemini 5 85183-2 (2). Ciccolini, O de
Paris, Serge Baudo

(B) * Sony (ADD) SB2K 89977 (2). Entremont, O du Capitole
Toulouse, Plasson

Piano Concertos 1–5; Africa Fantaisie, Op. 89;
Wedding-Cake Caprice-valse, Op. 76 (both for piano and
orchestra)

⊶ ✪ *** Hyp. CDA 67331/2 (2). Hough, CBSO, Oramo
(with *Allegro appassionato; Rhapsodie d'Auvergne*)

(B) *** EMI double forte CZS5 73356-2 (2). Collard, RPO,
Previn

Marvellous performances from Stephen Hough, full of joy,
vigour and sparkle, with Oramo and the CBSO accompanying spiritedly and with the lightest touch. The recording is in
the demonstration bracket, and this Hyperion set includes no
fewer than four encores. An easy first choice.

As always with Collard there is splendid character and a
dazzling technique. He brings panache and virtuosity to these
concertos, as well as impressive poetic feeling. At one point in
the *Fifth (Egyptian) Concerto* Collard exploits Saint-Saëns's
genius in manipulating the piano to suggest Eastern sonorities and makes his instrument sound exactly like an Arab
qunan or zither. Throughout, Previn and the Royal Philharmonic Orchestra are sensitive accompanists, and this set not
only includes the *Wedding-Cake Caprice-valse*, but also a
sparkling account of the exuberant, pseudo-exotic *Africa
Fantaisie*. Although in many respects allegiance to Pascal
Rogé on Decca remains strong, Collard with his greater
dynamic range and authority often makes even more of this
music. The digital sound is very good too, at times slightly
more transparent than the Decca, but there is a distinct touch
of hardness on top.

Pascal Rogé brings delicacy, virtuosity and sparkle to the
piano part and he receives expert support from the various
London orchestras under Dutoit. Altogether delicious playing
and excellent piano-sound from Decca, who secure a most
realistic balance.

The performances from Ciccolini and Baudo on EMI are
admirably spirited and emerge freshly on CD. The vibrant, at
times slightly brash, 1970 sound gives the music-making
strong character and projection.

Entremont is a vigorously persuasive interpreter of French
music, but here he is let down by the recording, which dates
from the late 1970s and did less than justice to the soloist's
gentler qualities, with the forward balance reducing the
dynamic range. The CD remastering has made matters worse,
with orchestral tuttis sounding crude and fierce and no
bloom given to the piano, which becomes clattery and aggressive under pressure. Stephen Hough's complete set on Hyperion leads the field.

(ii) *Piano Concertos 1 in D, Op. 17; 2 in G min., Op. 22; (i)*
Orchestral Suite in D, Op. 49

*** BIS CD 1040. (i) Tapiola Sinf., Kantorow; (ii) with Ogawa

BIS couples the *First* and *Second* piano concertos, which are
played with great charm and grace by Norika Ogawa and the
Tapiola Sinfonietta under Jean-Jacques Kantorow. As a makeweight it has added the *Suite in D major, Op. 49,* which was
originally conceived for the harmonium and later arranged
for orchestra. It is all attractive and engaging and excellently
recorded too. Ms Ogawa's many admirers can proceed with
confidence. All the same, it is well worth remembering that

you can get all five Saint-Saëns piano concertos for the same
money in Pascal Rogé's elegant and refreshing performances
on Decca.

Piano Concerto 2 in G min., Op. 22

(B) *** RCA 2CD (ADD) 74321 84606-2 (2). Rubinstein, Phd.
O, Ormandy – CHABRIER: *Pièces pittoresques;* DEBUSSY:
Estampes etc.; FAURE: *Nocturne No.3;* FRANCK:
Symphonic Variations; Prelude choral et fugue; RAVEL:
Valses nobles et sentimentales etc. ***

(***) Testament mono SBT 1029. Gilels, Paris Conservatoire
O, Cluytens (with SHOSTAKOVICH: *Prelude & Fugue in D,*
Op. 87/5) – RACHMANINOV: *Piano Concerto 3* (***)

(BB) (***) Naxos mono 8.110683. Moiseiwitsch, LPO,
Cameron – GRIEG: *Piano Concerto;* LISZT: *Fantasia on*
Hungarian Folk Themes (***)

Rubinstein, understandably, had a soft spot for the Saint-
Saëns *Second Piano Concerto*. He chose it for his début in
Berlin in 1900 and played it finally on his last TV show in
1979. Rubinstein's secret is that, though he appears at times
(especially in the *Toccata* finale) to be attacking the music, his
phrasing is full of little fluctuations so that his playing never
sounds stilted. The *Scherzo* scintillates. On the two-CD set the
couplings are very generous, and this RCA Double is highly
recommendable.

Gilels's celebrated account of the Saint-Saëns *G minor*
Concerto comes from 1954 and is masterly in every respect. Its
delicacy and refinement still come across in spite of the
limitations of the recording, and Gilels gets marvellous support from the Paris orchestra under André Cluytens. Excellent transfers.

On Naxos, a neat-fingered and characterful account of this
popular concerto and a welcome reminder of Moiseiwitsch's
art. Good transfer.

Piano Concertos 2 in G min.; 4, Op. 44

(B) *** Decca Eloquence (ADD) 467 471-2. Rogé, RPO or
Philh. O, Dutoit – POULENC: *Mouvements perpétuels;*
Napoli ***

(BB) **(*) Naxos 8.550334. Biret, Philh. O, Loughran

These have long been the two favourite Saint-Saëns piano
concertos, often coupled together on LP, and they are most
persuasively presented by Pascal Rogé in partnership with
Dutoit. No. 4 with its indelible main theme is particularly
attractive, and the Decca recording is first class. A bargain –
but one can get all five concertos played by these artists on a
Double Decca (see above).

Idil Biret makes rather heavy weather of the opening of the
G minor Concerto, and her performance sounds just a little
portentous and wanting in charm, though the scherzo is
played with delicacy and character. The accompaniment by
the Philharmonia Orchestra under James Loughran is very
good and so too is the recording. There are performances of
greater subtlety to be had – albeit not at this price.

Violin Concertos 1 in A, Op. 20; 2 in C, Op. 58; 3 in B min.,
Op. 61; Caprice andalou, Op. 122; Le Déluge, Op. 45: Prélude.
Havanaise, Op. 83; Introduction & Rondo capriccioso,
Op. 28; Morceau de concert, Op. 62; Romances: in D, Op. 37;
in C, Op. 48; La Muse et le poète, Op. 132 (Also includes:
YSAYE: *Caprice d'après l'étude en forme de valse, Op. 52/6*)

(BB) **(*) EMI (ADD) 5 72001-2 (2). Hoelscher, New Philh.
O, Dervaux; (i) with Kirshbaum

This two-CD box collects all Saint-Saëns's music for violin and orchestra (with a short bonus from Ysaÿe) in performances of excellent quality. Ulf Hoelscher is an extremely accomplished soloist who plays with artistry as well as virtuosity. The *Second Concerto* has a most attractive *Andante* and a catchy *Allegro scherzando* finale, while the first of the two *Romances* deserves to be much better known. The *Morceau de concert* is most engaging, as is the relatively ambitious extended duo concertante piece, *La Muse et le poète*, in which Hoelscher is admirably partnered by Ralph Kirshbaum and which seems much more substantial here than usual. In this EMI set Pierre Dervaux directs excellent accompaniments, and the recording (made at Abbey Road in 1977) is basically of excellent quality even though the forward balance of the soloist does not enhance Hoelscher's timbre in the upper range.

Violin Concertos 1–3
*** Hyp. CDA 67074. Graffin, BBC Scottish SO, Brabbins

Violin Concertos (i) 1; (ii) 3; (iii) Havanaise; Introduction & rondo capriccioso
(M) *** Decca (ADD) 460 008-2. Kyung Wha Chung, (i) Montreal SO, Dutoit; (ii) LSO, Lawrence Foster; (iii) RPO, Dutoit

Violin Concerto 1; Havanaise in E, Op. 83; Introduction & rondo capriccioso, Op. 28; Morceau de concert, Op. 62; Romance in C, Op. 48; Sarabande, Op. 93/1
*** BIS CD 860. Kantorow, Tapiola Sinf.

Though Saint-Saëns's *Third Concerto* is relatively well known, with its charming central *Andantino* set between two bravura movements, and the *First Concerto*, in a single movement, has not been neglected either, the *Second Concerto* is the earliest and longest, yet arguably the most memorable – full of the youthful exuberance of a 23-year-old. The French violinist Philippe Graffin, with rich, firm tone, gives performances full of temperament, warmly supported by Martyn Brabbins and the BBC Scottish Symphony Orchestra, and the recording cannot be faulted.

Kyung Wha Chung presents Saint-Saëns's *First Violin Concerto* delightfully and receives admirable support from Dutoit. She gives a passionate account of the *B minor Concerto*, so intense that even a sceptical listener will find it hard not to be convinced that this is a great work. Such music needs this kind of advocacy, and Miss Chung is splendidly backed up by the LSO under Lawrence Foster. The 1975 analogue recording is slightly less flattering than the 1980 digital sound in Montreal, but it remains full and clear.

It is a pleasure also to welcome this BIS collection which brings the short and early *First Violin Concerto* with such rightly popular display pieces as the *Introduction and Rondo capriccioso* and the *Havanaise*. Everything is expertly played and Kantorow has the right blend of panache and spontaneity. First-class sound, as one expects from this source.

Violin Concerto 3 in B min., Op. 61; Caprice andalous in G, Op. 122; Introduction & rondo capriccioso in A min., Op. 28; Morceau de concert in G, Op. 62
(BB) **(*) Naxos 8.550752. Kang, Polish Nat. RSO, Wit

Dong-Suk Kang brings out the delicate lyricism in Saint-Saëns's most popular violin concerto. The coupling of concertante works brings similar charm, and it is good to have

the rarer *Caprice andalous* included, a 10-minute piece with many typical Saint-Saëns felicities. If Kang's artistic personality is less strong than say, Perlman in this repertoire, these are still enjoyable accounts, and Wit provides sensitive accompaniments. The 1993 recording is good but not outstanding, lacking a degree of richness and depth.

(i) Violin Concerto 3 in B min., Op. 61; (ii) Havanaise; Introduction & Rondo capriccioso
(N) *** Decca 2-CD 475 6706 (2). Bell, Montreal SO, Dutoit (with CHAUSSON: *Poème*; MASSENET: *Thaïs: Méditation*; RAVEL: *Tzigane*; SARASATE: *Zigeunerweisen*; YSAYE: *Caprice*) – LALO: *Symphonie espagnole* **

Joshua Bell's performance of the *Concerto* is very attractive, with the Montreal sound casting a glow over the proceedings, so that even the brass chorale sounds genial. The *pianissimo* opening is full of atmosphere, and the *Andantino* has a pleasing lyrical simplicity, with the work's romanticism blossoming throughout. With a realistic balance for the soloist, the recording is one of Decca's most convincing.

Danse macabre, Op. 40; (i) Havanaise; Introduction & rondo capriccioso. La Jeunesse d'Hercule, Op. 50; Marche héroïque, Op. 34; Phaéton, Op. 39; Le Rouet d'Omphale, Op. 31
(M) *** Decca (ADD) 425 021-2. (i) Kyung Wha Chung, RPO; Philh. O; Dutoit

The symphonic poems are beautifully played, and the 1979 Kingsway Hall recording lends the appropriate atmosphere. Charles Dutoit shows himself an admirably sensitive exponent, revelling in the composer's craftsmanship and revealing much delightful orchestral detail in the manner of a Beecham. Decca have now added Kyung Wha Chung's equally charismatic and individual 1977 accounts of what are perhaps the two most inspired short display-pieces for violin and orchestra in the repertoire.

Havanaise, Op. 83
(M) *** EMI (ADD) 5 66058-2. Perlman, O de Paris, Barenboim – RAVEL: *Tzigane*; VIEUXTEMPS: *Violin Concertos 4 & 5* ***
(M) (***) RCA mono 09026 61753-2. Heifetz, RCA Victor SO, Steinberg – CHAUSSON: *Poème* **(*); LALO: *Symphonie espagnole* (**(*)); SARASATE: *Zigeunerweisen* (***)
*** Australian Decca Eloquence (ADD) 461 369-2. Ricci, LSO, Gamba – BRUCH; MENDELSSOHN: *Violin Concertos* **(*)
**(*) EMI 5 55026-2. Chang, Phd. O, Sawallisch – PAGANINI: *Violin Concerto 1* **(*)

Perlman plays with splendid panache and virtuosity on EMI; his tone and control of colour in the *Havanaise* are ravishing.

The Heifetz performances have quite extraordinary panache: his bowing in the coda of the *Havanaise* is utterly captivating. Indeed, this dazzling playing is unsurpassed on record and the 1951 mono recording, if closely balanced, is very faithful. Even if you have these works in more modern versions, this marvellous disc should not be passed by.

These famous violin showpieces are superbly played by Ricci, who has dash and sparkle in plenty, helped by Gamba's lively conducting. The 1959 recording is full and vivid, only just hinting at its age. A fine bonus for Ricci's very individual performances of the two concertos.

Although she misses some of the sultry seductiveness in

the *Havanaise*, the twelve-year-old Sarah Chang still captures the gleaming Spanish sunshine. She is well supported by Sawallisch but is not flattered by the close recording-balance.

Havanaise, Op. 83; Introduction & Rondo Capriccioso, Op. 28

⊕— (M) * EMI (ADD) 5 62599-2. Perlman, O de Paris, Martinon (with MASSENET: *Thaïs: Méditation*) – CHAUSSON: *Poème*; RAVEL: *Tzigane* ***

⊕— (M) **(*) Warner Elatus 2564 60013-2. Vengerov, Israel PO, Mehta – PAGANINI: *Violin Concerto 1* **(*); WAXMAN: *Carmen Fantasy* *

Perlman plays these Saint-Saëns warhorses with special panache. The digital remastering brings Perlman's gorgeous fiddling right into the room, at the expense of a touch of aggressiveness when the orchestra lets rip, but the concert-hall ambience prevents this from being a problem.

Maxim Vengerov really show his mettle in these Saint-Saëns *morceaux de concert*. He plays with much finesse and dazzles with his easy fireworks, the *Havanaise* in particular producing ravishing tone, yet no over-indulgence. Mehta stands back and gives his young soloist his head.

Henry VIII: ballet music

(BB) *** Naxos 8.553338/9. Razumovsky Sinfonia, Mogrelia – DELIBES: *Sylvia* ***

This ballet-divertissement, described as a '*fête populaire*', comes in Act II of the opera, and in the outer movements Saint-Saëns wittily introduces first a Scottish reel then an Irish jig with Gallic insouciance. But all six numbers, which are enjoyably tuneful, unashamedly incorporate a great many airs from both countries, and Mogrelia presents them affectionately and vividly. With excellent recording, this is a genuine bonus to a pleasing account of Delibes's *Sylvia*.

Javotte (ballet; complete); Parysatis (ballet; introduction & 3 scenes)

**(*) Marco Polo 8.223612. Queensland O, Mogrelia

It is a pity that Saint-Saëns did not write more ballet music outside his operas – his natural gift for melody and colour suits the medium perfectly. *Javotte* (1896) seems to be his only full-length ballet, and one can find out very little about its history. Nothing is mentioned in the booklet, although a detailed synopsis is provided. The rustic story, in the manner of *La Fille mal gardée*, provided plenty of opportunity for Saint-Saëns to prove that at the end of his career he had lost none of his ability for writing witty and tuneful music, all of it charmingly orchestrated. Curiously, the composer regarded this work as 'the *post scriptum* to my musical career', though in the event it proved nothing like it. The eight-minute *Parysatis* suite, incidental music for the play first performed in 1902, shows the composer in exotic mode, reflecting the imported nature of both the story and the country, Egypt, where the music was mainly written (during 1901). Excellent performances, though the recording is pretty average: the strings lack glow, with Saint-Saëns's colours slightly muted by the sound in general.

Le rouet d'Omphale

(M) (**(*)) BBC mono BBCL 4113. RPO, Beecham (with spoken introduction) – (with MOZART: *Divertimento in D, K.131*: excerpts). (**(*)) BERLIOZ: *The Trojans: Royal Hunt and Storm*; CHABRIER: *España; Gwendoline*

Overture; DEBUSSY: *L'Enfant prodigue: Cortège et Air de danse;* DELIUS: *Brigg Fair;* MASSENET: *La Vierge: Le dernier sommeil de la vierge*

Only Martinon equalled Beecham in this most delicately evoked of Saint-Saëns's tone-poems, but the present (1958) BBC recording lacks the transparency of texture and range to do Beecham's illustrious performance full justice.

Symphonies: in A; in F (Urbs Roma); Symphonies 1–3

(B) *** EMI (ADD)5 69683-2 (2). French Nat. RO, Martinon (with Gavoty, organ of the Église Saint-Louis des Invalides in 3)

The *A* and *F major* works were totally unknown and unpublished at the time of their recording and have never been dignified with numbers. Yet the *A major*, written when the composer was only fifteen, is a delight and may reasonably be compared with Bizet's youthful work in the same genre. More obviously mature, the *Urbs Roma Symphony* is perhaps a shade more self-conscious, and more ambitious too, showing striking imagination in such movements as the darkly vigorous Scherzo and the variation movement at the end.

The first of the numbered symphonies is a well-fashioned and genial piece, again much indebted to Mendelssohn and Schumann, but with much delightfully fresh invention. The *Second* is full of excellent ideas. Martinon directs splendid performances of the whole set, well prepared and lively. The account of the *Third* ranks with the best: freshly spontaneous in the opening movement, and the threads knitted powerfully together at the end of the finale. Here the recording could do with rather more sumptuousness. Elsewhere the quality is bright and fresh, with no lack of body.

Symphony in F (Urbs Roma); Symphony 2 in A min., Op. 55; (i) Africa for Piano & Orchestra, Op. 89

*** BIS CD 790. (i) Mikkola; Tapiola Sinfonietta, Kantorow

The *F major* '*Urbs Roma*' Symphony and the delightful *Second Symphony in A minor* are played with great spirit and zest by the Tapiola Sinfonietta and Jean-Jacques Kantorow. *Africa*, a fantasy for piano and orchestra, is a later piece, written after Saint-Saëns had returned from a trip to Ceylon (as Sri Lanka was then known) and Egypt. Laura Mikkola is the excellent pianist. If the coupling is suitable, these intelligent and well-recorded performances can be recommended.

Symphony 2; Phaéton, Op. 39; Suite algérienne, Op. 60

*** ASV CDDCA 599. LSO, Butt

Symphonies 2; (i) 3 in C min., Op. 78

*** Chan. 8822. Ulster O, Y. P. Tortelier; (i) with Weir

If you want the *Second Symphony*, it is particularly well played by the LSO under Yondani Butt, with the freshness of a major orchestra discovering something unfamiliar and enjoying themselves. The companion pieces are also thoroughly enjoyable and are just as attractively presented. The recording is warmly atmospheric.

Yan Pascal Tortelier's performance of the *Second* is also very attractive and very well recorded; but Butt's account of this work has greater freshness, and the slightly less reverberant ASV recording contributes to this. If, however, your main interest lies with the *Third Symphony*, this extra resonance proves no disadvantage and the Tortelier version is a 'best buy', both for the appeal of the performance overall and for the state-of-the-art Chandos recording.

Symphony 3 in C min., Op. 78

⊶ ❀ (M) *** RCA (ADD) **SACD** 82876 61357-2.
Zamkochian, Boston SO, Munch – DEBUSSY: *La Mer*
(*); IBERT: *Escales* *

*** DG 419 617-2. Preston, BPO, Levine – DUKAS: *L'Apprenti sorcier* ***

Symphony 3; (i) Carnival of the Animals

(BB) **(*) EMI Encore (ADD) 5 74753-2. Paris Conservatoire
O, Prêtre; (i) with Ciccolini, Weissenberg – POULENC: *Les Animaux modèles* **

(i) Symphony 3; (ii) Danse macabre; Le Déluge: Prelude, Op. 48; Samson et Dalila: Bacchanale

(B) *** DG Entrée (ADD) 474 612-2. (i) Litaize, Chicago SO;
(ii) O de Paris., Barenboim

(i) Symphony 3 in C min. (Organ), Op. 78. Danse macabre; Le rouet d'Omphale

(BB) (***) Warner Apex 8573 89244-2. Alain; O Nat. de
l'ORTF, Martinon – POULENC: *Organ Concerto in G min.*

(i; ii) Symphony 3; (ii) Danse macabre, Op. 40; Samson et Dalila: Bacchanale; (i) 3 Rhapsodies sur des cantiques bretons, Op. 7

*** BIS CD 555. (i) Fagius; (ii) Royal Stockholm PO, DePreist

Symphony 3; Phaéton, Op. 39; Le Rouet d'Omphale, Op. 31

(B) *** EMI Red Line 5 69833-2. O de France, Ozawa

Munch's Boston recording dates from 1959, yet in its currently remastered SACD form it still sounds spectacular. The performance is stunning, full of lyrical ardour and moving forward in a single sweep of great intensity. The couplings, showing Munch and his Bostonians at their peak, are equally valuable, if not quite so outstandingly recorded.

With the Berlin Philharmonic in cracking form, Levine's is a grippingly dramatic reading, full of imaginative detail. The great thrust of the performance does not stem from fast pacing: rather it is the result of incisive articulation, while the clarity of the digital recording allows the pianistic detail to register crisply. The thunderous organ entry in the finale makes a magnificent effect, and the tension is held at white heat throughout the movement. The Dukas coupling is equally memorable, and this remains among the first choices for modern, digital versions of the symphony.

DePreist is straight and unmannered, completely at the service of the music, and proves very persuasive. Hans Fagius plays the Stockholm Concert Hall organ so that, unlike some performances in which the organist is tacked on afterwards, this is a genuine performance. He plays the *Trois rhapsodies sur des cantiques bretons* on the splendid Marcussen instrument of St Jakobs Kyrka in Stockholm to striking effect. The recording of all these items is full-blooded and has plenty of impact yet it is beautifully and naturally balanced.

Ozawa's version is coupled with attractive performances of two of Saint-Saëns's most colourful symphonic poems, in which the conductor is in his element. The *Symphony* too is very enjoyable, and this performance certainly wears well. Ozawa's finale makes a splendidly opulent effect. The sound is in the demonstration class.

Barenboim's inspirational 1976 performance of the *Symphony* glows with warmth and vitality from beginning to end and has now, understandably, been reissued as one of DG's bargain Entrée CDs. Among the three attractive bonuses is an exciting account of the *Bacchanale* from *Samson et Dalila*.

However, although the remastering has brought an excitingly vivid impact, especially in the finale of the *Symphony*, the effect is not entirely advantagous. While detail is sharper, the massed violins sound thinner and less natural at *fortissimo* level.

At super-bargain price Prêtre's reading has much to recommend it. The recording is open to the charge of being over-reverberant, but the overall sound is vivid enough and the performance has vigour and commitment. In the refreshingly brilliant account of the *Carnival of the Animals* Ciccolini and Weissenberg make a contribution of some distinction. It opens a little heavily, but the characterization is nicely managed, with some very good orchestral playing. As Poulenc's *Les Animaux modèles* is based on the fables of La Fontaine, it makes a rather apt bonus, although here the sound is drier.

Martinon's performance of the *Symphony* is, not surprisingly, highly distinguished, the first movement alert and sparkling, the *Poco Adagio* warmly romantic, yet with a touch of nobility at the close. Marie-Claire Alain's powerful entry in the finale will disppoint no one. *Danse macabre* and *Le rouet d'Omphale* are also pieces that Martinon does almost better than anyone, except Beecham, although *Le rouet d'Omphale* here is taken rather fast. The snag is that, while the performances are three star, the CD transfer is certainly not. It has an artificially brightened upper range which brings shrillness to the violins and a fierce edge to the organ sound in the *Symphony*. It is a pity that Warner Classics did not take the trouble to remaster this CD for its reissue, for the Poulenc *Organ Concerto* is even worse!

CHAMBER MUSIC

Bassoon Sonata, Op. 168; Clarinet Sonata, Op. 167; Caprice on Danish & Russian Airs for Flute, Oboe, Clarinet & Piano, Op. 79; Feuillet d'album, Op. 81 (arr. Taffanel); Oboe Sonata, Op. 166; Odelette for Flute & Piano, Op. 162; Romance in D flat for Flute & Piano, Op. 37; Tarantelle for Flute, Clarinet & Piano, Op. 6

(B) *** Cala CACD 1017 (2). Bennett, Daniel, Campbell, Gough & Ens. – DEBUSSY: *Chamber Music* ***

The *Sonatas for Clarinet, for Oboe* and *for Bassoon* are elegantly finished but surprising pieces, with an unaccustomed depth of feeling. The *Caprice* is a diverting kind of pot-pourri, inspired by the composer's visit to Russia in 1876. Paul Taffanel's arrangement of the *Feuillet d'album*, Op. 81, for flute, oboe and two each of clarinets, bassoons and horns, is a first recording and, like almost everything on this record, refreshing and elegant. That goes for the performances too, which are well recorded, though the piano is occasionally overpowering. Strongly recommended – and outstanding value.

Carnival of the Animals (chamber version); Piano Trio in F, Op. 18; Septet in E flat for Trumpet, Strings & Piano, Op. 65

⊶ (BB) *** Virgin 2x1 5 61516-2 (2). Nash Ens. – DVORAK: *Piano Quintet, Op. 81; Piano Trio 4 (Dumky)* ***

In the sparkling Nash chamber version of the *Carnival of the Animals*, Ian Hobson is joined by Susan Tomes. Its humour is nicely captured without clumsiness, and these players make sure the listener does not miss the composer's witty quotations, with delightful results. The *Septet* too is presented with a similar geniality and lightness of touch, and the account of the first of Saint-Saëns's two piano trios is similarly persuasive. The acoustic has warmth and the balance between the instruments, particularly in the *Grande fantaisie zoologique*, is admirably judged. Coupled with fine performances of two of Dvořák's most appealing chamber works, this inexpensive Virgin Double is self-recommending.

Cello Sonatas 1 in C min., Op. 32; 2 in F, Op. 123; Le Cygne (trans. Godowski)

*** Hyp. CDA 67095. Lidström, Forsberg

Written thirty years apart, the two *Cello Sonatas* have an abundant and fluent invention, and are captivating when played with such fervour and polish. These artists radiate total conviction and a life-enhancing vitality and sensitivity.

Piano Quartet in B flat, Op. 41

(N) (M) *** Virgin 482061-2 (2). Kandinsky Qt –
   CASTILLON; CHAUSSON; LEKEU: *Piano Quartets* ***

The *B flat major Piano Quartet* comes from 1875, the period of the *Third* and *Fourth Piano Concertos*, *La Jeunesse d'Hercule* and *Danse macabre*, and is a masterly piece. There is a Mendelssohnian feel to it in places, and the score is characterized by lucidity of texture and the grace and fluency of the writing. Good playing and recording, and thoroughly rewarding couplings.

Piano Trio 1 in F, Op. 18

**(*) Ara. Z 6643. Golub-Kaplan-Carr Trio – DEBUSSY;
   FAURE: *Trios* ***

Piano Trios 1 in F, Op. 18; 2 in E min., Op. 92

(BB) *** Naxos 8.550935. Joachim Trio

No quarrels with the playing of the Joachim Trio (Rebecca Hirsch, Caroline Dearnley and John Lenehan). The pianist in particular has elegance and charm. This is delightful and inventive music, well recorded – and well worth the money.

David Golub, Mark Kaplan and Colin Carr also give a very good account of themselves in the *Piano Trio in F major*. They are intelligent and imaginative. The piano dominates in the right way, and David Golub makes a particularly strong and vital impression. They are very well recorded too.

(i) String Quartets 1 in E min., Op. 112; 2 in G, Op. 153; (ii) Violin Sonatas 1 in D min., Op. 75; 2 in E flat, Op. 102; Berceuse, Op. 38; Elégies Op. 143 & 160; Romance, Op. 37

(BB) **(*) Warner Apex 2564 61426-2 (2). (i) Viotti Qt; (ii)
   Charlier, Hubeau

Saint-Saëns was sixty-four years old when he wrote the *First Quartet*, and eighty-four when he composed its successor! Although neither finds him at his most inspired, a lifetime's experience and an effortless mastery are evident. As a glance at the opus numbers will show, the two violin sonatas are relatively late, the *First* coming from 1885 and the *Second* a decade later. Nevertheless, they are fresh and inventive and full of the composer's usual charm and fluency. Olivier Charlier makes a persuasive case for them. Although the recordings are not more than serviceable, this is a good way of getting to know some rewarding and neglected repertoire at little cost.

Violin Sonata 1 in D min., Op. 75

(N) *** EMI 5 57679-2. Chang, Vogt – FRANCK: *Violin Sonata*; RAVEL: *Violin Sonata* ***

(N) *** New Note Quartz QTZ 2002. Liebeck, Apekisheva –
   CHAUSSON: *Poème*; PROKOFIEV; YSAYE: *Violin Sonatas* ***
*** Essex (ADD) CDS 6044. Accardo, Canio – CHAUSSON:
   Concert ***

Sarah Chang and Lars Vogt make a winning partnership and give an infectiously vivacious account of this engaging sonata. Together with the Franck and the Ravel *G major Sonata* it makes for a strong contender in each work. Good recorded sound too.

Jack Liebeck and Katya Apekisheva find all Saint-Saëns's wistful charm, especially in the *Adagio*, while the Scherzo has the lightest rhythmic touch and the exhilarating finale is busy as a bee. The sound is good, although the violin's upper range can sometimes seem a little undernourished.

The performance of the *D minor Sonata* by Accardo and Canio is also marvellously played, selfless and dedicated. The recording too is very good, and this can be recommended strongly, if the coupling is suitable.

Violin Sonatas 1 in D min., Op. 75; 2 in E flat, Op. 102; Berceuse in B flat, Op. 38; Elégie, Op. 143; Triptyque, Op. 136

*** Hyp. CDA 67100. Graffin, Devoyon

Violin Sonatas 1; 2 in E flat, Op. 102; Berceuse, Op. 38; Introduction & rondo capriccioso, Op. 28 (arr. Bizet)

**(*) ASV CDDCA 892. Xue Wei, Lenehan

Of Saint-Saëns's two *Violin Sonatas* the second is especially appealing with its simple *Andante* and closing *Allegro grazioso*, in which Xue Wei seems thoroughly at home. He is also delightfully nimble in the Scherzo (as is his fine partner, John Lenehan) and he manages the *moto perpetuo* finale of the *First Sonata* with equal facility. Before that comes the lovely *Berceuse*, which shows Xue Wei's tone at its most appealing, but in the opening *Introduction and Rondo capriccioso*, played with real sparkle, the close microphones are unflattering to the violin's upper range.

Hyperion score over its competitors, not only in the up-to-date and beautifully balanced recorded sound but also artistically. Pascal Devoyon is the most imaginative pianist and like his Korean colleague Philippe Graffin has both style and charm. This is an enjoyable disc in every way and more generous than the ASV collection.

ORGAN MUSIC

Bénédiction nuptiale, Op. 9; Elévation ou Communion; Fantaisies: in E flat; in D, Op. 101; 2 Improvisations, Op. 150/1 & 7; Prélude & Fugue in E flat, Op. 99/3

☛ ✿ (N) *** Capriccio Surround Sound SACD 71 046.
   Dorfmüller (Doms Klais organ, Altenburg Cathedral)

In spite of the celebrated *Third Symphony*, one does not think of Saint-Saëns first and foremost as a composer of organ music; yet in 1853 he became the resident at the church at Sainte-Merry (an appropriate name) and four years later was appointed to play the Cavaillé-Coll instrument at Sainte-Madeleine, where he continued until 1877. This CD offers a representative survey of his organ music, and very enjoyable it is. The opening *Prélude and Fugue* exudes a characteristically genial spirit, and the composer's ready tunefulness bursts out in the jolly *Fantaisie in E flat*, which soon expands spectacularly; its companion in E flat major is more reflective. The *Elévation ou Communion* has an affectingly hushed, spiritual atmosphere, and the *Bénédiction*, using the tremolo *vox humana* stop, is gentle and touching. The two *Improvisations*, the highlight of the programme, ought to be much better known. The *F major* is a thoughtful processional with divisions, richly registered, which moves to a splendid climax and closes with a sombre comment on the pedals and celestial fluting. Then, in its *C major* companion, Saint-Saëns really lets himself go in a bouncing, bravura showpiece. Both are marvellously played here, and altogether this is a superb disc. Joachim Dorfmüller is completely at one with the composer, and his performances on this ideal organ are spontaneous and totally involving, especially when the surround sound gives the listener the impression of sitting in the cathedral itself. Altogether a most enjoyable recital, which will appeal to those listeners who (apart from Bach and one or two display pieces like the Widor *Toccata*) do not readily respond to organ music.

VOCAL MUSIC

Choral songs: *Calme des nuits; Des pas dans l'allée; Les Fleurs et les arbres*
*** Ph. 438 149-2. Monteverdi Ch., ORR, Gardiner – FAURE: *Requiem;* DEBUSSY; RAVEL: *Choral Works* ***

Three charming examples of Saint-Saëns's skill and finesse in drawing inspiration from early sources in a way remarkable at the time he was writing. Gardiner and his team give ideal performances, adding to the valuable list of rarities that he provides as coupling for the Fauré *Requiem*.

Mass, Op. 4
(BB) *** Warner Apex 8573 89235-2. Lausanne Vocal Ens., Corboz; Alain; Fuchs (organ) – GOUNOD: *Mass Chorale* ***

The Op. 4 *Mass* of Saint-Saens, like its Gounod coupling, is an early work (1855) but although it still draws on the alternation tradition of the French organ mass, the addition of soloists and orchestral accompaniment makes for a more modern larger-scale work, with only the organ preserving the plainsong tradition. Here the *Mass* is performed with the orchestral music transcribed for a second organ by Léon Rogues, which is less than ideal. Nevertheless this is generally a fine performance. Even if the soloists are not as impressive as the chorus, the choral alternation with the main organ (magnificently played by Marie-Claire Alain) in the *Sanctus* is very impressive, while the *O Salutaris* brings a memorable floating choral line against a gently pointed organ accompaniment, leading to a romantically seraphic *Agnus Dei*. At its modest cost this disc is well worth having.

OPERA

Samson et Dalila (opera; complete)
☛ *** Arthaus **DVD** 100 202. Domingo, Verrett, Wolfgang Brendel, San Francisco Opera Ch. & O, Rudel (Director: Nicolas Joel. V/D: Kirk Browning)
*** EMI 7 54470-2 (2). Domingo, Meier, Fondary, Courtis, L'Opéra-Bastille Ch. & O, Myung-Whun Chung
(M) **(*) DG (ADD) 477 5602-2 (2). Obraztsova, Domingo, Bruson, Lloyd, Thau, Ch. & O de Paris, Barenboim
(N) (M) **(*) Ph. 475 6239 (2). Carreras, Balta, Estes, Burchuladze, Bav. R. Ch. & RSO, C. Davis

(M) ** EMI (ADD) 5 67598-2 [567602] (2). Gorr, Vickers, Blanc, Diakov, René Duclos Ch., Paris Nat. Op. O, Prêtre

Recorded in 1981 at the San Francisco Opera House, this DVD of Saint-Saëns's biblical opera offers a heavily traditional production with realistic sets and costumes like those in a Hollywood epic. Sporting a vast bouffant wig like a tea-cosy (ripe for Dalila's shears in Act II), Plácido Domingo is in magnificent, heroic voice, with Shirley Verrett also at her peak as Dalila, at once seductive and sinister. Other principals are first-rate too, and the chorus, so vital in this opera, sings with incandescent tone in a riproaring performance under Julius Rudel, culminating in a spectacular presentation of the fall of the Temple of Dagon. Most enjoyable.

In the newer, EMI CD set, Domingo with Chung gives a deeper, more thoughtful performance than on DG, broader, with greater repose and a sense of power in reserve. When the big melody appears in Dalila's seduction aria, *Mon cœur s'ouvre*, Chung's idiomatic conducting encourages a tender restraint, where others produce a full-throated roar. Meier may not have an ideally sensuous voice for the role, with some unwanted harshness in her expressive account of Dalila's first monologue, but her feeling for words is strong and the characterization vivid. Generally Chung's speeds are on the fast side, yet the performance does not lack weight, with some first-rate singing in the incidental roles from Alain Fondary, Samuel Ramey and Jean-Philippe Courtis. Apart from backwardly placed choral sound, the recording is warm and well focused.

Barenboim proves as passionately dedicated an interpreter of Saint-Saëns here as he did in the *Third Symphony*, sweeping away any Victorian cobwebs. It is important, too, that the choral passages, so vital in this work, be sung with this sort of freshness, and Domingo has rarely sounded happier in French music, the bite as well as the heroic richness of the voice well caught. Renato Bruson and Robert Lloyd are both admirable too; sadly, however, the key role of Dalila is given an unpersuasive, unsensuous performance by Obraztsova, with her vibrato often verging on a wobble. The recording is as ripe as the music deserves.

When the role of Samson is not one naturally suited to Carreras, it is amazing how strong and effective his performance is, even if top notes under stress grow uneven. Even the very strain seems to add to the intensity of communication, above all the great aria in the last Act, when Samson, blinded, is turning the mill. Unevenness of production is more serious, with Agns Baltsa as Dalila. The microphone often brings out her vibrato, turning it into a judder, and the changes of gear between registers are also underlined. She remains a powerful, characterful singer, but hers is hardly the seductive portrait required in this role, and it is a shortcoming that, like the rest of the cast, she is not a native French-speaker. Both Burchuladze as the Old Hebrew and Simon Estes as Abimelech equally seem intent on misusing once fine voices, but Jonathan Summers as the High Priest of Dagon is far more persuasive. Despite all these reservations, the inspired conducting of Sir Colin Davis, coupled with a refined, atmospheric recording, makes this preferable to the old EMI.

Jon Vickers and Rita Gorr are in commanding voice, both recorded at their vocal peak. Ernest Blanc characterizes well as the High Priest, but the other soloists are undistinguished. The main snag is the conducting of Prêtre, which presents the big moments of high drama effectively enough, but is coarse-grained at too many points. The recording is basically atmospheric and vivid, but from the very opening the choral focus is far from sharp, and the new transfer still brings the occasional touch of distortion on vocal peaks. The overall effect is certainly red-blooded and the set is perhaps more enticing at mid-price, but is hardly an apt candidate for EMI's 'Great Recordings of the Century'.

SAINTE-COLOMBE (died c. 1700)

Concerts à deux violes: Bourrasque; La Dubois; La Raporté; Le Retour; Tombeau 'les regrets'
(B) *** Astrée ES 9968. Savall, Kuijken

Le Retour; Tombeau 'les regrets'
(BB) *** Naxos 8.550750. Spectre de la Rose – MARAIS: *Tombeau pour M. de Sainte-Colombe* etc. ***

The success of the film (*Tous les matins du monde*) about this reclusive composer and his relationship with his pupil, Marin Marais, has led to the soundtrack becoming a bestseller. However, this enterprising and inexpensive Naxos recital includes the 'hits' from the film. The two Saint-Colombe works included are austerely but certainly touchingly played by a fresh-sounding 'authentic' group led by Alison Crum (viola da gamba) and Marie Knight (baroque violin). The Naxos recording is vivid, but its forward balance means that for a realistic effect a modest setting of the volume control should be chosen.

Those who are then tempted to explore the music of Saint-Colombe further might invest in the excellent Auvidis CD featuring Jordi Savall, who was associated with this film. It is performed by artists who have this music in their bones, and the playing is more subtle and has even greater emotional depth. The CD is excellently recorded and is available separately at bargain price.

SALIERI, Antonio (1750–1825)

Overtures: Angiolina, ossia Il matrimonio per sussurro; Cublai, gran kan de'Tartari; Falstaff, ossia Le tre burle; La locandiera. Sinfonia Il giorno onomastico; Sinfonia Veneziana; 26 Variations on La folia di Spagna
*** Chan. 9877. LMP, Bamert

A fascinating disc demonstrating just why Salieri was such a successful composer in his day. The music here brings a profusion of ear-tickling ideas and the secondary themes for his concise and lively overtures are most engaging. Tuttis, with trumpets, are invariably bright and rather grand, but the lighter scoring shows a nice feeling for woodwind colour and there is much elegant phrasing for the violins. The *Larghetto* of the four-movement *Sinfonia Il giorno onomastico* is deliciously delicate, opening with gossamer strings over a pizzicato bass followed by delicate writing for flutes and oboes. The *Allegretto* finale brings an equally charming *moto perpetuo*, and this work could easily be mistaken for a ballet. Perhaps the most striking work is the kaleidoscopic set of *26 Variations on 'La folia'* which occupies eighteen minutes, continually changing colour and mood, often dramatically, sometimes bizarrely, but usually entertainingly (although there is an element of repetition). This piece dates from 1815 and deserves to be better known. The London Mozart Players play all this music most winningly, with vigour, polish and charm and the Chandos recording is state of the art.

Double Concerto in C for Flute & Oboe
*** Chan. 9051. Milan, Theodore, City of L. Sinf., Hickox – MOZART: *Flute & Harp Concerto; Oboe Concerto* ***

Salieri's innocently insubstantial *Double concerto* is quite transformed by the charisma and sheer style of the solo playing from Susan Milan and David Theodore. The exquisite playing of Theodore in the simple melody of the *Largo* and the perfect blending of the two soloists turn it into a really memorable slow movement, and the flute and oboe chase each other round engagingly in their winning decorations of the nicely poised Minuet finale. Hickox's accompaniment is both polished and genial, and the recording casts a pleasing glow over the whole proceedings.

Fortepiano Concertos: in B flat and C
(M) *** Warner Elatus 0927 49556-2. Staier, Concerto Köln – STEFFAN: *Fortepiano Concerto* ***

These two attractive works show Salieri as quite a dab hand at a keyboard concerto, with a distinct personality of his own. The rising arpeggio opening of the *C major Concerto* is a bit square, but its ideas are deftly handled and it has a charming minor-key serenade for its *Larghetto* that reminds one a little (at first) of the slow movement of the Mozart *A major*, K.488; but then it later produces an unusual pizzicato accompaniment. The spirited finale is in contrast to its sad little coda. The *B flat Concerto* opens strongly and has most agreeable secondary material; the *Adagio* brings the more conventional device of an Alberti bass and then closes with a winningly cheerful Minuet, almost a lollipop, with simple but effective variations, giving Staier plenty of opportunities to show the fortepiano's paces, contributing his own creative cadenzas, which the concertos clearly need. Overall the performances could hardly be more persuasive, with the bold, slightly abrasive tuttis from the Concerto Köln adding to the strength of characterization. The recording is first class.

Falstaff, or The Three Tricks (complete)
*** Chan. 9613 (2). Franceschetto, Myeounghee, De Filippo, Chialli, Luis Ciuffo, Bettoschi, Valli, Milan Madrigalists & Guido Cantelli, O, Veronesi

Like Verdi, Salieri and his librettist ignore the Falstaff of the histories. They tell the story within the framework of the conventional two-act opera of the period with crisp and brief numbers leading to extended finales. Though Fenton and Anne (Nannetta) are omitted, Mistress Page (here renamed Slender) is given her husband. Though it never comes near to matching Mozart, it is all great fun, particularly in performances as fresh and lively as these. The Chandos version takes priority over the Hungaroton (HCD 21789/91) – which in any case is currently not easily obtainable – when thanks to the brisk, alert pacing of Veronesi the opera is squeezed on to two discs instead of three. Though Romano Franceschetto in the title role is not so firmly commanding as Joszef Gregor in the Hungarian performance, he does sing characterfully. As for the rest, the Italian cast on Chandos is fresher and more idiomatic than the Hungarian, with fuller sound an added advantage.

'The Salieri Album': Arias from: *La cifra; La fiera Venezia; La finta scena; La grotta di Trofonio; Palmira, regina di Persia; Il ricco d'un guirno; La secchia rapida*
** Decca 475 100-2. Bartoli, OAE, Fischer

It is astonishing when this adventurous disc contains so much imaginative, brilliant and characterful singing, exploiting rare repertory, that it opens with an aria from Salieri's opera, *La secchia rapida*, in which Cecilia Bartoli's performance can only be described as grotesque. With fluttery tone she attacks this bravura piece with ugly squawking. That will be enough to turn off many listeners, but the rest is never less than characterful, often exciting and occasionally moving, even if some of the more demanding of these 13 arias bring some fluttering and roughness of tone that Bartoli would earlier have avoided. Though Salieri's inspiration may be thin compared with that of Mozart, these pieces are consistently lively and inventive, and Bartoli proves a passionate advocate, vigorously accompanied by Adám Fischer and the Orchestra of the Age of Enlightenment. Notes and full texts are provided in a handsome booklet.

SALLINEN, Aulis (born 1935)

(i; ii) *Cello Concerto, Op. 44;* (iii) *Chamber Music I, Op. 38;* (i; iii) *Chamber Music III, Op. 58;* (iii) *Some Aspects of Peltoniemi Hintrik's Funeral March;* (iv) *Sunrise Serenade (for 2 trumpets and chamber orchestra), Op. 63;* (ii) *Shadows, Op. 52; Symphonies 4, Op. 49; 5 (Washington Mosaics), Op. 57*

🔊 (B) *** Finlandia 4509 99966-2 (2). (i) Noras; (ii) Helsinki PO, or (iii) Finland Sinfonietta, Kamu; (iv) Harjanne, Välimäki, Avanti CO

This Finlandia Double brings an extensive survey of Sallinen's music and provides an inexpensive entry into the composer's world. Apart from the symphonies, the *Cello Concerto* of 1976 is the most commanding piece here. Sallinen's ideas resonate in the mind. Artos Noras has its measure and plays with masterly eloquence. *Shadows* is an effective short piece which reflects or 'shadows' the content of the opera *The King Goes Forth to France. Some Aspects of Peltoniemi Hintrik's Funeral March* is a transcription for full strings of the *Third Quartet* (1969), a one-movement work in five variations that never loses sight of its basic folk-inspired idea; not one of the composer's strongest works, but persuasively presented here. The middle movement of the *Fourth Symphony* is marked *Dona nobis pacem;* throughout the finale, bells colour the texture, as is often the case with Sallinen's orchestral writing. *Washington Mosaics* is a five-movement work in which the outer movements form the framework for three less substantial but highly imaginative intermezzi. There are Stravinskian overtones in the first movement and the intermezzi cast a strong spell. The work has a feeling for nature and a keen sense of its power. The performances, under Okko Kamu, are very impressive and the recording quite exemplary. Overall, excellent value.

(i) *Violin Concerto, Op. 18;* (ii) *Nocturnal Dances of Don Juanquixote, Op. 58. Some Aspects of Peltoniemi Hintrik's Funeral March, Op. 19; Variations for Orchestra (Juventas variations), Op. 8*

*** BIS CD 560. (i) Koskinen; (ii) Thedéen; Tapiola Sinf., Vänskä

The *Variations for Orchestra* is an imaginative and inventive piece which shows remarkable command of the orchestra. It is tonally ambiguous without being serial; indeed, at one point there is a reminder of Britten. The *Violin Concerto* is also rewarding and in the slow movement often beautiful, but its lyrical impulse is not strong enough for it to enter the standard repertoire. It has a powerful advocate in Eeva Koskinen. Excellent playing from Torleif Thedéen and the Tapiola Sinfonietta under Osmo Vänskä and a vivid, well-lit but not overbright BIS recording.

(i) *Symphonies 1, 3;* (ii) *Chorali;* (iii) *Cadenze for Solo Violin;* (iv) *Elegy for Sebastian Knight;* (v) *String Quartet 3*

*** BIS (ADD) CD 41. (i) Finnish RSO, Kamu; (ii) Helsinki PO, Berglund; (iii) Paavo Pohjola; (iv) Frans Helmerson; (v) Voces Intimae Qt

The *First Symphony*, in one movement, is diatonic and full of atmosphere, as indeed is the *Third*, a powerful, imaginative piece which appears to be haunted by the sounds and smells of nature. The performances under Okko Kamu are excellent. *Chorali* is a shorter piece, persuasively done by Paavo Berglund; and there are three chamber works, albeit of lesser substance. The recordings are from the 1970s and are all very well balanced. Highly recommended.

(i) *Symphonies 2 (Symphonic Dialogue for Solo Percussion Player & Orchestra), Op. 65; Sunrise Serenade, Op. 63*

*** BIS CD 511. (i) Mortensen; Malmö SO, Okko Kamu

The *Second Symphony*, like the *First*, is a one-movement affair lasting a quarter of an hour. Its sub-title, *Symphonic Dialogue for Solo Percussion Player and Orchestra*, gives an accurate idea of its character, pitting the fine soloist, Gerd Mortensen, against the remaining orchestral forces. The main work is the ambitious *Sixth Symphony*. Like the *Third Symphony*, it is powerfully evocative of natural landscape; indeed, it is one of the strongest and most imaginative of all Sallinen's symphonies. Okko Kamu gets very responsive playing from the Malmö Symphony Orchestra in both symphonies and in the slight but effective *Sunrise Serenade*. The recording is excellent.

Symphonies 4, Op. 49; 5 (Washington Mosaics), Op. 57; Shadows (Prelude for Orchestra), Op. 52

*** BIS CD 607. Malmö SO, James DePreist

Suffice it to say that these performances by the Malmö Symphony Orchestra under James DePreist are every bit as good as the Helsinki rivals listed above; if anything, the recording has more impressive range and definition.

Chamber Music I, Op. 38; (i) *II, for Alto Flute & Strings, Op. 41;* (ii) *III, for Cello & Strings (The Nocturnal Dances of Don Juanquixote), Op. 58. Some Aspects of Peltoniemi Hintrik's Funeral March (Quartet 3 arr. for strings); Sunrise Serenade for 2 Trumpets, Piano & Strings, Op. 63*

(BB) *** Naxos 8.553747. Finnish CO, Kamu, with (i) Juutilainen; (ii) Rondin

Aulis Sallinen's string music is tonal and accessible ('audience friendly'), and in no way forbidding. However, to our ears it is insubstantial, the invention thin and repetitive. Others may respond more warmly to this music, and those who do will find the playing and recording very good indeed.

Kullervo (opera)

*** Ondine ODE 780-3T. Hynninen, Sallinen, Jakobsson, Silvasti, Vihavainen, Finnish Nat. Op. Ch. & O, Söderblom

Although the theme will be familiar from Sibelius's early

symphony of the same name, Sallinen has based his *Kullervo* on the play by Aleksis Kivi and he wrote the libretto himself. The plot emerges from a mixture of narration, in which the chorus plays a central role, and dreams. The opera is a compelling musical drama. Sallinen's musical language has debts to composers as diverse as Britten (shadows of the 'Sunday morning' interlude in *Peter Grimes* briefly cross the score in Kullervo's Dream at the beginning of Act II), Puccini, Debussy even, though they are synthesized into an effective vehicle for a vivid theatrical imagination. There is impressive variety of pace and atmosphere, and the black voices of the Finnish Opera Chorus resonate in the memory. So, too, do the impressive performances of Jorma Hynninen as Kullervo and Anna-Lisa Jakobsson as the smith's young wife and, indeed, the remainder of the cast and the Finnish National Opera Orchestra under Ulf Söderblom. While *Kullervo* may not be a great opera, it is gripping and effective musical theatre, and the Ondine recording has excellent presence and detail.

SANDSTRÖM, Jan (born 1954)

Trumpet Concerto 2

*** BIS CD 1021. Hardenberger, Malmö SO, Varga – BORTZ: *Trumpet Concerto*; RABE: *Sardinsarkofagen* ***

Jan Sandström has just turned 50 and is the youngest of the three Swedish composers on this disc. His concerto, with its pert, if occasionally predictable syncopations, is often diverting and at times in the slow movement even touching. Bright and lively in every way, stunningly played and recorded.

SANTOS, Joly Braga (1924–88)

Symphonies 3 & 6

*** Marco Polo 8.225087. Neves, São Carlos Theatre Ch., Portuguese SO, Cassuto

José Manuel Joly Braga Santos is the leading Portuguese symphonist of his day. His *Third Symphony*, composed in 1949, when he was in his mid-20s, is strongly modal in idiom, with a strong sense of forward movement and a powerful feeling for architecture. It is imaginatively scored and at times suggests Vaughan Williams, and even at one point in the slow movement (about two and a half minutes in) the Shostakovich of the *Fifth Symphony*. The *Sixth Symphony* (1972) is a one-movement work with a closing choral section. The first two-thirds are purely orchestral and more expressionist in their musical language, non-tonal but without being dodecaphonic, the choral part being tonal. Very good performances and recordings.

SARASATE, Pablo (1844–1908)

Carmen Fantasy, Op. 25; Introduction et Tarantelle, Op. 43; Zigeunerweisen.

(M) *** EMI (ADD/DDD) 5 62594-2. Perlman, Abbey Road Ens., Foster – PAGANINI: *Violin Concerto 1* ***

Perlman's *Carmen Fantasy* makes a dazzling encore for his unsurpassed account of the Paganini *Concerto*, and for this reissue in the 'Perlman Edition' EMI have added more dazzling accounts of two other showpieces, the *Introduction et Tarantelle* and *Zigeunerweisen*, recorded digitally in 1995, in which Perlman's tone is even more luscious.

Carmen Fantasy, Op. 25

*** Claudio CB 5256-2. Jin, LSO, Wordsworth – LALO: *Symphonie espagnole*; PROKOFIEV: *Solo Violin Sonata* *** (with Kroll: *Banjo and Fiddle*, orch. Bradbury; Tarrega: *Recuerdos de la Alhambra*, arr. Ricci **(*))

Min Jin does not quite have Perlman's flamboyant panache in Saraste's brilliant arrangement of Bizet, but her airily fragile approach is equally spontaneous and refreshingly different. Against a strong backing from Barry Wordsworth and the LSO, the solo playing is still dazzling, but never uses effect for its own sake. Just sample her delicate harmonic slides (1'06" and 2'12") – and how seductive she is in the delicate *Habañera*, while throughout she clearly relishes Bizet's wonderful tunes. Very good recording, much more naturally balanced than Perlman.

Carmen Fantasy, Op. 25; Zigeunerweisen, Op. 20

*** Ph. (IMS) 464 531-2. Suwanai, Budapest Fest. O, Iván Fischer – DVORAK: *Violin Concerto; Masurek* ***

It takes a magnetic violinist like Akiko Suwanai – the youngest ever winner of the Tchaikovsky Competition in Moscow in 1990 – to bring off Saraste's brilliant showpieces, particularly the *Zigeunerweisen*, which can easily outstay its welcome. Suwanai's virtuoso flair comes out not just in bold bravura playing, but in the daring range of dynamic, with Suwanai communing with herself in extreme, hushed pianissimos. An unexpected if attractive coupling for the Dvořák concerto, very well recorded.

Zigeunerweisen, Op. 20

*** DG 431 815-2. Shaham, LSO, Foster – WIENIAWSKI: *Violin Concertos 1 & 2* etc. ***

(M) (***) RCA mono 09026 61753-2. Heifetz, RCA Victor SO, Steinberg – CHAUSSON: *Poème* **(*); LALO: *Symphony espagnole* (**(*)); SAINT-SAENS: *Havanaise* etc. (***)

(M) (***) EMI mono 7 64251-2. Heifetz, LPO, Barbirolli – SAINT-SAENS: *Havanaise* etc.; VIEUXTEMPS: *Concerto 4*; WIENIAWSKI: *Concerto 2* (***)

(BB) **(*) EMI Encore 5 74735-2. Mutter, O Nat. de France, Ozawa (with MASSENET: *Thaïs: Meditation*) – LALO: *Symphonie espagnole* **(*)

(B) **(*) EMI Debut 5 73501-2. Shapira, ECO, Hazlewood – BLOCH: *Baal Shem* ***; BRUCH: *Violin Concerto 1 in G min., Op. 26* **; BUNCH: *Fantasy* **

Gil Shaham plays Sarasate's sultry and dashing gypsy confection with rich timbre, languorous ardour and a dazzling display of fireworks at the close.

What can one say about the Heifetz performances except that they are unsurpassed: they are dazzling in the fireworks and with the most luscious tone and sophisticated colouring in the lyrical melody. The recording is dry but faithful. This is a marvellous disc.

A sparkling performance of Sarasate's gypsy pot-pourri from Anne-Sophie Mutter, given good support from Ozawa. There are some dazzling fireworks, but some may feel her playing in the famous principal lyrical melody too chaste. The balance places the solo violin well forward, and the timbre is very brightly lit.

Ittai Shapira is a twenty-four-year-old Israeli violinist, whose début recording this is. The closing part of the *Zigeunerweisen* shows that EMI's confidence in him is not misplaced, as does the splendid *Baal Shem*.

Navarra (for violin and piano)

*** Warner 0927 45664-2. Hanslip, Ovrutsky – BRUCH: *Violin Concertos 1 & 3* ***

The Sarasate showpiece with its jaunty Spanish dance-rhythms makes a sparkling extra on Chloë Hanslip's fine recording of the Bruch *Violin Concertos Nos. 1 and 3*. Here she is sensitively accompanied by Mikhail Ovrutsky.

SARUM CHANT

Missa in gallicantu; Hymns: A solis ortus cardine; Christe Redemptor omnium; Salvator mundi, Domine; Veni Redemptor omnium

*** Gimell CDGIM 017. Tallis Scholars, Phillips

Filling in our knowledge of early church music, the Tallis Scholars under Peter Phillips here present a whole disc of chant according to the Salisbury rite – in other words *Sarum Chant* – which, rather than the regular Gregorian style, was what churchgoers of the Tudor period and earlier in England heard at their devotions. The greater part of the record is given over to the setting of the First Mass of Christmas, intriguingly entitled *Missa in gallicantu* or *Mass at Cock-Crow*. Though this is simply monophonic (the men's voices alone are used), it is surprising what antiphonal variety there is. The record is completed with four hymns from the Divine Offices of Christmas Day. The record is warmly atmospheric in the characteristic Gimell manner.

SATIE, Erik (1866–1925)

PIANO MUSIC

Piano, 4 hands: *La Belle excentrique; Chapitres tournés en tous sens; En habit de cheval; 3 Morceaux en forme de poire; 3 Petites pièces montées.* Solo piano music: *Aperçus désagréables; Avant dernières pensées; Carnet d'esquisses et de croquis; Croquis et agaceries d'un gros bonhomme en bois; Descriptions automatiques; Danses gothiques; Embroyens desséchés; Enfantillages pittoresques; La fils des étoiles; 3 Gnossiennes (2 sets); 3 Gymnopédies; Heures séculaires et instananées; Jack in the Box; Menus propos enfantins; Musiques intimes et secrètes; 2 Nocturnes; 3 Nocturnes; Ogives; Pages mystiques; Les pantins dansent; Passacaille; Peccadilles importunes; 12 Petites chorals; Petite ouverture à danser; 6 Pièces de la période 1906–13; Pièces froides & Nouvellles pièces froides; Le piège de Méduse; Poudre d'or; Première menuet; Première pensée de la Rose + Croix & Sonneries de la Rose + Croix; 4 Préludes; Préludes flasques (pour un chien); Prélude et tapisserie; Rêveries de l'enfance de Pantagruel; 2 Rêveries nocturnes; 3 Sarabandes; Sonatine bureaucratique; Sports et divertissements; 3 Valses du précieux dégoûté; Véritable préludes flasques (pour un chien); Vieux sequins et viellies cuirasses*

(BB) **(*) EMI (ADD) 5 74534-2 (5) Ciccolini

Recorded between 1967 and 1971, Aldo Ciccolini's 5-CD survey of Satie's piano music is now the most comprehensive available, including a number of novelties and many works in revisions by Robert Cadby. Ciccolini's playing is certainly sympathetic and idiomatic, and he manages the four-handed pieces by pre-recording and playing in duet with himself. The

currrent remastering by EMI France has improved the realism of the piano image – it is firm, full and clear, just a bit hard at times, but fully acceptable. The notes, however, are sparse and only in French without translation. Those not wanting such an extensive coverage, inexpensive as it is, might turn to a single CD recorded during the 1980s where in the piano duet pieces Ciccolini is joined by Gabriel Tacchino, to even greater effect (see below).

La Belle excentrique; En habit de cheval (both for piano, four hands); Embryons desséchés; 6 Gnossiennes; 3 Gymnopédies; Jack in the Box; 3 Morceaux en forme de poire; 3 Nocturnes; Sports et divertissements

(N) (BB) *** EMI Encore (ADD) 6 86430-2. Ciccolini

This is an inexpensive, generous (78 minutes) and well-chosen collection which includes the earlier recordings of the two four-handed works in which Ciccolini plays both parts by electronic means. Here the sound is a bit brittle, but for the most part EMI's remastering of recordings made over a decade from 1965 onwards makes the very most of sound which has good sonority and excellent focus, and is only occasionally a trifle hard. With the favourite *Gymnopédies* and *Gnossiennes* included, this is excellent value for bargain hunters.

Piano, 4 Hands: (i) *La Belle excentrique; 3 Morceaux en forme de poire.* Solo piano: *Avant-dernières pensées; Caresse; Chapitres tournés en tous sens; Croquis et agaceries d'un gros bonhomme en bois; Danse de travers; Descriptions automatiques; Embryons desséchés; 6 Gnossiennes; 3 Gymnopédies; Heures séculaires et instantanées; Je te veux; 2 Oeuvres de jeunesse: Valse ballet; Fantaisie valse. Passacaille; Les pantins dansent; Le Piccadilly (Marche); Première Pensée Rose + Croix; Petite ouverture à danser; Pièces froides I: Airs à faire fuir. II: Danse de travers. Poudre d'or; Prélude de la porte héroïque du ciel; Prélude et tapisserie; Sonatine bureaucratique; 3 Valses distinguées du précieux*

(N) (BB) *** Virgin 5 62363-2 (4). Queffélec; (i) with Collard – RAVEL: *Piano Music* **(*)

Although we think Pascal Rogé is very special in this repertoire, Anne Queffélec has strong claims too. She can be quirky, as in the opening *Croquis et agaceries d'un gros bonhomme en bois* or, more particularly, the satirical *Valse ballet*; she is engagingly cool in the *Pièces froides*; her accounts of the *Caresse* and *Les Pantins dansent* are quite haunting, while the *Petite ouverture à danser* has much charm. In the *Trois morceaux en forme de poire* and the lively *La Belle excentrique* she is partnered by the late lamented Catherine Collard, and how brilliantly they end the first CD with that final quartet of sparkling vignettes, opening with the dazzling *Grande ritournelle* and ending with the irrepressible *Can-can 'grand-mondain'*.

The second disc includes the celebrated *Gnossiennes* and *Gymnopédies*, beautifully evoked, and fills out the collection to make it one of the most comprehensive in the catalogue. Throughout, her playing has much subtlety and character, and the music is despatched with great character and style. Nor does she possess less charm than Pascal Rogé. The piano sound is excellent: it is firm, clean and fresh, with a splendid tonal bloom. This is very recommendable, and her coupled Ravel collection is very rewarding too.

Piano, 4 hands: (i) *La Belle excentrique; 3 Morceaux en forme de poire.* Solo piano: *Descriptions automatiques; Embryons desséchés; 3 Gnossiennes; 3 Gymnopédies; 2 Valses*

(M) *** Virgin 5 61846-2. Queffélec; (i) with Collard

This mid-price reissue also includes solo items from the earlier recital above, dating from 1988, notably the celebrated *Gymnopédies* and *Gnossiennes*. All the music here is dispatched with great character and style, and these artists are exceptionally well served by the engineers. These solo items are also available on a budget disc (HMV 6 86761-2) together with a Debussy recital by Ciccolini.

Music for Piano, 4 hands: (i) *La Belle excentrique; 3 Morceaux en forme de poire.* Solo piano music: *Avant-dernières pensées; Embryons desséchés; 6 Gnossiennes; Croquis et agaceries d'un gros bonhomme en bois; 3 Gymnopédies; 5 Nocturnes; Sonatine bureaucratique; Véritables préludes flasques (pour un chien)*

(M) *** EMI 5 67239-2. Ciccolini; (i) with Tacchino

Aldo Ciccolini recorded this selection during the 1980s and he is completely in sympathy with their style. He is totally inside this music and makes the most of its (not particularly wide) contrasts of mood and atmosphere. The recorded sound, harder in outline and not as rich as afforded to Pascal Rogé in his complete survey on Decca, is still very good. And some may feel that the slight edge given to the sharply articulated pieces (the *Embryons desséchés* and the *Sonatine bureaucratique* for instance) adds to their witty vitality. Gabriel Tacchino joins his colleague for the four-handed pieces. In many ways this is one of the most distinctive Satie collections in the catalogue.

The Angora Ox; La Belle excentrique; La Diva de l'Empire, Dreaming Fish; L'enfance de Ko-Quo; 7 Gnossiennes; 3 Gymnopédies; 5 Grimaces pur le songe d'une nuit d'été; Jack-in-the-box; Je te veux; Le Piccadilly; Sonatine bureaucratique; Versets laïques et somptueux

** Decca 470 290-2. Thibaudet

Jean-Yves Thibaudet's disc includes some miniatures that have not been recorded before (*L'enfance de Ko-Quo* was discovered only a few years ago) but he is curiously heavy-handed. Expressive details are underlined with unidiomatic rubato while other pieces are gabbled without allowing their wit and subtlety to register. No challenge here to Decca's own Pascal Rogé.

Avant-dernières pensées; Caresse; Chapitres tournées en tous sens; 3 Gymnopédies; Jack-in-the-Box; 6 Pièces de la Période 1906–13; Préludes flasques (pour un chien); 2 Rêveries nocturnes; Sonata bureaucratique; Sports et Divertissements

(BB) **(*) Warner Apex 0927 41380-2. Legrand

Michel Legrand is an unpredictable Satie exponent. He opens his recital with a very measured performance of the *First Gymnopédie*, then rushes into the opening movement of the *Sonata bureaucratique* breathlessly; after taking a brief breath in the *Andante*, he plays the finale equally brilliantly. The *Sports et Divertissements* are very percussive. Yet he finds charm there too, and later, poise, especially in the rare *Pièces de la Période 1906–13*, the *Avant-dernières pensées*, and *Chapitres tournées*, all of which are individually characterized. He uses the other two *Gymnopédies*, played just as slowly, as peaceful interludes. The piano recording is faithful but a trifle hard, yet this remains a stimulating recital, lacking

innocence perhaps, but not bravura, commitment or understanding.

(i) *Avant-dernières pensées; Embryons desséchés; Gnossiennes 1–5; Gymnopédies 1–3; Nocturne 1; Sarabandes 1–3; Sonatine bureaucratique; 3 Valses distinguées du précieux dégoût;* (ii) *Croquis et agaceries d'un gros bonhomme en bois; Descriptions automatiques; Je te veux; Poudre d'or*

(B) **(*) Sony (ADD) SBK 48283. (i) Varviso; (ii) Entremont

Both recitals here were recorded in 1979. Daniel Varviso has the measure of these pieces and plays admirably. Perhaps the first of the *Embryons desséchés* could have greater delicacy and wit, and there could be greater melancholy in the second of the *Gymnopédies*. But one's main reservation concerns the closely balanced recording of the piano and the slightly dry sound. Philippe Entremont, too, is placed forwardly, but he brings some charm to *Je te veux* and *Poudre d'or*, while the *Descriptions automatiques* are engagingly crisp and witty.

Avant-dernières pensées; Embryons desséchés; 6 Gnossiennes; 3 Gymnopédies; Pièces froides; Sarabande 3; Sonatine bureaucratique; 3 Valses distinguées du précieux dégoût; 3 Véritables préludes flasques (pour un chien)

*** BIS CD 317. Pöntinen

Roland Pöntinen seems perfectly in tune with the Satiean world, and his playing is distinguished by sensibility and tonal finesse. He is very well recorded too.

Berceuse; Caresse; 6 Gnossiennes; 3 Gymnopédies; Nocturne 4; 2 Oeuvres de jeunesse; Peccadilles importunes; Petit prélude à la journée; Le Piccadilly; Poudre d'or; Prélude de la porte héroïque du ciel; Rêverie du pauvre; Sonatine bureaucratique

❿— *** Decca 458 105-2. Rogé

This generous compilation, taken from Pascal Rogé's uniquely distinguished Decca coverage of Satie's piano music, is entitled (reasonably enough) 'Piano Dreams'. The selection concentrates on the composer's gentler, haunting evocations, including – besides the *Gymnopédies* and *Gnossiennes* – several highlights from the third disc, which we especially enjoyed. The mood livens up towards the close, with the ragtime valse from the *Oeuvres de jeunesse*, and finally the cakewalk, *Le Piccadilly*. With first-class recording, this could well be a first choice for those wanting a single-disc Satie collection.

Chapitres tournés en tous sens; Croquis et agaceries d'un gros bonhomme en bois; Le Fils des étoiles; Gymnopédies; Je te veux (valse); Prélude et tapisserie; Le Piccadilly; Pièces froides; Le Piège de Méduse; Poudre d'or; Sonata bureaucratique; Sports et divertissements; Véritables préludes flasques pour un chien; Vexations

(M) *** RCA 09026 63976-2. Dickinson

Peter Dickinson has made Satie's music a centrepoint of his repertoire, and his thoughtful approach to this highly rewarding music is all his own, often more withdrawn than usual. By his side Ciccolini sounds almost brittle. The *Trois Gymnopédies*, taken very slowly, have a grave dignity, and Dickinson finds a captivating delicacy of feeling for the *Chapitres tournés en tous sens*. The *Sonata bureaucratique* is playful rather than ironic, its *Andante* most delicate, while the *Pièces froides* have a distinct air of nostalgia.

Of the two *valses*, *Je te veux* is attractively intimate, *Poudre d'or* more populist, though not without refined light and shade. *Piccadilly* is as perky as ever, and the charming rhythmic diversity of the dance vignettes which make up *Le Piège de Méduse* is matched by the *Sports et divertissements*, which have a much wider range of character and feeling here than in most performances. Throughout, Dickinson's variety of articulation and colour is fully at the service of the composer, and he departs in an air of mystery with his gentle account of the enigmatic *Vexations*. The recording, made at the Maltings in 1989, and engineered by the late Bob Auger, is very real indeed.

Embryons desséchés; 6 Gnossiennes; 3 Gymnopédies; Heures séculaires et instantanées; Nocturnes 1–5; Sonatine bureaucratique; Sports et divertissements
(N)(BB) *** Hyp. Helios CDH 55176. Seow

The Singapore-born pianist Yitkin Seow is a good stylist; his approach is fresh and his playing crisp and marked by consistent beauty of sound. Seow captures the melancholy of the *Gymnopédies* very well and the playing, though not superior to Rogé or Queffélec in character or charm, has a quiet reticence that is well suited to this repertoire. The recording is eminently truthful.

Embryons desséchés; 6 Gnossiennes; 3 Gymnopédies; Je te veux; Nocturne 4; Le Piccadily; 4 Préludes flasques; Prélude en tapisserie; Sonatine bureaucratique; Vieux séquins et vieilles cuirasses
*** Decca 410 220-2. Rogé

Rogé has real feeling for this music and conveys its grave melancholy as well as he does its lighter qualities. He produces, as usual, consistent beauty of tone, and this is well projected by the recording. Very well recorded, too.

'Rose + Croix': Danses gothiques; 4 Ogives; Prière; 4 Préludes; Prélude de la Porte héroïque du Ciel; Première pensée Rose Croix; Sonneries de la Rose Croix
(N) *** MDG 613 1064-2. Schleiermacher

During the 1890s Satie became involved in the mystical/religious Ordre de Temple de la Rose + Croix, and all these piece are associated with this encounter. The four *Ogives* were written earlier (in 1886) and act as a kind of 'liturgical' preparation. In each of these atmospheric pieces (inspired by the pointed arches in Notre Dame) a simple melody appears, first as a monody then in chordal style, with strong dynamic contrasts. The *Première Pensée* and *Sonneries de la Rose Croix* of 1891 are directly associated with the Rosicrucians, with whom Satie became briefly linked, and musically they follow on naturally from the *Ogives*. The *Sonneries* are more animated, but the serene chordal sequences still dominate the music. The *Prière* then acts as a gentle coda. But the four *Préludes*, although written much later (between 1888 and 1892) continue the simplicity and semi-religious mood of the Rosicrucian inspiration and are thematically reminiscent of the earlier music. The sombre *Danses gothiques* (1893), which are dances in name only, continue the block chords in a thoughtfully uneventful, melancholy fashion, with the *Prélude de la Porte héroïque du Ciel* acting as a final postlude. Steffen Schleiermacher plays this music sensitively and (remarkably) all but manages to avoid monotony. He is beautifully recorded, and this is a programme to dip into.

SAUER, Emil von (1862–1942)

Piano Concerto 1 in E min.
*** Hyp. CDA 66790. Hough, CBSO, Foster –
   SCHARWENKA: *Piano Concerto 4* ***

This potent coupling of Sauer and Scharwenka surely combines every feature of the 'Romantic concerto', from flamboyant display to beguiling lyricism. As a greatly admired virtuoso, Emil von Sauer was an able exponent of the Scharwenka concerto; and his own work, although lighter in feeling, makes comparable demands on the dexterity of the soloist. Its delightful melodic vein and style have much in common with Saint-Saëns. Stephen Hough sparkles his way through its glittering upper tessitura. Altogether this makes a perfect foil for the more ambitious concerto with which it is paired. Splendid recording, with a nice sense of scale.

SAUGUET, Henri (1901–89)

Mélodie concertante for Cello & Orchestra
*** Russian Disc (ADD) RDCD 11108. Rostropovich, USSR
   SO, composer – BRITTEN: *Cello Symphony* **(*)

Sauguet belongs at the heart of the Gallic tradition, and the opening of his *Mélodie concertante* has a dream-like pastoral. Its source of inspiration was an old, persistent memory of a young cellist from Bordeaux. It is an extended improvisation, based on a haunting, introspective theme heard at the beginning of the piece. The performance is, of course, authoritative in every way, and the 1964 analogue recording sounds every bit as good as it did in its fine LP format.

SCARLATTI, Alessandro (1660–1725)

(i) *Concerti grossi 1–6;* **(ii)** *Stabat Mater*
(M) **(*) DG (ADD) 459 454-2 (2). (i) Solisti from Scarlatti
   Orchestra of Naples, Gracis; (ii) Freni, Berganza, Paul
   Kuenz CO, Mackerras – PERGOLESI: *Stabat Mater* **(*)

Ettore Gracis's recording of these six fine *Concerti grossi* was made in the 1960s. The first three act as a postlude to Scarlatti's memorably searching setting of the *Stabat Mater*; the remainder are used in a similar way for the coupled Pergolesi setting. In the vocal work, recorded a decade later, there is fine singing from both soloists, and the beauty of the writing is never in doubt, even if the balance unduly favours the voices, while the orchestral playing could be more resilient. The accounts of the *Concerti grossi* are alive and workmanlike, but not as fresh or accomplished as those by I Musici.

Sonatas for Recorder, 2 Violins & Continuo in A min. & F. Cantatas: Bella Dama di nome Santa; Perché tacete, regolati concenti
(N) **(*) MDG 309 0632-2. Wessel, Musica Alta Ripa (with
   Francesco Scarlatti: *Cantata in un'ostante*) – DOMENICO
   SCARLATTI: *Cantata: Doppo lungo servire* **(*)

A well-planned record in that it not only includes music by Domenico Scarlatti, but also a charming pastoral cantata by Alessandro's brother, Francesco. The works by Alessandro include a pair of lively *Trio Sonatas* and two *Cantatas*, each with an instrumental obbligato to tickle the ear; *Bella Dama* uses a flute and *Perché tacete* a solo violin. Musica Alpa Ripa's instrumental contribution is first class, and Kai Wessel sings with espressivo and style. The only possible reservation is that his male alto timbre, which is slightly 'hooty', may not appeal to all listeners.

Cantatas

Cantatas: *Clori e Mirtillo; E pur vuole il cielo e amore; Ero e Leandro; Filli che esprime la sua fede a Fileno; Marc'Antonio e Cleopatra; Questo silenzio ombroso*

(B) **(*) VIRGIN 5 61803-2 (2). Lesne, Piau, Il Seminario Musicale – HANDEL: *Italian Cantatas* **(*)

As so often with this repertoire, the texts dramatize the problems of lovers who are unable to be together or who destiny insists must part. The most dramatic of these is the dialogue between Antony and Cleopatra at the moment when he has to leave for Rome. The opening, much shorter, pastoral cantata here, *Questa silenzio ombroso* ('This shady quietude'), is a deeply expressive duet which lightens as the soprano line describes the sweetly lamenting nightingale. *Filli che esprime la sua fede a Fileno*, an expression of steadfast love, has a long instrumental introduction for violin and flute which comes off well. Both vocal artists are on top form, and the simple continuo accompaniments are admirably played by Il Seminario Musicale. This is specialized repertoire, perhaps not to all tastes; but Lesne and Piau are exceptional artists. This disc now comes as a Virgin Double coupled inexpensively with *Italian Cantatas* by Handel. The snag is the absence of texts and translations.

Cantata per la Notte di Natale: Abramo, il tuo sembiante (Christmas Eve cantata)

*** Opus 111 OP 30-156. Bertini, Fedi, Cavina, Naglia, Foresti, Concerto Italiano, Alessandrini – CORELLI: *Christmas concerto grosso in G min., Op. 6/8* ***

This delightful semi-operatic cantata presents the Nativity through the eyes of five figures from the Old Testament, Abraham (bass), Ezekiel (soprano), Isaiah (tenor), Jeremiah (alto) and Daniele (soprano), who are all together in Limbo, where they await the Messiah. There is splendid music for all the soloists, and especially the excellent male alto, Claudio Cavina, who, as Jeremiah, foresees and laments the coming suffering and death of Christ. The whole performance bursts with life under Rinaldo Alessandrini, and makes a fine entertainment, touching, but never solemn. Corelli's most famous concerto grosso, with its *Pastorale* closing movement, is used as a vivacious introduction. The recording sparkles and this is very highly recommended.

Cantatas: *Il rossignuolo se scioglie il volo; Clori vezzosa e bella*

(*) Australian Decca Eloquence (ADD) 461 596-2. Watts, Dupré, Dart – HANDEL: *Italian Cantatas* *

Very attractive performances dating from the late 1950s in warm, vivid sound. The only curious thing is a low rumble which affects these two cantatas from time to time but which is noticeable with only viola de gamba and harpsichord accompaniments. The main Handel items (with orchestra) are unaffected.

Motets: *De tenebroso lacu; Infirmata, vulnerata;* (i) *Salve Regina. Totus amore languens*

(M) *** Virgin (ADD) 5 45103-2. Lesne; (i) Gens; Il Seminario Musicale

Alessandro Scarlatti wrote about a hundred motets. Often strikingly original, in many ways they are like vocal concerti grossi, contrasting slow and fast movements to suit the text; at the same time they combine an Italianate expressive melodic cantilena with an operatic feeling for drama. Lesne is right inside the music's expressive world and it is difficult to imagine this being better sung. In the setting of *Salve Regine* he is joined by Véronique Gens, and their voices blend admirably. Throughout, the accompaniments are creative, vital and warmly supportive – stimulating and beautiful in their own right. This is period-instrument performance at its most revealing. The recording is vivid, yet has just the right degree of warmth and spaciousness. Full translations are provided.

Motets: *Domine, refugium factus es nobis; O magnum mysterium*

(B) *** Double Decca (ADD) 443 868-2 (2). Schütz Ch. of L., Roger Norrington – BONONCINI: *Stabat Mater* ***; PERGOLESI: *Magnificat in C; Stabat Mater* **(*); DOMENICO SCARLATTI: *Stabat Mater;* CALDARA: *Crucifixus;* LOTTI: *Crucifixus* ***

These two motets are fine pieces that show how enduring the Palestrina tradition was in seventeenth-century Italy. They are noble in conception and are beautifully performed here and, given first-class sound, make a fine bonus for this enterprising Double Decca collection of Italian baroque choral music.

Oratorio per la Santissima Trinità

(N) *** Virgin 5 545666-2 (2). Invernizzi, Gens, Genaux, Agnew, Abbondanza, Europa Galante Ens., Biondi

When, in 1715 in Naples, Alessandro Scarlatti wrote this, one of the last of his 40 oratorios, his music was coming to be regarded as out of date. It did not help that, unlike most of his religious oratorios, based on Biblical sources, the subject was undramatic, a theological discussion on the doctrine of the Trinity, personalized in the allegorical figures of Faith, Divine Love, Theology, Time and Infidelity, that last improbably a tenor role, excellently taken here by Paul Agnew. What this fresh account of the oratorio under Fabio Biondi demonstrates throughout is the liveliness of Scarlatti's inspiration. The 49 sections last a little over an hour, with brief recitatives punctuating dozens of tiny arias and duets, almost all brisk. Outstanding in a first-rate team of soloists is the ravishing Véronique Gens as Divine Love.

(i) *Salve Regina;* (i; ii) *Stabat Mater;* (iii) Motet: *Quae est ista*

**(*) Virgin 5 45366-2. (i) Lesne; (ii) Piau; (i–iii) Novelli; Il Seminario Musicale

Gérard Lesne is heard at his finest in Scarlatti's eloquent A minor setting (one of five) of the *Salve Regina*, expressive and dramatic by turns. But when he joins with Sandrine Piau for the *Stabat Mater* the combination of voices is characterful in its contrast rather than a vocal symbiosis. Sandrine Piau's singing is pure, and tenderly touching, Lesne is more dramatic and brings a wider range of vocal colour, but his contribution is less moving. The two singers are successfully joined by the tenor Jean-François Novelli for the attractive closing motet, *Quae est ista*, which is widely varied in style; but again it is the soprano who stands out. Il Seminario give pleasing authentic support and this is a stimulating collection, but collectors primarily interested in the *Stabat Mater* will find that the performance by Gemma Bertagnolli and Sara Mingardo with the Concerto Italiano remains unsurpassed (see below).

Stabat Mater

⊶ **(N) (B)** *** Opus 111 OPS 30406. Bertagnolli, Mingardo, Concerto Italiano, Alessandrini – PERGOLESI: *Stabat Mater* *** ✪

If somewhat less theatrical than Pergolesi's setting, Scarlatti's music brings continual bursts of vitality to contrast with the rich flowing polyphonic lines when the soprano and alto voices are combined. There are memorably expressive solos for both singers and, as in the companion work, they combine touchingly for the work's closing benediction before the tension lifts at the coda. Once again both the radiant soprano, Gemma Bertagnolli, and the dark-voiced contralto, Sara Mingardo, rise fully to the challenge of this remarkable music, and Alessandrini's instrumental support could not be more persuasive or authentic.

Sedecia (oratorio; complete)

*** Virgin 5 45452-2 (2). Lesne, Pochon, Jaroussky, Harvey, Padmore, Il Seminario Musicale, Lesne

This superb première recording of *Sedecia, re di Gerusalemme* reveals a vital masterpiece written for Rome in 1705, where oratorio regularly took the place of secular opera. The most important of Scarlatti's oratorios on an Old Testament theme, *Sedecia* tells the story of the last king of Jerusalem and the punishment meted out to him at the hands of Nebuchadnezzar. Though it was dismissed as 'extremely tedious' by Edward J. Dent in his biography of the composer, that shallow judgement is absurd. The fast-moving sequence of 54 generally compact numbers, arias and recitatives, punctuated by the occasional duet and rounded off with a chorus, broadly follow the pattern later developed by Handel in his English oratorios, with a flexibility, energy and variety of invention found only in the finest religious music of the period. Gérard Lesne, himself taking the counter-tenor role of the king, directs a performance which with an excellent cast carries the listener forward – through the preparation of Part One, to a most moving climax in Part Two, with one deeply expressive aria after another. The work culminates in a duet marked by scrunching suspensions, where the blinded Sedecia bids farewell to his wife, Anna. Following Lesne's own example, each of the principals sings with clear, fresh tone and superb technique. Clear, well-balanced recording to match. Not to be missed.

SCARLATTI, Domenico (1685–1757)

The Good-humoured Ladies (ballet suite; arr. Tommasini)

(***) Testament mono SBT 1309. Paris Conservatoire O, Désormière (with IPPOLITOV-IVANOV: *Caucasian Sketches, Op. 10*; TCHAIKOVSKY: *Sleeping Beauty: Suite* (***))

(B) **(*) Sony (ADD) SBK 60311. Cleveland O, Lane – RESPIGHI: *The Birds; Church Windows* **(*)

The Good-humoured Ladies was a Diaghilev commission which enjoyed much success in its day; it draws on Scarlatti in much the same way as Stravinsky drew on Pergolesi in *Pulchinella*. Tommasini scores with great wit and character. Roger Désormière directs with unerring style and character. This 1951 performance, originally coupled with *Les biches*, is

unlikely to be surpassed except in recording quality. It was produced (like the rest of the programme) by John Culshaw, and readers should snap it up.

Scarlatti's music in Tommasini's witty arrangement chatters along very like a group of dear old ladies gossiping over tea. Louis Lane directs freshly an enjoyable account of this delightfully light-hearted music, so wittily scored. The Clevelanders respond with style and delicacy, and the 1970 Severance Hall recording is warm and pleasing, even if ideally it could be a little more transparent. However, the so-called '*Cats' Fugue*' is neatly and clearly articulated, and Lane scores a bonus point by including the *Overture*.

Keyboard Sonatas (complete)

(N) (B) *** Erato 2564 62092-2 (34), Ross, Huggett, Coin, Henry, Vallon

The outstanding integral recording of Scarlatti's 555 *Keyboard Sonatas* (originally issued for the composers tercentenary) has reappeared just as we go to press, complete with the accompanying 200-page book at less than half the original price. They include works for violin and continuo, and for the unlikely combination of violin and oboe in unison. Scott Ross at the keyboard (harpsichord and organ) is joined by Monica Huggett, Christopher Coin and others, and this excellently recorded set provides an endless source of interest and satisfaction.

Keyboard Sonatas, Kk.1, 20, 98, 159, 450, 487

(N) *** DG **DVD** 073 4045. Pogorelich (piano) (Director: Humphrey Burton) – BACH: *English Suites 2 & 3* **(*); BEETHOVEN: *Piano Sonata 11* **(*)

Ivo Pogorelich is at his most dazzling in these brilliant accounts of a well-chosen clutch of sonatas, crisply articulated on the piano. His tempi are brisk but never sound hurried. This is not the only way to play Scarlatti, but it is certainly involving, especially the well-known *C major* piece, K.159, which ends the recital infectiously. The camera watches his hands as well as taking overall shots, and the changes are not distracting. Good, clean, bright sound.

Keyboard Sonatas, Kk.1, 9, 14, 27, 38, 103, 114, 141, 208, 213, 296–9, 380, 490–92, 555

(M) **(*) Warner Elatus 2564 60030-2. Ross (harpsichord)

This is a well-chosen selection from Scott Ross's complete coverage of the *Keyboard Sonatas*, made in 1984–5 and just reissued. He plays freshly, perhaps a little didactically at times, but always very musically, and he is very well recorded. The harpsichord is not named.

Keyboard Sonatas, Kk.1, 3, 8–9, 11, 17, 24–5, 27, 29, 87, 96, 113, 141, 146, 173, 213–14, 247, 259, 268, 283–4, 380, 386–7, 404, 443, 519–20, 523

⊶ *** Virgin 5 61961-2 (2). Pletnev (piano)

This carefully chosen selection of some of Scarlatti's finest and most adventurous sonatas, stretches over two CDs, giving the fullest opportunity to demonstrate the extraordinary range of this music in a recital-length programme playing for 140 minutes. In the opening *D major Sonata*, Kk.443, Pletnev establishes a firm pianistic approach, yet the staccato articulation reminds us that the world of the harpsichord is not so far away. However, in the *G major Sonata*, Kk.283, and in the following Kk.284 his fuller piano sonority transforms the effect of the writing. The second CD opens with the almost orchestral Kk.96 *in D*, with its resonant horn calls, and later the lovely, flowing *C minor Sonata* and the even more expressive Kk.11 *in F sharp minor* bring a reflective poetic feeling, which could not have been matched in colour by the plucked instrument. The performances throughout are in the very front rank.

Keyboard Sonatas, Kk.1, 8–9, 11, 13, 20, 87, 98, 119, 135, 159, 380, 450, 487 & 529
*** DG 435 855-2. Pogorelich (piano)

Pogorelich plays with captivating simplicity and convinces the listener that this is music which sounds far more enjoyable on the piano than on the harpsichord. His dazzling execution, using the lightest touch, consistently enchants the ear with its subtle tonal colouring, and the music emerges ever sparkling and fresh. These performances can be measured against those of Horowitz and not be found wanting. Moreover Pogorelich is beautifully recorded in an ideal acoustic, and the hour-long programme is admirably chosen to provide maximum variety.

Keyboard Sonatas, Kk.8, 13, 44, 184, 246, 402, 421, 427, 430, 434, 446, 450, 487, 523, 531, 533, 544
(BB) (***) Naxos 8.553061. Andjaparidze (piano)

Naxos have planned their Scarlatti survey to include different pianists, and the Georgian pianist Eteri Andjaparidze, the youngest prize-winner in Moscow's Tchaikovsky competition, proves an excellent choice for the first collection. She plays with finesse, elegance and style and is at her finest in the reflective minor-key sonatas. The snag is that this recital was recorded over three days in June 1994, and for some reason the piano pitch is not consistent and changes disconcertingly between some items. Otherwise the recording is of high quality.

Keyboard Sonatas, Kk.8, 20, 32, 107, 109, 124, 141, 159, 234, 247, 256, 259, 328, 380, 397, 423, 430, 440, 447, 481, 490, 492, 515 & 519
(M) (***) EMI mono 7 64934-2. Landowska (harpsichord)

Landowska led the revival of interest in the harpsichord at a time when it was a relative rarity both in the recital room and in the recording studio. She used a thunderous Pleyel that was specially built to withstand the rigours of 1920s and '30s travel, but her playing has more character than most other modern players put together; it is electrifying in its sheer vitality and imagination. Lionel Salter's excellent notes quote her as saying she was 'sensitive to Scarlatti's bucolic mind, his rustic jauntiness … the elemental strength, the richness of his rhythmical power, as well as all that is Moorish in them. He has the genuine nobility, the heroism and the audacity of Don Quixote.' The first batch of sonatas was recorded in 1934 and the others in 1939 and 1940. Indispensable.

Keyboard Sonatas, Kk.9, 13 & 430
(M) **(*) Sony (ADD) SMK 87753. Gould (piano) – BACH: *Aria variata*; C. P. E. BACH: *Sonata* **(*)

Glenn Gould's precise articulation suits Scarlatti and these three varied sonatas are full of life. Good, clear (if rather dry) recording to match.

Keyboard Sonatas, Kk.9, 27, 33, 69, 87, 96, 159, 193, 247, 427, 492, 531; Fugue in G min., Kk.30
(BB) *** Warner Apex (ADD) 0927 44353-2. Queffélec (piano)

Anne Queffélec employs a modern Steinway with great character and aplomb. She immediately captures the listener in the dashing opening of the *D major Sonata*, Kk.96, with its lively fanfares and, in the gentler *B minor*, Kk.27, her rippling passage-work is Bach-like in its simplicity. She alternates reflective works with those sonatas calling for sparkling bravura and her choice is unerringly effective: the recital closes with the *Fugue*, which unfolds with calm inevitability. The 1970 recording is first class; the piano is naturally focused and has plenty of space without any resonant blurring.

Keyboard Sonatas, Kk.12, 25, 27, 45, 118, 183, 187, 197, 201, 213, 233, 409, 239, 340, 517, 545. Essercizi: 'Cats' Fugue' in G min., Kk.30
**(*) Lyrichord LEMS 8043. Comparone (harpsichord)

It was Clementi who nicknamed the last of Scarlatti's Essercizi the 'Cats' Fugue', which gives this Lyrichord collection its sobriquet. Fortunately, Elaine Comparone is not tempted to overdo such a pictorial suggestion. She uses a modern Hubbard copy of a 1646 Ruckers harpsichord, enlarged in 1780 by Taskin, which she plays with bold, clear articulation and plenty of rhythmic lift. However, we would have liked a little more relaxation at times in some of the minor-key works, where she makes little attempt to seduce the ear with a more gentle approach. The recording is real and vividly present.

Keyboard Sonatas, Kk.20, 24, 27, 30, 87, 197, 365, 426, 427, 429, 435, 448, 455, 466, 487, 492, 545, in G min.
(N) *** BIS-CD 1508. Sudbin (piano)

In his excellent note for this collection, this prize-winning young Russian pianist Yevgeny Sudbin quotes from a Preface to his published set of 30 sonatas in which Scarlatti wrote in 1738: 'Do not expect any profound Learning, but rather an ingenious gesting with Art, to accommodate you to the Mastery of the Harpsichord.' Sudbin then goes on to find, besides much to charm the ear, an infinite expressive depth in many of the minor key works, which are played here with appealing expressive freedom. (Sample Kk.87 or Kk.197 in B minor or the delicacy of Kk.466 in F minor.) From the very opening B flat major work we are aware that this is a modern piano, but how well it suits these innovative and infinitely diverse sonatas. There is sparkle and brilliance here too, and Sudbin can be both strong and delectably light-fingered. He is splendidly recorded, and this can be placed among the finest and most generous of recent single-disc Scarlatti collections (76 minutes).

Keyboard Sonatas, Kk.20, 32, 39, 79, 109, 124–5, 128, 342, 381, 394, 425, 454, 470, 491, 495, 547, 551
☛ (BB) *** EMI Encore 5 74969-2. Tipo (piano)

Maria Tipo's 18 Scarlatti sonatas first appeared in 1989 and sound every bit as good now as they did then. Tipo has not gained the wider recognition for which her artistry entitles her, but this recital shows her in the best possible light. Her range of keyboard colour is wide and her sense of dynamic contrast strong, but she never uses them simply to make effect. No fewer than seven of her sonatas are in G major and only three are in minor keys. There is a spontaneity and a sense of discovery here that is delightful, and the EMI sound is very faithful. She is not the equal of Horowitz or Pletnev in this repertoire, but she has undoubted grace and sparkle, and this record is an unmissable bargain.

Keyboard Sonatas, Kk.25, 33, 39, 52, 54, 96, 146, 162, 197–8, 201, 260, 303, 319, 466, 474, 481, 491, 525, 547

(N) (B) **(*) Sony (ADD) 517487-2. Horowitz (piano)

Provided you are prepared to accept sometimes less than flattering and often rather dry recorded sound, this is marvellous playing, which sweeps away any purist notions about Scarlatti having to be played on the harpsichord. The 20 sonatas were chosen by Horowitz after he had recorded nearly twice as many throughout 1964. The very opening, staccato *D major*, Kk.33, is made to sound very brittle by the close balance, but in the following *A minor*, Kk.54, the pianist's gentle colouring is fully revealed. Here, as in the two slow *F minor Sonatas*, Kk.466 and Kk.481, the music is particularly beautiful in a way not expected of Scarlatti. The playing time has been extended to 72 minutes by the addition of six more sonatas to the content of the original CD.

Keyboard Sonatas, Kk.32, 64, 69, 87, 133, 146, 160, 198, 208, 213, 380, 429, 466, 481, 511, 517; Toccata in D min.

(B) **(*) Cal. CAL 6670. Södergren (piano)

Inger Södergren gives an appealing recital of 16 well-contrasted *Sonatas* plus a brilliant account of the highly individual *Toccata in D minor*. Some might feel that her gentle, almost wistful treatment of the lyrical sonatas errs towards being too romantic, but her keen sensitivity and crisp articulation in the lively pieces are unimpeachable, and she is very well recorded.

Keyboard Sonatas, Kk.46, 87, 99, 124, 201, 204a, 490–92, 513, 520–21

(M) *** CRD (ADD) CRD 3368. Pinnock (harpsichord)

No need to say much about this: the playing is first rate and the recording outstanding in its presence and clarity. There are few better harpsichord anthologies of Scarlatti in the catalogue, although the measure is not particularly generous.

Keyboard Sonatas, Kk.64, 87, 96, 108, 118–19, 132–3, 141, 175, 198, 202–3, 213–14, 263–4, 277–8, 420–21, 454–5, 460–61, 490–92, 501–2, 516–19

(N) (B) *** DHM 82876 67375-2 (2). Staier (harpsichord)

We welcomed Andreas Staier's Haydn sonata collection with much enthusiasm. He seems equally at home with the music of Scarlatti, and he characterizes each of these sonatas vividly and with real imagination. This pair of CDs (originally published in 1991/2) may well have been planned to be part of an integral collection which was never completed. In any event the choice of repertoire is fruitful; playing (and recording) of this quality has no need to fear even the most exalted competition. A strongly recommended reissue.

Keyboard Sonatas, Kk.213/4, 248/9, 318/9, 347/8, 356/7, 380/1, 436, 454/5, 478/9, 524/7

(N) *** DG Blue (ADD) 477 5003. Kirkpatrick (harpsichord)

At the beginning of the 1970s when this recital first appeared on LP, Ralph Kirkpatrick's monumental study of Domenico Scarlatti's harpsichord music was the standard work on the subject, and it remains an enormously readable and erudite book. These performances, paired according to his theory, have all the panache and scholarship one would expect from

this artist, in addition to a welcome degree of freedom and poetry. Since then only Andreas Staier has chosen consistently to pair sonatas in the same way (though Pletnev makes up six doubles in his collection above). Nevertheless it is a pleasure to welcome this well-recorded collection back to the catalogue.

Keyboard Sonatas, Kk.159, 175, 208, 213, 322 & 380 (arr. for guitar)

(B) *** Sony (ADD) SBK 62425. Williams (guitar) –
GIULIANI: *Variations on a Theme by Handel;* PAGANINI: *Caprice; Grand Sonata;* VILLA-LOBOS: *5 Preludes* ***

Guitar arrangements of Scarlatti sonatas have their charms when played by an artist as imaginative as John Williams. He manages by percussive plucking to sound at times almost like a harpsichord, while his gentle playing is always beguiling, especially in the delightful *D major Sonata*, Kk.159. The recording is faithful, somewhat close and larger than life, but never unacceptably so. This diverse and well-planned recital (76 minutes) is very enjoyable indeed.

Collection: (i) *Keyboard Sonatas: Kk.208, 248, 412, 466, 492, 508, 511, 521 & 532.* (ii) Cantatas: *Piangete, occhi dolenti; Scrite con falso inganno; Tinte a note di sangue. Operatic Duets: L'Ottavia restituita al trono: Se l'alma non t'adora'. Tolomeo et Alessandro: Addio consorte amato*

(N) ** Virgin 5 45546-2. (i) Curtis (harpsichord); (ii) Ciofi, Bonitatibus, Il Complesso Barocco, Curtis

This collection aims to show the full range of Scarlatti's music and includes nine keyboard sonatas, which are each and all a delight (beautifully played by Alan Curtis and recorded on an ideal harpsichord). The rest of the programme includes three solo cantatas and two operatic duets. The cantatas are shared by Patrizia Ciofi (soprano) and Anna Bonitatibus, who sing eloquently but whose voices tend to spread and are somewhat unwieldy. However, they join together for the duets, of which the excerpt from *L'Ottavia restituita al trono* is particularly attractive, and which has the added interest of deriving from a libretto which is a sequel to Monteverdi's *L'Incoronazione di Poppea*. Full texts and translations are included.

VOCAL MUSIC

Cantatas: *Che vidi, oh Ciel, che vidi; O qual mecco Nice; Pur nel sonno almen tal'ora. Sinfonia*

(N) **(*) Astrée Naïve E 8673. Gerstenherber, Musique des Lumières, Frisch

Although these cantatas were written for the castrato voice, they suit a high soprano very well. Each is quite extended, but it is *Pur nel sonno almen tal'ora* ('Even in slumber, the lady of my heart appears to comfort me in my sorrow') with its flute obbligato which is especially delightful. The other two works are more theatrical, and Cyrille Gerstenberger sings them vividly, with plenty of temperament. However, Scarlatti's writing is often richly expressive too and her cantabile line is always affecting. The accompaniments, on period instruments, are at times curiously abrasive. Full texts and translations are provided.

Cantata: *Doppo lungo servire*

(N) **(*) MDG 309 0632-2. Wessel, Musica Alta Ripa (with Francesco Scarlatti: *Cantata in un'ostante*) – ALESSANDRO SCARLATTI: *Sonatas & Cantatas* **(*)

Scarlatti's pastoral cantata is about the troubles of Filenus, who cannot persuade the fickle Phyllis to respond to his advances, and it ends with his melancholy siciliana. It is very well performed, but not all will take to Kai Wessel's male alto timbre. The documentation is first class.

Stabat Mater

(B) *** Double Decca (ADD) 443 868-2 (2). Schütz Ch. of L., Norrington – BONONCINI: *Stabat Mater* ***; PERGOLESI: *Magnificat in C; Stabat Mater* **(*); A. SCARLATTI: *Domine, refugium factus es nobis; O magnum mysterium;* CALDARA: *Crucifixus;* LOTTI: *Crucifixus* ***

Norrington's performance is admirable, though not always impeccable in matters of tonal balance; and the recording is very good. Overall this well-designed Double Decca set combines three fine *Stabat Mater* settings with other comparable baroque choral music, all well performed and impressively recorded.

Stabat Mater; Magnificat; Te Deum; Laetatus sum (Psalm 121); Miserere in E min.

🎧— *** EMI 5 57498-2. King's College Ch., Cleobury

On EMI, King's College Choir offer a fine, representative collection of Scarlatti's church music, freshly and atmospherically performed in the reverberant acoustic of King's Chapel. The most ambitious piece here is the *Stabat Mater*, described as being in ten parts (though the full ten are reserved for special moments); and the work which most impressively demonstrates Scarlatti's skill with polyphony is the *Magnificat* in four parts, with its superb climax in the *Gloria*. The other works are also given dedicated performances and all are very well recorded.

SCHARWENKA, Franz Xaver
(1850–1924)

Piano Concertos 2 in C min., Op. 56; 3 in C sharp min., Op. 80

*** Hyp. CDA 67365. Tanyel, Hanover R. Philharmonie des NDR, Strugala

These two concertos bristle with technical challenges of which Seta Tanyel makes light. She has long championed this composer, and her fine records for the defunct Collins label are now resurfacing on Hyperion. She is fully equal to their technical demands and takes them comfortably in her stride, although she is not quite in the same league as Stephen Hough, whose recording of the *Fourth* on this label rightly won such acclaim. The *Second Concerto* comes from 1880, and the debt to both Chopin and Hummel can be clearly discerned. Eighteen years separate the two concertos, seven of which Scharwenka spent in the United States. He gave the first performance of the *Third* in Berlin in 1899 to much acclaim – understandably so, given the quality of the central *Adagio*. Tanyel not only copes with the virtuoso demands of Scharwenka's writing but is a very musical player. Excellent support from Tadeusz Strugala and the Hanover Radio Orchestra, and a first-class (1996) recording.

Piano Concerto 4 in F min., Op. 82

*** Hyp. CDA 66790. Hough, CBSO, Foster – SAUER: *Piano Concerto 1* ***

Scharwenka wrote four piano concertos; this, his finest, was very famous in its time. It is ambitiously flamboyant and on the largest scale. Its invention, which manages a potent mix of bravura and lyricism, readily holds the attention, with plenty of interest in the bold orchestral tuttis. The second-movement *Allegretto* has much charm and is very deftly scored; a full flood of romanticism blossoms in the *Lento* slow movement. The stormy *con fuoco* finale combines a touch of wit and more robust geniality with glittering brilliance and power; and all four movements make prodigious technical and artistic demands on the soloist, to which Stephen Hough rises with great technical aplomb and consistent panache; he also plays with fine poetic sensibility. He is given vigorously committed support by Lawrence Foster and the CBSO and a first-class Hyperion recording. Winner not only of the *Gramophone* Concerto Award, this was also that magazine's Record of the Year in 1996, and deservedly so.

SCHEIBE, Johann Adolph (1708–76)

Sinfonias in A; B min. (Mourning Cantata for Queen Louise); in B flat; D (Homage Cantata to Queen Juliana Maria, 'Der Tempel des Ruhmes'); in E flat (Mourning Cantata for King Frederik V)

(M) *** Chan. 0696. Concerto Copenhagen, Manze

Scheibe, who was German by birth, settled in Denmark in 1740. He gained notoriety for his dismissal of Bach's music as 'bombastic and confused' in *Der critische Musicus* which he briefly edited. He became court composer in Copenhagen and some of the sinfonias on this disc derive from works written for royal occasions. They date from the 1730s and 1740s and are all in fast–slow–fast form, with animated outer movements separated by slow movements of fair charm. The *D major Sinfonia à 16* probably receives its first performance here since the composer's lifetime. The sinfonias from the cantatas are different in character: the *Introduzzione in E flat* was played just before the funeral procession of King Frederik V and has solemn overtones; the *B minor Sinfonia* was written to mark the death of the British-born Queen of King Frederik V and is similarly grave in tone (the first movement in particular). The brass and woodwind writing in both these works is very effective. The *D major Sinfonia* for the cantata 'The Temple of Fame' is, by contrast, much more extrovert. If there is in this music more surface than substance, Andrew Manze and the Concerto Copenhagen play it all with a sprightly elegance and character that is persuasive. It is an interesting footnote on music in Denmark at the time of Telemann and Bach.

SCHEIDT, Samuel (1587–1654)

Samuel Scheidt was born in Halle and spent virtually all his life there, eventually (in 1620) becoming Kapellmeister of the Saxon Court. However, local disputes impeded his career and in 1636 the plague decimated his family of four children. The Court left the city from 1625 until 1638, when Scheidt's fortunes were restored.

Ludi musici (Hamburg, 1621): excerpts

(B) *** Virgin 2×1 5 62028-2 (2). Hespèrion XX, Savall – G. GABRIELI: *Canzoni da sonare;* SCHEIN: *Banchetto musicale* ***

(N) *** Astrée Naïve ES 9980. Hespèrion XX, Savall

Samuel Scheidt published four collections of instrumental music between 1621 and 1624 under the title *Ludi musici* but only the First Book survives, and all these pieces are drawn from it. For all its good nature, his music has a melancholy streak and has much in common with Dowland's *Lachrimae*. Scheidt actually draws on Dowland in his spirited *Battle galliard*, so characteristic of its time. Other English tunes are featured in his canzons, notably in the delightful five-part *Canzon* (from Cantus XXVI). All this music is played with characteristic finesse, nicely judged espressivo and plenty of vitality by the superb Jordi Savall and Hespèrion XX, and the viol sound is smooth and pleasingly natural, with none of that scratchiness which comes from too close microphones. The coupling with the music of Johann Schein could not be more apt, and this reissue is topped off with *Canzoni* by Giovanni Gabrieli and his contemporaries to make an altogether sumptuous Rennaisance feast.

Although it duplicates much material in the Virgin set, it is useful to have a separate collection of excerpts from the *Ludi musici* when it is played and recorded so persuasively. Here is both cheerful and more doleful authenticity by turns, excellent musicianship and a 62-minute programme of stimulating variety and range, and with a striking melodic content. The recording is excellent and, like the Virgin collection, the period instruments, without loss of character, are easy on the ear.

SCHEIN, Johann Hermann (1586–1630)

Banchetto musicale (1617): Suites a 5: 2, 6, 16, 20, 36, Canzon in A (Collarium)

(B) *** Virgin 2x1 5 62028-2 (2). Hespèrion XX, Savall – G. GABRIELI: *Canzoni da sonare*; SCHEIDT: *Ludi musici* ***

Johann Hermann Schein's instrumental music has much in common with that of his Italian contemporary Giovanni Gabrieli, although the interplay between various groups, usually brass and strings (or recorder), is much less spectacular. The *Canzon in A (Collarium)*, however, is a more ambitious piece, very much in the contrapuntal Gabrieli manner. The *Banchetto musicale* is intended as a background for meals, although the sonorous brass writing with occasional bravura roulades suggests that the banqueting hall would have needed to be very spacious. However, the very pleasing expressive music (especially the *Padouanas*) invites lower dynamic levels. The *Intradas* open the feast with a drumbeat suggesting the musicians marching in. The performances here are stylish and pleasing, responding well to the music's dolorousness. Perhaps they could have been more robust, but the result is very suitable for domestic listening and is very well recorded. The coupling with music by Schein's contemporary Samuel Scheidt is most appropriate, bringing the attention of the collector to a pair of talented early seventeenth-century composers, each with an individual musical personality.

SCHIERBECK, Poul (1888–1949)

The Chinese Flute, Op. 10

(**(*)) Bluebell mono ABCD 075. Nilsson, Swedish Radio O, Mann – BARTOK: *Bluebeard's Castle* (**(*))

The Chinese Flute, Op. 10; Queen Dagmar; The Tinder-Box, Op. 61

*** dacapo 224104. Dam-Jensen, Dolberg, Larsen, Van Hal, Dreyer, Odense SO, Bellincampi

Schierbeck belongs to the generation midway between Nielsen and Vagn Holmboe. Until recently he was unrepresented in the catalogue, now no fewer than three versions of his charming songs *The Chinese Flute*, to poems by Hans Bethge, which inspired many composers, not least Mahler in *Das Lied*, are available and the present issue also brings the cantata *Dronning Dagmar* ('Queen Dagmar'). The melodrama *Fyrtøjet* ('The Tinder-box'), based on Hans Andersen, is both inventive and imaginative. This is an excellent introduction to a gifted minor master. Inger Dam-Jensen is excellent in the Bethge settings, and the orchestral playing and recording are first class.

Nilsson's first recording was in 1946 of an aria from Berwald's *Estrella di Soria*, and this recording of *The Chinese Flute* comes from a Swedish Radio broadcast two years later. What a voice! It comes with a haunting but unaccountably cut *Bluebeard's Castle* under Fricsay.

SCHMELZER, Johann (c. 1620–80)

Balletto di centauri, ninfe e salvatici; Balletto di spiritelli; Sacro-Profans concentus musicus: Sonata I a 8; Sonata a 7 flauti; Sonata con arie der kaiserlichen Serenada

(B) *** Double Decca (ADD) 458 081-2 (2). New L. Consort, Pickett – BIBER: *Ballettae; Sonate; Serenade; Requiem* ***

Johann Schmelzer was apppointed Vice-Kapellmeister to the Viennese Imperial Court, and in 1679 he became Kapellmeister – almost too late, for he died of the plague a year later. One of his tasks was the provision of ballet music for use in pageants, and much of this survives. The *Balletto di spiritelli* is scored for recorders and curtal (an ancestor of the bassoon), violins and viols, and the *Balletto di centauri* uses cornetts and sackbuts, as well as recorders, strings and continuo. The even more robust *Sonata con arie zu der kaiserlichen Serenada* (with three trumpets, timpani plus a string ensemble and continuo) has six movements, including two *Arias* and a *Canario*, but still lasts only seven minutes. Philip Pickett himself leads the consort of recorders in the *Sonata a 7*, which is a fairly ambitious continuous piece, longer than either of the ballets, and the *Sonata a 8* highlights a trumpet duo against a group of violins and viols. This is agreeably inventive music, which is brought refreshingly to life by Pickett's instrumental ensemble, using original instruments to persuasive effect. The recording is both clear and spacious.

Sacroprofanus concentus musicus: Sonata. Vesperae sollennes

(BB) **(*) DHM 05472 77856-2. Soloists, Gradus ad Parnassum, Junghänel – BIBER: *Missa Alleluia* **(*)

Like the coupled Biber Mass, Schmelzer's *Vespers* is introduced by an instrumental piece, here for two clarini, two cornets, three trombones and two organs. His setting, again associated with church dedication, uses a double chorus and a wide range of brass and string instruments, but the writing itself is harmonically more simplistic than that of his celebrated colleague of a generation later. A fine performance, spectacularly if very resonantly recorded, and well worth its modest cost.

SCHMIDT, Franz (1874–1939)

Symphonies 1–4
☞ *** Chan. 9568 (4). Detroit SO, Järvi

Chandos have now boxed their individual releases of the symphonies into a 4-CD set, discarding the fill-ups. The *First Symphony* was composed during Schmidt's early to mid-20s and, as one might expect, is derivative, even if his orchestration is masterly. Right from the start, one is left in no doubt that Schmidt is a born symphonic composer with a real feeling for the long-breathed line and the natural growth flow of ideas. He began work on the *Second Symphony* on leaving the Vienna Philharmonic in 1911 and finished two years later. The *Third* (1927–8) is a richly imaginative score in the romantic tradition, though it yields pride of place among the symphonies to the elegiac, valedictory *Fourth* (1933–4), whose nobility and depth of feeling shine through every bar. The Detroit Symphony Orchestra under Neeme Järvi play with a freshness and enthusiasm that is totally persuasive. They almost sound Viennese and the recordings are very good indeed.

Clarinet Quintet 2 in A (for clarinet, piano & strings)
*** Marco Polo 8.223414. Jánoska, Mucha, Lakatos, Slávik, Ruso

The *Quintet in A major for Clarinet, Piano and Strings* is unusual: it begins like some mysterious other-worldly scherzo which immediately introduces a pastoral idea of beguiling charm. The second movement is a piano piece in ternary form; there is a longish scherzo, full of fantasy and wit, and there is an affecting trio, tinged with the melancholy of late Brahms. The fourth movement sets out as if it, too, is going to be a long, meditative piano piece, but its nobility and depth almost put one in mind of the Elgar *Quintet*. The fifth is a set of variations on a theme of Josef Labor, and is sometimes played on its own. The recording has freshness and bloom, though it could benefit from a bigger recording venue. This is a glorious work.

Piano Quintet in G (arr. Wührer)
(N) *** Australian Decca Eloquence (ADD) 476 2455. Mrasek, VPO Qt – BRUCKNER: *String Quartet in F* ***

Franz Schmidt's *Piano Quartet in G* is the first of three that he wrote for Paul Wittgenstein, the one-armed pianist for whom Ravel and Prokofiev both composed concertos. The piano parts were subsequently arranged for two hands by Felix Wührer. This is rewarding music, full of unexpected touches; it is also possessed of genuine nobility, as one would expect from the composer of the *Fourth Symphony*. The performance is elegant and beautifully recorded in the Sofiensaal in 1974, and has transferred well to CD.

Das Buch mit sieben Siegeln (The Book with 7 Seals)
☞ (BB) *** EMI Gemini 85782-2 (2). Oelze, Kallisch, Andersen, Odinius, Pape, Reiter, Bav. R. Ch. & SO, Welser-Möst; Winklhofer (organ)
**(*) Teldec 8573 81040-2 (2) Röschmann, Lipovšek, Lippert, Hawlata, Tachezi; Vienna Singverein, VPO, Harnoncourt

After finishing the *Fourth Symphony* in 1933, Schmidt devoted his remaining creative years to this setting of the *Revelation of St John the Divine*, completing it in 1937.

This newest version of Schmidt's *Book with Seven Seals* was recorded live by EMI in the Herculessaal in 1997 and is played by the magnificent Bavarian Radio Orchestra with the Bavarian Radio Chorus under Franz Welser-Möst, who shows great sympathy for the score. The soloists are excellent, and this now supplants both Harnoncourt's account with the Vienna Singverein and the VPO on Teldec, and also the earlier Calig version of 1996. However, no texts are included.

The version from Nikolaus Harnoncourt with the Wiener Singverein and Philharmoniker has a lot going for it: very good and full-bodied choral singing, fine soloists and impressive orchestral playing. Were it not for some didactic and intrusive expressive over-emphases from Harnoncourt, it could receive a stronger recommendation.

SCHMITT, Florent (1870–1958)

Symphony 2, Op. 137; La Danse d'Abisag, Op. 75; (i) Habeyssée (suite for violin and orchestra), Op. 110. Rêves, Op. 65
*** Marco Polo 8.223689. (i) Segerstam; Rheinland-Pfalz PO, Segerstam

La Danse d'Abisag, like the much earlier *Tragédie de Salomé*, has a biblical theme: unlike Salome, Abisag, despite her erotic dancing, fails to arouse the ageing monarch (King David). The *Symphony No. 2* was no mean achievement for a composer in his eighty-eighth year! In terms of orchestral expertise and flair, it is second to none, and the opulence of its palette and its imaginative vitality are remarkable. *Rêves* is an early piece, inspired by a poem by Léon-Paul Fargue and appropriately atmospheric; and *Habeyssée*, said to be inspired by an Islamic legend, is a three-movement suite for violin and orchestra. This is a rewarding issue which offers some good playing from the Rheinland-Pfalz Orchestra under Segerstam, who excels in this repertoire. Good recording too.

La Tragédie de Salomé (ballet; complete)
*** Marco Polo 8.223448. Fayt, Rheinland-Pfalz PO, Davin

Schmitt's skill as an orchestrator is such that the heady, exotic draft he prepared is hardly less potent than the more sumptuously scored, 1908 version. The piece is as long again as the more familiar ballet, and much of the music that was lost in the process is every bit as atmospheric and colourful. Patrick Davin and the Rheinland-Pfalz Philharmonic Orchestra cast a strong spell, and Marie-Paule Fayt is the off-stage nymphet. The Marco Polo recording has a good, spacious acoustic and plenty of detail. The documentation is of unusual interest and gives a detailed account of the action of the ballet.

Piano trio: Très lent
(BB) **(*) Naxos 8.550934. Joachim Trio – DEBUSSY; RAVEL: *Piano Trios* **(*)

This three-minute fragment, about which the notes are uninformative, is rather haunting and, like the rest of the programme, beautifully played and recorded.

SCHNABEL, Artur (1882–1951)

String Quartet 5; Piano Trio; 7 Piano Pieces
(N) **(*) CPO 999 881-2. Pellegrini Qt, Ravinia Trio, Benedikt Koehlen

Like other great interpreters of his generation, the pianist Artur Schnabel was also a composer; but, unlike most, he was anything but a traditionalist, wholeheartedly accepting the disciplines of Schoenbergian serialism. These three works from late in his career have a gritty quality, even if the earliest of the three, the *Fifth String Quartet* of 1940, sometimes sounds like romantic music with the wrong notes. He also allows himself passages of simple chordal writing and octave doubling, whereas the *Piano Trio* of 1945 hardly relaxes from its serial disciplines throughout, even though the slow-moving lines of the central *Larghetto* make for more lyrical results. The finale, the longest and most energetic of the three movements, also gives more freedom to the two stringed instruments, where Schnabel tended to think of piano trios as sonatas with trimmings. The *Piano Pieces*, written over 1945 and 1946, alternate slow and fast movements, leading up to the *Lento* fifth movement, the most deeply meditative. Excellent performances, promoted by West German Radio.

SCHNITTKE, Alfred (1934–98)

Concerto for Piano and Strings; (i) *Concerto for Piano Four Hands & Chamber Orchestra*

(M) ** Warner Elatus 0927 49811-2. Postnikova, (i) with Irena Schnittke; L. Sinf., Rozhdestvensky

Authoritative performances of two very thin pieces. In the *Concerto for Piano Four Hands* the quality of the musical invention is far from distinguished and, without putting too fine a point upon it, the *Concerto for Piano and Strings* is pretty empty. The playing time of the disc is 47 minutes, but it seems much longer. Victoria Postnikova plays with taste and authority as, in the *Concerto for Piano Four Hands,* does the composer's widow. The recording comes from the early 1990s and is very acceptable.

Viola Concerto

*** TDK **DVD** DV-VPOVG. Bashmet, VPO, Gergiev (includes Bashmet talking about Schnittke; Gergiev talking on Prokofiev and Stravinsky). Director and V/D: Brian Large –
PROKOFIEV: *Symphony 1 (Classical), Op. 25;*
STRAVINSKY: *Firebird Complete Ballet* ***

Schnittke's *Viola Concerto*, completed not long before his stroke, is generally thought to be among his finest compositions. It is made up of two *Largos* surrounding a fast, often violent, central movement, the mood swinging between a pensive brooding and frenetic activity. It is certainly written well for the viola, and Yuri Bashmet plays it with great intensity and dedication. Whether one warms to the music or not, it communicates very directly here to the viewer/listener. The orchestral tuttis are sometimes wildly explosive, and Gergiev's face registers their demonic force as his directs the orchestra with enormous conviction. The documentary is a considerable bonus, but it is for the fine performance of *The Firebird* that most collectors will seek out this DVD.

Violin Concertos 1–2

*** BIS CD 487. Lubotsky, Malmö SO, Klas

The *First Violin Concerto* inhabits a post-romantic era. Its lyricism is profoundly at variance with its successor of 1966, commissioned by Mark Lubotsky, the soloist on this record. Here the central concept is what Schnittke calls 'a certain drama of tone colours', and there is no doubt that much of it is vividly imagined and strongly individual. The double-bass

is assigned a special role of a caricatured 'anti-soloist'. There is recourse to the once fashionable aleatoric technique, but this is all within carefully controlled parameters. The Malmö orchestra under Eri Klas play with evident feeling in both works and are very well recorded. This is an altogether highly satisfactory coupling.

(i) *Gogol Suite* (compiled Rozhdestvensky); *Labyrinths*

*** BIS CD 557. Malmö SO, Markiz; (i) with Kontra

There is a surrealistic quality to the *Gogol Suite* reminiscent of Gogol's own words quoted in Jürgen Köchel's note: 'The world hears my laughter; my tears it does not see nor recognize.' *Labyrinths* is a ballet score composed in 1971, thin in development and musical ideas but sufficiently strong in atmosphere to survive the transition from stage to concert hall. The Malmö orchestra under Lev Markiz play very well and the recording is in the demonstration class.

Symphony 1

*** Chan. 9417. Russian State SO, Rozhdestvensky

Schnittke's *First Symphony* is a huge radical canvas lasting some 68 minutes. In his essay on 'The Symphony in the Soviet Union' in *A Guide to the Symphony*, David Fanning writes that it 'contains a whole lexicon of advanced devices – the theatricality of American happenings with the players entering one by one and leaving at the end only to enter again as if to restart the whole process, the aleatory (chance) elements of the Polish school, and the multiple quotations of Berio's *Sinfonia* plus a cadenza for jazz violin'. It is essentially a musical gesture, a tirade rather than a symphony of protest and anger which sounds pretty thin now. Rozhdestvensky's performance is committed, and the recording, made at a public performance in the Moscow Conservatoire in 1988, is well detailed. There is more rhetoric than substance here. The three stars are allotted for the performance and recording; for the composition the stars can be aleatoric!

(i) *Symphony 4;* (ii) *3 Sacred Hymns*

*** Chan. 9463. (i) Zdorov, Pianov; (i–ii) Russian State Symphonic Cappella; (i) Russian State SO; Polyansky

The *Fourth Symphony* draws on Christian (Catholic, Lutheran and Russian Orthodox) and Jewish chant and is avowedly religious in programme, reflecting episodes in the life of the Virgin Mary. It lasts 40 minutes and is scored for two singers, one a counter-tenor, chorus and orchestra; it also makes inventive and colourful use of keyboard sonorities. Both the performance and the recording are of high quality, but the piece seems too concerned with gesture and is essentially empty of musical substance. The *Three Sacred Hymns* for *a cappella* choir from 1983 are both eloquent and beautiful.

Symphony 8; The Census List: Suite

*** Chan. 9885. Russian State SO, Polyansky, with (i) Butenin (nar.)

Symphony 8; (i) *Concerto Grosso 6*

*** Chan. 9359. Stockholm RSO, G. Rozhdestvensky, with (i) S. Rozhdestvensky; Postnikova

Completed in 1964, just before he suffered the stroke that led to his terminal illness, the *Symphony No. 8* is one of the most moving of Schnittke's later works. In it he develops a sparer style, often angular but warmly lyrical, reflecting his inspiration over a five-movement structure in the sections of the Mass. Earlier works were similarly inspired from spiritual sources, but this most clearly of all, with a rising scale figure a symbolic element. The solemn *Moderato* first movement brings a massive central climax, leading to an angular *Allegro* second movement. The central slow movement, by far the most expansive, then emerges as the emotional heart of the work, with the last two movements rounding off the symphony in resonant brass. Polyansky directs a warmly expressive performance, opulently recorded, with the generous coupling providing a delightful contrast. The incidental music to a play drawn from Gogol, *The Census List*, dates from 1978; it is pastiche writing designed as a cheeky thrust at Soviet authority, with witty parodies over the eight movements. The fifth involves a narrator, Lev Butenin, reciting a satirical poem about Ferdinand VIII.

Rozhdestvensky and the Stockholm orchestra recorded Schnittke's *Eighth Symphony*, which they had commissioned, soon after the first performance in 1994. It is a powerful, warmly committed performance, if not quite so sharply focused as Polyansky's, also on Chandos. The fill-up is less generous but arguably more apt: written in 1993 for the Rozhdestvensky family in Schnittke's neo-classical manner, it is much drier than the *Symphony* and again is very well played by the dedicatees.

Cello Sonata
*** BIS CD 336. Thedéen, Pöntinen – STRAVINSKY: *Suite italienne*; SHOSTAKOVICH: *Sonata* ***

The *Cello Sonata* is a powerfully expressive piece, its avant-garde surface enshrining a neo-romantic soul. Torleif Thedéen is a refined and intelligent player who gives a thoroughly committed account of this piece with his countryman, Roland Pöntinen.

Piano Quintet
●━ (BB) *** Naxos 8.554830-2. Berman, Vermeer Qt – SHOSTAKOVICH: *Piano Quintet* ***
*** ECM 461 815-2. Lubimov, Keller Qt – SHOSTAKOVICH: *String Quartet 15* ***

Like the Shostakovich *Piano Quintet*, with which it is aptly coupled, the Schnittke *Piano Quintet* of 1972–5 is one of the composer's most poignant and haunting works. Dedicated to the memory of his mother, and darkly elegiac, it was finished in the year of Shostakovich's death. Its mood of gloom, unrelieved except for a painfully plaintive waltz in the second of the five movements, inspires Berman and the Vermeers to a performance as powerfully concentrated as that of the Shostakovich; if the CBC studios in Toronto do not always flatter their tone, this a real bargain.

There is no doubt that the anguished *Piano Quintet* is deeply felt and powerful in the hands of Lubimov and the Keller Quartet. Good recording too. But the Naxos version is much more competitively priced.

Piano Trio
*** Nim. NI 5572. V. Piano Trio – SHOSTAKOVICH: *Trios, Opp. 8 & 67* ***

Schnittke's *Piano Trio* has its origins in a string trio written in 1985. In 1987 it was transcribed as the *Trio Sonata for Chamber Orchestra* and then in 1992 put into its present form. The Vienna Piano Trio give as convincing a performance as you are ever likely to hear, and they certainly get superb recorded sound.

Prelude in Memoriam Shostakovich (for 2 solo violins)
*** Chan. 8988. Mordkovitch, Young – PROKOFIEV; SHOSTAKOVICH: *Violin Sonatas* ***

The Schnittke *Prelude* for two solo violins is the shortest of the works on Lydia Mordkovitch's excellent disc of Soviet violin music, but it is among the most moving in its intense, elegiac way. She is well matched by her partner, Emma Young.

Violin Sonata 1; Sonata in the Olden Style
*** Chan. 8343. Dubinsky, Edlina – SHOSTAKOVICH: *Violin Sonata* ***

Schnittke's *First Sonata* is a well-argued piece that seems to unify his awareness of the post-serial musical world with the tradition of Shostakovich. On this version it is linked with a pastiche of less interest, dating from 1977. Excellent playing from both artists, and very good recording too.

Piano Sonata
*** Chan. 8962. Berman – STRAVINSKY: *Serenade* etc. ***

Berman gives as persuasive an account of Schnittke's *Piano Sonata* as it is possible to imagine. He is very well recorded, too, and the three Stravinsky pieces with which it comes are also given with great pianistic elegance.

SCHOECK, Othmar (1886–1957)

(i) *Horn Concerto, Op. 65. Prelude for Orchestra, Op. 48*; (ii) *Serenade for Oboe, Cor Anglais & Strings, Op. 27. Suite in A flat for Strings*
(M) ** CPO 999 337-2. (i) Schneider; (ii) Zabarella, Zuchner; Coll. Musik, Winterthur, Albert

The major work here is the five-movement *Suite in A flat for Strings*, which Schoeck composed in 1945. Although it is not quite as poignant as *Sommernacht*, there is some imaginative and expressive writing. The second movement, *Pastorale tranquillo*, has that sense of melancholy and nostalgia so characteristic of Schoeck. In it he imagined 'the peace and deep stillness of the forests'. The slightly later *Concerto for Horn and Strings* (1951) is well played by Bruno Schneider and is an appealing piece that will strike a responsive chord among all who care for late Strauss. The *Serenade for Oboe, Cor Anglais and Strings* is a five-minute interlude which Schoeck composed for a much-truncated production of his opera, *Don Ranudo*, at Leipzig in 1930. The *Prelude for Orchestra* serves as a reminder that Schoeck was at one time a pupil of Reger. Its textures lack transparency, but this is in part due to the rather opaque recording, made in a radio studio. It is perfectly acceptable, but the strings could do with more bloom and tuttis need to open out a little more.

Violin Sonatas: in D, Op. 16; in E, Op. 46; in D, WoO22; Albumblatt, WoO70
** Guild GMCD7142. Barritt, Edwards

The two *D major Violin Sonatas* come from the first decade of the last century. The student essay of 1905 is of lesser interest, but Op. 16 has a strong vein of lyricism and a characteristic warmth of invention. The *Sonata in E major*, Op. 46, of 1931 inhabits a totally different world. Its musical language is less immediate and in this respect could possibly be compared with late Fauré, though there is no resemblance in idiom. Paul Barritt and Catherine Edwards give very capable and sensitive performances and, were the recording a little more spacious and less forward, this would gain three stars.

Elegie (song cycle), *Op. 36*

☺ (M) *** CPO 999 472-2. Schmidt, Winterthur Music Collegium, Albert

The *Elegie*, Op. 36, has been described as 'a narrative of a dying love' and to some extent charts the turbulent course of the composer's affair with the pianist Mary de Senger. The cycle comprises twenty-four short but concentrated settings of poems by Lenau and Eichendorff, and is for baritone and a small instrumental ensemble, used with great subtlety and resource. The songs are powerfully evocative and beautifully fashioned; each one immediately establishes its own atmosphere within a bar or two, and draws the listener completely into its world. Almost any would serve as an example but particularly potent is the third, *Stille Sicherheit*, which is extraordinarily concentrated in feeling, or the wonderfully haunting *Vesper*, with its tolling bells and almost tangible half lights. This is deeply felt music with a wonderful sense of line, and Andreas Schmidt sings with tremendous conviction. Werner Andreas Albert gets very sensitive and supportive playing from the Winterthur ensemble and the CPO recording is first class.

3 Lieder, Op. 35; 6 Lieder, Op. 51; Das Wandsbecker Liederbuch, Op. 52; Im Nebel; Wiegenlied

** Jecklin JD677-2. Banse, Henschel, Rieger

Das Wandsbecker Liederbuch is a latter-day equivalent of the Hugo Wolf Songbooks; they offer a portrait of a poet (in this case Mathius Claudius) rather than a thematically connected cycle, and the songs, though highly conservative in idiom, are full of subtleties and depth, as indeed are the remaining songs on this CD. They are decently sung and recorded, and admirers of Schoeck's art need not hesitate.

OPERA

Venus (complete)

*** MGB Musikszene Schweiz CD 6112 (2). Lang, Popp, O'Neal, Fassbaender, Skovhus, Alföldi, Heidelberg Kammer Ch., Basle Boys' Ch., Swiss Youth PO, Venzago

Venus is based on a libretto by Schoeck's school-friend, Armin Rüeger, and comes from Ovid, though Rüeger sets the action in a country castle in the south of France. Venzago's conducting radiates total dedication, and so does the playing of the young Swiss orchestra. The opening scene almost prompts one's thoughts to turn to the Strauss of *Ariadne*, but as the opera unfolds Venzago's view of the work as partly 'an enormous orchestral poem (exposition, development, Scherzo and recapitulation) with obbligato voices' seems more and more valid. The sheer quality of the invention is notable and many of the ideas, particularly the Venus motive, have great tenderness and delicacy. Schoeck's scoring is superb, and those who know *Penthesilea* should lose no time in acquiring this glorious score. The performance may not be absolutely ideal vocally, but it is worth putting up with that for the sake of such beautiful music. Good and atmospheric recording.

SCHOENBERG, Arnold (1874–1951)

Chamber Symphonies 1–2, Opp. 9 & 38; Verklaerte Nacht, Op. 4

☛ (BB) *** Warner Apex 0927 44399-2. COE, Holliger

Schoenberg's *Chamber Symphonies* are superbly performed by the COE, played with both warmth and thrust, with complex textual problems masterfully solved. *Verklaerte Nacht* in its orchestral version receives one of its most passionate performances on disc, reflecting 'the glow of inmost warmth' in the Richard Dehmel poem which inspired it. This new coupling makes an excellent bargain on the Apex label, and the sound is first-rate.

Chamber Symphony 1, Op. 9 (arr. Webern); (i) Ode to Napoleon. Verklaerte Nacht (string sextet version), Op. 4

(BB) **(*) Virgin 2x1 5 61760-2 (2). Nash Ens.; (i) with Allen
  – SHOSTAKOVICH: *Piano Quintet; Piano Trio 2; 4 Waltzes* ***

The Nash Ensemble give us Webern's arrangement of the *Chamber Symphony*, Op. 9, reduced to the same group of five instruments used in the *Ode to Napoleon*. Contrapuntal detail is certainly clarified, but the Nash players ensure that the work's emotional content comes over expressively in spite of the less opulent textures. Thomas Allen provides a congenial, characterful narration for the strange *Ode* and although the close balance in *Verklaerte Nacht* is less than ideally alluring, throughout the Nash Ensemble play with easy virtuosity, intensity and fine blending. As so often with bargain reissues, no text is provided for the *Ode*, and the notes are sparse. An intriguing issue, just the same, for the Shostakovich couplings are first class.

(i) Chamber Symphony 1; (ii) Verklaerte Nacht; (i–iii) Gurrelieder

(B) *** Double Decca 473 728-2 (2). (i) Concg. O; (ii) Berlin RSO; (iii) Jerusalem, Dunn, Fassbaender, Brecht, Haage, Hotter, St Hedwig's Cathedral Ch., Berlin, Düsseldorf State Musikverein; all cond. Chailly

Chailly's magnificent (1985) recording of Schoenberg's massive *Gurrelieder* is among the finest of modern versions and, if that weren't enough, for this Double Decca reissue the considerable bonus of *Verklaerte Nacht* and the *Chamber Symphony No. 1* have been added. If these performances are not in the same league as the *Gurrelieder*, they are still very worthwhile. The Berlin recording of *Gurrelieder* is full and rich, well detailed and balanced, and conveys a natural dramatic tension not easy to find in studio conditions. Siegfried Jerusalem as Waldemar is not only warmer and firmer of tone than most of his rivals but more imaginative too. Susan Dunn makes a sweet, touchingly vulnerable Tove, while Brigitte Fassbaender gives darkly baleful intensity to the message of the Wood-dove. Hans Hotter is a characterful Speaker in the final section. The impact of the performance is the more telling with sound both atmospheric and immediate, bringing a fine sense of presence, not least in the final choral outburst. Texts and translations are included, and this is an undoubted bargain.

(i) Piano Concerto, Op. 42; (ii) Pelleas und Melisande, Op. 5

(N) (M) *** Chan. 10285X. (i) Malling, Danish Nat. RSO, Schønwandt; (ii) SNO, Bamert

Amalie Malling proves an intelligent and sympathetic soloist who, if not more persuasive than some of her better-known rivals such as Pollini, is every bit as convincing. Michael Schønwandt gets very good results from the Danish orchestra and the texture is lucid and transparent, and splendidly recorded. The coupling is a finely shaped account of *Pelleas*, admirably played, and the sound is well blended, if a little recessed.

(i) *Piano concerto, Op. 42; Pieces, Opp. 11 & 19*

☛ *** Ph. 468 033-2. Uchida, (i) Cleveland O, Pierre Boulez
– BERG: *Piano Sonata;* WEBERN: *Variations* ***

Mitsuko Uchida is logically coupled, and she and Boulez and the Cleveland Orchestra give us a keenly articulate account of the *Piano Concerto* that may well reach home to a wider audience than before. There is both delicacy and lyrical feeling. Surprisingly, William Glock once asked way back in the 1960s, 'Why is it that Schoenberg's music always sounds so ugly?' But in Uchida's hands it doesn't. She is also very persuasive in the Opp. 11 and 19 *Klavierstücke* (not, incidentally, the same performance of the former that Philips included in her *Great Pianists of the Century* set). The Philips recording has both clarity and warmth. Those who have not responded even to the Brendel account should try this beautifully recorded piece.

(i) *Piano Concerto.* Piano Music: *3 Pieces, Op. 11; 6 Little Pieces, Op. 19; 5 Pieces, Op. 23; 2 Pieces, Op. 33a & b; Suite, Op. 25*

(M) **(*) DG (IMS) (DDD/ADD) 471 361-2. Pollini, (i) with
BPO, Abbado – WEBERN: *Variations for Piano* ***

Pollini is very persuasive in the *Piano Concerto*; his account has all the pianistic mastery one would expect and much refinement of keyboard colour, but he is not helped by a rather claustrophobic recording that is wanting in real transparency. Abbado gives devoted support and the Berlin orchestra play splendidly. In the solo piano music Pollini again plays with enormous authority and refinement of dynamic nuance and colour, making us perceive this music in a totally different light from other performers. Here the sound is excellent, very slightly on the dry side, but extremely clear and well defined.

(i) *Concerto for String Quartet & Orchestra after Handel's Concerto grosso, Op. 6/7*

(BB) *** Warner Apex 7559 79675-2. American Qt., NYCO,
Schwarz – R. STRAUSS: *Divertimento (after Couperin)* ***

*** Ara. Z 6723. San Francisco Ballet O, Lark Qt, Le Roux –
HANDEL: *Concerto grosso in B flat, Op. 6/7;* ELGAR:
Introduction & Allegro for Strings; SPOHR: *Concerto for
String Quartet & Orchestra* ***

Schoenberg virtually recomposed Handel's Op. 6/7 for string quartet and orchestra, offering a rich spicing of dissonance. The result, inflated to nearly twice the size of the original, is at times grotesque, but always aurally fascinating and entertaining. The performance by the excellent American Quartet with the New York Chamber Orchestra under Gerard Schwarz is spirited and given bright, lively sound. The coupling too is particularly desirable, and the price will surely tempt the collector to explore this excellent CD.

The San Francisco performance also has plenty of edge, vitality and colour and it was a bright idea to include Handel's original (in a performance for full modern strings) so the listener can switch back and forth between the two utterly different sound-worlds.

(i) *Pelleas und Melisande; Verklaerte Nacht*

☛ (M) *** DG 457 721-2. BPO, Karajan

The Straussian opulence of Schoenberg's early symphonic poem has never been as ravishingly presented as by Karajan and the Berlin Philharmonic in this splendidly recorded version. The gorgeous tapestry of sound is both rich and full of refinement and detail, while the thrust of argument is

powerfully conveyed. These are superb performances which present the emotional element at full power but give unequalled precision and refinement. They make an ideal candidate for separate reissue in DG's series of Originals.

(i) *5 Pieces for Orchestra, Op. 16*

(BB) *** EMI Encore 5 75880-2. CBSO, Rattle – BERG: *Lulu:
Suite;* WEBERN: *6 Pieces* ***

Rattle and the CBSO give an outstanding reading of this Schoenberg masterpiece, bringing out its red-blooded strength, neither too austere nor too plushy. With sound of demonstration quality and an ideal coupling, it makes an outstanding recommendation on EMI's bargain Encore label.

(i) *Variations for Orchestra, Op. 31*

☛ (M) *** DG (IMS) (ADD) 457 760-2. BPO, Karajan –
BERG: *Lyric Suite,* etc.; WEBERN: *Passacaglia* ***

(i) *Variations for Orchestra, Op. 31; Verklaerte Nacht, Op. 4*

☛ ✪ (M) *** DG 476 2201. BPO, Karajan

Karajan's version of *Verklaerte Nacht* is altogether magical and very much in a class of its own. There is a tremendous intensity and variety of tone and colour: the palette that the strings of the Berlin Philharmonic have at their command is altogether extraordinarily wide-ranging. Moreover, on CD the sound is firmer and more cleanly defined, and this is now a mid-priced bargain on Universal's 'Penguin ✪ Collection'.

(i) *Verklaerte Nacht*

*** Chan. 9616. Norwegian CO, I. Brown – SCHUBERT:
String Quartet 14 (Death and the Maiden), arr. Mahler
**(*)

*** ECM 465 778-2. Camerata Bern, Zehetmair – BARTOK:
Divertimento; VERESS: *4 Transylvanian Dances* ***

An eloquent and impressive *Verklaerte Nacht* from the splendid Norwegian Chamber Orchestra and Iona Brown. It comes with Mahler's transcription of *Death and the Maiden*, made when opportunities to hear Schubert's masterpiece were rare. Those who want to hear it need have no doubts as to the excellence of the playing or of the Chandos recording.

Thomas Zehetmair and the Camerata Bern recorded this account of *Verklaerte Nacht* in 1995, four years earlier than the Bartók and Sándor Veress couplings but in an equally good acoustic. Eloquent playing and very present and lifelike recording make this, while not necessarily a first choice, a highly recommendable version.

CHAMBER MUSIC

(i) *Chamber Symphony 1* (arr. Webern for piano quintet); (i) *Concerto for String Quartet and Orchestra (after Handel's Concerto grosso, Op. 6/7); (ii) Ode to Napoleon, Op. 41; Phantasy for Violin and Piano, Op. 47; String Quartet in D; String Quartets 1–4; String Trio, Op. 45; Wind Quintet, Op. 26; 6 Little Piano Pieces, Op. 19 (both arr. Guittart for strings); Verklaerte Nacht*

*** Chan. 9939 (5). Schoenberg Qt with Narucki, Grotenhuis,
(i) Arnhem PO, Benzi; (ii) Grandage

This ambitious five-disc set brilliantly brings together all of Schoenberg's chamber music for strings, including several arrangements. What is so persuasive is the expressive warmth of the Schoenberg Quartet. Even when the atonal Schoenberg is at his most abrasively intellectual, as in the *String Trio* of

1946, one is made to appreciate that this is music with an emotional core. So it is, too, in the four *String Quartets*, which form a central core to the collection, a splendid cycle stretching from the post-romantic No. 1 of 1904–5 through the mould-breaking No. 2 of 1907–8 with its evocative use of a soprano soloist in the third and fourth movements to the severity of Nos. 3 and 4, both commissioned by Mrs Sprague Coolidge, a great musical patron. The portrait of the composer is made all the more persuasive by having such a wide range of works including not just the early *Verklaerte Nacht*, wonderfully evocative, but the unnumbered string quartet of 1897. It is good, too, to find him relaxing in the *Concerto for String Quartet and Orchestra* of 1933, which he freely transcribed from Handel's *Concerto grosso* Op. 6, No. 7, which he wrote in France as a relaxation immediately after fleeing from Germany in 1933. One also welcomes the inclusion of the *Napoloen Buonaparte Ode* in its version for reciter and piano quintet. The recordings made in Holland are first-rate, warm and atmospheric.

String Trio, Op. 45

(N) *** Hyp. CDA 67429. Leopold String Trio – DOHNANYI: *Serenade in C; MARTINU: Trio 2****

Many critics have hailed the *String Trio* as Schoenberg's masterpiece. It is certainly one of his most intensely felt works, composed in the wake of a severe heart attack and the experience of being snatched back from the grave. The dreadful breathlessness of an asthmatic attack, the stopping of his heart, the injection into the heart itself that saved him, even the personalities of his nurses are said to be recorded in this music. (Calum MacDonald reproduces his masterly account of the piece in the excellent note.) The Leopold Trio play the work with consummate mastery and are superbly recorded. If you want this piece, you can't really do better than this.

String Quartets 1 in D min., Op. 7; (i) 2 in F sharp min., Op. 10. 3, Op. 30; 4, Op. 37

(***) Archiphon ARC mono 103/4. Kolisch Qt, (i) with Gifford

String Quartet (1897); String Quartet 1, Op. 7

*** MDG 307 0919-2. Leipzig Qt

String Quartets (i) 2, Op. 10; 4, Op. 37

*** MDG 307 0935-2. (i) Oelze; Leipzig Qt

No quartet has ever been more closely associated with these pieces than the Kolisch, and the present recordings were made at the turn of 1936–7. It is well worth putting up with surface noise for the sake of *real* music-making. Indeed, given phrasing of this quality there is more to the rigorously disciplined *Third* and *Fourth Quartets* than most later ensembles have found; and never have the two earlier *Quartets* sounded so eloquent. The set contains a short speech of thanks by Schoenberg.

MDG and the Leipzig Quartet do go in for extravagant layout. Their Schoenberg runs to three CDs – No. 3 is coupled with *Verklaerte Nacht* on a third disc which we have not heard. It is difficult to fault them in the two early quartets or for that matter in the *Second*, Op. 10, in which Christiane Oelze sings beautifully. They phrase with great naturalness, their ensemble is perfect and they have great warmth, richness and tonal beauty, though nothing is overstated or projected. If any ensemble or recording could win doubting listeners over to this repertoire, this is it. The recording balance is perfect.

Verklaerte Nacht, Op. 4 (string sextet version)

⊕ (***) Testament mono SBT 1031. Hollywood Qt, with Dinkin, Reher – SCHUBERT: *String Quintet* (***) ⊕

*** Hyp. CDA 66425. Raphael Ens. – KORNGOLD: *Sextet* ***

*** Nim. NI 5614. Brandis Qt, with Küssner, Schwalke – R. STRAUSS: *Metamorphosen; Capriccio: Prelude* ***

The 1950 Hollywood account was the first version of *Verklaerte Nacht* in its original sextet form ever to appear on records, and arguably it remains unsurpassed and possibly unequalled. This almost flawless performance enjoyed the imprimatur of Schoenberg himself, who supplied the sleeve-note for it (reproduced in the excellent booklet), the only time he ever did so. The sound is remarkably good and very musical. Recommended with enthusiasm.

For those wanting a modern, digital version, the Raphael Ensemble have the advantage of very good recorded sound and give a fine account of Schoenberg's score. They also have the advantage of a rarity in their coupling, the youthful *Sextet* of Korngold.

The Brandis Quartet with two colleagues from the Berlin Philharmonic are in excellent form. They possess an unforced eloquence and expressive beauty that is impressive. The Nimbus recording is well balanced and very lifelike and can be recommended alongside the Raphael version.

Piano music: 3 Pieces, Op. 11; 6 Little Pieces, Op. 19; 5 Pieces, Op. 23; 2 Pieces, Op. 33a & b; Suite, Op. 25

(BB) *** Naxos 8.553870. Hill – BERG: *Piano Sonata;* WEBERN: *Variations, Op. 27* ***

Peter Hill may not challenge Pollini's magisterial survey of the Schoenberg canon (currently withdrawn) but his is highly intelligent, thoughtful playing, acutely sensitive to dynamic and tonal shading. In some ways he is more persuasive than Pollini in that one feels more completely drawn into this musical world. In any event, given the low price tag and the high quality of the recorded sound, this is self-recommending.

VOCAL MUSIC

Gurrelieder (see also above under Chamber Symphony 1)

🎧 *** EMI 5 57303-2 (2). Mattila, Von Otter, Moser, Langridge, Quasthoff, Berlin R. Ch., Leipzig R. Ch., Ernest Senff Ch., BPO, Rattle

*** Teldec 4509-98424-2 (2). Moser, Voigt, Larmore, Weikl, Riegel, Brandauer, Saxon State Op. Ch., Dresden, Leipzig R. Ch., Prague Male Ch., Dresden State O, Sinopoli

(N) (BB) *** Naxos 8.557518/9. O'Mara, Diener, Lane, Wilson-Johnson, Hill, Haefliger (speaker), Simon Joly Ch., Philh. O, Craft

*** DG (IMS) 439 944-2 (2). Sweet, Jerusalem, Lipovšek, Wekler, Langridge, Sukowa, Vienna State Op. Ch., Schoenberg Ch., Slovak Phil Ch., VPO, Abbado

(M) **(*) Ph. 475 455-2 (2). McCracken, Norman, Troyanos, Werner Klemperer, Tanglewood Festival Ch., Boston SO, Ozawa

(i) Gurrelieder; (ii) Suite for Strings

(B) **(*) EMI double forte (ADD) 5 74194-2 (2). (i) Arroyo, Young, Baker, Woltad, Môller, Patzak, Danish State R. Ch., SO & Concert O, Ferencsik; (ii) Cond. Del Mar

(i) *Gurrelieder;* **(ii)** *4 Orchestral Songs*

(M) *** Sony (ADD) SM2K 48459 (2). (i) Jess Thomas,
Napier, Nimsgern, Bowen, Reich, BBC Singers & Ch. Soc.,
Goldsmith's Ch. Union, Men's voices of LPO Ch.; (i; ii)
Yvonne Minton, BBC SO; Boulez

Drawn from live performances given in the Philharmonie in
Berlin in September 2001, Rattle's version of Schoenberg's
opulent score is the most refined yet in its beauty, warmly
spontaneous from first to last, sweeping you away with its
richness and magnetism up to the final choral climax. The
soloists and massed choruses are all first-rate, with Karita
Mattila as Tove consistently warm and tenderly responsive,
opposite Thomas Moser in the key role of Waldemar, here
more firmly focused than usual, stronger than on Sinopoli's
Teldec version. As in Abbado's Vienna version on DG, Philip
Langridge is outstanding as Klaus-Narr, and though Anne
Sofie von Otter sings with grainy tone in the *Song of the
Wood-dove*, her performance is both dramatic and moving,
while Thomas Quasthoff is superb both as the Woodsman
(Bauer) and in the difficult role of the Speaker in the melodrama of the final section, sounding younger and fresher
than immediate rivals.

In his highly compelling live recording, Sinopoli conducts
a most sensuous reading of *Gurrelieder*, bringing out all its
high romantic voluptuousness. Speeds are spacious, thanks in
part to his expressive freedom, and anyone who has ever
thought of Schoenberg as cold should certainly hear this,
magnetic from first to last, helped by rich, immediate sound.
The soloists are excellent, even if Thomas Moser as Waldemar
is gritty at times in a Wagnerian way.

Recorded in October 2001 in the helpful acoustic of Watford Colosseum, Robert Craft's version of *Gurrelieder* is
among the most beautiful ever. The warmth and refinement
of the sound as well as its fine detail are instantly established
in the opening Prelude, atmospheric and evocative. Surprisingly for a specialist in twentieth-century music, Craft then
directs a performance which brings out the work's warmly
romantic qualities rather than its foretastes of later Schoenberg. He is helped by an outstanding team of soloists, headed
by the clear, strong tenor, Stephen O'Mara, as Waldemar and
the radiant, fresh Natalie Diener as Tove, with Jennifer Lane
firm and cleanly focused in the *Song of the Wood-dove*. David
Wilson-Johnson as the Peasant and Martyn Hill as Klaus-
Narr both characterize well, and the veteran tenor, now
retired from singing, Ernst Haefliger, copes with the sing-
speech of the Speaker's role in a high-pitched way that
Schoenberg himself evidently wanted. The Philharmonia
plays with passionate conviction throughout, with textures
consistently refined, and the Simon Joly Chorale provides a
glorious choral conclusion. Craft himself provides an
informative note, and Schoenberg's own detailed comments
on performing the work are given in full; but sadly there is no
detailed synopsis of the story and no texts. A remarkable
bargain, just the same.

Abbado's version begins magnetically with the most delicate tracery of sound, immediately capturing both atmosphere and dramatic intensity. Though Siegfried Jerusalem as
Waldemar is not quite as firmly focused as he was on Riccardo Chailly's Decca set, he conveys more passion, and
regularly Abbado's reading is freer and more volatile than
Chailly's, with a sense of wonder enhanced by the very
atmosphere of a concert. Susan Dunn as Tove in Chailly's
version is firmer and truer than Abbado's Sharon Sweet,
whose tight vibrato is often intrusive, but this is a strong,

characterful reading, and Marjana Lipovšek is deeply moving
as the Wood-dove, with the hushed tension behind her big
solo tellingly conveyed. Philip Langridge is outstanding as
Klaus-Knarr and Hartmut Welker makes a bluff if slightly
unsteady Peasant. The only soloist who is controversial is the
woman speaker, Barbara Sukowa, whose use of sliding
Sprech-Stimme, chattering in the style of *Pierrot lunaire*,
comes near to being comic.

Boulez's warm, expressive style using slow, luxuriating
tempi brings out the operatic quality behind Schoenberg's
massive score. With Boulez, the Wagnerian overtones are
richly expressive and, though Marita Napier and Jess Thomas
are not especially sweet on the ear, they show the big, heroic
qualities which this score ideally demands, while Yvonne
Minton is magnificent in the *Song of the Wood-dove*. Boulez
builds that beautiful section to an ominous climax and, at
mid-price, remains competitive, for the CBS/Sony recording
has attractively vivid and atmospheric sound, and this set also
offers a generous coupling of Yvonne Minton's fine account
of the *Orchestral Songs*.

Ozawa's gloriously opulent live performance *Gurrelieder*,
with a ravishing contribution from Jessye Norman, won the
Gramophone Choral Award in 1979. It is not now a first
choice, with Rattle and Sinopoli leading the list of current
recommendations, but its price advantage and the inclusion
of text and translation certainly make it more competitive,
even though the recording is obviously not up to the finest
studio standards.

Though the 1968 HMV recording of a live performance
given in Copenhagen is less precise of ensemble than the
studio versions, it is very dynamic musically. Janet Baker (as
she was then) was in glorious voice as the Wood-dove, giving
expressive weight to every word, and although Alexander
Young may seem too light a tenor for a Heldentenor role, the
result as heard on record is the more beautiful. Martina
Arroyo as Tove is also impressive, and it is good to hear the
veteran Patzak in the non-singing role of the narrator. But
above all it is the dramatic thrust of the performance that
comes over, with Ferencsik creating consistent tension and
spontaneity. The vividly atmospheric recording, well balanced, and clear in every detail, is here admirably transferred
to CD for the first time, with the closing chorus, *Seht die
Sonne*, resplendent.

Norman Del Mar then gives a polished and vibrantly
expressive account of the leonine *Suite for Strings*, the first
product of Schoenberg's American years and an attractive
example of his later style at its richest and most inventive.
This was recorded four years earlier at Abbey Road and is
equally successful in its CD format. The great snag is the
absence of texts and translations.

Die Jakobsleiter; Friede auf Erden, Op. 13 (Instrumental
Prelude & *a cappella* Choral Postlude)

(N) *** HM **SACD** 801821. Henschel, Kammer, Meier,
Kaufmann, Rügamer, Azesberger, Volle, Johnson, Berlin R.
Ch., Berlin SO, Nagano

Like the later opera, *Moses und Aron*, this oratorio, *Jacob's
Ladder*, another work devoted to the composer's thoughts on
God, remained unfinished at his death. Composition was
interrupted when the composer was called up for army
service in the First World War. Even as a torso it stands – like
the opera – as an exceptionally powerful piece, ending with
what was originally conceived as a symphonic interlude,
closing on the sound of the Soul (a soprano) and heavenly
woman's voices. The baritone, Dietrich Henschel, is superb in

the central role of Gabriel, with the Berlin Radio Choir bringing out the warmth as well as the power of the choral writing. It remains an enigmatic work, inspired as it was, not just by the Bible, but by the philosophy of Swedenborg and by Balzac's novel, *Seraphita*. *Friede auf Erden*, 'Joy on Earth', provides a prelude in its orchestral form (sounding surprisingly consonant) and a postlude in the original a cappella choral version. Brilliant performances and exceptionally full and vivid recording.

Pierrot lunaire ('One Night, One Life')
* Arthaus **DVD** 100 330. Schäfer, Ensemble
  InterContemporain, Boulez – SCHUMANN: *Dichterliebe* (*)

Under the title 'One Night, One Life', Christine Schäfer, with Boulez conducting, presents this realization of Schoenberg's masterpiece, against a surreal New York background, with close-ups of beetles crawling around and sides of meat hanging up. New York Central Station is used as a backcloth, and chases down endless corridors act as dream-like interludes. All the while Schäfer is shown with an expressionless face, for though the actual performance is musically impressive, it was recorded separately from the film. It may not be as pretentious as the realization of Schumann with which it is coupled but, with an interview in German as supplement, it is hardly recommendable at all.

Pierrot lunaire, Op. 21
♦— (M) *** Chan. 6534. Manning, Nash Ens., Rattle –
WEBERN: *Concerto* ***

(i) Pierrot lunaire; Herzgewächs, Op. 20. (ii) Ode to Napoleon Buonaparte
*** DG 457 630-2. (i) Schäfer; (ii) Pittman-Jennings; Soloists
  of Ensemble Intercontemporain, Boulez

Jane Manning is outstanding among singers who have tackled this most taxing of works, steering a masterful course between the twin perils of, on the one hand, actually singing and, on the other, simply speaking; her sing-speech brings out the element of irony and darkly pointed wit that is essential. Rattle draws strong, committed performances from the members of the Nash Ensemble and, apart from some intermittently odd balances, the sound is excellent.

For *Pierrot lunaire*, Boulez imaginatively chooses a sweet-toned soprano and the result is the more revealing, in an element of beauty and mystery usually missing while the dramatic point of this cabaret-like sequence is never underplayed. Balance is excellent, with the Ensemble InterContemporain playing with warmth and brilliance, as they do in the brief *Herzgewächs* (Schäfer again radiant) and in the *Ode to Napoleon*. David Pittman-Jennings takes an idiosyncratic view of the narration, reciting in a stylized way as though English is a foreign language, but it is good to have this neglected work so well played and recorded.

SCHREKER, Franz (1878–1934)

Ekkehard (Symphonic Overture), Op. 12; Fantastic Overture, Op. 15; Interlude from Der Schatzgräber; Nächtstuck (from Der ferne Klang); Prelude to a Drama; Valse lente
*** Chan. 9797. BBC PO, Sinaisky

Schreker reused material from his stage works to produce concert pieces such as the ones here, all demonstrating his gift for drawing sumptuous sounds from the orchestra. This sequence of six pieces presents a good cross-section of his

output, demonstrating Schreker's development from the *Symphonic Overture*, *Ekkehard*, and the charmingly unpretentious *Valse lente*, to the later works, which remain sumptuously late-romantic but which were regarded as daringly modern by early audiences. Both the *Nachtstück* from *Der ferne Klang* (1909) and the *Prelude to a Drama* (1913) – the drama in question being the opera *Die Gezeichneten* – are powerfully imaginative. Perhaps the most seductive piece is the *Valse lente*. Schreker had a wonderful sense of fantasy, a feeling for colour, and impressive mastery of the orchestra. The textures are lush and overheated. Sinaisky draws seductively beautiful playing from the BBC Philharmonic, heightened by gloriously rich Chandos sound, and the whole disc serves to advance Schreker's cause.

Ekkehard Overture; Fantastic Overture; Die Gezeichneten: Prelude. Der Schatzgräber, Act III: Interlude. Das Spielwerk: Prelude
(BB) ** Naxos 8.555246. Slovak PO, Seipenbusch

Prelude to Memnon; Romantic Suite
(BB) ** Naxos 8.555107. NOe. Tonkünstler O, Vienna, Mund

Both these issues first appeared on Marco Polo in the late 1980s, when Schreker's representation in the catalogue was relatively meagre. It is, of course, useful to have these (on the whole) adequate performances at bargain price, but it would be idle to pretend that they are of the highest order. Neither the Slovak Philharmonic under Edgar Seipenbusch nor the NOe. (Lower Austrian) Tonkünstler Orchestra with Uwe Mund are the equal of the BBC Philharmonic, nor do the recordings approach the Chandos Schreker series. On the Slovak disc neither the *Ekkehard Overture* nor the *Fantastic Overture* is the best Schreker; they are, in fact, less than distinguished. The Prelude to *Die Gezeichneten* is another matter, although the playing has more guts than finesse. The Chandos account of the *Romantic Suite* under Valery Sinaisky knocks spots off the Viennese rival and is altogether richer and more enjoyable. Incidentally, the *Prelude to Memnon* is identical to the *Prelude to a Drama* on Chan. 9797.

Der ferne Klang (opera; complete)
(BB) *** Naxos 8.660074/5 (2). Grigorescu, Harper, Haller, Hagen Op. Ch. & PO, Halász

Der ferne Klang's central character is an ambitious young dramatist, Fritz, who pursues his creative ambitions and his search for *Der ferne Klang* ('the distant sound') at the expense of his love for Grete, whom he abandons and who turns to prostitution. Schreker scores with chamber-like delicacy and has a Puccini-like finesse in the handling of colour, and great imagination in his handling of harmonic resource. And like Puccini, he was also aware of developments in French music. The skill with which he handles the orchestras in the pit and on the stage in the Venetian scene is impressive and obviously influenced Berg in *Wozzeck*. The score is quite gripping, its sound world at times astringent in its harmonies, at others lush and intoxicating. Good soloists, though it is a pity that the voices are rather prominently balanced in this 1989 recording and that the subtlety of Schreker's lavish scoring is not always heard to best advantage. Strongly recommended.

Prelude to a Grand Opera (Vorspiel zu einer grossen Oper)
(B) *** EMI double forte 5 75157-2 (2). Cologne PO, Conlon –
  BRUCH: *Symphonies 1–3* ***

Schreker's *Prelude to a Grand Opera*, a late work written in 1933, is quite a find, in essence an expansive (22-minute) and colourful symphonic poem presenting the opera in chrysalis. The planned work, which was never completed, was *Memnon* (in Greek mythology he was the son of Eos and nephew of King Priam). It is vividly scored and makes an impressive entity in its own right, with a sinuous and ear-catching oriental atmosphere in its lyrical melodic lines. It is very well played indeed and the recording is very good too, even if fortissimos are just a little fierce.

Prelude to a Grand Opera; Prelude to Das Spielwerk; Romantic Suite, Op. 14. (i) 5 Gesäng

*** Chan. 9951 (i) Katarina Karnéus; BBC PO, Sinaisky

The *Romantic Suite* comes from 1903, when Schreker was in his mid-twenties, though its third movement began life independently as an *Intermezzo for strings* a year earlier. It is a rather beautiful piece as, for that matter, is the opening *Idylle*, written at much the same time as he was making the first sketches for *Der ferne klang*. There is a lot of Strauss here and in the mercurial Scherzo, Reger – the latter is a highly inventive movement. Only the finale, *Tanz*, is routine. The *Five Songs*, imaginatively sung by the Swedish mezzo, Katarina Karnéus, are later; they were written in 1909, the year before the opera was finished, but were not scored until the early 1920s. They have plenty of atmosphere and mystery, and are well worth getting to know. The opening song, *Ich frag' nach dir jedwede Morgonsonne*, has a touch of Szymanowski about it, and certain moments elsewhere call the Chamber Symphony to mind. The disc covers the whole of Schreker's career: the Prelude to *Das Spielwerk* is a wartime piece while the *Vorspiel zu einer grossen Oper* comes from the last months of his life. This was after he had been hounded from his teaching post in Berlin by the Nazis, a trauma which is said to have induced the stroke which eventually killed him in March 1934. It is an ambitious piece, some twenty-four minutes in length and draws on material that he had intended for the opera *Memnon*, whose libretto he had completed in 1918 but which he never managed to complete. It is darker than his earlier pieces but despite its expert orchestration remains somewhat overblown. The playing of the BBC Philharmonic under Sinaisky is superb and the recording is in the demonstration class. Intelligent liner notes.

Der Geburtstag der Infantin

** Edition Abseits ED A013-2. Berlin Kammersymphonie, Bruns – TOCH: *Tanz-Suite, Op. 30* **

This is a first recording of the original (1910) version of Schreker's dance pantomime on Oscar Wilde's short story, *The Birthday of the Infanta*. It surfaced during the 1980s in a Vienna archive, having been misfiled. Good playing and recording.

Der Schatzgräber (opera): complete

**(*) Cap. 60010-2 (2). Protschka, Schnaut, Stamm, Haage, Hamburg State O, Albrecht

The attractions of Schreker's sweet-sour treatment of a curious morality fairy-story are fairly well conveyed in this first recording, made live at the Hamburg State Opera in 1989, though there are very few signs of the audience's presence, with no applause, even at the end. Josef Protschka sings powerfully as Elis, hardly ever over-strenuous, but Gabriele Schnaut finds it hard to scale down her very bright and powerful soprano and seems happiest when she is scything your ears with loud and often unsteady top notes; yet she is certainly dramatic in this equivocal role. Outstanding among

the others is Peter Haage as the court jester. *Der Schatzgräber* may be hokum, but it is enjoyable hokum, and, with Albrecht drawing committed performances from the whole company, this well-made recording is most welcome.

SCHUBERT, Franz (1797–1828)

ORCHESTRAL MUSIC

Concerto Movement for violin and Orchestra in D, D.345

(M) *** CRD (ADD) CRD 3369. Thomas, Bournemouth SO – BEETHOVEN: *Romances 1–2;* MENDELSSOHN: *Violin Concerto* ***

Schubert's *Konzertstück* is slight, but Ronald Thomas's refreshing playing and direction make it well worth having on disc, along with the excellent Beethoven and Mendelssohn. The recording is first class.

Rondo in A for Violin & Strings, D.438

*** EMI 7 49663-2. Kennedy, ECO, Tate – BRUCH; MENDELSSOHN: *Concertos* ***

The ideas in Schubert's *Rondo* flow very sweetly with Kennedy, making this an attractive bonus to the usual Bruch–Mendelssohn coupling.

Rosamunde: Overture (Die Zauberharfe), D.644, and incidental music (complete), D.797

(M) *** Decca (ADD) 470 261-2. VPO, Münchinger – WEBER: *Preciosa Overture;* SCHUMANN: *Genoveva: Overture* ***

It is right that these beautifully played and recorded performances are released on Decca's Legends series. This delightful music glows with affectionate warmth and understanding which places it as one of Münchinger's very best records, and the 1974 sound emerges fresher than ever in this new transfer. The two overtures, taken from a long-forgotten 'Romantic Overtures' LP, are similarly also beautifully played and recorded. Strongly recommended.

Symphonies 1–6; 8–9

(N) (B) *** RCA 82876 60392-2 (4). Dresden State O, C. Davis

(BB) **(*) Brilliant 99587 (4). Hanover Band, Goodman

(BB) *** Warner Apex 2564 60532-2 (5). Sinfonia Varsovia, Y. Menuhin (disc 5 includes conversation in German: Menuhin/Jurgen Seeger)

(B) **(*) DG (ADD) 471 307-2 (4). BPO, Boehm

Symphonies 1–6; 8–9; Grand Duo in C, D.812 (orch. Joachim); Rosamunde: Overture (Die Zauberharfe)

*** DG 423 651-2 (5). COE, Abbado

Symphonies 1–6; 8 (Unfinished); 9 (Great); Overtures: Fierrabras; In the Italian Style in C; Des Teufels Lustschloss

(B) **(*) Decca (ADD) 430 773-2 (4). VPO, Kertész

Abbado's is an outstanding set. Rarely has he made recordings of the central Viennese classics which find him so naturally sunny and warm in his expression. Speeds are often on the fast side but never feel breathless, and the recording is refined, with fine bloom on the string-sound. Textually too, the Abbado set takes precedence over its rivals and there are certain fascinating differences from what we are used to. The five CDs are now also available separately – see below.

Sir Colin Davis's Dresden cycle (on four bargain discs),

despite observing all repeats, makes a glowing tribute that regularly reveals Davis drawing magnetic and intense playing from the Dresden orchestra, with the polish of the ensemble adding to the impact, never making the results sound self-conscious. In the youthful symphonies, Nos. 1–3, Davis refuses to regard them as just elegantly Mozartian, but genuinely Schubertian. In the middle symphonies Davis seems happier bringing out the elegance and charm, but then crowns the cycle with a radiant reading of the *Unfinished*, marked by high dynamic contrasts. In the *Great C major* tensions are not quite so keen. This is a most distinguished cycle, helped by glowing sound.

Menuhin's more recent (1997) IMG set of the Schubert *Symphonies*, now reissued on Apex, offers performances electrically tense, generally at brisk speeds, with an easy feeling for Schubertian lyricism, helped by alert, warmly responsive playing from this leading Polish chamber orchestra and full, immediate recording. With Menuhin there is no question of the early symphonies – boyhood works often described as Haydnesque – being mistaken for eighteenth-century music. Modest in scale, these are interpretations that yet bite home with Beethovenian power. With the last two symphonies the result is equally fresh, with fast, steady speeds and high contrasts. Most radical of all is the *Great C major*, brisk and urgent. The disappointment is that the supplementary conversation is in German only.

Boehm does not smile as often as Schubert's music demands – especially by the side of Beecham in Nos. 3 and 5 – but he is always sympathetic. Certainly the Berlin wind are a joy to listen to, and it is only in the early symphonies that he does not quite capture the youthful sparkle of these delightful scores, although in its way No. 1 is brightly and elegantly done and No. 2 also is characteristically strong; both are classical in spirit. No. 4 offers splendidly disciplined playing, but this is not one of the more characterful interpretations of the set. Boehm's warmly graceful account of No. 5 and the glowing performance of No. 6, coupled together, show Boehm at his best, taking an easy-going view, with relaxed tempi that never grow heavy. Boehm capped his series with an outstanding account of the *Unfinished Symphony* and one of the finest of all recorded performances of the *Great C major*, to make an excellent coupling. The recording is very good indeed and the CDs are available together in a budget box in DG's Collector's Edition.

Kertész began his Schubert cycle with Nos. 8 and 9 and the overtures, and these two symphonies are the finest performances in the cycle. The *Ninth* is fresh, dramatic and often very exciting, the *Unfinished* is highly imaginative and comparably dramatic in its wide dynamic contrasts. In the two early symphonies Kertész scores with the spirited VPO playing and a light touch, and this also applies to Nos. 3 and 6, even if they are without the last ounce of character and distinction. The playing of the VPO is beyond reproach throughout, and it has a pervading freshness, helped by the transparent yet full Decca sound.

Goodman draws lively, beautifully sprung performances from the players of the Hanover Band. For anyone wanting an inexpensive set of period performances of these symphonies, they can be warmly recommended with the reservation that the (originally Nimbus) sound balance is very reverberant. The strings are attractively caught in a warm acoustic, but the resonance tends to obscure detail in tuttis, with the woodwind set very backwardly, and even the rasp of the natural horns is underplayed. However, this Brilliant reissue is in the lowest possible price range (cheaper than Naxos),

although documentation is non-existent. The four discs are in individual jewel-boxes within a slip case.

Symphonies 1–3; 4 (Tragic); 5–7; 8 (Unfinished); 9 (Great); 10 in D, D.936a; Symphonic Fragments: in D, D.615 and D.708a (completed & orch. Newbold)
(B) *** Ph. 470 886-2 (6). ASMF, Marriner

Marriner's excellent set gathers together not only the eight symphonies of the regular canon, but two more symphonies now 'realized', thanks to the work of Brian Newbold of Hull University. For full measure, half a dozen fragments of other symphonic movements are included, orchestrated by Professor Newbold. The set brings sparkling examples of the Academy's work at its finest, while the bigger challenges of the *Unfinished* (here completed with Schubert's Scherzo filled out and the *Rosamunde B minor Entr'acte* used as finale) and the *Great C major* are splendidly taken. These are fresh, direct readings, making up in rhythmic vitality for any lack of weight. The recordings, all digital, present consistent refinement and undistractingly good balance. Now reissued as a bargain box, this set is well worth any collector's attention.

Symphonies 1–4; Rosamunde: Ballet music 1 & 2
(N) (BB) **(*) EMI (ADD) 5 86064-2 (2). BPO, Karajan (with
    WEBER: *Der Freischütz Overture* ***)

Symphonies 5–6; 8 (Unfinished); 9 (Great); Rosamunde: Overture
(N) (BB) **(*) EMI (ADD) 5 86067-2 (2). BPO, Karajan

Karajan presents a most polished and beautiful set of Schubert symphonies, now reissued on a pair of Gemini CD doubles at budget price. The point and elegance of the Berliners' playing in the early symphonies is most persuasive, yet the results are never mannered. Undoubtedly many ears will react adversely to the reverberant acoustic for giving the impression of too large a band, one which rather lacks the brightness and transparency one associates with Schubert's songful writing; and the *Fourth Symphony*, the *Tragic*, finds Karajan less compelling. The *Unfinished*, dating from 1975, brings characteristic Berlin refinement. The first movement is the original first take restored; there were technical problems with it and so Karajan re-recorded the movement a month later. Those problems have now been solved by the current re-mix, with excellent results. The *Great C major* (1977) is also compelling. The overtures and ballet music make a fine bonus (the Weber, notable for its dramatic opening, is digital).

Symphonies 1 in D, D.82; 2 in B flat, D.125
☛ *** DG (IMS) 423 652-2. COE, Abbado
(BB) **(*) Naxos 8.553093. Failoni O of Budapest, Halász

The coupling of the two earliest *Symphonies* on DG brings bright and sparkling performances, reflecting the youthful joy of both composer and players. Abbado brings out the sunny relaxation of the writing, most exhilaratingly of all in the light-hearted finales. The recording of both captures the refined playing of the COE very vividly.

Michael Halász and the Failoni Orchestra are affectionately easy-going rather than overtly dramatic, but they play both these works most winningly. The recording too is full and naturally balanced, although the resonance of the Italian Institute in Budapest makes the tuttis spread and lose some of the sharpness of focus. But this is a most enjoyable disc nevertheless and well worth its modest cost.

Symphonies 1–2; 8 in B min. (Unfinished)
(M) (**(*)) Sony mono SMK 87876. RPO, Beecham

Beecham's versions of the first two Schubert symphonies originally appeared together on an American Columbia LP, and in Britain on Philips. Sony now add a moving account of the *Unfinished*, made in 1951. Artistically, this remains second to none, and the finale of the *Second Symphony* has rarely been given with greater vivacity or lightness of touch. However, the 1953 recording sounds less transparent and fresh than many LPs of the period. The *Unfinished* is quite special however, and among the best things Sir Thomas did in the early 1950s.

Symphonies 1 in D, D.82; 4 in C min. (Tragic)
(BB) **(*) Warner Apex 2564 60527-2. Sinfonia Varsovia, Y. Menuhin

Menuhin's *First Symphony* opens weightily (partly the effect of the resonant recording), but the allegro, fast and resilient, is graceful as well as lively, and the *Andante* has characteristic warmth. As throughout the cycle, the Minuet is briskly characterful and the finale captivates with energetic lightness of articulation from the strings. The *Tragic Symphony* opens powerfully, yet again the main allegro, like the finale, is resilient as well as boldly forward-looking, and the slow movement nobly expressive. The Trio of the Minuet is most engagingly done. The sound is full-bodied, with tuttis not completely transparent, but this is certainly a very recommendable series in the budget range.

(i) Symphony 1; (ii) Marche militaire, Op. 51/1; (iii) Overtures: Fierrabras; Des Teufels Lustschloss; (iv) 4 Waltzes & 4 Ecossaises (2 sets)
** Australian Decca Eloquence 466 908-2. (i) Israel PO, Mehta; (ii) VPO, Knappertsbusch; (iii) VPO, Kertész; (iv) Boskovsky Ens.

Mehta is no Beecham, but his account of the *First Symphony* is a fresh, straightforward account which gives pleasure. The Israeli orchestra lacks something in polish. But there are no such problems for the ensuing Viennese recordings, which give this bargain disc its appeal. Knappertsbusch's noble and trusty account of the *Marche militaire*, and the little-known overtures under Kertész are always a joy to hear. *Des Teufels Lustschloss* is a juvenile work. *Fierrabras* is more melodramatic, but lively in invention. To cap an imaginative programme, Boskovsky gives delectable accounts of the charming dance pieces, and all are well recorded.

Symphonies 2 in B flat; 6 in C
⊕ (BB) *** Warner Apex 2564 60529-2. Sinfonia Varsovia, Y. Menuhin

Menuhin's coupling is outstanding in every way, with first-movement allegros swiftly paced and fizzing with vitality. Both *Andantes* are beautifully played, each elegant and poised. With vigorous Scherzi (winning Trios) and jaunty finales, these performances are hard to beat, full of Schubertian character. The orchestral playing is first class, glowing and vivacious, and the recording is both full and transparent.

Symphonies 3 in D; 5 in B flat; 8 in B min. (Unfinished)
⊕ (BB) *** Warner Apex 2564 60530-2. Sinfonia Varsovia, Y. Menuhin

A truly outstanding triptych from Menuhin at his most inspired. No. 3 is bold, strong and forward-looking, yet the first movement's second subject could not be more enticingly Schubertian, and the *Allegretto* is delightful, as is the Trio of the vigorously rhythmic Scherzo. No. 5 too, has both strength and grace, although some listeners may feel that Menuhin moves the *Andante* on too briskly. However, one soon adjusts, for this is a movement that can too easily drag. The *Unfinished* then emerges as the most powerful, most romantic of the cycle, the *sotto voce* lower strings at the opening full of mystery and the climaxes thrillingly Beethovenian in their power; the second movment is then perfectly balanced in its lyrical serenity, while retaining its emotional puissance. Again superb playing from the Sinfonia Varsovia and first-rate recording.

Symphonies 3; 4 (Tragic)
*** DG (IMS) 423 653-2. COE, Abbado

Crisp, fast and light, No. 3 is given a delectable performance by Abbado. In No. 4, the *Tragic*, Abbado makes the slow C minor introduction bitingly mysterious before a clean, elegant *Allegro*, and with this conductor the other movements are also elegant and polished as well as strong. Textually, No. 4 eliminates the extra bars in the slow movement, which had been inserted originally by Brahms. The slow movement is outstandingly beautiful, with the oboe solo – presumably COE's Douglas Boyd – most tenderly expressive.

Symphonies 3; 5; 6
⊕ ✿ (M) *** EMI (ADD) 5 66984-2 [5669992]. RPO, Beecham

Beecham's are magical performances in which every phrase breathes. There is no substitute for imaginative phrasing and each line is shaped with affection and spirit. The *Allegretto* of the *Third Symphony* is an absolute delight. The delicacy of the opening of the *Fifth* is matched by the simple lyrical beauty of the *Andante*, while few conductors have been as persuasive as Beecham in the *Sixth 'little' C major Symphony*. The sound is now just a shade drier in Nos. 3 and 6 than in their last LP incarnation but is generally faithful and spacious. This is an indispensable record for all collections and a supreme bargain in the Schubert discography, now rightly reissued as one of EMI's 'Great Recordings of the Century'.

Symphonies 3 in D, D.200; 6 in C, D.589
(BB) *** Naxos 8.553094. Failoni O of Budapest, Halász

These are delightful performances, fully capturing the innocent charm of these youthful symphonies. Michael Halász is most sensitive, and in the *Allegretto* second movement of No. 3 his style is Beechamesque in its affectionate elegance. The economy of Schubert's scoring means that the resonant acoustic affects the clarity of the tuttis only marginally and it certainly lends an attractive bloom to the proceedings.

Symphonies 3; 8 (Unfinished)
(M) **(*) DG (ADD) 449 745-2. VPO, Kleiber

Carlos Kleiber is a refreshingly unpredictable conductor, as in the slow movement of No. 3, which is rattled through jauntily. The Minuet too becomes a full-blooded Scherzo, and there is little rest in the outer movements. The *Unfinished* brings a more compelling performance, but there is unease in the first movement, where first and second subjects are not fully co-ordinated, the contrasts sounding a little forced. The recording brings out the brass sharply, and is of wide range.

Symphony 4 in C min. (Tragic), D.417

(M) *** BBC (ADD) BBCL 4093-2 (2). New Philh. O, Giulini – BEETHOVEN: *Missa solemnis* **(*)

Recorded at the Edinburgh Festival in 1968, Giulini's reading of Schubert's *Tragic Symphony* brings a bitingly intense reading, more than usual making this early work live up to its nickname. It makes an attractive fill-up to Giulini's monumental reading of Beethoven's *Missa solemnis* recorded earlier in that year.

Symphony 4 (Tragic); Grand Duo in C, D.812 (orch. Joachim)

(BB) **(*) Naxos 8.553095. Failoni O of Budapest, Halász

Halász presents the *Tragic Symphony* sympathetically and, though this is not a strongly dramatic reading, the resonant acoustic adds a certain weight, and the *Andante* is warmly and expressively played. This inexpensive disc is valuable for its coupling, the orchestration of the large-scale *Grand Duo* for piano duet by Joachim. The work is convincingly played, with gravitas and freshness nicely balanced. The warm resonance of the Budapest Italian Institute suits this work very well.

(i) Symphonies 4 in C min.; 5 in B flat; (ii) 8 in B min. (Unfinished); (i) 9 in C (Great). Rosamunde: Entr'acte 3 & ballet music, 1 & 2

☛— (B) *** RCA (ADD/DDD) 74321 84607-2 (2). (i) N. German RSO, Wand; (ii) Chicago SO, Reiner

The freshness and robust, spirited vigour of Günter Wand's Schubert shines through all of his performances and cannot fail to give pleasure. The recordings are excellent (the *Fourth* is analogue; Nos. 5 and 9, plus the engaging *Rosamunde* excerpts, are digital). Reiner's *Unfinished*, however, dates from the early days of stereo (RCA is coy about its date) but hardly betrays its age. The performance is atmospheric and dramatic, especially so in the impulsive first movement, the second is richly lyrical. Good value if the programme suits.

Symphony 5 in B flat, D.485

(BB) *** DG (ADD) 447 433-2. VPO, Boehm – BEETHOVEN: *Symphony 6* ***

**(*) BBC (ADD) BBCL 4003-2. BBC SO, Kempe – BRAHMS: *Symphony 4* **(*)

(BB) (***) Dutton Lab. mono CDK 1208. Concg. O, Van Beinum (with BEETHOVEN: *Creatures of Prometheus: Overture* (LPO)) – BERLIOZ: *Symphonie fantastique, Op. 14* (***)

Boehm's VPO recording of the *Fifth Symphony* dates from the very end of his career. In his eighties he preferred a tauter, more incisive view than he had given in his 1967 Berlin performance, weightier, but still with a light rhythmic touch, while the slow movement is not lacking grace. The finale is strong and purposeful and this is Boehm at his finest, with superbly polished and responsive VPO playing in repertoire they know and love. The 1980 recording is full and warm, a live performance and rightly reissued now in DG's 'Legendary Recordings' series of 'Originals'.

Kempe's *Fifth Symphony* comes as a makeweight to an excellent 1974 concert performance of the Brahms *Fourth*. The Schubert was recorded at a Promenade Concert three years earlier, and is a delight from start to finish. Very musicianly, enjoyable, natural and full of life. Small wonder that Beecham thought so highly of Kempe. Very decent sound too.

From Eduard van Beinum and the Concertgebouw Orchestra come cultured playing and well-balanced sound. An enjoyable reminder of the fine results Eduard van Beinum achieved in Amsterdam.

Symphonies 5 in B flat; 6 in C

*** DG (IMS) 423 654-2. COE, Abbado

Abbado brings out the happy songfulness of the slow movements in these works, as well as the rhythmic resilience of the *Allegros*. As in No. 4, so also in No. 6 Abbado eliminates the extra bars added by Brahms in his original Schubert edition. Excellent recording, with fine bloom and good, natural contrasts.

Symphonies 5 in B flat; 8 (Unfinished)

(N) (***) BBC stereo/mono BBCL 4120-2. Hallé O, Barbirolli – MOZART: *Symphony 40* (***)

Barbirolli conducts a light, beautifully sprung reading of the *Fifth Symphony*, well paced, leading up to an exhilarating account of the finale. There is no exposition repeat in the first movement, and though the recording – from the Proms in 1968 – is in stereo, it is rather less atmospheric than the mono recording of the *Unfinished Symphony*, made in a BBC studio in 1965 with warmer sound. Characteristically, Barbirolli after a slow, deliberate first phrase offers a performance which combines warmly expressive phrasing and steady speeds, with magic in such passages as the big crescendo in the first-movement development.

Symphonies 5; 8 (Unfinished); 9 in C (Great)

☛— (B) *** Double Decca 448 927-2 (2). VPO, Solti

Symphonies 5; 8 in B min. (completed by Brian Newbold); 9 in C (Great); Rosamunde (Ballet Music), D.797: 2 in G

(B) *** Virgin 2x1 5 61806-2 (2). OAE, Mackerras

This Double Decca coupling of three favourite Schubert symphonies is one of the most attractive of all Solti's many reissues on the Decca label. There have been more charming versions of No. 5 but few that so beautifully combine freshness with refined polish. The *Unfinished* has Solti adopting measured speeds but with his refined manner keeping total concentration. The *Great C major Symphony* is an outstanding version, among the very finest, beautifully paced and sprung in all four movements, and superbly played. It has drama as well as lyrical feeling, but above all it has a natural sense of spontaneity and freshness. The recordings all confirm the Vienna Sofiensaal as an ideal recording location, and the glowing detail, especially in No. 9, is a source of consistent pleasure.

Mackerras was the first to use period instruments in Schubert's *Ninth*. The characterful rasp on the period brass instruments and the crisp attack of timpani are much more striking than any thinness of string-tone. It is a performance of outstanding freshness and resilience. The *Fifth* is not quite as magnetic as the *Ninth*, but still has comparable qualities. Tempi are only marginally brisker than conventional performances, and the slow movement has grace if not quite the degree of warmth that Boehm and Walter find. The special claim of this second disc is the inclusion of the *Unfinished Symphony* heard here as 'finished' by Brian Newbold. Mackerras opens in the mysterious depths with the darkest piano-pianissimo, and the plangent period timbres bring a real sense of *Sturm und Drang*, with powerful contrasts and strong, forceful accents in the second movement. The recording is excellent throughout.

Symphony 8 in B min. (Unfinished), D.759

⊖━ ✸ EMI **DVD** DVA 4928429. LPO, Stokowski (with DEBUSSY: *Prélude à l'après midi d'un faune.* WAGNER: *Die Meistersinger: Overture* (LSO)). Bonus: DUKAS: *L'apprenti sorcier*, LSO, Monteux) – BEETHOVEN: *Symphony 5* ***

⊖━ (M) *** DG 445 514-2. Philh. O, Sinopoli – MENDELSSOHN: *Symphony 4 (Italian)* ***

(B) (***) EMI mono 5 74801-2. Philh. O, Cantelli – MENDELSSOHN: *Symphony 4;* SCHUMANN: *Symphony 4* (***)

(*) Sony **SACD SS 6506. NYPO, Walter (with BEETHOVEN: *Symphony 5* **)

**(*) BBC (ADD) BBCL 4039-2. Philh. O, Boult – BIZET: *Jeux d'enfants;* RAVEL: *Daphnis et Chloé: Suite 2;* SIBELIUS: *Symphony 7* **(*)

(N) (B) **(*) DG (ADD/DDD) 477 5324 (2). VPO, C. Kleiber – BRAHMS: *Symphony 4;* WAGNER: *Tristan und Isolde: Act III: excerpts* ***

(N) (B) (**) BBC Classics mono BBCM 5014-2. BBC SO, Sargent (with MENDELSSOHN: *A Midsummer Night's Dream: Nocturne; Wedding March***(*)) – MOZART: *Clarinet Concerto* etc.

Symphony 8 (Unfinished); Grand Duo (orch. Joachim)
*** DG (IMS) 423 655-2. COE, Abbado

Historical DVDs – at their finest – re-create concert performances with such immediacy that the watching and listening experience all but matches being present in person, with the additional advantage of closer visual communication. So it is with these marvellous Stokowski performances with the LPO: an electrifying Beethoven *Fifth* and a naturally shaped, glowing Schubert *Unfinished*, the interpretation ideally paced, sensitive in every detail, and bringing out the fullest depth of Schubert's rich romanticism. It is a truly imaginative reading, full of subtle variations of light and shade, which the conductor seemingly does very little physically to achieve. As he has told E.G., 'It is all in the eyes.' The very opening, with its richly resonant double-basses, is extraordinarily compelling, and the first movement's progress has great drama to contrast with its lyrical warmth. The opening of the second movement is Elysian, with a quite perfect balance for the woodwind and horns, who play gloriously, and the secondary theme arrives with magical delicacy. The very close of the movement has wonderful serenity, and this is a performance that long resonates in the memory. The camera lets us watch the conductor in close-up a great deal of the time: the almost impassive face, the economy of the flowing hand-movements, a dramatic gesture when needed. This is Stokowski and Schubert (for the conductor never imposes his personality over that of the composer) at their most inspirational, and the wondrous originality of the Unfinished Symphony is revealed here as in no other version. Fortunately, the recording, made in the Fairfield Hall, Croydon, is superb: rich, expansive and naturally detailed. The bonus items, discussed under their Beethoven coupling, are also treasurable.

Sinopoli secures the most ravishingly refined and beautiful playing; the orchestral blend, particularly of the woodwind and horns, is magical. It is a deeply concentrated reading of the *Unfinished*, bringing out much unexpected detail, with every phrase freshly turned in seamless spontaneity. The contrast, as Sinopoli sees it, is between the dark tragedy of the first movement, relieved only partially by the lovely second subject, and the sunlight of the closing movement, giving an unforgettable, gentle radiance. The exposition repeat is

observed, adding weight and substance. Warmly atmospheric recording, made in the Kingsway Hall.

It is good to see Cantelli's beautifully shaped reading from the mid-1950s back in circulation, not that it has ever been long out of the catalogue. The *Unfinished* is one of the classic accounts of the symphony and, with its couplings, is among the finest performances ever committed to disc.

Abbado's outstandingly refined and sensitive version comes with a valuable coupling. The second subject in the *Unfinished* brings some slightly obtrusive agogic hesitations at the beginning of each phrase; but with such responsive playing they quickly sound fresh and natural.

Bruno Walter, too, brings special qualities of warmth and lyricism to the *Unfinished*. There is a rich humanity in this reading that marks it out from all but a few of its rivals. Affection and gentleness are the keynote of this performance, recorded in the St George Hotel, Brooklyn, in March 1958. The orchestra is well balanced and in this SACD the 'certain pallor of timbre' which we noticed on the original LP has been filled out and warmed by the remastering. Unfortunately, Walter's companion recording of Beethoven's *Fifth*, recorded with a specially chosen pick-up orchestra (all the finest West Coast musicians wanted to be included) two months earlier in California, has a civilized rather than a dramatic character, and is played with a mellow maturity which is far from electrifying. This is primarily of interest for Walter devotees.

Showmanship and flamboyance were alien to Sir Adrian's personality, which is perhaps why he remains underrepresented on CD and underrated by the wider public. In his BBC days he pioneered a varied repertoire that included Berg's *Wozzeck*, Schoenberg's *Variations for Orchestra* and Busoni's *Doktor Faust*, not to mention Bax, Vaughan Williams and many young British composers. This recording serves as a reminder of his stature and the quiet, natural dignity that informed his music-making. The Bizet, Schubert and Ravel come from a Promenade Concert in 1964 and the Sibelius from a Festival Hall concert given the preceding year. In the *Unfinished* there is the unforced eloquence that distinguished his famous *Great C major*.

Carlos Kleiber's account of the *Unfinished* was more compelling than the *Third Symphony* with which it was originally coupled; but here there is an unease in the first movement where first and second subjects are not fully coordinated, the contrasts sounding a little forced. Still, this is undoubtedly a performance of some stature which many will find compelling. The 1978 analogue recording brings out the brass well and is wide-ranging.

Sargent's performance, recorded live at a 1960s Promenade concert, is well played but not really distinctive, and the mono recording is rather limited in range.

Symphonies 8 (Unfinished); 9 in C (Great)

⊖━ ✸ (M) *** Decca (ADD) 476 1551. (i) VPO; (ii) LSO; Krips

⊖━ (B) *** RCA Twofer 09026 68314-2 (2). BPO, Wand

*** Telarc CD 80502. Sc CO, Mackerras

(M) **(*) Sony (ADD) SBK 48268. Cleveland O, Szell

(B) *** CfP (ADD) 574 8852. LPO, Pritchard

(N) (M) **(*) EMI (ADD) 4 76895-2. BPO, Karajan

(M) **(*) EMI (ADD) 5 67338-2. Philh. O, Klemperer

Krips recorded the *Unfinished* in the very early days of mono LP, a gentle, glowing performance; and here, in 1969 with the

VPO, he directs an unforced, flowing and wonderfully satisfying account, helped by excellent playing and splendid Sofiensaal recording, produced by Christopher Raeburn. This makes a splendid coupling for Krips's much earlier LSO recording of the *Ninth*, which has long been counted by us as one of his very finest records, perhaps *the* finest. The performance similarly has a direct, unforced spontaneity, which shows Krips's natural feeling for Schubertian lyricism at its most engaging. An ideal candidate for Universal's mid-priced 'Penguin ✿ Collection'.

Günter Wand offers visionary performances of both works, superbly played in live Berlin performances and glowingly recorded. Consistently he makes the playing sound spontaneous, even in the tricky problems of speed-changes in the *Great C major*. In the manner of his generation he does not observe exposition repeats in the outer movements or second-half repeats in the Scherzo, but this is a beautifully co-ordinated, strong and warm reading. The *Unfinished* is just as magnetic, again with no exaggeration, but with every interpretative problem solved as though it did not exist. An outstanding issue if you want this coupling.

Having earlier recorded both these symphonies for Virgin with the period instruments of the OAE (see above), Mackerras here gives his revised thoughts using modern instruments. The results are both intense and refreshing, with the benefits of period performance consistently apparent in the clarity of texture, but with warmer, sweeter string sound, which while yet on a chamber-scale has the necessary freshness. In the finale of the *Great C major* the sound is even more transparent, but where in the Scherzo he omits the second-half repeat, this time he does include the exposition repeat in the finale, omitted before. Broadly, Mackerras's readings remain the same but with more of the mystery of the *Unfinished* revealed than before.

Szell's, too, is a splendid performance of the *Unfinished*. Phrasing and general discipline are immaculate, but Szell never lacks warmth here, and drama and beauty walk hand in hand in the second movement. Apart from the lack of a real pianissimo, the 1960 recording is very good for its time. The *Ninth* dates from the previous year. Szell's control of tempo in the first movement brings a convincing onward flow, and the performance is notable for the alertness and rhythmic energy of the playing, yet there is no lack of resilience in the *Andante*. In the brilliant finale few rivals can match the precision of the hectic triplet rhythms. The sound is fuller in this remastered form than it was originally on LP.

Pritchard's reading of the *Unfinished* is magnetic, unusually direct, even in the melting lyricism of the incomparable second subject. The high dramatic contrasts – as in the development – are fearlessly presented with fine intensity, and the second movement, too, brings purity and freshness. The *Great C major* is as vital as it is refreshing. The opening brings a slightly square account of the introductory horn theme, but after that the resilience of the LPO playing is consistent, with the players often keenly challenged by the fast tempo and later able to relax into the lyricism of the beautiful slow movement. It is always significant when one welcomes repeats observed in this already long symphony, and at the time he made these recordings (1975), Pritchard observed repeats more than anyone else on record. Only the exposition repeat in the finale is omitted. Both recordings have the advantage of a warm ambience (Watford Town Hall) and are naturally balanced.

Karajan's EMI *Unfinished*, which dates from 1975, finds Berlin refinement at its most ethereal. The performance has

an other-worldly quality, rapt and concentrated. The *Great C major* is also compelling, but here some may find the reverberant acoustic gives the impression of too much weightiness. This is not a superficial reading, however; it has plenty of impetus and power, while the *Andante* has freshness too. The finale has undoubted thrust, although tuttis bring a degree of heaviness, caused as much by the sound itself as by the playing.

Klemperer's *Unfinished* is seen as a massive two-part symphonic structure, with keen, alert playing that never lets the attention flag. The quiet opening is deliberately purposeful, but when the second subject finally arrives there is no attempt to beautify the melody and it acquires an unusual purity. So it is at the opening of the second movement and through the whole performance, and it remains an outstanding example of Klemperer's interpretative genius. The *Ninth Symphony* is deliberately literal, but also rather heavy, particularly in the first movement. Yet once the speeds and severe approach are accepted, the power of the performance is matched by its fascination and there is some glorious playing from the Philharmonia. The Kingsway Hall recording from the early 1960s is rich and full and most realistically balanced.

Symphony 9 in C (Great), D.944

⊕ ✿ (M) *** Decca Legends (ADD) 460 311-2. VPO, Solti – WAGNER: *Siegfried Idyll* ***

⊕ (M) *** RCA 82876 59425-2. BPO, Wand

(M) *** EMI (ADD) 5 62791-2. LPO, Boult – BRAHMS: *Alto Rhapsody; Academic Festival Overture* ***

(BB) *** Warner Apex 2564 60531-2. Sinfonia Varsovia, Y. Menuhin

(M) (***) DG mono 447 439-2. BPO, Furtwängler – HAYDN: *Symphony 88* (***) ✿

(B) *** EMI double forte (ADD) 5 69364-2 (2). Cleveland O, Szell – BEETHOVEN: *Symphony 7* *** ✿; ROSSINI: *Overtures* **(*)

(M) *** BBC Legends BBCL 4140. LPO, Giulini – BRITTEN: *The Building of the House Overture;* WEBER: *Der Freischütz: Overture* ***

**(*) BBC stereo/mono BBCL 4072-2. BBC SO, Boult (with CHERUBINI: *Anacréon Overture;* CORNELIUS: *Barber of Baghdad Overture*)

(M) **(*) Warner Elatus 0927 46750-2. Concg. O, Harnoncourt (with MENDELSSOHN: *Fair Melusine Overture* (BPO) ***)

(M) (**(*)) Beulah mono 3PD12. BBC SO, Boult – MENDELSSOHN: *Hebrides Overture;* WAGNER: *Die Meistersinger: Overture* (**)

Symphony 9 in C (Great); Rosamunde: Overture (Die Zauberharfe), D.644

*** DG (IMS) 423 656-2. COE, Abbado

*** Häns. CD 93.044. Stuttgart RSO, Norrington

Günter Wand offers a visionary account of Schubert's *Great C major Symphony*, taken from superbly played, live, Berlin performances, glowingly recorded. Consistently he makes the playing sound spontaneous, even in the tricky problems of speed changes inherent in this work. In the manner of his generation, he does not observe exposition repeats in the outer movements or second-half repeats in the Scherzo, but this is a beautifully co-ordinated, strong and warm reading, well worthy of reissue in RCA's mid-priced 'Classic Library' series.

Solti's superb recording with the VPO (one of his finest

records) is also available as part of a Double Decca, which includes Nos. 5 and 8 (see above). Decca have rightly chosen it for reissue in their Legends series, coupled with Wagner's *Siegfried Idyll*. Both performances have comparable distinction and show that Solti could relax in music which he loved without sacrificing concentration and drama.

Though the COE is by definition an orchestra of chamber scale, the weight of Abbado's version, taken from his complete cycle, is ample, while allowing extra detail to be heard, thanks also to the orchestra's outstandingly crisp ensemble. Speeds are very well chosen, and the expressive detail is consistently made to sound natural. This version is important too for including textual amendments, and the Scherzo has four extra bars that were originally cut by Brahms in his early edition. The sound is beautifully refined, to match the point and polish of the playing. The *Rosamunde* (*Zauberharfe*) *Overture* makes a valuable and generous fill-up.

Older readers will welcome back to the catalogue this splendidly wise and magisterial account from the doyen of British conductors. There is not a whit of hyperbole; indeed, Sir Adrian's tendency to understate is evident in the slow movement, just as his feeling for the overall design is undiminished. The LPO respond with playing of high quality and the 1972 Kingsway Hall recording (like the Brahms coupling) is transferred admirably to CD.

Most listeners will surely do an aural double-take at the astonishing speed of the opening horn solo of Menuhin's highly individual and original interpretation. Yet the movement moves forward in a single thrust, gathering power, energy and momentum to its thrilling coda. The *Andante con moto* is also brisker than usual, but it comes naturally within Menuhin's conception, and the Scherzo rollicks forcefully and genially before the closing *Allegro vivace* sweeps all before it, the trombones helping to drive the music onwards. The sheer exuberance of this performance all but negates the idea of a work of 'heavenly' length and, with such vigour and zest, it is impossible to be bored for a moment, even if you resist the conception. Marvellous playing and splendid recording, leaving the listener on a high.

As with the coupled Haydn, Furtwängler gives the *Great C major* a glowing performance, if a highly individual one. The first movement brings an outstanding example of his wizardry, when he takes the recapitulation at quite a different speed from the exposition and still makes it sound convincing. In the beautifully played *Andante*, his very slow tempo is yet made resilient by fine rhythmic pointing. The mono recording dates from 1951 and the sound is remarkably fresh and very well balanced, with the dynamic range in the slow movement strikingly wide.

Szell's Cleveland account was his second in stereo with that orchestra (the first is discussed above, paired with the *Unfinished*). It has the hallmarks of an HMV recording from the beginning of the 1970s, with a wider dynamic range than Szell usually enjoyed and better overall balancing. Szell's powerful reading provides a reminder that the parallels between him and another great disciplinarian conductor, Toscanini, were sometimes significant. Szell's approach is similarly direct, but lyrical feeling underlies the surface brightness and the crisply sprung rhythms are exhilarating. In the hectic triplets of the finale the orchestra is unmatched in precision, with a sparkling lightness of articulation that is a joy to the ear.

Like his Stuttgart cycle of the Beethoven symphonies, also on Hänssler, Roger Norrington's second recording of the *Great C major Symphony* was taken live by Stuttgart Radio engineers, with modern instruments using period techniques. The first two movements are marginally faster even than Norrington's EMI recording with the London Classical Players. The clipped style of attack is made sharper by the warm, immediate recording, more open than on EMI. The interpretation is very similar, with rhythms lightly sprung. The main theme of the slow movement is more tense than before, although, as before, Norrington allows a degree of relaxation for the cello melody after the great central ostinato climax. In the last two movements speeds are similar but fewer repeats are observed, notably the exposition section of the finale. The *Die Zauberharfe Overture* (usually known as *Rosamunde*) makes a welcome extra, with a powerful introduction and a fast, light *Allegro*.

Giulini's live recording of Schubert's great *C major Symphony* was made at the Royal Festival Hall in London in May 1975, the principal work in one of the BBC Legends reissues celebrating the conductor's ninetieth birthday. It is a powerful reading, well recorded in full-bodied stereo. In the first two movements Giulini's speeds are broader than usual, so that he manages generally to avoid the traditional if unmarked speed-changes of most performances. So it is that in the slow movement he builds the central climax relentlessly with no speeding up; but then, for the yearning cello melody which follows, he does allow himself a degree of broadening, phrasing with characteristic warmth. The Scherzo is then infectiously sprung and the finale is beautifully articulated, even at high speed. As well as the two overtures, the extra items include a brief clip from a BBC interview, emphasizing the spiritual quality Giulini finds in music.

Sir Adrian's BBC version comes from a 1969 Prom. It has a grandeur and sense of space that compel admiration, not for Boult but for Schubert. Sir Adrian observes pretty well every repeat. It is a supremely classical performance, but the recording is not always ideally transparent; in fact, it is at times distinctly murky (the oboe is very reticently balanced in the opening of the second movement), and the Prom audience is unusually noisy and takes time to settle down at the beginning of every movement. The *Anacréon Overture* comes from a Royal Festival Hall Concert with the RPO from 1963, while the Cornelius *Barber of Baghdad Overture* is a mono recording taken from one of the studio concerts he conducted in the 1950s.

Like Abbado, Harnoncourt returned to Schubert's manuscripts to authenticate his recorded performances of the Schubert symphonies; yet there are differences, and he does not integrate Abbado's changes to the slow movement and Scherzo of the *Ninth Symphony*. What he does add, unexpectedly, is a diminuendo to the symphony's final chord. However, he manages the tempo changes of the opening movement with easy fluidity, creating a spring-like energy without any undue forcefulness. The Concertgebouw Orchestra plays beautifully for him, especially in the idyllic *Andante* and the crisply articulated finale. A fine performance, then, Viennese in its warmth and manner, but not a primary recommendation. The Mendelssohn *Overture*, which acts as an encore, is delicately Schubertian in feeling at its opening and close, but the allegro is comparatively bold and strongly motivated in Harnoncourt's more characteristic style. Excellent recording throughout.

When earlier in 1934 Sir Adrian Boult recorded the *Great C major Symphony* with the BBC Symphony Orchestra, it was only one of three versions then available, yet this reading, fresh and direct, certainly stands the test of time. Not surprisingly, speeds are a shade brisker than in his stereo version, yet in a similar way he solves the speed changes just as subtly, concealing problems with natural ease. Like the two overtures which come as fill-ups, the playing of the BBC Symphony, founded only in 1930, is a splendid tribute to Boult's genius as an orchestral trainer. Reflecting the limitations of short-playing 78 records, there are no repeats in the outer movements, and only the very first one in the Scherzo. The Beulah transfer involves a high but even surface hiss, which is generally easy to ignore when the sound has plenty of body, with fine presence and good detail, set against a dry acoustic, evidently with no added reverberation.

CHAMBER MUSIC

Arpeggione Sonata, D.821 (arr. for cello)
*** Ph. (IMS) 412 230-2. Maisky, Argerich – SCHUMANN: *Fantasiestücke* etc. ***
(BB) *** Naxos 8.550654. Kliegel, Merscher – SCHUMANN: *Adagio & Allegro* etc. ***
(M) **(*) Decca Legends (ADD) 460 974-2. Rostropovich, Britten – DEBUSSY: *Sonata:* SCHUMANN: 5 *Stücker in Volkston* ***

Mischa Maisky and Martha Argerich make much more of the *Arpeggione Sonata* than any of their rivals. Their approach may be relaxed, but they bring much pleasure through their variety of colour and sensitivity. The Philips recording is in the very best traditions of the house.

At super-bargain price, Maria Kliegel and Kristin Merscher are highly competitive. The performances are well shaped and sensitive, though perhaps lacking the last ounce of character you find in, say, the Rostropovich–Britten account. All the same, neither the Schubert nor the Schumann coupling will disappoint at this price, given the general high standard of playing and recording.

Rostropovich gives a curiously self-indulgent interpretation of Schubert's amiable *Arpeggione Sonata*. The playing of both artists is eloquent and it is beautifully recorded, but it will not be to all tastes.

Arpeggione Sonata; Cello Sonatinas 1–3, D.384–5 & D.408
*** Channel Classics CCS 9696. Wispelwey, Giacometti

The highly musical Pieter Wispelwey has the full measure of Schubert's innocent lyricism, and the pianist's light touch in the finale is especially persuasive. Paolo Giacometti makes a most convincing case for the use of the fortepiano in Schubert, and the restored has a remarkable range of colour. Pieter Wispelwey's tone, using gut strings, always sings and, even using a minimum of vibrato, he constantly cajoles the ear, while his phrasing has an appealing simplicity. Thus the three violin *Sonatinas* are made to sound convincing in these cello transcriptions, especially the *G minor*, D.408, in which the *Andante* and finale are endearing. The recording is forwardly but truthfully balanced. Recommended.

(i) *Arpeggione Sonata in A min., D.821* (arr. for cello); (ii) *Piano Quintet in A* (*Trout*)
(BB) **(*) RCA (ADD/DDD) 822876 55270-2. (i) Harrell, Levine; (ii) Ax, Guarneri Qt (members), Julius Levine (double bass)

(i) *Arpeggione Sonata;* (ii) *Piano Quintet in A* (*Trout*); (iii) *Die Forelle*
**(*) Sony SK 61964. (i–ii) Ma; (i–iii) Ax; (ii) Frank, Young, Meyer; (iii) Bonney

We have long praised Lynn Harrell's 1976 recording of the *Arpeggione Sonata* in partnership with James Levine. It is a refreshingly unmannered account and yet full of personality. Vital, sensitive playing, excellently recorded. It now comes coupled with a *Trout*, recorded digitally a decade later, yet less well balanced. The piano dominates throughout, not least because of the strong, though very musical contribtion of Emanuel Ax. The leader of the Guarneri Quartet is backwardly balanced and his timbre is small, yet this adds to the intimacy of what is undoubtedly a lively performance, with sympathtic accounts of both the *Andante* and Variations.

Emanuel Ax leads an impressive ensemble in this invigorating Sony account of the *Trout Quintet*. But, alas, there is a constant tendency to move onwards too quickly. This does not affect the famous theme and variations, which is done most imaginatively, but the Scherzo is very fast indeed, and the finale sounds rushed. A pity, as Yo-Yo Ma's performance of the *Arpeggione Sonata* is totally endearing, with all the warmth, joy and innocent Schubertian charm one could ask for. Barbara Bonney's account of the famous song is direct rather than innocently beguiling. No complaints about the recording balance.

Arpeggione Sonata, D.821 (arr. in G min. for clarinet & piano)
*** Chan. 8506. De Peyer, Pryor – SCHUMANN: *Fantasiestücke; 3 Romances;* WEBER: *Silvana Variations* ***

So persuasive is the performance of Gervase de Peyer and Gwenneth Pryor that the listener is all but persuaded that the work was actually written for this combination.

(i) *Arpeggione Sonata;* (ii) *Duo in A, D. 574; Fantaisie in C, D. 943; Violin Sonatinas 1–3, D. 384–5 & D. 408*
(B) *** Double Decca stereo/mono (ADD) 466 748-2 (2). (i) Gendron, Françaix; (ii) Goldberg, Lupu

Szymon Goldberg and Radu Lupu give us the complete violin and piano music (except for one small piece) in beautifully played and well-recorded performances, which have an unaffected Schubertian feeling. Indeed, Goldberg's account of the *Fantaisie* is particularly intimate and appealing. The presence of Lupu ensures that these performances give pleasure, and his playing has a vitality and inner life that are undoubtedly rewarding. These recordings date from the end of the 1970s, but the *Arpeggione Sonata*, which has a comparable intimacy and Schubertian affinity, is hardly less appealing even though the recording is mono (but very truthful mono) and dates from 1954.

(i) *Fantasia in C for Violin & Piano, D.934. Fantasia in C* (*Wanderer Fantasia*), D. 760
**(*) ECM 464 320-2. Schiff; (i) with Shiokawa

As might be expected, András Schiff's account of the *Wanderer Fantasia* is finely paced and highly sensitive, and entirely free from expressive exaggeration. He has the advantage of lifelike and full-bodied recorded sound. The coupling is another *C major Fantasia*, for violin and piano, with Yuuko Shiokawa, his partner in previous recordings. However, the piano is very dominant, and Shiokawa is very backwardly placed. At 50 minutes the disc is short measure anyway. A pity, since this is a distinguished *Wanderer*.

(i) *Fantasy in C, D.934;* (i; ii) *Piano Trio 2 in E flat, D.929;*
(iii) *String Quartets 8 in B flat, D.112 (Op. 168); 14 in D min.*
(Death and the Maiden), D.810; 15 in G, D.887 (Op. 161)

(***) HM Pearl mono GEMMCDS 9141 (2). (i) Adolf Busch,
Serkin; (iii) with Hermann Busch; (iii) Busch Qt

Some have spoken of the Busch Quartet's Schubert as the greatest ever committed to disc. Certainly the *G major Quartet* has never had so searching and powerful a reading, and the early *B flat Quartet*, which used to be known as Op. 168, sounds every bit as captivating as one remembers it from the days of shellac. The *E flat Trio* and the *C major Fantasy* are also in the highest class, and the Pearl transfers are very good indeed. These two CDs, packed economically in one jewelcase, encompass three LPs and are really excellent value for money. A lovely set.

Octet in F, D.803

0—◆ ✪ (M) *** Decca (ADD) 466 580-2. Vienna Octet –
SPOHR: *Octet in E* ***

(BB) *** HM Classical Express HCX 3957049. Music from
Aston Magna

*** Chan. 8585. ASMF Chamber Ens.

*** ASV CDDCA 694. Gaudier Ens.

*** Hyp. CDA 67339. Gaudier Ens.

(M) **(*) Cal. CAL 9314. Octuor de France

Octet in F, D. 803; Wind Octet, in F, D.72

(BB) **(*) Naxos 8.550389. Budapest Schubert Ens.

The Vienna Octet's 1958 recording of the Schubert *Octet* has stood the test of time. It has a magical glow with the group at its peak under the leadership of Willi Boskovsky. The horn has a Viennese fruitiness which helps to make the performance more authentic, and these fine players never put a foot wrong throughout. The recording only betrays its age in the upper registers, but is basically full and modern sounding. The delightful and unusual Spohr coupling makes this a fine addition to Decca's Legends series.

A wholly delightful account from the Aston Magna American group using period instruments with great finesse and affectionate warmth. Indeed, the music-making is pervaded with an American-styled geniality throughout, although the allegro of the first movement, like the jocular finale, is agreeably brisk and vivacious. All the playing is very personable, but the star of the occasion is the clarinettist, Eric Hoeprich, whose timbre is utterly seductive. He uses a pair of instruments, including a C clarinet in the fourth movement *Andante con variazioni*. The recording is first class and this is a real bargain.

The Chandos version brings a performance just as delightful as the earlier one by the ASMF, less classical in style, a degree freer in expression, with Viennese overtones brought out in Schubert's sunny invention. It has the benefit of excellent modern digital sound, cleaner on detail than before.

The Gaudier Ensemble give an entirely winning account of the *Octet*, essentially spontaneous yet very relaxed and catching all the ingenuous Schubertian charm. Excellent sound, vivid yet well balanced within a pleasing acoustic which gives a feeling of intimacy. An ideal record for a warm summer evening.

The Gaudier Ensemble can always be relied on in Schubert and their newest version of the *Octet* for Hyperion is no exception. As in their earlier version for ASV their approach is warm and relaxed, with a genuine Viennese *gemutlich*. Yet though the playing is always sunny, the relaxation here, especially in the second movement, is more pervasive than in

the ASV account, the overall effect slightly less spontaneous. So though the Hyperion disc is most enjoyable, the ASV performance is that bit more spirited.

A beautifully played and naturally recorded performance of the *Octet* from the French ensemble on Calliope, notable for its warmth and simplicity, and also for fine contributions from the clarinettist, Jean-Louis Sajot, and the horn player, Antoine Degremont. The overall effect is warmly spontaneous but there is no coupling.

A vivacious enough account from the Schubert Ensemble on Naxos provides a more than viable super-bargain version, particularly as the bonus, a little *Wind Octet* in the same key, has a winning finale. Good playing and lively recording ensure that this disc gives pleasure, although it is worth paying the extra money for the Decca Vienna version.

Piano Quintet in A (Trout) (DVD version)

(N) *** Opus Arte **DVD** OA CN 0903 D. Barenboim,
Perlman, Zukerman, Du Pré, Mehta. 'The Trout':
Documentary and performance; The Greatest Love and the
Greatest Sorrow – Documentary (V/D: Christopher Nupen)

Christopher Nupen, defying convention, in 1969 made his classic film, 'The Trout', combining documentary with musical performance. The performers, all emerging into international stardom, still in their twenties, provide an effervescent picture of musical preparation behind the scenes. Waiting for the performance at the newly opened Queen Elizabeth Hall in London, they simply have fun, with Jacqueline du Pré jazzing up the Mendelssohn *Violin Concerto* while pretending to be Pablo Casals, Zubin Mehta bowing Perlman's violin as he fingers the opening of that same work, and Perlman playing the *Flight of the Bumblebee* on the cello. Part of the challenge – realized in the exhilarating performance which follows – was that Pinchas Zukerman was playing the viola instead of the violin and the conductor, Zubin Mehta, was returning to his old instrument, the double-bass, just for the occasion, while another conductor, Lawrence Foster, turned the pages for Daniel Barenboim. Much more sombre, but moving too, is the other film on the disc, a survey of the remaining months of Schubert's short life after the death of Beethoven, when he wrote a sequence of supreme masterpieces.

Piano Quintet in A (Trout), D.667

(N) *** EMI 5 57664-2. Adès, Belcea Qt. (members) with C.
Long – ADÈS: *Piano Quintet* ***

*** BBC (ADD) BBCL 4009-2 (2). Curzon, Amadeus Qt,
Merret – BRAHMS: *Piano Quintet in F min., Op. 34* ***

*** Ph. 446 001-2. Brendel, Zehetmair, Zimmermann, Duven,
Riegelbauer – MOZART: *Piano Quartet 1* ***

(N) (M) **(*) Ph. (ADD) 476 7283. Brendel, Cleveland Qt

(B) **(*) Hyp. Dyad CDD 22008 (2). Schubert Ens. of L. –
HUMMEL: *Piano Quintet*; SCHUMANN: *Piano Quintet*;
Piano Quartet **(*)

(M) **(*) Sony (ADD) 512872-2. R. Serkin, Laredo, Naegele,
Parnas, J. Levine – SCHUMANN: *Piano Quintet* **(*)

Piano Quintet in A (Trout); Adagio & Rondo concertante in F, D.487

(BB) **(*) Naxos 8.550658. Jandó, Kodály Qt, with Tóth

Piano Quintet in A (Trout); Adagio & Rondo concertante; Notturno in E flat, D.897

(M) **(*) Classic fm 75605 570062. Berezovsky, Soloists of
ROHCG

Piano Quintet in A (Trout); Piano Trio 1 in B flat
(N) *** ASV Gold GLD 4000. W. Howard & Schubert Ens.

(i) *Piano Quintet in A (Trout);* (ii) *String Quartet 14 (Death and the Maiden)*
(M) *** DG Entrée 471 740-2. (i) Levine, Hetzel, Christ, Faust, Posch; (ii) Hagen Qt

(M) **(*) Sony (ADD) SBK 46343. (i) Horszowski, Budapest Qt (members), Levine; (ii) Juilliard Qt

(N) **(BB)** **(*)HMV 5 86763-2. (i) Lympany, LSO Principals; (ii) Gabrieli Qt

(M) **(*) DG (ADD) 449 746-2. Amadeus Qt, with (i) Gilels, Zepperitz

(i) *Piano Quintet in A (Trout); Fantasia in C (Wanderer), D.760*
(B) *** EMI Red Line CDR5 72567. Richter, (i) with Borodin Qt

(i) *Piano Quintet in A (Trout). Moments musicaux, D.780*
☛ **(M)** *** Decca 458 608-2. Schiff; (i) Hagen Qt

(i) *Piano Quintet in A (Trout);* (ii) *Der Hirt auf dem Felsen*
(BB) **(*) Regis RRC 1027. (i) Ian Brown, Nash Ens.; (ii) Lott, Brown, Collins

András Schiff and the Hagen Quartet give a delectably fresh and youthful reading of the *Trout Quintet*, full of the joys of spring, but one which is also remarkable for hushed concentration, as in the exceptionally dark and intense account of the opening of the first movement. The Scherzo brings a light, quick and bouncing performance, and there is extra lightness too in the other middle movements. Alongside Brendel's (but no other current rivals), this version observes the exposition repeat in the finale, and with such a joyful, brightly pointed performance one welcomes that. The *Moments musicaux* are also beautifully played and recorded, and make a considerable bonus.

The performance from Thomas Adès and the Belcea Quartet is in every way distinctive and, not surprisingly, full of fresh insights, while one is always aware of Colin Long's gentle double-bass contribution. Opening dramatically, tempi are brisk throughout, with the Scherzo making a vibrant centrepiece. The performance is generous on repeats and this brings its own sense of spaciousness. The players use the widest range of dynamic and there is great variety of lyrical expressive response in the *Andante* and the famous variations, which are beautifully played, the overall effect is pleasingly spontaneous. The recording was made at the Maltings so has the expected bloom.

Like the Brahms *Quintet*, with which it is coupled on a bonus disc, Curzon's live BBC recording of the *Trout Quintet* with the augmented Amadeus Quartet, made at the Royal Festival Hall in 1971, amply compensates in warmth and power for what it may lack in high studio polish, with all five artists at their most spontaneous. The Trout variations may be on the slow side, but the rhythmic pointing is a delight. Good radio sound, smoother on top than Curzon's famous Decca version.

ASV used the paired performances from the Schubert Ensemble to launch their 'Gold' label, and they are worthy of the promotion. These are vibrant accounts, full of life but not lacking charm, with the excellent pianist, William Howard, dominating artistically (although the piano is not unnaturally balanced). In the *Trout*, tempi are brisk but not excessively so, and the variations are full of attractive detail; in the

Piano Trio, the warm acoustic brings full textures without loss of clarity. Both accounts are seemingly spontaneous and if you want this coupling, the disc can receive a firm recommendation.

A first-class DG Entrée reissue from the early 1990s now rises to near the top of the list for those wanting the obvious coupling with Schubert's most popular string quartet. James Levine leads a highly spontaneous performance of the *Trout*, full of vigour, but also striking for its delicacy of lyrical feeling in the delightful account of the famous theme and variations, which contrasts so well with the vibrant Scherzo and crisply animated finale. Throughout the use of light and shade is most musical. Excellent, modern recording, with the piano dominating in the right way. The Hagen Quartet then give a vital, well-shaped and sensitive account of *Death and the Maiden*. They are generous in the matter of repeats and produce consistent beauty of sound. They are fully alive to the darker side of the work, and even if they rather overdo the pianissimo markings, reducing them to the faintest whisper in the slow movement, this remains one of the best modern accounts of the work, and they are very well recorded.

The Brendel/Cleveland performance may lack something in traditional Viennese charm, but it has a compensating vigour and impetus, and the work's many changes of mood are encompassed with freshness and subtlety. The second-movement *Andante* is radiantly played, and the immensely spirited Scherzo has a most engagingly relaxed Trio, with Brendel at his most persuasive. His special feeling for Schubert is apparent throughout: the deft pictorial imagery of the opening of the variations is delightful. The recording is well balanced and truthful. This is now reissued in Universal's 'Critics' Choice' series, but it would have benefited from a coupling, and is no longer a first choice.

The later Brendel performance is superbly recorded, the imagery rich and tangible, especially the piano, with Thomas Zehetmair's violin sweetly caught and the string bass gently resounding at the bottom. Like Brendel's previous Cleveland performance, which it easily displaces, this lacks something in traditional Viennese charm, but it has a compensating warmth and weight and certainly plenty of natural impetus, with Brendel consistently persuasive. The inclusion of a substantial Mozart coupling gives this Philips account an advantage, but the Decca version is in some ways even more endearing.

Richter dominates the EMI digital recording of the *Trout Quintet*, not only in performance but in balance. Yet this account has marvellous detail, with many felicities drawn to the attention that might have gone unnoticed in other versions. The first movement is played very vibrantly indeed, while the second offers a complete contrast, gently lyrical, and the variations have plenty of character. This is very satisfying, even though other versions are stronger on Schubertian charm. The performance of the *Wanderer Fantasia* comes from as long ago as 1963 but still sounds well. It is very distinguished indeed and makes a superb bonus, even if the piano-timbre is a shade hard.

Horszowski's contribution to the *Trout* is most distinguished, and his clean, clear playing dominates the performance which, although full of imaginative detail, is a little on the cool side – though refreshingly so, for all that. The Juilliard Quartet are far from cool in the *Death and the Maiden Quartet*, the unanimity of ensemble consistently impressive. In both works the sound is a little dry, but not confined.

Dame Moura Lympany's performance of the *Trout* sets off

in a brisk manner, the playing lively and fresh. In the second movement the interpretation relaxes and the variations are attractively done. The matter-of-fact approach is enhanced by the overall spontaneity of the music-making. The balance, however, is less than perfect, favouring the piano and not ideally sympathetic to the first violin (John Brown), with less body to his tone as recorded than the lower strings, while in his decorations of the 'Trout' theme he is too distant. But in most respects this is an enjoyable performance, if not a primary choice. For a coupling the Gabrielis give a sensitive and polished accout of Schubert's great *D minor Quartet*, not wearing their hearts on their sleeves, but genuinely touching in the slow movement. The recording here, made three years earlier than the *Trout*, is first class and has been smoothly transferred to CD.

In the 1975 DG recording of the *Trout* there is a masterly contribution from Gilels, and the Amadeus play with considerable freshness. The approach is very positive, not as sunny and spring-like as in some versions, but rewarding in its seriousness of purpose. The recording balance is convincing and the remastering creates a firm and vivid sound-image. The Amadeus's account of the *Death and the Maiden Quartet* was their first analogue recording of this work in 1959. The unanimity of ensemble is remarkable. The quartet play as one in dealing with the finer points of phrasing, for example at the very beginning of the variations. The early DG stereo, too, is very good.

On Classic fm, Boris Berezovsky leads a direct, spontaneous account, in which he makes a memorable contribution to the famous variations. If the performance (which includes the exposition repeat) had been imbued with the added expressive intensity which appears at the beginning of the *Adagio and Rondo concertante*, it would have been even more recommendable; but it is certainly fresh and well recorded. The *Notturno* also opens (and closes) with rapt concentration (and one recalls the slow movement of the *String Quintet*), but the playing is also just a little mannered.

A lively, immediate account from the Schubert Ensemble of London, strongly led by the pianist, William Howard. The first movement is brisk but committed, and the famous variations are well characterized. There are more touching accounts on record but few more vivaciously spontaneous, with a vivid recording to match.

The Jandó–Kodály *Trout* is above all bracing. The first movement is soon moving along briskly and at a concert one could well be swept along by the momentum of the performance, for there is relaxation in the *Andante* and the famous *Variations* are mellow and strongly characterized. The polish and impetus of this playing is never in doubt and the recording is excellent, but this account obviously comes from east of Vienna. The *Adagio and Rondo concertante* sounds a stronger work here than usual and the rondo is spirited and jolly.

The Serkin performance is distinguished, with some spontaneous if idiosyncratic playing from the master pianist. As a performance this is worth considering in the mid-price range, but the recommendation must be qualified, because the string tone of the 1967 recording is somewhat hard.

The account by the Nash Ensemble, previously on Carlton, now on Regis, brings a fill-up in the shape of *The Shepherd on the Rock*. They are rather forwardly recorded here, and their account is just a little wanting in the spontaneity that distinguishes the finest of current versions. Ian Brown is, as always, a sensitive artist, and Michael Collins provides an admirable clarinet obbligato for one of Schubert's most engaging songs.

Piano Trios 1 in B flat, D.898; 2 in E flat

(N) *** Praga **SACD** PRD/DSD 250 201. Guarneri Trio, Prague

(B) **(*) Double Decca 455 685-2 (2). Ashkenazy, Zukerman, Harrell

Piano Trios 1–2; Adagio in E flat ('Notturno') (for piano trio), D.897; Sonata in B flat (for piano trio), D.28

(BB) *** Arte Nova 74321 79424-2 (2). Trio Opus 8

(B) **(*) Teldec 4509 94558-2 (2). Trio Fontenay

(i–iii) Piano Trios 1–2; Notturno in E flat, D.897; Sonata Movement, D.28; (i, ii) Grand Duo in A, D.574

(B) **(*) EMI double forte 5 74197-2. (i) Collard; (ii) Dumay; (iii) Lodéon

(i) Piano trios 1–2; Notturno, D.897; Sonata in B flat, D.28; (ii) String Trios: in B flat (in one movement), D.471; in B flat, D.581

(B) *** Ph. Duo (ADD) 438 700-2 (2). (i) Beaux Arts Trio; (ii) Grumiaux Trio

The Beaux Arts set of the Schubert *Piano Trios* from the late 1960s is another of the extraordinary bargains offered on the Philips Duo label. The performances provide impeccable ensemble with the pianist, Menahem Pressler, always sharply imaginative and the cellist, Bernard Greenhouse, bringing simple dedication to such key passages as the great slow-movement melody of the *Trio No. 2 in E flat*. The *Notturno*, played here with great eloquence, recalls the rapt, hushed intensity of the glorious slow movement of the *String Quintet*. What makes the set doubly attractive is the inclusion of the two much rarer *String Trios*, also early works from 1816–17. Given such persuasive advocacy, both pieces cannot fail to make a strong impression.

Jean-Philippe Collard, Augustin Dumay and Frédéric Lodéon, all splendid performers in their own right, create a fully integrated ensemble that sounds as if the players enjoy chamber music at home. All these performances sparkle, and there is a true Schubertian spirit in the *Grand Duo*. The one reservation concerns the first movement (and to a lesser extent the finale) of the *Second Trio in E flat*. The balance here is rather dominated by the piano, and Collard adopts very brisk tempi. There is plenty of charm elsewhere, but this is a less easily recommendable performance than those of the *B flat Trio*, the *Notturno* and the *Sonatensatz*, where the balance is better integrated and the pacing can hardly be faulted. The recordings were made in a concert-hall acoustic (the Salle Wagram, Paris), and the early digital sound is bright and clearly focused, if a touch dry.

Arte Nova offer both trios at the most competitive of prices – less than the Hyperion accounts of the two Trios alone. No quarrels with the playing or recording. Neither of the Trio performances is touched by routine, though at the same time neither quite attains the level of distinction of the Florestan Trio (see below). If one bought a ticket for a concert one would feel very satisfied at this playing, and the present issue is well worth the money and well recorded too.

There are many felicities of detail in the performances from the Trio Fontenay and their affectionate lyricism certainly does not lack warmth. But at times they over-dramatize and at others there is a feeling that phrasing is indulgent, as for instance with Niklas Schmidt's beautifully timbred yet almost sensuous cello solo in the *Andante* of the *B flat Trio*. The rapt opening of the *Notturno* needs a greater feeling of Schubertian innocence: a serenity without too much *espressivo*. The first movement of the *B flat Trio* has a strong impulse, and the Scherzo is treated as an opportunity for extrovert virtuosity. Excellent recording, but these performances lack the spring-like freshness of the competing Viennese group, or indeed the famous Beaux Arts set on Philips.

Czech musicians often display a special feeling for Schubert; the Guarneri players are no exception, and they have a splendidly agile pianist in Ivan Klánsky. They set off into the *B flat Trio* with an attractive jauntiness of spirit and then find a nice delicacy for the opening of the lovely *Andante*. After the jolly Scherzo there is a comparably lightness of touch for the finale. The *E flat Trio* has a similar vivacious impetus, and the *Andante* with its gentle bouncing underlay is delightfully done; and the same rhythmic lift brings added joy to the rondo finale. In short these are wholly delightful accounts, with a true Schubertian spirit. They are truthfully recorded, although, surprisingly for a SACD, the upper range is a little dry, which affects the violin timbre. But both the performances are memorable.

Ashkenazy, Zukerman and Harrell give strong performances of both works, full of impetus and there is much subtlety of detail. But although the concentration of the playing in the slow movement of the *E flat Trio* is in no doubt and Ashkenazy produces scintillating passage work, in the last result the innocent charm which informs Schubert's inspiration is all but missed. The players are not helped by a vividly forward recording which tends to sound aggressive in fortissimos, though some reproducers will register this more strikingly than others. These are new digital recordings but the two discs are offered as a Double Decca.

Piano Trio 1 in B flat, D.898

(B) *** EMI double forte (ADD) 5 69367-2 (2). Oistrakh, Knushevitzky, Oborin – BEETHOVEN: *Archduke Trio* ***; BRAHMS: *Violin Sonatas 1–2* **(*)

(BB) (***) Naxos mono 8.110188. Thibaud, Casals, Cortot – BEETHOVEN: *Variations on 'Ich bin der Schneider Kakadu'*; HAYDN: *Piano Trio 39 in G* (***)

Schubert's music needs warmth and humanity, and this well-integrated Russian team on the bargain forte reissue give both these qualities in abundance. They imbue the music with just that essence of clarity and warmth that it demands by right. The tempi are sensitively chosen, and the Scherzo is handled in masterly fashion by all three players. Excellent piano-tone and a good round sound from the strings. The encores are beautifully played and, if the couplings are suitable, this makes a fine bargain.

The Thibaud–Casals–Cortot partnership made their famous recording of the Schubert *B flat Trio* in 1926, and it was long one of the classics of the gramophone. It still has a rich humanity and warmth that explain its reputation. The Ward Marston transfer is very good indeed, even if the sound now seems very dated and two-dimensional.

Piano Trio 1 in B flat, D.898; Sonata in B flat (for piano trio), D.28; Notturno, D.897

🔊 *** Hyp. CDA 67273. Florestan Trio

The Florestan Trio are among the latest to tackle the Schubert *B flat Piano Trio* and are among the finest on disc. This is highly musical playing, whose value is enhanced by the contributions of that fine pianist Susan Tomes. They have the benefit of excellent recording. A strong recommendation and arguably a first choice.

Piano Trio 2 in E flat, D.929 (includes both first and second versions of finale)

🔊 *** Hyp. CDA 67347. Florestan Trio

The Florestan Trio follow up their outstanding account of Schubert's *B flat major Trio* with another memorable performance of the more profound, yet still often light-hearted, *E flat Trio*, written in the same month (November) in which Schubert completed *Winterreise*. If once again the playing of the pianist, Susan Tomes, stands out, the cellist's (Richard Lester's) contribution is hardly less memorable. As before, the recording is completely lifelike and very well balanced, catching the widest range of dynamic with naturalness and fidelity. This, like its companion, is now a primary recommendation. As a bonus we are additionally offered Schubert's original finale, nearly two minutes longer without the two cuts in the development made by the composer, totalling 98 bars.

Piano Trio 2 in E flat, D.929; Sonatensatz, D.28

(BB) *** Virgin 2x1 5 62007-2 (2). Castle Trio –
BEETHOVEN: *Piano Trio 7 (Archduke); 10 (Variations) & 11 (Variations)* ***

Anyone seeking Schubert's *E flat Piano Trio* on period instruments will find it difficult to better this performance by the Castle Trio. Led by the nimble-fingered Lambert Orkis, playing a modern copy of an 1824 Graf fortepiano. The *Andante* is particularly fine, with a memorably refined contribution from the cellist, Kenneth Slovak, while the sparkling Scherzo and finale (full of rhythmic character) show the mettle of both Orkis (with crisply incisive articulation and his fortepiano never sounding clattery, and the violinist, Marilyn McDonald. The early *Sonatensatz* too has charming naivety and simplicity, and is presented with consummate style and freshness.

Rondo in B min. (for violin & piano), D.895

(M) *** EMI Debut 5 74017-2 Batiashvili, Chernyavska –
BACH: *Partita 1*; BRAHMS: *Violin Sonata 1 in G*

A pupil of Mark Lubotsky, the Georgian-born Elisabeth Batiashvili came to international attention when at the age of sixteen she won second prize at the Sibelius Competition in Helsinki. Now twenty-two, she makes her EMI debut with a mixed programme. She gives a vital and lyrical account of this Schubert piece and is expertly partnered by Milana Chernyavska.

String quartets

String Quartets 1–15; Quartet Movement in C min., D.103
(B) **(*) DG (ADD) 463 151-2 (6). Melos Qt of Stuttgart

String quartets 1 in G min./B flat, D.18; 2 in C, D.32; 3 in B flat, D.36; 4 in C, D.46; 5 in B flat, D.68; 9 in G min., D.173; 10 in E flat, D.87; 12 in C min. (Quartettsatz), D.703; 15 in G, D.887; in C min. (Overture), D.8a
*** CPO 999 410-2 (3). Auryn Qt

String Quartets 6 in D, D.74; 7 in D, D.94; 8 in B flat, D.112; 11 in E, D.353; 13 in A min., D.804; 14 in D min. (Death and the Maiden), D.810. 5 Minuets & 5 German Dances, D.89
**(*) CPO 999 409-2 (3). Auryn Qt

String Quartets 1; 13; Overture in B flat, D.470
*** MDG 307 0602-2. New Leipzig Qt

String Quartets 2; 11; Overture in C min. (for quintet), D.8; Fragment, D. 87a
*** MDG 307 0609-2. New Leipzig Qt

String Quartets 3; 8; in B flat (fragment), D.470
*** MDG 307 0606-5. New Leipzig Qt

String Quartets 4; 5 (including 1st & 2nd versions of Allegro maestoso); 2 Ländler for 2 Violins in D, D.354
*** MDG MDG 307 0608-2. New Leipzig Qt

String Quartets 6; 10; in C min. (fragment), D.103
*** MDG 307 0605-5. New Leipzig Qt

String Quartets 7; 9; Quartet movement in C min., D. 703
*** MDG 307 0607-2. New Leipzig Qt

String Quartet 14 (Death and the Maiden); Minuet, D.86; Minuets & German Dances, D.89
*** MDG 307 0604-2. New Leipzig Qt

String Quartet 15; Fragment, D.2c; String Trio, D.472
*** MDG 307 0601-2. New Leipzig Qt

(i) *String Quintet in C, D.956. Fragment, D.3; Overture, D.8a*
*** MDG 307 0603-2. (i) Sanderling; New Leipzig Qt

The New Leipzig Quartet offer an ideal approach. They have great sweetness of tone, yet they are not sugary; they give us a wide dynamic range without drawing attention to themselves, and they seem totally inside the Schubert tradition. They have much greater warmth than the Melos Quartet of Stuttgart on DG and are far removed from the overpowering jet-setting quartet-machines. Theirs is humane music-making which conveys some sense of period and naturalness of expression. The *Quintet* may not be as intense as some versions but it is still very rewarding. The recordings are very good and the set has the merit of including various less familiar fragments. A thoroughly musical and well-recorded series.

The Auryn Quartet also give eminently satisfactory accounts of the Schubert *Quartets* adding also some early minuets and trios, D.89. They are at their happiest in the earlier quartets, which they play with an unforced fluency that will delight listeners. They may not always penetrate the depths of the *G major*, D.887, as some of their rivals do, but generally speaking both performances and recordings are more than just serviceable. The package is far more economical than the Leipzig Quartet on Dabringhaus and Grimm, which stretches to nine CDs – and just as comprehensive. Those looking for a complete ready-made Schubert quartet cycle could find this a worthwhile investment. Not every performance is competitive with the finest, but they are all eminently musical.

The Melos Quartet give us an inexpensive survey. The early works have a disarming grace and innocence and some of their ideas are most touching (witness the *Adagio* introduction of No. 4 in C). The Melos Quartet give impressive, unmannered accounts of all these works, finding the drama as well as the music's inner tensions. They are, however, let down by the recording, which, although faithful, is rather too closely balanced. The remastering provides good presence, and conveys a wide dynamic range, but fortissimos can be a little fierce. Nevertheless, this well-documented set is value for money and worth considering when the full-priced competition costs twice as much.

String Quartets 1, D.18; 4, D.46; 8, D.112
☛ (BB) *** Naxos 8.555921. Kodály Qt

The Kodály Quartet are embarking with distinction on a complete Schubert cycle. Their playing has the same simplicity of style that they brought to early Haydn, yet the Schubertian colouring emerges immediately at the opening of the very *First Quartet*. This astonishingly confident work was written as early as 1810–11, yet it has a delightful, Ländler-like Minuet which calls for mutes, a graceful *Andante* and a busy, sparkling finale. No. 4, written two years later, opens with a grave echo of Mozart's *Dissonance Quartet* and has a delicate slow movement in siciliano rhythm, while the cheerful finale returns to the mood of a rustic Austrian dance. No. 8 has a G minor slow movement, again obviously influenced by Mozart, which lightens its mood later, but it never shakes off its seriousness entirely until the Haydnesque dancing Minuet and energetic finale. Altogether a splendid beginning, very naturally recorded.

String Quartets 3, D.36; 7, D.94; 9, D.173
☛ (BB) *** Naxos 8.550592. Kodály Qt

Schubert's *Third Quartet* was written in 1812–13. It is a cheerful work, with a dominating motif in the first movement to remind us of Haydn's *Fifths Quartet*. While Haydn remains Schubert's model throughout, the lyrical *Andante* has a darker, more personal tinge in the middle section. *No. 7 in D major*, written a year earlier, has a disarming opening movement, the effect astonishingly mature, and the *Andante* is comparably serene. The spirit of Haydn returns in the Minuet with its bouncing Trio, and the finale is sheer joy. The Kodály Quartet play this work marvellously and make it the highlight of the disc. *No. 9 in G minor* opens very positively, its argument both dramatic and serious, but the *Andantino* (though still Haydnesque) has a Schubertian theme. The Minuet then reminds us dramatically of the comparable movement in Mozart's *Symphony No. 40*, and the engaging finale echoes and quickens that same idea. Once again the playing is splendid, and the recording most naturally balanced throughout.

String Quartet 8 in B flat, D.112
(M) (***) EMI mono 5 65308-2 (4). Busch Qt (with MENDELSSOHN: *Capriccio in E min.*) – BEETHOVEN: *String Quartets.* *** ●

The excellence and lightness of spirit the Busch communicate in this quartet is exhilarating. There is an alternative transfer available on Pearl (see above, under *Fantasy in C major*).

String Quartets 8; 13 in A min., D.804
*** ASV CDDCA 593. Lindsay Qt

In the glorious *A minor* the Lindsays lead the field. It would be difficult to fault their judgement in both these works on tempi and expression, and dynamics are always the result of keen musical thinking. Excellent recording.

String Quartets 10 in E flat, D.87; 12 (Quartettsatz), D.703; 13 in A min., D.804
☛ (M) *** Virgin 5 61995-2. Borodin Qt
(B) *** EMI 5 557419-2. Belcea Qt

These Virgin recordings of the silken-toned Borodins playing Schubert come from 1991 and offer cultured performances that will give much pleasure. They are unforced readings, which are free from any interpretative point-making and are content to leave the music to speak for itself. Some might feel that the *E flat Quartet* could be more strongly characterized, but the *Quartettsatz* is as powerfully dramatic a reading as any in the catalogue. Though in the *A minor Quartet* they are not necessarily to be preferred to the Lindsays, the New Leipzig (in their MDG series), or the Quartetto Italiano (see below), they can certainly be recommended alongside them.

The Belcea made a strong impression with their début recording of Debussy and Ravel, and they now follow up with another of the best Schubert quartet discs to have appeared in recent months. Tempi are expertly judged and they command both feeling and concentration.

String Quartets 10 (7); 13, D.804

☞ ✪ *** Astrée E 8580. Mosaïques Qt

(BB) *** Naxos 8.550591. Kodály Qt

Above all, these period-instrument performances, so notable for their points of closely observed detail, are highly spontaneous. The very opening of the *E flat Quartet* (published posthumously as No. 10) is warmly inviting, and the players have the full measure of the songful serenity of its lovely *Adagio*. The profundities of the *A minor* are fully understood by this highly sensitive group, and the recapitulation is particularly memorable. There is dramatic intensity as well as charm in the famous (*Rosamunde*) *Andante*, with the finale following gracefully: the delicacy of the shading of the playing here is a marvel. A superb disc, beautifully recorded.

What strikes one immediately at the opening of the Kodály's account of the great *A minor Quartet*, D.804, is the guileless simplicity of their approach. There is drama too, but the innocent, lyrical feeling persists, and it enhances the lovely *Andante* with its *Rosamunde* theme. The restless opening of the Minuet/Allegretto is perfectly caught, and the good-natured finale maintains the finesse and warmth of what is a most rewarding performance. The earlier *E flat major Quartet* is presented with comparable geniality and again the ensemble is immaculate, with some delightful interchanges in the vigorous finale with its wistful secondary theme. Once again excellent recording.

String Quartets 10, D.87; 14 (Death and the Maiden)

☞ (M) *** Cal. Approche CAL 5234. Talich Qt

(M) (***) Telefunken mono 0927 42661-2. Calvet Qt

The Talich Quartet do not wear their hearts on their sleeves: the intensity of their performance of *Death and the Maiden* comes from within. There is a profundity in the theme and variations of the *Andante* which, together with the richness of texture that they create, is wonderfully heart-warming. The performance of the earlier *D major Quartet* is hardly less fine: more volatile, with the spirited finale concluding the disc unforgettably. Superb recording; string quartet discs do not come any better than this.

The Calvet's few records were not readily accessible in England before the war, but it is clear that they were a wonderful ensemble. Their Schubert has great finesse, a wide dynamic range and variety of tone-colour. They bring a controlled passion and an unerring rightness of tempo to both works: they carry a complete sense of conviction and a selfless absence of expressive exaggeration. As with the Busch, one feels one is gaining a more complete picture of the composer and learning something new about this glorious music. It goes without saying that these are technically immaculate performances, but the tonal sweetness does not disguise the pathos central to Schubert's art. No Schubertian should overlook this CD. Excellent transfers that soon make one forget the inevitable sonic limitations.

String Quartets 12 (Quartettsatz); 13; 14 (Death and the Maiden); 15 D.887

(B) *** Ph. (ADD) Duo 446 163-2 (2). Italian Qt

String Quartets 12–15; (i) String Quintet in C, D. 956

(M) *** Nim. NI 1770. Brandis Qt, (i) with Yang

(N) (B) **(*) Trio 477 045-2 (3). Emerson Qt. with (i) Rostropovich

The Brandis Quartet, a fine Central European group, have warmth and they bring a natural eloquence to all these quartets, which are all the more potent for being free of interpretative point-making. In the great *C major Quintet*, with beautiful matching, they again convey spontaneous expressiveness, and they are not afraid to linger a little over the first movement's lovely second-subject melody. Their slow movement, played freely, has rapt tension but, again, also conveys warmth, rather an ethereal, withdrawn atmosphere which communicates in a quite individual way. They are very naturally recorded.

The Italian Quartet's 1965 coupling of the *Quartettsatz* and the *Death and the Maiden Quartet* was counted the finest available in its day, with the famous variations played with great imagination and showing a notable grip in the closing pages. Technically the playing throughout is remarkable. These players' understanding of Schubert is equally reflected in their performance of the *A minor Quartet*, recorded a decade later. The familiar '*Rosamunde*' slow movement is beautifully paced, with an impressive command of feeling. The 1976 sound, too, is first class. The *G major Quartet* is, if anything, even finer. And the recording is extremely vivid, making this one of the most thought-provoking accounts of the *Quartet* ever. Excellent CD transfers throughout.

The Emersons certainly have an amazing technical address and are among the finest quartets playing now. Their attack and ensemble are impeccable; their tonal blend and finesse disarm criticism. Their approach is distinctly late twentieth-century Manhattan, rather than early nineteenth-century Europe with its gentler colours. Yet they spring from a different culture and have no want of intelligence and insight. There is tenderness at times and, in the *C major Quintet* with Rostropovich as second cello, an abundant eloquence. Good recording.

String Quartets 12 (Quartettsatz); 14 (Death and the Maiden)

☞ *** ASV CDDCA 560. Lindsay Qt

(BB) *** Naxos 8.550590. Kodály Qt

(BB) **(*) Naxos 8.550221. Mandelring Qt

The Lindsays' intense, volatile account of the *Death and the Maiden Quartet* is played with considerable metrical freedom and the widest range of dynamic, and the *Quartettsatz*, which acts as the usual filler, is unusually poetic and spontaneous in feeling. The recording is excellent.

The Kodály players are not renowned for wearing their hearts on their bow-arms, and their performance of the first movement of the *Death and the Maiden*, though not lacking in point and responsive intensity, is not as sharply extrovert in its associations with mortality as some. They find the heart of the work in the slow movement variations, which they open very intimately and they play with their usual humanity and feeling, if without quite the potency of the Lindsays. They then immediately warm to the Scherzo with its almost wistful Trio, and their bouncing account of the vigorous finale is second to none. This is certainly a performance to live with, even if it does not dwell on the tragedy of Schubert's inspiration and the playing in the *Quartettsatz*, agitated and lilting by turns, is also very fine. The recording, which has a natural presence, is well up to the high standard of this fine series.

The Mandelring Quartet are very good indeed. The performances are sensitively and sensibly played and very decently recorded, and anyone tempted by this Naxos disc will not be disappointed for so modest an outlay.

String Quartets 12 (Quartettsatz); 15, D.887

(B) **(*) HMA 1951409. Melos Qt

This is not to be confused with the set of Schubert quartets that the Melos recorded for DG in the late 1970s. These come from a set comprising the works written in 1820–26, of which the *G major Quartet*, D.887, is the most remarkable of all, powerfully searching and deeply personal. The Melos Quartet play with great commitment and power, and are decently recorded, but this is not a first choice.

String Quartets 13 in A min., D.804; 14 in D min. (Death and the Maiden), D.810

🕭 (B) *** Ph. (ADD) 426 383-2. Italian Qt

**(*) Ara. Z 6687. Guarneri Qt

This separate bargain Philips issue, taken from the above Duo, is most welcome. The sound is excellent.

The Guarneri record of *Death and the Maiden* was made in 1996 and, as one would expect from this fine ensemble, offers immaculate playing and, when required, dramatic intensity. There could perhaps be more tenderness in the A minor first movement, but this well-recorded account does not lack emotional power and freshness. However, the Italian Quartet's coupling of these two works remains a first choice.

String Quartets 13 in A min., D.804; 14 (Death and the Maiden), D.810; 15 in G, D.887; (i) String Quintet in C

(BB) **(*) EMI Gemini (ADD) 5 85526-2 (2). Hungarian Qt;
(i) with Varga

This economical EMI package brings all Schubert's last masterpieces in this genre. The performances have been in circulation on a number of occasions, most recently in the 'Rouge et Noir' series. The *Death and the Maiden* and the *A minor Quartet* were recorded in 1958, the early days of stereo (the former appeared in this country on the Vox label), while the *G major Quartet*, recorded in the Salle Wagram, comes from 1968, and the *Quintet*, with the fine Hungarian cellist László Varga as second cello, is from 1970. They are eminently serviceable performances, which will give pleasure even if – in the *Quartets* at least – they do not displace the Quartetto Italiano on Philips.

String Quartets 14 (Death and the Maiden); 15 in G

(M) (***) EMI (mono) 7 69795-2. Busch Qt

The Busch Quartet's account is more than fifty years old, but it brings us closer to the heart of this music than almost any other. The slow movement of the *Death and the Maiden Quartet* is a revelation, and the same must be said of the *G major*, which has great depth and humanity. For its age, the sound is still amazing.

String Quartet 14 (Death and the Maiden) (arr. for string orchestra by Mahler)

**(*) Chan. 9616. Norwegian CO, I. Brown – SCHOENBERG:
Verklaerte Nacht ***

Mahler made his transcription of *Death and the Maiden* when opportunities to hear Schubert's masterpiece were few and far between. In the days of its ready accessibility on

records and in the concert hall, the idea of recording it seems a false reverence (just as recording piano-duet versions of Glazunov symphonies would be). Its character is naturally changed in the orchestral medium, but those who want this transcription will find the playing of the Norwegian Chamber Orchestra and the Chandos recording both first class.

String Quartet 15 in G, D.887

🕭 (N) *** Naxos 8.557125. Kodály Qt

(M) (**(*)) Orfeo mono C604031B. Hungarian Qt –
BARTOK: *Quartet 5* (**(*))

A truly outstanding performance of Schubert's last and probably greatest *String Quartet* from the Kodály group, who open dramatically and encompass all the work's magical changing moods with consistent concentration and deep feeling. Spontaneity informs every bar: the *Andante* has an unforgettable atmosphere of gentle melancholy, yet there is a joyful simplicity in the dancing finale, which is brilliantly played. Indeed, this is one of the group's very finest records, for the infectious *German Dances* make a most engaging bonus, the closing Laendler particularly winning. First-class recording.

This performance comes from a concert given at the Salzburg Mozarteum in August 1961, some years before the Hungarian Quartet's commercial recording at the Salle Wagram. The live occasion prompts playing of tremendous intensity and heartfelt feeling. This has a higher emotional temperature than the latter, but the more refined EMI stereo recording will probably incline most readers towards the studio set, though the mono sound is perfectly acceptable.

String Quintet in C, D.956

(M) *** EMI 5 66890-2 [5 66942-2]. Alban Berg Qt with Schiff

❂ (***) Testament mono SBT 1031 Hollywood Qt, Reher –
SCHOENBERG: *Verklaerte Nacht* (***) ❂

*** Nim. NI 5313. Brandis Qt, Yang

*** Channel Classics CCS 6794. Orpheus Qt, Wispelwey

(***) Biddulph mono LAB 093. Pro Arte Qt, Pini – BRAHMS:
String Sextet 1 (***)

(M) **(*) DG (ADD) 453 668-2. Melos Qt, Rostropovich

(**) Testament mono SBT 1157. Amadeus Qt, Pleeth –
MOZART: *Sinfonia concertante, K.364* (**(*))

String Quintet in C; String Quartet 14 (Death and the Maiden); Quartettsatz, D. 703

🕭 ❂ (M) *** ASV CDDCS 243 (2). Lindsay Qt

String Quintet in C; String Trio in B flat, D.581

(BB) *** Naxos 8.550388. Villa Musica Ens.

(i) String Quintet in C; (ii) Lieder: An die Musik; An Sylvia; Auf dem Wasser zu singen; Ave Maria; Die Forelle; Gretchen am Spinnrade; Heidenröslein; Der Tod und das Mädchen

(N) (BB) *** EMI HMV 5 86762-2. (i) Chilingirian Qt, with Ward Clark; (ii) J. Baker, Parsons or Moore

(i) String Quintet in C, D.956; (ii) Auf dem Strom, D.943; (iii) Gretchen am Spinnrade; Nacht und Träume; Rastlose Liebe

(M) *** Sony SMK 60032. (i) Cleveland Qt, Ma; (ii) Valente, Bloom, Serkin; (ii) Te Kanawa, Amner

The Lindsay version gives the impression that one is eavesdropping on music-making in the intimacy of a private concert. They observe the first-movement exposition repeat and the effortlessness of their approach does not preclude intellectual strength. In the ethereal *Adagio* they effectively convey the sense of it appearing motionless, suspended, as it were, between reality and dream, yet at the same time they never allow it to become static. Their reading must rank at the top of the list; it is very well recorded. It now comes coupled at mid-price with an equally memorable version of the *Death and the Maiden Quartet* – a virtually unbeatable pairing, with the *Quartettsatz* thrown in for good measure.

The Cleveland Quartet and Yo-Yo Ma are scrupulous in observing dynamic markings (the second subject is both restrained and pianissimo) and they also score by observing all repeats. Their performance has feeling and eloquence, as well as a commanding intellectual grip. Moreover, they are admirably recorded and thus present a strong challenge at mid-price. For the reissue, some Schubert Lieder have been added. A fine performance from Benita Valente of *Auf dem Strom* is made memorable by Myron Bloom's glorious horn obbligato. Of the following three songs from Kiri Te Kanawa, *Gretchen am Spinnrade* has a delightful simplicity and *Nacht und Träume* is tonally ravishing. So this vocal music makes a considerable bonus.

Few ensembles offer timbre as full-bodied or as richly burnished as that produced by the Alban Berg and Heinrich Schiff, whose recording has impressive sonority, although there is just a touch of digital fierceness on top. This group has the advantage of wonderfully homogeneous tone, even in their raptly sustained pianissimo in the *Adagio*. Given the sheer polish and full sound that distinguishes their playing, this must rank high among current recommendations. However, unlike the Lindsays, they do not observe the first movement exposition repeat. This CD now returns to the catalogue in EMI's 'Great Recordings of the Century' series.

The Hollywood Quartet's 1951 version of the *Quintet* with Kurt Reher as second cello stands apart. Over 40 years on, its qualities of freshness and poetry, as well as an impeccably confident technical address, still impress as deeply as ever. This is the product of consummate artistry and remains very special indeed.

Vividly recorded (in 1980), with clear placing of instruments in a smallish but not dry acoustic (in fact a chapel), the Chilingirian version presents a most compelling account, totally unmannered and direct in style but full of concentration and spontaneity. So one has the consistent sense of a live performance, and the great melody of the first movement's second subject emerges without any intrusive nudging or over-expressiveness. The slow movement too has a natural intensity, though the closeness of the recording prevents one from observing a really soft *pianissimo*. Throughout, the string timbres and blending are most natural. For this inexpensive reissue Dame Janet Baker provides glorious performances of eight favourite songs, suitable for the female voice, admirably accompanied by either Geoffrey Parsons or Gerald Moore.

The Brandis Quartet with Wen-Sin Yang (cello) also give a very satisfying account which is also available coupled with *Quartets 12–15* (see above).

The Villa Musica players tackle the great *C major Quintet* with a freshness and concentration that are consistently compelling, even if the finale is neat and clean rather than urgently dramatic. The little *String Trio* makes an attractive and generous fill-up, another assured and stylish performance. With clear, well-balanced recording this super-budget issue makes another outstanding bargain.

The Orpheus Quintet offer a performance of communicated warmth and feeling, both in the slow movement and in the remarkable *Andante* central section of the Scherzo. The playing is fresh and feels alive, and the recording has striking body and realism.

Rostropovich plays as second cello in the Melos performance, and no doubt his influence from the centre of the string texture contributes to the eloquence of the famous *Adagio* which, like the performance as a whole, is strongly, even dramatically, characterized. The emphasis on the rhythmic articulation of the outer movements leaves no doubt as to the power of Schubert's writing, and there is no lack of atmosphere in the opening and closing sections of the slow movement. The recording is live and immediate. A fine version, but not a first choice.

The Pro Arte Quartet's 1935 account of the Schubert *Quintet*, with Anthony Pini as second cello, dominated the pre-war catalogues. Its humanity and warmth still tell, particularly in the slow movement. It comes with a fine account of the Brahms *B flat Sextet*, made in the same year. Needless to say, some allowance has to be made for the recording, eminently well transferred though it is.

EMI made their Amadeus Quartet's recording of the great *C major Quintet* before their long-term contract with DG. If the first movement is a degree warmer and more purposeful than in the later versions, the slow movement at a more flowing speed lacks the inner intensity of the later recordings, partly a question of pianissimos not being registered so gently. Also the finale at a marginally broader speed lacks the exuberance of later recordings, but the youthful freshness and strength of the whole performance are most winning, helped by an excellent transfer.

Violin Sonatinas, 1–3; Fantasy in C, D.934

(BB) *(**) Naxos 8.550420. Kang, Devoyon

Korean-born Dong-Suk Kang plays with style and panache and is given excellent support by Pascal Devoyon. Neither is well served by the recording, however, made in a cramped studio that robs the piano-tone of some of its timbre, while the close balance does less than complete justice to the sound this fine violinist makes in the flesh. Nevertheless it still gives pleasure. Performances three star; the recording one.

PIANO MUSIC

Piano music for four hands

Allegro in A min. (Lebensstürme), D.947; Divertissement à la française in E min., D.823; Divertissement à la hongroise in G min., D.818; Fantasia in F min., D.940; Grand Duo in C, D.812; 4 Ländler, D.814

(B) *** EMI double forte (ADD) 5 69770-2 (2). Eschenbach, Frantz

German Dance in G min., D.818; Grande marche funèbre, D.859; Grande marche héroïque, D.885; 6 Grandes marches et trios, D.819; Grand rondeau (allegretto quasi andantino), D.951; Kindermarsch in G min., D.928; 2 Ländler in E, D.618; 2 Marches caractéristiques, D.886; 2 Marches héroïques, D.602; 3 Marches militaires, D.733.

(B) *** EMI double forte (ADD) 5 69764-2 (2). Eschenbach, Frantz

Christoph Eschenbach and Justus Frantz made their extensive survey of Schubert's four-handed piano music in 1978 and 1979, and the Abbey Road recording was of high quality. The opening of the *F minor Fantasia* here may suggest that the performance is too reticent, but that is deceptive and this is as powerful a reading as any available with its rhythms well sprung; and the same comment applies to the *Grand Duo*, while the wide range of mood in the *Lebensstürme* is encompassed impressively. The delicate interplay between the two pianists is a constant delight, whether in the simple *Ländler*, the charming central *Andantino varié* of the *Divertissement à la française* or the cimbalom imitations in the companion Hungarian-style *Divertissement*, both extended three-movement works showing the composer at his most felicitously inventive and presented here joyfully.

The second collection includes a great many marches, but their expressive range is very much wider than might be expected. Much of it is jolly and extrovert, but there is delicacy and lyricism too. In the hands of Eschenbach and Frantz the third *Marche héroïque* of D.602 is quite charming, more like an impromptu. The *German Dance in G minor* opens with appealing restraint and the *Kindermarsch* brings a delightful, child-like simplicity, while the two *Marches caractéristiques* sparkle with brilliance. Most remarkable of all are the *Grande marche funèbre* and the *Grande marche héroïque*. The first is highly eloquent, but it is the second, in A minor, which is the more extended (17 minutes), with a characteristic lyrical strain as its centrepiece. The closing *Grand rondeau*, most touchingly played, was written in June 1828, only five months before the composer's death at the age of thirty-one. Overall Eschenbach and Frantz score in sheer freshness, but the EMI sound at times has a bright edge.

Allegro moderato & Andante, D.968; Fantasy in G min., D.9; 3 Marches militaires D.733; 4 Polonaises, D.599; Variations on 'Marie' by Herold.

(BB) **(*) Naxos 8.553441. Jandó, Kollar

This disc of some of Schubert's lesser works for piano duet begins most temptingly with the most famous of his *Marches militaires*, played by the Hungarian duo with crispness and vigour. Ranging from the very early *Fantasy* to the late *Allegro & Andante*, this well-recorded collection may be a little short on charm, but is winningly fresh throughout.

Andante varié in B min., D.823

(M) *** Decca (ADD) 466 821-2. Richter, Britten – MOZART: *Piano Sonata in C, K.521, etc.* DEBUSSY: *En blanc et noir.*

This inspired account of the Schubert *Divertissement* – labelled *Andantino varié* – was recorded at the same Jubilee Hall concert as the *Fantasie* and *Grand Duo*, also available in the Britten at Aldeburgh series. It may be just a charming trifle, but in their hands it is magnetic, revealing deeper expression.

Duo, D.947; Fantasia in F min., D.940; 6 Polonaises, D.824; Variations on an Original Theme, D.813

(BB) *** Warner Apex (ADD) 0927 49812-2. Queffélec, Cooper

The playing of Anne Queffélec and Imogen Cooper is hardly less eloquent than any of their rivals', and they also offer a commanding account of the *Fantasia in F minor*. The slighter pieces also come off well: the *Variations* are beautifully played and have an engaging innocence, while the six *Polonaises* are also worth having on disc when played so brightly and spontaneously. The 1978 analogue recording is well balanced, clear and natural, the acoustic neither over-reverberant nor too confined. There can be no doubting that this is a bargain in every way: these are excellent performances, well recorded, and provide an inexpensive way to explore Schubert's delightful piano music for four hands.

Fantasia in F min., D.940

🔊 *** Sony 517490-2. Perahia, Lupu – MOZART: *Double Piano Sonata* ***

*** Chan. 9162. Lortie, Mercier – MOZART: *Andante with Variations* etc. ***

(M) *** DG (ADD) 463 652-2. Emil & Elena Gilels – MOZART: *Piano Concerto 27; Double Piano Concerto* *** ●

Recorded live at The Maltings, the performance of Lupu and Perahia is full of haunting poetry, with each of these highly individual artists challenging the other in imagination. Warmly atmospheric recording.

The Louis Lortie–Hélène Mercier partnership is as impressive here as it is elsewhere. The Schubert holds its own even against such illustrious competition as the Lupu–Perahia recording on Sony, also coupled with Mozart. Very good recording.

On DG an apt and finely played bonus for a treasurable Mozart coupling.

Fantasia in F min., D.940; German Dance & 2 Ländler, D.618; 3 Marches héroïques, D.602; Overture in F; Variations on an Original Theme, D.968a

(BB) *** Naxos 8.554513. Jandó, Kollar

The Hungarian pianist Jenö Jandó first made his mark on disc when he recorded all 32 of Beethoven's *Sonatas* for Naxos, fresh, totally unmannered performances that were among the early treasures of that bargain label. Here, with his colleague Zsuzsa Kollar, he gives a similarly magnetic reading of what by any reckoning is the greatest of all piano duets, Schubert's haunting *F minor Fantasia*, with its inspired telescoping of a four-movement structure. With Jandö and partner, nothing distracts one from the beauty of Schubert's writing, and the lesser pieces, including the dramatic *Overture in F* and some delectable dances and marches, have comparable freshness, cleanly recorded.

Fantasia in F min.; Grand Duo; Variations, D.813

(M) *** Decca (ADD) 466 822-2. Richter, Britten

As these electrically intense performances demonstrate, Richter and Britten favoured fast speeds, which yet allowed crisply sprung rhythms and warmly lyrical phrasing, with phenomenally crisp articulation from both players. The two major works were recorded in 1965 in Jubilee Hall, Aldeburgh, the *Variations* in the Parish Church a year earlier, both with clear, immediate stereo-sound balanced for radio by BBC engineers.

Solo piano music

Adagio in E major, D.612; Adagio & Rondo in E, D.506; Allegretto in C minor, D.915; 3 Klavierstücke, D.946; 12 Ländler, D.790; Variations on a Theme by Anselm Hüttenbrenner, D.576

*** Chan. 9860. Edlina

Luba Edlina is better known as a chamber-music player than a soloist – she is the pianist of the Borodin Trio – although she has made a handful of very good solo recordings, including Russian repertoire and Mendelssohn's *Songs Without Words*. Her Schubert recital is satisfying and unaffected, and the searching *3 Klavierstücke* are well served. The Chandos recording is natural, and readers attracted to the repertoire need not hesitate.

Allegretto, D.915; Impromptus 1–4, D.899; 5–8, D.935; 3 Klavierstücke, D.946

**(*) DG 457 550-2 (2). Pires

Maria João Pires proves as impressive a Schubertian as she is a Mozart interpreter. The presentation reproduces various quotes from Goethe and does not tell us too much about Schubert, but Pires does! Despite the odd touch of prettification, this is satisfying playing and eminently well recorded. However the set is uneconomically laid out on a pair of full-priced CDs, the first of which plays for only 35 minutes 20 seconds!

Allegretto in C min., D.915; 3 Klavierstücke, D.946; Piano Sonata 20 in A, D.959.

(M) *** DG (IMS) 471 356-2. Pollini

DG have reissued the *A major Sonata* alone in their 'Pollini Edition'. The playing is characteristically strong. But his admirers will surely prefer the alternative mid-priced disc combining D.958 and D.959 (DG 427 327-2 – see below).

Fantasia in C (Wanderer), D.760

(M) *** EMI 5 66895-2 [5 66947-2]. Richter – DVORAK: *Piano Concerto ***

(M) *** Ph. (ADD) 420 644-2. Brendel – *Sonata 21 ***

(M) *** DG (ADD) 447 451-2. Pollini – SCHUMANN: *Fantasia, Op. 17 ***

◉ (M) (***) Decca mono 466 498-2. Curzon – SCHUMANN: *Fantasia in C, Op. 17; Kinderszenen, Op. 15 *** ◉

(M) **(*) DG 445 562-2. Kissin – BRAHMS: *Fantasias **(*);* LISZT: *Concert Paraphrases of Schubert Lieder, etc. ***

Fantasia in C (Wanderer), D.760; Der Wanderer (arr. Liszt)

**(*) MDG 312 0924-2. Tanski – SCHUMANN: *Kreisleriana; Widmung* (arr. Liszt) **(*)

Richter's 1963 performance is masterly in every way. The piano timbre is real and the remastering for EMI's 'Great Recordings of the Century' gives the pianist a compelling presence.

Brendel's playing too is of a high order, and he is truthfully recorded and coupled with what is perhaps Schubert's greatest *Sonata*, so this is excellent value at mid-price.

Pollini's account is outstanding and, though he is not ideally recorded and the piano timbre is shallow, the playing still shows remarkable insights. Moreover the Schumann coupling is equally fine.

Curzon's famous account of the *Wanderer fantasia* dates from 1949 and the clear, dry recording emphasizes his dramatic approach to the outer movements, putting his infinitely touching account of the sadly yearning central *Adagio* into bold relief. It is this movement which expresses the message of the song on which the work is based: *Dort, wo du nicht bist, dort ist das Glück!* ('Happiness is where you are not!').

Claudius Tanski first made a name for himself in the late 1980s with the Reubke *Piano Sonata*. His *Wanderer Fantasy* is well held together and sensitive and, though not a first choice, is well worth while. Good recording too.

Kissin gives a fine account of the *Wanderer*, though it is not quite as persuasive (perhaps he himself is not quite as persuaded by the music) as the finest rivals. Of course, there is some very fine pianism, but other artists, Kempff for instance, find greater depths. Good DG recording.

Fantasia in C (Wanderer), D.760; Piano Sonata 21 in B flat, D.960; Impromptus D 899/3–4

☛ ◉ (M) *** RCA 09026 63054-2. Rubinstein

This CD is among the very finest of all the Rubinstein reissues from the 1960s. He plays the *Wanderer fantasia* with sure magnificence. The extended structure needs a master to hold it together and, particularly in the variations section, Rubinstein is electrifying. He compels attention as though he is improvising the work himself, but even so avoids any sentimentality. The 1965 recording sounds surprisingly full, and it is even better in the two *Impromptus*, played with the most subtle shading of colour and delectable control of rubato, and in the superb account of the *Sonata*. Unaccountably, this has never been issued before, yet it shows Rubinstein as a magically persuasive Schubertian. The first movement is very relaxed (14 minutes 17 seconds as against Curzon's 13 minutes 18 seconds) yet the effect is wonderfully luminous, and a similar inspired and ruminative spontaneity infuses the essentially gentle *Andante*. Then the articulation in the final two movements is a joy, light and crisp in the Scherzo, bolder but never heavy in the finale. Throughout, the great pianist conveys his love for the music, and the playing is wonderfully refined in detail. The sound is remarkably real, with fine presence and almost no shallowness.

Impromptus 1–4, D. 899; 5–8, D.935

*** Sony SK 37291. Perahia

(M) *** Decca 460 975-2. Lupu

(BB) **(*) Naxos 8.550260. Jandó

Perahia's account of the *Impromptus* is very special indeed. Directness of utterance and purity of spirit are of the essence here, with articulation of sparkling clarity. The CBS recording is very good and truthful in timbre.

Lupu's *Impromptus* are of the same calibre as the Brendel analogue versions, and he is most beautifully recorded on CD. Indeed, in terms of natural sound this is a most believable image.

Though his set of the *Impromptus* is not ideally recorded (the microphones are rather too close, with unpleasing results in fortissimo passages), Jandó is a very musical player and his unaffected (and often perceptive) readings are more than acceptable.

Impromptus 1–8 (including original draft of 1); *Moments musicaux 1–6; 3 Klavierstücke D.946* (including original version of 1)

(B) *** Virgin 2x1 5 61797-2 (2). Orkis (fortepiano)

Those who think they are allergic to Schubert on the fortepiano in this repertoire should try this inexpensive set from Lambert Orkis. Both the *Impromptus* and the *Moments musicaux* are vital and fully attuned to the Schubertian sensibility, and the three *Klavierstücke* are full of character. This is exceptional playing in every way – living and responsive to every nuance – and although it is not a sole recommendation for either the *Impromptus* or the *Moments musicaux*, it is certainly a set that all Schubertians should consider as a supplement to modern grand piano recordings. It is made the more fascinating by the inclusion of Schubert's original version of the stormy first *Klavierstücke*, and more strikingly the pencil draft for the *C minor Impromptu*, in which the original arresting opening chord is omitted. The timbre of the fortepiano here certainly does not lack sonority or colour.

Impromptus 1–8; 3 Klavierstücke, D.946; 6 Moments musicaux, D.780

(B) *** Virgin 2x1 5 62233-2 (2). Tan (fortepiano) – BEETHOVEN: *Allegretto, etc. ***

Schubert on the fortepiano is, of course, quite unlike the Schubert we know from the modern pianoforte. Melvyn Tan's playing is refreshingly unmannered and for the most part very persuasive: he is at pains to avoid any sentimentality, yet he succeeds in conveying the music's tenderness. He has the measure of the scale of the *F minor Impromptu*, D.935/1, and brings both dramatic fire and poetic feeling to it. He is arguably a shade too brisk in D.935/4 and in the *B flat major*, D.935/3, but throughout there are valuable insights. In the *Moments musicaux* he has remarkable feeling for colour and never approaches the music with any excess of that judicious reverence which distinguishes some musicians using period instuments. His Schubert is consistently spirited and fresh and, throughout, this stimulating and lively playing casts new light on the composer. The recording is excellent.

Impromptus 1–8; 3 Klavierstücke, D.946; Moments musicaux 1–6, D.780; Allegretto in C min., D.915; 6 German Dances, D.820; Grazer Galopp, D.925; Hungarian Melody in B min., D.817; 12 Ländler, D.790

(B) *** Double Decca 458 139-2 (2). Schiff

Impromptus 1–8; 3 Klavierstücke (Impromptus), D.946; 6 Moments musicaux, D.780; 12 German Dances, D.790; 16 German Dances, D.783

🗝 ✹ (B) *** Ph. (ADD) Duo 456 061-2 (2). Brendel

Brendel's analogue set of the *Impromptus* is magical, and the *Moments musicaux* are among the most poetic in the catalogue. It is difficult to imagine finer Schubert playing than this; to find more eloquence, more profound musical insights, one has to go back to Edwin Fischer – and even here comparison is not always to Brendel's disadvantage. The *Klavierstücke* are searching, and in his hands the *German Dances*, although retaining their underlying charm, sound anything but trivial. The recordings offer Philips's very finest analogue quality.

András Schiff's playing is idiomatic, intelligent and humane, and the recording is more than acceptable. It is impossible to recommend his *Impromptus* in preference to those of Brendel, but no one will be disappointed with them. Schiff has the advantage of very natural digital recording, the effect lighter-textured than with Brendel.

Impromptus 1–8; Moments musicaux, D.780/3–6

🗝 (BB) *** Regis (ADD) RRC 1019. Brendel

This is the finest of Brendel's Vox (Turnabout) recordings made in the 1960s so far reissued on the Regis budget label. His playing has an unaffected simplicity that is utterly disarming, and the lightness of his articulation is a pleasure in itself. The fresh, natural eloquence is also very striking in the four favourite *Moments musicaux*, which are offered here as a bonus (the disc has a playing time of 71'). The recording, too, is suprisingly good. While his Philips Duo, which includes the later Philips analogue recordings of both complete sets, plus the *Klavierstücke*, D.946, and some delightful *German Dances*, remains very special (see above), this Regis CD is well worth having at its very modest price.

Impromptus 1–4, D.899; Impromptu in B flat, D.935/3; Moments musicaux, D.780/1, 2 & 6

(B) *** LaserLight 15609. Jandó

Jenö Jandó is here heard recorded in an acoustic that does justice to his talent. The sound, at least in the opening *B flat major Impromptu* of D.935, is fresh and truthful, the ambience is warm, and the playing is very good. The balance is not as good in the three *Moments musicaux* or in the D.899 *Impromptus*: it is closer and marginally drier.

Impromptus 1–4, D.899; Piano Sonata 21 in B flat, D.960

*** Cal. CAL 6689. Södergren

Inger Södergren's account of the first four *Impromptus* belongs in exalted company, and the *B flat Sonata* is hardly less fine. Her playing is marked throughout by sensitivity and a selfless and unostentatious dedication to Schubert. The recording is acceptable rather than outstanding.

3 Klavierstücke, D.946

(M) (***) BBC mono BBCL 4125. Claudio Arrau – BRAHMS: *Piano Concerto 2* (***)

Arrau's magisterial artistry is captured here in the BBC's Maida Vale Studios in 1959. These are searching accounts, which should be eagerly snapped up by admirers of Arrau. The later Schubert box that Philips issued in the 1990s did not include these pieces.

Moments musicaux 1–6, D.780; 3 Klavierstücke, D.946; Allegretto in C min., D.915

(BB) **(*) Naxos 8.550259. Jandó

Though the venue is the Italian Institute in Budapest, Jandó is much better recorded here than he often has been. He proves a thoroughly sympathetic and sensitive Schubertian, but he is still too upfront. The opening of the *Drei Klavierstücke* is a shade too fast (Jandó does not completely convey its dark, disturbing overtones) but the middle section is beautifully judged. Thoughtful and intelligent music-making, acceptably recorded, and very good value for money.

Moments musicaux, D.780; 2 Scherzi, D.593; Piano Sonata 14 in A min., D.784

*** DG (IMS) 427 769-2. Pires

Maria João Pires gives masterly accounts of the *Moments musicaux* and the *A minor Sonata*, distinguished throughout by thoughtful and refined musicianship, and she is fully aware of the depth of feeling that inhabits the *Moments musicaux*, without ever indulging in the slightest expressive exaggeration. The digital recording is exceptionally present and clear.

Piano sonatas

Piano Sonatas 1 in E, D.157; 2 in C, D.279; 3in E, D.459; 4 in A min., D.537; 5 in A flat, D.557; 6 in E min., D.566; 7 in E flat, D.568; 9 in B, D.575; 11 in F min., D.625; 12 in F min, D.625; 13 in A, D.664; 14 in A min., D.784; 15 in C, D.840 (Relique); 16 in A min., D.845; 17 in D, D.850; 18 in G, D.894; 19 in C min., D.958; 20 in A, D.959; 21 in B flat, D.960

(B) *** DG 463 766-2 (7). Kempff
(M) *** Decca 448 390-2 (7). Schiff

Wilhelm Kempff's cycle was recorded over a four-year period (1965–9) and has been much admired over the years. These are among the most consistently satisfying accounts of the sonatas, with a wisdom that puts them in a category of their own. Indeed their insights are very special indeed. The recording has a touch of shallowness, but is generally excellent. All seven CDs are now available in a convenient, inexpensive bargain box, and represent exceptional value.

With Schiff's collection (like Kempff's survey) including the *First Sonata*, D.157 (written when the composer was eighteen), and also the fragment of the *Eighth* (which Kempff omits), Schiff sets the seal on his seven-CD survey for Decca, which has excited golden opinions. In his note he calls them 'among the most sublime contributions written for the piano' – and he plays them as if they are, too. Yet Schiff's is a survey that blends pianistic finesse with keen human insights. He has a good feeling for the architecture of these pieces and he invests details with just the right amount of feeling. Good, modern, digital recordings, made in the Brahms-Saal of the Musikverein in Vienna. The CDs come conveniently packaged in a mid-priced box, and are still available separately at full price.

Piano Sonatas 14–21; German Dances; Impromptus; Moments musicaux; Wanderer fantasia
*** Ph. 426 128-2 (7). Brendel

Piano Sonatas 14 in A min., D.784; 17 in D, D.850
*** Ph. 422 063-2. Brendel

Piano Sonatas 16 in A min., D.845; 3 Impromptus, D.946
*** Ph. (IMS) 422 075-2. Brendel

Piano Sonatas 19 in C min., D.958; Moments musicaux 1–6, D.780
*** Ph. (IMS) 422 076-2. Brendel

Piano Sonatas 20 in A, D.959; Allegretto in C min., D.915; 16 German Dances, D.783; Hungarian Melody in B min., D.817
**(*) Ph. (IMS) 422 229-2. Brendel

Piano Sonata 21 in B flat, D.960; Wanderer fantasia, D.760
*** Ph. 422 062-2. Brendel

Brendel's later digital set is more intense than his earlier cycle of recordings for Philips, though there was a touching freshness in the earlier set, and he has the benefit of clean, well-focused sound. These are warm performances, strongly delineated and powerfully characterized, which occupy a commanding place in the catalogue. They are separately available, and all of them can be confidently recommended to Brendel's admirers.

'The Last Six Years, 1823–1828': Vol. 1: Piano Sonatas 14 in A min., D.784; 18 in G, D.894; 12 German Dances (Ländler), D.790
*** Priory/Ottavo OTR C68608. Cooper

Vol. 2: *Piano Sonatas 15 in C, D.840; 20 in C, D.959; 11 Ecossaises, D.781*
*** Priory/Ottavo OTR C58714. Cooper

Vol. 3: *Piano Sonata 16 in A min., D.845; 4 Impromptus, D.935*
*** Priory/Ottavo OTR C88817. Cooper

Vol. 4: *Piano Sonata 17 in D, D.850; 6 Moments musicaux, D.780*
*** Priory/Ottavo OTR C128715. Cooper

Vol. 5: *Piano Sonata 21 in B flat, D.960; Allegretto in C min., D.915; 3 Impromptus (Klavierstücke), D.946*
*** Priory/Ottavo OTR C88821. Cooper

Vol. 6: *Piano Sonata 19 in C min., D.958; 4 Impromptus, D.899*
*** Priory/Ottavo OTR C78923. Cooper

Imogen Cooper, in her outstanding set on the Dutch Ottavo label, has a true Schubertian sensibility; her feeling for this composer's special lyricism is second to none, yet her playing has both strength and a complete understanding of the music's architecture. The recordings were made in the Henry Wood Hall, London over a period of three years, between June 1986 and July 1989, using a Steinway for the first three volumes and a fine-sounding Yamaha for the later records. The balance is admirable and the sound full, with a convincing natural resonance. The playing has the spontaneity of live music-making, and the warm colouring and fine shading of timbre are as pleasing to the ear as the many subtle nuances of phrasing, which are essentially based on a strong melodic line. These performances can be recommended alongside those by artists with the most illustrious names, and they do not fall short. With their fine, modern, digital recording these CDs will give much delight and refreshment.

Piano Sonatas: 1 in E, D.157; 15 in C (Relique), D.894
*** Sony SK 89647. Volodos (with LISZT: *Concert paraphrase: Der Müller und der Bach*)

Arcadi Volodos's reputation as a dazzling virtuoso is now enhanced by his natural lyricism and keen musical insight. This Schubert recital has been greeted with well-deserved acclaim and shows this Russian artist as a real musician not just a brilliant showman. Sony offer very good recorded sound and this CD is highly recommended.

Piano Sonata 4 in A min., D.537
(M) ** DG 457 762-2. Michelangeli – BEETHOVEN: *Piano Sonata 4 in E flat, Op. 7 *; BRAHMS: *Ballades ***

Michelangeli rushes the opening theme of the *A minor Sonata* and rarely allows the simple ideas of the first movement to speak for themselves. Elsewhere his playing, though aristocratic and poised, is not free from artifice, and the natural eloquence of Schubert eludes him. Fine 1981 digital recording, but on this CD only the Brahms finds this artist at his best.

Piano Sonatas 4 in A min., D.537; 13 in A, D.664; 6 German Dances, D.820; 12 German Dances, D.790
*** Ph. 470 265-2. Uchida

There is no doubt as to the pianistic distinction of Mitsuko Uchida's Schubert. She makes a beautiful sound and is full of poetic feeling – and, moreover, the Philips recording is of a quite exceptional quality and naturalness. At the same time, naturalness is not the whole picture as far as her readings are concerned; there is a trace of self-awareness that may worry some listeners. However, admirers of this artist who are untroubled by this can rest assured as to its many excellences.

Piano Sonatas 4, D.537; 7, D.568; 9, D.575; 13, D.664; 14, D.784; 15 (Relique), D.840; 16, D.845; 17, D.850; 18, D.894; 19, D.958; 20, D.959; 21, D.960; German Dances, D.790 & 820; 8 Impromptus, D.899 & 935; 3 Klavierstücke, D.946; Moments musicaux, D.70
(N) (B) **(*) Ph. 475 6282 (8). Uchida

Mitsuko Uchida began her Schubert survey in 1997 and continued until 2002, then leaving the cycle incomplete. As can be seen from the separate reviews below, she did not have quite the same degree of success here that she did with the sonatas of Mozart. This is distinctive playing, sensitive and eloquent; moreover the Philips recording is exceptionally truthful. Certain sonatas, the *Relique* for instance, are outstanding in every way and the great *B flat Sonata, D.960* shows her at her very finest. But at other times she does not always leave the composer to speak for himself and Schubert's special quality of innocence all but eludes her. This criticism could be over-stated, she still has her own insights to offer, and her admirers will find this an inexpensive way of exploring the major Schubert keyboard repertoire in her hands.

Piano Sonata 7 in E flat, D.568; Moments musicaux, D.780
*** Ph. **SACD** 470 603-2; CD 470 164-2. Uchida

As with earlier issues in her Schubert series, Mitsuko Uchida offers wonderfully expressive and eloquent playing. She is unfailingly poetic and lyrical, and her admirers will not be disappointed. As piano playing this is consummate, though some may feel that she tends to beautify further what is already beautiful, and the innocence of Schubert succumbs to over-sophistication. The recordings are wonderfully realistic, indeed state-of-the-art sound, especially on SACD.

Piano Sonatas 9; 11; 13; Moment musical, D.780/1
*** BBC (ADD) BBCL 4010-2. Richter

This disc comprises a Schubert recital Richter gave at the Royal Festival Hall in 1979, and the dryish sound is perfectly acceptable. Richter recorded all three sonatas for EMI in Japan three years later, and there is little significant difference in approach between the two accounts. As always, his playing is magisterial and eloquent. Thoroughly recommendable.

Piano Sonatas 9 in B, D.575; 16 in A min., D.845
*** Ph. 462 596-2. Uchida

Mitsuko Uchida is beautifully recorded, and collectors who have admired the other issues in her Schubert recordings need not hesitate. Some may find her tendency to beautify this music a little intrusive, so this is not for every Schubertian, but this is still imaginative and distinguished playing.

Piano Sonatas 9 in B, D.575; 18 in G, D.894; 20 in A, D.959; 21 in B flat, D.960
**(*) Ph. 456 573-2 (2). Brendel

Issued to celebrate Brendel's 70th birthday in January 2001, these inspired Schubert performances were all recorded live, unlike his previous Schubert on disc. Brendel describes them as 'correctives, alternatives or supplements to my previous studio recordings', but they are more than that. Though Brendel's approach to Schubert remains broadly the same as in his 1971 series of late sonatas and the more individual digital versions of the late 1980s, there is an extra magnetism in these live accounts, intensifying the depth of what he has to say. He is more freely expressive than before, with speeds more flexible, and with rhythms given an extra lift. At times he seems improvisational in his flights of fantasy, while the depth of concentration conveyed in pianissimos is consistently greater than in his studio performances.

Three of the four last and greatest sonatas are included, with the early B major Sonata of 1817 as a supplement, a sonata not previously recorded by Brendel and one that, as he sees it, points forward to the late works. The opening of the great B flat Sonata is marred by intrusive coughing from a woman in the Festival Hall audience, but otherwise the sound is excellent, bright and full-toned, with acoustic differences between four different venues ironed out – the Alte Oper in Frankfurt, the Concertgebouw in Amsterdam, the Snape Maltings and the Royal Festival Hall.

Piano Sonatas 13 in A; 14 in A min.; Hungarian Melody, D.817; 12 Waltzes, D.145
☙ ✪ (M) *** Decca (ADD) 443 579-2. Ashkenazy

A magnificent record in every respect. Ashkenazy is a great Schubertian who can realize the touching humanity of this

giant's vision as well as his strength. There is an astonishing directness about these performances and a virility tempered by tenderness. This matches Ashkenazy's own high standards, and Decca have risen remarkably to the occasion. The 1966 analogue recording, reissued in Decca's Classic Sound series, has splendid range and fidelity.

Piano Sonatas 13, D.664; 21 in B flat
*** Decca (IMS) 440 295-2. Lupu

Radu Lupu's is one of the most searching of all his Schubert recordings and finds this masterly pianist at his most eloquent and thoughtful.

Piano Sonatas 14 in A min., D.784; 17 in D, D.850
**(*) Ph. 464 480-2. Uchida

Wonderful pianism and great delicacy of sound from Mitsuko Uchida and recording quality of great naturalness. This artist is occasionally an intrusive interpreter and does not always allow Schubert to speak for himself in the way that Kempff did. Some may find that her insights enhance their feeling for these wonderful pieces, but others may see them as a barrier. Recommended without qualification to Ms Uchida's admirers, but with caution to others.

Piano Sonata 15 in C, D.840 – see also under *Winterreise*

Piano Sonatas 15 (Relique); 18, D.894
*** Ph. 454 453-2. Uchida

The unfinished torso of the *Relique Sonata* is given an eloquent, inward-looking reading of great tonal beauty. The *G major Sonata* is masterly, combining careful thought with emotional depth. Another of the best Schubert sonata discs of the last few years. The Philips recording is excellent in every way.

Piano Sonatas 15 in C (Relique), D.840; 21 in B flat, D.960
(M) **(*) Sony mono/stereo 512874-2. Serkin

Although he opens the B flat major Sonata persuasively, Rudolf Serkin's rugged, less lyrical manner in Schubert will not be to all tastes, but it is undeniably strong in impact. The slow movement is squarer and less flowing than usual, and the interpretation registers the mature, uncompromising response of an artist intent on reading his Schubert very directly, and less intent on beguiling his audience. But there is no question of the patrician character of both these readings. The two-movement C major Sonata was recorded (in mono) in 1955, twenty years before the B flat major, and with very much the same positive manner, although the Andante has an apealing simplicity. In both, the recording is close, strikingly present, but rather hard.

Piano Sonata 16 in A min., D.845
☙ (M) *** DG (ADD) 463 676-2. Pollini – SCHUMANN: Sonata 1 ***

Pollini's playing of the A minor Sonata is searching and profound. He is almost without rival in terms of sheer keyboard control, and his musical insight is of the same order. The 1973 recording lacked presence in its LP format; the CD transfer has brought the piano-image forward, but in so doing has added a certain hardness to the timbre. Nevertheless, this remains pianism of an altogether exceptional order.

Piano sonatas 16 in A min., D.845; 18 in G, D.894
☙ ✪ (M) *** Decca (ADD) 476 2182. Lupu

Radu Lupu's version of the A minor Sonata of 1825 is searching and poetic throughout. He brings tenderness and classical discipline to bear on this structure, and his playing is musically satisfying in a very Schubertian way. The coupling is hardly less fine, a superb reading, relatively straight in its approach but full of glowing perception on points of detail; moreover, the exposition repeat is observed in the first movement. The analogue recordings date from 1975 and 1979 respectively and are of Decca's finest, with timbre of warm colour yet with a striking sense of presence overall. A fully worthy addition to Universal's 'Penguin ✪ Collection' (at mid-price).

Piano Sonatas 17; 20; 21; March in E, D.606; Moments musicaux, D.780

(M) (***) EMI mono 7 64259-2 (2). Schnabel

It was thanks to Schnabel's championship that the *Piano Sonatas* re-entered the repertory. Neither the *A major* nor the *B flat Sonata* was state-of-the-art piano-sound, but the *Moments musicaux* sound remarkably full-bodied. The playing is full of characteristic insights, and as always with this artist there is imagination of a remarkable order. These recordings are now fifty years old, but some of the playing Schnabel offers – at the opening of the *B flat* and in the slow movements of all three *Sonatas* – will never be less than special.

Piano Sonata 19; Moments musicaux, D.780

(M) *** Decca (IMS) 417 785-2. Lupu

Lupu's performance has a simple eloquence that is most moving. His *Moments musicaux* are very fine indeed. The Decca recording is very natural and, at mid-price, this is extremely competitive.

Piano Sonatas 19; 20 in A, D.959

*** DG (IMS) 427 327-2. Pollini

In Pollini's hands these emerge as strongly structured and powerful sonatas, yet he is far from unresponsive to the voices from the other world with which these pieces resonate. Perhaps with his perfect pianism he does not always convey a sense of human vulnerability, as have some of the greatest Schubert interpreters.

Piano Sonatas 19–21; Allegretto in C min., D.915; 3 Klavierstücke, D.944

(M) *** DG 474 613-2 (2). Pollini

Piano Sonatas 19–21; 4 Impromptus, D.899/1–4

☛ (B) *** Double Decca 475 184-2 (2). Schiff
(B) ** Ph. Duo (ADD/DDD) 473 895-2 (2). Arrau

Piano Sonatas 19–21; 3 Klavierstücke, D.946/1–3

(B) **(*) Ph. Duo (ADD) 438 703-2 (2). Brendel

In his note András Schiff calls Schubert's last three sonatas 'among the most sublime compositions written for the instrument' – and he plays them as if they are too. There is formidable competition, particularly in the *A major* and great *B flat Sonata* from Kempff and Kovacevich, but admirers of the present fine artist can rest assured that the finesse and insight of his playing are undiminished. The bold drama of the *C minor* work is set in contrast with the more ruminative approach to the *B flat Sonata*. Excellent, truthful recording.

Brendel's analogue recording of the *A major* suffers from rather more agogic changes than is desirable. Some listeners may find these interferences with the flow of the musical argument a little too personal. The *C minor Sonata* is not free

from this charge, but it remains an impressive performance. Brendel's account of the *B flat Sonata* is characteristically imposing and full of insight, as one would expect. Here his mood is both serious and introspective, and he is not unduly wayward; moreover he is at his very finest in the *Klavierstücke*. This is eloquent and profoundly musical playing. Throughout, the recording is well up to Philips's high standard of realism.

In Pollini's hands the three last sonatas emerge as strongly structured and powerful, yet he is far from unresponsive to the voices from the other world with which these pieces resonate. Perhaps with his perfect pianism he does not always convey a sense of human vulnerability, as have some of the greatest Schubert interpreters, but this pairing is certainly worthy of inclusion among DG's 'Originals'.

Arrau's performances on Philips, though rich in insights, often suffer from disruptive rubati which do not wear well on repetition – and indeed disturb on a first hearing – and this is noticeable here, especially in the great *B flat Sonata*. As always he produces distinctive, beautiful sonority and immaculate fingerwork, but this performance could not be a primary recommendation. A similar interference with the music's flow also applies, though to a lesser extent, to the *Adagio* of the *C minor Sonata*, D.958. Surprisingly, in the *A major*, D.959, where he often plays beautifully and his thoughts are far from unilluminating, the recording lets him down: the image is not in focus and the sound resonates around the Concertgebouw, where all these recordings were made (between 1978 and 1982). The *Impromptus* are given with aristocratic refinement, and here the recording is very fine, in both tone and timbre.

Piano Sonata 20 in A, D.959; 4 Impromptus, D.935/1–4

(M) **(*) Sony (ADD) 512873-2. Serkin

A much-praised performance in its day (1966), Rudolf Serkin's account of Schubert's *A major Sonata* seems somewhat less sensitive than one remembers and expects from an artist of this stature, although it has some moments of appealing lyricism. His command of the structure of the work is impressive enough, but the *fortissimos* are rather hard (partly the fault of the recording) and one would have liked more finesse in the phrasing. The *Impromptus*, recorded 13 years later, are a different matter, undoubtedly distinguished, and the recording, if slightly dry, is truthful and sounds even better in its new transfer. Serkin's manner may be more severe than Brendel's, but the playing is searching and has memorable insights. There is a sense of stature here, while the songful character of the writing is conveyed without a trace of sentimentality. The range of dynamic is matched by Serkin's sense of colour; the classical authority is balanced by the natural spontaneity of the music-making.

Piano Sonata 20 in A, D.959. Lieder: (i; ii) Auf dem Strom; Pilgerweise; Der Unglückliche; (ii) Die Sterne

☛ *** EMI 5 57266-2. Andsnes, with (i) T. Brown; (ii) Bostridge

The Schubert *A major Sonata* finds Leif Ove Andsnes at his most impressive. His is a thoughtful reading of this great piece, which unfolds with the naturalness we associate with this artist. Never does he interpose his own thoughts but is completely the servant of the composer. This is as fine an account as any we have had in recent years, and is magnificently recorded. The idea of coupling the *Sonata* with a handful of well-chosen songs will enhance the disc's appeal, and admirers of Ian Bostridge will not be disappointed, particularly by *Auf dem Strom*, written in the same year.

Piano Sonatas 20 in A, D.959; 21 in B flat, D.960
**** HM HMC 901800. Lewis

In the 2001–2 Wigmore Hall season Paul Lewis played a complete cycle of the Schubert *Sonatas* and in doing so received the South Bank Television Award for 2003. His performances of both these late masterpieces are completely individual and deeply felt, using the widest range of colour and dynamic and great variety of articulation. At one moment his playing is touchingly gentle, thoughtful and introspective, at others intensely dramatic; yet the result sounds totally spontaneous, as at a live recital. These are among the most stimulating and thoughtful Schubert performances of the last few years, and they are very well recorded. A disc to seek out, even if you already have this repertoire played by other, more famous names.

Piano Sonata 21 in B flat, D.960
(M) *** Ph. (ADD) 420 644-2. Brendel – *Wanderer fantasia* ***

(N) *(*)* RCA 82876 58462-2. Kissin – LISZT: *Concert Paraphrases* **

Piano Sonata 21 in B flat, D.960; Allegretto in C min., D.915; 6 Moments musicaux, D.780
● (M) *** EMI 5 62817-2. Kovacevich

Piano Sonata 21; 3 Klavierstücke, D.946
*** Ph. 456 572-2. Uchida

Piano Sonata 21 in B flat, D.960; (i) Lieder: Abschied von der Erde; Viola; Der Winterabend
(N) *** EMI 5 57901-2. Andsnes; (i) with Bostridge

Stephen Kovacevich made a memorable recording of the great *B flat major Sonata* for Hyperion which (in our 1988 edition) we called 'one of the most eloquent accounts on record of this sublime sonata and one which is completely free of expressive point-making. It is an account which totally reconciles the demands of truth and beauty.' One could well say the same of the later (1994) EMI version though, if anything, it explores an even deeper vein of feeling than its predecessor. Indeed, it is the most searching and penetrating account of the work to have appeared in recent years and, given the excellence and truthfulness of the recording, must carry the strongest and most enthusiastic recommendation. It certainly ranks Kovacevich among the 'Great Artists of the Century', and for this reissue EMI have added the six *Moments musicaux* which he recorded six months later, also at Abbey Road, and which have comparable insights.

EMI continue their Schubert series combining the sonatas played by Leif Ove Andsnes with a few songs in which he accompanies Ian Bostridge. The *Sonata* is impressive in its range and depth of emotion and fine musical discipline. Richard Wigmore's excellent sleeve-note speaks of the ethereal tranquillity of the first two movements, and Andsnes conveys this with simplicity and artistry. The fine recording, made at Potton Hall, Surrey, is an additional advantage. This account deserves to rank with the very finest of recent years.

Brendel's earlier analogue performance is as impressive and full of insight as one would expect. He is not unduly wayward, for his recording has room for the *Wanderer fantasia* as well, and he is supported by excellent Philips sound.

Mitsuko Uchida couples the last *Sonata* with the *Drei Klavierstücke*. Hers is a performance of considerable stature; she allows Schubert to speak for himself. There is a rapt concentration and an almost other-worldly quality about her playing that will repay the attentive listener. Some may feel that she lingers a little too long in the slow movement and allows the onward flow of the music to stagnate – and they will doubtless prefer Kovacevich or Brendel. In any event there is no doubt whatever as to the excellence of the Philips recording.

Kissin's pianism is second to none, but if it is depth and insight that you are looking for, his account will only disappoint. The young Russian master offers beautiful sound but little else, and there is an unappealing self-awareness and a want of spontaneous feeling. The Liszt paraphrases with which it is coupled are more successful.

Piano Transcriptions: Overture in D (trans. Busoni). Symphony 8 (Unfinished): Passacaglia (based on the first 8 bars; Godowsky). Waltzes (trans. Prokofiev). Lieder: Die Schöne Müllerin; Morgengruss Winterreise; Gute Nacht (both trans. Godowsky); Im Dorfe; Die Stürmische Morgen; Erlkönig; Der Lindenbaum (both trans. Liszt)
(BB) *** Naxos 8.555997. Siirala

A fascinating and splendidly played collection that serves to introduce the young Finnish pianist Antti Siirala, who (understandably) carried off first prize at the London International Piano Competition after replacing an indisposed finalist at the last minute. His playing, informed by a remarkable range of keyboard colour and dynamic and by genuine poetic feeling, is matched by an apparently effortless technique. He finds an Italian felicity within Busoni's rather Germanic transcription of the *D major Overture* and is then very commanding indeed in Busoni's spectacular *Passacaglia* based on the eight-bar introduction of Schubert's *Unfinished*. Siirala is also a master of the pause, which adds suspense to the Lieder, but he primarily seeks out their lyrical beauty, while rising to the bravura, of the Lisztian decorations. While *Erlkönig* is the most dramatic of these, it is the simplicity of the phrasing of the melodies of *Gute Nacht* and *Der Lindenbaum* that remains in the memory. The Naxos recording is first class.

VOCAL MUSIC

Dietrich Fischer-Dieskau: The EMI Recordings
The First Recital (1951): *Der Atlas; Ihr Bild; Fischermädchen; Die Stadt; Am Meer; Der Doppelgänger; Erlkönig; Nacht und Träume; Du bist die Ruh; Ständchen*

Vol. I (1955): *Der Wanderer an den Mond; Uber Wildemann; Der Einsame; Auflösung; Der Kreuzzug; Totengräbers Heimweh; Nachtviolen; Frühlingssehnseht; Geheimnes; Rastlose Liebe; Liebesbotschaft; Im Abendrot; Abschied*

Vol. II (1957): *Dem Unendlichen; Die Sterne; An die Musik; Wehmut; Kriegers Ahnung; Der Zwerg; Der Wanderer; Frühlingsglaube; Die Taubenpost; An Silvia; Im Frühling; Auf der Bruck*

Vol. IIIa (1958): *Ständchen; Alinde; Nähe des Geliebten; Normanns Gesang; In der Ferne*

Vol. IIIb (1958): *Aufenthalt; Lied des gefangenen Jägers; Greisengesang; Erlkönig; Nachtstück*
(all with Gerald Moore)

Vol. IV (1959): *Gruppe aus dem Tartarus; Die Götter Griechenlands; Ewartung; Sehnsucht; Der Taucher*

Vol. V (1959): *Der Sänger; Die Bürgschaft; Der Fischer; Einsamkeit*

Vol. VIa (1959): *Am Strome; Der Alpenjäger; Erlafsee; Wie Ulfru fischt; Beim Winde; Trost; Auf der Donau* (1959)

Vol. VIb (1959): *Abendstern; Liedesend; Sehnsucht; Heliopolis; Zum Punsche; Der Sieg; An die Freunde* (Vols. IV–VIb with Karl Engel)

Vol. VII (1962): *Der Atlas; Ihr Bild; Das Fischermädchen; Die Stadt; Am Meer; Der Doppelgänger; Lachen und Weinen; Dass sie hier gewesen; Sei mir gegrüsst; Du bist die Ruh; Im Walde (Waldesnacht)*

Vol. VIII (1965): *Seligkeit; Heidenröslein; Ständchen; Des Fischers Liebesglück; Fischerweise; Der Jüngling an der Quelle; An die Laute; Die Forelle; Auf der Riesenkoppe*

Vol. IX (1965): *An die Entfernte; Auf dem Wasser zu singen; Der Schiffer; Der Wanderer; Nachtgesang; Das Zügenglöcklein; Der Jüngling und der Tod; Das Heimweh; Das Lied im Grünen; Der Tod und das Mädchen; Der Winterabend; Der zürnende Barde; Der Strom; Litanei auf das Fest Aller Seelen*

(all with Gerald Moore)
(M) *** EMI mono/stereo 5 65670-2 (6). Fischer-Dieskau, Moore or Engel

This HMV set makes an admirable survey of Fischer-Dieskau's Schubert recordings for EMI over a decade and a half before he moved to Deutsche Grammophon to make the extensive survey listed below. It is particularly interesting to compare the earliest recordings (the first in mono), with the voice and manner still youthfully fresh, to the second generation, again with Gerald Moore but also with Karl Engel. The contrast is fascinating, with the voice still younger than on DG. The transfers are superbly managed and full translations are provided to make this an indispensable supplement to the DG sets.

Lieder, Vol. 1 (1811–17); Vol. 2 (1817–28); Song cycles: *Die schöne Müllerin; Schwanengesang; Die Winterreise*
(B) *** DG (ADD) 437 214-2 (21). Fischer-Dieskau, Moore (as below)

Fischer-Dieskau's monumental survey of all the Schubert songs suitable for a man's voice (some of the longer ones excepted) was made over a relatively brief span, with the last 300 songs concentrated on a period of only two months in 1969, yet there is not a hint of routine. The two big boxes of nine discs come at bargain price, whereas the smaller box, containing the song-cycles, comes at mid-price. Nor has the background information been skimped. Each box contains complete German texts and English translations (plus summaries in French) as well as introductory essays. The one serious omission is an alphabetical list of titles. It makes it unnecessarily hard to find a particular song – much the most likely way of using so compendious a collection.

This collection of 21 CDs is offered at bargain price, as are the two separate 9-disc collections of Lieder listed below. The three great song-cycles – also included here – cost more if purchased separately.

Lieder, Vol. I (1811–17): *Eine Leichenfantasie; Der Vatermörder* (1811); *Der Jüngling am Bache* (1812); *Totengräberlied; Die Schatten; Sehnsucht; Verklärung; Pensa, che questo istante* (1813); *Der Taucher* (1813–15); *Andenken; Geisternähe; Erinnerung; Trost, An Elisa; Die Betende; Lied aus der Ferne; Der Abend; Lied der Liebe;*

Erinnerungen; Adelaide; An Emma; Romanze: Ein Fräulein klagt' im finstern Turm; An Laura, als sie Klopstocks Auferstehungslied sang; Der Geistertanz; Das Mädchen aus der Fremde; Nachtgesang; Trost in Tränen; Schäfers Klagelied; Sehnsucht; Am See (1814); *Auf einen Kirchhof; Als ich sie erröten sah; Das Bild; Der Mondabend* (1815); *Lodas Gespenst* (1816); *Der Sänger* (1815); *Die Erwartung* (1816); *Am Flusse; An Mignon; Nähe des Geliebten; Sängers Morgenlied; Amphiaraos; Das war ich; Die Sterne; Vergebliche Liebe; Liebesrausch; Sehnsucht der Liebe; Die erste Liebe; Trinklied; Stimme der Liebe; Naturgenuss; An die Freude; Der Jüngling am Bache; An den Mond; Die Mainacht; An die Nachtigall; An die Apfelbäume; Seufzer; Liebeständelei; Der Liebende; Der Traum; Die Laube; Meeres Stille; Grablied; Das Finden; Wandrers Nachtlied; Der Fischer; Erster Verlust; Die Erscheinung; Die Täuschung; Der Abend; Geist der Liebe; Tischlied; Der Liedler; Ballade; Abends unter der Linde; Die Mondnacht; Huldigung; Alles um Liebe; Das Geheimnis; An den Frühling; Die Bürgschaft; Der Rattenfänger; Der Schatzgräber; Heidenröslein; Bundeslied; An den Mond; Wonne der Wehmut; Wer kauft Liebesgötter?* (1815); *Der Goldschmiedsgesell* (1817); *Der Morgenkuss; Abendständchen: An Lina; Morgenlied: Willkommen, rotes Morgenlicht; Der Weiberfreund; An die Sonne; Tischlerlied; Totenkranz für ein Kind; Abendlied; Die Fröhlichkeit; Lob des Tokayers; Furcht der Geliebten; Das Rosenband; An Sie; Die Sommernacht; Die frühen Gräber; Dem Unendlichen; Ossians Lied nach dem Falle Nathos; Das Mädchen von Inistore; Labetrank der Liebe; An die Geliebte; Mein Gruss an den Mai; Skolie – Lasst im Morgenstrahl des Mai'n; Die Sternenwelten; Die Macht der Liebe; Das gestörte Glück; Die Sterne; Nachtgesang; An Rosa I: Warum bist du nicht hier?; An Rosa II: Rosa, denkst du an mich?; Schwanengesang; Der Zufriedene; Liane; Augenlied; Geistes-Gruss; Hoffnung; An den Mond; Rastlose Liebe; Erlkönig* (1815); *Der Schmetterling; Die Berge* (1819); *Genügsamkeit; An die Natur* (1815); *Klage; Morgenlied; Abendlied; Der Flüchtling; Laura am Klavier; Entzückung an Laura; Die vier Weltalter; Pflügerlied; Die Einsiedelei; An die Harmonie; Die Herbstnacht; Lied: Ins stille Land; Der Herbstabend; Der Entfernten; Fischerlied; Sprache der Liebe; Abschied von der Harfe; Stimme der Liebe; Entzückung; Geist der Liebe; Klage: Der Sonne steigt; Julius an Theone; Klage: Dein Silber schien durch Eichengrün; Frühlingslied; Auf den Tod einer Nachtigall; Die Knabenzeit; Winterlied; Minnelied; Die frühe Liebe; Blumenlied; Der Leidende; Seligkeit; Erntelied; Das grosse Halleluja; Die Gestirne; Die Liebesgötter; An den Schlaf; Gott im Frühling; Der gute Hirt; Die Nacht; Fragment aus dem Aeschylus* (1816); *An die untergehende Sonne* (1816–17); *An mein Klavier; Freude der Kinderjahre; Das Heimweh; An den Mond; An Chloen; Hochzeitlied; In der Mitternacht; Trauer der Liebe; Die Perle; Liedesend; Orpheus; Abschied; Rückweg; Alte Liebe rostet nie; Gesänge des Harfners aus Goethes Wilhelm Meister: Harfenspieler I: Wer sich der Einsamkeit ergibt; Harfenspieler II: An die Türen will ich schleichen; Harfenspieler III: Wer nie sein Brot mit Tränen ass. Der König in Thule; Jägers Abendlied; An Schwager Kronos; Der Sänger am Felsen; Lied: Ferne von der grossen Stadt; Der Wanderer; Der Hirt; Lied eines Schiffers an die Dioskuren; Geheimnis; Zum Punsche; Am Bach im Frühling* (1816); *An eine Quelle* (1817); *Bei dem Grabe, meines Vaters; Am Grabe Anselmos; Abendlied; Zufriedenheit; Herbstlied; Skolie: Mädchen entsiegelten; Lebenslied; Lieden der Trennung* (1816); *Alinde; An die Laute* (1827); *Frohsinn; Die Liebe;*

Trost; Der Schäfer und der Reiter (1817); Lob der Tränen (1821); Der Alpenjäger; Wie Ulfru fischt; Fahrt zum Hades; Schlaflied; Die Blumensprache; Die abgeblühte Linde; Der Flug der Zeit; Der Tod und das Mädchen; Das Lied vom Reifen; Täglich zu singen; Am Strome; Philoktet; Memnon; Auf dem See; Ganymed; Der Jüngling und der Tod; Trost im Liede (1817)

(B) *** DG (ADD) 437 215-2 (9). Fischer-Dieskau, Moore

This remarkable project, with Volume 1 recorded between 1966 and 1968 and Volume 2 over two months of intensive sessions in 1969, is an astonishing achievement in bringing together the greatest Schubertian of our time and the finest accompanist in a wide survey of the Lieder for solo voice. Already in 1811, as a boy in his early teens, Schubert was writing with astonishing originality, as is shown in the long (19 minutes) opening Schiller setting, a *Funeral Fantasy* with its rough, clashing intervals of a second and amazing harmonic pointers to the future. Drama comes very much to the fore in the second song here, *Der Vatermörder* ('A father died by his son's hand'), while the composer's endearing, flowing lyricism makes both *Der Jüngling am Bache* and *Die Schatten* sound remarkably mature. *Totengräberlied* ('Dig, spade, dig on!') brings a characteristically light touch to a gravedigger's soliloquy as he reflects that rich and poor alike, handsome and noble, are all in the end reduced to bones. Throughout these nine well-filled CDs the diversity of Schubert's imagination holds the listener, and his melodic gift almost never disappoints, especially when the performances are so completely at home with the music. The songs are presented in broadly chronological order and the arrangement of items ensures that each disc of the nine makes a satisfying recital in its own right. The CD transfers are impeccable, adding a little in presence to what were originally very well-balanced recordings.

Lieder, Vol. II (1817–28): An die Musik; Pax vobiscum; Hänflings Liebeswerbung; Auf der Donau; Der Schiffer; Nach einem Gewitter; Fischerlied; Das Grab; Der Strom; An den Tod; Abschied; Die Forelle; Gruppe aus dem Tartarus; Elysium; Atys; Erlafsee; Der Alpenjäger; Der Kampf; Der Knabe in der Wiege (1817); Auf der Riesenkoppe; An den Mond in einer Herbstnacht; Grablied für die Mutter; Einsamkeit; Der Blumenbrief; Das Marienbild (1818); Litanei auf das Fest Allerseelen (1816); Blondel zu Marien; Das Abendrot; Sonett I: Apollo, lebet noch dein Hold verlangen; Sonett II: Allein, nachdenken wie gelähmt vom Krampfe; Sonett III: Nunmehr, da Himmel, Erde schweigt; Vom Mitleiden Mariä (1818); Die Gebüsche; Der Wanderer; Abendbilder; Himmelsfunken; An die Freunde; Sehnsucht; Hoffnung; Der Jüngling am Bache; Hymne I: Wenige wissen das Geheimnis der Liebe; Hymne II: Wenn ich ihn nur hab; Hymne III: Wenn alle untreu werden; Hymne IV: Ich sag es jedem; Marie; Beim Winde; Die Sternennächte; Trost; Nachtstück; Prometheus; Strophe aus Die Götter Griechenlands (1819); Nachthymne; Die Vögel; Der Knabe; Der Fluss; Abendröte; Der Schiffer; Die Sterne; Morgenlied (1820); Frühlingsglaube (1822); Des Fräuleins Liebeslauschen (1820); Orest auf Tauris (1817); Der entsühnte Orest; Freiwilliges Versinken; Der Jüngling auf dem Hügel (1820); Sehnsucht (1817); Der zürnenden Diana; Im Walde (1820); Die gefangenen Sänger; Der Unglückliche; Versunken; Geheimnes; Grenzen der Menschheit (1821); Der Jüngling an der Quelle (1815); Der Blumen Schmerz (1821); Sei mir gegrüsst; Herr Josef Spaun, Assessor in Linz; Der

Wachtelschlag Ihr Grab; Nachtviolen; Heliopolis I: Im kalten, rauhen Norden; Heliopolis II: Fels auf Felsen hingewälzet; Selige Welt; Schwanengesang: Wie klage'ich's aus; Du liebst mich nicht; Die Liebe hat gelogen; Todesmusik; Schatzgräbers Begehr; An die Leier; Im Haine; Der Musensohn; An die Entfernte; Am Flusse; Willkommen und Abschied (1822); Wandrers Nachtlied: Ein Gleiches; Der zürnende Barde (1823); Am See (1822–3); Viola; Drang in die Ferne; Der Zwerg; Wehmut; Lied: Die Mutter Erde; Auf dem Wasser zu singen; Pilgerweise; Das Geheimnis; Der Pilgrim; Dass sie hier gewesen; Du bist die Ruh; Lachen und Weinen; Greisengesang (1823); Dithyrambe; Der Sieg; Abendstern; Auflösung; Gondelfahrer (1824); Glaube, Hoffnung und Liebe (1828); Im Abendrot; Der Einsame (1824); Des Sängers Habe; Totengräbers Heimwehe; Der blinde Knabe; Nacht und Träume; Normans Gesang; Lied des gefangenen Jägers; Im Walde; Auf der Bruck; Das Heimweh; Die Allmacht; Fülle der Liebe; Wiedersehn; Abendlied für die Entfernte; Szene I aus dem Schauspiel Lacrimas; Am mein Herz; Der liebliche Stern (1825); Im Jänner 1817 (Tiefes Leid); Am Fenster; Sehnsucht; Im Freien; Fischerweise; Totengräberweise; Im Frühling; Lebensmut; Um Mitternacht; Uber Wildemann (1826); Romanze des Richard Löwenherz (1827); Trinklied; Ständchen; Hippolits Lied; Gesang (An Silvia); Der Wanderer an den Mond; Das Zügenglöcklein; Bei dir allein; Irdisches Glück; Wiegenlied (1826); Der Vater mit dem Kind; Jägers Liebeslied; Schiffers Scheidelied; L'incanto degli occhi; Il traditor deluso; Il modo di prender moglie; Das Lied im Grünen; Das Weinen; Vor meiner Wiege; Der Wallensteiner Lanznecht beim Trunk; Der Kreuzzug; Das Fischers Liebesglück (1827); Der Winterabend; Die Sterne; Herbst; Widerschein (1828); Abschied von der Erde (1825–6)

(B) *** DG (ADD) 437 225-2 (9). Fischer-Dieskau, Moore

Volume II of this great project brings the mature songs; performances and recording are just as compelling as in Volume I. In their Berlin sessions Fischer-Dieskau and Moore adopted a special technique of study, rehearsal and recording most apt for the project. The sense of spontaneity and new discovery is unfailing, since each take was in fact a performance. On a later occasion, both artists might have taken a different view but, using the ease of access possible with CD, this collection is a unique way of sampling the many different aspects of Schubert's genius. The collection opens appropriately with *An die Musik* of 1817 and, as before, the songs in this volume are laid out chronologically with certain obvious exceptions – on disc 4, for instance, *Orest auf Tauris* (1817) is placed alongside the highly contrasted *Der entsühnte Orest* ('Orestes purified') (1820) – and the closing recital on disc 9 is suitably concluded with *Abschied von der Erde* ('Farewell to the Earth'), dating from 1825–6. Once again there is much unfamiliar repertory to discover: the four *Hymnes* grouped together on the second disc are little known but show the composer's imaginative diversity in a specifically religious connotation, while the unexpected song dedicated to *Herr Josef Spaun, Assessor in Linz*, which closes the fourth CD, is strikingly operatic. Both booklets offer full translations and each includes also brief essays by Fischer-Dieskau and Walther Dürr on the composer.

Lieder, Vol. III: Song-cycles: Die schöne Müllerin; Schwanengesang; Winterreise

☛— (M) *** DG (ADD) 437 235-2 (3). Fischer-Dieskau, Moore

Fischer-Dieskau and Moore had each recorded these great

cycles of Schubert several times already before they embarked on this set in 1971–2 as part of DG's Schubert song series. It was no mere repeat of earlier triumphs. If anything, these performances – notably that of the darkest and greatest of the cycles, *Winterreise* – are even more searching than before, with Moore matching the hushed concentration of the singer in some of the most remarkable playing that even he has put on record. As in the extensive recitals listed above, Fischer-Dieskau is in wonderfully fresh voice, and the transfers to CD have been managed very naturally.

Lieder: *Abendbilder; Am Fenster; Auf der Bruck; Auf der Donau; Aus Heliopolis; Fischerweise; Im Frühling; Liebeslauschen; Des Sängers Habe; Der Schiffer; Die Sterne; Der Wanderer; Wehmut; Das Zügenglöcklein*

🔊 (M) *** DG (ADD) (IMS) 445 717-2. Fischer-Dieskau, Richter

Recorded live in 1977, this beautifully balanced selection of Schubert songs displays the singer's enormous range of expression, as well as the acute sensitivity of the pianist in responding. The songs have been grouped almost in a cycle, starting with a biting expression of self-torment (*Des Sängers Habe*). This is sung aggressively here (understandably so) but gradually the mood lightens from melancholy (*Wehmut*) to brighter thoughts (*Das Zügenglöcklein* – 'The little bell'). Not many of these songs are well known, but it is a programme to delight aficionado and newcomer alike, atmospherically recorded with remarkably little interference from audience noises.

The Graham Johnson Schubert Lieder Edition

Hyperion's complete Schubert song edition was masterminded by the accompanist, Graham Johnson. Each of the 37 Volumes has a theme or is centred on a particular artist. The series has been reviewed several times in past editions, but now for reasons of space we are retaining the listings, but giving a brief summary of the reviews, carrying the full reviews (plus the listings) into our 2006/7 Yearbook. We would wish now to guide the reader towards the outstanding collections, although that is very difficult, for almost every volume is remarkable in one way or another.

Lieder, Vol. 1: *Der Alpenjäger; Amalia; An den Frühling; An den Mond; Erster Verlust; Die Ewartung; Der Fischer; Der Flüchtling; Das Geheimnis; Der Jüngling am Bache; Lied; Meeres Stille; Nähe des Geliebten; Der Pilgrim; Schäfers Klagelied; Sehnsucht; Thekla; Wanderers Nachtlied; Wonne der Wehmut*

🔊 *** Hyp. CDJ 33001. Baker, Johnson

Lieder, Vol. 2: *Am Bach im Frühling; Am Flusse; Auf der Donau; Fahrt zum Hades; Fischerlied (two settings); Fischerweise; Der Schiffer; Selige Welt; Der Strom; Der Taucher; Widerschein; Wie Ulfru fischt*

*** Hyp. CDJ 33002. Varcoe, Johnson

Lieder, Vol. 3: *Abschied; An die Freunde; Augenlied; Iphigenia; Der Jüngling und der Tod; Lieb Minna; Liedesend; Nacht und Träume; Namenstagslied; Pax vobiscum; Rückweg; Trost im Liede; Viola; Der Zwerg*

*** Hyp. CDJ 33003. Murray, Johnson

Lieder, Vol. 4: *Alte Liebe rostet nie; Am See; Am Strome; An Herrn Josef von Spaun (Epistel); Auf der Riesenkoppe; Das*

war ich; Das gestörte Glück; Liebeslauschen; Liebesrausch; Liebeständelei; Der Liedler; Nachtstück; Sängers Morgenlied (2 versions); Sehnsucht der Liebe

*** Hyp. CDJ 33004. Langridge, Johnson

Lieder, Vol. 5: *Die Allmacht; An die Natur; Die Erde; Erinnerung; Ferne von der grossen Stadt; Ganymed; Klage der Ceres; Das Lied im Grünen; Morgenlied; Die Mutter Erde; Die Sternenwelten; Täglich zu singen; Dem Unendlichen; Wehmut*

*** Hyp. CDJ 33005. Connell, Johnson

Lieder, Vol. 6: *Abendlied für die Entfernte; Abends unter der Linde (two versions); Abendstern; Alinde; An die Laute; Des Fischers Liebesglück; Jagdlied; Der Knabe in der Wiege (Wiegenlied); Lass Wolken an Hügeln ruh'n; Die Nacht; Die Sterne; Der Vater mit dem Kind; Vor meiner Wiege; Wilkommen und Abschied; Zur guten Nacht*

*** Hyp. CDJ 33006. Rolfe Johnson, Johnson (with chorus)

Lieder, Vol. 7: *An die Nachtigall; An den Frühling; An den Mond; Idens Nachtgesang; Idens Schwanenlied; Der Jüngling am Bache; Kennst du das Land?; Liane; Die Liebe; Luisens Antwort; Des Mädchens Klage; Meeres Stille; Mein Gruss an den Mai; Minona oder die Kunde der Dogge; Naturgenuss; Das Rosenband; Das Sehnen; Sehnsucht (2 versions); Die Spinnerin; Die Sterbende; Stimme der Liebe; Von Ida; Wer kauft Liebesgötter?*

🔊 *** Hyp. CDJ 33007. Ameling, Johnson

Lieder, Vol. 8: *Abendlied der Fürstin; An Chloen; An den Mond; An den Mond in einer Herbstnacht; Berthas Lied in der Nacht; Erlkönig; Die frühen Gräber; Hochzeitslied; In der Mitternacht; Die Mondnacht; Die Nonne; Die Perle; Romanze; Die Sommernacht; Ständchen; Stimme der Liebe; Trauer der Liebe; Wiegenlied*

*** Hyp. CDJ 33008. Walker, Johnson

Lieder, Vol. 9: *Blanka; 4 Canzonen, D.688; Daphne am Bach; Delphine; Didone abbandonata; Gott! höre meine Stimme; Der gute Hirt; Hin und wieder Fliegen Pfeile; (i) Der Hirt auf dem Felsen. Ich schleiche bang und still (Romanze). Lambertine; Liebe Schwärmt auf allen Wegen; Lilla an die Morgenröte; Misero pargoletto; La pastorella al prato; Der Sänger am Felsen; Thekla; Der Vollmond strahlt (Romanze)*

🔊 *** Hyp. CDJ 33009. Augér, Johnson; (i) with King

Lieder, Vol. 10: *Adelwold und Emma; Am Flusse; An die Apfelbäume, wo ich Julien erblickte; An die Geliebte; An Mignon; Auf den Tod einer Nachtigall; Auf einen Kirchhof; Harfenspieler I; Labetrank der Liebe; Die Laube; Der Liebende; Der Sänger; Seufzer; Der Traum; Vergebliche Liebe; Der Weiberfreund*

*** Hyp. CDJ 33010. Hill, Johnson

Volume 1 features Dame Janet Baker in glorious voice singing Schiller and Goethe settings, above all those Schubert wrote in 1815, when he was 18 years old. Volume 2 introduces Stephen Varcoe in a delightful collection of men's songs. Volume 3 is devoted to Ann Murray with the intimate beauty of the voice consistently well caught. Volume 4 brings Philip Langridge and a rare collection of Schubert's setting of poets in his immediate circle. Volume 5 centres around the theme of 'Schubert and the Countryside' and Volume 6 is called 'Schubert and the Nocturne'. Volume 7, with Elly Ameling both charming and intense, offers a rewarding sequence of 24 songs all written in the composer's *annus mirabilis*, 1815. Volume 8 brings a second disc dedicated to 'Schubert and the Nocturne' demonstrating Sarah Walker's perfectly controlled mezzo at its most sensuous, while in Volume 9 Arleen Augér's heady contribution is called 'Schubert and the Theatre'. Volume 10 returns to the year 1815.

Lieder, Vol. 11: *An den Tod; Auf dem Wasser zu singen; Auflösung; Aus 'Heliopolis' I & II; Dithyrambe; Elysium; Der Geistertanz; Der König in Thule; Lied des Orpheus; Nachtstück; Schwanengesang; Seligkeit; So lasst mich scheinen; Der Tod und das Mädchen; Verklärung; Vollendung; Das Zügenglöcklein*
*** Hyp. CDJ 33011. Fassbaender, Johnson

Lieder, Vol. 12: *Adelaide; An Elise; An Laura, als sie Klopstocks Auferstehungslied sang; Andenken; Auf den Sieg der Deutschen; Ballade; Die Betende; Don Gayseros I, II, III; Der Geistertanz; Lied an der Ferne; Lied der Liebe; Nachtgesang; Die Schatten; Sehnsucht; Trost; Trost in Tränem; Der Vatermörder*
** Hyp. CDJ 33012. Thompson, Johnson

Lieder, Vol. 13: (i) *Eine altschottische Ballade. Ellens Gesang I, II & III (Ave Maria); Gesang der Norna; Gretchen am Spinnrade; Gretchens Bitte; Lied der Anna Lyle; Die Männer sind méchant; Marie; Das Marienbild;* (i) *Normans Gesang; Szene aus Faust. Shilrik und Vinvela; Die Unterscheidung*
*** Hyp. CDJ 33013. McLaughlin, Johnson; (i) with Hampson

Lieder, Vol. 14: *Amphiaraos; An die Leier;* (i) *Antigone und Oedip. Der entsühnte Orest; Freiwilliges Versinken; Die Götter Griechenlands; Gruppe aus dem Tartarus; Fragment aus dem Aeschylus;* (i) *Hektors Abschied. Hippolits Lied; Lied eines Schiffers an die Dioskuren; Memnon; Orest auf Tauris; Philoktet; Uraniens Flucht; Der Zürnenden Diana*
*** Hyp. CDJ 33014. Hampson, Johnson; (i) with McLaughlin

Lieder, Vol. 15: *Am Fenster; An die Sonne; An die untergehende Sonne; Der blinde Knabe; Gondelfahrer; Im Freien; Ins stille Land; Die junge Nonne; Klage an den Mond; Kolmas Klage; Die Mainacht; Der Mondabend; Der Morgenkuss; Sehnsucht; Der Unglückliche; Der Wanderer an den Mond; Der Winterabend*
☞ ✿ *** Hyp. CDJ 33015. M. Price, Johnson

Lieder, Vol. 16: *An die Freude; An Emma; Die Bürgschaft; Die Entzückung an Laura I & II; Das Geheimnis; Der Jüngling am Bache; Laura am Clavier; Leichenfantasie; Das Mädchen aus der Fremde; Die vier Weltalter; Sehnsucht; Der Pilgrim*
*** Hyp. CDJ 33016. Allen, Johnson

Lieder, Vol. 17: *Am Grabe Anselmos; An den Mond; An die Nachtigall; An mein Klavier; Aus 'Diego Manazares' (Ilmerine); Die Einsiedelei; Frühlingslied; Geheimnis; Der Herbstabend; Herbstlied; Die Herbstnacht; Klage; Klage um Ali Bey; Lebenslied; Leiden der Trennung; Lied; Lied in der Absenheit; Litanei; Lodas Gespenst; Lorma; Minnelied; Pflicht und Liebe; Phidile; Winterlied*
*** Hyp. CDJ 33017. Popp, Johnson

Lieder, Vol. 18: *Abendlied; An den Schlaf; An die Erntferne; An die Harmonie; An mein Herz; Auf den Tod einer Nachtigall; Auf der Bruck; 'Die Blume und der Quell'; Blumenlied; Drang in die Ferne; Erntelied; Das Finden; Das Heimweh (2 versions); Im Frühling; Im Jänner 1817 (Tiefes Lied); Im Walde; Lebensmut; Der Liebliche Stern; Die Nacht; Über Wildemann; Um Mitternacht*
*** Hyp. CDJ 33018. Schreier, Johnson

Volume 11 opens with a chilling account of *Death and the Maiden* and appropriately the theme of Brigitte Fassbaender's

somewhat ominous programme is 'Death and the Composer'. Volume 12 is by comparison disappointingly sung by Adrian Thompson. The next two Volumes are shared by Marie McLaughlin and Thomas Hampson. Volume 13 is broadly a survey of Schubert's inner conflicts and contradictions, with several songs centring on Gretchen the Spinner, but also including some translated Scottish ballads; Volume 14 is called 'Schubert and the Classics' (including Ancient Greece). Volume 15 then introduces Dame Margaret Price in songs on the theme of 'Night' and achieved a new peak (hence its well deserved Rosette). In Volume 16 Thomas Allen too, is challenged to some of his most sensitive singing in settings of Schiller.

It was fitting that Lucia Popp's contribution was made in Volume 17, for it was one of her last recordings before her tragic death in 1993, and her selection of songs written in 1816 inspire all her characteristic sweetness and charm. The 18th Volume represents the halfway point in this masterly series with Peter Schreier keenly illuminating in a group of strophic songs.

Lieder, Vol. 19: *Abendlied; Am See; Auf dem See; Auf dem Wasser zu singen; Beim Winde; Der Blumen Schmerz; Die Blumensprache; Gott im Frühling; Im Haine; Der liebliche Stern; Nach einem Gewitter; Nachtviolen; Die Rose; Die Sterne; Suleika I & II; Die Sternennächte; Vergissmeinicht*
*** Hyp. CDJ 33019. Lott, Johnson

Lieder, Vol. 20: 'Schubertiad' (1815) Songs and part-songs: *Abendständchen (An Lina); Alles um Liebe; Als ich sie erröten sah; Begräbnislied; Bergknappenlied; Der erste Liebe; Die Frölichkeit; Geist der Liebe; Grablied; Heidenröslein; Hoffnung; Huldigung; Klage um Ali Bey; Liebesrausch; Die Macht der Liebe; Das Mädchen von Inistore; Der Morgenstern; Nachtgesang; Ossians Lied nach dem Falle Nathos; Osterlied; Punschlied (Im Norden su singen); Schwertlied; Schwanengesang; Die Tauschung; Tischerlied; Totenkranz für ein Kind; Trinklied (2 versions); Trinklied vor der Schlacht; Wiegenlied; Winterlied; Der Zufriedene*
*** Hyp. CDJ 33020. Rozario, Mark Ainsley, Bostridge, George, Johnson; L. Schubert Ch., Layton

Lieder, Vol. 21: Songs from 1817–18: *Die abgeblühte Linde; Abschied von einem Freunde; An die Musik; An eine Quelle; Erlafsee; Blondel zu Marien; Blumenbrief; Evangelium Johannes; Der Flug der Zeit; Die Forelle; Grablied für die Mutter; Häbflings Liebeswerbung; Impromptu; Die Liebe; Liebhaber in allen Gestalten; Lied eines Kind; Das Lied vom Reifen; Lob der Tränen; Der Schäfer und der Reiter; Schlaflied; Schweizerlied; Sehnsucht; Trost; Vom Mitleiden Mariä*
*** Hyp. CDJ 33021. Mathis, Johnson

Lieder, Vol. 22: 'Schubertiad II': *Der Abend; Das Abendroth; An die Sonne; An Rosa I & II; An Sie; Das Bild; Cora an die Sonne; Cronnan; Die drei Sänger; Die Erscheinung; Furcht der Geliebten; Gebet wahrend der Schlacht; Genugsamkeit; Das Grab; Hermann und Thusnelda; Das Leben ist ein Traum; Lob des Tokayers; Lorma; Das Mädchen aus der Fremde; Morgenlied; Punschlied; Scholie; Selma und Selmar; Die Sterne; Trinklied; Vaterlandslied*
*** Hyp. CDJ 33022. Anderson, Wyn-Rogers, MacDougall, Keenlyside; Johnson

Lieder, Vol. 23: Songs from 1816: *Abendlied; Abschied von der Harfe; Am ersten Maimorgen; An Chloen; Bei dem Grabe meines Vater; Edone; Der Entfernten; Freude der*

Kinderjahre; Die frühe Liebe; Geist der Liebe; Gesänger des Harfners aus 'Wilhelm Meister' (Wer sich der Einsamkeit ergibt; Wer nie sein Brot mit Tränen ass; An die Türen will ich schleichen); Das Grab; Der Hirt; Julius an Theone; Der Jüngling an der Quelle; Klage; Die Knabenzeit; Der Leidende (2 versions); *Die Liebesgötter; Mailied; Pflügerlied; Romanze; Skolie; Stimme der Liebe; Der Tod Oscars; Zufriedenheit*

☞ ✱ *** Hyp. CDJ 33023. Prégardien, Johnson

Lieder, Vol. 24: *Goethe Schubertiad: An Mignon; An Schwager Kronos; Bundeslied; Erlkönig; Ganymed; Geistes-Gruss; Gesang der Geister über den Wassern* (2 versions); *Der Goldschmiedsgesell; Der Gott und die Bajadere; Hoffnung; Jägers Abendlied* (2 versions); *Mahomets Gesang; Mignon (So lasst mich scheinen); Rastlose Liebe; Der Rattenfänger; Schäfers Klagelied; Der Schatzgräber; Sehnsucht* (2 versions); *Sehnsucht (Nur wer die Sehnsucht kennt); Tischlied; Wer nie sein Brot mit Tränen ass*

*** Hyp. CDJ 33024. Schäfer, Mark Ainsley, Keenlyside, George, L. Schubert Ch., Layton; Johnson

Lieder, Vol. 25: (i) *Die schöne Müllerin* (song-cycle); (ii) with additional poems by Wilhelm Müller

☞ ✪ *** Hyp. CDJ 33025 (i) Bostridge, Johnson; (ii) read by Fischer-Dieskau

Lieder, Vol. 26: *'An 1826 Schubertiad': 2 Scenes from Lacrimas (Schauspiel); 4 Mignon Lieder of Wilhelm Meister. Lieder: Abschied von der Erde; An Sylvia; Das Echo; Der Einsame; Grab und Mond; Mondenschein; Nachthelle; Des Sängers Habe; Ständchen; Totengräberweise; Trinklied; Der Wanderer an den Mond; Widerspruch; Wiegenlied*

*** Hyp. CDJ 33026. Schäfer, Mark Ainsley, Jackson. L. Schubert Ch., Layton; Johnson

Lieder, Vol. 27: *Abendröte cycle of Friedrich von Schlegel* (complete). Other settings of Friedrich von Schlegel: *Blanka; Fülle der Liebe; Im Walde; Der Schiffer.* Settings of August von Schlegel: *Lebensmelodien; Lob der Tränen; Sonnets I–III; Sprache der Liebe; Wiedersehn*

*** Hyp. CDJ 33027. Görne, Schäfer, Johnson

Lieder, Vol. 28: *'Schubertiad' (1822): Am Flusse; An die Entfernte; Du liebst mich nicht; Frülingsgesang; Geheimes; Geist der Liebe; Ihr Grab; Im Gegenwärtigen Vergangenes; Johanna Sebus; Die Liebe hat gelogen; Mahomets Gesang; Mignon (Heiss mich nicht reden); Der Musensohn; Die Nachtingall; Schatzgräbers Begehr; Sei mir gegrüsst!; Selige Welt; Des Tages Weihe; Todesmusik; Versunken; Der Wachtelschlag; Willkommen und Abschied*

*** Hyp. CDJ 33028. Schäfer, Mark Ainsley, Koningsberger, Ch., Johnson

Lieder, Vol. 29: *Abendbilder; Blondel zu Marien; Einsamkeit* (cantata); *Frühlingsglaube; Himmelsfunken; Hoffnung; Hymne I–IV; Im Walde (Waldesnacht); Der Jüngling auf dem Hügel; Die Liebende schreibt; Morgenlied; Nachthymne; Trost*

*** Hyp. CDJ 33029. Lipovšek, Berg, Johnson

Lieder, Vol. 30: *Winterreise* (song cycle), *D.911*

☞ *** Hyp. CDJ 33030. Görne, Johnson

Graham Johnson's theme for Felicity Lott's Volume 19 is 'Schubert and Flowers' prompting a selection of charming, ever-lyrical songs, mostly neglected. Then Volume 20 brings a different kind of recital disc, the first of Johnson's simulated 'Schubertiads' with a range of singers performing no fewer than 32 brief songs and ensemble number, all written in 1815. Volume 21 then moves on to 1817/18 for a sequence sung with characteristic sweetness by the Swiss soprano, Edith Mathis. Volume 22 returns to the year 1815 and Johnson devises 'Schubertiad II' including vocal quartets and trios. Volume 23 turns back a year earlier to 1816, and the German lyric tenor, Christoph Prégardien, uses his lovely voice with its honeyed tone colours through a wide expressive range in a very varied selection. Volume 24 is another group recital all drawn from Goethe settings. Here some items are set more than once, notably *Erlkönig*, with three different singers taking part.

Volume 25 brings the first of the great song cycles, *Die schöne Müllerin*, sung by an artist now very closely associated with the work, Ian Bostridge, giving an eagerly detailed account, mesmeric at the close. The bonus here is the inclusion of the retired Fischer-Dieskau reciting the Müller poems which Schubert failed to set. Volume 26 is another 'Schubertiad', darker than before, relying entirely on songs written in 1825 and 1826. Volume 27 then introduces the outstanding young German baritone, Matthias Görne in settings of poems by the Von Schlegel brothers in which Christine Schäfer joins him in three items by Friederich.

Volume 28 brings an 1822 'Schubertiad' including concerted numbers and in particular, a miniature cantata, *Des Tages Weihe*. Another cantata is included in Volume 29, more ambitious this time, *Einsamkeit* with words by Mayrhofer sung by the Canadian baritone, Nathan Berg, who is joined in the rest of the programme by the velvet-voiced mezzo, Marjana Lipovšek. Volume 30 then provides a climax for the second part of the survey with Matthias Görne giving a truly outstanding account of the greatest of the song-cycles, *Winterreise*. He movingly brings out the point that this is the tragedy of a young lover, not an old one.

Lieder, Vol. 31: *Die Allmacht* (2nd version for chorus); *Die gestirne; Hagars Klage; Himmelsfunken; Im Abendrot; Das Mädchens Klage* (1st version); *Mirjams Siegergesang; Psalms 13; 23* (both trans. Mendelssohn); *Psalm 92* (unacc. in Hebrew); *Dem Unendlichen*

*** Hyp. CDJ 33031. Brewer, Holst Singers, Layton; Johnson

Lieder, Vol. 32: *'An 1816 Schubertiad': An die Sonne; Beitrag zur Fünfzigjährigen Jubelfeier des Herrn von Salieri: Der Entfernten; Entzückung; Der Geistertanz; Gott der Weltschöpfer; Gott im Ungewitter; Grablied auf einen Soldaten; Das grosse Halleluja; Licht und Liebe; Des Mädchens Klage; Naturgenuss; Ritter Toggenburg; Schlachtgesang; Vedi quanto adoro (Dido Abbandonata); Die verfehlte Stunde; Der Wanderer; Das war ich; Zufriedenheit; Zum Punsche*

*** Hyp. CDJ 33032. Dawson, Schäfer, Murray, Ainsley, Norman, Prégardien, Schade, Spence, Maltman, Varcoe, L. Schubert Ch. & Soloists, Layton; Johnson

Lieder, Vol. 33: (i) *Lebenstraum (Gesang in C min.); Lebenstraum; Pensa, che questo istante; Totengräberlied;* (ii) *Entra l'uomo allor che nasce (Aria di Abramo); L'incanto degli occhi; Misero pargoletto; O combats, o désordre extrême!; Ombre amene, amiche piante (La serenata); Quelle' innocente figlio (Aria dell' Angelo); Rien de la nature; Son fra l'onde;* (iii) *Klaglied;* (iv) *Entra l'uomo allor che nasce (Aria di Abramo); Erinnerungen; Geisternähe;* (v)

Serbate o dei custodi; (vi) *Die Befreier Europas in Paris*; (vii) *Der abend*; (viii) *Ammenlied; Die Nacht*; (ix) *Dithyrambe; Trinklied; Viel tausend Sterne prangen*

*** Hyp. CDJ 33033. McLaughlin, Murray, Wyn-Rogers, Langridge, Norman, Thompson, Koningsberger, Varcoe and soloists, L. Schubert Ch., Layton; Johnson

Lieder, Vol. 34: (i) *Abend*; (ii) *Das Abendrot*; (iii) *Der Alpenjäger*; (iv) *Atys*; (v) *Kantate zum Geburtstag des Sängers Michael Vogl*; (vi) *Das Dörfchen*; (vii) *Die Einsiedelei*; (viii) *Frohsinn*; (ix) *Die gefangenen Sänger*; (x) *Die Gesellligkeit (Lebenslust)*; (xi) *Das Grab*; (xii) *Grenzen der Menschheit; Der Kampf*; (xiii) *Das Mädchen*; (vi) *La pastorella al prato*; (xiv) *Prometheus*; (xv) *Sing-Ubungen*; (xvi) *Uber allen Zauber Liebe*; (iii) *Wandrers Nachtlied II*

*** Hyp. CDJ 33034. Anderson, Dawson, Lozario, Lipovšek, Hill, Langridge, Norman, Schade, Finley, Görne, Hampson, Keenlyside, Loges, Maltman, Davies (with Denley, Mark-Ainsley, Bostridge, MacDougall, George); Johnson; L. Schubert Ch., Layton

Lieder, Vol. 35: (1822–25): *Bootgesang; Coronach; Dass sie hier gewesen!; Du bist die Ruh; Gebet (Du Urquell aller güte); Gondelfahrer; Gott in der Natur; Greisengesang; Lachen und Weinen; Lied des gefangenen Jägers; Lied eines Kriegers; Pilgerweise; Schwestergruss; Der Sieg; Der Tanz; Totengräbers Heimwehe; Die Wallfahrt; Der zürnende Barde*

*** Hyp. CDJ 33035. Dawson, McGreevy, Langridge, Hampson, Konigsberger, Maltman; Johnson

Lieder, Vol. 36: *'Am 1827 Schubertiad': Cantata zur Feier der Genesung der Irene Kiesewetter; Fröhliches Scheiden; Frühlingslied; Heimliches Lieben; Der Hochzeitsbraten; Il mondo di prender moglie; Il traditor deluso; L'incanto degli occhi; Jägers Liebeslied; Der Kreuzzug; Romanze des Richard Löwenherz; Schiffers Scheideleid; Sie in jedem Liede; Die Sterne; Das Wallensteiner Lanznecht beim Trunk; Das Weinen; Wolke und Quelle*

*** Hyp. CDJ 33036. Banse, Schade, Finley, Dawson; Johnson; Holst Singers, Layton; Asti

Lieder, Vol. 37: *'The final year': Schwanengesang*, Parts I & II. (i) *Auf der Strom. Bei dir allein!; Herbst; Irdisches Glück; Lebensmut*

☞ *** Hyp. CDJ 33037. Mark Ainsley, Rolfe Johnson, Schade; (i) with Pyatt

In Volume 31, the American soprano, Christine Brewer, opens the final part of Graham Johnson's survey in a disc devoted to sacred songs. In the concerted numbers she is joined by other soloists and also the Holst Singers to show fascinatingly Schubert's equivocal approach to religious inspiration, too individual to follow Catholic dogma precisely. Volume 32 brings another (1816) 'Schubertiad' with few of the items well known, while Volume 33, entitled 'The Young Schubert' offers a mixed bag of songs from 1810–14, including what is now thought to be the very first Schubert song of 1810, now fitted with words – *Liebenstraume* ('Life's dream').

Volume 34 has a huge cast and collects together hitherto omitted songs that Schubert wrote between 1817 and 1821, presented in chronological order, while Volume 35 similarly harvests songs from the years of the composer's late twenties including four masterpieces with words by Rückert. The penultimate Volume 36 provides the last of the 'Schubertiads', from 1827, the year preceding the composer's death, with a major contribution from the baritone, Gerald Finley, in magnificent voice, clear, firm and dark.

Then the survey is superbly rounded off, not only with

Schwanengesang, but a carefully chosen group of other songs from 1828, the year Schubert died. Three fine Lieder singers are featured here, with the first song on the disc, *Auf der Strom*, with an opulent horn obbligato from David Pyatt, written as a heartfelt memorial to Beethoven. As a poignant postscript, after the darkness of *Der Döpperlganger*, stark and bare as though in anticipation of death, comes the last song that Schubert ever wrote, *Die Taubenpost* ('Pigeon Post') seemingly trivial. Here happy lyricism blossoms gloriously over an exhilarating accompaniment representing the clip-clopping of a horse.

Throughout the whole series Johnson in his inspired accompaniments consistently revels in Schubert's joyfully original piano writing, and his carefully detailed revelatory notes provide constant illumination. Few series of recordings so richly repay detailed study and all are a pleasure to return to, when the sound and balance too are consistently of such high quality. All collectors should dip into this remarkable anthology, and be encouraged to return again and again.

'The Songmakers' Almanac Schubertiade': I, 'Lebensmut': *Die junge Nonne; Der zürnende Diana; Vom Mitleiden Mariä; Lachen und Weinen; Selige Welt; Mignon und der Harfner; Auflösung; Lebensmut; Willkommen und Abschied*. II, 'Nacht und Träume': *An die Laute; Wiegenlied; Ellens Gesang I; Nacht und Träume; Licht und Liebe; Ständchen (Horch! horch! die Lerch); Der Tod und das Mädchen; Der Winterabend; Abschied von der Erde*. III, 'Das Lied im Grünen': *Fischerweise; Das Lied im Grünen; Der Schiffer; Nähe des Geliebten; Frühlingsglaube; Wandrers Nachtlied; Im Frühling; Wehmut; Auf der Bruck*. IV, 'An mein Klavier': *An mein Klavier; Zum Punsche; Geheimnis; Viola; Der Hochzeitsbraten*

(B) **(*) Hyp. Dyad CDD 22020 (2). Lott, Murray, Rolfe Johnson, Jackson; Johnson

Recorded in 1983, this two-disc collection presents over two hours of songs arranged by related groups – 'The Romantic Struggle', 'Serenades and Lullabies', 'Nature and Love', 'At home with the Schubertians'. That was the way Graham Johnson devised his immensely popular Songmakers' Almanac concerts, making this a forerunner of his brilliantly conceived recorded edition of the complete songs. Johnson's notes, including comments on individual items and full texts, observe a similar pattern to that adopted in the main edition, though a song like the Seidl *Wiegenlied* is allowed only three of its stanzas, not all five. The analogue recording, given an AAD transfer to CD, is not quite as clean as in the main edition, not quite sharply focused enough. Such inspired performance give a delightful impression of just such live events as the original Schubertiads. Left to the end are the two items which are by far the longest: the poignant *Viola*, a ballad telling of an abandoned flower, with Ann Murray a charming soloist, and the convivial *Hochzeitsbraten* ('Wedding dish'), featuring the other three soloists. All four singers are at their freshest, with Ann Murray in particularly fine voice, taking on many of the most challenging songs.

Miscellaneous vocal recitals

Abendlied der Fürstin; An die Nachtigall; An die Sonne; Blanca (Das Mädchen); Du bist die Ruh; Ellens Gesang I, II & III; Gesang der Norna; Gretchen am Spinnrade; Im Freien; Der Hirt auf dem Felsen; Die junge Nonne; Klage der Ceres; Klaglied; Die Liebende schreibt; Lied de Anne Lyle; Lied der

Mignon I, II & III; Das Mädchens Klage; Die Männer sind méchant; Mignons Gesang; Suleika I & II; Wiegenlied

- (B) *** DG Double (ADD) 453 082-2 (2). Janowitz, Gage

This attractive DG Double is self-recommending. Many of the songs here are favourites, although there are some novelties. They come from a comprehensive survey of Lieder suitable for female voice, originally issued on five LPs and recorded in 1976–7. They receive persuasive handling from Janowitz and, with a voice so naturally beautiful and used with such musical intelligence, the results are consistently compelling, helped by the sympathetic, concentrated accompaniments of Irwin Gage. If *Gretchen am Spinnrade*, which comes near the beginning of the recital, is somewhat idiosyncratic in its speed variations, Janowitz makes it very much her own, and her *Die junge Nonne*, which opens the second CD, is similarly appealing. Perhaps the most ravishing singing comes in the *Wiegenlied* and *Du bist die ruh* and, most memorably of all, the first Suleika song (*Was bedeutet die Bewegung?*) with its gentle closing pianissimo as the singer reflects that the soft whisper of the wind suggests the breath of love. The recital ends with the famous *Shepherd on the Rock* with its clarinet obbligato well played by Ulf Rodenhäuser, although it has been presented more seductively elsewhere. The recording is first rate and full translations are included.

'A Schubert Evening': (i) *Abendstern; Am Grabe Anselmos; An die Nachtigall; An die untergehende Sonne'; Berthas Lied in der Nacht; Delphine; Ellen's Gesang from The Lady of the Lake (Raste Krieger; Jäger von der Jagd; Ave Maria); Epistel an Herrn Josef von Spaun; Gondelfahrer; Gretchen am Spinnrade; Hin und wieder; Iphigenia; Die junge Nonne; Kennst du das Land; Liebe schwärmt; Das Mädchen; Das Mädchens Klage; Die Männer sind méchant; Mignon Lieder I–III (Heiss mich nicht reden; So lasst mich scheinen; Nur wer die Sehnsucht kennt); Schlummerlied; Schwestergruss; Strophe von Schiller (Die Götter Griechenlands); Suleika songs I–II (Was bedeutet die Bewegung; Ach, um deine feuchten Schwingen); Wiegenlied; Wiegenlied (Schlafe, schlafe).* 'Favourite Lieder': (ii) *An die Musik; An Sylvia; Auf dem Wasser zu singen; Du bist die Ruh'; Die Forelle; Frühlingslaube; Heidenröslein; Litanei; Der Musensohn; Nacht und Träume; Rastlose Lied; Der Tod und das Mädchen*

- ⚙ (B) *** EMI double forte (ADD) 5 69389-2 (2). Baker, with (i) Moore; (ii) Parsons

This very generous collection combines a pair of recitals recorded by Dame Janet at two different stages in her career, in 1970 and a decade later. The first collection ranges wide in an imaginative *Liederabend* of Schubert songs that includes a number of comparative rarities. They move from the delectably comic *Epistel* to the ominous darkness of *Die junge Nonne*. The two cradle songs are irresistible, the Seidl setting even more haunting than the more famous one; and throughout Baker consistently displays the breadth of her emotional mastery and her range of tone-colour. With Gerald Moore (who returned to the studio out of retirement especially for the occasion) still at his finest, this is a rarely satisfying collection. Only the opening *Gretchen am Spinnrade* brings a performance which one feels Baker could have intensified on repetition, but the rest could not be more treasurable. A very high proportion of favourite Schubert songs is included in the 1980 group. With a great singer treating each with loving, detailed care, the result is a charmer of a recital. The very first item, Dame Janet's

strongly characterized reading of *Die Forelle*, makes it a fun song, and similarly Parsons' naughty, springing accompaniment to *An Sylvia* (echoed later by the singer) gives a twinkle to a song that can easily be treated too seriously. One also remembers the ravishing *subito piano* for the second stanza of *An die Musik*. The later recording is of fine EMI vintage and catches the more mature voice naturally and with rather more presence than a decade earlier. It is a pity that, because the set is so economically priced, there are no translations, but this remains an unmissable reissue.

Lieder: *Abendstern; An die Entfernte; Atys; Auflösung; Ganymed; Der Musensohn; Nähe des Geliebten*

(B) (***) BBC (ADD) BBCB 8015-2. Pears, Britten –
BRITTEN: *On this Island*; WOLF: *7 Mörike Lieder* ***; (with ARNE: *Come Away death; Under the Greenwood Tree;* QUILTER: *O Mistress Mine;* WARLOCK: *Take, O Take Those Lips Away;* TIPPETT: *Come Unto These Yellow Sands* (***))

Britten as accompanist in Lieder regularly conveyed a sense of spontaneity and here – in a shrewdly chosen group of songs, not all well known – he seems almost to be improvising. The lightness and agility of his accompaniment in the best-known songs, *Der Musensohn*, is a marvel. Fine, sensitive singing from Pears in these 1969 performances.

Lieder, Vol. 1: *An den Mond; An die Musik; Auf dem Wasser zu singen; Du bist die Ruh; Erlkönig; Erster Verlust; Der Fischer; Fischerweise; Die Forelle; Ganymed; Geheimes; Frühlingsglaube; Heidenröslein; Im Frühling; Im Haine; Litanei auf das Fest Allerseelen; Der Musensohn; Nacht und Träume; Seimir gegrüst; Seligkeit; An Silvia; Wandrers Nachtlied I & II; Wehmut; Der Zwerg*

- (N) (M) *** EMI 4 76851-2. Bostridge, Drake

Few discs of favourite Schubert songs match this for sheer beauty. As in his prizewinning recording of *Die schöne Mullerin* for Hyperion, Ian Bostridge here not only sings with ravishing tenor tone but, with German words heightened, offers fresh revelation in even the best-known songs. So, with Julius Drake matching him in insight, *Die Forelle* ('The Trout'), opens the sequence in youthful eagerness, light and brisk, and lightness is also the keynote in such songs as *Heidenröslein*. The contrast is all the keener when in darker songs, such as *Wandrers Nachtlied*, Bostridge sings with such rapt intensity, the legato lines perfectly sustained on a mere thread of sound. A worthy inclusion among EMI's 'Great Artists of the Century' series.

Lieder, Vol. II: Goethe Lieder: *Am Flüsse; An die Entfernte; Geheimes; Schäfers Klagelied; Versunken; Wilkommen und Abschied; Maryrehoderlieder: Abendstern; Auf der Donau; Auflösung; Lied eines Schiffers; Nachtstuck; Lieder: Die Götter Griechenlands; An die Leier; Am See; Alinde; Wehmut; Uber Wildemann; Auf der Riesenkoppe; Sei mir gegrüsst; Dass sie hier gewesen; Geistertanz*
*** EMI 5 57141-2. Bostridge, Drake

This second volume of Schubert songs from Ian Bostridge and Julius Drake on EMI is divided neatly between songs to poems by Goethe and Mayrehoder, and miscellaneous songs, some of them favourites like *Die Götter Griechenlands* and *An die Leier*, but many less well known. In this wide-ranging selection Bostridge reveals his expanding mastery in the widest variety of expression, with the subtlest range of tone, and with a deliberate hardening of the characteristically sweet voice in some of the more dramatic songs, effectively so when the sense of strain adds to the intensity. In all this Drake is the perfect partner, ranging wide in his tonal palette too. Natural, beautifully balanced sound.

Lieder: *An die Musik; An Sylvia; Auf dem Wasser zu singen; Ave Maria; Du bist die Ruh'; Die Forelle; Ganymed; Gretchen am Spinnrade; Heidenröslein; Im Frühling; Die junge Nonne; Litanei; Mignon und der Harfner; Der Musensohn; Nacht und Träume; Sei mir gegrüsst; Seligkeit*

(BB) *** Regis RRC 1052. Lott, Johnson

At budget price, Felicity Lott's collection brings an ideal choice of songs for the general collector. With Graham Johnson the most imaginative accompanist, even the best-known songs emerge fresh and new, and gentle songs like *Litanei* are raptly beautiful.

Lieder: (i) *An die Musik; An Sylvia; Auf dem Wasser zu singen; Ganymed; Gretchen am Spinnrade; Im Frühling; Die junge Nonne; Das Lied im Grünen; Der Musensohn; Nachtviolen; Nähe des Geliebten; Wehmut;* (ii) *Der Einsame; Die Forelle; Heidenröslein; Der Jüngling an der Quelle; Liebe schwärmt auf allen Wegen; Liebhaber in allen Gestalten; Seligkeit; Litanei; Ungeduld; Die Vögel;* (iii) *An mein Klavier; Erlkönig*

☛ ✿ (M) (***) EMI mono/stereo 5 62754-2 [5 62773-2]. Schwarzkopf, with (i) Fischer; (ii) Moore; (iii) Parsons

Elisabeth Schwarzkopf had her doubts about taking many of the Schubert songs into her repertoire, most of which she felt were more suitable for the male voice; but the present survey includes some of those for which she felt a strong personal identification, including *Gretchen am Spinnrade* and the passionate *Die junge Nonne*. The main group here is drawn from an elysian selection she put on disc at the beginning of her recording career in partnership with Edwin Fischer, who was at the end of his. In spite of her reservations about lack of experience in this repertoire (in the early 1950s), she and Fischer create a magical partnership, full of intimate intercommunication, with even the simplest of songs inspiring intensely subtle expression from singer and pianist alike. Though Fischer's playing is not immaculate, he left few recordings more endearing than this, and Schwarzkopf's colouring of word and tone is masterly. So it is in the other songs now added to further extend this survey of her Schubertian career. Among the items accompanied by Gerald Moore, *Die Vögel* and *Liebhaber in allen Gestalten* date from 1948, *Litanei* and *Ungeduld* from 1954, and the others from 1965/6, including the two final songs accompanied by Geoffrey Parsons, of which *Erlkönig* was one of her favourites. With excellent transfers – the sound surprisingly consistent – and full texts and translations included, this collection makes an obvious choice for inclusion among EMI's 'Great Artists of the Century'.

Goethe Lieder: *An den Mond; An die Türen; An Mignon; Auf dem See; Erster verlust; Erlkönig; Der Fischer; Ganymed; Heidenröslein; Meeres Stille; Der Musensohn; Nachtgesang; Nahe des Gelibten; Prometheus; Rastlose Liebe; Schäfers Klaglied; Schwager Kronos; Versunken; Wandrers Nachtlied; Wer nie sein Brot mit Tränen ass; Wer sich der Einsamkeit ergibt*

☛ *** Decca 452 917-2. Goerne, Haefliger

Matthias Goerne here confirms his mastery as a Liedersinger, already revealed in his account of *Winterreise* and

other Schubert songs in Graham Johnson's collected edition on Hyperion. With Andreas Haefliger a deeply understanding accompanist – challenging as well as matching his partner – Goerne here tackles a beautiful sequence of Goethe settings, thrillingly powerful in *Prometheus*, youthfully exuberant in such a favourite as *Der Musensohn*, finding a rapt gravity rare in a young singer in such visionary songs as *Meeres Stille*. Even the understatement of his *Erlkönig* brings bonuses in extra beauty. Outstanding in every way.

Goethe Lieder: (i) *An den Mond; An schwager Kronos; Auf dem See; Erster Verlust; Ganymed; Gesänge des Harfners: Harfenspieler I, II & III; Jägers Abendlied; Meeres Stille; Der Musensohn; Prometheus; Wandrers Nachtlied I & II.* (ii) *Am Flusse; Erlkönig; Geheimes; Grenzen des Menschheit; Heidenröslein; Der König in Thule; Nähe des Geliebten; Rastlose Liebe; Wilkommen und Abscheid*

(M) *** DG (IMS) (ADD) 457 747-2. Fischer-Dieskau; (i) Demus; (ii) Moore

This reissued collection draws on three sets of recordings: Fischer-Dieskau's first stereo DG Goethe LP, recorded with Joerg Demus in 1960, and two subsequent groups with Gerald Moore dating from a decade later. Some of the very finest Goethe settings are here and Fischer-Dieskau is on top of his form, but the partnership with Demus is less than ideal. He proves a capable but not highly imaginative accompanist, although his artistry is not to be denied. But as for the singing, the spectrum of emotion takes on a new glow as each song begins. The two settings of *Wandrers Nachtlied* are particularly fine, as are the joyous *Der Musensohn* and the fiery *An schwager Kronos*. Needless to say the partnership with Gerald Moore is much more of a symbiosis, and these later performances are outstanding in every way. The recording too, is warmer and has a more pleasing ambience. A treasurable disc, just the same, well worthy of DG's Originals.

Lieder: *An den Mond* (2 versions); *Der Einsame; Erlkönig; Der Fischer; Ganymed; Im Abendrot; Die junge Nonne; Der Musensohn; Nachtstück; Nacht und Träume; Nachtviolen; Rastlose Liebe; Schäfers Klagelied; Die Sterne; Suleika I & II; Wandrers Nachtlied; Der Zwerg*

(M) *** CRD CRD 3464. Walker, Vignoles

Sarah Walker's début Lieder recital was made not long before she joined Graham Johnson for her contribution to Hyperion's Schubert Lieder Edition. Only *An den Mond* and *Erlkönig* are duplicated, and the CRD recital includes many favourites. Here she is accompanied by Roger Vignoles on a period piano of 1864. The attractive selection of songs, with many favourites, consistently draws warm, easily confident singing from her, full of charm, yet she is dramatic when required, as in *Erlkönig*. There she is not helped by the balance with the piano, which slightly favours the accompanist, masking the full intensity of her characterization, with power kept in reserve until the end. That contrasts beautifully with her easy-going lightness in such a song as *Der Einsame* and the poise of *Nacht und Träume*, with phrases sustained on a mere thread of sound. Despite the balance, words are clear thanks to the singer's fine diction and feeling for word-meaning. Roger Vignoles accompanies persuasively, full translations are included, and the playing-time is generous too: 74 minutes.

Goethe Lieder, Vol. 1: *An den Mond* (1st and 2nd versions); *An schwager Kronos; Bundeslied; Der Fischer; Ganymed; Geistes-Gruss; Gesang des Harfners* (1st, 2nd, and 3rd versions); *Der Gott und die Bajadere; Grenzen der Menschheit; Harfenspieler* (1st and 2nd versions); *Heidenröslein; Der König in Thule; Mahomets Gesang; Meeres Stille; Prometheus; Der Rattenfänger; Der Schatzgräber; Wandrers Nachtlied* (1st and 2nd versions)

(BB) *** Naxos 8.554665. Bästlein, Laux

This fine Goethe collection is one of the first of a proposed series of Schubert Lieder discs masterminded for Naxos by the pianists Stefan Laux and Ulrich Eisenlohr. They aim to choose only German-speaking singers from the younger generation, and Ulf Bästlein certainly qualifies. His is a firm, warm baritone, which he uses most sensitively, shading tone and dynamic with fine feeling for words, as in his rapt account of *Meeres Stille* ('Becalmed'). Though the selection includes the popular favourite *Heidenröslein*, and such masterly songs as *An den Mond* (both settings) and *Ganymed*, the choice is imaginative, and it is good to have such multiple settings of the same words, sensitively contrasted by singer and pianist. Unlike many bargain discs of Lieder, this offers full texts and translations.

Lieder: *An die Entfernte; Auf dem Wasser zu singen; Du bist die Ruh'; Erlkönig; Die Forelle; Heidenröslein; Das Heimweh; Der Jüngling an der Quelle; Der Jüngling und der Tod; Das Lied im Grünen; Litanei auf das Fest Allerseelen; Nachtgesang; Der Schiffer; Sei mir gegrüsst!; Ständchen; Der Strom; Der Tod und das Mädchen; Der Wanderer; Der Winterabend; Das Zügenglöcklein; Der zürnende Barde*

☛ (BB) *** EMI Encore (ADD) 5 74754-2. Fischer-Dieskau, Moore

EMI's Encore collection of vintage Fischer-Dieskau recordings makes an ideal sampler of favourite Schubert songs. Early in his career the voice was at its freshest and most beautiful and, though the comparatively early stereo recording is less atmospheric than on later issues, there is a face-to-face immediacy which with such an artist could not be more revealing. With Gerald Moore at the piano this is a supreme bargain among Schubert Lieder recitals.

Lieder: (i) *An die Freunde; Auf der Donau; Aus Heliopolis; Fischerweise; Freiwilliges Versinken; Gruppe aus dem Tartarus;* (ii) *Der Hirt auf dem Felsen;* (i) *Prometheus; Der Strom; Der Wanderer; Der Wanderer an den Mond*

(B) *** BBC (ADD) BBCB 8011-2. (i) Fischer-Dieskau; (ii) Harper, King, Britten – WOLF: 3 *Christmas Songs;* 3 *Michelangelo Lieder* ***

Fischer-Dieskau has rarely if ever been more inspired in his recordings of Schubert than here, in live performances given with Britten at the Snape Maltings in 1972 – the last year Britten was able to take an active part in the Aldeburgh Festival. The great baritone, then at his peak, was plainly inspired by the quality of his accompanist's playing, and the selection of songs, well contrasted, brings together an attractive mixture of rare and well known. Similarly, in the *Shepherd on the Rock*, with Thea King producing honeyed tone in the clarinet obbligato, the magnetism is irresistible. The Wolf songs from Pears and Shirley-Quirk make an attractive bonus.

Lieder: *An die Laute; An die Leier; An die Musik; An Silvia; Auf der Bruck; Du bist die Ruh'; Erlkönig; Das Fischermädchen; Die Forelle; Ganymed; Gruppe aus dem Tartarus; Heidenröslein; Lachen und Weinen; Litanei auf das Fest; Meeres Stille; Der Musensohn; Rastlose Liebe;*

Schäfers Klagelied; Ständchen; Die Taubenpost; Der Tod und das Mädchen; Der Wanderer; Wandrers Nachtlied

*** DG 445 294-2. Terfel, Martineau

Bryn Terfel's DG disc of Schubert was one of his first recordings to confirm his exceptional gift of projecting his magnetic personality with keen intensity, in Lieder, not just in opera. Terfel emerges as a positive artist, giving strikingly individual and imaginative readings of these 23 favourite songs. As you immediately realize in three favourite songs common to both collections, *Heidenröslein, An Silvia* and *Du bist die Ruh*, Terfel is daring in confronting you face to face, very much as the young Fischer-Dieskau did, using the widest range of dynamic and tone. You might argue that Terfel's characterization of the different characters in *Erlkönig* is too extreme, but it is a measure of his magnetism that the result is so dramatically compelling. Full, firm sound.

An die Laute; An die Musik; An Silvia; Der Einsame; Im Abendrot; Liebhaber in allen Gestalten; Lied eines Schiffers an die Dioskurern; Der Musensohn; Ständchen (Leise flehen meine Lieder)

(M) *** DG (ADD) 449 747-2. Wunderlich, Giesen –
BEETHOVEN: *Lieder;* SCHUMANN: *Dichterliebe* ***

Few tenors have matched the young Wunderlich in the freshness and golden bloom of the voice. The open manner could not be more appealing here in glowing performances, well coupled with other fine examples of this sadly short-lived artist's work. A very apt addition to DG's series of 'Legendary Performances'.

Goethe Lieder: *An Schwager Kronos; Erlkönig; Heidenröslein; Jägers Abendlied; Der König in Thule; Der Musensohn; Rastlose Liebe; Wandrers Nachtlied I & II.* Other Lieder: *An Silvia; Auf dem Wasser zu singen; Du bist die Ruh'; Der Einsame; Die Forelle; Im Abendrot; Lachen und Weinen; Der Lindenbaum; Sei mir gegrüsst; Seligkeit; Ständchen (2 versions); Der Wanderer*

☛ (M) *** DG Entrée (ADD) 474 173-2. Fischer-Dieskau, Moore

This superb collection makes the perfect entrée into the world of Schubertian song. Twenty-two items (67 minutes) with nine Goethe settings (including an unforgettable *Erlkönig*) and many lovely performances of top favourites: *Lachen und Weinen*, two different *Serenades, The Trout* and none more beautifully sung than *Der Lindenbaum*. The recordings come from 1969 and 1970 and throughout Gerald Moore is a superb partner. Texts and translations are included. Very highly recommended.

'Favourite Lieder': *An Sylvia; Auf der Bruck; Bei dir allein; Du bist die Ruh'; Der Einsame; Freiwilliges Versinken; Gondelfahrer; Die Götter Griechenlands; Gruppe aus dem Tartarus; Heidenröslein; Himmelsfunken; Im Haine; Der Jüngling an der Quelle; Lied eines Schiffers; Nachtviolen; Prometheus; Ständchen; Die Sterne; Waldesnacht; Der Wanderer an den Mond*

(B) *** CfP 585 6182. Keenlyside, Martineau

The velvety beauty of Simon Keenlyside's cleanly focused baritone goes with fresh, thoughtful readings of 20 favourite songs, perfectly judged, with ever-sensitive accompaniment from Malcolm Martineau. Now at bargain price, this disc makes another outstanding Schubert Lieder recommendation, which includes one or two unusual songs among many favourites.

Lieder: *Auf dem Wasser zu singen; Ave Maria; Die Forelle; Du bist die Ruh; Ganymed; Gretchen am Spinnrade; Gretchens Bitte; Heidenröslein; Heiss mich nicht reden;* (i) *Der Hirt auf dem Felsen. Im Abendrot; Kennst du das Land; Liebhaber in allen Gestalten; Nahe des Geliebten; Nur wer die Sehnsucht kennt; So lasst mich scheinen; Ständchen*

(M) *** Warner Elatus 0927 46741-2. Bonney, Parsons; (i) with Kam

Barbara Bonney here is at her freshest, and who better to accompany her than Geoffrey Parsons? The generous programme (well over an hour) includes many firm favourites, and Bonney not only sings with much beauty of tone and a flowing Schubertian line but with keen concern for word-meanings. Songs like *Die Forelle, Auf dem Wasser zu singen* and the lovely *So lasst mich scheinen* sound especially fresh; and it is always good to have *Der Hirt auf dem Felsen* ('The shepherd on the rock') with its fluid obbligato clarinet (here the persuasive Sharon Kam). Spontaneous-sounding expressiveness in a natural partnership between fine artists.

Auf der Riesenkoppe; Der blinde Knabe; Du bist die Ruh'; Die Forelle; Das Geheimnis; Gretchen am Spinnrade; Heidenröslein; (i) *Der Hirt auf dem Felsen; Der König in Thule; La pastorella; Schwanengesang; Die Wehmut*

(B) **(*) CfP (ADD) 575 7732 (2) M. Price, Lockhart; (i) with Brymer – (with LISZT; TCHAIKOVSKY: *Songs* ***) SCHUMANN: *Frauenliebe und Leben* **(*))

Dame Margaret Price was in fine voice when she made this record in 1971. Her singing of Schubert is full-throated in style, although she successfully fines down the tone for a song like *Du bist die Ruh.* The opening recitative of *Auf der Riesenkoppe* takes us straight into the opera house; *La pastorella* (a charming song) reminds us of Rossini, and in *The Shepherd on the Rock* the sheer breadth of the singing tends to dwarf even Jack Brymer's beguiling clarinet obbligato. *Die Forelle* is very attractively done, and *Der König in Thule* is serenely beautiful. *Heidenröslein* has a simple, affecting charm and in *Gretchen am Spinnrade* the soaring line is sensitively controlled, but Price's involvement is obvious. James Lockhart accompanies most sensitively but, maybe because of the recording balance, like Brymer he tends to be dwarfed by the voice. No translations are provided, but the notes give a synopsis of each song. This now comes on a two-disc set, coupled with Schumann's *Frauenliebe und Leben* and two well-chosen groups of songs by Tchaikovsky and Liszt, recorded two years later.

Auf dem Strom

(N) (BB) *** Naxos 8.557471. Kuhmeier, Tomboeck, Inui – BEETHOVEN: *Horn Sonata;* BRAHMS: *Horn Trio;* SCHUMANN: *Adagio and Allegro* ***

The Schubert song, *Auf dem Strom* ('*Upon the River*'), with its horn obbligato is parallel with another late song, *The Shepherd on the Rock,* with its clarinet obbligato. The pure, fresh-toned soprano, Genia Kuhmeier, matches the ripe-toned horn-player, Wolfgang Tomboeck, in the warmth and imagination of her phrasing. A valuable supplement to the instrumental works illustrating the Vienna horn.

Lieder: *Ave Maria (Ellens Gesang 3); Die Allmacht: An die Musik; Auf dem Wasser zu singen; Erlkönig; Fischerweise; Die Forelle; Frühlingsglaube; Ganymed; Gretchen am*

Spinnrade; (i) *Der Hirt auf dem Felsen. Lachen und Weinen; Litanei auf das Fest Allerseelen; Der Musensohn; Der Tod und das Mädchen*

(N) (M) *** EMI (ADD) 5 62896-2 [5 62897-2]. Ludwig, Parsons or Moore; (i) with de Peyer

Most of these songs, including some of Schubert's most justly popular, come from a 1959 recital with Geoffrey Parsons, who accompanies with great tact and sensitivity, although Gerald Moore takes his place sympathetically in *Die Allmacht* and *Fischerweise.* Christa Ludwig presents them with disarming dedication and to hear the hackneyed *Ave Maria* sung like this is to realize afresh the beauty which all too often is jellied over with sentiment. Perhaps at times the approach is too simple, not sufficiently characterized in *Der Erlkönig;* but when it comes to *Death and the Maiden* and *Gretchen am Spinnrade,* the depth of understanding and sympathy is unmistakable. Gervase de Peyer provides an engaging clarinet obbligato in *The Shepherd on the Rock* and in *Musensohn,* most exuberant of Schubert songs, the bouncing jollity is unbounded. With truthful recording this takes its place among EMI's 'Great Recordings of the Century'.

Italian songs: *Da quel sembiante appresi; Guarda, che bianca luna; Io vuo'cantar di Cadmo; Mi batte il cor!; Mio ben ricordati; Non t'accostar all'urna; La pastorella; Pensa, che questo istante; Se dall'Etra; Vedi quanto adoro ancora ingrato!*

*** Decca 440 297-2. Bartoli, Schiff – BEETHOVEN: *Che fa il mio bene?* etc.; HAYDN: *Arianna a Naxos;* MOZART: *Ridente la calma* ***

Bartoli is at her finest here in *Dido's lament,* but the other rare songs are also fresh and enjoyable, helped by sensitive accompaniments from András Schiff.

Song-cycles

Die schöne Müllerin (song-cycle), *D.795* (see also above, under Graham Johnson Schubert Lieder Edition, Vol. 25)

*** DG (ADD) (IMS) 415 186-2. Fischer-Dieskau, Moore

(M) *** Decca 475 211-2. Schreier, Schiff

(N) (B) *** CfP (ADD) 586 1812 (2). Ian & Jennifer Partridge – SCHUMANN: *Dichterliebe; Liederkreis* ***

*** Cap. 10 082. Protschka, Deutsch

(B) *** EMI Début 5 72824-2. Henschel, Schwinghammer

Fischer-Dieskau's classic 1972 version on DG remains among the very finest ever recorded, combining as it does his developed sense of drama and story-telling, his mature feeling for detail and yet spontaneity too, helped by the searching accompaniment of Gerald Moore. It is a performance with premonitions of *Winterreise.*

Rarely has a pianist played Schubert accompaniments with such individuality as András Schiff in this 1991 *Gramophone* award-winning performance of *Die schöne Müllerin.* He brings new illumination in almost every phrase, so that in *Wohin?* he transforms the accompaniment into an impressionistic fantasy on the flowing stream, and his rhythmic pointing regularly leads the ear on, completely avoiding any sense of sameness in the strophic songs. Peter Schreier, here challenged to produce his most glowing tone, matches his partner with his brightly detailed singing, transcending even his earlier versions of this favourite cycle, always conveying his response so vividly that one clearly registers his changes of vocal expresion from line to line. At times the voice develops a throaty snarl, purposely so for dramatic reasons. Outstandingly warm and well-balanced recording makes this mid-priced reissue very desirable.

Ian Partridge's is an exceptionally fresh and urgent account. Rarely has the dynamic quality of the cycle been so effectively conveyed, rising to an emotional climax at the end of the first half with the song *Mein'*, expressing the poet's ill-founded joy, welling up infectiously. Partridge's subtle and beautiful range of tone is a constant delight, and he is most imaginatively accompanied by his sister, Jennifer. An outstanding bargain coupling that should win many new friends for Lieder, although there are no texts and translations.

Josef Protschka gives an intensely virile, almost operatic reading, which is made the more youthful-sounding in the original keys for high voice. As recorded, the voice, often beautiful with heroic timbres, sometimes acquires a hint of stridency, but the positive power and individuality of the performance make it consistently compelling, with all the anguish behind these songs caught intensely. The timbre of the Bösendorfer piano adds to the performance's distinctiveness, well if rather reverberantly recorded.

The clear-toned young baritone, Dietrich Henschel, one of the most promising of German baritones today, on an EMI Début disc consistently finds freshness and intensity in an attractively spontaneous-sounding reading, with words vividly projected, matching his success in Gluck's *Alceste* in Gardiner's Philips recording. He is greatly helped by the sensitive, responsive accompanist, Fritz Schwinghammer.

Die schöne Müllerin, D.795 (with spoken Prologue & Epilogue), D.795

(M) *(**) EMI 5 66907-2 [566959]. Fischer-Dieskau, Moore

EMI have understandably chosen Fischer-Dieskau's 1961 recording of *Die schöne Müllerin* (which includes spoken versions in German of the *Prologue* and *Epilogue*) for their 'Great Recordings of the Century' series. But alas all their current remastering skill has not been able to improve the sound: the voice remains unpleasingly edgy. The later DG recording (also with Gerald Moore) remains far preferable.

Die schöne Müllerin; An die Musik; Du bist die Ruh; Erlkönig; Heidenröslein; Der Musensohn

☛─ ✿ (M) *** DG (ADD) 453 676-2. Fischer-Dieskau, Moore

Though Fischer-Dieskau had made several earlier recordings, this is no mere repeat of previous triumphs, now combining his developed sense of drama and story-telling, his mature feeling for detail and yet spontaneity too, helped by the searching accompaniment of Gerald Moore. It is a performance with premonitions of *Winterreise*. With extra Lieder added to fill out the recital, this is one of the most cherishable of Fischer-Dieskau's many superb Schubert CDs.

Die schöne Müllerin, D.795; Winterreise, D.911

(B) *** EMI double forte 5 74855-2 (2). Bär, Parsons

Die schöne Müllerin was the first of the cycles which Olaf Bär recorded in 1986 in Dresden, with the voice fresher and more velvety than later, especially when the digital recording is so flattering to Bär's warmly beautiful lyrical flow. In *Winterreise*, recorded two years later, again with Geoffrey Parsons a masterful accompanist, Bär finds a winning beauty of line and tone in singing which is both deeply reflective and strongly dramatic. If without quite the power of Fischer-Dieskau's poetic projection, or the sheer intensity of Britten

and Pears, these are most rewarding performances in their own right.

Schwanengesang, D.957

*** Amphion/Priory (ADD) PHI CD157. Hemsley, Wilde

Schwanengesang, D.957; Lieder: Am Bach in Frühling; An die Musik; Geheimes; Gruppe aus dem Tartarus; Im Abendrot; Im Frühling; Meeresstille; Sei mir gegrüsst; Wandrers Nachtlied I & II

(M) (***) EMI mono 5 65196-2. Hotter, Moore

As in his darkly searching account of *Winterreise*, also recorded in mono with Gerald Moore in the 1950s, this Schubert collection coupling *Schwanengesang* with other favourite songs reveals Hotter at his peak. The voice as recorded may not always be beautiful, but the gravity and intensity of the singing reveal a master Lieder-singer, as commanding here as in his Wagner interpretations.

Thomas Hemsley spent much of his career in opera houses in Germany and made few commercial Lieder records. This *Schwanengesang* from 1976 derives from live performances with David Wilde and serves as a welcome reminder of the artistry of this master singer.

Schwanengesang; 4 Seidl Lieder: Am Fenster; Bei dir allein; Die Taubenpost; Der Wanderer an den Mond

(N) (M) *** Decca 476 7103. Schreier, Schiff

Peter Schreier's voice may no longer be beautiful under pressure, but the bloom on this Decca recording is kind to him, and the range of tone and inflexion over word-meaning make this one of the most compelling recordings ever of *Schwanengesang*; it is not surprising that the disc won the *Gramophone* Solo Vocal Award in 1990. Enhancing the singing are the discreet but highly individual and responsive accompaniments of András Schiff. Schreier makes up a generous CD length by including not just the 14 songs published together as *Schwanengesang*, but four more, also from the last three years of Schubert's life. The recording is vividly real, bringing out Schreier's confidential directness in communicating, his mastery in conveying facial expression as he sings. For sample, try his chillingly intense account of *Der Doppelgänger*.

Schwanengesang; 5 Lieder: Am Fennster; Herbst; Sehnsucht; Der Wanderer an den Mond; Wiegenlied, D.867

☛─ ✿ (M) *** Decca 474 535-2. Fassbaender, Reimann

Winner of the *Gramophone* Solo Vocal Award in 1992, Brigitte Fassbaender's performance of *Schwanengesang* remains uniquely distinctive and now makes a welcome reissue at mid-price.

Winterreise (song-cycle), D.911

*** Warner NVC Arts **DVD** 8573 83780-2. Bostridge, Drake (Producer: Gordon Baskerville. V/D: David Alden)

(*) Arthaus **DVD 100 258. Hynninen, Gothoni (V/D: Julie Didier)

*** DG 415 187-2. Fischer-Dieskau, Moore

(N) *** EMI 5 57790-2. Bostridge, Andsnes

*** Ph. 464 739-2. Fischer-Dieskau, Brendel

(M) *** EMI (ADD) 5 62784-2 [5 62787-2]. Fischer-Dieskau, Moore

☛─ (M) *** DG 447 421-2. Fischer-Dieskau, Demus

✿ (M) *** Decca (ADD) 466 382-2. Pears, Britten

*** Hyp. CDJ 33030. Goerne, Johnson

(BB) *** EMI Encore 5 74988-2. Fassbaender, Reimann

(M) (***) EMI mono 5 66985-2 [5 67002]. Hotter, Moore

(M) (**(*)) EMI mono 5 67927-2 [5 67928-2].
  Fischer-Dieskau, Moore

(i; ii) *Winterreise, D.911;* (ii) *Piano Sonata 15 in C, D.840*

(M) *** Ph. 475 900-2 (2). (i) Schreier; (ii) S. Richter

These two admirably sung DVD recordings of Schubert's *Winterreise* demonstrate only too well the difficulties of 'staging' an extended song-cycle, however imaginative the producer and director. Ian Bostridge's revelatory way with Schubert is already familiar in two outstanding collections of favourite Lieder on EMI, and his youthfully radiant and eagerly detailed performance of *Die schöne Müllerin* is a key issue in Graham Johnson's Schubert Lieder Collection on Hyperion (CDJ 33025). His account of *Winterreise*, with a hardly less fine partner in Julius Drake, brings the same beautiful voice and even greater imaginative detail. The performance also has an extraordinarily powerful atmosphere – it is imbued with an air of desolation which we can see in his gaunt face as well as hear in his voice. David Alden's setting is an empty room, within which Bostridge, in his dark coat, can freely move about. There are occasional bursts of visual histrionics, which not all will take to, but on the whole the production works well, and the performance itself is gripping throughout, especially as the recording is so vivid. An additional documentary, rather facetiously titled 'Over the Top with Franz', details the background to the recording and filming and the artistic conflicts generated.

Jorma Hynninen and Ralf Gothoni recorded their fine account of *Winterreise* in 1994 at the Särestöniemi Museum in Finnish Lapland. The artist Reidar Särestöniemi (1925–81) designed the building so that he could draw inspiration in both winter and summer from the beauties of the Finnish countryside. The performance takes place before a small audience, and apart from the two artists themselves, we see some of Särestöniemi's impressions of Finnish landscape as well as nature itself. The visual side of the production is handled with both taste and imagination, and the musical balance is well focused and natural. Hynninen and his admirable partner convey the poignancy of this music to splendid effect, although some may well find that the pauses between each song could have been fractionally longer.

In some ways Ian Bostridge's latest (2004) account of *Winterreise* does not quite match his earlier DVD account in conveying the full underlying desolation of Schubert's masterly cycle. Here Bostridge, though not less sensitive, is more direct, more positive in projection, less bleak in feeling. Yet even so, it is a highly involving performance and is continually lifted by Leif Ove Andsnes's imaginative and atmospheric accompaniments. The delightful lilt at the opening of *Frülingstraume*, the galloping *Post*, and the very touching presentation of *Das Wirthaus* are matched by the simplicity of the penultimate *Die Nebensonnen*, and the delicate portrayal of *Der Leiermann*, to which Bostridge responds so tenderly. The recording is beautifully balanced, and this remains an unforgettable performance.

The effect, with Jorma Hynninen's warm baritone, is less bleak than with Bostridge (his richly resonant voice is especially telling in *Der Lindenbaum*), and it is anger, rather than desolation that registers so vividly in Hynninen's eyes and facial muscles. He is very well accompanied by Ralf Gothoni and the two artists give a moving performance, but are in the last resort less affecting than Bostridge and Drake, who leave an unforgettable impression with their deeply touching reading of that haunting final portrait of *Der Leiermann*.

In the early 1970s Dietrich Fischer-Dieskau's voice was still at its freshest, yet the singer had deepened and intensified his understanding of this greatest of song-cycles to a degree where his finely detailed and thoughtful interpretation sounded totally spontaneous, and this DG version is now freshened on CD. However on Philips, the collaboration of Fischer-Dieskau with one of today's great Schubert pianists, Alfred Brendel, brings endless illumination in the interplay and challenge between singer and pianist, magnetic from first to last. With incidental flaws, this may not be the definitive Fischer-Dieskau reading, but in many ways it is the deepest and most moving he has ever given. This has been reissued as one of Philips's '50 Great Recordings' at mid-price.

For their reissue in the 'Great Artists of the Century' series EMI have chosen Dietrich Fischer-Dieskau's 1962 *Winterreise*, which combines direct power of expression with rich vocal power. A great performance which has the virtue of striking freshness from singer and pianist alike. The recording scarcely shows its age. A full text and translation are included.

There are those who regard Fischer-Dieskau's third recording of *Winterreise* as the finest of all, such is the peak of beauty and tonal expressiveness that the voice had achieved in the mid-1960s, and the poetic restraint of Jörg Demus's accompaniment. The recording still sounds well, and as a mid-price reissue in DG's Legendary Recordings series it certainly makes an excellent alternative recommendation.

What is so striking about Pears's performance is its intensity. One continually has the sense of a live occasion and, next to it, even Fischer-Dieskau's beautifully wrought singing sounds too easy. As for Britten, he re-creates the music, sometimes with a fair freedom from Schubert's markings, but always with scrupulous concern for the overall musical shaping and sense of atmosphere. The sprung rhythm of *Gefror'ne Tränen* is magical in creating the impression of frozen teardrops falling, and almost every song brings similar magic. The recording and the CD transfer are exceptionally successful in bringing a sense of presence and realism, and this is certainly a proper candidate for reissue on Decca's Legends label.

Recorded live in the newly restored Semper Opera House in Dresden just after its reopening in February 1985, Peter Schreier's is an inspired version of *Winterreise*: dramatic, outstandingly beautiful and profoundly searching in its expression, helped by magnetic, highly individual accompaniments from Richter, a master of Schubert. Speeds are not always conventional, indeed they are sometimes extreme – but this only adds to the vivid communication which throughout conveys the inspiration of the moment. Rarely has the agonized intensity of the last two songs been conveyed so movingly on record, the more compellingly when the atmosphere of a live occasion is so realistically captured; it is a small price to pay that the winter audience makes so many bronchial contributions. A more serious snag is that the cycle (which is usually contained on a single CD) spreads over to a second, thanks to the slow speeds. It is surprising that for this reissue celebrating a Solo Vocal Award by the *Gramophone* in 1986, the recording was not remastered to fit on a single disc – for with modern technology that would almost certainly be possible.

Though the Schubert *C major Sonata* brings a comparably inspired performance from Richter (recorded live at Leverkusen in (then) West Germany in December 1979), not everyone will want the coupling. The sound in the *Sonata* recording – though, like the song-cycle, it has striking presence – is drier but is less troubled by audience noise.

Matthias Goerne's outstanding performance is discussed above as Volume 30 of Graham Johnson's Schubert Lieder Edition and is among the most magnetically perceptive of recent versions.

Brigitte Fassbaender gives a fresh, boyishly eager reading of *Winterreise*, marked by a vivid and wide range of expression; she demonstrates triumphantly why a woman's voice can bring special illumination to this cycle, sympathetically underlining the drama behind the tragic poet's journey rather than the more meditative qualities. Reimann, at times a wilful accompanist, is nevertheless spontaneous-sounding, matching the singer. A remarkable bargain Encore reissue.

Hans Hotter's 1954 mono recording of *Winterreise* has been reissued as one of EMI's 'Great Recordings of the Century'. It brings an exceptionally dark, even sepulchral performance, lightened by the imagination of Gerald Moore's accompaniment. Hotter scales down his great Wagnerian baritone so that only occasionally is the tone gritty. His concern for detail brings many moments of illumination, but the lack of animation makes this an unrelievedly depressing view.

Curiously, EMI have also chosen Dietrich Fischer-Dieskau's 1955 *Winterreise* for inclusion among their 'Great Recordings of the Century'. It is certainly a fine performance, and the recording, lovingly remastered, sounds admirably real and fresh. But his later versions (for DG and Philips as well as EMI) are even more revelatory.

Church music

Auguste jam coelestium, D.488; 6 Antophonen zu Palmsonntag, D.696; Deutsche Messe, D.872; Graduale in C, D.184; Hymnus an den heiligen Geist, D.964; Kyries: in D min., D.31; B flat, D.45; D min., D.49; F, D.66. Lazarus, D.689; Magnificat in D, D.486; Masses: 1 in F, D.105; 2 in G, D.167; 3 in B flat, D.324; 4 in C, D.452; 5 in A flat, D.678; 6 in E flat, D.950. Offertoriums: (Salve Regina) in F, D.223; (Salve Regina) in A, D.676; (Totus in corde) in C, D.136; (Tres sunt) in A min., D.181; in B flat, D.963. Psalms: 23, D.706; 92, D.953. Salve Reginas: in B flat, D.106, D.379 & D.386; in A, D.676. Stabat Maters: in G min., D.175; in F, D.383. Tantum ergos: in C, D.461, D.462, D.739 & D.811; in D, D.750; in E flat, D.962

(N) (BB) *** EMI (ADD/DDD) 5 87011-2 (7). Popp, Donath, Rüggerberg, Venuti, Hautermann, Falk, Fassbaender, Greindle-Rosner, Dallapozza, Araiza, Protschka, Tear, Lika, Fischer-Dieskau, Schreier, Capella Bavariae, Bav. R. Ch. & SO, Sawallisch

Sawallisch's highly distinguished survey of Schubert's church music – one of the most impressive gramophone achievements of this composer's music – was recorded in the late 1970s and early 1980s, and is now available in one bargain box set for the first time. The performances of the *Masses* are warm and understanding, even if, in his masterpiece in this form, the *Mass in E flat*, the chorus isn't always flawless. The earlier Mass settings bring superb, lively inspiration, not to mention the separate *Kyries* and *Salve Reginas*. Much of this glorious music is rare, but little or none of it is inconsequential. Even some of the shortest items – such as the six tiny *Antiphons*, allegedly written in half an hour – have magic and originality in them. Plainer, but still glowing with Schubertian joy, is the so-called *Deutsche Messe*. The *Magnificat*, too, is a strongly characterized setting, and even the settings of St Thomas Aquinas's *Tantum ergo* have their charm. There are many other surprises. The lovely setting of the *Offertorium in C (Totus in corde)* is for soprano, clarinet and orchestra, with

the vocal and instrumental lines intertwining delectably, while the no less appealing *Auguste jam coelestium* is a soprano–tenor duet. The *Salve Regina in C*, D.811, is written for four male voices, *a cappella*, and they again contribute to the performance of *Psalm 23*, where Sawallisch provides a piano accompaniment. Schubert left the religious drama *Lazarus* unfinished and, though no more dramatic than his operas, it contains much delightful music. Some of it is as touching as the finest Schubert, while other sections are little short of inspired; there are some thoroughly characteristic harmonic colourings and some powerful writing for trombones. With Robert Tear in the name-role, Helen Donath as Maria, Lucia Popp as Jemima, Maria Venuti as Martha, Joseph Protschka as Nathanael and Fischer-Dieskau as Simon, it is very strongly cast, and the performance is splendid; indeed, the singing throughout this set is outstanding from chorus and soloists alike, and the recordings, made in the Munich Hercules Hall, are warm and well balanced, adding to one's pleasure. An outstanding bargain.

Magnificat, D.486; Offertorium in B flat, D.963 (Intende voci)

*** Teldec 3984 26094-2. Oelze, von Magnus, Lippert, Finley, Arnold Schoenberg Ch., VCM, Harnoncourt – HAYDN: *Mass 13 in B flat: Schöpfungsmesse* ***

Harnoncourt's period performances, set in a warm church acoustic, were recorded live, like the Haydn Mass with which they are coupled, sounding similarly fresh and new. The *Magnificat* is relatively well known, with Christiane Oelze ravishingly beautiful in the central *Deposuit* section. By contrast the offertorium *Intende voci* for tenor soloist, choir and orchestra, written in 1828 within weeks of the composer's death, is surprisingly a rarity. Though the formalized style harks back to Haydn and Mozart, the gravity of the inspiration is clear. The recording is warmly atmospheric, even if the balance of the choir, slightly backward, prevents it from having quite the impact its incisive singing deserves. An unexpected coupling, but an illuminating one.

Masses 1 in F, D.105; 2 in G, D.167

*** Sony SK 68247. Nader, Puchegger, Leskovich, Hering, Azesberger, Van der Kamp, V. Boys' Ch., Ch. Viennensis, OAE, Bruno Weil

Masses 3 in B flat, D. 324; 4 in C, D. 452

*** Sony SK 68248. Nader, Puchegger, Leskovich, Hering, Van der Kamp, V. Boys' Ch. Viennensis, OAE, Weil

Bruno Weil draws incandescent performances of Schubert's *Masses* from his fine team, helped by sound that is clearer and more detailed than on direct rival recordings. The combination of Viennese choirs – with the trebles of the Vienna Boys' Choir outstandingly full and fresh – and of a British period orchestra works superbly, making one appreciate, even more than with the Sawallisch versions, how seriously this area of Schubert's œuvre has been underappreciated. In the earlier *Masses* the presence of boys adds to the impression of liturgical performances, fresh and dedicated. The one snag is the relatively short measure, but for such music-making that is relatively unimportant. As ever, he draws inspired playing and singing from his Austro-British team, with the bright, full treble sound of the Vienna Boys cleanly set against the period instruments of the OAE, both beautifully balanced in a recording with plenty of bloom on the sound, yet with good detail.

Masses (i–iv) *4 in C, D.452;* (ii; iv–vi) *5; 6.* (iii; vii)
Offertorium, D.963; (i–ii; iv; vii) *Tantum ergo, D.962*
⚏ (B) *** EMI double forte ADD/DDD 5 73365-2 (2). (i)
  Popp; (ii) Fassbaender; (iii) Dallapozza; (iv)
  Fischer-Dieskau; (v) Donath; (vi) Araiza; (vii) Schreier; Bav.
  R. Ch. & SO, Sawallisch

This inexpensive reissue from Sawallisch's excellent choral
series combines three settings of the Mass including the two
finest, *in A flat* and the masterly work *in E flat*; while the
Tantum ergo (*in C*) also undoubtedly has its charm. These
performances have stood the test of time, containing some
outstanding singing from soloists and chorus, although the
latter is not flawless in D.950. Sawallisch proves to be a
warmly understanding Schubertian and the recordings are
both vivid and atmospheric.

Masses 5 in A flat, D.678; 6 in E flat, D. 950
(B) *** Ph. Duo (ADD) 473 892-2 (2). Donath, Springer,
  Schreier, Rotzsch, Adam, Leipzig R. Ch., Dresden State O,
  Sawallisch

Sawallisch's glorious Philips recordings from 1971 have
remained submerged in the catalogue by his EMI versions,
which were made in the 1980s. Yet the earlier Dresden sound
is first class: spacious, with plenty of depth and a very good
overall balance. The conductor has chosen a superb team of
soloists, as is immediately apparent in their contribution to
the exultant *Gloria* of the *A flat Mass*, after the radiantly
serene opening *Kyrie*. The Leipzig Radio Chorus too makes a
thrillingly ardent contribution in the *Sanctus* and the soloists
return in the celestial *Benedictus* and *Agnus Dei*, where they
are led by Helen Donath who sings very beautifully. The
choral singing in the *Gloria* of the *E flat Mass* is even more
incisive, and equally impressive here is the dramatic contribution of the three orchestral trombones. The *Sanctus* is as
resplendent as in the earlier work, but the *Benedictus* is
graver, and the brass return to lead the powerfully solemn
and extended *Agnus Dei*, which is so forward looking in its
style and ends the work so movingly. The body of sound in
these performances, the use of women's voices and the gloriously full-textured Dresden Staatskapellen do not mean that
detail is obscured or that there is a lack of freshness, and
undoubtedly Sawallisch is at his most inspired throughout.
However the EMI double forte issue (see above) includes not
only the *C major Mass* but also the *Offertorium* and *Tantum
ergo.*

Mass 6 in E flat, D.950
*** BBC (ADD) BBCL 4029-2 (2) Scottish Festival Ch., New
  Philh. O, Giulini – VERDI: *Requiem* ***

Schubert's last and most ambitious setting of the Mass makes
a generous coupling for Giulini's inspired account of the
Verdi *Requiem*. It was recorded at the Edinburgh Festival in
1968 with radio sound remarkably free and full for a performance in the Usher Hall. As in the Verdi, Giulini directs a
dedicated performance, again with incandescent choral singing from the Scottish Festival Chorus.

OPERA

Alfonso und Estrella (complete)
*** Berlin Classics BC2156-2 (3). Schreier, Mathis, Prey,
  Adam, Fischer-Dieskau, Berlin R. Ch. & State Op. O,
  Suitner

It is strange that Schubert, whose feeling for words in lyric
poetry drew out emotions which have natural drama in
them, had little or no feeling for the stage. Had his operas
been produced, no doubt he would have learnt how to use
music more positively; as it is, this tale of royal intrigue in
medieval times never quite captures the listener as an opera
should. Even so, it contains a stream of delightful music,
Schubert at his most open and refreshing; under Suitner's
direction it here receives a sparkling performance, excellently
cast. Edith Mathis makes a sweet heroine, and Peter Schreier
sings radiantly, as if in an orchestrated *Schöne Müllerin*. The
reconciliation of the two principal male characters, Froila and
Mauregato, is most touching as sung by Fischer-Dieskau and
Prey. The recording is richly atmospheric and is splendidly
transferred to CD. A full translation is included.

Fierrabras (complete)
(M) *** DG 459 503-2 (2). Protschka, Mattila, Studer,
  Gambill, Hampson, Holl, Polgár, Schoenberg Ch., COE,
  Abbado

Schubert may have often let his musical imagination blossom
without considering the dramatic effect, but there are jewels
in plenty in this score. Many solos and duets develop into
delightful ensembles, and the influence of Beethoven's *Fidelio*
is very striking, with spoken melodrama and offstage fanfares
bringing obvious echoes. A recording is the ideal medium for
such buried treasure, and Abbado directs an electrifying
performance. Both tenors, Robert Gambill and Josef Protschka, are on the strenuous side, but have a fine feeling for
Schubertian melody. Cheryl Studer and Karita Mattila sing
ravishingly, and Thomas Hampson gives a noble performance as the knight, Roland. Only Robert Holl as King Karl
(Charlemagne) is unsteady at times. The sound is comfortably atmospheric, outstanding for a live recording. Now
reissued at mid-price this is even more attractive.

Rosamunde: Overture (Die Zauberharfe, D.644) &
Incidental Music, D.797 (complete)
*** DG 431 655-2. Von Otter, Ernst Senff Ch., COE, Abbado
(B) *** Australian Decca Eloquence (ADD) 466 677-2.
  Yachmi, Vienna State O Ch., VPO, Münchinger

Abbado and the COE give joyful performances of this magical incidental music. It is a revelation to hear the most
popular of the entr'actes played so gently: it is like a whispered meditation. Even with a slow speed and affectionate
phrasing, it yet avoids any feeling of being mannered. Glowing recording to match. Anne Sofie von Otter is an ideal
soloist.

Münchinger's performance of the delightful *Rosamunde*
music glows with an affectionate warmth and understanding
which places this as one of his very best records. Its unavail-
ability on CD until this Australian disc appeared is unaccountable: there is an unforced spontaneity, as well as
strength here, and the 1970s recording is rich and naturally
balanced. The vocal numbers are superbly done, and the VPO
is at its magnificent best. A real bargain.

Die Verschworenen (complete)
(M) *** CPO/EMI (ADD) 999 554-2. Moser, Fuchs,
  Dallapozza, Schary, Moll, Finke, Bav. R. Ch., Munich RO,
  Wallberg

Die Verschworenen ('The Conspirators') is a variant on the
old theme of Aristophanes' *Lysistrata*, with the wives of
returning crusaders withholding their favours from their

menfolk. Though the heroine's lovely minor-key *Romance* near the beginning with clarinet obbligato points to serious emotions, and there is a Weber-like storm sequence, this is predominantly light-hearted, with ensemble passages which for the Anglo-Saxon listener will recall Gilbert and Sullivan, as in the fourth number, a chorus in which men are set against women. Much the longest number is the extended finale, structured like a Mozart operatic finale and here, as in Schubert's other one-act operas, there are hints that he had studied Beethoven's *Fidelio*. In this very well-made recording there is no weak link in the Munich cast, with the bass, Kurt Moll, outstanding as Count Heribert. As in other issues in this CPO series of recordings originally made by EMI, there is no libretto but a good synopsis linked to the CD tracks.

Der vierjährige Posten (complete)
(M) *** CPO/EMI (ADD) 999 553-2. Donath, Schreier, Fischer-Dieskau, Brokmeier, Lenz, Bav. R. Ch. & O, Wallberg

Schubert wrote this one-act piece ('The Four-year Post') in 1815 at the age of eighteen. With little more than half an hour of music, including a substantial overture, its eight numbers have many characteristically Schubertian touches, not just in the flowing tunes but in foretastes of the *Rosamunde* music. Apart from the overture, the only extended number (and the only real aria) is the prayer of Kätchen, the heroine, which in its calm beauty seems to anticipate Agathe's aria, *Und ob die Volke*, in Weber's *Der Freischütz* of six years later. The cast in this recording, originally made by EMI-Electrola, is an outstanding one, with star singers forming a splendid team. Highly recommended, though the piece offers short measure for a whole disc. No libretto is provided, only a synopsis.

Die Zwillingsbrüder (complete)
(M) *** CPO/EMI (ADD) 999 556-2. Donath, Gedda, Moll, Fischer-Dieskau, Munich State Op. Ch., Bav. RSO, Sawallisch

Die Zwillingsbrüder ('The Twin Brothers'), completed in 1819, deftly tells the story of twin brothers, strikingly contrasted, both returning from serving in the army, the one a rough-diamond of a soldier, the other – thought to be dead – the devoted lover. Inevitably this leads to confusion, resolved only at the end in a conventional but winning way. When Fischer-Dieskau takes the roles of both twins – who never appear on stage together – the result is delightful, with Schubert inspired to sparkling music, and with the brothers' contrasting characters well conveyed in their respective arias. With Sawallisch drawing superb playing and singing from the whole team, this comes near to being an ideal performance, not just starrily cast but very well recorded.

Opera arias from Adrast; Alfonso und Estrella; Die Bürgschaft; Die Freunde von Salamanka; Der Graf von Gleichen; Des Teufels Lustschloss; Die Zwillingsbrüder
*** Hyp. CDA 67229. Widmer, Hungarian Nat. PO, Schultsz

This collection of arias from operas composed at various periods in Schubert's career points the contrast with his song-writing. Lively as these items are, with the two from the mature *Alfonso und Estrella* the most elaborate, they are generally less individual than his songs. Even so, there is much to enjoy, helped by the lively, characterful singing of the Swiss baritone Oliver Widmer, with sympathetic accompaniment from the Hungarian orchestra. Just occasionally one of the items will offer a magical orchestral effect, as in the

second of the *Alfonso und Estrella* excerpts, with airy harp arpeggios in 3/4 time, nearly but not quite a waltz song. The two contrasted arias from the comic *Die Zwillingsbrüder* ('The Twins'), are relatively well known, but most of the rest are rarities, some of them from operas not otherwise recorded. The collection is rounded off with five arias from the incomplete opera *Die Bürgschaft* ('The Bond'), four of them for the character Möros, one less serious for Dionysos, a comic tyrant like Mozart's Osmin in *Entführung*. Good characterization and clear recording.

SCHULHOFF, Erwin (1894–1942)

5 Pieces (for string quartet)
*** DG 469 066-2. Hagen Qt. – DVORAK: *String quartet 14;* KURTAG: *Hommage à Mihály András* ***

These five pieces are very slight indeed, witty and inventive but not the kind of music to which you would often want to return, even given the excellence of the performance and recording.

SCHULZ, Johann Abraham (1747–1800)

(i; ii; iii) The Death of Christ (Christe Dod). Overture, The Harvest Festival (Höstgildet). (iv) (Keyboard): Allegretto in C; Andante Sostenuto in A, Op. 1/2. (i; iv) Songs: Abendlied; An die Natur; Mailied; Neujahrslied. (ii; iii) Motet: Denk ich Gott an eine Güte (arr. from Haydn's Symphony 104)
*** Chan. 9553. (i) Dam-Jensen, Halling, Zachariassen, Mannov; (ii; iii) Danish National Ch. & RSO, Hogwood; (iv) Hogwood (fortepiano)

Born in north Germany in 1747, Johann Abraham Peter Schulz established himself in Copenhagen as the pioneer of Danish national music, dying in 1800. *The Death of Christ* is a 35-minute cantata, both moving and dramatic, which in its linked sequence of 13 sections moves from total darkness, mourning Christ's death, to blazing light in the exhilarating final chorus, *He lives!* In style Schulz echoes both Haydn and C. P. E. Bach with a fascinating anticipation of Beethoven's *Pastoral Symphony* in the storm music. Excellent performance under Hogwood, who also plays two fortepiano pieces as interludes. Inger Dam-Jensen, Cardiff Singer of the World, is outstanding among the soloists, both in the cantata and in the songs *Abendlied* and *Mailied*.

SCHUMAN, William (1910–92)

Piano Concerto
(*(**)) VAI mono VAIA 1124. Tureck, Saidenberg Little Symphony, Daniel Saidenberg – DALLAPICCOLA: *2 Studies for Violin & Piano* (**); DIAMOND: *Piano Sonata* (***)

William Schuman's *Piano Concerto*, written in 1938, but revised in 1942, is worthy of a modern recording, and we hope Naxos will soon oblige in their American series. There is no doubt about the power, expressive commitment and virtuosity of Rosalyn Tureck's première performance, recorded in New York's Town Hall in 1943, and the orchestra for the most part plays well enough, especially in the fine central slow movement, in which Tureck certainly observes the composer's marking, 'Deliberately'. Her virtuosity in the brilliant, glitteringly rhythmic finale is hardly less impressive. But the piano is placed well forward, and the dry recording is very unflattering to all concerned, especially the orchestral brass, while in the accompanied piano passages the strings are distant and ill-focused.

(i) *Violin Concerto. New England Triptych*

⊶ (BB) *** Naxos 8.559083. (i) Quint; Bournemouth SO, Serebrier – IVES: *Variations on America* ***

Schuman's powerfully expressive *Violin Concerto* (1959) underwent more than one transformation in its gestation, with the original three movements becoming two. After a strong, rhythmically angular opening (with the soloist immediately introducing the work's dominating motif) the first movement soon slips into a magically lyrical *molto tranquillo*. Later there is a sparkling scherzando section and an extended cadenza before the brilliant conclusion. Lyrical feeling also seeps through the finale, although there is plenty of vigour and spectacle too, and a fugue, before the bravura *moto perpetuo* display of the closing section. Altogether a splendidly rewarding work, given a first-rate performance here by Philip Quint and the strongly involved Bournemouth players under Serebrier.

They are no less persuasive in the *New England Triptych*, a folksy, immediately communicative work inspired by and drawing on the music of William Billings. First-class recording in an attractively spacious acoustic. The coupling, which Schuman orchestrated, could not be more apt.

In Praise of Shahn (Canticle for Orchestra); (i) *To Thee Old Cause (Evocation for Oboe, Brass, Timpani, Piano & Strings)*

(M) *** Sony (ADD) 516235-2 [SK 90390]. (i) Gomberg (oboe); NYPO, Bernstein – BARBER: *Adagio for Strings; Violin Concerto* ***

Both of these works are commemorative. *To Thee Old Cause* is dedicated to the memory of Dr Martin Luther King, and the score quotes from Walt Whitman ('Thou peerless, passionate, good cause, Thou stern, remorseless, sweet idea'). It features an oboe obbligato within its string textures which are reinforced by brass sonorities. In a single movement, its *Larghissimo* opening is intense and evocative, although poignant lyrical feeling predominates. *In Praise of* (Ben) *Shahn* remembers the New York artist. It is in two sections, both (drawing on Eastern European Jewish folk material) include dynamic and expressive writing. This is music which in its atmosphere and use of dissonance often looks back to Charles Ives, although Schuman's own individual voice is never submerged. Bernstein is in his element and neither piece could receive more passionate advocacy. The (1970) Avery Fisher Hall recording is very immediate but has plenty of atmosphere too.

Judith; New England Triptych; Symphony for Strings; Variations on America

*** Delos DE 3115. Seattle SO, Schwarz

The composer himself heard these performances and spoke of their combination of 'intellectual depth, technical superiority and emotional involvement'. The *Symphony for Strings*, his Fifth, is one of his strongest and most beautiful works. This Seattle account has the advantage of fresh recorded sound. The ballet, *Judith*, was written for Martha Graham. Powerful and atmospheric music, here given a performance with both these qualities. The *New England Triptych* makes use of New England themes by the Bostonian, William Billings (1746–1800), whose music served to fuel the cause of the American Revolution. This present account is superior to the version by Howard Hanson on Mercury.

Symphonies 3; 5 (for strings); 8

⊶ (M) *** Sony SMK 63163. NYPO, Bernstein

The *Third* (1941) is (to quote Bernstein) 'alive, radiant and optimistic', and it is without question a masterpiece. It has the sweep and power of Harris, the freshness of Copland and an entirely individual and compelling atmosphere. Bernstein's 1960 performance is superb, and superior to his later remake for DG. The *Symphony for strings* comes from 1943 and is consistently imaginative, with a highly developed and sophisticated harmonic vocabulary. The *Eighth Symphony*, on the other hand, was commissioned by the New York Philharmonic in 1962. Its inspiration gives the impression of being manufactured rather than composed, except in the impressive and beautiful *Largo* movement; but make no mistake, its two companions on this record are among the finest symphonies to come out of America. The performances are terrific and the recordings, all emanating from the 1960s are expertly restored, sounding much fresher and better defined than the LP originals.

SCHUMANN, Clara (1819–96)

4 Songs, Op. 12

*** Philadelphia Orchestral Association POA 2003 (3). Hampson, Sawallisch – R. SCHUMANN: *Violin Concerto; Symphonies 1–4*, etc. **(*)

The songs by Clara Schumann find Thomas Hampson in superb form, communicating vividly with every word, flawlessly supported by Wolfgang Sawallisch on the piano.

Piano Trio in G min., Op. 17

*** Hyp. CDA 66331. Dartington Piano Trio – FANNY MENDELSSOHN: *Trio* ***

Clara's *Piano Trio* moves within the Mendelssohn–Schumann tradition with apparently effortless ease and, when played as persuasively as it is hereby the Dartington Trio, makes a pleasing impression. If it does not command the depth of Robert, it has a great deal of charm to commend it. Excellent recording.

Hyperion Schumann Edition

Lieder Edition, Vol. 5: ***Ihr Bildnis; Lorelei; Sie liebten sich beide; Volkslied***

*** Hyp. CDJ 33105. Maltman, Johnson – R. SCHUMANN: *Lieder* ***

It adds to the value of this searching collection of Heine settings by Robert Schumann that four rival settings by his wife are appended, simpler and less distinctive in style as they are. As in the rest of the disc Maltman is at his finest, with Graham Johnson ever-illuminating both as accompanist and annotator.

Graham Johnson Lieder Edition

Lieder Edition, Vol. 6: ***6 Lieder from Jucunde***

*** Hyp. CDJ 133106. McGreevy, Johnson – R. SCHUMANN: *Lieder* ***

6 Lieder from Jucunde, Op. 23; 6 Lieder, Op. 13; Lieder, Op. 12: Er ist gekommen; Liebst du um Schönheit; Warum willst du. **Lieder:** ***Der Abendstern; Walzer; Am Strande; Beim***

Abschied; Die gute Nacht; Ihr Bildnis; Lorelei; Mein Stern; Oh weh des Schiedens; Sie lieben sich beide; Das Veilchen; Volkslied; Der Wanderer; Der Wanderer in der Sägemühle
*** Hyp. CDA 67249. Gritton, Loges, Asti

Clara Schumann wrote almost all her songs during her marriage to Robert, often inspired by special occasions such as birthdays and Christmases. When he died she wrote no more, which is greatly to be regretted when these charming inspirations have so many delightful qualities, generally light-hearted and lyrical. Her Rückert setting, *Liebst du um Schönheit*, in its folk-like innocence contrasts nicely with the well-known Mahler setting of the same words, and in addition to the mature songs from her married years it is good to have a group that date from her early girlhood, with *Der Wanderer* written when she was only 12, and thought until recently to have been composed by her father. Another of her early songs, *Der Wanderer in der Sägemühle* ('The Wanderer at the Sawmill'), has unexpected harmonic twists, rather in the manner of Schubert, as do many of her songs. Susan Gritton is a charming soloist in the *Jucunde* songs, also included in Graham Johnson's Schumann series, freer in expression than Geraldine McGreevy, if stylistically less pure. She and Stephan Loges are the excellent soloists in the whole programme, given inspired accompaniment by Eugene Asti, often more volatile than his former teacher, Graham Johnson.

SCHUMANN, Robert (1810–56)

Cello Concerto in A min., Op. 129
*** BIS CD 486. Thedéen, Malmö SO, Markiz – ELGAR: *Concerto* ***
(M) **(*) Sup. (ADD) SU 3667-2. Navarra, Czech PO, Ančerl – BLOCH: *Schelomo* **(*); RESPIGHI: *Adagio con variazioni* ***
☛ (BB) *** Naxos 8.550938. Kliegel, Nat. SO of Ireland, Constantine – BRAHMS: *Double Concerto* ***
(M) **(*) EMI (ADD) 5 62803-2. Du Pré, New Philh. O, Barenboim – DVOŘÁK: *Cello Concerto* **(*)
(M) **(*) BBC BBCL 4133-2. Tortelier, BBC SO, Dorati – HINDEMITH: *Cello Concerto* **(*)
(N) ** Virgin 5 45664-2. Mørk, Fr. R. PO, P. Jarvi – BLOCH: *Schelomo*; BRUCH: *Kol Nidrei* ***
(M) *(*) EMI (ADD) 5 66913-2 [5 66965]. Rostropovich, O Nat. de France, Bernstein – R. STRAUSS: *Don Quixote* ***

The young Swedish virtuoso, Torleif Thedéen, is splendidly recorded on BIS, and the Malmö orchestra give him sympathetic support. He plays with a refreshing ardour, tempered by nobility and a reticence that is strongly appealing. He couples it with an account of the Elgar that is every bit as attuned to the latter's sensibility as any in the catalogue. Strongly recommended.

Jacqueline du Pré's spontaneous style is well suited to this most recalcitrant of concertos and the slow movement is particularly beautiful. As in the coupling, the partnership with Daniel Barenboim is very successful, and the remastered 1968 recording has brought a firmer orchestral focus to match the realistic cello timbre.

The Schumann *Cello Concerto* is the more attractive for coming on the Naxos super-budget label in a warmly spontaneous-sounding performance, very well recorded. Kliegel takes a spacious, lyrical view of the first movement, using a soft-grained tone at the start, with wide vibrato. The

simple, dedicated approach to the central *Langsam* also brings dedicated playing, while the finale is wittily pointed, not least in the second subject.

André Navarra on his day is one of the most commanding of cellists and his performance here has real personality, rivalling some versions on dearer labels. The Supraphon sound has been made more vivid by the remastering, with the cello focus real and present, and the orchestra caught warmly and naturally.

Paul Tortelier's account comes from the dryish BBC Maida Vale studios in 1962 and the sound is perhaps less appealing than in many recordings from this label, though the ear quickly adjusts. It is a very spontaneous and finely shaped performance, which admirers of the great French cellist will want to have. The BBC Symphony Orchestra under Antal Dorati responds with vital and sensitive playing, and it comes with a fine account of Hindemith's *Cello Concerto* written in 1940.

Though Truls Mørk's reading of the Schumann, like those of the Bloch and Bruch rhapsodies with which it is coupled, is comparably warm, his freely expressive style with its flexible phrasing leads him to vary the beat so much that it becomes distracting, reducing the impact of the whole. Mørk's freedom does go with a sense of fantasy, and in the brisk finale there is less room for him to pull the tempo around, with rhythms lightly sprung. Though in *Schelomo* Järvi draws playing of admirable clarity from the orchestra, here in the Schumann the sound at times is congested and the playing less incisive. But this is still a compelling reading, well coupled with outstanding performances of Bloch and Bruch.

Except in the finale where energy triumphs, the collaboration of Rostropovich and Bernstein sounds disappointingly self-conscious. The great Russian cellist is at his most indulgent, not least in the lovely slow section, which is pulled about wilfully at a very slow basic tempo. The Strauss coupling is in an altogether different class, so this is a strange choice for EMI's 'Great Recordings of the Century' series.

(i) Cello Concerto; (ii) Adagio & Allegro, Op. 70; 3 Fantasiestücke; 5 Stücke im Volkston; Romanze 1 in A min., Op. 94/1; Marchenbilder, Op. 113/1
**(*) DG (IMS) 469 524-2. Maisky, with (i) Orpheus CO; (ii) Argerich

Mischa Maisky has never been an artist for half measures. It was he who earlier recorded the Schumann *Cello Concerto* with Leonard Bernstein, a big-scale reading, often wayward and self-indulgent. His new version, recorded with the conductorless Orpheus Chamber Orchestra brings a more purposeful reading, faster and marginally less wilful in the first movement, but with the slow movement pulled around even more than before, with exaggerated rubato. Like the first movement the finale gains in bite from the close-up sound. The concerto comes last on the disc as the culmination of Schumann's cello music. Like Yo-Yo Ma on Sony and Heinrich Schiff on Philips, Maisky also offers the other shorter pieces with piano which Schumann either wrote specifically for cello (the *Adagio & Allegro* and the *5 Stücke im Volkston*) or suggested the cello as an option. Unlike those rivals he adds two extra pieces, the *Romance* and the *Marchenbilder* movement as bonuses in his own adaptations, though that hardly compensates for the wilfulness. Maisky is well partnered by another great individualist, Martha Argerich. The sound is full and bright.

(i) *Cello Concerto in A min.*; (ii) *Piano Concerto in A min.*

(M) **(*) DG (IMS) (ADD) 449 100-2. (i) Rostropovich, Leningrad PO, Rozhdestvensky; (ii) Argerich, Nat. SO of Washington, Rostropovich

Rostropovich's DG performance of the *Cello Concerto* is superbly made, introspective yet at the same time outgoing, with a peerless technique at the command of a rare artistic imagination. The sound is vivid. In the *Piano Concerto* Rostropovich moves to the rostrum and Argerich takes on the role of soloist. The partnership produces a performance which is full of contrast – helped by a recording of wide dynamic range – and strong in temperament. There is an appealing delicacy in the *Andantino* and the outer movements have plenty of vivacity and colour. Yet in the last analysis the work's special romantic feeling does not fully blossom here, although the playing is not without poetry. The recording is admirably lifelike and well balanced.

(i; iii) *Cello Concerto*; (ii; iii) *Piano Concerto*; (ii) *Etudes symphoniques, Op. 13*

(M) *** Sony SMK 89716. (i) Ma; (ii) Perahia; (iii) Bav. RSO, C. Davis

The two concerto performances on Sony make a recommendable mid-priced coupling and this disc is undoubtedly good value. In the *Cello Concerto* Yo-Yo Ma's playing is characteristically refined, but keenly affectionate too, although at times he carries tonal sophistication to excess and suddenly drops into *sotto voce* tone and near inaudibility. But both he and Sir Colin Davis are thoroughly attuned to the sensibility of this composer and the recording balance is excellent. Similarly Davis makes a fine partner for Perahia, who in the *Piano Concerto* enjoys displaying his ardour and virtuosity, as well as his ability to invest a phrase with poetry and magic. The recording is live, but is full and spacious. The *Symphonic Etudes* are equally fine although here the balance is rather close.

(i) *Cello Concerto*; (ii) *3 Fantasiestücke, Op. 73; 3 Romanzen, Op. 94*

(***) Testament mono SBT 1310. Gendron, SRO, (i) Ansermet, (ii) Françaix – TCHAIKOVSKY: *Variations on a Rococo Theme* (***)

It is hard to believe that the Testament recording of the *Cello Concerto* is over half-a-century old for it has great freshness and presence. Maurice Gendron was rather overshadowed by his countrymen and contemporaries, Pierre Fournier and Paul Tortelier, but he was no less eloquent an artist and had much of the former's aristocratic finesse and the latter's intensity. His playing was quite personal and his tonal burnish reflects (as Tully Potter puts it in an excellent note) his admiration for Feuermann. When it first appeared, the authors of *The Record Guide* spoke of it as by far the best of the versions then available, and even if such master-cellists as Fournier and Rostropovich had not then committed it to disc, Gendron's remains an impressive account, well worth reviving. It makes its first appearance on CD. The Opp. 73 and 94 pieces, recorded in 1952, originally appeared coupled with Schubert's *Arpeggione Sonata* and serve as a reminder of the refined musicianship of the elegant composer-pianist, Jean Françaix.

(i) *Piano Concerto in A min., Op. 54. Carnaval, Op. 9*

*** EMI **DVD** DBV4 928399. Arrau, (i) LPO, Hurst (with BEETHOVEN: *Piano Sonatas 32 in C min., Op. 111*). (Also *Piano Sonata 23 in F min. (Appassionata), Op. 57* played by Solomon)

Claudio Arrau's *A minor Concerto* was filmed in a dryish BBC studio in London in June 1963 and *Carnaval* two years earlier, both produced by the legendary Walter Todds. His account of Beethoven's *C minor Sonata* comes from a Paris studio recital from 1970, and of these three works it best captures the distinctive Arrau sonority. Fine though his *Carnaval* is, it is Op. 111 that brings the wonderful range of tone and colour that readers who heard him in the concert hall will remember. In the *Piano Concerto* it is good to be reminded of the excellence of the underrated George Hurst's accompanying. Some of the footage is grainy in the concerto, but the camera-work is always unobtrusive. One of the most exciting things here is the so-called bonus which offers an altogether electrifying performance of the *Appassionata* by Solomon, recorded in January 1956 not long before he suffered the stroke that immobilized him. This is apparently the only example of Solomon's playing that exists on film and even his admirers who expect great playing will be astonished at the stature of this performance. An indispensable issue.

Piano Concerto in A min., Op. 54

☙ ✪ *** EMI 5 57562-2. Andsnes, BPO, Jansons – GRIEG: *Piano Concerto* *** ✪

☙ (M) *** Ph. (ADD) 464 702-2. Kovacevich, BBC SO, C. Davis – GRIEG: *Concerto* ***

*** EMI 5 57773-2. Argerich, Svizzera-Italiana O, Rabinovitch-Barakovsky – BEETHOVEN: *Triple Concerto* ***

*** EMI 7 54746-2. Vogt, CBSO, Rattle – GRIEG: *Concerto* ***

*** Sony 518810-2 [SK 92736]. Perahia, Bav. RSO, C. Davis – GRIEG: *Concerto* ***

(M) *** Decca (ADD) 458 628-2. Ashkenazy, LSO, Segal – TCHAIKOVSKY: *Concerto 1* **(*)

(M) *** Decca (ADD) 466 383-2. Lupu, LSO, Previn – GRIEG: *Piano Concerto* ***

(M) *** Warner Elatus 0927 49617-2. Grimaud, Berlin Deutsche SO, Zinman – BEETHOVEN: *Piano Concerto 4* ***

(M) (***) DG mono 474 024-2 (5). Kempff, LSO, Krips – BEETHOVEN: *Piano Concertos 1–5*; BRAHMS: *Piano Concerto 1*; MOZART: *Piano Concertos 9 & 15*; LISZT: *Piano Concertos 1 and 2* (***)

(BB) (***) Dutton CDEP 9719. Lipatti, Philh. O, Karajan – GREIG: *Concerto* (***)

(B) **(*) Decca (ADD) 433 628-2. Gulda, VPO, Andrae – FRANCK: *Symphonic Variations* *** ✪; GRIEG: *Concerto* ***

(B) **(*) EMI Red Line CDR5 69859. Ousset, LPO, Masur – GRIEG: *Piano Concerto* **(*)

(BB) (***) Naxos mono 8.110612. Cortot, LPO, Ronald – CHOPIN: *Piano Concerto 2 in F min., Op. 21*

Piano Concerto in A min.; Concert-allegro with Introduction in D min., Op. 134. Introduction & Allegro appassionato, Op.92

**(*) MDG 340 1033-2. Zacharias, Lausanne Chamber O

(i; ii) *Piano Concerto in A min.;* (i; iii) *Introduction &*
Allegro appassionato, Op. 92. Novellette in F, Op. 21/1;
Toccata in C, Op. 7; Waldszenen, Op. 82

(M) **(*) DG stereo/mono 447 440-2. Richter, with (i)
  Warsaw Nat. PO, (ii) Rowicki, (iii) Wislocki

The Schumann and Grieg *Concertos* make a perfect coupling
since the one is modelled on the other. As a student at
Leipzig, Grieg had fallen under Schumann's spell and had
heard Clara Schumann playing her husband's *Concerto*. Andsnes's Schumann is a performance of the highest poetic
feeling and distinction. Like the Grieg, it brings glorious
playing from both soloist and the orchestra under Jansons, a
performance similarly combining spontaneity and concentration, dedication and poetry, with no hint of self-
consciousness or routine. The pianistic virtuosity is
commanding but never overrides tenderness. A performance
of both authority and nobility, recorded in particularly lifelike and well-balanced sound. A classic version for our time.

EMI's live recording of the Schumann, made at the Lugano
Festival, has a rare vitality, thanks to the vividly characterful
playing of Martha Argerich. This account may not be as
polished as Argerich's studio version, when impulsively she
keeps taking her conductor by surprise, but the magnetism of
her playing is here irresistible, with high dramatic contrasts
between sparkling virtuosity and yearning lyricism. With the
Beethoven *Triple Concerto*, similarly animated, as an unusual
coupling, this makes an attractive recommendation.

Although Pires should not be forgotten (coupled with the
Piano Quartet), otherwise our primary recommendation for
this favourite Romantic concerto remains with the successful
symbiosis of Stephen Kovacevich and Sir Colin Davis, who
give an interpretation which is both fresh and poetic, unexaggerated but powerful in its directness and clarity, and the
spring-like element of the outer movements is finely presented by orchestra and soloist alike. This is now rightly
placed among the Philips '50 Great Recordings'.

Lars Vogt's sensitivity, an innate sense of style, and a keen
imagination, are strongly in evidence in this account of the
Schumann, in which he is well supported by Simon Rattle
and the CBSO. There is stiff competition, of course, but
among modern recordings Vogt acquits himself with honour.

Perahia's 1988 version also benefits from having the guiding
hand of Sir Colin Davis directing the orchestra. The recording is live. Perahia is never merely showy, but here he enjoys
displaying his ardour and virtuosity as well as his ability to
invest a phrase with poetry and magic. With its full and
spacious sound, the Perahia is among the finest current
versions of this favourite coupling, and it now comes at
mid-price with the finale of the Mendelssohn *Second Con-*
certo as a bonus.

Ashkenazy's performance, balancing the demands of
drama against poetry, comes down rather more in favour of
the former than one might expect, but it is a refined reading
as well as a powerful one, with the finale rather more spacious than usual. The recording, from the late 70s, is of
vintage quality and has been remastered most successfully.
However, Ashkenazy is less obviously attuned to the rhetoric
of the Tchaikovsky coupling.

The Lupu–Previn performance suits the music admirably,
with the piano lucidly and truthfully caught against a natural
orchestral backcloth. Lupu's clean boldness of approach in
the outer movements is appealingly fresh, with the finale
brilliant yet unforced, while the *Intermezzo* has both warmth
and the necessary tender delicacy. This reissue in Decca's

Legends series must move up to stand high alongside other
current mid-priced recommendations.

A most enjoyably spontaneous performance from Hélène
Grimaud in a very successful coupling with Beethoven's *G*
major Concerto. David Zinman proves a sympathetic partner
and, while the opening movement has a flexible, romantic
flamboyance, its delicate moments are thoughtfully poetic, as
is the gentle account of the *Intermezzo*, to be followed by an
exhilarating finale. The spaciously resonant recording has an
attractive concert-hall ambience, and altogether this ranks
high on the recommended list.

Kempff's first recording of the Schumann, made for Decca
in 1953, is unique in its magic, sparklingly transparent in its
textures, delicately pointed and consistently poetic. No pianist with such light pedalling could play with a smoother
legato, making the melodies sing. This mono recording,
unavailable for 40 years and more, is a wonderful addition to
Kempff's legacy on disc, helped by sparklingly clear sound,
engineered by the legendary Kenneth Wilkinson.

Dinu Lipatti's classic version of the Schumann *Concerto*, a
staple of the catalogue from when it was recorded in the late
1940s, now comes in this Dutton bargain issue with the sound
fuller and clearer than ever before, and superior to the newest
EMI transfer.

Gulda's account is refreshingly direct yet, with light, crisp
playing, never sounds rushed. The *Intermezzo* remains delicate in feeling, with nicely pointed pianism. The finale is just
right, with an enjoyable rhythmic lift, and the early stereo
(1956), though a little dated, is fully acceptable.

Cécile Ousset, with sympathetic support from Masur, gives
a spirited account of the Schumann *Concerto*, like the Grieg
coupling rather weightier than one might have expected but
not lacking sparkle, while the central dialogue with the
orchestra is delightfully done.

Zacharias, with chamber forces, offers a comparatively
small-scale approach, with textures exceptionally transparent,
and with his crisp articulation consistently adding sparkle in
the most elaborate passage-work. But both in the finale and
in the two rarer concertante works he takes a broad view,
avoiding pomposity in the rhetorical gestures of Op. 134, and
springing rhythms lightly, never letting the music drag, the
effect carefree if lacking flamboyance. With exceptionally
clear recording, it makes a refreshing and distinctive view,
certainly poetic.

Richter's reissue in DG's 'Originals' series does not always
represent him at his very finest. Perhaps the sluggishness of
the orchestral playing affected his concentration. Not that the
concerto or the *Introduction & Allegro appassionato* lack style
but the tension could be greater. The focus of the late-1950s
Polish recording has been improved in the concerto but in
Op. 92 remains a little fuzzy around the edges, not quite up to
the standard one expects from DG. The *Novellette* and *Toc-*
cata are fabulous performances, full of hair-raising virtuosity,
but shaped with an unerring sense of style and musical as
well as technical control. The piano tone is dry but clear. The
Waldszenen is a mono recording from 1956 and beautifully
played.

There is something quite special about Cortot. There is
lyrical warmth, poetic feeling and a wonderful freshness and
individuality. Mark Obert-Thorn gets a very good sound
from the shellac originals.

(i) *Piano Concerto in A min. Symphony 1*

(M) **(*) Warner Elatus 0927 49568-2. (i) Argerich; COE,
  Harnoncourt

In her live recording of the *Piano Concerto* Martha Argerich gives a vividly compelling, characteristically volatile reading, at once poetic and full of fancy, powerful and often wildly individual. The performance culminates in an account of the finale so daring that one wants to cheer at the end, so freely does the adrenalin flow. The orchestra is hard pressed to keep up with her at her fast basic speed, and the first movement takes some time to settle down (the woodwind ensemble at the start is a bit rough). Argerich plays with her usual concentration, there is a splendid swing to the rhythm and no sense of haste. The central *Andantino grazioso* too brings fantasy and flair, a freely spontaneous reading, and this remains an inspirational account that is hard to resist. Harnoncourt's account of the *Symphony* is very well played but is much less individual and it lacks the spontaneous thrust of the *Concerto*.

(i) Piano Concerto in A min., Op. 54; (ii) Piano Quintet in E flat, Op. 44

*** DG 463 179-2. Pires; (i) COE, Abbado; (ii) Dumay, Capuçon, Caussé, Wang

(N) (M) *** RCA 82876 65830-2. Alicia de Larrocha; (i) LSO, C. Davis; (ii) Tokyo Qt

It makes an excellent if unusual coupling to have the Schumann *Piano Concerto* alongside the most heroic of his chamber works. In both Pires is inspired to give freely spontaneous performances, at once powerfully persuasive and poetic. In the *Quintet* the interplay between musicians is delightful, each distinguished individually but who plainly enjoy working together. Consistently Pires leads the team to play with natural, unselfconscious rubato in all four movements, with speeds perfectly chosen and the structure firmly held together.

In the *Concerto* Pires is also at her most persuasive. With the ever-responsive Chamber Orchestra of Europe, Abbado matches the volatile quality in Pires's performance with beautifully transparent accompaniment. Two beautifully judged performances, both very well recorded.

Like Pires, Alicia de Larrocha made the rare coupling with the *Piano Quintet*, and she is hardly less successful. With Sir Colin Davis as partner, it is not surprising that the *Concerto* strikes a perfect balance between poetic feeling and drama, and the LSO players respond sensitively to both pianist and conductor. The Abbey Road recording is first class. Similarly, the *Quintet* brings a truly responsive performance, full of warmth, the engaging *In modo d'una marcia* making a perfect contrast to the joyously vigorous Scherzo. Here the recording is close but with piano and strings well balanced, to make a fine mid-priced alternative.

Piano Concerto in A min., Op. 54; (i) Carnaval, Op. 9; Waldszenen: Vogel als Prophet (only)

(BB) (***) Naxos mono 8.110604. Hess; (i) O, Goehr

Dame Myra Hess was admired particularly for her Schumann, which was both authoritative and sensitive. Nothing is ever overstated, and she is completely inside Schumann's poetic world. Virtuosity and display are bi-products of her dedication to the letter and spirit of the score. Her rubato seems completely right and tempos are judged perfectly. The recording of the *Piano Concerto* (in the 78 era, the preferred choice of most collectors) is a little dry, but the performance is fresher than her mono account with Rudolf Schwarz and the Philharmonia. Decent transfers.

Violin Concerto in D min.

☛ (N) (B) *** Decca 475 6703 (2). Bell, Cleveland O, von Dohnányi – BRAHMS; TCHAIKOVSKY; WIENIAWSKI: *Violin Concertos* ***

☛ (BB) *** Warner Apex 0927 49517-2. Zehetmair, Philh. O, Eschenbach – DVORAK: *Violin Concerto; Romance* **(*)

(N) *** Virgin 545663-2. Capuçon, Mahler CO, Harding – MENDELSSOHN: *Violin Concerto* ***

**(*) CBC SMCD 5197. Kang, Vancouver SO, Comisiona – WIENIAWSKI: *Violin Concerto 2 in D min.; Légende in G min.* **(*)

With Christoph von Dohnányi adding to the weight of the drama, Jamie Bell, in a commanding performance defies the old idea of this concerto as an impossibly flawed piece, bringing out the charm as well as the power. The central slow movement has a rapt intensity rarely matched, and the dance-rhythms of the finale have fantasy as well as jauntiness and jollity. With full-bodied, well-balanced recording this is a Double which offers three equally recommendable couplings, with the Brahms concerto among the very finest in the catalogue.

Thomas Zehetmair is perfectly cast for the Schumann *Concerto*. He understands the central European tradition and makes the very most of the comparatively weak first movement. The *Langsam* slow movement is glorious (Schumann seemingly at his most inspired) and even the erratic finale is made to sound jolly and not too disjointed. Eschenbach accompanies sympathetically, the recording is excellent, and this performance is outstanding in every way.

Renaud Capuçon's performance of Schumann's still underappreciated *Violin Concerto* is marked by lightness and transparency, not least in the chamber-scale orchestral accompaniment, with bright, crisp attack and a tender account of the second subject. With free, open sound, recorded in the Jugendstill theatre in Vienna, this makes an outstanding version of an apt and rare coupling.

It is a measure of the artistry of the young Canadian violinist Juliette Kang, winner of the Yehudi Menuhin International Competition, that she conceals the problems of the Schumann concerto, so much less grateful for the soloist than the Wieniawski. Playing with dazzlingly clean articulation even in the most taxing bravura passages, she gives a smaller-scale reading than most, which compensates for any lack of weight in fiery brilliance and thoughtful expressiveness. The slightly recessed CBC recording plays its part in giving that impression, with orchestral sound also less full-bodied than most.

Fantasy for Violin & Orchestra, Op. 131

(BB) *** Warner Apex 0927 4959-2. Zehetmair, Cleveland O, Dohnányi – BRAHMS: *Violin Concerto* **

Schumann's rarely heard *Fantasy* was presented to his wife for Clara's 34th birthday. The violin dominates reflectively throughout and has many solo passages which are improvisational in character. It is not a masterpiece, but its lyrical inspiration is strong and its loose structure surprisingly convincing. Both Zehetmair and Dohnányi are in total sympathy with the music and the recording is excellent. It is a pity that this was not reissued in harness with the *Violin Concerto* (above), for Zehetmair's Brahms, though warmly sympathetic, is less memorable.

SYMPHONIES

Symphony in G min. (Zwickau); Symphonies 1–3 (Rhenish), Op. 97; Symphony 4: original 1841 version and revised 1851 version; (i) Konzertstück for 4 Horns & Orchestra in F, Op. 86

🔊 ⊛ *** DG 457 591-2 (3). ORR, Gardiner

With his brilliant orchestra of period instruments Gardiner offers not just the four regular symphonies but a complete survey of Schumann as symphonist. He seeks specifically to explode the myth that Schumann was a poor orchestrator, pointing out how quick he was to learn from his own mistakes. Gardiner makes an exception over the 1851 revision of the *Fourth Symphony*, in which Schumann thickened the woodwind writing with much doubling. Illuminatingly, both versions of that symphony are included, with the contrasts well brought out. Gardiner himself, like Brahms, prefers the slimmer, more transparent first version, suggesting that the 1851 changes made it safer and less original. Yet paradoxically, in performance Gardiner is even more inspired in the later version, which here emerges as bitingly dramatic, working up to a thrilling coda. Like other cycles, this one offers the *Overture, Scherzo and Finale* of 1841 as a necessary extra, but still more fascinating is the *Konzertstück* of 1849 for four horns, with the ORR soloists breathtaking in their virtuosity on nineteenth-century instruments. Also included is the early, incomplete *Symphony in G minor* of 1832 (named after Schumann's home town of Zwickau). Under Gardiner the two completed movements emerge as highly original in their own right.

Symphonies 1–4

🔊 (BB) *** Arte Nova 8287657743-2 (2). Zurich Tonhalle O, Zinman

Symphonies 1–4; Scherzo in G min. (ed. Draheim)

🔊 (M) *** DG 429 672-2 (2). BPO, Karajan

(B) **(*) DG Double 453 049-2 (2). VPO, Bernstein

**(*) Classico CLASSCD 431/2. Czech Chamber PO, Bostock

Symphonies 1–4: Manfred Overture, Op. 115

(N) (B) **(*) Sony (ADD) 516027-2 (2). Cleveland O, Szell

Symphonies 1 in B flat (Spring), Op. 38; 2 in C, Op. 61

(B) *** Sony (ADD) SBK 48269. Bav. RSO, Kubelik

Symphonies 3 in E flat (Rhenish), Op. 97; 4 in D min., Op. 120; Overture Manfred, Op. 115

(B) *** Sony (ADD) SBK 48270. Bav. RSO, Kubelik

Symphonies 1–4; Overture, Scherzo & Finale, Op. 52

(M) *** EMI 567268-2 [567771] (2). Dresden State O, Sawallisch

Symphonies 1–4; Overture: Julius Caesar, Op. 128; Overture, Scherzo & Finale, Op. 52

(B) **(*) Double Decca (ADD) 448 930-2 (2). VPO, Solti

Symphonies 1–2 in C; Genoveva Overture

**(*) Australian DG Eloquence 463 200-2. BPO, Kubelik

Symphonies 3–4; Manfred Overture

**(*) Australian DG Eloquence 463 201-2. BPO, Kubelik

Karajan's interpretations of the Schumann *Symphonies* stand above all other recordings on modern instruments. No. 1 is a beautifully shaped performance, with orchestral playing of the highest distinction; No. 2 is among the most powerful ever recorded, combining poetic intensity and intellectual strength in equal proportions; and No. 3 is also among the most impressive versions ever committed to disc: its famous fourth-movement evocation of Cologne Cathedral is superbly spacious and eloquent, with quite magnificent brass playing. No. 4 can be classed alongside Furtwängler's famous record, with Karajan similarly inspirational, yet a shade more self-disciplined than his illustrious predecessor. However, the reissued complete set brings digital remastering which – as with the Brahms symphonies – has leaner textures than before, while in tuttis the violins above the stave may approach shrillness.

The Dresden CDs of the Schumann *Symphonies* under Sawallisch are as deeply musical as they are carefully considered; the orchestral playing combines superb discipline with refreshing naturalness and spontaneity. Sawallisch catches all Schumann's varying moods, and his direction has splendid vigour. These recordings have dominated the catalogue, alongside Karajan's, for some years. Although the reverberant acoustic brought a degree of edge to the upper strings, the sound-picture has the essential fullness which the Karajan transfers lack, and the remastering has cleaned up the upper range to a considerable extent. The set now appears in a mid-priced box.

As in his outstanding cycle of the Beethoven symphonies, David Zinman with the Tonhalle Orchestra offers modern-instrument performances which have taken on board the lessons learned from period-instrument performances. With speeds on the fast side, these are all readings which, with excellent sound, are at once fresh, resilient and transparent, defying the old idea of Schumann's thickness of orchestration. Among digital sets there is no finer cycle, whatever the price.

Kubelik's fine Sony set also remains fully competitive. The recording was made in the Hercules-Saal, Munich, in 1979, and the advantages of that glowing acoustic can be felt throughout. The orchestral playing is generally very fine (if not quite as polished as the Berlin Philharmonic) and is especially eloquent in the spacious slow movements. These are strongly characterized readings with plenty of vitality which display the same bright and alert sensitivity to Schumann's style as did his earlier set for DG. But the Sony recording is obviously more modern, and the latest CD transfer brings plenty of body to the sound and a better focus to the violins than in the Sawallisch set. That more logically includes the *Overture, Scherzo and Finale*, but many will count the *Manfred Overture* an equally desirable alternative.

No. 2, with which Szell began his cycle in October 1958, proves to be a thrilling performance of great power and strong forward thrust, yet the eloquent *Adagio* expands gloriously and brings the most ardent response from the Cleveland strings. Szell is at his most incisive and the orchestra are at their warmest in No. 1. The account of the *Rhenish* is even finer, marvellously full of life. The playing is breathtaking, with the horns gloriously full-blooded. No. 4 is strong and dramatic, not as weighty as some, but equally convincing. Szell proves himself an outstanding exponent of Schumann, able to stand alongside the finest interpreters of his day, and, were it not for the reduced range of dynamic, this set would have been even more recommended.

Kubelik's earlier Sony accounts of the symphonies are beautifully played and well recorded. The readings have not the drive of Karajan, notably in No. 4, but they undoubtedly have both eloquence and warmth. They are straightforward and unmannered and recorded in a spacious acoustic with good CD transfers. Kubelik's ear for balance removes all suspicions of heaviness in the orchestration, and the recordings, dating from the mid-1960s, still sound good. Two enjoyable overtures are offered as a bonus.

Bernstein's VPO recordings from 1984–5 have the extra voltage which comes with live music-making at its most compulsive, though he seems reluctant to let the music speak for itself. The first movement of the *Spring Symphony* is pushed very hard, and the *Second Symphony* also brings the same larger-than-life projection. Slow movements are obviously deeply felt and have both warmth and humanity. In the *Rhenish Symphony* Bernstein's expressive indulgences are less disruptive. The outer movements of the *Fourth* are not allowed to move forward at a steady pace, but the *Romanze* has warmth and charm, even if the phrasing at the opening has an element of self-consciousness. Even so, with splendid orchestral playing and much engaging detail, there is a great deal to admire throughout these performances, and the resonant acoustic of the Grossersaal of the Musikverein gives the music-making a robust immediacy.

Solti's Schumann interpretations are full of his personal brand of lyrical intensity. The most compelling performance of the cycle is the *Second Symphony*, with its passionate slow movement. And with a feeling of spontaneous lyricism paramount, this is a most compellingly individual reading. The performance of the *Spring Symphony* is played well enough but is just a shade disappointing. However the *Rhenish* is another memorable performance. Here Solti's sense of rhythm is strikingly alert so that the first movement hoists one aloft on its soaring melodies and, comparably, the drama of the *Fourth Symphony* is given full force without ever falling into excessive tautness: there is always room to breathe. The *Julius Caesar Overture* is no masterpiece, but makes an enjoyable bonus and the *Overture, Scherzo and Finale* is very successful. The late 1960s recordings are slightly dry, bright and forward, but one cannot complain that Schumann's scoring sounds too thick!

(i) *Symphonies 1–4; Manfred Overture*; (iii) *Andante & Variations*; (i; ii) *Violin Concerto in D min.*
(*) Philadelphia Orchestral Association POA 2003 (3). (i) Phd. O, Sawallisch; (ii) with Kavakos; (iii) Sawallisch, with Buchbinder and orchestral soloists – C. SCHUMANN: 4 Songs, Op. 12 *

In tribute to Wolfgang Sawallisch at the end of his ten years as music director, the Philadelphia Orchestra has published these live recordings of Schumann, made at concerts over his last season. For some 30 years Sawallisch's Dresden recordings of the Schumann symphonies for EMI (5 67268-2) have established themselves as benchmark versions, and the simple message here is that, with fuller, clearer, weightier digital sound, these new Philadelphia versions have every advantage, carrying exactly the same authority as before, enhanced by modern recording. These are the first issues of recordings made in the orchestra's fine new Verizon Hall, at once warm and clear. Sawallisch, like other great conductors, has long made nonsense of the old idea that Schumann's orchestration is thick and opaque and, even more than the more reverberant Dresden recordings, these new ones bear that out. At the very start in the slow introduction of the *Spring Symphony, No. 1*, the separation of the wind solos, the terracing of texture, is more clearly brought out, and the rhythmic spring in the main *allegro* is all the more infectious. Differences are slight, and broadly Sawallisch's approach to each of the symphonies remains very much the same, if with a tendency for speeds, fast and slow, to be not quite so extreme.

The third disc in the Philadelphia set is a mixed bag. After the incandescence of the symphonies, the relatively low-key account of the *Manfred Overture* is a disappointment. There is a similar lack of bite in the first movement of the *Violin Concerto*, despite the commanding virtuosity of Leonidas Kavakos. The slow movement is then beautifully tender and songful, leading to a bright, clean reading of the finale. For the other items Sawallisch demonstrates his mastery as a pianist. The 19-minute *Andante and Variations* involve the odd ensemble of two pianos, two cellos and horn, which works surprisingly well, and Sawallisch with his pianist colleague, Rudolf Buchbinder, and three fine Philadelphia players conveys the joy of such corporate music-making. Yet it is perhaps a pity that this Philadelphia set does not concentrate on just the symphonies.

Symphony 1 in B flat (Spring), Op. 38
(M) *** DG (ADD) 447 408-2. BPO, Karajan – BRAHMS: *Symphony 1* ***

Karajan is totally attuned to Schumann's sensibility and he provides a strong yet beautifully shaped performance of the *Spring Symphony*. The very opening is electrifying, with the Berlin Philharmonic giving of their finest. The sound is an obvious improvement on the previous CD incarnation of this well-balanced analogue recording from the early 1970s, adding body and weight to the clear, fresh detail.

Symphonies 1 in B flat (Spring), Op. 38; 4 in D min., Op. 120; Konzertstück for 4 Horns & Orchestra in F, Op. 86
(M) *** DG 474 551-2. ORR, Gardiner

These recordings were orginally part of a three-CD set, which included both versions of the *Fourth Symphony*. This midprice release gives us the familiar (1851) version of the *Fourth*, less bold than the original version, but still striking in this vivid performance. The *Spring Symphony*, too, is fresh and dynamic, and full of energy. But perhaps the most fascinating work here is the 1841 *Konzertstück for four horns*, virtually unplayable in Schumann's own time, but presented here with extraordinary panache, with the ORR soloists breathtaking in their virtuosity.

Symphony 2 in C
(N) *** Testament (ADD) SBT 1378. BPO, Szell (with BRAHMS: *Tragic Overture*; R. STRAUSS: *Don Juan*)

Szell's account of the *Second Symphony* is among the finest in the current catalogue. It is more spontaneous and highly charged than the Cleveland set he recorded in the early 1960s, good though that was. The performance comes from a concert given at the Philharmonie in June 1969 and, apart from the immaculate control which distinguished all his music making, has a powerful sense of line and in the slow movement great lyrical feeling and humanity. The Deutschland Radio recording is very faithful and communicates the sense of occasion. The other works on the programme, and in particular the *Don Juan*, are likewise performances of stature. Strongly recommended.

Symphony 2 in C, Op. 61; 4 Pieces from Carnaval, Op. 9 (arr. Ravel); 6 Pieces from Kinderjahr, Op. 68 (arr. Adorno)
**(*) BIS CD 1055. RPO, Joeres

Dirk Joeres offers an idiomatic and sensitive account of the *Second Symphony*. He has the advantage of excellent playing from the Royal Philharmonic and this is a performance of some quality. The extra items are undeniably enterprising:

there are four fragments that survive from Ravel's orchestration of *Carnaval*, never before recorded, which only came to light in the 1970s; with *Kinderjahr*, there is a transcription by the philosopher and once-composer Theodor Wiesengrund Adorno of six of the Op. 68 *Album for the Young*.

Symphony 3 (Rhenish); (i) Des Sängers Fluch, Op. 139
*** Chan. 9760. Danish Nat. RSO, Schonwandt; (i) with Fischer, Rorholm, Wagenführer, Henschel, Hansen, Danish Nat. R. Ch.

Schonwandt and the fine Danish orchestra also give a fresh, spontaneous-sounding, well-paced reading of Schumann's warmest symphony. Schonwandt lifts rhythms infectiously in a performance full of light and shade, giving rapt intensity to the inner meditation of the Cologne Cathedral movement. The playing of the fine Copenhagen Orchestra is unfailingly cultured. A strongly competitive and compelling account, beautifully recorded by the Danish Radio engineers. The rare and generous coupling is most welcome, the 40-minute long choral ballad *The Minstrel's Curse*. A late work, it comes from 1852 and is a setting of Ludwig Uhland's ballad, which Schumann's collaborator Richard Pohl interspersed with other Uhland poems. No less a Schumann authority than Joan Chissell rates it well above the companion choral pieces of the period, and it has some delightful moments. It may lack the lyrical freshness of the symphony, but in this dedicated performance it impressively reveals Schumann's dramatic side, with foretastes even of Wagner. Not all the soloists are ideally steady, but the chorus is outstanding. First-rate sound.

Symphonies 3 (Rhenish); 4, Op. 120
(M) *** Virgin 5 61734-2. L. Classical Players, Norrington

With Schumann's orchestration usually accused of being too thick, there is much to be said for period performances like this. Norrington not only clarifies textures, with natural horns in particular standing out dramatically, but, at unexaggerated speeds for the outer movements – even a little too slow for the first movement of No. 3 – the results are often almost Mendelssohnian. Middle movements in both symphonies are unusually brisk, turning slow movements into lyrical interludes. Warm, atmospheric recording.

Symphony 4 in D min., Op. 120
☻ (N) (M) (***) DG mono 474 988-2. BPO, Furtwängler – HAYDN: *Symphony 88* (***)☻
(B) (***) EMI mono 5 74801-2. Philh. O, Cantelli – MENDELSSOHN: *Symphony 4;* SCHUBERT: *Symphony 8* (***)
*** Orfeo (ADD) C 522 991 B. VPO, Boehm – MAHLER: *Lieder eines fahrenden Gesellen;* BEETHOVEN: *Symphony 4* ***
*** BBC (ADD) BBCL4058-2. BBC SO, Monteux – BRAHMS: *Symphony 3* *** (with ROSSINI: *L'italiana in Algeri Overture* **(*))

This has now been reunited with its original coupling (in a facsimile of the original LP sleeve), Furtwängler's inspired account of Haydn's *Symphony No. 88*.

Along with Furtwängler's recording, also made in 1953, Cantelli's is one of the really great accounts of Schumann's *Fourth Symphony*. It sounds first class in this excellent transfer and serves as yet another reminder of the loss music suffered by his untimely death. Everything is beautifully proportioned and feeling is finely controlled.

Boehm's thrilling account of Schumann's *Fourth*, incandescent from first to last, crowns what was a very special Salzburg Festival concert in August 1969. In his studio recordings Boehm was rarely so fiery as here, with biting attack and strong rhythmic emphasis from the Vienna Philharmonic in superb form. The second-movement *Romanze* is set in sharp contrast: the deeply meditative opening theme gives way to lightness and transparency. The mystery of the slow introduction to the finale maintains the high voltage too, and though the close is something of a scramble with its successive accelerandos, the result could not be more exciting. Good radio sound, if with some edge on high violins.

Monteux recorded the *Fourth Symphony* in his San Francisco days but this did not enjoy wide currency outside the United States. Those who remember the BBC Symphony Orchestra in the early 1960s when it had been in the hands of Sir Malcolm Sargent and Rudolf Schwarz will recall that strong though its wind section was, the string sonority was generally opaque and thick. By comparison, Monteux produces a lighter, more transparent sound, given the constraints of Schumann's much criticized scoring. Rhythmic accents are lighter and there is a sense of drama without any histrionics. A valuable memento of Monteux in repertoire that is not associated with him.

CHAMBER MUSIC

Abendlied, Op. 85/2; Adagio & Allegro in A flat, Op. 70; Fantasiestücke, Op. 73; 3 Romances, Op. 94; 3 Pieces in Folk Style, Op. 102/2–4
(M) *** Ph. (IMS) (ADD) 426 386-2. Holliger, Brendel

Adagio and Allegro in A flat, Op. 70
(N) (BB) *** Naxos 8.557471. Tomboeck, Inui –
BEETHOVEN: *Horn Sonata;* BRAHMS: *Horn Trio;* SCHUBERT: *Auf dem Strom* ***

(i) Adagio and Allegro, Op. 70; (ii) Fantasiestücke, Op. 73 (both for cello & piano)
(B) *** RCA 2-CD 74321 84598-2 (2). Starker; (i) Buchbinder; (ii) Neriki – BRAHMS: *Cello Sonatas 1 –2; in D* (arr. of *Violin Sonata, Op. 78*); RACHMANINOV: *Cello Sonata* **(*)

Adagio & Allegro, Op. 70; Fantasiestücke, Op. 73; 5 Stücke im Volkston, Op. 102
(BB) *** Naxos 8.550654. Kliegel, Merscher – SCHUBERT: *Arpeggione Sonata* ***

Adagio & Allegro in A flat, Op. 70; Fantasiestücke, Op. 73; 5 Stücke im Volkston, Op. 102 (all for cello & piano)
**(*) BIS CD 1076. Thedéen, Pöntinen – CHOPIN: *Cello Sonata* **(*)

In the *Adagio and Allegro*, Op. 70, the distinctively fruity sound of the Vienna horn is wonderfully caught on the superb Naxos disc, its programme perfectly designed to show off the instrument. Like the other works, the Schumann is warmly done, with Wolfgang Tomboeck producing the ripest tones and the hunting-horn rhythms of the Allegro have an infectious brilliance and swagger.

The three *Romances* are specifically for oboe, but Holliger suggests that the others too are suitable for oboe, since the composer himself gave different options. One misses something by not having a horn in the *Adagio and Allegro*, a cello in the folk-style pieces, or a clarinet in the *Fantasiestücke* (the oboe d'amore is used here); but Holliger has never sounded more magical on record and, with superbly real recording and deeply imaginative accompaniment, the result is an unexpected revelation.

Starker and Neriki give a quite splendid account of the three pieces which make up the *Fantasiestücke* and are very well recorded (in 1990). The *Adagio and Allegro* is also very fine – producing a passionate flow of ardour, but here (two years later) Starker's tone is less ripely captured. However, this is still very recommendable if the couplings are suitable.

Maria Kliegel and Kristin Merscher couple these charming Schumann miniatures with the Schubert *Arpeggione* and turn in fresh and musical performances and are recorded in very clean and well-focused sound.

The rather reverberant acoustic of the former Academy of Music, Stockholm, at Nybrokajen, does not help these fine artists, either here or in the Chopin *Sonata*. Torleif Thedéen and Roland Pöntinen are sympathetic exponents of this repertoire even if in the *Fünf Stücke im Volkston* they are just a bit too earnest and lacking in charm. Maria Kliegel and Kristin Merscher (on Naxos 8.550654) are fresher and more appealing and they couple these works successfully with the Schubert *Arpeggione Sonata*.

Adagio and Allegro, Op. 70; 3 Fantasiestücke, Op. 73; 3 Romanzen; Märchenbilder; (i) Märchenerzählungen, Op. 132

*** Zig-Zag Territoires ZZT 010401. Beranger, Gastaldi; (i) with Heau

This is above all a celebration of the viola in Schumann's chamber music, with the young French viola-player Vinciane Beranger fresh, incisive and full-toned in all five works. Schumann was always accommodating about the instrumentation of these pieces, with the viola regularly interchanged with the clarinet. This has no doubt led Beranger to also take on the *Fantasiestücke* and the *Romanzen*, where Schumann suggests clarinet and violin as options but not the viola. The *Adagio and Allegro*, originally with horn or cello, works beautifully here, and the two later 'fairy-tale' works, *Märchenbilder* and *Märchenerzählungen*, are among the glories of the viola repertoire. It is only in the latter work that the clarinettist Florent Heau appears, another sensitive artist.

Fantasiestücke, Op. 73; 3 Romances, Op. 94

*** Chan. 8506. De Peyer, Pryor – SCHUBERT: *Arpeggione Sonata*; WEBER: *Silvana Variations* ***

Fantasiestücke; 5 Stücke in Volkston

*** Ph. (IMS) 412 230-2. Maisky, Argerich – SCHUBERT: *Arpeggione Sonata* ***

With warmth of tone and much subtlety of colour, Gervase de Peyer gives first-class performances and is well supported by Gwenneth Pryor. The recording is most realistic.

Mischa Maisky on cello and Martha Argerich give relaxed, leisurely accounts of these pieces that some collectors will find a bit self-indulgent. Others will luxuriate in the refinement and sensitivity of their playing.

Fünf Stücke in Volkston (for cello and piano)

(M) *** Decca (ADD) 460 974-2. Rostropovich, Britten (as above) – DEBUSSY: *Sonata* ***; SCHUBERT: *Arpeggione Sonata* **(*)

Though simpler than either the Britten or Debussy sonatas with which it is coupled, this is just as elusive a work. Rostropovich and Britten show that the simplicity is not as square and solid as might at first seem and that, in the hands of masters, these *Five Pieces in Folk Style* have a rare charm,

particularly the last with its irregular rhythm. The excellent recording justifies the reissue.

Märchenbilder, Op. 113

**(*) Chan. 8550. Imai, Vignoles – BRAHMS: *Viola Sonatas* **(*)

The *Märchenbilder* are also persuasively played here by Nobuko Imai and Roger Vignoles. The recording acoustic is not ideal, but this does not seriously detract from the value of this coupling.

Märchenerzählungen, Op. 132; Kinderszenen: Träumerei

*** RCA 09026 63504-2. Collins, Isserlis, Hough – BRAHMS; FRUHLING: *Clarinet Trios* ***

It makes a delightful coupling on an outstandingly successful disc having Schumann's *Fairy-tale Suite* – an association not explained in the booklet, which leaves you simply with the daunting German title – with Steven Isserlis on the cello taking the original viola part. *Träumerei*, offered as an encore to the three main works on the disc, comes in an arrangement for the same forces by Stephen Hough.

Piano Quartet in E flat, Op. 47; Piano Quintet in E flat, Op. 44

(M) **(*) Berlin Classics (ADD) 0094032BC. Rösel, Gewandhaus Qt

(B) **(*) Hyp. Dyad CDD 22008 (2). Schubert Ens. of L. – HUMMEL: *Piano Quintet*; SCHUBERT: *Trout Quintet* **(*)

**(*) Chan. 0698. Michelangelo Piano Qt, with (i) De Secondi

(M) **(*) CRD (ADD) CRD 3324. Rajna, members of the Alberni Qt

These Leipzig performances both sound very good, though a little more amplitude round the aural image would perhaps be welcome. The playing of Peter Rösel and the Gewandhaus Quartet is keenly alive and very musical. Tempi are fairly brisk but phrasing is affectionate and sensitive. This is playing of quality and good value at mid-price.

Lively, committed performances from the Schubert Ensemble of London led by their excellent pianist, William Howard. There are more individual versions of both works but if this inexpensive Dyad compilation seems tempting, the overall standard of musicianship is commendable and their playing enjoyable. Good if not outstanding recording.

Recorded in Florence in 2000, the Michelangelo Piano Quartet gives stylish accounts of Schumann's two most popular chamber works; these are pioneer versions of these works on period instruments. Fairly enough, the players allow a degree of flexibility in the sonata-form movements, no doubt aiming to reflect romantic performance practice, even though Clara Schumann's pupils have suggested that she was strict over tempo. The fortepiano, a fine 1830 instrument from Vienna, cannot sustain legato lines as a modern piano would (notably in the warmly lyrical slow movement of the *Piano Quartet*), but the extra clarity of articulation is a delight, while the stilling of vibrato by the strings intensifies the mood of dedication in slow passages, with splendidly crisp attack in *Allegros*.

Though not flawlessly polished in their playing, Thomas Rajna and the Alberni give performances that in their way are urgent and enjoyable. The recording is brighter and crisper, which gives an extra (and not unlikeable) edge to the performances.

Piano Quartet, Op. 47; Piano Quintet, Op. 44; Adagio & Allegro, Op. 70; Andante & Variations, Op. 46; Fantasiestücke, Op. 73; Märchenbilder, Op. 113; Violin Sonata 2 in D min., Op. 121

*** EMI 5 55484-2 (2). Argerich, Schwarzenberg, Hall, Imai, Maisky, Neunecker, Gutman, Rabinovitch

These recordings were made at a series of informal concerts at Nijmegen, and they radiate a spontaneity and life that are more difficult to capture under studio conditions. The *Piano Quintet* with Martha Argerich, Dora Schwarzenberg, Lucy Hall, Nobuko Imai and Mischa Maisky must be numbered among the most vibrant on record, and the *Piano Quartet*, with Natalia Gutman replacing Maisky and with Alexandre Rabinovitch at the piano, is hardly less fine. Although this is an arbitrary collection, those whose needs are met by this particular compilation will not be disappointed.

(i) *Piano Quartet, Op. 47; Piano Quintet, Op. 44. Piano Trios 1 in D min., Op. 63; 2 in F, Op. 80; 3 in G min., Op. 110*

☛ (B) *** Ph. Duo (ADD) 456 323-2 (2). Beaux Arts Trio, (i) with Bettelheim and Rhodes

Once again Philips have compiled a particularly generous measure for this Duo of Beaux Arts Schumann performances from the 1970s. This illustrious trio (with associates) give splendid readings of the *Piano Quartet* and *Quintet*. The vitality of inspiration is brought out consistently, and with that goes their characteristic concern for fine ensemble and refined textures. They are also probably the safest bet for the three *Piano Trios*. Not that competition is exactly legion, but none that we have heard can outclass the Beaux Arts in terms of musicianship and finesse. Throughout, the set offers cultured and concentrated music-making, matched by truthful and present analogue recording.

Piano Quintet in E flat, Op. 44

(BB) *** Naxos 8.550406. Jandó, Kodály Qt – BRAHMS: *Piano Quintet* ***

(***) Testament mono SBT 3063. Aller, Hollywood Qt – BRAHMS: *Piano Quartets etc.* (***)

(M) **(*) Sony (ADD) 512872-2. Serkin, Budapest Qt – SCHUBERT: *Piano Quintet (Trout)* **(*)

A strongly characterized performance of Schumann's fine *Quintet* from Jenö Jandó and the Kodály Quartet. This is robust music-making, romantic in spirit, and its spontaneity is well projected by a vivid recording, made in an attractively resonant acoustic. An excellent bargain.

Exhilarating and masterly, the Hollywood Quartet and Victor Aller on Testament comes from the compilation of Brahms chamber music, recorded in the mid-1950s. A performance of some stature which transcends sonic limitations.

On Sony there is some masterly playing from Serkin, though the intonation of the Budapest Quartet is not above suspicion and their tone not of the warmest. But this remains a performance of stature, even if the sound is less than ideal.

(i) *Piano Quintet in E flat, Op. 44; String Quartets 1 in A min.; 2 in F; 3 in A, Op. 41/1–3*

☛ (B) *** EMI double forte 5 75175-2 (2). Cherubini Qt, with (i) Zacharias

A vital and intelligent account of the *Piano Quintet*, not perhaps as fine as some presently available – most notably the Beaux Arts – but very acceptable given the competitive price and the couplings. The *Quartets* are not generously represented in the current catalogues and some of the finest

recordings (the Vogler Quartet on RCA and the Quartetto Italiano on Philips) are not currently in circulation. The present recordings were first issued as part of a series coupling Schumann and Mendelssohn, and the performances date from 1989 to 1991. They are finely paced and well shaped, and as persuasive as any now before the public – so this double forte reissue is well worth considering.

Piano Quintet, Op. 44; Andante & Variations for 2 Pianos, 2 Cellos & Horn, Op. 46; Fantasiestücke for Cello and Piano, Op. 73; Märchenbilder for Viola & Piano, Op. 113

*** EMI 5 57308-2. Argerich, Rabinovitch, Hall, Imai, Gutman, Maisky, Neunecker

A very distinguished line-up. We have highly-praised the performance of the *Piano Quintet*, recorded at the Concertgebouw, Nijmegen, in 1994. We also spoke of the informality of the music-making, which had 'the enthusiasm and intimate inspiration of a house-party'. EMI has now detached it from the two-CD set issued in 1995 (see above), albeit without a reduction in price, but nonetheless giving it another lease of life. The other items are also finely done.

(i; ii) *Piano Quintet in E flat, Op. 44; (ii) String Quartet 1 in A min., Op. 41/1; (i) Arabeske, Op. 18; Blumenstück, Op. 19*

*** Linn CKD132. (i) d'Ascoli; (ii) Schidlof Qt

The pianist, Bernard d'Ascoli, is an inspirational artist whose playing on disc is regularly marked by a winning spontaneity. This Linn programme makes an attractive mixture, with two of the major Schumann chamber works from the magic year, 1842, linked to two shorter piano works. In the *Piano Quintet* it is d'Ascoli who leads the ensemble, maybe controversially in the first movement, when he unashamedly encourages marked changes of tempo – persuasively so, thanks to the feeling of spontaneity. The freshness and ease of the interchanges between players gives the performance a relaxed warmth, not least in the finale, which is not overdriven. There are similar qualities in d'Ascoli's performances of the *Arabeske* and *Blumenstück*, with textures fresh and clean.

The *String Quartet* brings another refined performance with plenty of light and shade, starting with a slow introduction that brings out the mystery of the writing, echoing late Beethoven. The recording, made in the Blackheath Concert Halls, is finely focused within a helpful acoustic.

Piano Trios 1–3; Fantasiestücke, Op. 88

**(*) Chan. 8832/3 (2). Borodin Trio

Piano Trio 1 in D min., Op. 63; Bilder aus Osten, Op. 66; Phantasiestücke, Op. 88;

*** MDG 303 0921-2. Trio Parnassus

Piano Trios 2 in F, Op. 80; 3 in G min., Op. 110; 6 Pieces in the Form of a Canon, Op. 56

*** MDG 303 0922-2. Trio Parnassus

Piano Trio 1 in D min., Op. 63

(M) **(*) CRD (ADD) CRD 3433. Israel Piano Trio – BRAHMS: *Piano Trio 2* **(*)

(BB) (***) Naxos mono 8.110185. Cortot, Thibaud, Casals – MENDELSSOHN: *Piano Trio 1* (***)

Piano Trios 2 in F, Op. 80; 3 in G min., Op. 110; Fantasiestücke, Op. 88

(M) **(*) CRD (ADD) CRD 3458. Israel Piano Trio

Piano Trios 1, Op. 63; 2, Op. 80

(BB) *** Naxos 8.553836. Vienna Brahms Trio

The Trio Parnassus are a very good ensemble and give characterful and sensitive accounts of the three *Piano Trios* and the other repertoire included here. The MDG recording is very natural and well focused.

On Chandos are full-hearted performances that give undoubted pleasure – and would give more, were it not for some swoons from Rostislav Dubinsky, who, at the opening of the *D minor Trio*, phrases with a rather ugly scoop. While too much should not be made of this, greater reticence would have been more telling throughout. The Chandos recording is vivid and faithful.

The Israel Piano Trio give a powerfully projected account of the *D minor Trio*; the pianist is at times rather carried away, as if he were playing a Brahms concerto. There are, however, some sensitive and intelligent touches, and the recording is first class. Nos. 2 and 3 are much the same: lively, articulate playing with a sometimes over-forceful pianist.

The Vienna Brahms Trio give eminently musical accounts of both scores and are satisfactorily recorded. The Beaux Arts Trio on Philips, however, are every bit as competitive (see above).

The partnership of Jacques Thibaud, Pablo Casals and Alfred Cortot made their recording of the *D minor Piano Trio* in 1928, so the sound is wanting the body and colour of later recordings. Coming to this set afresh one wonders if it has ever been surpassed in musical insight. They are immaculate, wonderfully singing in their phrasing, and their apparent spontaneity of feeling is born of a firm musical grip. Ward Marston's transfer is first rate.

Piano Trio 3 in G min.; Piano Quartet in E flat, Op. 47; Fantasiestücke, Op. 88
*** Hyp. CDA 67175. Florestan Trio (augmented)

The Florestan Trio is first rate in every way and gives thoughtful and spirited accounts of all three of these Schumann pieces. It is joined effectively in the *E flat Piano Quartet* by the violist Thomas Riebl.

String Quartets 1–3, Op. 41/1–3
*** HM HMU 907270. Eroica Qt
(N) (M) *** CRD 2-CD CRD 2414 (2). Alberni Qt –
   MENDELSSOHN: *Quartet 2* ***

String Quartets 1 in A min, Op. 41/1; 3 in A, Op. 41/3
*** ECM 1793. Zehetmair Qt

The Eroica is the only ensemble so far to have squeezed all three Schumann quartets onto a single CD. Schumann's writing benefits from the transparency of tone produced by the group's all first instruments. Tempos are judged well, and the overall impression is fresh and enjoyable.

Quite outstanding performances from the Zehetmair Quartet and arguably the best account of either work to have appeared in recent years. But the playing time is only 49 minutes, which would have left room for the remaining *Quartet in F*, Op. 41/2. The Eroica Quartet, playing on period-instruments, accommodate all three on their Harmonia Mundi CD but, good though they are, we would not prefer them to the Zehetmair. If you already have the *F major*, there is no need to hesitate.

The well-recorded and sympathetic performances by the Alberni Quartet have plenty of finesse and charm and are guided throughout by sound musical instinct. The Mendelssohn coupling is equally attractive.

Violin Sonatas 1 in A min., Op. 105; 2 in D min., Op. 121; 3 in A min., Op. posth
**(*) CPO 999 597-2. Faust, Avenhaus

Violin Sonatas 1; 2 in D min., Op. 121
*** DG (IMS) 419 235-2. Kremer, Argerich

Violin Sonata 1 in A min., Op. 105
(***) Biddulph mono LAB 165. Busch and Serkin – BRAHMS:
   String Quartets 1–2 (**(*)) (with REGER: *Violin Sonata 5, Op. 84: Allegretto* (***))

The first two *Violin Sonatas* both date from 1851 and are 'an oasis of freshness' in Schumann's last creative period. Kremer and Argerich are splendidly reflective and mercurial by turn and have the benefit of an excellent recording.

The Biddulph sleeve-note hails the 1937 Busch–Serkin account of the *A minor Sonata*, Op. 105, erroneously billed as No. 2 on the label and sleeve, as 'never having been equalled for its intensity and romantic ardour'. This is absolutely right. The disc throws in the only Reger that Busch recorded, the *Allegretto* from the *F sharp minor Sonata*, Op. 84.

The *Third Sonata* was composed on the brink of Schumann's breakdown. It was the last music he ever wrote, but was not published until the centenary year in 1956. In character the first movement is close to its D minor predecessor, but as a whole the piece is far from negligible. The CPO performances are a little assertive and not always prepared to let Schumann speak for himself, but this should not deter the reader from considering this well-recorded disc.

PIANO MUSIC

'Abegg' Variations, Op. 1; Arabeske, Op. 18; Blumenstück, Op. 19; Bunte Blätter, Op. 99; Carnaval, Op. 9; Davidsbündlertänze, Op. 6; Etudes symphoniques, Op. 13; Fantasie, Op. 17; Fantasiestücke, Op. 12; Faschingsschwank aus Wien, Op. 26; Humoreske, Op. 20; Kinderszenen, Op. 15; Kreisleriana, Op. 16; Nachtstücke; Novellette, Op. 21/1, 2 & 8; Papillons, Op. 2; 3 Romanzen, Op. 28; Sonatas 1–2; Waldszenen, Op. 82
(B) *** Decca 470 915-2 (7). Ashkenazy

Vladimir Ashkenazy's survey of the Schumann piano music comes from the late 1980s through to the mid-1990s and, like so many of these Decca collections (Jorge Bolet's Liszt and Katchen's Brahms), offers terrific value for money. Of course there are individual performances that have been surpassed by other artists (Perahia's *C major Fantasy* has perhaps the greater poetic intensity and spontaneity, and Lupu's unforgettable accounts of the *Humoreske* and *Kreisleriana* are performances of real distinction). But this is not to minimize the achievement of these thoughtful and intuitive performances or the artistry and excellence which Ashkenazy brings to bear on a composer for whom he obviously has great feeling. The recordings are generally very natural, and readers wanting a complete Schumann coverage will find much to reward them here.

Abegg Variations, Op. 1; Davidsbündlertänze, Op. 6
*** Ottavio OTRC 39027. Cooper – BRAHMS: *Fantasias, Op. 116* ***

Imogen Cooper plays the *Abegg Variations* with a rare combination of iridescent brilliance and poetic feeling, and she characterizes the *Davidsbündlertänze* with consistent imagination and colour. Her playing is spontaneous from first to last, and the recording most realistic.

Abegg Variations, Op. 1; Kreisleriana, Op. 16; 3 Romances, Op. 28

**(*) CPO 999 598-2. Banfield

Volker Banfield provides a thoughtfully musical account of *Kreisleriana* (although the ending of the third section is a bit scrambled and overpedalled) as well as the *Abegg Variations* and the three *Romances*. No challenge to the likes of Perahia or Lupu, but intelligent playing all the same.

Albumblätter, Op. 99; Arabeske, Op. 18; Etudes symphoniques, Op. 13

(BB) *** Naxos 8.550144. Vladar

Stefan Vladar intersperses the additional studies that Schumann published as an appendix into the *Etudes symphoniques*. His account is quite simply superb in every respect and deserves recording of comparable excellence. The *Albumblätter* is hardly less masterly. Artistically this rates three stars, with the compelling quality of the playing transcending the sonic limitations of the recording.

Album für die Jugend, Op. 68/21, 26 & 30; Davidsbündlertänze, Op. 6; Fantasia in C, Op. 17

(M) *** Virgin 5 62196-2. Hough

Stephen Hough comes into competition with Perahia in the *Davisdbündlertänze*, and with Pollini and Curzon in the *Fantasia* (both works inspired by Schumann's romantic feelings for Clara). But these fine readings stand up well to such searching comparisons, even if they do not supplant them. The three pieces from the set of forty-three, written for the seventh birthday of his eldest child, Marie, make a delightful bonus, and Hough plays the thirtieth and finest (marked *Sehr langsam*) very beautifully indeed. Fine natural, if resonant recording.

Allegro in B min., Op. 8; Concerto without Orchestra, Op. 14; Davidsbündlertänze, Op. 6; Gesänge der Frühe, Op. 133; Kreisleriana, Op. 16

⊕ ⌐ (N) (B) *** DG 471 3682 (2). Pollini

This Schumann reissue finds Pollini on his best form, with something of the spontaneity and freshness he showed when he first emerged on the scene in the early 1960s tempered with the wisdom of advancing years. Indeed, this *Kreisleriana* is among the very finest. Maurizio Pollini is wonderfully satisfying and is beautifully recorded; the only reservation to be made is that both discs offer short measure at 48 minutes. However as a Double the set remains good value.

Arabeske, Op. 18; Blumenstücke, Op. 19; Davidsbündlertänze; Etudes symphoniques, Op. 13

(M) *** Warner Elatus 0927 49612-2. Schiff

András Schiff opts for the original (1837) *Davidsbündlertänze*, rather than the more usual 1851 revision. Admittedly the differences are not earth-shattering, but the fewer repeats ensure the greater freshness of the ideas. Each of the pieces is strongly characterized and played with appropriate ardour. In the *Etudes symphoniques* he chooses the generally used late version of 1852 (posthumously revised to restore two rejected earlier numbers). The *Arabeske* and the *Blumenstücke* complete a satisfying and competitively priced recital.

Arabeske, Op. 18; Bunte Blätter, Op. 99; Carnaval, Op. 9; Kreisleriana, Op. 16; Novelletten, Op. 21/1 & 8; Papillons, Op. 2; Toccata, Op. 7

(B) *** EMI double forte (ADD) 5 74191-2 (2). Egorov

Yuri Egorov has the kind of temperament that makes him a highly volatile but always perceptive Schumann advocate. His playing offers many insights as well as superb pianism. There is no lack of delicacy in the *Arabeske*, a winningly flowing account, and he brings out the wide range of colour and attractive ideas in the elaborate set of *Bunte Blätter* (Various Leaves). His are among the finest versions of *Carnaval* and *Kreisleriana*, the latter full of poetic and dynamic contrast, to say nothing of impulsive bravura. *Papillons*, too, has a great deal to commend it. Egorov does it with real imagination and much sensitivity, and although artistically his version is not superior to Murray Perahia's Sony account, the EMI recording is incomparably better. Indeed, the piano is given full sonority and fine presence throughout.

Arabeske, Op. 18; Carnaval, Op. 9; Davidsbündlertänze, Op. 6; Fantasie in C, Op. 17; Humoreske, Op. 20; Kinderszenen; Kreisleriana, Op. 16; Nachtstücke, Op. 23; Novelette, Op. 99/9; Papillons, Op. 2; 3 Romances, Op. 28; Sonata 2 in G min., Op. 22; Symphonic Studies, Op. 13; Waldszenen, Op. 21

(B) *** DG (ADD) 471 312-2 (4). Kempff

Kempff began recording the major Schumann piano works in 1967 with *Papillons* and *Davidsbündlertänze*, and he completed his survey in the early 1970s. Not all the music suits him equally well. He is in his element in pieces like the *Arabeske*, the relatively little-known first and third *Romances*, and the *Novelette*, where he inspires an element of fantasy, of spontaneous re-creation, and he is also at his most inspirational in the *Fantasie in C major*. *Davidsbündlertänze*, the *Nachtstücke* and *Papillons* are all extremely fine.

On the other hand the comparatively extrovert style of *Carnaval* suits him less well. It certainly does not lack life, but there is no special degree of illumination. Kempff's thoughtful, intimate readings of two of the *Etudes symphoniques* and *Kreisleriana* are marvellously persuasive, giving a clear illusion of live performances, spontaneously caught and again well recorded. Similarly if the sharper contrasts of the *Humoreske* are toned down by charm and geniality, the *Waldszenen* are glowingly relaxed and both are comparably personal and individual.

The last time these recordings were gathered together they occupied six LPs, issued to commemorate Kempff's eightieth birthday, and we commented at the time that they were fully worthy of the occasion. The reissues still are, and on four bargain-priced CDs they are even better value.

Arabeske, Op. 18; Carnaval, Op. 9; Humoreske, Op. 20; Toccata in C, Op. 7

*** BIS CD-960. Kempf

A debut recital from Freddy Kempf. His Schumann blends the right amount of intelligence and intuitive feeling. He is at his best in the reflective and inward moments and his *Humoreske* is particularly successful. He has remarkable technical prowess and refined musicianship. The recorded sound is very lively and natural, and the disc as a whole gives much satisfaction.

Arabesque, Op. 18; Fantasy in C, Op. 17

(M) *** DG (IMS) (ADD) 471 358-2. Pollini – LISZT: *Sonata; La Lugubre gondola* ***

Pollini's 1973 account of the *C minor Fantasy* is most distinguished. It is as fine as Richter's, and the playing throughout has a command and authority on the one hand and deep poetic feeling on the other that instantly capture the listener spellbound. The *Arabesque*, too, is impressively played. The recording is good if not outstanding, but, with its riveting Liszt coupling, this is one of the very finest reissues in the 'Pollini Edition'.

Davidsbündlertänze, Op. 6

(N) (B) **(*) EMI Debut 5 85894-2. Biss – BEETHOVEN: *Piano Sonata 23; Fantasy in G min.*.**(*)

Jonathan Biss was only 23 when making this disc, and he has collected golden reviews and awards in his native America. A pupil of Leon Fleischer, his Beethoven–Schumann recital forms part of EMI's invaluable Debut series. He commands superb technical address and a keen dramatic sense, though his temperament seems more attuned to the wilder and more impulsive side of Schumann's sensibility rather than the inward-looking and poetic. Compelling playing all the same, without being totally satisfying. The recording captures the timbre and colour of the piano most truthfully.

Davidsbündlertänze, Op. 6; Fantasiestücke, Op. 12; Papillons, Op. 2

☞ (M) *** Sony (ADD) SMK 89714. Perahia

Perahia has a magic touch and his electric spontaneity is naturally caught in the studio. In the works of Schumann, which can splinter apart, this quality of concentration is enormously valuable, and the results could hardly be more powerfully convincing, despite recording quality which lacks something in bloom and refinement. The *Papillons*, added for this reissue, are unlikely to be surpassed, and it is a pity that the close balance robs the piano timbre of some of its allure.

Davidsbündlertänze, Op. 6; Sonata 2 in G min., Op. 22; Toccata, Op. 7

☞ (BB) *** Warner Apex 0927 40834-2. Berezovsky

Boris Berezovsky is a keyboard lion of the first order. Everything we have so far heard of his has been of exceptional artistry and great finesse. His formidable musicianship is allied to a technique of magisterial calibre, and this coupling is very impressive indeed. These performances are of the highest calibre. The *Davidsbündlertänze* is particularly charismatic and this bargain reissue cannot be too strongly recommended.

Etudes symphoniques

(B) *** EMI double forte 5 69521-2 (2). Alexeev – BRAHMS: *Fantasias* etc. ***

Dimitri Alexeev combines the virtuoso technique which the work demands with supreme musicality and poetic feeling, the performance providing a structural cohesion not always in evidence. The digital recording, made several years later than that of the coupling, is excellent in bringing out the warmth of the piano-tone. A first-rate bargain.

Fantasia in C, Op. 17

☞ (M) *** DG (ADD) 447 451-2. Pollini – SCHUBERT: *Wanderer fantasia* ***

*** Chan. 9793. Lortie – LISZT: *Concert Paraphrases of Beethoven's An die ferne Geliebte; Mignon; Schumann Lieder* ***

This is among the most distinguished Schumann performances in the catalogue. Pollini's playing throughout has a command and authority on the one hand and deep poetic feeling on the other that hold the listener spellbound. The recording is good but not outstanding. A welcome mid-priced reissue in DG's series of 'Originals'.

Lortie is an unfailingly thoughtful and thought-provoking artist of compelling utterance, who always has something new to say – and whose expressive eloquence is always at the service of the composer. This newcomer ranks alongside the finest and most satisfying versions of the *C major Fantasia* now around. And it is *very* well recorded.

Fantasia in C, Op. 17; Faschingsschwank aus Wien (Carnival Jest from Vienna), Op. 26; Papillons, Op. 2

(BB) *** EMI Encore (ADD) 5 75233-2. Richter

Richter's 1961 account of the *C major Fantasy* is a wonderfully poetic performance. His phrasing, his magnificent control of dynamics, his gift for seeing a large-scale work as a whole – all these contribute to the impression of unmatchable strength and vision. The recording is faithful, with genuine presence. The other two works included on this CD were recorded live during Richter's Italian concert tour a year later. Inevitably, the piano sound is somewhat less sonorous, shallower at fortissimo level, but fully acceptable. The account of *Papillons* is beguilingly subtle in its control of colour. Reissued at budget price, this is an unmissable bargain.

Fantasia in C, Op. 17; Kinderszenen, Op. 15

☞ ✪ (M) (***) Decca mono 466 498-2. Curzon – SCHUBERT: *Wanderer Fantasia* (***) ✪

The *Fantasia* is a work indelibly associated with the composer's love for Clara and the spell that she cast over him. Curzon's extraordinarily chimerical and romantic reading of the first movement is matched by the depth of poetic feeling and passion he finds in the finale. Surely in this instance, to use his own metaphor, he perfectly succeeded in 'catching the butterfly on the wing' in a performance which is so 'live' and spontaneous in feeling, that it is difficult to believe it was made in the studio. The gentle *Kinderszenen* (also inspired by Clara) are equally magical. The recording is dry but faithful.

Fantasia in C, Op. 17; Piano Sonata 1 in F sharp min., Op. 11

✪ *** EMI 5 56414-2. Andsnes

The young Norwegian pianist gives us the freshest and most vibrant account of the *C major Fantasy* since Murray Perahia, coupled with as fine an account of the *F sharp minor Sonata* as you could find. It is beautifully paced and shaped. This is both magisterial and subtle playing, and well served by the engineers.

Fantasiestücke, Op. 12; Kinderszenen, Op. 15; Kreisleriana, Op. 16

☞ (M) *** Ph. 434 732-2. Brendel

Fantasiestücke is strong as well as poetic. The *Kinderszenen* is also one of the finest performances of the 1980s and is touched with real distinction. Brendel's *Kreisleriana* is intelligent and finely characterized. He is better recorded (in 1981–2) than most of his rivals and the overall impression is highly persuasive.

5 Gesänge der Frühe, Op. 133; Kreisleriana, Op.16; 4 Nachtstücke, Op. 23 Variations on an Original Theme in E flat

(M) *** Warner Elatus 2564 600026-2. Schiff

This is very much a valedictory programme, but András Schiff has included the justly popular *Kreisleriana* to remind us of the younger composer at the height of his inspirational powers. The withdrawn and unostentatious *Five Gesänge der Frühe* were written in October 1853, only four months before Schumann committed suicide. He was anxious about the publication of this work, which he described as depicting 'the emotions on the approach and advance of morning, but more as an expression of feeling than painting'. One feels he was thinking of dawn in another world, and this applies particularly to the serene opening and closing pieces. Op. 133 is not obviously rewarding for the pianist; neither is the set of four *Nachtstücke* (originally entitled 'Funeral Fantasy'). This was written much earlier in 1839, also with the presentiment of death, in this case the composer's brother, Edward. Schiff is a thoroughly sympathetic exponent, and once again it is the first and last of the pieces that are the most characteristic and memorable.

Schiff's opening of *Kreisleriana*, which follows, seems a bit rushed, but overall it is finely played, as are the lovely Variations on a 'quiet and inward theme' (which Schumann also used in the *Violin Concerto*). The first four variations were completed on 27 February 1854; then Schumann suddenly left his house and, in a deeply disturbed state, threw himself into the Rhine. He was rescued and taken back home, where he completed the fifth variation, which ends without finality. Shortly afterwards he was incarcerated in the asylum where he died in July 1856. A collection like this needs good documentation, and there are no complaints on this score nor on the quality of the recording.

Humoreske in B flat, Op. 20

(BB) **(*) Naxos 8.550469. Harden – REGER: *Variations* **(*)

Wolf Harden's performance of the Schumann *Humoreske* is highly imaginative, idiomatic and full of sensitive touches. There is plenty of air around the aural image.

Humoreske, Op. 20; Kinderszenen, Op. 15; Kreisleriana, Op. 16

*** Decca 440 496-2. Lupu

Lupu is one of the few artists whose understanding of the composer can be measured alongside that of Murray Perahia. His account of the *Humoreske*, Op. 20, is both poetic and hardly less magical than the *Kreisleriana*. This is playing of great poetry and authority. The recording is excellent, albeit resonant.

Humoreske, Op. 20; Nachtstücke, Op. 23; 8 Novelletten, Op. 21; Sonata in F sharp min., Op. 14

*** ECM 472 119-2 (2). Schiff

András Schiff has moved on from Decca to the ECM label and makes an impressive debut with this live 1999 Schumann recital, which communicates strongly. His playing is refreshingly light-textured with much delicacy of colour plus a natural response to the music's mood swings. This especially applies to the eight *Novelletten*, by no means easy works to bring off, for they can easily seem inflated. The *Sonata* too is finely played, never hectoring, and imaginatively detailed, the *Variations on Clara's Andantino* especially so, followed by a

brilliantly articulated finale. The closing encore, the *Nachtstücke*, is quite magical. The recording is excellent, the piano image clear and realistic.

Kinderszenen, Op. 15

(BB) *** Naxos 8.550885. Biret – DEBUSSY: *Children's Corner Suite* **(*); TCHAIKOVSKY: *Album for the Young* ***
(BB) (*) Naxos mono 8.505189 (5). Schnabel – BEETHOVEN: *Concertos* (***); BRAHMS: *Concerto 1–2*, etc. (*(*))

Idil Biret was a pupil of Kempff and is completely at home in the delightful children's pieces of Schumann. The characterization is strong, sensitive and often touching, as in *Träumerei* and the lovely closing movement, *The Poet Speaks*. The piano recording, made in the Clara Wieck Auditorium, is forward but realistic.

This post-war recording is a makeweight to Schnabel's Beethoven and Brahms concertos. Nothing that this great pianist does is without quality or interest, but this does not rank among his most outstanding recordings.

Kinderszenen, Op. 15; Kreisleriana, Op. 16; Waldszenen, Op. 82

☛ (B) *** DG (ADD) 469 555-2. Kempff

Nothing that Kempff does is without insight, and the simplicity of his approach to the *Kinderszenen* is disarming. Even the famous *Träumerei* has an innocence to match the suite's overall conception. The *Waldszenen* too are delightfully evoked, especially the famous *Prophet Bird*; and if Kempff's thoughtfully intimate reading of the more ambitious *Kreisleriana* misses the element of heroism in the music, the playing is still marvellously persuasive, giving a clear illusion of live performance. The new transfers of recordings from the early 1970s have never sounded more natural and present.

Kinderszenen, Op. 15; Papillons, Op. 2

(B) ** EMI Début 5 73500-2. Slobodyanik – CHOPIN: *Piano Sonata 3*, etc. **(*)

Alex Slobodyanik's accounts of both *Papillons* and *Kinderszenen* are undoubtedly sensitive and distinguished by great beauty of touch. There are many imaginative touches but the performance is somewhat marred by moments of affectation, from which the Chopin is relatively free.

Kreisleriana, Op. 16; Widmung (arr. Liszt)

**(*) MDG 312 0924-2. Tanski – SCHUBERT: *Wanderer Fantasia*; *Die wanderer* (arr. Liszt) **(*)

Claudius Tanski first came to notice during the late 1980s with an impressive account of the Reubke *Piano Sonata*. In this Schumann–Schubert recital he gives thoroughly musical and thoughtful accounts both of the *Kreisleriana* and of the Liszt transcription of *Widmung*. Although his *Kreisleriana* may not be a first choice, given the range and quality of the competition, no one who invests in this disc will be greatly disappointed.

Piano Sonata 1 in F sharp min., Op. 11

(M) *** DG (ADD) 463 676-2. Pollini – SCHUBERT: *Sonata 16* ***

Pollini's playing has command and authority on the one hand and deep poetic feeling on the other that instantly capture the listener spellbound. The CD transfer of the 1973 recording is a little hard, but this coupling with Schubert is among Pollini's most distinguished records and an apt candidate for DG's 'Originals'.

Piano Sonata No.1 in F min., Op. 14 (2nd version); *Studies after the Caprices of Paganini, Op. 3/1–6; Op. 10/1–6*
**(*) MDG 604 0941-2. Lee

The Korean pianist Mi-Joo Lee gives us the 1853 version of the *F minor Sonata*, which had a complicated gestation, although she restores two of the variations which Schumann finally excised. She also performs the two sets of *Paganini Studies*, more rarities that Schumann lovers will want to investigate. Good playing and decent recording.

VOCAL MUSIC

The Graham Johnson Lieder Edition

Following up his monumental Schubert song series for Hyperion, Graham Johnson here sets out on his parallel Schumann project with the same inspired combination of scholarship and artistry.

Lieder, Vol. 1: *6 Gedichte und Requiem, Op. 90; 6 Gesänge, Op. 107; Aufträge; Die Blume der Ergebung; Er ist's; Heiss' mich nicht reden; Ihr Stimme; Mädchen-Schwermut; Melancholie; Die Meersee; Mignon (Kennst du das Land?); Nachtlied; Nur wer die Sehnsucht kennt; Röslein, Röslein!; Sängers Trost; Singet nicht in Trauertönen; So lasst mich scheinem; Das verlassene Mägdelein; Warnung; Zigeunerliedchen I & II*
*** Hyp. CDJ 33101. Schäfer, Johnson

For volume 1, Christine Schäfer is chosen to sing a collection of late songs, written between 1849 and 1852, which reflect the increasing disturbance of the composer's mind in bouts of depression. Though these songs – generally with writing more chromatic than earlier – have been seriously neglected, Schäfer and Johnson consistently show that Schumann's inspiration remained undiminished. The recording, forward and well-balanced, does not always bring out the full sweetness of Schäfer's voice, though the subtlety and beauty of her tonal shading is faithfully caught, in unfailingly sensitive response to word-meaning.

Lieder, Vol. 2: *3 Gedichte von Emanuel Geibel, Op. 30; 12 Gedichte von Justinus Kerner, Op. 35; 4 Husarenlieder, Op. 117; An die Türen will ich schleichen; Ballade des Harfners; Die Löwenbraut; Wer nie sein Brot mit Tränen ass; Wer sich der Eisamkeit ergibt*
☙ *** Hyp. CDJ 33102. Keenlyside, Johnson

The virility of Simon Keenlyside's strongly projected singing is thrilling. This selection of songs concentrates on four poets, starting with four powerful settings of Goethe from late in Schumann's career, contrasting with light, ballad-like *Hussar songs*, also late, to words by Lenau. The other two groups of early songs, including *Der Hidalgo* to words by Geibel, with sparkling Spanish dance rhythms, and the substantial set of twelve settings of Justinus Kerner, a figure who links the other three poets. Johnson's notes as ever, like his playing, could not be more illuminating.

Lieder, Vol. 3: *Frauenliebe und Leben, Op. 42* with poem; *Traum der eignen Tage, 7 Lieder of Elisabeth Kulmann, Op. 104; Songs of Mary Queen of Scots, Op. 135.* Lieder: *Blonde Lied; Geisternähe; Gesungen!; Himmel und Erde; Jasminenstrauch; Die Kartenlegerin; Loreley; Sag'an, o lieber Vogel mein; Schneeglöckchen; Die Soldatenbraut; Stiller Vorwuf*
☙ *** Hyp. CDJ 33103. Banse, Johnson

The young German soprano Juliane Banse, with her warm, vibrant voice beautifully controlled, makes an imaginative choice of artist for this third volume of Graham Johnson's Schumann series. The selection concentrates mainly on songs on the subject of women's life and loves, not just in the ever-popular *Frauenliebe und Leben*. In that cycle, the strong tonal contrasts in Banse's singing heighten the drama throughout, but most of all in the final tragic song. As an epilogue, Banse recites the final poem in Chamisso's cycle, which wisely Schumann did not set. She also reads the composer's superscriptions before touching songs to poems by Elisabeth Kulmann, a poet who died tragically at 17. Rounding off the disc is the late set of five poems to words by Mary Queen of Scots – as Johnson points out, another 'Frauenliebe' without the 'Leben'. Fine recording and excellent notes.

Lieder, Vol. 4: *5 Lieder und Gesange, Op. 51; 6 Romanzen und Balladen, Op. 45* including *O weh des Scheidens, das er tat* by C. SCHUMANN; *20 Poems from Liebesfrühling, Op. 37* (including 4 settings by C. SCHUMANN)
**(*) Hyp. CDJ 33104. Doufexis, Widmer, Johnson

In his fourth selection for the Hyperion Schumann Edition, Graham Johnson offers as centrepiece a sequence of twenty settings of poems from Rückert's *Liebesfrühling*, including four by Schumann's wife, Clara. Other Rückert settings are included too, as well as settings of Heine, Eichendorff and Goethe, all presented with the compelling scholarship that was associated with his monumental Schubert series. This time, instead of well-known singers, he has chosen to work with two relatively little known artists.

The German mezzo, Stella Doufexis, has a bright, girlish voice, which suits the songs for a woman's voice well, including those of Clara Schumann. The voice of the Swiss baritone, Oliver Widmer, is more problematic when, for all his feeling for word-meaning and musical shaping, a hint of flutter grows unpleasantly uneven under pressure, most notably in the first song of all, *Sehnsucht*, making an unpromising start. Otherwise, clear, well-balanced sound.

Lieder, Vol. 5: *Dichterliebe, Op. 48; Lieder: Der arme Peter* (2 settings); *Auf ihrem Grab da steht eine Linde; Die beiden Grenadiere; Belsazar; Dein Angesicht si lieb; Entflieh' mit mir und sei mein Weib; Es fiel ein Relf in der Frühlingsnacht; Es leuchtet meine Liebe; Die feindlichen Brüder; Der Hans und Grete tanzen; In meiner Brust; Lehn deine Wang' an mein Wang'; Die Lotosblume* (2 settings) *; Mein Wagen rollet langsam; Die Minnesïnger; Tragödie*
*** Hyp. CDJ 33105. Maltman, Polyphony, Johnson – C. SCHUMANN: *Lieder ***

Christopher Maltman's expressive baritone is not easy to capture gracefully on disc, with the microphone inclined to bring out an unevenness of production. It says much for Graham Johnson as inspirer as well as accompanist that he prompts Maltman to give his finest, best-focused recorded performances yet, not only in the sixteen well-loved songs of *Dichterliebe*, but in a score of others mostly little known. They include two which Schumann originally planned for that cycle but that he excised – *Dein Angesicht so lieb* and *Lehn deine Wang*. Over the whole range of songs Maltman uses sharp contrasts of tone and dynamic, with crystal clear diction. *Die beiden Grenadiere*, the best-known of the non-*Dichterliebe* songs, with its portrait of the two Napoleonic veterans, is powerfully and movingly dramatic, leading up to the quotation of the 'Marseillaise'. Johnson's notes, as in his

Schubert series for Hyperion, are a model of scholarly insight, bringing extra illumination on every level, as in his analysis of Schumann's own contacts with Heine, as well as those of his wife, Clara, four of whose songs are also included. It is also illuminating to have two *a cappella* choral settings of Heine poems, beautifully sung by Polyphony, including *Die Lotosblume*, a poem also set as a solo song. Excellent, beautifully balanced sound.

Lieder, Vol. 6: *Spanishes Liebespiel, Op. 74; Spanische Liebeslieder, Op. 138; 5 Lieder, Op. 40*

*** Hyp. CDJ 133106. McGreevy, Doufexis, Thompson, Loges, Johnson, Hough – C. SCHUMANN: *6 Lieder from Jucunde*

This sixth instalment in Graham Johnson's splendid Schumann Lieder series brings together two neglected Spanish-inspired cycles, important for having prompted Brahms to write his *Liebeslieder Waltzes*. Op. 138 offers an almost exact model when, like those popular Brahms pieces, it has piano-duet accompaniment, here with Stephen Hough as Johnson's partner. It was in these colourful cycles that Schumann pioneered the idea of treating a group of soloists in a quasi-operatic way, coupling this with his fondness for 'armchair travelling', so popular in the mid-nineteenth century. They involve not just solo songs but duets, trios and quartets too, generally lightweight inspirations made the more winning by a characterful team of soloists. The baritone of the group, Stephan Loges, also tackles the five Op. 40 songs, four of them settings of Hans Andersen poems in German translations by Adalbert von Chamisso, poet of *Frauenliebe und Leben*. As a coupling come six songs by Clara Schumann, setting poems contained in Hermann Rollett's novel, *Jucunde*, fresh and lyrical, beautifully sung here by Geraldine McGreevy. As with other issues in this and Johnson's Schubert series, the detailed notes are endlessly illuminating.

Other Lieder Recordings

Lieder from *Album für die Jugend, Op. 79; Gedichte der Königen Maria Stuart, Op. 135; Myrthen Lieder, Op. 25:* excerpts. *Abends am Strand; Die Kartenlegerin; Ständchen; Stille Tränen; Verratene Liebe*

☯— (M) *** CRD (ADD) CRD 3401. Walker, Vignoles

Sarah Walker's 1982 Schumann collection is most cherishable, notably the five Mary Stuart songs which, in their brooding darkness, are among Schumann's most memorable. With superb accompaniment and splendid recording, this is an outstanding issue.

(i) *Dichterliebe, Op. 48; Liederkreis, Opp. 24 & 39;* (ii) *Belsatzar, Op. 57; 3 Gedichte, Op. 30; 6 Gedichte aus dem Liederbuch eines Malers, Op 36; 3 Gesänge, Op. 31; 4 Gesänge, Op. 142; Lieder und Gesänge, Op. 27; 5 Lieder und Gesänge, Op. 127; Myrten, Op. 25; Romanzen und Balladen, Opp. 49, 53 & 64*

☯— (M) *** DG (ADD) 474 466-2 (2). Fischer-Dieskau; (i) Eschenbach; (ii) Demus

The Lieder of Robert Schumann were central to Fischer-Dieskau's repertoire. He first sang the Op. 48 *Dichterliebe* in 1956 and, when he bade farewell to Salzburg in the summer of 1992, the two Heine cycles, Opp. 24 and 48, were included in the programme. The recordings of the three cycles with Christoph Eschenbach were made in 1974, 1975 and 1976 and are most impressive when considered in detail against other versions of these much recorded works. The tone may not be

as fresh as it was earlier, but Eschenbach's accompaniments are superb, consistently imaginative. The other recordings, made between 1961 and 1979, span the early to middle years of the singer's career. As it developed, his readings acquired a sharper edge, with the darkness and irony in some of Schumann's songs more specifically contrasted against the poetry and expressive warmth. This is an incredibly generous reissue, over 150 minutes in total, and as can be seen, the second disc, with Jörg Demus – who was Fischer-Dieskau's friend as well as a highly musical partner – includes rarities alongside the more familiar repertoire. Yet almost all these songs date from 1840, the year in which their composer concentrated on Lieder to the virtual exclusion of all other genres. The recording is excellent; the only snag is the absence of texts and translations.

Dichterliebe, Op. 48

(M) *** DG (ADD) 449 747-2. Wunderlich, Giesen – BEETHOVEN; SCHUBERT: *Lieder* ***

(*) Arthaus **DVD** 100 330. Schäfer, Natascha Osterkorn – SCHOENBERG: *Pierrot Lunaire* *

Dichterliebe, Op. 48; Liederkreis, Op. 39.

(N) (B) *** CfP (ADD) 586 1812 (2). Ian & Jennifer Partridge – SCHUBERT: *Die schöne Müllerin* ***

Dichterliebe (song-cycle), *Op. 48; Liederkreis* (song-cycle), *Op. 39; Myrthen Lieder, Op. 25*

*** DG (ADD) 415 190-2. Fischer-Dieskau, Eschenbach

Fischer-Dieskau's earlier DG *Dichterliebe* (recorded between 1973 and 1977) is not quite as emotionally plangent as his later, digital version on Philips (416 352-2), but the contrasts between expressive warmth and a darker irony are still apparent. Eschenbach is always imaginative and the recording has fine presence.

As in the excellent Schubert coupling, Ian Partridge here shows himself a deeply sensitive Lieder singer, blessed with a radiant light voice. In both cycles his thoughtfulness illuminates every line, helped by superbly matched accompaniment from his sister and well-balanced, truthful recording.

Yet another outstandingly fine *Dichterliebe* comes at bargain price on DG, plus the magnificent Op. 39 *Liederkreis*, made the more attractive on CD by the generous addition of seven of the *Myrthen* songs. Eschenbach is imaginative without ever being intrusive. Very good sound for the period.

Wunderlich, had he lived, would no doubt have surpassed this early recording of a favourite Schumann song-cycle but, even with an often unimaginative accompanist here, his freshness is most endearing, irresistible with so golden a voice.

Quite apart from the oddity of having a soprano performing a song-cycle designed for male singers, the presentation of *Dichterliebe* on DVD with Christine Schäfer could not be more pretentious. The film starts with the singer in bed with her (male) partner, followed by her disappearing for ablutions. Other trivial incidents are then set in an aseptic modern apartment, a nightclub and (presumably) a recording studio. The sound of the piano is excruciating, more like a harp, and the interview with the singer (in German with the option of subtitles) is only moderate compensation, filmed in a coffee-bar and covering such subjects as her life, education and singing styles. There is, mercifully, a digital option of viewing the songs only.

Frauenliebe und Leben, Op. 42

(B) *** EMI Debut 5 85559-2. Coote, Drake – HAYDN: *Arianna a Naxos*; MAHLER: *Das Knaben Wunderhorn* (excerpts), etc. ***

(B) **(*) CfP 2-CD (ADD) 575 7732 (2). M. Price, Lockhart; (i) with Brymer (with LISZT: *Es muss ein Wunderbares sein; Kling leise, mein Lied; O lieb', so lang du lieben kannst; Die Lorelei; Die stille Wasserrose*; TCHAIKOVSKY: *None but the lonely heart; Do not believe my friend; At the Ball* ***) SCHUBERT: *Lieder* **(*)

(N) (BB) (**(*)) Naxos mono 8.11009. Ferrier, Newmark – BRAHMS: *Alto Rhapsody*, etc. (**(*))

EMI's Debut series has brought to disc a formidable list of young artists, but none finer than the mezzo, Alice Coote. Her choice of repertory could hardly be more challenging, inviting instant comparison with recordings by Dame Janet Baker at her very finest. Coote's voice may not have the velvety warmth of Dame Janet, but in its firmness and clarity it is strikingly distinctive, with a wide dynamic range perfectly controlled down to *pianissimos* of breathtaking intensity. One of Baker's very first recordings was of this Schumann song-cycle, and Coote comes very near that model in depth and range of feeling, with words finely pointed. A pity that, as in other EMI issues of Lieder in this series, no texts or translations are given.

Recorded two years after Margaret Price's Schubert coupling, this recital shows an advance on all fronts, not least the balance with the piano, which is admirable, as are James Lockhart's accompaniments. The performance of the famous *Frauenliebe* cycle brings most affecting and dedicated singing, particularly in the touching closing song, and the voice seems well suited to three of Tchaikovsky's best-known songs, and even more so to the equally well-chosen Liszt group, of which *O lieb', so lang du lieben kännst* is a setting of words to the composer's most famous piano piece, *Liebesträume*.

Ferrier was a deeply impressive Lieder singer, but there are more tender, more loving emotions in Schumann's cycle than she was able to convey at that stage of her career (1950). She is not helped by the limited accompaniment of John Newmark. Nevertheless, who will fail to be moved by her touching singing of the closing song, *Nun hast du mir den ersten Schmerz getan*, and the Brahms couplings make this reissue indispensable.

Frauenliebe und Leben, Op. 42; Liederkreis, Op. 39

(M) (***) Westminster (IMS) mono 471 269-2. Jurinac, Holetschek (with RESPIGHI: *Il tramonto* (Jurinac, Barylli Qt) ***)

Sena Jurinac's 1953 mono account of *Frauenliebe und Leben* on Westminster enjoyed great renown in its day, as indeed did its coupling on this disc, Respighi's lovely Shelley setting, *Il tramonto*, which Sena Jurinac sings with the Barylli Quartet. This is a disc whose return after almost half a century is a matter for celebration. It does not sound its age and offers glorious singing. Readers are urged to snap it up before it is again deleted.

Frauenliebe und Leben, Op. 42; Liederkreis, Op. 24; 3 Heine Lieder (Abends am Strand; Lehn' deine Wang' an meine Wang'; Mein Wagen rollet langsam); Tragödie, Op. 64/3

(N) **(*) Australian DG Eloquence 476 2386. Fassbaender, Gage

Positively characterized, with a wide range of expression and fine detail but little sense of vulnerability, Fassbaender's

reading conceals the underlying sentimentality of the poems of *Frauenliebe*. There is little attempt to beautify the voice, though it is a fine, consistent instrument, for a clear exposition of the words in the singing of the Heine *Liederkreis*, of which there are surprisingly few recordings. The three songs of *Tragödie* and the three separate Heine settings make an important supplement. Irwin Gage is the understanding accompanist. The recording is well balanced, with fine presence.

Frauenliebe und Leben, Op. 42; 5 Lieder, Op. 40 (Märzveilchen; Muttertraume; Der Soldat; Der Spielmann; Verratene Liebe). Lieder: Abendlied; Dein Angesicht; Die Kartenlegerin; Die Löwenbraut; Lust der Sturmnacht; Mein schöner Stern; Die Meersee; Rose, Meer und Sonne; Der Schätzgräber; Schneeglöckchen; Des Sennen Abscheid; Die Soldatenbraut; Stille Liebe; Volksliedchen; Vom Schlaraffenland

*** DG 445 881-2. Von Otter, Forsberg

Anne Sofie von Otter characterizes the contrasting songs in *Frauenliebe* with exceptional intensity, presenting a character, as in an opera, developing from youthful, eager girl to bereaved widow. By creating a character outside herself, von Otter may for some seem a shade detached compared with other, more personally involved singers, but that strengthens the cycle, minimizing the sentimentality of the poems. This is an exceptionally generous recital (79 minutes) and other songs on the disc are characterized commandingly, with dramatic contrasts heightened. Try the beautiful Heine setting, *Dein Angesicht* ('Your face'), sung with poise and flawless legato. Excellent sound and fine accompaniment from Forsberg. Highly recommended.

Frauenliebe und Leben, Op.42; Liederkreis, Op. 39; Aus den östlichen Rosen; Kennst du das Land; Meine Rose; Der Nussbaum; Requiem; Die Soldatenbraut; Widmung

(BB) *** Regis RRC 1051. Lott, Johnson

Felicity Lott is a connoisseur's artist, far greater than many more illustrious and publicized rivals, and she sings here with great poise and a completely unaffected artistry. The recording comes from 1990 and is not new, but the finesse and musicianship of this partnership, as well as the intelligence which guides everything they do, make it treasurable. The sound, too, is very good indeed.

Frauenliebe und Leben, Op. 42; Liederalbum für die Jugend, Op. 79 (excerpts): Der Abendstern; Schmetterling; Frühlingsbotschaft; Frühlingsgrüss; Vom Schlaraffenland; Sonntag; Des Knaben Berglied; Käuzlein; Hinaus ins Freie; Der Sandman; Marienwürmchen; Die Waise; Frühlings Ankunft; Kinderwacht. Lieder und Gesänge aus Wilhelm Meister, Op. 98a (excerpts): Mignons Gesang; Lied der Mignon I, II & III; Lied der Philine. Myrthen, Op. 25 (excerpts): Jemand; Mein Herz ist betrübt; Lied der Suleika: Wie mit innigstern Behagen. Die Hochländer-Witwe; Lied der Braut I & II; Hochlander Wiegenlied; Weit, weit; Im Westen

☛ (B) *** DG Eloquence (ADD) 469 767-2. Mathis, Eschenbach

An extraordinary bargain, even though no texts or translations are included. With her fresh tone and delicately poised manner, Edith Mathis brings out the girlish feelings implied by the *Frauenliebe* songs. Inevitably Mathis lacks a little weight in the last song of bereavement, but there is no lack of intensity. What makes this inexpensive Eloquence reissue indispensable is the generous collection of other songs for female voice taken from three major collections, Opp. 25, 79 and 98a, bringing consistently sensitive and imaginative singing, sustained by accompaniments from Eschenbach as responsive as those he provided on other records for Dietrich Fischer-Dieskau. Throughout, these are finely detailed performances, always refreshing and perceptive and in some of the less well-known songs Mathis often transforms what seems a simple idea into something magical. First-rate recording, vividly real with a perfect balance. Highly recommended.

Liederkreis, Op. 39
(B) *** EMI double forte (ADD) 5 73836-2 (2). Baker, Barenboim – LISZT; MENDELSSOHN: Lieder ***

With Barenboim an endlessly imaginative if sometimes reticent accompanist, this song-cycle is a classic example of Dame Janet Baker's art, the centrepiece in a superb recital which contrasts the high romantic and sometimes tragic world of Schumann with fine collections of hardly less fine settings of Liszt and Mendelssohn.

Liederkreis, Op. 39; 12 Kerner Lieder, Op. 35
(BB) *** Hyp. Helios CDH 55011. Price, Johnson

As a spin-off from Graham Johnson's Schubert recording with Dame Margaret Price (No. 15 in the series), Johnson partners her here in a superb Schumann disc, coupling the sequence of 12 Settings of Justinus Kerner, Op. 35, with the Eichendorff Liederkreis, Op. 39. The singer's presence, magnetism and weight of expression are superbly caught, and the tonal beauty and immaculate sense of line go with detailed imagination in word-pointing. Price may underplay the horror of such a song from Op. 39 as Waldesgesprach about meeting the Lorelei, but the moment of confrontation is sharply pointed when legato is suddenly abandoned. The lesser-known Kerner Lieder also contain many treasures. First-rate sound. Full notes and texts with translations are included in this bargain reissue.

(i) Mass in C min., Op. 147; (ii) Requiem in D flat, Op. 148
(N) (BB) *** EMI Encore 5 85819-2. Düsseldorf State Musikverein Ch., with (i) Shirai, Seiffert, Rootering, BPO, Sawallisch; (ii) Donath, Soffel, Gedda, Fischer-Dieskau, Düsseldorf SO, Klee

Schumann's Mass brings some of his finest flights of invention – not at all the tailing-off which has been ascribed to him in the period leading up to his mental illness. Of the soloists only the soprano has much to sing (the delectable Mitsuko Shirai, sensuously beautiful in the Offertorium solo) and the weight of the work rests on the chorus, here a fine body, warmly rather than clinically recorded. Few conductors today can match Sawallisch in Schumann's music, yet in the Requiem Klee also extracts a very sympathetic response from his distinguished solo team, and the fine Düsseldorf Chorus and Orchestra. Like Mozart, Schumann was unable to shake off the conviction that the Requiem was for himself, and the opening Requiem aeternam is affecting and dignified, while the final Benedictus has a haunting eloquence. Again the EMI recording is natural and well balanced and this is another real bargain on the budget Encore label.

Mass in C min., Op. 147; Requiem for Mignon, Op. 98b
(BB) *** Warner Apex 0927 49977-2. Michael, Bizimeche-Eisinger, Silveira, Schaeffer, Brodard, Lisbon Gulbenkian Foundation Ch. & O, Corboz

In 1852 Schumann had been proselytizing the music of Bach, including the B minor Mass, and perhaps that prompted the composition of his own Mass in C minor. It is a powerful work in which the chorus is all-important. The Lisbon singers rise to the challenge eloquently under Corboz, who is a persuasive exponent. He has good soloists, and Audrey Michael is particularly touching in the Offertorium, where she sings with treble-like purity. The Sanctus which follows is also very fine. The less ambitious Requiem für Mignon is also very attractively done, with the matching of the female solo voices particularly pleasing. Excellent digital recording gives a natural projection and focus to the performers, and the documentation about the music has been restored for this inexpensive reissue.

(i) Das Paradies und die Peri, Op. 50; (ii) Requiem für Mignon, Op. 98b; Nachtlied (for chorus & orchestra), Op. 108
*** DG 457 660-2 (2). (i) Bonney, Coku, Fink, Prégardien, Archer, Finley, Hauptman; (ii) Dazeley; Monteverdi Ch., ORR, Gardiner

It takes a conductor as perceptive and persuasive as Sir John Eliot Gardiner to transform Das Paradies und die Peri into something like a masterpiece. That he does with his period forces in this fine version on DG Archiv. For good measure he adds two other much shorter neglected works and similarly presents them in their full originality. Clara Schumann may have claimed Das Paradies as the most beautiful of her husband's works, and it seems to have been his first major piece to establish his international reputation; yet this secular oratorio on a Persian legend from Thomas Moore's oriental epic Lalla Rookh is by latterday standards sentimental, telling the story of the Peri who is refused entry into Paradise, having been the child of a fallen angel and a mortal.

With his period forces Gardiner brings out the clarity and subtlety of the choral and orchestral writing, moulding phrases warmly but with none of the syrupy sweetness that gave the piece a bad name. In such a performance the fairy choruses have a sparkle to match Mendelssohn. Barbara Bonney, pure and tender, is ideally cast as the Peri and she is well matched by the rest of the team, with the mezzo, Bernarda Fink, and the two tenors, Christoph Prégardien and Neill Archer, all outstanding. Yet most brilliant of all is the Monteverdi Choir, singing with freshness and clarity.

With William Dazeley as soloist, and with four trebles from the Hanover Boys Choir in key solo roles, the Requiem für Mignon is also most atmospherically done with wonderfully varied textures. To words by Hebbel, the Nachtlied, too, is revealed as more buried treasure. Refined, beautifully balanced recording made at the Watford Colosseum.

Der Rose Pilgerfahrt, Op. 112
*** Chan. 9350. Nielsen, Van der Walt, Møller, Paevatalu, Danish Nat. R. Ch. and SO, Kuhn

Schumann wrote his cantata, Der Rose Pilgerfahrt ('The Pilgrimage of the Rose') in 1851, towards the end of his career. The very opening has the lyrical openness of Schubert, its freshness enhanced by the interplay of solo voices and women's chorus. The idiom, as well as recalling Schubert, often suggests the folk-based writing of Humperdinck in Hänsel und Gretel, similarly innocent-seeming, but in fact subtle.

Gustav Kuhn conducts an aptly bright and atmospheric performance, very well recorded, with Inga Nielsen and Deon van der Walt in the two principal roles. The chorus and orchestra are first rate and the recording, sponsored by Danish Radio, is full-bodied and atmospheric. A valuable rarity. Sadly, the booklet contains no translation alongside the German text, though Richard Wigmore's note and summary are very helpful.

Scenes from Goethe's Faust
⊕ (M) *** Decca (ADD) 476 1548 (2). Harwood, Pears, Shirley-Quirk, Fischer-Dieskau, Vyvyan, Palmer, Aldeburgh Festival Singers, ECO, Britten

Britten's outstanding 1972 performance (see our main volume) now reappears in Universal's 'Penguin ⊕ Collection' at mid-price with full documentation included. Though the episodic sequence of scenes is neither opera nor cantata, the power and imagination of much of the music (not least the delightful garden scene and the energetic setting of the final part) are immensely satisfying. In 1972, soon after a live performance at the Aldeburgh Festival, Britten inspired his orchestra and his fine cast of singers to vivid performances which are outstandingly recorded against the warm Maltings acoustic. This is magnificent music, and readers are urged to explore it – the rewards are considerable.

SCHURMANN, Gerard (born 1928)

6 Studies of Francis Bacon for Large Orchestra; Variants for Small Orchestra
*** Chan. 9167. BBC SO, composer

Inspired by the fantastic, often violent or painful paintings of Francis Bacon, Schurmann here writes a virtuoso orchestral showpiece, full of colourful effects. The vigour of the writing is admirably caught both in this performance and in the often spiky writing of the Variants for a rather smaller orchestra, set against passages of hushed beauty. First-rate 1979 recording, made in the warm acoustics of All Saints', Tooting, and admirably transferred to CD.

SCHUSTER, Joseph (1748–1812)

Demofoonte (opera; complete)
*** BMG/RCA 74321 98282-2 (2). Post, Mields, Melnitzki, Waschinski, Buchin, Kobow, Schafferer, La Ciaccona, Rémy

Dresden-based throughout his career, Joseph Schuster had his training as an opera composer during several extended visits to Italy. He became court composer in Dresden in 1777, a much-respected figure. Having had early success writing opera buffa, he turned to opera seria, with Demofoonte appearing in 1786 while he was on one of his trips to Italy. To a libretto by Metastasio already set by Paisiello a couple of years earlier, Schuster decks the improbable story in an attractive series of lively and inventive numbers. The oracle has placed on the realm of King Demofoonte a curse: a virgin must be sacrificed each year as long as a usurper sits on the throne. The heroine, Dircea, daughter of the King's chief minister, Matusio, is secretly married to the King's eldest son, Timante, and that leads to her being condemned as the victim. The twists in the plot are many and complex, before the necessary happy ending is achieved through a double switch of parentage, a twist worthy of W. S. Gilbert.

In this recording, made in the Bavarian Music Academy, the period-performance group La Ciaccona, under Ludger Rémy, brilliantly brings out the strong colouring of Schuster's instrumental writing, with braying horns rasping away in almost every number from the hunting-rhythms of the Overture onwards, and with oboes adding bite. The casting is good, with Dorothee Mields sweet and tender as well as agile as Dircea, and with Joerg Waschinski, accurately described as a male soprano, taking on the formidable castrato role of Timante, her lover. Two incidental castrato roles are well taken by male altos, Werner Buchin and Bernhard Schafferer, though Marie Melnitzki's soprano (as recorded) sounds unpleasantly thin and shallow. Both the tenor roles are very well sung, with Andreas Post as Demofoonte and Jan Kobow equally fresh and unstrained as the minister, Matusio. Schuster's limitation is that, lively as his writing is in general, he seems to find it hard to express deep emotion. When the ill-fated Dircea sings the aria Padre perdona, it is only the first few bars that express pathos, before the aria switches to a jolly allegro. Deeper feelings tend to be consigned to recitative; disappointingly, the opera ends on a sequence of secco recitative, with only a final march from the orchestra to round things off. A welcome rarity nevertheless, well recorded.

SCHÜTZ, Heinrich (1585–1672)

Heinrich Schütz was born in Weissenfels in Saxony, a city haunted by the Plague at the turn of the sixteenth into the seventeenth century. During this period nearly 2,000 of its citizens were carried off, and while still young Schütz himself lost most of his family, including his parents, wife and two daughters. It is perhaps not surprising that his most celebrated work is his Requiem setting. Schütz also lived within the social havoc of the Thirty Years War, and besides making two visits to Italy and Venice he moved between German courts to make his living, although basing himself in Dresden, where he held the post of Kapellmeister. Remarkably, through all this turmoil, he did not lose his faith in the promises of Christianity, and many of his works offer eloquent praise to God and confidence in the hereafter.

Die Auferstehung unsres Herren Jesu Christi. (i) Meine Seele erhebt den Herren
*** HM HMC 90 1310. Concerto Vocale, Jacobs, (i) with Kiehr

Schütz's Resurrection has a purity of feeling and a depth that cleanses the spirit, and René Jacobs's wonderfully paced and unhurried account of the Passion story has the listener (or at least this listener) completely under his spell. The quality and imaginative playing of the instrumentalists are no less impressive than the vocal contributions, especially that of Maria Cristina Kiehr. The recording is very well balanced and real.

Christmas Day Vespers 1664 (including: Christmas Story; Magnificat with Christmas Interpolations; O bone Jesu, fili Mariae (Sacred Concerto); Warum toben die Heiden)
*** DG 463 046-2. (i) Daniels, Boys Ch. & Congregational Ch. of Roskilde Cathedral, Gabrieli Consort and Players, McCreesh

As in his earlier hypothetical recreation of Vespers, at St Mark's, Venice, Paul McCresh here celebrates Christmas Vespers as it might have been heard at the Dresden Court in 1664. The result is an immensely varied vocal and instrumental tapestry, ranging from congregational hymns, to Schütz's glorious *Magnificat* setting, including such familiar Christmas interpolations as the chorales *Lobt Gott, ihr Christen all zugleich* and *In dulci jubilo*, and ending with a burst of magnificence in the organ postlude, *Benedicamus Domino* by Samuel Scheidt. The centrepiece is a very fine performance of Schütz's *Christmas Story* with Charles Daniels a lyrical rather than a dramatic Evangelist. Other soloists are drawn from the Gabrieli Consort and the instrumental groups include wind instruments, cornetts and sackbutts, strings and a widely varied palette of continuo. The cathedral ambience adds to the sense of occasion, and the variety of the music here is matched by the colourful and dedicated response of the performers. A remarkable achievement.

Christmas Story (Weihnachthistorie)

🔘 (M) *** Virgin 5 61353-2. Kirkby, Rogers, Thomas, Taverner Cons., Taverner Ch., Taverner Players, Parrott – PRAETORIUS: *Christmas Motets* ***

Christmas Story (Weihnachthistorie); 3 Cantiones sacrae (1625); Psalm 100

(BB) *** Naxos 8.553514. Agnew, Crookes, MacCarthy, Oxford Camerata, Summerly

Virgin Veritas's version has the advantage of three first-class soloists, all of whom are in excellent voice. One is soon gripped by the narrative and the beauty and simplicity of the line. There is no sense of austerity here, merely one of purity, with the atmosphere of the music beautifully captured by these forces under Andrew Parrott. Apart from a rather nasal edge on the violin tone, it is difficult to fault either this moving performance or the well-balanced and refined recording.

On Naxos Summerly with his talented group of ten singers – two of them doubling as soloists – also give a compelling reading of Schütz's vivid and compact telling of the *Christmas Story*. Aptly austere in its overall manner, with clear instrumental accompaniment, it yet brings out the beauty and vigour of the numbers depicting the different groups, in turn the angels, the shepherds and the wise men. The scholarly credentials are impeccable, with excellent notes provided, and the recording, made in Hertford College, Oxford, is full and vivid. The motets and the psalm-setting make a welcome fill-up.

Kleine geistliche Konzerte & Symphoniae Sacrae: Bone Jesu; Bringt her dem Herrn; Eile, mich, Gott zu erretten; Habe deine Lust an dem Herren; Herr unser Herrscher; Herzlich lieb hab ich dich o Herr; Ihr Heigen lobsinget; O Jesu nomen dulce; O Süsser, O freundlicher; Was betrübst du dich, meine Seele; Was hast du verwirket; Wie ein Rubin; Wohl dem, der nicht wandelt

(N) ** HM HMC 901097. Hennig, Jacobs, with Christie, Coin, Junghänel, Kimura, Swierstra

It is good to encounter a lighter side of Schütz's musical personality. But only one of the 13 items here is secular. A pity more were not included, but *Wie ein Rubin* ('As a ruby gleams in fine gold') is charming and quite well sung by the treble soloist, Sebastian Hennig (although he is never one hundred per cent secure in intonation). These 'Little concertatos' and *Symphoniae sacrae* are otherwise concerned with sacred texts, offering praise, but with the texts concerned also with the penitence that comes with medieval apprehension concerning the insecurity of existence. However, the settings are lively and lyrical; they vary from monody to writing for two voices (with a bass continuo) and often engage in dialogue, with overlapping part-writing, as in *Ihr Heiligen lobsinget dem Herren* or *Bringt her dem Herren*, which is spiced with lively

'Alleluja's'. The music was intended to be performed by male singers, hence the choice of the treble soloist in duet with René Jacobs, and their voices blend well together. But a certain monotony results; one would like to hear this repertory with the treble line taken by a voice capable of more variety of colour.

Musicalische Exequien (German Requiem); Motets: Also hat Gott die Welt gelibt; Die Himmel erzählen; Ich bin die Auferstehung; O lieber Herre Gott; Selig sind die Toten; So fahr ich hin zu Jesu Christ

(N) *** HM HMC 901261. Mellon, de Reyghere, Zanetti, Crook, Fouchécourt, Lamy, Machart, Kooy, Lika, Chappelle Royale, Herreweghe

Herreweghe's account of the *Musicalische Exequien* seems to us particularly fine; it has deep feeling, without histrionics, and the quality of the unaccompanied singing is very high indeed. The work was commissioned by the noble Lord of Gera, appropriately named Heinrich Reuss Posthumus. He chose the selections of Biblical texts on which the work is based (and also had them inscribed on the inside of his coffin!). Herreweghe followed the composer's instructions in preparing this performance and uses six soloists and a six-voiced Capella for the first part, two equal choirs for the second, and a large choir plus three soloists for the third, the *Nunc Dimittis* (Song of Simeon), while in the latter a more distantly placed semi-chorus is used. Apart from the continuo bass for fugal entries, no other instruments are used and undoubtedly the work gains from this degree of austerity. The spatial effects are well captured in the recording. The motets which make up the rest of the programme come from the *Geistliche Chormusik* of 1648 and are all concerned with death, salvation and the promised resurrection. However, the settings are full of optimism and the interplay between solos, ensemble groupings and tutti, with modest backing instrumentation, brings a rich polyphonic dialogue, with the penultimate *O lieber Herre Gott*, and the closing 'heavens declaring the glory of God' especially fine. Full texts and translations are included.

Musicalische Exequien. Motets: Auf dem Gebirge; Freue dich des Weibes Jugend; Ist nicht Ephraim mein teurer Sohn; Saul, Saul, was verfolgst du mich

🔘 *** DG (IMS) 423 405-2. Monteverdi Ch., E. Bar. Soloists, His Majesties Sackbutts & Cornetts, Gardiner

Schütz's *Musical Exequien* contains music that is amazing for its period. The Monteverdi Choir respond with fiery intensity, making light of the complex eight-part writing in the second of the three *Exequies*. Four more superb motets by Schütz make an ideal coupling, with first-rate recorded sound.

Musicalische Exequien (German Requiem); The Seven Last Words of Christ on the Cross. Motets: Die mit Tränen säen; Si fahr ich hin zu Jesu Christ

(N) (BB) ** Naxos 8.555705. Soloists, Asfelder Volkalsemble, Himlische Cantorey, I Febiarmonici Bar. O, Helbische

It was an excellent idea for Naxos to combine their fine account of the *Musicalische Exequien* with Schütz's hardly less impressive version of the *Seven Words of Jesus Christ on the Cross* of 1645. Schütz's setting brings an opening and closing *Symphonia* but is introduced by the five-part *Introitus*, and ends with a confident chorale *Conclusio*. The five fresh-voiced soloists share the narrative, telling the gospel story, and also take the parts of the two Thieves, while Jesus is an additional tenor role. The programme is concluded with two well-chosen and richly eloquent motets 'They that sow in tears shall reap in joy' leading to 'I sleep and rest well, then Jesus Christ who will open Heaven's gate, will lead ne to eternal life'. The surprising snag is that the resonant acoustic of St Peter's, Bremen, seems to have defeated the resources of the Naxos engineer, Mike Clements, for although the sound is rich in texture, the choral focus is woolly.

Motets: Auf dem Gebirge; Der Engel sprach; Exultavit cor meum; Fili mi Absolon; Heu mihi Domine; Hodie Christus natus est; Ich danke Dir Herr; O quam tu pulchra es; Die seele Christi; Helige mich; Selig sind die Todten; Was mein Gott will

⊶ (BB) *** Regis (ADD) RRC 1168. Esswood, Keven Smith, Elliott, Griffet, Partridge, Etheridge, George, Pro Cantione Antiqua, L. Cornet & Sackbut Ens., Restoration Ac., Fleet

An eminently useful and well-recorded super-bargain anthology of Schütz motets that offers such masterpieces as Fili mi Absolon (for bass voice, five sackbuts, organ and violone continuo) and the glorious Selig sind die Todten in well-thought-out and carefully prepared performances under Edgar Fleet. These accounts have a dignity and warmth that make them distinctive. Moreover, the CD sound is excellently managed, rich and clear.

Musicalische Vesper
*** MDG 332 1170-2. Kölner Kammerchor, Coll. Cartusianum, Neumann

Taking Monteverdi's great 1610 set of Vespers as a model, Peter Neumann with his talented Cologne period group has here devised a thrilling German equivalent to Monteverdi's masterpiece, using appropriate Psalm settings and antiphons from Schütz's principal collections. So it is that we can appreciate with fresh ears some of the most inspired church music that Schütz ever wrote, given new perspectives when set against the model of Monteverdi. Vespers and Matins were the only elements of the Catholic liturgy fully retained in the Lutheran church, so that Schütz, who was studying in Venice with Giovanni Gabrieli just when Monteverdi published his work, was inspired to write church music which directly echoed his example, clearly designed for great cathedrals. The German sequence also gains greatly in cohesion from being relatively compact, at just over an hour, ending with a glorious setting of the Magnificat. The Psalm settings leading up to that are drawn from such collections as the composer's Psalms of David and Symphoniae Sacrae, some items already well known on disc, but others not otherwise available. Peter Neumann draws singing and playing from his Cologne forces of spectacular precision and clarity, and he gains greatly from the brilliant engineering of the record company, MDG, which, using only two channels, yet gives a vivid illusion of surround sound.

O bone Jesu, fili Mariae
(M) *** DG (IMS) 447 298-2. Monteverdi Ch., E. Bar.
   Soloists, Gardiner – BUXTEHUDE: Membra Jesu nostri ***

A wonderfully eloquent performance of this Spiritual Concerto by one of the greatest of baroque masters. Schütz juxtaposes stanzas of a poem ascribed to St Bernard of Clairvaux with prose passages of Latin devotional literature, treating the latter as recitative and the former set homophonically, and ending the cantata in concertato style. Beautifully recorded.

Psalm 150
(B) **(*) EMI double forte (ADD) 5 68631-2 (2). Cambridge University Musical Soc., Bach Ch., King's College Ch., Wilbraham Brass Soloists, Willcocks – G. GABRIELI: Motets etc. **(*); MONTEVERDI: Vespers *(*)

Schütz's setting of Psalm 150 is for double choirs and soloists, each used in juxtaposition against the others, with built-in antiphony an essential part of the composer's conception. The majesty of Schütz's inspiration certainly comes over vividly here, the closing Alleluja having remarkable weight and richness, though the overall focus of the recording is not absolutely clean. In the coupled Monteverdi Vespers there is actual distortion and the performance is disappointing.

Der Schwanengesang (Opus ultimum; reconstructed by Wolfgang Steude)
(M) *** Virgin 5 61306-2 (2). Hannover Knabenchor, Hilliard Ens., L. Bar., Hennig

Schütz's Opus ultimum is a setting of Psalm 119, the longest psalm in the psalter, which he divides into eleven sections. He finishes off this thirteen-part motet cycle with his final setting of Psalm 100, which he had originally composed in 1662, and the Deutsches Magnificat. Wolfram Steude's note recounts the history of the work, parts of which disappeared after Schütz's death; and his reconstruction of two of the vocal parts is obviously a labour of love. The performance is a completely dedicated one, with excellent singing from all concerned and good instrumental playing, and the conductor, Heinz Hennig, secures warm and responsive singing from his Hannover Knabenchor. The acoustic is spacious and warm and the recording balance well focused. The sound is firm, clear and sonorous.

The Seven Words of Jesus on the Cross. Magnificat. Motets: Ach, Herr, du Schöpfer aller Ding; Adjuro vos; Anima mea; Die mit Tränen säen; Erbarm dich mein, o Herre Gott; Meine Seele erheben den Herren; Quemadmodum desiderat
(B) ** HM HMA 1951255. Soloists, Clément Janequin Ens., Les Saqueboutiers de Toulouse, Visse

Schütz's Seven Last Words is a comparatively short work (17 minutes) and takes up only a small part of this programme, although the front of this Musique d'abord CD does not make this clear.

The concert opens with a Latin Magnificat setting, again alternating brass and solo voices, but sounding more like a secular madrigal than a religious celebration. The madrigal spirituel, Ach, Herr, du Schöpfer aller Ding, is also sung slowly and serenely. The excerpts from the Symphoniae sacrae, too, might again have been more spirited, although the closing concerted number from the Psalmen Davids is livelier. The actual singing here is of a high standard, and the brass-playing is superb, but one feels that the music-making could have been more eloquently extrovert. The recording is excellent, but only texts and no translations are provided. A fascinating disc, just the same.

Sinfoniae Sacrae, Op. 6/2–13, 15, 17–19, SWV 258–269, 271, & 273–5
⊶ (BB) *** Warner Apex 2564 61143-2. Dietschy, Bellamy, Lurens, Zaepfel, Elwes, Guy de Mey, Fabre-Garrus, Les Saqueboutiers de Toulouse

Schütz's 20 Sinfoniae Sacrae of 1629 (of which 16 are included here) are the result of the Dresden composer's second visit to Italy in 1628, when he was strongly influenced by Monteverdi and the Italian *concertato* style. These pieces fascinatingly combine voices and instruments in a single texture, usually with an interweaving interplay, and rarely with the instruments acting just as an obbligato. The performances are eminently stylish and freshly spontaneous, and the instrumentalists are expert – and, moreover, they play in tune. The balance is beautifully judged, with voices and instruments within the same perspective, and the recording is wholly realistic.

SCHWANTER, Joseph (born 1943)

From Afar … (Fantasy for Guitar and Orchestra)

(BB) ** Virgin 2×1 5 61627-2 (2). Isbin, Saint Paul CO, Wolf – RODRIGO: *Concierto de Aranjuez; Fantasia para un gentilhombre* ***; Recital: 'Latin Romances' ***

Sharon Isbin commissioned Schwanter's *From Afar …* and the insert note describes it as 'an intense fantasy which unfolds in a combination of brilliant passages and lyrical episodes'. So it does, but well played as they are, they are neither remarkably cohesive nor memorable, and the best part of the work by far is the cadenza, which the soloist sustains with brilliant playing and personal magnetism.

SCOTT, Cyril (1879–1970)

Aubade, Op. 77; 3 Symphonic Dances, Op. 22; 2 Passacaglias on Irish Themes; Suite fantastique

**(*) Marco Polo 8.223485. South Africa Broadcasting Corporation Nat. SO, Marchbank

Cyril Scott, born in Birkenhead, studied composition in Frankfurt at the Hoch Conservatoire. In 1895 his fellow students included Percy Grainger, Balfour Gardiner and Roger Quilter, and the group subsequently became known as the 'Frankfurt Group'. But Scott eventually went his own musical way.

Now he is best remembered for his piano piece *Lotus Land*, but at the very beginning of the last century his *First Symphony* was performed in Manchester and Liverpool under Hans Richter (who admired it) and the *Second* by Sir Henry Wood at the London Promenade Concerts. This was subsequently to be reworked as the *Three Symphonic Dances*.

The first of these opens with appealingly English pastoral flair, but its ideas become repetitive; the second (*Andante sostenuto e sempre molto cantabile*) is already anticipating the languorous, sequence-laden style of his later music, especially when the rather lovely winding main tune is reprised on the oboe and rapturously taken up by the violins.

By the time he came to write his *Aubade* for large orchestra in 1911, Scott's feeling for voluptuous colour and translucent textures had developed further, and although this very telling evocation is very like Debussy, it is most impressively scored. At the close one is also reminded of Delius, and the latter's influence is also to reappear in the *Neapolitan Rhapsody*.

If the ideas themselves are rather amorphous in the *Suite fantastique*, the 'Spectres', 'Goblins' and 'Elves' of the two final movements are imaginatively pictured, and in the two *Passacaglias* Scott effectively decorates and re-orchestrates the themes on which they are based, rather than developing them organically. These are all excellent, sympathetic performances, well recorded in a warm acoustic.

(i) *Piano Concerto 2; Neptune (Poem of the Sea);* (ii) *Symphony 3 (The Muses)*

*** Chan. 10211. BBC PO, Brabbins; with (i) Shelley; (ii) Huddersfield Ch. Soc.

The *Piano Concerto* has been recorded before (by John Ogdon for Lyrita in 1975), but the present performance by Howard Shelley is every bit as convincing and is certainly compelling. Although it has undoubted atmosphere, its shifting moods and rhapsodic chromaticism will not be to all tastes. The interplay between soloist and orchestra is not a clearly determined dialogue (it is rather like a baroque ritornello concerto, where soloist and accompanist play alternating passages). In the first movement, tempi fluctuate and there is a curious passage marked *Nobilmente tranquillo*, yet the nobilmente is elusive. After the brief slow movement (*Tranquillo pastoral*) the finale brings more contrasting episodes and, because of this, its *energico* easily dissipates.

The *Symphony No. 3*, subtitled *The Muses*, is not very coherent in symphonic terms either, although it has four clearly defined movements, devoted to 'Epic Poetry and Tragedy', 'Comedy and Merry Verse', 'Love and Poetry' and, finally, the 'Muse of Dance and Song'. It is scored for a huge orchestra, including a large percussion section with a wind machine, and in the finale a vocalising choir. The broad-spanned, powerfully dramatic first movement, although it opens gently on four muted violins, soon expands into a vast and complex score, with distinct reminders not only of Debussy's *La Mer* but also of Ravel's *Daphnis et Chloé*. The Scherzo becomes more like a bacchanale and the spirit of its title seems evasive. The slow movement is even more enigmatic, its melodic lines elusive, suggesting that love too is elusive. The finale opens dramatically with pounding timpani, and the spirit of the dance is orgiastic, the chorus becoming wilder and wilder, like the wailing of dervishes. But the movement reaches a positive if brief conclusion on a triumphant C major, and the listener is left breathless.

Undoubtedly the most successful work here is *Neptune* (*Poem of the Sea*). Here the constantly changing moods and tempi certainly evoke the restless ocean. No specific programme is intended, though the original plan was to describe the *Titanic* disaster pictorially. In response to criticism, Scott removed almost all the tangibly descriptive passages. Perhaps this is a pity, but the present work remains very evocative, and it is more cohesive than its two companions. It still depicts a central storm sequence and, after a despondent passage for three bassoons, the work ends with an elegiac lament, the sea now once again calm, creating a mood of twilight brooding.

The performances are very fine, Chandos has provided its most spectacular sound and, for all its diffuseness of ideas, Scott's music undoubtedly has a haunting quality which makes one want to return to it.

Piano Music Vol. 1: 2 Alpine Sketches, Op. 54/4; Autumn Idyll; Cherry Ripe; 3 Dances, Op. 20; Deuxième Suite, Op. 75; Handelian Rhapsody, Op. 17; Indian Suite; Miniatures; 3 Little Waltzes, Op. 58; Notturno, Op. 54/5; 3 Old Country Dances; A Pageant: 3 Dances. 3 Pastorals; Pastoral Suite; Requiescat; Sphinx, Op. 63; Soirée Japonaise, Op. 67/4; Twilight-tide; Valse caprice, Op. 74/7; Vesperale, Op. 40/2; Vistas (includes bonus tracks of Cyril Scott playing his own music)

(N) (M) *** Dutton CDLX 7150. De'Ath

Piano Music, Vol. 2: Piano Sonatas: in D, Op. 17; 1 (Original Version), Op. 66; 2–3

(N) (M) *** Dutton CDLX 7155. De'Ath

Cyril Scott suffered grievous neglect in the post-war years and his star had already begun to wane in the 1930s. Yet he was highly regarded at the beginning of the century when he was hailed by Debussy as no less than 'one of the rarest artists of the present generation'. Edmund Rubbra, who was a pupil of his, never lost his youthful admiration for him, even in his last years. His piano music is not generously represented these days in the concert hall or on CD, and these two discs, the first of a complete series, cover the *Suites* and *Miniatures* and *Sonatas*. Scott composed over 200 pieces. Leslie De'Ath himself provides discerning and judicious notes from which we quote: 'For those who wish to find echoes of other composers many may be heard: at times Elgar, Holst, Delius and MacDowell, and elsewhere Scriabin, Debussy and Stravinsky. Yet his music is distinct from all others – varied and difficult to pin down exactly, yet not to be dismissed as derivative.' Of particular interest and individuality is the *Deuxième Suite* of 1910. In addition to De'Ath's own sympathetic performances, there is an additional attraction in that Scott's own recordings (he was a formidable pianist) from 1928–30 are included as an appendix on the first disc.

The four *Sonatas* on the second CD were written over half a century. A truncated version of the *First* was arranged by Percy Grainger as the *Handelian Rhapsody*, included in Volume 1. The original version is twice as long but is still rhapsodical and does not seem greatly over-extended. Its themes are attractive, particularly the lyrical secondary melody. The sonata which Scott called No. 1, written in 1908, is a confident, interwoven four-movement work, with a characteristic slow movement, full of Scott's flowing, voluptuous English romanticism, yet also Straussian. The Scherzo which follows is more vibrant, but is hardly a scherzo, and the fugue of the finale continues the chromatic lyricism and reintroduces the material of the earlier movements. The *Second Sonata* of 1933 is a single-movement work, textually and harmonically rich, somewhat after the exotic manner of Scriabin, but with a touch of impressionism, a work which Gieseking admired and championed.

The *Third Sonata*, published in 1956, is marginally sparer in atmosphere; it has three distinct movements but remains harmonically oblique, yet its invention, like the earlier works, is both individual and quite haunting. The performances here are highly sympathetic and convincing, and are well recorded.

Piano Sonata 1, Op. 66; 3 Danses tristes, Op. 74; Over the Prairie: 2 Impressions; 2 Pieces, Op. 47; 2 Pierrot Pieces, Op. 35; Pierrette; Poems
**(*) Australian ABC Eloquence 465 737-2. Henning

Cyril Scott's piano music is at times Debussian, and if without that composer's genius it is certainly individual, atmospheric and attractive. The performances are good and the recording acceptable, if a touch brittle, and this Eloquence CD comes with helpful notes by the pianist.

SCRIABIN, Alexander (1872–1915)

Piano Concerto in F sharp min., Op. 20; Fantasy (arr. Rozhdestvensky); (i) *Prometheus*
**(*) Chan. 9728. Postnikova; Residentie O, Rozhdestvensky, (i) Hague Ch.

(i) *Piano Concerto in F sharp min., Op. 20. Poème de l'extase, Op. 54.* (i; ii) *Prometheus (Le Poème du feu), Op. 60. Rêverie, Op. 24. Symphonies Nos.* (ii; iii) *1, Op. 26. 2; 3 (Le Divin Poème)*
(M) **(*) Decca Trio 473 971-2 (3). Deutsches SO, Berlin, Ashkenazy; with (i) Jablonski; (ii) Berlin R. Ch.; (iii) Balleys, Larin

(i) *Piano Concerto;* (i; ii) *Prometheus;* (i) *Preludes, Op. 11/6, 10, 15, & 17; Fragilité, Op. 51/1; Sonata 1, Op. 6: Marche funèbre* (orch. Rogal-Levitsky)
(BB) *** Naxos 8.550818. (i) Scherbakov; (ii) Russian State TV and R. Ch.; Moscow SO, Golovschin

On Naxos Konstantin Scherbakov gives a most poetic account of the Chopinesque *F sharp minor Concerto*, which is as good as any in any price range. The improvisatory musings of the slow movement come over beautifully, and *Prometheus* is no less characterful. Of course, the Moscow Symphony are not in the same league as the Cleveland Orchestra, but they play with ardour and the sound is very natural without being in the demonstration category.

Victoria Postnikova and her husband, Gennadi Rozhdestvensky, replace *Le Poème de l'extase* with a transcription of the early *Fantasy*. The Chandos sound is exemplary and the performance of the *Piano Concertos* both sensitive and poetic. A good account of *Prometheus* even if it does not displace Ashkenazy.

Ashkenazy's set of the Scriabin *Symphonies* is also available on a Double Decca, together with his highly charged Berlin Radio version of the *Poème de l'extase* (460 299-2). They are beautifully recorded; the performances shimmer with sensuality, but are lacking in the last degree of dramatic intensity. The same comments apply here to the *Piano Concerto*, in which Jablonski is a sympathetic if rather self-effacing soloist (he is not very forwardly balanced). Nevertheless he and Ashkenazy find plenty of romantic poetry in the music, especially in the slow movement, and with such good sound this is certainly enjoyable.

Le Poème de l'extase, Op. 54
⊷ (M) *** BBC (ADD) BBCL 4121-2. USSR State SO, Svetlanov – RIMSKY-KORSAKOV: *Scheherazade; Procession of the Nobles* ***
*** BBC (ADD) BBCL 4018-2. New Philh. O, Stokowski (and conversation with Deryck Cooke) – BERLIOZ: *Symphonie fantastique* **(*)
*** Naïve V 4946. O Nat. de France, Svetlanov – DEBUSSY: *La Mer* ***
*** Australian Decca Eloquence (ADD) 466 904-2. LAPO, Mehta – NIELSEN: *Symphony 4* **

Svetlanov's powerful and enormously authoritative account was recorded with his own orchestra at a BBC Prom in the expansive acoustics of the Royal Albert Hall in August 1968. His reading is one of the most compelling accounts of Scriabin's extraordinary score that one is likely to encounter and is second to none (not even Stokowski). It has greater atmosphere and excitement than the commercial recording he made at the time, and it serves as a reminder of what a virtuoso body this orchestra was. The performance has much subtle light and shade but is underpinned by a Slavonic, extrovert passion that is very compelling indeed, leading to a tremendously exciting climax, with strings and horns at their absolute zenith, before the lush close. Like the coupling, the recording is more brilliant and has greater range than one expects from this source.

Stokowski conducted the American première of *Le Poème de l'extase* in 1917 and it is difficult to imagine a performance of greater luminosity and energy from an octogenarian over half a century later. This account comes from a 1968 Festival Hall concert with the New Philharmonia Orchestra. Orgiastic, no holds barred, totally abandoned and wonderfully dedicated playing. However, the BBC sound is less than ideally transparent in its handling of detail.

An impressive memento on Naïve of Svetlanov's last visit to Paris. He has, of course, recorded the *Poème de l'extase* commercially with the USSR Symphony Orchestra for Melodiya, and a 1968 performance at the Proms with the same orchestra on the BBC 'Legends' label coupled with Rimsky's *Scheherazade*.He seems to have established an excellent rapport with this great French orchestra, and he casts a powerful spell. A fine account, which comes with a no less atmospheric *La Mer*. Very good recorded sound.

This is Mehta on top form in his vintage Decca years. Recorded in the mid-1960s, it is still sonically very impressive, with the engineers doing ample justice to the complexity and opulence of this lavishly self-intoxicated and orgasmic score. It remains one of the most gripping performances available today, but is coupled with an extrovert and less recommendable account of Nielsen's *Fourth Symphony*.

Prometheus (The Poem of Fire), Op. 60
*** Ph. 446 715-2. Toradze, Kirov Op. Ch. & O, Gergiev –
STRAVINSKY: *Firebird* (complete ballet) ***

On Philips an *echt*-Russian account of *Prometheus*, with a suitably inflammable pianist in the person of Alexander Toradze. This is the only current recording by a Russian orchestra, and under Gergiev's masterly direction they give an outstanding account of this voluptous and gloriously decadent score. The recording, too, is in the demonstration class even if the pianist is perhaps slightly too forwardly placed in the aural picture. It comes with an appropriately incandescent *Firebird*, marvellously played and recorded.

Symphonies 1–3; Le Poème de l'extase; (i) Prometheus
&⟶ (M) *** EMI ADD 5 67720-2 (3). Toczyska, Myers, Westminster Ch. (in 1), Phd. O, Muti; (i) with Alexeev

(i; ii) *Symphonies 1 in E, Op. 26;* (i) *2 in C min., Op. 29;* (iii) *3 (Le Divin Poème); Le Poème de l'extase*
(B) **(*) Double Decca (IMS) 460 299-2 (2). (i) Berlin Deutsche SO; Ashkenazy; (ii) Balleys, Larin, Berlin R. Ch.; (iii) Berlin RSO

(i) *Symphonies 2;* (ii) *3 (Le Divin Poème);* (iii) *Le Poème de l'extase;* (i) *Rêverie, Op. 24*
(B) *** Chan. 2-for-1 241-5 (2). (i) RSNO; (ii) Danish Nat. RSO; (iii) Chicago SO; Järvi

Muti's complete set of the Scriabin symphonies can be recommended almost without reservation; overall the sound is as vivid and richly coloured as the performances. With the two later symphonies-cum-symphonic poems (*Le Poème de l'extase* white-hot with passionate intensity, yet masterfully controlled) now added, this is an impressive achievement.

The splendid account of the *Second Symphony* from Järvi, with its richly detailed recording, can be recommended strongly. There is something refreshingly unforced and natural about Järvi's version of the *Third*, which puts this score in a far better light than those conductors who play it for all they are worth. Järvi's version of *Le Poème de l'extase*, played superbly and recorded vividly and resonantly in Chicago's Orchestral Hall, emphasizes Scriabin's primary colours, with the trumpet solo penetrating boldly through the voluptuous texture and skirting vulgarity by a small margin. There have been more subtle performances, but this one certainly makes a strong impact.

If recording were the sole criterion, Ashkenazy's performances would be a first choice. The sound is extraordinarily well detailed in the *First Symphony*, with both allure and presence, and only slightly less well defined in the *Second*. But in the *First Symphony* one misses that wild-eyed demonic fire that is so strong an ingredient in Scriabin's make-up. The *Second Symphony* is more impetuously volatile and has a good deal more vigour and sense of internal combustion. There is an atmosphere of simmering passion in the *Andante*, which often wells ardently to the surface. The *Third* brings an even more highly charged feeling from the Berlin forces, which carries through into *Le Poème de l'extase*. Again the Decca engineers rise to the occasion and the recording is very impressive. Yet overall the performances do not have the sheer grip of Muti's Philadelphia accounts.

Symphony 1 in E, Op. 26
(N) *** Chan. 10311. Kostyuk, Dolgov, Russian State SO, Polyansky – RACHMANINOV: *Six Choruses* ***

Scriabin's 50-minute *First Symphony* in six movements was his first major work not written for the piano. It is a diffuse work with some inspired episodes. It needs a conductor with a very firm grip on its generally rhapsodic discourse. Polyansky proves a sympathetic guide, though Muti exercises an even stronger hold over its architecture. All the same, this account is very persuasive, the soloists in the last movement eminently acceptable and the sound warm and well defined.

PIANO MUSIC

Allegro Appassionato, Op. 4; Canon in D min.; Etude in D sharp min.; Fugue in E min.; Muzurkas in: B min. & F; Nocturnes in F sharp min., Op. 5/1; A, Op. 5/2; D flat, Op. 9/2; A flat. Prelude in C sharp min., Op. 9/1; Sonata in E flat min.; Sonate-fantaisie; Variations on a Theme by Mlle Egorova; Waltz in F min., Op. 1; Waltzes in G sharp min. & D flat
*** Hyp. CDA 67149. Coombs

Stephen Coombs concentrates on Scriabin's early period, when he had yet to escape from Chopin's magnetic field, which has received less attention than the late sonatas. The earliest piece here, a *Canon in D minor*, was written when he was only eleven years old, but many of these Chopinesque pieces are of real quality and do not deserve to be so completely overshadowed. Coombs has a genuine feel for this repertoire and is very well served by the recording team.

Etudes (complete): Etude in C sharp min., Op. 2/1; 12 Etudes, Op. 8; 8 Etudes, Op. 42 (1903); Etude in E flat, Op. 49/1; Op. 56/4 (1908); 3 Etudes, Op. 65
**(*) Hyp. CDA 66607. Lane

Piers Lane makes light of the various technical problems in which these pieces abound and he plays with an admirable sense of style. Yet he does not give us the whole picture. He has sensibility and produces a good sonority, aided in no small measure by an excellently balanced recording; but one misses the nervous intensity, the imaginative flair and the feverish emotional temperature that the later pieces call for.

Etudes, Op. 8/7 & 12; Op. 42/5; Preludes, Op. 11/1, 3, 9–10, 13–14, 16; Op. 13/6; Op. 15/2; Op. 16/1 & 4; Op. 27/1; Op. 48/3; Op. 51/2; Op. 59/2; Op. 67/1; Sonatas 3, Op. 23; 5, Op. 53; 9 (Black Mass), Op. 68

☞ (B) (***) RCA 2-CD mono 74321 84594-2 (2). Horowitz (with CLEMENTI: *Sonatas, Op. 14/3; Op. 34/2; Op. 47/2: Rondo* (***) – MUSSORGSKY: *Pictures at an Exhibition* (***)

The engineers have done wonders to these recordings from the 1950s, though some of the original shallowness and clatter remains. The *Preludes* and the legendary accounts of the *Third* and *Ninth* sonatas come from 1956, the *Fifth* is much later, coming from 1976, and has more bloom. The performances form an essential part of any good Horowitz collection, and the Mussorgsky and Clementi couplings are equally indispensable.

10 Mazurkas, Op. 3; 9 Mazurkas, Op. 25; 2 Mazurkas, Op. 40
*** ASV CDDCA 1066. Fergus-Thompson

Another impressive instalment of Scriabin's complete piano music from Gordon Fergus-Thompson, a masterly and underrated artist. Even when put alongside native Russian pianists he can hold his own.

Preludes: Op. 2/2; Prelude for the Left Hand, Op. 9/1; 24 Preludes, Op. 11; 6 Preludes, Op. 13; 5 Preludes, Op. 15; 5 Preludes, Op. 16; 7 Preludes, Op. 17; 4 Preludes, Op. 22; 2 Preludes, Op. 27; 4 Preludes, Op. 31; 4 Preludes, Op. 33; 3 Preludes, Op. 35; 4 Preludes, Op. 37; 4 Preludes, Op. 39; Op. 45/3; 4 Preludes, Op. 48; Preludes, Op. 49/2; Op. 51/2; Op. 56/1; Op. 59/2; 2 Preludes, Op. 67; 5 Preludes, Op. 74
*** Hyp. CDA 67057/8. Lane

Piers Lane has the measure of Scriabin's idiom and seems completely attuned to his musical language and sensibility. These preludes range from his formative Chopinesque years, around 1889, through to 1914, and Lane traverses them with flair. They are generally more successful than his complete set of *Etudes*.

Piano Sonatas 1–10; Sonate-fantaisie in G sharp min.
☞ *** Hyp. CDA 67131/2. Hamelin

Piano Sonatas 1–10; Etude in C sharp min., Op. 2/1; Feuillet d'album, Op. 58; 2 Morceaux, Op. 57; 2 Poèmes, Op. 63; 4 Preludes, Op. 48; 5 Preludes, Op. 64; 2 Preludes, Op. 67; Vers la flamme, Op. 72
(B) *** EMI (ADD) double forte 5 72652-2 (2). Ogdon

Piano Sonatas 1–10; 2 Danses, Op. 73; 4 Morceaux, Op. 51; 4 Morceaux, Op. 56; 2 Poèmes, Op. 32
(B) *** Double Decca ADD/DDD 452 961-2 (2). Ashkenazy

Piano Sonatas 1–10; Piano Sonata in E flat min. (1887–9); Sonata fantaisie in G sharp min.
(B) **(*) DG Trio 477 049-2 (3). Szidon

Marc-André Hamelin commands the feverish intensity, the manic vision, wide dynamic range and fastidious pedalling that Scriabin must have. There are other fine Scriabin cycles and, of course, celebrated accounts of single sonatas from Richter and others, but of newer cycles Hamelin's must now be a first recommendation.

Ogdon is nothing if not persuasive, and the only reservation one need feel about his playing is an occasional tendency to be less than scrupulous in observing dynamic indications and a certain lack of finish. His account of the *Tenth Sonata*,

however, is particularly fine, and if in the *Ninth* (*The Black Mass*) he does not match the demonic fury and power of Horowitz (and who, for that matter, does?) his is still a thoroughly felt and vividly realized reading. The shorter pieces are particularly appealing (the richly coloured *Etude in C sharp minor* which opens the first disc should tempt anyone to explore further). The piano is very well recorded throughout (at Abbey Road in 1971).

Ashkenazy's Scriabin set was made over a decade between 1972 and 1984, but the sound is remarkably consistent. Ashkenazy is clearly attuned to this repertoire: he is as thoroughly at home in the miniatures as in the sonatas, readily finding their special atmosphere and colour. He is at his very finest in the earlier sonatas – the last three are given with brilliance and vision – and there is no lack of awareness of the demonic side of Scriabin's personality.

Roberto Szidon recorded all ten *Sonatas* as well as the two early *Sonatas* and the Op. 28 *Fantasy* in 1971, and this DG Trio offers the whole set at bargain price. Szidon seems especially at home in the later works. His version of the *Black Mass Sonata* (No. 9) fares best and conveys real excitement. At its new price this is an attractive reissue and can be considered alongside Ashkenazy, who only offers the basic ten works, and John Ogdon, who offers extra music. But first choice rests with Marc-André Hamlin on Hyperion, who commands the feverish intensity that Scriabin must have.

Piano Sonatas 2 in G sharp min., Op. 19; 5 in F sharp, Op. 53
(N) (M) *** Praga (ADD) PR 54056. S. Richter – CHOPIN: *Etudes; Nocturnes, etc.* *

The two *Sonatas* are dazzling and as impressive as any of Richter's Scriabin on disc in the past; they were recorded in 1972. The overall appeal of the disc is diminished by the poor quality of the sound in the Chopin *Etudes* but this is much better.

Piano Sonatas 2 in G sharp min., Op. 19; 5 in F sharp, Op. 53; 6 in G, Op. 63; 7 in F sharp (White Mass), Op. 64; 9 in F (Black Mass), Op. 68; Fantaisie in B min., Op. 28
(BB) **(*) Naxos 8.553158. Glemser

Piano Sonatas 3 in F sharp min., Op. 23; 10 in C, Op. 70; in E flat (1890); Poème nocturne, Op. 61; Vers la flamme, Op. 72
(BB) **(*) Naxos 8.555468. Glemser

These performances are very good indeed. Bernd Glemser has an excellent feel for the Scriabin world. He commands a keen imagination, a wide range of keyboard colour and he possesses an impressive technical address. No one buying these sonatas will feel short-changed.

Piano Sonata 3 in F sharp min., Op. 23; 2 Poèmes, Op. 32; Vers la flamme, Op. 72
**(*) Kingdom KCLCD 2001. Fergus-Thompson – BALAKIREV: *Piano Sonata* **(*)

Gordon Fergus-Thompson gives a splendid account of Scriabin's overheated *F sharp minor Sonata* and sensitive, atmospheric performances of the other pieces here. A reverberant but good recording.

Piano Sonatas 4, Op. 30; 5, Op. 53; 9 (Black Mass) Op. 68; 10, Op. 70; Etude, Op. 2/1; 8 Etudes, Op. 42
**(*) ASV CDDCA 776. Fergus-Thompson

Fergus-Thompson is thoroughly inside this idiom. At the same time it must be conceded that his performances are not as individual as those of Ashkenazy and in the cruelly competitive world of recorded music would not be a first choice. Nevertheless, there is much musical nourishment to satisfy the collector.

Piano Sonatas 8, Op. 66; 9, Op. 68; 10, Op. 70; 2 Danses, Op. 73; 2 Poèmes, Op. 69; 2 Poèmes, Op. 71; 2 Preludes, Op. 67; 5 Preludes, Op. 74; Vers la flamme, Op. 72
*(**) Altarus AIR-CD 9020. Amato

Donna Amato seems wholly attuned to Scriabin's sensibility and plays all his late music (Opp. 66–74), including the last three *Sonatas*, to the manner born. Scriabin's world is claustrophobic – but unfortunately so is the recording, which sounds as if it was made in a small acoustic environment but with some echo added. The sound-quality diminishes the pleasure this CD gives but not, of course, Amato's artistry.

SCULTHORPE, Peter (born 1929)

Piano Concerto
**(*) Australian ABC Eloquence 426 483-2. Fogg, Melbourne SO, Fredman – EDWARDS: *Piano Concerto*; WILLIAMSON: *Concerto for 2 Pianos* **(*)

In many ways, Sculthorpe's *Piano Concerto* is the most difficult of the three works to get to grips with on this Australian Eloquence CD. Written during a very sad time in the composer's life, its mood reflects that. It is not a virtuosic showpiece for the pianist, but stands as an interesting modern concerto that repays listening. The performance here is excellent and the recording acceptable.

SEARLE, Humphrey (1915–82)

Symphonies 1–5; Night Music; Overture to a Drama
(N) *** CPO 777 131-2 (2). BBC Scottish SO, Francis

Searle's *First Symphony* was championed by Sir Adrian Boult and the LPO but never reissued on CD, the *Second* by Josef Krips; but his later symphonies have not enjoyed the exposure they deserve either in the concert hall or on CD. This two-CD set makes handsome amends: Searle's music is concentrated and powerful and it rewards study and attention. It is an unlikely candidate for popularity but, like Fricker's, is a strong contender for revaluation.

SEGERSTAM, Leif (born 1944)

Symphonies (i) 21 (September; Visions at Korpijärvi); (ii) 23 (Afterthoughts, Questioning Questionings)
**(*) Ondine ODE 928-2. (i) Finnish RSO; (ii) Tampere PO (both without conductor)

There are some refined and sensitive touches in the course of these shapeless and sprawling pieces. They seem more like the improvisational sketches a composer makes prior to composition than the finished work of art. There is no feeling of a distinctive musical personality. The heavily scored and seemingly interminable tutti subdue and overpower the listener but the overall impact is underwhelming. Very good performances and excellent recording. If you try these pieces, you may like them more than we do.

SEIBER, Mátyás (1905–60)

Clarinet Concertino
(BB) *** Hyp. Helios CDH 55068. King, ECO, Litton –
BLAKE: *Clarinet Concerto*; LUTOSLAWSKI: *Dance Preludes* ***

Mátyás Seiber's highly engaging *Concertino* was sketched during a train journey in 1926 (before the days of seamless rails) and certainly the opening *Toccata* has the jumpy, rhythmic feeling of railway line joints and points. Yet the haunting slow movement has a touch of the ethereal, while the Scherzo has a witty jazz element. Thea King has the measure of the piece; she is accompanied well by Andrew Litton, and very well recorded. On Hyperion's budget Helios label, this reissue is well worth seeking out.

String Quartet 3 (Quartetto lirico)
(M) (***) EMI mono 5 85150-2. (i) Amadeus Qt – TIPPETT: *String Quartet 2, etc.* (***)

Hungarian composer Matyas Seiber's *Third String Quartet* was completed in 1951 and dedicated to the Amadeus Quartet, who recorded this performance in 1954. It employs serial technique, with plenty of glissandi and *sul ponticello*, and if this style will not be to all tastes the music obviously springs from intense emotion, although it is the Tippett *String Quartet No. 2* on this CD which communicates more readily. This performance is a very good one indeed, and one enjoys the often very beautiful sounds for their own sake. The recording is astonishingly rich and full, with virtually no background noise at all.

SEREBRIER, José (born 1938)

(i) Partita (Symphony 2); Fantasia; Winterreise; (ii) Sonata for Solo Violin
*** Reference RR 90 CD. (i) LPO, composer; (ii) Acosta

The *Partita* (or *Symphony No. 2*) is attractive and its exuberant finale sparkles with Latin-American dance rhythms. The *Fantasia for Strings* convincingly combines energy with lyricism, while *Winterreise* titillates the listener's memory by ingeniously quoting, not from Schubert, but from seasonal inspirations of Haydn, Glazunov and Tchaikovsky's *Winter Daydreams Symphony*, using all three snippets together, plus the *Dies irae* at the climax. The *Solo Violin Sonata* is unashamedly romantic and very well played, as are the orchestral works under the composer. An enterprising and worthwhile issue.

SERLY, Tibor (1901–78)

Rhapsody for Viola & Orchestra
(BB) *** Naxos 8.554183. Xiao, Budapest PO, Kovacs –
BARTOK: *Viola Concerto* (2 versions; ed. Bartok & ed. Serly); *Two Pictures* ***

Tibor Serly, friend of Bartók and first editor of the unfinished *Viola Concerto*, here offers a closely related work, less individual than Bartók's own, but well worth hearing. Beautifully played by the Chinese viola-player, Hong-Mei Xiao, it provides a good makeweight for the disc containing both editions of the Bartók *Concerto*.

SESSIONS, Roger (1896–1985)

Concerto for Orchestra

(BB) *** Hyp. Helios CDH 55100. Boston SO, Ozawa –
PANUFNIK: *Symphony 8* ***

Sessions's *Concerto for Orchestra* finds him at his thorniest and most uncompromising, with lyricism limited to fleeting fragments of melody; but the playful opening leads one on finally to a valedictory close, sharply defined. Ozawa makes a powerful advocate, helped by superb playing from the Boston orchestra.

Symphony 4; Symphony 5; Rhapsody for Orchestra
*** New World NW 345. Columbus SO, Badea

Roger Sessions's musical language is dense and his logic is easier to sense than to follow. The performances by the Columbus Symphony Orchestra under Christian Badea appear well prepared, and there is no doubt as to their commitment and expertise. The sound ideally needs a larger acoustic, but every strand in the texture is well placed and there is no feeling of discomfort.

SÉVERAC, Déodat de (1872–1921)

Piano, 4 hands: L'Album pour les enfants petits et grands: Le Soldat de plomb (Histoire vraie en trois récits). Solo piano: Baigneuses au soleil (Souvenir de Banyuls-sur-mer); Cerdaña (5 Etudes pittoresques); Le Chant de la terre (poème géorgique); En Languedoc (suite); En vacances (petites pièces romantiques); Les Naïades et le faune indiscret; Pippiment-get (Valse brillante de concert); Premier Recueil (Au château et dans le parc); Deuxième Recueil (inachevé); Sous les lauriers roses ou Soir de Carnaval sur la Côte Catalane; Stances à Madame de Pompadour; Valse romantique

(B) **(*) EMI (ADD)5 72372-2 (3). Ciccolini

Déodat de Séverac came from the Pays d'Oc and always retained his roots in the region. He first studied law at Toulouse before deciding on music and becoming a pupil of Magnard and then d'Indy. He was a friend of Ravel, to whom his musical language is much indebted. All the music on these CDs is civilized and has great charm. The recordings were made between 1968 and 1977 and are serviceable rather than distinguished. But the set will give much pleasure.

Cerdaña (5 Etudes pittoresques pour le piano); En Languedoc
(BB) *** Naxos 8.555855. Masó

Aldo Ciccolini's set of Déodat de Severac's music has much to commend it, but three CDs may be too many for some collectors. Jordi Masó's lucid and sensitive accounts will make an excellent introduction to this delightful composer. His playing is finely characterized and there is a subtle use of keyboard colour. Good sound, too.

SGAMBATI, Giovanni (1841–1914)

Piano Concerto in G min., Op. 15; Overture Cola di Rienzo; Berceuse-rêverie, Op. 42/2 (orch. Massenet)
*** ASV CDDCA 1097. Caramiello, Nuremberg PO, Ventura

Giovanni Sgambati grew up in Rome as a musical prodigy. But from his earliest years he was not interested in Italian opera, his tastes turning instead to the music of the nineteenth-century German masters. He conducted the first Italian performances of the *Eroica Symphony* and *Emperor Concerto*, and in 1886 premièred Liszt's *Dante Symphony*. All these influences can be found in his music, yet he was his own man, and his *Piano Concerto* is a real find, genuinely inspired, with the solo part marvellously conceived to work in harness with the orchestra, both heroically and poetically. The concerto opens not with a grand gesture, but evocatively and thoughtfully, and a little forlornly. The piano entry is bold and strong, but soon slips into the lyrical secondary material, which it decorates with brilliant roulades. The movement is on the largest scale and produces continuous rhapsodical mood changes, a remarkable variety of invention and orchestral re-colourings, always holding the listener by its flowing spontaneity and structural security. Schumann and Brahms hover over the remaining two movements. The *Andante* is like an intermezzo, at first hesitant, but soloist and woodwind soon enter into a gentle romantic dialogue. The finale opens on the brass and soon galumphs away with a syncopated theme, but with underlying lyrical warmth to counter the coruscating brilliance of the solo writing. Altogether it is a splendid work, and it could hardly be played with more confidence and understanding than it is here by Francesco Caramiello in his excellent Nuremberg orchestral partnership with Fabrizio Ventura.

It is they who then give a completely convincing account of the Lisztian symphonic poem, which is designated the *Cola di Rienzo Overture*. One of the composer's earliest works, written in 1866, it opens with appealingly romantic melodic evocation and proceeds to describe an undocumented narrative, often excitingly, sometimes melodramatically, but with lovely orchestral colouring and powerful expressive feeling. The closing section is quite haunting. The delightful *Berceuse-Rêverie*, originally a piano piece, but lusciously scored by Massenet, makes a delightful closing lollipop. With first-class recording, this disc is really worth exploring; the concerto is as fine as any in Hyperion's 'Romantic Piano Concerto' series.

SHANKAR, Ravi (born 1920)

Sitar Concertos (i) 1; (ii) 2 (Rāga Mālā: A Garland of Ragas). Morning Love (based on the Rāga Nata Bhairov); Rāga Purlyā Kalyan; (iii) Prabhāti (based on the Rāga Gunkali); Rāga Piloo. Swara-Kākali

(N) (BB) **(*) EMI Gemini (ADD/DDD) 5 86555-2 (2). Ravi Shankar, with (i) LSO, Previn; (ii) LPO, Mehta; (iii) Y. Menuhin

This collection is an oddity. It would be easy to dismiss this pair of concertos, particularly as they are in four movements each and seem very long (the first runs for 40 minutes, the second for nearly 52 minutes!) and, except for aficionados, will undoubtedly outstay their welcome. Fairly evidently they are neither very good Western music nor good Indian music. The idiom is sweet – arguably too sweet and unproblematic – but at least they represent 'crossover' in the real sense – a painless tour over the geographical layout of the raga. It also prompts brilliant and atmospheric music-making from both Previn and the LSO, and from Mehta (himself Indian-born) and the LPO. Not to mention the composer himself, who launches into solos which he makes sound spontaneous in the authentic manner, however prepared they may actually be. He opens the first CD with a very Westernized raga, which he calls *Morning Love*, and in the ragas *Piloo* and *Prabhāti*, when he is joined by Menuhin (who is also on very good form), the latter's contribution draws an obvious parallel with East European folk music.

SHAPERO, Harold (born 1920)

Symphony for Classical Orchestra; Nine-minute Overture
**(*) New World NW 373-2. LAPO, Previn

Stravinsky and Copland are the major influences on Shapero's exhilarating and masterly *Symphony for Classical Orchestra*. Copland spoke of his 'wonderfully spontaneous musical gift' and the listener is held throughout by his powerful sense of momentum. Although he is perhaps almost too much in thrall to Stravinsky, this is a gripping and inspiriting score, which benefits greatly from Bernstein's advocacy. Previn gets good results from the Los Angeles orchestra but does not bring the sheer vitality that distinguished Bernstein's pioneering record (now deleted).

SHCHEDRIN, Rodion (born 1932)

Carmen (ballet, arr. from Bizet: complete); *Concertos for Orchestra 1 (Naughty Limericks) and 2 (The Chimes)*
⌐━ *** DG 471 136-2. Russian Nat. O, Pletnev

(i) *Carmen* (ballet; arr. from Bizet): *Suite; Concerto for Orchestra (Naughty Limericks)*
(BB) **(*) Naxos 8.553038. Ukrainian State O, Kuchar

(i) *Carmen* (ballet; arr. from Bizet): *Suite; Humoresque. In Imitation of Albéniz; Stalin Cocktail*
*** Chan. 9288. I Musici de Montréal, Turovski; (i) with Ens. Répercussion – TURINA: *La oración del torero* ***

Shchedrin's brilliantly original *Carmen* ballet has never sounded more dramatically vivid than in this new Pletnev recording, which is now top choice for this piece. The *Concerto for Orchestra No. 1 (Naughty Limericks)*, is a vibrant scherzo, a fun piece, brightly scored and full of character in this performance. The *Second Concerto (The Chimes)* (referring to the historical significance of bells in Russia) could hardly be more contrasted. It begins broodingly with tremolo strings, which leads on to an array of orchestral effects and, of course, quite a few bells (18 tubular bells are used). It is not especially inspired but has its moments. Superlative playing and recording throughout.

The Chandos version by I Musici de Montréal was recorded in the richly resonant acoustic of the Eglise de la Nativité de la Sainte-Vierge, La Prairie, Quebec. The sound is very much in the demonstration bracket, with glittering percussion effects (marimba and vibraphone particularly well caught) and dramatic use of sidedrum snares. Yuli Turovski's performance opens evocatively and is highly dramatic, winningly expressive and subtle in its use of the wide range of string colour and dynamic. The pastiche, *In Imitation of Albéniz*, and the grotesque, Shostakovich-like *Humoresque* are offset by a malignant parody-evocation of Stalin, full of creepy special effects and with a shout of horror at the end. They are very well presented here, but one would not want to return to them very often.

Kuchar's version is also vividly played, with wit as well as high drama and atmosphere. The Naxos recording is excellent. The brief *Concerto for Orchestra* with its curious subtitle is a kaleidoscopic scherzando, a whirlwind presentation of Russian folk-motives over a minimalist ostinato. It is played with great verve but rather outstays its welcome.

Concerto Cantabile
*** EMI 5 56966-2. Vengerov, LSO, Rostropovich –
STRAVINSKY: *Violin Concerto*; TCHAIKOVSKY: *Sérénade mélancolique* ***

Shchedrin has said that he understands the term *cantabile* to express 'firstly a certain tension in the "soul" of the notes, and also the manner in which they are produced. The term also refers to the juxtaposition, interweaving, conflict and resolution of the soloist's singing lines against the orchestra.' The serene opening is deceptive, for the composer's arch-like structure forms a complex and at times dissonant work, even if 'in the finale the sound of the solo violin should come to resemble that of a shepherd's pipe'. With the vibrant support of Rostropovich, Maxim Vengerov's performance combines a powerful lyricism with the composer's required 'tonal variety'. The dancing centrepiece brings splendid bite of bow on strings, combined with a genuine sense of fantasy, and the finale produces a burst of radiance in the orchestral strings which the soloist follows with a ruminative soliloquy. The Abbey Road recording is first class.

Stihira
(M) *** Warner Elatus 0927 49014-2. Nat. SO, Rostropovich
– GLAZUNOV: *Violin Concerto in A min.*, Op. 82;
PROKOFIEV: *Violin Concerto 1 in D, Op. 19* ***

Shchedrin here celebrates the millennium of the introduction of Christianity into Russia with a measured passacaglia-like piece based on Russian Orthodox chant, which builds up to a central climax of Mussorgskian splendour. The recording, made in the Kennedy Center, Washington, is more airy and spacious than many from this venue.

Piano Concerto 2
*** Hyp. **SACD**: SACDA 67425; CD: CDA 67425. Hamelin, BBC Scottish SO, Litton – SHOSTAKOVICH: *Piano Concertos 1–2* ***

The *First* of Shchedrin's concertos was a graduation piece from 1954, very much in the Kabalevsky or Khachaturian mould. In the *Second Concerto* in 1966, Shchedrin experimented with 12-note technique and jazz. It teems with energy and there is some pretty angular keyboard writing, though much of the activity seems to be to little purpose. Shchedrin himself recorded it with Svetlanov in the late 1970s, but this newcomer supersedes it in sheer virtuosity and panache, not to mention the clarity and presence of the Hyperion recording.

Balalaika; Echo Sonata for Solo Violin
*** EMI 5 57384-2. Vengerov – BACH: *Toccata & Fugue in D min.*; YSAYE: *Solo Violin Sonatas Nos 2, 3, 4 & 6* ***

Shchedrin's party-piece encore, *Balalaika*, has Vengerov the perfect showman in this live recording of a solo recital, playing pizzicato throughout with the violin held like a balalaika, to the great amusement of the audience. The *Echo Sonata* is far more formidable, again with Vengerov an intense communicator, always spontaneous.

SHENG, Bright (born 1955)

China Dreams; (i) Nanking! Nanking! (A Threnody for Orchestra and Pipa); (ii) 2 Poems from the Sung Dynasty
☀︎— (BB) *** Naxos 8.555866. Hong Kong PO, Wong; with (i) Quiang; (ii) Gondek

Bright Sheng was born in Shanghai, experienced living through the Chinese Cultural Revolution as a child and later studied composition at the local Conservatory of Music. In 1982 he moved to New York where he studied further, under Bernstein among others, winning various awards both in his homeland and in the USA. His highly accessible music has an individual voice and a vividly unpredictable orchestral palette. The spectacular *China Dreams* was composed between 1992 and 1995 and its attractive themes draw on Chinese folk music. *Fanfare*, the second of the four movements, a brilliant toccata well laced with percussion, is immediately arresting, and the following evocation for strings, *The Stream Flows* is lyrically haunting. The finale, picturing the *Three Gorges of the Yangtze River* develops ideas introduced in the *Prelude*, and builds to a powerful motoric climax, perhaps suggesting the spectacular dam construction, then ends with a peaceful evocation of lapping waters. Juliana Gondek joins the orchestra for the *Two Poems*, early works from 1985, the first short and exotic including some expert vocal glissandi, the second, longer, more a symphonic poem, with atmospheric orchestral writing and startling percussion.

Nanking! Nanking!, completed in 2000 and depicting the massacre, when the Japanese swept into that ancient city in 1937, opens powerfully and stridently with remorseless rhythms and echoes of the *Rite of Spring*. The pipa (a short-necked Chinese lute) provides a ruminative retrospective narration, remembering both the darkness and the heroism of the survivors. But the music again generates considerable violence before, in a warm postlude for the strings, both elegiac and hopeful, the composer celebrates the resilience of the human spirit. The work's peaceful conclusion, with a final soliloquy from the pipa – so sensitively played here by Zhang Qiang – is interrupted by a brief but desperate final warning from the orchestra. These are surely definitive performances, with the Hong Kong orchestra responding superbly to the dedicated direction of Samuel Wong, and the recording is outstanding too.

SHEPPARD, John (c. 1515–c. 1559)

Aeterne rex altissime; Audivi vocem de coelo; Beata nobis gaudia; Dum transisset Sabbatum (1st & 2nd settings); In manus tuas (2nd & 3rd settings); Gaude, gaude, gaude Maria; Hostis Herodes impie; Impetum fecerunt unanimes; In manus tuas (3rd setting); Libera nos, salva nos (2nd setting); Sacris solemniis; Sancte Dei pretiose; Spiritus sanctus procedens (2nd setting). Second Service: Magnificat; Nunc dimittis. Te Deum laudamus. Western Wynde Mass
(B) *** Hyp. Dyad CDD 22022 (2). The Sixteen, Christophers

Ave maris stella. Cantate Mass. Motets: Deus tuorum militum (1st setting); Filiae Hierusalem venite; Haec dies; In manus tuas Domine (1st setting); In pacem in idipsum; Jesu salvator saeculi, redemptis; Jesu salvator saeculi verbum; Justi in perpetuum vivent; Laudem dicite Deo; Libera nos,

salva nos (1st setting); Paschal Kyrie; Regis Tharsis et insulae; Salvator mundi, Domine; Spiritus sanctus procedens (1st setting); Verbum caro factus est
☀︎— ✿ (B) *** Hyp. Dyad CDD 22021 (2). The Sixteen, Christophers

The first collection listed (CD 22022) is especially attractive as it includes Sheppard's *Western Wynde Mass*. However, this is a less elaborate setting of this famous theme than some others, notably that of John Taverner, for until the closing *Agnus Dei* Sheppard consistently places the melodic line on top, whereas Taverner moves the tune about within the lower parts. Nevertheless, Sheppard's setting has an appealingly simple beauty, while the extended *Te Deum laudamus* is even richer in its harmonic progressions. The soaring second version of *Dum transisset Sabbatum* and the third version of the sombre *In manus tuas* (with their characteristic dissonances) are also memorable. The set includes ten more responsories, all of high quality and offering considerable variety, from the flowing antiphon *Libera nos, salva nos* to the gently serene second setting (for Palm Sunday) of *In manus tuas Domine*.

However, we have given our Rosette to the companion set (CDD 22021), for it includes Sheppard's glorious six-voiced *Cantate Mass*, much more complex than *Western Wynde* and, with its glowingly textured polyphony, surely among his most inspired works. There are also eleven responsories, all showing the composer at his most concentrated in inspiration. The Sixteen consistently convey the rapturous beauty of Sheppard's writing, above all in the ethereal passages in the highest register, very characteristic of him. Even there, the Sixteen's sopranos seem quite unstressed by the tessitura. There are not many more beautiful examples of Tudor polyphony than this.

Christe redemptor omnium; In manus tuas; Media vita; Reges Tharsis; Sacris solemniis; Verbum caro
*** Gimell CDGIM 016. Tallis Scholars, Phillips

All the music here is based on chant, and much of it is for the six-part choir, which produces a particularly striking sonority. The *Media vita* ('In the midst of life we are in death') is a piece of astonishing beauty, and it is sung with remarkable purity of tone by the Tallis Scholars under Peter Phillips. Glorious and little-known music: the recording could hardly be improved on.

Motets: *Gaude, gaude, gaude Maria; In manus tuas* (1st setting); *In pace; Laudem dicite Deo; Verbum caro*
(B) **(*) CfP (ADD) 575 982-2. Clerkes of Oxenford, Wulstan
   – TALLIS: *Motets* **(*)

The performances by the Clerkes of Oxenford under David Wulstan are full of fervour, particularly in the inspired *Gaude, gaude, gaude Maria* and the closing *Verbum caro*. Wulstan presses on very strongly, and some might feel there is a lack of contrasting repose and not enough subtlety in the sheer thrust of his direction. But the commitment of the singing will surely convince anyone who buys this CD on impulse that this is great music and that its composer's name should be more familiar. The 1978 analogue recording has plenty of body and atmosphere.

SHIELD, William (1748–1829)
Rosina
*** ABC Classics (ADD) 461 922-2. Elkins, Harwood, Sinclair, Tear, Macdonald, Ambrosian Singers, LSO, Bonynge –
   ELGAR: *Sea Pictures* **(*)

Shield's rustic comedy *Rosina* is a delight from beginning to end. First heard at Covent Garden in 1782, it is crammed full of delights. Even the overture, with its witty interjections from the woodwind, threatens to upstage the main work, but the engaging and piquant arias that follow easily match it. The dialogue rings through with crystal clarity, the country-accents delivered with relish. The performance is lively and fun, with Bonynge allowing the singers to embellish their vocal lines while the orchestra provides a stylish and vivid accompaniment.

Margreta Elkins is superb as Rosina, and she is matched by the rest of the team; whether they be joyful rustic arias, or sentimental ballads, each is characterized beautifully. The full English text is provided in the lavishly illustrated booklet, and with vintage Decca sound (1966) this CD is a winner. The unexpected couplings are well worth having too.

SHOSTAKOVICH, Dmitri (1906–75)

'The Film Album': *Alone, Op. 26* (extended excerpts). *The Counterplan, Op. 33* (excerpts). *The Gadfly: Romance. The Great Citizen, Op. 55: Funeral March. Hamlet, Op. 116* (excerpts). *Pirogov, Op. 76a: Scherzo & Finale. Sofia Perovskaya, Op. 132: Waltz. The Tale of the Silly Little Mouse, Op. 56* (arr. Andrew Cornhall)
☛ *** Decca 460 792-2. Concg. O, Chailly

Shostakovich's ready fund of melody and exotic orchestral palette spiced with touches of wit make here for a kaleidoscope of memorable vignettes. The delightful opening *Presto* of the music from *The Counterplan* leads to a wistful romantic concertante violin episode, not unlike the more famous *Romance* from *The Gadfly*, which is also included. The continuous sequence illustrating *The Tale of the Silly Little Mouse* (an animated cartoon) is full of delicate charm; the engaging *Valse* from *Pirogov* is rather more robust, and *Hamlet* brings music of more pungency and dramatic power. But the most substantial set of excerpts is taken from the composer's second film score, *Alone* (1930). It opens roisterously, follows up with a Kabalevsky-like *Galop*, and the other numbers, with avant-garde flair, bring a wide range of picaresque and touching evocations, describing a barrel organ, schoolchildren and a tempest, and ending with an eerie calm after the storm. First rate Concertgebouw playing and the most vivid Decca recording ensure the success of this entertaining collection.

Ballet Suites 1–5; Festive Overture, Op. 96; Katerina Ismailova: Suite
*** Chan. 7000/1. RSNO, Järvi

This highly entertaining set again represents Shostakovich in light-hearted, often ironic mood, throwing out *bonnes-bouches* like fireworks and with a sparkling vividness of orchestral colour. The *Ballet Suites* reuse material from earlier works: the *Fifth Suite* draws entirely on music from the 1931 ballet, *The Bolt* (see below). This is the most extended of the five suites, and typical of the young Shostakovich. The *Suite* from *Katerina Ismailova* (*Lady Macbeth of Mtsensk*) consists of entr'actes from between the scenes, which effectively act as emotional links. Järvi is entirely at home in all this music and clearly relishes its dry humour. The recording is spectacular and resonantly wide-ranging in the Chandos manner.

The Bolt (ballet; complete recording)
*** Chan. 9343/4 (2). Stockholm PO, Stockholm Transport Band, Rozhdestvensky

The Bolt dates from 1931 and in its original form sank without trace, largely thanks to the feeble, cumbersome propagandist libretto. Yet the dances are so sharp and colourful in their inspiration that over the years suites of movements have been heard, and now, in this vivid, full-blooded recording, Rozhdestvensky resurrects the complete score of 43 movements, lasting two and a half hours. Even if it is no masterpiece it demonstrates how dazzlingly inventive the young Shostakovich was, even when faced with an indifferent subject. Rozhdestvensky plainly believes passionately in this score, and he draws an electrifying performance from the Swedish orchestra. Demonstration sound.

'The Dance Album': *The Bolt: Ballet Suite, Op. 27a* (1934 version); *The Gadfly* (extended excerpts from the film score), *Op. 97* (original orchestration);
Moscow-Cheryomushki (suite from the operetta), *Op. 105*
☛ *** Decca 452 597-2. Phd. O, Chailly

Chailly offers 13 items from *The Gadfly* and reveals it to be far finer music than hitherto suspected, partly by using the original scoring. For all his sophistication of detail and expressive expansiveness, Chailly does not miss out on the witty audacity. The opening number of *Moscow-Cheryomushki, A Spin through Moscow* (when the chauffeur borrows the boss's car), has great energy and élan, the *Polka* from *The Bolt* combines wit with narrowly avoided vulgarity, and the boisterous opening of the following *Variations* will disappoint nobody. But, apart from the tunefulness, what one remembers most here is the superb playing of the Philadelphia Orchestra: the sonorous brass and vivid woodwind, while the strings have not sounded like this in decades. It is a joy to hear the luscious violins in *The Tango* from *The Bolt*, or *Montanelli* from *The Gadfly*; while the full body of tone in melancholy response to *The Slap in the Face* and the soft-voiced cellos and violas in *Gemma's Room* recall the Stokowskian era.

The Bolt: Suite; Jazz Suites 1 & 2; Tahiti Trot
(BB) **(*) Naxos 8.555949. Russian State SO, Yablonsky

The *Jazz Suites* show a light-hearted Shostakovich at his witty best, with some delightful melodies, colourfully orchestrated, with the composer's ironic tang adding a piquant spice. Likewise, the dances from *The Bolt*, not quite so inconsequential, but just as enjoyable, have an edge, which makes Shostakovich in popular mode so enticing. Yablonsky directs enjoyable, straightforward accounts of these works. Chailly's account of *The Bolt Suite* on Decca is obviously superior, but, that said, this CD is still good value, especially at its super-bargain price, and the inclusion of Shostakovich's arrangement of 'Tea for Two' as the *Tahiti Trot* is a real bonus.

Chamber Symphony, Op. 83a (String Quartet 4, orch. Barshai); *Symphony for Strings & Woodwinds* (String Quartet 3, orch. Barshai)
(N) *** BIS CD 1180. Tapiola Sinf., Kantorow

Shostakovich did authorize the transcription for full strings of the *Eighth* and *Tenth Quartets* and did apparently give Rudolf Barshai permission to arrange some of the other quartets for larger forces. Naturally, something of their original character is lost, and we well understand those who simply prefer to stick with the originals. However, those willing to try these powerful works in this form will not be disappointed by the playing of the Tapiola Sinfonietta, who are superbly recorded by BIS.

Chamber Symphony 1, Op. 110a; Symphony for Strings, Op. 118a (both arr. Barshai); (i) From Jewish folk poetry

(M) *** Chan. 6617. I Musici de Montreal, Turovsky; (i) with Pelle, Hart, Nolan

A fine record. The transcriptions for strings of the *Eighth* and *Tenth Quartets* were made by Rudolf Barshai, and if the performances here do not quite match their arranger's own recording (now withdrawn), they have plenty of bite and intensity and top-quality Chandos sound. The eleven vignettes, which Shostakovich based on Jewish folk music, have the widest diversity of mood and are splendidly sung here, the dialogue songs especially idiomatic. They are surprisingly upbeat, with the final concerted number, *Happiness*, ending the cycle robustly. Turovsky's framing accompaniments, too, are colourful and vividly caught by the engineers.

Chamber Symphony 1, Op. 110a; Symphony for Strings, Op. 118a; (i) Suite on Finnish Themes

*** BIS CD 1256. (i) Komsi, Nyman; Ostrobothian CO, Kangas

The *Suite on Finnish Themes* was written in 1939 in the immediate wake of the *Sixth Symphony* (indeed Shostakovich had to miss the Moscow première of the symphony in order to finish the piece) in response to a commission from the Leningrad Military District. This was, of course, the year of the first Winter War between the Soviet Union and Finland. It is slight (lasting less than twelve minutes) and yet often very characteristic, and it is scored for soprano, tenor, flute, oboe, clarinet, trumpet, triangle, tambourine, side-drum, piano and strings. For some reason it was never performed at the time (Shostakovich did not add the words himself) and the score has only recently come to light in a private collection in St Petersburg. It comes with two of the so-called *Chamber Symphonies*, transcriptions for full strings of the *Eighth* and *Tenth Quartets* by Rudolf Barshai and was made with the approval of the composer. Dedicated playing and exemplary recording.

Chamber Symphony 1, Op. 110a; (i) Symphony 14 in G min., Op. 135

(B) ** Virgin 2x1 5 62050-2 (2). Kastrashvili, Krutikov, Lausanne CO, Lazarev – DEBUSSY: *Danse; Sarabande*; MILHAUD: *La création du monde*; PROKOFIEV: *Symphony 1 (Classical)* ***

In the *Chamber Symphony* Lazarev gets off to a sluggish start from which the performance never fully recovers, though it is very well played. He is obviously at home in the *Symphony*, creating a powerful atmosphere, but the contribution of his very Russian soloists is uneven. Although she sings with much intensity of feeling (and is especially moving in *The Suicide*), the rich-toned Makvala Kastrashvili has a troublesome vibrato and moments of squalliness, notably in *The Death of a Poet*. The bass, Mikhail Krutikov, is very impressive and *In the Santé Prison* is really memorable. But in this symphony one badly needs texts and translations, which are not forthcoming. The recording is excellent.

Cello Concerto 1 in E flat, Op. 107

☞ ✿ *** EMI **DVD** DVA 4901209. Rostropovich, Monte Carlo Nat. Op. O, Kamu – PROKOVIEV: *Sinfonia Concertante*. Bonus: MUSSORGSKY: *Songs and Dances of Death* ***

*** Chan. 8322. Wallfisch, ECO, Simon – BARBER: *Cello Concerto* ***

When he came to befriend Shostakovich in the 1950s, Rostropovich obviously wanted to ask him for a cello concerto, but prudently withheld a request. The composer's wife later told him that only if he withheld any such prompting might Shostakovich produce something especially for him. She was right and in 1959 the great cellist's restraint was rewarded. Here is the result, and Rostropovich recorded it in London two years later. It is tersely scored for quite a small orchestra, double woodwind, celesta, but just one horn (here the splendid Barry Tuckwell) with whom the solo cello often duets. There is a magical central *Moderato*, where the cello shares an exquisite passage on high harmonics with the celesta, followed by a virtuoso cadenza which leads into the fiendish, virtuoso finale. As with the Prokofiev coupling, one watches engrossed at the way Rostropovich shares the work with his orchestral colleagues; but the camera, rightly, often centres on the cellist and gives him great presence. The filming is in black and white, but the 1961 recording of the orchestra is better than the dry Monte Carlo sound, although acceptable rather than outstanding. Fortunately there are no complaints about the recording of the great cellist himself, who often seems to come right into the listener/watcher's room.

Wallfisch handles the first movement splendidly and he gives a sensitive account of the slow movement and has thoughtful and responsive support from the ECO. The Chandos recording is outstandingly fine.

Cello Concertos 1; 2 in G, Op. 126

(BB) *** Naxos 8.550813. Kliegel, Polish Nat. RSO (Katowice), Wit

(M) *** BIS CD 300626. Thedéen, Malmö SO, DePreist

☞ (BB) *** Warner Apex 0927 40604-2. Noras, Norwegian RO, Rasilainen (with R. STRAUSS: *Romanze ***)

Maria Kliegel and the Polish National Radio Orchestra at Katowice under Antoni Wit also give a very good account of both concertos that can be confidently recommended at this price, and on all counts is well worth considering.

The fine Swedish cellist, Torleif Thedéen, has a lot going for him, and his passionately committed performances would honour any collection. He has the advantage of excellent engineering, which gives a very alive sound, plus good orchestral support from the Malmö orchestra under James DePreist.

Arto Noras is an aristocratic artist with a beautiful tone, and his playing is wonderfully flexible with intelligent phrasing and an instinctive feel for this repertoire. He never plays to the gallery, and his performances are all the more effective as a result. Not a first choice, then, but eminently recommendable in terms of value for money, as is the Apex alternative.

Cello Concerto 1 in E flat, Op. 107

☞ (M) (***) BBC Legends mono BBCL 4143-2. Rostropovich, Leningrad PO, Rozhdestvensky – TCHAIKOVSKY: *Symphony 4* (***)

The Times 'special Correspondent', whose by-line disguised the identity of William Mann, is quoted by the notes as saying that 'Rostropovich's tone has to be heard to be believed, so mighty is its strength, so richly varied its colour, and so beautiful its quality throughout its range. His technique is that of the effortless kind that enables him to carry out every feat of bowing, chording or violin-like dexterity with thought not for the means but only the artistic end' – and the virtuosity and tonal homogeneity of the Leningrad Philharmonic is astonishing. An exceptionally compelling musical document, coupled with an equally high-voltage account of Tchaikovsky's *Fourth Symphony*, given 11 years later at the Royal Albert Hall.

(i) *Cello Concerto 1; Piano Concertos Nos.* (ii) *1, Op. 35;* (iii) *2, Op. 102*
(M) *** Sony (DDD/ADD) SMK 89752. (i) Ma, Phd. O, Ormandy; (ii) Previn, Vacchiano, NYPO, Bernstein; (iii) Bernstein (piano & cond.), NYPO

Yo-Yo Ma plays with an intensity that compels the listener, the Philadelphia Orchestra give eloquent support, and the digital recording is excellent. This couples aptly with the shrewd, much earlier pairing of Bernstein's radiant account of the *Second Piano Concerto* with Previn's equally striking reading of No. 1. If these recordings are far from recent they are transferred most vividly.

(i) *Cello Concerto 1;* (ii) *Violin Concerto 1 in A min., Op. 99*
☞— ✿ (M) (***) Sony stereo/mono MHK 63327. (i) Rostropovich, Phd. O, Ormandy; (ii) D. Oistrakh, NYPO, Mitropoulos

Rostropovich's recording première of the Shostakovich *First Cello Concerto* was made in 1959 and has for long enjoyed legendary status. It has probably not been surpassed, even by Rostropovich himself in subsequent recordings. David Oistrakh's mono recording of the *Violin Concerto* with Mitropoulos conducting the New York Philharmonic still sounds stunning. The presentation brings alive memories of the original issues and induces much nostalgia. This reissue is comparatively expensive but well worth it.

Cello Concerto 2, Op. 126
(M) (**(*)) BBC mono BBCL 4073-2. Rostropovich, LSO, Hurst (with KHACHATURIAN: *Concerto Rhapsody;* TCHAIKOVSKY: *Rococo Variations* **(*))

The BBC recording of the Shostakovich *Second Cello Concerto* was made at the Festival Hall in October 1966, not long after its Soviet première in Moscow, with Colin Davis conducting. The sound has less transparency than in the much later DG studio version but against that there is, of course, the intensity of a première performance and the consequent excitement. The Khachaturian *Concerto Rhapsody* of 1963 is also captured at its première with the LSO and George Hurst, and the 1964 *Rococo Variations*, again with Colin Davis but at the Albert Hall, is a performance of no mean mastery. All in all, well worth having as a document of both the master cellist and two new works to which he is so deeply committed.

Piano Concerto 1 for Piano, Trumpet & Strings, Op. 35
(***) British Music Society mono BMS 101 CDH. Mewton-Wood, Sevenstern, Concert Hall O, Goehr – BLISS: *Concerto* (***) ✿; STRAVINSKY: *Concerto for Piano and Wind* (***)

(i; ii) *Piano Concerto 1 for Piano, Trumpet and Strings: Symphonies Nos.* (ii) *1 in F min.;* (iii) *10 in E min.*
(B) ** EMI double forte 5 75178-2. (i) Rudy, Antonsen; (ii) BPO; (iii) Phd. O; Jansons – MUSSORGSKY: *Songs and Dances of Death* ***

(i) *Piano Concerto 1;* (ii) *Symphony 5 in D min., Op. 47*
**(*) Australian Decca Eloquence (ADD) 466 664-2. (i) Ogdon, ASMF, Marriner; (ii) SRO, Kertész

The Shostakovich concerto was the last commercial recording made by Noel Mewton-Wood, in 1953, and the sound is the finest of the three concertos reissued on this British Music Society CD, the orchestral strings lustrous in the delicately romantic *Largo*, warm and full in the *Moderato* and with plenty of bite in the outer movements, with Harry Sevenstern's crisply articulated trumpet-playing cleanly caught. The performance is full of wit, gently ironic in the first movement, sharply brilliant in the dazzlingly played finale.

John Ogdon's clean, stylish performance of the *First Piano Concerto* – which encompasses both the humour and romanticism of the score – was one of his best records. He keeps a little more detached than Marriner in the tender slow movement, but the trumpet playing of John Wilbraham is masterly in the finale. Though the balance gives the performance a chamber quality, the sound is full and vivid.

Making its CD debut, Kertész's *Fifth Symphony* was recorded in the early 1960s, though you would hardly guess it. It is a thoroughly musical reading, but others find much more tension and colour in the climax of the *Largo*. The finale is taken steadily, but there is a splendid outburst of controlled exuberance for the coda, and the excellent recording – with some impressive timpani – projects the reading effectively. An enterprising coupling.

This EMI double forte reissue is something of a mixed offering. In Mikhail Rudy's hands the *Concerto for Piano, Trumpet and Strings* starts off very slowly for an *Allegro moderato*, and the effect is ponderous, although he does proceed at a more normal tempo at the second *Più mosso* marking. In the slow movement Jansons is also a shade slower than most rivals, but he draws ravishing sound from the Berlin Philharmonic strings. Ole Edvard Antonsen plays the trumpet part with impeccable musicianship and taste. Altogether a well thought-out but not wholly convincing performance and much the same verdict must be returned on the *First Symphony*. Wonderful playing from the Berliners, but the overall impression is a little studied, something wanting in spontaneity.

The *Tenth Symphony* is another matter and is highly recommendable. Jansons draws a splendid response from the Philadelphia Orchestra and the playing has tremendous fervour. Karajan's interpretation (see below) remains preeminent, but the EMI sound is generally preferable. The Mussorgsky coupling is also well worth having, so this collection is by no means to be dismissed.

Piano Concerto (i) *1 for Piano, Trumpet & Strings in C min., Op. 35. 2 in F, Op. 102*
☞— *** Hyp. **SACD**: SACDA 67425; CD: CDA 67425. Hamelin, (i) O'Keeffe; BBC Scottish SO, Litton – SHCHEDRIN: *Piano Concerto 2* ***

(i; ii) *Piano Concertos 1–2;* (iii) *The Gadfly: Barrel-Organ Waltz; Romance;* (iv) *Jazz Suite 1: Waltz; Polka; Foxtrot. Jazz*

Suite 2: Waltz 2. Tahiti Trot (Tea for Two), Op 16; (i) The Unforgettable Year 1919: The Assault on the Beautiful City of Gorky

☛ (N) (BB) *** EMI HMV 5 86765-2. (i) Alexeev, ECO, Maksymiuk; (ii) Philip Jones; (iii) ASMF, Marriner; (iv) Phd. O, Jansons

(i) *Piano Concertos 1–2; Piano Sonata 2 in B min., Op. 61*

(BB) *** Warner Apex 8573 89092-2. Leonskaya; (i) Saint Paul CO, Wolf

Marc-André Hamelin gives a vibrant, superbly articulate and dazzling account of both *Concertos*. These are stunning performances, which fully deserve the plaudits that have been showered on them. The listener is on the edge of the seat throughout, with both poetic insights and the right kind of excitement. Both works are splendidly characterized, though the trumpeter really rather overdoes things in the 'Poor Jenny is a Weeping' section of the finale. The recording, made in the Caird Hall, Dundee, is in the demonstration class. There is no better version of the two piano concertos coupled together on the market.

Otherwise Alexeev is a first choice among couplings of both concertos and his record would sweep the board even at full price. The digital recording is excellent in every way and he offers a fill-up in the form of a miniature one-movement concerto from a film score called *The Unforgettable Year 1919*. Moreover, for this reissue on their HMV budget label EMI have included some delightful miniatures from the two *Jazz Suites*, plus Shostakovich's lollipop arrangement of *Tea for Two*, all beautifully played and recorded. Unmissable!

We know from her fine Tchaikovsky recordings that Elisabeth Leonskaya is thoroughly at home in Russian music, and so it proves in her sparkling and wittily pointed accounts of these two concertos of Shostakovich. The Saint Paul Chamber Orchestra, too, provide admirable backing. The strings play with striking beauty in both slow movements, the *Andante* of No. 2 is ravishing, and the solo trumpeter, Gary Borden, brings a nice sense of humour to his solos in the finale of No. 1. What makes this disc doubly attractive is Leonskaya's distinctive account of the *B minor Piano Sonata*, with thoughtful playing not only in the slow movement but in the finale, which is in essence a set of variations. Vivid recording, with a touch of hardness on the piano tone, which does not come amiss in this repertoire.

(i) *Piano Concertos 1–2; Symphony 1*

(BB) ** EMI Encore 5 75886-2. (i) Rudy, Antonsen, BPO or LPO, Jansons

The performances of the *First Concerto* and *Symphony No.1* are discussed above. The *Second Concerto* is admirably done but, like the double forte collection above, this is a mixed offering.

Piano Concertos: (i) 1 for Piano, Trumpet & Strings in C min., Op. 35; (ii) 2 in F, Op. 102. 3 Fantastic Dances, Op. 5; Preludes and Fugues, Op. 87 1 in C; 4 in E min.; 5 in D; 23 in F; 24 in D min.

(M) (**(*)) EMI mono 5 62646-2 [5 62648-2]. Composer, with (i) Vaillant; (i; ii) O Nat. de l'ORTF, Cluytens

Shostakovich made his mono recordings of the two piano concertos and the solo piano pieces in Paris in 1958. In his youth he was an accomplished player and was good enough to enter the first Warsaw Piano Competition in 1924, though he did not gain a prize. By the time he made these recordings his keyboard prowess had passed its peak and he did not play very much in public. Despite intensive practice he was not totally in command (he was experiencing a mysterious and debilitating weakness of the right hand – as well as his usual nerves), but the performances are still valuable in giving an authoritative idea of his own conception of his music. He gets a supportive accompaniment from Cluytens and the French National Radio Orchestra. The concertos appeared in EMI's 'Composer as Performer' series but, if memory does not deceive, the mono sound is improved in Simon Gibson's new transfer for the 'Great Recordings of the Century'.

Piano Concerto 2 in F, Op. 102

(BB) *** EMI Encore (ADD) 5 74991-2. Ogdon, RPO, Foster – BARTOK: *Piano Concerto 3*, etc. **(*)

John Ogdon, at the height of his powers, gives a splendidly idiomatic account of this concerto written originally for Shostakovich's son, Maxim. The playing is full of character, the outer movements striking for their wit and dash, and the beautiful slow movement richly romantic without being sentimentalized. This remains one of the finest versions available, and the 1971 sound is excellent.

Violin Concerto 1 in A min., Op. 99

*** Sony SK 68338. Midori, BPO, Abbado – TCHAIKOVSKY: *Violin Concerto* ***
**(*) Simax PSC 1159. Tellefsen, RPO, Berglund – BACH: *Violin Concerto 2* **(*)

Having the Tchaikovsky concerto together with this twentieth-century Russian masterpiece brings out the parallels between the two, a point enhanced by Midori's readings, recorded live, with rhythm and phrasing freely expressive. At the start of the *Moderato* first movement of the Shostakovich her tone is so withdrawn that one has to prick the ears, and in the *Passacaglia* third movement she also conveys an ethereal poignancy in her pianissimo playing. Abbado is a powerful and sympathetic, yet discreet accompanist, with recording that is both warm and well detailed.

Arve Tellefsen gives a fine account of the concerto and brings fine musicianship and no lack of passion to it. Berglund proves a supportive accompanist and the RPO play well for him. Moreover the sound is very well balanced. But this is not a first choice.

(i) *Violin Concerto 1 in A min., Op. 99; (ii) 3 Violin Duets*

(M) **(*) EMI (DDD/ADD) 5 62593-2. Perlman, with (i) Israel PO, Mehta; (ii) Pinchas Zukerman – GLAZUNOV: *Violin Concerto* **(*)

Perlman's version of the Shostakovich *First Violin Concerto* was recorded live in the Mann Auditorium in Tel Aviv, and though that involves some roughness in the sound, particularly in tuttis, the flair and electricity of this modern wizard of the violin are more compellingly caught. Excitement is the keynote: Perlman and Mehta put the work in the light of day and, in the two fast movements and the cadenza, that brings tremendous dividends. There is no violinist in the world who can quite match Perlman in sheer bravura, particularly live, and the ovation which greets this dazzling performance of the finale is richly deserved. Yet some of the mystery and fantasy which Russian interpreters have found – from David Oistrakh onwards – is missing, and the close balance of the solo instrument, characteristic of Perlman's concerto recordings, undermines hushed intensity. The three *Violin Duets* which act as an encore are entertaining trifles (there is a salon piece, a gavotte and some waltzes), all betraying some measure of wit. They are, of course, marvellously played.

Violin Concertos 1; 2 in C sharp min., Op. 129

⊶ (M) *** Warner Elatus 0927 46742-2. Vengerov, LSO, Rostropovich

(BB) *** Virgin 2x1 5 61633-2. Sitkovetsky, BBC SO, Davis

*** Chan. 8820. Mordkovitch, SNO, Järvi

(BB) *** Naxos 8.550814. Kaler, Polish Nat. RSO (Katowice), Wit

**(*) BBC (ADD) BBCL 4060. D. Oistrakh, (i) Philh. O, Rozhdestvensky, (ii) USSR State O, Svetlanov – YSAYE: *Amitié* **(*)

Vengerov comes into direct competition with Sitkovetsky on Virgin, yet his playing can dazzle the ear equally tellingly; he also really gets under the skin of both concertos and finds an added depth of poetic feeling, while fully retaining the music's thrust and spontaneity. The haunting intensity, both at the opening of the *Second Concerto* and in its *Adagio* slow movement, is totally memorable. Rostropovich and the LSO give splendid support, and this mid-priced Warner Elatus disc now becomes a first recommendation.

Virgin's coupling by Sitkovetsky and the BBC Symphony Orchestra under Andrew Davis is impressive and intense; there is no doubt as to its excellence, it has tremendous bite. It is splendidly recorded, and also takes its place at the top of the list.

Mordkovitch's concentrated reading of No. 2 is matched by Järvi and the orchestra in their total commitment. She even outshines the work's dedicatee and first interpreter, David Oistrakh, in the dark reflectiveness of her playing, even if she cannot quite match him in bravura passages. In the better-known concerto (No. 1) the meditative intensity is magnetic, with a fullness and warmth of tone that have not always marked her playing on record before.

Ilya Kaler's technique is flawless, with playing that is not only brilliant but consistently beautiful tonally. The *Second Violin Concerto*, the more wayward, more problematic work, is particularly fine and Kaler relishes the key role given to the cadenzas. The haunting beauty of the performance may be measured by the gentle cadenza and final ghostly coda of the first movement, leading to a wonderfully rarefied account of the central *Adagio* and a mercurial, quicksilver one of the finale. If in the better-known *First Concerto* Kaler's performance does not quite have the same intensity, that is partly a question of the marginally less taut orchestral accompaniment and of the recording balance.

David Oistrakh's recording of the *First Violin Concerto* comes from the Edinburgh Festival of 1962 and the *Second* from a Prom in 1968. Both are performances to cherish alongside the commercial recordings that the great violinist (the dedicatee of both works) made in the 1950s. Although neither performance supersedes these, there is the electricity of a live occasion that gives something extra, and the first movement (*Nocturne*) of the *First* has an atmosphere that is as powerful as it was under Mitropoulos. The sound is very good.

The Golden Age (ballet; complete)

**(*) Chan. 9251/2. Stockholm PO, Rozhdestvensky

This is the first complete recording of Shostakovich's first ballet, with its extraordinary plot of Soviet and capitalist sportsmen and women. The famous *Polka* is meant to satirize a disarmament meeting in Geneva. The music as a whole is

remarkably potent and full of succulent ideas (even *Tea for Two* arrives during Act II), and the big set-pieces are expansively and sometimes darkly symphonic. The score is well played in Stockholm, but the warm orchestral style does not always readily bring out the music's plangent character and moments of barbed wit.

Hamlet (1932 production; complete incidental music), Op. 32; (1954 production; incidental music); King Lear (1941 production; complete incidental music), Op. 58a

(M) *** Cala CACD 1021. Winter, Wilson-Johnson, CBSO, Elder

An enterprising release, which offers Shostakovich's music for Nikolai Akimov's 1932 production of *Hamlet*. Akimov altered and extended Shakespeare's conception, even interpolating bits of Erasmus. Shostakovich's score has many biting and sarcastic episodes, and listening to the 30 short numbers – some only a few seconds long – makes for unsettled listening. There are spoken interpolations from the player-king and queen. Also included here is a gigue and finale from a 1954 production of *Hamlet*, and the Fool's songs, brilliantly sung by David Wilson-Johnson, from a 1941 production of *King Lear*, full of inventive things. This is not top-drawer Shostakovich, but congratulations are in order for Cala's enterprise in recording all this and to the City of Birmingham Orchestra under Mark Elder for the vital and alert performances. The recording too is expertly and tastefully balanced.

The Limpid Stream (complete ballet; revised Rozhdestvensky)

** Chan. 9423. Stockholm PO, Rozhdestvensky

Shostakovich's ballet enjoyed much the same fate as *Lady Macbeth of the Mtsensk District* for, after a successful run of eight months, *The Limpid Stream* was denounced in *Pravda*. It is not vintage Shostakovich nor complete, for as presented here it is a revision by Rozhdestvensky. Some of the numbers are familiar from *The Bolt*, but there is nothing that is as good as, say, the polka from *The Age of Gold*. Good recording, and the playing is very good if a little wanting in abandon.

New Babylon (film score); (i) From Jewish Folk Poetry (song-cycle)

*** Chan. 9600. Russian State SO, Polyansky with (i) Sharova, Kuznetsova, Martynov

It makes an unusual and revealing coupling having Shostakovich's long-buried music for the satirical silent film, *New Babylon*, paired with the moving sequence of Jewish song-settings. Polyansky and an excellent trio of soloists bring out the expressive depth of these deceptively simple, lyrical songs, regularly reflecting the composer's sympathy with the suffering of the Jews. *New Babylon* was the composer's very first film score, with sharp parodies, 1920s-style, of French models reflecting the Parisian background of the story. Colourful, atmospheric orchestration beautifully caught in full-bodied, well-balanced sound.

Symphonies

Symphonies 1–15; (i; ii) From Jewish Folk Poetry; (ii) 6 Poems of Marina Tsvetaeva

(B) *** Decca DDD/ADD 444 430-2 (11). Varady, Fischer-Dieskau, Rintzler; (i) Söderström, Karczykowski; (ii) Wenkel; Ch. of LPO or Concg. O; LPO or Concg. O, Haitink

No one artist or set of performances holds all the insights

into this remarkable symphonic canon, but what can be said of Haitink's set is that the playing of both the London Philharmonic and the Concertgebouw orchestras is of the highest calibre and is very responsive; moreover the Decca recordings, whether analogue or digital, are consistently of this company's highest standard, outstandingly brilliant and full. If without the temperament of a Mravinsky, Haitink proves a reliable guide to this repertoire, often much more than that, and sometimes inspired. All in all, a considerable achievement. The eleven discs are now offered together at bargain price, but they also remain available separately at mid-price – see below.

Symphony 1 in F min., Op. 10

(**N**) ** EMI **DVD** (ADD) 4901109. O Nat. de l'ORTF, Markevitch – WAGNER: *Tannhäuser: Overture* etc. STRAVINSKY: *Symphony Of Psalms* **

Those who saw Markevitch in the concert hall will remember the clarity and precision of his beat and what in the excellent booklet Alan Sanders calls his 'cool, slightly clinical, yet also intense approach' to his scores. In the 1950s he spent a good deal of time with the Orchestre Lamoureux, but by the 1960s he was a frequent visitor to the French Radio. The *First Symphony* featured in Markevitch's repertory fairly often and this slightly dry 1963 account with the Orchestre National de l'ORTF is very characteristic.

(i) *Symphony 1 in F min., Op. 10;* (ii) *Festive Overture.* Collection: *The Age of Gold: Polka. Ballet Suite 1: Galop; Music-box Waltz; Dance. Ballet Suite 2: Polka; Galop. The Gadfly: Introduction; Barrel Organ Waltz; Nocturne; Folk Festival; Galop. Moscow-Cheryomushki: Overture Waltz; Galop*

🔑 ❁ (B) *** Sony (ADD) SBK 62642. (i) Phd. O, Ormandy; (ii) Columbia SO, Kostelanetz

Ormandy and the Philadelphia Orchestra recorded this version of the *First Symphony* in the presence of the composer in 1959. It is a beautifully proportioned, tense and vivid account. The sound, too, is excellent. Still, after 40 years, a front-runner in spite of some excellent successors. The coupling could not have been better chosen: a suite of Shostakovichian orchestral lollipops selected by Kostelanetz, a dab hand at this kind of audacious light music. Readers who know the *Polka* from *The Age of Gold* will know what to expect. Kostelanetz opens with a fizzing account of the *Festive Overture*, Op. 96. Then comes the series of miniatures – mixed up to provide maximum contrast. Many of the pieces were virtually unknown when these performances first appeared in 1965, and even today few of them are familiar to the wider public. The fast numbers (like the Offenbachian *Galop* from *The Gadfly*) are redeemed from vulgarity by momentum and brilliant scoring, many of them suggesting the composer thumbing his nose at the Soviet authorities, and there is no better example than the *Moscow-Cheryomushki Overture Waltz* with its trombone glissandi accompanying a very Russian dance-accelerando, followed by the equally infectious potpourri called *Folk Festival*. But the gentler pieces are more memorable still: the hauntingly tender *Nocturne* from *The Gadfly* and the delicious *Barrel Organ Waltz* from the same source, matched by the *Music-box Waltz* from the *Ballet Suite No. 1*. Kostelanetz plays this music for all it is worth, and if again the recording is brash, this time it fits the music like a glove.

Symphonies (i) *1;* (ii) *5*

(**N**) (BB) **(*) LPO LPO 0001. LPO, Masur

(**N**) (BB) ** EMI (ADD) HMV 5 86764-2. (i) Philh. O, Kurtz; (ii) Chicago SO, Previn

These live recordings from the first batch of the LPO's own-label discs demonstrate the orchestra at its finest. The crispness and point of the ensemble and the refined beauty of the strings are most impressive, recorded in full, forward sound at Royal Festival Hall concerts early in 2004. Masur as the orchestra's music director has perfect control, even if his reading of the *First Symphony* is more remarkable for its brilliance than for its wit; for all the beauty, refinement and precision of the *Fifth*, it remains a little straight-faced, contemplative in the first and third movements, and genuinely jubilant in the rumbustious finale, ignoring the element of irony.

Kurtz's account of No. 1 has the distinction of being one of EMI's very first stereo recordings – and very good it still sounds, as does the excellent performance, with the Philharmonia on top form. Unfortunately, Previn's account of the *Fifth Symphony*, which is also extremely well played and recorded, is disappointing by comparison, for the reading has little sense of freshness or urgency.

***Symphonies 1; 5 in D min., Op. 47;* (i) *7 (Leningrad); Prelude 14 in E flat min., Op. 34* (arr. Stokowski)**

(***) Pearl GEMM CDS 9044 (2). Phd. O; (i) NBC SO, Stokowski

Stokowski's *First Symphony* was recorded in 1934, less than a decade after its première under Malko. The sound is dryish, but there is tremendous atmosphere and concentration, and the transfers are excellent. Stokowski's (1939) pioneering *Fifth* is an electrifying performance, impeccably played and splendidly transferred. The slow movement has a gripping intensity that is quite exceptional. The famous transcription of the *E flat minor Prelude*, Op. 34, has a brooding, Mussorgskian menace all its own, while Stokowski's *Leningrad Symphony* is hardly less gripping. This *Leningrad* for all its sonic defects makes for exciting listening.

Symphonies 1; 6 in B min., Op. 54

*** Chan. 8411. SNO, Järvi

Järvi's account of the *First Symphony* is more volatile than Haitink's in the outer movements – there is no lack of quirkiness in the finale, while the *Largo* is intense and passionate. The *Sixth* has comparable intensity, with an element of starkness in the austerity of the first movement. The Scherzo is skittish at first but, like the finale, has no lack of pungent force.

Symphonies 1, Op. 10; 9 in E flat, Op. 70

🔑 (M) *** Warner Elatus 2564 60121-2. Nat. SO of Washington, Rostropovich

In Rostropovich's hands the youthful *First Symphony* begins very promisingly indeed and continues well. Indeed, there is plenty of fulfilment. The reading is free from exaggeration, even if the Scherzo is rushed off its feet. The *Ninth*, too, is well served: the slow movement is shapely, and there is only one moment of agogic exaggeration. Rostropovich is also given a decently balanced recording, and this can certainly be recommended to those looking for this particular coupling.

(i) *Symphonies 2 (To October), Op. 14; 3 in E flat (The First of May), Op. 20; The Bolt: Suite, Op. 27a*
*** DG (IMS) 469 525-2. Gothenburg SO, Järvi; (i) Gothenburg Ch.

Apart from the radical and imaginative opening of the *Second*, neither of these symphonies shows the composer at his most individual or inspired. The *Third* must rank alongside the *Twelfth* as Shostakovich's least compelling work. Similarly *The Bolt* is not the best vintage, but it is still well worth having! Neeme Järvi benefits in having the excellent Gothenburg acoustic (and very good sound engineering from the Gothenburg team), and he secures eminently satisfactory playing from his orchestra.

Symphonies (i) *2 (October);* (ii) *14, Op 135*
(N) (M) **(*) Warner Elatus 2564 61374-2. (i) London Voices, LSO; (ii) Vishnevskaya, Reshetin, Moscow Ac. SO (members); Rostropovich

The two Rostropovich performances were recorded 20 years apart, No. 2 in London in 1993 and No. 14 much earlier in Moscow. In No. 2 the LSO respond to his direction with real fervour, everything is well prepared and well thought out. The performance of No. 14 is dark and intense, with expressive detail sometimes underlined. Vishnevskaya will not be to all tastes (she is thin and shrill above the stave at the top of her register), but Reshetin is most impressive. The soloists are balanced a little too close, but otherwise the sound has fine presence and definition in both recordings.

Symphony 4 in C min., Op. 43
(N) *** EMI 5 57824-2 Bav. RSO, Jansons
(N) *** Ph. 470 842 Kirov O, Gergiev
(N) *** DG 446 759-2 Phd. O, Chung
*** Chan. 8640. SNO, Järvi

Järvi draws from the SNO playing which is both rugged and expressive, consistently conveying the emotional thrust of the piece and making the enigmatic ending, with its ticking rhythm, warmer than usual, as though bitterness is finally evaporating. He is helped by exceptionally rich, full recording.

Ever since Kondrashin's pioneering record in 1961, we have been spoilt for choice in this symphony, and recent CDs of the work are all impressive. The Bavarian Radio Orchestra is one of the finest in Europe and under Mariss Jansons it produces a wonderful range of sonorities and finely blended tone. The EMI recording is very detailed and present, and Jansons is completely inside the work and conveys his intentions in masterly fashion.

Valery Gergiev's account has enormous intensity and a wide expressive range. Like Jansons, he is more expansive than Myung-Whun Chung. And his orchestra produces the rougher, rawer, pained sonorities. By comparison the Jansons account has the more cultured and finely blended sonority and the recording is more truthfully balanced. Gergiev's players are closer and although honours are pretty evenly divided, it is perhaps Gergiev who brings the terror of this score more vividly before one's eyes.

Myung-Whun Chung's performance was recorded in 1994 but not published until 2002. It has had little or no attention from the monthlies, and this neglect is undeserved. The Philadelphia Orchestra has a long association with Shostakovich, going back to the days of Stokowski and Ormandy, and Chung is a sound guide. Perhaps he misses the frenetic quality in the opening of the finale but, generally speaking,

this fine version gives pleasure and deserves to rank high in the ample discography of this symphony.

Symphonies 4, Op. 43; 10, Op. 93
(B) *** Sony (ADD) SB2K 62409 (2). Phd. O, Ormandy

Ormandy pioneered the *Fourth Symphony* in the West. His reading of this strange and powerful symphony is less refined than Haitink, but it is thoroughly convincing and has the Philadelphia Orchestra playing both brilliantly (witness the frenzied string passage at the climax of the first movement) and with real depth of feeling. The combination of irony, anguish and plangent lyricism is remarkably well caught. The 1963 recording, made in Philadelphia Town Hall, is spaciously full and vivid; it sounds excellent in the current CD transfer.

Ormandy went on to record No. 10 with equal success in the same venue in 1968, and again he makes a case for treating the work with a passion that is apt for Tchaikovsky. The result is not as refined in its effect as Karajan's DG version, but it still makes a compelling, indeed massive, impact, notably in the long first and third movements. Ormandy's control of string phrasing is again immaculate and his great orchestra is never less than convincing and is often superbly brilliant in the precision of its virtuosity. This makes a thoroughly worthwhile bargain coupling.

Symphony 5 in D min., Op. 47 (see also under *Cello Concerto 1*)
🎕 **(N)** *** BBC (ADD) BBCL 4165-2. LSO, Stokowski – VAUGHAN WILLIAMS: *Symphony 8* ***
(N) (BB) ** LSO Live LSO 058. LSO, Rostropovich

(i) *Symphony 5;* (ii) *Hamlet* (film incidental music), *Suite, Op. 116*
🎕 (M) *** RCA (ADD/DDD) 82876 55493-2. (i) LSO, Previn; (ii) Belgian RSO, Serebrier

Previn's celebrated RCA version, dating from early in his recording career (1965), remains at the top of the list for this often recorded symphony, sounding excellent in this new transfer. This is one of the most concentrated and intense readings ever, superbly played by the LSO at their peak. In the third movement, Previn sustains a slower speed than anyone else, making it deeply meditative in its dark intensity, while the build-up in the central development section brings playing of white heat. The bite and urgency of the second and fourth movements are irresistible. Only in the hint of tape-hiss and a slight lack of opulence in the violins does the sound fall short of the finest modern recordings, but it is more immediate than many more modern versions. The coupling is appropriate. *Hamlet* obviously generated powerful resonances in Shostakovich's psyche and he produced vivid incidental music: the opening Ball scene is highly reminiscent of *Romeo and Juliet*. The playing of the Belgian Radio Orchestra under Serebrier is eminently serviceable without being really distinguished but, with an atmospheric recording, this 28-minute suite makes a considerable bonus.

Stokowski's performance, recorded live in the Royal Albert Hall in the 1964 Prom season, vividly demonstrates that even in his eighties Leopold Stokowski had few rivals in inspiring performances of the highest voltage. The Shostakovich *Fifth Symphony* was his favourite, and here the biting tensions of the opening are masterfully contrasted with the pure, sinuous lines of the second subject in a performance of exceptional refinement and dedication, with each movement bringing fresh revelations, fully faithful to the score. Excellent stereo sound, remarkably vivid for a radio broadcast of the period. Very well coupled with another revelatory performance of the Vaughan Williams *Symphony No. 8.*

Rostropovich conducts the LSO in a rugged account of the *Fifth*, recorded live at the Barbican in July 2004. More than usual in the LSO Live series, the acoustic of the hall leads to limitations in the recorded sound, with a lack of bloom on the strings which too often sound curiously distant, so that the *pianissimo* at the start of the slow movement is barely audible if a reasonable volume is chosen for the *fortissimo* outbursts. This appeared at very much the same period as the LPO's live recording of Nos. 1 and 5 under Masur, with ensemble far crisper and fuller sound. With no coupling, the LSO disc is poor value, even at super-budget price.

Symphonies (i) 5; (ii) 6 in B min., Op. 54
(M) *** Warner Elatus 0927 46732-2. (i) Leningrad PO,
   Mravinsky; (ii) Nat. SO of Washington, Rostropovich
(BB) *** Regis RRC 1075. Cologne RSO, Barshai

Mravinsky conducted the première of the *Fifth Symphony* in 1937 and so brings a special authority to this work. This Erato Elatus account emanates from a concert performance almost half a century later (in 1984) and, like his recording made at the 1978 Vienna Festival, is far from impeccable. The other suffered from some vulnerable woodwind intonation and the present version is not free from the odd untidiness; but there is still evidence of a commanding personality and, even though the recording itself is not in the luxury bracket, this performance must figure high on any list. It comes coupled with Rostropovich's *Sixth*, recorded ten years later in the Washington Kennedy Center. In his spacious account of the opening *Largo*, Rostropovich does not wear his heart on his sleeve, but the quiet, poignant intensity of his simple approach, with no underlining, is very telling and the burlesque Scherzo which follows is pointed with nice ironic geniality, while the following finale bursts with witty high spirits. Excellent orchestral playing and fine recording make this a coupling to reckon with.

Rudolf Barshai's coupling comes from concert performances in the Cologne Philharmonie in 1995–6. (It was apparently included in a complete cycle issued on the super-economy Brilliant label but until now has not enjoyed wide currency in Britain.) Barshai's credentials in this repertoire are well known. He conducted the first recording of the *Fourteenth Symphony* and has, of course, arranged the *Fourth*, *Eighth* and *Tenth Quartets* for full strings with the composer's blessing. These are very well-prepared and expertly played accounts, which may not equal Mravinsky but are finely shaped and felt. At the price, and given the clarity of the recording, these can certainly be recommended.

Symphonies 5 in D min.; 9 in E flat, Op. 70
(BB) *** Naxos 8.550427. Belgian R. & TV O, Rahbari
(M) *** Decca 425 066-2. (i) Concg. O; (ii) LPO, Haitink

Both in the hushed intensity of the lyrical passages and in the vigour and bite of Shostakovich's violent *Allegros* Rahbari's reading is most convincing, with dramatic tensions finely controlled in a spontaneous-sounding way. In No. 9 Rahbari opts for a controversially slow *Moderato* second movement but sustains it well, and the outer movements are deliciously witty in their pointing. The playing of all sections is first rate, and the sound is full and brilliant. An outstandingly generous coupling makes this a most attractive issue, even with no allowance made for the very low price.

In No. 5 Haitink is eminently straightforward, there are no disruptive changes in tempo, and the playing of the Concertgebouw Orchestra and the contribution of the Decca engineers are beyond praise. There could perhaps be greater intensity of feeling in the slow movement but, no matter what small reservations one might have, it is most impressive both artistically and sonically. The coupled No. 9 is superb. Without inflation Haitink gives it a serious purpose, both in the poignancy of the waltz-like second movement and in the equivocal emotions of the outer movements. The recording is outstanding in every way.

Symphony 6, Op. 54; (i) The Execution of Stepan Razin, Op. 119
** Chan. 9813. Russian State SO, Polyansky; (i) with Lochak,
   Russian State Symphonic Capella

Valery Polyansky has given us some splendid things, but his account of the *Sixth Symphony* does neither him nor Shostakovich full justice. The performance is touched by routine. *The Execution of Stepan Razin* is given with much greater character, and Polyansky has greater conviction than in the symphony; but although Anatoly Lochak is a fine soloist, memories of Vitaly Gromadsky with Kondrashin in 1966 are not banished.

(i) Symphonies 6; (ii) 9, Op. 70
**(*) Everest (ADD) EVC 9005. (i) LPO, Boult; (ii) LSO,
   Sargent

Boult secures very good playing from the LPO and the late-1950s Walthamstow recording is excellent, but he is wanting a little in intensity. Sargent's account of the *Ninth* is lyrical and attractive, with infectious vitality in the odd-numbered of the five movements. Again the recording is very good indeed. This is undoubtedly an enjoyable coupling.

Symphonies 6; 12 (The Year 1917)
☛ (M) *** Decca 425 067-2. Concg. O, Haitink

Haitink's structural control, coupled with his calm, taut manner, is particularly impressive in the slow movement of No. 6. As a work, No. 12 is more problematic. There is much of the composer's vision and grandeur here but also his crudeness. However, the sheer quality of the sound and the superb responsiveness and body of the Concertgebouw Orchestra might well seduce many listeners. As with the *Sixth* the slow movement has a marvellous sense of atmosphere; the Amsterdam orchestra play as if they believe every crotchet, although not even their eloquence can rescue the finale.

Symphony 7 in C (Leningrad), Op. 60
☛ (N) *** MDG **Surround Sound SACD** 937 1203-6.
   Beethoven O, Bonn, Hofman
*** Chan. 8623. SNO, Järvi
(BB) *** Regis RRC 1074. Cologne RSO, Barshai
**(*) Ph. 470 845-2. Kirov O, Rotterdam PO, Gergiev
(M) **(*) Decca 425 068-2. LPO, Haitink
(B) **(*) Sony (ADD) SBK 89904. NYPO, Bernstein

This superbly realistic and spectacular new recording from the unlikely source of the Beethoven Orchestra, Bonn, rather sweeps the board. Roman Hofman has the full measure of this remarkable symphony. He builds the famous first-movement ostinato with unremitting concentration into an overwhelming climax, and his reading creates a satisfying combination of passion and irony in the work as a whole, with raptly beautiful playing and great intensity from the strings in the *Adagio* and jubilant triumph at the work's close. Yet he still retains the composer's underlying perception, which pervades the work, that victory does not come without cost. The recording is very much in the demonstration bracket, whether using two speakers or four. Shostakovich's extra brass ('banda'), used to heighten the climax of the opening movement, is positioned at the rear, but (by using the controls judiciously) it can be placed however the listener wishes to balance the extraordinary *fortissimo* at the peak.

Järvi's is a strong, intense reading, beautifully played and recorded, which brings out the full drama of this symphony in a performance that consistently gives the illusion of spontaneity in a live performance, as in the hushed tension of the slow, expansive passages. There have been more polished versions than this, but, with its spectacular Chandos sound, it makes an excellent alternative choice as a single-disc version.

Barshai's recording comes from a concert performance in the Cologne Philharmonie in 1992. EMI also issued a very fine *Eighth Symphony* with the Bournemouth Orchestra in the late 1980s, but this newly released Cologne version of the *Leningrad* has a great deal going for it. There is no bombast, yet the understatement does not entail loss of character and impact, and the sound quality is very good indeed, thanks to the excellent Cologne acoustic. An eminently viable choice and not only in this price bracket.

Gergiev's live recording of the *Leningrad* brings out the purely musical qualities of a score which from its very conception has invited programmatic treatment. Bartók may have parodied in his *Concerto for Orchestra* the ironic ostinato sequence in the first movement of the symphony, but Gergiev, rather like Haitink on Decca, sets the passage logically in place, if at a faster tempo. By contrast, the other movements are slower than usual, with a live occasion enhancing the concentration of the performance, and with high dramatic contrasts well caught, if not quite with ideal sharpness. The linking of the two orchestras specially associated with Gergiev works well, even if it seems not to add greatly to the weight of sound.

Haitink is here eminently straightforward. There could perhaps be greater intensity of feeling in the slow movement, and the long first-movement *ostinato* is not presented histrionically; but the deep seriousness which Haitink finds in the rest of the work challenges comparisons with the other wartime symphony, the epic *Eighth*. The playing of the Concertgebouw Orchestra is beyond praise.

Bernstein brings a certain panache and fervour to his reading, particularly in the inspired slow movement, so that one is tempted to look indulgently at its occasional overstatements.

Symphonies 7 (Leningrad); 11 (1905)
(B) **(*) EMI double forte (ADD) 5 73839-2 (2). Bournemouth SO, Berglund

Berglund directs a strong, powerful performance of the *Seventh*. Though he is not always sensitive to finer points of expressiveness, it is still a reading that holds together convincingly, especially when the sound is so full as well as vivid. In the *Eleventh*, too, Berglund lets the music speak for itself, keeping the long opening *Adagio* at a very steady, slow tread, made compelling by the high concentration of the Bournemouth playing. Indeed, he is at his finest here, again helped by exceptionally vivid, full-bodied recording.

Symphony 8 in C min., Op. 65
**(*) BBC (ADD) BBCL4002-2. Leningrad PO, Mravinsky – MOZART: *Symphony 33 in B flat, K.319* **
(M) *** Decca (IMS) 425 071-2. Concg. O, Haitink
(N) (BB) *** CfP 587 034-2. Bournemouth SO, Barshai

Mravinsky's BBC recording comes from the Festival Hall Concert given on the Leningrad Orchestra tour in 1960 at which Shostakovich himself was present. This transfer reproduces the occasion with great realism and a wide dynamic range. This reading has tremendous intensity and authenticity of feeling. It comes with a bonus – the first half of the concert, which was given over to an elegant performance of the Mozart *Symphony No. 33*. Even among modern recordings this more than holds its own and the sound is very good indeed. Mandatory listening.

Haitink characteristically presents a strongly architectural reading of this war-inspired symphony, at times direct to the point of severity. After the massive and sustained slow movement which opens the work, Haitink allows no lightness or relief in the Scherzo movements, and in his seriousness in the strangely lightweight finale (neither fast nor slow) he provides an unusually satisfying account of an equivocal, seemingly uncommitted movement.

Barshai holds up surprisingly well against the competition he faces from Haitink. The noble symphonic *Adagio* which opens the work is marvellously sustained, and the playing of the Bournemouth orchestra is extremely fine in all departments. In one or two exposed passages the strings do not match the bloom and lustre of their celebrated Dutch colleagues, but this is a finely paced and powerful reading which, particularly in the first movement, has a wonderful brooding intensity and eloquence. In the *Allegretto*, Barshai adopts the recommended crotchet = 132, and some listeners will think this too slow. However, it is what the composer asks for, and the result inevitably seems weightier. In the third movement Barshai is less successful in sustaining tension and momentum. The *Passacaglia* is very powerful and has a real epic sweep. As far as sound quality is concerned, the balance of this 1985 recording could hardly be improved upon, and the excellent acoustic is used to splendid and thrilling effect. The perspective is consistent and well judged, and detail is admirably present. This budget reissue is a genuine bargain.

Symphony 9 in E flat, Op. 70; Festive Overture, Op. 96; Katerina Ismailova (Lady Macbeth of Mtsensk): 5 Entr'actes. Tahiti Trot (arr. of Youmans's Tea for Two), Op. 16
*** Chan. 8587. SNO, Järvi

Järvi's version of the *Ninth* brings a warmly expressive, strongly characterized reading in superb, wide-ranging sound. The point and wit of the first movement go with bluff good humour, leading on to an account of the second-movement *Moderato* that is yearningly lyrical yet not at all sentimental, contrasted with the fun and jokiness of the final *Allegretto*. The mixed bag of fill-up items is both illuminating and characterful, ending with the jolly little chamber arrangement that Shostakovich did in the 1920s of Vincent Youmans's *Tea for Two*, the *Tahiti Trot*.

Symphony 10 in E min., Op. 93
(M) **(*) Warner Elatus 2564 60660-2 Leningrad PO, Mravinsky (with WAGNER: *Tristan: Prelude and Liebestod* **(*))
🎮 *** DG 439 036-2. BPO, Karajan

(M) (***) DG mono 463 666-2. Czech PO, Ančerl –
STRAVINSKY *Violin Concerto* ***

(M) ** EMI 7 64870-2. Philh. O, Rattle – BRITTEN: *Sinfonia da Requiem* ***

Symphony 10 in E min., Op. 93; Ballet Suite 4
*** Chan. 8630. SNO, Järvi

Already in his 1967 recording Karajan had shown that he had the measure of this symphony; this newer version is, if anything, even finer. In the first movement he distils an atmosphere as concentrated as before, bleak and unremitting, while in the *Allegro* the Berlin Philharmonic leave no doubts as to their peerless virtuosity. Everything is marvellously shaped and proportioned, and the early (1981) digital sound is made firmer by this 'original-image' bit reprocessing.

Mravinsky conducted the work's première. This Elatus recording was made at a 1976 concert performance and it has no want of intensity or power. The recording is less than ideal, but this is a performance to reckon with, and the Wagner bonus (also recorded live, two years later) also rises to a passionate climax.

Though recorded in 1955, Karel Ančerl's DG recording still makes a very considerable impact, as it did on its original release. The sense of brooding atmosphere in the opening movement is superbly caught, and it carries a sense of momentum that is utterly compelling. The ensuing *Allegro* is fast and furious, rather clipped, but extremely exciting and provides striking contrast with the succeeding *Allegretto*; the tension is superbly maintained throughout. The finale is electrifying, bursting through all the limitations of the mono sound. The transfer is excellent, and so too is the coupling. Karajan may reign supreme among stereo recordings of this work (DG 439 036-2), but this Czech version is also unforgettable.

Järvi, too, conducts an outstandingly strong and purposeful reading in superb sound, full and atmospheric. In the great span of the long *Moderato* first movement he chooses an ideal speed, which allows for moments of hushed repose but still builds up relentlessly. The curious little *Ballet Suite No. 4*, with its sombre *Prelude* leading to a bouncy *Waltz* and a jolly *Scherzo Tarantella*, makes a delightful bonus.

Rattle's Philharmonia version is curiously wayward in the two big slow movements, first and third in the scheme. In the first, Rattle is exceptionally slow, and tension slips too readily. So too in the third movement. The Scherzo and energetic finale are much more successful. The recording does not help, with the strings sounding thin and lacking body.

(i) Symphony 10 in E min., Op. 93 (arr. for piano duet); (ii) 4 Preludes from Op. 34 (arr. for violin & piano)
(M) (***) Revelation mono RV 70002. Composer, with (i) Vainberg; (ii) Kogan

The recording may be primitive but this is of great documentary interest, capturing Shostakovich and his fellow composer Moisei Vainberg playing the *Tenth Symphony* in a piano-duet arrangement only a few months after its completion and not long before Mravinsky made the première recording. They play with great fervour and strain the instrument to the limit. The performance is surprisingly brisk (47 minutes as opposed to the usual 50) and completely involving. The transcriptions of the *Preludes* are wonderfully played by Kogan and the composer, and there are also a few bars from *The Gadfly* too.

Symphonies 10; (i) 13 (Babi-Yar)
(B) *** EMI double forte DDD/ADD 5 73368-2 (2). LSO, Previn; (i) with Petrov, LSO Ch.

Previn's is a strong and dramatic reading of No. 10, marked by a specially compelling account of the long first movement. At marginally slower speeds than usual, Previn's rhythmic lift, both in the Scherzo and in the finale, brings exhilarating results, sparkling and swaggering. The digital recording is early (1982) but strikingly firm and full. The *Thirteenth Symphony*, inspired by the often angry poems of Yevtushenko, is presented at its most stark and direct. Previn takes a relatively literal view of the sprung rhythms in the ironic second movement, *Humour*, and makes the picture of peasant women queueing for food in the snow less atmospheric than it sometimes is. The result is that the work becomes a genuine symphony, rather than an orchestral song-cycle, but ending in wistfulness on a final Allegretto, *A Career*, with weaving flutes and gentle lolloping pizzicato rhythms. Playing and analogue recording are superb, among the very finest from this source, making this a very attractive pairing on all counts.

Symphony 11 (The Year 1905), Op. 103
*** Testament SBT 1099. French R. O, Cluytens
*** Delos D/CD 3080. Helsinki PO, DePreist

1905 was the year of the first Russian uprising, which foreshadowed the revolution to come rather more than a decade later. The result is a programme symphony conceived on a fairly large scale and, as in the *Leningrad Symphony*, its style is sometimes repetitive.

Cluytens's performance was recorded in Paris in the presence of the composer. It appears now in stereo for the very first time and sounds quite astonishing. Indeed, it stands up to modern competition very well. Shostakovich called the *Eleventh* his 'most Mussorgskian work' and it was clear to Soviet audiences that its 'sub-text' was not so much the abortive February rebellion of the title as the events in Budapest, where the Soviet Union had just suppressed the Hungarian uprising.

The DePreist version won golden opinions: it certainly has the benefit of magnificent recording. The Helsinki orchestra may lack the weight and richness of sonority of the greatest orchestras but it plays with great intensity and feeling. A performance that has striking atmosphere and expressive power.

Symphonies 11 (1905); 12 (1917); Age of Gold (suite); Hamlet (suite); October (symphonic poem), Op. 131; Overture on Russian & Kirghiz Folk Themes, Op. 115
(B) **(*) DG Double 459 415-2 (2). Gothenburg SO, Järvi

This is a generous package and besides the appropriately paired symphonies this DG Double has four additional inducements which are all brought off impressively. Neeme Järvi's account of the *Eleventh Symphony*, too, has much to recommend it, including good orchestral playing and very fine recorded sound. However, good though it is, the performance misses the last ounce of intensity, and the same comments must apply to Järvi's performance of No. 12 (even though here the recording has rather less transparency and sharpness of focus). If this symphony is to come off it has to be played with 200 per cent conviction and panache, and Järvi's performance does not really challenge Mravinsky or Rozhdestvensky.

Symphony 13 in B flat min. (Babi-Yar)

☞ (N) *** EMI 5 57902-2. Aleksashkin, Bav. R. Ch. & SO,
  Jansons

(M) *** Decca 425 073-2. Rintzler, Concg. Male Ch. & O,
  Haitink

*** Sup. SU 0160-2 231. Mikuláš, Prague Philharmonic Ch.,
  Prague SO, M. Shostakovich

The often brutal directness of Haitink's way with Shostakovich works well in the *Thirteenth Symphony*, particularly in the long *Adagio* first movement, whose title, *Babi-Yar*, gives its name to the whole work. That first of five Yevtushenko settings, boldly attacking anti-Semitism in Russia, sets the pattern for Haitink's severe view of the whole. Rintzler with his magnificent, resonant bass is musically superb but, matching Haitink, remains objective rather than dashingly characterful. The resolution of the final movement, with its pretty flutings surrounding a wry poem about Galileo and greatness, then works beautifully. Outstandingly brilliant and full sound, remarkable even for this series.

With the superb Russian bass Sergi Aleksashkin dominating the performance, so that the Bavarian Radio Chorus too are encouraged to sing with intense Slavonic fervour, Jansons's new EMI recording is very powerful indeed. The work's dark, forceful irony is well caught in the *Allegretto* second movement, yet it is in the third movement that the performance reaches its merciless climax which is so well resolved in the epilogue-like finale, strangely uplifting with its celestial flutes. Jansons holds the work together more passionately than Haitink and he secures splendid playing from the Bavarian orchestra. The EMI recording has great vividness and atmosphere, and many will feel that this account is even more telling bcause of Jansons's obvious personal involvement.

Maxim Shostakovich's Supraphon version, with sound so vivid you hear some alien noises, is menacingly atmospheric, one of the finest of his recordings of his father's symphonies. Helped by the immediate sound, he sustains each movement with fine concentration, with each movement heightened by characterful singing from the superb Czech bass, Peter Mikuláš. So in the second movement, *Humour*, brutal and tense, he conveys a gleam of manic menace in the music and brings out the full chilling horror of the third movement with its picture of women queueing. The chorus with its Slavonic timbres sounds totally idiomatic too, not balanced too close, making this one of the most convincing versions of this moving and atmospheric song-cycle symphony.

Symphonies Nos. (i) 13 (Babi Yar), Op. 113; (ii) 14, Op. 135. 15, Op. 141

(M) **(*) DG 474 469-2 (2). Gothenburg SO, Järvi, with (i)
  Kotscherga, Estonian Nat. Male Ch.; (ii) Kazarnovskaya,
  Leiferkus

Järvi has a good feeling for Shostakovich and this two-CD DG reissue offers a generally recommendable set of performances. In *Babi Yar*, Anatoly Kotscherga proves a resonantly theatrical bass soloist and the Estonian choir sing confidently and idiomatically. While *Fears* (with its bold tuba solo) is emotionally strong, Järvi seeks to bring out, above all, the work's ironic satire, especially in the second movement, but also in the finale, although the actual close is poignantly moving. In No. 14, which in inspiration is so closely linked with Mussorgsky's *Songs and Dances of Death*, Järvi is more overtly expressive, less darkly biting than most rivals. But he has a powerfully intense and idiomatic soloist in Leiferkus, and he and Ljuba Kazarnovskaya bring out the vivid operatic

elements in their interchanges of Apollinaire's *Lorelei*. If Järvi could be more sharply expressive in the more dramatic songs, he again demonstrates his ability to bring out Shostakovich's wry humour. No. 15, which was the first to be recorded, is also a characterful account, and it is again very well played by the Gothenburg orchestra. Throughout all three symphonies, the recording is impressively spacious and, as full texts and translations are included, this set is well worth considering,

Symphony 14 in G min., Op. 135

(BB) *** Naxos 8.550631. Hajóssyová, Mikuláš, Slovak RSO
  (Bratislava), Slovák

(B) **(*) BBC (ADD) BBCB 8013-2. Vishnevskaya, Rezhetin,
  ECO, Britten − BRITTEN: *Nocturne* **(*)

(i) *Symphony 14;* (ii) *6 Poems of Marina Tsvetaeva, Op. 143a*

☞ (M) *** Decca 425 074-2. (i) Varady, Fischer-Dieskau;
  (ii) Wenkel; Concg. O, Haitink

The *Fourteenth* is Shostakovich's darkest and most sombre score, a setting of poems by Lorca, Apollinaire, Rilke, Brentano and Küchelbecker, all on the theme of death. Haitink's version gives each poem in its original language. It is a most powerful performance, and the outstanding recording is well up to the standard of this fine Decca series. The song-cycle, splendidly sung by Ortrun Wenkel, makes a fine bonus.

Slovák's account of No. 14 is one of the finest in his Shostakovich series for Naxos, strongly characterized in each of the eleven contrasted movements with the help of two superb soloists. Mikuláš is just as strong and individual as in No. 13, and Hajóssyová, with her firm, Slavonic mezzo, is equally idiomatic. Regularly, Slovák and his performers bring out the menace behind the composer's inspiration on the theme of death, with the fourth song, 'The Suicide', particularly moving in its tenderness. The booklet gives a summary of each poem, but no texts or translations. Full, immediate sound.

This was the symphony which Shostakovich dedicated to Britten, and this Snape Maltings performance of 1970 with the ECO conducted by Britten was the very first outside Russia. Galina Vishnevskaya's sharply distinctive soprano has rarely sounded so rich or firmly focused on disc, and the bass, Mark Rezhetin, firm and dark, sings gloriously too. The tensions of a live performance add to the drama, poignantly so, when both Britten and Shostakovich were facing terminal illness. Sadly, this mid-priced issue gives none of the important texts.

(i) Symphony 15; (ii) From Jewish Folk Poetry (song-cycle), Op. 79

(M) *** Decca (ADD/DDD) 425 069-2. (i) LPO; (ii)
  Söderström, Wenkel, Karczykowski, Concg. O; Haitink

Symphony 15 in A, Op. 141; (i) Piano Sonata 2 in B min., Op. 61

☞ ✪ (M) *** RCA 09026 63587-2. Phd. O, Ormandy; (i)
  Gilels

Ormandy gave the American première of the *Fifteenth Symphony* as well as a number of other Shostakovich works, including the *Fourth*, *Thirteenth* and *Fourteenth Symphonies* and the *First Cello Concerto* with Rostropovich. He was not so much underrated as taken for granted during the early 1970s when this recording was made, but there is no doubt as to his authority and mastery. The playing could hardly be surpassed, and the recording originally appeared in RCA's brand of Quadrophony, when it sounded pretty spectacular. Even now it sounds superb and stands up well against subsequent versions. Its coupling, Gilels's incomparable account of the wartime *Second Sonata*, recorded at Carnegie Hall in January 1965, is one of the classics of the gramophone. An indispensable reissue.

Haitink makes the first movement sound genuinely symphonic, bitingly urgent. He underlines the purity of the bare lines of the second movement; after the Wagner quotations which open the finale, his slow tempo for the main lyrical theme gives it heartaching tenderness, not the usual easy triviality. The playing of the LPO is excellent, with refined tone and superb attack, and the recording is both analytical and atmospheric. The CD includes a splendidly sung version of *From Jewish Folk Poetry*, settings which cover a wide range of emotions including tenderness, humour and even happiness as in the final song. Ryszard Karczykowski brings vibrant Slavonic feeling to the work which, with its wide variety of mood and colour, has a scale to match the shorter symphonies.

CHAMBER MUSIC

Adagio and Allegretto for String Quartet; (i) *Piano Quintet, Op. 57;* (ii) *2 Pieces for String Octet, Op. 1/1;* (i) *5 Pieces for 2 Violins and Piano* (arr. Atovmian)

*** Challenge CC 72093. Brodsky Qt (members), with (i) Blackshaw; (ii) Shave, Theaker, Atkins, Baillie (available from www.challengeclassics.com)

A superb collection. Like the Brodsky's equally recommended coupling of string quartets by Britten and Tchaikovsky, the sense of spontaneous, live music-making inhabits every bar here. The range of mood is remarkably wide. The early *Pieces for String Octet*, Op. 1 are as wild and uninhibited as the delightful *Pieces for Two Violins and Piano* are elegantly tuneful. The deeply expressive *Adagio* and quirky *Allegretto* are arrangements of Katerina's aria from *Lady Macbeth of the Mtsensk District* and the famously witty *Polka* from *The Golden Age* ballet. But the key work here is the *Piano Quintet*, a marvellously concentrated performance. The second movement *Fugue-Adagio* and the *Intermezzo* both open with a rapt pianissimo framing the bold, jaunty central *Scherzo* and leading on to the puissant finale. Excellent recording throughout, although some might think the acoustic for the quintet gives the piano a rather too resonant image.

Cello Sonata in D min., Op. 40

(N) (BB) *** Virgin 2x1 4 82067-2 (2)-2. Mørk, Vogt – MIASKOVSKY; RACHMANINOV; PROKOFIEV: *Cello Sonatas;* STRAVINSKY: *Suite italienne* ***

*** Chan. 8340. Turovsky, Edlina – PROKOFIEV: *Sonata* ***

*** BIS CD 336. Thedéen, Pöntinen – SCHNITTKE: *Sonata;* STRAVINSKY: *Suite italienne* ***

Cello Sonata in D min., Op. 40; Moderato in A min.

(*) Chant du Monde LDC 2781112. Hoffman, Philippe Bianconi – PROKOFIEV: *Adagio; Ballade; Cello Sonata, Op. 119, etc.* *

Truls Mørk and Lars Vogt can more than hold their own with the best. The performances are very vital and intelligent, and eminently well recorded and the couplings are astonishingly generous.

Yuli Turovsky and Luba Edlina play the *Cello Sonata* with great panache and eloquence, if in the finale they almost succumb at times to exaggeration in their handling of its humour – no understatement here.

The Swedish cellist, Torleif Thedéen, has a real feeling for its structure and the vein of bitter melancholy under its ironic surface. Roland Pöntinen gives him excellent support and the BIS recording does justice to this partnership.

There is expert and elegantly fashioned playing from Gary Hoffman and Philippe Bianconi. There are some exaggerations and some listeners may find the inward, withdrawn tone of the cellist in the third movement a bit affected. Still, the playing has enormous finesse and accomplishment and gives great pleasure. The *Moderato* is a slight piece composed in the same year, disinterred only after the composer's death.

(i) *Cello Sonata in D min., Op. 40; Moderato* for cello & piano; (ii) *Piano Quintet;* (iii) *2 Pieces*

☛ (BB) *** Double Decca 473 807-2 (2). (i) Harrell; (i; ii) Ashkenazy; (ii; iii) Fitzwilliam Qt – PROKOFIEV: *Cello Sonata;* RACHMANINOV: *Cello Sonata, etc.* ***

Lynn Harrell and Vladimir Ashkenazy give a convincing account of the *Cello Sonata*, though they slow down rather a lot for the second group of the first movement. All the same, their brisk tempo and their freedom from affectation are refreshing. The short *Moderato* for cello and piano was discovered in the Moscow State Archives only in the 1980s; it could at some stage have been intended for the *Sonata* itself, though its brevity and its quality make one doubtful. The *Piano Quintet*, with Ashkenazy and the Fitzwilliam Quartet, cannot be seriously faulted and withstands comparison with the illustrious Richter and Borodin Quartet version, and the recording is superb. With the highly attractive *Two Pieces* – the first mysteriously haunting, the second delightfully quirky – also included, this set, with its excellent couplings, is an undoubted bargain.

Cello Sonata in D min., Op. 40; (i) *Piano Trio 2 in E min., Op. 67*

**(*) Sony MK 44664. Ma, Ax; (i) with Stern

The *Trio* receives a deeply felt performance, one which can hold its own with any issue, past or present. The *Sonata* is another matter; the playing is as beautiful as one would expect, but here Yo-Yo Ma's self-communing propensity for reducing his tone is becoming a tiresome affectation. Ax plays splendidly and the CBS recording is very truthful.

Piano Quintet in G min., Op. 57

☛ (M) *** Warner Elatus 2564 60813-2. Leonskaja, Borodin Qt

☛ (BB) *** Naxos 8.554830-2. Berman, Vermeer Qt – SCHNITTKE: *Piano Quintet* ***

(***) Testament mono SBT 1077. Aller, Hollywood Qt – FRANCK: *Piano Quintet* (***)

(M) **(*) CRD (ADD) CRD 3351. Benson, Alberni Qt – BRITTEN: *Quartet 1* ***

Piano Quintet in G min., Op. 57; Piano Trio 2 in E min., Op. 67

**(*) Chan. 8342. Borodin Trio, Zweig, Horner

Piano Quintet in G min., Op. 57; Piano Trio 2 in E min., Op. 67; 4 Waltzes for Flute, Clarinet & Piano

(BB) *** Virgin 2x1 5 61760-2 (2). Nash Ens. – SCHOENBERG: *Chamber Symphony, Op. 9, etc.* **(*)

The Nash Ensemble on Virgin offer the ideal coupling – plus an interesting makeweight – of two of Shostakovich's key chamber works, written before his quartet series developed, when he had completed only the first, relatively trivial work.

The *Piano Trio* is a particularly painful and anguished work, dedicated to the memory of a close friend, Ivan Sollertinsky, who died in the year of its composition. The Nash players bring out the dedicated intensity in this very personal writing, with refined readings which can be warmly recommended, even if they are not quite as characterfully individual as the very finest, and the new pairing with Schoenberg makes for a highly intriguing collection, well worth its modest cost.

With Leonskaja leading, yet still very much a partner, this Teldec performance of the *Piano Quintet* is very fine indeed, with inspired playing from all concerned. The very wide range of dynamic and string timbre of the *Fugue*, with the music initially sustained on a thread of tone, moving to a climax and back, has enormous concentration, and the spikier humour of the *Scherzo* is splendidly pointed. After the poignant *Intermezzo*, the close of the finale is most subtly managed.

It is luxury casting to have on the Naxos budget label the Vermeer Quartet, one of the finest in America, in partnership with another star artist, Boris Berman. This is a dedicated performance, recorded for Canadian radio, which with fearlessly extreme dynamic contrasts brings out the full greatness of the piece. The Schnittke *Piano Quintet* of 1972–5 makes an apt and unusual coupling, similarly one of the composer's finest chamber works. The CBC studio recording is acceptable, and if the sound is somewhat wanting in warmth and bloom this is a still a formidable bargain.

On Testament is a magisterial account of the *Piano Quintet* if ever there was one. This belongs among the finest of interpretations. Its praises were sung by the authors of *The Record Guide* in the mid-1950s when they spoke of it in their down-to-earth manner as 'a dazzling performance and their tone, though often extremely delicate, is never skinny'. Those readers who care about Shostakovich should find it an indispensable issue and need make few allowances for the 1952 sound.

The Chandos version is bold in character and concentrated in feeling. Alternatively, there is a vigorous and finely conceived account from Clifford Benson and the Alberni Quartet, vividly recorded; if the Britten coupling is wanted, this will be found fully satisfactory.

(i) Piano Quintet; Piano Trio 2. String Quartet 1, Op. 49
(N) * Hyp. CDA 67158. St Petersburg Qt, with (i) Uryash

The St Petersburg Quartet give a perfectly acceptable account of the innocent, neo-classical *C major Quartet*, Op. 49, but both the *Piano Trio* and the *Piano Quintet* fall short of real distinction; indeed, they are distinctly routine. There are intonation problems in the Scherzo of the *Quintet* and neither work receives a really authoritative performance.

Piano Trios 1, Op. 8; 2, Op. 67
*** Simax PSC 1147. Grieg Trio – BLOCH: *3 Nocturnes;*
  MARTIN: *Piano Trio on Irish Folktunes ****
*** Nim. NI 5572. V. Piano Trio – SCHNITTKE: *Trio ****

Piano Trios 1, Op. 8; 2 in E min., Op. 67; (i) 7 Romances to Poems by Alexander Blok, Op. 127
*(*) Orfeo C465 991A. Munich Piano Trio; (i) Ablaberdyeva

The first of the Shostakovich *Piano Trios* remained in the obscurity of manuscript, until one of Shostakovich's students, the composer Boris Tischenko, put it into performable shape (as twenty bars had gone missing). The Grieg Trio play it with vital feeling and sensitivity; its dreamy opening,

a kind of impressionistic Schumann, sounds exceptionally convincing in their hands. Moreover, they give as fine an account of the wartime *Piano Trio in E minor* as any now before the public. The couplings further enhance the value of this issue.

The Vienna Piano Trio on Nimbus also give cogently argued and finely paced accounts of both the Shostakovich trios. The Vienna is among the best and are naturally and vividly recorded. If the 1985 Schnittke *Trio* appeals as a coupling, this is an eminently desirable recommendation.

Although obviously a highly accomplished ensemble, the Munich Piano Trio do not convey much of the atmosphere of the eerily enigmatic and powerful *E minor Trio*, Op. 67, and Alla Ablaberdyeva is not wholly successful in the *Romances to Poems by Alexander Blok*.

Piano Trio 2 in E min., Op. 67
(N) (B) * Decca 475 6712 (2). Bell, Mustonen, Isserlis –**
  PROKOFIEV: *Violin Concertos & Sonatas ****

The Decca is a marvellously telling and perceptive account of Shostakovich's masterpiece and is very truthfully balanced. The only snag is the very wide dynamic range of the recording. The opening *pianopianissimo* has ethereal concentration, but registers so quietly that the listener is tempted to turn up the volume. If one does, the *fortissimos* are not quite comfortable, for the microphones are fairly close. But it is possible to get it right and the rewards of the playing are very considerable.

19 Preludes, from Op. 34 (arr. Tikanov for violin & piano)
**(*) Avie AV0023. Gleusteen, Ordronneau – JANACEK:
  Violin Sonata; PROKOFIEV: *Violin Sonata 1 **(*)*

The transcription of Shostakovich's *Preludes* for violin and piano works surprisingly well in this mixed bag of Slavonic works. The composer himself gave full approval to this arrangement of his original piano versions, readily persuaded by his friend, Dmitri Tikanov, a violinist as well as a composer. Tikanov was leader of the Beethoven Quartet for over half a century, the group that gave the first performances of all but the last of the Shostakovich Quartets. He chose 19 out of the *24 Preludes*, putting them in a different order and concentrating on those that were the most melodic. The result is that, though the violin versions bring out the lyrical element more clearly, they sound less sharply original, if still very characteristic of Shostakovich. Kai Gleusteen plays them with obvious love, giving extra power to some of the more dramatic preludes.

Preludes and Fugues, Op. 87/1–9, 12, 15–17 & 19 (arr. Alban Wesly)
**(*) MDG 619 1185. Calefax Reed Quintet

The *Preludes and Fugues* are intelligently arranged, most expertly played and superbly recorded. The Calefax give us 14 (just over half) of the set, omitting those that are too pianistic. Readers should turn first and foremost to Tatiana Nikolaeva in this repertoire (Regis RRC 3005 – see below) though there are other highly desirable alternatives. This does not strike us as one of them. This will doubtless attract some wind enthusiasts, but it is of somewhat specialist and limited appeal.

2 Pieces for String Octet, Op. 11
*** Chan. 9131. ASMF Chamber Ens. – ENESCU: *Octet in C;*
  R. STRAUSS: *Capriccio: Sextet ****

The Academy of St Martin-in-the-Fields Chamber Ensemble play splendidly and with conviction; they are beautifully recorded and also offer a highly recommendable version of the Enescu *Octet*.

String Quartets

String Quartets 1–13
(M) *** Chan. (ADD) 10064 (4). Borodin Qt

String Quartets 1–15; 3 Pieces for String Quartet, Op. 36
(N) (BB) *** Regis (ADD) 5001 (5). Shostakovich Qt

String Quartets 1 in C, Op. 49; 2 in A, Op. 68; 3 in F, Op. 73; 4 in D, Op. 83; 5 in B flat, Op. 92; 7 in F sharp min., Op. 108; 3 Pieces, Op. 36
(N) (BB) *** Regis (ADD) 2028 (2). Shostakovich Qt

String Quartets 6 in G, Op. 101; 8 in C min., Op. 110; 9 in E flat, Op. 117; 10 in A flat, Op. 118; 11 in F min., Op. 122; 15 in E flat min., Op. 144
(N) (BB) *** Regis (ADD) 2029 (2). Shostakovich Qt

String Quartets 12 in D flat, Op. 133; 13 in B flat min., Op. 138; 14 in F sharp, Op. 142
(N) (BB) *** Regis (ADD) 1024. Shostakovich Qt

String Quartets 1–15; Adagio (Elegy after Katerina's Aria from Scene 3 of Lady Macbeth of the Mtsensk District); Allegretto (after Polka from The Age of Gold ballet, Op. 22)
**(*) DG 463 284-2 (5). Emerson Qt

The Shostakovich *Quartets* thread through his creative life like some inner odyssey and inhabit terrain of increasing spiritual desolation.

The classic Borodin series appeared in the late 1960s and was issued in a well presented six-LP HMV/Melodiya box. It was this illuminating mono-LP cycle of Quartets 1–13 only on Melodiya records that reigned supreme in the early 1960s, but unfortunately their CD transfer some years ago did not do them justice. No such grumbles here, and readers who do not have their deleted later set of all 15, packaged with the *Piano Quintet* with Richter, can settle for this transfer without hesitation. The Chandos performances are unfailingly fresh and musically compelling. However, they omit Quartets 14 and 15.

The eponymous Shostakovich Quartet recorded a cycle over the period 1978 to 1985 and bring a special intensity to this repertoire as well as effortless technical address, and a tonal blend that gives their readings a strong claim on the collector's allegiance. It is no longer possible to talk of an out-and-out first choice in this repertoire, but this set has now been reissued by Regis well documented at budget price, either in a super bargain box or a pair of doubles plus one single disc. The *Two Pieces Op. 36* are also included.

If sheer brilliance and virtuosity were all that mattered, the Emerson Quartet would lead the field. They offer us all fifteen quartets in chronological order on five CDs, plus two attractive encores, thus scoring over their main rivals who all take six. (Of course, both the Borodins enjoy a price advantage.) In terms of recorded sound, the Emersons are wonderfully realistic, if a trifle too closely balanced. Their playing is immaculate technically, with spot-on intonation, accuracy and unanimity of ensemble, but they bring an unrelieved intensity to everything they touch and offer little real repose, when that is called for.

Gleaming and dazzling then, but they don't get very far under the surface here. There is infinitely more of Shostakovich's inner spirit to be found in the old Beethoven Quartet,

who premièred nearly all these works. If it is an exaggeration to say that the Emersons see the cycle as a vehicle for their own virtuosity, they certainly set great store by superb execution. These are public rather than private communications and one is not left feeling close to the anguish of most of this music.

String Quartets 1; 4; 9
(N) *** HM HMC 891865. Jerusalem Qt

Although we are well served in this repertoire, this new version by the Jerusalem Quartet is arguably the finest to appear since the days of the Borodin and Fitzwilliam sets in the 1970s. This young group brings tremendous concentration and commitment to the three *Quartets* recorded here, and even if you have either of the classic sets mentioned above – or indeed the eponymous group on Regis – you should try to hear this illuminating and brilliantly recorded newcomer.

String Quartets 1; 8 & 9
(BB) *** Naxos 8.550973. Eder Qt

String Quartets 2 in A, Op. 68; 12 in D flat, Op. 133
(BB) *** Naxos 8.550975. Eder Qt

String Quartets 4; 6–7
(BB) *** Naxos 8.550972. Eder Qt

If the Naxos discs are not necessarily a first choice, no one investing in them need fear they are getting short-changed. The Eder Quartet is a very distinguished ensemble and have a very good feeling for this repertoire. They are better recorded than the Borodins, and those for whom economy is a primary concern should consider this.

If anything, the Eder coupling of Nos. 2 and 12 is even more impressive than the first disc. The account of the third-movement *Adagio: Recitativo and Romance* of No. 2, with its intense, improvisatory feeling, is particularly fine, and the closing *Theme and Variations* is strongly characterized. Similarly the extended *Allegretto* second movement of No. 12 is powerfully argued and these performances have compelling concentration throughout.

Quite apart from its cost, this series is emerging as one of the most competitive of the newer versions of this powerful music. The recorded sound is superior and offers a serious challenge.

String Quartets 2–3
**(*) Hyp. CDA 67153. St Petersburg Qt

String Quartets 4; 6 & 8
** Hyp. CDA 67154. St Petersburg Qt

String Quartets 5; 7 & 9
** Hyp. CDA 67155. St Petersburg Qt

The St Petersburg Quartet's performances display appropriate intensity and enthusiasm even if *piano* and *pianissimo* markings are at times a little exaggerated. The leader plays with evident feeling in the *Recitative and Romance* movement of the wartime *Second Quartet*, though intonation is not always impeccable. Some will find the first movement a little rushed. A promising start but the playing in tutti can be rough and the recording lends a certain hardness and glassiness to the leader's tone.

In the *Fourth Quartet* the St Petersburg group would not be a first choice. The leader's rapid rubato will not be to all tastes and the performance throughout is far too self-conscious. These Russian players give a good account of the

Sixth (1956), but the *Eighth* is too full of emotion and vehemence: the greater reticence of the Borodins is the more telling. The St Petersburg group are decently recorded, though there is just a touch of wiriness above the stave.

They play with impressive virtuosity and intensity in all three works on the third disc. They are not free from expressive exaggeration and the leader's rapid vibrato will not give universal pleasure.

String Quartets 2; 3; 7; 8; 12
(BB) *** Virgin 5 61630-2 (2). Borodin Qt

The third series of Borodin accounts now on a Virgin Double have the benefit of far better and more refined recording than their earlier, Melodiya versions now on Chandos. The sound is richer, cleaner and has a pleasing bloom, as one would expect from the Snape Maltings. As far as the performances are concerned, some things come off better than others so that on balance there is little to choose between the earlier and newer sets; those who have the former need not make a change. This is one of the greatest quartets now before the public and they are completely inside this music.

String Quartets 2; 14
(N) *** Chan. 10114. Sorrel Qt
String Quartets 5; 15
(N) *** Chan. 10248. Sorrel Qt

The earlier issues in the Sorrel Quartet's Shostakovich cycle have not impressed quite as much as these recent issues, which are very well played and perceptive. The *Fifth Quartet*, one of the composer's greatest works, balances architectural strength and expressive eloquence perfectly. The Sorrel players have the advantage of almost ideal recording, made in the fine acoustic of the Snape Maltings. Recommended, even if it would not necessarily be a first choice.

String Quartets 3; 7 & 8
*** BIS CD 913. Yggdrasil Qt

The Yggdrasil Quartet are a young Swedish group who are now embarking on a Shostakovich cycle. This first issue is an auspicious start with a bold and searching account of the autobiographical *Eighth*, and intelligent and satisfying readings of its companions.

String Quartets 4; 8 & 11
*** ASV CDDCA 631. Coull Qt

The *Fourth Quartet* is a work of exceptional beauty and lucidity, one of the most haunting of the cycle; the *Eleventh Quartet* is a puzzling, almost cryptic work in seven short movements. The Coull are among the most gifted of the younger British quartets and give eminently creditable accounts of all three pieces. Good if slightly overlit recording.

String Quartets 7, Op. 108; 8, Op. 110; 9, Op. 117
(BB) **(*) Warner Apex 8573 89093-2. Brodsky Qt

The Brodskys are recorded in good, well-detailed digital sound with an attractive ambience. These are well-prepared and committed accounts, and if the playing is generally less searching than the Borodin Quartet, these three performances do not lack depth of feeling (witness the slow movement of No. 8). The characteristically ambivalent mood changes in No. 9 are also thoroughly absorbed to make the performance seemingly spontaneous.

String Quartet 8, Op. 110
(M) *** Classic fM 75605 57027-2. Chilingirian Qt –
  BORODIN: *Quartet 2*; DVORAK: *Quartet in F, Op. 96* ***
(M) (**(*)) BBC mono BBCL 4063-2. Borodin Qt –
  BORODIN: *Quartet 2*; RAVEL: *Quartet* (**(*))

On Classic fM the Chilingirians also give a tautly controlled performance, not as flexible as some but with the power enhanced by the rich, immediate, digital recording.

This BBC performance (currently deleted) is not quite as fine as the Borodins' earlier, Decca version, but it is still well worth having and sounds very good for its age. The Borodins recorded the Shostakovich on three further occasions after 1962, as part of their complete cycles in 1974 and 1978 and again in 1990. In the very opening bars, their tempo is fractionally brisker here than in their 1978 recording, and the vibrato is more intense. A well worthwhile memento of an important musical event.

String Quartets 10; 12; 14
(N) ** Hyp. CDA 67156. St Petersburg Qt

As with earlier issues in their cycle, the St Petersburg Quartet do not challenge, let alone displace, the Borodins or Shostakovich Quartet, which offer far greater musical rewards.

String Quartet 15
*** ECM 461 815-2. Keller Qt. – SCHNITTKE: *Piano Quintet* ***

Sorrow drained to the bitterest dregs is how one eminent critic described the *Fifteenth Quartet*. The Keller Quartet make out a strong case for the work, and they are superbly recorded.

Violin Sonata, Op. 134
*** Chan. 8988. Mordkovitch, Benson – PROKOFIEV: *Sonatas*; SCHNITTKE: *In Memoriam* ***
*** Chan. 8343. Dubinsky, Edlina – SCHNITTKE: *Sonata 1* etc. ***

The *Violin Sonata* can seem a dry piece, but Mordkovitch's natural intensity, her ability to convey depth of feeling without sentimentality, transforms it. Clifford Benson is the understanding pianist. In first-rate sound it makes a fine central offering for Mordkovitch's well-planned disc of Soviet violin music.

Rostislav Dubinsky's account is also undoubtedly eloquent, and Luba Edlina makes a fine partner. The recording is excellent too, although it is balanced a shade closely.

PIANO MUSIC

Aphorisms, Op. 13; 3 Fantastic Dances, Op. 5; Lyric Waltz (from Dances of the Dolls); Nocturne (from The Limpid Stream); Piano Sonata 2, Op. 61; 5 Preludes; Short Piece & Spanish Dance (from The Gadfly)
*** Decca **SACD** 470 469-2. Ashkenazy

Although he was an accomplished pianist, Shostakovich wrote comparatively little for his instrument. Apart from the two concertos and the music on the present disc, there are only the *First Sonata*, the *Preludes*, Op. 34, and the Op. 87 *Preludes and Fugues*. Vladimir Ashkenazy is a trusted guide in this repertoire and benefits from outstanding and natural recorded sound. His version of the *Sonata* does not efface memories of the classic Gilels account (or, way back in the days of LP, Menahem Pressler) but, as one would expect, there are none of the affectations of Mustonen's recent Op. 87, to which we have just been listening, but an appropriate dedication to and respect for the composer's intention.

Aphorisms, Op. 13; 3 Fantastic Dances, Op. 5; Piano Sonata 1; 24 Preludes, Op. 34

(BB) *** Naxos 8.555781. Scherbakov

Beautifully recorded at Potton Hall in Suffolk, Konstantin Scherbakov gives thought-provoking and wonderfully controlled accounts of the Op. 34 *Preludes*. By comparison with Nikolayeva he is at times a little too sophisticated in matters of tonal finesse, and dynamic markings are a shade exaggerated; but this has such imaginative and masterly pianism that readers can afford to overlook the occasional affectation (which we have not encountered in this artist before). He plays the whole recital with the keyboard mastery we associate with him. Strongly recommended.

24 Preludes, Op. 34

(M) *** Decca 475 212-2. Mustonen – ALKAN: 25 Preludes ***

Of the recordings of the Shostakovich *Preludes*, Op. 34, currently available, the Decca record by the Finnish pianist Olli Mustonen is as strong as any, although since this record won its *Gramophone* Instrumental Award in 1992, Hyperion have issued another outstanding set by Tatiana Nikolayeva (CDA 66620 – see below). However, Mustonen scores over his rivals by offering an apt Alkan rarity, the 25 Preludes, Op. 34, some 47 minutes of highly interesting music, which makes a highly satisfying coupling, very well recorded.

24 Preludes, Op. 34; Prelude & Fugue in D min., Op. 87/24; Piano Sonatas 1, Op. 12; 2 in B min., Op. 61

*** Athene ATH CD 18. Clarke

24 Preludes; Piano Sonata 2, Op. 61; 3 Fantastic Dances, Op. 5

*** Hyp. CDA 66620. Nikolayeva

Raymond Clarke generously couples the two sonatas with the aphoristic and witty *Preludes*, Op. 34, and these new performances are a viable first-choice for anyone coming to this repertoire afresh.

Tatiana Nikolayeva is very well recorded indeed. She is one of the authentic advocates of Shostakovich, and her CD will be a must for most collectors. Recommended alongside Clarke and Mustonen.

24 Preludes & Fugues, Op. 87

☛ ❀ (BB) *** Regis RRC 3005 (3). Nikolayeva
*** Hyp. CDA 66441/3. Nikolayeva
**(*) Decca 466 066-2. Ashkenazy
(BB) **(*) Naxos 8.554745-46. Scherbakov

In this repertoire, the first choice must inevitably be Tatiana Nikolayeva, 'the onlie begetter', as it were, of the *Preludes and Fugues*. Her reading has enormous concentration and a natural authority that is majestic. There is wisdom and humanity here, and she finds depths in this music that have eluded most other pianists who have offered samples. No grumbles about the Hyperion recording, which is very natural.

However, her Melodiya set, made in 1987 and now reissued in the budget range on the enterprising Regis label, is if anything cleaner and better focused (if a bit dry). In neither reading will readers be disappointed, but the Regis set has a huge price advantage.

Ashkenazy's set has the advantage of good Decca sound; there is a pleasing ambience and great clarity and warmth. His playing is very fine – that goes almost without saying – though he traverses the cycle in 141 minutes as opposed to Nikolayeva's 168. In comparing individual pieces, Nikolayeva always seems to find so much more in this music. She has been inside it, and it shows in the subtlety of her colouring and depth of tone, and the sense of space. On its own terms the Ashkenazy is recommendable but he does not perhaps tell the whole story.

Konstantin Scherbakov commands a formidable technical address and much refinement of colour. Of course there are some formidable rivals in this repertoire, notably Tatiana Nikolayeva, but none is anywhere near as competitively priced. Scherbakov is often insightful, although there is some want of *Innigkeit* and some of the contemplative numbers find him almost on auto-pilot. All the same there is a lot to admire, and readers will find much that is rewarding. Nikolayeva's set on RCA/Melodiya remains a first choice.

Preludes & Fugues, Op. 87, 1; 5 & 24

(***) Testament mono SBT 1089. Gilels – CHOPIN: Sonata 2; MOZART: Piano Sonata 17 (***)

These three *Preludes and Fugues* were recorded in New York in 1955. The sound is a little dry and close, but the playing is magisterial.

VOCAL MUSIC

(i) The Fall of Berlin, Op. 82; (ii) The Unforgettable Year 1919, Op. 98a

** Marco Polo 8.223897 Moscow SO, Adriano, with (i) Moscow Capella & Youth Ch.; (ii) Alekseyeva

Composed in the immediate wake of the Zhdanov affair when Shostakovich, Prokofiev, Miaskovsky and others were subjected to official Soviet abuse, these film scores are hack work but fill in the picture of the composer. Reasonably good performances in decent sound. A disc for completists.

OPERA

Lady Macbeth of Mtsensk (complete)

☛ ❀ (M) *** EMI (ADD) 5 67776-2 [567779] (2). Vishnevskaya, Gedda, Petkov, Finnilä, Krenn, Tear, Malta, Valjakka, Amb. Op. Ch., LPO, Rostropovich
*** DG (IMS) 437 511-2 (2). Ewing, Haugland, Larin, Langridge, Ciesinski, Moll, Kotcherga, Zednik, Paris Bastille Op. Ch. & O, Chung

Rostropovich, in his finest recording ever, proves with thrilling conviction that this first version of Shostakovich's greatest work for the stage is among the most original operas of the century. Vishnevskaya is inspired to give an outstanding performance and provides moments of great beauty alongside aptly coarser singing; Gedda matches her well, totally idiomatic. As the sadistic father-in-law, Petkov is magnificent, particularly in his ghostly return, and there are fine contributions from Robert Tear, Werner Krenn, Birgit Finnilä and Alexander Malta. With an enhanced transfer this now rightly takes its place as one of EMI's 'Great Recordings of the Century'.

If ever Rostropovich's classic EMI recording of this opera is unavailable, then Chung's provides an alternative, not quite as violent or powerful, but even more moving. The biggest contrast comes in the portrayal of the heroine. Where Vishnevskaya makes her a ravening fire-eater, with the voice abrasive and aggressive, Maria Ewing's portrait is much more vulnerable, with moods and responses subtly varied, her feminine charms more vividly conveyed in singing far more sensuous, with the beauty of hushed pianissimos most tenderly affecting. Sergei Larin as Katerina's labourer-lover equally gains over his EMI rival, Nicolai Gedda, by sounding more aptly youthful, with his tenor both firm and clear yet Slavonic-sounding. His touch is lighter than Gedda's, with a nice vein of irony. Aage Haugland is magnificent as Boris, Katerina's father-in-law, and Philip Langridge sings sensitively as her husband, Zinovi, while Kurt Moll as the Old Convict provides an extra emotional focus in his important solo at the start of the last Act.

SIBELIUS, Jean (1865–1957)

Andante festivo; The Bard; Canzonetta, Op. 62a; En Saga; Finlandia; Karelia Suite; King Christian II (Suite), Op. 27; Kuolema: Valse triste; Scene with Cranes; Op. 44/1–2; 4 Legends, Op. 22; (i) *Luonnotar, Op. 70; Night Ride and Sunrise, Op. 55; 4 Legends, Op. 22; The Oceanides, Op. 73; Pohjola's Daughter; Spring Song, Op. 16 ; Tapiola, Op. 112; Valse romantique, Op. 62b*

⊶ (N) (B) *** DG Trio 477 5522 (3). Gothenberg SO, Järvi;
(i) with Isokoski

This impeccably recorded, bargain-priced Trio groups together three separate CD collections of Sibelius's orchestral works, each of which has been highly praised by us. It includes one of the best accounts of *The Oceanides* we have had since the celebrated Beecham version, and a first-class *Luonnotar*. *The Bard* is brooding and mysterious, the *Canzonetta* for strings and *Valse triste* have great poetry, and the *Scene with Cranes* is full of atmosphere. Järvi gives a passionate and atmospheric reading of the first *Legend*, and his account of *The Swan of Tuonela* is altogether magical, one of the best in the catalogue. He takes a broader view of *Lemminkäinen in Tuonela* than many of his rivals and builds up an appropriately black and powerful atmosphere. The disappointment is *Lemminkäinen's Homeward Journey*, which lacks the possessed, manic quality of Beecham's very first record (see below), which sounded as if a thousand demons were in pursuit. However, *Tapiola* is a great success: Järvi produces a performance of commanding power, and the unhurried (and all the more terrifying) storm is judged excellently. *En Saga*, on the other hand, fares less well and at times seems almost matter of fact, although the introspective, quieter sections in the middle and closing paragraphs are evocative. *Spring Song* also borders on the routine – but then so does the music. Certainly overall this is an estimable survey, especially suitable as a basis for any collection of Sibelius's orchestral music, and the modern digital sound and truthful balance are equally commendable.

Andante festivo for Strings; Canzonetta, Op. 62a; The Dryad, Op. 45/1; Dance Intermezzo, Op. 45/2; In Memoriam, Op. 59; 4 Legends, Op. 22; Pan and Echo, Op. 53a; Romance in C for Strings, Op. 42; Spring Song, Op. 16; Suite Mignon for 2 Flutes & Strings, Op. 98a; Suite champêtre for Strings, Op. 98b; The Tempest: Prelude; Suites 1 & 2, Op. 109/1–3; Valse romantique, Op. 62b

(BB) **(*) EMI Gemini (ADD) 5 85532-2 (2). RLPO, Groves

This Gemini double draws together the recordings Sir

Charles Groves made of rare Sibelius miniatures in the early 1970s. Much of this is lightweight Sibelius, but none the worse for that when it is so beautifully played. However, *The Dryad*, which comes from the same period as the *Fourth Symphony*, is rather impressive. *Spring Song* is an early piece and not particularly strong, yet its sonority catches the ear readily. The two *Suites*, Op. 98 are charming, and so are the *Canzonetta, Dance Intermezzo* and *Valse romantique*. The better-known *Romance in C* is most eloquently played, as is the *Andante festivo*, while *In Memoriam* has nicely judged gravitas. Always a sympathetic Sibelian, Groves succeeds in generating both atmosphere and tension in the *Four Legends*, which are often exciting, even if they could not be considered a primary recommendation. The same comment applies to the music from *The Tempest*. In *The Oak-tree* and *The Chorus of the Winds* Groves fails to distil the magic that distinguished Beecham's famous mono set, but the performances are by no means to be dismissed. The recording is well balanced and vividly detailed, and its warmth of sonority is striking, with rich string-textures – some of the recordings were originally made in quadraphony. Altogether this inexpensive reissue gives considerable pleasure, not least because of the splendid sound.

(i) *Andante festivo;* (ii) *En Saga;* (iii) *Pohjola's Daughter;* (iv) *Rakastava; Impromptu*

(***) Ondine mono/stereo ODE 992-2. (i) Finnish RSO, Composer; (ii) Swedish RSO, Franck; (iii) Tampere PO, Ollila; (iv) Virtuosi di Kuhmo, Czaba (with: Kajanus: *Aino* *******)

Though, unlike Svendsen and Nielsen, Sibelius was not a conductor by profession, he was a highly effective interpreter of his own music. The *Andante festivo* is the only surviving recording of him conducting and he draws playing of great intensity. (An earlier account attributed to him was in fact a recording of a rehearsal under Tauno Hannikainen.) Mikko Franck's version of *En Saga* is both concentrated and atmospheric. There is a more than serviceable account of *Pohjola's Daughter* and an affecting *Rakastava*, while the *Impromptu* is an arrangement for strings of two early piano pieces, Op. 5. The bonus is a rarity, the 1991 recording under Jorma Panula of *Aino* by Sibelius's great champion, Robert Kajanus, which was the spark that kindled the flame that led to Sibelius's *Kullervo Symphony*.

Autrefois (Scène pastorale), Op. 96b; The Bard, Op. 64; Presto in D for Strings; Spring Song, Op. 16; Suite caractéristique, Op. 100; Suite champêtre, Op. 98b; Suite mignonne, Op. 98a; Valse chevaleresque, Op. 96c; Valse lyrique, Op. 96a

*** BIS CD 384. Gothenburg SO, Järvi

A mixed bag. *The Bard* is Sibelius at his greatest and most powerful, and it finds Järvi at his best. The remaining pieces are all light: some of the movements of the *Suite mignonne* and *Suite champêtre* could come straight out of a Tchaikovsky ballet, and Järvi does them with great charm. The last thing that the *Suite*, Op. 100, can be called is *caractéristique*, while the three pieces, Op. 96, find Sibelius in Viennese waltz mood. The rarity is *Autrefois*, which has a beguiling charm and is by far the most haunting of these pastiches. Sibelius introduces two sopranos and their *vocalise* is altogether captivating. The *Presto in D major for Strings* is a transcription – and a highly effective one – of the third movement of the *B flat Quartet*, Op. 4. Excellent recording, as one has come to expect from BIS.

The Bard; Dance-Intermezzo; The Dryad; En saga; Legend: Night Ride and Sunrise; The Oceanides; Pohjola's Daughter
**(*) BIS CD 1225. Lahti SO, Vänskä

Osmo Vänskä has already recorded *The Wood-Nymph*, *Tapiola* and the 1892 version of *En saga*. This CD brings the remaining tone poems – with the exception of *Pan and Echo*. This conductor, much and rightly admired in this repertoire, is unfailingly sure of instinct. In *En saga* phrasing is so natural and unforced, though the *pianissimo sul ponticello* string passage (18 bars before M: track 1, 8:14 mins) is exaggerated to the point of inaudibility. *Pohjola's Daughter* is very impressive, though the affected dynamic exaggerations (the *pianopianissimi* at 7:30 mins and again at the very end) are irritating. In *Night Ride and Sunrise* pacing is superb and the final sunrise is magnificent and beautifully sustained. But ultimately in both *The Oceanides* and *Night Ride* the LSO and Sir Colin Davis remain unchallenged, and among very recent issues we liked Oramo and the CBSO, who give very convincing accounts of *The Bard* and *Pohjola's Daughter*.

The Bard, Op. 64; En Saga, Op. 9; Finlandia, Op. 26; Legend: Lemminkaïnen's Return, Op. 22; Symphony 4 in A min., Op. 63
(N) (BB) (***) Naxos mono 8.110867. LPO, Beecham

The merits of these classic recordings are too well known to require further exegesis. The transfers by Mark Obert-Thorn are very good indeed (though so were the earlier, HMV issues by Anthony Griffith) and can be confidently recommended.

The Bard, Op. 64; En Saga, Op. 9; The Oceanides, Op. 73; Pohjola's Daughter, Op. 49; Tapiola, Op. 112
(BB) **(*) Naxos 8.555299. Iceland SO, Sakari

Petri Sakari is comparatively direct and straightforward and gets good playing from the Iceland orchestra, even if the strings lack richness of timbre. *Pohjola's Daughter* is finely shaped, though, like *Tapiola*, wanting in intensity. There is plenty of atmosphere in *En saga* and *The Oceanides*. No one wanting a bargain set of Sibelius tone-poems is likely to be disappointed by these musicianly and unaffected readings, decently performed and well recorded. All the same, there are finer individual performances around.

The Bard; Four Legends, Op. 22; Pohjola's Daughter, Op. 49
**(*) RCA 74321 68945-2 LSO, Davis

The first *Legend* is finely paced and one feels, as with any great conductor, that there is always something left in reserve. But at almost twelve minutes Sir Colin's *Swan* is excessively ruminative: his Boston version was just over nine! Moreover, while the sense of menace in *Lemminkäinen in Tuonela* is very striking and it is enormously atmospheric, it is *far* too slow. In *Lemminkäinen's Homeward Journey* Davis is not as headlong as Beecham or Vänskä. Their hero is altogether rougher and in very much of a hurry while Davis's is a more thoughtful chap. *The Bard* is magical, every bit as mysterious and inward-looking as the recent CBSO version under Oramo. Sir Colin recorded *Pohjola's Daughter* with the Boston Orchestra way back in 1981, though it was never transferred to CD. Though they actually differ by only a few seconds, this newcomer feels even slower: many collectors will find it far too measured. Vänskä offers the earlier 1896 versions of Nos. 1 and 4 and the alternative 1897 ending of No. 4, and Mikko

Franck on Ondine has *En Saga*. Mike Hatch produces exceptionally fine recorded sound for Davis, but this collection, which we overpraised in our last main volume, must be approached with a degree of caution.

Belshazzar's Feast (suite), Op. 54; Dance Intermezzo, Op. 45/2; The Dryad, Op. 45/1; Pan and Echo, Op. 53; Swanwhite, Op. 54
*** BIS CD 359. Gothenburg SO, Järvi

Belshazzar's Feast, a beautifully atmospheric piece of orientalism, and the incidental music for Strindberg's *Swanwhite* may not be Sibelius at his most powerful, but both include wonderful things. Neeme Järvi's collection with the Gothenburg orchestra is first class in every way.

The Breaking of the Ice on the Oulo River; Press Celebrations Music; Song of the Athenians
*** BIS CD 1115. Lahti SO, Vänskä

A recording which will be of compelling interest for all Sibelians. It contains the music Sibelius composed for a pageant in 1899, the so-called *Press Celebrations Music*, from which he later fashioned the first set of *Historic Scenes* and *Finlandia*. In all there is some 40 minutes of music. Here we have Sibelius's original thoughts, as well as a *Prelude for Wind Instruments* and two movements which he left in manuscript. Not all of it is top-drawer Sibelius, but the fifth tableau is powerful and atmospheric, and it is surprising that he made no effort to re-shape it and include it with the other *Historic Scenes*. The third tableau is the original version of the *Boléro*, which Sibelius revised in 1900 and then again in 1911 as *Festivo*. There are other rarities from the same period, including *The Breaking of the Ice on the Oulo River*, all worth hearing and given an excellent performance by Osmo Vänskä and the Lahti Symphony Orchestra and first-rate recorded sound.

Cassazione, Op. 6 (first version); Coronation March; Cortège; Morceau romantique sur un motif de Monsieur Jakob de Julin; Musik zu einer Scene; The Oceanides, Op. 73 (Final and Yale Versions). Spring Song. Trad.: March of the People of Pori (arr. Sibelius)
*** BIS CD 1445. Lahti SO, Vänskä

Osmo Vänskä and the Lahti Symphony Orchestra add to their outstanding Sibelius series with this fascinating collection of rarities, centring on *The Oceanides*, the only item here that has been recorded before. When Sibelius was invited to America in 1914, he was commissioned to compose a new work by his host, Carl Stoeckel. He posted the score in advance, entitling it *Rondo of the Waves*, but as soon as he had done so he began re-working its material into what was to become *The Oceanides*. The original MS. eventually found its way into the Yale University Library and, although its existence has long been known to scholars, it makes its début on record. So, too, do two further MS. pieces which Sibelius himself called 'Fragments for a Suite for Orchestra/Predecessor of *The Oceanides*'.

The Oceanides is one of Sibelius's greatest tone-poems and the Yale MS. gives a fascinating glimpse of its gestation. The whole collection offers the most illuminating picture of Sibelius's creative process. Curiously, he eventually went back to the original order of the material that he had had in the finale of the *Suite*, but he expanded it and refined it out of all recognition. The Yale version, on the other hand, originally called *Rondo of the Waves*, presents the material in an unexpected order, with what became the main theme set nearer the middle and with the stormy climax even more of a culmination than in the final version, making the result more dramatic.

Otherwise, the most substantial work here is the *Cassazione*, which in this original version of 1904 uses a bigger orchestra than what became Op. 6. The first version contains a quite ethereal episode for wind, though Sibelius was undoubtedly right to cut the opening. The tiny *Morceau romantique*, written for a charity concert, whose opening bars sound almost like Rachmaninov, becomes a jolly waltz movement, using material written by a rich relative of Marshal Mannerheim, the Finnish President. The *Coronation March* of 1896, which comes from the music Sibelius composed for Tsar Nicholas II, is unlike any coronation march you have ever heard. *Spring Song* of 1895 is uninhibitedly melodic, and *Cortège* in a polonaise rhythm is Sibelius working in the light of day, with mystery removed, rather like the *Karelia Suite*. Trivial or not, it makes compelling listening, helped by masterly performances and beautifully balanced recording. This is a most interesting and rewarding issue, excellently annotated.

Cassazione, Op. 6; Preludio; The Tempest: Prelude & Suites 1–2, Op. 109; Tiera
*** BIS CD 448. Gothenburg SO, Järvi

Järvi's recording of Sibelius's incidental music to *The Tempest* is among the most atmospheric since Beecham and, though it does not surpass the latter in pieces like *The Oak-Tree* or the *Chorus of the Winds*, it is still very good. The *Cassazione* resembles the *King Christian II* music in character, but it is well worth having on disc. Neither *Tiera* nor the *Preludio*, both from the 1890s, is of great interest or particularly characteristic.

Violin Concerto in D min. (1903–4 version); Violin Concerto in D min., Op. 47 (1905; published version)
(M) *** BIS CD 300500. Kavakos, Lahti SO, Vänskä

The first performance of the *Violin Concerto* left Sibelius dissatisfied, and he immediately withdrew it for revision. This CD presents Sibelius's initial thoughts so that for the first time we can see the familiar final version struggling to emerge from the chrysalis. Comparison of the two concertos makes a fascinating study: the middle movement is the least affected by change, but the outer movements are both longer in the original score, and the whole piece takes almost 40 minutes. The Greek violinist, Leonidis Kavakos, proves more than capable of handling the hair-raising difficulties of the 1904 version and is an idiomatic exponent of the definitive concerto. The Lahti orchestra under Osmo Vänskä give excellent support and the balance is natural and realistic. An issue of exceptional interest and value.

Violin Concerto in D min., Op. 47
** Arthaus **DVD** 100 034. Vengerov, Chicago SO, Barenboim – FALLA: *Nights in the Gardens of Spain*. ** (Producer: Bernd Hellthaler; V/D: Bob Coles.)

☛ ❂ *** Sony SMK 89748. Lin, Philh. O, Salonen – NIELSEN: *Violin Concerto* *** ❂

*** HM Naïve V 4959. Sergey Khachaturian, Sinfonia Varsovia, Krivine – KHACHATURIAN: *Violin Concerto* ***

☛ (M) *** Decca (ADD) 425 080-2. Chung, LSO, Previn – TCHAIKOVSKY: *Violin Concerto* ***

(N) (M) *** RCA (ADD) 82876 66372-2. Heifetz, Chicago SO, Hendl – GLAZUNOV: *Concerto*; PROKOFIEV: *Concerto 2* ***

*** EMI 5 56418-2. Chang, BPO, Jansons – MENDELSSOHN: *Violin Concerto in E min* ***

(M) *** Ph. 464 741-2. Mullova, Boston SO, Ozawa – TCHAIKOVSKY: *Violin Concerto* **(*)

(M) *** EMI (ADD) 5 62590-2. Perlman, Pittsburgh SO, Previn – KORNGOLD: *Concerto*; SINDING: *Suite* ***

*** EMI 7 54127-2. Kennedy, CBSO, Rattle – TCHAIKOVSKY: *Concerto* **(*)

*** Erato 4509-98537-2. Repin, LSO, Krivine – TCHAIKOVSKY: *Violin Concerto* ***

(M) (***) EMI mono 7 61011-2. Neveu, Philh. O, Susskind – BRAHMS: *Concerto* (***)

(BB) *** Naxos 8.550329. Kang, Slovak (Bratislava) RSO, Leaper – HALVORSEN: *Air norvégien* etc.; SINDING: *Légende*; *** SVENDSEN: *Romance* ***

(BB) (**(*)) Naxos mono 8.110938. Heifetz, LPO, Beecham – TCHAIKOVSKY: *Violin Concerto*; WIENIAWSKI: *Violin Concerto 2 in D min.* (***)

(M) (***) EMI mono 7 64030-2. Heifetz, LPO, Beecham – GLAZUNOV: *Violin Concerto* (***) ❂; TCHAIKOVSKY: *Violin Concerto* (***)

(M) **(*) Warner Elatus 0927 46743-2. Vengerov, Chicago SO, Barenboim – TCHAIKOVSKY: *Violin Concerto* ***

(i) Violin Concerto; (ii) Andante festivo; Finlandia; Kuolema: Valse triste; Legend: The Swan of Tuonela
☛ (N) (BB) *** EMI HMV 5 86767-2. (i) Tasmin Little, RLPO, Handley; (ii) Oslo PO, Jansons

Violin Concerto in D min., Op. 47; 4 Humoresques, Op. 89
(N) *** DG 464 814-2. Gringolts, Gothenburg SO, Järvi – PROKOFIEV: *Violin Concerto 1* ***

(i) Violin Concerto; Karelia Suite; Belshazzar's Feast (suite)
**(*) Ondine ODE 8782. (i) Suusisto; Helsinki PO, Segerstam

Violin Concerto; 2 Serenades, Op. 69; Humoresque 1 in D min., Op. 87/1
*** DG 447 895-2. Mutter, Dresden State O, Previn

Violin Concerto; Serenade 2 in G min.
(N) (BB) **(*) Naxos 8.557266. Kraggerud, Bournemouth SO, Engeset – SINDING: *Violin Concerto*, etc. ***

Violin Concerto; Humoreske 5 in E flat, Op. 89/3; 2 Serenades, Op. 69
(BB) **(*) EMI Encore (ADD) 5 75236-2. Haendel, Bournemouth SO, Berglund

(i) Violin Concerto; (ii) Symphony 2
(N) (BB) (***) Dutton mono 9733. (i) Neveu, Philh. O, Susskind; (ii) NYPO, Barbirolli

(i) Violin Concerto. The Tempest: Prelude; Suites 1 & 2, Op. 109
*** Häns. 98353. (i) Sitkovetsky; ASMF, Marriner

On DVD a 1997 recording made while the Chicago orchestra and Vengerov were in Germany. Pretty stunning virtuosity and much *zigeuner* brilliance and glitz, though much less of the silvery, aristocratic restraint that is called for in the slow movement. But if you warm to this glamorous player – and he has a strong following – this DVD can be recommended. Barenboim accompanies sensitively and Vengerov dashes off the Bach *Sarabande* from the *D minor Partita* and the *Third Solo Sonata (Ballade)* of Ysaÿe as encores. The equivalent CD is coupled with an inspired performance of the Tchaikovsky *Violin Concerto*.

Cho-Liang Lin's playing is distinguished not only by flawless intonation and an apparently effortless virtuosity but also by great artistry. He produces a glorious sonority at the opening and the slow movement has tenderness, warmth and yet restraint with not a hint of over-heated emotions. Lin encompasses the extrovert brilliance of the finale and the bravura of the cadenza with real mastery. The Philharmonia Orchestra rise to the occasion under Esa-Pekka Salonen, and the recording is first class.

Sergey Khachaturian comes from a famous Armenian musical family and in 2000 he won first prize in the Jean Sibelius competition in Helsinki. His account of the *Concerto*, although opening ethereally, is full of Slavic feeling, with the slow movement passionately intense. It is a powerfully spontaneous performance, very well accompanied by the excellent Polish Sinfonia Varsovia, and excellently recorded. The coupling is an outstanding account of the (underrated) Khachaturian *Violin Concerto*.

Kyung-Wha Chung has inimitable style and an astonishing technique, and her feeling for the Sibelius *Concerto* is second to none. André Previn's accompanying cannot be praised too highly: it is poetic when required, restrained and full of controlled vitality and well-defined detail. The 1970 Kingsway Hall recording is superbly balanced and produces an unforced, truthful sound. This is a most beautiful account, poetic, brilliant and thoroughly idiomatic, and must be numbered among the finest versions of the work available.

Tasmin Little's outstanding account, rapt in its intensity, is very highly recommendable. Her hushed and mysterious account of the opening theme leads to a performance that is both poised and purposeful, magnetic in her combination of power and poetry. Kyung Wha Chung's reading with André Previn may be more overtly passionate, but Little's is just as deeply felt, with an even wider tonal range, and her virtuosity culminates in an account of the finale in which she finds an element of wit in the pointing of insistent dance rhythms. Throughout she is splendidly matched by the colourful playing of the RLPO under Vernon Handley. Jansons's performances of the coupled orchestral works are hardly less distinctive. There is an aristocratic feel to the *Andante festivo* and *The Swan of Tuonela*, both of which are distinguished by string-playing of great intensity. Jansons whips *Valse triste* into something of a frenzy towards the climax, but elsewhere these performances are totally free from exaggeration. Excellent recording throughout.

Heifetz's stereo performance of the Sibelius *Concerto* with the Chicago Symphony Orchestra under Walter Hendl set the standard by which others have come to be judged. It is one of his finest recordings; in remastered SACD form the sound is vivid, the Chicago ambience making an apt setting for the finely focused violin line.

In her live recording, made at a concert in the Philharmonie, Sarah Chang gives an astonishingly mature reading of the Sibelius. She may not be as passionate as her fellow-Korean, Kyung-Wha Chung, but with sweet, refined tone the thoughtfulness and spontaneous poetry of the playing make her comparably magnetic. Warm, atmospheric sound.

Viktoria Mullova made the headlines during the 1980s by winning the Sibelius competition and subsequently making a dramatic escape to the West. Not surprisingly her account of the concerto is very successful, capturing its magical element right from the very opening, while the slow movement has a cool dignity that is impressive. What this concerto needs above all else is finesse and a certain aristocratic feeling, as well as warmth, which is free of the *Zigeuner* element, and

Mullova meets these combined needs admirably. The recording is excellent.

Where most violinists treat the opening as a deep meditation, Mutter makes it tougher than usual, less beautiful, using momentarily a vibratoless, slightly steely tone. Not that her reading lacks inner qualities for, despite the close balance, the opening of the slow movement finds Mutter playing in rapt meditation on a half-tone. In the finale, taken fast, power is again the keynote. Previn draws a committed performance from an orchestra not noted for playing Sibelius. In the two *Serenades*, Mutter, at her most inspired, beautifully captures the wayward, quasi-improvisatory quality of these pieces.

Perlman's second (1978) version is now restored to the catalogue in the 'Perlman Edition'. Here he plays the work as a full-blooded virtuoso showpiece, and the Pittsburgh orchestra under Previn support him to the last man and woman. In the first movement his tempo is broader than that of Heifetz, and in the rest of the work he is more expansive than he was on the earlier record. This new version takes 32 minutes, whereas the Boston performance took 29 minutes 15 seconds. Perlman is at his stunning best in the first cadenza and he makes light of the fiendish difficulties with which the solo part abounds. He takes a conventional view of the slow movement, underlining its passion, and he gives an exhilarating finale. As usual with this artist, the balance places him rather forward, but the sound is marvellously alive, the CD transfer making the forward balance even more apparent.

With the *Violin Concerto* again not coupled with another violin work, the Hännsler CD makes a unique and imaginative Sibelius issue, recorded in full, clear, spectacular sound. Sitkovetsky's is a fine reading, positive, powerful and direct, with no suspicion of self-indulgence. With Marriner and the Academy in fresh, clear partnership, this is a performance that, warmly expressive as it is, keeps tempi steadier and less volatile than most. In terms of length, the incidental music for *The Tempest*, with 18 brief movements, is the major item here. Thanks to the vividness of the recording, the originality of this late Sibelius inspiration comes over even more strikingly than usual, with echoes of other late Sibelius works brought out, not just the obvious links with *Tapiola* in the storm movements. Marriner reveals the charm of the dance rhythms in such colourful genre movements as *Caliban's Songs* in the *Suite No. 1* and the *Dance of the Nymphs* in the *Suite No. 2*

Throughout, Nigel Kennedy's intonation is true and he takes all the technical hurdles of this concerto in his stride. There is a touch of the *zigeuner* throb in the slow movement, but on the whole he plays with real spirit and panache. This can be confidently recommended if the coupling with the Tchaikovsky, a rather more indulgent performance, is suitable. The playing of the Birmingham orchestra is excellent throughout as, indeed, is the EMI recording.

The purity and refinement of Vadim Repin's playing are what strike one first in his earlier recording with Krivine. The withdrawn darkness at the very start quickly opens out thrillingly to reveal his total command, the tautness of his control, with tone sharply focused. Here is a young artist who, for all the brilliance of his virtuosity, regularly keeps a degree of emotion in reserve, his very restraint adding to the intensity. The speed in the finale is thrillingly fast, yet Repin with light attack brings out the scherzando element as well as the passion.

Gringolts gives a thoughtful account of the *Concerto*. He takes the finale somewhat slower than usual to rather striking effect. A pity that he doesn't give us also the two *Humoresques*, Op. 87, but never mind; this is an impressive account of these lovely pieces.

The magnetism of Neveu in this, her first concerto recording, is inescapable from her opening phrase onwards, warmly expressive and dedicated, yet with no hint of mannerism. The EMI transfer is not as impressive as Dutton's coupled with Barbirolli's outstanding account of the Second Symphony.

Heifetz made his first historic recording of the Sibelius *Violin Concerto* with Beecham in 1935, a reading that set standards in virtuosity for generations to come. Next to many later recordings, it may be short on mystery, but the passion as well as the brilliance of the playing is very clear, with Beecham a challenging partner. The Naxos transfer is well balanced but the surface hiss is intrusive at times. But despite Sir Thomas's direction, Heifetz gave the more powerful account of it in his later, Chicago, recording with Walter Hendl in the early days of stereo. (The reverse was the case with the Glazunov.) A good transfer nevertheless from EMI with different couplings, although this CD costs more than the Naxos alternative.

Dong-Suk Kang chooses some popular Scandinavian repertoire pieces, such as the charming Svendsen *Romance in G*, as makeweights. His version of the concerto is very fine, though the slow movement could do with more tenderness as opposed to passion. There is splendid virtuosity and authoritative playing in the outer movements. The orchestral playing is very acceptable too. In the bargain basement, this enjoys a strong competitive advantage, but even if it were at full price it would feature quite high in the current lists.

Ida Haendel brings great attack to the *Violin Concerto*, and there is a refreshing want of egocentricity to her interpretation. She plays with dash and authority, though others have brought to it greater poetic refinement (Kyung-Wha Chung, for example). Berglund accompanies sympathetically, although the finale could go with greater panache. The two *Serenades* are marvellously atmospheric, and Miss Haendel does them proud in this, their première recording. The 1975 sound is good for its period and has been well transferred; had Berglund created greater atmosphere in the *Violin Concerto*, this would be one of the top recommendations.

Helped by a close balance and a full, rich and immediate recording, the Finnish violinist Pekka Suusisto, barely twenty, gives a strong and passionate reading, very outward-going, lacking some of the meditative, inner qualities that others find but compensating in his volatile imagination. His speeds are on the broad side, but the urgency and concentration are never in doubt. With a Finnish conductor and orchestra too, the result is both powerful and idiomatic. The playing is equally positive in the two suites. The exotic colours of *Belshazzar's Feast* are vividly caught.

Henning Kraggerud also gives a powerful, red-blooded reading of the Sibelius *Violin Concerto*, treating it as a work very much in the great Romantic tradition. He may lack some of the deeper, more inward qualities that the very finest versions possess, but, with an unusual and very attractive coupling, it stands out among the bargain recommendations. The poignant *G minor Serenade* is also well served.

Among the profusion of recordings of the Sibelius *Concerto*, Maxim Vengerov's Chicago account is dazzling and brilliant. He is much and rightly admired, but here he seems insensitive to the special atmosphere of this work. It is all too glib and flashy. Barenboim draws good playing from the Chicago orchestra, and the recording is very full-bodied and pleasant. The Tchaikovsky coupling is a different matter – inspired in every way.

(i; iii) *Violin Concerto in D minor, Op. 47;* (i) *Finlandia; Karelia Suite, Op. 11; Kuolema: valse triste, Op. 44/1; Legend: the Swan of Tuonela, Op. 22/2;* (i) *Symphonies 2 in D, Op. 43;* (ii) *5 in E flat, Op. 82*

(B) **(*) DG Panorama (ADD) 469 201-2 (2). BPO; (i) Kamu;
(ii) Karajan; (iii) Ferras

There are several performances of stature in this Panorama package, notably Karajan's celebrated account of the *Fifth Symphony* from 1965 and his hardly less masterly performances of *Swan of Tuonela*, *Finlandia* and *Valse triste* from the same time. Okko Kamu's account of the *Second Symphony* is a good performance, eminently recommendable though not particularly special. Christian Ferras is impressive in the *Violin Concerto*, but there is some wiriness of tone. Even so, many will prefer him to Mutter, also on DG, though not to Lin or Kyung-Wha Chung. All the same, a useful introduction to some deservedly popular Sibelius.

(i–ii) *Violin Concerto in D min., Op. 47;* (ii) *Symphonies 1–7; En Saga, Op. 9; Finlandia, Op. 26/7; Karelia Suite, Op. 11; Kuolema: Valse triste, Op. 44/1. Romance for Strings in C, Op. 42;* (i–ii) *2 Serenades, Op. 69; 2 Serious Melodies, Op. 77;* (iii–iv) *Luonnotar*

(B) *** Decca ADD/DDD 473 590-2 (5). (I) Belkin; (ii) Philh.
O; (iii) Söderström; (iv) Boston SO; all cond. Ashkenazy

Ashkenazy's cycle of the *Symphonies*, a top recommendation in its Double Decca format, has been packaged even more attractively in a bargain box, together with the *Violin Concerto* and other shorter works. The *Symphonies* are notable for the excellence of the digital recording; but on performance grounds, too, these readings are very rewarding (see below). In the *Violin Concerto*, Boris Belkin – a powerful and sensitive player – brings a fiery temperament to this work. There are moments of exaggeration that might prove irritating to some listeners; although his Slavonic ardour and flamboyance bring a boldness of attack and a spontaneity that are appealing, there are infelicities that do not improve on repetition: an ugly scoop at fig. 1 in the finale, and some less than true intonation in the sixths just after fig. 10 in the first movement. He inspires warm support from Ashkenazy and his orchestra, and he is very well recorded (1978). But Belkin resorts to an expressive distortion at the very beginning and he suddenly exaggerates the earthiness of the G-string writing a couple of dozen bars later. However, the pair of *Serenades* and *Serious Melodies* are beautifully played, the popular tone-poems are impressively done, and Söderström is on good form in *Luonnotar*, even if some ears may find her wide vibrato and hard-edged tone not entirely sympathetic. But overall this set makes a worthwhile investment for the *Symphonies* and tone-poems alone.

(i) *Violin Concerto;* (ii) *Symphony 7; Tapiola*

(***) Ondine mono ODE 809-2. (i) Oistrakh, Finnish RSO,
Fougstedt; (ii) Helsinki PO, Beecham

David Oistrakh's account of the *Violin Concerto* has a marvellous strength and nobility as well as an effortless virtuosity that carries all before it. His artistry inspires a warm response from the Finnish Radio Orchestra under Nils-Eric Fougstedt, who give magnificent support. There was always a special sense of occasion, too, at any Beecham concert, and the opening of the *Seventh Symphony* is more highly charged than his EMI commercial recording with the RPO. *Tapiola* also has great intensity, though the orchestral playing does not have the finesse, magic and tonal subtlety of the RPO recording. Subfusc recording, but a coupling well worth investigating all the same.

**(i) *En saga; Finlandia; Karelia Suite;* (ii) *Four Legends,*
Op. 22; (i; iii) *Luonnotar;* (ii) *Night Ride and Sunrise,*
Op. 55; Pohjola's Daughter, Op. 49; (i) *Tapiola***
(B) *** Double Decca (ADD) 452 576-2 (2). (i) Philh. O,
  Ashkenazy; (ii) SRO, Stein; (iii) with Söderström

This Double Decca combines Ashkenazy's mid-priced digital collection from the 1980s as listed below with more distinguished and finely calculated performances from Horst Stein. *Night Ride and Sunrise* and *Pohjola's Daughter* date from 1971. At the time, we thought they showed the Suisse Romande Orchestra in much better form than usual, and the *Legends*, too, are impressive, with a hell-for-leather account of *Lemminkäinen's Return*. The 1980 analogue sound is first class, having fine weight and definition. Again the Suisse Romande Orchestra plays very well. Even if the body of string tone does not match that of the Philharmonia, the brooding atmosphere of *The Swan of Tuonela* is well caught, and both the first and third *Legends* are well shaped and exciting. All in all, excellent value.

**(i) *En Saga, Op. 9; Finlandia, Op. 26; Karelia Suite, Op. 11;*
(ii) *Legend: The Swan of Tuonela***
(B) *** Ph. Eloquence 468 201-2 (2). Philh O, Ashkenazy; (ii)
  ASMF, Marriner – GRIEG: *Holberg Suite* etc. **

Ashkenazy's superb Sibelius recordings – a fresh-sounding yet exciting *Finlandia*, an impressively evocative *En Saga* and an enjoyably vivid *Karelia Suite* – remain top choices, and the early digital recordings are superb in every way. Marriner's *Swan of Tuonela* is most sensitive, with the cor anglais solo beautifully played by Barry Griffiths. However, the Grieg couplings are not quite so recommendable.

**(i) *En Saga, Op. 9; Finlandia;* (ii) *Karelia Suite;* (i) *Legend:*
The Swan of Tuonela, Op. 22/2; (ii) *Tapiola, Op. 112***
(M) **(*) EMI ADD/DDD EMI 7 64331-2. BPO, Karajan
(BB) *** Belart 450 018-2 (without *Tapiola*). (i) SRO, Stein;
  (ii) VPO, Maazel – GRIEG: *Peer Gynt* ***

Karajan's *En Saga* is more concerned with narrative than with atmosphere to start with; the climax is very exciting and the *lento assai* section and the coda are quite magical. *Tapiola* is broader and more expansive than the first DG version; at the storm section the more spacious tempo is vindicated, and the climax is electrifying. *The Swan of Tuonela* is most persuasively done. These recordings date from 1977. The later, digital recording of *Karelia* has been added for the current reissue.

Horst Stein shows a gift for the special atmosphere of Sibelius, and these distinguished and poetic performances offer some of the finest playing we have had from the Suisse Romande Orchestra. Moreover Decca's 1972 recording approaches the demonstration class, especially in *En Saga*. Maazel's *Karelia* is also first rate.

En Saga; Karelia Suite; Kuolema: Valse triste. Pohjola's
Daughter; Tapiola
(N) *** Australian Ph. Eloquence (ADD) 476 2817. Boston
  SO, C. Davis

Beautifully refined and imaginative performances from the Boston orchestra, with a particularly distinguished account of *Pohjola's Daughter*; indeed, it ranks with the very finest ever recorded; Sir Colin's maiden has real allure, Väinämöinen's struggles with his various tasks have never been more heroic.

The relaxed pace of the *Karelia Suite* works very well, the *Intermezzo* delightful with its unforced yet genuine rhythmic lift which carries one along. On LP, the *En Saga* sounded rather opaque compared to other recordings, largely as a result of the sound, which is much improved on CD. There is tremendous atmosphere in these recordings; *Tapiola* is full of mystery and power and, like the rest of the programme, is superbly done. Colin Davis is a born Sibelian and the Boston orchestra play magnificently for him. A very welcome return to the catalogue.

En Saga; Scènes historiques, Opp. 25, 66
*** BIS CD 295. Gothenburg SO, Järvi

Järvi has the advantage of modern digital sound and the Gothenburg orchestra is fully inside the idiom of this music and plays very well indeed. *En Saga* is exciting and well paced.

Finlandia; Karelia Suite; Kuolema: Valse triste; Legend: The
Swan of Tuonela; Scènes historiques: Festivo; Tapiola
(M) (***) DG mono 447 453-2. BPO, Rosbaud

Karajan was not the only champion of Sibelius's music in post-war Germany. Hans Rosbaud, the high priest of the Second Viennese School and the 1950s avant-garde, also included it in his repertoire and indeed insisted on conducting the *Fourth Symphony* when he came to the BBC Symphony Orchestra some months before his death in 1962. These recordings come from the mid-1950s, and although some allowance must be made for the mono sound, the performances themselves have the ring of conviction. The *Tapiola* is something special, among the most terrifying evocations of that dark Nordic forest, and worthy to keep company with those of Beecham, Koussevitzky and Karajan. *The Swan of Tuonela* is a little brisk, but it is not wanting in atmosphere. The *Alla marcia* of the *Karelia Suite* is a bit sedate, heavy-footed even, but Sibelians will want this disc for Rosbaud's intensely cold *Tapiola*.

Finlandia; Karelia Suite; Kuolema: Valse triste; Nightride
and Sunrise; The Oceanides; Tapiola
*** RCA 09026 68770-2. LSO, C. Davis

The two performances of special interest here are *Night Ride and Sunrise* and *The Oceanides*, neither of which Sir Colin Davis has recorded before. *The Oceanides* holds up alongside the celebrated Beecham in atmosphere and poetic feeling, and *Night Ride and Sunrise*, with its difficult transition from the trochaic ride to the stillness and grandeur of sunrise, is splendidly realized. Sir Colin's account of *Tapiola* is even more impressive and terrifying than his earlier Boston version. Very good sound.

**'The World of Sibelius': (i; ii) *Finlandia; Karelia Suite,*
Op. 11; Symphony 3 in C, Op. 52; (i–iii) *Serenade for Violin*
and Orchestra, Op. 69/2; (i; iv) *Valse triste;* (v) *Flickan kon*
*ifran sin älsklings möte; Var det dröm?***
(B) *** Decca (ADD/DDD) 473 144-2. (i) Ashkenazy; (ii)
  Philh. O; (iii) Belkin; (iv) Boston SO; (v) Nilsson, V. Op. O,
  Bokstedt

Ashkenazy's superb Sibelius recordings are self-recommending, and it is good that Decca chose a less-played symphony rather than the ever-popular No. 2 for their 'World of Sibelius' CD. Ashkenazy's is a volatile reading, in many ways a very Russian view of Sibelius, with the conductor finding a clear affinity with Tchaikovsky. At the very opening, the quick, flexible treatment of the repeated crotchet motif is urgent, not weighty or ominous as it can be. Ashkenazy's control of tension and atmosphere makes for the illusion of a live performance in the building of each climax, and the rich recording adds powerfully to that impression. Ashkenazy's vibrant accounts of the popular orchestral works are superbly played in similarly brilliant sound. With Belkin's excellent account of the hauntingly charming *Serenade*, and some magnificent singing from Birgit Nilsson, this CD is worth considering if the repertoire appeals.

Finlandia; Kuolema: Valse triste; Legend: The Swan of Tuonela, Op. 22/2

*** DG 439 010-2. BPO, Karajan – GRIEG: *Holberg Suite*, etc. ***

Coupled with Grieg, this is Karajan at his very finest in the early 1980s, and the remastered digital recording is impressively real and present, particularly in the languorous *Valse triste* and in *The Swan*, Karajan's third and final account on record, powerful in its brooding atmosphere. There is a touch of brashness in the brass in *Finlandia*, but generally this Berlin–Karajan partnership has never been surpassed.

Finlandia, Op. 26; Kuolema, Op. 44: Valse triste. Legend: The Swan of Tuonela, Op. 22/2; Pelléas et Mélisande: Suite, Op. 46; Tapiola, Op. 112

☞ (B) *** DG (ADD/DDD) 2-CD 474 269-2 (2). BPO, Karajan – GRIEG: *Holberg Suite*, etc. ***

For the reissue of their 'Karajan Collection' DG have added the digital *Pelléas et Mélisande Suite* and the hardly less outstanding mid-1960s *Tapiola*. Karajan's *Pelléas* can compare with the classic Beecham version. Indeed, in certain movements, *By the spring in the park* and the *Pastorale*, it not only matches Sir Thomas but almost surpasses him. The *Pastorale* is altogether magical and there is plenty of mystery in the third movement, *At the seashore*, omitted by Beecham. The recording here is in the demonstration bracket and this bargain coupling with Grieg cannot be recommended too highly.

Finlandia; Legend: The Swan of Tuonela; The Oceanides; Pohjola's Daughter, Op. 49; Tapiola

(M) **(*) Chan. 6508. RSNO, Gibson

The Oceanides is particularly successful and, if Karajan finds even greater intensity in *Tapiola*, Gibson's account certainly captures the icy desolation of the northern forests. He is at his most persuasive in an elusive piece like *The Dryad*, although *En Saga* is also evocative, showing an impressive overall grasp. The RSNO are on peak form.

(i) Six Humoresques, Opp. 87 & 89; 2 Serenades, Op. 69; 2 Serious Melodies, Op. 79; Ballet Scene (1891); Overture in E (1891)

*** BIS CD 472. (i) Kang, Gothenburg SO, Järvi

The *Humoresques* are among Sibelius's most inspired smaller pieces. They are poignant as well as virtuosic and have a lightness of touch, a freshness and a sparkle. The two *Serenades* have great poetic feeling and a keen Nordic melancholy. They are wonderfully played by this distinguished Korean artist, who is beautifully accompanied. The two orchestral works are juvenilia, which predate the *Kullervo Symphony*. There are some characteristic touches, but Sibelius himself did not think well enough of them to permit their publication. All the violin pieces, however, are to be treasured, and the recording is top class.

Karelia suite: Intermezzo; Alla marcia; Finlandia; The Oceanides; Scènes historiques: Suite 1; Tapiola; (i) Kullervo Symphony, Op. 7; (ii) Serenades 1–2, Op. 69a/b

(B) *** EMI double forte (ADD) 5 74200-2 (2). Bournemouth SO, Berglund; (i) Soloists, Helsinki University Male Voice Ch., (ii) Haendel

This was the first recording of *Kullervo*, the work with which Sibelius made his breakthrough in Finland in 1892 and which was not heard again until 1958, the year after his death. Berglund's account, recorded in 1971, comes up surprisingly well. The orchestral playing is full of enthusiasm and is well disciplined, and this re-issue (its first CD transfer) comes with a well-filled and desirable programme. Both *Tapiola* and *The Oceanides* are eminently competitive, and the two *Serenades* have the benefit of Ida Haendel, whose playing has elegance and poetry. The *Serenades* were composed in 1913 and 1914, when Sibelius was toying with the idea of a second violin concerto. Good transfers, with the chorus fractionally more forward than on the original LP; the cellos and basses are cleaner and better focused but less weighty. Those wanting a bargain *Kullervo* need have no misgivings, however, particularly in view of the excellence of the rest of the programme.

King Christian II (suite); Pelléas et Mélisande (suite), Op. 46; Swanwhite (suite: excerpts), Op. 54

*** Chan. 9158. Iceland SO, Sakari

The *King Christian II* music is a winner and full of the most musical touches. It also includes a previously unrecorded *Minuet* and the *Fool's Song*, excellently sung by Sauli Tiilikainen. Although the *Pelléas et Mélisande* suite does not displace either Beecham or Karajan, it makes a useful alternative to either – and that is praise indeed! It has plenty of atmosphere and, though tempi are on the slow side, there is always plenty of inner life. The *Swanwhite* (five movements only) is attentive to refinements of phrasing and dynamics and at the same time free from the slightest trace of narcissism. Beautifully natural recording, warm and well balanced.

Four Legends from the Kalevela (Lemminkäinen suite), Op. 22. Lemminkäinen and the Maidens of Saari; Lemminkäinen's Homeward Journey (1896 versions); Second ending of Lemminkäinen's Homeward Journey (1897 version); Excerpt from Lemminkäinen in Tuonela (1896 version)

☞ *** BIS Dig. CD 1015. Lahti SO, Vänskä

As is well known, the *Four Legends* that make up the *Lemminkäinen suite* (1895–6) were revised twice – in 1897 and then in 1900 – and, in the case of *Lemminkäinen and the Maidens of Saari* and *Lemminkäinen in Tuonela*, retouched for publication in 1939. BIS continues its exploration of the first version of Sibelius's orchestral scores by bringing us the 1896 version of the former and also the first, much longer score of *Lemminkäinen's Homeward Journey*. This is very nearly twice as long as the definitive version and considerably less effective. The first *Legend* underwent a particularly fascinating transformation. The disc also offers the alternative 1897 ending of *Lemminkäinen's Homeward Journey* and an excerpt from *Lemminkäinen in Tuonela*, which Sibelius excised. The finished work is played in exemplary fashion by Osmo Vänskä and his Lahti Orchestra and superbly recorded. *The Swan of Tuonela* is highly evocative and way up there among the best.

Four Legends, Op. 22
*** BIS CD 294. Gothenburg SO, Neeme Järvi

Four Legends; The Bard; (i) Luonnotar
(M) *** Chan. (ADD) 6586. SNO, Gibson, (i) with Bryn-Johnson

Four Legends, Op. 22; En Saga
*** Ondine 953-2. Swedish RSO, Franck

Four Legends; Finlandia; Karelia Suite
(BB) **(*) Naxos 8.554265. Iceland SO, Sakari

4 Legends, Op. 22; Night Ride and Sunrise, Op. 55
(M) **(*) Warner Elatus 2564 60621-2. Toronto SO, Saraste

Four Legends; Tapiola
☉━ *** Ondine ODE 852-2. Helsinki PO, Segerstam

Although Segerstam perversely ignores Sibelius's instructions about the order of the Legends (so, for that matter, did Salonen), this is of little moment, given the fact that collectors can easily reprogramme the disc. The performances of both the Legends and Tapiola are first class and are infinitely preferable to the symphony cycle Segerstam recorded in Copenhagen for Chandos. This is now a first recommendation for the Legends, while Tapiola is one of the best since Karajan.

Neeme Järvi has the advantage of fine, modern digital sound and a wonderfully truthful balance. He gives a passionate and atmospheric reading of the first Legend, and his account of The Swan of Tuonela is altogether magical, one of the best in the catalogue. He takes a broader view of Lemminkäinen in Tuonela than many of his rivals and builds up an appropriately black and powerful atmosphere. The disappointment is Lemminkäinen's Homeward Journey, which lacks the possessed, manic quality of Beecham's very first record, which sounded as if a thousand demons were in pursuit.

Mikko Franck is a thoughtful interpreter and is obviously steeped in the atmosphere of this score and fresh in his musical responses. He is expansive in the bigger movements, too much so in Lemminkäinen in Tuonela, which does not wholly sustain tension. He does not match Beecham's hell-for-leather account of Lemminkäinen's Homeward Journey, but he is impressive nonetheless. His account of En Saga has a strong narrative feel and plenty of atmosphere. The Swedish Radio Orchestra play well for him, and there is plenty of personality. Recommended.

Gibson comes at mid-price and offers sensitive performances of The Bard and Luonnotar, where the soprano voice is made to seem like another orchestral instrument. The Scottish orchestra play freshly and with much commitment. The Swan of Tuonela has a darkly brooding primeval quality, and there is an electric degree of tension in the third piece, Lemminkäinen in Tuonela. The two outer Legends have ardent rhythmic feeling, and altogether this is highly successful. The recorded sound is excellent.

Petri Sakari's account of the Legends with the Iceland orchestra has a lot going for it and is very decently recorded. Why he reverses the order of the middle two is something of a mystery. The Karelia Suite and Finlandia are well played, and most CD machines can reprogramme the order of the Legends. On the whole, good value for money but not a first choice.

Saraste re-recorded the Four Legends in 1998, only six years after his set with the Finnish Radio Orchestra for RCA, and it is reasonable to wonder whether we need his views on this wonderful score again so soon! However, while his 1992 recording was very good, it must be admitted that this Canadian account is better in both the quality of the orchestral playing and the recorded sound. Like Sakari on Naxos, Saraste reverses the order of the two central movements and those who wish to follow Sibelius's wishes have to programme their machines accordingly (tracks 1, 3, 2, 4). No lack of atmosphere all the same, particularly in Lemminkäinen in Tuonela, and no want of passion, even if Saraste does not match the urgent momentum and level of excitement in Lemminkäinen's Homeward Journey that Beecham, Segerstam or Vänskä achieve, and Night Rise and Sunset sounds pedestrian by the side of Sir Colin Davis.

The Oceanides; Night Ride and Sunrise; The Tempest (Suites 1 & 2)
**(*) Ondine ODE 914-2. Helsinki PO, Segerstam

This is Segerstam's second recording of the first suite from The Tempest music; his earlier version on Chandos came as a fill-up to the Fourth Symphony. The newcomer is very fine indeed, full of atmosphere and power and free from expressive exaggeration. The Oceanides is another matter: a generally rushed and breathless main section is preceded by an insufferably slow opening. Night Ride and Sunrise is much finer: it is difficult to bring off well, but Segerstam paces it convincingly. State-of-the-art recording.

Rakastava (suite), Op. 14; Scènes historiques, Opp. 25, 66; Valse lyrique, Op. 96/1
☉━ (M) *** Chan. 6591. RSNO, Gibson

Derived from music for a patriotic pageant, the first set of Scènes historiques are vintage Sibelius. In the Love Song Gibson strikes the right blend of depth and reticence, while elsewhere he conveys a fine sense of controlled power. Convincing and eloquent performances that have a natural feeling for the music. Gibson's Rakastava is beautifully unforced and natural, save for the last movement, which is a shade too slow. The Valse lyrique is not good Sibelius, but everything else certainly is. Gibson plays this repertoire with real commitment, and the recorded sound is excellent, with the orchestral layout, slightly distanced, most believable. At mid-price this is a specially desirable collection.

Scaramouche, Op. 71; The Language of the Birds: Wedding March
*** BIS CD 502. Gothenburg SO, Järvi

Scaramouche, Sibelius's only ballet, is scored for relatively small forces, including piano (not unlike Strauss's music for Le Bourgeois Gentilhomme), and at its best it reminds one of the luminous colourings of the Humoresques of five years later. A wistful, gentle and haunting score, often inspired though slightly let down by its uneventful second act. Sibelius did not think highly enough of the Wedding March to Adolf Paul's play, The Language of the Birds, to give it an opus number, but it is in fact quite an attractive miniature. The playing of the Gothenburg orchestra under Neeme Järvi is altogether excellent and so, too, is the BIS recording.

SYMPHONIES

(i) Symphonies 1 in E min., Op. 39; 2 in D, Op. 43; 5 in E flat, Op. 82; 7 in C, Op. 105
(N) (M) (*) DG 474 936-2 (3). VPO, Bernstein — ELGAR: Enigma Variations *(*); BRITTEN: 4 Sea Interludes *

Symphonies 1–7; (i) Kullervo. En Saga; Rakastava

☞– (B) *** RCA 74321 54034-2 (5). LSO, C. Davis; (i) with Martinpelto, Frederiksson, L. Symphony Ch.

Symphonies 1–7; (i) Kullervo. The Bard, Op. 22; Finlandia, Op. 26; Karelia Suite, Op. 11; Kuolema: Valse triste. 4 Legends, Op. 22; Night Ride and Sunrise, Op. 55; The Oceanides, Op. 73; Pohjola's Daughter, Op. 49; Rakastava Tapiola, Op. 112

☞– (B) *** RCA 82876 55706-2 (7). LSO, C. Davis; (i) with Martinpelto, Frederiksson, LSO Ch.

Symphonies 1–7

(M) **(*) Chan. 6559 (3). SNO, Gibson

(M) (**) Finlandia mono 3984-22713-2 (3). Stockholm PO, Ehrling

Symphonies 1 in E min., Op. 39; 2 in D, Op. 43; 4 in A min., Op. 63; 5 in E flat, Op. 82

(B) *** Ph. Duo (ADD) 446 157-2 (2). Boston SO, C. Davis

Symphonies 3 in C, Op. 52; 6 in D min., Op. 104; 7 in C, Op. 105; (i) Violin Concerto. Finlandia; Legend: The Swan of Tuonela; Tapiola

(B) *** Ph. Duo (ADD) 446 160-2 (2). (i) Accardo; Boston SO, Davis

Symphonies 1, 2 & 4; Finlandia; Karelia Suite

(B) *** Double Decca 455 402-2 (2). Philh. O, Ashkenazy

Symphonies 3, 5, 6 & 7; En Saga; Tapiola

(B) *** Double Decca 455 405-2 (2). Philh. O, Ashkenazy

Symphonies 1–7; Finlandia; Karelia Suite, Op. 11; Kuolema: Valse triste; Legends: The Swan of Tuonela; Lemminkäinen's Return; Pelléas et Mélisande: Suite; Pohjola's Daughter; Rakastava; Romance for Strings in C, Op. 42; Scènes historiques: All'overtura; The Hunt; Scena

(M) **(*) EMI (ADD) 5 67299-2 (5). Hallé O, Barbirolli

(i) Symphonies 1–7; (ii) Night Ride and Sunrise; (i) The Oceanides; Scene with Cranes

(M) **(*) EMI (ADD) 7 64118-2 (4). (i) CBSO, (ii) Philh. O, Rattle

Symphonies 1–7; Night Ride and Sunrise, Op. 55; Pelléas et Mélisande: Suite, Op. 46; Pohjola's Daughter, Op. 49

(M) (***) Beulah mono 1-4PD 8 (4). LSO, Collins

Sir Colin Davis's RCA set of the *Symphonies* has now been reissued together with his other major LSO recordings of the principal orchestral works on 7 CDs. The excellence of the LSO playing is matched by the consistently fine RCA recordings, made in the Blackheath Concert Halls, Watford Town Hall or Walthamstow, between 1992 and 2000. It is a totally authoritative survey, and nearly all the symphonic poems are of a similar calibre, with the magical account of *The Bard, Night Ride and Sunrise, The Oceanides* and a riveting *Tapiola* standing out. The alternative set (on 5 discs) includes only *Kullervo, En Saga* and *Rakastava*. One of these collections should be at the centre of any representative Sibelius collection.

Otherwise Ashkenazy's Sibelius cycle takes precedence. A rich and strong, consistently enjoyable cycle. Ashkenazy by temperament brings out the expressive warmth, colour and drama of the composer rather than his Scandinavian chill, reflecting perhaps his Slavonic background. The recordings – made between 1979 and 1984, either at Walthamstow or in the Kingsway Hall – are full and rich as well as brilliant, most of

them still of demonstration quality. For those wanting a complete set, they make a most attractive alternative recommendation, although the newest cycle from Sir Colin Davis and the LSO on RCA takes pride of place.

Sir Colin Davis's earlier Boston set of the symphonies, recorded during the second half of the 1970s, is not only very economical but three tone-poems and an estimable account of the *Violin Concerto* are thrown in for good measure. Indeed Accardo's performance of the latter is very high on the recommended list. *Tapiola*, too, is atmospheric and superbly played. Nos. 1, 2, 5 and 7 were the first to be recorded (in 1975–6). The idiomatic playing Davis secures from the Boston orchestra is immediately apparent. Tempi are well judged and there is a genuine sense of commitment and power, though the recording is not quite as fine as Ashkenazy's on Decca. However, the remastering has undoubtedly improved its overall depth. Davis's Philips accounts of the *Third, Fourth* and *Sixth Symphonies* are among the best on disc and are excellently recorded. In the *Third* Davis judges the tempi in all three movements to perfection; no conductor has captured the elusive spirit of the slow movement or the power of the finale more effectively. The *Fourth* is arguably the finest of the cycle; there is a powerful sense of mystery, and the slow movement in particular conveys the feeling of communication with nature that lies at the heart of its inspiration. The *Fifth* is no match for Karajan, the *Seventh* is not as fine as with Rattle. The *Sixth* is altogether more impressive and much more vivid as sound.

Barbirolli favoured spacious tempi, but almost always held the listener in his spell. This certainly applies to the present account of the *First Symphony*, which has a freshness and ardour that are very appealing. It is undoubtedly gripping, even if, compared with his enthusiastic account of the *Second*, it is just a little lacking in panache. All seven symphonies were recorded in the Kingsway Hall. The first two date from 1966, but in No. 1 in the present remastering string fortissimos are made fierce. No. 2 is in every way more successful. The Hallé play particularly well and give a warm-hearted account, romantic in approach. In No. 3, tempi are well judged, but the inner tension is less well maintained than in No. 2. Even so, there is some very fine wind-playing in the *Andante* and the transition to the finale is very convincingly managed. In Barbirolli's account of No. 4 the Hallé strings produce an admirably chilling quality, far removed from the well-nourished string sound in Karajan's Berlin Philharmonic versions. Unfortunately, things come adrift in the development of the first movement where the wind and strings are out of step for quite a few bars. The *Fifth*, like the *Second*, is one of the finest of the series and has great breadth and nobility. Sir John draws playing of high quality from the orchestra, who are on top form throughout. The *Seventh* makes a fine culmination for the cycle, bringing a feeling of power and a sense of inevitability which increases as the work progresses. The build-up to its climax is well paced. The recording is very fine.

Barbirolli included the *Sixth Symphony* in the last concert he conducted in Manchester on 3 May 1970, and he recorded it three weeks later, only two months before he died. It is easy to sense an elegiac feeling in the performance, which remains most compelling, especially in the beautiful closing passage for the strings, given the benefit of radiant sound.

The shorter orchestral works were recorded at Abbey Road during the same period and the charismatic 1966 collection was for some years one of Barbirolli's most successful discs. The suite from *Pelléas et Mélisande* is powerfully atmospheric, as is *The Swan of Tuonela*, but here Sir John's rather endearing vocalizations are clearly audible. *Pohjola's Daughter* is very strongly characterized, as are the *Scènes historiques*. *Rakastava*, and especially the touching *Romance for Strings*, are much rarer, originally having a short catalogue life. They are very well played and recorded. All in all, this is a cherishable box, attractively illustrated with some of the original LP sleeve pictures.

Simon Rattle's performances with the City of Birmingham Symphony Orchestra are available as a four-CD boxed set but no longer as individual discs. The best advice is probably to opt for his *Seventh*, coupled with the *Fifth* and the highly atmospheric *Scene with Cranes* (see below). As a set the box is worth considering, but it would not be first choice.

Sir Alexander Gibson's Sibelius cycle is impressive, both musically and from an engineering point of view; there are no weak spots anywhere. (Indeed, one respected critic chose Gibson's version of No. 1 as his first choice on a BBC 'Record Review' some years ago.) The performances are eminently sane, sound and reliable, and no one investing in the set is likely to be at all disappointed. Taken individually, none would be an absolute first choice.

Sibelians should also note that Anthony Collins's highly distinguished accounts of the symphonies (with the fill-ups) make a four-disc set in a slip-case at a saving on the price of the individual records.

On Finlandia comes the very first survey of the symphonies, which dates from 1952–3 and was conducted by Sixten Ehrling. Their handsome sleeves are reproduced here. (Incidentally, the original LPs speak of the 'Stockholm Radio Symphony Orchestra'.) Sibelius himself is said to have heard and liked them. Ehrling is an admirably sound interpreter. In the first two symphonies the playing has more temperament than polish. In the *Third*, Ehrling – giving the symphony its first recording since the pioneering Kajanus set – is more measured than Collins, who set very brisk tempi in both the first and second movements. The *Fourth* is impressively dark, and in the *Fifth* the transition between the body of the first movement and its Scherzo section is well negotiated. Not a real challenge to Collins, but though it lacks finesse and has some vulnerable wind intonation, it provides an interesting insight into how these symphonies sounded at the time.

With the best will in the world, Bernstein's digital Sibelius recordings with the VPO are hardly among his best recordings – not a patch on his earlier, CBS/Sony accounts. The first movement of the *First* is so frustratingly pulled about and mannered it puts you off almost straight away, despite some beautiful sounds coming from the orchestra. The *Second* is insupportably inflated, while his tendency to linger over cadential phrases undermines the music's sense of impetus. He dwells excessively on incidental moments of splendour and grandeur, and he pulls the slow movement completely out of shape. If the *Fifth* is not as idiosyncratic as that, it is terribly slow: it lacks both power and atmosphere, and so too does the *Seventh*, which is curiously deficient in electricity. There are equally perverse Elgar and Britten couplings to match.

Symphonies (i) 1–3; (ii) 4–7
(M) **(*) DG Trio ADD 474 353-2 (3). (i) Helsinki R. O or
(No. 2) BPO, Okko Kamu; (ii) BPO, Karajan

As Karajan did not record a complete Sibelius cycle in the 1960s for DG, that company has created the present Trio by ingeniously filling in the missing early works with performances from Okko Kamu recorded in the early 1970s. Alas, the resulting collection is far from ideal, for the account of No. 1 rarely rises above the routine, and in No. 2 Kamu indulges in some impulsive touches – the odd speed-up or slow-down. These are not destructive, and the Berlin Philharmonic provides highly polished and superbly refined playing. The pick of Kamu's three performances is undoubtely the *Third*, which still has strong claims to be considered among the finest on record. Tempi are well judged and the atmosphere is thoroughly authentic, particularly in the slow movement, whose character seems to have eluded so many conductors. The recordings, whether made in Berlin or Helsinki, are excellent and most musically balanced.

When one turns to the last four symphonies, one moves into an inspired Sibelian world, with Karajan securing playing of astonishing tonal beauty and virtuosity from the Berlin Philharmonic and performances of great intensity and power. The most obvious way to acquire them is with the separate DG, mid-priced couplings of Nos. 4 and 7 (given a ✹ below) and 5 and 6.

Symphonies 1–3; 5; *Belshazzar's Feast* (incidental music); *Karelia Suite; Pohjola's Daughter; Tapiola*
(M) (***) Finlandia mono 4509 95882-2 (3). LSO, Kajanus

When the Finnish government sponsored recordings of the first two symphonies in 1930, Sibelius insisted on having Kajanus as the most authentic interpreter. These performances were all made in 1930 and 1932 and sound amazingly good for the period. The celebrated storm in *Tapiola*, taken at a much slower and more effective tempo than is now usual, still has the power to terrify, despite the inevitable sonic limitations, and no conductor has ever given a more spell-binding and atmospheric account of the suite from *Belshazzar's Feast*. The broader, more leisurely view Kajanus takes of the *Third Symphony* comes as a refreshing corrective to the later, more hurried account by Anthony Collins. No performer, save Beecham and Karajan, came closer to Sibelius's intentions. Essential listening for all Sibelians.

Symphonies 1–4
(B) *** EMI double forte 5 68643-2 (2). Helsinki PO,
Berglund

Berglund's rugged, sober but powerful readings bring a good feeling for the architecture of the music and no want of atmosphere. Both the playing and the interpretation of the *First* are involving in their breadth and concentration (even if in the first movement the climactic timpani echo of the main theme does not come through). In the *Second*, Berglund is scrupulously faithful to the letter of the score as well as to its spirit, although the Scherzo and finale are of a lower voltage than in the finest versions. The Helsinki Philharmonic respond with no mean virtuosity and panache, but the last degree of intensity eludes them. In the *Third*, Berglund adopts sensible tempi throughout and shapes all three movements well; he evokes a haunting feeling of tranquillity in the withdrawn middle section of the slow movement, a passage where Sibelius seems to be listening to quiet voices from another planet. This was Berglund's third account of the *Fourth* and it is a performance of considerable stature: it has a stark grandeur that resonates in the mind. There is not a great deal of *vivace* in the second movement but Berglund's finale is superb, even if some may find the closing bars not sufficiently cold and bleak. The digital recording throughout the set is excellent.

Symphonies 1 in E min.; 3 in C, Op. 52

(***) Testament mono SBT 1049. Philh. O, Kletzki

(BB) *** Naxos 8.554102. Iceland SO, Sakari

Symphonies 1; 3; Finlandia, Op. 26

**(*) Warner 0927 43500-2. CBSO, Oramo

Kletzki is tauter than the traditional Kajanus school yet far less headlong (or headstrong) than Collins. In both scores he and the Philharmonia Orchestra strike the right balance between the romantic legacy of the nineteenth century and the more severe climate of the twentieth. The recordings are beautifully balanced and have great warmth, and they come up splendidly in these transfers.

Sakari Oramo is thoughtful and perceptive, and completely inside the mind of his great countryman. Of the present two symphonies, the *First* is particularly fine, with well-judged tempi and playing that is full of spirit and feeling. The *Third*, too, has a good deal going for it, though in Oramo's hands the first movement is more allegro than moderato. Momentum is well sustained, however, without the result being as headlong as in Anthony Collins's pioneering LP. The slow movement, though only a few seconds longer than Kajanus, feels slower, and although the atmosphere is finely conveyed, Oramo allows the tension to sag. The wind are not as impeccably tuned and blended as they might be, and in the finale the balance gives the horns rather too much prominence, and they sound blustery. But there are many sensitive touches.

Petri Sakari proves a sound and straightforward interpreter. The playing of the Iceland orchestra in both symphonies is spirited and vital, even if they do not command the virtuosity and polish of the major international ensembles. The *Third Symphony* is very well paced indeed and the playing has conviction. The recording, too, is natural and vivid, with a good balance between the various sections of the orchestra. In any event, good value for money.

Symphonies 1; 4 in A min., Op. 63

*** BIS BIS CD 861. Lahti SO, Vänskä

In the *First Symphony* the Finnish conductor, Vänskä, secures a marvellously controlled and splendidly executed performance from his dedicated players. There is that sense of inevitability and of an irresistible forward movement throughout, though never at the expense of incidental beauty. The Scherzo is among the most exciting on disc, very fast and full of controlled abandon. The *Fourth Symphony* receives a perceptive and deeply intelligent reading. The Lahti orchestra play with keen concentration and intensity and though tempi are very slow (perhaps too much so in the case of the slow movement), the performance is marvellously sustained. The recording is natural and eminently well balanced. A distinguished issue.

Symphonies 1; 4; 5; 6; Karelia Suite

(B) *** EMI double forte (ADD) 5 74858-2 (2). Berlin PO, Karajan

In the *First Symphony*, Karajan, a great Tchaikovsky interpreter, identifies with the work's inheritance. But there is a sense of grandeur and vision here, and the opulence and virtuosity of the Berliners helps to project the heroic dimensions of Karajan's performance. The early digital recording (1981) is not top-drawer; the bass is over-weighted, but the full upper strings sing out gloriously, with the richest amplitude in the finale, which has an electrifying climax and the brass is comparably rich and resonant.

In Karajan's second recording of the *Fourth* (1976), he courts controversy in his spacious tempi, especially in the first and third movements – much slower than his earlier DG version – but it is all highly atmospheric. He conveys eloquently the haunting quality of the landscape in the third movement, and the first undoubtedly has great mystery and power. Again, in the *Fifth*, recorded the same year, the opening movement is broader than in his earlier DG account, achieving a remarkable sense of strength and majesty. The transition to the Scherzo is slightly more abrupt than in the 1965 recording, and indeed tempi in the first half of the work are generally rather more extreme in this version. Both the slow movement and finale are glorious, demonstrating real vision, and the recording is excellent.

The 1980 recording of the *Sixth* brings to life the other-worldly qualities of this score, in particular the long white nights of the northern summer and their 'fragile melancholy', conjured by the slow movement (or, for that matter, the opening polyphony). While this is a spacious account (though actually marginally quicker than his 1967 DG performance), we are always aware of the sense of forward movement. In short, this is Karajan at his finest, and this inexpensive double forte reissue can be very strongly recommended, especially with a strong, weighty performance of the *Karelia Suite* included too.

Symphonies 1; 7; Karelia Overture

(***) Beulah mono IPD 8. LSO, Collins

There are those who (justly) count Anthony Collins's magnificent account of the *First Symphony* of 1952, with its haunting, otherworldly opening clarinet solo, as the finest ever put on disc, for the tension throughout the performance is held at the highest level. The closely integrated *Seventh* is also well understood by Collins, and once again the closing moments of the symphony are drawn together very impressively. The Decca recording remains remarkably vivid and, if the fortissimos are more one-dimensional than we expect today and the massed violins could ideally be fuller, the brass certainly makes a fine impact. The comparatively rare *Karelia Overture*, which was recorded later (1955), makes a brief bonus.

Symphony 2 in D, Op. 43

(N) (***) BBC mono BBCL 4154-2. BBC SO, Beecham – DVORAK: *Symphony 8* (***)

(***) BBC mono BBCL 4115-2. BBC SO, Stokowski (with BEETHOVEN: *Overture Egmont* ***) – TCHAIKOVSKY: *Sleeping Beauty: Suite* (***)

Symphony 2; Finlandia

(N) (M) * Telarc CD 80095. Cleveland O, Levi

Symphony 2; Finlandia; Legends: Lemminkäinen's Return; The Swan of Tuonela; Pohjola's Daughter

(BB) (**) Naxos mono 8.110810. NBC SO, Toscanini

Symphony 2; Romance in C

*** BIS CD 252. Gothenburg SO, Järvi

Symphony 2; The Tempest Suite 1, Op. 109/2

(BB) **(*) Naxos 8.554266. Iceland SO, Sakari

Sir Thomas Beecham's famous broadcast account of the *Second Symphony* comes from a BBC Symphony concert on the occasion of the composer's 89th birthday on 8 December 1954 and relayed to Finland. The knowledge that Sibelius was listening lent an added frisson to the occasion, for the playing is very intent and exciting. The microphones picked up various whoops and other vocal exhortations from Sir Thomas, and the playing is of pretty high voltage. He conducted this work more than 40 times between the 1930s and 1950s, but his only commercial recording in 1946 was with his newly formed Royal Philharmonic Orchestra and has not yet been transferred to CD. The playing may be more cultured, but this has an electricity and immediacy of impact that are quite special. The transfer does not reproduce the earlier HMV ALP issue but is a new one taken from the original tapes.

Järvi is very brisk in the opening *Allegretto*: this Gothenburg version has more sinew and fire than its rivals, and the orchestral playing is more responsive and disciplined than that of the SNO on Chandos (see below). Throughout, Järvi has an unerring sense of purpose and direction and the BIS performance is concentrated in feeling and thoroughly convincing. The *Romance for Strings* is attractively done.

Surprisingly, Stokowski's 1964 Sibelius *Second* is a mono recording, but the warmth of the Royal Albert Hall acoustic adds ambience and sonority so that one does not miss the stereo too much (though the bronchial afflictions of the audience are a deterrent). It is a widely contrasted reading, using constantly flexible tempi as only Stokowski can, without loss of tension. He thought of the symphony as 'free and rhapsodic' but kept the horizon always in view. The *Andante* generates a grave melancholy towards the close, then the eruption of energy (though not of volume) at the *vivacissimo* makes a dynamic contrast. The great tune of the finale is superbly prepared, and Stokowski builds steadily towards the expansive final peroration (often slowing down on the way without the slightest loss of concentration). A remarkable if unpredictable reading of a masterly symphony (which the conductor very unfashionably thought 'more inspired than the Seventh').

Petri Sakari's Sibelius is natural and unaffected in the *Second Symphony*. When Sibelius himself conducted it in 1916 we know he was brisker even than Kajanus, whose performance took a little over 39 minutes, six less than Sakari's. Sakari scores points with his fine musicianship and by not playing to the gallery, but his first movement really could have had a little more sense of thrust. Throughout the piece there is a certain want of the fire and the high voltage one needs in this most 'public' of the Sibelius symphonies. The recording is more recessed in the symphony than in *The Tempest*, which has greater presence and a more forward balance. Sakari gets a splendidly concentrated atmosphere and has a special feeling for the otherworldly qualities of *The Oak Tree* and the *Berceuse*, which come off beautifully. This visionary score is brought to life most imaginatively, and Sakari's is as good an account as any among recent recordings.

In December 1940, at the time of the Russian invasion of Finland, Toscanini conducted these Sibelius performances, tautly controlled but emotional too, reflecting the feelings of the time. The first movement of the symphony is unusually fast, a true allegro, and speeds are never leisurely, yet more than was usual for him. Toscanini allows expressive freedom to his orchestral soloists, notably the cor anglais in the *Swan of Tuonela*. Dry, limited sound, but transferred better than with some in this series.

Yoel Levi's is a plainspun reading, essentially spacious, though with moments when he forces the pace. The Cleveland Orchestra play well for him, but the electricity sparks only fitfully, and overall the result fails to grip the listener. *Finlandia* too is unimpressive, though the characteristically rich Telarc sound gives a fine body and bloom to strings and brass alike.

Symphonies 2; 3 in C, Op. 52
**(*) BIS CD 862. Lahti SO, Vänskä

Osmo Vänskä's accounts of the *Second* and *Third Symphonies* are as thought-provoking as his remarkable pairing of Nos. 1 and 4, though they are not quite deserving of the same star rating. The dynamic markings are sometimes a little too extreme, the second theme of the slow movement marked *pianopianissimo* is almost whispered rather than played, and to readers playing the disc at less than full-room volume, it will be barely audible. It is just a shade self-conscious. Everything is carefully thought out, and the general effect is impressive. The *Third Symphony* is generally well paced and has the right atmosphere. Those following the series will not be disappointed. Very wide-ranging but expertly balanced sound.

Symphonies 2; 5 in E flat, Op. 82
(M) *** Chan. (ADD) 6556. SNO, Gibson

(N) (BB) * EMI HMV 5 86766-2. (i) BPO, Karajan; (ii) Philh. O, Rattle

(N) (M) **(*) EMI (ADD) 4 76882-2. Philh. O, Karajan

The *Second* is among the best of Gibson's cycle and scores highly, thanks to the impressive clarity, fullness and impact of the 1982 digital recording. Gibson's reading is honest and straightforward, free of bombast in the finale. Tempi are well judged: the first movement is neither too taut nor too relaxed – it is well shaped and feels right. Overall this is most satisfying, as is the *Fifth*, which has similar virtues. At no time is there any attempt to interpose the personality of the interpreter, and the finale has genuine weight and power.

Karajan's 1981 digital version of the *Second Symphony* with the Berlin Philharmonic is marginally more spacious than his earlier, Philharmonia version. Tempi for all four movements are fractionally broader; nevertheless, the first movement is still a genuine *Allegro* – basically in the tradition of Kajanus, whose pioneering (1930) set was probably closer to Sibelius's intentions than most others. Throughout all four movements there is splendour and nobility – and some glorious sounds from the Berlin brass. The oboe theme in the Trio section of the Scherzo is moulded most expressively, but not all listeners will warm to the grand and measured approach to the finale, though there is no lack of lyrical fervour. It is not as beautifully recorded as, say, Ashkenazy's Decca, but is undoubtedly a performance of stature.

Simon Rattle's prize-winning account of the *Fifth Symphony* with the Philharmonia makes an appropriate coupling. Everything about it feels right: the control of pace and texture, and the balance of energy and repose. The development of the first movement has a compelling sense of mystery and the transition to the Scherzo section is very beautifully judged. The Philharmonia Orchestra play splendidly and the EMI recording is very good indeed. Altogether this budget reissue is one of the most remarkable bargains in the Sibelius discography.

Karajan's Philharmonia coupling, produced by Walter Legge and recorded in the Kingsway Hall in 1960, makes a comparison coupling, for in spite of the superb playing from the Philharmonia (especially the strings), the problem of the earlier interpretations is one of concentration in the earlier movements. While his long-drawn paragraphs, dramatic and solemn, strong and personal, are particularly suitable for Sibelius's idiom, at times the concentration slips. Even so, he brings off the slower-than-usual tempo for the finale of the *Second* because of the sheer intensity of the orchestral response. The *Fifth Symphony*, too, has a superbly graduated finale: the first appearance of the swinging horn tune is a glorious moment. Excellent sound, well transferred; not a first choice for either symphony, but a reissue not to be missed by admirers of this conductor.

Symphonies 2; 6 in D min., Op. 104
⊕–⊤ *** RCA 09026 68218-2. LSO, C. Davis
(***) Beulah mono 2PD 8. LSO, Collins

The *Sixth* is a work for which Colin Davis has always shown a special affinity and understanding. Sir Colin's earlier recording with the Boston orchestra (see above) was one of the best in that magisterial cycle, and this newcomer is if anything even finer. There is 'nothing of the circus' (to quote the composer's own words apropos the *Fourth Symphony*) in his reading of the *Second* and no playing to the gallery. There is a grandeur and a natural distinction about the playing.

The Decca sound in Collins's 1953 recording of the *Second Symphony* is fuller than in the *First Symphony*. The performance is superb, held together with a tension that carries the listener through from the first bar to the last. The closing pages of the finale, with the timpani again making a telling contribution, are particularly satisfying. The *Sixth* was recorded in 1955, and again the ear notices a further improvement in the sound, particularly at the radiant pastoral opening. The LSO play with much sensitivity, and woodwind and string detail is ever luminous; the conductor's special feeling for Sibelian colour and atmosphere is especially apparent in this work, with the beautiful final coda sustained with moving simplicity. Altogether a lovely performance.

Symphony 3; King Kristian II (suite)
*** BIS CD 228. Gothenburg SO, Järvi

Symphony 3; Night Ride and Sunrise; Pelléas et Mélisande: Suite; Pohjola's Daughter
(***) Beulah mono 3PD8. LSO, Collins

With the *Third Symphony* there is a sense of the epic in Järvi's hands, and it can hold its own with any in the catalogue. In Gothenburg, the slow movement is first class and the leisurely tempo adopted here by the Estonian conductor is just right. Järvi's coupling is the incidental music to *King Khristian II*. This is very beautifully played and recorded.

More outstanding performances from Anthony Collins: only *Night Ride and Sunrise*, although dramatically effective, is slightly less memorable than the other works here. The other reservation concerns the tempo for the second movement of the symphony. Some listeners find it too fast, but the playing has much delicacy of feeling and texture. Collins's approach matches the whole reading, which has a strong momentum overall, and the build-up of tension to the work's climax is satisfyingly controlled. The account of *Pohjola's Daughter* is imaginative and colourful, and the excerpts from the incidental music to *Pelléas et Mélisande* are beautifully played. All the recordings, except *Night Ride* (1955), were made in the Kingsway Hall in 1954 and absolutely no apologies need be made for the mono sound, which in this admirable CD transfer is remarkable for its vivid immediacy and fullness.

Symphonies 3; 5 in E flat, Op. 82
(N) ** Ondine ODE 1035-2. Helsinki PO, Leif Segerstam

Leif Segerstam's 2004 account of the *Third Symphony* is a good deal better than his Chandos recording with the Danish National Radio Orchestra from the early 1990s. This suffered

from the disruptive gear-changes and other idiosyncratic touches. The Helsinki account is much more straightforward, as in fact is the *Fifth*, which is relatively free from expressive exaggeration. Segerstam handles the transition between the main section of the first movement and the scherzo-like second half in masterful fashion, though he inflates the return of the big tune in the finale. The orchestra play well for him, and the recording is finely detailed and decently balanced. But we are spoilt for choice these days, and neither performance challenges existing recommendations.

Symphonies 3; 6; 7
(M) *** Chan. (ADD) 6557. SNO, Gibson

With three symphonies offered, some 74 minutes overall, this is a fine bargain and an excellent way to experience Gibson's special feeling for this composer. The SNO is in very good form. The first movement of the *Third* has real momentum. The *Andantino* is fast, faster than the composer's marking. Such a tempo, while it gives the music-making fine thrust, 'means that Gibson, like Collins before him, loses some of the fantasy of this enigmatic movement. But there is more here to admire than to cavil at. The *Sixth* is impressive too, with plenty of atmosphere and some radiant playing from the Scottish violin section; the *Seventh* has a rather relaxed feeling throughout, but it does not lack warmth and, as in No. 1, Gibson draws the threads together at the close with satisfying breadth.

Symphonies 4 in A min.; 5 in E flat
(***) Beulah mono 4PD 8. LSO, Collins
(BB) *** Naxos 8.554377. Iceland SO, Sakari

Collins's opening to the *Fourth Symphony* with its desolate, Nordic atmosphere is remarkably restrained, yet the work as a whole has extraordinary underlying intensity. With Collins, every phrase breathes naturally and the lightening of mood in the Scherzo, with wind and string playing of great delicacy, is merely an interlude, before the powerfully sombre feeling of the *Il tempo largo* gives birth to a climax of compulsive power. In the finale the flux of mood and feeling that comes with its surge of animation is handled with great subtlety. The performance of the *Fifth Symphony* carries all before it, with the reading moving forward in a single sweep. In both symphonies the LSO is marvellously responsive. The 1954–5 Kingsway Hall mono recordings were among the finest in terms of balance and truthfulness that Decca made throughout the mono LP era, and this CD reproduces superbly.

Had one heard either of Sakari's performances in the concert hall, one would have left feeling very satisfied. Both grip the listener. They are straightforward and unaffected, dedicated and selfless, and free from interpretative point-making. Tempi are for the most part uncommonly well judged, and you feel that Sakari really sees the works as a whole, rather than as a sequence of wonderful episodes. The first movement of the *Fifth* has splendid breadth, and the transition into the Scherzo section is expertly handled. The Iceland orchestra may not be in the luxury league but their responses are keen and alert, and the performances have much greater inner life than, say, Paavo Berglund's set on EMI. Moreover, the sound is truthfully balanced and well detailed.

Symphonies 4 in A min., Op. 63; 5 in E flat; Finlandia
(N) (M) (***) EMI Legend mono 557754. Philh. O, Karajan
(with bonus **DVD**: BERLIOZ: *Symphonie fantastique: 1st movt only ****)

These mono performances with Karajan and the Philharmonia Orchestra are of special interest. Erik Tawaststjerna (in *Sibelius*, Vol. 3) notes that when Sir Thomas Beecham telephoned in response to a number of detailed criticisms that the composer had made of his 78s of the *Fourth Symphony* in 1937, Sibelius was overwhelmed by the flood of English which he only dimly grasped. He hastily agreed the Beecham recording. Walter Legge, however, showed Sibelius's tempo and other suggestions to Karajan before he made this 1954 recording. After hearing it, Sibelius drafted a telegram, speaking of Karajan's 'deep insights and great artistic grip' and went so far as to tell Legge that 'Karajan is the only one who really understands my music'. Certainly these performances are of stature and carry the composer's imprimatur. The *Fourth* was always a favourite of Karajan's, and in some ways this is even finer than the subsequent Berlin accounts: the sound is leaner and more spare and it conveys the sense of desolation at the core of its bleak, wintry terrain. The *Fifth*, recorded in 1952, has great breadth and majesty and is undoubtedly an impressive reading. *Finlandia* is very fine too, full of the right temperament, building up to a truly exciting climax. The bonus DVD of the *Symphonie fantastique* was filmed in 1970 with the Orchestre de Paris, and is compelling enough to make one regret that only the first movement is included (equally impressive is the visual line-up of the orchestra).

Symphonies 4 in A min., Op. 63; 6 in D min., Op. 104
⚫ (M) *** DG (ADD) 476 220-2. BPO, Karajan

Karajan's nearly 40-year-old recording of the *Fourth Symphony* is a performance of real stature, notable for its great concentration and tension. It is coupled with a glorious account of the *Sixth Symphony*, which remains almost unsurpassed among modern versions. Although these recordings do not have quite the range of the very best newer versions, the sound is considerably improved now over earlier releases, and this readily finds its place in Universal's 'Penguin ⚫ Collection'.

Symphonies 4–7; Legend: The Swan of Tuonela; Tapiola
(M) *** DG (ADD) 457 748-2 (2). BPO, Karajan

This set is a convenient way of collecting Karajan's splendid DG performances of Sibelius's last four symphonies, including his outstanding version of the *Fourth*. All but the *Sixth* are available separately in other formats (see below) and his glorious 1967 account of the latter remains almost unsurpassed by more recent accounts. So with a brooding *Swan of Tuonela* and a thrilling *Tapiola* thrown in for good measure, this can be strongly recommended.

Symphonies 4; 7; Kuolema: Valse triste
⚪ ⚫ (M) *** DG (ADD) 439 527-2. BPO, Karajan

Karajan's celebrated 1965 account of the *Fourth Symphony* wears well. For many it remains the finest version of the *Fourth* on record. The plush sonority of the Berlin Philharmonic at first deceives one into thinking that Karajan has beautified the symphony's landscape, but he comes closer to the spirit of the score than most others. It is a performance of great concentration, deep thought and feeling. Although the new DG transfer of the recording does not have quite the body of violin-tone of the finest digital recordings, the acoustics of the Jesus-Christus-Kirche give weight and depth and a fine resonance to the bass. The performance is undoubtedly a great one. The *Seventh Symphony* is perhaps less successful

though it comes off better than in Karajan's Philharmonia version, and the *Valse triste* is seductive. An indispensable record.

Symphonies 4; 7; Pelléas et Mélisande Suite; Swanwhite; Tapiola; The Tempest (incidental music): Dance of the Nymphs
(***) BBC mono BBCL 4041-2 (2). RPO, Beecham (with British and Finnish National anthems, and speeches by Beecham, including Beecham on Sibelius)

Beecham never re-recorded the *Fourth Symphony* commercially after his 1938 recording but, judging from this 1955 performance, his basic approach remained little changed. He also never recorded the *Swanwhite* suite. Here he omits only *The Prince Alone*. He did make stereo versions of the *Pelléas et Mélisande* music (without the brief *By the Seashore* movement) and *Tapiola* a few days on either side of the birthday concert. He also recorded the *Seventh* commercially at the same time, but this performance comes from a Royal Albert Hall concert of the previous year and is slightly higher in voltage than his Abbey Road recording. There is a tremendous sense of occasion here, which is supplemented by his famous talk describing his long friendship with Sibelius and recounting his hilarious visit to his home the previous year.

Symphony 5 (1915 version); En Saga (1892 version)
*** BIS CD 800. Lahti SO, Vänskä

Symphony 5 (1915 version & definitive 1919 version)
*** BIS CD 863. Lahti SO, Vänskä

Not long after Sibelius's death, the orchestral material for the first version of the *Fifth Symphony* was discovered in the attic at Ainola. To reconstruct the actual score was a simple matter. It offers an invaluable insight into the workings of the creative process and is testimony to Sibelius's refusal to rest content until he had fully realized his vision. The work is in four (not three) movements, the opening horn-call is yet to be discovered; and there are no final hammer-blow chords. But there is much else that is different, and to study these differences offers an endless source of fascination. The *En Saga* we know from 1901, when it was extensively revised for Busoni to conduct in Berlin. There are some Brucknerian touches in one or two places, and the orchestration is less expert. Totally dedicated performances. An essential disc for all Sibelians, and magnificently recorded into the bargain.

BIS have also recoupled the original 1915 four-movement version of the *Fifth Symphony* with the definitive 1919 version, as part of their ongoing cycle from Osmo Vänskä and the Lahti orchestra. Vänskä has a great feeling for the general architecture of the piece and paces it superbly. Our only reservation is his penchant for extreme *pianissimos* – the development section in the finale drops beyond a whisper to virtual inaudibility.

Symphony 5 in E flat, Op. 82
(M) *** EMI 7 64737-2. Philh. O, Rattle – NIELSEN: *Symphony 4* etc. ***

Symphony 5; The Bard; Karelia Suite; The Bard; Pohjola's Daughter
**(*) Teldec 8573 85822-2 CBSO, Oramo

Symphony 5; Finlandia; Kuolema: Valse triste. Tapiola, Op. 112
(B) *** DG (ADD) 439 418-2. BPO, Karajan

Symphonies 5; 6; Legend: The Swan of Tuonela

⊘— (M) *** DG (ADD) 439 982-2. BPO, Karajan
(N) (BB) *** LSO Live LSO 0037. LSO, C. Davis

Symphonies 5 in E flat, Op. 82; 6 in D min., Op. 104; Tapiola

(B) **(*) Ph. Eloquence 468 198-2. Boston SO, C. Davis

Colin Davis's performances come from 2002–3 and, like the cycle he recorded with the LSO in the 1990s, are at bargain price. The first movement of the *Fifth* has a magnificent breadth and a powerful atmosphere, and he handles the transition into the Scherzo section, always a crucial test, with masterly control. Tempi feel just right, and both the symphonic architecture and the musical atmosphere emerge to eloquent effect. The final chords are splendidly paced and powerfully delivered. The opening of the *Sixth* seems slightly more relaxed than before, and the strange, other-worldly atmosphere of the second movement registers perfectly. This *Sixth* ranks alongside Davis's RCA records and those of Karajan in both his Philharmonia and Berlin recordings. Very good sound.

Such is the excellence of the classic Karajan DG *Fifth* that few listeners would guess its age. It is a great performance, and this 1964 version is indisputably the finest of the four he made. The fillers are familiar performances, also from the mid-1960s. *Tapiola* is a performance of great intensity and offers superlative playing; *Finlandia* is also one of the finest accounts available, but *Valse triste* is played very slowly and in a somewhat mannered fashion.

The alternative mid-priced reissue is obviously even more attractive, coupled with his glorious 1967 account of the *Sixth*, which remains almost unsurpassed by more recent accounts. The brooding *Swan of Tuonela* is placed between the two symphonies and is played just as admirably by the Berlin Philharmonic on their finest form.

Simon Rattle's account of the *Fifth Symphony* with the Philharmonia was to the 1980s what Karajan's Berlin account was to the 1960s. Everything about it feels right: the control of pace and texture and the balance of energy and repose. The development of the first movement has a compelling sense of mystery and the transition to the Scherzo section is beautifully judged. The Philharmonia Orchestra play splendidly, and the EMI recording is very good indeed.

Sakari Oramo is a Sibelian of sound instinct. He conveys the awe and majesty of the symphony's opening paragraphs to perfection as well as the sense of mystery of the development. In fact, this is highly impressive, even if in the scherzo section he is a fraction headlong. The slow movement and finale are well paced and the Birmingham Orchestra give him excellent support. Of the remaining works *Pohjola's Daughter* is taut and highly charged. *The Bard*, one of Sibelius's most concentrated and profound utterances, is wonderfully atmospheric; indeed it is among the very finest accounts ever recorded (not forgetting Beecham). The recording is state-of-the-art – spacious, well defined and transparent. But for the symphony, this is not a first choice.

Sir Colin Davis's mid-1970s account of the *Fifth* still sounds extremely good and the performance, if without quite the resplendence of his later LSO version for RCA, is still compelling and very well-played (as is *Tapiola*). The account of the *Sixth* is very fine indeed, so this is excellent value, if the coupling is wanted.

Symphonies 5–7; Finlandia; The Oceanides; Tapiola

(B) **(*) EMI double forte 5 68646-2 (2). Helsinki PO, Berglund

This double forte completes Berglund's Sibelius cycle. Nos. 1–4 are on a companion reissue (see above). They are sober, straightforward, powerful readings which maintain the high standards of performance and recording that have consistently distinguished Berglund's EMI Sibelius records. There is a good feeling for the architecture of this music and no want of atmosphere. In the *Fifth Symphony*, the development section of the first movement has a mystery that eluded Berglund first time round, and there is splendid power in the closing pages of the finale. The *Sixth* is particularly fine, though the Scherzo may strike some listeners as too measured. The *Seventh* has real nobility and breadth, and Berglund has the full measure of all the shifting changes of mood and colour. Moreover the Helsinki orchestra play magnificently and seem to have a total rapport with him. Berglund's account of *The Oceanides* is splendidly atmospheric and can be put alongside Rattle's, which is praise indeed! The recording is well detailed and truthful, and the perspective is natural. *Tapiola* is given its impact by a spacious ruggedness, and the very close of the work has a moving intensity. All the same, despite the very good recorded sound and the economical price and packaging, these cannot be recommended in preference to the earlier Colin Davis set with the Boston Symphony, which is similarly priced and packaged on a pair of Philips Duos (see above).

Symphonies 5; 7; Kuolema: Scene with Cranes. Night Ride and Sunrise

(M) *** EMI (ADD) 7 64122-2. CBSO, Rattle

What is particularly impressive in Rattle's account of the *Fifth Symphony* is the control of the transition between the first section and the Scherzo element of the first movement. There is a splendid sense of atmosphere in the development and a power unmatched in recent versions, save for the Karajan. The playing is superb, with recording to match. The *Seventh* is hardly less powerful and impressive: its opening is slow to unfold and has real vision. With the addition of an imaginative and poetic account of the *Scene with Cranes* from the incidental music to *Kuolema*, this is the finest single disc in Rattle's Birmingham cycle.

Symphonies 6; 7; Tapiola

*** BIS CD 864. Lahti SO, Vänskä

Symphony 6–7; The Tempest: Suite 2, Op. 109/3

(BB) *** Naxos 8.554387. Iceland SO, Sakari

Osmo Vänskä's account of the *Sixth* and *Seventh Symphonies* brings his cycle to a fitting climax. The *Sixth* is serene yet taut, and the *Seventh* particularly fine, both in pacing and character. Vänskä's reading of *Tapiola* has a thrilling intensity and if it is not the equal of Karajan or Beecham, it is certainly among the very best of the others. The Lahti orchestra always plays with enthusiasm and fire, and the BIS recording is first class.

Petri Sakari's Icelandic Sibelius cycle is admirably straightforward and unaffected. The *Sixth Symphony* is the best we have had since Vänskä: it is thoughtful, well prepared and dedicated, and even if the Iceland Orchestra is not in the same league as the Vienna Philharmonic or the Concertgebouw, they are a very good ensemble. The *Seventh* is powerful and has breadth and majesty; not the equal of Colin Davis, perhaps, but eminently satisfying all the same. The second suite from *The Tempest* is magnificent (the *Chorus of the Winds* sounds quite magical) and full of mystery and atmosphere. This is Sakari's finest Sibelius disc yet, and the well-balanced sound does credit to all concerned.

Symphony 7 in C, Op. 150

**(*) BBC (ADD) BBCL 4039-2. Philh. O, Boult – BIZET: *Jeux d'enfants*; RAVEL: *Daphnis et Chloé: Suite 2*. SCHUBERT: *Symphony 8 (Unfinished)* **(*)

Symphony 7 in C; Canzonetta, Op. 62a; Kuolema: Valse triste; Scene with Cranes; Night Ride and Sunrise; Valse romantique, Op. 62b

*** BIS CD 311. Gothenburg SO, Järvi

(i) *Symphony 7 in C, Op. 105*; (ii) *Pohjola's Daughter; Swanwhite: The Maiden with the Roses. Tapiola*

(BB) (***) Naxos mono 8.110168. (i) BBC SO; (ii) Boston SO; Koussevitzky (with GRIEG: *The Last Spring* (***))

Koussevitzky's pioneering (1933) recording of the *Seventh Symphony* with the then newly formed BBC Symphony Orchestra has rarely been challenged and never surpassed and, together with his *Pohjola's Daughter* and *Tapiola* from 1936 and 1939 respectively, is among the classics of recorded music. One critic spoke of the Boston Symphony Orchestra under Koussevitzky as one of the great achievements of Western civilization and, listening to them in these splendid new transfers, this scarcely seems an exaggeration.

Neeme Järvi and the Gothenburg orchestra bring great energy and concentration to the *Seventh Symphony*. The only disappointment is the final climax, which is perhaps less intense than the best versions. However, it is a fine performance, and the music to *Kuolema* is splendidly atmospheric; *Night Ride* is strongly characterized. The recording exhibits the usual characteristics of the Gothenburg Concert Hall and has plenty of body and presence.

Anyone who remembers Sir Adrian's set of the Sibelius tone-poems on Pye Records from the 1950s or his broadcasts from the 1940s and 1950s will have high expectations of his *Seventh Symphony* and will not be disappointed. It is finely shaped and superbly paced. A Festival Hall performance from 1963, it is well worth rescuing from oblivion. Good sound too.

The Wood Nymph (tone-poem), *Op. 15*; (i) *The Wood Nymph* (melodrama) (1895); *A Lonely Ski-trail. Swanwhite, Op. 54*

*** BIS CD 815. (i) Pöysti; Lahti SO, Vänskä

Sibelius composed *The Wood Nymph* in 1894–5, when the four *Lemminkäinen Legends* were taking shape in his mind. It is a reworking of the melodrama written for two horns, piano and strings to accompany the recitation of verses by the mainland Swedish poet, Viktor Rydberg. It is stirring stuff and begins with echoes of the *Karelia* music and in places comes close to both the first of the *Legends* and *Lemminkäinen's Homeward Journey*. It improves with every hearing: its main ideas haunt the listener and are difficult to dislodge from the brain! *A Lonely Ski-trail* is slight, but *The Wood Nymph* melodrama is imaginative and highly unusual. The original music to *Swanwhite* has some poetic ideas that did not find their way into the suite, though for the most part there is not a great deal that is unfamiliar. Superb playing from the Lahti orchestra under Osmo Vänskä, and spacious, impeccably balanced recording.

The Wood-Nymph (Melodrama), *Op. 15*

(N) *** Warner 2564 61992-2 Pöysti, Nordic SO,Tali – RACHMANINOV: *3 Russian Songs*; TUUR: *Zeitraum; Action, Passion, Illusion* ***

This *Wood-Nymph* is not the tone-poem for full orchestra that Osmo Vänskä recorded (see above) but the thematically

related melodrama of 1894 to the Rydberg text and scored for narrator, two horns, piano and strings. The speaker on this CD is Lasse Pöysti, who also took part in the earlier, rather more atmospheric 1996 BIS recording above.

CHAMBER MUSIC

(i) *Adagio in D min.*; (ii, iii) *Duo in C for Violin & Viola*; (i) *Fugue for Martin Wegelius*; (iii, iv, v) *Piano Trio in C (Lovisa)*; (vi, vii) *Suite in E for Violin & Piano*; (iii, iv) *Water Drops for Violin & Cello*

*** Ondine ODE 850-2. (i) Sibelius Qt; (ii) Hirvikangas; (iii) Kimangen; (iv) Arai; (v) Lagerspetz; (vi) Kuusisto; (vii) Kerppo

These are all slight pieces from Sibelius's youth and student years: *Water Drops* was written when he was ten and is of no artistic interest. The *Fugue* for his teacher, Martin Wegelius, of 1888 was originally intended as the finale for his *A minor Quartet*, just as the *Adagio in D minor* (1890) was probably to have-formed part of the *B flat Quartet, Op. 4*. This is the most individual of the pieces on this well-played and well-recorded set. With the exception of the *Lovisa Trio* of 1888, these are all first recordings.

Danses champêtres, Op. 106; 3 Pieces, Op. 116; 4 Pieces, Op. 78; 5 Pieces, Op. 81; 4 Pieces, Op. 115 (all for Violin & Piano)

(N) *(*) Ondine 1046-2. Kuusisto, Kärkkäinen

This disc is entitled 'Musical Soirée at Ainola', as it has been recorded at Ainola, the villa Sibelius named after his wife in 1904. The piano is the Steinway Sibelius was given for his 50th birthday in 1915; its timbre is surprisingly fresh, and it is expertly played here. Naturally the sound is dryish, as you would expect from a domestic environment, but is perfectly acceptable. These miniatures cover the period 1915–29 at the time when Sibelius's thoughts were turning in earnest to the projected *Eighth Symphony*. Some are slight, like the *Romance* from the Op. 78 set, a kind of Nordic *Salut d'amour*; but others, like the *Religioso*, strike a deeper note. Pekka Kuusisto is a highly accomplished player, but his approach is far too sophisticated in these pieces. He brings too wide a range of dynamic shading to them and loses sight of their affecting simplicity. This music gains from being allowed to speak for itself.

Piano Quartets: in C min. for 2 violins, cello & piano; in D min. for 2 violins, cello & piano; in G min. for violin, cello, piano & harmonium; (i) *Andante Cantabile in E flat (for piano & harmonium). Scherzo in E min. (for violin, cello & piano, four hands). Ljunga Wirginia (for violin, cello & piano, four hands)*

(N) **(*) BIS CD 1182. Kuusisto, Satu Vänskä, Turunen, Gräsbeck, Lönnqvist; (i) Viitanen

The various works and fragments recorded here come from 1884–91, when Sibelius was yet to find his voice. None is written for the combination of instruments one would expect (string trio and piano) and only one, the eight-minute *C minor Quartet*, has been recorded before (see below). There are unusual ensembles: violin, cello, piano and harmonium in the *G minor quartet* of 1887. (This was composed for the Sucksdorff family in Lovisa whose music room accommodated both a piano and a harmonium.) In fact, all these pieces originate in evenings of domestic entertainment. The fragments for violin, cello and piano four hands (*Ljunga*

Wirginia), intended for a projected dramatic venture Sibelius planned with his friend Walter von Konow, are completely new, if unimportant. Indeed, it would be idle to pretend that any of these slight pieces gives us the slightest glimpse of the real Sibelius; but the performances and the recorded sound are excellent.

(i) *Piano Quartet in C min.* (for piano, two violins and cello); (ii) *String Trio in G min.; Suite in A for String Trio;* (iii) *Violin Sonata in F*
*** Ondine ODE 826-2. (i) Novikov, Quarta, Miori, Rousi; (ii) Söderblom, Angervo, Gustafsson; (iii) Kovacic, Lagerspetz

These are all early and uncharacteristic works. The *Violin Sonata in F major* (1889) shows Sibelius still under the spell of Grieg. Only three movements of the *Suite in A major* for string trio (1888) survive (these artists give us what remains of the fourth movement, a *Gigue*); and its companion, the *String Trio in G minor*, is also unfinished. Only the *Lento* survives intact, though the disc also gives a realization of what remains of the sketches of two other movements. The *Quartet in C minor* for piano, two violins and cello is a set of variations from the composer's Vienna year, 1891. All this is largely uncharacteristic and, save for the opening of the *A major Suite*, offers few glimpses of the mature Sibelius. The performances are dedicated and beautifully recorded.

(i) *Piano Quintet in G min.; Piano Trio in C (Lovisa); String Quartet in E flat*
*** Finlandia 4509 95858-2. Sibelius Academy Qt, (i) with Tawaststjerna

(i) *Piano Quintet in G min.; String Quartet in D min. (Voces intimae), Op. 56*
*** Chan. 8742. (i) Goldstone; Gabrieli Qt

The *Piano Quintet* is a long and far from characteristic piece in five movements. Anthony Goldstone and the Gabrielis reverse the order of the second and third movements so as to maximize contrast. The first movement is probably the finest, and Goldstone, an impressive player by any standards, makes the most of Sibelius's piano writing to produce a very committed performance. The *Voces intimae Quartet* is given a reflective, intelligent reading, perhaps at times wanting in momentum but finely shaped. Good recording.

The early *Quartet in E flat* is Haydnesque and insignificant, and the *Lovisa Trio*, so called because it was written in that small town in the summer of 1888, offers only sporadic glimpses of things to come. The *Piano Quintet* is given a fine performance on Finlandia, and there is little to choose between it and the more expansive Goldstone/Gabrieli account on Chandos.

Piano Trios in A min.; in A min. (Hafträsk); in G for 2 Violins & Piano; Piano Trio movements: *Allegro in C; Andantino in A; Allegro in D; Andante – Adagio – Allegro maestoso; Minuet in D min.; Minuet in F for 2 Violins & Piano; Moderato in A min.*
*** BIS CD 1282. Kuusisto, Vänskä, Ylönen, Gräsbeck

All these pieces are still unpublished and the autographs are in Helsinki University Library. All are new to the catalogue and will naturally be of keen interest to Sibelians. They were all composed in Sibelius's late teens, before he began his formal studies in Helsinki with Wegelius. In his study of Sibelius's juvenilia John Rosas quotes Sibelius's secretary, Santeri Levas, as saying that in all his correspondence with the Sibelius Museum in Turku (Åbo), the composer was at pains to emphasize that these chamber works were *neither to be published nor performed – even after his death!* This CD brings to the attention of the wider musical public music that has been available heretofore only to scholars. The opening of the family vaults has revealed the full extent of the composer's early activity, which finds him flexing his creative muscles in the shadow of the Viennese masters. The earliest work is the *G major Trio* for two violins and piano, a fluent and attractive piece, which reflects Sibelius's own youthful experience as a player. As always, the writing is well schooled though the ideas give scant indication of what was to come. Perhaps the most striking work is the *A minor Trio* of 1884, whose provenance Folke Gräsbeck explores in his well-researched notes. It owes something to Haydn in its layout, and its *Trio* has distinctly rustic accents. The *Andantino in A major* of 1886 is a rather lovely piece, too. No one would make exaggerated claims for these pieces, some of which have scant merit; but to observe the composer's complete ban on them would have deprived us of the opportunity of hearing at first hand the extraordinary transformation of Sibelius's talent into genius only a half a dozen years later. The performances are alert and intelligent and the recording exemplary and wonderfully present.

Piano Trios in D (Korpo) (1887); in C (Lovisa). Alla Marcia in C; Andantino in G min.; Allegretto in A flat; Allegro in D min. (completed Aho); *Allegretto in E flat* (completed Kuusisto)
*** BIS CD 1292. Kuusisto, Ylönen, Gräsbeck

The second volume of music for piano trio covers the period 1887–95 and thus follows chronologically on the first. Together they represent Sibelius's complete output in this medium for, although he never returned to it in later life, the piano trio was almost his favourite chamber form in the 1880s. The '*Lovisa*' *Trio*, so called because it was written in the family summer home in Lovisa, is available in two alternative versions, but otherwise this music is all new. The '*Korpo*' *Trio* (1887) is by far the most substantial piece here running to over 35 minutes. Korpo is an island in the southwest archipelago of Finland, and the estate on which the manor house (designed by Charles Bassi and reproduced on the sleeve) is where Sibelius composed his *Trio*. Few coming to it with innocent ears would guess the identity of the composer but it evinces a natural feeling for form. There are other rarities too, some of which are in fragmentary form. The most engaging is the *March in C major*, which almost calls to mind the Saint-Saëns of the *Carnival of the Animals!* Expert performances.

String Quartets in E flat (1885); A min. (1889); B flat, Op. 4 (1890); D min. (Voces intimae), Op. 56
⊶ (M) *** Finlandia (ADD/DDD) 4509 95851-2. Sibelius Academy Qt

Sibelius's youth was dominated by chamber music: opportunities to hear an orchestra in provincial Finland were few. The *E flat Quartet* is an exercise, modelled on the Viennese classics, and shows that Sibelius knew his Haydn. The *A minor* (1889) is another matter. Long thought lost, as only the first violin part survived, it was found among his brother Christian's papers, and it is highly inventive. Sibelius first thought well enough of it to list it as Op. 2, though he later had second thoughts and never published it. The *B flat Quartet* (1891), is a fine piece whose slow movement bears a resemblance to one of the themes from *Rakastava*, which was to follow in 1894. Sibelius was undoubtedly harsh in his judgements on both, for they are well worth a place in the repertoire. The Scherzo of the *A minor Quartet* is wonderfully exhilarating. The performances are first rate and are generally well served by the engineers. There is only one mature Sibelius quartet, *Voces intimae* (1909), and this performance is arguably still the finest now available. An outstanding bargain, and strongly recommended.

String Quartet in D min. (Voces intimae), Op. 56

(***) Biddulph mono LAB 098. Budapest Qt – GRIEG:
  Quartet; WOLF: *Italian Serenade.* (***)

**(*) HM HMA 1951671. Melos Qt – VERDI: *String Quartet*
  **(*)

A welcome transfer – the first on CD – of the 1933 pioneering *Voces intimae*, still unbeaten. It briefly appeared on LP (on the World Record label) and is newly (and well) transferred here by Ward Marston. Sibelians will need no reminders of its excellence – and the same goes for the couplings.

The Melos Quartet give an impeccably well-turned-out performance of *Voces intimae* and one which will give satisfaction to their admirers. But briefly returning to it, we were reminded of how the famous Budapest version of 1933 remains incomparable. The recording is very truthful but (at 50 minutes or so) the issue is short measure, given its price-tag.

Music for violin and piano

Adagio in D min.; Allegretto in C; 2 Pieces; 3 Pieces; Sonata Exposition: Allegro in A min.; Grave (Fragment) in D min.; Largamente (Fragments) in E min.; in D min.; Sonata in F; Suite in E; Tempo di valse in A. Music for solo violin: *Allegretto in A; Etude in D; A Happy Musician; Romance in G*

*** BIS CD 1023. Kuusisto, Gräsbeck

This is the companion disc to BIS's complete youthful production for violin and piano (see below) and covers the years 1885–9, when Sibelius was in his early 20s. Always sensitive about his early music, Sibelius (except for one occasion) forbade both the performance and publication of such works as the *String Quartet*, Op. 4, and the *Kullervo Symphony*. All the material recorded here is completely new. None has been performed publicly or recorded until these artists played them in 1999. We have known about them solely from John Rosas's pioneering study from the early 1960s and the first volume of Erik Tawaststjerna's biography, but most of Sibelius's unpublished juvenilia is a closed book. The *A minor Sonata* has echoes of early Beethoven and comes from his school years; the *Suite in D minor* (1887–8) shows that his writing for the violin was naturally fluent and idiomatic even then. It seems that the composer was sufficiently taken with it to show it to his first biographer, Erik Furujhelm. The performances here are expert and accomplished in every way. Good, well-balanced recorded sound.

Andante grazioso in D major (1884–5); *5 Pieces* (1886–7); *Violin Sonata in A minor* (1884); *Sonata Movement* (1885); *Sonata Fragment in B minor* (1887); *Suite in D minor* (1887-8); Various short movements and fragments

*** BIS CD 1022. Kuusisto, Gräsbeck

This disc collects some of Sibelius's youthful output for violin and piano, and covers the years 1884–8, from his school years through to his time at Helsinki. The violin was his chosen instrument and his writing for it is totally idiomatic with a natural fluency. None of the music has been heard before. The *A minor Sonata* of 1884, from his school years, is redolent of the early Beethoven sonatas: it is highly accomplished but totally derivative. There are a number of short movements, some mere fragments, and not all of them are worth committing to disc. The *Suite in D minor* (1887–8) is another matter and shows just how good his writing for the instrument was. Very good playing from Jaakko Kuusisto and Folke Gräsbeck, as well as good and scholarly sleeve notes from the latter. Excellent sound.

5 Danses champêtres, Op. 106; Novellette, Op. 102; 5 Pieces, Op. 81; 4 Pieces, Op. 115; 3 Pieces, Op. 116

*** BIS CD 625. Sparf, Forsberg

Many of the items here, such as the delightful *Rondino* from Op. 81, are little more than salon music, but some of the others are rewarding pieces. Indeed the first of the *Danses champêtres* almost suggests the music to *The Tempest*, written at much the same time. Both the Opp. 115 and 116 pieces contain music of quality. As in the companion disc, Nils-Erik Sparf and Bengt Forsberg prove as imaginative as they are accomplished.

2 Pieces, Op. 2 (2 versions); Scaramouche: Scène d'amour. 2 Serious melodies, Op. 77; 4 Pieces, Op. 78; 6 Pieces, Op. 79; Sonatina in E, Op. 80

*** BIS CD 525. Sparf, Forsberg

This CD offers the first recording of the 1888 versions of the *Grave* and the *Perpetuum mobile*, the two pieces which Sibelius assigned to Op. 2, together with the 1911 versions, in which the former was revised as *Romance in B minor* and the latter overhauled as *Epilogue*. The former bears a certain affinity to the slow movement of the *Violin Concerto* and the prevalence of the tritone in the latter acts as a reminder that it was reworked in the wake of the *Fourth Symphony*. Exemplary performances of the later pieces, including *Laetare anima mea* and the 1915 *Sonatina*, Op. 80.

PIANO MUSIC

Andante in E flat; Aubade in A flat; Au crépuscule; A Catalogue of Themes, 50 Short Pieces; Con moto, sempre una corda; 3 Pieces; Scherzo in E & Trio in E min.; 3 Short Pieces; 5 Short Pieces; Trio in E min. (arr. for piano); Trånaden (Yearning); 11 Variations on a Harmonic Formula

*** BIS CD 1067. Gräsbeck

As part of its ambitious scheme to record every note that Sibelius ever wrote, BIS has turned its attention to the early piano pieces Sibelius composed in his study years. They reaffirm how great were the strides he had taken by the time of the *B flat Quartet*, Op. 4, and the *Kullervo Symphony*. All these are unpublished and give no hint of what was to come. Perhaps the most imaginative is *Trånaden* to accompany a recitation of Stagnelius's poem. Folke Gräsbeck plays very well, and the recording is natural and lifelike.

Complete Youthful Production of Music for the Piano I
*** BIS CD 1067. Folke Gräsbeck

Complete Youthful Production of Music for the Piano II
*** BIS CD 1202 Folke Gräsbeck

There is a natural curiosity about the kind of music Sibelius was composing as a student in Helsinki and Berlin, though recording his 1889 student exercises for Albert Becker is carrying reverence too far. Some of the pieces, such as the *Moderato – Presto in D minor* (1888) are worth hearing, but none can be said to be remotely characteristic. Some are fragments only, a few seconds in duration; some have no title. Two of the scraps he composed while studying in Vienna under Goldmark and Robert Fuchs are only 20 seconds. None are in print and the performances are based on the autograph material held in the Helsinki University Library. All, with the exception of the *Florestan Suite* of 1889, are first recordings. Folke Gräsbeck plays them with fluent grace, and the BIS recording and documentation are exemplary.

10 Bagatelles, Op. 34; Barcarole, Op. 24/10; Esquisses, Op. 114; Kyllikki, Op. 41; 5 Pieces, Op. 75; **Piano transcriptions:** *Finlandia, Op. 26; Valse triste, Op. 44/1*
(***) Ondine ODE 847-2. Gothoni

Gothoni makes the most of every expressive gesture and every gradation of keyboard colour, without indulging in any exaggeration. These performances make out a stronger case for Sibelius's piano music than almost any other. Unfortunately, they are badly let down by the recording, which is reverberant and clangorous; the piano itself hardly sounds in ideal shape. A pity about the sound.

10 Bagatelles, Op. 34; The Cavalier; Dance Intermezzo; 6 Finnish Folk Songs; Kyllikki (3 Lyric Pieces), Op. 41; Mandolinato; Morceau romantique; Pensées lyriques, Op. 40; Spagnuolo; To Longing
(BB) *** Naxos 8.554808. Gimse

The Norwegian pianist Håvard Gimse here includes two important sets of the piano pieces, Opp. 34 and 40, and the *6 Finnish Folk Songs*, the fifth of which, *Fratricide*, is slightly Bartókian. Sibelius's contemporary and countryman Selim Palmgren put it perfectly when he wrote that 'even in what for him were alien regions, [Sibelius] moves with an unfailing responsiveness to tone colour', and Gimse brings finesse and distinction to this repertoire. This and the companion disc are first recommendations.

6 Bagatelles, Op. 97; 5 Characteristic Impressions, Op. 103; 5 Esquisses, Op. 114; 8 Little Pieces, Op. 99; 5 Romantic Pieces, Op. 101; 5 Sketches, Op. 114
(N) (BB) *** Naxos 8.555853. Gimse

Håvard Gimse's Naxos series, of which this is the fifth issue, goes from strength to strength. All the pieces recorded here come from the 1920s, the period of the *Sixth* and *Seventh Symphonies*, and are rarities. Among the finest are the *Five Sketches*, which come from the very end of the decade and are among Sibelius's last published works. They may be slight but they are highly individual and have great finesse. *Village Church* from Op. 103 has overtones of the *Andante festivo* for strings, and *The Oarsman* seems to ruminate on ideas in the *Seventh Symphony*. Sibelius's piano-writing may have evoked little enthusiasm during his lifetime and it is true that, by the exalted standards he set elsewhere, it is limited in resource and scale. But pieces like *In Mournful Mood* and *Landscape* from Op. 114 are curiously haunting. So is the rest of the Op. 114 set, and its neglect has been our loss.

5 Characteristic Pieces, Op. 103; 5 Sketches, Op. 114; Finlandia, Op. 26/7; 3 Lyric Piaces, Op. 41; Piano Sonata, Op. 12; 5 Pieces (Flowers), Op. 85; Rondinos, Op. 68
(BB) **(*) Warner Apex 2564 60114-2. Heinonen

Eminently sensitive and serviceable accounts of these underrated and charming pieces from Eero Heinonen, well recorded. The Gimse Naxos series in the same price range is even finer, but this disc is worth its modest cost.

5 Characteristic Pieces, Op. 103; 5 Sketches, Op. 114; 5 Pieces (The Trees), Op. 75; 5 Pieces (The Flowers), Op. 85; 5 Romantic Pieces, Op. 101
*** Chan. 9833. Tabe

By the exalted standards Sibelius set elsewhere, his keyboard writing is limited both in range and resource, but when it is played as sensitively as by Kyoko Tabe, the effect can be quite persuasive. She makes the most of these miniatures without making too much of them. Opp. 75 and 85 come from the period 1914–15 and the remainder from the 1920s. She conveys some of their charm and individuality with expertise and is recorded with a lifelike and natural sound.

6 Impromptus, Op. 5; Sonata in F, Op. 12; 10 Pieces, Op. 24
(BB) *** Naxos 8.553899. Gimse

The *Sonata* and *Impromptus* are early and come from the year in which the first version of *En Saga* was composed. The *Sonata* has a genuine sense of forward movement and some of its ideas are appealing. The Op. 24 *Pieces* were written at various times between 1894 and 1903. The Norwegian pianist Håvard Gimse has consistent tonal beauty and unfailing musicianship. He is imaginative and has the kind of natural eloquence which allows the music to speak for itself yet still makes it sound fresh and unsentimental. This is distinguished playing and a strong recommendation at any price level.

3 Lyric Pieces, Op. 41; 5 Characteristic Impressions, Op. 103; 6 Impromptus, Op. 5; 5 Pieces, Op. 75; 5 Pieces, Op. 85; Finlandia (arr. composer)
(BB) *** Naxos 8.553661. Lauriala

Perfectly good playing and decent recording make this a useful alternative to the complete survey by Annette Servadei. Its price advantage will incline some readers to give it preference, and it also enjoys the benefit of decent recorded sound.

4 Lyric Pieces, Op. 74; 5 Pieces (The Flowers), Op. 35; 5 Pieces (The Trees), Op. 75; 6 Pieces, Op. 94; 13 Pieces, Op. 76
(N) (BB) *** Naxos 8.555363. Gimse

This latest issue in Håvard Gimse's survey lives up to the high expectation aroused by earlier issues in this series. He is a highly imaginative and sensitive player and is given excellent sound by the Naxos team.

10 Pieces, Op. 58; 2 Rondinos, Op. 68; 3 Sonatinas, Op. 67
(BB) *** Naxos 8.554814. Gimse

The *Ten Pieces* of Op. 58 date from 1909, the year of the *String Quartet (Voces intimae)*. They are delightful and by no means just trivial. Each has its own sobriquet and shows real keyboard character. The final rather solemn *Summer Song* is memorable, as is the wistful mood of the first of the *Two Rondinos*, written two years later; the second sparkles most pianistically.

The three *Sonatinas*, written together in the summer of 1912, are also full of charming ideas, giving the impression of a composer relaxing in holiday mood. Håvard Gimse plays all this music freshly, and finds its simple beauty. He is very well recorded and this Naxos disc more than bears out the promise of its companions.

ORGAN MUSIC

Intrada, Op. 111a; Masonic Music, Op. 113/1 & 10; Surusoitto, Op. 111b

*** BIS CD 1101. Ericsson – DVORAK: *Preludes & Fugues* **(*); GLAZUNOV: *Preludes & Fugues*, etc. ***

After the death of Sibelius's old friend and drinking companion, the artist Akseli Gallen-Kalela, the composer was forced not only to break with custom by attending the funeral (which he usually refused to do) but also after much arm-twisting, to compose something at short notice for the ceremony. *Surusoitto* was the result. In the late 1960s the composer Joonas Kokkonen put forward the theory that given the pressure of time, Sibelius might have drawn on material from the *Eighth Symphony*, on which he was working throughout 1931. Aino Sibelius, the composer's widow, also thought this likely. Not that this short piece gives many clues as to how the symphony would have sounded, any more than would the string threnody of the *Seventh Symphony* if it were taken out of context and played on the piano. The *Intrada* (1925) is powerful, but the *Funeral March* from the *Masonic Music* (1927) betrays its proximity to the *Tempest* music. Superb playing from Hans-Ola Ericsson on a magnificently powerful instrument.

VOCAL MUSIC

Academic March (1919); Andante festivo (1922); (i) Cantata for the Conferment Ceremony of 1894; (ii) Coronation Cantata (1896); Finlandia, Op. 26/7

**(*) Ondine ODE 936-2. (ii) Isokoski, Kortekangas; (i & ii) Finnish Ph. Ch.; Helsinki PO, Segerstam

These two early cantatas are completely new to the repertoire. Only two sections of the *Academic Cantata* or *Cantata for the Conferment Ceremony of 1894* survive. It is hardly top-drawer Sibelius, though there are occasional flickers of individuality in the orchestral writing. The *Coronation Cantata*, written for the accession of Tsar Nicholas II, has not been heard since 1896 and its inspiration is thin and commonplace. Good solo singing from Soile Isokoski and Jaakko Kortekangas and decent performances from all concerned. Segerstam's *Finlandia* was recorded in 1994, five years before the rest of the programme. It is a particularly striking account and the whole programme is very well recorded.

Academic March; Finlandia (arr. composer); Har du mod?, Op. 31/2; March of the Finnish Jaeger Battalion, Op. 91/1; (i) The Origin of Fire, Op. 32; Sandels, Op. 28; Song of the Athenians, Op. 31/3

**(*) BIS CD 314. (i) Tiilikainen, Laulun Ystävät Male Ch.; Gothenburg SO, Järvi

The Origin of Fire is by far the most important work on this record. Sauli Tiilikainen is very impressive indeed, and the playing of the Gothenburg Symphony Orchestra under Neeme Järvi has plenty of feeling and atmosphere. None of the other pieces is essential Sibelius. The singing of the Laulun Ystävät choir is good rather than outstanding, and the Gothenburg orchestra play with enthusiasm. A fine recording in the best BIS traditions.

(i) Belshazzar's Feast (complete score), Op. 51; The Countess's Portrait (Grefvinnans konterfej); (ii) Jedermann (Everyman) (incidental music), Op. 83

☛ *** BIS CD 737. (i) Passikivi; Lahti SO, Vänskä; (ii) with Lehto, Tiilikainen, Pietiläinen, Lahti Chamber Ch.

The incidental music to Hugo von Hofmannsthal's morality play, *Everyman*, comes from the autumn of 1916, when Sibelius was also working on the second version of his *Fifth Symphony*. The score runs to 16 numbers and takes 40 minutes. A lot of the music is fragmentary, wisps of sound; all of it is atmospheric and the best of it (the *Largo* section from track 12 onwards) finds Sibelius at his most inspired. The complete score for Hjalmar Procopé's *Belshazzar's Feast* brings us some seven minutes of extra music. The scoring is different from and less effective than the concert suite. There is, for example, no oboe in the original; the seductive descending oboe theme in *Khadra's Dance* is assigned to the clarinet. *Grefvinnans konterfej (The Countess's Portrait)* is a short, wistful piece for strings which comes from 1906 and was originally designed to accompany a recitation of *Porträtterna*, a poem by the mainland Swedish poet, Anna-Maria Lenngren. Dedicated, sensitive performances from the Lahti Symphony Orchestra and excellent recording. An indispensable disc for all Sibelians.

(i) Karelia (complete incidental music); (ii) Kuolema, Op. 44; Valse triste (1904 version)

☛ *** BIS CD 915. (i) Laitinen, Hoffgren; (i; ii) Laukka; (ii) Tiilhonen; Lahti SO, Vänska

Although the *Karelia Suite* is familiar enough, few readers will have heard the complete score. It has only recently been put into performable shape. However, a set of parts survived, albeit incomplete, and the composer, Kalevi Aho, has prepared an edition which Osmo Vänskä and his musicians use for this score. Some things are disconcerting: the familiar cor anglais melody in the *Ballade* is given to a tenor, and the movement is far too long. But there is much of interest here that makes this essential listening for Sibelians. The incidental music to *Kuolema* ('Death'), written ten years later, was revised the following year (1904) and rescored. The original second section, *Paavali's Song*, is quite inspired, though Sibelius was quite right to add wind to represent the bird cries in the following scene (he conflated scenes 3 and 4 to form *Scene with Cranes*). The disc also affords an opportunity to contrast the 1903 and 1904 versions of *Valse triste*, the differences will bring you up with a start. Superb playing and recording.

(i) Karelia Suite, Op. 11 (original scoring); (ii) King Christian II, Op. 27 (complete original score); (iii) Pelléas et Mélisande (original scoring)

*** BIS CD 918. (i; ii) Laukka; (iii) Jakobsson; Lahti SO, Vänskä

Sibelius rescored all three works for larger forces when he made his *King Christian* concert suite the following year, his first orchestral work to be published. It is particularly good to hear the *Musette* from that suite in such a characterful form, just for wind. The changes in the score Sibelius composed for Bertel Gripenberg's Swedish translation of Maeterlinck's *Pelléas et Mélisande* are less extensive but we do have an additional section that has never been published. The *Karelia Suite* is drawn from BIS CD 915. A highly successful issue of great interest to all Sibelians.

Kullervo Symphony, Op. 7

☛ *** BIS CD 1215. Paasikivi, Laukka, Helsinki University Ch., Lahti SO, Vänskä

**(*) Chan. 9393. Isokoski, Laukka, Danish Nat. RSO, Segerstam

**(*) Virgin 5 45292-2. Stene, Mattei, Nat. Male Voice Ch., Royal Stockholm PO, P. Järvi

Having completed an impressive cycle of the symphonies Osmo Vänskä and the Lahti Orchestra give us a finely paced reading of Sibelius's groundbreaking work, with plenty of dramatic intensity and a strong atmosphere. There is the same sense of grip and epic sweep that distinguishes Sir Colin Davis's RCA recording. Apart from two fine soloists, he has the advantage of a Finnish male choir. Incidentally, some small errors in the published score have been corrected. This is the best performance of this wonderful symphony since Davis's version, and it is a strong challenger, in that the LSO version spreads over on to a second disc, which accommodates the *Seventh Symphony* and *En saga*. For many this BIS CD will be a first choice.

Segerstam gives what is for him an uncharacteristically straightforward account of this remarkable work. There are none of the idiosyncrasies that have proved so disruptive elsewhere. His soloists are good, and both the playing of the Danish Radio Orchestra and the skill of their engineers are admirable. But this is not a first choice.

There is a lot right about Paavo Järvi's fine reading with the Royal Stockholm Philharmonic and his Swedish choir. The first two movements are admirably paced and in the central movement the Norwegian mezzo-soprano Randi Stene and the Swedish baritone Peter Mattei make admirable soloists. No reservations about the excellent EMI/Virgin recording. The big snag is the finale, *Kullervo's Death*, which Järvi *fils* drags out to almost 15 minutes while most others get through it in about ten. The result is to make it sound bombastic and overblown.

Cantatas: *Laulu Lemminkäiselle (Song to Lemminkäinen), Op. 31/1; Maan virsi (Hymn to the earth), Op. 95; Oma Maa (Our native land), Op. 92; Sandels, Op. 28; Snöfrid, Op. 29; Väinön virsi (Väinö's Song), Op. 110; Finlandia, Op. 26*
*** Virgin 5 45589-2. Ellerhein Girls' Ch., Estonian Nat. Male Ch. & SO, P. Järvi

Three of these cantatas come from Sibelius's last period: *Our native land*, probably the best known of these pieces, comes from 1918, but if you didn't know you would think it came from the 1890s. Much the same goes for the other two. *Hymn to the earth* from 1919 is very conventional and, although *Väinö's Song* is a neighbour of *The Tempest* and *Tapiola*, it betrays nothing of their vision or mastery. *Our native land* certainly sounds stronger and more appealing in this performance than in any other version on disc. Paavo Järvi makes the most of Sibelius's evocative description of the aurora borealis and the white nights of the Nordic summer. These cantatas are well worth hearing, even if they are not Sibelius at his most original. Järvi gives a totally committed account of them and has a fine body of singers. Excellent sound.

(i; ii) *Snöfrid, Op. 29; (i) Coronation Cantata, JS104; Oma maa, Op. 92.Andante festivo, JS34b; Overture in A min., JS144; Rakastava, Op. 14*
(N) *** BIS CD 1265. Lahti SO, Vänskä, with (i) Jubilate Ch.; (ii) Stina Ekblad (narr.)

Snöfrid is an 'improvisation' for narrator, mixed choir and orchestra, dating from 1900, and it accompanies lines from Rydberg's poem of that name. It is characteristic of early Sibelius, often powerful and consistent in quality. The *Overture* was written at high speed two years later to fill out the programme which included the première of the *Second Symphony*, and is a rewarding piece. It looks forward to the period of the *Voces intimae Quartet*, which one of its themes

actually anticipates. Tawaststjerna called the *Coronation Cantata* of 1896 'banal' and certainly, by Sibelius's exalted standards, it is pretty routine stuff. *Oma maa* ('My own Land') is an altogether different matter and comes from the last year of the First World War, at a time when Sibelius was working on the final version of the *Fifth Symphony*. The 1912 transcription of the early choral suite, *Rakastava* ('The Lover') for strings and percussion is Sibelius at his most inspired and poignant. Fine performances and recording.

The Tempest (incidental music), Op. 109 (complete)
⊶ *** BIS CD 581. Tiihonen, Passikivi, Hirvonen, Kerola, Heinonen, Lahti Opera Ch. & SO, Vänskä
**(*) Ondine ODE 813-2. Groop, Viljakainen, Hynninen, Silvasti, Tiilikainen, Op. Festival Ch., Finnish RSO, Saraste

Sibelius's original score for the 1926 Copenhagen production of Shakespeare's play is extensive: it runs to some 34 numbers in all for soloists, mixed chorus, harmonium and orchestra, and takes about 65 minutes. There are some unfamiliar effects here: the muted strings with which we are familiar in the *Berceuse* were an afterthought. In the original, their music is allotted to the harmonium; and although this is at first startling, the effect is otherworldly in a completely unexpected way. There are other master-strokes that are missing (the insinuating bass clarinet in *The Oak-tree*) but much else that will be new. The *Chorus of the Winds* with a real chorus is also quite magical – in fact the vocal writing is often highly imaginative – and the singers on the BIS CD are all good. The atmosphere is very strong and puts one completely under its spell. The BIS recording, though good, needs to be reproduced at a higher than usual level setting.

If clarity and definition are a first priority, the Ondine version under Saraste is the one to go for. There is good singing here, too, from Monica Groop, Jorma Hynninen and the rest of the cast. The performance is given in Danish (as it would have been in the 1926 version, rather than the Finnish text used by BIS). However, Saraste is nowhere near as sensitive as Vänskä and does not have his sense of mystery or atmosphere. His *Prospero* is too fast, almost routine by comparison with Vänskä, who draws the listener more completely into Sibelius's and Shakespeare's world. Both accounts are recommendable and either is to be acquired rather than none. But the BIS makes a clear first choice.

Songs

Complete Songs: *5 Christmas Songs, Op. 1; Arioso, Op. 3; 5 Songs of Runeberg, Op. 13; 7 Songs, Op. 17; Jubal, Teodora, Op. 35; 6 Songs, Op. 36; 5 Songs, Op. 37; 5 Songs, Op. 38; 6 Songs, Op. 50; 8 Songs of Josephson, Op. 57; 4 Songs, Op. 72; 6 Songs, Op. 86; 6 Songs of Runeberg, Op. 90; Serenade (1888); Segelfahrt (1899); Souda, souda, sinisorsa (1899); Hymn to Thaïs (1900); Erloschen (1906); Narcissen (1918); Små flickorna (1920); King Christian II, Op. 27; Serenade to the Fool. Pelléas et Mélisande, Op. 46; Les Trois Soeurs aveugles. Two Songs from 'Twelfth Night', Op. 60*
⊶ ✿ (M) *** Decca (ADD) 476 17259 (4). Söderström, Krause, Ashkenazy or Gage; Bonell (guitar)

Many of these songs had never been recorded before this collection arrived and won the 1985 *Gramophone* Solo Vocal Award. Sibelius the symphonist has, understandably enough, overshadowed the achievement of the song composer. Indeed, in the past his songs have been written off by many music-lovers whose knowledge of them does not extend far beyond the popular handful: *Black Roses, The Maid Came from her Lover's Tryst (Flickan kom ifrån sin älsklings möte)* and *Sigh, Sedges, Sigh (Säv, säv, susa)*. As with Grieg, the most popular of his songs are not necessarily the best and may have served to hinder the collector from exploring the rest. Another cause for their neglect is the relative inaccessibility of the Swedish language as far as non-native singers are concerned, for again (like those of Grieg or Mussorgsky) the songs of Sibelius do not sound well in translation. Only a handful (quite literally five) of the songs are in Finnish; the bulk are inspired by the great Swedish nature romantics: Runeberg, Rydberg, Fröding and Tavaststjerna. Apart from the familiar handful, there are so many riches here to take one by surprise: songs like *Soluppgang* ('Sunrise') and *Lasse Liten* ('Little Lasse') are finely characterized, with some of the concentration and atmosphere one finds in his finest miniatures. *På verandan vid havet* ('On a Balcony by the Sea'), more familiar from Flagstad's recording, is almost a miniature tone-poem; it shows a very different side of the Sibelius world and its dark, questioning lines look forward to the bleak contours and landscape of the *Fourth Symphony*. Both *Autumn evening (Höstkväll)* and *On a Balcony by the Sea* are great songs by any standards and can be mentioned in the most exalted company, but neither is new to record, whereas both *Jubeland* and *Teodora*, the two songs comprising Op. 35, were, at the time of this set's original release. The first, *Jubel*, is to a poem of the Swedish poet and painter, Josephson, who inspired the Op. 57 settings. As so often in Sibelius, the piano part is fairly simple, and the burden of the musical argument rests with the voice – the reverse of Wolf. But what a vocal part it is! It ranges with great freedom over a compass of almost two octaves; indeed, so intense is this writing and that of its companion, *Teodora*, and so full of dramatic fire that, in spite of *The Maiden in the Tower*, one wonders whether Sibelius could not have become an operatic composer. *Teodora* will come as a revelation to many Sibelians, for in its over-heated expressionism it comes close to the Strauss of *Salome* and *Elektra*. Krause is superb here and indeed throughout this set. The vast majority of these songs falls to him and Irwin Gage, the remaining dozen or so coming from Södeström and Ashkenazy. Krause's voice has lost some of its youthful freshness and bloom, but none of its black intensity. If you put his earlier accounts of, say, *Vilse* ('Astray') or *Narcissen* ('Narcissus'), both delightful songs, alongside the new, you will notice the firmer focus of the voice in the earlier items, but you will find this offset by the keener interpretative insight and feeling for their character in the complete set. The performances throughout are authoritative and majestic. Apart from Swedish and Finnish, Sibelius set a number of German poets before the First World War. They are not in the same class as the best of the Runeberg settings, but none of them is second rate: *Im Feld ein Mädchen singt* is undoubtedly an eloquent song. However, the real masterpiece in this set is its companion, *Die stille Stadt*, which has the concentration of mood and the strong atmosphere of a miniature tone-poem; indeed, its serenity, beauty of line and sense of repose mark it out from the others. It is a song of great distinction and refinement of feeling. The Op. 61 set, composed in close proximity to the *Fourth Symphony*, has some of Sibelius's most searching thoughts. One song here is grievously neglected; it alone is almost worth the price of this set: *Låndsamt som kvällsyn* ('Slowly as the Evening Sun'), which haunts the listener with its intensity and concentration of mood. It is a setting of Karl August Tavaststjerna, to whom Sibelius turns for four other poems in this set. None is quite so searching and inward in feeling, but nevertheless they all find the composer at his most individual. *Romeo*, for example, is a most subtle and brilliant song, which shows that he knew his Debussy well; and the *Romans* has strong atmosphere too. (His diaries from this period record that Sibelius had been studying both Debussy and Rachmaninov.) This is one of the pleasures of this set, that one finds new delights in the songs each time one turns to them, and a piece that one at first thought unremarkable turns out to be very special. In terms not just of ambition but also of achievement, this set is a landmark recording. Very few of the songs (*Segelfahrt* is an example) are wanting in interest; most of them are very rewarding indeed, and there are many more masterpieces than is commonly realized. This is a veritable treasure-house which will be a revelation to many who think they already know their Sibelius. Music lovers should be very grateful to Universal Classics for making this set available again (it has previously been issued on CD only in Japan), and is now released on their *Gramophone* Award Collection at mid-price with – thank heavens – full texts and translation. Anyone who cares about Sibelius and songs simply must seek out this set.

Songs: *Arioso, Op. 3; Den judiska flickans sång (The Jewish Maiden's Song); Belshazzars gästabud (Belshazzar's Feast); Höstväll (Autumn Evening); Luonnotar; Sancta Maria (Jungfrun på tornet) (The Maiden in the Tower); Se'n har jag ej frågat mera (And I questioned her no further); Soluppgång (Sunrise); Våren flyktar hastigt (The Spring is Flying)*

(N) *** Warner 8573 8.0243-2. Mattila, CBSO, Oramo (with GRIEG: *Songs* ***)

Karita Mattila is in powerful, expressive form. She has a splendid breadth in the *Arioso*, a much later song than its early opus number would indicate, and her *Luonnotar* is second to none. These are marvellous songs and Mattila deserves much credit for including an aria from the early (and unsuccessful) opera, *The Maiden in the Tower*, which the composer subsequently withdrew. Sakari Oramo and the Birmingham orchestra give splendid support throughout, and the recording has great naturalness and presence.

Arioso, Op. 3; Narcissus; Pelléas et Mélisande: The Three Blind Sisters. 7 Songs, Op. 17; 6 Songs, Op. 36; 5 Songs, Op. 37; 6 Songs, Op. 88; Souda, souda, sinisorsa
*** BIS CD 457. Von Otter, Forsberg

Miss von Otter always makes a beautiful sound, but she has a highly developed sense of line and brings great interpretative insight to such songs as 'My bird is long in homing' and 'Tennis at Trianon', which has even greater finesse than Söderström's. And what a good accompanist Bengt Forsberg is. The recording is good if a bit reverberant.

Songs with orchestra: *Arioso; Autumn evening; Come away, Death!; The diamond on the March snow; The fool's song of the spider; Luonnotar, Op. 70; On a balcony by the sea; The rapids-rider's brides; Serenade; Since then I have questioned no further; Spring flies hastily; Sunrise*
*** BIS CD 270. Hynninen, Häggander, Gothenburg SO, Panula

Jorma Hynninen is a fine interpreter of this repertoire: his singing can only be called glorious. Mari-Anne Häggander manages the demanding tessitura of *Arioso* and *Luonnotar* with much artistry, and her *Luonnotar* is certainly to be preferred to Söderström's. Jorma Panula proves a sensitive accompanist and secures fine playing from the Gothenburg orchestra. In any event, this is indispensable.

Belshazzar's Feast; Den judiska flickans sång (The Jewish Girl's Song); 6 Songs, Op. 36; Svarta Rosor (Black Roses); Men min fågel märks dock icke (But my Bird is Long in Homing); Bollspelet vid Trianon (Tennis at Trianon); Säv, säv, susa (Sigh, Sedges, Sigh); Marssnön (The March Snow); Demanten på marssnön (The Diamond on the March Snow). 5 Songs, Op. 37: Den första kyssen (The First Kiss); Lasse liten (Little Lasse); Soluppgång (Sunrise); Var det en dröm? (Was it a dream?); Flickan kom ifrån sin älsklings möte (The Tryst). 6 Songs, Op. 50: Lenzgesang (Spring Song); Sehnsucht (Loneliness); Im Feld ein Mädchen singt (In the Field a Maiden Sings); Aus banger Brust (From anxious heart); Die stille Stadt (The Silent Town); Rosenlied (Rose Song). Illale (To Evening); Jag är ett träd (I am a Tree), Op 57/5; Näcken (The Watersprite or The Elf King), Op 57/8; Under strandens granar (Beneath the Fir Trees), Op 13/1; Våren flyktar hastigt (Spring is Flying) Op 13/4; Norden (The North), Op 90/1; Vem styrde hit din väg? (Who Brought you Here?), Op 90/6
*** Hyp. CDA 67318. Karnéus, Drake

Of Sibelius's 100 or so songs, all but a handful are to texts by Swedish poets, a quarter of them are to settings of Runeberg. The only Finnish song here is *Illale (To Evening)*, among the most lyrical and affecting of his songs. Katarina Karnéus offers the Opp. 36 and 37 sets, which include some of the best loved (and best) songs like *Säv, säv susa* and *Men min fågel märks dock icke*, and one of the subtlest, *Bollspelet vid Trianon*. She also includes the German settings, Op. 50, written in 1906. It was natural that at a time when the composer's music was beginning to find a welcome in Germany that he should turn to a major language (Sibelius spoke little French or English). Two of them, *Im Feld ein Mädchen* ('In the Field a Maiden Sings') and *Die stille Stadt* ('The Silent Town') are among his greatest songs.

Karnéus possesses a glorious voice and sings with real interpretative insight, and in these inspired performances she and Julius Drake find new dimensions in these jewels of songs, performances that sharply bring out the contrasts of mood, the range of emotion and the sense of drama, as in the overpowering tragic climax of *The Tryst*. The eerie originality of such a song as *Näcken* ('The Watersprite') is perfectly caught, with Drake at the piano drawing out the beauty of sound, just as Karnéus does in the vocal line. It is a magical partnership, giving fresh insights in every item. Those who have yet to explore Sibelius's songs should start right here. And no one should miss the orchestral songs on BIS CD 270, discussed above.

7 Songs, Op. 13; 6 Songs, Op. 50; 6 Songs, Op. 90; Resemblance; A song; Serenade; The wood-nymph; The Jewish girl's song; (i) The Thought
☚— (M) *** BIS CD 757. Von Otter, Forsberg, (i) with Groop

The Opp. 13 and 90 songs are all settings of Runeberg, Sibelius's favourite poet, but there are rarities such as *Skogsrået* ('The Wood-nymph') – totally unrelated, by the way, to the melodrama and tone-poem of the same name which Sibelius wrote in the early 1890s – and never before recorded. Also new are the duet, *Tanken* ('The Thought'), *Resemblance* and *A song*. Von Otter and her partner characterize each song with the consummate artistry one expects from them, and the only possible reservation concerns the balance, which in some of the early songs favours the piano.

OPERA

The Maiden in the Tower (opera); Karelia Suite, Op. 11
*** BIS CD 250. Häggander, Hynninen, Hagegård, Kruse, Gothenburg Ch. and SO, Järvi

(i) The Maiden in the Tower (opera; complete); Pelléas et Mélisande (incidental music), Op. 46; Kuolema: Valse Triste
*** Virgin 5 45493-2. (i) Kringelborn, Jonsson, Passikivi, Magee, Estonian Girls' Ch. & Nat. Male Ch.; Estonian NSO, Järvi

The Maiden in the Tower falls into eight short scenes. The orchestral interlude between the first two scenes brings us the real Sibelius, and the second scene is undoubtedly impressive; there are echoes of Wagner, such as we find in some of the great orchestral songs of the following decade. All the same, it lacks something we find in all his most characteristic music: quite simply, a sense of mastery. Yet there are telling performances here from Mari-Anne Häggander and Jorma Hynninen and the Gothenburg orchestra. Neeme Järvi's account of the *Karelia Suite* is certainly original, with its *Intermezzo* too broad to make an effective contrast with the ensuing *Ballade*.

The Virgin issue is more generously filled than the rival version from Gothenburg and Neeme Järvi and comes with the *Pelléas* suite, which was composed a decade later. Jorma Hynninen is an imposing villain in the Gothenburg version, and of the two heroines, Margareta Häggander is perhaps the more convincing. This is a useful alternative to the BIS account, even if it does not completely displace it.

SIMPSON, Robert (1921–97)

Energy; Introduction & Allegro on a Theme by Max Reger; The Four Temperaments; Volcano; Vortex
*** Hyp. CDA 66449. Desford Colliery Caterpillar Band, Watson

The Four Temperaments is a four-movement, 22-minute symphony of great imaginative power, and ingeniously laid out for the band. Simpson played in brass bands as a boy, and this is doubtless where he acquired some of his expertise in writing for them. *Energy* came in response to a commission from the World Brass Band Championships. The *Introduction and Allegro on a Theme by Max Reger* is awesome and impressive. Together with *Volcano* and his most recent piece, *Vortex*, it makes up his entire output in this medium. The Desford Colliery Caterpillar Band under James Watson play with all the expertise and virtuosity one expects, and the recording has admirable clarity and body, although the acoustic is on the dry side.

Symphony 1
(M) (***) EMI mono 5 75789-2. LPO, Boult – FRICKER: *Symphony 2* **(*); ORR: *Symphony* ***

Both the Fricker and Simpson symphonies were composed in 1951 and originally appeared on ten-inch LPs and were subsequently coupled together on a twelve-inch LP in the 1960s. Neither performance has ever appeared before on CD. The one-movement *First Symphony* served as a 'dissertation' for the degree of Doctor of Music at Durham University, and is a powerful and finely wrought work with strong resonances. Nielsen and Bruckner, about whom Simpson wrote extensively, are influences; but Simpson is already very much his own man. It carries particular conviction in this pioneering record, and an amazing amount of detail comes through in this expertly done transfer.

Symphonies 1; 8
*** Hyp. CDA 66890. RPO, Handley

Robert Simpson's *First Symphony* is a one-movement work, albeit in three sections, powerfully constructed and forcefully argued. It holds up to the test of time remarkably well and better than much other music of the 1950s. Vernon Handley gives a spacious and magisterial account of it, and the Hyperion recording illuminates the music splendidly. Like the *First Symphony*, the *Eighth* received its première from a Danish orchestra (the former under Launy Grøndahl, the latter under Jerzy Semkow). One critic has pointed to the *Eighth* as seeming to embody some 'colossal inner rage' and, like the *Fifth*, it undoubtedly has a combative tumult that rarely passes into tranquillity. Handley makes out a strong case for both scores, and the sound is absolutely first class. An indispensable issue for anyone who cares about the post-war symphony in Britain.

Symphonies 2; 4
⊕ *** Hyp. CDA 66505. Bournemouth SO, Handley

The *Second*, composed in 1956 for Anthony Bernard's London Chamber Orchestra, is one of the very best; its opening is one of Simpson's most mysterious and inspired ideas, lean and sinuous but full of poetic vision. The variation slow movement is one of the most virtuosic and remarkable exercises in the palindrome, yet such is the quality of Simpson's artistry in concealing his ingenuity that no one coming to it innocently would be aware of this. The *Second* is a work of enduring quality, music that is both accessible yet of substance. The *Fourth Symphony* is the more extended piece. Powerful and inspiriting music in totally dedicated performances by Vernon Handley, and excellent recording quality.

Symphonies 3; 5
*** Hyp. CDA 66728. RPO, Handley

Vernon Handley brings us the première recording of the *Fifth Symphony* (1971), a work of striking power and range. It is combative and intense and enjoys at times an almost unbridled ferocity that enhances the admittedly few moments of repose. No admirer of the composer – and no one who cares about twentieth-century music in general – should pass these performances by, for it is music of a vital and forceful eloquence. Fine playing by the RPO under Handley, and exemplary recording.

Symphonies 6; 7
*** Hyp. CDA 66280. RLPO, Handley

The *Sixth* is inspired by the idea of growth: the development of a musical structure from initial melodic cells in much the same way as life emerges from a single fertilized cell in nature. The *Seventh*, scored for chamber orchestral forces, is hardly less powerful in its imaginative vision and sense of purpose. Both scores are bracingly Nordic in their inner landscape and exhilarating in aural experience. The playing of the Liverpool orchestra under Vernon Handley could hardly be bettered, and the recording is altogether first class.

Symphony 9
⊕ ✪ *** Hyp. CDA 66299. Bournemouth SO, Handley
(with talk by the composer)

What can one say about the *Ninth* of Robert Simpson, except

that its gestures are confident and its control of pace and its material are masterly? It is a one-movement work, but at no time in its 45 minutes does it falter – nor does the attention of the listener. The CD also includes a spoken introduction to the piece that many listeners will probably find helpful. It is played superbly by the Bournemouth Symphony Orchestra under Vernon Handley, and is no less superbly recorded.

Symphony 10
*** Hyp. CDA 66510. RLPO, Handley

The *Tenth Symphony* (1988) will be a tough nut to crack for many collectors. Its musical argument is unfailingly concentrated. Like its predecessor, it has a Beethovenian strength and momentum. The symphony lasts almost an hour and is not the ideal starting place from which to explore this composer's world. But make no mistake: it is a work of stature, and it is very well played and recorded here.

Symphony 11; Variations on a Theme by Nielsen
(N) *** Hyp. CDA 67500. City of L. Sinfonia, Taylor

The *Eleventh Symphony* comes from 1990 and is a two-movement work: an *Andante* followed by an *Allegro*. It was written for Matthew Taylor, who had much impressed the composer when he conducted his *Seventh Symphony*. Scored for smaller forces than its two immediate predecessors, Simpson said he wanted to create a sort of luminosity of texture not unlike that of Sibelius's *Sixth Symphony*. It has the powerful and uncompromising logic that shapes all the composer's best music; indeed, many may feel that it is his finest symphony. The *Variations on a Theme by Nielsen* was written in 1983 and includes some highly evocative and resourceful invention. The theme itself comes from some incidental music Nielsen was composing at the time of the *Sixth Symphony*. An essential acquisition for anyone who cares about the modern British symphony, and very well-detailed sound indeed.

(i) Canzona for Brass; (i & ii) Media morte in vita sumus; (ii) Tempi; (iii) Eppur si muove
*** Hyp. CDA 67016. (i) Corydon Brass Ens.; (ii) Corydon Singers, Best; (iii) Quinn

The *Canzona for Brass* from 1957 has never sounded more impressive on CD. It has the dignity and grandeur of Gabrieli. The *Media morte in vita sumus* ('In the midst of death we are in life') comes from 1975, between the *Fifth* and *Sixth Symphonies*, and is for voices and brass. It has a depth and eloquence completely at variance with so much contemporary music. *Tempi* (1988) is a setting for *a cappella* choir of various Italian tempo indications, written for a choral competition in the composer's adopted Eire. Such is its beauty that it makes one regret that it is Simpson's only contribution to the medium. *Eppur si muove* (1988) is an imposing 30-minute piece for organ, not dissimilar in scope and ambition to Nielsen's *Commotio*. It derives its title from Galileo's response when he was compelled by the Church to recant his view that the earth revolved round the sun: 'But it *does* move.' Iain Quinn plays it with consummate mastery on the organ of Winchester Cathedral. The brass playing is superb and the Corydon Singers cope with Simpson's demanding vocal writing admirably even if the sopranos are obviously taxed at times above the stave. State-of-the-art recording. Not to be missed.

(i) Clarinet Quintet; String Quartet 13; (ii) String Quintet 2
*** Hyp. CDA 66905. (i) King; (ii) Van Kampen; Delmé Qt

The *Clarinet Quintet* is arguably the most searching example of the genre to have appeared since the war and not just in this country. From the opening, with the model of Beethoven's *C sharp minor Quartet*, Op. 131, not far from view, right to the ending, this is a subtle, concentrated and profoundly original – and profound – work. It is one of those pieces which is more than the sum of its parts and which resonates long in the memory. The *Thirteenth Quartet* is a concentrated piece and the Delmé Quartet are ideal exponents.

Horn Quartet (for horn, violin, cello & piano); Horn Trio (for horn, violin & piano)
*** Hyp. CDA 66695. Watkins, Lowbury, Armytage, Dearnley

The *Quartet for Horn, Violin, Cello and Piano* of 1976 is of unfailing quality and imagination, and its development is magnificently sustained. The composer's command of large-scale musical thinking is much in evidence – but so, too, is his feeling for sonority. He draws some extraordinary sounds from these four instruments. In some ways this is one of his most deeply original and compelling works. The later *Horn Trio*, written for Anthony Halstead, Frank Lloyd and Carol Slater, immediately pre-dates the *Ninth Symphony*. These are most impressive pieces, and the performances are completely dedicated and highly imaginative. Excellent recording too.

String Quartets 1; 4
*** Hyp. CDA 66419. Delmé Qt

The *First Quartet* opens in as innocent a fashion as the Haydn *Lark Quartet* or Nielsen's *E flat*, but the better one comes to know it the more it is obvious that Simpson is already his own man. The second movement is a palindrome (many modern composers do not know how to write forwards, let alone backwards as well) but its ingenuity is worn lightly. The *Fourth* is part of the trilogy which Simpson conceived as a kind of commentary on Beethoven's *Rasumovsky Quartets*, yet they live very much in their own right. Excellent performances from the Delmé Quartet, and fine recording too.

String Quartets 2; 5
*** Hyp. CDA 66386. Delmé Qt

The *Second Quartet* is thought-provoking and full of character. The *Fifth*, composed over 20 years later in 1974, is one of the three modelled on Beethoven's *Rasumovsky Quartets* – in this case, Op. 59, No. 2 – and even emulates the phrase structure of the Beethoven. It is a long and powerfully sustained piece, which receives expert advocacy from the Delmé Quartet and excellent Hyperion sound.

String Quartets 3 & 6; String Trio (prelude, adagio & fugue)
*** Hyp. CDA 66376. Delmé Qt

The *Third Quartet* is a two-movement piece. Its finale is a veritable power-house, with its unrelenting sense of onward movement which almost strains the medium. Its first movement is a deeply felt piece that has a powerful and haunting eloquence. The *Sixth* is further evidence of Simpson's remarkable musical mind. The *String Trio* is a marvellously stimulating and thoughtful piece. Dedicated performances and excellent recording.

String Quartets 7 & 8
*** Hyp. CDA 66117. Delmé Qt

The *Seventh Quartet* has a real sense of vision and something of the stillness of the remote worlds it evokes, 'quiet and

mysterious yet pulsating with energy'. The *Eighth* turns from the vastness of space to the microcosmic world of insect-life, but, as with so much of Simpson's music, there is a concern for musical continuity rather than beauty of incident. Excellent playing from the Delmé Quartet, and very good recorded sound, too.

String Quartet 9 (32 Variations & Fugue on a Theme of Haydn)
*** Hyp. CDA 66127. Delmé Qt

The *Ninth Quartet* is a set of thirty-two variations and a fugue on the minuet of Haydn's *Symphony No. 47*. Like the minuet itself, all the variations are in the form of a palindrome. It is a mighty and serious work, argued with all the resource and ingenuity one expects from this composer. A formidable achievement in any age, and a rarity in ours. The Delmé Quartet cope with its difficulties splendidly, and the performance carries the imprimatur of the composer. The recording sounds very good in its CD format.

String Quartets 10 (For Peace); 11
*** Hyp. CDA 66225. Coull Qt

The subtitle of No. 10, *For Peace*, refers to 'its generally pacific character' and aspires to define 'the condition of peace which excludes aggression but not strong feeling'. Listening to this *Quartet* is like hearing a quiet, cool voice of sanity that refreshes the troubled spirit after a long period in an alien, hostile world. The one-movement *Eleventh* draws on some of the inspiration of its predecessor. It is a work of enormous power and momentum. Excellent performances and recording.

String Quartet 12 (1987); (i) String Quintet (1987)
*** Hyp. CDA 66503. Coull Qt, (i) with Bigley

Robert Simpson's *Twelfth Quartet* is a masterly and absorbing score. His *String Quintet* is another work of sustained inventive power. We are unlikely to get another recording, so this is self-recommending; but it must be noted that the heroic demands this score makes on the players keep them fully stretched. The intonation and tone of the leader is not always impeccable, but the playing has commitment and intelligence.

String Quartets 14 & 15; (i) Quintet for Clarinet, Bass Clarinet & Strings
*** Hyp. CDA 66626. (i) Farrall, Cross; Vanbrugh Qt

The *Fourteenth Quartet* comes from 1990, and the *Fifteenth*, written when Simpson was seventy (in 1991), was his last. This is surely the greatest quartet cycle produced in the last half of the twentieth century, and in terms of contrapuntal ingenuity and musical depth belongs with Bartók, Shostakovich and Holmboe. The *Clarinet Quintet* is not to be confused with the 1968 work listed above; it is an arrangement for clarinet, bass clarinet and string trio of a 1983 quintet intriguingly scored for clarinet, bass clarinet and three double basses. These are powerful Beethovenian scores whose stature and musical processes are easier to recognize than describe. Dedicated performances, superbly recorded.

Piano Sonata; Michael Tippett, his Mystery; Variations & Finale on a Theme by Beethoven; Variations & Finale on a Theme by Haydn
*** Hyp. CDA 66827. Clarke

The *Piano Sonata* is a concentrated, craggy, powerfully

argued piece, not obviously pianistic but bristling with challenges and difficulties. The *Variations and Finale on a Theme
of Haydn* (1948) evince Simpson's lifelong interest in the
palindrome. The slow movement of the *Second Symphony* is a
palindrome, and the theme he uses here (that of the minuet
of Haydn's *Symphony No. 47*) also forms the basis of the
mighty variations which comprise the *Ninth String Quartet*.
The short piece written for Tippett was a contribution to a
birthday tribute. The *Variations and Finale on a Theme of
Beethoven* are based on a little-known *Bagatelle*, WoO 61a,
and were written for Charles Burney's granddaughter, and
with the present pianist in mind. The performances are
authoritative and, apart from a certain over-resonance, the
recording is satisfactory.

SINDING, Christian (1856–1941)

Violin Concerto 1 in A, Op. 45; Romance in D, Op. 100
(N) (BB) *** Naxos 8.557266. Kraggerud, Bournemouth SO,
Engeset – SIBELIUS: *Violin Concerto*, etc. **(*)

Henning Kraggerud's powerful reading of the Sibelius *Violin
Concerto* comes here with an unusual and attractive coupling
in another Scandinavian violin concerto, the first of the three
written by the Norwegian, Christian Sinding. Though the
opening theme in this work is a barefaced crib from the finale
of the Brahms *Violin Concerto*, Sinding's individual voice is
quickly established in the full-blooded first movement, leading to a darkly intense slow movement and dance-like finale.
The shorter piece nicely points the contrast of character
between the two composers. Full, vivid sound.

Suite in A min., Op. 10
(M) *** EMI (ADD) 5 62590-2. Perlman, Pittsburgh SO,
Previn– KORNGOLD; SIBELIUS: *Concertos* ***

Heifetz recorded this dazzling piece in the 1950s, and it need
only be said that Perlman's version (restored to the catalogue
as part of the 'Perlman Edition') is not inferior. The blend of
archaism and fantasy in Sinding's *Suite* sounds distinctly
Scandinavian of the 1890s yet is altogether fresh and quite
delightful. Such is the velocity of Perlman's first movement
that one wonders whether the recording transfer is playing at
the right speed. Stunning virtuosity and vivid recording.

Légende, Op. 46
(BB) *** Naxos 8.550329. Dong-Suk Kang, Slovak (Bratislava)
RSO, Leaper – HALVORSEN: *Air norvégien* etc.; SIBELIUS:
Violin Concerto; SVENDSEN: *Romance* ***

Dong-Suk Kang plays Sinding's *Légende* with great conviction
and an effortless, songful virtuosity. It is by no means as
appealing as the Halvorsen and Svendsen pieces but makes a
good makeweight for an excellent collection in the lowest
price range.

Symphonies 1 in D min., Op. 21; 2 in D, Op. 83
*** CPO 999 502-2 Hanover NDR PO, Dausgaard
(BB) *** Warner Apex 0927 48310-2. Norwegian R. O,
Rasilainen

Symphonies 3 in F, Op. 121; 4 (Winter and Spring), Op. 129
(N) *** CPO 999 596-2. N. German R. PO, Porcelijn
*** Finlandia 8573 82356-2. Norwegian R. O, Rasilainen

Most Norwegian composers after Grieg and Svendsen are
steeped in their rich storehouse of folk song, but an exception
is Christian Sinding of *Rustle of Spring* fame. He began the

First of his four symphonies in 1887, though it did not reach
its final form until the mid-1890s, while the *Second* followed a
decade later. Both symphonies are well crafted, though the
scoring is often opaque. Thomas Dausgaard is a persuasive
advocate and gets good playing from the excellent Hanover
Orchestra. On balance, this is to be preferred to the rival
Norwegian Radio accounts under Ari Rasilainen; however,
readers wanting to explore the first two symphonies will
surely be tempted by the low price of the Apex disc.

Sinding's *Symphony No. 3*, his longest and most ambitious
work, was completed in 1919 when he was 73, and was first
performed the following year under the great Arthur Nikisch.
In a leaping 9/8 compound-time the first theme enters at
once, with horns whooping exuberantly, leading to a second
subject which echoes the Rhine motif in Wagner's *Ring* cycle.
This is the music of a young-sounding composer rather than
of a septuagenarian, and though the slow movement with its
gentle flow of themes is less striking, the skipping dance-
rhythms of the Scherzo and the strong, *Meistersinger*-like
tread of the celebratory finale again bring exhilaration. The
Symphony No. 4, like *No. 3* warmly and colourfully performed
under the Dutch conductor, David Porcelijn, is structurally
more adventurous, with its linked sequence of seven sections
offering a satisfying one-movement symphonic structure.
Amazingly, the piece was produced for Sinding's 80th birthday. Like the performances, the North German Radio recording is first rate, and it is again preferable to the alternative
Finlandia coupling.

*Scenes of Life, Op. 51; Sonata in F, Op. 73; Romance in E
min., Op. 9; Suite in the Old Style, Op. 99* (all for violin &
piano)
(N) *** CPO 999 931-2. Bratchkova, Meyer-Hermann

Dora Bratchkova and Andreas Meyer-Hermann admirably
catch the light-hearted spirit of these agreeable works, with
the central *Cantabile* of *Op. 73* and the *Andante doloroso* of
the *Suite in the Old Style* played most touchingly. The rhythmic feeling of the *Allegretto* in 5/4 tempo of the same piece is
nicely caught, and the long-breathed early *Romance*, Op. 9, is
pleasingly contoured. There is plenty of vivacity here too, and
the four *Scènes de la vie* are both colourful and zesty. Good,
lifelike recording.

Violin Sonatas in C, Op. 12; in F, Op. 74; Suite in F, Op. 14
(N) *** ASV CDDCA 1166. Rogliano, Paciariello

All three of the violin works on this ASV disc date from early
in Sinding's long career but have similar qualities. Like the
Symphony No. 3, the *C major Violin Sonata* starts with
another surging theme, leaping in compound-time, while the
F major work is warmly Brahmsian in its positive sequence of
attractive ideas. The *Suite*, written at the same time as the *C
major* work, is like a sonata with a shortened first movement:
a strong opening theme with baroque violin flourishes leads
to a lyrical second subject which then, instead of developing
in sonata form, takes you straight back to the opening theme.
An amiable piece, like the sonatas very well performed and
recorded by the Italian duo of Marco Rogliano and Maurizio
Paciariello.

SIRMEN, Maddalena Lombardini
(1745–1818)

String Quartets 1–6
*** Cala CACD 1019. Allegri Qt

Maddalena Lombardini was born in Venice. She proved so talented that she was sent to study with Tartini, and it was primarily as a violinist, in his view 'absolutely without equal', that she first made her reputation, although she also trained as a singer.

Her *String Quartets* were published in Paris in 1769 by another enterprising woman, Madame Berault. The string quartet medium was at that time in its infancy (the present contribution is approximately contemporary with Haydn's Op. 9 set) and thus her easy skill in handling the medium is the more remarkable. The Allegri Quartet obviously lived with this music for some time before this record was made, and they play it with much style and conviction, conveying their own pleasure in part-writing which is obviously enjoyable to play. With excellent recording, admirably present but naturally balanced, this is very much worth exploring.

String Quartets 2 in B flat; 3 in G min.

*** CPO 999 679-2. Basle Erato Qt – E. MAYER: *Quartet 14;* F. MENDELSSOHN: *String Quartet* ***

Many collectors will be satisfied with just two of these enjoyable quartets, particularly as the couplings here are so enterprising. They are two-movement works and fit rather well together: the catchy finale of the *B flat major* nicely complements the elegant opening *Tempo giusto* of the *G minor*. The performances here are excellent and so is the recording.

SKROUP, František (1801–62)

The Tinker Overture

(**) Sup. mono SU 1914 011. Czech PO, Sejna – DVORAK: *The Cunning Peasant Overture* (**); SMETANA: *Festive Symphony*, etc. (***)

The author of the sleeve-note speaks of 'the stunning melodic spontaneity' of Skroup's *The Tinker Overture*, which is no small claim. It is not a bad piece, but its melodic invention, while pleasant, is far from stunning. Sejna's performance is marvellously spirited, but the recording was made in 1951 and is rather thin on top.

SLAVICKY, Klement (1910–99)

Moravian Dance Fantasias; Rhapsodic Variations

(N) (M) (**(*)) Sup. mono SU 3688-2. Czech PO, Ančerl – NOVÁC: *In the Tatra Mountains* (**(*))

Klement Slavicky was a member of the Czech Radio's Music Department until 1951, when he left to pursue a freelance career. His *Moravian Dance Fantasias*, written the same year, wear well. They were originally coupled with Janáček's *Lachian Dances*, appropriately enough, since Slavicky's father had been one of his pupils. We enjoyed them then – rather more than the Janáček coupling – and still do. They are colourful, and the folk-like invention is full of character and individuality. The *Rhapsodic Variations* followed a couple of years later and are also rewarding. The sound comes up very well in both works.

SMETANA, Bedřich (1824–84)

Festive Symphony in E, Op. 6; Festive Overture, Op. 4

(M) (***) Sup. stereo/mono SU1914 011. Czech PO, Sejna – DVORAK: *Cunning Peasant Overture*; SKROUP: *The Tinker Overture* (**)

Smetana's *Festive* or *Triumphal Symphony* from 1853 is best known for its effervescent Scherzo, which is often performed on its own. It is also by far the best of the four movements. Karel Sejna's account was recorded in 1966, though the orchestral texture is so well balanced that it can hold its own with more modern recordings. The *Festive Overture*, Op. 4, recorded in 1955, is amazingly good for its period.

Má Vlast (complete)

☞– *** Sup. 11 1208-2. Czech PO, Kubelik

(BB) *** Naxos 8.550931. Polish Nat. RSO (Katowice), Wit

*** Telarc CD 80265. Milwaukee SO, Macal

*** Chan. 9366. Detroit SO, Järvi

(M) *** Sup. SU 3672-2 901. Czech PO, Ančerl

*** Sup. SU 3465-2 031. Czech PO, Mackerras

(N) (BB) *** EMI HMV 5 896768-2. RLPO, Pešek

(B) **(*) Sony SBK 89776. Israel PO, Mehta

(N) ** RCA 2-CD 82876 54331-2 (2). VPO, Harnoncourt

In 1990 Rafael Kubelik returned to his homeland after an enforced absence of 41 years to open the Prague Spring Festival with this vibrant performance of *Má Vlast*. He had recorded the work twice before in stereo, but this Czech version is special, imbued with passionate national feeling, yet never letting the emotions boil over. At the bold opening of *Vyšehrad*, with the harp strongly profiled, the intensity of the music-making is immediately projected, and the trickling streams, which are the source of *Vltava*, have a delicacy almost of fantasy. *Sárka*, with its bloodthirsty tale of revenge and slaughter, is immensely dramatic, contrasting with the pastoral evocations of the following piece; the Slavonic lilt of the music's lighter moments brings the necessary contrast and release. The recording is vivid and full but not sumptuous, yet this suits the powerful impulse of Kubelik's overall view, with the build-up to the exultant close of *Blaník* producing a dénouement of great majesty.

Antoni Wit and his excellent Polish National Radio Orchestra give us a superbly played and consistently imaginative account. The spacious opening of *Vyšehrad*, marginally slower than usual, glows with romantic evocation; equally the flutes, trickling down from the sources of the *Vltava*, captivate the ear and the famous string-tune is unusually gracious and relaxed. The opening of *Sárka* brings tingling melodrama, which subsides naturally for the jaunty theme which follows. *From Bohemia's Woods and Fields* opens with opulent expansiveness, and later the ethereal high string entry is exquisitely made. *Tábor* develops great weight and gravitas. The warm resonance of the Concert Hall of Polish Radio in Katowice seems right for this very individual reading, full of fantasy, which goes automatically to the top of the list alongside Kubelik's distinguished, and justly renowned, 1990 Czech Philharmonic version on Supraphon, which is rather special.

Macal's Telarc version offers the finest recording of all; indeed it approaches the demonstration bracket. He provides a highly spontaneous and enjoyable performance, imaginatively conceived and convincingly paced. Other accounts, notably Kubelik's, have greater Slavic fire and find a more red-bloodedly patriotic feeling, but the excellent orchestral playing is responsive to his less histrionic view. *Sárka* has a folksy flavour, the melodrama good-humoured, while in *From Bohemia's Woods and Fields*, after the radiant high string passage, the horns steal in magically with their chorale. Throughout the brass are full and sonorous, mitigating any rhetorical bombast in the last two symphonic poems; and

Macal's Czech nationality ensures that the performance has idiomatic feeling.

Järvi's, too, is an enjoyably vivid performance, and he has the double advantage of first-class playing from the highly committed Detroit orchestra and the splendid acoustics of Symphony Hall. The romantic *Vyšehrad* is fresh and immediate, and the mountain streams of *Vltava* gleam brightly in the sunlight before the string-tune arrives and moves on with plenty of lyrical impetus. *Šárka* is very dramatic indeed, with great melodramatic gusto and a heartfelt response from the strings. The opening of *Tábor* is tellingly ominous, and the weight of the Detroit brass makes a powerful contribution to both of the final two sections of the score; the zest of the Detroit music-making is always compelling, and the culminating climax is thrilling rather than expansively grandiloquent.

The CD of Karel Ančerl's 1963 performance is something of a revelation. We dismissed the original LP for its unattractive sound, which appeared to be artificially brightened, but the quality is now transformed by the CD transfer, full, warmly atmospheric yet still brilliant. The performance is full of character and the playing of the Czech Philharmonic is superb, with glowing woodwind detail and much beautiful string-playing. Ančerl clearly relishes the folk-like inspiration and colour of the melodic writing, and his account of *Šárka* is one of the most attractive on record. *Tábor* and *Blaník* are highly dramatic, but less self-consciously patriotic than usual, and the music itself seems closer to the symphonic poems of Dvořák.

Mackerras's affinity with Czech music is well known, and although his version of *Má Vlast* does not displace existing recommendations it ranks high among them. The sound has presence and body, and the warm, reverberant acoustic is pleasing yet allows plenty of detail to register.

Pešek's idiomatic account of *Má Vlast* is very well played and recorded. Pešek's reading does not miss the music's epic patriotic feeling, yet never becomes bombastic. There is plenty of evocation, from the richly romantic opening of *Vyšehrad* to the more mysterious scene-setting in *Tábor*, while the climax of *Šárka*, with its potent anticipatory horn-call, is a gripping piece of melodrama. The two main sections of the work, *Vltava* and *From Bohemia's Woods and Fields*, are especially enjoyable for their vivid characterization, while at the very end of *Blaník* Pešek draws together the two key themes – the *Vyšehrad* motif and the Hussite chorale – very satisfyingly.

It would be easy to undervalue Mehta's Israel performance, for he clearly enjoys the music and so do the Israeli players; the recording is fuller and somewhat more atmospheric than we often experience in Tel Aviv, although it is at times unrefined and string detail is husky. Mehta's tempi are close to Järvi's in the first three symphonic poems, rather more expansive in the second triptych. *Vyšehrad* comes off quite effectively. But after an attractively delicate opening, the great string-tune of *Vltava* fails really to take off, and the climax needs a more expansive acoustic. The opening of *Tábor* isn't very arresting either, and both here and in *Blaník*, although the adrenalin runs freely, there is an element of bombast (the comparatively dry acoustic does not help) and Mehta seldom displays the imaginative flair of his competitors.

Harnoncourt's live performance is in every way a disappointment. It is well played, of course, and the central movements, *Šárka* and *Tábor*, are more strongly characterized than usual. But the flowing tune of *Vltava* does not really take off, and the normally expansive acoustics of the Vienna Musikverein are deadened by the presence of an audience; the sound is lacking in range and is inclined to be opaque.

Má Vlast: From Bohemia's Woods and Fields; Vltava; Vyšehrad. The Bartered Bride: Overture & Dances

(BB) *** DG 474 565-2. VPO, Levine

The three *Má Vlast* excerpts, taken from Levine's complete set, are quite splendid, full of momentum and thrust, aptly paced, with much imaginative detail. The opening of *Vyšehrad* immediately shows the impulse of the music-making, yet it is warmly romantic too; while the two most famous pieces, *Vltava* and *From Bohemia's Woods and Fields*, are full of flair and are most beautifully played. The *Bartered Bride Overture* and *Dances* are highly infectious: Levine offers the usual numbers, plus the *Skočná*. The sound is full-blooded and vivid, with a wide amplitude and range to give the music plenty of atmosphere. A good bargain for those just wanting the popular numbers of *Má Vlast*.

Má Vlast: Vltava

(M) *** DG 463 650-2. BPO, Fricsay – DVORAK: *Symphony 9 (New World)*; LISZT: *Les Préludes* ***
**(*) DG 439 009-2. VPO, Karajan – DVORAK: *Symphony 9 (New World)* **(*)
(M) (***) EMI mono 5 62790-2. VPO, Furtwängler – R. STRAUSS: *Death and Transfiguration* etc. (***)

With Fricsay the *Vltava* river is obviously in full flood, yet every episode is freshly and characterfully detailed, with the lake twinkling in the moonlight, contrasting with the spectacle of the St John's rapids. A splendid bonus for a memorably individual account of the *New World Symphony*.

Karajan's VPO performance is characteristically well structured, and the recorded sound sounds quite expansive in this remastered format, even if the balance is not quite natural.

Furtwängler's recording of *Vltava* was made in the Musikvereinsaal in 1951 with Walter Legge producing, a guarantee of a finely balanced musical sound which does justice to the tonal finesse of the Vienna orchestra. It serves as an introduction and makeweight to three Strauss tone-poems that were given performances of commanding eloquence and which remain in the memory long after the record ends.

Má Vlast: Vltava. The Bartered Bride: Overture; Polka; Furiant

(N) (B) *** Decca (ADD) 476 2453. Israel PO, Kertész – DVORAK: *Slavonic Dances*; ENESCU: *Romanian Rhapsody 1* ***

With Kertész, these pieces are exceptionally vivid. The separate entries in the overture are beautifully clear and the ambience makes the background rustle of the strings all weaving away at their fugato theme sound quite captivating. *Vltava* too is very brilliant, with fast tempi, yet not losing its picturesque qualities. Vivid sound and exciting music-making make this disc something of a classic.

CHAMBER MUSIC

Duo for Violin & Piano (From the Homeland)

*** Praga PRD 250 153. Remeš, Kayahara – DVORAK: *Sonatina*; JANACEK; MARTINU; SMETANA: *Violin Sonatas* ***
(N) (M) *** Sup. SU 3772. Suk, Panenka – DVORÁK: *Romantic Pieces, Sonatina*; SUK: *Ballade; 4 Pieces* ***

Smetana's two-movement *Duo* (*From the Homeland*) is, not surprisingly, full of endearing Czech folk influences, with the dumka-style hovering over the first movement. The lyrical second part at first has something of a domestic atmosphere, yet the infectious spirit of the *Skočná* soon asserts itself. It is marvellously played by these two fine artists, who are thoroughly immersed in its local atmosphere. The recording is vividly live and present.

They are also admirably played by Suk and Panenka, who are just as idiomatic in feeling, and are most naturally recorded.

Piano Trio in G min., Op. 15

☞ *** Chan. 8445; Borodin Trio – DVORAK: *Dumky Trio* ***

(BB) *** Warner Apex 7559 79679-2. Boston Symphony Chamber Players – DVORAK: *String Sextet in A* ***

*** Ara. Z6661. Golub-Kaplan-Carr Trio – TCHAIKOVSKY: *Piano Trio* ***

**(*) MDG MDGL 3247. Trio Parnassus – ARENSKY: *Piano Trio in D min* **(*)

Writing the *Trio* was a cathartic act, following the death of the composer's four-year-old daughter, so it is not surprising that it is a powerfully emotional work. The writing gives fine expressive opportunities for both the violin and cello, which are taken up eloquently by Rostislav Dubinsky and Yuli Turovsky, and the pianist, Luba Edlina, is also wonderfully sympathetic. In short, a superb account, given a most realistic recording balance. Highly recommended.

The 1983 Boston performance on Warner Apex brings a distinguished line-up, Joseph Silverstein, the cellist Jules Eskine and the pianist Gilbert Kalisch. This sensitive and vital account ranks among the most competitive of Smetana's *Piano Trio*, particularly given its price bracket. It comes with a warm and affectionate account of the Dvořák *Sextet*.

Although the balance may place the listener a bit too close to the players for some tastes, the Arabesque CD offers a perfectly pleasing sound and the performance is eminently musical and unaffected. This is the kind of chamber-music playing to inspire confidence in the future: nothing overdriven, mechanized or attention-seeking. While it does not necessarily displace the Borodin Trio, it can be ranked among the best and is the only recording to offer so substantial a partner as the Tchaikovsky Trio – completely uncut, too.

The Trio Parnassus play very much in the nineteenth-century manner and tend to underline and italicize, but they give a likeable and convincing performance, very alive and vivid. Their coupling, the Arensky *D minor Trio*, may well sway some readers in their favour.

String Quartet 1 in E min. (From My Life)

*** EMI 7 54215-2. Alban Berg Qt – DVORAK: *String Quartet 12* ***

(***) Testament mono SBT 1072. Hollywood Qt – DVORAK; KODALY: *Quartets* (***)

(M) (***) BBC mono BBCL 4137-2. Smetana Qt – BEETHOVEN: *String Quartet 1* (**); MOZART: *String Quartet 20* (**(*))

(M) **(*) DG (IMS) (ADD) 437 251-2. Amadeus Qt – DVORAK: *String Quartet 12* **(*)

The Alban Berg Quartet sound just a shade too polished and professional. There is not quite enough spontaneity. All the same, there is much more to admire in the Alban Berg's reading than to cavil at: the first movement comes off well,

and the EMI recording is very truthful and present. There is no cause to withhold a third star, particularly as their Dvořák is very successful.

This Hollywood Quartet recording was never issued in the UK in the 1950s when it was made. It is a performance of tremendous fire and passion, with an exhilarating rhythmic drive and a powerful sense of momentum. Yet everything sounds perfectly natural and not overdriven. Great quartet playing – and perfectly acceptable sound, given the mid-1950s date.

The Smetana Quartet's performance of the *E minor Quartet* (*From my Life*) comes from a BBC relay from the Royal Festival Hall in June 1965, and the mono sound is very acceptable indeed. The Smetanas recorded it commercially, but their playing here has equal polish, ardour and freshness. Recommended, alongside the best of its rivals.

A strongly felt and purposeful account from the Amadeus, who are on top form: their ensemble, matching of timbre and unanimity of attack, is peerless. At times one feels that Norbert Brainin wears his heart too openly on his sleeve; but there is no doubt that the performance overall is gripping, and the 1977 recording is vividly realistic.

String Quartet 1 (From My Life) (orchestral version by George Szell); The Bartered Bride: Overture & Dances

*** Chan. 8412. LSO, Simon

The Czech feeling of Szell's scoring is especially noticeable in the *Polka*, but overall there is no doubt that the fuller textures add a dimension to the music, though inevitably there are losses as well as gains. The powerful advocacy of Geoffrey Simon and the excellent LSO playing, both here and in the sparkling excerpts from *The Bartered Bride*, provide a most rewarding coupling. The recording is well up to the usual high Chandos standards.

String Quartets 1 in E min. (From My Life); 2 in D min. (plus Documentary)

(*) Sup. **DVD SU 7004-2. Smetana Qt – DVORAK: *Sextet in A* **(*)

From the Smetana Quartet, straightforward performances and equally straightforward presentation for the camera. Perhaps they are not quite as fresh as the recordings they made commercially in the 1960s or the BBC broadcast reviewed below, but they still bring a special authority to this repertoire. However, the documentary in which the members of the quartet look back over their career is curiously stiff and it is difficult to imagine oneself replaying it. Recommended for the performances, however.

String Quartets 1 (From My Life); 2 in D min.

☞ *** ASV CDDCA 777. Lindsay Qt (with DVORAK: *Romance; Waltzes 1–2* ***)

(N) (B) **(*) Virgin 2x1 5 26347-2 (2). Endellion Qt – DVORAK: *String Quartet 12* **(*); MARTINU: *Concertos* ***

(M) **(*) Telarc CD 80178. Cleveland Qt – BORODIN: *Quartet 1* **(*)

(M) **(*) Sup. SU 3450-2 131. Panocha Qt

** Sup. 3740-2. Skampa Qt

The Lindsay Quartet bring dramatic intensity to the *E minor Quartet* and play with great fire and vitality. Their (perhaps slightly forward) recording is very good indeed, and readers wanting both the Smetana *Quartets* together need look no further.

The Endellion Quartet give a spirited account, strongly characterized, but it does not always speak with wholly idiomatic accents. Their playing is always vitally musical, rich in sonority and strongly passionate, however. They are very well recorded, but there is a small reservation about the Dvořák coupling.

The Cleveland Quartet play magnificently but, as in the coupled Borodin, their performance is a bit short on spontaneity. The recording is first class.

The two string quartets from the Panocha Quartet are short measure at 45 minutes! These are well-played and intelligently shaped performances, but there are finer, more spirited versions in the catalogue.

The Skampa coupling was made in 2003 and should surely accommodate more. Although this group is highly regarded among Czech quartets, their account of the *E minor Quartet* falls short of distinction when placed alongside the Alban Berg or the Hollywood (on Testament). The *Second* is another matter, and receives a performance of quality. However, the Supraphon recording is curiously dry and for those wanting both Quartets the Lindsays remains first choice.

PIANO MUSIC

Memories of Bohemia in the Form of Polkas, Op. 12; Op. 13; 3 Poetic Polkas, Op. 8; Polkas in F min.; A; E; G min.; 3 Salon Polkas, Op. 7

(N) (M) ** Warner Elatus 2564 61734-2. Schiff

This issue serves as a reminder of the excellence and freshness of Smetana's keyboard music. Two-thirds of his output is for the piano. András Schiff is as sympathetic an interpreter as one could wish for, but the attractions of the disc are somewhat diminished by the claustrophobic acoustic, which lends a brittle tone to the instrument.

OPERA

The Bartered Bride (complete, in Czech)

☞ *** Sup. 10 3511-2 (3). Beňačková, Dvorský, Novák, Kopp, Jonášová, Czech Philharmonic Ch. and O, Košler

The digital Supraphon set under Košler admirably supplies the need for a first-rate Czech version of this delightful comic opera. The performance sparkles from beginning to end, with folk rhythms crisply enunciated in an infectiously idiomatic way. The cast is strong, headed by the characterful Gabriela Beňačková as Mařenka and one of the finest of today's Czech tenors, Peter Dvorský, as Jeník. Miroslav Kopp in the role of the ineffective Vašek sings powerfully too. As Kecal the marriage-broker, Richard Novák is not always steady, but his swaggering characterization is most persuasive. The CDs offer some of the best sound we have yet had from Supraphon, fresh and lively. The discs are fairly generously banded, but this could now be fitted on a pair of CDs, so the set is unnecessarily expensive. The libretto, however, has been improved and is clear and easy to use.

The Bartered Bride: Overture

(N) (M) *** RCA (ADD) **SACD** 82876 66376-2. Chicago SO, Reiner – DVORAK: *Symphony 9 (New World)*; WEINBERGER: *Schwanda: Polka & Fugue ***

The easy, bustling virtuosity of the Chicago strings makes this vivacious performance of Smetana's famous overture hard to beat, when the remastered recording is so full on SACD, while retaining its clear inner detail.

The Brandenburgers in Bohemia (complete)

**(*) Sup. (ADD) 11 1804-2 (2). Zídek, Otava, Subrtová, Kalaš, Joran, Vich, Prague Nat. Theatre soloists, Ch. & O, Jan Hus Tichý

Though much of the drama centres on the fate of the heroine, Liduše, abducted by a Prague burgher with the mercenary Germanic name of Tausendmark, the love interest which must sustain any romantic opera is sketched in only cursorily. The main duet between Liduše and her beloved, Junoš, is charming and jolly rather than heartfelt, an opportunity missed. Nevertheless there is much to enjoy in a performance as lively as this, with stirring patriotic choruses sung with a will, even if their melodic invention is hardly distinguished. Milada Subrtová sings with appealingly sweet, firm tone as Liduše, and the young Ivo Zídek makes a fresh-voiced hero, strained only a little on top. Tausendmark is sung by a stalwart veteran, Zdeněk Otava, making up in bite what he lacks in vocal quality. A collector's item.

Dalibor (complete)

*** Sup. (ADD) 11 2185-2 (2). Přibyl, Kniplová, Jindrák, Svorc, Horáček, Prague Nat. Theatre Ch. & O, Krombholc

In the development of the plot, when the imprisoned hero's lover is disguised as the gaoler's assistant, *Dalibor* readily evokes associations with *Fidelio*, and the subject prompted Smetana to write some of his most inspired music. The confrontations between hero and heroine also inspire Smetana to some glorious writing, richly lyrical, most notably the love duet in the prison scene of Act II. This vintage set of 1967, sounding more vivid and full-blooded than many more recent recordings, features in those roles two of the most distinguished Czech singers of their time, both in their prime, the tenor Vílém Přibyl and the dramatic soprano, Nadezda Kniplová. The other principals are not so consistent, but Krombholc proves a most persuasive advocate, consistently bringing out the red-blooded fervour of the writing. Highly recommended to anyone who wants to investigate beyond *The Bartered Bride*. A full translation is provided.

Libuše

**(*) Sup. 11 1276-2 633 (3). Beňačková, Zítek, Svorc, Vodička, Děpoltová, Prague Nat. Theatre Ch. & O, Košler

Recorded live, the cast here is even stronger than that of the previous recording under Krombholc, with Gabriela Beňačková-Cápová as Libuše memorable in her prophetic aria in Act III. Václav Zítek as Přemysl, her consort, provides an attractive lyrical interlude in Act II, which, with its chorus of harvesters, has affinities with *The Bartered Bride*. In Act I there is some Slavonic wobbling, notably from Eva Děpoltová as Krasava, but generally the singing is as dramatic as the plot-line will allow. Košler directs committedly; with the stage perspectives well caught, an unintrusive audience and no disturbing stage-noises with such a static plot, the recording is very satisfactory. The cues still provide poor internal access for an opera playing for not far short of three hours. Twelve extra index points have been added to the 14 bands – not nearly enough for a work of this kind.

The Two Widows (complete)

** Sup. (ADD) 11 2122-2 (2). Sormová, Machotková, Zahradníček, Horáček, Prague Nat. Theatre Ch. & O, Jílek

The Two Widows is a tale of country life in the big house rather than among the peasantry, with the plot centring on two cousins, both widows, and inconsequential confusions over which of them is going to marry the hero, Ladislav. That said, Smetana offers much delightful music and there are some charming numbers in between, not least an aria for the hero, '*When Maytime arrives*', at the beginning of Act II. Jiří Zahradníček is at his best there, singing lustily, though in gentler moments Slavonic unsteadiness develops. Jaroslav Horáček is effective in the *buffo* bass role of Mumlal but, sadly, the casting of the two widows, both sopranos, involves the major role of Karolina going to the shrill and wobbly Nǎda Sormová, while Marcela Machotková, who is altogether sweeter and firmer, with a mezzo-ish quality, is consigned to the role of Anežka with far less to sing, even though it is she who gets the hero. Recorded in 1975, this lively performance under Frantisek Jílek is on the whole well transferred to CD, though in a dryish acoustic the Prague Theatre violins sound undernourished. The libretto includes a very necessary translation.

SMYTH, Ethel (1858–1944)

(i) *Concerto for Violin, Horn & Orchestra. Serenade in D*
♠— *** Chan. 9449. (i) Langdon, Watkins; BBC PO, De la Martinez

The *Concerto for Violin, Horn and Orchestra* is a highly successful piece in every respect. The first movement begins with an ambitious string melody, then the soloists enter alternately with the endearing secondary idea (one of the composer's very best tunes), which is imaginatively developed in a free fantasia of flowing and dancing melody and varying moods; only at the recapitulation do the soloists share the opening theme. The romantic central *Elegy* brings a touchingly beautiful and nostalgic exchange between the two soloists.

The *Serenade in D major* might well be Brahms's. Not only does the rich string writing of the first movement have a glorious sweep, but the harmonic thinking and progressions are *echt*-Brahms. Yet Smyth's invention is of high quality, for all its eclecticism. With superb performances and warm, sumptuous recording, both these colourful and tuneful works will give great pleasure. This is easily the most impressive Smyth offering yet to have appeared on CD, and it is conducted with understanding and commitment.

The Wreckers: Overture
(B) *** CfP (ADD) 767 7532. RSNO, Gibson – GERMAN: *Welsh Rhapsody*; HARTY: *With the Wild Geese*; MACCUNN: *Land of the Mountain and Flood* ***

Ethel Smyth's *Overture* for her opera, *The Wreckers*, is a strong, meaty piece, which shows the calibre of this remarkable woman's personality for, while the material itself is not memorable, it is put together most compellingly and orchestrated with real flair. The recording is full and the CD has refined detail.

String Quartet in E min.; (i) String Quintet in E, Op. 1
♠— **(B)** *** CPO 999352-2. Mannheim Qt, with (i) Griesheimer

The *Quintet* of 1884 may suggest Dvořák's *American Quartet* and *New World Symphony* in its first movement, but the Smyth *Quintet* was written before either of those works, a strongly built piece with substantial outer movements framing three interludes, including a brief, magical *Adagio* which breathes the air of late Beethoven. Even more delightful and refreshing is the *Quartet*, begun in 1902 but not completed until ten years later. Instead of an allegro first movement, Smyth opts for an easy-going *Allegretto*, while the beautiful, peacefully lyrical slow movement equally belies the composer's political image.

SOMERVELL, Arthur (1863–1937)

Violin Concerto in G
(N) *** Hyp. CDA 67420. Marwood, BBC Scottish SO, Brabbins – COLERIDGE-TAYLOR: *Violin Concerto* **(*)

Sir Arthur Somervell is best remembered for his settings of *A Shropshire Lad* and Tennyson's *Maud*. He was Inspector of Music at the Board of Education (as the Department or Ministry was then known). Like the Coleridge-Taylor concerto with which it is coupled, it was its composer's last work. Written for Adila Fachiri (Jelly d'Aranyi's sister), it was first broadcast by the BBC Symphony Orchestra under Sir Adrian Boult in 1933 and then promptly forgotten. In its easy late-romantic style, it makes a strong impression, a more persuasive piece than the Coleridge-Taylor concerto. The long first movement in traditional layout includes an opening orchestral tutti and a big cadenza, with a warmly Elgarian theme for second subject. The central *Adagio* is richly lyrical and beautifully orchestrated (a song-composer's inspiration), leading to a jaunty, brightly inventive finale rather like a pastoral dance. This is its first performance since the 1930s and, although the debt to Elgar must be noted, it is well worth hearing. Superbly played and brilliantly recorded, it makes a most attractive rarity. Anthony Marwood is a fine soloist and more committed than the orchestra under Martyn Brabbins. An interesting and worthwhile coupling.

Clarinet Quintet in G
(BB) *** Hyp. Helios (ADD) CDH 55110. King, Aeolian Qt – JACOB: *Clarinet Quintet* ***

Sir Arthur Somervell first studied composition under Stanford and, later, Parry, but his dominating musical influences came from the German school and in particular from Brahms, whose voice can be heard at the very opening of this rather lovely *Quintet*. It is just the sort of work that deserves resurrection on record when fashion no longer matters. The *grazioso* first movement and touching *Adagio* (*Lament*) are in contrast to the bubbling finale which is a special delight, with Thea King and the Aeolian Quartet at their most persuasive, helped by very good (1979) recording, well transferred to CD.

SORABJI, Khaikhosru (1892–1988)

Fantaisie Espagnole; Fantasiettina sul nome illustre dell'egregio poeta Christopher Grieve ossia Hugh M'Diarmid (Tiny Little Fantasy on the Illustrious Name of the Distinguished Poet Christopher Grieve, i.e. Hugh M'Diarmid); Fragment for Harold Rutland; Gulistán (The Rose Garden): Nocturne for Piano; Introito and Preludio-Corale from Opus Clavicembalisticum; Le Jardin parfumé (Poem for Piano); Nocturne: Djâmî. 3 Pastiches: Chopin's Valse, Op. 64/1; Habanera from Bizet's Carmen; Hindu Merchant's Song (Rimsky-Korsakov). Piano Pieces: In the Hothouse; Prelude, Interlude & Fugue; Toccata.

Quaere relique hujus materiei inter secretiora; St Bertrand de Comminges: 'He was Laughing in the Tower'; Valse Fantaisie (Hommage à J. Strauss)

*** British Music Society BMS 427-9 (3). Habermann (with HABERMANN: *A la manière de Sorabji: 'Au clair de la lune'* ***)

This three-CD set collects the remarkable recordings that Michael Habermann has made of Sorabji's piano music over the years. It is well known that after a performance of his *Opus Clavicembalisticum* Sorabji banned further performance of his music – or, rather, insisted that it should be given only with his expressed permission. Yonty Solomon in Britain and Michael Habermann in America were his chosen interpreters. Habermann proves an extraordinarily persuasive advocate of this music: he has all the virtuosity it needs, as well as the musical and imaginative insight. When Sorabji played his *First Sonata* to Busoni in London in 1919, Busoni observed that it was like 'a tropical forest' and it is for its luxuriant, hothouse textures that it has gained a reputation. The *Fantaisie espagnole* (1918) is an extraordinarily fantastic evocation of the sights and sounds of Spain and *Le Jardin parfumé*, which earned Delius's admiration, has all the sensuous loveliness of the latter but with an added vivid luxuriance of texture and colour. Sorabji's musical world derives inspiration from Busoni, Scriabin and middle-period Szymanowski, and some have seen it as foreshadowing Messiaen. (He had little time for Messiaen, as R.L. can testify; having written without enthusiasm about one of Messiaen's larger works, he received a card from Sorabji memorably describing the French master as 'Scriabinated Franck'. Be that as it may, these three discs leave no doubt as to the uniqueness and originality of Sorabji's music. Habermann's excellent notes are worth quoting for they sum the composer up well: 'The interaction of imaginative rhythms, melodies, harmonies and textures in his music is fascinating – perhaps even awe-inspiring. Moods are varied. The nocturnal pieces explore mystical trance states. The energetic pieces grab the listener by their sheer obstinacy and determination, and massive climaxes encompass the entire arsenal of the piano (and pianist).' Habermann is a splendid exponent of the pyrotechnical wizardry and the richness of imagination of these scores, and he gives us an admirable entry point into Sorabji's world. The recordings are eminently acceptable.

Fantaisie espagnole
*** Altarus AIR-CD 9022. Amato

Sorabji's *Fantaisie espagnole* comes from 1919 and shows his preoccupation with exotic, Szymanowskian keyboard textures and voluptuous, Ravel-like harmonies. Donna Amato seems completely attuned to the idiom. It is a short work (just under 18 minutes) and is brilliantly played and recorded on this Altarus single.

SOUSA, John Philip (1854–1932)

Marches: *The Ancient and Honourable Artillery Company; The Black Horse Troops; Bullets and Bayonets; The Gallant Seventh; Golden Jubilee; The Glory of the Yankee Navy; The Gridiron Club; High School Cadets; The Invincible Eagle; The Kansas Wildcats; The Liberty Bell; Manhattan Beach; The National Game; New Mexico; Nobles of the Mystic Shrine; Our Flirtation; The Piccadore; The Pride of*

Wolverines; Riders for the Flag; The Rifle Regiment; Sabre and Spurs; Sesqui-Centennial Exposition; Solid Men to the Front; Sound Off

(N) (M) *** Mercury **SACD** (ADD) 475 6182. Eastman Wind Ens., Fennell

Fennell's Mercury collection of 24 Sousa marches (73 minutes) has characteristic American pep and natural exuberance, and the zest of the playing always carries the day. One of the more striking items is *The Ancient and Honourable Artillery Company*, which incorporates *Auld Lang Syne* as its middle section. The sound is brilliant in the Mercury way and will be even more impressive for those with SACD equipment. The most vivid Sousa collection around.

SPOHR, Ludwig (1784–1859)

(i) *Clarinet Concertos 1 in C min., Op. 26; 3 in F min., WoO19;* **(ii)** *Potpourri for Clarinet & Orchestra in F, Op. 80*
(BB) *** Naxos 8.550688. Ottensamer; (i) Slovak State PO (Košice); (ii) Slovak RSO (Bratislava), Wildner

Clarinet Concertos: 1 in C min.; 2 in E flat; Potpourri in F; Variations in B flat
(N) *** Hyp. CDA 67509. Collins, Swedish CO, O'Neill

Clarinet Concertos 2 in E flat, Op. 57; 4 in E min.; Fantasia & Variations on a Theme of Danzi, Op. 81
⊶ (BB) *** Naxos 8.550688. Ottensamer, Slovak RSO (Bratislava), Wildner

Spohr's four concertos were written between 1908 and 1929 for the clarinettist Johann Simon Hermstedt, but although they are all in a traditional three-movement format, each work has a character of its own. The *First* opens with a delightful chorale-like theme on the woodwind, which then becomes the basis for the first movement.

The *Second Concerto* brings a bustling first movement with an engagingly dotted marching theme, very like Hummel.

The very dramatic opening tutti of the *Third Concerto* introduces a charmingly doleful lyrical melody in the violins over a pizzicato accompaniment, to balance a dramatic restlessness in the orchestra. The lovely *Adagio* is deeply expressive, all but worthy of Mozart.

The *Fourth Concerto* is in many ways the finest of all, opening with a solemn minor-key exposition, and even the secondary theme is lyrically restrained, with the orchestral tuttis reflecting a more searching mood than in the earlier works, and the lyrical interludes make it plain that Spohr is determined to avoid any suggestion of triviality.

The *Danzi Fantasia* opens very dramatically, but its basic theme is simple and ingenuous, its treatment histrionically operatic.

The four works on Hyperion are perfect vehicles for the dazzling virtuosity of Michael Collins, superbly accompanied by the Swedish Chamber Orchestra under Robin O'Neill. The treatment is always nicely pointed and inventive. The *Second Concerto* in particular is a delight, with jaunty martial rhythms in the outer movements. The *Potpourri* is a double set of variations on themes from a long-forgotten opera by Peter von Winter, and the *Variations in B flat* similarly use a theme from Spohr's own opera, *Alruna*. Spohr was still in his twenties when he wrote these works, and that is reflected in the consistent freshness of the writing. Full, immediate sound.

Ernst Ottensamer is a most sensitive artist and a superb

player with an appealingly warm, liquid tone. Apart from sailing through all Spohr's decorative roulades and technical extravagances with aplomb, he plays over the widest range of dynamic, often fining down his tone to a pianissimo to echo a phrase with magical effect. Johann Wildner provides lively, polished accompaniments, and the recording is first rate. It is difficult to imagine these performances being surpassed, and this pair of discs would be highly recommendable if they cost far more.

Clarinet Concerto 1 in C min., Op. 26

(M) *** Classic fM 75605 57019-2. Lawson, Hanover Band, Goodman – WEBER: Clarinet Concertos 1–2 etc. ***

On Classic fM the first of Spohr's Clarinet Concertos provides a generous bonus on an outstanding disc. Colin Lawson, principal clarinet of the Hanover Band, plays most imaginatively with attractively reedy tone to match the period instruments of his colleagues. Full and vivid sound.

Concerto for String Quartet & Orchestra in A min., Op. 131

*** Ara. Z 6723. San Francisco Ballet O, Lark Qt, Le Roux – HANDEL: Concerto grosso in B flat, Op. 6/7; SCHOENBERG: Concerto for String Quartet & Orchestra after Handel's Concerto grosso, Op. 4/7; ELGAR: Introduction & Allegro for Strings ***

This is a consistently engaging work (Spohr's very last concerto), inventive and tuneful – the slow movement is particularly fine – using the players in the solo quartet individually as well as in consort. It is very persuasively played, and with the proviso that the solo group are balanced rather forwardly, the recording is very good too. With imaginative couplings this is very much worth trying.

Violin Concertos 7 in E min., Op. 38; 12 in A min., Op. 79

(BB) **(*) Naxos 8.555101. Nishizaki, Bratislava Philharmonic CO, Pešek

The key of Spohr's E minor Concerto brings a certain Mendelssohnian affinity, especially in the passage work. Its lyrical ideas are attractive, especially the rather lovely Adagio, and the bouncing finale dances in a fast waltz tempo.

The more rhapsodic Twelfth Concerto, written over a decade later (and actually designated a concertino), is in a single movement of three linked sections, with a closing Polacca. Takako Nishizaki plays both works affectionately and very stylishly, and she is warmly accompanied by Pešek and the Bratislava orchestra. The recording is pleasingly resonant, but the microphones are perhaps a fraction too close to the solo violin.

(i) Overture, Op. 12; (i; ii) Quartet Concerto, Op. 131; (iii) Nonet in F, Op. 31

(N) **(*) MDG 307 0849-2. (i) Leipzig CO, Weigle; (ii) Leipzig Qt; (iii) Ens. Villa Musica

This collection is a disappointment. The Overture is rather bland, and the players are not helped by the resonant acoustic. Nor does the opening movement of the Quartet Concerto come off well texturally for similar reasons, although the Adagio is beautiful. So too is the Adagio of the better-known Nonet; indeed, it is gloriously played and the finale is neat and delightfully spirited. However, the Gaudier and Nash Ensembles both offer equally fine performances, more attractively coupled with the Octet – see below.

Symphonies 1 in E flat, Op. 20; 5 in C min., Op. 102

**(*) Marco Polo 8.223363. Slovak State PO (Košice), A. Walter

Spohr wrote ten symphonies in all: the First when he was in his mid-twenties and still in thrall to Mozart; the Fifth comes from the late 1830s and was much admired by Schumann. Although he is no great symphonist, Spohr is an eminently civilized composer, and the case for him is well put by Alfred Walter and the Košice orchestra, who are decently served by the engineers.

Symphonies 2 in D min., Op. 49; 9 in B min. (The Seasons), Op. 143

** Marco Polo 8.223454. Slovak State PO (Košice), A. Walter

The Second Symphony (1820) has dramatic undertones, but emerges here an amiable, Mendelssohnian work with a neat Scherzo and much Schubertian charm in the finale. Walter's performance is warm and polished, but one feels the music could be given a stronger profile. At the opening of The Seasons, the Schumanesque depiction of Winter entirely lacks icicles, but the Transition to Spring brings some delightful birdsong and leads to a charming Ländler, which later becomes more animated. Summer is hazily somnolent with 'distant sounds of thunder', then simple horn-calls lead into the more exuberant hunting and drinking scene of autumn, with some colourful orchestral effects. In imaginative force this is not a patch on Haydn, but one feels a really strongly characterized performance could make more of it than does the rather literal-minded Alfred Walter.

Symphonies 3 in C min., Op. 78; 6 in G (Historical Symphony in the Style and Taste of Four Different Periods), Op. 116

*** Marco Polo 8.223349. Slovak State PO (Košice), A. Walter

This coupling, which so far is the best of Walter's Spohr series, is well worth getting. The Historical Symphony is a fascinating pastiche, and the C minor is one of the finest of Spohr's early symphonies, inspiring Walter to give one of his most vigorous and committed performances. The Larghetto has genuine depth, but the most ambitious movement is the highly inventive finale, both life-enhancing and energetic, and with plenty of contrapuntal interest, including a full-scale central fugue. It is very well played indeed. The Historical Symphony is most endearing in its respect for the great masters. It opens with a solemn, full-orchestral treatment of the C major fugue from Book I of Bach's '48', and also introduces pastoral reminders of Handel's Messiah, including an allusion to 'He shall feed his flock'. The slow movement, richly scored, remembers both Mozart's 39th and Prague Symphonies, and in the curiously lyrical Scherzo the timpani (rather too muted here) recall the Beethoven of the Seventh Symphony. The inappropriately but agreeably frivolous finale, 'the latest of the new', then bursts with energy, drawing on the vivacious ideas of Adam and Auber, in particular the Muette de Portici Overture. Walter is a convincing exponent of this curiously balanced work, and his orchestra respond with enthusiasm.

Symphonies 7 in C (The Earthly and Divine in Human Life), Op. 121; 8 in G, Op. 137

** Marco Polo 8.223432. Slovak State PO (Košice), A. Walter

In contrasting his Irdisches und Göttliches im Menschenleben, Spohr uses the concerto grosso principal, with an eleven-piece concertino representing the 'divine', while the full orchestra are the 'earthly'; here both elements are fairly fully integrated. He charmingly and successfully depicts The World of Childhood, but the profounder sentiments of The Age of

Passion defeat him, and the *Final Triumph of the Heavenly*, moves from melodrama to a serene but complacent sentimentality. The *Eighth Symphony*, although conservative, is an altogether better proposition. The work's kernel is a fine, sombre *Poco Adagio*, with the strings effectively underpinned by trombone sonorities. The Scherzo opens with a romantic horn-call and features an obbligato solo violin in the Trio. Together with the engagingly songful finale, it almost turns the symphony into a serenade. Alfred Walter is clearly at home here and the Slovak orchestra creates a Bohemian bonhomie in the two final movements. Good, smooth, warm sound.

Nonet in F, Op. 31

(***) Testament mono SBT 1261. Augmented Vienna Octet – BEETHOVEN: *Septet* (***)

It is good to see this 1952 Decca recording of Spohr's delightful *Nonet* – full of tunes and good humour – return to the catalogue. The playing here is superb, full of unforced charm, with a lovely Viennese glow. The transfers are excellent, the mono sound unbelievably warm and rich for the period.

CHAMBER MUSIC

Double Quartet 1 in D min., Op. 65

(BB) ** Warner Apex 8573 89089-2. Kreuzberger Qt & Eden Qt – MENDELSSOHN: *Octet; String Quartet 1 in E flat, Op. 12* **

The Kreuzberger and Eden Quartets join together to give a well-integrated and felicitous performance of Spohr's *Double Quartet*, which is distinctly enjoyable, especially the vivacious *Allegro molto* finale. The snag is that the remastered recording from the early 1980s has just a touch of edge on the string sound.

Double Quartets 1 in D min., Op. 65; 2 in E flat, Op. 77; 3 in E min., Op. 87; 4 in G min., Op. 136

*** Hyp. Dyad CDD 22014 (2). ASMF Chamber Ens.

The opening of the first *Double Quartet* is inviting (as again is the rather solemn introduction of the *Third*, which then lightens, yet retains its nostalgic feeling). While this is all essentially amiable music, the standard of Spohr's invention is quite high throughout all four works, and the scoring cleverly makes the most of the antiphony between the two groups. So does the recording here, with a natural interplay within a pleasingly warm acoustic. The playing is predictably fluent and spontaneous-sounding, well blended and polished.

Nonet in F, Op. 31; Octet in E, Op. 32

☛ *** Hyp. CDA 66699. Gaudier Ens.

(M) *** CRD (ADD) CRD 3354. Nash Ens.

The Gaudier Ensemble give us a performance of the *Octet* as imaginative as it is spontaneous, and the work's finale with its lolloping main theme is joyously spirited. The *Nonet* is also very attractive. Spohr's invention is again at its freshest and his propensity for chromaticism is held reasonably in check. The Hyperion recording is fresh and warm, clearly detailed against a resonant acoustic, although this means that the first violin is given a fractional hint of wiriness by the fairly close microphones.

The sound on the competing CRD disc is that bit more mellifluous, yet it remains natural and lifelike; some may prefer the greater suavity of the analogue tonal blend in this urbane music. The Nash Ensemble play both works with much elegance and style, and these performances are very civilized and hardly less spontaneous.

Octet in E, Op. 32

(M) *** Decca (ADD) 466 580-2. Vienna Octet – SCHUBERT: *Octet in F, D.803* ***

Spohr's Octet is a particularly charming work, and the variations on Handel's *Harmonious Blacksmith*, which forms one of the central movements, offer that kind of naïveté which, when so stylishly done as here, makes for delicious listening. The playing is expert throughout, with the five strings blending perfectly with the two horns and clarinet, and altogether this is a winning performance. The 1960 recording is fresh and open and leaves little to be desired.

Piano Quintet in D min., Op. 130; Septet, Op. 147

☛ *** MDG 304 0534-2. Ens. Villa Musica

The *Piano Quintet* is a dashingly amiable work and its first movement has a primary theme which includes a bravura passage of hair-raising filigree, which the pianist of the excellent Villa Musica Ensemble, Kalle Randalu, manages with a nimbleness that the first violin's comparable arabesques can only just match. The following Scherzo, too, is full of virtuoso bonhomie, and its middle section produces more glittering pianistic roulades. The *Adagio* at last brings a mood of serenity to provide a peaceful interlude before the rollicking finale. The spirited MDG performance is most enjoyable and the much better-known *Septet* for piano and wind is played with comparable relish and warmth. Excellent, vividly present recording makes this a most enjoyable coupling.

Piano & Wind Quintet in C min., Op. 52; String Quintet 6, Op. 130; Septet, Op. 147; String Sextet, Op. 140

(N) *** MDG 304 1263-2. Ens. Villa Musica

These are all attractive works, a little garrulous at times but always fluently melodic and well crafted. In the two works with piano, the pianist at times is called upon to play some hair-raising runs, which Kalle Randalu manages with aplomb. Both the *String Sextet* and *Quintet* have fine slow movements, and the *Piano and Wind Quintet* has a sparkling finale, with a particularly winning secondary theme. Fine performances throughout and natural reording, although rather resonant.

Piano Trios 1 in E min., Op. 119; 2 in F, Op. 123; 3 in A min., Op. 124; 4 in B flat, Op. 133; 5 in G min., Op. 142

(B) *** CPO 999 246-2 (3). Ravensburg Beethoven Trio

Piano Trios 3 in A min., Op. 124; 4 in B flat, Op. 133

**(*) Chan. 9372. Borodin Trio

Piano Trios 1-5; (i) Piano Quintet in D, Op. 130

(BB) ** Naxos 8.553206 (1 & Quintet); 8.553205 (2 & 4); 8.553164 (3 & 5). Hartley Piano Trio; (i) with Outram

Spohr's five *Piano Trios* are among his freshest, most appealing chamber works, full of attractive ideas and fine craftsmanship. The Ravensburg Trio give fine performances, mellow, with slightly more gravitas than sparkle, although they too have an excellent pianist in Inge-Susann Römchild, whose touch is often pleasingly light. The CPO recording is warm and full to suit the playing. The five *Trios* are just too long to fit on a pair of CDs, and the third plays for only 31 minutes.

The Borodin Trio offers plenty of life and the Chandos recording is pleasingly open and vivid. But Luba Edlina's vibrant temperament and timbre do not so readily match Spohr's relatively suave writing, and this coupling is less enjoyable than either of the complete sets.

The Naxos acccounts (available separately) are well played and serviceable, and have the advantage of including the *Piano Quintet*, which has a remarkable, sparkling *Scherzo*, changing mood in the Trio. Its pensive *Adagio* is one of the composer's most expressively telling, and the finale then trips along gaily. Caroline Clemmov generally rises to the occasion. The recording is fully acceptable, and this first disc of the three is worth sampling, and after that the third (with Nos. 3 and 5) for these players, if not having a particularly strong collective personality, are thoroughly musical and at home in this composer's idiom.

Piano & Wind Quintet in C min., Op. 52; Septet in A min. for Flute, Clarinet, Horn, Bassoon, Violin, Cello & Piano, Op. 147
(M) *** CRD (ADD) CRD 3399. Ian Brown, Nash Ens.

These two pieces, the sparkling *Quintet* and the more substantial but still charmingly lighthearted *Septet*, are among Spohr's most delightful. Ian Brown at the piano leads the ensemble with flair and vigour, and the recording quality is outstandingly vivid.

String Quartets 1 in C; 2 in C min., Op. 4/1-2; 5 in D, Op. 15/2
*** Marco Polo 8.223253. New Budapest Qt

If you enjoy the earlier and middle-period Haydn Quartets, you might well try Spohr. He seems also to have an almost inexhaustible fund of ideas and writes enjoyably smooth, well-crafted works, which every so often produce a movement which is quite memorable – like the gentle *Adagio* of his very first essay in the medium, strikingly fresh, written when the composer had just turned twenty. Op. 4/2 has an opening movement which is worthy of Haydn and the *Poco Adagio* is just as thoughtful as its predecessor. The Rondo finale, with its dotted main theme is very catchy. Op. 15/2 is without a slow movement. However the accomplished fugal finale has a brief *Adagio* introduction. The performances here are always persuasive and well recorded too: it is a pity that this series does not appear on the Naxos label, when it would be even more recommendable. However, praise is due for the excellent documentation.

String Quartets 7 in E flat; 8 in C, Op. 29/1-2
**(*) Marco Polo 8.22355. New Budapest Qt

The Op. 29 *Quartets* are associated with Johann Tost (dedicatee of Haydn's Opp. 54/5 and 65). Both are written in Spohr's friendly, accomplished style; the first ingeniously bases its opening movement on a two-note motto theme and has an outstanding set of variations for its slow movement. The tender *Adagio* of the *C major* is even finer, daring in its expressive chromaticism. Both performances are spontaneous and this is vibrant, felt quartet-playing, without artifice, and the recording is lively and present.

String Quartets 11 in E (Quatuor brillant), Op. 43; 12 in C, Op. 45/1
**(*) Marco Polo 8.223257. New Budapest Qt

String Quartets 13 in E min.; 14 in F min., Op. 45/2-3
*** Marco Polo 8.223258. New Budapest Qt

The *Quatuor brillant* dates from 1817, and its subtitle is deceptive, for, as its engaging opening suggests, it is essentially a lyrical work, although the closing Minuet sparkles brightly enough. The Op. 45 quartets are more romantic in feeling, suaver in texture, moving further away from the classical Haydn idiom. The melancholy introduction to the *F minor Quartet* certainly catches the listener up, but the clouds lift with the key change to *A major* and the first movement is essentially amiable, although the hymn-like *Adagio* returns to the mood of the opening. The 'fantasy' *Scherzo* is then most welcome, and the brilliant finale soon produces a lollipop lyrical idea, which then dominates the movement. The Budapest players are at their very best in these two fine works.

String Quartets 15 in E flat; 16 in A, Op. 58/1-2
*** Marco Polo 8.23256. New Budapest Qt

The two Op. 58 *Quartets* written in 1821 show a new maturity, especially the noble *Adagio* of the *E flat major*, which reminds one of Mozart, after a cheerful first movement laced with effective pizzicatos. The light-hearted Scherzo, with its Viennese, Ländler-influenced Trio has much charm, and the work is capped by a springy closing Rondo. A splendid disc in every way.

String Quartets 20 in A min.; 21 in B flat, Op. 74/1-2
*** Marco Polo 8.223259. New Budapest Qt

The Op. 74 *Quartets*, dating from 1826, are further evidence of Spohr's increasingly deft integration of his ideas in finely argued first movements, essentially lyrical but not lacking dramatic elements. The players here again respond very sympathetically to these attractive quartets and capture their spirit admirably. Fine, natural recording.

String Quartets 27 in D min.; 28 in A flat, Op. 84/1-2
**(*) Marco Polo 8.223251. New Budapest Qt

These two works, written in 1831-2, exemplify Spohr's smooth, finely integrated quartet-writing at its most characteristic. The slow movement, sustaining a mood of serene simplicity, is the most memorable in each case, although the lyrical finale of the *A flat major Quartet* is also rather appealing. Good performances, lively enough, but capturing the suaveness of the idiom. The recording is truthful.

String Quartets 29 in B min., Op. 84/3; 30 in A, Op. 93
**(*) Marco Polo 8.223252. New Budapest Qt

In many ways *No. 29 in B minor* is the finest of the Op. 84 set, with its touch of melancholy in the first movement, a lively minuet and a pensive slow movement. Op. 93, written in 1835, is more extrovert in atmosphere in the first movement (after a sombre introduction), but it offers another thoughtfully intense slow movement and a very jolly finale. It brings out the best in these players – and there is plenty of bravura for the first violin – and, again, good tonal matching plus a smooth, warm recording combine effectively for this slightly suave music.

String Quintets 1 in E flat; 2 in G, Op. 3/1–2
(BB) *** Naxos 8.555965. Augmented Danubius Qt

String Quintets 3 in B min., Op. 69; 4 in A min., Op. 91
**(*) Naxos 8.223599. Augmented Danubius Qt

Spohr's *String Quintets* feature a second viola, which gives them a characteristically full, slightly bland texture. But the suave opening theme of the *E flat major Quartet* is deceptive, for it is strong enough to influence the two following movements including the near-melancholy *Larghetto* and the attractive Minuet and Trio. In the *G major* work a similarly mild opening theme is to dominate. Both quintets are warmly and sympathetically played by the Danubius Quartet, augmented by Sándor Papp, and smoothly and pleasingly recorded. Originally on Marco Polo, this reissue is eminently competitive at its Naxos price.

String Quintet 4, Op. 91; String Sextet in C, Op. 140; Pot-pourri on Themes of Mozart, Op. 22
**(*) Chan. 9424. ASMF Chamber Ens.

To be candid, the *A minor String Quintet*, although as always with this composer well crafted, is rather bland, a characteristic the well-rehearsed ASMF performance does very little to counteract. The Mozartian *Potpourri* is much more entertaining. The fine *String Sextet in C major*, one of the composer's last chamber works, from 1848, has a particularly endearing Brahmsian main theme in the first movement, a hymn-like slow movement and a brilliant finale. The ASMF Chamber Ensemble give a fine, polished account of it, well recorded.

String Quintets 5 in G min., Op. 106; 6 in E min., Op. 129
(BB) **(*) Naxos 8.555967. Augmented Budapest Haydn Qt

The *G minor Quintet* has a disarmingly winsome opening movement, followed by a simple *Larghetto*, rich in texture. Then, after the vigorous Scherzo, the finale has a rustic character with a drone-like accompaniment for the main theme. The *E minor Quintet* brings a busy but blander opening movement, with an underlying melancholy lyricism, which is dispelled by the Mendelssohnian Scherzo, with the gracious Trio coming twice, but in different keys. The calm of the reflective *Adagio* then contrasts with the energetic, even agitated finale. These are two fine works, very persuasively played, even if the ensemble is not always absolutely immaculate. Good recording too, and value for money at Naxos price.

String Quintet 7 in G min., Op. 144; Potpourri (for solo violin and string quartet), Op. 22; Sextet in C, Op. 140
*** Marco Polo 8.223600. Augmented New Haydn Qt

The *Seventh Quintet* is, like its odd-numbered predecessor, Op. 106, also in G minor, but its character is more recessive, and the feeling of unease that permeates the first movement is at times reflected in the essentially serene and beautiful *Larghetto*. The Minuetto, too, is less extrovert than usual, and while the finale has the undulating rhythm of a barcarole, it does not wholly resolve earlier uncertainties.

The *Sextet* is much sunnier, opening warmly, and even its rather grave *Larghetto* has a hint of geniality in its secondary material. The Scherzo, which includes a charming *con grazia* section, leads straight into the finale, and the two movements are cunningly intermingled, with a very positive but brief *prestissimo* coda.

Spohr used the *Potpourri* as a show-off piece to act as an encore at his own concerts. A Russian folk tune, with variations, is contrasted with a hit tune of the time, *Là ci darem la mano* from Mozart's *Don Giovanni*. Very good performances here and first-rate recording. Let us hope this soon reappears on the Naxos label, but it is worth its asking price.

SPONTINI, Gasparo (1774–1851)

Olympie (opera): complete
**(*) Orfeo C 137862H (3). Varady, Toczyska, Tagliavini, Fischer-Dieskau, Fortune, Berlin RIAS Chamber Ch., German Op. Male Ch., Berlin RSO, Albrecht

In Spontini's *Olympie*, based on an historical play by Voltaire about the daughter of Alexander the Great, the writing is lively and committed and, despite flawed singing, so is this performance. Julia Varady is outstanding in the name-part, giving an almost ideal account of the role of heroine, but Stefania Toczyska is disappointingly unsteady as Statire and Franco Tagliavini is totally out of style as Cassandre. Even Dietrich Fischer-Dieskau is less consistent than usual, but his melodramatic presentation is nevertheless most effective. The text is slightly cut.

STAINER, John (1840–1901)

The Crucifixion
(N) (BB) *** Naxos 8.557624. Gilchrist, Bailey, Clare College, Cambridge, Ch., T. Brown; S. Farr (organ)
(B) *** CfP (ADD) 575 7792 (2). Hughes, Lawrenson, Guildford Cathedral Ch., Rose; Williams – MAUNDER: *Olivet to Calvary* ***

(i) *The Crucifixion; Come Thou Long Expected Jesus* (hymn); *I Saw the Lord* (anthem); (ii) *Love Divine, all Loves Excelling* (hymn)
(M) *** Decca (ADD/DDD) 470 379-2. (i) Lewis, Brannigan, St John's College, Cambridge Ch., Guest; (ii) King's College, Cambridge Ch., Cleobury

It is good to have an outstanding new digital recording of *The Crucifixion*, with excellent soloists (the tenor James Gilchrist outstandingly eloquent); and Clare College Choir, directed by Timothy Brown, sings very beautifully, catching the music's devotional simplicity movingly, without sentimentality. Stephen Farr's organ contribution is supportive but not intrusive. The recording, made in Guildford Cathedral, is first class. With the congregational hymns included, this must now take pride of place, although we still have a soft spot for the old St John's version with Owen Brannigan and Richard Lewis.

All five hymns in which the congregation is invited to join are included on the Decca (originally Argo) record. Owen Brannigan is splendidly dramatic and his voice makes a good foil for Richard Lewis in the duets. The choral singing is first-class, and the 1961 recording is of Argo's best vintage, even finer than its CfP competitor. Moreover, the latest Decca reissue includes three bonuses: a fine eight-part anthem, *I Saw the Lord*, and two hymns, one of which is a favourite, sung by King's College Choir.

The Classics for Pleasure version (from the late 1960s) is of high quality and, although one of the congregational hymns is omitted, in every other respect this can be recommended. John Lawrenson makes a movingly eloquent solo contribution and the choral singing is excellent. The remastered recording sounds first class, but the Decca version is finer still. This reissue, very aptly coupled with Maunder's *Olivet to Calvary*.

STAMITZ, Carl (1745–1801)

Cello Concertos 1 in G; 2 in A; 3 in C
☞— (BB) *** Naxos 8.550865. Benda, Prague CO

These three delightful concertos are admirably played by Christian Benda, who also directs his own accompaniments. He is a present member of a well-known family of Czech musicians, a dynasty which reaches back to the court of Frederick the Great. The *First G major Concerto* is particularly winning, and the spirited allegros of the other two works are hardly less amiable and each has a slow movement with a yearning contour, with the closing *Rondo* of the *C major* work the most infectious of all. The recording is excellent, and if you enjoy cello concertos this group is not to be missed. A small reservation is that the cadenzas, composed by another member of the Benda family, could with advantage have been more succinct.

Clarinet Concertos 3 in B flat; 10 in B flat; 11 in E flat
*** EMI 7 54842-2. Meyer, ASMF, Brown – J. STAMITZ: *Concerto in B flat* ***

Clarinet Concertos 7 in E flat; 8 in B flat (Darmstadt 1-2); 10 in B flat; 11 in E flat
(BB) *** Naxos 8.554339. Berkes, Nicholas Esterházy Sinfonia

Clarinet Concerto 10 in B flat
*** EMI CDC5 55155-2. Meyer, ASMF, Brown – MOZART: *Clarinet Concerto*, etc.; WEBER: *Clarinet Concerto 1* ***

Sabine Meyer's performances are highly musical and she is given characteristically polished and elegant accompaniments by Iona Brown and the Academy. However Kálmán Berkes on Naxos is by no means a lesser soloist. He finds a Bohemian sense of fun in the closing Rondos, which is less obvious with Meyer, although she still plays them lightheartedly and her collection remains very enjoyable. The accompaniments on Naxos are also warm and stylish and the recording is excellent.

In No. 10 the slow movement is plain beside that of its Mozart coupling, but Sabine Meyer presents it persuasively and makes much of the genial passage-work of the outer movements, and especially the roulades of the dancing finale. She is stylishly accompanied and excellently recorded.

Symphonies: in D (La Chasse); in C & G, Op. 13/16, 4 & 5; in F, Op. 24/3
*** Chan. 9358. LMP, Bamert

Carl Stamitz wrote over fifty symphonies and the present examples are most attractive examples of his three-movement 'Italian overture' style. His slow movements are Haydnesque and quite gracious; his finales are witty: that for the *F major* work is particularly catchy. *La Chasse* is the earliest work here and the outer movements have plenty of energy and whooping horn-calls, with a rather wistful *Andante* to separate them. Excellent performances, very well played and recorded.

STAMITZ, Johann (1717–57)

Clarinet Concerto 1 in F; (i) Double Clarinet Concerto in B flat; (ii) Double Concerto for Clarinet & Bassoon in B flat
☞— (BB) *** Naxos 8.553584. Berkes, with (i) Takashima; (ii) Okazaki; Nicholas Esterházy Sinfonia

The *F major* solo *Concerto* is a delightful work with a vigorous first movement leading to a lyrical minor-key *Andante* and a jig finale. The double concerto was a favourite form with Stamitz, with long opening tuttis in the slow movements as well as the first. Both works are linked to the sinfonia concertante format as well as to the earlier form of the concerto grosso with its strongly contrasted, lightly scored passages for the solo instruments. Both are built on attractive material, but the work for clarinet and bassoon is the more successful, with instruments sharply contrasted. As soloist as well as director, Berkes, with his reedy clarinet tone, is well matched by his Japanese partners, helped by full, open recording.

Clarinet Concerto 2 in B flat
*** EMI 7 54842-2. Meyer, ASMF, Brown – C. STAMITZ: *Concertos* ***

Johann Stamitz's *Concerto* has a rather fine slow movement and an elegantly good-natured closing rondo. It is most persuasively played here and excellently recorded.

Trumpet Concerto in D (arr. Boustead)
(B) *** Ph. Duo 464 028-2 (2). Hardenberger, ASMF, Marriner – HAYDN; HERTEL; HUMMEL: *Concertos* *** (with concert: 'Famous Classical Trumpet Concertos' *** ☯)

This *Concerto* was written either by Stamitz or by a composer called J. G. Holzbogen. The writing lies consistently up in the instrument's stratosphere and includes some awkward leaps. It is quite inventive, however, notably the finale, which is exhilarating on the lips of Håken Hardenberger. There is no lack of panache here and Marriner accompanies expertly. Good if reverberant recording, with the trumpet given great presence. This now comes as part of a Duo anthology, which is very highly recommendable.

Symphonies: in A; B flat; G (Mannheim); in D, Op. 3/2; in E flat, Op. 11/2; Orchestral Trio in E, Op. 5/3
(BB) *** Naxos 8.553194. New Zealand CO, Armstrong

The bold opening chords and immediately following crescendo of the *D major Symphony*, Op.3/2 (from the early 1750s) immediately establish its Mannheim credentials, as do the elegantly sophisticated scoring of the Andantino and the effective use of horns in the *Minuet* and *Trio*. The *E flat Symphony*, one of the composer's last, follows a similar pattern, but the three earlier works (from the 1740s), which are actually designated as 'Mannheim' Symphonies are altogether simpler, each with only three movements.

The *E major Trio* is much more ambitious, with a searchingly expressive *Adagio*, all but worthy of Haydn. The excellent New Zealand Chamber Orchestra under Donald Armstrong, play with finesse and vitality and are persuasive advocates of music which so far proves not especially adventurous. But this disc is described as Volume I, so perhaps they will make even more interesting discoveries later in their Naxos series.

(Orchestral) Trios, Op. 1/1-4
(BB) **(*) Naxos 8.553213. New Zealand CO, Armstrong

Although designated Op. 1, the six *Orchestral Trios* appear to be relatively late works (1755–6) and were designated by the composer to be performed optionally either as trios or by a fuller chamber orchestra, as here. They are each in four movements, elegant, simply constructed, with a divitimento-like character, but not trivial. The most striking is *No.4 in C minor*, which explores a wider range of expressive feeling than its companions, but the Siciliana-like *Larghetto* of the *F major* (No. 3), followed by a rather striking *Minuet* and robust finale, also sets that work apart. They are very well played here, polished in ensemble with musical phrasing and good use of light and shade. The recording is very natural. But one cannot pretend this is anything but pleasing wallpaper music, although it must have been rewarding for talented amateurs to play.

STANFORD, Charles (1852–1924)

Clarinet Concerto in A min., Op. 80
(BB) *** Hyp. Helios CDH 55101. King, Philh. O, Francis – FINZI: *Concerto* ***

The Stanford *Clarinet Concerto* finds Thea King bringing a firm, sharp attack. In the finale too King is strong and forthright, but she is warmer and more flexible in the slow movement, and at bargain price the Helios reissue remains competitive.

Piano Concerto 1 in G, Op. 59
*** Hyp. CDA 66820. Lane, BBC Scottish SO, Brabbins – PARRY: *Piano Concerto* ***

Written in 1894, the first of Stanford's two piano concertos brings even clearer Brahmsian echoes than usual, but the finesse of the writing and the ravishing beauty of the slow movement make it almost as enjoyable as the second and better-known concerto, particularly in a performance by turns as brilliant and poetic as Piers Lane's. Full, warm sound.

(i) Piano Concerto 2, Op. 126; Down among the Dead Men, Op. 71. Irish Rhapsodies 1; 2 (The Lament for the Son of Ossian); (ii) 3 (for Cello & Orchestra); 4 (The Fisherman of Loch Neagh and What He Saw); 5; (iii) 6 (for Violin & Orchestra)
(M) *** Chan. X10116 (2). (i) Fingerhut; (ii) Wallfisch; (iii) Mordkovitch; Ulster O, Handley

Stanford's ambitious *Second Piano Concerto*, although in three rather than four movements, is a work on the largest scale, recalling Brahms's *B flat Concerto*. Yet Stanford asserts his own melodic individuality and provides a really memorable secondary theme for the second movement, even if the finale is perhaps a little inflated. Margaret Fingerhut is a first-rate soloist, both here and in her apt and entertaining account of the *Down among the Dead Men Variations*, for Stanford was a dab hand at this format. The new coupling is with the six *Irish Rhapsodies* (two of them also concertante pieces with highly responsive soloists), which are the more impressive when heard as a set. They too are splendidly played and recorded.

Violin Concerto in D, Op. 74; Suite for Violin & Orchestra, Op. l32
☛ *** Hyp. CDA 67208. Marwood, BBC Scottish SO, Brabbins

Starting magically with the violin entering over an impressionistic twitter on woodwind, the Stanford *Violin Concerto* provides an important link between the Brahms concerto of 1878 and the Elgar of 1909–10. After that poetic start, Stanford builds his expansive structure in a strong Brahmsian manner, using clear, positive themes. He ends with an Irish jig finale,

the nationalistic equivalent of Brahms's Hungarian finale. Anthony Marwood gives a warm, clean-cut reading, as he also does in the *Suite*, an attractive if heavyweight example of 19th-century neo-classicism. A splendid addition to Hyperion's 'Romantic Violin Concerto' series, following up their brilliantly successful set of romantic piano concertos.

Symphonies 1–7
*** Chan. 9279/82 (4). Ulster O, Handley

Now available in a box of four CDs, with the fill-ups which accompanied the original CDs now put aside for separate reissue, this is obviously the most attractive way to approach this generally impressive if uneven British symphonic canon. Handley and his Ulster Orchestra are completely at home in this repertoire, and the Chandos recording is consistently of this company's best quality.

Symphony 1 in B flat, Op. 78; Irish Rhapsody 2: The Lament for the Son of Ossian, Op. 84
*** Chan. 9049. Ulster O, Handley

Stanford's mature musical studies had been in Berlin and Hamburg, and he came back to England profoundly influenced by the German symphonic style. Now we can discover for ourselves that, although he could assemble a convincing structure, his melodic invention was not yet strong enough to achieve real memorability. Handley and the Ulster Orchestra do their persuasive best for a piece which is certainly not a silk purse. The *Irish Rhapsody* has distinctly more melodramatic flair. Excellent recording.

Symphony 2 in D min. (Elegiac); (i) Clarinet Concerto
*** Chan. 8991. Ulster O, Handley; (i) with Hilton

In the *Second Symphony* the influences of German masters are still strong but the work still has its own individuality, for the most part in the scoring. The delightful *Clarinet Concerto* makes a splendid coupling, with Janet Hilton at her most seductive, both in timbre and in warmth, and articulating with nimble expertise. A delightful performance.

Symphony 3 (Irish), Op. 28; Irish Rhapsody 5, Op. 147
☛ *** Chan. 8545. Ulster O, Handley

This *Third* and most celebrated of the seven symphonies of Stanford is a rich and attractive work, none the worse for its obvious debts to Brahms. The ideas are best when directly echoing Irish folk music, as in the middle two movements, a skippity jig of a Scherzo and a glowing slow movement framed by harp cadenzas. The *Irish Rhapsody No. 5* dates from 1917, reflecting perhaps in its martial vigour that wartime date. Even more characteristic are the warmly lyrical passages, performed passionately by Handley and his Ulster Orchestra, matching the thrust and commitment they bring also to the *Symphony*.

Symphony 4 in F, Op. 31; Irish Rhapsody 6 for Violin & Orchestra, Op. 191; Oedipus Rex Prelude, Op. 29
*** Chan. 8884. Ulster O, Handley, (i) with Mordkovitch

The *Fourth Symphony*, like the *Third*, is a highly confident piece and an effective symphony, even if it runs out of steam before the close of the finale despite attractive invention. The *Irish* concertante *Rhapsody* is a much later work, its nostalgia nicely caught by the soloist here, Lydia Mordkovitch, who is obviously involved. Handley, as ever, takes the helm throughout with ardent commitment and makes the most of the many nice touches of orchestral colour. Excellent recording.

Symphony 5 in D (L'Allegro ed Il Penseroso), Op. 56; Irish Rhapsody 4 (The Fisherman of Lough Neagh and What He Saw)
*** Chan. 8581. Ulster O, Handley

Stanford's *Fifth Symphony* is colourfully orchestrated and full of easy tunes, illustrating passages from Milton's *L'Allegro* and *Il Penseroso*. The last two movements readily live up to Stanford's reputation as a Brahmsian, representing the *Penseroso* half of the work, and the slow epilogue brings reminders of Brahms's *Third*. The *Irish Rhapsody* is more distinctive, bringing together sharply contrasted, colourful and atmospheric Irish ideas under the title *The Fisherman of Lough Neagh and What He Saw*. Excellent recording of the finest Chandos quality.

Symphony 6 in E flat (In Memoriam G. F. Watts), Op. 94; Irish Rhapsody 1 in D min., Op. 78
*** Chan. 8627. Ulster O, Handley

Stanford's *Sixth Symphony* is not the strongest of the set, but it has a rather lovely slow movement, with a pervading air of gentle melancholy. The first movement has some good ideas but the finale is too long, in the way finales of Glazunov symphonies tend to overuse their material. Nevertheless Vernon Handley makes quite a persuasive case for the work and an even better one for the enjoyable *Irish Rhapsody No. 1*, which features and makes rather effective use of one of the loveliest of all Irish tunes, the *Londonderry Air*. Excellent sound.

Symphony 7 in D min., Op. 124; (i) Concert Piece for Organ & Orchestra, Op. 181; (ii) Irish Rhapsody 3 for Cello & Orchestra, Op. 137
*** Chan. 8861. Ulster O, Handley; with (i) Weir; (ii) R. Wallfisch

The *Seventh Symphony* sums up its composer as a symphonist – structurally sound, yet not now so heavily indebted to Germany, and with the orchestration often ear-catching. It is not a masterpiece, but it could surely not be presented with more conviction than here by Handley and his excellent orchestra. The *Irish Rhapsody* is very Irish indeed and makes the use of several good tunes. It is most sensitively played by Wallfisch, and Gillian Weir makes a strong impression in the *Organ 'Concertino'*, where the composer uses only brass, strings and percussion in the accompaniment. The music has a touch of the epic about it.

CHAMBER MUSIC

2 Fantasies (for clarinet & string quartet)
(BB) *** Hyp. Helios CDH 55076. King, Britten Qt – ROMBERG: *Clarinet Quintet* ***

Stanford's pair of *Fantasies* are miniature quartets, the first in three contrasted movements, the second in four. They are agreeably inventive, if not really memorable. Thea King and the Britten Quartet blend beautifully together and make the very most of them.

Serenade (Nonet) in F, Op. 95
(BB) *** Hyp. Helios CDM 55061. Capricorn – PARRY: *Nonet* ***

Like the Parry *Nonet*, with which it is coupled, the *Serenade* is an inventive and delightful piece, its discourse civilized and the Scherzo full of charm. Capricorn play this piece with evident pleasure and convey this to the listener. The recording

is very natural and truthfully balanced, and this disc is most reasonably priced.

Violin Sonatas 1 in D, Op. 11; 2 in A, Op. 70; Irish Fantasy 1 (Caoine), Op. 54 1; 5 Characteristic Pieces, Op. 93
*** Hyp. CDA 67024. Barritt, Edwards

One expected these to be enjoyably well-crafted works but they are a great deal more than that, teeming with memorable ideas, to make consistently delightful listing. Paul Barritt and Catherine Edwards play all this music with a spring-like freshness, and obviously enjoy every bar. They are beautifully recorded.

PIANO MUSIC

24 Preludes, Set 1, Op. 163; 6 Characteristic Pieces, Op. 132
*** Priory PRCD 449. Jacobs

The *24 Preludes* are not bravura works like those of Chopin and Rachmaninov. Written in 1918, their chromatic key-sequence would suggest that they are more readily associated with Bach's *Well-tempered Clavier*. The variety of Stanford's invention brings a continuing freshness throughout the set, which can be enjoyed as a progression as well as by selecting individual items. The *Characteristic Pieces* were written six years earlier and are also of high quality, with the engaging *Rondel* (No. 4) dedicated to the Schumann of *Kinderszenen*. Peter Jacobs almost never disappoints and his performances here are accomplished, stylish, spontaneous and thoroughly sympathetic, while the recording is first class.

VOCAL MUSIC

(i) Agnus Dei; (ii) Beati Quorum Via, Op. 38/3; The Bluebird; (ii) The Fairy Lough; (iv or v) Magnificat; Nunc Dimittis; (vi) O Praise God In His Holiness; O Sing Unto the Lord a New Song; (iii) A Soft Day; (vii) Songs of the Sea, Op. 91; (iv) Te Deum Laudamus
(M) *** Decca (ADD/DDD) 470 384-2. (i) Royal School of Church Music Ch., Dakers; (ii) New College Oxford Ch., Higginbottom; (iii) Ferrier, Stone; (iv) Winchester Cathedral Ch., Bournemouth SO, Hill; (v) King's College Cambridge Ch., Ord; (vi) St John's College Ch., Guest; (vii) Allen, LPO Ch. & O, Norrington

John Allen is excellent in this 1996 recording of the superbly briny *Songs of the Sea*, beautiful and commanding, with fine support from the LPO chorus and orchestra, and a first-rate Decca recording. David Hill's 1990 performances with his Bournemouth forces are similarly enjoyable – these enormously attractive works are very exciting in their full symphonic form (they were originally for, and usually recorded with voices and organ), especially in the swelling climaxes of the music. The choral works are well executed, and the Ferrier items make an attractive bonus. Good value in Decca's British Music Collection.

3 Motets, Op. 38: Beati quorum via; Cœlos ascendit; Justorum animae. Anthems: For lo, I raise up; Glorious and powerful God; How beautiful are their feet; If ye then be risen with Christ; The Lord is my Shepherd; Ye choirs of new Jerusalem; Ye holy angels bright. (Organ) Preludes & Fugues in B & C, Op. 193/2–3
☛ (M) *** CRD CRD 3497. New College, Oxford, Ch., Higginbottom; Plummer or Smith (organ)

Edward Higginbottom and his splendid choir never made a finer record than this. All this music shows Stanford at his most confidently inspired, readily carrying the listener with him, when the performances are so secure and committed and superbly recorded in the Chapel of New College, Oxford.

3 Motets, Op. 38: Beati quorum via; Cœlos ascendit; Justorum animae. Anthems: *For lo, I raise up, Op. 145; The Lord is my Shepherd. Bible Songs: A song of peace; A song of wisdom, Op. 113/4 & 6.* Hymns: *O for a closer walk with God; Pray that Jerusalem. Magnificat for Double Chorus, Op. 164; Morning, Communion & Evening Services in G, Op. 81: Magnificat & Nunc dimittis. Morning, Communion & Evening Services in C, Op. 115: Magnificat & Nunc dimittis. (Organ) Postlude in D min.*

- 🔾 (B) *** EMI 5 55535-2. Mark Ainsley, King's College, Cambridge, Ch., Cleobury (organ); Vivian (organ accompaniments)

Framed by eloquently beautiful settings of the *Magnificat* and *Nunc dimittis* from 1902 and 1909 respectively (Alastair Hussain the radiantly secure treble soloist in the former), this 75-minute collection celebrates Stanford's remarkable achievement within the Anglican tradition over a quarter of a century. James Vivian, the current organ scholar, impressively provides some of the accompaniments, which are usually important in their own right and make bravura demands on the player. Highly recommended alongside the CRD collection above. Both CDs are well worth having, even though some duplication is involved.

Communion Service in C, Op. 115: Kyrie; Credo. Evening Service in G, Op. 81: Magnificat; Nunc dimittis. Evening Service in C, Op. 115: Magnificat; Nunc dimittis. Morning Service in C, Op. 115: Te deum and Benedicus. For lo, I raise up, Op. 145; 3 Latin Motets: Beati quorum via; Coelos ascendit hodie; Justorum animae. (Organ) (i) Postlude in D min.; Prelude in G min.

- 🔾 (BB) *** Naxos 8.555794. St John's College Ch., Robinson; (i) Whitton

The copious church music of Sir Charles Villiers Stanford stands at the very heart of the Anglican tradition, and Christopher Robinson with his splendid, fresh-voiced choir of St John's, Cambridge, offers an ideal cross-section. When Stanford tended to concentrate on setting the *Magnificat* and *Nunc dimittis* of the *Evening Service*, it is good to have two examples represented, the G major with its opening treble solo more intimate and less dramatic than the C major. Having the C major *Morning Service* (but without the *Jubilate*) as well as the *Communion Service* gives a broader perspective, with the traditional Cranmer words for the Mass ending with the *Gloria*, where nowadays Anglo-Catholics follow the Roman order in their devotions. As in other issues in the excellent Naxos series, the chapel acoustic is warmly atmospheric, while allowing lightness and transparency in the choral textures, with words commendably clear.

(i) *Requiem, Op. 63;* (ii) *The Veiled Prophet of Khorassan* (excerpts)

(N) (BB) *** Naxos 8.555201/2. (i) Lucy, McGahon, Kerr, Leeson-Williams, RTE Philharmonic Ch.; (ii) Kerr; Nat. SO of Ireland, cond. (i) Leaper; (ii) Pearce

Stanford's magnificent *Requiem* (1897) was composed in honour of the painter, Lord Leighton, who died in 1896. It is a

powerfully conceived and moving work, integrating the soloists as a team with the choir in a particularly satisfying way. The contrasts of the writing, from the ethereal opening of the *Kyrie* to the blazing fortissimo of the *Tuba mirum*, are superbly caught here, one of the best recordings we have had from Naxos and surely in the demonstration bracket. With fine solo singing to match the fervour of the chorus, Adrian Leaper can be congratulated on the great success of the first recording of a work that should surely be in the general choral repertoire. The exotic suite from Stanford's first opera, *The Veiled Prophet of Khorassan*, makes an agreeable if not distinctive encore, and this set is a real bargain.

(i) *Stabat Mater, Op. 96; Te Deum* (from *Service in B flat, Op. 10);* (ii) *6 Bible Songs, Op. 113*

*** Chan. 9548. (i) Attrot, Stephen, Robson; (i; ii) Varcoe; (ii) Watson; Leeds Philharmonic Ch., BBC PO, Hickox

Stanford, Irish to the core, here offers a Protestant setting of the deeply Catholic text of the *Stabat Mater*. In its directness and vigour, this relates to Stanford's healthily Anglican church music on the one hand and to his symphonic writing on the other. Like his *Requiem*, this is a piece, long-neglected, that richly deserves revival, and Hickox with his excellent forces directs a performance, atmospherically recorded, that demands its return to the repertory. The six settings of biblical texts for baritone and organ (warmly done by Stephen Varcoe and Ian Watson) are fresh and forthright, leading to the stirring *Te Deum in B flat*, one of the glories of English church music.

STANLEY, John (1712–86)

6 Organ Concertos, Op. 10

(M) *** CRD (ADD) CRD 3365. Gifford, N. Sinfonia

These bouncing, vigorous performances, well recorded as they are on the splendid organ of Hexham Abbey, present these *Concertos* most persuasively. No. 4, with its darkly energetic C minor, is particularly fine. The recording is natural in timbre and very well balanced.

Concertos for Strings, Op. 2/1–6

*** Chan. 0638. Coll. Mus. 90, Standage

These six highly engaging *Concertos for Strings* are concerti grossi in the style of Corelli and, most closely, Handel. For Stanley shares the latter's gift for a noble melodic contour. No. 3 is a fine example and also has a buoyant fugue of the kind Handel would have written. No. 2 is equally memorable and brings a solo cello contribution in the second movement. The period-instrument performances here are wonderfully spirited – vitality without abrasive edge – as well as bringing the right degree of expressive warmth. The recording is first class.

Organ Voluntaries, Op. 5/1, 5, 8 & 9; Op. 6/2, 4, 5 & 6; Op. 7/6–9

*** Chan. 0639. Marlow (organ of Trinity College Chapel, Cambridge)

John Stanley wrote three sets of ten *Organ Voluntaries*. Opp. 5–7 were published in the 1740s and 1750s. Most are in two or three movements, although Op. 5/1 and Op. 6/6 (two of the most attractively diverse) extend to four. Richard Marlow presents four from each set. No pedals are used, but Stanley's published registrations are colourful (often quite orchestral, as in the *Vivace* of Op.7/6), and as they are French-influenced it is right than a fine English organ should be used, one which has a colourful palette, sometimes piquant, but which is not too plangent in timbre. Op.7/9 closes with a lively fugue, but the invention throughout is engaging, sometimes using echo passages and alternating fast and slow passages. The recording is very real and vivid, but not overwhelming, which makes for enjoyably relaxed listening. Recommended.

STEFAN, Joseph Anton (1726–97)

Fortepiano Concerto in B flat

(M) *** Warner Elatus 0927 49556-2. Staier, Concerto Köln – SALIERI: *Fortepiano Concertos* ***

The Bohemian-born Joseph Stefan's *Concerto* (from the 1780s) is fluent and musical, if slightly overlong, but with a rather fine slow movement; the concerto also opens with an extended and quite touching Adagio in D minor. Staier's performance is highly persuasive, and he is given alert and sympathetic support by the excellent Concerto Köln.

STENHAMMAR, Wilhelm (1871–1927)

(i) *Piano Concerto 1 in B flat min., Op. 1; Symphony 3* (fragment)

*** Chan. 9074. (i) Widlund; Royal Stockholm PO, Rozhdestvensky

(i) *Piano Concerto 1;* (ii) *Florez och Blanzeflor, Op. 3;* (iii) *2 Sentimental Romances, Op. 28*

*** BIS CD 550. (i) Derwinger; (ii) Mattei; (iii) Wallin, Malmö SO, Järvi

Stenhammar's *First Piano Concerto* is full of beautiful ideas and the invention is fresh. Love Derwinger proves an impressive and sympathetic intepreter and gets good support from Paavo Järvi. The early *Florez och Blanzeflor* ('Flower and Whiteflower'), a ballad by Oscar Levertin, brings a certain Wagnerian flavour but has a charm that is sensitively sung by the young Swedish baritone Peter Mattei.

Chandos offer the less substantial coupling, a three-minute fragment from the *Third Symphony*, on which Stenhammar embarked in 1918–19. In itself it is too insignificant a makeweight to affect choice. But in the *Concerto* Mats Widlund proves the more imaginative soloist and brings just that little bit more finesse to the solo part. Rozhdestvensky gives excellent support and the Stockholm orchestra (and in particular their strings) have greater richness of sonority. The Chandos recording also has the edge on its BIS competitor in terms of depth and warmth.

2 Sentimental Romances, Op. 28

(BB) **(*) Naxos 8.554287. Ringborg, Swedish CO, Willén – AULIN; BERWALD: *Violin Concertos* **(*)

These two charming Stenhammar pieces are played to excellent effect in Tobias Ringborg's hands. Decent and well-balanced recorded sound.

Serenade for Orchestra, Op. 31

☞ ✿ (BB) *** Warner Apex 0927 43075-2. Royal Stockholm PO, A. Davis (with GRIEG: *Holberg Suite* (Helsinki Strings, Szilvay); NIELSEN: *Little Suite* (Norwegian R. O, Rasilainen) ***)

The Stenhammar was recorded in 1998 and originally coupled with the Brahms *D major Serenade*. We can only reiterate

our wonder at this glorious work; its invention is rich and its harmonies subtle. Nothing more perfectly enshrines the spirit of the Swedish summer night than its *Notturno*, but throughout the level of inspiration is uniformly high. Andrew Davis shapes the score with scrupulous attention to detail and evident sensitivity and feeling. In this bargain-basement refurbishment it is coupled with fine performances of the Grieg *Holberg Suite* from Helsinki and the enchanting Nielsen *Little Suite* from Norway. A terrific bargain.

(i) *Serenade in F, Op. 23;* (ii) *Symphony 2, in G minor, Op. 34*

*** Swedish Soc. SCD1115. Stockholm PO; (i) Kubelik; (ii) Mann

Rafael Kubelik's pioneering recording from 1964 of the *Serenade for Orchestra*, is an excellent account. It wears its years lightly and is fresh and full of poetry. Kubelik obviously loved this marvellous score, though now the Neeme Järvi and Andrew Davis versions (and in particular the BIS account, which includes the rejected *Reverenza* movement) constitute strong competition. However, this reissue sounds astonishingly good. It is a pity that it is at full price, as this will diminish the competitive appeal of what is an historically important CD. Mann's performance of the *Second Symphony* is refreshingly straightforward and is held together well and imaginative in its handling of detail. It sounds much better than it did in its last incarnation when it was presented on its own.

(i) *Symphonies 1 in F; 2 in G min., Op. 34; Serenade for Orchestra, Op. 31* (with *Reverenza* movement); *Excelsior Overture, Op. 13; The Song (Sången): Interlude, Op. 44; Lodolezzi Sings (Lodolezzi sjunger): suite;* (ii) *Piano Concertos 1;* (iii) *2 in D min., Op. 23;* (iv) *Ballad: Florez och Blanzeflor;* (v) *2 Sentimental Romances;* (vi) *Midwinter, Op. 24; Snöfrid, Op. 5*

(M) *** BIS (DDD/ADD) CD 714/716. (i) Gothenburg SO, Järvi; (ii) Derwinger; (iii) Ortiz; (iv) Matthei; (v) Wallin; (vi) Gothenburg Ch.; (ii–v) Malmö SO, P. Järvi

Paavo Järvi's performances are now repackaged at a distinctly advantageous price. The *First Piano Concerto* makes use of Stenhammar's own orchestration, which came to light only recently in America; and this is the most comprehensive compilation of Stenhammar's orchestral music now on the market. All the performances and recordings are of high quality, and the only serious criticism to make affects the first movement of the *Second Symphony*, which Järvi takes rather too briskly. In the *Second Piano Concerto* Cristina Ortiz is a good soloist. All the recordings are digital save for that of the *First Symphony*, which comes from a 1982 concert performance and has great warmth and transparency.

Symphony 2 in G min., Op. 34

*** Cap. (ADD)CAP 21151. Stockholm PO, Westerberg

Symphony 2; Overture, Excelsior!, Op. 13

(BB) **(*) Naxos 8.553888. RSNO, Sundkvist

This is a marvellous symphony. It is direct in utterance; the melodic invention is fresh and abundant, and the generosity of spirit it radiates is heart-warming. The Stockholm Philharmonic under Stig Westerberg play with conviction and eloquence; the strings have warmth and body, and the wind are very fine too. The recording is vivid and full-bodied even by the digital standards of today: as sound, this record is absolutely first class.

Petter Sundkvist's account too is absolutely first class interpretatively, though it is rather let down by the quality of sound, which does not match that of his Stockholm rivals. It is a meticulous, dedicated account, which radiates an understanding of and love for this music. The Royal Scottish National Orchestra respond with enthusiasm.

CHAMBER MUSIC

String Quartets (i) *1 in C, Op. 2;* (ii) *2 in C min., Op. 14;* (iii) *3 in F, Op. 18; 4 in A min., Op. 25;* (i) *5 in C (Serenade), Op. 29;* (ii) *6 in D min., Op. 35*
(M) *** Cap. (ADD) CAP 21536 (3). (i) Fresk Qt; (ii) Copenhagen Qt; (iii) Gotland Qt

The *First Quartet* shows Stenhammar steeped in the chamber music of Beethoven and Brahms, though there is a brief reminder of Grieg; the *Second* is far more individual. By the *Third* and *Fourth*, arguably the greatest of the six, the influence of Brahms and Dvořák is fully assimilated, and the *Fourth* reflects that gentle melancholy which lies at the heart of Stenhammar's sensibility. The *Fifth* is the shortest; the *Sixth* comes from the war years when the composer was feeling worn out and depressed, though there is little evidence of this in the music. Performances are generally excellent, as indeed is the recording, and it is good to have this thoroughly worthwhile set at mid-price.

PIANO MUSIC

Allegro con moto ed appassionato; 3 Fantasies, Op. 11; Impromptu; Impromptu-Waltz; Late Summer Nights, Op. 33; 3 Small Piano Pieces
*** BIS CD-554. Negro

Although he was by all accounts a wonderful pianist, Stenhammar wrote relatively little piano music of real quality. Brahms is a dominant influence in the early *Allegro con moto ed appassionato* and in the Op. 11 *Fantasies*, but there is a strong individual personality at work too, and the *Sensommarnätter* ('Late summer nights'), which come from the period of the *Serenade for Orchestra*, are wonderfully thoughtful and atmospheric pieces that inhabit a wholly personal world. Lucia Negro is thoroughly at home in this repertoire and is very persuasive, and the BIS recording is altogether first rate.

3 Fantasies, Op. 11; Impromptu in G flat; Late Summer Nights, Op. 33; 3 Small Piano Pieces; Sonata in G min.
(BB) *** Naxos 8.553730. Sivelöv

Niklas Sivelöv proves a thoroughly idiomatic interpreter and is as much at home in the quasi-impressionistic third movement of the *Late Summer Nights* and the delicate *Poco allegretto* as he is in the virtuosic, big-boned, penultimate movement. He is very well served by the recording engineers. Well worth the money.

Piano Sonatas 1 in C; 2 in C min.; 3 in A flat; 4 in G min.; Fantasie in A min.
**(*) BIS CD634. Negro

The *Fantasie in A minor* and the *First Sonata* were written when Stenhammar was nine and were followed a year later by another sonata. The *A flat Sonata* comes from 1883 when he was twelve (not two years later as stated on the sleeve-note). All these juvenilia are in the style of Mozart, Weber and Mendelssohn – and it is puzzling why they should be thought worth recording. The *Sonata No. 4 in G minor* is another matter, and in it one recognizes the profile of the real Stenhammar. It comes from 1890, when he was nineteen, and has the breadth and scale of the mature composer. The ideas are long-breathed and the piano writing far more virtuosic and big-boned. The performances could not be more beguiling. Lucia Negro brings great charm and intelligence to the smaller pieces and she gives the *G minor Sonata* with total conviction. Good recording too.

VOCAL MUSIC

30 Songs
*** MSVE (ADD) MSCD 623. Von Otter, Hagegård, Forsberg, Schuback

These songs cover the whole of Stenhammar's career: the earliest, 'In the forest', was composed when he was sixteen, while the last, *Minnesang*, was written three years before his death. The songs are unpretentious and charming, fresh and idyllic, and nearly all are strophic. Hagegård sings the majority of them with his usual intelligence and artistry, though there is an occasional hardening of timbre. Anne Sofie von Otter is in wonderful voice and sings with great sensitivity and charm. Bengt Forsberg and Thomas Schuback accompany with great taste, and the recording is of the highest quality.

7 Songs from Thoughts of Solitude, Op. 7; 5 Songs to Texts of Runeberg, Op. 8; 5 Swedish Songs, Op. 16; 5 Songs of Bo Bergman, Op. 20; Songs and Moods, Op. 26; Late Harvest
**(*) BIS CD 654. Mattei, Lundin

Only two of the three-dozen Stenhammar songs on this disc last longer than four minutes: *Jungfru Blond och Jungfru Brunett* ('Miss Blonde and Miss Brunette') and *Prins Aladin av Lampan* ('Prince Aladdin of the Lamp'), both of which are to be found on the set of thirty songs recorded by Anne Sofie von Otter and Håkan Hagegård. As a song composer Stenhammar was often inspired and his craftsmanship is always fastidious and in the posthumously published *Efterskörd* ('Late Harvest') and the 'Thoughts of Solitude', Op. 7, he brings to light some songs of great eloquence and beauty that are not readily available outside Sweden. Peter Mattei is an intelligent singer, well endowed vocally; the voice is beautiful, but he has a tendency to colour the voice on the flat side of the note, and on occasion (in *Prins Aladin*, for example) is flat. Bengt-Åke Lundin deserves special mention for the sensitivity and responsiveness of his accompanying, and the recording is excellent.

Lodolezzi Sings: suite, Op. 39; (i) *Midwinter, Op. 24;* (ii) *Snöfrid, Op. 5; The Song* (interlude)
*** BIS CD 438. (i; ii) Gothenburg Concert Hall Ch., (ii) with Ahlén, Nilsson, Zackrisson, Enoksson; Gothenburg SO, Järvi

Snöfrid is an early cantata. The young composer was completely under the spell of Wagner at this time and it offers only occasional glimpses of the mature Stenhammar. *Midwinter* is a kind of folk-music fantasy or potpourri on the lines of Alfvén's *Midsummer Vigil*, though not quite so appealing. *Lodolezzi Sings* has much innocent charm. None of this is great Stenhammar but it is well worth hearing; the performances under Neeme Järvi are very sympathetic, and the recording is natural and present.

(i) *The Song (Sången), Op. 44;* (ii) *2 Sentimental Romances, Op. 28;* (iii) *Ithaca, Op. 21*

*** Cap. (ADD) CAP 21358. (i) Sörenson, Von Otter, Dahlberg, Wahlgren, State Ac. Ch., Adolf Fredrik Music School Children's Ch., (ii) Tellefsen, (iii) Hagegård, Swedish RSO; (i) Blomstedt; (ii) Westerberg; (iii) Ingelbretsen

The first half of *The Song* has been described as 'a great fantasy' and is Stenhammar at his best and most individual: the choral writing is imaginatively laid out and the contrapuntal ingenuity is always at the service of poetic ends: the second half is less individual. The solo and choral singing is superb and the whole performance has the total commitment one might expect from these forces. The superbly engineered recording does them full justice. The *Two Sentimental Romances* have great charm and are very well played, and Hagegård is in fine voice in another rarity, *Ithaca*.

Tirfing (opera): excerpts

*** Sterling CDO 1033-2. Tobiasson, Morling, Taube, Stockholm Royal Op. O, Segerstam

Tirfing is a 'mystical saga-poem', based on the Hervarar Saga, and tells of the warrior Angantyr, his valkyrie daughter Hervor and Tirfing, a sword with the magical power to destroy everything. It is all terribly Wagnerian, but even so, the music has the power and sweep of Stenhammar. There are characteristic modulations (one is reminded of *Excelsior!* among other things). Above all, even at its most Wagnerian, the music grips the listener from start to finish. Leif Segerstam gets first-rate results from the Royal Opera Orchestra and the same from the three soloists, in particular Ingrid Tobiasson as Hervor. Good wide-ranging recording. The growing band of Stenhammar's admirers will want this.

STEVENSON, Ronald (born 1928)

Passacaglia on D.S.C.H.
🎵 *** Divine Art 25013. McLachlan

It was the appearance of John Ogdon's remarkable LP set of the *Passacaglia on D.S.C.H.* in 1967 that alerted collectors to Ronald Stevenson's music. He composed the *Passacaglia* between 1960 and 1962 and, like Sorabji's *Opus clavicembalisticum* or Busoni's *Fantasia contrappuntistica* (Stevenson is a keen and persuasive advocate of that composer), it is something of a *tour de force*. It is a mighty set of variations on the four-note motif D-S-C-H derived from Shostakovich's monogram, lasting without a break for some 80 minutes. Later on in the score Stevenson introduces another four-note anagram, B-A-C-H, perhaps a reference to Busoni's *Fantasia contrappuntistica*. When he presented Shostakovich with the score at the 1962 Edinburgh Festival, he said that the combination of Russian and German motifs symbolized his hope that the two nations, and mankind generally, would live in harmony. The twelfth section cleverly alludes to the microtonal scale of the Highland bagpipes and incorporates a seventeenth-century Pibroch *Cumha ne Cloinne* ('Lament for the Children') and there is a formidable climactic triple fugue in which the *Dies irae* surfaces. In the 1960s Sir William Walton hailed the pieces as 'really tremendous – magnificent – I can't remember having been so excited by a new work for a very long time'. Murray McLachlan is an impressive exponent of this score and he is very well recorded. (Some years ago he recorded the two piano concertos that Stevenson

wrote at about this time, so he is completely attuned to this music.) An earlier version by Raymond Clarke (Marco Polo 8.223545), though a formidable musical achievement, is rather let down by the boxy recording, and neither of the composer's own accounts is easily available.

STILL, William Grant (1895–1978)

Symphony 2 (Song of a New Race) in G min.
*** Chan. 9226. Detroit SO, Järvi – DAWSON: *Negro Folk Symphony;* ELLINGTON: *Harlem* ***

Stokowski conducted the première of this attractive piece in 1937, seven years after the composer's *First Symphony* had been the first work by an Afro-American composer to be played by a major orchestra (the NYPO). Still worked as an arranger, so he knew how to score, and he had a fund of tunes: the slow movement is haunting, the high-spirited Scherzo whistles along like someone out walking on a spring morning. The idiom is totally American and, if the score is more a suite than a symphony, it remains very personable. It is played most persuasively here and is given a richly expansive recording.

STRADELLA, Alessandro (1644–82)

Christmas Cantatas: (i) *Ah, ah, troppo è ver;* (ii) *Si apra al riso* (both *per Il Santissimo natale*)
🎵 (BB) *** DHM 05472 77463 2. (i) Bach, Ziesak, Prégardien, (i–ii) Wessel, Schopper; (ii) Schlick; La Stagione Frankfurt, Schneider

With a freshness and originality one expects from the composer of *San Giovanni Battista*, Stradella's Christmas cantata, *Ah, ah, troppo è ver*, is a great deal more than a serene pastorella. Lucifer (Michael Schopper) appears at the very opening, strenuously to interrupt the good-natured *Sinfonia*, to announce his determination to thwart the influence of the Christ child. Then come three scenas, in turn depicting the Annunciation, the Nativity and the Adoration of the Magi with the Angel and Mary (Mechthild Bach), followed by the Shepherd (Ruth Ziesak), each given beautiful narrative arias, all of which are sung ravishingly here. Joseph (Christoph Prégardien) then rounds off the story-telling, and the work closes with an engagingly happy madrigal in which all participate. *Si apra al riso* is less dramatic but musically just as inspired, with two duets and a madrigal trio interspersed among the solo numbers, here with Barbara Schlick standing out from her excellent colleagues. Michael Schneider paces the music admirably and the instrumental playing is first class. Vivid recording in a pleasing acoustic completes the listener's pleasure. A real bargain.

Motets: (i) *Benedictus Dominus Deo; Chare Jesu suavissime. Crocifissione e morte di N. S. Giesù Christo; Lamentatione per il Mercoledì Santo; O vos omnes qui transitis*
(BB) **(*) Virgin 2×1 5 61588-2 (2). Lesne, Il Seminario Musicale; (i) with Piau – CALDARA: *Sonatas; Cantatas* **(*)

Alessandro Stradella wrote church music which combined drama with remarkable serenity and expressive beauty. *Benedictus Dominus Deo* is a particularly beautiful duet cantata in which God is thanked for sending his son to earth to redeem mankind. *O vos omnes*, a solo cantata, is shorter but no less potent. The text first expresses a languishing adoration of Jesus, with sensuous use of descending chromatics, and the work ends with lively *Alleluias*. Lesne is a master of this repertoire, and in the former cantata he is radiantly joined by Sandrine Piau, who then goes on to dominate the joyously lyrical *Chare Jesu suavissime*, sweetly praising Saint Philip Neri. These works are framed by the more austere *Crocifissione e morte di N. S. Giesù Christo* (which has a memorably eloquent instrumental introduction, after which the solo line is both grave and plaintive) and the closing *Lamentatione for Ash Wednesday*, which is also restrained but touchingly beautiful. The accompaniments, by a small, authentic-instrument group, are very sensitive indeed. This is perhaps specialist repertoire, but Gérard Lesne has made it his own and his artistry is unsurpassed. Now reissued very inexpensively indeed, aptly coupled to dramatic cantatas and sonatas of Caldara, this is very recommendable – with the very important proviso that now no texts are included.

San Giovanni Battista (oratorio)

♏ ✿ (M) *** Warner Elatus 2564 60444-2. Bott, Batty, Lesne, Edgar-Wilson, Huttenlocher, Musiciens du Louvre, Minkowski

Stradella's oratorio on the biblical subject of John the Baptist and Salome is an amazing masterpiece and offers unashamedly sensuous treatment of the story. Insinuatingly chromatic melodic lines for Salome (here described simply as Herodias's daughter) are set against plainer, more forthright writing for the castrato role of the saint, showing the composer as a seventeenth-century equivalent of Richard Strauss. There is one amazing phrase for Salome, gloriously sung here by Catherine Bott, which starts well above the stave and ends after much twisting nearly two octaves below with a glorious chest-note, a hair-raising moment, Herod's anger arias bring reminders of both Purcell and Handel, and at the end Stradella ingeniously superimposes Salome's gloating music and Herod's expressions of regret, finally cutting off the duet in mid-air as Charles Ives might have done, bringing the whole work to an indeterminate close. Quite apart from Catherine Bott's magnificent performance, at once pure and sensuous in tone and astonishingly agile, the other singers are most impressive, with Gerard Lesne a firm-toned countertenor in the title-role and Philippe Huttenlocher a clear if sometimes gruff Herod. Marc Minkowski reinforces his claims as an outstanding exponent of period performance, drawing electrifying playing from Les Musiciens du Louvre, heightening the drama. Excellent sound. Not to be missed – especially at mid-price.

STRAUSS Family, The

Strauss, Johann Sr (1804–49)
Strauss, Johann Jr (1825–99)
Strauss, Josef (1827–70)
Strauss, Eduard (1835–1916)

(all music listed is by Johann Strauss Jr unless otherwise stated)

Strauss, Johann Sr: The Complete Edition

As with the music of Johann Jr and Josef Strauss, Marco Polo are planning a complete edition of all Johann Sr's music, most of it totally unknown and much of it underrated,

conducted by the excellent Christian Pollack or Märzendorfer. So far, the series has reached Volume 6, all full of interest. But this survey, for reasons of space is being taken forward into our 2006/7 Yearbook.

Johann Strauss Jr: The Complete Edition

All played by the CSSR State PO (Košice) unless indicated otherwise)

The Complete Edition of the music of Johann Strauss on Marco Polo covers 53 CDs and is also to be included in our 2006/7 Yearbook. This collection has great documentary value, but only some of the CDs can be recommended to the general collector: Volumes 17 (8.223217), 27, to which we gave a Rosette (8.223227), 34 (8.223234), 37 (8.223237), 46 (8.223246), 47 (8.223247), 50 (8.223276) and 51 (8.223279), which earned the series its second Rosette. These CDs have all been discussed in previous editions of the *CD Guide* but must now be carried forward for reasons of space.

Boskovsky Strauss Edition

Galops: *Aufs Korn; Banditen.* Marches: *Egyptischer; Franz Joseph I Rettungs-Jubel; Napoleon; Persischer; Russischer; Spanischer. Perpetuum mobile.* Polkas: *Annen; Auf der Jagd; Bitte schön!; Champagner; Demolirer; Eljen a Magyar; Explosionen; Freikugeln; Im Krapfenwaldl; Leichtes Blut; Lob der Frauen; Ohne Sorgen; Pizzicato* (with Josef); *Neue Pizzicato; So ängst sind wir nicht; 'S gibt nur a Kaiserstadt, 's gibt nur a Wien!; Stürmisch in Lieb' und Tanz; Tik-Tak; Tritsch-Tratsch; Unter Donner und Blitz (Thunder and Lightning); Vernügungszug.* Quadrilles: *Fledermaus; Orpheus; Schützen* (with Josef & Eduard). Waltzes: *Accelerationen; An der schönen blauen Donau (Blue Danube); Bei uns z'Haus; Carnavals-Botschafter; Du und du; Errinerung an Covent-Garden; Freuet euch des Lebens; Frühlingsstimmen (Voices of Spring); Geschichten aus dem Wienerwald (Tales from the Vienna Woods); Kaiser (Emperor); Künstlerleben (Artist's Life); Lagunen; Liebslieder; Mephistos Höllenrufe; Morgenblätter (Morning Papers); Nordseebilder; Rosen aus dem Süden (Roses from the South); Seid umschlungen, Millionen!; Schneeglöckchen; Tausend und eine Nacht; Wein, Weib und Gesang (Wine, Women and Song); Wiener Blut (Vienna Blood); Wiener Bonbons; Wo die Citronen blüh'n!.* JOHANN STRAUSS SR: Galops: *Sperl; Wettrennen.* Radetzky march. Polka: *Piefke und Pufka.* Waltz: *Loreley-Rhein-Klänge.* JOSEF STRAUSS: Polkas: *Auf Ferienreisen; Brennende Liebe; Eingesendet; Die Emancipirte; Extempore; Feuerfest; Frauenherz; Heiterer Mut; Im Fluge; Jokey; Die Libelle; Moulinet; Rudolfsheimer; Die Schwätzerin.* Waltzes: *Aquarellen; Delirien; Dorfschwalben aus Osterreich (Village swallows); Dynamiden; Mein Liebenslauf ist Lieb und Lust; Sphärenklänge (Music of the spheres); Transactionen.* EDUARD STRAUSS: Polkas: *Bahn Frei!; Mit Extrapost.* Waltz: *Fesche Geister*

(B) **(*) Decca (ADD) 455 254-2 (6). VPO, Boskovsky

These six vintage CDs (offering 86 titles) span Willi Boskovsky's long (analogue) recording career for Decca, stretching over two decades from the late 1950s onwards, when his records dominated the LP discography in the Strauss family repertoire. In 1979 he directed the first of the now famous VPO New Year Concerts (see below) and that recording tradition has continued until the present day. It has now become an annual event shared by different record companies and various conductors, capped in 1987 by Karajan, after he had set aside a period of his musical life to re-evaluate his interpretations. Since then there have been a series of fine discs from Abbado, Kleiber, Lorin Maazel, Mehta and Riccardo Muti, all of whom have risen to the occasion and been given admirable support by the various recording teams.

Even so, Boskovsky's achievement in this repertoire remains unique, both in its range – the output of Josef, particularly his polkas, is notably well covered – and the almost unfailing sparkle of the performances. Following a sequence begun by Decca in the days of mono LPs with Clemens Kraus, he showed a unique feeling for the Straussian lilt in the waltzes and the fizzing élan and exuberance of the polkas and marches, while the playing he drew from the Vienna Philharmonic Orchestra was consistently persuasive. The Decca engineers rose to the occasion (notably so when special effects were required, as in the *Explosion* and *Thunder and Lightning Polkas*) and the Sofiensaal provided an ideal ambience, with plenty of warmth and bloom. The one snag is the thinness of violin-tone, especially on the earlier records – it is immediately noticeable here on *An der schönen blauen Donau*, which rightly opens the first disc. The present CD transfers are very vivid and immediate, and their brightness has also served to add a hint of coarseness to some of the lively music. The ear adjusts, however, when the music-making is so zestful and alive; in spite of such reservations, there is no finer or more all-embracing collection of the best of the output of the Strauss family than in this box. Appropriately, the Decca recording producer, John Parry, has provided a biographical essay, and the documentation includes Edward Hanslick's obituary, which records that Johann Jr was not only a great composer but 'an extremely charming, genuine and benevolent person'. This is surely reflected in the life-enhancing geniality of his music.

Waltzes: *Accelerationen; An der schönen, blauen Donau (Blue Danube); Du und du; Frühlingsstimmen (Voices of Spring); Geschichten aus dem Wiener Wald (Tales from the Vienna Woods); Kaiser (Emperor); Künstlerleben (Artist's Life); Liebeslieder; Morgenblätter (Morning Papers); Rosen aus dem Süden (Roses from the South); Tausend an eine Nacht; Wein, Weib und Gesang (Wine, Women and Song); Wiener Blut (Vienna Blood); Wiener Bonbons; Wo die Zitronen blühn (Where the Lemon Trees Bloom).* JOSEF STRAUSS: *Dorfschwalben aus Österreich; Sphären-Klange (Music of the Spheres)*

🔊 (B) *** Double Decca (ADD) 443 473-2 (2). VPO, Boskovsky

One might think that such a succession of Strauss waltzes spread over two discs might produce a degree of listening fatigue, but that is never the case here, such is Johann's resource in the matter of melody and freshness in orchestration. The earliest recordings show their age a bit in the violin tone, but on CD it is remarkable just how well these vintage recordings sound. With 145 minutes of music offered this is excellent value.

Boskovsky EMI recordings

Johann Strauss Sr: *Radetzky March; Seufzer-Galopp.* Johann Strauss Jr: *Banditen-Galopp.* Overtures: *Blindekuh; Cagliostro in Wien; Der Carneval in Rom; Eine Nacht in Venedig; Die Fledermaus; Das Spitzentich der Königin; Der Zigeunerbaron.* Polkas: *Auf der Jagd; Champagne; Eljen a Magyar!; Explosions; Express, Op. 311; Gruss aus Österreich;*

Im Krapfenwald'l; Im Sturmschritt; I-Tipfel; Kreuzfidel!; Leichtes Blut; Neue Pizzicato-Polka; Unter Donner und Blitz; Vom Donaustraume. Waltzes: *Accelerationen; An der schönen Carnevalsbilder; Carnevals-Botschafter; Donau; Donauweibchen; Frühlingsstimmen; Du und du; Feuilleton-Walzer; Flugschiften; Gedankenflug; G'schichten aus dem Wienerwald; Immer heiterer; Kaiser-Walzer; Künstlerleben; Kuss-Walzer; Morgenblätter; Lagunen-Walzer; Leitartikel; Neu-Wien; Rosen aus dem Süden; Schatz-Walzer; Wein, Weib und Gesang; Wiener Blut; Wiener Frauen; Wo die Zitronen blüh'n.* JOSEF STRAUSS: Polkas: *Allerlei; Auf Ferienreisen; Buchstaben; Feuerfest!; Frauenherz; Im Fluge; Jokey; Künster-Gruss; Masken; Ohne Sorgen!; Plappermäulchen; Die Schwätzerin; Sport; Vorwärts!* Waltzes: *Aquarellen; Delirien; Dorfschwalben aus Österreich; Geheime Anziehungskräfte; Mein Labenslauf ist Lieb' und Lust; Perlen der Liebe.* EDUARD STRAUSS: Polkas: *Alpenrose; Ausser Rand und Band; Faschingsbrief; Nahn frei!; Mit Vergnügen; Ohne Aufenthalt; Ohne Bremse; Reiselust; Unter der Enns; Wo man lacht und lebt*

(N) (BB) **(*) EMI (ADD/DDD) 586019 (6). Johann Strauss O of V., Boskovsky

Willi Boskovsky's recordings date from 1971 to 1985 and this is a pretty complete survey. By any standards, these are excellent performances, with many of the popular works (and just about all the popular works are here) showing Boskovsky at his best: from the very opening of the *Blue Danube*, the playing of Boskovsky's Johann Strauss Orchestra balances an evocative Viennese warmth with the right sort of vigour; and other major waltzes, such as *Morning Papers*, are very enjoyable too. Other familiar numbers like the vivacious *Morgenblätter, Du and du* and *Wein, Weib und Gesang* all sound splendid too. There are a number of less familiar items here, and in many ways these come off best: the two concerning ladies, *Donauweibchen* and *Wiener Frauen*, are winning examples. All the various overtures are full of attractive tunes and are highly entertaining overall, it must be admitted the playing is not as uniformly memorable as his classic Decca accounts; just occasionally a hint of blandness creeps in here. But the resonant, warm EMI sound makes for enjoyable listening.

Overtures: *Cagliostro in Wien; Carnival in Rom'; Das Spitentuch der Königin.* Polkas: *Banditen; Episode; Explosionen; Express; Grüss aus Österreich; I-Tipferl; Karnevalotschafter; Karnevalsbilder; Kreuzfidel!; Maskenzug; Im Sturmschritt; Unter Donner und Blitz; Vom Donaustrande.* Waltzes: *Accelerationen; An den schönen, blauen Donau; Donauweibchen; Du und Du; Feuilleton; Flugschriften; Gedankenpflug; Geschichten aus dem Wienerwald; Kaiser; Künstlerleben; Küss; Lagunen; Leichtes Blut; Die Leitartikel; Morgenblätter; Rosen aus dem Süden; Schatz; Wein, Weib und Gesang; Wiener Blut; Wiener Frauen; Frühlingsstimmen.* EDUARD STRAUSS: Polkas: *Alpenrose; Ausser Rand und Band; Faschingsbrief; Mit Vergnügen; Reiselust; Unter der Enns; Wo man Lacht und lebt*

(B) **(*) EMI 5 74528-2 (5). Johann Strauss O of V., Boskovsky – JOSEF STRAUSS: *Polkas and Waltzes* ***

Willi Boskovsky's digital re-recordings of many of the best-known Strauss waltzes and polkas were made between 1982 and 1987 with a pick-up orchestra in a Viennese studio, but one with a warmly attractive ambience. The performances are affectionate, lively, idiomatic and well played. With good sound this generous and inexpensive anthology is certainly enjoyable, if for the most part without quite the distinction and sheer character of the conductor's earlier, Decca recordings. There are some attractive novelties too. Why for instance are the three shrewdly chosen novelty waltzes on the fourth disc, *Flugschriften*, *Gedankenpflug*, and *Die Lietartikel*, not better known? Virtually all the Josef Strauss items are on the fifth disc in the box – see below.

Waltzes: *Accelerationen; An der schönen Donau; Donauweibchen; Du und Du; Flugschriften; Frühlingsstimmen; Gedankenflug; Geschichten aus dem Wienerwald; Kaiser; Künstlerleben; Lagunen; Leitartikel; Morgenblätter; Rosen aus dem Süden; Schatz; Wein, Weib und Gesang; Wiener Blut; Wiener Frauen*

(N) (B) **(*)HMV 5 86769-2 (2). Johann Strauss O of V., Boskovsky

There are some novelties here that are not included in Boskovsky's Decca survey, notably *Flugschriften, Gedanken-flug and Leitartikel* and *Wiener Frauen.* Some of the favourites are very successful here, notably the *Emperor, Roses from the South, Tales from the Vienna Woods* and *Voices of Spring,* sounding freshly minted, rhythmic nuances flexibly stylish and obvious spontaneity. Those preferring digital sound (which here is full and resonant) should certainly consider this set.

Waltzes: *An der schönen, blauen Donau; Frühlingstimmem; Geschichten aus dem Wiener Wald; Kaiser; Künstlerleben Rose aus dem Süden; Wiener Blut; Wein, Weib und Gesang*

(BB) *** EMI Encore 5 75239-2. V. Strauss O, Boskovsky

This 1982 compilation was Boskovsky's most impressive Strauss collection since his Decca era. From the very opening of the *Blue Danube* the playing balances an evocative Viennese warmth with vigour and sparkle. Rhythmic nuances are flexibly stylish and the spontaneity is enjoyably obvious. The digital sound is agreeably rich – there is no digital edge on top – yet detail is realistic, within the resonant acoustic. Highly recommendable as a sample of the mature Boskovsky at its new budget price.

NEW YEAR CONCERTS

1963–1979 New Year's Concerts: excerpts; 1974 New Year Concert (complete): *Czárdás: Ritter Pásmán* (1967) *Einzugmarsch* from '*Zigeunerbaron*' (1969); *Galopp: Banditen* (1972); *Overture 'Die Fledermaus'* (1972); *Perpetuum mobile* (1978); Polkas: *Annen* (1966); *Auf der Jagd* (1979); *Bitte schön* (1972); *Leichtes Blut* (1975); *Unter Donner und Blitz* (1967); *Vergnügungszug* (1970). Waltz: *Kaiser* (1975);* JOSEF STRAUSS: Polkas: *Auf Ferienreisen* (1964); *Eingesendet* (1968); *Feuerfest* (1971); *Jockey* (1972); Waltzes: *Dorfschwalben aus Osterreich* (1963); *Sphärenklänge* (1964). 1974 Concert: *Galopp: Wetrennen;* Polkas: *Explosions; Pizzicato* (with Josef); *Tritsch-Tratsch; Rasch in der Tat; Künsterguss;* Waltzes: *An der schönen blauen Donau; Freut euch des Lebens; Geschichten aus dem Wienerwald.* JOSEF STRAUSS: Polkas: *Frauenherz; Künstlergruss; Ohne Sorgen; Plappermälchen.* JOHANN STRAUSS SR: *Radetzky Marsch*

(N) (***) DG **DVD** mono 073 4002 (2). VPO, Boskovsky (with Bonus: *Boskovsky Portrait*)

Willi Boskovsky took over the direction of the Vienna Philharmonic's traditional New Year's concert in 1955 and continued for 25 years. Apart from being the orchestra's leader, he was a superb solo fiddler and so he continued to direct the concerts in Strauss's own style, leading and conducting from his violin bow and often participating, nowhere more impressively than in the *Ritter Pásmán Csárdás* (1967), when the VPO assumes a Hungarian mantle; nowhere more charmingly than in *Tales from the Vienna Woods* (1974), when in the introduction he plays an engaging little duet with the orchestra's concert master. Even in the *Pizzicato Polka* he opens the piece alongside his players.

The first of the two DVDs here gives us the complete 1974 Concert, a surprisingly mellow affair, not helped by the mono recording which (presumably deriving from a telecast) has a restricted range of sound, although the acoustic of the Golden Hall of the Musikverein, so visually pleasing, brings plenty of warmth and atmosphere. The programme is relatively short by today's standards, but Boskovsky in his frock coat sustains his patrician image seductively with his Viennese charm and natural feeling for Straussian inflexion and rubato. Especially beguiling is the introduction to the two most famous waltzes, *The Blue Danube* and *Tales from the Vienna Woods*, where it is fascinating to watch the zither player in close-up, with his subtle finger-vibrato. The orchestra itself makes a robust vocal contribution in *Ohne Sorgen*. The camerawork is effective enough, although in the latter piece the producer misses picturing a horn solo by focusing on the wrong player!

The second DVD assembles 19 items from various other concerts of which seven are in black-and-white. If visually these are less attractive, musically they certainly are not, for in the earlier concerts the obviously younger Boskovsky is often at his most vivacious and, throughout, the sound (still mono) is much brighter and more vivid. There are many highlights here, not least the two great Josef Strauss waltzes, while the side-drummer in the percussion department enjoys himself with various jokes and explosive effects in *Unter Donner und Blitz*, the *Banditen Galop*, and notably *Auf der Jagd*, where he presents Boskovsky with the results of the shoot. But he amuses the audience most with his pair of anvils in *Feuerfest*. On both discs, every now and then the orchestral visuals are interrupted by dancing from members of the Vienna State Opera and Volksoper Ballets, but for the most part we watch the conductor and his players, all so obviously enjoying themselves. While this second DVD is a fascinating historical record and gives much pleasure, it could have been more skilfully edited so that we do not constantly watch the conductor coming on and taking a bow before each performance.

'*New Year's Day Concert in Vienna (1979)*'. Polkas: *Auf der Jagd* (with encore); *Bitte schön! Leichtes Blut; Pizzicato* (with Josef); *Tik-Tak.* Waltzes: *An der schönen blauen Donau; Bei uns zu Haus; Loreley-Rheine-Klänge; Wein, Weib und Gesang.* JOSEF STRAUSS: *Moulinet Polka; Die Emanzipierte Polka-Mazurka; Rudolfsheimer-Polka; Sphärenklänge Waltz.* JOHANN STRAUSS SR: *Radetzky March.* E. STRAUSS: *Ohne Bremse Polka.* ZIEHRER: *Herreinspaziert! Waltz.* SUPPE: *Die schöne Galathee Overture*

(M) *** Decca 468 489-2. VPO, Boskovsky

Decca chose to record Boskovsky's 1979 New Year's Day concert in Vienna for their very first digital issue on LP. The clarity, immediacy and natural separation of detail are very striking throughout, and the strings of the Vienna Philharmonic are brightly lit. There is some loss of bloom and not quite the degree of sweetness one would expect today on a record made in the Musikvereinsaal, but the ear soon adjusts. The music-making itself is another matter. It gains much from the spontaneity of the occasion, reaching its peak when the side-drum thunders out the introduction to the closing *Radetzky March*, a frisson-creating moment that, with the audience participation, is quite electrifying. The whole concert is now fitted on to a single mid-priced CD playing for five seconds over 81 minutes.

'1987 New Year Concert in Vienna': Overture: *Die Fledermaus*. Polkas: *Annen; Pizzicato* (with Josef); *Unter Donner und Blitz; Vergnügungszug.* Waltzes: *An der schönen blauen Donau;* (i) *Frühlingsstimmen.* J. STRAUSS SR: *Beliebte Annen* (polka); *Radetzky March.* JOSEF STRAUSS: *Ohne Sorgen Polka.* Waltzes: *Delirien; Sphärenklänge*

⊕― * DG 419 616-2. VPO, Karajan; (i) with Battle**

In preparation for this outstanding concert, which was both recorded and televised, Karajan restudied the scores of his favourite Strauss pieces; the result, he said afterwards, was to bring an overall renewal to his musical life beyond the scope of this particular repertoire. The concert itself produced music-making of the utmost magic; familiar pieces sounded almost as if they were being played for the first time. Kathleen Battle's contribution to *Voices of spring* brought wonderfully easy, smiling coloratura and much charm. *The Blue Danube* was, of course, an encore, and what an encore! Never before has it been played so seductively on record. In the closing *Radetzky March*, wonderfully crisp yet relaxed, Karajan kept the audience contribution completely in control merely by the slightest glance over his shoulder. This indispensable collection makes an easy first choice among Strauss compilations. Unfortunately the current presentation is without proper musical documentation, which is a disgrace. We have consequently removed our Rosette.

'1989 New Year Concert in Vienna': Overture: *Die Fledermaus; Ritter Pásmán: Czárdás.* Polkas: *Bauern; Eljen a Magyar; Im Krapfenwald'l; Pizzicato* (with Josef). Waltzes: *Accelerationen; An der schönen blauen Donau (Blue Danube); Bei uns z'Haus; Frühlingsstimmen; Künstlerleben.* JOSEF STRAUSS: Polkas: *Jockey; Die Libelle; Moulinet; Plappemäulchen.* JOHANN STRAUSS SR.: *Radetzky March*

****(*) DG DVD 073 024-9. VPO, C. Kleiber. (Producer: Horst Bosch. V/D: Brian Large.)**

Carlos Kleiber's pursuit of knife-edged precision prevents the results here from sounding quite relaxed enough, although the advantage of the DVD is that being able to watch his flexible and often graceful arm-movements makes his rather precise style with Viennese rhythms easier to accept. But in one or two numbers Kleiber really lets rip, as in the Hungarian polka, *Eljen a Magyar*, and in the *Ritter Pásmán Czárdás*. With well-judged camera-work the viewer is made to feel closely involved with the orchestra's music-making, making this an enjoyably spontaneous concert. The recording is both vivid and warmly atmospheric, although the violin timbre is brightly lit to match Kleiber's style.

'1996 & 1999 New Year Concerts': excerpts: *Kaiser Franz-Joseph Rettungs-Jubel-Marsch, Op. 126;* Polkas: *Bitt Schön; Ein Herz, ein Sinn; Spleen; Tritsch-Tratsch.*

Fledermaus Quadrille; Waltzes: *An der schönen blauen Donau; A la Paganini; Geschichten aus dem Wiener Wald; Kaiser.* JOHANN STRAUSS SR: *Radetzky March*

(M) * 09026 63983-2. VPO, Maazel**

This is a one disc-selection from the two Vienna New Year Concerts (currently withdrawn) which Lorin Maazel directed so vivaciously in 1996 and 1999, containing (alas) few of the novelties which made those collections valuable, yet embracing some items not included on the orginal issues. On both occasions Maazel was in relaxed form, obviously enjoying himself, and this is reflected in the orchestral response. In the *Walzer à la Paganini* he takes up his solo violin, entering fully into the fun of the occasion, as he did in several other pieces, not included here. With 70 minutes of music, this brilliantly recorded selection is certainly value for money if the programme is suitable. The *Blue Danube* and *Radetzky March* by Johann Senior were two of the encores and they are used to end the present concert.

'2000 New Year Concert': *Csárdás* from *Ritter Pásmán;* March: *Persischer.* Polkas: *Albion; Eljen a Magyar; Hellenen; Process; Vom Donaustrande.* Waltzes: *An der schönen blauen Donau; Lagunen; Liebeslieder; Wein, Weib und Gesang.* EDUARD STRAUSS: Polkas: *Mit Extrapost; Gruss an Prag.* JOSEF STRAUSS: Polkas: *Die Libelle; Künstler-Gruss.* Waltz: *Marien-Klänge.* JOHANN STRAUSS SR: *Radetzky March*
**** EMI DVD DVB4 92361-9; (M) *** EMI 5 67323-2 (2).**
VPO, Muti (with SUPPE: *Overture: Morning, Noon and Night in Vienna*)

Like Lorin Maazel before him, Riccardo Muti loses any prickly qualities, concentrating on charm rather than bite, as is obvious from the very opening number in the 2000 concert. The *Lagunen Waltz* of Johann Strauss Jr makes the gentlest possible start, leading to a couple of sparkling novelties, never heard at these concerts before, the brisk *Hellenen Polka* and the feather-light *Albion Polka*, dedicated to Prince Albert. That sets the pattern for the whole programme. For all the brilliance of the playing, it is the subtlety of the Viennese lilt (as in Josef Strauss's *Marien-Klänge*, another novelty) that one remembers, or the breath-taking delicacy of the *pianissimo* which opens the first of the encores, the *Blue Danube*, perfectly caught by the EMI engineers. For its Millennium concert the Vienna Philharmonic could not be more seductive. The two-disc CD format at mid-price, with the first half shorter than the second, allows the whole programme to be included without cuts.

Two tracks, the *Ritter Pásmán Csárdás* and Josef's *Marien-Klänge Waltz* have optional, fairly unimaginative ballet sequences provided by members of the Vienna State Opera Ballet, but one can stay with Muti. During the splendid performance of the *Blue Danube*, we are taken on a visual tour of the building, inside and out, and there are other shots of Vienna, plus an introduction to those famous Viennese white horses. Muti's New Year speech (in English) is brief and simple and he controls his audience firmly and adeptly in the closing *Radetzky March*.

'New Year Concert 2002': March: *Zivio! Overture Die Fledermaus.* Polkas: *Beliebte Annen; Elisen; Tik-Tak.* Waltzes: *An der schönen blauen Donau; Carnevalsbotschafter; Künsterleben; Wiener Blut.* JOSEF STRAUSS: Polkas: *Aquarellen; Im Fluge; Die Libelle;*

Plappermäulchen!; Die Schwäzerin; Vorwärts! JOHANN STRAUSS SR: *Radetzky March* (with HELLMESBERGER: *Danse diabolique*)

*** TDK **DVD** DV-WPNK02. VPO, Ozawa. (V/D: Brian Large)

*** Ph. **SACD** 470 615-2; CD 468 999-2. VPO, Ozawa
(without *Arm in Arm; Beliebte Annen & Elisen Polkas; Perpetuum mobile; Carnevalsbotschafter Waltz*)

Ozawa's 2002 Concert was certainly a great success, and he made a special feature of including no fewer than six memorable polkas by Josef Strauss. The background took the form of a large sign over the organ pipes celebrating the arrival of the Euro on that very day. Among the special extras on the DVD is a second performance of *Perpetuum mobile*, with illustrations of the new currency being manufactured and printed. Also among the 'specials' are the Vienna State Opera Ballet dancing to the *Blue Danube* and the Spanish Riding School demonstrating against the background of a pair of polkas. These items are all included in the main concert, which Brian Large and his cameras follow with his usual expertise. Ozawa proves a warmly flexible Straussian, even without the aid of a baton, and his performances are consistently enjoyable, if perhaps not as individual as those of Harnoncourt. The end-of-concert joke is the New Year greeting offered in a host of different languages by orchestral members (who are not all Viennese), with Ozawa himself contributing in Japanese and Chinese, and the German version coming from the orchestra *en masse*. Altogether a most enjoyable occasion.

As can be seen above, the equivalent SACD/CD, although it plays for 79 minutes, omits five items, but it can certainly be recommended, if you fancy the programme.

'New Year Concert 2003': *Kaiser Franz Joseph I: Rettungs-Jubel-Marsch.* Polkas: *Bauern; Furioso; Hellenen; Leichtes Blut; Lob der Frauen; Niko; Scherz; Secunden.* Waltzes: *An der Schönen blauen Donau; Kaiser; Krönungs-Lieder; Schatz.* JOSEF STRAUSS: *Delirien Waltz; Pélé-Méle Polka.* JOHANN STRAUSS SR: *Chinese Galop; Radetzky March* (with WEBER/BERLIOZ: *Invitation to the Dance.* BRAHMS: *Hungarian Dance 5 & 6)*

🕭— *** TDK **DVD** DV-WPNK03. VPO, Harnoncourt. (V/D: Brian Large) (Bonus includes Soloists of V. St. Op. Ballet in the *Hellenen Polka*; and Kirov Ballet in the *Krönungs-Lieder Waltz*)

Harnoncourt's 2003 DVD is really special – the most memorable New Year celebration since the famous 1987 occasion, which saw the return of Karajan to the Musikverein. What is so striking with Harnoncourt is the seductive combination of relaxed warmth (with some leisurely tempi in the Polkas) and the laid-back refinement of the orchestral playing. Even the trombone raspberry in the *Scherz Polka* is delicately done. Highlights include the beautifully played *Schatz* and *Emperor Waltzes*, especially the gentle coda of the latter, and Josef's sparkling *Pélé-Méle Polka*. The ravishing account of the Weber/Berlioz *Invitation to the Dance* is equally memorable.

Harnoncourt himself is a joy to watch. Never more so than when he comes back for the encores, and, with flashing eyes, unleashes an extraordinary bravura performance of the *Furioso Polka*. Then, after sailing on the *Blue Danube*, he has the audience totally under control for the clapping in the very theatrical account of the *Radetzky March*.

Although the camera does occasionally stray away from the musicians to roam outside the concert hall, the ballet dancing

and the visit to the Chinese Chamber at the Schönbrunn Palace are kept as special features at the end.

'New Year Concert, 2004': JOHANN STRAUSS SR: Galopps: *Cachucha; Indiana;* March: *Radetzky;* Polkas: *Beliebte-Sperl; Frederika;* Waltz: *Philomelen.* JOHANN STRAUSS JR: *Czárdás (Die Fledermaus).* March: *Es war so wunderschön.* Overture: *Das Sitzentuch der Königin.* Polkas: *Champagne; Im Sturmschritt; Satanella.* Quadrille: *Zigeunerin.* Waltzes: *Accelerationen; An der schönen blauen Donau.* JOSEF STRAUSS: Polkas: *Eislauf; Stiefmütterchen.* Waltz: *Sphärenklänge.* EDUARD STRAUSS: *Polka: Mit Vergnügen* (with LANNER: *Tarantel Galopp; Hofball-Tänze Waltz*)

(N) *** DG **DVD** 073 079-9. VPO, Muti (V/D Brian Large); CD 474 900-2 (2)

Riccardo Muti once again presents his programme with an authentic Viennese glow. The concert in 2004 was designed to celebrate the bicentenary of Johann Strauss Sr, father of the waltz-king we most revere. Normally the final encore, the *Radetzky March*, is his most notable contribution, but here we have four rare pieces by him, including the delectable *Philomena Waltz*, leading to two seductive items by his contemporary, Josph Lanner, presented with an endearing, gentle touch of Viennese schmaltz in the more modern Schrammeln style that we remember from the early recordings of the Boskovsky Ensemble.

Johann Strauss Jr and his siblings take over again in the second half, with more rarities and an ecstatic account of the *Sphärenklänge Waltz* to match an equally ravishing account of the *Accelerationen Waltz* in the first half, where the increase in tempo is managed most engagingly. While the *Champagne Polka* fizzes appropriately, it cannot be said that visually the 2004 concert is as electrifying as Harnoncourt's 2003 proceedings. Muti's visual image is dapper; curiously, his bespectacled countenance reminds one a little of Glenn Miller, though there is nothing jazzy about his affectionately cultivated conducting style. With Brian Large in command, the camera angles are almost always impeccable, and only very occasionally do we leave the auditorium. The sound is excellent. There are optional filmed sequences of the Vienna State Opera Ballet for *Accelerations* and the *Champagne Polka* and for Josef Strauss's *Eislauf Polka*, and we are offered a choice of figure-skating impressions. But it is much more rewarding to be caught up in the music-making itself.

'New Year Concert, 2005': Marches: *Indigo; Russische.* Polkas: *An der Jagd; Die Bajadere; Bauern; Ein Herz, ein Sinn; Fata Morgana; Haut-Volée; Klipp-Klapp; Nordseebilder; Pizzicato* (with Josef); *Vergnügungszug.* Waltzes: *An der schönen blauen Donau; Geschichten aus dem Wienerwald; 1001 Nacht.* JOSEF STRAUSS: Polkas; *Die Emancipirte; Winterlust.* Waltzes: *Lustschwärmer.* EDUARD STRAUSS: *Electrisch Polka* (with SUPPÉ: Overture 'Die schöne Galathee'. Joseph HELLMESBERGER: *Auf Wiener Art*)

(N) *** DG **DVD** 073 4020. VPO, Maazel (V/D: Brian Large)

It is fascinating how the New Year's Day concert in Vienna seems to mellow even the severest disciplinarians among conductors. Lorin Maazel has never been so warm as when conducting this event, yet throughout his face registers (and his body movements confirm) an extraordinary kaleidoscopic range of emotions, from relaxed geniality and a hint of a smile to the strongest forcefulness and determination, communicated directly to the players and, of course, to us (one of the fascinations of DVD). The discipline underlies every performance, the playing has consistently precise ensemble without a hint of stiffness, and there is always plenty of lift. Maazel zips through over a dozen polkas with consistent exhilaration but saves his greatest affection for waltzes, and also the opening of the Suppé overture – a truly *schöne* Galatea – with magical playing from the Vienna strings (and an engaging bouquet of roses appearing on the screen). As a superb violinist, he has already followed Boskovsky's example in joining the orchestra to lead the *Pizzicato Polka*, and in *Geschichten aus dem Wiener Wald* he takes up the violin again to play the delightful gentle passage in the introduction normally given to the zither.

Because of the tsunami catastrophe only a few days before the concert, it was decided it would be inappropriate to end the concert with the *Radetzky March* so, after the speeches and multi-language 'Happy New Year's, it was the *Blue Danube Waltz* which ended the concert, played quite gloriously and with infinite flexibility. Indeed, in the coda, Maazel manages an extra touch of indulgent rubato, quite impermissible, of course, but totally captivating in this instance because it was seemingly spontaneous on a very special occasion. Brian Large, as usual, supervised the visuals expertly, and allowed himself to take the camera outside the Musikverein into the Vienna Woods at the appropriate time to show how they mirror the beauty of Strauss's waltz. Otherwise, in three optional filmed sequences, the viewer can choose to watch the Vienna State Opera Ballet. But we prefer the orchestra. Excellent sound.

OTHER COLLECTIONS

Marches: *Egyptischer; Persischer.* **Polkas:** *Auf der Jagd; Pizzicato* (with Josef); *Unter Donner und Blitz; Postillon d'amour; Leichtes Blut.* **Waltzes:** *G'schichten aus dem Wienerwald; Morgenblätter; Wiener Blut.* JOSEF STRAUSS: *Sphärenklänge*

⊘—¬ (M) *** DG (ADD) 449 768-2. BPO, Karajan

The present collection is based on an LP originally published in 1971. A few prize items have been added, notably the engaging *Postillon d'amour* polka, which is bounced in true dance rhythm, and Josef's *Sphärenklänge,* which Karajan shapes most affectionately, particularly the lovely opening. But the original disc is most notable for the central section of the *Egyptian March* when the Berlin orchestral players make a robust vocal contribution to the middle section. The piece is then charmingly pared down, like a patrol disappearing into the distance. Of the waltzes, *Wiener Blut* lilts attractively, and *Tales from the Vienna woods* is coaxed most seductively, with a particularly delicate zither solo. The sound is excellent, and altogether this is the best Karajan Johann Strauss disc in the DG catalogue, apart from his famous (1987) New Year concert in Vienna, which is unsurpassable.

Overture: Die Fledermaus; Emperor Waltz; Perpetuum mobile; Tritsch-Tratsch Polka

⊘—¬ *** BBC (ADD) BBCL 4038. Hallé O, Barbirolli –
   HAYDN: *Symphony 83 in G min. (La Poule)*; LEHAR: *Gold and Silver*; R. STRAUSS: *Der Rosenkavalier Suite* ***

Barbirolli's performance exudes the full communicative atmosphere of this 1969 Prom, and one can hear Sir John himself vocalizing in the overture. The performance of the *Emperor Waltz* is ravishing, and an outrageous fun performance of *Tritsch-Tratsch* follows, with sudden pauses to bring bursts of laughter from the promenaders.

Overtures: *Die Fledermaus; Waldmeister; Perpetuum mobile.* **Polkas:** *Eljen a Magyar!; Pizzicato* (with Josef); *Tritsch-Tratsch; Unter Donner und Blitz; Vergnügungszug.* **Waltzes:** *Accelerationen; An der schönen, blauen Donau; G'schichten aus dem Wienerwald; Kaiser; Morgenblätter; Rosen aus dem Süden.* JOSEF STRAUSS: **Polkas:** *Frauenherz; Die Libelle; Ohne Sorgen; Die tanzende Muse.* **Waltzes:** *Aquarellen; Delirien; Sphärenklänge; Transaktionen.* JOHANN STRAUSS SR: *Radetzky March*

(B) **(*) DG Double 453 052-2 (2). VPO, Maazel

The presence of a New Year's Day audience is most tangible in the *Pizzicato Polka,* where one can sense the intercommunication as Maazel manipulates the rubato with obvious flair. He also gives a splendid account of *Transaktionen,* which has striking freshness and charm. The *Waldmeister Overture* is a delightful piece and readily shows the conductor's affectionate response in its detail, while the opening of the *Aquarellen Waltz* brings an even greater delicacy of approach and the orchestra responds with telling *pianissimo* playing. For the rest, these are well-played performances of no great memorability. The digital sound is brilliant and clear, somewhat lacking in resonant warmth.

Perpetuum mobile. Polkas: Annen; Auf der Jagd; Pizzicato (with Josef); Tritsch-Tratsch; Unter Donner und Blitz. Waltzes: An der schönen, blauen Donau; G'schichten aus dem Wienerwald; Kaiser; Wiener Blut. JOSEF STRAUSS: Delirien Waltz

(M) **(*) DG (IMS) (ADD) 437 255-2. BPO, Karajan

Here is a selection taken from two analogue LPs which Karajan made in 1966 and 1969 respectively. The performances have characteristic flair and the playing of the Berlin Philharmonic has much ardour as well as subtlety, with the four great waltzes of Johann II all finely done (the *Emperor* has a particularly engaging closing section) and the polkas wonderfully vivacious. The current remastering is satisfactory, brightly lit, but with the Jesus-Christus-Kirche providing ambient fullness.

Pappacoda polka; Der lustige Kreig (quadrille); Klug Gretelein (waltz). JOSEF STRAUSS: Defilir marsch. Polkas: Farewell; For ever. EDUARD STRAUSS: Weyprecht-Payer marsch. Polkas: Mädchenlaune; Saat und Ernte. Waltzes: Die Abonnenten; Blüthenkranz Johann Strauss'scher. J. STRAUSS III (son of Eduard): Schlau-Schlau polka

*** Chan. 8527. Johann Strauss O of V., Rothstein, with Hill Smith

This programme is admirably chosen to include unfamiliar music which deserves recording; indeed, both the *Klug Gretelein waltz,* which opens with some delectable scoring for woodwind and harp and has an idiomatic vocal contribution from Marilyn Hill Smith, and *Die Abonnenten* (by Eduard) are very attractive waltzes. *Blüthenkranz Johann Strauss'scher,* as its title suggest, makes a pot-pouri of some of Johann's most famous melodies. The polkas are a consistent delight, played wonderfully infectiously; indeed, above all this is a cheerful concert, designed to raise the spirits; the CD sound sparkles.

Polka: Pariser. Waltz: Wiener Blut. J. STRAUSS SR: Polkas: Eisele und Beisele-Sprünge; Salon. Waltz: Kettenbrücke; JOSEPH STRAUSS: Polka: Sehnsucht

(BB) **(*) Naxos 8.555689. V. Tanzquartett – LANNER: *Polkas & waltzes* **(*)

The waltzes and polkas of the Strauss family, usually recorded in their full-blown orchestral versions, were more often heard in their day in the countless coffee-houses, restaurants and beer-halls throughout Austria in much smaller arrangements, as recorded here for a string quartet. These are sympathetic performances, which readily evoke nineteenth-century Austria. The waltzes are well contrasted with the polkas (the minor-keyed *Sehnsucht Polka*, a sentimental and charming piece, is a highlight). Perhaps the string tone, alongside the highest standards, isn't as sophisticated as it might be, but, most importantly, the right style is conveyed. Not perhaps a disc to listen to all in one go, but ideal background or late-night listening. The recording is essentially good, with the slight thinness of tone not a serious fault.

Waltz transcriptions: *Kaiser; Rosen aus dem Süden* (both trans. Schoenberg); *Schatz Waltz* (from *Der Zigeunerbaron*; trans. Webern); *Wein, Weib und Gesang* (trans. Berg)

(M) **(*) DG (IMS) (ADD) 463 667-2. Boston SO Chamber Players – STRAVINSKY: *Octet for Wind Instruments; Pastorale, etc.* ***

A fascinating curiosity. Schoenberg, Berg and Webern made these transcriptions for informal private performances. Schoenberg's arrangements of the *Emperor* and *Roses from the South* are the most striking, though Berg's *Wine, Woman and Song* is sweetly appealing with its scoring for harmonium. As might be expected, Webern's *Schatz Waltz* is aptly refined. With the Boston Chamber Players taking rather too literal a view and missing some of the fun, the lumpishness of some of the writing is evident enough, but the very incongruity and the obvious love of these three severe atonalists for music with which one does not associate them is endearing. The recording and balance are excellent, and remains so in this transfer with its new Stravinsky couplings.

VOCAL MUSIC

Vocal waltzes

(i) *Auf's Korn! Bundesschützen-Marsch.* (ii) *Hoch Osterreich! Marsch.* Polkas: (i) *Burschenwanderung (polka française); 'S gibt nur a Kaiserstadt! 'S gibt nur ein Wien!;* (ii) *Sängerslust.* Waltzes: *An der schönen, blauen Donau;* (i) *Bei uns z'Haus;* (ii) *Gross-Wien;* (i) *Myrthenblüthen;* (ii) *Neu-Wien; Wein, weib und gesang!*

**(*) Marco Polo 8.223250-2. V. Männergesangverein, Czecho-Slovak RSO (Bratislava); (i) Track; (ii) Wildner

A most enjoyable collection. Wildner is occasionally a bit strong with the beat, but the *Blue Danube* with chorus is much more enjoyable than his performance with orchestra alone. The singers are Viennese, so they have a natural lilt, and the recording has an ideal ambience.

OPERA AND OPERETTA

Die Fledermaus (complete)

(*) DG **DVD 073 007-9. Coburn, Perry, Fassbaender, Waechter, Brendel, Hopferwieser, Bav. State Op. Ch. & O, C. Kleiber (Director: Otto Schenk)

☛ (B) *** Ph. Duo 464 031-2 (2). Te Kanawa, Gruberová, Leech, W. Brendel, Bär, Fassbaender, Göttling, Krause, Wendler, Schenk, V. State Op. Ch., VPO, Previn

(B) *** EMI double forte (ADD) 5 73851-2 (2). Scheyrer, Lipp, Dermota, Berry, Ludwig, Terkal, Waechter, Kunz, Philh. Ch. & O, Ackermann

☛ (BB) (***) Naxos mono 8.110180/181 (2). Gueden, Lipp, Patzak, Dermota, Poell, Wagner, Preger, Vienna State Op. Ch., VPO, Krauss

(M) *** EMI (ADD) 7 66223 (2). Rothenberger, Holm, Gedda, Dallapozza, Fischer-Dieskau, Fassbaender, Berry, V. State Op. Ch., VSO, Boskovsky

(M) (***) EMI mono 5 67074-2 [567153] (2). Schwarzkopf, Streich, Gedda, Krebs, Kunz, Christ, Philh. Ch. & O, Karajan

(N) (B) **(*) Decca (ADD) 475 6216 (2). Wächter, Janowitz, Holm, Holocek, Kunz, Windgassen, Kmentt, V. State Op. Ch., VPO, Boehm

Recorded live at the Bavarian State Opera in 1987, Carlos Kleiber's film version of *Die Fledermaus* is preferable to his audio recording, also for DG (457 765-2), in fair measure because of the superb assumption of the role of Prince Orlofsky by Brigitte Fassbaender, a fire-eater who makes the most positive host in the party scene of Act II, singing superbly, where the audio recording has a feeble falsettist. Though Janet Perry's soprano is shallow and bright, she has the agility and sparkle for the role of Adèle, with Patricia Coburn as a warm, positive Rosalinde, whoopsing away persuasively in the waltz numbers, and entering into the spirit of the party, despite a violently unconvincing red wig. Eberhard Waechter sounds too old and unsteady as Eisenstein, and Josef Hopferwieser is also unconvincingly old as the philandering tenor, Alfred, both shown up by the dark, firm Wolfgang Brendel as Falke. As on CD, Kleiber directs a taut performance, which yet has plenty of sparkle, helped by full-bodied sound.

Dame Kiri Te Kanawa's portrait of Rosalinde brings not only gloriously firm, golden sound but also vocal acting with star quality. Brigitte Fassbaender is the most dominant Prince Orlofsky on disc. Singing with a tangy richness and firmness, she emerges as the genuine focus of the party scene. Edita Gruberová is a sparkling, characterful and full-voiced Adèle; Wolfgang Brendel as Eisenstein and Olaf Bär as Dr Falke both sing very well indeed, though their voices sound too alike. Richard Leech as Alfred provides heady tone and a hint of parody. Tom Krause makes a splendid Frank, the more characterful for no longer sounding young. Anton Wendler as Dr Blind and Otto Schenk as Frosch the jailer give vintage Viennese performances, with Frosch's cavortings well tailored and not too extended. Vivaciously directed, this now goes to the top of the list of latterday *Fledermaus* recordings, though with one serious reservation: the Philips production in Act II adds a layer of crowd noise as background throughout the Party scene, even during Orlofsky's solos and in the lovely chorus, *Bruderlein und Schwesterlein*, yearningly done. Otherwise the recorded sound is superb. Like Kleiber on DG, Previn opts for the *Thunder and Lightning Polka* instead of the ballet. Its reissue at bargain price is welcome and retains all the qualities of the original (except texts and translations).

Like Gui's Glyndebourne *Nozze di Figaro*, Ackermann's vintage *Die Fledermaus* has been promoted from Classics for Pleasure to EMI's own double forte bargain label. It remains splendid value, for the singing sparkles, and the opera has an infectious sense of Viennese style. Wilma Lipp is a delicious Adèle and Crista Ludwig's Orlofsky is a real surprise, second only to Brigitte Fassbaender's assumption of a breeches role that is too often disappointing. Karl Terkal's Eisenstein and Anton Dermota's Alfred give much pleasure, and Erich Kunz's inebriated Frosch in the finale comes off even without a translation. The recording is excellent.

Die Fledermaus was one of the first Decca mono sets to show us what operatic treats the LP was to bring, and signalled a breakthrough in the recording of both opera and operetta, freed from the tyranny of the short-playing 78-r.p.m. side. It also demonstrated the extraordinary quality of the Vienna State Opera company in that post-war period, and many would claim that this version of *Fledermaus* has never been matched, let alone bettered. Clemens Krauss conducts an irresistibly sparkling account of the score with the starry cast forming a wonderfully co-ordinated ensemble. Hilde Gueden with her golden tones makes a deliciously minxish Rosalinde, with a naughty, provocative smile implied, and Julius Patzak as a tenor Eisenstein has never been surpassed, totally idiomatic, well contrasted with the equally fine Alfred of Anton Dermota. Add to that Wilma Lipp's bright, agile Adèle and the firm, clear if very feminine Orlofsky of Sieglinde Wagner. The original snag was the thin violin-timbre which became even more 'whistly' in the old Ace of Clubs reissue. In the latest Naxos transfer the voices are very well caught, set very much in front of the orchestra, and Davis Lennick's remastering tames the sound, even if the violins remain a little fizzy. This is a gramophone classic by any standards.

Those wanting a fairly modern, mid-priced version should consider EMI's Boskovsky set. Though he sometimes fails to lean into the seductive rhythms as much as he might, his is a refreshing account of a magic score. Anneliese Rothenberger is a sweet, domestic-sounding Rosalinde, relaxed and sparkling if edgy at times, while, among an excellent supporting cast, the Orlofsky of Brigitte Fassbaender must again be singled out as the finest on record, tough and firm. The entertainment has been excellently produced for records, with German dialogue inserted, though the ripe recording sometimes make the voices jump between singing and speaking. The remastering is admirably vivid.

The mono recording of Karajan's 1955 version has great freshness and clarity, along with the polish which for many will make it a first favourite. Schwarzkopf makes an enchanting Rosalinde, not just in the imagination and sparkle of her singing but also in the snatches of spoken dialogue (never too long) which leaven the entertainment. As Adèle, Rita Streich produces her most dazzling coloratura; Nicolai Gedda and Helmut Krebs are beautifully contrasted in their tenor tone, and Erich Kunz gives a vintage performance as Falke. The original recording, crisply focused, has been given a suitable facelift as one of EMI's 'Great Recordings of the Century'.

Boehm may not have the instant sparkle of the finest versions of this work, but what he does possess is an affection and warmth which are very endearing. From the word go, one marvels at the richness of playing (and vintage Decca sound from 1971) and his weightier approach, combined with a robust swagger, gives this set a unique – and attractive – quality. The stars of the performance are undoubtedly Gundula Janowitz, in rich voice as Rosalinde, and Renate Holm as Adèle (she is also on the EMI/Boskovsky set). The male principals are less impressive: the use of a male Orlofsky has less dramatic point on record than it would on stage, and Windgassen is vocally far from impressive. The recording is without dialogue (and that will be an advantage for some) and the ballet is replaced by the *Thunder and Lightning Polka*.

Die Fledermaus (complete, in English)

*** Arthaus **DVD** 100 134 (2). Gustafson, Howarth, Kowalski, Otey, Michaels-Moore, Bottone, ROHCG Ch. & O, Bonynge (Director: John Cox)

Lasting well over three and a quarter hours, this version of *Die Fledermaus*, in an English version by John Mortimer, stretches to two DVDs, largely because in this gala performance at Covent Garden on New Year's Eve 1989/90 a half-hour of performances by the 'surprise guests' is included in the party scene: Luciano Pavarotti, Marilyn Horne and – making her farewell to the opera stage – Dame Joan Sutherland. For Sutherland devotees it is an essential item, with the two duets specially cherishable, the *Semiramide* duet with Horne and *Parigi o cara* from *La Traviata* with Pavarotti.

Under Richard Bonynge's light, beautifully sprung direction, the gala fizzes splendidly with a first-rate cast, even though at the start of Act II Falke (Michaels-Moore) unwittingly loses his monocle. The countertenor, Jochen Kowalski, makes a characterful, distinctive Orlofsky with baritone speaking voice contrasted with his singing. Nancy Gustafson is a warm Rosalinde and Judith Howarth a sweet Adèle, and the others all sing well, despite the pressure of the occasion.

Die Fledermaus: highlights

(B) *** EMI Red Line 5 69839. Popp, Baltsa, Lind, Seiffert, Domingo, Bav. R. Ch., Munich RSO, Domingo

It was not originally intended that Plácido Domingo should sing the role of Alfred as well as conducting EMI's newest digital recording of *Fledermaus*, but the tenor who had originally been engaged cancelled at the last minute, and Domingo agreed to do the double job, singing over accompaniments that had already been recorded. The happiness of the occasion is reflected in a strong and amiable, rather than an idiomatically Viennese, performance. Lucia Popp makes a delectable and provocative Rosalinde and Peter Seiffert a strong tenor Eisenstein, with Agnes Baltsa a superb, characterful Orlofsky. With ensembles vigorous and urgent, this is a consistently warm and sympathetic selection.

A Night in Venice (Eine Nacht in Venedig); Wiener Blut: complete

(M) (***) EMI mono 5 67532-2 (2). Schwarzkopf, Gedda, Köth, Kunz, Klein, Loose, Dönch, Philh. Ch. & O, Ackermann

A Night in Venice, in Erich Korngold's revision, is a superb example of Walter Legge's Philharmonia productions, honeyed and atmospheric. As a sampler, try the jaunty little waltz duet in Act I between Schwarzkopf as the heroine, Annina, and the baritone Erich Kunz as Caramello, normally a tenor role. Nicolai Gedda as the Duke then appropriates the most famous waltz song of all, the *Gondola Song*, but, with such a frothy production, purism would be out of place. The digital remastering preserves the balance of the mono original admirably. This now comes attractively coupled with *Wiener Blut*. In *Wiener Blut* to have Schwarzkopf at her most ravishing, singing a waltz song based on the tune of *Morning Papers*, is enough enticement for this Philharmonia version of the mid-1950s, showing Walter Legge's flair as a producer at its most compelling. Schwarzkopf was matched by the regular team of Gedda and Kunz and with Emmy Loose and Erika Köth in the secondary soprano roles. The original mono recording was beautifully balanced, and the facelift given here is achieved most tactfully.

Wiener Blut (complete)

(M) **(*) EMI (ADD) 7 69943-2 (2). Rothenberger, Gedda, Holm, Hirte, Putz, Cologne Op. Ch., Philh. Hungarica, Boskovsky

The EMI set conducted by Willi Boskovsky makes a delightful entertainment, the performance authentic and with a strong singing cast. The recording is atmospherically reverberant, but there is no lack of sparkle. However, for some people there will be too much German dialogue, which also involves two CDs.

Der Zigeunerbaron (The Gipsy Baron): complete

(M) (***) EMI mono 5 67535-2 (2). Schwarzkopf, Gedda, Prey, Kunz, Köth, Sinclair, Philh. Ch. & O, Ackermann

This superb Philharmonia version of *The Gipsy Baron* from the mid-1950s, recently restored to the catalogue, has never been matched in its rich stylishness and polish. Elisabeth Schwarzkopf as the gypsy princess sings radiantly, not least in the heavenly Bullfinch duet (to the melody made famous by MGM as *One day when we were young*). Nicolai Gedda, still youthful, produces heady tone, and Erich Kunz as the rough pig-breeder gives a vintage *echt*-Viennese performance of the irresistible *Ja, das Schreiben und das Lesen*. The CD transcription from excellent mono originals gives fresh and truthful sound, particularly in the voices.

Der Zigeunerbaron (arr. Harnoncourt; Linke: complete)

*(**) Teldec 4509 94555-2 (2). Coburn, Lippert, Schasching, Hamari, Holzmair, Oelze, Von Magnus, Lazar, Arnold Schoenberg Ch., VSO, Harnoncourt

When *Zigeunerbaron*, second only to *Fledermaus* among Strauss operettas, has been so neglected on disc, this new Teldec set, offering a more expanded text than ever before, fills an important gap. Harnoncourt, as a Viennese and with a Viennese orchestra, ensures that the Strauss lilt is winningly and authentically observed from the pot-pourri overture onwards, and Harnoncourt's concern (as a period specialist) for clarity of texture gives the whole performance a sparkling freshness. Sadly, the casting is seriously flawed, when the central character of the gypsy princess, Saffi, is taken by a soprano, Pamela Coburn, who, as recorded, sounds strained and unsteady. The others are better, with Rudolf Schasching catching the fun behind the comic role of the pig-breeder, Zsupán, authentically but without exaggeration, and the light tenor, Herbert Lippert, is charming as the hero, Barinkay. Among the rest, the mezzo, Elisabeth von Magnus, sings in cabaret style in the supporting role of Mirabella, given a major point-number here, often omitted. Christiane Oelze as Arsena, the girl who does not get the hero, sings far more sweetly than Coburn, and Julia Hamari as Saffi's foster-mother, Czipra, sounds younger than her daughter. The recording is full and vivid, but many will feel that there is too much German dialogue – largely accounting for the extended length of two and a half hours.

STRAUSS, Franz (1822–1905)

Horn Concerto in C min., Op. 8

(B) **(*) Double Decca (ADD) 460 296 (2). Tuckwell, LSO, Kertész – R. STRAUSS: *Concertos* **(*)

This concerto by Franz Strauss, Richard's father, at times half-anticipates the lyrical style his son was to favour a generation later. But the quality of the musical material is undistinguished, and with its florid ornamentation the writing shows a tendency to fall into the manner of the cornet air with variations. Barry Tuckwell's performance is responsive and secure, but it fails to convince the listener that the work should not be put back in the attic where it rightly belongs.

STRAUSS, Josef (1827–70)

Strauss, Josef: The Complete Edition

As with the music of Johann Sr and Johann Jr, Marco Polo are planning a complete edition of all Josef's music, much of it totally unknown. So far the series has reached Volume 26, all full of interest. But, for reasons of space, our survey is being taken forward into our 2006/7 Yearbook.

Polkas: *Auf Ferienreisen; Buchstaben; Feuerfest; Frauenherz; Im Fluge; Jockey; Ohn Sorgen; Sport; Vorwärtz; Die Schwätzerin.* Waltzes: *Aquarellen; Delirien; Dorfschwalben aus Osterreich; Dynamiden; Jockey; Mein Lebenslauf is Lieb' und Lust*

(B) *** EMI 5 74528-2 (5). Johann Strauss O of V., Boskovsky – JOHANN STRAUSS JR: *Overtures, Polkas and Waltzes* **(*)

As always, orchestras respond to the lesser-known music of Josef which at its best can easily match Johann in melodic distinction. All six waltzes included here are delightful and are presented with much spirit, finesse and affection, with *Delirien, Dorfschwalben aus Osterreich* and *Dynamiden* standing out. This is the most attractive of the five CDs in EMI's reissued Strauss box and it ought to be available separately.

STRAUSS, Richard (1864–1949)

Symphonic poems: *An Alpine Symphony, Op. 64; Death and Transfiguration, Op. 24; Don Juan, Op. 20; Ein Heldenleben, Op. 40*

(M) *** Chan. 7009/10. RSNO, Järvi

Symphonic poems: *Also sprach Zarathustra, Op. 30; (i) Don Quixote, Op. 35. Macbeth, Op. 23; Symphonia domestica, Op. 53; Till Eulenspiegel, Op. 38*

(M) *** Chan. 7011/12. RSNO, Järvi; (i) with R. Wallfisch

Järvi's generally distinguished survey of the Strauss symphonic poems was recorded in the sumptuous acoustics of the Caird Hall, Dundee, between 1986 and 1989. If occasionally the resonance prevents the sharpest internal clarity, the skilled Chandos engineering ensures that the orchestral layout is very believable, heard within a natural perspective. The account of *An Alpine Symphony* is ripely enjoyable, with the reverberant acoustic here very helpful. Järvi seeks to present a general scenic view within a performance that is not as electrically taut or crisp of ensemble as, say, Karajan's but which is very effective in giving a genial description of the changing landscapes. *Death and Transfiguration* shows the orchestra at its finest and here detail is revealed well, within a reading which has impressive control. *Don Juan* is portrayed as a bluff philanderer and the reading seeks sentience and amplitude rather than searing brilliance. *Ein Heldenleben* is strongly characterized and warmly sympathetic from first to last, marked by powerful, thrustful playing, lacking only the last degree of refinement in ensemble.

Järvi's *Symphonia domestica* is particularly successful, as indeed is his joyful portrait of *Till*. *Macbeth*, less than a masterpiece, is also presented very persuasively; few if any recorded performances make a better case for it. *Don Quixote* then takes a rather leisurely journey, although an amiable one. Raphael Wallfisch, the solo cellist, plays splendidly but, like the excellent violist, John Harrington, is very forwardly balanced, while inner orchestral detail is less than ideally clear. *Also sprach Zarathustra*, which closes the programme, is the least successful of the series, with the reverberant acoustic rather muddying the sound, without bringing compensating richness; moreover the organ pedal at the opening is much too dominant. At mid-price they are undoubtedly competitive, particularly for collectors who enjoy Chandos's rich tapestries of sound.

An Alpine Symphony, Op. 64; Also sprach Zarathustra, Op. 30

⊶ *** EMI (ADD) **Audio DVD** DVC4 92396-9. Dresden State O, Kempe

The *Alpine Symphony* has all the rhetoric, confidence and opulence of the great Strauss tone-poems, and if its melodic invention is not up to the best of them, its visual imagination more than compensates when the performance and recording are as good as this. Kempe brings a glowing warmth and humanity to the score and there is no doubt that in his hands it sounds a greater work than it is. He moulds each phrase with great sensitivity and life, observing all the pictorial detail yet retaining a strong sense of forward movement. The Dresden orchestra is a magnificent body, here at its finest and producing rich, cultured yet essentially vital playing throughout. The 1971 EMI recording was made in quadraphony and is sensational in this Audio DVD transfer, offered either in high-resolution stereo or multi-channel surround sound. There is remarkable depth and splendid detail; although the upper strings date the sound just a little, the horns and heavy brass are superb and the concert-hall illusion is remarkable.

Also sprach Zarathustra is transferred at a somewhat lower level, no doubt to encompass the huge expansion of dynamic at the opening, with the organ pedal becoming almost overwhelming. The contrasting gentle string passage that follows is wonderfully mellow yet radiant. Kempe's performance is always convincingly paced, and the strings produce a sumptuous tone throughout. The work's climax, with its tolling bell, expands magnificently. A superb reissue in every way.

An Alpine Symphony, Op. 64

*** DG 439 017-2. BPO, Karajan
*** Australian Decca Eloquence 466 670-2. LAPO, Mehta

This DG reissue in the Karajan Gold series is one of the most remarkable in its improvement of the sound over the original CD issue. The acoustic boundaries of the sound seem to have expanded. Detail is not analytically clear, but the sumptuous body of tone created by the orchestra is glorious, with the violins glowing and soaring as they enter the forest. Undoubtedly this performance is very distinguished, wonderfully spacious and beautifully shaped – the closing *Night* sequence is very touching – and played with the utmost virtuosity.

Mehta's version is perhaps the best of his Decca Strauss recordings. It is a virtuoso performance, and he is supported by a superb recording which is wide in range and rich in

detail. It is not overlit, yet the Decca engineers allow every strand of the texture to 'tell' without ever losing sight of the overall perspective, and it has transferred strikingly well to CD.

(i) An Alpine Symphony; (ii) Also sprach Zarathustra; (i) Death and Transfiguration; Don Juan; Ein Heldenleben; (ii) Festliches Praeludium, Op. 61; Der Rosenkavalier: waltzes from Act III. Salome: Dance of the Seven Veils; Till Eulenspiegel

(B) *(**) DG mono/stereo 463 190-2 (3). (i) Dresden State O, (ii) BPO; Boehm

Boehm's Strauss is impressive, and this bargain box, comprising some mono but mainly stereo recordings, is a fine tribute to his natural affinity with this composer. *An Alpine Symphony*, *Don Juan* and *Ein Heldenleben* are mono, but are excellent performances: it is Boehm's attention to detail which one most enjoys, though there is excitement too, even if this music ideally requires stereo to make its full impact. The rest of the performances are stereo. *Also sprach Zarathustra* dates from 1958 and the sound is good if a little thin; it is a spacious and satisfying account, with splendid playing to support the conductor's conception. The rustic portrayal of *Till* and the *Waltzes* from *Der Rosenkavalier* are both effective, as is the highly sensuous account of *Salome's Dance*. The *Prelude*, written in 1913 for the opening of the Konzerthaus in Vienna, is a fascinating bonus: it is a somewhat inflated work, for organ and a huge orchestra, in which the composer piles sequence upon sequence to produce a climax of shattering sonority. Boehm manages to give the work a dignity not really inherent in the music. All these were recorded a few years after *Also sprach Zarathustra* and have fuller sound. For *Death and Transfiguration*, Boehm's 1972 live Salzburg Festival recording was used; it is a performance of excitement and strong tensions (despite a couple of irritating coughs at the beginning), even if the recording is slightly overweighted at the top. At bargain price, this set is worth considering, and an essential purchase for admirers of this distinguished conductor.

(i) An Alpine Symphony; (ii) Also sprach Zarathustra, Don Juan, (iii) Ein Heldenleben; (ii) Till Eulenspiegel

(B) *** Double Decca (ADD) 440 618-2 (2). (i) Bav. RSO; (ii) Chicago SO; (iii) VPO; Solti

The Bavarian Radio Orchestra recorded in the Herculessaal in Munich could hardly sound more opulent in the *Alpine Symphony* and the superb quality of the 1979 analogue recording tends to counterbalance Solti's generally fast tempi. The performances of *Also sprach Zarathustra*, *Don Juan* and *Till Eulenspiegel* come from analogue originals, made in Chicago a few years earlier. Solti is ripely expansive in *Zarathustra*, and throughout all three symphonic poems there is the most glorious playing from the Chicago orchestra in peak form. For *Ein Heldenleben* Solti went (in 1977–8) to Vienna, and this is another fast-moving performance, tense to the point of fierceness in the opening tutti and elsewhere. It underlines the urgency rather than the opulence of the writing but Solti is at his finest in the final coda after the fulfilment theme, where in touching simplicity he finds complete relaxation at last, helped by the exquisite playing of the Vienna Philharmonic concertmaster, Rainer Küchl. The Decca recording is formidably wide-ranging to match this high-powered performance and, as with the rest of the programme, the transfers to CD are full-bodied and vividly detailed.

An Alpine Symphony; Also sprach Zarathustra; Don Juan; Till Eulenspiegel; Salome: Dance of the 7 Veils; (i) Vier letzte Lieder (4 Last Songs)
(B) **(*) DG 2-CD (DDD/ADD) 474 261-2 (2). BPO, Karajan, (i) with Tomowa-Sintow

Karajan's outstanding *Alpine Symphony* is digital, as are Anna Tomowa-Sintow's *Four Last Songs*, beautifully sung with creamy tone, if without the final touch of imagination that such inspired music cries out for. The rest of the recordings are analogue and are discussed below. Certainly this new compilation in DG's Karajan Collection is value for money.

An Alpine Symphony; Don Juan; Suite for 13 Wind Instruments, Op. 4; Symphonia domestica; Till Eulenspiegel
(BB) **(*) Virgin 2x1 5 61460-2 (2). Minnesota O, De Waart

An excellent and inexpensive anthology, very well played and recorded, over which there are only minor reservations. There is no lack of spectacle in the *Alpine Symphony*, which ends with an impressive storm and a rich-hued sunset: only the echoing horns on the way up seem rather too far away; but nothing is inflated needlessly. Similarly, anyone who feels that Strauss's domestic revelations need tempering with a little discretion will enjoy this performance, which is also very well played by the excellent Minnesota Orchestra. The *Suite in B flat* is beautifully blended and comparably refined. In *Don Juan* the orchestra may not succeed in producing quite the same sophisticated opulence of texture as is achieved by such Straussians as Reiner in Chicago or Karajan in Berlin, but they still play very well indeed; and throughout, the sound has both depth and clarity. Good value.

An Alpine Symphony; Festival Prelude (Festliches Praeludium)
(BB) *** Arte Nova 74321 92779-2. Zurich Tonhalle O, Zinman

David Zinman and his Zurich Tonhalle Orchestra have now followed up their exceptionally successful Beethoven cycle on the Arte Nova budget label with a fine Strauss series. Here they offer two of the most extravagant orchestral works that even Strauss created. More than usual, Zinman finds clarity and refinement in the *Alpine Symphony*. It has space as well as real poetic feeling and imagination. The effect may be less opulent than some versions, vividly recorded as it is, but there is no lack of passion or emotional thrust in presenting a score which is not just a musical picture postcard of a mountain-ascent, but a tautly conceived structure in which the spectacular orchestral effects are controlled with masterly finesse. The rarely heard *Festival Prelude*, written for Vienna in 1913, uses even bigger forces, an occasional piece which in this ripe performance makes a sumptuous fill-up.

Also sprach Zarathustra – see also under Four Last Songs
Also sprach Zarathustra, Op. 30
*** Sony **DVD** SVD 46388. BPO, Karajan– MOZART: Divertimento 17 **(*)

By the time Karajan conducted the concert celebrating the 750th anniversary of the founding of Berlin, he was already ailing, as one registers from his painful progress to the podium each time; once there, however, the electric intensity of his conducting never falters in passionate commitment to this great Strauss work, always a favourite of his. It is as though he realizes that this may be the last time he will ever conduct it. Though the hushed close makes this a subdued sort of celebration. Karajan's control is emphasized in the total silence at the end, until his subtle signal of release for the applause to begin, at which the audience responds with fervour. One myth which the performance tends to undermine is that Karajan consistently had his eyes shut when conducting. There are certainly moments when that happens, but in this work above all, his eye, when you see it, drills like a gimlet, ever observant. It is a help that the DVD offers ample index points separating the sections. This DVD is short measure but is still indispensable.

Also sprach Zarathustra, Op. 30
(M) *** DG (ADD) 463 627-2. Boston SO, Steinberg – HOLST: The Planets ***

Steinberg's 1972 *Also sprach Zarathustra* now reappears as one of DG's Originals. It is sumptuously recorded with the orchestra slightly recessed within a warm Boston acoustic, which adds to the sentient feeling of what is essentially a lyrical account of considerable ardour, reaching a superb climax. It is very well transferred indeed and will satisfy Steinberg admirers attracted to his fine and individual account of *The Planets* (equally impressively remastered).

(i) Also sprach Zarathustra; (i) Burleske for Piano & Orchestra. Der Rosenkavalier: 1st & 2nd Waltz Sequence. Die Liebe der Danae (symphonic fragment); Metamorphosen for 23 Solo Strings
(B) *** Delos Double DE 3707 (2) (i) Rosenberger; Seattle Symphony, Schwarz

Throughout this programme the Seattle orchestra plays splendidly, with warmth, passion and finish, and the concert hall acoustic is just right for this richly scored music. With no loss of definition, there is a degree of sumptuousness and bloom here missing in Lorin Maazel's otherwise technically impressive RCA Bavarian CDs (see above), Gerard Schwarz's earlier recordings have already proved him a dedicated and idiomatic Straussian. His version of *Metamorphosen* (see below) is sustained at a very spacious tempo indeed, But it is unfailingly eloquent and holds the listener in its grip throughout. So does *Also sprach Zarathustra*, which has a fine forward sweep but plenty of imaginative detail. The *Burleske* is an affectionately fanciful performance, rather loosely held together, but with Carol Rosenberger an endearingly nimble and romantic soloist. The two *Waltz Sequences* from *Der Rosenkavalier* are spirited enough, but add up to nearly 22 minutes and would outstay their welcome if not cued into two separate groups. However, the *symphonic fragment* from *Die liebe der Danae*, Strauss's penultimate opera, is sombrely and movingly powerful and makes an excellent foil for the seductive *Salome's Dance*, as voluptuosly involving an account as any on record, closing with thrilling abandon. With such fine playing and superb sound this pair of discs, offered for the cost of one, is worthy of any collector's outlay.

Also sprach Zarathustra; Death and Transfiguration; Don Juan
*** DG (IMS) 439 016-2. BPO, Karajan
*** Telarc CD 80167. VPO, Previn

As a performance the 1983 Karajan *Also sprach Zarathustra* (coupled with an exciting account of *Don Juan*) will be hard to beat and could very well be first choice. And the newly remastered CD has great dynamic range and presence, particularly at the extreme bass and treble, and the massed violins produce wonderfully radiant textures, as in the section marked *Von der grossen Sehnsucht* ('of the great longing'). The soaring main theme of *Don Juan* is hardly less sumptuous and the playing is electrifying in its energy.

Previn draws magnificent playing from the Vienna Philharmonic in powerful, red-blooded readings of the symphonic poems, and the recording is among Telarc's finest. Strongly recommended for anyone wanting this particular coupling, and enjoying spectacularly voluptuous sound-quality.

Also sprach Zarathustra; Death and Transfiguration; Till Eulenspiegel; Salome: Dance of the Seven Veils

(M) *** Decca (ADD) 466 388-2. VPO, Karajan

(BB) *** EMI Encore (ADD) 5 74756-2 Dresden State O, Kempe

Karajan's Decca version of *Also sprach Zarathustra* was a famous early stereo demonstration disc in its day (1959), with its wide dynamic range and thrilling orchestral virtuosity; all its tonal opulence is restored in the CD transfer. The other works were recorded a year later and sound freshly minted, amazingly full and sharply detailed. *Till* is irrepressibly cheeky and full of wit, and *Salome's Dance* is decadently sensuous. *Don Juan* brings a similar, richly voluptuous response from the Vienna strings. Again the playing is superb, as beguiling in the love music as it is exhilarating in the chase.

Kempe's *Also sprach Zarathustra* is powerful in its emotional thrust, without going over the top. It is admirably paced, and while the Dresden orchestra may yield in virtuosity – though not much – to the Berlin Philharmonic under Karajan, whose analogue version was made in the same year, the HMV digital remastering retains the opulence of the Dresden acoustic. The rather mellow portrait of *Till* is particularly attractive and *Salome's Dance* is also superbly played. Excellent value.

(i) Also sprach Zarathustra, Op. 30; (ii) Don Juan, Op. 20; (iii) Salome: Dance of the Seven Veils, Op. 54

(BB) **(*) DG Entrée 474 566-2. (i) NYPO; (ii) Dresden State O; (iii) Deutsche Oper, Berlin, O; Sinopoli

Sinopoli is at his most warmly and passionately persuasive in this Strauss triptych and all three orchestras play with virtuosity and conviction. But in *Also sprach Zarathustra* the conductor's special relationship with the New York Philharmonic is let down by the recording, brilliant and spectacular but harsh in *fortissimos*. The Dresden and Berlin acoustics are more sympathetic, and both *Don Juan* and the *Dance of the Seven Veils* have very powerful climaxes.

Also sprach Zarathustra; Don Juan; Till Eulenspiegel; Salome: Salome's Dance

(M) *** DG (ADD) 447 441-2. BPO, Karajan

Karajan's 1974 DG analogue version of *Also sprach Zarathustra* is coupled with his vividly characterized performance of *Till Eulenspiegel* and a thrillingly ebullient *Don Juan*, plus his powerfully voluptuous account of *Salome's Dance*. The Berlin Philharmonic plays with great fervour (the timpani strokes at the very opening are quite riveting) and creates characteristic

body of tone in the strings, although the digital remastering has thrown a much brighter light on the violins.

Also sprach Zarathustra; (i) Don Quixote, Op. 35

(B) **(*) Sony (ADD) SBK 47656. Phd. O, Ormandy; (i) with Munroe

Ormandy's 1963 Sony *Also sprach Zarathustra*, if not as overwhelming as his later, EMI version, has much virtuoso orchestral playing to commend it and many felicities of characterization. His (1961) *Don Quixote* will also give considerable pleasure. There is some marvellous orchestral playing and the two soloists play splendidly with plenty of character but without the 'star soloist' approach favoured by so many record companies. A very competitive coupling.

Also sprach Zarathustra, Op. 30; Ein Heldenleben, Op. 40

🔊 ✹ (M) *** RCA **SACD** (ADD) 82876 61389-2. Chicago SO, Reiner

🔊 (***) Testament mono SBT 1183. VPO, Krauss

These were the first stereo sessions the RCA engineers arranged with Fritz Reiner, after the company had taken over the Chicago orchestra's recording contract from Mercury. It must be said – to their enormous credit – that the RCA recording team 'got it right' from the very beginning, and the series of records they made with Reiner and his players in Orchestra Hall remain a technical peak in the history of stereo recording and the impressive feeling of space it conveyed. Later reissues have improved on its definition but none has done so with the stunning success of the present transfer. *Ein Heldenleben* shows Reiner in equally splendid form. There have been more incisive, more spectacular and more romantic performances, but Reiner achieves an admirable balance and whatever he does is convincing. If anything, the recording sounds even better than *Also sprach* and the warm acoustics of Orchestra Hall help convey Reiner's humanity in the closing pages of the work.

Clemens Krauss brings the heroic sweep, the contrasts and delicacy of texture and the breadth of *Ein Heldenleben* before one's eyes. There is a nobility here (and, for that matter, in *Zarathustra* too) that not every Strauss conductor conveys. Straussians will naturally have Karajan, Reiner and Kempe in this repertoire, but Krauss still has special claims on the serious collector and he has a warmth and humanity that are enormously rewarding.

Aus Italien; Die Liebe der Danae (symphonic fragment); Der Rosenkavalier: waltz sequence 2

(BB) *** Naxos 8.550342. Slovak PO, Košler

On Naxos, a very well-recorded and vividly detailed account of *Aus Italien* with an excellent sense of presence. The orchestra plays very well for Zdeněk Košler both here and in the ten-minute symphonic fragment Clemens Krauss made from *Die Liebe der Danae* and in the *Rosenkavalier* waltz sequence. The Slovak Philharmonic is a highly responsive body, with cultured strings and wind departments and, given the quality of the recorded sound, this represents a real bargain.

Aus Italien, Op. 16; Metamorphosen for 23 Solo Strings

(N) (M) *** Chan. 10218X. RSNO, Järvi

Järvi offers an apt coupling of early and late Strauss. *Aus Italien* is early and does not do the composer the fullest justice, but it does have marvellous moments, including the beautiful slow movement. The finale quotes a famous Neapolitan tarantella by Denza but does not make a great deal of it. Järvi takes a spacious view of the work, and the Chandos sound is full-bodied, with a natural perspective, and there is plenty of warmth. The orchestra seems at home in the score, giving the finale a certain Celtic lilt. *Metamorphosen* is a late masterpiece. Järvi's account is deeply felt and ardent, and the Scottish strings convey the underlying angst of the music with moving passion: they also play very well indeed. The recording is rich, expansive and natural. All in all, a great success and attractively priced.

Le Bourgeois Gentilhomme: Suite, Op. 60. Symphonia domestica, Op. 53

⊖ (***) Testament mono SBT 1184. VPO, Krauss

Remarkably few allowances need be made for the 1951 recording of the *Symphonia domestica*, a Cinderella among Strauss tone-poems and curiously unloved. If any performance should transform its status, this is it. Krauss had given it its Viennese première in 1922, and this was its first (and for many years only) LP recording. The authors of *The Record Guide* noted that many critics 'have been so bothered by the mundane details of the programme that they have failed to appreciate the beauties as well as the dazzling cleverness of the score'. There have been impressive versions from Reiner, Karajan, Kempe, Sawallisch and others; this one has a special authenticity of feeling and richness of response that disarm criticism. Krauss conducted many early performances of the suite from *Le Bourgeois Gentilhomme* and this unforgettable (1952) account has wonderful lightness of touch and delicacy of feeling. Its charm is quite irresistible. This ranks alongside the great recordings by Fritz Reiner and Sir Thomas Beecham.

Burleske for piano and orchestra

(M) *** Warner Elatus 0927 46768-2. Grimaud, Berlin State O, Kurt Sanderling – BRAHMS: *Piano Concerto 1 in D min.* ***

Hélène Grimaud is not only an impressive Brahms interpreter but a virtuoso of no mean order. She dispatches the Richard Strauss *Burleske* with great aplomb and, with the help of Sanderling, finds much character in the music. Good recording too.

(i; ii; iii) Burleske for Piano & Orchestra; (iv; v) Duet Concertino for Clarinet & Bassoon; (vi; ii; vii) Horn Concertos 1 in E flat, Op. 11; 2 in E flat; (viii; v) Oboe Concerto; (ix; v) Violin Concerto in D min., Op. 8

(B) **(*) Double Decca mono/stereo ADD/Dig. 460 296-2 (2). (i) Gulda; (ii) LSO; (iii) Collins; (iv) D. Ashkenazy, Walker; (v) Berlin RSO, V. Ashkenazy; (vi) Tuckwell; (vii) Kertész; (viii) Hunt; (ix) Belkin – FRANZ STRAUSS: *Horn Concerto* **(*)

For the *Burleske*, Decca have turned back to a first-rate 1954 mono performance in which Gulda, on top form, is vivaciously partnered by Anthony Collins. They respond readily to its scherzando wit, while the muted ending is quite touching. The recording is very good for its period, although with Strauss one ideally needs more opulence in the orchestral violin tone. The *Duet Concertino* is an elusive work and here the timbres of the clarinet and bassoon soloists are rather too sharply individual to gel, and the conductor holds the orchestral reins rather slackly: the result is characterful but lacks an ongoing fluency and grip. Barry Tuckwell's essentially lyrical approach to the two horn concertos misses some of the

music's character and the more florid *Second Concerto* also needs a stronger impulse, although the finale brings engaging light-hearted bravura. Boris Belkin's performance of the *Violin Concerto* isn't technically flawless, yet is distinctly enjoyable (see below). But the highlight of the set is Gordon Hunt's superb account of the *Oboe Concerto*. His creamy tone is ideally suited to Strauss's songful late masterpiece, and its technical hazards are surmounted with easy aplomb. There is no finer version.

Burleske; Parergon, Op. 73; Stimmungsbilder, Op. 9

**(*) Ara. Z 6567. Hobson, Philh. O, Del Mar

Ian Hobson's account, on its own terms, is eminently satisfactory, and he is well supported by Norman Del Mar and the Philharmonia, and is well recorded. The *Parergon* for left hand is again very well played. The *Stimmungsbilder* are early, rather Schumannesque pieces, written in 1884: Hobson gives a rather touching account of *Träumerei*, and though one can imagine a performance of the *Intermezzo* with greater charm, there is still much to admire here. Decent recording.

Horn Concertos 1 in E flat, Op. 11; 2 in E flat

⊖ ✪ (M) (***) EMI mono 5 67782-2 [Angel 5 67783-2]. Brain, Philh. O, Sawallisch – HINDEMITH: *Horn Concerto; Concert Music* ***

(i) Horn Concertos 1 & 2. Andante for Horn and Piano, Op. posth; Capriccio: Introduction to the finale scene. Introduction, Theme and Variations in E flat (for horn and piano). (ii) Alphorn, Op. 15/3 (for soprano, horn and piano).

(N) (B) **(*) Australian Decca Eloquence 476 2699. Tuckwell with (i) RPO; (ii) McLaughlin; Ashkenazy (pianist and cond.)

(i) Horn Concertos 1; (ii) 2; (iii) Oboe Concerto; (iv) Duet Concertino for Clarinet & Bassoon

*** DG (IMS) 453 483-2. (i) Janezic, (ii) Stransky; (iii) Gabriel; (iv) Schmidl, Werba; VPO, Previn

(i) Horn Concertos 1-2; (ii) Duet Concertino for Clarinet & Bassoon. Wind Serenade in E flat, Op. 11

⊖ (B) *** CfP 573 5132. (i) Pyatt; (ii) Farrall, Andrews; Britten Sinfonia, Cleobury

Dennis Brain's performances are incomparable and almost certainly will never be surpassed. Sawallisch gives him admirable support, and fortunately the latest EMI CD transfer captures the full quality of the 1956 mono recording. This coupling certainly deserves a place among EMI's 'Great Recordings of the Century' and for the reissue an extra Hindemith work has been added.

David Pyatt gives a ripely exuberant performance of the first of Strauss's two *Horn Concertos*. The more elusive first movement of the *Second Concerto* is shaped – often quite subtly – in an attractively rhapsodical style, while the finale brings heady, lightly tongued bravura. The outer movements of the gently rapturous *Duet Concertino* are presented with enticing delicacy of texture, and the slow movement again brings a most touchingly doleful opening solo, this time from the bassoonist, Julie Andrews. Cleobury and the Britten Sinfonia give sensitive support throughout, and the early *Serenade* is always fresh, never congealing, helped by the naturally balanced recording, made in the Henry Wood Hall, Southwark.

On DG some glorious music-making, relaxed, unforced and full of expressive delights. The virtuosity is at no time self-regarding and everybody appears to be enjoying themselves. The sound, too, is as natural as the music-making. A most welcome addition to the catalogue.

Barry Tuckwell's essentially lyrical approach to the two horn concertos misses some of the music's character, and the more florid *Second Concerto* also needs a stronger impulse, although the finale brings engaging light-hearted bravura. They are, of course, still very enjoyable, and this CD brings the advantage of some rarities: all of them pleasingly attractive, rather than momentous, with the *Op. 15 Alphorn*, with the pleasing combination of soprano, horn and piano, most attractive. Warm recording.

(i; ii) *Oboe Concerto*; (ii) *Metamorphosen for 23 Solo Strings*; (iv) *Violin Sonata in E flat*; (ii; iii) Orchestral Lieder: *Befreit; Freundliche Vision; Die Heiligen drei Könige aus Morgenland; Meinem Kinde; Morgen!; Ruhe, meine Seele; Waldseligkeit; Wiegenlied; Winterweihe*
(BB) **(*) Virgin 2x1 5 61766-2 (2) (i) Still; (ii) Academy of L., Stamp; (iii) Janowitz; (iv) Sitkovetsky, Gililov

Ray Still, the principal oboe of the Chicago Symphony Orchestra, is fully equal to the technical and lyrical demands of Strauss's florid concerto. His accompaniment is warmly supportive, but Richard Stamp could be subtler in controlling the work's complex detail. However, the Academy play the *Metamorphosen* confidently, and with refinement and ardour. They also provide a rich backcloth for Gundula Janowitz's creamily sensuous performances of nine of Strauss's most beautiful Lieder. There is a certain uniformity about her approach to all these songs, but she certainly feels the words, and her rich timbre and flowing lines are so beautiful that criticism is disarmed. Dimitry Sitkovetsky also makes a comparably ardent lyrical response to the *Violin Sonata*. Pavel Gililov too is a perceptive artist, but his playing is not quite the equal of Krystian Zimerman (see below). Nevertheless the Virgin sound balance is praiseworthy throughout this disc and this anthology is excellent value at its modest asking price.

Violin Concerto in D min., Op. 8
*** ASV CDDCA 780. Xue Wei, LPO, Glover – HEADINGTON: *Violin concerto* *** ●

With Jane Glover and the LPO warmly sympathetic accompanists, Xue Wei makes a very persuasive case for this very early work of Strauss, with its echoes of Mendelssohn and Bruch.

Death and Transfiguration; Don Juan; Till Eulenspiegel
●➤ (M) (***) EMI mono 5 62790-2. VPO, Furtwängler – SMETANA: *Vltava* ***
(N) (***) Testament mono SBT 1383. Philh. O, Karajan (with WAGNER: *Tannhäuser: Venusberg music* ***)

Don Juan and *Till Eulenspiegel* come from 1954, some months before the onset of deafness brought Furtwängler's career to an end, while *Death and Transfiguration* was recorded in Vienna in 1950. They are performances of commanding stature and have the glowing sonorities, naturalness of utterance and mastery of pace that characterized Furtwängler at his best. The EMI recordings still sound glorious despite their age, though climaxes in *Death and Transfiguration* are distinctly opaque; Walter Legge produced the 1950 sessions and Laurance Collingwood the 1954 ones, and it is hard to imagine any mono discs of *Don* and *Till* being better balanced or more natural. Of course, they were soon superseded by the

Karajan records, but these earlier performances have a special place in any Strauss collection.

Karajan's *Till* and the *Don* were recorded in the Kingsway Hall in 1951 with Walter Legge producing, and *Death and Transfiguration* followed eighteen months later. The former were issued on Columbia's first LP (33CX 1001) and enjoyed the imprimatur of the editors of 'The Record Guide'. Rightly so! The transfers by Paul Baily are a tribute to the instinctive and masterly balances that Legge and his superb engineer, Douglas Larter achieved. Sound that is over half-a-century old can still convey a sense of freshness and sparkle. The Wagner makeweight (with the same venue and recording team) comes from 1954 and is of the same order of inspiration. Excellent notes by Richard Osborne. Strongly recommended.

Death and Transfiguration; Metamorphosen for 23 Solo Strings
● ➤ (M) *** DG 474 889-2. BPO, Karajan

Karajan's digital coupling of *Death and Transfiguration* and the *Metamorphosen* is one of his very finest records and deservedly won the *Gramophone* Orchestral Award in 1983. This famous CD is now available at mid-price.

Death and Transfiguration; Ein Heldenleben; Salome: Dance of the 7 Veils
(M) *** EMI 5 67891-2 [567892]. Dresden State O, Kempe

Kempe and the great Dresden orchestra at their finest are admirably represented here for EMI's 'Great Recordings of the Century'. *Death and Transfiguration* is marvellously characterized. Its drama is powerfully conveyed, yet the transfiguration theme emerges with wonderful simplicity at the close, with its nobility of feeling unsurpassed, not even by Karajan. Similarly *Salome's Dance* is sinuously compelling but less voluptuous than with some versions, while *Ein Heldenleben* glows with life, and the closing pages have a special kind of rapt intensity. The excellent recordings from the early 1970s, made in the Dresden Lukaskirche, have been splendidly remastered by Andrew Walter. Readers will note that *Death and Transfiguration* and *Salome's Dance* in their earlier remastering are also available on the super-bargain Encore disc above. But the present CD is the one to go for.

Death and Transfiguration; Metamorphosen for 23 Solo Strings; (i) Vier letzte Lieder (Four Last Songs)
(M) **(*) DG 447 422-2. BPO, Karajan, (i) with Janowitz

Karajan's earlier versions are still powerful and convincing. In the *Four Last Songs*, Janowitz produces a beautiful flow of creamy tone while leaving the music's deeper and subtler emotions under-exposed. The transfers are very impressive, and *Death and Transfiguration* can still be regarded as a showpiece among Karajan's earlier Berlin recordings.

(i) Death and Transfiguration; Symphonia domestica; (ii) Salome's Dance of the Seven Veils
●➤ (B) *** Sony (ADD) SBK 53511. (i) Cleveland O, Szell; (ii) Phd. O, Ormandy

Szell's *Death and Transfiguration* has the most compelling atmosphere and the triumphant closing pages are the more effective for Szell's complete lack of indulgence. The recording has been vastly improved in the present transfer, with Cleveland's Masonic Temple providing a richly expansive ambience. The *Symphonia Domestica*, recorded in 1964, is less naturally balanced but the performance brings such powerful orchestral playing, with glorious strings especially in the passionate *Adagio*, that criticism is disarmed: there is certainly no lack of body here. The programme ends with an extraordinarily voluptuous Philadelphia performance of *Salome's Dance*, which conjures up a whole frieze of naked female torsos. Ormandy directs with licentious abandon, and the orchestra responds with tremendous virtuosity and ardour, unashamedly going over the top at the climax.

(i; ii) *Death and Transfiguration*; (iii) *4 Last Songs*; (i; iv) *Der Rosenkavalier*: Highlights

(N) *** EMI (ADD/DDD) HMV 5 86770-2. (i) Dresden State O; (ii) Kempe; (iii) Lucia Popp, LPO, Tennstedt; (iv) Te Kanawa, Von Otter, Rydl, Hendricks, cond., Haitink

An admirable 80-minute budget collection. Lucia Popp gives a ravishingly beautiful account of the *Four Last Songs*. With the voice given an ethereal glow, naturally balanced in a warmly atmospheric digital recording, the radiance of texture is paramount. This is an orchestral performance rather than a deeply illuminating Lieder performance, and that matches the coupling, the early tone poem of death, *Death and Transfiguration*, which is quoted by the dying composer in the last of the songs. Kempe's performance is from the mid-1970s, marvellously characterized and sumptuously recorded, while the Dresden Staatskapelle, common to all three recordings here, is in superb form. Finally we are offered four key scenes from Haitink's 1991 *Der Rosenkavalier* with Kiri Te Kanawa in glorious voice in the Marschallin's Monologue, and Anne Sofie von Otter believably boyish in the scene of the *Presentation of the Silver Rose*. Kurt Rydl is equally well cast as Baron Ochs and the excerpts include the great final Trio and lovers' duet. No texts, but a brief, useful synopsis makes this a superb collection overall.

Divertimento (after Couperin) for Small Orchestra, Op. 86

(BB) *** Warner Apex 7559 79675-2. NYCO, Schwarz – SCHOENBERG: *Concerto for String Quartet & Orchestra after Handel* ***

Strauss's *Divertimento* draws on sixteen of the keyboard pieces of François Couperin and scores them for small orchestra. The result is expressive, witty and tangy by turns in this very spirited account by the New York Chamber Orchestra under Gerard Schwarz. With vivid recordings and an unexpectedly entertaining Schoenberg/Handel coupling, this is well worth exploring.

Don Juan; Ein Heldenleben

(BB) (***) Dutton Lab. mono CDEA 5025. Concg. O, Mengelberg

(i) *Don Juan*; (ii) *Ein Heldenleben*; (iii) *Till Eulenspiegel*

(M) *** Sony (ADD) SBK 48272. (iii) Cleveland O, Szell; (ii) Phd. O, Ormandy

Don Juan, Op. 20; Feuersnot: Love Scene

(**(*)) Testament mono SBT 1255. VPO, Cluytens – WAGNER: *Siegfried idyll*, etc. (**(*))

Don Juan; Till Eulenspiegel; Salome: Dance of the Seven Veils

*** Everest EVC 9004. NY Stadium SO, Stokowski – CANNING: *Fantasy on a Hymn Tune* ***

Szell's *Don Juan* delights ear and senses by its forward surge of passionate lyricism, the whole interpretation founded on a bedrock of virtuosity from the remarkable Cleveland players.

Till is irrepressibly cheeky and here the recording acoustic is almost perfect, with a warm glow on the tone of the players and every detail – and Szell makes sure one can hear every detail – crystal clear, without any loss of momentum or drama.

Ormandy's *Ein Heldenleben* is an engulfing performance, and the composite richness of tone and the fervour of the playing, from the Battle section onwards, bring the highest possible level of orchestral tension, finally relaxing most touchingly for the fulfilment sequence. The 1960 recording is more two-dimensional, less full, than the Cleveland recordings (which, surprisingly, were made as early as 1957) but is still appropriately spacious.

This justly famous Stokowski triptych from the late 1950s, with the spacious recording cleaned up, now sounds very well indeed. Not surprisingly with the old magician in charge, Salome is made to languish more voluptuously than ever before, and even *Till* in his posthumous epilogue has a languishing mood on him. *Don Juan* indulges himself with rich sensuality, yet leaps off into the fray with undiminished vitality, while the great unison horn-call is held back with a compellingly broadened thrust. As ever, Stokowski is nothing if not convincing, and those looking for really ripe versions of these pieces need not hesitate. The Canning coupling is also worth having.

André Cluytens was rather taken for granted (at least on this side of La Manche) during the 1950s when these recordings were made. He took the Vienna Philharmonic on tour to the United States, making this inspiriting account of *Don Juan* with them in 1958. It was not released in Britain at that time (no doubt the catalogues were awash with alternatives), but it is well worth while catching up with it now, particularly in this splendid new transfer.

Willem Mengelberg and the Concertgebouw Orchestra were jointly the dedicatees of Richard Strauss's most ambitious orchestral work, *Ein Heldenleben*. They give a heartfelt performance, freely spontaneous and expansive, with old-fashioned string portamento intensifying the warmth. The splendid Dutton transfer is clear on detail with plenty of body and fair bloom on top. The *Don Juan* recording of 1938 is even more cleanly focused.

Don Quixote, Op. 35

(M) *** EMI (ADD) 5 66913-2 [566965-2]. Rostropovich, BPO, Karajan – SCHUMANN: *Cello Concerto* *(*)

🔊 ✪ *** EMI (ADD) 5 55528-2. Du Pré, New Philh. O, Boult – LALO: *Cello Concerto in D min* ***

(i) *Don Quixote*; (ii) *Horn Concerto 2*

(M) *** DG (IMS) (ADD) 457 725-2. (i) Fournier; (ii) Hauptmann; BPO, Karajan

(i) *Don Quixote; Don Juan, Op. 20; Till Eulenspiegel, Op. 28*

(***) Testament mono SBT 1185. (i) Fournier, Moraweg; VPO, Krauss

The Karajan/Rostropovich account of *Don Quixote* is predictably fine. The recorded sound (1975) is impressively remastered, spectacular in its realism, with well-defined detail, superb warmth and body, and fine perspective, its only failing a tendency for Rostropovich to dominate the aural picture. He dominates artistically, too. His Don is superbly characterized, and the expressiveness and richness of tone he commands are a joy in themselves. This now comes recoupled with Schumann's *Cello Concerto* as one of EMI's 'Great Recordings of the Century' series, which the latter performance (with Bernstein) certainly is not. A sad mismatching!

Fournier's partnership with Karajan is also outstanding and so is the 1966 recording. It is of DG's very finest quality, with remarkable transparency, yet plenty of warmth and a believable perspective. The great cellist brings infinite subtlety and (when required) repose to his part, and Karajan's handling of the orchestral detail is quite splendid. The finale and Don Quixote's death are very moving. Norbert Hauptmann's account of the more florid of Strauss's two horn concertos is ripely assured with a most eloquent and touching *Andante*.

A magnificent *Don Quixote* from Clemens Krauss and his eminent soloist which encapsulates the essence of Strauss's score. RL recalls Egon Wellesz in the early 1950s singing the praises of Krauss as a Straussian ('unsurpassed even by Sir Thomas Beecham'), and this performance with that aristocrat of cellists, Pierre Fournier, has a special nobility and authority. Both *Don Juan* and *Till Eulenspiegel* were recorded in 1950 (the *Don Quixote* in 1953) and are superbly characterized. In the latter, Krauss clearly does not regard this as just a conductor's showpiece but puts characterization before orchestral display.

Jacqueline du Pré's *Don Quixote* comes in a studio recording, dating from 1968, which has been lovingly pieced together from long-buried tapes. No doubt du Pré with more time would have sharpened up some of the bravura passages, but in its tenderness and poignancy this reading is unsurpassed. The lyrical dialogue between Sancho Panza and Quixote in the third variation has a heartfelt warmth, with Herbert Downes a fine partner on the viola. Above all, the final death scene is more yearningly tender than on any rival recording, a magical example of her art.

(i) Don Quixote. Ein Heldenleben; Symphonia domestica

(N) (M) *** EMI (ADD) 4 76903-2 (2). BPO, Karajan; (i) with Rostropovich

The Karajan/Rostropovich *Don Quixote* is predictably fine. The recorded sound (1975) is impressively remastered, spectacular in its realism, with well-defined detail, superb warmth and body, and fine perspective, its only failing a tendency for Rostropovich to dominate the aural picture. He dominates artistically too. His Don is superbly characterized, and the expressiveness and richness of tone he commands are a joy in themselves. *Ein Heldenleben*, superbly recorded a year earlier, again offers a performance which shows a remarkable consistency of approach on Karajan's part and an equal virtuosity of technique, and even greater sumptuousness of tone on the part of the Berlin Phiharmonic compared with the earlier DG performances, while the playing is gloriously ardent. The *Symphonia domestica* is equally admirably served by a recording from one more year earlier. The playing is stunningly good and the sumptuous Berlin strings produce tone of great magnificence. Altogether a superb triptych for reissue in EMI's Karajan Collection, the only snag being that the *Symphonia domestica* involves a side-break immediately before the finale.

(i) Don Quixote, Op. 35; Romance in F; (ii) Cello Sonata in F, Op. 6

*** RCA 74321 75398-2. (i) Isserlis, Bavarian Radio SO, Maazel; (ii) Hough, Maazel (piano)

Steven Isserlis on RCA is an ardent soloist and is even more impressive than he was in his earlier recording with Edo de Waart (Virgin). He makes a glorious sound and characterizes

each variation with flair and is well partnered by an anonymous Sancho Panza, presumably the first violist of the Bavarian Orchestra. It is among the best of the recent *Dons* though it does not displace the likes of Rostropovich or Fournier (both with Karajan). One of the other attractions of the disc is a vibrant account of the early *Cello Sonata* with Stephen Hough as a splendid partner. Very good sound.

Ein Heldenleben, Op. 40

(N) *** RCO Live **DVD** RCO 04103, or **Surround Sound SACD** RCO 04005. Concg. O, Jansons (DVD – V/D: Hans Hulscher – with Documentary 'The Sixth Maestro' – introducing Mariss Jansons as the orchestra's conductor)

(M) *** DG (ADD). 449 725-2 BPO, Karajan – WAGNER: *Siegfried Idyll* ***

(B) *** EMI double forte (ADD) 5 69349-2 (2). LSO, Barbirolli – MAHLER: *Symphony 6* **(*)

Ein Heldenleben; Death and Transfiguration, Op. 24

**(*) DG (IMS) 439 039-2. BPO, Karajan

Ein Heldenleben; Feuersnot: Liebszene; Intermezzo: Träumerei am Kamin; Salome: Dance of the Seven Veils

(***) Testament mono SBT 11147. RPO, Beecham

Ein Heldenleben, Op. 40; Metamorphosen.

**(*) Avie 0017. WDR SO, Bychkov

Ein Heldenleben, Op. 40; Till Eulenspiegel

(N) (M) *** RCA 82876 62313-2. Bav. RSO, Maazel

(M) *** Warner Elatus 0927 49555-2. Chicago SO, Barenboim

(i) Ein Heldenleben; (ii) Till Eulenspiegel; (iii) Salome: Dance of the Seven Veils

(BB) (***) Dutton CDBP 9737. (i) Bav. State O; (ii) Berlin State Op. O; (iii) BPO; composer

Jansons's magnificent Concertgebouw performance of *Ein Heldenleben* comes in a superb SACD recording in natural surround sound which, with four speakers, captures the richness of the Concertgebouw acoustic and gives the orchestra the most sumptuous and detailed presentation in a live performance which is unsurpassed in adrenalin flow, refinement of detail, and glorious playing. The DVD offers the special visual treat of the magnificent Concertgebouw as a backcloth for great music-making and at the same time provides first-class sound (though not quite as opulent as the CD) plus a vivid pictorial survey of the performance, which is both rewarding and interesting in a score as diverse and detailed as *Ein Heldenleben*, as the camera follows the orchestra's involvement.

Although Karajan's 1959 *Heldenleben* cannot quite match his later EMI version (currently withdrawn) in sumptuousness it still sounds remarkably impressive. Playing of great power and distinction emanates from the Berlin Philharmonic and, in the closing section, an altogether becoming sensuousness and warmth. The remastering makes the most of the ambient atmosphere and, while not losing body, firms up the orchestral detail.

Karajan's digital *Heldenleben* has tremendous sweep and all the authority and mastery we have come to expect – and indeed to take for granted. Nor is the orchestral playing anything other than glorious – indeed, in terms of sheer virtuosity, the Berlin players have never surpassed this. However, in spite of the 'original-image bit re-processing' the early (1983) digital recording falls short of the highest present-day standards. Since Karajan's superb *Death and Transfiguration* (recorded only three years later) has been added to it, the ear is drawn to notice that *Ein Heldenleben*, although firmly focused, has less warmth and the strings by comparison lack bloom, while the violins have a certain glassiness in the high treble, characteristic of the early digital era.

Originally issued within a boxed set, Maazel's performances demonstrate a pleasing freshness of approach, besides showing that the Bavarian Radio Orchestra has a natural affinity with Richard Strauss. *Ein Heldenleben* has plenty of impetus and intensity, and *Till* is equally strongly characterized, portrayed as a robustly dynamic figure, unrepentantly humorous in his fashion, who comes to a really spectacular end and then endearingly floats off to the next world without any regrets. Both works were recorded in the studio but certainly do not lack ambience, although there is a degree of unnatural digital brightness in the *fortissimo* high violins.

Recorded in 1990, shortly before Barenboim took over the Chicago orchestra, this is an extremely worthwhile account, particularly at its mid-price. Barenboim propels the music onwards and never allows the tension to sag: the *Battle* is fast, almost Scherzo-like, and the whole performance is both splendidly conceived and brilliantly executed. In a field which includes the likes of Beecham, Reiner, Karajan and Kempe, this holds its own. The same goes for *Till*. A very well-balanced and richly detailed recorded sound, too.

Barbirolli recorded *Ein Heldenleben* at Abbey Road in 1969, not long before his death, and here he sets the seal on his Indian summer in the recording studio. All the tempi are slow, even by his latter-day standards. He luxuriates in every moment of this opulent score (his occasional groans of pleasure sometimes punctuating the score) and the LSO, in superb form, follows him with warmth and ardour through every expressive rallentando. The result has the inescapable electricity of a great occasion. The CD transfer has lost some of the original opulence, but there was enough and to spare, and the sound now has greater focus and detail.

Dutton made a superb transfer of the 1941 *Alpine Symphony* that Strauss recorded for Electrola (CDBP 9720 – now deleted). Later the same year Strauss returned to DG to record this wonderfully humane account of *Ein Heldenleben* with the Munich orchestra. Siemens had developed a new recording process which extended the frequency range, and no previous transfer has ever reproduced its sound quite so vividly. The playing Strauss produces is characterized by such unforced virtuosity and naturalness of feeling that it is put quite in a class of its own. Even if you possess Karajan, Kempe and Beecham, this is a mandatory purchase, for it really carries the ring of truth. *The Dance of the Seven Veils* and *Till Eulenspiegel* both come from the late 1920s and are less revelatory.

Beecham's 1947 account remains a model of its kind: authoritative, marvellously paced and beautifully transparent in its textures. A glorious performance which long held sway until Karajan's 1959 account came along. The other Strauss excerpts were recorded in the late 1940s before the advent of the mono LP.

Semyon Bychkov gets a very good sound out of his Cologne orchestra and he is a Straussian through and through. However, it must be conceded that the orchestral playing is by no means as virtuosic as that of the Chicago Symphony for Barenboim. *Metamorphosen* is played with eloquence and feeling, but such great Straussians as Karajan and Kempe are not challenged or displaced.

Josephslegende (ballet suite): *Suite*; *Symphonia domestica, Op. 53*

**(*) Delos DE 3082. Seattle SO, Schwarz

Josephslegende, based on the Old Testament story, was written for Diaghilev's Ballet Russes, and first produced in Paris in May 1914, the worst possible timing on the eve of the First World War. It did not help that Nijinsky was not available as planned to take the title role. Strauss offers a sumptuous feast of sound in a score using an enormous orchestra, which is over twice as long as the *Symphonic Fragment* of 1947 in which Strauss salvaged some of the music.

Gerard Schwarz gives us the suite from the ballet in addition to a very idiomatic account of the *Symphonia domestica*. There is very good playing from the Seattle orchestra: cultured, thoroughly idiomatic and with splendid sweep; the recording, too, is splendidly detailed, if perhaps just a bit too brightly lit to be ideal.

Metamorphosen for 23 Solo Strings

*** Chan. 9708. Norwegian CO, I. Brown – TCHAIKOVSKY: *Souvenir de Florence* ***

(M) *** EMI (ADD) 5 67036-2 (2). Philh. O, Klemperer – MAHLER: *Symphony 9*; WAGNER: *Siegfried idyll* ***

*** EMI 5 56580-2. VPO, Rattle – MAHLER: *Symphony 9* ***

*** Delos DE 3121. Seattle SO, Schwarz – HONEGGER: *Symphony 2*; WEBERN arr. SCHWARZ: *Langsamer satz* ***

Iona Brown's performance has a powerfully passionate impetus that is wholly spontaneous, with intense valedictory feeling in the shading down of the closing pages, which has wonderful concentration. The Chandos recording is outstandingly fine.

With Klemperer, *Metamorphosen* has a ripeness that exactly fits Strauss's last essay for orchestra, helped by the superb Philharmonia string-playing, rich in texture but with striking refinement of detail. The remastering of the 1961 Kingsway Hall recording for the 'Klemperer Legacy' is very impressive.

Rattle with the Vienna Philharmonic, producing string sounds of magical beauty, brings out the visionary intensity behind this late flowering of Strauss's genius, sustaining its long span masterfully. Warm, atmospheric sound. An excellent coupling for Mahler's *Ninth*.

Gerard Schwarz's account of Strauss's elegiac threnody is as deeply felt and dignified as it is unhurried, and it should be heard. The listener is completely drawn into its world and, although it does not supersede the Kempe or any of the the Karajan accounts except perhaps in terms of recorded realism, it deserves to be recommended alongside them. At 32 minutes it may be the slowest *Metamorphosen* on disc, but it is certainly one of the best.

Serenade for Wind; *Sonatina 1 in F for Wind (From an Invalid's Workshop)*; *Suite in B flat for 13 Wind Instruments*; *Symphony for Wind (The Happy Workshop)*

(B) *** Hyp. Dyad CDD 2015. London Winds, Collins

The London Winds on Hyperion are fairly closely observed by the microphone-balance and the effect is clearly defined and dramatic. The playing has the strongest impulse, the autumnal feeling less apparent in the *Serenade*. But one cannot help being caught up by playing that is so vividly robust and vital, and by no means lacking in warmth and affection. Even if there is a touch of over-projection, inner detail is clear and many will like the extra bite on the sound.

Symphony 2 in F min.; (i) *Romance in F* (for cello & orchestra); (ii) *6 Lieder, Op. 68*

(N) (M) *** Chan. 10236X. (i) Wallfisch; (ii) Hulse; RSNO, Järvi

Like Korngold a generation later, Strauss was a composing prodigy. This early symphony may give little idea of the mature composer's style, but the skill of the writing is astonishing, not least the instrumentation. The *F minor* brings an admixture of Brahms, with just occasional Wagnerian hints. Järvi paces the score with real mastery and gets very good playing from the Royal Scottish National Orchestra. The glorious Brentano *Lieder*, Op. 68, date from 1918 and Strauss transcribed them for orchestra in 1941. Eileen Hulse produces some beautiful tone and is sensitively supported throughout. The *Romance* was another early work which Strauss abridged when he scored it for orchestra. It is charmingly nostalgic, and most persuasively played here. Not core repertory this, but a disc for Straussians.

Till Eulenspiegel

(B) (***) Dutton Lab. mono CDEA 5013. Boston SO, Koussevitzky – BERLIOZ: *Harold in Italy* (**(*))

Till Eulenspiegel, recorded in 1945, makes a spectacular fill-up to Koussevitzky's pioneering account of the Berlioz, another fizzing performance, both warm and brilliant, very well transferred in sound both full-bodied and airy.

CHAMBER MUSIC

Piano Quartet in C min., Op. 13

*** Black Box BBX 1048. Lyric Piano Qt – TURINA: *Piano Quartet in A min., Op. 67* ***

By general consent the *Piano Quartet in C minor* is not great Strauss, but it is well played and recorded here and coupled with another rarity by Turina. A disc for those with a taste for offbeat repertoire.

Serenade in E flat, Op. 7; Sonatina in F (From an Invalid's Workshop). Suite in B flat, Op. 4

(N) *** MDG 304 1173 Ens. Villa Musica

These civilized and genial pieces are a joy and splendidly played here by the Villa Musica Ensemble. One marvels afresh at the inventiveness, skill and culture of Strauss's writing for wind instruments. Demonstration sound.

String Quartet in A, Op. 2

(BB) **(*) Hyp. Helios CDH 55012. Delmé Qt – VERDI: *Quartet* **(*)

The Strauss *Quartet* is early and derivative, as one might expect from a sixteen-year-old, but it is amazingly assured and fluent. The Delmé version is well played; however, although the basic acoustic is pleasing, the sound-balance remains a little on the dry side.

(i) Metamorphosen (arr. for string septet). Capriccio: Prelude

*** Nim. NI 5614. Brandis Qt., with Küssner, Schwalke – SCHOENBERG: *Verklaerte Nacht* ***

The first ideas for *Metamorphosen* came to Strauss as a string septet. In 1990, Strauss's pencil sketch came to light and, with the aid of that and the definitive score, Rudolf Leopold has carefully reconstructed the original. The Brandis Quartet and three Berlin colleagues play with magnificent artistry and eloquence, both here and in the opening sextet from *Capriccio*. The Nimbus sound is first class.

Flute Sonata in E flat (trans. of Violin Sonata)

(N) *** EMI 557 813-2. Pahud, Le Sage – FRANCK: *Flute Sonata*; WIDOR: *Suite* ***

Flute-players have long taken the Franck *Violin Sonata* as a suitable work for adaptation, but here Emmanuel Pahud goes one further in similarly taking over Richard Strauss's early *Violin Sonata*. Linking the two comes the charming Widor *Suite*, and though the three composers represent three successive generations, the works themselves were written within a span of only three years, ample justification for the unexpected mixture of repertory. If in the Franck few would suggest that the flute is actually preferable to the violin, there is a strong case in the Strauss for preferring this flute arrangement to the original. After the dramatic contrasts of the long first movement the lyrical second movement is even more beautiful on the flute, losing the hint of salon music that even a fine violin performance brings, and the finale in Pahud's hands has a winning swagger, again relying on his wide tonal range.

Violin Sonata in E flat, Op. 18

*** Erato 8573-85769-2 Repin, Berezovsky – BARTOK: *Romanian folk dances*; STRAVINSKY: *Divertimento* ***

(M) *** Decca 474 558-2. Chung, Zimerman – RESPIGHI: *Sonata* ***

The sheer sweep and intensity of the extraordinary Repin–Berezovsky partnership brings a captivating reading which is unlikely to soon be surpassed. It is arguably the best we have had since the days of Neveu and Heifetz.

Among modern versions Kyung Wha Chung is also oustanding and her version of the Strauss scores over most rivals also in the power and sensitivity of Krystian Zimerman's contribution and the excellence of the DG recording. There is, however, a cut of 42 bars in the coda of the first movement (Universal Edition) which appears to be sanctioned.

Enoch Arden, Op. 38 (Melodrama for narrator and piano)

**(*) VAI Audio (ADD) VAIA 1179-2 (2). Vickers, Hamelin

Jon Vickers, the narrator on VAIA, recommends (in English) how so 'soul-satisfying' a piece gives a powerful reminder of 'the timeless truths of Love, Patience, Fidelity and Steadfastness'. In his declamation he makes a persuasive case for the piece, but even Marc-André Hamelin, equally persuasive, cannot mask the fact that the piano-writing in its illustrative naivety has much in common with the accompaniments for silent films, which soon after became so popular. The live recording (with much applause beforehand) is aptly atmospheric.

CHORAL MUSIC

(i) An den Baum Daphne; (ii) Der Abend; Hymne, Op. 34/1–2; (iii) Deutsche Motette, Op. 62; (iv) Die Göttin im Putzzimer

*** Chan. 9223. (i) Lund, Lisdorf, Copenhagen Boys' Ch.; (iii) Kiberg, Stene, Henning-Jensen, Cold; (i–iv) Danish Nat. R. Ch., Parkman

This disc brings very good performances of some very beautiful and curiously little-known music. The engineers produce a realistic sound too.

VOCAL MUSIC

8 Lieder, Op. 10; 5 Lieder, Op. 15; 6 Lieder, Op. 17; 6 Lieder, Op. 19; Schlichte Weisen, Op. 21; Mädchenblumen, Op. 22; 2 Lieder, Op. 26; 4 Lieder, Op. 27; Lieder, Op. 29/1 & 3; 3 Lieder, Op. 31; Stiller Gang, Op. 31/4; 5 Lieder, Op. 32; Lieder, Op. 36/1-4; Lieder, Op. 37/1-3 & 5-6; 5 Lieder, Op. 39; Lieder, Op. 41/2-5; Gesänge älterer deutscher Dichter, Op. 43/1 & 3; 5 Gedichte, Op. 46; 5 Lieder, Op. 47; 5 Lieder, Op. 48; Lieder, Op. 49/1 & 2; 4-6; 6 Lieder, Op. 56; Krämerspiegel, Op. 66; Lieder, Op. 67/4-6; Lieder, Op. 68/1 & 4; 5 kleine Lieder, Op. 69; Gesänge des Orients, Op. 77; Lieder, Op. 88/1-2; Lieder ohne Opuszahl

(M) *** EMI (ADD) 7 63995-2 (6). Fischer-Dieskau, Moore

Fischer-Dieskau and Moore made these recordings of the 134 Strauss songs suitable for a man's voice between 1967 and 1970, tackling them in roughly chronological order. With both artists at their very peak, the results are endlessly imaginative, and the transfers are full and immediate, giving fine presence to the voice.

Four Last Songs; Lieder: Das Bächlein; Befreit; Cäcilie; Freundliche Vision; Die heiligen drei Könige aus Morgenland; Mein Auge; Meinem Kinde; Morgen; Muttertändelei; Ruhe, meine Seele!; Waldseligkeit; Wiegenlied

**(*) Chan. 9054. Lott, SNO, Järvi

Drei Hymnen, Op. 71. Orchestral songs: Des Dichters Abendgang; Frühlingsfeier; Gesang der Apollopriesterin; Liebeshymnus; Das Rosenband; Verführung; Winterliebe; Winterweihe; Zueignung

*** Chan. 9159. Lott, SNO, Järvi

Felicity Lott's two discs bring together a whole series of recordings of Strauss songs in their orchestral versions which originally appeared as couplings for Järvi's discs of the Strauss symphonic poems. She sings them beautifully, though the voice is not always caught at its most golden, notably in the *Four Last Songs* which yet are movingly done. The second CD includes the first recording of *Drei Hymnen*, Hölderlin settings composed in 1921, pantheistic poems about love of nature which are full of ardour and are provided with the most opulent accompaniments. Lott's voice, for the most part well focused, rides over the rich orchestral textures impressively, and throughout both discs there is agreeably warm, full, orchestral sound.

Four Last Songs

(M) *** Ph. 464 742-2. Norman, Leipzig GO, Masur – WAGNER: *Wesendonck Lieder* **(*)

Four Last Songs; Lieder: Allerseelen; Freundliche Vision; Geduld; Die Georgine; Meinem Kinde; Morgen!; Muttertändelei; Die Nacht; Nichts; Das Rosenband; Ruhe, meine Seele!; Die Verschwiegenen; Wiegenlied; Die Zeitlose; Zueignung

**(*) Decca 460 812-2. Bonney, Martineau

Four Last Songs; Orchestral Lieder: Das Bächlein; Freundliche Vision; Die heiligen drei Könige; Meinem Kinde; Morgen; Muttertändelei; Das Rosenband; Ruhe, meine Seele; Waldseligkeit; Wiegenlied; Winterweihe; Zueignung

⏻ ✹ *** EMI (ADD) 566908-2 [5669602]. Schwarzkopf, Berlin RSO or LSO, Szell

Four Last Songs; Orchestral Lieder: Das Bächlein; Freundliche Vision; Die heiligen drei Könige; Meinen Kinde;

Morgen; Muttertändelei; Das Rosenband; Ruhe, meine Seele; Waldseligkeit; Wiegenlied; Winterweihe; Zueignung

✹ (N) (M) *** EMI Legend (ADD) 5 57752. (With **Bonus DVD**: *Der Rosenkavalier: Act I finale*). Schwarzkopf, Berlin RSO or LSO, Szell

(i) *Four Last Songs; Orchestral Lieder: Befreit; Cäcilie; Muttertändelei; Waldseligkeit; Wiegenlied. Der Rosenkavalier: suite*

(N) (M) **(*) RCA 82876 59408-2. (i) Fleming; Houston SO, Eschenbach

(i) *Four Last Songs. Orchestral Lieder: Befreit; Morgen; Muttertändelei; Ruhe meine Seele; Wiegenlied; Zueignung.* (ii) *Also sprach Zarathustra*

(M) **(*) Sony SMK 89881. (i) Te Kanawa; LSO, A. Davis; (ii) Tilson Thomas

(i) *Four Last Songs;* (ii) *Du meines Herzens Krönelein; Ruhe, meine Seele; Zueignung*

(M) (***) BBC mono BBCL 4107-2. (i) Jurinac, BBC SO, Sargent; (ii) Ludwig, Parsons (with BRAHMS: *Ständchen; Wiegenlied* *** – MAHLER: *Lieder eines fahrenden Gesellen*, etc.

(i) *Four Last Songs;* (ii) *Arabella* (opera): excerpts; (i) *Capriccio* (opera): *Closing Scene*

(N) (M) (***) EMI mono 5 85825-2. Schwarzkopf (i) Philh. O, Ackermann; (ii) Metternich, Gedda, Philh. O, Von Matačic

Four Last Songs; (i) *Arabella: excerpts. Ariadne auf Naxos: Ariadne's Lament. Capriccio: Closing scene*

(M) (***) Decca mono 467 118-2. Lisa della Casa; (i) with Gueden, Schoeffler Poell; VPO, Boehm, Moralt; Hollreiser

(i; ii) *Four Last Songs (Vier letzte Lieder).* (i; iii; iv) *Arabella: Er ist der Richtige nur für mich . . . Aber der Richtige;* (i; iii; v) *Der Richtige so hab'ich still zu mir gesagt . . . So wie Sie sind . . . Und du wirst mein Geliebter sein;* (i; iii; vi) *Das war sehn gut, Mandryka;* (i; ii; iv; vi) *Ariadne auf Naxos: Ein schönes war; Es gibt ein Reich;* (vii) *Capriccio: Intermezzo & Closing Scene*

(N) (BB) (*(**)) Regis mono RRC 1192. Lisa della Casa; (i) VPO; (ii) Boehm; (iii) Moralt; (iv) Gueden; (v) Schoeffler; (vi) Poell; (vii) Elderling, O cond. den Hertog.

For the Legend version of Schwarzkopf's raptly beautiful recording of the *Four Last Songs* (1965), EMI have added not just the old coupling of Strauss orchestral songs but also the seven extra she recorded in 1968, also with George Szell conducting, but with the LSO instead of the Berlin Radio Orchestra. There are few recordings in the catalogue which so readily capture the magic of a great performance, with the intensity of Schwarzkopf's singing in all its variety of tone and meaning perfectly matched by inspired playing. The current remastering seems to add even more lustre to voice and orchestra alike. This is also available as one of EMI's 'Great Recordings of the Century' (5 66908-2) with texts and translations included, but this Legend release, although without texts, includes a bonus DVD of Schwarzkopf in the Act I finale of *Der Rosenkavalier*, with Hertha Töpper, Philharmonia Orchestra under Mackerras (1961).

Schwarzkopf's 1953 mono version of the *Four Last Songs* comes with both its original coupling, the closing scene from *Capriccio*, also recorded in 1953, and the four major excerpts from *Arabella* which she recorded two years later. The *Four Last Songs* are here less reflective, less sensuous, than in

Schwarzkopf's later version with Szell, but the more flowing speeds and the extra tautness and freshness of voice bring equally illuminating performances. Fascinatingly, this separate account of the *Capriccio* scene is even more ravishing than the one in the complete set, and the sound is even fuller, astonishing for its period.

Strauss's publisher, Ernest Roth, says in the score of the *Four Last Songs* that this was a farewell of 'serene confidence', which is exactly the mood that Jessye Norman conveys. The start of the second stanza of the third song, *Beim Schlafengehen*, brings one of the most thrilling vocal crescendos on record, expanding from a half-tone to a gloriously rich and rounded forte. In concern for detail, Norman is outshone only by Schwarzkopf, but the stylistic as well as the vocal command is irresistible, and the radiance of the recording matches the interpretations. Unfortunately, for this reissue Philips have exchanged the six other orchestral songs on the original CD (which included a powerfully operatic account of *Cäcile*) for Norman's earlier (mid-1970s) recording of Wagner's *Wesendonck Lieder*, which were rather less successful.

Lisa della Casa with her creamily beautiful soprano was a radiant Straussian, as these precious excerpts demonstrate. Her account of the *Four Last Songs* (given in the original order, not that usually adopted) has a commanding nobility. *Ariadne's Lament* also receives a heartfelt performance, soaring to a thrilling climax, and the *Arabella* duets with Gueden, Schoeffler and Poell are hauntingly tender. For this superb reissue in Decca's Legends series, the transfer has been vastly improved; both voice and orchestra and the ambience of the Grosser Saal in the Musikverein are faithfully caught, with no lack of bloom.

In the alternative Regis collection the transfers have smoothed the original Decca mono sound, although Decca's own remastering is preferable. The main interest of this CD is that the live (1953) *Capriccio* excerpts with Anton Elderling and conducted by Johannes den Hertog are new. Here the sound is more restricted, with thin, papery violins. An intriguing disc nevertheless, for the glorious voice comes over in its full richness. This collection is without texts and translations but is enticingly inexpensive.

Renée Fleming with her rich, mature soprano gives warmly sympathetic readings of the *Four Last Songs*, thrilling in climaxes as the voice is allowed to expand, and full of fine detail, even if these readings lack the variety of a Schwarzkopf. The five separate orchestral Lieder also bring a wide expressive range, with *Waldseligkeit* beautifully poised, and ending boldly on *Cäcilie*. The singer is not helped by the way that Eschenbach makes the accompaniments seem a little sluggish, polished though the playing is. Something of the same lack of thrust marks his account of Strauss's own arrangement of the *Rosenkavalier* excerpts, despite beautiful playing from the Houston orchestra. How much more welcome would it have been to have had extra items from the singer.

Coupled with outstanding items from Christa Ludwig, Sena Jurinac's historic version of the *Four Last Songs* was recorded at a Prom in 1961 with Sargent conducting the BBC Symphony Orchestra. All four songs are faster than usual, even faster than in Jurinac's earlier live broadcast performance of ten years before, recorded in Stockholm and issued by EMI. Defying rather rough mono sound, the result is ardent and animated rather than meditative, almost operatic and not at all valedictory. The Strauss songs with Christa Ludwig accompanied by Geoffrey Parsons come from a Wigmore Hall recital of 1978, with the glorious voice flawless in legato.

As a first encore, *Zueignung* wins storms of applause.

Dame Kiri Te Kanawa gives an open-hearted, warmly expressive reading of the *Four Last Songs*. If she misses the sort of detail that Schwarzkopf uniquely brought, her commitment is never in doubt. Her tone is consistently beautiful, but might have seemed even more so if the voice had not been placed rather too close in relation to the orchestra. The orchestral arrangements of the other songs make an excellent coupling and Andrew Davis directs most sympathetically. No complaints about the balance in *Also sprach Zarathustra* which has a fine concert hall layout producing lustrous strings and sonorous brass. The LSO again plays very well indeed and this makes a generous (if hardly apt) bonus, even if the performance does not quite maintain the intensity of the Kempe and Karajan versions.

Barbara Bonney uses her creamy soprano with great sensitivity and concern for detail in this generous selection of Strauss Lieder, even if the tonal range could be wider. With a high proportion of favourite songs, the disc can be fairly warmly recommended, though the *Four Last Songs* are not entirely successful with piano instead of orchestral accompaniment. Even the keenly imaginative Malcolm Martineau cannot conceal the problems in the last two songs, which cry out for a sustained legato beyond anything possible on the piano, notably in the long link between stanzas in *Beim schlafengehen*. Warm, well-balanced sound.

Lieder: *Allerseelen; All' mein' Gedanken; Befreit; Cäcilie; Efeu; Heimliche Aufforderung; Herr Lenz; Hochzeitlich; Junggesellenschwur; Liebeshymnus; Mein Auge; Meinem Kinde; Nachtgang; Nichts; Das Rosenband; Sehnsucht; Ständchen; Traum durch die Dämmerung; Waldseligkeit; Wasserrose; Weihnachtsgefühl; Winternacht*

●── (B) *** CfP 585 9032. Keenlyside, Martineau

Simon Keenlyside follows up the success of his fine Schubert recital (now also reissued on CfP) with this excellent collection of Strauss Lieder, beautifully sung, again with Malcolm Martineau a most sensitive accompanist. Try the highly distinctive, intimate reading of *Ständchen* ('Serenade'), with Keenlyside singing almost in a half-tone and with Martineau playing magically. The fine-spun legato of *Waldseligkeit* and the poise of *Meinem Kinde* are equally impressive. Keenlyside uses a head voice for the gentle top notes of *Allerseelen* ('All Souls' Day') but then finds plenty of power, sharply focused, in songs like *Befreit*. The sequence is rounded off with two exhilarating songs, *Cäcilie* and *Herr Lenz* (with its pun on the name Strauss – nosegay). No texts are provided in its new Classics for Pleasure release; even so, it is well worth its bargain price.

Lieder: *Allerseelen; Am Ufer; Aus den Lindern der Trauer; Heimkehr; Liebeshymnus; Lob des Leidens; Madrigal; Morgen Die Nacht; Winternacht; Zueignung*

(M) *** Decca 474 536-2. Fassbaender, Gage – LISZT: *Lieder* ***

Coupled with an equally perceptive group of Liszt songs, Fassbaender's Strauss selection, winner of the *Gramophone* Solo Vocal Award for 1987, brings singing of exceptional command and intensity; always she communicates face to face, and the musical imagination – as in the very slow account of the popular *Morgen* – adds to the sharply specific quality she gives to each song. The voice is beautiful as recorded, but that beauty is only an incidental. Warmly understanding accompaniment; well-balanced recording.

OPERA

Die Aegyptische Helena (complete)

*** Telarc CD 80605 (2). Voigt, Tanner, Shafer, Grove, Robertson, NY Concert Chorale, American SO, Botstein

If till now *Die Aegyptische Helena* has failed to make its mark in the regular repertory, the fault lies rather with the libretto of Hugo von Hofmannsthal than with the music of Strauss. It is a point that comes over vividly with this Telarc version, made live in New York in 2002, the finest yet. This is the third of a trilogy of marriage operas, following up the massively symbolic *Die Frau ohne Schatten* and the lightly autobiographical *Intermezzo*. Hofmannsthal's suggestion was to write an opera about the mythical Helen after she returned from Troy to Menelaus, the husband she had left, though the failure to make Menelaus into a rounded character tends to undermine that, in face of the sensuous warmth of Strauss's score. Even so, the role of Menelaus is arguably the finest he ever gave to a tenor, very well sung here by Carl Tanner. The relationship between Helen and the Egyptian princess and sorceress Aithra is far more revealing, prompting Strauss into the sort of duetting between sopranos that drew from him so much of his finest operatic inspirations. What the New York recording triumphantly brings out is the melodic richness of Strauss's score. It has even been described as a bel canto opera, though that is to underestimate the complexity of the work's structure, wonderfully crafted throughout, with orchestral writing of a richness that even Strauss never surpassed. Where the conductor, Leon Botstein, scores even over Antal Dorati in the previous studio recording, made for Decca, and over Josef Krips in the live recording of 1970 from the Vienna State Opera (RCA) is the extra warmth he finds in the score, helped by rich, digital sound, with the engineers overcoming the acoustic problems of recording in the Avery Fisher Hall in Lincoln Center. The new set also scores heavily over those previous versions in not having Gwyneth Jones in the title-role, always given to squally moments. This time it is Deborah Voigt, whose richness and command are a joy, with even the most challenging top notes firm and pure. She is well matched by Celena Shafer as Aithra, singing with consistent freshness and clarity. Jill Grove is the wonderfully resonant contralto in the improbable role of the Omniscient Seashell (adviser to Aithra), with Christopher Robertson as Altair, prince of the Atlas Mountains, and Eric Cutler as his son, Da-ud.

Arabella (complete DVD versions)

⊕–▪ *** Warner DVD 0630-16912-2. Putnam, Brocheler, Rolandi, Sarfaty, Korn, Lewis, Bradley, LPO, Haitink (Dir.: John Cox; DVD Dir.: John Vernon)

*** DG DVD 073 005-9. Te Kanawa, Wolfgang Brendel, McLaughlin, Dessay, Kuebler, Dernesch, McIntyre, Met. Op. Ch. and O, Thielemann (Producer: Otto Schenk. V/D: Brian Large)

Arabella (complete CD versions)

**(*) Decca (ADD) 460 230-2 (2). della Casa, Gueden, London, Edelmann, Dermota, V. State Op. Ch., VPO, Solti

(M) (***) DG mono (IMS) 445 342-2 (3). Reining, Hotter, Della Casa, Taubmann, VPO, Boehm

The Warner DVD offers a live recording of a classic Glyndebourne production of *Arabella* with handsome, realistic sets by Julia Trevelyan Oman. In this 1984 performance Bernard Haitink, then music director at Glyndebourne, draws ravishing playing from the LPO in support of an outstanding cast with not a single flaw. Ashley Putnam makes a tall and imposing Arabella, at once pretty and girlishly eager, yet with a natural dignity and a vocal command that makes her performance magnetic, with the set-piece solos and duets deeply moving. Opposite her, John Brocheler is a formidable Mandryka, handsome and heavily bearded, with a clean-cut voice that has just a hint of grit in it, aptly so. As Zdenka Gianna Rolandi cuts a vivacious, eager figure, even if her tiny stature next to the imposing Putnam makes it unlikely that even the simple-minded Matteo (superbly sung by Keith Lewis) would mistake her for Arabella even in bed. As Arabella's parents, Regina Sarfaty and Artur Korn both characterize well, and Gwendolyn Bradley makes the most of the brief if spectacular role of the Fiakermilli in Act II. John Vernon's video direction, using many helpful close-ups, adds to the impact. The irritation of this issue is that the printed documentation does not include a list of cast and characters: that appears only on screen at the end, as each character takes a bow. It is inadequate too that only the briefest synopsis is given on the box, with no booklet provided.

It would be hard to think of a starrier line-up of soloists for *Arabella* than in the live account recorded at the Met in New York in November 1994. One of the great strengths of the production is the conducting of Christian Thielemann, who was then just emerging as a new star among Strauss conductors. He is at once thrustful and emotional, drawing ripe sounds from the orchestra.

Dame Kiri Te Kanawa gives a convincing dramatic account of the title role and is in glorious voice, producing ravishing sounds in her big numbers, even more charming when observed in close-up. She obviously relishes the sumptuous production, which is as traditional as could be, with grandly realistic sets by Gunther Schneider-Siemssen. The stage direction is by Otto Schenk, who shows appropriate respect for Hofmansthal and Strauss's wishes, and the intelligence of the public.

The Mandryka of Wolfgang Brendel carries conviction even if he looks somewhat older than he should (mid-thirties). His voice is strong, firm and unstrained in a rather intimidating yet ultimately vulnerable characterization, and Marie McLaughlin is poignantly convincing as Zdenka, the younger sister forced to adopt the role of boy. Donald McIntyre and Helga Dernesch are vividly characterful as Arabella's parents, and in the second act Natalie Dessay as the Fiakermilli is full of character, and she makes much of her brief appearance at the ball, bright and brilliant in her showpiece.

The balance favours the voices and not all the wealth of orchestral detail registers, but the recording is aptly rich and full-bodied. The visual side of the production is first rate (and a great improvement on the Laserdisc). As usual Brian Large's camera is pointing exactly where one wants it to point. On the videotape there were no subtitles at all, and on the LaserDisc there were English subtitles which could not be removed. Here not only are there subtitles in English, French and Mandarin, but the original Hofmannsthal text is also accessible. Strongly recommended.

On the Decca CD set Della Casa soars above the stave with the creamiest, most beautiful sounds and constantly charms one with her swiftly alternating moods of seriousness and gaiety. Perhaps Solti does not linger as he might over the waltz rhythms, and it may be Solti too who prevents Edelmann from making his first scene with Mandryka as genuinely humorous as it can be. Edelmann otherwise is superb, as fine a Count as he was an Ochs in the Karajan *Rosenkavalier*. Gueden, too, is ideally cast as Zdenka and, if anything, in

Act I manages to steal our sympathies from Arabella, as a good Zdenka can. George London is on the ungainly side, but then Mandryka is a boorish fellow anyway. Dermota is a fine Matteo, and Mimi Coertse makes as much sense as anyone could of the ridiculously difficult part of Fiakermilli, the female yodeller. The sound is brilliant. It has now been impressively remastered onto two discs with the break coming just before Milli begins her yodelling song. However, this set is no longer at mid-price.

Recorded live in August 1947 at the Salzburg Festival, the Boehm recording is a radiant account with an outstanding cast. Maria Reining is here in firm, true voice, conveying not just the dignity of the heroine but the depth of feeling behind her often imperious manner. Hans Hotter too in his early maturity is in splendid voice, a superb Mandryka, characterful and well focused. Lisa della Casa, destined to make the role of Arabella a speciality, is here a charming Zdenka, fresh and girlish; and the rest of the cast includes many Viennese stalwarts of the period. Despite the limitations of the orchestral sound and some very rough playing, it is a most cherishable set.

Ariadne auf Naxos (complete DVD versions)

(***) Arthaus **DVD** 100 170. Anthony, Martinez, Koch, Villars, Junge, Adam, Semper Oper Ch., Dresden State O, C. Davis (Producer: Marco Arturo Marelli. V/D: Felix Breisach)

** DG **DVD** 073 028-9. Norman, Battle, Troyanos, King, Netwig, Dickson, Laciura, Met. Op. Ch. & O, Levine (V/D: Brian Large)

Ariadne auf Naxos (complete CD versions)

(N) (M) *** Ph. 475 6674 (2). J. Norman, Varady, Gruberová, Asmus, Bär, Frey, Leipzig GO, Masur

⊶ ✪ (M) (***) EMI mono 5 67077-2 [5671562]. Schwarzkopf, Schock, Rita Streich, Dönch, Seefried, Cuénod, Philh. O, Karajan

*** DG 471 323-2 (2). Voigt, Dessay, Von Otter, Heppner, Dohmen, Dresden State O, Sinopoli

(BB) *** Arte Nova 74321 77073-2 (2). Wachutka, Woodrow, Komlosi, Kutan, San Carlo, Naples O, Kuhn

(M) **(*) Decca (ADD) 460 233-2 (2). Price, Troyanos, Gruberová, Kollo, Berry, Kunz, LPO, Solti

(B) **(*) DG Double 453 112-2 (2). Tomowa-Sintow, Battle, Baltsa, Lakes, Rydl, Prey, Zednik, VPO, Levine

(M) **(*) EMI (ADD) 7 64159-2 (2). Janowitz, Geszty, Zylis-Gara, King, Schreier, Prey, Dresden State Op. O, Kempe

(M) (*(**)) DG (IMS) 445 332-2 (2). Della Casa, Gueden, Seefried, Schock, Schöffler, VPO, Boehm

We are at odds about the Arthaus DVD *Ariadne auf Naxos*, recorded live at the Semper Oper in Dresden. R.L. feels that for most collectors it will be a complete turn-off. The setting is in a present-day museum of modern art whose visitors wander in and out of the gallery throughout the whole opera to mightily distracting effect. It contributes nothing to an opera whose creators knew what they were doing. They were masters of their art and in no need of 'interpretation' from an attention-seeking director. The performance is not particularly distinguished vocally either, save for Sophie Koch's Composer. The best of the others are John Villars's Bacchus and Theo Adam's Music Master, and the orchestra make a pretty sumptuous sound under Sir Colin Davis. The intrusive silliness of the production makes it difficult to sit through this performance once, let alone a second time!

E.G. on the other hand feels that Sir Colin Davis, at his most inspired, directs a glowing performance with a cast of young singers who respond superbly, both to the conducting and to the imaginative stage direction of Marco Arturo Marelli. The Prologue, updated to the twentieth century, takes you behind the scenes of an impromptu theatre, with a piano centre-stage and with a washroom half visible behind.

The costumes, also designed by Marelli, add to the atmosphere of fantasy. The Composer, characterfully sung by Sophie Koch, heartfelt in the final solo, rightly provides the central focus, with his new passion for Zerbinetta well established. The main opera follows without an interval. The scene is neatly changed before our eyes to a picture gallery during a private view.

The composer (silent in this half) again provides a focus, with Ariadne and the others performing the opera as an impromptu charade. Central to the performance's success is the radiant singing of Susan Anthony as Ariadne with her firm, creamily beautiful voice. The sparky Zerbinetta of Iride Martinez, vivaciously Spanish-looking, unashamedly shows off in her big aria, both vocally in her dazzling coloratura and in her acting.

Jon Villars is a powerful, unstrained Bacchus in the final scene, with the commedia dell'arte characters all very well taken too. Though this is not as starry a cast as some, it is unusually satisfying, with no weak link. Clear, full-bodied sound, and, as in other Arthaus operas, a helpful booklet is provided.

Your Editor had not better enter the fray, as he hates almost all modern opera productions which make a time-change, and do not follow the original intentions of the composer and librettist. Readers can make up their own minds as to whose side they are on.

There is some impressive singing in the 1988 Metropolitan production of *Ariadne*. Levine's DG recording of the opera had been made only a year earlier in Vienna with Anna Tomowa-Sintow as Ariadne, Agnes Baltsa as the Composer and Kathleen Battle as Zerbinetta. Jessye Norman had only recently recorded the title-role with Masur for Philips, and Tatiana Troyanos had been the Composer in Solti's Decca set from the late 1980s. Recordings of *Ariadne* are legion and some (like the Karajan, Kempe and Solti versions) are in their way indispensable, but there is only one DVD alternative, marvellously conducted by Sir Colin Davis but in an intrusively updated production. This is straight and unfussy in its staging, and the video production by Brian Large could not be more expert and unobtrusive (save for one or two close-ups of Norman's larynx). Troyanos's Composer is quite superb, and neither Battle nor Norman can be faulted vocally, even if some will find the former's charm a bit overdone. No complaints about the men either, even if James King's Bacchus is a mite strained on some of his top notes. James Levine is a fine musician, but the orchestral playing has all too little of the finesse and subtlety of Kempe or Karajan and the orchestral textures are nowhere near as refined as they achieve.

In the Philips CD version, Jessye Norman's is a commanding, noble, deeply felt performance, ranging extraordinarily wide; if she does not find the same raptness, the inner agony that still makes Elisabeth Schwarzkopf's performance unique, she yet provides the perfect focus for a near ideal cast. Julia Varady as the Composer brings out the vulnerability of the character as well as the ardour in radiant singing. The Zerbinetta of Edita Gruberová adds an extra dimension to previous recordings in the way she translates the panache of her stage performance into purely aural terms for recording. It is a thrilling performance and, even if the voice is not always ideally sweet, the range of emotions Gruberová conveys, as in her duet with the Composer, is enchanting. Paul Frey is the sweetest-sounding Bacchus on record yet, while Olaf Bär as Harlekin and Dietrich Fischer-Dieskau in the vignette role of the Music-Master are typical of the fine team of artists here in the smaller character parts. Masur proves a masterly Straussian and he is helped by the typically warm Leipzig recording, with sound rich and mellow to cocoon the listener, yet finely balanced to allow you to hear the interweaving of the piano as never before in twentieth century imitation of a continuo.

Elisabeth Schwarzkopf makes a radiant, deeply moving Ariadne, giving as bonus a delicious little portrait of the Prima Donna in the Prologue. Rita Streich was at her most dazzling in the coloratura of Zerbinetta's aria and, in partnership with the harlequinade characters, sparkles engagingly. But it is Irmgard Seefried who gives perhaps the supreme performance of all as the Composer, exceptionally beautiful of tone, conveying a depth and intensity rarely if ever matched. Rudolf Schock is a fine Bacchus, strained less than most, and the team of theatrical characters includes such stars as Hugues Cuénod as the Dancing Master. The fine pacing and delectably pointed ensemble add to the impact of a uniquely perceptive Karajan interpretation. Though in mono and with the orchestral sound a little dry, the voices come out superbly.

Sinopoli's version offers an opulent view of this most delicate of the Strauss operas. The full-bodied sound goes with an outstandingly strong and characterful cast with no weak link. In the *Prologue* Anne Sofie von Otter is at once tender and vulnerable as the Composer. Encouraged by Sinopoli she brings out an urgently volatile element in the character, leading up to the passionate outburst of the closing solo glorifying this *heilige Kunst*, 'the Holy Art of music'. Deborah Voigt brings power as well as warmth and flexibility to the role of Ariadne, and Natalie Dessay as Zerbinetta is similarly commanding and characterful, even if both of them have their moments of edginess. Ben Heppner is a superb Bacchus, both pure and heroic with no hint of strain, and one big benefit of a studio recording is that the harlequinade ensembles are so light and crisp.

The modestly priced Arte Nova version can also be strongly recommended, offering a warmly enjoyable live recording made at the San Carlo opera-house in Naples in February 2000. With Gustav Kuhn an urgent Straussian, this is a passionate and persuasive reading, very well recorded, if with occasional stage noises. The cast is a strong one, with Elisabeth-Marie Wachutka outstanding as Ariadne, sweet and pure over the widest range, and bringing girlish passion to the role, culminating in a heartwarming account of Ariadne's final solo in response to Bacchus, the excellent clear-voiced Alan Woodrow. Aline Kutan is a similarly impressive Zerbinetta, matching more starry rivals, brilliant in coloratura with a winning sparkle. Though the harlequinade characters are inevitably less polished in their ensembles than in a studio recording, the fun of the piece comes over well, as well as the atmospheric beauty of the Naiads' music. The one snag is the miscasting of Ildiko Komlosi as the Composer. It is a rich, warm contralto rather than a mezzo, satisfying enough vocally except under pressure, but too feminine for this trouser role. Yet the thrust of a live performance makes this a highly competitive version at super-budget price. The German libretto is included but, alas, no translation.

Brilliance is the keynote of Solti's set of *Ariadne*. What the performance is short of is charm and warmth. Nevertheless, Leontyne Price makes a strong central figure, memorably characterful. Tatiana Troyanos is affecting as the composer, and Edita Gruberová establishes herself as the unrivalled Zerbinetta of her generation, though here she is less delicate than on stage. René Kollo similarly is an impressive Bacchus. The new Decca CD transfer is characteristically vivid, although it is not wanting in warmth and atmosphere.

As Ariadne, on DG, Tomowa-Sintow with her rich, dramatic soprano adds to the sense of grandeur and movingly brings out the vulnerability of the character. But ultimately she fails to create as fully rounded and detailed a character as her finest rivals, and the voice, as recorded, loses its bloom and creaminess under pressure, marring the big climaxes. Both Agnes Baltsa as the Composer and Kathleen Battle as Zerbinetta are excellent: the one tougher than most rivals with her mezzo-soprano ring, little troubled by the high tessitura, the other delectably vivacious, dazzling in coloratura, but equally hard finding the unexpected tenderness in the character. The *commedia dell'arte* characters and the attendant theatrical team are strongly taken by stalwarts of the Vienna State Opera, among them Kurt Rydl, Hermann Prey and Heinz Zednik, while the Heldentenor role of Bacchus, always hard to cast, is strongly taken by Gary Lakes, clear-toned and firm, at times pinched but never strained. The very reasonable cost of this set should tempt many collectors to sample this very rewarding opera, particularly when the recording is so warmly flattering to both singers and orchestra.

Kempe's relaxed, languishing performance of this most atmospheric of Strauss operas is matched by opulent recording, warmly transferred to CD. Gundula Janowitz sings with heavenly tone-colour (marred only when hard-pressed at the climax of the Lament), and Teresa Zylis-Gara makes an ardent and understanding Composer. Sylvia Geszty's voice is a little heavy for the fantastic coloratura of Zerbinetta's part, but she sings with charm and assurance. James King presents the part of Bacchus with forthright tone and more taste than do most tenors.

Boehm's affection for this elegant, touching score glows through the whole performance. Lisa della Casa is a poised, tender Ariadne, totally rapt in the final duet with Bacchus. Even though her later studio recordings of the *Lament* are more assured than this, the passion of the climax of that key solo is most involving. As in Karajan's studio recording, Irmgard Seefried as the Composer and Rudolf Schock as Bacchus have few equals; but what crowns the whole performance is the charming Zerbinetta of Hilde Gueden, not just warmly characterful but fuller-toned than almost any. The snag is the recording, fizzy in the orchestral sound, with even the voices rather thinly recorded.

(i) *Ariadne auf Naxos* (excerpts). Lieder: (ii) *Befreit; Einerlei; Hat gesagt; Morgen!; Schlechtes Wetter; Seit dem dein Aug'; Waldseligkeit*
*** Testament (ADD) SBT 1036. della Casa, with (i) Schock, BPO, Erede; (ii) Peschko

The 1959 stereo recording is full and immediate, bringing out the glories of della Casa's creamy soprano but failing to convey the full, atmospheric beauty of the music, notably in the echo chorus of Naiads. Della Casa had earlier recorded *Ariadne's Lament* for Decca, but this is even more powerful. The first excerpt is of the opening of the entertainment from the overture through to Ariadne's first solo. There follow her second solo, *Ein Schönes war*, and the *Lament*, while the last extended excerpt has the whole of the final scene from the entry of Bacchus. Rudolf Schock, as in the Karajan version, sings nobly, and Erede brings out the lyrical warmth of the writing. Della Casa is less imaginative in the Strauss Lieder but still sings very beautifully and persuasively. The faithful and full Testament transfers bring out the wide range of the recording, tending to emphasize sibilants in the singing.

Ariadne auf Naxos: Prelude & Final Duet; Elektra: Recognition Scene & Finale

(M) (***) Preiser mono 90341. Cebotari, Friedrich; Schluter, Schöffler, Widdop, Welitsch, Ch. & RPO, Beecham

These two historic opera recordings were made by RCA at the time of the Strauss festival that Beecham organized in London in October 1947. The *Elektra* excerpts, bitingly dramatic, were issued on 78 straight away, but the *Ariadne* excerpts have been kept in limbo, with the ill-fated Maria Cebotari in one of her very rare recordings joined by Karl Friedrich, a stalwart tenor of the Vienna State Opera at the time, otherwise totally neglected on disc. It makes a generous package, with Beecham not only persuasive in his direction of Strauss but urgently dramatic, adopting speeds in *Elektra* faster than have become the norm, with electrifying results, not least in Elektra's moving recognition of her brother, Oreste. Erna Schluter, singing the title role, may not have had the most beautiful voice, but it is consistently fresh, incisive and accurate. The *Ariadne* excerpts generously offer the final scene from the first offstage entry of Bacchus to the end, though it is a pity that Cebotari was not recorded in *Ariadne's Lament*. Excellent, undistracting transfers.

Capriccio (complete)

*** Arthaus **DVD** 100 354. Te Kanawa, Hagegård, Troyanos, Braun, Kuebler, Keenlyside, Sénéchal, Travis, San Francisco Op. O, Runnicles (Dir.: Lawless; DVD Dir.: Maniura)

⊖– ✪ (M) (***) EMI mono 5 67394-2 (2) [567391-2]. Schwarzkopf, Waechter, Gedda, Fischer-Dieskau, Hotter, Ludwig, Moffo, Philh. O, Sawallisch

*** Forlane UCD 268052 (2). Lott, Allen, Kunde, Genz, von Kannen, Vermillion, SWR Stuttgart Vocal Ens. & Radio SO, Prêtre

(M) **(*) DG (ADD) 445 347-2 (2). Janowitz, Troyanos, Schreier, Fischer-Dieskau, Prey, Ridderbusch, Bav. RSO, Boehm

**(*) Orfeo C 518 992 1 (2). Tomowa-Sintow, Schöne, Büchner, Grundheber, Jungwirth, Schmidt, Ridder, Scarabelli, Ballo, Minth, VPO, Stein

With evocative sets by Mauro Pagano and in-period eighteenth-century costumes by Thierry Bosquet, Stephen Lawless's production for the San Francisco Opera will delight traditionalists. In this live (1993) performance, Donald Runnicles is the deeply sympathetic conductor inspiring an outstanding cast with no weak link. Kiri Te Kanawa not only sings gloriously with a continuous flow of full, warm sound, she acts most movingly. Vivacious at the start of this 'conversation piece', her deepening of feeling is vividly conveyed, first when she hears the sonnet written for her, and then throughout in the way she uses her deep-set, haunted eyes with their hooded lids, fully exploited in Peter Maniura's video direction. Håkan Hagegård as the Count, her brother, is a big, burly figure, bumbling enough in his overacting to make the rehearsal scene with Tatiana Troyanos as a characterful Clairon both funny and believable. The rival duo of poet and composer is superbly taken by David Kuebler as Flamand and

Simon Keenlyside as Olivier, vocally and visually handsome, with Victor Braun as La Roche, Maria Fortuna and Craig Estep as the Italian soprano and tenor ideally cast, and with even the role of the Major Domo very strongly sung by Dale Travis, and with the veteran Michel Sénéchal masterly in the cameo role of the prompter, Monsieur Taupe. For sheer Straussian beauty, evocatively presented, it would be hard to match the rendering here of the final scene. First-rate sound and excellent documentation in the accompanying booklet, as usual with Arthaus DVDs.

In the role of the Countess in Strauss's last opera, Elisabeth Schwarzkopf has had no equals on CD. This recording, made in 1957 and 1958, brings a peerless performance from her, full of magical detail both in the pointing of words and in the presentation of the character in all its variety. Not only are the other singers ideal choices in each instance, they form a wonderfully co-ordinated team, beautifully held together by Sawallisch's sensitive conducting. As a performance this is never likely to be superseded. This is truly one of EMI's 'Great Recording of the Century' and Andrew Walter's new translation reveals the naturalness and beauty of the mono sound, both of the voices and the orchestra relatively backwardly balanced. Excellent documentation and a full libretto.

Recorded at a series of concert performances in Mannheim in 1999, the Forlane set, with Prêtre an understanding Straussian, offers vivid, immediate sound, giving extra intensity to this inspired 'conversation-piece' on the subject of opera. Central to the set's success is the inspired portrayal of the Countess by Dame Felicity Lott in one of her great roles. Her feeling for the idiom is unerring, and though the closeness of the recording brings out the occasional unevenness under pressure, this will delight Dame Felicity's many admirers. Schwarzkopf may offer an even more thoughtful, more deeply reflective portrayal on the classic EMI set under Sawallisch, and Gundula Janowitz with Boehm on DG is even more radiantly beautiful, but there is a bite to Lott's reading that brings out how formidable the character is. With Thomas Allen ideally cast as the Count, with Gregory Kunde as the composer, Flamand, and Stephan Genz as the poet, Olivier, the supporting cast is first rate, with voices cleanly focused, and conversational exchanges beautifully timed. This team yields only to the even more sharply characterful one on EMI.

On DG, Gundula Janowitz is not as characterful and pointful a Countess as one really needs (and no match for Schwarzkopf), but Boehm lovingly directs a most beautiful performance of a radiant score, very consistently cast, beautifully sung and very well recorded for its period (1971). There is full documentation, including translation.

The Austrian Radio recording from Orfeo offers a warm, rich performance in satisfyingly full sound, made the more compelling for being taken live at a Salzburg Festival performance in August 1985. Tomowa-Sintow sings with poise and tenderness, with the rest of the cast making a strong team. Outstanding is Trudeliese Schmidt as the flamboyant actress Clairon, and Horst Stein is inspired by the beauty of the score to conduct with more passion than in studio recordings. Though the jewel-case promises German and English texts, no libretto is provided, only a detailed synopsis, a serious shortcoming in this of all operas with its complex interchanges.

Capriccio, Op. 85: String Sextet

*** Hyp. CDA 66704. Ens. – BRUCKNER: *String Quintet* ***

*** Chan. 9131. ASMF Chamber Ens. – ENESCU: *Octet in C;*
SHOSTAKOVICH: 2 *Pieces for String Octet* ***

The opening sextet from Strauss's last opera, *Capriccio*, makes
an excellent fill-up to the Bruckner *String Quintet*. Obviously
readers are unlikely to buy the Bruckner for the sake of such a
short work, even though it is of great beauty, but those who
do will be rewarded by some fine music-making and recording.

The autumnal preface to *Capriccio* is also the expertly
played fill-up to Enescu's remarkable *Octet*; very well
recorded it is, too.

Capriccio: Prelude. Feuersnot: Love scene. Guntram: Prelude
*** DG 449 571-2. German Opera, Berlin, O, Thielemann –
PFITZNER: *Das Herz*, etc **(*)

These Strauss items, two of them rare, make an excellent
coupling for the Pfitzner which Thielemann chose for his
début recording with DG. Though in the *Feuersnot* Love
scene the orchestra of the Deutsches Oper in Berlin is not
quite as poised or refined as the Staatskapelle in Dresden for
Sinopoli, the thrust and passion are even greater, with a freer
expressiveness. Excellent sound.

Elektra (complete)
*** Arthaus **DVD** 100 048. Marton, Fassbaender, Studer,
King, Grundheber, V. St. Op. Ch. & O, Abbado
⊶ ✪ *** DG 453 429-2 (2). Marc, Schwarz, Voigt,
Jerusalem, Ramey, V. State Op. Konzertvereinigung, VPO,
Sinopoli
*** Decca (ADD) 417 345-2 (2). Nilsson, Collier, Resnik,
Stolze, Krause, V. State Op. Ch., VPO, Solti

Eva Marton recorded *Elektra* with Wolfgang Sawallisch in
1990, but the present account comes from a Vienna performance of the preceding year with Abbado conducting. It
appeared on laser disc on the Pioneer label in 1993 and now
makes a welcome appearance on DVD.

The performance has enormous intensity: both Marton's
Elektra and Fassbaender's Klytemnestra stay long in the
memory, and all the remaining characters are triumphantly
realized, not least Franz Grundheber's blood-thirsty Orest.
Marton makes the most of the intent, obsessive, powerfully
demonic Elektra and has enormous dramatic presence.

Harry Kupfer's production is gripping. The setting is dark
though not quite as dismal as Götz Friedrich's 1981 production with Rysanek and Varnay under Boehm on a Decca LD.
Musically, this is an exciting and concentrated account, and
the camera is musically handled by Brian Large. He has an
unerring feel for directing our attention where it needs to be,
and many collectors will feel that this is an essential acquisition, alongside the Sinopoli CD set.

On CD Sinopoli directs an incandescent performance of
Elektra, at once powerful and sensuous, vividly recorded in
full-bodied sound. Alessandra March is here aptly cast in the
title-role, instantly establishing her command in the opening
monologue, magnetically done. Where she scores even over
Nilsson is in the warmth and beauty of tone. Not only are the
dramatic outbursts thrillingly projected with firmly focused
tone, she is just as compelling in gentler moments, whether
reflecting the creepily sinister side of Elektra's character or in
her radiant ecstasy following her recognition of her brother,
Orestes. The glorious solo ending with the rapturous cry of
'*Seliger*' ('happier') has never been caught so seductively on
disc as here, with Sinopoli drawing glowing playing from the
Vienna Philharmonic. Deborah Voigt as Chrysothemis is

clear and firm too, well contrasted, and Hanna Schwarz is a
powerful Klytemnestra, with bitingly well-focused tone. Having such a fine, heroic tenor as Siegfried Jerusalem in the
small role of Aegist is another tribute to the casting, crowned
by the choice of Samuel Ramey as a warm and strong Orest, a
perfect foil for Alessandra Marc. The performance is rounded
off with a thrilling account of the final scene, capturing
Elektra's hysterical joy with rare intensity.

Nilsson is almost incomparable in the name-part, with the
hard side of Elektra's character brutally dominant. Only when
– as in the Recognition scene with Orestes – she tries to
soften the naturally bright tone does she let out a suspect flat
note or two. As a rule she is searingly accurate in approaching
even the most formidable exposed top notes. One might draw
a parallel with Solti's direction – sharply focused and brilliant
in the savage music which predominates, but lacking the
languorous warmth one really needs in the Recognition
scene, if only for contrast. The brilliance of the 1967 Decca
recording is brought out the more in the newest digital
transfer on CD, aptly so in this work. The fullness and clarity
are amazing for the period.

Feuersnot (complete)
(B) *** Arts 47546-2 (2). Varady, Weikl, Bergere-Tuna, Tölz
Boys' Ch., Bav. R. Ch., Munich RO, Fricke

Feuersnot, Strauss's second opera, which was first given in
1901, is an allegory with an element of satire, set in medieval
times. Like his first (*Guntram*) it is opulently scored, and in
three compact Acts tells its story of Kunrad, a young sorcerer
who, when rejected and ridiculed, puts a curse on the town,
extinguishing all fire and light. This Bavarian Radio recording
made in 1985 fills an important gap and is the more welcome
on a bargain label. The performance is a fine one, with Bernd
Weikl as Kunrad and Julia Varady as Dimut, his beloved, the
Mayor's daughter - both outstanding. Heinz Fricke directs a
warmly expressive performance in well-balanced digital radio
sound. Recommended.

Die Frau ohne Schatten
⊶ ✪ *** Decca 436 243-2 (3). Behrens, Varady, Domingo,
Van Dam, Runkel, Jo, VPO, Solti
(M) (**(*)) DG mono 457 678-2 (3). Rysanek, Hoffman,
Ludwig, Thomas, Berry, Popp, Wunderlich, V. State Op. Ch.
& O, Karajan

In the Heldentenor role of the Emperor, Plácido Domingo,
the superstar tenor, gives a performance that is not only
beautiful to the ear beyond previous recordings but which
has an extra feeling for expressive detail, deeper than that
which was previously recorded. Hildegard Behrens as the
Dyer's wife is also a huge success. Her very feminine vulnerability is here a positive strength, and the voice has rarely
sounded so beautiful on record. Julia Varady as the Empress
is equally imaginative, with a beautiful voice, and José van
Dam with his clean, dark voice brings a warmth and depth of
expression to the role of Barak, the Dyer, which goes with a
satisfyingly firm focus. Reinhild Runkel in the key role of the
Nurse is well in character, with her mature, fruity sound. Eva
Lind is shrill in the tiny role of the Guardian of the Thresh-
old, but there is compensation in having Sumi Jo as the Voice
of the Falcon. With the Vienna Philharmonic surpassing
themselves, and the big choral ensembles both well disciplined and warmly expressive, this superb recording is
unlikely to be matched, let alone surpassed, for many years.
Solti himself is inspired throughout.

The 1964 Karajan recording from Austrian Radio captures the intensity of the live occasion, with ecstatic applause for each of the Acts. With orchestral sound in mono thin and limited (a serious shortcoming in Strauss) the voices are paramount, with words made the clearer by the closeness. The cast is an outstanding one, with Leonie Rysanek powerful as the Empress and Jess Thomas exploiting his cleanly focused Heldentenor as the Emperor. The young Walter Berry is firmly commanding as Barak, the Dyer; and best of all is Christa Ludwig as the Dyer's Wife, here early in her career singing with a freshness and intensity that she retained in her later studio recording with Solti for Decca. The mono sound is limited, but with voices well caught. The usual stage-cuts are made in this epic score.

Guntram (complete)
(BB) ** Arte Nova 74321 61339-2 (2). Woodrow, Wachutka, Konsulov, Scheidegger, Marchigiana PO, Kuhn

Strauss's very first opera, set in the age of chivalry, is an opulent piece, unashamed in its high romanticism. On the Arte Nova label Gustav Kuhn conducts a warm, thrustful performance, recorded live at Garmisch-Partenkirchen, with the rich orchestral tapestries beautifully caught in open, refined sound, only occasionally disturbed by audience noises. Alan Woodrow makes a strong Guntram, with his firm Heldentenor tone only occasionally strained. Elisabeth Wachutka with her fruity soprano sounds too mature for the heroine, Freihild, and none of the other singers quite matches those in the currently withdrawn rival version on Sony, but this makes an excellent super-bargain set for those wanting to sample this opera inexpensively, although we hope the preferable CBS/Sony set will soon return to the catalogue.

Intermezzo (complete)
*** EMI (ADD) 7 49337-2 (2). Popp, Brammer, Fischer-Dieskau, Bav. RSO, Sawallisch

The central role of Intermezzo was originally designed for the dominant and enchanting Lotte Lehmann; but it is doubtful whether even she can have outshone the radiant Lucia Popp, who brings out the charm of a character who, for all his incidental trials, must have consistently captivated Strauss and provoked this strange piece of self-revelation. The piece inevitably is very wordy, but with this scintillating and emotionally powerful performance under Sawallisch, with fine recording and an excellent supporting cast, this set is as near ideal as could be, a superb achievement. The CD transfer is well managed but – unforgivably in this of all Strauss operas – no translation is given with the libretto, a very serious omission.

Intermezzo: Symphonic Interludes
*** Chan. 9357. Detroit SO, Järvi – SCHMIDT: Symphony 1 ***

Neeme Järvi is an underrated Straussian and here he proves equal to the very best. He and his Detroit musicians give a thoroughly persuasive account of the interludes Strauss extracted from Intermezzo, and this comes as a generous fill-up to Schmidt's derivative but delightful First Symphony. Strongly recommended.

Die Liebe der Danae (complete)
*** CPO 999 967-2 (3). Grundheber, Schöpflin, McNamara, Uhl, Zach, Chafin, Behle, Fleitmann, Kiel Op. Ch. & PO, Windfuhr

**(*) Telarc CD 80570 (3). Flanigan, Coleman-Wright, Smith, Lewis, Saffer, NY Concert Chorale, American SO, Botstein

Die Liebe der Danae is an ingenious conflation – originally suggested by Hugo von Hofmannsthal – of two myths involving gold, the legend of Midas and the golden touch, and Jupiter's seduction of Danae in the guise of golden rain. The scale is formidable, with a climactic final duet between Danae and Jupiter of Wagnerian grandeur, echoing the farewells of Wotan and Brünnhilde. The love duets too between Danae and Midas – true love more valuable than gold – are movingly tender, with the tenor for once in Strauss an equal partner. Their duet in Act II ends terrifyingly, when Midas, embracing Danae, unwittingly turns her into a golden statue.

Recorded live at the Kiel Opera in April 2003, the CPO set of this late opera of Strauss, follows on the success of this same company's recording of Alfano's Cyrano de Bergerac. It comes into direct competition with the Telarc version under Leon Botstein, also recorded live but in a concert performance. Where the account under Ulrich Windfuhr consistently scores is in the dramatic bite of the performance, with singers on stage conveying each confrontation of character more convincingly than is ever likely in a concert performance. The recording helps, made by the engineers of North German Radio. Though the voices on stage are balanced in front of the orchestra, they are well separated, and the extra bloom on the orchestral sound compared with the rather boxy sound on Telarc makes all the difference in this luscious score with its evocative passages like the 'golden rain' interlude in Act I. Though Botstein is a formidable Straussian, Windfuhr is even more warmly idiomatic, conveying a surge of warmth at the big climaxes, and his singers too seem to understand the idiom far more clearly than their American counterparts. Standing out from an excellent cast is the magnificent Jupiter of Franz Grundheber, weightily Wagnerian like a latter-day Wotan; and Robert Chafin in the tenor role of Midas is also splendid. Manuela Uhl as Danae has a bright, clear soprano, which she shades down seductively in gentler passages such as the meeting with Midas, but she tends to sound inflexible under pressure. Her counterpart on Telarc is sweeter and easier on the ear. Though in precision of ensemble the chorus on stage cannot match the American chorus in concert, the singers regularly convey an extra warmth in compensation, adding to the impact of the big choral moments.

Leon Botstein, a dedicated advocate of the piece, conducts a loving performance with his excellent cast. As Danae, Lauren Flanigan has ample richness and power, yet remains girlish, while Hugh Smith makes an engaging Midas, fresh and unstrained, with Peter Coleman-Wright in the difficult role of Jupiter repeating his formidable Garsington interpretation. The quartet of queens – all of them, like Leda and Semele, seduced by Jupiter in their time – and the quartet of kings are beautifully integrated, and Lisa Saffer is outstanding as Xanthe, Danae's maid, who has just one ravishing and very demanding duet with her mistress in Act I. First-rate chorus work. Though the clean if rather dry recording fails to do justice to the sumptuous scoring, with voices to the fore, the result is still magnetic, although the CPO set is a clear first choice.

Der Rosenkavalier (complete DVD versions)
⊕—• ✪ *** DG DVD 073 4072 (2). Lott, Von Otter, Bonney, Moll, Hornik, V. State Op. Ch. & O, Carlos Kleiber (Producer: Otto Schenck. V/D: Horant Hohlfeld)

(N) *** EMI **DVD** 5 44258-9 (2). Nina Stemme, Kasarova, Hartelius, Muff, Zurich Op., Ch. & O, Welser-Möst. (Producer: Sven-Eric Bechtolf. V/D Director: Chloé Perlemuter. Sets: Rolf Glittenberg)

Der Rosenkavalier (complete; CD versions)

☛ ✿ (M) *** EMI (ADD) 5 67605-2 (3) [5 67609-2]. Schwarzkopf, Ludwig, Stich-Randall, Edelmann, Waechter, Philh. Ch. & O, Karajan

*** EMI 7 54259-2 (3). Te Kanawa, Von Otter, Rydl, Grundheber, Hendricks, Dresden Op. Ch., Dresden Boys' Ch., Dresden State O, Haitink

**(*) Decca (ADD) 417 493-2 (3). Crespin, Minton, Jungwirth, Donath, Wienr, V. State Op. Ch., VPO, Solti

**(*) DG (IMS) 423 850-2 (3). Tomowa-Sintow, Baltsa, Moll, Perry, Hornik, VPO Ch. & O, Karajan

(M) (**(*)) Decca mono 467 111-2 (3). Reining, Jurinac, Gueden, Weber, Poell, Dermota, V. State Op. Ch., VPO, Erich Kleiber

(N) (BB) (**(*)) Naxos mono 8.111011/13 (3) Reining, Jurinac, Gueden, Weber, Dermota, V. State Op. Ch, VPO, Erich Kleiber

(N) (BB) ** Regis mono RRC 3007 (3) Reining, Jurinac, Gueden, Weber, Dermota, V. State Op. Ch, VPO, Erich Kleiber

This celebrated DG DVD production, recorded in Vienna in March 1994, appeared on videotape and laser disc the following year. Carlos Kleiber has spoken of Felicity Lott as his ideal Marschallin, and she is probably currently as unrivalled in this role as was Schwarzkopf in the 1950s. She does not wear her heart on her sleeve, and her reticence makes her all the more telling and memorable. The other roles are hardly less distinguished, with Anne Sofie von Otter's Octavian splendidly characterized and boyish, while Barbara Bonney's Sophie floats her top notes in the Presentation of the Rose scene with great poise and impressive accuracy. Kurt Moll's Ochs, a splendidly three-dimensional and subtle reading, is one of the highlights of the performance. Otto Schenck's production deserves the praises that have been lavished on it, and Rudolf Heinrich's sets are handsome. Carlos Kleiber gets some ravishing sounds from the Vienna Philharmonic, and his reading of the score is as Straussian and as perfect as you are likely to encounter in this world. It is even finer than the version he did in Munich in 1979 with Dame Gwyneth Jones as the Marschallin, Fassbaender as Octavian and Popp, which was issued on video and laser disc and which will presumably find its way onto DVD in the fullness of time. The sound is very natural and lifelike, not too forward, and with a good perspective. On the video there were no subtitles, although they were on laser disc. Things look up here, as not only are subtitles given in English, French and Mandarin but Hofmannsthal's original is also available.

The competing Zurich Opera production, recorded a decade later, is also outstanding in every way. Nina Stemme is a superb Marschallin, a sophisticated portrayal, but with deep underlying feeling which is so affecting in the great closing trio. Vesselina Kasarova's Octavian has a most engaging boyish quality while her richly contrasted mezzo blends perfectly with Malin Hartelius, an enchanting Sophie, whose exquisite singing in the Silver Rose scene is unforgettable. Alfred Muff is a splendid three-dimensional Baron Ochs, clumsily oaffish, yet believably real in his portrayal of a character totally unaware that his behaviour is hopelessly unacceptable, or

that anyone could possibly think of 'cuckolding' him. Moreover he has a rich, deep bass voice.

But there are many other plus points. As a backcloth for Marianne Glittenberg's lavish costumes, Rolf Glittenberg's sets are a visual delight, from the Marschallin's elegant bedroom of Act I to the colourful following kitchen scene where the nervous Sophie hides in the cupboard until her Cavalier persuades her to step out. Chloé Perlemuter's direction is unerring, with the camera focusing in close-up, connected to the dialogue to convey the feelings and reactions of the principal characters. The moment when Octavian and Sophie take that first astonished close look at each other is magically caught, and in the ravishingly sung final trio, one is made well aware of the conflicting emotions of the Marschallin, and the two lovers, who cannot believe what it is happening. Franz Welser-Möst conducts comparably elegantly, yet with ardour (the Waltz music is gorgeous), and the orchestral playing is richly responsive. The opening prelude is not as overtly passionate as with some conductors, and when the curtain rises there is almost a sense of *coitus triste*, before the arrival of the Baron lightens the mood. But the opera's close is very moving indeed. Excellent sound and the all-essential subtitles are splendidly managed.

On CD Karajan's 1956 version, one of the greatest of all opera recordings, is in a class of its own, with the patrician refinement of Karajan's spacious reading combining with an emotional intensity that he has rarely equalled, even in Strauss, of whose music he remains a supreme interpreter. Matching that achievement is the incomparable portrait of the Marschallin from Schwarzkopf, bringing out detail as no one else can, yet equally presenting the breadth and richness of the character, a woman still young and attractive. Christa Ludwig with her firm, clear mezzo tone makes an ideal, ardent Octavian and Teresa Stich-Randall a radiant Sophie, with Otto Edelmann a winningly characterful Ochs, who yet sings every note clearly. This has now rightly been reissued (at mid-price) as one of EMI's 'Great Recordings of the Century', with sound further enhanced.

Vocally the biggest triumph of Haitink's beautifully paced reading is the Octavian of Anne Sofie von Otter, not only beautifully sung but acted with a boyish animation to make most rivals sound very feminine by comparison. If the first great – and predictable – glory of Dame Kiri's assumption of the role of the Marschallin is the sheer beauty of the sound, the portrait she paints is an intense and individual one, totally convincing. The portrait of Sophie from Barbara Hendricks is a warm and moving one, but less completely satisfying, if only because her voice is not quite so pure as one needs for this young, innocent girl. Kurt Rydl with his warm and resonant bass makes a splendid Baron Ochs, not always ideally steady, but giving the character a magnificent scale and breadth. Whatever the detailed reservations over the singing, it is mainly due to Bernard Haitink that this is the most totally convincing and heartwarming recording of *Rosenkavalier* since Karajan's 1956 set. This recording, unlike the Karajan, opens out the small stage cuts sanctioned by the composer.

The current remastering of the Solti *Der Rosenkavalier* from the late 1960s has brought the most striking improvement in the sound among all the Decca reissues of his Strauss opera series and there is now body and ambient warmth, so essential for this gloriously ripe score. The VPO strings have a lovely sheen, yet inner detail is glowingly clear. Crespin is here at her finest on record, with tone well focused; the slightly maternal maturity of her approach will appear for many ideal. Mandfred Jungwirth makes a firm and virile, if not always imaginative Ochs, Yvonne Minton a finely projected Octavian and Helen Donath a sweet-toned Sophie. Solti's direction is fittingly honeyed, with tempi even slower than Karajan in the climactic meoments. The one serious disappointment is that the great concluding Trio does not quite lift one to the tear-laden height one ideally wants. Even so this *Rosenkavalier* offers much to ravish the ear.

Karajan's digital set brings few positive advantages. For the principal role he chose Anna Tomowa-Sintow; the refinement and detail in her performance present an intimate view of the Marschallin, often very beautiful indeed, but both the darker and more sensuous sides of the character are muted. The Baron Ochs of Kurt Moll, firm, dark and incisive, is outstanding, and Agnes Baltsa as Octavian makes the lad tough and determined, if not always sympathetic. Janet Perry's Sophie, charming and pretty on stage, is too white and twittery of tone to give much pleasure.

Now reissued in the Legends series, Decca's set conducted by Erich Kleiber was the first ever complete recording of *Rosenkavalier*, and it has long enjoyed cult status. Sena Jurinac is a charming Octavian, strong and sympathetic, and Hilde Gueden a sweetly characterful Sophie, not just a wilting innocent. Ludwig Weber characterizes deliciously in a very Viennese way as Ochs; but the disappointment is the Marschallin of Maria Reining, very plain and lacking intensity. She is not helped by Kleiber's refusal to linger; with the singers recorded close, the effect of age on what was once a fine voice is very clear, even in the opening solo of the culminating trio. And ensemble is not good, with even the prelude to Act I a muddle. Decca's own CD transfer in the Legends series of this classic first complete recording of *Rosenkavalier* offers full, forward sound, very good for a mono recording of 1954 if with surprising variations of level.

The Naxos transfer, meticulously made by Mark Obert-Thorn, irons out some of those inconsistencies as well as some electronic clicks and some distortion, and also offers full sound, a little more detailed but with some fizz occasionally and some veiling of voices in places.

The Regis version offers full, warm sound, less detailed and with a more noticeable surface-hiss, making it rather less recommendable. None of the three gives the strings of the Vienna Philharmonic their full bloom. Only the Decca Legends issue offers the libretto, with Naxos and Regis providing instead detailed synopses linked to the index points.

Der Rosenkavalier (highlights)

(M) *** EMI 5 65571-2. Schwarzkopf, Ludwig, Stich-Randall, Edelmann, Waechter, Philh. Ch. & O, Karajan

On EMI we are offered the Marschallin's monologue to the end of Act I (25 minutes); the Presentation of the silver rose and finale from Act II; and the Duet and Closing scene, with the Trio from Act III, flawlessly and gloriously sung and transferred most beautifully to CD. A superb disc in every way.

Der Rosenkavalier (abridged); highlights from early recordings

(BB) (***) Naxos mono 8.110191-2 (2). Lehmann, Olszewska, Schumann, Mayr, VPO, Heger

Mark Obert-Thorn's meticulous transfer of the original 78s of this classic opera set has the voices just as vivid as on EMI's own transfer, tending to being out more clearly the variable balances and volume-levels which marked the original. The

performance remains peerless, with all four principal soloists at their peak. That makes the substantial 43-minute appendix specially valuable, with alternative performances by Lehmann and Richard Mayr set against recordings by such rivals at the time as Barbara Kemp a superb Marschallin, Alexander Kipnis an Ochs even more powerful than Mayr, with Richard Tauber masterly in the tenor aria of Act I (omitted in the main set of excerpts) and Conchita Supervia a delectable Octavian opposite the Sophie of Maria Ferraris singing in Italian. The selection is rounded off with live recordings of the final trio and part of the duet made at the Theater der Unter den Linden in 1928 with Barbara Kemp, Delia Reinhardt and Marion Claire – a wonderful historic document.

Der Rosenkavalier (highlights in English)

(M) **(*) Chan. 3022. Kenny, Montague, Joshua, Tomlinson, Shore, Mitchell Ch., Kay Children's Ch., LPO, Parry

This generous 80-minute selection from *Der Rosenkavalier* sung in English, reflects the strength of English National Opera's highly successful stage production. David Parry paces the score most persuasively, and the orchestral sound is aptly sumptuous, if a little clouded on detail. The selection of items, concentrating on the beginnings and endings of Acts, cannot be faulted, except that John Tomlinson's strongly characterized Baron Ochs – with nobility part of the mixture – is represented only by the end of Act II, with its great Waltz theme. One snag is that the recording tends to exaggerate the singers' vibratos, intrusively so only with Yvonne Kenny as the Marschallin. She is strong but not very warm with such a noticeable flutter in the voice. On the other hand, Diana Montague is a winningly expressive Octavian, and Rosemary Joshua a sweet-toned Sophie. The booklet includes full text in the English version of Alfred Kalisch.

Der Rosenkavalier Suite

*** BBC (ADD) BBCL 4038. Hallé O, Barbirolli – HAYDN: Symphony 83 in G min. (La Poule); LEHAR: Gold and Silver; JOHANN STRAUSS JR: Emperor Waltz, etc. ***

A glorious performance from Barbirolli with the kind of affectionate attention to detail which all but disguises the fact that this is a musical patchwork. The Hallé horns and strings excel themselves in a performance that is full of uninhibited ardour, yet the *Presentation of the Rose* sequence is lovingly tender, and the final *Trio* full of bliss.

Salome (complete)

☻─➤ *** DG 431 810-2 (2). Studer, Rysanek, Terfel, Hiestermann, German Opera, Berlin, Ch. & O, Sinopoli

*** Decca (ADD) 414 414-2 (2). Nilsson, Hoffman, Stolze, Kmentt, Waechter, VPO, Solti

*** Chan. 9611 (2). Nielsen, Hale, Goldberg, Silja, Danish National RSO, Schonwandt

(M) *** EMI 567080-2 (2) [5671592]. Behrens, Bohme, Baltsa, Van Dam, VPO, Karajan

(N) (B) *** Decca 476 7223 (2). Malfitano, Terfel, Riegel, Schwarz, Begley, VPO, Von Dohnányi

(M) **(*) DG (IMS) (ADD) 445 319-2 (2). Jones, Fischer-Dieskau, Dunn, Cassilly, Hamburg State Op. O, Boehm

(N) (BB) (**(*)) Naxos mono 8.111014/5. Goltz, Kenny, Patzak, Dermota, Braun, VPO, Krauss

(M) (*(**)) Decca mono 475 6087 (2). Goltz, Kenny, Patzak, Dermota, Braun, VPO, Krauss

The glory of Sinopoli's DG version is the singing of Cheryl Studer as Salome, producing glorious sounds throughout. Her voice is both rich and finely controlled, with delicately spun pianissimos that chill you the more for their beauty, not least in Salome's attempted seduction of John the Baptist. Sinopoli's reading is often unconventional in its speeds, but it is always positive, thrusting and full of passion, the most opulent account on disc, matched by full, forward recording. As Jokanaan, Bryn Terfel makes a compelling recording début, strong and noble, though the prophet's voice as heard from the cistern sounds far too distant. Among modern sets this makes a clear first choice, though Solti's vintage Decca recording remains the most firmly focused, with the keenest sense of presence, especially in the newly remastered version.

Birgit Nilsson is splendid throughout; she is hard-edged as usual but, on that account, more convincingly wicked: the determination and depravity are latent in the girl's character from the start. Of this score Solti is a master. He has rarely sounded so abandoned in a recorded performance. Waechter makes a clear, young-sounding Jokanaan. Gerhardt Stolze portrays the unbalance of Herod with frightening conviction, and Grace Hoffman does all she can in the comparatively ungrateful part of Herodias. The vivid CD projection makes the final scene, where Salome kisses the head of John the Baptist in delighted horror (*I have kissed thy mouth, Jokanaan!*), all the more spine-tingling, with a close-up effect of the voice whispering almost in one's ear.

With an outstanding cast, the Chandos version, superbly recorded in co-operation with the Danish Broadcasting Corporation, stands out among modern digital versions. Inga Nielsen is a superb Salome, pingingly precise in her vocal attack, with an apt hint of acid in the voice but always firm, with no shrillness. The result is a portrayal with all the strength needed, not least for the unrelenting malevolence at the end, but leaving one with the impression of a character still young. Robert Hale is a characterful and expressive, if at times gruff, Jokanaan, and the Heldentenor, Reiner Goldberg, and the veteran Anja Silja, make an exceptionally strong, well-characterized duo as Herod and Herodias. Smaller roles are also well cast.

Hildegard Behrens is also a triumphantly successful Salome. The sensuous beauty of tone is conveyed ravishingly, but the recording is not always fair to her fine projection of sound, occasionally masking the voice. All the same, the feeling of a live performance has been captured well, and the rest of the cast is of the finest Salzburg standard. In particular José van Dam makes a gloriously noble Jokanaan, and in the early scenes his offstage voice from the cistern at once commands attention. Karajan – as so often in Strauss – is at his most commanding and sympathetic, with the orchestra, more forward than some will like, playing rapturously. This is a performance which, so far from making one recoil from perverted horrors, has one revelling in sensuousness.

Dohnányi's is a clear, sharply focused reading in full ranging sound more refined than any. With the orchestra set further behind the voices than usual in Decca opera recordings, the violence is to a degree underplayed and the chamber quality of the score (intended by Strauss) enhanced. Catherine Malfitano brings out the girlish element in Salome, also bringing out the malevolence. The beat in her voice can be distracting, occasionally turning into a wobble, but she rises superbly to the final scene, with full power and precision. As Jokanaan, Bryn Terfel is even finer than he was for Sinopoli, rich and firm, with the voice of the prophet from the cistern clearly focused. Kenneth Riegel as a neurotic

Herod, Hanna Schwarz as a powerful, sharply dramatic Herodias, and Kim Begley as a ringing Narraboth are all outstanding. The set is reissued as part of Universal's 'Critics' Choice' series as it was chosen for the BBC Radio 3 'Building a Record Library'.

In this violent opera Boehm conducts a powerful, purposeful performance which in its rhythmic drive and spontaneity is most compelling, not least in *Salome's Dance*, which seems a necessary component rather than an inserted showpiece. Gwyneth Jones, though squally at times, is here at her most incisive, and her account of the final scene is chilling, above all when she drains her voice for the moment of pianissimo triumph, having kissed the dead lips of Jokanaan. Fischer-Dieskau characteristically gives a searchingly detailed, totally authoritative performance as John the Baptist: one believes in him as a prophet possessed. With Richard Cassilly as a powerful Herod, the rest of the cast is strong, making this a fair contender among live recordings.

The glory of the Decca set, dating from 1954, is the loving direction from Clemens Krauss, the composer's close friend. The drawback is the unlovely performance of the heroine's music by Christel Goltz, who was a magnetic artist in the opera house but with a voice that took very badly to the microphone. Even so, with Patzak and Dermota in the cast the performance was certainly worth putting on Decca's excellent 'Original Masters' series, especially as all of Krauss's 1950s Decca recordings (courtesy of Testament Records) are now available. The orchestral sound is not especially rich but good enough for its vintage (without the harsh quality which affects some Decca mono recordings from this period) and with the voices well caught and with surprisingly little distortion.

However on Naxos Mark Obert-Thorn has made one of his miraculous transformations of the sound, somehow adding lustre and body to the strings, and without losing vividness of wind and brass detail, giving the whole recording, voices and orchestra alike, added ambient warmth. The set comes with a cued synopsis, costs less than the Decca, and is much preferable. It certainly demonstrates what a great conductor Krauss was.

Salome: Dance of the Seven Veils; Closing Scene. Lieder: *Cäcilie; Ich liebe dich; Morgen; Wiegenlied; Zueignung*

(N) ** Australian DG Eloquence (ADD) 476 2467. Caballé, French Nat. O, Bernstein – BOITO: *Mefistofele: Prologue* **

One of Caballé's earliest and most refreshingly imaginative opera sets was Strauss's *Salome* with Leinsdorf conducting. This version of the final scene, recorded over a decade later (1977) with a very different conductor, has much of the same imagination, the sweet innocent girls still observable next to the blood-thirsty fiend. The Lieder are not quite so recommendable, party because Caballé underlines the expressiveness of works that remain Lieder even with the orchestral accompaniment. Bernstein directs an over-weighted account of the *Dance of the Seven Veils*. The recording is warm and full.

Die schweigsame Frau (complete)

(M) (***) DG mono 445 335-2 (2). Gueden, Wunderlich, Prey, Hotter, VPO, Boehm

**(*) Orfeo C 516 992 (2). Böhme, Mödl, McDaniel, Kusche, Grobe, Grist, Schädle, Loulis, Peter, Proebstl, Bellgardt, Strauch, Horn, Schreiber, Bav. State Ch. and O, Sawallisch

(M) **(*) EMI 5 66033-2 (3). Adam, Scovotti, Burmeister, Trudeliese Schmidt, Dresden State Op. Ch. & State O, Janowski

With a cast that could hardly be bettered, Boehm masterfully relishes the high spirits as well as the classical elegance of this late Strauss opera and, though the acoustic is dry and stage noises are often fearsomely intrusive, the sense of presence on the voices makes it consistently involving. Hans Hotter in his prime makes a wonderfully bluff curmudgeon, pointing every word characterfully. Hilde Gueden – greeted with wild applause on her first entry along with Fritz Wunderlich – is a deliciously minx-ish heroine, using her distinctive golden tone, while the young Wunderlich gives a glorious performance. As the barber who aids the conspiratorial young couple against the old man, Hermann Prey has rarely sounded stronger or more beautiful on disc.

Recorded live at the Bavarian State opera in July 1971, the Orfeo performance consistently demonstrates the mastery of Sawallisch as a Strauss interpreter. The orchestral sound is atmospheric if rather thin, and stage noises are often intrusive, but one can still readily appreciate how perfectly Sawallisch paces this adaptation of Ben Jonson's The Silent Woman to bring out not just the humour and vigour but the beauty of the score. Reri Grist is a charming heroine, with the edge on her bright soprano making her the more compelling as a scold. Kurt Böhme right at the end of his long career sings most characterfully as the old man, Sir Morosus, with the supporting team consistently strong. An enjoyable alternative to Karl Boehm on DG and Marek Janowski on EMI, though only the latter (on three discs, not two) offers the score without cuts. Disappointingly, despite the promise of German, English and French texts, no libretto is provided, only a synopsis.

Janowski conducts an efficient rather than a magical performance, and Theo Adam's strongly characterized rendering of the central role of Dr Morosus is marred by his unsteadiness. Jeanette Scovotti is agile but shrill as the Silent Woman, Aminta. A valuable set of mixed success. The CD transfer brings the usual advantages but underlines the oddities of the recording. The reissue (unlike the previous full-priced set) includes a libretto/booklet with full English translation.

COLLECTIONS

Arias from: (i) Die Aegyptische Helena; (ii) Ariadne auf Naxos; (i) Die Frau ohne Schatten; Guntram; Der Rosenkavalier; Salome. (iii) Lieder: Allerseelen; Freundliche Vision; Schlangende hertzen; Wie Sollten wir geheim
(B) *** RCA 2-CD 74321 88687-2. L. Price with (i) Boston SO or New Philh. O, Leinsdorf; (ii) LSO, Cleva; (iii) Garvey (piano) – PUCCINI: Arias ***

Leontyne Price, always at her finest in Strauss, here gives generous performances of an unusually rich collection of Strauss scenes and arias, strongly accompanied by Leinsdorf (or by Cleva in Ariadne). Recorded between 1965 and 1973, Price was still at her peak, even if occasionally the voice grows raw under stress in Strauss's heavier passages. It is particularly good to have rarities as well as such regular favourites as the Empress's awakening in Die Frau ohne Schatten, one of the finest of all the performances here. The four Lieder make an attractive encore, although no translations are provided, and the documentation is poor.

'Strauss's Heroines': Arabella, Act I: Duet. Capriccio: Moonlight Music and closing scene. Der Rosenkavalier, Act I: closing scene, Act III, Trio and finale
*** Decca 466 314-2. Fleming, Bonney, Graham, VPO, Eschenbach

Under the title 'Strauss's heroines', this ravishing disc offers a generous collection of the most seductive scenes in the Strauss operas. In the end of Act I of Rosenkavalier, Renée Fleming and Susan Graham come near to matching the example of Elisabeth Schwarzkopf and Christa Ludwig as the Marschallin and Octavian. Then, sadly, the Act III Trio has Christoph Eschenbach opting for an absurdly sluggish speed, but the singing is superb, and so it is in the lovely duet between the sisters in Arabella and the magical closing scene of Capriccio, where Fleming is at her most moving. Opulent sound to match.

Arias and scenes from: Ariadne auf Naxos; Capriccio; Die Liebe der Danae; Salome
*** Orfeo C 511991A. Varady, Bamberg SO, Fischer-Dieskau

Recorded just before Julia Varady's retirement in 1999, still at the height of her powers, this wide-ranging collection of excerpts contains some of the most magnificent Strauss singing in years. The wonder is that any soprano can range so wide, while producing the most beautiful, full and even stream of sound, whether in the closing scene of Salome, in Ariadne's monologue and lament, in the heroine's big Act III solo from Die Liebe der Danae or as the Countess in the closing scene of Capriccio. Helped by the understanding conducting of her husband, Dietrich Fischer-Dieskau – who contributes a solitary line of singing as major domo at the end of Capriccio – she sings with consistent fervour. This Salome may not be as sinister as many in kissing the lips of John the Baptist – the sound is too beautiful for that – but the poise as well as the power and the detailed expressiveness are magnetic. Excellent sound to match.

STRAVINSKY, Igor (1882–1971)

The Stravinsky Edition: Vol. 1, Ballets, etc.: (i) The Firebird; (i) Fireworks; (iii) Histoire du soldat; (i) Petrushka; (iv, iii) Renard the Fox; (i) The Rite of Spring; (i) Scherzo à la russe; (ii) Scherzo fantastique; (v) The Wedding (Les Noces) (SM3K 46291) (3)

Vol. 2, Ballets, etc.: (vi) Agon; (i) Apollo; (i) Le Baiser de la fée; (i) Bluebird (pas de deux); (vii) Jeu de cartes; (viii) Orphée; (ix, i) Pulcinella; (ii) Scènes de ballet (SM3K 46292) (3)

Vol. 3, Ballet Suites: (i) Firebird; Petrushka; Pulcinella (SMK 46293)

Vol. 4, Symphonies: (i) Symphony in E; (ii) Symphony in C; (i) Symphony in 3 movements; (x, ii) Symphony of Psalms; (i) Stravinsky in rehearsal: Apollo; Piano Concerto; Pulcinella; Sleeping Beauty; Symphony in C; 3 Souvenirs (SM2K 46294)

Vol. 5, Concertos: (xi, i) Capriccio for Piano & Orchestra (with Robert Craft); Concerto for Piano & Wind; (xii, i) Movements for Piano & Orchestra; (xiii, i) Violin Concerto in D (SMK 46295)

Vol. 6, Miniatures: (i) Circus Polka; Concerto in D for String Orchestra; Concerto for Chamber Orchestra, 'Dumbarton

Oaks'; (ii) *4 Etudes for Orchestra*; (i) *Greeting Prelude*; (ii) *8 Instrumental miniatures*; *4 Norwegian moods*; *Suites 1–2 for Small Orchestra* (SMK 46296)

Vol. 7, Chamber music and historical recordings: (iii) *Concertino for 12 Instruments*; (xiv; xv) *Concerto for 2 solo Pianos*; (xv; xvi) *Duo concertante for Violin & Piano*; (xvii; xviii) *Ebony Concerto (for Clarinet & Big Band)*; (iii) *Octet for Wind*; (xix; iii) *Pastorale for Violin & Wind Quartet*; (xv) *Piano Rag Music*; (xviii) *Preludium*; (xx; iii) *Ragtime* (for 11 instruments); (xv) *Serenade in A*; (iii) *Septet*; (xii) *Sonata for Piano*; (xxi) *Sonata for 2 Pianos*; (xviii) *Tango*; (xxii) *Wind Symphonies* (SM2K 46297)

Vol. 8, Operas and songs: (xxiii; iii) *Cat's cradle songs*; (xxiii; xxiv) *Elegy for J. F. K.*; (xxv; ii) *Faun and shepherdess*; (xxvi; iii) *In memoriam Dylan Thomas*; (xxvii; iii) *3 Japanese Lyrics* (with Robert Craft); (xxvii; xxix) *The owl and the pussycat*; (xxvii; iii) *2 poems by K. Bal'mont*; (xxx; i) *2 poems of Paul Verlaine*; (xxiii; i) *Pribaoutki (peasant songs)*; (xxiii; i) *Recollections of my childhood*; (xxviii; xxxi) *4 Russian songs*; (xxxvii) *4 Russian peasant songs*; (xxiii; iii) *3 songs from William Shakespeare*; (xxvii; i) *Tilim-Bom (3 stories for children)*; (xxxii) *Mavra*; (xxxiii) *The Nightingale* (SM2K 46298)

Vol. 9, (xxxiv) *The Rake's progress* (SM2K 46299)

Vol. 10, Oratorio and Melodrama: (xxxv; i) *The Flood* (with Robert Craft); (i) *Monumentum pro Gesualdo di Venosa (3 madrigals recomposed for instruments)*; (vii) *Ode*; (xxxvi) *Oedipus Rex*; (xxxvii; xxxviii, i) *Perséphone* (SM2K 46300)

Vol. 11, Sacred works: (x) *Anthem (the dove descending breaks the air)*; (x) *Ave Maria*; (xxxix; x, i) *Babel*; (xxviii; xxvi; x, iii) *Cantata*; (xl) *Canticum sacrum*; (x; ii) *Credo*; (x, iii) *Introitus (T. S. Eliot in Memoriam)*; (xli) *Mass*; (x; i) *Pater noster*; (xlii; i) *A Sermon, a narrative & a prayer*; (xliii; i) *Threni*; (x, i) *Chorale: Variations on: Vom Himmel hoch, da komm ich her* (arr.); *Zvezdoliki* (SM2K 46301)

Vol. 12, Robert Craft conducts: (xliv, i) *Abraham and Isaac*; (iii) *Danses concertantes*; (xlv) *Double Canon: Raoul Dufy in memoriam*; (xlvi) *Epitaphium*; (i) *Le Chant du rossignol* (symphonic poem); (i) *Orchestral Variations: Aldous Huxley in memoriam*; (xlvii) *Requiem Canticles*; (i) *Song of the Nightingale* (symphonic poem) (SM2K 46302)

Complete Stravinsky Edition

(B) *** Sony SX22K 46290 (22). (i) Columbia SO; (ii) CBC SO; (iii) Columbia CO; (iv) Shirley, Driscoll, Gramm, Koves; (v) Allen, Sarfaty, Driscoll, Barber, Copland, Foss, Sessions, American Chamber Ch., Hills, Columbia Percussion Ens.; (vi) Los Angeles Festival SO; (vii) Cleveland O; (viii) Chicago SO; (ix) Jordan, Shirley, Gramm; (x) Festival Singers of Toronto, Iseler; (xi) Entremont; (xii) Rosen; (xiii) Stern; (xiv) Soulima Stravinsky; (xv) Igor Stravinsky; (xvi) Szigeti; (xvii) Goodman; (xviii) Columbia Jazz Ens.; (xix) Baker; (xx) Koves; (xxi) Gold, Fizdale; (xxii) N. W. German RSO; (xxiii) Berberian; (xxiv) Howland, Kreiselman, Russo; (xxv) Simmons; (xxvi) Young; (xxvii) Lear; (xxviii) Albert; (xxix) Craft; (xxx) Gramm; (xxxi) Di Tullio, Remsen, Almeida; (xxxii) Belinck, Simmons, Rideout, Kolk; (xxxiii) Driscoll, Grist, Picassi, Smith, Beattie, Gramm, Kolk, Murphy, Kaiser, Bonazzi, Washington, D. C., Op. Society Ch. & O; (xxxiv) Young, Raskin, Reardon, Sarfaty, Miller, Manning, Garrard, Tracey, Tilney, Sadler's Wells Op. Ch., Baker, RPO;

(xxxv) Harvey, Cabot, Lanchester, Reardon, Oliver, Tripp, Robinson, Columbia SO Ch., Smith; (xxxvi) Westbrook (nar.), Shirley, Verrett, Gramm, Reardon, Driscoll, Chester Watson Ch., Washington, D. C., Op. Society O; (xxxvii) Gregg Smith Singers, Smith; (xxxviii) Zorina, Molese, Ithaca College Concert Ch., Fort Worth Texas Boys' Ch.; (xxxix) Calicos (nar.); (xl) Robinson, Chitjian, Los Angeles Festival Ch. & SO; (xli) Baxter, Albert, Gregg Smith Singers, Columbia Symphony Winds & Brass; (xlii) Verrett, Driscoll, Hornton (nar.); (xliii) Beardslee, Krebs, Lewis, Wainner, Morgan, Oliver, Schola Cantorum, Ross; all cond. composer. (xliv) Frisch; (xlv) Baker, Igleman, Schonbach, Neikrug; (xlvi) Anderson, Bonazzi, Bressler, Gramm, Ithaca College Concert Ch., Gregg Smith; cond. Craft

On these 22 bargain-price discs (some volumes are also available separately at mid-price) you have the unique archive of recordings which Stravinsky left of his own music. Presented in a sturdy plastic display box that enhances the desirability of the set, almost all the performances are conducted by the composer, with a few at the very end of his career – like the magnificent *Requiem canticles* – left to Robert Craft to conduct, with the composer supervising. In addition there is a handful of recordings of works otherwise not covered, mainly chamber pieces. With some recordings of Stravinsky talking and in rehearsal (included in the box devoted to the symphonies) it makes a vivid portrait. Currently the separate issues are still available, except for Volume 2 (*Ballet Suites*), Volume 7 (*Chamber Music*), Volume 10 (*Oratorio and Melodrama*) and Volume 12 (*Robert Craft conducts*).

Of the major ballets, *Petrushka* and *The Firebird* are valuable, but *The Rite* is required listening: it has real savagery and astonishing electricity. (It is also available in a separate issue – see below.) The link between *Jeu de cartes* from the mid-1930s and Stravinsky's post-war opera, *The Rake's Progress*, is striking, and Stravinsky's sharp-edged conducting style underlines it, while the *Scènes de ballet* certainly have their attractive moments. If *Orpheus* has a powerful atmosphere, *Apollo* is one of Stravinsky's most gravely beautiful scores, while *Agon* is one of the most stimulating of Stravinsky's later works, and here the orchestra respond with tremendous alertness and enthusiasm to Stravinsky's direction. The recording of *Le Baiser de la fée* is a typical CBS balance with forward woodwind. However the splendid performance overcomes such a technical drawback. Stravinsky's recording of *Pulcinella* includes the vocal numbers, while in the orchestra the clowning of the trombone and the humour generally is strikingly vivid and never too broad. Similarly with the chamber scoring of the suite from *The Soldier's Tale*, the crisp, clear reading brings out the underlying intense emotion of the music with its nagging, insistent little themes. There is a ruthlessness in the composer's own reading of *Les Noces* which exactly matches its primitive Russian feeling, and as the performance goes on so one senses the added alertness and enthusiasm of the performers. *Renard* is a curious work, a sophisticated fable which here receives too unrelenting a performance. The voices are very forward and tend to drown the instrumentalists.

In the early *Symphony in E flat*, Op. 1, the young Stravinsky's material may be comparatively conventional, but in this definitive performance the music springs to life. Each movement has its special delights to outweigh any shortcomings, while in the *Symphony in Three Movements* Stravinsky shows how, by vigorous, forthright treatment of the notes, the emotion implicit is made all the more compelling. The Columbia Symphony plays superbly and the recording is full and brilliant. Stravinsky never quite equalled the intensity of the pre-war 78-r.p.m. performance of the *Symphony of Psalms*, but the later, stereo version is still impressive. It is just that, with so vivid a work, it is a shade disappointing to find Stravinsky as interpreter at less than maximum voltage. Even so, the closing section of the work is very beautiful and compelling. The CD transfers of the American recordings are somewhat monochrome by modern standards but fully acceptable.

The iron-fingered touch of Philippe Entremont has something to be said for it in the *Capriccio for Piano and Wind*, but this performance conveys too little of the music's charm. The *Movements for Piano and Orchestra* with the composer conducting could hardly be more compelling. Stern's memorable account of the *Violin Concerto in D* adds a romantic perspective to the framework. But an expressive approach to Stravinsky works marvellously when the composer is there to provide the bedrock under the expressive cantilena.

The *Dumbarton Oaks Concerto* with its obvious echoes of Bach's *Brandenburgs* is one of the most warmly attractive of Stravinsky's neo-classical works, all beautifully played and acceptably recorded. The *Octet for Wind* of 1924 comes out with surprising freshness and if the *Ragtime* could be more lighthearted, Stravinsky gives the impression of knowing what he wants. The *Ebony Concerto*, in this version conducted by the composer, may have little of 'swung' rhythm, but it is completely faithful to Stravinsky's deadpan approach to jazz.

In *Le Rossignol* the singing is not always on a par with the conducting, but it is always perfectly adequate and the recording is brilliant and immediate. *Mavra* is sung in Russian and, as usual, the soloists – who are good – are too closely balanced, but the performance has punch and authority and on the whole the CD quality is fully acceptable. The songs represent a fascinating collection of trifles, chips from the master's workbench dating from the earliest years. There are many incidental delights, not least those in which the magnetic Cathy Berberian is featured.

The Rake's Progress has never since been surpassed. Alexander Young's assumption of the title-role is a marvellous achievement, sweet-toned, accurate and well characterized. In the choice of other principals, too, it is noticeable what store Stravinsky set by vocal precision. Judith Raskin makes an appealing Anne Trulove, John Reardon is remarkable more for vocal accuracy than for striking characterization, but Regina Sarfaty's Baba is marvellous on both counts. The Sadler's Wells Chorus sings with great drive under the composer, and the Royal Philharmonic play with warmth and a fittingly Mozartian sense of style to match Stravinsky's surprisingly lyrical approach to his score. The CDs offer excellent sound.

The *Cantata* of 1952 is a transitional piece between Stravinsky's tonal and serial periods. However, of the two soloists, Alexander Young is much more impressive than Adrienne Albert, for her voice brings an unformed choirboy sound somehow married to wide vibrato. The *Canticum sacrum* includes music that some listeners might find tough (the strictly serial choral section). But the performance is a fine one and the tenor solo from Richard Robinson is very moving. The Bach *Chorale Variations* has a synthetic modernity that recalls the espresso bar, though one which still reveals underlying mastery. The *Epitaphium* and the *Double canon* are miniatures, dating from the composer's serial

period, but the *Canon* is deliberately euphonious.

The *Mass* is a work of the greatest concentration, a quality that comes out strongly if one plays this performance immediately after *The Flood*, with its inevitably slack passages. As directed in the score, trebles are used here, and it is a pity that the engineers have not brought them further forward: their sweet, clear tone is sometimes lost among the lower strands. In *The Flood*, originally written for television, it is difficult to take the bald narrations seriously, particularly when Laurence Harvey sanctimoniously keeps talking of the will of 'Gud'. The performance of *Oedipus Rex*, too, is not one of the highlights of the set. *Perséphone*, however, is full of that cool lyricism that marks much of Stravinsky's music inspired by classical myths. As with many of these vocal recordings, the balance is too close, and various orchestral solos are highlighted.

Of the items recorded by Robert Craft, the *Requiem canticles* stands out, the one incontrovertible masterpiece among the composer's very last serial works and one of the most deeply moving works ever written in the serial idiom. Even more strikingly than in the *Mass* of 1948, Stravinsky conveys his religious feelings with a searing intensity. The *Aldous Huxley variations* are more difficult to comprehend but have similar intensity. Valuable, too, is the ballad *Abraham and Isaac*. However, as we go to press, volumes 10 and 12 are no longer available separately.

Apollo (Apollon musagète); Le Baiser de la fée (complete ballet & *Divertimento*); (i) *Capriccio for Piano & Orchestra; Concerto for Piano & Wind Instruments. Le Chant du rossignol; Circus Polka; 4 Etudes; The Firebird* (complete ballet); *Petrushka* (1911 version; complete); *Pulcinella* (suite and (ii) complete ballet); *Rite of Spring; Scherzo à la russe; Soldier's Tale* (suite); *Suites 1 & 2; Symphony in C; Symphony in 3 Movements; Symphonies of Wind Instruments;* (iii) *Les Noces* (ballet-cantata); (iv) *Symphony of Psalms;* (v) *Mavra;* (vi) *Renard*

(B) **(*) Decca (ADD) 467 818-2 (8) SRO, Ansermet, with (i) Magaloff; (ii) Tyler, Franzini, Carmeli; (iii) Retchitzka, Devallier, Cuénod, Rehfuss, Diakoff, Geneva Motet Ch. (iv) Choeur des Jeunes & Ch. of R. Lausanne; (v) Carlyle, Watts, Sinclair, Macdonald; (vi) English, Mitchinson, Glossop, Rouleau

Having begun his Stravinsky recordings for Decca during the days of ffrr 78s, Ansermet finally undertook his major survey with the coming of stereo. *Apollon Musagète*, the complete *Firebird* ballet and the two piano concertos – with Nikita Magaloff in fine form – date from as early as 1955, yet the recording still sounds remarkably well, and if in the concertante works Ansermet's direction lacks some of the bite and sharp wit that this neoclassical music needs, they follow an authentic tradition from Parisian music-making between the wars.

The Firebird was highly praised by us for its clarity of detail when it first appeared, although we commented on the lack of body to the upper strings. Undoubtedly Ansermet's later Philharmonia recording (not included here) is finer still, better played and with richer sound, but this remains impressive for its time.

Le Chant du rossignol and the *Pulcinella Ballet Suite* followed in 1956, both showing Ansermet at his interpretative best. The recordings, too, were considered demonstration-worthy in their day, with *The Song of the Nightingale* showing how clearly and beautifully Decca could cope with a big

Stravinsky orchestra, while *Pulcinella* showed even more impressively how a small chamber group of instruments could be projected with vivid realism.

The 1957 *Petrushka* also set high standards of clarity and vividness, although the Swiss violins were not flattered by the close microphones and, fine as it was, Ansermet's performance did not quite match his earlier 78 version (available in a fine Dutton transfer – see below) in dramatic and emotional vividness. It was soon to be upstaged by Dorati's famous Mercury version. *The Rite of Spring*, however, recorded in the same year, was a performance of great integrity. Ansermet's scrupulous insistence on maintaining the score's natural balance brought an awe-inspiring relentlessness and a wild primitive beauty.

In 1960 came the *Symphony in C*, strongly played, and often incisive, but the companion *Symphony in Three Movements* lacks a feeling of strong rhythmic vitality, and is without the fullest impetus. However, the clean stylish account of *The Soldier's Tale*, given (1961) sound of tingling immediacy, is matched by the fine performance of the haunting *Symphonies for Wind Instruments*, where Ansermet's warmth more than compensates for any lack of tautness.

The *Quatre Etudes* (from 1962) have considerable subtlety, and the *Suites* are enjoyable in a spontaneous, extrovert way. Both show the lighter side of Stravinsky, and Ansermet plays them with spirit and style. However, there is something curiously heavy and lethargic about his account of the *Symphony of Psalms*, even though this account is better than the earlier version on 78s. Fortunately the well-projected recording adds sharpness to a reading which might otherwise have sounded flat.

In *Les Noces*, recorded that same year, Ansermet fails to capture the essential bite in Stravinsky's sharply etched portrait of a peasant wedding. The hammered rhythms must sound ruthless and here they are merely tame. This was followed with complete versions of *Le Baiser de la fée* (in 1963), and *Pulcinella* (with vocal numbers) in 1965, neither of which was as successful as the earlier recordings of the *Fairy's Kiss Divertimento* and the *Pulcinella Ballet Suite*, primarily because of moments of slackness and under-par orchestral playing. However, yet again Ansermet's warmth, and the splendidly vivid recording help to project the music in spite of the inadequacies of the playing.

The series culminated in 1964 with *Mavra* and *Renard* (where one enjoys the clear English). Both were a great success, vividly performed and brilliantly recorded. Here more than usual Ansermet caught the sort of toughness one recognizes in the composer's own performances of his music, and the haunting yet light-hearted *Scherzo à la russe*, with its bouncing main theme, is a splendid bonus.

(i) *Apollo (Apollon musagète)* complete ballet
(M) *** DG 463640-2. (i) BPO, Karajan – BARTOK: *Music for Strings, Percussion and Celeste* **(*)

(i) *Apollo;* (ii) *The Firebird; Petrushka* (1911 score); *The Rite of Spring* (complete ballets)
☛ ✪ (B) *** Ph. Duo (ADD) 438 350-2 (2). (i) LSO, Markevitch; (ii) LPO, Haitink

Apollo (Apollon musagète) (1947 version); *Firebird: Suite* (1945 version); *Jeu de cartes; Petrushka* (1947 version); *The Rite of Spring*
(B) **(*) Double Decca 473 731-2 (2). Concg. O, or Cleveland O; Chailly

Apollo; Orpheus (ballets)
*** ASV CDDCA 618. O of St John's, Lubbock

Apollo is a work in which Karajan's moulding of phrase and care for richness of string texture make for wonderful results, especially in the glorious *Pas de deux*. The 1972 recording is of DG's highest quality and in no way sounds its age. It now comes coupled with Bartók's *Music for Strings, Percussion and Celeste* on one of DG's Originals at mid-price.

The ASV issue offers an ideal coupling, with refined performances and excellent recording. The delicacy of the rhythmic pointing in *Apollo* gives special pleasure, and there is a first-rate solo violin contribution from Richard Deakin.

Markevitch's gravely beautiful reading of *Apollon musagète* here comes with Haitink's strikingly refined account of the other key ballets. In *The Firebird* the sheer savagery of *Katschei's Dance* may be a little muted, but the sharpness of attack and clarity of detail make for a thrilling result, while the magic and poetry of the whole score are given a hypnotic beauty. In *Petrushka* the rhythmic feeling is strong, especially in the Second Tableau and the finale, where the fairground bustle is vivid. The natural, unforced quality of Haitink's *Rite* also brings real compulsion. Other versions may hammer the listener more powerfully, thrust him or her along more forcefully; but the bite and precision of the LPO playing here are most impressive, as throughout the set, while the recording's firm definition and the well-proportioned and truthful aural perspective make it a joy to listen to. Outstanding value.

The Double Decca anthology is rather more notable for Decca's demonstration-quality sound than for Chailly's interpretations, but the orchestral playing itself remains outstanding throughout. In this somewhat indulgent reading of *Apollo*, the score's refined neo-classicism is muted in favour of opulent warmth, and some of the ballet's rhythmic profile is lost, especially in the celebrated *Pas de deux*, which is far more voluptuous here than with Karajan. Chailly is more naturally at home revelling in the rich Rimskian colours of the extended 1945 *Firebird Suite*, which includes the delectable *Pantomimes*. The explosive entry of *Katschei* is riveting and the expansive finale could not be more voluptuous.

Jeu de cartes, recorded in 1996, is released here for the first time. The performance is impressive. Chailly's *Petrushka* is vividly characterized, and he brings a genuine pathos to Petrushka's cell scene. The Decca engineers provide glittering detail, yet make full use of the warm Concertgebouw ambience.

This 1985 recording of *The Rite of Spring*, has also been accepted as one of the most spectacular versions of the digital age. With speeds faster than usual – markedly so in Part Two – Chailly's taut and urgent reading is gripping throughout, and bass-drum enthusiasts will find that it plays its part with a precision and resonance to startle the listener. If, with Chailly's urgent pacing in Part Two, there is less contrast than usual in the final *Sacrificial Dance*, there is no doubting the intrinsic power of the reading overall. Moreover, Decca have given it sufficient cueing points for the first time. For audiophiles, this collection is a real Stravinskian bargain: the second CD lasts over 81 minutes.

(i–ii) *Le Baiser de la fée* (ballet; complete); (i; iii) *Ode;* (iv) *Symphonies of Wind Instruments;* (i; ii) *Symphony in E flat, Op. 1;* (i; iii) *Symphony in C; Symphony in 3 Movements*
(B) *** Chan. 2-for-1 ADD/DDD 241-8 (2). (i) RSNO; (ii) Järvi; (iii) Gibson; (iv) Nash Ens., Rattle

(i) *Le Baiser de la fée (divertimento); Le Chant du rossignol;*
(ii) *Dumbarton Oaks Concerto;* (iii) *Petrushka* (1911); *The Rite of Spring*

(B) **(*) RCA 2CD stereo/mono 74321 84609-2. (i) Chicago SO, Reiner; (ii) NDR SO, Wand; (iii) Boston SO, Monteux

(i) *Le Baiser de la fée (Divertimento);* (ii) *Petrushka:* excerpts: *(Danse russe; Chez Petrushka; La Fête populaire);* (i) *Pulcinella* (suite); (ii) *The Rite of Spring* (complete ballet)

(B) (***) EMI mono CZS5 69674-2 (2). (i) French Nat. R. O;
(ii) Philh. O, Markevitch – PROKOFIEV: *Love for 3 Oranges,* etc. (**)

On Chandos Strauss's deft scoring of *Le Baiser de la fée* is a constant delight, much of it on a chamber-music scale; and its delicacy, wit and occasional pungency are fully appreciated by Järvi, who secures a wholly admirable response from his Scottish orchestra. The ambience seems exactly right, bringing out wind and brass colours vividly. As for the symphonies, even when compared with the composer's own versions, the performances by the Royal Scottish National Orchestra – in excellent form under Sir Alexander Gibson – stand up well, with Järvi directing the early *E flat* work equally impressively. The vivid naturalness of the splendid 1982 digital recordings compensates for any slight lack of bite. The cool, almost whimsical beauty of the *Andante* of the *Symphony in Three Movements* is most subtly conveyed, and the inner movements of the *Symphony in C* are beautifully played. Moreover the Nash Ensemble's perceptive account of the *Symphonies of Wind Instruments* under Rattle does not let the side down. It is good to have also as a bonus the *Ode* in memory of Natalia Koussevitzky, which has an extrovert, rustic scherzo section framed by short elegies.

Reiner's Chicago recordings of *Le Baiser de la fée* and *Le Chant du rossignol* are legendary. The latter is praised below, where it is coupled with Rimsky's *Scheherazade;* the equally delightful *Fairy's Kiss Divertiment* has character and life as well as much charm, with the *Pas de deux* beautifully done. The overall performance has great atmosphere, with distinguished woodwind and brass contributions, helped by the astonishingly vivid 1958 Chicago recording.

Wand's hardly less engaging account of the *Dumbarton Oaks Concerto,* played with great geniality and finesse, is also most naturally recorded in an attractive acoustic.

For *Petrushka* and *The Rite of Spring* RCA have turned to Monteux, who conducted the première of the latter. But they have not selected his Paris Conservatoire stereo performances. Instead they have chosen the alternative Boston versions, which are much better played. *The Rite* dates from 1951 and is mono, with a recording which harshens at climaxes. But the performance powerfully captures the wild intensity of the ballet's violent pagan ritual, and, just as tellingly, projects the hauntingly mysterious evocation of the opening of the second part.

The Boston recording of *Petrushka* is stereo and dates from 1959. There is still an edge to the sound at climaxes, but the Boston acoustic adds its ambient glow throughout, and the performance is extremely lively, with memorable solo contributions in the central tableaux and a particularly exciting and dramatic account of the final scene, all the bustle of the Shrovetide carnival brilliantly conveyed.

Markevitch's electrifying 1959 recording of *The Rite of Spring* has long been famous, even though the documentation suggests that it is mono. The Philharmonia playing is superbly exciting, and the conductor's rhythmic vitality and

ruthless thrust are matched by an amazingly spectacular recording which hardly sounds dated even now. In the elegant *Divertimento,* which Stravinsky culled from his Tchaikovskian ballet *Le Baiser de la fée,* the French orchestral playing here has both finesse and flair. The three excerpts from *Petrushka* are similarly lively and colourful, and only *Pulcinella* is slightly disappointing: the trombones blow raspberries in their famous *Vivo* duet with the double basses, and elsewhere Markevitch dilutes the music's charm by his forcefulness. However this is certainly value for money.

(i) *Capriccio for piano and orchestra; Concerto for Piano and Wind Instruments; Movements for piano and orchestra.* **Piano Music:** *Les cinq doigts; 4 Etudes, Op. 7; 3 Movements from Petrushka; Piano-Rag Music; Scherzo; Serenade in A; Sonata for Piano* (1924); *Sonata in F sharp min.; Souvenir d'une marche boche; Tango; Valse pour les enfants*

(N) (B) *** EMI (ADD) 5 86973-2 Michel Béroff; (i) Orchestre de Paris, Ozawa

This classic set comes from the 1970s when Béroff was astonishing the musical world with his dazzling virtuosity and musicianship. Althought most of this repertoire is well represented on disc, this issue remains a highly satisfying and competitive one, still a first choice. The three concertos (or rather the two concertos and a capriccio) are also first rate and well accompanied by Seiji Ozawa and the Orchestre de Paris.

Le Chant du rossignol (Song of the Nightingale): **symphonic poem** (see also under *The Firebird* below)

✿ (M) *** DG (ADD) (IMS) 449 769-2 (2). Berlin RSO, Maazel – RAVEL: *L'heure espagnole; L'enfant et les sortilèges;* RIMSKY-KORSAKOV: *Capriccio espagnol ***

☛ (N) (M) *** RCA SACD (ADD) 82876 66377-2. Chicago SO, Reiner – RIMSKY-KORSAKOV: *Scheherazade *** ✿

Le Chant du rossignol, which Stravinsky made from the material of his opera, deserves a much more established place in the concert repertoire; Maazel's justly famous DG version dates from 1958. Maazel is nothing if not dramatic, but above all he revels in the glittering orchestral detail and the marvellous atmosphere this score commands. The Berlin Radio Orchestra produces a feast of chimerical glowing colours, and the DG engineers of the time surpassed themselves. It is well coupled with Ravel's two delightful neoclassical operas and Maazel's superb Berlin Philharmonic version of Rimsky-Korsakov's *Capriccio espagnol* from the same period.

On its new SACD format Reiner's 1956 *Chant du rossignol* brings astonishingly vivid sound, full of presence, an excellent coupling for his strong and dramatic reading of *Scheherazade.* Where this transitional work – composed over two separate periods – can seem lacking something in thrust, Reiner's virile, sharply focused reading relates it more clearly to the *Rite of Spring.* The virtuosity of the playing and the clarity of the direction are arresting, while the glittering detail of the orchestral palette in the work's five titled (and here cued) closing sections is most evocative.

Le Chant du rossignol; **Complete ballets:** *The Firebird; Petrushka* (1911 version); *The Rite of Spring*

(B) **(*) Delos Double DE 3702 (2). Seattle SO, Schwarz

The Delos Schwarz performances are finely played, and the extremely vivid and well-focused internal detail heard against an attractively resonant acoustic will thrill audiophiles with equipment capable of making the most of the projection and clarity of these first-class digital recordings. *Le Chant du rossignol* and *The Firebird* both glow luminously, but in *Petrushka* one would liked more bite in the articulation, and the picture of the Shrovetide Fair is a broad canvas rather than a sharply dramatic sequence of events. *The Rite of Spring* could not be more different from the Mehta version, except that the drums make a fine impact. But it is not ferocious, yet gathers tension as it proceeds, and the great horn entry in the *Ancestors' Ritual* is splendidly bold, leading to an exciting concluding *Sacrifice*.

(i) *Le Chant du rossignol;* (ii) *Pulcinella* (ballet; complete)
(N) (BB) **(*) Warner Apex 2564 62088-2.(i) French Nat. O;
(ii) Murray, Rolfe Johnson, Estes, Ens. InterContemporain;
Boulez

Boulez's Erato performance of *Le chant du rossignol* is impressively atmospheric if a little cool. The French National Orchestra captures detail vividly and have the advantage of a fine (1982) recording. Boulez also gets some superb playing from the Ensemble InterContemporain, and his singers are first class in every way. His is a keen performance too, although at times he sems personally uninvolved. His pacing is more extreme than some, with contrasts between movements almost overcharacterized. However, some will like the periodic added edge, and again the recording has been excellently transferred to CD.

(i) *Concerto for Piano and Wind; Fireworks*
*** Arthaus **DVD** 100 314. (i) Toradze; Rotterdam PO,
Gergiev (with DEBUSSY – *Le Martyre de Saint-Sébastien* ***)
(Director: Rob van der Berg. V/D: Peter Rump) –
PROKOFIEV: *Scythian Suite, Op. 20* (with Rehearsal) ***
❂

Alexander Toradze is as impressive an exponent of Stravinsky as he was of the Prokofiev concertos he recorded with Gergiev and the Kirov Orchestra for Philips, and while the main interest of this DVD is the Prokofiev coupling, this well-planned concert is very rewarding throughout and stimulating to watch.

Concerto for Piano & Wind
(***) British Music Society mono BMS 101 CDH.
Mewton-Wood, Hague Residentie O, Goehr – BLISS:
Concerto *** ❂; SHOSTAKOVICH: *Piano Concerto 1* (***)

Edward Sackville-West placed this record as one of two recordings that serve as the 'best memorial of his [Mewton-Wood's] style', and certainly the partnership here with Walter Goehr is very impressive indeed. It is the central *Largo* one especially remembers, wonderfully cool and beautiful, immediately offset by the brilliance of the finale. In reviewing the original LP in *Gramophone* Lionel Salter wrote: 'Clarity and balance of forces here are exemplary; but what takes one's breath away is the uncanny and faultless accuracy in this very taxing work.' The recording of the piano is very good, and the orchestra has more body than in the Bliss coupling.

Concerto for Strings in D
(M) *** DG (ADD) 447 435-2. BPO, Karajan – HONEGGER:
Symphonies 2–3 *** ❂

Karajan's version of the *Concerto in D for Strings* – written within a few months of the Honegger *Symphonie Liturgique*, with which it is coupled – may strike some listeners as not quite acerbic or biting enough, but the finesse and lightness

of touch of the Berlin strings and their rhythmic legerdemain are a delight. The recording is first class.

(i) *Concerto in D for Strings; Danses concertantes; Dumbarton Oaks Concerto in E flat; 4 Etudes;* (ii) *4 Norwegian Moods;* (iii) *Orchestral Suites 1–2.* Chamber music: (iv) *Concertino for 12 instruments; Epitaphium; L'Histoire du soldat* (suite for violin, clarinet and piano); *Octet; Ragtime; Pastorale; 3 Pieces for Solo Clarinet; Septet;*
(v) *Concerto for 2 Pianos*
☛ ❂ (B) *** Double Decca (DDD/ADD) 473 810-2 (2). (i) Montreal SO, Dutoit; (ii) Cleveland O, Chailly; (iii) SRO, Ansermet; (iv) European Soloists Ens., Ashkenazy; (v) Ashkenazy & Gavrilov

Here is a unique and imaginative package of off-beat Stravinsky, expertly compiled by Raymond McGill of Universal Records, that will give great pleasure. Apart from the two *Suites for Orchestra*, which Ansermet recorded in 1961, these performances come from various times between 1987 and 1996, and apart from their musical excellence, are superbly recorded. Of particular value is the *Concerto for Two Pianos*, written in the early 1930s, with Ashkenazy and Gavrilov. The European Soloists are a first-class group who give wonderfully alert and vital accounts of the *Octet* and the *Concertino for Twelve Instruments*. Dutoit and his Montreal players are on very good form, too, in the *Dumbarton Oaks Concerto* and the *Danse concertantes*. In every respect this collection cannot be recommended too highly.

(i) *Concerto for Strings in D; Dumbarton Oaks Concerto for Chamber Orchestra;* (ii) *Violin Concerto;* (iii) *Petrushka* (ballet; 1911 version); (iv) *Pulcinella* (ballet; complete)
(B) **(*) Artemis Vanguard (ADD/DDD) ATM-CD 1515 (2). (i) Zurich CO, with Wind of Zurich Tonhalle O, Edmond de Stoutz; (ii) Spivakovsky, Utah SO, Abravanel; LSO, Mackerras; (iv) (iii) Cullen, Edmunds, Dickson, Australian CO, Lyndon-Gee

The *Dumbarton Oaks Concerto*, scored for wind as well as strings, was written in 1938, the year Stravinsky settled in America, and the *String Concerto* in 1946. Both are among the composer's most light-hearted works, and the highly original scoring of the former is a constant delight. Indeed Stravinsky himself has admitted that the Bach *Brandenburgs* were his starting point. These Zurich performances could hardly be bettered: polished, warm, and with neat touches of irony. The early 1960s recording too is excellent. Christopher Lyndon-Gee has already given us an outstanding version of Respighi's *Ancient Airs and Dances*, and his account of *Pulcinella* is affectionately detailed and well played by the Australian Chamber Orchestra. He has good soloists, even if they are not individually distinctive, and with warmly atmospheric, digital recording made (in 1987) in the Concert Hall of Sydney Opera House, this is very enjoyable, if not as dramatically characterized as Abbado's version.

Spivakovsky's performance of the *Violin Concerto*, however, is less appealing, brilliantly efficient but lacking charm, with the soloist's rather literal approach emphasized in the recording by his forward projection. Mackerras's lively *Petrushka* is also available separately on a Vanguard SACD (see below); but the CD version is hardly less telling; despite the backward balance and lack of sharp inner detail, the performance still makes a good impact.

Violin Concerto in D

⊶ (M) *** Decca (ADD) 425 003-2. Chung, LSO, Previn – PROKOFIEV: *Concertos 1–2* ***

(M) *** Sony SMK 89983. Lin, LAPO, Salonen – PROKOFIEV: *Violin Concertos 1–2* *** **◎**

(M) *** Warner Elatus 2564 6572-2. Perlman, Chicago SO, Barenboim – PROKOFIEV: *Violin Concerto 2* ***

(N) (M) *** DG 477 5376. Mutter, Philh., Paul Sacher – BARTOK: *Violin Concerto 2* **(*); DUTILLEUX: *Sur le même accord* ***

(M) *** DG (ADD) 463 666-2. Schneiderhan, Czech PO, Ančerl – SHOSTAKOVICH: *Symphony 10 in E min., Op. 93* (***)

(M) *** DG (ADD) 447 445-2. Perlman, Boston SO, Ozawa – BERG: *Concerto*; RAVEL: *Tzigane* ***

*** Sony SK 89649. Hahn, ASMF, Marriner – BRAHMS: *Violin Concerto* ***

Kyung Wha Chung is at her most incisive in the spicily swaggering outer movements which, with Previn's help, are presented here in all their distinctiveness; tough and witty at the same time. In the two movements labelled *Aria*, Chung brings fantasy as well as lyricism, less overtly expressive than Perlman but conveying instead an inner, brooding quality. Brilliant Decca recording, the soloist diamond-bright in presense but with plenty of orchestral atmosphere.

As in the two Prokofiev concertos, so in the Stravinsky Cho-Liang Lin plays with power and warmth, while Salonen terraces the accompaniment dramatically, with woodwind and brass bold and full. The Prokofiev coupling is outstanding.

Though Perlman's coupling of the Stravinsky *Concerto* and Prokofiev No. 2 on Warner Elatus is most ungenerous, this performance, recorded live in 1994, is more compelling than his earlier studio recording, with Barenboim adding to the urgency and energy. Far more Stravinskian wit is conveyed in the outer movements, with rhythms more bouncy and with phrasing more seductively individual. In the two slow inner movements, Arias I and II, Perlman opts for speeds marginally more flowing, with Aria II more inward than before, more reflective even at a faster speed.

DG restore Anne-Sophie Mutter's brilliant 1988 account of the Stravinsky and her 1991 Bartók to circulation, coupling it with a new work by Dutilleux. The Stravinsky was originally coupled with Lutoslawski, and the recording is spacious and well focused with Ms Mutter not too prominently placed in the aural picture. A very good performance and recommended alongside though not necessarily in preference to Kyung-Wha Chung (also coupled with Bartók), Cho-Liang Lin (coupled with the Prokofiev concertos) and Perlman.

Schneiderhan is just the man to bring out the work's neo-classicism and his sprightly playing in the outer movement is contrasted with a touch of restraint in the cantilena of the central *Arias*, which are nevertheless shaped most sensitively. The performance, dating from 1962, projects splendidly in this new Originals transfer, which is both warm and full, and the excellent support the soloist receives from Ančerl in an important factor. The coupling – the main work on this CD – is quite superb.

Perlman's precision, remarkable in both concertos on the DG disc, underlines the neo-classical element in the outer movements of the Stravinsky, while the two *Aria* movements are more deeply felt and expressive. The balance favours the soloist, but no one will miss the commitment of the Boston orchestra's playing, vividly recorded. The Ravel *Tzigane* has now been added for good measure.

The opening of Hilary Hahn's reading of the Stravinsky *Concerto* is the more striking in its power because of the close balance of the violin, intensifying the impact of the very fast tempo she adopts. Her playing is phenomenal in its precision, but anyone used to more conventional readings such as Mullova's or, in particular, Chung's, will find it sounding very hectic, rather lacking in the rhythmic bounce which can so readily warm this neoclassical writing. Hahn's reading of the finale brings a similarly urgent speed, again intensifying the power of the work, but with little of its geniality conveyed. It is certainly a valid view, but will not please everyone used to other readings. Hahn, needless to say, in the two arias brings out the full meditative depth of the music. The result is to underline the toughness of the work, making it more clearly an apt coupling for the epic Brahms *Concerto*, plainly as she intends.

(i) Dumbarton Oaks Concerto; (ii) The Firebird (suite; 1919); (iii) Petrushka; (iv) Pulcinella (suite); (v) The Rite of Spring; Circus Polka; (vi) Symphony of Psalms

(B) *** DG Panorama (ADD) 469 205-2 (2). (i) InterContemporain Ens., Boulez; (ii) Berlin RSO, Maazel; (iii) LSO, Dutoit; (iv) ASMF, Marriner; (v) BPO, Karajan; (vi) Russian State Ch. & O, Markevitch

This set begins with Maazel's glittering *Firebird Suite* – one of the finest versions ever – then goes on to Karajan's smoothly powerful *Rite*, and Markevitch's vibrant if somewhat rough and ready account of the *Symphony of Psalms* (with plenty of Russian wobble in the brass). Dutoit's *Petrushka* is splendidly alive and atmospheric, and Marriner's superbly etched *Pulcinella* suite (originally on Argo), sounds as fresh as paint. This is of the very best compilations in the not always well-chosen Panorama series.

Dumbarton Oaks Concerto; 8 Instrumental Miniatures; (i) Ebony Concerto

(M) *** DG (ADD) 447 405-2. (i) Arrignon; Ens. InterContemporain, Boulez – BERG: *Chamber Concerto* ***

The playing of the Ensemble InterContemporain is very brilliant indeed. There is much to enjoy in these performances, which are spiced with the right kind of wit and keenness of edge, and even those who do not normally respond to Boulez's conducting will be pleasantly surprised with the results he obtains here.

Complete ballets: (i) The Firebird; (ii) Orpheus; (i) Petrushka (1947 version); The Rite of Spring

(M) **(*) Ph. 464 744-2 (2) (i) Concg. O; (ii) LSO, C. Davis

An outstanding set. Sir Colin Davis directs a magically evocative account of the complete *Firebird*, helped not just by the playing of the Concertgebouw Orchestra (the strings outstandingly fine) but by the ambience of the hall, which allows inner clarity yet gives a bloom to the sound, open and spacious, superbly co-ordinated. Similarly the Philips recording of *Petrushka* (although not so well balanced as *Firebird*) reveals details of the rich texture that are often obscured. Again Davis draws brilliant playing from the orchestra, rarely if ever forcing the pace, though always maintaining the necessary excitement. The piano starts a little cautiously in the *Russian Dance* but that is an exception in an unusually positive reading.

Davis also has his idiosyncrasies in *The Rite of Spring* (one of them his strange hold-up on the last chord), but generally he takes a direct view and the result is strong, forthright and powerful. *Orpheus* is much less frequently heard. It is a post-war ballet, written in 1974, and its mellow classical lines mark a return to the manner of *Orpheus*. But the material is never quite so memorable, or for that matter so varied, and even Davis's excellent account cannot create a richness of colour to match its companions. The recording is warm and very natural, if not so lustrous at those made in the Concertgebouw, but that is partly the effect of the composer's scoring.

(i) *The Firebird* (ballet; complete. Choreography: Mikhail Fokine.); (ii) *Les Noces* (Choreography: Bronislava Nijinska.)

⊶ ❀ *** Opus Arte **DVD** OA 0832 D. (i) Benjamin, Cope, Rosato, Drew; (ii) Yanowsky, Pickering and members of Royal Ballet; ROHCG O, or 4 Pianos, cond. Carewe. (V/D: Ross MacGibbon.)

A moving and well-directed visual record, totally free from attention-seeking camerawork, brings these two marvellous ballets in their original choreography back to life, as if one had the privilege of visiting Diaghilev's Ballets Russes. The dancing is of the highest standard, led by Leanne Benjamin's Firebird, and costumes and sets are visually equally memorable. There are two important bonuses, in addition to the rehearsal footage. Those who have treasured their TV recordings of Stravinsky's own appearance with the New Philharmonia Orchestra at the Royal Festival Hall in 1965 when he was eighty-three will cherish the DVD transfer, which has much-enhanced definition, both visually and aurally. Finally there is a hilarious description by David Drew of Nijinska's visit to Covent Garden to mount *Les noces* in the late 1960s.

(i) *The Firebird*; (ii) *Pulcinella* (complete ballets)

** Arthaus **DVD** 100 130 (i) Hønningen, Jeppesen, Damsgaard, Royal Danish Ballet; Royal Danish O, Jørgensen, Glen Tetley, Choreography, Dir.: Grimm. (ii) Scapino Ballet, NOS choreography, Christe, Berganza, Davies, Shirley-Quirk, LSO, Abbado. Dir.: Hullscher

The performance of *Firebird* comes from a production mounted in Copenhagen in 1982, the centenary of Stravinsky's birthday, with choreography by Glen Tetley. The principals and in particular the Firebird of Mette Hønningen are excellent, as are the *corps de ballet* and the excellent Royal Danish Orchestra under Poul Jørgensen give a good account of the score. Glen Tetley's choreography will interest his many admirers and is undoubtedly inventive. Others may find it wanting in atmosphere and the fact that the Firebird herself is on stage at the very beginning makes a nonsense of her entry. The *Pulcinella* comes from a 1988 Dutch TV broadcast which uses Abbado's commercial record with the LSO and not live musicians. All the same this is colourful and entertaining, and offers some fine dancing from the company. Nils Christe worked for many years with the celebrated Nederlands Dans Theater before becoming a director of the Scapino Ballet of Rotterdam. Of the two, he comes closer to the spirit of the score. As far as *Firebird* is concerned, Arthaus has announced (as we go to press) that they are releasing the Royal Ballet's version coupled with *Les noces* with Nijinska's original choreography, together with attractive bonuses: Stravinsky himself conducting the *Firebird Suite* with the BBC Symphony Orchestra at the Festival Hall and rehearsal material from the Royal Ballet.

The Firebird (complete ballet)

*** TDK **DVD** DV-VPOVG. VPO, Gergiev (includes Gergiev talking on Prokofiev and Stravinsky). Director and V/D: Brian Large – PROKOFIEV: *Symphony 1 (Classical), Op. 25*; SCHNITTKE: *Viola Concerto* ***

This is, of course, not the performed ballet as above, but an orchestral performance of Stravinsky's glittering score, filmed at the Salzburg Festival in 2000. Gergiev has an excellent rapport with his players and the performance is most impressive, both musically and, thanks to an excellent balance, aurally. The complete score is recorded here, and if there are times when one feels Gergiev could give his players just a little more time (the *Dance of the Princesses*), this is still a very fine reading, with superb playing from the Viennese. The performance is enhanced by the visual direction which, as so often with Brian Large, directs the listener's eyes where his ears want them to be. The sound itself is extremely vivid.

The Firebird (complete ballet)

*** Ph. 446 715-2. Kirov O, Gergiev – SCRIABIN: *Prometheus* ***

(N) **(*) Australian Decca Eloquence 476 2700. VPO, Dohnányi – BARTOK: *Two Portraits, Op. 5* ***

The Firebird (complete ballet); *Le Chant du Rossignol; Fireworks; Scherzo à la russe; Tango*

❀ (N) (M) *** Mercury **SACD** (ADD) 470 643-2. LSO, Dorati

Dorati's electrifying 1959 recording of *The Firebird* is perhaps Dorati's finest recording, and one of the great recordings of all time. It sounds as fresh and as vivid as the day it was made; the brilliantly transparent detail and enormous impact suggest state of the art modern sound, rather than something which in the not too distant future will be 50 years old! Only the sound of the massed upper strings reveals the age of the original master, although this does not spoil the ravishing final climax: the bite of the brass and the transient edge of the percussion are thrilling. The performance sounds completely spontaneous and the LSO wind playing is especially sensitive. The recording of Stravinsly's glittering symphonic poem *The Song of the Nightingale* is hardly less compelling – urgent and finely pointed – and the shorter piece come up in a blaze of colour and energy, especially on SACD, but even on CD equipment the sound is amazing by any standards.

The complete *Firebird* (on Philips) played by Russian artists has, as one might expect, a strong sense both of atmosphere and theatre, and Valery Gergiev manages the transitions between sections, dramatic characterization and contrasts with consummate mastery. The orchestra play with effortless virtuosity and are recorded with remarkable realism and definition. Although it is difficult to speak of a first choice in so hotly contested a field, Gergiev's would also be a viable contender alongside Dorati. The coupling, Scriabin's *Prometheus*, can hold its own alongside most rivals.

For a score as magical as *The Firebird* a recording can be too clear, and the digital sound in Dohnányi's version tends to be too analytical. Separating the threads in a way which prevents the music from making its full evocative effect. That said, there are many good things in this performance, and those who enjoy sound for sound's sake will like it for that reason, for it is indeed impressive, and it is good to have it available again.

The Firebird (complete); *4 Etudes; Petrushka* (1947 version; complete); *Scherzo à la russe* (2 versions: for jazz band; for orchestra); *Symphony in 3 Movements*
(BB) **(*) EMI Gemini 5 85538-2 (2). CBSO, Rattle

Strong, clean and well played, Rattle's CBSO version of *The Firebird* is forthright and positive rather than atmospheric, looking forward to the *Rite of Spring* rather than back to Russian nationalism. So the lovely melody of Khorovod, the *Round Dance of the Princesses*, has a plain, folk-like quality, and *Katshchei's Dance*, firmly controlled, is straightforward and direct, not as fiercely exciting as it can be. The recording is warm and full, but this is not one of Rattle's most inspired recordings. His reading of *Petrushka* brings out the sturdy jollity of the ballet, contrasting it with the poignancy of the puppet's own feelings. The full and brilliant recording here is beefy in the middle and bass, and Rattle and his players benefit in clarity by their use of the 1947 scoring, finely detailed to bring out many points that are normally obscured. In the *Symphony in Three Movements*, done with comparable power, colour and robustness, Rattle brings out the syncopations and pop references with great panache. The two versions of the *Scherzo à la russe* then make a fascinating comparison – both given with Rattle's usual flair, infectiously bouncy. The *Four Studies* provide another light-hearted makeweight.

The Firebird; Petrushka (1947) (complete ballets)
(N) (BB) *** Naxos 8.557500 Philh. O, Craft

Vividly recorded and played with fire and warmth by the Philharmonia, Robert Craft's generous coupling of the complete *Firebird* and *Petrushka* ballets makes an outstanding bargain on the Naxos label. The clarity of sound brings out the extra transparency of *Petrushka* in the revised 1947 scoring, with well-sprung rhythms in the dance movements, and with the *Russian Dance* biting in its impact. The complete *Firebird* of 1910 is advertised as the first recording of the original version, but the differences with the usual 1910 score amount to no more than the inclusion of two long valveless trumpets on stage playing a single note in places. Nonetheless, Craft inspires a taut performance which holds the structure together, while bringing out the atmospheric beauty of this warmest of Stravinsky's scores, as in the *Khorovod* or Round Dance where the Philharmonia brass is vividly caught, not least the horn solo in the final apotheosis, while *Katshchei's Infernal Dance* has all the bite and weight you need. Helpfully, there are copious tracks to help identify the narrative, 22 in *Firebird* and 17 in *Petrushka*.

The Firebird (complete: ballet); *Symphonies of Wind Instruments*
(M) *** Virgin 5 61848-2. LSO, Nagano

Kent Nagano's vividly detailed LSO recording of the original Stravinsky *Firebird* score was produced by Andrew Keener and recorded at Abbey Road in 1991/2. We missed it on its original appearance but the mid-priced reissue must go to the very top of the recommended list. From the very opening the brilliantly detailed kaleidoscope of orchestral colour reminds the listener of Dorati's famous Mercury record, but the new Virgin sound balance (engineered by Mark Vigars) is even more realistic, slightly softer-grained in its etching, warmer, more lustrous. At the opening the intensity of the LSO playing is slightly less tangible than with Dorati, but the concentration steadily increases and the orchestral colour glows. Katshchei's venomous *Danse infernale* contrasts with

the glowing *Princesses' Round Dance* and the *Berceuse;* all are superbly played. The final climax expands gloriously, yet has plenty of bite. The original 1920 score of the *Symphonies of Wind Instruments* makes a diverting coupling, with sonorities and textures keenly balanced.

(i) *The Firebird* (complete); (ii) *The Rite of Spring* (complete)
●—● ✿ (M) *** Sony SMK 89875. Columbia SO, composer
(B) *** Decca Penguin (ADD) 460 644-2. Detroit SO, Dorati

Stravinsky's own (1961) version of *Firebird* is of far more than documentary interest, when the composer so tellingly relates it to his later work, refusing to treat it as merely atmospheric. What he brings out more than others is the element of grotesque fantasy, the quality he was about to develop in *Petrushka*, while the tense violence with which he presents such a passage as *Katshchei's Dance* clearly looks forward to *The Rite of Spring*. That said, he encourages warmly expressive rubato to a surprising degree, with the line of the music always held firm. But the revelatory performance here is *The Rite of Spring*, for Stravinsky's own (1960) reading has never been surpassed as an interpretation of this seminal twentieth-century score. Over and over again, one finds passages which in the balancing and pacing (generally fast) give extra thrust and resilience, as well as extra light and shade. The digital transfer may be on the bright side, but brass and percussion have thrilling impact, sharply terraced and positioned in the stereo spectrum. This is a CD that should be in every basic collection.

Dorati's Detroit version of *The Firebird* has the benefit of spectacular digital recording. The clarity and definition of dark, hushed passages are amazing, with the contra-bassoon finely focused, never sounding woolly or obscure, while string tremolos down to the merest whisper are uncannily precise. The performance is very precise, too; though Dorati's reading has changed little from his previous versions with London orchestras, there is just a little more caution. Individual solos are not so characterful and *Katshchei's Dance* lacks just a degree in excitement; but overall this is a strong and beautiful reading, even if the Mercury LP account is not entirely superseded.

Similarly, in terms of recorded sound, Dorati's *Rite* with the Detroit orchestra scores over almost all its rivals. This has stunning clarity and presence, exceptionally lifelike and vivid sound, and the denser textures emerge more cleanly than ever before. It is a very good performance too, almost but not quite in the same league as those of Karajan and Muti, generating plenty of excitement. The only let-down is the final *Sacrificial Dance*, which needs greater abandon and higher voltage. Yet too much should not be made of this. The performance is so vivid that it belongs among the very best. Its release on Penguin Classics makes it an undoubted bargain. The personal essay is by Philip Hensher.

The Firebird: Suite (1919 version)
*** DG (IMS) 437 818-2. O de l'Opéra Bastille, Chung – RIMSKY-KORSAKOV: *Scheherazade* ***
(*) Sony (ADD) **SACD SS 89415. Cleveland O, Szell – MAHLER: *Symphony 10: Adagio; Purgatorio;* WALTON: *Partita* ***

Myung-Whun Chung gets very musical results from his players and there are many imaginative touches. The sound has great warmth and richness, but the perspective is absolutely right too.

Szell's 1961 *Firebird Suite* first appeared in the UK on the EMI Columbia label. It was celebrated at the time for its vividness and strength of character, and it is certainly superbly played. The opening immediately brings atmospheric tension, and from the *Ronde des Princesses* onwards there is all the colour and warmth you could want, while the finale, with superb brass playing, is riveting.

Ballets: The Firebird (suite; 1919 version); *Jeu de cartes; Petrushka* (1911 version); (i) *Pulcinella* (1947 version); *The Rite of Spring*
(B) *** DG Double (ADD) 453 085-2 (2). LSO, Abbado; (i) with Berganza, R. Davies, Shirley-Quirk

The highlight on this DG Double is *Petrushka*, while both the *Firebird Suite* and *Jeux de cartes* are given stunning performances. The LSO plays with superb virtuosity and spirit. The neoclassical score of *Pulcinella* is given a surprisingly high-powered reading, and not just the playing but the singers too are outstandingly fine. Abbado's feeling for atmosphere and colour is everywhere in evidence, heard against an excellently judged perspective. There is a degree of detachment in Abbado's reading of *The Rite of Spring*, although his observance of markings is meticulous and the orchestra obviously revels in the security given by the conductor's direction.

The Firebird: Suite (1919 version); *Petrushka* (1947 version; complete); *Scherzo à la Russe*
🔾➤ *** Telarc CD 80587. Cincinnati SO, P. Järvi

Paavo Järvi's new Telarc coupling of the *Firebird Suite* and *Petrushka* is outstanding in every way, with the Cincinnati orchestral playing superb throughout. In the *Firebird* the glowingly translucent Rimskian colouring is richly conveyed, while the ferocious entry of Katshchei and the *Infernal Dance* which follows is hugely arresting. The finale expands gloriously, with the bass drum which introduced Katshchei thrillingly underlining the climactic chords. In its vividness, *Petrushka* has much in common with Ansermet's early recordings. Of course Ansermet used the original (1911) score, and Järvi the 1947 version. But Järvi, like Ansermet, relishes every detail of Stravinsky's sparkling orchestral palette, while the natural concert-hall balance within the superb acoustics of Cincinnati's Music Hall adds extra ambient warmth and atmosphere, yet still achieves remarkable woodwind (and trumpet) detail and a rich patina to the strings. The important piano roulades too, brilliantly played by Michael Chertock, glitter cheekily. Järvi's reading certainly does not lack histrionic qualities, yet it has added pathos, particularly in the scene in the Moor's Room; and at the very end of the ballet Järvi chooses a distanced effect for the appearance of Petrushka's ghost, to create a haunting atmosphere of melancholy. The robust and jolly (1945) *Scherzo à la Russe*, following after *Petrushka*, echoes the ballet in more than one respect. The Telarc recording, balanced by Jack Renner, offers demonstration sound which can be enjoyed for its natural perspective as well as for its impressive amplitude and range of dynamic.

(i) *The Firebird* (suite; 1919 score); (ii) *The Rite of Spring*
(N) (B) **(*) Sony (ADD) 516240 [SK 93076]. (i) NYPO, (ii) LSO; Bernstein (with PROKOFIEV: *Scythian Suite* (*))

Bernstein's *Rite* (1972) was recorded with quadraphonic 'surround sound' in mind. Although it does not have the pin-point precision of some other versions, the electric intensity is never in doubt. Bernstein is more consciously romantic in

expressiveness than is common, but conveys the illusion of a live performance – it was this recording which convinced him of the advantages of recording live from then on. It still makes an impact on CD, but is not in the demonstration bracket. The *Firebird Suite* (1957) is in most ways better recorded: more open, better defined and with rather greater depth. It is an exciting, beautifully played performance but lacks something in atmosphere. Prokofiev's *Scythian Suite*, which comes as a bonus, is a splendidly savage account of his vivid score, let down by strident recording. However, the Stravinsky ballets show Bernstein at his most charismatic.

(i) *Les Noces;* (ii) *Oedipus Rex*
(N) (BB) **(*) Naxos 8.557499. (i) Wells, Bickley, Ewing, International Piano Qt, Tristan Fry Percussion Ens.; (ii) Lane, Cornwell, Wilson Johnson, Greenan, Fox (speaker); (i; ii) Simon Joly Ch., Philh. O, Craft

This first issue in the Robert Craft collection to be issued on Naxos provides an exceptionally generous coupling of two of Stravinsky's supreme masterpieces in excellent versions superbly recorded. Craft, the composer's amanuensis in his later years, began conducting as a loyal helper of Stravinsky, but here he reveals himself as much more, an inspired interpreter who can reveal the fire and freshness of these two works, in performances of high voltage superbly recorded. The distinctive timbre of *Les Noces* with its four pianos and percussion is vividly caught, and the Western singers capture the Russian idiom well with a rustic tinge. *Oedipus Rex* is just as powerfully projected with Edward Fox as narrator in English and Martyn Hill in the title role dramatic if under strain at times, as is Jennifer Lane as Jocasta. But Colin Davis's vintage Sadler's Wells version on CfP, though not so generously coupled is in almost every way superior (see below).

Petrushka (1911 score; complete)
(***) Testament mono SBT 1139. Philh. O, Stokowski – RIMSKY-KORSAKOV: *Scheherazade* **
(M) (***) Somm mono SOMMCD 027. SRO, Ansermet – ROSSINI: *La boutique fantasque* *** ●
(M) (***) RCA mono 09026 63303-2. Boston SO, Monteux – FRANCK: *Symphony in D min.* *** ●

(i) *Petrushka* (ballet; complete, 1911 version); (ii) *The Firebird* (arr. for piano by Agosti): excerpts: *Katshchei's Infernal Dance; Berceuse; Finale*
(M) ** Artemis Vanguard **SACD** ATM CD 1505. (i) LSO, Mackerras; (ii) Robin McCabe

Mackerras's *Petrushka* was an eight-track recording, made in Watford Town Hall in 1973, but the original LP brought an unnatural balance which Tracy Martinson's SACD remastering is unable to improve very greatly. The backward strings now have more bite, but the violins still sound thin, and although the hall's warm resonance is ambiently full, inner detail is not really sharp enough for this brilliant score. The performance is confident in manner, and fully alive, but the playing lacks the last degree of precision and drama. The CD version (see above) if anything has a brighter image and comes with a much more lavish programme on a Vanguard Double. The present coupling of Robin McCabe's performance of three key movements from the *Firebird* ballet suite in Guido Agosti's ingenious piano transcription is ungenerous, and again is not helped by an over-resonant acoustic.

Stokowski's *Petrushka* with the Philharmonia Orchestra is

also superb. The orchestral playing is exciting and full of colour. It is almost as impressive as his famous pre-war set with the Philadelphia Orchestra – and that is saying something. It is coupled, however, with a somewhat idiosyncratic *Scheherazade*.

In November 1949, when Ansermet's ffrr Decca recording of *Petrushka* was made, the Suisse Romande Orchestra was in better shape than when he made his stereo Stravinsky discs in the later 1950s. Overall the performance, besides being better played, is more gutsy than Ansermet's later stereo version. Its strikingly vivid quality and sense of the dramatic is brought about by everything being sharply focused in strong primary colours, a tribute to the engineering as well as the performance, and it is only the inherent thinness in the upper range of the violins that gives cause for complaint.

As he conducted the ballet's première, it is good to have Monteux's 1931 Boston recording at last satisfactorily remastered, with the sound now vivid and the Boston ambience more of an advantage than a drawback. The performance has undoubted flair and is very well played.

Petrushka (1911 score; complete); *The Rite of Spring* (complete ballets)

(N) (B) (***) Sanctuary Living Era AJC 8554. SRO, Ansermet

(BB) ** RCA 74321 68020-2. RPO, Temirkanov

Older readers re-encountering Ansermet's famous pioneering 1949 version of *Petrushka* in this very faithful transfer will share our astonishment at the way this extraordinarily vivid performance and recording has remained in the memory in every detail. It is a true classic of the gramophone. On its original issue the authors of *The Record Guide* declared (in 'The Record Year') 'The sound of the orchestra is wonderfully lifelike, with plenty of aural perspective ... many moments are among the most dramatic yet achieved by the gramophone.' Indeed, the sense of the drama inherent in the engineering and performance alike is unforgettable. Everything is sharply focused in strong primary colours in front of the listener, and more than half-a-century after the LP first appeared, the immediacy of the sound in this remarkable score remains unsurpassed, so that one soon puts aside the well remembered thin, 'whistly' edge on the fortissimo upper strings. The *Rite of Spring*, recorded a year later, is a lesser performance perhaps, but it still retains the stereoscopic detail, sense of drama and spontaneity for which the conductor was famous in the recording studio.

There is nothing intrinsically wrong with Yuri Temirkanov's 1988 readings of these two masterful scores – they are well played and well recorded – but there is nothing especially outstanding about them either. *Petrushka* lacks the character of the best performances, and although there is some nice detail in *The Rite*, it lacks the sheer overwhelming impact that the score should generate.

Petrushka (1947 score; complete)

(N) (B) **(*) Australian Decca Eloquence 476 2686. VPO, Dohnány – BARTOK: *The Miraculous Mandarin* **(*)

Dohnány directs a genial and well-paced reading, slightly lacking in sparkle and imagination but revealing the VPO as a band very sympathetic to repertoire not normally associated with it. Though the piano and trumpet might with advantage have been placed closer, the (1977) sound is generally of Decca's best late analogue quality.

(i) Petrushka (1947 score); (ii) *Pulcinella* (suite)

**(*) Testament SBT 1156. (i) New Philh O; (ii) Philh. O; Klemperer

Following a concert performance in 1967, Klemperer insisted on recording *Petrushka*. EMI initially edited together a finished copy that was rejected. What Stewart Brown of Testament has done is to investigate the original tapes, and put together a recording drawn from the first day's sessions instead of the third – sharper and more intense. The result is a fascinating version, strong and symphonic rather than atmospheric, and magnetic from first to last. Vivid recording, full of presence. The *Pulcinella Suite* of four years earlier has already appeared on CD, an attractively fresh performance, not quite as biting as that of *Petrushka*.

(i) Petrushka (1947 version); (ii; iii; iv) *Pulcinella*; (i) *The Rite of Spring*; (ii; iii) *Suites 1 & 2*; (v; iii) *Danses concertantes*

(BB) **(*) EMI ADD/DDD CZS5 74305-2 (2). (i) Phd. O, Muti; (ii) ASMF; (iii) Marriner; (iv) with Kenny, Tear, Lloyd; (v) Los Angeles CO

Muti's 1978 *Rite* is as red-blooded as you could wish for, with the fast tempi highlighting the brutal qualities of the score to the full. The orchestra relishes the virtuosity of the performance, which is certainly exciting. (This is also available separately on EMI's new Encore label – see below.) *Petrushka*, dating from 1981, is not quite so successful. Once again Muti achieves stunning playing from the Philadelphians, but if their response is breathtaking, his reading can be best described as breathless. There is an unremitting drive here with the *Danse russe* taken at break-neck speed and everything far too regimented. The recording has splendid impact and clarity, but there is too little tenderness and magic.

Marriner directs the rest of the programme and it is good to have these excellent ASMF recordings back in the catalogue. Their playing is very fine indeed. Some might feel that a more astringent bouquet is called for in *Pulcinella*, and here the voices are a bit forward, but the singing is good enough for that not to matter, and Marriner's approach brings out the geniality. The fine often witty response of the Academy is no less beguiling in the delectably scored orchestral *Suites*. They are no less successful in the *Danses concertantes*, one of Stravinsky's most light-hearted pieces, where the highly original scoring is a constant delight, particularly when recorded as vividly as here. The sound in all these recordings has a natural balance with plenty of air around the instruments and no want of depth.

Petrushka (1947 score); *The Rite of Spring*

(M) **(*) Sup. SU 3665-2 011. Czech PO, Ančerl

(i) Petrushka (1947 score); (ii) *The Rite of Spring; Circus Polka; Fireworks*

(N) (BB) **(*) HMV 5 86771-2. (i) CBSO, Rattle; (ii) LPO, Mackerras

Recorded in 1962–3 Ančerl's Czech Philharmonic versions are superbly played, particularly the *Rite of Spring*. *Petrushka* begins relatively undramatically, but by the middle of Scene 2 the tension has increased. The colourful music for the Moor's scene is crisply pointed, the recording focus here outstandingly clear, and the final Shrovetide Fair tableau is really vivid, especially the fiercely dramatic appearance of Petrushka's ghost at the close. The recording gives the violins a bright edge; obviously the Czech engineers were familiar with

Ansermet's recording. *The Rite of Spring* is even finer. Ančerl sheds any restraint and, while keeping everything under control, maintains tension, to produce a consistently gripping reading which is still atmospheric in the score's lyrical moments. The recording is resonant but has bite too, and the powerful closing sequence leads to a thrilling sacrificial dance. Not perhaps a first choice for either work, but very stimulating.

Rattle's bold and strongly characterized CBSO recording of *Petrushka* is also available in a 2-CD Gemini set (see above), coupled with the complete *Firebird* and other music. Mackerras's *Rite of Spring* is powerful and spacious, recorded in opulent and finely textured, if slightly distanced sound. The weight of the recording adds to the dramatic impact, though it is a pity that the timpani are backward and less sharply focused than they might be. The pair of trifles are presented by Mackerras with delectable point and wit.

(i) Pulcinella (complete); Danses concertantes
(BB) *** Naxos 8.553181. (i) James, Bostridge, Herford; Bournemouth Sinf., Sanderling

The Naxos complete *Pulcinella* ballet, is fresh and alert and with the impact of the crisp, clean ensemble reinforced by full and immediate sound on an apt chamber scale. This was one of the very first recordings made (in 1993) by the tenor, Ian Bostridge, and the heady beauty of his voice is superbly caught in such vocal numbers as the *Serenata*. The other soloists are also good. A full text and English translation are given, and it is good to have the far later *Danses concertantes* (1941–2) as a valuable makeweight, done with equal point and polish. Strongly recommended.

The Rite of Spring (complete ballet) (see also above, under Petrushka)
☛ (BB) *** EMI Encore 5 74742-2. Phd. O, Muti – MUSSORGSKY: *Pictures* ***
(M) **(*) DG (ADD) 463 613-2. BPO, Karajan – PROKOFIEV: *Symphony 5* ***
(BB) (**) Dutton Lab. mono CDK 1206. Concg. O, Van Beinum – BARTOK: *Concerto for Orchestra* (***) ●

The Rite of Spring; Symphony in 3 Movements
(BB) **(*) Warner Apex 8573 89095-2. NYPO, Mehta

The Rite of Spring; Symphony of Psalms
(M) **(*) Warner Elatus 2564 60120-2. Ch. & O de Paris, Barenboim

Muti generally favours speeds a shade faster than usual, and arguably the opening bassoon solo is not quite flexible enough, for metrical precision is a key element all through, and the performance presents the violence with a red-blooded forcefulness that is very compelling. The recording, not always as analytically clear as some rivals, is strikingly bold and dramatic, with brass and percussion caught exceptionally vividly. At super-bargain price, coupled with an equally outstanding version of Mussorgsky's *Pictures*, this is very competitive indeed.

Barenboim's coupling of an exciting and atmospheric *Rite of Spring* and a bitingly eloquent *Symphony of Psalms* dates from 1987 but has only recently reappeared on Elatus. The resonant recording, if not sharply detailed, brings spectacular results in the ballet, including impressive contributions from the timpani and bass drum, and is even better focused and balanced in the *Symphony of Psalms*, where the Paris Choir sings powerfully and committedly, with the lovely closing

Hallelujahs particularly telling. The orchestral contribution, too, with its French woodwind colouring, is full of character, and this fine performance can be considered alongside Bernstein's (see below), although the latter is still a first choice.

Karajan's approach may have excitement but, next to other more extrovert accounts, it sounds a bit too smooth and civilized. His attention to detail is striking, but at the expense of sheer elemental strength, though it is interesting to hear such a sophisticated reading of this score. The recording is technically outstanding, with its vivid projection counteracting the high degree of reverberation. Not a top recommendation, but an interesting performance with integrity, which will not disappoint Karajan admirers, and those coming new to it will certainly see the work in a different light. The Prokofiev coupling is outstanding in every way.

The Decca version (now reissued on Dutton) conducted by Edward van Beinum was the first *Rite of Spring* to appear in Europe after the war, when Stravinsky's own set on five 78s, and Stokowski's on four, still held sway. The sound is pretty remarkable for its period and shows how far ahead the Decca engineers were in 1946, but the overall impression is not as exciting as the astonishing Bartók with which it is coupled.

Although the effect is often rhythmically ferocious – some might say crude – no one could suggest that Mehta's New York *Rite of Spring* isn't exciting, partly because the NYPO play very well indeed, but are also obviously caught up in Mehta's impulsive forward thrust. It is also very brilliantly recorded, with spectacular use of the drums, and the acoustics of New York's Manhattan Center providing a spacious dimensional layout. If the bold horn entry in the penultimate movement echoes resonantly rather than having a biting forward projection, the final *Sacrificial dance* could not be more brutal. The *Symphony in Three Movements* also has forceful accents, and makes its progress very purposefully, yet the central *Andante* is neatly done, and has charm.

The Soldier's Tale (L'histoire du soldat; complete)
(N) (M) *** Vanguard (ADD) **SACD** ATMSC 1559. Madelaine Milhaud, Aumont, Singher, Instrumental Ens., Stokowski
*** Chan. 9189. Haugland, SNO, Järvi

(i) The Soldier's Tale (complete); (ii) Dumbarton Oaks Concerto in E flat
(BB) *** Naxos 8.55366-2. D. Thomas, Soames, Keeble, & Instrumental Ens.; (ii) N. Ch. O; Ward

This surprisingly neglected score is heard here for the first time on CD as the composer intended. It might be questioned why Vanguard chose a woman as narrator, but Milhaud's wife had already acted in a similar role in a concert performance of Stravinsky's *Persephone* under the composer's direction, and she received his imprimatur. She was also able to record the piece in the original French as well as English, and her diction is both clear and histrionically involving, even reminding one a little of Dame Edith Sitwell in Walton's *Façade*. The rhyming libretto was the work of the Swiss writer Charles Ferdinand Ramuz, who had provided the French text for *Les Noces*. The two actors playing the Soldier (Jean Pierre Aumont) and the Devil (a dominating Martial Singhier) are excellent; the latter produces a remarkable falsetto while in the guise of the old clothes woman. Whether the piece works or not only the listener can decide, but the performance is certainly first rate and full of life. Throughout, Stokowski magics Stravinsky's vivid score, making the most of its lyrical warmth as well as the more abrasive Devil's music, which has plenty of rhythmic bite. The septet of expert instrumentalists was recorded (in 1967) on three tracks – the narration separately, as it had to be bilingual. The solo violinist (Charles Tarrack) and the trumpeter (Theodore Weis) are fully up to the considerable demands placed on them (the *Tango*, *Waltz* and *Ragtime* are delightfully played), and here everything is expertly combined to make a most convincingly balanced SACD, with each item of music separately cued. This may be an eccentric artistic amalgamation, but it includes the whole of Stravinsky's score, and is aurally fascinating. The sound is remarkably vivid and immediate.

With recording ideally balanced, intimate but not too dry, with fair bloom on voices and instruments, Nicholas Ward on Naxos offers a crisp and well-lifted account, with seven stylish players from the Northern Chamber Orchestra. Using the idiomatic English version of Michael Flanders and Kitty Black, the three actors characterize well without exaggeration. From the full chamber orchestra the *Dumbarton Oaks Concerto* makes a generous and apt coupling, similarly crisp and persuasive

Aage Haugland takes a forthright view, with the Devil given a crypto-French accent as a very oily character. Where the Chandos scores is in the sharp focus of the performance, generally brisk and taut at fast speeds, helped by a close recording which yet has plenty of air round the sound.

Symphony in 3 Movements
*(*) Arthaus **DVD** 100 320. Bavarian RSO, Solti –
BRUCKNER: *Symphony 3* *(*)

Symphony in 3 Movements; Symphonies of Wind Instruments; (i) Symphony of Psalms
**(*) DG 457 616-2. BPO, Pierre Boulez; (i) with Berlin R. Ch.

The *Symphony in Three Movements* brings a violent approach from Boulez, with the Berliners relishing the jazzy outbursts of the outer movements and the warmth of the central slow movement. An unexpected but revelatory disc. Refined recording to match. The results are refined rather than biting in the *Symphony of Psalms* and *Wind Symphonies*, where Boulez's restraint combined with beautifully moulded ensemble gives way to dramatic power only at key climaxes. The poignancy of the *Wind Symphonies* is reinforced, and the beauty of the *Symphony of Psalms* culminates in a glowing account of the final apotheosis, one of Stravinsky's most sublime inspirations.

In this Bavarian Radio recording on DVD of the Stravinsky *Symphony in Three Movements* there is nothing light or witty in Solti's approach to this neoclassical work. The first movement is heavy and chunky, made to seem unremitting and abrasive, with jagged rhythms underlined. Even in the central Andante, again on the slow side, Solti is too heavy, and in the finale, again jagged and relentless, there is none of the tongue-in-cheek quality which lead the composer to end on a jazz chord. Textures are clear, with the important piano and harp parts – the players credited – brought out both aurally and visually. What cannot be denied is the power of Solti's reading and the brilliance of the orchestral playing.

CHAMBER MUSIC

Ballad; Chanson russe; Danse russe; Divertimento; Duo concertante; Pastorale; Suite italienne
*** Chan. 9756. Mordkovitch, Milford

Lydia Mordkovitch, truly Russian, defies the idea of Stravinsky as a cold composer, finding radiant intensity even in the

neoclassical *Duo concertante*, notably in the lovely final *Dithyrambe*. This was a work Stravinsky wrote for himself to play with the violinist Samuel Dushkin, and the other pieces, all lighter, are arrangements he also made for their recitals, based on some of his most approachable works. So the ballets *Pulcinella* and *The Fairy's Kiss* prompted respectively the *Suite italienne* and the *Divertimento*, while the other shorter pieces culminate here in a fizzing account of the *Danse russe* from *Petrushka*.

Concertino; Double Canon; 3 Pieces for String Quartet
(M) *** EMI 5 67550-2 [5675512]. Alban Berg Qt – DEBUSSY;
RAVEL: *String Quartets* **(*)
(BB) *** Naxos 8.554315. Goldner Qt – SZYMANOWSKI:
String Quartets 1–2 ***

Stravinsky's original titles for the *Three Pieces* were *Danse*, *Excentrique* and *Cantique*, with the second an etching of the contortions of the famous clown, Little Tich, and the third a Russian chant. The playing of the Alban Berg Quartet has tremendous bite and grip, and the music's spare lyricism and irony is indelibly caught, as is the rhythmic energy and bustle of the *Concertino*. The economic *Double Canon* is dedicated to the memory of the painter Raoul Dufy, and this short valediction is touchingly realized. First class, vividly present recording certainly gives these performances the right to be considered as among the 'Great Recordings of the Century', although we are much less sure about the claims of the Debussy and Ravel couplings.

On Naxos Stravinsky's bright and brittle miniatures for string quartet, with their compressed and cryptic arguments, make a striking contrast with the rich and exotic quartets of Szymanowski. The excellent Goldner quartet play them with dramatic bite, underlining that contrast. Excellent sound.

Concertino for 12 Instruments; Octet for Wind Instruments; Pastorale for Violin & Wind Quartet; Ragtime for 11 Instruments
(M) *** DG (IMS) (ADD) 463 667-2. Boston SO Chamber
Players – J. STRAUSS: *Waltz Transcriptions* **(*)

The *Pastorale*, a vocalise for voice and piano, is an early piece, written in 1907, which Stravinsky arranged for Samuel Dushkin in 1934. All these pieces are musically rewarding and full of Stravinsky's wit and intelligence, and they are given exemplary performances by this distinguished group. The recording too, lively and well-detailed, comes up well in its new Originals transfer.

Divertimento
*** Erato 8573-85769-2. Repin, Berezovsky – BARTOK:
Romanian folk dances; STRAUSS: *Violin Sonata* ***

On Erato Repin and Berezovsky also give a performance of immense character and elegance, and ideally balanced.

3 Pieces for String Quartet
*** ASV CDDCA 930. Lindsay Qt – DEBUSSY; RAVEL:
Quartets **(*)

A vital, finely etched performance of these delightful pieces from the Lindsays. A good fill-up to thoughtful and vigorous accounts of the Debussy and Ravel *Quartets*. Good recordings.

Suite italienne for Cello & Piano
(N) (BB) *** Virgin 2x1 4 82067-2. Mørk, Vogt –
MIASKOVSKY; PROKOFIEV; RACHMANINOV: *Cello Sonata in C, Op. 119*; SHOSTAKOVICH: *Cello Sonata* ***

Suite italienne for Violin & Piano

*** BIS CD 336. Thedéen, Pöntinen – SCHNITTKE: *Sonata;*
SHOSTAKOVICH: *Sonata* ***

Stravinsky made several transcriptions of movements from *Pulcinella*, including the *Suite italienne* for both cello and alternatively violin and piano. The performances by Torleif Thedéen and Roland Pöntinen, are felicitous and spontaneous, and they are afforded strikingly natural recording.

Truls Mørk and Lars Vogt also give a very lively account. It is a welcome makeweight for their eloquent accounts of the Shostakovich, Miaskovsky, Rachmaninov and Prokofiev sonatas, and this budget reissue is very strongly recommended.

PIANO MUSIC

Solo piano music

Circus Polka; 4 Etudes; Piano Rag Music; Ragtime; Scherzo; Serenade; Sonata; Sonata in F sharp min.; Tango; Valse pour les enfants. Piano transcriptions: *Le Chant du rossignol* (probably made by Arthur Lourié); 3 *Movements from The Firebird* (trans. Agosti); 3 *Movements from Petrushka; Symphonies for Wind Instruments* (arr. Arthur Lourié)
(B) *** Nim. NI 5519/20. Jones

A fascinating and immensely valuable survey. The piano was Stravinsky's indispensable work-tool. He thought of it as 'a utility instrument which sounds right only as percussion', but Rubinstein convinced him otherwise, and it was for Rubinstein that he transcribed the *Three Movements from Petrushka*. Martin Jones plays them vividly, and is particularly evocative in the central *Chez Pétrouchka* (as he is in the *Firebird* finale). The other piano transcriptions, wanted for use at ballet rehearsals, were made by others. *Le Chant du rossignol* is very orchestral and prolix, but again Martin Jones finds atmospheric magic in the third and final tableau.

The earliest work here is the charming *Scherzo* with its rhythmic hoppity-jump, while Jones relishes the full-blooded Tchaikovskian romanticism of the *F sharp minor Sonata*, an entirely uncharacteristic but very enjoyable student work from 1903-4: its simple *Andante* is touching. The *Etudes* of 1908 move into the world of Scriabin and the *Valse pour les enfants* is rather like Poulenc, but the *Piano Rag Music* and the engaging *Ragtime* (1918–19) are harder-edged and more typical.

The *Sonata* (1924) with its cool, almost Ravelian *Adagietto* and the delightful *Serenade* (1925) are perhaps Stravinsky's two finest solo works, and ought to be much better known. The much later and beguiling *Tango* (1940) contrasts with the *Circus Polka* (1942), which, with its parody of Schubert's *Marche militaire*, brings an element of the bizarre. Martin Jones readily encompasses the wide range of these pieces, and even if his playing is less percussive than the composer's own drier approach, it remains fully authoritative, as well as giving much enjoyment when so well (if fairly resonantly) recorded.

3 Movements from Petrushka

(M) *** DG (IMS) (ADD) 471 360-2. Pollini – BARTOK: *Piano Concertos 1–2* ***

Pollini's electrifying performance of Stravinsky has here been (less suitably) recoupled with Bartók's *Piano concertos* instead of other twentieth-century piano music.

Piano Sonata; Piano-rag Music; Serenade in A

*** Chan. 8962. Berman – SCHNITTKE: *Sonata* ***

Boris Berman is an artist of powerful intelligence who gives vivid and alertly characterized accounts of all these pieces. Excellent piano sound, too, from the Chandos engineers. Strongly recommended.

VOCAL MUSIC

Symphony of Psalms (1948 version)

** EMI **DVD** DVB 4901 109. French Nat. R. Ch. & O., Markevitch (with SHOSTAKOVICH: *Symphony 1;* WAGNER: *Tannhäuser Overture; Tristan: Prelude & Liebestod* (both with O Nat. de l'ORTF **) BONUS: STRAVINSKY: *Firebird Suite:* New Philh. O, composer
(B) *** Sony (ADD) SBK 61703. E. Bath Festival Ch., LSO, Bernstein – ORFF: *Catulli Carmina* **(*)
(N) (M) *(*) Telarc CD 80643. Atlanta Ch. & SO, Shaw – POULENC: *Gloria*, etc. *(*)

The *Symphony of Psalms* was televised a week before the commercial recording, made at the Théâtre des Champs-Elysées, Paris, in June 1967. Markevitch was usually clear and business-like as a conductor, often rather cool even to he point of detachment. In a sense, he was ideally suited to this work, though this particular performance does him and his Parisian forces less than full justice. The Shostakovich *Symphony* comes from a broadcast concert made in the Paris Studios of the French Radio in 1963 and is clean-cut but not special. The Wagner excerpts come from the Besançon Festival and are also rather cool. These accounts come with a bonus of Stravinsky himself conducting the *Firebird Suite* (filmed in black and white) on his last visit to the New Philharmonia Orchestra in London in 1965 (also included in the BBC DVD of *Firebird* and *Les Noces*). An interesting and instructive DVD rather than a great musical experience.

Bernstein's *Symphony of Psalms* ranks among the finest ever recorded, though his view of the work is not as austere and ascetic as the composer's own. Yet there is grandeur and a powerful sense of atmosphere as well as first-class singing and playing from the chorus and orchestra. The recording is distinguished by clarity and range, and with few alternatives available this is an essential purchase for all Stravinskians.

Like the Poulenc *Gloria* with which it is coupled, Robert Shaw's Atlanta version of the *Symphony of Psalms* is well disciplined and brilliantly recorded, but it misses the energetic bite and sharpness of focus so necessary in this work, before it finds its resolution at the end in the heavenly *Alleluias*.

OPERA

Oedipus Rex (with narration in English)

⊕–⊛ (B) *** CfP 585 0112. Dowd, Herincx, Blackburn, Johnson, Remedios, Richardson (nar.), Sadler's Wells Op. Ch. (men's voices), RPO, C. Davis

In 1960 the Sadler's Wells Opera Company (predecessor of the ENO) had one of its most spectacular successes when Colin Davis as Music Director conducted a revelatory production of *Oedipus Rex*, directed by the legendary Michel St Denis. What till then had generally been regarded as a dry, over-intellectual piece, not helped by using a Latin text, was triumphantly revealed as an overwhelming, vitally dramatic opera, defying convention. Davis and his team went into the recording studio the following year – with the opera company's orchestra replaced by the RPO – and this thrilling account of Stravinsky's score resulted. In full, immediate sound, vividly transferred to CD, there is a hit-you-between-the-eyes quality which reflects the original stage experience, with each member of the cast singing challenging music with heartfelt commitment. The involvement is intensified by the nobly formalized narrations of Sir Ralph Richardson, preparing one for the colourful, energetic performance from orchestra and chorus under the young Colin Davis. There is no more red-blooded version of this opera than this, with Ronald Dowd a powerful, cleanly focused Oedipus, deeply affecting in his two climactic solos, *Invidia fortunam odit*, and the final, agonized *Lux facta est* – all is revealed. Patricia Johnson is similarly firm as Jocasta, with a balefully dark chest register, and Raimund Herincx as Creon, Harold Blackburn as Tiresias and the young Alberto Remedios in the tiny role of the Shepherd all bear witness to the vocal and dramatic strengths of the company at that time. It is astonishing that this superb recording has been buried for many decades, making this vividly immediate CD transfer doubly welcome on the CfP label.

(i) *Oedipus Rex* (with narration in French). *Symphony of Psalms*

(M) **(*) Sup. SU 3674-2 11. (i) Desailly (nar.), Zidek, Soukupová, Bermann, Haken, Kroupa; Prague Philharmonic Ch., Czech PO, Ančerl

Ančerl's account of the *Symphony of Psalms* is beautifully sung but suffers from rhythmic heaviness in all three movements, for he fails to sustain his rather slow tempi, notably in the finale. The phrasing is not as flexible as it might be but, with good choral recording, the result is still moving, especially at the close.

Oedipus Rex is a different matter, and it understandably won a Grand Prix du Disque in 1968. Ančerl is at his finest, and the Czech performers give a far more convincing and moving account of Stravinsky's compressed operatic masterpiece than the composer himself did in his stereo version. There is a degree of expressiveness in the phrasing that might not please the composer himself but Ančerl has at his disposal a large group of virtuoso singers, and the result is sharp and committed: the precision of discipline is much more acute than in Stravinsky's performance. The Czech soloists too are not only movingly eloquent but bring a Slavonic timbre which is not at all inappropriate in this work with its lingering traces of Russian influence. The recording quality is very natural, and so is the CD transfer. Moreover the work's last two notes, which were snipped off at the end of the LP, are now restored, ending the piece properly after the gradual diminuendo on repeated triplets. There are two snags: the text is provided but no translation, and there are no internal cues to separate out the spoken narrative, only a single band between Acts I and II.

Stravinsky Edition, Vol. 9: *The Rake's Progress* (complete)

⊶ (M) *** Sony (ADD) SM2K 46299 (2). Young, Raskin, Reardon, Sarfaty, Miller, Manning, Sadler's Wells Op. Ch., RPO, composer

The Rake's Progress (complete)

*** DG 459 648-2 (2). Bostridge, York, Terfel, Robson, Howells, Von Otter, Monteverdi Ch., LSO, Gardiner

*** Erato 0630 12715-2 (2). Hadley, Upshaw, Lloyd, Ramey, Collins, Bumbry, Lyon Opéra Ch. & O, Nagano

(N) (M) **(*) Decca 475 7005 (2). Langridge, Pope, Walker, Ramey, Dean, Dobson, L. Sinf. Ch. & O, Chailly

Arthaus DVD 100 254. Upshaw, Hadley, Pederson, Henschel, Banks, Ormison, Best, Tuff, V. State Op. Ch., Camerata Academica, Cambreling. Producer: Mussbach; Video producer: Large

Stravinsky's own recording of *The Rake's Progress* has many elements of the original Sadler's Wells production. The casting is uniformly excellent with the Rake of Alexander Young dominating but Judith Raskin an attractive heroine. Regina Sarfaty's Baba is superbly characterized and her anger at being spurned just before the 'squelching' makes a riveting moment. The composer conducts with warmth as well as precision, both chorus and orchestra respond persuasively, and the CD transfer is excellent.

Gardiner's incisive direction, with brilliant, polished playing from the LSO confirms this as the finest of modern versions, when Gardiner at speeds often faster than usual, brings extra sparkle to the rhythmic neoclassical writing and conveys a hushed intensity in the many tender moments of this moral tale. Ian Bostridge's lyric tenor might seem light for the role of Tom but with fine pointing of words he underlines the Rake's vulnerability, the ease with which he gives way to temptation. Bryn Terfel makes a seductive Nick Shadow, strong and sardonic, singing superbly, and the young American, Deborah York, sings with golden tone and dazzling flexibility as Anne, untroubled by high tessitura. The rest of the team is equally strong, with Anne Sofie von Otter making Baba the Turk the most eloquent nagger. Well-balanced recording – the point on which other modern versions fall short – with well-defined sound staging.

Kent Nagano, with his Lyon Opera forces and an outstanding cast of soloists, directs a fresh and crisp account. In the title-role Jerry Hadley, with his fresh, clear tone, is aptly youthful-sounding and brings out the pathos of the final scenes when struck insane by Nick Shadow. Samuel Ramey is powerful and sinister in that devilish role, as he was in the earlier, Chailly version, and Dawn Upshaw makes a tenderly affecting Anne Trulove, bringing out the heroine's vulnerability. Robert Lloyd as Trulove and Anne Collins as Mother Goose are both very well cast, and the veteran, Grace Bumbry, makes a fruity Baba the Turk. Excellent ensemble from the Lyon Opera chorus, though the balance is a little backward. Otherwise first-rate sound.

Richard Chailly draws from the London Sinfonietta playing of a clarity and brightness to set the piece aptly on a chamber scale without reducing the power of this elaborately neo-classical work. Philip Langridge is excellent as the Rake himself, very moving when Tom is afflicted with madness. Samuel Ramey as Nick, Stafford Dean as Trulove, and Sarah Walker as Baba the Turk are all first rate, but Cathryn Pope's soprano as recorded is too soft-grained for Anne. Charming as the idea is of getting the veteran, Astrid Varnay to sing Mother Goose the result is out of style. The recording is exceptionally full and vivid but the balances are sometimes odd: the orchestra recedes behind the singers and the chorus sounds congested, with little air round the sound.

The DVD production is highly intrusive and more concerned with presenting the 'ideas' of Peter Mussbach than offering a straightforward account of Stravinsky's score. Nick Shadow has a checker board painted on one side of his face, is dressed in jeans and the other accoutrements of the modern-day lout. Shadow arrives in a cardboard aeroplane which remains on stage – and so on! There is some good playing from the pit and the singers do their best, but, as so often with going to the opera these days, you are far better off with any of the CDs and the theatre of the imagination. Not recommended and no stars!

(i) *Le Rossignol* (complete)

⊶ ✿ (***) Testament mono SBT 1135. Micheau, Moizan, Giraudeau, Lovano, Roux; French R. Ch. & O, Cluytens – DELAGE: *4 Poèmes hindous* **

(i) *Le Rossignol* (complete); (ii) *Renard* (histoire burlesque)

*** EMI 5 56874-2. Paris Nat. Opéra Ch. & O, Conlon; (i) Dessay, McLaughlin, Urmana, Schagidullin; (i; ii) Grivnov, Naouri, Mikhailov; (ii) Caley, Naouri, Mikhailov

Stravinsky's early opera, *Le Rossignol*, in three compact acts, is a problematic work, and Conlon here provides a near-ideal reading. Evocative and atmospheric in Act I, the work is then transformed into something far more tautly dramatic, even while its Russian roots are still clear. Natalie Dessay with her bright soprano is very well suited to the role of the Nightingale, with the tenor Vsevolod Grivnov producing honeyed tones as the Fisherman who acts as commentator. Warm playing and singing from the whole company. The relatively brief burlesque *Renard* brings a performance just as committed, though it lacks the rustic bite and bluff humour that ideally are needed. Warm sound to match.

Apart from the powerful atmosphere that Cluytens evokes from his fine orchestra, the performance is unforgettable on account of the superlative singing of Janine Micheau in the title role and the general excellence of the other soloists. It has something of the same quality of sheer perfection that distinguished Ernest Bour's recording of Ravel's *L'enfant et les sortilèges*, which Testament restored to circulation some years ago.

STROZZI, Barbara (c. 1619–64)

Secular Cantatas: *Appresso a i molli argenti (Lamento); L'Astratto; Moralità amorosa; Non pavento lo ti de; Su'l Rodano severo (Lamento)*

(N) (B) *** HM HMX 2901114. Nelson, Christie, Coin, Hutchinson

Barbara Strozzi was a singer and composer, who left us eight volumes of vocal music. Alongside Francesca Caccini she was the only woman composer in 17th century Italy. Born in Venice she was celebrated mainly as a writer of opera libretti, but she studied with Cavalli and wrote lyrical music of real quality. Although we discovered her from a beautiful CD of sacred music (now deleted), she was best known for her arias and cantatas, six of which are included on this disc. They are often operatic in style, alternating recitative and aria, and her characteristic use of a doleful descending scale familiar from her sacred music is again found in the *Lamento, Appresson a i molli argenti* ('Beside the silver liquid of a mumuring little stream sat lovelorn Phileno'). But, if anything, its lovely companion, *Su'l Rodano severo* is even more ambitious and expressively telling: its principal melody totally memorable and including moments of high drama. Other cantatas are lighter and sung vivaciously, like the opening *L'Astratto viglio si vì cantar* ('I want, yes I want to sing') which is most engaging here. Judith Nelson, like Maria Kiehr, has the full measure of the Strozzi style, singing with a ravishing vocal

line and changing moods spontaneously, and she is splendidly accompanied by a continuo featuring William Christie, Christophe Coin and John Hutchinson (harp).

SUK, Josef (1874–1935)

Asrael Symphony, Op. 27

⊶ ☰ ✿ *** Chan. 9042. Czech PO, Bělohlávek

(***) Sup. mono 11 1902-2 (2). Czech PO, Talich (with DVORAK: *Stabat Mater* (*))

(N) ** CPO 777 001-2. Berlin Comic Opera O, Kirill Petrenko

Jiří Bělohlávek, the principal conductor of the Czech Philharmonic, draws powerfully expressive playing from the orchestra in a work which in its five large-scale movements is predominantly slow. Next to Pešek's fine Liverpool performance, the speeds flow a degree faster and more persuasively, and the ensemble, notably of the woodwind, is even crisper, phenomenally so.

Václav Talich's pioneering mono account from the early 1950s has great intensity of utterance and poignancy and provides a link with the composer himself. Talich knew him well and conducted many Suk premières. The sound is very acceptable for the period, and it is a pity that it comes harnessed to a less successful Dvořák *Stabat Mater*.

Good though it is to have an alternative to the wonderful performances by Talich and Bělohlávek, the CPO version although well played and recorded does not displace any of them interpretatively.

A Fairy-Tale, Op. 16

(**) Biddulph mono WHL 048. Czech PO, Talich – DVORAK: *Symphony 9 (New World); Polonaises* (**)

A Fairy-Tale; Praga, Op. 26

*** Sup. 10 3389-2. Czech PO, Libor Pešek

A Fairy-Tale is full of charm and originality. Talich was a friend of Suk, and he conveys its character with great poignancy and warmth. The sound is very acceptable, given its period, and the disc is worth having for this piece alone.

It is also persuasively played under Pešek. It is coupled with *Praga*, a patriotic tone-poem reflecting a more public, outgoing figure than *Asrael*, which was to follow it. Libor Pešek secures an excellent response from the Czech Philharmonic; the recordings, which date from 1981–2, are reverberant but good.

Fantasy in G min. (for violin and orchestra), *Op. 24*

(M) *** Sup. (ADD) SU 1928-2 011. Suk, Czech PO, Ančerl – DVORAK: *Violin Concerto*, etc. ***

Suk's playing is refreshing and the orchestral accompaniment under Ančerl is no less impressive. Good remastered 1960s sound.

Fantastic Scherzo, Op. 25

*** Chan. 8897. Czech PO, Bělohlávek – MARTINU: *Symphony 6;* JANACEK: *Sinfonietta* ***

This captivating piece brings playing from the Czech Philharmonic under Bělohlávek which is even finer than any of the earlier performances and it cannot be too strongly recommended, particularly in view of the excellence of the couplings.

Serenade for Strings in E flat, Op. 6

(BB) *** Virgin 2×1 5 61763-2 (2). LCO, Warren-Green – DVORAK: *Serenade for Strings;* ELGAR: *Introduction &*

Allegro; Serenade; TCHAIKOVSKY: *Serenade;* VAUGHAN
WILLIAMS: *Fantasia on Greensleeves,* etc. ***
(BB) *** Naxos 8.550419. Capella Istropolitana, Krěchek –
DVORAK: *String Serenade* **(*)

Warren-Green and his LCO also give a wonderfully persuasive account of Suk's *Serenade,* making obvious that its inspiration is every bit as vivid as in the comparable work of
Dvořák. The recording, made in All Saints', Petersham, is
fresh, full and natural without blurring from the ecclesiastical
acoustic. This now comes as part of an incredibly generous
Virgin Double, one of the most desirable bargain collections
of string music in the catalogue.

On Naxos another entirely delightful account of Suk's
Serenade. The innocent delicacy of the opening is perfectly
caught and the *Adagio* is played most beautifully and then,
with a burst of high spirits (and excellent ensemble), the
finale bustles to its conclusion with exhilarating zest. The
recording is first class, fresh yet full-textured, naturally balanced and transparent.

A Summer Tale, Op. 29; A Winter's Tale, Op. 9
(BB) **(*) Naxos 8.553703. Slovak RSO, Mogrelia

Good, very musical performances, with fine sound to boot.
The Slovak Orchestra are not the equal of the Czech Philharmonic but they produce eminently decent results. This is
lovely music and the performances are enjoyable and well
worth the modest outlay.

CHAMBER MUSIC

Ballade, Op. 30; 4 Pieces, Op. 17 (for violin & piano)
(N) (M) ** Sup. SU 3772. Suk, Panenka – DVORAK: *Romantic
Pieces; Violin Sonatina;* SMETANA: *From the Homeland* ***

The *Four Pieces* are quite well known and very attractive,
given the persuasive advocacy of these fine artists; the early
Ballade is comparatively unmemorable, if by no means without interest. But this reissue is desirable for the highly idiomatic accounts of the Smetana pieces and the delightful
Dvořák *Violin Sonatina.*

4 Pieces for Violin and Piano, Op. 17
(BB) (***) Dutton mono CDBP 9710. G. Neveu, J. Neveu –
BRAHMS: *Violin Concerto in D, Op. 77;* RAVEL: *Tzigane;
Encores* (***)

Ginette Neveu's fiery temperament is shown at its most
compelling in these lively genre pieces by Josef Suk with the
closing moto perpetuo *Burleska* scintillating on her nimble
bow. Her brother Jean accompanies attentively and the
recording sounds most real and present in this first-class
Dutton transfer.

Piano Quartet in A min., Op. 1
(B) *** Virgin 2×1 5 61904-2 (2). Domus – MARTINU: *Piano
Quartet 1,* etc.; DOHNANYI: *Serenade;* DVORAK: *Bagatelles;*
KODALY: *Intermezzo* ***

Suk's early *Piano Quartet* shows this master below his
inspired best, but it is still worth having in so sympathetic a
performance as Domus gives us. It is a well-filled set and well
worth having in particular for the Martinů pieces which are
not generously represented on disc.

*String Quartets 1 in B flat, Op. 11; 2, Op. 31; Ballade;
Barcarolle; Meditation on the Czech Choral, St Wenceslas,
Op 35a; Minuet*
➤ ✹ (M) *** CRD CRD 3472. Suk Qt

The early *B flat Quartet* is essentially a sunny work, yet its
Adagio has a remarkable potency of elegiac feeling, which is
very affecting in a performance as ardently responsive as that
by the eponymous Suk Quartet on CRD. The *Second Quartet*
is far more concentrated than its predecessor, its thematic
material is curiously haunting and in some ways its boldness
and forward-looking writing suggest that Janáček's quartets
are just around the corner. The performance here is not only
deeply moving and seemingly spontaneous, it is wonderfully
full of observed detail. Of the other works here the simple
Meditation is played very touchingly, while the *Barcarolle* is a
charming piece of juvenilia, a real lollipop, to show the
composer's ready melodic facility. CRD have never made a
better record than this superb collection. The beauty and
internal transparency of string texture is matched by the
natural presence of the group itself.

PIANO MUSIC

*About Mother, Op. 28; Lullabies, Op. 33; 4 Piano Pieces,
Op. 7; Spring, Op. 22a; Summer, Op. 22b; Things Lived and
Dreamed, Op. 30*
*** Chan. 9026/7 (2). Fingerhut

It is striking how the earliest works here have a carefree,
sweetly lyrical character, gentler than Dvořák but typically
Czech. Then, after the death in 1904 and 1905 of his mentor,
Dvořák, and his wife (Dvořák's daughter), even these fragmentary inspirations, like the massive *Asrael Symphony,*
become sharp, sometimes even abrasive. The second disc
brings the finest and most ambitious of the suites in which
Suk generally collected his genre pieces, *Things Lived and
Dreamed.* Margaret Fingerhut proves a devoted advocate,
playing with point and concentration, helped by full-ranging
Chandos sound.

*About Mother (O matince), Op. 28; Moods (Nálady), Op. 18;
6 Pieces, Op. 7*
(BB) **(*) Naxos 8.553762. Lauriala

Although we associate Suk more with large-scale orchestral
canvases, like *Asrael* and *A Fairy-Tale,* his piano music is also
of the highest quality, as readers who have sampled the
two-CD set made by Margaret Fingerhut on Chandos, which
includes Op. 7 and Op. 28, will know. The Finnish pianist
Risto Lauriala has a strong affinity with this music and gives a
sympathetic account of the five pictures, Op. 28, *O matince
(About Mother),* composed for Suk's son in 1907, two years
after Otilie's death. The recording is generally well balanced if
a little close, so that there is a touch of glare in fortissimo
passages.

SULLIVAN, Arthur (1842–1900)

L'Ile enchantée (complete ballet); *Thespis:* suite
**(*) Marco Polo 8.2234560. RTE Concert O, Dublin, Penny

L'Ile enchantée, using lyrical brass solos as well as engaging
woodwind, is quite lively, with a splendid final *Galop. Thespis*
was an early Gilbert and Sullivan creation which did not
survive, and the very introduction of the ballet suite unmistakably establishes the jolly rhythmic pattern we associate

with the Savoy Operas, while its closing *Galop* has a character which draws on both influences. Andrew Penny secures bold, lively playing from the Dublin orchestra, and the resonant recording is very suitable, if without the lustrous glow we associate with Decca's ballet records.

King Arthur (incidental music): suite; *Macbeth* (incidental music): suite; *The Merry Wives of Windsor* (incidental music): suite
*** Marco Polo 8.223635. MacDonald, RTE Chamber Ch. & Concert O, Dublin, Penny

The opening *Chorus of Lake Spirits* in *King Arthur* might well have come out of *Patience* (they sound very much like lovesick maidens). But the following, more confident *Unseen Spirits* would have fitted more readily into *Iolanthe*. The music for *Macbeth* brings a fine Overture with some striking brass writing, and the *Introduction to Act IV* has a rather good tune (though hardly with the flavour of Shakespearean tragedy). But easily the finest number is the deliciously fairy-like, Mendelssohnian *Chorus of the Spirits in the Air*. All the music for *The Merry Wives of Windsor* sounds as if it were part of an operetta, and the closing *Dance* with chorus rounds the whole programme off in exhilarating fashion. Sullivan's flow of attractive ideas makes for a most enjoyable 50 minutes, and all the performers rise to the occasion. The recording is excellent.

Overtures: *Di Ballo; The Gondoliers; HMS Pinafore; Iolanthe; Macbeth; The Mikado; Patience; The Pirates of Penzance; The Yeomen of the Guard*
(N) (M) ** Decca 476 2094. ASMF, Marriner

Marriner's performances are as well played and recorded (originally by Philips) as one would expect. What these performances lack is a feeling of the theatre, a certain character and adrenalin which this music should instantly conjure up. One enjoys the refinement and elegance of the playing of course, notably in *Di Ballo* (and the rare *Macbeth Overture*) – but this is not Marriner at his uniformly sparkling best.

Overtures: (i; iii) *The Gondoliers*; (ii) *HMS Pinafore*; (i; iii) *Iolanthe*; (i; iv) *Patience*; (i; iii) *The Mikado; The Pirates of Penzance*; (i; iv) *Princess Ida*; (ii) *Ruddigore* (2 versions); (i; iii) *The Yeomen of the Guard; Di Ballo*
**(*) TER CDVIR 8316. (i) D'Oyly Carte Op.; (ii) New Sadler's Wells Op. O, Phipps; (iii) Pryce-Jones; (iv) Edwards

The majority of Sullivan's overtures are not original compositions, but arrangements by the hands of others, though are all enjoyable pots-pourris of Sullivan's splendid tunes. These recordings are taken from TER's excellent complete opera recordings, and in that context they are enjoyable and offer very good sound. However, collected together in this way, with some of the tempi on the slow side, they sometimes lack the sparkle that brings out the full exhilaration of the music; *Di Ballo* is rather heavy going here too. The orchestral playing is very good. However, those who must have everything of Sullivan available will enjoy two versions of the *Ruddigore* overture.

Pineapple Poll (ballet; arr. Mackerras)
(B) *** Decca Double 473 653-2 (2). Philh. O, Mackerras – *Princess Ida* ***
(B) *** CfP (ADD) CD-CFP 4618. LPO, Mackerras – VERDI: *Lady and the Fool* ***

On Decca Mackerras conducts with warmth as well as vivacity, and the elegantly polished playing of the Philharmonia

Orchestra gives much pleasure. The record was made in the Kingsway Hall with its glowing ambience, and the CD transfer, though brightly vivid, has a pleasing bloom. Indeed the quality is in the demonstration bracket, with particularly natural string textures.

Mackerras's LPO version of the suite on CfP, made in the London Henry Wood Hall in 1977, is striking for its affection and vivacity. With an apt Verdi coupling, this is excellent value, very well transferred to CD.

Symphony in E (Irish); In memoriam Overture; The Tempest: Suite, Op. 1
*** Chan. 9859. BBC PO, Hickox

Richard Hickox makes a strong and persuasive case for these Sullivan pieces, notably the attractive *Irish Symphony*, which at last receives a first-class recording. The BBC Philharmonic respond with alert and sensitive playing. Sullivan wrote the *In memoriam Overture* in the space of ten days following the sudden death of his father. *The Tempest* music, composed when he was only 18, is not otherwise available. The recording is in the best traditions of the house and serves to enhance this CD's appeal.

CHAMBER MUSIC

(i; ii) *An Idyll* (for cello & piano); *Duo Concertante Op. 2* (for cello & piano). (iii) *Romance for String Quartet*. (i; ii) *Slowly, Slowly* (for cello & piano). (iii) *String Quartet*. (ii) *Allegro Risoluto; Berceuse; Daydreams 1–6; Thoughts 1 & 2; Twilight*
** Somm CD 223. (i) Walton; (ii) McLachlan; (iii) Yeomans String Qt

Sullivan's early *String Quartet*, written when the composer was studying in Leipzig, is the earliest chamber work to come down to us (it came to light as recently as 1995), and it has the youthful charm and energy of a budding sixteen-year-old composer, although not a great deal of substance. The *Romance for String Quartet* is rather more memorable, with a simple, lilting, minor-keyed theme, which remains in the mind. The piano works have a certain nostalgic charm; they are mainly in a simple reflective mode, unpretentious and innocent-sounding. The works for cello and piano show an understanding of how to write a long-breathed melodic line, anticipating Sullivan's later talent for writing for the voice. *An Idyll* is especially attractive, with a lovely, tender theme, and deserves to be better known. Murray McLachlan and Jamie Walton play with understanding and feeling, though the Yeoman String Quartet is not the last word in accuracy of intonation. The recording is not of the highest standard, but this collection will surely be of interest to the composer's admirers.

ORATORIO

The Golden Legend
**(*) Hyp. CDA 67280 (2). Watson, Rigby, Wilde, Brown, Black, L. Ch., New L. O, Corp

Appearing in 1886, *The Golden Legend*, based on a Longfellow poem, promptly overtook *Elijah* as the second most popular oratorio in Britain, with only Handel's *Messiah* clocking up more performances. The prologue finds Lucifer and his minions at the height of the storm seeking to tear down the cross from Strasburg Cathedral, but then the bold musical gestures evaporate, with the writing for chorus surprisingly tame, punctuating the plot with set-piece anthems like the evening hymn, *O Gladsome Light*, sung unaccompanied. By contrast the orchestral writing is bright, colourful and imaginative. Sullivan's portrayal of the fiendish Lucifer is then relatively mild; he introduces him over tripping rhythms closer to Wagner's music for the Apprentices in *Meistersinger* than to anything devilish. Nonetheless, the free lyricism of the writing carries one along very agreeably, even if one misses the sort of tunes the composer so consistently provided for his operettas. The Victorian soppiness of the story remains a barrier, with Elsie's prayer glutinous in its sentiment, as she prepares to sacrifice her life for that of the Prince. She even likens herself, almost blasphemously, to Christ, aiming to 'more nearly dying thus, resemble Thee'.

Ronald Corp draws alert playing and singing from the chorus and orchestra, but sadly, in the casting of soloists there is a serious flaw. Jeffrey Black's portrayal of Lucifer – the only soloist in the Prologue – brings strained and ill-focused singing, with the very pitch in doubt. Happily, the other principals are all first-rate, not just Janice Watson as the heroine, Elsie and Jean Rigby as Ursula, her mother, but Mark Wilde as Prince Henry, with his clear, unforced, distinctive tenor.

OPERA

The Contrabandista (opera); *The Foresters* (Incidental Music)

(N) **(*) Hyp. CDA 67486. Rutter, McCafferty, Catling, Maxwell, Suart, Moses, L. Ch., New L. O, Corp

Two Sullivan rarities: *The Contrabandista* (*The Chieftain*), a short comic opera from 1867, and *The Foresters*, incidental music for a play written in 1892 with text by Lord Tennyson. *The Contrabandista* has the same librettist, Francis Cowley Burnand, as *Cox and Box* (1866), though the earlier work has an immediate wit and sparkle – and certainly memorable tunes – which the opera of a year later lacks; and comic moments are few. Not that musically it is dull: it is throughout a pleasantly enjoyable score, with numbers such as the quintet, *Hand of Fate*, looking forward to the mature composer. Other items, such as *Only the night wind sighs alone*, are fairly memorable too. Francis McCafferty posses a rich, deep alto, but she should have been encouraged to characterize her role more vividly. The men are variable: Geoffrey Moses (bass) is rather good, but the tenor, Ashley Catling is somewhat thin-voiced, and, more surprisingly, Richard Suart is not very stable, though his comic inflection is excellent: the swaggering 'From rock to rock' is a highlight.

Tennyson's *The Forresters* (a tale of Robin Hood and Maid Marian) 'is not a great play – it is not even a good play', as the *Pall Mall Gazette* wrote at its premiere. What is worth listening to is Sullivan's music, written with the craftsmanship which we would expect from the then experienced composer. The score includes some lively choruses (*Long Live Richard*), characteristic patriotic songs (*There is no land like England*) and some good tunes. Claire Rutter is once again excellent, though Ashley Catling is, again, hardly a singer who generates blazing excitement – indeed, he sounds somewhat fey. The rest of the cast is adequate. Ronald Corp conducts with his usual feeling for this repertoire, but a bit more verve, especially in the comic opera, would have made it a more theatrical experience. However, the interest of the music is considerable, and the booklet notes from the Sir Arthur Sullivan Society are excellent. A libretto is included.

DVD Collection: (i) *Cox and Box;* (ii) *The Gondoliers;* (iii) *HMS Pinafore;* (iv) *Iolanthe;* (v) *The Mikado;* (vi) *Patience;* (vii) *The Pirates of Penzance;* (viii) *Princess Ida;* (ix) *Ruddigore;* (x) *The Sorcerer;* (xi) *Trial by Jury;* (xii) *The Yeomen of the Guard*

(N) (M) *(**) Universal **DVD** 8228651-11 (10). Amb. Ch., LSO, Faris; with (i) Russell Smythe, Fryatt, Lawlor; (ii) Michell, Shilling, McDonnell, Egerton, Collins; (iii) Marshall, Frankie Howerd, Drower, Della Jones, Bulman, Watt; (iv) Stroud, Van Allen, Oliver, Hemsley, Flowers, Mills, Collins; (v) Conrad, Revill, Collins, Stewart, Dean, Flowers; (vi) Hammond Stroud, Fryatt, Dugdale, Jenkins, Collins, Kennedy, Adams; (vii) Mitchell, Oliver, Knight, Kelly, Hudson; (viii) Gorshin, Christie, Dale, Collins, Dickenson, Powell, Jackson; (ix) Treleaven, Howard, Adams, Peters, Hudson; (x) Revill, Kerman, Oliver, Christie, Adams, Willis, (xi) Frankie Howerd, Flowers, Ryland Davies, McDonell, Bryson, Donlan; (xii) Gale, Powell, Marks, Hillman, Bainbridge (V/D: Dave Heather)

Producer George Walker made this series of Gilbert and Sullivan recordings for television in the early 1980s and they have now appeared on DVD for the first time. The critical reception was mixed – and remains so – but as a whole the series succeeds more than it fails. Firstly, it has the advantage of being filmed on a studio set which ensures that lighting and sound are of uniformly good quality. Secondly, producer Judith de Paul has provided attractive sets, with little of the gratuitous 'souping up' which often mars modern production. Thirdly, Alexander Faris paces the music well and has the support of the LSO and the Ambrosian Chorus, which ensures a good basis of quality. The casting of the smaller roles is usually more than adequate, but the controversy comes with some of the major casting: whilst Frankie Howerd is always a delight to see, his personality does not sit happily in *HMS Pinafore* as Sir Joseph Porter, though, if anything, Peter Marshall as Captain Corcoran is worse: an embarrassingly over-acted caricature. These two leads diminish the otherwise attractive performance. Frankie Howerd is better in *Trial by Jury*, but again his personality is not really suited to the piece. On the other hand, the ballet which has been contrived before the opening of this work, set to the *Overture di Ballo*, is a delight. Joel Grey as Jack Point is an irritant that mars a decent *Yeomen of the Guard*, prompting one unkind critic to remark that his insensible collapse at the end comes as a relief for all the wrong reasons. The *Pirates of Penzance* is bright and breezy but the snag is Peter Allen camping it up as the Pirate King (not to mention his grating voice). The celebrity casting is much better in *Ruddigore*, which has Vincent Price as Sir Despard Murgatroyd who (almost) manages to make one forget his lack of singing ability through sheer personality. In *Princess Ida*, uniquely in the series, the original G&S conception is tampered with so that you have a play within a play; you may or may not like the idea, but why did they bother? The performance is quite a good one, though Frank Gorshin as King Gama is a big let down, with little flair for the idiom. The most successful performances – mainly the ones with fewer celeb casting – include *Patience, The Sorcerer, The Gondoliers* and *Iolanthe* (ideal for a television production to aid the supernatural qualities of the story) which offer generally unalloyed delight. *The Mikado*, too, is generally good, with television star William Conrad as the Mikado far more integrated into the performance than many of the other stars. *Cox and Box* (not a Gilbert libretto, by the way) is one of the set's gems, an exhilarating early one-acter from 1867, which brims with sparkling ideas and memorable tunes. The sound and picture quality have been dramatically improved on DVD and each disc comes with full texts. As on the videos – for better or worse – Douglas Fairbanks Jr.'s introduction are included though can be skipped. For all these annoying faults, there is still plenty to enjoy.

(i) *Cox and Box;* **(ii)** *Trial by Jury* **(both complete)**
(N) *** Chan. 10321. (i; ii) Evans, Brook, Maxwell; (ii) Gilchrist, RMCM Chamber Ch.; BBC Nat. O of Wales, Hickox

Cox and Box, Sullivan's collaboration with F. C. Burnand, is here well-coupled with his first collaboration with W. S. Gilbert. Never on disc before has the sparkle of this preparatory piece been caught so brilliantly, bringing out the fact that this is already vintage Sullivan, superbly orchestrated. The text is fuller too, even though the Gambling Duet has had to be omitted for lack of space. The trio of soloists is first rate, with the resonant Donald Maxwell as the landlord, Bouncer, acting as narrator in the well-tailored spoken links, a crisp and effective alternative to the dialogue. James Gilchrist as Box and Neal Davies as Cox make an excellent duo, and the same three soloists are qually impressive in *Trial by Jury*, particularly Donald Maxwell who relishes the exhilarating speed set by Hickox for the Judge's Song, setting a brilliant pattern for patter-numbers in G&S to follow. Rebecca Evans maks a charming Plaintiff, and in both pieces the vividly atmospheric recording brings out the beauty and point of the writing.

Haddon Hall (complete without dialogue)

🎧 ⭐ *** Divine Art 21201 (2). Timmons, Griffin, Lawson, Smart, Main, Borthwick, Boyd, Thomson, Edinburgh Prince Consort Ch. & O, Lyle

In 1892 Sullivan needed a new source of income, yet had fallen out with Gilbert. So he decided to collaborate with a different librettist, Sidney Grundy, with a considerable reputation in the field of light opera.

The result was *Haddon Hall*, based on a true story about the elopement of Lady Dorothy Vernon with her Royalist lover, John Manners, from her ancestral home. But Grundy resourcefully predated the action so that he could use period costumes, and bring in a chorus of Puritans who in the last act, in true topsy-turvy fashion, renounce 'being thoroughly miserable' and instead plan to 'merry-make the livelong day'.

At the beginning of Act II Grundy also introduces an unforgettable Scottish character, The McCrankie, from the Isle of Rum, and he appears to an extraordinarily convincing orchestral evocation of bagpipes. *My name is McCrankie* is followed by his duet with Rupert, *There's no one by*, a wittily dour exposition of their Puritan creed ('We'd supervise the plants and flowers, prescribe them early-closing hours'). Then follows *Hoity-toity*, a delightful trio with Dorcas, the heroine's maid (who sings most engagingly in her own solos), to make three of the most delightful numbers in the whole opera.

Sir John Manners's servant, Oswald (the excellent Alan Borthwick), arrives disguised as traveling salesman and introduces himself with the engagingly lively *Come simples and gentles*, full of musical quotations, and this leads to a heavenly duet with Dorcas, *The sun's in the sky*. But it is Rupert, the heroine's Roundhead cousin, splendidly sung by Ian Lawson, who is the key humorous figure. He only wants Lady Dorothy's hand as it comes with the Haddon Hall estates, and his very winning *I've heard it said* is an inimitable patter style we all recognize; he also has a fine number with chorus, *When I was but a little lad*.

The performance by the semi-professional Prince Consort, from the Edinburgh Festival Fringe, but using a professional orchestra, may have its rough patches, but it is very well cast, with Mary Timmons a pleasing heroine, who blends appealingly with Steven Griffin as her lover, John Manners. He sings very strongly, especially when he dominates the opera's spectacular finale, when everything is happily resolved. Davis Lyle's conducting is full of vigour and the opera comes vividly to life in this excellent recording, well balanced and with a fine, full theatrical ambience.

The Savoy Operas

The Savoy Operas; EMI Recordings: (i) *The Gondoliers;* **(ii)** *HMS Pinafore;* **(iii)** *Iolanthe;* **(iv)** *The Mikado;* **(v)** *Patience;* **(vi)** *The Pirates of Penzance;* **(vii)** *Ruddigore;* **(viii)** *Trial by Jury;* **(ix)** *The Yeomen of the Guard* **(all without dialogue). Orchestral Music: (x)** *Cello Concerto in D* **(reconstructed Mackerras & Mackie); (xi)** *Overtures: Cox and Box; Di ballo; Princess Ida.* **(xii)** *In Memoriam;* **(xiii)** *Symphony in E (Irish);* **(xii)** *The Merchant of Venice: Suite. The Tempest* **(incidental music):** *Suite*
(BB) *** EMI (ADD/DDD) 5 74468-2 (16). (i) Graham; (i; vi) Milligan; (i; iii; v; ix) Young; (i; iv; ix) G. Evans; (i; ii; iv; vi–ix) Lewis; (i–iv; vi; viii; ix) Cameron; (i–ix) Brannigan, Morison; (i–vi; ix) Thomas; (i–vii; ix) Sinclair; (ii; iii; v–viii) G. Baker; (iii) Cantelo; (iii; vi) Harper; (iii; iv) Wallace; (v) Shaw, Anthony, Harwood, Harper; (vii) Blackburn, Bowden, Rouleau; (ix) Dowling; Glyndebourne Festival Ch., Pro Arte O, Sargent; (x) Lloyd Webber, LSO, Mackerras; (xi) Pro Arte O or BBC SO, Sargent; (xii) CBSO, Dunn; (xiii) RLPO, Groves

The distinguished Sargent EMI series of the Savoy Operas are not available separately, but this generously filled box is at super-budget price and is first-class value for money. The performances are uniformly notable for the quality of the soloists (and, indeed, the excellent chorus). Sargent was a long-experienced advocate and he conducts with consistent authority, if not always with the 'first-night' zest that Isidore Godfey managed consistently to achieve in his D'Oyly Carte recordings.

The Gondoliers is a case in point. Sargent chose a curiously slow tempo for the *Cachucha*, while the long opening scene is rather relaxed and leisurely. At the entrance of the Duke of Plaza Toro (Sir Geraint Evans, no less) things wake up considerably and Owen Brannigan, whose larger-than-life vocal personality dominates the whole series, is a perfectly cast Don Alhambra. Edna Graham only sang in this one recording, but she is a charmingly small-voiced Casilda, and there is much else to enjoy.

It was to Owen Brannigan's credit that, little as he has to do in *HMS Pinafore* without the dialogue, he conveys the force of Dick Deadeye's personality so strongly. George Baker is splendid as Sir Joseph and John Cameron, Richard Lewis and (especially) Monica Sinclair as Buttercup make much of their songs. Elsie Morison is rather disappointing: she spoils the end of her lovely song in Act I by singing sharp. The whole of the final scene is musically quite ravishing, and if Sir Malcolm fails to find quite all the wit in the music he is never less than lively.

There is much to praise, too, in *Iolanthe*. The climax of Act I, the scene in which the Queen of the Fairies lays a curse on members of both Houses of Parliament, shows most excitingly what can be achieved with the 'full operatic treatment'. George Baker is an excellent Lord Chancellor: the famous *Nightmare Song* is very well and clearly sung; however, for some ears John Cameron's dark timbre may not readily evoke an Arcadian Shepherd. The two Earls and Private Willis are excellent, and all of Act II – except perhaps Iolanthe's recitative and ballad near the end (which is always a bit of a problem) – goes well. The famous Trio with the Lord Chancellor and the two Earls is a joy.

The Sargent set of *The Mikado* was the first to be recorded, in 1957, but it has been given remarkable vividness and presence by the digital remastering. The grand operatic style for the finales of both acts, the trio about the 'death' of Nanki-Poo, and the glee that follows are characteristic of the stylish singing, even if the humour is less readily caught than in the D'Oyly Carte version. Owen Brannigan makes a fine Mikado, but the star performance is that of Richard Lewis, who sings most engagingly throughout as Nanki-Poo. Elsie Morison is back on form as a charming Yum-Yum, and Monica Sinclair is a generally impressive Katisha, although she could sound more convinced when she sings *These Arms shall Now Enfold You.*

Patience was one of the great successes of the Sargent cycle. It is pity that there is no dialogue, which is so important to establish the character of Bunthorne, the 'fleshly poet'. But there is more business than usual from this EMI series and a convincing theatrical atmosphere. The chorus is a strong feature throughout, and Elsie Morison's Patience, George Baker's Bunthorne and John Cameron's Grosvenor are all admirably characterized, while the military men are also excellent.

Once again in *Pirates*, the EMI recording has more atmosphere than usual, and the performance is (for the most part) highly successful, stylish as well as lively, conveying both the fun of the words and the charm of the music. Undoubtedly the star of this piece is George Baker: he is a splendid Major-General, and Owen Brannigan is his inimitable self as the Sergeant of the Police. The performance takes a little time to warm up, and in *Poor Wandering One*, Mabel's opening cadenza, Elsie Morison, is angular and over-dramatic. However, elsewhere she is much more convincing, especially in the famous duet, *Leave Me not to Pine Alone.* The choral contributions are pleasingly refined yet have no lack of vigour. *Hail Poetry* is resplendent, while the choral finale is vigorously done and with a balance which allows the inner parts to emerge effectively.

In most respects *Ruddigore* crowned the EMI series. Sargent's essentially lyrical approach brings out the associations this lovely score has with Schubert. The performance is beautifully sung. Perhaps George Baker sounds a little old in voice for Robin Oakapple, but he manages his 'character' transformation later in the opera splendidly. Pamela Bowden is a first-class Mad Margaret, and her short Donizettian scene is superbly done. Equally Richard Lewis is an admirably bumptious Richard. Owen Brannigan's delicious Act II duet with Mad Margaret has irresistible gentility. The drama is

well managed too; the scene in the picture gallery (given a touch of added resonance by the recording) is effectively sombre. Altogether a superb set, probably unsurpassed on record.

Sargent's *Trial by Jury* (with George Baker as the Judge) is by general consent the best there is, splendidly spirited and very well sung and recorded; and *The Yeomen of the Guard* is also very fine. The trios and quartets with which this score abounds are most beautifully performed and skilfully balanced, and the ear is continually beguiled. Owen Brannigan's portrayal of Wilfred again comes up trumps, and Monica Sinclair is a memorable Dame Carruthers. The finales to both acts have striking breadth, and the delightfully sung trio of Elsie, Phoebe and the Dame in the finale of Act II is a charming example of the many felicities of this set. *Strange Adventure*, too, is beautifully done. There is very little feeling of humour, but the music triumphs and, as with the rest of the series, the sound is excellent, with fine presence and definition.

It might have been better had EMI not included the fillers which accompanied the individual issues of the operas. The most interesting and most disappointing is the *Cello Concerto*, written when Sullivan was nineteen, after he returned from study in Leipzig. It was given a few performances and then forgotten. In 1964 the one surviving score was destroyed in the fire at Chappell's publishing house; but the work was reconstructed in the late 1980s with the help of the solo cello part. Sadly, the end result hardly justifies such labours. Curiously proportioned, with the first movement too brief for any symphonic pretensions and with themes less than memorable, it is a lightweight divertissement, pleasant but undistinguished. However, Julian Lloyd Webber and Mackerras, very well recorded, do all they can to give the flimsy inspiration some bite.

The *Symphony* is a far better proposition, pleasingly lyrical, with echoes of Schumann as much as the more predictable Mendelssohn and Schubert. The jaunty *Allegretto* of the third movement with its 'Irish' tune on the oboe is nothing less than haunting. Groves and the RLPO give a fresh and affectionate performance, and the 1986 recording has emerged freshly on CD.

The pair of Shakespeare-inspired suites are also well worth having. The longer selection from *The Tempest* dates from 1861, the same year as the *Cello Concerto*, but shows distinctive flair and orchestral confidence. The shorter *Merchant of Venice Suite* was composed five years later; almost immediately, the writing begins to anticipate the lively style which was so soon to find a happy marriage with Gilbert's words. The performance here is highly infectious and the sound is first class. Of the overtures, *Di ballo* is the most useful, well worth having in Sargent's performance, but *In Memoriam*, a somewhat inflated religous piece, written for the 1866 Norwich Festival, is for Sullivan aficionados only.

The Major Decca Analogue Stereo Sets

Complete Decca D'Oyly Carte Recordings: *Cox and Box; The Gondoliers; The Grand Duke; HMS Pinafore; Iolanthe; The Mikado; Patience; The Pirates of Penzance; Princess Ida; Ruddigore; The Sorcerer; Trial by Jury; Utopia Ltd; The Zoo;* plus *Overtures: Di Ballo; Macbeth; Marmion; Pineapple Poll* (ballet, arr. Mackerras); excerpts: *Henry VIII; Victoria and Merrie England*

(B) *** Decca (ADD) 473 631-2 (24). Artists & orchestras listed below, cond. Godfrey; Nash; Sargent; Mackerras

(i) *Cox and Box* (libretto by F. C. Burnand) complete; (ii) *Ruddigore* (complete; without dialogue)

(B) *** Double Decca (ADD) 473 656-2 (2). (i) Styler, Riordan, Adams; New SO of L.; (ii) Reed, Round, Sandford, Riley, Adams, Hindmarsh, Knight, Sansom, Allister, D'Oyly Carte Op. Ch., ROHCG O, Godfrey

The Gondoliers (complete; with dialogue)

(B) *** Decca Double (ADD) 473 632-2 (2). Reed, Skitch, Sandford, Round, Styler, Knight, Toye, Sansom, Wright, D'Oyly Carte Op. Ch., New SO of L., Godfrey

(i; ii) *The Grand Duke*. (ii) *Henry VIII: March & Graceful Dance*. (iii) *Overture Di Ballo*

(B) *** Double Decca (ADD) 473 635-2 (2). (i) Reed, Reid, Sandford, Rayner, Ayldon, Ellison, Conroy-Ward, Lilley, Holland, Goss, Metcalfe, D'Oyly Carte Op. Ch.; (ii) RPO, Nash; (iii) Philh. O, Mackerras

HMS Pinafore (complete; with dialogue)

⊕━ ✪ (B) *** Double Decca (ADD) 473 638-2. Reed, Skitch, Round, Adams, Hindmarsh, Wright, Knight, D'Oyly Carte Op. Ch., New SO of L., Godfrey

Iolanthe (complete; with dialogue)

(B) *** Double Decca (ADD) 473 641-2 (2). Sansom, Reed, Adams, Round, Sandford, Styler, Knight, Newman, D'Oyly Carte Op. Ch., Grenadier Guards Band, New SO, Godfrey

The Mikado (complete; without dialogue)

⊕━ (B) *** Double Decca (ADD) 473 644-2 (2). Ayldon, Wright, Reed, Sandford, Masterson, Holland, D'Oyly Carte Op. Ch., RPO, Nash

Patience (complete; with dialogue)

(B) *** Double Decca (ADD) 473 647-2 (2). Sansom, Adams, Cartier, Potter, Reed, Sandford, Newman, Lloyd-Jones, Toye, Knight, D'Oyly Carte Op. Ch. & O, Godfrey

The Pirates of Penzance (complete; with dialogue)

⊕━ (B) *** Double Decca (ADD) 473 650-2. Reed, Adams, Potter, Masterson, Palmer, Brannigan, D'Oyly Carte Op. Ch., RPO, Godfrey

(i) *Princess Ida* (complete; without dialogue); (ii) *Pineapple Poll* (ballet; arr. Mackerras)

(B) *** Double Decca (ADD) 473 653-2 (2). (i) Sandford, Potter, Palmer, Skitch, Reed, Adams, Raffell, Cook, Harwood, Palmer, Hood, Masterson, D'Oyly Carte Op. Ch., RPO, Sargent; (ii) Philh. O, Mackerras

(i) *The Sorcerer* (complete; without dialogue); (ii) *The Zoo* (libretto by Bolton Rowe)

(B) *** Double Decca (ADD) 473 659-2 (2). (i) Adams, D. Palmer, Styler, Reed, C. Palmer, Masterson; (ii) Reid, Sandford, Ayldon, Goss, Metcalfe; nar. Shovelton; (i; ii) D'Oyly Carte Op. Ch., RPO; (i) Godfrey; (ii) Nash

(i) *Utopia Ltd* (complete). Overtures: *Macbeth; Marmion. Victoria and Merrie England*

(B) **(*) Double Decca (ADD) 473 662-2 (2). (i) Sandford, Reed, Ayldon, Ellison, Buchan, Conroy-Ward, Reid, Broad, Rayner, Wright, Porter, Field, Goss, Merri, Holland, Griffiths, D'Oyly Carte Op. Ch.; RPO, Nash

(i) *The Yeomen of the Guard* (complete; without dialogue); (ii) *Trial by Jury*

⊕━ (B) *** Double Decca (ADD) 473 665-2. Hood, Reed, Sandford, Adams, Raffell; (i) Harwood, Knight; (ii) Round; D'Oyly Carte Op. Ch.; (i) RPO, Sargent; (ii) ROHCG O, Godfrey

As can be seen, there are two basic sets of recordings of the major Savoy Operas, nearly all from Godfrey (on Decca) and Sargent (on EMI). However, the individual EMI sets have all been withdrawn, except for *The Mikado* (on EMI 5 64403-2), although they are still all available in a budget box (see above). Decca have now additionally provided their twelve major sets in a slip-case; and they have restored the splendid original artwork on each separate reissue, which are offered at a new lower price. The Decca series usually has the advantage (or disadvantage, according to taste) of including the dialogue. Certain of the operas are available only in D'Oyly Carte versions, and of these the most fascinating is *Cox and Box*. This pre-Gilbertian one-Acter was written in 1867 and thus pre-dates the first G&S success, *Trial by Jury*, by eight years. The D'Oyly Carte performance is splendid in every way. It is given a recording which, without sacrificing clarity, conveys with perfect balance the stage atmosphere.

The Grand Duke, on the other hand, was the fourteenth and last of the Savoy operas. The present recording, the only complete version, came after a successful concert presentation in 1975, and the recorded performance has both polish and vigour, although the chorus does not display the crispness of articulation of ready familiarity. The recording is characteristically brilliant. The bonuses are well worth having, with Mackerras's account of the *Overture Di Ballo* showing more delicacy of approach than usual, though certainly not lacking sparkle.

The 1960 Godfrey set of *HMS Pinafore* is in our view the finest of all the D'Oyly Carte analogue stereo recordings. Donald Adams's assumption of the role of Dick Deadeye on Decca (which does have the dialogue) is little short of inspired, and his larger-than-life characterization underpins the whole piece. The rest of the cast make a splendid team: Jean Hindmarsh is a totally convincing Josephine – she sings with great charm – and John Reed's Sir Joseph Porter is a delight.

In the D'Oyly Carte set of *The Gondoliers* the solo singing throughout is consistently good, the ensembles have plenty of spirit and the dialogue is for the most part well spoken. As a performance this is on the whole preferable to the Sargent account.

With *Iolanthe*, the 1960 Decca set was given added panache by the introduction of the Grenadier Guards Band into the *March of the Peers*. Mary Sansom is quite a convincing Phyllis, and if her singing has not the sense of style that Elsie Morison brought to the part, she is completely at home with the dialogue. Also Alan Styler makes a vivid and charming personal identification with the role of Strephon, an Arcadian shepherd. John Reed is very good as the Lord Chancellor: dryly whimsical, and he provides an individual characterization. Godfrey's conducting is lighter and more infectious than Sargent's in the Act I finale, and there is much to delight the ear in the famous Trio of Act II with the Lord Chancellor and the two Earls.

The 1973 stereo remake of *The Mikado* by the D'Oyly Carte Company directed by Royston Nash is a complete success in every way and shows the Savoy tradition at its most attractive. It is a pity no dialogue is included, but the choral singing is first rate, and the glees are refreshingly done, polished and refined, yet with plenty of vitality. John Reed is a splendid Ko-Ko, Kenneth Sandford a vintage Pooh-Bah and Valerie Masterson a charming Yum-Yum. John Ayldon as the Mikado provides a laugh of terrifying bravura, and Lyndsie Holland is a formidable and commanding Katisha.

Owen Brannigan was surely born to play the Sergeant of Police in *The Pirates of Penzance*, and he does so unforgettably. On Decca there is a considerable advantage in the inclusion of the dialogue, and here theatrical spontaneity is well maintained. Donald Adams is a splendid Pirate King. John Reed's portrayal of the Major General is one of his strongest roles, while Valerie Masterson is an excellent Mabel. Godfrey's conducting is as affectionate as ever, and the dialogue undoubtedly adds an extra sense of the theatre.

Patience and *Ruddigore* were the two greatest successes of the Sargent series. However, the extra card in the D'Oyly Carte hand in *Patience* is the dialogue, so important in this opera above all, with its spoken poetry; if Mary Sansom does not give the strongest portrayal vocally, of the main role, both Bunthorne and Grosvenor are well played, while the military numbers, led by Donald Adams in glorious voice, have an unforgettable vigour and presence.

The D'Oyly Carte *Ruddigore* comes up surprisingly freshly, in fact better than we had remembered it, though it is a pity the dialogue was omitted. The performance includes *The battle's roar is over*, which is (for whatever reason) traditionally omitted. There is much to enjoy here (especially Gillian Knight and Donald Adams, whose *Ghosts' high noon* song is a marvellous highlight). Isidore Godfrey is his inimitable sprightly self and the chorus and orchestra are excellent. A fine traditional D'Oyly Carte set, then, brightly recorded.

Princess Ida is fake feminism with a vengeance. Elizabeth Harwood in the name-part sings splendidly, and John Reed's irritably gruff portrayal of the irascible King Gama is memorable; he certainly is a properly 'disagreeable man'. The rest of the cast is no less strong and, with excellent teamwork from the company as a whole and a splendid recording, spacious and immediate, this has much to offer, even if Sullivan's invention is somewhat variable in quality. The CD transfer is outstanding and the 1965 recording has splendid depth and presence. As a bonus we are offered Mackerras's vivacious and polished 1982 digital recording of his scintillating ballet score, *Pineapple Poll*.

The Sorcerer is the Gilbert and Sullivan equivalent of *L'elisir d'amore*, only here a whole English village is affected, with hilarious results. John Reed's portrayal of the sorcerer himself is one of the finest of all his characterizations. The plot drew from Sullivan a great deal of music in his fey, pastoral vein. By 1966, when the set was made, Decca had stretched the recording budget to embrace the RPO, and the orchestral playing is especially fine, as is the singing of the D'Oyly Carte chorus, at their peak. John Reed gives a truly virtuoso performance of his famous introductory song, while the spell-casting scene is equally compelling. The final sequence in Act II is also memorable. The sound is well up to Decca's usual high standard .

Both recordings of *The Yeomen of the Guard*, Decca's and EMI's set, were conducted by Sir Malcolm Sargent. The later Decca account has marginally the finer recording and Sir Malcolm's breadth of approach is immediately apparent in the Overture. Both chorus and orchestra (the RPO) are superbly expansive and there is again consistently fine singing from all the principals (and especially from Elizabeth Harwood as Elsie). This Decca *Yeomen* is unreservedly a success,

with its brilliant and atmospheric recording. In any case, the considerable bonus is the inclusion of Godfrey's immaculately stylish and affectionate *Trial by Jury* with John Reed as the Judge.

Utopia Ltd was revived for the D'Oyly Carte centenary London season in 1974, which led to this recording. Its complete neglect is unaccountable. Royston Nash shows plenty of skill in the matter of musical characterization, and the solo singing is consistently assured. When Meston Reid as Captain FitzBattleaxe sings 'You see I can't do myself justice' in *Oh, Zara*, he is far from speaking the truth – this is a performance of considerable bravura. The ensembles are not always as immaculately disciplined as one is used to from the D'Oyly Carte, and *Eagle high* is disappointingly focused: the intonation here is less than secure. However, the sparkle and spontaneity of the performance as a whole are irresistible.

The Zoo (with a libretto by Bolton Rowe, a pseudonym of B. C. Stevenson) dates from June 1875, only three months after the success of *Trial by Jury* – which it obviously seeks to imitate, as the music more than once reminds us. Although the libretto lacks the finesse and whimsicality of Gilbert, it is not without humour, and many of the situations presented by the plot (and indeed the actual combinations of words and music) are typical of the later Savoy Operas. As the piece has no spoken dialogue it is provided here with a stylized narration, well enough presented by Geoffrey Shovelton. The performance is first class, splendidly sung, fresh as paint and admirably recorded, and it fits very well alongside *The Sorcerer*. The CD transfer is more brightly lit than its companion, and the opera has animal noises to set the scene and close the opera.

The Earlier Decca Mono Recordings

(i) *Iolanthe* (complete, without dialogue). (ii) *Pineapple Poll* (ballet, arr. Mackerras: complete)
(BB) (**) Naxos mono 110231/2. (i) Green, Halman, Mitchell, Drummond-Grant, Styler, Osborn, Thornton, Morgan, D'Oyly Carte Op. Ch. & O, Godfrey; (ii) Sadler's Wells O, Mackerras

The joy of this 1951 recording (one of the last of the first Decca series) is of course Martyn Green's Lord Chancellor, particularly when set against Ella Halman's resonantly fruity Queen of the Fairies, one of her most celebrated characterizations. Although ensemble is not always ideally polished, the performance is certainly spirited and is at its best in the long Act I Finale. Margaret Mitchell's Phyllis is certainly fresh and Ann Drummond-Grant sings Iolanthe's Act II aria very touchingly, so there is much to enjoy. But the transfer retains the accentuated treble that dogged the Ace of Clubs mono LPs, and this makes the orchestral violins thin and shrill and even affects the voices at times. Mackerras's early recording of *Pineapple Poll* is more successfully transferred.

The Mikado (complete; without dialogue)
☛ (BB) (***) Naxos mono 8.110176/7. Fancourt, Green, Mitchell, Osborn, Watson, Halman, Styler, Gillingham, Wright, D'Oyly Carte Op. O, New Promenade O, Godfrey

Decca's 1950 set of *The Mikado* appeared at the very beginning of the mono LP era, and did as much as any recording, apart from Ansermet's *Petrushka*, to establish the credentials of the new medium. The clarity of the sound, coupled with the convenience of having the whole opera complete on four sides, immediately made converts, including I.M., who revisited the set countless times.

The performance was to be preferred to both its later full-priced Decca/Godfrey and EMI stereo competitors (but not the 1973 D'Oyly Carte stereo remake under Royston Nash). Not only does it cast Martyn Green in his best part (his *Little List* and the charming *Tit willow* are unsurpassed), but it has Darrell Fancourt in splendid form singing his Mikado's song superbly, with that great gusty laugh between verses.

Leonard Osborn was perhaps just past his best, but *A wand'ring minstrel* shows what a fine singer he was, especially in the contrasting middle verses. Ella Halman's Katisha was incomparably magisterial, and if her intonation had become slightly suspect at the top, her lower register was still superb and her Act II lament, *Alone and yet alive*, is most affecting. Margaret Mitchell was a charmingly petite Yum-Yum and Richard Watson a splendid Pooh-Bah and the glees *Brightly dawns* and *Here's a how-de-do* (in which on stage Martyn Green used to provide hilarious business for up to five encores) still sound as fresh as ever.

Over the whole proceedings presides the sparkling conducting of Isidore Godfrey. The vivid recording makes every word clear. It always had moments of excess sibilance, but the present transfer (like Decca's earlier Ace of Clubs LP set) loses some of the bloom and slightly exaggerates the upper range.

Patience (complete; without dialogue)

O—➤ (BB) (***) Naxos mono 8.11023. Green, Mitchell, Styler, Fancourt, Pratt, Osborn, Griffiths, Halman, Drummond-Grant, Harding, D'Oyly Carte Op. Ch. & O, Godfrey

The quality of the Naxos transfer of the 1951 *Patience* is unbelievably better than the companion set of *Iolanthe*, and the performance is much more polished, from the lively Overture onwards. Darrell Fancourt is magnificent as Colonel Calverly (wonderful diction) and almost – but not quite – upstages Martyn Green's memorable Bunthorne. Margaret Mitchell's Patience is fresh and charming, if perhaps a little over-sophisticated, as Alan Styler's Grosvenor is a shade precious. But Ella Halman is a splendid Lady Jane, and her duet with Bunthorne, *So Go to Him and Say to Him*, is a highlight. Throughout the chorus is excellent and the whole performance is full of spirit. Alongside *The Mikado* it was one of the very finest of Godfrey's first series of recordings for Decca and in this excellently managed and well-documented Naxos reissue is very enjoyable indeed.

(i; ii) *The Pirates of Penzance* (complete; without dialogue); (ii; iii) *Trial by Jury*

(BB) (**) Naxos mono 8.110196/7. (i) Green, Fancourt, Halman; (ii) Harding, Osborn; Watson; (ii) Rands, Flyn; D'Oyly Carte Op. Ch. & O, Godfrey

Alas, this 1949 Decca *Pirates*, which appeared first on 78s and later on LP, is lacklustre, with even Godfrey not as sprightly as usual. None of the principals are at their best, and Murial Harding is below form as Mabel. Of course Martyn Green and Darrell Fancourt have their moments, and the performance picks up and becomes more spirited in Act II, with Richard Watson an excellent Sergeant of the Police. It is he who, as the Learned Judge, is at the centre of *Trial by Jury* which shows all concerned in a far better light. Fine singing all round, especially from the chorus, makes this enjoyable, and the recording too has transferred most vividly. But overall this set is primarily of historical interest.

Ruddigore (complete; without dialogue)

(N) (**) Naxos mono 8.110295. Green, Osborn, Mitchell, Watson, Fancourt, Drummond-Grant, D'Oyly Carte Op. Ch. & O, Godfrey

This vintage performance dates from 1950 and now appears on a single CD. If Martyn Green is the star, Darrell Fancourt's famous ghost song (*When the night wind howls*) is memorable too, and the surprise is Ann Drummond-Grant's key number in Act I as Mad Margaret, which is splendidly sung. (She was to move up in the company to take over the various contralto roles very successfully when Ella Halman retired and, later, in real life married Isidore Godfrey.)

Martyn Green as Robin sings the Schubertian lyrical numbers appealingly, disguising his lack of sustained vocal timbre with warmth of personality and brilliant vocal projection. Leonard Osborn is suitably brash and boisterous as Richard. Alas, Margaret Mitchell is ill-cast as Rose Maybud, missing the character's petite innocence, and despite her obvious vocal competence has little charm. Unfortunately the concerted items are also much less successful. The chorus sounds under-rehearsed, with ensemble often ragged, and even the soloists let the side down with doubtful intonation in the great madrigal at the end of Act I. The current CD transfer, however, is very well managed and the quality of the original recording is restored (Decca's own earlier Ace of Clubs LP remastering was very poorly done).

(i) *The Sorcerer* (complete; without dialogue); (ii) Highlights from 1933 recording

(N) (BB) (***) Naxos mono 8.110785/6. (i) Peter Pratt, Harding, Griffiths, Morgan, Skitch, Dixon, Dean, Drummond-Grant, Adams, D'Oyly Carte Op. Ch., New SO; (ii) G. Baker, Dickson, Oldham, Fancourt, Rands, Bethell, Moxton, Gill, Robertson, Ch. & O; both cond. Godfrey

Chronologically the second of the Gilbert and Sullivan collaborations, following (in 1877) *Trial by Jury*, *The Sorcerer* was initially successful enough, but it never sustained that success permanently. Yet music and text offer many pointers to the future, often tickling the ear with now familiar devices. So this is a fascinating and indispensable set for all keen Savoyards. Not only does it make available again the excellent 1953 D'Oyly Carte Decca mono recording of *The Sorcerer*, not previously reissued, but as a bonus it gives us the previous (1933) set, described as Highlights, but more of an abridged version of the opera, originally issued on a series of 10-inch HMV 78s.

The very well-recorded Decca set emerges with uncanny immediacy, especially the chorus, though the earlier version has a limited range, giving less presence to the ensemble numbers. There is not really a weak link in either cast, and Peter Pratt, Ann Drummond-Grant, Muriel Harding, Neville Griffiths and Fisher Morgan all shine in the D'Oyly Carte production. Yet if anything the earlier team of Savoyards is even more distinguished, with the tenor, Derek Oldham as the hero, Alexis, more characterful than his successor, Neville Griffiths, and Darrel Fancourt as Sir Marmaduke even more striking than Fisher Morgan in 1953. In the title role of John Wellington Wells, each time the casting could hardly be stronger, with the opening patter song a hit number in each set, George Baker in 1933 just as fluent and characterful as Peter Pratt in 1953. What Isidore Godfrey brings out in each recording is the liveliness of the early examples of the G&S genre, springing rhythms delectably, while both casts sing with immaculate diction. Amazingly in David Lennick's transfers the 1933 solo voices are just as clear and full in the CD transfer as those recorded on LP 20 years later, and the orchestra does not have the edge which the 1953 Decca gives to the strings.

The Yeomen of the Guard (complete, without dialogue)

(BB) (**) Naxos mono 8.110293/4 (2). Green, Fancourt, Watson, Osborn, Harding, Drummond-Grant, Halman, D'Oyly Carte Op. Ch., New Promenade O, Godfrey (with orchestral selections from the operas: British Light SO, Moore *)

This was another of the best of Decca's first-generation mono sets of the Savoy Operas, recorded in the summer of 1950. Dominated by Martyn Green's inimitable Jack Point, it is strongly cast, with Ella Halman at her commanding best as Dame Carruthers, Richard Watson a formidable Wilfred Shadbolt and Darrel Fancourt in the relatively minor role of Sergent Merryll. Ann Drummond-Grant returned to the company that year to sing the mezzo role of Phoebe very stylishly. (She was to take over the principal contralto roles the following year, when Halman retired.) Muriel Harding is a charming Elsie and the merits of the female cast as a team come out attractively in the closing numbers of Act II, *A Man who would Woo a Fair Maid*, *When a Wooer Goes a Wooing*, and the infinitely touching finale, when Martyn Green shows he can play a tragic role, without overdoing the sentiment, as well as a comic one. (His patter songs are all irresistible.) Godfrey conducts with his usual dedication and vitality, and the chorus sings ardently (the opening of Act II is especially fine). If the ensembles are not always immaculate, that shows the recording conditions of the time, with limited rehearsal and a scratch orchestra. Excellent, vivid mono sound, splendidly transferred: every word is clear. The nostalgic orchestral selections from six operas which follow (including, surprisingly, an excerpt fom *Utopia Ltd*) come from 1935 78s on the Columbia label. The ensemble is very small, with single wind and brass, reminiscent of a pier orchestra, but Stephen Moore's conducting is lively enough and the studio-ish recording is incredibly good and expertly remastered: one could hardly guess the recording date, except that occasionally one can hear some background rustle.

Telarc Mackerras Series
HMS Pinafore
⊛ ✹ *** Telarc CD 80774. Suart, Allen, Evans, Schade, Palmer, Adams, Ch. & O of Welsh Nat. Op., Mackerras

The Mikado
⊛ ✹ *** Telarc CD 80284. Adams, Rolfe Johnson, Suart, McLaughlin, Palmer, Van Allan, Folwell, Ch. & O of Welsh Nat. Op., Mackerras

The Pirates of Penzance
*** Telarc CD80353. Mark Ainsley, Evans, Suart, Van Allan, Adams, Knight, Ch. & O of Welsh Nat. Op., Mackerras

(i) The Yeomen of the Guard; (ii) Trial by Jury
*** Telarc 80404 (2). (i) Mellor, Archer, Palmer; (i; ii) Suart, Adams, Maxwell; (ii) Evans, Banks, Savidge; Ch. & O of Welsh Nat. Op., Mackerras

HMS Pinafore; The Mikado; The Pirates of Penzance; Trial by Jury; The Yeomen of the Guard
⊛ ✹ (M) *** Telarc CD 80500 (5). Above five complete recordings; cond. Mackerras

As can be seen, the five Telarc operas also come together in a slip-case, with five CDs offered for the cost of three – in every way a superb bargain.

Sir Charles Mackerras here gives an exuberant reading of the first operetta of the cycle, *HMS Pinafore*. The lyricism and transparency of Sullivan's inspiration shine out with winning freshness. The casting is not just starry but inspired. Even such a jaunty number as the 'encore' trio, *Never mind the why and wherefore*, gains in point when so well sung and played as here, with Allen joined by Rebecca Evans as an appealing Josephine and Richard Suart as a dry Sir Joseph Porter. Michael Schade is heady-toned as the hero, Ralph Rackstraw, while among character roles Felicity Palmer is a marvellously fruity Little Buttercup, with Richard van Allan as Bill Bobstay and the veteran, Donald Adams, a lugubrious Dick Deadeye. As with the previous CDs of *Mikado* and *Pirates of Penzance*, Telarc squeezes the whole score on to a single CD, vividly recorded.

With the overture again omitted (not Sullivan's work) and one of the stanzas in Ko-Ko's 'little list' song (with words unpalatable today), the whole fizzing Mackerras performance of *The Mikado* is fitted on to a single, very well-filled disc. The cast has no weak link, and Mackerras is electrically sharp at brisk speeds, sounding totally idiomatic and giving this most popular of the G&S operettas an irresistible freshness at high voltage. The tingling vigour of Sullivan's invention is constantly brought out, with performances from the WNO Chorus and Orchestra at once powerful and refined. With that sharpness of focus Sullivan's parodies of grand opera become more than just witty imitations. So Katisha's aria at the end of Act II, with Felicity Palmer the delectable soloist, has a Verdian depth of feeling. It is good too to hear the veteran Savoyard, Donald Adams, as firm and resonant as he was in his D'Oyly Carte recording made no less than 33 years earlier.

The Pirates of Penzance is characteristic of the rest of this splendid Telarc series. Mackerras's exuberant direction often brings fast tempi (as in *How beautifully blue the sky*) but the underlying lyricism is as ardently conveyed as ever, especially by John Mark Ainsley, who is a really passionate Frederic. Rebecca Evans makes him a good partner and sings with great charm as Mabel. Needless to say, Richard Suart is a memorable Major General (his patter song is thrown off at great speed) and Donald Adams has not lost his touch. His vintage portrayal of the Pirate King is well matched by Gillian Knight's Ruth in their engaging 'Paradox' duet of Act II. While memories of Owen Brannigan are far from banished, Richard van Allan is a suitably bumptious Sergeant of the Police, and the Welsh Opera Chorus are splendidly fervent in *Hail poetry!* The recording has fine depth and realism and as a single-disc modern digital version this will be hard to beat.

The Yeomen of the Guard, the fourth Telarc issue of G&S, is very involving as a performance, conveying most exuberantly the sparkle as well as the emotional weight of this most serious of the canon. Alwyn Mellor makes an appealing heroine. Among the others, Felicity Palmer makes a delectably fire-snorting Dame Carruthers, and the veteran, Donald Adams, an incomparable Sergeant Merryll. (His cries of 'Ghastly, ghastly' when cornered by the Dame are wonderful.) Richard Suart as Jack Point characterizes vividly in authentic style, and the only weak link is the Fairfax of Neil Archer, who too often sounds strained. Even so, the final bringing-together of Fairfax and Elsie could not be more touching. The absence of spoken dialogue allows *Trial by Jury* to be included as a fill-up, with Suart even more aptly cast and Adams again incomparable as the Usher, while the WNO Chorus again sings with ideal clarity. Otherwise it involves different singers, with Rebecca Evans golden-toned as the Plaintiff and Barry Banks firm if light as the Defendant.

Other complete recordings

Cox and Box (original, full-length, 1866 version)
*** Divine Arts 2-4104. Berger, Kennedy, Francke, Barclay

This lively and enjoyable performance re-creates the original version of *Cox and Box*, first heard at a private gathering at the librettist Burnand's own house in May 1866, with Sullivan himself improvising the accompaniment at the piano. The orchestration came a year later for the work's prèmiere at the Adelphi Theatre, and the Overture and the duet *Stay Bouncer stay*, were also added subsequently.

The present account (based on a professional production for London Chamber Opera) is spirited and polished, and its considerable length (over an hour) serves to demonstrate the reasons for Sullivan's own shortened version in 1894. It was further truncated in 1921 to produce the concise version which remained in the D'Oyly Carte Company's repertoire until the late 1970s. However, the performance on the present disc is most enjoyable and does not outstay its welcome. Donald Francke is a splendidly rumbustious Bouncer. The charming original compound-time version of the *Bacon lullaby* is considerably different from the song known in the revised score. *Stay Bouncer stay* is added in for good measure. Of course, one misses the orchestra, but the piano accompaniment, using a suitable period instrument, is well managed. The words are admirably clear, a consideration which would surely have been just as important to Burnand as to Gilbert. It is good to see that the production is dedicated to the memory of the late Arthur Jacobs, biographer of Sullivan, at whose insistence this recording (sponsored by the Sullivan Society) was issued commercially.

The Gondoliers (complete; without dialogue)
(BB) (***) Naxos mono 8.110196/7. Green, Osborn, Styler, Mitchell, Harding, Dean, Wright, Goodier, Watson, Halman, D'Oyly Carte Op. Ch., New Promenade O, Godfrey

This vintage *Gondoliers* from the D'Oyly Carte Decca mono era was recorded in 1950, the same year as the similarly excellent *Mikado*. Although originally issued on shellac, both were to be highlights of the early LP catalogue. Even though Decca only gave him a small orchestra, noticeably thin on strings, Godfrey conducts with verve throughout, and he has a splendid cast. Apart from the inimitable Martyn Green as the recalcitrant Duke of Plaza Toro, admirably partnered by Ella Halman as the Duchess, there is a strong Don Alhambra in Richard Watson.

The two Gondolieri, Leonard Osborn and Alan Styler, are perfectly cast and if Osborn (as usual at this period) sounds a bit strained in his higher register, his 'Sparkling Eyes' is still very spirited. The younger women are uniformly good. Margaret Mitchell is a strong Casilda, and Tessa's *When a merry maiden marries*, nicely sung by Yvonne Dean, is as charming as Gianetta's *Kind Sir, you cannot have a heart*, with Muriel Harding in particularly sweet voice. Henry Goodier is not the strongest Luiz, but his meeting duet in Act I with Casilda comes off well. Throughout, the vigorous ensembles have plenty of life, and the *Cachucha* sparkles under Godfrey in a way that it never did with Sargent. The quartet *In a contemplative fashion* is delightfully sung. All-in-all a most entertaining set, cleanly transferred with clear words, even if the orchestra is less full-bodied than one would wish.

The Gondoliers (complete; without dialogue); Overture Di Ballo
*** That's Entertainment CD-TER2 1187 (2). Suart, Rath, Fieldsend, Oke, Ross, Hanley, Woollett, Pert, Creasy, D'Oyly Carte Op. Ch. & O, Pryce-Jones

The That's Entertainment set of *The Gondoliers* was recorded at Abbey Road studios in 1991, offers very good sound and speaks well for the standards of the resuscitated D'Oyly Carte company. The men are very good indeed. Richard Suart's Duke of Plaza Toro is as dry as you could wish, while the voice itself is resonant, and his duet in Act II with the equally excellent Duchess (Jill Pert), in which they dispense honours to the undeserving, is in the best Gilbertian tradition. Perhaps Gianetta (Lesley Echo Ross) and Casilda (Elizabeth Woollett) are less individually distinctive and slightly less vocally secure than their counterparts on the Godfrey and Sargent versions, but they always sing with charm. The chorus is first class – the men are especially virile at the opening of Act II. The orchestral playing is polished, and the ensembles are good, too; John Pryce-Jones conducts with vigour and an impressive sense of theatrical pacing. The finale brings an exhilarating closing *Cachucha* to round the opera off nicely. The acoustic of the recording has both warmth and atmosphere

HMS Pinafore (complete; with dialogue)
*** TER CDTER 1259 (2). Sandison, McVeigh, Boe, Barclay, McCafferty, Wilding, D'Oyly Carte Op. Ch. & O, Edwards

HMS Pinafore (complete; without dialogue)
*** TER CDTER2 1150 (2). Grace, Sandison, Gillett, Ritchie, Ormiston, Lawlor, New Sadler's Wells Op. Ch. & O, Phipps

The comparatively recent series of D'Oyly Carte stage revivals at London's Savoy Theatre, the natural home of G&S, have brought a breath of fresh air into the company's traditional style of performance, with an imaginative new approach to production values. The set changed to that of an early steamship, looking more like the deck of a cruise-ship than a navy frigate, and this lighter touch to the proceedings is helped by Frances McCafferty's engagingly individual Scottish Buttercup.

Gordon Sandison here moved on from his casting as Captain Corcoran in the 1987 Sadler's Wells production to an avuncular, less aristocratic portrayal of Sir Joseph, an infectiously spirited characterization which is vivaciously caught in this recording. Tom McVeigh's crisply enunciated portrayal of the Captain makes an excellent foil. The two lovers are vocally perfectly matched, with Alfred Boe's pleasingly ardent tenor paired with the simplicity of Yvonne Barclay's delightfully sweet-voiced Josephine. In short, it is difficult to imagine this opera being more effectively cast, while with John Owen Edwards at the helm, the sheer zip of the briny choruses in Act I is matched by the vibrant ensembles which close both Acts.

The dialogue interchanges between the principal characters are increasingly engaging, especially Buttercup and the Captain, while Dick Deadeye's colloquial accent underlines the common sense of his observations without losing the gruffness. An interesting novelty is the reinstatement of Hebe's dialogue (cut, for reasons explained in the booklet, just before the opera's original premiere) and a section of abandoned recitative for the principals in the finale. Also included is a reconstructed duet, *Reflect My Child*, between the Captain and Josephine in Act I. All-in-all this sparkling set cannot be too highly praised and the vivid recording projects the voices with such clarity that every word is clear.

As with the new generation of D'Oyly Carte recordings, the 1987 Sadler's Wells set has a fine theatrical atmosphere. It is consistently well cast, with Linda Ormiston a pleasing Buttercup, if not so individual as Frances McCafferty, and Nickolas Grace making a traditionally aristocratic Sir Joseph Porter. The lovers sing well together and the choral numbers of Act I have plenty of zest. Simon Phipps paces the music fluently, if without quite the unerring timing of Godfrey or the sheer zest of John Owen Edwards, and this is very likeable from first to last, especially if no dialogue is required. While the famous Godfrey set is not upstaged, nor the more recent D'Oyly Carte version, this is still very enjoyable. Moreover it offers three fascinatingly different endings (separately cued), so that listeners can choose their own. One includes Arne's *Rule Brittania* as used for Queen Victoria's Jubilee celebrations.

Iolanthe (complete; without dialogue). Thespis (orchestral suite)

**(*) That's Entertainment CD-TER2 1188 (2). Suart, Woollett, Blake Jones, Richard, Creasy, Pert, Rath, Hanley, D'Oyly Carte Op. Ch. & O, Pryce-Jones

After the success of the new D'Oyly Carte *Gondoliers*, this fresh look at *Iolanthe* is something of a disappointment. John Pryce-Jones obviously sees it as a very dramatic opera indeed, and he ensures that the big scenes have plenty of impact (the *March of the Peers* is resplendent with brass). But his strong forward pressure means that the music feels almost always fast-paced, and the humour is completely upstaged by the drama, especially in the long Act I Finale, which is certainly zestful. The Lord Chancellor's two patter songs in Act I, *The law is the true embodiment* and *When I went to the bar*, are very brisk in feeling, and Richard Suart, an excellent Lord Chancellor, is robbed of the necessary relaxed delivery so that the words can be relished for themselves. Jill Pert is certainly a formidable Queen of the Fairies, but elsewhere the lack of charm is a distinct drawback.

(i) Iolanthe: highlights; (ii) The Mikado (complete; without dialogue)

○━ (B) *** CfP (ADD) 575 9902 (2). (i) Shilling, Harwood, Moyle, Dowling, Begg, Bevan, Greene, Kern; (ii) Holmes, Revill, Wakefield, Studholme, Dowling, Allister, John Heddle Nash; Sadler's Wells Op. Ch. & O, Faris

The Sadler's Wells *Iolanthe* is stylistically superior to Sargent's earlier EMI recording and is often musically superior to the Decca/D'Oyly Carte versions. Alexander Faris often chooses untraditional tempi. *When I went to the bar* is very much faster than usual, with less dignity but with a compensating lightness of touch. Eric Shilling is excellent here, as he is also in the *Nightmare song*, which is really *sung*, much being made of the ham operatic recitative at the beginning. The lovers, Elizabeth Harwood as Phyllis and Julian Moyle as Strephon, make a charming duo, and the Peers are splendid. Their entry chorus is thrilling and their reaction to the Fairy Queen's curse is delightfully, emphatically horrified, while the whole Act I finale (the finest in any of the operas) goes with

infectious stylishness. All the solo singing is of a high standard and Leon Greene sings the Sentry song well. But one has to single out for special praise Patricia Kern's really lovely singing of Iolanthe's aria at the end of the opera. The recording has splendid presence and realism.

The Sadler's Wells *Mikado* is traditional in the best sense, bringing a humorous sparkle to the proceedings which gives great delight. Clive Revill is a splendid Ko-Ko; John Heddle Nash is an outstanding Pish-Tush, and it is partly because of him that the *Chippy chopper* trio is so effective. Denis Dowling is a superb Pooh-Bah, and Marion Studholme a charming Yum-Yum. Jean Allister's Katisha is first rate in every way; listen to the venom she puts into the word '*bravado*' in the Act I finale. Even the chorus scores a new point by their stylized singing of *Mi-ya-sa-ma*, which sounds engagingly mock-Japanese. The one disappointment is John Holmes in the name-part. He sings well but conveys little of the mock-satanic quality. But this is a small point in an otherwise magnificent set, which has a vivacious new overture arranged by Charles Mackerras.

The Mikado (complete; without dialogue)

**(*) TER CDTER 1178 (2). Ducarel, Roberts, Bottone, Rees, Rivers, Gorton, D'Oyly Carte Op. Ch. & O, Pryce-Jones

The newest D'Oyly Carte *Mikado* dates from 1989 so it is a comparatively distant relative of the very successful 2001 production at the Savoy, revived in 2002. What is common to both is the superb choral and orchestral contributions (the latter with its arresting opening bass drum and splendidly regal trumpets to announce the Lord High Executioner). The cast is uniformly strong, with Bonaventura Bottone a fine Nanki-Poo and Deborah Rees a pleasing if not memorable Yum-Yum. Eric Roberts is a fairly traditional Ko-Ko, though his extended 'little list' now sounds very dated. Alas, additional lyrics for this famous number seldom match Gilbert's wit, and their topicality soon evaporates. Moreover Roberts's darker baritone has less charm than, say, Martyn Green, when he woos Katisha with *On a Tree by a River*.

Michael Ducarel is an authoritative Mikado, but his repeated guttural laugh (following in the Fancourt tradition) rather goes over the top, especially second time round. However, John Pryce-Jones paces the ensembles admirably and directs the whole proceedings with vigour and aplomb. The drama of both Act finales, with Susan Gorton a splendidly venemous Katisha, leading both ensembles very powerfully, is indeed memorable. A fine performance then, with excellent teamwork, very well recorded with a real theatrical atmosphere; but overall the cast shows rather less individuality than in the other recent D'Oyly Carte recordings.

The Mikado (slightly abridged)

**(*) TER CDTER 1121. Angus, Idle, Bottone, Garrett, Van Allan, Palmer, ENO Ch. & O, Robinson

This selection from the 1986 ENO production includes all the important numbers. As is normal, the performance is dominated by Ko-Ko and Eric Idle takes the role effectively enough, although his 'little list' is, understandably, even more dated than Eric Roberts's additions in the newest D'Oyly Carte version. Bonaventura Bottone is a rather stylized Nanki-Poo, but Lesley Garrett anticipates her later fame with her charming portrait of Yum-Yum. There are some memorable moments here, and the recording is vivid, but this will appeal primarily to those wanting a memento of the English National Opera production.

The Pirates of Penzance (complete; without dialogue)
*** TER CDTER2 1177 (2). Roberts, Creasy, Hill Smith, Rivers, Gorton, Jones, D'Oyly Carte Op. Ch. & O, Pryce-Jones

This D'Oyly Carte production, like the companion set of *The Mikado*, dates back to 1989, but its verve and panache recognizably carried through to the much more recent revival at the Savoy. It is splendidly paced and could hardly be better cast. Even Samuel (Gareth Jones), who opens the show with *Pour, Oh Pour the Pirate Sherry*, is strong-voiced enough to take a more leading role, and Susan Gorton immediately shows her versatility as a very personable Ruth, with fine characterization and crisp diction. She is partnered by Malcolm Rivers's commanding Pirate King, while the lovers, Philip Creasy as Frederic and the charming Marilyn Hill Smith, are equally well matched (especially in the lovely *Oh Leave me Not to Pine Alone*). Eric Roberts's bold portrayal of the Major General will disappoint no one, and in Act II Simon Masterton Smith makes a winningly colloquial Sergeant of Police. The whole of the second Act has tremendous pace and gusto, with the choral numbers from both Pirates and Police superbly sung, given an exhilarating lift by the conductor. The recording is first class and altogether this might be counted the most vividly theatrical *Pirates* on record. One returns to it with unalloyed pleasure.

Ruddigore (complete recording of original score; without dialogue)
*** That's Entertainment CDTER2 1128. Hill Smith, Sandison, Davies, Ayldon, Hillman, Innocent, Hann, Ormiston, Lawlor, New Sadler's Wells Op. Ch. & O, Phipps

What is exciting about the New Sadler's Wells production of *Ruddigore* is that it includes the original finale, created by the logic of Gilbert's plot which brought *all* the ghosts back to life, rather than just the key figure. The opera is strongly cast, with Marilyn Hill Smith and David Hillman in the principal roles and Joan Davies a splendid Dame Hannah, while Harold Innocent as Sir Despard and Linda Ormiston as Mad Margaret almost steal the show. Simon Phipps conducts brightly and keeps everything moving forward, even if his pacing is not always as assured as in the classic Sargent version. The recording is first class, with fine theatrical atmosphere.

The Yeomen of the Guard (complete; without dialogue)
*** TER CDTER2 1195 (2). Maxwell, Pert, Gray, Ross, Roebuck, Fieldsend, Montaine, D'Oyly Carte Op. Ch. & O, Edwards

This 1992 D'Oyly Carte production of *The Yeomen of the Guard* is outstanding in every way, with the splendidly authoritative and formidable Dame Carruthers (Jill Pert) dominating the action by the force of her vocal personality. Her nobly sung *When our Gallant Norman Foes* is a sombre highlight of Act I, and she gets excellent support from Terence Sharpe's Sergeant Meryll. The consistently vibrant choral singing, from men and women alike, is often viscerally thrilling, and gives splendid weight and bite to the finales of both Acts, admirably paced by John Owen Edwards. And how beautifully the women sing the lovely melody which opens the second act, *Night has Spread her Pall*.

There is no weak link in the cast. Janine Roebuck is a most appealing Phoebe, even if perhaps she could have found more wit in *Were I thy Bride*, Lesley Echo Ross rises to her big moments as a sympathetic Elsie Maynard, and the pleasingly-voiced David Fieldsend is a convincingly gallant Colonel

Fairfax. It was an excellent idea to include the spirited snatch of dialogue with which Jack Point (Fenton Gray) and Elsie make their entry, and Point not only delivers his patter songs with aplomb but the comic duets he shares with Wilfred Shadbolt (Gary Montaine) are the more telling for being sung colloquially. But above all it is the superb theatrical atmosphere of the recording which tells, after a spacious account of the Overture played by an expanded orchestra, with the strings again sounding richly full-bodied at the Introducion to Act II.

There are bonuses too, including an additional verse for the third and fourth Yeomen in the Act I finale, and, as an appendix, extra numbers for Sergeant Meryll and Wilfred Shadbolt (*A Joyous Torment*) and an earlier version of Fairfax's *Is Life a Boon?* Highly recommended.

Collections

Arias from: *The Beauty Stone; The Chieftain; The Emerald Isle; Haddon Hall; Ivanhoe; The Martyr of Antioch; The Rose of Persia*
**(*) TER CDTER 1248. Davies, Jones, Knight, Masterson, McCafferty, Stuart, Nat. SO, Steadman

While Sullivan's most successful works are undoubtedly found in his collaboration with W. S. Gilbert, their ten-year quarrel of 1890 led the composer to use other collaborators and to venture into more 'serious' works. The arias on this disc date from that period, and, as recent performances of the complete works have shown, they contain music of much quality and fine invention, if less consistency. This disc gathers some of the best numbers. *In Days of Old* (from *Haddon Hall*), *The Gay Hussar* (from *The Chieftain*), and *I Care Not if the Cup I Hold* (from *The Rose of Persia*) are all rollicking, lively songs in the best Sullivan manner, while there is characteristic lyrical appeal in such arias as *O Moon Art Thou Clad* (from *Ivanhoe*).

If You Wish to Appear as an Irish Type (from *The Emerald Isle*) is a patter-song and would fit easily into any of the Savoy operas, while *Since it Dwelt in That Rock* (from *The Beauty Stone*) is another first-class melody, embellished with piquant detail. *Ah, Oui, J'étais une pensionnaire* (from *The Chieftain*) is sung in both French and English, to charming effect, as if the ghost of André Messager had suddenly taken over its composition. There are some splendid choruses too: the opening *Now Glory to the God Who Breaks* (from *The Martyr of Antioch*) sounds almost like Weber with its flurry of brass. With some typically enjoyable ensembles, such as *On the Heights of Glentaun* (another item from *The Emerald Isle*), the programme is varied and well designed. The performances are generally of quality, though occasionally an obtrusive vibrato mars the singing, notably Gillian Knight's acccount of *Io Paean* (from *The Martyr of Antioch*), but with such G&S stalwarts as Valerie Masterson, the character of the music is well captured. The recording is very good and full texts are included.

'Gilbert and Sullivan Favourites': Excerpts from: *The Gondoliers; The Grand Duke; Haddon Hall; HMS Pinafore; Iolanthe; The Mikado; Patience; The Pirates of Penzance; Ruddigore; The Sorcerer; The Yeomen of the Guard*
☛ (N) (BB) *** EMI HMV 5 86728-2. Masterson, Tear, Bournemouth Sinf., Alwyn; or Armstrong, Tear, Luxon, N. Sinfonia, Hickox

This is perhaps the most attractive and generous single-disc Gilbert and Sullivan anthology in the catalogue (73 minutes).

It is drawn from a pair of LPs originally issued in the mid-1980s. The first features Valerie Masterson and Robert Tear with sparkling accompaniments ably directed by Kenneth Alwyn. It is notable for the clever choice of material, with items from different operas engagingly juxtaposed instead of being gathered together in sequence. The singing is enchantingly fresh and spontaneous. Valerie Masterson's upper range is ravishing, clear and free. Robert Tear's *A wand'ring minstrel* is wonderfully stylish, while in the duets the two artists consistently project their response to the words as well as the music – the final cadence of *Leave me not to pine alone* is very touching. The second collection also includes Robert Tear, now joined by Benjamin Luxon and Sheila Armstrong, and it is Luxon who introduces the principal novelty, *I've heard it said* from *Haddon Hall*, a vintage Sullivan number, even though the words are not by Gilbert. Luxon is no less personable in *When you find you're a broken-down critter* from *The Grand Duke* and he partners well with Robert Tear in duets from *Ruddigore* and *The Gondoliers*. Sheila Armstrong is heard at her best in *For love alone* from *The Sorcerer*, and if, when the three artists sing together in *Here's a how-de-do!*, some of the polish is missing, there is no lack of spirit. The compilation is underpinned by understanding accompaniments from Hickox, and given vivid recording throughout which however tends at times to exaggerate the vocal consonants. A very real bargain nevertheless.

'The Gold Collection': extracts from: (i; iv) *The Gondoliers; HMS Pinafore; Iolanthe.* (ii; v) *The Mikado.* (i; iv) *Patience.* (ii; iv) *The Pirates of Penzance.* (ii; vi) *Princess Ida; Ruddigore.* (ii; iv) *The Sorcerer.* (iii–iv) *Trial by Jury;* (ii; vi) *The Yeomen of the Guard*

〄 ➤ ✪ (B) *** Double Decca (ADD) 460 010-2 (2). Reed, Masterson, Knight, Round, Adams, Sandford, Wright, Brannigan, Toye, Styler and soloists, D'Oyly Carte Op. Ch., (i) New SO; (ii) RPO; (iii) ROHCG O; cond. (iv) Godfrey; (v) Nash; (vi) Sargent

If you are looking for a CD to cheer you up on a dull day, either of the pair which make up this Double Decca will serve admirably. The overall selection earns full marks for perception and variety. *The Mikado* is (understandably) the most generously treated, including ten items, and the only real miscalculation was to end the second disc with the trio, *This helmet I suppose* from *Princess Ida*, which, following immediately after John Reed's delicious *Whene'er I spoke sarcastic joke*, comes as an anticlimax. The joyous trio, *If you go in, you're sure to win*, from *Iolanthe* (which comes earlier) would have been more effective or, better still, the Act I finale, which is omitted and for which there would have just about been room. Yet this is carping. The consistent wit of Gilbert's words, the delightful Sullivan melodies and the sparkle of Godfrey's conducting are a constant joy.

'The Best of Gilbert and Sullivan': highlights from *The Gondoliers; HMS Pinafore; Iolanthe; The Mikado; Patience; The Pirates of Penzance; Ruddigore; Trial by Jury; The Yeomen of the Guard*

(B) *** EMI (ADD) 5 73869-2 (3). Morison, M. Sinclair, Thomas, G. Baker, Lewis, Brannigan, Young, Wallace, Cameron, Evans, Milligan, Glyndebourne Festival Ch., Pro Arte O, Sargent

This three-disc EMI set makes a good supplement for the comparable Double Decca collection (see above). The Sargent recordings are generally more grandly operatic in style

and at times they are rather less fun. But, as one might expect from the starry cast list, there is some outstandingly fine solo and concerted singing from the principals in the lyrical numbers. Obviously with the film *Topsy-Turvy* in mind, the major selection is from *The Mikado* (some 20 items), and Sargent's expansive manner has much in common with Carl Davis's approach (especially in the Finale). With Owen Brannigan as The Mikado, Monica Sinclair as Katisha, Richard Lewis as Nanki-Poo, Elsie Morison as Yum-Yum and Ian Wallace as Pooh-Bah, the results will surely please those who enjoyed the movie.

Princess Ida and *The Sorcerer* are not represented, but the other key operas (apart from the single Learned Judge's number from *Trial by Jury*) have between five and eight items each, including the substantial and treasurable finales from *Iolanthe* and (to conclude the programme) *The Yeomen of the Guard*. Besides taking the role of the Judge in *Trial*, George Baker is a stalwart of the series and he delivers the famous patter songs with aplomb.

No less a figure than Sir Geraint Evans takes his place as the Duke of Plaza Toro (*Gondoliers*), and Jack Point (*Yeomen*). Owen Brannigan is an unforgettable Sergeant of Police (*Pirates*) and is hardly less memorable as Private Willis (*Iolanthe*) and Sir Despard (*Ruddigore*). The choral contribution is first class, and Sir Malcolm Sargent conducts freshly throughout, although not always with the sparkle that Godfrey commanded, as is instanced by his curiously measured *Cachucha* in *The Gondoliers*. But the selections from *Patience* and *Ruddigore* show him and this talented company (Elsie Morison especially) at their very finest.

'The Best of Gilbert and Sullivan': excerpts from: *The Gondoliers; HMS Pinafore; Iolanthe; The Mikado; Patience; The Pirates of Penzance; The Yeomen of the Guard*

(M) **(*) Sony SMK 89248. Soloists, D'Oyly Carte Op. Ch. & O, Edwards or Pryce-Jones

Intended as a companion selection to *Topsy-Turvy* below, these present-day D'Oyly Carte recordings have plenty of life and vigour. Indeed, both conductors favour very brisk tempi, and often there is a sense that the music is being driven very hard, with the *Tripping thither* chorus in *Iolanthe* rhythmically almost over-pointed. Simon Butteriss's *Am I alone and unobserved* is very dramatic indeed, but this certainly gives the number a fresh impetus. There is plenty of good singing, and among the other principals Richard Suart does not disappoint in the Lord Chancellor's patter songs in *Iolanthe* and in *From the sunny Spanish shore* from the *Gondoliers*. Eric Roberts takes over effectively as the Major-General, and Eric Rogers is an engaging Ko-Ko for *Tit-willow* in *The Mikado*. Marilyn Hill-Smith's *Poor wand'ring one* is pleasingly fresh and Donald Maxwell provides a military zest for his two numbers in *Patience*. The disc is generously full, but each selection is rather meagre. *The Yeomen of the Guard* has only two items, and the second, *Here's a man of jollity*, cuts off rather suddenly. Better to have omitted the two overtures (beautifully played as they are) and perhaps to have concentrated on fewer operas and offered more music from each. Still, this is all enjoyable enough and vividly recorded.

Highlights from: *The Gondoliers; HMS Pinafore; Iolanthe; The Mikado; The Pirates of Penzance; The Yeomen of the Guard*

(B) **(*) CfP (ADD) CD-CFP 4238. Soloists, Glyndebourne Festival Ch., Pro Arte O, Sargent

An attractive selection of highlights offering samples of six of Sargent's vintage EMI recordings. There is some distinguished solo singing and, if the atmosphere is sometimes a little cosy, there is a great deal to enjoy. The recordings have transferred well.

Highlights from: (i; ii) *HMS Pinafore*; (iii; iv) *The Mikado*; (ii; iv; v) *The Pirates of Penzance*; (ii; vi) *Trial by Jury*; (vii) *The Yeomen of the Guard*

*** Telarc CD 80431. Suart, with (i) Allen, Palmer; (ii) Evans; (iii) Rolfe Johnson, McLaughlin, Howells, Watson; (iv) Van Allan, Folwell; (v) Mark Ainsley, Gossage; (vi) Banks, Garrett, Savidge, Rhys Davies; (vii) Archer, Mellor, Stephen; Welsh Nat. Op. Ch. & O, Mackerras

Even with 76 minutes' playing time, this can be no more than a sampler of Mackerras's effervescent G&S series for Telarc, dominated by the dry-timbred Richard Suart in the key patrician roles. As can be seen, most of the other soloists change with each opera, but the standard remains extraordinarily high. The choice of excerpts is inevitably arbitrary, with about half a dozen items from each of the two-Act operas and three from *Trial by Jury*. If you buy this, you will inevitably be tempted to go on to one or other of the complete sets. Nevertheless it is a splendid collection in its own right. Characteristically first-class Telarc sound.

'Topsy-Turvy' (music from the film soundtrack, with interludes arr. Carl Davis): includes excerpts from: *The Grand Duke* (orchestral only); *The Mikado*; *Princess Ida*; *The Sorcerer*; *The Yeomen of the Guard*; *The Lost Chord*; *The Long Day Closes* (arr. Davis)

**(*) Sony SK 61834. Soloists Ch. & O, Carl Davis

Mike Leigh's film *Topsy-Turvy* was a personal indulgence. The choice of music is also personal and arbitrary, and not all of it works especially effectively in the cinema. But the film centres on the conception, writing and première of *The Mikado*. The excerpts from this masterpiece are as splendidly sung as they are extravagantly costumed, although, considering its importance as the emotional climax of the plot, it is surprising that the Mikado's famous Act II solo is not heard complete. Carl Davis's arrangements used as interludes are pleasing if not charismatic, but for many the principal weakness of this collection will be Davis's often over-deliberate tempi. Yet the quality of the singing triumphs over this drawback, with Timothy Spall and Louise Gold splendid as the Mikado and Katisha respectively, while Martin Savage is in his element in the patter songs. But why, oh why, was *Tit-willow* omitted? The recording is outstanding, often approaching demonstration quality, and the accompanying booklet is handsomely colour-illustrated and includes full texts.

SUPPÉ, Franz von (1819–95)

Complete overtures

Vol. 1: Overtures: *Carnival; Die Frau Meisterin; Die Irrfahrt um's Glück (Fortune's Labyrinth); The Jolly Robbers (Banditenstreiche); Pique Dame; Poet and Peasant; Des Wanderers Ziel (The Goal of the Wanderers). Boccaccio: Minuet & Tarantella. Donna Juanita: Juanita march*

** Marco Polo 8.223647. Slovak State PO (Košice), A. Walter

Vol. 2: Overtures: *Beautiful Galate (Die schöne Galatee); Boccaccio; Donna Juanita; Isabella; Der Krämer und sein Kommis (The Shopkeeper and His Assistant); Das Modell (The Model); Paragraph 3; Tantalusqualen. Fatinitza March*

** Marco Polo 8.223648. Slovak State PO (Košice), A. Walter

Vol. 3: Overtures: *Fatinitza; Franz Schubert; Die Heimkehr von der Hochzeit (Homecoming from the Wedding); Light Cavalry; Trioche and Cacolet; Triumph. Boccaccio: March. Herzenseintracht polka; Humorous Variations on 'Was kommt dort von der Höhv'; Titania Waltz*

** Marco Polo 8.223683. Slovak State PO (Košice), A. Walter

Alfred Walter's performances here are unsubtle, but they have a rumbustious vigour that is endearing and, with enthusiastic playing from the Slovak orchestra, who are obviously enjoying themselves, the effect is never less than spirited. Many of the finest of the lesser-known pieces are already available in more imaginative versions from Marriner. But Walter has uncovered some attractive novelties, as well as some pleasing if inconsequential interludes and dances. On Volume 1 *Carnival* (nothing like Dvořák's piece), opens rather solemnly, then introduces a string of ideas, including a polka, a waltz and a galop. *Des Wanderers Ziel* begins very energetically and, after brief harp roulades, produces a rather solemn cello solo and brass choir; later there is an attractive lyrical melody, but there are plenty of histrionics too, and the dancing ending brings distinctly Rossinian influences.

In Volume 2 *Isabella* is introduced as a sprightly Spanish lady, but Viennese influences still keep popping up, while *Paragraph 3* summons the listener with a brief horn-call and then has another striking lyrical theme, before gaiety takes over. *Der Krämer und sein Kommis* proves to be an early version (the ear notices a slight difference at the dramatic opening) of an old friend, *Morning, Noon and Night in Vienna*. *Donna Juanita* brings a violin solo of some temperament; then, after some agreeably chattering woodwind, comes a grand march.

On the third CD, *Trioche and Cacolet* immediately introduces a skipping tune of great charm and, after another of Suppé's appealing lyrical themes, ends with much rhythmic vigour. The biographical operetta about *Schubert* opens with an atmospheric, half-sinister reference to the *Erlkönig* and follows with further quotations, prettily scored; however, the writing coarsens somewhat vulgarly at the end. But the prize item here is a set of extremely ingenious variations on a local folksong, which translates as *What comes there from on high?* It seems like a cross between 'A Hunting we will Go' and 'The Grand Old Duke of York'.

Vol. 4: Overtures: *Dame Valentin oder Frauenräuber und Wanderbursche; Dolch und Rose oder Das Donaumädchen; Der Gascogner; Die G'frettbrüderln; Die Hammerschmidin aus Steiermark oder Folgen einer Landpartie; Kopf und Herz; Reise durch die Märchenwelt; Unterthänig und Unabhängig; Zwei Pistolen*

**(*) Marco Polo 8.223865. Slovak State PO (Košice), Pollack

The intriguing titles here provide the entrée to music of much charm and inexhaustible melody – little of the music here is dull. The opening *Der Gascogner* ('The Man from Gascogny') begins with a rather haunting series of held notes on the horn, and the melodramatic opening of *Dolch und Rose* ('The Dagger and the Rose') is not quite what we expect from this composer. *Dame Valentin oder Frauenräuber* ('Dame Valentin or Lady Robber') has a piquant opening, complete with triangle, before melting into some delightful melodies, including, of course, some spirited waltzes and galops. There is plenty to enjoy here, especially some of

Suppé's more ambitious writing – *Reise durch die Märchen-welt* ('Journey through the World of Fairies') has passages which sound almost Wagnerian. The performances here are sympathetic, although the recording lacks ideal richness.

Beautiful Galathea: Overture

(M) *** Sony (ADD) SMK 61830. NYPO, Bernstein – BIZET: *Symphony in C*; OFFENBACH: *Gaîté parisienne*, etc. **

An excellent performance of the *Beautiful Galathea overture* from Bernstein: frothy in the fast sections, but sensitive in the quiet passages – especially in the strings. The 1967 recording is warm and vivid, though the couplings are not quite so recommendable.

Overtures: Beautiful Galathea; Boccaccio; Light Cavalry; Morning, Noon and Night in Vienna; Pique Dame; Poet and Peasant

(N) (M) *** Mercury **SACD** (ADD) 470 638-2. Detroit SO, Paray – AUBER: *Overtures: The Bronze Horse; Fra Diavolo; Masaniello* ✪

Paray injects plenty of verve and exhilaration in his Suppé performances, which sound totally fresh and convincing. His chimerical approach to *Beautiful Galathea* (with a wonderfully luminous passage from the Detroit strings near the very opening) is captivating, and the bravura violin playing to match the resplendent brass in *Light Cavalry* is remarkably deft. With the splendid Auber coupling, this is one of Mercury's most desirable CDs, sounding superb, with a degree of extra warmth on SACD.

OPERETTA

Die schöne Galathea

*** CPO 999 726. Bogner, Rickenbacher, Heyn, Kupfer, Koblenz State Theatre Ch., Rhenish State Op. O, Eitler

Starting with the famous galumphing overture, Suppe's one-act operetta on a classical theme is a delight. Pygmalion may still fall in love with his statue of Galathea, when she comes to life – a marvellous moment for the bright, clear soprano, Andrea Bogner – but in this comic retelling she is just a provocative coquette, who much prefers the young Ganymed, taken here by another soprano, Juliane Heyn. First heard in Vienna in 1865, this starts like Offenbach in German, but turns into a precursor of Viennese operetta the moment that waltz-time is engaged. Based on a production in Koblenz on the Rhine, this is a sparkling, well-balanced recording, with the comic persona characterfully taken by Hans-Jurg Rickenbacher and Michael Kupfer. It might have been even more fun had a sprinkling of spoken dialogue been included. As it is, the single disc comes with libretto and translation in a cumbersome double-disc jewel-case.

SURINACH, Carlos (1915–97)

Piano Concerto

(N) *** Australian Decca Eloquence (ADD) 476 2971. Larrocha, RPO, Burgos – ALBENIZ: *Rapsodia española*; MONTSALVATGE: *Concerto brève*; TURINA: *Rapsodia sinfónica* ***

Carlos Surinach's *Piano Concerto*, like its Montsalvatge companion on this disc, was written for Alicia de Larrocha, and, as with that work, she plays it with total conviction. If, once

again, the writing is short on really memorable themes, it is made enjoyable through its colourful orchestration, plus a fine performance, backed up by first class Decca (1977) sound. Anyone who enjoys a dash of Spanish colour in their music will enjoy this rare concerto, and offered with imaginative couplings too.

SUSSMAYR, Franz (1766–1803)

Requiem

(N) **(*) Avie AV 0047. Jette, Larmore, Taylor, Owens, St Olaf Ch., St Paul CO, Delfs – MOZART: *Requiem* **(*)

All credit to the recording producer, Malcolm Bruno, for searching out the long-forgotten *Requiem* of Franz Sussmayr, written about the time he made his completion of the Mozart *Requiem*. Though it is no masterpiece it is a fascinating curiosity, a setting in German written for one of the Austrian duchies which by a special papal dispensation were allowed to sing the Requiem in the vernacular. The choral writing is plain and direct in a simple homophonic idiom, influenced by the cadences of Austrian folk music. It is a style well suited to this paraphrase of the usual Latin text. Andreas Delfs' direction, as in the Mozart with which it is coupled, is on the square side, but with fresh, alert singing by the St Olaf Choir under their director, Anton Armstrong, that matches the music well. Full, open sound.

SVENDSEN, Johann Severin (1840–1911)

Romance in G, Op. 26

(BB) *** Naxos 8.550329. Kang, Slovak (Bratislava) RSO, Leaper – HALVORSEN: *Air Norvégien* etc.; SIBELIUS: *Violin Concerto*; SINDING: *Légende* ***

Dong-Suk Kang plays Svendsen's once-popular *Romance in G* without sentimentality but with full-hearted lyricism. The balance places him a little too forward, but the recording is very satisfactory.

Symphonies 1 in D, Op. 4; 2 in B flat, Op. 15

(BB) *** EMI Encore 5 85069-2. Oslo PO, Jansons

(BB) *** Naxos 8.553898. Bournemouth SO, Engeset

(BB) **(*) Warner Apex 0927 40621-2. Norwegian R. O, Rasilainen

Symphonies 1 in D, Op. 4; 2 in B flat, Op. 23; Polonaise, Op. 28

*** Chan. 9932 Danish Nat. R SO, Dausgaard

Symphonies 1-2; 2 Swedish Folk-Melodies, Op. 27

*** BIS CD 347. Gothenburg SO, Järvi

Svendsen's *D major Symphony* is a student work of astonishing assurance and freshness, in some ways even more remarkable than the *B flat*. Neeme Järvi gives first-class performances, sensitive and vital, and the excellent recordings earn them a strong recommendation.

The performances from Mariss Jansons and the Oslo Philharmonic are also distinguished by first-rate ensemble, alert rhythms and keenly articulated phrasing. They have much the same enthusiasm and relish as their Gothenberg rivals, who offer a bonus in the transcription for strings of two *Swedish folk melodies*. But although there is not much to choose between the two recordings, the Oslo orchestra has the richer sonority and the EMI disc is now reissued in the lowest price category.

Thomas Dausgaard and the Danish Radio Orchestra also capture the youthful exuberance of the one and the warmth and generosity of spirit of the other. This is captivating music and the Danes, among whom Svendsen spent so much of his life, respond with enthusiasm. Tempi are well judged though the scherzo of the D major would benefit from being brisker. The *Polonaise* of 1881 is not the equal of the famous *Fest-Polonaise*. Recommended alongside though not necessarily in preference to Järvi.

Järvi's recording is also strongly challenged by Bjarte Engeset and the Bournemouth orchestra. These players are obviously encountering this music with enthusiasm and they are well served by both the acoustic and the engineering. At the Naxos price it is a real bargain.

There is nothing wrong with the Finlandia version from the Norwegian Radio Orchestra under Ari Rasilainen either (though the recording is not as good as BIS for Järvi) and at Apex price remains fully competitive.

Symphony 2; Carnival in Paris, Op. 9; Norwegian Artists' Carnival, Op. 14; Norwegian Rhapsody 2, Op. 19; (i) Romance in G, for Violin & Orchestra, Op. 26
** Chatsworth FCM 1002. Stavanger SO, Llewelyn; (i) with Thorsen

Decent performances from Stavanger of the *Second Symphony* and other popular Svendsen pieces under the Welsh conductor, Grant Llewelyn. The strings do not have the depth of sonority of their immediate rivals, but the orchestra plays with freshness and enthusiasm.

(i) Octet in A, Op. 3; (i) Romance in G for Violin & Strings, Op. 26
*** Chan. 9258. ASMF Chamber Ens. (i) with Sillito –
NIELSEN: *String Quintet in G* ***

(i) Octet; String Quartet in A min., Op. 1
*** BIS CD753. Kontra Qt; with (i) Bjørnkjaer, Madsen, Rasmussen, Johansen

Svendsen's youthful *Octet, Op. 3* is a product of his student years at Leipzig, and was obviously inspired by Mendelssohn. But, it has a strong personality of its own and is full of lively and attractive invention. The scherzo is particularly delightful. The Kontra Quartet and their colleagues give a spirited account of it, coupling it with another student work, the *A minor Quartet, Op. 1*. A good well-balanced sound.

However, those primarily wanting the *Octet* should turn to the Academy of St Martin-in-the-Fields Chamber Ensemble whose leader, Kenneth Sillito plays the G major *Romance* as a fill-up. First-rate performances and recording.

String Quartet in A min., Op. 1; (i) String Quintet in C, Op. 5
*** CPO 999 858-2. Olso String Qt, (i) with Graggerud

Two early works, composed while Svendsen was at the Leipzig Conservatoire. Both show a natural feeling for form and an unfailing sense of proportion. Svendsen thinks in long musical paragraphs, and his ideas have a strong, lyrical momentum as well as astonishing assurance and freshness. Both Op. 1 and Op. 5 were coupled together many years ago by the Hindar Quartet, but these Oslo players have much greater tonal blend and refinement, as well as unanimity of attack.

Two delightful and rewarding scores that have been absurdly neglected, now very persuasively played and well recorded.

SWEELINCK, Jan (1562–1621)

ORGAN MUSIC

Allein Gott in der Höh sei Ehr; Ballo del granduca; Christe qui lux est et dies; Echo Fantasia (Ionian); Engelsche Foruyn; Erbarme dich mein; Est-ce Mars?; O Herre Gott; Fantasia (a-Phrygian); Fantasia Chromatica; Ich ruf zu dir, Herr Jesu Christ; Ick voer al over Rhijn; Ik heb den Heer lief (Psalm 116); Malle Sijmen; Mein junges Leben hat ein End; More palatino; Nun freut euch, lieben Christen gemein; Onder een linde groen; Ons is gheboren een kindekijn; Onse Vader hemelrijck; Pavana hispanica; Pavana Lachrimae; Pavana Philippi; Poolsche dans; Ricerar (Aeolian); Toccata (Ionian)
⊶ *** Hyp. CDA 67421/2 (2). Herrick (organ of the Norrfjärden Kyrka, Norrfjärden, Piteå, Sweden)

Sweelinck exerted enormous influence during his lifetime. Christopher Herrick has chosen the organ of the Norrfjärden Kyrka, Piteå, on the northeastern coast of Sweden. It is based on a reconstruction of the 1609–84 organ of the Tyskakyrkan in Stockholm, an instrument closely associated with one of Sweelinck's pupils. Herrick is completely attuned to the flavour and style of this repertoire and draws a consistently characterful sound from this lovely instrument. Koopman notwithstanding, collectors should investigate this fine set of a composer who remains seriously underrated outside the Netherlands. The recording is in the best traditions of the house.

Ballo del Granduca; Echo fantasia; Engelsche Fortuyn; Puer nobis nascitur
*** Chan. 0514. Klee (organ of St Laurens Church, Alkmaar) –
BUXTEHUDE: *Collection* ***

Sweelinck lived during the Dutch Golden Age and was a contemporary of Rembrandt. His music is colourful and appealing, and it could hardly be better represented than in this engaging 'suite' of four contrasted pieces, three of which are based on melodies by others. Piet Klee is a very sympathetic advocate and he is given a recording of demonstration standard.

Ballo del Granduca; Chorale variations: Erbarm dich mein, O Herr Gott; Mein junges Leben hat ein End'. Echo fantasia in A min.; Malle Sijmen; Onder een linde groen; Poolsche dans; Ricercar; Toccatas: in A min. & C
(BB) *** Naxos 8.550904. Christie (C. B. Fisk organ, Houghton Chapel, Wellesley College, USA)

Those wanting a larger, more fully representative collection of Sweelinck's organ music can turn to Naxos, who do not usually let us down with their one-disc surveys. Certainly the Wellesley College organ sounds right, James David Christie is a persuasive exponent, and his pacing is convincing. The two *Toccatas* are the most commanding pieces here, the C major quite virtuosic. Sweelinck's chorale variations repeat the cantus firmus clearly with embellishments of increasing complexity. The secular variations are simpler. Those based on a Dutch song are derived from an English ballad, *All in a garden green*, and the jolly *Malle Sijmen* ('Simple Simon') is based on an old English dance-tune, and is piquantly registered. *Poolsche dans* ('Polish dance') is much more elaborate.

It is in the middle section of the *Echo Fantasia* that the cuckoo-like echoes finally appear and the piece concludes like a toccata. Excellent recording.

Cantiones sacrae (1619)
*** Hyp. CDA 67103 (Nos. 1–21); CDA 67104 (Nos. 22–37).
Trinity College Chapel Ch., Cambridge, Marlow

Sweelinck wrote a great deal of vocal music (though none in his own language), including French chansons and Psalm settings, and Italian madrigals. The 37 *Cantiones sacrae*, which date from 1691, are in Latin, for five-part choir, and surely represent him at a peak of inspiration. The range of texts is wide, but most pertain to major feasts of the liturgical year. This pair of Hyperion discs (each available separately) offers glorious music, gloriously sung. The simplicity and underlying vitality of the very first piece, *Non omnis qui dicit mihi, Domine*, captures the listener's ear, and the opening sequence of some half-a-dozen fairly serene settings is then interrupted by three exuberant motets of praise, *Ecce nunc benedicte Dominum, Cantate Domino* and the exultant *Venite exultemus Domino*. But the sequence which opens the second disc, beginning with *In illo tempore*, celebrating the naming of Jesus, is hardly less fine. The resonant acoustic is right for the music, but brings some distinct blurring of the upper focus. Nevertheless this is an outstanding set.

SZYMANOWSKI, Karol (1882–1937)

(i; ii) *Concert Overture, Op. 12*; (iii; iv) *Harnasie, Op. 55*; *Symphonies Nos.* (i; ii) *2 in B flat, Op. 19*; (i; iv–vi) *3 (Song of the Night), Op. 27*; (i; v; vii) *4 (Symphonie concertante), Op. 60*. (viii) *20 Mazurkas for Solo Piano, Op. 50/1 & 2. Theme & Variations for Solo Piano, Op. 3*
(BB) **(*) EMI Gemini (ADD) 585539-2 (2). (i) Polish R. Nat. SO; (ii) Kaspszyk; (iii) Bachleda, Kwasny, Polish R. O of Kraków, Wit; (iv) Polish R. Ch. of Kraków; (v) Semkow; (vi) Ochman; (vii) Paleczny; (viii) Blumenthal

This is an excellent and inexpensive way to explore this often marvellous composer. The *Second Symphony* is not as rewarding as the *Third*, but it is unusual in form: there are only two movements, the second being a set of variations, culminating in a fugue. The influences of Richard Strauss and Scriabin are clearly audible, if not altogether assimilated. The *Third Symphony (Song of the Night)*, however, is one of the composer's most beautiful scores, with a heady, intoxicated – and intoxicating – atmosphere. These performances date from 1982, and they remain full and atmospheric, even if the quality of the orchestral playing, though good, has been superseded in more recent versions (the vibrato on the brass instruments will not be to all tastes). The gripping account of the ambitious *Concert Overture*, which sounds for all the world like an undiscovered symphonic poem by Richard Strauss, is highly enjoyable. In the *Symphonie concertante*, Piotr Paleczny is no mean artist and he has all the finesse and imagination as well as the requisite command of colour that this work calls for; Wit provides him with admirable support, and this 1979 account, as a whole, makes a stronger impression than the more recent Naxos version, similarly priced. *Harnasie* is also very successful; it reflects Szymanowski's discovery of the folk music of the Tatras. It calls for large forces, including a solo violinist as well as a tenor and full chorus, and poses obvious practical production problems. As always with this composer, there is a sense of rapture, the soaring, ecstatic lines and the

intoxicating exoticism that distinguish the mature Szymanowski, and it comes across most tellingly here. The sound is spaciously wide-ranging and full, but it is made a bit fierce on top by the CD mastering. Blumenthal's accounts of the piano items are reasonably persuasive, though they are sound rather than inspired performances; however, they make a nice bonus.

Violin Concerto 1
(N) *** DG 987 0577. Benedetti, LSO, Harding (with
CHAUSSON: *Poème*; MASSENET: *Thaïs: Méditation*;
SAINT-SAENS: *Havanaise*; TAVENER: *Fragment for the Virgin* ***)

This is a most impressive début recording from Nicola Benedetti, at 17 the 2004 BBC 'Young Artist of the Year', now with a lucrative recording contract from DG. Born in Scotland of Italian stock, she studied at the Menuhin School before deciding at 15 to study on her own. Centring on the Szymanowski, the work she played at the BBC final, she already displays in each of these items the temperament, concentration and imagination of a great artist in the making, quite apart from her virtuoso technique. The passion of her performance of the *Concerto* is remarkable, even suggesting a parallel with the young Jacqueline du Pré. Daniel Harding draws comparably passionate and intense playing from the LSO, and the impact of the performance is heightened by the relatively close balance of soloist and orchestra, hitting home very hard in the exotic climaxes. She may miss the otherworldly quality that other, more mature artists find in this work, but the thrust of imagination is irresistible. Her performances of the other works are just as impressive, not just the Chausson, Massenet and Saint-Saëns, but the piece John Tavener wrote specially for her, inspired by the range of her playing.

(i) *Violin Concertos 1–2. Concert Overture, Op. 12*
*** Chan. 9496. (i) Mordkovitch; BBC PO, Sinaisky

(i) *Violin Concertos 1–2, Op. 61*; (ii) *Romance, Op. 23; 3 Paganini Caprices, Op. 40*
☛ *** EMI 5 55607-2. Zehetmair, (i) CBSO, Rattle; (ii) Avenhaus

Thomas Zehetmair's deeply felt versions with Rattle and the CBSO conjure up the Szymanowskian sound-world with real flair, and the soloist characterizes each phrase with impeccable instinct. The engineers deliver first-rate sound in both works and in the four violin and piano makeweights, in which Zehetmair is well supported by the young German pianist, Silke Avenhaus.

Lydia Mordkovitch is also admirably suited, full-toned and red-blooded, for these exotic concertos, helped by playing, richly recorded, from the BBC Philharmonic under Vassily Sinaisky, the orchestra's Principal Guest Conductor. Both works are strongly contrasted with the early and extrovert *Concert Overture*, an illuminating coupling.

(i) *Violin Concertos 1–2*; (ii) *Symphony 4 (Symphonie concertante)*
☛ *** EMI 5 57777-2. (i) Zehetmair; (ii) Andsnes; CBSO, Rattle

Zehetmair's versions of the two *Violin Concertos* are now joined by Leif Ove Andsnes's outstanding account of the *Symphonie concertante*. Both he and Rattle capture the sensuous luminosity of the central movement, and Rattle unleashes the wildness of the finale with great vigour. Throughout, the CBSO conjures up the exotic Szymanowskian sound-world, and the engineers deliver spectacularly wide-ranging recording.

(i) Harnasie (ballet pantomime), Op. 55; (ii) Mandragora (pantomime), Op. 43; Etude for Orchestra in B flat min., Op. 3 (orch. Fitelberg)

(BB) *** Naxos 8.553686. Polish State PO (Katowice), Stryja; (i) with Grychnik, Polish State PO Ch.; Meus

Harnasie, like the Op. 50 *Mazurkas*, is the fruit of Szymanowski's encounter with the Polish folk music of the Góral mountains, and its heady exoticism is quite captivating. Stryja's recording is a good one and, though not quite as intoxicating as the full-price Satanowski on Koch, runs it pretty close. Like its rival, it is coupled with *Mandragora*, a harlequinade for chamber forces from 1920 – not Szymanowski at his most fully characteristic but a cultivated and intelligent score. Worth the money.

Symphonies 1 in F min., Op. 15; 2, Op. 19

(BB) *** Naxos 8.553683. Polish State PO (Katowice), Stryja

The two-movement *First Symphony* (1906–7) was first performed in 1909 and was received coolly. Alistair Wightman called it heavily overscored even by the standards of the period. The *Second* (1911) is heavily indebted to Reger, Scriabin and Strauss. It is overlong and overscored, but it contains original and memorable passages. Given the price asked, it justifies the modest expense involved.

Symphony 2 in B flat, Op.19; Concert Overture, Op. 12; (i) Slopiewnie (Wordsong), Op. 46; Songs of the Infatuated Muezzin, Op. 42

*** Telarc CD 80567. LPO, Botstein (i) with Kilanowicz

Neither of the orchestral pieces are quite *echt*-Szymanowski, the *Symphony* and *Overture* being still very much under the influence of Strauss and Reger. All the same, both are heard to best advantage in this finely detailed recording with highly persuasive performances. The two sets of songs are rarities; indeed, *Slopiewnie* is not otherwise available on disc in its orchestral form and the *Songs of the Infatuated Muezzin* – composed at the height of the composer's interest in the oriental and the exotic in 1918 (four of which he later scored in 1934) – are not generously represented on disc. Zofia Kilanowicz has just the right blend of purity and seductiveness and the orchestral playing under Leon Botstein is first class.

Symphonies 2; (i) 4 (Sinfonia concertante)

*** Chan. 9478. (i) Shelley; BBC PO, Sinaisky

The *Second* and *Fourth Symphonies* are two decades apart. The soft-focus Chandos recording of No. 2 is less clearly defined than, say, Dorati's brightly lit, well-detailed account on Decca (currently withdrawn), but it presents a more atmospheric aural picture. Vassily Sinaisky is a highly sympathetic interpreter of the piece, and this BBC version must be a prime recommendation. So, too, is the coupling, the *Sinfonia concertante* (1932). Howard Shelley produces a quality of sound that is luminous, refined and velvet-toned. The balance between piano and orchestra is particularly well managed, and the lush orchestral textures are more lucid than we have heard them elsewhere.

Symphonies (i) 3 (Song of the Night), Op. 27; (ii) 4, Concert Overture, Op. 12

(BB) *** Naxos 8.553684. (i) Ochmann, Polish State Philharmonic Ch.; (ii) Zmudzinski; Polish State PO (Katowice), Stryja

(i) Symphony 3 (Song of the Night), Op. 27; (ii) Litania do Marii Pany, Op. 59; (iii) Stabat Mater, Op. 53

☛ *** EMI 5 55121-2. (i) Garrison; (ii-iii) Szmytka; (iii) Quivar, Connell; CBSO Ch., CBSO, Rattle

Szymanowski has that fastidious ear for texture and heightened sense of vision that distinguish mystics, and nowhere is atmosphere more potent than in the *Third Symphony*, the *Song of the Night*. Sir Simon is equally committed and persuasive in the *Stabat Mater*, these days a standard coupling, and one of the unequivocally great choral works of the century. These are very good performances and the sumptuous and finely detailed recording is absolutely state-of-the-art.

Stryja's set of the *Song of the Night* and the *Fourth Symphony* offers a well-filled disc that is worth its asking price. He uses a tenor in the *Third Symphony* and Taduesz Zmudzinski is an effective soloist in the *Fourth Symphony* or *Sinfonia concertante* for piano and orchestra. The performance of the Straussian and derivative *Concert Overture* is as persuasive as it can be. The sound in the *Third Symphony* is good, in the remaining pieces rather less impressive but still acceptable.

Symphony 4 – see under King Roger

CHAMBER MUSIC

3 Mythes, Op. 30

*** HM HMC90 1793. Faust, Kupiec – JANACEK: *Violin Sonata*; LUTOSLAWSKI: *Partita, Subito* ***

The Szymanowski *Mythes* (dating from 1915, like the Janáček *Sonata*), bring a sharp contrast with the rest of this mixed bag in the shimmeringly evocative opening of *The Fountain of Arethusa*, at once reflective and urgent, here presented with a magical lightness by the pianist as well as the violinist, who produce magical *pianissimos*. The mystery, the ethereal quality, in these three classically inspired pieces is beautifully brought out, when the technical demands on the violinist can easily result in heavy-handed, earthbound playing. That applies not only to the first two pieces but to the energetic third piece, *Dryades et Pan*, with its buzzing trills suggesting insect music.

Mythes, Op. 30; Kurpian Folk Song; King Roger: Roxana's Aria (both arr. Kochanski)

☛ ✪ (M) *** DG (IMS) (ADD) 431 469-2. Danczowska, Zimerman – FRANCK: *Violin Sonata* ***

Kaja Danczowska brings vision and poetry to the ecstatic, soaring lines of the opening movement of *Mythes, The Fountains of Arethusa*. Her intonation is impeccable, and she has the measure of these other-worldly, intoxicating scores. There is a sense of rapture here that is totally persuasive, and Krystian Zimerman plays with a virtuosity and imagination that silence criticism. An indispensable reissue.

String Quartets 1–2

☛ (BB) *** Naxos 8.554315. Goldner Qt – STRAVINSKY: *Concertino; 3 Pieces; Double Canon* ***

Even within the comparatively limited medium of the string

quartet, Szymanowski creates characteristically rich and exotic textures in these original and tautly constructed works. They were written ten years apart in 1917 and 1927, demonstrating the way his style was developing ever more personally over that period. Occasionally echoing Debussy and Ravel, they make a pointful contrast with Stravinsky's characteristically cryptic essays in the genre, sharp and often brittle. The Goldner Quartet prove understanding, refined interpreters of both composers, playing with rapt intensity in the hushed slow movements of the Szymanowski works. Excellent sound.

Violin Sonata in D min., Op. 9
(B) *** EMI Début 5 72825-2. Zambrzycki-Payne, Presland –
  BRITTEN: *Suite for Violin & Piano, Op. 6;* GRIEG: *Violin Sonata 3* ***

Violin Sonata; Mythes, Op. 30; Nocturne & Tarantella, Op. 28
**(*) Chan. 8747. Mordkovitch, Gusk-Grin

Rafal Zambrzycki-Payne more than earns a place in the Szymanowski discography. He has a strong musical personality and intelligence, and gets splendid support from his pianist, Carole Presland. The Abbey Road recording is expertly balanced and sounds very natural.

Lydia Mordkovitch is ideally attuned to this sensibility and plays both the *Sonata* and the later works beautifully, and she is sensitively partnered by Marina Gusk-Grin. This can be recommended, though this account of the *Mythes* does not displace Danczowska and Zimerman.

PIANO MUSIC

Complete piano music
Disc 1: *9 Preludes, Op. 1; Variations in B flat min., Op. 3; 4 Etudes, Op. 4; Sonata 1 in C min., Op. 8* (NI 5405)
Disc 2: *Variations on a Polish Theme in B min., Op. 10; Fantasia in C min., Op. 14; Prelude & Fugue in C sharp min., (1909); Sonata 2 in A, Op. 21* (NI 5406)
Disc 3: *Métopes (3 Poèmes), op. 29; 15 Etudes, Op. 34; Sonata 3, Op. 36* (NI 5435)
Disc 4: *20 Mazurkas, Op. 50; 2 Mazurkas, op. 62; 4 Polish Pieces (1926); Romantic Waltz (1925)* (NI 5436)
*** Nim. NI 1750 (4). M. Jones

This complete Nimbus survey invites enthusiasm, particularly as the music is presented in historical sequence. The *Nine Preludes* of Op. 1, although published in 1906, were composed much earlier and are simple, romantic miniatures, with at times a flavour of Chopin. The two sets of *Variations* of Op. 3 and Op. 10, although appealingly inventive, are in the received German tradition; but the *Four Etudes* of Op. 4 and the opening movement of the impressive *First Sonata* already suggest Scriabin. The *Second Sonata* (1910/11) is much more complex in both its structure and use of chromaticism. The later pieces, *Masques* and *Métopes*, written at about the time of the *First Violin Concerto*, show Szymanowski responding to French influences and early Stravinsky, and evolving a sophisticated exoticism all his own. The beautiful and always imaginative *Etudes* (1916) draw on a whole range of styles from Ravel and Debussy, and even Bartók, but they are well assimilated. The *Third Sonata* (1917) is wholly impressionistic and Martin Jones manages its quixotic changes of mood and atmosphere most compellingly. The *Mazurkas*, from the

1920s, find Symanowski seeking to create an authentic Polish idiom in contemporary terms. The advantage of listening to this rewarding music in sequence means that one senses the composer gradually forging his own individuality. Martin Jones is a consistently persuasive advocate and he is naturally recorded. A most rewarding set.

4 Etudes, Op. 4; Fantasy, Op. 14; Masques, Op. 34; Métopes, Op. 29
⊶ (BB) *** Hyp. Helios CDH 55081. Lee

Dennis Lee not only encompasses the technical hurdles of *Masques* and *Métopes* with dazzling virtuosity but also provides the keenest artistic insights. His Hyperion CD is quite simply the finest record of Szymanowski's piano music to have appeared to date; he conveys the exoticism and hot-house atmosphere of these pieces; moreover he handles the early Chopinesque *Etudes* and the *Fantasy* with much the same feeling for characterization and artistry. The Hyperion sound is very good indeed. An excellent bargain.

4 Etudes, Op. 4; Mazurkas, Op. 50/1–4; Metopes, Op. 29; Piano sonata 2 in A, Op. 21
(BB) *** Naxos 8.553016-2. Roscoe

Fantasia in C, Op. 14; Masques, Op. 34; Mazurkas, Op. 50/5–12; Variations on a Polish theme, Op. 10
(BB) *** Naxos 8.553300. Roscoe

Martin Roscoe proves a perceptive and sensitive interpreter of Szymanowski and the first two discs augur well for this ongoing series. In the four *Mazurkas*, Op. 50, that open the first CD he shows real feeling and insight. He is equally persuasive in the early Chopinesque *Etudes*, Op. 4, and the refined impressionism of *Metopes*. The *Second Sonata* is a problematic piece, full of virtuosic hurdles, romantic gestures and Regerian ingenuity. The second disc gives us the *C major Fantasy*, Op. 14, and the Op. 10 *Variations*, in which the debts to Scriabin and Chopin have yet to be fully discharged. A fine account of the *Masques*, too. This is playing of quality. As far as recording is concerned, Martin Roscoe is well served.

20 Mazurkas, Op. 50; 2 Mazurkas, Op. 62; 4 Polish Dances; Valse Romantique
*** Hyp. CDA 67399. Hamelin

The Szymanowski *Mazurkas* are late works and are among his best and certainly his most haunting piano pieces. They are without doubt the finest mazurkas after Chopin. Their inward qualities and their sense of mystery elude many pianists, but Marc-André Hamelin gives as perceptive and authoritative an account of these extraordinary pieces as any. In this music Szymanowski was entering new territory, and their significance in his development cannot be underestimated. Hyperion give Hamelin natural and truthfully balanced sound, and no readers interested in this once neglected but now rightly appreciated master should overlook this fine issue.

Piano Sonatas 1 in C min., Op. 8; 2 in A, op. 21; 3, Op. 35; Prelude & Fugue in C sharp min.
*** Athene ATHCD 19. Clarke

Readers who want to explore just the three piano sonatas should consider this excellently played offering. No less than Martin Jones, Raymond Clarke has an intuitive grasp of – and affinity with – Szymanowski's sound-world. He is second to none in terms of sensibility and keyboard command. His version of the *First Sonata* is particularly convincing. Good recording, though not in the demonstration class.

VOCAL MUSIC

(i) *Demeter, Op. 37b;* (ii) *Litany to the Virgin Mary;* (iii) *Penthesilea;* (iv) *Stabat Mater, Op. 53;* (v) *Veni Creator, Op. 57*

(BB) *** Naxos 8.553687. Polish State PO (Katowice), Stryja, with (i) Malewicz-Madej; (iii) Owsinska; (iv) Gadulanka, Szostek-Radkowa, Hiolski; (v) Zogórzanka; (i–ii; iv–v) Polish State Ch., Katowice

Szymanowski's *Stabat Mater* is not only one of his greatest achievements but one of the greatest choral works of the twentieth century. This welcome account has the advantage of highly sensitive conducting and an excellent response from the orchestra, but some of the solo singing is less distinguished, and Jadwiga Gadulanka's intonation is less than perfect. The *Litany to the Virgin Mary* is another late work of great poignancy, but *Demeter* is exotic, almost hallucinatory textures. It is all heady and intoxicating stuff, and not to be missed by those with a taste for this wonderful composer.

(i) *3 Fragments of the Poems by Jan Kasprowicz;* (ii) *Love Songs of Hafiz;* (iii) *Songs of the Fairy-Tale Princess;* (iv) *Songs of the Infatuated Muezzin;* (v) *King Roger: Roxana's Song*

(BB) **(*) Naxos 8.553688. (i) Malewicz-Madej; (ii; iv) Ryszard Minkiewicz; (iii) Gadulanka; (v) Zagórzanka; Katowice Polish State PO, Stryja

In the *Songs of the Fairy-Tale Princess*, one feels that Szymanowski must have known Stravinsky's *Le Rossignol*. On Naxos, both the *Songs of the Infatuated Muezzin* and the *Love Songs of Hafiz* are sung by a tenor (Ryszard Minkiewicz) with impressive insight, but the 1989 recording is resonant and does not flatter him. Jadwiga Gadulanka is hardly less impressive in the extraordinary *Songs of the fairy-tale princess* and Barbara Zagórzanka sings the famous *Chant de Roxane* beautifully, and both she and Anna Malewicz-Madej in the Kasprowicz songs are very well balanced.

STAGE WORKS

King Roger, Op. 46 (complete)

(N) *** Accord ACD 131-2. Drabowicz, Pasiecznik, Beczala, Tesarowicz, Toczyska, Szymt, 'Alla Polacca' Youth Ch., Polish Nat. Op. Ch. & O, Kaspszyk

(i) *King Roger* (complete); (ii) *Symphony 4*

🎧 ⊛ *** EMI 5 56824/25-2 (2). (i) Hampson, Szmytka, Minkiewicz; CBSO Ch. & Youth Ch.; (i; ii) CBSO, Rattle; (ii) Andsnes

King Roger stands on the borderline between opera and music drama. The opening in Palermo Cathedral is of awesome opulence, and given such sounds one hardly needs a stage representation. All the singers are first-rate: Thomas Hampson has what one can only call magisterial presence, and the Roksana is quite ethereal. Only Ryszard Minkiewicz's Shepherd is, perhaps, wanting in tonal bloom. Of course, the glorious orchestral tapestry is the centre-piece of attention: the opening of the Hellenic Third Act is inspired and atmospheric. Sir Simon Rattle shows great feeling for Szymanowski.

He is accorded excellent recording. There have been three earlier recordings, all Polish: Mierzejewski's set from the 1960s has long disappeared, Robert Satanowski's 1988 Warsaw version (Koch) and Karol Stryja's 1990 Katowice account (Marco) were recently reissued on Naxos. But this sweeps the board and has much more refined sound. Incidentally, there is a bonus, for, at the end of the first CD, Roksana's famous aria is given with its concert ending. An even more important bonus comes in the shape of the *Fourth Symphony*, the *Sinfonia concertante for Piano and Orchestra*. This has greater lucidity of textures than any of its previous rivals and brings magical playing from the soloist.

Jacek Kaspszyk's set is finer than any of the three earlier Polish versions. Indeed, it is possible to prefer it to Sir Simon Rattle's. In the title-role Wojtek Drabowicz is every bit as authoritative as Thomas Hampson and arguably is better characterized, and in vocal quality the Roksana of Olga Pasiecznik sounds even purer than Rattle's Elzbieta Szmytka. Her famous aria is quite ravishing. Indeed, the whole performance is strong vocally and the choral singing is magnificent. Kaspszyk paces the work in masterly fashion: the opening in Palermo Cathedral is one of the most glowing and atmospheric in all Szymanowski, and its sense of mysticism is conveyed with authority. It scores over the EMI in accommodating the whole opera on one disc. The recording, too, has impressive range and definition, though the EMI set has greater space round the aural image, giving slightly greater refinement and atmosphere. But this new Polish set is very powerful and makes a highly competitive alternative.

TAKEMITSU, Toru (1930–96)

Fantasma/cantos

*** EMI 5 56832-2. Meyer, BPO, Abbado – DEBUSSY: *Première rapsodie;* MOZART: *Clarinet Concerto* ***

In this sequence of works designed to bring out the full artistry of Sabine Meyer, the hypnotic 16-minute span of this Takemitsu work seems to develop out of the evocative Debussy piece, similarly inhabiting a dream-like world of sound, with ravishing clarinet tones over the widest range. An unusual but revealing coupling.

A Flock Descends into the Pentagonal Gardens; (i) *Quatrain*

(N) *** DG 477 5381. Boston SO, Ozawa; (i) with Tashi

In *Quatrain* Takemitsu contrasts his solo concertino of clarinet, violin, cello and piano with the full orchestra in a way that might suggest neoclassicism, except that Takemitsu's music is essentially sensuous and evocative; one might almost count him a Japanese Debussy. The other piece, which is purely orchestral, is overtly impressionistic. Both are superbly played; the outstanding Tashi group is ideally suited to *Quatrain.*

Quotation of Dream

(N) (M) *** DG 476 7114. Crossley, Peter Serkin; L. Sinf., Knussen

Takemitsu suggested that his music endeavoured 'to create a perspective of sound – music that forever strides the border between dream and reality'. As an overall work *Quotation of Dream* has something in common with Schubert's *Schwanengesang* in that the individual items which make up the whole were not composed as an entity, but were compiled by Oliver Knussen, a great admirer of the composer. They are extremely varied in scoring and in the size of the ensemble used, but are held together stylistically by the composer's 'enigmatic, murmuring, ever flowing currents of sound . . . drifting into being at the time of performance'. The five pieces are framed by *Day* and *Night Signals from Heaven*, each an antiphonal fanfare for brass, and the following segment, for two pianos and orchestra, which bears the title of the whole work, not only dominates what follows, but epitomizes the character of what is to follow. Its evocation of the sea subtly draws on wisps of Debussy's *La Mer*, and throughout the other sections the listener has the feeling that Takemitsu is haunted by memories of music from the recent past, which are woven into his textures. The other movements are *How slow the wind* (for chamber orchestra), the gently rocking *Twill by Twilight* for a larger orchestra, the antiphonal *Archipelago G* (for 21 wind players, including horn and trumpet), and *Dream Window*, with its Buddhist ambiguity. The performance (from Oliver Knussen, his two piano soloists, Paul Crossley and Peter Serkin, and members of the London Sinfonietta) is remarkably fine, and the recording, made in two different venues, is richly atmospheric. The *Gramophone*, giving the disc its Contemporary Award in 1999, suggested that 'this is the best single CD of Takemitsu's music so far issued', and it certainly has not been surpassed since.

TALLIS, Thomas (c. 1505–85)

The Complete Vocal and Instrumental Music of Tallis: Volumes 1–9

(N) (M) *** Signum SIGCD 060 (10). Chapelle du Roi, Alistair Dixon, with Soloists, Instrumentalists and Charivari Agréable

Alistair Dixon and his Chapelle du Roi (plus other contributors) have now completed their distinguished integral coverage of the music of the great Elizabethan composer, Thomas Tallis. The complete series is currently available in a mid-priced box with full documentation, but the discs are all available separately and are praised individually below.

*** SIGCD 001. Vol. 1: **The Early Works**

*** SIGCD 002. Vol. 2: **Music at the Reformation**

(*) SIGCD 003. Vol. 3: **Music for Queen Mary

*** SIGCD 010. Vol. 4: **Music for the Divine Office – I**

*** SIGCD 016. Vol. 5: **Music for the Divine Office – II**

*** SIGCD 022. Vol. 6: **Music for a Reformed Church**

*** SIGCD 029. Vol. 7: **Music for Queen Elizabeth**

(N) *** SIGCD 036. Vol. 8: **Lamentations & English Motets**

(N) *** SIGCD 042 (with bonus CD). Vol. 9: **Instrumental Music & Songs**

Just looking at the titles of the individual volumes underlines the dramatic period of English history through which Tallis lived and composed, successfully moving from a Latin liturgy to English settings, then back again. Finally, during the reign of Elizabeth I (the fourth monarch to sit on the throne in Tallis's lifetime), in the best spirit of English compromise, he created new from the old in setting English words to music originally written to serve Latin texts. Even the famous *Spem in Alium* was heard anew as *Sing and glorify*, although generations later it reverted to its original Latin format.

The first disc augurs extremely well for the project. The programme is framed by three Marian votive antiphons, the first two comparatively immature and rather similar: *Ave Dei patris filia* (in a reconstructed text) and *Ave rosa sine spinis*;

the second is rather more purposeful than the first. *Salve intemerata*, however, is masterly in its concisely integrated part-writing (with some soaring treble solos, beautifully sung here). It can surely be compared with the famous *Spem in alium*, and becomes remarkably complex and yet very succinct at the closing *Amen*. The mass sharing its name uses much of the same material: the *Gloria* and *Sanctus* are particularly fine. The *Alleluia* and *Euge celi porta* are less ambitious, but still serenely beautiful, four-part plainchant settings used as part of the Ladymass.

Most, and possibly all of the music in Volume 2 dates from the 1540s and reflects the remarkable diversity of musical response that came directly from the profound change in reformed religious procedures that developed in England within a single decade. Much liturgical music was still sung in Latin, notably the splendid *Magnificat* and the deeply felt *Sancte Deus*, but already there are settings in English, including three fine early anthems, an extended English *Benedictus* and a remarkable five-part *Te Deum*, all very different from the music on Volume 1 of this series. The surprisingly homophonic setting of the Latin *Mass* is forward-looking, too, and very telling.

Volume 3 returns to the Latin rite and all the works here date from the reign of Mary Tudor (1553–8). The collection opens with the Psalm setting, *Beati immaculati*, and includes also the glorious, large-scale votive antiphon, *Gaude gloriosa*, magnificently sung. The key work, however, is the seven-part Mass *Puer natus est nobis*, which is incomplete. Here the *Gloria*, *Sanctus* and *Agnus Dei* are performed with the plainchant Propers for the third Mass of Christmas. As usual the singing is splendid, but there is a good deal of monodic chant here, beautifully phrased certainly, but which will reduce the appeal of this volume for some collectors.

Volume 4 in this ever-rewarding series is the first to concentrate on music for the cycle of eight services, Matins, Lauds, Prime, Terce, Sext, None, Vespers and Compline, sung daily in Latin Christendom. The riches of the polyphony here are unending. *Dum transisset sabbatum* and the six-part *Videte miraculum* are particularly fine, while the seven-part *Loquebantur variis linguis* with its recurring *Alleluias* spins an even more complex contrapuntal web. Even the simplest of the settings here, *Quod chorus vatum*, is moving by its comparative austerity.

Volume 5 of Alistair Dixon's invaluable survey continues the music that Tallis wrote for the Divine Office begun in Volume 4. There are some particularly beautiful examples, notably the opening responsory for All Saints Day, *Audivi vocem de coelo* (set for three trebles and an alto), the following, even richer *Candidi facti sunt* and the even more imaginative *Honor virtus et potestas*, all gloriously sung here.

But the special interest of this CD is the inclusion of the organ music, simply written and based on plainchant melismas. Tallis generally used the organ as a substitute for voices, interchanging instrumental with sung text. In this aurally appealing alternation, the organist played the odd-numbered verses, usually providing – as in *Veni redemptor genitum* – a piquant introduction to contrast with the sonorous vocal entry. The organ used for the recordings, in the private chapel at Knole, is the oldest playable organ in England, so its choice seems admirable, and Andrew Benson Wilson's contribution to the success of this CD is considerable, since all the organ music is most appealing.

Volume 6 of the excellent Signum coverage of Tallis's output is devoted to music which he composed for use in the reformed services promulgated by *The Booke of the Common*

Prayer, which came into effect in 1549, here presented in the normal liturgical sequence. Much of the music is simple and homophonic, but it has an unadorned beauty of its own. The anthems are richer in the interplay of parts but are still brief, and the collection ends with the nine even briefer psalm-tune harmonizations which Tallis contributed to Archbishop Matthew Parker's *Psalter*, published in about 1567.

Elizabeth was the fourth monarch to sit on the throne in Tallis's lifetime, and Tallis was by then in his sixties. Undoubtedly both greatly regretted the destruction of choir books and partbooks of the older generations of church music which the Reformation had brought about. Both composer and monarch also appear to have been equally determined that the new Elizabethan Latin motets should seek new expressive approaches, while drawing on the best of the past. Their success is confirmed by the fact that cathedral musicians fitted English words to much of Tallis's music. *Absterge Domine* therefore also becomes *Discomfort them O Lord*. The two Psalm settings included, *Domine, quis habitat* (Psalm 15) and the shorter but no less impressive *Laudate Dominum* (Psalm 117), are both memorable, and often Tallis has a way of catching the ear with a soaring opening phrase, as in both settings of *Salvator mundi*, and particularly in the beautiful *Salutaris hostia*. The most celebrated of these motets is of course *Spem in Alium*, with its incredibly dense part-writing still able to astonish the ear. It was first heard in the early 1570s and remains one of the greatest achievements of English vocal music. It is sung gloriously here, its ebb and flow and rich climaxes splendidly controlled.

Tallis's two richly expressive settings of the *Lamentations of Jeremiah* are given in Volume 8 in serene and dedicated performances, followed by what are known as *contrafacta*, English versions of Latin motets rewritten by Tallis by the post-Reformation English Church. The music itself, usually in five parts, seems to adapt very well to its linguistic transformation; the first piece here, *Wipe away my sins (Absterge Domine)*, described as 'A Prayer' is particularly beautiful. *With all our hearts and mouths* and the lovely *Arise, O Lord* both derive from Tallis's first setting of *Salvator mundi, while I call and cry to Thee (O sacrum convivium)*, very popular in its day, was to lay the basis for Tallis's English anthems. The most familiar work here is *Sing and glorify*, an adaptation of Tallis's most famous, 40-part *Spem in alium*, for eight choirs. Altogether a fine and revealing collection, with the recording well up to standard.

The fascination of the final volume in Signum's comprehensive survey is the virtually unknown instrumental music, consisting of a small collection of works for viols and some fine pieces for keyboard, which we hear variously on virginals, harpsichord or organ. In his excellent notes, John Milsom suggests that while Tallis's official duties involved him only as a church musician, he may have written some of this music for the Tudor Court, and the keyboard pieces could conceivably been written for Queen Elizabeth I, who was a celebrated amateur performer. Certainly they are attractive enough.

The consort manuscripts give no indication of the instrumentation, but viols (as used here) seem a likely choice, and Tallis's pair of *In nomines* are the first known examples of this form (settings using the *Gloria tibi Trinitas* as a basis).

As far as is known, Tallis did not write for the lute, so the impressively complex work based on the plainsong 'Felix namque' is almost certainly an arrangement by an unknown lutenist. This is heard alongside the less virtuosic keyboard version written two years earlier. *Mr Tallis's Lesson* (which we hear both on harpsichord and on organ) is a very agreeable

pedagogic piece based on a decorated canon, and was no doubt intended as a study for the composer's choirboy pupils.

As for the songs, they make a wonderful closing section. The very touching *When shall my sorrowful sighing* might well have been composed by Dowland, and *Ye sacred music*, a tribute to Byrd, is fully worthy. They are sung sympathetically by Stephen Taylor (counter-tenor), and the instrumental pieces from Charivari Agréable, Laurence Cummings (virginals and harpsichord) and Andrew Benson Wilson (organ) are expertly played, while Lynda Sayce gives a virtuoso account of the arrangement of *Felix namque*.

The bonus disc includes a complete setting of the *Litany*, omitted from Volume 6, two brief organ Versets, and a further performance of the earlier, less complex version of *Felix Namque*. As with the other organ pieces, Benson Wilson uses the oldest playable organ known in England – at the private chapel in Knole in Kent (owned during Tallis's lifetime by both Archbishop Cranmer and Henry VIII). All in all, Volume 9 makes a fitting conclusion to a splendid project, admirably realized, and as before full texts and translations are included.

Anthems; *Lamentations of Jeremiah I & II; Motets* including *Spem in alium* (as listed below on GDGIM 006, 007 and 025)

⊘ (M) *** Gimell 2-CD CDGIM 203 (2). Tallis Scholars, Phillips

This collection from the eponymous Tallis Scholars directed by Peter Phillips now includes, on a pair of CDs, the music from three earlier issues (each still available separately and listed and discussed below). The performances are outstanding, wonderfully secure and very beautiful, recorded in an ideal acoustic. This mid-priced set has as its highlight a quite glorious account of the famous 40-part motet, *Spem in alium*; so this would be an admirable basis for any collection, small or large.

Anthems: *Blessed are those that be undefiled; Christ, rising again; Hear the voice and prayer; If ye love me; A new commandment; O Lord, in Thee is all my trust; O Lord, give thy holy spirit; Out from the deep; Purge me; Remember not, O Lord God; Verily, verily I say: 9 Psalm Tunes for Archbishop Parker's Psalter*

⊘ *** Gimell CDGIM 007. Tallis Scholars, Phillips

This disc collects the complete English anthems of Tallis and is thus a valuable complement to the discs listed below. Here women's voices are used instead of boys', but the sound they produce has boyish purity, and the performances could hardly be more committed or idiomatic. Strongly recommended.

***Gaude gloriosa; Loquebantur variis linguis; Miserere nostri; Salvator mundi, salva nos, I & II; Sancte Deus; Spem in alium* (40-part motet)**

⊘ ⊛ *** Gimell (ADD) CDGIM 006. Tallis Scholars, Phillips

Within the ideal acoustics of Merton College Chapel, Oxford, the Tallis Scholars give a thrilling account of the famous 40-part motet *Spem in alium*, in which the astonishingly complex polyphony is spaciously separated over a number of point sources, yet blending as a satisfying whole to reach a massive climax. The *Gaude gloriosa* is another much recorded piece, while the soaring *Sancte Deus* and the two very contrasted settings of the *Salvator mundi* are hardly less beautiful. The vocal line is beautifully shaped throughout, the singing combines ardour with serenity, and the breadth and depth of the sound are spectacular.

Lamentations of Jeremiah I & II. Motets: *Absterge domine; Derelinquat impius; In jejunio et fletu; In manus tuas; Mihi autem nimis; O sacrum convivium; O nata lux de lumine; O salutaris hostia; Salve intemerata virgo*

⊕–↠ *** Gimell CDGIM 025. Tallis Scholars, Phillips

This, the third of the Tallis Scholars' discs devoted to their eponymous composer, is centred on the two great settings of the *Lamentations*. They have often been recorded before, but never more beautifully than here, performances that give total security. As well as the eight fine motets, the collection also has a rare Marian antiphon, *Salve intemerata*, that is among Tallis's most sustained inspirations. Clear, atmospheric recording of striking tangibility.

Lamentations I & II. Audivi vocem de caelo

(N) (M) *** CRD 3499 Clerks of New College, Oxford, Ch., Higginbottom – BYRD: *Lamentations; Mass for 4 Voices* ***

The performance by the Clerks of New College, Oxford, Choir (16 strong) directed by Edward Higginbottom is no less serenely beautiful and deeply felt. It is appropriately coupled with Byrd's only surviving setting of the *Lamentations* and an equally rewarding account of the Tallis responsory, *Audivi vocem de caelo* with its interchange of polyphony and plainchant, which makes an admirable postlude. The recording is first class, with a richly appealing ambience.

Absterge Domine; Candidi facti sunt; Nazareri; Derelinquat impius; Dum transisset sabbatum; Gaude gloriosa Dei Mater; Magnificat & Nunc dimittis; Salvator mundi

(M) *** CRD (ADD) 3429. New College, Oxford, Ch., Higginbottom

The performances by the Choir of New College, Oxford – recorded in the splendid acoustic of the College Chapel – are very well prepared, with good internal balance, excellent intonation, ensemble and phrasing. The *Gaude gloriosa* is one of Tallis's most powerful and eloquent works.

Absterge Domine: Derelinquat impius; Gaude gloriosa; Jesu salvator saeculi; Loquebantur variis linguis; Magnificat a 5; Mihi autem nimis; Nunc dimittis a 5; O nata lux; Sermone blando angelus; Suscipe quaeso Domine

(N) **(*) Hyp. CDA 67548. Cardinall's Musick, Carwood

The large-scale antiphon, *Gaude gloriosa*, is the highlight here, celestial in its paean to the Virgin Mary, and the *Magnificat* and *Loquebantur variis linguis* with its repeated *Alleluias* are joyous too. But many of the other motets here are penitential, and both *Jesu salvator* and *Sermone blando angelus* are homophonic, alternating plainsong with composed music. Listening to this programme through, beautifully sung as it is, one feels the need for more celebration, less supplication.

Audivici vocem de caelo; Candidi facti sunt Nazarei eius a 5; Dum transisset sabbatus; Gaude gloriosa, Dei Mater; Hodie nobis celorum rex; Homo quidam fecit cenam magnam; Honor, virtus et potestas; In jejunio et fletu; In pace in idipsum; Lamentations of Jeremiah I & II; Loquebantur variis linguis; Miserere nostri; O nata lux de lumine; O

sacrum convivium; Salvator mundi I & II; Spem in alium; Suscipe quaeso Domine; Te lucis ante terminum (Procul recedante somnia) I; Videte miraculum

(B) *** Virgin 2×1 5 62230-2 (2). Taverner Consort, Parrott

The Taverner style is brighter and more abrasive than we are used to in this often ethereal music but, apart from the scholarly justification, the polyphonic cohesion of the writing comes over the more tellingly. Our listing is in alphabetical order, but the programme – as presented here – was planned as two separate collections, the first disc containing Tallis's most elaborate and most celebrated choral piece, the 40-part motet, *Spem in alium*, as well as nine other magnificent responsories, some of them – like *Videte miraculum* and *Dum transisset sabbata* – almost as extended in argument. The second of the two discs has two magnificent *Lamentations of Jeremiah* as well as an even more expansive motet, which Tallis wrote early in his career, *Gaude, gloriosa, Dei Mater*, and a number of the shorter *Cantiones sacrae*. This reissue is warmly recommendable and very well recorded.

(i) *Audivi vocem;* (ii; iii) *Derelinquat impius;* (ii; iv) *Dum transisset sabbatum;* (ii; iii) *Ecce tempus idoneum;* (ii; iv) *Honor, virtus et potestas;* (ii; iii) *In ieiunio et fletu; In manus tuas;* (ii; iii) *Lamentations of Jeremiah I & II;* (ii) *Loquebantur variis linguis;* (ii; iii) *O nata lux de lumine; Salvator mundi; Sancte Deus; Spem in alium* (40-part motet); *Te lucis ante terminum* (2 settings); *Veni Redemptor gentium; Videte miraculum;* (i) *Te Deum.* (Organ) (v) *Clarifica me, pater; Fantasy; Iam lucis;* (vi) *Lesson*

(B) **(*) Double Decca ADD/DDD 455 029-2 (2). (i) St John's College, Cambridge, Ch., Guest; (ii) King's College, Cambridge, Ch.; (iii) Willcocks; (iv) Cleobury; (v) White; (vi) A. Davis

The King's College Choir are in their element in music mostly written for Waltham Abbey or the Chapel Royal, whether conducted by Willcocks or Cleobury. The highlight of their programme is the magnificent 40-part motet, *Spem in alium*, in which the Cambridge University Musical Society joins forces with King's. The *Lamentations* are performed authentically, using men's voices only. The motets, *Sancte Deus* and *Videte miraculum*, are for full choir, and here the balance gives slight over-prominence to the trebles. The choir of St John's College under George Guest sing well in the *Te Deum* but sound happier in their motet, *Audivi vocem*. Andrew Davis is an excellent advocate of the *Organ Lesson*; the other two organ pieces are musically less interesting but are well played by Peter White. The (originally Argo) recording is full and atmospheric throughout, although the choral focus is not always sharp.

Audivi vocem de Caelo; Honor virtus et Postestas; O sacrum convivium; Salvator mundi; Sancte Deus

(M) *** CRD 3372, Ch. of New College, Oxford, Higginbottom – TAVERNER: *Western Wynde*, etc. ***

This collection of votive antiphons, motets and responds makes up an attractive group, and the Choir of New College, Oxford, produces a clean and well-blended sound. Given the attractions of the coupling this disc has a strong appeal.

Ecce tempus idoneum; Gaude gloriosa Dei Mater; Loquebantur variis linguis; O nata lux de lumine; Spem in alium

(B) **(*) CfP (ADD) 575 9822. Clerkes of Oxenford, Wulstan – SHEPPARD: *Motets* **(*)

A useful reissue, since it not only juxtaposes motets by Tallis against those of his great (but less familiar) contemporary, John Sheppard, but also gives us a strongly sung bargain version of the famous forty-part motet, *Spem in alium*. Here the resonance of Merton College Chapel means that definition could be more refined, and throughout the programme David Wulstan's tempi are somewhat brisk, while at times there is also some sense of strain among the women. Reservations notwithstanding, there are fine things on this inexpensive CD, and it can be recommended.

Magnificat (4 vv); Mass Puer natus est nobis; Motets: Audivi vocem; Ave Dei patris filia

☛ *** Gimell CDGIM 034-2. Tallis Scholars, Phillips

The performance by the Tallis Scholars of the reconstructed Tallis Christmas Mass has an appealing directness and simplicity and is well up to the standard of its competitors. The four-part *Magnificat* is an early work, but is again very impressively sung here, and the programme is completed with two votive antiphons. *Ave Dei patris filia* is particularly appealing. It has a striking, soaring opening from the trebles emphasizing the word '*Ave*', which illuminates the music throughout its seven stanzas. Excellent recording, but there would have been room for more music here.

Mass for 4 Voices; Motets: Audivi vocem; In manus tuas Domine; Loquebantur variis linguis; O sacrum convivium; Salvator mundi; Sancte Deus; Te lucis ante terminum; Videte miraculum

☛ (BB) *** Naxos 8.550576. Oxford Camerata, Summerly

The Oxford Camerata with their beautifully blended timbre have their own way with Tallis. Lines are firm, the singing has serenity but also a firm pulse. In the *Mass* (and particularly in the *Sanctus*) the expressive strength is quite strongly communicated, while the *Benedictus* moves on spontaneously at the close. The motets respond particularly well to Jeremy Summerly's degree of intensity. The opening *Loquebantur variis linguis* has much passionate feeling, and this (together with the *Audivi vocem* and, especially, the lovely *Sancte Deus*) shows this choir of a dozen singers at their most eloquent. The recording, made in the Chapel of Wellington College, is very fine indeed. Excellent value.

Spem in alium (40-Part Motet)

(N) (**) NMC mono D 103. Morley College Ch., Tippett – TIPPETT: *Concerto for Double String Orchestra, etc.* **(*)

As a delightful supplement to the early recordings of Tippett's works, issued by NMC to celebrate his centenary, comes his own first recording as a conductor, not of his own music but of Thomas Tallis's astonishing 40-part motet, *Spem in alium*, a first ever recording, mushy in its choral sound but full of warmth.

Spem in alium (40 Part Motet); Salve intemerata (Mass & Motet); I call and cry to thee, O Lord; Discomfort them O Lord; With all our heart

✿ (☛) (M) **** Naxos **SACD** 6.110111; CD 8.55770; **Audio DVD** 5.110111. Oxford Camerata, Summerly

This is one of the most remarkable recordings of 2005 and is fully worthy of the celebration of the 500th anniversary of Tallis's birth. Some of his greatest masterpieces are here, written for eight choirs of five voices. *Spem in alium* is justly the most famous. In order to replicate the circular effect

intended by the composer, the producer here, Andrew Walton, and engineer, Mike Clements, have created a surround sound effect with four choirs positioned in the form of four sides of a huge St Chad Cross. Reproduced through four speakers, the result (especially at the climax of *Spem in alium*) is overwhelming. But the extended motet, *Salve intemerata*, and its associated Mass are superb too, while the three English motets which complete the programme are by no means an anticlimax. The performances here are beyond praise, as is the skill of the Naxos recording team, while the acoustic of All Hallows, Gospel Oak, London, was ideally chosen for this remarkable enterprise. We have awarded four stars for this unique achievement, as three seemed insufficient, since this mid-priced disc pioneers the technology of the future. This recording comes in 3 versions: SACD (for SACD players with surround sound); ordinary CD; and for DVD Audio and DVD Video player.

TANEYEV, Sergei (1856–1915)

Symphonies 2 in B flat; 4 in C min., Op. 12

*** Chan. 9998. Russian State SO, Polyansky

Symphony 4 in C min., Op. 12; Overture The Oresteia, Op. 6

*** Chan. 8953. Philh. O, Järvi

Valeri Polyansky's account of the *Fourth Symphony* is more generously coupled with the earlier *B flat Symphony* than is Neeme Järvi's excellent account on the same label. The *Fourth*, the first symphony to be published in the composer's lifetime, is a long piece of over 40 minutes. It comes from 1898, twenty years later than No. 2. The outer movements were scored, but the central *Andante* was left in short score, and the work was put into performable shape by Vladimir Blok. There is a certain nobility about Taneyev's writing, although his ideas do not have the personality of a Glazunov or a Rachmaninov, and that applies to both symphonies offered here by Polyansky. But the *Fourth* has a particularly inventive and delightful Scherzo, which shows his keenness of wit. The Russian performances are very good, though Järvi's CD of the *Fourth* with the Philharmonia Orchestra is not displaced. He gets very good playing from the Philharmonia and similarly first-class recording.

Piano Quartet in E, Op. 20

**(*) Pro Arte CDD 301. Cantilena Chamber Players

The *Piano Quartet* is a finely wrought and often subtle work. With a superbly sensitive contribution from Frank Glazer, the performance is altogether first rate, though the acoustic in which it is recorded is not quite big enough.

(i) Piano Quartet in E, Op. 20. Piano Trio in D min., Op. 22

(N) (M) *** Dutton CDSA 6882. Barbican Piano Trio, (i) with J. Boyd

The Barbican Trio is a fine ensemble and excellently recorded. Theirs is a well-shaped account of the Op. 22 *Trio*, albeit not quite as commanding as the Repin–Harrell–Pletnev partnership. Their excellent pianist, highly musical though he is, does not command the range of colour and dynamics, or the clarity of articulation of Pletnev. Their coupling is the slightly earlier but equally rewarding *E major Piano Quartet*, which is not otherwise currently available on CD. Taneyev's melodic invention may not be of the quality of Tchaikovsky's, but his music is full of subtleties and surprises and gives much delight.

Piano Quintet in G min., Op. 30

*** Ara. Z 6539. Lowenthal, Rosenthal, Kamei, Thompson, Kates

Not only is the *Piano Quintet* well structured and its motivic organization subtle, but its melodic ideas are strong and individual. It is arguably the greatest Russian chamber work between Tchaikovsky and Shostakovich. The recording is not in the demonstration bracket, but it is very good, and the playing, particularly of the pianist Jerome Lowenthal, is excellent. Strongly recommended.

Piano Quintet, Op. 30; Piano Trio in D min., Op. 22

⊕— *** DG 477 5419. Repin, Gringolts, Imai, Harrell, Pletnev

Both the *Piano Trio* (1908) and the *Quintet* (1911) are long works but, played as they are here, belie their length. There have been imposing performances of both from Jerome Lowenthal and colleagues (Arabesque) and from the Borodin Trio (Chandos), but this newcomer, coupling both together, displaces them. The *Piano Trio* contains a set of variations (following the example of Tchaikovsky). Taneyev's have breadth and nobility, as do the companion movements. The *Piano Quintet* is an even more magnificent score (Professor David Brown calls its *Passacaglia* 'Taneyev at his greatest, fashioning a magisterial and wonderfully original movement'), and its remarkable Scherzo he rightly calls 'magical'. Mikhail Pletnev is mercurial here. In fact these are performances which are in every respect masterful, and they are hardly likely to be surpassed. The warmest welcome to them and the strongest recommendation!

Piano Trio in D, Op. 22

*** Chan. 8592. Borodin Trio

This *Trio* is a big, four-movement work. The invention is attractive – and so, too, are the excellent performance and recording. Strongly recommended.

String Quartets 1 in B flat Min., Op. 4; 2 in C, Op. 5

*** OCD 697. Krasni Qt

This fine coupling offers yet more evidence that, in his chamber music especially, Taneyev was a more important figure in Russian music than has hitherto been suspected. The *First Quartet*, written in 1890 and dedicated to his former teacher, Tchaikovsky, is a distinctly individual piece in five movements, alternating slow and fast tempi. The beautiful Largo is searching, with an almost improvisatory feel, the Scherzo dances along spiritedly, and a delicately nostalgic Intermezzo intervenes before the light-hearted *Giocoso* finale, which has a charming secondary theme.

The *Second Quartet* (1895) has a pervading folksy quality and is certainly Slavic in feeling, especially the melody that forms the centrepiece of the Scherzo. The Adagio espressivo is very intense, but also restless; the finale (*vigorosamente*) resolves matters cheerfully, and halfway through introduces a double fugue, gathering together the work's principal ideas. Then the tempo quickens, the texture lightens, and the movement ends jokingly, with a *moto perpetuo* over growling low scales from the cello. These performances are first class, and the recording is truthful (even if perhaps a little close). Recommended.

Cantata 2, Op. 36 (At the Reading of a Psalm)

⊕— (N) *** PentaTone SACD PTC 5186 038. Semenina, Tarassova, Gubsky, Baturkin, St Petersburg State Ac. Ch., Glinka Choral College Boys' Ch., Russian Nat. O, Pletnev

In March 2005 Pletnev and the Russian National Orchestra broke a lance for Taneyev by bringing two of his big choral works and the *Fourth Symphony* to London's Barbican Hall – and to packed houses! This account of *At the Reading of a Psalm* is every bit as dedicated and committed as their London concert, and the choral singing is wonderfully full-blooded and rich in tone. This will come as a revelation to those who think of the composer as 'the Russian Brahms' (the same epithet is applied to Medtner) for this music speaks with a completely individual voice.

John of Damascus

*** DG 471 029-2. Mescheriakov, Larin, Chernov, Moscow State Ch. O, RNO, Mikhail Pletnev – RACHMANINOV: *The Bells* ✪ ***

Taneyev was the teacher of Glière, Scriabin, Medtner and Rachmaninov. His mastery of counterpoint was legendary and (as Calvocoressi and Gerald Abraham remind us in their *Masters of Russian Music* (Duckworth, London, 1936)) he would make countless drafts and preparatory exercises, fugues and canons and the like, so as to master every possibility and potential of his ideas before he embarked on a score. Taneyev's *John of Damascus* is his Op. 1 and a noble piece, whose long neglect on the gramophone is at last remedied. An earlier version from Valéry Polyansky on Chandos made a strong impression but was encumbered with a perfectly adequate but unwanted performance of Tchaikovsky's *Fourth Symphony*. In any event this is vastly superior in every way.

TARTINI, Giuseppe (1692–1770)

(i; ii) *Cello Concerto in A*; (iii; ii) *Violin Concertos in D min., D.45*; (iv; ii) *in E min., D.56; in G, D.82*; (iii; v) *Violin sonatas* (for violin & continuo): *in A; in G min.; in F, Op. 1/1, 10 & 12; in C, Op. 2/2; in G min. (Devil's Trill)*

(N) (BB) *** Warner Apex 2564 61693-2 (2). (i) Zannerini; (ii) Sol. Ven.; (iii) Toso; (iv) Amoyal; (v) Farina

Here is a collection to make the listener understand why Tartini was so admired in his day. Spanning both halves of the eighteenth century as he did, he possesses the lyrical purity of Corelli and Vivaldi with a forward-looking sensibility that is highly expressive. Indeed, his invention is almost romantic at times and there are moments of vision which leave no doubt that he is underrated. The first work on the opening disc is the *Violin Concerto in D minor, D.45*, which opens with a richly winning orchestral ritornello and has a very beautiful central *Grave*, which Piero Toso plays exquisitely. The other concertos also have memorable slow movements to which Amoyal and Zannerini both respond persuasively. The orchestral playing is committed, and the fresh, warm analogue recording from the 1970s is pleasingly transferred. Tartini's sonatas take their virtuosity for granted; even the *Devil's Trill* does not flaunt its bravura until the finale with its extended trills – considered impossibly difficult in his day. Instead these works call for playing of the greatest technical finesse and musicianship. Pierre Amoyal plays them superbly; he makes no attempt to adapt his style to period-instrument practice. Instead his performances have a sweetness of tone and expressive eloquence to commend them, and though he is forwardly placed, the (unimportant) harpsichord continuo just comes through to give support. The violin is beautifully recorded. A most desirable pair of CDs.

Cello Concerto in D

(M) *** Warner Elatus 0927 49839-2. Rostropovich, St Paul
CO, Wolff – C. P. E. BACH; VIVALDI: *Concertos* ***

A commanding performance by Rostropovich of the Tartini
concerto, originally written for viola da gamba and transcribed for cello in the late 1920s by Rudolf Hindemith and
revised here by Hugh Wolff. It is a mellifluous and beautiful
work, played with great eloquence not only by the distinguished soloist, but also the fine Saint Paul orchestra. Excellent recorded sound.

Violin Concertos, Op. 1/1, 4–5 & 12; in C

☞ *** Hyp. CDA 67345. Wallfisch, Raglan Bar. Players,
Kraemer

Tartini's Op. 1 was published in Amsterdam in 1728, but only
included Nos. 1, 4 & 5 of the present set. No matter what their
provenance, they are all most engaging works in three movements, although the first includes an additional and modestly
paced *Fugue à la breve*. The performances here are splendid.
Elizabeth Wallfisch may be playing a period instrument, but
her timbre is smooth and polished, with no edginess, and the
Adagio or *Cantabile* slow movements could not be sweeter.
She is splendidly athletic in allegros as are her alert accompanying group and they are very well balanced in recording.

Violin Concertos in C, D.2; F, D.67; A, D.96; A min. (A Lunardo Venier), D.115; B min., D.125

☞ (BB) *** Warner Apex (ADD) 2564 60152-2. Toso, Sol.
Ven., Scimone

Tartini is a much underrated composer, as the many beautiful
slow movements of these concertos will readily show. Pierre
Toso, who recorded a number of them in the early 1970s,
responds with admirable feeling, his timbre consistently
sweet. The *Adagio* of the *C major*, D.2 (*Se mai saprai*), is
particularly beautiful, but for Toso the 'senza splendor' of the
concerto's finale is not ostentatious. Yet his approach is
consistently stylish and pleasing: the *Adagio* of the *A major* is
most gracious, and the *Largo/Andante* finale (which has the
inscription 'Flow bitter tears until my anguish is consumed')
is movingly played. No less touching is the *Larghetto* of the *B
minor Concerto*, which brings another inscription, '*Lascia
ch'io dica addio*', while the *Andante cantabile* of the *F major* is
a charming siciliano with the indication '*Misterio anima mea*'.
Scimone and I Solisti Veneti accompany sympathetically and,
while the balance tends to favour the solo violin a little, it
otherwise produces excellent results, with the overall sound
most natural and pleasing.

(Unaccompanied) Violin Sonatas: in A min., B:a3; in G min.; (Sonata de Diavolo), B:g5; L'arte del arco, B:f11; 14 Variations on the Gavotte from Corelli's Op. 5/10; Pastorale for violin in scordatura, B:a16

☞ ✿ *** HM HMU 907213. Manze

Andrew Manze plays those genuinely fiendish trills in the
finale of the *Devil's Trill Sonata* quite hair-raisingly. He
re-creates here the electrifying effect Tartini's playing must
have had on his own generation. Manze calls the opening
Largo an 'infernal siciliana' (yet presents it with great poise
and refined espressivo), and the central movement (hardly
less remarkable) becomes a 'demonic moto perpetuo'. Yet
Corelli's gavotte is played with engaging delicacy, the bravura
left for the variations. The *A minor Sonata* also includes a set
of variations, which again offers an amazing range of musical

and technical opportunities, as does the colourful hurdy-
gurdy finale of the *Pastorale* which ends so hauntingly. These
works were left with a written bass line – omitted here
because, according to Manze, this was the composer's stated
'true intention' and own practice. Manze's playing is totally
compelling and certainly confirms that the music is 'complete' without a continuo. The recording is very real and
immediate.

Violin sonata in G min. (Devil's Trill), arr. Zandonai for violin and strings

**(*) DG 463 259-2. Mutter; Trondheim Soloists – VIVALDI:
The 4 Seasons ***

Mutter, as in her previous recording of the sonata – one of
the items on a virtuoso showpiece disc (*Carmen Fantasy*) –
uses Zandonai's string arrangement, this time with harpsichord and cello rather than piano continuo. As in the Vivaldi,
Mutter takes an unashamedly romantic view of the piece,
providing an inauthentic but interesting makeweight to a
version of *The Four Seasons* which, whatever its controversial
points, is magnetic from first to last.

TAVENER, John (born 1944)

(i) Eternal Memory for Cello and Strings; (ii) The Hidden Treasure (for String Quartet); Svyati (O Holy One) for Cello & Chorus; (iv) Akhmatova Songs for Soprano & Cello. Chant for Solo Cello

(N) (M) *** RCA 82876 64278-2. Isserlis, with (i) Moscow
Virtuosi, Spivakov; (ii) Philips, Feeney, Phillips; (iii) Kiev
Chamber Ch., Gobdych; (iv) Rosario

All this music is constructed simply (simplistically, some
might say) and is based for the most part on a straightforward rising and falling scalic sequence, in the case of *Svyati*
and *Eternal Memory* linked thematically. Their atmosphere is
magnetic. *Eternal Memory* moves on from *The Protecting Veil*,
and the composer describes its evocation as 'the remembrance of death; the remembrance of Paradise lost'; its serene
outer sections frame a more troubled centrepiece, 'grotesque,
dance-like and rough'. *The Hidden Treasure* for string quartet
still has a dominating cello role and might be described as a
religious pilgrimage, closing with a mystical transformation.
In the *Akhmatova Songs* the rising and falling sequence is
floridly ornamented, and the singer is required to soar up
ecstatically to the top of her range, which Patricia Rosario
manages confidently. *Svyati* returns to a simple but radiant
dialogue, alternating cello soliloquy with a mystical choral
response. Steven Isserlis has never made a finer record than
this, and he gives the feeling of quiet improvisation (especially in his solo *Chant*); the singing and playing throughout
capture the music's atmosphere superbly. The beautiful
recording has a natural presence.

(i) The Protecting Veil; (ii) The Last Sleep of the Virgin (a Veneration for Strings & Handbells)

**(*) Telarc CD 80487. (i) Springuel; (ii) Willems; I
Flamminghi, Werthen

(i) The Protecting Veil; Thrinos

(M) *** Virgin 5 61849-2. Isserlis, (i) LSO, Rozhdestvensky –
BRITTEN: *Cello Suite 3* ***

(i) The Protecting Veil; (ii) Wake up ... and die

*** Sony SK 62821. Ma, with (i) Baltimore SO; (ii) cellos of
Baltimore SO; Zinman

(i) *The Protecting Veil*; (ii) *In alium* (for soprano, tape and orchestra)

⊶ (BB) *** Naxos 8.554388. (i) Kliegel; (ii) Hulse; Ulster O, Yuasa

In the inspired performance of Steven Isserlis, dedicatedly accompanied by Rozhdestvensky and the LSO, *The Protecting Veil* has an instant magnetism, at once gentle and compelling. The 'protecting veil' of the title refers to the Orthodox Church's celebration of a tenth-century vision, when in Constantinople the Virgin Mary appeared and cast her protecting veil over the Christians who were being attacked by the Saracen armies. Tavener, himself a Greek Orthodox convert at the time, echoes the cadences of Orthodox chant, ending each section with passages of heightened lyricism for the soloist. Each time that guides the ear persuasively on into the next section, leading at the end to the work's one sharply dramatic moment, when a sudden surge represents Christ's Resurrection. Much is owed to the performance, with Isserlis a commanding soloist. He is just as compelling in the other two works on the disc, not just the Britten but also the simple lyrical lament, *Thrinos*, which Tavener wrote especially for him. Excellent recording.

Yo-Yo Ma, rather more withdrawn, is equally concentrated, daringly adopting an even slower tempo in the central section, *Lament of the Mother of God*. He is helped by the sympathetic accompaniment of David Zinman and the Baltimore orchestra, with recording a degree more transparent than the original RCA. The fill-up is a new work, similarly visionary, commissioned from Tavener by Sony, in which, using a palindromic motif, the spacious cello solo is enhanced by cellos from the orchestra.

Using a warm, wide vibrato, Maria Kliegel gives a dedicated performance. With Yuasa drawing superb playing from the Ulster Orchestra, this is an unusually spacious reading that sustains its length well. What makes it specially attractive is the coupling, *In Alium*, a piece for soprano, tape and orchestra which is at once devotional and sensuous. The layering of textures, with dramatic contasts, is vividly caught in the excellent Naxos recording. Warmly recommended.

The cello soloist in the Telarc version is relatively reticent emerging out of the orchestra, but the playing is beautiful in its gentle way. *The Last Sleep of the Virgin*, written originally for string quartet in memory of Dame Margot Fonteyn, makes an apt coupling in the conductor's enriched version for string orchestra.

(i) *The Protecting Veil* (for Cello & Orchestra). (ii; iii) *Angels*. (iv) *Funeral Ikos; 2 Hymns for the Mother of God; The Lamb*; (ii) *Song for Athene*

⊶ (N) (BB) *** EMI HMV 5 86772-2. (i) Isserlis, LSO, Rozhdestvensky; (ii) Winchester Cathedral Ch., Hill; (iii) D. Dunnett (organ); (iv) Vasari Singers, Backhouse

As a single budget disc offering some of Tavener's key works, this HMV compilation is hard to beat. It includes the key Isserlis/Rozhdestvensky account of *The Protecting Veil* (see above), Tavener's justly celebrated carol *The Lamb*, plus the *Funeral Ikos* and *Two Hymns for the Mother of God* from the excellent Vasari Singers, and the fine Winchester account of the equally famous *Song for Athene*. Excellent recording makes this a real bargain.

Diódia (String Quartet 3) – see below under *Akhmatova Songs*

String Quartets: *The Hidden Treasure*; (i) *The Last Sleep of the Virgin*

*** Virgin VC5 45023-2. Chilingirian Qt, (i) with Simcock (handbells) – PART: *Fratres; Summa* ***

'Quiet and intensely fragile' is Tavener's guide to performances of *The Last Sleep of the Virgin*, a work which might be described as an ethereal suggestion, using the simplest means (string quartet and tolling bell) to convey both the reality and the implications of the death and burial of 'the Mother of God'. *The Hidden Treasure* in its seeking for Paradise offers more violent contrasts (a brief cello cadenza-soliloquy a key factor) interrupting the flow of the spiritual journey. Tavener's world is all his own and the artists convey the music's logic with hypnotic concentration, helped by a resonant acoustic. The mystical close of *The Hidden Treasure* brings a shimmering *pianissimo-diminuendo* of remarkable intensity.

VOCAL MUSIC

(i) *Akhmatova Songs; Many Years; The World* (all for soprano and string quartet); *Diódia (String Quartet 3)*

⊶ *** Hyp. CDA 67217. (i) Rozario; Vanbrugh Qt

Tavener's six *Akhmatova Songs* are among the most beautiful and directly communicative of all his settings. Originally written for soprano and cello, here they are rearranged even more tellingly, using a string quartet but still relying a great deal on a solo cello. Patricia Rozario is now completely at home in the soaring melisma and surpasses her earlier performance for RCA, with her account of the exotic melody of *The Muse*, sounding like a celestial Russian folksong. However, it is the hauntingly passionate closing evocation of *Death* which gains most from the new instrumentation. *The World* depends much on sustained high notes for the voice over a gentle pedal and 'should be performed at maximum intensity throughout', which it certainly is here. The simply harmonized *Many Years* is a brief but melodious prayer of supplication for the longevity of the Prince of Wales, given as a present on his fiftieth birthday.

But the most ambitious work here is the *Third String Quartet, Diódia*, which in a series of very similar episodes, considers 'the posthumous states of being of the soul'. Tavener is directly concerned with the balance between heaven and hell in music which is predominantly reflective and serene, but with dramatic and sometimes savagely violent interruptions. The performance has great concentration, achieving a remarkable closing pianissimo over a beating drum (perhaps a fading heartbeat). The recording is of Hyperion's best quality.

(i) *Angels*; (ii) *Collegium regale: Magnificat & Nunc Dimmitis*; (i; iii) *God is with us (A Christmas Proclamation)*; (iv) *Funeral Ikos; 2 Hymns to the Mother of God; The Lamb*; (i) *Lament of the Mother of God*; (i) *Song for Athene*; (v) *The Protecting Veil* (excerpt): 1st section only

⊶ (B) *** CfP 585 9152. (i) Winchester Cathedral Ch., Hill; (ii) King's College, Cambridge, Ch., Cleobury; (iii) with Kendall, Dunnet (organ); (iv) Vasari Singers, Backhouse; (v) Isserlis, LSO, Rozhdestvensky

Like the companion Classics for Pleasure introduction to the music of Arvo Pärt, this compilation draws on a number of similar sources, all of high quality, both musically and as recordings. The items from the Vasari Singers include Tavener's justly famous and haunting carol, *The Lamb*. Jeremy Backhouse enhances his performance with an effective ritardando at the end of each verse, while he links the melancholy simplicity of the *Funeral Ikos* naturally to the ethereality of the *Two Hymns to the Mother of God*. The items from the Winchester choir conducted by David Hill (with David Dunnet at the organ in *God is with us*) are all atmospherically recorded: each one presents a sharply distinctive vision, culminating in the magnificent Christmas proclamation, *God is with us*. The choir then closes the programme with the beautiful and intense *Song for Athene*, heard at the funeral of Princess Diana. However, it seems a curious idea to include only the first section from Tavener's most famous instrumental work, *The Protecting Veil*, impressive though it is in the performance from Steven Isserlis, conducted by Rozhdestvensky.

'Choral Ikons': Annunciation; As One who has Slept; The Hymn of the Unwaning Light; A Hymn to the Mother of God; The Lamb; The Lord's Prayer; Magnificat and Nunc Dimittis; A Parting Gift for Tom Farrow; Song for Athene; The Tyger

🔴 *** **DVD** BBC Opus Arte OS 0854 D. The Choir, Whitbourn

This collection of some of John Tavener's most attractive choral pieces is not only beautifully sung by The Choir, a professional group founded in 1999, but imaginatively presented. Using virtual-reality techniques, the fourteen singers, recorded in a Dutch television studio in Hilversum, are placed against the background of Hagia Sophia in Istanbul (what was in medieval times the church of St Sophia). With heavy reverberation added, some of the items suggest a far bigger choir, as in the longest item, *The Hymn of the Unwaning Light*, marred slightly by the wobbly contributions of the baritone soloist. The hypnotically repetitious *Song for Athene* has become popular thanks to its use at the end of Princess Diana's funeral service, and the two Blake settings, *The Lamb* and *The Tyger*, are widely heard too, but the dedication behind all the pieces is very clear, each of them introduced visually by an ikon or an ikon-like illustration. A fine DVD première for Tavener's music. As supplementary items the disc offers a long and illuminating interview with the composer, who provides a spoken commentary on each piece (not the most convenient method of providing programme notes), and a Dutch expert talking about the sources of ikon painting.

Annunciation; 2 Hymns to the Mother of God; (i) Innocence; The Lamb; (ii) Little Requiem for Father Malachy Lynch; Song for Athene; The Tyger

*** Sony SK 66613. Westminster Abbey Ch., Neary; with (i) Rozario, Titus, A. Nixon, M. Neary, Baker; (ii) ECO

With Martin Neary drawing incandescent singing from the Westminster Abbey Choir, this CD offers a sequence of Tavener's best-known short works – such as the Blake settings, *The Lamb* and *The Tyger*, and the *Hymns to the Mother of God* – as well as longer pieces in which he movingly exploits spatial effects. *Innocence* encapsulates in its 25-minute ritual what many of his more expansive pieces have told us, with multi-layered elements atmospherically contrasted, near and far, starting with apocalyptic organ-sounds and ending with a surging climax. The elegiac *Song for Athene*, heard at the funeral of Princess Diana, is also among Tavener's most beautiful and touching inspirations, a ritual inspired by Orthodox chant over a drone bass. The Sony recording vividly captures the Abbey acoustic, with extreme dynamics used impressively to convey space and distance.

As one who has slept; Birthday Sleep; The Bridal Chamber; Butterfly Dreams; Exhortation and Kohima; Schuon Hymnen; Schûnya; The Second Coming
(N) *** Hyp. CDA 67475. Polyphony, Layton

Stephen Layton's superb professional choir, Polyphony, does wonders in bringing variety to a sequence of Sir John Tavener's recent works for small chorus which might easily have seemed too persistently slow and meditative. Layton magnetically sustains Tavener's obsessively repetitious writing, even in the longest and least varied of the pieces, *Shunya*, with that Sanskrit word for 'void' endlessly repeated over Tibetan gong-beats. Most impressive of the longer works is *Schuon Hymnen*, setting German words by the Sufi sheikh, Frithjof Schuon, with verses and refrains bringing sharp contrasts between powerful unisons and distant choral comment, punctuated by mantra-like phrases for solo tenor. *Birthday Sleep*, setting a Vernon Watkins poem, brings attractively scrunching harmonies, and the eight tiny movements of *Butterfly Dreams* include one which delightfully captures the fluttering of a butterfly.

As one who has slept; Funeral Ikos; God is with us (Christmas Proclamation); 2 Hymns to the Mother of God; The Lamb; The Lord's Prayer; Love bade me welcome; Magnificat & Nunc dimittis; Song for Athene; (i) Svyati (O Holy One); The Tyger
🔴 (BB) *** Naxos 8.555256. Choir of St John's College, Cambridge, Robinson; (i) with Hugh

The Christmas Proclamation, *God is with us*, is the striking first item in this collection of John Tavener's shorter choral pieces. It was inspired, like so many of Tavener's works, by Greek Orthodox liturgy, rising in thrilling crescendo and punctuated at the end by fortissimo organ chords. The *Song for Athene* is here presented as an anthem rather than a processional. The longest work, *Svyati*, with its cello solo magnetically played by Tim Hugh, echoes the example of Tavener's visionary cello work *The Protecting Veil*, while the shorter pieces include most of the favourite Tavener items. Superb singing throughout and vividly atmospheric sound.

(i; ii) Canticle of the Mother of God; (i; ii) Ikon of the Nativity; (iii) Out of the Night (Alleluia); (iv) Threnos
*** Sony SK 61753. (i) Tavener Ch., Parrott; (ii) McFadden; (iii) Atkins, Nixon; (iv) Walsh – PART: *Fratres* ***

Tavener's music is here effectively juxtaposed with works by his Estonian contemporary, Arvo Pärt, with the sustained but brief *Out of the Night* (for tenor voice and viola) acting as an evocative repeated refrain as it is heard (and performed) four times throughout this programme. The *Canticle of the Mother of God*, with its strange soprano melisma and choral dissonance, is ecstatically powerful and contrasts with the ruminative cello solo of *Threnos*, while the *Ikon of the Nativity* (which ends the concert ardently) is a set of three variations heard within a long melodic arch. The performances are undoubtedly compelling, the resonant sound just right for the music.

(i) Eternity's Sunrise; (ii) Funeral Canticle; Petra; A Ritual Dream; (i; iv) Sappho: Lyrical Fragments; (i; v) Song of the Angel
*** HM HMU 907231. (i) Rozario, (ii) Mosely, AAM Ch., (iv) Gooding, (v) Manze; with AAM, Goodwin

Eternity's Sunrise is an elegiac setting of words by Blake in Tavener's rapt and intense style, with the soprano, Patricia

Rozario, both pure and sensuous in singing the soaring cantilena. The final work on the disc *Funeral Canticle* for baritone and chorus is related in being written in memory of the composer's father; 'calm and mesmeric' as Paul Goodwin says in his note, over an extended span, one of the finest, most intense examples of Tavener's religious minimalism. Of the rest, *Sappho* represents Tavener at an earlier period, grittier in expression, while *Petra* and the *Song of the Angel* bring ethereal violin solos from Andrew Manze set against the voices. Radiantly atmospheric sound to match.

Fall and Resurrection

*** Chan. 9800. Rozario, Chance, Hill, Richardson, Peacock, BBC Singers, St Paul's Cathedral Ch., City of L. Sinf., Hickox

Fall and Resurrection is the hour-long work which Tavener wrote for the Millennium celebrations in January 2000. Heard first in the echoing expanses of St Paul's Cathedral, it was simultaneously televised, and here comes in a sound recording of that première which in important ways brings advantages. Not only is there greater clarity, with clean directional stereo effects heightening the impact of the writing in massive blocks of sound, with chords endlessly sustained, but the inclusion of a full text in the booklet lets one follow the slow progress of the piece more closely.

Tavener's ambitious aim is to 'encompass in brief glimpses the events which have taken place since the beginning of time and before time'. Using broad brush-strokes in illustrative effects, both choral and instrumental, this becomes a physical experience rather than a musical argument. So, after the slow emergence of the prelude out of silence, darkness and the representation of Chaos (with massive banks of timpani), the voice of Adam is heard against a chill flute solo, a simple dedicated vision. The first of the three parts is then devoted to the fall of Adam and Eve, with the Serpent illustrated by a whining saxophone. The second section, representing prediction, leads from the fall to a quotation from Psalm 121, *I lift my eyes to the hills*, movingly sung by the counter-tenor, Michael Chance. The final part, *The Incarnation of the Logos*, in telegraphic brevity encompasses the birth of Jesus, the Crucifixion and finally the Resurrection in a Cosmic dance, when 'all is transfigured'. The final sustained chord fades away to reveal the sound of the bells of the cathedral outside, ringing out to the world, a theatrical coup underpinned by a heartfelt performance here under Richard Hickox with a superb team of choirs and soloists.

Funeral Ikos; (i) Ikon of Light. Carol: The Lamb

*** Gimell CDGIM 005. Tallis Scholars, (i) Chilingirian Qt (members), Phillips

Ikon of Light is a setting of Greek mystical texts, with chant-like phrases repeated hypnotically. The string trio provides the necessary textural variety. More concentrated is *Funeral Ikos*, an English setting of the Greek funeral sentences, often yearningly beautiful. Both in these and in the brief setting of Blake's *The Lamb*, the Tallis Scholars give immaculate performances, atmospherically recorded in the chapel of Merton College, Oxford.

We Shall See Him as He Is

*** Chan. 9128. Rozario, Ainsley, Murgatroyd, Britten Singers, Chester Festival Ch., Hickox

We Shall See Him as He Is is a sequence of what Tavener describes as musical ikons, setting brief, poetic texts based on the Epistle of St John, each inspired by a salient event in the life of Christ: His baptism, the Wedding Feast at Cana, the cleansing of the Temple, and on to the Last Supper, the Crucifixion and the Resurrection. Each ikon is punctuated by a choral refrain, setting the words of the work's title in Greek. Though at first the inspiration may seem painfully thin, the simple ritual becomes magnetic, with its structured, highly atmospheric use of large-scale choral forces progressing towards rapt contemplation of the Resurrection, the ultimate ikon. The recording was made live at a dedicated Prom performance. The tenor, John Mark Ainsley, in the central solo role of St John, sings with deep feeling, while Patricia Rozario makes her brief, wide-ranging solo a soaring climax.

Mary of Egypt (complete)

(BB) *** Regis RRC 2026 (2). Rozario, Varcoe, Goodchild, Ely Cathedral Ch., Britten–Pears Chamber Ch., Aldeburgh Festival Ens., Friend

Mary of Egypt was recorded live at the Aldeburgh Festival first performances in June 1992 and, characteristically, Tavener compels you to accept his slow pacing and paring down of texture. In many ways the disc works better than the live staging, when with the help of the libretto the developments in the bald, stylized plot can be more readily followed. The musical landmarks are sharply defined in clear-cut, memorable motifs, with moments of violence set sharply against the predominant mood of meditation. What is disconcerting is the disembodied voice representing the Mother of God: Chloe Goodchild, using weird oriental techniques, sounds like a raw baritone. Under Lionel Friend the performance has a natural concentration, with Patricia Rozario as Mary and the baritone, Stephen Varcoe, as Zossima both outstanding. Their confrontation in Act III brings a radiant duet that acts as a climactic centrepiece to the whole work. A synopsis and libretto are provided, but instead of notes there is a 15-minute interview with the composer, informative but disconcertingly overamplified.

The Veil of the Temple

(N) *** RCA 8287 666 154-2 (2). Rozario, Temple Church Ch., Holst Singers, Layton

Tavener describes *The Veil of the Temple* as an all-night vigil, which it literally is, when in its full form it lasts eight hours, a choral sequence in eight cycles. It represents a journey from darkness to light, from death to rebirth, ending on the eighth cycle, which represents a new week and a new creation. He has taken his inspiration not just from Greek Orthodox rituals (a regular source for him) but from Russian church music too, and more particularly from eastern sources, Sufi, Hindu, Tibetan and Sanskrit, a meeting of east and west. Even the Lord's Prayer is taken from various sources, English, Greek and Church Slavonic, interwoven. In its full form it ran the risk of seeming sprawling and repetitive in Tavener's devotional style of spiritual minimalism. Yet with dedicated performances from all the forces, this disc, recorded live at two performances in the summer of 2003, makes for magnetic results over the span of two and a half hours. Only the second of the eight cycles is presented complete, but the progress from the simple dedication of the opening cycles to the grandeur of the last three, increasingly involving massive percussion sounds with gongs of different kinds and weighty choral interventions, is most compelling. The ending brings obsessive cries of 'Shantih', Peace, from the basses as the choir moves off. Spectacular recording, vividly capturing the atmosphere of the Temple Church, with an SACD option.

COLLECTION

'A Portrait'. *Zodiacs* (for piano). Choral/Vocal: *Ikon of Eros: Idon of Light; In Alium; The Lamb; Prayer of the Heart; Song for Athene; The Tyger.* Excerpts from: *The Protecting Veil* (for Cello and Orchestra); *Chant* (for Guitar); *Diodia* (for String Quartet); *Mandolin* (for organ); *Akhmatova; Mary of Egypt; Mother and Child; To a Child Dancing in the Wind*

(N) (BB) *** Naxos 8.558152-53 (2). Rozario, Hulse, Kliegel, St John's College, Cambridge, Ch., Robinson, The Sixteen, Christophers, Vanbrugh Qt, Ulster O, Yuasa, etc.

John Tavener may not have won over the entire musical world with his brand of music, but he has undoubtedly won a sincere and popular following with his obvious gift for communicating directly to his audience. This disc offers a broad cross section of his work, from the early *In Alium* (1968) which features a pre-recorded tape of people making irritating noises (to this listener's ears) to some of his most recent works. It features many of his obvious hits (such as an excerpt from The *Protecting Veil*), and embraces genres from solo piano and organ music to his opera (or 'moving icon' as the composer calls it), *Mary of Egypt*. As one would expect, there are many beautiful sounds on this CD and the performances are very good. What makes this disc so recommendable, however, is that it has been put together so well by the project editor, Genevieve Helsby, making this two CD set equally enjoyable as an introduction to Tavener's music, or as an enjoyable compilation for those who have already succumbed. The booklet notes are lavish and the second CD includes a forty-five minute interview with the composer.

TAVERNER, John (c. 1495–1545)

Missa Corona Spinea; Responsory: *Audivi vocem de caelo*
*** Proud Sound PROUCD 1149. Ch. of King's College, London, Trendell – BYRD: *Laetentur caeli; Tristitia et anxietas* ***

The 28 young singers in this choir from King's College, London, tackle a formidable programme of polyphonic music, centred on the magnificent setting of the Mass which Taverner wrote for Cardinal College, Oxford, to which he had been appointed choirmaster in 1526. The 16 sopranos with their fresh tone confidently tackle the exuberant writing for trebles in its wonderfully varied contrasts of timbre, even if their matching is not always as polished as it might be. Like Christ Church Cathedral Choir on the rival ASV version they establish this as yet another long-buried masterpiece of early Tudor polyphony. The responsory, *Audivi*, using a similar combination of high voices, provides an apt tail-piece for a programme also celebrating the mastery of William Byrd in two superb motets. Warmly atmospheric recording.

Missa Corona spinea; Motets: *Gaude plurium; In pace*
⊶ ✿ (BB) *** Hyp. Helios CDH 55051. The Sixteen, Christophers

Missa Corona spinea; Motet: *O Wilhelme, pastor bone*
**(*) ASV CDGAU 115. Christ Church Cathedral Ch., Grier

As with the *Missa Mater Christi sanctissima* (see below), we are offered a choice of performance style for the inspired *Missa Corona spinea*, perhaps the most thrilling of all the Taverner Mass settings. In the Christ Church performance

Francis Grier has transposed the music up, and his choir, although always eloquent, have to try very hard to cope with the highest tessitura. The Sixteen, using professional singers (and secure female trebles), have no such problems and they sing gloriously throughout. Taverner's inspiration is consistent and his flowing melismas are radiantly realized, with fine support from the lower voices; indeed, the balance and blend are nigh perfect. The two motets are no less beautifully sung, and the recording, made in St Jude's Church, Hampstead, is outstanding both in clarity and in its perfectly judged ambience. A superb disc and an astonishing bargain.

Missa Gloria tibi Trinitas; Audivi vocem (responsory); anon.: *Gloria tibi Trinitas*
⊶ (BB) *** Hyp. Helios CDH 50552. The Sixteen, Christophers

Missa Gloria tibi Trinitas; Dum transisset sabbatum; Kyrie a 4 (Leroy); Western Wynde Mass (with song: *Western Wynde*)
*** Gimell CDGIM 004. Tallis Scholars, Phillips

This six-voice setting of the *Gloria tibi Trinitas* Mass is richly varied in its invention (not least in rhythm) and expressive in a deeply personal way very rare for its period. Harry Christophers and The Sixteen underline the beauty with an exceptionally pure and clear account, superbly recorded and made the more brilliant by having the pitch a minor third higher than modern concert pitch.

Peter Phillips and the Tallis Scholars give an intensely involving performance of this glorious example of Tudor music. The recording may not be as clear as on the rival Hyperion version, but Phillips rejects all idea of reserve or cautiousness of expression; the result reflects the emotional basis of the inspiration the more compellingly. The motet, *Dum transisset sabbatum*, is then presented more reflectively, another rich inspiration. To make this reissue even more attractive, Gimell have now added first-class accounts of the famous *Western Wynde Mass* and the song on which it is based.

(i) *Missa Mater Christi sanctissima; Hodie nobis coelorum rex; Magnificat a 4: Nesciene mater; Mater Christi sanctissima;* (ii) *In nomine a 4; Quemadmodum a 6*
(BB) *** Hyp. Helios CDH 55053. (i) The Sixteen, Christophers; (ii) Fretwork

Continuing their outstanding Taverner survey The Sixteen here offer the *Missa Mater Christi sanctissima* plus the votive anthem on which it is based. Christophers presents the Mass as it stands, and the music itself is all sung a tone up, which certainly makes it sound brighter. His pacing is rather restrained, and that adds a touch of breadth. The Helios disc includes extra music, including the Christmas responsory *Hodie nobis*, a fine four-part *Magnificat* and, a surprise, two rather grave pieces for viols from Fretwork to frame the Mass itself. The recording is outstandingly fine, spacious yet clear.

Mass, O Michael; Dum transisset sabbatum; Kyrie a 4 (Leroy)
(BB) *** Hyp. Helios CDH 55054. The Sixteen, Christophers

The *Missa O Michael* is an ambitious six-part Mass lasting nearly 40 minutes which derives its name from the respond, *Archangeli Michaelis interventione*, which prefaces the performance. The chant on which the Mass is built appears no fewer than seven times during its course. The so-called Leroy *Kyrie* (the name thought to be a reference to *le roi* Henry) fittingly precedes it: the *Missa O Michael* has no Kyrie. The Easter motet, *Dum transisset sabbatum*, completes an impressive disc.

Missa Sancti Wilhelmi; Dum transisset Sabbatum; Ex eius tumba; O Wilhelme, pastor bone
⊕━ (BB) *** Hyp. Helios CDH 55055. The Sixteen, Christophers

The *Missa Sancti Wilhelmi* (known as 'Small Devotion' in two sources and possibly a corruption of *S. Will devotio*) is prefaced by the antiphon, *O Wilhelme, pastor bone*, written in a largely syllabic, note-against-note texture, and the second of his five-part settings of the Easter respond, *Dum transisset Sabbatum*, and washed down, as it were, by the Matins responds for the Feast of St Nicholas, *Ex eius tumba*, believed to be the only sixteenth-century setting of this text. The singing of The Sixteen under Harry Christophers is expressive and ethereal, and the recording impressively truthful. Recommended with confidence.

Mass: The Western Wynde. Mater Christi
(M) *** CRD CRD 3372, Ch. of New College, Oxford, Higginbottom – TALLIS: *Audivi vocem de Caelo*, etc. ***

Mass: The Western Wynde; Christe Jesu pastor bone; Dum transisset Sabbatum; Kyrie Leroy; Mater Christie
(B) *** Double Decca (ADD) 452 170-2 (2). King's College, Cambridge, Ch., Willcocks – BYRD: *Masses for 3, 4 & 5 Voices*, etc. ***.

Mass: The Western Wynde; Alleluia, Veni, electa mea; O splendor gloria; Te Deum
⊕━ (BB) *** Hyp. Helios CDH 55056. The Sixteen, Christophers

John Taverner's remarkable individuality is admirably shown by this excellent King's concert. The *Western Wynde Mass* (so called because of its use of this secular tune as a constantly recurring ground) is a masterpiece. Its lines soar to express rich expressive feeling, particularly in the *Sanctus*, and overall it is hauntingly memorable. The other music here also shows the composer's wide range of expressive power: the motets, works of great beauty, match the Mass in their inspiration. With first-class King's performances, appropriately more extrovert in feeling than the coupled music of Byrd, this makes an outstanding collection, with the highly evocative 1961 (originally Argo) recording giving the trebles an abundant body of tone.

This CRD version of Taverner's *Mass* was the first to appear after the King's College, Cambridge, recording of 1961. Since then there have been others, but it was a worthy successor and the acoustic of New College, Oxford, is, if anything, superior to King's, producing greater clarity and definition. Higginbottom's choir sings with great feeling but with restraint and splendid control, both of line and ensemble.

Western Wynde Mass is also beautifully sung and recorded by Harry Christophers' Sixteen in what must be regarded as an ideally paced and proportioned performance. But what makes this inexpensive Helios reissue doubly attractive is the collection of other works included. *O splendor gloria* carries the exulted mood inherent in its title (referring to Christ and the Trinity) and the *Alleluia* is equally jubilant. Most remarkable and individual of all is the masterly five-part *Te Deum*, a profoundly poignant setting, harmonically and polyphonically, even richer than the Mass, and using those momentary

shafts of dissonance that can make music of this period sound so forward-looking. The recording is superb and this CD is obviously the place to start for those wanting to explore this excellent Helios series.

TCHAIKOVSKY, Peter (1840–93)

Andante cantabile for Strings (arr. Serebrier); *Capriccio italien; 1812 Overture; Elégie for Strings in G; Fatum, Op. 77; Marche slave*
*** BIS CD 1283. Bamberg SO, Serebrier

In this, the third of José Serebrier's Tchaikovsky discs for BIS, the popular coupling of *Capriccio italien*, the *1812 Overture* and *Marche slave* brings a fresh, distinctive approach that underlines the purely musical qualities of works that are easily vulgarized. There is special benefit here in the *Capriccio italien*, in which refined textures eliminate any feeling of coarseness, so that the Italianate themes emerge with a light-hearted spring. In the *1812* and *Marche slave*, both with their bold quotations from the tsarist national anthem, there is more to be said for a flamboyant, larger-than-life approach. Yet there, too, it is a revelation to find the conductor's refining process bringing out beauties in the instrumentation that are normally plastered over. Although the cannon and bell effects at the end of *1812* are not identified as coming from anywhere but the orchestra, the excellent BIS recording gives them plenty of punch. *Marche slave* also gains clarity, even in the heaviest passages, with a swaggering spring given to the march rhythms.

The popular *Andante cantabile* comes in the arrangement that Serebrier made when he recorded the piece earlier for ASV with the Scottish Chamber Orchestra, with parts at times redistributed to suit a string orchestra rather than a quartet. This version is a degree more refined than before, as is the surprisingly neglected *Elégie*, a lovely late work written in a single day. The rarity on the disc, the symphonic fantasia *Fatum*, dates from 1868, soon after Tchaikovsky left the St Petersburg Conservatory, and there the clarity and precision of Serebrier's performance in places exposes the weaknesses of this early work. Nevertheless it has a spontaneity and thrust that point forward to Tchaikovsky's later fate-obsessed works, making it a welcome addition to a well-contrasted collection.

Andante cantabile, Op. 11; Nocturne, Op. 19/4; Pezzo capriccioso, Op. 62 (1887 version); 2 Songs: Legend; Was I not a little blade of grass; Variations on a Rococo Theme, Op. 33 (1876 version)
*** Chan. 8347. Wallfisch, ECO, Simon

Andante cantabile; Nocturne (both arr. for cello & orchestra); Pezzo capriccioso; Variations on a Rococo Theme (original versions)
(BB) *** Virgin 2×1 5 61490-2(2). Isserlis, COE, Gardiner – BLOCH: *Schelomo*; ELGAR: *Cello Concerto*; KABALEVSKY: *Cello Concerto 2*; R. STRAUSS: *Don Quixote* ***

The delightful Chandos record gathers together all of Tchaikovsky's music for cello and orchestra, including his arrangements of such items as the famous *Andante cantabile* and two songs. The major item is the original version of the *Rococo Variations* with an extra variation and the earlier variations put in a more effective order, as Tchaikovsky wanted. Geoffrey Simon draws lively and sympathetic playing from the ECO, with Wallfisch a vital if not quite flawless soloist. Excellent recording, with the CD providing fine presence and an excellent perspective.

On this bargain Virgin Double, not only are all the performances of high quality, but Isserlis offers Tchaikovsky's original versions of both the *Pezzo capriccioso* and the *Rococo Variations*. The solo playing has at times a slight reserve, but also an elegant delicacy, most noticeable in the *Andante cantabile*. Throughout, Gardiner provides gracefully lightweight accompaniments and the Virgin recording is faithfully balanced, fresh in texture and warm in ambience. Although there is some sparkling and flawless bravura in the variations, the performance here has less extrovert feeling than with Rostropovich, but many will feel that its lightness of touch has a special appeal.

Capriccio italien, Op. 45

🕪 ✿ (M) *** RCA (ADD) 09026 63302-2. RCA Victor SO, Kondrashin – KABALEVSKY: *The Comedians Suite*; KHACHATURIAN: *Masquerade Suite*; RIMSKY-KORSAKOV: *Capriccio espagnol* ***

Kondrashin's 1958 recording of Tchaikovsky's *Capriccio italien* has never been surpassed. The arresting opening still surprises by its impact, the brass fanfares – first trumpets, then horns, then the full tutti – sonically riveting. The music is alive in every bar and a model of careful preparation, with the composer's dynamic markings meticulously terraced. Kondrashin's pacing throughout is absolutely right and the closing section is highly exhilarating. This is a stereo demonstration disc if ever there was one. And the couplings are pretty good too.

Capriccio italien; (i) 1812 Overture

(M) **(*) DG (ADD) 463 614-2. BPO, Karajan; (i) with Don Cossack Ch. – RIMSKY-KORSAKOV: *Scheherazade* **(*)

Karajan's *1812* is very well presented and very exciting, with fine orchestral playing, and the Russian chorus used to open the piece certainly adds an extra dimension, sonorously recorded. If the closing pages have the cannon added in a calculated fashion rather than showing a touch of engineering flair, the result is still impressive. Although Karajan takes a while to get going, the *Capriccio italien* is also impressive, with the Berlin brass particularly telling. The recording is bright and vividly resonant, but there are more genuinely idiomatic accounts available.

Capriccio italien, Op. 45; 1812 Overture, Op. 49; Fate, Op. 77; Festival Overture on the Danish National Anthem, Op. 15; Francesca da Rimini, Op. 32; Hamlet, Op. 67a; Manfred Symphony, Op. 58; Marche slave, Op. 31; Overture in F, Op. 67; Romeo and Juliet (Fantasy Overture); The Tempest, Op 18; The Voyevoda, Op. 87

(N) ✿ (🕪) (B) *** DG Trio 477 053-2 (3). Russian Nat. O, Pletnev

On these three CDs Deutsche Grammophon have assembled the orchestral pieces previously offered when the Tchaikovsky symphonies appeared separately. The set therefore makes an excellent companion for the five-CD box set of the symphonies. Whatever other versions you may have, and irrespective of whether you have the symphonies, this issue is a *must*. Pletnev has a quite special feeling for Tchaikovsky's music, gauging its highly charged emotional content and dramatic flair to perfection, and never losing sight of the disciplined mind which oversaw the musical design. There is

no shortage of great performances of *Romeo and Juliet* and *Francesca da Rimini*, and Pletnev's account with his Russian National Orchestra certainly ranks among them. But the special value of this set is that it offers rarities like *The Voyevoda* and the *F major Overture* in performances which are unlikely to be bettered for a very long time. When it first appeared, we placed his *Manfred* among the finest in the catalogue, and that judgement still holds. An essential purchase, particularly at so competitive a price.

Capriccio italien; 1812 Overture; Francesca da Rimini; Marche slave

(N) *** Capriccio **Surround SoundSACD** 71 042. ASMF, Marriner

Marriner's performances are very fine, perhaps lacking the very last drop of adrenalin at the climaxes of *Capriccio* and *Francesca*, but still involvingly enjoyable for the polish and commitment of the orchestral response. Indeed, the beauty of the wind- and string-playing in the central section of *Francesca* and in the folksy, lyrical themes in *1812* is memorable. *Marche slave* is sturdy and rather grand, but both these very Russian works end with a fair burst of excitement, even if overall they are not as vital as Sian Edwards's accounts (see below). The Capriccio surround sound is very impressive indeed. The back speakers add just enough ambience to give a concert-hall illusion; the orchestra is naturally balanced and the effect vividly dramatic, while the cannon in *1812* are really spectacular, without dwarfing the orchestra.

Capriccio italien; 1812 Overture; Marche slave; Romeo and Juliet (fantasy overture)

(BB) *** Naxos 8.550500. RPO, Leaper

Adrian Leaper proves a natural Tchaikovskian: whether in the colourful extravagance of the composer's memento of his Italian holiday, the romantic ardour and passionate conflict of *Romeo and Juliet*, the sombre expansiveness of *Marche slave* with its surge of adrenalin at the close, or in the extrovert celebration of *1812*, he draws playing from the RPO that is spontaneously committed and exciting. The brilliantly spectacular recording, with plenty of weight for the brass, was made in Watford Town Hall, with realistic cannon and an impressively resonant imported carillon to add to the exciting climax of *1812*.

Capriccio italien; 1812 Overture; Mazeppa: Cossack Dance

(N) **(*) Telarc **SACD** SACD 60646. Cincinnati SO, Kunzel – GERSHWIN: *American in Paris; Rhapsody in Blue* **(*)

The original compact disc of the Telarc performances gave due warning that the cannon in *1812* might damage speakers and windows if the disc was played at too high a level! So if you need a recording of cannon plus *1812*, and your speakers can accommodate the dynamic range and amplitude, both impressively wide on SACD, this issue is for you. In the *Capriccio Italien* there are no cannon, so the engineers substitute the bass drum, which is very prominent. The orchestral contribution throughout is lively but not memorable, and the playing simply does not generate enough adenalin to compensate for the lack of projection of the orchestral tone. At the end of *1812*, Tchaikovsky's carefully contrived climax, with its full-blooded scalic descent, lacks weight. The most enjoyable item is the sparkling *Cossack Dance*, a favourite item in the days of 78s.

Capriccio italien, Op. 45; 1812 Overture, Op. 49; Marche slave; Romeo and Juliet: Fantasy Overture; The Snow Maiden: Dance of the Tumblers

(BB) *** Naxos 8.550500. Nat. SO of Ukraine, Kuchar

Theodore Kuchar and the excellent Ukraine orchestra follow up their highly recommendable Mussorgsky disc with an almost equally impressive Tchaikovsky collection. Once again the recording is spectacular, with striking depth and resonance. The orchestra is set slightly back, so you need to set the volume a little higher than usual. The playing is most impressive. After the opening fanfare, Kuchar's *Capriccio italien* relaxes warmly, yet, like the perky coda of *Marche slave*, brings a vivid accelerando in the closing pages. *Romeo and Juliet* is very well laid out. Spacious and exciting, the reading is not individually distinctive but has plenty of romantic feeling. Like the *Gopak* in the Mussorgsky programme, the *Dance of the Tumblers* from *The Snow Maiden* makes a lively central interlude, and the closing *1812* generates plenty of Russian colouring, at the same time reminding the listener how characterfully tuneful it is. Kuchar presses forward excitingly to a very spectacular climax, where the superbly resonant carillon all but dwarfs the cannon. While there are other more distinctive versions of some of these pieces, this collection is very enjoyable overall and excellent value.

(i) *Capriccio italien; 1812 Overture; Romeo and Juliet;* (ii) Song: *None but the lonely heart; Eugene Onegin: Lensky's Aria*

(N) (BB) **(*) EMI Encore 5 86443-2. (i) Philh. O, Domingo; (ii) Domingo, Philh. O, Behr

Here we have Domingo in his latter-day role as conductor giving heartfelt and individual readings of three popular orchestral favourites, with plenty of drama and with the passion worn on the sleeve. *1812* is ceremonially measured, with the organ adding breadth and spectacle at the close. The recording is appropriately spacious and resonant. Any lack of sharp co-ordination of ensemble is compensated for by the impact. The vocal items show that Domingo can still tug at the emotions in his more familiar role. The recording, made in All Saints', Tooting, is expansively resonant.

Capriccio italien; Overture 1812; Hamlet (Fantasy Overture), Op. 67; Marche slave; Romeo and Juliet (Fantasy Overture).

✺ (N) (M) *** Sony 516329-2. NYPO, Bernstein

This is one of Bernstein's very finest Sony compilations, showing him consistently at his most imaginative and charismatic. *Capriccio Italien* (1960) may have freely fluctuating tempi, but the structure holds together, and Bernstein gives the fullest character to each theme in turn, with the closing pages matching splendour with weight. The equally gripping (1962) *1812* brings one or two personal idiosyncrasies but is always spontaneous-sounding, and the orchestral playing throughout is expert and totally committed. At the end, the fusillade is impressively spectacular. The coda of *Marche slave* (1963) has a similar projection of adrenalin, yet the central section is invested with genial high spirits. The performance of *Romeo and Juliet*, dating from 1957, is thrillingly intense and dramatically unforgettable. The recording of the strings lacks sumptuousnes but otherwise these new transfers sound much more impressive than the original LP incarnations. But what caps this reissue is the bonus of *Hamlet* from a decade later, which was a new discovery for us. This is a totally gripping account, perhaps the only performance on record to

match Stokowski's famous version. It is stunningly played and excellently recorded. A reissue not to be missed by aficionados of Bernstein or Tchaikovsky, or both.

Concert Fantasy, Op. 56; Piano Concertos 1–3

☞ (BB) **(*) EMI Gemini 85540-2 (2). Donohoe, Bournemouth SO, Barshai

Peter Donohoe's account of the *B flat minor Concerto*, although thoroughly sympathetic and spaciously conceived, lacks the thrust and indeed the electricity of the finest versions. The *Third Concerto* is altogether more successful, dramatic and lyrically persuasive, and held together well by Barshai. The *Concert Fantasia* is even more in need of interpretative cohesion. A little more poise would have been welcome, but there is no denying the spontaneous combustion of the music-making here, and the recording – but for a little too much resonance for the solo cadenza in the opening movement – is effectively spectacular. But what makes this inexpensive Gemini Double distinctive is the inclusion of Donohoe's much praised account of the *Second Concerto*, which was given a ✺ on its original separate issue and deserves to retain it. This superb recording of the full original score in every way justifies the work's length and the unusual format of the slow movement. Its extended solos for violin and cello are played with beguiling warmth by Nigel Kennedy and Steven Isserlis. The first movement goes with splendid impetus, and the performance of the finale is a delight from beginning to end. Donohoe plays with infectious bravura, and he is well supported by sparkling playing from the Bournemouth orchestra under Barshai.

Piano Concertos (i) *1 in B flat min.;* (ii) *2 in G;* (iii) *3 in E flat;* (iv) *Violin Concerto in D;* (v) *Variations on a Rococo Theme for Cello & Orchestra*

(B) **(*) EMI ADD/DDD 5 69695-2 (2). (i) Cziffra, Philh. O, Vandernoot; (ii) Kersenbaum, Fr. R. O, Martinon; (iii) Donohoe, Bournemouth SO, Barshai; (iv) Kogan, Paris Conservatoire O, Silvestri; (v) Fournier, Philh. O, Sargent

(i; ii) *Piano concertos 1–3; Concert Fantasy, Op. 56;* (iii) *Symphony 6 (Pathétique); Marche slave;* (i) *The Seasons; 6 Pieces, Op. 21; Sleeping Beauty* (excerpts), arr. Pletnev

(N) (BB) *** Virgin 5 62358-2 (4). (i) Pletnev (piano); (ii) Philh. O, Fedoseyev; (iii) Russian Nat. O, cond. Pletnev

An outstanding bargain collection, Mikhail Pletnev's masterful account of the *First Concerto* has all the qualities we associate with his remarkable pianism. This high-voltage account, together with that of the *Concert Fantasy*, is among the very finest of modern recordings in the catalogue. Vladimir Fedoseyev and the Philharmonia Orchestra give excellent support and the recording is exemplary. The *Second Concerto* brings comparably commanding playing from Pletnev, but it also brings a small but unnecessary cut in the slow movement. It would be difficult to improve on the *Third Concerto*, which is characterized strongly and interestingly. The recording is very good, but not in the demonstration bracket.

The way in which Pletnev launches us into the development of the first movement of the *Pathétique* in his earlier Virgin recording still takes one aback, even when one knows what to expect. His hand-picked orchestra is as virtuosic as Pletnev himself can be on the keyboard, with a challengingly fast tempo for the Scherzo. There is a stirring account of

Marche slave too, and a very fine recording, perfectly balanced, although the effect is a little recessed.

Tchaikovsky's twelve *Seasons* (they would better have been called 'months') were written to a regular deadline for publication in the St Petersburg music magazine, *Nuvellist*. Mikhail Pletnev has exceptional feeling for Tchaikovsky, revealing depths that are hidden to most interpreters. He grips one from first note to last, not only in *The Seasons* but also in the charming and touching *Six morceaux*, Op. 21. Fresh and natural recorded sound.

Although Cziffra's *B flat minor Piano Concerto* is disappointingly idiosyncratic, everything else on the EMI double is very valuable indeed, notably Leonid Kogan's splendid account of the *Violin Concerto* and Pierre Fournier's distinctive and stylish *Rococo Variations*. After Cziffra, brilliant but wilful in the *B flat minor Concerto*, Sylvia Kersenbaum's 1972 account of the *Second Piano Concerto* with Martinon is a different matter, absolutely complete in its text. The tempo for the opening movement is perfect, and Martinon's opening has a sweep to compare with that of the *B flat minor Concerto*. The violin and cello soloists in the slow movement play most sensitively, as does the pianist, and she is splendidly ebullient in the finale. One's only slight reservation concerns the recording, full but very resonant. Peter Donohoe provides a totally satisfying account of the *Third Concerto*, in an excellent, modern, digital recording. The compilation is crowned by Kogan's warm and spontaneous-sounding 1959 version of the *Violin Concerto*, and Fournier's aristocratic and elegant account of the *Rococo Variations*, dating from 1956 but with sound still full and brilliant.

Piano Concerto 1 in B flat min., Op. 23

☛ *** EMI **DVD** DVA4 901 249. Gilels, French R. & TV O, Cluytens (with PROKOFIEV: *Piano Sonata 3*; MUSSORGSKY: *Pictures at an Exhibition* (orch. Ravel); RAVEL: *Daphnis et Chloe: Suite 2* (with O Nat. de l'RTF))

** Sony **DVD** SVD 45986. Kissin, BPO, Karajan (with PROKOFIEV: *Classical Symphony* **(*))

*** Häns. CD 98.932. Ohlsson, ASMF, Marriner – RACHMANINOV: *Piano Concerto 2* ***

*** Ph. 446 673-2. Argerich, Bav. RSO, Kondrashin – RACHMANINOV: *Piano Concerto 3* ***

(BB) *** EMI 5 73765-2 (3). Rudy, St Petersburg PO, Jansons – RACHMANINOV: *Piano Concertos 1–3; Rhapsody on a Theme of Paganini* ***

(N) (M) *** RCA SACD (ADD) 82876 61392-2. Cliburn, RCA SO, Kondrashin – RACHMANINOV: *Piano Concerto 2* ***

(*) DG 474 291-2. Lang Lang, Chicago SO, Barenboim – MENDELSSOHN: *Piano Concerto 1* *

☛ ⚫ (BB) (***) Naxos mono 8.110671. Horowitz, NBC O, Toscanini – BRAHMS: *Piano Concerto 2* (**)

☛ (B) (***) RCA mono 82876 56052-2. Horowitz, NBC SO, Toscanini – RACHMANINOV: *Piano Concerto 3; Recital: 'Legendary RCA Recordings'* (***)

*(**) Chan. 9913. Judd, Moscow PO, Lazarev – PROKOFIEV: *Piano Concerto 3* *(**).

(N) (BB) (**(*)) Sanctuary Living Era mono AJC 8550. Rubinstein, LSO, Barbirolli – BRAHMS: *Piano Concerto 1* (**(*))

(M) (**) DG (ADD) 447 420-2. Richter, VSO, Karajan – RACHMANINOV: *Piano Concerto 2* ***

(i) *Piano Concerto 1*; (ii) *Nutcracker Suite, Op. 71a* (arr. Economou, for 2 pianos)

*** DG (ADD/DDD) 449 816-2. Argerich, (i) BPO, Abbado; (ii) with Economou

The sheer sweep of Gilels's playing in the Tchaikovsky is awesome. His concentration, freshness and lyrical spontaneity strike the listener forcefully, as does his rapport with André Cluytens (who was himself a fine pianist in his youth). Gilels's entry in the opening of the second movement has that melting quality for which his touch was renowned, and one can see as well as hear the way in which these two artists shape its final cadence. Gilels produces a clarity of articulation and an unostentatious brilliance that are immensely commanding. Cluytens's *Daphnis* is characterized by great finesse, respect for the score and freedom from any kind of expressive exaggeration. When the camera focuses on him at the end of *Lever du jour* you can see how he achieved such fluidity and grace, and how supportive he was as an accompanist in the great flute solo in *La Danse de Pan*. By the time this television broadcast was made in 1960, there were many LP versions of the *Pictures at an Exhibition* so one can see why Cluytens never recorded it commercially. The conception is fine but the actual playing is not distinguished. There is a bonus in the form of the Prokofiev *Third Piano Sonata*, which Gilels recorded in a BBC Studio in 1959: suffice it to say that his playing is mesmeric and breathtaking.

Both works on the Sony DVD were recorded at a New Year's Eve concert at the end of 1988, and the concerto was issued on DG 427 485-2 as well as on video. Kissin was 16 at the time of this performance, though he looks even younger, and the whole occasion must have been rather an awesome experience for him. His playing has great elegance and tremendous poise – his pianissimo tone is quite ravishing – but he tends not to let himself go, and there is a slight feeling that he is playing safe, particularly in the finale. The performance as a whole, for all its finesse, lacks abandon.

The strings in the DVD of Prokofiev's *Classical Symphony* have the characteristic Berlin sheen, and the slow movement has great tonal sweetness. The *Scherzo* is a bit heavy-handed, but it is offset by an altogether captivating finale, perfectly judged in pace and character. The camera work is unobtrusive, and although the piano is rather forward, the balance is well judged, though the overall sound is a shade dry.

It is good to have a really splendid, modern coupling of these two most popular romantic concertos from Ohlsson and Marriner that can measure up to the finest versions from the past, presented in naturally balanced, modern, digital recording of the very highest quality. The Tchaikovsky opens with a commanding melodic sweep, and the first-movement allegro is as full of poetic detail as it is exciting, leading on to the cadenza in the most spontaneous way. The *Andante semplice* is charmingly light-hearted and, after the scintillating centrepiece, is very tender at its reprise. The dancing finale brings all the bravura you could ask for, with weight and power as well as excitement.

Argerich's 1994 live performance with the Berlin Philharmonic under Abbado is undoubtedly the finest of her three recordings. It has prodigious virtuosity, while in the first movement, after a richly commanding opening, conductor and pianist find a perfect balance between dynamism and magically gentle poetry. Even though Argerich's impetuosity is famous, on first hearing the listener will surely be astonished by her two tempestuous octave entries, where she carries all before her. And the cadenza, like the barnstorming closing pages of the finale, brings a thrilling, all-out bravura of the kind one normally only associates with Horowitz. Yet the *Andante semplice* has wonderful delicacy with the central *Prestissimo* glittering like a shower of meteorites. The first-class analogue recording is fully worthy of the music-making, and the audience is astonishingly silent. However, one wonders about the wisdom of DG's choice of coupling. Economou's arrangement of the *Nutcracker Suite* for two pianos works well enough, though it does not banish memories of the dazzling transcription made by Pletnev (recorded by him for HMV and now deleted). However, if the present 1983 performance is not quite so breathtaking, it is still playing of a high order. The digital recording is good but rather dry. This CD, fine as it is, should have been reissued at mid-price.

Argerich's Philips issue comes from a live performance given in October 1980, full of animal excitement, with astonishingly fast speeds in the outer movements. The impetuous virtuosity is breathtaking, even if passage-work is not always cleanly articulated. The CD version clarifies and intensifies the already vivid sound, which is fuller than her DG version of nine years earlier (see below), and the new coupling with her even more sensational account of Rachmaninov's *Third Concerto* from earlier makes this a very desirable issue.

Like the Rachmaninov collection with which it is coupled, Mikhail Rudy's account of the Tchaikovsky *Concerto* treats it less as a warhorse than as a fresh, unhackneyed masterpiece, with poetry and refinement set alongside bravura display. As always, Rudy exhibits much artistry and taste in this eloquent St Petersburg account, partnered by Mariss Jansons. His playing is not short on virtuosity and command, but never at the expense of poetic feeling; the warmly idiomatic orchestral playing under Jansons has great character and personality. The recording balance too does justice to both soloist and orchestra. Altogether it makes a refreshing alternative version, here offered in a bargain package with equally illuminating accounts of the Rachmaninov concertos. Excellent sound, full and vivid.

Van Cliburn and the Russian conductor Kondrashin give an inspired performance with much warmth and glitter. The 1958 sound-balance is forward and could have done with more atmosphere; the tuttis reveal that this is not a modern recording, but in this transfer it sounds better than before, with piano-tone much improved from its LP days. The SACD playback brings marginally greater warmth. Outstanding coupling.

Recorded in Chicago's Orchestra Hall in 2003, Lang Lang's performance bears out the glowing reports of his youthful brilliance and sensitivity. He is totally at ease, if with breathtaking virtuosity, in the notorious bravura passages of the Tchaikovsky; his tempos tend to be broader than usual, only occasionally sounding self-conscious, for in general he is masterly in his control of rubato. The opening instantly establishes this as a big-scale performance, strongly rhythmic and sharply accented, though – with the piano balanced close – the big melody on the first violins sounds surprisingly weak, hidden behind the pianist's monumental chords: the reason for our reservation, when this is one of the composer's most eloquent themes. The outer sections of the slow movement, like the lyrical passages of the first movement, are daringly broad, with Barenboim helping to sustain tension, while in the finale Lang Lang, again encouraged by Barenboim, himself a keyboard virtuoso, varies the tempo boldly, while sustaining a purposeful thrust. The Mendelssohn makes an unusual but attractive coupling.

Horowitz's famous wartime Carnegie Hall recording of the B flat minor Concerto has since remained the yardstick by which all subsequent versions have been judged. Somehow the alchemy of the occasion was unique and the result is unforgettable. In spite of the Carnegie Hall ambience, the recording is confined and lacking bass, but the Naxos transfer engineer, Mark Obert-Thorn, has achieved impressive results from a single post-war set of 78s in mint condition. Such is the magnetism of the playing, however, that the ear forgets the sonic limitations within moments. Toscanini's accompaniment is remarkable not only for matching the adrenalin of his soloist (particularly in the visceral thrill of the finale's climax), but for the tenderness he finds for the lyrical passages of the first movement. The powerful cadenza becomes its apex, with one passage in which there seem to be two pianists in duet, rather than just one pair of human hands. Toscanini's moments of delicacy extend to the *Andantino*, which is truly *semplice*, even when accompanying the coruscating pianistic fireworks of the central section. The finale carries all before it, with Horowitz's riveting octaves leading to a tremendously exciting statement of the big tune before storming off furiously to the coda.

Horowitz's RCA reading of the *Tchaikovsky Concerto* with his father-in-law, Toscanini, is the 1941 performance given at Carnegie Hall, even faster and more exciting than the better-known 1943 version. The playing is not always immaculate, but it is wonderfully incisive in articulation. The sound is confined, with shallow piano-timbre, but acceptable. This now comes coupled on a bargain double with his unsurpassed 1951 version of the Rachmaninov *Third Concerto* and a recital assembled mainly from miscellaneous 78-r.p.m. discs of the same era, but with a few more recent recordings added.

Terence Judd contributed his powerful and urgent reading at the 1978 Tchaikovsky Piano Competition in Moscow, and though it has its moments of roughness and the recording is limited and badly balanced, the compulsion and urgency of the playing are hard to resist. This is hardly a competitive version for general listening, especially at full price, but, with the equally magnetic Prokofiev, it is a splendid reminder of a fine pianist who died tragically young.

During the 1940s, Rubinstein's early account of the concerto vied for the collector's attention alongside the famous Toscanini/Horowitz version. But Rubinstein's recording was more primitive, dating back to 1932, which accounts for the backward balance of the orchestra and the relatively thin massed strings. Yet the performance itself had its own attractions: not barnstorming like Horowitz, but characteristically patrician, with the young Barbirolli ensuring that there was plenty of excitement from the orchestra, to match Rubinstein's brilliantly sparkling articulation, while the work's lyrical qualities were not submerged. The transfer is clear and clean, and the Brahms coupling is of comparable historical interest.

The element of struggle for which this work is famous is all too clear in the Richter/Karajan performance; not surprisingly, these two musical giants do not always agree: each chooses a different tempo for the second subject of the finale and maintains it, despite the other. In both the dramatic opening and the closing pages of the work the approach is mannered and self-conscious, not easy to enjoy. The recording is full-blooded, with a firm piano image.

(i) *Piano Concerto 1;* (ii) *Violin Concerto in D, Op. 35*

(N) (BB) * EMI HMV 5 86775-2. (i) Pletnev, Philh. O, Fedoseyev; (ii) Chang, LSO, C. Davis

*** Pentatone **SACD**/CD PTC 5186 022. (i) Lugansky; (ii) Tetzlaff; Russian Nat. O, Nagano

(B) *** DG (ADD) 439 420-2. (i) Argerich, RPO, Dutoit; (ii) Milstein, VPO, Abbado

(BB) **(*) Warner Apex 8573 89096-2. (i) Berezovsky; (ii) Suwanai, Moscow PO, Kitaenko

(BB) **(*) RCA (ADD) 09026 63979-2. (i) Browning; (ii) Friedman; LSO, Ozawa

The budget HMV disc tends to sweep the board, coupling Pletnev's high-voltage account of the *First Piano Concerto* (see above) with Sarah Chang's wonderfully fresh and natural account of the *Violin Concerto*, persuasively accompanied by Sir Colin Davis (see below), making a bargain difficult to match, let alone surpass.

Nicolai Lugansky was a pupil of Tatiana Nikolaeva, and his is a far from barnstorming performance of the *B flat minor Concerto*. The famous opening is broad and weighty, and the vividly Russian first subject of the allegro is given a bold, rhythmic character, yet it is not pressed too hard. In both the exposition and recapitulation the beauty of the lyrical secondary material is relished. The *Andantino*, introduced exquisitely by the flute, is played by Lugansky with comparable delicacy, followed by a scintillating central scherzando section. The finale then bursts forth with irrepressible impetus, and the coda would certainly bring the house down at a concert. In his warmly romantic but never sentimental account of the *Violin Concerto*, Tetzlaff's beguiling introduction of the two main themes is invested with a natural lyrical feeling. Nagano follows the flowing cantabile style of his soloist, yet he brings a surge of rhythmic energy when Tchaikovsky turns the main theme into an exuberant polacca; the recapitulation then brings a wonderfully warm reprise, with a gently ecstatic climax, followed by a quicksilver coda. Not surprisingly, the orchestral colouring of the slow movement is very Russian, and this ripely nostalgic palette carries through to the contrasting woodwind interludes in the exuberant finale. Tetzlaff's bravura playing, almost unbelievably polished and secure, is thrilling in its sparkling virtuosity, the closing bars dazzling in their exuberance.

On CD Martha Argerich's 1971 version of the *First Piano Concerto* with Dutoit has long been among the top recommendations. The sound is firm, with excellent presence. The weight of the opening immediately sets the mood for a big, broad performance, with the kind of music-making in which the personalities of both artists are complementary. Argerich's conception encompasses the widest range of tonal shading. Milstein's 1973 performance of the *Violin Concerto* is equally impressive, undoubtedly one of the finest available, while Abbado secures playing of genuine sensitivity and scale from the Vienna Philharmonic, with a recording that is also well balanced.

The Berezovsky/Suwanai coupling was made at the prizewinner's concert after the 1990 Moscow Tchaikovsky Competition, and the recording balances (and occasional coughs) reflect that. Berezovsky's account of the *Piano Concerto* shows a dazzling ease of execution, but poetry too, especially in the *Andantino*. Unfortunately, Kitaenko provides him with a routine accompaniment. Akiko Suwanai (only 18 at the time) fares much better. Even though her approach to the first movement is relaxed, she responds to Tchaikovsky's lyricism with great warmth, and revels in the first movement cadenza, which is marvellously detailed. There is spontaneity in every bar. The microphones are rather too near and do not flatter her upper tessitura but she has a glorious tone. The slow

movement is again richly lyrical, and in the sparkling finale Kitaenko is obviously inspired by her playing, and gives her a totally supportive accompaniment and the orchestra, carried away in the sheer animation of the coda, drop a brick at the very end. Even so this is a very rewarding coupling and well worth its modest cost.

John Browning's mid-1960s interpretation of the solo role in the *Piano Concerto* is remarkable, not only for his power and bravura but also for the wit and point in the many scherzando passages, and in the finale he adopts a fast and furious tempo to compare with Horowitz. Erick Friedman, Heifetz's pupil, is a thoughtful violinist who gives a keenly intelligent performance of the companion work, imbued with a glowing lyricism; the slow movement is particularly poetic and beautiful. His timbre is small but true, and there is plenty of dash and fire in the finale, and Ozawa gives first-rate support to both soloists. Here are two performances to match those of almost any rival. The recording is excellent, although in the *Violin Concerto* the orchestral strings are just a little lacking in body.

(i) *Piano Concerto 1; Symphony 6 in B min. (Pathétique)*
(B) (**(*)) Naxos mono 8.110807. (i) Horowitz; NBC SO, Toscanini

This is Horowitz's 1941 performance, given at Carnegie Hall, even more brilliant than the better-known 1943 version. This version of the *Pathétique Symphony* comes from the same concert, taut and urgently exciting rather than warmly emotional, marginally broader in the outer movements than his 1947 reading on RCA. Typically limited sound, not quite as dry as many from this source.

Piano Concerto 2 in G, Op. 44; Concert Fantasy, Op. 56
☛— (BB) *** Naxos 8.550820. Glemser, Polish Nat. RSO, Wit

This Naxos coupling can be strongly recommended on all counts, quite irrespective of cost. Bernd Glemser and the Polish National Radio Symphony Orchestra give an outstanding account of Tchaikovsky's underrated *G major Concerto*, flamboyant and poetic by turns. The unnamed orchestral principal cellist introduces the *Andante* gently and tenderly and his two string colleagues join him with equal sensitivity. The finale has plenty of sparkle and gusto and the whole account is very enjoyable indeed.

The *Concert Fantasy* too, is treated as a large-scale work. Both pianist and orchestra play it with total conviction, and much virtuosity (the cadenza very impressive). The *Contrasts* of the second movement are most tellingly made, with the lyrical minor key *cantabile* touching, and the Russian dance element as vigorous as one could wish. Excellent, well-balanced, full-bodied recording.

Piano Concertos 2 in G, Op. 44; 3 in E flat, Op. 75
*** Ara. Z 6583. Lowenthal, LSO, Comissiona
(N) (BB) *** Warner Apex 2564 61913-2. Leonskaya, NYPO, Masur

In an attractive coupling of two unjustly neglected works, the energy and flair of Lowenthal and Comissiona combine to give highly spontaneous performances, well balanced and recorded. If the *G major Concerto* has not quite the distinction of Donohoe's EMI version (now withdrawn), it is still satisfyingly alive; the soloist brings an individual, poetic response as well as bravura. With very good sound, this is well worth investigating, as the account of the *Third Concerto* is comparably spontaneous.

Leonskaya is a splendid Tchaikovskian and she finds a sympathetic partner in Kurt Masur. Their account of the elusive *Second Piano Concerto* is very fine, weighty, expansive and compelling. The red-blooded orchestral tuttis are matched by Leonskaya's bold, forwardly balanced pianism, and if in the (uncut) slow movement she misses some of its delicacy, she is ardently lyrical. The finale is forceful in its exuberance, powerful and exciting, and the rich Leipzig recording matches the style of the performance. The *Third Concerto* follows on with equal success, and offers brilliant playing with plenty of zest and ardour from soloist and orchestra alike. Outstanding value.

Piano Concerto 3

(*) Chan. 9130. Tozer, LPO, Järvi – *Symphony 7* *

It was a good idea to record the *Third Piano Concerto* alongside the *Seventh Symphony*, on whose first movement it is based (see below). Geoffrey Tozer is an excellent soloist and, as in his Medtner performances for Chandos, plays with sympathy as well as powerful bravura. The playing of the London Philharmonic is not so consistent, with violin tone as recorded often thin, not opulent enough for big Tchaikovsky melodies.

Violin Concerto in D, Op. 35

☛— *** Ph. 473 343-2. Repin, Kirov O., Gergiev – MIASKOVSKY: *Violin Concerto* *** ◐

(M) *** Warner Elatus 09027 46743-2. Vengerov, BPO, Abbado – SIBELIUS: *Violin Concerto* **(*)

*** Erato 4509 98537-2. Repin, LSO, Krivine – SIBELIUS: *Violin Concerto* ***

(M) *** Decca (ADD) 425 080-2. Chung, LSO, Previn – SIBELIUS: *Violin Concerto* ***

(N) (B) *** Decca 475 6703. Bell, Cleveland O, Von Dohnányi – BRAHMS; SCHUMANN; WIENIAWSKI: *Violin Concertos* ***

(N) *** DG 474 874-2. Mutter, VPO, Previn – KORNGOLD: *Violin Concerto* ***

*** DG (IMS) 471 428-2. Garrett, Russian Nat. O, Pletnev – CONUS: *Violin Concerto* ***

*** Sony SK 68338. Midori, BPO, Abbado – SHOSTAKOVICH: *Violin Concerto 1* ***

*** EMI 7 54753-2. Chang, LSO, C. Davis – BRAHMS: *Hungarian Dances* ***

(BB) *** Naxos 8.550153. Nishizaki, Slovak PO, Jean – MENDELSSOHN: *Concerto* ***

(B) *** DG (IMS) Double (ADD) 453 142-2 (2). Milstein, VPO, Abbado – BEETHOVEN: *Concerto* ***; BRAHMS: *Concerto* **(*); MENDELSSOHN: *Concerto* ***

(M) *** Sony SACD (ADD) SS 6062. Stern, Phd. O, Ormandy – SIBELIUS: *Violin Concerto* ***

(***) Testament mono SBT 1038. Haendel, RPO, Goossens – BRAHMS: *Violin Concerto* (***)

(M) (***) EMI mono 7 64030-2. Heifetz, LPO, Barbirolli – GLAZUNOV: *Violin Concerto* (***) ◐; SIBELIUS: *Violin Concerto* (**)

(BB) (***) Naxos mono 8.110938. Heifetz, LPO, Barbirolli – SIBELIUS: *Violin Concerto*; WIENIAWSKI: *Violin Concerto 2 in D min.* (***)

*** Sup. SU 3709-2. Sporcl, Czech PO, Bělohlavek– DVORAK: *Violin Concerto in D* ** (*)

(BB) (***) Naxos mono 8.110977. Milstein, Chicago SO, Stock – BRUCH: *Violin Concerto 1*; MENDELSSOHN: *Violin Concerto* (***)

(M) **(*) EMI (ADD) 5 62591-2. Perlman, Phd. O, Ormandy – MENDELSSOHN: *Concerto* ***

(BB) **(*) CfP 585 6192. Kennedy, LPO, Kamu – CHAUSSON: *Poème* **(*)

(M) **(*) Ph. 464 741-2. Mullova, Boston SO, Ozawa – SIBELIUS: *Violin Concerto* ***

**(*) Globe GLO 5174. Lubotsky, Estonian Nat. SO, Volmer – ARENSKY: *Violin Concerto*; RIMSKY-KORSAKOV: *Concert Fantasy* **(*)

**(*) Testament (ADD) SBT 1337. Ferras, Philh. O, Silvestri – BRAHMS: *Double Concerto* **(*)

(i) *Violin Concerto in D; Méditation for Violin & Orchestra, Op. 42/1; Romeo and Juliet* (fantasy overture)

**(*) Häns. 98346. (i) Sitkovetsky; ASMF, Marriner

Violin Concerto in D; Sérénade mélancolique, Op. 26; Souvenir d'un lieu cher, Op. 42/3: Mélodie; Valse-scherzo, Op. 34

*** ASV CDDCA 713. Xue-Wei, Philh. O, Accardo

Violin Concerto in D; Sérénade mélancolique; String Serenade: Waltz

(M) **(*) RCA (ADD) 09026 61743-2. Heifetz, Chicago SO, Reiner – MENDELSSOHN: *Concerto* ***

(i) *Violin Concerto in D*; (ii) *Méditation, Op. 42/1*; (iii) *Sérénade mélancolique, Op. 26*

(***) Testament mono/stereo SBT 1224. Kogan; (i; ii) Paris Conservatoire O, (i) Vandernoot; (ii) Silvestri; (iii) Philh. O, Kondrashin – PROKOFIEV: *Violin Concerto 2* ***

Vadim Repin is one of the most notable violinists of the day either in Russia or elsewhere and his newest account of the Tchaikovsky concerto with the Kirov Orchestra under Gergiev has effortless virtuosity and a compelling dramatic fire and nobility of feeling. His account would stand high in the lists even if it were uncoupled but it has the additional attraction of a masterly account of Miaskovsky's glorious 1939 *Violin Concerto*, which is not to be missed.

Vengerov gives an inspired performance, with magic inspiration breathing new life into well-known music. This Tchaikovsky reading immediately establishes itself as a big performance, both in the daring manner and in the range of dynamic of the playing. For all his power and his youthfully eager love of brilliance, Vengerov is never reluctant to play really softly. The central *Canzonetta* is full of Russian temperament, and the finale is sparklingly light, with articulation breathtakingly clean to match the transparency of the orchestral textures. What a pity the original coupling was not retained for this reissue, for the Sibelius concerto is much less successful.

In his first recording with the LSO under Krivine, Repin's withdrawn tone in moments of meditation and his fondness for the gentlest pianissimos are as remarkable as his purity and sharpness of focus in bravura. He brings many moments of magic, such as the gentle lead-in to the second subject and the whispered statement of the main theme in the central *Canzonetta*, enhanced by the natural balance of the soloist in a refined and well-detailed Erato recording, making this a highly recommendable alternative.

Kyung Wha Chung's earlier recording of the Tchaikovsky *Concerto* with Previn conducting has remained one of the strongest recommendations for a much-recorded work ever since it was made, right at the beginning of her career. Although she recorded it later with Dutoit, anyone should be well satisfied with Chung's 1970 version with its Sibelius coupling. With Previn a most sympathetic and responsive accompanist, this has warmth, spontaneity and discipline, every detail is beautifully shaped and turned without a trace of sentimentality. The recording is well balanced and detail is clean.

Joshua Bell plays with an expressive warmth which is generally kept within a relatively steady pulse. The symphonic strength of the work is brought out without any loss of excitement rather than the opposite. Bell may not have quite the fantasy of a version like Chung's, but it is an outstanding account, nevertheless, very recommendable if the very generous couplings are suitable (all outstanding). In the finale of the Tchaikovsky, Bell does not open out the tiny cuts in the passage-work that until recently have been traditional, brilliant recording, with the soloist well balanced.

Mutter, accompanied by her husband in a live recording, gives a notably free, spontaneous-sounding performance. Some may find the results too extreme, but the natural warmth of the playing, enhanced by a phenomenal range of tone-colours (something which Mutter claims has developed over the years), makes the result magnetic. Like the majority of players, she observes the brief statutory cuts in the semi-quaver passage-work of the finale.

David Garrett was still only seventeen when he recorded this fluent and sweet-toned account of the Tchaikovsky with Mikhail Pletnev and the Russian National Orchestra for DG. Beautifully balanced it is too, with the violin in an ideal relationship with the orchestra. His technique is immaculate and so too (one or two expressive emphases in the cadenzas apart) is his taste. In the slow movement his playing has great feeling and a high emotional temperature that is at the same time restrained. Mikhail Pletnev gives finely judged and sympathetic support. Undoubtedly one of the most enjoyable modern accounts of this masterly score in which new things are always to be discovered. Don't be put off by the gushing autobiographical notes by the young soloist.

In her live recording, Midori, with the solo instrument naturally balanced, gives a reading that makes its impact as much in hushed poetry as in virtuoso display, with rhythms and phrasing freely expressive. Though the central *Canzonetta* is taken dangerously slowly, the rapt intensity is most compelling. As in the Shostakovich, Abbado and the Berlin Philharmonic give warm and powerful support, very well recorded. Midori adopts the tiny traditional cuts in the finale, arguably the preferable course.

Sarah Chang plays with exceptionally pure tone, avoiding heavy coloration, and her individual artistry does not demand the wayward pulling-about often found in this work. In that she is enormously helped by the fresh, bright and dramatic accompaniment provided by the LSO under Sir Colin Davis, always a sensitive and helpful concerto conductor, and here encouraging generally steady speeds. The snag is the ungenerous coupling, but Chang's performances of the four Brahms *Hungarian Dances* are delectable.

Kogan's account of the Tchaikovsky concerto was made in Paris in 1956, three years before his better known (and generally speaking better) version with Constantin Silvestri conducting the same orchestra. (He had also recorded a version in 1950 with Vassily Nebolsin, which was briefly available in the U.K. on the short-lived Saga label.) However, any performance by this aristocrat of violinists is worth having and his effortless virtuosity and purity of tone is heard to excellent effect in this well-balanced mono recording. The *Sérénade mélancolique* and the *Méditation*, both recorded in 1959, are in stereo and among the finest performances of the pieces on disc.

Xue-Wei gives a warmly expressive reading of this lovely concerto, missing some of the fantasy and mystery. With rich, full tone, he brings out the sensuousness of the work, while displaying commanding virtuosity. The central *Canzonetta* is turned into a simple song without words, not over-romanticized. The coupling will be ideal for many, consisting of violin concertante pieces by Tchaikovsky, not just the *Sérénade mélancolique*, but the *Valse-scherzo* in a dazzling performance, and *Mélodie*, the third of the three pieces that Tchaikovsky grouped as *Souvenir d'un lieu cher*, freely and expressively done. The orchestral playing under another great violin virtuoso is warmly sympathetic but could be crisper, not helped for detail in tuttis by the lively acoustic.

There can be no real reservations about the sound of the present remastering of Heifetz's 1957 stereo recording, both full and brilliant. Heifetz is closely balanced, but the magic of his playing can be fully enjoyed. There is some gorgeous lyrical phrasing, and the slow movement marries deep feeling and tenderness in an ideal performance. The finale is dazzling but is never driven too hard. Reiner always accompanies understandingly, producing fierily positive tuttis. The Mendelssohn coupling is equally desirable, and the *Sérénade mélancolique* makes a splendid bonus.

Takako Nishizaki gives a warm and colourful reading, tender but purposeful and full of temperament. As in the Mendelssohn with which this is coupled, the central slow movement is on the measured side but flows sweetly, while the finale has all the necessary bravura, even at a speed that avoids breathlessness. Unlike many, Nishizaki opens out the little cuts which had become traditional. With excellent playing and recording, this makes a first-rate recommendation in the super-bargain bracket.

Milstein's fine (1973) version with Abbado remains among the more satisfying recordings. It now comes as part of a DG Double with three other concertos, although it is Zukermann rather than Milstein who plays the Beethoven (and very impressively too).

Stern was on peak form when he made his first stereo recording with Ormandy. It is a powerfully lyrical reading, rich in timbre and technically immaculate. The playing is poetic, but it is not helped by the very close balance of the soloist, so that pianissimos consistently become *mezzo fortes*. However, the new SACD fills out the orchestral sound and the overall effect is greatly improved.

Sitkovetsky gives an immaculate reading, with every note in place, crisply articulated in bravura passages, and with no hint of haste in the finale, lacking just a little in fire. Both in the slow movement and in the *Méditation* there is a purity in the approach, a hint of detachment, even though Sitkovetsky's tone is warm with vibrato, carefully controlled. This may not be a front-runner in a keenly competitive field for the concerto, but the disc is worth considering by those who want this unique triptych, with the overture as a welcome coupling, similarly fresh and direct.

Recorded in mono in 1953, Ida Haendel's red-bloodedly romantic account is such a distinctive, positive and powerful reading, one is grateful to Testament for bringing back so unjustly neglected a recording, and in such a vivid transfer. With speeds on the broad side in the first two movements, and generally kept steady, Haendel's warmly expressive style is the more compelling, leading to a fast and muscular account of the finale. It is generously and ideally coupled with Haendel's masterly reading of the Brahms, similarly neglected.

Heifetz's first (mono) recording of the Tchaikovsky *Violin*

Concerto, made in 1937, has tremendous virtuosity and warmth. The sound is opaque by modern standards but the ear quickly adjusts, and the performance is special even by Heifetz's own standards. The EMI transfer, too, is very good and, coming as it does with a classic account of the Glazunov and a fascinating Sibelius, this is a fine bargain.

Though the alternative Naxos transfer has rather high surface hiss, it captures the violin well, with the central *Canzonetta* sweet yet unsentimental, and the finale marked by dazzlingly clean articulation. A generous triptych.

The young Czech virtuoso Pavel Sporcl is a colourful, charismatic artist. It helps that the performances were recorded live, in the Rudolfinum in Prague, with the electricity of each occasion vividly conveyed. Sporcl brings not only dashing virtuosity but tonal variety and tender expressiveness to the Tchaikovsky, with speed changes always sounding natural and spontaneous. The central *Canzonetta* has a hushed poignancy, with the recording beautifully capturing the subtlety of Sporcl's *pianissimo* playing. In the finale his clarity of articulation is a delight, with the coda irresistibly exciting.

Milstein recorded the Tchaikovsky in Chicago in March 1940 with Frederick Stock, an underrated maestro (as indeed was his successor, Desiré Defauw). It is a more classical reading than his later versions, though the finale is a remarkably dashing *tour de force* on the part of soloist and orchestra. The recording is also very fine, for at this time American Columbia had begun to record on to 33⅓ rpm lacquer master discs. The recordings sound as well as 1950s early tape masters. This may not be Milstein's best account of the Tchaikovsky, but it has a lot going for it, and comes with two superb performances of the Bruch and Mendelssohn *Concertos*.

The expressive warmth of Perlman's 1978 recording goes with a very bold orchestral texture from Ormandy and the Philadelphia Orchestra. The focus of sound is not quite as clean as this work ideally needs, but Perlman's panache always carries the day.

Nigel Kennedy gives one of the most expansive readings of the first movement ever put on disc. In ample sound, it is consistently beguiling, though equally its idiosyncrasies will not please everyone. The result would sound self-indulgent, except that Kennedy's total commitment vividly conveys the impression of a live experiance, naturally free in expression. The *Canzonetta* is taken at a flowing speed, while the finale brings extremes of expression similar to those in the first movement. Okko Kamu and the LPO are recorded in exceptionally rich and full sound, and the playing is excellent. But their style does not always match that of the soloist; it sometimes sounds a little stiff in the tuttis, though the final coda is thrilling. A bargain at its new, CfP price.

This was Viktoria Mullova's first commercial recording and it is a resounding success. Her performance is immaculate and finely controlled – as is the coupling – but she does not always succeed in achieving the combination of warmth and nobility that this score above all requires. However, her playing has an undeniable splendour and an effortless virtuosity. Ozawa and the Boston Orchestra give excellent support and the recording is exemplary.

Mark Lubotsky's performance with Arvo Volmer and the fine Estonian National Orchestra is wonderfully musical and natural. Not perhaps as high-powered or flamboyant as many rivals, but everything unfolds naturally and effortlessly. It comes with enterprising couplings, including the endearing Arensky *Concerto*.

Christian Ferras recorded his better-known account of the Tchaikovsky *Concerto* with Karajan for DG in 1967, but he made this version earlier in his short career, in 1957 with Constantin Silvestri and the Philharmonia. This shines perhaps with less lustre but has greater feeling and individuality. Some collectors worry at Ferras's rather sinewy nervous vibrato – though it was surely less worrying than Francescatti's; but by any standards this is a performance natural in style and direct in utterance which finds the Philharmonia responding to their soloist with playing of great enthusiasm and fire. The *Concerto* is erroneously described as being in D minor, an unusual slip for Testament, whose presentation is always scrupulous.

(i) Violin Concerto; (ii) Variations on a Rococo Theme, Op. 33

**(*) EMI 7 54890-2. (i) Kennedy, LPO, Kamu; (ii) P. Tortelier, N. Sinfonia, Y. P. Tortelier

Nigel Kennedy gives a warmly romantic and very measured reading of the *Concerto*, full of temperament. For all his many *tenutos* and *rallentandos*, however, Kennedy is not sentimental, and his range of tone is exceptionally rich and wide, so that the big moments are powerfully sensual. This performance is available coupled to an outstanding version of the Sibelius *Concerto* with Sir Simon Rattle (EMI 7 54559-2) and also with the Chausson *Poème* (see above) as well as in this pairing with Paul Tortelier's finely wrought account of the *Rococo Variations*, with excellent analogue recording.

1812 Overture, Op. 49

(BB) **(*) EMI Encore 5 74751-2. Phd. O, Muti – RIMSKY-KORSAKOV: *Scheherazade* **(*)

(BB) *(**) EMI Encore 5 85460-2. Phd. O, Muti – LISZT: *Les Préludes* **(*); RAVEL: *Boléro* *(*)

(i) 1812 Overture; Capriccio italien

●━● ✿ (M) *** Mercury (ADD) **SACD** 475 6609-2. (i) Bronze French cannon, bells of Laura Spelman Rockefeller Memorial Carillon, Riverside Church, New York City; Minneapolis SO, Dorati (with separate descriptive commentary by Deems Taylor) – BEETHOVEN: *Wellington's Victory* *** ✿

Just as in our listing of this famous Mercury record we have placed *1812* first, so in the credits the cannon and the glorious sounds of the Laura Spelman Carillon take precedence, for in the riveting climax of Tchaikovsky's most famous work the effects completely upstage the orchestra. On this remastered SACD the balance is managed spectacularly, with the 'shots' perfectly timed, while the Minneapolis orchestra clearly enjoy themselves both in *1812* and in the brilliant account of *Capriccio italien*. Deems Taylor provides an avuncular commentary on the technical background to the original recording.

Muti gives an urgent, crisply articulated account of *1812*, concentrated in its excitement. The Philadelphia Orchestra takes the fast speed of the main allegro in its stride, and the coda produces a spectacularly thrilling climax. Those who enjoy the bass drum will find it very much in evidence here, and the sonics include a mêlée of bells and an impressive cannonade at the close. The snag lies in the fierceness of the early digital recording of the strings above the stave, the brilliance artificially achieved.

(i) *1812 Overture; Francesca da Rimini; Marche Slave; Romeo and Juliet* (fantasy overture); (ii) *Eugene Onegin: Tatiana's Letter Scene*

(B) *** CfP 575 5672. (i) RLPO, (ii) LPO; Edwards; (ii) with Hannan

An outstanding reissue, which shows Sian Edwards as an instinctive Tchaikovskian. In *Romeo and Juliet* the love-theme is ushered in very naturally and blossoms with the fullest ardour, while the combination of the feud music with the Friar Lawrence theme reaches a very dramatic climax. *Marche Slave*, resplendently high-spirited and exhilarating, makes a splendid foil. The emotional ebb and flow of *Francesca da Rimini* is persuasively managed, and this performance is the highlight of the disc. Francesca's clarinet solo is melting, and the work's middle section has a Beechamesque feeling for woodwind colour. The passionate climax could hardly be more eloquent, while the spectacular recording gives great impact to the closing whirlwind sequence and despair-laden final chords, where the tam-tam makes its presence felt very pungently.

The inclusion of *Tatiana's Letter Scene*, Tchaikovsky's greatest inspiration for soprano – originally coupled with the *Fifth Symphony* – was a capital idea. This is freshly and dramatically sung in a convincingly girlish impersonation by the Australian Eileen Hannan. *1812*, which closes the concert, is also very enjoyable indeed. Full of vigour and flair, it has a majestic final sequence, with superbly resounding cannon.

(i) *1812 Overture; Francesca da Rimini; Romeo and Juliet (Fantasy Overture)*; (ii) *Nutcracker (ballet; complete), Op. 71*

(N) (BB) **(*) EMI Gemini 586076-2 (2). (i) Oslo PO; (ii) LPO; Jansons

This is a rather good budget package for the small collection, including as it does a complete performance of the Tchaikovsky ballet which has now become a Christmas favourite. *1812* combines brilliance with a rather dignified grandiloquence and, if the last degree of fervour is missing in the orchestral response, the recording is quite spectacular. In *Francesca* there is a frenzied evocation of Dante's Inferno in the outer sections of the work, with the orchestral evocation of the whirlwinds in the reprise very telling; the idyllic central section, too, is beautifully played. However, the overwhelming passion of the lovers and Tchaikovsky's complex polyphonic representation of their discovery and murder does not communicate here with the power of Stokowski's famous performances. The highlight of the 1987 Oslo triptych is the *Romeo and Juliet Overture*, which has genuine breadth, the love theme shaped with real eloquence by the Oslo strings. The main allegro may lack the last degree of physical excitement, but there is plenty of vigour. The one idiosyncrasy is Jansons's interpolation of a tam tam alongside the explosive timpani roll in the dramatic coda, an effect which suits *Francesca da Rimini* more readily than *Romeo and Juliet*.

Jansons's 1991 complete *Nutcracker* is also highly dramatic, the histrionic effect emphasized by the spectacular recording – especially of the brass, which sounds almost Wagnerian at times in its amplitude. Overall, this is certainly a lively, often very beautiful account; the famous Characteristic Dances of the second Act divertissement (the haunting *Arab Dance*, for example) are delightful, and it is all stylishly played. Other versions, such as Ansermet and Ashkenazy, have offered more magic at the glowing climax of the first Act, but this is still an impressive account, and the Gemini reissue is worth having for the ballet alone.

1812 Overture; Hamlet (fantasy overture); *The Tempest*

*** Delos D/CD 3081. Oregon SO, DePreist

The Oregon orchestra show their paces in this vividly colourful triptych, and James DePreist is a highly sympathetic Tchaikovskian. In *1812*, the cannon are perfectly placed and their spectacular entry is as precise as it is commanding. The performance overall is highly enjoyable, energetic but with the pacing unforced. The performances of both *Hamlet* and *The Tempest* are passionately dramatic, the latter generating comparable intensity to (but more melodrama than) Dorati's Decca version.

(i) *1812 Overture*; (ii) *Romeo and Juliet* (fantasy overture); (iii) *Serenade for Strings in C, Op. 48*

(B) **(*) DG 439 468-2. (i) Gothenburg SO, Järvi; (ii) Philh. O, Sinopoli; (iii) Orpheus CO

Järvi's *1812* is exciting – and not just for the added Gothenburg brass and artillery or for the fervour of the orchestra at the opening. He clearly knows how to structure the piece, and he obviously enjoys the histrionics, and so do we. Sinopoli's reading of *Romeo and Juliet* brings a hint of self-consciousness at the first entry of the big love theme, but there is plenty of uninhibited passion later. In the *Serenade for Strings* no one could accuse the Orpheus Chamber Orchestra of lack of energy in the outer movements. Overall it is an impressive performance, even if the problems of rubato without a conductor are not always easily solved. The sound is first class.

(i) *1812 Overture* (arr. Buketoff); *Sleeping Beauty, Op. 66* (ballet; excerpts); *The Voyevoda* (symphonic ballad), *Op. 78*; (i; ii) *Moscow* (coronation cantata)

**(*) Delos DE 3196. Dallas SO, (i) and Ch.; (ii) with Furdui and Gerello; Litton

Tchaikovsky's *Voyevoda* was underrated, even by the composer, who, soon after he had written it, destroyed the score. Fortunately the orchestral parts survived. Taken from Pushkin, it has a rather similar plotline to *Francesca da Rimini*. Its Tchaikovskian melancholy is most persuasively brought out by the excellent Dallas Symphony under Andrew Litton. He is equally impressive in a rather arbitrary set of excerpts from the *Sleeping Beauty* ballet. The programme opens with a choral *1812* in Ivor Buketoff's arrangement, which returns to the words of the original folksongs on which the music is based. At the close the Dallas chorus sings with an expansiveness that almost overwhelms cannon and carillon. Tchaikovsky's cantata *Moscow* was an 1883 commission for the coronation of Alexander III, a lyrical work, sung here with feeling by the chorus and two ardently Slavonic soloists. The recording is rich and spacious.

Festival Overture on the Danish National Anthem, Op. 15; (i) *Hamlet: Overture & Incidental Music, Op. 67a*

(M) *** Chan. X10108. (i) Kelly, Hammond-Stroud; LSO, Simon

Festival Overture on the Danish National Anthem, Op. 15; (i) *Hamlet: Overture & Incidental Music, Op. 67a; Mazeppa: Battle of Poltava & Cossack Dance; Romeo and Juliet* (fantasy overture; 1869 version); *Serenade for Nikolai Rubinstein's Saint's Day*

*** Chan. 8310/11. LSO, Simon, (i) with Kelly, Hammond-Stroud

Tchaikovsky himself thought his *Danish Festival Overture*

superior to the *1812*, and though one cannot agree with his judgement it is well worth hearing. The *Hamlet Incidental Music*, however, shows the composer's inspiration at its most memorable. The *Overture* is a shortened version of the *Hamlet Fantasy Overture*, but much of the rest of the incidental music is virtually unknown, and the engaging *Funeral March* and the two poignant string elegies show the composer at his finest. *Ophelia's Mad Scene* is partly sung and partly spoken, and Janis Kelly's performance is most sympathetic, while Derek Hammond-Stroud is suitably robust in the *Gravedigger's Song*. A translation of the vocal music is provided. It is sung in French (as in the original production of *Hamlet*, performed in St Petersburg). The digital recording has spectacular resonance and depth to balance its brilliance, and there are excellent notes by Noel Goodwin.

The music from *Mazeppa* and the tribute to Rubinstein make engaging bonuses, but the highlight of the two-disc set is the 1869 version of *Romeo and Juliet*. It is fascinating to hear the composer's early thoughts before he finalized a piece that was to become one of the most successful of all his works. The performances here under Geoffrey Simon are excitingly committed and spontaneous.

Francesca da Rimini

(N) (**(*)) BBC Legends mono BBCL 4163-2. Leningrad PO, Rozhdestvensky – BERLIOZ: *Symphonie fantastique* (**(*))

It was in 1960 that the Leningrad Philharmonic first visited Britain, giving spectacular concerts, conducted not just by the long-time music director, Evgeni Mravinsky, but also by Gennadi Rozhdestvensky, then still in his twenties. Here, in an Edinburgh Festival performance at the Usher Hall, we can hear that the younger colleague inspired playing of comparable fire and refinement in Tchaikovsky's *Francesca da Rimini*. This is a weighty and impulsive reading which holds this episodic piece tautly together, and the 1960 mono recording is surprisingly warm and full, if not ideally detailed. Now that Stokowski's Everest coupling with *Hamlet* is temporarily unobtainable, this is all the more attractive.

(i) Hamlet: Overture & Incidental Music, Op. 67a; Romeo and Juliet (fantasy overture; original (1869) version)

*** Chan. 9191. (i) Kelly, Hammond-Stroud; LSO, Simon

An admirable recoupling. The (1869) original version of *Romeo and Juliet*, a most enjoyable rarity, is very different from the 1880 revision we all know, with a completely different opening section. After a less well-organized development of the feud and love music, it ends sombrely but rather less tellingly than Tchaikovsky's final masterpiece. Geoffrey Simon is a committed advocate and the performances here are exciting and spontaneous. The *Hamlet Incidental Music* is hardly less valuable. The overture is a shortened version of the *Hamlet Fantasy Overture*, but much of the rest of the incidental music is unknown, and the engaging *Funeral March* and the two poignant string elegies show the composer at his finest. *Ophelia's Mad Scene* is partly sung and partly spoken, and Janis Kelly's performance is most sympathetic, while Derek Hammond-Stroud is suitably robust in the *Gravedigger's Song*. A translation of the vocal music is provided, here sung in French as in the original production of *Hamlet* at St Petersburg. The digital recording has spectacular resonance and depth.

Hamlet (fantasy overture); Romeo and Juliet (fantasy overture); The Tempest, Op. 18

*** BIS CD 1073. Bamberg SO, Serebrier

José Serebrier follows up the first impressive disc in his Tchaikovsky series for BIS (*Francesca da Rimini* and the *Fourth Symphony*) with this fine Shakespeare triptych. It is typical of Serebrier's performance that he makes *The Tempest* sound so fresh and original. *Hamlet*, dating from much later, is treated to a similarly fresh and dramatic reading, with Serebrier bringing out the yearningly Russian flavour of the lovely oboe theme representing Ophelia. He may not quite match the thrusting power of his mentor, Stokowski, but he is not far short.

In *Romeo and Juliet* he is just as careful over observing Tchaikovsky's relatively modest markings, so that the central development section, built on the conflict music, is rightly restrained, mainly *mezzo forte* but down to *pp* for the violins in places. This is the opposite of a 'wham-it-home' approach, with *fortissimos* coming far too easily, yet the playing of the Bamberg orchestra, incisive as in the earlier BIS disc, both wonderfully drilled and warmly committed, with outstanding solos from wind and brass, ensures that there is no lack of power. It is good to welcome so refreshing a Tchaikovsky compilation.

Manfred Symphony, Op. 58

*** Chan. 8535. Oslo PO, Jansons

(***) Testament mono SBT 1048. Philh. O, Kletzki – BORODIN: *Symphony 2* (***)

(*) BBC (ADD) BBCL 1007-2. Bournemouth SO, Silvestri – RESPIGHI: *Pines of Rome* *

Manfred Symphony; The Tempest, Op. 18

*** DG (IMS) 439 891-2. Russian Nat. O, Pletnev

Except in a relatively relaxed view of the *vivace* second movement, Jansons favours speeds flowing faster than usual, bringing out the drama but subtly varying the tensions; his warmly expressive phrasing never sounds self-conscious when it is regularly given the freshness of folksong. The performance culminates in a thrilling account of the finale, leading up to the entry of the organ, gloriously resonant and supported by luxuriant string sound. The Chandos recording is among the finest in the Oslo series.

Pletnev identifies with the ongoing sweep of the work, yet he can relax glowingly in the pastoral evocation of the slow movement. In *The Tempest* Pletnev again carries the piece through on a wave of passionate romantic feeling. The recording is first class and this is one of his finest Tchaikovsky records.

Though Kletzki makes cuts and one or two amendments of orchestration, this is another reading which, far more than usual, carries you warmly and thrustfully through music that can seem unduly episodic. So the electricity which Kletzki generates in the central *Allegro con fuoco* section of the finale is remarkable, with the playing throughout marked by superfine clarity of articulation and subtle rubato. As to the mid-1950s recording and transfer, the brass and wind have thrilling immediacy, and the dynamic range is astonishing for the time.

Silvestri at Bournemouth does bring a highly charged emotional current to this score and much spontaneity of feeling, but the music is still pulled about in a way that will not enjoy universal acclaim. The recording is very good and the Respighi coupling outstanding.

Manfred Symphony (abridged); *Romeo and Juliet (Fantasy Overture)*

(M) (**(*)) Music and Arts mono CD 4260. NBC SO, Toscanini

Toscanini had an on–off relationship with Tchaikovsky, first introducing many of his works to Italy in the 1890s but later losing interest in the Russian composer for more than 30 years. It was with *Manfred*, in 1933, that his interest revived and he conducted it several times, recording it for RCA in 1949. However, the present recording was made during a January 1953 concert, broadcast within the flattering acoustics of Carnegie Hall, so different in ambience from his infamous broadcasting studio. However, Toscanini took Tchaikovsky too seriously when the composer not only fell out of love with his own work, but said so. Toscanini used this as an excuse to truncate the piece, making major cuts, mostly in the outer movements. Certainly *Manfred* does suffer from a certain amount of inflation, and there is no doubt that the Toscanini version is more succinct than the composer's original. It makes a powerful impact throughout, even if the cymbal clashes the conductor added in the last seven bars of the coda of the first movement may not be to all tastes. Yet adrenalin runs free and the performance is undoubtedly thrilling, while the lyrical music (especially in the centrepiece of the Scherzo) shows the conductor's affection and warmth in a very positive and endearing way. The orchestral playing itself is not always as immaculate as we expect from Toscanini, but its passionate thrust carries the listener along with it. Moreover, the actual sound is amazingly good, with a richness and depth that are only too rare in this conductor's recordings.

Romeo and Juliet dates from only two months later and shows Toscanini and his orchestra right back on form; indeed, this is a splendid performance, as perceptively structured as it is exciting, and again the sound is remarkably full-bodied. With all the reservations, this is a Toscanini reissue with a wide appeal, for all its idiosyncrasies.

Marche slave

(M) **(*) Cala (ADD) CACD 0536. LSO, Stokowski – RIMSKY-KORSAKOV: *Scheherazade* (***)

This Cala version of Stokowski's Phase Four account of Rimsky-Korsakov's *Sheherazade* comes with this thrilling live performance of Tchaikovsky's *Marche slave*, given as an encore at his ninetieth birthday concert in 1972 in London, with a spoken introduction by himself. It even outshines his studio recording in high-voltage electricity. It is charismatic, very Russian in feeling, but with an unexpected elegance and charm in the Trio and the captivating coda, in which Stokowski holds back the flow of adrenalin until the thrilling *accelerando* at the closing section. The sound of the strings is a bit fierce, but the recording overall is forwardly vivid.

Méditation, Op. 42/1

☛ ✹ *** RCA 74321 87454-2. Znaider, Bav. RSO, Jansons – GLAZUNOV: *Violin Concerto*; PROKOFIEV: *Violin Concerto 2* *** ✹

This piece comes from the *Souvenir d'un lieu cher* for violin and piano which Tchaikovsky composed while staying on the estate of his patroness, Madame von Meck. It had originally been planned as the slow movement of the *Violin Concerto*, and it fell to Glazunov to put it into orchestral form. It is beautifully played and comes here as a fill-up to Nikolaj Znaider's outstanding set of the Glazunov and Prokofiev concertos.

(i) *The Nutcracker, Op. 71;* (ii) *The Sleeping Beauty, Op. 66;* (iii) *Swan Lake, Op. 20* (complete ballets)

(B) **(*) Decca (ADD) 460 411-2 (6). Nat. PO, Bonynge

(B) **(*) EMI (ADD) 5 73624-2 (6). LSO, Previn

(N) (B) **(*) DG (ADD/DDD) 477 5153-2 (5). (i) Boston SO, Ozawa; (ii) Russian Nat. O, Pletnev

Bonynge's Tchaikovsky performances are all recommendable. *Swan Lake* receives a red-blooded performance in which the forward impulse of the music-making is immediately striking. The 1975 recording is vivid and bright, though a little dry, producing a leonine string-tone sound rather than a feeling of sumptuousness. If the full romantic essence of this masterly score is not totally conveyed (partly as a result of the recording), the commitment of the orchestral playing is never in doubt. *The Sleeping Beauty* was recorded a year later with similarly vivid sound. Bonynge secures brilliant and often elegant playing from the National Philharmonic, and his rhythmic pointing is always characterful. He is especially good at the close of Act II when, after the magical *Panorama*, the Princess is awakened – there is a frisson of tension here and the atmosphere is most evocative. Bonynge's *Nutcracker* is finely done too, with plenty of colour in the characteristic dances. The recording from 1974 is rich and brilliant. All are packed in one of Decca's space-saving 'Collector Boxes', and this set is undoubtedly a bargain.

Previn's 1972 *Nutcracker* is superbly played by the LSO – it is a wonderfully warm account which gets more involving as it goes along. If *The Sleeping Beauty* is not as vital as it could be (though never slack), it makes up for it with the superb playing of the orchestra: the *Panorama* is beautifully done. The recording (1974) could sparkle a little more though. *Swan Lake* (1976) is given a similarly warm performance, though the overall effect is at times just that bit too 'cosy' for such dramatic writing. The music never drags though, and the excellence of the orchestral playing does much to enhance one's pleasure. The choice between these two bargain boxes is a matter of personal taste: Bonynge offers the more vivid performances (thanks also to the sound), while Previn has more opulence. However, both are equally enjoyable and well packaged.

The Ozawa/Pletnev package is placed economically on 5 discs by beginning the *Nutcracker* at the end of *Swan Lake* on disc 2. Pletnev's very Russian *Sleeping Beauty* is unsurpassed on CD. Ozawa's *Swan Lake* has plenty of life and is beautifully played. Both are spectacularly recorded (see below). In the *Nutcracker* Ozawa's light ballet touch again produces playing of much elegance and grace, and the recording is remarkably transparent as well as warm and full. There is sometimes a hint of blandness with Ozawa, but the great Boston Orchestra is consistently on top form.

The Nutcracker, Op. 71 (ballet; complete)

☛ ✹ *** Warner NIVC Arts DVD 0630 19394-2. Collier, Dowell, Coleman, Rose, Niblett, Royal Ballet, ROHCG O, Rozhdestvensky. (Producer: Peter Wright. V/D: John Vernon, in association with Peter Wright. Choreography: Lev Ivanov and Peter Wright)

☛ ✹ *** BBC Opus Arts DVD OA 087 D. Yoshida, Cope, Dowell, Cojocaru, Putrov, Royal Ballet, ROHCG O, Svetlanov (Producer: Peter Wright; V/D: Ross MacGibbon; Choreography: Lev Ivanov & Peter Wright)

(*) TDK **DV DV-BLCNUT. Lindqvist, Nordström, Nisen, Rosén, Kastrinos, Carlsson, Royal Swedish Ballet & Op. O, Salavatov (V/D: Gunilla Wallin; Choreography: Pär Isberg)

*(*) Arthaus **DVD** 100 118. Saidova, Malakhov, Matz, Knop, Kirillova, Neumann, Deutsche State Op. Ballet, Berlin State O, Barenboim (Choreography: Patrice Bart; Producer: François Duplat; V/D: Alexandre Tarta)

*** Ph. 462 114-2. Kirov O & Ch., Gergiev

*** Telarc CD 8137 (2). L. Symphony Ch., LSO, Mackerras

(B) *** Sony SB2K 89778 (2). Philh. O & Ch., Tilson Thomas

(B) *** CfP CD-CFPD 4706 (2). Amb. S., LSO, Previn

(B) *** Double Decca (ADD) 476 7220 (2). Nat. PO, Bonynge

– OFFENBACH: *Le Papillon* ***

(i) *The Nutcracker* (complete); (ii) *Orchestral Suites 3 in G; 4 (Mozartiana)*

(M) *** Ph. (ADD) 464 747-2 (2). (i) Concg. O, with boys' Ch.; (ii) New Philh. O, Dorati

Here, side by side, we have two separate DVDs of Sir Peter Wright's outstanding production of Tchaikovsky's magical Christmas ballet. They are both wonderfully realized, and it is impossible to choose between them. In the first, from 1985, Lesley Collier, who has already enchanted us in *La fille mal gardée*, is ideally cast as the Sugar Plum Fairy. Her Prince is elegantly characterized and finely danced by Anthony Dowell, and her romantic partner in the earlier ballet, Michael Coleman, now takes a more dramatic and slightly sinister role as Herr Drosselmeyer.

In the later (1996) BBC Opus Arte version, Anthony Dowell takes over as the strangely benign Drosselmeyer (whose nephew has been transformed into a grotesque Nutcracker Doll). In Peter Wright's production Droselmeyer is always at the background of the narrative to remind us that his aim is to break the spell (through Clara – a non-dancing role) and have his nephew return to human form. Jonathan Cope, who was the Mouse King in the earlier production, is now an elegant Prince. His new partner, Miyako Yoshida, is an enchanting Sugar Plum Fairy, and the Nutcracker is Ivan Putrov.

If anything, the transformation scene when the Christmas Tree grows to a huge height is even more spectacularly managed in the later set, and we have a very soft spot for the moment when Clara deftly comes to the Nutcracker's rescue by hitting the Mouse King over the head with her shoe. But in the earlier version the Christmas party scene is especially endearing in its detail. In both versions the sequence where Clara and the transformed Nutcracker journey together in a sleigh, through the Pine Forest and among the waltzing Snowflakes, to the Land of Snow – against a musical background of two of Tchaikovsky's finest melodic inspirations – and on to the Kingdom of Sweets is delightfully managed.

Here, in the great Act II Divertissement, come the enchanting characteristic dances (familiar in the suite), capped by *Waltz of the Flowers*, the passionate *Pas de deux*, the bravura solo numbers for the Sugar Plum Fairy and her Prince and the *Waltz* finale. Peter Wright's production is gloriously traditional, brilliantly choreographed, lavishly spectacular, while Julia Oman's costumes (especially for the battling Mice) are no less imaginative. The camera is always in the right place – one is hardly aware of it – and the orchestral recording is wonderfully vivid, full and immediate. Tchaikovsky's miraclouly inspired score, of which one could never tire, is marvellously played by the Covent Garden Orchestra, regardless of whether it is conducted by Rozhdestvensky or by Svetlanov.

The version from the Royal Swedish Ballet, choreographed by Pär Isberg, brings a transformation of Hoffmann's characters, to match others from Swedish folklore. They are taken from *Petter and Lotta's Christmas* (a famous Swedish children's book by Elsa Beskow). Brother and sister together replace Clara, and Drosselmeyer becomes a character called Uncle Blue. The Nutcracker is replaced by a charcoal-burner, who still turns into a prince, and it is the Housemaid who dances in place of the Sugar Plum Fairy in the Land of the Sweets. Dances by gingerbread men, sticks of peppermint rock, and (engagingly personified) Christmas crackers add to the festivities. The battle with the mice (with splendid costumes) remains in the story, and three of the mice, held in reins by the transformed Nutcracker, join the spirit of the finale by dancing a *Pas de trois*. It is all charmingly small-scale, but great fun, and the standard of the dancing and the orchestral playing is high. Enjoyable, for a change, but not a substitute for the Covent Garden spectacle.

Patrice Bart's perverse re-writing of Hoffmann's tale is even more wilful than the companion version of *Swan Lake* (see below). There is an extra prologue in which we see Marie (the equivalent role of Clara) abducted as a young girl in the Russian Revolution, losing touch with her mother. This is choreographed to Tchakovsky's battle music, so the latter is not available for the mice battle (although there are no mice in this version), so in the second Act its reprise loses all point. Marie is adopted by the family who give the party of Act I and, traumatized, she cannot get on with her two siblings. The Nutcracker is a puppet toy which Marie had as a child, and the narrative then has Drosselmeyer leading her to find her mother in the land of ice and snow, where her puppet Nutcracker changes into a Prince. It is all very Freudian and very contrived, but is partially saved by some splendid dancing, sets and costumes, plus superb orchestral playing, although Barenboim takes the famous *Waltz of the Flowers* much too slowly. Not recommended.

Gergiev's complete CD recording is on a single disc (over 81 minutes) and it is magnificently played and recorded. Tchaikovsky's inspired score emerges pristine and fresh as one of his most perfect masterpieces. The great *Adagio* for the two principal dancers has a passionate Russian ardour; the lively characteristic dances are simply bursting with Slavonic fervour. If there is a certain want of magic and charm, Gergiev everywhere displays a keen ear for Tchaikovsky's vivid orchestral detail. There are no pauses between numbers in the *Divertissement*, and this may well be dictated by the single-disc format. But it also increases the feeling that the score overall is a composite whole, and this is emphasized by the sense of apotheosis in the finale. Unless you are looking for a more relaxed spacious approach, this can be highly recommended.

The Telarc set was recorded in Watford Town Hall, which adds glamour to the violins and a glowing warmth in the middle and lower range. When the magic spell begins, the spectacularly wide dynamic range and the extra amplitude make for a physical frisson in the climaxes, while the glorious climbing melody, as Clara and the Prince travel through the pine forest, sounds richly expansive. Before that, the battle has some real cannon-shots interpolated but is done good-humouredly, for this is a toy battle. The great *Pas de deux* brings the most sumptuous climax, with superb sonority from the brass. The Telarc presentation is ideal, with a detailed synopsis.

Michael Tilson Thomas has the advantage of fine Philharmonia playing, recorded in an attractive acoustic. The Sony balance is very good too, and this account lies between Previn and Mackerras, with a touch more spectacle than the former. The clock striking midnight makes for quite a sinister effect after a feeling of skilfully created tension. The party scene before this has been pressed on strongly, but there is a pleasing relaxation after the battle, and the *Waltz of the Snowflakes* has real radiance. Tempi are generally a fraction brisk, but the brighter rhythmic feeling often pays dividends. If this would not be a first choice it is excellent value, although the documentation is meagre.

Dorati's 1975 complete *Nutcracker* with the Concertgebouw Orchestra makes a good first choice in the bargain category. The playing of the Concertgebouw Orchestra is most refined as well as very dramatic. The CD transfer brings less sumptuous sound than on the old LPs, but the Concertgebouw ambience ensures body as well as vividness. The set has been reissued, reasonably enough, as one of Philips's 'Great Recordings' re-coupled with what are perhaps the two most attractive *Orchestral Suites* (reviewed below). The remastering is excellently done.

Previn's earlier (1972) analogue set with the LSO has been freshly remastered. As in his later, digital version (only available combined with the other two ballets), the famous dances in Act II are given with refinement and point, and the orchestral playing throughout is of very high quality. With Act I sounding brighter and more dramatic than in its original LP format, this CfP reissue makes a fine bargain alternative.

Bonynge's set is made the more attractive by its rare and substantial Offenbach coupling. His approach is sympathetic and the orchestral playing is polished, even if in the opening scene he misses some of the atmosphere. With the beginning of the magic, as the Christmas tree expands, the performance becomes more dramatically involving and Bonynge is at his best in the latter part of the ballet, with fine passion in the Act II *Pas de deux*. The Decca Kingsway Hall recording is brilliant on top, yet has a glowing ambient warmth.

The Nutcracker (excerpts)

** Chan. 9799. Danish Nat. RSO, Temirkanov – RAVEL: *Ma mère l'Oye (suite); La Valse* ** (with GADE: *Tango Jalousie*)

This CD offers only some of *The Nutcracker*, and the Ravel coupling is hardly a rarity. The fine Danish Radio Orchestra plays excellently, but Temirkanov is, as so often, all too idiosyncratic. No complaints about the sound.

Nutcracker Suite; Romeo and Juliet (fantasy overture)

**(*) DG (IMS) 439 021-2. BPO, Karajan

Nutcracker; Sleeping Beauty; Swan Lake: Highlights

(B) **(*) EMI double forte (ADD) 5 74308-2 (2). Phil. O, Kurtz

(N) (BB) **(*) EMI HMV 5 86776-2. Philh. O, Lanchbery

Kurtz was a persuasive Tchaikovskian, and these excerpts from *Sleeping Beauty* and *Swan Lake* are nicely turned, fresh performances dating from the late 1950s, with the advantage of particularly beautiful Philharmonia wind playing. The recording is good, set in a natural, theatrical acoustic, and its early date only hinted at in the slight thinness of violin sound. *The Nutcracker*, though enjoyable, falls just below this fine quality, both as a performance and as a recording (it is not quite so open) and, inexplicably, the *Chinese Dance* is omitted from the otherwise complete 'suite'. With the bonus of a star violin soloist, Yehudi Menuhin (though he doesn't

have a great deal to do until it comes to *Swan Lake*), this two-disc compilation remains good value.

Those wanting a budget disc of highlights from Tchaikovsky's three major ballets will surely find that Lanchbery's selection fits the bill readily enough, although it was a pity that the whole *Nutcracker Suite* was not included. The favourite items are here, and there are eight popular excerpts from *Swan Lake* and seven from the *Sleeping Beauty* score, 77 minutes of music in all, played with great flair, warmth and polish, and given first-class EMI digital sound.

Originally designed to accompany a picture biography of Karajan, this not very generous Tchaikovsky coupling brings superbly played performances. The suite is delicate and detailed, yet perhaps lacks a little in charm, notably the *Arab Dance* which, taken fairly briskly, loses something of its gentle sentience. The performance of *Romeo and Juliet* is both polished and dramatic, but Karajan draws out the love theme with spacious moulding, and there is marginally less spontaneity here than in his earlier recordings.

Nutcracker Suite

(N) **(*) Telarc **SACD** 60650. Cleveland O, Maazel – BERLIOZ: *Symphonie fantastique* **

With vivid orchestral playing and bright, crisply focused recording within a natural ambience, now somewhat enhanced on compatible SACD, Maazel's *Nutcracker Suite* is enjoyably colourful. His manner is affectionate (especially in the warmly lilting *Waltz of the Flowers*) and the only idiosyncrasy is the sudden accelerando at the close of the *Russian Dance*.

Nutcracker Suite; Sleeping Beauty: Suite; Swan Lake: Suite

●➤ ● (M) *** DG (ADD) 449 726-2. BPO, Rostropovich

(BB) *** EMI Encore (ADD) 5 74758-2. LSO, Previn

(M) *** Decca (ADD) 466 379-2. VPO, Karajan

Rostropovich's triptych of Tchaikovsky ballet suites is very special. His account of the *Nutcracker Suite* is enchanting: the *Sugar Plum Fairy* is introduced with ethereal gentleness, the *Russian Dance* has marvellous zest and the *Waltz of the Flowers* combines warmth and elegance with an exhilarating vigour. The *Sleeping Beauty* and *Swan Lake* selections are hardly less distinguished, and in the former the *Panorama* is gloriously played. The CD remastering now approaches demonstration standard, combining bloom with enhanced detail. Sixty-nine minutes of sheer joy and at mid-price.

The digital remastering has also been very successful on the EMI disc, freshening the sound of the excellent recordings, taken from Previn's analogue complete sets (which means that the *Dance of the Sugar Plum Fairy* in *The Nutcracker* has the longer coda rather than the ending Tchaikovsky devised for the *Suite*). The performances are at once vivid and elegant, warm and exciting. Previn's *Panorama* from *Sleeping Beauty* is hardly less beguiling than Rostropovich's and the recording has comparable warmth.

As reissued in Decca's Legend series, the Karajan recording is very impressive indeed; tuttis are well focused by the digital transfer, and the glowing ambience of the Sofiensaal flatters the strings and adds to the woodwind colourings, particularly in the *Nutcracker Suite*, which is less bland here than in Karajan's later re-recording with the BPO. Overall this disc offers very fine playing from the VPO and, although the atmosphere is generally relaxed (especially in *Sleeping Beauty*), there is a persuasive warmth.

Nutcracker Suite; Sleeping Beauty: Introduction & Waltz;
Swan Lake: Suite
(N) **(BB)** **(*)** ASV Resonance CDRSN 3047. RPO, Bátiz

Bátiz's selection was made in the attractive acoustics of the
Henry Wood Hall, and his performances are characteristically
spontaneous, well paced and fresh. Yet the effect has a certain
lack of idiosyncrasy, though enjoyable enough, and the RPO
play very well indeed. At budget price, this is quite competitive.

Romeo and Juliet (fantasy overture)
(M) *** Classic fM 75605 57047. RPO, Gatti – PROKOFIEV:
Romeo and Juliet (ballet: excerpts) ***
(BB) **(*)** EMI Encore (ADD) 5 74961-2. Philh. O, Muti –
DVORAK: *Symphony 9 (From the New World)* **
(*) Pentatone **SACD** PTC 5186 019. Netherlands PO,
Kreizberg – DVORAK: *Symphony 9 (From the New World)*
(*)
(B) **(*)** CfP 575 5652. Hallé O, Kamu – RACHMANINOV:
Symphony 2 in E min., Op. 27 **(*)**

Daniele Gatti's performances could not be more highly
charged romantically, and with a vividly passionate (if not
always immaculate) response from the RPO, the climaxes are
thrilling, with the horns and trumpets ringing out superbly at
the climax of the duel sequence. The recording too is splendidly full and sumptuous, and the rare coupling with
Prokofiev could not be more apt. This is one of Classic fM's
finest issues so far.

In his Philharmonia period Muti was an outstanding
Tchaikovskian, and his 1977 *Romeo and Juliet* is a very fine
performance, full of imaginative touches. The opening has
just the right degree of atmospheric restraint and immediately creates a sense of anticipation; the great romantic climax is noble in contour yet there is no lack of passion, while
the main allegro is crisply and dramatically pointed. The
repeated figure on the timpani at the coda is made to suggest
a tolling bell and the expressive woodwind that follows gently
underlines the feeling of tragedy. The recording is good
although rather light in the bass, and it is a pity that the
coupling is not a performance of distinction.

A strong, incisive performance of Tchaikovsky's *Romeo
and Juliet* from Kreizberg to match the Dvořák *Symphony*,
very well played and brilliantly recorded. The SACD is compatible and, if played on a normal CD player, reproduces at a
slightly lower level than usual.

Okko Kamu's account of *Romeo and Juliet* is impressive,
well paced and exciting. There is no lack of thrust, although
there is a curious momentary broadening – it barely lasts a
bar – at the climax of the love theme which some might find
intrusive on repetition. But the sombre opening and closing
sections evoke a powerful and very Russian melancholy.

*The Seasons, Op. 37b; Chanson triste; Mazurka, Chant sans
paroles; Danse russe, Op. 40/2, 4, 6 & 10; Rêverie
interrompte* (arr. for violin & orchestra by Breiner)
(BB) **(*)** Naxos 8.553510. Nishizaki, Queensland SO,
Breiner

Tchaikovsky's twelve *Seasons* are slight but winsome in their
original piano format (see below), but if they are to be
arranged for violin, Takako Nishizaki is surely their ideal
exponent, for she plays with delicacy and charm. She readily
catches their moments of nostalgia as in *January* ('By the
Fireside'), Russian melancholy, as in *March* ('Song of the
Lark') and their miniaturism, as in the *April* portrait of a

'Snowdrop', and she is in her element in the engaging 'Barcarolle', which Tchaikovsky chose for *June*. The scherzando for
August, picturing 'The Harvest', is also neatly scored, and in
all the gentle numbers Peter Breiner's orchestrations are
felicitous. If the fully scored items (the *February* 'Carnival'
and the brassy picture of the *September* 'Hunt') are rather
inflated by the resonant acoustic, these arrangements overall
can be counted a modest success, alongside those of the
piano pieces from Op. 40 (the *Danse russe* will be recognized
from *Swan Lake*), while the closing *Rêverie* has a proper salon
daintiness.

Sérénade mélancólique (for violin and orchestra), *Op. 26*
*** EMI 5 62607-2. Menuhin, RPO, Boult – BEETHOVEN:
Violin Concerto in D; Romance 1 in G ***
*** EMI 5 56966-2. Vengerov, LSO, Rostropovich –
SHCHEDRIN: *Concerto cantabile;* STRAVINSKY: *Violin
Concerto* ***

Recorded in 1959 as a filler for a version of the Tchaikovsky
Violin Concerto never completed, Menuhin's account of the
Sérénade mélancolique, previously unpublished, conveys a
gravity beyond its modest span. It is a welcome coupling for
the superb Beethoven performances.

The disarmingly simple lyricism of Tchaikovsky's gentle,
yet ardent Serenade is well caught by Vengerov and Rostropovich in a refined reading that catches the composer's Russian
melancholy to perfection. It makes a perfect encore for
Vengerov's superb account of the spikier Stravinsky concerto.

Serenade for Strings in C, Op. 48
(BB) *** Virgin 2x1 5 61763-2 (2). LCO, Warren-Green –
DVORAK: *Serenade for Strings in E, Op. 22;* ELGAR:
Introduction & allegro; Serenade; SUK: *Serenade;*
VAUGHAN WILLIAMS: *Fantasia on Greensleeves*, etc. ***
(M) *** Decca (ADD) 470 262-2. ASMF, Marriner – GRIEG:
Holberg Suite ***; DVORAK: *Serenade* **(*)**
Serenade for Strings; Souvenir de Florence. Op. 70
(BB) **(*)** Naxos 8.550404. V. CO, Entremont

Not surprisingly, Christopher Warren-Green's reading of
Tchaikovsky's *Serenade* with the excellent London Chamber
Orchestra is full of individuality. The first movement's secondary idea has an appealing feathery lightness, and when
the striding opening theme reappears at the end of the
movement it brings a spontaneous-sounding burst of expressive intensity characteristic of this group. The *Waltz* lilts
gently, with the tenutos nicely managed, the *Elégie* has delicacy as well as fervour, and the finale develops plenty of
energy. Very well recorded, it is a performance to give pleasure for its freshness and natural impetus, and the couplings
are amazingly generous and equally stimulating.

Marriner's classic 1968 version holds its place among the
best. Although Tchaikovsky asked for as big a body of strings
as possible in his delectable *Serenade*, there is much to be
said, in these days of increased string resonance and clever
microphone placing, for having a more modest band like the
Academy of St Martin's-in-the-Field. However, one does
notice the lack of sheer tonal weight that a larger group
would afford. Marriner's performance compensates with
expressive phrasing (most striking in the slow movement),
imaginative and fresh playing from the Academy, and the
finest pointing and precision of ensemble. The original coupling of the *Souvenir de Florence* now lives on a Double Decca
CD with the *String Quartets* (452 614-2), but the couplings
here are excellent. A fine transfer in this Legends reissue.

Philippe Entremont's performances of Tchaikovsky's two major string works communicate above all a feeling of passionate thrust and energy. After the ardour of the *Elégie*, the finale steals in persuasively, with dance-rhythms bracing and strong. The *Souvenir de Florence* has comparable momentum and eagerness. The dashing main theme of the first movement swings along infectiously, while the wistful secondary idea also takes wing. Entremont brings out the charm in writing inspired by Russian folksong. The VCO are committed, persuasive advocates to make one wonder why the *Souvenir* does not have a more central place in the string repertoire.

The Sleeping Beauty, Op. 66 (ballet; complete)

☞ *** Arthaus **DVD** 100 312. (Choreography: Petipa, revised Konstantin Sergeyev) Lezhnina, Ruzimatov, Makhalina, Guliayev (Carabosse), Kirov Ballet Co. & O, Fedotov (V/D: Bernard Picard)

☞ ✿ (M) *** BBC (ADD) BBCL 4091-2 (2). BBC SO, Rozhdestvensky

*** DG 457 634-2 (2). Russian Nat. O, Pletnev

(BB) *** Naxos 8.550490/2. Slovak State PO (Košice), Mogrelia

*** Ph. (IMS) 434 922-2 (3). Kirov O (St Petersburg), Gergiev

(BB) **(*) EMI Gemini (ADD) 5 85788-2 (2). LSO, Previn

This DVD performance was recorded and filmed in June 1989 during the Kirov's guest appearance in Canada at the Place des Arts in Montreal. It was first issued on Philips video tape and on a laser disc set. The present transfer represents an improvement over both. The dancing is pretty virtuosic and both the character dances and the main roles are flawless: the performance lingers in the memory long afterwards. The production, too, conveys an appropriate sense of magic, and the visual direction is well handled. The orchestral playing under Viktor Fedotov is first class (save for an unappealing clarinet quality) but the recording is inconsistent in balance, with a very prominent piano at one point. Things settle down, however, and the bulk of the last act is in good perspective. This does not detract from the overall satisfaction and sheer delight these dancers give.

Rozhdestvensky's recording, made in 1979, was part of the BBC Symphony Orchestra's fiftieth anniversary celebrations and is fully worthy of the occasion. The great Russian conductor (using the original Russian score which is absolutely complete) shows just how to hold Tchaikovsky's ballet together as a symphonic entity by creating a consistent narrative pulse. Yet his pacing can never be faulted: this always remains music to be danced to. It could not be entrusted to more caring or sensitive direction, and the ear is continually amazed by the quality of Tchaikovsky's invention. Rozhdestvensky's loving attention to detail and his response to the vivid colouring are matched by his feeling for the narrative drama. He is masterly in building his climaxes, while his lyrical phrasing brings flowing rubato beautifully controlled, so that the wonderful *Panorama* floats elegantly over its rocking bass.

In Tchaikovsky's inspired series of characteristic dances the conductor's light rhythmic touch and delicacy of feeling draw a wonderfully refined yet vividly coloured response from the BBC players. The ballet ends majestically, and the BBC recording has plenty of amplitude, warm strings, glowing woodwind and a natural concert-hall balance. Climaxes have brilliance and full dynamic impact, and this is every bit as enjoyable as Pletnev's DG studio recording, with the additional magnetism of live music-making.

Pletnev's is a performance of individuality and high quality. It is a strongly narrative and dramatic account that has tenderness (as in the opening of the *Pas de six* in the Prologue) and much the same virtuosity that Pletnev exhibits at the keyboard. The articulation is pretty dazzling throughout and there is plenty of wit in the Act III *Divertissement*. Even though there are times when tempi seem too brisk for dancing, everything sounds fresh. The recording is very good, wide in dynamic range and well balanced, though not in the demonstration bracket (perhaps wanting a shade in amplitude). DG accommodate the set on two CDs (of 79 and 80 minutes respectively).

Andrew Mogrelia conducts Tchaikovsky's score with a fine combination of warmth, grace and vitality. Moreover, the Slovak State Philharmonic prove to be an excellent orchestra for this repertoire, with good wind-players and equally impressive string principals for the important violin and cello solos. The Naxos digital recording is full and brilliant without being overlit, and the acoustics of the House of Arts in Košice bring a spacious ambience, with vivid orchestral colours.

The Kirov recording of Tchaikovsky's complete ballet is in every way satisfying. The playing – from an orchestra completely inside the music – is warmly sympathetic and vital, with no suggestion that familiarity has bred any sense of routine. Gergiev is a subtle interpreter, and his performance of the Act III *Pas de Quatre* for all four fairies is a highlight of the sparkling Act III *Divertissement*. The Philips recording is sumptuous without being cloudy, and it expands magnificently for Tchaikovsky's rhetorically exciting climaxes without assaulting the ears.

With warm, polished orchestral playing and recording to match (though it expands at climaxes), Previn conveys his affection throughout; but too often – in the famous *Waltz*, for instance – there could be more sparkle. On the other hand, the *Panorama* shows Previn and the LSO at their very best, the tune floating over its rocking bass in the most magical way. There is also much delightful wind-playing but, with Previn's tempi sometimes indulgently relaxed, it has been impossible to get the complete recording on a pair of CDs and the penultimate number (29) in Act III (included in the original three-disc LP issue) has been cut. Never mind, the CD transfer of the 1974 Abbey Road recording is admirable, and with such a flow of marvellous tunes and inspired orchestral colouring this makes very relaxing listening. And the set is very inexpensive.

Sleeping Beauty: Aurora's Wedding (suite selected and edited by Diaghilev)

✿ (M) *** Cala CACD 0529 (ADD) Nat. PO, Stokowski (with 'Encores', all arr. Stokowski: DEBUSSY: *Clair de lune; Soirée dans Grenade.* ALBENIZ: *Ibéria: Fête-Dieu à Seville.* NOVACEK: *Perpetuum mobile.* SHOSTAKOVICH: *Prelude in E flat min.* RIMSKY-KORSAKOV: *Flight of the Bumble-bee.* TCHAIKOVSKY: *Humoresque in G, Op. 10/2.* CHOPIN: *Mazurka in B flat min.; Prélude in D min. Op.28/24* ***)

Diaghilev staged the first performance of Tchaikovsky's *Sleeping Beauty* outside Russia in a London season in 1921. The result was a financial disaster. The public, used to the usual Diaghilev triptych of three different ballets, found the work too long and stayed away. The following year the great impresario devised a one-act version centring on the Act III

Divertissement, framed by the Introduction and final *Apothéose*. It is a perceptively chosen selection, with *Panorama* the only obvious omission.

Stokowski was attracted to the score and recorded it twice. His stereo version, made when he was 94, dates from 1976, yet, as with so many of the recordings he made during his 'Indian summer', the electricity crackles throughout, and his charisma is felt in every bar. The Sony recording is vividly brilliant, lacking sumptuousness in the violins, but otherwise very good.

It was an inspired idea of Edward Johnson of the Stokowski Society to link *Aurora* with his even more charismatic collection of encores, recorded three months later. Here the sound is even better, approaching demonstration quality, and there is no finer programme on record to show Stokowski's genius as an orchestral arranger (indeed 're-creator'), and his ability to rethink piano music in orchestral terms.

Even the lusciously seductive *Clair de lune* is surpassed by the spectacular excerpt from *Ibéria*, the sombre *E flat minor* Shostakovich *Prelude*, and the delightful Tchaikovsky *Humoresque*, which Stravinsky also scored, quite differently, using horns, in *Le Baiser de la fée*. Most astonishing of all are the two Chopin items, the *Mazurka* totally transformed, and the fiercely dramatic *Prélude* almost unrecognizable. The sparkling orchestral bravura in Nováček's *Perpetuum mobile* and Rimsky's *Bumble-bee* provide light relief and altogether this is a wonderfully entertaining concert, superbly played.

Souvenir de Florence, Op. 70 (string orchestra version)
*** Channel Classics **SACD**: CCS SA 21504. Amsterdam Sinf., Thompson – VERDI: *String Quartet* ***
*** Chan. 9708. Norwegian CO, Brown – R. STRAUSS: *Metamorphosen* ***

The Amsterdam Sinfonietta, formerly called the Nieuw Sinfonietta Amsterdam, here offers outstanding performances of two works originally written for solo strings which, played like this by a string orchestra, are if anything even more impressive. This was Candida Thompson's first recording with them after she was appointed the Sinfonietta's leader/conductor, and the unanimity of the playing, the immaculate precision of ensemble, is phenomenal, yet it is never a cold precision. The warmth of the performances is just as remarkable, with the bounding rhythms of the first movement of the Tchaikovsky – one of his most purely happy inspirations – given an exuberant thrust. That goes with total homogeneity in the subtle shaping of rubato, so that in that first movement the entry of the second subject brings a *pianissimo* which is ravishing in its tenderness. The slow movement too has a breathtaking purity. The resonance of the playing is also exceptional too, involving a strikingly wide dynamic range and a meticulous observance of markings. The opulent recording helps, with a helpful ambience allowing ample detail, with the opportunity of 'surround sound' if you have the additional speakers.

Iona Brown and the Norwegian Chamber Orchestra give us a splendid account of the full orchestral version of Tchaikovsky's invigorating and captivating *Souvenir de Florence*, bouncingly rhythmic in the opening movement, and buoyantly exuberant in the swinging secondary theme of the finale. There is both warmth and subtlety in the inner movements; and it is given one of Chandos's most brilliant and full-bodied recordings. The result is irresistible.

Souvenir d'un lieu cher, Op. 42; Valse scherzo in C, Op. 34 (orch. Glazunov)
*** DG 457 064-2. Shaham, Russian Nat. O, Pletnev – GLAZUNOV; KABALEVSKY: *Concertos* ***

Eloquent and dazzling playing of these Tchaikovsky pieces by Gil Shaham and the Russian National Orchestra under Pletnev are an additional inducement to get this fine disc of the Glazunov and Kabalevsky *Concertos*.

Suites 1 in D min., Op. 43; 2 in C; 3 in G, Op. 55; 4 in G, (Mozartiana), Op. 56
*** Chan. 9676 (2). Detroit SO, Järvi
(B) *** Ph. Duo (ADD) 454 253 (2). New Phil. O, Dorati
(BB) *** Naxos 8.550644 *(Nos. 1–2)*; **(*) 8.550728 *(Nos. 3–4)*. Nat. SO of Ireland, Sanderling

Tchaikovsky's four *Orchestral Suites*, for which the composer had a great affection, are full of good things. Their extraordinary range of colour demands recording of the very highest quality and that is just what Chandos for the most part provides, which gives Järvi's set a place at the top of the list.

Järvi generally adopts somewhat brisk tempi, especially in No. 1, but the Detroit orchestral response in both the two earliest suites is consistently winning. The performance of the *Fourth Suite* also has an agreeable warmth, aptly Tchaikovskian even more than it is elegantly Mozartian. In No. 3, the most ambitious of the set, Järvi continues to draw warmly expressive playing from his Detroit musicians even if his treatment here is a little heavy-handed (as it is just occasionally in No. 2). The performance is well characterized – not least in the colourfully diverse variations that make up the last and longest movement and that are given an ebullient finale – but lacks something in charm. In this the acoustic of the Detroit hall is not as helpful as it might be to high fortissimo violins.

Dorati's sound has some lack of transparency and ultimate vividness alongside the Detroit recording, but it is pleasingly naturally balanced. Dorati was a masterly ballet conductor, and he brings out the balletic feeling, in the first two suites especially, revelling in the infinitely inventive orchestral detail which shows the composer consistently seeking new orchestral colourings. *Mozartiana* is neatly and stylishly done. Dorati is thoroughly at home in the *Theme and Variations*, capped by a splendid closing *Polacca*; the Philips recording expands impressively here and rises to the occasion.

On Naxos, Stefan Sanderling (son of Kurt) gives nicely turned performances of the first two suites, neatly characterized and with much charm and colour. The *Third* and *Fourth Suites* are slightly less successful. Sanderling shows much delicacy of feeling, both in the opening *Gigue* of *Mozartiana* and in the *Elégie*, the first movement of the *Third Suite* and it is a pity that one has reservations about the sets of variations which Tchaikovsky uses for his final movements. In *Mozartiana* Sanderling is very romantic. The masterly *Theme and Variations* which end the *Third Suite* are splendidly done until the finale, which refuses to take off: Sanderling is that bit too grandiose and measured.

Suites (i) 3 in G, Op. 55; (ii) 4 (Mozartiana) in G, Op. 61
(N) **(*) Australian Decca Eloquence (ADD) 476 2723. (i) VPO, Maazel; (ii) SRO, Ansermet

The first thing one notices about Maazel's 1977 recording of the underrated *Third Suite* with its superb closing set of variations is the ravishing playing of the VPO, with the strings sounding gloriously rich and glowing in the Decca sound, and with Maazel relaxed and unforced. The performance is not as strongly characterized as some, but it is far from bland, especially the woodwind detail, having a pleasing individuality of colour. All the things one expects from a classic Ansermet performance are here in the *Fourth (Mozartiana) Suite*: vivid sound (with a lovely, warm ambience), felicity of detail, especially in the pointing of the strings, but less than ideally polished orchestral playing for a work drawing on Mozart. However, it remains enjoyable for its distinct character and spontaneity.

Swan Lake, Op. 20 (ballet; complete)

(⊶) ✪ (N) *** DVD 073 4044. Fonteyn, Nureyev, V. State Op. Ballet, VSO, Lanchbery (Choreography: Rudolf Nureyev; Director: Truck Branss)

⊶ *** Opus Arte DVD OA 0865 D. (Choreography: Peter Wright, after Petipa and Ivanov.) Nordquist, Nordström, Kaila, Rambe, Ohman, Swedish Ballet School, Royal Swedish Op. O, Quéval (V/D: Kirsty Garland)

**(*) Arthaus DVD 100 001. Scherzer, Matz, Händler, Ballet of the Deutsche Oper, Berlin, Berlin St. O, Barenboim (Choreography: Patrice Bart)

(N) (M) *** Naxos Surround Sound SACD 6.110005/6. Russian State SO, Yablonsky

*** Decca 436 212-2 (2). Montreal SO, Dutoit

*** ROH 301/2 (2). ROHCG O, Ermler

(B) **(*) DG Double 453 055-2 (2). Boston SO, Ozawa

(BB) **(*) EMI Gemini 5 85541-2 (2). Phd. O, Sawallisch

There is little one needs to say about the 1966 Fonteyn/Nureyev *Swan Lake* except that it is one of the great ballet films of all time and looks marvellous on DVD. Moreover, the sound is excellent, as is the photography, with the camera angles well judged so that there are frequent close-ups of the most famous ballet dance partnership of our time. Nureyev's choreography (based on Ivanov/Petipa), like the production, décor and costumes, is satifyingly traditional, which means it is what Tchaikovsky and Petipa envisaged, without spurious additions. The story is told simply and dramatically and, apart from the unforgettable and moving dancing of the two principals, the whole company give outstanding support in the many colourful individual dances. Highlights include the touching scene in Act II when Prince Siegfried, crossbow at the ready, is disconcerted to meet and fall in love with Odette, and the following *Danses des cygnes* (with some lovely, tender playing from the solo violin of the orchestra's principal violin). After the delightful divertissement, Siegfried's great *pas de deux* of Act III, with Odile, is breathtaking, and the ballet's tragic end when, after parting from Odette, Siegfried sinks between the swirling waters of Rotbart's lake is most imaginatively achieved. John Lanchbery conducts the excellent Vienna Symphony Orchestra with great flair, and altogether this is unbeatable.

The Royal Swedish Ballet's *Swan Lake*, recorded on 24 May 2002, is elegant and sumptuous, inventively choreographed and beautifully staged by Sir Peter Wright and Galina Samsova, with particularly splendid sets and costumes. Peter Wright stages it as a Gothic tragedy concentrating on the role of the Prince and honouring the 1895 Petipa/Ivanov original. In Nathalie Nordquist and Anders Nordström it has a fine and expressive partnership, and the cast as a whole has no weaknesses. Indeed, one of the strengths of the performance is the excellence of the teamwork of the company. (It is tastefully and imaginatively lit, too, by Martin Säfström.) It is very well danced, though the Odette/Odile is not perhaps as

strongly characterized as Steffi Scherzer in the Berlin performance under Daniel Barenboim, available on Arthaus.

In the (1998) Deutsche State Opera Ballet version with the Berlin State Orchestra, playing splendidly and conducted warmly but indulgently by Barenboim, the period is shifted nearer our own time, and the spectacular costumes and ladies' hats in Act I evoke the Ascot scene in *My Fair Lady*. There are, of course, many plus points, notably the huge, graceful, superbly disciplined corps de ballet, creating patterned groupings of the Swans, often effectively seen from above. Both Steffi Scherzer as Odette/Odile and Oliver Matz as Prince Siegfried dance very beautifully, but the Prince assumes a permanent air of despondency. He goes hunting with a rifle given him by his mother, and he seems to cheer up only when he meets and dances spectacularly with Odile in Act III. This is because in François Duplat's production (we are told in the booklet) the Prince has not only a dominating mother-fixation but also a less conventional attachment for his best friend, Benno von Sommerstein. The Queen does not want to lose her son to a swan, so she is involved in the plot with her Prime Minister (Rotbart, no less) to have Siegfried seduced by his daughter (Odile). The dramatic dénouement extends the original story, and after Siegfried hopelessly returns to seek Odette, with the Robart figure sinisterly waving his cloak in the background, they fight and the Prince murders the Prime Minister before, engulfed by mist, he dies himself, ending in his mother's arms.

On CD Dutoit offers the original score virtually complete, as Tchaikovsky conceived it. The Montreal orchestra play it beautifully, rising to the plot's histrionic moments and while not lacking the final apotheosis, Dutoit's reading, while not lacking drama, emphasizes the warmth and grace of the music and its infinite variety.

A very Russian performance of *Swan Lake* on Naxos, superbly recorded. It is easy to get the balance right between rear and front speakers in order to achieve a full concert-hall effect (with added ambience), but the discs still sound very impressive through a normal CD reproducer. The playing is idiomatic, polished and exciting, with the unnamed solo violinist making an excellent contribution; but the whole orchestra are on their toes. This is not a relaxed performance but one in which there is plenty of charm and character, and free-running adrenalin too.

Mark Ermler's deeply sympathetic direction has both refinement and red-blooded commitment, and one is constantly aware of the idiomatic feeling born of long acquaintance. The sound is exceptionally full and open, with the brass in particular giving satisfying weight to the ensemble without hazing over the detail. The set has now been reissued on a pair of CDs with the break coming in Act II after the *Dance of the Little Swans*. Ermler's broad speeds consistently convey, more than most rivals', the feeling of an accompaniment for dancing, as in the great andante of the Act I *Pas de deux*. This is a set to have you sitting back in new enjoyment.

Ozawa's version omits the Act III *Pas de deux* but otherwise plays the complete original score. His performance is alive and vigorous (as at the opening *Allegro giusto*), but it has not quite the verve of Lanchbery's deleted CfP version; Ozawa's approach is more serious, less flexible. Yet with polished, sympathetic playing from the Boston orchestra there are many impressive and enjoyable things here, with wind (and violin) solos always giving pleasure. The end result is a little faceless, in spite of a spectacular, wide-ranging analogue recording, as vivid as it is powerful.

Sawallisch directs Tchaikovsky's greatest ballet score with pleasing freshness, and the Philadelphia Orchestra play superbly. But, as so often in the past, they are let down by the choice of venue for the recording, in this instance the Memorial Hall, Fairmount Park, whose apparently intractible acoustics have led to close microphone placing, creating an unnatural effect. There is no lack of atmosphere, but very soon it becomes apparent that *fortissimos* are unrefined, with fierce cymbals, grainy violins, even an element of harshness. This orchestra's fine string section does not sound like this at a concert. Yet there is much to enjoy: the first and most famous *Waltz* is played gorgeously, and how engaging are the Cygnets, tripping in very precisely, while in the famous *Pas de deux* of Odette and the Prince the violin and cello duet brings ravishingly serene yet voluptuous solo playing. There are many instances of Sawallisch's nicely judged pacing and the consistently responsive solo playing, while the thrilling final climax (with gorgeously full horn-tone at the restatement of the famous *idée fixe*) makes an overwhelming apotheosis, even if the shrillness added to the violins, who play with enormous fervour, is not a plus factor. A very stimulating set, nevertheless, and singularly inexpensive in this reissued format.

Swan Lake, Op. 20 (ballet; slightly abridged recording of the European score)

(B) **(*) Double Decca (ADD) 440 630-2 (2). SRO, Ansermet
 – PROKOFIEV: *Romeo and Juliet* **

Returning to Ansermet's 1959 recording of *Swan Lake*, one is amazed by the vigour of the playing and the excellence of the recording. The Drigo version of the score, which Ansermet uses, dates from 1895; Drigo added orchestrations of his own, taken from Tchaikovsky's piano music (Op. 72), yet he left out some 1,600 bars of the original score. Ansermet offers the Act I introduction and Nos. 1–2, 4, 7 and 8; Act II, Nos. 10–13; Act III, Nos. 15, 17–18 and 20–23, with No. 5 (the *Pas de deux*) then interpolated before Nos. 28 and 29 from Act IV. Despite the obvious gaps, most of the familiar favourites are included here, and the music-making has such zest and colour that one revels in every bar. The solo wind playing is not always as sweet-timbred as in some other versions, but the violin and cello solos are well done. The transfer is well managed, full-blooded and bright. It was a happy idea to couple this on its Double Decca reissue with a selection of 15 items from the two suites from Prokofiev's *Romeo and Juliet* ballet, even if here the orchestral playing is less impressive.

Variations on a Rococo Theme for Cello & Orchestra, Op. 33

(***) Testament mono SBT 1310. Gendron, SRO, Ansermet –
 SCHUMANN: *Cello Concerto*, etc. (***)

When it first appeared in 1954, the authors of *The Record Guide* spoke of 'a wonderful display of consummate cello playing' and indeed so it is! Although Maurice Gendron was rather overshadowed in the 1950s and 1960s by Fournier and Tortelier, he was no less eloquent an artist, who brought an aristocratic finesse and tonal richness to everything he did. The virtuosity is effortless and his phrasing seamless; Gendron's artistry gives unalloyed pleasure. As always with this label, the transfer does justice to the 1953 Decca recording.

SYMPHONIES

Symphonies 1–6

(M) *** DG (ADD) 429 675-2 (4). BPO, Karajan
**(*) DG (IMS) 449 967-2 (5). Russian Nat. O, Pletnev

Symphonies 1–6; Capriccio italien; Manfred Symphony

⊛ (M) *** Chan. 8672/8 (7). Oslo PO, Jansons

Jansons's Tchaikovsky series, which includes *Manfred*, is self-recommending. The full romantic power of the music is consistently conveyed and, above all, the music-making is urgently spontaneous throughout, with the Oslo Philharmonic Orchestra always committed and fresh, helped by the richly atmospheric Chandos sound. The seven separate CDs offered here are packaged in a box priced as for five premium discs.

Karajan offers the six symphonies fitted on to four mid-priced CDs, the only drawback being that Nos. 2 and 5 are split between discs. From both a performance and a technical point of view, the accounts of the last three symphonies are in every way preferable to his later, VPO digital versions; all offer peerless playing from the Berlin Philharmonic.

Pletnev's readings have all the innate aristocratic feeling Tchaikovsky could ask for, but at no time does Pletnev wear his heart on his sleeve. Some may feel that the emphasis in the *First Symphony* is too much on the *rêveries* of the title, and Tchaikovsky's rhetoric might be handled more convincingly; but, for the most part, Pletnev's approach throughout the cycle is the reverse of overblown. Indeed, the highly charged, high-voltage sound which we associate with Mravinsky surfaces in the *Pathétique*, but otherwise he sets greater store by classicism, carefully balanced proportions and a masterly sense of line. DG have accorded the cycle very fine and well-detailed sound.

Symphonies 1–6; (i) Piano Concerto 1; (ii) Violin Concerto; Capriccio italien; Eugene Onegin: Polonaise & Waltz; Marche slave; The Nutcracker Suite; 1812 Overture; Romeo and Juliet (fantasy overture); Sleeping Beauty: Suite; String Serenade; Swan Lake: Suite; (iii) Variations on a Rococo Theme

(B) *** DG (ADD) 463 774-2 (8). (i) Richter, VSO; (ii) Ferras;
 (iii) Rostropovich; BPO; all cond. Karajan

These Berlin performances of the symphonies are fine in every way; perhaps a bit of over-refinement creeps in from time to time, but by any standards they are a magnificent achievement, especially the symphonies. The *Violin Concerto* is superbly shaped by Karajan, though some will find Ferras's tone lacking charm – his close vibrato in lyrical passages tends to emphasize schmaltz on the G string. Richter and Karajan are, to say the least, controversial in the *Piano Concerto*. In the first movement, both artists play havoc with any sense of forward tempo (though there are occasional bursts of real excitement), and Richter's excessive rubato in the lyrical second subject sounds unspontaneous. Clearly two major artists at work, but the result is none too convincing. The *Rococo Variations* with Rostropovich is a breath of fresh air after all that – lovely glowing accounts – and the orchestral music is generally fine, but not outstanding, and a hint of glossiness creeps in from time to time (though the *Sleeping Beauty* and *Swan Lake* suites are quite superb). The sound throughout the set is of a generally high standard.

Symphonies 1–6; Manfred Symphony; Capriccio italien; Romeo and Juliet (fantasy overture); Serenade for Strings; The Tempest; Eugene Onegin: Polonaise

(BB) *** Virgin 5 61893-2 (6). Bournemouth SO, Litton

Andrew Litton's set of the Tchaikovsky symphonies, including *Manfred*, is in many ways his finest achievement on record, and this super-super-bargain Virgin box is very desirable indeed. The cycle gets off to a splendid start with the first two symphonies, which are very successful. With warm and full recording, less distanced than many on this label, these urgently spontaneous performances rival any in the catalogue. Litton reveals himself as a volatile Tchaikovskian, free with accelerandos and slowings yet never sounding self-conscious or too free. The hushed pianissimos of the Bournemouth strings in the slow movement of No. 1 are ravishing, and the *Second Symphony* too brings a beautifully sprung reading, allowing plenty of rhythmic elbow-room in the jaunty account of the syncopated second subject in the finale.

Again in the outer movements of No. 3 Litton challenges his players to the limit, setting fast speeds, but the clean, purposeful manner is very satisfying, even if some other versions spring rhythms more infectiously. Litton's finesse comes out impressively in the *Andante elegiaco*, where he chooses a flowing tempo needing no modification for the broad melody that follows, which is then nobly moulded.

No. 4 is essentially spacious, both in choice of tempi and the rather backward balance of the orchestra. Ideally one needs a brighter focus in this symphony, yet Litton, with crisp ensemble, builds the structure of the first movement steadily and unerringly. The dotted clarinet theme of the second subject opens with an enticing tenuto, then the tension is carried through the development to make a strong climax before the recapitulation. The slow movement, warmly lyrical, is similarly purposeful with a delightfully decorated reprise, while the finale is weighty as well as athletic, with the secondary theme bringing another striking expressive contrast.

The first movement of the *Fifth* is surprisingly slow and steady, and here the reading lacks the high voltage of Litton's finest Tchaikovsky performances. But the slow movement brings a beautiful horn solo, and the Waltz is delightfully fresh and delicate. The finale is again on the broad side, warm rather than ominous, with very clean articulation in the playing.

The *Pathétique* caps the cycle impressively: an outstanding performance, full of temperament, not just fiery but tender too, arguably the finest of the whole cycle. The Bournemouth playing has never been more clearly articulated.

Manfred is both individual and satisfying. The Astarte theme in the first movement has rarely been moulded so affectionately and throughout Litton controls the tension to bring out the narrative sequence and heighten the dramatic cohesion. He points the chattering semi-quavers of the 'Alpine Fairy' *Scherzo* with engaging wit and fantasy, and the spacious treatment of the third-movement *Andante* allows the oboist to play his opening solo with a tender expressiveness to make most others seem prosaic. The sound is clean cut and well balanced, with the organ entry at the end of the finale among the most dramatic on record.

The encores are substantial and add much to the attractions of the set. In the *Capriccio italien* both playing and recording display the dramatic contrasts of texture and dynamic to the full, while the *Eugene Onegin Polonaise* brings an even more infectiously rhythmic lift. On the other hand the *String Serenade* is warmly romantic, with the *Waltz elegant* and the *Elégie* expressively intense, and the finale bursts with energy.

The *Tempest* is given an outstanding performance, while *Romeo and Juliet* is similarly fine. All in all, this is an astonishing bargain (to match Menuhin's equally generous Mozart collection from the same label) with – at the time of going to press – the six discs offered at well under twenty pounds.

Symphonies 1–3; Capriccio italien; Marche slave

⊶ (M) *** DG 459 518-2 (2). BPO, Karajan

Having recorded the last three Tchaikovsky symphonies three times in little more than a decade, Karajan then, at the end of the 1970s, turned to the early symphonies and brought to them the same superlative qualities. With his great orchestra finely honed in ensemble the playing throughout proved marvellous and the performances equally illuminating. It is typical that even though the opening *tranquillo* of No. 1 is taken fast there is no feeling of breathlessness, it is genuinely *tranquillo*, although the rhythmic bite of the syncopated passages, so important in these early symphonies, could hardly be sharper. In the *Little Russian Symphony* the tempo for the *Andante* is very nicely judged and the outer movements have plenty of drama and fire. In No. 3 Karajan even finds an affinity with Brahms in the second movement (which Tchaikovsky would not have acknowledged), yet the climax of the *Andante* is full of Tchaikovskian fervour and in the less tractable finale the articulation of the *Polacca* (which gave the symphony its sobriquet 'Polish') is both vigorous and joyful. The recording is bold, full-bodied, brilliant and clear.

(i) *Symphonies 1–3;* (ii) *Francesca da Rimini*

(B) *** Ph. Duo (ADD) 446 148-2 (2). (i) LSO; (ii) New Philh. O; Markevitch

(B) *** Double Decca (ADD) 467 264-2 (2). VPO, Maazel

Markevitch is a good Tchaikovskian and his readings have fine momentum and plenty of ardour. In the *First Symphony* he finds the Mendelssohnian lightness in his fast pacing of the opening movement, while there is real evocation in the *Adagio* and a sense of desolation at the reprise of the *Andante lugubre*, before the final rousing peroration. In the *Little Russian Symphony* the opening horn solo is full of character and the allegro tautly rhythmic. The *marziale* marking of the *Andantino* is taken literally, but its precise rhythmic beat is well lifted. The finale is striking for its bustling energy rather than its charm. The *Polish Symphony* has a comparably dynamic first movement, but the central movements are expansively warm, the ballet-music associations not missed. *Francesca da Rimini* is very exciting too, and there is some lovely wind playing from the New Philharmonia in the central section. Excellent sound, warmly resonant and full-bodied.

Maazel's performances, made with the VPO in the 1960s, clearly look forward to the emotional tautness of the mature symphonies from the *Fourth* onwards. But if the first movement of the *Winter Daydreams Symphony* is driven hard and the Mendelssohnian quality of the opening is not as evocative as in some versions, with the slow movement not as dreamy as one might ask, it is not without atmosphere and the strong, thrusting horns in the final statement of the tune are very telling. Maazel also gets some splendidly crisp and rhythmic playing from the VPO strings in the allegros of the *Little Russian* and *Polish Symphonies* to create an exciting brio, while the *Andantino marziale* of the former is nicely pointed (as are the *Scherzos* of all three symphonies). Much felicitous detail emerges throughout all three symphonies and Maazel is clearly at home in Tchaikovsky's rhetoric, especially in the finale of No. 3. In short, although charm is not Maazel's strong suit, the vitality of this music-making is compelling. The spectacularly resonant and brilliantly engineered recording suits the performances.

Symphony 1 in G min. (Winter Daydreams)
*** Chan. 8402. Oslo PO, Jansons

Symphony 1; Hamlet (fantasy overture)
(BB) *** Naxos 8.550517. Polish Nat. RSO, Leaper

Symphony 1 (Winter Daydreams); Romeo and Juliet (Fantasy Overture); The Snow Maiden: excerpts
(N) *(*) BIS SACD 1398. Gothenburg SO, Järvi

Refreshingly direct in style, Mariss Jansons with his brilliant orchestra gives an electrically compelling performance of this earliest of the symphonies. Structurally strong, the result tingles with excitement, most of all in the finale, faster than usual, with the challenge of the complex fugato passages taken superbly. The recording is highly successful.

Adrian Leaper conducts a taut and sympathetic reading of Winter Daydreams, with excellent playing from the Polish orchestra enhanced by vivid recording, fresh and clear, with plenty of body and with refined pianissimo playing from the strings in the slow movement. This is among the finest Tchaikovsky recordings on the Naxos list, with all four movements sharply characterized. The overture too comes in a tautly dramatic reading. An outstanding bargain.

The performances here are strangely uncharacteristic of Neeme Järvi. Where warmth and spontaneity have regularly marked his many recordings, his thrustful manner here too often involves clipped, unsprung rhythms and speeds so fast as to make the result sound perfunctory. Even the excellent players of the Gothenburg Symphony Orchestra are in places hard pressed to articulate the notes accurately, as in the running quavers in the finale. Tchaikovsky's First Symphony is full of magic moments, a piece still under-rated, yet Järvi gives very few signs of affection, whether in the very plain account of the second subject in the first movement, the cool, fast account of the slow movement — turned into an Andante rather than an Adagio — and the fast and fierce reading of the third-movement Scherzo. Much of the playing is crisp and refined, and the hectic tempo in the main section of the finale does bring a kind of excitement at the end, but too much is missing. Sadly, a similar pattern marks the four excerpts from the Snow Maiden and Romeo and Juliet. As ever, the BIS recording is full, brilliant and clear.

Symphonies 1 (Winter Daydreams); 2 (Little Russian)
*** Delos DE 3087. Seattle Symphony, Schwarz

This Delos coupling has the sobriquet 'The Young Tchaikovsky', but the effect of Schwarz's performances, both expansive and exciting, is to make each symphony sound more mature than usual. He brings a free rubato style to both readings, but he is a natural Tchaikovskian, and the result is very enjoyable indeed, particularly when the spacious Seattle acoustic and superbly wide-ranging Delos recording bring the finest sound yet given to these symphonies, with particularly rich strings, while one must mention especially the glorious horns at the end of the lovely Adagio of the Winter Daydreams. Every detail of Tchaikovsky's scoring is glowingly revealed and the ear revels in the charm of the Andantino marziale of the Little Russian and the kaleidoscopic variations at the beginning of the finale. Here the gutsy middle strings too are splendidly caught, as is the spectacular closing hyperbole of both finales. In short if you want a modern digital pairing of these two splendid symphonies, it is hard to better this.

Symphony 2 in C min. (Little Russian), Op. 17 (original (1872) score); Festive Overture on the Danish National

Anthem, Op. 15; Serenade for Nikolai Rubinstein's Saint's Day; Mazeppa: Battle of Poltava; Cossack Dance
*** Chan. 9190. LSO, Simon

This was the first recording of Tchaikovsky's original score of the Little Russian Symphony and probably the first performance outside Russia. In 1879 Tchaikovsky retrieved the score and rewrote the first movement. He left the Andante virtually unaltered, touched up the scoring of the Scherzo, made minor excisions and added repeats, and made a huge cut of 150 bars (some two minutes of music) in the finale. He then destroyed the original. (The present performance has been possible because of the surviving orchestral parts.) Though this first attempt cannot match the reworked first movement, and the finale — delightful though it is — needs no extra bars, it is fascinating to hear the composer's first thoughts, and this is an indispensable recording for all Tchaikovskians. Geoffrey Simon secures a committed response from the LSO, and the recording is striking in its inner orchestral detail and freshness. The music from Mazeppa, the Danish Festival Overture and the tribute to Rubinstein make engaging bonuses.

Symphony 2; Capriccio italien, Op. 45
*** Chan. 8460. Oslo PO, Jansons

Jansons prefers a fastish speed for the Andantino second movement, but what above all distinguishes this version is the joyful exuberance both of the bouncy Scherzo — fresh and folk-like in the Trio — and of the finale, and the final coda brings a surge of excitement, making most others seem stiff. The coupling is a fizzing performance of the Capriccio italien. With some edge on violin tone, this is not the finest of the Chandos Oslo recordings, but it is still fresh and atmospheric.

Symphonies (i) 2 (Little Russian); (ii) 4 in F min.
(B) *** DG (ADD) 429 527-2. (i) New Philh. O; (ii) VPO; Abbado

Abbado's account of the Little Russian Symphony is very enjoyable, although the first movement concentrates on refinement of detail. The Andantino is nicely pointed, and the Scherzo is admirably crisp and sparkling. The finale is superb, with fine colour and thrust and a memorably spectacular stroke on the tam-tam before the exhilarating coda. The 1967 recording still sounds excellent. The account of the Fourth Symphony is almost unsurpassed on record. Abbado's control of the structure of the first movement is masterly. The Andantino, with its gentle oboe solo, really takes wing in its central section, followed by a wittily crisp Scherzo, while the finale has sparkle as well as power. It was recorded in 1975 in the Musikverein and still sounds very good indeed.

Symphonies 2 (Little Russian); 6 (Pathétique); Francesca da Rimini; Romeo and Juliet (Fantasy Overture)
(N) (BB) *** EMI Gemini (ADD) 5 86531-2 (2). Philh. O, Giulini

Giulini's very distinguished recordings were made between 1956 and 1962 when the Philharmonia was at its peak and the conductor on top form. The Little Russian Symphony was the first version to appear on CD, and it still ranks among the finest. The performance is full of vitality, with brisk tempi throughout, except for the engagingly wistful little march of the Andantino, which makes a perfect foil. The kaleidoscopic finale is very fast indeed and is marvellously articulated, yet the second subject has an appropriately gracious delicacy. The coda with its terrific accelerando is breathtaking. The Pathétique is comparatively spacious, and equally memorable.

There is a degree of restraint in the way Giulini interprets the big melodies of the first and last movements, which are given an almost Elgarian nobility. Yet passionate intensity is conveyed by the purity and concentration of the playing, which equally builds up electric tension and excitement without hysteria. The performances of *Francesca da Rimini* and *Romeo and Juliet* are in a similar mould, full of impetus, colour and passion; in *Romeo*, Giulini brings out the dignity of the opening and closing pages, and the first appearance of the great love theme is superbly managed. The Kingsway Hall recordings are spectacular, but there is a degree of harshness and fierceness in tuttis, to show the age of the *Little Russian Symphony* (1956). The *Pathétique* sounds magnificent, as does *Romeo and Juliet*, and this set is a superb reminder of Giulini and the Philharmonia at their greatest.

Symphony 3 in D (Polish), Op. 29
🔗 *** Chan. 8463. Oslo PO, Jansons

Tchaikovsky's *Third* is given a clear, refreshingly direct reading by Jansons, but it is the irresistible sweep of urgency with which he builds the development section of the first movement that sets his performance apart, with the basic tempo varied less than usual. The second movement is beautifully relaxed, the *Andante elegiaco* heartwarmingly expressive, tender and refined, and the Scherzo has a Mendelssohnian elfin quality; but it is the swaggering reading of the finale that sets the seal on the whole performance. Though the recording does not convey a genuinely hushed pianissimo for the strings, it brings full, rich and brilliant sound.

Symphonies 4–6 (Pathétique)
(B) *** DG Double (ADD) 453 088-2 (2). BPO, Karajan
(B) *** Double Decca (ADD) 443 844-2 (2). Philh. O, Ashkenazy
(M) (***) DG mono 447 423-2 (2). Leningrad PO; (i) K. Sanderling; (ii) Mravinsky
(B) **(*) DG 2-CD (ADD) 474 284-2 (2). BPO, Karajan

Karajan's 1977 analogue version of No. 4 (the most atmospherically recorded of the three) is more compelling than his previous recordings and also is preferable to the newer, digital, Vienna version. Similarly the 1976 reading of the *Fifth* stands out from his other recordings. The Berlin Philharmonic string-playing is peerless. Karajan had a special affinity with Tchaikovsky's *Pathétique Symphony*, and of his five stereo versions this one from 1977 is the finest. The digital remastering of the analogue recordings is first rate.

Ashkenazy's set makes a fine alternative bargain on Double Decca. Apart from the emotional power and strong Russian feeling of the readings, the special quality that Ashkenazy conveys is spontaneity. The freshness of his approach, his natural feeling for lyricism on the one hand and drama on the other is consistently compelling. The late-1970s Kingsway Hall recording quality is full and atmospheric.

Mravinsky re-recorded the three last symphonies of Tchaikovsky with his Leningrad orchestra for DG in stereo, but these legendary earlier, mono performances, without loss of concentration, were less exaggeratedly histrionic, and Sanderling's speeds for the finale of the *Fourth Symphony* particularly, but also Mravinsky's for the *Fifth*, were not as frenetic as in the latter's stereo versions. The opening of the *Fifth* again brings an added dimension of Russian melancholy, and Mravinsky sustains a lyrical intensity throughout the symphony characteristic of all his Tchaikovsky readings. The slow movement brings a performance of great dramatic

extremes, the only drawback for Western ears being the solo horn sounding like a euphonium. The emotional power of Mravinsky's *Pathétique* has never been surpassed and the finale is deeply eloquent, genuinely touching rather than hysterical, with a characterful rasp from the Russian trombones.

The reissue in the Karajan Collection (474 284-2) offers the mid-1960s recordings of all three symphonies, and they are well worth hearing, even if No. 4 takes a little while to generate its full tension in the opening movement, and No. 5 also has an element of restraint. The *Pathétique*, however, is very closely matched to the later recording. But the versions from the 1970s remain consistently more stimulating.

Symphony 4 in F min., Op. 36
(M) (***) BBC Legends mono BBCL 4143-2. Leningrad PO, Rozhdestvensky – SHOSTAKOVICH: *Cello Concerto 1* (***)

A particularly valuable reminder of the days when orchestras from the then Soviet Union were heard relatively rarely in the West. This high-voltage account of the *Fourth Symphony* was recorded at one of three Promenade Concerts this great orchestra gave in the 1971 season, and it has the compelling quality and excitement that live music-making generates. The BBC recording does justice to the rich sonority this great orchestra produced at that period.

Symphony 4 in F min., Op. 36
(N) 🔗 *** Ph. SACD 476 6196. VPO, Gergiev
*** Chan. 8361. Oslo PO, Jansons
**(*) DG (IMS) 439 018-2. VPO, Karajan

Symphony 4; Capriccio italien
(M) *** DG (ADD) 419 872-2. BPO, Karajan

Symphony 4; Francesca da Rimini
*** BIS CD 1273. Bamberg SO, Serebrier

Gergiev's account of No. 4 was recorded live in the orchestra's home, the Musikverein in Vienna, and the performance captures many of the vital qualities that made his earlier reading of No. 5 so magnetic. The opening fanfare motif calls us compellingly to attention; but then, after the slow introduction, the start of the main *Moderato con anima* with its lilting compound time is surprisingly relaxed, yet very convincing. Typically for Gergiev, the tension mounts magnetically, when the balletic waltz-rhythms develop into the movement's big climaxes. In all this, Gergiev's subtle tempo changes sound totally idiomatic and spontaneous, as they do throughout the performance. The oboe theme at the start of the *Andante* slow movement is warmly expressive and leads up to a satisfying broadening at the *fortissimo* peak of the movement, before the main theme returns, delicately decorated with woodwind scales. The Vienna Philharmonic plainly love working with Gergiev, for the playing is wonderfully taut in the pizzicato Scherzo, with the 'drunken peasant' passage wittily pointed, while the finale culminates in a subtle accelerando in the closing bars of the coda, with thrilling results. There is no applause at the end, suggesting, as is usual in 'live recordings' in the Musikverein, that a modest amount of patching was conceded.

Jansons conducts a dazzling performance, unusually fresh and natural in its expressiveness, yet with countless subtleties of expression, as in the balletic account of the second-subject group of the first movement. The *Andantino* flows lightly and persuasively, the Scherzo is very fast and lightly sprung, while the finale reinforces the impact of the whole performance: fast and exciting, but with no synthetic whipping-up of tempo. That is so until the very end of the coda, which finds Jansons pressing ahead just fractionally as he would in a concert, a thrilling conclusion made the more so by the wide-ranging, brilliant and realistic recording.

On the Swedish BIS label, surprisingly for a company best-known for rarities, comes this impressive foray into mainstream repertory, with the *Fourth Symphony* superbly played and recorded. Consistently textures are clarified, helped by the thoughtful, finely judged reading of José Serebrier. The Bamberg orchestra boasts an exceptional line-up of refined wind soloists, phrasing subtly. Not that in this concern for detail there is any lack of excitement, for the incisive attack and Serebrier's preference for steady speeds brings a structural strength too rarely achieved in Tchaikovsky. *Francesca da Rimini*, inspired by Dante, makes an apt coupling, a work written in very much the same period as the *Symphony*. Again with full, clear sound, the orchestral outbursts have biting impact, with the Bamberg wind soloists once more phrasing seductively in the love music. While Szell (currently deleted) and Jansons still hold their place, this can be ranked alongside them.

Karajan's 1977 analogue version with the BPO is more compelling than any of his other versions. It is the vitality and drive of the performance as a whole that one remembers above all, but also the beauty of the wind playing at the opening and close of the slow movement. The CD transfer is extremely vivid. The *Capriccio italien* makes a good filler.

Although the playing of the VPO under Karajan does not match that of the Berlin Philharmonic in earlier versions, the performance itself has greater flexibility and more spontaneity. The freer control of tempo in the first movement brings a more relaxed second-subject group, while in the *Andantino* the phrasing is less calculated. The warmly resonant acoustic is attractive; even if detail is not absolutely clear, there is no lack of fullness.

Symphony 5 in E min., Op. 64
● ✿ *** Ph. **SACD** 475 6718; CD 462 905-2. VPO, Gergiev
*** Chan. 8351. Oslo PO, Jansons
(M) **(*) Warner Elatus 2564 60035-2. Leningrad PO, Mravinsky
**(*) DG (IMS) 439 019-2. VPO, Karajan

Symphony 5; Overture 1812
(M) *(**) Warner Elatus 2564 61777-2. Chicago SO, Barenboim

(i) **Symphony 5**; (ii) **1812 Overture; Marche slave**
(N) ● (BB) *** EMI HMV 5 86774-2. (i) LPO; (ii) RLPO; Edwards

Symphony 5; Francesca da Rimini
(B) **(*) EMI Red Line 5 69842. Phd. O, Muti

(i) **Symphony 5**; (ii) **Nutcracker Suite, Op. 71a**
(B) *** DG (ADD) 439 434-2. (i) Leningrad PO, Mravinsky; (ii) BPO, Karajan

Symphony 5; Romeo and Juliet (Fantasy Overture)
● *** HM HMU 907381. RPO, Gatti

Symphony 5; Serenade for Strings
(B) *** Sony SBK 46538. Phd. O, Ormandy
(M) **(*) Sony SMK 89795. (i) Chicago SO, Abbado; (ii) Ma, Pittsburgh SO, Maazel

Valery Gergiev's account of the *Fifth Symphony* is really quite special. It is a performance of real stature, totally electrifying. No wonder the audience went wild at the end. It certainly belongs among the best *Fifths* on record. Some collectors will find full price a bit steep for 46 minutes, no matter how marvellous the performance and excellent the recording; but if you can put economy to one side, you will be rewarded with out-of-the-ordinary music-making. Unlike the companion version of the *Pathétique*, the SACD is compatible two-channel only and is very little different from the CD.

Sian Edwards conducts an electrifying and warm-hearted reading of Tchaikovsky's *Fifth* to which we gave a Rosette when it first appeared. It still matches almost any version in the catalogue. Edwards's control of rubato shows her to be a natural Tchaikovskian, and she is exceptionally persuasive, notably so in moulding the different sections of the first movement of the symphony, while the great horn solo of the slow movment is played with exquisite delicacy by Richard Bissell. The Waltz third movment is most tenderly done, while the finale brings a very fast and exciting allegro, challenging the orchestra to brilliant, incisive playing. *1812* is also very enjoyable indeed, full of vigour and flair, and *Marche slave*, too, is resplendently high-spirited and exhilarating. The full-bodied recording is well balanced and thrilling in the proper Tchaikovskian way. A superb bargain.

Daniele Gatti often chooses tempi that are brisker than usual and that are closer to the composer's own metronome markings. The result in the first movement, with crisp rhythmic pointing, is an invigorating forward thrust from beginning to end, with the primary second subject theme on the violins romantic in its rubato, rather than impassioned, as with Gergiev. The elegiac melancholy of the slow movement, with its evocative horn solo most sensitively played by Martin Owen, brings climaxes which are spaciously affecting but not as passionately overwhelming as with Gergiev, the forceful interruptions of the motto theme less histrionic, and the movement brings a gently touching close. The Waltz is elegant and graceful, with neatly decorative violins, a contrasting interlude before the excitingly strong, direct finale. Here the brass is crisp and urgent, especially in the repeated reprise of the Fate theme, which is very sharply focused. Once again Gatti takes the movement forward in a single sweep, with free-running adrenalin, pausing only briefly to reflect Tchaikovsky's moment of self-doubt before pressing onwards to the triumphant coda with its blazing trumpets. Gatti offers in addition a superb account of *Romeo and Juliet*. The Abbey Road recording throughout both symphony and overture is excellent, full-bodied, with vivid, weightily sonorous bass.

In the first movement, Jansons's refusal to linger never sounds anything but warmly idiomatic, lacking only a little in charm. The slow movement again brings a steady tempo, with climaxes built strongly and patiently but with enormous power, the final culmination topping everything. In the finale, taken very fast, Jansons tightens the screw of the excitement without ever making it a scramble, following Tchaikovsky's notated slowings rather than allowing extra rallentandos. The sound is excellent, specific and well focused within a warmly reverberant acoustic, with digital recording on CD reinforcing any lightness of bass.

Mravinsky's earlier stereo version of the *Fifth* with the Leningrad Philharmonic on DG would occupy a distinguished place in any collection. The performance is full of Slavonic vitality and the reading is romantic as well as red-blooded. The solo horn has a faint wobble in the famous solo in the slow movement, and the trumpets in the final peroration of an exhilaratingly fast finale also have a vibrato, but these details are unimportant when the reading has such fire and individuality. The recording, made in Watford Town Hall in 1960, is resonant and full, if not always absolutely clean in focus. By comparison Karajan's 1966 *Nutcracker Suite* sounds a little cool, but it is marvellously polished and vivid, and the *Waltz of the Flowers* is most elegant.

Ormandy's *Fifth*, splendidly recorded in the spacious acoustics of Philadelphia's Broadwood Hotel, is early (1959) stereo and is one of his very finest Tchaikovsky performances. There is not a suspicion of routine, and the Philadelphia strings play gloriously, particularly in the *Andante cantabile*, which generates great passion. Again the weight of string-tone at the opening of the *Serenade* (recorded the following year) establishes the full-blooded character of Ormandy's approach. The finale opens delicately but soon generates great bustle. Overall this coupling is a magnificent demonstration of the Ormandy regime in Philadelphia at its very peak.

Abbado's Chicago *Fifth* is admirably fresh and superbly played. All Tchaikovsky's markings are scrupulously yet imaginatively observed and the reading is full of contrast. Other versions of the slow movement have more extrovert passion, but Abbado shows that the climaxes can be involving without being histrionic. After an elegant Waltz, with the orchestra in sparkling form, the finale has fine energy and momentum. If it does not have quite the gripping excitement of Jansons or Gergiev, the moment of the composer's self-doubt, before the *Poco più animato*, is the more effectively characterized. The recording is made in a convincingly resonant acoustic, the balance is very good with full strings and a supporting weight in the bass, but it is less rich than the Philips and Chandos versions.

As an encore Yo-Yo Ma's *Rococo Variations* are characteristically refined, and although his playing is at times just a little mannered (and one longs for the full-timbred Rostropovich approach), Ma always engages the listener's sympathy by his delicacy and grace. Maazel's less than inspired accompaniment does, however, diminish the appeal of the performance, which is again very well recorded.

Mravinsky's account of the *Fifth Symphony* on Elatus comes from a concert performance on 19 March 1983. It is his last recording of the symphony that survives and is perhaps less 'possessed' than his famous DG accounts issued in 1956 and 1961 or the subsequent deleted performances from 1965 and 1973 on Olympia and RCA/BMG. Yet it is hardly less compelling and if anything more human.

The oddity of Muti's Philadelphia version is that, though the first two movements have the disappointingly over-relaxed manners that marked his *Pathétique* earlier, often with surprisingly slack ensemble, the last two movements are played with the high voltage one expects of this conductor and orchestra at their finest. The fill-up is also played at white heat, a powerful performance. It makes a rare and worthwhile coupling. The sound, not as clear as it might be, has warmth and weight beyond most recent Philadelphia issues.

Barenboim's 1995 live performance brings a compelling reading, passionately expressive, yet warm too and convincingly impulsive. The Chicago orchestra play magnificently, with refined detail and a memorable horn solo in the slow movement. Alas, the presence of the audience has damped down the hall acoustic so that the strings lack bloom and the brass needs a greater richness of resonance. *1812*, another exciting performance, but recorded without an audience, sounds much richer and more spacious. This would be

higher on the list of recommendations had the recording of the symphony matched that of the overture.

Karajan's last VPO version of the *Fifth* brings a characteristically strong and expressive performance; however, neither in the playing of the Vienna Philharmonic nor even in the recorded sound can it quite match his 1976 Berlin Philharmonic version for DG, which is currently not available individually.

Symphony 5; (i) *Piano Concerto 1*

(***) Biddulph mono WHL 051. BPO, Mengelberg; (i) with Hansen

This is not the famous Mengelberg *Fifth Symphony*, which we all knew in the 78s era, which was recorded with the Concertgebouw Orchestra (and issued by Columbia), but a later version with the Berlin Philharmonic from 1940, and first issued on Telefunken. Yet the interpretation is similar in every detail. It is an extraordinary performance. Mengelberg takes Tchaikovsky's marking for the slow movement, 'con alcuna licenza', to apply to the whole symphony (even the Waltz). For him every bar is open to constant twists of personal rubato and fluctuations of tempo. Also he feels able to adjust the harmony if needed, and make two major cuts in the finale.

Yet it is a great performance. For Mengelberg had both the will to impose his own personality on Tchaikovsky's music and the charisma to carry it off. His passionate response remains so compelling that the listener is taken along with him, even when, as in the last movement, he adopts a comparatively modest pacing for the main allegro. The recording has an element of harshness but is fully acceptable in this excellent Biddulph transfer.

The performance of the concerto is not in this league. Conrad Hansen, a pupil of Edwin Fischer, has his moments, but in the finale (rather like the Richter/Karajan version) he and Mengelberg tend to press the music along at different degrees of forcefulness. A fascinating reissue nonetheless.

Symphony 6 in B min. (Pathétique), Op. 74

*** Chan. 8446. Oslo PO, Jansons
(N) *** Ph. **SACD** 475 6197; CD 456 580-2. Kirov O, Gergiev
(M) **(*) EMI (ADD) 5 67336-2. Philh. O, Klemperer – SCHUMANN: *Symphony 4* ***
(**(*)) BBC mono BBCL 4023-2. Philh. O, Giulini – MUSSORGSKY: *Pictures at an Exhibition* (**(*))
(***) Biddulph mono WHL 046. Phd. O, Ormandy – MUSSORGSKY: *Pictures at an Exhibition* (orch. Cailliet) (***)
(N) (M) *(**) RCA **SACD** (ADD) 82876 61397-2. Boston SO, Monteux

Symphony 6 (Pathétique); Capriccio italien; Eugene Onegin: Waltz & Polonaise

(B) **(*) Sony (ADD) SBK 47657. Phd. O, Ormandy

Symphony 6 (Pathétique) in B min., Op. 74; Francesca da Rimini, Op. 32

(M) **(*) Warner Elatus (ADD) 0927 46733-2. Leningrad PO, Mravinsky

(i) Symphony 6 (Pathétique); (ii) Romeo and Juliet (Fantasy Overture)

⊙ (M) *** DG 471 742-2. Russian Nat. O, Pletnev
(N) (BB) *** EMI HMV 5 86773-2. (i) Bournemouth SO, Litton; (ii) ASMF, Marriner

Pletnev's account of the *Pathétique* with the Russian National Orchestra comes from the complete cycle he recorded in

November 1995, four years after the Virgin recording he made shortly after the orchestra's formation. That was acclaimed as a worthy successor to the famous Mravinsky, Furtwängler and Karajan accounts. This is no less impressive and its level of dramatic intensity and emotional concentration are even higher. The *Allegro* is a shade steadier perhaps but the March is every bit as breathtaking. The dark colourings of the finale and the soulful lyricism of the strings resonate in the memory. The *Romeo and Juliet* is both exciting and moving, and the DG recording is even more detailed, present and realistic than the Virgin version.

Valery Gergiev's *Pathétique* has a similar intensity and dramatic power to his *Fifth*. Some may find it hard-driven at times, but there is great excitement and firmness of grip. Gergiev is by no means as subtle – certainly in matters of dynamic nuance – as Pletnev. The recording on CD has impressive depth and resonance and in surround sound it is tremendously exciting, especially the climax of the headlong Scherzo. On SACD this is certainly the finest recording the symphony has ever received, and the sense of ambience, of sitting in the hall, is uncanny. The performance, especially in the impulsively passionate finale, will not appeal to everyone, but it is I.M.'s first choice.

Mariss Jansons and the Oslo Philharmonic crown their magnetically compelling Tchaikovsky series with a superbly concentrated account of the last and greatest of the symphonies. It is characteristic of Jansons that the great second-subject melody is at once warm and passionate yet totally unsentimental, with rubato barely noticeable. The very fast speed for the third-movement *March* stretches the players to the very limit, but the exhilaration is infectious, leading to the simple dedication of the slow finale, unexaggerated but deeply felt. Fine, warm recording as in the rest of the series.

Litton's too is an outstanding performance. The only idiosyncrasy is that in the big second-subject melodies of the outer movements Litton prefers speeds broader than usual, but with no hint of self-indulgence in the finely moulded phrasing. With an account of *Romeo and Juliet* that builds up powerfully from a restrained start, the disc makes a splendid culmination, a match even for the earlier version with Pletnev, and more fully and cleanly recorded. Moreover, Marriner and his Academy play the *Andante cantabile* most beautifully to make a pleasing interlude between the two major works. This disc is a very real bargain.

This electrifying performance of the *Pathétique Symphony* on Biddulph, one of the fastest ever on disc, was Ormandy's first Philadelphia recording, begun in December of 1936 and completed the following month. So in the first movement Ormandy is more volatile than in his later recordings, tending to press on faster after setting a tempo. The result is very powerful and exciting, not at all sentimental. First-rate transfer.

Like Mravinsky's companion account of *Symphony No. 5* on Warner's Elatus label, the Russian conductor's approach to this repertoire has mellowed a little since his blazing DG recordings from the early 1960s, though this live 1982 account of the *Pathétique* is only marginally less emotionally tense and generates plenty of excitement. The audience is reasonably well behaved (although the coughs at the beginning of the second movement are a bit irritating), and the sound is generally very good, if a bit raucous in the climaxes. With the characteristic Leningrad brass, *Francesca da Rimini* (coming from the same concert as the *Pathétique*) sounds particularly Russian, and has white-hot emotional intensity. Considering its provenance, the sound is good, and one can put aside the imperfections of a live occasion listening to this immensely vivid and exciting music-making.

Ormandy's fine 1960 performance on Sony is a reading of impressive breadth, dignity and power, with no suggestion of routine in a single bar. The orchestra makes much of the first-movement climax and plays with considerable passion and impressive body of tone in both outer movements; yet there is an element of restraint in the finale which prevents any feeling of hysteria. In short, this is most satisfying, a performance to live with; the CD transfer, while brightly lit, avoids glare in the upper range. Ormandy's panache and gusto give the *Capriccio italien* plenty of life without driving too hard, and the dances are rhythmically infectious.

Klemperer's *Pathétique* was recorded in the Kingsway Hall in 1960. Nobility rather than agonized intensity is the keynote, and the climax of the first movement carries that hallmark (with a superb contribution from the Philharmonia trombones). The Scherzo/March is much more of a march than a scherzo but the neatly articulated playing prevents heaviness, and the finale is given a spacious dignity, even if the emotional thrust sounds consciously under control. But with such an impressive response from the Philharmonia strings the closing pages have great poignancy.

Giulini conducted his live performance at the 1961 Edinburgh Festival. As in the studio, Giulini preserves a degree of restraint, finding nobility in Tchaikovsky's great melodies. But here the adrenalin of a live occasion brings a slightly more passionate treatment. Although this is not the most overwhelming of recorded *Pathétiques*, it still represents Giulini at his most impressive, but the snag, almost as much as in the coupled Mussorgsky, is the dryness of the mono sound, recorded in the unhelpful acoustic of the Usher Hall, Edinburgh. Alas the audience is never quite silent, and the beginnings of movements are especially prone to various noises.

If the sound of Monteux's performance is not 'state of the art', it is still amazing for 1955; and it is well balanced, full in texture, with a decent amount of warmth for the strings. The performance, while not lacking in excitement, is essentially no-nonsense in approach, while in the 5/4 movement there is some lack of graciousness (especially with the increase in pace of the close). The brass come through vividly, and if their distinctive, rather French-sounding vibrato will not to be all tastes, the playing still has character. The Scherzo is crisply pointed; the finale is heart-felt and passionate. Unlike most RCA Living Stereo recordings reissued on SACD, the gains are not very apparent. What is apparent, however, is the short playing time of under 45 minutes.

Symphony 7 (arr. Bogatyryev)
*** Chan. 9130. LPO, Järvi – *Piano Concerto 3* **(*)

This reconstructed symphony, abandoned not long before Tchaikovsky wrote his culminating masterpiece in the *Pathétique Symphony*, may be no match for the regular canon, but it brings many Tchaikovskian delights. Having symphony and concerto, on which the first movement was based, side by side makes it very easy to compare Bogatyryev's reconstruction of the original version, in structure identical except for the central solo cadenza. In the *Symphony* Järvi finds poetry and fantasy, and the modern digital recording allows far more light and shade over a much wider dynamic range. Apart from the thinness on the upper strings, the recorded sound is satisfyingly full and warm. Geoffrey Tozer – see above – gives a fine performance of the *Concerto*.

The Tempest, Op. 18

(BB) *** Virgin Classics 2x1 5 61751-2 (2). Bournemouth SO, Litton – BORODIN: *Prince Igor: Overture & Polovtsian dances* ***; MUSSORGSKY: *Night on the Bare Mountain*, etc. **; RIMSKY-KORSAKOV: *Scheherazade* **(*)

The Shakespearean symphonic fantasy *The Tempest* – not to be confused with the much less ambitious overture of the same name, written for Ostrovsky's play – is given a glowing performance under Litton, passionately committed, yet refined, to suggest a forgotten masterpiece. It is a pity that the rest of the performances here do not measure up to this standard, although all are very well played and recorded.

Variations on a Rococo Theme for Cello & Orchestra, Op. 33

🔊 🎵 *** EMI 5 56126-2. Chang, LSO, Rostropovich – BRUCH: *Kol Nidrei;* FAURE: *Elégie;* SAINT-SAENS: *Cello Concerto 1* ***

(M) *** DG (ADD) 447 413-2. Rostropovich, BPO, Karajan – DVORAK: *Cello Concerto* *** 🎵

(N) (M) **(*) Mercury **SACD** 475 6608. Starker, LSO, Dorati – DVORAK: *Cello Concerto;* BRUCH: *Kol Nidrei* **(*)

(M) **(*) Virgin 5 61838-2. Mørk, Oslo PO, Jansons – DVORAK: *Cello Concerto* **(*)

The phenomenally gifted 13-year-old, Korean-born cellist Han-Na Chang has the most ravishing tone and a wonderfully musical sense of line. Rostropovich as conductor sets the scene with an affectionate elegance, and then Chang introduces Tchaikovsky's theme with disarming simplicity. *Andante grazioso*, introduced very gently, is quite ethereal and the finale has the expected dash, and the crispest articulation. The LSO are inspired by Chang to give a wonderfully sensitive accompaniment, and the recording is in the demonstration class.

Like Chang, Rostropovich uses the published score rather than the original version which more accurately reflects the composer's intentions. But this account, with Karajan's glowing support, is so superbly structured in its control of emotional light and shade that one is readily convinced that this is the work Tchaikovsky conceived. The recording (made in the Jesus-Christus Kirche) is beautifully balanced and is surely one of the most perfect examples of DG's analogue techniques.

Starker's relaxed, elegant performance may lack romantic urgency, but with Dorati accompanying sympathetically it has a relaxed, ruminative quality which is endearing. It never sounded more warmly persuasive than in this new SACD remastering, which has quite transformed the recording, making it warmer and fuller, more flattering to the cello timbre.

A fine performance from Truls Mørk, with plenty of energy and finesse, and the *Andante* of Variation 11 played with an appealingly Slavonic, plaintive feeling. Very good recording too, but in sheer elegance and panache this is no match for Rostropovich.

CHAMBER MUSIC

Piano Trio in A min., Op. 50

🔊 *** BIS CD 1302. Kempf Trio – RACHMANINOV: *Trio élégiaque 1* ***

*** Ara. Z 6661. Golub–Kaplan–Carr Trio – SMETANA: *Piano Trio* ***

**(*) EMI (ADD) 7 47988-2. Ashkenazy, Perlman, Harrell

(BB) **(*) Warner Apex 0927 48728-2. Amoyal, Lodeon, Rogé

(B) *(**) EMI double forte (ADD) 5 73650-2 (2). Zukerman, Barenboim, Du Pré – BEETHOVEN: *Violin Sonatas* **(*)

Tchaikovsky's *Piano Trio* is dominated by the piano part, which has moments of bold (sometimes repetitive) rhetoric, which must ring out triumphantly yet not be allowed to usurp the work's underlying elegiac feeling. In this respect the new performance on BIS carries all before it. Freddy Kempf leads with great conviction, yet can pull back whenever necessary; moreover he provides some dazzlingly light-fingered playing during the kaleidoscopic variations of the second movement, which are presented with sparkling panache. The work's very beginning is lyrically seductive, and in the romantically expansive opening of the *Adagio* (the second half of the 'Pezzo elegiaco') the violinist, Pierre Bensaid, and the cellist, Alexander Chaushian, share a ravishingly romantic duet. Later they are appealing in a less extrovert way in the *Andante flebile* (Variation 9). The recording is very well balanced, although under moments of passionate stress in the Tchaikovsky trio it catches a touch of wiriness in the upper register of the violin. But the effect overall is convincingly realistic.

The Golub/Kaplan/Carr account of the Smetana *G minor Piano Trio* is well matched in the Tchaikovsky, which has the merit of being completely uncut. The balance places the listener rather too close to the players, but the sound is perfectly pleasing and the performance refreshingly unaffected. Nothing is overdriven, mechanized or attention-seeking. While it does not necessarily displace the Chung Trio or Ashkenazy, Perlman and Harrell, it can be ranked alongside them.

With the keyboard dominating, the first movement of Tchaikovsky's *Piano Trio* can so easily sound too rhetorical, and that is not entirely avoided by Ashkenazy, Perlman and Harrell. The *Variations* which form the second part of the work are very successful, with engaging characterization and a great deal of electricity in the closing pages. Generally this group carry all before them, with their sense of artistic purpose and through their warmth and ardour. The sound is on the dry side, with the digital remastering increasing the sharpness of focus, not ideally atmospheric. This is still at full price and comes without a coupling.

The Apex team give an eloquent performance which finds Pierre Amoyal in impressive form. The same must be said of Pascal Rogé whose account of the piano part is hardly less brilliant and sensitive than that of Ashkenazy on EMI. Frédéric Lodeon completes a fine team and though the recording is a bit close, artistically these dedicated French players give much satisfaction. A good bargain.

The Zukerman, Barenboim, Du Pré performance has great ardour and all the immediacy of a live concert, and that more than compensates for the odd inelegance that might have been corrected in the recording studio. There is nothing routine about Barenboim's playing: he takes plenty of risks and is unfailingly imaginative; it is a pity that the instrument itself is not worthy of him, for it sounds less than fresh. Zukerman also sustains a high level of intensity and at times is close to schmaltz. However, this is without doubt a high-voltage performance, though the sound quality is very average. Incidentally, the traditional cut sanctioned by the composer is observed here.

(i) *Souvenir de Florence, Op. 70* (string sextet)

🔊 *** Hyp. CDA 66648. Raphael Ens. – ARENSKY: *String Quartet in A min.* ***

*** Chan. 9878. ASMF Chamber Ens. – GLAZUNOV: *String Quintet* ***

** Mer. CDE 84211. Arienski Ens. – ARENSKY: *String Quartet 2* ***; BORODIN: *Sextet movements* **

*(**) EMI 5 57243-2. Chang, Hartog, W. Christ, T. Christ, Faust, Maninger – DVORAK: *String Sextet* *(**)

A first-rate performance from the Raphael Ensemble. They play with total unanimity of ensemble and richness of tone. Their coupling, the Arensky *Quartet with Two Cellos* is magnificently played. The recording may be a snag for some collectors – it is all a bit too forward and we are very much in the front row – but there is no reason to withhold a third star given its artistry and authority.

From the ASMF Chamber Ensemble, a very sympathetic and well-recorded account which deserves a warm recommendation. Its coupling, which brings a Glazunov rarity, strengthens its claims.

A very good rather than a distinguished performance of Tchaikovsky's eloquent *Souvenir de Florence* on Meridian, very decently recorded. The strength of the issue lies in the interest of its coupling, an Arensky rarity, the *A minor Quartet*, from which the well-known *Variations on a Theme of Tchaikovsky* derive, and two Mendelssohnian movements from the Borodin *Sextet*.

Sarah Chang and her starry team of string-players drawn from the Berlin Philharmonic, past and present, give the most joyfully exuberant performance of one of Tchaikovsky's happiest works, perfectly coupled with another great sextet by a Slavonic composer. The opening movement's bouncy rhythms in compound time set the pattern, with the second subject hauntingly seductive in its winning relaxation. Chang's individuality is matched throughout by her partners, each challenging the others, yet in a manner plainly developed from orchestral work keeping the ensemble perfectly crisp and polished, so that inner textures are beautifully clear. The *Adagio cantabile* second movement is tenderly beautiful, with the central section sharply contrasted, and the folk-dance rhythms of the last two movements are sprung with sparkling lightness. The snag is the recording, which in tuttis has a fierce treble response unsupported by a full, expansive bass, so necessary in Tchaikovsky. On some reproducers the sound is tiring to the ears.

String Quartet in B flat; String Quartets 1–3; (i) Souvenir de Florence

☛ (N) (M) *** Warner Elatus 2564 61774-2 (2). Borodin Qt, (i) with Yurov, Milman

String Quartet Movement in B flat; String Quartets 1–3; 4 Early Pieces; (i) Souvenir de Florence

(N) *** CRD CRD 3501 (*Nos. 1 & 2; Movement*); CRD 3502 (*No. 3; Early Pieces; Souvenir*). Endellion Qt; (i) with T. Boulton & R. Cohen

String Quartets 1–3; (i) Souvenir de Florence, Op.70

(B) **(*) Nim. NI 5711/2. Schubert Qt

The Elatus set, made in 1993 in the Berlin Teldec studios, is digital and the sound is a shade dry. It includes the early *B flat Movement* and is a superb, unassailable recommendation for a complete set.

The Endellion Quartet are completely at home in Tchaikovsky's special chamber-music idiom, and they give very persuasive and understanding performances of all this music. They are less vibrant, more intimate, than the Borodin or Brodsky Quartets, but their mellower approach brings its

own rewards; their playing certainly does not lack vitality or spontaneity. They open the *First Quartet* with appealing warmth, and yet there is plenty of bite in the Scherzo. All the slow movments, not just the *Andante cantabile* of No. 1 and *Andante funèbre* of No. 3, are played with deep feeling, using a wide range of dynamic: the hushed opening of the *Quartet Movement in B flat* perfectly captures the composer's *misterioso* marking. The quirky rhythm of the Scherzo of the *Second Quartet* is most engagingly pointed, as is the *Allegretto* of the *Souvenir de Florence*, while there is plenty of verve in the outer movements of this happy and often rumbustious work. But what makes this set especially desirable is the closing bonus of the four brief but characterful *Early Pieces*, and especially the gentle final *Andante molto*, which remains in the memory after the second disc has faded into silence. Excellent recording: close, but full-bodied and real. The two CDs are available separately.

The Nimbus set from the early 1990s has been issued as a two-for-the-price-of-one Double. The Franz Schubert Quartet are throughly sympathetic and produce smooth, beautifully balanced sound and good ensemble. Indeed, this is one of the best chamber-music recordings Nimbus have given us. All the same, the performances yield to the Borodin versions on Elatus made at about the same time.

String Quartet 1 in D, Op. 11

☛ ⊚ *** Challenge Classics CC 72106. Brodsky Qt – BRITTEN: *String Quartet 1; Divertimenti* ⊚ ***

(M) *** Cal. 6202. Talich Qt – BORODIN: *Quartet 2* **(*)

(***) Testament mono SBT 1061. Hollywood Qt – GLAZUNOV: *5 Novelettes*; BORODIN: *String Quartet 2 in D* (***)

(M) **(*) Decca (ADD) 425 541-2. Gabrieli Qt – BORODIN; SHOSTAKOVICH: *Quartets* **(*)

The Brodsky Quartet seem to find an affinity between the gently lyrical opening theme of Tchaikovsky's *D major Quartet* and the luminous magic at the beginning of the coupled Britten work in the same key; in both there is an elliptical reprise, but although Britten ends his movement hauntingly, Tchaikovsky characteristically provides a dashing coda. The Brodskys are completely at home in both works, and after a superb account of Tchaikovsky's opening movement, passionate yet full of dynamic contrast and delicately observed detail, they provide a ravishingly tender *Andante cantabile*. The vigorous bite of the Scherzo is followed by a bustling, joyous, yet always essentially rhythmic finale, with its elated lyrical theme carrying all before it in an exhilarating close. The performance has all the spontaneity of live music-making and the Brodskys are given a superb presence by the recording, made at The Maltings.

A glorious account of Tchaikovsky's best-loved quartet from the Talich group. They play the opening movement with an unassertive, lyrical feeling that is quite disarming, while the famous *Andante cantabile* has never sounded more beautiful on record, shaped with a combination of delicacy of feeling and warmth that is wholly persuasive. The Scherzo has plenty of verve, and the finale winningly balances the music's joyful vigour and its underlying hint of melancholy with a typical lightness of touch. The 1987 digital recording is beautifully balanced. Highly recommended.

The Hollywood Quartet's LP first appeared in 1953 and their fervent account has a persuasive eloquence that still puts one under its spell. The sound has been improved, and the addition of the Glazunov, which is new to the catalogue, enhances its value. The disc runs to one second short of 80 minutes, and the sleeve warns that some older CD players may have difficulty in tracking it.

The Gabrielis give a finely conceived performance, producing well-blended tone-quality, and the 1977 recording is clean and alive; but ideally the upper range could be less forcefully projected.

String Quartet 1 in D; 2 in F, Op. 22

(BB) **(*) Naxos 8.550847. New Haydn Qt

Very well-played accounts of both quartets from the New Haydn Quartet, which, taken on their own merits, have much to recommend them – warmth, intelligence and some finesse. In the slow movement of the D major the group has real eloquence, and in the finale it scores by observing the exposition repeat. However, it is not in the same league as the Borodin (see above), which remains a strong first choice.

String Quartets 2 in F, Op. 22; 3 in E flat min., Op. 30.

☛ (N) *** Brodsky Records BRD 3500. Brodsky Qt

The Brodsky Quartet have already given us a superb account of Tchaikovsky's *First Quartet* – see above. Now they have followed up on their own label with an equally memorable coupling of the two remaining works. They fully understand and respond to the passionate ebb and flow of this music, and these are wonderfully ardent and compelling performances. Indeed, the first movement of the *E flat Quartet* has an enormous surge of lyrical impetus, and the *Andante funèbre* has comparable depth of intensity. The recording has great immediacy, which suits the performances.

String Quartet 3 in E flat min., Op. 30

(B) *** EMI Début 5 85638-2. Atrium Qt – MOZART: *String Quartet 15*; SHOSTAKOVICH: *String Quartet 7* ***

The *E flat minor Quartet* is strongly elegiac in feeling, and was dedicated to the memory of Ferdinand Laub, who led the first performances of Tchaikovsky's *First* and *Second Quartets*. The performance serves as recording début for the young Atrium String Quartet from St Petersburg (their teacher was Iosif Levinzon, cellist of the Taneyev Quartet). Their programme is admirably chosen. Like its immediate predecessor, the *Quartet* is a rarity in the concert hall, though it has strong musical claims on the music lover. The Atrium play it as well as any of the many ensembles in the catalogue: their performance is deeply felt, they make a beautiful sound and the EMI team serve them well. Strongly recommended.

PIANO MUSIC

Album for the Young, Op. 39

(BB) *** Naxos 8.550885. Biret – DEBUSSY: *Children's Corner Suite*; SCHUMANN: *Kinderszenen* ***

Album for the Young, Op. 39: (i) original piano version; (ii) trans. for string quartet by Dubinsky

*** Chan. 8365. (i) Edlina; (ii) augmented Borodin Trio

These 24 pieces are all miniatures, but they have great charm; their invention is often memorable, with quotations from Russian folksongs and one French, plus a brief reminder of *Swan Lake*. Here they are presented twice, in their original piano versions, sympathetically played by Luba Edlina, and in effective string quartet transcriptions arranged by her husband, Rostislav Dubinsky. The Borodin group play them with both affection and finesse. The CD has plenty of presence.

This is perhaps the highlight of Idil Biret's apt triptych of suites of piano music for children. She has the full measure of Tchaikovsky's two dozen vignettes and plays them all with affection and charm. They range from miniature portraits of *Maman*, *Dolly*, a *Lark* and even a witch (*Baba-Yaga*) to a *Toy Soldier's March* and an *Organ-grinder's Song*, as well as folksy pieces from Italy, France, Germany and Russia's own *Kamarinskaya*. The recording cannot be faulted.

Capriccioso in B flat, Op. 19/5; Chanson triste, Op. 40/2; L'Espiègle, Op. 72/12; Humoresque in G, Op. 10/2; Méditation, Op. 72/5; Menuetto-scherzoso, Op. 51/3; Nocturne in F, Op. 10/1; Rêverie du soir, Op. 19/1; Romances: in F min., Op. 5; in F, Op. 51/5; The Seasons: May (White Nights), June (Barcarolle), November (Troika), January (By the fireplace); Un poco di Chopin, Op. 72/15; Valse de salon, Op. 51/2; Waltz in A flat, Op. 40/8; Waltz-scherzo in A min., Op. 7

☛ (BB) *** Regis (ADD) RRC 1093. Richter

It is good to hear Richter (recorded in 1983 by Ariola-Eurodisc) given first-class, modern sound and on top technical form, showing that he had lost none of his flair. These miniatures are invested with enormous character in playing of consistent poetry; there is never a whiff of the salon. The opening *Nocturne in F major*, the charming neo-pastiche called *Un poco di Chopin* and the haunting *Rêverie du soir* readily demonstrate Richter's imaginative thoughtfulness, while the apparently simple *Capriccioso in B flat* produces a thrilling burst of bravura at its centre piece. They are all captivating, and the bolder *Menuetto-scherzoso* also shows Tchaikovsky at his most attractively inventive. With its very truthful sound-picture, this is a first recommendation for anyone wanting a single CD of Tchaikovsky's piano music.

18 Pieces, Op. 72

(N) ❂*** DG 477 5378. Pletnev (with CHOPIN: *Nocturne, op. posth.*)

Mikhail Pletnev has made these late, marvellous and neglected Tchaikovsky pieces very much his own. R.L. was bowled over by a 1981 recital in Prague, when Pletnev was in his early twenties, in which he played 12 of them. He subsequently gave the same 12 in a BBC recital in London and recorded them for Melodiya. The present recording was made at a recital at the Tonhalle, Zurich, in 2004. It is a stunning performance which shows not only transcendental virtuosity but great tenderness and poignancy when called for. These pieces are rich in melodic invention, and many are hauntingly beautiful. What a composer and what a pianist! The Chopin *Nocturne in C sharp minor* (No. 20) acts as a final encore.

The Seasons, Op. 37a (see also above, in orchestral music)

**(*) Chan. 8349. Artymiw

The Seasons, Op. 37b; 6 Pieces, Op. 21; Sleeping Beauty (excerpts; arr. Pletnev)

(N) ❂(BB) *** Virgin 2x1 4 82055-2 (2). Pletnev – MUSSORGSKY: *Pictures at an Exhibition* *** ❂

The Seasons; Aveu passioné; Berceuse, Op. 72/2; Méditation, Op. 72/5; Polka peu dansante, Op. 51/2; Tendres reproches, Op. 72/3

*** Decca 466 562-2. Ashkenazy

Tchaikovsky's 12 *Seasons* (they would have been better called 'Months') were written to a regular deadline for publication in a St Petersburg music magazine, *Nuvellist*. Like the Opus 72

Pieces, above, and the touching *Morceaux*, Op. 21, Pletnev reveals depths that are hidden to most interpreters and he grips one from first note to last. Then, in the present transcription, he gives us about 30 minutes of *The Sleeping Beauty* in a dazzling performance. In sheer clarity of articulation and virtuosity this is pretty remarkable – also in poetry and depth of feeling. An altogether outstanding reissue, very well recorded, and in every way a *tour de force*.

Vladimir Ashkenazy gives a poised and finely prepared account of *The Seasons* which is very well recorded. At the same time it does not match Pletnev in terms of poetic insight or tenderness. The charming numbers from the *Eighteen Pieces*, Op. 72, are beautifully done too.

It is the gentler, lyrical pieces that are most effective in the hands of Lydia Artymiw, and she plays them thoughtfully and poetically. Elsewhere, she sometimes has a tendency marginally to over-characterize the music. The digital recording is truthful.

Piano Sonata in G, Op. 37; Deux morceaux; Dumka (Scène rustique russe); Méditation; Nutcracker Suite: Andante maestoso (arr. Pletnev); *Valse; Valse-Scherzo 1*
*** EMI 5 57719-2. Uehara

Ayako Uehara was the first prize winner in the Tchaikovsky Competition of 2002, placing her in the company of Vladimir Ashkenazy, Andrei Gavrilov and Mikhail Pletnev. She was in fact the first woman to gain this distinction, as well as the first Japanese pianist. This recital shows her to be a sympathetic as well as brilliant exponent of Tchaikovsky. In the *Sonata* she has awesome competition from the likes of Richter and Pletnev; though they are not superseded, she is certainly a serious contender in this repertoire and, moreover, is blessed with an excellent recorded sound.

VOCAL MUSIC

4 Duets: *Dawn; Evening; In the Garden by the River; Tears*
(B) *** BBC (ADD) BBCB 8001-2. Harper, Baker, Britten –
  BRAHMS: *Liebeslieder Waltzes, Op. 52*; ROSSINI: *Soirées musicales* ***

Heather Harper and Janet Baker, recorded at the Aldeburgh Festival in 1971, make a dream duet partnership in these tenderly sentimental duets, sung in English. Britten's inspired accompaniment adds poetry to Tchaikovsky's distinctive piano writing. No texts are given, but James Bowman writes movingly of such 'family music-making' at Aldeburgh.

Liturgy of St John Chrysostom, Op. 41
(BB) **(*) Naxos Dig 8.553854.2. Ovdiy, Mezhulin, Kiev Chamber Ch., Hobdych

Liturgy of St John Chrysostom; Anthem: An angel crying; 9 Sacred Pieces (for unaccompanied chorus)
*** Hyp. CDA 66948. Corydon Singers, Best

Liturgy of St John Chrysostom; 6 Sacred Pieces: Blessed are they whom Thou hast chosen; The hymn of the Cherubim; It is meet; Now the angels are with us; Our Father; To Thee we sing
⊶ (B) *** EMI double forte (ADD) 5 68661-2 (2). Soloists, Bulgarian a Cappella Ch., Robev

The a cappella *Liturgy of St John Chrysostom*, which dates from 1878, was not commissioned but written simply to reflect Tchaikovsky's devotion to the Russian Orthodox

Church. Best and the Corydon Singers in their refined, dedicated performances bring out the freshness and energy in this inspired music, with basses cleanly focused down to subterranean depths, echoing authentic Russian examples. The disc also contains the sequence of *9 Sacred Choruses* which Tchaikovsky wrote five or six years after the *Liturgy*, even simpler in style, but showing his ready melodic gift, and a separate piece, a dramatic Easter Day anthem, *An angel crying*, which is a miniature masterpiece. Warm, clear sound.

The alternative Bulgarian performances (although the cost is about the same) stretch to a pair of CDs and include only six of the nine choruses. Yet the Bulgarian singing has an added idiomatic Slavonic colouring and great intensity of feeling, and aided by the cathedral acoustic, the effect is wonderfully spacious. Indeed, this music could hardly be performed more convincingly and the recording is superb.

In contrast with rival versions of this masterpiece of Russian Orthodox music, which offer substantial couplings, the Naxos issue presents a liturgical performance complete with the priests' solos, almost 70 minutes long. Not all collectors will want such a format for repeated listening, but for those who prefer such an authentic course, this Naxos disc can be warmly recommended, strongly and idiomatically performed with fine solos, and atmospherically recorded in a church in Kiev.

The Snow Maiden, Op. 12 (complete incidental music)
⊶ *** Chan. 9324. Mishura-Lekhman, Girshko, Michigan University Ch. Soc., Detroit SO, Järvi
(M) *** Chant du Monde RUS 788090. Erasova, Arkipov, Vassiliev, Sveshnikov Russian State Ch., Bolshoi Theatre O, Chistiakov
(BB) **(*) Naxos 8.553856. Okolysheva, Mishenkin, Moscow Capella, Moscow SO, Golovschin

Ostrovsky's play *The Snow Maiden*, based on a Russian folktale, prompted Tchaikovsky to compose incidental music, no fewer than 19 numbers, lasting 80 minutes, a cherishable rarity. Much of it is vintage material, very delightful, bringing reminders of *Eugene Onegin* in the peasant choruses and some of the folk-based songs, and of the later Tchaikovskian world of *The Nutcracker* in some of the dances. He himself thought so well of the music that he wanted to develop it into an opera, but was frustrated when Rimsky-Korsakov wrote one first.

The consistent freshness and charm of invention comes out in Järvi's reading of the 19 numbers, lasting just under 80 minutes. It makes a delightful, undemanding cantata, very well played and sung, and is a clear first choice.

Chistiakov's fine 1994 performance, now reissued on Chant du Monde's mid-priced Russian label, is in every way recommendable at mid-price. The three excellent soloists are characterfully Slavonic, rather too forwardly balanced but well caught by the recording, and the fine singing of the chorus is given both sonority and plenty of bite. The orchestral playing is highly persuasive in a pleasingly atmospheric acoustic.

Tchaikovsky's engaging score also inspires Golovschin and his Moscow forces to a warmly idiomatic performance on Naxos, richly and colourfully recorded, if without quite the same degree of vividness. This may not match the Chant du Monde version in vitality, which at generally faster speeds sparkles more and offers crisper ensemble, but it is similarly persuasive. The conductor's affection is obvious. There are only two soloists to share the vocal music, but they are convincingly Slavonic and they are balanced slightly less forwardly. This Naxos disc is well worth its more modest cost. Both recordings offer full translations. However, Järvi's Chandos version is even finer.

Songs

Songs: *Amid the noise of the ball; Behind the window; The canary; Cradle song; The cuckoo; Does the day reign?; Do not believe; The fearful minute; If only I had known; It was in the early spring; Last night; Lullaby in a storm; The nightingale; None but the lonely heart; Not a word, O my friend; Serenade; Spring; To forget so soon; Was I not a little blade of grass?; Why?; Why did I dream of you?*
*** Hyp. CDA 66617. Rodgers, Vignoles

The warmly distinctive timbre of Joan Rodgers' lovely soprano has been heard mainly in opera but she is equally compelling in this glowing disc of songs. Her fluency with Russian texts as well as the golden colourings of her voice make this wide-ranging collection a delight from first to last. Though the voice is not quite at its richest in the most celebrated song of all, *None but the lonely heart*, the singer's subtle varying of mood and tone completely refutes the idea that Tchaikovsky as a song-composer was limited. One of the finest discs issued to mark the Tchaikovsky centenary in 1993.

OPERA

Eugene Onegin (complete)
☛ *** Decca **DVD** 071 124-9. Kubiak, Weikl, Burrows, Reynolds, Ghiaurov, Hamari, Hartle, Sénéchal, Van Allan, Mason, John Alldis Ch., ROHCG O, Solti (Stage/Video Director: Petr Weigl)
(*) TDK **DVD DV-OPEON (2). Gavrilova, Udalova, Novak, Redkin, Baskov, Martirosyan, Bolshoi Ch. and O, Ermler (V/D: Nikhita Tikhonov)
** Arthaus **DVD** 100 126. Boylan, Gluschak, König, Burford, Schelomianski, EU Opera Ch. & O, Rozhdestvensky (Producer: Nikolaus Lehnhoff.)
☛ *** Decca (ADD) 417 413-2 (2). Kubiak, Weikl, Burrows, Reynolds, Ghiaurov, Hamari, Sénéchal, Alldis Ch., ROHCG O, Solti
**(*) DG 423 959-2 (2). Freni, Allen, Von Otter, Shicoff, Burchuladze, Sénéchal, Leipzig R. Ch., Dresden State O, Levine
(BB) (***) Naxos mono 8.110216/17 (2). Nortsov, Kruglikova, Antonova, Kozlovsky, Mikhailov, Bolshoi Ch. & O, Melik-Pashaev, Orlov

Solti, characteristically crisp in attack, has plainly warmed to the score of Tchaikovsky's colourful opera, allowing his singers full rein in rallentando and rubato to a degree one might not have expected of him. The Tatiana of Teresa Kubiak is most moving – rather mature-sounding for the *ingénue* of Act I, but with her golden, vibrant voice rising most impressively to the final confrontation of Act III. The Onegin of Bernd Weikl may have too little variety of tone, but again this is firm singing that yet has authentic Slavonic tinges. The rest of the cast is excellent, with Stuart Burrows as Lensky giving one of his finest performances on record yet. Here, for the first time, the full range of expression in this most atmospheric of operas is superbly caught, with the Decca CDs vividly capturing every subtlety – including the wonderful off-stage effects.

The DVD of the same performance represents a fascinating experiment by Decca, and may augur the future process,

by which an outstanding older audio recording can be laminated on to a newer production, acted out visually. In the present instance, the brilliant Czech director, Petr Weigl, has in his 1988 film illustrated the familiar Decca audio recording, conducted by Sir Georg Solti, with the most evocative visual realization of the narrative. Actors mime to the words in settings as nearly as possible those of the original Pushkin story, whether in the Russian countryside or in St Petersburg. The result is all the more moving, when the agonizing of the young Tatiana or of the disillusioned Onegin is presented by actors who so accurately look the part, as do all the authentically costumed cast. The contrast between the country ball of Act II with the grand ball of Act III set in a St Petersburg palace is brought out in a way that could never be achieved on stage, and the chill of the duel scene is all the more involving when the scene is of genuine snow in a genuine forest. Musically, the oddity is that the Prelude and first scene (the Tatiana–Olga duet) are presented in audio recording only, for Weigl starts his film most atmospherically with the peasants' chorus which opens the second scene of Act I, with the reapers observed from afar wending their way in the mist down a winding country path.

But because the action is filmed in various locations, including the open air, with actors miming the singers, the Kingsway Hall acoustic in which Decca recorded the original in the mid-1970s does not quite match up with what we see, and though the direction and the sets are always imaginative, the free-ranging camera does not (and cannot) match the evidence of the ear, so that the acoustic disparity is obvious.

Weigl was the original producer at Covent Garden and ideally should have filmed his Covent Garden production. But he didn't, and this is what he has designed in its place. The cast are handsome and mime for the most part successfully. But some collectors, like R.L., may be unable to sustain the suspension of disbelief, and will find the result here ultimately unconvincing. R.L. feels that here is a case where the collector is better served by the original CD set, which sounds splendid.

But both E.G. and I.M. find the DVD totally compelling and convincing, even though there are cuts in the music, and are only too delighted that the recording was made in such an attractive acoustic ambience, with the disparity soon forgotten. With the surtitles so easy to follow, the viewer/listener can be totally caught up in the action and at the same time enjoy not only the glorious singing, but also the inspired orchestral detail of Solti's accompaniment through which Tchaikovsky is conveying the emotions of the characters as one watches them. The sound itself is superb. So while R.L. has his doubts, for E.G. and I.M. this set is a triumph.

In 2000, the Bolshoi in Moscow revived one of its oldest productions, first seen in 1944. The director Boris Pokrovsky in this film maintains tradition, encouraging the principal singers to adopt melodramatic gestures. What makes the result visually enjoyable is the atmospheric realism of the extravagant sets, with full-scale trees dotted around in the open-air scenes and strongly contrasted (if equally lavish) scenery for the two Ball scenes, the one at the Larins' house grandly provincial, the one in St Petersburg glitteringly palatial, easily coping with the very large corps de ballet. Though Maria Gavrilova as Tatiana and Vladimir Redkin as Onegin characterize well, their singing is flawed, the one with a harsh edge to her voice, the other often pitching too vaguely. Nikolai Baskov's thoaty tenor sounds very Russian in the role of Lensky; but most satisfying of the principals is the vintage contralto, Irina Udalova, as Mme Larina. Mark Ermler conducts with idiomatic warmth. The film comes extravagantly spread over two discs.

Rozhdestvensky's DVD performance, which was staged at the 1998 Baden-Baden Festival, has the advantage of an excellent Onegin in Vladimir Glushchak, but the cast is otherwise not wholly convincing. (Ineke Vlogtman's Larina looks far too young to be a mother, let alone the mother of Orla Boylan and Anna Burford!) There are good things, of course, among which the conducting ranks high. But there is little sense of period, and the chorus certainly don't sound Russian, despite the presence of a Russian conductor. Above all, there is little sense of atmosphere, and the bright, overlit opening scene, with its abundance of kites, hardly induces confidence.

The DG CD version brings a magnificent Onegin in Thomas Allen, the most satisfying account of the title-role yet recorded. It is matched by the Tatiana of Mirella Freni, even at a late stage in her career readily conveying girlish freshness in her voice. The other parts are also strongly taken. The tautened-nerves quality in the character of Lensky comes out vividly in the portrayal by Neil Shicoff, and Anne Sofie von Otter with her firm, clear mezzo believably makes Olga a younger sister, not too mature a character. Paata Burchuladze is a satisfyingly resonant Gremin and Michel Sénéchal, as on the Solti set, is an incomparable Monsieur Triquet. What welds all these fine components into a rich and exciting whole is the conducting of James Levine. The Leipzig Radio Choir sings superbly as well. The snag is that the DG recording is dry and studio-bound, with sound close and congested enough to undermine the bloom on both voices and instruments. In every way the more spacious acoustic in the Solti set is preferable.

Recorded in Moscow in 1937 on forty short-playing 78 r.p.m. discs, this historic version of *Eugene Onegin* on Naxos was the first complete recording of the opera ever made, and it is remarkable not just for the idiomatic warmth of the conducting – with Alexander Orlov replacing Alexander Melik-Pashaev for some passages – but for the fine singing of the principals, with not a Slavonic wobbler among them. Panteleimon Nortsov in the title role sings with a firmness and clarity that is most moving, his tone rather darker than usual in this role. Elena Kruglikova is equally moving as Tatiana, even though the voice, generally warm and clear, acquires an edginess when under pressure at the top. Elizaveta Antonova sings with rich, velvet tone as Olga, and though Ivan Kozlovsky as Lensky has the nasal twang that is typical of many Russian tenors, his firmly focused expressiveness is equally compelling. The transfers of Ward Marston are astonishingly fine, firm and full bodied, an achievement the more remarkable when, in a Soviet recording made over a relatively long period, the inconsistencies of sound between the 80 original sides have so satisfyingly been countered and surface noise so well controlled.

The Queen of Spades (Pique Dame) (complete)

☛ *** Ph. **DVD** 070 434-9. Grigorian, Gulegina, Leiferkus, Gergalov, Filatova, Borodina, Kirov Op. Ch. & O, Gergiev (Producer: Temirkanov; V/D: Brian Large)

(*) Arthaus **DVD 100 272-2. Marusin, Gustafson, Leiferkus, Khartinov, Palmer, Todorovich, Glyndebourne Fest. Ch., LPO, A. Davis (Producer: Vick; V/D: Peter Maniura)

*** Ph. 438 141-2 (3). Grigorian, Putilin, Chernov, Solodovnikov, Arkhipova, Gulegina, Borodina, Kirov Op. Ch. & O, Gergiev

(M) *** DG (ADD) 463 679-2 (3). Gougaloff, Vishnevskaya, Resnik, Schwarz, Weikl, Petkov, Popp, Tchaikovsky Ch. & O Nat. de France, Rostropovich

Pushkin's dark story of a gambler's growing obsession with discovering the secret that will bring him riches is taut and concentrated. It unfolds with a gripping psychological intensity, all the more powerful for its understatement. Modest Tchaikovsky's libretto differs in many respects from Pushkin's story. In the opera Lisa becomes a romantic figure who meets a melodramatic end; in the original she is the down-trodden ward of the Countess, not her granddaughter, whose ideas are conditioned by romantic novelettes and who fastens on Herman as a deliverer. There is no fiancé: the figure of Prince Yeletsky was written into the plot by Modest. Lisa's fate, too, is very different, for in the original she marries a pleasant enough young man, a civil servant with a comfortable income. Herman, for whom Tchaikovsky felt such compassion, ends his days in an asylum and is an altogether colder figure than in the opera, where his love for Lisa is genuine and only gradually subsumed in his obsession.

Dating from 1992, the Philips DVD, with the conductor, Valery Gergiev, looking very young, is a live recording of the Kirov Company's grandly traditional production. It is handsome to look at and very well staged, a joy to watch as well as listen to. Yuri Temirkanov (Gergiev's predecessor at the Kirov) produces and does not lose sight of the rococo component in this wonderful opera. Yet it is a straightforward and clean-cut presentation, deftly using massive choruses to match the opulent costumes and scenery, and nearly all the cast is first-rate. Incidentally, this cast differs from the CDs, with Irina Arkhipova's Countess being replaced by Ludmila Filatova and Nikolai Putilin giving way to Leiferkus as Tomsky, who appeared in the Ozawa set on RCA and also in the Glyndebourne production reviewed below.

Gegam Grigorian's Herman makes an unromantic figure, a predator rather than an ardent lover. He is a little stiff to start with and rarely sings below *forte*, but he improves as the opera unfolds and his performance acquires intensity, the characterization deepens, and he sings powerfully and cleanly. Maria Gulegina is superb as the heroine, Lisa, impressively dramatic and vocally powerful. The others are first-rate with the sad exception of Ludmila Filatova as the Countess, with a voice that is too thin and tremulous even to be acceptable in that aged role. This shortcoming is serious in her big scenes, which should be the climax of the whole drama, though she is certainly affecting, and makes up for it in vocal characterization.

Leiferkus is the soul of elegance, both vocally and as an actor. Nor should Olga Borodina's outstanding Pauline go unmentioned. Above all the hero is Gergiev himself who paces this marvellous score with depth and passion, and Brian Large's visual direction is superb. The eyes are directed to where the action and sound naturally dictate. The video recording was made after the CD and without the audience.

In the CD set Gergiev and his talented team from the Kirov Opera in St Petersburg have also produced a winner. The very opening, refined and purposeful, sets the pattern, with Gergiev controlling this episodic work with fine concern for atmosphere and dramatic impact, unafraid of extreme speeds and telling pauses. Though the engineers fail to give a supernatural aura to the voice of the Countess when she returns as a ghost, the recorded sound is consistently warm and clear. It is good to have the veteran Irina Arkhipova singing powerfully and bitingly in that key role, while the other international star,

Olga Borodina, is unforgettable as Pauline, singing gloriously with keen temperament. Otherwise Gergiev's chosen team offers characterful Slavonic voices that are yet well focused and unstrained, specially important with the tenor hero, Herman, here dashingly sung by Gegam Grigorian. As the heroine, Lisa, Maria Gulegina sings with warm tone and well-controlled vibrato, slightly edgy under pressure.

After the Gergiev–Temirkanov DVD, Graham Vick's Glyndebourne production is a distinctly lesser pleasure, albeit a pleasure nonetheless. The smaller stage (this was recorded in 1992 before the renovation) naturally imposes constraints, and the set, a slanted black box whose walls are daubed with paint, is a self-imposed limitation. Vick changes the angle of his box to reflect Herman's psychological state. Since Tchaikovsky so eloquently shows this in the music, this is supererogatory. (How right the late Hans Keller was to describe the opera producer as 'one of music's unnecessary professions'.) Yuri Masurin's Herman is if anything more impressive than Grigorian's; he is the part from beginning to end. Nancy Gustafson is an expressive Lisa, who conveys her bewilderment and anguish with much artistry and the cast in general is first-rate. Felicity Palmer's Countess is particularly fine. Andrew Davis holds all the threads together magnificently and gets an impressive response from his singers and the LPO. Gergiev perhaps gets the greater sweep and depth of tone and has of course the most sumptuous and authentic staging.

Recorded by Radio France in the winter of 1976–7, this DG version is among the finest of the opera sets conducted by Mstislav Rostropovich. Warmly idiomatic and well recorded, in clear, well-balanced analogue sound, it has been seriously neglected in the CD era and now emerges at mid-price in DG's series of vintage 'Originals'. With a strong cast which – with a stiffening of non-Russian stars – avoids the penalties of Slavonic wobblers, it is even a contender for first choice against Gergiev's Philips version with the Kirov Opera. In the mid-1970s Galina Vishnevskaya was still at her peak, here proving a strong and vibrant Lisa, not young-sounding but with plenty of temperament. The firm velvet tones of Hanna Schwarz's mezzo as her sister, Pauline, provide a fine contrast. Schwarz is also well-matched in the duet which is the high point of the Act II *Intermezzo*, with Lucia Popp as a starry soprano partner, a charming pastiche sequence. Peter Gougaloff is a characterful Herman, the key figure in this story based on Pushkin. His very Russian tenor lacks beauty, but it is firm and full toned, with words expressively brought out. As the Countess Regina Resnik gives an aptly over-the-top performance, biting and incisive, not only in her death scene but in the Countess's ghostly reappearance, atmospherically presented using an echo chamber. The rest of the large cast assembled in Paris includes such leading singers in incidental roles as Bernd Weikl and Dimiter Petkov.

Yolanta (complete)
*** Ph. (IMS) 442 796-2 (2). Gorchakova, Alexashkin, Hvorostovsky, Grigorian, Kirov Op. Ch. & O, Gergiev

Gergiev and his outstanding Kirov team give a warm, idiomatic reading of Tchaikovsky's charming fairy-tale opera of the blind princess. Bringing out the atmospheric beauty of the score, it completely outshines the Rostropovich version on Erato, Galina Gorchakova gives the most moving portrait of the heroine, tender and vulnerable, with words delicately touched in. As Vaudémont, the knight who falls in love with her, Gegam Grigorian sings with rather tight, very Russian tenor-tone, not always pleasing but with a fine feeling for the

idiom and a natural ease in high tessitura. Dmitri Hvorostovsky sings nobly and heroically as Robert, his more vigorous friend and rival, while Sergei Alexashkin sings with dark, grainy – again very Russian – tone as King René, Iolanta's father. Above all, the exchanges between characters consistently convey the feeling of stage-experience. The recording, not ideally clear but well balanced, was made in the theatre but under studio conditions.

Vocal Collection

Prelude: The Battle of Poltava. Arias from: *Eugene Onegin; The Maid of Orleans* (with *Prelude*); *Mazeppa* (with *Gopak*); *The Queen of Spades; The Sorceress; Yolanta*
** Orfeo C540 011 A. Varady, Munich R. O, Kofman

Julia Varady gives commanding performances of this wide-ranging collection of Tchaikovsky arias, even if the voice sounds very mature for the young Tatiana in the *Letter Scene* of *Eugene Onegin*. What sadly undermines the impact of the performances is that the recording, made in collaboration with Bavarian Radio, lacks the warmth and fullness usually associated with this source, with Varady's voice lacking its characteristic bloom. The three orchestral pieces make a useful supplement.

TCHEREPNIN, Alexander (1899–1977)

Piano Concertos 2, Op. 26; 4 (Fantaisie), Op. 78; Magna mater, Op. 41; Symphonic Prayer, Op. 93
*** BIS CD 1247. Ogawa, Singapore SO, Lan Shui

Tcherepnin bridged so many different musical cultures. He grew up in St Petersburg, from which he was forced to flee during the Revolution: first to the Georgian capital of Tbilisi and subsequently to Paris in 1921. His career as a pianist-composer took him to many parts of the world, and he spent some time teaching in Shanghai. The *Piano Concerto No. 2* is 'European' in style, while the *Fourth Concerto*, written shortly before he emigrated to the USA, is full of Chinese influence. Neither *Concerto* is new to the catalogue but the present versions supersede their predecessors. Eminently serviceable recording.

(i) *Piano Concerto 5, Op. 96. Symphonies 1 in E, Op. 42; 2 in E flat, Op. 77*
*** BIS CD 1018. Singapore SO, Shui (i) with Ogawa

(i) *Piano Concerto 6, Op. 99. Symphonies 3 in F sharp, Op. 83; 4 in E , Op. 91*
*** BIS CD 1017. Singapore SO, Shui (i) with Ogawa

Alexander Tcherepnin was the son of the composer Nikolai, who conducted when the Diaghilev Ballet made its Paris début. The *First Symphony* of 1927 caused a stir, not so much on account of its radical musical language as the fact that its Scherzo was written for percussion only. It is inventive and stimulating and full of personality. The *Second Symphony* did not follow until the end of the 1939–45 war, and two successors followed in the 1950s: the *Third* in 1952, and the *Fourth*, commissioned by Charles Munch and the Boston Symphony Orchestra, in 1958–9.

It is with the *Fourth* that the newcomer to Tcherepnin's music should start. Its invention is wonderfully alert and fresh, and the control of pace masterly. It is neoclassical in feeling with a great sense of wit and style. The two piano concertos are from the 1960s and are elegantly played by Noriko Ogawa. The Singapore orchestra has greatly improved since its early Marco Polo records under Choo Hoey, and the Chinese conductor Lan Shui gets generally good results from them.

Symphony 4; Romantic Overture, Op. 67; Russian Dances, Op. 50; Suite for Orchestra, Op. 87

**(*) Marco Polo 8.223380. Czech-Slovak State PO (Košice), Yip

The *Fourth Symphony* is among Tcherepnin's finest works. Written in the mid-1950s, it is colourful and tautly compact, neo-classical in idiom, very well organized and full of lively and imaginative musical invention. The *Suite*, Op. 67, is less individual and in places recalls the Stravinsky of *Petrushka* and *Le Chant du rossignol*. Like the much earlier *Russian Dances*, it is uneven in quality but far from unattractive. The *Romantic Overture* was composed in wartime Paris. Generally good performances, decently recorded too under the young Chinese conductor Wing-Sie Yip, who draws a lively response from her players.

TCHEREPNIN, Nikolai (1873–1945)

Narcisse et Echo, Op. 40

*** Chan. 9670. Hague Chamber Ch., & Residentie O, Rozhdestvensky

This endearing and atmospheric choral ballet, *Narcisse et Echo* for much of the time sounds more French than Russian, with fascinating anticipations of *Daphnis*, not least in obbligato choral passages. Other sections mirror what the young Stravinsky was writing, but toned down. There also is a lot of Rimsky-Korsakov in it, and if you respond to that Russian master as well as Scriabin and Ravel, you will like this. It is somewhat static and in the last part of the ballet Narcissus is simply absorbed in gazing at his own reflection. However, though it is emphatically not great music, there is much that enchants. Rozhdestvensky is the ideal advocate, helped by ripe Chandos sound.

Le Pavillon d'Armide (ballet; complete)

**(*) Marco Polo 8.223779. Moscow SO, Shek

Le Pavillon d'Armide was the ballet with which Diaghilev opened his first *Ballets russes* season introducing Nijinsky. Its invention is fluent, owing much to Tcherepnin's teacher, Rimsky-Korsakov and to Glazunov and Tchaikovsky. It runs to well over an hour and the inspiration is uneven. At its best, though, it has real charm, and the scoring is always full of colour. It is very well recorded.

TELEMANN, Georg Philipp

(1681–1767)

Concertos: for 2 Chalumeaux in D min.; for Flute in D; for 3 Oboes, 3 Violins in B flat; for Recorder & Flute in E min.; for Trumpet in D; for Trumpet & Violin in D

🕭 (N) (M) *** DG (IMS) 476 7253-2. Soloists, Col. Mus. Ant., Goebel

As Reinhard Goebel points out, Telemann 'displayed immense audacity in the imaginative and ingenious mixing of the colours from the palette of the baroque orchestra', and these are heard to excellent effect here. Those who know the vital *B flat Concerto* for three oboes and violins from earlier versions, will find the allegro very fast indeed and the slow movement quite thought-provoking. The chalumeau is the

precursor of the clarinet, and the concerto for two chalumeaux recorded here is full of unexpected delights. Marvellously alive and accomplished playing, even if one occasionally tires of the bulges and nudges on the first beats of bars. This has been reissued at mid-price in Universal's 'Critics' Choice' series.

Concerto for 2 Chalumeaux in D min.; Sonata for 2 Chalumeaux in F; in G; Viola Concerto in G; Overture des Nations anciennes et modernes in G; Völker Overture (Suite in B flat)

*** Chan. 0593. Lawson, Harris, Standage, Coll. Mus. 90

Colin Lawson and Michael Harris with their 'liquid' timbres find a delicate charm in the two works for chalumeaux and the *Sonata* has a rather touching *Grave*, which is played very serenely. Standage himself takes the solo part with distinction and pleasingly full timbre in the famous *Viola Concerto*, and his characterization of the *Ancient and Modern Overture*, is alert and strong, finding dignity in *Les Allemands* and not overdoing the closing parody lament for *Les Vieilles Femmes*. He is equally positive in the so-called 'Folk' Overture, played vibrantly: Its last five movements each draw on a different culture – Turkish, Russian and so on – but with their rhythms given a Western overlay.

Concertos: for 2 Corni da caccia in F, TWV 52:F3; for Violin & 3 Corni di caccia in D, TWV 54:D2. Overtures for 2 Corni di caccia in D. TWV 55:D17; for 2 Corni di caccia & 2 Oboes in F, TWV 55:F3

🕭 *** MDG 605 1045-2. Deutsch Natural Horn Soloists, New Dusseldorf Hofmusik

The Deutsch Natural Horn Soloists are a superb group. They play here expertly using hand horns without valves and demonstrating the most thrilling bravura, whether in partnership with oboes, where the interplay of the *Réjouissance* in the *F major Overture* (or Suite) is a real hit number, or in the *Concerto in F*, which reminds one a little of Handel's *Water Music*. In the concerto scored for three horns, the solo violin in the *Grave* slow movement gives expressive contrast before sharing the exuberant finale. With excellent recording, this is outstanding in every way, but not to be played all in one go!

Flute Concertos: in B min.; C; D (2); E; E min.

*** VAI Audio VAIA 1166. Stallman, Phd. Concerto Soloists CO

Every one of these fine concertos, *galant* and Italianate by turns, shows the composer's invention at its most fertile and imaginative. All but one is in four movements. The *E minor*, which is in five, is perhaps finest of all. The Vivaldian *Dolce e staccato* opening movement of the *E major* is also particularly striking. The *D major's* finale is a bouncing Minuet, with delicious bird trills in the Trio, while in the extended first movement of the B minor work Telemann heralds the return of the final tutti with a repeated 'posthorn' call from the soloist emerging distinctly from his running roulades. Robert Stallman is a stylish and elegant player and he is given crisply sympathetic modern instrument accompaniments from the Philadelphia Chamber Orchestra. Excellent recording too.

Flute Concertos in D, TWV:51:D2; in G, TWV:51:G2. Concerto for 2 Flutes, Violone in A min., TWV:53:a; Concerto for Flute, Oboe d'amore & Viola d'amore in E, TWV:53:E; Tafelmusik: Concerto for Flute & Violin in A, TWV:53:A2

*** EMI 5 57397-2. Pahud, Berlin Bar. Soloists, Kussmaul

An enchanting disc. Everything Emmanuel Pahud plays seems to turn to gold, and he has admirable support from his solo colleagues (including Albrecht Meyer, oboe d'amore and Wolfram Christ, viola d'amore). For magical phrasing, sample the lovely opening *Andante* of the reconstructed G major solo concerto; for exquisite elegance, try the lovely *Loure* of the A minor triple concerto; for delicacy and haunting atmosphere, turn to the *Andante* and *Siciliana* of the *Concerto for Flute, Oboe d'amore and Viola d'amore*. Throughout allegros are wonderfully nimble and light-hearted. The Berlin Baroque Soloists directed by Rainer Kussmaul accompany with wonderful finesse and warmth and the recording is in the demonstration bracket.

Horn Concerto in D

*** Ara. Z 6750. Rose, St Luke's Chamber Ens. – FORSTER; HAYDN; L. MOZART: *Horn Concertos* ***

Telemann's *D major Horn Concerto* (designated for the *corno di caccia* or hunting horn) is one of his best, and indeed one of the most attractive of all concertos for the instrument, other than those of Mozart. It opens with a catchy, swiftly articulated *moto perpetuo* which puts any soloist on his mettle; then follows a melancholy *Largo*, which reaches up into the instrument's highest tessitura. The finale is a Minuet with plenty of decorative passages and trills again taking the horn up to its highest register (all excellently managed here). Stewart Rose's broad, open tone suits this robust music admirably and he plays with confident finesse; the crisply stylish accompaniment provides an excellent backcloth and the recording is excellent.

Triple Horn Concerto in D; Alster (Overture) Suite; La Bouffonne Suite; Grillen-Symphonie

🔊 *** Chan. 0547. Coll. Mus. 90, Standage

This collection offers some of Telemann's most colourful and descriptive music, often quite bizarrely scored. The *Triple Horn Concerto* opens the programme with the hand-horns rasping boisterously. Then comes *La Bouffonne Suite*, with its elegant *Loure* and the extremely fetching *Rigaudon*, while the work ends with a touchingly delicate *Pastourelle*, beautifully played here. The *Grillen-Symphonie* ('cricket symphony') brings a piquant dialogue between upper wind and double-basses in the first movement, while the second has unexpected accents and lives up to its name *Tändeln* ('flirtatious'). The horns (four of them) re-enter ambitiously at the colourful *Overture* of the *Alster Suite*, add to the fun in the *Echo* movement and help to simulate the Hamburg glockenspiel that follows. The entry of the Alster Shepherds brings a piquant drone effect, but best of all is the wailing *Concerto of Frogs and Crows*, with drooping bleats from the oboe and then the principal horn. Standage and his group make the very most of Telemann's remarkable orchestral palette and play with great vitality as well as finesse.

Oboe Concertos: in C min. (2); D (Concerto grazioso); D min.; E; E flat; F; F min.; Oboe d'amore Concertos: E; E min.; G; (i) Triple Concerto for Oboe d'amore, Flute & Viola d'amore

🔊 (BB) *** Regis RRC 2057 (2). Francis, L. Harpsichord Ens.; (i) with Mayer, Watson

Sarah Francis's survey of Telemann's *Oboe* and *Oboe d'amore Concertos* brings modern-instrument performances, which are a model of style. The *G major Oboe d'amore Concerto* on the first disc is most gracious (with colouring dark-timbred

like a cor anglais in the *soave* first movement). The *Concerto grazioso*, too, is aptly named. The *C minor Oboe Concerto* begins with a *Grave*, then the main Allegro brings a witty dialogue between soloist and violins, with the theme tossed backwards and forwards like a shuttlecock. But it is the works for oboe d'amore that are again so striking. Most imaginative of all is the *Triple Concerto* with its sustained opening *Andante* (rather like a Handel aria) and *Siciliano* third movement with the melody alternating between oboe d'amore and viola d'amore, and nicely decorated by flute triplets. The performances are full of joy and sparkle as well as expressive. They are beautifully recorded and make a very good case for playing this repertoire on modern instruments. Now reissued as a budget Double on Regis they are even more highly recommended.

(i) Oboe Concertos: in D min.; E min.; F min.; (ii) Sonatas: E min. (from Esercizi musici); in G (from Sonata metodiche, Op. 13/6); G min. (from Tafelmusik, Part III)

(BB) *** Virgin 2×1 5 61878-2 (2). De Vries; (i) Amsterdam Alma Musica, Van Asperen; (ii) Van Asperen, Möller – ALBINONI: *Concerti a cinque, Op. 9* ***

Hans de Vries is a fine player and he produces an attractively full timbre on his baroque oboe. All three concertos are characteristically inventive, with alert and stylish accompaniments, but the three *Sonatas* are a delight, the work from the *Tafelmusik* particularly diverse. The slight snag is the very forward balance of the solo instrument, which reduces the overall range of dynamic, but apart from that the sound is vivid, and the harpsichord image in the *Sonatas* is pleasing. This comes as part of an inexpensive Double, but the present CD only plays for just over 40 minutes and one wonders what has happened to the fourth concerto in C minor which was on the original CD.

Oboe d'amore Concerto in E min., TWV 51:E2; Double Horn Concerto in F, TWV 52:F4; Viola Concerto in G, TWV 51:G9; Double Viola Concerto in G, TWV 52:G3; Violin Concertos: in A (Die Relinge), TWV 51:A4; in G, TWV 51:G6; Double Violin Concerto in B flat, TWV 52:B2; Concerto for 2 Violins & 2 Horns in D, TWV 52:D4

🔊 ✿ *** EMI 5 57232-2 Mayer, Christ, Kussmaul, Dohr, Schreckenberger, Berlin Baroque Soloists

This compilation is described as 'unknown works', but that does not apply to the *Viola Concerto*, which Wolfgang Christ plays so beautifully. These are period instrument performances, but the Berlin Soloists have a particularly light, graceful style of playing and the dainty articulation of their oboist, Albrecht Mayer, is captivating. The *Violin Concerto* nicknamed *Die Relinge* pictures pond frogs, but their croaking here is engagingly delicate. The first movement of the *Concerto for 2 Violas* is a Minuet marked *Douceur*, the second *Gay*, and these superb players catch both moods delightfully, while the *Double Violin Concerto* is hardly less felicitous. The works including horns are obviously more robust, but the Vivace finale of TWV52:F4 is wonderfully lighthearted and polished. Indeed, all the performances have an unusual elegance, the solo playing of the very highest calibre. With splendidly natural recording and a concert-hall balance, this is one of the very finest of all Telemann collections.

Double Concertos: for 2 Oboes d'amore in A; for Recorder & Flute in E min.; Violin Concerto in B flat; Overtures (Suites): in F sharp min.; D

*** Chan. 0661 Holtslag, Brown, Robson, Eastaway, Coll. Mus. 90, Standage

The title of this Chandos disc, 'Ouverture comique', refers to the last of the five Telemann works included in this delightful programme. It is a weirdly surreal musical portrait – eighteenth-century style – of a hypochondriac afflicted with gout. Over seven movements he, in turn, finds remedies in dancing – cue for inserted dance-fragments – in a coach-ride, and even a visit to a brothel. Telemann wrote this sparkling piece in his eighties with his imagination still working overtime. The other works, more conventional but just as inventive, include another overture/suite and three refreshing concertos, all beautifully done.

Concerto in B flat for 3 Oboes & 3 Violins; Concerto in E for Flute, Oboe d'amore & Viola d'amore. Tafelmusik, Part I: Concerto in A for Flute, Violin & Cello; Part II: Concerto in F for 3 Violins

*** Chan. 0580. Soloists, Coll. Mus. 90, Standage

The triple concertos here are among the composer's most colourful works and the period wind-instruments here are piquant in their mixed colours, the strings lithe, yet not abrasive. The opening of the *E major Concerto* (which comes last in the programme) tickles the ear engagingly with its opening *Andante*, and the third movement *Siciliano* is equally diverting. The lively opening movement of the *Tafelmusik Triple Violin Concerto* momentarily recalls Handel's *Queen of Sheba*, and it has a particularly eloquent *Largo*. First-class playing and recording throughout.

Concertos in B flat for 3 Oboes, 3 Violins & Continuo, TWV 44:43; F for Recorder, Bassoon & Strings; for 4 Violins in G, TWV 40:201. Overture in F for 2 Horns & Strings, TWV 44:7

🎵➡ (BB) *** Warner Apex 2564 60523-2. Soloists, VCM, Harnoncourt

When this collection was first issued on LP in 1966 on Telefunken's Das Alte Werk label we suggested it was one of the best Telemann discs in the catalogue, and it still is. The *Overture* featuring a pair of solo horns (natural horns are used here) shows the composer at his most characteristic, using all the open notes possible on these valveless instruments with striking melodic ingenuity. In the *B flat Concerto* the oboes also sound splendidly in tune, which was not always the case with earlier recordings using baroque instruments, and phrasing is alive and sensitive. In the *Concerto for Recorder and Bassoon*, featuring Frans Brüggen and Otto Fleischmann as soloists, the combination of woody bassoon timbre and the piping recorder is most effective. Indeed, all the performances here are extremely fine; the recording, made in a warm acoustic, is excellent, and at budget price this disc still deserves a strong recommendation.

Recorder Concertos: in C & E major; Double Concerto for Recorder & Flute; Suite in A min. for Recorder & Strings

🎵➡ (BB) *** Naxos 8.554018. Rothert, Umbach, Cologne CO, Müller-Brühl

It is a pity that Naxos do not provide TWV identification as do EMI and DG Archiv, but the *Suite in A minor* is an irresistible masterpiece if ever there was one, and is easily identified. It is played here as winningly and stylishly as anywhere else on disc. The two named soloists share the *Double Concerto* (which has a delightful *Largo* that starts off like Handel's 'Where'er you walk'), but it is not clear who plays elsewhere. However it is of no moment; all the solo playing here is expert and personable, and there is some delicious virtuoso piping in the second movement of the *E*

major Concerto. Indeed all four works show Telemann on top form, Helmut Müller-Brühl's accompaniments are polished and equally stylish, and the recording is first class.

(i) Recorder Concertos: in C; in F; (ii) Suite in A min. for Recorder & Strings; (i) Sinfonia in F

(BB) **(*) Hyp. Helios CDH 55091. (i) Holtslag, Parley of Instruments; (ii) cond. Goodman

The three solo concertos here are a delight. Peter Holtslag's piping treble recorder is truthfully balanced, in proper scale with the authentic accompaniments, which are neat, polished, sympathetic and animated. The *Sinfonia* is curiously scored, for recorder, oboe, solo bass viol, strings, cornett, three trombones and an organ, with doubling of wind and string parts. Even with Roy Goodman balancing everything expertly the effect is slightly bizarre. About the great *Suite in A minor* there are some reservations: it is played with much nimble bravura and sympathy on the part of the soloist, but the orchestral texture sounds rather thin. However, at budget price this remains an attractive proposition.

Recorder Concerto in C; (i) Double Concerto for Recorder & Bassoon

*** BIS CD 271. Pehrsson, (i) McGraw; Drottningholm Bar. Ens. – VIVALDI: Concertos ***

Clas Pehrsson and Michael McGraw are most expert players, as indeed are all their colleagues of the Drottningholm Baroque Ensemble; the recordings are well balanced and fresh.

Double Concertos: for 2 Tenor Recorders in A min. & B flat; for Recorder & Bassoon in F; in E min. for Recorder & Flute; in A min. for Recorder, Gamba & Strings

**(*) BIS CD 617. Pehrsson, Laurin, McCraw, Evison, Larsson, Drottningholm Bar. Ens., Spark

Among what is claimed are the 'complete double concertos with recorder' the most attractive work here is for recorder and flute, with its engaging drone finale, using a Polish folk dance. Here Telemann contrasts 'ancient and modern' baroque flute types effectively against each other. The combination of recorder and bassoon is effective too, but the writing for recorder and gamba works less well. The performances here are expert, authentic and stylish, but not all the solo playing is strong in personality and this is an agreeable rather than an indispensable collection.

(i–iii) Double Concerto in E min. for Recorder & Transverse Flute; (iv) Viola Concerto in G; (i; v) Suite in A min. for Flute & Strings; (iii) Overture des nations anciens et modernes in G

(BB) *** Warner Apex (ADD) 0927 40843-2. (i) Brüggen; (ii) Vester; (iii) Amsterdam CO, Rieu; (iv) Doctor, Concerto Amsterdam, Brüggen; (v) Southwest German CO, Tilegant

All these works show Telemann as an original and often inspired craftsman. His use of contrasting timbres in the *Double Concerto* has considerable charm; the *Overture des nations anciens et modernes* is slighter but is consistently and agreeably inventive, and the *Suite in A minor*, one of his best-known works, is worthy of Handel or Bach. Frans Brüggen and Franz Vester are expert soloists and Brüggen shows himself equally impressive on the conductor's podium accompanying Paul Doctor, the rich-timbred soloist in the engaging *Viola Concerto*. The 1960s sound, splendidly remastered, is still superb, with excellent body and presence, and this Apex reissue is a fine bargain.

Concerto in A min. for 3 Treble Recorders & Strings; Paris Quartet 6 in E min.; Quadro in G min.; Sonata in F (Corellisierende); Trio Sonata in B flat

(*) Channel Classics CCS 5093. Florilegium

Instead of recording groups of categorized works, Florilegium often prefer to take a varied cross-section of a composer's output and create an ongoing concert. This works pleasingly here, with a fair amount of instrumental variety, and playing which is sensitive and vigorous by turns. If the well-known *Triple Concerto in A minor* sounds more effective with a larger ripieno, the *Quadro* with its whirlwind *allegros* and memorable central *Adagio* is very successful, as is the opening Corellian pastiche. The group are very well recorded but this is not one of their more memorable collections.

Concertos for Strings: in B flat (Concerto polonaise); in G (Concerto polonaise); Divertimento for Strings in A & B flat; Viola Concerto in G; Double Concerto in G for 2 Violas; Chamber Concerto in G for 2 Solo Violins, 2 Ripeno Violins & Viola

(*) DG 463 074-2. Col. Mus. Ant., Goebel

Both the string concertos with the sobriquet *polonaise* are through-composed, and each is based on a Polish folk dance, although the effect is very German, for here, as in the *Double Viola Concerto*, the ear is often aware of the heavy accenting that Goebel seems to favour. The *Divertimenti* are lighter, each consisting of a series of scherzi, although varying greatly in tempi. The B flat piece includes a *Tempi di minuetto tedesco* and a *Tempo di minuetto francese.*

Easily the finest work here is the *Viola Concerto*, given an impressive period-instrument performance by Florian Deuter, while the delicately textured *Chamber Concerto for Two Solo Violins, Two Ripeno Violins and Viola* is also very engaging, the textures beautifully transparent.

(i) Viola Concerto in G; (ii) Suite in A min. for Recorder & Strings; Tafelmusik, Part 2: (iii) Triple Violin Concerto in F; Part 3: (iv) Double Horn Concerto in E flat

⊛ ✹ (BB) *** Naxos 8.550156. (i) Kyselak; (ii) Stivín; (iii) Hoelblingova, Hoelbling, Jablokov; (iv) Z. & B. Tylšar; Capella Istropolitana, Edlinger

It is difficult to conceive of a better Telemann programme for anyone encountering this versatile composer for the first time and coming fresh to this repertoire, having bought the inexpensive Naxos CD on impulse. Ladislav Kyselak is a fine violist and is thoroughly at home in Telemann's splendid four-movement concerto; Jiři Stivín is an equally personable recorder soloist in the masterly *Suite in A minor*, his decoration is a special joy. The *Triple Violin Concerto* with its memorable *Vivace* finale and the *Double Horn Concerto* also show the finesse which these musicians readily display. Richard Edlinger provides polished and alert accompaniments throughout. The digital sound is first class.

Violin Concertos: in C, D, E, E min., F & G, TWV51:C2; D9 & D10; E2; E3; F2; G8.

(N) *** CPO 999 900-2. Wallfisch, Orfeo Bar. O

Telemann was an excellent fiddler, and he tells us in his autobiography that when preparing to play a concerto he had to lock himself up 'some days before, with the violin in my hand, my shirt sleeve rolled up on my left arm, and with a supply of fortifying (alcoholic) lubrications of the nerves'. Probably some of these concertos were composed for his own use; others must have been intended for his admired older

colleague at the Eisensach Court, Pantaleon Hebenstreit. They require a fair degree of virtuosity and, if less individually original than those of Vivaldi, their invention is consistently stimulating. The opening *Affetuoso* of the C major work here, with the oboe prominent in the orchestra, is particularly appealing, its melody almost Handelian. The other four-movement concertos here are similarly inviting, the D major opening *Con contento* and the E major again marked *Affetuoso*. The three-movement concertos are more conventional, but Telemann's ideas never desert him: the E minor has a fine *Soave* slow movement, framed by lively allegros, and the D major completes the programme engagingly with its galloping finale. Elizabeth Wallfisch is a complete master of this repertoire, playing with plenty of authentic dash and an agreeable expressive lyricism, and at the same time directing vivacious accompaniments from her excellent Baroque Orchestra. The balance is just as it should be.

(i) Violin Concerto in A (Les Rainettes); Overtures (Suites) in B flat (Les Nations); in D TWV 55; in G (La Bizarre)

*** HM HMC 901744. (i) Seiler; Berlin Akademie for Alte Musik

The bluff good humour of Telemann and his fondness for a musical joke are splendidly illustrated in this delightful disc of three of his *Overture/Suites* and a *Violin Concerto* equally spirited with its joky imitation of frogs ('rainettes' in French), which the note suggests might be a take-off of Vivaldi. The *B flat Overture* with its sequence of brief movements celebrating different nations is well enough known, but the jolliest work of all here is the one nicknamed *La Bizarre*, with its deliberate rule-breaking in the fugue of the opening movement. The players of the Berlin Academy of Early Music bring out the fun all the more effectively with the brilliance, precision and energy of their playing, vividly recorded.

Darmstadt Overtures (Suites): for 3 Oboes, Bassoon, & Strings: in C, TWV 55/C6; in D, TWV 55/D15; in G min., TWV 55/G4

(BB) *** Naxos 8.554244. Cologne CO, Müller-Brühl

The modern-instrument performances on Naxos are delightfully vivacious and elegant. This is a first-class chamber orchestra and Müller-Brühl's light rhythmic touch keeps the dance movements sparkling. The recording is excellent. A most entertaining collection.

Don Quixote (Suite burlesque) in G; Concerto for Strings in D; Suite in A for Violin & Strings, TWV 55:A8; Suite in A min. for strings, TWV 55:A7; Suite in D for Viola da gamba & Strings, TWV 55:D6

(*) BIS CD 1226. Drottningholm Bar. Ens.

Don Quixote (Suite burlesque in G); Concerto in D for 2 Violins & Bassoon; Overtures in B min.; G

*** Chan. 0700. Coll. Mus. 90, Standage

Don Quixote (Suite burlesque); Overtures (Suites) in F (Alster); in B flat (La Bourse)

☛ *** Analekta Fleur de Lys FL2 3138. Tafelmusik, Lamon

The *Don Quixote Burlesque* is scored for strings without wind, but Telemann is as resourceful as ever and the portrayal of Sancho Panza is as striking as the gallop of Sancho's donkey. The lively *Windmills* sequence contrasts with the Don's gentle sighs for *Dulcinée*. Not surprisingly the performance of the *Alster Suite* by the superb Tafelmusik under Jean Lamon upstages all the competition, with superbly exuberant horn-playing and especially imaginative echo effects. The pictorial characterization, too, is remarkably vivid, with the frogs leaping and shepherds enjoying their raucous dance music. The vivid performance of *La Bourse* is equally memorable. With outstanding recording, this is one of the most winning of all Telemann orchestral discs.

The Drottningholm performance of *Don Quixote* again shows just how effective period instruments are in etching the music's burlesque portraits, from the Don's ferocious attack on the windmills to his amorous sighing for Dulcinée. The *Suite in A major* also brings a *Passepied burlesque* and the *A minor Suite* offers both a sparking *Rejouissance* and a jolly closing *Harlequinade*. But perhaps the most striking work on the BIS CD after *Don Quixote* is the *Suite with concertante* for *viola da gamba*. All the performance have great vitality, and the rasp of the lower range gives fine support to the bravura of the upper strings. But if you like your baroque music to sound genial, this is not the disc for you, and in any case the Tafelmusic collection is even more enjoyable.

The descriptive *Don Quixote* burlesque is well covered in the catalogue, but this account from Collegium Musicum 90 is among the best; and the other two *Suites*, if not especially individual, are very well played too. The engaging little *Concerto in D* with its string–bassoon solo interplay is also played and recorded most elegantly.

Overtures (Suites) in F (Alster); in F (La Chasse); in G min. (La Musette); in D (for the Jubilee of the Hamburg Admiralty); in D (Ouverture jointe d'une suite tragi-comique)
*** HM HMC 901654. Berlin Akademie für Alte Musik

The opening *Overture in D*, written for the Hamburg Admiralty's centenary celebration, is remarkably like Handel's *Fireworks Music* and makes a festive start to this very attractive Harmonia Mundi period-instrument collection. (The complete work for which it is the prelude is also available – see below.) We have had the *Alster Suite* before, with all its pictorial effects (from the Collegium Musicum 90 on Chandos and Tafelmusik – see above). Sufficient to say that the bravura horn playing is exciting here too, in the *Overture* and *Echo* movement, and the bizarre characterization strong, especially the *Dorfmusik* ('shepherds' music') with its drone, and the balancing delicate evocation of Pan.

In the *Musette Suite* Telemann reuses a drone effect for his fifth movement (hence the sobriquet), but this is otherwise a collection of lively dance vignettes from various national sources, of which the most attractive are the Italian *Napolitaine* and *Harliquinade*.

La Chasse is scored for wind instruments alone, again featuring horns, who have plenty to do. But there is engaging writing for oboes too, and they echo the horns in the *Sarabande*. The *Minuet* closing movement, *Le Plaisir*, pictures the hunting party gathered for drinks when the chase is over.

The atmosphere of the witty *Tragi-comique Suite* depicts human aches and pains, from the gout-stricken *Loure* to a hypochondriac, cured by being forced to dance in swiftly changing style and time-signature, while the brass dauntlessly depict the only general remedy available (apart from a suggested alternative visit to a brothel): *'souffrance héroïque'*. Excellent, lively playing and vivid recording.

Overtures (Suites): La Changeante; Les Nations anciens et modernes; in D
(BB) **(*) Naxos 8.553791. N. CO, Ward

These are agreeably mellow performances on modern instruments, which come into their own in the warmly Handelian lyrical melodies, like the *Avec douceur* from *La Changeante* and the *Plainte* from the *D major Suite for Strings and Horns* (which is the highlight of the disc), and in neatly making the contrasts between the *Ancient and Modern* pairs of movements, the first slow, the second more animated.

Tafelmusik (Productions 1–3) complete
*** DG (IMS) 427 619-2 (4). Col. Mus. Ant., Goebel
(B) **(*) Naxos 8.553724/5 & 8.553731. O of the Golden Age
**(*) MDG 311 0580-2 (3). Camerata of the 18th Century, Hünteler

The playing of the Musiqua Antiqua is distinguished by dazzling virtuosity and unanimity of ensemble and musical thinking. They also have the advantage of very vivid and fresh recording quality; the balance is close and present without being too forward and there is a pleasing acoustic ambience.

The Orchestra of the Golden Age is a new chamber group based in Manchester, playing with a good sense of style, plenty of life and a convincing linear manner in expressive music. They represent one of Naxos's first excusions into period-instrument music-making and are very well recorded. While Harnoncourt and Reinhard Goebel's versions have something special to offer in this music, this Naxos set is excellent value and will give considerable satisfaction.

The Camerata of the 18th Century are based in Amsterdam. They too give expert performances of this repertoire which show an appealing affectionate warmth. But they are recorded in a fairly resonant church acoustic and, although this gives a pleasing added warmth and makes the overall effect more orchestral, with less chamber intimacy, inner detail is less readily revealed. But the solo playing is highly felicitous and many listeners will enjoy the fuller string textures here.

Water Music (Hamburger Ebb' und Fluth)
*** Hyp. CDA 66967. King's Cons., King – HANDEL: *Water Music* ***

Telemann's *Water Music* is rightly one of his most popular works, and it is good to have a thoroughly recommendable period-instrument performance available and aptly coupled with Handel.

The King's Consort performance is most enjoyable. There is exhilarating playing from the oboes in the Overture and the following Sarabande (with recorders) is seductive, as is the later Minuet (*Der angeneheme Zephir*). In short, this is excellent in every way. It is coupled with the *Water Music* of Handel.

CHAMBER MUSIC

6 Concertos & 6 Suites (1734) for Flute, Violin, Viola da gamba, or Cello & Harpsichord (Lute or Organ)
*** CPO 999 690-2 (3). Camerata Köln

This remarkable set of four-movement *Concertos* and seven- or eight-movement *Suites*, published by Telemann in Hamburg in 1734, was resourcefully written so that in each case the four parts could be played by a varying combination of instruments, which is what happens here, with sometimes only three instruments in use, sometimes four. This adds variety and freshness to music which constantly shows the composer's astonishing musical fertility. Throughout, the ear is always entertained, when the period-instrument playing is so expert, with the musicians clearly enjoying themselves. As an example, the four *Airs* that conclude *Suite No. 1* (*Dolce, Allegro, Spiritoso*, the charming *Piacevole* and the closing *Allegro*) are all ear-tickling, and, throughout, the more expansive concerto slow movements always have memorable expressive content, as in the *Adagio* of *Concerto No. 3*, the engaging *Dolce* of *Concerto No. 4* or the delicate *Gratioso* of *Concerto No. 5*. The recording is excellent.

Fantasias for Solo Treble Recorder in C; D min.; G min.; A min.; B flat, TWV 40/2, 4, 9, 11 & 12. Sonatas for Treble Recorder & Continuo: Esercizi musici. Sonatas in C, TWV 41:C5; D min., TWV 41:d4; Der getreue Music-Meister: Canonic Sonata in B flat, TWV 41:B3; Sonatas in C, TWV 41:C2; F, TWV 41:F2; F min., TWV 41:f1

(BB) *** Warner Apex 2564 60368-2. Brüggen, Bylsma, Leonhardt

The 12 solo *Fantasias* were actually written for transverse flute, but Frans Brüggen plays them very effectively on the treble recorder, transposing them up a minor third in order to do so. The *Sonatas for Treble Recorder and Continuo* are all most winning and well chosen to show the composer at his most inventive, and are played with breathtaking virtuosity and a marvellous sense of style. The sound is excellent.

12 Fantasias for Unaccompanied Violin (complete)

(M) *** Maya MCD 9302. Homburger

Telemann's *12 Fantasias* for solo violin are a decade later than Bach's *Partitas* and *Sonatas*, and they are less ambitious and less demanding. Each is in either three or four movements, usually opening with a *Largo* or *Grave*, alternating with *Allegros*. With striking invention, they make very enjoyable listening, especially when played with such life and style. Maya Homburger uses a baroque violin and has joined in recordings with the Academy of Ancient Music, English Baroque Soloists and the English Concert. This is cheerful music and it would be difficult to imagine these works being played more freshly or with a more sensitive espressivo. Homburger is recorded most naturally against a warm but not too resonant acoustic, and there is not a trace of vinegar in her timbre.

Der getreue Music-Meister (complete)

⌐ ✪ (M) *** DG 476 1852 (4). Mathis, Töpper, Haefliger, Unger, McDaniel, Würzburg Bach Ch., Instrumental soloists, including Linde, Tarr, Melkus, Schäffer, Van der Ven, Ulsamer

We award a ✪ for sheer enterprise to DG's Archiv division for recording (in 1966–7) a 'complete' version of Telemann's *Der getreue Music-Meister* ('The Constant Music Master'), which has been called the first musical periodical. Other composers were invited to contribute, thus the present box includes a lute piece by Weiss, a *Gigue sans basse* by Pisandel and an ingenious choral canon by Zelenka. There is also a great deal of refreshing instrumental music of Telemann with the widest variety of instrumentation, with various combinations of recorder, flute, oboe, chalumeau, bassoon, trumpet and various stringed instruments, including a *Burlesque suite* for two violins ingeniously depicting scenes from *Gulliver's Travels*. The operatic arias from *Eginhard, Belsazar* and *Sacio* are of considerable interest, while the comic fable from *Aesopus* concerns 'The she-goat's wooing of the lion'. Sixty-two pieces are recorded here. Performances are almost invariably of

excellent quality, and Edith Mathis and Ernst Haefliger stand out among the vocal soloists. Excellent documentation includes full vocal texts. The recording sounds delightfully fresh and natural, and it is now most welcome back to the catalogue in Universal Classics' 'Penguin ✪ Collection' at mid-price.

Kleine Cammermusic (6 Partitas for Violin, Flute or Oboe Continuo)

(M) *** CPO 999 497-2. Camerata Köln

The six *Partitas* of the *Kleine Cammermusik*, published in 1716, were written – as was the composer's policy – to be playable by three alternative solo instruments with harpsichord. Each consists of an opening slow introduction, followed by a group of six *Arias* (or airs), varying in style and tempo. As ever, Telemann never seems to run out of attractive ideas and here the works are allotted in turn to oboe (Nos. 1 and 3, both delightful, the latter with a lovely opening *Adagio*), flute (No. 2, which opens *dolce* with a charming *Siciliana*, and is worthy of comparison with Bach), viola da gamba (No. 4 and very well chosen), violin (No. 5) and recorder (No. 6, with organ continuo, and another of the most attractive). The performances here could hardly be bettered and they are beautifully balanced and recorded. The variety of instrumentation makes this one of the most enticing of all the Telemann chamber music CDs.

Overtures (Suites) for 2 Oboes, 2 Horns, Bassoon and Double Bass in F: (La Joie); in F (La Fortune); in F (La Chasse), TWV55:F5; F8; F9; in F, TWV55: F15 & F18

*** MDG 301 1109-2. Consortium Classicum

Telemann wrote many works for wind ensemble but only ten Overture/Suites have survived, five of which are offered here. They are all essentially in the same pattern of five or six movements although the dances vary between them. One would have expected the work nicknamed *La Chasse* to have the most spectacular horn parts, but in the event *La Fortune* and *La Joie* are the most impressive in this respect and the two works without nicknames are just as inventive as those with a sobriquet, with TWV 55:F18 the most attractive of all. The playing here is expert and full of life, but with similar sonorities throughout and all the works in the key of F, this is a CD to dip into rather than play right through. Excellent recording.

Paris Flute Quartets 1–6 (1730) (for flute, violine, viola da gamba & continuo)

⌐ *** HM HMC 901787. Freiburg Bar. Cons.

The splendid Freiburg Baroque Consort (including the exceedingly nimble flautist Karl Kaiser), drawn from the excellent orchestra of that name, give first-class period-instrument performances of these delightful works, and the recording is excellent. An outstanding disc in every way.

6 Nouveaux Paris Flute Quartets (1738)

(B) *** Virgin 2x1 5 61812-2 (2). Trio Sonnerie

In 1730 Telemann published in Hamburg a set of six quartets for violin, flauto traverso, viola da gamba and bass continuo, and these were sufficiently popular to be pirated by the French publishing house, Le Clerk, and reprinted in 1736 – without the composer's permission. Telemann learned by this experience: during a long and fruitful visit to Paris in 1737–8, by virtue of a Privilège du Roi, he was able himself to publish a new and even finer set, which he called *Nouveaux quatuors*.

The performances on Virgin are of a high calibre and are representative of modern practice, using original instruments and bringing lighter textures and greater delicacy of style. Thus, they have a different kind of charm. Tempi with this group are almost always brisker, with both losses and gains. The Trio Sonnerie are led by the expert Monica Huggett, and their timbre is cleaner, more transparent, perhaps slightly less substantial than that of Quadro Amsterdam, but who can say which is the more authentic? Certainly, the results on Virgin Veritas are refreshingly different, while the sound is truthful and again very well balanced.

Paris Quartets (1730): 2, Concerto secondo in D; 3, Sonata prima in A; 4, Sonata seconda in G min.; 5, Première suite in E min. Fantasias: 5 in A for (solo) Violin; 7 in D for (solo) Flute; 8 in G min. for Harpsichord
𝄞⟶ *** Channel Classics CCS 13598. Florilegium

Instead of providing a set, Florilegium have chosen four of the earlier quartets and set them in the context of a concert, interspersed with solo *Fantasias*. They play with affectionate warmth, readily bringing out shades of melancholy in slow movements, to contrast with the busy allegros, played with real virtuosity, with the tone of Ashley Solomon's period flute particularly enticing. But the timbre and clean articulation of the two string players, Rachel Podger (violin) and Daniel Yeadon (viola da gamba), are hardly less appealing, and the overall blend of tone in a warm but intimate acoustic could not be more attractive. These players convey a deep expressive feeling.

6 Flute Quartets or Trios (Hamburg, 1733). Der Getreu Musikmeister: Cello Sonata (for cello and continuo) in D
**(*) Lyrichord LEMS 8028. Mélomanie

Telemann himself published his *Six quatuors ou trios*, ensuring their success by making them available for performance on various alternative combinations of flutes, violins, bassoon and cello, with a flexible continuo. This is their first complete recording. The collection divides into two groups. The first three works are three- or four-movement sonatas in an elegant conversational style; the last three each open with a slow movement followed by three unpredictable 'Divertimenti', showing the composer imaginatively trying out different dance forms. The four-movement *Cello sonata* offered as bonus also shows the composer at his best. It is very well played, as are the Quartets (favouring two period flutes – not always absolutely immaculate in tuning – cello and harpsichord).

Paris Flute Quartets, Book 4 (c.1752): Sonatas 1–6
**(*) Globe GLO 5146. Hazelzet, Stuurop, Have, Ogg, Scheifes

Although they are listed in the *New Grove*, there is some doubt about the authenticity of these simple, four-movement works, which the composer designated as *Sonatas*. They are not trivial, but pleasingly inventive, with a charming simplicity. If they are Telemann's, he probably wrote them earlier than the published date. Wilbert Hazelzet uses a modern copy of a mid-eighteenth-century flute, and his nimble playing, with immaculate tuning, and decorative flourishes (never overdone) readily tweak the ear. His supporting group provide a somewhat insubstantial (though not edgy) backing, but the solo playing is so adept and full of personality that one accepts Hazelzet's ready domination of the proceedings.

Quartets (Concertos) for Flute, Bassoon, Viola da gamba & Continuo: in B min., TWV 43:b3; in C TWV 43:C2; Quartet in G for Flute, 2 Violas da gamba, TWV 43:G12; Trio Sonatas: in F for Violin, Viola da gamba & Continuo, TWV 42:F10 in G min., for Flute, Viola da gamba & Continuo, TWV42:G7 (from Darmstadt manuscripts)
*** Astrée Auvidis E 8632. Limoges Bar. Ens., Coin

All these manuscripts come from the Darmstadt Library, and the two most attractive quartets (which include a bassoon) bear the additional title *Concerto*. All five works here are in the four-movement Italian *sonata di chiesa* form (slow-fast-slow-fast), although the *Trio Sonata in G minor* has additionally a characteristic opening *Siciliana*. Although the allegros are lively enough, the pervading mood is often attractively dolorous, and the intimacy of the excellent performances enhances that impression. Very good recording.

Quadros (Quartets): in A min. for Recorder, Oboe, Violin & Continuo, TWV 43:a3; in G, for Recorder, Oboe, Violin & Continuo, TWV 43:g6; in G min. for Oboe, Violin, Viola da gamba & Continuo, TWV43:g92; in G min. for Recorder, Violin, Viola da gamba & Continuo, TWV43:g94. Esercizi musici: Trio Sonatas: in C min. for Recorder, Oboe & Continuo, TWV 42:c2; in F for Recorder, Viola da gamba & Continuo, TWV 42:f3. Trio Sonata in D min. for Recorder, Violin & Continuo, TWV 42:d10
𝄞⟶ *** Globe GLO 5154. Ens. Senario

These *Quadros* (or Quartets) are among Telemann's very finest chamber music, every bit as inventive and diverting as the more famous *Paris* quartets. Telemann writes parts of equal interest for all three of his solo instruments, and provides slow movements of considerable expressive intensity, framed by winningly virtuosic allegros. Perhaps finest of all is the G major Quartet, with its solemn central *Grave*, but the G minor Quartet (TWV 43:g94), which opens the programme, is hardly less seductive. Telemann subtitles the A minor work 'Concerto', and indeed there is plenty of opportunity for virtuoso display here, and its four movements also include a pair of touching *Adagios*. The Trio Sonatas, slighter in texture, are also very enjoyable when presented so freshly. Indeed, the performances here could hardly be bettered. The brilliant recorder playing of Saskia Coolen is well matched by the oboist, Peter Frankenberg, and the group overall integrates splendidly. The balance and recording could hardly be improved on.

Sonatas for 2 Flutes, TWV 40: 130–35
**(*) Lyrichord LEMS 8019. Reighley, Moore

Telemann wrote four sets of sonatas for two flutes, all designed for amateurs to play and enjoy, for they do not make too many bravura demands. However, this fourth series (which remained unpublished but which probably dates from the end of the 1730s or the beginning of the 1740s) uses keys that were more difficult for the one-keyed flute of that time, so these works were clearly aimed at players with fair performance skills. They are each in four movements, and the slow movement is usually marked *Dolce* or *Amoroso*. They are well presented here on period instruments although, amiable as it is, this is music to take in small doses.

Recorder Sonatas: Esercizi musici: in C, TWV 41:C5; D min., TWV 41:D2. Der Getreue Musikmeister: in A/B flat TWV41:B3 (Canonic Sonata), TWV 41:A3; in C, TWV 41:C2;

in F, TWV 41:F2; in F min., TWV 41:F1; Neue Sonatinen; in A min., TWV 41:A4; in C min., TWV 41:C2. Sonatina in F min., TWV41:D4

(N) *** Cap. 67 070. Michael & Annette Schneider, Beuse, Imamura, Bauer

**(*) Globe GLO 5151. Ehrlich, Egarr, Levy

Both Capriccio and Globe offer what are described as Telemann's 'complete sonatas for recorder and continuo', two of which derive from the *Esercizi musici* and four from *Der Getreue Musikmeister*. Like the comparable Naxos collection of recorder concertos, there is the danger here of unvarying sameness of timbre. Both sets of performances are stylish and the recorder playing is nimble and highly musical. But on the whole we are inclined to give our vote to the Capriccio set, which features a bassoon in the excerpts from *Der Getreue Musikmeister* and employs a continuo using a lute and clavierorganum.

On Globe, Robert Ehrlich's authentic recorder image is small, which partly limits his range, while the use of a viola da gamba, while it makes an effective interplay with the recorder in the *Canonic Sonata*, offers less variety of colour. Both recordings are well balanced and truthful.

Sonatas for 2 Recorders 1–6; Duetto in B flat
*** BIS CD 334. Pehrsson, Laurin

Canon Sonatas 1–6; Duettos 1–6
*** BIS CD 335. Pehrsson, Laurin

All the *Duet Sonatas* are in four movements, the second being a fugue; the *Canon Sonatas* are for two flutes, violins or bass viols. Needless to say, listening to two recorders for longer than one piece at a time imposes a strain on one's powers of endurance, no matter how expert the playing – and expert it certainly is. The BIS versions can be recommended. However, although it is good to have the two treble recorders blending so well together, a clearer degree of separation would have helped in the imitative writing.

Sonata Metodiche 1–6 (1728); 7–12 (1732)
*** Accent ACC 94104/5D (2). B. and W. Kuijken, Kohnen

Telemann's *Methodical Sonatas* were written in two sets of six, the first designated 'for violin or flute', the second 'for flute or violin', which is a curious alternation of emphases, the more so as the second set sometimes uses keys that are less comfortable for the baroque flute. Not that this is apparent in these expert performances, lively and expressive by turns, and there is plenty of variety in the music itself. One of the purposes of these sonatas was to instruct amateurs in the art of ornamentation, so Telemann wrote out ornaments in the French style for each first movement, while mixing French and Italian styles in the writing itself. A worthwhile addition to the catalogue, very well recorded.

6 Trios (1718): 1 (Oboe & Violin); 2 (Recorder & Violin); 3 (Flute & Violin); 4 (2 Violins); 5 (Violin & Viola da gamba); 6 (2 Violins), TWV:42:B1, a1, G1, D1, g1, & F1
(N) *** CPO 999 957-2 Camerata Köln

Trio Sonatas 1–6, TWV43:G3, c1, A2, d2, e1, D4; Trio Sonata in B flat for Violin, Bassoon & Continuo, TWV42:B5; Bassoon Quartet in E min., TWV43:E3.
(N) *** CPO 999 934-2. Parnassi Musici, with Azzolini

The two CPO collections above are linked, for the composition of the *6 Trios of 1718* served Telemann as a prototype for establishing the format of the *Trio Sonatas* which followed in

the 1720s. Each work has a different instrumental combination, and Telemann resourcefully finds suitable ideas to match his lead instrument. All but two of the six are in the four-movement *sonata da chiesa* format, which brings an opportunity for extra variety. The work for oboe is an exception, with a central *Siciliana*, but the sprightly *Trios* for flute and recorder each begin with a characteristic *Affetuoso*. The use of the viola da gamba brings darker textures, especially in the *Grave* slow movement, and the very fluent work for a pair of violins also has more depth and gravitas. The three-movement *Trio* for the violin, cello and continuo brings a particularly stimulating dialogue between the two string soloists in the opening movement, to anticipate the regular use of this combination by many other composers in the future. Performances are excellent.

Having experimented with various instrumentations, Telemann settled on the combination of two violins (or two flutes as a possible alternative) and wrote trio sonatas essentially derived from Corelli's Italian style (and advertised as such on publication). These *Sonatas* show Telemann at his finest. Allegros are full of bouncing vitality and the slow movements are often delicately charming, as in the *Dolce* opening of No. 1 or the *Cantabile* of No. 3. The employment here of an organ continuo makes its mark most attractively in the delicate *Lento* of No. 2. The two works with bassoon bring a jaunty geniality and another winning *Cantabile* in TWV43, while the closing *Presto* of the *F major Sonata* ends the concert vivaciously. The performances are outstandingly fine, full of life and with a graceful elegance, and they are ideally recorded in a friendly but not too resonant acoustic. The only irritating feature of this latter disc is the absence of dividing bands for the individual movements (as indicated in the documentation).

6 Trio Sonatas in the Italian Style (Sonates en Trios dans le Goût Italien) TWV 42: g3; c1; a2; d2; e1; d4; Trio Sonata in G, TWV 42: g12
*** Lyrichord LEMS 8035. Moore, Myford, Fournier, Palumbo

Telemann had altogether greater success with his *Trio Sonatas in the Italian Style* than he did with his Corelli imitations. They are pleasingly lightweight, sunny works, played here with the second part authentically given to the violin rather than a flute. The *C minor* and *A major* works are particularly attractive, but the standard of invention is high, and particularly striking in the minor-key works. They are most felicitously played by this very musical period-instrument group, who know all about elegance, and very well balanced. Tom Moore's baroque flute has a most agreeably watery timbre that is wholly authentic.

COLLECTIONS

Music for Flute: *Der Getrue Musikmeister: Capriccio for Flute & Continuo; Concertos in A min. & B min. for Harpsichord, Flute, Cello & Lute; Dolce & Largo e misurato for Flute and Cello. Fantasias 3 in B min.; 10 in F sharp min.; Solo in B min. (all for flute); Sinfonie à la française in B min. for Flute & Continuo*
(B) **(*) Glossa 2-CD GCD 2KO803 (2). Hazelzet, Ter Linden, Junghänel, Ogg

It is difficult to fault the playing on this disc by this esteemed group of musicians who are well versed in baroque repertoire. They play vivaciously, expertly and expressively (Hazelzet's solos are a highlight as are the *Gayment* and the brief *Sinfonie à la française*). They are well recorded, too. Yet at times one feels that there could be more charm.

Music for Oboe & Continuo: (i) *'Dresden' Sonata for Oboe & Bassoon, TWV 41:g10. Esercizi musici: Sonatas in B flat, TWV 41:B6; E min., TWV 41:e6. Trio Sonata in E flat. Der getrue Musikmeister: Sonata in A min., TWV 41:a3. Tafelmusik: Sonata in G min. for Oboe & Bassoon, TWV 41:g6*

● (M) *** Somm SOMMCD 236. Francis, Jordan, Powell, Dodd; (i) with Beach

This admirable Somm collection, in which Sarah Francis is the star performer, draws on both the *Esercizi musici* and *Der getrue Musikmeister* (see below) and includes an extra sonata found in a Dresden manuscript. It has an engaging *Alla breve* second movement where the interplay between oboe and bassoon is particularly felicitous. The *Trio Sonata* is comparably winning with an obbligato harpsichord part, played here delightfully by Howard Beach. Of the sonatas for oboe and a normal continuo the B flat work from the *Esercizi musici* includes a lovely *Cantabile* in which the cellist, Margaret Powell, plays beautifully, while the *A minor Sonata* from *Der getrue Musikmeister* has a delightful opening *Siciliana*. In short, this is an ideal way of sampling this repertoire which shows the composer at his freshest and most inventive, and the use of the bassoon rather than the cello continuo in two of the sonatas makes for a pleasing diversity. Excellent, very well-balanced recording.

Music for Oboe and Continuo: *Esercizi musici: Solo V in B flat; Solo XI in E min.; Trio 12 in E. XXI. Der getreue Music-Meister: Lesson 17, Sonata in A min. Harmonischer Gottes-Dienst: 26, Am Sonntage Jubilate in C min.; 31, Am ersten Pfingstfeiertage in G. Kleine Cammermusic: Partita 2*

(*) HM HMU 907152. Goodwin, North, Sheppard, Toll, Cranham

Music for Oboe and Continuo: *Esercizi musici: Trio Sonata in E flat. Der getreue Music-Meister: Lesson 17, Sonata in A min. Kleine Cammermusic: Partita 4 in G min. Tafelmusic: Trio Sonata in G min. Concerto in D for Trumpet, 2 Oboes & Continuo; Sonata in G min. for 2 Oboes & Continuo*

(*) Accent ACC 9511OD. Ponseele, Kitazato, Lindeke, Jacobs, Richte Van Der Meer, Hantal

After the success of *Kleine Cammermusic* (see above) in 1716, Telemann went on in 1725 to publish the *Harmonischer Gottes-Dienst*, twenty-seven sacred cantatas, accompanied by violin, oboe, flute or recorder with continuo. Here the vocal line is effectively allotted to a baroque cello. In 1728 he offered the first instalment of *Der getreue Music-Meister*, a kind of music magazine, including a varied anthology of solos, duets, trios, suites *et al.*, which invited contributions from other composers, of which Bach was one.

The very ambitious *Esercizi musici* followed in 1739, and probably represents the peak of Telemann's output of solos and trio sonatas. Paul Goodwin's selection from these various publications has been well made, notably the *Esercizi musici*, while the excerpts from *Harmonischer Gottes-Dienst* (each of two movements) are especially characterful, and both the *Sonata in A minor* from *Der getreue Music-Meister* and the *Partita No. 2* from *Kleine Cammermusic* include memorable *Sicilianas*, which suit the baroque oboe so well. The performances are of high musical quality and are very well recorded. But it was a pity that other solo instruments could not have been included to provide more diversity.

The Accent collection offers a similar repertoire, again very well played and recorded in authentic style, and the programme does mitigate the lack of variety of timbre by including a work featuring a baroque trumpet (with a timbre of the 'throttled' kind), and also a charming *Trio Sonata*, including a pair of oboes who converse animatedly together. Even so the Harmonia Mundi performances have rather more personality and are marginally to be preferred.

Esercizi musici: Solo 2: Flute Sonata in D; Solo 4: Recorder Sonata in D min. Solo 5: Chalumeau Sonata in B flat; Solo 8: Flute Sonata in G. Der getreue Musick-Meister: Bassoon Sonata in F min. Tafelmusik, Part III: Oboe Sonata in G min. Harpsichord Fantasias: in E min. & F, Set 1/4–5; Harpsichord Overture in G min.

*** Mer. CDE 84347. Badinage

This is an ideal way of assembling a concert of Telemann's chamber and instrumental music, not centring on a single instrument, but making a hand-picked selection of music (much of it from the *Solos* in the *Esercizi musici*) featuring a wide range of instrumental colour, from the dolorous bassoon and the piquantly watery timbre of the primitive chalumeaux to the brighter recorder and flute. All the soloists here are expert, and the fine harpsichordist provides interludes, lively and *dolce* at three strategic points in the programme. The recording is excellent.

KEYBOARD MUSIC

6 Overtures for Harpsichord, TWV 32:5/10

(M) ** CPO 999 645-2. Hoeren (harpsichord)

Telemann's six *Overtures* were published between 1745 and 1749. Each is in three movements, beginning grandly in the French style (the rhythm dotted) and moving on to a toccata-like fugato. The central movement is usually marked *Largo e scherzando*, and each work ends with a lovely presto. This layout was regarded as a feature of the 'Polish style', often incorporating local rhythmic influences, for Telemann said: 'A Polish song sets the whole world a-jumping.' Harald Hoeren plays boldly on a modern copy of a Flemish harpsichord from around 1750. He is suitably vigorous in allegros, yet is inclined to be rhythmically metric elsewhere.

Music for harpsichord and chamber organ: (i) *Overture in G min.; Fantasias II in C; VII in G min.; IX in B min.; X in D; XII in E flat; Suite in A; Esercizi musici: Solo in F.* (ii) *6 Chorale Preludes; 3 Little Fugues*

*** Mer. CDE 84333. Gifford (i) harpsichord; (ii) chamber organ

Gerald Gifford has already given us an attractive compilation of the keyboard repertoire of Johann Krebs. The lion's share of the music here is for harpsichord, played on a modern copy (by Philip Smart of Oxford) of a Hemsch instrument dating from 1756. While Gifford cannot wholly be absolved from a metrical approach to the opening *Overture in G minor*, elsewhere his playing is attractively buoyant, helped by the vivid sound of the instrument itself.

The splendid *A major Suite* was admired by Bach, for it was found copied into the *Klavierbüchlein* for Wilhelm Friedman, while the *Solo* from the *Esercizi musici* is an even more generous collection of dances, prefaced by a *Cantabile* rather than a French overture. The three-movement *Fantasias* are each attractively inventive, and all this keyboard music is played spiritedly and in fine style.

The organ *Chorale Preludes* are much less elaborate than Bach's, but they are piquantly registered, and the presentation of the three simple *Fugues* is similarly colourful. All in all, this makes an excellent survey, very well recorded, which can be highly recommended.

Organ music: 6 Chorale Preludes; Fantasia in D; Pasacaille in B min.; Sonata in D for 2 Manuals & Pedal; Concerto in G min. (trans. Bach as *BWV 985*); **Concerto per la chiesa on G** (trans. J. G. Walther)
(*) MDG 320 0078-2. Baumgratz (Bach organ, Bremer Dom)

This collection opens commandingly with the *Concerto in G minor*, attributed to Telemann, and transcribed by Bach. But it is such a magnificent tripartite piece that one is tempted to believe that there is more Bach in it than Telemann. The *Passacaglia* that follows, with its decoration increasingly florid, moves to a fair climax, and the four *Chorale Preludes* that come next (each in two sections) are agreeably managed, *Komm heiliger Geist* easily the most telling, especially the jaunty second part. However, the pair of chorales based on *Nun freut euch lieben Christen g'mein*, brief as they may be, show Telemann nearer to Bach in his manipulation of variations around a clear cantus firmus.

The *D major Sonata* sounds like an arrangement of a trio sonata, and the three-part *Fantasia*, with its characteristic central *Dolce*, is much more impressive. Finally comes J. G. Walther's transcription of the *G major Concerto per la chiesa*, which has an effective opening fugato, but springs fully to life, in organ terms, only in the finale. Wolfgang Baumgratz makes the most of all this music by registering brightly and imaginatively, and he is very well recorded. But this collection serves to confirm that Telemann's talent lay not with the organ, but with the baroque orchestra and in the world of chamber music.

VOCAL MUSIC

Ach, Herr, straf mich nicht in deinem Zorn; Ach wie nichtig, ach wie flüchtig; Du, aber, Daniel, gehe hin; Sei getreu bis in den Tod. (In Festo Penticost): Schaffe in mir, Gott ein reines Herz (Trauer-Actus Cantatas)
*** HM HMC 901768. Koslowsky, Popoen, Jochens, Mammel, Shreckenberger, Cantus Cölln, Junghänel

These cantatas date from Telemann's earliest composing years (1697–1708), and although they are simple in style, they already show his remarkable skill and melodic talent. The adagio close of the funeral cantata, *Du aber, Daniel, gehe hin*, is introduced by flute and oboe, *Schlaft wohl, ihr seligen Gebeine* is wonderfully serene while in *Sei gettreu bis in den Tod*, the lovely alto aria *Dich lieb ich allein* is in no way immature. It is followed by a light-hearted soprano aria and another expressive aria for tenor. In the five-movement Pentecost Cantata a tenor aria and a touching soprano/alto duet are framed and interwoven by three simple choruses. The performances here are dedicated and the soloists are excellent, and this well-recorded and enterprising collection throws new light on a truly remarkable composer.

Die Auferstehung (The Resurrection): Easter Oratorio; Cantata: De Danske, Norske og Tydske Undersaaters Glaede (The Joy of the Danish, Norwegian and German Citizens)
*** CPO 999 634-2. Mields, Schwarz, Post, Mertens, Decker, Magdeburg Chamber Ch., Michaelstein Telemann CO, Rémy

Telemann's *Easter Oratorio* of 1761 has an appealing simplicity. It opens without preamble with a solo lament from the soprano, and only then does the chorus enter, joyfully asserting 'The Lord Has Risen'. The bass then tells of the angel arriving 'fast as a flash of lightning' (illustrated by a brilliant violin obbligato) and the narrative continues with the alto and chorus dramatically describing the despair of Hell, while the reappearance of the risen Christ is depicted in a lovely soprano aria (beautifully sung here by Dorothee Mields). The Resurrection is then further celebrated in fine expressive arias from tenor and bass, before the joyful closing chorus with trumpets.

The reconstructed cantata celebrating the birthday of the Danish King Frederick V, written four years earlier, was a curious choice of coupling, but it is a happy work. The text alternates verses in Danish, German and Latin with lyrical solos, pleasingly small-scale choruses and a rather engaging soprano-bass duet before the closing chorus. Both performances here are first class, with a sensitive team of soloists and excellent support from the fine chorus and orchestra. The recording is very well balanced, spacious and natural.

Betrachtung der 9 Stunde an dem Todstage Jesu (Passion Oratorio); Cantatas: Ein Mensch is in seinem Leben wie Gras, TWV 4:18; Herr, ich habe lieb die Stätte deines Hauses, TWV 2:2
*** CPO 999 500-2. Zádori, Jochens, Wessel, Cordier, Wimmer, Schreckenberger, Van der Kamp, Rheinisch Kantorei, Kleine Konzert, Max

Telemann's *Passion Cantata, Reflection of the Ninth Hour on the Day of Jesus's Death* (with a text by Joachim Zimmerman) is an unusual conception, in that the figure who is involved in these personal reflections is not a biblical character but a poetic creation, who provides a reflective meditation on the events surrounding the Crucifixion. Telemann added three chorales to create a binding structure and the vocal observations are not centred on a single soloist but four, with tenor, alto and two basses together providing the introduction. The first bass aria, *Whither then in vain you impudent people*, boldly accompanied by horns, dramatically sets the scene, and each soloist continues the reflective commentary, the work ending with a philosophical bass aria of acceptance, and a reassuring closing chorale. If the musical result is less imaginative than the conception, the work is still well worth hearing, as are the pair of contrasted canatatas with which it is coupled, which show Telemann's invention at its freshest. All three pieces are very well sung and accompanied, and the recording is well up to the high standard of this excellent CPO series.

Cantatas for the first Sunday of Advent: Saget den verzagten Herzen, TWV 1:1233; Saget der Tochter Zion, TWV 1: 1235. Cantatas for the first day of Christmas: Auf Zion! Und lass in geheilgten Hallen, TWV 1: 109; Kündlich gross ist das Gottselige Geheimnis, TWV 1: 1020
*** CPO 999 515-2. Mields, Schwarz, Jochens, Schmidt, Magdeburg Chamber Ch., Michaelstein Telemann CO, Rémy

This is marginally the finest of Ludger Rémy's series of Telemann's festive cantatas so far. The opening of *Saget den verzagten Herzen* brings a splendid interchange between soloists and chorus, and the following alto aria (marked *Affettuoso*), *So komm den auch*, is touchingly eloquent, while the bass and tenor soloists both have lively arias to follow. The bravura bass aria, *Zerstreuet euch*, which opens *Saget der Tochter Zion*, has even more brilliant trumpet parts, and the opening bass aria of *Auf Zion*, decorated with flutes, is equally memorable. The Christmas story is then told in a series of brief recitatives and choruses, much more atmospheric and dramatic than the so-called 'Christmas Oratorio' (see below). The second of the two Christmas Day cantatas, *Kündlich gross ist das Gottselige Geheimnis*, is even more dramatic and has a remarkable soprano aria punctuated by trumpets and drums. The alto air *Göttlich Kind* is a Handelian alto and trumpet duet, and the trumpets stay for the bass aria. Rémy directs with flair, and with strikingly good male soloists, fine choral singing and first-rate playing from his period-instrument accompanying group, this is well worth seeking out. The documentation (as throughout the series) is impeccable, including full translations.

Christmas Oratorio: *Die Hirten on der Krippe zu Bethlehem*, TWV 1:797; *Christmas Cantatas: Siehe, ich verkündige Euc* (1761), TWV 1:1334; *Der Herr hat offenbaret* (1762): TWV 1: 262

**(*) CPO 999 419-2. Backes, George, Post, Mertens, Michaelstein Chamber Ch. & Telemann CO, Rémy

The so-called 'Christmas Oratorio' opens with the chorale we know as *In dulci jubilo*, fully scored with trumpets, to the words, *O Jesu parvule* – and is simply structured and comparatively unambitious, with the chorus interleaving the arias with chorales. Flutes and trumpets are used to decorate the pastoral scenes. There is a fine bass aria welcoming the shepherds. But the cantatas are much more ambitious. The 1761 work opens arrestingly with a brilliant soprano aria when the angel sings those famous words '*Behold I bring you glad tidings*' with trumpets blazing, and she is answered dramatically by the choral heavenly host, who return to praise God after fine contributions from both the tenor and bass. The 1762 cantata opens and closes with a chorus, and the following arias for soprano and bass (again using trumpets and flutes) are both rather fine. Fortunately, the soloists here are again excellent and if the conductor of the small period-instrument ensemble is at times rhythmically a bit emphatic in the oratorio, he keeps the music alive and flowing. The recording is excellent.

Cornett cantatas: *Cantata for the 2nd Sunday after Epiphany: Sehet an die Exempel der Alten*, TWV 1: 1259; *Cantata for Exaudi Sunday: Ich halte aber dafür*, TWV 1: 840; *Cantata for Rogation Sunday: Erhöre mich, wenn ich rufe*, TWV 1: 459

*** CPO 999 542-2. Spägele, Vass, Jochens, Mertens, Leipzig Bläser Collegium, Michaelstein Telemann CO, Rémy

The rich textures Telemann creates are very much his own, not like Gabrieli, rather nearer to Schütz. In consequence, he does not demand a chorus, and the chorales are sung by the soloists, never more effectively than at the end of the *Epiphany cantata*, following a fine soprano aria. Telemann uses his colourful ripieno imaginatively throughout, especially so in the *Rogation cantata*, which is shared by tenor and bass. Wilfried Jochens and Klaus Mertens are in splendid form and make the most of all their opportunities, especially their fine penultimate duet, richly embroidered by the brass and wind, *Herr, auf dein Wort verlass ich mich*, which is again followed by the closing chorale. The *Cantata for Exaudi Sunday* opens with a spectacular polyphonic interplay, shared by singers and orchestra, and after an alto recitative the

cornetti decorate the bass aria, while oboes are used later for the alto solo, and the work closes with a serene Martin Luther hymn. If the invention in these works is less dramatic than in the *Advent* and *Christmas cantatas*, many of the individual numbers are lyrically very persuasive, especially when they are so well sung and so musically accompanied by this strikingly well-balanced period-instrument ensemble under the excellent Ludger Rémy.

(i) *Fortsetzung des Harmonischen Gottesdienstes: Cantatas 5: Ein Jammerton, en schluchzend Ach*, TWV1:424; 35: *Ertrage nur das Joch des Mängel*, TWV1:479; 42: *Die Glut des Zorns*, TWV1:331; 48: *Da, Jesu, Deinen Ruhm zu mehren*, TWV1:531:67; *Mein Glaube ringt in letzten Zügen*, TWV:184; (ii) *20 Little Fugues for Organ*, TWV30:6, 8, 20 & 30

(N) *** CPO 999 764-2. (i) Ziesak, Camerata Köln; (ii) Bauer

The *Harmonischen Gottesdienstes* ('Harmonous Divine Service') of 1731/2 consists of no fewer than 72 cantatas, of which these five are typical examples, each consisting of two arias (usually one fast and the other slow) with a brief linking recitative (in effect a miniature vocalized sermon). The settings depend a great deal for their appeal on their use of obbligato solo instruments, in No. 5 flute and oboe, in No. 35 (very attractive) and 67 two flutes, in No. 48 (the most engaging of all) recorder and oboe. Ruth Ziesak sings throughout with true baroque freshness, matching her woodwind partners most expertly, and the accompaniments have plenty of life. One of Telemann's *Little Fugues for Organ*, also dating from 1731, is effectively used as a brief interlude between each cantata. The recording is excellent, and full texts and translations are provided.

Hamburg Admiralitätsmusik (1723); Water Music (Hamburger Ebb' und Fluth)

(M) *** CPO 999 373-2 (2). Van der Sluis, Pushee, Müller, Mertens, Thomas, Schopper, Alsfeder Vokalensemble, Bremen Baroque O, Helbich

CPO took advantage of a live performance in Bremen in 1995 to make this excellent recording of a work that otherwise would have been an unlikely choice for CD. Telemann's occasional piece, which he called a *Serenade*, was written for the Hamburg Admiralty's centenary celebration of the founding of the local Naval College in 1723. It was first performed at a gala concert, together with the composer's much better known *Water Music*, hence the coupling.

As the main work is set to a poem by Michael Richey in praise of Hamburg, the allegorical characters represented by the soloists are all associated with the city. The soprano (as Hammonia) embodies Hamburg itself and the principal bass (as Neptunus) symbolizes the North Sea, and he has a memorable lyrical aria celebrating Hamburg's prosperity. More remarkably, the two tenors, as Themis and Mercurius, represent the prospering economy, and the privileges and rights of the constitution.

One of the other two basses symbolizes Mars, and sings a dramatic aria of defiance of lightning and stormy blasts. The third bass as Albis (the Elbe) celebrates his flowing currents and then has a charming tête-à-tête with Hammonia. Not surprisingly, there is a chorus of Nymphs and Tritons and the finale, *Long live the Admiralty*, is almost worthy of Sullivan! The performance is full of life, and of high quality, with no weak link in the cast, and with excellent recording, overall this is a delightful surprise.

THOMAS, Ambroise (1811–96)

Mignon; Overture & Gavotte
*** Chan. 9765. BBC PO, Y. P. Tortelier (with Concert:
  'French bonbons' ***)

Thomas's opera *Mignon* has one of the most delectable of all
French overtures, with its opening woodwind and harp solos
followed by a romantic horn tune. It is beautifully played and
recorded on Chandos in this first-rate concert of French
lollipops.

Hamlet (complete)
☛ *** EMI 7 54820-2 (3). Hampson, Anderson, Ramey,
  Graves, Kunde, Garino, Le Roux, Trempont, Amb. S., LPO,
  Almeida

Thomas's *Hamlet* may be an unashamed travesty of Shakespeare, complete with happy ending (in its original form),
but it remains a strong and enjoyable example of French
opera of its period. So much was evident from Richard
Bonynge's 1983 Decca set. If the EMI set is even more strikingly successful, it is not just that it provides an unusually full
text – with the tragic, so-called Covent Garden ending and
the ballet music in an appendix – but that Thomas Hampson
gives such a commanding performance in the title-role. One
no longer finds the aria *Etre ou ne pas être* sounding conventional or trivial, and consistently Hampson magnetizes the
attention the moment he begins to sing. June Anderson is not
so happily cast as Ophelia. The voice is inclined to sound too
edgy, and she is hardly more successful at sounding girlish
than Sutherland, but the singing is felt and expressive.
Almeida is understanding, and the presentation of the full
text, with a recently discovered duet for Claudius and Ger-
trude as a bonus, makes it invaluable.

Mignon (complete)
(M) *** Sony (ADD) SM3K 34590 (3). Horne, Vanzo, Welting,
  Zaccaria, Von Stade, Méloni, Battedou, Hudson,
  Ambrosian Op. Ch., Philh. O, Almeida

Thomas's once-popular adaptation of Goethe has many vocal
plums, and here a very full account of the score is given, with
virtually all the alternatives that the composer devised for
productions after the first, not least one at Drury Lane in
London where recitatives were used (as here) instead of
spoken dialogue; an extra aria was given to the soubrette
Philine and other arias were expanded. The role of Frédéric
was given to a mezzo-soprano instead of a tenor, and here the
appropriately named Frederica von Stade is superb in that
role, making one rather regret that she was not chosen as the
heroine. However, Marilyn Horne is in fine voice and sings
with great character and flair, even if she hardly sounds the
frail figure of the ideal Mignon. Nonetheless, with Alain
Vanzo a sensitive Wilhelm, Ruth Welting a charming Philine
and colourful conducting from Almeida, this is an essential
set for lovers of French opera. The 1977 recording has a
pleasingly warm ambience and the voices are naturally
caught in the present transfer.

THOMPSON, Randall (1899–1984)

Symphony 2 in E min.
*** Chan. 9439. Detroit SO, Järvi – CHADWICK: *Tam
  O'Shanter*, etc. ***

Randall Thompson's *Second Symphony* (1931) does not have
the strongly distinctive personality of Harris or Piston.
Neeme Järvi and the Detroit orchestra give an eminently
satisfying account and have a finely detailed and luxurious
recording. Those for whom sound is very important can
safely invest in this, for the Chadwick coupling is well worth
having.

*Alleluia; Choose something like a Star; The best of Rooms;
The Eternal Dove; Felices ter*
☛ *** ASV CDDCA 1125. Harvard University Ch.,
  Somerville; Johnson (organ) – BEACH: *Choral Music* ***

Commissioned by Koussevitzky in 1940 for the opening of
the Tanglewood Music Center, Randall Thompson's *Alleluia*
is for choral societies the American vocal equivalent of Barber's *Adagio* for string orchestras. Built on that single word it
rises to a climax of comparable intensity, never losing its grip
on the listener during its imaginative forward progress. *The
Eternal Dove* and *Choose something like a Star* are much later
works and in many ways equally fine and almost as memorable. Thompson is an individual writer, and all these works are
very rewarding when so committedly sung.

THOMSON, Virgil (1896–1989)

*Film music: Louisiana Story: Arcadian Songs & Dances &
Suite. The Plow that Broke the Plains: Suite. Power among
Men: Fugues & Cantilenas*
**(*) Hyp. CDA 66576. New L. O, Corp

Apart from his opera *Four Saints in Three Acts* (available on
two separate recordings in the USA), Virgil Thomson is best
known for his film score to Flaherty's *Louisiana Story*. Here
we are offered both the four-movement suite and a series of
brief vignettes, called *Arcadian Songs and Dances*, of which
the first (*Sadness*) and last (*The Squeeze Box*) are the most
striking. The *Fugues and Cantilenas* from *Power among Men*
are also not what one might expect from the titles, but are
atmospheric and imaginatively scored. All this music is quite
appealing, even if only very occasionally does one feel it is
first rate. The performances by Ronald Corp and the New
London Orchestra, are deft, evocatively played, and well
recorded.

THUILLE, Ludwig (1861–1907)

Piano Quintets: in E flat; G min.
(N) *** ASV CDDCA 1171. Tomer Lev, Falk Qt

Ludwig Thuille, Austrian-born, became an academic in
Munich who, as well as writing operas on a Wagnerian scale,
composed finely wrought chamber works at a time when
close contemporaries like Strauss and Reger were ignoring
the genre. The more ambitious of these two attractive piano
quintets, the *E flat* of 1901, opens with an exhilaratingly
thrustful *Allegro* in compound time, leading via a darkly
intense *Adagio* and jaunty *Scherzo* to a vigorous finale.
Written much earlier, when Thuille was still in his teens, the
G minor work in three movements is equally inventive, far
more than a student piece, demonstrating the composer's
innate lyrical gift. The Israeli pianist Tomer Lev and the Falk
Quartet give warmly persuasive readings.

TIPPETT, Michael (1905–98)

Concerto for Orchestra; (i) Triple Concerto
(M) *** Ph. 476 7144. LSO, C. Davis, (i) with Pauk, Imai, Kirshbaum

*** Chan. 93842. (i) Chilingirian, Rowland-Jones, De Groote; Bournemouth SO, Hickox

In 1979 when the *Triple Concerto* was first heard – with this same conductor and soloists – Tippett's new, more exuberantly lyrical style represented an important development in his career. The *Concerto for Orchestra* was associated with the opera *King Priam* and, even more successfully than the opera, it exploits his thorny style, tough and sinewy, hardly at all lyrical in the manner of its coupling. But to study such a piece on record is certainly stimulating. The transfer is first class; the upper string timbre has a touch of astringency but the ambient fullness remains.

Hickox's coupling of these two major orchestral works is a fine supplement to his set of the four Tippett symphonies, also with the Bournemouth orchestra, warmly recorded in well-focused sound. Levon Chilingirian makes a powerful leader for the trio of soloists, heightening the sharp contrasts of the elliptical argument in Tippett's late return to lyricism. The *Concerto for Orchestra* is presented with similar concentration and concern for lyrical warmth.

(i) Concerto for Double String Orchestra; (ii–iv) Piano Concerto; (i) Fantasia concertante on a Theme of Corelli; Little Music for Strings; (v; iv) Praeludium for Brass, Bells & Percussion; Suite for the Birthday of Prince Charles; (vi; iii–iv) Triple Concerto for Violin, Viola, Cello & Orchestra; (vii) The Blue Guitar (sonata for solo guitar). Vocal music: (viii; ix) Bonny at morn (Northumbrian folksong for unison voices and 3 recorders); (viii) A Child of Our Time: 5 Negro Spirituals. (viii; x) Crown of the Year (cantata); (viii) Dance, Clarion Air (madrigal); (xi) Evening Canticles; (viii) Music (unison song); Plebs Angelica (motet for double choir); The Weeping Babe (motet for soprano and choir). The Midsummer Marriage: (v; iv) Ritual Dances; (xii) Sososis's Aria
(BB) *** Nim. NI 1759 (4). (i) E. String O, Boughton; (ii) Tirimo; (iii) BBC PO; (iv) cond. composer; (v) E. N. Philh. O; (vi) Kovacic, Causé, Baillie; (vii) Ogden; (viii) Christ Church Cathedral Ch., Oxford (members), Darlington; (ix) Copley, Hodges, Nallen; (x) Medici Qt, with wind soloists, Jones (piano) and percussion; (xi) St John's College, Cambridge, Ch., Guest; (xii) Hodgson

This bargain collection of Tippett, issued to commemorate the composer's death in 1998, is specially valuable for containing two discs of recordings made by Tippett himself. When he did them, he was already in his late eighties, and the performance of the *Ritual Dances* from *The Midsummer Marriage* is not as incisive as most other versions, but the warmth of expressiveness and the sense of occasion conveyed are most compelling, the more so in Alfreda Hodgson's rich and resonant performance of Sososis's aria from the same opera, even though the voice is backwardly balanced. It is good too to have Tippett offering a rare example of his occasional music in the uncomplicated *Prince Charles Suite*. Even more valuable is the concerto disc, again more relaxed at more spacious speeds than rival versions, but with outstanding soloists revealing Tippett at his most warmly magnetic. Martino Tirimo is particularly impressive in the

elaborate figuration of the *Piano Concerto*, which can easily sound empty. Broad speeds, well sustained, also mark William Boughton's readings of the string pieces on the fourth disc; the *Guitar Sonata*, tautly played by Craig Ogden, and *Evening Canticles* sung by the St John's College Choir under George Guest (for whom they were written) make a splendid supplement. The choral singing from Christ Church Cathedral Choir on the second disc is also excellent, with the school cantata, *The Crown of the Year*, revealing the composer at his most open and least enigmatic. Warm, atmospheric sound, characteristic of Nimbus.

(i) Concerto for Orchestra; (ii) Concerto for Double String Orchestra; (ii; iii) Concerto for Violin, Viola, Cello and Orchestra; (i) Fantasia concertante on a Theme of Corelli; (iv) Byzantium; (v) Fanfare for Brass; (i) Little Music for String Orchestra; (vi) Dance, Clarion Air
☛ (M) *** Decca (ADD/DDD) 470 196-2 (2). (i) LSO, Davis; (ii) ASMF, Marriner; (iii) Pauk, Imai, Kirshbaum; (iv) Robinson, Chicago SO, Solti; (v) Philip Jones Brass Ens., Snell; (vi) Kelly, Eckersley, Cave, Cann, Schola Cantorum of Oxford, Cleobury

'Tippett Collection': (i) Concerto for Orchestra; (ii) Concerto for Double String Orchestra; (ii; iii) Triple Concerto for Violin, Viola, Cello & Orchestra; (i) Fantasia Concertante on a Theme of Corelli; (iv) Fanfare for Brass; (i) Little Music for Strings; (v) Suite for the Birthday of Prince Charles. Symphonies (i) 1–2; (i; vi) 3; (v) 4; (vii) Sonata for 4 Horns; (viii) String Quartets 1–3; (ix) Piano Sonatas 1–3; (x) Midsummer Marriage; Ritual Dances
(N) (B) *** Decca 475 6750 (6). (i) LSO, C. Davis; (ii) ASMF, Marriner; (iii) with Pauk, Imai, Kirshbaum; (iv) Philip Jones Brass Ens.; (v) Chicago SO, Solti; (vi) with Harper; (vii) Tuckwell Horn Qt; (viii) Lindsay Qt; (ix) Crossley; (x) ROHCG O, Pritchard

This double CD is an ideal way to begin an exploration of Tippett's music. The *Triple Concerto* was recorded (by Philips) in 1981, and was nominated 'Record of the Year' by *Gramophone* magazine. This beautiful recording presents a near-ideal performance of one of Tippett's later works. The *Concerto for Double String Orchestra* is surely one of the finest twentieth-century works for strings. With utter commitment Marriner and his colleagues allow the jazz inflections of the outer movements to have their lightening effect on the rhythm, and in the heavenly slow movement the slowish tempo and hushed manner display the full romanticism of the music without ever slipping over the edge into sentimentality. The *Corelli Fantasy*, a similarly sumptuous work but without the same lyrical felicity, and the *Little Music* are both equally well done, and the early 1970s sound remains excellent. The *Concerto for Orchestra* was a by-product of the opera *King Priam* and the performance is excellent. This 1964 (Philips) recording remains warm and vivid, though with a little tape hiss.

Byzantium was written to celebrate Solti's 30-year association with the Chicago Symphony Orchestra and is an extended setting for soprano of the Yeats poem of the same name. This is Tippett at his most exotic, responding vividly to the words, and the live 1991 recording can hardly be faulted. Faye Robinson, taking over from Jessye Norman at the last minute, gives a radiant performance, triumphantly breasting the problems of the often stratospheric and angular vocal line. Equally, Solti draws brilliant, responsive playing from the orchestra. With the vibrant *Fanfare* and the striking choral work *Dance, Clarion Air* included, this British Collection set makes an excellent general recommendation.

For those wanting to explore Tippett's music in depth, Decca have provided, for the centenary of his birth, an even more extensive collection, which includes the four symphonies, the first three conducted by Sir Colin Davis with the LSO fully committed, and the *Fourth* by Sir Georg Solti, who also offers the agreeable if less substantial *Suite for the Birthday of Prince Charles*. The *First* is the most concentrated of the four, organically conceived and relatively accessible. When one first encounters the *Second*, its proliferation of ideas seems almost to undermine the sense of forward direction, but closer aquaintance shows this to be misleading; the parts fit into an integrated and logical whole, while the slow movement explores the 'magical' side of Tippett's personality.

Tippett himself described the *Third* as a hybrid symphony and he consciously follows the example of Beethoven's *Ninth* in the transition to the final vocal section, in which the soprano sings three blues numbers and a dramatic scene to words by the composer. Some listeners find that the latter part of the work, which comes after a busy Scherzo, is far less cogent than the powerful first section, although Colin Davis, as in the two earlier symphonies, is as powerful as any conductor could be, while Heather Harper almost manages to mute the comparative crudities of Tippett's text. Solti's brilliantly played account of the *Fourth Symphony* is comparably powerful, although there are depths and tenderness in this score yet to be uncovered. Some of its quieter sonorities spring from much the same soil as one glimpses in the sudden moments of repose in Henze's symphonies, moments of a poignant melancholy that resonate long after the tumult surrounding them has subsided. Certainly these recordings and performances have a special place in the catalogue, although (as Hickox has since shown) there are other dimensions to these scores which are not uncovered here.

The Lindsays' recordings of the first three *String Quartets* carry the composer's imprimatur and are also available separately alongside the remaining two – see below. Paul Crossley's recordings of the *Piano Sonatas* come from the 1970s, and his playing could hardly be more persuasive or committed. With full documentation, this compilation certainly does Tippett full justice.

Concerto for Double String Orchestra

(B) *** CfP (ADD) 575 9782. (i) Friend; (ii) Partridge; (iii) Busch; LPO, Pritchard – BRITTEN: *Violin Concerto; Serenade* ***

(***) BBC BBCL mono 4059-2. LSO, Stokowski – GABRIELI: *Sonata pian e forte*; LISZT: *Mephisto Waltz 1*; NIELSEN: *Symphony 6* ***

The Classics for Pleasure reissue makes an outstanding bargain in coupling Handley's strong, committed performance with two key works by Britten. No one could here miss the passion behind the sharp rhythmic inspirations of the *Concerto's* outer movements and the glorious lyricism of the *Adagio cantabile*. The early 1970s recording sounds remarkably vivid and is admirably transferred to CD.

As far as we know Stokowski did not conduct any other Tippett and this eloquent account of the *Double Concerto* is a 'must', particularly as it comes with another rarity, a studio performance of Nielsen's *Sixth Symphony*. Commanding accounts, recorded in vivid and well-balanced mono sound.

Concerto for Double String Orchestra; Divertimento on 'Sellinger's round'; Little Music for Strings; (i) The Heart's Assurance (orch. Meirion Bowen)

**(*) Chan. 9409. City of L. Sinf., Hickox, (i) with Mark Ainsley

Hickox draws warm and energetic performances from his chamber orchestra, opulently recorded with fine definition. The first movement of the *Concerto* may lack a little in bite, but the slow movement is ravishing and the finale fizzes with energy. The playing may not always be quite as polished as that of the Academy on the rival Decca disc, but the big bonus is the first recording of the song-cycle *The Heart's Assurance* in the orchestration prepared by Meirion Bowen with the composer's express approval. What with piano accompaniment can seem a gritty, uncompromising piece here emerges with warmth and beauty, thanks also to the fine singing of John Mark Ainsley.

(i) Concerto for Double String Orchestra; Divertimento on 'Sellinger's Round' (for chamber orchestra); Little Music for String Orchestra; (ii) The Midsummer Marriage: Ritual Dances; (iii) Sonata for Four Horns

(N) (B) **(*) EMI 5 86587-2. (i) ASMF, Marriner; (ii) Bournemouth String O, Barshai; (iii) Michael Thompson Horn Qt

Marriner conducts the Academy in immaculate performances of these fine chamber works which yet have plenty of energy and bounce. Consistently they bring out the joyful exuberance of Tippett's inspiration in his first full maturity, and the sound, from the mid-1990s, is full and well balanced. However, Rudolf Barshai's account of the *Ritual Dances* from a decade earlier was an ill-conceived bonus for this reissue. The performance sounds cautious, and the weight of brass obscures the detail in other sections, even though the recording is again full and realistic. The account of the *Sonata for Four Horns* rights the balance: it is splendidly played and recorded.

Concerto for Double String Orchestra; Fantasia concertante on a Theme of Corelli; (i) The Midsummer Marriage: Ritual Dances

●━ ✿ (BB) *** Warner Apex 8583 89098-2. BBC SO, A. Davis; (i) with BBC Symphony Ch.

This outstanding bargain disc offers superb performances from Sir Andrew Davis and the BBC Symphony Orchestra of Tippett's two string masterpieces, both in the great tradition of English string-writing, coupled with an equally inspired account of the vividly atmospheric *Ritual Dances* from *A Midsummer Marriage*. The *Concerto* and *Fantasia* are warmly passionate, yet wonderfully detailed, helped by a spaciously resonant recording which is internally clear, yet has a wide dynamic range to match the dynamic contrasts of the playing. In the third of the *Ritual Dances*, *The air in spring*, the chimerical delicacy of the orchestral playing makes the bold entry of the BBC Chorus, near the close, the more arresting and thrilling. If you buy only one Tippett CD, this is the one to have; for apart from being ridiculously inexpensive, it makes an ideal introduction to his music and the sound could hardly be more vivid.

Concerto for Double String Orchestra; Fantasia Concertante on a theme of Corelli; (i) Songs for Dov

(N) (B) *** EMI 5 86588-2. SCO, composer, (i) with Robson

Among the many reissues to celebrate the Tippett centenary,

none is more welcome than this heart-warming triptych of the composer conducting his own music, originally issued on Virgin in 1988. It is particularly valuable to have the richest and most immediately appealing of his works, the *Concerto for Double String Orchestra*. Interpreting his own youthful inspiration, the octogenarian gives delightfully pointed readings of the outer movements, bringing out the jazzy implications of the cross-rhythms, not taking them too literally, while the lovely melody of the slow movement has never sounded more warmly expressive. The Scottish Chamber Orchestra plays with comparable passion in the *Fantasia Concertante*, a related work from Tippett's middle period, while Nigel Robson is a wonderfully idiomatic and convincing tenor soloist in the difficult vocal lines of the *Songs for Dov*. This is a generous coupling (71 minutes) representing the composer at all periods. Warm, full recording, with fine range and definition.

(i) *Concerto for Double String Orchestra;* (ii) *String Quartet 2;* (iii) *Fantasy Sonata*

(N) (***) NMC mono D 103. (i) O, Goehr; (ii) Zorian Qt; (iii) Sellick – TALLIS: *Spem in alium* (**)

Also issued to celebrate the centenary of the composer's birth, the disc, 'Remembering Tippett', opens with a piano recording of 1941 so vivid in the CD transfer that it is hard to believe that date. Phyllis Sellick, a pianist who was always magnetic in new or difficult music, gives an inspired reading of Tippett's *Fantasy Sonata*, a work he later revised as the *Sonata No. 1*. Walter Goehr, one of Tippett's earliest advocates then conducts his warmest and most approachable work, the *Concerto for Double String Orchestra*. In mono the recording cannot convey the true spread of sound, and the strings are on the edgy side, but the warmth of the writing comes over compellingly in this performance by an unnamed orchestra. The third work included is the *String Quartet No. 2*, played brilliantly by the Zorian Quartet in a recording from 1947, while as a delightful supplement comes Tippett's own first recording as a conductor, not of his own music but of Thomas Tallis's astonishing 40-part motet, *Spem in alium*.

(i) *Piano Concerto 1. Piano Sonatas 1 & 2*

(N) (B) **(*) EMI (ADD) 5 86586-2. Ogdon; (i) Philh. O, C. Davis

The *Piano Concerto* represents Tippett's complex, rich-textured earlier style, and the analogue recording copes with it well enough without being sharply detailed, its clarity enhanced by the remastering. It is essentially a lyrical and undoubtedly inspired piece, and John Ogdon and Sir Colin Davis present it persuasively enough. But Ogdon is at his best in the *First sonata*, which the composer rightly prized as the first work he felt able to publish, soon after it received its première in 1937. It has great vitality of invention, is harmonically direct and well suited to Ogdon's forthright approach. He plays it superbly and is movingly simple in his presentation of the *Andante molto tranquillo*, yet he readily catches the lighter, syncopated mood of the *Rondo giocoso* finale. The single-movement *Second Sonata*, written nearly three decades later, is more intractable. The argument is by way of reshuffling tiny motifs rather than by conventional development, but few of the ideas are especially memorable. Without being as uninhibited as he might be, John Ogdon displays his usual virtuosity.

(i) *Piano Concerto. Piano Sonatas 1 & 2*

(N) (B) *** EMI (ADD) 5 86596-2. Ogdon; (i) Philh. O, C. Davis

These are the pioneering recordings of the *Piano Concerto* and the *Second Sonata*, and they have strong claims on the collector even if Howard Shelley's and Paul Crossley's later accounts (see below) have more more up-to-date sound and are every bit as well performed.

Little Music for String Orchestra

(M) **(*) Chan. 6576. Soloists of Australia, Thomas – BLISS: *Checkmate*; RUBBRA: *Symphony 5* ***

Tippett's *Little Music* was written in 1946 for the Jacques Orchestra. Its contrapuntal style is stimulating but the music is more inconsequential than the *Concerto for Double String Orchestra*. It receives a good if not distinctive performance here, truthfully recorded.

(i) *The Rose Lake;* (ii) *The Vision of St Augustine*

🎵 ✪ *** Conifer 75605 51304-2. LSO; (i) C. Davis; (ii) with Shirley-Quirk, L. Ch., composer

As Sir Colin Davis's superb recording with the LSO demonstrates from first to last, *The Rose Lake* is arguably the most beautiful of all Tippett's works. It was in 1990 on a visit to Senegal that the 85-year-old composer visited a lake, Le Lac Rose, where at midday the sun transformed its whitish-green colour to translucent pink. It led to this musical evocation of the lake from dawn to dusk, centred round the climactic mid-moment when the lake is in full song. The 12 sections, sharply delineated, form a musical arch, with the lake-song represented in five of them on soaring unison strings in free variation form.

That culminating masterpiece is well coupled with Tippett's own 1971 recording, never previously available on CD, of his cantata *The Vision of St Augustine*. First heard in 1965, it is a work which can now be recognized as the beginning of his adventurous Indian Summer. His reading is expansively atmospheric rather than tautly drawn, bringing out the mystery of the piece.

Symphonies 1–4; New Year Suite

(N) (M) *** Chan. 10330X (3). Robinson, Bournemouth SO, Hickox

Symphony 1; (i) *Piano Concerto*

*** Chan. 9333. (i) Shelley; Bournemouth SO, Hickox

Those who thought that Sir Colin Davis's pioneering recordings of the first three Tippett symphonies were definitive will find fresh revelation in Richard Hickox's readings, not least in the *First Symphony*. Hickox gives an extra spring to the chattering motor rhythms at the start, and from then on the Bournemouth performance is regularly warmer and more expressive, as in the distinctive trumpet melody in the slow movement. In the last two movements too, Hickox finds more fun and jollity in Tippett's wild inspirations. The *Piano Concerto*, with Howard Shelley a superb soloist, brings another revelatory performance, warm and affectionate but purposeful too, rebutting any idea that with their fluttering piano figurations these are meandering arguments. Warm, full, atmospheric sound, with the piano balanced within the orchestra instead of in front of it. This must now be a first recommendation, although all four symphonies are now available in a box at mid-price.

Symphony 2; New Year (opera): Suite
*** Chan. 9299. Bournemouth SO, Hickox

As in the *First Symphony*, Hickox brings out the joy behind Tippett's inspirations without ever losing a sense of purpose. This may be a less biting performance than Sir Colin Davis's was on Decca, but it is consistently warmer, with extra fun and wit in the third-movement Scherzo. The coupling is also valuable, when Tippett's own suite from his last opera, *New Year*, brings out the colour and wild energy of this inspiration of his mid-eighties. If anything, the music seems the more telling for being shorn of the composer's own problematic libretto. The obbligato instruments – saxophones, electric guitars and kit drums – are most evocatively balanced in the warm, atmospheric recording.

Symphonies 2; 4
(N) *** NMCD D 104. BBC SO, composer

Though Tippett's conducting was decidedly eccentric, the evidence of his natural magnetism is readily borne out in his accounts of these two symphonies, recorded for the BBC at the time of his 90th birthday. Comparing these performances with others by such conductors as Sir Colin Davis (Tippett's most devoted advocate) and Richard Hickox, they are not nearly as precise. Speeds also tend to be a degree slacker, but the warmth and concentration hold each movement firmly together, conveying logic even in the thorniest textures. After all, there is an element of wildness in almost all of Tippett's writing, not least in his later work, and these rugged performances reflect that.

The *Second Symphony* of 1958 begins memorably with pounding bass arpeggios, inspired by Tippett hearing a Vivaldi concerto, with the four movements, in the composer's words, reflecting in turn 'joy, tenderness, gaiety and fantasy'. The *Fourth Symphony*, written in 1977 for Sir Georg Solti and the Chicago Symphony Orchestra, is in a single massive movement of seven major sections with elements of sonata form, as Tippett described it, 'a birth-to-death piece'.

(i) Symphony 3. Praeludium for Brass, Bells & Percussion
*** Chan. 9276. Bournemouth SO, Hickox; (i) with Robinson

In two long movements, each lasting nearly half an hour, the *Third Symphony* is not easy to hold together and, though Richard Hickox and the Bournemouth orchestra cannot match the original performers, Sir Colin Davis and the LSO, in power, they find more light and shade. Hickox gives wit to the Stravinskian syncopations in the first section and then dedicatedly carries concentration through the pauses of the slow second half of the movement. Though Faye Robinson's voice in the blues sections of the second movement is not as warm or firm as Heather Harper's was, she is more closely in tune with the idiom, helping to build the sequence to a purposeful conclusion in the long final scena. The recording is full and warm to match. The *Praeludium for Brass, Bells and Percussion* was written in 1962 for the 40th anniversary of the BBC, a gruff, angular piece hardly suggesting celebration, but none the less welcome in a well-played performance.

Symphony 4; Fantasia concertante on a Theme of Corelli; (i) Fantasia on a Theme of Handel (for piano and orchestra)
*** Chan. 9233. (i) Shelley; Bournemouth SO, Hickox

In the *Fourth Symphony* Richard Hickox and the Bournemouth Symphony are less weighty than the work's originators, but they are generally warmer and more atmospheric. In place of Solti's fiery brilliance, Hickox brings an element of wildness to the fast sections, and he also finds a vein of tenderness in the meditative sections. The well-known *Corelli Variations* have never sounded quite as sumptuous and resonant as here, and the disc is generously rounded off with a welcome rarity: the early *Handel Fantasia for Piano and Orchestra*. Howard Shelley is most convincing in the weighty piano-writing, like his accompanists giving the music warmth. Full-blooded sound to match.

String Quartets 1–5
*** ASV (ADD/DDD) CDDCS 231 (2). Lindsay Qt

String Quartet 4
*** ASV CDDCA 608. Lindsay Qt – BRITTEN: *Quartet 3* ***

This set neatly brings together the première recordings of Tippett's last two quartets with the recordings the same players made in the 1970s for L'Oiseau-Lyre of the first three quartets in the series, long unavailable. The notes include the composer's own commentary on the first three quartets, written for the original issue. He explains that he regards these works, written between 1935 and 1946, as a sequence, each developing out of the other. The Lindsays give performances as near definitive as could be, making one realize why they inspired the composer so positively. The analogue sound for Nos. 1–3, as transferred, is brighter, with less body than the digital recordings for Nos. 4 and 5.

As can be seen, the *Fourth Quartet* is also available separately, well coupled with Britten's *Third*.

(i) String Quartet 2 in F sharp; (ii; iii) Boyhood's End; The Heart's Assurance; (ii; iv) Songs for Ariel
(M) (***) EMI mono/stereo 5 85150-2. (i) Amadeus Qt; (ii) Pears; (iii) Wood; (iv) Britten – SEIBER: *String Quartet 3* (***)

A fascinating disc in which some historic Decca recordings (the vocal items) seem to have escaped on to EMI. *Boyhood's End* is a setting of a passage from W. H. Hudson's autobiography, *Far Away and Long Ago*. Its evocation of Hudson's boyhood past – seen from the perspective of him as an old man – in which he recalls his fear of losing his close contact with nature is subtly done, with the vocal line in very expressive arioso style, with much florid decoration. There is great atmosphere, too, with Pears making the very most of all the nuances. *The Heart's Assurance* occupies very much the same world, though with even more brilliant and difficult accompaniments, and the tragic spirit of the poems is beautifully caught. These historic recordings (Pears premièred both these works) dating from 1953 suffer from a little distortion, but are perfectly acceptable. The three short *Songs for Ariel*, written for a 1962 production of *The Tempest*, are short but effective, and are recorded here in stereo. Tippett's *Second String Quartet*, with its opening movement rich in polyphony, a very haunting fugal second movement, a bracing Scherzo and the emotional fervour of the finale, has much to recommend it. This very eloquent performance, in amazingly good (1954) sound, makes a welcome return to the catalogue. An important historical disc, with an unusual coupling.

Piano Sonatas 1 (Fantasy-Sonata); 2–3
*** Chan. 9468. Unwin

Piano Sonatas 1 (Fantasy Sonata); 2–4
(M) *** CRD CRD 34301 (2). Crossley

Paul Crossley has been strongly identified with the Tippett

sonatas; he recorded the first three for Philips in the mid-1970s: indeed, No. 3 was written for him. The *Fourth* and last (1983–4) started life as a set of five bagatelles. Crossley contributes an informative and illuminating note on the sonata and its relationship with, among other things, Ravel's *Miroirs*; his performance has all the lucidity and subtlety one would expect from him. These masterly accounts are matched by truthful and immediate sound-quality.

Nicholas Unwin has an exceptionally wide range of colour, though at times Crossley has more subtlety and delicacy when Tippett's fantasy takes wing. The Chandos recording is superb. Crossley's set takes two CDs but, if you happen not to need or want the *Fourth*, this is a viable alternative.

VOCAL MUSIC

Boyhood's End

(N) ** Hyp. CDA 67459. Padmore, Vignoles – BRITTEN: *Who are these children?*; *6 Holderlin Fragments*; FINZI: *A Young Man's Exhortation* ***

Mark Padmore, in his first solo song-recital disc, makes an inspired choice, bringing together four cycles on the theme of youth and friendship. Warmly accompanied by Roger Vignoles, he sings with a heady beauty and deep understanding, not least in this unusual Tippett cycle. Asked by his friends Benjamin Britten and Peter Pears to write a piece for them when they returned from America in 1943, Tippett chose to set not verse but prose passages by W. H. Hudson. The result is very characteristic of his early style, with often craggy vocal lines, which Padmore copes with superbly, and awkwardly written piano accompaniment, which Vignoles equally masters with apparent ease.

A Child of Our Time (oratorio)

❂– *** Chan. 9123. Haymon, Clarey, Evans, White, L. Symphony Ch., LSO, Hickox

(BB) *** Naxos 8.557570. Robinson, Walker, Garrison, Cheel, CBSO Ch. & O, composer

Hickox's version of Tippett's oratorio, *A Child of Our Time*, establishes its place against severe competition largely through the exceptionally rich recording and its distinctive choice of soloists, a quartet of black singers. Not only do Cynthia Haymon, Cynthia Clarey, Damon Evans and Willard White make the transitions into the spirituals (used in the way Bach used chorales) seem all the more natural, their timbres all have a very sensuous quality. The London Symphony Chorus, though not at its most incisive, sings well, responding to Hickox's warmly expressive style, often even more expansive than the composer himself on his recent recording.

Sir Michael Tippett in his mid-eighties may not secure the best-disciplined performance on record of the earliest of his oratorios, but it is undoubtedly very moving. The spirituals which punctuate the story like chorales in a Bach Passion have a heart-easing expressiveness, warmly idiomatic, while the lightness and resilience of *Nobody knows* allows the syncopations to be pointed with winning jazziness. Next to Sir Colin Davis's taut, tough reading (now reissued on Decca) this may be relatively slack, taking a full five minutes longer overall, but the sound on the Naxos disc (originally Collins) is fuller and warmer than that on the Davis set. The soloists are placed well forward, an outstandingly characterful team of singers especially associated with Tippett's music.

Although overall the Hickox version on Chandos must be counted first choice, at Naxos price the composer's own version can certainly be recommended alongside it.

(i) *A Child of Our Time*; **(ii)** *5 Negro Spirituals*. Choral music: *Magnificat and Nunc Dimittis*; *4 Songs from the British Isles*. *Bonny at Morn*; *Dance, Clarion Air*; *Lullaby*; *Music*; *Piebs angelica*; *The Source*; *The Weeping Babe*; *The Windhover*

❂– **(M)** *** Decca (ADD) 473 421-2. (i) J. Norman, J. Baker, Cassilly, Shirley-Quirk, BBC Singers, BBC Ch. Soc., C. Davis; (ii) Oxford Schola Cantorum, Cleobury

Sir Colin Davis's Philips account of *A Child of Our Time*, though more detached in style with a fairly old recording, offers a sharply focused performance with by far the finest quartet of soloists on record. Davis's speeds tend to be on the fast side, both in the spirituals and in the other numbers. He may miss some of the tenderness; by avoiding all suspicion of sentimentality, however, the result is incisive and very powerful, helped by excellent solo and choral singing. This is now reissued in Decca's British Music Collection with more choral music added, recorded three years later in Oxford for the Argo label. This demonstrates the awkward quality in the composer's choral writing: the music rarely progresses in anything like a predictable way. However, the Oxford Schola Cantorum has the music's full measure under Cleobury, and they sound fresh and spontaneous. Always Tippett has some illumination of words, whether in Edith Sitwell (*The Weeping Babe*), Yeats (*Lullaby*) or more traditional texts. The spirituals from *A Child of Our Time* are duplicated here in their concert version, to make an apt conclusion, though out of context they do not sound as effective as in the oratorio.

The Ice Break (opera-oratorio; complete)

(N) **(B)** *** EMI 5 86585-2. Sylvan, Harper, Wilson-Johnson, Page, Tear, Clarey, Randle, L. Sinf., Atherton

The *Ice Break* is presented here more as a modern dramatic oratorio than as an opera. The music has the physical impact characteristic of the later Tippett, but with less of the wildness that developed in his works of the 1980s. Centrally in Act II comes a lament for one of the principal black characters, the nurse Hannah (beautifully sung by Cynthia Clarey). In its bald simplicity that solo provides a vital, touching moment of repose, warmly emotional, to contrast with the tensions of a plot that centres on the Cold War period, with violence, racial conflict and student demonstration part of the scheme. David Atherton directs an electrically tense performance, with the American baritone Sanford Sylvan singing superbly in the central role of Yuri, a second-generation immigrant, set against Heather Harper as his mother Nadia, full-voiced and characterful, and David Wilson-Johnson as Lev, the father who in the first scene arrives after 20 years of prison and exile. The single disc comes with a keyed synopsis and retains the excellent notes by Meirion Bowen.

OPERA

King Priam (complete)

*** Chan. 9406/7 (2). Bailey, Harper, Allen, Palmer, Langridge, Minton, Tear, Roberts, L. Symphony Ch., LSO, Atherton

'The future of any twentieth-century opera depends quite a lot on recording,' Sir Michael Tippett said on the appearance of this superb set, and it is no exaggeration that it set the seal on the acceptance of a masterly work that seemed disconcerting when it first appeared in 1962. The dry fragmentation of texture and choppy compression of the drama then seemed at odds with an epic subject, particularly after the lyrical, expansive warmth of Tippett's preceding opera, *The Midsummer Marriage*. With an outstanding cast of the finest British singers of the time, Atherton in this 1980 recording brings out the sharp cogency of the writing, the composer's single-mindedness in pursuing his own individual line. The Wagnerian, Norman Bailey, sounds agedly noble in the title-role, with Robert Tear a shiningly heroic Achilles and Thomas Allen a commanding Hector, illuminating every word. The digital recording, originally made by Decca, comes out brilliantly on CD, with each Act fitted conveniently on a single disc.

TJEKNAVORIAN, Loris (born 1937)

Piano Concerto, Op. 4
*** ASV CDDCA 984. Babakhanian, Armenian PO, composer
– BABADZHANIAN: *Heroic Ballade; Nocturne* ***

A highly coloured work, very much in the tradition of Khachaturian, but rather more dissonantly pungent, Tjeknavorian's *Fourth Concerto* certainly makes an immediate impact on the listener. There is a central pianistic soliloquy at the centre of the first movement, sinuously Armenian in flavour, which leads to a huge climax, ridden by the pianist's thundering bravura, before the wildly obstreperous orchestra returns to add to the mêlée. Introduced by a yearning horn theme, the *Andante* wears its romantic heart on its sleeve, even though the soloist ruminates; and the rumbustious, syncopated finale also has a sinuous lyrical interlude, before the orchestra returns for the riotous race to the winning post. Babakhanian is surely an ideal soloist, producing explosions of virtuosity whenever needed, yet persuasively sensitive to the work's lyrical side. With the composer conducting and the orchestra on their toes, the result surely is definitive, for the recording is extremely vivid.

TOCH, Ernst (1887–1964)

Symphonies 1, Op. 72; 4, Op. 80
(N) *** CPO 999 774-2. Berlin R. O, Francis

Toch first studied medicine and philosophy but, after winning the Frankfurt Mozart prize in 1909, he settled on a musical career. He was a distinguished teacher, one of his pupils being Vagn Holmboe; but like so many of his contemporaries he emigrated in the early 1930s to settle in America. He came to the symphony late in life, and his *Third* was recorded in the days of LP by Steinberg and the Pittsburgh orchestra. After a long period of neglect there is a renewal of interest in his work and it is evident that he has the instincts and breadth of a real symphonist. Those who admire Holmboe or Robert Simpson will find much that is congenial about Toch's thinking. The *First Symphony* was written in 1950, by which time he was 63; it is exhilarating and highly inventive. Like Holmboe, the music does not proceed along predictable lines but derives its logic from the natural evolution of its thematic substance. Eminently acceptable performances and recording.

(i) Symphony 5 (Jephtha); (ii) Cantata of the Bitter Herbs
(N) ***(BB) Naxos 8.559417. (i) Seattle SO; (ii) Bikel, Meyer, Shammash, Clement, Christopher, Prague Philharmonic Ch., Czech PO; Schwarz

What an interesting and rewarding composer Toch is! The *Cantata of the Bitter Herbs* for narrator, soloists, chorus and orchestra comes from 1938, four years after he had left Nazi Germany to settle in the United States. It is neo-romantic and at times even Straussian (he had, incidentally, gone with Strauss to Florence in 1934 to a musical conference). No doubt prompted by the death of his mother in Vienna, it is a work of much inventive resource and undoubted expressive eloquence. The *Fifth* of his seven symphonies comes from 1962–3 and, like the cantata, is based on Exodus. It is subtitled 'Rhapsodic Poem' and is altogether freer in style than Nos. 6 and 7, to which he turned in the last year of his life. Both works are of quality and are very well performed and recorded: at a fraction of the price of a concert ticket, this is a real bargain which will well repay curiosity.

String Quartets: 8 in D flat, Op. 18; 9 in C, Op. 26
*** CPO 999 686-2. Verdi Qt

One of the casualties of the 1930s, Toch's music is receiving welcome attention from the CPO label. Widely played in the 1920s, Toch lost no time in emigrating when the Nazis seized power and spent the rest of his life writing for Hollywood and teaching in the University of Southern California. (Incidentally, his pupils in Berlin included the young Vagn Holmboe.) Toch was largely an autodidact, copying out the expositions of Mozart quartet movements and then trying to complete them. He was drawn early on to the quartet medium, and the two works recorded here are in the Strauss–Reger tradition: the *Eighth Quartet* comes from 1909 just after he had won the Mozart Prize in Frankfurt, and the *Ninth* was composed in 1920, and though indebted to Strauss is more radical in language. As the post-war symphonies show, Toch was a composer of real substance, and these two quartets reward acquaintance. Good performances and decent recording.

TOMASINI, Luigi (1741–1808)

Baryton Trios, K.19, 20, 27, 33 & 34
(N) ** CPO 999 973-2, Esterházy Ens.

Luigi Tomasini was the leader/concert master of Haydn's orchestra at Esterháza, although apparently he began his employment there as a valet! He was also the first violin Haydn had in mind when he composed his string quartets. As is well known, Prince Nicholas was very partial to the baryton. He made insatiable demands for new music for his favourite instrument to which Tomasini (who also wrote more than 20 string quartets) was asked to contribute. They are ably crafted but conventional, and the performances here reflect that in their musically straightforward response. There is nothing here to set the blood racing.

TOMKINS, Thomas (1572–1656)

Thomas Tomkins came from a distinguished Pembrokeshire family of practising musicians: his father and three brothers were all professional organists, but Thomas junior was the only one to make a lasting reputation as composer. Receiving his initial instruction at home from his father, at the age of 22 he went to London to study under Byrd. Two years later he moved to Worcester Cathedral as Master of the Choristers, where he stayed until he died. His compositions soon attracted royal commissions from London, to which he travelled frequently; but in the last years of his life he found time to collect his major manuscripts together so that they could be published posthumously as his *Musica Deo Sacra*.

Music for viols: Almain in F (for 4 viols); Fantasias 1, 12 & 14 (for 3 viols); Fantasia (for 6 viols); Galliard: Thomas Simpson (5 viols & organ); In Nomine II (for 3 viols); Pavane in A min. (for 5 viols & organ); Pavane in F; Ut re mi (Hexachord fantasia) (both for 4 viols); (Keyboard) (i) Fancy for two to play. Pavan & Galliard: Earl Strafford. (Organ) In nomine; Miserere; Voluntary; Verse anthems: Above the stars; O Lord, let me know mine end; Thou art my King

⚷ ✿ (BB) *** Naxos 8.550602. Rose Consort of Viols, Red Byrd; Roberts; (i) with Bryan

This well-planned Naxos programme is carefully laid out in two parts, each of viol music interspersed with harpsichord and organ pieces and ending with an anthem. It gives collectors an admirable opportunity to sample, very inexpensively, the wider output of Thomas Tomkins, an outstandingly fine Elizabethan musician whose music is still too little known. Though he is best known for his magnificent church music, it is refreshing to discover what he could do with viols, experimenting with different combinations of sizes of instrument, usually writing with the polyphony subservient to expressive harmonic feeling, as in the splendid and touching *Fantasia for six viols*. Perhaps the most remarkable piece here is the *Hexachord fantasia*, where the scurrying part-writing ornaments a rising and falling six-note scale (hexachord). The two five-part verse anthems and *Above the stars*, which is in six parts, are accompanied by five viols, with a fine counter-tenor in *Above the stars* and a bass in *Thou art my King*.

KEYBOARD MUSIC

Music for harpsichord and virginals: Barafostus Dreame; 2 Fancies; Fancy for Two to Play; Fortune my Foe; Galliard of 3 Parts; Galliard Earl Stafford; 2 Grounds; In nomine; Lady Folliott's Galliard; Miserere; Pavan; Pavan Earl Strafford with its devision; Pavane of 3 parts; A Sad Pavane for these Distracted Times; Toy made at Poole Court; What if a Day; Worcester Brawls

*** Metronome METCD 1049. Cerasi

Carole Cerasi offers here the finest available collection of the keyboard music of the last of the great English virginalists, Thomas Tomkins. Indeed, it is the repertoire played on the virginals that stands out, especially her exquisitely spontaneous performance of *A Sad Pavane for these Distracted Times*, and her equally sensitive response to the dolorous *Fortune my Foe* (the two most extended pieces here). In contrast, the charmingly good-humoured *Toy made at Poole Court* is given the lightest rhythmic lift. She uses a modern copy of an early seventeenth-century Ruckers and it could hardly be more realistically recorded. The harpsichord pieces (using a copy of an instrument by Bartolomeno Stephanini) are more robust and often have exuberant decoration, as in the disc's title piece 'Barafostus Dreame'. Earl Strafford's Galliard is another splendid example of her exciting bravura on the latter instrument and the closing *Ground* with extended variations is a *tour de force*. The recording venue has a

pleasing ambience and the balance is ideal if you set the volume level carefully.

Barafostus's Dream; Fancy; Fortune my Foe; Galliard & Pavane Earl Strafford; Ground; Hunting Galliard; Pavan and Galliard; Perpetual Round; Prelude; A Sad Pavane for the Distracted Times; Ut, Mi, Re; Voluntary; Worcester Brawls

(N) ** MDG 607 0563-2. Klapprott (harpsichord or virginal)

Tomkins's variations on *Barafostus's Dream, Fortune my Foe* and the extended *Ground* (with the bass figure presented 24 times) show the quality of his invention, besides demanding much virtuosity from the performer. They receive that readily from Bernhard Klapprott, although his manner tends to over-deliberation. One would have liked a sense of revelling in the bravura. He is more enthusiastic in *Worcester Brawls*, which reflects the chaos during the repeated sieges the city suffered during the years following 1640. The *Sad Pavane for the Distracted Times* has a comparable connection with English history, a *tombeau* for King Charles I, written in February 1649, two weeks after his execution. Both *Pavans* are expressively played, but again are somewhat cautious. The recording of both harpsichord and virginals is faithful but a trifle over-resonant. This cannot compare with Carole Cerasi's outstanding collection.

Fancy; Fancy (for Viols); Galliard; Ground; In Nomine, In Nomine Versions I–II; 4 Pavans; Prelude; Robin Hood; Toy – Made at Poole Court; Voluntary

(N) *** MDG 607 0704-2. Klapprott (harpsichord or virginal)

In his second collection, Bernhard Klapprott is well attuned to Tomkins's often measured tread, especially in the *Pavans*, which are given a noble dignity. Yet he also seems much more outgoing than on his first disc, and in the single *Galliard* included here he obviously revels in the fast passage-work. *The Toy – Made at Poole Court* is a most engaging little tune, while the *Robin Hood* variations, using a memorable basic theme, suggest a horse-riding hero. Both this and the closing *Ground* are similarly lively. Excellent recording, not too close and not too resonant.

The Great Service (No. 3); Anthems: Know you not; Oh, that the Salvation; O Lord, let me know mine end; (i) Organ Voluntaries: in A; C; G

(M) *** CRD CRD 3467. New College, Oxford, Ch., Higginbottom; (i) Burchell

The Great Service (No. 3); When David Heard; Then David Mourned; Almighty God, the Fountain of All Wisdom; Woe is Me; Be Strong and of a Good Courage; O Sing unto the Lord a New Song; O God, the Proud are then Risen Against Me

⚷ *** Gimell CDGIM 024. Tallis Scholars, Phillips

The *Great Service*, in no fewer than ten parts, sets the four canticles – *Te Deum, Jubilate, Magnificat* and *Nunc dimittis* – with a grandeur rarely matched, using the most complex polyphony. The following motets bring comparable examples of his mastery. These complex pieces bring the flawless matching and even tone for which the Tallis Scholars are celebrated, and with recording to match.

Many will prefer the more direct and throatier style of the Choir of New College, Oxford; even if the choral sound (recorded in the chapel of New College) is less sharply defined, the effect is very satisfying and real. The service is given added variety by the inclusion of three organ voluntaries, well played by David Burchell. What makes this record especially attractive is the inclusion of three of Tomkins's most beautiful anthems. The treble solos in *Know you not* and *Oh, that the Salvation* are ravishingly done, and the alto soloist in *O Lord, let me know mine end* is hardly less impressive.

ANTHEMS AND MOTETS

Above the stars my Saviour dwells; Almighty God, the fountain of all wisdom; Arise O Lord, lift up thine hand; Behold the hour cometh and now is; Funeral Sentences; Great and marvellous are Thy works; My Shepherd is the living Lord; O sing unto the Lord a new song; A Sad Psalm; Then David mourned; When David heard; Fifth Service: Magnificat and Nunc dimittis; (i) *Organ Voluntary in D; Pavan & Galliard*
(N) **(BB)** *** Naxos 8.553794. Oxford Camerata, Summerly;
   (i) L. Cummings (organ)

Not surprisingly, Jeremy Summerly and his Oxford Camerata give us an outstanding collection of Tomkins's sacred vocal music, very well laid out. Among the highlights are the beautiful *Funeral Sentences*, and the following glorious *Above the stars my Saviour dwells*, the group which begins with *When David heard that Absolom was slain* and ends with the serene *Almighty God, the fountain of all wisdom* and the glowing *O sing unto the Lord a new Song*. Laurence Cummings adds *A Sad Pavan for these distracted times* to this melancholy sequence, but elsewhere he plays a cheerful *Pavan and Galliard* as another interlude. The choir (with fine soloists) are vividly recorded, with the acoustic resonance of Hertford College Chapel well controlled so that words are clear. An outstanding disc in every way.

Songs of 3, 4, 5 & 6 Parts (1622): Adieu, ye city-prisoning towers; Cloris, when as I woo; Come, shepherds, sing with me; Fond men that do so highly prize; Fusca, in thy starry eyes; How great delight from those sweet lips I taste; It is my well beloved's voice; Love, cease tormenting; Music divine, proceding from above; No more I will thy love importune; Oft did I mark how in thy eyes; O let me live for true love; Phyllis, yet see him dying; Phyllis, now cease to move me; See, see the shepherds' Queen; Sure, there is no God of Love; Too much I once lamented; To the shady woods now wend we; Turn unto the Lord our God; Was ever wretch tormented; Weep no more, thou sorry boy; When David heard that Absolom was slain; When I observe those beauty's wonderments; Woe is me! that I am constrained
(N) *** Chan. 0680. I Fagiolini, Hollingworth

This enterprising Chandos disc introduces us to a side of Tomkins which, for the most part, is very different from his sacred music. Certainly this collection includes a few deeply religious settings, such as the meltingly beautiful *Woe is me! that I am constrained* (from Psalm 120) and its companion *Turn unto the Lord our God*. But many of these songs are madrigals concerned with more earthly love, even though they remain just as richly expressive, like *Weep no more thou sorry boy*. Others are jolly: *Oyez! Has any found a lad* and the delightful *To the shady woods now wend we*, with its 'fa-la-la-la-las' not as innocent as they seem. The charming, lightweight *See, see the Shepherds' Queen* is a glee which might almost have been written by Sullivan. I Fagiolini sing this nicely varied prograame expertly, with a neat rhythmic touch and an attractive blending of voices. They are beautifully recorded.

TORELLI, Giuseppe (1658–1709)

Giuseppe Torelli, born in Verona, centred his career on Bologna but travelled in his middle years, visiting Amsterdam and Vienna, besides serving briefly as leader/concertmaster at the Court of George Friedrich, Margrave of Brandenburg-Ansbach. As a composer he belonged to the generation before Vivaldi, but he too made a major contribution to the birth of the solo concerto.

(i) *Violin Concertos, Op. 8/8, 9 & 11;* (i; ii) *Double Violin Concertos, Op. 8/2, 4, 5, 6;* (iii) *Sinfonias for Trumpet in D (G 8);* (iii; iv) *for 2 Trumpets, (G 23).*
(N) *** Chan. 0716. (i) Standage; (ii) Weiss; (iii) Steele-Perkins; (ii) Blackadder; Coll. Mus. 90

While Torelli's earlier concertos remain in the world of the concerto grosso, by the time he came to write Op. 8 (published in 1709), he had moved away to give his soloists independence. The lustrous, busy opening of Op. 8/2 is immediatialy enticing, but these are all attractive works, particularly Nos. 4 (where the pointed theme of the finale reminds one of 'All we like sheep') and 6, with its *Largo e staccato* central movement anticipating Vivaldi. The solo *Concerto in E minor, Op. 8/11*, is also a particularly fine work. Not surprisingly, the period performances here are first class, with gleaming string tuttis and nothing edgy about the immaculate, sensitive solo playing. The rather more conventional trumpet concertos are in also confident hands, and throughout the accompaniments are characteristically stylish and the Chandos recording first rate.

TOVEY, Donald (1875–1940)

Piano Concerto in A, Op. 15
*** Hyp. CDA 67023. Osborne, BBC Scottish SO, Brabbins –
   MACKENZIE: *Scottish Concerto* ***

Hyperion in its imaginative series of Romantic piano concertos here offers two Scottish works. Sir Donald Tovey is best known for his analytical essays, and his *Concerto*, if less distinctively Scottish, is the grander work, with weighty textures and a strongly controlled structure. The young Scottish pianist Steven Osborne is a brilliant advocate.

TRUSCOTT, Harold (1914–92)

Symphony in E; Elegy for String Orchestra; Suite in G
*** Marco Polo 8.223674. Nat. SO of Ireland, Brain

Harold Truscott broadcast as a pianist for the BBC, specializing in Schubert, and this record suggests that his own music, for all its eclectic influences, has genuine individuality and power. The moving *Elegy* for strings, elliptical in structure, is a near-masterpiece, and the three-movement *Symphony*, which dates from the end of the 1940s, is a powerfully argued piece. The *Suite in G* has a *Molto Andante* which confirms the intensity of feeling the composer could create with string textures. Gary Brain has an instinctive feel for all these works and holds together the turbulent moods of the first movement of the *Symphony* coherently, while the Dublin orchestra rise to the occasion and play with much conviction throughout. The recording is full-bodied, with the resonance at the service of the music but without clouding textures.

(i; ii) *Cello Sonata in A min.*; (iii; ii) *Clarinet Sonata 1 in C*; (iv; v; vi) *Flute Trio* (for flute, violin and viola) *in A*; (i) *Meditation for Solo Cello on Themes from Emmanuel Moór's Suite for 4 Cellos*; (v) (Solo) *Violin Sonata in C*
*** Marco Polo 8.223727. (i) Domonkos; (ii) Lugossy; (iii) Varga; (iv) Kovács; (v) Eckhart; (vi) Bársony

This fine collection of Truscott's chamber music bears out the promise of the orchestral disc above. The *Flute Trio* (1950) is strikingly fresh, with a spirited, spikily colourful ostinato-like opening movement, followed by a charming *quasi allegretto*. But the heart of the work is the third movement, a simple Elegy. The finale is then a winning *Tempo di menuetto*, characteristically quirky.

The lyrical writing in the *Clarinet Sonata* of nine years later immediately makes full use of the instrument's *chalumeau* range and then contrasts an engaging repeated-note scherzo with a serene *Adagio*, maintaining the romantic, lyrical flow in the finale. Both the rather serious-minded single-movement *Solo Violin Sonata* and the darker *Cello Meditation* (1946) are short but memorable. The *Cello Sonata* dates from much later and the writing style is more concentrated, with a bravura finale. Yet the central *Allegretto scherzando* and searching *Adagio* have much in common with the earlier music. Fine, eloquent performances throughout, and truthful if reverberant recording, although the resonance is most troubling in the *Clarinet Sonata*.

TUBIN, Eduard (1905–82)

(i) *Balalaika Concerto; Music for Strings; Symphony 1*
⌿— *** BIS CD 351. (i) Sheynkman; Swedish RSO, Järvi

The opening of the *First Symphony* has a Sibelian breadth, but for the most part it is a symphony apart from its fellows. The quality of the musical substance is high; its presentation is astonishingly assured for a young man still in his twenties, and the scoring is masterly. Emanuil Sheynkman's account of the *Balalaika Concerto* with Neeme Järvi is first class, both taut and concentrated. Excellent recording.

(i) *Ballade for Violin & Orchestra*; (ii) *Double-bass Concerto*; (i) *Violin Concerto 2; Estonian Dance Suite; Valse triste*
*** BIS CD 337. (i) Garcia; (ii) Ehren; Gothenburg SO, Järvi

Tubin's highly imaginative *Double-bass Concerto* has an unflagging sense of momentum and is ideally proportioned; the ideas never outstay their welcome and one's attention is always held. The *Second Violin Concerto* has an appealing lyricism, is well proportioned and has a strong sense of forward movement. The *Ballade* is a work of gravity and eloquence. *Valse triste* is a short and rather charming piece, while the *Dance Suite* is the Estonian equivalent of the *Dances of Galánta*. Splendid performances from both soloists in the *Concertos* and from the orchestra under Järvi throughout, and excellent recording.

Symphonies (i) *1 in C min.; 2 (The Legendary); 3 in D min.*; (ii) *4 in A (Sinfonia lirica)*; (iii) *5 in B min.*; (ii) *6*; (iv) *7*; *8*; (iv) *9 (Sinfonia semplice); 10*; (ii) *Suite from the ballet, Kratt*; (iv) *Toccata for Orchestra*
⌿— ◉ (M) *** BIS CD 1402/06 (5). (i) Swedish RSO; (ii) Bergen PO; (iii) Bamberg SO; (iv) Gothenburg SO; Järvi

Neeme Järvi's survey of the Tubin symphonies is here packaged shorn of some of its couplings and presented in an attractive and competitive format (five CDs for the price of three). These are marvellous works, rich in invention and with the real breadth of the symphonist about them. Anyone who is attuned to the symphonies of Sibelius or Prokofiev will find themselves at home in this world. This handsomely produced set whose individual issues have given enormous satisfaction over the years is mandatory listening. Presumably BIS will collect the various odds and ends, such as the *Balalaika Concerto* and the *Concertino for Piano and Orchestra* and reissue them separately.

Symphonies *2 (The Legendary); 6*
*** BIS CD 304. Swedish RSO, Järvi

The opening of the *Second Symphony* is magical: there are soft, luminous string chords that evoke a strong atmosphere of wide vistas and white summer nights, but the music soon gathers power and reveals a genuine feeling for proportion and of organic growth. If there is a Sibelian strength in the *Second Symphony*, the *Sixth*, written after Tubin had settled in Sweden, has obvious resonances of Prokofiev – even down to instrumentation – and yet Tubin's rhythmic vitality and melodic invention are quietly distinctive. The Swedish Radio Symphony Orchestra play with great commitment under Neeme Järvi, and the recorded sound is magnificent.

Symphonies *3; 8*
(M) *** BIS CD 300342. Swedish RSO, Järvi

The first two movements of the wartime *Third Symphony* are vintage Tubin, but the heroic finale approaches bombast. The *Eighth* is his masterpiece; its opening movement has a sense of vision and mystery, and the atmosphere stays with you. This is the darkest of the symphonies and the most intense in feeling, music of great substance. Järvi and the Swedish orchestra play it marvellously, and the recording is in the demonstration bracket.

Symphonies (i) *4 (Sinfonia lirica)*; (ii) *9 (Sinfonia semplice); Toccata*
*** BIS CD 227. (i) Bergen SO; (ii) Gothenburg SO; Järvi

The *Fourth* is a highly attractive piece, immediately accessible, the music well argued and expertly crafted. The opening has a Sibelian feel to it but, the closer one comes to it, the more individual it seems. The recording comes from a concert performance with an exceptionally well-behaved audience. The *Ninth Symphony* is in two movements: its mood is elegiac and a restrained melancholy permeates the slower sections. Its musical language is direct, tonal and, once one gets to grips with it, quite personal. If its spiritual world is clearly Nordic, the textures are transparent and luminous, and its argument unfolds naturally and cogently. The playing of the Gothenburgers under Järvi is totally committed in all sections of the orchestra. The performances are authoritative and the recording, altogether excellent.

Symphony *5 in B min.; Kratt* (ballet suite)
*** BIS CD 306. Bamberg SO, Järvi

The *Fifth* makes as good a starting point as any to investigate the Tubin canon. Written after he had settled in Sweden, it finds him at his most neo-classical; the music is finely paced and full of energy and invention. The ballet suite is a work of much character, tinged with folk-inspired ideas and some echoes of Prokofiev.

Symphony 7; (i) *Concertino for Piano & Orchestra;* *Sinfonietta on Estonian Motifs*
*** BIS CD 401. (i) Pöntinen; Gothenburg SO, Järvi

The *Seventh* is a marvellous work and it receives a concentrated and impressive reading. As always with Tubin, you are never in doubt that this is a real symphony, which sets out purposefully and reaches its goal. The ideas could not be by anyone else and the music unfolds with a powerful logic and inevitability. Neeme Järvi inspires the Gothenburg orchestra with his own evident enthusiasm. The *Concertino for Piano and Orchestra* has some of the neo-classicism of the *Fifth Symphony*. Roland Pöntinen gives a dashing account of the solo part. The *Sinfonietta* is a fresh and resourceful piece, a Baltic equivalent of, say, Prokofiev's *Sinfonietta*, with much the same lightness of touch and inventive resource. Superb recording.

Symphonies 9 (Sinfonia semplice); 10; 11
*** Alba ABCD 172. Estonian Nat. SO, Volmer

It is good that there should be an alternative to Neeme Järvi's fine cycle of the symphonies on BIS. This did not include the one-movement *Eleventh Symphony*, left incomplete on Tubin's death, though Paavo Järvi subsequently recorded it for Virgin. Both the *Ninth* and *Tenth* belong among Tubin's very finest works, and the former is particularly haunting. The first 541 bars of No. 11 were completed and fully scored, and the Estonian-born Canadian composer Kaljo Raid scored the remaining 70-odd measures. Arvo Volmer conducted its première in Tallinn in 1988 and recorded it in the early 1990s (on Koch). The present recordings were made in 2002 and are strong performances, not superior to Järvi in Nos. 9 and 10, but worthy of recommendation alongside them.

Symphony 10; (i) *Requiem for Fallen Soldiers*
*** BIS CD 297. Gothenburg SO, Järvi; (i) with Lundin, Rydell, Hardenberger, Lund Students' Ch., Järvi

Tubin's *Requiem*, austere in character, is for two soloists (a contralto and baritone) and male chorus. The instrumental forces are merely an organ, piano, drums, timpani and trumpet. The simplicity and directness of the language are affecting and the sense of melancholy is finely controlled. The final movement is prefaced by a long trumpet solo, played here with stunning control and a masterly sense of line by the young Håkan Hardenberger. It is an impressive and dignified work, even if the choral singing is less than first rate. The *Tenth Symphony* is a one-movement piece that begins with a sombre string idea, which is soon interrupted by a periodically recurring horn call – and which resonates in the mind long afterwards. The recordings are absolutely first class.

(i; iii) *Ballade; Capricci 1 & 2; The Cock's Dance;* *Meditation; 3 Pieces; Prelude.* (i) *Sonata for Unaccompanied Violin.* (ii; iii) *Violin Sonatas 1 & 2; Suite of Estonian Dance Tunes; Suite on Estonian Dances.* (ii; iii) *Viola Sonata; Viola Sonata (arr. of Alto Saxophone Sonata)*
*** BIS CD 541/542 (2). (i) Leibur; (ii) Vahle; (iii) Rumessen

Although the smaller pieces are finely wrought, Tubin seems to come into his own on a larger canvas. Particularly impressive are the *Second Violin Sonata* (*In the Phrygian Mode*), the visionary *Second Piano Sonata*, and the two sonatas for viola, one a transcription of the alto-saxophone sonata with its foretaste of the *Sixth Symphony* (1954) in which that instrument plays a prominent, almost soloistic role, and the later *Viola Sonata* (1965). As so often with Tubin's non-symphonic

music, there is much of interest to reward the listener. Highly accomplished performances from Arvo Leibur and Petra Vahle, and exceptionally thorough documentation from the pianist Vardo Rumessen, with over 40 music-type examples. The recording is truthful, but the acoustic lends a shade too much resonance to the piano, which is often bottom-heavy.

Complete piano music: *Album leaf; Ballad on a Theme by Maat Saar; 3 Estonian folk-dances; 4 Folksongs from my Country; A Little March for Rana; Lullaby; 3 Pieces for Children; Prelude 1; 7 Preludes; Sonatas 1-2; Sonatina in D min.; Suite on Estonian Shepherd Melodies; Variations on an Estonian folk-tune*
*** BIS CD 414/6. Rumessen

Tubin's first works for piano inhabit a world in which Scriabin, Ravel and Eller were clearly dominant influences but in which an individual sensibility is also to be discerned. The resourceful *Variations on an Estonian folk-tune* is a lovely work that deserves a place in the repertoire, as does the *Sonatina in D minor*, where the ideas and sense of momentum are on a larger scale than one would expect in a sonatina. The *Second Sonata* is a key work in Tubin's development. It opens with a shimmering figure in free rhythm, inspired by the play of the aurora borealis, and is much more concentrated than his earlier piano works. Vardo Rumessen makes an excellent case for it and it is impressive stuff. The performances are consistently fine, full of understanding and flair, and the recording is very natural.

OPERA

Barbara von Tisenhusen
*** Ondine ODE776-2 (2). Raamat, Sild, Kuusk, Puurabar, Kollo, Estonian Op. Company & O, Lilje

Tubin's opera with its theme of illicit passion is not long, consisting of three acts of roughly 30 minutes each. It has pace and a variety of dramatic incident and musical textures, and the main roles in the action are vividly characterized. The musical substance of the opera is largely based on a chaconne-like figure of nine notes heard at the very outset, yet the theme changes subtly and skilfully to meet the constantly shifting dramatic environment so that the casual listener will probably not be consciously aware of the musical means Tubin is employing. All the singers are dedicated and serve the composer well and, though the orchestra is not first class, it too plays with spirit and enthusiasm under Peeter Lilje. The recording produces a sound comparable to that of a broadcast relay rather than the opulent sound one can expect from a commercial studio recording. A strong recommendation.

The Parson of Reigi; (i) *Requiem for Fallen Soldiers*
*** Ondine ODE783-2 (2). Maiste, Eensalu, Tônuri, Kuusk, Estonian Op. Company & O, Mägi; (i) Tauts; Deksnis, Leiten; Tiido, Roos, Estonian Nat. Male Ch., Klas

After the success of *Barbara von Tisenhusen*, the Estonian Opera immediately commissioned Tubin to compose *The Parson of Reigi*, and it, too, concerns an illicit relationship. Tubin's music powerfully evokes the claustrophobic milieu of a small, closely knit fishing community and is particularly successful in conveying its atmosphere. The dawn scene, where the parson, Lampelius, blesses the departing fishermen, is particularly imaginative, as is the evocation of the white summer nights in the garden scene, where the heroine confesses her illicit passion. As in *Barbara von Tisenhusen*,

Tubin's powers of characterization of both the major and supporting roles are striking, and there is a compelling sense of dramatic narrative as well as variety of pace. The performance of the three principal singers is very good – especially the parson, splendidly sung by the baritone, Teo Maiste – and the only let-down is in the quality of the orchestral playing, which is little more than passable.

The coupled *Requiem for Fallen Soldiers* is generally to be preferred to the rival account on BIS coupled with the *Tenth Symphony* (see above). The Estonian singers produce better focused and darker tone than their Swedish colleagues, though the BIS recording has some amazingly lyrical playing by Håkan Hardenberger. The Estonian player, Urmas Leiten, is very eloquent too. Strongly recommended.

TURINA, Joaquin (1882–1949)

Danzas fantásticas, Op. 22; La Procesión del Rocio, Op. 9; Sinfonia sevillana, Op. 23

☛— *** Telarc CD 80574. Cincinnati SO, López-Cobos – DEBUSSY: *Ibéria* ***

As we have already discovered with his earlier Decca recording of the *Danzas fantásticas*, Jesús López-Cobos is at his finest in these alluring and exotically orchestrated pieces. The *Sinfonia sevillana*, which was written in the same year as the *Danzas fantásticas*, is dominated by the Flamenco dance spirit, yet unified by a motto theme heard at the opening on flute and oboe. The central movement depicts the *Guadalquivir River*, with a cor anglais solo heard against a richly undulating backcloth, but the later appearance of the castanets confirms the Spanish ambience. The closing *Fiesta* brings more sparkling dance rhythms but is lyrical, too, and closes with a sense of grandeur. The Cincinnati orchestra play throughout with voluptuous brilliance and are especially exciting in the closing *Orgía* of the *Danzas fantásticas*. The recording is of Telarc's finest quality, a rich, glittering tapestry of sound.

La oración del torero (version for string orchestra)

*** Chan. 9288. I Musici di Montréal, Turovsky – SHCHEDRIN: *Carmen ballet suite*, etc. ***

The composer's string-orchestral version of the haunting *Oración del torero* is warmly and sensitively played and very well recorded here, and if the quartet version is even more subtle (see below) this makes an enjoyable foil for Shchedrin's brilliant arrangement of music from Bizet's *Carmen*.

Rapsodia sinfónica (arr. Halfter)

(B) *** Decca 448 243-2. De Larrocha, LPO, Frühbeck de Burgos – ALBENIZ: *Rapsodia española*; RODRIGO: *Concierto de Aranjuez*, etc. ***

(N) *** Australian Decca Eloquence 476 2971. De Larrocha, LPO, Burgos – ALBENIZ: *Rapsodia española*; MONTSALVATGE: SURINACH: *Piano Concerto* ***

(BB) *** Warner Apex 8573 89223-2 Heisser, Lausanne CO, López-Cobos – ALBENIZ: *Concierto fantástico*; *Rapsodia española*; FALLA: *Nights in the Gardens of Spain* ***

Turina's *Rapsodia sinfónica* has been recorded by others, but in the hands of Alicia de Larrocha it is played with such éclat that it becomes memorable and thoroughly entertaining. This performance is also available on an Australian Decca reissue, coupled to rare concertos by other lesser-known composers.

The performance by Jean-François Heisser (with López-Cobos a brilliantly idiomatic partner) is also first class in every way, combining seductive poetic feeling, brilliant colouring and excitement. The digital recording is vividly balanced and the couplings are no less attractive.

CHAMBER MUSIC

La oración del torero

(***) Testament mono SBT 1053. Hollywood Qt – CRESTON: *Quartet*; DEBUSSY: *Danses sacrées*; RAVEL: *Introduction & Allegro*; VILLA-LOBOS: *Quartet 6* (***)

It is difficult to imagine Turina's famous piece being played with greater expressive eloquence or more perfect ensemble than by the incomparable Hollywood Quartet, and it comes as part of a valuable and beautifully transferred anthology.

Piano Quartet in A min., Op. 67

*** Black Box BBX 1048. Lyric Piano Qt – STRAUSS: *Piano Quartet in C min., Op. 13* ***

Turina's *Piano Quartet in A minor* comes from 1931, and though it is not great music it is far from negligible. It is well played and recorded here, and the coupling is equally rare.

TURNAGE, Mark-Anthony (born 1960)

(i) *Blood on the Floor*; (ii) *Dispelling the Fears*; (iii) *Night Dances*; (iv) *Your Rockaby* (for saxophone and orchestra); (v) *Some Days*

☛— (M) *** Decca 468 814-2 (2). (i) Ens. Modern, Rundel; (ii) Hardenberger, Wallace, Philh. O, Harding; (iii) Hulse, Tunstall, Constable, Wallace, L. Sinf., Knussen; (iv) Robertson, BBC SO, Davis; (v) Clarey, Chicago SO, Haitink

Turnage is a natural communicator who can happily draw on the widest range of influences and produce music that, for all its modernity, is immediately enjoyable to more than the specialist. These five works offer an impressive survey of his progress from 1981, when he wrote *Night Dances*, to his most recent collaboration with the established jazz soloists of the Ensemble Modern, when he rescored a shortened version of *Dispelling the Fears* as the final movement of the ambitious nine-movement suite, *Blood on the Floor*.

Dispelling the Fears for two trumpets and orchestra is also included here in its longer original version, with the atmospheric passage, with its undoubled blues influence at the end providing a welcome resolution to what is otherwise a comparatively tough piece.

Throughout, jazz and popular music provide an underlying strand in Turnage's writing. *Night Dances* has a movement directly drawing on Miles Davis, and *Your Rockaby* is in effect a saxophone concerto, with a percussive background. Improvisatory, and powerfully expressive, kaleidoscopic in mood, it is based on a Beckett monologue centring on a woman in a rocking-chair hauntingly rethinking her life.

The poetry on which the mezzo-soprano song-cycle *Some Days* draws has a despondently black voice, reaching despair in its haunting closing, 'I am absolutely alone forever'. It has an awkward vocal line which is powerfully sung by Cynthia Clarey, and there is a curiously ambivalent *Tango* as a central orchestral interlude, where Haitink, who directs the work confidently and fluently, seems slightly less rhythmically at home.

Throughout the collection there is no doubt about Turnage's genuine originality, but it is in the ambitious *Blood on the Floor* that his different sources of inspiration coalesce most readily into a satisfying whole, with the jazz influences made especially strong by the starry cast of players. The opening movement combines a kind of complex, vibrant minimalism with something approaching a jam session, and the following sections move from the melodic, bluesy *Junior Addict* through an extraordinary mélange of orchestral colours to a lively saxophone break (*Needles*), an *Elegy for Andy* (the composer's brother) on the electric guitar, and a highly rhythmic interlude (*Cut-up*), which draws boldly and unashamedly on Stravinsky's *Rite of Spring*.

A free-drumming sequence, ornamented instrumentally, then leads to the finale; but whether it was wise to use the earlier *concertante* trumpet piece here is open to question. Turnage obviously wanted to end with the remarkably atmospheric coda that resolves that work, where the two soloists ruminate freely and hauntingly together. But even in abbreviated form it takes the overall length of the suite to nearly 69 minutes. However, the quality of performance and recording is in no doubt.

Scorched (with John Scofield)
*** DG 474 729-2. Scofield, Patitucci, Erskine, Frankfurt RSO, HR Big Band, Wolff

In sound that comes up and hits you, *Scorched* is a prime example of 'musical fusion', with Mark-Anthony Turnage developing jazz pieces by the American guitarist and composer, John Scofield, using not only a jazz trio (led by Scofield on a prominent electric guitar) but a big band and symphony orchestra. The title itself, *Scorched*, was designed to reflect that: SCofield ORCHestratED. The result, recorded live at the Alte Oper in Frankfurt and later developed by Turnage and Scofield, is certainly ear-catching, with most of the 14 pieces – some separate and some linked – vigorously upfront, with Scofield's playing magnetic, but including strongly contrasted pieces for strings. The wildest piece of all, which rounds off the concert, is improbably called *Protocol*. Recommended for anyone who, like Turnage from a classical base, is fascinated by jazz.

CHAMBER MUSIC

An Invention on Solitude; Cortège for Chris; 2 Elegies Framing a Shout; 3 Farewells; 2 Memorials; Sleep On; True Life Stories: Tune for Toru
*** Black Box BBM 1065. Nash Ens. (members)

Anyone coming new to Turnage could not do better than start here, for all this music is intensely expressive and instantly communicative. Its overriding character is thoughtful and contemplative, although *An Invention of Solitude* is the exception, for while inspired by the Brahms *Clarinet Quintet*, the writing, for the same combination, 'fluctuates between stillness and violence'. The *Cortège for Chris* (Christopher Van Kempen, the Nash Ensemble's cellist who died in 1998) features both cello and clarinet, as well as a ruminative piano, while the *Two Memorials* are commemorated with haunting soliloquizing from the solo saxophone.

The *Three Farewells* are strangely obsessive: each has a hidden text, the second, *Music to Hear*, for viola and muted cello, a Shakespeare sonnet. The finale, *All will be well*, was written as a wedding piece, and the composer observes ironically 'the marriage didn't last'.

Not surprisingly, some of the most peaceful and serene writing comes in *Sleep On*, for cello and piano, a triptych framed by a lovely *Berceuse*, and a restful *Lullaby*. The solo saxophone returns for the first of the *Two Elegies* and after being exuberantly interrupted by the *Shout* – a spiky and restlessly energetic boogie – the piano (with the saxophone) 'searches for and finds repose'.

The reflective closing *Tune for Toru* (a gentle piano piece) was written in response to the death of the Japanese composer Toru Takemitsu and readily finds the stillness the composer was searching for in his *Invention on Solitude*. Superbly responsive performances throughout and vividly real recording, within an attractively spacious acoustic.

TURNBULL, Percy (1902–76)

Piano music: *Character Sketches 2–4 & 7; 3 Dances; Fantasy Suite; 3 Miniatures; Pasticcio on a Theme by Mozart; 2 Preludes; Sonatina; 3 Winter Pieces*
*** Somm SOMMCD 1015. Jacobs

Percy Turnbull, born in Newcastle upon Tyne, is yet another of the lost generation of English composers whose virtually forgotten music is now being rescued by the gramophone. His student contemporaries at the Royal College of Music included Tippett, Maconchy and Rubbra, yet at the time (the early 1920s) his talent shone out from among them. He was a fine pianist and is a natural-born composer of piano music, his style a beguiling diffusion of many influences, from Delius and John Ireland in England, to Fauré and Ravel among his French contemporaries. Yet his musical personality has its own individuality and his writing gives great refreshment and pleasure, his style notable for its gentle colouring, clarity and lightness of texture, without any hint of triviality.

The delightful *Pasticcio on a Theme of Mozart* displays his classical background, for each of the 12 variations absorbs the manner of another composer, from Bach to Brahms, Fauré and Ravel to Delius and Bartók. The *Sonatina* is entirely his own, moving from gentle English lyricism to a witty, syncopated finale. The other miniatures continually delight the ear and the *Three Winter Pieces* (1956), which were his last completed works for piano, are typical of his easy and innocent inventiveness at its most sophisticated and communicative. Throughout, Peter Jacobs is an admirable and persuasive advocate, and he is beautifully recorded. Well worth exploring.

TÜÜR, Erkki-Sven (born 1959)

Action, Passion, Illusion for Strings; Zeitraum for Orchestra
*** Warner 2564 61992-2. Pöysti, Nordic SO, Tali –
RACHMANINOV: *3 Russian Songs*; SIBELIUS: *The Wood-Nymph* ***

The Estonian Erkki-Sven Tüür is still in his mid-40s and is already well represented in the catalogue. *Zeitraum* has already been recorded by Paavo Järvi and the Stockholm Philharmonic (on Virgin 5 4521-2) and the third panel of the string trilogy, *Illusion*, is also available in an alternative version. And what a fine composer he is too. *Zeitraum* is rich in resource and imagination, and its 'glittering woodwind figurations, slow moving pulses in the strings [giving] way to leaping minimalist patterns' (to quote Martin Anderson's excellent note) exert a strong fascination. The three string pieces offer some reminders of Honegger and Bartók, though, as in its companions, Tüür speaks with a totally individual voice. The conductor Anu Tali is in her early 30s and founded the Estonian-Finnish Orchestra (now the Nordic Symphony) so as to develop cultural contacts between Estonia and Finland. She has studied with the celebrated Ilya Musin in St Petersburg and has already made appearances with other orchestras in Estonia, Finland, Latvia and further afield. She gets very good results from her forces and her enterprising programme is well recorded.

TVEITT, Geirr (1908–81)

Piano Concertos (i) *1, Op. 1;* (ii) *4 (Northern Lights), Op. 130;* (iii) *The Turtle*
(N) *** BIS CD 1397. Stavangar SO, Ruud, with (i) Bjelland; (ii) Austbø; (iii) Kosmo

Tveitt's opus list runs into the 300-s, much of it unpublished and a good deal of it destroyed in 1970 in a fire. He studied with Florent Schmitt, Honegger and Egon Wellesz (in his Vienna, not his Oxford, days); when his *Fifth Piano Concerto,* Op. 156, was performed in Paris in the early 1950s, a French critic spoke of him as 'a Norwegian Bartók'. But it is the suites of folk-music arrangements dazzlingly scored that have made so strong a claim on the wider musical public, for he had a real flair for the orchestra. The *First Piano Concerto,* written in his early 20s, has a natural fluency and a certain Gallic charm. The opening of *The Turtle,* a setting of a passage from Steinbeck's *The Grapes of Wrath,* once again leaves no doubt as to the vividness of his orchestral imagination. Like our own Robert Simpson, Tveitt was a keen amateur astronomer, and the *Fourth Concerto,* inspired by the Aurora Borealis, shows his strong fascination with the heavens. It is imaginative if diffuse and wanting in concentration; but there are flashes of colour and inspiration that really reward investigation. Exceptionally wide-ranging recorded sound.

Piano Concertos 1 in F, Op. 1; 5, Op. 156
(BB) *** Naxos 8.555077. Gimse, RSNO, Engeset

Geirr Tveitt (pronounced with a soft 'G' and surname as in 'Tate') was obviously an accomplished pianist as, when he gave the first performance of the *Fifth Piano Concerto* in 1954 in Paris under Jean Martinon, he also played the *B flat minor Concerto* of Tchaikovsky and Brahms's *D minor Concerto!* Håvard Gimse is an artist of quality and well supported by the Royal Scottish National Orchestra under Bjarte Engeset.

Piano Concerto 4 (Aurora borealis), Op. 130; (i) *Variations on a Folksong from Hardanger for Two Pianos & Orchestra*
☞ **(BB)** *** Naxos 8.555761. Gimse, RSNO, Engeset, with (i) Süssmann

Geirr Tveitt was a virtuoso of both the piano and the orchestra (not for nothing was he chief orchestral arranger for NRK, the Norwegian Radio), and his music encapsulates the spirit of Norway's folk tradition as completely as does that of Grieg and Sæverud. His *Fourth Piano Concerto* of 1947 is highly original and, as its subtitle suggests, evokes the extraordinary display and movement of the *Northern Lights.* It is superbly played by Håvard Gimse and the Scottish Orchestra under Bjarte Engeset. The *Variations,* in which Gimse is joined by Gunilla Süssmann, are also full of character and colour, even if they somewhat outstay their welcome. Strongly recommended.

A Hundred Hardanger Tunes, Op. 151: Suites 1, 1–15; 4 (Nuptials) 46–60.
☞ **(BB)** *** Naxos 8.555078. RSNO, Engeset

A Hundred Hardanger Tunes: Suites 2: 15 Mountain Songs (Nos. 16–30); 5: Troll Tunes (61–75)
(BB) *** Naxos 8.555770. RSNO, Engeset

If Tveitt's musical schooling was cosmopolitan (he studied with Honegger, Wellesz, Florent Schmitt and Villa-Lobos), his musical outlook was steeped in the Hardanger music of western Norway. Even though almost 80 per cent of his output was destroyed in a fire, he can almost rival Milhaud, Niels Viggo Bentzon or Villa-Lobos in fecundity. The *Fourth Suite of Hardanger Tunes* was the first Tveitt work to be recorded on LP, way back in the 1960s, albeit in a much less complete form than it is here. Try 'So stilt dei ror på glitrefjord' (*How silently they row on the glittering fjord*), and you will understand why Tveitt enjoyed such an enviable reputation as an orchestrator. His sound world is highly original and imaginative, and unfailingly inventive. Each of these suites comprises fifteen numbers, which some may find too much of a good thing, and there is something to be said for making one's own shorter compilations. The Royal Scottish National Orchestra play with evident enthusiasm for Bjarte Engeset, who has collated the various different sources in preparing his edition. Nearly all these pieces are delightful and many are quite captivating. The second selection is every bit as imaginative and colourful as the earlier sets. Something of a find.

Prillar, Op. 8 (**completed Jon Øivind Ness**); *Solgud-Symfonien (The Sun God Symphony), Op. 81* (**re-created by Kaare Dyvyk Husby**)
(M) **(*) BIS CD 301027. Stavanger SO, Ruud

Both pieces come from the thirties and the *Sun God Symphony,* originally part of a ballet, *Baldur's Dreams,* has been restored thanks to the existence of a piano score and two recordings, one from 1938 and the other of a revision from 1958. It is much indebted to folksong and brilliantly scored. There are some attractive ideas, even if the middle movement, *The Gods Forget the Mistletoe,* goes on too long.

Prillar refers to the Norwegian folk instrument, the *Prillarhorn,* and is very much in his post-Grieg nationalist vein. The second movement is distinctly Gallic and the piece was actually given in Paris in 1938 by the Orchestre National under Manuel Rosenthal. Decent performances though the Stavanger strings are a bit thin and a good (if not characteristically spectacular) BIS recording.

TYE, Christopher (c. 1505–c. 1572)

Complete instrumental music: *Amavit a 5; Christus Resurgens a 5; Dum Transisset a 5* (4 versions); *In Nomines a 4, a 5, a 6* (21 settings); *Lawdes Deo a 5; Sit fast a 3*
(M) **(*) Astrée ES 9939. Hespèrion XX, Savall

Tye is associated as a vocal composer with Ely Cathedral and the Chapel Royal, but his consort music is unjustly neglected. The present collection includes all of his surviving instrumental pieces. Virtually all the music is slow and expressive; many of the *In nomine* pieces have biblical allusions in their simple titles. The performances here make a very strong impression; the viol timbre unexpectedly full-bodied. Indeed, the playing of Hespèrion XX has been criticized for being too rich in timbre for the period. We have no quarrel with the sound, but would have liked greater dynamic contrast in the playing. Excellent recording.

Euge bone; Kyrie: Orbis factor; Motets: Miserere mei, Deus; Omnes gentes, plaudite minibus; Peccavimus cum patribus nostris; Quaesumus omnipotens Deus
☛ (BB) *** Hyp. Helios CDH 55079. Winchester Cathedral Ch., Hill

Masses: Euge bone; Peterhouse; Western Wind
(M) *** ASV CDGAU 190 (2). Ely Cathedral Ch., Trepte

Christopher Tye spent most of his musical life in Cambridge and Ely and became master of the chorus and organist at Ely Cathedral in 1543; he retired to take holy orders in 1560 but remained living near Ely. So the soaring acoustics of Ely Cathedral and performances by its present-day choir could not be more apt for his three greatest masses, of which the large-scale *Euge bone* is the most splendid. The passionate singing on ASV is fully worthy, the choral sound glorious. With a playing time of 83 minutes, the three works would not fit onto a single CD, but the two discs are offered for the price of one.

The performance from the splendid Winchester Cathedral Choir under David Hill is no less eloquent; the contrast between the *Gloria*, pressed on ardently, and the serene *Sanctus* is particularly telling. Moreover, the four accompanying motets are also very fine, especially the exuberant *Omnes gentes* (a setting of Psalm 46 from the Vulgate), and the extended and very beautiful supplication, *Peccavimus cum patribus nostris*, which soars up to the heavens. Fine atmospheric recording makes this bargain reissue particularly tempting.

VACHON, Pierre (1731–1803)

String Quartets, Op. 5/2; Op. 7/2
*** ASV CDGAU 151. Rasumovsky Qt – JADIN: *Quartets* ***

Although none of the works on this disc are masterpieces, the music provides us with an interesting and enjoyable sampler of the French school of quartet writing at the end of the eighteenth century. Vachon, born in Arles, was a frequent visitor to London, playing in his own concertos at the Haymarket Theatre. He wrote his quartets in a *galant* style which the French called the *quatuor concertant ou dialogué*. Op. 5 and Op. 7 were both published in London during the composer's first visit, at the beginning of the 1770s. The performances here are polished and well recorded. Enjoyable in an innocuous way.

VAINBERG, Moishei (1919–96)

Violin Concerto
(BB) *** Naxos 8.557194. Grubert, Russian PO, Yablonsky – MIASKOVSKY: *Violin Concerto* ***

The Lithuanian violinist Ilya Grubert on Naxos couples Miaskovsky's glorious concerto with the relatively little known concerto of Mieczyslaw (or Moishei) Vainberg, composed in 1958 for Leonid Kogan. His pioneering Melodiya account (still available on Olympia OCD 622) has a special authority, but Grubert is hardly less persuasive and the competitive price may well encourage collectors, who have

hesitated to acquire the Kogan, to investigate this. The concerto owes a lot to Shostakovich, but an individual voice can be discerned as one comes closer to it.

Sinfonietta 1, Op. 41; Symphony 5, Op. 76
*** Chan. 10128. Polish Nat. RSO, Chmura

Most of Vainberg's symphonies have been recorded at one time or another. There are touches of Hindemith, Prokofiev and even Mahler. All the symphonies we have heard also betray a debt to Shostakovich, without being entirely overwhelmed by him. The *Fifth* is a long piece dating from 1962, and it holds the listener even when it doesn't wholly satisfy him or her. The slow movement is a little too long, given the quality of its ideas, but generally speaking the work has considerable power and eloquence. It has thoroughly committed players in Gabriel Chmura and his fine Polish orchestra – and superb Chandos recording. The *Sinfonietta No. 1* (1948) makes use of Jewish melodies, which Vainberg fashions in a style influenced by Bartók. Well worth investigating. Incidentally, Vainberg is variously transliterated as Vaynberg or Weinberg, though Chandos opts for the latter (as in the most recent Grove).

VALEN, Fartein (1887–1952)

(i) *Violin Concerto*; (ii) *Symphony 1*; (iii) *Le Cimetière marin, Op. 20*; (iv) *Nachtstücke; Ode to Solitude, Op. 35; Pastorale, Op. 11; Song without Words*
*** Runegrammofon RCD 2013. (i) Tellefsen, Trondheim SO, Ruud; (ii) Bergen PO, Ceccato; (iii) Oslo PO, Caridis; (iv) Torgersen

The Norwegian composer Fartein Valen enjoyed cult status for a few years after the Second World War, but interest has waned since his death in the early 1950s. He grew up in Madagascar, where his father was a missionary, and he studied philology and languages before turning to music. As early as the 1920s he developed a kind of 12-note technique, but for much of his life he was something of an outsider in Norwegian music. At times there is a strong sense of nature and refinement of texture, as if he were a mildly atonal Delius; at others there is a feeling of claustrophobia, as if the fjords are shutting out light. After a time the ear tires of the concentration of activity above the stave.

The *Violin Concerto* is Valen's masterpiece; it is short and intense and, like the Berg concerto, an outpouring of grief on the death of a young person. It ends like the Berg by quoting a Bach chorale. Incidentally, Valen was adamant that he had never heard the Berg. (Music did not travel easily in 1940, and Valen lived in a particularly isolated part of Norway.) His own concerto is played marvellously here by Arve Tellefsen.

The longest work here is the *First Symphony*, which began life as a piano sonata but reached its definitive orchestral form two years later in 1939. The textures are fairly dense, though the opening of the second movement is an exception: the pale, luminous colouring is distinctly northern. *Le Cimetière marin* is one of the better known of Valen's works and is highly evocative. All are given well-prepared and dedicated performances and eminently serviceable recordings, made between 1972 and 1997. The presentation is impossibly pretentious. The CD label contains no information of any kind and appears to come from the Tate Modern: the front cover reads 'fartein valen – the eternal' (all lower case) and the backing slip gives, in absolutely microscopic print, the titles of the works – again lower case, black on a darkish red. You need to consult the booklet for track information, which is all in funereal black. That apart, this anthology serves as a useful introduction to this intriguing composer.

VALI, Reza (born 1952)

(i) *Flute Concerto*; (ii) *Deylâmân*; (iii) *Folksongs*

(BB) **(*) Naxos 8.557224. Boston Modern O, Rose; with (i) Almarza; (ii) Bárbát; (iii) Baty

Persian composer Reza Vali's *Flute Concerto*, written in 1998, uses the technique involving the playing of the flute and singing simultaneously, bringing out the overtones and altering the timbre of the instrument in order to imitate the sound of the Persian bamboo flute (the ney). There is quite a lot of Persian 'mood' music here, but also some more jolly sections too: not a profound work, but quite an entertaining modern concerto, even if the 17 minutes of the final movement are too long. In the *Folksongs*, which are based on Persian folk music, the vocal line is bolstered by Vali's brightly colourful accompaniments (the third movement is a lament, full of bells and gongs, and lots of references to birds, appropriate for a piece composed in memory of Olivier Messiaen). *Deylâmân* (1995), named after a region in north-west Persia, employs two Persian instruments, the ney (or, rather, the flute imitating it here, as in the *Flute Concerto*, above) and the bárbát (or oud, a short-necked lute) and uses a mode which originates (and is named after) that region. It is a curious (if not terribly gripping) work, with more exotic 'mood' music, beginning and ending all very mysteriously with what the composer describes as a special type of 'Persian polyphony', in between which there are quotes from various classical composers: Beethoven, Bruckner, Mahler and Wagner, though why is not explained. The performances and recording are first class.

VALS, Francisco (1665–1747)

Missa Scala Aretina

(BB) **(*) DHM 05472 77842-2. Piau, Van der Sluis, Lettinga, Elwes, Van der Kamp, Netherlands Bach Fest. Bar. O, Leonhardt – BIBER: *Requiem in F min* **(*)

Francisco Vals, another name to spring suddenly out of the past, was choirmaster at Barcelona Cathedral, and the *Missa Scala Aretina* (1702) is the only one of his ten Masses to have gained any kind of fame outside Spain. It is a powerfully expressive piece, not always with conventional harmony. It is laid out for four separate groups of performers, containing, respectively, the soloists, instrumentalists (including harp in the continuo) and two choral ensembles. Leonhardt delivers a committed spontaneous performance, but the choral singing does not convey the impression that the Netherlanders are thoroughly at home in the Spanish idiom nor is it ideally crisp in ensemble. Nevertheless, with rich recording, this is by no means unimpressive and it is certainly not dull.

VAŇHAL, Jan (1739–1813)

Double-bass Concerto in D

*** Hyp. CDA 67179. Nwanoku, Swedish CO, Goodwin – DITTERSDORF: *Double-bass Concertos 1 & 2*

Vaňhal, an exact contemporary of Dittersdorf, was equally prompted to write concertos for the virtuoso double-bass

player, Johann Matthias Sperger, himself a composer. This charming work makes an idea supplement to the two fine Dittersdorf works, with Chi-Chi Nwanoku making light of the problems presented by such a cumbersome solo instrument. First-rate sound.

(i) *Double Bassoon Concerto in F; Sinfonias: in A min.; F*

**(*) BIS CD 288. (i) Wallin, Nilsson; Umeå Sinf., Saraste

The best work here is the *Concerto*, an arresting and inventive piece, with the slow movement touching a deeper vein of feeling than anything else on the disc. The two *Sinfonias* are less musically developed but very interesting: the minuet of the *F major* has a *Sturm und Drang* feel to it: Vaňhal's symphonies may well have paved the way for Haydn at this period; they were certainly given by Haydn while Kapellmeister at the Esterházy palace. The recording is good, as one has come to expect from this source, even if the acoustic is on the dry side. Very good playing by the Umeå ensemble.

Violin Concerto in B

(B) *** Discover DICD 920265. Zenaty, Virtuosi di Praga, Oldrich Vlček – MYSLIVECEK: *Violin Concerto* ***

Vaňhal was born in Bohemia, almost a generation before Mozart; he similarly wrote inventive, lively music, of which this *Violin Concerto* is an appealing example, with the central slow movement a nostalgic intermezzo. On this well-recorded bargain issue Ivan Zenaty with his clean, full tone proves an outstanding advocate, with the Virtuosi di Praga providing lively support on modern instruments. Excellent recording.

Symphonies: in A min. (Bryan a2); in C (Sinfonia Comista); in D min. (Brian d1); in E min. (Bryan e1); in G min. (Bryan g1)

(M) **(*) Warner Elatus 2564 60340-2. Concerto Köln

Vaňhal (or Wanhal, as he himself signed his name) was born in Bohemia but spent the greater part of his life in Vienna, where these works were composed during the 1760s and 1770s. This was the period of the so-called *Sturm und Drang* symphonies, works in a minor key with a keen, driving intensity, of which Haydn's *La Passione* is a good example. Vaňhal's symphonies were widely heard at this time, and the great French Mozart scholar Georges de Saint-Foix cited his *D minor Symphony* (albeit not the one on this disc) as an influence on Mozart's little *G minor Symphony*, K.183. These are works of vivid and lively invention, which also embrace a wide diversity of approach. The *C major Sinfonia Comista*, one of the later symphonies, differs from its companions in its richness of scoring and its programmatic inspirations. The Concerto Köln play with tremendous spirit, enthusiasm and style, but the recording is too forwardly balanced so that tuttis are at times a little rough. Not that this greatly inhibits a three-star recommendation for what is a very interesting recording of repertoire which is not otherwise available at present.

Symphonies in A, Bryan: A9; in C, Bryan: C3; in C, Bryan: C11; in D, Bryan: D17

🔜 (BB) *** Naxos 8.554341. Esterházy Sinfonia, Grodd

Symphonies in B flat, Bryan B3; in D min., Bryan D2; in G, Bryan G11

🔜 (BB) *** Naxos 8.554138. City of L. Sinfonia, Watkinson

Among the many new discs of forgotten music by Mozart's contemporaries this Naxos issue stands out. These four compact symphonies are all winningly colourful and inventive, often bringing surprises that defy the conventions of the time. The Esterházy Sinfonia under Uwe Grodd give attractively lively performances with some stylish solo work, vividly recorded.

The second disc in the Naxos Vaňhal series is hardly less impressive than the first. The *B flat Symphony* (from the early 1760s) reminds the listener of both Haydn and Mozart. The *D minor Symphony* in only three movements, written a decade later, is scored for five horns, yet the main string theme of the first movement is quite haunting. The *G major work* (1775) also has an endearingly gracious first movement, although horns are still prominent in the scoring. Excellent, polished performances from the City of London Sinfonia under Andrew Watkinson and very good recording.

Symphonies in D, Bryan D2; C min., Bryan C2; A flat, Bryan Ab1; G, Bryan G6

**(N) (BB) ** Naxos 8.557483. Toronto Camerata, Mallon

Vaňhal's symphonies are never less than interesting, and this third volume from Naxos (each with a different orchestra and conductor) offers more examples of the composer's bold and imaginative writing (the *C minor Symphony*, as one might expect, is especially original). The Toronto orchestra is competent, of course, and plays musically, but they have neither the dramatic bite of period-performance groups (such as Concerto Köln on Warner Elatus) nor the beauty and polish of orchestral playing of the best modern-instruments groups (such as the London Mozart Players on Chandos) – there is at times a hint of blandness and a lack of sure-footedness about this music-making.

Symphonies in C min., Bryan Cm2; in D, Bryan D4; in G min., Bryan Gm2

*** Chan. 9607. LMP, Bamert

The *G minor Symphony*, the second of Vaňhal's symphonies in that key, is an absolute delight, full of good ideas and comparable with the *Sturm und Drang* of Haydn's No. 39 or Mozart's No. 25 in the same key. The *C minor Symphony* (1770) is also a work of originality with an occasional foreshadowing of Beethoven. Matthias Bamert and the London Mozart Players give an excellent account of themselves, and are recorded with great clarity and warmth.

Oboe Quartets, Op. 7

(B) **(*) Hyp. Helios CDH 55033. Francis, Tagore String Trio

These six *Oboe Quartets* bubble along with tuneful amiability, with little of the *Sturm und Drang* writing we know from Vaňhal's stormy, minor-keyed symphonies. The performances are eminently enjoyable rather than distinctive, and the recording is bright and vivid.

Missa pastoralis in G; Missa solemnis in C

(BB) *** Naxos 8.555080. Haines, Ainsworth, Pitkanen, Tower Voices, New Zealand Arcadia Ens., Grodd

Vaňhal's *Pastoral Mass* has a delightfully lyrical *cantabile* feeling, which gives the music a warmth and Arcadian simplicity that is very beguiling. Not all the solo contributions are absolutely secure, especially when two female voices are combined, but the choral response is very persuasive and the result is most rewarding. The *Missa solemnis* is rather more conventional, but Vaňhal's setting is still richly enjoyable with the *Benedictus* and *Agnus Dei* particularly lovely. And he always makes the most of his 'Amens'. The spacious recording

adds to one's enjoyment, and any minor reservations are swept aside when the disc is so inexpensive.

VARÈSE, Edgar (1883–1965)

Tuning Up; Amériques (original version); *Arcana; Dance for Burgesses;* (i) *Density 21.5. Déserts;* (ii) *Ecuatorial;* (iii; iv) *Un grand sommeil noir* (original version). (iii) *Un Grand sommeil noir* (orch. Beaumont); *Hyperprism; Intégrales; Ionisation;* (v; vi) N*octurnal, Octandre;* (v) *Offrandes; Poème électronique*

⌐ ❂ (M) *** Decca 475 487-2 (2) Concg. O or ASKO Ens., Chailly; with (i) Zoon; (ii) Deas; (iii; iv) Delunsch; (iv) Kardoncuff; (v) Leonard; (vi) Prague Philharmonic Male Ch.

This comprehensive coverage of the music of Varèse was given the 1999 *Gramophone* Award for Twentieth-Century Music. He first came to public notice in the 1930s when Percy Scholes chose him to represent the last word in zany modernity in his 'Columbia History of Music', but his mockery backfired. *Octandre* (one movement then recorded) sounds as quirkily original now as it did then (it is played marvellously here). The witty opening *Tuning Up* sets the mood for writing which is ever ready to take its own course regardless of tradition and set new musical paths. *Amériques*, which follows, is heard in its original (1921) version, lavishly scored, with reminiscences of music by others, not least the Stravinsky of *The Rite of Spring*. It makes fascinating listening. *Ionisation*, less ear-catching, stands as a historic pointer towards developments in percussion writing. *Poème électronique* originated at the 1958 Brussels World Fair, where it was played through more than 400 loudspeakers inside the Philips pavilion. The montage of familiar and electronic sounds (machine noises, sonorous bells, etc.) comes from the composer's own original four-track tape. But all the works here are sharply distinctive and show the composer as a true revolutionary, usually decades ahead of his time. The vocal pieces are among the most fascinating aurally, not least *Ecuatorial*, a setting in Spanish with bass soloist of a Maya prayer, brightly coloured and sharp with brass, percussion, organ, piano and ondes martenot. *Un Grand sommeil noir* is a rare surviving early song, lyrically Ravelian in feeling, heard here in both the original version with piano, and in an orchestration by Antony Beaumont. *Nocturnal*, Varèse's haunting last piece, was left unfinished. Completed by Professor Chou, it is as extravagant and uninhibited as ever, featuring male chorus and a solo soprano voice, used melodically to evoke a mysterious dream-world. All the performances here are superbly definitive and this set will be hard to surpass. The recording acoustic, too, is open, yet everything is clear.

Amériques (revised version); Arcana; (i) Densité. Déserts; Hyperprism; Intégrales; Ionisation; Octandre; (ii) Ecuatorial; (iii; iv) Nocturnal; (iii) Offrandes

(N) (BB) * Warner Apex 2564 62087-2. O de France, Nagano; with (i) Philippe Pierlot; (ii) Isherwood; (iii) Bryn-Johnson; (iv) Male Ch. of R. France

Anyone wanting an inexpensive voyage through Varèse's extraordinary sound-world can turn to Nagano and his team on Apex. The Erato recording is both strikingly vivid and atmospheric. The Stravinsky associations (and in one instance a virtual quotation) in *Arcana* and *Amériques* come over dramatically and with plenty of vitality. The latter gains from its revision: more concise and orchestrally hardly less luscious. *Ionisation* (for percussion) is surprisingly listener-friendly, and *Octandre* even has an element of wit. Both soloists are excellent, Nicholas Isherwood in *Ecuatorial*, with its weirdly exotic jungle background including two ondes martenot and organ, all but out-Loboses Villa-Lobos, and Phyllis Bryn-Johnson is engagingly refined, especially in *Offrandes*; while the choral contribution to *Nocturnal* is quite extraordinary. *Déserts* ends the programme even more spectacularly. What Nagano achieves here (helped by the excellent performances and often sensational sound) is to make this music seem just as audaciously new and uncompromisingly avant garde as when it first astonished the musical public. And no one could say, when it is presented so vitally spontaneously, that it is not stimulating – though not heard all at once!

VAUGHAN WILLIAMS, Ralph (1872–1958)

(i) *Concerto accademico. Fantasia on Greensleeves; 5 Variants of Dives and Lazarus; 2 Hymn-Tune Preludes*; (i) *The Lark Ascending; Oboe Concerto. Old King Cole* (ballet); *The Poisoned Kiss: Overture; 49th Parallel: Prelude; Prelude on an Old Carol Tune; 2 Preludes on Welsh Hymn Tunes; The Running Set; Sea Songs: Quick march. Serenade to Music* (orchestral version); (ii) *5 Mystical Songs*

(B) *** EMI 5 73986-2 (2). (i) Creswick; (ii) Roberts; E. N. Sinfonia, Hickox

This disc comprises the bulk of three LPs Richard Hickox made in the mid-1980s. It includes some rarities and occasional pieces written for particular events or projects, such as the *Prelude* to the film, *49th Parallel*. The ballet music for *Old King Cole* is lively and full of charm, as is the tuneful overture to the sadly neglected opera, *The Poisoned Kiss*. Bradley Creswick's account of the *Concerto accademico* is one of the finest available, with the complex mood of the *Adagio*, both ethereal and ecstatic, caught on the wing, and he seems equally at home in *The Lark Ascending*. Roger Wingfield is hardly less engaging in the *Oboe Concerto*, his timbre full of pastoral colour, while he displays a deliciously light touch in the finale. *Greensleeves* is taken spaciously, but Hickox brings out the breadth as well as the lyrical beauty of the melody. *Dives and Lazarus*, rich in sonority, and the two *Hymn-Tune Preludes* have their elegiac mood judged perfectly. The *Five Mystical Songs* are sensitively done, though Stephen Roberts displays a rather gritty vibrato. All in all, an excellent bargain collection, very well recorded. The *Serenade to Music*, however, loses a dimension in its orchestral version.

(i) *Concerto accademico for Violin. Concerto grosso for Strings*; (ii) *Oboe Concerto*; (iii) *Piano Concerto in C*; (iv) *Tuba Concerto. 2 Hymn-Tune Preludes*; (v) *The Lark Ascending. Partita for Double String Orchestra*; (vi) *Towards the Unknown Region*

*** Chan. 9262/3. (i) Sillito; (ii) Theodore; (iii) Shelley; (iv) Harrild; (v) M. Davis; (vi) L. Symphony Ch.; LSO, Thomson

Chandos offer here as a separate compendium the series of mostly concertante works that were used as fillers for Bryden Thomson's set of the *Symphonies*, and with generous measure and characteristically fine recording this pair of CDs is very attractive. With immaculate LSO string ensemble, the *Concerto grosso* under Thomson's persuasive direction shows how

in glowing sound its easy, unforced inspiration brings it close to the world of the *Tallis Fantasia*. While many performances of the *Concerto accademico* make the composer's neo-classical manner sound like Stravinsky with an English accent, Thomson and Sillito find a rustic jollity in the outer movements very characteristic of Vaughan Williams. David Theodore's plangent tones in the *Oboe Concerto* effectively bring out the equivocal character of this highly original work, making it far more than just another pastoral piece. Howard Shelley addresses the neglected *Piano Concerto* with flair and brilliance, making light of the disconcerting cragginess of the piano writing and consistently bringing out both the wit and the underlying emotional power. The bluff good humour of the *Tuba Concerto* is beautifully caught in Patrick Harrild's rumbustious account, and this outstanding tuba soloist plays with wit and panache. Michael Davis makes a rich-toned soloist in *The Lark Ascending*, presenting it as more than a pastoral evocation. The *Hymn-Tune Preludes* are unashamedly pastoral in tone; then the *Partita* finds the composer in more abrasive mood, less easily sympathetic. *Towards the Unknown Region* is the only relative disappointment – a setting of Whitman that antedates the *Sea Symphony*. The choral sound is beautiful, but this early work really needs tauter treatment.

(i) *Concerto grosso for Strings*; (i; ii) *Oboe Concerto*; (i) *English Folksongs Suite* (trans. Gordon Jacob); *Fantasia on Greensleeves* (arr. Greaves); (iii) *Fantasia on a Theme by Thomas Tallis*; (i; iv) *The Lark Ascending*; (iii) *5 Variants of Dives and Lazarus; In the Fen Country; Norfolk Rhapsody 1*; (v) *Partita for Double String Orchestra*; (i; vi) *Romance for Harmonica, Strings & Piano*

(B) **(*) Double Decca ADD/DDD 460 357-2 (2). (i) ASMF, Marriner; (ii) Nicklin; (iii) New Queen's Hall O, Wordsworth; (iv) Brown; (v) LPO, Boult; (vi) Reilly

This Double Decca offers a fascinating comparison in that the first disc brings modern-instrument recordings (from Marriner and his Academy) and the second a special kind of period-instrument performance, although it is Boult and the LPO who give us the *Partita*. With the ASMF, Celia Nicklin gives a most persuasive account of the elusive *Oboe Concerto*, while the *Concerto grosso* is lively and polished. The atmospheric *Romance*, although not one of the composer's most inspired works, is still worth having, and the *Folksongs* could hardly be presented more breezily; *The Lark Ascending* is superbly balanced and refined, with Iona Brown an inspirational soloist. The performances on the second disc are given by the re-formed New Queen's Hall Orchestra playing instruments in use at the turn of the century. *Portamento* is featured in the string style but here it is applied very judiciously, and for the most part the ear notices the fuller, warmer sonority of the violins, the treble less brilliant in attack. In works like the *Tallis Fantasia* and *Dives and Lazarus* one can readily wallow in the richly refined textures, but Wordsworth's performance of *Tallis* misses the final degree of intensity at the climax, and the opening of *Dives and Lazarus* is also rather relaxed, even indulgent in relishing the sheer breadth of sonority achieved, though the closing pages are ethereally lovely. The performers are at their finest in the evocative opening of the *Norfolk Rhapsody*, while *In the Fen Country* has a fine idyllic ardour, with some very sensitive playing from wind and brass in the coda. The Wordsworth recording, made in Walthamstow Assembly Hall, is splendidly expansive and natural.

Concerto grosso; Fantasia on Greensleeves; Fantasia on a Theme of Thomas Tallis; In the Fen Country; Norfolk Rhapsody 1

(BB) **(*) Naxos 8.555867. New Zealand SO, Judd

As music director of the New Zealand Symphony Orchestra, James Judd draws warmly expressive performances from his players in this attractive group of favourite Vaughan Williams works, helped by richly resonant recording. A sequence of recordings by this orchestra has demonstrated what a fine body it has become, and there are outstanding solo contributions from the leading string-players in the *Tallis Fantasia*. The folk-based writing of the *Norfolk Rhapsody* and the impressionistic study *In the Fen Country* are given a satisfying firmness of purpose, with climaxes surging passionately. The *Greensleeves Fantasia* is treated with a degree of reserve, avoiding all sentimentality, and although the *Concerto grosso*, with its contrasted groups of players (originally designed to be played by the members of the Rural Schools Music Association), is a degree less polished in ensemble, the warmth and impulsiveness make ample amends, helped by the full-bodied sound.

(i; ii) *Concerto grosso*; (iii; iv) *Fantasia on a Theme by Thomas Tallis*; (i; ii; v) *The Lark Ascending*; (i; ii) *Partita*; (vi; iv) *Romance in D flat*; (i; ii; vii; viii) *Dona nobis pacem*; (i; ii; vii; ix) *Fantasia on the Old 104th Psalm Tune*; (x) *Magnificat*; (i; ii; vii; viii) *Towards the Unknown Region*

(B) **(*) EMI mono/stereo 5 74782-2 (2). (i) LPO; (ii) Boult; (iii) Philh. O; (iv) Sargent; (v) with Pougnet; (vi) Adler, Gritton, BBC SO; (vii) LPO Ch.; (viii) Armstrong, Carol Case; (ix) Katin; (x) Watts, Amb. S., O Nova of London, Davies

This self-recommending Vaughan Williams anthology includes some unexpected items, notably the atmospheric *Romance*, beautifully performed by Larry Adler, its dedicatee, in 1952. Boult's affinity with this composer is well known, and it is good to hear again just how well he presents the powerful and sustained climax in the *Dona nobis pacem*. As for the *Fantasia on the Old 104th* (for piano, chorus and orchestra) – far from the composer's greatest work – Boult's team (with Peter Katin as the pianist) makes it sound better than it really is. The *Partita* and *Concerto grosso* are beautifully done, and *Towards the Unknown Region* is similarly impressive. The *Lark Ascending* is the only Boult item not dating from the 1970s: it was recorded (in mono) with Jean Pougnet as the soloist in 1952 and made its CD début here. It's a good performance, though some allowances have to made for the sound. Also, it was a pity that Boult's 1970s version of the *Tallis Fantasia* was not chosen; Sargent doesn't quite produce the spiritual quality this work ideally needs, despite the beautiful playing and good 1959 sound. The Holstian *Magnificat* is performed with sympathy and imagination by Meredith Davies's team, and the 1970 recording has transferred well. This set is well worth considering, even though no texts are offered.

(i; ii) *Oboe Concerto*; (i; iii) *Tuba Concerto*. (iv) *Fantasia on Greensleeves; 5 Variants of Dives and Lazarus; Sinfonia antartica (No. 7); The Wasps: Overture*

(M) (***) EMI mono 5 66543-2 (2). (i) LSO; with (ii) Rothwell; (iii) Catelinet; (iv) Hallé O, Barbirolli — ELGAR: *Cockaigne; Introduction & Allegro; Serenade.* (***)

Vividly transferred, this double-disc collection brings together Barbirolli's superb readings of Vaughan Williams

and Elgar from the early 1950s. Strong and warmly expressive, these performances reflect the quality of the Hallé in the early 1950s, with the LSO equally responsive in the concertos. Central to the collection is the première recording of the *Sinfonia antartica*, made only five months after Barbirolli had conducted the first performance in January 1953. The thrust and power have never been surpassed, and the clear, immediate recording brings out the originality of the orchestration. Evelyn Rothwell, Lady Barbirolli, plays the *Oboe Concerto* with heartfelt warmth and understanding, while the *Tuba Concerto* is superbly characterized, bluff in the outer movements, tender in the slow movement. With the coupled Elgar items, an outstanding reissue.

'*Portrait of Vaughan Williams*': (i–iii) *Oboe Concerto*; (i; ii) *Fantasia on Greensleeves; Fantasia on a Theme by Thomas Tallis; 5 Variants of Dives and Lazarus*; (i; ii; iv) *The Lark Ascending*. (i; ii) *The Wasps Overture*. (v; vi) *Phantasy Quintet*; (v) *String Quartets 1–2*. (vii; viii; i) *Flos campi*; (vii) *Mass in G min.*; (vii; i) *O, clap your hands; The Old Hundredth Psalm Tune*; (viii; i; ix) *An Oxford Elegy*. (vii) *3 Shakespeare Songs*. Sacred and secular songs: *Blessed Son of God; Lord, Thou hast been our refuge; No sad thought his soul affright; O taste and see; Valiant for truth*; (vii; i) *Te Deum*

(BB) *** Nim. NI 1754 (4). (i) English String O, (ii) Boughton; (iii) with Bourge; (iv) with Bochman; (v) Medici Qt; (vi) with Rowland-Jones; (vii) Christ Church Cathedral Ch., Oxford, Darlington; (viii) with Best; (ix) with May (narrator)

This super-budget Nimbus boxed set offers a wonderfully illuminating cross-section of Vaughan Williams's music, showing its consistent inspiration, and both its diversity and its linkages. The orchestral and concertante music included here is all very familiar, but is most sympathetically played under William Boughton (with sensitive soloists) and presented amply and atmospherically, and with a rich amplitude of string tone. The chamber music shows a more intimate side of the composer: the special atmosphere of these works, with moments of haunting delicacy, is warmly and idiomatically caught, but with no lack of concentration and intensity. The Medici players were recorded in The Maltings, which means a sympathetic ambience, but also that the microphones are rather close. The glorious sonorities of the unaccompanied *Mass in G minor*, with its double choir and four soloists, draw an immediate vocal parallel with the *Tallis Fantasia*. The *Mass* opens with a *Kyrie* which looks back to the Elizabethan era and beyond, and then blossoms polyphonically in the *Gloria* and swaying *Sanctus* before the beautiful closing *Agnus Dei*. The *Oxford Elegy* brings more fine music, but the narrative, confidently and clearly delivered here by Jack May, remains as intrusive as ever (its inclusion was not one of the composer's best ideas). With Roger Best a fine viola soloist, *Flos campi* is particularly successful, as are the *Te Deum* and the shorter unaccompanied choral songs, especially the three imaginative Shakespeare settings. All in all this is a cornucopia of musical joys, worth getting, even if you already have recordings of the better-known orchestral pieces.

(i) *Oboe Concerto. Fantasia on Greensleeves; Fantasia on a Theme of Thomas Tallis; 5 Variants of Dives and Lazarus*; (ii) *The Lark Ascending. The Wasps: Overture*

(M) *** Nim. NI 7013. (i) Bourgue; (ii) Bochmann; E. String O or SO, Boughton

Opening with an exuberant account of *The Wasps Overture*, this is a very attractive and generous 70-minute collection of favourite Vaughan Williams orchestral pieces, most sympathetically played under William Boughton and presented atmospherically. The spacious acoustic of the Great Hall of Birmingham University ensures that the lyrical string-tune in the overture is properly expansive without robbing the piece of bite and that both the deeply felt *Tallis Fantasia*, with its passionate climax, and *Dives and Lazarus* have a rich amplitude of string-sound. Michael Bochmann, the sympathetic soloist in *The Lark Ascending*, playing simply yet with persuasive lyrical freedom, is nicely integrated with the warm orchestral backing. More questionable is the *Oboe Concerto*, with the superb French soloist Maurice Bourgue balanced too close. Bourgue's playing, sharply rhythmical and with a rich, pastoral timbre, is ideally suited to the piece.

(i) *Oboe Concerto. Fantasia on Greensleeves;* (ii) *The Lark Ascending*

(M) *** DG (ADD) 439 529-2. (i) Black; (ii) Zukerman, ECO, Barenboim – DELIUS: *Aquarelles*, etc.; WALTON: *Henry V* ***

Neil Black's creamy tone is ideally suited to Vaughan Williams's *Oboe Concerto* and he gives a wholly persuasive performance. Zukerman's account of *The Lark Ascending* is full of pastoral rapture – not always quite idiomatic but totally ravishing. The recordings, from the late 1970s, are warmly atmospheric in the digital remastering.

Piano Concerto in C

(B) *** CFP 575 9832. Lane, RLPO, Handley – DELIUS: *Piano Concerto;* FINZI: *Eclogue* ***

Piers Lane defies the old idea of this as a grittily unpianistic work, giving it a powerful, refreshing reading, helped by fine playing from the RLPO under Handley, always a sympathetic Vaughan Williams interpreter, while the apt and unusual coupling can be warmly recommended.

(i) *Piano Concerto; Symphony 9 in E min.*

*** Chan. 8941. (i) Shelley, LPO, Thomson

The most strikingly original of the three movements of the *Piano Concerto* is the imaginative and inward-looking *Romanza*, which has some of the angularity of line one finds in *Flos campi*, while the finale presages the *Fourth Symphony*. The piece abounds in difficulties, which Howard Shelley addresses with flair and brilliance. He makes light of the disconcerting cragginess of the piano writing and consistently brings out both the wit and the underlying emotional power. Bryden Thomson conducts a powerful performance of the last of Vaughan Williams's symphonies. Though the playing may not be ideally incisive, it brings out an extra warmth of expression. Both performances are greatly helped by the richness and weight of the Chandos sound, warmly atmospheric but with ample detail and fine presence.

(i; ii) *English Folksongs Suite; Fantasia on Greensleeves;* (iii) *Fantasia on a Theme by Thomas Tallis;* (ii; iv; v) *The Lark Ascending;* (ii; v) *Norfolk Rhapsody 1;* (vi) *5 Variants of Dives and Lazaras;* (ii; vii) *The Wasps (Aristophanic Suite): Overture*

(N) (BB) *** EMI (ADD/DDD) 5 86778-2. (i) LSO, (ii) Boult; (iii) Sinfonia of L., Barbirolli; (iv) Hugh Bean; (v) New Philh. O; (vi) CBSO, Del Mar; (vii) LPO

All the music here is beautifully performed and recorded.

Hugh Bean understands the spirit of *The Lark Ascending* perfectly and his performance is wonderfully serene. Barbirolli's account of the *Tallis Fantasia* is the finest available, and the other Boult performances are warmly sympathetic too.

(i) *English Folksongs Suite;* (ii) *Fantasia on a Theme by Thomas Tallis; The Lark Ascending;* (iii) *Partita for Double String Orchestra;* (iv; v) *6 Studies in English Folksong;* (iv; vi) *3 Vocalises for Soprano and Clarinet*

(M) **(*) ASV Platinum (DDD/ADD) PLT 8520. (i) London Wind O; (ii) ASMF, Marriner; with Brown; (iii) London Fest. O, Pople; (iv) Johnson; (v) Martineau; (vi) Howarth

The London Wind Orchestra's 1980 account of the *English Folksongs Suite* is the only analogue recording here, but the sound is extremely bright and vivid, and the *Suite* is given a comparably zestful performance. If the slow movement might have been played more reflectively, the bounce of *Seventeen Come Sunday* is irresistible. Iona Brown has recorded *The Lark Ascending* before with Marriner and the ASMF but this newer, digital version is both eloquent and evocative, although the great clarity of the recording does rob it of a little atmosphere. However, Marriner's ASV version of the *Tallis Fantasia*, though beautifully played, is relatively bland beside his classic Argo account (now on a Double Decca). Ross Pople's fresh yet relaxed reading of the *Partita* is a very good one indeed, even if it can't match the sheer beauty of sound of the ASMF. The *6 Studies in English Folksong* are excellently played and recorded, and are delightful, as are the brief *3 Vocalises*, a curiously haunting work.

English Folksongs Suite; Flourish for Wind Band; Toccata marziale

*** Chan. 9697. Royal N. College of Music Wind O, Reynish – HOLST: *Hammersmith*, etc. ***

Vaughan Williams's music for wind band is less inspired than that of Holst, but the jaunty *English Folksongs Suite* certainly sounds more vivid in its original scoring than it does in the orchestral version. It could hardly be played more breezily than it is here, and the other two pieces also come off splendidly. Demonstration sound.

Fantasia on Greensleeves; Fantasia on a Theme of Thomas Tallis

◄━━ ⦿ (M) *** EMI (ADD) 5 67240-2 [567264]. Sinfonia of L.; (i) with Allegri Qt; Barbirolli – ELGAR: *Introduction & Allegro for Strings*, etc. *** ⦿

(BB) **(*) RCA 74321 68018-2. Philh. O, Slatkin – HOLST: *The Planets* **

Fantasia on Greensleeves; Fantasia on a Theme of Tallis; (i) *The Lark Ascending*

(BB) *** Virgin 2x1 5 61763-2 (2). LCO, Warren-Green; (i) with Warren-Green (violin) – DVORAK: *Serenade for Strings;* ELGAR: *Introduction & Allegro; Serenade;* SUK: *Serenade;* TCHAIKOVSKY: *Serenade* ***

(B) *** Sony (ADD) SBK 62645. (i) Phd. O, Ormandy; (ii) Druian; Cleveland Sinf., Lane – DELIUS: *Brigg Fair*, etc. ***

Barbirolli's inspirational performance of the *Tallis Fantasia* now rightly takes its place among EMI's 'Great Recordings of the Century'. His ardour combined with the magically quiet playing of the second orchestra is unforgettable. The recording has magnificent definition and sonority, achieving dramatic contrasts between the main orchestra and the distanced solo group, which sounds wonderfully ethereal.

Christopher Warren-Green and his London Chamber Orchestra give a radiant account of *The Lark Ascending*, in which Warren-Green makes a charismatic solo contribution, very free and soaring in its flight and with beautifully sustained true *pianissimo* playing at the opening and close. For the *Tallis Fantasia*, the second orchestra (2.2.2.2.1) contrasts with the main group (5.4.2.2.1) and here, though the effect is beautifully serene, Warren-Green does not quite match the ethereal, otherworldly *pianissimo* that made Barbirolli's reading unforgettable. The performance overall has great ardour and breadth, almost to match the coupled *Introduction and Allegro* of Elgar in its intensity. The recording, made at All Saints' Church, Petersham, has resonant warmth and atmosphere yet sharp definition. This now comes as part of one of the most desirable of all the Virgin 2×1 Doubles, offering a remarkably generous programme of string music, all very well played and recorded.

The excellent performances from 1963 on Sony demonstrate the special feeling American musicians can find for English music. In the *Tallis Fantasia* Ormandy (like Barbirolli) characteristically underlines the drama of a work that is often regarded as delicate and atmospheric. The recording of *The Lark Ascending* was made during the period when Louis Lane was a colleague of George Szell at Cleveland and the orchestra was at the peak of its form. Rafael Druian is the intensely poetic violin soloist, producing the most delicate sustained *pianissimos*, even though the balance is close. The orchestral playing is both polished and characterful. The CD transfers have expanded the original sound most strikingly. With expressive Delius performances as coupling, this is one of the most desirable of Sony's 'Essential Classics'.

Beautifully played and very well-recorded accounts of the two *Fantasias* from Slatkin, with the contrasts between the main string group and the smaller 'concertino' in the *Tallis Fantasia* well brought out. If not in the Barbirolli league, these performances are still enjoyable. Unfortunately, the main work on this disc, Holst's *Planets*, is less recommendable.

**(i) *Fantasia on Greensleeves*; (ii) *Fantasia on a Theme by Thomas Tallis*; 5 Variants on Dives and Lazarus; In the Fen Country; (i; iii) *The Lark Ascending*; (ii) *Norfolk Rhapsody 1*
*** Chan. 9775. (i) LSO; (ii) LPO; Thomson; (iii) with M. Davis**

It is good to have *In the Fen Country* and the *First Norfolk Rhapsody* in such beautiful modern digital sound and played so sympathetically. Indeed, Bryden Thomson is a most persuasive guide in all this repertoire, although in the *Tallis Fantasia* he is rather more concerned with sonority, beauty and contrasts of texture than with subtlety. Michael Davis makes a rich-toned soloist in *The Lark Ascending*, presenting it as more than a gentle pastoral invocation. Although these recordings are now nearly a decade old, the generous measure (79 minutes) almost compensates for the continued premium price.

(i; ii) *Fantasia on Greensleeves*; (iii; iv) 2 Hymn-Tune Preludes; Overtures: *The Poisoned Kiss*; (v; ii) *The Wasps*: Overture. (vi) *Romance for Harmonica & Orchestra*; (iii; iv) *The Running Set*; (iii; iv) Sea Songs (march); (iii; vii; viii) *Suite for Viola & Orchestra*; (ix) 6 Studies in English Folksong; (iii; vii; viii; x) *Flos campi*; (xi) Linden Lea; (xii) *The House of Life*: Love-sight; Silent noon; Heart's haven. (ii; v) Serenade to Music
(B) **(*) Chan. 2-for-1 ADD/DDD 2419 (2). (i) BBC PO; (ii) Handley; (iii) Bournemouth Sinf.; (iv) Hurst; (v) LPO; (vi)

Reilly, ASMF, Marriner; (vii) Riddle; (viii) Del Mar; (ix) Hilton, Swallow; (x) Bournemouth Sinf. Ch.; (xi) Huddersfield Ch., Kay; (xii) Varcoe, City of L. Sinfonia, Hickox

A generally attractive, if rather bitty, anthology, including a fair proportion of lesser-known Vaughan Williams. Exceptionally well recorded and vividly impressive, Vernon Handley's readings of the *Wasps Overture*, the *Greensleeves Fantasia* and the *Serenade to Music* in its orchestral version are most sympathetically done. The *Overture* to the opera *The Poisoned Kiss* is merely a potpourri, but it is presented most persuasively here. *The Running Set* is an exhilarating fantasy on jig rhythms. Fine performances under George Hurst, who also includes the two very characteristic *Hymn-Tune Preludes*. The evocation of the Song of Solomon contained in *Flos campi* shows Vaughan Williams at his most rarefied and imaginative, while the *Suite for Viola and Orchestra* is lightweight but engagingly unpretentious music with its charming *Carol* and quirky *Polka mélancolique*. Frederick Riddle is an eloquent soloist, even if the playing is not always technically immaculate, and Norman Del Mar directs sympathetically. Tommy Reilly, with Marriner, gives a haunting account of the *Romance for Harmonica and Orchestra*, while the attractive arrangements for clarinet and piano of the *Folksong Studies* are also played most sensitively by Janet Hilton and Keith Swallow. Roger Varcoe is the generally sympathetic soloist in three of the songs from the Rossetti cycle, *The House of Life* (orchestrated by Maurice Johnson), of which the most famous is *Silent noon*. His vibrato is occasionally intrusive, but the warmth of Hickox's accompaniment is a considerable plus point. *Linden Lea* is heard in its choral arrangement, pleasingly sung a cappella by the Huddersfield Choral Society under Brian Kay.

Fantasia on a Theme of Tallis
◑ (N) (BB) *** Warner Apex 2564 61437-2. RPO, Warren-Green − BRITTEN: *Simple Symphony*; BUTTERWORTH: *Banks of Green Willow*; ELGAR: *String Serenade*; HOLST: *St Paul's Suite* ***

Christopher Warren-Green's rich-textured RPO performance is even finer than his earlier, Virgin version in creating the necessary dynamic contrast between the opposing string groups, with the tension in *pianissimos* raptly sustained and climaxes richly expansive. This is part of an outstanding anthology of English music, all excellently played and recorded.

Fantasia on a Theme of Thomas Tallis; 5 Variants of Dives and Lazarus; In the Fen Country; Norfolk Rhapsody
*** Chan. 8502. LPO, Thomson

(i) *Fantasia on a Theme by Thomas Tallis*; 5 Variants of Dives and Lazarus; Norfolk Rhapsody 1; (ii) *In Windsor Forest*; (i; iii) *Toward the Unknown Region*
(M) *** EMI (ADD) 5 65131-2. (i) CBSO; (ii) Bournemouth Symphony Ch. & Sinf.; (iii) with CBSO Ch.; Del Mar

*Fantasia on a Theme by Thomas Tallis; In the Fen Country; (i) *The Lark Ascending*. Norfolk Rhapsody 1; (ii) *On Wenlock Edge* (cycle)*
(M) **(*) EMI 5 85151-2. (i) Chang; (ii) Bostridge; LPO, Haitink

Norman Del Mar's strong and deeply felt account of the *Tallis Fantasia* is given a splendid digital recording, with the second orchestral group creating radiant textures. The direct approach, however, lacks something in mystery, and not all of the ethereal resonance of this haunting work is conveyed. The early (1907) cantata, *Toward the Unknown Region*, set to words of Walt Whitman, and *In Windsor Forest*, which the composer adapted from his *Falstaff* opera, *Sir John in Love*, make a perfect coupling. Norman Del Mar directs warmly sympathetic performances, given excellent sound.

Bryden Thomson is a most persuasive guide in all this repertoire and more than holds his own with most of the opposition.

An appealing anthology assembled from fill-ups originally offered with Haitink's set of the symphonies. The comparatively rare *Norfolk Rhapsody* is particularly welcome when it is so beautifully played. In the *Tallis Fantasia*, Haitink's straight rhythmic manners make the result sensitively unidiomatic, but very powerful in its monumental directness, helped by a recording of spectacular range. Sarah Chang proves an intensely poetic soloist in *The Lark Ascending*, volatile at the start in the bird-like, fluttering motif and magnetically concentrated to match. With Ian Bostridge the sensitive, honey-toned soloist, the six songs of the Housman cycle make a welcome closing section. First-class recording throughout.

Film Music: *Coastal Command* (suite); *Elizabeth of England: Three Portraits. 49th Parallel: Prelude. The Story of a Flemish Farm* (suite)

**(*) Marco Polo 8.223665. RTE Concert O, Dublin, Penny

Vaughan Williams's wartime film music was of the highest quality. The Powell/Pressburger movie *49th Parallel* (1941), made in the early years of the war, inspired a *Prelude* with a nostalgic patriotic feeling. *Coastal Command* (1942) was a dramatized documentary which centred on the romantic profiles of the Catalina flying-boats, resulting in warmly evocative music, with echoes from the composer's symphonic writing. The even more imaginative (1943) score for *The Story of a Flemish Farm* (a true story about personal sacrifice which enabled a wartime escape to England) brings similar resonances. The masterly evocation of *Dawn in the Barn* clearly anticipates the *Sixth Symphony*, while the haunting sequence *The Dead Man's Kit* evokes the *Sinfonia antartica*. *Elizabeth in England* (1955–7), another documentary, narrated by Alec Clunes, has its Elizabethan hey-nonny flavour, but there is a haunting *Poet* sequence which introduces a magically gentle tune, also used in the *Sea Symphony*. Finally comes a celebration of *The Queen*, not just regal but thoughtful in restrained nobility. Andrew Penny is a splendid advocate in performances eloquent in their mood-painting. The recording is bright and full, if rather two-dimensional.

Film Music: *Coastal Command; The People's Land; Scott of the Antarctic*

*** Chan. 10007. M. Gamba, Sheffield Philh. Ch., BBC PO, R. Gamba

When, in 1947, Vaughan Williams was asked to write the music for Michael Balcon's film *Scott of the Antarctic*, he was so enthusiastic about the idea that he composed a great deal of the score before he had even seen the script. The result was that little more than half the music he wrote was used in the film. He was later moved to use much of that material in his seventh symphony, the *Sinfonia antartica*. This 40-minute suite brings together virtually all the music he wrote, including much striking material not used in either the film or the symphony. It is astonishing that a composer in his mid-seventies could conceive such totally original musical ideas and sonorities in one movement after another. Helped by

vividly atmospheric sound, Rumon Gamba draws superb playing from the BBC Philharmonic, and there are haunting vocal effects from Merryn Gamba and the Sheffield Philharmonic Choir. Suites from two other characterful film scores make a colourful supplement.

Film Music: *The Dim Little Island; The England of Elizabeth; 49th Parallel* (all ed. Stephen Hogger)

*** Chan. 10244. Soloists, Chetham's Chamber Ch., BBC PO, Gamba

The magnetic *nobilmente* theme for the title and closing sequence of *49th Parallel* is totally memorable, to match the outstanding film it illustrated, and much of the rest of this score shows the composer at his most pictorially imaginative. For the ten-minute short, *The Dim Little Island*, however, VW effectively reworked his *Variants on Dives and Lazarus*. The documentary *Elizabeth of England*, with its generous folk-song and folk-dance influences, shows how he felt completely at home in the musical world of Tudor England. Yet in its elaborate colouring the music has much in common with the *Eighth Symphony*, although the score also quotes ideas from two other works. Splendidly restored by Stephen Hogger, the music is superbly played, sung and recorded.

Job (A Masque for Dancing)

(BB) *** Warner Apex 0927 444 394-2. BBC SO, A. Davis – WALTON: *Belshazzar's Feast* ***

Job (A Masque for Dancing); Fantasia on a Theme by Thomas Tallis; 5 Variants on Dives and Lazarus

(B) *** CfP (ADD/DDD) 575 3142. LPO, Handley

Job (A Masque for Dancing); (i) *The Lark Ascending*

— (BB) *** Naxos 8.553955. E. N. Philh., Lloyd-Jones, (i) with Greed

David Lloyd-Jones – at super-budget price on Naxos – upstages all competition. He gives a performance tingling with drama, yet with great delicacy. The opening scene is particularly atmospheric and the *Saraband of the Sons of God* brings a noble dignity, especially when it returns expansively on the full brass. There is much fine orchestral playing. The big climaxes bring a superb brass contribution, almost submerging the organ at the vision of Satan. The dance rhythms are caught superbly – bitingly so in *Satan's Dance of Triumph*, genially Holstian in the *Galliard of the Sons of the Morning*. The Epilogue is touchingly ethereal. The recording, made in Leeds Town Hall, has an ideal spaciousness, yet combines vivid detail with glowing textures. For an encore the orchestral leader, David Greed, provides an exquisitely delicate portrayal of *The Lark Ascending*, with a beautifully sustained closing *pianissimo*.

Handley's performance of *Job* too is outstandingly fine. His dedicated approach shows the composer's inspiration at its most deeply characteristic and most consistently noble. The breadth of dynamic of the EMI analogue recording is used to enormous effect to increase the drama: the organ entry representing Satan enthroned in heaven has great presence and is overwhelming in impact. Comparably the ravishingly luminous *espressivo* playing in the work's quieter lyrical pages is movingly beautiful, with the music's evocative feeling memorably captured. The other works also show Handley at his best, especially *Dives and Lazarus*.

It was an imaginative idea to re-couple Vaughan Williams's early 1910 ballet score (intended for Diaghilev, but rejected as being 'too English') with Andrew Davis's fine recording of

Belshazzar's Feast taken from the last night of the 1994 Promenade Concerts – both the '*Masque for Dancing*' (as the composer described it) and Walton's famous choral work vividly depict Bible narratives. The BBC Symphony Orchestra plays *Job* splendidly, and the recording is spacious. As in Davis's other Vaughan Williams records, the orchestra is set back and some of their power is lost. However, no one could say that the spectacular organ entry (recorded earlier by Andrew Davis in King's College Chapel, Cambridge, and effectively dubbed in) does not make a huge impact, while Job's comforters are strongly characterized and the serene closing music, including the lovely *Pavane of the Sons of the Morning*, is radiantly presented.

The Lark Ascending

☛– *** EMI 5 56413-2. Kennedy, CBSO, Rattle – ELGAR: *Violin Concerto* ***

(M) *** EMI 5 62813-2. Kennedy, CBSO, Rattle – WALTON: *Viola Concerto; Violin Concerto* ***

(N) ** DG 474 504-2. Hahn, LSO, Davis – ELGAR: *Violin Concerto* **

Kennedy provides a valuable and welcome fill-up to his fine remake of the Elgar *Concerto* in this spacious and inspirational account of Vaughan Williams's evocative piece.

Vaughan Williams's piece also makes a fine bonus for the two Walton concertos chosen to represent Nigel among EMI's 'Great Artists of the Century'. It is beautifully recorded.

Though *The Lark Ascending* suffers less than the Elgar *Violin Concerto* from a cool approach such as Hilary Hahn adopts, the result misses the work's atmospheric magic, making it disappointing, like the *Concerto*.

(i) The Lark Ascending; (ii) Fantasia on Greensleeves; Fantasia on a Theme by Thomas Tallis

(B) **(*) CfP 574 8802. (i) Nolan, LPO, Handley; (ii) RLPO, Handley – ELGAR: *Enigma Variations; Serenade for Strings* ***

Handley gives an essentially rhapsodic account of the *Tallis Fantasia*, relaxing in its central section and then creating an accelerando to the climax. The inner string group creates radiantly ethereal textures, but ideally the recording needs a little more resonance – the work was written to be performed in Gloucester Cathedral – although it is rich-textured and truthful. The immediacy of the recording allows no mistiness in *The Lark Ascending*, but it is still a warm, understanding performance.

(i) The Lark Ascending; The Wasps: Overture and Aristophanic Suite; Prelude and Fugue in C min.

(B) *** CfP (ADD/DDD) 575 3162. (i) Nolan; LPO, Handley – DELIUS: *Collection* ***

This attractive pairing of favourite items by Vaughan Williams and Delius is aptly entitled '*A Lark and a Cuckoo*'. David Nolan gives a warm, understanding performance of *The Lark Ascending*, projected in clear yet atmospheric digital sound. Then the *Wasps Overture* buzzes in lively fashion. It is spaciously conceived, and leads to charming, colourful accounts of the other four pieces which make up the suite, among which the engaging *March Past of the Kitchen Utensils* stands out. The spectacular *Prelude and Fugue* is an orchestral arrangement of an organ piece (made by the composer) for the Three Choirs Festival, Hereford, in 1930: its style has something in common with *Job*.

Preludes on 3 Welsh Hymn-Tunes

(N) (BB) **(*) Hyp. Helios CDH 55070. L. Brass Virtuosi, Honeyball – ELGAR: *Severn Suite*; IRELAND: *Comedy Overture* **(*)

The three hymn-tunes which Vaughan Williams favours and which are united here are Ebenezer, Calfaria amd Hyfrydol, and the result is quite short and very effective, if not memorable, on a brass group.

Serenade to Music (orchestral version); The Wasps Overture

(M) ** Chan. 10174X. LPO, Handley – DELIUS: *Air and Dance; On Hearing the First Cuckoo in Spring*, etc. **

Exceptionally well recorded, Handley's readings of *The Wasps Overture* and the *Serenade to Music* in its orchestral version are most sympathetically done and, although the *Serenade* lacks a dimension without voices, it is most persuasive and is beautifully played by the LPO. However, at 46 minutes overall, this mid-priced reissue is distinctly ungenerous.

SYMPHONIES

Symphonies 1–9

(N) (B) (***) Decca mono 473 241-2 (5). LPO, Boult, with I. Baillie, Cameron, Ritchie, Gielgud, LPO Ch. in No. 1

In some ways Boult's mono set of the Vaughan Williams symphonies (No. 8 is in stereo) is unsurpassed and the recording still sounds amazingly realistic, especially in the *Sea Symphony*, a demonstration LP in its day. The composer was present at the recording sessions, and the orchestral playing was notable for its inspirational intensity. The five discs come in a strong cardboard box. A set which is as indispensable as it is inexpensive. Boult's first recording of No. 9 is an Everest recording.

Symphonies 1–9

**(*) Chan. 9087/91. LSO, Thomson (with Kenny, Rayner Cook in 1; Kenny in 3; Bott in 7; L. Symphony Ch. in 1 & 7)

(i) Symphonies 1–9; (ii) Concerto accademico in D min.; (iii) Tuba Concerto in F min.; 3 Portraits from Elizabeth in England; The Wasps: Overture

☛– ✿ (B) *** RCA 82876 55708-2 (6). LSO, Previn; with (i) Harper, Shirley-Quirk, Amb. S., L. Symphony Ch., R. Richardson (speaker); (ii) J. O. Buswell; (iii) J. Fletcher

Symphonies 1–9; Oboe Concerto; English Folksongs Suite; Fantasia on Greensleeves; Fantasia on a Theme by Thomas Tallis; 5 Variants on Dives and Lazarus; Flos Campi; Job; Partita for String Orchestra; Serenade to Music

(N) (B) *** CfP (DDD/ADD) 575 7602 (7). Soloists, incl. Christopher Balmer, RLPO Ch. & O, Handley

Symphonies 1-9; (i) Double Piano Concerto. English Folk Song Suite; Fantasia on Greensleeves; Fantasia on a theme by Thomas Tallis; In the Fen Country; Job; (ii) The Lark Ascending. Norfolk Rhapsody; The Wasps: Overture & Suite; (iii) Serenade to Music

(N) (B) *** EMI 5 73924-2 (8). (i) Vronsky & Babin; (ii) Bean; (iii) 16 Vocal Soloists; LPO Ch., LPO, New Philh. O, or LSO Boult

Symphonies 1–9; Fantasia on a Theme by Thomas Tallis; In the Fen Country; (i) The Lark Ascending; (ii) On Wenlock Edge

(N) (B) **(*) EMI 5 86026-2 (7). Soloists, including (i) Sarah Chang; (ii) Bostridge; LPO Ch., LPO, Haitink

Previn recorded the Vaughan Williams *Symphonies* over a five-year span from 1968 to 1972, and his achievement in this repertoire represented a peak in his recording career at that time. Here the nine symphonies plus their original fill-ups have been neatly compressed on to six CDs. The most striking performances are those which were recorded last, Nos. 2, 3 and 5; for these Previn achieves an extra depth of understanding, an extra intensity, whether in the purity of *pianissimo* or the outpouring of emotional resolution. For the rest there is only one performance that can be counted at all disappointing, and that is of the symphony one might have expected Previn to interpret best, the taut and dramatic *Fourth*. Even that is an impressive account, if less intense than the rest. Otherwise, the great landscape of the whole cycle is presented with richness and detail in totally refreshing interpretations, brilliantly recorded and impressively transferred to CD. The extra items are worth having too, notably the two concertos with responsive soloists.

For its reissue, Handley's set has been expanded to seven bargain CDs to include more of the extra works he recorded so sympathetically. It will especially suit those requiring modern digital sound, for only the *Sinfonia Antartica* is analogue – and that is still a fine, modern recording, offering also the orchestral version of the *Serenade to Music* as a fill-up. In all his Vaughan Williams recordings Handley shows a natural understanding for expressive rubato and is totally sympathetic. Many of his performances are first or near first choices. No. 5 is also outstanding in every way and was given a Rosette by us on its first appearance. Its original coupling, a very successful account of *Flos Campi*, is also included here, as is his memorable version of *Job*.

Boult's late 1960s vintage stereo performances remain very satisfying indeed. Boult's approach to Vaughan Williams was firmly symphonic rather than evocative, and many lovers of the composer will like them for their warmly consistent view, patiently studied and broadly presented. If at times the playing is not so electrically urgent as with, for instance, Previn, the maturity of Vaughan Williams's vision has never been more convincingly presented. This newest collection includes also the shorter pieces originally included as fill-ups on LP, plus some extra and important bonuses including the *Double Piano Concerto* and *Job*, a work dedicated to Boult and for which he had a special affinity, and which is superbly recorded. But overall the sound is full-bodied and well focused, and this set presents a comprehensive portrait of the composer, unmatched by any other single issue.

Haitink recorded the nine symphonies and various supporting works for EMI between 1984 and 1997, establishing what to traditional English ears may seem not idiomatic but strong and forthright. At the time of going to press, only the *Sea Symphony, London Symphony* and No. 5 are available separately (and are discussed below), so this bargain box is very welcome indeed, for undoubtedly Haitink throws a new 'international' light on all these works. In the jaunty themes of the *London Symphony* his straight manner at times brings an unexpected Stravinskian quality, and his expansively serene handling of the lovely melodies of the slow movement brings elegiac nobility rather than romantic warmth.

Undoubtedly Haitink is deeply involved in the *Pastoral Symphony*. With expansive tempi he maintains the concentration throughout the *Lento moderato* slow movement, through the powerfully conceived *Moderato pesante* third movement and on to the intensity of the finale. No. 4 too has similar concentrated power held throughout; and again in the *Sixth* he takes a direct, literal view, bringing out the power and thrust of the argument at steady speeds. It may miss some of the mystery of the piece, as in the contrapuntal writing of the hushed epilogue, but the purposefulness is tellingly conveyed.

That same seriousness of purpose and dedication also permeate the *Eighth* and *Ninth Symphonies*, catching the nobility of the composer's vision, with the finale of the *Ninth* making a real apotheosis, when the playing of the LPO is so responsive, involved and involving.

But, perhaps surprisingly, Haitink is at his very finest in the *Sinfonia Antartica*, a revelatory performance of a programmatic work magnificently recorded which, as Haitink shows, can stand powerfully as an original inspiration in absolute terms. Among the fill-ups, the straight rhythmic manner of the *Tallis Fantasia* makes the result sensitively idiomatic and again very powerful in its monumental directness, with superb playing from the LPO and firm, refined sound. Among the other fill-ups is *On Wenlock Edge*, with Ian Bostridge the sensitive, honey-toned soloist.

By omitting the various fillers, Chandos have fitted the nine Vaughan Williams symphonies on to five CDs; each work is offered without a break. However, Bryden Thomson's achievement is somewhat uneven through the cycle. In the *Sea Symphony* the chorus lacks the sharpest focus and the microphone is not kind to Brian Rayner Cook, the baritone soloist. In the *Pastoral Symphony* the orchestral sound is almost too tangible, losing some of the more gentle atmospheric feeling, and this applies also to the *Sinfonia Antartica*. Generally there is no lack of power, and the readings have both individuality and warmth as well as wide-ranging digital recording.

A Sea Symphony (1)

☞ (B) *** CfP 575 3082. Rodgers, Shimell, RLPO & Ch., Handley

(BB) (***) Belart mono 450 144-2. Baillie, Cameron, LPO Ch. & O, Boult

(N) (BB) *** EMI HMV 586777-2. Lott, Summers, LPO Ch., LPO, Haitink

(M) *** EMI 7 64016-2. Armstrong, Carol Case, LPO Ch., LPO, Boult

Vernon Handley conducts a warmly idiomatic performance, which sustains relatively slow speeds masterfully. The reading is crowned by Handley's rapt account of the slow movement, *On the Beach at Night Alone*, as well as by the long duet in the finale, leading on through the exciting final ensemble, *Sail Forth*, to a deeply satisfying culmination in *O my Brave Soul!* Joan Rodgers makes an outstandingly beautiful soprano soloist, with William Shimell drier-toned but expressive. The recording, full and warm, has an extreme dynamic range, placing the two soloists rather distantly.

As a performance, Boult's (early 1952) Decca mono recording with outstanding soloists and incisive and sympathetic singing from the LPO Choir has never been surpassed. This conveys the urgency of a live performance, with the dramatic opening astonishingly vivid and real in the vintage sound. Boult was at his most inspired. This Belart CD makes the very most of the master tape, and only the lack of body of the massed upper strings betrays the age of the original. The choral sound is full and well focused and the Kingsway Hall acoustic spacious and warm; the closing section, *Away O soul*, is particularly beautiful.

As in the rest of his Vaughan Williams series, Bernard Haitink takes what to traditional English ears may seem a very literal view. Speeds are almost all unusually spacious, making this (at well over 70 minutes) the slowest version on record; but Haitink sustains that expansiveness superbly. It is the nobility of the writing, rather than its emotional warmth, that is paramount. The recording is the fullest and weightiest yet given to this work, with the orchestra well defined in front of the chorus. Felicity Lott and Jonathan Summers are both excellent.

Boult's stereo version demonstrates his affectionate style, drawing consistently expressive but never sentimental phrasing from his singers and players. John Carol Case's baritone does not sound well on disc with his rather plaintive tone-colour, but his style is right, and Sheila Armstrong sings most beautifully. The set has been remastered with outstanding success.

A London Symphony (2) (original 1913 version)
☺ ✱ *** Chan. 9902. LSO, Hickox (with
   G. BUTTERWORTH: *The Banks of Green Willow* (***))

A London Symphony was Vaughan Williams's own favourite among his symphonies (and I. M.'s too). It was the one he revised most often, first between 1918 and 1920, and later even more radically in the 1930s, with the definitive score finally published in 1936. What this revelatory recording demonstrates is that the 20 minutes or so of music that were excised include many passages that represent the composer at his most magically poetic. There is even a case for saying that in an age which now thrives on expansive symphonies – the examples of Bruckner, Mahler and Shostakovich always before us – the original offers the richer experience. Vaughan Williams undoubtedly made the work structurally tauter, but discursiveness in a symphony is no longer regarded as a necessary fault.

No one could make the case for this 1913 version more persuasively than Hickox. He draws ravishing sounds throughout from the LSO, with an unerring feeling for idiomatic rubato and a powerful control of massive dynamic contrasts. In this first version the first movement is no different, but each of the other movements here includes substantial sections completely eliminated later, some of them echoing the Ravel of *Daphnis and Chloé*, including an extended one in the Scherzo. The sumptuous Chandos sound, with an extraordinarily wide dynamic range, adds to the impact of the performance, which comes with a short but valuable and beautifully played fill-up.

A London Symphony (2) (1920 version)
(***) Biddulph mono WHL 016. Cincinnati SO, Goossens –
   WALTON: *Violin Concerto* (***) (with Concert (***))

This is the only recording ever made of the 1920 version of Vaughan Williams's *London Symphony*. That involves three minutes of intensely poetic music, later excised in RVW's definitive 1936 edition. The sessions immediately followed the first recording of the Walton *Violin Concerto* with Heifetz in 1941 in which Eugene Goossens and the Cincinnati orchestra provided the accompaniment. The coupling (together with other British music) is among the most valuable of all the reissues in the Biddulph catalogue, with excellent CD transfers.

A London Symphony; Fantasia on a Theme of Thomas Tallis
(M) *** EMI (ADD) 7 64017-2. LPO, Boult
*** EMI (ADD) 7 49394-2. LPO, Haitink
A London Symphony; The Wasps: Overture
(BB) *** Naxos 8.550734. Bournemouth SO, Bakels

The Naxos version of Vaughan Williams's *London Symphony*, coupled with the *Wasps Overture*, is powerful and dedicated. Kees Bakels draws ravishing sounds from the Bournemouth Symphony Orchestra, notably the strings, with the Scherzo cleanly pointed and the slow movement both warm-hearted and refined, and with *pianissimos* that have you catching the breath. The problem is the extreme range of dynamic in the recording. A thrilling experience nonetheless.

The sound is spacious on Boult's splendid 1970 version and the orchestra produces lovely sounds in deeply committed playing. With Boult's noble, gravely intense account of the *Tallis Fantasia* offered as a coupling, this remains a very viable option. The CD transfer is very successful indeed.

In jaunty themes, Haitink's straight manner at times brings an unexpected Stravinskian quality, and his expansively serene handling of the lovely melodies of the slow movement brings elegiac nobility rather than romantic warmth. In the *Tallis Fantasia*, the straight rhythmic manners make the result sensitively unidiomatic too but very powerful in its monumental directness. The recording has spectacular range.

(i) *A London Symphony (2); Fantasia on Greensleeves; The Wasps Overture;* **(ii)** *Serenade to Music*
(BB) (***) Dutton Lab. mono CDBP 9707. (i) Queen's Hall O; (ii) Baillie, Allen, Suddaby, Turner, Balfour, Desmond, Brunskill, Jarred, Nash, Widdop, Jones, Titterton, Henderson, Easton, Williams, Allin, BBC SO; Wood

The historic Decca recording of Vaughan Williams's *London Symphony*, with the specially assembled group of musicians designated as the 'Queen's Hall Orchestra', conducted by Sir Henry Wood, brings a most striking discrepancy of pace with modern performances. The first movement alone takes over three minutes less than in most latter-day recordings. The not-so-slow introduction may lack mystery but there has never been a more passionate account of the work than this on record, and even with limited dynamic range – no true *pianissimo* is caught – the hushed intensity of the slow movement is tellingly conveyed. The *Symphony* comes coupled with shorter Vaughan Williams works: *The Wasps Overture*, *Greensleeves* and, best of all, the original (1938) Columbia recording of the *Serenade to Music*, with the 16 soloists specified in the score, a stellar group. The gently soaring phrase 'of sweet harmony' has never sounded so sweetly angelic as when sung here by Isobel Baillie. The Dutton Laboratory transfers are outstandingly true to the originals.

A London Symphony (2); Symphony 8 in E min.
(B) *** CfP 575 3092. RLPO, Handley

Vernon Handley gives a beautifully paced and well-sprung reading of the *London Symphony*, although not as crisp in ensemble as some and with sound diffused rather than sharply focused. The result is warmly sympathetic and can be strongly recommended if the generous coupling of the *Eighth Symphony*, an underestimated work, is preferred.

A Pastoral Symphony (3); Norfolk Rhapsodies 1 in E min.; 2 in D min.; The Running Set
*** Chan. 10001. LSO, Hickox; (i) with Evans

As in his other recordings of Vaughan Williams symphonies, Richard Hickox here demonstrates his rare gift for drawing out the warmth of this evocative music, moulding phrases and rhythms with a natural spontaneity. The *Pastoral Symphony*, inspired not by the English countryside as much as by the composer's experiences on the Western Front in the First World War, is among his most elusive works, yet here, with Rebecca Evans a radiant soprano soloist in the melismatic writing of the finale, the magnetism of Vaughan Williams's spacious inspirations is irresistible. The three folk-based works make an apt coupling. The *Norfolk Rhapsody No. 1* has remained in the regular repertory over the years, but the *Norfolk Rhapsody No. 2*, just as warmly attractive in its use of folk material, was here receiving its first performance since 1914, with two missing pages of the score judiciously reconstructed by Stephen Hogger.

(i) *A Pastoral Symphony (3); Symphonies 4 in F min.; 5 in D; 6 in E min.*
☮⊶ (B) *** RCA (ADD) 74321 88680-2 (2). LSO, Previn; (i) with Harper

The most striking of Previn's performances is the *Fifth Symphony*, and the only performance that can be accounted at all disappointing is the dramatic *Fourth*. This is a work, the tautest and most dramatic of the cycle, that one might have expected Previn to interpret best. It is an impressive account, but the somewhat ponderous tempo he adopts for the first movement lets it down. Nevertheless, on the whole it is a powerful reading and is vividly recorded.

Previn draws an outstandingly beautiful and refined performance from the LSO of the *Pastoral Symphony*, the bare textures sounding austere but never thin and the few climaxes emerging at full force with purity undiminished. In the third movement the final coda – the only really fast music in the whole work – brings a magic tracery of pianissimo in this performance, lighter, faster and even clearer than achieved by Boult. The recording adds to the beauty in its atmospheric distancing, not least in the trumpet cadenza of the second movement and the lovely melismas for the soprano soloist in the last movement.

The *Sixth Symphony*, with its moments of darkness and brutality contrasted against the warmth of the second subject or the hushed intensity of the final, otherworldly, slow movement, is a work for which Previn has an innate affinity. In the first three movements his performance is superbly dramatic, clear-headed and direct, with natural understanding. His account of the mystic final movement with its endless pianissimo is not, however, on the same level, for – whether on not the fault of the recording – the playing is not quite hushed enough and the tempo is just a little too fast. In its closely wrought contrapuntal texture, this is a movement that may seem difficult to interpret but that should be allowed to flow along on its own intensity.

In the *Fifth* there are no such reservations. In this most characteristic – and many would say greatest – of the Vaughan Williams symphonies Previn refuses to be lured into pastoral byways. His tempi may – rather surprisingly – be consistently on the slow side, but the purity of tone he draws from the LSO strings, the precise shading of dynamic and phrasing and the sustaining of tension through the longest, most hushed passages produce results that will persuade many not normally convinced of the greatness of this music. In the first movement Previn builds the great climaxes of the second subject with much warmth, but he reserves for the climax of the slow movement his culminating thrust of emotion, a moment of visionary sublimity, after which the gentle urgency of the *Passacaglia* finale and the stillness of the *Epilogue* seem a perfect happy conclusion. It is some tribute to Previn's intensity that he can draw out the diminuendi at the ends of movements with such refinement and no sense of exaggeration. Special tribute must also be paid to the uncredited remastering engineer and to the producer of this reissue, Lionel Falleur, for the sound really is superb throughout the set.

(i) *A Pastoral Symphony (3);* (ii) *Symphony 5 in D*
(M) *** EMI (ADD) 7 64018-2. (i) M. Price, New Philh. O; (ii) LPO; Boult

(BB) (***) Belart mono 461 118-2. (i) Ritchie; LPO, Boult
** Decca (IMS) 458 357-2. LPO, Norrington

On EMI, in the *Pastoral Symphony* Boult is not entirely successful in controlling the tension of the short but elusive first movement, although it is beautifully played. The opening of the *Lento moderato*, however, is very fine, and its close is sustained with a perfect blend of restraint and intensity. In a generous coupling Boult gives a loving and gentle performance of No. 5, easier and more flowing than most rivals', and some may prefer it for that reason, but the emotional involvement is a degree less intense, particularly in the slow movement. Both recordings have been very successfully remastered.

It is good to have Boult's earlier, Kingsway Hall recordings back in the catalogue. They were made in 1952/3 with the composer present; although some allowances have to be made for the lack of amplitude in the upper string climaxes, the CD transfer is impressively full and the recording luminous. The translucent textures Boult creates in the *Pastoral Symphony*, with its ethereal opening, and his delicacy later are balanced by his intensity in the *Fifth*, where the climax of the first movement has wonderful breadth and passion. The LPO of the time play with great sympathy and warmth.

Norrington takes a cool view of these two symphonies. Textures are exceptionally clean, the playing of the LPO most refined, but Norrington's preference for a very steady beat, rarely allowing himself much rubato even at climaxes, prevents these performances from having full emotional impact, a degree of restraint that might be approved by those who prefer an objective view. But there is a dimension missing here, especially in No. 5. Refined Decca sound to match.

A Pastoral Symphony (3); Symphony 6 in E min.
(BB) **(*) Naxos 8.550733. Bournemouth SO, Bakels

Kees Bakels's serenely expressive account of the *Pastoral* has moments of drama to heighten its quiet, atmospheric intensity. There is much lovely orchestral playing, with the soloists in the Bournemouth Symphony Orchestra very sympathetic to the music's subtle, lyrical resonance. The account of the *Sixth* does not catch the degree of underlying menace in the *Lento* second movement, but the performance has plenty of life and vigour, and Bakels sustains the epilogue with an ethereal, glowing *pianissimo*. First-rate Naxos recording in both works.

Symphony 4 in F min.
(M) (***) Cala mono CACD 0528. NBC SO, Stokowski – ANTHEIL: *Symphony 4* (***); BUTTERWORTH: *Shropshire Lad* (**)

Symphony 4; Fantasia on Greensleeves; Fantasia on a Theme by Thomas Tallis; (i) ***Serenade to Music***
(B) **(*) Sony SBK 89779. NYPO, Bernstein; (i) with vocal soloists

Symphony 4; Norfolk Rhapsody 1; (i) ***Flos Campi***
(N) (BB) *** Naxos 8.557276. Bournemouth SO, Daniel; (i) with Silverthorne, Bournemouth SO Ch.

Symphony 4 in F min.; (i) ***Mass in G min.;*** (ii) ***6 Choral Songs to be Sung in Time of War***
🔑 ❁ *** Chan. 9984. (i) Hickox Singers; (ii) L. Symphony Ch.; LSO, Hickox

Richard Hickox's searing reading of the *Fourth Symphony* matches, and even outshines in its fury, the première recording conducted by the composer in 1937. Hickox even manages to match the very fast speed RVW set, angry to the very last bar. The intensity of the LSO's playing, brilliant from first to last, has one magnetized in all four movements, chill in the slow movement with its eerie polytonal writing, and unrelenting even in the skipping rhythms of the *Scherzo* and the oompah sequences of the finale. Like the composer, Hickox never relaxes into mere jauntiness, but does not sound rigid either, moulding the great melodies that, in defiance of the overall mood, surge up in each movement. This work, written in 1935 and designed by Vaughan Williams to shock his contemporaries and possibly even himself, emerges fresher than ever. The *Mass in G minor* makes a fine and unusual coupling, here given sharper focus than usual, with dramatic contrasts underlined, and with the precision of ensemble compensating for having women's rather than boy's voices in the upper parts. The six unison *Songs to be Sung in Time of War*, which come as a unique supplement, were written at the outbreak of war in 1939 to texts by Shelley, miniatures that in their natural lyrical intensity rise beyond the limits of scale. Superb Chandos sound in both the symphony and the choral works.

No longer shocking, Vaughan Williams's abrasive *Fourth Symphony* (which has much in common with the Hickox version) emerges in Paul Daniel's powerful performance as one of the most vital of Vaughan Williams's works, at once chilling and lyrical in its forward thrust. The impact of the opening has never been sharper than here, helped by the weighty and atmospheric recording. The *Symphony* is superbly contrasted with a masterpiece from the 1920s, the visionary piece, *Flos campi*, for viola and orchestra, inspired over its six sections by the Song of Solomon, with Paul Silverthorne a superb soloist. Covering the full range of Vaughan Williams's achievement, the disc also includes the *Norfolk Rhapsody No. 1* of 1906, representing the composer's early pastoral style at its most attractive.

The only time that Stokowski ever conducted Vaughan Williams's provocative *Fourth Symphony* was in March 1943, when this high-powered, red-blooded reading was recorded, the first to be made outside Britain. The violently dissonant opening is broad and emphatic, leading to a warm, passionate account of the lyrical second subject, and throughout the performance one marvels that Stokowski could draw sounds from the NBC Orchestra so different from those the same players produced under Toscanini. The chill and poignancy of the slow movement and the bluff humour of the *Scherzo*, each strongly characterized, lead to a comparably positive account of the finale, making one regret that Stokowski never returned to this work. The sound, limited in range, is yet satisfyingly full-bodied.

Bernstein's account is strangely impressive. His first movement is slower than usual but very well controlled; he captures the flavour and intensity of the score as well as the brooding quality of the slow movement. The New York orchestra plays extremely well and the 1965 recording is full and vivid. The *Serenade to Music* is less successful: the solo singers are too forwardly balanced and the sound in general is unimpressive, though the performance itself is not without interest. The two *Fantasias* are expansively done (American performances of *Greensleeves* are always slow), and the *Tallis* certainly has plenty of tension. Well worth trying at bargain price.

Symphonies (i) ***4 in F min.;*** (ii) ***6 in E min.;*** (i) ***Fantasia on a Theme of Thomas Tallis***
🔑 (B) (***) Retrospective Sony mono/stereo RET 011. NYPO, (i) Mitropoulos; (ii) Stokowski

The recordings of Vaughan Williams's two apocalyptic symphonies made by the New York Philharmonic – No. 4 conducted in 1956 by Dmitri Mitropoulos (in a reading approved by the composer himself) and No. 6 in 1949 by Stokowski (directing with unsentimental thrust) – make a fascinating coupling. As transferred to CD they sound far better than they ever did on LP. Both demonstrate what idiomatic power and brilliance American players could bring to the composer's two most abrasive symphonies. Stokowski's reading is the more controversial, disconcertingly fast in the slow movement and unpointed in the slow, visionary finale. Mitropoulos in a generous fill-up shows equal understanding of the rarefied *Tallis Fantasia*.

Symphony 5 in D; (i) ***Oboe Concerto;*** (ii) ***Flos campi***
(B) *** CfP 575 3112. (i) Small; (ii) Balmer, RLPO Ch.; RLPO, Handley

Symphony 5 in D; Hymn-Tune Prelude; Prelude & Fugue in C min.; (i) ***The Pilgrim Pavement; Psalm 23; Valiant for Truth***
🔑 ❁ *** Chan. 9666. (i) Hickox Singers; LSO, Hickox

Symphony 5 in D; (i) ***The Lark Ascending. Norfolk Rhapsody***
*** EMI 5 55487-2. LPO, Haitink, (i) with Chang

Hickox with the LSO captures a visionary fervour in this most characteristic of the series. Hickox's style is warmly expressive, moulding phrases and tempo affectionately, always sounding spontaneous, building climaxes with shattering power. The LSO respond with playing both rich and refined, helped by the wide-ranging Chandos sound. Equally, the rarities on the disc are most persuasively done, three of them première recordings. *The Pilgrim Pavement* is a touchingly direct devotional motet written for the Church of St John the Divine in New York, and the setting of *Psalm 23* for soprano is adapted from his opera *The Pilgrim's Progress*, while the *Prelude and Fugue* is an amplification of an organ work of 1930, which anticipates the abrasive Vaughan Williams of *Job*.

Vernon Handley's disc is outstanding in every way, a spacious yet concentrated reading, superbly played and recorded, which masterfully holds the broad structure of this symphony together, building to massive climaxes. The warmth and poetry of the work are also beautifully caught. The rare and evocative *Flos campi*, inspired by the Song of Solomon, makes a generous and attractive coupling, equally well played if rather closely balanced. The sound is outstandingly full, giving fine clarity of texture. For this reissue Jonathan Small adds a delectable account of the charmingly lyrical *Oboe Concerto*.

Haitink's measured, dedicated view of VW, broad and steady in tempo, goes with beautiful playing from the LPO, notably in refined *pianissimos* from the string section. This may not be as passionate as some other versions in climaxes, but it compensates in monumental strength. After the measured speeds in earlier movements, the finale brings extra purposefulness in a flowing tempo. Haitink draws out comparable qualities in the rare *Norfolk Rhapsody*, while Sarah Chang proves an intensely poetic soloist in *The Lark Ascending*, volatile at the start in the bird-like fluttering motif and magnetically concentrated throughout. Full, atmospheric recording to match.

Symphonies 5 in D; 9 in E min.

(BB) *** Naxos 8.550738. Bournemouth SO, Bakels

Kees Bakels and the Bournemouth Symphony follow up their earlier issues with a superb coupling of No. 5, arguably the peak of the series, and the very last symphony, long underestimated. Drawing the most refined playing from the Bournemouth orchestra, not least the strings, he finds in a relatively direct reading an extra purity and nobility, pointing the big emotional climaxes of the first and third movements most tellingly. Speeds are on the fast side, but the visionary beauty is perfectly caught. No. 9, with its original structure flouting convention, emerges strong and fresh, with the *Andante tranquillo* finale bringing echoes of the comparable movement of No. 6. Clear, refined recording to match.

Symphony 6 in E min.

(**(*)) Cala mono CACD 0537. NYPO, Stokowski, Thomas Jefferson (with TCHAIKOVSKY: *Romeo and Juliet* (abridged version); MOZART: *Symphony 35 (Haffner)*; SCOTT: *From the Sacred Harp*; WEINBERGER: *Schwanda the Bagpiper: Polka & Fugue* (**))

Symphony 6 in E min.; Fantasia on a Theme of Thomas Tallis; (i) The Lark Ascending

(BB) *** Warner Apex 0927 49584-2. (i) Little; BBC SO, A. Davis

Andrew Davis's reading of the *Sixth* is taut and urgent, with emotions kept under firm control. The two shorter works which come as supplement are given more warmly expressive, exceptionally beautiful performances, with Tasmin Little an immaculate soloist in *The Lark Ascending*. Warner Apex's wide-ranging sound, setting the orchestra at a slight distance, blunts the impact of the symphony in the first three movements, but then works beautifully in the chill of the hushed *pianissimo* meditation of the finale, as it does too in the fill-ups.

Cala offer the same recorded performance of the *Sixth Symphony* as is available on Retrospective Sony, but the 1949 Carnegie Hall recording is vastly improved in the present transfer, with fuller textures and a more realistic conveyance of the Carnegie Hall ambience. The performance has a riveting foward impetus and, characteristically, Stokowski relishes the big tune on the strings in the first movement; but the slow movement is controversially fast. Also, whether the couplings offered here can match the appeal of Mitropoulos's *Fourth*

Symphony and *Tallis Fantasia* on Sony is doubtful. The *Haffner* is Stokowski's only recording of any Mozart symphony: it is certainly lively and has a beautifully pointed *Andante* and a sparkling finale. But it suffers badly from audience noises. *Romeo and Juliet* is well played but hardly riveting, and the recording lacks range. Moreover, Stokowski substitutes a quiet ending for the composer's dramatic final chords, doubtfully claiming that such an alteration had Tchaikovsky's sanction. Thomas Jefferson Scott's folksy *From the Sacred Harp* is hardly one of the conductor's major discoveries, but the Weinberger *Polka and Fugue* is certainly successful, and the only time Stokowski conducted any music by this composer. Good transfers, but not really a satisfying collection, except perhaps for the Stokowski aficionado.

(i) Symphony 6 in E min.; (ii) The Lark Ascending; (iii) A Song of Thanksgiving

(BB) (***) Dutton Lab. mono CDBP 9703. (i) LSO; (ii) Pougnet; (ii, iii) LPO; (iii) with Dolemore, Speight, Luton Choral Soc. & Girls' Ch., all cond. Boult

Boult Conducts Vaughan Williams is the title of this valuable issue in Dutton's excellent bargain series of historic reissues. Boult's pioneer 1949 recording of the *Sixth Symphony* with the LSO, vividly transferred from 78s, has the original, heavily scored version of the *Scherzo* included as a supplement. It remains among the finest ever versions of this bitingly dramatic work. The total chill of the slow finale has never been more tellingly conveyed, even though the relatively close-up sound cannot convey an extreme *pianissimo*. Jean Pougnet, then leader of the LPO, proves a most understanding soloist in *The Lark Ascending*, with *A Song of Thanksgiving* providing an attractive makeweight, a piece with narrator, soprano soloist and chorus, written to celebrate victory in the Second World War.

Symphonies 6 in E min.; 8 in D min.; (i) Nocturne

*** Chan. **SACD** CHSA 5016; CD CHan. 10103. LSO, Hickox; (i) with Roderick Williams

As in the rest of this Vaughan Williams cycle, Richard Hickox draws warmly idiomatic playing from the LSO in this coupling of Nos. 6 and 8. He is particularly fine in the dedicated slow finale of No. 6 with its visionary overtones; yet in the first three movements of that darkly intense work the abrasiveness of the writing is a little muted, thanks to the mellow recording acoustic of All Saints', Tooting. It does not help either that the transfer level is on the low side, so that the heavy brass passages, for all their weight, lack something in bite. In No. 8 the acoustic is less of a problem, even if the Scherzo for wind alone could be even more jaunty. The slow movement for strings brings tender refinement and the rumbustious finale a swaggering conclusion. The *Nocturne* for baritone and orchestra makes a most valuable supplement. Written in 1908 but not discovered until 2000, it is a warmly evocative setting of the composer's favourite, Walt Whitman. He was about to study with Ravel in Paris, but demonstrates here what mastery he already had over orchestral colour, giving forecasts of *A London Symphony*.

Symphonies 6 in E min.; 9 in E min.; Fantasia on Greensleeves

(B) *** CfP 575 3122-2. RLPO, Handley

Handley, with rich, full recording, gives warm-hearted readings of Nos. 6 and 9. The two works can be seen as related not only by key, but also in their layout – both end on measured, visionary slow movements. Next to Previn's now withdrawn recording in the same coupling, Handley lacks some of the darker, sharper qualities implied. Though his speeds are consistently faster, his is a more comfortable reading, and the recording adds to that impression. Handley's approach is a valid one as the slow pianissimo finale, here presented as mysterious rather than desolate, was inspired not by a world laid waste by nuclear war (as was once thought), but by Prospero's 'cloud-capp'd towers' in Shakespeare's *The Tempest*. The *Greensleeves Fantasia* is now added as a contrasting encore.

Sinfonia Antartica (7)
(*) Pangaea **DVD PDVD 5401. New Zealand SO, Judd
(BB) *** RCA Navigator (ADD) 74321 29248-2. Harper, Richardson, L. Symphony Ch., LSO, Previn – WALTON: *Cello Concerto* ***

(i) *Sinfonia Antartica (7)*; (ii) *Serenade to Music* (choral version); *Partita for Double String Orchestra*
(B) *** CfP (ADD) 573 3132. (i) Hargan; (ii) RLPO Ch.; RLPO, Handley

(i) *Sinfonia Antartica (7)*; *The Wasps* (incidental music): *Overture & Suite*
(M) **(*) EMI (ADD) 7 64020-2. (i) Armstrong; LPO, Boult

The ideas for the *Sinfonia Antartica* began life in the film music Vaughan Williams composed for *Scott of the Antarctic*, which were refashioned in symphonic form in 1949–52. The work does not really escape from its cinematic origins, and in this DVD the tables are reversed and the symphony becomes an aural backcloth against which some imposing shots of the Antarctic are presented. There are one or two tiresome clichés of current TV practice – time-lapse photography, for example, in which clouds scud hysterically across the horizon – but for the most part the visual images are of much beauty, and there is also some striking underwater photography. The 1999 performance under James Judd is well shaped, although it does not challenge recommended CD rivals. The documentaries are of interest and include historic footage from before the First World War. It is at least pleasant viewing and listening during a heat wave: the Antarctic vistas are cooling.

Previn's interpretation concentrates on atmosphere rather than drama in a performance that is sensitive and literal. Because of the recessed effect of the sound, the portrayal of the ice-fall (represented by the sudden entry of the organ) has a good deal less impact than in Vernon Handley's version. Before each movement Sir Ralph Richardson speaks the superscript written by the composer on his score. As can be seen, Previn's *Sinfonia Antartica* is coupled with Walton's *Cello Concerto* – a real bargain on RCA's super-budget Navigator label.

Handley shows a natural feeling for expressive rubato and draws refined playing from the Liverpool orchestra. At the end of the epilogue Alison Hargan makes a notable first appearance on disc, a soprano with an exceptionally sweet and pure voice. In well-balanced digital sound it makes an outstanding bargain, particularly when it offers an excellent fill-up, the *Serenade to Music* (though in this lovely score a chorus never sounds as characterful as a group of well-chosen soloists). Also added for this latest reissue is the rare *Partita*, very well played and sonorously recorded.

Sir Adrian gives a stirring account and is well served by the EMI engineers. The inclusion of Vaughan Williams's Aristophanic suite, *The Wasps*, with its endearing participation of the kitchen utensils plus its tuneful *Overture*, is a bonus,

although in the *Overture* the upper strings sound a bit thin.

(i) *Sinfonia Antartica (7)*; *Symphony 8 in D min.*
☛ (BB) *** Belart mono/stereo 461 116-2. LPO, Boult; (i) with Ritchie, LPO Ch. (superscriptions spoken by Gielgud)
(BB) *** Naxos 8.550737. Bournemouth SO, Bakels; (i) with Russell, Waynflete Singers (superscriptions read by Timson)

Boult's 1953 mono performance of the *Sinfonia Antartica* has never been surpassed; the atmospheric recording, with its translucent icy vistas and Margaret Ritchie's floating, wordless soprano voice sounding ethereal, remains a model of balancing. Boult and the LPO achieve keen concentration throughout, and the evocation of the frozen landscapes and the shifting ice-floes is as compelling as his control of the structure of a work that is never easy to hold together. Sir John Gielgud's superscriptions (from the score) act as moving preludes. The recording of the *Eighth Symphony* is early stereo (1956). The LPO plays beautifully, and the Decca engineers have relished the challenge of balancing the exotic sounds of glissando tubular bells, tuned gongs, vibraphone and xylophone. The string-tone sounds far fuller than it did when this recording last appeared, crowning this remarkably successful series of Belart super-bargain reissues.

Kees Bakels gives powerful, intense performances of two of the more problematic works, written towards the end of the composer's career, when he deliberately defied symphonic convention. The *Antartica* is particularly impressive, helped by vividly atmospheric recording that, with superb separation, clarifies textures – not least the percussion and wind-machine – and beautifully captures the ethereal sound of Lynda Russell singing off-stage. Bakels's fast speed for the opening movement tautly draws together a structure which can seem dangerously episodic, and the thrust is maintained through the other movements. Sensibly, the superscriptions are included on separate tracks at the end of the disc. No. 8 is excellently done too, with an element of wildness brought out in the sharp contrasts of the first movement, bouncing humour in the Scherzo and refinement in the slow movement and finale.

Symphony 9 in E min.
(N) (***) Cala mono CACD 0539. O, Stokowski (with:
RIEGGER: *New Dance*; HOVHANESS: *Symphony 2*;
CRESTON: *Toccata, Op. 68 (***)*)

Stokowski was a fervent advocate of Vaughan Williams (and of much other English music – even of Rubbra's *Fifth Symphony*). His accounts of the *Fourth* and *Sixth* are also available on Cala, and the *Eighth* was briefly on the BBC label but the present disc comprises a 1958 Carnegie Hall concert in September which also included three American composers whose work Stokowski had consistently championed. All three performances are well worth having on CD; the *Symphony* is given with great dedication and authority and is a reading that is second to none despite some slight tape imperfection at the beginning of the first movement. Those who have not grasped the stature of this work from the records by Sir Adrian Boult and Bernard Haitink will surely be convinced by this commanding and gripping interpretation. Percy Grainger, who was in the audience, wrote of its beauty and cosmic quality, and the 76-year-old Stokowski certainly conveyed its power and nobility. The American works have comparable authority and vitality, and there need be no reservations concerning the quality of the mono sound, given the period.

CHAMBER MUSIC

Piano Quintet in C min.; Quintet in D for Clarinet, Horn, Violin, Cello & Piano; String Quartet; Nocturne & Scherzo; 3 Preludes on Welsh Hymn-Tunes; Romance; Romance & Pastorale; Scherzo; Suite de Ballet
⊕— *** Hyp. CDA 67381/2 (2). Nash Ens.

Although most of the chamber works in this revelatory collection were, until the 1990s, kept under wraps, they richly deserve revival, for they are full of distinctive ideas confidently developed. On the first of the two discs the *Piano Quintet* of 1903 opens strikingly with sharp discords and then whirls you into a vigorous movement with French overtones. The *String Quartet* of 1898, with its folk-like pentatonic writing, sounds more like the RVW we know, and again his mastery in handling a difficult medium is perfectly clear, as it is even more strikingly in the *Quintet* for the difficult and unusual combination of piano, clarinet, horn, violin and cello. Each movement is sharply conceived, ending in a jaunty finale echoing Dvořák. The *Nocturne and Scherzo* (1906) for string quintet clearly anticipate the song-cycle *On Wenlock Edge*, and other shorter works for various combinations from later in his career help to fill out the musical portrait of a composer whose music seems to grow in vitality with the years, largely thanks to brilliant performances like these. The recording is well up to house standards.

6 Studies in English Folksong for Clarinet & Piano
*** Chan. 8683. Hilton, Swallow – BAX: *Sonata* **(*); BLISS: *Quintet* ***

These *Folksong Studies*, which Vaughan Williams published in arrangements for the viola and cello, come from the mid-1920s and are very beautiful, most sensitively played by Janet Hilton and Keith Swallow.

String Quartets 1 in G min.; 2 in A min.; (i) Phantasy Quintet
⊕— ⊛ (BB) *** Naxos 8.555300. Maggini Qt, with (i) Jackson

The Maggini Quartet, even more responsive than on their previous discs of British music, give revelatory performances of works that too often have been underestimated, regarded as mere diversions from the composer's regular path. The Magginis find a rare clarity and warmth in both quartets. The *First* was written soon after Vaughan Williams's studies with Ravel in Paris, with obvious echoes not just of Ravel but of the Debussy *Quartet*. The *Second Quartet* dates from 1942 to 1943, written in the crucial gap between the lyrical *Symphony No. 5* and the abrasive *No. 6*. Most revelatory of all is the Maggini performance of the *Phantasy Quintet* of 1912, a masterpiece long neglected, weighty and compressed. A slow prelude as intense as that of a Purcell Fantasy leads to three comparably strong and sharply characterized sections.

VOCAL MUSIC

Benedicite; Let Us Now Praise Famous Men; O Clap Your Hands; Old Hundreth Psalm; O Taste and See; Toward the Unknown Region
**(*) Australian Decca Eloquence 467 613-2. Byram-Wigfield, Winchester Cathedral Ch., Waynflete Singers, Bournemouth SO, Hill – WALTON: *Coronation March & Te Deum*, etc. **(*)

Enthusiastic performances, set in a reverberant acoustic and

well recorded. They may not be the most polished available but the infectious quality of the music-making is very involving. The *Benedicite*, a strong sixteen-minute work, which is too often overlooked, is hugely enjoyable. Well worth considering.

(i; ii) Dona nobis pacem; (i; iii) Fantasia (quasi variations) on the Old 104th Psalm Tune; (iv) Magnificat; (i) Toward the Unknown Region
(B) *** EMI (ADD) 5 74782-2 (2). (i) LPO Ch., LPO, Boult; (ii) with Armstrong, Carol Case; (iii) Katin; (iv) Watts, Amb. S., O Nova, Davies – *Concerto grosso*, etc. **(*)

Dona nobis pacem, which appeared in 1936 as a direct response to the dark uneasy peace of the 1930s, is a work that was obviously relevant but is still elusive. The central setting of a Whitman poem, 'Dirge for Two Veterans', may not be stylistically quite consistent with the rest, but in a performance as sensitive and understanding as this, the whole scheme emerges powerfully. In its simplicity, the 'Dirge' presents a stirring and sustained climax, while the more austere settings of biblical texts have a dark simplicity that is most compelling. The *Magnificat* shows Vaughan Williams in his most Holstian vein. It dates from the early 1930s and has strong suggestions of *Flos Campi*. Its inspiration is of high quality, and it is performed here with sympathy and imagination. The *Psalm Tune Fantasia*, however, is not one of the composer's most successful works, although these artists do their best for it. The early setting of Whitman, *Toward the Unknown Region*, is much more rewarding and is finely sung.

Dona nobis pacem; 4 Hymns; Lord, Thou hast been our refuge (Psalm 90); O clap your hands (Psalm 47); Toward the Unknown Region
*** Hyp. CDA 66655. Howarth, Mark Ainsley, Allen, Corydon Singers & O, Best

Dona nobis pacem; 5 Mystical Songs
*** Chan. 8590. Wiens, Rayner Cook, LPO Ch., LPO, Thomson

(i; ii) Dona nobis pacem; (ii; iii) Sancta civitas
⊕— *** EMI 7 54788-2. (i) Kenny; (ii) Terfel; (iii) Langridge, St Paul's Cathedral Choristers; L. Symphony Ch., LSO, Hickox

These two visionary masterpieces, both seriously neglected, both with Latin titles and both dating from the interwar period, make an ideal and generous coupling on EMI. Drawing passionate performances from his choir and soloists (notably from Bryn Terfel in both works), Hickox brings out not only the visionary intensity and atmospheric beauty – as in the offstage trumpets and 'Alleluias' near the start of *Sancta civitas* – but also the dramatic power. Both these works may be predominantly meditative, but they have moments of violence which relate directly to the dark side of VW, as expressed in the *Fourth Symphony*, such as the chorus *Beat! Beat! Drums!*, the second section of *Sancta civitas*. In that same work it is fascinating to have the words 'Babylon the great is fallen' set as a hushed lament instead of as a shout of triumph, as in Walton's *Belshazzar's Feast*. Hickox is a degree broader in his speeds than previous interpreters on disc, but is all the warmer for it.

Using a relatively small choir and orchestra, Best takes an intimate view of *Dona nobis pacem* but one which, as a result, is even sharper in focus, capturing the dramatic contrasts as a big performance would, with words unusually clear. The sweet-toned Judith Howarth and the warmly expressive

Thomas Allen are ideal soloists. *Toward the Unknown Region* was VW's first big choral work, not as distinctive as his later music but with many typical fingerprints. Best brings out the beauty of the choral writing, as he does in the even rarer *Four Hymns* for tenor, viola and strings, which the composer intended as a counterpart to the *Five Mystical Songs*. Ainsley is the clear tenor soloist, though strained a little at the top. The setting of *Psalm 90* is the more effective here for having, instead of a semi-chorus, the optional baritone soloist, with Allen again singing with deep dedication.

The *Dona nobis pacem* is also performed well on the Chandos disc, with Edith Wiens and Bryan Rayner Cook as soloists. The latter gives an eloquent account of the much earlier *Five Mystical Songs*, with Bryden Thomson drawing committed playing from the LPO. The recording is warmly resonant, with clear orchestral detail.

(i) *Fantasia on Christmas Carols*; (ii) *Flos campi*; (i) *5 Mystical Songs*; (iii) *Serenade to Music*
⊕— *** Hyp. CDA 66420. (i) Allen, (ii) Imai & Corydon Singers; (iii) 16 soloists; ECO, Best

This radiant record centres round the *Serenade to Music* and, as in the original performance, sixteen star soloists are here lined up; though the team of women does not quite match the stars of 1938, the men are generally fresher and clearer. Above all, thanks largely to fuller, modern recording, the result is much more sensuous than the original, with ensemble better matched and with Matthew Best drawing glowing sounds from the English Chamber Orchestra. The other items are superbly done too, with Nobuko Imai a powerful viola soloist in the mystical cantata *Flos campi*, another Vaughan Williams masterpiece. Thomas Allen is the characterful soloist in the *Five Mystical Songs*. Warmly atmospheric sound to match the performances.

(i) *Flos campi. Household Music (3 Preludes on Welsh Hymn-Tunes)*
*** Chan. 9392. (i) Dukes, N. Sinfonia, Hickox – *Riders to the Sea* ***

Philip Dukes proves a rich and eloquent viola soloist in *Flos campi*, in which the Northern Sinfonia Chorus is balanced more forwardly and powerfully than usual, and this is a remarkably successful performance on all counts. The *Household Music*, never recorded before, offers three delightful miniatures, written in 1941 as a wartime exercise, intended for amateur musicians as well as professionals.

(i) *Hodie (Christmas Cantata)*; (ii) *Fantasia on Christmas Carols*
⊕— (M) *** EMI (ADD) 5 67427-2. (i) Baker, Lewis, Shirley-Quirk, Bach Ch., Westminster Abbey Ch., LSO, Willcocks; (ii) Barrow, Guildford Cathedral Ch. & String O, Rose

Hodie; Fantasia on Christmas Carols
**(*) EMI 7 54128-2. Gale, Tear, Roberts, L. Symphony Ch., LSO, Hickox

In 16 separate numbers, lasting close on an hour, the Christmas cantata *Hodie* brings one of Vaughan Williams's late, characteristically rumbustious inspirations. It is, above all, bluff and jolly, not very subtle in its effects, but full of open-hearted humanity. Those qualities are splendidly realized in this fine performance, not just by the choir, but most of all by the excellent trio of soloists, with Dame Janet as ever

giving heartfelt intensity to Vaughan Williams's broad melodic lines. The *Fantasia on Christmas Carols*, easy and approachable, makes a generous and apt coupling. The transfers of both recordings are newly done and give an excellent example of mid-1960s EMI sound.

Though the three soloists cannot match the original trio in Sir David Willcocks's pioneering version, Hickox directs a more urgent and more freely expressive reading of the big Christmas cantata, *Hodie*, helped by refined and incisive choral singing. As on the earlier disc, the *Christmas Carols Fantasia* proves an ideal coupling, also warmly done.

The House of Life; Songs of Travel
(B) *** EMI (ADD) 5 74785-2 (2). Rolfe Johnson, Willison (with BUTTERWORTH: *A Shropshire Lad* (song-cycle). GURNEY: *Black Stitchel; Desire in Spring; Down by the Salley Gardens; An Epitaph*. IRELAND: *The Land of Lost Content* (song-cycle). WARLOCK: *My Own Country; Passing by; A Prayer to St Anthony; Pretty Ring Time; The Sick Heart ***)

This outstanding two-disc song collection, dating from the mid-1970s, includes both the *Songs of Travel* and the much rarer early Rossetti cycle of 1903, which is the source of the familiar *Silent Noon* (beautifully sung here). But the other Rossetti settings, often ballad-like in their treatment of the theme of love, even if uncharacteristic, are well worth having on disc, and the lyrical flow of the closing *Love's Last Gift* is very appealing. Anthony Rolfe Johnson, in splendidly fresh voice, memorably sings both this cycle and the more familiar, generally more robust *Songs of Travel*, with a natural understanding of their style. The second disc is hardly less valuable in offering not only Ireland's *Land of Lost Content* and Butterworth's *Shropshire Lad* cycles, but four lovely Gurney songs for which Rolfe Johnson shows a special affinity, as he does the five Warlock settings, with much charm displayed in the two lighter songs that end the programme. Throughout, David Willison accompanies most sensitively and the excellent recordings have transferred most vividly to CD.

The House of Life (6 sonnets); Songs of Travel; 4 Poems by Fredegond Shove; 4 Last Songs: 2, Tired; Songs: In the spring; Linden Lea
**(*) Chan. 8475. Luxon, Williams

Though Benjamin Luxon's vibrato is distractingly wide, the warmth and clarity of the recording help to make his well-chosen collection of Vaughan Williams songs very attractive, including as it does not only the well-known Stevenson travel cycle but the Rossetti cycle, *The House of Life* (including *The water mill*), as well as the most famous song of all, *Linden Lea*.

Lord Thou hast been our refuge; Prayer to the Father of Heaven; A Vision of Aeroplanes
*** Chan. 9019. Finzi Singers, Spicer – HOWELLS: *Requiem*, etc. ***

These three choral pieces make an apt coupling for the Howells choral works on the Finzi Singers' disc. *A Vision of Aeroplanes* improbably but most imaginatively uses a text from Ezekiel.

Mass in G min.
⊕— (M) *** EMI (ADD) 5 65595-2. King's College, Cambridge, Ch., Willcocks – BAX; FINZI: *Choral Music* ***

Here, with the finest band of trebles in the country, Sir David Willcocks captures the beauty of the Vaughan Williams *Mass* more completely than any rival, helped by the fine, atmospheric, analogue recording. This is a work that, on the one hand, can easily seem too tense and lose its magic or, on the other, can fall apart in a meandering style; Willcocks admirably finds the middle course. Although recorded two decades before the Bax and Finzi couplings, the remastered analogue sound is still full and fresh.

5 Mystical Songs; O Clap Your Hands

(M) *** EMI (ADD) 5 65588-2. Shirley-Quirk, King's College, Cambridge, Ch., ECO, Willcocks – FINZI: *Dies natalis*; HOLST: *Choral Fantasia; Psalm 86* ***

In the *Five Mystical Songs* to words by George Herbert, John Shirley-Quirk sings admirably, and the motet *O Clap Your Hands* makes a fine bonus for a recommendable triptych of English vocal works.

(i) 5 Mystical Songs; (i; ii) 5 Tudor Portraits

(BB) **(*) Hyp. Helios CDH 55004. (i) Herford; (ii) Walker; Guildford Ch. Soc., Philh. O, Davan Wetton

The contrast of the religious pastoralism of the *Five Mystical Songs* and the rumbustious vigour of the *Tudor Portraits* is well understood by Hilary Davan Wetton. Henry Herford is the rather restrained but sympathetic soloist in the former (an early work, concurrent with the *Sea Symphony*); his vocal style is less well suited to the portrait of *Pretty Bess* in the latter, written a quarter of a century later. Sarah Walker touchingly sings her *Lament* for her pet sparrow (the victim of her cat), and although she is a little strained at the climax, the chorus opens up powerfully and then paints a touching epitaph. She also paints a robust picture of *The Tunning of Elinor Running*. The chorus are boldly enthusiastic both here and in the burlesque *Epitaph on John Jayberd of Diss*. The Philharmonia play sensitively and enter fully into the spirit of the bawdy Elizabethan frolics, playing with colourful vigour in the brilliant closing *Scherzo, Jolly Rutterkin*, with its lively cross-rhythms. Henry Herford, too, is more vociferous here. The recording is truthful, although the chorus could have been given more bite, for the words are not ideally clear. Otherwise an enjoyable and recommendable bargain coupling, which supplies full texts and even a brief glossary of unfamiliar Elizabethan terms.

On Wenlock Edge (song-cycle from A. E. Housman's A Shropshire Lad); (i) 10 Blake Songs for Voice & Oboe. 4 Hymns: (Lord, come away!; Who is this fair one?; Come love, come Lord; Evening hymn); Songs: Merciless beauty; (ii) The new ghost; The water mill

⊕ (M) *** EMI (ADD) 5 65589-2. I. Partridge, (i) Craxton, Music Group of L.; (ii) J. Partridge

This EMI mid-priced CD is an outstandingly beautiful record, with Ian Partridge's intense artistry and lovely individual tone-colour used with compelling success in Vaughan Williams songs both early and late. The Housman cycle has an accompaniment for piano and string quartet, which can sound ungainly but which here, with playing from the Music Group of London, matches the soloist's sensitivity; the result is atmospheric and moving. The *Ten Blake Songs* come from just before the composer's death: bald, direct settings that with the artistry of Partridge and Craxton are darkly moving. The tenor's sister accompanies with fine understanding in two favourite songs as a welcome extra. The other rare items make an attractive bonus, with the *Four Hymns* distinctively accompanied by viola and piano.

(i) On Wenlock Edge; (ii) Songs of Travel (song-cycles)

(M) *** EMI 7 64731-2. (i) Tear; (ii) Allen, CBSO, Rattle – BUTTERWORTH; ELGAR: *Songs* ***

Vaughan Williams's own orchestration of his Housman song-cycle, made in the early 1920s, has been curiously neglected. It lacks something of the apt, ghostly quality of the version for piano and string quartet, but some will prefer the bigger scale. The orchestral version brings home the aptness of treating the nine songs as a cycle, particularly when the soloist is as characterful and understanding a singer as Thomas Allen. The Housman settings in the other cycle are far better known, and Robert Tear, as in his earlier recording with Vernon Handley, proves a deeply perceptive soloist. Warm, understanding conducting and playing, and excellent sound.

(i; ii) An Oxford Elegy; (i; iii) Flos campi; (iv) Sancta civitas; (i) Whitsunday Hymn

(M) *** EMI (ADD) 5 67221-2. King's College, Cambridge, Ch., Willcocks, with (i) Jacques O; (ii) Westbrook (speaker); (iii) Aronowitz; (iv) Partridge, Shirley-Quirk, Bach Ch., LSO

An Oxford Elegy, written in 1949, is an example of a work that rises well above its original commission, its richly flowing inspiration characteristic of the composer's ripe Indian summer. The spoken quotations from Matthew Arnold are effectively presented by John Westbrook, while the Cambridge choir is admirable in its words of tribute to Oxford. *Flos campi*, with its inspiration in the Song of Solomon, is one of the composer's most sensuously beautiful works, with its deeply expressive solo for the viola, here beautifully played by Cecil Aronowitz. It needs a persuasive interpretation, and that it certainly receives. *Sancta civitas* ('The holy city') is a product of the composer's visionary years in the early 1920s. A masterpiece, elusive in its apparent meandering, but in fact as sharply focused as his *Pastoral Symphony* of the same period. The words are mostly from the Book of Revelation and are set to sublime, shifting choral textures (with the main chorus set against a semi-chorus and an off-stage boys' chorus) and the whole effect is evocatively captured on this CD. The *Whitsunday Hymn* is a short but beautiful piece composed for the Leith Hill Festival at Dorking in 1929, yet it somehow remained unpublished at the time; this performance provides its CD début and, like the rest of the programme, is a tribute to the conductor in his eightieth birthday year. A valuable and stimulating release.

The Pilgrim's Progress (incidental music, ed. Palmer)

*** Hyp. CDA 66511. Gielgud, Pasco, Howells, Corydon Singers, City of L. Sinfonia, Best

Vaughan Williams had a lifelong devotion to Bunyan's great allegory, which fired his inspiration to write incidental music for a BBC radio adaptation of the complete *Pilgrim's Progress*. Much of the material, but not all, then found a place in the opera. Christopher Palmer has here devised a sequence of twelve movements, which – overlapping with the opera and the *Fifth Symphony* – throws up long-buried treasure. Matthew Best draws warmly sympathetic performances from his singers and players, in support of the masterly contributions of Sir John Gielgud, taking the role of Pilgrim as he did on radio in 1942, and Richard Pasco as the Evangelist.

The Shepherds of the Delectable Mountains; 3 Choral Hymns; Magnificat; A Song of Thanksgiving; Psalm 100

*** Hyp. CDA 66569. Gielgud, Dawson, Kitchen, Wyn-Rogers, Mark Ainsley, Bowen, Thompson, Opie, Terfel, Best, Corydon Singers, L. Oratory Junior Ch., City of L. Sinfonia, Best

With Sir John Gielgud as narrator and Lynne Dawson as the sweet-toned soprano soloist, Best gives *A Song of Thanksgiving* a tautness and sense of drama, bringing out the originality of the writing, simple and stirring in its grandeur, not for a moment pompous. The *Magnificat* brings more buried treasure, a massive setting designed not for liturgical but for concert use. With its haunting ostinatos it is closer to Holst's choral music than most Vaughan Williams. The *Three Hymns* and the setting of *Psalm 100* are comparably distinctive in their contrasted ways, and it is good to have a recording of the Bunyan setting, *The Shepherds of the Delectable Mountains*. Most of the solo singing is excellent, and the chorus is superb, helped by warmly atmospheric recording.

OPERA

A Cotswold Romance (adapted by Maurice Jacobson in collaboration with the composer from *Hugh the Drover*); *Death of Tintagiles*

*** Chan. 9646. Mannion, Randle, Brook, LPO Ch., LSO, Hickox

This makes a splendid supplement to Hickox's outstanding recording of Vaughan Williams's last opera, *The Pilgrim's Progress*. Saddened towards the end of his life that this tuneful ballad opera, *Hugh the Drover*, was seriously neglected, he adapted some of the most winning sequences to produce this cantata, *A Cotswold Romance*, never recorded before. Even though some striking items from the opera are omitted, it helps that the role of the chorus is expanded, with the colour and vigour of the original enhanced. The *Death of Tintagiles*, even more neglected, is drawn from Vaughan Williams's incidental music for a Maeterlinck play, six dark and spare fragments anticipating later Vaughan Williams works.

Hugh the Drover (complete)

(M) *** Hyp. Dyad CDD 22049 (2). Bottone, Evans, Walker, Van Allan, Opie, New L. Children's Ch., Corydon Singers & O, Best

Described as a ballad opera, *Hugh the Drover* uses folk-themes with full-throated Puccinian warmth. The Hyperion version in atmospheric digital sound offers a fresh, light view, resilient and urgent in the first act, hauntingly tender in the second. Rebecca Evans is superb as the heroine, Mary, with Bonaventura Bottone an amiable Hugh, only occasionally strained, well supported by a cast of generally fresh young singers.

The Poisoned Kiss (complete)

*** Chan. **SACD** 5020 (2); CD 10120 (2). J. Watson, Gilchrist, Helen Stephen, Williams, N. Davies, Collins, Adrian Partington Singers, BBC Nat. O of Wales, Hickox

When in 1927 Vaughan Williams began writing *The Poisoned Kiss*, his forgotten opera, he was already at work on his Falstaff work, *Sir John in Love*, and was beginning to make sketches for *Job*. Consistently this far-fetched setting of a fairy-tale reflects the exuberance of his inspiration, yet that subject and its treatment explains why *The Poisoned Kiss* has been so consistently neglected, not just in performance but on disc too, for this is its very first complete recording. Evelyn Sharp, sister of Cecil Sharp, leader of the folksong movement, wrote a libretto based on short stories by Richard Garnett and Nathaniel Hawthorne; it centres round a beautiful princess who lives on poison. The trouble is that the treatment of that idea both in the plot and, even more seriously, in deplorably bad versification, undermines the lightness originally intended. Sharp and the composer had in mind among other sources the operettas of Gilbert and Sullivan, yet the choice of anachronisms is never pointed in a Gilbertian way. Despite two bouts of revision, in 1936 and 1955, there are still too many unfunny lines.

Whatever the obvious shortcomings of the piece, no lover of Vaughan Williams's music should miss hearing this wonderful set, with a strong and characterful cast superbly led by Richard Hickox, and with warmly atmospheric sound enhancing the musical delights. Janice Watson as Tormentilla sings with sweetness and warmth, while giving point to the literally poisonous side of the character, and James Gilchrist makes an ardent Amaryllus, with Pamela Helen Stephen as Angelica and Roderick Williams totally affecting in their love music, given many of the most charming moments of all. Neal Davies is firm and strong as the magician, Dipsacus, and, though the Empress does not arrive until Act III, she then dominates things, following the G&S tradition of formidable contraltos: in that role the veteran Anne Collins is aptly larger than life. The incidental trios of Hobgoblins and Mediums are also cast from strength with leading singers, the chorus is fresh and bright, and the BBC National Orchestra of Wales plays throughout with winning warmth. Outstandingly atmospheric recording, especially on SACD.

The Pilgrim's Progress (complete)

⊶ ✺ (B) *** Chan. 9625 (2). Finley, and soloists, ROHCG Ch. & O, Hickox

(M) *** EMI (ADD) 7 64212-2 (2). Noble, Burrowes, Armstrong, Herincx, Carol Case, Shirley-Quirk, Keyte, LPO Ch., LPO, Boult

Richard Hickox not only brings out the visionary intensity of much of the writing – notably in the ideas drawn from the *Fifth Symphony* – but also the passion and urgency, pacing the music to bring out the underlying drama in heightened contrasts. As in his recording of that symphony, Hickox is masterly in moulding phrases to magnetize the ear, always a warm interpreter, reflected in the unfailing ardour of the Covent Garden Chorus and Orchestra. The big cast is a strong one, mainly of young singers, led by Gerald Finley as a firm, fresh-voiced Pilgrim, and with Peter Coleman-Wright introducing the opera strongly as John Bunyan. The Chandos recording is superb, spacious and atmospheric, with the many offstage effects beautifully balanced, yet with words always clear. It is one of the many delights of this opera to register the heightened moments when the libretto quotes a Psalm or other familiar sources. Vaughan Williams may not have been a practising Christian, but the depth of his humanitarian faith was never more powerfully demonstrated than here, supremely so in this overwhelming recording.

On EMI John Noble gives a dedicated performance in the central role of Pilgrim, and the large supporting cast is consistently strong. Vanity Fair may not sound evil here, but Vaughan Williams's own recoil is vividly expressed, and the jaunty passage of Mr and Mrs By-Ends brings the most delightful light relief. Boult underlines the virility of his performance with a fascinating and revealing half-hour collection of rehearsal excerpts, placed at the end of the second CD. The outstanding recording quality is confirmed by the CD transfer, which shows few signs of the passing of two decades.

Riders to the Sea (complete)

*** Chan. 9392. Finnie, Daymond, Dawson, Attrot, Stephen, N. Sinfonia, Hickox – *Flos campi*, etc. ***

As in other Vaughan Williams works, Hickox takes a broad, warmly idiomatic view, less urgent than the previous EMI recording, more timeless and mysterious, helped by opulently atmospheric recording. He is helped too by an excellent cast. Even if Linda Finnie as the old woman, Maurya, who loses all her sons to the sea, cannot quite match Helen Watts on the original recording, her final monologue of lament and resignation provides a moving, deeply expressive culmination. Among the others, Karl Daymond as Bartley, the last son to drown, is a newcomer to note, as impressive here as he was in Hickox's recording of Purcell's *Dido*. The generous coupling adds to the disc's attractions.

Sir John in Love (complete)

*** Chan. 9928 (2). Maxwell, Gritton, Claycomb, Connolly, Owens, Padmore, Thompson, Best, Williams, Varcoe, Sinfonia Ch., Northern Sinf., Hickox

(M) *** EMI (ADD) 5 66123 (2). Herincx, Bainbridge, Watts, English, Eathorne, Tear, John Alldis Ch., New Philh. O, M. Davies

Richard Hickox follows up his long list of Vaughan Williams recordings, not least the original version of the *London Symphony*, with a warm, dramatic reading of the opera that Vaughan Williams, conscious of Verdi's example, based on *The Merry Wives of Windsor*. In his own relatively complex libretto he sticks much closer to Shakespeare than Verdi and Boito do, and as Ursula Vaughan Williams has said, he wrote the piece 'just to please himself'.

While this is the opera that provided the material for the *Greensleeves Fantasia* and uses other folk material, it has been wrongly dismissed as just a collection of folk-tunes. In fact, as Hickox's incisive account of the *Prelude* with its cross-rhythms instantly establishes, there are many links here with the sharper Vaughan Williams of *Flos campi* (written at the same period) and the later symphonies.

As an opera this may not match Verdi's *Falstaff* in polish or sophistication, but in its more relaxed, more lyrical way it offers a comparably individual slant on Shakespeare, with the title, *Sir John in Love*, clearly indicating a different emphasis on the character of Falstaff. With Vaughan Williams he is not just comic but a believable lover, more genial and expansive than in Boito's portrait.

The 1974 EMI set of the opera remains a formidable competitor, but quite apart from the extra fullness of the digital Chandos sound, Hickox's reading is a degree more warmly expressive, more sharply dramatic than Meredith Davies's on EMI.

In the casting the central strength of the Chandos set is the Falstaff of Donald Maxwell, with his full, dark bass fatter-sounding than that of Raimund Herincx. Susan Gritton is also outstanding as Anne, rich and golden, relishing the glorious duet she sings with Fenton in the very first scene, with Mark Padmore fresh and youthful too. Not all the others are as characterful as their predecessors, good as they are, as for example Laura Claycomb as Mistress Page. Yet the very large cast works together splendidly, with clear differentiation of the many extra characters that Vaughan Williams includes.

In the EMI set Meredith Davies relishes the colourfulness of the score. Raimund Herincx is a positive and sympathetic Falstaff, and Helen Watts as Mrs Quickly and Elizabeth Bainbridge as Mrs Ford rise ripely to the occasion. Wendy Eathorne as Anne Page and Robert Tear as Fenton make a delightful pair of lovers, and such singers as Gerald English as Dr Caius add to the stylishness. The 1974 Abbey Road recording is vivid and warmly atmospheric and beautifully balanced, and this is still very much worth considering at mid-price.

VEALE, John (born 1922)

Violin Concerto

*** Chan. 9910. Mordkovitch, BBC SO, Hickox – BRITTEN: *Violin Concerto* ***

Surgingly lyrical in a melodic idiom echoing Mahler on the one hand and Walton on the other, John Veale's *Violin Concerto* of 1984 makes an unusual, highly enjoyable coupling for Lydia Mordkovitch's searching account of the Britten. Seriously neglected, with not a note of his music otherwise available on disc, John Veale, born in Kent in 1922, writes in a confident tonal idiom, which with its colourful orchestration reflects his work as a film composer in the post-war period. His development was strongly influenced by his consultations with Walton, and the vigorous finale of this concerto with its swinging Cuban rhythms directly echoes not only Walton but Lambert too. That prompts Mordkovitch to a dazzling performance, with Hickox drawing brilliant, vigorous playing from the BBC orchestra.

Yet the first two movements, both more expansive, are the ones that bear the main emotional weight, with Mordkovitch's passionate intensity heightening the impact. The first movement sets yearning lyricism against sharply rhythmic writing, rather as Walton does, yet the specific echoes are more from Mahler, occasionally from Vaughan Williams, culminating in a long, brilliant cadenza before a tarantella coda. The central slow movement is entitled *Lament*, but the mood is sensuous rather than elegiac, with ecstatic outpouring of melody high above the stave from the soloist at the beginning and end, and with a passionate climax in the middle. On one plane one might regard this as a self-indulgent work, yet the heartfelt commitment is never in doubt. A most rewarding coupling for the Britten for anyone who enjoys post-romantic writing, superbly recorded in the richest Chandos sound.

VECCHI, Orazio (1550–1605)

L'amfiparnaso (commedia harmonica)

(BB) *** Naxos 8.553312. Cappella Musicale di Petronio di Bologna, Vartolo

L'amfiparnaso (commedia harmonica); Il convito musicale (musical banquet; excerpts): O Giardiniero; Lunghi danni; Bando del asino

(B) **(*) HM HMA 1951461. Ens. Clément Janequin, Visse

Unlike Lassus, Vecchi, although earning his living as a *maestro di capella* in the church, leaned in his own music towards the secular. Described as a 'madrigal comedy', *L'amfiparnaso*, first performed in 1594, fascinatingly points forward to the development of opera as a new genre in the following decade. The text in a Prologue and three brief acts develops a comic plot stocked with *commedia dell'arte* characters, but, instead of solo voices representing different characters, here each scene is set as a madrigal for a small group of voices. Each madrigal, three in the first act, five in both the other two, is preceded by a brief spoken summary, the whole making up a taut entertainment that still sounds fresh and charming after 400 years. Much is owed to the liveliness of the Naxos performance, using a first-rate ensemble from Bologna under Sergio Vartolo. With splendidly crisp ensemble the singers consistently bring out the sharply rhythmic quality of Vecchi's writing, with clear, well-balanced sound. Full texts and an English translation are provided.

L'amfiparnaso is also brought vividly to life by the solo and ensemble singing on Harmonia Mundi. *Il convito musicale* (of which we are given only excerpts) is an innocent pastoral sequence set in a garden. A touching lament, *Lunghi danni*, follows, but it is the closing section, with its engaging vocal imitations of instruments and animals croaking together, that makes the piece memorable. The recording is first class and so is the basic documentation, but the texts are now given in only two languages, French and Italian, so the Naxos disc is the preferable choice.

VERDI, Giuseppe (1813–1901)

The Lady and the Fool (ballet suite; arr. Mackerras)

(B) *** CfP CD-CFP 4618. LPO, Mackerras – SULLIVAN: *Pineapple Poll* ***

The Lady and the Fool (ballet; arr. Mackerras); Overtures: *Alzira; La forza del destino; Nabucco.*

(***) Testament mono/stereo SBT 1326. Philh. O, Mackerras

Three of Verdi's finest overtures come in a coupling with the ballet score, *The Lady and the Fool*, which Mackerras drew from the lesser-known operas of Verdi. To choreography by John Cranko, it tells the story of the beautiful La Capricciosa choosing the clown, Moondog, as her lover in preference to three rich and eligible suitors. Mackerras's aim was to follow up the brilliant success of his earlier ballet score, *Pineapple Poll*, which in a very similar way uses material drawn from Sullivan's operettas and other works. This is the only complete recording ever made, demonstrating what a superb sequel it is. Not only has Mackerras drawn on dozens of delectable Verdian ideas, he has woven them into a scintillating tapestry. Ingeniously, Mackerras often superimposes one theme contrapuntally on another, just as Sullivan did in some of his most brilliant ensembles. Some of the movements draw on as many as six or seven different operas over a brief span. The orchestration too is far more adventurous than the originals, while remaining broadly faithful to Verdi's distinctive timbre. Though the recording is in mono only, the sense of presence is most impressive, at least as vivid as in the stereo recordings of the three overtures which come as bonus to the 50-minute ballet, all of them combining brilliance and expressive warmth.

Those content with the *Ballet Suite* only can choose Mackerras's later stereo recording which is equally vivacious and appropriately coupled with *Pineapple Poll*.

Ballet music from: (i) *Il trovatore; I vespri siciliani;* (ii) *Otello;* (i) Overture: *Luisa Miller*

(***) Testament (ADD) SBT 1327. Mackerras with (i) Philh. O; (ii) Rohcg O – PONCHIELLI: *La Gioconda: Dance of the Hours* ***; WOLF-FERRARI: *Overtures, Intermezzi and Dances* (***)

This mixed bag of Mackerras's recordings from the mid-1950s has as its centrepiece his brilliant recordings of the *Luisa Miller Overture* and three examples of the ballet music which Verdi provided for Paris productions of his operas. It is striking, even in the *Otello* ballet music with its corny orientalism, how Verdi regularly harks back to a much earlier, less sophisticated style than he uses in the main body of the opera in question, perhaps a reflection on Parisian taste. The results may have their banalities – even the more ambitious *Four Seasons*, written for the original production of *Les Vêpres siciliennes* – but Mackerras's springing of rhythm and the sparkle of the Philharmonia playing fully bring out their unassuming delights. He is helped by the finely balanced stereo sound in all but the *Otello* music, which curiously seems only ever to have been issued on a 45-r.p.m. EP.

String Quartet in E min. (arr. for string orchestra)

*** Channel Classics **SACD** CCS SA 21504. Amsterdam Sinf., Thompson – TCHAIKOVSKY: *Souvenir de Florence* ***

The Amsterdam Sinfonietta, recording for the first time under its new name and with its new leader/conductor Candida Thompson, plays with phenomenal unanimity, demonstrating what gains there are in having a full string orchestra performing the Verdi *String Quartet*. As in the Tchaikovsky *Souvenir de Florence*, with which it is aptly coupled, speeds are ideally chosen, with the second movement clearly an *Andantino*, light and elegant, and the chattering quavers of the fugal finale shaped more clearly. The thrust and warmth of the performance is enhanced by the wide dynamic range of the playing, well caught in the opulent recording (with the option of 'surround sound').

String Quartet in E min.

**(*) HM HMA 1951671 Melos Qt – SIBELIUS: *String Quartet in D min.* **(*)

This distinguished ensemble give a suitably well-turned-out performance of the Verdi, though they tend to underplay its pure lyricism. We are not so well served in this repertoire at present that new Verdi *Quartets* can be lightly passed over. The recording is truthful but with the *Voces intimae* as its sole companion, the 50 minutes or so of this issue makes for relatively short measure.

Complete Overtures, Preludes and Ballet Music

Vol. 1: Overtures and Preludes: *Alzira* (Overture); *Attila* (Prelude); *La battaglia di Legnano* (Overture); *Il corsaro; I due Foscari; Ernani* (Preludes); *Un giorno di regno (Il finto Stanislao); Giovanna d'Arco* (Overtures); *Macbeth* (Prelude with ballet music); *I Masnadieri* (Prelude); *Nabucco; Oberto* (Overtures)

*** Chan. 9510. BBC PO, Downes

Vol. 2: *Jérusalem* (Overture and ballet music); *Luisa Miller* (Overture); *Rigoletto* (Prelude); *Il trovatore* (ballet music)

*** Chan. 9594. BBC PO, Downes

Vol. 3: *Un ballo in maschera* (Prelude); *Simon Boccanegra* (Prelude: 1st version, 1857); *La traviata* (Preludes to Acts I & III); *Les Vêpres siciliennes: Ballet of the Four Seasons*

*** Chan. 9696. BBC PO, Downes

Vol. 4: *Aida* (Prelude for Cairo première, 1871; Overture for Italian première, 1872; 2 Dances & Act II ballet music); *Don Carlos* (Prelude to Act III and ballet music: *La peregrina*); *La forza del destino* (Prelude, 1862); *Otello* (ballet music, Act III)

*** Chan. 9788. BBC PO, Downes

Preludes, Overtures and Ballet Music (as above)
*** Chan. 9787 (4). BBC PO, Downes

Overtures and Preludes: *Aida* (Prelude); *Alzira; Aroldo* (Overtures); *Attila; Un ballo in maschera* (Preludes); *La battaglia di Legnano; Il corsaro* (Sinfonias); *Ernani* (Prelude); *La forza del destino* (Overture); *Un giorno di regno; Giovanna d'Arco* (Sinfonias); *Luisa Miller* (Overture); *Macbeth; I Masnadieri* (Preludes); *Nabucco* (Overture); *Oberto, Conte di San Bonifacio* (Sinfonia); *Rigoletto; La traviata* (Preludes); *I vespri siciliani* (Overture)
(B) *** DG Double (ADD) 453 058-2 (2). BPO, Karajan

Overtures and Preludes: *Aida* (Prelude); *Alzira* (Sinfonia); *Aroldo* (Sinfonia); *Attila* (Prelude); *Un ballo in maschera* (Prelude); *Il corsaro* (Prelude); *Luisa Miller* (Sinfonia); *Oberto, Conte di San Bonifacio* (Sinfonia); *La traviata* (Preludes to Acts I & III); *I vespri siciliani* (Sinfonia)
(BB) **(*) Naxos 8.553018. Hungarian State Op. O, Morandi

Overtures: *Aida* (reconstructed and arr. Spada); *La forza del destino; I vespri siciliani*
(BB) *** RCA 74321 68012-2. LSO, Abbado – ROSSINI: *Overtures* ***

Overtures and Preludes: *La battaglia di Legnano* (Sinfonia); *Don Carlos* (Prelude to Act III); *I due Foscari* (Prelude); *Ernani* (Prelude); *La forza del destino* (Sinfonia); *Un giorno di regno* (Sinfonia); *Giovanna d'Arco* (Sinfonia); *Macbeth* (Sinfonia); *I Masnadieri* (Prelude); *Nabucco* (Overture); *Rigoletto* (Prelude)
(BB) **(*) Naxos 8.553089. Hungarian State Op. O, Morandi

Edward Downes's Verdi survey covers virtually all the overtures, preludes and ballet music, the latter full of charm when so elegantly played and beautifully recorded. Original versions are chosen where available, so we get the first 1857 score of the *Prelude* to *Simon Boccanegra* and the brief 1862 *Overture* to *La forza del destino*, rather than the familiar expanded, 1869 version. The outstanding novelty is Verdi's extended 1872 overture written for the Italian première of *Aida*. The shorter Prelude heard at the opera's Cairo première was substituted at the last moment. The 1872 piece was never heard of again. The ballet music was, of course, an essential requirement if a work was to be performed at the Paris Opéra. Verdi often rises to the occasion and produces charming, tuneful music, felicitously scored. In the suite from *Il trovatore* (an unlikely subject for a balletic diversion), the delightful third section, *La Bohémienne*, is worthy of Delibes in its use of the graceful violins and piquant woodwind. Not surprisingly Edward Downes has the full measure of this music. The finer overtures are played with bold characterization and dramatic fire, *Nabucco*, with its dignified sonority, and *Giovanna d'Arco* both show the BBC Philharmonic brass at their finest in quite different ways, and *Luisa Miller* is another very strong performance. The strings play most beautifully in the *Traviata Preludes*. With such richly expansive recording, showing Chandos engineering at its most spectacular, the effect is less bitingly leonine than in Karajan's electrifying two-disc survey. But even if not all of this music is top-class Verdi, the Chandos set offers much to enjoy, and the spontaneity and elegance of the music-making are never in doubt.

Karajan's 1975 complete set of Overtures and Preludes was one of the very best analogue recordings made in the Philharmonie: the sound combines vividness with a natural balance and an attractive ambience. The performances have an electricity, refinement and authority that sweep all before them. The little-known overtures *Alzira*, *Aroldo* and *La battaglia di Legnano* are all given with tremendous panache and virtuosity. Try the splendid *Nabucco* or the surprisingly extended (8-minute) *Giovanna d'Arco* to discover the colour and spirit of this music-making, with every bar spontaneously alive, while there is not the faintest suggestion of routine in the more familiar items.

Morandi has served his time conducting at La Scala and he gives ripely robust accounts of these colourful overtures and sinfonias, with excellent playing from his Hungarian musicians, notably from the strings in the *Traviata* and *Aida Preludes* and from the brass in *Nabucco*. *La forza del destino* ends the second disc strongly. Full-bloodedly resonant sound (with the second collection at times marginally sharper in definition) makes this an excellent bargain, even if the readings are not as individual as those of Chailly, Downes and Karajan.

Abbado also included the *Overture* which Verdi originally wrote for the first Italian performance of *Aida*. It is a considerably extended piece in Spada's reconstruction and one can hear why the composer decided against anticipating effects in instrumental terms far more telling in the full operatic setting. But heard independently it is most entertaining and deftly scored. Together with the other two familiar overtures it is given a strong and brilliant performance with the conductor's magnetism felt not only in the *pianissimo* string playing but especially in the exciting account of *La forza del destino*. The sound is bright, but has supporting weight and a concert-hall resonance.

String Quartet in E min.
(M) *** CRD 3366. Alberni Qt – DONIZETTI: *Quartet 13*; PUCCINI: *Crisantemi* ***
(B) **(*) Hyp. Helios CDH 55012. Delmé Qt – R. STRAUSS: *Quartet* **(*)

The Alberni Quartet's performance is strong and compelling, and it is most imaginatively and attractively coupled with the Puccini and Donizetti pieces.

The Delmé are not a 'high-powered', jet-setting ensemble and they give a very natural performance of the Verdi, which will give much pleasure: there is the sense of music-making in the home among intimate friends, refreshingly unforced, even if the sound is on the dry side.

CHORAL MUSIC

Ave Maria; Laudate pueri; Libera me (Messa per Rossini 1869); Messa solenne (Messa di Gloria); Pater noster; Qui tollis; Tantum ergo in F; Tantum ergo in G
*** Decca (IMS) 467 280-2. Scano, Gallardo-Domas, Diego, Florez, Tarver, Aliev, Pertusi, Milan Ch. & SO, Chailly

What Riccardo Chailly has done is to record a series of Verdi's student works, all of them sacred, which have been unearthed in recent years in his native Busseto. They provide a fascinating view of the young composer's development, led as he was towards operatic models, notably Rossini, by his teacher, an anti-clerical choirmaster. The major item is the *Messa solenne*, which after a weighty, almost Beethovenian opening, sadly lacking in distinctive ideas, has a vigorously rhythmic second *Kyrie* and chirpy woodwind writing. There are also echoes of Mozart and Bellini. If none of this offers insights in the manner of Berlioz's youthful inspirations, it is all enjoyable, warmly performed under Chailly by the Milan choir and orchestra and a fine line-up of soloists, fresh and clear. In addition to the student works there are three rarities from later on. More revelatory are the linked but contrasting settings of the *Pater noster* and *Ave Maria*, first performed at La Scala in 1880, which deserve to be far better known, with their anticipations of the last scene of *Otello*.

Requiem Mass

🔊 *** EMI **DVD** DVB4 92693-9. Gheorghiu, Barcellona, Alagna, Konstantinov, Swedish R. Ch., Eric Ericson Chamber Ch., BPO, Abbado

(N) *** DG **DVD** 730 055. L. Price, Cossotto, Pavarotti, Ghiaurov, La Scala, Milan, Ch. & O, Karajan

(*) Arthaus **DVD 100 146. Price, Norman, Carreras, Raimondi, Edinburgh Fest. Ch., LSO, Abbado

*** EMI 5 57168-2 (2). Gheorghiu, Barcellona, Alagna, Konstantinov, Swedish R. Ch., BPO, Abbado

*** Chan. 9490. Crider, Hatziano, Sade, Lloyd, L. Symphony Ch., LSO, Hickox

🔊 (N) (B) *** EMI Gemini (ADD) 5 86239-2 (2). Scotto, Baltsa, Luchetti, Nesterenko, Amb. Ch., Philh. O, Muti – CHERUBINI: *Requiem in C min.* ***

*** BBC (ADD) BBCL 4029-2 (2). Shuard, Reynolds, Lewis, Ward, Philh. Ch. & O, Giulini (with *Overture: La forza del destino* ***) – SCHUBERT: *Mass in E flat* ***

(M) (***) DG mono 447 442-2. Stader, Radev, Krebs, Borg, St Hedwig's Cathedral Ch., Berlin RIAS O, Fricsay

**(*) Ph. 468 079-2 (2). Fleming, Borodina, Bocelli, D'Arcangelo, Kirov Ch. & O, Gergiev

**(*) Decca (ADD) 411 944-2 (2). Sutherland, Horne, Pavarotti, Talvela, V. State Op. Ch., VPO, Solti

(N) (M) **(*) RCA 82876 62318-2 (2). L. Price, J. Baker, Luchetti, Van Dam, Chicago Symphony Ch. & O, Solti

(N) (B) **(*) Sony (ADD) 516028-2 (2). Arroyo, Veasey, Domingo, Raimondi, LSO Ch. & O, Bernstein

(i) Requiem Mass; (ii) 4 Sacred Pieces

*** Ph. 442 142-2 (2). (i) Orgonasova, Von Otter, Canonici, Miles; (ii) D. Brown; Monteverdi Ch., ORR, Gardiner

*** DG (IMS) 435 884-2 (2). Studer, Lipovšek, Carreras, Raimondi, V. State Op. Ch., VPO, Abbado

(M) **(*) EMI 5 67560-2 [56250]. (i) Schwarzkopf, Ludwig, Gedda, Ghiaurov; (ii) J. Baker; Philh. Ch. & O, Giulini

(BB) **(*) Naxos 8.550944/5 (2). Filipova, Scalchi, Hernández, Colombara, Hungarian State Op. Ch. & O, Morandi

(B) **(*) Decca (ADD) 467 118-2 (2). (i) L. Price, Elias, Björling, Tozzi, V. Musikverein, VPO, Reiner; (ii) Minton, Los Angeles Master Ch., LAPO, Mehta

** Sony **SACD** SS 707. Amara, Forrester, Tucker, London, Westminster Ch., Phd. O, Ormandy

Requiem Mass. La forza del destino: Overture

(M) (**(*)) BBC Legends mono BBCL 4144-2 (2). (i) Ligabue, Bumbry, Kónya, Arié, Philh. Ch.; Philh. O, Giulini (also Interview: Giulini in Conversation wih Michael Oliver)

(i) Requiem Mass. Choruses from: Aida; Don Carlo; Macbeth; Nabucco; Otello

*** Telarc CD 80152 (2). (i) Dunn, Curry, Hadley, Plishka; Atlanta Ch. & SO, Shaw

The EMI DVD offers the video version, very well presented, of Abbado's superb live recording of the Verdi *Requiem* made at the Philharmonie in Berlin in January 2001 to commemorate the 100th anniversary of the composer's death. The visual element adds significantly to the impact with the chorus full-toned and weighty, and with the four soloists an outstanding team of singers, all still young. The power and beauty of Gheorghiu's singing are even more striking when one can see as well as hear the vibrant intensity with which she attacks her key solos.

On CD, too, Abbado is at his most powerful, helped by full, weighty sound. The Swedish Radio Chorus and the Berlin Philharmonic, challenged by the drama of a live event, add to a performance of electric intensity. Among the soloists, Angela Gheorghiu stands out in a reading which repeatedly brings new revelation, as in her high, floating entry in the *Offertorio*, leading finally to an account of the concluding *Libera me* – where the soprano reigns supreme – which is at once tender and commanding, conveying to the full the disturbing emotions of the liturgy. The other soloists are excellent too, not just Alagna, but a rich-toned young mezzo in Daniela Barcellona and a characterfully Slavonic bass in Julian Konstantinov. With no fill-up, this comes as a two-discs-for-the-price-of-one package.

Karajan, for his performance at La Scala in 1967, chose the starriest possible quartet of soloists, and all four are at their peak, even the still-young Luciano Pavarotti, who, beardless, is barely recognizable visually, even if the voice is already glowingly distinctive. The firmness and focus of all four is a joy to the ear, and the 1967 recording is surprisingly full and bright, which makes it marginally more recommendable than Abbado's Edinburgh Festival recording, below. Karajan, conducting without a baton, is at once incisive and warmly expressive, looking like a priest in agonized meditation. The great French film director Henri-Georges Clouzot is relatively conservative in his camerawork but regularly uses his shots for beautifully stylized pattern-making, with the members of the chorus and the orchestra often symmetrically placed.

As a performance, Abbado's earlier live DVD recording, made for television at the Edinburgh Festival in 1982, outshines his regular audio recordings of the *Requiem*, not least thanks to the extraordinary line-up of soloists, with Jessye Norman taking the mezzo role against Margaret Price as the soprano. All four soloists are in superb voice, with Ruggiero Raimondi almost sinister in *Mors stupebit* when viewed in close-up, his villainous expressions projected, quite apart from the power and precision of his singing. Similarly, José Carreras has never sounded more powerful, with the big solo *Ingemisco* flawlessly delivered. Jessye Norman sings gloriously too, in such solos as the *Liber scriptus* and the *Recordare*, and she makes a fine match with Margaret Price in their duetting, equally firm and secure, distinct yet blended.

Yet it is Margaret Price who crowns the whole performance in the final *Libera me*, deeply moving and keenly dramatic, the more so when seen in close-up. The Edinburgh Festival Chorus sing as though possessed, and Abbado draws passionate playing from the LSO, with none of the coolness that can mark this conductor's work in the studio. The sound cannot match the finest modern recordings, and it is not helped by the dryness of the Usher Hall, where the performance was recorded, but, as transferred to DVD, the result is still full and vivid, with powerful impact.

It says much for Richard Hickox's recording for Chandos with the LSO and London Symphony Chorus that in important ways – not just practically as the only modern single-disc version – it marked the first of a new generation of readings of Verdi's choral masterpiece. His pacing flows more freely than has become the rule in latterday performances, yet there is never a feeling of haste, simply of heightened intensity when his control of rubato and phrase is so warmly idiomatic. These are very much the speeds which made the vintage Serafin recording of 1939 so compelling, but with singing from the London Symphony Chorus infinitely finer than that of Serafin's Italian chorus. In their fire they rival Giulini's classic Philharmonia set, even outshining that in luminosity, thanks in part to the spacious and full recording which, in a reverberant church acoustic, yet reveals ample detail. The warm-toned soprano, Michele Crider, has a glorious chest register, and the mezzo, Markella Hatziano, is equally warm and characterful, while the tenor, Gabriel Sade, sings with clear, heady beauty, not least in a radiant *Ingemisco*, and Robert Lloyd gives one of his noblest, most commanding performances. A winning set in every way.

Gardiner, using period forces, is searingly dramatic and superbly recorded, with fine detail, combining transparent textures, weight and atmospheric bloom. It can still be recommended as a fine alternative among modern digital recordings even to collectors not drawn to period performance. The soloists make a characterful quartet, with the vibrant Orgonasova set against the rock-steady von Otter, and with Canonici bringing welcome Italianate colourings to the tenor role. The *Four Sacred Pieces* are equally revealing. The longest and most complex, the final *Te Deum*, is the most successful of all, marked by thrillingly dramatic contrasts, as in the *fortissimo* cries of '*Sanctus*'.

With spectacular analogue sound – not always perfectly balanced, but vividly wide in its tonal spectrum – Muti's 1979 Kingsway Hall performance makes a tremendous impact and is in almost all respects preferable to his later version, recorded live eight years later at La Scala. Characteristically, he prefers fast speeds, and in the *Dies irae* he rushes the singers dangerously, making the music breathless in its excitement. Unashamedly, from first to last this is an operatic performance, with a passionately committed quartet of soloists, underpinned by Nesterenko, in glorious voice, giving priestly authority to the *Confutatis*. Scotto is not always sweet on top, but Baltsa is superb, and Luchetti sings freshly. Now offered, very inexpensively, and aptly coupled with a splendid (digital) account of Cherubini's *C minor Requiem*, so admired by Berlioz, this makes an outstanding bargain.

Giulini's performances of the Verdi *Requiem* in the early 1960s have become legendary, electrifying occasions that led to a benchmark studio recording of 1964. Here the BBC Legends series puts an important gloss on that in offering a Prom recording of 1963, even more dramatically involving for the extra spontaneity of a live performance. The stereo sound is first-rate, and though the British soloists may not be such stars as their studio counterparts, they sing beautifully, with firm, clear tone. The Schubert *Mass*, recorded at the Edinburgh Festival of 1968, makes a welcome and generous coupling.

Six months later he performed the *Requiem* once more, again with Philharmonia forces, but this time at the Royal Festival Hall and with a starrier international quartet of soloists. This second live recording comes as a valuable supplement, though it hardly replaces the earlier BBC version. Sadly, it comes in mono only, with the dry Festival Hall acoustic unhelpful, not nearly as warm or atmospheric as the stereo recording from the Prom. The biting drama of Giulini's performance comes over thrillingly, but with some harshness in such passages as the *Dies irae*, and, though the singing of the international quartet is more strongly characterized than that of the fine British one at the Prom, they are no more imaginative. The *Overture* makes a good supplement, and Michael Oliver's interview with Giulini on the subject of recording is

more valuable still (how easy to create a 'beautiful corpse' in the studio, he says), but the extras on the rival BBC version are much more generous (BBCL 4029-2).

Robert Shaw, in the finest of his Atlanta recordings, may not have quite the same searing electricity as Toscanini's classic NBC recording (for which he trained the chorus), but it regularly echoes it in power and the well-calculated pacing. In the *Dies irae*, for example, like Toscanini he gains in thrust and power from a speed marginally slower than usual. With sound of spectacular quality, beautifully balanced and clear, the many felicities of the performance, not least the electricity of the choral singing and the consistency of the solo singing, add up to an exceptionally satisfying reading. The fill-up of five Verdi opera choruses is colourful, and again brings superb choral singing.

Fricsay's superb earlier mono studio recording of Verdi's *Requiem* caused a sensation when it first appeared on LP in 1954. Its tingling drama anticipated the later version, and though tempi are generally faster than in that live account there is marginal extra precision and polish. This makes a worthy reissue in DG's 'Legendary Recordings' series, with the full, spacious mono recording already showing that the DG engineers, using mono techniques, could achieve a combination of clarity and atmosphere. The solo team is first class with the contribution of Kim Borg standing out, as in the live performance.

Claudio Abbado's DG CD live recording was taken from performances at the Vienna Musikverein with the Vienna Philharmonic and Vienna choirs, as well as Cheryl Studer, Marjana Lipovšek, José Carreras and Ruggero Raimondi, all in superb voice and finely matched, even if Carreras has to husband his resources. In detail Abbado's reading is little different from his earlier, La Scala version, but the sense of presence, of the tension of a live occasion, makes the later account far more magnetic, from the hushed murmurings of the opening onwards. The Vienna forces are not only more expressive but more polished, too. The *Four Sacred Pieces* are also superbly done in another live recording.

Recorded during the Kirov Company's visit to Covent Garden in 2000, Gergiev's reading is one of high contrasts. Though the chorus often sounds misty and distant in hushed passages, the fervour of the singing is never in doubt in the big dramatic moments, as in the opening of the *Dies irae*. Yet what above all makes a powerful impact is the orchestra recorded close, so that the instrumental fire of the *Dies irae* has rarely come over so vividly, complete with shattering bass drum. Renée Fleming and Olga Borodina could hardly be bettered as the two women soloists, both characterful and well-contrasted, yet with a fine blend in their duets. Borodina's firm, tangy chest register is a special delight, and the involvement of Fleming in the soul-searching of the final *Libera me* is most moving, as on the words *Tremens factus*, 'I am seized with fear and trembling'. Andrea Bocelli produces a fine flow of sweet tenor-tone controlling the *Ingemisco* well, if at times with excessive portamento, but Ildebrando d'Arcangelo sounds rather underpowered in the bass role, with *Mors stupebit* intimate rather than commanding. Gergiev is wonderfully fiery in the big dramatic moments, but with phrasing elaborately moulded, he, too, often seems to make the music drag in slow numbers. Not a first choice but a characterful one.

What Giulini on EMI proved was that refinement added to power can provide an even more intense experience than the traditional Italian approach. In this concept a fine English chorus and orchestra prove exactly right. The array of soloists could hardly be bettered. Schwarzkopf caresses each phrase, and the exactness of her voice matches the firm mezzo of Christa Ludwig in their difficult octave passages. Gedda is at his most reliable, and Ghiaurov with his really dark bass actually manages to sing the almost impossible *Mors stupebit* in tune without a suspicion of wobble. Giulini's set also finds space to include the *Four Sacred Pieces* in polished and dramatic performances which bring out the element of greatness in often uneven works. This has been carefully remastered as one of EMI's 'Great Recordings of the Century' but the otherwise excellent new transfer of the 1963/4 recording still reveals roughness in heavy climaxes of the *Dies irae* in the *Requiem*.

Well recorded, with first-rate Hungarian chorus and orchestra, the Naxos version offers an enjoyable account which may lack something in dramatic intensity but which consistently brings out the work's lyrical warmth. Though the tenor, César Hernández, is at times coarse, the other three soloists are very good, notably the Bulgarian soprano, Elena Filipova, with her opulent tone. This is a performance which gains in intensity as it progresses and, if anything, the *Four Sacred Pieces*, an apt fill-up, bring performances even more dedicated, with refined choral singing, with the chorus set slightly behind the orchestra. A good bargain version, though it is worth remembering that Richard Hickox's outstanding Chandos version of the *Requiem*, coming on a single full-priced disc, is also a bargain, with much more sharply detailed recording of the chorus.

Reiner's opening of the *Requiem* is very slow and atmospheric. He takes the music at something like half the speed of Toscanini and shapes everything very carefully. Yet as the work proceeds the performance soon sparks into life, and there is some superb and memorable singing from a distinguished team of soloists. The recording has a spectacularly wide dynamic range, enhanced by the CD format, and, with the chorus singing fervently, the *Dies irae* is overwhelming. Mehta's performance of the *Sacred Pieces* is enhanced by brilliant, sharply focused recording.

There is little or nothing reflective about Solti's Decca account, and those who criticize the work for being too operatic will find plenty of ammunition here. The team of soloists is a very strong one, though the matching of voices is not always ideal. It is a pity that the chorus is not nearly as incisive as the Philharmonia on the EMI Giulini set. But if you want an extrovert performance, the firmness of focus and precise placing of forces in the Decca engineering of 1967 make for exceptionally vivid results on CD.

On RCA, with an unusually sensitive and pure-toned quartet of soloists – Luchetti perhaps not as characterful as the others, Leontyne Price occasionally showing strain – and with superb choral singing and orchestral playing, Solti's 1977 Chicago version has all the ingredients for success. The set is well worth having for Dame Janet Baker's deeply sensitive singing, but the remastered recording – less than ideally balanced – tends to be fierce on climaxes; and in other ways too, Solti's earlier Decca/Vienna set is preferable.

Ormandy's is a sincere, warm-hearted performance, with ardent choral singing and plenty of drama. The snag lies with the soloists, who all fall short of their rivals. One has only to sample their contributions to the *Kyrie* to hear that this is not really distinguished singing. The SACD remastering has certainly given the sound added depth, but this cannot carry a strong recommendation at SACD price in view of the competition.

Bernstein's 1970 *Requiem* was recorded in the Royal Albert Hall. By rights, the daring of the decision should have paid off, but with close balancing of microphones the result is not as full and free as one would expect. Bernstein's interpretation remains persuasive in its drama, exaggerated at times, maybe, but red-blooded in a way that is hard to resist. The quartet of soloists is particularly strong. At bargain price, many collectors will feel this is worth considering.

Te Deum (from *Quattro pezzi sacri*)

(BB) *** Warner Apex 8573 89128-2. Soloists, Bielefeld Musikvereins Ch., Philh. Hungarica, Stephani – BRUCKNER: *Te Deum* ***

Although Verdi's *Te Deum* was published as the last of the *Four Sacred Pieces*, Verdi did not expect them to be performed as a group, and the *Te Deum* for double chorus makes a fine independent work. Supported by spectacular orchestration, Verdi's dramatic setting, from the *pianissimo* opening onwards, makes frequent use of bold dynamic contrasts, which are well realized here. The choral singing is first class, the brass resplendent and the conductor, Martin Stephani, keeps everyone on their toes. The recording has a warmly resonant acoustic against which the singing projects thrillingly. Aptly coupled with Bruckner's much more devotional setting, this can be strongly recommended, especially at such a modest cost. Text and translation are included.

OPERA

Aida (complete; DVD versions)

*** DG **DVD** 073 001-9. Millo, Domingo, Zajick, Milnes, Burchuladze, Kavrakos, Met. Op. Ch. & O, Levine

(N) *** NVC Arts **DVD** 0630 198389-2. Chiara, Cossotto, Martinucci, Scandola, Zanazzo, Ch., O & Corps de Ballet of Verona Arena, Guadagno (Producer: Giancarlo Sbragia; V/D: Brian Large)

Recorded live at the Metropolitan in New York in October 1988, James Levine's powerful and starrily cast DVD of *Aida* brings a grandly traditional staging. The sets and costumes are so lavish that the unveiling of the same scene in Act II prompts enthusiastic applause. In that same scene Plácido Domingo is encumbered not only with his golden armour but with a ridiculously tall egg-shaped headdress. Yet he still manages to sing superbly throughout, a believable hero, and though Aprile Millo has her edgy moments, her poise as well as her power are impressive, not least in the Nile Scene. Dolora Zajick is a vibrant, powerful Amneris, and Sherrill Milnes, only just past his peak, is a magnificent Amonasro. Luxury casting brings Paata Burchuladze in as Ramfis, though Dimitri Kavrakos is less impressive as the King. Levine is in his element, drawing warm and dramatic playing and singing from his formidable team at the Met. Good, bright sound.

This new series, recorded in the Verona Arena, from which we have already had a splendid *Tosca*, is proving equally impressive in Verdi. The spectacle of *Aida* with its dignified Triumphal March (with a surprise at the climax) is ideal for the spaciousness available, and Vittorio Rossi has designed a superb set, geometrically based round a pyramid to provide a satisfying backcloth. The costumes are exotic, with only the hats for the ladies not quite believable; the Egyptian crown, which often features in the narrative, is also curiously designed. But the singing is superb. Maria Chiara, whom we remember affectionately from her Decca début recital disc, sings gloriously in the title-role and never more affectingly than in the great closing duet. Fiorenza Cossotto is a memorable foil as Amneris, Nicola Martinucci is a properly heroic Radames, with a strong voice to match a striking presence, and the others complete a fine team, with Amonasro (Giuseppe Scandola) standing out. Brian Large deals with the huge set by varying between long shots and intimate close-ups for the main solos and duets. Anton Guadagno conducts with consistent vitality, the ballet is visually pleasing, and the huge chorus is very impressive indeed. The excellent stereo brings out the antiphonal trumpets in the March, yet strangely the camera fails to do so. Nevertheless, this is both vocally and visually a feast, and the applause is fully acceptable in the context of a live performance so powerful and finely sung by all concerned.

Aida (complete; CD versions)

☞ (M) *** EMI (ADD) 7 69300-2 (3). Freni, Carreras, Baltsa, Cappuccilli, Raimondi, Van Dam, V. State Op. Ch., VPO, Karajan

(B) *** Double Decca (ADD) 460 765-2 (2). L. Price, Gorr, Vickers, Merrill, Tozzi, Rome Op. Ch. & O, Solti

(M) *** Decca (ADD) 460 978-2 (3). Tebaldi, Simionato, Bergonzi, MacNeil, Van Mill, Corena, V. Singverein, VPO, Karajan

(N) (***) Testament (mono) SBT2 1355 (2). Callas, Baum, Simionato, Walters, Neri, ROHCG Ch. & O, Barbirolli

(BB) (***) Naxos 8.110156/7. Caniglia, Gigli, Tajo, Stignani, Bechi, Pasero, Rome Op. Ch. & O, Serafin

On EMI, Karajan's is a performance of *Aida* full of splendour and pageantry, which is yet fundamentally lyrical. On disc there is no feeling of Freni lacking power even in a role normally given to a larger voice, and there is ample gain in the tender beauty of her singing. Carreras makes a fresh, sensitive Radames, Raimondi a darkly intense Ramfis and Van Dam a cleanly focused King, his relative lightness no drawback. Cappuccilli gives a finely detailed performance as Amonasro, while Baltsa as Amneris crowns the whole performance with her fine, incisive singing. Despite some over-brightness on cymbals and trumpet, the Berlin sound for Karajan, as transferred to CD, is richly atmospheric, both in the intimate scenes and, most strikingly, in the scenes of pageant, reflecting the Salzburg Festival production which was linked to the recording. The set has been attractively re-packaged and remains a first choice, irrespective of price.

Leontyne Price is an outstandingly assured Aida on Decca, rich, accurate and imaginative, while Solti's direction is superbly dramatic, notably in the Nile Scene. Merrill is a richly secure Amonasro, Rita Gorr a characterful Amneris, and Jon Vickers is splendidly heroic as Radames. Though the digital transfer betrays the age of the recording (1962), making the result fierce at times to match the reading, Solti's version otherwise brings full, spacious sound, finer, more open and with greater sense of presence than most versions since. As a Double Decca reissue this is a formidable bargain, and the new-style cued synopsis with 'listening guide' is a fair substitute for a full libretto.

On Decca, as on EMI, Karajan was helped by having a Viennese orchestra and chorus; but most important of all is the musical teamwork of his soloists. Bergonzi in particular emerges here as a model among tenors, with a rare feeling for the shaping of phrases and attention to detail. Cornell MacNeil too is splendid. Tebaldi's creamy tone-colour rides beautifully over the phrases and she too acquires a new depth of imagination. Among the other soloists Arnold van Mill and

Fernando Corena are both superb, and Simionato provides one of the finest portrayals of Amneris. The recording has long been famous for its technical bravura and flair. It has now been impressively remastered for Decca's current Legend series, and remains a remarkable technical achievement.

Though Maria Callas was one of the most inspired interpretative musicians of the twentieth century, yet on almost all her studio recordings the flaws in her vocal production (early on, a heavy beat; later in her career, great flapping wobbles) severely undermine enjoyment of her towering artistry, if not for her devotees. It was in 1953, during the Coronation season at Covent Garden, that she took the title-role in Verdi's *Aida*, with John Barbirolli conducting; as this CD set of the live broadcast vividly demonstrates, it was in many ways a performance that outshines almost all her studio recordings. With the voice securely focused in every register, she thrusts home a thrilling assumption of the role of the Ethiopian princess, magnetic in every way. Though inevitably the mono sound has its limitations, with background noise at times and odd balances, what matter are the voices – not just Callas's – and they come over vividly, with the stage atmosphere well caught. It is a joy to hear her effortlessly floating the dauntingly taxing high phrases in her big aria, *O patria mia*, in the Nile scene. Barbirolli too is a winningly warm and sympathetic Verdian, just as idiomatic as Tullio Serafin in Callas's studio recording of two years later. The rest of the cast is first rate too. The Czech tenor Kurt Baum, as Radames, may not have an Italianate voice, but he sings clearly, without strain or exaggeration, and Giulietta Simionato is a superb Amneris, searingly powerful. As Amonasro, the American baritone Jess Walters sings firmly and incisively, not as evil-sounding as Tito Gobbi in the studio version but strong and dramatic, with Giulio Neri as Ramfis and Michael Langdon as the King both excellent. As a curiosity, the tiny role of the Priestess who sings off-stage at the start of the second scene is taken by the young Joan Sutherland, sounding very distant but perfectly identifiable.

Serafin's 78-r.p.m. version was recorded in July 1948, the last of the complete opera sets from HMV that featured Beniamino Gigli as the hero. It is an electrifying performance, with Serafin at his most magnetic leading an outstanding cast of principals, all with voices firm and true. Heralded by trumpets that vividly leap out of the speakers, Gigli launches into *Celeste Aida* at the start with a clarity and bravura that mark his whole performance. Maria Caniglia in the title-role is at her very finest, using the widest range of expression, a fire-eater who knows tenderness too, while Gino Bechi is a superbly sinister Amonasro with a natural snarl in the voice. The others characterize strongly too, with the close balance of the voices and natural dryness of acoustic vividly bringing out words and expression. The transfers by Ward Marston are outstanding, making this one of the very finest of the impressive Naxos historic opera series.

Aida (complete; in English)

(M) **(*) Chan. 3074 (2). Eaglen, Plowright, O'Neill, Yurisich, Rose, Alistair Miles, Geoffrey Mitchell Ch., Philh. O, Parry

Though this account of *Aida* in English starts unpromisingly with Dennis O'Neill over-stressed in Radames' opening aria (in Edmund Tracey's translation '*Goddess Aida Fair as a Vision*'), this is overall a strong and dramatic reading. Central to the set's success is the formidable assumption of the title-role by Jane Eaglen, here sounding more comfortable singing in English than she often has in international original-language recordings. The voice is rich and warm, better focused than it often has been, with fearless attack above the stave, and fine poise in reflective moments. After his strenuous start O'Neill sings most sensitively, so that even by the end of his first aria he achieves a quiet top B flat such as Verdi wanted, and sustains it impressively using a head-voice. Rosalind Plowright, gravitating down to the mezzo register, makes a suitably fruity and vehement Amneris, not quite steady enough, with Gregory Yurisich an incisive Amonasro, and Peter Rose and Alastair Miles strongly cast as Pharaoh and Ramfis respectively. Though David Parry does not always keep dramatic tensions as taut as they might be, the rich and vividly atmospheric Chandos sound regularly compensates.

Aida (highlights)
(BB) **(*) EMI Encore 5 74759-2. Caballé, Domingo, Cossotto, Ghiaurov, ROHCG Ch., New Philh. O, Muti

(M) (***) EMI mono 5 66668-2 (from above complete recording, with Callas, Tucker, Barbieri, Gobbi; cond. Serafin)

On Muti's set of highlights, Caballé's portrait of the heroine is superb, full of detailed insight into the character and with plenty of examples of superlative singing, while Cossotto makes a fine Amneris. Domingo produces a glorious sound, but this is not one of his most imaginative recordings. The sound is relatively small-scale, underlining the fierceness of Muti's reading.

The set of highlights from the Callas *Aida* includes the Nile scene and is slightly more generous, at 58 minutes, than many other reissues in this series. It certainly conveys the overall strength of the cast.

Alzira (complete)
** Orfeo (ADD) CO 57832 (2). Cotrubas, Araiza, Bruson, Rootering, Bav. R. Ch., Munich RO, Gardelli

Alzira, dating from 1845, is at once the least cherished and the most compact of Verdi's operas, yet on disc, when brevity is often an asset, it emerges as far from perfunctory. Indeed, it can stand comparison with any of the other operas Verdi wrote in his years 'in the galleys'.

Gardelli recorded the piece for Orfeo with an excellent cast, helped by warm and well-balanced recording supervised by Munich Radio engineers, with Cotrubas flexible in coloratura, Francisco Araiza as the Inca hero, Zamoro, and Renato Bruson as Gusmano, Governor of Peru. Though the Orfeo recording is excellent, the earlier, deleted Philips set was finer on all counts.

Attila (complete)
(M) *** Ph. (ADD) 475 6766-2 (2). Raimondi, Deutekom, Bergonzi, Milnes, Amb. S., Finchley Children's Music Group, RPO, Gardelli

With its dramatic anticipations of *Macbeth* and musical ones of *Rigoletto*, and the compression which (on record if not on the stage) becomes a positive merit, *Attila*, in a fine performance under Gardelli on this Philips set, is an intensely enjoyable experience. Deutekom, not a sweet-toned soprano, has never sung better on record, and the rest of the cast is outstandingly good. The 1973 recording is well balanced and atmospheric, and this reissue in the Classic Opera series comes with a full libretto.

Un ballo in maschera (complete)
(B) *** DG Double 453 148-2 (2). Ricciarelli, Domingo, Bruson, Obraztsova, Gruberová, Raimondi, La Scala, Milan, Ch. & O, Abbado

(M) *** EMI 5 66510-2 (2). Arroyo, Domingo, Cappuccilli, Grist, Cossotto, Howell, ROHCG Ch., New Philh. O, Muti

(***) EMI mono 5 56320-2 (2). Callas, Di Stefano, Gobbi, Ratti, Barbieri, La Scala, Milan, Ch. & O, Votto

(B) **(*) Double Decca (IMS) (ADD) 460 762-2 (2). Tebaldi, Pavarotti, Milnes, Resnik, Donath, St Cecilia Academy, Rome, Ch. & O, Bartoletti

Abbado's powerful reading, admirably paced and with a splendid feeling for the sparkle of the comedy, remains highly recommendable at bargain price. The cast is very strong, with Ricciarelli at her very finest and Domingo sweeter of tone and more deft of characterization than on the Muti set of five years earlier. Bruson as the wronged husband Renato (a role he also takes for Solti) sings magnificently, and only Obraztsova as Ulrica and Gruberová as Oscar are less consistently convincing. The analogue recording clearly separates the voices and instruments in different acoustics, which, though distracting at first, brings the drama closer.

The quintet of principals on Muti's earlier set is unusually strong, but it is the conductor who takes first honours in a warmly dramatic reading. Muti's rhythmic resilience and consideration for the singers go with keen concentration, holding each act together in a way he did not quite achieve in his earlier recording for EMI of *Aida*. Arroyo, rich of voice, is not always imaginative in her big solos, and Domingo rarely produces a half-tone, though the recording balance may be partly to blame. The sound is full and vivid, and for the present reissue a new booklet has been provided with full translation.

Votto's 1956 mono recording, with voices set close but with a fair amount of space round them, is among the best of the sets with Callas from La Scala, and the CD focuses its qualities the more sharply. Cast from strength, with all the principals – notably Gobbi and Giuseppe di Stefano – on top form, this is indispensable for Callas's admirers.

The main interest in the earlier Decca set rests in the pairing of Tebaldi and Pavarotti. The latter was in young, vibrant voice but Tebaldi made her recording in the full maturity of her career. She gives a commanding performance, but there is no mistaking that her voice here is not as even as it once was. The supporting cast is strong, not only Milnes as Renato and Donath as Oscar, but Resnik a dark-voiced Ulrica. Bartoletti directs the proceedings dramatically, and the (1970) Decca recording remains strikingly vivid and atmospheric. Now reissued as a Double Decca with new-style cued synopsis, this makes a good bargain recommendation.

Un ballo in maschera (sung in English)
(N) (M) ** Chan. 3116 (2). O'Neill, Patterson, Michaels-Moore, Grove, Richardson, Geoffrey Mitchell Ch., LPO, Parry

Verdi in English has its problems, when other associations keep bursting in, not least Gilbert and Sullivan. Here in David Parry's lively reading of *A Masked Ball*, using Amanda Holden's crisp translation and with the action moved back from colonial Boston to the Sweden of Gustavus III, the witty finale to Act I irresistibly echoes Offenbach, though again the complications of the plot are wonderfully clarified, thanks to the clear diction of the soloists. Sadly, Dennis O'Neill as the King now sounds strained, and even Anthony Michaels-Moore as Anckarstroem is less warm than usual. Otherwise a reliable cast, with Susan Patterson as Amelia, Linda Richardson as Oscar and Jill Grove a resonant Ulrike (Azucena).

Il Corsaro (complete)
(N) (M) *** Ph. 475 6769. Norman, Caballé, Carreras, Grant, Mastromei, Noble, Amb. S., New Philh. O, Gardelli

In Il Corsaro, although the characterization is rudimentary, the contrast between the two heroines is effective, with Gulnara, the Pasha's slave, carrying conviction in the *coup de foudre* which has her promptly worshipping the Corsair, an early example of the Rudolph Valentino figure. The rival heroines are splendidly taken here, with Jessye Norman as the faithful wife, Medora, actually upstaging Montserrat Caballé as Gulnara. Gardelli directs a vivid performance, with fine singing from the hero, portrayed by José Carreras. Gian-Piero Mastromei, not rich in tone, still rises to the challenge of the Pasha's music. Excellent, firmly focused and well-balanced, mid-1970s Philips sound, well transferred in this mid-priced reissue, with full libretto included.

Don Carlos (complete)
🔾🏷 *** Warner DVD 0630 16318-2. Alagna, Hampson, Van Dam, Mattila, Meier, Halfvarson, Théâtre du Châtelet Ch., O de Paris, Pappano
*** EMI 5 56152-2 (3). Alagna, Van Dam, Hampson, Mattila, Meier, Théâtre du Châtelet Ch., O de Paris, Pappano
(M) *** EMI (ADD) 7 69304-2 (3). Carreras, Freni, Ghiaurov, Baltsa, Cappuccilli, Raimondi, German Op. Ch., Berlin, BPO, Karajan
(M) *** EMI 5 67401-2 (3) [567397]. Domingo, Caballé, Raimondi, Verrett, Milnes, Amb. Op. Ch., ROHCG O, Giulini
**(*) DG 415 316-2 (4). Ricciarelli, Domingo, Valentini Terrani, Nucci, Raimondi, Ghiaurov, La Scala, Milan, Ch. & O, Abbado
(BB) **(*) Naxos 8.660096/8. Cleveman, Ryhänen, Mattei, Rundgren, Martinpelto, Tobiasson, Sörensen, Hedlund, Wallén, Leidland, Royal Swedish Op. Ch. & O, Hold-Garrido

This fine Warner issue provides one of the clearest instances where DVD scores on almost every level over the equivalent CD set. Here you have a full three and half hours of music on a single disc, as against the three-CD set from EMI. That also offers a live recording made in the Théâtre du Châtelet in Paris with an identical cast of principals. The sound on DVD may be marginally less full than on CD, but it would take someone with an exceptional ear to feel short-changed. The chorus is rather less crisply disciplined in places, but rises splendidly to the big challenge of the *Auto da fé* scene of Act III. And where too many DVDs skimp on the number of index points, this one follows the normal CD practice of having them at every crucial point.

All that plus the advantage of having a visual presentation of Luc Bondy's production. Though the sets are simple and stylized, the production never gets in the way of the music, with the costumes of Moidele Bickel (coloured black, white or crimson) close enough to seventeenth-century fashion not to distract from the drama. The score is tautly and warmly presented, as on CD, by Antonio Pappano and the principals are as fine a team as have ever been assembled for this opera

on disc – here using the original French text and the full five-act score complete with Fontainebleau scene. Karita Mattila gives the most masterly performance as the Queen, with one inspired passage after another culminating in a supreme account of her Act V aria. Roberto Alagna is in superb voice too, firm and heroic, well-matched against Thomas Hampson, noble as Rodrigo. José van Dam may not have the deep bass normal for the role of Philip II, but having a more lyrical voice brings compensating assets, and he contrasts well with the Grand Inquisitor of Eric Halfvarson. One of the few controversial points in the production is the way that the Grand Inquisitor's entry prompts a few fiery flashes of lightning round him. Otherwise the simple sets add to the speed of the production, with the gantry used in the garden scene of Act III, quickly opening up before one's eyes to make a gallery for the chorus in the *Auto da fé* scene. An outstanding issue.

In the five-act CD version Pappano may not include as much of the extra and optional material as Abbado has on his four-disc DG La Scala set (the only rival in French), but his judgement on the text is good, with one or two variants included. The whole performance sounds more idiomatic, helped by a cast more fluent in French than Abbado's. Regularly Pappano conveys the dramatic thrust more intensely. Naturally impetuous as well as expressive, he inspires his players as well as his singers, an exceptionally strong team. Waltraud Meier is not caught at her best as Eboli, but relishes the drama of *O don fatale*. As the Grand Inquisitor, Eric Halfvarson is not quite steady enough, even if (thanks to Pappano) the confrontation with the King is thrilling. The live recording brings some odd balances, with the sound transferred at a lowish level, but the opera-house atmosphere, vividly caught, amply compensates for any shortcoming.

Karajan opts for the four-act version of the opera, merely opening out the cuts he adopted on stage. The *Auto da fé* scene is here superb, while Karajan's characteristic choice of singers for refinement of voice rather than sheer size consistently pays off. Both Carreras and Freni are most moving. Baltsa is a superlative Eboli and Cappuccilli an affecting Rodrigo. Raimondi and Ghiaurov as the Grand Inquisitor and Philip II provide the most powerful confrontation. The sound is both rich and atmospheric and is made to seem even firmer and more vivid in its current remastering, giving great power to Karajan's uniquely taut account, full of panache.

Yet it is Giulini's 1971 set that EMI have chosen as one of their 'Great Recordings of the Century'. He uses the full, five-act text. Generally the cast is strong; the only vocal disappointment among the principals lies in Caballé's account of the big aria *Tu che le vanità* in the final act. The CD transfer of the analogue recording brings astonishing vividness and realism, a tribute to the original engineering of Christopher Parker. Even in the big ensembles the focus is very precise, yet atmospheric too, not just analytic. Excellent documentation and a full libretto and translation.

Abbado's set was the first recording to use the language which Verdi originally set, French, in the full five-act text. The first disappointment lies in the variable quality of the sound, with odd balances, yet the cast is a strong one. Domingo easily outshines his earlier recording with Giulini (in Italian), while Katia Ricciarelli as the Queen gives a tenderly moving performance, if not quite commanding enough in the Act V aria. Ruggero Raimondi is a finely focused Philip II, nicely contrasted with Nicolai Ghiaurov as the Grand Inquisitor in the other black-toned bass role. Lucia Valentini Terrani as Eboli is warm-toned if not very characterful, and Leo Nucci makes a noble Posa.

Edited together from three live performances, the Naxos set offers a lively, incisive account of the five-act version of *Don Carlo*, with the Swedish Opera's Spanish music-director, Alberto Hold-Garrido, drawing out the formidable talents of his company in a warmly idiomatic reading. It is the more impressive that this is a repertory performance without imported stars. Hillevi Martinpelto, commanding as Elisabetta, and Peter Mattei, the powerful Rodrigo, have both had great success outside Sweden, not least on disc, but the others in the cast equally demonstrate the company's tradition, ever since the days of Jussi Björling and Birgit Nilsson, in encouraging singers with firm, clear voices at a time when too many ill-focused wobblers are being accepted elsewhere.

In the title-role, Lars Cleveman may not be a match for such a star as Plácido Domingo in imagination, but this is a fresh, gripping performance which in Carlo's duets with Rodrigo can live up to almost any comparison. As Philip II, Jaakko Ryhänen sings magnificently, movingly so in his monologue, carrying on the Finnish tradition of Martti Talvela, while Ingrid Tobiasson makes a feisty Eboli. The only snag is that the singers so impress the Stockholm audience that the performance is frequently interrupted by applause. It is a tribute to the singers that even with close-up sound, set in a relatively dry acoustic and with the orchestra forwardly placed, there is no roughness in the singing, just evidence of well-honed technique. As usual with this opera – of which Verdi devised four alternative versions, four-act and five-act – the text is an amalgam, mainly drawn from the 1886 Modena version with a shortened Fontainebleau scene preceding the final revision of the other four acts, and with elements of the original Paris version brought in. An outstanding bargain issue that even includes the full Italian libretto.

Don Carlos (highlights)

(M) *** EMI 7 63089-2 (from above complete recording, with Domingo, Caballé; cond. Giulini)

Giulini's disc of highlights can be highly recommended. In selecting from such a long opera, serious omissions are inevitable, but the *Auto da fé* scene is included. Vivid sound; the only reservation concerns Caballé's *Tu che le vanità*, which ends the selection disappointingly.

(i) Don Carlo, Act III, Scene 2; (ii) Simon Boccanegra, Act I, Scene 2

(M) *** EMI 5 62777-2. Gobbi, (i) Filippesci; (ii) De los Angeles; (i) Rome Op. O, Santini – PUCCINI: *Gianni Schicchi* ***

Rodrigo in *Don Carlo* and his golden-voiced Simon Boccanegra were two of Tito Gobbi's most famous roles, and they are well celebrated in this dramatic pair of excerpts, with honeyed support from De los Angeles as Amelia and Mario Filippesci as Don Carlo. Texts and translations are included.

Ernani (complete)

(M) *** RCA (ADD) GD 86503 (2). L. Price, Bergonzi, Sereni, Flagello, RCA Italiana Op. Ch. & O, Schippers

**(*) EMI 7 47083-8 (3). Domingo, Freni, Bruson, Ghiaurov, La Scala, Milan, Ch. & O, Muti

At mid-price, Schippers's set, recorded in Rome in 1967, is an outstanding bargain. Leontyne Price may take the most celebrated aria, *Ernani involami*, rather cautiously, but the voice is gloriously firm and rich, and Bergonzi is comparably strong and vivid, though Mario Sereni, vocally reliable, is dull, and Ezio Flagello gritty-toned. With Schippers drawing

the team powerfully together, it remains a highly enjoyable set, with the digital transfer making voices and orchestra sound full and vivid.

The great merit of Muti's set, recorded live at a series of performances at La Scala, is that the ensembles have an electricity rarely achieved in the studio, even if the results may not always be so precise and stage noises are often obtrusive. The singing, generally strong and characterful, is yet flawed. The strain of the role of Elvira for Mirella Freni is plain from the big opening aria, *Ernani involami*, onwards. Even in that aria there are cautious moments. Bruson is a superb Carlo and Ghiaurov a characterful Silva, but his voice now betrays signs of wear. As Ernani himself, Plácido Domingo gives a commanding performance, but under pressure there are hints of tight tone. The CD version gives greater immediacy and presence, but also brings out the inevitable flaws of live recording the more clearly.

Ernani (complete; in English)

(M) *** Chan. 3052 (2). Gavin, Patterson, Opie, Wedd, Rose, ENO Ch. & O, Parry

Early Verdi in English can sound like an anticipation of Gilbert and Sullivan, particularly in the jolly choruses, but in a lively, vibrant performance like this, recorded soon after the ENO production in 2000, it is in some ways even more vital than a performance in Italian. The principals are first rate, with Susan Patterson a formidable Elvira, tackling her big aria in Act I firmly and confidently, at once rich-toned and agile with a perfect trill. The Australian tenor Julian Gavin is also well cast in the title-role, with a cleanly focused voice and clear diction, while Alan Opie gives a vintage performance in the baritone role of the King. Full, vivid recording. A welcome if unexpected addition to the Peter Moore/Chandos Opera in English series.

Falstaff (complete)

(*) BBC Opus Arte **DVD OA 0812D. Terfel, Frittoli, Rancatore, Manca di Nissa, Montague, Frontali, Tarver, Leggate, Howell, ROHCG Ch. & O, Haitink

⊕ *** DG 471 194-2 (2). Terfel, Pieczonka, Diadkova, Hampson, Röschmann, Shtoda, Berlin R. Ch., BPO, Abbado

*** EMI 5 67083-2 (2). Gobbi, Schwarzkopf, Zaccaria, Moffo, Panerai, Philh. Ch. & O, Karajan

(N) (BB) *** LSO 0055 (2). Pertusi, Alvarez, Ibarra, Domashenko, Henschel, L. Symphony Ch., LSO, C. Davis

(N) (M) *** Decca (ADD) 475 6677 (2). G. Evans, Ligabue, Freni, Kraus, Elias, Simionato, RCA Italiana Op. Ch. & O, Solti

(M) **(*) Sony (ADD) SM2K 91181 (2). Fischer-Dieskau, Panerai, Ligabue, Sciutti, Oncina, Resnik, Rössl-Majdan, V. State Op. Ch., VPO, Bernstein

(M) **(*) DG (IMS) 447 686-2 (2). Taddei, Kabaivanska, Perry, Ludwig, Panerai, Araiza, De Palma, Zednik, V. State Op. Ch., VPO, Karajan

(BB) (***) Naxos mono 8.110198/9 (2). Rimini, Tassinari, Tellini, Buades, D'Alessio, Monticone, Ghirardini, La Scala Ch. and O, Molajoli (with arias by MASCAGNI, MASSENET, MOZART, PUCCINI, WAGNER (***))

Graham Vick's provocative DVD production with crudely coloured toy-town sets by Paul Brown was the opening attraction in the newly refurbished Covent Garden operahouse. It is powerfully conducted by Bernard Haitink as

Music Director who, in a brief interview, rightly suggests that this is a score with not a superfluous note. The production's principal asset is the strong, characterful Falstaff of Bryn Terfel, musically and dramatically most satisfying despite his grotesquely exaggerated costume and pot-belly. In the tradition of the finest Falstaffs, he is at once comic and dignified and ultimately moving, while the voice is in splendid form. Barbara Frittoli also makes an excellent Alice, and the rest of the cast is consistently fine. The problem lies in the sets with their aggressive primary colours and simplistic lines, though the false perspectives have a vaguely medieval look.

The costumes, although equally garish, are in Elizabethan style, and Vick allows Falstaff to be tipped into the Thames in a genuine laundry basket, but he removes all magic from the final Windsor Forest scene, with a tower of bodies (intrepid members of the chorus) taking the place of Herne's Oak. In an interview (one of the extra features) Vick explains that he wanted to bring out the physicality of the piece, emphasizing that this is an Italian opera, not a Shakespeare play. The interview with Terfel is not helped by the questioner who is rather too pleased with himself, but the singer's warm personality overrides that drawback. There is also a 10-minute tour backstage of the newly refurbished opera-house, and an illustrated synopsis of the opera. Unlike many operas on DVD this one has ample index points, with 31 chapters or tracks.

Abbado's is a big-scale view of *Falstaff*, helped by the weighty recorded sound and upfront balance of voices, matching the larger-than-life characterization of the fat knight by the charismatic Bryn Terfel. Terfel gives a vital, three-dimensional reading as one might expect, but uses tone-colours that do not generally have you picturing a fat character, a point that also applies to the classic portrayal by Tito Gobbi in the first Karajan recording on EMI. The darkness of Falstaff's Act III monologue after his ducking is as intense as you will ever hear it, while the final fugue at a very fast tempo is thrillingly precise, thanks to a team of leading singers who respond brilliantly to Abbado's strong, thoughtful direction. Adrianna Pieczonka is a superb Alice, full-toned and characterful, and Dorothea Röschmann a charming Nannetta, with Larissa Diadkova a fruity Mrs Quickly. The male characters are well contrasted too, and though Thomas Hampson's velvety baritone hardly conveys the meanness of Ford, the sensitive detail in his characterization is magnetic. For most collectors this will now be the primary recommendation, although Giulini's famous version is not eclipsed.

The earlier (1956) Karajan recording presents not only the most pointed account orchestrally of Verdi's comic masterpiece (the Philharmonia Orchestra at its very peak) but the most sharply characterful cast ever gathered for a recording. If you relish the idea of Tito Gobbi as Falstaff (his many-coloured voice, not quite fat-sounding in humour, presents a sharper character than usual), then this is clearly the best choice. The rest of the cast too is a delight, with Schwarzkopf a tinglingly masterful Mistress Ford, Anna Moffo sweet as Nannetta and Rolando Panerai a formidable Ford. On CD the digital transfer is sharply focused.

Particularly after the disappointment of Davis's 1992 version of Falstaff for RCA, made in Munich, it is a joy to have as exhilarating an account as this live recording, made with the LSO at the Barbican in May 2004, with an outstanding cast led by the Italian baritone, Michele Pertusi. The extra resilience of the LSO's playing, matched by the singers, makes all the difference in this new version. More than in Munich,

Davis springs rhythms infectiously, bringing out the sparkle and wit in this magical score, as well as the dramatic contrasts, with tender Verdian lyricism a vital element. Davis is masterly too in timing the climaxes. The recording helps, with voices cleanly separated so that, though this was taken from concert performances, the sense of live drama is irresistible. Pertusi is brilliant in the title-role, bluff and powerful, with voice cleanly focused over the widest expressive range. Carlos Alvarez as Ford is nicely contrasted, his dark anger coming over powerfully in his Act II monologue, while Ana Ibarra as Alice Ford leads a superb team of women soloists, phenomenally precise in their chattering ensembles, with Jane Henschel a wonderfully fruity Mistress Quickly. Maria José Moreno as Nannetta and Bulent Bezduz as Fenton make a winning pair of lovers. Above all, the liveness of the experience adds to the electricity, as it does in the classic Toscanini version. Like all LSO live issues, this one comes at budget price, making it an astonishing bargain, with libretto and translation included in the booklet, as well as a thoughtful essay by Rodney Milnes.

Sir Geraint Evans's 1963 assumpion of the role of Verdi's Falstaff in partnership with Sir George Solti was originally issued by RCA, and here it returns to the catalogue in Decca's Classic Opera series, in a mid-priced box (with libretto), as sparkling as ever. There is an energy, a sense of fun and vivacity that outshines most rival versions, outstanding though they may be. Evans never sounded better on record, and the rest of the cast live up to his example admirably. Solti drives hard, but it is an exciting and well-pointed performance, and the rest of the cast is well contrasted.

Bernstein's mid-1960s set, with Fischer-Dieskau in the title-role, is flawed by Sony's inept presentation, without either a libretto/translation (so essential in this opera), or even a cued synopsis. Nevertheless, collectors will surely want to snap it up before it disappears again. It is based on a production at the Vienna State Opera, and the fleetness of execution at hair-raisingly fast speeds suggests that Bernstein was intent on out-Toscanini-ing Toscanini. The allegros may be consistently faster than Toscanini's, but they never sound rushed, and always Bernstein conveys a sense of fun, while in relaxed passages, helped by warm Viennese sensitivity, he allows a full rotundity of phrasing, at least as much as any rival. It does not really matter here, any more than it did with the Toscanini set, that the conductor is the hero rather than Falstaff himself.

Fischer-Dieskau does wonders in pointing the humour. In his scene with Mistress Quickly arranging an assignation with Alice, he can inflect a simple 'Ebben?' to make it intensely funny, but he finally suffers from having a voice one inevitably associates with baritonal solemnity, whether heroic or villainous. Just how noble Falstaff should be is a matter for discussion.

The others are first rate – Panerai singing superbly as Ford, Ilva Ligabue as Mistress Ford, Regina Resnik as Mistress Quickly, and Graziella Sciutti and Juan Oncina as the young lovers. Excellent engineering (by a Decca recording team) together with effective remastering have produced a very satisfactory sound-balance. But this set is let down by its inadequate documentation.

Anthony Michaels-Moore is compellingly thoughtful and self-searching as Ford, and the quartet of women is outstanding, with Hillevi Martinpelto fresh and bright as Alice, Sara Mingardo wonderfully resonant as Mistress Quickly, and Rebecca Evans singing ravishingly as Nannetta. As Fenton, Antonetto Palombi may not quite be quite so secure as Evans, but his voice is headily youthful to make a good match. A sparkling version quite distinct from others in a very strong field of contenders and well worth considering as a supplemental purchase if you already have either the Giulini or Karajan recordings.

Karajan's second (1980) recording of Verdi's last opera, made over twenty years after his classic EMI Philharmonia version with Gobbi and Schwarzkopf, is far less precise in a relaxed and genial way. With the exception of Kabaivanska, whose voice is not steady enough for the role of Alice, it is a good cast, with Ludwig fascinating as Mistress Quickly. Most astonishing of all is Taddei's performance as Falstaff himself, full, characterful and vocally astonishing from a man in his sixties. The digital sound is faithful and wide-ranging, and the CD transfer vividly captures the bloom of the original reverberant recording.

Recorded in 1930 for Italian Columbia, the La Scala version of *Falstaff* in Naxos's historical series was the first ever made and is here superbly restored on CD by Ward Marston, with voices vividly caught and surface hiss generally well subdued. Toscanini's historic concert performance for RCA has dimmed memories of this equally urgent and idiomatic reading. It features a fine, well-coordinated team of soloists noted for their performances at La Scala at the time, who bring out the words with astonishing clarity. Giacomo Rimini, with his firm, dark voice, not only articulates well but also conveys the humour of the fat knight, and Pia Tassinari, then not quite thirty years old, is a fresh, characterful Alice. Aurora Buades is a fruity Mrs Quickly with a formidable chest register, and the casting of the rest is also near-ideal. The first two acts are contained complete on the first disc, leaving room for a 35-minute supplement on the second, gathering together arias and ensembles with Pia Tassinari, mostly dating from 1941–3 when her voice was weightier but still fresh and pure. It is remarkable to have an Italian soprano of the period singing with such stylishness in Mozart (Susanna's *Deh vieni* from *Figaro*), Wagner (Elsa's two arias from *Lohengrin* in Italian) and Massenet (Charlotte's letter-song from *Werther*, also in Italian). A cherishable supplement, with Tassinari's husband, Ferruccio Tagliavini, joining her in the concluding quartet from Act III of Puccini's *La Bohème*.

Falstaff (complete; in English)

(M) *** Chan. 3079 (2). Shore, Kenny, Gritton, Holland, Banks, Kale, De Pont, Davies, Coote, ENO Ch. & O, Daniel

Taken straight from the ENO stage at the Coliseum to the recording studio, Paul Daniel's brilliant version of *Falstaff* is among the finest of the Opera in English series sponsored by the Peter Moores Foundation. Ensemble is consistently crisp and pointed, yet the feeling of a live experience is vividly caught, with sound-production creating an illusion of a staged performance, so getting the best of both worlds. The role of Falstaff is a speciality of Andrew Shore, and he delivers a vivid portrait, at once comic and weighty, but with lightness and sparkle part of the mixture, and with the Act III monologue of disillusion after his ducking ('*Your World is Crumbling*' in the excellent translation of Amanda Holden) a high point. The voice grows rough in places, but Shore is unfazed by the high-lying passages, which come over well. There is no weak link in the rest of the cast, with Yvonne Kenny as Alice and Susan Gritton as Nannetta both outstanding. Yet above all, it is the taut and finely paced conducting of Paul Daniel and the playing of the orchestra, superbly recorded, which

make this set musically competitive with the finest versions in Italian. As they sing in the final fugue, '*Life is a burst of laughter*'.

La forza del destino (1862 version; complete)

*** Arthaus **DVD** 100 078. Gorchakova, Putilin, Grigorian, Tarasova, Kirov Ch. & O, Gergiev (Producer: Elijah Moshinsky; V/D: Brian Large)

☛ (M) *** RCA (ADD) 74321 39502-2 (3). L. Price, Domingo, Milnes, Cossotto, Giaiotti, Bacquier, Alldis Ch., LSO, Levine

(M) *** DG 474 903-2 (3). Plowright, Carrres, Bruson, Burchuladze, Baltsa, Amb. Op. Ch., Philh. O, Sinopoli

(M) **(*) EMI (ADD) 7 64646-2 (3). Arroyo, Bergonzi, Cappuccilli, Raimondi, Casoni, Evans, Amb. Op. Ch., RPO, Gardelli

The DVD production of the 1862 version of *La forza* comes from St Petersburg, where the opera had its première. In discussing the differences between the 1862 and 1869 versions of the opera itself, Julian Budden says that there is 'not a change in the revision which is not an improvement,' but all the same it is good to have Verdi's first thoughts together with some music that is unfamiliar.

In 1862 the overture was replaced by a short prelude, but otherwise the changes concern the final scenes of Act III, where the duo between Don Alvaro and Don Carlo follows rather than precedes the encampment scene. The finale is also different: the Alvaro–Carlo duel takes place on stage and Alvaro does not survive, but takes his own life. Of particular interest is the fact that the Kirov reproduce the original sets, which look quite handsome, even if the staging is at times a bit hyperactive.

The performance is much stronger than in the version that the Kirov brought to Covent Garden in the summer of 2001, and Valéry Gergiev here proves a more idiomatic Verdi conductor than he was during the London season. The cast is strong, with Gorchakova in good form as Leonora, singing with great dramatic eloquence.

Philips have recorded it under Gergiev on three CDs (446 951-2) with substantially the same cast, the major changes being Marianna Tarasova (instead of Olga Borodina) as Preziosilla and Sergei Alexashin (instead of Mikhail Kit) as the Padre Guardiano. Otherwise the main characters are the same.

Gegam Grigorian is an impressively confident Alvaro, and Nikolai Putilin's Don Carlo is every bit as good as on CD. Tarasova's Preziosilla does not disappoint, and Sergei Alexashin's Guardiano is better focused than Mikhail Kit in the 1996 CD. The opera looks very good – and sounds very good: the audio balance is first class. Brian Large's video direction is first class, too, and although Moshinsky's direction is busy, it is for the most part effective. Subtitles are in English, German, French and Dutch.

Leontyne Price recorded the role of Leonora in an earlier RCA version made in Rome in 1956, but the years hardly touched her voice. The roles of Don Alvaro and Don Carlo are ideally suited to the team of Plácido Domingo and Sherrill Milnes so that their confrontations are the cornerstones of the dramatic structure. Fiorenza Cossotto makes a formidable rather than a jolly Preziosilla, while on the male side the line-up of Bonaldo Giaiotti, Gabriel Bacquier, Kurt Moll and Michel Sénéchal is far stronger than on rival sets. In a vivid transfer of the mid-1970s sound, this is a strong, well-paced version with an exceptionally good and consistent cast.

Sinopoli's performance is notable for the creamy soprano of Rosalind Plowright, Agnes Baltsa's splendidly assured Preziosilla and Paata Burchuladze's resonant portrayal of the Padre Guardiano. Although this recording won the *Gramophone* Opera Reward in 1987, it is not now a first choice. Sinopoli draws out phrases lovingly, sustaining pauses to the limit, putting extra strain on the singers. Happily, the whole cast thrives on the challenge, and the spaciousness of the recording acoustic not only makes the dramatic interchanges the more realistic, it brings out the bloom on all the voices. Though José Carreras is sometimes too conventionally histrionic, even strained, it is a strong, involved performance. Renato Bruson is a thoughtful Carlo, while some of the finest singing of all comes from Agnes Baltsa as Preziosilla.

Gardelli, normally a reliable recording conductor in Italian opera, here gives a disappointing account of a vividly dramatic score. The cast is vocally strong and each member of it lives up to expectations. Moreover the recording – made in 1969 in Watford Town Hall – is first rate, vivid, full and atmospheric. But it is vital in so long and episodic a work that overall dramatic control should be firm. Admirers of the individual artists will find much to enjoy when the sound is so flattering to the voices. The layout places Acts I and II on the first disc, while Acts III and IV are each allotted a CD apiece.

La forza del destino (slightly abridged)

(***) EMI mono 5 56323-2 (3). Callas, Tucker, Tagliabue, Nicolai, Rossi-Lemeni, Capecchi, La Scala, Milan, Ch. & O, Serafin

Though there are classic examples of Callas's raw tone on top notes, they are insignificant next to the wealth of phrasing which sets a totally new and individual stamp on even the most familiar passages. Apart from his tendency to disturb his phrasing with sobs, Richard Tucker sings superbly; but not even he – and certainly none of the others (including the baritone Carlo Tagliabue, well past his prime) – begin to rival the dominance of Callas. Serafin's direction is crisp, dramatic and well paced, again drawing the threads together. The 1955 mono sound is less aggressive than many La Scala recordings of this vintage and has been freshened on CD.

Un giorno di regno (complete)

(N) (BB) *** Ph 475 67722 (2). Cossotto, Norman, Carreras, Wixell, Sardinero, Ganzarolli, Amb. S., RPO, Gardelli

Un giorno di regno may not be the greatest comic opera of the period, but this scintillating performance under Gardelli clearly reveals the young Verdi as more than an imitator of Rossini and Donizetti, and there are striking passages that clearly give a foretaste of such numbers as the duet *Si vendetta* from *Rigoletto*. Despite the absurd plot, this is as light and frothy an entertainment as anyone could want. Excellent singing from a fine team, with Jessye Norman and José Carreras outstanding. The recorded sound is vivid, and the Philips reissue includes full libretto.

Giovanna d'Arco (complete)

(M) **(*) EMI (ADD) 7 63226-2 (2). Caballé, Domingo, Milnes, Amb. Ch., LSO, Levine

The seventh of Verdi's operas, based very loosely indeed on Schiller's drama, is typical of the works which the master was writing during his 'years in the galleys', exuberantly melodic.

James Levine, a youthful whirlwind in his very first opera recording, presses on too hard in fast music, with the rum-ti-tum hammered home, but is warmly sympathetic in melodic writing, particularly when Caballé is singing. What had become a standard trio of principals for the 1970s here gives far more than a routine performance. With fine recording there is much to enjoy, even when the plot – involving merely Joan, her father (who betrays her) and the King – is so naïve.

Jérusalem (complete)

*** Ph. 462 613-2 (3). Mescheriakova, Giordani, Scandiuzzi, SRO Ch. & O, Luisi

TDK **DVD** DV-OPJER. Momirov, Villaroel, Bragaglia, Fondary, Teatro Corlo Felice Ch. & O of Genoa, Plasson (Director: Piergiorgio Gay; V/D: Paola Longobardo)

To have a long-buried Verdi opera dusted down and given a brilliant first recording like this is a rare joy, particularly when it confounds the adverse verdict trumpeted for 150 years. *Jérusalem* is the radical reworking of Verdi's second big success, *I Lombardi*, which he made for the Paris Opéra in 1847, his first essay in setting French.

The general view, with one glowing exception, has been that *Jérusalem* is a failure, even dottier in its plot than *I Lombardi*. Yet Julian Budden, that most perceptive of Verdi scholars, has voiced the opposite view in his comprehensive survey of the operas, and it is here triumphantly justified. Where in *I Lombardi* the tenor hero is excluded from Act I and dies before Act IV – in which he is absurdly brought back as a heavenly voice – the layout of *Jérusalem* is clearly preferable. The big hit number, the trio for the three principals, which in *I Lombardi* comes at the end of Act III, is placed far more effectively in *Jérusalem* at the end of Act IV, with only a brief dénouement to follow, and with its saccharine solo violin removed. Other changes are also in favour of the later work.

This première recording offers brilliant sound and fine, incisive playing from the Suisse Romande Orchestra, with electrifying singing from the Geneva Chorus. The principals are more variable. Roberto Scandiuzzi in the principal baritone role, Roger, sounds too old, but Marcello Giordani as the hero, Gaston, is youthfully fresh and Marina Mescheriakova is a sweetly vibrant heroine, if rather taxed in coloratura.

Jérusalem, Verdi's reworking of *I Lombardi* for Paris, is a welcome rarity on DVD, but this video (made in 2000 for Italian television) is put out of court by having the singers miming inexactly to a pre-recorded film in an uninspired traditional production from the opera-house in Genoa. No stars.

I Lombardi (complete)

*** Decca 455 287-2 (2). Pavarotti, Anderson, Leech, Ramey, Met. Opera Ch. and O, Levine

(M) *** Ph. (ADD) 422 420-2 (2). Deutekom, Domingo, Raimondi, Amb. S., RPO, Gardelli

With the help of brilliant Decca recording, Levine consistently brings out this early work's adventurousness, its striking anticipations of *La forza del destino*. Based on the staging of the opera at the Met in New York, the chief glory of the set is the casting of Pavarotti as the hero, Oronte. As Oronte does not appear until Act II and dies at the end of Act III (signal for the *Great Trio*, much the finest number in the opera), it is not a role one would have expected Pavarotti to take on at this stage of his career. He does it masterfully, on the whole, with even more imagination than the young Domingo on the rival Philips set under Gardelli. Unfortunately, the visionary appearance of the dead hero in Act IV (*Benedetto del cielo*) has the singer placed far too close, a very corporeal ghost. Samuel Ramey sings strongly in the baritone role of the evil brother, Pagano (who appears later as a Hermit), but vocally cannot quite match Ruggero Raimondi on Philips. On the other hand June Anderson as the heroine, Giselda, is both sweeter and more sympathetic than Cristina Deutekom on Philips.

I Lombardi reaches its apotheosis in the famous *Trio*, well known from the days of 78-r.p.m. recordings. By those standards, Cristina Deutekom is not an ideal Verdi singer: her tone is sometimes hard and her voice is not always perfectly under control. Domingo as Oronte is in superb voice, and the villain Pagano is well characterized by Raimondi. Impressive singing too from Stafford Dean and Clifford Grant. Gardelli conducts dramatically, heightening the impact of the plot.

Luisa Miller (complete)

(M) *** Decca 473 365-2 (2). Caballé, Pavarotti, Milnes, Reynolds, L. Op. Ch., Nat. PO, Maag

(B) *** DG Double (ADD) 459 481-2 (2). Ricciarelli, Obraztsova, Domingo, Bruson, Howell, ROHCG Ch. & O, Maazel

On Decca, Caballé, not flawless vocally, yet gives a splendidly dramatic portrait of the heroine, and Pavarotti's performance is full of creative, detailed imagination. As Federica, Anna Reynolds underlines the light and shade, consistently bringing out atmospheric qualities. Vividly transferred to CD. This is now reissued at mid-price, neatly repackaged in Decca's Compact Opera Collection, with a cued synopsis and the libretto obtainable via a CD-ROM, which is provided with the set.

Maazel's 1979 Covent Garden set returns to the catalogue as a DG Double and would have been very competitive indeed had it included a full libretto and translation instead of just a synopsis. Though taut in his control, Maazel uses his stage experience of working with these soloists to draw them out to their finest, most sympathetic form. Ricciarelli gives one of her tenderest and most beautiful performances on record, Domingo is in glorious voice, and Bruson as Luisa's father sings with a velvet tone. Gwynne Howell is impressive as the Conte di Walter, and Wladimiro Ganzarolli's vocal roughness is apt for the character of Wurm. The snag is the abrasive Countess Federica of Elena Obraztsova.

Macbeth (1847 version; complete)

*** Opera Rara ORCV 301 (2). Glossop, Hunter, Tomlinson, Collins, BBC Singers & Concert O, Matheson

What till now have been seriously neglected on disc have been Verdi's first thoughts, the versions of operas which he went on to revise, none more radically than his first Shakespearean venture, *Macbeth*. This fascinating recording of the original version will be a revelation to most Verdians. Taken from a BBC studio broadcast of 1979, masterminded by the Verdi scholar Julian Budden, it demonstrates very clearly how many of the most strikingly original passages were already there in Verdi's first version. Act I is already in place as we know it, with just a few tiny changes, and Lady Macbeth's great sleepwalking scene of Act IV, one of the most memorable passages of all, is already fully developed. Yet the revisions, involving almost a third of the score, are radical, the more strikingly so as the opera progresses. So in Act II, instead of the dramatic aria, *La luce langue*, Lady Macbeth sings a more conventional display piece which, like her Brindisi later in the

act, involves a jolly oompah rhythm, while in Act III, the scene of Macbeth's hallucinations is quite different. Act IV is what Verdi changed most. Here it opens with a bold chorus involving a big tune sung in unison on the lines of *Va pensiero*, the chorus of Hebrew Slaves from *Nabucco*. Like almost all of Verdi's other first thoughts, it is not as refined musically as the magnificent chorus of lamentation with which it was replaced in 1865, but stylistically it is more consistent with the rest of the opera. The final scene too is quite different in this first version. A sequence of fanfares instead of a fugato represents the battle, with the whole opera ending on a death scene for Macbeth instead of a victory chorus.

This set is the more cherishable when the performance, incisively conducted by John Matheson, is so strongly cast. In this version the central roles of Macbeth and Lady Macbeth are vocally even more demanding than in Verdi's revision, and the baritone, Peter Glossop, here gives a searingly powerful performance as Macbeth. Rita Hunter is equally commanding as Lady Macbeth, for her massive soprano, Wagnerian in scale, is surprisingly flexible in coloratura, with a perfectly controlled trill. The young John Tomlinson is magnificent as Banquo, and the tenor Kenneth Collins makes a fine Macduff.

Macbeth (complete; DVD versions)

(*) Arthaus **DVD 100 140. Bruson, Zampieri, Morris, O'Neill, Deutsche Op. Ch. & O, Sinopoli (Director: Luca Ronconi)

(N) **(*) Arthaus **DVD** 101 895. Paskalis, Barstow, Morris, Erwin, Glyndebourne Ch., LPO, Pritchard (V/D: Dave Heather)

In his second recording, on DVD, made at the Deutsche Oper in Berlin in 1987, Giuseppe Sinopoli conducts a dramatic reading of *Macbeth*, dominated by the fine Macbeth of Renato Bruson, his self-searching the more compelling in close-up on DVD, and the powerful, if sometimes hooty, Lady Macbeth of Mara Zampieri, perfectly looking the part, young and handsome still. She points the drinking-song well, and although she avoids the final top note of the sleepwalking scene, it is still a magnetic performance. The rest of the cast is strong too, with Dennis O'Neill as Macduff and James Morris as Banquo. The chorus sings splendidly, with a line-up of dozens of witches in the opening scene, gathered behind the long table that dominates a fair proportion of scenes in Luca Ronconi's bare production, with sets and costumes by Luciano Damiani. Excellent, well-separated sound.

It was at Glyndebourne in the 1930s that Verdi's Macbeth was first produced in Britain, and the 1972 television recording demonstrates what power the piece has when presented in an intimate setting. Dominating the performance is the young Josephine Barstow as Lady Macbeth, singing powerfully and acting with venom and malice mixed with humour. Hers is hardly a beautiful voice as recorded, but the bite and edge add greatly to the impact. As Macbeth, Paskalis sings powerfully too, presenting in Michael Hadjimischev's production a worryingly equivocal character. The young James Morris as Banquo focuses his voice cleanly and incisively, and Keith Erwin as Macduff provides a refreshing contrast. Strong choral work and atmospheric sets by Emanuele Luzzati.

Macbeth (complete; CD versions)

(M) *** DG (ADD) 449 732-2 (2). Cappuccilli, Verrett, Ghiaurov, Domingo, La Scala, Milan, Ch. & O, Abbado

(M) (*(**)) EMI mono 5 66447-2 (2). Callas, Mascherini, Tajo, Penno, Della Pergola, La Scala, Milan, Ch. & O, De Sabata

At times Abbado's tempi are unconventional, but with slow speeds he springs the rhythm so infectiously that the results are most compelling. Together making a fine team, each of the principals is meticulous about observing Verdi's detailed markings, above all those for *pianissimo* and *sotto voce*. Verrett, powerful above the stave, makes a virtue out of necessity in floating glorious half-tones, and with so firm and characterful a voice she makes a highly individual Lady Macbeth. Cappuccilli has never sung with a finer range of tone or more imagination on record than here, and Plácido Domingo makes a real, sensitive character out of the small role of Macduff. Excellent recording, splendidly remastered as one of the first operas to be included in DG's 'Legendary Recordings' series, and now at mid-price on two discs.

The role of Lady Macbeth could hardly have been more perfectly suited to Maria Callas, and though there are serious flaws in this live recording of 1952 – evidently taken off a radio relay – the commanding presence, the magnetic musical imagination and the abrasive tones make this a unique experience. In 1952 the vocal flaws that beset Callas were largely in the future, and there is a thrilling sound in every register. Also Victor de Sabata, despite some odd misjudgements like his brisk tempo for the sleepwalking scene, is comparably incisive. Sadly, nothing else in the performance matches such mastery, with Enzo Mascherini a dull, uncharacterful Macbeth and only the resonant Italo Tajo as Banquo otherwise commanding attention. Scrubby, limited sound, which most ears will still accommodate for the sake of such a performance.

Nabucco (complete; DVD version)

(N) *** NVC Arts **DVD** 0630 19390-2. Bruson, Dimitrova, D'Artegna, Petkov, Baglioni, Garaventa, Ch. & O of Verona Arena, Maurizio Arena (Producer: Renzo Giacchieri; V/D: Brian Large)

In some ways Verdi's *Nabucco*, dealing as it does with the conflict between a pagan religion and Christianity, is half-opera, half histrionic-oratorio, and Renzo Giacchieri's somewhat stylized production – the clashes between the rival groups of soldiers are symbolic rather than realistic – against a comparatively primitive rocky set is highly effective, with the costumes providing plenty of colour. Yet in the two 'miracles', when Nabucco is struck down by a thunderbolt and, later, the destruction of the statue of Baal, are simply and effectively managed. The opera is cast from strength, with Renato Bruson's Nabucco dominating the action powerfully and the High Priest (Ellero D'Artegna) singing nobly. Dimitrova is hardly less commanding as Abigaille; her big Act II aria and her scene with Nabucco in Act III are equally memorable. But, above all, *Nabucco* grips its audience with its big choruses, and they are splendidly sung here. The orchestra too plays vibrantly under the appropriately named Maurizio Arena, and altogether this is visually and vocally first class.

Nabucco (complete; CD versions)

☞ *** DG 410 512-2 (2). Cappuccilli, Dimitrova, Nesterenko, Domingo, Ch. & O of German Op., Berlin, Sinopoli

*** Decca (ADD) 417 407-2 (2). Gobbi, Souliotis, Cava, Previdi, V. State Op. Ch. & O, Gardelli

With Sinopoli one keeps hearing details normally obscured. Even the thrill of the great chorus *Va, pensiero* is the greater when the melody first emerges at a hushed *pianissimo*, as marked. Dimitrova is superb in Abigaille's big Act II aria, noble in her evil, as is Cappuccilli as Nabucco, less intense than Gobbi was on Gardelli's classic set for Decca, but stylistically pure. The rest of the cast is strong too, including Domingo in the unusually small tenor role and Nesterenko superb as the High Priest, Zaccaria. Bright and forward digital sound, less atmospheric than the 1965 Decca set with Gobbi and Souliotis, conducted by Gardelli.

On Decca, the Viennese chorus lacks bite in *Va, pensiero*; but in every other way this is a masterly performance, with dramatically intense and deeply imaginative contributions from Tito Gobbi as Nabucco and Elena Souliotis as the evil Abigaille. Souliotis made this the one totally satisfying performance of an all-too-brief recording career, wild in places but no more than is dramatically necessary. Though Carlo Cava as Zaccaria is not ideally rich of tone, it is a strong performance, and Gardelli, as in his later Verdi recordings for both Decca and Philips, showed what a Verdian master he is, whether in pointing individual phrases or whole scenes, simply and naturally. Vivid and atmospheric 1965 Decca recording.

Nabucco (highlights)

(M) *** Decca (ADD) 458 246-2 (from above recording, with Souliotis, Gobbi; cond. Gardelli)

Souliotis's impressive contribution is well represented on the Decca highlights disc, and there are fine contributions too from Gobbi. Needless to say the chorus *Va, pensiero* is given its place of honour and the reissued selection now runs for 69 minutes. As in other Opera Gala reissues, a full translation is now included.

Otello (complete; DVD versions)

(N) *** NVC Arts **DVD** 4509 99214-2. Te Kanawa, Atlantov, Cappuccilli, Bevacqua, Schiavon, Rafanelli, Ch. & O of Verona Arena, Peskó (Producer: Gianfranco de Bosio; V/D: Preben Montell)

*** DG **DVD** 073 092-9. Domingo, Fleming, Morris, Bunnell, Croft, Anthony, Metropolitan Ch. & O, Levine (Producer: Louisa Briccetti; V/D: Brian Large)

(*) DG **DVD 073-006-9. Vickers, Freni, Glossop, Malagu, Bottion, Senechal, Van Dam, Deutsche Op. Ch., BPO, Karajan

Otello is one of the most powerful indictments of human evil in Shakespeare, and Verdi's opera captures its essence in a work that depends on the intimate but dramatic interplay of the principal characters: scheming, credulous, jealous or innocent. The opera does not call for spectacle; the storm at the opening is in the orchestra, so the Verona producer Gianfranco de Bosio and designer Vittorio Rossi have chosen a very plain set, yet they used the full resources of Verona for the one big scene at the end of Act III, which is magnificently staged. Vladimir Atlantov is a very real, believable Otello, often grim-faced yet obviously melted in Act I by Desdemona's love. Kiri Te Kanawa is at her glorious best as Desdemona, ravishingly clear-voiced and true, and her final *Willow Song* is infinitely touching before the opera's terrible close. Piero Cappuccilli is an obsequiously wily Iago. As we discover in his Creed, his voice is less strong than Atlantov's powerful Otello, but his false-friendly *Era la notte* is superbly characterized, and in the big duet with Otello at the end of Act II the two voices are naturally blended. In short there are no flaws here, and the video direction centres on the principal characters very vividly, while Zoltan Peskó keeps the tension at a high level. Another Verona triumph, which is very compelling.

It is good to have so telling a reminder on DVD of Plácido Domingo's masterly assumption of the role of Otello: commanding in every way, particularly when at the Met. in New York in 1996 he was singing opposite Renée Fleming as Desdemona, then at her freshest and purest, yet also with power, looking and sounding girlish. James Levine's direction is high-powered from beginning to end, matching the singing of his principals, controlling the massive forces provided in this lavish production directed by Elijah Moshinsky with sets by Michael Yeargan and costumes by Peter J. Hall. Though James Morris is not the most sinister of Iagos, his singing is clean and firm, well varied in the two big monologues of Act II. Excellent singing too from Jane Bunnell as a very positive Emilia and Richard Croft as Cassio, a tenor well contrasted with Domingo. The only bonuses on DVD are a picture gallery and trailer.

As well as conducting, Karajan himself directed this glamorous DG film version of *Otello* on DVD, presenting it in spectacular settings, with effects going far beyond what is possible on stage, as in the opening storm scene. The singers mime their parts to an audio recording, with mouthmovements not always well synchronized.

That is a small price to pay for a fine, bitingly dramatic performance, characterfully cast and beautifully sung. Jon Vickers was still at his peak when the recording was made in 1974, thrilling in the title-role with not a hint of strain and backed up by powerful acting. Similarly, Peter Glossop has never been finer on disc, whether in his singing or his acting, a plausible yet uncompromising Iago, and Mirella Freni gives a radiant performance as Desdemona, rising superbly to the challenge of the final scene, both sweet and powerful.

The balance of the voices frequently follows the closeness or distancing of the camerawork, which can be distracting, but this is an involving presentation of the Verdi masterpiece, intelligently re-thought for the camera. The sound is good, though not as vivid as in the latest fully digital recordings.

Otello (complete; CD versions)

☛— *** DG 439 805-2 (2). Domingo, Studer, Leiferkus, Ch. & O of Bastille Opera, Chung

(M) *** RCA (ADD) 74321 39501-2 (2). Domingo, Scotto, Milnes, Amb. Op. Ch., Nat. PO, Levine

*** Decca 433 669-2 (2). Pavarotti, Te Kanawa, Nucci, Rolfe Johnson, Chicago SO & Ch., Solti

(M) *** EMI 7 69308-2 (2). Vickers, Freni, Glossop, Ch. of German Op., Berlin, BPO, Karajan

(B) **(*) HM Music & Arts CD 1043 (2). Domingo, Freni, Cappuccilli, Ciannella, Raffanti, La Scala, Milan, Ch. & O, C. Kleiber

On CD, Plácido Domingo's third recording of *Otello* proves to be more freely expressive, even more involved than his previous ones; the baritonal quality of his tenor has here developed to bring extra darkness, with the final solo, *Niun mi tema*, poignantly tender. Cheryl Studer gives one of her finest performances as Desdemona, the tone both full and pure, while Sergei Leiferkus makes a chillingly evil Iago, the more so when his voice is the opposite of Italianate, verging on the gritty, which not everyone will like. With plenty of light and shade, Myung-Whun Chung is an urgent Verdian, adopting free-flowing speeds yet allowing Domingo full

expansiveness in the death scene. The Chorus and Orchestra of the Bastille Opera excel themselves, setting new standards for an opera recording from Paris, and the sound is first rate.

On RCA, Domingo as Otello combines glorious heroic tone with lyrical tenderness. Scotto is not always sweet-toned in the upper register, and the big ensemble at the end of Act III brings obvious strain; nevertheless, it is a deeply felt performance which culminates in a most affecting account of the all-important Act IV solos, the *Willow Song* and *Ave Maria*. Milnes makes a powerful Iago, a handsome, virile creature beset by the biggest of chips on the shoulder. In the transfer of the 1977 analogue original the voices are caught vividly and immediately, and the orchestral sound too is fuller and cleaner than in many more recent versions.

In the Decca Chicago set the key element is the singing of Pavarotti, new to his role of Otello, as was Nucci as Iago. In obedience to Solti, Pavarotti often adopts faster speeds than usual. Whatever the detailed reservations, this is a memorable reading, heightened by Pavarotti's keen feeling for the words and consistently golden tone. With a close microphone-balance, like the others he is prevented from achieving genuine *pianissimos*; but above all he offers a vital, animated Otello, always individual. Dame Kiri Te Kanawa produces consistently sumptuous tone; the *Willow Song* is glorious. The impact of the whole is greatly enhanced by the splendid singing of the Chicago Symphony Chorus, helped by digital sound that is fuller and more vivid than on any rival set.

On EMI, Karajan directs a big, bold and brilliant account, for the most part splendidly sung and with all the dramatic contrasts strongly underlined. There are several tiny, but irritating, statutory cuts, but otherwise on two mid-price CDs this is well worth considering. Freni's Desdemona is delightful, delicate and beautiful, while Vickers and Glossop are both positive and characterful, only occasionally forcing their tone and losing focus. The recording is clarified on CD.

Music and Arts offers a live recording of the legendary performance in December 1976. If Carlos Kleiber can often sound cold or even uninvolved in his studio recordings, this demonstrates the high voltage electricity he can produce on a big occasion, here matching the searing intensity of Toscanini in this work. Plácido Domingo, having just completed a series of performances in Hamburg and Paris, is in superb form, with the voice at its finest, and his personal magnetism as an actor is heightened by the conductor's challenge. Mirella Freni as Desdemona is at her freshest, sweet and vulnerable, while Cappuccilli sings with keen incisiveness as Iago, not always sinister-sounding but musically superb. Stage noises are endlessly intrusive, but the atmosphere of a great occasion is vividly caught.

Otello (complete; in English)

(M) **(*) Chan. 3068 (2). Craig, Plowright, Howlett, Bottone, ENO Ch. & O, Elder

Recorded live at the London Coliseum in 1983 and now reissued on Chandos, the ENO version of *Otello* is flawed both vocally and in the sound; but those who seek recordings of opera in English need not hesitate, for almost every word of Andrew Porter's translation is audible, despite the very variable balances inevitable in recording a live stage production. Less acceptable is the level of stage noise, with the thud and ramble of wandering feet all the more noticeable on CD. The performance itself is most enjoyable, with dramatic tension building up compellingly. Charles Craig's Otello is most moving, the character's inner pain brought out vividly, though top notes are fallible. Neil Howlett as Iago may not have the most distinctive baritone, but finely controlled vocal colouring adds to a deeply perceptive performance. Rosalind Plowright makes a superb Desdemona, singing with rich, dramatic weight but also with poise and purity. The death scene reveals her at her finest, radiant of tone, with flawless attack.

Rigoletto (complete)

(*) BBC Opus Arte **DVD OA 0829D. Gavanelli, Schäfer, Alvarez, Halfvarson, ROHCG Ch. & O, Downes

•━ (B) *** Ph. Duo 462 158-2 (2). Bruson, Gruberová, Shicoff, Fassbaender, Lloyd, St Cecilia Ac., Rome, Ch. & O, Sinopoli

*** Decca (ADD) 414 269-2 (2). Milnes, Sutherland, Pavarotti, Talvela, Tourangeau, Amb. Op. Ch., LSO, Bonynge

*** DG 447 064-2 (2). Chernov, Pavarotti, Studer, Scandiuzzi, Graves, Met. Op. Ch. & O, Levine

(***) EMI mono 5 56327-2 (2). Gobbi, Callas, Di Stefano, La Scala, Milan, Ch. & O, Serafin

(M) **(*) DG (ADD) 457 753-2 (2). Cappuccilli, Cotrubas, Domingo, Obraztsova, Ghiaurov, Moll, Schwarz, V. State Op. Ch., VPO, Giulini

David McVicar's Covent Garden production of *Rigoletto* was one of the offerings leading towards the Verdi centenary in January 2001, strongly cast with Paolo Gavanelli firm and powerful in the title-role. As McVicar explains in an interview (one of the extra DVD features) he perceives the piece as a concentrated howl of pain, evoking the atmosphere of the once-banned play, *Le Roi s'amuse* by Victor Hugo, on which Verdi and his librettist, Piave, based the opera. McVicar incidentally points out that the opera dates from the period of Marx and the Communist Manifesto, though the menace in the production has as much to do with sado-masochistic violence as with politics, helped by Tanya McCallin's costumes (with a leather clown costume making Rigoletto into a gnome-like figure and the Duke's leather outfit when he meets Gilda underlining his role as predator). The setting is rough too in what looks like an old junk-yard with much wire-netting and corrugated-iron sheets. However, this twentieth-century touch hardly gets in the way of the drama, with the costumes broadly traditional in period.

The casting is first rate, with Gavanelli well matched by the girlish Gilda of Christine Schäfer (not previously known as a coloratura but admirably flexible) and the menacingly seductive Duke of Marcelo Alvarez. Edward Downes as ever is a masterly Verdi interpreter, pacing the drama strongly and purposefully. The extra features include a BBC documentary celebrating the Verdi centenary, with atmospheric shots of Busseto, doing for Verdi what Salzburg has done for Mozart.

Edita Gruberová might have been considered an unexpected choice for Gilda, remarkable for her brilliant coloratura rather than for deeper expression, yet here she makes the heroine a tender, feeling creature, emotionally vulnerable yet vocally immaculate. Similarly, Renato Bruson as Rigoletto does far more than produce a stream of velvety tone, detailed and intense, responding to the conductor and combining beauty with dramatic bite. Even more remarkable is the brilliant success of Neil Shicoff as the Duke, more than a match for his most distinguished rivals. Here the *Quartet* becomes a genuine climax. Brigitte Fassbaender as Maddalena is sharply unconventional but vocally most satisfying. Sinopoli's speeds, too, are unconventional at times, but the

fresh look he provides is most exciting, helped by full and vivid recording, consistently well balanced.

Just over ten years after her first recording of this opera, Sutherland appeared in it again, this time with Pavarotti, who is an intensely characterful Duke: an unmistakable rogue but a charmer, too. Thanks to him and to Bonynge above all, the *Quartet*, as on the Sinopoli set, becomes a genuine musical climax. Sutherland's voice has acquired a hint of a beat, but there is little of the mooning manner that disfigured her earlier assumption, and the result is glowingly beautiful as well as supremely assured technically. Milnes makes a strong Rigoletto, vocally masterful rather than strongly characterful. The digital transfer is exceptionally vivid and atmospheric.

With an excellent cast James Levine conducts a thrustful, exceptionally high-powered reading of *Rigoletto*, vividly dramatic. The sound is full and immediate, with the solo voices in sharp focus, enhancing the power. Vladimir Chernov is a firm, clear, virile Rigoletto, not as searchingly characterful as some, but maybe because he sings with no hint of strain, with the beauty and accuracy of the singing consistently satisfying. Cheryl Studer is a tenderly affecting Gilda, singing with a bright, girlish tone, at once youthful and mature, defying age. Pavarotti was fresher in his earlier recording with Bonynge, but heard in close-up his is a thrillingly involving performance still, and the rest of the cast are first-rate too. Not a first choice perhaps, but a strong and sound one.

There has never been a more compelling performance of the title-role in *Rigoletto* than that of Gobbi on his classic La Scala set of the 1950s. At every point, in almost every single phrase, Gobbi finds extra meaning in Verdi's vocal lines, with the widest range of tone-colour employed for expressive effect. Callas, though not naturally suited to the role of the wilting Gilda, is compellingly imaginative throughout, and Di Stefano gives one of his finest performances. The transfer of the original mono recording is astonishingly vivid in capturing the voices. This remains at full price.

Unlike Solti, Giulini, ever thoughtful for detail, seems determined to get away from any conception of *Rigoletto* as melodrama; however, in doing that he misses the red-blooded theatricality of Verdi's concept, the basic essential. Although it may be consistent with Giulini's view, the dramatic impact is further reduced by the fact that Cappuccilli (with his unsinister voice) makes the hunchback a noble figure from first to last, while Domingo, ever intelligent, makes a reflective rather than an extrovert Duke. Cotrubas is a touching Gilda, but the close balance of her voice is not helpful, and the topmost register is not always comfortable. The recording, made in the Musikverein in Vienna, has the voices well to the fore, with much reverberation on the instruments behind, an effect emphasized by the CD transfer.

Rigoletto (complete; in English)

(M) *** Chan. 3030 (2). Rawnsley, Field, A. Davies, Tomlinson, ENO Ch. & O, Elder

The flair of the original English National Opera production, setting *Rigoletto* in the Little Italy area of New York in the 1950s and making the Mafia boss the 'Duke', is superbly carried through to this originally EMI studio recording. The intensity and fine pacing of the stage performances are splendidly caught, thanks to Mark Elder's keenly rhythmic conducting, making this one of the most successful of the ENO's Verdi sets. Outstanding vocally is the heady-toned Duke of Arthur Davies, and though neither John Rawnsley as Rigoletto nor Helen Field as Gilda has a voice so naturally beautiful, they too sing both powerfully and stylishly. Excellent recording, clean and full, and the production of the opening scene includes an effective crowd ambience of the kind pioneered by Decca.

Rigoletto (excerpts)

**(*) Claremont CDGSE 1567. Fourie, Goodwin, Gabriels, Andrews, EOAN Group, Cape Town Municipal O, Manca

A historic recording with a difference, this offers generous excerpts from a live recording made in Cape Town in 1960, when for the first time in South Africa an Italian opera was performed complete by an all-black cast. Most of these singers were amateurs, with little or no formal vocal training, and despite the lively conducting of Joseph Manca, the mastermind behind the EOAN Group, ensembles and choruses are often ragged.

Yet the performance has a thrust and energy that reflect an occasion which plainly moved the audience in the City Hall as much as the cast. Its success rests to a great degree on the qualities of the three principals, all of them intelligent singers, not always polished, who use fresh clear voices with admirable technique. Joseph Gabriels, a tenor with an attractively Italianate quality, who sings the role of the Duke, went on to study in Milan and make a successful career in Europe, notably in Germany.

As Gilda, Ruth Goodwin uses her light, bright, flexible soprano most stylishly, with coloratura presenting no problems for her. The Rigoletto of Lionel Fourie is comparably secure, a firm, cleanly focused baritone, finely controlled. He may not be ideally characterful but delivers the big solos with fine attack and plenty of feeling. The three Gilda-Rigoletto duets are among the highlights of the whole performance. The sound is limited, with balances sometimes odd, but generally with voices well forward, so that words are clear. An unusual offering that provides a fascinating insight into music-making in South Africa during apartheid.

Rigoletto (highlights)

(M) (***) EMI mono 5 66667-2 (from above complete recording, with Callas, Gobbi, di Stefano; cond. Serafin)

The 58-minute selection from the Gobbi/Callas Rigoletto is well chosen to represent an extremely compelling performance, and the synopsis is properly cued.

Simon Boccanegra (1857 version; complete)

**(*) Opera Rara ORCV 302 (2). Bruscanti, Ligi, Turp, Elvin, Howell, Hudson, BBC Singers, BBC Concert O, Matheson

The revision of Simon Boccanegra which, prompted by Boito's rewriting of the libretto, Verdi produced in 1881 has now firmly been accepted as one of the composer's supreme masterpieces, defying the old idea that it could never be popular. This valuable Opera Rara issue, like that company's recording of the original version of Verdi's Macbeth, is taken from a BBC recording made in 1976. The sound is satisfyingly vivid and well balanced, and the performance under John Matheson is warmly idiomatic, with the BBC Concert Orchestra rivalling the work of the other BBC orchestras. Casting is strong, with Sesto Bruscantini (towards the end of his career) as characterful as ever, with the voice still lyrical, set in striking contrast against the powerful Fiesco of the bass, Gwynne Howell, singing magnificently. Josella Ligi, little known on disc, makes an appealing Amelia, with the Canadian tenor André Turp singing strongly as Gabriele.

Even so, the set is rather of specialist than of general interest, when in every significant way, certainly at every key moment in the involved story, this first version is disappointingly conventional. So even the great Recognition scene, when Boccanegra realizes that Amelia is his daughter, fails in its timing and structure to have the overwhelming impact of the revised version, and the scene which was later replaced by the great Council Chamber scene seems astonishingly flat and perfunctory by comparison. One of the passages omitted in the revision is a cabaletta for Amelia, attractive enough but dramatically inappropriate; and Amelia's lovely nocturnal aria lacks the evocative orchestral introduction and distinctive accompaniment which make it so striking in the revision. Roger Parker's essay in the lavish booklet and libretto makes as strong a case as possible for this first version as being more consistent stylistically, but then fails to specify the differences with the revision, a sad omission. Even so, dedicated Verdians will welcome the chance to study just how Verdi translated a relatively workaday example of his music into a towering masterpiece.

Simon Boccanegra (complete)

⊶ ❀ ⚙ (M) *** DG (ADD) 449 752-2 (2). Freni, Cappuccilli, Ghiaurov, Van Dam, Carreras, La Scala, Milan, Ch. and O, Abbado

(M) (***) EMI mono 5 67483-2 (2). Gobbi, Christoff, De los Angeles, Campora, Monachesi, Dari, Rome Op. Ch. & O, Santini

(BB) **(*) Discover DICD 920225/6. Tumagian, Gauci, Aragall, Mikulas, Sardinero, BRTN Philharmonic Ch. and O, Rahbari

Abbado's 1977 recording of Simon Boccanegra is one of the most beautiful Verdi sets ever made. The playing of the orchestra is brilliantly incisive as well as refined, so that the drama is underlined by extra sharpness of focus. The cursing of Paolo after the great Council Chamber scene makes the scalp prickle, with the chorus muttering in horror and the bass clarinet adding a sinister comment, here beautifully moulded. Cappuccilli, always intelligent, gives a far more intense and illuminating performance than the one he recorded for RCA earlier in his career. He may not match Gobbi in range of colour and detail, but he too gives focus to the performance; and Ghiaurov as Fiesco sings beautifully too. Freni as Maria Boccanegra sings with freshness and clarity, while Van Dam is an impressive Paolo. With electrically intense choral singing as well, this is a set to outshine even Abbado's superb Macbeth, and it is superbly transferred to CD. The set is now all the more desirable at mid-price.

Tito Gobbi's portrait of the tragic Doge of Genoa is one of his greatest on record, and it emerges all the more impressively when it is set against equally memorable performances by Boris Christoff as Fiesco and Victoria de los Angeles as Amelia. The recognition scene between father and daughter has never been done more movingly on record; nor has the great ensemble, which crowns the Council Chamber scene, been so powerfully and movingly presented, and without the help of stereo recording. The transfer is full and immediate, giving a vivid sense of presence to the voices.

On the Discover bargain label Alexander Rahbari's well-paced reading is newly recorded in good digital sound with strong casting. Excellent East European principals are joined by the long-established Spanish tenor, Giacomo Aragall, and the baritone, Vincente Sardinero. Miriam Gauci is a vibrant, sympathetic Amelia, and though Eduard Tumagian is not the most characterful Boccanegra and Peter Mikulas could be darker-toned in the bass role of Fiesco, their voices are clear and well focused, despite backward balance. Libretto in Italian only. Good value.

Stiffelio (complete)

(N) (M) *** Ph. 475 6775-2 (2). Carreras, Sass, Manuguerra, Ganzarolli, Austrian R. Ch. & SO, Gardelli

Coming just before the great trio of masterpieces, *Rigoletto, Il trovatore* and *La traviata, Stiffelio* is still a sharply telling work, largely because of the originality of the relationships and the superb final scene in which Stiffelio reads from the pulpit the parable of the woman taken in adultery. Gardelli directs a fresh performance, at times less lively than Queler's of *Aroldo* but with more consistent singing, notably from Carreras and Manuguerra. First-rate recording from Philips, typical of this fine series, and including a full libretto.

La traviata (complete)

●— ✿ *** Decca **DVD** 071 431-9. Gheorghiu, Lopardo, Nucci, ROHCG Ch. & O, Solti (Director: Richard Eyre; V/D: Humphrey Burton & Peter Maniura)

●— ✿ *** Decca 448 119-2 (2). Gheorghiu, Lopardo, Nucci, ROHCG Ch. & O, Solti

*** Arthaus **DVD** 100 112. McLaughlin, MacNeil, Ellis, LPO & Glyndebourne Ch., Haitink (Director & V/D: Peter Hall)

*** Warner NVC **DVD** 4509 92409-2. Gruberová, Shicoff, Zancanaro, La Fenice Ch. & O, Rizzi

*** Decca 430 491-2 (2). Sutherland, Pavarotti, Manuguerra, L. Op. Ch., Nat. PO, Bonynge

(M) **(*) EMI 7 47538-8 (2). Scotto, Kraus, Bruson, Amb. Op. Ch., Philh. O, Muti

(N) (M) **(*) DG **SACD** 477 0772. Cotrubas, Domingo, Milnes, Bav. State Op. Ch. & O, C. Kleiber

(B) **(*) EMI double forte (ADD) 5 73824-2 (2). De los Angeles, Del Monte, Sereni, Rome Op. Ch. & O, Serafin

(B) **(*) Double Decca (ADD) 460 759-2 (2). Sutherland, Bergonzi, Merrill, Ch. & O of Maggio Musicale Fiorentino, Pritchard

(B) **(*) DG Double (ADD) 453 115-2 (2). Scotto, Raimondi, Bastianini, La Scala, Milan, Ch. & O, Votto

(BB) (***) Naxos mono 8.110115/6 (2). Steber, Di Stefano, Merrill, Met Ch. & O, Antonicelli (with Steber Recital (***))

(M) (**) Fonit mono 3984 29354-2 (2). Callas, Albanese, Savarese, Turin R. Ch. & O, Santini

(BB) (**(*) Naxos mono 8.110300/01. Callas, Albanese, Savarese, Turin R. Ch. & O, Santini

(M) (*(**)) EMI mono 5 66450-2 (2). Callas, Di Stefano, Bastianini, La Scala Ch. & O, Giulini

(B) **(*) Ph. Duo 464 982-2 (2). Te Kanawa, Kraus, Hvorostovsky, Maggio Musicale (Florence) Ch. & O, Mehta

As the DVD rightly claims, this famous Solti performance of *La traviata* captures one of the most sensational debuts in recent operatic history. Singing Violetta for the first time, Angela Gheorghiu made the part entirely her own. But the DVD can also claim a special plaudit for the magical opening, when the camera focuses closely on Solti while he conducts the *Prelude*, with every movement of his hands and the concentration in his eyes creating the music in front of us. He holds the tension at the highest level throughout, with the strings playing marvellously, and recorded with absolute realism. Then the curtain goes up and Bob Crowley's superb

stage spectacle spreads out in front of our eyes. The singing is glorious, and this is one of the DVDs that should be a cornerstone in any collection.

Defying the problems of recording opera live at Covent Garden, the Decca engineers here offer one of the most vivid and involving versions ever of *La traviata*. As on stage, Gheorghiu brings heartfelt revelations, using her rich and vibrant, finely shaded soprano with consistent subtlety. Youthfully vivacious in Act I, dazzling in her coloratura, she already reveals the depths of feeling which compel her later self-sacrifice. In Act II she finds ample power for the great outburst of *Amami, Alfredo*, and in Act III almost uniquely uses the second stanza of *Addio del passato* (often omitted) to heighten the intensity of the heroine's emotions. Frank Lopardo emerges as a fresh, lyrical Alfredo with a distinctive timbre, passionate and youthful-sounding too. Leo Nucci, a favourite baritone with Solti, provides a sharp contrast as a stolid but convincing Germont.

Sir Peter Hall's production of *La traviata* for Glyndebourne in 1988, powerfully directed for television by Sir Peter himself, makes a very satisfying DVD version. The camera is used to disguise the relative smallness of the stage in the old Glyndebourne, with the necessary grandeur of the two party scenes, both at the start and at the end of Act II, vividly conveyed. At the same time, the intimacy of the drama of the dying Violetta is made the more affecting in close-up. Marie McLaughlin sings beautifully, yet too often fails to convey her deepest emotions in facial expressions, although arguably understatement is a fault on the right side. Only in the coloratura at the end of Act I does she have moments of vocal uncertainty, for this was a role that drew out her finest qualities. One is glad to have both verses of the *Addio del passato*. Walter MacNeil is a winningly lyrical Alfredo, and Brent Ellis is a strong, if slightly gruff Germont. Bernard Haitink is refreshingly direct in bringing out the drama of Verdi's score. The video direction is the more effective when this was recorded on stage but not in a live performance.

Recorded in December 1992 in the beautiful theatre of La Fenice in Venice before the disastrous fire, the alternative Warner DVD offers a moving performance, well cast and with sympathetic conducting from Carlo Rizzi, despite an excessively slow opening prelude. Though Neil Shicoff as Alfredo is made to look like a Victorian bank-clerk, hardly a romantic figure in metal-framed spectacles, the production is traditional, with colourful costumes and evocative sets. Romantic or not, Shicoff is in splendid voice, phrasing and shaping his big set-pieces sensitively, and Edita Gruberová makes a moving Violetta, jolly and vivacious in Act I, taking to the coloratura like a bird before gradually transforming into the haggard tragic figure of Act IV, crowning her performance with the most tender singing. Just as Giorgio Zancanaro as a strong, forthright Germont sings both verses of *Di Provenza al mar* in Act II, Gruberová sings both verses of the *Addio del passato*, surpassing herself in the whispered half-tone, perfectly controlled, of the second stanza. Though this must come second to the superb Decca Solti DVD, it is still very much worth having.

Sutherland's second recording of the role of Violetta has a breadth and exuberance beyond her achievement in the earlier version of 1963, conducted by John Pritchard, and the richness and command of the singing put this among the very finest of her later recordings. Pavarotti too, though he overemphasizes *Di miei bollenti spiriti*, sings with splendid panache as Alfredo. Manuguerra as Germont lacks something in authority, but the firmness and clarity are splendid.

Bonynge's conducting is finely sprung, the style direct, the speeds often spacious in lyrical music, generally undistracting. The digital recording is outstandingly vivid and beautifully balanced but the CD booklet is not ideal.

Muti has no concern for tradition; at the start of the Act I party music, he is even faster than Toscanini, but the result is dazzling; and when he needs to give sympathetic support to his soloists, above all in the great Act II duet between Violetta and Germont, there is no lack of tenderness. Overall, it is an intensely compelling account, using the complete text (like Bonynge), and it gains from having three Italy-based principals. Scotto and Kraus have long been among the most sensitive and perceptive interpreters of these roles, and so they are here; with bright digital recording, however, it is obvious that these voices are no longer young, with Scotto's soprano spreading above the stave and Kraus's tenor often sounding thin. Bruson makes a fine, forthright Germont, though it does not add to dramatic conviction that his is the youngest voice. Small parts are well taken, and the stage picture is projected clearly on CD in a pleasantly reverberant acoustic.

Carlos Kleiber's 1977 set is a fascinating early example of multi-microphone recording now being used for SACD. Cotrubas makes an ideal heroine in this opera, but what was disappointing in the original DG recording was that the microphone exaggerated technical flaws, so that not only was her breathing too often audible, but also her habit of separating coloratura with intrusive aitches was underlined, the vibrato becoming too obvious at times. Such is her magic that many will forgive the faults, for her characterization combines strength with vulnerability. But Kleiber's direction is equally controversial, with more than a hint of Toscanini-like rigidity in the party music, and an occasional uncomfortable insistence on discipline. The characteristic contributions of Domingo and Milnes, both highly commendable, hardly alter the issue. However, played back in surround sound, the sense of presence in a three-dimensionsal acoustic is very impressive, particularly in the party scenes where the 'off-stage' orchestra is cunningly repositioned, as indeed is Domingo. There is still spotlighting of soloists, but Cotrubas projects very realistically and vividly. While the balance still underlines the fierce side of Kleiber's conducting, which contrasts strongly with his ripely romantic side, the overall effect is highly involving, indeed thrilling, and this reissue must be counted an outstanding success.

Even when Victoria de los Angeles made this EMI recording in the late 1950s, the role of Violetta lay rather high for her voice. Nevertheless it drew from her much beautiful singing, not least in the coloratura display at the end of Act I which, though it may lack easily ringing top notes, has delightful sparkle and flexibility. As to the characterization, De los Angeles is a most sympathetically tender heroine. Though neither the tenor nor the baritone can match her in artistry, their performances are both sympathetic and feeling, thanks in part to the masterly conducting of Serafin. All the traditional cuts are made, not just the second stanzas. The CD transfer is vivid and clear and at bargain price a fair recommendation, though only a synopsis is provided.

In Sutherland's 1963 recording of *La traviata*, it is true that her diction is poor, but it is also true that she has rarely sung on record with such deep feeling as in the final scene. The *Addio del passato* (both stanzas included and sung with an unexpected lilt) merely provides a beginning, for the duet with Bergonzi is most winning, and the final death scene, *Se una pudica vergine*, is overwhelmingly beautiful. This is not a sparkling Violetta, but it is vocally close to perfection. Bergonzi is an attractive Alfredo and Merrill a clean-cut Germont. This is excellent value as a Double Decca, although now the libretto has been replaced with Decca's cued synopsis and 'listening guide'.

It is worth having the 1962 DG La Scala set for the moving and deeply considered singing of Renata Scotto as Violetta, fresher in voice than in her later, HMV set. In a role which has usually eluded the efforts of prima donnas on record, she gives one of the most complete portraits, with thrilling coloratura in Act I and with the closing scene unforgettably moving. It is sad that the rest of the cast is largely undistinguished. Gianni Raimondi as Alfredo is stirring if not refined, and Bastianini is a coarse Germont *père*. The conductor, Antonino Votto, gives routine direction but keeps the music alive. The usual stage cuts are observed. The recording is vividly atmospheric, a fair bargain on a DG Double. There are good notes and a well-cued synopsis.

Few singers on disc can match Eleanor Steber as Violetta in the historic live recording of *La traviata*, made at the Met in New York on New Year's Day 1949, and now reissued on Naxos. The beauty and precision as well as the power of Steber's singing are phenomenal, with each note clearly defined down to ornamentation of diamond clarity. With the eager and youthful Giuseppe di Stefano as Alfredo, and Robert Merrill as a rock-steady, intense Germont, the emotional thrust of the drama comes over at full force, with Giuseppe Antonicelli drawing playing and singing from his Met forces to match even a Toscanini. Limited radio sound clearly transferred. As a very welcome supplement come a series of Steber's commercial recordings of different arias, showing her versatility, from Verdi, Rossini and Puccini to Romberg and Richard Rodgers.

Like the companion Cetra set of *La gioconda*, this Fonit set was made by Callas very early in her career (in 1952). She was to record it again three years later with Giulini and Di Stefano, and that is still available, showing her at her very peak, but the sound of the transfer deteriorates towards the end. The 1952 recording is more consistent, noticeably fierce at the opening (affecting both the orchestral strings and the vocal *fortissimos*), but it seems to settle down (with occasional peakiness) and in the present transfer the overall effect is quite open. Callas's characterization of Violetta had not fully reached maturity, but the fresh youthfulness of the voice more than compensates. All the singing is very characteristic (including an odd mistake in the vocal flurries before *Sempre libera* – otherwise an excitingly brilliant account). Francesco Albanese is a sympathetic Alfredo, especially in the closing act, but Ugo Savarese as Germont *père* is no more distinguished than Bastianini in the later La Scala set. However, Callas admirers will surely find this reissue worth having alone for Callas's very moving closing scene. The Italian libretto, though, is without a translation.

However, Naxos have now made available a superior transfer by Ward Marston, still shrill at the opening but catching the voices well. The documentation includes a cued synopsis and this is a super-bargain issue.

Callas's version with Giulini was recorded in 1955. There is no more vividly dramatic a performance on record than this, unmatchable in conveying Violetta's agony; sadly, the sound, always limited, grows crumbly towards the end. It is sad too that Bastianini sings so lumpishly as Germont *père*, even in the great duet of Act II, while di Stefano also fails to match his partner in the supreme test of the final scene. The transfer is fair.

Though both Alfredo Kraus as Alfredo and Dmitri Hvorostovsky as Germont sing well on Philips, they offer an unconvincing partnership. Kraus's musical imagination is masked by a dry tone and strain on top, with a very gusty entry, for example, in the duet *Parigi o cara*. Equally the rich-toned Hvorostovsky hardly sounds fatherly, though he does his best in a firm, spacious account of the aria *Di Provenza*. Dame Kiri Te Kanawa is tenderly beautiful as Violetta, finely poised in *Ah fors'è lui* and the Farewell, as well as in a hushed, intense account of the Act II duet with Germont.

La traviata (highlights)

(M) *** Decca (ADD) 458 211-2 (from above complete set, with Sutherland, Bergonzi, Merrill; Pritchard)

(B) **(*) DG 439 421-2. Cotrubas, Domingo, Milnes, Bav. State Op. Ch. & State O., C. Kleiber

Decca's highlights from Sutherland's first (1963) recording make a clear first choice. They come handsomely packaged in Decca's Opera Gala series, with a generous selection (73 minutes) and including a full translation. Sutherland is in ravishing voice, and Bergonzi is also in excellent form. The set is discussed more fully above.

Muti's complete set is hardly a first choice at full price, so many will be glad to have this 61-minute, mid-price disc of highlights, including both the Act I and Act III *Preludes* and a well-balanced selection from each of the three Acts, with most of the key numbers included.

For many, Cotrubas makes an ideal star in *Traviata*, but unfortunately the microphone-placing in Carlos Kleiber's complete set over-emphasizes technical flaws and the vibrato is exaggerated. The strong contributions of Domingo and Milnes make this bargain-priced Classikon highlights CD recommendable, with 71 minutes of music, including the two *Preludes*. The documentation is well thought out, except that it omits a track-by-track synopsis of the narrative.

La traviata (complete; in English)

(M) *** Chan. 3023 (2). Masterson, Brecknock, Du Plessis, E. Nat. Op. Ch. & O, Mackerras

Mackerras directs a vigorous, colourful reading which brings out the drama, and Valerie Masterson is given the chance on record she has so long deserved. The voice is caught beautifully, if not always very characterfully, and John Brecknock makes a fine Alfredo, most effective in the final scene. Christian Du Plessis's baritone is less suitable for recording. The conviction of the whole enterprise is infectious – but be warned: Verdi in English has a way of sounding rather like Gilbert and Sullivan on record.

Il Trovatore (complete; DVD versions)

(N) **(*) NVC Arts **DVD** 4509 99215-2. Plowright, Cossotto, Bonisolli, Zancanaro, Ch. & O of Verona Arena, Giovaninetti (Video Producer: Robin Scott; V/D: Brian Large)

(*) Arthaus **DVD 100 276. Sutherland, Collins, Summers, Elms, Shanks, Australian Op. Ch., Elizabethan Sydney O., Bonynge (Director Elijah Moshinsky)

** DG **DVD** 073 002-9. Marton, Zajick, Pavarotti, Milnes, Met. Ch. & O, Levine

At the opening of the Verona *Il Trovatore*, the camera focuses on the audience, then moves forward and turns to show the Count de Luna's soldiers with their siege machine and the wooden set which is obviously connected with the planned attack in Act III. Thereafter Brian Large ensures that we are drawn closely into the interplay of the characters. However, this opera (as Caruso told us) is concerned with great voices, and one welcomes in the opening scene the richness of Ferrando's timbre as he relates to the soldiers the grim tale on which the opera is based. The three principal characters soon arrive, the fine Leonora of Rosalind Plowright clear and true, the richly dramatic baritone of the Count di Luna (Giorgio Zancanaro) and the bold but less distinctive tenor of Manrico (Franco Bonisolli) who, later in Act III, almost shouts *Di quella pira*. If Leonora were to choose her lover on vocal power alone, it would have to be the Count, unattractive though his character may be. Fiorenza Cossotto is the ever reliable, intensely dramatic Azucena, and the chorus are splendidly drilled in their crisply dotted numbers. Under the baton of Reynald Giovaninetti the whole opera goes forward with a vibrant propulsion, with the various duets and unforgettable trios splendidly gutsy. All in all, a most enjoyable DVD, very well recorded, but not the finest performance on record.

Recorded live in July 1983, the Australian Opera DVD presentation of *Il trovatore* offers a bravura display from Dame Joan Sutherland as Leonora, bringing the rarest combination of weight and flexibility to the role, surpassing in mastery her Decca studio recording of six years earlier, gloriously free over the widest range. Though the rest of the cast may not be so starry, they all sing with firmness and clarity to make it an exceptionally satisfying performance, with Richard Bonynge persuasively idiomatic in his conducting. Kenneth Collins is far more sensitive than many more celebrated Manricos – even though he is made to look like a Sicilian bandit – and Jonathan Summers is a strong, handsome di Luna, with Lauris Elms as Azucena making one wonder why she was never used as she should have been in recordings. Elijah Moshinsky's production updates the story to the time of Verdi, with characterful backcloths by Sydney Nolan colourful if not always helpful to the story. The sound on DVD has an edge to it that does not help the voices, but the magnetism of the occasion has one forgetting that.

Recorded in October 1988 at the Metropolitan in New York, this DG DVD offers an effective presentation of the production by Fabrizio Melano with typically grand, traditional sets by Ezio Frigerio and costumes by Franca Squarciapino. This will please those who resist modern trendy 'concept' productions, but sadly the singing, even with a starry cast of principals, is flawed. Luciano Pavarotti as the Duke is in ringing voice, giving a gloriously full-throated performance with words sharply focused, but the others are disappointing. Sherrill Milnes is sadly past his best, with the voice no longer as rock-steady as in his earlier career, yet he cuts a splendid figure as the Count. Dolora Zajick as Azucena is not as steady as she can be either, with a flutter in the voice, but the principal drawback is the casting of Eva Marton as Leonora, not a singer one would have expected in this role which requires velvet legato and bright flexibility rather than sheer power. She controls the voice better than in Wagner, but too often the focus of such a fruity, gusty soprano is approximate, with pitching vague, disastrously so in coloratura. James Levine directs a typically thrustful, dramatic reading of score.

Il trovatore (complete; CD versions)

*** EMI 5 57360-2 (2). Gheorghiu, Alagna, Hampson, Diadkova, D'Arcangelo, L. Voices, LSO, Pappano

⊶ ✿ (M) *** RCA (ADD) 74321 39504-2 (2). L. Price, Domingo, Milnes, Cossotto, Amb. Op. Ch., New Philh. O, Mehta

*** DG 423 858-2 (2). Plowright, Domingo, Fassbaender, Zancanaro, Nesterenko, Ch. & O of St Cecilia Academy, Rome, Giulini

⊶ (BB) (***) Naxos mono 8.110240/1 (2) Milanov, Bjorling, Warren, Barbieri, Robert Shaw Ch., RCA Victor O, Cellini (with: *6 Songs of Yugoslavia*; Milanov, with piano & violin)

(BB) (***) Regis mono RRC 2060 (2). Milanov, Björling, Warren, Barbieri, Moscona, Robert Shaw Ch., RCA Victor O, Cellini

(***) EMI mono 5 56333-2 (2). Callas, Barbieri, Di Stefano, Panerai, La Scala, Milan, Ch. & O, Karajan

(B) *** DG Double (ADD) 453 118-2 (2). Stella, Bergonzi, Cossotto, Bastianini, La Scala, Milan, Ch. & O, Serafin

(BB) (***) Naxos mono 8.110162.63 (2). Scacciati, Molinari, Zinetti, Merli, Zambelli, La Scala Ch. & O, Molajoli

(M) **(*) EMI (ADD) 7 69311-2 (2). L. Price, Bonisolli, Cappuccilli, Obraztsova, Raimondi, German Op. Ch., Berlin, BPO, Karajan

The problem for the two principals on EMI CD, Angela Gheorghiu and Roberto Alagna, is rather greater than in their previous recordings with Pappano, when their lyric voices might not seem weighty enough for the roles of Leonora and of Manrico. Gheorghiu characteristically capitalizes on the problem, bringing a rare tenderness to her big arias, floating her top notes ravishingly, and exploiting her formidable coloratura powers in cabalettas, always stylish in ornamentation. Only in the bravura aria *Tu vedrai che amore in terra* and the final scenes does she press the voice, so that it flickers in emotion. Though in the heroic outburst of *Di quella pira* Alagna tends to force his tone, holding on provocatively to his final top C, that is rather the exception, and generally this is a performance marked, like Gheorghiu's, by individual phrasing to bring out the warmth of emotion along with the meaning of the words. Thomas Hampson as di Luna is at once sinister and ardently sincere in his love for Leonora, giving a warmly involved performance, while Larissa Diadkova with a Slavonic tang in her mezzo tone is a formidable and moving Azucena. Ripely atmospheric recording beautifully balanced, with fine playing and singing from the LSO and London Voices. This is now a pretty clear first choice, though the mid-priced RCA set is still very strongly recommendable.

The soaring curve of Leontyne Price's rich vocal line is immediately thrilling in her famous Act I aria, and it sets the style of the RCA performance, full-bodied and with dramatic tension consistently high. The choral contribution is superb; the famous *Soldiers'* and *Anvil Choruses* are marvellously fresh and dramatic. When *Di quella pira* comes, the orchestra opens with great gusto and Domingo sings with a ringing, heroic quality worthy of Caruso himself. There are many dramatic felicities, and Sherrill Milnes is in fine voice throughout; but perhaps the highlight of the set is the opening section of Act III, when Azucena finds her way to Conte di Luna's camp. The ensuing scene with Fiorenza Cossotto is vocally and dramatically electrifying.

Giulini flouts convention at every point. The opera's whitehot inspiration comes out in the intensity of the playing and singing, but the often slow tempi and refined textures present the whole work in new and deeper detail. Rosalind Plowright, sensuous yet ethereal in *Tacea la notte*, confidently brings together not just sweetness and purity but brilliant coloratura, flexibility and dramatic bite. Plácido Domingo sings Manrico as powerfully as he did in the richly satisfying Mehta

set on RCA, but the voice is even more heroic in an Otello-like way, only very occasionally showing strain. Giorgio Zancanaro proves a firm and rounded Count di Luna and Evgeny Nesterenko is a dark, powerful Ferrando, while Brigitte Fassbaender, singing her first Azucena, sings with detailed intensity, matching Giulini's freshness. The recording is warm and atmospheric with a pleasant bloom on the voices, naturally balanced and not spotlit.

The classic RCA recording of 1952, with four of the reigning stars of the Metropolitan Opera at their peak, remains among the very finest recorded versions. The transfers by Mark Obert-Thorn bring out the full beauty and character of all four principals very vividly and are particularly valuable when Zinka Milanov, always an iconic figure at the Met, is here recorded with a purity and firmness that transcends many of her later, all-too-rare recordings. Bjorling is, as ever, superb in his heroic projection, though in a performance with the usual cuts he is allowed only one stanza of *Di quella pira*. Leonard Warren and Fedora Barbieri are also perfectly focused, with Renato Cellini drawing lively playing and singing from the RCA Victor Orchestra and the hand-picked Robert Shaw Chorale. A recording to treasure and not to be missed at Naxos price. The bonus items of six songs from Milanov's native Yugoslavia, recorded in New York in 1944, give a different perspective on the voice: closer and earthier if just as characterful.

The new Regis transfer seems to us to give the voices marginally more presence, although there is not a great deal in it, and the Naxos sound is a little more rounded. Both sets are very enjoyable indeed, so choice can be made by considering whether or not you require the Naxos bonus of six Yugoslavian folksongs sung by Milanov. Incidentally, we omitted to mention the superb contribution of Nicola Moscona as Ferrando in the opera's first scene.

The combination of Karajan and Callas is formidably impressive. There is toughness and dramatic determination in Callas's singing, whether in the coloratura or in the dramatic passages, and this gives the heroine an unsuspected depth of character which culminates in Callas's fine singing of an aria that used often to be cut entirely – *Tu vedrai che amore in terra*, here with its first stanza alone included. Barbieri is a magnificent Azucena, Panerai is a strong, incisive Count, and Di Stefano is at his finest as Manrico. On CD the 1956 mono sound, now greatly improved, is one of the more vivid from La Scala at that period.

There is room for a recommendable bargain set of *Il trovatore*, and Serafin's splendidly red-blooded La Scala version on a DG Double fits the bill well. For the present DG Double reissue, the documentation has been improved with the synopsis well cued, but with no libretto. The performance is most enjoyable, with the contributions of Cossotto as Azucena and Carlo Bergonzi, splendid as Manrico, matching almost any rival. Stella and Bastianini give flawed performances, but they have many impressive moments; as Leonora's opening aria readily demonstrates, Stella is in full voice and identifies strongly with the heroine. The conducting of Serafin is crisp and stylish, and the 1963 recording is vividly transferred to CD with plenty of atmosphere.

Recorded by Columbia in 1930, the Naxos issue offers a lustily red-blooded reading typical of Italian performances at that period dominated by verismo. As Leonora Bianca Scacciati has a distinctive timbre, slightly throaty. She is occasionally gusty in her production, but technically secure beyond what one can expect in latterday recordings. Similarly Francesco Merli, a tenor much-admired by Toscanini, with his baritonal timbre is a strong and satisfying Manrico. Enrico Molinari is a reliable Count, sounding a little old at times, and Giuseppina Zinetti is a fruitily resonant Azucena, rich and firm throughout her register, making one appreciate how at that period few leading singers had the sort of wobbles so common today. The performance under Lorenzo Molajoli is lusty and red-blooded to match, and is exceptionally well-transferred by Ward Marston, marrying 78 r.p.m. pressings from different sources. The usual cuts of the period are observed, which leaves room for a supplement of fine recordings by Scacciati, four of the five with Merli as well, including rare items from Marchetti's *Ruy Blas*, Gomes's *Guarany* and Catalani's *Loreley*, as well as the Trio from Verdi's *I Lombardi*, all very well sung.

The later Karajan set with Leontyne Price promised much but proves disappointing, largely because of the thickness and strange balances of the recording, the product of multi-channel techniques exploited over-enthusiastically. So the introduction to Manrico's aria *Di quella pira* provides full-blooded orchestral sound, but then the orchestra fades down for the entry of the tenor, Bonisolli, who is in coarse voice. In other places he sings more sensitively, but at no point does this version match that of Mehta on RCA. CD clarifies the sound but makes the flaws in the original recording all the more evident.

I vespri siciliani (complete)

**(*) EMI (ADD) 7 54043-2 (3). Merritt, Studer, Zancanaro, Furlanetto, Ch. & O of La Scala, Milan, Muti

This EMI set is among the most successful of the live recordings made by Muti at La Scala, Milan, plagued by a difficult acoustic. The atmosphere is well caught and, though Muti can be too tautly urgent a Verdian, his pacing here is well geared to bring out the high drama. Outstanding in the cast is Cheryl Studer as the heroine, Elena, singing radiantly; while the tenor Chris Merritt as Arrigo sounds less coarse and strained than he has in the past. Giorgio Zancanaro also responds to the role of Monforte – the governor of Sicily, discovered to be Arrigo's father – with new sensitivity, and though Ferruccio Furlanetto as Procida lacks the full weight to bring out the beauty of line in the great aria, *O tu Palermo*, his is a warm performance too.

Les Vêpres siciliennes (original, French version)

(N) *** Opera Rara ORCV 303 (3). Brumaire, Bonhomme, Taylor, Baran, BBC Concert O, Rossi (or Lawrence in ballet)

Like the other Opera Rara issues in the 'Verdi Original' series, this set fills an important gap, when this opera is almost always performed in the Italian translation which Verdi sanctioned after the Paris première in 1855. Very well cast, the recording is taken from a BBC broadcast of May 1969, with the stereo sound full and clear and voices well caught. Verdi was prompted by his Paris commission to write a full-scale five-act piece, complete with a substantial ballet, *The Four Seasons*, in Act III. Musically, the differences between this and *I vespri siciliani* are relatively small, but the use of French does alter the feel of Verdi's big melodies, even in the famous bass aria for the rebel, Procida, *Et toi, Palerme*, instead of '*O tu Palermo*', well sung by Ayhan Baran, if with some flutter. As the hero, Henri, Jean Bonhomme is ideally cast with his very French-sounding tenor and stylish phrasing. As the Duchess Hélène, Jacqueline Brumaire sounds equally French with her warm, vibrant and agile soprano, and Neilson Taylor is excellent in the baritone role of the Sicilian Governor, Guy de Montfort. Mario Rossi conducts a lively, very well-paced reading of the score, totally idiomatic – though, oddly, the Act III ballet is conducted not by him but by Ashley Lawrence.

COLLECTIONS

Arias and Scenes: *Aida: Se quel guerrier io fosi! . . . Celeste Aida. Alzira: Miserandi avanzi; Vieni, ed a tempi men rei* (Chorus); *Irne lungi. Aroldo: Sotto il sol di Siria ardente. Attila: Qual notte!* (Chorus); *Qui, qui sostiamo; Oh! ma Odabella! . . . Ella in poter del barbaro!; Cara patria, già madre e reina; Dall'alghe di questi marosi* (Chorus); *O mio furore! Qui del convegno è il loco; Che non avrebbe il misero. La battaglia di Legnano: O magnanima, e prima . . . La pia materna mano. Un ballo in maschera: Di' tu se fedele; Sull'agile prora; Forse la soglia attinse . . . Ma se m'è forza perderti* (with Chorus). *Il Corsaro: Eccomi prigionieri! I due Foscari: Notte, perpetua notte . . . Non maledirmi, o prode. Don Carlo: Fontainebleau! Foresta immensa e solitaria! Ernani: Mercè, diletti amici . . . Come rugiada al cespite. Falstaff: Dal labbro il canto estasiato vola. La forza del destino: La vita è inferno . . . Oh, tu che in seno agli angeli. Un giorno di regno: Pietoso al lungo pianto. Giovanna d'Arco: Amici v'appressate . . . Teste prostrato a terra . . . Sotto una quercia parvemi; La rue parole* (with Chorus). *I Lombardi: La mia letizia infondere . . . Sien miei sensi . . . Come poteva un angelo. Luisa Miller: Oh! fede negar potessi . . . Quando le sere al placido. Macbeth: O figli, figli meie! . . . Ah, la paterna mano. I Masnadieri: Quando io leggo in Plutarco . . . O mio castel paterno; Ecco un figlio a te diretto . . . Fiere umane . . . Nell'argilla maledetta* (with Chorus). *Come splendido e grande . . . Di ladroni attorniato. Oberto, Conte di Bonifacio: Ciel che feci! . . . Ciel pietoso. Otello: Dio! mi potevi scagliar tutti i mali; Nun mi tema. Rigoletto: Questa o quella. Ella mi fu rapita! . . . Parmi veder le lagrime. La donna è mobile. Simon Boccanegra: I inferno! . . . Sento avvampar nell'anima. La Traviata: Lunge da lei . . . De'miei bollenti spiriti. Il Trovatore: Il presagio funesto . . . Ah si ben mio . . . Del quella pira. I vespri siciliani: E di Monforte il cenno! . . . Giorno di pianto*

(N) (M) * Decca (ADD) 475 6169 (3). Bergonzi, with Riccardo Cassinello & William Elvin, Amb. S., New Philh. O, Santo, or RPO, Gardelli

Bergonzi's remarkable survey was originally recorded by Philips in 1972 and 1974. It must be the most comprehensive Verdi anthology by a single singer ever put on disc, spanning the whole of the composer's career, and it makes an admirable offering. Philips used a chorus when essential for any particular aria or scene, and though Bergonzi almost inevitably fails to contrast the characters very distinctly, few tenors of his generation (or indeed any other) could have undertaken such an exacting project with such consistently satisfying musicianship. Good, clear, analogue recording, but with plenty of atmosphere, faithfully transferred, and generally stylish accompaniments. Full texts and translations are included. But this is not a set to be listened to at a single sitting.

Arias from: (i) *Aida;* (ii & iii) *Don Carlo;* (ii) *Ernani; Macbeth;* (i) *Otello;* (ii) *Nabucco* (with bonus DVD: 1965 Paris recital, arias by Massenet; Bellini; Puccini)

(N) (M) * EMI Legends (ADD) 5 57760-2. Callas, with (i) Paris Conservatoire O; (ii) Philh. O; Rescigno

The Philharmonia recordings, made in 1958, marked Callas's only visit to record at Abbey Studios. Much of the content shows the great diva at her very finest. Dismiss the top-note wobbles from your mind, and the rest has you enthralled by the vividness of characterization as well as musical imagination. It is sad that Callas did not record the role of Lady Macbeth complete. Here *La luce langue* is not as intense as the Act I aria and sleepwalking scene, which are both unforgettable, while she holds the tension masterfully in the long *Don Carlos* scene. Abigaille, Elvira and Elisabetta all come out as real figures, sharply individual. Finely balanced recordings, sounding good in their Legends transfer. The Paris recordings (with the orchestra's distinctive timbre) are exciting too, with the Desdemona from *Otello* commandingly taken, Aida's *Ritorna vincitor* vehemently done, and *O don fatale* as theatrical as you might expect. With the bonus DVD of arias filmed in 1965 with the Orchestre National de l'ORTF under Prêtre, this is one of the most tempting Callas collections about, though no texts are included.

Arias, Vol. II: *Aroldo: Ciel ch'io respir! … Salvami, salvami tu gran Dio! O Cielo! Dove son io. Don Carlos: Non pianger, mia compagna; O don fatale. Otello: Mia madre aveva una povera ancella … Piangea cantando … Ave Maria piena di grazia*
(M) **(*) EMI (ADD) 5 66461-2. Callas, Paris Conservatoire O, Rescigno

Arias, Vol. III: *Aida: Ritorna vincitor. Attila: Liberamente or piangi! … Oh! nel fuggente nuvolo. Un ballo in maschera: Ecco l'orrido campo; Morrò, ma prima in grazia. Il corsaro: Egli non riede ancor … Non so le tetre immagini; Né sulla terra … Vola talor dal carcere … Verrò … Ah conforto è sol la speme. Il trovatore: Tacea la notte placida … Di tale amor. I vespri siciliani: Arrigo! ah parli a un core*
(M) **(*) EMI (ADD) 5 66462-2. Callas, Paris Conservatoire O or Paris Opéra O, Rescigno

For her second and third collections of Verdi arias, Callas went to Paris in December 1963 and February 1964 (Volume II); and then she began a third compilation in April 1964, returning in 1965 and 1969. She approved some of the tracks for release in 1972, and the rest first appeared in 1978. In the second volume, the Shakespearean challenge of the Desdemona sequence from *Otello* is commandingly taken, very distinctive, and all the singing is dramatic. Allowances have to be made, but there is much here to cherish. The third is much more uneven, with the later items coming from a period when the voice had deteriorated, particularly in the items recorded as late as 1969. There are exceptions: Aida's *Ritorna vincitor*, vehemently done, is magnificent, and the two arias from *Il corsaro*, although among her last recordings, show the vocal technique at its most assured (particularly in the legato phrasing) and the artistry at its most commanding. This third disc is essential for Callas devotees only.

Arias from: *Aida; Un ballo in maschera; Ernani; Otello*
(N) (M) **(*) Decca (ADD) 475 6810. L. Price, Israel PO, Mehta

Decca's key opera producer, Christopher Raeburn, must have been pleased to take this opportunity to record Leontyne Price in Tel Aviv in 1980, singing a selection of spinto roles specially suited to her. But in each instance earlier recordings show the voice in finer, fresher form, and her admirers will do better to invest in the RCA reissue below.

Arias: *Aida; Ernani; La forza del destino; Otello; Il trovatore; I vespri siciliani*
(B) (***) Naxos mono 8.110728. Ponselle (with various partners and accompanists including Martinelli, Pinza and Stracciari)

This splendid disc celebrating the glories of Rosa Ponselle's unique voice and interpretative powers brings excellent CD transfers of her most celebrated electrical recordings made for RCA in 1928, including the heroine's big aria from *Ernani*, spectacularly well done, and the sequence of *Forza* recordings with Martinelli and Pinza – as well as Columbia recordings from the pre-electric period, made between 1918 and 1924 – all chosen by Ward Marston as being the finest Ponselle versions of each item. The result is a wonderful gallery of perfection, beautifully transferred with the voice vividly caught.

Arias: *Aida: Ritorna vincitor!; Qui Radamès verrà! O patria mia. Il trovatore: Che più t'arresti; Tacea la notte; (i) Di tale amor. Timor di me?; D'amor sull'ali rosee*
(N) (M) *** RCA SACD 82876 61395-2. L. Price, Rome Op. O, De Fabritiis or Basile; (i) with Londi – PUCCINI: *Arias* **(*)

This 1959 recital, known as the 'blue album' (the colour of the original LP is reproduced on the CD), has justly become a collectors' item – the glorious flow of tone makes one understand why, even if tension is lower than in Price's performances of the complete operas. The SACD brings added bloom to the excellent recording.

Arias from: (i) *Alzira;* (ii) *Aroldo; Attila; I corsaro; I due Foscari; Un giorno di regno; I Lombardi*
(N) (M) *** RCA (ADD) 82876 62309-2 (2). Caballé, RCA Italian Op. Ch. & O, with (i) Sunara; (ii) Kozma – ROSSINI; DONIZETTI: *Arias* ***

As in the Rossini and Donizetti arias, recorded around the same time (1967), these Verdi items (originally called 'Verdi Rarities') find Caballé at her finest. Re-listening to these performances, one can understand why Caballé's career really took off, when around this time she also had enormous stage success in America. Her bel canto has a fine-spun purity, and in these excerpts of Verdi's early genius she conveys the melodic freshness, against the conventional rum-ti-tum accompaniments: there is both brilliance and beauty in plenty here. Good accompaniments from the Italian orchestra, and vivid sound. Texts and translations – not to be taken for granted these days – are included.

Arias: *Don Carlos: Tu che la vanità. La traviata: Ah fors è lui. Il trovatore: Timor di me*
(M) *** Sony SMK 60975. Te Kanawa, LPO, Pritchard, or LSO, Maazel – PUCCINI: *Arias* *** (with MOZART: *Don Giovanni: Ah! Fuggi il traditor; In quali eccessi … Mi tradì;* HUMPERDINCK: *Der kleine Sandmann bin ich;* DURUFLE: *Requiem: Pie Jesu* ***)

The Verdi part of Kiri Te Kanawa's Verdi–Puccini recital brings three substantial items, less obviously apt for the singer, but in each the singing is felt as well as beautiful. The coloratura of the *Traviata* and *Trovatore* items is admirably clean, and it is a special joy to hear Elisabetta's big aria from *Don Carlos* sung with such truth and precision. Good recording, enhanced on CD. However these same excerpts are also available as part of a more generous mid-priced recital.

Scenes and duets: *Aida; Don Carlos; I Lombardi; I masnadieri; Otello; Rigoletto; Simon Boccanegra; La traviata; Il trovatore; I vespri siciliani; etc.*

*** EMI 5 56656-2. Gheorghiu, Alagna, L. Voices, BPO, Abbado

Whatever the hype surrounding this starry operatic couple, this is an imaginatively planned collection of relative rarities as well as favourites, which inspires some ravishing singing. It helps that the presentation is lavish, with the chorus contributing far more than is common on such a disc, setting each duet in context. Dramatically and musically, Gheorghiu is very much the dominant partner, using the widest range of dynamic and tone-colour, not just exploiting her voice in every register, but turning each phrase with memorable individuality. Though Alagna is not quite so inspired, and such a role as Otello is not quite his yet, there are few tenors today who could match him. The disc is crowned by the ripe and responsive playing of the Berlin Philharmonic under Abbado, opulently recorded. An operatic feast!

Choruses: *Requiem* excerpts: *Dies irae; Tuba mirum; Sanctus.* Choruses: *Aida; Un ballo in maschera; Don Carlo; Ernani; I Lombardi; Macbeth; Nabucco; Otello; Simon Boccanegra; Il trovatore*

(M) *** DG (IMS) (ADD) 463 655-2. Ch. & O of La Scala Milan, Abbado

The basic collection here, of nine opera choruses, was welcomed by us with enthusiasm (and a ❍) when it was first issued in 1975. The combination of precision and tension is riveting and the analogue recording is of DG's highest standard, offering a wide dynamic range, fine detail in the pianissimos, and splendid weight in the moments of spectacle. The diminuendo at the end of the *Anvil Chorus* is most subtly managed, while the fine rhythmic bounce of *Si, redesti* (from *Ernani*) is matched by the expansive brilliance of the excerpts from *Aida* (lovely fruity trumpets) and *Don Carlo*, and by the atmospheric power of *Patria oppressa* from *Macbeth*.

For the reissue, as one of their 'Originals', DG have expanded the contents to a more realistic 68 minutes, by adding some more items from Abbado's complete recordings, including *Un ballo in maschera* and *Simon Boccanegra*. The snag is that the collection ends with three excerpts from Abbado's 1980 set of the *Requiem*, where, compared with what has gone before, there is a degree of slackness and lack of bite. In the *Dies irae* the chorus sounds too small and there is little excitement. However, the recording is excellent and the rest of the programme remains highly desirable.

Choruses: *Aida; La battaglia di Legnano; Don Carlo; Ernani; La forza del destino; Macbeth; Nabucco; Otello; La traviata; Il trovatore*

(BB) *** Naxos 8.550241. Slovak Philharmonic Ch. & RSO, Dohnányi

Under Oliver Dohnányi's lively direction the chorus sings with fervour. The collection ends resplendently with the triumphal scene from *Aida*, omitting the ballet but with the fanfare trumpets blazing out on either side most tellingly. With a playing time of 56 minutes this is an excellent bargain, with naturally balanced recording from the Bratislava Radio Concert Hall.

'The World of Verdi': (i) *Aida: Celeste Aida;* (ii) *Grand March & Ballet.* (iii) *La forza del destino: Pace, pace, mio Dio.* (iv) *Luisa Miller: O! Fede negar potessi … Quando le sere al placido.* (v) *Nabucco: Va pensiero.* (vi) *Otello: Credo. Rigoletto:* (vii) *Caro nome;* (viii) *La donna è mobile;* (vii; viii; ix) *Quartet: Bella figlia dell'amore.* (x) *La traviata: Prelude, Act I;* (vii; xi) *Brindisi: Libiamo ne'lieti calici. Il trovatore:* (xii) *Anvil Chorus;* (xiii) *Strida la vampa;* (viii) *Di quella pira. I vespri siciliani:* (xiv) *Mercè, diletti amiche*

(M) *** Decca (ADD) 433 221-1. (i) Vickers; (ii) Rome Op. Ch. & O, Solti; (iii) Jones; (iv) Bergonzi; (v) Amb. S., LSO, Abbado; (vi) Evans; (vii) Sutherland; (viii) Pavarotti; (ix) Tourangeau, Milnes; (x) Maggio Musicale O, Fiorentino, Pritchard; (xi) Bergonzi; (xii) L. Op. Ch., Bonynge; (xiii) Horne; (xiv) Chiara

Opening with the *Chorus of the Hebrew Slaves* from *Nabucco* and closing with Pavarotti's *Di quella pira* from *Il trovatore*, this quite outstandingly red-blooded Verdi compilation should surely tempt any novice to explore further into Verdi's world, yet at the same time it provides a superbly arranged 74-minute concert in its own right. The choice of items and performances demonstrates a shrewd knowledge of both popular Verdi and the Decca catalogue, for not a single performance disappoints. Joan Sutherland's melting 1971 *Caro nome* with its exquisite trills is the first of three splendid excerpts from *Rigoletto*, ending with the famous *Quartet*, and other highlights include Dame Gwyneth Jones's glorious *Pace, pace, mio Dio* from *La forza del destino*, Sir Geraint Evans's superb account of Iago's evil *Credo* from *Otello* and Marilyn Horne's dark-timbred *Strida la vampa* from *Trovatore*. Solti, too, is at his most electric in the great March scene from *Aida*. The stereo throughout is splendidly vivid.

VERESS, Sándor (1907–92)

4 Transylvanian Dances

*** ECM 465 778-2. Camerata Bern, Zehetmair – SCHOENBERG: *Verklaerte Nacht*; BARTOK: *Divertimento* ***

Unlike Bartók, whose colleague he was, Sándor Veress remained in Budapest during the years of the pro-Nazi Horthy régime, succeeding Kodály at the Budapest Academy in 1943, when three of these *Transylvanian Dances* were written. Not long after Rákosi seized power in 1948 he settled in Switzerland where he added the much darker *Lejtös* movement. These are first-rate pieces, strongly Bartókian in feeling, but nonetheless distinctive. RL remembers being much impressed by a broadcast of a highly imaginative Violin Concerto in the early 1950s. Let us hope that these excellently played and vividly recorded pieces will presage more of his music on CD.

VERHULST, Johannes (1816–91)

Symphony in E min., Op. 46; Overtures in B min., Op. 2; C min. (Gijsbrecht van Aemstel); D min., Op. 8

*** Chan. 10179. Residentie O, The Hague, Bamert

Bamert has given us much attractive music in his Dutch music survey on Chandos (notably the music of Voormolen, Chan. 9815), and here is another excellent addition. Verhulst occupied an important position in Dutch musical life for many years, although his intrinsic conservatism in the face of the 'new' music of Liszt and Wagner ultimately led to his withdrawal from musical life, both voluntarily and not, and he died, embittered and increasingly forgotten. However, there is nothing embittered in his music: the composer who most readily springs to mind in the 1841 *E minor Symphony* is Mendelssohn (the finale reminds one especially of the *Octet*), though Schubert and Schumann are here too. It is full of vitality and good tunes among its drama and is well worth anyone's 35 minutes. The three early *Overtures*, though not quite as inspired as the *Symphony*, have the same qualities and are all highly enjoyable. Warm Chandos sound makes this an excellent CD for anyone who responds to music of the first half of the nineteenth century.

Mass, Op. 20

*** Chan. 10020. Oostenrijk, Van Reisen, Reijans, Claessens, Netherlands Concert Ch., Hague Residentie O, Bamert

It is good to have a disc that so boldly disposes of the idea that there were no significant Dutch composers between Sweelinck and Diepenbrock. Verhulst, a professional violinist and budding composer by the time he was twenty years old, was spotted by Mendelssohn, who persuaded him to study in Leipzig where, over six or seven years, he established a formidable reputation as a composer. He returned to Holland in 1843 and was promptly offered the directorship of the royal music by King Willem II, when he completed the *Mass* that he had begun in Leipzig. Over the years he gathered other important posts in Holland, but sadly his unbending conservatism – which involved totally ignoring the music of Berlioz and Wagner – led to his downfall in 1883, after which his music was neglected. The *Mass* is on an impressive scale, reflecting in its purposeful idiom not only the influence of his mentor, Mendelssohn, but even more strikingly that of Beethoven. So the *Credo* leads from a gently flowing opening to boldly dramatic effects, emphatic in the use of timpani and with the *Crucifixus* bringing a striking unison passage for tenors and basses. There is excellent singing from the chorus and young soloists alike, with Matthias Bamert drawing comparably committed playing from the Residentie Orchestra.

VERMEULEN, Matthijs (1888–1967)

Symphonies 2 (Prelude à la nouvelle journée); 6 (Les Minutes heureuses); 7 (Dithyrambes pour les temps à venire)

*** Chan. 9735. Residentie O, Rozhdestvensky

Matthijs Vermeulen's reputation as a wild man of Dutch music, likened by some to Charles Ives in America, is largely borne out by this group of three of his seven symphonies, very well performed and recorded by the Residentie Orchestra under Rozhdestvensky. Vermeulen's career as a composer was not helped by the sharpness of his pen in his other role of critic, and the *Symphony No. 2* had to wait for its first full performance until 1956, thirty-six years after it was completed. That delay was directly due to the scandal of Vermeulen's outspoken public protest in the Concertgebouw at the conservatism of Mengelberg's artistic policy, which resulted in a total boycott of his music at the famous Dutch concert hall. The wildness of the very start, brassy with timpani banging away, is deliberately provocative, certainly striking, if not fully matched by the distinction of the thematic material. Nonetheless, the five sections make a well-contrasted whole. The 1956 performance under van Beinum directly inspired Vermeulen to write his *Sixth Symphony*, a comparatively restrained piece, more intellectual and formulaic, with even the *amoroso* second movement hardly sensuous. In the *Symphony No. 7*, written when the composer, by then in his

mid-seventies, was terminally ill, the energy of No. 2 returns in a defiant work, which in its compression and often simplified textures is arguably the finest of the three symphonies here. The persistent and aggressive ostinatos of the third movement finale unexpectedly resolve on a concluding consonance. Sadly, the composer was too ill to attend the first performance under Bernard Haitink in 1967.

VICTORIA, Tomás Luis de (c. 1548–1611)

Ascendens Christus (motet); Missa Ascendis Christus in altum; O Magnum mysterium (motet); Missa O Magnum mysterium

*** Hyp. CDA 66190. Westminster Cathedral Ch., Hill

Missa Ave Maris stella; O quam gloriosum est regnum (motet); Missa O quam gloriosum

⊶ ⊛ *** Hyp. CDA 66114. Westminster Cathedral Ch., Hill

The Latin fervour of the singing is very involving; some listeners may initially be surprised at the volatile way David Hill moves the music on, with the trebles eloquently soaring aloft on the line of the music. The spontaneous ebb and flow of the pacing is at the heart of David Hill's understanding of this superb music. *Ave maris stella* is particularly fine. Hill's mastery of the overall structure produces a cumulative effect as the choir moves towards the magnificent closing *Agnus Dei.*

On the companion disc, the spirited presentation of the motet, *Missa Ascendis Christus in altum* prepares the way for a performance of the Mass that is similarly invigorating. The recording balance is perfectly judged, with the Westminster acoustic adding resonance (in both senses of the word) to singing of the highest calibre, combining a sense of timelessness and mystery with real expressive power.

Antiphons; Motets; excerpts from Masses: Missa Gaudeamus; Missa Quam pulchra sunt; O magnum mysterium; Lute & Vihuela solos

(N) (M) **(*) HM HMI 987042. Mena; Rivera, Gallego

There are sixteenth-century precedents for transcribing this repertoire for solo voice, accompanied by either the vihuela or lute. More conjecturally, a brass instrument could be featured in duet with the soloist, perhaps a period cornet as Francisco Gallego plays here. Carlos Mena has a beautiful and individual counter-tenor voice; he is accompanied intimately and authentically by Juan Carlos Rivera and is atmospherically recorded. The repertoire here is varied and all of high calibre. This is a disc which is suitable for late evening listening, but will probably not appeal to everyone.

Ave Maria; Ave Maris stella (hymn). Missa Vidi speciosam. Ne timeas, Maria; Sancta Maria, succurre miseris; Vidi speciosam (motets)

*** Hyp. CDA 66129. Westminster Cathedral Ch., Hill

An outstanding collection of some of Victoria's most beautiful music celebrating the Virgin Mary. The four-part *Ave Maria* may not be authentic, but the composer would surely not be reluctant to own it. The Westminster Choir again show their flexibly volatile response to this music with that special amalgam of fervour and serenity that Victoria's writing demands. The acoustics of Westminster Cathedral add the right degree of resonance to the sound without clouding.

Missa Ave Regina caelorum (with motet: *Ave Regina caelorum* for 8 voices); *Ave Maria* (for 4 Voices); *Ave Maria* (for 8 Voices); *Dixit Dominus; Laetatus sum; Laudate Dominum omnes gentes; Laudate pueri Dominum; Magnificat septimi toni; Nisi Dominus*

🎵 (N) *** Hyp. CDA 67479. Westminster Cathedral Ch., Martin Baker

Although it does not have the advantage of 'surround sound' like the account of the *Officium Defunctorum* by The Sixteen (see below), this Hyperion collection also stands out among recent recordings of Victoria's music. Under the direction of Martin Baker the Westminster style is volatile and strikingly passionate (their account of the *Dixit Dominus* arrestingly so), yet there is serenity too in the lovely *Missa Ave Regina caelorum*, a parody mass based on Victoria's two motet settings of which the eight-part version is used here to introduce the mass. But it is the shorter works that stand out even more strikingly, especially the joyous *Laetatus sum* for twelve voices and the richly blended eight-part setting of *Ave Maria*, which closes the concert. The recording, made in the Cathedral, is not crystal clear, but otherwise is in every way first class.

Canta Beata Virginis: Ave Maria a 4; Ave Regina caelorum; Gaude, Maria virgo a 5; Magnificat Primi toni; Ne timeas, O magnun mysterium a 4; Maria a 4; Sancta Maria, succurre miseris a 4; Trahe me post te; Salve Regina a 8; Vidi speciosam sidcut columbam; (Instrumental) *Senex, Puerum portabat a 4*

(N) *** Astrée Naive ES 9975. La Capella Reial de Catalunya, Hespèrion XX, Savall

This admirable collection of some of Victoria's most beautiful, and often celestially serene, Marian motets has as its highlights two eight-part works for double choir – the memorable antiphon, *Salve Regina*, and the glorious *Magnificat Primi toni*, the *Canticle of the Blessed Virgin*, sung at the end of Vespers. But the four-part settings are hardly less memorable in these spontaneous, deeply felt and impressively blended performances, where the brass of Hespèrion XX are well integrated into the vocal textures, and indeed have the sombre *Senex, Puerum portabat* to themselves. The resonance casts a lovely aura over the sound, but it does blur innner definition and the words. However, full texts and translations are included.

Missa Gaudeamus; Missa Pro Victoria. Motets: *Cum beatis Ignatius; Descendit Angelus Domini; Doctor bonus, amicus Dei Andreas; Ecce sacerdos magnus; Estote fortes in bello; Hic vir despiciens mundum; O decus apostolicum; Tu es Petrus; Vieni sponsa Christis*

🎵 ✪ *** ASV CDGAU 198. Cardinall's Musick, Carwood

Happily the name of the opening *Missa Gaudeamus*, for six voices, celebrates the label on which it is issued. It is a relatively serene 'backward-looking' work, yet with the closing *Sanctus* and *Agnus Dei* richly memorable. The shorter *Missa Pro Victoria* is even finer, indeed one of Victoria's most powerful and expressive utterances, and unique in being based on a secular chanson, *La guerre, escoutez lous gentilz* by Janequin. Andrew Carwood's performance moves forward with true Latin passion and grips the listener from first to last. Among the nine very varied additional motets, *Tu es Petrus* and *O decus apostolicum* and the remarkable *Descendit Angelus Domini* stand out. The recording is of the very highest quality.

Mass and motet: *O magnum mysterium.* Mass and motet: *O quam gloriosum. Ardens est cor meum; Ave Maria*

(BB) *** Naxos 8.550575. Oxford Camerata, Summerly (with
A. LOBO: *Versa est in luctum ***)

Like David Hill, Jeremy Summerly moves the music of each Mass on fairly briskly until the *Sanctus* and *Agnus Dei*, when the spacious *espressivo* of the singing makes a poignant contrast. The two motets on which the Masses are based are sung as postludes, and very beautiful they are, especially the idyllic *O magnum mysterium.* Finally, the short *Versa est in luctum* (a setting of a section of the Requiem Mass) by Alonso Lobo, a Spanish contemporary, ends the concert serenely. The recording is excellent and this is a fine bargain.

Officium defunctorum (*Requiem*, 1605)
*** Gimell CDGIM 012. Tallis Scholars, Phillips (with A. LOBO: *Versa est in luctum ***)
*** Hyp. CDA 66250. Westminster Cathedral Ch., Hill

The *Officium defunctorum* is a work of great serenity and beauty. Honours are fairly evenly divided between the Westminster Cathedral Choir on Hyperion and the Tallis Scholars under Peter Phillips. The Westminster Choir has the advantage of boys' voices and larger forces; they are recorded in a warmer, more spacious acoustic. By comparison with the Gimell recording, the sound seems a little less well focused, but on its own terms it is thoroughly convincing. They permit themselves greater expressiveness, too. Moreover the *Requiem* is set in the wider liturgical context by the use of some chants.

The Tallis Scholars achieve great clarity of texture; they are twelve in number and, as a result, the polyphony is clearer, and so too are their words. They offer also a short and deeply felt motet by Alonso Lobo (*c.* 1555–1617). The recording has a warm, glowing sound which almost persuades you that you are in the imperial chapel.

Officium defunctorum (*Requiem; including Taedet animam meam vitae meae*). *Ave Regina caelorum a 8; Nigra sum; Quam pulchri sunt; Salve Regina; Trahe me post te*

🎵 (N) *** Coro Surround Sound SACD CORSACD 16033.
The Sixteen. Christophers

Harry Christophers and his Sixteen give a gloriously expressive performance of Victoria's *Requiem*, his supreme masterpiece, written in 1605 for the Dowager Empress Maria of Austria, and they have every advantage over their competitors above in the superb recording made in the Church of Saint Silas the Martyr, London, engineered in 'surround sound' by Mike Hatch. This compatible SACD is pretty impressive heard in the normal CD format, but when the rear speakers are brought into use and carefully balanced, the effect is of sitting in the Church itself; moreover not only is the sound more expansive but the range of dynamic is increased. The performance is prefaced by *Taedet animam meam vitae*, a Lesson from Matins setting a bleak text from the Book of Job, and the performance closes with the funeral motet *Versa est in luctum* and the responsory *Libera me.* The music of the Mass is supplemented by the proper plainsong intonations and verses (monody, beautifully sung by the sopranos). Before the mass we are offered six other shorter works in which the eight-voice *Ave Regina* and *Salve Regina* both stand out. Altogether this is the most impressive of recent issues in the Victoria discography and it is strongly recommended.

Officium decorum (1592): *Libera me Domine; Peccantem me quotidie. Officium decorum* (1605): *Taedet animam meam. Libera me Domine* (with Plainchant taken from Graduale Romanum)

**(*) ECM 457 851-2. James, Covey-Crump, Potter, Jones –
PALESTRINA: *Responsories* **(*)

This CD combines music by Palestrina and Victoria for the Office and Matins for the Dead and the Burial service, including one text, *Libera me Domine*, set by both composers. The four singers blend their voices persuasively and are beautifully recorded, but the prevailing mood is of unremitting deep melancholy.

Responsories for Tenebrae

☛ *** Hyp. CDA 66304. Westminster Cathedral Ch., Hill
(N) (M) *** Virgin 5 61221-2. The Sixteen, Christophers
** Gimell CDGIM 922. Tallis Scholars, Phillips

The *Tenebrae Responsories* are so called because of the tradition of performing them in the evening in increasing darkness as the candles were extinguished one by one. The Westminster Cathedral Choir under David Hill on Hyperion find atmosphere in this music and bring a sense of spontaneous feeling to their performance. Of recent versions, this can be welcomed without reservation.

Harry Christophers and the Sixteen too are fully in sympathy with Victoria's *Tenebrae Responsories*, combining serenity, beautiful blending of timbres and a willingness to be volatile when the music demands it. Excellent recording in a suitably warm acoustic.

The Tallis Scholars are flawless in both blend and intonation but are curiously uninvolving. They are beautifully recorded and technically immaculate but lack intensity of feeling.

VIERNE, Louis (1870–1937)

Piano Quintet in C minor

*** Hyp. CDA 67258. Coombs, Chilingirian Qt – HAHN:
Piano Quintet in F sharp minor ***

An interesting coupling: both Hahn and Vierne turned to the piano quintet within a few years of each other, though we associate Hahn mostly with song and Vierne with the organ. Vierne composed his *Piano Quintet* in 1917 after the death of his second son, killed in action at only seventeen during the Great War. It is finely structured and its slow movement is particularly searching and thoughtful. The sleeve note draws a parallel with Frank Bridge, and its dark chromaticism is bleak and its world altogether harsher than the more familiar organ. Its centrepiece is the haunting and powerful *Andante*, the emotional core of the work. Stephen Coombs and the Chilingirians play with conviction and character, and are given the benefit of excellently vivid recorded sound. If you enjoy the Franck *F minor Piano Quintet* or the Chausson *Concert*, you will feel very much at home here.

Suite 3, Op. 54: Carillon de Westminster

*** DG 413 438-2. Preston (organ of Westminster Abbey) –
WIDOR: *Symphony 5* ***

The Vierne *Carillon de Westminster* is splendidly played by Simon Preston and sounds appropriately atmospheric in this spacious acoustic and well-judged recording. It makes an attractive makeweight to the Widor *Fifth Symphony*.

ORGAN SYMPHONIES

Symphonies 1 in D min., Op. 14; 2 in E min., Op. 20; 3 in F sharp min., Op. 28; 4 in G min., Op. 32; 5 in A min., Op. 47; 6 in B min., Op. 32

☛ ⊕ *** MDG 316 0732-2 (4). Ben van Oosten
(Cavaillé-Coll organs in Saint-François-de-Sales, Lyons (*Symphonies 1 & 4*); St Ouen, Rouen (*Symphonies 2 & 6*); Basilica Saint-Sernin, Toulouse (*Symphonies 3 & 5*)
**(*) Mer. (ADD) CDE 84192 (1–2); CDE 84176 (3–4); CDE 84171 (5–6). Sanger (organ of La Chiesa Italiana di San Pietro, London) (available separately)

Symphonies 1 & 3
*** Telarc CD 80239. Murray (Cavaillé-Coll organ of Saint Ouen, Rouen)

Symphonies 2–3
**(*) Priory PRCD 446. Walsh (organ of Lincoln Cathedral)

Symphonies 3 & 6
(BB) *** Naxos 8.553524. Mathieu (Dalstein-Haerpfer organ of Eglise Saint-Sébastien de Nancy)

Symphonies 4 & 6
**(*) Priory PRCD 425. Simcock (organ of Westminster Cathedral)

In the second half of the nineteenth century the organ-builder Ariste Cavaillé-Coll (1811–99) created a special kind of organ in France, with the richest diversity of colour, underpinned by firm yet expansive pedals. These instruments proved as suitable for the earlier organ masses of Couperin as for the semi-orchestral canvases of César Franck, whose *Grande Pièce symphonique* initiated a whole new approach to organ-writing which was to find its peak in the organ symphonies of Vierne and Widor.

Widor's symphonies certainly have their impressive moments, but Vierne's are far more consistent in quality, and if you have not already explored them, this new survey from Ben van Oosten, superbly recorded on three different Cavaillé-Coll organs, provides an admirable opportunity to do so.

Vierne's *First Symphony* dates from 1899 and was written for the organ of Saint-Sulpice. It opens with a monumental *Prélude*, which Ben van Oosten plays very commandingly indeed, and he provides glowing registration for the *Pastorale* and *Andante* – although, in the clearly laid out *Fugue* and more particularly the *Allegro vivace* scherzo (which is very orchestral in conception), while the playing is certainly lightly *vivace*, the Lyons resonance brings slight blurring to the detail. But these are minor criticisms of performances of outstanding quality. The magnificent finale, obviously influenced by Widor (its main theme on the pedals with a carillon effect above), makes an overwhelmingly spectacular close.

The cyclic *Second Symphony* (admired by Debussy) came three years later, with its marcato opening movement balanced by a lyrical secondary theme. The Franckian *Choral* and engaging *Scherzo*, followed by a delicate, mellifluous *Cantabile*, make a perfect foil for the powerful sonorities of the finale.

The *Third* (1911) has been the most popular of the six, until now, with its bold *maestoso* first movement ending with great dynamism, the *Cantilène* featuring the *hautbois* and reprised calmly on the *trompette harmonique*. The piquant *Intermezzo* (like a *marche miniature* but in triple time) is followed by a meditative but romantic *Adagio*, already full of chromatic influences from both Franck and Wagner. The *Toccata* finale, which has a memorable chorale-like secondary figure, builds to another overpowering final climax.

The last three symphonies are all cyclical. The *Fourth*, composed in 1914, took a long time to make its mark and was not premièred until 1923. Until its finale, it is the least flamboyant of the six. The dominating theme of the *Prélude* is introduced dolefully on the pedals, and that mood is maintained, even through a sequential apex. The sturdy *Allegro* eventually expands to a big climax to make way for a dainty *Minuet* and a freely lyrical *Romance*, enhanced by a restrained underlying rapture. The finale, at last, unleashes the composer's more usual exuberance and the closing section is tumultuous, with a very affirmative coda.

The *Fifth Symphony* (1924), the most ambitious of the six, is one of Vierne's two final masterpieces. It is the most Wagnerian, developing its two main themes almost like *leit-motifs*, and opens gravely with a powerfully chromatic and very orchestral 'Tristan-like' *Prelude*. The inner movements are then argued and contrasted like an orchestral symphony, with the extended *Larghetto* passionately expansive, while the joyful finale opens like a peal of bells. But the great culmination, with the principal tune thundering forth, all stops open, is as thrilling a climax as in many more famous nineteenth-century orchestral symphonies.

The Franckian chromaticism at the opening of the *Sixth Symphony*, written in 1934 in sight of – and obviously inspired by – the Mediterranean, is immediately apparent, and the agitated introduction brings a tremendous surge of energy from which the symphonic argument develops a momentum flowing ever forward. The *Aria* has a calming effect, but the highly imaginative *Scherzo* swirls in, and a pointed diabolic rhythm (not to be taken too seriously) dances bizarrely (one inevitably thinks here of Saint-Saëns). The mood darkens perceptibly as the *Larghetto* opens sombrely over a sustained pedal to create a darker, other worldly atmosphere, its mysterious concentration steadily increasing until the stygian mood is forcibly shattered by the sheer joy of the *fortissimo* opening of the finale, with its exuberant main theme bringing the waves sweeping over the listener, and the work storms to its tempestuous close.

Ben van Oosten's performances cannot be too highly praised. He is deeply committed, has a wonderful ear for sonority and detail (witness his uniquely grotesque playing in the *Scherzo* of No. 6), and every performance creates the thrill and spontaneity of live music-making, while the recording of all three organs is magnificent.

Until now we have recommended David Sanger's recordings on Meridian, and many organ enthusiasts will enjoy the very appealing sound of the San Pietro organ. The quality throughout is of a very high standard: the resonance of the pedals is very telling without muddying the overall sound picture. But overall this set is now completely upstaged by the new one from MDG.

Among the individual CDs, Michael Murray's pairing of *Symphonies 1* and *3* can also be strongly recommended. He has the full measure of this music, and ensured the success of his coupling by also choosing the superb Rouen organ. Not surprisingly, the Telarc recording is both spectacular and naturally balanced – very much in the demonstration bracket.

The Naxos pairing is also more than worth its modest price. Bruno Mathieu is a pupil of Marie-Claire Alain, and a splendid organist in his own right. Moreover, he chooses the 'historic' organ at Nancy, which still has mechanical traction,

and provides a very characterful baroque palette of its own, richly displayed in the *Cantilène* of No. 3. But the pedals are very telling, too, and the finale of No. 6 is powerfully spectacular; yet overall, inner detail is remarkably clear. The only small disappointment is the *Scherzo* of No. 6, where the diabolic rhythmic figure is not as ironically piquant as with Van Oosten.

On Priory, both Colin Walsh at Lincoln Cathedral and Ian Simcock at Westminster (the more suitable organ of the two) show their mettle and understanding of this repertoire, and Vierne's music is projected powerfully and colourfully. But the Vierne symphonies gain much from being recorded on Cavaillé-Coll instruments, so these discs must take second place to the others.

VIEUXTEMPS, Henri (1820–81)

(i) *Violin Concertos 1 in E, Op. 10;* **(ii)** *4 in D min., Op. 31*
(BB) *** Naxos 8.554506. Keylin, (i) Janáček PO, Burkh; (ii) Arnhem PO, Yuasa

Misha Keylin couples the unfamiliar *First* with the much better-known *D minor Concerto*, which we are told he plays on a famous Stradivarius violin. Certainly its *Andante religioso* brings a generous-toned romanticism. But the solo timbre in the E major work is sweet and full, and he plays the dazzling lightweight finale with charm as well as sparkle. This is an excellent coupling, very well recorded, and both accompanying groups, Czech and Dutch respectively, are very supportive indeed.

Violin Concertos 2 in F sharp min., Op. 19; 3 in A, Op. 25
(BB) *** Naxos 8.554114. Keylin, Janáček PO, Burkh

Nos. 2 and 3 are by no means inferior to the better known Nos. 4 and 5. They are full of good tunes, both slow movements are warmly touching, and the finales have lyrical as well as histrionic appeal. Misha Keylin gives highly persuasive performances that constantly tickle the ear in their subtlety of bowing and colour, easy rubato and imaginative dynamic shading. Dennis Burkh provides the strongest backing: his spirited introductions for both works (and especially the *Third*, with its throbbing drama) are arresting, and the orchestral playing, somewhat leonine in timbre, is excellent. So too is the recording, made in the Janáček Concert Hall, Ostrava.

Violin Concertos 4 in D, Op. 31; 5 in A min., Op. 37
(M) *** EMI (ADD) 5 66058-2. Perlman, O de Paris, Barenboim – RAVEL: *Tzigane;* SAINT-SAENS: *Havanaise* ***
(BB) (***) Naxos mono 8.110943. Heifetz; (i) LPO, Barbirolli; (ii) LSO, Sargent (with SAINT-SAENS: *Introduction & Rondo capriccioso; Havanaise;* SARASATE: *Zigeunerweisen* (with LPO or LSO, Barbirolli); WAXMAN: '*Carmen' Fantasy* (with RCA Victor SO, Voorhees) (***))

(i) *Violin Concertos 4–5;* **(ii)** *Ballade et Polonaise, Op. 38*
(B) *** Ph. (IMS) Eloquence (ADD) 468 204-2. Grumiaux; (i) LAP, Rosenthal; (ii) Varsi

Violin Concerto 4 in D min., Op. 31
(M) (***) EMI mono 7 64251-2. Heifetz, LPO, Barbirolli – SAINT-SAENS: *Havanaise* etc.; SARASATE: *Zigeunerweisen;* WIENIAWSKI: *Concerto 2* (***)

Perlman is both aristocratically pure of tone and intonation and passionate of expression. In his accompaniments Barenboim draws warmly romantic playing from the Paris orchestra. The 1976–7 recording, as usual with Perlman, balancing the soloist well forward, now sounds a little dated, with a touch of shrillness on the upper range of the violin. However, this remains a three-star record, the more so for its inclusion of two of Perlman's very finest recordings as couplings.

Heifetz was the first leading violinist to revive the long-neglected concertos of the nineteenth-century Belgian violinist-composer, Henri Vieuxtemps, recording No. 4 in 1935 and No. 5 in 1947. Both are compact works, rhapsodic in structure, which brilliantly exploit violin technique, making an attractive centrepiece for this disc of showpieces. The two Saint-Saëns pieces inspire Heifetz to much witty pointing and seductive phrasing, as do the Sarasate firework piece and the *Fantasy on Themes from Bizet's Carmen*, written for the film *Intermezzo* by the Hollywood composer, Franz Waxman. Each has remarkably good recorded sound for the period, well transferred, if with some surface hiss.

Both these concertos are worth hearing when they receive such eloquent and persuasive readings as Grumiaux provides, his timbre both silvery and warm, and with plenty of dash in the brief *con fuoco* finale of No. 5. He is well accompanied, too, and although the orchestra is weightily recorded (in the mid-1960s), the balance is excellent and the solo violin most truthfully caught. The engaging *Ballade et Polonaise* for violin and piano, which was recorded a decade later, makes an attractive encore when the partnership between Grumiaux and Dinorah Varsi is so felicitous.

Violin Concerto 5 in A min., Op. 37

*** EMI 5 55292-2. Chang, Philh. O, Dutoit – LALO: *Symphonie espagnole* ***

(M) *** Sony SMK 89715. Lin, Minnesota O, Marriner – BRUCH; MENDELSSOHN: *Concertos* ***

(M) *** DG (IMS) 457 896-2. Mintz, Israel PO, Mehta – LALO: *Symphonie espagnole*; SAINT-SAENS: *Introduction & Rondo capriccioso* ***

(M) *** RCA (ADD) 09026 61745-2. Heifetz, New SO of L, Sargent – BRUCH: *Violin Concerto 1*, etc. ***

(B) **(*) Sony (ADD) SBK 48274. Zukerman, LSO, Mackerras – BRUCH: *Concerto 1*; LALO: *Symphonie espagnole* **(*)

Sarah Chang's recording, coupling a scintillating account of the Lalo *Symphonie espagnole*, goes readily to the top of the list. It is beautifully recorded, with a perfect balance, in an agreeably warm acoustic. Chang's vitality is matched by Dutoit and her playing has a magically gentle tenderness in presenting the engaging lyrical themes of the first movement and the *Adagio*. The brief finale has splendid élan.

Cho-Liang Lin plays with flair and zest and is well supported by Sir Neville Marriner and the Minnesota Orchestra. The recording is first class, and the couplings of the more famous concertos of Bruch and Mendelssohn could not be more appropriate.

Mintz's performance has enormous dash and also real lyrical magic. Mehta, obviously caught up in the inspiration of the solo playing, provides an excellent accompaniment. This is another example of a memorable live performance 'recorded on the wing' and, if the acoustic is not very flattering, the sound is truthful and well balanced.

The quicksilver of Heifetz is well suited to the modest but attractive *Fifth Concerto* of Vieuxtemps, and Sir Malcolm again provides a musical and well-recorded accompaniment. The balance of the soloist is rather close, but the digital

remastering is successful, and the couplings are both attractive and generous.

Zukerman provides here an enjoyable bonus to his dazzling accounts of the Bruch and Lalo works. There is a comparable dash for Vieuxtemps, yet he coaxes the *Adagio* tenderly. Again a very forward balance, but the ear adjusts.

Violin Concertos (i) 5, Op. 37; 6 in G, Op. 47; (ii) 7 in A min., Op. 49

☛ (BB) *** Naxos 8.557016. Keylin, (i) Slovak RSO, Mogrelia; (ii) Arnhem PO, Yuasa

Mischa Keylin here completes his valuable set of the Vieuxtemps Concertos with a fine, fully competitive version of the popular No. 5, and he also gives première recordings of Nos. 6 and 7. They belong to the last year of the composer's life and show no diminution of his melodic facility. The *G major* is in four movements and, in addition to the lovely *Pastoral* slow movement, has a charming *Intermezzo siciliano* before the sparkling *Allegretto* Rondo finale. Keylin is a very persuasive advocate, equally at home and accomplished in the *A minor Concerto*, with its *Mélancholie* central movement and dashing closing *Allegro vivo*. He plays a 1715 Stradivarius, and his elegantly warm lyricism shows its timbre off to seductive effect. The recording is very good, too.

Violin Concertos 6–7; Salut à l'Amérique, Op. 56

(N) *** Audivis Valois V 4797. Poulet, Liège R. PO, Bartholomée

Gérard Poulet has a small tone, but his playing is polished and warmly cultivated, and it suits these charmingly elegant works admirably. He is well accompanied, and is recorded in a pleasing acoustic. The novelty here is the engaging concertante fantasy, *Greeting to America*, written by Vieuxtemps for his first tour of the USA in 1844. It opens genially, featuring the American National Anthem intimately rather than flamboyantly. Poulet has its full measure, as he has the variations on 'Yankee doodle dandy' which follow.

Viola Sonata in B flat, Op. 36; Elégie, Op. 30; Morceaux, Op. 61

*** Chan. 8873. Imai, Vignoles – FRANCK: *Viola Sonata in A* ***

*** Simax PSC 1126. Tomter, Gimse – FRANCK: *Viola Sonata in A* ***

The Vieuxtemps *Sonata* is expertly crafted and well laid out for the instruments but it is no masterpiece. Nobuko Imai and Roger Vignoles give an exemplary account of it and are given expert recording from the Chandos engineers.

The Norwegian, Lars Anders Tomter, is hardly less accomplished and every bit as eloquent a player as his celebrated rival and countryman, Håvard Gimse, is a first-rate pianist. There is absolutely nothing to choose between them, and both couple the Vieuxtemps with the Franck sonata arranged for viola.

Viola Sonata in B flat, Op. 36; Unfinished Sonata, Op. Posth.: Allegro con fuoco; Scherzo: Grazioso (only); Capriccio, Op. Posth. Elégie, Op. 30

(B) **(*) Naxos 8.555262. Diaz, Koenig

As well as being known as one of the finest violinists and composers of his time, Vieuxtemps also excelled as a viola player and wrote expressively for that instrument, favouring its rich middle register. None of this music is quite of the calibre of his violin concertos, but the central *Barcarolla con* melancolilia of the *B flat major Sonata* is rather endearing, and the *Unfinished Sonata* has an engaging *Grazioso Scherzo* (a curious contradiction in musical terms) with a pair of Trios. The other pieces have a certain romantic flair, but the most indelible is the arrangement of Félicien David's *La nuit* (which is extracted from the *Ode-symphonie, La désert*), a quite delectable *morceaux de concert*. The performances by Roberto Diaz and Robert Koenig are of quality, without being truly memorable.

VILLA-LOBOS, Heitor (1887–1959)

Amazonas; Dawn in a Tropical Forest; Erosão; Gênesis
*** Marco Polo 8.223357. Czecho-Slovak RSO (Bratislava), Duarte

These are imaginative scores with tropical colouring and exotic textures, all sounding rather similar in their luxuriance – but who cares! *Amazonas* is the earliest and most astonishing score, dating from the First World War, and in its vivid sonorities affirms Villa-Lobos's contention that his first harmony book was the map of Brazil. The Bratislava strings could be more opulent, but the performances under a Brazilian conductor are very good indeed, as is the recording.

Bachianas brasileiras 1–9; Chôros 2 (for flute & orchestra); 5 (for piano, Alma brasileira); 10 (for chorus & orchestra); (i) 11 (for piano & orchestra). 2 Chôros (bis) (for violin & cello); (i) Piano Concerto 5. Descobrimento do Brasil; Invocação em defesa da Patria; (i) Mômoprecóce (fantasy for piano & orchestra). Symphony 4. Qu'est-ce qu'un Chôros? (Villa-Lobos speaking)
(M) (**(*)) EMI mono 7 67229-2 (6). De los Angeles, Kareska, Basrentzen, Braune, Tagliaferro, Du Frene, Plessier, Cliquennois, Bronschwak, Neilz, Benedetti; (i) Blumental; Chorale des Jeunesses Musicales de France, Fr. Nat. R. & TV Ch. & O, composer

This six-CD box is a colourful, warm-hearted collection, not helped by dull mono recordings and ill-disciplined performances, but full of a passionate intensity that plainly reflects the personality of a composer of obvious charisma, if of limited ability as a conductor. Endearingly, there is a 10-minute track spoken in French by Villa-Lobos himself. All nine of the *Bachianas brasileiras* are recorded here, including the celebrated No. 5 for soprano and eight cellos, with Victoria de los Angeles a radiant soloist. That recording is already well known, but most of the others have had very limited circulation. Despite the dull sound, the warmth of the writing never fails to come over.

Bachianas brasileiras 1 for Cellos; 2 for Orchestra; (i) 5 for Soprano & 8 Cellos; 9 for String Orchestra
(M) (**(*)) EMI mono 5 66912-2 [S 66964]. Fr. Nat. R. & TV O, composer; (i) with de los Angeles

Understandably, this EMI 'Great Recordings of the Century' reissue opens with No. 5, with its floating melodic line so delicately and ravishingly sustained by Victoria de los Angeles. Elsewhere the dry, lustreless orchestral recording will limit the appeal of this disc for the general, rather than the historically minded collector, for the composer's direction is of documentary rather than inspirational interest.

Bachianas brasileiras (iii) 1; (i; iii) 5; (i; ii) Suite for Voice & Violin. (iii) Arr. of BACH: *The Well-Tempered Clavier:*

Prelude in D min., BWV 583; Fugue in B flat, BWV 846; Prelude in G min., BWV 867; Fugue in D, BWV 874
☞ *** Hyp. CDA 66257. (i) Gomez, (ii) Manning, (iii) Pleeth Cello Octet

Jill Gomez is outstanding in the popular *Bachianas brasileiras No. 5* and with the violinist, Peter Manning, in the *Suite* (1923). Villa-Lobos's favourite 'orchestra of cellos' produce sumptuous sounds in both the *Bachianas brasileiras*, and an added point of interest is the effective transcriptions for cellos of unrelated Bach preludes and fugues. A most attractive introduction to this most colourful of composers.

(i; ii) Bachianas brasileiras 3; Mômoprecóce; (iii) Guitar Concerto; (iv) Fantasia for Soprano Saxophone & Chamber Orchestra; (i) Piano music: A próle do bébé 1 (suite); A lenda de caboclo; Alma brasileira (Chorus 5); Ciclo brasileiro: Festa no sertão; Impressões seresteiras
☞ (B) *** EMI double forte 5 72670-2 (2). (i) Ortiz; (ii) New Philh. O, Ashkenazy; (iii) A. Romero, LPO, López-Cobos; (iv) Harle, ASMF, Marriner

In many ways this is the finest Villa-Lobos collection in the catalogue, certainly the most varied. His rather melancholy piano piece *A lenda de caboclo* ('Legend of a half-caste') gives a clue to the unique identity of this music, for the composer's mother was Hispanic, his father of Indian descent. No. 3 of the *Bachianas brasileiras*, which dates from 1938, is the only one of the series to involve the piano. The *Mômoprecóce* began life in 1920 (while the composer was living in Paris) as the set of piano pieces called *Carnaval das Crianças*, and it was reworked in its concertante form later. Like so much of Villa-Lobos's music, the score is rowdy and colourful. Cristina Ortiz, herself Brazilian, is a natural choice for this repertoire. She plays with appropriate vigour, reflective feeling and colour, and Ashkenazy gives splendid support. The late-1970s recording is excellent, with the CD transfer adding a little edge to high violins. Ortiz is equally impressive in the solo piano pieces (again very well recorded), which she plays with flair and at times with touching tenderness, as in Villa-Lobos's portraits of the *Clay* and *Rag Dolls*, the third and sixth members of *A próle do bébé* ('baby's family'). Angel Romero makes the very most of the comparatively slight *Guitar Concerto*, bringing out its Latin feeling. The *Fantasia for Soprano Saxophone* is a more substantial piece with three well-defined movements, contrasted in invention. John Harle is a perceptive soloist with a most appealing timbre; one of the highlights of the set. The recordings in both these concertante works (made in 1984 and 1990 respectively) are well up to the best Abbey Road analogue standards.

Chôros 8; 9
(BB) *** Naxos 8.555241. Hong Kong PO, Schermerhorn

The *Chôros No. 8* (1925) is what we think of as quintessential Villa-Lobos, exotic, full of colour and superbly evocative insect, bird and forest sounds, all effectively conveyed by the Hong Kong orchestra under Kenneth Schermerhorn. Villa-Lobos himself spoke of the *Chôros* as 'representing a new form of musical composition synthesizing different kinds of Brazilian Indian and folk-music, having as their principal elements rhythm and all kinds of typical folk melody that appear accidentally from time to time, always transformed by the personality of the composer'. Like No. 8, the *Chôros No. 9* (1929) calls for a huge orchestra, including Brazilian percussion instruments. There is an exuberance, exoticism and an abundance of musical ideas clamouring for attention. The recordings were made in the 1980s and are very good indeed.

Guitar Concerto

(M) *** Sony (ADD) SMK 89753. Williams, ECO, Barenboim
– CASTELNUOVO-TEDESCO: *Concerto*; RODRIGO: *Concierto de Aranjuez; Invocación y danza* ***

(BB) *** Naxos 8.550729. Kraft, N. CO, Ward –
CASTELNUOVO-TEDESCO: *Concerto*; RODRIGO: *Concierto de Aranjuez* ***

*** Guild GMCD 7176. Jiménez, Bournemouth Sinf., Frazor –
ANGULO: *Guitar Concerto 2 (El Alevín)*; RODRIGO: *Concierto de Aranjuez* ***

(i) Guitar Concerto. 12 Etudes; 5 Preludes

(M) *** RCA (ADD) 09026 61604-2. Bream, (i) LSO, Previn

A highly distinguished account of the *Guitar Concerto* from Bream, magnetic and full of atmosphere in the slow movement and finale. Previn accompanies sympathetically and with spirit. The rest of the programme also shows Bream in inspirational form. He engages the listener's attention from the opening of the first study and holds it to the last. The recording has a nice intimacy in the concerto and the solo items have fine presence against an attractive ambience.

John Williams's compulsive performance makes the very most of the finer points of Villa-Lobos's comparatively slight concerto, and especially the rhapsodic quality of the *Andantino*. The recording is bright and fresh, the soloist characteristically close, but the effect is vividly present.

An excellent account from Norbert Kraft, spontaneous and catching well the music's colour and atmosphere. If it is not quite as individual as Bream's version, it has the advantage of vivid, well-balanced, modern, digital recording and excellent couplings. Another genuine Naxos bargain.

Rafael Jiménez also proves a natural soloist for Villa-Lobos's intimate concerto, and Terence Frazor and the Bournemouth Sinfonietta make the very most of the orchestral colouring, which sounds more vivid than usual. Yet the balance integrates the soloist appealingly within the orchestral texture.

Piano Concertos 1–5

(B) *** Double Decca 452 617-2 (2). Ortiz, RPO, Gómez-Martínez

What emerges from the series of concertos, as played here by Cristina Ortiz, is that the first two are the most immediately identifiable as Brazilian in their warm colouring and sense of atmosphere, even though the eclectic borrowings are often more unashamed than later, with many passages suggesting Rachmaninov with a Brazilian accent. No. 3, the work Villa-Lobos found it hard to complete, tends to sound bitty in its changes of direction. No. 4, more crisply conceived, has one or two splendid tunes, but it is in No. 5 that Villa-Lobos becomes most warmly convincing again, returning unashamedly to more echoes of Rachmaninov. With Ortiz articulating crisply, there is much to enjoy from such colourful, undemanding music, brilliantly recorded and sympathetically performed.

Discovery of Brazil: Suites 1–3; (i) 4

**(*) Marco Polo 8.223551. Slovak RSO (Bratislava), Duarte; (i) with Blazo, Slovak Philharmonic Ch.

The *Discovery of Brazil* derives from an ambitious film project and Villa-Lobos fashioned three orchestral suites from it, plus a fourth which employs a soloist and choir. Though there are good things in this music and some exotic

orchestral effects, the colours are not quite as vivid and dazzling as one would have expected from this prolific Brazilian master. Enjoyable performances.

Symphonies 4 (A Vitória); 12

*** CPO 999 525-2. SWR German RSO, Stuttgart, St Clair

The *Fourth Symphony* (1919) evokes the composer's feelings at the conclusion of the First World War and calls for extravagant musical forces, including a small internal group of E flat clarinet, saxophone quartet and percussion, and another brass fanfare group. Exuberant, rumbustious, larger than life – Gallic influences are strong but there are some lovely individual touches in parts of the second movement and the inspired elegiac third movement. The *Twelfth* (1957) was completed on the composer's seventieth birthday. Although its finale is overscored, there is a great deal of lively invention and luxuriant orchestration to enjoy. Very good performances by Carl St Clair and the Südwestfunk Orchestra of Stuttgart and exemplary recording, well-detailed and vivid.

Symphonies 6 (Sobre a linha das montanhas do Brasil); 8; Suite for Strings

*** CPO 999 517-2. SWR RSO Stuttgart, St Clair

The subtitle of the *Sixth Symphony* of 1944 (*On the Profiles of the Mountains of Brazil*) has a more than programmatic significance. Villa-Lobos supposedly used the contours of the mountain peaks in Rio de Janeiro (drawn on graph paper) to create some of his melodic lines. The most memorable of its four movements is arguably the lush, atmospheric slow movement with its imaginative orchestration, reminiscent of Ravel and Respighi.

The *Eighth Symphony*, written six years later, is more concerned with symphonic purpose than local geography. It has striking themes and the first movement thrusts forward with infectious momentum.

The *Suite for Strings* is an orchestral version of what was originally a work for double string quintet. Its three movements are entitled *Timide*, *Mysterious* and *Restless (Air de ballet)*, but the music has much more depth than such a description would suggest and the opening section is quite haunting. All three works are splendidly played and recorded, and this CD is well worth exploring, if you enjoy symphonies which are genuine, are garbed in unusual colours, and move in unexpected directions. Very good playing from the Südwestrundfunk Orchestra of Stuttgart under Carl St Clair and well-balanced recording.

Symphony 7; Sinfonietta

(N) *** CPO 999 713-2. SW German RSO, Stuttgart, St Clair

The opening of Villa-Lobos's *Seventh Symphony*, with its extravagant orchestration, exotic jungle noises and contrary-motion glissandi all bursting out from a big orchestra, is aurally fascinating, while at the same time the work has an undoubted symphonic structure. The themes are bony and interrelated, and the outer movements have plenty of propulsion. Yet the first movement has a striking invention, with a fine seconday lyrical interlude. The *Lento*, introduced by a haunting bassoon call, is a yearning evocation based on the word AMERICA (the Southern continent), its theme resourcefully using substitutions (with the note F for letter 'M', D for 'R' and B for 'I'). The music gathers impulse and excitement before returning on the woodwind to the withdrawn nostalgia of the opening. The Scherzo is again exotically scored, and is based on a four-note figure which vigorously explores the large gathering of instruments; and the finale brings an engaging syncopated theme on the horns, which then becomes more lyrical. With woodwind and strings again creating jungle simulations, the symphony moves with increasing animation to its life-assertive, but sudden, conclusion. It is very well played by the Stuttgart Radio Orchestra and the studio recording is vivid, though forwardly balanced. However, the sound lacks sumptuousness, which is a distinct drawback in such a colourful score.

The *Sinfonietta* suits the small acoustic more readily. Scored for a classic chamber ensemble plus trombone, it is based on two (unidentified) Mozartian motives. The writing is genially spontaneous, with a very winning main theme in the first movement, a cultivated extended *Andante* which opens moodily but soon changes style and tempo, and a finale which is marked *Andantino* but which gathers energy, with a 'giusto' ending. It is excellently played, the orchestra and conductor obviously responsive, and here the studio recording is first class.

GUITAR MUSIC

Chôros 1 (Typico); 12 Etudes; 5 Préludes; Suite populaire brésilienne

☞— (BB) *** Naxos 8.553987. Kraft

Norbert Kraft show his absolute mastery of his instrument in his dazzling account of the *Twelve Etudes*, which have contrasting moments of reflection. He plays the *Five Préludes* beautifully, too, with a fine control of atmosphere and rubato. The *Chôros* and *Suite populaire brésilienne* are marginally less spontaneous-sounding, and the latter is not as colourfully idiomatic as in the hands of Julian Bream. But this inexpensive disc gathers together all the composer's important music for solo guitar, and by any standards this is fine playing. The recording is naturally balanced and has a vivid but not exaggerated presence.

5 Preludes for Guitar

(B) *** Sony (ADD) SBK 62425. Williams (guitar) –
  GIULIANI: *Variations on a Theme by Handel*; PAGANINI:
  Caprice 24; Grand Sonata; D. SCARLATTI: *Sonatas* ***

Although John Williams is balanced a shade too closely, he is very well recorded; his playing, improvisationally spontaneous and full of magical evocation, is of the highest level of mastery. A lower level setting compensates for the balance and enables this artist's playing to register effectively. These are as perfect and as finely turned as any performances in the catalogue.

CHAMBER MUSIC

Assobio a jato (for flute & cello); Bachianas brasileiras 6 (for flute & bassoon); Canço do amor (for flute & guitar); Chôros 2 (for flute & clarinet); Modinha; Distribuição do flores (both for flute & guitar); Quinteto en forma e chôros (for wind); Trio for Oboe, Clarinet & Bassoon

☞— (BB) *** Hyp. Helios CDH 55057. Bennett, Tunnell, O'Neill, Wynberg, King, Black, Knight

Although it was originally published in 1999, we have not before encountered this winning collection of Villa-Lobos's chamber music for wind, superbly played and recorded, and now an inestimable bargain. Indeed, there are few more inviting introductions to the exotic colours and indelible invention that this Brazilian composer has made his own. With the superb flautist William Bennett at the centre of the group, the performances could hardly be more enticing, or indeed more polished. For the engaging Parisian *Quinteto en forma de chôros* of 1928, with its wild mood changes, there is equally expert playing from Thea King (clarinet), Neil Black (oboe), Robin O'Neill (bassoon) and Janice Knight (cor anglais). Among the various duos in the improvisatory duet style of Rio's street musicians (to which Charles Tunnell, guitar, also contributes) the romantic *Modinha*, the lovely *Distribution of Flowers*, the *Song of Love* and the chirping flute and fluid cello lines of the *Jet Whistle*, with its touching centrepiece, contrast with the witty *Chôros No. 2*. The most ambitious Brazilian piece is the unpredictable Trio with its raw jungle voicings, dextrous rhythms and syncopations and lyrical *Languisamente*. This slow central section and the *Vivo* finale are faintly Stravinskian, but with an added touch of witty geniality. First-class recording, present but not too close. Not to be missed.

String Quartets 2 (1915); 7 (1941)
**(*) Marco Polo 8.223394. Danubius Qt

The *Seventh Quartet* comes from 1941 – a good vintage for Villa-Lobos – and is conceived on an ambitious scale, not far short of 40 minutes. Unlike Villa-Lobos's music from the 1930s, this is less exotic in feel, and his discovery of Bach in the *Bachianas brasileiras* also makes itself felt here. There is an abundance of melodic invention and contrapuntal vitality, even if his musical thinking remains essentially rhapsodic. The Danubius Quartet give a straightforward if rather languid account of the piece. The *Second Quartet* of 1915 is much shorter and of less interest.

String Quartets 4 (1917); 6 (Quarteto brasileiro) (1938); 14 (1953)
*** Marco Polo 8.223391. Danubius Qt

The three quartets recorded here are all well crafted and their ideas are of quality. The *Fourth* is perhaps the most Gallic; the *Sixth* (*Quarteto brasileiro*) is one of the most individual and rewarding. It makes intelligent use of Brazilian folk material. The *Fourteenth*, like so much of Villa-Lobos, is not entirely free from note-spinning. The Danubius Quartet are an accomplished ensemble and play with evident commitment. The recording places them rather forward in the aural picture.

String Quartet 6 (Quarteto brasileiro)
(***) Testament mono SBT 1053. Hollywood Qt – CRESTON:
  Quartet; DEBUSSY: *Danses sacrées*; RAVEL: *Introduction & Allegro*; TURINA: *La oración* (***)

The *Sixth Quartet* is a slight but amiable score, ultimately facile but pleasing and well crafted. It would be hard to imagine a finer performance than this.

PIANO MUSIC

Music for Piano, 2 & 4 Hands: Carnaval das Crianças (Children's Carnival); Solo Piano Music: A Fiandeira (The Spinning Girl); A Legenda do Cabocio (The Legend of the Cabocio); New York Skyline (2nd version); Rudepoèma; Saudades das Sélvas Brasileiras (Yearning after the Brazilian Jungles)

(N) (B) *** DG 2-CD 477 5439 (2). Szidon, LPO, Downes –
  GERSHWIN: *Piano Concerto in F*; IVES: *Piano Sonatas*;
  MACDOWELL: *Piano Concerto 2* ***

Bright, attractive music that is unfailingly inventive and enjoyable, and excellently played by Robert Szidon. *Rude-poèma*, written in the first half of the 1920s, is one of Villa-Lobos's best pieces in this medium. Szidon is a brilliant player, and in the *Carnaval das Crianças*, for piano, four hands (although some of the pieces are for only one pianist), he is well supported by Richard Metzler. The recording is a shade close but eminently realistic, and the couplings are all thoroughly worthwhile.

Alma brasileira, Bachianas brasileiras 4; Ciclo brasileiro; Chôros 5; Valsa da dor (Waltz of Sorrows)
*** ASV CDDCA 607. Petchersky

Alma Petchersky's style is romantic, and some might find her thoughtful deliberation in the *Preludio* of the *Bachianas Brasileiras No. 4* overdone. Her very free rubato is immediately apparent in the *Valsa da dor*, which opens the recital. Yet she clearly feels all this music deeply, and the playing is strong in personality and her timbre is often richly coloured. She is at her finest in the *Brazilian Cycle*. The recording is excellent.

As três Marias; Bachianas Brasileiras 4: Preludio. Prole do bèbe (The Child's Doll): Suite; Rudepoèma
(BB) **(*) Warner Apex (ADD 0927 40837-2). Freire

Excellent playing and eminently satisfactory recording of some delightfully colourful piano music. But at 40 minutes the measure is short, even at Apex price.

Cirandas; Rudepoèma
*** ASV CDDCA 957. Petchersky

Not only is the playing here first class, but the music itself is of much interest. *Rudepoêma* (1921–6) is a musical portrait of Artur Rubinstein and is full of temperament and virtuosity. Alma Petchersky rises to its innumerable challenges with great spirit and panache. The *Cirandas* (1926), which make formidable technical demands on the pianist, are dispatched with great brilliance and poetic feeling. Alma Petchersky is very well recorded and, if the standards of this series are maintained, future issues will be self-recommending.

VOCAL MUSIC

Bachianas brasileiras 5 for Soprano & Cellos
(B) *** Double Decca 444 995-2 (2). Te Kanawa, Harrell and instrumental ens. – CANTELOUBE: *Songs of the Auvergne* ***

The Villa-Lobos piece makes an apt fill-up for the Canteloube songs, completing Kiri Te Kanawa's recording of all five books. It is, if anything, even more sensuously done, well sustained at a speed far slower than one would normally expect. Rich recording to match.

VINTER, Gilbert (1909–69)

Hunter's Moon
(N) (M) (***) BBC mono BBCL 4164-2. Dennis Brain, BBC Concert O, Tausky – BEETHOVEN: *Quintet* (**); HINDEMITH: *Horn Sonata;* JACOB: *Sextet* (***)

One of Dennis Brain's favourite encores, Gilbert Vinter's infectious miniature, *Hunter's Moon*, is played here with characteristic charm and easy virtuosity.

VIOTTI, Giovanni Battista (1755–1824)

Violin Concerto 13 in A
(BB) *** Hyp. Helios CDH 55062. Oprean, European Community CO, Faerber – FIORILLO: *Violin Concerto 1* ***

Viotti wrote a great many violin concertos in much the same mould, but this is one of his best. Adelina Oprean's quicksilver style and light lyrical touch give much pleasure – she has the exact measure of this repertoire and she is splendidly accompanied and well recorded. The measure, though, is short.

VISÉE, Robert de (1650?–1732)

Robert de Visée was among the last representatives of the French school of lute and theorbo playing, for the lute was soon to be replaced by the guitar in public favour in the way that the viola da gamba was to be superseded by the cello. In his day de Visée was both a celebrated lutenist and a respected composer, and at the height of his career he was summoned to the French court, where he gave guitar lessons to the Dauphin, and played for the King (Louis XIV) after supper in the evening.

Suites de danses: in A min.; B min.; C min.; D min.
(M) *** Virgin 5 61541-2. Monteilhet (theorbo)

(Suites) *Pièces in G; in C. Le Bergeries de Mr Couperin; Les Sylvaines de Mr Couperin; Chaconne des Harlequinnes de Mr Lully; Entrée des espagnoles de Mr Lully; Logistille de Mr Lully*
(N) *** Glossa GCD 2K0104. Moreno (theorbo)

It is significant that all the chosen suites here are in the minor key, for while each, after an introductory *Prélude*, includes a set of dances – allemande, courante, gavotte, sarabande and gigue – their atmosphere is not as light-hearted as you would expect. It is the sarabande in each case that finds the composer writing with a particularly haunting melancholy, whereas the style of the allemandes is consistently serious. That in the *A minor Suite* is dedicated to *La Royale*, and in the *C minor* it is in the form of a *Plainte* ('for the tomb of the composer's daughters'), a noble commemoration of a personal tragedy.

The theorbo could be supplemented by a set of very low-sounding strings which added support to the harmony with their rich tone and added resonance, as Pascal Monteilhet shows here in these remarkably evocative performances, warmly recorded, which transport the listener back to a different age.

The sympathetic harmonic vibration of the longer strings of the theorbo also provides José Miguel Moreno with a pleasingly warm and resonant timbre without blurring the focus of the sound. He offers a pair of C major Suites (called *Pièces*) with the same mixture of dances as the minor-key works; but to match their generally upbeat character, each also includes a genial chaconne. They are through-composed (i.e. they draw on the same basic material throughout), and so are the two groups of tributes to Couperin and Lully. A fine supplement to the Virgin collection.

VIVALDI, Antonio (1675–1741)

Philips Vivaldi Edition, Vol. 1: Concertos: (i) *L'estro armonico, Op. 3;* **(ii)** *La stravaganza, Op. 4;* **(iii)** *6 Violin Concertos, Op. 6.* **Chamber music: (iv)** *12 Sonatas for 2 Violins, Op. 1;* **(v)** *12 Violin Sonatas, Op. 2;* **(vi)** *6 Sonatas for 1 or 2 Violins, Op. 5*

(B) *** Ph. (ADD) 456 185-2 (10). (i) Michelucci; (ii) Ayo; (iii) Carmirelli; (i–iii) I Musici; (iv–vi) Accardo, Canino, De Saram; (iv) Gulli; (vi) Gazeau

Philips Vivaldi Edition, Vol. 2: Concertos: (i; ii) *12 Concertos for Oboe or Violin, Op. 7;* **(iii)** *Il cimento dell'armonia e dell'invenzione (The Trial between Harmony and Invention, including The Four Seasons), Op. 8; La cetra, Op. 9;* **(i)** *6 Violin Concertos, Op. 11; 6 Violin Concertos, Op. 12*

(B) *** Ph. (ADD) 456 186-2 (9). I Musici, with (i) Accardo (ii) Holliger; (iii) Ayo; (iv) Gazzelloni

Philips's Vivaldi Edition is very competitively priced, and any reservations tend to be swept aside when the coverage is so uniquely comprehensive and the music-making so warmly enjoyable. These are refreshing and lively performances, and the current transfers offer gleaming tuttis, while the soloists are realistically placed and cleanly focused. The reissue of the chamber music is particularly welcome, as these sonatas are not otherwise readily obtainable. In any case it is unlikely that Accardo's performances, so ably supported by Franco Gulli (in Op. 1), Rohan de Saram (cello) and Bruno Canino (harpsichord) could be surpassed in terms of fluency, musicianship and sheer beauty of tone. The Opp. 11 and 12 *Violin Concertos* were recorded in 1974–5. The best of them are very rewarding indeed and, played by Salvatore Accardo, they are likely to beguile the most reluctant listener.

L'Estro armonico, Op. 3; La Stravaganza, Op. 4; Il Cimento dell'armonia e dell'invenzione (The Trial of Harmony and Invention), Op. 8, including The Four Seasons, Op. 8/1–4; La Cetra, Op. 9. Bassoon Concerto, RV 498; Flute Concerto, RV 441; Oboe Concerto, RV 456; Double Horn Concerto, RV 539; Double Oboe Concerto, RV 535; Concertos for 2 Oboes, Bassoon, 2 Horns & Violin, RV 569 & RV 574; Piccolo Concerto, RV 443

🔊➔ (N) (B) *** Decca (ADD) 475 471-2 (7). Loveday, Iona Brown, Kaine & Soloists, ASMF, Marriner or (in Op. 9) Brown

During the 1970s, starting with Alan Loveday's ground-breaking account of *The Four Seasons*, the Academy of St Martin-in-the-Fields recorded the four major sets of Vivaldi's violin concertos with great distinction, first directed by Marriner, and then (in *La Cetra*) by Iona Brown. In these gleaming new transfers the performances come up as freshly as ever, as do the eight sparkling wind concertos which act as makeweights. This could prove a splendid and inexpensive basis for any Vivaldi collection, large or small.

L'estro armonico (12 Concertos), Op. 3

🔊➔ *** Chan. 0689 (2). Guglielmo & soloists, L'Arte dell'Arco, Hogwood

(M) *** Virgin 5 45315-2 (2). Biondi, Longo, Casazza, Negri, Naddeo, Europa Galante

L'estro armonico, Op. 3; **(i)** *Bassoon Concerto in A min., RV 498;* **(ii)** *Flute Concerto in C min., RV 441;* **(iii)** *Oboe Concerto in F, RV 456;* **(i; iii; iv)** *Concerto in F for 2 Oboes, Bassoon, 2 Horns & Violin, RV 574*

(B) *** Double Decca (ADD) 443 476-2 (2). ASMF, Marriner; with (i) Gatt; (ii) Bennett; (iii) Black; (iv) Nicklin, T. Brown, Davis, I. Brown

(i) *L'estro armonico, Op. 3;* **(ii)** *6 Flute Concertos, Op. 10*

(B) *** Double Decca 458 078-2 (2). (i) Holloway, Huggett, Mackintosh, Wilcock; (ii) Preston; AAM, Hogwood

(B) *** DG 477 5421 (2). (i) Standage & soloists, E. Concert, Pinnock; (ii) with Beznosiuk

Using a new edition, based on the earliest printed manuscripts, Christopher Hogwood has returned to *L'estro armonico*, using a group of Italian musicians and, in particular, their *maestro al violino*, Federico Guglielmo. Although he was born in Padua, he studied in Venice where, encouraged by Hogwood, he devoted himself to the performance of baroque music on period instruments. The fruitful results are borne out here in a glowing performance, with one instrument to a part, combining (unexaggerated) vitality with gleaming Italian expressive warmth. The quality of sonority is nearer to the ASMF style than some of the abrasive sounds we hear from some 'authentic' performances, and this new set is very enjoyable indeed. It is virtually impossible to talk about a best version of these twelve concertos, but this new Chandos set certainly goes to the top of the list.

Pinnock's *l'estro armonico* (with one instrument to a part) brings together the best features from past versions: there is as much sparkle and liveliness as with Hogwood, for rhythms are consistently resilient, the ensemble crisp and vigorous. Yet in slow movements there is an expressive radiance and sense of enjoyment of beauty without unstylish indulgence. In the *Flute Concertos* Beznosiuk is a superb soloist and the sound is first class throughout.

There is no question about the sparkle of Christopher Hogwood's earlier performance with the Academy of Ancient Music. The captivating lightness of the solo playing and the crispness of articulation of the accompanying group bring music-making that combines joyful vitality with the authority of scholarship. Hogwood's continuo is first class, varying between harpsichord and organ, the latter used to add colour as well as substance. The balance is excellent, and the whole effect is exhilarating. In Op. 10 Stephen Preston plays a period instrument, a Schuchart, and the Academy of Ancient Music likewise play old instruments. Their playing is eminently stylish, but also spirited and expressive, and they are admirably recorded, with the analogue sound enhanced further in the CD format.

Fabio Biondi and Europa Galante start with No. 2, whose arresting opening *Adagio e spiccato* is very dramatic. Indeed, these performances are tremendously alert, crisply rhythmic and marvellously played, with the lyrical writing always winningly expressive. Almost all of these works are for two or more soloists, and here the concertino work splendidly together. But when Biondi plays alone his contribution is very stylish indeed and the *Largo* of the solo concerto, RV 356 (No. 6), is exquisite. Equally Biondi and Isabella Longo make a captivating partnership in the *Double Violin Concerto*, RV 519 (No. 7). Period-instrument playing of Vivaldi has clearly matured and, with first-class modern recording, this offers a strong challenge to both Pinnock and Hogwood.

Those who have not been won over to the more abrasive

sound of period instruments will find Marriner's set no less stylish. As so often, he directs the Academy in radiant and imaginative performances of baroque music and yet observes scholarly good manners. The delightful use of continuo – lute and organ as well as harpsichord – the sharing of solo honours and the consistently resilient string playing of the ensemble make for compelling listening. The 1972 recording, made in St John's, Smith Square, is immaculately transferred, and as a bonus come four of Vivaldi's most inventive concertos, each with its own special effects.

(i) L'estro armonico, Op. 3 (complete); (ii) 6 Flute Concertos, Op. 10. Miscellaneous concertos:

CD 1: Double Mandolin Concerto, RG 532; Oboe Concertos, RV 548 & 461; Concerto for Strings (alla rustica), RV 151; Con molti stromenti, RV 558; Double Violin Concerto, RV 516

CD 2: Concertos for Bassoon, RV 484; for Flute, RV 436; for Oboe & Bassoon, RV 545; for Strings, RV 159; for Viola d'amore & Lute, RV 540; for Violin (L'amoroso), RV 271

(B) *** DG 471 317-2 (5). (i) Standage, Wilcock, Golding, Comberti, Jaap ter Linden; (ii) Beznosiuk; & Soloists, E. Concert, Pinnock

Pinnock's performances of L'estro armonico and the Op. 10 Flute Concertos with Lisa Beznosiuk are among our top recommendations. The two separate single-CD collections, one entitled Alla rustica the other L'amoroso, offer lively, communicative performances, using period instruments in the most enticing way. The sheer variety of Vivaldi is constantly established, totally contradicting the old idea that he wrote one concerto hundreds of times over. The playing time of these two discs is not particularly generous (53 and 57 minutes respectively), but now they come within a bargain box in DG Archiv's Collectors Edition this seems less important than the consistently high quality of the performances and recordings. The documentation is excellent.

L'estro armonico, Op. 3/1, 2, 4, 7, 8 & 10–11
(BB) *** Naxos 8.550160. Capella Istropolitana, Kopelman

Jozef Kopelman and the Capella Istropolitana are robustly competitive with their bargain disc. The performances are lively, and the recording has warmth and presence. Good value for money.

Violin Concertos: L'estro armonico, Op.3/3; (i) 5, 6, 9 & 12. Il cimento dell'armonia e dell'invenzione, Op. 8/7, 9 & 12. Double Concertos: (i) for 2 Violins, RV 529; (ii) for Violin & Cello, RV 547; (iii) for Violin and Oboe, RV 548; (iv) for Violin & Organ, RV 541 & 542
(BB) *** EMI Gemini 5 85544-2 (2). Y. Menuhin, Polish CO, Maksymiuk; with (i) Chen; (ii) Mørk; (iii) Black; (iv) Bell

This reissue combines two CDs (from 1986 and 1990 respectively) which we have not encountered before, to make a most attractive pairing, especially at budget price. The first combines four solo violin concertos from L'estro armonico with three from Il cimento dell'armonia e dell'invenzione (missing out, of course, the first four, which are known as The Four Seasons). They are all fine works and Menuhin is in excellent form; his expressive playing is often very beautiful indeed. Moreover, Jerzy Maksymiuk directs lively and stylish accompaniments. These are modern-instrument performances of high quality, but the crisp rhythms and bright, clean recording offer no suggestion of inflation.

The second collection, which Menuhin directs from the bow, concentrates on double concertos and includes the A major work from L'estro armonico, Op. 3/5. With Truls Mørk an erstwhile partner, the two concertos with cello are certainly enjoyable, and the combination of violin and organ also brings a most engaging interplay. But it is the B flat Concerto for Violin and Oboe that is most winning of all, and here Neil Black makes a truly memorable contribution.

La stravaganza (12 Concertos), Op. 4 (complete)
(N) *** Channel Classics **SACD** CCS SA 19503 (2). Podger, Arte Dei Suonatori

☛ ✹ (B) *** Double Decca 444 821-2 (2). Soloists, ASMF, Marriner

(BB) **(*) Naxos 8.55323 (Nos. 1–6); 8.55324 (Nos. 7–12). Watkinson, City of L. Sinfonia, Kraemer

Rachel Podger and the splendid Polish period-instrument group, Arte Dei Suonatori, recorded in a warm ecclesiastical acoustic, give La Stravaganza a superb SACD début. Podger's solo playing is full of vitality and imaginative, expressive feeling, and the orchestra and continuo players all combine to give her a richly persuasive and detailed backcloth. Whether played using only the front speakers or also the third channel at the back (the fourth is silent) the recording has a spacious realism. Because of the ambient resonance of the Polish church, the overall focus is not sharply defined, but the sound itself is naturally balanced and gloriously full. While Rachel Podger's gleaming timbre dominates, the other soloists, drawn from the orchestra, are all excellent, as is the ensemble, apparently achieved without a conductor. The continuo too – archlute, guitar, theorbo, harpsichord and organ – comes through believably.

Marriner's performances make the music irresistible. The solo playing of Carmel Kaine and Alan Loveday is superb and, when the Academy's rhythms have such splendid buoyancy and lift, it is easy enough to accept Marriner's preference for a relatively sweet style in the often heavenly slow movements. The contribution of an imaginatively varied continuo (which includes cello and bassoon, in addition to harpsichord, theorbo and organ) adds much to the colour of Vivaldi's score. The recording, made in St John's, Smith Square, in 1973–4, is of the highest quality, with CD transfers in the demonstration class.

Nicholas Kraemer has fully absorbed period-instrument manners, and these athletic performances, full of vitality, on modern instruments, certainly have an authentic feel and sound. However, Andrew Watkinson's solo personality is not strong in individuality and while this set, which is very well recorded, is excellent value, those looking for the very best in an inexpensive format should turn to Marriner.

The Trial between Harmony and Invention (12 Concertos), Op. 8: (i) 1–4: The Four Seasons; (ii) 5–12 (complete); (ii; iii) Double Violin Concerto in D, RV 513
✹ (N) (BB) (***) Naxos mono 8.110297/8. Kaufman; (i) Concert Hall CO, Swoboda; (ii) Winterthur SO, Dahinden; (iii) with Rybar

This is a very special Four Seasons. Recorded in Carnegie Hall in December 1947 by Louis Kaufman, a soloist of distinction, very famous in America in his day, and the Concert Hall Chamber Orchestra directed by Henry Swoboda, it was the work's recording première. Some 3,000 sets were pressed – and so too was re-established the reputation of Antonio Vivaldi. All but forgotten for over two centuries, he was soon to become renowned as the composer of the most familiar and most popular classical piece in the entire concert repertory. Kaufman went on to record the other eight concertos of Op. 8 in Zurich in 1950 with the Winterthur Symphony Orchestra conducted by Clemens Dahinden, who was a natural Vivaldian and supported him well.

Kaufman was thus a key pioneer in promoting the Vivaldi revival, which came with the long-playing record. What is astonishing is how like modern-day performances these are, with apt tempi and a style which is athletic and expressive by turns. Indeed, all this music sounds as fresh as ever and, with excellent transfers, the sound too is astonishingly good, the *Four Seasons* limited in range but well balanced (with even a hint of the continuo now and then) and aurally pleasing. The sound in the remaining concertos is fresher and brighter; although there is an occasional hint of minor pitch fluctuation, it is brief and not too disturbing, when the overall effect is so pleasing. Kaufman is then joined by Peter Rybar for the *Concerto for Two Violins*, which makes a sprightly and engaging encore, and the continuo comes through well.

The Trial between Harmony and Invention (12 Concertos), Op. 8

🕭⇥ (M) *** Virgin 5 61980-2 (2) Biondi, Europa Galante

(B) *** Sony (ADD) SB2K 89980 (2). Zukerman, Black, ECO, Ledger (continuo)

(B) **(*) Ph. (IMS) Duo 438 344-2 (2). Ayo, I Musici

The Trial between Harmony and Invention (12 Concertos), Op. 8; (i) Double Concertos: for Violin, Cello & Strings in A, RV 546; for 2 Violins in G, RV 516

(BB) *** Virgin 2×1 5 61668-2 (2). Huggett, Raglan Bar.
Players, Kraemer; (i) with E. Wallfisch and Mason (cello)

Fabio Biondi and Europa Galante have already recorded the *Four Seasons* and their period-instrument performance is highly praised below. The new version, within the complete Op. 8, is just as fresh and certainly as vibrant, with some dazzling solo playing full of dynamic subtlety. One notices a few small differences in these new performances. In *Spring* the viola can surely never have barked more commandingly, and in the finale the ripieno achieves a very striking drone effect. In *Autumn* (and elsewhere) the continuo comes through especially tellingly in the slow movement, while the *pianissimo* opening of *Winter* moves from mysterious evocation to a strong climax. Clearly this particular winter is going to be a hard one.

The recording claims to use 'original manuscripts', and after considerable research (following Standage and Pinnock's example), Biondi used the recently discovered set of parts of the *Four Seasons* held in Manchester's Henry Watson Music Library. But for the other eight concertos in the set he has consulted alternative manuscripts held in libraries in Dresden and Turin. The reasons for this are well documented in the notes, and certainly Europa Galante make a dramatic case for the Dresden score of No. 5, *La tempesta di mare*.

They begin the second CD with an arresting account of *Concerto No. 11*, which Biondi considers is 'the richest in material of the whole collection', and very fine it is. *La caccia* (No. 10) follows, for which Biondi has turned to Turin, and the rest of the set has involved a great deal of detective work to determine the full detail of Vivaldi's intentions.

All the remaining concertos are played with the same energy and imaginative vitality which make the *Four Seasons* so enjoyable, and this new look is very stimulating indeed, for the recording is first class, and Europa Galante avoid all those linear excesses that can sometimes spoil period-instrument performances.

Kraemer's complete Op. 8 concertos with Monica Huggett make a fine alternative bargain recommendation in its new Virgin 2×1 format. In the *Four Seasons*, a lovely spontaneous feeling emerges: the light textures and dancing tempo of the finale of *Spring* are matched by the sense of fantasy in the central movement of *Summer*, while the rumbustious energy of the latter's last movement is gloriously invigorating. The *Adagio* of *Autumn* has a delicate, sensuous somnambulance, and only the opening of *Winter* is relatively conventional, though certainly not lacking character. The rest of the concertos are hardly less imaginative, with no exaggeration of phrasing, which used to haunt early-music performances, and the recording is excellent. With two other enjoyable concertos thrown in for good measure, this is very highly recommendable.

Sony have now restored Pinchas Zukerman's complete set of Op. 8 to the catalogue, with six concertos allotted to each of the two discs. Those wanting Zukerman's *Four Seasons* will find the performances of those celebrated works bring out all the drama, and their expressive qualities are in no doubt, with the solo movements offering playing that is both thoughful and searching. *Concerto No. 9* on the second CD is allotted to the oboe, and admirably played by Neil Black. The ECO provide alert and resilient accompaniments and the early 1970s recording is full and lively, with a close balance for the soloists.

Felix Ayo recorded the first four concertos (*The Four Seasons*) in 1959 and his was one of the finest of the early versions, although the recording was rather resonant. The remaining concertos in the set – full of typically Vivaldian touches which stamp these works as among the best of their time – date from 1961–2 and the recording, though still full-bodied, is less reverberant. The solo playing is attractively fresh, although Maria Teresa Garatti's continuo fails to come through adequately. Good value.

The Trial between Harmony and Invention (Il Cimento dell'armonia e dell'invenzione) (12 Concertos), Op. 8; La Cetra (12 Concertos), Op. 9

🕭⇥ (BB) *** Virgin 5 62260-2 (4). Huggett & Soloists, Raglan Baroque Players, Kraemer

Anyone wanting *Il Cimento dell'armonia* (including a highly recommendable set of *The Four Seasons*) and *La Cetra* together, admirably played on period instruments, could hardly better this Virgin budget box. Monica Huggett has already give us *La Stravaganza* on Oiseau-Lyre (although this currently awaits reissue) and her Vivaldian credentials are impeccable. The present performances are so accomplished and in such good style that they are unlikely to be surpassed by other authentic-instrument versions. She is in excellent form throughout and her virtuosity always appears effortless. Notably in *The Four Seasons*, her expressive flexibility extends to quite personal touches of rubato, which some might find a little mannered, but they give her solo playing added individuality. The Raglan Baroque Players are of the same size as the Academy of Ancient Music and some players are common to both groups. First-class recording throughout.

The Four Seasons, Op. 8/1–4

🕭⇥ *** BBC Opus Arte **DVD** OA 0818D. Fischer, ASMF, Sillito (Producer: Gethin Scourfield; V/D: Ferenc van Damme)

** EMI **DVD** 4 92498-9. Kennedy, ECO

** Sony **DVD** SVD 46380. Mutter, BPO, Karajan

(BB) *** Regis RRC 1160. Laredo, SCO (with *Concert – String Masterpieces* *** – see below)

*** DG 463 259-2. Mutter, Trondheim Soloists – TARTINI: *Devil's Trill Sonata* **(*)

(BB) **(*) DG (ADD/DDD) 474 567-2. Kremer, LSO, Abbado – HAYDN: *Trumpet Concerto*, etc. ***

**(*) EMI 5 57015-2. Chung, St Luke's Chamber Ens.

**(*) BIS CD 275. Sparf, Drottningholm Bar. Ens.

(B) **(*) CfP 574 8872 [5748872]. Sillito, Virtuosi di E., Davison – ALBINONI: *Concerti a cinque, Op. 7/3 & 6* **(*)

**(*) EMI 7 49557-2. Kennedy, ECO

(N) (B) *(**) Cala 2-CD CACD 0538. Bean, New Philh. O, Stokowski – HANDEL: *Messiah: Highlights* **

The Four Seasons (with sonnets in Italian and English)

(BB) *** Hyp. Helios CDH 88012. Bruni, Edwards (readers), Oprean, European Community CO, Faerber

(N) *(**) Decca **SACD Surround Sound** 475 6188. Jansen, with Instrumental Ens.

The Four Seasons

(N) * Simax Classics PSC 1247. Tønnesen, Norwegian CO

(i) *The Four Seasons;* (ii) *Bassoon Concerto in A min., RV 498;* (iii) *Double Concerto for 2 Oboes in D min., RV 535;* (iv) *Piccolo Concerto in C, RV 443*

(M) *** Decca (ADD) 466 232-2. (i) Loveday; (ii) Gatt; (iii) Black, Nicklin; (iv) Bennett; ASMF, Marriner

The Four Seasons; Cello Concerto in B min., RV 424; Double Oboe Concerto in D min., RV 535; Concerto for Strings in G (Alla Rustica), RV 151; (i) Double Trumpet Concerto in C, RV 337

(M) *** Sony SMK 89987. Lamon, Tafelmusik; (i) with Steele-Perkins, Thiessen

(i) *The Four Seasons;* (ii) *Oboe Concertos in C, RV 447; in F, RV 457*

(B) **(*) Sony (ADD) SBK 60711. (i) S. Kuijken, La Petite Bande; (ii) Haynes, O of 18th Century, Brüggen

(i) *The Four Seasons;* (ii) *Oboe Concertos: in D min., Op. 8/9 (RV 454); in A min., RV 461.*

(N) (M) *** Warner Elatus 0927 46726-2. (i) Manze; (ii) Ponselle; Amsterdam Bar. O, Koopman

The Four Seasons, Op. 8/1–4; Double Violin Concerto in G, RV 516; Double Concerto for Violin & Oboe Concerto in F, RV 548

(M) *** DG 474 616-2. Standage, E. Concert, Pinnock

The Four Seasons; Violin Concerto in D, RV 171; Concerto for Strings in B flat (Concha), RV 163

*** Opus 111 OPS 569120. Biondi, Europa Galante

The Four Seasons; Violin Concertos: in E flat (La tempesta di mare), RV 253; in C (Il piacere), RV 108, Op. 8/5–6

(BB) *** Warner Apex 8573 89097-2. Blankestijn, COE

(N) *** DHM/BMG 82876 60158-2. Von der Goltz, Freiburg Bar. O & Harp Consort (with Vivaldi's *Four Descriptive Sonnets in Italian and English*)

The Four Seasons; Violin Concertos: L'estro armonico, Op. 3/1, 4, 7, & 10

(B) *** DG (IMS) 2-CD 474 287-2 (2). Schwalbé & string soloists, BPO, Karajan – BACH: *Brandenburg Concertos 3 & 5; Orchestral Suite 3* **

(i) *The Four Seasons;* (ii) *Violin Concertos: L'estro armonico: in A min., Op. 3/6. La stravaganza: in A, Op. 4/5. Concerto in C min. (Il sospetto), RV 199*

(BB) *** EMI Encore (ADD) 5 74761-2. Perlman, (i) LPO; (ii) Israel PO

(i) *The Four Seasons;* (i; ii) *L'estro armonico: Concerto for 2 Violins & Cello in D min., Op. 3/11, RV 565;* (iii) *Double Oboe Concerto in D min., RV 535. Concerto for Strings in A, RV 158*

(BB) *** RCA 74321 68001-2. (i) Spivakov; (ii) Futer & Milman; (iii) Utkin & Evstigneev; Moscow Virtuosi

(i) *The Four Seasons; Concerto for Strings in G (Alla rustica), RV 151;* (ii) *Violin Concerto in E (L'amoroso), RV 271; Sinfonia in B min. (Al Santo Sepolcro), RV 169*

(B) *** DG (ADD) 439 422-2. (i) Schwalbé; (ii) Brandis; BPO, Karajan

The Four Seasons, Op. 8/1–4; Violin Concertos: in D, RV 211; in E flat, RV 257; in B flat, RV 276

*** Sony SK 51352. Carmignola, Venice Bar. O, Marcon

The Four Seasons; Violin Concerto in E (L'amoroso), RV 271

(M) **(*) Ph. (ADD) 464 750-2. Ayo, I Musici

Over the years there have been various ways of promoting a new record of Vivaldi's *Four Seasons*, but Janine Jansen's début in this work must be unique in being marketed with a presentation including eight CD-size full-page photographs of her in glamorous décolletage. Vivaldi is nowhere to be seen, and the brief note on the music receives only three-quarters of a descriptive page! As well as looking more than presentable, Miss Jansen is a fine player and she is accompanied here vigorously and stylishly by a string quintet plus continuo. However, although the performance has some fine moments (*Summer* is impressive), it tends to be over-characterized, with moments of exaggerated phrasing and dynamics. One feels that both soloist and accompanying group were trying too hard: the shepherd's dog, for instance, is nearly on one's lap.

The other newest version comes from Simax (PSC 1247) in which, inside the cover of Terje Tønnesen's version with the Norwegian Chamber Orchestra, the soloist writes ominously that his 'Four Seasons is a project the intent of which is to bridge the gap in time between the year 2000 and 1700 . . . a form of time travel in which we attempt a "correct" reading of history while at the same time interpreting it freely from our own perspective'. Upon trying the CD itself, we were immediately confronted with electronic wind noise and atmospheric effects; then, within the next 90 seconds, there was, first, a curious cadenza featuring mainly violin harmonics, then the performance was interrupted by thunderous drums. At that point we stopped listening. Fortunately the catalogue is well stocked with fine accounts of Vivaldi's masterpiece in which the performers are willing to let the music speak for itself.

It seems rather appropriate that, as with LP and CD, the first really outstanding DVD of *The Four Seasons* should come from the Academy of St Martin-in-the-Fields, this time directed and led vivaciously by Kenneth Sillito, and with a brilliant young soloist in Julia Fischer. She plays with remarkable freshness, obviously inspiring the Academy players also to give of their very best. The result is remarkably spontaneous, and one feels one is hearing this baroque masterpiece anew. The recording was made in the dome of the National Botanic Gardens of Wales, which has surprisingly good acoustics. All four of the *Seasons* were recorded separately, Miss Fischer choosing a new (but simple) dress for each of the four occasions. The performers are filmed alongside nature's own changing backcloth. So the viewer watches the musicians in close-up or enjoys the pictorial splendour of the changing Welsh countryside, lakeland and glowing sunsets. Although the camera is on a crane and roves around the players, which can be a little unsettling, one soon adjusts, for the close-ups mean that the performers' bows on strings are as tangible as the music itself. (You cannot possibly miss Vivaldi's barking shepherd's dog.) There are 'director's cut' and 'performance edit' options and the bonuses include a series of brief interviews with the soloist.

No one could say that Kennedy's DVD of *The Four Seasons* is dull; the only snag is that he talks a lot about it, not very illuminatingly, in his special kind of vernacular, and then introduces each movement as well. The performance itself is certainly spectacular in conveying the picturesque imagery (except for the viola's barking shepherd's dog, which is rather feeble). The total running time, including all the documentary bits, is still only 48 minutes.

On DVD, Karajan sits and directs the Berlin Philharmonic from the harpsichord for Mutter, but, beautifully as she plays, the result is plushy and in the last resort rather bland.

Marriner's 1970 Academy of St Martin-in-the-Fields version with Alan Loveday still remains at the top of the list of CD versions. The performance is as satisfying as any and will surely delight all but those who are ruled by the creed of authenticity. It has an element of fantasy that makes the music sound utterly new; it is full of imaginative touches, with Simon Preston subtly varying the continuo between harpsichord and organ. The opulence of string tone may have a romantic connotation, but there is no self-indulgence in the interpretation, no sentimentality, for the contrasts are made sharper and fresher, not smoothed over. Decca have reissued this performance on the Legends label including, as a bonus, concertos for bassoon, piccolo and two oboes.

Salvatore Accardo's is a version with a difference. Recorded in live performances at the 1987 Cremona Festival, it is of particular interest in that Accardo uses a different Stradivarius for each of the four concertos – period instruments with a difference! Thanks to this aristocrat of violinists, the sounds are of exceptional beauty, both here and also in the two multiple concertos which are added as a bonus. The performances are much enhanced, too, by the imaginative continuo playing of Bruno Canino. The recording itself is a model of fidelity and has plenty of warmth; it must rank very high in the Vivaldi discography and now justly reappears as part of Universal's 'Penguin ✿ Collection'.

Tafelmusik offers another superbly imaginative version, but on period instruments. The playing is at once full of fantasy and yet has a robust gusto that is irresistible. The opening of *Spring*, with its chirruping bird calls, sets the scene, and the second movement brings a lovely cantilena from Jeanne Lamon, while the barking dog is as musical as he is gruff. The performances throughout are full of dramatic contrasts, and the new bonuses are as varied as they are attractive. The Sony recording is first class, with most refined detail.

Not surprisingly, Andrew Manze's bravura performance is hugely dramatic, fiercely energetic and full of individuality. In *Spring*, the shepherd's dog really means to be heard; in *Summer* the storms must be the worst for more than a

decade, yet *Autumn*, while opening boldly, has a lusciously sensuous *Adagio*, followed by a very boisterous hunting party. The slow movement of *Winter* is similarly seductive, with very gentle raindrops, and the finale opens in a temperate, improvisatory mood, before dashing away impetuously to its riotous conclusion. Koopman matches Manze's virtuosity and feeling for atmosphere throughout and provides many subtle touches in the continuo (on harpsichord and organ). The bonus of two of Vivaldi's finest *Oboe Concertos* is the more winning for the sunny geniality of Marcel Ponselle's playing on a baroque oboe with a particularly attractive timbre. First-class recording.

Fabio Biondi and his similarly excellent period-instrument group, L'Europa Galante, have already given us an outstanding set of *L'estro armonico*, and their account of *The Four Seasons* is equally fresh. There is not a hint of routine anywhere, the solo playing is often exquisite; and even if the soloist nearly gets blown away by the gusto of the summer winds, the central reverie in *Autumn* is hauntingly gentle and serene. *Winter* opens very dramatically indeed and the solo roulades have great bravura; the central movement makes a charmingly relaxed contrast. The bonuses are imaginative and include another of Vivaldi's most individual violin concertos and the *Concerto for Strings* given the nickname *Concha* because it is supposed to simulate a primitive instrument made from a seashell, notably in the central *Andante* with its echoing fifth (B flat and F). Again the performances are strongly characterized and very well recorded.

Gottfried von der Goltz is a highly sensitive soloist on DHM, but it is the sheer personality of the justly renowned Freiburg Baroque Orchestra that dominates this music-making. It is a performance of contrasts – indeed of extremes, with great energy in allegros and very measured tempi in slow movements. In *Spring* the continuo at times suggests a hurdy-gurdy, while shepherd's dog barks to a crisp abrasive staccato, and there is a similar sharpness of attack in the orchestral *Presto* at the centre of the slow movemnt of *Summer*, and again in the *impetuoso* finale. In the *Adagio* of *Autumn* the violin soloist floats delicately and languorously over an ethereal accompaniment with a delicate continuo; and *Winter* has similar evocative contrasts. The two additional concertos are equally vibrant, their central *Largos* again ravishing in gentle *espressivo*. Here, perhaps more than in the *Seasons*, one registers that the Harp Consort is providing a most subtle and varied continuo. At the close we hear the four sonnets Vivaldi appended to his score, delightfully read in fluid yet theatrical Italian, but with a translation provided.

Trevor Pinnock directs his 1981 Archiv version from the keyboard, with Simon Standage leading the English Concert. Although a relatively intimate sound is produced, their approach is certainly not without drama, while the solo contributions have impressive flair and bravura. The result finds a natural balance between vivid projection and atmospheric feeling. With two highly attractive (if not generous) double concertos added to this mid-priced Originals release – all in fine sound – authenticists should be well satisfied.

The Sony version, with Giuliano Carmignola the breathtakingly brilliant soloist, is another period performance with no holds barred. Incredibly fast tempi for allegros contrast with gently lyrical, highly atmospheric slow movements in which one is given the feeling almost of ruminative improvisation. Certainly the performances are full of imagination and there are many new touches (witness the *sotto voce* opening of *Winter*). It is impossible not be gripped by the magnetic concentration and visceral excitement of this playing. But one wonders if Vivaldi would not have been astonished by such bravura, from the orchestra as well as the soloist. Carmignola offers as his bonus similarly dazzling accounts of what are described as première recordings of three more violin concertos, all very attractive, the D major, RV 211 (which comes last), especially so, with its siciliana *Larghetto* and striking finale. The brilliant yet transparent recording matches the performances admirably. The CD offers texts and translations of the poems with which the works are associated.

For those still preferring the fuller texture of modern instruments, the Apex version with the COE provides the perfect alternative and at super-bargain price too. The chimerical solo playing of Marieke Blankestijn is a delight and her clean style shows that she has learned from authentic manners. There is more imaginative delicacy here, particularly in the improvisatory central movement of *Summer* and the gentle haze of *Autumn*, where the gutsy finale has splendid bite and energy.

Jaime Laredo's performance with the Scottish Chamber Orchestra – originally issued on Carlton – was always one of the most recommendable lower-priced versions, and now it comes with a well-chosen collection of baroque string lollipops, which is excellent in every way. The performance of *The Four Seasons* has great spontaneity and vitality, emphasized by the forward balance, which is nevertheless admirably realistic, as the bright upper range is balanced by a firm, resonant bass. Laredo plays with bravura and directs polished, strongly characterized accompaniments. Pacing tends to be on the fast side; although the reading is extrovert and the lyrical music – played responsively – is made to offer a series of interludes to contrast with the vigour of the allegros, the effect is exhilarating rather than aggressive. A first-class bargain.

Mutter on DG is above all deeply reflective, reacting emotionally to each movement, allowing herself a free expansiveness at generally broad speeds. Not surprisingly, this is a far more intimate reading than her previous version with Karajan and the Vienna Philharmonic, with sound bright and immediate so that dynamic contrasts are dramatically underlined, with Mutter less spotlit than most violin virtuosos tackling this work. With the Norwegian players consistently reacting as chamber-music partners, the result is a performance which repeatedly brings out mystery in these atmospheric sound-pictures. She takes a similarly romantic view of the Tartini, using Zandonai's string arrangement, as she did in her previous recording.

Perlman's imagination holds the sequence together superbly, and there are many passages of pure magic, as in the central *Adagio* of *Summer*. The digital remastering of the 1976 recording is managed admirably, the sound firm, clear and well balanced, with plenty of detail. Now this recording has been made much more competitive by the addition of three extra violin concertos, all fine works. Although the acoustic is somewhat dryish, this does not prevent these extra works from sounding very good.

Vladimir Spivakov's highly enjoyable 1988 account of Vivaldi's *Four Seasons* comes high on the list of bargain recommendations, and is made the more attractive by the inclusion of three other appealing and varied concertos. Indeed all three concertos are played with much sophistication and grace, as is the more famous main work, which, like its companions, is given an essentially chamber-scaled account; the very opposite of a larger-than-life full orchestral

version and yet not lacking in robust moments. *Spring* is tinglingly fresh, with much use made of light and shade, and Spivakov's sweet, classically focused timbre. There is plenty of vigour for the summer storms, and altogether this is highly refreshing, with the recording vivid and well balanced within the attractive background ambience of L'Église du Liban, Paris.

Karajan's 1972 recording of *The Four Seasons* was a popular success and remains very enjoyable. Its tonal beauty is not achieved at the expense of vitality and, although the harpsichord hardly ever comes through, the overall scale is acceptable. Michel Schwalbé is a memorable soloist; his playing is neat, precise and imaginative, with a touch of Italian sunshine in the tone. The remastering for DG's bargain label, Classikon, has restored the body and breadth of the original, and in the additional works (recorded in the St Moritz Französische Kirche in Switzerland two years earlier) the string-sound is glorious. The charismatic BPO playing, notably in the expressive *Sinfonia al Santo Sepolcro*, is difficult to resist, and the *Concerto alla rustica* sounds sumptuous.

The fine Schwalbé/Karajan version of the *Seasons* also comes as a DG Double as part of the 'Karajan Collection'; it is coupled with four concertos from *L'Estro armonico*, similarly recorded in 1972 but never issued until now. The string sound is gloriously, richly opulent, and the three soloists, with Thomas Brandis and Leon Spierer joining Schwalbé, play like richly haloed angels. However, the Bach coupling is less recommendable.

The novelty of the Helios issue is the inclusion of the sonnets which Vivaldi placed on his score to give his listeners a guide to the illustrative detail suggested by the music. Before each of the four concertos, the appropriate poem is read, first in a romantically effusive Italian manner and then in BBC English (the contrast very striking). On CD one can conveniently programme out these introductions. The performances are first class. Adelina Oprean is an excellent soloist, her reading full of youthful energy and expressive freshness; her timbre is clean and pure, her technique assured. Faerber matches her vitality, and the score's pictorial effects are boldly characterized in a vividly projected sound-picture.

In the DG version with Gidon Kremer and the LSO under Claudio Abbado, it is obvious from the first bar that Abbado is the dominating partner. The dramatization of Vivaldi's detailed pictorial effects is extremely vivid. The vigour of the dancing peasants is surpassed by the sheer fury and violence of the summer storms. Yet the delicacy of the gentle zephyrs is matched by the hazy somnolence of the beautiful *Adagio* of *Autumn*. After a freezingly evocative opening to *Winter*, Abbado creates a mandolin-like pizzicato effect in the slow movement (taken faster than the composer's marking) to simulate a rain shower. The finale opens delicately, but at the close the listener is almost blown away by the winter gales. Kremer matches Abbado's vigour with playing that combines sparkling bravura and suitably evocative expressive moments.

Kyung Wha Chung's joyful performance stands out for its freshness and spontaneity, with the soloist directing the St Luke's Chamber Ensemble. Here she seems totally relaxed in the studio, springing rhythms infectiously, defying period practice in warmly expressive phrasing at speeds that avoid extremes. This is music-making among friends, made the more vivid by the richness and immediacy of the recorded sound. The absence of a coupling makes it poor value, but admirers of Chung may not mind.

The BIS recording by Nils-Erik Sparf and the Drottningholm Baroque Ensemble has astonishing clarity and presence, and the playing is remarkable in its imaginative vitality. These Swedish players make the most of all the pictorial characterizations without ever overdoing them: they achieve the feat of making one hear this eminently familiar repertoire as if for the very first time.

The earlier performance by Kenneth Sillito, with the Virtuosi of England, stands out for its bold, clear sound, well focused and full of presence. Indeed the soloist is a shade too present, and this detracts a little from the gentler expressiveness. Yet Sillito's playing is both poetic and assured and, with such vivid projection, is full of personality. The same comments apply to the Albinoni concertos now offered as a fill-up.

La Petite Bande, with Kuijken as soloist and director, offers an authentic version of considerable appeal. Although the accompanying group can generate plenty of energy when Vivaldi's winds are blowing, this is essentially a small-scale reading, notable for its delicacy, and the result is refreshing. The new coupling is a pair of *Oboe Concertos* played on a characterfully squawky and not entirely tractable period instrument by Bruce Haynes. If the end result is less refined than the main work, the duck-like noises occasionally bring a smile.

Philips have returned Ayo's 1960 version with I Musici to the catalogue as one of their 'Great Recordings'. It is hardly that, and ought by rights to be restored to its previous bargain category. But the warm recording still sounds well and this will be enjoyed by those for whom sustained richness of string textures is paramount, even at the cost of vitality. Felix Ayo produces lovely tone, both here and in the bonus concerto, and he certainly plays stylishly. But at 57 minutes this CD seems expensive.

Kennedy's CD account is among the more spectacular in conveying the music's imagery, with *Autumn* involving controversially weird special effects, including glissando harmonics in the slow movement and percussive applications of the wooden part of the bow to add rhythmic pungency to the hunting finale. There is plenty of vivid detail elsewhere. The ECO's playing is always responsive, to match the often very exciting bravura of its soloist, and allegros have an agreeable vitality. However, at 41 minutes, with no fillers, this is not generous and it would not be our first choice for repeated listening.

Our early reaction to Stokowski's 1966 Phase 4 recording was to describe the conductor's 'wilful unstylishness' as 'endearingly wrong-headed'. It still is, and the result will be anathema to authenticists; but now we are inclined to take a more indulgent view. Stokowski always cared about the lavishness of his string-textures, and here they are lusciously rich, with radiant *pianissimos*. The mellowness of the approach – with sensuous warmth in *Spring* and *Summer* alike, and *Winter* far from freezing – tends to act against Vivaldi's intended contrasts, and additionally there are unmarked ritenutos at the end of each allegro. But Hugh Bean is a highly sensitive soloist, and it is only too easy to wallow in Stokowski's glorious opulence of texture when the CD transfer is so sympathetically managed by Pascal Byrne, in the true spirit of the conductor's intentions.

(i) *The Four Seasons; Bassoon Concerto in E min., RV 484; Flute Concerto in G min. (La notte), RV 439; Double Mandolin Concerto in G, RV 575; Double Concerto for Oboe & Violin in B flat, RV 548; Concerto for Orchestra 'con molti

instromenti', RV 550; Concerto for Strings in G (Alla rustica), RV 151; Concerto for 4 Violins (from L'estro armonico), RV 549; (ii) Gloria in D, RV 589*
(B) *** DG Panorama 469 220-2 (2). (i) Standage; (ii) Smith, Argenta, Wyn Rogers, E. Concert Ch.; E. Concert & Soloists, Pinnock

Pinnock's Archiv performance of *The Four Seasons* was always among the top contenders for the period-instrument crown (see above). It had the advantage of using a newly discovered set of parts found in Manchester's Henry Watson Music Libary which additionally brought the correction of minor textual errors in the La Cène text in normal use. The overall effect is essentially refined, treating the pictorial imagery with subtlety. Now it is joined by a collection of half a dozen favourite concertos in lively, refreshing performances with fine solo playing from wind and string players alike, again using period instruments in the most enticing way. As an added bonus we are offered a lively and vivid account of the favourite Vivaldi choral work, very well sung and played, with excellent soloists. An admirable introduction to the composer and thoroughly worthwhile for the experienced collector as well as the newcomer. Excellent recording too.

The Four Seasons, Op. 8/1–4 (arr. for flute and strings)
(M) *** RCA (ADD) GD 60748. Galway, Zagreb Soloists

James Galway's sensitive transcription is so convincing that at times one is tempted to believe that the work was conceived in this form. The playing is marvellous, full of detail and imagination, and the recording is excellent, even if the flute is given a forward balance, the more striking on CD.

Violin Concertos, Op. 8: 5 in E flat (La tempesta di mare), RV 253; 6 in C (Il piacere), RV 108; 10 in B flat (La caccia), RV 362; 11 in D, RV 210; in C min. (Il sospetto), RV 199
(B) *** CfP 767 2662. Menuhin, Polish CO, Maksymiuk

Menuhin's collection of five concertos – four of them with nicknames and particularly delightful – brings some of his freshest, most intense playing. Particularly in slow movements – notably that of *Il piacere* ('pleasure') – he shows afresh his unique insight in shaping a phrase. Fresh, alert accompaniment and full digital recording.

La cetra (12 Violin Concertos), Op. 9
(BB) *** Virgin 2x1 5 61594-2 (2). Huggett, Raglan Bar. Players, Kraemer
(B) ** Ph. (ADD) 473 310-2 (2). I Musici

(i) *La cetra; (ii) Double Oboe Concerto in D min., RV 535; (iii) Piccolo Concerto in C, RV 443*
☞ ✿ (B) *** Double Decca 448 110-2 (2). (i) I. Brown, ASMF; (ii) Black; (iii) Nicklin; both with ASMF, Marriner

Iona Brown here acts as director in the place of Sir Neville Marriner. So resilient and imaginative are the results that one detects no difference from the immaculate and stylish Vivaldi playing in earlier Academy Vivaldi sets. There is some wonderful music here; the later concertos are every bit the equal of anything in *The Trial between Harmony and Invention*, and they are played gloriously. The recording too is outstandingly rich and vivid, even by earlier Argo standards with this group, and the Decca transfer to CD retains the demonstration excellence of the original analogue LPs, with a yet greater sense of body and presence. For the Double Decca reissue, two of Vivaldi's most engaging wind concertos have been added, winningly played by two fine Academy soloists. The sound is just as fine as in the concertos for violin.

Monica Huggett and the Raglan Baroque Players offer performances so accomplished and in such good style that they are unlikely to be surpassed in authentic-instrument versions of *La cetra*. She is in excellent form and her virtuosity always appears effortless. The Raglan Baroque Players are of the same size as the Academy of Ancient Music and some players are common to both groups. First-class recording.

I Musici's 1964 set of Vivaldi's Op. 9 concertos remains an agreeable modern-instrument set, with full sound and a realistic balance. With Ayo as the principal soloist, the playing is lively and expressively rich, although by modern standards it is sometimes stylistically rather over-ample and heavy in slow movements. The continuo part is played on an organ throughout.

6 Flute Concertos, Op. 10; Flute Concertos: in A min., RV 108; in D, RV 429; in G, RV 438; in A min., RV 440; in C min., RV 441; (i) Double Flute Concerto in C, RV 533. Piccolo Concerto in A min., RV 445

(B) *** Ph. (IMS) Duo (ADD) 454 256-2 (2). Gazzelloni, I Musici; (i) with Steinberg

This Duo set purports to contain Vivaldi's 'complete flute concertos', but it is an unlikely claim: the works for sopranino recorder, RV 443 and 444, are not here, nor is the arrangement of *La notte* (RV 104) which includes also a bassoon. However, the solo flute version is (Op. 10/2) and, with its movements representing ghosts (*Fantasmi*) and sleep (*Il sonno*), is a masterpiece by any standards. A Duo collection entirely made up of concertante works for flute might be thought a rather daunting prospect, but Gazzelloni is an artist of such quality and poetry that such doubts are banished. And it must be added that these concertos all show Vivaldi in the best light, not only in the best known, *La tempesta di mare* and *Il gardellino*, from Op. 10, but in many of the miscellaneous concertos, too: witness the delicate slow movement of the *A minor*, RV 440, the touching *Largo* of the *C minor*, RV 441, or the lively opening movements of the *D major*, RV 429, and *A minor*, RV 108. In these modern-instrument performances Gazzelloni's tone is admirably fresh and clean, with I Musici giving him splendid support. The analogue recordings (from the 1960s and 1970s) are first rate.

6 Flute Concertos, Op. 10

⊕— *** DG (IMS) 437 839-2. Gallois, Orpheus CO

(BB) *** Regis RRC 1077. Hall, Divertimenti of L., Barritt

(BB) **(*) Naxos 8.553101. Drahos, Nicolaus Esterházy Sinf.

The Patrick Gallois/Orpheus version on DG is the lightest and most spirited of any, be they on period instruments or not. Collectors who recall Gallois's dazzling account of the Nielsen *Concerto* will know what to expect: effortless virtuosity, refined musicianship, intelligence and taste. He has an excellent rapport with the splendid Orpheus Chamber Orchestra and is very well served too by the engineers. A most distinguished issue.

Judith Hall's record of the Op. 10 *Flute Concertos* is fresh and brightly recorded, and she plays with great virtuosity and fine taste. The Divertimenti of London is a modern-instrument group and the players are both sensitive and alert. At budget price this is distinctly competitive.

Béla Drahos is an excellent soloist on Naxos, and he phrases very musically: the *siciliana* slow movement of *Il gardellino* is beautifully played. He gets lively support from the Nicolaus Esterházy Sinfonia, who are also suitably gentle

and evocative in the dream world of *La notte*. The *C minor Concerto* makes a welcome bonus, for in the finale the Goldfinch of *Il gardellino* appears to have flown back in through the window.

Flute Concertos Op. 10/1–6; Flute Concertos in: A min., P.80; G, P.118; E min., P.139; G, P.140; G, P.141; E min., P.142; D, P.203; D, P.205; C min., P.440; Concerto for Flute & 2 Violins in A min.; Double Flute Concerto, P.76; Piccolo Concertos in C, P.78 & P.79

(B) **(*) Sony (ADD) SB2K 89981 (2). Rampal, I Sol. Ven., Scimone

Jean-Pierre Rampal is without a doubt the aristocrat of the modern flute, with a silvery timbre which sets him apart. His art is much in evidence in these performances in which his vitality and superb sense of style is matched by Vivaldi's seemingly inexhaustible invention. The Op. 10 set of flute concertos is self-recommending, but there is always fresh delight in exploring the less well-known works. Especially enjoyable are the minor key concertos – and just sample the *Double Concerto* for sheer effervescence (Sony do not reveal the other player's identity), or the short, cheerful one-movement of the *G major Concerto*, P.141. The principal reservation on this release is the variable quality of the sound: the flute tone is generally truthful, but the string quality is not particularly ingratiating, rather glassy and unyielding, which is a bit wearing after a while. This is a pity as Scimone secures some lively playing from I Solisti Veneti. Sony are also coy about the recording dates, but it is assumed that they emanate from the 1960s.

Flute Concertos: Op. 10/1-6; in G, RV 414; in D, RV 427.

(N) (BB) **(*) Warner Apex 2564 60373-2. Rampal, Sol. Ven., Scimone

Jean-Pierre Rampal was an aristocrat among flautists and it is surprising that his set of Op. 10, dating from 1966, has not resurfaced until now. His performances of the enigmatic *Fantasmi* of *La Notte*, the delightful *Cantabile siciliana* of *Il Gardellino*, the charmingly elegant opening movement of the *F major Concerto* (No. 5), and the rollicking and echoing finale of the last concerto of the set show him at his masterly best. His playing in the two additional concertos offered as a bonus is no less delectable. Scimone and I Solisti Veneti provide more than acceptable accompaniments, and the sound is good, if not as transparent as we would expect today.

Flute Concertos, Op.10/1 (Tempesta di mare); 2 (La Notte); 3 (Il Gardellino); in G, A min. & C min., F VI/6, 7 & 11.

(N) (M) ** Häns. 94.007. Dambrine, Ens. La Partita

Sylvia Dambrine, brightly recorded, plays nimbly in allegros, but she tends to languish in slow movements, notably so in the *Cantabile* of *Il Gardellino*, which loses much of its *siciliana* character. Otherwise these performances are enjoyable enough, if not distinctive, and La Partita accompany her stylishly enough on modern instruments.

(i; ii) *Flute Concertos. Op. 10: 1 in F (La tempesta di mare), RV 433; 2 in G min. (La notte), RV 439; 3 in D (Il gardellino), RV 428; (i; iii) 5 in F, RV 434. Flute Concerto in A min., RV 108s; Sopranino Recorder (Piccolo) Concertos: in C, RV 553.*

(BB) *** Naxos 8.554053. Soloists; (i) Capella Istropolitana, (ii) Krechek; (i; iii) Dohnányi; (iv) City of L. Sinfonia, Kraemer

An attractive regrouping of Naxos recordings (78 minutes)

brings a particularly generous clutch of modern-instrument performances that will especially suit those who want only the most famous named concertos from Op. 10. They are most persuasively played and the recording is excellent throughout.

Complete bassoon concertos

Bassoon Concertos: in C, RV 466; in C, RV 467; in C, RV 469; in C, RV 470; in C, RV 471; in C, RV 472; in C, RV 473; in C, RV 474; in C, RV 475; in C, RV 476; in C, RV 477; in C, RV 478; in C, RV 479; in C min., RV 480; in D min., RV 481; in E flat, RV 483; in E min., RV 484; in F, RV 485; in F, RV 486; in F, RV 487; in F, RV 488; in F, RV 489; in F, RV 490; in F, RV 491; in G, RV 492; in G, RV 493; in G, RV 494; in G min., RV 495; in G min., RV 496; in A min., RV 497; in A min., RV 498; in A min., RV 499; in A min., RV 500; in B flat (La notte), RV 501; in B flat, RV 502; in B flat, RV 503; in B flat, RV 504

(M) *** ASV CDDCS 552 (5). Smith, ECO, Ledger; Zagreb Soloists, Ninic

The bassoon brought out a generous fund of inspiration in Vivaldi, for few of his 37 concertos for that instrument are in any way routine. Daniel Smith plays with constant freshness and enthusiasm. His woody tone is very attractive and he is very well caught by the engineers. This set can be welcomed almost without reservation and, dipped into, the various recordings will always give pleasure. Even if some of the more complicated roulades are not executed with exact precision, Smith's playing has undoubted flair. For the last three CDs of the series the Zagreb Soloists take over the accompaniments and offer alert, vivacious playing that adds to the pleasure of these warm, affectionate performances. Daniel Smith, too, responds with vigour and polish.

Bassoon Concertos, RV 471/473; 481/2; 484; 491/497; 499/500; 503/4

(B) *** Ph. Duo 475 233-2 (2). Thunemann, I Musici

Apart from the complete cycle by Daniel Smith on ASV, which has some rough edges, this is the most impressive survey of Vivaldi's bassoon concertos on CD. Moreover, Klaus Thunemann makes every work seem a masterpiece. His virtuosity is remarkable and it is always at the composer's service, while the polish of the playing is matched by its character and warmth. I Musici are on their finest form, and all the slow movements here are touchingly expressive, with Thunemann's ease of execution adding to the enjoyment. With the Philips recording in the demonstration bracket, this reissue demonstrates just how well Vivaldi's music can sound on modern instruments.

Complete Bassoon Concertos, Vol. 1: Concertos, RV 471, RV 476, RV 480, RV 487, RV 493, RV 498, RV 503

(N) (BB) *** Naxos 8.555937. Benkócs, Nicolaus Esterházy Sinfonia, Drahos

Complete Bassoon Concertos, Vol. 2: Concertos, RV 467, RV 475, RV 486, RV 488 (La Notte), RV 501, RV 504

(N) (BB) *** Naxos 8.555938. Benkócs, Nicolaus Esterházy Sinf., Drahos

This excellent new Naxos survey seems set eventually to upstage Daniel Smith on ASV, and certainly to match the excellent recordings of Klaus Thunemann on Philips. Tamás Benkócs is a splendid, personable bassoonist, his expressive

colouring matching his easy but sometimes remarkable bravura. Moreover, Béla Drahos supports him with accompaniments that are warmly phrased in slow movements and full of vitality in allegros. If anything, the second collection (which includes the solo version of *La Notte*) is more stimulating and lively than the first, and both make a good case for playing Vivaldi on modern instruments. The recording too is resonantly full without clouding detail; the balance, with the bassoon given a real presence, is very satisfactory.

Bassoon Concerto in F, RV 485; (i) *Double Concerto in G min., for Recorder & Bassoon (La notte), RV 104*

*** BIS CD 271. McGraw, (i) Pehrsson; Drottningholm Bar. Ens. – TELEMANN: *Concertos* ***

The concerto subtitled *La notte* exists in three versions: one for flute (the most familiar), RV 439; another for bassoon, RV 501; and the present version, RV 104. Clas Pehrsson, Michael McGraw and the Drottningholm Baroque Ensemble give a thoroughly splendid account of it, and the *Bassoon Concerto in F major* also fares well. Excellent recording.

Complete cello concertos

Cello Concertos: in C, RV 398 & 399; in C, RV 400; in C min., RV 401/402; in D, RV 403/404; in D min., RV 405/406/407; in E flat, RV 408; in F, RV 410/411/412; in G, RV 413/414; in G min., RV 416/417; in A min., RV 418/419/420/421/422; in B flat, RV 423; in B min., RV 424; Concerto Movement in D min., RV 438; Double Cello Concerto in G min., RV 531; (i) *Double Concerto in E min., for Cello & Bassoon, RV 409;* (ii) *Double Concerto: in B flat for Violin & Cello, RV 544; (Il Proteo o sia il mondo al rovesco), RV 547*

(N) (BB) *** Naxos 8.550907 (*RV 398–9; 404; 406; 410; 412; 419*); 8.550908 (*RV 400–401; 408; 413; 422; 531*, with Keith Harvey); 8.550909 (*RV 402–3; 407; 409*, with Joanna Graham; *418; 423–4*); 8.550910 (*RV 405; 411; 414; 416–17; 420–21*) (available separately). Wallfisch, City of L. Sinfonia, Kraemer

(N) (B) *** RCA 82876 67886-2 (4) (without *RV 398, 400, 421, 531*). Harnoy, Toronto CO, Robinson; with (i) James MacKay; (ii) Igor Oistrakh

Vivaldi liked to write for instruments playing in the middle and lower register, favouring both the bassoon and cello (the latter a relatively new instrument in his time, having taken the place of the viola da gamba as a favoured solo instrument). Here are two highly recommendable recordings of Vivaldi's 'complete' *Cello Concertos*; neither is quite complete, but if it is the 27 solo concertos you are most concerned with, then Raphael Wallfisch offers them all, including the sole *Double Cello Concerto*, RV 531 (which Ofra Harnoy omits), and the *Concerto for Cello and Bassoon*, RV 409. Harnoy, however, includes the pair of *Double Concertos with Violin* (which the Naxos set omits). Here she achieves an excellent partnership with Igor Oistrakh, and in the work with the subtitle 'Il Proteo' the *Adagio* is particularly touching. Hers are traditional performances with modern instruments; she plays with style, impeccable technique and eloquence. In short, she is a first-rate artist with a good lyrical sense. Her strength lies not so much in her tone, which is not big, but in her selfless approach to this repertoire. She does not regard this music as a vehicle for her own personality, but plays it with agreeable dedication and a delight in its considerable felicities. She is given good support from the Toronto Chamber Orchestra and is very well recorded.

The Naxos series is part of a planned overall survey, and in the solo concertos the choice of Raphael Wallfisch could hardly have been bettered. He forms an admirable partnership with the City of London Sinfonia, directed from the harpsichord or chamber organ by Nicholas Kraemer, so that, although not using period instruments, the effect is as authentic as you could want. Kraemer's use of the organ continuo, both in tutti and to underpin the solo cello line (in RV 419, for instance), is most effective, while in allegros the alert, resilient orchestral strings are a pleasure in themselves. Wallfisch plays with a restrained use of vibrato and a nicely judged expressive feeling, and in the *Double Concerto* (which he shares with Keith Harvey), there is much bustling interchange in the outer movements, with the soloists answering each other eloquently in the *Largo*.

Volume 3 (8.550909) is a particularly fine collection, including the *E minor Double Concerto*, RV 409, where the cello is joined by a subservient and somewhat doleful solo bassoon; but Volume 4 brings a further batch of concertos notable for their vitality and the vigorous bravura demanded from the soloist. Throughout these four Naxos discs there is never a hint of routine; the recording is vividly realistic and the balance very well judged indeed. We originally awarded a token Rosette to Volume 3, but the accolade could surely apply to any of the four discs here which all stand up very high indeed in the Vivaldi discography.

Cello Concerto in D min., RV 406.

(M) *** Warner Elatus 0927 49839-2. Rostropovich, St Paul CO, Hugh Wolff – C. P. E. BACH; TARTINI: *Concertos* ***

Who says that modern chamber orchestras cannot achieve the same transparency as period ensembles? Admittedly the Saint Paul Chamber Orchestra have had the advantage of Christopher Hogwood's presence, but the sound they produce blends transparency of texture with warmth and subtlety of colouring. Rostropovich is as masterly and eloquent as one could imagine, and he is accorded excellently balanced sound.

Flute concertos, Vol. 1: *Chamber Concertos: in C, for Flute, Oboe, Violin, Bassoon & Continuo, RV 88; in D, for Flute & 2 Violins, RV 89; in D, for Flute, Violin, Bassoon & Continuo (Il gardellino), RV 90; in D, RV 91; in D min., RV 96 (both for Flute, Violin, Bassoon & Continuo); in F, RV 99; in G min., RV 107 (both for Flute, Oboe, Violin, Bassoon & Continuo)*

(BB) *** Naxos 8.553365. Drahos and soloists, Nicolaus Esterházy Sinf.

This Naxos disc collects multiple concertos, but with a continuo instead of an orchestra. Although not to be played at a single sitting, these works offer a great deal of pleasure, stemming from their rich textural interplay with plenty of imitation among the soloists. The quality of invention is astonishingly high. *Il gardellino* (which opens the programme) is justly famous, but the *G minor* work, RV 107, is also remarkable, with a touching *siciliano* slow movement; it ends with a chaconne which maintains the minor key. RV 88 has a strikingly cheerful opening movement, then gives prominence to the flute both in its central *Largo cantabile* and in another chirping finale. RV 89 effectively brings a change of colour in the use of a pair of violins in juxtaposition to the flute. The performances here are admirable and the recording is most effectively balanced.

Flute Concertos: in A min., RV 108; in F, RV 434; Double Flute Concerto in C, RV 533; Sopranino Recorder Concertos: in C, RV 443 & RV 444; in A min., RV 445

(BB) *** Naxos 8.550385. Jálek, Novotny, Stivin, Capella Istropolitana, Dohnányi

The Capella Istropolitana, who are drawn from the excellent Slovak Philharmonic, play with vitality and sensitivity for Oliver Dohnányi and the soloists show appropriate virtuosity and flair. As always, there are rewards and surprises in this music. The sound is very good indeed, and so is the balance.

Flute Concertos: in D, RV 427 & RV 429; in E min., RV 431 & RV 432; in G, RV 436; RV 438 & RV 438 bis; in A min., RV 440; in C, RV 533

(N) *** Naïve Opus 111 OP 30298. Barthold Kuijken, Academia Montis Regale

If Jean-Pierre Rampal was the patrician among flautists of the 1950s and 1960s, it was Barthold Kuijken who took his place in the 1960s and 1970s, after discovering and mastering an original baroque instrument. For the present recordings he plays a copy of a Belgian transverse flute of 1735, while the Academia Montis Regale accompany him smoothly, proficiently and spiritedly on comparable period instruments. For the programme here he turned to a collection of manuscripts in the Turin Library, from which the *A minor Concerto*, RV 440, stands out, while Vivaldi's sole *Concerto for Two Flutes*, RV 533, is made doubly charming by the use of a bassoon continuo throughout. The *Concerto in G major*, K. 438, also features the bassoon in duet with the flute in the *Andante*, and the *Largo* of RV 436 proves to be rather similar, but with a cello in place of a bassoon. The other concertos here are all elegant and attractive works. None is as spectacular as the Op. 10 set, but their simplicity is also their virtue. The two E minor works, RV 431 and 432, have come down to us incomplete: the sprightly finale of the former is used to end the programme vivaciously. The performances could hardly be more authentic, and the recording is excellent.

Guitar Concertos in C, RV 82; in D, RV 93

(M) *** DG (IMS) (ADD) 439 984-2. Behrend, I Musici – CARULLI: *Concerto in A*; GIULIANI: *Concerto in A, Op. 30* ***

Both these concertos are transcriptions of chamber works intended for the lute. They work well on guitar and are most elegantly played here. Although – as the opening of the *D major* shows – there is no lack of life in these smooth, elegant performances, a more robust and sinewy approach can be more telling in this repertoire.

Guitar Concertos: in D, RV 93 (arr. Malipiero); in A (arr. Pujol from *Trio Sonata in C, RV 82*); (i) *Double Concerto for Guitar & Viola d'amore in D min., RV 540* (arr. Malipiero)

(B) **(*) Decca 448 709-2. Fernández, ECO, Malcolm, (i) with Blume – GIULIANI: *Concerto*; PAGANINI: *Sonata* **(*)

Eduardo Fernández is a musician's guitarist whose playing is consistently refined and sensitive, always responsive to the composer's needs, if at times perhaps a little too self-effacing. The performance of the *Double Concerto for Guitar and Viola d'amore* is winningly intimate, particularly in the very gentle central *Largo*, in which Fernández is perfectly balanced with Norbert Blume. The solo concertos are similarly refined, with bravura unexaggerated and Malcolm always providing the most understanding and polished accompaniments. The recording is first class and beautifully balanced.

Mandolin Concertos in D, RV 93; C, RV 425; (i) Double Mandolin Concerto in G, RV 532; Concerto for 2 Flutes, 2 Chalumeaux, 2 Violins ('In tromba marina'), 2 Mandolins, 2 Theorbos & Cello in C, RV 558

● (BB) *** Warner Apex 2564 61264-2. Orlandi; (i) Frati; soloists, Sol. Ven., Scimone

It is good to have a budget CD with excellent performances of the two solo *Mandolin Concertos* and the *Double Mandolin Concerto*, presented with style and delicacy and with the colourful *Concerto con molti istromenti* thrown in for good measure. The recording is very good indeed.

Mandolin Concerto in C, RV 425; Double Mandolin Concerto in G, RV 532; (Soprano) Lute Concerto in D, RV 93; Double Concerto in D min. for Viola d'amore & Lute, RV 540. Trios: in C, RV 82; in G min., RV 85

*** Hyp. CDA 66160. Jeffrey, O'Dette, Parley of Instruments, Goodman and Holman

These are chamber performances, with one instrument to each part, providing an ideal balance for the *Mandolin Concertos*. An organ continuo replaces the usual harpsichord, and very effective it is; in the *Trios* and the *Lute Concerto* (but not in the *Double Concerto*, RV 540) Paul O'Dette uses a gut-strung soprano lute. The delightful sounds here, with all players using period instruments, are very convincing. The recording is realistically balanced within an attractively spacious acoustic.

(i) Mandolin Concerto in C, RV 425; (ii) Double Concerto for 2 Mandolins in G, RV 532. Concerti con molti strumenti: Concerto for Violin & 2 Flutes diritti; 3 Oboes & Bassoon (Dedicated to a Sua Altezza Reale di Sassonia), RV 576; Concerto for 2 violins in tromba marina, 2 Flutes diritti, 2 Mandolins, 2 Salmoe, 2 Theorbos & Cello, RV 558; Concerto for Violin Solo, 2 Oboes & Bassoon (dedicated to S. Pisandel) (Dresden version), RV 319; Concerto for 2 Violins & 2 Cellos in D, RV 564; Concerto in C for 3 Violins, Oboe & 2 Flutes diritti; 2 Viole all'inglese, Salmoe, 2 Cellos, 2 Harpsichords & 2 Violins in tromba marina, RV 555

● *** Virgin 5 45527-2. (i) Scaramuzzino; (ii) Maurer; soloists, Europa Galante, Biondi

Another excellent disc from Fabio Biondi and his outstanding period-instrument group. The two simple *Mandolin Concertos* are played intimately and are perfectly balanced. The *Concerti con molti strumenti* offer an extraordinary range of tone colour, especially the extravagantly scored *C major Concerto*, RV 555. In the *Largo* of this work the violin plays an obbligato line to the two solo harpsichords, which are given alternating arpeggios in a pendulum style, embroidering them *a piacimento* ('as they please'). Toussaint Loviko, who provides the excellent notes, tells us that Vivaldi's girl musicians were hidden by grilles curtained with black gauze, so they were able to exchange instruments at will and were thus able to surprise their listeners.

Oboe Concertos in C, RV 447 & RV 451; in F, RV 455 & RV 457; in A min., RV 461 & RV 463

(BB) *** Naxos 8.550860. Schilli, Budapest Failoni CO, Nagy

Oboe Concertos in C, RV 450 & RV 452; in D, RV 453; in D min., RV 454; (i) Double Oboe Concertos in C, RV 534; D min., RV 535; A min., RV 536

(BB) *** Naxos 8.550859. Schilli; (i) with Jonas; Budapest Failoni CO, Nagy

Excellent playing from these Budapest musicians. The second of these two discs offers the three *Double Concertos*, and the two CDs between them include half the solo works. They are often surprisingly florid, requiring considerable bravura from the soloist. A good example is the Minuet finale of RV 447, which is a cross between a Rondo and a theme and variations. Vivaldi is never entirely predictable, except that his invention never seems to flag, and many of the simple *Grave*, *Larghetto* and *Largo* slow movements are very pleasing indeed.

The oboe's syncopated theme in the *D minor Concerto*, heard against chromatically swerving strings, is especially diverting and the following *Largo*, with its organ continuo, is quite lovely. The *Allegro molto* which opens RV 451 shows Dombrecht's virtuosity (and that of the orchestra) at its most sparkling, and the piquant finale is no less diverting. This CD, very well recorded, is a real collector's item.

Oboe Concertos in A min., RV 461; B flat, RV 464; C, RV 64, RV 447 & RV 452; D, RV 453; D min., RV 454; F, RV 456

(BB) **(*) Warner Apex 0927 48724-2 (ADD). Pierlot, I Sol. Ven., Scimone

Pierre Pierlot generously offers eight well-recorded concertos at budget price, and they are played neatly, with stylish accompaniment by Scimone. If the last degree of individuality is missing, this is still a worthwhile and enjoyable collection.

Recorder Concertos for Alto Recorder in D (Il gardellino), RV 428; in G, RV 425; for Flautino in C, RV 443 & RV 444; in A min., RV 445. Chamber Concertos in D for Alto Recorder, Violin & Continuo, RV 92; in A min., for Alto Recorder, 2 Violins & Continuo, RV 108

**(*) BIS CD 865. Laurin, Bach Collegium, Japan, Masaaki Suzuki

The BIS Collection, with Dan Laurin as soloist, includes three concertos for flautino ('little flute'). This is not a piccolo, but a minor member of the recorder family, with a small, piquant timbre, which balances well with period strings, as the three quite engaging but very similar concertos here effectively demonstrate. The performance of *Il gardellino* (from Op. 10) is the highlight of the programme, very effectively using an organ continuo in the siciliana *Largo*, and the *G major Concerto*, RV 425, is hardly less impressive. Of the other two chamber works with continuo, the *Double Concerto* with violin is rather pale and lacking in profile, but the *A minor Concerto* with two violins is stronger with an attractive finale. Even so this well-recorded anthology is not nearly as vivid as the Hyperion collection of chamber concertos for recorder (see below).

Recorder Concertos: for Treble Recorder, RV 441 & 442; for Sopranino Recorder, RV 443, 444 & 445; Chamber Concerto for Recorder, Bassoon, Oboe, Cello, & Violin Continuo (La Pastorella), RV 95

(N) (BB) *** Naxos 8.553829. Kecskeméti, Czidra & Soloists, Nicolaus Esterházy Sinfonia, Zalay

Another collection in the outstanding Naxos series of wind concertos, this purports to include all those for solo recorder, which it doesn't. However, the performances from László Kecskeméti of the three works for the sopranino instrument are dazzling (though not to be played in a row); then follow the two fine works for treble recorder, the first of which is played by László Czidra with equal skill. Kecskeméti then takes over for the rest of the programme, which ends with the chamber concerto, *La Pastorella*. This is the highlight of the collection, one of the composer's masterpieces, delightful in its range of colour and imitative echo effects, and indeed its *siciliano* slow movement and ingenious fugal finale. Splendid contributions from the players of the Nicolaus Esterházy Sinfonia throughout, and excellent recording.

**Concertos for Strings, Vol. 1: Paris Concertos 1 in G min.
(with woodwind), RV 157; 2 in E min., RV 133; 3 in C min.,
RV 119; 4 in F, RV 136; 5 in C (with woodwind), RV 114; 6 in
G min., RV 154; 7 in A, RV 160; 8 in D min., RV 127; 9 in B
flat, RV 164; 10 in D, RV 121; 11 in G (with woodwind), RV
150; 12 in A, RV 159**
*** Chan. 0547. Col. Mus. 90, Standage

Vivaldi wrote over forty *concerti a quattro* for strings alone, without a soloist, and the present group were gathered together in a single manuscript, written in the hand of Vivaldi's father, and have been preserved in the Paris Conservatoire Library ever since. They are each in three movements, with the central slow movement quite brief and acting as an expressive interlude linking the two vivacious framing allegros. The exception is RV 114, which is in two movements, the first moving from a sharply dotted *Allegro* to *Adagio*, with a jolly *Chaconne* to round things off. RV 133 has a striking *Rondeau* finale, and it is thought that these two works may have been composed separately from the others. They are all freshly inventive and played here with springing rhythms and plenty of vitality. In three concertos, though not specified by the composer, woodwind have been added to give extra colour. The touch of abrasiveness on the string sound is aurally bracing, and slow movements have a nicely ruminative improvisatory feel. The recording is first class.

**Concertos for Strings, Vol. 2: in C, RV 109; in C (with flutes),
RV 112; in C (with flutes), RV 117; in C min., RV 120; in D,
RV 124; in D min., RV 128; in F min., RV 143; in G min.
(Concerto ripieno; with woodwind), RV 152; in G min., RV
153; in B flat (with woodwind), RV 162; Conca, RV 163; in B
min., RV 168.**
(N) *** Chan. 0668. Col. Mus. 90, Standage

**Concertos for Strings, Vol. 3: in C, RV 110; in C (Concerto
ripieno; with woodwind), RV 115; in C min. (with
woodwind), RV 118; in D min. (Concerto madrigalesco), RV
129; in E min., RV 134; in F, RV 142; in G, RV 145; in G
(Concerto alla rustica), RV 151; in G min., RV 156; in C
(Concerto ripieno), RV 158; in A min., RV 161; in B flat, RV
166; in B flat, RV 167**
(N) *** Chan. 0687. Col. Mus. 90, Standage

Volumes 2 and 3 continue to demonstrate the amazing variety of invention in these concertos for strings, some of which have added woodwind, with the pair using additional flutes. In Volume 2, RV 112 and RV 117 are particularly attractive. But the works using strings alone are by no means second best, as RV 153 in *G minor* readily shows. The concerto subtitled *Conca* rather bizarrely seeks to portray a Bohemian 'conch', a primitive folk instrument which in the last movement simulates a 'hee-haw'. Elsewhere, more seriously, Vivaldi often uses a contrapuntal style to stimulating effect, as in the first

movement of RV 143, while the finales of RV 120 and RV 124 both introduce a fugato based on a scalic figure, falling in the D major work, and rising in the *C minor Concerto*.

Volume 3 opens with a *Concerto ripieno* (RV 158), but Simon Standage has chosen to present this without additional woodwind, although two other concertos are augmented. Some of the concertos here are rather plain, but this third collection includes two well-known masterpieces, the *Concerto alla rustica* and the *Concerto madrigalesco*. The performances from Standage and his Collegium Musicum 90 are full of life and expressively penetrating throughout both discs; the recording is as fine as ever.

**Concertos for Strings: in C, RV 113 & RV 114; in D min., RV
127; in F, RV 138; in G (Alla rustica), RV 151; in G min., RV
153, RV 156 & RV 157; in A min., RV 161; in B flat, RV 167**
(BB) **(*) Naxos 8.553742. Accademia I Filarmonici, Martini

The Accademia I Filarmonici is a conductorless chamber orchestra, to some extent led from the bow by Alberto Martini. They do not use period instruments, but their style, brisk and athletic, with comparatively lean textures, is well removed from that of I Musici. They make the most of this group of Vivaldi's string concertos – which might equally well have been called sinfonias. The only famous one is *Alla rustica*, which is vigorously done. Slow movements are delicate in texture, with the harpsichord continuo coming through naturally. Not all this music is equally appealing, but the best movements are memorable, for instance the jogging opening allegro of RV 113 and its minor-key *Grave* slow movement. Excellent recording.

**Concertos for Strings: in D, Op. 12/3, RV 124; in D min.
(Madrigalesco), RV 129; Sinfonia and Sonata al Santo
Sepolcro, RV 130; (i) In furore iustissimae irae, RV 626;
Laudate pueri Dominum, RV 601.**
☛ (N) (M) *** Chan. 0714X. (i) Bott; Augmented Purcell Qt

Framed by the *Sonata a quattro* and *Sinfonia al Santo Sepolcro*, which are among Vivaldi's most dramatically intense and poignant string works, this collection includes also two of his most original concertos, including the 'Madrigalesco' (which draws its material from his sacred vocal works) and the harmonically abrasive *Concerto a quattro*, which closes with a passionate fugue. The playing here is fully worthy of this remarkable music, uniting rigour with expressive fervour.

But this is Catherine Bott's record, and she gives a superb performance of the motet, *In furore iustissimae irae*, moving from fiery vocal bravura in expressing heaven's righteous anger to the limpid beauty of the lament, *Tunc meus fletus*. Her performance of *Laudate pueri Dominum*, Vivaldi's third setting of the Vesper Psalm (112) is equally memorable, dramatic and ravishing by turns, especially in her touching duet with the solo flute (Stephen Preston) in the *Gloria Patri*.

**Concertos for Strings in D min. (Concerto madrigalesco), RV
129; in G (Alla rustica), RV 151; in G min., RV 157. (i) Motet:
In turbato mare irato, RV 627; Cantata: Lungi dal vago volto,
RV 680. Magnificat, RV 610**
☛ (N) (BB) *** Hyp. Helios CDH 55190. (i) Kirkby; Leblanc,
Forget, Cunningham, Ingram, Tafelmusik Ch. & Bar. O,
Lamon

Mingling vocal and instrumental items, and works both well-known and unfamiliar, Jean Lamon provides a delightful collection, with Emma Kirkby a sparkling, pure-toned soloist in two items never recorded before: the motet, *In turbato mare irato*, and the chamber cantata, *Lungi dal vago volto*. The performance is lively, with fresh choral sound. The Tafelmusik performers come from Canada, and though the use of period instruments has some roughness, their vigour and alertness amply make up for that. Good, clear recorded sound.

Viola d'amore Concertos in D, RV 392; in D min., RV 393, RV 394 & RV 395; in A, RV 396; in D min., RV 397
(N) (BB) **(*) Hyp. Helios CDH 55178. Mackintosh, OAE

The viola d'amore was greatly admired in Vivaldi's time for its tone, apparently sweeter than that of the contemporary violin. Yet to today's ears its character is more plangent, and that especially applies to performance style on a baroque instrument. As can be seen, Vivaldi favoured the key of D minor above others for his concertos for that instrument, which are generally less striking than most of his violin concertos. Catherine Mackintosh gives expert performances with the Orchestra of the Age of Enlightenment, using rather astringent tone.

Violin concertos

'Dresden Violin Concertos', Vol. 1: Violin Concertos: in C, RV 170; in G, RV 314a; in G min., RV 319; in A, RV 341; in B flat (Il carbonelli), RV 366; in B flat, RV 383
(BB) * Naxos 8.553792. Martini, with Accademia I Filarmonici

This series concentrates on concertos which survive in manuscript in the Dresden Saxony Landesbibliothek, and which were used by the Court Orchestra. They do not derive from the composer's residence in the city, and the sleeve note suggests that their existence may be connected with Vivaldi's association with an influential group of Dresden musicians, most notably the violinist, Johanne Pisendel, who visited and studied under the composer during the latter part of 1716, and to whom Vivaldi dedicated a number of his concertos. The quality of these works is often remarkably high, reflecting the calibre of the orchestra and indeed Pisendel's virtuosity and musicianship. They sound extremely well in these excellent modern-instrument performances. Volume 1 gets off to very good start indeed. Alberto Martini directs bright, resilient performances, aptly paced, and he also proves a splendid soloist. There is nothing routine about any of these six works, as is demonstrated by the haunting *Largo* of the *A major*, RV 341, where the soloist plays over a gentle quasi-tremolando; the result is exquisite.

'Dresden Violin Concertos', Vol. 2: Violin Concertos: in C, RV 184; in D min., RV 241; in E, RV 267; in F, RV 292; in G min., RV 329; in B flat (Posthorn), RV 363
(BB) * Naxos 8.553793. Baraldi, Accademia I Filarmonici, Martini

The concertos on the second disc are full of surprises, and Roberto Baraldi gives them the strongest profile. He is a very positive soloist, with a bolder sound image than Martini, which is not to say he is in the least insensitive. He likes to echo phrases, followed by the orchestra. His strength of purpose is especially telling in the *Posthorn Concerto*, which features octave rhythmic figures on B flat, and also just right for the *D minor Concerto*, RV 241. But perhaps the most striking work here is the *F major*, RV 292, where the six-minute first movement interpolates a slow central section and is virtually a miniature concerto in itself. The *E major Concerto* goes one further with four tempo changes, *Allegro-Adagio-Largo-Allegro*, while the *C major*, not to be outdone,

has its opening and closing ritornello interrupted by a two-bar *Adagio* from the soloist; it also has a very lively and highly inventive finale. Again excellent sound.

'Dresden Violin Concertos', Vol. 3: Violin Concertos in D, RV 228; in D min., RV 245; in E flat, RV 262; in F, RV 285; in G min., RV 323; in B min., RV 384
(BB) * Naxos 8. 553860. Fornaciari, Accademia I Filarmonici, Martini

One is struck by the vigour of the *Allegros* in Volume 3, emphasized by Marco Fornaciari's extrovert style and very open timbre. Yet in slow movements he fines down his tone most beautifully. The *Largo* of the *B minor Concerto*, accompanied solely by the basso continuo, is particularly fine, while RV 262 brings a memorable central siciliana. The first movement of the *F major*, RV 285, introduces a second solo violin to echo the first, and the central melody of the slow movement is framed by a remarkable chromatic series of repeated descending chords.

'Dresden Violin Concertos', Vol. 4: Violin Concertos in D, RV 213; in D, RV 219; in D, RV 224; in D min., RV 240; in E flat, RV 260; in A, RV 344; in B min., RV 388
(BB) * Naxos 8.554310. Rossi, Accademia I Filarmonici, Martini

The use of a different soloist for each of these Naxos Dresden collections adds to their variety and interest. Cristiano Rossi's style is more intimate than that of Marco Fornaciari, yet his playing is by no means without personality and rhythmic flair. *Allegros* bustle with life in the orchestra, and Vivaldi's slow movements never fail to bring textural interest, apart from their melodic appeal. The last three of the seven concertos on this disc are all in D major, yet there is no sense of monotony, and RV 213 brings a stimulating close. Excellent recording.

Violin Concertos in C, RV 177 & RV 191; D, RV 222; E min., RV 273; F, RV 295; B flat, RV 375
☛ * Sony SK 89362. Carmignola, Venice Bar. O, Marcon

Violin Concertos in D min., RV 235; E flat, RV 251 & RV 256; F, RV 296; B min., RV 386; B min., RV 389
☛ * Sony SK 87733. Carmignola, Venice Bar. O, Marcon

The modern-instrument style of *I Musici* has recently been overtaken by new Italian string groups, which choose to play on period instruments, not in a thin, colourless manner, but creating full, gleaming timbres, which still retain an overall transparency. The excellent Venice Baroque Orchestra, directed by Andrea Marcon, demonstrate this new stylistic development in these two very enjoyable compilations of 'late' violin concertos by Vivaldi. The playing combines resilience and unashamed beauty of line with lyrical finesse and the widest range of dynamic. Slow movements can often be exquisitely gentle, so that the continuo, often using lute or theorbo, comes through engagingly. Giuliano Carmignola is a superbly assured and imaginative soloist throughout, and the recording is first class.

Violin Concertos: in C, RV 187; in D (Grosso Mogul), RV 208; in D (L'Inquietudine), RV 234; in E (Il Favorito), RV 277. L'estro armonico: (i) Concerto for 4 Violins & Cello in B min., Op. 3/10, RV 580
(N) * Onyx 4001. Mullova, Il Giardino Armonico, Antonini, (i) with Barneschi, Bianchi, Minasi

First-rate playing from Viktoria Mullova throughout, at her finest in the slow movement of *Il Favorito*. The accompaniments from Il Giardino Armonico attack allegros turbulently, especially in the fiery opening movement of *Grosso Mogul* and the furious *Allegro molto* of *L'Inquietudine* ('Restlessness'). Indeed, the period-instrument style here is far removed from the mellow I Musici manners, emphasized by the vividly forward recording. It cannot really be faulted, yet charm isn't the strong point of these performances.

Violin Concertos in C, RV 187; in D, RV 209

(BB) *** RCA 74321 68002-2. Zukerman, ECO – BACH:
   Violin Concertos, BWV 1041–2, BWV 1056; Double Violin Concerto ***

Two of Vivaldi's most attractive concertos played with great vitality and warmth, make a splendid coupling for Bach, particularly as the finale of the *C major* recalls the *Third Brandenburg Concerto*. Excellently vivid sound too.

'Music for the Chapel of the Pietà': (i) *Violin Concerto fatto per la Solennità della S. Antonio in Padova, RV 212; Violin Concerto in F, RV 292; (i; ii; iii) Concerto for Violin, Cello, Organ & Continuo, RV 554a; (i; iii) Concerto for Violin & Organ in F, RV 542; (iv) Laudate pueri Dominum, RV 600; (iv) i Salve Regina, RV 617.*

(N) *** Avie AV 2063. (i) Chandler; (ii) McMahon; (iii) Howarth; (iv) Lawson; La Serenissima

The most strikingly original work here is the *Violin Concerto fatto per la Solennità della S. Antonio in Padova*, RV 212, which, like the *F major Concerto*, RV 292, with its multi-tempo opening movement, survives in Dresden. Unfortunately the manuscript of the former suffered from water damage during the Second World War and, though the solo part remains almost entirely legible, the ritornelli had to be reconstructed by Adrian Chandler for this recording and he plays it superbly. It is a remarkable work, with a gutsy first movement and a dark, freely expressive *Grave*, where the soloist seems almost to be meditating; then the mood becomes buoyant for the virtuosic finale, including an extraordinary cadenza in which the soloist is taken up to the highest point of the normal violin register and then back down again. In the two concertos featuring the organ, the violin dominates throughout, although the organ contibution (nicely played and balanced here) adds an extra palette of colour.

The *Laudate pueri Dominum* of 1713 is an earlier, less elaborate setting of Psalm 112 than the masterpiece (RV 601) included in Volume 7 of the Hyperion survey, above. But it is also a superior work and is eloquently and even dramatically sung by Mhairi Lawson, whose vocal line is clear and true. Yet she is even finer in the *Salve Regina* (which, unusually, has a violin obbligato), singing the lovely closing *Et Jesum benedictum* blissfully. Throughout, La Serenissima provide strongly characterized accompaniments under their excellent violinist/conductor, and the recording has splendid presence and detail.

Miscellaneous concerto collections

(i) *The Trial between Harmony and Invention: Violin Concertos 5 in E flat (La tempesta di mare); 6 in C (Il piacere), Op. 8/5–6; (ii) Bassoon Concertos: in C, RV 472; in C min., RV 480; in A min., RV 498; in B flat, RV 504*

(M) *** Chan. 6529. (i) Thomas, Bournemouth Sinf.; (ii) Thompson, LMP, Ledger

The two concertos included here from *The Trial between Harmony and Invention* were among the best of the complete set recorded by Ronald Thomas in 1980. The use of modern instruments does not preclude a keen sense of style, and the balance is convincing. The bassoonist Robert Thompson turns a genial eye on his four concertos. He is rather forwardly projected but the performances are, like the sound, agreeably fresh, among the most attractive accounts of Vivaldi's bassoon concertos available on CD.

Bassoon Concerto in E min., RV 484; Flute Concerto in G min. (La notte), Op. 10/2, RV 439; Double Mandolin Concerto in G, RV 532; Concerto con multi instrumenti in C, RV 558; Double Concerto for Oboe & Violin in B flat, RV 548; Concerto for Strings (Alla rustica), RV 151; Concerto for 2 Violins & 2 Cellos in G, RV 575; L'estro armonico: Concerto for 4 Violins in D, Op. 3/1, RV 549

(M) *** DG (IMS) 447 301-2. Soloists, E. Concert, Pinnock

This generous 72-minute collection of varied works is very enticing at mid-price, showing Pinnock and the English Concert at their liveliest and most refreshing, although not always so strong on charm. The *Concerto for Four Violins* is very lithe, and throughout the concert the solo playing is most expert. The orchestral concerto, RV 558, involves an astonishing array of instruments.

Bassoon Concertos in A min., RV 497; in B flat (La notte), RV 501; Double Mandolin Concerto in G, RV 532; Piccolo Concerto in C, RV 443; Viola d'amore Concerto in D min., RV 394; Double Violin Concerto for Violin & Violin per eco lontano in A, RV 552

(M) *** Vernay PV 730052. Soloists, Paul Kuentz CO, Kuentz

Although described as 'six rare concertos', this most enjoyable, 71-minute collection is made up entirely of favourites, all played with much character. The two mandolinists, Takashi and Sylvia Ochi, are as personable as the sprightly bassoonist, Fernand Corbillon, with his woody French timbre, while the *Echo Violin Concerto* (the echoes feature in the ripieno as well as the solo writing) comes off to great effect. Fine accompaniments from Kuentz and first-rate digital sound, naturally balanced.

Bassoon Concerto in A min., RV 498; Flute Concerto in C min., RV 108; Double Horn Concerto in F, RV 539; Oboe Concerto in F, RV 456; Double Oboe Concerto in D min., RV 535; 2 Concertos for 2 Oboes, Bassoon, 2 Horns & Violin in F, RV 569 & RV 574; Piccolo Concerto in C, RV 208

(B) *** Double Decca (ADD) 452 943-2 (2). Soloists, ASMF, Marriner – BELLINI: *Oboe Concerto in E flat*; HANDEL: *Oboe Concertos*, etc. ***

Marriner's modern-instrument performances of favourite Vivaldi wind concertos, made between 1965 and 1977, have long been praised. The soloists are all distinguished and the playing here is splendidly alive and alert, with crisp, clean articulation and well-pointed phrasing, full of imagination, yet free from over-emphasis. The *A minor Bassoon Concerto* has a delightful sense of humour. Although the musical substance may not be very weighty, Vivaldi was never more engaging than when writing for wind instruments, particularly if he had more than one in his team of soloists, as in the two attractive composite works included in the programme. The vintage recordings remain in the demonstration bracket.

Concerti 'con molti istromenti': *Concerto funèbre in B flat for Oboe, Chalumeau, Violin, 3 Viole all'inglese, RV 579;*

Concerto in C for 2 Recorders, Oboe, Chalumeau, Violin, 2 Viole all'inglese; 2 Violins 'in tromba marina', 2 Harpsichords, RV 555; Concerto in D min. for 2 Oboes, Bassoon, 2 Violins, RV 566; Double Trumpet Concerto in D, RV 781; Concerto in F for viola d'amore, 2 Horns, 2 Oboes & Bassoon, RV 97; Concerto in F for Violin, 2 Oboes, Bassoon, 2 Horns, RV 574; Concerto in D for Violin, 2 Oboes, 2 Horns, RV 562

*** Hyp. CDA 67073. Soloists, King's Consort, King

This is one of the most attractive of all the CD groupings of Vivaldi's often extraordinarily scored multiple concertos, in which the period-instrument playing is not only expert, but constantly tweaks the ear. The braying horns often dominate, especially in the pair of concertos, RV 562 and RV 574, either rasping buoyantly or boldly sustaining long notes. The oboes are used to decorate the *Grave* of the latter, and elegantly open the finale of the former, before a bravura violin sends sparks flying. The horns again return spectacularly for the outer movements of RV 97, but the central *Largo* brings a delightful interplay between the languishing viola d'amore, and the oboes. The *Concerto funèbre*, not surprisingly, opens with a *Largo* and combines the remarkable solo combination of muted oboe, tenor chalumeau, a trio of viole all'inglese accompanied by muted strings. Then (in RV 555) comes the most remarkable array of all. Vivaldi even throws in a pair of harpsichords for good measure, and they are given some most attractive solo passages and used to provide a gentle rocking background for a most engaging violin soliloquy in the central *Largo*. Throughout the solo playing is wonderfully stylish and appealing, and Robert King maintains a fine vigour in allegros and an often gentle espressivo in slow movements. The recording is first class. Very highly recommended.

Concerto funèbre con molti istromenti for muted Oboes, Chalumeaux (Salmoè), Violin & Viola da gamba; Double Concertos: for Violin & Cello in F (Il Proteo o sia il mondo al rovescio); for Violin & Viola da gamba in A, RV 546; Triple Concertos for 2 Violins & Viola da gamba: in D min., RV 565; in G min., RV 578; Concerto for 4 Violins & Cello in B Min., RV 580

☛ *** Alia Vox AV 9835. Savall & soloists, Le Concert des Nations

This splendid collection centres on the vibrant presence of Jordi Savall, who contributes instrumentally to half the concertos included here, and directs them all. The highly original *Funeral Concerto* (based on a *Sinfonia* from the opera *Tito Manlio*) creates most colourful sonorities by including muted oboes, tenor chalumeaux, and three viole all'inglese. The *Il Proteo* (upside-down) concerto is written with the violin solos written in the bass clef while the cello reads from the treble clef. This is a joke aimed at the players, for it makes no difference to the resulting sound. These are all aurally fascinating works, and they are superbly played and recorded, with characteristic Savall gusto in allegros and warmly lyrical slow movements.

'Concerti con molti strumenti': Concerto in G min. for Oboe solo, Violin solo, 2 Flutes & 2 Oboes, RV 576; Concerto in G min. for Oboe solo, Violin solo, 2 Flutes & 2 Oboes, RV 577; Concerto in F for Violin, 2 Oboes & 2 Horns, RV 574; Concerto in F for Violin, 2 Oboes & 2 Horns, RV 569; Sinfonia for Strings in C, RV 192

☛ *** Opus 111 OP 30283. Soloists, Freiburg Bar. O, Von Der Goltz

We know of the excellence of Gottfried von der Goltz's period-instrument Freiburg Baroque Orchestra from their outstanding DVD of the Bach *Brandenburg Concertos*. They are no less stimulating in these Vivaldi concertos, written for Dresden, to which they bring a remarkable range of instrumental colour and dynamic, much vitality and expressive finesse. Slow movements, usually played gently, are always memorable, as in the *Grave* of RV 569 or the *Larghetto* of RV 576, and the excellence of their horn players is demonstrated vigorously in RV 574. A splendid collection, vividly recorded.

Double Cello Concerto in G min., RV 531; Concerto for Flute, Oboe, Bassoon & Violin in F (La tempesta di mare), RV 570; Concerto funèbre in B flat for Violin, Oboe, Salmoé & 3 Viole all'inglese, RV 579; Flute Concerto in G min. (La notte), RV 439; Violin Concertos: in D (L'inquietudine), RV 234; in E (Il riposo – per il Natale), RV 270; in A (Per eco in lontano), RV 552

*** Virgin 5 45424-2. Europa Galante, Biondi

This collection of some of Vivaldi's most imaginative concertos, played on period instruments, is just as attractive as its looks. All the special effects, from the ghost and sleep evocations in *La notte* to the echoing second violin in RV 552, are neatly managed, and the atmosphere of the *Concerto funèbre* is well sustained. This concerto features a theme taken from *Tito Manlio* where it was used as part of a procession to execution, and the scoring is very telling (see above). Fabio Biondi leads an excellent team of soloists and directs sparkling accompaniments, with a touch of vintage dryness to the bouquet of string timbre. Excellent recording.

Double Cello Concerto in G min., RV 531; Lute (Guitar) Concerto in D, RV 93; Oboe Concerto in F, F.VII, 2 (RV 455); Double Concerto for Oboe & Violin; Trumpet Concerto in D (trans. Jean Thilde); Violin Concerto in G min., Op. 12/1, RV 317

*** Naxos 8.550384. Capella Istropolitana, Kreček

This is a recommendable disc from which to set out to explore Vivaldi concertos, especially if you are beginning a collection. Gabriela Krcková makes a sensitive contribution to the delightful *Oboe Concerto in F major* F.VII, No. 2 (R. 455), and the other soloists are pretty good too.

Double Concertos for 2 Cellos in G min., RV 531; for Violin, Cello & Strings in F (Il Proteo ò sia il mondo rovescio), RV 544; for 2 Violins in A (per eco in lontano), RV 552. Triple Concertos: for 3 Violins in F, RV 551; for Violin & 2 Cellos in C, RV 561. Quadruple Concerto for 2 Violins & 2 Cellos: in C, RV 561; in D, RV 564

☛ *** Teldec 4509 94552-2. Coin and soloists, Il Giardino Armonico, Antonini

An exceptionally rewarding collection of concertos for multiple, stringed instruments, made the more striking by the inclusion of RV 544 with its curious subtitle evoking Proteus and an upside-down world. Christophe Coin leads an excellent team of soloists and the imaginative continuo (organ, harpsichord and archlute) adds to the colour of performances which are full of life, yet which also reveal the music's more subtle touches and are remarkably free from the exaggerated stylistic devices often associated with period instruments. The recording is excellent.

Double Concertos for 2 Cellos in G min., RV 531; for 2 Oboes in D min., RV 523; for 2 Violins in C, RV 505; in D, RV 511. Triple Concerto for Oboe & 2 Violins, RV 554

*** Chan. 0528. Coe, Warkin, Robson, Latham, Standage, Comberti, Coll. Mus. 90, Standage

Period-instrument performances are increasingly identified with the style of their performing groups, and that of Simon Standage's Collegium Musicum 90 is most invigorating, stylish with no lack of expressive feeling. The rhythmic crispness and buoyancy and the plangent string-sound make for characterful performances. The ripe sound of the baroque oboes and the crunchy cello timbre are particularly attractive, although the tingling astringency characteristic of the accompanying group is even more strongly focused in the solo playing for the concertos for two violins, and especially in the busy finale of RV 511. Outstanding Chandos sound.

Flute Concerto in G min. (La Notte), Op. 10/2, RV 439; Oboe Concerto in A min., RV 463; Concertos for Strings: in G min., RV 156; in D min. (Madrigalesco), RV 129; Double Trumpet Concerto in C, RV 537; Violin Concerto in G, Op. 1/4, RV 308; Quadruple Violin Concerto, Op. 3/10, RV 580

(N) (B) **(*) CfP 586 0512. Soloists, Hanover Band, Halstead

An attractive and generous clutch of concertos, including several of Vivaldi's best, although it is a pity that the version of *La Notte* was not chosen which includes a bassoon. The period performances are lively, spick and span, but the soloists from the Hanover Band are a little lacking in individuality of personality. The recording is excellent.

Double Concertos for 2 Flutes in C, RV 533; for 2 Horns in F, RV 538 & RV 539; for 2 Trumpets in C, RV 537; for Oboe & Bassoon in G, RV 545. Concerto (Sinfonia in D) for Strings, RV 122; Quadruple Concerto for 2 Oboes & 2 Clarinets, RV 560

(BB) *** Naxos 8.553204. Soloists, City of L. Sinfonia, Kraemer

A lively clutch of concertos, very well recorded in All Saints' Church, East Finchley. The opening double concertos for two horns, RV 539, two flutes, RV 533, and two trumpets, RV 537, all go well enough and make expert solo contributions, but then at the arrival of the *Quadruple Concerto for Two Oboes and Two Clarinets* the playing suddenly sparks into extra exuberance, and one senses the musicians' enjoyment of one of Vivaldi's most imaginatively scored multiple works. The *Concerto for Two Horns* which follows (RV 538) has a similar ebullience, and the concert is rounded off by a captivating account of RV 545, where both the oboe and bassoon clearly relish every bar of their engaging dialogue. Kraemer's accompaniments are polished and spirited.

Fourteen concertos: Disc 1: (i; ii) *Lute Concerto in D, RV 93; Double Concerto for 2 Mandolins in G, RV 532;* (i; iii) *Recorder Concertos in A min., RV 108; in G min. (La notte);* (iv) *Violin Concerto in D (Grosso Mogul), RV 208.* Disc 2: Double concertos: (v) *Double Concertos for 2 Cellos in G min., RV 531; 2 Flutes in C, RV 533; 2 Trumpets in C, RV 443. Concertos for Strings in D min. (Madrigalesco), RV 129; in G (Alla rustica), RV 151; in G min., RV 153. Quadruple*

Concerto for 2 Violins & 2 Cellos in D, RV 564; L'estro armonico: Quadruple Violin Concerto in B min., Op. 3/10, RV 580

(B) *** O-L Double (DDD/ADD) 455 703-2 (2). (i) New L. Cons., Pickett, with (ii) Finucane; (iii) Pickett; (iv) Ritchie, Bach Ens., Rifkin; (v) Soloists, AAM, Hogwood

The 14 concertos on this Oiseau-Lyre Double readily demonstrate the extraordinary diversity of Vivaldi's musical ideas, and in many cases his originality too. None more so than the remarkable *Violin Concerto*, RV 208 (written about 1710), nicknamed – probably not by the composer – 'Grosso Mogul'. The outer movements with their *moto perpetuo* arpeggios demand great virtuosity from the soloist, and the slow movement is a long recitativo, more like an improvisation. The remarkable seven-minute finale, perhaps the longest in any Vivaldi concerto, has a central cadenza which demands and is given a performance of dazzling virtuosity by the soloist here, Stanley Ritchie. An unforgettable performance, very well recorded. The concertos for lute, mandolins and recorder are also expertly and pleasingly played by Philip Pickett and his group, whose brand of authenticity is rather less abrasive than Hogwood's. The digital sound is first class. The *Concerto for Two Flutes* has great charm and is dispatched with vigour and aplomb. Performances and recording alike are first rate. For the reissue, three extra works have been added, most notably the famous *Quadruple Violin Concerto* from *L'estro armonico*, taken from the Academy's splendid complete set, with John Holloway, Monica Huggett, Catherine Mackintosh and Elizabeth Wilcock the excellent soloists.

Double Mandolin Concerto in G, RV 532. Oboe Concertos in A min., RV 461; in B flat, RV 548. Concertos for Strings in G (alla rustica), RV 151; in C (Con molti istromenti), RV 558. Double Violin Concerto in G, RV 516

(M) *** DG (IMS) 457 897-2. E. Concert, Pinnock

Taking its title, *Alla rustica*, from the charming little *G major Concerto*, RV 151, with its drone in the finale, this collection is a straight reissue of a 1986 CD, offering only six concertos and a playing time of barely 53 minutes. Nevertheless, it makes up in quality for what it lacks in quantity, finding Pinnock and English Concert at their liveliest and most refreshing. Outstanding in a nicely balanced programme is the *C minor Concerto*, RV 558, involving a remarkable array of concertino instruments including two violins (in 'tromba marina') and pairs of recorders, mandolins and theorbos, plus one cello. Excellent recording, giving a most realistic perspective.

CHAMBER MUSIC

Cello Sonatas: 1 in B flat, RV 47; 2 in F, RV 41; 3 in A min., RV 43; 4 in B flat, RV 45; 5 in E min., RV 40; 6 in B flat, RV 46

(N) *** Sony SK 51350. Bylsma, Galligioni, Zanenghi, Sbrogio, Marcon

Cello Sonatas 1–9, RV 39/47

(N) (B) *** CRD CRD 34401 (2). L'Ecole d'Orphée

Vivaldi wrote ten sonatas for cello and continuo, of which one is lost. These recordings use an edition published in Budapest in 1995. Their four-movement format probably derives from the *sonate da chiese*, but they were surely designed for concert performance for they afford the soloist both expressive and bravura opportunities, although they are not virtuoso works.

All nine *Sonatas* are given highly musical performances on CRD; they do not set out to impress by grand gestures but succeed in doing so by their dedication and sensitivity. Susan Sheppard is a thoughtful player and is well supported by her continuo team, Lucy Carolan and Jane Coe. The CRD recording is well focused with fine presence.

Although offering only the first six sonatas, Anner Bylsma proves an ideal soloist and he has fine continuo support. He was recorded in 1999 and we must hope that the remainder will follow.

Chamber Concertos in D, RV 84; (Sonata) in A, RV 86; in D, RV 94; in D (La pastorella), RV 95; in F, RV 99; in G min., RV 103 & 105

(B) *** HM Classical Express HCX 3957046. Verbruggen, Goodwin, Holloway, Godburn, Toll, Comberti

Vivaldi was at his most imaginatively inventive in his chamber concertos. The spicy, chirping opening of *La pastorella* (RV 95) is scored for recorder, oboe and bassoon to depict a shepherd piping. RV 94 opens with a simulated hurdy-gurdy effect, and RV 99 depicts a hunt (without horns!) and has a very rustic central *Largo*, while the slow movement of RV 105 is an almost bucolic duet for recorder and bassoon, with oboe added spiritedly in the finale. RV 84 was written for performance by the Dresden Orchestra and includes the composer's chromatic 'Sleep' motif in its finale, though it is not in the least somnambulant. The *Sonata* (for recorder and bassoon with continuo) provides a piquant further change of texture. The soloists group together for the tutti and the playing is vividly colourful and the recording excellent. Most delectable.

Chamber Concertos in C for Recorder, Oboe, 2 Violins, Cello, Harpsichord & Lute, RV 87; in D for Flute, Violin, & Cello, RV 92; in G min. for Flute, Oboe, Bassoon, Cello, Organ & Lute, RV 107; in D min. for Solo Organ & Flute, 2 Violins, Viola, Cello, Violone & Lute, RV 541; in F for Organ & Violin solo, 2 Violins, Viola, Cello, Violone & Lute, RV 542. Trio Sonata in D min. (La folia), RV 65

🔊 🎵 *** Channel Classics CCS 8495. Florilegium

These concertos could hardly be played more persuasively (one instrument to each part) than they are by Florilegium, an outstanding period-instrument ensemble. The concertos, which include a solo organ, are enchanting in their piquant colouring, and are full of splendid ideas. The finale of RV 107, for instance, is a kaleidoscopic chaconne, in effect a chimerical set of variations. But every work here is inspired and aurally stimulating, and they could hardly be better played. The programme ends with Vivaldi's extensive variations on *La folia* in the form of a *Trio Sonata*, which is presented with bravura, a wide range of dynamic and a sense of fantasy. The group, led by Ashley Solomon (flute/recorder), are all masters of their instruments and play infectiously together as a team. The recording is ideally balanced, within an acoustic with just the right feeling of ambient space.

Chamber Concertos for Treble Recorder in A min., RV 108; in C min., RV 441; in F, RV 442; for Sopranino Recorder in C, RV 443 & RV 444; in A min., RV 445

(BB) *** Hyp. Helios CDH 55016. Holstag, Parley of Instruments, Holman

These are all treated as chamber concertos, with one instrument to each part, and by alternating treble and sopranino recorders Peter Holman provides variety, although this is not a CD to undertake all in one session. But the *C major Sopranino Concerto*, played with sparkling virtuosity, cannot fail to cheer you up. Even the *Largo* is perky, and the trilling finale is projected with superb aplomb. The same might be said for its two companions here.

The mellower sound of the treble recorder still gives pleasure too, of course, especially in the *A minor Concerto*, RV 445, while the *Rondo* finale of the *C major*, RV 443, is also very diverting. Excellent recording and good value.

Trio Sonatas, Op. 1/1–12. Trio Sonatas in C, RV 60; in G min., RV 72. Cello Sonata in A min., RV 43; Double Violin Sonata in F, RV 70; Sonata for Violin & Cello in C min., RV 83

(M) *** CPO 999 511-2 (2). Sonnerie

Trio Sonatas Op. 1/1–12. Trio Sonatas in B flat; in G min., Op. 5/17–18; 2 Sonatas (Al Santo Sepolcro) in E flat, RV 130; in B min., RV 169. Violin Sonata in C, RV 114

*(**) BIS CD 1025/26. L. Bar., Medlam

Vivaldi's Op. 1 *Trio Sonatas* were published during 1712–13, just after *L'estro armonico* had appeared and made its composer famous. It is unlikely that this dates their composition, and many of them could have been written up to a decade earlier. While Corelli was a major influence on these works, Vivaldi's own voice and originality come through again and again, and these sonatas are every bit as rewarding musically as his concertos of this period.

There is no problem here as to choice. Both performances are from expert period-instrument performers. But whereas the bright violin timbre of Monica Huggett of Sonnerie is smoothly caught within an attractively warm acoustic, and her colleagues too are naturally recorded and balanced. Ingrid Seifert, who leads London Baroque, has no such good fortune. The BIS engineers (perhaps because they were recording in a church) have put their microphones close, and the result is unattractively edgy and aurally tiring. So the CPO set is the one to go for, and if you acquire it you will especially enjoy the final sonata of the set, Vivaldi's brilliant set of nineteen ostinato variations on the famous *La folia*, which is brilliantly played. The various bonuses are enjoyable too.

12 Violin Sonatas, Op. 2

**(*) Signum SIGCD 014 (2). Cordaria (Reiter, Ad-El, Sharman or Sayce)

Vivaldi's Op. 2 was first published in 1709. In 1712 the sonatas were republished, more elegantly printed in Amsterdam, so they must have been a success. They are early rather than mature Vivaldi, but pleasingly inventive all the same, with the bass line fairly free, sometimes detaching itself from the continuo and engaging in dialogue with the violin. The performances on Signum are lively and musical, not distinctive, but Walter Reiter is certainly up to the bravura demanded of him in some of fizzing *Presto* finales. Good, clear recording.

Violin Sonatas, Op. 2/1–6

(N) *** Hyp. CDA 67467. Wallfisch, Tunnicliffe, Proud

Elizabeth Wallfisch, with her colleagues Richard Tunnicliffe (cello) and Malcom Proud (harpsichord), offers only the first six *Sonatas*. But we must hope the others will follow, for their performances of these three- and four-movement works are captivating, light-hearted and sparkling in allegros, expressively appealing in the comparatively simple *Sarabandes* and *Adagios*. They are beautifully recorded.

'Manchester' Violin Sonatas (for violin and continuo) 1–12 (complete)

(*) Arcana A 4/5. Biondi, Alessandri, Naddeo, Pandolfo, Lislevand
(B) ** HM HMX 2907342/3 (2). Romanesca

The so-called 'Manchester' *Sonatas* were discovered as recently as 1973 in Manchester's Henry Watson Music Library. Within simple structures Vivaldi wrote fine music offering much refreshment. Neither disc is ideal. Romanesca are recorded fairly dryly, though they are very well balanced. Nigel North's archlute, theorbo or guitar makes a very pleasing contribution and John Toll's harpsichord is nicely in the picture, but the sound of Andrew Manze's baroque violin is rather raw. On the other hand, the Romanesca phrasing has marginally less of that curious accented lunging often favoured by period groups, which is at times more noticeable on the Arcana set. However, one adjusts to this when Fabio Biondi's tone is so much sweeter and his colleagues are afforded an altogether warmer sound by the more expansive Arcana recording. Tempi are generally faster with Romanesca, appreciably so in the Correntes. Overall the Arcana disc is the more persuasive but the Harmonia Mundi set has a considerable price advantage.

VOCAL MUSIC

Sacred music, Vol. 1: *Credo in unum Deum, RV 591; Dixit Dominus, RV 594; Kyrie eleison, RV 587; Lauda Jerusalem, RV 608; Magnificat, RV 610*

*** Hyp. CDA 66769. Gritton, Milne, Denley, Atkinson, Wilson-Johnson, Choristers and Ch., King's Consort, King

Hyperion's series aims to cover all the key sacred choral works of Vivaldi, and this first volume could not be more promising. All the music here is for double choir except the simple *Credo*, which is without soloists but has great intensity of feeling expressed in the *Et incarnatus est* and *Crucifixus*. Apart from the splendidly grand and masterly *Dixit Dominus*, RV 594 (gloriously sung here), there are two fine, shorter works which also include double string orchestra: the *Kyrie eleison* and the *Lauda Jerusalem*. But most striking of all is Vivaldi's first setting of the *Magnificat* – in G minor, dating from around 1715 although revised in the 1720s – made memorable by its highly individual chromatic writing, but also adding to the poignancy of the *Et misericordia*. Robert King has gathered an excellent team of soloists for this collection (witness the following soprano duet, *Esurientes*, which is delightful), but it is the stirringly eloquent choral singing one remembers most, vividly directed by King and splendidly balanced and recorded.

Sacred music, Vol. 2: Motets: (i) *Canta in prato, ride in monte, RV 623;* (ii) *Clarae stellae, scintillate, RV 625; Filiae maestae Jerusalem, RV 638;* (i) *In furore iustissimae irae, RV 626;* (iii) *Longe mala, umbrae, terrores, RV 629;* (i) *Nulla in mundo pax sincera, RV 630*

*** Hyp. CDA 66779. (i) York; (ii) Bowman; (iii) Denley; King's Consort, King

All the appealing works here are very well sung indeed, with those for the soprano, the very agile Deborah York, the most

memorable. The opening of *In furore iustissimae irae* ('In wrath and most just anger') is delivered with dramatic venom, but then the *Largo, Tune meus fletus* ('Then shall my weeping'), follows exquisitely. The other highlight of the collection is James Bowman's *Filiae maestae Jerusalem*, which brings a touching *Larghetto, Silenti Zephyri* ('Let the winds be hushed'). The closing soprano cantata opens with a gentle siciliana with a typically evocative string accompaniment. The nimble following aria depicts a hidden snake waiting for the unwary, and the closing, fast-flowing *Alleluia* requires virtuosity from the singer, sparklingly delivered here. A first-class collection, excellently recorded.

Sacred music, Vol. 3: *Beatus vir* (two versions), *RV 597 & RV 598; Crediti propter quod, RV 605; Dixit Dominus, RV 595; Domine ad adjuvandum, RV 593*

*** Hyp. CDA 66789. Gritton, Wyn-Davies, Denley, Daniels, N. Davies, George, Ch. King's Consort, King

Vivaldi's two settings of the *Beatus vir* are quite different. RV 597 is for double choir and is on an ambitious scale, with a refrain that reappears in various sections of the work. RV 598 is in a single movement and is written for soloists and a single choir, rather in the manner of a concerto grosso. The present setting of *Dixit Dominus* is for single chorus (but with sopranos sometimes divided). *Domine ad adjuvandum* is a superbly concentrated short work for double choir, based on Psalm 69. The performances here are well up to the standard of this excellent series, and the soloists sing with bravura, especially in duets. The Hyperion recording is of high quality, although ideally one would have welcomed more choral bite.

Sacred music, Vol. 4: *Juditha triumphans* (complete)

*** Hyp. CDA 67281/2. Murray, Bickley, Kiehr, Connolly, Rigby, Ch. & King's Consort, King

Juditha triumphans, Vivaldi's only surviving oratorio, works well on disc, with its elaborate instrumental textures. Written for the Ospedale di Pietà in Venice, a home for foundlings, it involves only women's voices in the solo roles and here is exceptionally well cast. Anne Murray, in one of her most beautiful performances on disc, is seductive as Judith rather than sharply dramatic, and it is left to Susan Bickley as the tyrannical general, Holofernes, to steal first honours, strong and incisive. The others are excellent too, with the chorus (involving male voices as well as female) heightening the drama from the opening martial chorus onwards. Robert King relishes the rich instrumentation with its brilliant and original obbligato solos, beautifully caught in vivid, atmospheric recording.

Sacred music, Vol. 5: *Confitebor tibi, Domine; Deus tuorum militum; In turbato mare, RV 627; Non in pratis aut in hortis, RV 641; O qui coeli terraeque serenitas, RV 631; Stabat Mater, RV 621*

*** Hyp. CDA 66799. Gritton, Rigby, Blaze, Daniels, N. Davies, King's Consort, King

Volume 5 of this excellent Hyperion series offers two solo motets, a simple Vesper hymn (*Deus tuorum militum*) sung as a contralto/tenor duet, and ends with a very fine three-voice setting of Psalm 110, *Confitebor tibi, Domine*, which in its final movement draws on a sparkling terzet from Vivaldi's opera *La fida ninfa*. It makes a satisfying close to a programme which has as its centrepiece the glorious *Stabat Mater* (1712), very beautifully sung here by the male alto, Robin Blaze. As an ideal prelude to this masterpiece Jean Rigby sings most movingly the 'Introduzione to the Miserere', *Non in pratis aut in hortis*, which has a beautiful lament as its solo aria. To open the concert Susan Gritton dispatches *In turbato mare irato* with biting bravura, but is later able to show her lovely lyrical style in *O qui colei terraeque serenitas*.

Sacred music, Vol. 6: *Beatus vir, RV 795; In exitu Israel, RV 604; Laudate Dominum, RV 606; Nisi Dominus, RV 608; Salve Regina, RV 617*

**(*) Hyp. CDA 66809. Gritton, Stutzmann, Summers, Gibson, Ch. & King's Consort, King

While the two motets *In exitu Israel* and *Laudate Dominum* are for choir alone, the ambitious setting of *Beatus vir* (only comparatively recently confirmed as authentic Vivaldi), which alternates extended solos with a brief repeated chorale, involves Susan Gritton immediately in spectacularly florid solo singing. Later she is joined by Hilary Summers and Alexandra Gibson in the seraphic trio *In memoria aeterna*, and both contraltos then make major solo contributions. Gritton is at her finest in the *Salve Regina*, where Simon Jones provides elaborate violin obbligatos. In *Nisi Dominus* further bravura is demanded from Nathalie Stutzmann and she nimbly rises to the occasion. The soaring *Gloria* brings more instrumental embroidery from Katherine McGillivray (viola d'amore) and the closing *Amen* is another virtuoso display. The microphones are kinder to Stutzmann's voice than Gritton's and for some reason the choral sound in the motets is edgy.

Sacred music, Vol. 7: *Gloria, RV 688; Laetatus sum, RV 607; Laudate pueri, RV 601; Jubilate, o amoeni chori, RV 639; Vespro Principi divino, RV 633*

(N) *** Hyp. CDA 66819. Gritton, Sampson, Stutzmann, Daniels, Ch. and King's Consort

Although opening with the choral *Laetatus sum*, the kernel of Volume 7 is a pair of solo works of which *Laudate pueri* (Psalm 112) is the more ambitious. It is a true virtuoso piece for soprano (originally a castrato) able to reach D *in alt*. Carolyn Sampson sings it gloriously, radiant in *A solis ortu usque ad occasum*, and ethereally beautiful in the *Gloria Patri* which she sings in duet with an obbligato flute. This is followed by an outstanding performance by Nathalie Stutzmann of the motet *Vespro Principi divino* (a paraphrase of Psalm 23), sung with comparable virtuosity. She then leads the way into the lesser-kown Vivaldi setting of the *Gloria* by way of an introductory motet, *Jubilate o amoeni chori*, whose second and final aria leads straight into the opening chorus of the *Gloria*. This work is superbly sung by soloists and double chorus alike, and the slightly backward balance of the chorus is here beneficial to the work's overall layout. Hyperion offer top quality sound, and this is one of the very finest of their Vivaldi series.

Cantatas: (i) *All'ombra di sospetto, RV 678;* (ii; iii) *Amor hai vinto, RV 651;* (i) *Lungi dal vago volto, RV 680; Vengo a voi, luci adorate, RV 682.* (iv) *Gloria in D, RV 589;* (v; iii) *Nisi Dominus (Psalm 127), RV 608;* (ii; iii) *Nulla in mundo pax sincera, RV 630.* (vi) *Trio Sonata (La folia), RV 63*

(B) *** O-L Double (ADD/DDD) 455 727-2 (2). (i) Bott, New L. Cons., Pickett; (ii) Kirkby; (iii) AAM, Hogwood; (iv) Nelson, Kirkby, Watkinson, Christ Church Cathedral Ch., AAM, Preston; (v) Bowman; (vi) Standage, Mackintosh, Hogwood

Vivaldi's secular cantatas are lightweight but have much charm. Combining recitative and a pair of arias, they usually express the dolours of unrequited love in an Arcadian setting. In each case the words are written from the male point of view, yet here they are treated as soprano solos – delightfully so, for, after Emma Kirkby has opened the programme with a characteristically fresh-voiced *Amor hai vento*, Catherine Bott takes over with her softer focus and more plaintive style. As a central instrumental interlude we are offered a lively and stylish account of the *Trio Sonata* which Vivaldi based on *La folia*. The first CD opens with the familiar *Gloria*. The choristers of Christ Church Cathedral excel themselves and the recording is remarkably fine. The solo motet, *Nulla in mundo pax sincera*, brings back Emma Kirkby, who copes splendidly with the bravura writing for soprano. James Bowman is also a persuasive soloist in the more extended, operatic-styled setting of Psalm 127. But since Vivaldi probably wrote *Nisi Dominus* for the Pietà, a Venetian orphanage for girls, there is a case here for preferring a woman soloist.

Cantatas: (i) *Amor hai vinto, RV 683; Cesssate, omai cessate, RV 684.* La stravaganza: (ii) *Violin Concerto in D min., Op. 4/8, RV 429.* (iii) *Cello Concerto in A min., RV. 422; Concertos for Strings in C & E min., RV 117 & RV 134; in G (Alla rustica), RV 151*

*** Opus 111 OPS 30-181. (i) Mingardo; (ii) Vicari; (iii) Piovano; Concerto Italiano, Alessandrini

Rinaldo Alessandrini opens this concert with an exhilaratingly crisp account of the bouncing allegro of *Concerto for Strings in C major* and sets the scene for *Amor hai vinto*, the first of the two pastoral cantatas sung with comparably bracing vocal virtuosity. The singer alternately languishes in unrequited love or looks back despairingly in 'immeasurable grief' and then in revengeful anger, after betrayal. There are plenty of dramatic and expressive opportunities, well taken here by the fine alto soloist, but also long passages of bravura runs when the lover obsessively repeats the indignant admonishments.

In effect these are concertos for voice, and Sarah Mingardo's virtuosity brings an instrumental ease of execution, the keenly honed articulation quite exhilarating. The two cantatas are framed and interleaved by the five instrumental concertos, all with excellent soloists, and the concert ends as invigoratingly as it began with the best-known work, ingenuously subtitled *Alla rustica*.

Motets: *Canto in prato, ride in monte, RV 623; Invicti, bellate, RV 68; Longe mala, umbrae, terrores, RV 629; Nulla in mundo pax sincera, RV 630; O qui coeli terraeque serenitas, RV 631; Vestro Principi divino, RV 633*

(N) *** Opus 111 OP 30340. Herrman, Polverelli, Academia Montis Regalis, De Marchi

The four-section sacred motets here (*Aria–Recitativo–Aria–Allegro*) have non-liturgical texts alternating between the fresh and sweet-voiced soprano Anke Herrman and the nimble and well-focused contralto, who finds both bravura and drama for the opening *Longe mala, umbrae, terrore* ('Begone, evils, shadows and terrors') and sings with special eloquence in *Invicti, bellate*, which ends with a virtuoso *Alleluia*. The soprano motets end with *Alleluias* too, and they are often meltingly lyrical in both arias, notably so in *O qui coeli terraeque serenita* and the lovely closing *Nulla in mundo pax sincera*, which Herrman sings so delightfully with the *Alleluia* close quite remarkable. The Academia Montis Regalis, directed by Alessandro de Marchi, accompany warmly and sympathetically, using modern instruments, and the recording is excellent.

(i–v) *Beatus vir in G, RV 597;* (vi) *Introduction to Gloria, RV 639;* (i; iv; vi; vii) *Gloria in D, RV 588;* (i; ii; viii) *Gloria in D, RV 589;* (i; iii; vi; vii; ix) *Magnificat in G min., RV 611;* (x) *Nulla in mundo pax sincera, RV 630;* (xi) *Stabat Mater, RV 621*

🎜— (B) *** Ph. Duo (ADD) 462 170-2 (2). (i) Marshall; (ii) Murray; (iii) Collins; (iv) Rolfe Johnson; (v) Holl; (vi) Finnie; (vii) Lott; (viii) Finnilä; (ix) Burgess; (x) Ameling; (xi) Kowalski; Alldis Ch., ECO, Negri

This Philips Duo offers a splendid selection of Vivaldi's choral work taken over from Negri's survey, above. It includes the two *Glorias* and the double-choir version of the *Magnificat*, while the *Beatus vir*, also for two choirs, is a similarly stirring piece. The collection opens with striking vocal bravura from Linda Finnie, who sings the *Introduction* to *Gloria*, RV 639, with spectacular virtuosity; later there is a comparable display from Elly Ameling in *Nulla in mundo pax sincera*, with the brilliant upper tessitura of the closing *Alleluia* testing her to the limit of her powers. Jochen Kowalski is the fine soloist in the touching *Stabat Mater*. The other soloists are also splendid, while the choir, vividly recorded, captures the dark, Bach-like intensity of many passages, contrasted with more typical Vivaldian brilliance. The analogue recordings are transferred to CD most impressively. A splendid introduction to Vivaldi's inspired writing for voices.

Beatus vir, RV 597; Gloria in D, RV 589

(BB) **(*) Naxos 8.550767. Crookes, Quitaker, Lane, Trevor, Oxford Schola Cantorum, N. CO, Ward

This Naxos coupling of what are probably the two favourite Vivaldi choral works is beautifully recorded and well worth its modest cost. Although some listeners will want greater attack in the famous opening and closing sections of the *Gloria* and in the *Potens in terra* in the companion work, these spacious performances, directed by Nicholas Ward, are still warmly enjoyable, partly because of the freshness of the solo contributions, but also because the choral singing has considerable intensity, especially in the continual return of the haunting *Beatus vir* chorale in RV 589. The *Paratum cor eius*, too, brings a surge of choral feeling, and the chorus rises to the occasion for the splendid closing *Gloria patri*. Full translations are included.

(i) Motets: (i) Clarae stella, scintillate, RV 625; Nisi Dominus, RV 608; Salve Regina, RV 616; Vespro Principi divino, RV 633. Concertos for Strings: in C, RV 109; in F, RV 141

🎜— *** Decca 466 964-2. (i) Scholl; Australian Brandenburg O, Dyer

This splendidly varied compilation of Vivaldi's sacred motets has claims to being Andreas Scholl's finest recital so far. Moreover, the Australian balance engineer, Allan Maclean, has caught his voice with the utmost naturalness.

Scholl's account of the Vesper psalm *Nisi Dominus* catches to the full the lyrical beauty of *Vanum est vobis* and the volatility of the following lively *Surgite sagittae in manu potentis*.

Cum dederit delectis suis somnum opens very mysteriously (Vivaldi asks his strings to play with *piombi* – lead mutes – instead of the normal wooden *sordini*) and Scholl sings his slowly rising chromatic scale with seraphic, sensuous beauty, a moment of sheer magic. The work's expressive climax,

Gloria patri, with its viola da gamba obbligato, is transcendent, followed by the bravura release of *Sicut erat*.

Not surprisingly *Clarae stellae* gleams and sparkles, but the other highlight here is Vivaldi's highly imaginative setting of the *Salve Regina*, with its antiphonal accompaniment for double orchestra, especially striking in the *Ad te clamamus*. But again it is the lyrical music which is so memorable, with the touching *Ad te suspiramus* poignantly accompanied by a 'sighing' flute, and the closing *O clemens, op pia* softly coloured by a pair of recorders: the final *O dulcis virgo Maria* is exquisite. The period-instrument Australian Brandenburg Orchestra contribute much to the success of this record, providing (as interludes) vibrantly infectious accounts of two of Vivaldi's *String Concertos*, of which the *C major*, with its lovely central *Adagio*, is particularly memorable. We shall surely hear more from this group and their impressive conductor, Paul Dyer.

Dixit Dominus in D, RV 594; Gloria in D, RV 589; Magnificat in G min., RV 610

**(*) EMI 5 57265-2. Fox, Norman, Chance, Gilchrist, Lemalu, King's College, Cambridge, Ch., AAM, Cleobury

These are fine performances, with an excellent team of soloists (and a most sensitive oboe solo in the *Domine deus* of the *Gloria*). The King's College Choir are on fine form too, but in the last resort the performances, though committed and musical, are a shade lacking in the spontaneous feel of live music-making. In the *Gloria*, too, one would have liked a brighter sound from the period violins. Otherwise the recording is spacious and well balanced.

(i) Gloria in D, RV 588; Gloria in D, RV 589; (ii) Concerto for Guitar & Viola d'amore, RV 540

(B) *** Decca 448 223-2. (i) Russell, Kwella, Wilkens, St John's College, Cambridge, Ch., Wren O, Guest; (ii) Fernández, Blume, ECO, Malcolm

(i) Gloria in D, RV 588; Gloria in D, RV 589; (ii; iii) Beatus vir in C, RV 597; Dixit Dominus in D, RV 594; (iv; iii) Magnificat in G min., RV 610

🎜— (B) *** Double Decca (DDD/ADD) 443 455-2 (2). (i) Russell, Kwella, Wilkens, Bowen, St John's College, Cambridge, Ch., Wren O, Guest; (ii) J. Smith, Buchanan, Watts, Partridge, Shirley-Quirk, ECO, Cleobury; (iii) King's College, Cambridge, Ch.; (iv) Castle, Cockerham, King, ASMF, Ledger

The two settings of the *Gloria* make an apt and illuminating pairing. Both in D major, they have many points in common, presenting fascinating comparisons, when RV 588 is as inspired as its better known companion. Guest directs strong and well-paced readings, with RV 588 the more lively. Good, warm recording to match the performances. *Dixit Dominus* cannot fail to attract those who have enjoyed the better known *Gloria*. Both works are powerfully inspired and are here given vigorous and sparkling performances with King's College Choir in excellent form under Philip Ledger. The soloists are a fine team, fresh, stylish and nimble, nicely projected on CD. What caps this outstanding Vivaldi compilation is the earlier King's account of the inspired *Magnificat in G minor*. Ledger uses the small-scale setting and opts for boys' voices in the solos such as the beautiful duet, *Esurientes*, which is most winning. The performance overall is very compelling and moving, and the singing has all the accustomed beauty of King's. The transfer of an outstanding (1976) analogue recording to CD is admirable, even richer than its digital companions.

As can be seen, those seeking an inexpensive disc of the two *Glorias* will find the Eclipse CD a satisfactory alternative, and the *Concerto for Guitar & Viola d'amore* makes an attractively lightweight interlude between the two.

Gloria in D, RV 589

- *** EMI 7 54283-2. Hendricks, Murray, Rigby, Heilmann, Hynninen, ASMF Ch. & O, Marriner – BACH: *Magnificat* ***
- (M) *** Decca (ADD) 458 623-2. Vaughan, Baker, Partridge, Keyte, King's College, Cambridge, Ch., ASMF, Willcocks – HANDEL: *Coronation Anthem: Zadok the Priest;* HAYDN: *Nelson Mass* ***
- (BB) *** Naxos 8.554056. Oxford Schola Cantorum, N. CO, Ward – BACH: *Magnificat* ***

Gloria in D, RV 589; Kyrie in G min., RV 587

- (BB) *** Warner Apex (ADD) 0927 48681-2. Smith, Staempfli, Rossier, Schaer, Lausanne Vocal & Instrumental Ens., Corboz – BACH: *Magnificat in D, BWV 243* ***

Gloria, RV 589; Magnificat, RV 611

- (M) EMI (ADD) 5 66987-2 [5 760002]. Berganza, Valentini, Terrani, New Philh. Ch. & O, Muti

(i) Gloria, RV 589; Magnificat, RV 611; Concerto for Strings in D min., RV 243; (ii) Double Concerto for Trumpet & Oboe, RV 563

- *** Opus 111 OP 3019 S. (i) York, Biccire, Mingardo, Champagne & Ardene Regional Vocal Ens., (ii) Soloists, Concerto Italiano, Alessandrini

Gloria, RV 589; Ostro picta, armata spina, RV 642

- *** Chan. 0518. Kirkby, Bonner, Chance, Coll. Mus. 90, Hickox – BACH: *Magnificat* ***

Hickox and Marriner couple the more popular of the two *D major Glorias* with the Bach *Magnificat* and offer a clear choice between period and modern instruments. Honours are evenly divided between them: Hickox's purposeful account has the benefit of a fine team of soloists and good Chandos recording; Marriner's performance with the Academy on modern instruments is well paced, as is the Bach *Magnificat*. His soloists are also very fine, and the recording has warmth and immediacy. Both can be strongly recommended.

Rinaldi Alessandrini's dazzling speed for the opening of Vivaldi's more famous setting of the *Gloria* must be just about the fastest on record, and it is just as exciting in the reprise for the *Quoniam*. Yet ensemble remains remarkably crisp, and later the pair of sopranos revel in their virtuosity in the *Laudamus te*. Elsewhere, while there is plenty of vigour there is no feeling of the music being hurried. The *Domine Deus* and *Qui tollis* bring a contrasting element of calm, and the closing *Cum Sanctos Spiritu* makes a fittingly joyous conclusion.

The *Magnificat*, too, combines spaciousness with vitality. The mysteriously evocative *Et misericordia* contrasts dramatically with the dynamic *Deposuit potentes*; but, throughout, the essential Italianate warmth of Alessandrini's reading comes through, and the rich choral response is at its most embracing in the closing *Gloria Patri*.

The bonuses include a *Concerto for Strings* (which acts as a spirited intermezzo between the main works) and a lively *Double Trumpet Concerto* as an end-piece, arranged from a work for trumpet and oboe, with the oboe retained for just the slow movement.

Willcocks's version authentically uses comparatively small forces and has an excellent team of soloists. It is very stylish and very well recorded. Some might feel that consonants are too exaggerated but, in consequence, words are admirably clear.

Corboz, a fine choral conductor, gives a lively performance of the famous *Gloria*, and his super-bargain version includes another richly rewarding liturgical work by Vivaldi alongside an equally spontaneous account of Bach's *Magnificat*. The *Kyrie* is magnificent, with its four soloists, double chorus and double string orchestra spread spaciously across the sound stage. The CD transfer is excellent.

On Naxos it is most refreshing to have a performance of Vivaldi's most popular choral work that with modern instruments and a relatively small choir clarifies textures, revealing inner detail usually obscured. With Jeremy Summerly directing the choir and Nicholas Ward conducting the orchestra, the rhythmic point of the writing is reinforced, helped by superb sound, fresh, clear and immediate.

Muti offers the more expansive version of the *Magnificat*, including extended solo arias. His approach, both in that work and in the *Gloria*, is altogether blander than the authentic style adopted by Pinnock. Muti's expansiveness undoubtedly suits the larger-scaled *Magnificat* better than the *Gloria*, which lacks incisiveness. The 1977 analogue recording has been effectively remastered, but this is a curious choice for EMI's 'Great Recordings of the Century' series.

Juditha triumphans (oratorio; complete)

*** Opus 111 OP 30314 (3). Koxená, Trullu, Comparato, Herrman, Carraro, Santa Cecilia Academy, Chamber Ch., Academia Montis Regalis, De Marchi

Juditha triumphans, Vivaldi's only surviving oratorio, has been recorded a number of times, and this Italian version, recorded in Mondovi in Italy in October 2000, offers a vigorous and scholarly account, meticulously prepared. With fair justification De Marchi has transposed the tenor and bass parts of the chorus up an octave, as Vivaldi is believed to have done with his female chorus at the Ospedale della Pietà in Venice. The result is fresh and brilliant, and the team of female soloists, two sopranos and three mezzos, adds to that impression, except that the recording balance sets them at a slight distance, seriously reducing their impact. Even so, the brilliant and rich-toned Slovakian soprano stands out in the title-role, with the mezzo Maria Jose Trullo bringing variety to the role of her adversary, Holofernes.

Laudate pueri Dominum, RV 601; Nisi Dominus, RV 608

*** Mer. CDE 84129. Dawson, Robson, King's Consort, King

The present setting of Psalm 113, RV 601, is a strong, consistently inspired work. Lynne Dawson sings with an excellent sense of style and is given splendid support. The coupling, the *Nisi Dominus*, a setting of Psalm 127, is much better known but makes an attractive makeweight. It is also given an excellent performance by Christopher Robson. Good recording.

Longe mala, umbrae, terrores, RV 629; Nisi Dominus (Psalm 126), RV 608; Stabat Mater, RV 621

- *** Virgin 5 45474-2. Daniels, Europa Galante, Bondi

A superb triptych. David Daniels has not made a finer solo record than this, and he receives splendid support from Fabio Bondi and Europa Galante. The warmth of expressive feeling from singer and accompaniment alike is apparent from the very opening of the *Stabat Mater*, which is superbly sung, and the performance of *Nisi Dominus* is both dramatic and moving. How beautiful is the *Beatus vir*, sung seraphically over the continuo accompaniment, while there is splendid bravura in *Sicut erat* without any loss of lyrical feeling. The motet *Longe mala* ('Long-standing ills, shadows, terrors') opens very dramatically, with more virtuosity demanded and relished, while the closing section *Descende o coeli vox* ('Descend O voice of heaven') again makes warm lyrical contrast; then the piece ends with an excitingly florid *Alleluia*.

Nisi Dominus (Psalm 127), RV 608; (ii) Nulla in mundo pax sincera, RV 630

(M) *** O-L (ADD) 443 199-2. (i) Bowman; (ii) Kirkby; AAM, Preston – BACH: *Magnificat*; KUHNAU: *Der Gerechte kommt um* ***

The solo motet *Nulla in mundo pax sincera* has Emma Kirkby as soloist coping splendidly with the bravura writing for soprano. James Bowman is also a persuasive soloist in the more extended, operatic-styled setting of Psalm 127. But since Vivaldi probably wrote *Nisi Dominus* for the Pietà, a Venetian orphanage for girls, readers might prefer a soprano voice.

(i) Stabat Mater in F min., RV 621; Cessate omai cessate, RV 684; Filiae mestae in C min., RV 638. Concerto for Strings in C, RV 114; Sonata al Santo Sepolcro in E flat, RV 130

⊕ *** HMC 901571. (i) Scholl; Ens. 415, Banchini

Chiara Banchini and Ensemble 415 have given us some fine period-instrument performances, but none is finer than this, thanks to the superb contribution of counter-tenor Andreas Scholl. His tenderly expressive account of the *Stabat Mater* is infinitely touching, while the pastoral cantata, *Cessate omai cessate*, is, dramatically and lyrically, no less involving. Here Vivaldi's imaginative accompaniments are relished by the instrumental ensemble, and they are equally on their toes in the similarly contrasted string works. Strongly communicative music-making, very well recorded, though the programme lasts less than an hour.

(i) Stabat Mater, RV 621; Clarae stella scintillate (Motet), RV 625. Concerto funèbre in B flat for violin, oboe, salmoè & 3 viole all'inglese. Concerto sacra in D for violin & cello, with organ obbligato, RV 554a; Sonata 4 al Santo Sepolcro in E flat for Strings, RV 124

(N) *** Opus 111 OP 30367. Mingardo, Concerto Italiano, Alessandrini

The deep contralto timbre of Sara Mingardo is especially telling in Vivaldi's *Stabat Mater*, and she is very moving in the agonized closing section. This performance is appropriately framed by the *Concerto funèbre* and similarly solemn *Santo Sepolcro Sonata*. The other concertos which frame the contrasting motet, 'O bright stars shine forth', match its very different mood, and Mingardo successfully lightens her voice and style. Fine performances throughout from the excellent Concerto Italiano under Alessandrini, and vivid recording. However, we would not prefer the performance of the *Stabat Mater* to Andreas Scholl's outstanding version on Harmonia Mundi.

Vespers for the Assumption of the Virgin Mary (arr. Alessandrini)

*** Opus 111 OP 30383 (2). Bertagnolli, Invernizzi, Simboli, Mingardo, Ferrarini, Bellotto, De Secondi, Concerto Italiano, Alessandrini

Taking Monteverdi's great 1610 set of *Vespers* as a model, Rinaldo Alessandrini, in collaboration with the scholar Frederic Delamea, has devised a sequence of Psalm settings and antiphons parallel to Monteverdi's, choosing works by Vivaldi such as might have been used for the Vespers service. Though Vivaldi never wrote music for the vast basilica of St Mark's in Venice, as Monteverdi had done a century earlier, he did write Psalm settings employing double choirs, works which cry out for spatial separation. Starting with a double concerto as overture with similarly divided forces, Alessandrini has included in the sequence such masterly examples of Vivaldi's church music as the *Dixit Dominus* (Psalm 109), *Lauda Jerusalem* (Psalm 147) and the superb *Magnificat* setting, RV 610a, rounded off with a cantata for solo contralto with two orchestras, *Salve Regina*. It makes a most compelling sequence. The challenge of over two and a half hours of music prompts Alessandrini to draw from his choir and period orchestra, Concerto Italiano, consistently fresh and incisive performances, brilliantly recorded. The soloists have bright, clear voices, apt for this music, with none of the vocal fruitiness typical of Italian singers.

OPERA

Opera Overtures: Armida al campo d'Egito; Arsilda, regina di Ponto; Bajazet (Tamerlano); Dorilla in Tempe; Farnace; Il giustino; Griselda; L'incoronazione di Dario; L'Olimpiade; Ottone in Villa; La verità in cimento

(BB) *** Warner Apex 2564 60537-2. I Sol. Ven., Scimone

Vivaldi's 'opera overtures' were conceived as sinfonias, scarcely related to the character of each work. But these 11 make a lively and surprisingly varied collection, splendidly played and recorded. But it may be as well not to play them all in sequence.

Opera Overtures or Sinfonias: Bajazet; La Dorilla; Farnace; Il Giustino; L'Olimpiade; Ottone in Villa; La verità in cimento. Chamber Concerto in D min., RV 128; Concerto in F, for Violin, 2 Oboes, Horn & Bassoon, RV 571; Sinfonia in G, RV 149

(N) (B) **(*) DHM/BMG 74321 935602. L'Arte del Arco, Hogwood

Although little of this music is top-drawer Vivaldi, all of it is of interest. Except for *L'Olimpiade* (which includes a tempesta di mare and is in four sections) and *Ottone in Villa* (which is a concertante piece for violins and oboes and is in two), these are all typical three-movement Italian overtures. *Bajazet* (because of the plot) features hunting horns in the outer sections, but they are used even more spectacularly in the *Concerto in F* (which is associated with a Venetian performance of the opera, *Arsilda, Regina di Ponto*), while its finale is based on the storm from *Ottone in Villa*. The finale of the *Sinfonia for La Dorilla* brings a surprise appearance of the introduction of *Spring* from *The Four Seasons*. The period performances here are highly energetic and certainly stylish, but a bit gruff. One might have thought Harnoncourt rather than Hogwood was in charge (perhaps because Federico Guglielmo, the lead violin, is credited with rehearsing the orchestra).

Il giustino (dramma per musica; abridged)

*** Virgin 5 45518-2 (2). Labelle, Comparato, Provvisionato, McGreevy, De Lisi, Cherici, Il Complesso Barocco, Curtis

Written for Rome in 1724, Vivaldi's *Il giustino* is based on a libretto that had already been set by Domenico Scarlatti and Albinoni, while twelve years later in London Handel also used it with modifications. Taking his cue from some of the simplifications made by the composer, Alan Curtis has introduced judicious cuts, preserving what he regards as the most inspired numbers. The result in this live recording made in Rotterdam is a sparkling entertainment, with one brief number after another advancing the involved plot about the Emperor Justinian with winning speed. The mood is consistently light, fresh and lively, with Curtis an inspired director. He consistently relishes the instrumental colouring, as in the ceremonial trumpets and timpani, as well as the occasional reference to music we know, as in the quotation from the *Four Seasons* in the *Sinfonia* introducing the fifth scene of Act I. Among the most striking numbers are a pastoral aria for Giustino in Act I, an extended minor-key aria for Anastasia, full of side-slipping chromatic harmonies, and a magnificent aria for Arianna ending Act I. The bird-song aria for Arianna in Act II is also remarkable, with Curtis introducing various eighteenth-century bird whistles, which, as he says, are played with great enthusiasm by the group's oboe and recorder players. The casting is strong, with fresh, clear voices in all the parts except one, and that sadly the title-role of Giustino, in which the mezzo, Francesca Provvisionato, sings with a distracting judder. Despite that blemish, this is a set to transform one's ideas of Vivaldi and his mastery as an opera-composer, so long ignored. Light, transparent sound.

Ottone in Villa (complete)

*** Chan. 0614 (2). Groop, Gritton, Argenta, Padmore, Daneman, Coll. Mus. 90, Hickox

Ottone in Villa was Vivaldi's very first opera, produced in 1713. It follows the conventions of the day in a sequence of da capo arias linked by recitatives, with no ensemble up until the final number for the characters in unison. With only five singers required, the scale of the piece is modest in treating the subject of the Emperor Ottone and the way he is fooled by the flirtatious Cleonilla. Vivaldi is here at his most tuneful and inventive, and Richard Hickox with an excellent cast of soloists and his fine period-instrument group, Collegium Musicum 90, presents the opera with a freshness and vigour that make one forget the work's formal limitations. Susan Gritton sings charmingly as the provocative Cleonilla, and Nancy Argenta brings flawless control to the castrato role of Caio Sillo, with the mezzo, Monica Groop, strong and firm in the title-role of the Emperor. Fine production and sound add to the compulsion of the performance.

La verita in cimento

**(*) Opus 111 OP 30365. Bertagnolli, Laurens, Mingardo, Stutzmann, Jaroussky, Rolfe Johnson, Ens. Matheus, Spinosi

La verita in cimento ('Truth on Trial'), Vivaldi's thirteenth opera, was first heard in Venice in 1720, but like almost all his other operas it has since been totally neglected. Then in 2002, using a score prepared from various scholarly sources, the enterprising French conductor Jean-Christophe Spinosi and his group, Ensemble Matheus, gave a very successful series of twenty-five performances of what emerges as an exceptionally lively piece. With six soloists and no chorus, it is a piece that defied the conventions of the Venetian establishment, led by Benedetto Marcello, and after it Vivaldi was prevented from writing more operas for some years. Yet, as recorded by Spinosi and his excellent team, this is a piece that sparkles with life.

After the dramatic overture, at the start of Act I all six soloists are given, in turn, an aria (all but one vigorous), setting the pattern for a fast-moving piece. The typically involved story of love and inheritance in neighbouring sultanates is made more complicated by being dependent on a Gilbertian switching of babies years earlier. It all ends happily, largely through the selfless generosity of the legitimate heir, Zelim, a castrato role, here taken superbly by the brilliant young French counter-tenor Philippe Jaroussky. There is no weak link among the others either, with the contralto, Sara Mingardo, not just ripely resonant but wonderfully agile in the other castrato role of the rival, Melindo. Vigorous music predominates, often with offbeat accenting and sharp dynamic contrasts. Many of the numbers, including a trio and a quintet as well as arias, are in minor keys, and the use of baroque guitar and theorbo lute among the continuo instruments adds a poetic quality to the gentler arias. The very brief final ensemble for all six soloists brings an exuberant closing number topped by a trumpet solo. The recording has the instruments set in an apt acoustic, but the solo voices, reasonably balanced in arias, are distractingly close in recitatives.

'Viva Vivaldi': Arias: (i) *Agitata da due venti La Griselda, RV 718. Gloria in D, RV 589: Domine Deus. Opera arias: Bajazet (Il Tamerlano): Anch'il mar par che sommerga. Farnace: Gelido in ogni vedo. La fida Ninfa: Dite, Oimè. Giustino: Sventurata Navicelli. Juditha Triumphans: Armatae face et Angibus. L'Olimpiade, Tra la follie divers ... Siam navi all'onde algenti. Ottone in villa, Gelosia, tu già rendi l'alma mia. Teuzzone: Di due rai languir costante; Zeffiretti che sussurrate. Tito Manlio: Non ti lusinghi la crudeltade. Concertos in C for flautino, RV 443; in D for lute, RV 93*

⇒ *** Arthaus **DVD** 100 228. (i) Bartoli; Il Giardino Armonico, Antonini (V/D: Brian Large)

Although Vivaldi is known to have composed 90 operas, only 20 have survived. For this programme Cecilia Bartoli has drawn on autograph material in the Turin Library and has come up with some valuable additions to the repertory. The recital was recorded in September 2000 at the Théâtre des Champs-Elysées and is presented very unobtrusively, albeit with a limited repertoire of shots.

In the two concertos, the *Domine Deus* and a couple of the arias, the score is available, though it must be said that its superimposition all but obliterates the visual image. As in her handsomely presented Decca *Vivaldi Album* (see below), Bartoli sings effortlessly and magnificently – and she duplicates one or two arias here.

Il Giordano Armonico are full of virtuosity and delicacy, and the presence of Brian Large prevents the kind of ostentatious visual 'cleverness' that wrecked their recital. The music is left to speak for itself, and the presence of Bartoli's Decca producer, Christopher Raeburn, ensures an excellent and musical balance. It is a tribute to Vivaldi's spectacular fund of invention that there is so much of quality yet to be discovered. Subtitles of the aria texts are in German, French, English and Spanish, and are also available in the original Italian.

Opera Arias and Scenas: *Bajazet (Il Tamerlano): Anch'il mar par che sommerga. Dorilla in Tempe: Dorilla'aura al sussurrar. Farnace: Gelido in ogni vena. La fida ninfa: Alma opressa; Dite, oimè. Griselda: Dopo un'orrida procella. Il giustino; Sorte, che m'invitasti ... Ho nel petto un cor sì forte. L'olimpiade: Tra le follie ... Siam navi all'onde algenti. L'Orlando finto pazzo: Qual favellar? ... Anderò volerò*

griderò. Teuzzone: Di trombe guerrier. Arias with unidentified sources: *Di due rai languir costante; Zeffiretti, che sussurrate*
- *** Decca 466 569-2. Bartoli, Il Giardino Armonico (with Arnold Schoenberg Ch.)

This remarkable collection is valuable as much for its exploration of unknown Vivaldi operas as for coloratura singing of extraordinary bravura and technical security. It is a pity that the programme (understandably) opens with the excerpt from *Dorilla in Tempe*, with its echoes of *Spring* from *The Four Seasons*, as the chorus, although enthusiastic in praising those seasonal joys, is less than sharply focused. But the following aria from *Griselda*, with its stormy horns and fiendish leaps and runs, shows just how expertly Cecilia Bartoli can deliver the kind of thrilling virtuosity expected by Vivaldi's audiences at their famous castrato soloists. Farnace's tragic aria, *Gelido in ogni vena* (based on the *Winter* concerto) shows the other side of the coin with some exquisite lyrical singing of lovely descending chromatics. Similarly, while *Alma opressa* (from *La fida ninfa*) brings a remarkable display of melismatic runs with its almost unbroken line of semiquavers, the following *Dite, oimè*, very movingly sung, has an almost desperate melancholy. In short, this is dazzling singing of remarkable music, most stylishly and vividly accompanied. Indeed, the Storm aria from *Bajazet* brings a delivery of such speed and sharpness of articulation that the rapid fire of a musical machine-gun springs instantly to mind. Moreover, Decca have done their star mezzo proud with fine documentation, full translations and a presentation more like a handsomely bound hardback book than a CD.

VOORMOLEN, Alexander (1895–1980)

Baron Hop Suites 1–2; (i) *Double Oboe Concerto; Eline (Nocturne for Orchestra)*
*** Chan. 9815. Hague Residentie O, Bamert; (i) with Oostenrijk; Roerade

Apart from Diepenbrock, late-nineteenth- and early-twentieth-century Dutch orchestral music still remains a virtually unexplored area. All the more reason to welcome this highly entertaining collection. Alexander Voormolen was born in Rotterdam, but his musical life centred on The Hague. His maternal grandmother was a Rameau (a descendant of Jean-Philippe's brother), which accounts for the French influences in his musical genes that were to attract the attention of Ravel, who became his sponsor, and whose personal recommendation ensured that the music was published.

Voormolen sought to create a truly Dutch style in his writing, but his genes thwarted him, and its charming eccentricity and unpredictability give a very un-Dutch impression. Indeed, one might think of him as a Netherlands equivalent of Lord Berners. His orchestral skill and witty humour are ideally suited to his musical evocations of the world of Baron Hop, a genial larger-than-life eighteenth-century Dutch diplomat and *bon viveur*, who so loved coffee that he had a famous sweetmeat made of it called 'Haagsche Hopjes'.

The two *Baron Hop Suites* (1924 and 1931) draw on material from an aborted *opéra comique*, and their spirited neoclassicism is well nourished by a richly coloured orchestral palette, and sprightly rhythms. There are Dutch popular tunes, and others too. In the first suite the witty opening overture (it has a false ending) quotes a snatch of the *Marseillaise*, and the closing *March of the Hereditary Prince-Stadtholder* even

includes *The British Grenadiers.* In between come a slightly sensuous *Sarabande* and an engaging *Polka.*

The *Concerto for Two Oboes* is quaintly colourful with a unique 'quacking' closing Rondo. *Eline* (originally a piano work) is languorous and faintly Delian, but has other influences too. All this music is played very persuasively indeed by the composer's home orchestra, directed with complete understanding, the nicest touches of rubato and neat rhythmic pointing by Bamert. The Chandos recording is glowingly full and vivid. A real find.

VOŘÍŠEK, Jan Václav (1791–1825)

Symphony in D, Op. 24
- *** Hyp. CDA 66800. SCO, Mackerras – ARRIAGA: *Symphony in D min.* etc. ***
(M) (**) Sup. mono SU 3678-2 001. Czech PO, Ančerl – MOZART: *Bassoon Concerto; Violin Concerto 3* (**(*))

Voříšek is as close as the Czechs got to producing a Beethoven, and this remarkably powerful work has many fingerprints of the German master everywhere while displaying some individuality. The slow movement is impressive and, after an attractive Scherzo, the finale has something in common with that of Beethoven's *Fourth*. Mackerras offers the finest account this work has received on record so far. The Hyperion recording is warmly reverberant, but this serves to increase the feeling of Beethovenian weightiness, and the Scherzo is particularly imposing. The Arriaga coupling is indispensable.

Ančerl's performance is amiable and polished, at its most characterful in the *Andante*, and very well played throughout, with a vigorous finale. The 1950 mono recording, too, is fully acceptable, but there is an even finer Supraphon stereo version by the conductorless Prague Chamber Orchestra, which rather puts this one in the shade and which we hope may be reissued soon. It would have been a better coupling for the fine Mozart performances that are offered here.

Fantasia in C, Op. 12; Impromptus 1–6, Op. 7; Piano Sonata in B flat min., Op. 19; Variations in B flat, Op. 19
*** Opus 111 OPS 30241. Tverskaya

The Russian-born but London-domiciled Olga Tverskaya is an eloquent advocate of this always interesting and often highly original music, and plays with great flair and conviction. She uses a period instrument, a copy of an 1823 Broadmann fortepiano by David Winston. The instrument comes from the exact period of the works included on this disc. The recording is altogether excellent and the disc in every respect, a success.

WAGNER, Richard (1813–83)

Siegfried Idyll
- (M) *** DG (ADD) 449 725-2. BPO, Karajan – R. STRAUSS: *Ein Heldenleben* ***
○ (M) *** Decca (ADD) 460 311-2. VPO, Solti – SCHUBERT: *Symphony 9* *** ○
(M) *** EMI (ADD) 5 67036-2 (2). Philh. O, Klemperer – MAHLER: *Symphony 9*; R. STRAUSS: *Metamorphosen* ***
(M) *** EMI (ADD) 5 62815-2. Philh. O, Klemperer – BRUCKNER: *Symphony 4* ***
(M) (***) BBC Legends mono BBCL 4076-2. Hallé O, Barbirolli – BEETHOVEN: *Symphony 7*; MOZART: *Symphony 35* ***

Karajan's account of Wagner's wonderful birthday present to

Cosima is unsurpassed; it has never sounded better than in this transfer, aptly coupled with Strauss's *Ein Heldenleben*, Karajan's very first stereo recording for DG.

So rich is the sound that Decca provided for Solti (in 1965) that one can hardly believe that this is a chamber performance. The playing is similarly warm and committed and this coupling with Schubert's *Great C major Symphony*, is one of Solti's finest recordings.

Klemperer also favours the original chamber-orchestra scoring and the Philharmonia players are very persuasive, especially in the score's gentler moments. The balance is forward and, although the sound is warm, some ears may crave a greater breadth of string tone at the climax.

Barbirolli's account of the *Siegfried Idyll*, recorded in the BBC's Manchester studios, comes in mono sound only, with obvious limitations. The use of reduced strings means that the woodwind solos come over very clearly, with a glorious horn outburst at the climax (track 9, 11'30"), and though the tempo for the central episode is on the slow side, with Barbirolli letting it get slower still in ecstasy, the magic of this birthday gift to Cosima Wagner comes over superbly, with thrilling climaxes. With the Beethoven and Mozart symphonies as coupling, one welcomes a splendid portrait of this ever-characterful conductor.

Siegfried Idyll; A Faust Overture; Götterdämmerung: Siegfried's Rhine Journey. Lohengrin: Prelude to Act III. Overtures: Die Meistersinger; Rienzi

(M) **(*) RCA 82876 59414-2. BPO, Maazel

For the Berlin Philharmonic's Wagner programme directed by Lorin Maazel, now reissued as part of the 'Classic Collection', RCA has returned to the Berlin Jesus-Christus-Kirche, where so many of the orchestra's most celebrated recordings were made. The *Siegfried Idyll* is beautifully played, the ebb and flow of tension admirably controlled, and the closing section quite lovely. *Rienzi* and the *Lohengrin Third Act Prelude* are vivid and brilliant, and the *Faust Overture* has plenty of character. But in the *Prelude* to *Die Meistersinger*, which Maazel paces convincingly, the ear craves rather more amplitude in the recording itself, in a deeper, more resonant bass. The principal horn (who also contributed impressively to the *Siegfried Idyll*) plays with panache (slightly distanced) in the closing *Siegfried's Rhine Journey* which, after an atmospheric opening and a sudden, impulsive accelerando, certainly makes a spectacular and gripping end to the concert. The digital sound-picture is cleanly focused, fresh, clear and well balanced, but a little more reflection of the hall acoustics would have made the recording even finer.

Siegfried Idyll. Der fliegende Holländer: Overture. Götterdämmerung: Siegfried's Rhine Journey & Funeral March. Lohengrin: Preludes to Acts I & III. Die Meistersinger: Overture; Dance of the Apprentices; Entry of the Masters. Parsifal: Prelude. Das Rheingold: Entry of the Gods into Valhalla. Siegfried: Forest Murmurs. Tannhäuser: Overture; Prelude to Act III. Tristan und Isolde: Prelude & Liebestod. Die Walküre: Ride of the Valkyries

☛ (M) *** EMI (ADD) 5 67893-2 [567896] (2). Philh. O, Klemperer

Two of the LPs from which this Klemperer programme is compiled were recorded and released in 1960 to celebrate Klemperer's 75th birthday. The balance, including the *Siegfried Idyll*, followed a year later. Klemperer chose to record the latter work in the original chamber scoring that Cosima heard at Triebschen on her Christmas birthday morning in 1870. It is also available separately, coupled with Mahler and Strauss – see above. All these performances have the kind of incandescent glow one associates with really great conductors, and the Philharmonia play immaculately. The remastered recording is very impressive indeed. This set now takes its place among EMI's 'Great Recordings of the Century'.

Siegfried Idyll; Der fliegende Holländer: Overture. Götterdämmerung: Siegfried's Funeral March. Lohengrin: Prelude to Act I; Hymn. Parsifal: Prelude to Act I. Rienzi: Overture. Tannhäuser: Overture & Bacchanale. Tristan und Isolde: Prelude to Act I

(B) *** Double Decca 440 606-2 (2). VPO, Solti

Solti's way with Wagner is certainly exciting: some may find the early 1960s performances of the *Rienzi* and *The Flying Dutchman* overtures a little hard-driven. But the *Siegfried Idyll*, played in its chamber version by members of the VPO, is most beautifully done, and the *Lohengrin Prelude* is similarly relaxed until its climax – two welcome moments of repose amid such drama.

Elsewhere one is easily caught up in the sheer force of Solti's music-making, and in the later recordings in the 1970s Solti has mellowed a little and the *Meistersinger Overture* has genuine grandeur and nobility. The VPO play splendidly, of course, and Decca has supplied brilliant sound to match. An inexpensive way to explore Solti's special charisma in orchestral Wagner.

(i; ii) *Siegfried Idyll.* (iii; iv) *Overture: Der fliegende Holländer.* (i; v) *Götterdämmerung: Siegfried's Rhine Journey. Lohengrin:* (i; ii) *Prelude to Act I;* (vi; iv) *Prelude to Act III. Die Meistersinger:* (vi; iv) *Overture;* (vii; viii) *Prelude to Act III.* (ix; viii) *Parsifal: Prelude & Good Friday Music. Overtures:* (vi; iv) *Rienzi;* (vii; x) *Tannhäuser. Tristan und Isolde:* (iii; iv) *Preludes to Acts I & III;* (vi; iv) *Death of Isolde.* (i; v) *Die Walküre: Ride of the Valkyries*

(B) *** DG Double (ADD) 439 687-2 (2). (i) BPO; (ii) Kubelik; (iii) Bayreuth Festival O; (iv) Boehm; (v) Karajan; (vi) VPO; (vii) German Op., Berlin , O; (viii) Jochum; (ix) Bav. RSO; (x) Gerdes

The *Siegfried Idyll* is beautifully shaped by Kubelik and equally beautifully played by the Berlin Philharmonic. He also conducts an impressive *Lohengrin Act I Prelude*, again with the BPO. Boehm not only provides a richly sustained opening for Rienzi but is exciting in *Der fliegende Holländer* and at his finest in the *Tristan Preludes* – taken from his 1966 Bayreuth complete set – which glow with intensity. Karajan contributes only two items, but both surge with adrenalin. The highlight of the set comes last, Jochum's electrifying performance of the *Prelude* and *Good Friday* music from *Parsifal*. Recorded in the Munich Herculessaal, it is not only a demonstration record from the earliest days of stereo, but the playing has a spiritual intensity that has never been surpassed. The recordings, dating from the late 1950s to the early 1980s, have all been transferred vividly, mostly with fuller and more refined sound. The documentation is sadly inadequate.

Siegfried Idyll. Tannhäuser: Overture. (i) *Tristan: Prelude & Liebestod*

*** DG 423 613-2. (i) Norman; VPO, Karajan

This superb Wagner recording was taken live from a unique concert conducted by Karajan at the Salzburg Festival in August 1987. The *Tannhäuser Overture* has never sounded so noble, and the *Siegfried Idyll* has rarely seemed so intense and dedicated behind its sweet lyricism; while the *Prelude and Liebestod*, with Jessye Norman as soloist, bring the richest culmination, sensuous and passionate, remarkable as much for the hushed, inward moments as for the massive building of climaxes.

ORCHESTRAL EXCERPTS AND PRELUDES FROM THE OPERAS

Der fliegende Holländer: Overture. Götterdämmerung: Funeral Music; Siegfried's Rhine Journey. Lohengrin: Act I Prelude. Die Meistersinger: Overture; Dance of the Apprentices; Entry of the Masters. Parsifal: Good Friday Music

(M) (***) Sony mono SMK 89889. RPO, Beecham

The 1954 recordings here – *Der fliegende Holländer*, the *Meistersinger* excerpts (the three items linked together) and *Siegfried's Rhine Journey* – come in fuller and weightier sound than Beecham generally enjoyed at that final period of mono recording with CBS, with splendid brass but an occasional edge on strings. The swagger and panache of Beecham in Wagner comes out superbly, and though the other recordings are not quite so full, with edginess more obtrusive, they are most enjoyable. In the manner of the time concert endings are provided where necessary.

Der fliegende Holländer: Overture. Götterdämmerung: Siegfried's Funeral Music; Finale. Die Meistersinger: Prelude, Act I. Tristan und Idolde: Preludes, Acts I & III; Liebestod. Die Walküre: The Ride of the Valkyries

(BB) **(*) DG Entrée 474 568-2. O de Paris, Barenboim

Barenboim's is a warm and sympathetic collection of overtures and preludes, plus the instrumental version of Isolde's *Liebestod*. The only snag is that the Paris orchestra – particularly its brass section, with its excessive vibrato – does not sound quite authentic, and the acoustic is not always helpful, failing to give the necessary resonance to the deeper brass sounds. These recordings derive from two LPs dating from 1983–4, though it's a pity there was no room for the delightful rarity included on one of the LPs, *La Descente de la Courtille*, a jolly processional piece sounding more like Offenbach and great fun.

Der fliegende Holländer: Overture; Lohengrin: Preludes to Acts I & III; Die Meistersinger: Overture; Parsifal: Preludes to Acts I & III; Overtures: Rienzi; Tannhäuser

**(*) Chan. 9870. Danish Nat. RSO, Albrecht

Splendidly full-blooded and expansive Chandos recording and first-class playing from the Danish Orchestra. They are at their finest in the beautifully shaped *Lohengrin: Prelude* to Act I, which has a superb cymbal-capped climax and an impressive closing diminuendo. But this is repertoire already available in outstanding performances from the likes of Karajan, Solti, Szell and Bruno Walter. Gerd Albrecht's very direct and well-detailed readings do not stand comparison with such exulted names. However, if you want straightforward accounts in top-quality sound, this disc may well be for you.

(i) Der fliegende Holländer: Overture. (ii) Lohengrin: Prelude to Act I. Die Meistersinger: Overture. (i) Rienzi: Overture; (ii) Tannhäuser: Overture. (i) Tristan und Isolde: Prelude; (i) Die Walküre: Ride of the Valkyries

(M) **(*) Decca (ADD) 458 214-2. (i) VPO; (ii) Chicago SO: Solti

Recorded between 1960 (*Rienzi*) and 1986 (*Lohengrin Prelude*) these performances were newly made in the studio, not taken from complete opera sets. So this is the self-contained *Tannhäuser Overture* from the Dresden version, and exciting it is with brilliant sound. The following *Meistersinger Prelude* is fuller and more expansive, but all the music-making here demonstrates Solti's characteristic Wagnerian flair and brings a high degree of tension. In *Der fliegende Holländer* the VPO are driven too hard and the effect is fierce, but *Rienzi* is mellower, with the big tune at the opening obviously relished. The CD transfers are vivid, if not always refined.

Der fliegende Holländer Overture. Lohengrin: Preludes to Acts I & III Die Meistersinger: Overture; (i) Tannhäuser: Overture and Venusberg Music. Tristan und Isolde: Prelude & Liebestod

⊙━ *** EMI (ADD) **Audio DVD** DVC4 92397-9. BPO, Karajan; (i) with German Op. Ch.

⊙━ (M) *** EMI 5 62756-2 [5 62771-2]. BPO, Karajan; (i) with German Op. Ch.

All in all, Karajan's 1974 collection is perhaps the finest single disc of miscellaneous Wagnerian overtures and preludes in the catalogue, recommendable alongside Szell's Cleveland collection of orchestral music from the *Ring*. Karajan's CD is fully worthy of inclusion as one of EMI's 'Great Recordings of the Century'. The body of tone produced by the Berlin Philharmonic gives a breathtaking amplitude at climaxes and the electricity the conductor generates throughout the programme is unforgettable. As with the other EMI Audio DVDs the recording was originally made in quadrophony, and there is a choice between multi-channel surround sound or high-resolution stereo. The results are spectacular with greater depth, a wider dyamic range and a remarkable sense of the ambience of the Berlin Philharmonie. But this much less expensive CD can be recommended with equal enthusiasm.

Der fliegende Holländer: Overture. Die Meistersinger von Nürnberg: Overture. Tannhäuser: Overture. Lohengrin: Preludes to Acts I & III, and (i) Ortrud's aria. Tristan und Isolde: Liebestod

*** Testament SBT 1256. Paris Opéra O, Cluytens with (i) Gorr

André Cluytens was the first French conductor to appear at Bayreuth. In 1955 he stepped in to replace an indisposed Eugen Jochum and during that period conducted *Tannhäuser*, *Lohengrin* and *Die Meistersinger*. It is obvious from the response of the Paris Opéra Orchestra in these stereo recordings of 1959–60 that he was not only a dedicated Wagnerian, but a Wagner conductor of stature. Both these discs are strongly recommended, and the sound (stereo for the Overtures and Preludes; mono on its companion) is in every way satisfying.

Overtures: Der fliegende Holländer; Die Meistersinger; Tannhäuser; Tristan: Prelude to Act I

(M) *** Sup. (ADD) SU 3469-2 011. Czech PO, Konwitschny (with R. STRAUSS: *Till Eulenspiegel* (mono) ***)

Konwitschny's collection was highly regarded in its day (1960) for the excitement and spontaneity of the readings, with *Die Meistersinger* particularly well shaped and *Tannhäuser* bringing thrilling cascades from the Czech Philharmonic strings as well as fine brass playing. *Der fliegende Holländer* creates a vivid image of the storm-tossed ship. The analogue recording, made (like most of the other current Supraphon reissues) in the Dvořák Hall in Prague, is impressively spacious. The transfer is bright and full, if not in the demonstration bracket. What makes the disc especially attractive is the 1952 mono coupling, a great credit to the sound engineer, František Burda. Konwitschny's performance takes off racily from the very opening bars. It has great zest, warmth and humour, plus spontaneous bursts of excitement. The closing section ends with a spectacular execution, before the touching little epilogue on the strings. (However be warned: there are some curious ticking noises on the tape at the very opening of *Till.*)

Götterdämmerung: Dawn and Siegfried's Rhine Journey; Siegfried's Death and Funeral Music. Lohengrin: Preludes to Acts I & III. Die Meistersinger: Overture. Das Rheingold: Entry of the Gods into Valhalla. Rienzi: Overture. Siegfried: Forest Murmurs. Tannhäuser: Overture. Die Walküre: Ride of the Valkyries; Wotan's Farewell and Magic Fire Music

(N) (BB) *** EMI Gemini 5 86248-2 (2). BPO, Tennstedt

This new bargain Gemini two-CD set comprises two early digital recordings (1981 and 1983) of Wagner's orchestral music which were quite a revelation in the early days of compact disc. In the music from the *Ring*, notably the *Entry of the Gods into Valhalla*, the sense of spectacle is in no doubt, and *Wotan's Farewell* and *Magic Fire Music* are also very impressive. The sound could ideally have greater amplitude (the brass is a bit dry), but the climax of *Siegfried's Funeral March* has massive penetration – and there is fine detail too, especially in the atmospheric *Forest Murmurs*. The playing throughout is of the finest quality, always maintaining a high level of tension. As can be seen, the non-*Ring* items are also available on a separate bargain HMV disc, discussed below.

Götterdämmerung: Dawn; Siegfried's Rhine Journey & Funeral March. Die Meistersinger: Prelude to Act I. Rienzi: Overture; Tannhäuser: Overture and Venusberg Music. Die Walküre: Ride of the Valkyries

(N) (BB) *** LPO Live LPO 003. LPO, Tennstedt

This 1988 recording of a live concert makes a fascinating comparison with Tennstedt's EMI discs, above and below. As before, his readings are characteristically broad, with the *Meistersinger Prelude* warmly and weightily expansive and the *Götterdämmerung* excerpts spaciously powerful. However, the live occasion also makes its mark, and the thundering chords of the *Funeral Music* are sinisterly overwhelming, while *Rienzi* is more volatile here than in the Berlin studio. The LPO are on their toes and play splendidly throughout; they are gorgeously sensuous in the *Venusberg Music*, helped by the rich amplitude of the recording. Indeed, the acoustic of the Royal Festival Hall has never sounded more opulent on CD, although because this almost certainly came from a broadcast the dynamic range is narrower than the Berlin Philharmonic studio recording. But the only real minus point is that the programme ends unexpectedly at the end of the *Venusberg Music*, when the exciting *Ride of the Valkyries*, with its enthusiastic applause, would have made a much more upbeat conclusion.

(i) *Götterdämmerung: Siegfried's Rhine Journey & Funeral March;* (ii) *Die Meistersinger: Prelude to Act III; Procession of the Meistersingers;* (iii) *Das Rheingold: Entrance of the Gods into Valhalla;* (ii) *Rienzi: Overture. Tristan und Isolde: Prelude and Liebestod. Die Walküre:* (ii) *Magic Fire Music;* (iii; iv) *Ride of the Valkyries*

(M) *(**) RCA (ADD) 82876 55306-2. Stokowski, with (i) LSO; (ii) RPO; (iii) Symphony of the Air; (iv) Arroyo; Ordassy; Parker

Three orchestras are here unified by Stokowski's brand of magnetism. At a flick of the wrist, he creates electric tension, the dynamic contrasts and climaxes made more all the more effective when heard alongside the richly sensuous playing in the slow numbers, with the conductor adopting tempos which might seem indulgent in less gifted hands. The opening of the *Die Meistersinger Prelude* is rich in Wagnerian amplitude, while the *Tristan Prelude and Liebestod* is glowingly atmospheric in the high strings. The *Entry of the Gods into Valhalla* and a vocal version of the *Ride of the Valkyries* are predictably exciting, as is the *Rienzi Overture*, which builds up to a fine climax. The two *Götterdämmerung* items with the LSO bring a real frisson, with *Siegfried's Funeral March* suitably sombre and the dramatic interjections from the full orchestra powerfully placed. The sound is surprisingly uniform throughout the programme (dating from between 1961 and 1974), generally full and certainly vivid, but not always refined, with the brass coarsening under pressure, though Stokowski's string sonorities come over well.

Götterdämmerung: Dawn & Siegfried's Rhine Journey; Siegfried's Death & Funeral Music. Die Meistersinger: Prelude. Das Rheingold: Entry of the Gods into Valhalla. Siegfried: Forest Murmurs. Tristan und Isolde: Prelude & Liebestod. Die Walküre: Wotan's Farewell & Magic Fire Music

⊕→ ✿ *** Sony **SACD** SS 89035; **(B)** CD (ADD) SBK 48175. Cleveland O, Szell

The orchestral playing here is breathtaking in its virtuosity. Szell generates the greatest tension, particularly in the two scenes from *Götterdämmerung*, while the *Liebestod* from *Tristan* has never been played on record with more passion and fire. The *Tristan* and *Meistersinger* excerpts (from 1962) have been added to the contents of the original LP, which contained the *Ring* sequences made later (in 1968), much improved on CD. This is well worthy of Szell's extraordinary achievement in Cleveland in the 1960s, even if the forward balance of the recording places a limit on the dynamic range. It is also available as a SuperAudio CD which has expanded the range, especially at the lower end.

Lohengrin: Preludes to Acts I & III

*** Australian Decca Eloquence (ADD) 467 235-2. VPO, Mehta – MAHLER: *Symphony 4* **

These beautifully and excitingly played and recorded preludes make a good bonus for Mehta's fresh account of Mahler's *Fourth Symphony*. There is something of an explosive thrill about the Act III *Prelude* which is really quite memorable.

(i) *Lohengrin: Preludes to Acts I & III; Die Meistersinger: Prelude to Act I. Rienzi: Overture; Tannhäuser: Overture;* (ii) *Tristan und Isolde: Prelude; Liebestod.* (i) *Die Walküre: Ride of the Valkyries*

(⊕→) (N) (BB) *** EMI HMV 5 86785-2. (i) BPO; (ii) Norman, LPO; Tennstedt

This outstanding budget reissue combines an early digital collection, made in the Philharmonie in the early 1980s, with the *Prelude* and Jessye Norman's splendidly sung *Liebestod* from *Tristan*, recorded five years later. The orchestral recordings could be more opulent in the middle and bass, but the brilliance is demonstrable and there is weight, too. Moreover, the orchestral playing is superb and the sense of spectacle is in no doubt. Tennstedt amalgamates something from the combined Furtwängler and Klemperer traditions in his broad, spacious readings, yet the voltage is consistently high. The opening and closing sections of the *Tannhäuser Overture* are given a restrained nobility of feeling without any loss of power or impact. Similarly, the gorgeous string melody at the opening of *Rienzi* is elegiacally moulded, and later when the brass enter in the allegro there is no suggestion of the bandstand. In the Act I *Lohengrin Prelude*, Tennstedt lingers in the *pianissimo* sections, creating radiant detail, then presses on just before the climax. The Berlin Philharmonic are on top form throughout.

Die Meistersinger: Overture

(M) (**) Beulah mono 3PD12. BBC SO, Boult –
  MENDELSSOHN: *Hebrides Overture* (**); SCHUBERT: *Symphony 9 in C (Great)* **(*)

In this recording of 1933, constricted by the length of short-playing 78 r.p.m. discs, Boult takes an urgent and biting view of the *Meistersinger Overture*, fresh and dramatic. Surface hiss is high but even, with full-bodied sound set in a dry acoustic with no added reverberation. A good supplement to the Schubert.

Die Meistersinger: Prelude to Act III. Tannhäuser: Overture & Venusberg Music. Tristan und Isolde: Prelude & Liebestod

**(*) DG (IMS) 439 022-2. BPO, Karajan

In Karajan's digital concert the orchestral playing is superlative. But, in spite of the reprocessing, the upper strings lack space, and climaxes should be freer. The overall effect is rather clinical in its detail, instead of offering a resonant panoply of sound, but the playing is eloquent and powerful. The measure is not very generous for a reissued premium-price CD.

Parsifal, Act III: Symphonic Synthesis. Tristan und Isolde: Symphonic Synthesis. Die Walküre: Wotan's Farewell & Magic Fire Music (all arr. Stokowski)

*** Chan. 9686. BBC PO, Bamert

Stokowski's recordings of Wagner excerpts always treated the voices as a kind of adjunct to the orchestra, and he loved best to play the orchestral music without them. So he made a series of symphonic syntheses, joining scenes together in a continuous sensuous and dramatic melodic flow, leaving the orchestra to convey the full narrative. *Parsifal* includes tolling bells and rich mysticism, and in *Tristan* Stokowski frames the *Liebesnacht* (including the distant hunting horns heralding the return of Tristan) with the passionate *Prelude* and *Liebestod*. Best of all he creates a symphonic poem out of Wotan's sad, loving farewell to his beloved Brünnhilde, making a great climax out of the *Fire Music*. Bamert is passionate and tender by turns and the BBC Philharmonic readily respond to the luscious orchestration. Perhaps the last degree of Stokowskian intensity is missing here, but with superbly spacious Chandos sound this is easy to enjoy.

Tannhäuser: Overture & Venusberg Music

(N) (**) BBC mono BBCL 4161-2. Hallé O, Barbirolli –
  BRUCKNER: *Symphony 3* (**)

Though the radio recording, made in the Free Trade Hall in Manchester in 1969, is relatively harsh, the warmth of Barbirolli's reading is persuasive, making an apt coupling for the glowing performance of the Bruckner, if you can accept the restricted sound.

VOCAL MUSIC

Wesendonck Lieder

(M) **(*) Ph. (ADD) 464 742-2. Norman, LSO, C. Davis – R.
  STRAUSS: *Four Last Songs* ***
(M) ** EMI (ADD) 5 67037-2. Ludwig, Philh. O, Klemperer –
  BRUCKNER: *Symphony 6* ***

The poised phrases of the *Wesendonck Lieder* drew from Jessye Norman in this 1976 recording a glorious range of tone colour, though in detailed imagination this falls short of some of the finest rivals on record. Good, refined recording, made vivid on CD with an excellent transfer.

Christa Ludwig is less successful here in her partnership with Klemperer than in the Brahms *Alto Rhapsody* also dating from 1962. In Wagner she seems to be thinking in operatic terms. She has a rich and beautiful vocal quality, but seems unable or unwilling to always reduce the tone sufficiently for the more intimate effect required in Lieder. The orchestral accompaniment is very well done.

Wesendonck Lieder: Der Engel; Stehe still; Im Treibhaus; Schmerzen; Träume. Götterdämmerung: Starke Scheite schichet mir dort. Siegfried: Ewig war ich. Tristan: Doch nun von Tristan?; Mild und leise

⊶ (M) (***) EMI mono 7 63030-2. Flagstad, Philh. O,
  Furtwängler, Dobrowen

Recorded in the late 1940s and early 1950s, a year or so before Flagstad did *Tristan* complete with Furtwängler, these performances show her at her very peak, with the voice magnificent in power as well as beautiful and distinctive in every register. The *Liebestod* (with rather heavy surface noise) may be less rapt and intense in this version with Dobrowen than with Furtwängler but is just as expansive. For the *Wesendonck Lieder* she shades the voice down very beautifully, but this is still monumental and noble rather than intimate Lieder-singing.

OPERA

Solti Wagner Edition

Der fliegende Holländer

(M) **(*) Decca (ADD) 470 792-2 (2). Bailey, Martin, Talvela, Kollo, Krenn, Isola Jones, Chicago Ch. & O, Solti

Lohengrin

(M) *** Decca 470 795-2 (4). Domingo, Norman, Nimsgern, Randová, Sotin, Fischer-Dieskau, V. State Op. Concerto Ch., VPO, Solti

Die Meistersinger von Nürnberg

⊶ (M) *** Decca 470 800-2 (4). Van Dam, Heppner, Mattila, Opie, Lippert, Vermillion, Pape, Chicago SO Ch. & O, Solti

Parsifal

(M) *** Decca (ADD) 470 805-2 (4). Kollo, Ludwig, Fischer-Dieskau, Hotter, Kelemen, Frick, V. Boys' Ch., V. State Op. Ch., VPO, Solti

Tannhäuser (Paris version)

(M) *** Decca (ADD) 470 810-2 (3). Kollo, Dernesch, Ludwig, Sotin, Braun, Hollweg, V. State Op. Ch., VPO, Solti

Tristan und Isolde

(M) *** Decca (ADD) 470 814-2 (4). Uhl, Nilsson, Resnik, Van Mill, Krause, VPO, Solti

Solti Wagner Edition (complete)

(M) *** Decca (ADD/DDD) 470 600-2 (21)

Following on after the box containing Solti's unsurpassed *Ring* cycle (455 555-2), Decca have handsomely repackaged his other Wagner recordings, which are now available separately at mid-price for the first time, or together, in a slip case, at a further reduced price. Those who invest in the Complete Edition receive a free bonus CD of rehearsal sequences from the *Tristan* recording, which was included in the original LP set. Many of these recordings remain among the top recommendations, and have the advantage of Decca's finest vintage opera sound. With the exception of the digital recordings they have been remastered for this release.

Among the highlights must be the 1972 *Parsifal* which is, by any standards, a magnificent recording, with universally excellent singing and Solti sustaining the right sort of tension throughout the performance. Hardly less impressive is *Tannhäuser*, with superlative playing from the VPO, and Christa Ludwig as Venus outshining all rivals. The 1971 sound remains impressive. Solti is less flexible in the 1960 *Tristan*, but he does relax in the more expansive passages, and he generates superb thrust in the exciting moments, such as the end of Act I, and the opening of the *Love Duet*, which has knife-edged dramatic tension.

The digital 1986 *Lohengrin* finds Domingo on magnificent form, and if Jessye Norman is not ideally suited to the role of Elsa, she is always commandingly intense, full of character. The rest of the cast and the VPO are superb. Throughout these recordings, Decca employ, almost always successfully, plenty of Culshaw-like production effects, but curiously, in the 1976 *Der fliegende Holländer*, there are none, so that characters 'halloo' at one another when they are obviously standing elbow to elbow. However, the cast on this recording is generally impressive, and though Kollo is a little coarse as Erik, it is an illuminating portrayal.

Decca rightly chose Solti's later (digital) recording of *Die Meistersinger* where the conductor's characteristic urgency is counterbalanced by a great warmth, and the cast is generally outstanding – a fine conclusion to an impressive achievement. This is now a clear first recommendation.

Der fliegende Holländer (Original, Paris version)

(N) (M) **(*) DHM/BMG 82876 64071-2 (2). Stensvold, Weber, Selig, Durmüller, WDR R. Ch., Prague Chamber Ch., Cappella Coloniensis, Weil

Using an orchestra of period instruments, Bruno Weil on DHM offers the first ever recording of Wagner's original score, the Paris version of 1841. Wagner prepared it for a performance that never took place, and the actual première had to wait until January 1843 in Dresden, for which Wagner made his first set of alterations. He made at least three sets of revisions in his lifetime, and he planned more, but this first version firmly presents the piece (as latter-day productions have tended to do) as a big, one-act work in three sections, joined by brief interludes. There are also different endings for the overture and the final scene. Dramatically, the big difference is that the opera is set in Scotland, not Norway, with Donald (not Daland) and Georg (not Erik) as the huntsman who loves the heroine, Senta. Musically, one notes instantly the extra clarity of textures and the fact that the orchestra does not so easily overwhelm the singers, who are lighter than those usually cast in these roles. The role of Senta is taken by Astrid Weber with her bright, fresh voice, biting at times but shading down to a beautiful thread of sound for the *pianissimo* top notes of *Senta's Ballad*, set in A, a full tone higher than usual. Terje Stensvold is a comparably clean-cut Dutchman, precisely focused, though Franz-Josef Selig has his woolly moments as Donald. Jorg Durmüller is excellent as Georg, Germanic in tone yet free from strain. Lively conducting and first-rate sound.

Der fliegende Holländer (complete)

⊶ *** DG 437 778-2 (2). Weikl, Studer, Sotin, Domingo, Seiffert, Ch. & O of German Op., Berlin, Sinopoli

(M) *** Ph. 434 599-2 (2). Estes, Balslev, Salminen, Schunk, Bayreuth Festival (1985) Ch. & O, Nelsson

(B) *** Naxos 8.660025/6. Muff, Haubold, Knodt, Seiffert, Budapest R. Ch., Vienna ORF SO, Steinberg

(M) **(*) EMI 64650-2 (2). Van Dam, Vejzovic, Moll, Hofmann, Moser, Borris, V. State Op. Ch., BPO, Karajan

(M) **(*) Decca (ADD) 470 792-2 (3). Bailey, Martin, Talvela, Kollo, Krenn, Isola Jones, Chicago S & O Ch. O, Solti

(M) **(*) EMI (ADD) 5 67408-2 [567405-2] (2). Adam, Silja, Talvela, Kozub, Burmeister, Unger, BBC Ch., New Philh. O, Klemperer

(BB) (***) Naxos mono 8.110189/90 (2). Hotter, Varnay, Svanholm, Nilsson, Metropolitan Ch. & O, Reiner

Sinopoli's is an intensely involving performance, volatile in the choice of often extreme speeds, slow as well as fast, but with fine playing from the orchestra of the Deutsche Oper, Berlin, it never sounds forced, with rhythms crisply sprung, making others seem dull or even pedestrian. The choral singing too is electrifying, and the line-up of principals is arguably finer than any. Cheryl Studer is a deeply moving Senta, not just immaculate vocally but conveying the intense vulnerability of the character in finely detailed singing. Bernd Weikl is a dark-toned, firmly focused Dutchman, strong and incisive. Hans Sotin is similarly firm and dark, nicely contrasted as Daland, and the luxury casting may be judged from the choice of Plácido Domingo as an impressive, forthright Erik and Peter Seiffert (the fine *Lohengrin* in Barenboim's Teldec set) as a ringing Steersman. Full, vivid sound. A clear first choice.

Woldemar Nelsson conducts a performance glowingly and responsively. The cast is more consistent than almost any, with Lisbeth Balslev as Senta firm, sweet and secure, raw only occasionally, and Simon Estes a strong, ringing Dutchman, clear and noble of tone. Matti Salminen is a dark and equally secure Daland and Robert Schunk an ardent, idiomatic Erik. The veteran Anny Schlemm, as Mary, though vocally overstressed, adds pointful character, and the chorus is superb, wonderfully drilled and passionate with it. Though inevitably stage noises are obtrusive at times, the recording is exceptionally vivid and atmospheric. On two mid-priced discs only, it makes an admirable first choice.

Pinchas Steinberg here proves a warmly sympathetic Wagnerian. More than most rivals, he brings out the light and shade of this earliest of the regular Wagner canon, helped by the refined, well-balanced recording, and by brilliant, sharply dramatic playing from the orchestra. The chorus too sings with a bite and precision to match any rival. Alfred Muff as the Dutchman attacks the notes cleanly, with vibrato only occasionally intrusive. The vibrato of Ingrid Haubold is more of a problem but, except under pressure, it is well controlled, and she begins *Senta's Ballad* with a meditative *pianissimo*. Both tenors are excellent, Peter Seiffert as Erik and Joerg Hering as the Steersman, and though Erich Knodt, rather gritty in tone, is an uncharacterful Daland, his Act II aria is light and refreshing, thanks to Steinberg's fine rhythmic pointing. The recording is both atmospheric and clear, and the set comes with libretto, translation, notes and detailed synopsis, an outstanding bargain.

The extreme range of dynamics in EMI's recording for Karajan, not ideally clear but rich, matches the larger-than-life quality of the conductor's reading. He firmly and convincingly relates this early work to later Wagner, *Tristan* above all. His choice of José van Dam as the Dutchman, thoughtful, finely detailed and lyrical, strong but not at all blustering, goes well with this. Van Dam is superbly matched and contrasted with the finest Daland on record, Kurt Moll, gloriously biting and dark in tone, yet detailed in his characterization. Neither the Erik of Peter Hofmann, nor – more seriously – the Senta of Dunja Vejzovic matches this standard; nevertheless, for all her variability, Vejzovic is wonderfully intense in *Senta's Ballad* and she matches even Van Dam's fine legato in the Act II duet. The CD transfer underlines the heavyweight quality of the recording, with the *Sailors' Chorus* made massive, but effectively so, when Karajan conducts it with such fine spring.

What will disappoint some who admire Solti's earlier Wagner sets is that this most atmospheric of the Wagner operas is presented as a concert performance with no Culshaw-style production whatever. Even the Dutchman's ghostly chorus sounds close and earthbound. But with Norman Bailey a deeply impressive Dutchman, Janis Martin a generally sweet-toned Senta, Martti Talvela a splendid Daland, and Kollo, for all his occasional coarseness, an illuminating Erik, it remains well worth hearing.

Klemperer's recording is perhaps a controversial candidate for inclusion as one of EMI's 'Great Recordings of the Century', but at least this means that it has returned to the catalogue at mid-price and on two well-filled CDs instead of three full-priced ones. Moreover, it is very well documented, with an essay by Richard Osborne, plenty of sessions photographs and a full libretto and translation. The reading is predictably spacious in its tempi, and the drama hardly grips you by the throat. But Klemperer's symphonic approach is compelling, and the underlying intensity is irresistible. This could hardly be recommended as a first choice, but any committed admirer of the conductor should take the opportunity of hearing it. It is a pity that Anja Silja was chosen as Senta, even though she is not as squally in tone here as she can be. Otherwise, the vocal cast is strong, and there is much beautiful orchestral playing (particularly from the wind soloists), and the lively recording sounds much more full-bloodedly expansive and vivid in its newest CD transfer by Andrew Walter.

Dating from December 1950, the Naxos historical version offers a radio recording of a searingly dramatic performance under Fritz Reiner with a cast as starry as one could imagine.

Reiner's conducting is urgent and intense from start to finish, with Hans Hotter in his prime as the Dutchman, uniquely characterful and fresher and more cleanly focused vocally than he became later. His towering performance is matched by the masterly singing of Astrid Varnay as Senta, with the great ballad bringing pinging attack and precision over the widest intervals. She, too, was in her prime, with her voice pure and clear, only occasionally acquiring an edge on top, largely thanks to the recording. Svanholm with his clear heroic tenor makes a powerful, warmly expressive Erik, and Sven Nilsson is a strong, firm Daland. Although the solo voices are balanced close, the chorus and orchestra add to the power of the performance, despite the limitations of original recording on 7½-inch tape, taken off the air.

The Flying Dutchman (sung in English)
(N) (M) *** Chan. 3119 (2). Tomlinson, Stemme, Begley, Halfvarson, LPO, Parry

Ever since Peter Moores' Opera in English series was initiated, some 30 years ago with a version of the *Ring* cycle conducted by Reginald Goodall, Wagner has been neglected until this fine account of *The Flying Dutchman*. John Tomlinson, a favourite in the title-role at Bayreuth, now a veteran, is masterful as the Dutchman, exploiting his wide tonal and expressive range, with few signs of wear on the voice. Opposite him as the self-sacrificing heroine, Senta, is Nina Stemme, who in 2002 had such a resounding success as Isolde at Glyndebourne, fresh and true, to outshine almost any rival on disc. The tenor, Kim Begley, is strongly cast as Erik, and though Eric Halfvarson as Senta's father, Daland, has his moments of roughness, it is a characterful performance. Most striking of all is the richness of the recorded sound, vividly capturing the fine playing of the LPO under David Parry.

Götterdämmerung (complete)
☛ *** Decca (ADD) 455 569-2 (4). Nilsson, Windgassen, Fischer-Dieskau, Frick, Neidlinger, Watson, Ludwig, V. State Op. Ch., VPO, Solti
(M) *** DG (ADD) 457 795-2 (4). Dernesch, Janowitz, Brilioth, Stewart, Kelemen, Ludwig, Ridderbusch, German Op. Ch., BPO, Karajan
(M) (***) Testament mono SBT 4175 (4). Varnay, Aldenhoff, Uhde, Mödl, Weber, Bayreuth Fest. Ch. & O, Knappertsbusch
(BB) *** Arte Nova 74321 80775-2 (4). Woodrow, Silberbauer, Del Monte, Adami, Ottenthal, Wolak, Martin, Tyrol Fest. Ch. & O, Kuhn

Solti's *Götterdämmerung* represented the peak of his achievement in recording the *Ring* cycle. There is not a single weak link in the cast. Nilsson surpasses herself in the magnificence of her singing: even Flagstad in her prime would not have been more masterful as Brünnhilde. As in *Siegfried*, Windgassen is in superb voice; Frick is a vivid Hagen, and Fischer-Dieskau achieves the near impossible in making Gunther an interesting and even sympathetic character. As for the recording quality, it surpasses even Decca's earlier achievement, and the current remastering has further improved the sound.

Karajan's singing cast is marginally even finer than Solti's, and his performance conveys the steady flow of recording sessions prepared in relation to live performances. Ultimately he falls short of Solti's achievement in the thrusting, orgasmic quality of the music. Dernesch's Brünnhilde is warmer than Nilsson's, with a glorious range of tone. Brilioth as Siegfried is fresh and young-sounding, while the Gutrune of Gundula Janowitz is far preferable to that of Claire Watson on Decca. The matching is otherwise very even. The new transfer has both freshened and filled out the sound.

The legendary Knappertsbusch recording made in 1951 during the first Bayreuth Festival after the war has produced for his Testament label a set astonishing in its vividness. This live recording was supervised by the Decca producer John Culshaw (later to mastermind Solti's complete *Ring* cycle) and the mono sound is even fuller and weightier than on the recording of *Parsifal* he also made at Bayreuth in 1951. Both operas were conducted by Hans Knappertsbusch, who in *Götterdämmerung* is even more electrifying than in *Parsifal*, defying his reputation as a relaxed, expansive Wagnerian. Vocally the star is Astrid Varnay, shiningly firm and incisive as Brünnhilde, rising magnificently to the final challenge of the immolation scene. Siegfried is sung by the short-lived Bernd Aldenhoff, strained at times like most Heldentenoren, but generally lyrical and boyish. Hermann Uhde as Gunther and Ludwig Weber as Hagen are both outstanding too, with the immediacy and sense of presence carrying one on from first to last.

Recorded live at the 2000 Tyrol Festival in Erl, this is the finest of the four *Ring* recordings made by Gustav Kuhn over successive years, with a more consistent cast than *Rheingold* and *Die Walküre*. Alan Woodrow, excellent in the title-role of Siegfried, here excels himself – his death scene is most moving – while in the role of Brünnhilde Eva Silberbauer sings with warmth and absence of strain, unlike her two rivals in *Die Walküre* and *Siegfried*. A young singer, she yet finds ample power in what is evidently a relatively intimate setting, helped by full, immediate recording. Duccio del Monte, overparted as Wotan in *Die Walküre*, here makes a strong, firm Hagen, while the roles of Gunther and Gutrune are well-taken by Herbert Adami and Gertrud Ottenthal, and Andrea Martin is excellent as Alberich, as he is in both *Rheingold* and *Siegfried*. It is a pity that the other three sections of Kuhn's *Ring* cycle do not measure up to this, which can be strongly recommended in the budget range.

The Twilight of the Gods (*Götterdämmerung*; complete; in English)

(M) *** Chan. (ADD) 3060 (5). Hunter, Remedios, Welsby, Haugland, Hammond-Stroud, Curphey, Pring, ENO Ch. & O, Goodall

Goodall's account of the culminating opera in Wagner's tetralogy may not be the most powerful ever recorded, and certainly it is not the most polished, but it is one that, paradoxically, by intensifying human as opposed to superhuman emotions, heightens the epic scale. The very opening may sound a little tentative (like the rest of the Goodall English *Ring*, this was recorded live at the London Coliseum), but it takes no more than a few seconds to register the body and richness of the sound. The few slight imprecisions and the occasional rawness of wind-tone actually seem to enhance the earthiness of Goodall's view, with more of the primeval saga about it than the studio-made *Ring* cycles.

Both Rita Hunter and Alberto Remedios were more considerately recorded on the earlier Unicorn version (now Chandos – see below) of the final scenes, with more bloom on their voices, but their performances here are magnificent in every way. In particular the golden beauty of Remedios's tenor is consistently superb, with no Heldentenor barking at all, while Aage Haugland's Hagen is giant-sounding to focus

the evil, with Gunther and Gutrune mere pawns. The voices on stage are in a different, drier acoustic from that for the orchestra, but considering the problems the sound is impressive. As for Goodall, with his consistently expansive tempi he carries total conviction – except, curiously, in the scene with the Rhinemaidens, whose music (as in Goodall's *Rheingold*) lumbers along heavily.

The Twilight of the Gods (*Götterdämmerung*): Act III (excerpts in English)

(M) *** Chan. (ADD) 6593. Hunter, Remedios, Bailey, Grant, Curphey, Sadler's Wells Opera Ch. & O, Goodall

Originally recorded by Unicorn in the early 1970s, this single Chandos CD brings an invaluable reminder of Reginald Goodall's performance of the *Ring* cycle when it was in its first flush of success, covering the closing two scenes. It is good too to have this sample, however brief, of Clifford Grant's Hagen and Norman Bailey's Gunther, fine performances both. Fresh, clear recording, not as full as it might be. At mid-price this CD is well worth investigating.

Lohengrin (complete; DVD version)

🔊➔ *** Arthaus **DVD** 100 956 (2). Domingo, Studer, Vejzovic, Welker, Lloyd, Vienna State Op. Ch., VPO, Abbado (Director: Wolfgang Weber; V/D: Brian Large)

Lohengrin (complete; CD versions)

*** DG 437 808-2 (3). Jerusalem, Studer, Meier, Welker, Moll, Schmidt, V. State Op. Ch., VPO, Abbado

(M) *** Decca 470 795-2 (4). Domingo, Norman, Nimsgern, Randová, Sotin, Fischer-Dieskau, V. State Op. Concert Ch., VPO, Solti

*** Teldec 3984 21484-2 (3). Seiffert, Magee, Struckmann, Polaski, Pape, Ch. & O of German Op.,Berlin, Barenboim

(M) *** EMI 5 67415-2 (3). Jess Thomas, Grümmer, Fischer-Dieskau, Ludwig, Frick, Wiener, V. State Op. Ch., VPO, Kempe

(M) **(*) EMI (ADD) 5 66519-2 [567411] (3). Kollo, Tomowa-Sintow, Vejzovic, Nimsgern, Ridderbusch, German Op. Ch., Berlin, BPO, Karajan

The Arthaus DVD offers the grandly traditional Vienna State Opera production of *Lohengrin* with Plácido Domingo at his peak in the title role, at once masterfully heroic and lyrical to a degree rare among Wagner tenors. His big solos inspire him to a glorious range of tone and dynamic. Cheryl Studer is an affecting Elsa, innocent and wide-eyed in contrast to the superbly sinister Ortrud of Dunja Vejzovic, exuding evil from every pore and with a wonderfully revealing glare. Her singing is masterful too, making the Telramund of Hartmut Welker seem relatively bland. Robert Lloyd is a powerful King Heinrich. Claudio Abbado and the Vienna Philharmonic are in glowing form, with dedicated singing from the chorus enhancing the ceremonial splendour of Wolfgang Weber's production. Although the staging is grandly expansive, there is a directness in the designs that helps to clarify the story, notably in the presentation of the swan as a great silver object, which appears and disappears in a flash. Such a traditional production brings obvious advantages in a DVD designed for repeated watching.

Abbado keeps Wagner's square rhythms flowing freely, allowing himself a great measure of rubato. That Abbado's speeds are generally faster than Solti's (with the Act III *Prelude* a notable exception) means that the complete opera is squeezed on to three instead of four discs, giving it the clearest advantage. As Elsa, matching her earlier, Bayreuth performance on Philips, Cheryl Studer is at her sweetest and purest, bringing out the heroine's naïvety more touchingly than Jessye Norman, whose weighty, mezzo-ish tone is thrillingly rich but is more suited to portraying other Wagner heroines than this. Though there are signs that Siegfried Jerusalem's voice is not as fresh as it once was, he sings commandingly, conveying both beauty and a true Heldentenor quality. Where Plácido Domingo for Solti, producing even more beautiful tone, tends to use a full voice for such intimate solos as *In fernem Land* and *Mein lieber Schwann*, Jerusalem sings there with tender restraint and gentler tone. Among the others, Waltraud Meier as Ortrud and Kurt Moll as King Heinrich are both superb, as fine as any predecessor, and though in the role of Telramund Hartmut Welker's baritone is not ideally steady, that tends to underline the weakness of the character next to the positive Ortrud.

It is Plácido Domingo's achievement singing Lohengrin that the lyrical element blossoms so consistently, with no hint of Heldentenor barking; at whatever dynamic level, Domingo's voice is firm and unstrained. Jessye Norman, not naturally suited to the role of Elsa, yet gives a warm, commanding performance, always intense, full of detailed insights into words and character. Eva Randová's grainy mezzo does not take so readily to recording, but as Ortrud she provides a pointful contrast, even if she never matches the firm, biting malevolence of Christa Ludwig on the Kempe set. Siegmund Nimsgern, Telramund for Solti, equally falls short of Fischer-Dieskau, his rival on the Kempe set; but it is still a strong, cleanly focused performance. Fischer-Dieskau here sings the small but vital role of the Herald, while Hans Sotin makes a comparably distinctive King Heinrich. Radiant playing from the Vienna Philharmonic, and committed chorus work too. This is one of the crowning glories of Solti's long recording career.

The first glory of Barenboim's set is the sound, full and upfront, with the voices clearly focused and with plenty of bloom, set against a rich, incandescent orchestra. Having voices relatively close adds immediacy to the drama, and Barenboim's pacing adds warmth and often urgency, even if Elsa's dream sounds a little sluggish. Emily Magee's full, rich tone makes the heroine sound rather too mature, and the voice is not well contrasted with the Ortrud of Deborah Polaski, a soprano rather lacking the sinister chest-tones apt for this evil character, hardly conveying her full villainy. Peter Seiffert makes an outstanding Lohengrin, lyrical as well as heroic, with no hint of strain. One merit of the set is that the text is absolutely complete, including the extended solo after that Act III aria. The Telramund of Falk Strickmann is rather gritty, lacking weight, and Roman Trekel is a strained Herald, but René Pape is magnificent as the King, a fine successor to Kurt Moll.

Kempe directs a rapt account of *Lohengrin*, a fine monument to a great Wagnerian. The singers seem uplifted, Jess Thomas singing more clearly and richly than usual, Elisabeth Grümmer unrivalled as Elsa in her delicacy and sweetness, Gottlob Frick gloriously resonant as the king. But it is the partnership of Christa Ludwig and Fischer-Dieskau as Ortrud and Telramund that sets the seal on this superb performance, giving the darkest intensity to their machinations in Act II, their evil heightening the beauty and serenity of so much in this opera. This is a now awarded an honourable place among EMI's 'Great Recordings of the Century'. The new CD transfer has greatly improved the sound; ensembles are still rather close and airless, but not congested. Solo voices are naturally caught, and the glow and intensity of Kempe's reading come out all the more involvingly in the new format. The set is also very economically contained on three CDs instead of the four for most rivals, though the first break between discs comes in the middle of Act II.

Karajan, whose DG recording of *Parsifal* is so naturally intense, fails in this earlier but related opera to capture comparable spiritual depth. So some of the big melodies sound a degree over-inflected and the result, though warm and expressive and dramatically powerful, with wide-ranging recording, misses an important dimension. Nor is much of the singing as pure-toned as it might be, with René Kollo too often straining and Tomowa-Sintow not always able to scale down to the necessary purity her big, dramatic voice. Even so, with strong and beautiful playing from the Berlin Philharmonic, it remains a powerful performance, and it makes a fair mid-priced version on three CDs.

Die Meistersinger von Nürnberg (complete; DVD versions)

(*) Arthaus **DVD 100 122. Doese, McIntyre, Frey, Pringle, Doig, Shanks, Gunn, Allman, Australian Op. Ch., Elizabethan PO, Mackerras (Producer/Director: Peter Butler & Virginia Lumsden; V/D: Michael Hampe)

(*) Arthaus **DVD 100 152 (2). Johansson, Brendel, Winbergh, Von Halem, Schulte, Peper, Walther, Deutsche Oper Ch. & O, Frühbeck de Burgos (Director: Gotz Friedrich; TV Director: Brian Large)

Die Meistersinger von Nürnberg (complete; CD versions)

⊛━ (M) *** Decca 470 800-2 (4). Van Dam, Heppner, Mattila, Opie, Lippert, Vermillion, Pape, Chicago SO Ch. & O, Solti

*** DG (ADD) 415 278-2 (4). Fischer-Dieskau, Ligendza, Lagger, Hermann, Domingo, Laubenthal, Ludwig, German Op. Ch. & O, Berlin, Jochum

*** Calig (ADD) CAL 50971-74 (4). Stewart, Crass, Hemsley, Konya, Unger, Janowitz, Fassbaender, Bav. R. Ch. & O, Kubelik

*** EMI (ADD) 5 55142-2 (4). Weikl, Heppner, Studer, Moll, Lorenz, Van der Walt, Kallisch, Bav. State Op. Ch., Bav. State O, Sawallisch

(M) **(*) EMI (ADD) 5 67086-2 [567148]. Adam, Kollo, Donath, Ridderbusch, Evans, Schreier, Hesse, Leipzig R. Ch., Dresden State Op. Ch. & O, Karajan

(BB) (**(*)) Naxos mono 8.110872-2 (4). Schwarzkopf, Edelmann, Kunz, Hopf, Unger, Bayreuth Fest. Ch. & O, Karajan

(N) (M) **(*) 475 6680 (4). Bailey, Bode, Moll, Weikl, Kollo, Dallapozza, Hamari, Gumpoldskirchner Spätzen, V. State Op. Ch., VPO, Solti

(M) (**(*)) Andante mono AND-3040 (4). Nissen, Reining, Wiedemann, Noort, Thorborg, Ch. & VPO, Toscanini

Recorded in 1990 in the relatively small opera-theatre of the Sydney Opera House, this Australian Opera production brilliantly overcomes the limitations of a theatre with very little space in the wings and orchestra pit and a relatively dry acoustic. Only in the overture and the orchestral link into the final scene of Act III does the relative thinness of the string-sound obtrude, and even then the electricity and vitality of Sir Charles Mackerras's conducting makes one readily forget any shortcomings. The production by Michael Hampe is very traditional, with sets by John Gunter which exploit the depth of the stage rather than its width, and ethnic German costumes by Reinhard Heinrich. The acting too is geared to old conventions, at times obtrusively so when viewed close on video (as when the girl–boy apprentices scamper about), but

Donald McIntyre is magnificent as Sachs, both vocally and dramatically, and the Swedish soprano Helena Doese is radiant as Eva, with her creamy soprano flawlessly even, most moving in the great quintet of Act III. After a rather rough start, Paul Frey emerges as an engaging Walther, rising to the challenge of the *Prize Song* with little strain, and the other principal tenor, Christopher Doig, effortlessly sails through the lighter role of David. Rosemary Gunn projects firmly and strongly as Magdalena, and John Pringle is a splendidly prim Beckmesser, singing and acting most convincingly. The test of any *Meistersinger* comes in the emotional impact of the big moments, and here, thanks to excellent singing and masterly conducting, the impact of Wagner's great score catches you as it would in the theatre. A booklet is included with ample information and a good essay, with copious index points on the two DVDs.

Updated to the early 20th century, Gotz Friedrich's production of *Meistersinger* for the Deutsche Oper in Berlin is introduced by shots of a toytown Nuremberg with houses set at rakish angles, and to the designs of Peter Sykora; the final scene is backed by the toytown city set in an upended semicircle. Otherwise this is a relatively straightforward presentation of Wagner's warmest opera, well produced on video by Brian Large, and enjoyable despite detailed flaws in the singing. Wolfgang Brendel, made up to look like the Polish leader, Lech Walesa, with a big moustache, is not always steady enough as Hans Sachs, but characterizes well, and is at his finest in the concluding monologue. Eva Johansson is a buxom Eva, sometimes squally under pressure, but rising beautifully to the challenge of the big *Quintet* in Act III. Gösta Winbergh, while not a conventional Heldentenor, sings the role of Walther with no strain, even though he is given to unstylish sliding up to notes. Beckmesser is presented by Eike Wilm Schulte as a pompous little shrimp, singing impressively despite the clowning, and Uwe Peper as David, also singing well, plays the role as a comic part, exaggerating archly. Finest of the Masters is Victor von Halem as Pogner, imposing in every way. The chorus sings well, but it is a pity that the younger Apprentices look so very feminine, not even attempting to seem boyish. Frühbeck de Burgos is a sympathetic Wagnerian, never letting the music drag.

This is the only Wagner opera that Sir Georg Solti has recorded a second time. By comparison, his earlier, Vienna recording is stiff and metrical, often fierce, with bright, upfront recording, where this new live recording, made in Orchestra Hall, Chicago, is mellower, with plenty of air round the sound, enhancing the extra warmth, relaxation and subtlety of the performance. Central to the success of the later performance is the singing of Ben Heppner as Walther, not just heroic but clear and unstrained, ardently following Solti's urgency in the *Prize Song*, a performance more beautiful than any of recent years except his own for Sawallisch. Karita Mattila sings with comparable beauty as Eva. Though she is still young, her firm, clear voice is more mature, almost mezzo-ish at times, than one expects of an Eva, and she too naturally surges forward in the great solo of the *Quintet*. For some the controversial element will be the Sachs of José van Dam, clean and sharply focused rather than weighty, not quite the wise, old, genial Sachs in his duet with Eva in Act II. This is again unconventional casting, which yet brings new beauty and new revelation, as in the hushed *pianissimo* at the end of the *Fliedermonolog* when he tells of the bird singing. With René Pape a powerful Pogner, Alan Opie a clean-cut, unexaggerated Beckmesser with plenty of projection, and Herbert Lippert and Iris Vermillion excellent as David and

Magdalene, it is a cast to rival any on disc, making this a clear recommendation if you want a digital recording.

Above all, Jochum is unerring in building long Wagnerian climaxes and resolving them – more so than his recorded rivals. The cast is the most consistent yet assembled on record. Though Caterina Ligendza's big soprano is a little ungainly for Eva, it is an appealing performance, and the choice of Domingo for Walther is inspired. The key to the set is the searching and highly individual Sachs of Fischer-Dieskau, and Horst Laubenthal's finely tuned David matches this Sachs in applying Lieder style. There is a lovely bloom on the whole sound and, with a recording which is basically wide-ranging and refined, the ambience brings an attractively natural projection of the singers.

The Calig issue, belatedly issued on commercial disc, is a radio recording, made in Munich in October 1967, and the vividness of the sound is astonishing, with more realism and presence than in almost any digital recording. This is also one of Kubelik's most inspired recordings, incandescent in the way it builds up to the big emotional climaxes, just as in a live performance. When it comes to the casting, every single voice has been chosen not only for its firmness and clarity, with no wobbling or straining, but also for the central aptness of voice to character. It would be hard to think of a more radiant and girlish Eva than Gundula Janowitz, and the Hungarian tenor, Sandor Konya, too little heard on record, is a glowing Walther, beautiful in every register if not quite as subtle as the leading Walther today, Ben Heppner. Thomas Stewart as Hans Sachs is similarly unstrained, using his firm, dark baritone with warm expressiveness, while Thomas Hemsley has rarely been so impressive on disc, a sharp-focused Beckmesser who conveys the ironic humour but who never guys the role. Franz Crass is a fine, dark Pogner, and it would be hard to find a match for Gerhard Unger as David or Brigitte Fassbaender as Magdalene, with the upfront sound heightening their subplot. A Wagner production as consistent as this is rare, the more surprising to find in a radio recording.

Sawallisch also paces the work in reflection of his long experience of performing it in the opera house with the same musicians. Add to that the most radiant and free-toned Walther on disc, the Canadian, Ben Heppner, and you have a superb set. In tonal beauty Heppner matches Plácido Domingo on Jochum's DG set, as he does in variety of expression and feeling. Cheryl Studer's contribution is hardly less remarkable than Heppner's, at once powerful and girlishly tender, with the voice kept pure. If she is less affecting than she might be in the poignant duet with Sachs in Act II and in the great *Quintet* of Act III, that has something to do with a limitation in Sawallisch's reading, fine as it is. It rarely finds the poetic magic that this of all Wagner's operas can convey. Bernd Weikl makes a splendid Sachs, firm and true of voice, but something of the nobility of the master-shoemaker is missing. Deon van der Walt is a strong David, clear-cut and fresh, with Cornelia Kallisch making a traditionally fruity yet firm Magdalene. Siegfried Lorenz is a well-focused Beckmesser who refuses to caricature the much-mocked Town Clerk, and Kurt Moll is a magnificent Pogner. The chorus (balanced a little backwardly) and orchestra play with the warmth and radiance associated with recordings made in the Herkulessaal in Munich.

In setting up their later star-studded stereo version, EMI fell down badly in the choice of Sachs. Theo Adam, promising in many ways, has quite the wrong voice for the part, in one way too young-sounding, in another too grating, not focused enough. However, after that keen disappointment there is much to enjoy, for in a modestly reverberant acoustic (a smallish church was used) Karajan draws from the Dresden players and chorus a rich performance which retains a degree of bourgeois intimacy. Donath is a touching, sweet-toned Eva, Kollo here is as true and ringing a Walther as one could find today. Sir Geraint Evans is an incomparably vivid Beckmesser, and Ridderbusch is a glorious-toned Pogner. Anyone wanting a widely expansive sound will be disappointed, but Karajan's thoughtful approach and the presence of perhaps the finest Eva on any current set makes this a good choice for those who are not upset by Adam's ungenial Sachs. However, whether this is one of the 'Great Recordings of the Century' is much less sure. This description might much more readily have been applied to Karajan's earlier mono version (currently withdrawn).

The Naxos set of Karajan's classic 1951 recording of *Meistersinger* provides a useful super-bargain alternative to EMI's own issue. Mark Obert-Thorn has opted to transfer this live recording, made over five performances and a rehearsal, at a higher level than the EMI engineers, and this has tended to bring out the inevitable inconsistencies and flaws, with voices not always well focused, particularly in the big ensembles. Yet the electric atmosphere of a historic occasion is thrillingly caught. Where EMI provides a complete libretto in German but no translation, Naxos relies on a detailed synopsis with references to the numbered tracks.

The great glory of Solti's first (1975) set of *Die Meistersinger* is not the searing brilliance of the conductor, but rather the mature and involving portrayal of Sachs by Norman Bailey. For his superb singing the set is well worth investigating. Indeed, Decca have returned it to the catalogue in their mid-priced Classic Opera series after many requests from collectors. But there is much else to enjoy, not least the bright and detailed sound which the Decca engineers have obtained with the Vienna Philharmonic, recording Wagner in the Sofiensaal. Kurt Moll as Pogner, Bernd Weikl as Beckmesser (really singing the part) and Julia Hamari as Magdalene (refreshingly young-sounding) are all excellent, but the short-comings are comparably serious. Both Hannelore Bode and René Kollo fall short of their far-from-perfect contributions to earlier sets and Solti, for all his energy, gives a surprisingly routine reading of this most appealing of Wagner scores, exaggerating the four-square rhythms with even stressing, pointing his expressive lines too heavily and failing to convey real spontaneity. It remains an impressive achievement, and those who must at all costs hear Bailey's marvellous Sachs should not be deterred, for the Decca sound comes up very vividly on the curent CD transfer. A full libretto is enclosed, although, as with the rest of this series, the print is very small.

When Toscanini's commercial recordings never included a complete Wagner opera, it is exciting to get a flavour of what it was like to attend one of his legendary Salzburg Festival performances. Dating from 1937, this one of *Meistersinger* demonstrates very clearly how at that period Toscanini was far from rigid in his conducting, with the high-voltage electricity of the moment leading him forward in urgency, while equally letting him and his performers expand in warmth. Hans Hermann Nissen makes a noble Sachs, as he does on EMI's historic Boehm recording of Act III made at the same period, and Maria Reining is a touching Eva, far fresher than in her later recordings. The others make a fine team. The radio sound is very limited, with the orchestra thin and dry. For most of the time the voices come over well, but they periodically fade into the distance, with the balances of voices on stage variable. Happily, the long first scene of Act III

comes over best, no doubt the result of forwardly placed scenery. The wonder is that the CD transfer by Ward Marston does so much to make the sound acceptable, with Andante offering its typically luxurious packaging.

Parsifal Documentary: 'The Seach for the Grail'

(N) *** Arthaus **DVD** 100 610. Domingo, Urmana, Salminen, Putilin, Mojhaey, Kirov Ch. & O, Gergiev (Dir: Tony Palmer)

Tony Palmer's 1998 film is much more documentary than musical performance, but it does bring the great benefit of letting us hear Plácido Domingo as Parsifal in several key passages from the opera. He also provides a commentary on the opera and its plot, as well as on the Grail legend. There are interviews with, among others, the Biblical scholar Karen Armstrong (in English) on the background and Wolfgang Wagner (in German) on the traditions of Bayreuth with special reference to the influence on Hitler and the Nazis. There are also clips from various Grail-inspired films, even including those involving Monty Python and 'Crocodile' Dundee. The musical performances were recorded, not only at the Mariinsky theatre in St Petersburg with Gergiev conducting, but also in Ravello, where Wagner first conceived the idea of writing the opera. As always with Palmer, it is a film both thoughtful and provocative.

Parsifal (complete; DVD version)

(N) *(**) Opus Arte **DVD** OA 0915 D (3). Ventris, Meier, Salminen, Hampson, Fox, Baden-Baden Festival Ch., Deutsches SO, Berlin, Nagano

Nikolaus Lehnhoff's production of *Parsifal* has been seen in opera houses from London (ENO) to Chicago and San Francisco, prompting much praise. For the video version it was felt better to transfer it to a smaller house, and that is why this film was recorded in the Festival Theatre in Baden-Baden, using a local chorus with the Deutsches Symphony Orchestra from Berlin and a starry cast, conducted by Kent Nagano. The opening scene is set in a bare box, with stylized medieval robes for most characters, and with Parsifal himself looking like a cross between a hippie and a John-the-Baptist lookalike. The symbolism then escalates, with the basic set for the remaining scenes involving a plain curved wall at the back suggesting a space-age design. At one point, railway track runs through a gap leading nowhere. Klingsor's Palace has to be imagined and the Flower-Maidens are all in grey, with long floppy extensions to their sleeves possibly suggesting petals. Titurel is in carapace-like Chinese armour, a figure returned from the dead, and Parsifal as a black knight looks like a metal beetle with a touch of Darth Vader. All this is distracting but barely gets in the way of the music, which is well played and well sung, notably by Matti Salminen as Gurnemanz, Waltraud Meier as Kundry and Thomas Hampson as Amfortas. Christopher Ventris is an upstanding, unstrained Parsifal and Tom Fox an incisive Klingsor. Each Act comes on a separate disc, with the third disc also containing an hour-long film directed by Reiner Moritz with interviews (in English) with Hampson, Ventris and Fox and (in German) with Lehnhoff and Meier. One wonders whether most collectors will want to watch this production very often and will prefer the sound without the video!

Parsifal (complete; CD versions)

☛ ✿ *** DG 413 347-2 (4). Hofmann, Vejzovic, Moll, Van Dam, Nimsgern, Von Halem, German Op. Ch., BPO, Karajan

*** Teldec 9031 74448-2 (4). Jerusalem, Van Dam, Hölle, Meier, Von Kannen, Tomlinson, Berlin State Op. Ch., BPO, Barenboim

(M) *** Decca (ADD) 470 805-2 (4). Kollo, Ludwig, Fischer-Dieskau, Hotter, Kelemen, Frick, V. Boys' Ch., V. State Op. Ch., VPO, Solti

**(*) DG 437 501-2 (4). Domingo, Norman, Moll, Morris, Wlaschiha, Rootering, Met. Op. Ch. & O, Levine

(M) **(*) DG (ADD) 435 718-2 (3). King, Jones, Stewart, Ridderbusch, McIntyre, Crass, (1970) Bayreuth Festival Ch. & O, Boulez

(BB) (***) Naxos mono 8.110221/24. Windgassen, London, Weber, Mödl, Uhde, Van Mill, 1951 Bayreuth Fest. Ch. & O, Knappertsbusch

Communion, musical and spiritual, is what this intensely beautiful Karajan set provides. The playing of the Berlin orchestra is consistently beautiful, enhanced by the clarity and refinement of the recording. Kurt Moll as Gurnemanz is the singer who, more than any other, anchors the work vocally, projecting his voice with firmness and subtlety. José van Dam as Amfortas is also splendid. The Klingsor of Siegmund Nimsgern could be more sinister, but the singing is admirable. Dunja Vejzovic makes a vibrant, sensuous Kundry who rises superbly to the moment in Act II when she bemoans her laughter in the face of Christ. Only Peter Hofmann as Parsifal brings any disappointment; at times he develops a gritty edge on the voice, but his natural tone is admirably suited to the part and he is never less than dramatically effective. He is not helped by the relative closeness of the solo voices, but otherwise the recording is near the atmospheric ideal, a superb achievement.

With Siegfried Jerusalem a superb Parsifal, one of the finest ever, both characterful and mellifluous, Daniel Barenboim's is a dedicated version with an excellent cast. Like Karajan, Barenboim draws glorious sounds from the Berlin Philharmonic, even if he cannot quite match his predecessor in concentrated intensity, well sustained as his control of long paragraphs is. Waltraud Meier, as in rival versions, is an outstanding, darkly intense Kundry, and José van Dam is superb as Amfortas, clean of attack, as he was for Karajan. John Tomlinson is a resonant, if young-sounding Titurel, and Gunther von Kannen a clear and direct, if unvillainous, even noble Klingsor. The relatively weak link is the Gurnemanz of Matthias Hölle, warm-toned but slightly unsteady, not quite in character.

Solti's singing cast could hardly be stronger, every one of them pointing words with fine, illuminating care for detail; and the complex balances of sound, not least in the Good Friday Music, are beautifully caught; throughout, Solti shows his sustained intensity in Wagner. What is rather missing is a rapt, spiritual quality. The remastering for CD, as with Solti's other Wagner recordings, opens up the sound, and the choral climaxes are superb.

James Levine's speeds outstrip almost anyone in slowness, with the New York studio performance at times hanging fire – as in the transformation scene of Act I. Many will find it a small price to pay for a performance, vividly recorded, involving a cast as starry as any that could be assembled. Jessye Norman as Kundry and Plácido Domingo in the title-role give performances that in every way live up to their reputations, not just exploiting beauty of sound but backing it with keen characterization and concern for word-meaning. Kurt Moll as Gurnemanz and Ekkehard Wlaschiha as Klingsor are both magnificent, firm and characterful, while James Morris

as Amfortas gives a powerful performance, with a slightly gritty tone adding to the character's sense of pain. Jan-Henrik Rootering's bass as Titurel is atmospherically enhanced by an echo-chamber, pointing the relative lack of reverberation in the main, firmly focused recording, one of the most vivid yet made in the Manhattan Center.

By contrast, Boulez's speeds are so consistently fast that in the age of CD it has brought an obvious benefit in being fitted – easily – on three discs instead of four, yet Boulez's approach, with the line beautifully controlled, conveys a dramatic urgency rarely found in this opera, and never sounds breathless, with textures clarified in a way characteristic of Boulez. Even the flower-maidens sing like young apprentices in *Meistersinger* rather than seductive beauties. James King is a firm, strong, rather baritonal hero, Thomas Stewart a fine, tense Amfortas, and Gwyneth Jones as Kundry is in strong voice, only occasionally shrill, but Franz Crass is disappointingly unsteady as Gurnemanz.

Hans Knappertsbusch was the inspired choice of conductor made by Wagner's grandsons for the first revival of *Parsifal* after the Second World War. The Naxos historical reissue of a recording originally issued by Decca, taken from the first season in 1951, makes a striking contrast with the later Knappertsbusch recording, made in stereo for Philips eleven years later. The 1951 performance is no less than 20 minutes longer overall, with Knappertsbusch, always expansive, even more dedicated than in his later reading.

The cast is even finer, with Wolfgang Windgassen singing with warmth as well as power and making other Heldentenors seem rough by comparison. Ludwig Weber is magnificently dark-toned as Gurnemanz, much more an understanding human being than his successor, Hans Hotter, and less of a conventional noble figure. Martha Mödl is both wild and abrasive in her first scenes and sensuously seductive in her long Act II duet with Parsifal. Hermann Uhde is bitingly firm as Klingsor. Although the mono sound remains limited in Mark Obert-Thorn's new transfer, the orchestral texture is full and pleasing, the sense of atmosphere is palpable, voices come over well, and the chorus is well caught. The other distractions, including moments of swish at the opening at Act II, could not be corrected, but the pitch drop at the end of Act III has been 'fixed', and the producer has restored a missing chord (just before the appearance of the Knights of the Grail). There is a brief synopsis. This set can be very highly recommended at its modest new price.

Parsifal, Act III: Good Friday Spell: Symphonic Synthesis (arr. Stokowski)

🔑 (M) (***) Cala mono CACD 0535. SO, Stokowski – MUSSORGSKY: *Boris Godunov: Scenes* (***)

In 1952, the same year as he recorded scenes from *Boris Godunov* in San Francisco, Stokowski recorded these selections from Act III of Wagner's *Parsifal* with a hand-picked orchestra of leading players in New York. The result has a similar incandescence, and the RCA engineers matched Stokowski's brilliance with sound of astonishing warmth and breadth, here superbly transferred to CD.

Das Rheingold (complete)

🔑 *** Decca (ADD) 455 556-2 (2). London, Flagstad, Svanholm, Neidlinger, VPO, Solti

*** Teldec 4509 91185-2 (2). Tomlinson, Brinkmann, Schreibmayer, Clark, Finnie, Johansson, Svendén, Von Kannen, Pampuch, Hölle, Kang, Liedland, Küttenbaum, Turner, (1991) Bayreuth Festival O, Barenboim

(M) **(*) DG (ADD) 457 781-2 (2). Fischer-Dieskau, Veasey, Stolze, Kelemen, BPO, Karajan

(B) (***) Naxos mono 8.110047-48 (2). Schorr, Huehn, Clemens, Maison, Habich, Laufkötter, Cordon, List, Branzell, Manski, Doe, Andreva, Petina, Met. Op. O and Ch., Artur Bodanzky

The first of Solti's cycle was recorded in 1958. The immediacy and precise placing are thrilling, while the sound-effects of the final scenes, including Donner's hammer-blow and the Rainbow Bridge, have never been matched since. Solti gives a magnificent reading of the score, crisp, dramatic and direct. Vocally, the set is held together by the unforgettable singing of Neidlinger as Alberich. He vocalizes with wonderful precision and makes the character of the dwarf develop from the comic creature of the opening scene to the demented monster of the last. Flagstad learned the part of Fricka specially for this recording, and her singing makes one regret that she never took the role on the stage. George London is sometimes a little rough, but this is a dramatic portrayal of the young Wotan. Svanholm could be more characterful as Loge, but again it is a relief to hear the part really sung. An outstanding achievement.

When Barenboim as Wagnerian has at times seemed lethargic, what is particularly surprising is the dramatic tension of the performance. Even with slow speeds, the sense of flow carries the ear on. Even with often-thunderous stage noises, the Barenboim performances magnetize you much more consistently, with the atmosphere of the Festspielhaus well caught by the engineers. It is very satisfying, too, to have on disc John Tomlinson's magnificent performance as Wotan, Graham Clark as an electrifying, dominant Loge and Linda Finnie a thoughtful, intense Fricka.

Karajan's reflectiveness of approach has its less welcome side, for the tension rarely varies. One finds such incidents as Alberich's stealing of the gold or Donner's hammer-blow passing by without one's pulse quickening as it should. On the credit side, however, the singing cast has hardly any flaw at all, and Fischer-Dieskau's Wotan is a brilliant and memorable creation, virile and expressive. Among the others, Veasey is excellent, though obviously she cannot efface memories of Flagstad; Gerhard Stolze with his flickering almost *Sprechstimme* as Loge gives an immensely vivid, if (for some) controversial interpretation. The 1968 sound has been clarified and further opened up in the new transfer.

The briskness of Artur Bodanzky as a Wagnerian, often disturbing in other operas, works well in the narrative of *Rheingold*, with the dramatic bite of each scene strongly conveyed. The recording was made in April 1937 not at the Met itself but at the Boston Opera House, with sound still limited but capturing the voices well. It is specially valuable to have the great Friedrich Schorr as Wotan, firm as a rock, strong and purposeful throughout, up to the magnificent final solo. Karin Branzell is a warm, clear Fricka, Eduard Habich an incisive Alberich and Emanuel List a magnificent Fafner, with the whole cast firm and clear if not always subtle. Even the neighing tone of Rene Maison as Loge can be regarded as characterful. A fascinating document, the more welcome at super-bargain price.

The Rhinegold (Das Rheingold); complete, in English
(M) **(*) Chan. (ADD) 3054 (3). Bailey, Hammond-Stroud, Pring, Belcourt, Attfield, Collins, McDonnall, Lloyd, Grant, ENO O, Goodall

Goodall's slow tempi in *Rheingold* bring an opening section where the temperature is low, reflecting hardly at all the tensions of a live performance, even though this was taken from a series of Coliseum presentations. Nevertheless, the momentum of Wagner gradually builds up so that, by the final scenes, both the overall teamwork and the individual contributions of such singers as Norman Bailey, Derek Hammond-Stroud and Clifford Grant come together impressively. Hammond-Stroud's powerful representation of Alberich culminates in a superb account of the curse. The spectacular orchestral effects (with the horns sounding glorious) are vividly caught by the engineers and impressively transferred to CD, even if balances (inevitably) are sometimes less than ideal.

Rienzi (complete)
(M) ** EMI (ADD) 5 67131-2 (3). Kollo, Wennberg, Martin, Adam, Hillebrand, Vogel, Schreier, Leipzig R. Ch., Dresden State Op. Ch., Dresden State O, Hollreiser

It is sad that the flaws in this ambitious opera prevent the unwieldy piece from having its full dramatic impact. This recording is not quite complete, but the cuts are unimportant and most of the set numbers make plain the youthful exuberance of the ambitious composer. Except in the recitative, Heinrich Hollreiser's direction is strong and purposeful, but much of the singing is disappointing. René Kollo sounds heroic, but the two women principals are poor. Janis Martin in the breeches role of Adriano produces tone that does not record very sweetly, while Siv Wennberg as the heroine, Rienzi's sister, slides unpleasantly between notes in the florid passages. Despite good recording, this is only a stop-gap.

Der Ring des Nibelungen: an introduction to The Ring by Deryck Cooke, with 193 music examples
(M) *** Decca (ADD) 443 581-2 (2). VPO, Solti

The reissue of Deryck Cooke's fascinating and scholarly lecture is most welcome. Even though the CD reissue omits the printed text, the principal musical motives are all printed out in the accompanying booklet and they demonstrate just how the many leading ideas in *The Ring* develop from one another, springing from an original germ. The discourse is riveting, though even dedicated Wagnerians may not want to hear it many times over. The music examples, many of them specially prepared, are clumsily inserted, but this is still a thoroughly worthwhile acquisition for those who already have recordings of the operas.

Der Ring des Nibelungen (complete; DVD versions)
⊕━ *** DG **DVD** 073 043-9 (7). Behrens, Jerusalem, Lakes, Ludwig, Morris, Norman, Rootering, Met. Op. Ch. & O, Levine (Stage Director: Otto Schenk; V/D: Brian Large)

*** Ph. **DVD** 073 4057 (8). Jones, McIntyre, Becht, Schwarz, Zednik, Bayreuth Fest. O, Boulez (Producer: Patrice Chéreau; V/D: Brian Large)

(N) * Opus Arte **DVD** *Das Rheingold* OA 0910D (2); *Die Walküre* OA 911D (3); *Siegfried* OA 912D (3); *Götterdämmerung* OA 912D (3) (available separately). Struckmann, Von Kannen, Clark, Polanski, Treleaven, Liceu Theatre Ch. & O, De Billy (V/D: Noemi Cuni)

Das Rheingold
*** DG **DVD** 073 036-9. Morris, Held, Baker, Jerusalem, Wlaschiha, Zednik, Rootering, Salminen, Met. Op. Ch. & O, Levine

*** Ph. **DVD** 070 4058. McIntyre, Zednik, Becht, Schwarz, Altmeyer, Salminen, Hübner, Bayreuth Fest. O, Boulez

Die Walküre
*** DG **DVD** 073 049-2 (2). Norman, Lakes, Moll, Morris, Behrens, Luwig, Met. Op. Ch. & O, Levine (V/D: Brian Large)
*** Ph. **DVD** 070 4059 (2). Jones, Altmeyer, Schwarz, Hormann, Salminen, McIntyre, Bayreuth Fest. O, Boulez

Siegfried
*** DG **DVD** 073 037-9 (2). Jerusalem, Behrens, Morris, Zednik, Wlaschiha, Salminen, Svenden, Upshaw, Met. Op. Ch. & O, Levine
*** Ph. **DVD** 070 4062 (2). Jung, McIntyre, Jones, Zednik, Becht, Hübner, Bayreuth Fest. O, Boulez (V/D: Brian Large)

Götterdämmerung
*** DG **DVD** 073 040-9 (2). Behrens, Jerusalem, Raffell, Salminen, Wlaschiha, Lisowka, Ludwig, Met. Op. Ch. & O, Levine
*** Ph. **DVD** 070 4065 (2). Jones, Jung, Hübner, Altmeyer, Becht, Mazura, Killebrew, Bayreuth Fest. O, Boulez

In 1989 the Metropolitan Opera in New York, celebrating the centenary of its first production of Wagner's *Ring* cycle in 1889, presented a new production with an American conductor in charge for the first time, James Levine. This reading, with the same cast, is familiar from the studio recordings on CD, but the DVD version, recorded live, adds an extra dimension and sense of involvement, with Brian Large adapting the spectacular staging by the Austrian actor-turned-producer, Otto Schenk. With lavish sets and costumes by Gunther Schneider-Siemssen (who designed the Karajan production earlier seen at the Met), this is a full-bloodedly realistic production in the romantic tradition, defying fashionable trends towards Wieland Wagner spareness and abstraction on the one hand and towards updated concept productions on the other. For a video version designed for repeated watching there is everything to be said for this approach, when the complex story is told so lucidly, with splendid camera-work. The aim was to modify the traditional approach, using all the theatrical effects available in a modern theatre. Indeed, the illusion of the Rhinemaidens swimming in water is very vivid at the start of *Rheingold*, and in the final scene of *Götterdämmerung*, after the Gibichung Hall has collapsed (realistically portrayed) and Brünnhilde has flung herself into the fire, you are briefly shown the bottom of the Rhine again and finally Valhalla in flames, reflecting what the music tells you. Hildegard Behrens as Brünnhilde and James Morris as Wotan are both even more convincing when seen as well as heard, and Siegfried Jerusalem as Siegfried makes a handsome hero. There is a picture-gallery as a bonus, with each opera given its own trailer; but nothing else.

When it first appeared in 1976, the centenary year of the tetralogy, the Patrice Chéreau/Pierre Boulez *Ring* caused public outrage, with boos (and even fisticuffs) in the auditorium. The late Harold Rosenthal called it 'France's long-delayed revenge for the Franco-Prussian war' and wrote that 'Boulez in his attempt to purge Wagner of bombast and grandiosity merely succeeded in making him sound dull, small scale and absolutely lacking in magic'. Musically speaking, there is an objectivity to this reading that is at the other end of the spectrum to Furtwängler, Karajan, Levine and Barenboim, and Boulez's meticulous attention to detail and the fact that he does not linger unduly will, for many, be distinct advantages. Perhaps there is a lack of atmosphere that would be

more unappealing in sound alone, but the eye to some extent compensates. On the musical side we have discussed the merits of the set in earlier editions, and the performances are identical. Chéreau's production divests *The Ring* of any tradition, whether it be to pre-war stagings or to the famous post-war Wieland Wagner productions, and forces the viewer to re-think afresh the meaning of the powerful mythology. His view is almost Shavian in seeing the characters as children of the industrial revolution, and the designs by Richard Poduzzi are arresting, even if they have little to do with Wagner's original intentions. All in all, this is an historic set that serious Wagnerians will want to add to their collections, while ordinary mortals will undoubtedly turn to Levine and the convincing attempt of the Met to provide what Wagner himself envisaged. In the Boulez version, Brian Large's handling of the cameras once again places the eye where the ear tells us it wants to be. This set now includes a documentary on the making of the recording which is also available separately on DG 073 406-8.

Harry Kupfer's surreal production of the *Ring* cycle for the Deutsche Oper in Berlin is presented on Opus Arte in performances given at the Liceu Theatre in Lisbon. With sound bright to the point of harshness and a variable cast, it is hardly competitive with the finest versions on DVD.

Der Ring des Nibelungen (complete; CD versions)
⊕► ☾ (M) *** Decca (ADD) 455 555-2 (14). Nilsson, Windgassen, Flagstad, Fischer-Dieskau, Hotter, London, Ludwig, Neidlinger, Frick, Svanholm, Stolze, Böhme, Höffgen, Sutherland, Crespin, King, Watson, Ch. & VPO, Solti
(B) *** Ph. (ADD) 446 057-2 (14). Nilsson, Windgassen, Neidlinger, Adam, Rysanek, King, Nienstedt, Esser, Talvela, Böhme, Silja, Dernesch, Stewart, Höffgen, (1967) Bayreuth Festival Ch. & O, Boehm
(B) *** EMI (ADD) 5 72731-2 (14). Behrens, Varady, Lipovšek, Schwarz, Hale, Kollo, Wlaschiha, Schunk, Tear, Rootering, Bav. State Op. Ch. & O, Sawallisch
(B) *** RCA 74321 45417-2 (14). Altmeyer, Kollo, Adam, Schreier, Nimsgern, Vogel, Minton, Wenkel, Salminen, Popp, Jerusalem, Norman, Moll, Studer, Leipzig R. Ch., Dresden State Op. Ch. & O, Janowski
(M) *** DG (ADD) 457 780-2 (14). Veasey, Fischer-Dieskau, Stolze, Kelemen, Dernesch, Dominguez, Jess Thomas, Stewart, Crespin, Janowitz, Vickers, Talvela, Brilioth, Ludwig, Ridderbusch, BPO, Karajan
(B) (M) **(*) EMI 7 64775-2 (14). Marton, Morris, Lipovšek, Sednik, Adam, Haage, Jerusalem, Te Kanawa, Rydl, Rappé, Studer, Goldberg, Meier, Salminen, Hampson, Tomlinson, Bundschuh, Bav. R. Ch. & SO, Haitink
(M) (***) EMI mono 7 67123-2 (13). Suthaus, Mödl, Frantz, Patzak, Neidlinger, Windgassen, Konetzni, Streich, Jurinac, Frick, RAI Ch. & Rome SO, Furtwängler

Solti's was the first recorded *Ring* cycle to be issued. Whether in performance or in vividness of sound, it remains the most electrifying account of the tetralogy on disc, sharply focused if not always as warmly expressive as some. Solti himself developed in the process of making the recording, and *Götterdämmerung* represents a peak of achievement for him, commanding and magnificent. Though CD occasionally reveals bumps and bangs inaudible on the original LPs, this is a historic set that remains as central today as when it first appeared. The latest remastering is very impressive and the layout is improved, with the set now on 14 discs. The original artwork is used throughout on the boxes.

Recorded at the 1967 Bayreuth Festival, Boehm's fine set captures the unique atmosphere and acoustic of the Festspielhaus very vividly. Birgit Nilsson as Brünnhilde and Wolfgang Windgassen as Siegfried are both a degree more volatile and passionate than they were in the Solti cycle. Gustav Neidlinger as Alberich is also superb, as he was too in the Solti set; and the only major reservation concerns the Wotan of Theo Adam, in a performance searchingly intense and finely detailed but often unsteady of tone even at that period. The sound, only occasionally constricted, has been vividly transferred. In the UK Philips are offering this version of the Ring in a 14-disc limited edition (in effect for a limited time) at bargain price.

On 14 discs also at bargain price, the Sawallisch version of the Ring makes an excellent recommendation. This is the sound-track of the Bavarian State Opera production by Nikolaus Lehnhoff, as recorded in 1989 for television. The cast is as fine as any in rival versions of the digital age, the performances gain in dramatic momentum and expressive spontaneity from being recorded live, and – rather surprisingly – the sound is outstandingly rich, warm and spaciously atmospheric, in many ways outshining rival digital recordings. Sawallisch conducts with a thrust and energy not always present in his studio recordings, with speeds often faster than have become common. One minor quibble is that both Walküre and Siegfried could each have been fitted easily on to three CDs instead of four. As to the casting, Robert Hale proves a noble Wotan, virile and strong. The voice may not be beautiful, but the range of expression is great, so that in Walküre the final moment of his kissing Brünnhilde's godhead away could hardly be more tender.

Dedication and consistency are the hallmarks of the RCA Ring, a series of studio recordings made between 1980 and 1983 with German thoroughness by the then East German record company, Eurodisc. Voices tend to be balanced well forward of the orchestra, but the digital sound is admirably full as well as clear. The clarity has one concentrating on the words, helped by Janowski's vividly direct approach to the score. Overall this is more rewarding than many of the individual sets that have been issued at full price over the years since it first appeared. The documentation is first class.

Karajan's DG recording originally followed close on the heels of Solti's for Decca, providing a good alternative studio version which equally stands the test of time, even if Siegfried has its disappointments. The manner is smoother, the speeds generally broader, yet the tension and concentration of the performances are maintained more consistently than in most modern studio recordings. Casting is not quite consistent between the operas, with Régine Crespin as Brünnhilde in Walküre, but Helga Dernesch at her very peak in the last two operas. The casting of Siegfried is changed between Siegfried and Götterdämmerung, from Jess Thomas to Helge Brilioth, just as strong but sweeter of tone.

Strong and purposeful, Haitink takes a thoughtful view which in each music-drama nevertheless builds up unerringly in tension and power, with the beauty of Wagner's orchestration consistently brought out. The recordings are warm and full, if not as sharply defined as they might be, and the principal snags lie in some of the casting, notably with Eva Marton as Brünnhilde, too often gusty and ill-focused. Theo Adam too is a disappointing Alberich, dramatically intense but unable any longer to sustain a steady line. James

Morris as Wotan yields to other singers in the role. For the rest, a strong and compelling issue, still (arguably) technically the best studio recording of the Ring in digital sound.

In its digital transfer, the boxiness of the studio sound and the closeness of the voices still take away some of the unique Furtwängler glow in Wagner, but the sound is acceptable and benefits in some ways from extra clarity.

'The Ring Without Words': Orchestral Excerpts from The Ring
(N) (M) ** Telarc CD 80154. BPO, Maazel

This Telarc CD offers 1987 recordings of a series of linked orchestral eposodes from the four Ring operas, with the scoring left to Wagner but with the linking sometimes dovetailed unconvincingly. The accompanying notes tell the listener what is going on, relating to the 20 cued tracks. The recording is spectacular and the Berlin Philharmonic playing is always powerful, but the special effects (from the hammering dwarfs of Rheingold to Donner's thunderbolt) are not very sophisticated. The highlights are, predictably, the Ride of the Valkyries and Wotan's passionate farewell to Brünnhilde. Maazel keeps the tension up by pressing on urgently, and at times there is a touch of coarseness in the sound-picture, but overall there is plenty of spectacle.

'The Best of The Ring': excerpts from Das Rheingold; Die Walküre; Siegfried; Götterdämmerung
(B) * Ph. Duo (ADD) 454 020-2 (2) (from (1967) Bayreuth Festival recordings; Boehm)**

The Ring: 'Great Scenes': Das Rheingold: Prelude & Scene 1; Entry of the Gods into Valhalla. Die Walküre: Winterstürme; Ride of the Valkyries; Wotan's Farewell & Magic Fire Music. Siegfried: Forging Scene; Forest Murmurs. Götterdämmerung: Siegfried's Rhine Journey; Siegfried's Funeral March; Brünnhilde's Immolation Scene
(B) * Double Decca (ADD) 448 933-2 (2). Nilsson, Windgassen, Kotter, Stolz, King, Crespin, VPO, Solti**

Although the Solti and Karajan selections have their appeal, as potted 'Rings' go, the Philips Duo is probably the best buy. Taken from Boehm's outstanding complete recording, it can be warmly enjoyed as a summary of Wagner's intentions, with most of the key scenes included. The only snag is that Bernard Jacobson's very brief synopsis of the narrative fails to relate each track to the story.

With 144 minutes of music included on this Decca Double, the excerpts from Solti's Ring are quite extended. Das Rheingold begins with the Prelude and the sequence continues for 24 minutes, the Entry of the Gods into Valhalla opens spectacularly and offers some 10 minutes of music, while the excerpts from Die Walküre include the Sieglinde/Siegmund Winterstürme duet (15 minutes) and the whole of Wotan's Farewell and Magic Fire Music. Götterdämmerung leads with Siegfried's Rhine Journey and closes with the Immolation Scene – some 20 minutes for each excerpt, with the tailoring expertly done in between. The only snag is the absence of any narrative cues within the sparse documentation; but the music itself is thrillingly projected.

The Ring: highlights: Das Rheingold: Lugt, Schwestern! Die Wenken lacht in den Grund; Zur Burg führt die Brücke. Die Walküre: Der Männer Sippe sass hier im Saal; Ride of the Valkyries; Wotan's Farewell & Magic Fire Music. Siegfried: Forest Murmurs; Aber, wie sah meine Mutter wohl aus?; Nun

sing! Ich lausche dem Gesang; Heil dir, Sonne! Heil dir, Licht!. Götterdämmerung: Funeral Music; Fliegt heim, ihr Raben!

🎞— (M) *** DG (ADD) 476 7254-2 (from complete recording; cond. Karajan)

The task of selecting highlights to fit on a single disc, taken from the whole of the *Ring* cycle, is daunting. But the DG producer of this bargain issue has extended the previous selection to 77 minutes and managed to assemble many key items, either very well tailored or ending satisfactorily. The whole of Wotan's great farewell scene with the *Magic Fire Music* is included, and much else besides. Moreover the *Funeral Music* from *Götterdämmerung* (where the previous CD ended) is now followed by *Brünnhilde's Immolation* and continues to the end of the opera. The transfers are extremely brilliant, making this a most attractive 'Critics' Choice' reissue.

'The Golden Ring' (BBC Documentary Film)
(includes audio excerpts from the Solti recordings of all four Ring Operas)

*** DVD 071 153-9. Produced and narrated and directed by Humphrey Burton. Film Cameraman: Peter Sargent. Decca Recording Team: John Culshaw, Gordon Parry, James Brown, Christopher Raeburn, Jack Law, Eric Smith

The legendary 1965 BBC film (made in Vienna in cooperation with the Austrian Television Service) of the making of Solti's unsurpassed recording of *The Ring* was filmed during the later stages of recording *Götterdämmerung*. It has unique documentary value, and for recording buffs it is fascinating to see vivid film of so many famous names, recording engineers and the recording production team, headed by John Culshaw, as well as the operatic stars of the great project, with Solti himself looking astonishingly young. Apart from the documentary interest, this remains one of the most fascinating and entertaining films of its kind ever made, and the audio bonus is the inclusion of famous key scenes from each of the four *Ring* operas, splendidly reproduced in surround-sound stereo.

Siegfried (complete)
🎞— *** Decca 455 564-2 (4). Windgassen, Nilsson, Hotter, Stolze, Neidlinger, Böhme, Hoffgen, Sutherland, VPO, Solti

(BB) (***) Naxos mono 8.110211 (3). Melchior, Flagstad, Thorborg, Schorr, List, Habich. Met. Op. O, Bodanzky

(BB) *(**) Arte Nova 74321 72116-2 (4). Woodrow, Wachutka, Uusitalo, Harper, Singers of the Montegral Academy, Tyrol Fest. O, Kuhn

(M) ** DG 457 790-2 (4). Dernesch, Dominguez, Jess Thomas, Stolze, Stewart, Kelemen, BPO, Karajan

Siegfried has too long been thought of as the grimmest of the *Ring* cycle, but a performance as buoyant as Solti's reveals that, more than in most Wagner, the message is one of optimism. Each of the three acts ends with a scene of triumphant joy. Solti's array of singers could hardly be bettered. Windgassen is at the very peak of his form, lyrical as well as heroic. Hotter has never been more impressive on record, his Wotan at last captured adequately. Stolze, Neidlinger and Böhme are all exemplary, and predictably Joan Sutherland makes the most seductive of Woodbirds. With singing finer than any opera house could normally provide, with masterly playing from the Vienna Philharmonic and with Decca's most vivid recording, this is still unsurpassed. As with the rest of

the series, the present newly remastered and enhanced CDs have cleaned up background noises.

Taken from a radio transmission from the Metropolitan in New York on 30 January 1937, this Naxos Historical Met. issue offers an astonishingly vivid view of a classic occasion with a cast unlikely ever to be equalled. Both Lauritz Melchior and Kirsten Flagstad were at their peak, and the firmness, clarity and absence of strain of their singing offers a lesson to all latter-day exponents of this music. Melchior is a Heldentenor without a hint of roughness in his tone, freely confident, while the noble Flagstad brings not only a comparable power to the role of Brünnhilde, but an element of tenderness that may surprise some. Kirsten Thorborg makes for luxury casting in the role of Erda, and Friedrich Schorr as the Wanderer sings with comparable firmness and clarity, virile rather than elderly. Artur Bodanzky, the Met's chief conductor at the time in the German repertory, is a brisk but understanding Wagnerian, and though there are statutory cuts, as was customary at the time, it means that each act is contained on a single CD. All the voices are superbly caught, but the orchestra is much dimmer, not helped by variable surface-noise, which is yet intrusive only occasionally, mainly in *pianissimo* passages. The voices are what matter, and they sound glorious, thanks to the excellent transfers of Ward Marston. An astonishing bargain.

The super-budget issue from Arte Nova is taken live from performances in the Tyrol festival in Austria in July 1999. The excitement of a live performance comes over well, with each act leading to a thrilling conclusion. Gustav Kuhn directs a clean-cut, well-structured performance, set in a relatively dry acoustic, with ample orchestral detail caught. The result may not be as weighty as usual, but is certainly compelling, with Alan Woodrow an outstanding, energetic Siegfried, fresh and clear, unstrained, characterizing vividly. By contrast, though Juha Uusitalo sings well as the Wanderer (Wotan), similarly firm and clear, he is not commanding as a character. Thomas Harper is an incisive Mime, and Elisabeth-Maria Wachutka is fresh and bright as Brünnhilde in Act III. If at first she seems rather lightweight, her clarity of attack is ample compensation with the closing duet rising to a fine, warm climax. The booklet provides notes and synopsis, and the full libretto is in German only. But this remains a welcome bargain.

When Siegfried is outsung by Mime, it is time to complain, and though Karajan's DG set has many fine qualities – not least the Brünnhilde of Helga Dernesch – it hardly rivals the Solti or Boehm versions. Windgassen on Decca gave a classic performance, and any comparison highlights the serious shortcomings of Jess Thomas. Even when voices are balanced forward, the digital transfer helps little to make Thomas's singing as Siegfried any more acceptable. Otherwise, the vocal cast is strong, and Karajan provides the seamless playing which characterizes his cycle. Recommended only to those irrevocably committed to the Karajan cycle, even though the current remastering is very successful.

Siegfried (complete, in English)
(M) *** Chan. 3045 (4). Remedios, Hunter, Bailey, Dempsey, Hammond-Stroud, Grant, Collins, London, Sadler's Wells Op. O, Goodall

More tellingly than in almost any other Wagner opera recording, Goodall's spacious direction here conveys the genuine dramatic crunch that gives the experience of hearing Wagner in the opera house its unique power, its overwhelming force; this is unmistakably a great interpretation caught on the wing. Remedios, more than any rival on record, conveys not only heroic strength but clear-ringing youthfulness, caressing the ear as well as exciting it. Norman Bailey makes a magnificently noble Wanderer, steady of tone, and Gregory Dempsey is a characterful Mime, even if his deliberate whining tone is not well caught on record. The sound is superbly realistic, even making no allowances for the conditions. Lovers of opera in English should grasp the opportunity of hearing this unique set. This original EMI recording has now been reissued by Chandos under the auspices of the Peter Moores Foundation.

Love duets: *Siegfried, Act III, Scene 3. Tristan, Act II, Scene 2*
⊕ *** EMI 5 57004-2. Voigt, Domingo, ROHCG O, Pappano

The great novelty here is the concert version of the *Tristan* love duet. Before *Tristan* was ever staged, Wagner prepared this concert version of the love duet, but it was never performed. Only recently has James Levine unearthed it in the Bayreuth archives, and here generously allowed Antonio Pappano to make this first recording. What is fascinating is that instead of the duet being cut off unceremoniously on the arrival of King Mark, the music merges seamlessly into the closing pages of the whole opera, the final minutes of the *Liebestod*, but with a part for Tristan included too. As performed by Plácido Domingo as Tristan and Deborah Voigt as Isolde, with Pappano an exceptionally warm Wagnerian, the result is sensuously beautiful, radiantly played and recorded. The closing scene from *Siegfried* too, with Voigt and Domingo strong and full-toned, makes one long to hear Pappano in complete Wagner performances.

Tannhäuser (Paris version; complete)
☞ *** DG 427 625-2 (3). Domingo, Studer, Baltsa, Salminen, Schmidt, Ch. & Philh. O, Sinopoli

(M) (**(*)) DG mono 457 682-2 (3). Beirer, Wächter, Frick, Brouwenstijn, Kmentt, Ludwig, Janowitz, V. State Op. Ch. & O, Karajan

Plácido Domingo as Tannhäuser for Sinopoli brings balm to the ears, producing sounds of much power as well as beauty. Sinopoli here makes one of his most passionately committed opera recordings, warmer and more flexible than Solti's Decca version, always individual, with fine detail brought out, always persuasively and never wilful. Agnes Baltsa is not ideally opulent of tone as Venus, but she is the complete seductress. Cheryl Studer – who sang the role of Elisabeth for Sinopoli at Bayreuth – gives a most sensitive performance, not always ideally even of tone but creating a movingly intense portrait of the heroine, vulnerable and very feminine. Matti Salminen in one of his last recordings makes a superb Landgrave and Andreas Schmidt a noble Wolfram, even though the legato could be smoother in *O Star of Eve*.

Tannhäuser was the one Wagner opera in the central canon which Karajan did not record for a regular record company. That makes this Austrian Radio recording in mono the more valuable, dry and limited in sound as it is, with voices well forward and with little bloom on either voices or instruments. Using the revised and expanded Paris version of the score, the recording dates from January 1963, revealing how Karajan varied his approach to each Act. With a hectic account of the *Venusberg Music* he is urgent and passionate in Act I, but that leads to a more measured manner in Act II, and an unusually spacious one in the tragedy of Act III. In the title-role the Heldentenor Hans Beirer is variable, with no bark in his powerful voice but with some juddery unevenness

to spoil the focus, more happily cast in Acts II and III than in Act I. As in her later recording for Solti, Christa Ludwig is a magnificent Venus, and the Dutch soprano Gré Brouwenstijn, too little recorded, an impressive Elisabeth. Gottlob Frick is a powerful, dark-toned Hermann, and Eberhard Wächter a lyrical Wolfram, with fine legato in *O Star of Eve*.

Tannhäuser (Dresden version; complete)
(M) **(*) EMI (ADD) 7 63214-2 (3). Hopf, Grümmer, Fischer-Dieskau, Schech, Frick, German State Op., Berlin, Ch. & O, Konwitschny

(M) ** DG Trio (ADD) 471 708-2 (3). Windgassen, Nilsson, Fischer-Dieskau, Adam, Laubenthal, Berlin Deutsch Op. Ch. & O, Gerdes

** Teldec 8573 88064-2 (3). Seiffert, Eaglen, Meyer, Hampson, Deutsch Op. Ch, Berlin State O, Barenboim

The Konwitschny set is a fine one, marred by one serious flaw: the coarse singing of Hans Hopf in the title-role; he fails to convey the joyous lyricism of the part, straining much of the time and with plenty of intrusive aitches. The opening scene with Venus is particularly daunting since Marianne Schech is the other disappointing member of the cast and, when they wobble together, the result is not far from comic. Happily things improve rapidly. Elisabeth Grümmer, Fischer-Dieskau and Gottlob Frick are all magnificent, and Konwitschny draws enthusiastic playing and singing from everyone. The chorus, important in this opera, is especially good, and the atmospheric recording adds to the warmth of the performance.

Appearing for the first time on CD is this 1969 recording of *Tannhäuser*, conducted by Otto Gerdes, who was formerly one of DG's recording managers. He gives a crisp, dramatic account of the Dresden version of *Tannhäuser*, which may be lacking in finer points of interpretation but is spirited enough in support of an excellent singing cast. Windgassen is not ideally sweet-toned, but Fischer-Dieskau makes a superb Wolfram, deeply expressive in *O Star of Eve*. The controversial point for many will be the choice of Birgit Nilsson, undoubtedly the leading Wagner soprano of her generation, to sing the roles of both Venus and Elisabeth. Vocally, the result is firmly satisfying, but Nilsson is suited neither by temperament not quality of voice to either the voluptuous Venus or the pure Elisabeth. She copes very intelligently – but one admires, rather than being moved. Good, atmospheric recording, vividly transferred. This has been out of the catalogue since the 1980s and is something of a collector's item.

This Teldec set does not add up to the sum of its parts. Though the casting is starry, arguably as fine a team as could be assembled today, and Barenboim's credentials as a Wagnerian have long been tested at Bayreuth and elsewhere, the performance lacks the dramatic thrust needed to bring together one of the more problematic of Wagner's operas. For many it will be in the set's favour that the text used is the original Dresden form with the more elaborate version of Act I, Scene 2, the big duet between Tannhäuser and Venus, taken from the much later Paris version. It does not help that Barenboim's speeds tend to be on the slow side, yet with little of the hushed tension that marks his finest Wagner performances, while occasionally by contrast he will choose a frenetic speed. The impression is of a carefully prepared studio run-through, and indeed the solo singing is beautifully controlled as though for a concert, so when Thomas Hampson as Wolfram sings his song to the evening star the emphasis is on beauty of tone and phrase. In the title-role Peter Seiffert sings with clean, firm projection with no sign of strain, yet the sound is hardly beautiful and his vocal acting is unconvincing. Waltraud Meyer is a formidable Venus, but again the sound as recorded is unrelenting rather than sensuous. Jane Eaglen as Elisabeth controls her massive soprano well, but one really wants a more tender, lyrical sound. The recording, faithful enough, tends to confirm the feeling of a concert performance.

Tannhäuser: Highlights

(N) (BB) **(*) Warner Apex 2564 61738-2. Kollo, Te Kanawa, Hagegård, Meier, Amb. S., Philh. O, Janowski

After a very fine account of the *Overture* (wonderful cascades from the Philharmonia violins at the close), Warner provide an enjoyable hour-long selection with the Ambrosian Singers, very well recorded, contributing impressively in the March scene and Pilgrims' Chorus. Kiri Te Kanawa's warm portrayal of Elisabeth is a little soft-centred, and René Kollo's Tannhäuser is also a romantic view. Wolfram's *O du mein holder Abendstern* ('O Star of Eve') is sung simply and affectingly by Håkan Hagegård. Throughout, the experienced Wagnerian, Marek Janowski, directs without too much pressure, but the closing scene comes off dramatically. The recording is vividly natural and well balanced and, since this is a mid-priced reissue, texts and a translation are included.

Tristan und Isolde (complete; DVD versions)

(N) *** DG **DVD** 073 044-9. Heppner, Eaglen, Pape, Ketelsen, Dalayman, Met. Op. Ch. & O, Levine (Producer: Dieter Dorn; Design: Jürgen Rosel; V/D: Brian Large)

(*) Hardy **DVD (ADD) HCD4009 (2). Nilsson, Vickers, Hesse, Rundgren, Berry, New Philh. Ch., O Nat. de l'ORTF, Boehm

Tristan und Isolde (complete; CD versions)

(N) (☞) ✪ *** EMI 5 58006-2 (3) (plus Audio DVD). Stemme, Domingo, Fujimora, Pape, Bär, ROHCG Ch. & O, Pappano

☞ (M) *** EMI (ADD) 7 69319-2 (4). Vickers, Dernesch, Ludwig, Berry, Ridderbusch, German Op. Ch., Berlin, BPO, Karajan

*** Teldec 4509 94568-2 (4). Meier, Jerusalem, Lipovšek, Salminen, Struckmann, Berlin State Op. Ch., BPO, Barenboim

(M) *** DG (ADD) 449 772-2 (3). Windgassen, Nilsson, Ludwig, Talvela, Waechter, Bayreuth Festival (1966) Ch. & O, Boehm

(M) *** Decca (ADD) 470 814-2 (4). Uhl, Nilsson, Resnik, Van Mill, Krause, VPO, Solti

(N) (BB) **(*) Naxos 8.660152/4 (3). Fassbender, Millgram, Dike, Forsen, Lundberg, Royal Swedish Op. Ch. & O, Segerstam

(M) (***) EMI mono 5 67621-2 (4). Flagstad, Suthaus, Fischer-Dieskau, Thebom, Philh., Furtwängler

☞ (BB) (***) EMI mono 5 85873-2 (4). Flagstad, Suthaus, Thebom, Greindl, Fischer-Dieskau, Philh., Furtwängler

(BB) (**(*)) Naxos 8.110321 (4) Flagstad, Suthaus, Thebom, Greindl, Fischer-Dieskau, Philh., Furtwängler

(N) (M) **(*) DG 477 5355 (3). Kollo, M. Price, Fassbaender, Fischer-Dieskau, Moll, Leipzig R. Ch., Dresden State O, Carlos Kleiber

Dieter Dorn's inspired production for the Met. in New York,

here filmed in 1999, uses stylized and geometric sets by Jürgen Rosel, each with decking for base and each with powerful diagonals. The lighting adds greatly to the atmospheric power of the production, with silhouettes used throughout. When both Ben Heppner as Tristan and Jane Eaglen as Isolde are bulkily unromantic figures, Dorn cleverly uses the lighting to minimize any problem, regularly creating striking stage pictures for their dueting. What matters is that both are vocally at their peak, singing like angels, totally unstrained and finely focused. The young René Pape as King Mark is formidably impressive too, with Katarina Dalayman a superb Brangäne, while Hans-Joachim Ketelsen is a powerful if at times less well-focused Kurvenal. James Levine brings out the power and concentration of this epic, drawing brilliant playing from the Met. Orchestra.

The DVD on the Hardy label offers a live recording made at the Orange Festival in France in July 1973, with the title-roles taken by the unchallenged leaders among Wagner singers of the day, Birgit Nilsson and Jon Vickers, with Karl Boehm conducting. That line-up alone makes this well worth investigating, and Nikolaus Lehnhoff's simple, stylized staging in the great amphitheatre at Orange is undistractingly effective. The circular stage contains merely two curved stairways, moved around in different positions for each act. It matters little that in Act I there is no hint of a ship or the sea; thanks to the music and the singing, one simply imagines the necessary scene. Nilsson and Vickers may not be the greatest actors, statuesque rather than dynamic, but their vocal command is irresistible, with not a hint of strain from either of them. Among the others Ruth Hesse is an uneven Brangäne, but both Walter Berry as Kurwenal and Bengt Rundgren as King Mark are superb, as commanding as Nilsson and Vickers. The chorus is the visiting New Philharmonia of London but, thanks to the staging, they are never visible. The big disappointment is that the video sound is so limited and thin, not nearly as full as one might have expected of a 1973 recording. The presentation, mostly in Italian, is also limited, with a simple leaflet giving an outline background to the opera and a simple synopsis.

When Plácido Domingo suggested to EMI that as a culmination to his unique career he would like to record *Tristan und Isolde*, the record company boldly took up the challenge and with luxury casting produced what is instantly recognizable as a classic recording, worthy successor to the great Furtwängler version of 1952 with Flagstad as Isolde. The glory of the set is not only the radiant singing of Domingo, still in glorious, full-throated voice in his sixties, but the warmly understanding conducting of Antonio Pappano with the Covent Garden Orchestra, more volatile than that of Furtwängler but just as concentrated. The modern digital recording offers enormous benefits in bringing out the rich beauty of the score, with the gradation of dynamic from hushed *pianissimo* to full *fortissimo* finely controlled by engineers and conductor alike. Domingo, at once heroic and lyrical, not only offers the most beautiful assumption on disc since Windgassen for Boehm at Bayreuth in 1966, but he sings with a passion beyond that of most Heldentenors, and he is matched by the tenderly girlish Isolde of Nina Stemme. Hers may not be a big, noble soprano like those of Flagstad or Birgit Nilsson, and in Act II she comes to sound a little stressed, but with fine projection and subtle shading her portrait is the more passionate and more feminine. Mihoko Fujimora as Brangäne is clear and tender too – her warnings in the love duet creep exquisitely on the ear – and René Pape as King Mark is unmatched by any contemporary. Olaf Bär with his lieder-like command of detail is a fine Kurwenal, with such stars as Ian Bostridge as the Shepherd and Rolando Villazon as the Young Sailor filling smaller parts. This set may well mark the end of an era, not just individually for Domingo but as one of the last big studio recordings of opera likely to be made. The set includes as a bonus an audio DVD of the complete performance in surround sound, with an on-screen libretto in German, English and French.

Karajan's is a sensual performance of Wagner's masterpiece, caressingly beautiful and with superbly refined playing from the Berlin Philharmonic. Dernesch as Isolde is seductively feminine, not as noble as Flagstad, not as tough and unflinching as Nilsson; but the human quality makes this account if anything more moving still, helped by glorious tone-colour through every range. Jon Vickers matches her in what is arguably his finest performance on record, allowing himself true *pianissimo* shading. The rest of the cast is excellent too. The recording has been remastered again for the present reissue and the 1972 sound has plenty of body, making this an excellent first choice, with inspired conducting and the most satisfactory cast of all. The set has also been attractively repackaged.

Barenboim's cast is an exceptionally strong one, with Waltraud Meier as Isolde graduating from mezzo soprano to full soprano, breasting the top Cs easily, showing no sign of strain, and bringing a weight and intensity to the role that reflect her earlier experience. The vibrato sometimes grows obtrusive, and even in the final *Liebestod* there is a touch of rawness under pressure; but the feeling for line is masterly, always with words vividly expressed. Siegfried Jerusalem, with a more beautiful voice than most latterday Heldentenoren, makes a predictably fine Tristan, not quite as smooth of tone as he once was and conveying the poignancy of the hero's plight in Act III rather than his suffering. Marjana Lipovšek is among the most characterful of Brangänes, strong and vehement, while Matti Salminen is a resonant, moving King Mark. Only the gritty tones of Falk Struckmann as Kurwenal fall short. With weighty, full-ranging and well-balanced sound, this is a first-rate recommendation for a modern digital set. Highlights are also available (76 minutes) on a budget Apex CD (2564 61505-2).

Boehm's Bayreuth performance offers one great benefit in presenting this without any breaks at all, with each act uninterrupted. Boehm is on the urgent side in this opera and the orchestral ensemble is not always immaculate; but the performance glows with intensity from beginning to end, carried through in the longest spans. Birgit Nilsson sings the *Liebestod* at the end of the long evening as though she was starting out afresh, radiant and with not a hint of tiredness, rising to an orgasmic climax and bringing a heavenly *pianissimo* on the final rising octave to F sharp. Opposite Nilsson is Wolfgang Windgassen, the most mellifluous of Heldentenoren; though the microphone balance sometimes puts him at a disadvantage to his Isolde, the realism and sense of presence of the whole set bathes you in the authentic atmosphere of Bayreuth. Making up an almost unmatchable cast are Christa Ludwig as Brangaene, Eberhard Waechter as Kurwenal, and Martti Talvela as King Mark, with the young Peter Schreier as the Young Sailor.

Solti's performance is less flexible and sensuous than Karajan's, but he shows himself ready to relax in Wagner's more expansive periods. On the other hand the end of Act I and the opening of the love duet have a knife-edged dramatic tension. Nilsson is masterly in her conviction and she never attacks below the note, so that at the end of the love duet the impossibly difficult top Cs come out and hit the listener crisply and cleanly, dead on the note; and the *Liebestod* is all the more moving for clean attack at the climax. Fritz Uhl is a sensitive Heldentenor, rather lightweight, but his long solo passages in Act III are superb. The Kurwenal of Tom Krause and the King Mark of Arnold van Mill are both excellent, and it is only Regina Resnik as Brangäne who gives any disappointment. The production has the usual Decca/Culshaw imaginative touch, and the recording matches brilliance and clarity with satisfying co-ordination and richness.

Strong as the Royal Swedish Opera cast is for the Naxos version, the singing hardly matches that of the earlier versions now available. Even so, Leif Segerstam offers an account that in its freshness and clarity proposes a keen alternative, the more attractive not just because of the full, transparent sound but because of the magnetism and urgency of the performance. Outstanding in the cast is Hedwig Fassbender as Isolde, singing with a beauty and evenness that stand as a moving alternative to grandly noble performances. Her example rather shows up those around her, for though Wolfgang Millgram as Tristan is a Wagnerian tenor who never barks, his control of legato is limited. As Brangäne, Martina Dike's mezzo, light for this role, acquires an edge at the top, and Gunnar Lundberg as Kurwenal grows rough in places. By contrast, the bass Lennart Forsen as King Mark sings with admirable evenness of tone. The one serious blot on the set is that Segerstam allows a substantial cut in the first, urgent section of the Act II love duet, an outdated practice. As usual with Naxos, instead of a libretto there is a detailed synopsis linked to the separate tracks.

Wilhelm Furtwängler's concept is spacious from the opening *Prelude* onwards, but equally the bite and colour of the drama are vividly conveyed, matching the nobility of Flagstad's portrait of Isolde. The richly commanding power of her singing and her always distinctive timbre make it a uniquely compelling performance. Suthaus is not of the same calibre as Heldentenor, but he avoids ugliness and strain. Among the others, the only remarkable performance comes from the young Fischer-Dieskau as Kurwenal, not ideally cast but keenly imaginative. One endearing oddity is that – on Flagstad's insistence – the top Cs at the opening of the love duet were sung by Elisabeth Schwarzkopf. The Kingsway Hall recording was admirably balanced, catching the beauty of the Philharmonia Orchestra at its peak. It stands among Furtwängler's finest memorials, still unsurpassed by later versions in its spacious concentration and intensity. Now reissued in EMI's 'Great Recordings of the Century' series, the mono sound in a superb transfer is astonishingly vivid, fuller than before with wonderful immediacy, often giving the illusion of stereo. The rest of the cast, including Ludwig Suthaus as an unstrained Tristan and the youthful Fischer-Dieskau as Kurwenal, gives strong support to the dominant Flagstad. At mid-price the set comes with lavish packaging and notes.

To forestall the imminent transfer of the same recording by Naxos, this alternative super-budget version was issued, minus libretto but with a very detailed synopsis linked to copious index points on the discs. The mono sound is amazingly full and immediate, transferred from the original tapes with more presence than the Naxos version and with less background noise.

In default of the EMI super-budget version, the Naxos set in the same price-bracket, lovingly transferred from carefully chosen LPs, offers a good alternative, not quite so vivid, also without a libretto and with fewer index points linked to the synopsis.

Kleiber directs a compellingly impulsive reading, crowned by the glorious Isolde of Margaret Price, the most purely beautiful of any complete interpretation on record. Next to more spacious readings, Kleiber's at times sounds excitable, almost hysterical, with fast speeds tending to get faster, for all his hypnotic concentration. But the lyricism of Price's Isolde, feminine and vulnerable, is well contrasted against the heroic Tristan of Kollo, at his finest in Act III. Kurt Moll makes a dark, leonine King Mark, and Fischer-Dieskau is at times gritty as Kurwenal and Brigitte Fassbaender is a clear but rather cold Brangaene. On CD the oddities and inconsistencies of sound (including odd bumps) are the more apparent, but, with voices set well back in a spacious acoustic, the sound is still sensuously beautiful. This is now reissued at mid-price as one of DG's 'Originals'.

(i) *Tristan und Isolde* (abridged); (ii) *Act III* (excerpts)

(BB) (**(*) Naxos mono 8.110200/02 (3). (i) Larsen-Todsen, Graarud, Bockelman, Andresen, Bayreuth Fest. Ch. and O, Elmendorff; (ii) Ljungberg, Widdop, Andresen, LSO, Coates or Collingwood, or Berlin State O, Blech

At the Bayreuth Festival in 1928 the English Columbia company made the first attempt to record a complete version of *Tristan und Isolde*, using tried and tested members of the company under the baton of Karl Elmendorff. Cuts were made in all three acts, particularly Act III, which was reduced to under half an hour, or less than a third of the whole. Yet what emerges here in this superb transfer by Ward Marston, with wonderfully silent surfaces, is warmly convincing and atmospheric enough to give one a clear idea of Bayreuth performances in the 1920s. Both Nanny Larsen-Todsen as Isolde and Gunnar Graarud as Tristan have clear, fresh voices, with their singing only occasionally marred by swooping attack, though Anny Helm as Brangaene slides around so much it makes you seasick. The young Rudolf Bockelman is a superb Kurwenal, and Ivar Andresen is a fine King Mark. Interestingly, the talk by Ernest Newman designed for the original issue is included as a supplement. The other bonus is much more substantial: the 40-minute collection of excerpts from Act III recorded by HMV with varied forces over the two previous years, with Gota Ljungberg and Walter Widdop even finer as the protagonists than their Bayreuth counterparts. A most valuable extra.

Tristan und Isolde, Act III, Scene 3: Tod und Hölle!; Mild und leise wie er lächelt

(N) (B) *** DG (ADD/DDD) 477 5324. M. Price, Fischer-Dieskau, Fassbaender, Götz, Moll, Dresden State O, C. Kleiber – BRAHMS: *Symphony 4* ***; SCHUBERT: *Symphony 8 (Unfinished)* **(*)

Two scenes from Carlos Kleiber's compelling *Tristan und Isolde*: the highly dramatic opening to the third scene of Act III, *Tod und Hölle!*, and a rich sample of Margaret Price's glorious Isolde – as beautiful as any on record, both offered as a bonus on this Carlos Kleiber tribute CD.

Die Walküre (complete)

*** DG **DVD** 073 011-9 (2). Behrens, Norman, Ludwig, Lakes, Morris, Moll, Met. Op. O, Levine (Dir: Otto Schenk)
*** Decca (ADD) 455 559-2 (4). Nilsson, Crespin, Ludwig, King, Hotter, Frick, VPO, Solti
(M) (***) EMI mono 7 63045-2 (3). Mödl, Rysanek, Frantz, Suthaus, Klose, Frick, VPO, Furtwängler
(BB) (***) Naxos mono 8.110058/60 (3). Traubel, Melchior, Schorr, Kipnis, Varnay, Thorborg, Met Op. O, Leinsdorf

(M) **(*) DG (ADD) 457 785-2 (4). Crespin, Janowitz, Veasey, Vickers, Stewart, Talvela, BPO, Karajan

Recorded live at the Met. in New York in April 1989, two years after the DG audio recording with the same personnel, the DVD film offers an even more compelling experience, with James Levine more thrustfully dramatic and drawing more spontaneous-sounding performances from his team. To have the gloriously voiced Jessye Norman as Sieglinde is luxury casting. She is totally secure and consistently intense and so commanding you feel that, far from being afraid, this Sieglinde could eat any of the Valkyries alive, including the Brünnhilde of Hildegard Behrens.

Solti sees Act II as the kernel of the work, with the conflict of wills between Wotan and Fricka making for one of Wagner's most deeply searching scenes. That is the more apparent when the greatest of latterday Wotans, Hans Hotter, takes the role, and Christa Ludwig sings with searing dramatic sense as his wife. Before that, Act I seems a little underplayed. This is partly because of Solti's deliberate lyricism – apt enough when love and spring greetings are in the air – but also (on the debit side) because James King fails both to project the character of Siegmund and to delve into the word-meanings as all the other members of the cast consistently do. As Sieglinde Crespin has never sung more beautifully on record. As for Nilsson's Brünnhilde, it has grown mellower, the emotions are clearer. Newly remastered, the sound is more vivid than ever and the layout is admirable.

Furtwängler, an excellent cast and the Vienna Philharmonic in radiant form match any of their successors. Ludwig Suthaus proves a satisfyingly clear-toned Heldentenor, never strained, with the lyricism of *Winterstürme* superbly sustained. Neither Léonie Rysanek as Sieglinde nor Martha Mödl as Brünnhilde is ideally steady, but the intensity and involvement of each is irresistible, classic performances both. Similarly, the mezzo of Margarete Klose may not be very beautiful, but the projection of words and the fire-eating character match the conductor's intensity. Gottlob Frick is as near an ideal Hunding as one will find, sinister but with the right streak of arrogant sexuality; while the Wotan of Ferdinand Frantz may not be as deeply perceptive as some, but to hear the sweep of Wagner's melodic lines so gloriously sung is a rare joy. The 1954 sound is amazingly full and vivid, with voices cleanly balanced against the inspired orchestra. The only snag of the set is that, to fit the whole piece on to only three CDs, breaks between discs come in mid-act.

Recorded live at the Met. in New York in December 1941, the Naxos historical set offers an electrifying performance, starrily cast, with radio sound giving clear focus to the voices. With Astrid Varnay as Sieglinde making her début at the Met. and Helen Traubel as Brünnhilde also making her début in that role, it was a great occasion, with Lauritz Melchior plainly intent on not being outshone. He is in heroic voice, the master Wagner tenor of his generation, daring to hold on to his cries of '*Walse, Walse*' for extraordinary lengths.

Varnay is a warm Sieglinde, producing Flagstad-like overtones. Equally, Helen Traubel sings with a rock-like firmness that is all too rare in latter-day Wagner sopranos, clear and incisive, never fluffing a note. Kirsten Thorborg is a magnificent Fricka, and Alexander Kipnis a thrilling Hunding, with his dark, incisive attack.

It is sad that next to these, the other great Wagnerian, Friedrich Schorr, as Wotan, reveals a sadly worn voice, strained and dry on top. It may be as well that his Act II monologue is severely cut. Yet the nobility of his portrayal still comes over powerfully, as in his final half-tone phrase, kissing away Brünnhilde's godhead. Leinsdorf draws incandescent playing from the Met. Orchestra in a performance wilder than his RCA studio account but just as compelling.

The great merits of Karajan's version are the refinement of the orchestral playing and the heroic strength of Jon Vickers as Siegmund. With that underlined, one cannot help but note that the vocal shortcomings here are generally more marked, and the total result does not add up to quite so compelling a dramatic experience: one is less involved. Thomas Stewart may have a younger, firmer voice than Hotter, but the character of Wotan emerges only partially; it is not just that he misses some of the word-meaning, but that on occasion – as in the kissing away of Brünnhilde's godhead – he underlines too crudely. Josephine Veasey as Fricka conveys the biting intensity of the part. Gundula Janowitz's Sieglinde has its beautiful moments, but it is not a dynamic performance. Crespin's Brünnhilde is impressive, but nothing like as satisfying as her study of Sieglinde on the Decca set. The DG recording is very good, but not quite in the same class as the Decca.

Die Walküre: Act I (complete)

☙— (M) (***) EMI mono 7 61020-2. Lehmann, Melchior, List, VPO, Walter

(M) (**(*)) Orfeo mono C 019991 Z. Schech, Völker, Dalberg, Bav. State O, Solti

(i) Die Walküre: Act I (complete). Götterdämmerung: Siegfried's Funeral March
**(*) Australian Decca Eloquence 466 678-2. VPO, Knappertsbusch; (i) with Svanholm, Flagstad, Van Mill

One is consistently gripped by the continuity and sustained lines of Walter's reading and by the intensity and beauty of the playing of the Vienna Philharmonic. Lotte Lehmann's portrait of Sieglinde, arguably her finest role, has a depth and beauty never surpassed since, and Lauritz Melchior's heroic Siegmund brings singing of a scale and variety – not to mention beauty – that no Heldentenor today can match. Emanuel List as Hunding is less distinguished but reliable.

All Solti devotees (and other Wagnerians) should hear his historic recording, made live at the Prinzregentem Theatre in Munich in 1947, when the young maestro was new to the post of principal conductor in Munich. Though at that time he had had remarkably little experience of conducting opera, this is already an electrifying example of his work as a Wagner conductor, culminating in a thrilling close to the act. The passionate build-up includes a cry of delight from Schech as Sieglinde when Siegmund retrieves the sword. The sound is close and unatmospheric, with stage noises obtrusive at times, but there is plenty of solid detail. Though the closeness does not help the singers, Marianne Schech is an impressive, vibrant Sieglinde, firmer than she later became, and Franz Völker as a veteran of the Vienna State Opera is a clear, heroic Siegmund, if strained at times at the top. Friedrich Dalberg makes an aptly sinister Hunding.

It was Kirsten Flagstad's wish that she should be able to record Sieglinde in Act I of Walküre, and she also wanted to work with the great Wagner conductor, Hans Knappertsbusch. If Flagstad is a bit too matronly for the role, it hardly matters, for there is an electric tension in this performance which makes it compellingly moving. The 1958 recording, though a bit tubby, is amazingly detailed, rich and full, and allows the inimitable Vienna glow to come through. With

Siegfried's funeral march thrown in too, this Australian CD is well worth seeking out.

The Valkyrie (Die Walküre; complete; in English)

(M) *** Chan. 3038 (4). Hunter, Remedios, Curphey, Bailey, Grant, Howard, ENO Ch. & O, Goodall

Recorded by EMI at the London Coliseum in 1975 and now reissued by Chandos the glory of the ENO performance lies not just in Goodall's spacious direction but in the magnificent Wotan of Norman Bailey, noble in the broadest span but very human in his illumination of detail. Rita Hunter sings nobly too, and though she is not as commanding as Nilsson in the Solti cycle she is often more lyrically tender. Alberto Remedios as Siegmund is more taxed than he was as Siegfried in the later opera (lower tessituras are not quite so comfortable for him) but his sweetly ringing top register is superb. If others, such as Ann Howard as Fricka, are not always treated kindly by the microphone, the total dramatic compulsion is irresistible. The CD transfer increases the sense of presence and at the same time confirms the relative lack of sumptuousness.

VOCAL COLLECTIONS

'Wagner Singing on Record': Excerpts from: (i) Der fliegende Holländer; (ii) Götterdämmerung; (iii) Lohengrin; (iv) Die Meistersinger von Nürnberg; (v) Parsifal; (vi) Das Rheingold; (vii) Siegfried; (viii) Tannhäuser; (ix) Tristan und Isolde; (x) Die Walküre

(M) (***) EMI mono/stereo (ADD) 7 640082 (4). (i) Hermann, Nissen, Endrèze, Fuchs, Beckmann, Rethberg, Nilsson, Hotter; (ii) Austral, Widdop, List, Weber, Janssen, Lawrence; (iii) Rethberg, Pertil, Singher, Lawrence, Spani, Lehmann, Lemnitz, Klose, Wittrisch, Rosavaenge; (iv) Schorr, Thill, Martinelli, Bockelmann, Parr, Williams, Ralf, Lemnitz; (v) Leider, Kipnitz, Wolff; (vi) Schorr; (vii) Nissen, Olszewska, Schipper, Leider, Laubenthal, Lubin; (viii) Müller, Lorenz, Janssen, Hüsch, Flagstad; (ix) Leider, Marherr, Larsen-Todsen, Helm, Melchior, Seinemeyer, Lorenz; (x) Lawrence, Journet, Bockelmann

This collection, compiled in Paris as 'Les Introuvables du chant wagnerien', contains an amazing array of recordings made in the later years of 78-r.p.m. recording, mostly between 1927 and 1940. In 49 items, many of them substantial, the collection consistently demonstrates the reliability of the Wagner singing at that period, the ability of singers in every register to produce firm, well-focused tone of a kind too rare today. Some of the most interesting items are those in translation from French sources, with Germaine Lubin as Isolde and Brünnhilde and with Marcel Journet as Wotan, both lyrical and clean-cut. The ill-starred Marjorie Lawrence, a great favourite in France, is also represented by recordings in French, including Brünnhilde's immolation scene from Götterdämmerung. Not only are such celebrated Wagnerians as Lauritz Melchior, Friedrich Schorr, Frida Leider, Lotte Lehmann and Max Lorenz well represented, but also singers one might not expect, including the Lieder specialist Gerhard Husch, as Wolfram in Tannhäuser and Aureliano Pertile singing in Italian as Lohengrin. Meta Seinemeyer, an enchanting soprano who died tragically young, here gives lyric sweetness to the dramatic roles of Brünnhilde and Isolde; and among the baritones and basses there is none of the roughness or ill-focus that marks so much latter-day Wagner singing. It is a pity that British-based singers are poorly represented, but the Prologue duet from *Götterdämmerung* brings one of the most impressive items, sung by Florence Austral and Walter Widdop. First-rate transfers and good documentation.

Der fliegende Holländer: Overture; Die Frist ist um. Die Meistersinger: Wahn! Wahn!; Fliedermonolog. Parsifal: Amfortas's Monologues. Tannhäuser: O du mein holder Abendstern. Die Walküre: Wotan's Farewell
*** DG **SACD** 471 638-2; CD 471 348-2. Terfel, BPO, Abbado

The challenge of Wagner plainly suits Bryn Terfel to perfection both musically and dramatically. Though when he made these recordings in Berlin he had yet to sing the roles on stage (with the exception of the least demanding, Wolfram in *Tannhäuser*) the impression of fully formed characterizations is irresistible, with none of the run-through quality of too many recital discs. This is helped by the generosity of the settings, with the feeling of 'bleeding chunks' avoided, while Abbado and the orchestra are plainly inspired by their soloist to give incandescent performances, full and intense. The *Flying Dutchman Overture* and the Dutchman's monologue were recorded live, and arguably the latter is on the slow side, but the illumination of words is as revelatory here as elsewhere on the disc. All of the items are vividly realized, making one long to see Terfel in these roles on stage, notably the two Hans Sachs monologues from *Meistersinger* and the wonderfully expressive portrait of Wotan in the *Walküre* monologue. This final item brings the most daring half-tone phrases from Terfel as he kisses Brünnhilde's godhead away, the culminating moment of the whole opera, here with the agony intensified by the intimacy of expression. The sound is among the richest from this source, with brass gloriously full and rich, especially in the new surround sound compatible SACD format.

Götterdämmerung: (i) *Prelude: Dawn;* (i) *Love Duet; Siegfried's Rhine Journey; Siegfried's Monologue and Funeral March. Siegfried:* (ii) *Forging Scene; Forest Murmurs;* (iii) *Closing Scene with Woodbird*
*** EMI 5 57242-2. Domingo, ROHCGO, Pappano; (i) with Urmana; (ii) Cangelosi; (iii) Dessay

This superb issue follows up Plácido Domingo's earlier prize-winning Wagner disc with Deborah Voigt, Antonio Pappano and the Covent Garden Orchestra in duets from *Tristan* and *Siegfried* (EMI 5 57004-2). Here he amplifies his portrait of Siegfried in powerfully heroic singing in these substantial sections of *Siegfried* and *Götterdämmerung*. It is astonishing that a tenor now 60 should retain a voice at once so full and sharply focused. As a Heldentenor he may not produce such honeyed sounds as in Italian opera, but there is never a suspicion of the ugly barking that disfigures so much Wagner singing, with pitching clear and firm. As on the earlier disc, Pappano proves a sympathetic partner, drawing from the orchestra playing at once rich and powerful, helped by the warm acoustic of the Colosseum, Watford. Urmana as Brünnhilde and David Cangelosi as Mime make excellent foils for the hero, though Natalie Dessay is less well cast as the Woodbird, not as fresh and bright as one really wants. The items are very well presented, with generous orchestral sections helping to avoid any suspicion of this as a collection of 'bleeding chunks'.

WAGNER, Siegfried (1869–1930)

Die Heilige Linde (opera; complete)
*** CPO 999 844-2 (3). Wegner, Schellenberger, Lukic, George, Scharnke, Kruzel, Horn, Heidbüchel, Halmai, West German RSO, Cologne Ch. & O, Albert

It says much for Siegfried Wagner that, even in face of the towering position held by his father, he was still determined to become a composer himself. *Die Heilige Linde* ('The Holy Linden Tree'), first heard in 1924, is the fourteenth of his 18 operas, with a substantial *Prelude* generally counted one of his finest works. The easy tunefulness of the very opening instantly establishes that the musical idiom preferred by the son is more straightforwardly diatonic, not nearly so radical as the chromatic style his father developed. One might relate it to the music of Humperdinck, or among Richard Wagner's works, *Die Meistersinger*, with a similar concern for German folksong.

That is apt, for this involved tale from the third century AD, tells of Arbogast, king of a German tribe, his wife Hildegard, and Fritigern, son of the king of a neighbouring tribe. The villain is Philo, described as a soldier instigator, in fee to the Roman Emperor, intent on getting Arbogast to forge an alliance with Rome. The second act, lighter and brighter than the first and third, is set in that city, but throughout the opera the involved story prompts the composer to produce an attractive series of episodes, colourfully orchestrated with some fine choral passages, which yet fail to add up dramatically. It makes agreeable listening, but the ends of the first two acts bring no sense of drama, and the end of the whole opera, when Arbogast has been killed in battle, is effective as a warmly patriotic ensemble rather than as a dramatic resolution.

Recorded in Cologne in collaboration with West German Radio, this CPO recording offers a warmly idiomatic performance under Werner Andreas Albert, very well sung. As Arbogast, John Wegner exploits a clear, forthright baritone, with Dagmar Schellenberger fresh and firm as Hildegard, and the tenor Schorsten Scharnke aptly heroic as Fritigern, the role with which the composer identified. As the sinister Philo, Volker Horn characterizes well with his bleating voice. The booklet contains a complete libretto and translation, with various essays and background material, but no synopsis of the difficult plot.

Sternengebot (opera; complete)
*(*) Marco Polo 8.225150-51 (2). Kruzel, Roberts, Lukic, Horn, Kinzel, Wenhold, Sailer, Bav. Ch. & Youth O, Albert

Tutored in composition by Humperdinck, Siegfried Wagner wrote no fewer than 18 operas, some of them unfinished, which rather than echoing his father's music turn rather to the example of his tutor in easily romantic fairy-tale pieces. This one, *The Commandment of the Stars*, completed in 1906, draws on astrology in its story from the age of chivalry, dated around the time of King Henry the Fowler. The writing is easily lyrical, far less radical than that of his father, but with the occasional nod of acknowledgement to Richard's example in his own, very involved libretto, as for example in the tournament for the heroine's hand, when the hero, Helferich, is defeated.

Apart from a thinness on exposed violins, the playing of the Bavarian Youth Orchestra is strong and expressive under the vigorous direction of Werner Andreas Albert, helped by full, clear recording. The role of Helferich is well taken by the tenor Volker Horn, if with some strain at times. Sadly, the other soloists are disappointing, notably Ksenija Lukic as the heroine, Agnes, whose shrill hooting tone in her opening scene is almost comical, even though she later improves slightly. In the principal baritone roles Karl-Heinz Kinzel as Adalbert and Andre Wenhold as Kurzbold are both very uneven. It is good to have on disc such a major score of Siegfried Wagner, but this set has to be approached with caution. A German libretto is provided, but no English translation, only a detailed synopsis.

WALLACE, William (1860–1940)

Symphonic Poems 1, The Passing of Beatrice; 3, Sister Helen; 5, Sir William Wallace; 6, Villon

*** Hyp. CDA 66848. BBC Scottish SO, Brabbins

Like Hamish McCunn, William Wallace was born in Greenock, near Glasgow. The fifth of his symphonic poems was premièred at Sir Henry Wood's Queen's Hall Promenade Concerts in 1905. The composition's full title is *Sir William Wallace, Scottish Hero, Freedom-fighter, Beheaded and Dismembered by the English*. The music is not as melodramatic as it sounds. Its Scottish character is immediately obvious at the brooding opening; the main theme, 'Scots wha' hae', emerges only slowly but is celebrated more openly towards the end. *Villon*, an irreverent medieval poet, was a hero of a different kind, and Wallace's programme draws on the thoughts of his philosophical ballads (which are named in the synopsis) in music that is both reflective and vividly colourful. The very romantic *Passing of Beatrice* is a sensuous vision of Paradise, lusciously Wagnerian with an unashamedly Tristanesque close, reflecting the heroine's final transformation. The scoring is sensuously rich, yet it retains also the spiritually ethereal quality of the narrative, rather as Wagner does in *Parsifal*. The final piece here is based on Rossetti, and its full title is *Sister Helen, Villainess, Murdering by Sorcery; Insane with Jealous and Frustrated Love*. What is so remarkable is not only the quality of the musical material throughout these works, but also the composer's skill and confidence in handling it: they are musically every bit as well crafted as the symphonic poems of Liszt. Clearly the BBC Scottish Symphony Orchestra enjoy playing them, and Martyn Brabbins shapes the musical episodes skilfully to balance the warm lyricism and drama without becoming too histrionically melodramatic. The result is remarkably satisfying.

WALLACE, William Vincent (1812–65)

Maritana (opera; complete)

**(*) Marco Polo 8.223406-7. Cullagh, Lee, Clarke, Caddy, RTE Philh. Ch. and Concert O, O Duinn

Along with Balfe's *Bohemian Girl* and Benedict's *Lily of Killarney*, Wallace's *Maritana* marked a breakthrough in opera in Britain, and it held the stage for over 50 years. This lively recording, with Irish artists celebrating this nineteenth-century Irish composer, helps to explain the work's attractions, regularly reminding the modern listener of Gilbert and Sullivan. The big difference is that where G & S present a parody of grand opera, with tongue firmly in cheek, Wallace is intensely serious, with the big melodramatic moments quickly becoming unintentionally comic. To compound the similarity with G & S, the story, like that of the *Yeomen of the Guard*, depends on the heroine, by contract, marrying a man condemned to death who then escapes his punishment. What

matters is that there are many more good tunes than that of the still-remembered aria for the heroine, *Scenes that are Brightest*, and the ensembles in this winning performance are always fresh and lively. The soloists too all have voices which focus cleanly, even if they are not specially distinctive. The recording is bright and forwardly balanced, with words crystal clear. Worth investigating as a period piece.

WALTON, William (1902–83)

'*At the Haunted End of the Day*': Television Profile directed by Tony Palmer

*** Decca **DVD** 074 150-9

Tony Palmer's Italia Prize-winning television profile of William Walton, is among the most moving ever made of a composer. The approach is both direct and evocative, starting with Walton himself nearing 80 and plainly rather frail, musing at the keyboard of the piano in his work room as he composes the solo cello *Passacaglia* for Rostropovich, one of his very last works. This moment brings several of his wrily humorous *obiter dicta* with which the film is delightfully dotted. He admits to composing at the piano, but being no pianist, he finds 'has rather boogered the whole thing oop' (resorting to the Lancashire accent he promptly dropped when as a boy treble he joined the choir of Christ Church Cathedral, Oxford).

The story of his career with its extraordinary sequence of lucky breaks, with one protector or helper after another coming along, is then told for the most part chronologically. We see the house where he was born, by Oldham standards relatively grand, (although as he points out, with an outside loo), and evocative shots follow of Oldham (including the 'very rough' board school he attended and his church), Oxford and later London and Amalfi in Italy. The impact of *Belshazzar's Feast* is fully brought out, not least thanks to Simon Rattle's conducting.

Later, Rattle also directs the passages from the *First Symphony*, which comes into the story not in its proper place in the 1930s, but in a sequence on the loves of Walton's life, when he is safely married to Susana and living comfortably on the isle of Ischia. The film was made within a couple of years of the composer's death in 1983 and has a vein of melancholy running through it, explaining Palmer's title, '*At the Haunted End of the Day*', taken from one of the most striking of the arias in the opera *Troilus and Cressida*.

Even so, the impact of the film is anything but depressing, with the effervescent personality of Susana taking over towards the end. A unique career, vividly re-created.

(i) *Anniversary Fanfare; Coronation Marches: Crown Imperial; Orb and Sceptre; (ii; v) Cello Concerto; (v) Symphony 1 in B flat min.; (iii–v) Belshazzar's Feast; (iv; v) Coronation Te Deum*

(B) ** Chan. 2-for-1 (ADD/DDD) 241-10 (2). (i) Philh. O, Willcocks; (ii) Kirshbaum; (iii) Milnes; (iv) RSNO Ch.; (v) RSNO, Gibson

The *Anniversary Fanfare* is designed to lead directly into *Orb and Sceptre*, which is what it does here. However, the Kirshbaum–Gibson reading of the *Cello Concerto* is disappointing, lacking the warmth, weight and expressiveness that so ripe an example of late romanticism demands. And while Gibson's is a well-paced, convincingly idiomatic view of the *First Symphony*, ensemble is not always bitingly precise enough for this darkly intense music (malice prescribed for the Scherzo, melancholy for the slow movement). The recording is first rate, but with less body than usual from Chandos and with timpani resonantly obtrusive. Gibson's view of Walton's brilliant oratorio *Belshazzar's Feast* tends towards brisk speeds, but is no less dramatic for that. It remains individually competitive, particularly with so magnificent a baritone as Sherrill Milnes as soloist, but overall this is not one of the more enticing issues in Chandos's 2-for-1 series.

Anniversary Fanfare; Crown Imperial; March for the History of the English-speaking Peoples; Orb and Sceptre; A Queen's Fanfare; (i) Antiphon; 4 Christmas Carols: All this time; King Herod and his cock; Make we now this feast; What cheer?; In honour of the City of London; Jubilate Deo; Where does the uttered music go?
*** Chan. 8998. (i) Bach Ch.; Philh. O, Willcocks

Sir David Willcocks conducts performances of the two *Coronation Marches* full of panache, with the brass superbly articulated and inner detail well caught. Also the *March for the History of the English-speaking Peoples*. The *a cappella* choral items are very well done too, if less intimately than on the Conifer disc of Walton choral music from Trinity College Choir. With the original organ parts orchestrated, the *Jubilate* and *Antiphon* gain greatly from having full instrumental accompaniment. The brief fanfares, never previously recorded, are a welcome makeweight, with the *Anniversary Fanfare*, designed to lead directly into *Orb and Sceptre*, which is what it does here.

5 Bagatelles for Guitar and Chamber Orchestra
*** Chan. 9963. Ogden, N. Sinf., Hickox – ARNOLD: *Guitar Concerto; Serenade;* L. BERKELEY: *Guitar Concerto* ***

It was the bright idea of Patrick Russ to mix together the set of *Five Bagatelles for Solo Guitar* which Walton wrote for Julian Bream and his very last work, *Varii capricci*, a brilliant orchestration of those same five pieces. The result is a guitar concerto which in many ways – rather surprisingly – transcends those two original sources, creating a work as effective as the fine guitar concertos of Sir Malcolm Arnold and Sir Lennox Berkeley.

What Russ has done is to retain as far as possible the substance of the solo guitar part of the *Bagatelles*, and use Walton's orchestral version mainly for comment, with the strands often alternating rather than playing together. This has involved a modest expansion of the fast outer movements, a positive gain when, without altering their character, it gives them added weight. The three genre pieces in between, all briefer and more relaxed, then together take on the role of a conventional slow movement. The composite work seems less lightweight than either the solo *Bagatelles* or *Varii capricci*, a genuine concerto rather than a suite of miniatures. Craig Ogden is a brilliant, persuasive advocate, warmly supported by Hickox and the Northern Sinfonia.

Capriccio burlesco; Coronation Marches: Crown Imperial; Orb and Sceptre. Hamlet: Funeral March; Johannesburg Festival Overture; Richard III: Prelude & Suite; Scapino (comedy overture); Spitfire Prelude & Fugue
(M) **(*) EMI (ADD) 5 67222-2. RLPO, Groves

The 1969 collection of Walton's shorter orchestral pieces was made in Studio 2 (EMI's hi-fi-conscious equivalent of Decca's Phase 4) and now seems slightly over-bright with its digital remastering. The sound tends to polarize, with a lack of

opulence in the middle range, so necessary in the nobilmente of the big tunes of the stirring *Spitfire Prelude and Fugue* and *Crown Imperial*. The Shakespearean film music was recorded much later (1984) and the quality is fuller, more warmly atmospheric. Although the two *Coronation Marches* could do with a little more exuberance, Groves is otherwise a highly sympathetic interpreter of this repertoire, and the playing of the Liverpool orchestra is excellent.

(i) Capriccio burlesco; (ii; iii) Violin Concerto; (i) Johannesburg Festival Overture; (iv) Partita; Symphony 2; Variations on a Theme by Hindemith; (iii; v) Belshazzar's Feast
⊕➔ (B) *** Sony (ADD) SB2K 89934 (2). (i) NYPO, Kostelanetz; (ii) Francescatti; (iii) Phd. O, Ormandy; (iv) Cleveland O, Szell; (v) with Cassel, Rutgers University Ch.

Sony's celebration for the Walton Centenary in 2002 brings together an outstanding batch of high-powered American performances such as no other British composer has ever received. Well transferred in typical CBS up-front sound in recordings dating as far back as 1959, they come at bargain price in the Essential Classics series. The three performances with Szell and the Cleveland Orchestra of the *Symphony No. 2*, the *Hindemith Variations* and the *Partita* are all stunning in every way, not just brilliant and powerful but passionately intense too. Ormandy is a warmly persuasive conductor with the Philadelphia Orchestra in both *Belshazzar's Feast* (with the Rutgers University Choir and baritone soloist, Walter Cassel) and in the *Violin Concerto*, with Zino Francescatti the flamboyant soloist. Andre Kostelanetz conducts the New York Philharmonic in comparably brilliant performances both of the *Johannesburg Festival Overture* and the work he was the first to conduct, the *Capriccio burlesco*, a comedy overture in all but name.

Capriccio burlesco; The First Shoot (orch. Palmer); Granada (prelude for orchestra); Johannesburg Festival Overture; Music for Children. Galop Finale (orch. Palmer); Portsmouth Point: Overture; Prologo e fantasia; Scapino
*** Chan. 8968. LPO, Thomson

The *Capriccio burlesco* is ravishingly orchestrated, with some apt echoes of Gershwin, and the *Prologo e fantasia* completes an American group. The *Granada Prelude*, written for the television company, taps Walton's patriotic march vein in a jaunty way. *The First Shoot* comes in Christopher Palmer's brilliant orchestration of the brass band suite. The opening *Giocoso* is a re-run of *Old Sir Faulk*, and the other movements bring more echoes of *Façade*. As for the other novelty, the ten brief movements of *Music for Children* are here supplemented by a *Galop Final*. Palmer has here orchestrated the piano score. Though the opulent Chandos recording tends to take some of the bite away from Walton's jazzily accented writing, the richness of the orchestral sound is consistently satisfying.

(i) Cello Concerto; (ii) Viola Concerto; (iii) Violin Concerto. Scapino; Coronation Marches: Crown Imperial; Orb and Sceptre; Façade Suites 1 & 2; Henry V: Suite; Symphonies 1 & 2; Variations on a Theme of Hindemith; (iv) Coronation Te Deum; Belshazzar's Feast
(M) *** Decca 470 508-2 (4). (i) Cohen; (ii) Neubauer; (iii) Little, (iv) Terfel; L'inviti, Waynflete Singers, Winchester Cathedral Ch.; Bournemouth Ch. & SO, Litton or Hill

Decca's four-disc Walton Edition offers consistently fine versions of all of the composer's most important orchestral works, some of them unsurpassed by rival versions, with Andrew Litton an idiomatic Waltonian with a natural feeling for the jazzy syncopations. This brings together the three Litton discs previously issued by Decca but with important additions. The third of the four discs, never originally issued with the others, contains outstanding versions of the *Viola Concerto* and *Hindemith Variations*, plus the two *Façade Suites*.

Where most latter-day interpreters of the *Viola Concerto* have taken a very expansive view of the lyrical first movement, *Andante comodo*, Paul Neubauer comes nearer than anyone to following the example of the original interpreters on disc, Frederick Riddle and William Primrose, in adopting a flowing tempo, encouraged by the composer. It makes Neubauer's and Litton's far more persuasive than other modern versions with no expressive self-indulgence, and with the brisker passages in this movement also taken faster than has become usual. Neubauer's tone is taut and firm to match, clean rather than fruity, with the central Scherzo taken excitingly fast and the finale again kept moving but without losing a spring in the jaunty rhythm of the main theme. He then relaxes beautifully for the hauntingly lovely epilogue, ending on a whispered *pianissimo*. Litton also encourages wide dynamic contrasts, with the big tuttis bringing an element of wildness in brassy syncopations.

The *Hindemith Variations* also delivers a performance with contrasts heightened, not just of dynamic but of speed, extreme in both directions. This goes with an exceptional transparency in the orchestral textures, well-caught in the recording and bringing out the refinement of Walton's orchestration. *Façade*, predictably, is a fun performance, although the warm acoustic runs the danger of taking some edge off these witty parodies.

Two of the other discs are the same as before, with Tasmin Little's heartfelt reading of the *Violin Concerto* very well coupled with Litton's outstanding account of the *Second Symphony* and *Scapino*, and Robert Cohen's thoughtful reading of the *Cello Concerto* in coupling with the *First Symphony*. Litton's powerful account of *Belshazzar's Feast* with Bryn Terfel as the most dramatic of baritone soloists, brings fresh, cleanly focused choral sound that, with the help of keenly atmospheric recording, points up more clearly than usual the terracing between the different groupings of voices. This disc also includes the two coronation marches, the *Coronation Te Deum* and the *Henry V Suite*, with David Hill, chorus-master in *Belshazzar*, ably standing in for Litton in *Orb and Sceptre* and the *Te Deum*.

Cello Concerto

☞ *** EMI **DVD** 492840-9. Piatigorsky, BBC SO, Sargent – MENDELSSOHN: *Violin Concerto* **; BEETHOVEN: *Piano Concerto 4* **(*)

(N) (☞) (M) *** RCA **SACD** 82876 66375-2. Piatigorsky, Boston SO, Munch – DVORAK: *Concerto* ***

(M) *** Sony SMK 89712. Ma, LSO, Previn – ELGAR: *Cello Concerto* ***

(BB) *** RCA Navigator (ADD) 74321 29248-2. Piatigorsky, Boston SO, Munch – VAUGHAN WILLIAMS: *Sinfonia Antartica* ***

(i; ii) *Cello Concerto*; (ii) *Improvisations on an Impromptu of Benjamin Britten*; *Partita for Orchestra*; (i) *Passacaglia for Solo Cello*

*** Chan. 8959. (i) Wallfisch; (ii) LPO, Thomson

Walton's *Cello Concerto* was commissioned by Piatigorsky, who subsequently premièred and recorded it with the Boston

Symphony and Charles Munch (see below). This was its British première, at the Royal Albert Hall in February 1957 with Sir Malcolm Sargent conducting the BBC Symphony Orchestra, whose chief conductor he still was. Those who remember hearing the broadcast or who were fortunate enough to have been there will find Piatigorsky's aristocratic account a particularly moving document; and those coming to it without any nostalgic baggage can hardly fail to respond to his blend of virtuosity and restraint. The camerawork is pleasingly restrained and totally free from the intrusive changes of perspective that are inescapable nowadays.

On CD Piatigorsky plays the *Cello Concerto* with a gripping combination of full-blooded eloquence and subtlety of feeling, readily capturing the bitter-sweet melancholy of its flowing lyrical lines. The closing pages of the final variations are particularly haunting. Munch provides a totally understanding accompaniment, with the strings of the Boston Symphony finding the lyrical ecstasy which is such a distinctive part of this concerto.

The 1957 recording is close, but the improvement in sound on the new SACD is astonishing, the cello-tone full and the ambience of the Boston hall adding a warmth and resonance to the orchestra. This is an indispensable performance, and the Dvořák *Concerto* is also highly attractive. Those preferring other couplings will find the CD transfer also comparably improved, and they can choose between either the Vaughan Williams *Sinfonia Antartica* on RCA's budget label or, more suitably, the excellent complete collection of Walton's concertante music on the RCA Double below, which includes also Previn's outstanding account of the *First Symphony*.

Yo-Yo Ma and Previn give a sensuously beautiful performance. With speeds markedly slower than usual in the outer movements, the meditation is intensified to bring a mood of ecstasy, quite distinct from other Walton, with the central allegro becoming the symphonic kernel of the work, far more than just a scherzo. In the excellent CBS recording, the soloist is less forward and more faithfully balanced than is common.

With his rich, even tone, Wallfisch is just as warm and purposeful in the solo *Passacaglia* as in the *Concerto*, while Thomson relishes the vivid orchestral colours in both the *Improvisations*, here wider ranging in expression than usual, and the brilliant *Partita*. Excellent Chandos sound.

(i) *Cello Concerto*; (ii; iii) *Viola Concerto*; (iv) *Violin Concerto*; (v) *Sinfonia concertante*; (iii) *Symphony 1*

☞ (B) *** RCA Double (mono/stereo) 74321 92575-2 (2). (i) Piatigorsky, Boston SO, Munch; (ii) Bashmet; (iii) LSO, Previn; (iv) Heifetz, Philh. O, composer; (v) Stott, RPO, Handley

The RCA two-disc collection includes the première recording of the *Cello Concerto* with Piatigorsky. It is given up-front recording, which for 1957 is commendably full and open. Similarly, Heifetz as the virtuoso who commissioned the *Violin Concerto* remains in his way supreme as an interpreter, urgent beyond any rival, here with the composer conducting the Philharmonia Orchestra. The 1950 mono recording has been opened up to put more air round the sound.

The other two concertante works come in modern digital versions – Kathryn Stott, in a recording made for Conifer, performs the original, more elaborate version of the *Sinfonia concertante*, and Yuri Bashmet brings his yearningly Slavonic temperament and masterly virtuosity to the *Viola Concerto* – see under its alternative coupling below (09026 63292-2).

Bashmet's partners are the ideal combination of Previn

and the LSO, and it is Previn's vintage version of the *First Symphony* with the LSO of an earlier generation that sets the seal on the whole package, a reading that has never been matched, let alone surpassed. What is also remarkable here is the clarity, definition and sense of presence of the 1966 recording, with the stereo spectrum even more sharply focused than in the later digital recordings. For I.M. this bargain-priced RCA Double stands out among the special offerings for the Walton Centennial.

(i) *Cello Concerto;* (ii) *Violin Concerto in B min.*

☞ (BB) *** Naxos 8.554325. (i) Hugh; (ii) Kang; E. N. Philh. O, Daniel

(i–iii) *Cello Concerto;* (iv; ii; iii) *Violin Concerto;* (v) *Overtures: Portsmouth Point; Scapino. Symphonies Nos.* (vi) *1 in B flat min.;* (v) *2*

(B) **(*) EMI (ADD) double forte 5 73371-2 (2). (i) Paul Tortelier; (ii) Bournemouth SO; (iii) Berglund; (iv) Haendel; (v) LSO, Previn; (vi) Philh. O, Haitink

In many ways Tim Hugh's reading of the *Cello Concerto* is the most searching yet. He finds an intense thoughtfulness, a sense of mystery, of inner meditation in the great lyrical ideas of all three movements, daring to play with a more extreme *pianissimo* than any rival. The bravura writing finds him equally concentrated, always sounding strong and spontaneous in face of any technical challenge. As in their previous Walton recordings, Paul Daniel and the English Northern Philharmonia equally play with flair and sympathy, so that the all-important syncopations always sound idiomatic, even if the strings lack a little in weight. In the *Violin Concerto* Dong-Suk Kang here follows up the success of his Naxos recording of the Elgar *Violin Concerto*, playing immaculately with a fresh, clean-cut tone, pure and true above the stave. If this is a degree more objective than more overtly romantic readings, Kang makes a virtue of opting for speeds rather faster than usual, evidently aware of the example of the dedicatee, Jascha Heifetz.

Tortelier's account of the *Cello Concerto* is characteristically passionate. After the haunting melancholy of the first movement, the central Scherzo emerges as a far weightier piece than most such movements, while the final variations have seldom on record developed with such a sense of compulsion. Ida Haendel's version of the *Violin Concerto* is warmly appealing. Previn is at his finest in the *Second Symphony*, sparkling in the outer movements, warmly romantic in the central slow movement, while in the two overtures he finds more light and shade than usual. However, Haitink's reading of the *First Symphony* is more controversial. The malevolent demon that inhabits the first two movements is somewhat tamed, and in the opening movement some will feel that the lack of the relentless forward thrust demonstrated in the finest versions (including Previn's RCA reading) underplays the music's character. However, Haitink's directness leads to spacious and noble accounts of the slow movement and finale. The bright, digital recording is a little lacking in bass and not as impressive as the fine analogue sound that EMI provide for Previn in No. 1.

(i; ii) *Cello Concerto;* (iii) *Façade suites (excerpts): Old Sir Faulk; Popular Song; Tango-pasodoble; Tarantella Sevillana;* (iii) *Variations on a Theme on Hindemith;* (iv) *Coronation Te Deum;* (iv; v) *The Twelve*

(M) (***) BBC mono/stereo BBCL 4098-2. (i) Fournier; (ii) RPO; (iii) BBC SO; (iv) LPO Ch., LPO; (v) with Dowdall, Minty, Tear, Wakeham; composer

This BBC Legends disc is especially valuable in giving us the composer's recordings of live performances of works which Walton did not otherwise record in the studio, filling in important gaps. It is good too to have a mono recording of Pierre Fournier as soloist in a 1959 Edinburgh Festival performance of the *Cello Concerto*, a work he did not otherwise record. Though sadly in the opening section he has an uncharacteristic lapse in intonation, it is a fine reading, sensitive and brilliant, with the soloist going along with the conductor in a far more flowing treatment than usual of the predominantly slow variations of the finale, shaving over two minutes off the regular timing, making it a much tauter conclusion. The *Hindemith Variations*, also with the RPO, come from a Festival Hall performance of 1963, antedating George Szell's studio recording. Walton's own reading has a keener sense of fun in scherzando variations, and is a degree more warmly expressive in lyrical passages, even if the ensemble is not quite so polished. The four favourite movements from *Façade* come from a Prom at the Royal Albert Hall in 1968, and also surprisingly are mono recordings, but show Walton as a supreme master of witty pointing, bringing out the fun of these delectable parodies. In some ways the greatest revelation comes in the two choral works, recorded in Westminster Abbey in 1966, with the BBC engineers skilfully getting round the problem of heavy reverberation to produce glowingly atmospheric sound with ample weight for the chorus. The *Coronation Te Deum* was, of course, written for the Abbey, and is made all the more ripely dramatic with antiphonal brass. Yet best of all is *The Twelve*, which in its usual form with organ accompaniment can sound bitty, whereas here with massive forces this 'Anthem for the Feast of Any Apostle' to words by Auden relates directly to the major Walton choral works including *Belshazzar*, weighty and dramatic.

Viola Concerto

*** RCA 09026 63292-2. Bashmet, LSO, Previn – BRUCH: *Concerto for Violin & Viola; Kol Nidrei; Romance* ***

*** EMI 5 57510-2. Vengerov, LSO, Rostropovich – BRITTEN: *Violin Concerto* ***

Yuri Bashmet with his opulent viola tone warmly relishes the ripe romanticism of the Walton concerto as well as the high-voltage electricity of its jazz-based writing. Like other latter-day interpreters he opts for a daringly spacious speed for the haunting opening melody, but avoids any hint of sluggishness, relishing the bravura of the contrasting sections. The central Scherzo brings a dazzling display, with the fun of the scherzando passages winningly brought out, as it is too in the finale. Bashmet ends with another daringly slow speed for the wistful epilogue, again superbly sustained, thanks also to the ideal accompaniment of Previn and the LSO. First-rate sound. The coupling may seem odd, but all three Bruch works will delight anyone who enjoys romantic viola music.

With Vengerov and Rostropovich unexpectedly tackling English music, some of the most ravishing string-playing results: this is music-making as a love-affair. As in the Britten coupling, Vengerov brings out the fun of the brilliant bravura passages, jazzing the syncopated rhythms, but the outer movements are taken far more slowly than is usual. Playing the viola for the very first time, Vengerov shows himself the complete master technically, so that the very measured speed for the first movement has a purity and rapt intensity that removes any feeling of self-indulgence. After the dazzling Scherzo, Vengerov, with Rostropovich's encouragement, changes the whole character of the finale with his consistently slow speeds. Its jaunty opening theme on the bassoon is made to sound like a cakewalk from *Façade*, while the tender recollections of the epilogue are hypnotically dreamlike, with the timing for that movement alone no less than six minutes longer than in early recordings from Riddle and Primrose. Hardly a definitive reading – for that try the Neubauer on Decca among modern versions – but a magical one that demands to be heard, not just by devotees of the composer.

Viola Concerto; Violin Concerto

(M) *** EMI 5 62813-2. Kennedy, RPO, Previn – VAUGHAN WILLIAMS: *The Lark Ascending* ***

(i) *Viola Concerto in A min.*; (ii) *Violin Concerto in B min.*; (iii) *Sinfonia concertante*

(M) (**(*)) Avid mono AMSC 604. (i) Primrose; (ii) Heifetz; Cincinnati SO, Goossens; (iii) Sellick, CBSO, Composer

Kennedy's achievement in giving equally rich and expressive performances of both works makes for an ideal coupling, helped by the unique insight of André Previn as Waltonian. Kennedy on the viola produces tone as rich and firm as on his usual violin. The Scherzo has never been recorded with more panache than here, and the finale brings a magic moment in the return of the main theme from the opening, hushed and intense. In the *Violin Concerto* too, Kennedy gives a warmly relaxed reading, in which he dashes off the bravura passages with great flair. He may miss some of the more searchingly introspective manner of Chung in her 1971 version, but there are few Walton recordings as richly rewarding as this, helped by warm, atmospheric sound, and with the bonus of Vaughan Williams's *Lark Ascending* this makes an excellent representation for Nigel Kennedy among EMI's 'Great Artists of the Century'.

In many ways, Heifetz's pioneering wartime version of the *Violin Concerto*, recorded in Cincinnati in 1941 at speeds far faster than we are used to now, has never been surpassed – even finer than his later remake with Walton and the Philharmonia, more fiery, with even more flair and spontaneity. This account of the *Viola Concerto* was the first of two which Primrose recorded, markedly cooler than the première recording on Decca, with the young Frederick Riddle accompanied by Walton and the LSO. The central Scherzo is taken at an astonishingly fast speed, on the verge of sounding breathless. By contrast, the première recording of the *Sinfonia concertante* with Phyllis Sellick is exceptionally warm and expressive, an interpretation never quite matched since. Despite the rough Avid transfers, such historic performances offered in a coupling on a bargain disc are self-recommending.

(i) Viola Concerto. Johannesburg Festival Overture; Symphony 2

(BB) *** Naxos 8.553402. (i) Tomter; E. N. Philh. O, Daniel

(i) Viola Concerto; Sonata for String Orchestra; Variations on a Theme of Hindemith

*** Chan. 9106. (i) Imai; LPO, Latham-Koenig

Pride of place on Naxos goes to the thoughtful, deeply felt reading of the *Viola Concerto* with the Norwegian viola-player, Lars Anders Tomter. Though Tomter's tight vibrato is at times prominent, he brings out the tender poetry of this most elusive of Walton's string concertos, with its mixture of melancholy and wit. More than others, Tomter observes *pianissimo* markings, and rightly he adopts a flowing speed for the first movement while refusing to be rushed in the

Scherzo and finale, which with delectable pointing acquire extra scherzando sparkle. The overture is given the most exuberant performance, rivalling the composer's own, with the orchestra's soloists playing brilliantly. In the *Symphony No. 2* Paul Daniel gives extra transparency to the often heavy orchestration, making the work less weighty than usual but just as warmly expressive. A superb bargain.

Imai is satisfyingly firm and true in all her playing, keenly confident in the virtuoso passages, with the central Scherzo not at all breathless-sounding. Imai uses a very broad *Andante* to bring out the full lyrical warmth, but it means that the following bravura section enters with a jolt rather than developing naturally. The movement is not helped either by the forward balance of the soloist. Jan Latham-Koenig secures crisply rhythmic playing from the orchestra in all three movements. The main theme of the finale is even jauntier than usual, again at a speed fractionally slower than normal.

The warmth of the LPO string-tone comes over impressively in the *Sonata for Strings*, but the contrast between the passages for solo string quartet (echoing the original quartet version) and the full string ensemble is too extreme. Latham-Koenig is also warmly expressive in the *Hindemith Variations*, which is not as lightly pointed or cleanly detailed as it might be, partly a question of the recording. The three works on the disc not only make an exceptionally generous triptych, but one which reflects Walton's mastery throughout his long career.

Violin Concerto

(M) *** Decca 476 1723. Bell, Baltimore SO, Zinman – BLOCH: *Baal Shem*; BARBER: *Violin Concerto* ***

(***) Biddulph mono WHL 016. Heifetz, Cincinnati SO, Goossens – VAUGHAN WILLIAMS: *A London Symphony (No. 2)* (***) (with Concert (***))

(BB) (***) Naxos (ADD) 8.110939. Heifetz, Cincinnati SO, Goossens – ELGAR: *Violin Concerto* (***)

(*) Classico CLASSCD 233. Azizjan, Copenhagen PO, Bellincamp – BRITTEN: *Violin Concerto* *

Violin Concerto; 2 Pieces for Violin & Orchestra; Sonata for Violin & Orchestra (both orch. Palmer)

*** Chan. 9073. Mordkovitch, LPO, Latham-Koenig

From an American perspective, Walton's *Violin Concerto* can well be seen as a British counterpart of the Barber, similarly romantic, written at exactly the same period. This prize-winning Decca disc has Bell giving a commanding account of the solo part, even matching Heifetz himself in the ease of his virtuosity. Playing with rapt intensity, Bell treats the central cadenza of the first movement expansively, making it more deeply reflective than usual. Rich and brilliant sound, with the violin balanced forward, but not aggressively so. It won the 1998 *Gramophone* Concerto Award and now reappears at mid-price on Universal's *Gramophone* Award Collection.

Lydia Mordkovitch gives the most expansive account of the Walton *Violin Concerto* on disc, sustaining spacious speeds warmly and persuasively. Latham-Koenig may not have quite the spark that Previn brings to the orchestral writing in both the Chung and Kennedy versions, but he is keenly idiomatic, both in his feeling for sharply syncopated rhythms and in flexible rubato for Walton's romantic melodies. The characteristically warm Chandos recording is also a help. Christopher Palmer's scoring of the *Sonata* offers a sensuousness of sound comparable with that in the opera *Troilus and Cressida*. Though his use of the harp or pizzicato strings for arpeggio accompaniments is not always comfortable, Palmer is right in seeing much of the piano part as already implying orchestration. With Mordkovitch just as powerful and rich-toned as in the regular concerto, the work makes a far bigger impact than in its original chamber form, a valuable addition to the Walton repertory. The two shorter pieces make an agreeable supplement, with Palmer's lush orchestration removing them even further from their medieval source-material.

Jascha Heifetz made the very first recording in 1941 with Eugene Goossens and the Cincinnati orchestra, and it has never quite been matched since for its passionate urgency as well as its brilliance. Speeds are much faster than has latterly become the norm, but the romantic warmth of the work has never been more richly conveyed. On Biddulph in an excellent CD transfer it is coupled with the early recording of the original score of Vaughan Williams's *London Symphony*, plus other British music.

The alternative Naxos transfer, less bright than RCA's original, is well balanced, making for comfortable listening. The generous Elgar coupling confirms this as in every way a winner.

Sergej Azizjan, the Leningrad-trained concertmaster of the Copenhagen Philharmonic, has a superb technique, marked by flawless intonation and a wide tonal range. His reading of the Walton is passionate in an aptly extrovert way, an excellent choice for anyone wanting this coupling, though the orchestra is a degree recessed, and such passages as the rhythmic opening of the Walton finale lack something in bite.

Coronation March: *Orb and Sceptre;* **(i)** *Coronation Te Deum; Jubilate Deo; A Litany; Set me as a Seal upon thine heart*
(*) Australian Decca Eloquence 467 613-2. Bournemouth SO, Hill; (i) with Winchester Cathedral Ch., Waynflete Singers – VAUGHAN WILLIAMS: *Benedicite,* **etc. **(*)

A swaggering vivacious *Orb and Sceptre* is marred by a rather over-reverberant acoustic, though the effect is certainly exciting. The choral items are sympathetically sung, and the *Coronation Te Deum* is gutsy, with the recording surprisingly well managed in the resonance.

Façade (an Entertainment; complete)
⊕━ ☼ (M) *** Decca mono 468 801-2. Sitwell, Pears, English Op. Group Ens., Collins – BRITTEN: *Serenade for Tenor, Horn & Strings, Op. 31; Folksongs* *******
*** Hyp. CDA 67239. Bron, Stilgoe, Nash Ens., Lloyd-Jones – LAMBERT: *Salome: suite* *******

Façade (complete, including Façade 2)
**(*) ASV CDDCA 679. Scales, West, LMP (members), Glover
**(*) Chan. 8869. Walton, Baker, City of L. Sinfonia (members), Hickox

Façade (complete, including Façade 2) & Other Edith Sitwell Poems
*** Ara. Z 6699. Redgrave, Chamber Music Society of Lincoln Center, Shifrin

Anthony Collins's 1954 recording of *Façade* is a gramophone classic, sounding miraculously vivid and atmospheric in a CD transfer that seems like modern stereo. Dame Edith Sitwell has one of the richest and most characterful of speaking voices and here she recited her early poems to the masterly witty music of the youthful Walton with glorious relish. Peter Pears is splendid too in the fast poems, rattling off the lines like the *grande dame* herself, to demonstrate how near-nonsense can be pure poetry.

It is the first great merit of this excellent Hyperion version that not only has the conductor gathered together all the surviving *Façade* settings, written between 1922 and 1928, a dozen more than in the regular Entertainment, but provides a valuable commentary on when and how they were written. *Popular Song*, the best known of all *Façade* items, was one of the last two to be composed. The Hyperion issue provides the printed texts of the poems for which the music is lost, leaving room for the newly discovered Lambert music for *Salome* as an attractive makeweight. Eleanor Bron and Richard Stilgoe make an excellent pair of reciters, and the recording in a natural acoustic balances them well – not too close – with no discrepancy between voices and instruments. They inflect the words more than Edith Sitwell and early interpreters did, but still keep a stylized manner, meticulously obeying the rhythms specified in the score, with Stilgoe phenomenally fluent, while Bron in slow poems adopts an effective trance-like manner. Under David Lloyd-Jones the brilliant sextet of players from the Nash Ensemble, including John Wallace on trumpet and Richard Hosford on clarinet, could not be more idiomatic, with rhythms delectably pointed.

With Lyn Redgrave an excellent reciter, characterful and sharply rhythmic, the ensemble from Lincoln Center under Joseph Silverstein give a virtuoso performance of the quirky score, both crisply disciplined and idiomatic. Far more than usual, the recording gets the balance right between voice and instruments, with words splendidly clear yet with no unnatural highlighting of the reciter. She also recites eleven *Façade* poems without music, a random choice, not those which Walton set, but for which the music is lost. Some may feel that Redgrave overdoes the characterizations, but she gets a very acceptable balance between expressive word-pointing and formality, characterizing precisely in different, stylized accents, as in the Noël Coward accent she adopts for the *Tango* and *Popular Song*.

Scales and West as a husband-and-wife team are inventive in their shared roles, and generally it works well. *Scotch Rhapsody* is hilariously done as a duet, with West intervening at appropriate moments, and with sharply precise Scots accents. Regional accents may defy Edith Sitwell's original prescription – and her own example – but here, with one exception, they add an appropriate flavour. The exception is *Popular Song*, where Prunella Scales's cockney accent is quite alien to the allusive words, with their 'cupolas, gables in the lakes, Georgian stables'. For fill-up the reciters have recorded more Sitwell poems, but unaccompanied.

Susana Walton, widow of the composer, makes a bitingly characterful reciter, matching with her distinctive accent – she was born in Argentina – the exotic character of many numbers. Richard Baker, phenomenally precise and agile in enunciating the Sitwell poems, makes the perfect foil, and Hickox secures colourful and lively playing from members of the City of London Sinfonia, who relish in particular the jazzy inflexions. *Façade 2* consists of a number of Sitwell settings beyond the definitive series of twenty-one. All of them are fun and make an apt if not very generous coupling for the regular sequence. Warm sound, a little too reverberant for so intimate a work.

Façade: Suites 1–3; Overture Portsmouth Point (arr. Lambert); Siesta; (i) Sinfonia concertante.
WALTON/ARNOLD: *Popular Birthday*
*** Chan. 9148. (i) Parkin; LPO, Latham-Koenig or Thomson

Adapted from a ballet score written for Diaghilev (but then

rejected), the *Sinfonia concertante*, with its sharply memorable ideas in each movement and characteristically high voltage, has never had the attention it deserves. Eric Parkin as soloist is perfectly attuned to the idiom, warmly melodic as well as jazzily syncopated, making this a most sympathetic account, even if the *Maestoso* introduction is hardly grand enough. The recording sets the piano a little more backwardly, no doubt to reflect the idea that this is not a full concerto. Jan Latham-Koenig gives the witty *Façade* movements just the degree of jazzy freedom they need. The third suite, devised and arranged by Christopher Palmer, draws on three apt movements from the *Façade* entertainment, ending riotously with the rag-music of *Something Lies Beyond the Scene*. That is a first recording, and so is Constant Lambert's arrangement for small orchestra of the *Overture Portsmouth Point*, clearer than the original. *Siesta* is given an aptly cool performance under Bryden Thomson, and the *Popular Birthday* is Malcolm Arnold's fragmentary linking of 'Happy birthday to you' with the *Popular Song* from *Façade*, originally written for Walton's twentieth birthday.

Façade: Suites 1 & 2

☞ (BB) *** Hyp. Helios CDH 55099. E. N. Philh. O,
  Lloyd-Jones – BLISS: *Checkmate ***; LAMBERT:
  Horoscope *** ✿.

Brilliantly witty and humorous performances of the two orchestral suites that Walton himself fashioned from his 'Entertainment'. This is music which, with its outrageous quotations, can make one chuckle out loud. Moreover it offers, to quote Constant Lambert, 'one good tune after another', all scored with wonderful felicity. The playing here could hardly be bettered, and the recording is in the demonstration bracket with its natural presence and bloom. A very real bargain.

Filmscores

As You Like It: Suite. The Battle of Britain: Suite. Henry V: Suite. History of the English-Speaking Peoples: March. Troilus and Cressida (opera): *Interlude*
(M) *** EMI 5 65585-2. LPO Ch. & O, Davis

The Battle of Britain Suite presents the music that (for trumpery reasons) was rejected for the original film, including a Wagnerian send-up and a splendid final march. Another vintage Walton march here was written for a television series based on Churchill's history, but again was never used. It is a pity that the *Henry V Suite* does not include the Agincourt charge, but it is good to have the choral contributions to the opening and closing sequences. Most welcome is the long-buried music for the 1926 Paul Czinner film of *As You Like It*. Warm, opulent recording.

As You Like It (poem for orchestra); *Hamlet* (Shakespeare scenario in 9 movements) (both arr. Palmer)
(BB) **(*) Naxos 8.553344. Sheen, Dublin RTE Concert O,
  Penny

In adaptations of film music for concert performance by the late Christopher Palmer, both Penny and the RTE Concert Orchestra give warm, sympathetic performances. Michael Sheen recites the Hamlet soliloquies with the ardour of youth, and the unnamed soprano soloist in the *As You Like It* song, *Under the greenwood tree*, sings with fresh, girlish tone. With recording a little recessed, and with thinnish strings,

this cannot match the Chandos issue of the same coupling at full-price, but it makes a good bargain.

Scenes from Shakespeare (compiled Palmer): As You Like It; Hamlet; Henry V; Richard III
(M) **(*) Chan. 7041. Gielgud, Plummer, ASMF, Marriner

This makes an apt and attractive compilation, putting together well-chosen selections from the recordings of Walton's Shakespeare film music, first issued in the complete Chandos edition, not just for the three masterly films directed by Laurence Olivier, but also for the pre-war *As You Like It*. Roughly two-thirds of the *Henry V* music is included here, and about half of each of the other three. However, many collectors will opt to have more music and will prefer to hear the Shakespearean text in the theatre or cinema.

The Battle of Britain (suite); *Escape Me Never* (suite); *The First of the Few: Spitfire Prelude & Fugue; Three Sisters; A Wartime Sketchbook*
*** Chan. 8870. ASMF, Marriner

The Spitfire Prelude and Fugue, from *The First of the Few*, was immediately turned into a highly successful concert-piece, but we owe it to Christopher Palmer that there is the *Wartime Sketchbook*, drawing material from three of the wartime films, plus scraps that Colin Matthews did not use in the suite from the much later *Battle of Britain* film music and not least in the stirring theme from the credits of the film, *Went the Day Well*. The brief suite from the music for Olivier's film of Chekhov's *The Three Sisters*, from much later, brings more than one setting of the *Tsar's Hymn* and a charming imitation of *Swan Lake*. Earliest on the disc is *Escape Me Never*, the first of Walton's film scores, written in 1935 in a more popular idiom; but the war-inspired music is what this delightful disc is really about. Marriner and the Academy give richly idiomatic performances, full of panache. Aptly opulent recording.

Hamlet (film score)
** Carlton DVD 37115 00183. Olivier, Herlie, Sydney,
  Simmons, Aylmer, Philh. O, Mathieson (Director: Laurence
  Olivier)

Although Laurence Olivier's film of *Hamlet* was made in 1948, four years after *Henry V*, the sound of Walton's evocative film score, as transferred to DVD, is greatly inferior to that in the earlier film, with far less body and less sense of space. Though it is not nearly as crumbly as the soundtrack of Eisenstein's *Ivan the Terrible*, it is not even as full-bodied as the sound on the VHS equivalent and, like that, offers only a truncated version of the most substantial section of the score, the final *Funeral March*. Muir Mathieson again conducted, but this time with the newly founded Philharmonia Orchestra. Needless to say, for all the lack of focus in the sound, the evocative camerawork in black and white, with swirling mists around the castle of Elsinore, is beautifully caught in sharp focus, and Olivier's truncated version of Shakespeare works very well as film.

Henry V: Suite (arr. Mathieson) and (i) *Scenes from the Film; Richard III: Prelude & Suite; Spitfire Prelude & Fugue*
☞ (M) *** EMI stereo/mono 5 65007-2. (i) Olivier
  (speaker); Philh. O, composer

This reissue includes the 1963 recordings of the *Henry V Suite*, *Richard III Prelude and Suite* and the *Spitfire Prelude and Fugue*. The performances are vital and exciting, and with the sound vivid and full the result is hugely enjoyable. Also included is the complete 1946 *Henry V* sequence with Laurence Olivier, as recorded on four 78s, and originally issued on LP by RCA with seven minutes of cuts. This is the restored complete version, and it has been excellently transferred, though the mono sound lacks body. The recording has great atmosphere though, with Olivier at his magnificent best, and the orchestra responding with tremendous energy: the sound of the arrows at the climax of the Agincourt sequence has never seemed more chilling. A wonderful CD.

Henry V: A Shakespeare Scenario (arr. Palmer)

*** Chan. 8892. Plummer (nar.), Westminster Cathedral Ch., ASMF, Marriner

Few film scores can match Walton's for the Olivier film of *Henry V* in its range and imagination, the whole of the 'Scenario' devised by Christopher Palmer lasting just over an hour. The most controversial change is to 'borrow' the first section of the march that Walton wrote much later for a projected television series on Churchill's *History of the English-Speaking Peoples*; otherwise, the chorus's call to arms, *Now all the youth of England is on fire*, would have had no music to introduce it. As an appendix, three short pieces are included which Walton quoted in his score. Sir Neville Marriner caps even his previous recordings in this series, with the Academy and Westminster Choir producing heartfelt playing and singing in sumptuous sound. As narrator, Christopher Plummer makes an excellent substitute for Olivier, unselfconsciously adopting a comparably grand style.

Henry V (filmscore)

** Carlton **DVD** 37115 00193. Olivier, Newton, Banks, Asherson, LSO, Mathieson (Director: Laurence Olivier)

Walton's music for Laurence Olivier's film of *Henry V* has never been surpassed in the way it adds so vividly both to the dramatic impact and to the atmospheric beauty. The very opening, with a play-bill fluttering to a flute figure and a panoramic view of Elizabethan London to a haunting off-stage chorus, sets the pattern even before the drama starts. Although the sound from a mono soundtrack is necessarily limited, it has been beautifully cleaned up for DVD, so that such effects are vividly atmospheric, giving a satisfying sense of space.

Much of Walton's music is well known in concert form, but the film brings home just how much more there is than that and how it is even more effective in its original context. Even the Agincourt charge music, a uniquely effective set-piece, is more effective still when seen as well as heard.

Olivier's concept, with the film moving from the Globe Theatre at the start to an idealized setting in France, with medieval false perspectives, remains masterly. An extraordinarily starry line-up of leading British actors of the time brings a whole gallery of characterful portrayals, not least from Olivier himself, unforgettable in the title-role.

Henry V: Passacaglia; The Death of Falstaff; Touch her Soft Lips and Part

(M) *** DG (ADD) 439 529-2. ECO, Barenboim – DELIUS: *Aquarelles*, etc.; VAUGHAN WILLIAMS: *Oboe Concerto* etc. ***

These fine Walton string pieces make an admirable complement to a sensuously beautiful collection of English music, with Barenboim at his most affectionately inspirational and the ECO very responsive, and with the 1975 recording retaining its warmth and bloom.

Macbeth: Fanfare & March; Major Barbara (suite); Richard III (Shakespeare scenario)

*** Chan. 8841. Gielgud (nar.), ASMF, Marriner

Disappointingly, Sir John Gielgud underplays Richard III's great 'Now is the winter of our discontent' speech, but working to the underlying music – much of it eliminated in the film – may have cramped his style. The performance generally has all the panache one could wish for, leading up to the return of the grand Henry Tudor theme at the end. The six-minute piece based on Walton's music for Gielgud's wartime production of *Macbeth* is much rarer and very valuable too, anticipating in its Elizabethan dance-music the *Henry V* filmscore. *Major Barbara* also brings vintage Walton material. Marriner and the Academy give performances just as ripely committed as in their previous discs in the series, helped by sonorous Chandos sound.

Partita for Orchestra

*** Sony (ADD) **SACD** SS 89415. Cleveland O, Szell –
MAHLER: *Symphony 10: Adagio; Purgatorio.* STRAVINSKY: *Firebird Suite* ***

The *Partita* was commissioned by the Cleveland Orchestra and first performed in 1958. The writing is typical of the composer's earlier style, the first movement *Toccata* having something of the hurly-burly of *Portsmouth Point*, and the finale, *Giga burlesca*, more than once reminds us of *Scapino*. The central *Pastorale Siciliana* is the weakest movement, simply for its lack of melodic distinction – not that the outer movements are any better, only there the skill of the writing all but carries the day. The Cleveland Orchestra, at their peak in 1959, give a superlative, dashing performance, and the gleaming recording helps to make this seem a more impressive piece than it is. The remastering for SACD makes the very most of the original master, but this is an expensive way to acquire such a mixed programme.

The Quest (ballet; complete); The Wise Virgins (ballet; suite)

*** Chan. 8871. LPO, Thomson

The Quest (complete ballet; original score); The Wise Virgins (ballet suite); Siesta

(BB) *** Naxos 8.555868. E. N. Philh. O, Lloyd-Jones

In 1943, at the height of the war, Walton was commissioned to write a full-length ballet for the Sadler's Wells Company to the choreography of Frederick Ashton. The 40-minute score of *The Quest* had to be completed while Ashton was on five weeks' leave from the RAF, forcing Walton to abandon his usual meticulous mode of working. Despite a starry cast, including Margot Fonteyn, Moira Shearer and Robert Helpmann, and beautiful sets by John Piper (one of which is reproduced on the cover of the disc), the ballet was a failure, largely because of the confusing allegorical plot derived from Spenser's *Faerie Queene* about St George fighting the forces of evil.

The ballet was never revived and the score was lost for many years, only to be brought out for a recording for the Chandos Walton Edition in 1990 with Bryden Thomson conducting. That used elaborated scoring by Christopher Palmer designed to counter the composer's feeling that the original spare orchestration, the result of wartime limitations, could be improved. What Lloyd-Jones has done with this fine Naxos version is to go back to Walton's original with only a modest expansion of forces, and the result in his brilliant performance, helped by refined recording, is greater transparency. Far from seeming thin the impact is sharper than in the earlier, more opulent version. This is vintage Walton, consistently fresh, defying any unevenness of invention, culminating in a radiant *Passacaglia*. One hopes the success of the disc will encourage the revival of the original ballet with its Piper sets.

Like Thomson, Lloyd-Jones couples *The Quest* with the suite from a ballet that Walton wrote earlier in the war, *The Wise Virgins*, orchestrating movements from Bach cantatas, including *Sheep may Safely Graze*. Again Lloyd-Jones's performance, at faster speeds, more effectively brings out the sharpness of orchestration which, so far from being inflated, gives off electric sparks. The brief interlude for strings, *Siesta*, one of Walton's earliest orchestral pieces, makes an attractive supplement.

Quite apart from the dramatic power of Thomson's performance, the recording is superb, among the fullest and clearest from Chandos. The sound for *The Wise Virgins* is more reverberant and the performance has less electricity, though Walton's distinctive arrangements of Bach cantata movements – including *Sheep may Safely Graze* – remain as fresh as ever.

The Wise Virgins (ballet; complete)

(N) *** ASV CDDCA 1168. BBC Concert O, Wordsworth –
   LAMBERT: *Horoscope* ***

The Wise Virgins, like Lambert's *Horoscope*, comes from a vintage period of the Sadler's Wells Ballet Company at the beginning of the Second World War. Till now they have appeared on disc only in truncated form as orchestral suites. The Walton ballet, using movements from Bach cantatas, was quickly dropped in the theatre, with the score of three of the movements lost or destroyed. Philip Lane has now re-orchestrated those three movements, using the original Bach scores, in a style near enough to Walton's sharply distinctive manner. Though the newly restored movements are not as striking as those we already know, Barry Wordsworth's warmly sympathetic readings make a strong case for the revival of the original ballets.

(i) Sinfonia concertante. Spitfire Prelude & Fugue; Variations on a Theme of Hindemith; March: The History of the English-Speaking Peoples

☛ (BB) *** Naxos 8.553869. (i) Donohoe, E. N. Philh., Daniel

Paul Daniel conducts the English Northern Philharmonia in electrifying performances of this varied group of orchestral works. As before he is splendid at interpreting Walton's jazzy syncopations with the right degree of freedom. Following the composer's own suggestion, the original version of the *Sinfonia concertante* is preferred to the revision, fuller and more brilliant. The performance is excellent, despite the placing of the soloist, Peter Donohoe, too far forward. Daniel draws playing both warm and scintillating from the orchestra in the *Hindemith Variations* – no finer version exists – while the *March* and the *Spitfire* music hit home all the harder through Daniel's refusal to dawdle.

Symphony 1: see also under Cello Concerto above
Symphony 1 in B flat min.; (i) Belshazzar's Feast

(M) (***) BBC mono/stereo BBCL 4097-2. (i) RPO; (ii) McIntyre, BBC Ch. & Choral Soc, Christchurch Harmonic Ch., BBC SO, composer

Symphony 1; Partita for Orchestra

(BB) *** Naxos 8.553180. E. N. PO, Daniel

Symphony 1; Overture Scapino; Siesta

(BB) *** Arte Nova 74321 39124-2. Gran Canaria PO, Leaper

Symphony 1; Varii Capricci

*** Chan. 8862. LPO, Thomson

Though Walton recorded both these major works in the studio for EMI, these live radio recordings are invaluable in amplifying his interpretative ideas. Neither performance replaces the (deleted) studio version, when the sound in each is more limited, but the vitality of a live occasion in each case gives an extra dramatic thrust to the readings. The *First Symphony* was recorded in mono at the Usher Hall at the 1959 Edinburgh Festival, and inevitably suffers from the dryness of the acoustic, as well as from a restless audience. The finale was clearly less well rehearsed than the rest, but there as in the earlier movements Walton on a live occasion consistently gives a lift to the jazzy syncopations, encouraging a degree of freedom that stamps them as totally idiomatic. Speeds are a shade faster than in the studio, and the grinding dissonances at the climax of the slow movement bite even harder, while the elegiac trumpet solo just before the final coda in the finale is more tender as well as more spacious.

Belshazzar's Feast comes in a stereo recording of 1965 from the Royal Festival Hall, with the chorus more backwardly balanced and less clear than in the studio version. One clear gain is the choice of soloist, with Donald McIntyre bitingly dramatic, and the points where the live account scores over the studio version include the description of the writing on the wall, more sinister in its pausefulness, and the lovely passage for semi-chorus in the finale, *The Trumpeters and pipers are silent*.

In the *First Symphony* Paul Daniel knows unerringly how to build up tension to breaking point before resolving it and then building again. He is also freer than many in his use of rubato, as well as in the degree of elbow-room he allows for jazzy syncopations, always idiomatic. The *Scherzo* is sparkily witty, not just full of malice. In the slow movement, after the poised opening, Daniel tends to press ahead slightly for the sections which follow, agonizingly intense. The finale with its brassy, more extrovert manner has plenty of panache, and the weight and bite of the sound are excellent. This is a version that vies with even the finest at whatever price, and it outshines most. Daniel's reading of the *Partita* brings out above all the work's joyfulness, with the outer movements relaxed in their brilliance and the central slow movement warmly expressive.

Leaper's disc of Walton's *First* also competes very well with almost any version in the catalogue. With finely disciplined playing, the reading is fresh and alert, idiomatic in its rhythmic pointing and with intense poetry in such key moments as the distant trumpet-call in the final coda. Starting almost inaudibly at the very start, Leaper seems intent on making the music emerge from mists, then he quickly builds up tension and momentum, even if in the first movement his reading is not as weighty as many. The clarity of the recording compensates and there is no lack of weight in the heavy brass, which has impressive bite. The slow movement brings inspired wind solos, and the Scherzo and finale are crisp and resilient, with busy ensembles made unusually clear, even transparent, a point that also marks Leaper's witty and sparkling account of the *Scapino Overture*, in which the cello solo is most beautifully done. *Siesta* is aptly dreamy, not literal or chilly, making this a disc to recommend to Waltonians and newcomers alike.

Thomson's is a warmly committed, understandingly idiomatic account of the work, weighty and rhythmically persuasive, if not as biting as some. In the slow movement his tender expressiveness goes with a flowing speed, well judged to avoid exaggeration. If the Scherzo is a degree less demonic than it might be, at a speed fractionally slower than usual, it is infectiously sprung. The Chandos coupling brings the first recording of *Varii capricci*, the orchestral suite in five compact movements which Walton developed from his set of guitar *Bagatelles*, written for Julian Bream. With a brilliant performance and sumptuous sound, it makes a fine supplement.

Symphony 2; Overtures: Portsmouth Point; Scapino; (i) Belshazzar's Feast

☾ ☞ * EMI Audio DVD** DVC4 92402-9. LSO, Previn; (i) with Shirley-Quirk, L. Symphony Ch.

André Previn and the LSO give a brilliant performance, which in some ways gets closer to the heart of the music than in any other version, with its overtones of the romantic opera, *Troilus and Cressida*. Previn is less sparkling in the outer movements, warmly romantic in the central slow movement of this still underrated symphony. In the two *Overtures* Previn, the shrewdest and most perceptive of Waltonians, finds more light and shade than usual. *Portsmouth Point* is attractively spirited, and *Scapino* affectionately light-hearted as well as brilliantly played. The recording from the early 1970s is outstandingly fine, enhanced further in this DVD remastering and this applies even more strikingly in the choral work.

Previn's 1972 Kingsway Hall *Belshazzar's Feast* on EMI still remains among the most powerful yet recorded. The digital remastering has not lost the body and atmosphere of the sound and now the DVD transfer further increases its impact and range. The splendid performance was recorded with Walton present on his seventieth birthday and, though Previn's tempi are slower than those set by Walton himself in his two recordings, the authenticity is clear, with consistently sharp attack and with dynamic markings meticulously observed down to the tiniest hairpin markings. Chorus and orchestra are challenged to their finest standards, and John Shirley-Quirk proves a characterful and imaginative soloist, with every word clear. To sample the demonstration standard of the CD transfer try track 5: *Praise Ye the God of Gold*. The DVD offers alternative two-speaker stereo and surround sound versions of the recordings.

CHAMBER MUSIC

(i) 5 Bagatelles for Solo Guitar; (ii; iii) Duets for Children; (iv; ii) 2 Pieces for Violin & Piano; Toccata for Violin & Piano; (ii) (Piano) Façade: Valse; (v; i) Anon in Love (for tenor & guitar); (v; ii) 2 Songs for Tenor: The Winds, The Tritons

*** Chan. 9292. (i) Bonell; (ii) Milne; (iii) Dowdeswell; (iv) Sillito; (v) Mark Ainsley

The *Toccata for Violin and Piano* is a curious mixture of cadenza and rhapsody of 15 minutes in a disconcertingly un-Waltonian style. The two songs for tenor are fascinating too, with a rushing accompaniment for *The Winds*, while *The Tritons* is chaconne-like, with a melody quite untypical of Walton. Milne and Dowdeswell bring out what charming, sharply focused ideas are contained in the ten *Duets for Children*. The piano arrangement of the *Valse* from *Façade* is

so thorny that even Hamish Milne has to go cautiously. The two violin pieces – using French troubadour songs – are spin-offs from the *Henry V* incidental music and, in the second, *Scherzetto*, reflect what their composer had learnt, writing for Heifetz. The two works with guitar are well known in Julian Bream's performances and recordings. Bonell is lighter and more delicate than Bream, both in the *Bagatelles* and in *Anon in Love*, but is no less persuasive. Similarly, John Mark Ainsley lacks some of the punch of Peter Pears, for whom the cycle was written, but in a gentler way taps the wit and point of these Elizabethan conceits. A delightful collection, full of revealing insights into the composer's complex character.

Passacaglia for Solo Cello

*** Chan. 8499. Wallfisch – BAX: *Rhapsodic Ballad*; BRIDGE: *Cello Sonata*; DELIUS: *Cello Sonata* ***

William Walton's *Passacaglia* for solo cello was composed in the last year of his life. It has restraint and eloquence, and Raphael Wallfisch gives a thoroughly sympathetic account of it. Excellent recording.

Piano Quartet; Violin Sonata

*** Chan. 8999. Milne, Sillito, Smissen, Orton

Piano Quartet; String Quartet in A min.

(BB) *** Naxos 8.554646. (i) Donohoe; Maggini Qt

This performance of the *Piano Quartet* with Hamish Milne as pianist makes one marvel that such music could have been the inspiration of a 16-year-old. Admittedly Walton revised the piece, but here is music that instantly grabs the ear, with striking ideas attractively and dramatically presented in each movement. The two principal performers from the quartet make a warmly sympathetic rather than high-powered duo for the *Violin Sonata* of 1949. Yet the combination of Sillito's ripely persuasive style and Milne's incisive power, clarifying textures and giving magic to the phrasing, keeps tensions sharp. The satisfyingly full sound helps too.

The young players of the Maggini Quartet – who earlier recorded Elgar for Naxos – give performances both refined and powerful of both works. The opening of the 1947 *String Quartet* is presented in hushed intimacy, making the contrast all the greater when Walton's richly lyrical writing emerges in full power. There is a tender, wistful quality here, which culminates in a rapt, intense account of the slow movement, with the world of late Beethoven much closer than most interpreters have appreciated. The poignancy of those two longer movements is then set against the clean bite of the second movement Scherzo and the brief hectic finale, with textures clear and transparent.

With Peter Donohoe a powerful, incisive pianist, the early *Piano Quartet* is also given a performance of high contrasts. The echoes of Stravinsky's *Petrushka* are colourfully brought out in the finale, a movement that looks forward more clearly than the rest to the mature Walton, even though the pentatonic writing in the earlier movements is here most persuasively presented. First-rate recording, even if the piano is a shade too forwardly balanced.

String Quartet in A min.

*** Hyp. CDA 66718. Coull Qt – BRIDGE: *3 Idylls* ***; ELGAR: *Quartet* **(*)

(BB) *** Regis RRC 1015. Britten Qt – ELGAR: *Quartet*

♦ *** Testament mono SBT 1052. Hollywood Qt – HINDEMITH: *Quartet 3*; PROKOFIEV: *Quartet 2* (***) ♦

String Quartet in A min; String Quartet 1
*** Chan. 8944. Gabrieli Qt
*** Black Box BBM 1035. Emperor Qt

Coupled ideally on Chandos with the mature *String Quartet in A minor*, completed in 1946, is the atonal *First Quartet*, long thought to be lost, which Walton wrote when an under-graduate at Oxford. The result, edited by Christopher Palmer, is hardly recognizable as Walton at all but is full of fire and imagination. The first movement is 'pastoral-atonal', lyrical in its counterpoint, but the Scherzo, built on vigorously rhyth-mic motifs and jagged ostinatos, has much more of Bartók in it than of Schoenberg, while the fugue of the finale seeks to emulate Beethoven's *Grosse Fuge* in its complexity and mas-sive scale, alone lasting almost 16 minutes. The Gabrieli performance brings out all the latent power and lyrical warmth, often implying an underlying anger. It provides a fascinating contrast with the highly civilized *A minor* work of 25 years later. That comes in a red-blooded Gabrieli recording of 1986, earlier available in coupling with the Elgar *Quartet*. Both recordings were made in the warm, rich acoustic of The Maltings, Snape, with little discrepancy between them.

The young members of the Emperor Quartet also give brilliant, incisive performances of both Walton's *String Quar-tets*. For the early work – which points forward to an atonal style very different from later Walton – the Emperor Quartet have had access to extra material involving editing and cuts, observing those that plainly were the composer's own. In addition to those minor differences of text, the Emperor Quartet's speeds are consistently faster than those of the Gabrieli Quartet on the rival version in the Chandos Walton Edition (Chan. 8944), notably in the fugal finale of the 1922 work, which here more clearly echoes Beethoven's *Grosse Fuge*. Helped by drier recording, the attack is more biting too, the approach more direct, less warmly expressive. A valid alternative, though in the 1947 work many Waltonians will miss the fuller romantic thrust of the Gabrielis and others.

The Elgar and Walton *Quartets* also makes an apt and attractive coupling, and here the Coulls, unlike their direct rivals, offer as bonus a fine example of Frank Bridge's quartet-writing. In the Walton, the reading captures mov-ingly the spirit of Waltonian melancholy, bringing out the elegiac intensity of the extended *Lento* slow movement, taken at a very measured pace. The Coulls are splendid too in capturing the element of fun in Walton's scherzando ideas.

The Britten Quartet, bitingly powerful, bring out the emo-tional intensity of the *A minor*, playing with refinement and sharp focus, finding a repose and poise in the slow movement that bring it close to late Beethoven. The contrasts of wistful lyricism and scherzando bite in the first movement make most other versions sound clumsy by comparison, and the incisiveness of Walton's jaggedly rhythmic writing is a delight.

In many ways the pioneering account by the Hollywood Quartet, made in 1950, has still not been surpassed. It first appeared on a Capitol LP in harness with the Villa-Lobos *Sixth Quartet*. The sound comes up very well, though it is not, of course, state of the art. Moreover, it comes with equally strong couplings and cannot be too strongly recommended.

Violin Sonata
*** Nim. NI 5666. Hope, Mulligan – ELGAR: *Violin Sonata;* FINZI: *Elegy* ***
(**(*)) Testament mono SBT 1319. Rostal, Horsley – DELIUS: *Violin Sonata 2;* ELGAR: *Violin Sonata in E min.* (**(*))

As in the Elgar, Daniel Hope gives a big-scale, virtuoso reading of the Walton sonata, using the widest dynamic range. The warmth and thrust of Hope's performance brings out the purposefulness of the writing in a work that can seem wayward. So, with understanding support from his fellow Menuhin protégé, Simon Mulligan, Hope brings tautness to the wide-ranging variation movement that rounds off the two-movement structure. With Hope's sweet, finely focused violin tone beautifully caught in the Nimbus recording – full and warm but less reverberant than some – and well balanced against the piano, it makes an outstanding recommendation.

The Walton *Violin Sonata* was still only five years old when Max Rostal and Colin Horsley made this recording for the fledgling Argo company. The original interpreters, Menuhin and Louis Kentner, had already recorded it for EMI, but Rostal, German-born but the most understanding interpreter of English music, and Horsley are even more persuasive, with Rostal overcoming the problems of the dry acoustic, subtly shading his tone as in the haunting recollection of the main theme in the coda of the first movement. Opting generally for faster speeds than Menuhin, Rostal then holds the argument together more tautly in the long set of variations that make up the second movement, playing with rapt concentration, not least in his warmly persuasive reading of the seventh and last variation, *Andante tranquillo*. The clarity of the clean, fresh Testament transfer quickly allows one to forget the sonic limitations.

CHORAL MUSIC

Antiphon; Cantico del sole; 4 Carols; Coronation Te Deum; Jubilate; A Litany (3 versions); *Magnificat and Nunc dimittis; Missa brevis; A Queen's Fanfare; Set Me as a Seal; The Twelve; Where Does the Uttered Music Go?*
*** Hyp. CDA 67330. Polyphony, Wallace Collection, Layton; Vivian (organ)

This collection of Walton's shorter choral pieces from Polyphony brings important advantages, which all Walton admirers will value. The inclusion of the Wallace Collection in the ensemble brings an immediate advantage in the first choral item, the *Coronation Te Deum*, when the extra bite of brass adds greatly to the power of a piece originally designed for far bigger forces in Westminster Abbey. That is preceded dramatically by the *Fanfare for the Queen* from 1959, and the use of brass also adds to the impact of the final item, *Antiphon*, one of Walton's very last works, setting George Herbert's hymn, *Let All the World in Every Corner Sing*. The other big advantage of this new disc is that it offers three contrasted versions of *A Litany*, the motet setting of Phineas Fletcher, which Walton wrote at Christ Church in his early teens. The original, conceived in 1916 when the boy was only 14, was for four treble voices and pitched a minor third higher than the definitive version, while the second version, made in 1917, introduced a full range of voices and was pitched slightly lower. What comes out from the three performances on this disc is the growing complexity of the writing, though from the start the young Walton obviously relished scrunching discords. Also included here are the *Four Carols*, making this as comprehensive a collection of Walton's shorter choral pieces as could be imagined. The fine professional group, Polyphony, with sopranos very boyish, sound very like a cathedral choir, set in an ecclesiastical atmosphere, though the acoustic of Hereford Cathedral is rather washy, with balance favouring the organ and brass.

Antiphon; Cantico del sole; Coronation Te Deum; Jubilate Deo; Magnificat & Nunc dimittis; A Litany; Missa brevis; Set Me as a Seal Upon thine Heart; The Twelve; Where Does the Uttered Music Go? Organ solos: *Henry V: Touch her Soft Lips and Part; Passacaglia: Death of Falstaff*

☼— (BB) *** Naxos 8.55579. St John's College Ch., Robinson

This disc of Walton's church music and smaller choral pieces is another in Naxos's superb series of English choral music from St John's College, Cambridge. It gains over rival collections of these pieces not just in price, but in using boys' rather than women's voices. With Walton himself trained as a boy chorister at Christ Church Cathedral, Oxford, his writing gains positively from that brighter, fresher sound, not just in the liturgical pieces. Even the *Coronation Te Deum* of 1953, designed for a big choir on the grandest of ceremonial occasions, benefits from the extra sharpness of focus, revealing not just a brilliant compression of a long text, but a taut musical structure. The pieces stretch over the widest span of Walton's career, from the setting of Phineas Fletcher in *A Litany*, the amazing inspiration of a 14-year-old but, anticipating the mature Walton, to *Antiphon*, one of his last works, a stirring setting of George Herbert's hymn, *Let All the World in Every Corner Sing*.

Belshazzar's Feast

(BB) *** Warner Apex 0927 444 394-2. Terfel, BBC Singers, BBC Ch. & SO, A. Davis – VAUGHAN WILLIAMS: *Job* ***

(B) ** CfP 2-CD (ADD) 575 7642 (2). Rippon, Hallé Ch. & O, Loughran – ELGAR: *Dream of Gerontius* **

(B) (**) CfP mono 585 9042. Milligan, Huddersfield Ch. Soc., RLPO, Sargent – ELGAR: *The Dream of Gerontius* (***)

(i) *Belshazzar's Feast. Coronation Marches: Crown Imperial; Orb and Sceptre*

(BB) ** Naxos 8.555869. (i) Purves, Lindley, Laudibus, Huddersfield Ch. Soc., Leeds Philharmonic Soc. Ch.; English N. Philh., Daniel

(i) *Belshazzar's Feast. Improvisations on an Impromptu of Benjamin Britten; Overtures: Portsmouth Point; Scapino*

☼— (M) *** EMI (ADD) 7 64723-2. LSO, Previn, (i) with Shirley-Quirk, L. Symphony Ch.

Belshazzar's Feast; Coronation Te Deum; Gloria

**(*) Chan. 8760. Howell, Gunson, Mackie, Roberts, Bach Ch., Philh. O, Willcocks

Previn's EMI version of *Belshazzar's Feast* still remains among the most spectacular yet recorded. The *Improvisations*, given a first recording, make a generous fill-up alongside the two overtures in which Previn, the shrewdest and most perceptive of Waltonians, finds more light and shade than usual. Again the remastered sound is excellent.

In Andrew Davis's dramatically eloquent account of *Belshazzar's Feast*, taken from the last night of the 1994 Promenade Concerts, the glorious choral contribution demonstrates how perfectly suited Walton's masterly oratorio is to the Royal Albert Hall's famous and sometimes intractable acoustics. From the powerful trombone opening and the riveting '*Thus spake Isaiah*' from the BBC Singers and Chorus, the listener is held under the music's spell, and Bryn Terfel's resonant '*If I forget thee*' is as compelling as his cry '*Babylon is a great city*', while the choral responses to '*Praise ye*' are as thrilling as the '*writing hand*' sequence is creepily sinister. The apt coupling with *Job*, another biblical work, makes this a most desirable reissue.

Willcocks scores over some rivals in his pacing. Speeds tend to be a degree faster, as in *By the Waters of Babylon* which flows evenly yet without haste. The soloist, Gwynne Howell, firm and dark of tone, is among the finest of all exponents but, with the Bach Choir placed rather more distantly than in most versions, this is not as incisive as its finest rivals. The *Coronation Te Deum* receives a richly idiomatic performance, and Willcocks also gives weight and thrust to the *Gloria*, with the tenor, Neil Mackie, outstanding among the soloists. The microphone unfortunately catches an unevenness in Ameral Gunson's mezzo. The recording is warmly reverberant, not ideally clear on choral detail but easy to listen to.

The Huddersfield Choral Society made the very first, ground-breaking recording of *Belshazzar's Feast* in 1943 at the height of the Second World War. Here on Naxos, today's choir returns to Walton's colourful masterpiece, joined not only by colleagues from Leeds but by the chamber choir, Laudibus, yet the impression on disc – with the singers set very much behind the orchestra – is regrettably not of massed choirs. That is a disappointment in what in so many ways is a powerful reading, with Paul Daniel a vigorous and generally idiomatic Waltonian, as he has demonstrated in his earlier Walton recordings for Naxos. The vividness of the orchestral sound is most impressive, notably the brass, a valuable asset in this highly coloured work, and the choral balance certainly improves in the central sections, involving praise to the Gods and the actual feast. Yet in the closing, exuberant chorus, *Then Sing Aloud*, the trouble is intensified, for distancing brings disconcertingly cloudy textures, not helped by the extraordinarily fast tempo that Daniel adopts, which also minimizes the rhythmic lift of the jazzy syncopations. Unlike the chorus, the baritone soloist, Christopher Purves, is balanced close, and is generally clean of attack. The two *Coronation Marches* on Naxos make an ungenerous coupling. Taken from a 1996 disc of Prom favourites, they are very well played and recorded.

Loughran's version is forthright and dramatic, helped by brilliant analogue recording from 1973. The orchestra is particularly well caught, and so is the excellent soloist, Michael Rippon, firm and clear in attack. The snag is the work of the chorus, which is relatively small and placed rather close to the microphones, so that details of imperfect ensemble and intonation tend to be exaggerated. The result is still a convincingly gripping account of Walton's choral masterpiece, although, like the Elgar coupling, it would not be a primary choice.

Sargent was present at the gestation of *Belshazzar's Feast* and conducted the first performance at the Leeds Festival in 1931, thereafter making it his own for a considerable period. His interpretation was authoritative, but he does not seem to have taken care over detail for this 1958 recording. (Among other things, the anvil to represent the God of Iron is missing.) The rich acoustic of Huddersfield Town Hall adds weight to the sound but robs the choral words of any kind of clarity and bite. James Milligan is a strong soloist, the orchestra plays very well indeed, and the recording is impressively transferred to CD, but overall this was not a jewel in Sargent's choral crown.

Christopher Columbus (A Musical Journey); Hamlet and Ophelia (A Poem for Orchestra (arr. Mathieson)

(N) *** Chan. **SACD** CHSA 5034. Carragher, Rigby, Randle, Williams, Julian Glover, Jamie Glover, Ogden, Ch. & BBC Nat. O of Wales, Hickox

Commisioned by the BBC in 1942 to write the incidental music for a radio play by Louis MacNeice, Walton composed a score which in many ways anticipates the masterly film score he wrote two years later for Olivier's *Henry V*. Walton himself refused to acknowledge that it had any value outside the play and he allowed the publication of only one brief song from it, *Beatriz's Song*, sung here by Jean Rigby. For the Chandos complete Walton Edition, Christopher Palmer drew a brief suite from the score, but in 2002 Carl Davis and Patrick Garland devised an hour-long entertainment, with the main musical items illustrating an abbreviated version of MacNeice's text. Not surprisingly, it does not work as well as the comparable sequence using the *Henry V* film music alongside Shakespeare, but many of these illustrative fragments have the true Waltonian ring, not just songs and orchestral links but evocative choral chants and several fine choruses, like the one near the end of Part 1, *Granada has fallen*, *Henry V*-like, and the final chorus of Part 2 which echoes *Belshazzar's Feast*. The *Song of Queen Isabella* has a direct Spanish flavour, and a Shanty neatly brings together echoes of Spanish music as well as sea songs. With Julian Glover taking the spoken role of Columbus opposite Jamie Glover as the Ironic Spirit, Richard Hickox conducts a warmly idiomatic reading with an excellent quartet of vocal principals – Caroline Carragher, Jean Rigby, Tom Randle and Roderick Williams – and the first-rate BBC National Chorus and Orchestra of Wales. Vivid sound in Hybrid SACD. Muir Mathieson's *Poem for Orchestra – Hamlet and Ophelia* is drawn directly from Walton's film music for Olivier's *Hamlet*, a sombre piece with fine string-writing and sinister fanfares in the middle.

(i) *Christopher Columbus* (suite of incidental music); (ii) *Anon in Love*; (iii) *4 Songs After Edith Sitwell: Daphne; Through gilded trellises; Long Steel Grass; Old Sir Faulk. A Song for the Lord Mayor's Table; The Twelve (an anthem for the Feast of any Apostle)*
*** Chan. 8824. (i) Finnie, Davies; (ii) Hill; (iii) Gomez; Westminster Singers, City of L. Sinfonia, Hickox

The composer's own orchestral versions of his song-cycles *Anon in Love* (for tenor) and *A Song for the Lord Mayor's Table* (for soprano) are so beautifully judged that they transcend the originals, and the strength and beauty of these strongly characterized songs is enormously enhanced, particularly in performances as positive as these by Martyn Hill and Jill Gomez. The anthem, *The Twelve*, also emerges far more powerfully with orchestral instead of organ accompaniment. The four Sitwell songs were orchestrated by Christopher Palmer, who also devised the suite from Walton's incidental music to Louis MacNeice's wartime radio play, *Christopher Columbus*, buried for half a century. It is a rich score which brings more happy anticipations of the *Henry V* film music in the choral writing, and even of the opera *Troilus and Cressida*, as well as overtones of *Belshazzar's Feast*. Warmly committed performances, opulently recorded.

OPERA

The Bear (complete)
*** Chan. 9245. Jones, Opie, Shirley-Quirk, N. Sinfonia, Hickox

The one-Acter *The Bear*, based on Chekhov, matches in its point and flair Britten's own chamber operas also written for Aldeburgh, with Walton producing textures that are sumptuous rather than spare. It is a masterly score, with the farcical element reflected in dozens of parodies and tongue-in-cheek musical references, starting cheekily with echoes of Britten's own *Midsummer Night's Dream*. Richard Hickox with members of the Northern Sinfonia paces the music superbly, flexibly heightening the moments of mock-melodrama that punctuate this tale of a mourning widow who faces the demands of one of her dead husband's creditors. The casting of the three characters is ideal, with Della Jones commanding as the affronted widow, all her words crystal clear, Alan Opie clean-cut and incisive as the creditor or 'Bear' of the title, and with John Shirley-Quirk as the old retainer. In many ways this is a piece – with its climactic duel scene leading to an amorous *coup-de-foudre* – which comes off even better on disc than on stage.

Troilus and Cressida (complete)
❀ *** Chan. 9370/1 (2). A. Davies, Howarth, Howard, Robson, Opie, Bayley, Thornton, Owen-Lewis, Opera North Ch., E. N. Philh. O, Hickox

Few operas since Puccini have such a rich store of memorable tunes as *Troilus and Cressida*. As Chandos's magnificent recording shows, based on Opera North's 1995 production – using Walton's tautened score of 1976 but with the original soprano register restored for Cressida – this red-bloodedly romantic opera on a big classical subject deserves to enter the regular repertory. Judith Howarth portrays the heroine as girlishly vulnerable, rising superbly to the big challenges of the love duets and final death scene. Arthur Davies is an aptly Italianate Troilus, an ardent lover, and there is not a weak link in the rest of the characterful cast, with Nigel Robson a finely pointed Pandarus, comic but not camp, avoiding any echoes of Peter Pears, the originator. As Evadne, Cressida's maid, Yvonne Howard produces firm, rich mezzo tone, and the role of Calkas, Cressida's father, is magnificently sung by Clive Bayley. The role of Diomede, Cressida's Greek suitor, can seem one-dimensional, but Alan Opie, in one of his finest performances on record, sharpens the focus, making him a genuine threat, a noble enemy. Richard Hickox draws magnetic performances from chorus and orchestra alike, bringing out the many parallels with the early Walton of *Belshazzar's Feast* and the *Symphony No. 1*. As for the recorded sound, the bloom of the Leeds Town Hall acoustic allows the fullest detail from the orchestra, enhancing the Mediterranean warmth of the score, helped by the wide dynamic range. The many atmospheric effects, often offstage, are clearly and precisely focused, and the placing of voices on the stereo stage is also unusually precise.

WARD, John (1571–1638)

Madrigals: *Come sable night; Cruel unkind; Die not, fond man; Hope of my heart; If heaven's just wrath; If the deep sighs; I have retreated; My breast I'll set; Oft have I tender'd; Out from the vale; Retire, my troubled soul; Sweet Philomel*
*** Hyp. CDA 66256. Consort of Musicke, Rooley

Ward's music speaks with a distinctive voice. He chooses poetry of high quality, his music is always finely proportioned, and such is the quality of this music and the accomplishment with which it is presented, these settings represent the madrigal tradition at its finest.

WARLOCK, Peter (1894–1930)

Capriol Suite (orchestral version); *Serenade for Strings* (for the sixtieth birthday of Delius)

*** Chan. 8808. Ulster O, Handley – MOERAN: *Serenade*, etc. ***

The effect of the present full orchestral score of the *Capriol Suite* is to rob the music of some of its astringency. A dryish wine is replaced with one with the fullest bouquet, for the wind instruments make the textures more rococo in feeling as well as increasing the colour. Handley's fine performance, is made to sound opulent by the acoustics of Ulster Hall, Belfast. The lovely *Serenade*, for strings alone, is also played and recorded very beautifully.

(i) *Capriol Suite; Serenade for Strings;* (ii) *Lullaby My Jesus.* Songs: (iii) *After Two Years; As Ever I Saw; The Bayley Berith of Bell Away; The Birds; The Cricketers of Hambledon; The Droll Lover; Eloré Lo; Fair and True; The Fox; The Frostbound Wood; Ha'nacker Mill; Julian of Berry; My Own Country; 12 Oxen; Passing By; Pretty Ring Time; Robin Goodfellow; Roister Doister; Romance; Sigh No More, Ladies; Sleep; There is a Lady Sweet and Kind; To the Memory of a Great Singer; When as the Rye Reach to the Chin; Yarmouth Fair; Youth*

(M) **(*) Decca (ADD/DDD) 470 199-2. (i) ASMF, Marriner; (ii) Winchester Cathedral Ch., Hill; (iii) Bailey, Parsons

This collection of over two dozen of Warlock's songs displays his art as a miniaturist, whether in the brisk items with their crisp pay-offs (not always so lightly pointed here as they should be) or in such intense songs as *The Frostbound Wood.* Though Norman Bailey is consistently thoughtful in his singing, charm is not one of his great qualities, and the vocal tone is somewhat lacking in variety. But with superb accompaniments and an effective five-voiced chorus joining in for two numbers (originally the ends of each LP side) this is a valuable and attractive anthology. Marriner's stylish and polished accounts of the orchestral items are always a joy to hear, and the sound throughout is of Decca's best late-1970s quality (the pleasing *Lullaby My Jesus* is digital).

Adam lay ybounden; As dew in Aprylle; Benedicamus Domino; Bethlehem down; The Birds; Born is the babe; Balulalow; Carillon, Carilla; A Cornish Christmas carol; A Cornish carol; Corpus Christi; The first mercy; The five lesser joys of Mary; The frostbound wood; I saw a fair maiden; My little sweet darling; Out of the Orient crystal skies; The rich cavalcade; Song for Christmas Day; Sweet was the song the Virgin sang; The sycamore tree; Tyrley Tyrlow; What cheer? Good cheer!; Where riches is everlastingly

*** Somm SOMMCD 011. Allegri Singers, Halsey; with Cable, Empett; Rosamunde Qt; M. Barnes; R. Barnes

Most of these Christmas settings are little known, many are quite simple, but all are quite lovely. Among the more extended pieces the *Cornish Christmas carol* is strophic but the harmonic setting is constantly varied, while the ravishing *Corpus Christi* carol and simpler *Born is the babe* are set for solo voices and string quartet. *Out of the Orient crystal skies* and the gentle *Bethlehem down* are particularly haunting and the concert ends with the brief *Sycamore tree,* as joyful as an English carol can be. Fine, lively, dedicated performances throughout, with excellent accompaniments from all concerned.

Songs: *As ever I saw; Autumn twilight; The bachelor; The bayly berith the bell away; Captain Stratton's fancy; First mercy; The fox; Hey, trolly, loly lo; Ha'nacker Mill; I held love's head; The jolly shepherd; Late summer; Lullaby; Milkmaids; Mourne no more; Mr Belloc's fancy; My gostly fader; My own country; The night; Passing by; Piggesnie; Play-acting; Rest, sweet nymphs; Sleep; Sweet content; Take, o take those lips away; There is a lady sweet and fair; Thou gav'st me leave to kiss; Walking the woods; When as the rye; The wind from the west; Yarmouth Fair*

*** Chan. 8643. Luxon, Willison

Songs like *Autumn twilight,* the powerfully expressive *Late summer* and *Captain Stratton's fancy* are appealing in utterly different ways, and there is not a single number either in this programme that does not show the composer either in full imaginative flow or simply enjoying himself, as in *Yarmouth Fair.* Luxon's performances are first class and David Willison provides sensitive and sparkling accompaniments. The recording is first class.

Songs: *Away to Twiver; The Bachelor; Bethlehem Down; Captain Stratton's Fancy; The Cloths of Heaven; The Curlew; Lilligay, Sets I & II; Peterisms, Sets I & II; Mr Belloc's Fancy; My ghostly Father; Sweet and Twenty; Savdades; Peter Warlock's Fancy*

(BB) ** Naxos 8.557115. Thompson, Maltman, Constable, Davies, Pendrill, Duke Qt

First issued on the Collins Classics label, this Naxos issue offers a well-chosen selection, characterfully performed to bring out the contrasting flavours, vigorous on the one hand, evocative on the other. It is good to have his masterpiece, *The Curlew,* an extended setting of Yeats, as the main item, even if Adrian Thompson has moments of roughness, which are exaggerated by close recorded balance. Although the instrumental accompaniment is beautifully played, there, too, the closeness prevents the full atmospheric beauty of the writing from being appreciated. Thompson is more successful in songs that require less sustained lines, and similar reservations have to be made about the singing of Christopher Maltman in the baritone songs, though he is rousingly convincing in such characteristic items as *Fancy, Mr Belloc's Fancy* and (best known of all) *Captain Stratton's Fancy.*

WASSENAER, Unico Wilhelm (1692–1766)

Concerti armonici 1–6

○━ (BB) *** Hyp. Helios CDH 55155. Brandenburg Cons., Goodman

(BB) ** Warner Apex 0927 49571-2. Amsterdam Bar. O, Koopman

(BB) ** Naxos 8.555384. Ardia Ens., Mallon

Long attributed to Pergolesi, these splendid concertos were in truth written by Unico Wilhelm, Graf von Wassenaer, a Dutch part-time composer of remarkable accomplishment. Their invention, vigorous and expressive, is sustained by a remarkably harmonic individuality: in short they are first-class works, almost on a par with the *concerti grossi* of Handel. These fine performances from the Brandenburg Consort are most presentable, and Hyperion's recording is very good indeed, to eclipse previous issues of this rewarding repertoire.

Koopman's performances are also spirited and have

expressive delicacy, but only a small string group is used, and the textures at times sound very meagre, in spite of the ecclesiastic ambience.

These are reasonably well-played accounts on period instruments in good sound on Naxos. However, a feeling of blandness creeps in from time to time, and it all sounds rather too much on the same dynamic and emotional plane. Roy Goodman's Hyperion disc better conveys the full diversity of these works and is well worth the extra money.

WATERHOUSE, Graham (born 1962)

(i) *Celtic Voices, Op. 36/1;* (i; ii) *Chieftain's Salute;* (iii) *Hale Bopp, Op. 36/2;* (iv) *Hymnus, Op. 49;* (i) *Jig, Air & Reel, Op. 8;* (iv) *Mouvements d'Harmonie, Op. 29;* (i) *Sinfonietta*
*** Mer. CDA 84510. (i) ECO, Traub; (ii) with Waller; (iii) Funnel (treble); (iv) Endymion Ens.

The novelty here is the opening *Chieftain's Salute*, a spectacular concertante work for 'great highland bagpipe' (played with much panache by Graham Waller) and strings. After the introductory 'Scottish Snap', the distant piper moves forward to a set of variations on the seventeenth-century lament, *Lady Doyle's Salute*. Most dramatic is the piquant harmonic clash between the pipes, with their three underlying drones, and the orchestra, which increases as the piper comes nearer, to produce a lively Scottish jig, before the return of the Lament as he departs.

In the works for strings, Graham Waterhouse writes very much within the broad tradition of English string music in a harmonic style that is essentially diatonic, but, by injecting pungent atonal dashes, the composer brings stimulating touches of abrasiveness to the textures. The deftly concise *Sinfonietta* has athletic and delectably astringent outer movements framing a neo-romantic *Adagio* and a fiddle-dominated folksy Scherzo. *Celtic Voices* similarly balances bravura with even warmer lyricism by adding a harmonic flavour of the Phrygian mode.

Hale Bopp mystically celebrates the appearance of the famous comet, then, after gaining momentum, introduces the melody, 'How Brightly Shines the Morning Star', sung hauntingly in the distance by a boy treble, acccompanied by just four string players. Waterhouse's writing for woodwind and horns in the *Mouvements d'Harmonie* has a distinct Gallic flavour, harmonically tangy, while the grave chorale of *Hymnus* recalls a famous carol. The concert ends richly with comparatively simple arrangements of three famous folk tunes, *Roger de Coverley*, the ravishing *Star of the County Down* and the sparkling *Devil among the Tailors*. First-rate playing throughout and excellent recording, bright but with an attractively spacious acoustic, which adds to the distinction of this collection, another memorable example of Meridian's current exploration of twentieth-century British composers.

WAXMAN, Franz (1906–67)

Carmen Fantasy
☛ (M) *** Warner Elatus 2564 60013-2. Vengerov, Israel PO, Mehta – PAGANINI: *Violin Concerto 1 in D, Op. 6* **(*); SAINT-SAENS: *Havanaise; Intro & Rondo Capriccioso* ***

Waxman's *Carmen* confection invites the flamboyance that the young Russian emigré Maxim Vengerov can readily provide. He dazzles and seduces the ear by turns, and even if he is forwardly balanced, the orchestral backing is well in the picture.

Film Music: Suites: (i) *The Bride of Frankenstein;* (ii) *The Invisible Ray; Prince Valliant; Rebecca; Suspicion; Taras Bulba*
*** Silva Screen FILMCD 726. Westminster PO, Alwyn; (ii) City of Prague PO, Bateman

With a flamboyant introduction that sweeps one into 1930s Hollywood, *The Bride of Frankenstein* – regarded by many as one of the finest 'horror' films ever made – is one of Waxman's most imaginative scores, very colourfully orchestrated, including the use of an ondes martenot – the effect provided here by a synthesizer – to create supernatural effects. There are moments of wit and parody too (Gounod's *Faust* crops up), and one especially enjoys the *Minuet*, most charmingly orchestrated by Clifford Vaughan. As an organist himself, he uses that instrument most effectively, especially in the delightfully quirky *Danse macabre* – a number that should have a lease of life of its own. Kenneth Alwyn and his orchestra fully re-create the music's evocation.

The more famous suites from *Prince Valliant*, *Taras Bulba* and *Suspicion* are included, as well as *Rebecca* (Waxman's most hauntingly memorable score) and the less familiar *The Invisible Ray*, with the suite assembled by the composer's son, John Waxman. Many of the Waxman manuscripts did not survive, and here Stephen Bernstein orchestrated it completely by ear after listening to the film's soundtrack. Very good performances, and excellent sound too.

WEBER, Carl Maria von (1786–1826)

Andante & Hungarian Rondo in E flat, Op. 35; Bassoon Concerto in F, Op. 75
*** Chan. 9656. Popov, Russian State SO, Polyansky – HUMMEL; MOZART: *Bassoon Concertos* ***

Valeri Popov is in his element here. There is some astonishing spiccato bravura in the finale of the *Hungarian Rondo*, and both he and his accompanying orchestra under Polyansky capture the grand manner of the first movement of the concerto and are quite touching in the romantic cantabile of the *Andantino*. The finale then brings both a genial wit and more solo fireworks. The recording is full-bodied and resonant, but clearly detailed in the Chandos manner.

Clarinet Concertino in E flat, Op. 26
*** ASV CDDCA 559. Johnson, ECO, Groves – CRUSELL: *Concerto 2* *** ✪; BAERMANN: *Adagio* ***; ROSSINI: *Introduction, Theme & Variations* ***

Emma Johnson is in her element here. Her phrasing is wonderfully beguiling and her use of light and shade agreeably subtle, while she finds a superb lilt in the final section, pacing the music to bring out its charm rather than achieve breathless bravura. Sir Charles Groves provides an admirable accompaniment, and the recording is eminently realistic and naturally balanced.

Clarinet Concerto 1 in F min., Op. 73
*** EMI 55155-2. Meyer, Dresden State O, Blomstedt – MOZART; STAMITZ: *Concertos* ***

Sabine Meyer gives a lusciously seductive account of the *F minor Concerto*, accompanying herself with aplomb. She is beautifully recorded.

Clarinet Concertos 1 in F min., Op. 73; 2 in E flat, Op. 74;
Clarinet Concertino

*** DG (IMS) 435 875-2. Neidlich, Orpheus CO (with
ROSSINI: *Introduction, Theme & Variations in E flat* ***)

(M) *** Classic fM 75605 57019-2. Lawson, Hanover Band,
Goodman – SPOHR: *Clarinet Concerto 1* ***

(BB) *** Virgin 2×1 5 61585-2 (2). Pay, OAE – CRUSELL:
Clarinet Concertos 1–3 ***

(BB) *** Naxos 8.550378. Ottensamer, Slovak State PO
(Košice), Wildner

**(*) Chan. 8305. Hilton, CBSO, Järvi

If you want these concertos on modern instruments, Charles
Neidlich meets every need. His tone is beautiful, his phrasing
warmly musical, he swings along most beguilingly in the
Andante of the *Concertino* and the *Romanze* of the *F minor*
Concerto is shaped with much delicacy. He lollops delightfully
in the finales of all three works. He plays his own cadenzas
and the Orpheus Chamber Orchestra, rather resonantly
recorded, provide accompaniments of substance which are
both polished and supportive. The Rossini *Variations* make a
witty and elegantly appealing bonus. However, the performances on the super-bargain Warner Apex collection below are
also first class in every way and every bit as well recorded, and
this disc includes also the *Grand duo concertant*.

Stylish and imaginative period performances of all three
works from Colin Lawson with the Hanover Band, vividly
recorded, generously supplemented by the Spohr *First Con-*
certo. With his attractively reedy tone Lawson is a most
persuasive soloist, moulding Weber's melodies seductively
and pointing rhythms jauntily, with brilliant feats of tonguing in the light-hearted finales of each work.

Antony Pay uses a copy of a seven-keyed clarinet by Simiot
of Lyons from 1800. The sonority is cleaner and less bland
than can be the case in modern performances, and the solo
playing is both expert and sensitive. A further gesture to
authenticity is the absence of a conductor; however, the
ensemble might have been even better and the texture more
finely judged and balanced had there been one. The recordings are vivid and truthful and those attracted to the coupling
with Crusell should be well satisfied.

Ernst Ottensamer is a highly sensitive clarinettist, who is a
member of the Vienna Wind Ensemble. His account of the
two *Clarinet Concertos* can hold its own against nearly all the
competition, the Košice orchestra also responds well to
Johannes Wildner's direction, and the recorded sound is very
natural and well balanced. A real bargain.

Polished and understanding performances of both concertos from Janet Hilton, spirited and rhythmic (particularly in
No. 1), but erring a little on the side of caution next to her
finest virtuoso rivals. The *Concertino*, however, is very successful and with full, well-balanced recording and nice
matching between soloist and orchestra, this is certainly
recommendable for its sound quality. But the original recordings date from 1982 and this should have been reissued at
mid-price.

(i; ii) *Clarinet Concertos 1 in F min.; 2 in E flat. Clarinet*
Concertino in E flat, Op. 26; (iii) Grand duo concertant for
Clarinet & Piano, Op. 48

♦━ ✿ *** ASV (ADD) CDDCA 747. (i) Johnson, (ii) ECO,
cond. Tortelier, Schwarz or Groves; (iv) with Black

(BB) *** Warner Apex 8573 89246-2. (i) Boeykens; (ii)
Rotterdam PO, Conlon; (iii) P. Meyer, Duchable

(i) *Clarinet Concertos 1–2; (ii) Grand duo concertant for*
Clarinet & Piano

(M) **(*) Warner Elatus 0927 46744-2. Kam, (i) Leipzig GO,
Masur; Black

Emma Johnson's scintillating accounts of these three Weberian showpieces were made at different times and with different conductors, all of whom prove to be highly sympathetic
to their young soloist. Her subtlety of expression is remarkable, with *pianissimos* more daringly extreme and with distinctly persuasive phrasing in slow movements treated
warmly and spaciously. In the sparkling finales she is wittier
than almost any, plainly enjoying herself to the full. The
Concertino, in some ways the most delightful work of the
three, especially its delicious finale, is hardly less beguiling;
and as a bonus we are offered a brilliant and individually
expressive account of the *Grand duo concertant* for clarinet
and piano. Here she finds an admirable partner in Gordon
Black, who accompanies with equal flair.

However, if you are looking for a bargain alternative,
Walter Boeykens will be hard to beat. He is a most sensitive
player and phrases the expressive music meltingly, with a
lovely tone, as the slow movement of the *F minor Concerto*
readily demonstrates; and there are some subtle touches of
rubato in the *Concertino*. James Conlon and the Rotterdam
Orchestra provide firm, yet flexible accompaniments. Weber's
chortling *Rondos* in all three works are delightfully presented,
with the *Polacca* finale of the *E flat Concerto* very neatly
pointed. Paul Meyer takes over in the romantic *Grand duo*
concertant, quite perfectly balanced with Duchable, and they
make a fine partnership. An excellent disc, given first-class
recording.

As the opening movement of the *First Concerto* demonstrates, Sharon Kam has the gift of magicking a phrase,
regularly holding tension over an exaggerated pause or
tenuto. Most remarkable of all is the dark intensity of Kam's
account of the slow, minor-key *Romanza* of the *Second Con-*
certo, taken at a measured tempo. She is similarly impressive
in the *Grand duo concertant*, though there the piano tone of
Itamar Golan is on the shallow side. The orchestral sound is
warm, if rather opaque in tuttis. Emma Johnson's rival disc
on ASV, with the *Clarinet Concertino* as an extra, remains
marginally preferable.

(i) *Clarinet Concertos 1–2; Clarinet Concertino; (ii) Clarinet*
Quintet (version for string orchestra)

(M) *** EMI 5 67988-2 [56799]. S. Meyer; (i) Dresden State
O, Blomstedt; (ii) Württemberg CO, Heilbronn, Faerber

Clarinet Quintet, Op. 34 (arr. for clarinet and string orch.)

*** EMI 5 57359-2. S. Meyer, ASMF, Sillito – BAERMANN:
Clarinet Quintet No.3 in E flat, Op. 23; MENDELSSOHN: *2*
Concert Pieces for Clarinet & Basset Horn ***

Weber, inspired by the playing of his friend, Heinrich Baermann, began writing his *Clarinet Quintet* while on holiday in
Switzerland in 1811, completing it the following year, a labour
of love following the two concertos and concertino he had
earlier written for Baermann. It is just as inspired and just as
demanding technically, which makes it an ideal candidate to
be translated, as here, into a full concerto for clarinet and
strings.

To represent Sabine Meyer in their 'Great Recordings of the
Century' series EMI have combined her fine recordings of the
Concertos – notable for particularly eloquent accounts of the
two slow movements – and her delectable, light-hearted

version of the *Concertino*, with her inspired account of the orchestral arrangement of the *Clarinet Quintet*. The orchestral accompaniments are on a larger scale than with Emma Johnson, but both Blomstedt and Faerber prove admirable accompanists, and the recording is excellent. While Emma Johnson has a special place in our affections, Meyer's performances are hardly less memorable. They are subtle and have wonderful finesse, and the EMI reissue is in the mid-price range and no less recommendable.

(i) *Clarinet Concertos 1 in F min.; 2 in E flat;* (ii) *Konzertstück in F min. for Piano & Orchestra;* (iii) *Invitation to the Dance* (orch. Berlioz), *Op. 65; Overtures: Abu Hassan;* (iv) *Euryanthe; Der Freischütz; Oberon.* (v) *Symphony 1 in C., Op. 19;* (vi) *Clarinet Quintet*
(B) ** Ph. Duo (ADD) 462 868-2 (2). (i) Michallik, Dresden State O, Sanderling; (ii) Magaloff, LSO, C. Davis; (iii) LSO, Mackerras; (iv) Concg. O, Dorati; (v) New Philh. O, Boettcher; (vi) Stahr, Berlin Philharmonic Octet (members)

The two *Clarinet Concertos* are well played by Oskar Michallik, with good support from Sanderling and the fine Dresden orchestra. But, as in Herbert Stahr's Berlin account of the *Quintet*, these artists are at their best in slow movements. Elsewhere, though thoroughly musical, the playing could do with more dash. However, Magaloff's poised and well-characterized account of the *Konzertstück* is most satisfying, well recorded and altogether one of the best versions on the market. The two performances under Mackerras are also a delight: *Abu Hassan* light and sparkling, and an elegant *Invitation to the Dance.* But in the other three overtures, the Concertgebouw string sound as recorded is brilliant to the point of fierceness and the effect is to emphasize Dorati's concentration on drama rather than atmosphere (though there is some beautiful horn playing). However, the engaging *First Symphony* is well served both by the New Philharmonia and by Boettcher, who favours a weighty approach but does not lack a lighter touch when needed. Overall this is fair value.

Piano Concertos 1–2; Konzertstück; Polacca brillante (L'Hilarité), Op. 72 (orch. Liszt)
(BB) *** Naxos 8.550959. Frith, Dublin R. & TV Sinf., O'Duinn

Benjamin Frith's accounts are first class and he receives splendid support from O'Duinn and the excellent Dublin Sinfonietta. In consequence, these performances all have real depth (the *Konzertstück* is particularly fine). Frith's playing has plenty of dash, yet its impetuosity is never inclined to run away with itself. The Naxos CD is not only very well recorded and inexpensive, it also includes the appropriately named *L'Hilarité – Polacca brillante*, which Frith plays with attractive panache.

(i–iii) *Piano Concertos 1–2;* (iv) *Symphonies 1 & 2 in C;* (ii, v) *Overtures: Abu Hassan; Der Beherrscher der Geister; Euryanthe; Der Freischütz; Jubel; Oberon; Preziosa*
(N) (BB) ** Brilliant 99935 (3). (i) Rösel; (ii) Dresden State O; (iii) Blomstedt; (iv) ASMF, Marriner; (v) Kuhn

The *Piano Concertos* are rarely heard, but they are melodically appealing and full of delightful touches. The performances are very good, but the 1984 recording is rather ordinary: the orchestra sounds a little unfocused and the piano timbre is a bit clattery at times. The marvellous *Konzertstück* comes off well too, though the same reservations on the sound apply. It has to be said that Frith's performances on Naxos are far

superior. Although both of Weber's *Symphonies* are in C major, each has its own individuality, and neither lacks vitality or invention. Sir Neville Marriner's performances (see below) are eminently recommendable, fresh and pleasing, and the 1982 (originally ASV) recording is clear and well balanced. The Overtures date from 1985 and are also available (much more expensively) in demonstration sound on a Capriccio SACD (see below). The performances are excellent, although they project much less vividly here. But this set is very inexpensive.

Konzertstück in F min.
(N) (M) *** EMI (ADD) 5 62884-2. Arrau, Philh. O, Galliera –
    CHOPIN: *Fantasy*, etc. ***

Arrau is superb. He gives one of the freshest performances imaginable of the unusual piece with its programme of knights and ladies. The orchestra responds splendidly and the recording is excellent. The couplings are equally fine and there is a seductive bonus of Mendelssohn's *Andante and Rondo capriccioso.*

Overtures: Abu Hassan; Der Beherrscher der Geister (Ruler of the Spirits); Euryanthe; Der Freischütz; Jubel; Oberon; Preziosa
(N) ( ) *** Capriccio Surround Sound SACD 71 045.
    Dresden State O, Kuhn

Some years back, Gustav Kuhn gave us an RCA/Eurodisc of Suppé *Overtures* with the RPO, not racy, but notable for his care over every detail. This collection of Weber *Overtures* has the same virtues. They are marvellously played by the superb Dresden Staatskapelle, and if as performances they do not quite match Karajan for panache or Sawallisch for sheer orchestral excitement, they certainly do not lack style and vitality. Indeed, their breadth plus a certain dignity increases their stature. But what makes this disc so thrilling is the magnificent recording, far finer than with any of their competitors. It is very much in the demonstration bracket, wonderfully real and full-blooded, especially when using four speakers, which provide a superb concert-hall illusion in the sitting room. There is no better example than *Jubel*, splendidly grandiloquent, especially when 'God save the Queen' arrives spectacularly and thrillingly at the close.

Overtures: Abu Hassan; Der Beherrscher der Geister (Ruler of the Spirits); Euryanthe; Der Freischütz; Jubel; Oberon; Peter Schmoll; Preziosa; Silvana; Turandot: Overture & March
*(**) Chan. 9066. Philh. O, Järvi

Overtures: Abu Hassan; Der Beherrscher der Geister (Ruler of the Spirits); Euryanthe; Der Freischütz; Oberon; Peter Schmoll. Invitation to the Dance, Op. 65 (orch. Berlioz)
(M) *** DG 419 070-2. BPO, Karajan

Overtures: Abu Hassan; Der Beherrscher der Geister (Ruler of the Spirits)
(N) *** Australian Decca Eloquence (ADD) 476 2745. VPO, Stein – BRUCKNER: *Symphony 6* ***

Overtures: Abu Hassan; Der Beherrscher der Geister (Ruler of the Spirits); Euryanthe; Der Freischütz; Jubel; Oberon; Preciosa
(BB) **(*) EMI Encore 5 75644-2 [575645]. Philh., O, Sawallisch

Chandos offer the most comprehensive collection of Weber overtures on CD and the performances certainly have plenty of vitality. But these recordings did not stem from one session, but three, and those made in the very resonant acoustic of St Jude's Church in April 1989 suffer from thick orchestral textures and unclear inner detail. They include *Der Beherrscher*, *Euryanthe* and *Der Freischütz*, the two latter both fine performances, but with tuttis made to sound very heavy. *Turandot* is even more opaque, *Oberon* rather less so. The others, using All Saints, Tooting, fare better, and throughout there is an impressive Philharmonia response, especially from the horns. But at times Järvi drives too hard, and by doing so loses much of the charm of *Abu Hassan*. In his efforts to keep the pot on the boil he also makes an unwritten accelerando at the end of *Oberon*, and presses on even more forcefully for the coda of *Peter Schmoll*. Fortunately, the novelty, *Silvana*, is the finest performance on this disc, and has recording to match.

Sawallisch (in 1958) had the advantage of the Philharmonia at their peak. The orchestral playing is superb and the excitement of *Der Freischütz*, the Turkish colouring of *Abu Hassan* and the contrasts of *Euryanthe* (the timpanist notable) are presented with a strong sense of the individual character of each piece. There is real orchestral virtuosity in *The Ruler of the Spirits* and the spectacular appearance of *God save the Queen* as the apotheosis of *Jubel* will cheer anyone up. The snag is the over-bright, sharply focused recording with a very light bass.

As it is, the less generous DG collection is the one to go for. Karajan's performances have great style and refinement and the Berlin Philharmonic playing in the two finest overtures, *Oberon* and *Der Freischütz*, is peerless (especially the horns). Both admirably epitomize the romantic spirit of the operas which they serve to introduce, while Karajan's elegant account of another Weberian innovation, the *Invitation to the Dance* (in Berlioz's brilliant orchestration), makes a valuable bonus. On CD the sound is brighter than the original LP, with some loss of weight in the bass, but it is still fuller than Sawallisch's EMI alternative.

Warm, lively and superbly played versions of two sparkling Weber overtures from Horst Stein, making an enjoyable bonus to a fine account of Bruckner's *Sixth Symphony*.

Symphonies 1 in C; 2 in C, J.50/51
**(*) ASV CDDCA 515. ASMF, Marriner

Symphonies 1 in C; 2 in C. Die drei Pintos: Entr'acte. Silvana: Dance of the Young Nobles; Torch Dance. Turandot: Overture; Act II: March; Act V: Funeral March
●—● ✺ (BB) *** Naxos 8.550928. Queensland PO, Georgiadis

Weber wrote his two symphonies in the same year (1807) and, though both are in C major, each has its own individuality. The witty orchestration and operatic character of the writing are splendidly caught in these sparkling Queensland performances, while in the slow movements the orchestral soloists relish their solos, for all the world like vocal cantilenas. The Naxos recording is in the demonstration class, and the disc is made the more attractive for the inclusion of orchestral excerpts from two little-known operas and incidental music from *Turandot*. The *Entr'acte* from the incomplete *Die drei Pintos* was put together by Mahler from Weber's sketches.

Sir Neville Marriner also has the full measure of Weber's two symphonies; these performances combine vigour and high spirits with the right degree of gravitas (not too much) in the slow movements. The recording is clear and full in the bass, but the bright upper range brings a touch of digital edge to the upper strings.

CHAMBER AND INSTRUMENTAL MUSIC

Cello Sonata in A; Adagio & Rondo
(***) Testament mono SBT 2158. Piatigorsky, Newton – BEETHOVEN: *Cello Sonatas*; BRAHMS: *Sonata 1* (***)

These records were made in 1934–5 and are arrangements by Piatigorsky of the *Fifth* of Weber's *Violin Sonatas*, Op. 10. The playing has an impressive eloquence.

Clarinet Quintet in B Flat, Op. 34
*** ASV CDDCA 1079. Johnson, Takacs-Nagy, Hirsch, Boulton, Shulman – MOZART: *Clarinet Quintet*; *Allegro in B flat*, K.516c **(*)
(N) *** Australian Decca Eloquence (ADD) 476 2447. De Peyer, Melos Ens. – HUMMEL: *Piano Quintet*; *Piano Septet****

(i) Clarinet Quintet; Introduction, Theme & Variations for Clarinet & String Quartet, Op. posth.; (ii) Grand duo concertant in E flat, Op. 48; 7 Variations on a Theme from Silvana in B flat, Op. 33 (both for clarinet and piano)
(BB) *** Naxos 8.553122. Berkes, with (i) Auer Qt; (ii) Jandó

(i) Clarinet Quintet; Flute Trio in G min., Op. 63 (for flute, cello and piano)
(M) *** CRD (ADD) CRD 3398. Nash Ens.

(i) Clarinet Quintet; (ii) Grand duo concertant, Op. 48; 7 Variations on a Theme from Silvana, Op. 33
(N) *** Praga PRD 250 164. Moraguès; (i) Pražák Qt; (ii) Izuha
**(*) Chan. 8366. Hilton, (i) Lindsay Qt; (ii) Swallow

This Praga disc is sheer delight, full of Bohemian spirit, with superbly elegant playing from everyone concerned. The very opening pair of string chords of the *Quintet* have a gentle, inviting warmth. We hear them twice, then the clarinet steals in seductively and announces the jaunty main theme with winning geniality. The allegro then springs to life, the secondary theme delightfully romantic. The slow movement opens pensively on the cello, and Pascal Moraguès's solo line is gently ravishing. A deliciously witty Scherzo leads naturally to the irresistibly perky finale. The *Duo concertant* is equally winning, with Moraguès's easy rubato given persuasive support by the pianist, Mari Izuha, the flowing *Andante* followed by a debonair, pointed finale. The *Silvana Variations*, based on another genially dotted theme, are again delightfully presented, with bravura flourishes and rollicking roulades from the clarinet and nimble accompanying pianism, and the recording could hardly be more truthful or better balanced.

Emma Johnson, always a characterful player with her distinctive reedy tone, gives a scintillating account of the *Quintet*, with brilliant support from her team of experienced chamber players. In this less well-known work she is more spontaneous-sounding than in the Mozart, full of sparkle and fun in the outer movements as well as the Scherzo, finding a rare depth of expression in the hushed writing of the second movement *Fantasia*, marked *Adagio*. The clarinet is forwardly balanced, but less obtrusively so than in the Mozart.

Gervase de Peyer, too, is in his element in the *Quintet*, immaculate and brilliant, and given superb support from the Melos Ensemble. The 1959 recording hardly sounds its age, remarkably warm and vivid, so if the Hummel couplings are wanted this is very recommendable.

On the CRD version, Antony Pay (playing a modern instrument) makes the very most of the work's bravura, catching the exuberance of the *Capriccio* third movement and the breezy gaiety of the finale. The Nash players provide an admirable partnership and then adapt themselves readily to the different mood of the *Trio*, another highly engaging work with a picturesque slow movement, described as a *Shepherd's Lament*. The recording is first class, vivid yet well balanced.

However, Naxos conveniently gather together expert and winning performances of all Weber's major chamber works featuring the clarinet, even if the amiable *Introduction, Theme and Variations* is now considered spurious. The *Quintet* is particularly successful with a lusciously appealing account of the *Adagio* and the finale chortles with great zest in its sparkling virtuosity. With Jandó an admirable partner, the *Grand duo concertant* is hardly less successful, and the two sets of variations are presented with both elegance and panache. The recording is realistic if too resonant, but the charisma and spontaneity of this Hungarian music-making carry the day in spite of this.

Janet Hilton plays with considerable authority and spirit though she is not always as mellifluous as her rivals. However, her account of the *Grand duo concertant* is a model of fine ensemble, as are the *Variations on a Theme from Silvana* of 1811, in both of which Keith Swallow is an equally expert partner.

7 Variations on a Theme from Silvana in B flat, Op. 33

*** Chan. 8506. De Peyer, Pryor – SCHUBERT: *Arpeggione Sonata*; SCHUMANN: *Fantasiestücke*, etc. ***

These engaging Weber *Variations* act as a kind of encore to Schubert's *Arpeggione Sonata* and with their innocent charm they follow on naturally. They are most winningly played by Gervase de Peyer; Gwenneth Pryor accompanies admirably. The recording is first class.

PIANO MUSIC

Piano Sonatas 1–2; Rondo brillante in E flat (La Gaîté), Op. 52; Invitation to the Dance, Op. 65
(M) *** CRD CRD 3485. Milne

Piano Sonata 3 in D min., Op. 49; 4 in E min., Op. 70; Polacca brillante in E (L'Hilarité) (with LISZT: Introduzione (Adagio))
(M) *** CRD CRD 3486. Milne

These two Weber *Sonatas* are not easy to bring off, with their classical heritage and operatic freedom of line. Hamish Milne's performances have a lightness of touch that is most appealing, without ever being superficial, and his playing in the slow movements has attractive lyrical feeling. Moreover he also provides a sparkling account of the *Rondo brillante* and, as a final encore, a totally captivating account of the charming *Invitation to the Dance*. He makes a sterner approach to the opening *Allegro feroce* of *No. 3 in D minor*, cast in an almost Beethovenian mould, while the last sonata is more introspective in its colouring and feeling, and concludes with a ruthless Tarantella, driven on by its own restless energy. The *Polacca brillante* returns to the world of dazzling articulation and sparkling display. Hamish Milne's playing is thoroughly inside Weber's world and technically equal to the composer's prodigious demands. He is very well recorded.

OPERA

Abu Hassan (complete)
(M) *** CPO/EMI (ADD) CPO 999 551-2. Forster, Gedda, Edda Moser, Moll, Bav. State Op. Ch. & O, Sawallisch

(i) Abu Hassan. Symphony 1 in C
🔊━ *** DHM/BMG 054 72 7779-2. (i) Völz, Dürmüller, Stojkovic, Selig, Werk Ruhr Ch.; Cappella Coloniensis of West Deutsche TV & R., L. Weil

Abu Hassan is a delightful one-act opera, an early work written in 1811, which, like Mozart's *Entführung*, exploits the fashion for 'Turkish' subjects. In a crisp series of brief numbers – two choruses, two arias, two duets and two trios – it lasts a mere 50 minutes, allowing it to be coupled in this sparkling performance on Deutsche Harmonia Mundi with Weber's equally delightful *Symphony No. 1*. Using period instruments, Bruno Weil gives the score all the lightness and transparency it needs, with a first-rate trio of soloists, all with clear, fresh voices, plus a Narrator who doubles in the role of the Caliph. The only snag for the non-German speaker is that the spoken dialogue separating the musical numbers may prove excessive, but there is generous indexing of tracks to allow it to be omitted, and the well-planned booklet gives German text and English translation. The *Symphony* too gains in point and transparency in this lively performance with period instruments.

Sawallisch too conducts a brilliant performance, with Nicolai Gedda in the title-role pointing his music lightly, with Edda Moser vibrantly expressive as his wife, and with Kurt Moll superb as the grasping money-lender, Omar. First-rate sound, engineered in 1975 by an EMI-Electrola team.

Der Freischütz: Overture
(M) (***) BBC Legends mono BBCL 4140. New Philh. O, Giulini – BRITTEN: *The Building of the House Overture*; SCHUBERT: *Symphony 9* ***

Recorded in mono at the Royal Festival Hall in December 1970, Giulini's reading of the Weber overture brings a performance of extremes, at once dedicated and dramatic, a valuable addition to the conductor's discography on this disc issued to celebrate his ninetieth birthday.

Der Freischütz (complete)
🔊━ *** Teldec 4509 97758-2 (2). Orgonasova, Schäfer, Wottrich, Salminen, Berlin R. Ch., BPO, Harnoncourt
(M) *** EMI (ADD) 7 69342-2 (2). Grümmer, Otto, Schock, Prey, Wiemann, Kohn, Frick, German Op. Ch., Berlin, BPO, Keilberth
(N) (B) *** DG 477 5611 (2). Seefried, Streich, Holm, Waechter, Peter, Bohme, Bav. R. Ch. & O, Jochum
(M) *** DG (ADD) 457 736-2 (2). Janowitz, Mathis, Schreier, Adam, Vogel, Crass, Leipzig R. Ch., Dresden State O, Carlos Kleiber
**(*) DHM 05472 77536-2 (2). Schnitzer, Stojkovic, Prégardien, Zeppenfeld, Röhlig, John (nar.), Capella Coloniensis & WDRO of Cologne, Weil
(N) (BB) ** Decca (ADD) 477 5611 (2). Behrens, Donath, Kollo, Moll, Brendel, Meven, Bav. R. Ch. & SO, Kubelik

Harnoncourt's electrifying and refreshing version of this operatic warhorse was recorded live at concert performances in the Philharmonie in Berlin in 1995 and the engineers have done wonders in conveying the atmosphere of a stage performance rather than a concert one, not least in the *Wolf's Glen* scene, helped by recording of a very wide dynamic range. Harnoncourt clarifies textures and paces the drama well, making it sound fresh and new. The cast is first rate, with Orgonasova singing radiantly as Agathe, not just pure but sensuous of tone, floating high *pianissimos* ravishingly. Christine Schäfer, sweet and expressive, makes Annchen into far more than just a soubrette character, and Erich Wottrich as Max is aptly heroic and unstrained, if hardly beautiful. The line-up of baritones and basses is impressive too, all firm and clear, contrasting sharply with one another, a team unlikely to be bettered today. A clear first choice among modern, digital recordings.

Keilberth's is a warm, exciting account of Weber's masterpiece, which makes all the dated conventions of the work seem fresh and new. In particular the *Wolf's Glen* scene on CD acquires something of the genuine terror that must have struck the earliest audiences. The casting of the magic bullets with each one numbered in turn, at first in eerie quiet and then in crescendo amid the howling of demons, is superbly conveyed. Elisabeth Grümmer sings more sweetly and sensitively than one ever remembers before, with Agathe's prayer exquisitely done. Lisa Otto is really in character, with genuine coquettishness. Schock is not an ideal tenor, but he sings ably enough. The Kaspar of Karl Kohn is generally well focused, and the playing of the Berlin Philharmonic has plenty of polish. The overall effect is immensely atmospheric and enjoyable.

Reissued in DG's Opera House series at budget price, Jochum's fine version makes a welcome return to the catalogue after many years in limbo. The warmth of Jochum's conducting and his understanding of how to pace this high romantic piece puts his among the finest versions with its outstanding cast, even if he cannot quite match Keilberth in re-creating the horror of the *Wolf's Glen* scene. Irmgard Seefried may be on the light side for the role of Agathe, but the golden purity of her voice, her projection and her flawless control of legato make hers a memorable performance; and few can match Rita Streich in brilliance as Annchen. Richard Holm sings with free, unstrained tone as Max, and Eberhard Waechter is outstanding as Otakar, with Kurt Bohme gruff but characterful as Kaspar. First-rate, well-balanced sound, remarkable for 1959. Well worth getting as a second version of this delightful opera.

Kleiber's fine, incisive account of Weber's atmospheric and adventurous score fulfilled all expectations. With the help of an outstanding cast, excellent work by the recording producer, Eberhard Geller, and transparently clear recording, this is a most compelling version of an opera which transfers well to the gramophone. Only occasionally does Kleiber betray a fractional lack of warmth, but the full drama of the work is splendidly projected in the enhancement of the newly remastered sound.

Bruno Weil conducts a recording of *Der Freischütz* with a difference. Not only does he bring his experience of period performance to the score, clarifying textures in a reading less grandly romantic than usual, often at crisply moving speeds, he uses in place of the usual spoken dialogue linking passages written by Steffen Kopetzy and spoken by an actor, Markus John, taking the role of Samiel. These are comments on the action rather than conventional narrations telling the story, and they work well in eliminating what has generally been regarded as the weakness of the usual dialogue. They are all brief and are optional, being separately banded. For the

non-German-speaker that may be less important, but the freshness of the whole production is reinforced, using an excellent cast of mainly young singers, with only Christoph Prégardien a star already established. As Max he is first rate, but so is Petra-Maria Schnitzer a fresh and girlish Agathe. As Annchen Johanna Stojkovic's soprano, less soubrettish than usual in this role, provides less contrast with the heroine, but hers too is a fresh, winning performance, with Georg Zeppenfeld excellent in Kaspar's drinking song. The climax of the *Wolf's Glen* scene at the end of Act II is splendidly biting in Weil's reading, but with clean-cut recording less atmospheric than it can be.

Kubelik takes a direct view of Weber's high romanticism. The result has freshness but lacks something of dramatic bite and atmosphere. There is far less tension than in the finest versions, not least in the *Wolf's Glen* scene, which in spite of the full-ranging 1979 recording seems rather tame. The singing is generally good, René Kollo as Max giving one of his best performances on record, but Hildegard Behrens, superbly dramatic in later German operas, here as Agathe seems clumsy in music that often requires a pure lyrical line. The bargain price (without texts) makes the set reasonable value, but the Keilberth mid-priced EMI set is altogether finer.

Overture: *Oberon*

**(N) (M) **(*) Dresden Staatskapelle Live VKJK 0414. Dresden Staatskapelle, Haitink –BRAHMS: *Symphony 1* **(*)

Haitink's Dresden recording of the Brahms symphony may be on the heavy side, but Weber's overture is quite different, magically refined in the slow introduction and lithe and athletic in the main allegro. A good coupling, if hardly a generous one on a mid-price disc.

Oberon (complete recording in the original English)

⊶ ✪ (N) * Ph. 475 6563-2 (2). Davislim, Martinpelto, Kaufmann, Dazeley, Monteverdi Ch., ORR, Gardiner, Allam (nar.)

Weber's *Oberon* is one of the great problem works of opera. Written for Covent Garden in 1825, it is based not on Shakespeare but on the fairy epic of Wieland which, using an English translation, Robinson Planche turned into an ungainly libretto. Its oddities effectively prevented Weber from developing the piece consistently, but he was inspired to write some of his most magical music, full of what John Eliot Gardiner defines as 'fire, fantasy and finesse'. How to present *Oberon* effectively has long presented almost intractable problems, but here Gardiner on disc, pioneering a recording in the original English, opts for what might be counted an ideal answer, using a narrator to link numbers instead of Planche's dialogue. The result in a superb performance is magnetic, letting one appreciate to the full the uniqueness of Weber's inspiration, with period instruments helping to clarify the fairy-light orchestral textures, plainly a model for Mendelssohn.

The singing cast is excellent, with the two main tenor roles splendidly taken – Oberon lyrically by the Australian tenor, Steve Davislim, and Huon, with his big spectacular aria full of formidable florid writing, by Jonas Kaufmann. Hillevi Martinpelto is fresh and clear as Raiza, another challenging role, and Roger Allam is unobtrusively effective speaking the narration. The Monteverdi Choir too plays an important part in bringing out the magic of the music, with beautifully balanced recording.

WEBERN, Anton (1883–1945)

(i) *Concerto for 9 Instruments, Op. 24; 5 Movements for String Quartet* (orchestral version), *Op. 5; Passacaglia, Op. 1; 6 Pieces for Large Orchestra, Op. 6; 5 Pieces for Orchestra, Op. 10; Symphony, Op. 21; Variations for Orchestra, Op. 30.* Arrangements of: Bach: *Musical Offering: Fugue* (1935). (ii) Schubert: *German Dances* (for small orchestra), *Op. posth.* Chamber Music: (iii) *6 Bagatelles for String Quartet, Op. 9; 5 Movements for String Quartet, Op. 5;* (iv; v) *4 Pieces for Violin & Piano, Op. 7;* (v; vi) *3 Small Pieces for Cello & Piano, Op. 11;* (v; vii) *Quartet, Op. 22* (for piano, violin, clarinet & saxophone); (iii) *String Quartet, Op. 28; String Trio, Op. 20;* (v) *Variations for Piano, Op. 27.* (Vocal) (viii; i) *Das Augenlicht, Op. 26;* (ix; x) *5 Canons on Latin Texts, Op. 16;* (viii; ix; i) *Cantata 1, Op. 29;* (viii; ix; xi; i) *Cantata 2, Op. 31;* (viii) *Entflieht auf leichten Kähnen, Op. 2;* (ix; x) *5 Sacred Songs, Op. 15;* (xii; v) *5 Songs, Op. 3; 5 Songs, Op. 4;* (xii; x) *2 Songs, Op. 8;* (xii; v) *4 Songs, Op. 12;* (xii; x) *4 Songs, Op. 13; 6 Songs, Op. 14;* (ix; x; xiii) *3 Songs, Op. 18;* (viii; i) *2 Songs, Op. 19;* (xii; v) *3 Songs, Op. 23;* (ix; v) *3 Songs, Op. 25;* (ix; x) *3 Traditional Rhymes, Op. 17*

(M) *** Sony SM3K 45845 (3). (i) LSO (or members), Boulez; (ii) Frankfurt R. O, composer (recorded December 1932); (iii) Juilliard Qt (or members); (iv) Stern; (vi) Piatigorsky; (vii) Majeske, Marcellus, Weinstein; (viii) John Alldis Ch.; (ix) Lukomska; (x) with Ens., Boulez; (xi) McDaniel; (xii) Harper; (xiii) with Williams. Overall musical direction: Boulez

What Pierre Boulez above all demonstrates in the orchestral works (including those with chorus) is that, for all his seeming asceticism, Webern was working on human emotions. The Juilliard Quartet and the John Alldis Choir convey comparable commitment; though neither Heather Harper nor Halina Lukomska is ideally cast in the solo vocal music, Boulez brings out the best in both of them in the works with orchestra. A rare recording of Webern himself conducting his arrangement of Schubert dances is also included. There are excellent notes, every item is cued, and perhaps it is carping to regret that the *Passacaglia* and *Variations for Orchestra* were not indexed.

(i) *Concerto for 9 Instruments, Op. 24;* (ii) *6 Orchestral Pieces, Op. 6; Symphony, Op. 21;* (i) *Quartet, Op. 22; Trio, Op. 20; 3 Pieces for Cello & Piano, Op. 11; 4 Pieces for Violin & Piano Op. 7; Variations for Piano, Op. 27;* (iii) *5 Canons for Soprano & 2 Clarinets; 3 Songs, Op. 18; 3 Traditional Rhymes, Op. 17.* (i) SCHUBERT, orch. WEBERN: *German Dances*

(N) (BB) *** Naxos 8.557330. (i) 20th Century Classics Ens. (members); (ii) Philh. O, Craft; (iii) Welch-Babidge

As an important issue in the 'Robert Craft Collection', Naxos here offers an exceptionally generous selection of Webern's mature works. Eight brief pieces for various forces frame the three central works, the *Six Pieces*, Op. 6, the most powerful example of his early atonal period, exploiting a very large orchestra, the *Symphony*, Op. 21, for chamber orchestra, one of the finest works of his later, fully serial period, and the *Concerto* for nine soloists, the most popular of his chamber works. The Philharmonia plays warmly in Opus 6, with the 20th Century Classics Ensemble from New York giving virtuoso performances of the other two, also supplying players

for the smaller-scale piece. Jennifer Welch-Babidge's bright, clear soprano, precisely focused, is ideal for the craggy lines of the vocal pieces. Full texts and English translations are given. As a charming supplement, the Philharmonia also plays the set of six tiny *German Dances* by Schubert which, soon after they were discovered in 1929, Webern set sensitively for small orchestra. Excellent sound in recordings from both London and New York.

Collected works:

Disc 1: (i) *Im Sommerwind; 5 Movements for String Quartet* (orchestral version), *Op. 5; Passacaglia, Op. 1; 6 Pieces for Large Orchestra, Op. 6.* Arrangements of: Bach: *Musical Offering: Fugue;* Schubert: *German Dances, D.820*

Disc 2: (i) *5 Pieces for Orchestra* (1913); *Symphony, Op. 21; Variations for Orchestra, Op. 30;* (iii; iv; v) *Das Augenlicht, Op. 26; Cantatas 1, Op. 29; 2, Op. 31; 3 Orchesterlieder* (1913–24)

Disc 3: (ii; vi) *Concerto for 9 Instruments, Op. 24;* (ii) *5 Pieces for Orchestra, Op. 10;* (ii; vi) *Piano Quintet; Quartet, Op. 22* (for piano, violin, clarinet & saxophone); (ii; iii; v; vii) *5 Canons on Latin Texts, Op. 15; Entflieht auf Leichten Kähnen, Op. 2; 2 Lieder, Op. 8; 4 Lieder, Op. 13; 6 Lieder, Op. 14; 5 Geistliche Lieder, Op. 15; 3 Lieder, Op. 18; 2 Lieder, Op. 19; 3 Volkstexte, Op. 17*

Disc 4: (iii; viii) *3 Gedichte* (1899–1903); *8 frühe Lieder* (1901–4); *3 Avenarius Lieder* (1903–4); *5 Dehmel Lieder* (1906–8); *5 St George Lieder; 5, Op. 4; 4 St George Lieder* (1908–9); *4 Lieder, Op. 12; 3 Jone Gesänge, Op. 23; 3 Jone Lieder, Op. 25*

Disc 5: (ix; x) *6 Bagatelles for String Quartet, Op. 5; (Langsamer) Slow Movement for String Quartet* (1905); *5 Movements for String Quartet, Op. 5; 3 Pieces for String Quartet* (1913); *Rondo for String Quartet* (1906); *String Quartet* (1905); *String Quartet, Op. 28; String Trio, Op. 20; Movement for String Trio, Op. posth.* (1925)

Disc 6: (xi; xii) *Cello Sonata* (1914); *2 Pieces for Cello & Piano* (1899); *3 Small Pieces for Cello & Piano, Op. 11;* (xiii; xiv) *4 Pieces for Violin & Piano, Op. 7;* (xv) Piano: *Kinderstück* (1924 & 1925); *Piece* (1906); *Sonata Movement (Rondo)* (1906); (xiv) *Variations, Op. 27*

(M) *** DG 457 637-2 (6). (i) Berlin PO, or (ii) Ens. Intercontemporain, Boulez; (iii) Oelz; (iv) Finley; (v) BBC Singers; (vi) Aimard; (vii) Pollet; (viii) Schneider; (ix) Emerson Qt; (x) McCormick; (xi) Hagen; (xii) Maisenberg; (xiii) Kremer; (xiv) Zimerman; (xv) Cascioli

This monumental DG set goes far further than the earlier Sony collection in its illumination of Webern as one of the great musical pioneers of the twentieth century. The first point is that where the earlier set limited itself to the numbered works, this one covers so much more (on six discs instead of three) with a far fuller portrait presented not only in the early works but also in such offerings as the incidental chamber works and his arrangements of Bach (the *Ricercar* from the *Musical Offering*) and Schubert (a collection of waltzes). Boulez's interpretations of the numbered works have developed too, with the Berlin Philharmonic exceptionally responsive, bringing out often unsuspected warmth and beauty. The point and purposefulness of these performances is particularly helpful in making such thorny late inspirations as the two *Cantatas* so much more readily approachable. The vocal soloists have been ideally chosen, with the fresh-toned

Christiane Oelze taking on the majority of songs, but with Françoise Pollet and Gerald Finley equally assured. The starry list of instrumental contributors could not be bettered either, including as it does such luminaries of DG as the Emerson Quartet and Krystian Zimerman, and the recordings made over a period of years are uniformly excellent.

Concerto for 9 Instruments, Op. 24

(M) *** Chan. 6534. Nash Ens., Rattle – SCHOENBERG: *Pierrot Lunaire* ***

This late Webern piece, tough, spare and uncompromising, makes a valuable fill-up for Jane Manning's outstanding version of Schoenberg's *Pierrot Lunaire*, a 1977 recording originally made for the Open University. First-rate sound and a beautifully clean CD transfer.

Langsamer Satz (arr. Schwarz)

*** Delos DE 3121. Seattle SO, Schwarz – HONEGGER: *Symphony 2*; R. STRAUSS: *Metamorphosen* ***

The slow movement Webern composed in 1905 for string quartet sounds even more Mahlerian in Gerard Schwarz's transcription for full strings, which is eloquently played and sumptuously recorded.

Passacaglia for Orchestra, Op. 1

⌐ (M) *** DG (IMS) (ADD) 457 760-2. BPO, Karajan – BERG: *Lyric Suite*, etc.; SCHOENBERG: *Variations* ***

This is a beautifully played and recorded version of Webern's *Passacaglia*, which will disappoint no one. It sounds especially haunting – even magical – in Karajan's hands, and has been superbly transferred.

6 Pieces for Large Orchestra, Op. 6

⌐ (BB) *** EMI Encore 5 75880-2. CBSO, Rattle – BERG: *Lulu: Symphonic Suite*; SCHOENBERG: *5 Orchestral Pieces* ***

Rattle and the CBSO bring out the microcosmic strength of the six Webern *Pieces*, giving them weight and intensity without inflation. Warmth is rightly implied here, but no Mahlerian underlining. The superb performance given sound of demonstration quality makes this bargain triptych an ideal introduction to the three key composers of the Second Viennese School.

CHAMBER MUSIC

(i) *6 Bagatelles, Op. 9; 5 Movements, Op. 5; 3 Little Pieces, Op. 11; 4 Pieces, Op. 7; Rondo, Op. posth.; Slow Movement, Op. posth.; String Quartet, Op. 28; String Quartet, Op. posth.* (1905); *String Trio, Op. 20;* (ii) *Piano Sonata, Op. posth.*

(N) *** Chan. 10083. (i) Schoenberg Qt; (ii) Grotenhuis (piano)

This outstanding collection, superbly performed, gives an excellent idea of the range of Webern's genius, from early works to such seminal masterpieces as the *Five Movements*, Op. 5, the late *String Trio* and *String Quartet*, Op. 28. Thanks to the warmth and expressive intensity of the playing of the Schoenberg Quartet, even the unprepared listener will find illumination here, with the early works providing a helpful introduction to the more daunting serial pieces.

6 Bagatelles for String Quartet, Op. 9; Langsamer Satz; 5 Movements for String Quartet, Op. 5; Rondo for String

Quartet (1906); *String Quartet* (1905); *String Quartet, Op. 28; Movement for String Trio, Op. posth.; String Trio, Op. 20.*

*** Nim. NI 5668. Vienna Artis Qt

With warm, purposeful performances recorded in full, close sound, the Artis Quartet present Webern's collected music for string quartet and string trio as a most persuasive survey of this problematic composer's creative career. The three works from 1905 and 1906 (those without opus number) represent his early post-romantic style at its ripest, while such works as the *Five Movements*, Op. 5, vividly illustrate the imaginative leap he made when adopting free atonality. Equally representative are the more astringent works of his later years, the *String Trio*, Op. 20 and the *String Quartet*, Op. 28, all presented with a purposefulness and commitment that readily helps to overcome any problems the listener may have. An excellent disc for anyone who wants to investigate a key twentieth-century figure.

Slow Movement for String Quartet (1905)

*** DG (IMS) 437 836-2. Hagen Qt – DEBUSSY; RAVEL: *Quartets* ***

The single-movement Webern *Quartet* was composed in Carinthia in the summer of 1905 and was first heard in the 1960s. It has an intense and chromatic study, and is played with great refinement by the Hagen Quartet and beautifully recorded. An excellent *bonne bouche*, if that term is appropriate, for a superb Debussy and Ravel coupling.

Variations for Piano, Op. 27

*** Ph. 468 033-2. Uchida – BERG: *Piano Sonata;* SCHOENBERG: *Piano Concerto; Klavierstücke* ***

(M) *** DG (IMS) (ADD) 471 361-2. Pollini– SCHOENBERG: *Piano Concerto & solo piano music* **(*)

(BB) *** Naxos 8.553870. Hill – BERG: *Piano Sonata;* SCHOENBERG: *Piano Pieces; Suite* ***

The *Variations*, Op. 27, Webern's only mature piano piece, dates from the mid-1930s and calls for the most eloquent playing if it is to persuade the listener. Webern himself stressed that the music's structural intricacies must give rise to a 'profound expressiveness'. They are very impressive in Pollini's hands and make a well-chosen bonus for his coverage of Schoenberg's piano music. However, Peter Hill can hold his own against any of the competition.

Uchida gives a highly imaginative and refined account, recorded with great clarity and presence in the Herkulessaal, Munich, and this *Gramophone* Award-winning performance is as fine as this piece has ever received. Moreover, the Philips couplings, too, are very highly recommendable.

WEILL, Kurt (1900–50)

Concerto for Violin & Winds, Op. 12

(B) *** Virgin 2×1 5 62053-2 (2). Tetzlaff, Deutsche Kammerphilharmonie Wind – BARTOK: *Violin Concerto 2; Violin Sonata;* JANACEK: *Violin Concerto; Sonata* ***

Weill's *Concerto for Violin and Winds* has a seriousness of purpose and an originality that are persuasive, no doubt much helped by the highly sensitive and imaginative performance given by Christian Tetzlaff and the winds of the Deutsche Kammerphilharmonie; it is coupled with most interesting repertoire. It will surely convert any who doubt the quality of this work.

The Eternal Road (abridged)

(N) (BB) *** Naxos 8.559402. Hauman, Rearick, DeNolfo, Dent, Rideout, Christopher, Maddalena, Berlin R. Children's Ch., Ernst Senff Ch., Berlin RSO, Schwarz

Conceived as a Biblical pageant, *The Eternal Road* is Kurt Weill's most ambitious work. In a massive sequence of words and music – lasting (if uncut) around five hours – the piece links the stories of Biblical characters with the latter-day persecution of Jews in Europe. Originally presented in New York in 1937, it proved too cumbersome for its own good and was quickly forgotten. Yet it contains some of the most inspired music that Weill ever wrote, demonstrating that after he fled from Europe to America his genius remained as fertile and original as ever. This generous selection of musical items, lasting 73 minutes, gives an excellent idea of the piece, very well performed and recorded in Berlin with American soloists and conductor. The vigour of the writing brings a most attractive image of the Broadway style that Weill was developing. That includes such numbers as the fine chorus representing the Israelites' Dance around the Golden Calf, while the duet between Ruth and Naomi effectively avoids sentimentality in its gentle dance rhythms, and the duet between Ruth and Boaz, similarly popular in style, develops passionately. First-rate sound.

STAGE WORKS

The Ballad of Magna Carta; Der Lindberghflug

*** Cap. 60012. Henschel, Tyl, Calaminus, Clemens, Cologne Pro Musica Ch. & RSO, Latham-König; Wirl, Schmidt, Feckler, Minth, Scheeben, Berlin R. Ch. & O., Scherchen

Der Lindberghflug ('The Lindbergh Flight') is a curiosity. Brecht wrote the text, but only later did Weill set the complete work, and that is how it is given in this excellent Cologne recording. A historic 1930 performance of the original Weill-Hindemith version, conducted by Hermann Scherchen, is given as an appendix, recorded with a heavy background roar but with astonishingly vivid voices. The fine, very German tenor who sang Lindberg in 1930 was Erik Wirl and the tenor in the new recording is not nearly so sweet-toned, and the German narrator delivers his commentary in a casual, matter-of-fact way. Otherwise the performance under Jan Latham-König fully maintains the high standards of Capriccio's Weill series; and the other, shorter item, *The Ballad of Magna Carta* is most enjoyable too, a piece never recorded before. Clear, if rather dry, recording with voices vivid and immediate.

Die Dreigroschenoper (The Threepenny Opera; complete)

☞ *** Decca 430 075-2. Kollo, Lemper, Milva, Adorf, Dernesch, Berlin RIAS Chamber Ch. & Sinf., Mauceri

*** Sony (ADD) MK 42637. Lenya, Neuss, Trenk-Trebisch, Hesterberg, Schellow, Koczian, Grunert, Ch. & Dance O of Radio Free Berlin, Brückner-Rüggeberg

On Decca there are obvious discrepancies between the opera-singers, René Kollo and Helga Dernesch, and those in the cabaret tradition, notably the vibrant and provocative Ute Lemper (Polly Peachum) and the gloriously dark-voiced and characterful Milva (Jenny). That entails downward modulation in various numbers, as it did with Lotte Lenya, but the changes from the original are far less extreme. Kollo is good, but Dernesch is even more compelling. The co-ordination of

music and presentation makes for a vividly enjoyable experience, even if committed Weill enthusiasts will inevitably disagree with some of the controversial textual and interpretative decisions.

The CBS alternative offers a vividly authentic abridged recording, darkly incisive and atmospheric, with Lotte Lenya giving an incomparable performance as Jenny. All the wrong associations, built up round the music from indifferent performances, melt away in the face of a reading as sharp and intense as this. Bright, immediate, real stereo recording, made the more vivid on CD.

The Rise and Fall of Mahagonny (complete)

(M) ** Sony SM2K 91184 (2). Lenya, Litz, Günter, Mund, Gollnitz, Sauerbaum, Markwort, Roth, Murch (speaker), NW German R. Ch. & O, Brückner-Rüggeberg

Though Lotte Lenya, with her metallic, rasping voice, was more a characterful *diseuse* than a singer, and this bitterly inspired score had to be adapted to suit her limited range, it remains a most memorable performance. The recording lacks atmosphere, with voices (Lenya's in particular) close balanced. Yet even now one can understand how this cynical piece caused public outrage when it was first performed in Leipzig in 1930. The one great drawback to this reissue is the lack of any documentation except a single paragraph giving a summary of the plot. Moreover the set has not been remastered.

Der Silbersee (complete)

*** Cap. 60011-2 (2). Heichele, Tamassy, Holdorf, Schmidt, Mayer, Korte, Thomas, Cologne Pro Musica Ch., Cologne RSO, Latham-König

Led by Hildegard Heichele, bright and full-toned as the central character, Fennimore, the Capriccio cast is an outstanding one, with each voice satisfyingly clean-focused, while the 1989 recording is rather better-balanced and kinder to the instrumental accompaniment than some from this source, with the voices exceptionally vivid.

Street Scene (opera; complete)

* Arthaus **DVD** 100 098. Putnam, Wellbee, Handen, Wilborn, Rheinland-Pfalz State Philh., Holmes

*** TER CDTER2 1185 (2). Ciesinski, Kelly, Bottone, van Allan, ENO Ch. and O, Davis

This video version of Kurt Weill's 'American Opera' was recorded in Ludwigshafen in 1995, with a German orchestra and chorus but with the cast and production translated from an earlier presentation by the Houston Grand Opera company, directed by Francesca Zambello. The result is strong and idiomatic, with realistic sets by Adrianne Lobel, and with Ashley Putnam warmly sympathetic in the central role of Mrs Maurrant. Unfortunately, there is no synopsis provided in the booklet, and no identification of which character is performing at what point. The 4 x 3 format also cuts off the sides of what was originally a wide-screen production, and the sound is abrasively loud.

The TER set was made with the cast of the ENO production at the Coliseum, and the idiomatic feeling and sense of flow consistently reflect that. Some of the solo singing in the large cast is flawed, but never seriously, and the principals are all very well cast – Kristine Ciesinski as the much-put-upon Anna Maurrant, Richard van Allan as her sorehead husband, Janis Kelly sweet and tender as the vulnerable daughter, and Bonaventura Bottone as the diffident young Jewish neighbour who loves her. Those are only a few of the sharply drawn characters, and the performance on the discs, with dialogue briskly paced, reflects the speed of the original ENO production. Warm, slightly distanced sound.

Der Zar lässt sich Photographieren (complete)
**(*) Cap. 60 007-1. McDaniel, Pohl, Napier, Cologne R. O, Latham-König

This curious one-act *opera buffa* is a wry little parable about assassins planning to kill the Tsar when he has his photograph taken. Angèle, the photographer, is replaced by the False Angèle, but the Tsar proves to be a young man who simply wants friendship, and the would-be assassin, instead of killing him, plays a tango on the gramophone, before the Tsar's official duties summon him again. Jan Latham-König in this 1984 recording directs a strong performance, though the dryly recorded orchestra is consigned to the background. The voices fare better, though Barry McDaniel is not ideally steady as the Tsar.

WEINBERGER, Jaromir (1896–1967)

Schwanda the Bagpiper (complete; in Czech)
(N) (BB) ** Naxos 8.660146/7 (2). Robavs, Monogarova, Choupenitch, Kostyuk, Wexford Festival Op. Ch., Belarus Nat. PO, Reynolds

Recorded at the Wexford Festival in Ireland in 2003, this Naxos set offers a lively account of a colourful opera very much in the tradition of Smetana's *Bartered Bride*, with the *Polka* a hauntingly memorable centrepiece. It helps that forces from another Slavonic country, Belarus, are involved, with Julian Reynolds drawing idiomatic singing and playing from the whole company. The title-role is well taken by the baritone, Matjaz Robavs, and so is the role of his wife, Dorota, by the bright, clear, agile soprano, Tatiana Monogarova. The fruity mezzo, Larisa Kostyuk, is well cast as the Queen, even if the Slavonic beat in her voice is often obtrusive. Sadly, the other important role, that of the mysterious Babinsky, is given to a tenor, Ivan Choupenitch, whose voice is so ill-focused it is hard to tell which notes he is singing. The recording, made in the tiny Wexford Theatre Royal, is inevitably limited on orchestral sound, but voices come over well.

Schwanda the Bagpiper: Polka & Fugue
(N) (M) *** RCA **SACD** 82876 66376-2. Chicago SO, Reiner –
SMETANA: *Bartered Bride: Overture* – DVORAK:
Symphony 9 (New World); Overture Carnival ***

This infectious orchestral display-piece was better known in the days of 78s. Reiner and his fine orchestra give a bravura performance, building to a big climax. The Chicago recording is suitably brilliant, enhanced by its SACD format, if not as strikingly as its principal Dvořák coupling.

WEINER, Leó (1885–1960)

Hungarian Folkdance Suite, Op. 18
(M) *** Chan. 6625. Philh. O, Järvi – BARTOK: *Hungarian Pictures*. ENESCU: *Romanian Rhapsodies 1–2* ***

Weiner here remained orientated towards the German and French schools, and this lively and attractive suite represents a Hungarian folk style more Westernized than Bartók's; but with purposeful direction from Järvi, fine dramatic playing from the orchestra and ripely resonant recording, the full range of colour is brought out in these four movements, which last almost half an hour.

Violin Sonatas 1 in D, Op. 9; 2 in F sharp min., Op. 11
**(*) Biddulph LAW 015. Shumsky, Lipkin – DOHNANYI:
Violin Sonata in C sharp min., Op. 21; Andante **(*)

The two violin sonatas of Leó Weiner were composed in 1911 and 1919 respectively, and they are heard here in good performances by Oscar Shumsky and Seymour Lipkin. They were recorded in New York in 1993 and if Shumsky's playing does not have the effortless mastery it possessed in the early 1980s, he still performs a service in restoring these enjoyable works to the wider musical public. A most worthwhile issue.

WEINGARTNER, Felix (1863–1942)

Symphony 1; King Lear (Symphonic Poem)
(N) *** CPO 999 981-2. Basel SO, Letonja

Felix Weingartner, noted Beethovenian, the first conductor to record a Beethoven symphony cycle complete, was also a prolific composer. This delightful symphony brims with one charming melody after another. So far from seeking to emulate Beethoven, this work comes closer to Dvořák, with a charmingly easy-going pastoral first movement, predominantly lyrical. Instead of a slow movement, Weingartner then has a flowing, march-like *Allegretto* with a surging violin melody in the middle. The third movement is a jolly folkdance with oboe and flute piping away, leading to a swaggering finale. Weingartner had a special relationship with Switzerland and with Basel in particular, inspiring Marko Letonja and the orchestra to a superb performance, vividly recorded. The symphonic poem, *King Lear*, more Lisztian than the *Symphony*, makes an excellent coupling in this first issue of a projected Weingartner series.

WEISS, Silvius (1686–1750)

Silvius Weiss, virtuoso lutenist, composer of the front rank, and contemporary of Bach was born at Breslau and centred his career as a court chamber musician, first at Düsseldorf, then at Dresden. He travelled frequently in Europe, where his playing was widely renowned, and during his excursions he met Corelli and both Alessandro and Domenico Scarlatti in Italy, and Quantz and Graun in Prague. In 1739 in Leipzig he was a guest of Bach, who subsequently arranged his *A major Sonata* for violin and harpsichord (BWV 1025). At the height of his fame, the Imperial Viennese Court offered him a huge monetary inducement to move to Vienna. But Weiss chose instead to end his career in Dresden, where he was completely at home.

Lute Sonatas (transcribed for guitar): 1–2, 4–6, 14, 17, 21, 25 & 29. Allegro in D (Duet); Fantasia in E min.; Menuet; (Trio)
(N) (B) *(*) Arte Nova 74321 77063-2 (10). Schneeweiss (guitar)

In layout Weiss's *Lute Sonatas* are very much like the suites and partitas of Bach, usually beginning with a Prelude, followed by a group of dance movements: *Allemande, Courante, Bourrée, Sarabande, Menuet* and *Gigue*. Sometimes Weiss closes with a *Chaconne* (Suite 6), *Passacaglia* (Suite 14) or an unusual movement, like the striking *Paysane* which ends Suite 25. The music is invariably through-composed, so that every movement is interrelated, and although each has an independent thematic existence one sometimes has a sense of a set of variations.

The Arte Nova box offers some of the early and middle-period sonatas, but the project to record all 29 of the surviving works appears to have halted. In any case there are considerable drawbacks to this survey. First, the music is recorded using the guitar instead of the lute, which means key transcriptions in certain instances. Also, ominously, the introduction to the survey in the note tells us that 'what we have here is not baroque music in the traditional sense, but an interpretation which makes use of all the modern playing techniques of the 21st-century guitar'.

In the event, Kurt Schneeweiss plays this music very freely indeed. The composer was famous for his improvisatary skills and expected his pupils to develop this technique. But Schneeweiss's style is so ruminatively improvisational in manner that, while the Sarabandes are effective enough, he all but loses the rhythmic character of the livelier dance movements, notably the *Menuets*, *Bourrées*, and especially the closing *Gigues*. He is at his best in the *Seventeenth, F minor, Sonata* where the music responds to his constant freedom with the metre; but elsewhere these performances must be approached with caution. The additional *Allegro* and *Menuet*, included on disc 2 after the *25th Sonata*, are played more robustly, the duet and trio apparently achieved electronically.

Lute Sonatas: 2 in D; 27 in C min.; 35 in D min.
(N) (BB) * Naxos 8.554350. Barto (Baroque lute)

Lute Sonatas: 5 in G; 25 in G min.; 50 in B flat
(N) (BB) * Naxos 8.553988. Barto (Baroque lute)

Lute Sonatas: 7 in C min.; 23 in B flat; 45 in A
(N) (BB) * Naxos 8.555772. Barto (Baroque lute)

Lute Sonatas: 21 in F min.; 37 in C; 46 in A
(N) (BB) * Naxos 8.554557. Barto (Baroque lute)

Lute Sonatas: 36 in D min.; 42 in A min.; 49 in B flat
(N) (BB) * Naxos 8.553773. Barto (Baroque lute)

Lute Sonatas: 38 in C; 43 in A min.; Tombeau sur la mort de M. Cajeran Baron d'Hartig
(N) (BB) * Naxos 8.554833. Barto (Baroque lute)

On Naxos, Robert Barto, playing a Baroque lute, shows us the breadth of Weiss's achievement and how naturally the music suits the lute, rather than the guitar. On almost all the discs offered so far he combines one early, one mid-period and one late sonata. He begins Volume 1 (8.553773) with the *D minor Sonata* from the 1720s (No. 36), opening with a short *Fantasia* which immediately invites an improvisatory freedom leading us naturally into the *Allemande*. Like the expansive *Sarabande*, this demonstrates the composer's celebrated Italianate cantabile style. Yet the *Bourrée* and, especially, the lively closing *Gigue* bring plenty of bubbly virtuosity. Both *Sonatas* 42 (probably a later work from the 1730s) and 49 open with pensive *Allemandes*, but there is plenty of variety later, and No. 42 has two consecutive fast movements (including a vigorous *Bourrée* marked 'Posato'), the essence of which reappears in the moto perpetuo finale.

The manuscript of the *Sonata in G major* (No. 5), which opens the second disc, was found in London. It is a most winning work, spontaneously integrating its basic musical material throughout, with the central *Courante* and *Bourrée* particularly infectious, and a jaunty finale. The opening Prelude of *No. 25 in G minor* is no more than a very brief

introduction to the *Allemande* and, after the lively *Passepied* and *Bourrée*, its *Sarabande* is nobly serene. However, No. 50 is a late work, and it has an extended *Introduzzione* which acts as Prelude and *Allemande* combined. After the light-hearted central movements, the *Sarabande* is thoughtful and searching, one of the composer's finest; the work ends with a brilliant finale which in its harmonic progressions is compellingly unpredictable.

But the quality of Weiss's invention seems inexhaustible throughout all these works, and he has a worthy exponent in Robert Barto, a virtuoso lutenist of a high order and a fine musician. He understands this repertory perfectly, never seeking to impose his personality over that of the composer, and the first-class Naxos recording gives him a natural presence.

WELLESZ, Egon (1885–1974)

During the 1920s and '30s Wellesz worked as a scholar – he was a leading authority on Baroque opera, on Byzantine and early Christian hymnology, and Professor of Musicology in Vienna, which consumed much of his energies. His main creative preoccupation at that period and after he settled in Oxford in 1938 was with opera but wartime conditions and the British indifference to opera led to a creative hiatus.

(i) *Violin Concerto, Op. 84. Prospero's Spell (Prosperos Beschwörungen), Op. 53*
*** Orfeo C478 981A. V. RSO, Albrecht; (i) with Löwenstein

Egon Wellesz pursued a dual career as a scholar and composer. *Prosperos Beschwörungen* (1935) is a highly imaginative score; Wellesz had toyed with the idea of writing an opera on *The Tempest* but these five orchestral pieces were the result. They are quite individual, though they are closer to Hindemith than to the Second Viennese school. The *Violin Concerto* (1961) is a made of sterner stuff and it provides a formidable challenge to the soloist, to which Andrea Duka Löwenstein rises triumphantly. Good playing from the ORF (Oesterreiches Rundfunk) or Vienna Radio Orchestra under Gerd Albrecht. Good sound, though perhaps a little studio bound.

Symphonies 2 in E flat (English), Op. 65; 9, Op. 111
*** CPO 999 997-2. V. RSO, Rabl

Wellesz did not turn to the symphony until he was sixty in 1945. No. 2 dates from 1947–8 and was first given in Vienna under Karl Rankl. RL recalls hearing the BBC première by the BBC Symphony Orchestra under Sir Adrian Boult (though he does not recall it ever being called 'The English'). Its subtitle apparently derived from the fact that Wellesz had steeped himself in English literature at the time of its composition. It is the longest of the nine and is consistently tonal, and the theme of its Scherzo stays with you, once heard. The *Ninth* comes from 1970, when Wellesz was eighty-five, and shows him losing none of his mastery, despite his frail health. Wellesz was also a master of the orchestra (his musical calligraphy, incidentally, resembled Strauss in its clarity) and he understood the symphonic process inside out. Gottfried Rabl and the Vienna Radio Symphony Orchestra do justice to these scores, and the recording is admirably balanced.

Symphonies 4, Op. 70; 6, Op. 95; 7, Op. 102
*** CPO 999 808-2. Vienna RSO, Rabl

The *Fourth* (*Sinfonia austrica*), which was written in Oxford during 1952–4, recalls Wellesz's former home, its beauty and also its tragedy and darker side. As with its immediate predecessors it is predominantly tonal. The *Sixth Symphony* comes from 1965, his eightieth year, and its successor from two years later, written for the Birmingham Symphony Orchestra. They are densely argued and finely wrought pieces by a master of the orchestra who understood the symphonic process inside out. They are given dedicated performances from Gottfried Rabl and the Vienna orchestra.

Die Bakchantinnen
*** Orfeo Musica Rediviva C136012H (2). Mohr, Burt,
   Stamm, Alexander, Barainsky, Breedt, Aschenbach,
   Gottschick, Berlin R. Ch., Deutsches SO, Albrecht

During the 1920s and 1930s Wellesz was better known as an operatic musicologist than as a composer. In England, to which he came at the time of the Anschluss, it was his eminence as a scholar in the field of early Christian and Byzantine hymnology and as a historian of opera that overshadowed his creative work. It was for his research on Giuseppe Bonno (a contemporary of Gluck), Cavalli and Venetian opera, Antonio Cesti and the development of opera and oratorio in Vienna that his reputation rested. True, Oxford put on his charming opera *Incognita* in a student performance under Sir Jack Westrup in 1951, but otherwise, apart from the rare broadcast from Austria, his operas remain unknown, and *Die Bakchantinnen* is the first of his operas to reach CD.

He wrote five operas between 1921 and 1931, and *Die Bakchantinnen*, for which he supplied his own libretto in 1930, was his last. Premièred in Vienna under Clemens Krauss the following year, it leaves no doubts about his mastery of dramatic pacing and momentum nor about the quality of his musical imagination. Wellesz's musical language is tonal and direct in appeal, and though he was close to the Schoenberg–Berg–Webern circle (he was Schoenberg's first biographer), he is very different from them. He is a master of the orchestra and writes effectively for the voice, as in Agave's exchanges with Ino in Act II. Almost the most impressive thing is the extensive (and often high-lying) choral writing. The choir plays a prominent role throughout, and Wellesz's choral writing is consistently powerful. What impresses – more than the dramatic characterization – is the sense of line, which is so much stronger than in Schreker, whose refined palette and exotic scoring are far removed from his world. Unlike Schreker, Wellesz never set great store by pure harmonic effect. Melodic lines are often angular but always move purposefully, and there is atmosphere and a strong responsiveness to dramatic mood. The cast is strong, in particular Roberta Alexander's Agave, even if Thomas Mohr's Dionysos shows the occasional sign of strain. The chorus and orchestra give a good account of themselves under Gerd Albrecht. The recording balance is well judged and the overall sound is very good. The notes are in German and English, but not in French, and the libretto is not offered in translation. Let us hope that Orfeo will go on to record *Alkestis* and the often enchanting *Incognita*.

WERT, Giaches de (1535–96)

Madrigals: *Ahì, come soffirò; Amor che sai; L'anima mia ferita; Con voi giocando, Amor; Crudelissima doglia; Del vago Mincio; Dica chi vuoi; Dolci spoglie; Forsennata grivada; Giunto a la tomba; Io non son però; M'ha punt'Amor; Misera, che farò; Non sospirar, pastor; Nova amor, nove fiamme, e nova legge; Occhi, de l'alma mia; O come vaneggiate, Donna; Questi odorate fiori; Soccorete, bem mio; Solo e pensoso; Sorgi e rischiara; Vago augeletto; Vezzosi augelli; Voglia mi vien; Voi ch'ascoltate*
(B) **(*) HM HMX 2901621. Cantus Cöln, Junghänel

Giaches de Wert was one of the most notable of the Flemish composers who travelled abroad to work in Italy. He was Monteverdi's predecessor in Mantua at the court of Count Alfonso. Over half a century, between 1558 and 1608, he published 16 books of madrigals, and the present well-contrasted selection dips into nearly all of them, but concentrates mainly on Book 7, published in 1581. The opening madrigal, *Vezzosi augelli* ('Graceful Birds among the Green Branches') is charmingly light-hearted, but many of the other settings are concerned with the trials and disappointments of love. *Forsennata grivada 'O te che porte'* ('Frantically she cried: "O you who bear away part of me with you"') is passionately declamatory and strongly sung here, but *Dolci spoglie* and *Misera, che farò* are very doleful indeed. Yet there is light relief too, and *Con voi giocando, Amor* is a charming scherzando. As in a previous (deleted) selection from Anthony Rooley's Consort of Musicke, De Wert certainly emerges here as a composer of expressive depth and personality, with a fine feeling for words. The Cologne performances, like their English predecessors, are richly blended, expressive and animated. Perhaps they are a shade too refined, not Italianate enough in feeling, but they are still very enjoyable and are excellently recorded.

WEYSE, Christoph Ernst Friedrich (1774–1842)

Symphonies 1 in G min., DF117; 2 in C, DF118; 3 in D, DF119
**(*) da capo 8.224012. Royal Danish O, Schønwandt

The example of Haydn affected Weyse strongly, and the minor-key symphonies in particular are reminiscent of Haydn's *Sturm und Drang* symphonies. Michael Schønwandt gives vital yet sensitive accounts of all three symphonies and is well served by the engineers. This lively music is worth investigating.

Piano Sonatas 5 in E; 6 in B flat; 7 in A min.; 8 in G min.
** da capo 8.224140. Trondhjem

The German-born Weyse played a key role in the development of song in Denmark, but he was also a fine pianist and, among other things, introduced some of the Mozart concertos to Copenhagen. These sonatas come from 1799, though the *Eighth in G minor* was not published until 1818. They are very much in the tradition of Clementi, Haydn and C. P. E. Bach, whose pupil Weyse nearly became. The *Eighth* even suggests the Beethoven of Op. 26. They employ a limited range of pianistic devices but have a certain grace. Thomas Trondhjem gives very acceptable performances and is decently recorded.

Sovedrikke (The Sleeping Draught)
**(*) da capo 8.224149. Soloists, Sokkelund Ch., Danish R.
   Sinf., Bellincampi

The Sleeping Draught was mounted in 1809 to great acclaim: the present issue is its first recording and indeed the first of any of Weyse's operas. The action is not easily summarized and calls for nine characters who are all pretty two-dimensional. There is scant opportunity for characterization and perhaps the most impressive things are the multi-movement finales: that of the first act runs for some 19 minutes. The cast is generally very good and the singing never falls below a decent level of accomplishment, and the sole aria (a kind of catalogue aria) of the baritone Guido Paëvatalu gives much pleasure. The Danish Radio Sinfonietta under Giordano Bellincampi are lively and enthusiastic, and the recording is eminently well balanced and warm. It comes with extensive and authoritative essays by Jørgen Hansen on the historical background and the development of the singspiel in Denmark as well as on Weyse himself. *Sovedrikke* is a fresh and pleasing entertainment for which few would make great claims but which has a lot of charm and is well worth hearing.

WHITE, Robert (c. 1538–74)

Motets: *Christe qui lux es; Domine quis habitavit; Portio mea Domine; Regina coeli*

◉ (M) *** Cal. CAL 6623. Clerkes of Oxenford, Wulstan – TALLIS: *Mass Puer natus est* etc. *** ◉

Robert White's style of writing has a basic restraint and often shows a gentle, Dowland-like melancholy, so striking at the opening of *Domine quis habitavit*. But this is often offset by the soaring trebles, especially in the ravishing *Portio mea Domine*, while *Christe qui lux es*, the last motet on this record, is very touching indeed. Glorious performances by Wulstan and the Clerkes of Oxenford, who have the full measure of this repertoire. The analogue recording could hardly be bettered. Not to be missed.

WIDOR, Charles-Marie (1844–1937)

Symphony 3 for Organ & Orchestra, Op. 69

*** Chan. 9785. Tracey (organ of Liverpool Cathedral), BBC PO, Tortelier – GUILMANT: *Symphony 2 for Organ & Orchestra, Op. 91*; FRANCK: *Choral 2* ***

Widor's *Third Symphony* for organ and orchestra, although in two sections, moves in a series of episodes: *Adagio – Andante* (introducing a luscious string tune) – *Allegro* (end of first movement); *Vivace – Tranquillamente – Allegro* (which with its horn calls and galloping energy brings a curious reminder of Franck's *Chasseur maudit*); finally comes an overwhelmingly majestic *Largo* with the chorale melody shared by organ and orchestra, bursting at the seams in sheer amplitude. The decibels of the coda are worthy of the finest speakers. Ian Tracey makes the most of his opportunities, as does Tortelier. Certainly the huge Liverpool organ and the resonant cathedral acoustics seem custom made for such spectacle and the Chandos engineers capture it all with aplomb.

Suite for Flute & Piano, Op. 34

(N) *** EMI 5 57813-2. Pahud, Le Sage – FRANCK: *Flute Sonata*; STRAUSS: *Flute Sonata* ***

Widor's *Suite for Flute and Piano* is his most popular work outside his organ music. In four charming movements it provides a delightful makeweight on Pahud's outstanding disc for the unusual coupling of the Franck and Strauss *Violin Sonatas* transcribed for flute.

SOLO ORGAN MUSIC

Bach Memento (Suite); Marche Nuptiale, Op. 64; 3 Nouvelles Pièces, Op. 87; Early versions of movts from the Symphonies: 1 (Allegro & Finale); 2 (Prélude); 3 (Marcia & Finale)

(N) **(*) Van Oosten (Cavaillé-Coll Organ in Saint-Sermin, Toulouse)

This disc will be of interest primarily to organists and the composer's admirers. Widor wrote anything from three to (mainly) five versions of his organ symphonies, often making significant changes, with the examples here only a few of many alternatives. Of the three *Nouvelles Pièces*, the second, *Mystique*, is the most colourful and interesting; the last brings the maximum bravura, as does the *Marche Nuptiale*. Easily the most attractive music here is the *Bach Memento*, creative transcriptions of keyboard and instrumental pieces, plus a chorale (*Wachet auf*) and the final chorus from the St Matthew Passion. Ben van Oosten is a sympathetic exponent and the superb organ is recorded spectacularly.

Symphonies 1 in C min.; 2 in D, Op. 13/1–2

(N) **(*) ASV CDDCA 1165. Nolan (organ of Liverpool Metropolitan Cathedral)

Widor's two early symphonies have seven and six movements respectively and, as the composer tends to meander, one feels a single, more succinct work could have been created by using the best movements from each. The scalic writing of the opening *Prelude* of the *First* is not very memorable; the following *Allegretto* is gentle and relaxed, but it is only in the third-movement *Intermezzo* that the work really springs to life, dancing over a strong theme in the pedals. The following *Adagio* makes a typical calm interlude, before the bold *March Pontificale* arrives, easily the most memorable movement in either work, and sounding splendid here. Then we have another *Meditation* before the robust fugal finale.

The *Praeludium circulaire* which opens the *Second Symphony* certainly goes round in circles, but the following *Pastoral* has genuine charm. The *Andante* is another of those movements which are like the music an organist plays while the collection is being taken; but the following plainsong-based *Salve Regina* brings more movement, before leading to the penultimate, spacious but uneventful *Adagio*, before the joyous, buoyant finale brings music which at last memorably blazes with vigour and has a catchy ostino for its main theme. Joseph Nolan obviously has none of our misgivings about Widor's meandering, and he plays both works with a fine mixture of robust vigour and well-sustained calm. The fine Liverpool organ is very well recorded and obviously suits this repertoire in Nolan's hands.

Symphonies 2 in D, Op. 13/2; 8 in B, Op. 42/4

*** BIS CD-1007. Fagius (organ of Kallio Church, Helsinki)

The Swedish organist Hans Fagius plays two Widor symphonies, the *Second in D major* and the *Eighth in B major*, on a new instrument made by the Swedish makers Akerman and Lund. The instrument itself is five years old and is modelled on the symphonic organs of Cavaillé-Coll tradition with which César Franck and Widor were so closely associated. Its disposition was the work of Kurt Lueders of Paris. Hans Fagius serves the music well and the engineers produce particularly impressive results. The opening *Allegro* of the *Eighth Symphony* gives a good idea of the impressive range this disc covers.

Symphonies 3 in E min., Op. 13/2: excerpts: Prélude; Adagio; Finale. 4 in F min., Op. 13/4; 9 (Gothique), Op. 70

(M) *** Warner Elatus (ADD) 2564 60341-2. Alain (Cavaillé-Coll organ of L'Eglise St-Germain, St Germain-en-Laye)

In the hands of Marie-Claire Alain, the St Germain organ sounds very orchestral, and the colouring of the gentle *Adagio* (a perpetual canon) of the *Third Symphony*, and the *Andante cantabile* of No. 4 are quite haunting. The spectacular Wagnerian finale of this *E minor Symphony* (played in the revised, 1901 version) with its cascading sextuplets is not musically as well focused as the more famous *Toccata*, which closes its successor, but it sounds very exciting here and, as it ends gently, the opening *Toccata* of No. 4 makes a bold contrast. The *Gothic Symphony* has a notable third movement in which a Christmas chant (*Puer natus est nobis*) is embroidered fugally. The final section is a set of variations, and the Gregorian chant is reintroduced in the pedals. These are classic performances, given spacious, analogue sound, with just a touch of harshness to add a little edge to *fortissimos*.

Symphonies 3 in E min., Op.13/2; 6 in G min., Op. 42/2; 3 Nouvelles pièces, Op. 87

*** ASV CDDCA 1106. Patrick (Coventry Cathedral organ)

For the second issue in their spectacular Widor series, ASV have turned to David Patrick and the organ of Coventry Cathedral, of which he is obviously a master. If less obviously suited to this repertoire than a French organ, it still sounds very impressive. Unlike Marie-Claire Alain he plays the *Third Symphony* complete, but he and the organ are at their finest in the *Sixth*, with its grand opening and equally bold *Marcia* finale. They frame a gentle *Adagio* and a hushed *Cantabile*, with the most characteristic movement, a brilliant scherzando-like *Intermezzo*, as the work's centrepiece. Patrick plays this superbly, effectively exploiting his organ's wide range of dynamic.

Symphony 5 in F min., Op. 42/1

*** Chan. 9271. Tracey (organ of Liverpool Cathedral), BBC PO, Tortelier – GUILMANT: *Symphony 1 for Organ & Orchestra* ***; POULENC: *Concerto* **(*)

The long reverberation-period of Liverpool Cathedral gives a special character to Widor's *Fifth Symphony*, especially the mellow central movements. Ian Tracey makes the most of the colouristic possibilities of his fine instrument and also uses the widest possible range of dynamics, with the tone at times shaded down to a distant whisper. Yet the famous *Toccata* expands gloriously if without the plangent bite of a French instrument.

Symphony 5; Marche pontificale (from *Symphony 1*); *Mystique, Op. 67/2*

(N) (BB) ** Hyp. Helios CDH 55144. Hill (organ of Westminster Abbey)

David Hill gives a fine performance of the *Symphony*, and his pair of encores are well chosen and well contrasted. However, the Westminster Abbey organ as recorded is very recessed and the quieter detail does not always come through too well, although the famous *Toccata* sounds magnificently full-blooded.

Symphonies 5; 6 in G min., Op. 42/1–2

(N) *** Discovery Cypres CYP 1631. Sehnhave (organ of Katarina Church, Stockholm)

The new Van den Heuvel organ in the Katarina Church, Stockholm, is admirably suited to Widor, having weighty pedals and a wide range of colourful registration, while the church acoustic provides an ambience which affords clarity of detail. Both of Kristiaan Sehnhave's performances are full of life and employ a wide dynamic range, and no one could complain that the famous finale of No. 5 and the tumultuous closing movement of the *Sixth Symphony* are in any way lacking in energy or spectacle.

Symphonies 5 in F min.; 7 in A min., Op. 42/3

☞ *** ASV CDDCA 958. Parker-Smith (Van den Heuvel organ), St Eustache, Paris

Jane Parker-Smith is a complete master of this repertoire (and she shows that it does not always have to be played on a traditional Cavaillé-Coll instrument). The organ at St Eustache, Paris is new (1967), and is Netherlands-built. It is magnificent. Not only are the big tuttis, as in the finale of the *Seventh Symphony*, superbly expansive, but the organ has a ravishingly rich palette and a warm sonority to deal with Widor's gentler ideas, like the *Andante cantabile* and *Adagio* of the *Fifth* and the inner movements of No. 7, and particularly the *Allegro ma non troppo*, where the gently murmuring semiquavers flow along sensuously like a warm summer breeze. Because of this natural clarity of internal focus Jane Parker-Smith is able to use a very wide dynamic range and in the supreme test, the masterly *Toccata* which closes the *Fifth*, the calm at the centre of the storm does not lose contact with the listener, and the great reprise of the main theme, with thundering pedals, is unforgettable.

Symphonies 5; 10 (Romane), Op. 73

(N) (BB) **(*) Arte Nova 74321 79587-2. Von Blohn (Späth organ of Hildegardskirche, St Gilbert)

Christian von Blohn has chosen to couple the *Fifth Symphony* with the *Tenth*, based on Gregorian plainchants and providing another spectacular finale, although after all the excitement there is a a closing relaxation. Both performances have plenty of rhythmic energy and the Hildegardskirche organ brings a reedy patina to the climax of the famous *Toccata* to sound more like a French organ than its competitors, even if it loses something in richness of sonority. A fine bargain just the same.

Symphony 8 in B, Op. 42/4

*** ASV CDDCA 1109. Fisell (organ of Liverpool Metropolitan Catholic Cathedral) (with COCHEREAU: *Variations sur un vieux Noël*)

It is good that the fine organ in Liverpool's Catholic Cathedral is at last receiving attention from the recording companies. Even if the circular building provides a very generous 8-second reverberation, even when the pedals get going, detail is not too muddied, and the reeds have a remarkably spicy French character. This is obvious at the powerful opening of the *B flat Symphony*, and even more so in the variations of the *Andante*. The pungent brilliance of the closing peroration is remarkable.

For his encore Jeremy Fisell has skilfully transcribed Pierre Cochereau's improvised variations on an old French carol, as played live by the composer and recorded on LP on Christmas Eve 1972. His own performance is thrillingly spontaneous, as if he were himself improvising. The animated first variation sets off exuberantly. Variation 4 is particularly eartickling, and the *Toccata* finale is a *tour de force*.

Symphony 10 in D (Romane), Op. 73; Suite Latine, Op. 86
*** MDG. 316 0406-2. Van Oosten (Cavaillé-Coll organ, at Sermin, Toulouse)

Ben van Oosten's gleaming registration at the opening of the *Symphonie Romane* is quite dazzling, yet the central *Choral* and *Cantilène* (both based on plainchant from the Easter liturgy) are wonderfully serene. The cascading finale achieves a spectacular climax (still featuring the plainsong) then makes an extended diminuendo, culminating when the opening theme is reintroduced. The *Suite Latine*, one of Widor's last works and written when he was 83, again uses plainsong, but more introspectively. In van Oosten's hands the central *Beatus vir*, *Lamento* and *Adagio* are gently withdrawn in colour and feeling, so that the exuberant finale is the more telling. These are undoubtedly distinguished performances, very well recorded on an impressively sonorous Cavaillé-Coll organ.

WIENIAWSKI, Henryk (1835–80)

(i) *Violin Concertos 1–2;* (ii) *Caprice in A min.* (arr. Kreisler); *Obertass-Mazurka, Op. 19/1; Polonaise de concert 1 in D, Op. 4; Polonaise brillante 2, Op. 21; Scherzo-tarantelle, Op. 16*
☞ (M) *** EMI (ADD) 5 66059-2. Perlman; (i) LPO, Ozawa; (ii) Sanders

Violin Concertos 1–2; Fantaisie brillante on Themes from Gounod's Faust, Op. 20
(BB) *** Naxos 8.553517. Bisengaliev, Polish Nat. RSO, Wit

Violin Concertos 1–2; Légende, Op. 17
*** DG 431 815-2. Shaham, LSO, Foster – SARASATE: *Zigeunerweisen* ***

The Paganinian pyrotechnics in the first movement of Wieniawski's *First Violin Concerto*, as Shaham readily demonstrates can be made to dazzle. Both soloist and orchestra are equally dashing, and lyrically persuasive in the better known *D minor Concerto*, while making an engaging encore out of the delightful *Légende*. With first-class DG recording this record is very recommendable.

Perlman also gives scintillating performances, full of flair, and is excellently accompanied. The recording, from 1973, is warm, vivid and well balanced. It is preferable to Perlman's digital re-make of the *Second Concerto*. The mid-priced reissue includes a mini-recital of shorter pieces, often dazzling, but losing some of their appeal from Perlman's insistence on a microphone spotlight. Samuel Sanders comes more into the picture in the introductions for the two *Polonaises*, although the violin still remains far too near the microphone.

Antoni Wit handles the long opening ritornello of the *F sharp minor Concerto* most impressively, and Marat Bisengaliev proves a natural, understanding soloist in both concertos, playing slow movements with warmly romantic feeling and sparkling with brilliance in the display passages and especially in the finales. The *Faust Variations* make a substantial (19-minute) and attractively tuneful bonus. Marat Bisengaliev has a fairly small, but sweet and beautifully focused tone; he is balanced naturally in relation to the orchestra, and both are very well recorded in the Polish Radio Concert Hall, which has an attractively warm acoustic.

Violin Concerto 2 in D min., Op. 22
(N) (B) *** Decca 475 6703-2 (2). Bell, Cleveland O, Ashkenazy – BRAHMS; SCHUMANN; TCHAIKOVSKY: *Violin Concertos* ***
**(*) CBC SMCD 5197. Kang, Vancouver SO, Comisiona – SCHUMANN: *Violin Concerto* **(*)
(M) (***) EMI mono 7 64251-2. Heifetz, LPO, Barbirolli – SAINT-SAENS: *Havanaise*, etc.; SARASATE: *Zigeunerweisen*; VIEUXTEMPS: *Concerto 4* (***)
(BB) (***) Naxos mono 8.110938. Heifetz, LPO, Barbirolli – SIBELIUS: *Violin Concerto;* TCHAIKOVSKY: *Violin Concerto* (***)

Wieniawski's *Second Concerto* makes an unusual but apt bonus for Joshua Bell's outstanding triptych of concertos by Brahms, Schumann and Tchaikovsky. It is a masterly performance full of flair, even if he does not find quite the same individual poetry in the big second-subject melody or in the central *Romance* as Itzak Perlman. Excellent recording, brilliant and full, and overall a remarkable bargain.

The Canadian violinist Juliette Kang, winner of the Menuhin International Competition, plays with quicksilver brilliance. Dazzlingly clear as the playing is, this is a smaller scale reading than most, largely a question of recording balance, with both violin and orchestra slightly distanced. What matters is that the performance, like that of the Schumann, is very persuasive. So Kang, light and volatile in the rapid passage-work, relaxes sweetly into the songful beauty of the motto theme, playing with a natural, unexaggerated lyricism. Both the slow movement and the outer sections of the *Légende* have a similar songful flow, natural and unaffected, while the finale has Kang and Comisiona choosing a speed that is fast and brilliant, allowing the dance rhythms to spring infectiously. A good recommendation for those who want this unique coupling.

Heifetz is in a class of his own. The concerto was recorded in 1935 with the young John Barbirolli, with whom Heifetz formed a strong rapport. It finds him at his most spontaneously lyrical, revelling in the rhapsodic argument. The central *Romance* in particular is magnetic in its hushed, meditative intensity, with the finale swaggering confidently. The sound is perhaps less vivid than the best recordings of the day, but both transfers are very good.

Capriccio-waltz, Op. 7; Gigue in E min., Op. 27; Kujawiak in A min.; Légende, Op. 17; Mazurka in G min., Op. 12/2; 2 Mazurkas, Op. 19; Polonaise 1; Russian Carnival, Op. 11; Saltarello (arr. Lenehan); Scherzo-tarantelle; Souvenir de Moscou, Op. 6; Variations on an Original Theme, Op. 15
(BB) **(*) Naxos 8.550744. Bisengaliev, Lenehan

All the dazzling violin fireworks are ready to bow here, from left-hand pizzicatos in the *Russian Carnival* to multiple stopping (and some lovely, warm lyricism) in the *Variations on an Original Theme*, plus all the dash you could ask for in the closing *Scherzo-tarantelle*, while the beautiful *Légende* (which Wieniawski dedicated to his wife as a nuptial gift) is both touchingly gentle and passionately brilliant. Marat Bisengaliev is without the larger-than-life personality of a Perlman, but he is a remarkably fine player and a stylist. John Lenehan provides his partner with admirable support throughout. The snag is the very reverberant acoustic of the Rosslyn Hill Chapel, Hampstead – so obviously empty; otherwise the sound and balance are natural enough.

WIKMANSON, Johan (1753–1800)

Johan Wikmanson is even more neglected than Berwald – though more understandably so. He spent some 30 years working for the Royal Lottery in Sweden and studied with both Kraus and the Abbé Vogler. He attained some eminence as an organist, translated Tartini's *Traité des agréments de la musique* into Swedish, and towards the end of his short life became Director of the Swedish Royal Academy of Music's conservatory.

String Quartet 2 in E min., Op. 1/2

(M) *** CRD (ADD) CRD 3361. Chilingirian Qt – BERWALD: *Quartet* ***

(M) *** CRD (ADD) CRD 33123 (2). Chilingirian Qt – ARRIAGA: *String Quartets 1–3* ***

Wikmanson was a cultured musician, but little of his music survives. His three quartets are all modelled on Haydn and were published thanks to the latter's acceptance of their dedication. While the Chilingirians do not always observe every dynamic nuance of the 1970 Critical Edition, they play the work with genuine commitment and, in the case of the slow movement, charm – though it is for the interesting 1818 Berwald *Quartet* that collectors will investigate this. The 1979 recording stands up well. The Chilingirian make out a persuasive case for this piece and are very well recorded. As can be seen, this work is available coupled with either Arriaga or Berwald.

WILBYE, John (1574–1638)

Madrigals (First Set, 1598): excerpts: *Adieu sweet Amaryllis; Alas what a wretched life; Cruel behold my ending; Die hapless man; Lady when I behold the roses* (2 versions); *Lady, your words do spite me; My throat is sore; Of joys and pleasing pains; Thus saith my Cloris bright; Thou art but young; Weep O mine eyes; When shall my wretched life; Why dost thou shoot.* (Second Set, 1609): excerpts: *Ah cannot sighs, nor tears; Draw on sweet night; O wretched man; Softly, o softly, drop my eyes; Stay, Corydon; Sweet honey-sucking bee; Yes sweet, take heed; Ye that do live in pleasures*

⊙━ (B) *** Double Decca (ADD) 476 7227 (2). Consort of Musicke, Rooley – GIBBONS; MORLEY: *Madrigals* ***

John Wilbye was one of the major figures in the English music of the period and this selection made from both his major sets of madrigals must be counted the best current available introduction to his art. The most famous madrigals such as *Draw on sweet night* and *Stay, Corydon* are matched by other sad settings like *O wretched man* and *Softly, o softly, drop mine eyes*, and while a lighter note is caught with *Adieu sweet Amaryllis* and *Sweet honey-sucking bees*, it is the melancholic nature of his finest works that give them their special character. The performances here are appealingly fresh rather than profound in their depth, but they are beautifully recorded and this anthology overall is a most important addition to the catalogue, reissued in Universal's 'Critics' Choice' series.

WILLAERT, Adrian (c. 1490–1562)

Ave Maria; Magnificat sexti toni; Missa Christus resurgens

(BB) *** Naxos 8.553211. Oxford Camerata, Summerly – RICHAFORT: *Motet: Christus resurgens* ***

Over the first half of the sixteenth century this Flemish composer was one of the key figures in Western music, instrumental in the development both of the madrigal and of church music for double chorus. From 1527 until his death he was *maestro di capella* at St Mark's in Venice, but this music dates mainly from his earlier years, when he achieved nine settings of the Mass. This splendid offering from Summerly and his Oxford camerata is the only one available, a magnificent 'parody mass', using as its base a motet by Jean Richafort, a piece included here as a prelude. Willaert's setting rises to a sublime conclusion in the extended *Agnus Dei*, in flowing polyphony. The *Magnificat* and *Ave Maria* offer inspired music too, performed with equal freshness and dedication. Vividly atmospheric sound. At Naxos price, not to be missed.

WILLAN, Healey (1880–1968)

Behold, the Tabernacle of God; Brighest and best of the Sons of the Morning; Gloria Deo per immensa saecula; Hail gladdening light; Hodie, Christus natus est; Immortal, invisible, God only wise (St Basil); Here we are in Bethlehem; How they so softly rest; Look down, O Lord; Lord enthroned in heavenly splendour; Missa brevis 4: Corde natus ex parentis (with Christmas Propers, motet, carol, and hymn); *Missa brevis 11 (Sancti Johannis Baptiste); Motets in honour of Our Lady, the Blessed Virgin Mary: I beheld her, beautiful as a dove; Fair in the face; Rise up my love; O King, all glorious; O King to whom all things do live; O Saving Victim; O Trinity most blessed Light; Preserve us, O Lord; Very Bread, Good Shepherd tend us*

*** Virgin 5 45109-2. St Mary Magdelene, Toronto Choirs, Hunter Bell

Healey Willan was born in Balham, Surrey. His musical education and training were not at a cathedral choir school but at the modest St Saviour's Church School, Eastbourne. By 1910 he had joined the London Gregorian Association and was already organist at St John the Baptist, Holland Park, which celebrated the Anglo-Cathlic ritual, and these combined experiences were profoundly to shape his musical life. In 1913 he emigrated to Canada and by 1919 he had become organist, choirmaster, musical director and composer-in-residence of one of Canada's finest churches, St Mary Magdelene's in Toronto.

Here he developed the celebration of the full Catholic ritual, teaching his choir of men and boys' choir to sing Plainsong and the Propers of the Mass in English. He then trained a second choir of men and women to sing unaccompanied, and soon this choir was moved to the rear gallery of the church – which has marvellous acoustics – and began to use the two choirs antiphonally. In 1931 the organ console was also moved to the gallery and everything was in place to create an ongoing musical tradition which became famous all over North America.

He continued as musical director for nearly fifty years and left behind him a choir of outstanding quality and an enormous amount of music. The present recording was made in 1995 to remember him tangibly on the twenty-fifth anniversary of his death. It includes the celebrated trio of 'Our Lady' motets, and some of his finest shorter works, but centres on a complete Christmas Midnight Mass with Proper and a wonderfully vibrant setting of *Hodie, Christus natus est*, but also the lovely, simple *Kyrie, Sanctus, Benedictus* and *Agnus Dei* of the *Fourth Missa brevis*. The closing *Gloria Deo* is wonderfully exultant. Willan's music exists in a tradition of Anglican and

Catholic church music which stretches back to Byrd, and the singing of the St Mary Magdalene choir reminds the listener of the great English Choirs at King's College, Cambridge, and other regional centres.

WILLIAMS, John (born 1932)

Film Music: *Close Encounters of the Third Kind; E.T.; Raiders of the Lost Ark; Star Wars Trilogy; Superman* (with COURAGE: *Star Trek: theme*)

(M) **(*) Telarc CD 80094. Cincinnati Pops O, Kunzel

The Telarc recording is certainly spectacular and the concert has a synthesized prologue and epilogue to underline the sci-fi associations. The inclusion of the famous *Star Trek* signature theme (a splendid tune) is wholly appropriate. The orchestra plays this music with striking verve, and the sweeping melody of *E.T.* is especially effective; but the overall effect is very brash, with the microphones seeking brilliance in the sound-balance (though for some that will be its attraction).

WILLIAMSON, Malcolm (1931–2003)

Double Concerto for 2 Pianos & Strings

**(*) Australian ABC Eloquence 426 483-2. Williamson, Campion, Tasmanian SO, Tuckwell – EDWARDS: *Piano Concerto* **(*); SCULTHORPE: *Piano Concerto* **(*)

Williamson's *Concerto for Two Pianos* has been recorded before (by EMI), but that is not currently available. This performance of this distinctive, but fairly tough – though by no means unapproachable – work is committed, well performed and reasonably well recorded, and is part of a valuable trilogy of rare concertos.

The Growing Castle

(*) Universal ABC Classics, Australia (ADD) 461 922-2. Elkins, Bamberg SO, Gierster – SHIELD: *Rosina*; ELGAR: *Sea Pictures* *

This recording of *The Growing Castle* was part of a project, aborted owing to illness, to record a collection of arias, of which this was all that was completed. It was forgotten for thirty years but resurrected for this Australian Heritage release. A short work, it opens very dramatically before a rather beautiful lyricism takes over, and was specially re-orchestrated by the composer at the request of the singer, Margreta Elkins, for this recording. The performance is excellent, though the recording, while quite full and vivid, sounds a bit dated, with Margreta Elkins too closely miked. It makes an unexpected bonus for Shield's sparkling *Rosina* and a fine Elgar *Sea Pictures*.

WILMS, Johann Wilhelm (1772–1847)

Symphonies 6 in D min., Op 58; 7 in C min.

(N) *** DG 474 508-2. Concerto Köln, Ehrhardt

The German-born Dutch composer, Johann Wilhelm Wilms, was an almost exact contemporary of Beethoven, as one quickly appreciates in these last two of Wilms's symphonies. He settled in Amsterdam when still in his teens, and became a key figure in Dutch music-making up to his death in 1847. Wilms's first four symphonies, completed before 1800, reflect the example of Haydn, but by the time he wrote his *D minor Symphony*, No. 6, in 1821, he had adopted a far weightier style, with prominent timpani and elaborate writing for horn, with

clean-cut themes and powerfully syncopated rhythms. The result is more like early rather than later Beethoven, and so is his *C minor Symphony*, No. 7, with hints of romanticism to come in storm-like writing. Sadly, in 1836, when it was first performed, it failed to please either the traditionalists or the romantic avant garde. The score was lost until Werner Ehrhardt and Concerto Köln resurrected the piece, two years ago, and recorded it along with its predecessor, two attractively vigorous rarities.

WIRÉN, Dag (1905–86)

Serenade for Strings in G, Op. 11

☛ (BB) *** Naxos 8.553106. Bournemouth Sinf., Studt (with Concert: *Scandinavian String Music.* ***)

The engaging *String Serenade* is Dag Wirén's one claim to international fame, and it is good to welcome an outstanding super-bargain version. The finale certainly earns its hit status, full of spontaneous, lilting energy. First-rate recording within an entirely recommendable concert of Scandinavian string music, not all of it familiar.

(i; ii) *Miniature Suite* (for cello & piano), *Op. 8b*; (ii) (Piano) *Improvisations; Little Suite; Sonatina, Op. 25; Theme & Variations, Op. 5*; (iii) *3 Sea Poems*; (iv; ii) *2 Songs from Hösthorn, Op. 13*

*** BIS CD 797. (i) Thedéen; (ii) Bojsten; (iii) Jubilate Ch., Riska; (iv) Högman

Dag Wirén was a miniaturist *Par Excellence* and few of the individual movements recorded here detain the listener for more than two or three minutes. The early (and inventive) *Theme and Variations*, Op. 5, is the longest work. Although it is slight, the *Sonatina for Piano* often touches a deeper vein of feeling than one might expect to encounter. Good performances from all concerned, and the usual truthful BIS recording.

Symphonies 2, Op. 14; 3 in C, Op. 20; Concert Overtures 1 & 2

*** CPO 999 677-2. Norrköping SO, Dausgaard

Apart from the celebrated *Serenade for Strings* (for years the signature-tune of the BBC's *Monitor* TV programme) and the *Sinfonietta Op. 7*, little of Dag Wirén's music is heard nowadays. In some ways the most appealing and natural Swedish composer of his generation, he lacks the breadth and sense of scale of the born symphonist. The *Third* (1944) was broadcast frequently during the 1940s, but even at the time it seemed thin and short-breathed and the idiom in thrall to Sibelius. The *Second Symphony* (1939) is the finer of the two, though ultimately deficient in motivic vitality and too reliant on ostinato figures. Good performances and recordings of likeable but flawed works.

WITT, Friedrich (1770–1836)

(i) *Flute Concerto in G. Symphony 6 (Sinfonie Turque) in A min.; Symphony 9 in D min.*

(N) *** MDG 329 1299-2. Hamburg SO, Moesus, (i) with Barner

Friedrich Witt is primarily famous for his so-called *Jena Symphony*, which was at one time erroneously attributed to Beethoven. The *Symphony No. 6* (printed in 1808–9), with its battery of Turkish instruments woven into the work's classical structure, is certainly a novelty. The opening movement has plenty of hearty rumbustiousness and the following slow movement (without percussion) makes an attractive lyrical contrast. The *Minuetto* has a lively rustic flavour, and the finale, with more Turkish flavourings, is enjoyable too. The *Ninth Symphony* (printed in 1818) has the lusty vigour of the *Sixth*, without the Turkish condiments, with Beethoven being an obvious model. Despite its minor key, the work is essentially optimistic and, like the *Sixth*, it has a vivacious finale. The *Flute Concerto* of 1806 is lighter in character, with plenty of classical charm and easy-going melody. The performances throughout this CD are sympathetic and the sound decent. Witt was essentially a conservative composer and, if no masterpieces have been uncovered here, his writing explores pleasing musical byways. He was one of the many composers buried beneath the weight of Beethoven's greatness.

Piano & Wind Quintet in E flat, Op. 5

*** CBC MCVD 1137. Kuerti, Campbell, Mason, Sommerville, McKay – BEETHOVEN; MOZART: *Quintets* ***

The German cellist Friedrich Witt modelled his *Quintet* with uncanny closeness on those of Beethoven and Mozart, though the *Adagio cantabile* – which opens with a bassoon solo – also brings a dash of Hummel. Unlike his predecessors, Witt also includes a *Minuet* whose Ländler-like trio is particularly engaging. Indeed, the quality of the invention is by no means to be sniffed at, with the good-humoured finale particularly successful in this vivid performance. The recording is first class – remarkably present and realistic.

WOLF, Hugo (1860–1903)

Italian Serenade in G

(***) Biddulph mono LAB 098. Budapest Qt – GRIEG; SIBELIUS: *Quartets* ***

A welcome reissue on Biddulph – the first on CD – of the 1933 pioneering *Italian Serenade*. It has a spring in its step and a lightness of touch that are almost unique, and it is well transferred here by Ward Marston. The couplings also show how special this ensemble was in the 1930s.

Italian Serenade; Penthesilea (Symphonic Poem); Scherzo and Finale; Der Corregidor (opera): Prelude and Intermezzo

(BB) *** Warner Apex 0927 49582-2. O de Paris, Barenboim

For those who only know Wolf's *Italian Serenade* and enjoy the subtle word-painting of the Lieder, this orchestral collection will come as something of a shock. The early three-part symphonic poem, *Penthesilea* (1883–5), is turbulently and voluptuously romantic in a style of post-Lisztian hyperbole, while the Prelude to *Der Corregidor* is Wagnerian in its expansive opulence. Barenboim plays both with uninhibited exuberance and almost convinces the listener that *Penthesilea* is worthy of standing alongside the music of Strauss. The *Intermezzo*, however, is almost in the style of French ballet music, and the well-known *Serenade*, of course, is similarly lightweight and sunny. The *Scherzo and Finale* of 1876–7 show the precocious skill of an eighteen-year-old: it is music of more than a little substance and felicitously scored, although Wagner briefly raises his head again in the *Finale*. Barenboim makes the very most of all these pieces, and they are played with much conviction. The recording is rather resonant but otherwise very good, and this collection is certainly recommendable at Apex price.

String Quartet in D min.; Intermezzo in E flat; Italian Serenade in G

(M) *** CPO CPO 999 529-2. Auryn Qt

String Quartet in D min.; Italian Serenade

*** Häns. C.93024. Fine Arts Qt

Hugo Wolf's massive *String Quartet* may be a student work, but in its concentration and complexity it harks back to late Beethoven, as well as to Wagner. The formidable first movement leads to a slow movement of heavenly length, here interpreted with hushed intensity by the young Auryn Quartet. Both in the *Quartet* and in the other two works, including the winningly exuberant *Italian Serenade*, the playing amply makes up in its warmth and spontaneity for any slight lack of polish. Warm, full sound.

This Hänssler Fine Arts performance is the only other version of the *Quartet* currently available, and it is well played by this long-established American group in the pleasing acoustics of the SudWestfunk Studios in Baden-Baden. However, the CPO disc is even finer and offers more music.

Goethe Lieder: Als ich auf dem Euphrat schiffte; Anakreons Grab; Die Bekehrte; Blumengruss; Dank des Paria; Epiphanias; Frühling über Jahr; Ganymed; Gleich und Gleich; Gretchen vor dem Andachtsbild der Mater dolorosa; Gutmann und Gutweib; Hoch beglückt in deiner Liebe; Kennst du das Land; Mignon Lieder I–III; Nimmer will ich dich verlieren; Phänomen; Philine; St Nepomuks Vorabend; Der Schäfer; So lang man nüchtern ist; Die Spröde; Wandrers Nachtlied

*** Hyp. CDA 67130. McGreevy, Johnson

Geraldine McGreevy, winner of the 1996 Kathleen Ferrier Award, makes a fresh and pure-toned partner for Graham Johnson in a challenging selection of Wolf's settings of Goethe, with all but two of the twenty-four songs coming from the great Goethe songbook of his maturity in 1888–9. As ever, Johnson provides the most searching and illuminating notes on each song, enhancing enjoyment greatly with his words as well as his playing, but it is good to welcome so sensitive and responsive a young Lieder-singer as McGreevy, who here triumphs over even the most demanding of challenges. So it is good to have readings of the four *Mignon* songs (the three regular ones plus *Kennst du das Land*), which bring out the mystery of the writing with the benefit of girlish tone, apt for Goethe's heroine. *Kennst du das Land* is the more moving for that, with McGreevy providing a thrilling crescendo in the last stanza, perfectly controlled. Yet she responds to the lighter songs beautifully too, with a fine feeling for word-meaning. Excellent, well-balanced sound.

Goethe Lieder: Anakreons Grab; Blumengruss; Erschaffen und Beleben; Gleich und gleich; Harfenspieler I, II & III; Ob der Koran von Ewigkeit sei?; Phänomen; Der Rattenfänger; Sie haben wegen der Trunkenheit; So lang man nüchtern ist; Spottlied; Trunken müssen wir alle sein!; Was in der Schenke waren heute. Mörike Lieder: Abschied; An die Geliebte; An eine Äolsharfe; Auf ein altes Bild; Bei einer Trauung; Elfenlied; Er ist's; Fussreise; Der Gärtner; Gebet; Gesang Weylas; Heimweh; Jägerlied; Nimmersatte Liebe; Der Tambour; Verborgenheit

(BB) *** Virgin 2×1 5 61418-2 (2). Allen, Parsons – BRAHMS: *Lieder* ***

This is an exceptionally generous (74-minute) collection of Wolf's Goethe and Mörike settings, which are much rarer, both on disc and in the recital room. Thomas Allen enters fully into the spirit of each song, and Geoffrey Parsons accompanies with characteristic imagination. Whether the words convey ardour (as in one of the best known, *An die Geliebte*), are hauntingly evocative (as in the remarkable *Harfenspieler* settings) or are exuberantly extrovert (*Der Rattenfänger*), these artists unerringly project their mood. Alas, this inexpensive reissue includes neither translations nor song summaries, but the vocal treasure offered here and the excellence both of performances and of Andrew Keener's recording balance at Abbey Road carries the day.

Goethe Lieder: *Anakreons Grab; 3 Harfenspieler Lieder*
*** Decca (IMS) 458 189-2. Goerne, Concg. O, Chailly –
  BRUCKNER: *Symphony 6 in A* ***

The three *Harfenspieler* songs, setting verses from the novel, *Wilhelm Meister*, as well as *Anakreons Grab* make a valuable and generous fill-up for Chailly's superb, refined reading of the Bruckner symphony. Matthias Goerne with his headily lyrical baritone makes an ideal, thoughtful interpreter, well balanced in the warmly atmospheric recording.

Mörike Lieder: *An eine Äeolsharfe; Bei einer Trauung; Denk' es, o Seele!; Heimweh; Im Frühling; Jägerlied; Lied eines Verliebten*
(M) *** BBC (ADD) BBCB 8015-2. Pears, Britten – BRITTEN: *On his island*, etc.; SCHUBERT: *7 Lieder* *** (with ARNE: *Come away death; Under the greenwood tree*; QUILTER: *O mistress mine*; WARLOCK: *Take, o take those lips away*; TIPPETT: *Come unto these yellow sands* ***)

In the BBC's sensitive performances of seven of Wolf's Mörike settings – recorded at the Snape Maltings in 1972, not long before Britten was stricken by terminal illness – these unfailingly convey a sense of spontaneity, capturing the inspiration of the moment in a way that is rare on disc, thanks above all to Britten's accompaniments. Excellent radio sound.

(i) *3 Christmas Songs:* *Auf ein altes Bild; Nun wandre, Maria; Schlafendes Jesuskind;* (ii) *3 Michelangelo Lieder: Alles endet, was entstehet; Fühlt meine Seele; Wohl denk' ich oft*
(M) *** BBC (ADD) BBCB 8011-2. (i) Pears; (ii) Shirley-Quirk, Britten – SCHUBERT: *11 Lieder****

John Shirley-Quirk in his singing of three of Wolf's Michelangelo settings at the 1971 Aldeburgh Festival has never been more mellifluous on disc, just as sensitive in his treatment of Lieder as the others, and the whole programme is delightfully rounded off by Pears's charming performances of the three Wolf Christmas songs. Excellent sound.

Italienisches Liederbuch (complete)
⊶ *** Hyp. CDA 66760. Lott, Schreier, Johnson
⊶ (M) *** EMI (ADD) 5 62650-2 [5 62651-2]. Schwarzkopf, Fischer-Dieskau, Moore
(*) Ondine ODE 998-2D. Isokoski, Skovhus, Viitasalo

Graham Johnson conjures up music-making full of magic, compelling from first to last. Yet, so far from being intrusive in his playing, he consistently heightens the experience, drawing out from Felicity Lott one of her most intense and detailed performances on record, totally individual. Peter Schreier, one of the supreme masters of Lieder today, also responds to this characterful accompanist; and having a tenor instead of the usual baritone brings many benefits in this sharply pointed sequence. The triumph of this issue is

crowned by the substantial booklet provided in the package, containing Johnson's uniquely perceptive commentary on each song – alone worth the price of the disc. Excellent sound.

The classic Schwarzkopf–Fischer-Dieskau set now reappears – rightly – as one of EMI's 'Great Recordings of the Century'. Few artists today can match the searching perception of these two great singers in this music, with Fischer-Dieskau using his sweetest tones and Schwarzkopf ranging through all the many emotions inspired by love. Gerald Moore is at his finest, and the well-balanced (1969) recording sounds better than ever.

The Ondine version offers a well-mannered reading, generally well sung but undercharacterized to the point of blandness. One could never imagine that either of the singers in their painstaking politeness might represent a character close to the soil. The accompaniments of Marita Viitasalo are similarly faithful but dull.

Spanisches Liederbuch (complete)
⊶ (M) *** DG (ADD) 457 726-2 (2). Schwarzkopf, Fischer-Dieskau, Moore
(B) *** EMI double forte 5 75181-2 (2). von Otter, Bär, Parsons

In this superb DG reissue, the sacred songs provide a dark, intense prelude, with Fischer-Dieskau at his very finest, sustaining slow tempi impeccably. Schwarzkopf's dedication comes out in the three songs suitable for a woman's voice; but it is in the secular songs, particularly those which contain laughter in the music, where she is at her most memorable. Gerald Moore is balanced rather too backwardly – something the transfer cannot correct – but gives superb support.

Completed barely six months before Geoffrey Parsons's untimely death, the EMI set of the *Spanish Songbook* makes a superb memorial to that great accompanist, here working with two of the most searching and stylish Lieder singers of the present generation. They opt for an order of the songs quite different from the original published order, seeking to find 'a dramatic shape that worked in the atmosphere of a concert'. Quite apart from Parsons's superb contribution, the performances of both soloists vie with those on the classic DG set with Schwarzkopf and Fischer-Dieskau. For the lighter songs von Otter uses a much brighter tonal range than elsewhere, though in such a song as *In dem Schatten meiner Locken* she remains more intimate than Schwarzkopf, pointing the words and phrases with comparable character. The double forte reissue is a fine bargain, though no texts and translations are included.

WOLF-FERRARI, Ermanno
(1876–1948)

L'amore medico: Overture. Il campiello: Intermezzo; Ritornello. La dama bomba: Overture. I gioielli della Madonna (suite). I quattro rusteghi: Prelude & Intermezzo. Il segreto di Susanna: Overture
*** ASV CDDCA 861. RPO, Serebrier

L'amore medico: Overture & Intermezzo; Il Campiello: Intermezzo; Ritornello; La dama bomba: Overture; I gioielli della Madonna: Suite; I quattro rusteghi: Prelude & Intermezzo; Il segreto di Susanna: Overture & Intermezzo
⊶ (B) *** EMI double forte 5 75160-2 (2). ASMF, Marriner
  – CHERUBINI: *Overtures* ***

Although the situation is currently changing, Wolf-Ferrari has long held a permanent place in the catalogue only with recordings of his operatic *intermezzi* – not surprising, perhaps, when they are so readily tuneful and charmingly scored. Serebrier conjures at times exquisite playing from the RPO (especially the strings) and, even though he takes Susanna's sparkling overture slightly slower than usual, it is hardly less successful. What is specially memorable is his delicate treatment of the gossamer string-pieces from *I quattro rusteghi* and the *Ritornello* from *Il Campiello*, which almost have a Beecham touch. The ASV recording, made in the Henry Wood Hall, is slightly more open and indeed marginally more transparent and fresh.

Marriner and the Academy are only marginally below their finest form here, and this concert makes a delightful entertainment with everything elegantly played and warmly (if resonantly) recorded. In the concertante *Intermezzo* from *L'amore medico*, Stephen Orton takes the cello solo most winningly.

Il Campiello: Prelude; Ritornello; Intermezzo. The Inquisitive Woman: Overture. Jewels of the Madonna: Neapolitan Dance. The School for Fathers: Intermezzo. Susanna's Secret: Overture. Serenade for Strings

(M) *** Berlin Classics 0091772BC. Berlin RSO, Rögner

Rögner's collection comes from the late 1970s and has the advantage of natural, warmly resonant analogue sound which gives these attractive pieces a pleasing hall ambience. He offers an aptly paced, sparkling account of *Susanna's Secret*, while the sprightly *Inquisitive Woman Overture*, with its songful theme for the oboe, is hardly less winning, and a real find. The Berlin Orchestra play it with the lightest rhythmic touch, and are hardly less persuasive in the *Neapolitan Dance*, a brilliant show-piece of which they take full advantage. The charming *Intermezzo* from *The School for Fathers* is given with fragile delicacy and the music from *Il Campiello* is just as delectable; both the *Prelude* and *Ritornello* have a haunting atmosphere. The programme ends with a captivating account of the *String Serenade*, which charms and touches the listener by turns.

(i) Cello Concerto in C (Invocazione), Op. 31. Sinfonia Brevis in E flat, Op. 28

(BB) *** CPO CPO 999 278-2. (i) Rivinius; Frankfurt RSO, Francis

Wolf-Ferrari's *Cello Concerto*, like the *Violin Concerto*, is a considerable work and its title *Invocazione* is well chosen. The opening movements are both marked *Tranquillo*, and even the use of a theme very like 'Three blind mice' does not rob the first of its serenity. The gay, dancing finale maintains the work's lightness of texture and feeling. The first movement of the *Sinfonia brevis* tries to sustain this tranquil mood, and finally does so at the close, after frequent interruptions, often quite boisterous. The jaunty *Capriccio* which follows acts as a colourful scherzo and might well be another of those intermezzi. The *Adagio* is both a barcarolle and a threnody, and again features a solo cello, pensive and darker voiced than in the concerto. The finale dances away in a jiggy tarantella rhythm and ends in cheerful buoyancy. The performances here are full of life and feeling, and are given a vividly spacious recording.

(i) Violin Concerto in D, Op. 26; Serenade for Strings

(BB) *** CPO CPO 999 271-2. (i) Hoelscher, Frankfurt RSO, Francis

Wolf-Ferrari's warmly romantic *Violin Concerto* captures the listener's ear from the very opening, and Ulf Hoelscher is a superbly responsive soloist. The *Romanza* opens with ethereal delicacy, but passion soon comes to the surface and is always ready to burst into the *Improviso* third movement. The jolly, sparkling Rondo finale is in the best traditional mode of classical concerto finales. Again Hoelscher is on his mettle: he never made a better recording than this, and his exquisite playing of the long cadenza-soliloquy towards the movement's close is especially fine. The *String Serenade* is an extraordinarily accomplished and individual four-movement student work, genuinely inspired, and it is most persuasively played here, with a more passionate less innocent performance than Heinz Rögner gives in his collection above. First-class recording.

The Jewels of the Madonna: Dances and Intermezzi. School for Fathers: Overture & Intermezzo. Susanna's Secret: Overture

(***) Testament mono SBT 1327. Philh. O, Mackerras –
PONCHIELLI: *La Gioconda: Dance of the Hours* ***;
VERDI: Overtures and ballet music (***)

As the opening section in this mixed bag of Mackerras's recordings from the 1950s, the charming Wolf-Ferrari pieces are delectably done, not just popular favourites like the overture to *Susanna's Secret* and the second *Intermezzo* from *The Jewels of the Madonna*, but the other miniatures too. The mono recording is clear and well balanced.

CHAMBER MUSIC

Duo in G min., Op. 33b; Introduzione e balleto, Op. 35 (both for violin and cello); String Trios: in B min. (1894); in A min., Op. 32

(M) *** CPO 999 624-2. Deutsch String Trio (members)

The early *String Trio* of 1894 sounds not in the least immature and has a nostalgic lyricism that reminds one a little of Schubert. Many years later, in 1947, Wolf-Ferrari wrote the *Duo in G minor* (originally intended for viola d'amore and viola da gamba). It is a delightfully inventive work, also in three movements, with a charming barcarolle as its centrepiece and a light-hearted finale, which suddenly darkens and becomes almost despondent, until the composer recovers his spirits.

The mature *A minor Trio* of 1945 is also ambivalent in mood, although it has a tranquil central *Pastorale*. Once again the finale opens wittily and energetically but has its moments of hesitancy, and a passage of strange bitter-sweet melancholy appears at its heart, which brings an uncertain close. The Deutsch String Trio are right inside this music and play it very persuasively indeed.

The *Introduzione* is much lighter in style and feeling, with a charming folksy element: the *Ballet* is a sentimental Viennese waltz, treated with great delicacy, yet expresses that underlying *fin de siècle* insecurity that characterizes all these remarkably rewarding works. It is marvellously played: the two instruments blend into a perfect partnership and their rubato sounds absolutely natural and spontaneous. First-class recording, too.

Piano Trios 1 in D, Op. 5; 2 in F sharp, Op. 7

*** ASV CDDCA 935. Raphael Trio

Wolf-Ferrari wrote these two ambitious *Piano Trios* at the very beginning of his career. They may not be masterpieces, but the large-scale first movements show him as a fine craftsman, and more importantly, his themes already show the gift of easy memorability which marks his other major works. So the slow movement of No. 1 is like a Mascagni lament, and the chattering finale might be a sketch for an operatic interlude. No. 2 is odder in its layout, with the first movement twice as long as the other two put together, but with well-disciplined performances from the Raphael Trio, an American group, the colour and charm of the writing is persuasively brought out.

WOOD, Charles (1866–1926)

Anthems and Hymn Anthems: *Ascension Hymn; The Earth trembled; Expectans expectavi; God omnipotent reigneth; Haec dies; I am risen; I will call upon God; Jesu, the very thought is sweet; O King most high; O Lord rebuke me not; O Lord that seest from yon starry Heights; O Most Merciful; O thou sweetest source; Sunlight all golden; This is the Day; 'Tis the Day of Resurrection; True love's the gift.* (i) **(Organ)** *Preludes: Martyrs; Old 104th; Old 132nd; Old 136th; Psalm 23; York Tune*

*** Priory PRCD 754. Gonville & Caius College, Cambridge Ch., Webber; Roberts; (i) Unglow (organ)

The career of the Anglo-Irish composer Charles Wood ran parallel with that of his better-known colleague, Stanford, whom he succeeded as Professor of Composition at the Royal College of Music. Wood's music is less flamboyant, less innovatory than Stanford's but his anthems and hymn anthems form a rich part of the fabric of Anglican church music. If the opening *O thou sweetest source* is impressive in its very simplicity, the gleaming brightness of *Sunlight all golden* does not belie its title, and *God omnipotent reigneth*, underpinned by the organ, is boldly arresting. Yet one of the most memorable items, the unaccompanied *Jesu, the very thought is sweet*, is quite brief, eloquently setting a melody from the *Piae Cantiones* of 1582. If Wood's harmonic language is not forward-looking, his music is of quality and often individual, as in his Latin settings, the jubilant *Haec dies* and the very touching *Expectans expectavi*, written in memory of his son, killed in the First World War. The Organ *Preludes* draw on old church melodies and are comparatively conventional in style, but very well played, and here used effectively as interludes. Indeed the presentation could hardly be bettered, the choir singing with fervour and rich tonal blending. The recording is excellent.

WOOD, Haydn (1882–1959)

Apollo Overture; A Brown Bird Singing (paraphrase for orchestra); *London Cameos* (suite); *Miniature Overture: The City; St James's Park in the Spring; A State Ball at Buckingham Palace. Mannin Veen* (Manx tone-poem); *Moods* (suite): *Joyousness* (concert waltz). *Mylecharane* (rhapsody); *The Seafarer (A nautical rhapsody); Serenade to Youth; Sketch of a Dandy*

⊕ *** Marco Polo 8.22340-2. Czech-Slovak RSO (Bratislava), Leaper

Haydn Wood, an almost exact contemporary of Eric Coates and nearly as talented, spent his childhood on the Isle of Man, and much of his best music is permeated with Manx folk-themes (original or simulated). *Mannin Veen* ('Dear Isle of Man') is a splendid piece, based on four such folksongs.

The companion rhapsody, *Mylecharane*, also uses folk material, if less memorably, and *The Seafarer* is a wittily scored selection of famous shanties, neatly stitched together. The only failure here is *Apollo*, which uses less interesting material and is over-ambitious and inflated. But the English waltzes are enchanting confections and *Sketch of a Dandy* is frothy and elegant. Adrian Leaper is clearly much in sympathy with this repertoire and knows just how to pace it; his Czech players obviously relish the easy tunefulness and the sheer craft of the writing. With excellent recording in what is surely an ideal acoustic, this is very highly recommendable.

A Day in Fairyland Suite: Dance of a Whimsical Elf; An Evening Song; Frescoes suite; London Landmarks: Horse Guards March; A Manx Rhapsody; May-Day Overture; Paris Suite; Roses of Picardy; Soliloquy; Variations on a Once Popular Humorous Song

*** Marco Polo 8.223605. Czech-Slovak RSO (Bratislava), Tomlinson

The second CD opens with the charming *May-Day Overture*, with its dreamy sound-picture of dawn, giving way to the day's festivities. The *Variations* are effective, and the composer's *Paris Suite* introduces a distinct Gallic flavour: the *Montmartre March* is especially enjoyable. Wood's beloved Isle of Man inspired the *Manx Rhapsody*, which finds the composer again in his attractive folksy-mode, and the composer's most famous piece, *Roses of Picardy*, is a slightly dated highlight of this volume. The rest of the programme is equally enjoyable, and the performances, this time with Ernest Tomlinson, are excellent. The recording is a bit richer than in Volume 1.

Piano Concerto in D min.

*** Hyp. CDA 67127. Milne, BBC Scottish SO, Brabbins – HOLBROOKE: *Piano Concerto 1* ***

Haydn Wood writes fluently and attractively throughout both for the piano and the orchestra, and in its echoes of Grieg and Rachmaninov. With an English accent, it establishes itself as one of the more striking British piano concertos of the period. The orchestral introduction provides a grand fanfare for the entry of the piano with a strong main theme and, even when melodies enter which might have developed into drawing-room ballads, Wood ensures that they avoid banality. The slow movement is a tenderly beautiful interlude with muted strings, and the finale, built on a bold motif, leads to two grandiloquent climaxes based on the one theme which skirts banality. The result is exciting none the less, suggesting that this could become a viable repertory piece. Brilliant playing from Hamish Milne and warm, well-balanced recording.

WOOD, Hugh (born 1932)

Symphony; (i) *Scenes from Comus*

*** NMC NMCD 070. BBC SO, A. Davis; (i) with McGreevy, Norman

Hugh Wood's powerful *Symphony*, written in the late 1970s and early 1980s, is a major addition to British symphonic repertoire, in a direct line from Walton's *First*. If not so immediately approachable, it readily responds to repeated listening, for it is cogently argued and gripping from the first note to the last. Drama of a semi-theatrical nature is the composer's springboard and the opening *Tempesta* is violently histrionic, yet has an underlying dark lyricism directly related to Wagner's *Die Walküre* and the passion of Siegmund and Sieglinde. Their love motif is quoted to make the derivation clear and the long *Elegia* slow movement is headed by a classical Greek quotation which draws a connection with Siegmund's *Todesverkündigung*. Later there is an unexpected fragment from Mozart: the flute-and-drum 'ordeal' sequence in *Die Zauberflöte*. The throbbing Scherzo draws on the work's basic ideas, but fragmented into a powerful *con fuoco*. The energy subsides and with delicate colouring from horns, piccolo flute and glockenspiel we are led to the disconsolate calm of the opening of the passacaglia finale, which is finally to end the work with a passionate, triumphantly positive acclamation.

The *Scenes from Comus* are not incidental music for Milton's masque, but a highly atmospheric symphonic narrative in eight sections with vocalizations, confidently sung by Daniel Norman (Comus) and Geraldine McGreevy. As the 'Lady' of the narrative, she is enchanted by the son of Circe after being abducted in *The Wild Wood*, where in Wood's setting she responds willingly to the following orgiastic dances. The finale duet *Sabrina Fair* brings a mood of ecstatic serenity and this remarkably imaginative work ends with a peaceful epilogue. Sir Andrew Davis conducts throughout with mastery and a total identification with the music of both works, each of which resonates in the memory, but especially the symphony. The recording is splendid.

WRIGHT, Margot (1911–2000)

(i; ii) *Cello Sonata;* (iii) *Improvisation for Solo Clarinet;* (iv; ii) *3 Northumbrian Folksongs for Viola & Piano;* (ii; v) *Piano Quintet in D minor.* (vi; ii; iii) *Fear no more the heat o' the sun; 3 Songs with Clarinet Obbligato*

(M) *** Dutton CDLX 7109 (i) Phelps; (ii) Moll; (iii) Braithwaite; (iv) Wright; (v) Camilli Qt; (vi) Morgan

The earliest piece here is the *Cello Sonata* (1930) and perhaps the finest the *Piano Quintet*. Margot Wright was much in demand as a pianist and was Kathleen Ferrier's partner. Eventually her role as a practising musician and a teacher displaced composition at the centre of her life. Her language is conservative and diatonic but she has a natural feeling for line and development, as the first movement of the *Quintet* shows. There are many imaginative things in her music, which makes one regret that recognition was never sufficient to encourage her to pursue her own creative path. The *Piano Quintet* is a work of quality and played with evident dedication: the violist, incidentally, is the daughter of the composer. Very natural recorded sound.

YOST, Michél (1754–86)

Clarinet Concertos 7 in B flat; 8 in E flat; 9 in B flat; 11 in B flat

⊶ *** MDG 301 0718-2. Klöcker, Prague CO

Not many collectors will have heard of Yost before discovering this CD. But here are four delightfully bubbly concertos, brimming with excellent tunes and plenty of wit, with any moments of drama soon pushed away with sunny abandon. Like the more substantial, but no less effervescent concertos of Cartellieri on the same label, this is a delightful CD and it is hard to imagine better performances or recordings.

YSAŸE, Eugène (1858-1931)

Amitié, Op. 26

(*) BBC mono BBCL4060-2. D. Oistrakh, I. Oistrakh, LPO, Sargent – SHOSTAKOVICH: *Violin Concertos 1 & 2* *

Amitié, for two violins and orchestra, is the last of Ysaÿe's six tone-poems and is a piece steeped in the post-Wagnerian tradition which he had assimilated so completely by this time. David and Igor Oistrakh play with great eloquence and were recorded at the Royal Albert Hall in 1961 with very good sound for the period.

6 Sonatas for Solo Violin, Op. 27

⊶ (BB) *** Naxos 8.555996. Kaler
(M) *** Oehms OC 236. Schmid
*** BIS CD 1046. Kavakos
*** Chan. 8599. Mordkovitch
(B) *** Nim. 1735 (3). Shumsky – BACH; MOZART: *Violin Concertos* ***

As is well known, the six sonatas Ysaÿe published in 1924 were written for the six greatest virtuosi of the day: Szigeti, Kreisler, Enescu, Jacques Thibaud and (less well remembered nowadays) Manuel Quiroga and Matthieu Grickboom. They are held in special regard by violinists who enjoy overcoming the technical challenges they pose. Ilya Kaler was a gold medallist in the Sibelius, Paganini and Tchaikovsky competitions and is a virtuoso of the first order. These are commanding accounts, which characterize the particular qualities of each *Sonata* to impressive effect; even if it did not enjoy a competitive price advantage it would be our preferred first choice.

No one investing in Benjamin Schmid's recording (and the outlay is modest) will be disappointed, for these performances are full of imagination and this is satisfying in its own right. However, Kaler makes one see these pieces in a fresher light.

Leonid Kavakos came to notice when he recorded the first version of the Sibelius concerto for BIS, and he impresses every bit as much here.

Lydia Mordkovitch also plays with great character and variety of colour and she characterizes No. 4 (the one dedicated to Kreisler, with its references to Bach and the *Dies Irae*) superbly. These *Sonatas* can seem like mere exercises, but in her hands they sound really interesting. Natural, warm recorded sound. Recommended.

Oscar Shumsky is a player of the old school. His artistry is everywhere in evidence in this 1982 recording, in the authority and naturalness of his phrasing, the sweetness of his tone and the security of his technique. True, there are one or two moments of imperfect intonation, but there are very few performances (as opposed to recordings) where every note in these impossibly demanding pieces is in perfect place. It is all wonderfully musical and splendidly free as if Shumsky is improvising these pieces. These performances now come in a bargain box celebrating his supreme artistry which can be strongly recommended.

Solo Violin Sonatas, Op. 27/2, 3, 4 & 6

*** EMI 5 57384-2. Vengerov – BACH: *Toccata & Fugue in D min.;* SHCHEDRIN: *Balalaika; Echo Sonata* ***

Maxim Vengerov gives dazzling performances of the four Ysaÿe *Solo Sonatas*, making light of the technical problems in warmly spontaneous readings, which are plainly a labour of love. It is a pity that the other two sonatas could not be included, although the Bach *Toccata* and the Shchedrin *Balalaika* are so full of flair one would not want to do without them.

ZELENKA, Jan (1679–1745)

Complete Orchestral Works: *Capriccios 1–5; Concerto a 8 concertanti; Hipocondrie a 7 concertanti; Melodrama de St Wenceslao: Symphonia. Ouverture a 7 concertanti; Symphonie a 8 concertanti*
(M) *** CPO 999 897-2 (3). Neu-Erffönete O, Sonnentheil

A contemporary of Bach and Handel, Jan Dismas Zelenka was among the most original composers of the period but is still something of a mystery figure when no portrait survives. Unlike his great contemporaries, he remained an underling in the world of his time. Happily, his music has survived, and this fine collection of his complete orchestral works, compiled from three separate discs issued earlier, reinforces the impact made twenty-five years ago when the Berne Camerata made pioneering recordings of all but one of the pieces here, the *St Wenceslao Symphonia*. All the works, including the five multi-movement *Capriccios* and the oddly named *Hipocondrie*, involve elaborate concertante writing, and although the soloists here are not as starry as those on the earlier set (which involved Heinz Holliger and Barry Tuckwell), the use of period instruments instead of modern adds to the freshness and bite, with the natural horns, above all, breathtakingly brilliant in music that ranges wide in its emotions.

Trios Sonatas 1–6
*** ECM 462 542-2 (2). Holliger, Bourgue, Zehetmair, Thuneman, Stoll, Rubin, Jaccotte

With such a starry team it is not surprising that these performances of Zelenka's *Trio Sonatas* are so spirited and accomplished. They are scored for various colourful combinations of (almost always) two oboes and bassoon, with continuo, the violin taking the upper voice in No. 3. Zelenka's movements proceed with breathless polyphony of mounting intensity, granting neither players nor listeners any respite. So these works are better approached one at a time, stimulating as they are. Excellent if forward recording.

Trio Sonatas for 2 Oboes, Bassoon & Continuo 2, 5 & 6
*** Astrée E 8511. Ens. Zefiro

Here are three of the above sonatas which favour the scoring for a pair of oboes and bassoon and very piquant they are, although not to be taken all at one go. The playing of Ensemble Zefiro is lively, expressive and polished, and the recording is naturally balanced, with the continuo providing good support. A good choice if you want just a selection of these works.

Lamentations Jeremiae Prophete (Lamentations for Maundy Thursday, Good Friday and Easter Eve)
🎵 (BB) *** Hyp. Helios CDH 55106. Chance, Mark Ainsley, George, Chandos Bar. Players

These solo settings of the six *Lamentations* for the days leading up to Easter reinforce Zelenka's claims as one of the most original composers of his time. The spacious melodic lines and chromatic twists in the harmonic progressions are often very Bachian, but the free-flowing alternation of arioso and recitative is totally distinctive, as is the melismatic obbligato writing for oboes and recorders. The fine Deutsche Harmonia Mundi under René Jacobs has now been withdrawn, but fortunately Hyperion have reissued this hardly less moving account on their bargain Helios label. Here, too, all three soloists are excellent: Michael Chance singing with

great beauty in the setting for Maundy Thursday and in the closing music, the bass Michael George distinguishing himself on Good Friday, and the tenor John Mark Ainsley equally impressive in the music for Easter Eve. The continuo is aurally beguiling, placed in an atmospheric acoustic, and the relaxed pacing very diverting.

Litaniae de Venerabili Sacramento; Officium Defunctorum: Invitatorium; 3 Lectiones. Motets: Regina coeli laetare; Salve Regina
*** Hyp. CDA 67350. Sampson, Outram, Blaze, Gilchrist, George, Harvey, King's Ch. & Consort, King

As his instrumental music has demonstrated, Jan Dismas Zelenka was one of the most original and inspired contemporaries of Bach. However, at the Saxon court in Dresden, where he was employed for most of his career, he was kept in a subservient role. Whether that was because of his difficult personality, the music he has left to posterity provides ample reason for revering him as a master, just as Bach himself did. Like Bach, Zelenka favoured what in the early eighteenth century was coming to be regarded as the 'old-fashioned' contrapuntal style – one reason he fell out of favour with his patron. But as this fine music demonstrates, it regularly resulted in daring harmonic progressions worthy of Bach himself.

Though these works were designed for practical use in church and so are rather less radical than much of Zelenka's instrumental music, the substantial introductions demonstrate his skill and inventiveness with instruments, while the writing for voices is consistently fresh and lively. That is particularly so in the two choral works here, the *Litanies* in twelve brief sections and the final *Invitatorium* with counter-tenor soloist and chorus, which like the three *Lectiones* – each, in effect, a recitative and aria – comes from the valedictory *Officium defunctorum*, which Zelenka wrote at the time of the death of Prince August the Strong of Saxony.

The magnificent *Litanies*, for four soloists and chorus with two oboes and strings, range wide in mood and expression, with the lively theme of the second *Kyrie* returning in the final *Agnus Dei*. The motet, *Regina coeli*, is in a simpler style but has a comparable freshness, and the *Salve Regina*, reworked from music by an anonymous composer in a manner distinctive of Zelenka, is a fine extended solo cantata for soprano. With excellent soloists, led by the soprano Carolyn Sampson, Robert King, with his King's Consort and Choir, directs performances that are both moving and exhilarating.

Magnificats in C & D, ZWV 107–8
🎵 *** BIS CD 1011. Persson, Nonoshita, Tachikawa, Türk, Urano, Bach Collegium, Japan, Masaaki Suzuki – BACH: *Magnificat in D;* KUHNAU: *Magnificat in C* ***

These two *Magnificats* are quite delightful, very fresh and inventive. They are not otherwise available on CD. Masaaki Suzuki and his fine team of singers and players serve them with enthusiasm and affection, and the recorded sound is absolutely first class.

(i) Missa in D: Missa gratias agimus tibi. 5 Responsoria pro Hebdomada Sancta; Antiphon: Su tuum praesidium
*** Sup. 11 0816-2. (i) Jonášová, Mrázová, Doležal, Mikuláš, Czech PO, (i; ii) Czech Philharmonic Ch., Bělohlávek

This *Mass* (1730) is a splendid work; the *Responsoria* (for Maundy Thursday and Good Friday), were composed seven years earlier. The programme is completed with a movingly simple Marian antiphon, written after the *Mass*. These works could hardly be more authentically or persuasively presented than in these very fine Supraphon recordings from 1984. Remarkably individual music, distinctively performed and very well recorded.

Missa Dei Filii, ZWV 20; Litaniae Laurentanae, ZWV 152

☛— (M) *** DHM/BMG 82876 60159-2. Argenta, Chance, Prégardien, G. Jones, Stuttgart Chamber Ch., Tafelmusik, Bernius

This fine reissue offers not only one of Zelenka's late masses, but also a splendid *Litany*, confirming him – for all the obscurity he suffered in his lifetime – as one of the most inspired composers of his generation. The *Missa Dei Filii* ('Mass for the Son of God') is a 'short' Mass, consisting of *Kyrie* and *Gloria* only. Some of the movements into which the two sections are divided are brief to the point of being perfunctory, but the splendid soprano solo in the *Christe eleison* points forward to the magnificent setting of the *Gloria*, in which the first two sections and the last are wonderfully expansive, ending with a sustainedly ingenious fugue. It seems that Zelenka never heard that Mass, but his *Litany*, another refreshing piece, was specifically written when the Electress of Saxony was ill. Zelenka, like Bach, happily mixes fugal writing with newer-fangled concertato movements. Bernius provides well-sprung support with his period-instrument group, Tafelmusik, and his excellent soloists and choir.

I Penitenti Sepolcro del Redentore (The Penitents at the Tomb of the Redeemer)

(M) *** Sup. SU 3785-2. Kožená, Prokeš, Pospíšil, Capella Regia Musicalis, Hugo

Bach himself understood that, though this second of Zelenka's oratorios, written in 1736 but apparently never performed then, hardly matches his instrumental music in daring, though its five arias and linking recitatives are both lively and inventive. The poem of Stefano Palavicini, with an Italian text, brings linked meditations from three biblical figures, not just Mary Magdalene and St Peter from Christ's own lifetime but his ancestor, the Psalmist, King David. When the arias are extended pieces, drama plays little part in the piece, and this performance recorded in Prague in 1994, is not helped by the rather colourless timbre of the tenor Martin Prokeš as King David, making the first aria with its da capo repeat seem very long indeed. The mezzo, Maddalena Kožená, then at the beginning of her career, is quite different, singing superbly in Mary's two big arias as well as the recitatives, already an outstanding artist. As St Peter Michael Pospíšil sings vehemently in his characterful defiance aria, *Lingua perfida*, condemning the slander which made this outspoken disciple deny Christ, at the expense in places of clean vocalizing. A fascinating rarity.

ZEMLINSKY, Alexander von

(1871–1942)

(i) *Cymbeline* (incidental music): Suite; Die Seejungfrau; Sinfonietta, Op. 23; Ein Tanzpoem; (ii) Frühlingsbegräbnis (cantata)

☛— (B) *** EMI double forte 5 75184-2 (2). (i) Kuebler; (ii) Voigt, Albert, Düsseldorf State Musikverein Ch.; Gürzenich O or Cologne PO, Conlon

James Conlon, a devotee of Zemlinsky's music, here conducts an admirable cross-section of his output. *Die Seejungfrau* is a ripely sensuous symphonic poem based on Hans Christian Andersen's fairy-tale about the mermaid. Conlon's reading is tender and poetic. At speeds rather more expansive than those in Chailly's brilliant and finely detailed Concertgebouw version, he brings out the evocative beauty with a more affectionate manner. The recording (as throughout the set) is atmospheric rather than sharply focused again giving warmth to the sensuous writing in the much later *Sinfonietta* of 1934.

With neo-classicism framing what is still essentially a late-Romantic work, it has a linking motif and opens with a wild Scherzo, a malevolent burlesque mixed with hope and despair. The central *Ballade* is both questing and ironic, rising more than once to a passionate entreaty but ending in resignation. The Rondo finale returns to and amplifies the nightmare burlesque of the first movement, but at the last minute produces a positive closing flourish.

Ein Tanzpoem and the suite from the incidental music for *Cymbeline* are altogether lighter in feeling and more diverting. Both are imaginatively scored, with luminous textures and colourful use of trumpets and horns as well as strings and woodwind. The central movement of *Cymbeline* is an attractive setting of '*Horch, horch! Die Lerche*' winningly sung by David Kuebler.

Ein Tanzpoem is an ambitious one-act ballet based on an aborted larger scale mime drama of 1901, planned by Hofmannsthal, called *Der Triumph der Zeit* ('The Triumph of Time'). Although the writing is more luscious, Zemlinsky's music has more than a little in common with Glazunov's *The Seasons*, but with its four sections evoking the changing moods of the hours of the day. It is hardly less spontaneous and tuneful and played here with much grace and a natural feeling for its seductive dance rhythms.

Frühlingsbegräbnis ('The Burial of Spring') is a fantasy cantata in seven brief movements, each richly memorable. Using soprano and baritone soloists, and with succulent choral writing, Zemlinsky's scenario involves a funeral procession of fairies and animals, a handsome youth struck down by the brightness of the dawn light, a preaching woodpecker, and a thunderstorm. It is admirably sung and played here. Indeed all this music could hardly be presented with more dedication or more flatteringly recorded, and this is one of the most worthwhile and stimulating of all EMI's double fforte reissues. Don't miss it.

(i) *Cymbeline*: incidental music; (ii) *Lyrische Symphonie, Op. 18*

*** Chan. 10069. Czech PO, Beaumont with (i) Brezina, members of the Bremen Shakespeare Co. (ii) Karlsen, Grundheber

Along with *Die Seejungfrau*, the *Lyric Symphony* is the most performed and recorded of Zemlinsky's works, but this newcomer has a special claim to attention in that it is based on the new critical edition of the score by Beaumont himself. This clears up the odd engravers' and copyists' errors and expunges a few cymbal crashes, which Zemlinsky himself removed during rehearsals. Textual matters aside, this performance is very fine indeed, and in the Norwegian soprano Turid Karlsen and Jaroslav Brezina it has dedicated soloists. A further attraction is the incidental music to Shakespeare's *Cymbeline*, dating from 1913–15 and also edited by the conductor. Scored for a full-scale orchestra, including triple wind, harp, harmonium, celesta and a substantial array of off-stage instruments, it is full of resource and inventive sonorities. Recommended.

Sinfonietta, Op. 23; Symphony 2 in B flat (1897); *Prelude to 'Es war einmal ...'* (original version). *Der Konig Kandaules: Prelude to Act III* (orch. Beaumont)

(N) *** Chan. 10204. Czech PO, Beaumont

Zemlinsky's *Symphony in B flat* is rich textured and full of luscious ideas, the four movements linked by a haunting motto theme, with which the work begins and ends. The *Sinfonietta*, a late work of 1934, was written just after the composer was forced to leave Germany for Switzerland, after the Nazis had taken over. Both these works are highly stimulating and played with great conviction.

In between comes a passionately sensuous Mahlerian prelude for the opera *Once upon a Time*, with a radiant close from the strings and oboe, which is balm to the senses. The darkly passionate Act III Prelude to Zemlinsky's *Der König Kandaules* has been added for this Chandos reissue of a CD previously available on Nimbus.

(i) *Symphonies 1 in D min.;* (ii) *2 in B flat*
(BB) **(*) Naxos 8.557008. (i) Slovak RSO, Rajter; (ii) Slovak PO, Siepenbusch

This apt coupling of the two symphonies that Zemlinsky wrote in the 1890s is drawn from two earlier Marco Polo discs, differently coupled. The *Symphony No. 1* of 1892 moves from an amiably lyrical *Allegro* and a nicely pointed *Scherzo* to a measured, deeply expressive finale, anticipating the similarly lyrical last movements of Mahler in some of his symphonies. The performance is not helped by the slightly distanced recording. The much more ambitious *Symphony No. 2* of 1897 makes a far sharper impact, both through the performance and the fuller, brighter recording. A slow introduction, brassily Wagnerian, leads to an urgently exhilarating *Allegro*, full of good thematic ideas. The jagged *Scherzo* and lyrical slow movement, again Wagnerian, based on a theme like an Austrian folk-tune, lead to a variation finale in strongly contrasted sections. It is a fine work that richly deserves revival.

Lyrische Symphonie, Op. 18
(BB) *** Arte Nova 74321 27768-2. Vlatka Orsanic, Johnson, SWFSO, Gielen – BERG: *Lyric Suite: 3 Pieces,* etc. ***

At speeds markedly faster than usual, Michael Gielen conducts an exceptionally powerful and purposeful account of Zemlinsky's *Lyric Symphony*. Here the work emerges as very fresh and distinctive in its own right. The playing of the orchestra is outstanding and the two soloists are ideal, singing with clean attack and fresh tone. First-rate recording too. An outstanding bargain, well coupled with the Berg works. The only snag is that the booklet is totally inadequate, with poor notes and no texts or translations, and not even any identification of the seven Tagore poems used by Zemlinsky in the symphony.

(i; ii) *Lyrische Symphonie, Op. 18*; (i; iii) *Eine florentinische Tragödie, Op. 16*; (iv) *Psalms 13, Op. 24; 23, Op. 14*; (v) *83*; (i; vi) *Symphonische Gesänge, Op. 20*
☛ **(B)** *** Double Decca 473 734-2 (2). (i) Concg. O; (ii) Marc, Hagegard; (iii) with Kruse, Dohmen, Vermillion; (iv) Ernst Senff Ch., Berlin RSO; (v) Slovak Phil. Ch., VPO; (vi) White; all cond. Chailly

With the help of Decca's opulent and finely detailed recording of vivid immediacy, Chailly's 1994 account of the *Lyrische Symphonie* is moving and passionate on the one hand, rapt

and poetic on the other, with the Concertgebouw producing ravishing sounds in playing marked by pinpoint ensemble. Haken Hagegard is an outstanding baritone soloist, illuminating in his pointing of words; Alessandra Marc may not have quite such clear diction, but she combines warmth and power with an ability to produce the most beautiful *pianissimos*. Zemlinsky's setting of the words in his *Symphonische Gesänge*, from the anthology of black poets in German translation, *Afrika singt*, brings a much more astringent style, which yet conveys powerful emotions, helped by the fine, intense singing of Willard White. The composer's aptly dramatic setting of *Psalm 83* is beautifully performed and richly recorded. *Psalm 13* reveals the urgency of Zemlinsky's inspiration – never a revolutionary in the same way as Schoenberg but always inventive and imaginative. *Psalm 23* is warm in expression, airy and beautiful, but do not expect a religious atmosphere: this is sensuous music, beautifully played and sung. The rather disagreeable love-triangle story that is the basis of *Eine florentinische Tragödie* is persuasively done here with three excellent soloists, though one equally enjoys the richly textured score, and it is in some ways better suited to CD than the opera house. The only drawback to this Double release is the lack of texts.

String Quartets 1–4; 2 Movements for String Quartet; Malblumen blühten überall
*** Chan. 9772 (2). Schoenberg Qt

This set of the four Zemlinsky quartets is very good indeed and the Dutch-based Schoenberg Quartet have the measure of this strange music. They convey the darker world of the *Adagio misterioso* of the *Two Movements* and the *Fourth Quartet*, composed two years before the Anschluss, as well as the post-Brahmsian gestures of the *First*. The *Malblumen blühten überall* is a setting for soprano and string sextet of Dehmel which the Schoenberg Quartet premièred (together with the *Two Movements*). Very good recordings on which much care has been lavished and altogether warmer than the long-serving set by the LaSalle Quartet on DG.

VOCAL MUSIC

Choral Music: (i) *Aurikelchen;* (ii; iii) *Frühlingsbegräbnis; Frühlingsglaube; Geheimnis; Minnelied;* (ii; iv) *Hochzeitgesang. Psalms 13, 23 & 83.* **Orchestral Lieder:** (v) *2 Gesänge* (for baritone & orchestra); (vi) *6 Maeterlinck Gesänge, Op. 13;* (vii) *Malblumen blühten überall;* (viii) *Symphonic Gesänge, Op. 20;* (vii) *Waldgespräch*
(N) (B) *** EMI Gemini 5 86079-2 (2). (i) Mülheimer Kantorei; (ii) Düsseldorf State Musikvereins Ch.; (iii) with Voight, Albert; (iv) Blum; (v) Schmidt; (vi) Urmana; (vii) Isokoski; (viii) Volle; Gürzenich O & Cologne PO, Conlon

The major choral works here are Zemlinsky's passionate and intense settings of the three *Psalms*. In a manner recognizable from his operas, the first two bring sensuous writing more apt for the *Song of Solomon* than the *Psalms*; the third (No. 83) brings dramatic martial music. Those three items as well as the cantata, *The Burial of Spring*, in seven compact movements, were recorded live in Cologne and bring warm, committed performances under Conlon as a dedicated Zemlinsky interpreter. The other lighter items were recorded later in the studio.

The two major solo works are both for soprano: *Waldgespräch* an Eichendorf/Loreley ballad, accompanied by a pair of horns, harp and strings, and *Malblumen blühten überall* inspired by Schoenberg's *Verklaerte Nacht* and supported no less alluringly by string sextet. Soile Isokoski responds with passion to both works, and Andreas Schmidt is no less responsive in the *Zwei Gesänge*, orchestrated by Antony Beaumont, both very Wagnerian in feeling. Michael Volle proves boldly dramatic in the *Symphonische Gesänge*, and if Violeta Urmana is less than ideally seductive in the Maeterlinck cycle, as always with Zemlinsky the orchestral sounds are as luscious as ever, with Conlon a splendidly supportive accompanist. Opulent sound throughout to match means that this is a highly recommendable (and inexpensive) coverage of Zemlinsky's choral and orchestral songs. No texts and translations are included, but these may be available on the EMI Website (www.musicfromemi.com).

6 Maeterlinck Lieder, Op. 13
(B) *** Double Decca (IMS) (ADD) 444 871-2 (2). Van Nes, Concg. O, Chailly – MAHLER: *Symphony 6* ***

Beautifully sung by Jard van Nes in her finest recording to date, these ripely romantic settings of Maeterlinck make an unusual but valuable fill-up for Chailly's rugged and purposeful reading of the Mahler *Symphony*. The rich, vivid recording captures van Nes's full-throated singing with new firmness.

OPERA

Eine florentinische Tragödie (complete)
*** Schwann CD 11625. Soffel, Riegel, Sarabia, Berlin RSO, Albrecht

A Florentine Tragedy presents a simple love triangle: a Florentine merchant returns home to find his sluttish wife with the local prince; but the musical syrup which flows over all the characters makes them repulsive, with motives only dimly defined. The score itself is most accomplished; it is compellingly performed here, more effective on disc than it is in the opera house. First-rate sound.

Der Zwerg (Der Geburtstag der Infantin)
☛ (M) *** EMI 5 66247-2 (2). Isokoski, Martinez, Kuebler, Collis, Cologne PO, Conlon

Der Zwerg, 'the dwarf', is the preferred title for the definitive edition of this most striking yet most disturbing of Zemlinsky's operas. The text here was prepared for Conlon from the autograph score, revised in detail by the composer. Deeply moving as Kenneth Riegel's performance is on the earlier recording below, David Kuebler here has the advantage of a more beautiful, younger sounding voice, making the portrait more tenderly moving, bringing out the character's vulnerability. Nor is passion lacking, and Soile Isokoski makes an excellent Princess, with Iride Martinez also singing beautifully as her favourite maid. The live recording is on the dry side, but still vivid and full.

ZWILICH, Ellen (born 1939)

Symphony 2
** First Edition LCD 002. Louisville O, Leighton Smith – HINDEMITH: *Piano Concerto* **(*) (with LAWHEAD: *Aleost* *(*))

Ellen Taaffe Zwilich was a pupil of Dohnányi. Her *First Symphony* (1982) won a Pulitzer Prize and prompted the San Francisco Orchestra to commission the *Second Symphony* in 1985. The work is called a 'cello symphony', since the cellos play a dominant role in the musical argument. The invention is solid and well argued, rather than inspired; it is music that commands respect, though it is not easy to discern a voice of strong individuality. Good playing and decent recording.

	Figaro	Cosi	Giovanni	Idomeneo	Entführung
Gardiner			HAVE	HAVE	HAVE
Solti			HAVE		HAVE
Böhm	HAVE				
Karajan	HAVE HARWOOD				
Davis	HAVE	HAVE			
Harnonc.					
Mackerras		HAVE		HAVE HUNT LIEBERSON	
Norrington			HAVE		
Marriner	HAVE				
Abbado	HAVE				
Gibson		HAVE BAKER HARWOOD			